CHILTON®

GENERAL MOTORS
SERVICE MANUAL
2008 EDITION
VOLUME II

CENGAGE
Learning™

Australia • Brazil • Japan • Korea • Mexico • Singapore • Spain • United Kingdom • United States

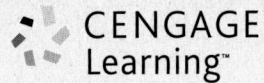

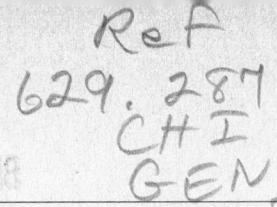

CHILTON®
General Motors Service Manual
2008 Edition
Volume II

Vice President,
Technology Professional Business Unit:
  Gregory L. Clayton

Publisher,
Technology Professional Business Unit:
  David Koontz

Director of Marketing:
  Beth A. Lutz

Production Director:
  Patty Stephan

Editorial Assistant:
  Jason Yager

Production Manager:
  Andrew Crouth

Marketing Specialist:
  Jennifer Stall

Marketing Assistant:
  Rachael Conover

Publishing Coordinator:
  Paula Baillie

Sr. Content Project Manager:
  Elizabeth C. Hough

Managing Editor:
  Terry L. Blomquist

Editors:
  Ken Burdette
  Joe Defrancesco
  Matt Frederick
  Eugene F. Hannon Jr.
  Will Kesseler
  Tom Mellon
  David G. Olson
  Christine Sheeky
  Jon Wallace
  Lance Williams

Graphical Designer:
  Melinda Possinger

For more information contact:
Cengage Learning
Executive Woods
5 Maxwell Drive, PO Box 8007,
Clifton Park, NY 12065-8007
Visit us at **www.chiltononline.com**
For more learning solutions, visit **www.cengage.com**
For permission to use material from
the text or product, contact us by
Tel. (800) 730-2214
Fax (800) 730-2215
www.cengage.com/permissions

Cengage Learning products are represented in Canada by Nelson Education, Ltd.

ISBN 10: 1-4283-2213-2
ISSN 13: 978-14283-2213-4
ISSN: 1939-621X

NOTICE TO THE READER

Printed in the United States of America
1 2 3 4 5 xx12 11 10 09 08 07

Table of Contents

Model Index

USING THIS INFORMATION

Organization

To find where a particular model section or procedure is located, look in the Table of Contents. Main topics are listed with the page number on which they may be found. Following the main topics is an alphabetical listing of all of the procedures within the section and their page numbers.

Manufacturer and Model Coverage

This product covers 2005–2008 General Motors models that are produced in sufficient quantities to warrant coverage, and which have technical content available from the vehicle manufacturers before our publication date. Although this information is as complete as possible at the time of publication, some manufacturers may make changes which cannot be included here. While striving for total accuracy, the publisher cannot assume responsibility for any errors, changes, or omissions that may occur in the compilation of this data.

Part Numbers & Special Tools

Part numbers and special tools are recommended by the publisher and vehicle manufacturer to perform specific jobs. Before substituting any part or tool for the one recommended, you must be completely satisfied that neither your personal safety, nor the performance of the vehicle will be endangered.

ACKNOWLEDGEMENT

Portions of materials contained herein have been reprinted with permission of General Motors Corporation, Service and Parts Operations under License Agreement #0510757.

PRECAUTIONS

Before servicing any vehicle, please be sure to read all of the following precautions, which deal with personal safety, prevention of component damage, and important points to take into consideration when servicing a motor vehicle:

- Always wear safety glasses or goggles when drilling, cutting, grinding or prying.
- Steel-toed work shoes should be worn when working with heavy parts. Pockets should not be used for carrying tools. A slip or fall can drive a screwdriver into your body.
- Work surfaces, including tools and the floor should be kept clean of grease, oil or other slippery material.
- When working around moving parts, don't wear loose clothing. Long hair should be tied back under a hat or cap, or in a hair net.
- Always use tools only for the purpose for which they were designed. Never pry with a screwdriver.
- Keep a fire extinguisher and first aid kit handy.
- Always properly support the vehicle with approved stands or lift.
- Always have adequate ventilation when working with chemicals or hazardous material.
- Carbon monoxide is colorless, odorless and dangerous. If it is necessary to operate the engine with vehicle in a closed area such as a garage, always use an exhaust collector to vent the exhaust gases outside the closed area.
- When draining coolant, keep in mind that small children and some pets are attracted by ethylene glycol antifreeze, and are quite likely to drink any left in an open container, or in puddles on the ground. This will prove fatal in sufficient quantity. Always drain the coolant into a sealable container.
- To avoid personal injury, do not remove the coolant pressure relief cap while the engine is operating or hot. The cooling system is under pressure; steam and hot liquid can come out forcefully when the cap is loosened slightly. Failure to follow these instructions may result in personal injury. The coolant must be recovered in a suitable, clean container for reuse. If the coolant is contaminated it must be recycled or disposed of correctly.
- When carrying out maintenance on the starting system be aware that heavy gauge leads are connected directly to the battery. Make sure the protective caps are in place when maintenance is completed. Failure to follow these instructions may result in personal injury.
- Do not remove any part of the engine emission control system. Operating the engine without the engine emission control system will reduce fuel economy and engine ventilation. This will weaken engine performance and shorten engine life. It is also a violation of Federal law.
- Due to environmental concerns, when the air conditioning system is drained, the refrigerant must be collected using refrigerant recovery/recycling equipment. Federal law requires that refrigerant be recovered into appropriate recovery equipment and the process be conducted by qualified technicians who have been certified by an approved organization, such as MACS, ASI, etc. Use of a recovery machine dedicated to the appropriate refrigerant is necessary to reduce the possibility of oil and refrigerant incompatibility concerns. Refer to the instructions provided by the equipment manufacturer when removing refrigerant from or charging the air conditioning system.
- Always disconnect the battery ground when working on or around the electrical system.
- Batteries contain sulfuric acid. Avoid contact with skin, eyes, or clothing. Also, shield your eyes when working near batteries to protect against possible splashing of the acid solution. In case of acid contact with skin or eyes, flush immediately with water for a minimum of 15 minutes and get prompt medical attention. If acid is swallowed, call a physician immediately. Failure to follow these instructions may result in personal injury.
- Batteries normally produce explosive gases. Therefore, do not allow flames, sparks or lighted substances to come near the battery. When charging or working near a battery, always shield your face and protect your eyes. Always provide ventilation. Failure to follow these instructions may result in personal injury.
- When lifting a battery, excessive pressure on the end walls could cause acid to spew through the vent caps, resulting in personal injury, damage to the vehicle or battery. Lift with a battery carrier or with your hands on opposite corners. Failure to follow these instructions may result in personal injury.
- Observe all applicable safety precautions when working around fuel. Whenever

servicing the fuel system, always work in a well-ventilated area. Do not allow fuel spray or vapors to come in contact with a spark, open flame, or excessive heat (a hot drop light, for example). Keep a dry chemical fire extinguisher near the work area. Always keep fuel in a container specifically designed for fuel storage; also, always properly seal fuel containers to avoid the possibility of fire or explosion. Do not smoke or carry lighted tobacco or open flame of any type when working on or near any fuel-related components.

• Fuel injection systems often remain pressurized, even after the engine has been turned OFF. The fuel system pressure must be relieved before disconnecting any fuel lines. Failure to do so may result in fire and/or personal injury.

• The evaporative emissions system contains fuel vapor and condensed fuel vapor. Although not present in large quantities, it still presents the danger of explosion or fire. Disconnect the battery ground cable from the battery to minimize the possibility of an electrical spark occurring, possibly causing a fire or explosion if fuel vapor or liquid fuel is present in the area. Failure to follow these instructions can result in personal injury.

• The EPA warns that prolonged contact with used engine oil may cause a number of skin disorders, including cancer! You should make every effort to minimize your exposure to used engine oil. Protective gloves should be worn when changing oil. Wash your hands and any other exposed skin areas as soon as possible after exposure to used engine oil. Soap and water, or waterless hand cleaner should be used.

• Some vehicles are equipped with an air bag system, often referred to as a Supple-mental Restraint System (SRS) or Supplemental Inflatable Restraint (SIR) system. The system must be disabled before performing service on or around system components, steering column, instrument panel components, wiring and sensors. Failure to follow safety and disabling procedures could result in accidental air bag deployment, possible personal injury and unnecessary system repairs.

• Always wear safety goggles when working with, or around, the air bag system. When carrying a non-deployed air bag, be sure the bag and trim cover are pointed away from your body. When placing a non-deployed air bag on a work surface, always face the bag and trim cover upward, away from the surface. This will reduce the motion of the module if it is accidentally deployed.

• Electronic modules are sensitive to electrical charges. The ABS module can be damaged if exposed to these charges.

• Brake pads and shoes may contain asbestos, which has been determined to be a cancer-causing agent. Never clean brake surfaces with compressed air. Avoid inhaling brake dust. Clean all brake surfaces with a commercially available brake cleaning fluid.

• When replacing brake pads, shoes, discs or drums, replace them as complete axle sets.

• When servicing drum brakes, disassemble and assemble one side at a time, leaving the remaining side intact for reference.

• Brake fluid often contains polyglycol ethers and polyglycols. Avoid contact with the eyes and wash your hands thoroughly after handling brake fluid. If you do get brake fluid in your eyes, flush your eyes with clean, running water for 15 minutes. If eye irritation persists, or if you have taken brake fluid internally, immediately seek medical assistance.

• Clean, high quality brake fluid from a sealed container is essential to the safe and proper operation of the brake system. You should always buy the correct type of brake fluid for your vehicle. If the brake fluid becomes contaminated, completely flush the system with new fluid. Never reuse any brake fluid. Any brake fluid that is removed from the system should be discarded. Also, do not allow any brake fluid to come in contact with a painted or plastic surface; it will damage the paint.

• Never operate the engine without the proper amount and type of engine oil; doing so will result in severe engine damage.

• Timing belt maintenance is extremely important! Many models utilize an interference-type, non-freewheeling engine. If the timing belt breaks, the valves in the cylinder head may strike the pistons, causing potentially serious (also time-consuming and expensive) engine damage.

• Disconnecting the negative battery cable on some vehicles may interfere with the functions of the on-board computer system (s) and may require the computer to undergo a relearning process once the negative battery cable is reconnected.

• Steering and suspension fasteners are critical parts because they affect performance of vital components and systems and their failure can result in major service expense. They must be replaced with the same grade or part number or an equivalent part if replacement is necessary. Do not use a replacement part of lesser quality or substitute design. Torque values must be used as specified during reassembly to ensure proper retention of these parts.

PONTIAC

12

G6

SPECIFICATIONS AND MAINTENANCE CHARTS

VEHICLE AND ENGINE IDENTIFICATION CHART

Engine								Model Year	
Code ①	Liters	Cu. In.	Cyl.	Fuel Sys.	Engine Type	Eng. Mfg.		Code ②	Year
B	2.4	146	4	MFI	DOHC	General Motors		5	2005
8	3.5	214	6	SEFI	OHV	General Motors		6	2006
1	3.9	238	6	SEFI	OHV	General Motors		7	2007
N	3.5	214	6	SEFI	OHV	General Motors			
7	3.6	217	6	SEFI	DOHC	General Motors			

MFI: Multi-port Fuel Injection

SEFI: Sequential Multi-port Fuel Injection

① 8th position of VIN

② 10th position of VIN

22116_GMG6_C0001

GENERAL ENGINE SPECIFICATIONS
All measurements are given in inches.

Year	Model	Engine Displacement Liters	Engine Series (ID/VIN)	Net Horsepower @ rpm	Net Torque @ rpm (ft. lbs.)	Bore x Stroke (in.)	Com-pression Ratio	Oil Pressure @ rpm
2005	G6	3.5	8	201@5600	222@3200	3.70x3.31	9.8:1	50-80@1000
2006	G6	2.4	B	169@6300	162@4500	3.81x3.39	10.0:1	30-45@1850
		3.5	8	201@5600	222@3200	3.70x3.31	9.8:1	50-80@1000
		3.9	1	240@6000	241@2800	3.90x3.31	9.8:1	30-45@1850
2007	G6	2.4	B	169@6300	240@6000	3.81x3.39	10.0:1	30-45@1850
		3.5	N	224@5800	220@4000	3.90x2.99	9.8:1	30-45@1850
		3.6	7	252@6300	251@3200	3.70x3.37	10.2:1	20@2000
		3.9	1	240@6000	240@4600	3.90x3.31	9.8:1	30-45@1850

22116_GMG6_C0002

GASOLINE ENGINE TUNE-UP SPECIFICATIONS

Year	Engine Displacement Liters	Engine VIN	Spark Plugs Gap (in.)	Ignition Timing (deg.) MT	Ignition Timing (deg.) AT	Fuel Pump (psi)	Idle Speed (rpm) MT	Idle Speed (rpm) AT	Valve Clearance In.	Valve Clearance Ex.
2005	3.5	8	0.060	①	①	50-60	①	①	HYD	HYD
2006	2.4	B	0.042	①	①	50-60	①	①	HYD	HYD
	3.5	8	0.060	①	①	50-60	①	①	HYD	HYD
	3.9	1	0.040	①	①	50-60	①	①	HYD	HYD
2007	2.4	B	0.040	①	①	50-60	①	①	HYD	HYD
	3.5	N	0.040	①	①	50-60	①	①	HYD	HYD
	3.6	7	0.043	①	①	50-60	①	①	HYD	HYD
	3.9	1	0.040	①	①	50-60	①	①	HYD	HYD

NOTE: The Vehicle Emission Control Information label often reflects specification changes changes made during production.

The label figures must be used if they differ from those in this chart.

HYD: Hydraulic

① Controlled by the Powertrain Control Module (PCM) and cannot be manually adjusted.

22116_GMG6_C0003

CAPACITIES

Year	Model	Engine Displacement Liters	Engine ID/VIN	Engine Oil with Filter (qts.)	Transmission (pts.)			Drive Axle		Fuel Tank (gal.)	Cooling System (qts.)
					4-Spd	6-Spd	Auto.	Front (pts.)	Rear (pts.)		
2005	G6	3.5	8	4.0	—	6.2	①	—	—	16.3	7.7
2006	G6	2.4	B	5.0	—	6.2	①	—	—	16.3	9.9
		3.5	8	4.0	—	6.2	①	—	—	16.3	7.7
		3.9	1	4.0	—	6.2	①	—	—	16.3	9.8
2007	G6	2.4	B	5.0	—	6.2	①	—	—	16.3	7.5
		3.5	N	4.0	—	6.2	①	—	—	16.3	9.7
		3.6	7	5.5	—	6.2	①	—	—	16.3	9.7
		3.9	1	4.0	—	6.2	①	—	—	16.3	9.7

NOTE: All capacities are approximate. Add fluid gradually and check to be sure a proper fluid level is obtained.

① 4T65-E: 14.8 pts.

4T45-E/4T46-E: 13.8 pts.

6T70/6T75: 19 pts

22116_GMG6_C0004

FLUID SPECIFICATIONS

Year	Model	Engine Displacement Liters	Engine ID/VIN	Engine Oil	Auto. Trans. ①	Drive Axle	Power Steering Fluid	Brake Master Cylinder
2005	G6	3.5	8	5W-30	Dexron VI	75W-80	GM PS Fluid	DOT 3
2006	G6	2.4	B	5W-30	Dexron VI	75W-80	GM PS Fluid	DOT 3
		3.5	8	5W-30	Dexron VI	75W-80	GM PS Fluid	DOT 3
		3.9	1	5W-30	Dexron VI	75W-80	GM PS Fluid	DOT 3
2007	G6	2.4	B	5W-30	Dexron VI	75W-80	GM PS Fluid	DOT 3
		3.5	N	5W-30	Dexron VI	75W-80	GM PS Fluid	DOT 3
		3.6	7	5W-30	Dexron VI	75W-80	GM PS Fluid	DOT 3
		3.9	1	5W-30	Dexron VI	75W-80	GM PS Fluid	DOT 3

DOT: Department Of Transpotation

① Manual Transmission GL-4 75W-80

22116_GMG6_C0011

VALVE SPECIFICATIONS

Year	Engine VIN	Engine Displacement Liters	Seat Angle (deg.)	Face Angle (deg.)	Spring Test Pressure (lbs. @ in.)	Spring Installed Height (in.)	Stem-to-Guide Clearance (in.)		Stem Diameter (in.)	
							Intake	Exhaust	Intake	Exhaust
2005	8	3.5	46	45	234@1.30	1.740	0.0010-0.0027	0.0010-0.0027	NA	NA
2006	B	2.4	NA	NA	220@1.32	NA	0.0012-0.0022	0.0020-0.0026	0.2344-0.3140	0.2337-0.2343
	8	3.5	46	45	234@1.30	1.740	0.0010-0.0027	0.0010-0.0027	NA	NA
	1	3.9	46	45	230@1.26	1.701	0.0010-0.0027	0.0010-0.0027	NA	NA
2007	B	2.4	NA	NA	220@1.32	NA	0.0012-0.0022	0.0020-0.0026	0.2344-0.3140	0.2337-0.2343
	N	3.5	46	45	234@1.30	1.740	0.0010-0.0027	0.0010-0.0027	N/A	NA
	7	3.6	45	45.25	N/A	1.740	0.0010-0.0026	0.0014-0.0030	0.2344-0.2352	0.2341-0.2348
	1	3.9	46	45	230@1.26	1.701	0.0010-0.0027	0.0010-0.0027	NA	NA

NA: Not Available

22116_GMG6_C0008

CAMSHAFT AND BEARING SPECIFICATIONS CHART

All measurements are given in inches.

Year	Engine Displ. Liters	Engine VIN	Journal Dia.	Brg. Oil Clearance	Shaft End-play	Runout	Journal Bore	Lobe Height	
								Intake	Exhaust
2005	3.5	8	1.8680-1.8690	1.8710-1.8720	—	0.001	NA	0.2727	0.2727
2006	2.4	B	1.0604-1.0614	—	0.0016-0.0057	0.0024	NA	NA	NA
	3.5	8	1.8680-1.8690	1.8710-1.8720	—	0.001	NA	0.2727	0.2727
	3.9	1	1.0614-1.0620	—	0.0016-0.0035	0.0024	NA	1.6981-1.7020	1.6933-1.6972
2007	2.4	B	1.0604-1.0614	—	0.0016-0.0057	0.0024	NA	NA	NA
	3.5	8	2.0240-2.0250	2.0280-2.0290	—	0.001	NA	0.2727	0.2727
	3.6	7	①	②	0.0018-0.0085	0.002	0.0016-0.0033	1.6687-1.6805	1.6703-1.6821
	3.9	1	1.0614-1.0620	—	0.0016-0.0035	0.001	NA	1.6981-1.7020	1.6933-1.6972

NA: Not Available

① Front Number 1: 1.3754-1.3764 Middle and Rear 2-4: 1.0605-1.0614

② Front Number 1: 1.3779-1.3787 Middle and Rear Number 2-4: 1.0630-1.0638

22116_GMG6_C0006

CRANKSHAFT AND CONNECTING ROD SPECIFICATIONS

All measurements are given in inches.

Year	Engine Displ. Liters	Engine VIN	Crankshaft				Connecting Rod		
			Main Brg. Journal Dia.	Main Brg. Oil Clearance	Shaft End-play	Thrust on No.	Journal Diameter	Oil Clearance	Side Clearance
2005	3.5	8	2.6473-2.6483	0.0008-0.0025	0.0024-0.0083	3	2.2489-2.2495	0.0007-0.0024	0.0078-0.0094
2006	2.4	B	2.2045-2.2050	0.012-0.0026	0.0012-0.0150	NA	1.9291-1.9297	0.0011-0.0027	0.0028-0.0146
	3.5	8	2.6473-2.6483	0.0008-0.0025	0.0024-0.0083	3	2.2489-2.2495	0.0007-0.0024	0.0078-0.0094
	3.9	1	2.6473-2.6483	①	0.0024-0.0083	3	2.2488-2.2495	0.0007-0.0024	0.0078-0.0094
2007	2.4	B	2.2045-2.2050	0.012-0.0026	0.0012-0.0150	NA	1.9291-1.9297	0.0011-0.0027	0.0028-0.0146
	3.6	7	2.6768-2.6775	0.0004-0.0024	0.0039-0.0130	NA	2.2044-2.205	0.0004-0.0028	0.0374-0.014
	3.5	N	2.6473-2.6483	0.0008-0.0025	0.0024-0.0083	3	2.2489-2.2495	0.0007-0.0024	0.0078-0.0094
	3.9	1	2.6473-2.6483	①	0.0024-0.0083	3	2.2488-2.2495	0.0007-0.0024	0.0078-0.0094

① 0.0008-0.0025 except no. 3
  0.0012-0.0030 on no. 3

22116_GMG6_C0007

PISTON AND RING SPECIFICATIONS

All measurements are given in inches.

Year	Engine Displ. Liters	Engine VIN	Piston Clearance	Ring Gap			Ring Side Clearance		
				Top Comp.	Bottom Comp.	Oil Control	Top Comp.	Bottom Comp.	Oil Control
2005	3.5	8	①	0.0070-0.0150	0.0190-0.0290	0.0100-0.0290	0.0010-0.0030	0.0020-0.0030	0.004
2006	2.4	B	0.0004-0.0016	0.0060-0.0120	0.0080-0.0180	0.0060-0.0200	0.0015-0.0031	0.0012-0.0030	0.0011-0.0069
	3.5	8	①	0.0070-0.0150	0.0190-0.0290	0.0100-0.0290	0.0010-0.0030	0.0020-0.0030	0.004
	3.9	1	②	0.0059-0.0118	0.0098-0.0177	0.0059-0.0255	0.0011-0.0025	0.0007-0.0021	0.004
2007	2.4	B	0.0004-0.0016	0.0078-0.0157	0.0137-0.0216	0.0098-0.0299	0.0015-0.0031	0.0012-0.0027	0.004
	3.5	N	①	0.0007-0.0153	0.0188-0.0291	0.0098-0.0291	0.0011-0.0299	0.0015-0.0307	0.0035
	3.6	7	0.0010-0.0021	0.0059-0.0118	0.0110-0.0189	0.0059-0.0236	0.0012-0.0026	0.0006-0.0024	0.0012-0.0067
	3.9	1	②	0.0059-0.0118	0.0098-0.0177	0.0059-0.0255	0.0011-0.0025	0.0007-0.0021	0.004

① -0.0011-+0.0011
② -0.0003-+0.0018

22116_GMG6_C0005

TORQUE SPECIFICATIONS
All readings in ft. lbs.

Year	Engine VIN	Engine Displacement Liters	Cylinder Head Bolts	Main Bearing Bolts	Rod Bearing Bolts	Crankshaft Damper Bolts	Flywheel Bolts	Manifold Intake	Manifold Exhaust	Spark Plugs	Oil Pan Drain Plug
2005	3.5	8	①	②	③	118	52	④	12	11	19
2006	2.4	B	⑤	⑥	③	⑦	⑧	⑨	⑩	15	18
	3.5	8	①	②	③	⑬	52	④	12	11	19
	3.9	1	①	②	③	⑬	52	④	15	11	19
2007	2.4	B	⑤	⑥	③	⑦	⑧	⑨	⑩	15	18
	3.5	N	①	②	③	⑬	52	④	12	11	19
	3.6	7	⑰	⑯	⑮	⑭	⑫	⑪	18	13	15
	3.9	1	①	②	③	⑬	52	④	15	11	19

① Step 1: 44 ft. lbs.
   Step 2: plus 90 degrees

② Step 1: 37 ft. lbs.
   Step 2: plus 77 degrees

③ Step 1: 18 ft. lbs.
   Step 2: plus 110 degrees

④ Lower manifold center bolt: 15 ft. lbs.
   Lower manifold corner bolt: 18 ft. lbs.
   Upper manifold: 18 ft. lbs.

⑤ Step 1: 22 ft. lbs.
   Step 2: plus 155 degrees

⑥ Step 1: 15 ft. lbs.
   Step 2: plus 70 degrees

⑦ Step 1: 74 ft. lbs.
   Step 2: plus 125 degrees

⑧ Step 1: 39 ft. lbs.
   Step 2: plus 25 degrees

⑨ Stud 53 INCH lbs.
   Nut/bolts: 89 INCH lbs.

⑩ Step 1: 52 ft. lbs.
   Step 2: plus 72 degrees

⑪ Lower and Upper manifold bolts: 17 ft. lbs.

⑫ Step 1: 22 ft. lbs.
   Step 2: plus 45 degrees

⑬ Step 1: 92 ft. lbs.
   Step 2: plus 130 degrees

⑭ Step 1: 74 ft. lbs.
   Step 2: plus 150 degrees

⑮ Step 1: 22 ft. lbs.
   Step 2: Loosen Bolts
   Step 3: 18 ft. lbs.
   Step 4: plus 110 degrees

⑯ Step 1: 22 ft. lbs.
   Step 2: plus 60 degrees

⑰ Step 1: 33 ft. lbs.
   Step 2: plus 120 degrees

22116_GMG6_C0009

WHEEL ALIGNMENT

Year	Model			Caster Range (+/-Deg.)	Caster Preferred Setting (Deg.)	Camber Range (+/-Deg.)	Camber Preferred Setting (Deg.)	Toe-in (Deg.)
2005	G6	Front	Left	0.75	+3.10	0.75	-0.90	0.20+/-0.20
			Right	0.75	+3.10	0.75	-0.70	0.20+/-0.20
		Rear		—	—	0.50	-0.80	0.20+/-0.20
2006	G6	Front	Left	0.75	+3.10	0.75	-0.90	0.20+/-0.20
			Right	0.75	+3.10	0.75	-0.70	0.20+/-0.20
		Rear		—	—	0.50	-0.80	0.20+/-0.20
2007	G6	Front	Left	0.75	+3.10	0.75	-0.90	0.20+/-0.20
			Right	0.75	+3.10	0.75	-0.70	0.20+/-0.20
		Rear		—	—	0.50	-0.80	0.20+/-0.20

22116_GMG6_C0010

TIRE AND WHEEL SPECIFICATIONS

Year	Model	OEM Tires Standard	OEM Tires Optional	Tire Pressures (psi) Front	Tire Pressures (psi) Rear	Wheel Size	Wheel Lug Nut Torque (Ft. Lbs.)
2005	G6	P215/60R16	None	30	30	6.5J	100
	G6 GT	P225/50R17	None	30	30	6.5J	100
	G6 GTP	P225/50R18	None	35	35	6.5J	100
2006	G6	P215/60R16	None	30	30	7J	100
	G6 GT	P225/50R17	None	30	30	7J	100
	G6 GTP	P225/50R18	None	35	35	7J	100
2007	G6	P195/60R15	P205/55R16	30	30	6.5J/7J	100
		P215/60R16	P225/50R17	30	30	7J	100
	G6 GT Conv.	P225/50R18	None	32	30	7J	100
	G6 GT	P225/50R17	P225/50R17	30	30	7J	100
	G6 GTP	P225/50R18	None	30	30	7J	100

OEM: Original Equipment Manufacturer

PSI: Pounds Per Square Inch

STD: Standard

OPT: Optional

22116_GMG6_C0013

BRAKE SPECIFICATIONS

All measurements in inches unless noted

Year	Model		Brake Disc Original Thickness	Brake Disc Minimum Thickness	Brake Disc Maximum Runout	Minimum Lining Thickness Front	Minimum Lining Thickness Rear	Brake Caliper Bracket Bolts (ft. lbs.)	Brake Caliper Mounting Bolts (ft. lbs.)
2005	G6	F	1.023	0.898	0.002	①	—	96	26
		R	0.551	0.465	0.002	—	①	96	26
2006	G6	F	1.023	0.898	0.002	①	—	96	26
		R	0.551	0.465	0.002	—	①	96	26
2007	G6	F	1.023	0.898	0.002	①	—	96	26
		R	0.551	0.465	0.002	—	①	96	26

① Not available

22116_GMG6_C0012

MAINTENANCE I AND II SERVICE SCHEDULES
2005-07 Pontiac G6

When the CHANGE ENGINE OIL light appears, certain services and inspections are required. Required services are described as Maintenance I and Maintenance II.

The first service on a vehicle should be Maintenance I, and the second service should be Maintenance II. Alternate between the 2 thereafter. However, in some cases, Maintenance II may be required more often.

Maintenance I: Use Maintenance I if the CHANGE ENGINE OIL light comes on within 10 months since vehicle was purchased or, if Maintenance II was performed.

Maintenance II: Use Maintenance II if the previous service performed was Maintenance I.

Always use Maintenance II whenever the CHANGE ENGINE OIL light comes on 10 months or more since the last service, or, if the CHANGE ENGINE OIL light has not come on at all for one year.

Service	Maintenance I	Maintenance II
Change the engine oil and filter. Reset the oil life system.	✓	✓
Visually inspect the vehicle for leaks or damage. A fluid loss in the vehicle system could indicate a problem. Inspected, repair and add fluid to the system if necessary.	✓	✓
Inspect the engine air cleaner filter. If necessary, replace the filter.	✓	✓
Rotate the tires. Inspect the tire inflation pressures and the tire wear.	✓	✓
Visually inspect the brake lines and hoses for proper hook-up, binding, leaks, cracks, chafing, etc. Inspect the disc brake pads for wear and the rotors for surface condition. Inspect the drum brake linings for wear or cracks. Inspect other brake parts, including drums, wheel cylinders, calipers, parking brake, etc. Inspect the parking brake adjustment.	✓	✓
Inspect the engine coolant and the windshield washer fluid levels. Add fluid as needed.	✓	✓
Inspect the suspension and steering components. Inspect the front and rear suspension and the steering system for damaged, loose or missing parts, or signs of wear. Inspect the power steering lines and the hoses for proper hook-up, binding, leaks, cracks, chafing, etc.	--	✓
Visually inspect the coolant hoses and replace the hoses if they are cracked, swollen or deteriorated. Inspect all pipes, fittings and clamps; replace with GM parts as needed. To help ensure proper operation, a pressure test of the cooling system and pressure cap and cleaning the outside of the radiator and air conditioning condenser is recommended at least once a year.		✓
Inspect the wiper blades for wear or cracking.	--	✓
Inspect the restraint system components. Ensure the safety belt reminder light and all the belts, buckles, latch plates, retractors and anchorages are working properly. Look for any other loose or damaged safety belt system parts. If you see anything that might keep a safety belt system from working correctly, repair or replaced the damaged part. Replace torn or frayed safety belts, refer to Operational and Functional Checks in Seat Belts. Inspect for any opened or broken air bag coverings, and repair or replace as needed. The air bag system does require regular maintenance.	--	✓

22116_GMG6_C0014

MAINTENANCE I AND II SERVICE SCHEDULES
2005-07 Pontiac G6

Lubricate the body components.Lubricate all key lock cylinders, hood latch assemblies, secondary latches, pivots, spring anchor and release pawl, hood and door hinges, rear folding seats and liftgate hinges. Frequent lubrication may be required when exposed to a corrosive environment, refer to Fluid and Lubricant Recommendations . Applying dielectric silicone grease GM P/N 12345579 (Canadian P/N 1974984) or equivalent on the weatherstrips with a clean cloth.	--	✓
Inspect the transaxle fluid level and add fluid as needed.	--	✓
Inspect the suspension and steering components.Inspect the front and rear suspension and the steering system for damaged, loose or missing parts, or signs of wear. Inspect power steering lines and hoses for proper hook-up, binding, leaks, cracks, chafing, etc.	--	✓
Inspect the throttle system for interference or binding and for damaged or missing parts. Replace the parts as needed. Replace any components that have high effort or excessive wear. Do not lubricate the accelerator or the cruise control cables.	--	✓
Replace the passenger compartment air filter.	--	✓

22116_GMG6_C0015

ADDITIONAL REQUIRED SERVICES
2005-07 Pontiac G6

TO BE SERVICED	TYPE OF SERVICE	VEHICLE MILEAGE INTERVAL (x1000)					
		25	50	75	100	125	150
Inspect fuel system for damage or leaks	S/I	✔	✔	✔	✔	✔	✔
Inspect exhaust system for loose or damaged components	S/I	✔	✔	✔	✔	✔	✔
Replace engine air filter	R		✔		✔		✔
2.4L (Code B) and 3.5L (Code N) Change automatic transmission fluid and filter (severe service only)	R		✔		✔		✔
3.9L (Code 1) Change automatic transmission fluid and filter (severe service only)	R		✔		✔		✔
3.9L (Code 1) Change automatic transmission fluid and filter (normal service)	R				✔		
3.6L (Code 7) Change automatic transmission fluid (severe service)	R		✔		✔		✔
3.6L (Code 7) Change automatic transmission fluid (normal service)	R		✔		✔		✔
Replace spark plugs. Inspect spark plug wires	R				✔		
Engine cooling system service (or every five years whichever occurs first)	S/I						✔
Replace engine drive belt	S/I						✔

R: Replace   S/I: Service or Inspect

22116_GMG6_C0016

PRECAUTIONS

Before servicing any vehicle, please be sure to read all of the following precautions, which deal with personal safety, prevention of component damage, and important points to take into consideration when servicing a motor vehicle:

• Never open, service or drain the radiator or cooling system when the engine is hot; serious burns can occur from the steam and hot coolant.

• Observe all applicable safety precautions when working around fuel. Whenever servicing the fuel system, always work in a well-ventilated area. Do not allow fuel spray or vapors to come in contact with a spark, open flame, or excessive heat (a hot drop light, for example). Keep a dry chemical fire extinguisher near the work area. Always keep fuel in a container specifically designed for fuel storage; also, always properly seal fuel containers to avoid the possibility of fire or explosion. Refer to the additional fuel system precautions later in this section.

• Fuel injection systems often remain pressurized, even after the engine has been turned **OFF**. The fuel system pressure must be relieved before disconnecting any fuel lines. Failure to do so may result in fire and/or personal injury.

• Brake fluid often contains polyglycol ethers and polyglycols. Avoid contact with the eyes and wash your hands thoroughly after handling brake fluid. If you do get brake fluid in your eyes, flush your eyes with clean, running water for 15 minutes. If eye irritation persists, or if you have taken brake fluid internally, IMMEDIATELY seek medical assistance.

• The EPA warns that prolonged contact with used engine oil may cause a number of skin disorders, including cancer. You should make every effort to minimize your exposure to used engine oil. Protective gloves should be worn when changing oil. Wash your hands and any other exposed skin areas as soon as possible after exposure to used engine oil. Soap and water, or waterless hand cleaner should be used.

• All new vehicles are now equipped with an air bag system, often referred to as a Supplemental Restraint System (SRS) or Supplemental Inflatable Restraint (SIR) system. The system must be disabled before performing service on or around system components, steering column, instrument panel components, wiring and sensors. Failure to follow safety and disabling procedures could result in accidental air bag deployment, possible personal injury and unnecessary system repairs.

• Always wear safety goggles when working with, or around, the air bag system. When carrying a non-deployed air bag, be sure the bag and trim cover are pointed away from your body. When placing a non-deployed air bag on a work surface, always face the bag and trim cover upward, away from the surface. This will reduce the motion of the module if it is accidentally deployed. Refer to the additional air bag system precautions later in this section.

• Clean, high quality brake fluid from a sealed container is essential to the safe and proper operation of the brake system. You should always buy the correct type of brake fluid for your vehicle. If the brake fluid becomes contaminated, completely flush the system with new fluid. Never reuse any brake fluid. Any brake fluid that is removed from the system should be discarded. Also, do not allow any brake fluid to come in contact with a painted surface; it will damage the paint.

• Never operate the engine without the proper amount and type of engine oil; doing so WILL result in severe engine damage.

• Timing belt maintenance is extremely important. Many models utilize an interference-type, non-freewheeling engine. If the timing belt breaks, the valves in the cylinder head may strike the pistons, causing potentially serious (also time-consuming and expensive) engine damage. Refer to the maintenance interval charts for the recommended replacement interval for the timing belt, and to the timing belt section for belt replacement and inspection.

• Disconnecting the negative battery cable on some vehicles may interfere with the functions of the on-board computer system(s) and may require the computer to undergo a relearning process once the negative battery cable is reconnected.

• When servicing drum brakes, only disassemble and assemble one side at a time, leaving the remaining side intact for reference.

• Only an MVAC-trained, EPA-certified automotive technician should service the air conditioning system or its components.

BRAKES

ANTI-LOCK BRAKE SYSTEM (ABS)

GENERAL INFORMATION

When wheel slip is detected during a brake application, the antilock brake system (ABS) enters antilock mode. During antilock braking, hydraulic pressure in the individual wheel circuits is controlled to prevent any wheel from slipping. A separate hydraulic line and specific solenoid valves are provided for each wheel. The ABS can decrease, hold, or increase hydraulic pressure to each wheel brake. The ABS cannot, however, increase hydraulic pressure above the amount which is transmitted by the master cylinder during braking.

During antilock braking, a series of rapid pulsations is felt in the brake pedal. These pulsations are caused by the rapid changes in position of the individual solenoid valves as the electronic brake control module (EBCM) responds to wheel speed sensor inputs and attempts to prevent wheel slip. These pedal pulsations are present only during antilock braking and stop when normal braking is resumed or when the vehicle comes to a stop. A ticking or popping noise may also be heard as the solenoid valves cycle rapidly. During antilock braking on dry pavement, intermittent chirping noises may be heard as the tires approach slipping. These noises and pedal pulsations are considered normal during antilock operation.

Vehicles equipped with ABS may be stopped by applying normal force to the brake pedal. Brake pedal operation during normal braking is no different than that of previous non-ABS systems. Maintaining a constant force on the brake pedal provides the shortest stopping distance while maintaining vehicle stability.

PRECAUTIONS

• Certain components within the ABS system are not intended to be serviced or repaired individually.

• Do not use rubber hoses or other parts not specifically specified for and ABS system. When using repair kits, replace all parts included in the kit. Partial or incorrect repair may lead to functional problems and require the replacement of components.

• Lubricate rubber parts with clean, fresh brake fluid to ease assembly. Do not use shop air to clean parts; damage to rubber components may result.

• Use only DOT 3 brake fluid from an unopened container.

• If any hydraulic component or line is removed or replaced, it may be necessary to bleed the entire system.

• A clean repair area is essential. Always clean the reservoir and cap thoroughly before removing the cap. The slightest amount of dirt in the fluid may plug an orifice and impair the system function. Perform repairs after components have been thoroughly cleaned; use only denatured alcohol to clean compo-

nents. Do not allow ABS components to come into contact with any substance containing mineral oil; this includes used shop rags.

• The Anti-Lock control unit is a microprocessor similar to other computer units in the vehicle. Ensure that the ignition switch is **OFF** before removing or installing controller harnesses. Avoid static electricity discharge at or near the controller.

• If any arc welding is to be done on the vehicle, the control unit should be unplugged before welding operations begin.

SPEED SENSORS

REMOVAL & INSTALLATION

The wheel speed sensors are part of the hub and bearing assembly. Refer to Wheel Hub and Bearing in the SUSPENSION Section..

BRAKES

BLEEDING THE BRAKE SYSTEM

BLEEDING PROCEDURE

BLEEDING PROCEDURE

1. Place a clean shop cloth beneath the brake master cylinder to catch brake fluid spills.

2. With the ignition OFF and the brakes cool, apply the brakes 3-5 times, or until the brake pedal effort increases significantly, in order to deplete the brake booster power reserve.

3. If you have performed a brake master cylinder bench bleeding on this vehicle, or if you disconnected the brake pipes from the master cylinder, or if you have disconnected the brake pipes from the proportioning valve assembly or the brake modulator assembly, you must perform the following steps to bleed air at the ports of the hydraulic component:

   a. Ensure that the brake master cylinder reservoir is full to the maximum-fill level. If necessary, add Delco Supreme 11, or equivalent DOT 3 brake fluid from a clean, sealed brake fluid container. If removal of the reservoir cap and diaphragm is necessary, clean the outside of the reservoir on and around the cap prior to removal.

   b. With the brake pipes installed securely to the master cylinder, proportioning valve assembly, or brake modulator assembly, loosen and separate one of the brake pipes from the port of the component. For the proportioning valve assembly or the brake modulator assembly, perform these steps in the sequence of system flow; begin with the fluid feed pipes from the master cylinder.

   c. Allow a small amount of brake fluid to gravity bleed from the open port of the component.

   d. Connect the brake pipe to the component and tighten securely.

   e. Have an assistant slowly press the brake pedal fully and maintain steady pressure on the pedal.

   f. Loosen the same brake pipe to purge air from the open port of the component.

   g. Tighten the brake pipe, then have the assistant slowly release the brake pedal.

   h. Wait 15 seconds, then repeat the steps until all air is purged from the same port of the component.

   i. With the brake pipe installed securely to the master cylinder, proportioning valve assembly, or brake modulator assembly, after all air has been purged from the first port of the component that was bled, loosen and separate the next brake pipe from the component, then repeat the steps until each of the ports on the component has been bled.

   j. After completing the final component port bleeding procedure, ensure that each of the brake pipe-to-component fittings are properly tightened.

4. Fill the brake master cylinder reservoir with Delco Supreme 11 or equivalent DOT 3 brake fluid from a clean, sealed brake fluid container. Ensure that the brake master cylinder reservoir remains at least half-full during this bleeding procedure. Add fluid as needed to maintain the proper level. Clean the outside of the reservoir on and around the reservoir cap prior to removing the cap and diaphragm.

5. Install a proper box-end wrench onto the RIGHT REAR wheel hydraulic circuit bleeder valve.

6. Install a transparent hose over the end of the bleeder valve.

7. Submerge the open end of the transparent hose into a transparent container partially filled with brake fluid from a clean, sealed brake fluid container.

8. Have an assistant slowly press the brake pedal fully and maintain steady pressure on the pedal.

9. Loosen the bleeder valve to purge air from the wheel hydraulic circuit.

10. Tighten the bleeder valve, then have the assistant slowly release the brake pedal.

11. Wait 15 seconds, then repeat the until all air is purged from the same wheel hydraulic circuit.

12. With the right rear wheel hydraulic circuit bleeder valve tightened securely, after all air has been purged from the right rear hydraulic circuit, install a proper box-end wrench onto the LEFT FRONT wheel hydraulic circuit bleeder valve.

13. Install a transparent hose over the end of the bleeder valve, then repeat the procedure.

14. With the left front wheel hydraulic circuit bleeder valve tightened securely, after all air has been purged from the left front hydraulic circuit, install a proper box-end wrench onto the LEFT REAR wheel hydraulic circuit bleeder valve.

15. Install a transparent hose over the end of the bleeder valve, then repeat the procedure.

16. With the left rear wheel hydraulic circuit bleeder valve tightened securely, after all air has been purged from the left rear hydraulic circuit, install a proper box-end wrench onto the RIGHT FRONT wheel hydraulic circuit bleeder valve.

17. Install a transparent hose over the end of the bleeder valve, then repeat the procedure.

18. After completing the final wheel hydraulic circuit bleeding procedure, ensure that each of the 4 wheel hydraulic circuit bleeder valves are properly tightened.

19. Fill the brake master cylinder reservoir to the maximum-fill level with Delco Supreme 11, or equivalent DOT 3 brake fluid from a clean, sealed brake fluid container.

20. Slowly press and release the brake pedal. Observe the feel of the brake pedal.

21. If the brake pedal feels spongy, repeat the bleeding procedure again. If the brake pedal still feels spongy after repeating

the bleeding procedure, perform the following steps:

    a. Inspect the brake system for external leaks.

    b. Pressure bleed the hydraulic brake system in order to purge any air that may still be trapped in the system.

    c. Turn the ignition key ON, with the engine OFF. Check to see if the brake system warning lamp remains illuminated.

22. If the brake light is on, DO NOT allow the vehicle to be driven until it is diagnosed and repaired.

BLEEDING THE ABS SYSTEM

1. Raise the vehicle on a suitable support.

2. Remove all four tire and wheel assemblies.

3. Inspect the brake system for leaks and visual damage.

4. Inspect the battery state of charge.

5. Install a scan tool.

6. Turn ON the ignition, with the engine OFF.

7. With the scan tool, establish communications with the EBCM. Select Special Functions. Select Automated Bleed from the Special Functions menu.

8. Bleed the base brake system.

9. Follow the scan tool directions until the desired brake pedal height is achieved.

10. When the desired pedal height is achieved, press the brake pedal in order to inspect for firmness.

11. Remove the scan tool.

12. Install the tire and wheel assemblies.

13. Inspect the brake fluid level.

14. Road test the vehicle while inspecting that the pedal remains high and firm.

BRAKES

FRONT DISC BRAKES

❋❋ CAUTION

Dust and dirt accumulating on brake parts during normal use may contain asbestos fibers from production or aftermarket brake linings. Breathing excessive concentrations of asbestos fibers can cause serious bodily harm. Exercise care when servicing brake parts. Do not sand or grind brake lining unless equipment used is designed to contain the dust residue. Do not clean brake parts with compressed air or by dry brushing. Cleaning should be done by dampening the brake components with a fine mist of water, then wiping the brake components clean with a dampened cloth. Dispose of cloth and all residue containing asbestos fibers in an impermeable container with the appropriate label. Follow practices prescribed by the Occupational Safety and Health Administration (OSHA) and the Environmental Protection Agency (EPA) for the handling, processing, and disposing of dust or debris that may contain asbestos fibers.

BRAKE CALIPER

REMOVAL & INSTALLATION

1. Remove enough brake fluid from the reservoir to reach the half fill mark.

2. Raise and support the vehicle.

3. Remove the tire and wheel.

4. Install and firmly hand tighten 2 wheel nuts to opposite wheel studs in order to retain the rotor to the hub.

5. Install a large C-clamp over the body of the brake caliper with the C-clamp ends against the rear of the caliper body and against the outer brake pad.

6. Tighten the C-clamp until the caliper piston is compressed into the caliper bore enough to allow the caliper to slide past the brake rotor.

7. Remove the C-clamp from the caliper.

8. Remove the brake hose from the brake caliper.

9. Cap or plug the opening in the brake caliper and the brake hose to prevent fluid loss and contamination.

10. Remove the brake caliper guide pin bolts.

11. Remove the brake caliper from the caliper bracket.

To install:

12. Install the brake caliper to the brake caliper bracket.

13. Install the brake caliper guide pin bolts and tighten to 26 ft. lbs. (35 Nm).

14. Remove the caps or plugs from the brake caliper opening and the brake hose.

15. Install new copper brake hose gaskets to the brake hose-to-caliper bolt and to the brake hose.

16. Install the brake hose and the brake hose-to-brake caliper bolt to the brake caliper and tighten to 37 ft. lbs. (50 Nm).

17. Bleed the hydraulic brake system.

18. Remove the wheel nuts retaining the brake rotor to the wheel hub.

19. Install the tire and wheel assembly.

20. Lower the vehicle.

21. With the engine off, gradually apply the brake pedal to approximately 2/3 of its travel distance.

22. Slowly release the brake pedal.

23. Wait 15 seconds, then repeat the steps until a firm brake pedal apply is obtained; this will properly seat the brake caliper piston and brake pads.

DISC BRAKE PADS

REMOVAL & INSTALLATION

1. Remove enough brake fluid from the reservoir to reach the half fill mark.

2. Raise and support the vehicle.

3. Remove the tire and wheel.

4. Install and firmly hand tighten 2 wheel nuts to opposite wheel studs in order to retain the rotor to the hub.

5. Remove the brake caliper lower guide pin bolt.

6. Push the disc brake caliper piston into the caliper bore using an old inner disc brake pad and a disc brake piston installation tool.

7. Without disconnecting the hydraulic brake flexible hose, pivot the caliper upward and secure the caliper with heavy mechanics wire.

8. Remove the brake pads from the caliper mounting bracket.

9. Remove the brake pad retainers from the caliper bracket.

10. Thoroughly clean the brake pad hardware mating surfaces of the caliper bracket, of any debris and corrosion.

To install:

11. Ensure the brake pad hardware mating surfaces are clean.

12. Install the brake pad retainers to the brake caliper bracket.

➡**The wear sensor equipped disc brake pad must be mounted inboard of the rotor with the leading edge of the sensor facing the brake rotor during forward wheel rotation, or at the top of the pad when installed in vehicle position.**

13. Install the brake pads to the caliper bracket.

14. Remove the support, and rotate the brake caliper into position over the disc

brake pads and to the caliper mounting bracket.

15. Install the lower brake caliper guide pin bolt and tighten to 26 ft. lbs. (35 Nm).

16. Remove the wheel nuts retaining the brake rotor to the hub.

17. Install the tire and wheel.

18. Lower the vehicle.

19. With the engine OFF, gradually apply the brake pedal approximately 2/3 of its travel distance.

20. Slowly release the brake pedal.

21. Wait 15 seconds, then gradually apply the brake pedal approximately 2/3 of

its travel distance again until a firm brake pedal apply is obtained. This will properly seat the brake caliper pistons and brake pads.

22. Fill the master cylinder auxiliary reservoir to the proper level.

23. Burnish the pads and rotors.

BRAKES

✳✳ CAUTION

Dust and dirt accumulating on brake parts during normal use may contain asbestos fibers from production or aftermarket brake linings. Breathing excessive concentrations of asbestos fibers can cause serious bodily harm. Exercise care when servicing brake parts. Do not sand or grind brake lining unless equipment used is designed to contain the dust residue. Do not clean brake parts with compressed air or by dry brushing. Cleaning should be done by dampening the brake components with a fine mist of water, then wiping the brake components clean with a dampened cloth. Dispose of cloth and all residue containing asbestos fibers in an impermeable container with the appropriate label. Follow practices prescribed by the Occupational Safety and Health Administration (OSHA) and the Environmental Protection Agency (EPA) for the handling, processing, and disposing of dust or debris that may contain asbestos fibers.

BRAKE CALIPER

REMOVAL & INSTALLATION

1. Remove enough brake fluid from the reservoir to reach the half fill mark.

2. Raise and support the vehicle.

3. Remove the tire and wheel.

4. Install and firmly hand tighten 2 wheel nuts to opposite wheel studs in order to retain the rotor to the hub.

5. Install a large C-clamp over the body of the brake caliper with the C-clamp ends against the rear of the caliper body and against the outer brake pad.

6. Tighten the C-clamp until the caliper piston is compressed into the caliper bore enough to allow the caliper to slide past the brake rotor.

7. Remove the C-clamp from the caliper.

8. Remove the brake hose from the brake caliper.

9. Cap or plug the opening in the brake caliper and the brake hose to prevent fluid loss and contamination.

10. On rear brakes, disconnect the parking brake cable from the caliper.

11. Remove the brake caliper guide pin bolts.

12. Remove the brake caliper from the caliper bracket.

To install:

13. Install the brake caliper to the brake caliper bracket.

14. Install the brake caliper guide pin bolts and tighten to 26 ft. lbs. (35 Nm).

15. Remove the caps or plugs from the brake caliper opening and the brake hose.

16. Install new copper brake hose gaskets to the brake hose-to-caliper bolt and to the brake hose.

17. Install the brake hose and the brake hose-to-brake caliper bolt to the brake caliper and tighten to 37 ft. lbs. (50 Nm).

18. On rear brakes, connect the parking brake cable to the caliper.

19. Bleed the hydraulic brake system.

20. Remove the wheel nuts retaining the brake rotor to the wheel hub.

21. Install the tire and wheel assembly.

22. Lower the vehicle.

23. With the engine off, gradually apply the brake pedal to approximately 2/3 of its travel distance.

24. Slowly release the brake pedal.

25. Wait 15 seconds, then repeat the steps until a firm brake pedal apply is obtained; this will properly seat the brake caliper piston and brake pads.

DISC BRAKE PADS

REMOVAL & INSTALLATION

1. Remove enough brake fluid from the reservoir to reach the half fill mark.

2. Raise and support the vehicle.

3. Remove the tire and wheel.

4. Install and firmly hand tighten 2 wheel nuts to opposite wheel studs in order to retain the rotor to the hub.

5. Remove the brake caliper lower guide pin bolt.

6. Push the disc brake caliper piston

REAR DISC BRAKES

into the caliper bore using an old inner disc brake pad and a disc brake piston installation tool.

7. Without disconnecting the hydraulic brake flexible hose, pivot the caliper upward and secure the caliper with heavy mechanics wire.

8. Remove the brake pads from the caliper mounting bracket.

9. Remove the brake pad retainers from the caliper bracket.

10. Thoroughly clean the brake pad hardware mating surfaces of the caliper bracket, of any debris and corrosion.

To install:

11. Ensure the brake pad hardware mating surfaces are clean.

12. Install the brake pad retainers to the brake caliper bracket.

➡The wear sensor equipped disc brake pad must be mounted inboard of the rotor with the leading edge of the sensor facing the brake rotor during forward wheel rotation, or at the top of the pad when installed in vehicle position.

13. Install the brake pads to the caliper bracket.

14. Remove the support, and rotate the brake caliper into position over the disc brake pads and to the caliper mounting bracket.

15. Install the lower brake caliper guide pin bolt and tighten to 26 ft. lbs. (35 Nm).

16. Remove the wheel nuts retaining the brake rotor to the hub.

17. Install the tire and wheel.

18. Lower the vehicle.

19. With the engine OFF, gradually apply the brake pedal approximately 2/3 of its travel distance.

20. Slowly release the brake pedal.

21. Wait 15 seconds, then gradually apply the brake pedal approximately 2/3 of its travel distance again until a firm brake pedal apply is obtained. This will properly seat the brake caliper pistons and brake pads.

22. Fill the master cylinder auxiliary reservoir to the proper level.

23. Burnish the pads and rotors.

BRAKES

PARKING BRAKE

PARKING BRAKE CABLES

REMOVAL & INSTALLATION

See Figure 1.

1. Ensure that the park brake lever is in the fully released position.
2. Remove the floor console.
3. Remove the rear carpet.
4. Remove the right rear park brake cable or the left rear park brake cable from the console park brake bracket and the front park brake cable equalizer.
5. Raise and support the vehicle.
6. Remove the plastic retainer clip from the body.
7. Remove the tire and wheel assembly.
8. Remove the rear park brake cable retainer bolt.
9. Remove the rear park brake cable from the caliper park brake lever.
10. Lower the vehicle
11. Remove the plastic retainer clip from the stud.
12. Remove the park brake cable and pass-thru grommet from the body and remove the cable from the vehicle.

To install:

13. Install the park brake cable to the vehicle.
14. Install the park brake cable and pass-thru grommet to the body.
15. Install the plastic retainer clip to the stud.
16. Raise the vehicle.
17. Install the rear park brake cable to the caliper park brake lever.

18. Install the rear park brake cable retainer bolt.
19. Tighten the bolt to 89 inch. lbs. (10 Nm).
20. Install the plastic retainer clip to the body.
21. Install the tire and wheel assembly
22. Lower the vehicle.
23. Install the right rear park brake cable or the left rear park brake cable to the console park brake bracket and the front park brake cable equalizer.
24. Install the rear carpet.
25. Install the floor console.
26. Cycle the park brake lever 3—5 times.

ADJUSTMENT

1. Apply and fully release the park brake lever several times. Verify that the park brake lever releases completely.
2. Turn ON the ignition. Verify the red BRAKE warning lamp is not illuminated.
3. If the red BRAKE warning lamp is illuminated, verify the park brake lever is in the fully released position and against the stop and there is no slack in the park brake cables.
4. Turn OFF the ignition.
5. Raise and support the vehicle.
6. With the park brake lever fully released, check the park brake apply levers on the rear calipers. The apply levers should be against the stops on the caliper housings. If the apply levers are not against the stops, binding may exist.
7. Fully apply and release the park brake lever 3—5 times in order for the cable tensioner to take up any slack in the park brake cables.
8. Fully apply the park brake lever, tension should be felt on the lever by pulling the lever less than one full pull.
9. Attempt to rotate the rear brake rotors. There should be no rotation forward or rearward.
10. Fully release the park brake lever.
11. Verify the park brake is released by rotating the rear brake rotors. The rotors should rotate freely and exhibit no brake drag.
12. Lower the vehicle.

LEVER ASSEMBLY

REMOVAL & INSTALLATION

See Figure 2.

1. Remove the park brake bezel and the park brake lever boot.
2. Remove the front floor console.
3. Ensure that the park brake lever is in the fully released position.
4. Remove the console support bracket.
5. Remove the shift assembly
6. Disconnect the electrical connector from the park brake warning lamp switch.
7. Remove the 4 park brake lever retaining nuts.
8. Remove the right rear cable and the left rear cable from the park brake lever equalizer.
9. Remove the park brake lever assembly from the vehicle.

To install:

10. Install the park brake lever assembly to the vehicle. Do not tighten the 4 retaining nuts.
11. Install the right rear cable and the left rear cable to the park brake lever equalizer.
12. Install the 4 park brake lever assembly retaining nuts.
13. Tighten the front 2 nuts to 20 ft. lbs. (27 Nm).
14. Tighten the rear 2 nuts to 89 inch. lbs. (10 Nm).
15. Install the shift assembly
16. Connect the electrical connector (1) to the park brake warning lamp switch.
17. Install the console support bracket.
18. Install the front floor console.
19. Fully apply and release the park brake lever 3—5 times.

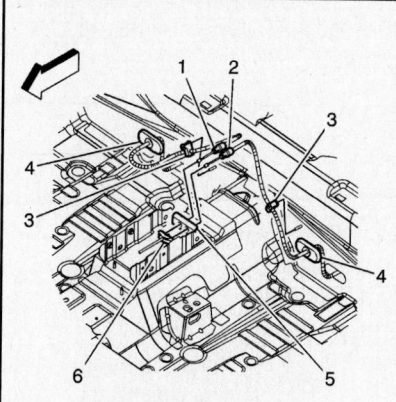

1. Right rear park brake cable
2. Console park brake bracket
3. Plastic retainer clip
4. Grommet
5. Console park brake bracket
6. Front park brake cable equalizer

22116_GMG6_G0085

Fig. 1 Inside vehicle parking brake cable components view

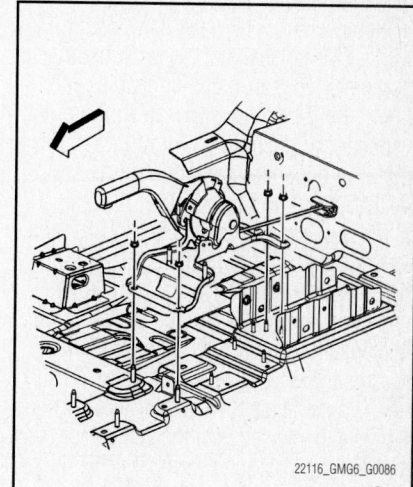

22116_GMG6_G0086

Fig. 2 Parking brake lever assembly and retaining nuts

GENERAL INFORMATION

✳✳ CAUTION

These vehicles are equipped with an air bag system. The system must be disarmed before performing service on, or around, system components, the steering column, instrument panel components, wiring and sensors. Failure to follow the safety precautions and the disarming procedure could result in accidental air bag deployment, possible injury and unnecessary system repairs.

SERVICE PRECAUTIONS

Disconnect and isolate the battery negative cable before beginning any airbag system component diagnosis, testing, removal, or installation procedures. Allow system capacitor to discharge for two minutes before beginning any component service. This will disable the airbag system. Failure to disable the airbag system may result in accidental airbag deployment, personal injury, or death.

Do not place an intact undeployed airbag face down on a solid surface. The airbag will propel into the air if accidentally deployed and may result in personal injury or death.

When carrying or handling an undeployed airbag, the trim side (face) of the airbag should be pointing towards the body to minimize possibility of injury if accidental deployment occurs. Failure to do this may result in personal injury or death.

Replace airbag system components with OEM replacement parts. Substitute parts may appear interchangeable, but internal differences may result in inferior occupant protection. Failure to do so may result in occupant personal injury or death.

Wear safety glasses, rubber gloves, and long sleeved clothing when cleaning powder residue from vehicle after an airbag deployment. Powder residue emitted from a deployed airbag can cause skin irritation. Flush affected area with cool water if irritation is experienced. If nasal or throat irritation is experienced, exit the vehicle for fresh air until the irritation ceases. If irritation continues, see a physician.

Do not use a replacement airbag that is not in the original packaging. This may result in improper deployment, personal injury, or death.

The factory installed fasteners, screws and bolts used to fasten airbag components have a special coating and are specifically designed for the airbag system. Do not use substitute fasteners. Use only original equipment fasteners listed in the parts catalog when fastener replacement is required.

During, and following, any child restraint anchor service, due to impact event or vehicle repair, carefully inspect all mounting hardware, tether straps, and anchors for proper installation, operation, or damage. If a child restraint anchor is found damaged in any way, the anchor must be replaced. Failure to do this may result in personal injury or death.

Deployed and non-deployed airbags may or may not have live pyrotechnic material within the airbag inflator.

Do not dispose of driver/passenger/curtain airbags or seat belt tensioners unless you are sure of complete deployment. Refer to the Hazardous Substance Control System for proper disposal.

Dispose of deployed airbags and tensioners consistent with state, provincial, local, and federal regulations.

After any airbag component testing or service, do not connect the battery negative cable. Personal injury or death may result if the system test is not performed first.

If the vehicle is equipped with the Occupant Classification System (OCS), do not connect the battery negative cable before performing the OCS Verification Test using the scan tool and the appropriate diagnostic information. Personal injury or death may result if the system test is not performed properly.

Never replace both the Occupant Restraint Controller (ORC) and the Occupant Classification Module (OCM) at the same time. If both require replacement, replace one, then perform the Airbag System test before replacing the other.

Both the ORC and the OCM store Occupant Classification System (OCS) calibration data, which they transfer to one another when one of them is replaced. If both are replaced at the same time, an irreversible fault will be set in both modules and the OCS may malfunction and cause personal injury or death.

If equipped with OCS, the Seat Weight Sensor is a sensitive, calibrated unit and must be handled carefully. Do not drop or handle roughly. If dropped or damaged,

replace with another sensor. Failure to do so may result in occupant injury or death.

If equipped with OCS, the front passenger seat must be handled carefully as well. When removing the seat, be careful when setting on floor not to drop. If dropped, the sensor may be inoperative, could result in occupant injury, or possibly death.

If equipped with OCS, when the passenger front seat is on the floor, no one should sit in the front passenger seat. This uneven force may damage the sensing ability of the seat weight sensors. If sat on and damaged, the sensor may be inoperative, could result in occupant injury, or possibly death.

DISARMING THE SYSTEM

See Figure 3.

➡**All Air Bag electrical wiring harnesses and connectors are covered with YELLOW outer insulation. Do not use electrical test equipment on any circuit related to the Air Bag sensors. When installing Air Bag components, always install with the arrow marks facing the front of the vehicle.**

1. Before servicing the vehicle, refer to the precautions in the beginning of this section.

2. Place the front wheels in the straight ahead position.

3. Turn the ignition switch to the **OFF** position and remove the key.

4. Remove the Body Control Module (BCM) fuse cover and remove the AIR BAG (IGN) and AIR BAG (BATT) fuses from the fuse block.

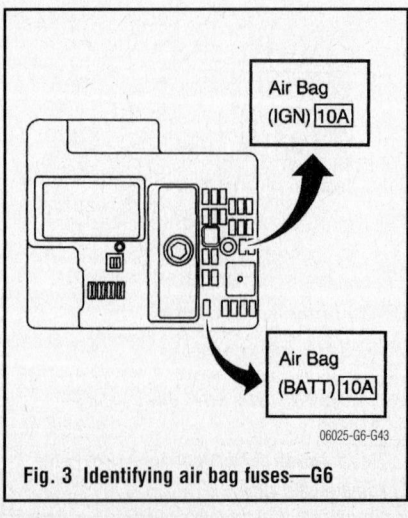

Air Bag (IGN) 10A

Air Bag (BATT) 10A

06025-G6-G43

Fig. 3 Identifying air bag fuses—G6

5. Open the hood and locate the front end sensor, also known as the Electronic Frontal Sensor (EFS) on the radiator support.

6. Remove the Connector Position Assurance (CPA) from the EFS connector.

7. Remove the EFS connector from the EFS (2).

ARMING THE SYSTEM

1. Turn the ignition switch to the **OFF** position.

2. Connect the EFS connector to the EFS.

3. Connect the CPA to the EFS connector.

4. Install the AIR BAG (IGN) and AIR BAG (BATT) fuses into the BCM fuse center.

5. Use caution while reaching in and turn the ignition switch to the ON position. The AIR BAG indicator will flash then turn OFF.

6. Perform the SIR Diagnostic System Check if the AIR BAG warning indicator does not operate as described.

CLOCKSPRING CENTERING

See Figure 4.

1. Verify the following conditions before centering the supplemental inflatable restraint (SIR) steering wheel module coil:

   a. The wheels on the vehicle are straight ahead.

   b. The block tooth and the centering mark (1) of the steering shaft is in the 12 o'clock position. If available, remove the yellow retaining tab (1) from the SIR steering wheel module coil and save the tab for reassembly.

2. Hold the SIR steering wheel module coil face up by the casing (2).

   a. Slowly turn the SIR steering wheel module coil hub (3) clockwise until the coil ribbon stops.

   b. Slowly rotate the SIR steering wheel module coil hub (3) counterclockwise 2.5 revolutions until the centering window (4) turns yellow. This indicates the CENTER position.

➡**If the retaining tab is not available, the use of tape to secure the SIR**

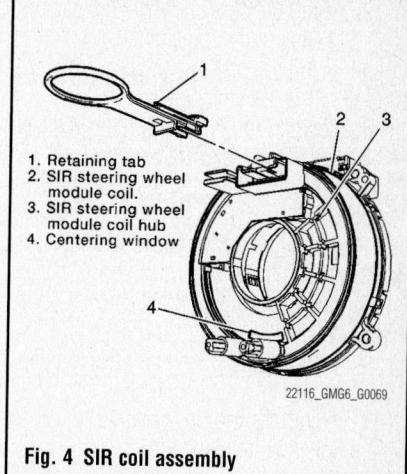

1. Retaining tab
2. SIR steering wheel module coil.
3. SIR steering wheel module coil hub
4. Centering window

22116_GMG6_G0069

Fig. 4 SIR coil assembly

steering wheel module coil is recommended for installation to the steering column.

3. Install the yellow retaining tab (1) to the SIR steering wheel module coil.

4. Slide the centered SIR steering wheel module coil onto the steering shaft.

DRIVETRAIN

AUTOMATIC TRANSAXLE ASSEMBLY

REMOVAL & INSTALLATION

4T40—E/4T45—E

1. Before servicing the vehicle, refer to the precautions in the beginning of this section.

2. Drain the transaxle fluid.

3. Disconnect the negative battery cable.

4. Raise and support the vehicle.

5. Spray penetrating oil on the exposed threads of both lower ball joint bolt to facilitate their removal.

6. Lower the vehicle.

7. Remove the air intake duct.

8. Disconnect the transaxle wiring harness from the transaxle and the Park Neutral Position (PNP) switch.

9. Remove the shift cable bracket and shift cable from the lever.

10. Remove the transmission wiring harness from the retainer on the transmission.

11. Disconnect the Bank 2 O2 sensor electrical connector.

12. Remove the left exhaust manifold heat shield.

13. Remove the front exhaust pipe nuts.

14. Remove the upper transmission to engine bolts and stud.

15. Install the engine support fixture.

16. Support the radiator and condenser from above using the condenser tabs on each side.

17. Raise the vehicle.

18. Remove the front wheels and tires.

19. Disconnect the Bank 2 O2 sensor electrical sensor.

20. Remove the left catalytic converter to right catalytic converter nuts.

21. Remove the left catalytic converter.

22. Remove the steering gear intermediate shaft .

23. Remove the frame.

➡**It is only necessary to remove the control arms when the frame is replaced.**

24. Disconnect the wheel drive shafts from the transaxle.

25. Remove the 3 bolts from the transmission brace near the right axle shaft.

26. Remove the 3 oil pan to bellhousing bracket bolts.

27. Remove the flywheel inspection cover.

28. Remove the starter.

29. Mark the relationship of the flywheel to the torque converter for reassembly

30. Remove the torque converter to flywheel bolts.

31. Remove the transmission oil cooler

lines by removing the nut holding the bracket to the transaxle case.

32. Disconnect the Vehicle Speed Sensor (VSS) wiring harness from the sensor.

33. Disconnect the rear Heated Oxygen Sensor (HO2S) harness from the bracket on the rear transaxle mount

34. Remove the remaining rear bolt from the shift cable bracket.

35. Remove the front transmission mount bracket from the transmission

36. Use a transmission jack in order to support the transmission.

37. Remove the remaining bellhousing bolts and studs and separate the transmission from the engine.

38. Lower the transmission with the transmission jack far enough to remove the transmission.

39. If the transmission is being replace or installed in a holding fixture, remove the rear transmission mount bracket from the transmission.

40. If the transmission is being replaced, remove the PNP switch from the transmission

41. If the transmission is being replaced, remove the transmission mount.

To install:

42. If the transmission is being replaced, install the transmission mount.

43. Install the side cover transmission mount bracket to the transmission.

44. Install the rear transmission mount bracket to the transmission

45. Position the transaxle in the vehicle.

46. Install the lower transmission to engine bolts and nuts, tighten to 66 ft. lbs. (90 Nm).

47. Install the front transmission mount bracket to the transmission.

48. Install the wheel drive shafts to the transaxle.

49. Connect the wiring harness to the VSS.

50. Install the torque converter to flywheel bolts and tighten to 46 ft. lbs. (62 Nm).

51. Install the starter and mounting bolts tighten to 30 ft. lbs. (40 Nm).

52. Install the flywheel inspection cover bolts and tighten to 89 inch. lbs. (10 Nm).

53. Connect the transaxle oil cooler pipes to the transaxle. Tighten the pipes to 71 inch. lbs. (8 Nm).

54. Install the 3 oil pan to bellhousing bracket bolts. Tighten the bolts to 53 ft. lbs. (72 Nm).

55. Install the 3 bolts to the transmission brace at the final drive area and tighten.

56. Remove the transmission jack.

57. Install the frame.

58. Tighten the frame to body bolts to 74 ft. lbs. (100 Nm) plus 90 degrees.

59. Tighten the frame support to body bolts to 74 ft. lbs. (100 Nm).

60. Install the engine splash shields.

61. Install the front wheels and tires.

62. Lower the vehicle.

63. Remove the radiator and condenser support and the engine support fixture.

64. Install the upper transmission to engine bolts and stud. Tighten the bolts and stud to 66 ft. lbs. (90 Nm).

65. Install the shift cable bracket and shift cable to the lever.

66. Install the left catalytic converter exhaust pipe.

67. Connect the Bank 2 O2 sensor electrical connector.

68. Install the left exhaust manifold heat shield.

69. Install the heat shield bolts and tighten to 89 inch. lbs. (10 Nm).

70. Connect the Bank 2 O2 sensor electrical connector

71. Connect the electrical connectors to the PNP switch and transaxle.

72. Connect the negative battery cable.

73. Install the air intake duct.

74. Add automatic transmission fluid DEXRON VI and verify the proper fluid level of the transaxle.

➡️ **It is recommended that Transmission Adaptive Pressure (TAP) information be reset. Resetting the TAP values using a scan tool will erase all learned values in all cells. As a result, The ECM, PCM or TCM will need to relearn TAP values. Transmission performance may be affected as new TAP values are learned.**

75. Reset the TAP values.

76. Road test the vehicle.

4T65—E

See Figure 5.

1. Raise and support the vehicle.

2. Spray penetrating oil on the exposed threads of both lower ball joint bolt to facilitate their removal later in this procedure.

3. Lower the vehicle.

4. Remove the air cleaner outlet duct.

5. Disconnect the negative battery cable.

6. Disconnect the transaxle wiring harness from the transaxle and the park neutral position (PNP) switch.

7. Remove the shift cable bracket and shift cable from the lever.

8. Remove the transmission wiring harness from the retainer on the transmission.

9. Remove the upper transmission to engine bolt and studs.

10. Install the engine support fixture.

11. Convertible ONLY, remove the transmission mount.

12. Support the radiator and condenser from above using the condenser tabs on each side.

13. Raise the vehicle.

14. Remove the front wheels and tires.

15. Remove the steering gear intermediate shaft.

16. Separate the control arm from the frame and the outer tie-rod end from the steering knuckles. Support the lower control arm with mechanic wire.

17. Remove the frame.

18. Remove the bolts from the transmission brace near the right axle shaft.

19. Remove the oil pan to bellhousing bracket bolts.

20. Remove the flywheel inspection cover.

21. Remove the starter.

22. Mark the relationship of the flywheel to the torque converter for reassembly.

23. Remove the torque converter to flywheel bolts.

24. Remove the transmission oil cooler lines by removing the nut holding the bracket to the transaxle case.

25. Disconnect the Vehicle Speed Sensor (VSS) wiring harness from the sensor.

26. Disconnect the rear Heated Oxygen Sensor (HO2S) harness from the bracket on the steering gear.

27. Disconnect the wheel drive shafts from the transaxle.

28. Remove the front transmission mount from the transmission.

29. Use a transmission jack in order to support the transmission.

30. Remove the remaining bellhousing bolts and studs and separate the transmission from the engine.

31. Lower the transmission with the transmission jack far enough to remove the transmission.

32. If the transmission is being replace or installed in a holding fixture, remove the rear transmission mount from the transmission.

33. Remove the PNP switch from the transmission.

34. Remove the transaxle to engine bolts

35. Separate the engine and the transaxle.

36. Remove the transaxle from the vehicle.

37. Remove the PNP switch.

38. Remove the shifter cable bracket.

39. Remove the lower transmission to engine stud.

40. Remove the left transmission mount bracket.

To install:

41. Install the PNP switch.

42. Install the torque converter clutch (TCC) lock up clutch O-ring.

43. Install the torque converter.

44. Transfer the transaxle from the bench fixture to the transmission jack.

45. Install the left transmission mount bracket to the transmission.

46. Install the rear transmission mount to the transmission.

47. Position the transaxle in the vehicle.

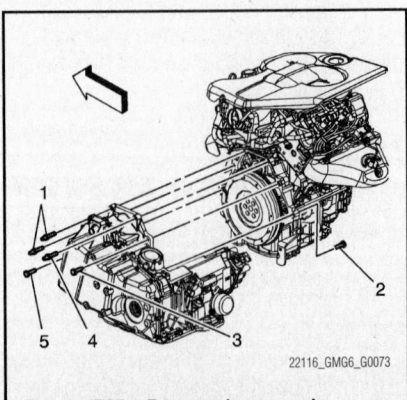

22116_GMG6_G0073

Fig. 5 4T65—E transaxle removal

48. Install the lower transmission to engine bolts and tighten to 66 ft. lbs. (90 Nm).

49. Install the front transmission mount to the transmission.

50. Install the wheel drive shafts to the transaxle. Tighten the shaft nuts to 159 ft. lbs. (215 Nm).

51. Connect the wiring harness to the VSS.

52. Install the torque converter to flywheel bolts and tighten to 46 ft. lbs. (62 Nm).

53. Install the starter and mounting bolts tighten to 30 ft. lbs. (40 Nm).

54. Install the flywheel inspection cover bolts and tighten to 89 inch. lbs. (10 Nm).

55. Connect the transaxle oil cooler pipes to the transaxle. Tighten the pipes to 71 inch. lbs. (8 Nm).

56. Install the 3 oil pan to bellhousing bracket bolts. Tighten the bolts to 53 ft. lbs. (72 Nm).

57. Install the 3 bolts to the transmission brace at the final drive area and tighten.

58. Remove the transmission jack.

59. Install the frame.

60. Tighten the frame to body bolts to 74 ft. lbs. (100 Nm) plus 90 degrees.

61. Tighten the frame support to body bolts to 74 ft. lbs. (100 Nm).

62. Install the engine splash shields.

63. Install the front wheels and tires.

64. Lower the vehicle.

65. Convertible ONLY, install the transmission mount.

66. Remove the radiator and condenser support and the engine support fixture.

67. Install the upper transmission to engine bolts and stud. Tighten the bolts and stud to 66 ft. lbs. (90 Nm).

68. Install the shift cable bracket and shift cable to the lever.

69. Install the exhaust pipe upper bolts and heat shield.

70. Connect the electrical connectors to the PNP switch and transaxle.

71. Connect the negative battery cable.

72. Install the air cleaner outlet duct.

73. Add automatic transmission fluid DEXRON VI and verify the proper fluid level of the transaxle.

➡ **It is recommended that Transmission Adaptive Pressure (TAP) information be reset. Resetting the TAP values using a scan tool will erase all learned values in all cells. As a result, The ECM, PCM or TCM will need to relearn TAP values. Transmission performance may be affected as new TAP values are learned.**

74. Reset the TAP values.

75. Road test the vehicle.

6T70/6T75

1. Disconnect the negative battery cable.

2. Remove the battery tray.

3. Remove the transmission range select lever cable and bracket.

4. Drain the transmission fluid.

5. Remove the wire harness retainer from the control valve body cover stud.

6. Disconnect the control valve body Transmission Control Module (TCM) electrical connector.

7. Remove the transmission fluid cooler pipe retainer nut.

8. Remove the transmission fluid cooler inlet hose and seal from the transmission.

9. Plug and/or cap the hose and transmission to prevent contamination.

10. Remove the transmission fluid cooler pipe retainer nut.

11. Remove the transmission fluid cooler outlet hose and seal from the transmission.

12. Plug and/or cap the hose and transmission to prevent contamination.

13. Remove the upper transmission to engine bolts.

14. Remove the frame.

15. Disconnect the wheel drive shafts from the transmission.

16. Remove the intermediate drive shaft.

17. Remove the transmission brace bolts.

18. Remove the transmission brace.

19. Remove the rear transmission mount from the transmission.

20. Remove the front transmission mount from the transmission.

21. Remove the starter.

22. Mark the relationship of the flywheel to the torque converter for reassembly.

23. Remove the torque converter to flywheel bolts.

24. Use a transmission jack in order to support the transmission.

25. Remove the flywheel inspection cover bolts.

26. Remove the flywheel inspection cover.

27. Remove the remaining transmission bolts.

➡ **Insure the torque converter remains securely in place on the transmission input shaft while separating and removing the transmission.**

28. Separate the transmission from the engine.

29. Lower the transmission with the

transmission jack far enough to remove the transmission.

To install:

30. Raise the transmission with the transmission jack and position the transmission to the engine.

31. Install the transmission bolts and tighten to 55 ft. lbs. (75 Nm).

32. Install the flywheel inspection cover and bolts, tighten to 55 ft. lbs. (75 Nm).

33. Remove the transmission jack.

34. Install the torque converter to flywheel bolts at starter motor hole. Tighten the bolts to 46 ft. lbs. (62 Nm).

35. Install starter motor and tighten the mounting bolts to 37 ft. lbs. (50 Nm).

36. Install the front transmission mount to the transmission.

37. Install the rear transmission mount to the transmission.

38. Install the transmission brace.

39. Install the transmission brace bolts tighten to 37 ft. lbs. (50 Nm).

40. Install the intermediate drive shaft.

41. Install the wheel drive shafts to the transmission. Tighten the shaft nuts to 159 ft. lbs. (215 Nm).

42. Install the frame

43. Install the upper transmission to engine bolts and tighten to 55 ft. lbs. (75 Nm).

44. Install the transmission fluid cooler outlet hose and seal to the transmission.

45. Install the transmission fluid cooler pipe retainer nut and tighten to 16 ft. lbs. (22 Nm).

46. Install the transmission fluid cooler inlet hose and seal to the transmission.

47. Install the transmission fluid cooler pipe retainer nut and tighten to 16 ft. lbs. (22 Nm).

48. Connect the control valve body TCM electrical connector.

49. Install the wire harness retainer to the control valve body cover stud. Tighten the nut to 106 lb inch. lbs. (12 Nm).

50. Install the transmission range select lever cable and bracket.

51. Install the battery tray.

52. Connect the negative battery cable.

53. Adjust the automatic transmission range selector lever cable.

54. Add automatic transmission fluid DEXRON VI and verify the proper fluid level of the transaxle.

✳✳ WARNING

Use DEXRON VI transmission fluid only. Failure to use the proper fluid may result in transmission internal damage.

➡️**After an internal transmission repair or internal part replacement the service fast learn adapt procedure should be performed.**

55. Perform the service fast learn adapt procedure. Use the scan tool to navigate to service fast learn adapts.

56. Road test the vehicle.

MANUAL TRANSAXLE ASSEMBLY

REMOVAL & INSTALLATION

See Figure 6.

1. Drain the transaxle fluid.
2. Disconnect the negative battery cable.
3. Remove the air cleaner assembly.
4. Disconnect the clutch actuator line from the clutch actuator.
5. Disconnect the select cable from the transaxle select lever.
6. Disconnect the shift cable from the transaxle shift lever.
7. Remove both cables from the cable bracket.
8. Remove the cable bracket bolt, nuts and bracket.
9. Disconnect the vehicle speed sensor (VSS) electrical connector and position the harness out of the way.
10. Disconnect the backup lamp switch electrical connector and position the harness out of the way.
11. Tie the radiator to the upper hood latch panel.
12. Install an engine support fixture.
13. Remove the upper transaxle mounting studs and bolt.
14. Raise and support the vehicle.
15. Remove the front wheels and tires.
16. Remove the left front fender liner.
17. Disconnect the 2 front wheel speed sensor connectors.
18. Unclip the wheel speed sensor wire harness and position the harness out of the way.
19. Remove the suspension frame.
20. Remove the starter.
21. Remove the transaxle front and rear mounts.
22. Remove the wheel driveshaft.
23. Lower the engine and transaxle assembly with the engine support fixture enough to clear the left side inner body panel.
24. Remove the front transaxle brace bolts and brace.
25. Remove the rear transaxle brace bolt and brace.

26. Remove the lower transaxle mounting bolts.
27. Support and remove the transaxle from the vehicle.

To install:

28. Support and raise the transaxle into the vehicle.
29. Install the lower transaxle mounting bolts. Hand-tighten only.
30. Lower the vehicle.
31. Install the upper transaxle mounting bolts. Hand-tighten only.
32. Tighten bolts (1, 4) in to 89 inch lbs. (10 Nm), then to 44 ft. lbs. (60 Nm).
33. Tighten the remaining bolts (2, 3, 5) to 44 ft. lbs. (60 Nm).
34. Install the rear transaxle brace and tighten the bolt to 22 ft. lbs. (30 Nm).
35. Install the front transaxle brace and bolts and tighten to 37 ft. lbs. (50 Nm).
36. Raise the engine and transaxle assembly with the engine support fixture into position.
37. Install the wheel driveshaft to the vehicle.
38. Install the transaxle front and rear mounts to the transaxle and tighten to 66 ft. lbs. (90 Nm).
39. Install the starter.
40. Install the suspension frame.
41. Route the wheel speed sensor wire harness to the speed sensor.
42. Connect the wheel speed sensor electrical connectors.
43. Install the left front fender liner.
44. Install the front wheels and tires.
45. Lower the vehicle.
46. Remove the engine support fixture.
47. Connect the backup lamp switch electrical connector.
48. Connect the VSS electrical connector.
49. Install the cable bracket and tighten the fasteners to 18 ft. lbs. (25 Nm).

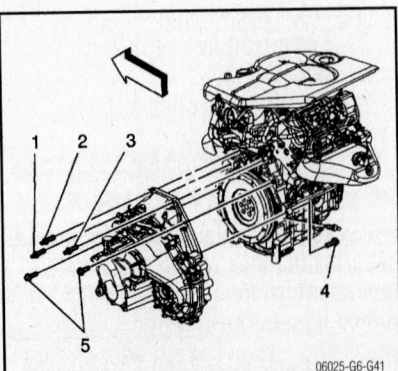

Fig. 6 Manual transaxle mounting bolt identification—G6

06025-G6-G41

50. Install both cables into the cable bracket.
51. Connect the shift cable to the transaxle shift lever.
52. Connect the select cable to the transaxle select lever.
53. Connect the clutch actuator line to the clutch actuator.
54. Install the air cleaner assembly.
55. Connect the negative battery cable.
56. Fill the transaxle to the proper level.

➡️ **Manual Transmission fluid part number 88861800 U.S. (88861801 Canada) is currently available through GMSPO. Current and past model vehicles listed above with either a manual transmission or transfer case that REQUIRE Dexron® III should use the above listed manual transmission fluid. This fluid is a direct replacement for Dexron®III in manual transmissions and transfer cases. DO NOT use Dexron®®®®®®®®®VI in place of the manual transmission fluid in any manual transmissions or transfer cases as a failure may result.**

57. Start the vehicle, check for leaks and repair if necessary.

CLUTCH DRIVEN DISC & PRESSURE PLATE

REMOVAL & INSTALLATION

See Figure 7.

1. Disconnect the negative battery cable.
2. Raise and support the vehicle safely.
3. Remove the transaxle.
4. Remove the clutch cover bolts one turn at a time, until spring pressure is relieved.
5. Remove the clutch cover and the clutch disc.

To install:

6. Align the heavy side of the flywheel assembly, stamped with an X, with the clutch cover light side, marked with paint.
7. Install an alignment tool in order to support the clutch cover to the flywheel assembly.
8. Install the clutch cover to flywheel bolts and tighten in sequence to 18 ft. lbs. (25 Nm).
9. Remove the alignment tool.
10. Lubricate the inside diameter of the bearing grease.
11. Install the transmission.
12. Bleed the hydraulic system.
13. Connect the negative battery cable.

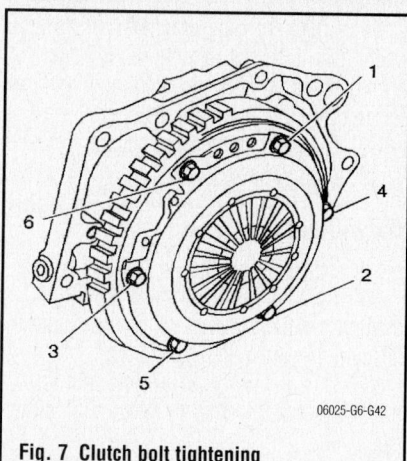

Fig. 7 Clutch bolt tightening sequence—G6

06025-G6-G42

PRESSURE PLATE ADJUSTMENT

See Figures 8 and 9.

1. Place the clutch pressure plate, flat surface down, on a press.

2. Compress the pressure plate diaphragm spring fingers until tension is released from the stepped adjusting r ing.

3. Hold 2 screwdrivers, or other suitable tools, and place them against 2 of the 3 stepped adjusting ring tension spring stops (1), just ahead of the adjusting ring tension springs.

4. Using the screwdrivers, rotate the stepped adjusting ring counterclockwise, compressing the tension springs, until the adjusting ring steps are fully adjusted out, then continue to hold in position.

5. Release the press pressure from the pressure plate diaphragm spring fingers.

6. Release the adjusting ring tension spring stops.

7. Remove the pressure plate from the press.

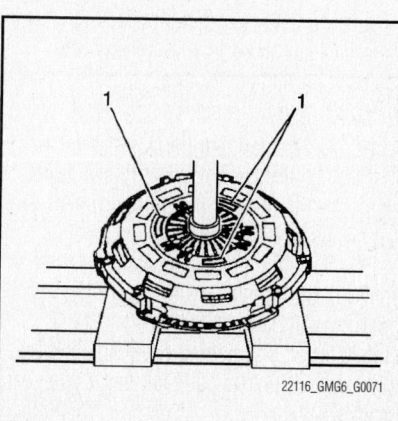

Fig. 8 Pressure plate, flat surface down, on a press

22116_GMG6_G0071

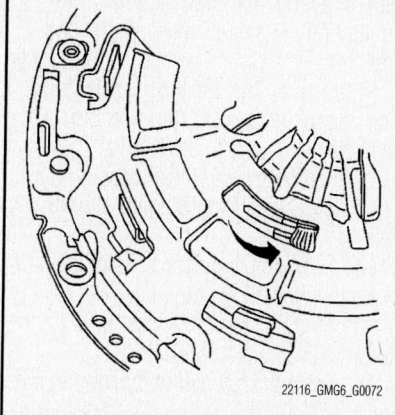

Fig. 9 Pressure plate adjusting ring steps view

22116_GMG6_G0072

CLUTCH MASTER CYLINDER

REMOVAL & INSTALLATION

1. Remove the driver side instrument panel insulator.

2. Disconnect the clutch master cylinder push rod from the clutch pedal pin.

3. Remove the clutch fluid reservoir retaining nut.

4. Remove the clutch fluid reservoir from the strut tower stud.

5. Remove the air cleaner outlet duct.

6. Remove the clutch hose retaining clip.

7. Disconnect the clutch hydraulic hose from the clutch master cylinder.

8. Rotate the clutch master cylinder clockwise 1/8 turn.

9. Remove the clutch master cylinder from the cowl.

To install:

10. With the clutch fluid reservoir connection at 2 o'clock position, insert the clutch master cylinder into the cowl.

11. Align the keys of the clutch master cylinder housing with the tabs on the cowl.

12. Rotate the clutch master cylinder counter clockwise approximately 1/8 turn until fully seated. The clutch fluid reservoir hose connection will be at vertical 12 o'clock position when the clutch master cylinder is properly installed.

13. Connect the clutch hydraulic hose.

14. Install the air cleaner outlet duct.

15. Install the clutch fluid reservoir to the strut tower stud.

16. Install the clutch fluid reservoir nut and tighten to 15 ft. lbs. (21 Nm).

17. Position the clutch master cylinder push rod to the clutch pedal pin.

18. Push the clutch master cylinder push rod onto the clutch pedal pin to secure.

19. Install the driver side instrument panel insulator.

20. Bleed the clutch hydraulic system.

CLUTCH CONCENTRIC ACTUATOR (SLAVE CYLINDER)

REMOVAL & INSTALLATION

1. Disconnect the clutch actuator cylinder line.

2. Remove the transmission.

3. Remove the clutch actuator cylinder body bolts.

4. Remove the upper line retainer bolt.

5. Remove the actuator.

To install:

6. Lubricate the inside diameter of the bearing.

7. Install the clutch actuator cylinder and the body bolts, tighten to 89 inch. lbs. (10 Nm).

8. Install the upper line retainer bolt.

9. Install the transmission.

10. Connect the clutch actuator cylinder line.

11. Bleed the hydraulic system.

CLUTCH

HYDRAULIC SYSTEM BLEEDING

1. Clean dirt and grease from the cap in order to ensure that no foreign substances enter the system.

2. Attach a hose to the bleeder screw on the clutch actuator assembly. Submerge the other end of the hose in a container of clutch fluid.

3. Depress the clutch pedal slowly and hold.

4. Loosen the bleeder screw to purge air.

5. Tighten the bleeder screw.

6. Repeat until air is purged.

7. Fill the reservoir to the top with fluid.

8. Check the clutch operation and repeat if necessary.

FRONT HALFSHAFTS

REMOVAL & INSTALLATION

1. Raise and support the vehicle safely.

2. Remove the front wheel.

3. Remove the halfshaft nut.

4. Disconnect the outer tie rod assembly from the steering knuckle.

5. Separate the ball joint from the steering knuckle.

6. Separate the front wheel drive axle from the drive shaft bearing using a slide hammer and appropriate puller. The nut can be partially re-installed to protect the threads.

7. Remove the halfshaft from the transaxle.

To install:

8. Install the halfshaft into the transaxle.

9. Verify that the front wheel drive shaft retaining ring is properly seated by grasping the inner housing and pull the inner housing outward. Do not pull on the front wheel drive axle shaft.

10. The front wheel drive axle will remain in place when the front wheel drive shaft retaining ring is properly seated.

11. Install the front wheel drive shaft into the front wheel bearing.

12. Connect the ball joint to the steering knuckle.

13. Connect the outer tie rod assembly to the steering knuckle.

14. Install a new wheel drive shaft nut. Insert a drift or a flat-bladed tool into the caliper and the rotor to prevent the rotor from turning. Tighten the nut to 159 ft. lbs. (215 Nm).

15. Install the wheel and tire.

16. Lower the vehicle.

17. Inspect the transaxle fluid level.

18. Inspect the wheel alignment.

CV-JOINTS OVERHAUL

Inner Joint

1. Disassemble the joint as follows:

2. Disconnect the swage ring from the halfshaft bar using a hand grinder to cut through the ring, taking care not to damage the halfshaft bar.

3. Remove the large seal retaining clamp from the tripot joint with side cutters. Discard the large seal retaining clamp.

4. Separate the inboard seal from the trilobal tripot bushing at the large diameter.

5. Slide the seal away from the joint along the halfshaft bar.

6. Remove the housing from the tripot joint spider and the halfshaft bar.

7. Spread the spacer ring.

8. Remove the spacer ring, spider assembly, spacer ring and tripot boot. Discard the boot and rings.

9. Clean the halfshaft bar Use a wire brush in order to remove any rust in the boot mounting area (grooves).

10. Inspect the needle rollers, needle bearings, and trunnion. Check the tripot housing for unusual wear, cracks, or other damage. Replace any damaged parts with the appropriate kit.

To install:

11. Place the new small swage ring or eared clamp onto the small end of the joint seal. Slide the joint seal and the small swage ring or eared clamp onto the halfshaft bar.

12. Position the small end of the joint seal into the joint seal groove on the halfshaft bar.

13. For swage ring installation, mount Drive Axle Swage Ring Clamp J-41048 in a vise.

14. Position the inboard end of the halfshaft assembly in the tool.

15. Align the top of the seal neck on the bottom die using the indicator.

16. Place the top half of the tool on the lower half.

17. Before proceeding, ensure there are no pinch points on the halfshaft inboard seal. This could cause damage to the halfshaft inboard seal.

18. Insert the bolts and tighten the bolts by hand until snug.

19. Align the halfshaft inboard seal, the halfshaft bar and the swage ring.

20. Tighten each bolt of the tool 180 degrees at a time using a ratchet wrench. Alternate between each bolt until both sides are bottomed.

21. For eared clamp installation, mount the halfshaft into a vise.

22. Slide the tripot seal to the corresponding groove on the halfshaft bar.

23. Crimp the eared clamp using clamping pliers, a torque wrench, and a breaker bar.

24. If equipped, install the spacer ring into the groove of the halfshaft bar.

25. Slide the tripot joint spider assembly as far as it will go on the halfshaft bar.

26. Install the spacer ring into the groove of the halfshaft bar.

27. Place approximately half of the grease from the service kit in the halfshaft inboard seal. Use the remainder of the grease to repack the housing.

28. Ensure the trilobal tripot bushing is flush with the face of the housing.

29. Install the trilobal tripot bushing to the housing.

30. Position the larger new seal retaining clamp on the halfshaft inboard seal.

31. Slide the housing over the tripot joint spider assembly on the halfshaft bar.

32. Slide the large diameter of the halfshaft inboard seal, with larger clamp in place, over the outside of the trilobal tripot bushing and locate the lip of the seal in the groove.

33. Align the halfshaft inboard seal, tripot housing and large seal retaining clamp.

34. Crimp the seal retaining clamp with to 130 ft. lbs. (176 Nm). Add the breaker bar and the torque wrench if needed.

35. Check the gap dimension on the clamp ear. If the gap dimension is larger than 0.102 inch (2.6mm), continue tightening until the dimension is reached.

36. Fully stroke the joint several times to disperse the grease.

Outer Joint

1. Disassemble the joint as follows:

2. Remove the large seal retaining clamp from the CV joint with a side cutter. Discard the seal retaining clamp.

3. Use a hand grinder to cut through the swage ring in order to remove the swage ring.

4. Separate the halfshaft outboard seal from CV joint outer race at the large diameter.

5. Slide the seal away from joint along the halfshaft bar.

6. Wipe the grease from the face of the CV joint inner race.

7. Spread the ears on the race retaining ring with snap ring pliers.

8. Remove the CV joint assembly from the halfshaft bar.

9. Remove and discard the halfshaft outboard seal.

10. Place a brass drift against the CV joint cage.

11. Tap gently on the brass drift with a hammer in order to tilt the cage.

12. Remove the first chrome alloy ball when the CV joint cage tilts.

13. Tilt the CV joint cage in the opposite direction to remove the opposing chrome alloy ball.

14. Repeat this process to remove all 6 of the balls.

15. Pivot the CV joint cage and the inner race 90 degrees to the centerline of the outer race. At the same time, align the cage windows with the lands of the outer race.

16. Lift out the cage and the inner race.

17. Remove the inner race from the cage by rotating the inner race upward.

18. Clean all parts with solvent and replace any damaged parts.

To install:

19. Assemble the joint as follows:

20. Install the new swage ring or eared clamp on the neck of the outboard seal. Do not swage or crimp.

21. Slide the outboard seal onto the halfshaft bar and position the neck of the outboard seal in the seal groove on the halfshaft bar. The largest groove below the sight groove on the halfshaft bar is the seal groove.

22. For swage ring installation, position the outboard end of the halfshaft assembly Drive Axle Swage Ring Clamp J-41048.

23. Align the swage ring.

24. Place the top half of the clamp tool onto the lower half.

25. Align the outboard seal, halfshaft bar and swage ring.

26. Insert the bolts and tighten by hand until snug.

27. Tighten each bolt 180 degrees at a time using a ratchet wrench. Alternate between each bolt until both sides are bottomed.

28. Loosen the bolts and separate the dies.

29. Check swaged ring for any lip deformities. If present, place the ring back into the tool making sure the ring covers the whole swaging area. If necessary, re-swage the ring.

30. For eared clamp installation, mount the halfshaft into a soft-jawed vise.

31. Install the new eared clamp on the neck of the seal. Do not crimp.

32. Slide the seal onto the halfshaft bar and position the neck of the seal in the seal groove on the bar.

33. Crimp the eared clamp using seal clamping pliers, a breaker bar, and a torque wrench.

34. Tighten the eared clamp to 100 ft. lbs. (136 Nm).

35. Check the gap dimension and continue tightening until the gap is 0,085 inch (2.15mm).

36. Put a light coat of grease from the service kit on the ball grooves of the inner race and the outer race.

37. \Hold the inner race 90 degrees to centerline of cage with the lands of the inner race aligned with the windows of the cage and insert the inner race into the cage.

38. Hold the cage and the inner race 90 degrees to centerline of the outer race and align the cage windows with the lands of the outer race.

39. Ensure that the retaining ring side of the inner race faces the halfshaft bar.

40. Place the cage and the inner race into the outer race.

41. Insert the first chrome ball then tilt the cage in the opposite direction to insert the opposing ball.

42. Repeat this process until all 6 balls are in place.

43. Place approximately half the grease from the service kit inside the outboard seal and pack the CV joint with the remaining grease.

44. Push the CV joint onto the halfshaft bar until the retaining ring is seated in the groove on the halfshaft bar.

45. Slide large diameter of the outboard seal with the large seal retaining clamp in place over the outside of the CV joint outer race and locate the seal lip in the groove on the CV joint outer race.

46. Crimp the seal retaining clamp to 130 ft. lbs. (174 Nm).

47. Check the gap dimension on the clamp ear. Continue tightening until the gap dimension is 0.074 inch (1.9mm).

CV-BOOTS INSPECTION

1. Raise and support the vehicle safely.
2. Spin drive axles by hand at the wheel.
3. Check for loose clamps, cracks, or open boots.
4. Check inner and outer boots.
5. Look for signs of grease leaking from axle boots.
6. Repair as needed.

INTERMEDIATE DRIVE SHAFT

REMOVAL & INSTALLATION

See Figure 10.

1. Remove right wheel drive shaft.
2. Remove intermediate drive shaft mounting bolts.
3. Remove intermediate drive shaft.

➡**Use care when removing the intermediate drive shaft from the transmission as not to damage the seal.**

To install:

4. Install intermediate drive shaft.
5. Install intermediate drive shaft mounting bolts and tighten to 44 ft. lbs. (60 Nm).
6. Install right wheel drive shaft and tighten shaft nut to 159 ft. lbs. (215 Nm).

CV-JOINTS OVERHAUL

Inner Joint

1. Disassemble the joint as follows:
2. Disconnect the swage ring from the halfshaft bar using a hand grinder to cut through the ring, taking care not to damage the halfshaft bar.
3. Remove the large seal retaining clamp from the tripot joint with side cutters. Discard the large seal retaining clamp.
4. Separate the inboard seal from the trilobal tripot bushing at the large diameter.
5. Slide the seal away from the joint along the halfshaft bar.
6. Remove the housing from the tripot joint spider and the halfshaft bar.
7. Spread the spacer ring.
8. Remove the spacer ring, spider assembly, spacer ring and tripot boot. Discard the boot and rings.
9. Clean the halfshaft bar Use a wire brush in order to remove any rust in the boot mounting area (grooves).
10. Inspect the needle rollers, needle bearings, and trunnion. Check the tripot housing for unusual wear, cracks, or other damage. Replace any damaged parts with the appropriate kit.

To install:

11. Place the new small swage ring or eared clamp onto the small end of the joint seal. Slide the joint seal and the small swage ring or eared clamp onto the halfshaft bar.
12. Position the small end of the joint

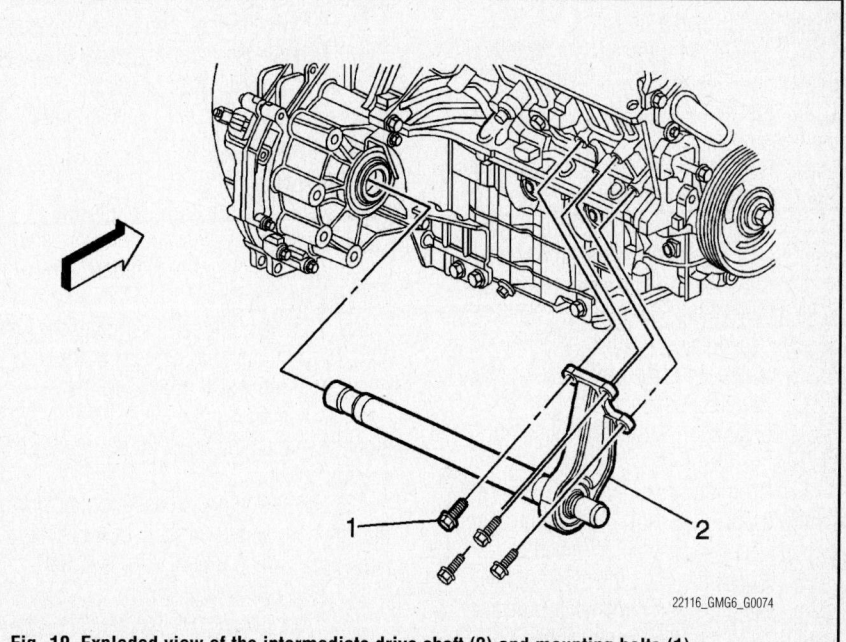

Fig. 10 Exploded view of the intermediate drive shaft (2) and mounting bolts (1)

22116_GMG6_G0074

seal into the joint seal groove on the half-shaft bar.

13. For swage ring installation, mount Drive Axle Swage Ring Clamp J-41048 in a vise.

14. Position the inboard end of the half-shaft assembly in the tool.

15. Align the top of the seal neck on the bottom die using the indicator.

16. Place the top half of the tool on the lower half.

17. Before proceeding, ensure there are no pinch points on the halfshaft inboard seal. This could cause damage to the half-shaft inboard seal.

18. Insert the bolts and tighten the bolts by hand until snug.

19. Align the halfshaft inboard seal, the halfshaft bar and the swage ring.

20. Tighten each bolt of the tool 180 degrees at a time using a ratchet wrench. Alternate between each bolt until both sides are bottomed.

21. For eared clamp installation, mount the halfshaft into a vise.

22. Slide the tripot seal to the corresponding groove on the halfshaft bar.

23. Crimp the eared clamp using clamping pliers, a torque wrench, and a breaker bar.

24. If equipped, install the spacer ring into the groove of the halfshaft bar.

25. Slide the tripot joint spider assembly as far as it will go on the halfshaft bar.

26. Install the spacer ring into the groove of the halfshaft bar.

27. Place approximately half of the grease from the service kit in the halfshaft inboard seal. Use the remainder of the grease to repack the housing.

28. Ensure the trilobal tripot bushing is flush with the face of the housing.

29. Install the trilobal tripot bushing to the housing.

30. Position the larger new seal retaining clamp on the halfshaft inboard seal.

31. Slide the housing over the tripot joint spider assembly on the halfshaft bar.

32. Slide the large diameter of the half-shaft inboard seal, with larger clamp in place, over the outside of the trilobal tripot bushing and locate the lip of the seal in the groove.

33. Align the halfshaft inboard seal, tripot housing and large seal retaining clamp.

34. Crimp the seal retaining clamp with to 130 ft. lbs. (176 Nm). Add the breaker bar and the torque wrench if needed.

35. Check the gap dimension on the clamp ear. If the gap dimension is larger than 0.102 inch (2.6mm), continue tightening until the dimension is reached.

36. Fully stroke the joint several times to disperse the grease.

Outer Joint

1. Disassemble the joint as follows:

2. Remove the large seal retaining clamp from the CV joint with a side cutter. Discard the seal retaining clamp.

3. Use a hand grinder to cut through the swage ring in order to remove the swage ring.

4. Separate the halfshaft outboard seal from CV joint outer race at the large diameter.

5. Slide the seal away from joint along the halfshaft bar.

6. Wipe the grease from the face of the CV joint inner race.

7. Spread the ears on the race retaining ring with snap ring pliers.

8. Remove the CV joint assembly from the halfshaft bar.

9. Remove and discard the halfshaft outboard seal.

10. Place a brass drift against the CV joint cage.

11. Tap gently on the brass drift with a hammer in order to tilt the cage.

12. Remove the first chrome alloy ball when the CV joint cage tilts.

13. Tilt the CV joint cage in the opposite direction to remove the opposing chrome alloy ball.

14. Repeat this process to remove all 6 of the balls.

15. Pivot the CV joint cage and the inner race 90 degrees to the centerline of the outer race. At the same time, align the cage windows with the lands of the outer race.

16. Lift out the cage and the inner race.

17. Remove the inner race from the cage by rotating the inner race upward.

18. Clean all parts with solvent and replace any damaged parts.

To install:

19. Assemble the joint as follows:

20. Install the new swage ring or eared clamp on the neck of the outboard seal. Do not swage or crimp.

21. Slide the outboard seal onto the half-shaft bar and position the neck of the outboard seal in the seal groove on the halfshaft bar. The largest groove below the sight groove on the halfshaft bar is the seal groove.

22. For swage ring installation, position the outboard end of the halfshaft assembly Drive Axle Swage Ring Clamp J-41048.

23. Align the swage ring.

24. Place the top half of the clamp tool onto the lower half.

25. Align the outboard seal, halfshaft bar and swage ring.

26. Insert the bolts and tighten by hand until snug.

27. Tighten each bolt 180 degrees at a time using a ratchet wrench. Alternate between each bolt until both sides are bottomed.

28. Loosen the bolts and separate the dies.

29. Check swaged ring for any lip deformities. If present, place the ring back into the tool making sure the ring covers the whole swaging area. If necessary, re-swage the ring.

30. For eared clamp installation, mount the halfshaft into a soft-jawed vise.

31. Install the new eared clamp on the neck of the seal. Do not crimp.

32. Slide the seal onto the halfshaft bar and position the neck of the seal in the seal groove on the bar.

33. Crimp the eared clamp using seal clamping pliers, a breaker bar, and a torque wrench.

34. Tighten the eared clamp to 100 ft. lbs. (136 Nm).

35. Check the gap dimension and continue tightening until the gap is 0,085 inch (2.15mm).

36. Put a light coat of grease from the service kit on the ball grooves of the inner race and the outer race.

37. \Hold the inner race 90 degrees to centerline of cage with the lands of the inner race aligned with the windows of the cage and insert the inner race into the cage.

38. Hold the cage and the inner race 90 degrees to centerline of the outer race and align the cage windows with the lands of the outer race.

39. Ensure that the retaining ring side of the inner race faces the halfshaft bar.

40. Place the cage and the inner race into the outer race.

41. Insert the first chrome ball then tilt the cage in the opposite direction to insert the opposing ball.

42. Repeat this process until all 6 balls are in place.

43. Place approximately half the grease from the service kit inside the outboard seal and pack the CV joint with the remaining grease.

44. Push the CV joint onto the halfshaft bar until the retaining ring is seated in the groove on the halfshaft bar.

45. Slide large diameter of the outboard seal with the large seal retaining clamp in place over the outside of the CV joint outer race and locate the seal lip in the groove on the CV joint outer race.

46. Crimp the seal retaining clamp to 130 ft. lbs. (174 Nm).

47. Check the gap dimension on the clamp ear. Continue tightening until the gap dimension is 0.074 inch (1.9mm).

ENGINE COOLING

ENGINE FAN

REMOVAL & INSTALLATION

1. Partially drain the cooling system.
2. Remove the air cleaner air duct.
3. Remove the upper radiator air deflector.
4. Remove the transmission oil cooler pipes from the radiator.
5. Loop a rope around each of the upper 2 tabs of the condenser and tie a rope around the upper tie bar.
6. Remove the upper radiator support bracket bolts.
7. Remove the upper radiator support brackets.
8. Pry upward on the fan shroud tabs at the radiator clips to release the fan shroud from the radiator.
9. Remove the lower radiator air deflector.
10. Lower the vehicle.
11. Remove the radiator inlet hose from the radiator.
12. Remove the radiator outlet hose from the radiator.
13. Disconnect the cooling fan wire harness connectors.
14. Remove the A/C compressor hose assembly.
15. Raise the vehicle.
16. Remove the lower radiator support bracket bolts.
17. Remove the lower radiator support brackets.
18. Remove the transmission oil cooler pipe clip from the fan shroud.
19. Remove the fan shroud assembly.

To install:
20. Install the fan shroud assembly.
21. Install the transmission oil cooler pipes to the radiator.
22. Install the transmission oil cooler pipe clip to the fan shroud.
23. Install the lower radiator support brackets.
24. Install the lower radiator support bracket bolts to 44 ft. lbs. (60 Nm).
25. Install the cooling fan wire harness connectors.
26. Install the radiator outlet hose to the radiator.

27. Install the lower radiator air deflector.
28. Lower the vehicle.
29. Snap fan shroud tabs into the radiator clips.
30. Remove the rope attached to the condenser and upper tie bar.
31. Install the upper radiator support brackets.
32. Install the upper radiator support bracket bolts and tighten to 89 inch lbs. (10 Nm).
33. Install the radiator inlet hose to the radiator.
34. Install the A/C compressor hose assembly.
35. Install the upper radiator air deflector.
36. Install the air cleaner air duct.
37. Fill the cooling system.
38. Inspect the transmission fluid level.

RADIATOR

REMOVAL & INSTALLATION

2.4L Engine

1. Remove the cooling fan and shroud assembly.
2. Remove and discard the condenser mounting bolts.
3. Push upward on the condenser and downward on the radiator to unsnap the condenser mounting tabs from the radiator clips.
4. Remove and discard the condenser mounting nuts from the radiator.
5. Remove the radiator from the vehicle.

To install:
6. Install the radiator to the vehicle.
7. Push upward on the radiator and downward on the condenser to snap the condenser mounting tabs into the radiator clips.
8. Install new condenser mounting nut to the radiator and tighten to 53 inch lbs. (6 Nm).
9. Install new condenser mounting bolts to the radiator and tighten to 53 inch lbs. (6 Nm).
10. Install the cooling fan and shroud assembly.

CV-BOOTS INSPECTION

1. Raise and support the vehicle safely.
2. Spin drive axles by hand at the wheel.
3. Check for loose clamps, cracks, or open boots.
4. Check inner and outer CV—boots.
5. Look for signs of grease leaking from axle boots.
6. Repair as needed.

3.5L and 3.9L Engines

1. Drain the coolant.
2. Remove the headlamps.
3. Loop a rope around each of the upper 2 tabs of the condenser and tie the rope around the upper tie bar.
4. Remove the upper radiator support bracket bolts.
5. Remove the upper radiator support brackets.
6. Reposition the surge tank outlet hose clamp at the radiator.
7. Remove the surge tank outlet hose from the radiator.
8. Raise the vehicle.
9. Remove the lower radiator air deflector retainers.
10. Remove the lower radiator air deflector.
11. Remove the right front fender liner.
12. Remove the right radiator air deflector retainers.
13. Remove the right radiator air deflector.
14. Remove the left radiator air deflector retainers.
15. Remove the left radiator air deflector.
16. Remove the radiator outlet hose from the radiator.
17. Place a drain pan under the transmission oil cooler pipes.
18. Remove the transmission oil cooler pipe attachment nut from the transmission.
19. Remove the transmission oil cooler pipes from the transmission.
20. Remove the lower radiator support bracket bolts.
21. Remove the lower radiator support brackets.
22. Remove the radiator lower mounts.
23. Remove and discard the condenser mounting bolts from the radiator.
24. Push upward on the radiator and downward on the condenser to unsnap the condenser mounting tabs from the radiator clips.
25. Remove and discard the condenser mounting nuts from the radiator.
26. Remove the radiator air side seals.
27. Remove the radiator, cooling fan shroud and transmission oil cooler pipe assembly.

28. Remove the transmission oil cooler pipes from the radiator.

29. Pry upward on the fan shroud tabs at the radiator clips.

30. Remove the cooling fan and shroud assembly.

To install:

31. Install the cooling fan and shroud assembly to the radiator.

32. Snap the fan shroud tabs into the radiator clips.

33. Install the transmission oil cooler pipes to the radiator.

34. Install the radiator, cooling fan shroud and transmission oil cooler pipe assembly.

35. Install the radiator air side seals onto the condenser mounting tabs on the radiator.

➡**The bolt retaining the condenser to the radiator end tank is a special length and should be the ONLY bolt used upon reinstallation. The use of a longer bolt will damage the radiator end tank.**

36. Install the condenser mounting nuts to the radiator.

37. Insert the condenser mounting tabs into the radiator clips.

38. Install the condenser to the radiator bolts and tighten to 53 inch lbs. (6 nm).

39. Bend the radiator air side seals and insert the seals into the channel of the intake air splash shields.

40. The radiator air side seals must be in the proper position for proper air flow.

➡**Replace the radiator lower mounts as a pair or vibration may result.**

41. Install the radiator lower mounts.

42. Install the lower radiator support brackets.

43. Install the lower radiator support bracket bolts and tighten to 44 ft. lbs. (60 Nm).

44. Install the transmission oil cooler pipes to the transmission.

45. Install the transmission oil cooler pipes attachment nut to the transmission.

46. Install the radiator outlet hose to the radiator.

47. Radiator air deflectors must be properly installed or reduced A/C and engine cooling system performance could occur.

48. Install the left radiator air deflector.

49. Install the left radiator air deflector retainers.

50. Install the right radiator air deflector.

51. Install the right radiator air deflector retainers.

52. Install the right front fender liner.

53. Install the lower radiator air deflector.

54. Install the lower radiator air deflector retainers.

55. Lower the vehicle.

56. Install the radiator inlet hose to the radiator.

57. Install the surge tank outlet hose to the radiator.

58. Reposition the surge tank outlet hose clamp at the radiator.

59. Remove the rope attached to the condenser and upper tie bar.

60. Install the upper radiator support brackets.

61. Install the upper radiator support bracket bolts and tighten to 89 inch lbs. (10 Nm).

62. Install the headlamps.

63. Fill the coolant.

64. Inspect the transmission fluid level.

3.6L Engines

See Figures 11 through 14.

1. Drain the coolant.

2. Loop a rope around each of the upper 2 tabs of the condenser and tie the rope around the upper tie bar.

3. Remove the upper radiator support brackets.

4. Reposition the radiator inlet hose clamp at the radiator.

5. Remove the radiator inlet hose from the radiator.

6. Remove the front air dam.

7. Remove the right engine splash shield retainers.

8. Remove the right engine splash shield.

9. Remove the left engine splash shield retainers.

10. Remove the left engine splash shield.

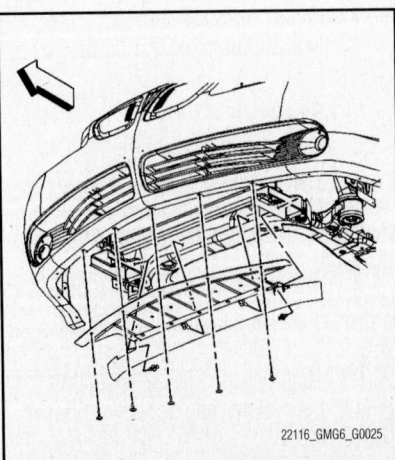

Fig. 11 Front air dam removal shown

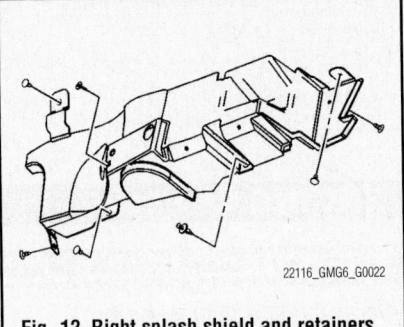

Fig. 12 Right splash shield and retainers

11. Reposition the radiator outlet hose clamp at the radiator.

12. Remove the radiator outlet hose from the radiator.

13. Remove the transmission oil cooler pipes from the radiator.

14. Remove the lower radiator support bracket bolts.

15. Remove the lower radiator support brackets.

16. Remove the radiator lower mounts.

17. Remove and discard the condenser mounting bolts from the radiator.

18. Push upward on the radiator and downward on the condenser to unsnap the condenser mounting tabs from the radiator clips.

19. Remove and discard the condenser mounting nuts from the radiator.

20. Remove the radiator air side seals.

21. Remove the radiator and cooling fan shroud assembly from the vehicle.

22. Pry upward on the fan shroud tabs at the radiator clips.

23. Remove the cooling fan and shroud assembly from the radiator.

To install:

24. Install the cooling fan and shroud assembly to the radiator.

25. Snap the fan shroud tabs into the radiator clips.

26. Install the radiator and cooling fan shroud assembly to the vehicle.

27. Install the radiator air side seals onto the condenser mounting tabs on the radiator.

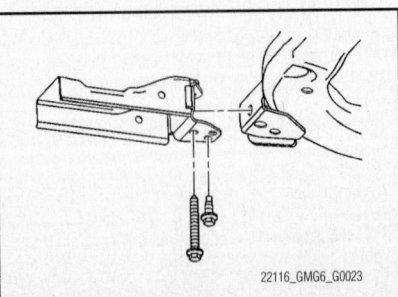

Fig. 13 Lower radiator support bracket and bolts

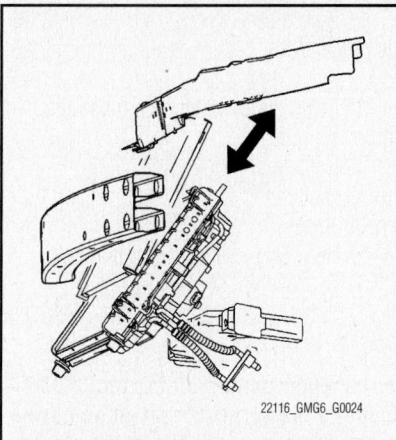

Fig. 14 Radiator and cooling fan shroud assembly removal

➡ **The bolt retaining the condenser to the radiator end tank is a special length and should be the only bolt used upon reinstallation. The use of a longer bolt will damage the radiator end tank.**

28. Install the condenser mounting nuts to the radiator.

29. Insert the condenser mounting tabs into the radiator clips.

30. Install the condenser to the radiator bolts and tighten to 53 inch. lbs. (63 Nm).

31. Bend the radiator air side seals and insert the seals into the channel of the intake air splash shields.

➡ **The radiator air side seals must be in the proper position for proper air flow.**

32. Install the radiator lower mounts.

✳✳ WARNING

If replacing the radiator lower mount replace as a pair or vibration may result.

33. Install the lower radiator support brackets.

34. Install the lower radiator support bracket bolts and tighten to 44 ft. lbs. (60 Nm).

35. Install the transmission oil cooler pipes to the radiator.

36. Install the radiator outlet hose to the radiator.

37. Reposition the radiator outlet hose clamp at the radiator.

✳✳ WARNING

Engine splash shields must be properly installed or reduced A/C and engine cooling system performance could occur.

38. Install the left engine splash shield.

39. Install the left engine splash shield retainers.

40. Install the right engine splash shield.

41. Install the right engine splash shield retainers.

42. Install the front air dam.

43. Lower the vehicle.

44. Install the radiator inlet hose to the radiator.

45. Reposition the radiator inlet hose clamp at the radiator.

46. Remove the rope attached to the condenser and upper tie bar

47. Install the upper radiator support brackets.

48. Fill and bleed cooling system.

49. Inspect the transmission fluid level and add if needed.

50. Check all connections for leaks.

THERMOSTAT

REMOVAL & INSTALLATION

2.4L Engine

1. Drain the cooling system.

➡ **A drain has been provided at the bottom of the water pump for engine block coolant drainage.**

2. Remove the water pump drain plug and drain the coolant from the engine block at the water pump drain.

3. Lower the vehicle.

4. Disconnect the engine coolant temperature (ECT) sensor electrical connector.

5. Disconnect the heated oxygen sensor (HO2S) electrical connector clip from the bracket.

6. Remove the ECT sensor.

7. If the vehicle is not equipped an engine oil cooler proceed with the following steps, otherwise proceed to step 12.

8. Reposition the radiator outlet hose clamp at the surge tank.

9. Remove the radiator outlet hose from the surge tank.

10. Reposition the radiator outlet hose clamp at the thermostat housing.

11. Remove the radiator outlet hose from the thermostat housing.

12. If the vehicle is equipped with an engine oil cooler, reposition the surge tank outlet hose clamp at the thermostat housing.

13. Remove the surge tank outlet hose from the thermostat housing.

14. Reposition the radiator outlet hose clamp at the thermostat housing.

15. Remove the radiator outlet hose from the thermostat housing.

16. Remove the exhaust heat shield bolts.

17. Remove the exhaust heat shield.

18. Reposition the heater inlet and outlet hose clamps at the thermostat housing pipes.

19. Disconnect the heater inlet and outlet hoses from the thermostat housing pipes.

20. Remove the thermostat housing bolts.

21. Twist the water transfer pipe while pulling in order to remove it from the water pump.

22. Remove the thermostat housing from the vehicle.

23. Remove the water transfer pipe from the thermostat housing, if necessary.

24. Remove and discard the water transfer pipe O-ring seals, if necessary.

25. Remove the thermostat housing cover bolts and cover, if necessary.

26. Remove the thermostat, if necessary.

27. Remove and discard the thermostat housing O-ring seal, if necessary.

28. Remove all debris and thread sealant from the engine coolant temperature sensor and bolt holes if the housing is being re-used.

To install:

29. Install a NEW thermostat housing cover O-ring seal into the recess groove.

30. Install the thermostat, if necessary.

31. Install the thermostat housing cover bolts to 89 inch lbs. (10 Nm).

32. Install a NEW thermostat housing to engine O-ring seal onto the thermostat housing.

33. Load the thermostat housing assembly into position while the vehicle is lowered.

34. The water feed pipe seals can be lightly lubricated with coolant to aid during installation.

35. Install NEW O-ring seals onto the water feed pipe.

36. Lubricate the O-rings with coolant.

37. Install the water feed pipe into the thermostat housing aligning locator tab.

38. Align the water pipe to water pump.

39. Seat the water feed O-ring seal by pushing inward toward the water pump. Take care not to tear or damage the O-ring.

40. Position the thermostat housing against the engine.

41. Install the thermostat housing bolts and tighten to 89 inch lbs. (10 Nm).

42. Connect the heater inlet and outlet hoses to the thermostat housing pipes.

43. Position the heater inlet and outlet hose clamps at the thermostat housing pipes.

44. Install the exhaust heat shield.
45. Install the exhaust heat shield bolts and tighten to 17 ft. lbs. (23 Nm).
46. If the vehicle is equipped with an engine oil cooler proceed with the following steps.
47. Install the radiator outlet hose to the thermostat housing.
48. Position the radiator outlet hose clamp at the thermostat housing.
49. Install the surge tank outlet hose to the thermostat housing.
50. Position the surge tank outlet hose clamp at the thermostat housing.
51. If the vehicle is not equipped an engine oil cooler, install the radiator outlet hose to the thermostat housing.
52. Position the radiator outlet hose clamp at the thermostat housing.
53. Install the radiator outlet hose to the surge tank.
54. Position the radiator outlet hose clamp at the surge tank.
55. Apply sealant to the threads of the ECT sensor.
56. Install the ECT sensor and tighten to 15 ft. lbs. (20 Nm).
57. Connect the ECT sensor electrical connector.
58. Connect the HO2S electrical connector clip to the bracket.
59. Apply sealant to the water pump drain plug.
60. Install the water pump drain plug and tighten to 15 ft. lbs. (20 Nm).
61. Verify the drain valves at the radiator and water pump are closed.
62. Fill the cooling system.
63. Verify the repair and inspect for any leaks.

3.5L and 3.9L Engines

1. Drain the cooling system.
2. Remove the air cleaner outlet duct.
3. Disconnect the surge tank hose from the coolant outlet.
4. Remove the thermostat housing to intake manifold bolts.
5. Remove the thermostat housing outlet and thermostat.

To install:

6. Install the thermostat and housing outlet.
7. Install the thermostat housing bolts and tighten to 18 ft. lbs. (25 M,).
8. Install the air cleaner outlet duct.
9. Fill the cooling system.
10. Inspect the system for leaks.

3.6L Engines

See Figure 15.

1. Partially drain the cooling system.

❊❊ WARNING

Do NOT separate the upper and lower intake manifolds.

2. Remove the upper intake manifold with the lower intake manifold. Refer to Lower Intake Manifold Replacement.
3. Disconnect the surge tank hose from the thermostat.
4. Remove the coolant pipe/thermostat housing bolt
5. Remove the coolant pipe bolt.
6. Remove the coolant inlet pipe from the thermostat housing.
7. Remove and discard the coolant pipe O-ring seal.
8. Remove the thermostat bolts.
9. Remove the thermostat and discard the thermostat seal.

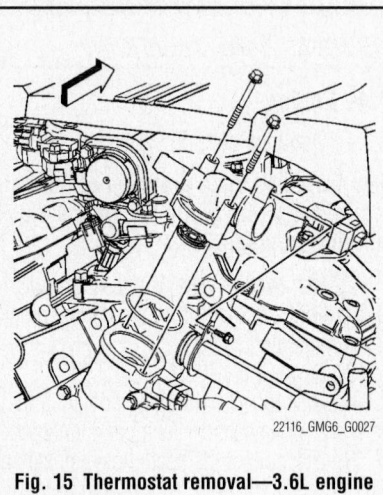

Fig. 15 Thermostat removal—3.6L engine

To install:

10. Install the thermostat with a new thermostat seal.
11. Install the thermostat bolts and tighten to 89 inch. lbs. (10 Nm).
12. Install the coolant pipe, new seal, and fasteners (1 and 3).
13. Install the surge tank hose to the thermostat.
14. Install the upper intake manifold with the lower intake manifold.
15. Fill and bleed the cooling system.
16. Inspect the system for leaks.

WATER PUMP

REMOVAL & INSTALLATION

2.4L Engine

See Figure 16.

1. Before servicing the vehicle, refer to the precautions in the beginning of this section.
2. Drain the coolant from the radiator and engine block.
3. Remove the drive belt.
4. Disconnect the water pump and thermostat hoses.
5. Remove the thermostat housing.
6. Remove the coolant heater.
7. Remove the water pump access plate from the front cover.

➡ **The water pump holding tool J-43651 supports the sprocket and chain during water pump service. The tool must be used or the balance shaft must be re-timed.**

8. Install the tool into position.
9. Tighten the bolts on the water pump holding tool into the threads on the water pump sprocket.
10. Install the access cover bolts that were removed earlier to secure the water pump holding tool to the front cover assembly.
11. Remove the 3 inner water pump sprocket to water pump bolts through the holes in the water pump holding tool.
12. Remove the 2 front and 2 rear water pump bolts.
13. Remove the engine wiring harness clip nut from the water pump stud.
14. Remove the engine wiring harness clip from the stud.
15. Remove the water pump.

To install:

16. Apply sealant to the water pump drain plug.
17. Install the water pump drain plug and tighten to 15 ft. lbs. (20 Nm).

➡ **A guide pin can be created to aid in water pump alignment. Use a**

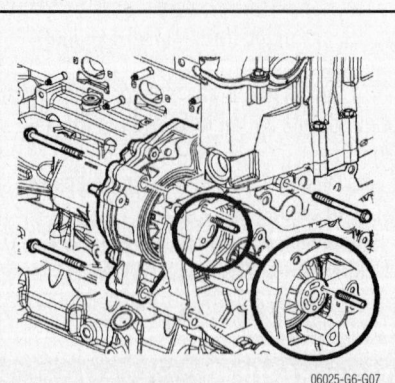

Fig. 16 Exploded view of the water pump mounting and guide pin installation—2.4L engine

M6 m x 6 mm stud. Thread the pin into the water pump sprocket.

18. Align the guide pin with the water pump holding tool.

19. Position the water pump against the engine block and hand tighten the water pump bolts.

20. Install the inner water pump sprocket bolts. After 2 are snug, remove the guide pin and install the 3rd bolt and tighten all bolts to 18 ft. lbs. (25 Nm).

21. Tighten the water pump sprocket bolts last to 89 inch lbs. (10 Nm).

22. Remove the holding tool and install the coolant heater.

23. Install the water pump access plate and bolts and tighten to 89 inch lbs. (10 Nm).

24. Install the thermostat housing.

25. Install the drive belt.

26. Connect the water pump and thermostat hoses.

27. Fill and bleed the cooling system.

28. Start the vehicle, check for leaks and repair if necessary.

3.5L Engine

See Figure 17.

1. Drain the cooling system.
2. Disconnect the radiator hoses.
3. Loosen the water pump pulley bolts.
4. Remove the drive belt.
5. Remove the water pump pulley bolts and pulley.
6. Remove the water pump bolts, pump, and gasket.
7. Clean the water pump mating surfaces.

To install:

8. Install the water pump gasket and pump.

9. Install the water pump bolts and tighten to 89 inch lbs. (10 Nm).

10. Install the water pump pulley and bolt until snug.

11. Install the drive belt.

12. Tighten the pulley bolts to 18 ft. lbs. (25 Nm).

13. Connect the radiator hoses.

14. Connect the negative battery cable

15. Fill and bleed the cooling system.

16. Start the vehicle, check for leaks and repair if necessary.

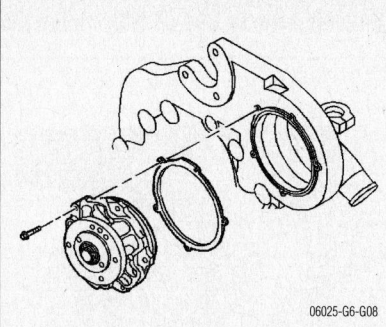

Fig. 17 Exploded view of the water pump mounting—3.5L engine

3.6L Engine

See Figure 18.

1. Drain the cooling system.
2. Loosen the water pump pulley bolts.
3. Remove the drive belt.
4. Remove the water pump pulley bolts and pulley.
5. Remove the water pump bolts, pump, and gasket.
6. Clean the water pump mating surfaces.

To install:

7. Install the water pump gasket and pump.

8. Install the water pump bolts and tighten to 89 inch lbs. (10 Nm).

9. Install the water pump pulley and bolts until snug.

Fig. 18 Exploded view of the water pump mounting—3.6L engine

10. Install the drive belt.

11. Tighten the pulley bolts to 106 inch lbs. (12 Nm).

12. Fill and bleed the cooling system.

13. Start the vehicle, check for leaks and repair if necessary.

3.9L Engine

See Figure 19.

1. Drain the cooling system.
2. Disconnect the radiator hoses.
3. Loosen the water pump pulley bolts.
4. Remove the drive belt.
5. Remove the water pump pulley bolts and pulley.
6. Remove the water pump bolts, pump, and gasket.
7. Clean the water pump mating surfaces.

To install:

8. Install the water pump gasket and pump.

9. Install the water pump bolts and tighten to 89 inch lbs. (10 Nm).

10. Install the water pump pulley and bolts until snug.

11. Install the drive belt.

12. Tighten the pulley bolts to 18 ft. lbs. (25 Nm).

13. Connect the radiator hoses.

14. Connect the negative battery cable

15. Fill and bleed the cooling system.

16. Start the vehicle, check for leaks and repair if necessary.

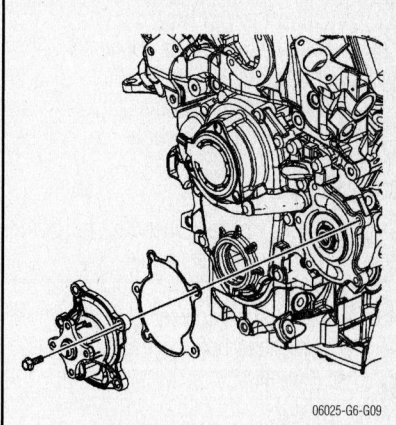

Fig. 19 Exploded view of the water pump mounting—3.9L engine

ALTERNATOR

REMOVAL & INSTALLATION

2.4L Engine

See Figure 20.

1. Remove or disconnect the following:
   - Negative battery cable
   - Air cleaner resonator
   - Drive belt
   - Alternator harness connectors
   - Alternator

To install:

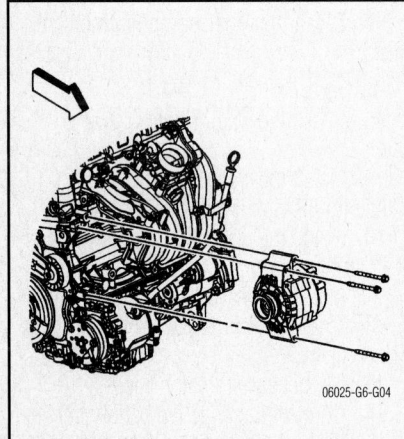

Fig. 20 Alternator mounting—2.4L engine

2. Install or connect the following:
   - Alternator and tighten the bolts to 16 ft. lbs. (22 Nm).
   - Alternator harness connectors
   - Drive belt
   - Air cleaner resonator
   - Negative battery cable

3.5L Engine

1. Remove or disconnect the following:
   - Negative battery cable
   - Drive belt
   - Alternator harness connector
   - Alternator bolts and nuts
   - Alternator

To install:

2. Install or connect the following:
   - Alternator and tighten the bolts to

Fig. 21 Alternator mounting—3.5L engine

37 ft. lbs. (50 Nm), and the nuts to 22 ft. lbs. (30 Nm).
   - Alternator harness connectors
   - Drive belt
   - Negative battery cable

3.6L Engine

See Figure 22.

1. Remove or disconnect the following:
   - Negative battery cable
   - Drive belt
   - Idler pulley
   - Alternator harness connector
   - Alternator bolts and nuts
   - Alternator

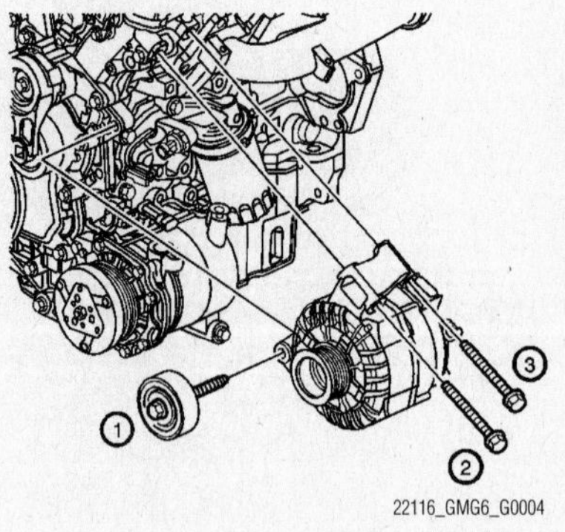

Fig. 22 Alternator mounting—3.6L engine

To install:

2. Install or connect the following:
   - Alternator, and tighten the bolts to 37 ft. lbs. (50 Nm), and the nut to 15 ft. lbs. (20 Nm).
   - Alternator harness connector
   - Idler pulley
   - Drive belt
   - Negative battery cable

3.9L Engine

See Figure 23.

1. Remove or disconnect the following:
   - Negative battery cable
   - Drive belt
   - Engine harness connector
   - Alternator harness connector
   - Upper and lower alternator bolts and stud
   - Alternator

To install:

2. Install or connect the following:
   - Alternator
   - Lower bolt and stud and tighten until snug.
   - Upper bolt and tighten to 37 ft. lbs. (50 Nm)
   - Alternator harness connectors
   - Engine harness connectors
   - Drive belt
   - Negative battery cable

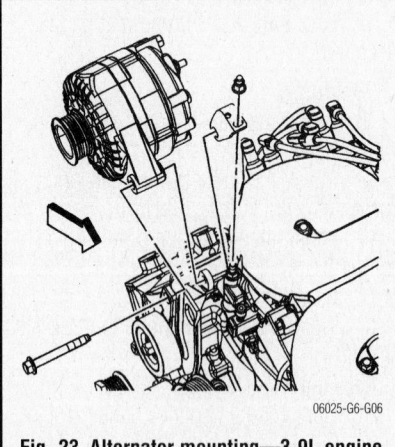

Fig. 23 Alternator mounting—3.9L engine

ENGINE ELECTRICAL   **IGNITION SYSTEM**

FIRING ORDER

2.4L L4 engine firing order: 1–3–4–2
3.5L, 3.6L, 3.9L V6 engines firing order:
1–2–3–4–5–6

IGNITION COIL

REMOVAL & INSTALLATION

2.4L Engine

1. Remove the intake manifold cover.
2. Disconnect the ignition coil electrical connector.
3. Remove the ignition coil bolts.
4. Remove the ignition coil

To install:

5. Install the ignition coils.
6. Install the ignition coil bolts and tighten to 89 inch lbs. (10 Nm).
7. Connect the ignition coil electrical connectors.
8. Install the intake manifold cover.

3.5L Engine

1. Remove the intake manifold cover.
2. Remove the 4 screws securing the ignition coil and module assembly to the bracket.
3. Remove the ignition coil and module assembly.

To install:

4. Install the ignition coil and module assembly to the bracket.
5. Install the ignition coil and module assembly screws and tighten to 40 inch lbs. (4.5 Nm).
6. Connect the spark plug wires.
7. Install the intake manifold cover.

3.9L Engine

1. Remove the intake manifold cover.
2. Disconnect the Manifold Absolute Pressure (MAP) sensor electrical connector.
3. Disconnect the ignition coil electrical connector.
4. Disconnect the spark plug wires from the ignition coils.
5. Remove the ignition coil bolts.
6. Remove the ignition coil nuts.
7. Remove the ignition coil.
8. Remove the ignition coil studs, if necessary.

To install:

9. Install the ignition coil studs, if necessary.
10. Install the ignition coil.

11. Install the ignition coil nuts and tighten to 15 ft. lbs. (20 Nm).
12. Install the ignition coil bolts and tighten to 15 ft. lbs. (20 Nm).
13. Connect the spark plug wires to the ignition coils.
14. Connect the ignition coil electrical connector.
15. Connect the MAP sensor electrical connector.
16. Install the intake manifold cover.

IGNITION TIMING

ADJUSTMENT

The ignition timing is controlled by the Powertrain Control Module (PCM). No adjustment is necessary or possible.

SPARK PLUGS

REMOVAL & INSTALLATION

2.4L Engine

1. Remove the ignition coils.

✷✷ WARNING

Make sure that any water and/or debris is blown out of the spark plug holes prior to removing the spark plugs.

2. Remove the spark plugs using a ⅝ inch spark plug socket.

➡**Do not coat spark plug threads with anti-seize compound. If anti-seize compound is used and spark plugs are over-torqued, damage to the cylinder head threads may result.**

3. Check spark plug gap for specification, 0.042 inch. (1.06 mm).

To install:

4. Install the spark plugs.
5. Tighten spark plugs to 15 ft. lbs. (20 Nm).
6. Install the ignition coils and tighten mounting bolts to 89 inch. lbs. (10 Nm).

3.5L Engine

➡**Allow the engine to cool before removing the spark plugs. Attempting to remove spark plugs from a hot engine can cause the spark plugs to seize. This can damage the cylinder head threads. Clean the spark plug recess area before removing the spark plug. Failure to do so can result in engine damage due to dirt or foreign material entering the**

cylinder head, or in contamination of the cylinder head threads. Contaminated threads may prevent proper seating of the new spark plug.

1. If you are replacing the engine left bank spark plugs, remove the air cleaner outlet duct.
2. Remove the spark plug wires from the spark plugs.
3. Remove the spark plugs from the engine.

To install:

➡**It is important to check the gap of all new and reconditioned spark plugs before installation. Pre-set gaps may have changed during handling. Use a round wire feeler gauge to be sure of an accurate check, particularly on used plugs. Installing plugs with the wrong gap can cause poor engine performance and may even damage the engine.**

4. Gap the spark plugs to the specifications, 0.040 inch. (1.02 mm).
5. Install the spark plugs to the engine.
6. Tighten spark plugs to 11 ft. lbs. (15 Nm).

➡**For new cylinder head tighten plugs to 15 ft. lbs. (20 Nm).**

7. Install the spark plug wires to the spark plugs.

3.6L Engine

➡**Allow the engine to cool before removing the spark plugs. Attempting to remove the spark plugs from a hot engine may cause the plug threads to seize, causing damage to cylinder head threads.**

1. Remove ignition coils.
2. Use compressed air in order to remove debris from the spark plug cavity.
3. Remove the spark plugs.

To install:

4. Ensure that the spark plug gap is equivalent to the spark plug gap specification. 0.043 inch. (1.10 mm).

➡**Be sure that the spark plug threads smoothly into the cylinder head and the spark plug is fully seated. Use a thread chaser, if necessary, to clean threads in the cylinder head. Cross-threading or failing to fully seat the spark plug can cause overheating of the plug, exhaust blow-by, or thread damage.**

5. Install the spark plugs.

6. Tighten spark plugs to 15 ft. lbs. (20 Nm).

7. Install ignition coils and tighten mounting bolts to 89 inch. lbs. (10 Nm).

3.9L Engine

➡ Allow the engine to cool before removing the spark plugs. Attempting to remove spark plugs from a hot engine can cause the spark plugs to seize. This can damage the cylinder head threads. Clean the spark plug recess area before removing the spark plug. Failure to do so can result in engine damage due to dirt or foreign material entering the cylinder head, or in contamination of the cylinder head threads. Contaminated threads may prevent proper seating of the new spark plug.

1. Remove the air cleaner outlet duct, if required.

2. Remove the intake manifold cover, if required.

3. Remove the left side spark plug wires from the spark plugs.

4. Remove the right side spark plug wires from the spark plugs.

5. Remove the spark plugs.

To install:

6. Ensure that the spark plug gap is equivalent to the spark plug gap specification. 0.040 inch. (1.02 mm).

7. Install the spark plugs.

8. Tighten spark plugs to 11 ft. lbs. (15 Nm).

9. Install the right side spark plug wires to the spark plugs,

10. Install the left side spark plug wires to the spark plugs,

11. Install the intake manifold cover, if required.

12. Install the air cleaner outlet duct, if required.

ENGINE ELECTRICAL

STARTER

REMOVAL & INSTALLATION

2.4L Engine

See Figure 24.

1. Remove or disconnect the following:
   - Negative battery cable
   - Solenoid terminal nut
   - Starter engine harness lead
   - Positive battery cable
   - Starter mounting bolts
   - Starter.

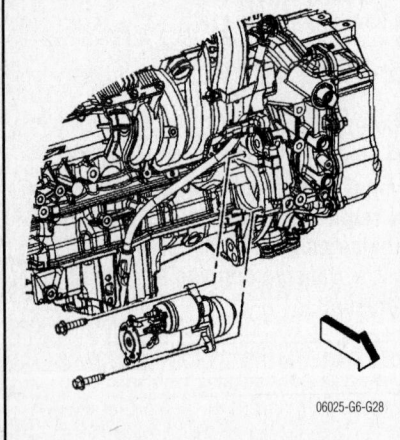

Fig. 24 Starter mounting—2.4L engine

To install:

2. Install or connect the following:
   - Starter. Torque the bolts to 30 ft. lbs. (40 Nm).
   - Positive battery cable
   - Starter engine harness lead
   - Solenoid terminal nut
   - Negative battery cable

3.6L Engine

See Figure 25.

1. Disconnect the negative battery cable.
2. Raise the vehicle.
3. Remove the front catalytic convertor.
4. Remove the knock sensor Bank 2.
5. Remove the starter solenoid BAT terminal nut.
6. Disconnect the engine harness electrical connector.
7. Disconnect the starter motor bolts and starter.

To install:

8. Position the starter motor in the engine block.

9. Install the mounting bolts and tighten to 37 ft. lbs. (50 Nm).

10. Connect the engine harness electrical connector to the starter.

11. Install the starter solenoid BAT terminal nut and tighten to 115 inch. lbs. (15 Nm).

12. Install knock sensor and tighten to 17 ft. lbs. (23 Nm).

13. Install the catalytic converter to right catalytic converter and tighten nuts to 18 ft. lbs. (25 Nm).

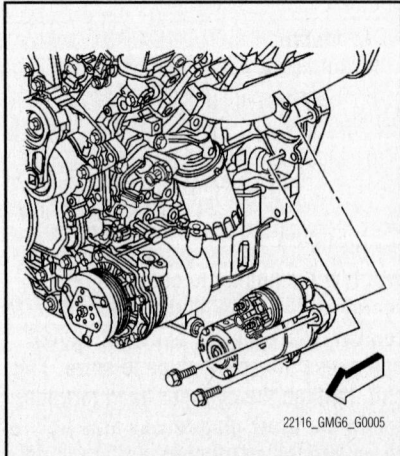

Fig. 25 Starter mounting—3.6L engine

STARTING SYSTEM

14. Install the front catalytic converter to exhaust manifold nuts tighten to 33 ft. lbs. (45 Nm).

15. Lower the vehicle

16. Connect the negative battery cable.

3.5L and 3.9L Engines

See Figure 26.

1. Remove or disconnect the following:
   - Negative battery cable
   - Raise the vehicle
   - Flywheel inspection cover
   - Starter harness
   - Both starter bolts
   - Starter.

To install:

2. Install or connect the following:
   - Starter
   - Both starter bolts. Tighten the bolts to 30 ft. lbs. (40 Nm).
   - Starter harness
   - Flywheel inspection cover
   - Negative battery cable

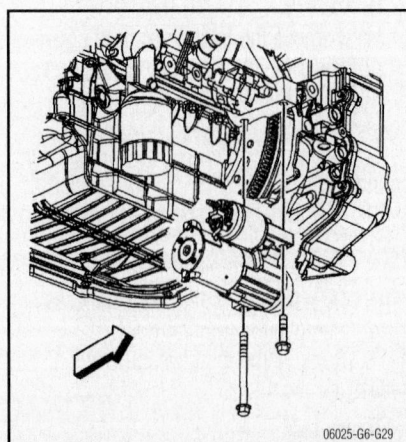

Fig. 26 Starter mounting—3.5L and 3.9L engines

ENGINE MECHANICAL

➡️Disconnecting the negative battery cable may interfere with the functions of the on board computer systems and may require the computer to undergo a relearning process, once the negative battery cable is reconnected.

ACCESSORY DRIVE BELTS

ACCESSORY BELT ROUTING

See Figures 27 through 30.

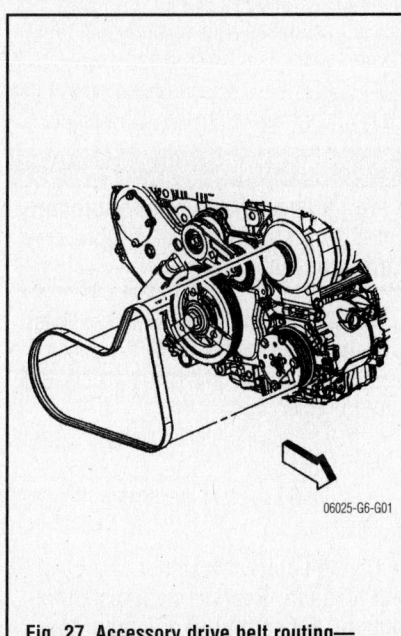

Fig. 27 Accessory drive belt routing—2.4L VIN B (CODE LE5) engine

Fig. 28 Accessory drive belt routing—3.5L VIN 8 (CODE LX9) and VIN N (CODE LZ4) engines

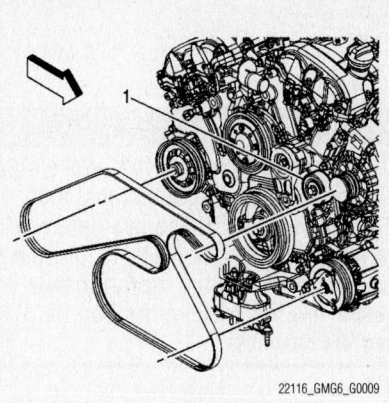

Fig. 29 Accessory drive belt routing—3.6L VIN 7 (CODE LY7) engine

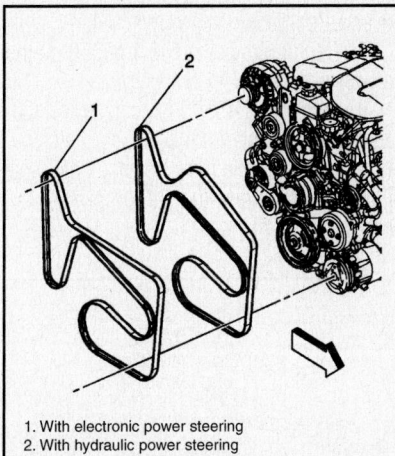

1. With electronic power steering
2. With hydraulic power steering

Fig. 30 Air conditioning drive belt routing—3.9L VIN 1 (CODE LZ9) engine

INSPECTION

Inspect the drive belt for signs of glazing or cracking. A glazed belt will be perfectly smooth from slippage, while a good belt will have a slight texture of fabric visible. Cracks will usually start at the inner edge of the belt and run outward. All worn or damaged drive belts should be replaced immediately.

ADJUSTMENT

Drive belts on this model have automatic adjusters.

REMOVAL & INSTALLATION

2.4L Engine

1. Remove the air cleaner outlet resonator.
2. Remove the right front fender liner.

3. Install Belt Tensioner Unloader J-44811 to the drive belt tensioner.
4. Using the tool, rotate the tensioner counterclockwise in order to release the tensioner from the drive belt.
5. Remove the drive belt.
6. Slowly rotate the tool and the tensioner clockwise in order to allow the tensioner to rest.
7. Remove the tool from the drive belt tensioner.

To install:

8. Install and position the drive belt around all of the pulleys except for the drive belt tensioner.
9. Install the tool to the drive belt tensioner.
10. Using the tool, rotate the tensioner counterclockwise.
11. Position the drive belt under the tensioner pulley.
12. Using the tool, rotate the tensioner clockwise in order to seat the tensioner pulley onto the drive belt.
13. Install the right front fender liner.
14. Install the air cleaner outlet resonator.

3.5L Engine

1. Remove the air cleaner assembly.
2. Remove the engine mount strut.
3. Rotate the drive belt tensioner counterclockwise to release the spring tension.
4. Remove the drive belt.

To install:

5. Rotate the drive belt tensioner counterclockwise to release the spring tension.
6. Install the drive belt.
7. Install the engine mount strut.
8. Install the air cleaner assembly.

3.6L Engine

1. Remove the air cleaner assembly.
2. Remove the engine mount strut bracket.
3. Rotate the drive belt tensioner clockwise to release the drive belt tension.
4. Slide the drive belt off of the belt idler pulley.
5. Slowly release the drive belt tensioner.
6. Remove the drive belt from the accessory drive pulleys.

To install:

7. Install the drive belt to the crankshaft pulley, the tensioner and the generator.
8. Rotate the drive belt tensioner clockwise.
9. Install the drive belt to the idler pulley.
10. Slowly release the drive belt tensioner.

➡️**Ensure the drive belt is properly aligned and seated into the grooves of the accessory drive pulleys.**

11. Install the air cleaner assembly.

3.9L Engine

Coupe

1. Remove the air cleaner.
2. Remove the intake manifold cover.
3. Remove the engine mount strut.
4. Rotate the drive belt tensioner counterclockwise in order to release the tensioner spring tension.
5. Remove the drive belt.

To install:

6. Rotate the drive belt tensioner counterclockwise in order to release the tensioner spring tension.
7. Install the drive belt.
8. Install the engine mount strut.
9. Install the intake manifold cover.
10. Install the air cleaner.

Convertible

1. Remove the air cleaner assembly.
2. Remove the intake manifold cover.
3. Remove the engine mount bracket bolt and spacer.
4. Rotate the drive belt tensioner counterclockwise in order to release the tensioner spring tension.
5. Remove the drive belt

To install:

6. Rotate the drive belt tensioner counterclockwise in order to release the tensioner spring tension.
7. Install the drive belt.

➡️**The spacer has a nominal length of 36.0 mm (1.42 in). If the spacer cannot be reinstalled, the spacer will require the ends to be buffed slightly using a crocus cloth or emery paper in order to bring the length to a minimum of 35.80 mm (1.41 in).**

8. Install the engine mount bracket spacer.
9. Install the engine mount bracket bolt and tighten to 37 ft. lbs. (50 Nm).
10. Install the intake manifold cover.
11. Install the air cleaner assembly.

BALANCE SHAFT

REMOVAL & INSTALLATION

2.4L Engine

See Figures 31, 32 and 33

1. Remove engine assembly.

2. Remove engine front cover and timing components.
3. Remove the balance shaft bearing carrier bolts.
4. Remove the balance shaft assemblies.

❄️ WARNING

It is possible to install the intake side balance shaft into the exhaust side and vice versa. Please use care not to install the balance shafts into the wrong bores. Engine vibration will result. Do not remove the bolt holding the sprocket.

5. Install the J 43650 into the balance shaft hole. Insert the tool with the foot parallel to the shaft.
6. When the J 43650 is inserted in the block turn the J 43650 so that the foot becomes perpendicular to the shaft.
7. Center the foot of the J 43650 on the balance shaft bushing.
8. Once the J 43650 is centered on the balance shaft bushing, then insert the centering guide into the front balance shaft bore and tighten the nut with an appropriate wrench

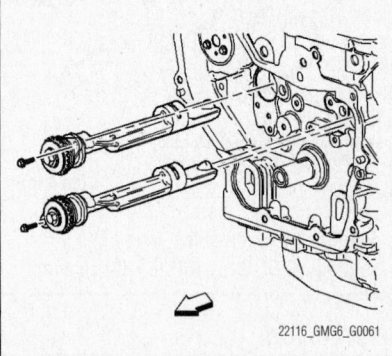

Fig. 31 Removal of balance shafts—2.4L engine

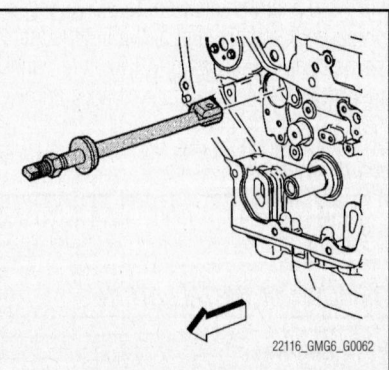

Fig. 32 J 43650— Balance shaft bushing removal tool

9. When the J 43650 is properly installed, before removing the bushing, the end of the tool should be 4.6 inch. (116 mm) from the block face.
10. If the J 43650 is less than approximately 4.5 inch. (114 mm) recheck the tool alignment.
11. Tighten the nut on the J 43650 until the tension releases. When the tension releases, remove the J 43650 and the balance shaft bushing.

To install:

12. Install the balance shaft bushing using the J 43650.
13. Seat the balance shaft bushing into the bore using the J 43650 and a wrench.
14. When the J 43650 is fully seated in the engine block, remove it with a wrench.

❄️ WARNING

If the balance shafts are not properly timed to the engine, the engine may vibrate or make noise.

15. Install the balance shaft assemblies to the engine using the following steps:

   a. Place the number one piston at top dead center (TDC).

   b. Lubricate the balance shaft lobes with engine oil.

   c. Install the balance shafts into their bores.

➡️ **Use the correct fastener in the correct location. Replacement fasteners must be the correct part number for that application. Fasteners requiring replacement or fasteners requiring the use of thread locking compound or sealant are identified in the service procedure. Do not use paints, lubricants, or corrosion inhibitors on fasteners or fastener joint surfaces unless specified. These coatings affect fastener torque and joint clamping force**

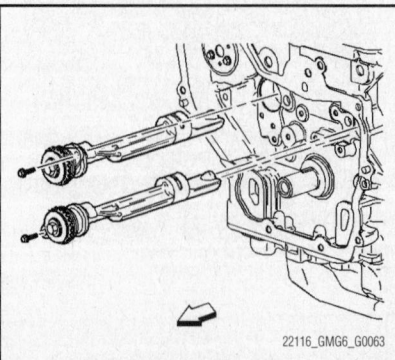

Fig. 33 Balance shaft bushing installation—2.4L engine

and may damage the fastener. Use the correct tightening sequence and specifications when installing fasteners in order to avoid damage to parts and systems.

16. Install the balance shaft retaining bolts.

17. Tighten the balance shaft retaining bolts to 89 inch. lbs. (10 Nm).

CAMSHAFT AND VALVE LIFTERS

INSPECTION

2.4L Engine

1. Inspect the camshaft journals and lobes for wear or scoring.

2. Inspect the camshaft sprocket alignment notch for damage.

3. Inspect the camshaft cover for damage or loose oil control baffles.

4. Clean the camshaft cover.

5. Wash the camshaft in solvent.

6. Oil the camshaft.

7. Inspect the camshaft cover for cracks or other signs of damage.

3.5L and 3.9L Engines

1. Remove and discard the camshaft position actuator filter.

2. Clean the camshaft with cleaning solvent.

3. Inspect the camshaft for scored bearing journals, damaged lobes or damaged position sensor reluctor areas.

4. Measure the camshaft journals using a micrometer. If the camshaft journals are not within 1.868-1.869 in (47.443-47.468mm) on 3.5L or 2.024-2.025 in (51.415-51.440mm) on 3.9L, replace the camshaft.

5. Measure the camshaft run out. If run out exceeds 0.001 in (0.025mm), replace the camshaft.

6. Measure the camshaft lobe lift using a dial indicator. Lubricate the camshaft and set the camshaft on V-blocks. If lobe lift exceeds 0.2727 in (6.9263mm), replace the camshaft.

7. Install a new camshaft position actuator filter.

3.6L Engine

See Figure 34.

1. Clean the camshaft in solvent.

2. Dry the camshaft with compressed air.

3. Inspect the camshaft oil feed holes (1) to the camshaft position actuator for dirt, debris or blockage.

4. Inspect the threaded hole (2) for damage.

5. Inspect the camshaft position actuator locating notch (3) for damage or wear.

6. Inspect the camshaft sealing grooves (4) for damage.

7. Inspect the camshaft thrust surface (5) for damage.

8. Inspect the camshaft lobes (6) and journals (7) for the following conditions:

   a. Excessive scoring or pitting.

   b. Discoloration from overheating.

   c. Deformation from excessive wear, especially the camshaft lobes.

9. If any of the above conditions exist on the camshaft, replace the camshaft.

10. Measure the camshaft journals for diameter and out-of-round using an outside micrometer.

   a. If the diameter is smaller than specifications, replace the camshaft.

   b. If the out-of-round exceeds specifications, replace the camshaft. Refer to Engine Mechanical Specifications.

11. Measure the camshaft run out using a magnetic base dial indicator. Refer to Engine Mechanical Specifications.

12. Measure the camshaft thrust width for wear using a depth micrometer. Refer to Engine Mechanical Specifications.

13. Measure the camshaft thrust wall surface for run out using a magnetic base dial indicator. Refer to Engine Mechanical Specifications.

14. If the camshaft is damaged or worn beyond specifications, replace the camshaft. No machining of the camshaft is allowed.

15. Measure the camshaft lobes for wear using a magnetic base dial indicator.

16. Place the magnetic base dial indicator with the indicator tip on the base circle (1) of the camshaft lobe.

17. Place the dial indicator at zero.

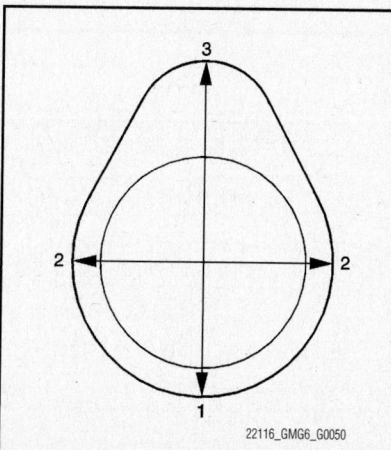

Fig. 34 Camshaft lobe reference points

22116_GMG6_G0050

18. Rotate the camshaft until the indicator tip is at the highest point (3) on the lobe. This reading is the lift of the camshaft lobe. Refer to Engine Mechanical Specifications.

19. If the indicated measurement is significantly lower than these specifications, replace the camshaft or engine performance will be reduced.

LIFTERS

20. Inspect the Stationary Hydraulic Lash Adjuster (SHLA) in the following areas:

   - A plugged oil passage
   - A scored or worn camshaft follower pivot area
   - A damaged or broken retainer, some applications
   - A severely scuffed or worn SHLA body

21. Replace the SHLA or SHLAs as necessary.

REMOVAL & INSTALLATION

2.4L Engine

1. Relieve the fuel system pressure.

2. Disconnect the negative battery cable.

3. Remove the valve cover.

4. Remove the intake and/or exhaust camshaft position actuator.

➡**Remove each bolt on each cap one turn at a time until there is no spring tension pushing on the camshaft.**

5. Mark the bearing caps to ensure they are installed in the original position.

6. Remove the bearing cap bolts and the bearing caps.

7. Remove the exhaust and/or intake camshaft.

➡**Keep all of the roller followers and hydraulic adjusters in order so that they can be reinstalled in their respective locations.**

8. Remove the camshaft roller followers.

9. Remove the lash adjusters.

To install:

10. Install the hydraulic element adjusters into their bores in the cylinder head.

11. Lubricate the hydraulic lash adjusters and valve tips.

12. Position the roller followers on the tip of the valve stem and on the lash adjuster.

13. Lubricate the camshaft(s) and install.

14. Install the camshaft bearing caps. Hand tighten the cap bolts.

15. Tighten the bearing cap bolts in increments of 3 turns to 89 inch lbs. (10 Nm) until they are seated.

16. Install the camshaft actuator(s).

17. Install the valve cover.

3.5L and 3.9L Engines

1. Drain the engine oil and cooling system.

2. Relieve the fuel system pressure.

3. To remove the valve lifters, remove the valve covers.

4. Remove the intake manifolds.

5. Remove the rocker arm bolts.

6. Remove the rocker arms.

7. Remove the pushrods.

8. Remove the intake manifold oil splash shield.

9. Remove the lifter guide bolts.

10. Remove the valve lifter guides.

11. Remove the valve lifters.

12. Clean all gasket surfaces with degreaser.

13. Clean the valve train parts.

14. Inspect the valve lifters and the cam lobes for wear.

15. To remove the camshaft, remove the engine front cover, timing chain and sprockets.

16. Remove the camshaft position sensor.

17. Remove the camshaft thrust plate.

18. Install the camshaft sprocket bolt into the camshaft. Tighten finger tight only.

19. Carefully rotate and remove the camshaft from the engine block.

To install:

20. Coat the camshaft journals with clean engine oil.

21. Coat the camshaft lobes with pre-lube.

22. Install the camshaft sprocket bolt into the camshaft. Tighten finger tight only.

23. Carefully rotate and install the camshaft to the engine block.

24. Install the camshaft thrust plate and tighten to 89 inch lbs. (10 Nm).

25. Install the camshaft position sensor and tighten to 89 inch lbs. (10 Nm).

26. Install the timing chain, sprockets and front cover.

27. Coat the valve lifters with prelube and install them.

28. Install the valve lifter guides and tighten to 89 inch lbs. (10 Nm).

29. Install the intake manifold oil splash shield.

30. Install the pushrods in their original locations.

➡**The intake pushrods are identified with yellow stripes and are 5-3/4**

inches long. Exhaust pushrods are identified with green stripes and are 6 inches long.

31. Install the rocker arms and tighten to 24 ft. lbs. (32 Nm).

32. Install the intake manifolds.

33. Install the valve covers.

34. Connect the negative battery cable.

35. Fill the cooling system.

36. Start the vehicle, check for leaks and repair if necessary.

3.6L Engine

Left Camshaft & Lifters

See Figures 35 through 40.

1. Disconnect the negative battery cable.

2. Remove the lower intake manifold.

3. Remove the left bank camshaft cover.

4. Remove the camshaft sensors.

5. Remove the camshaft position actuator solenoid.

6. Remove the crankshaft balancer

7. Rotate the crankshaft with the EN 46111 until the camshafts are in a neutral (low tension) position.

8. The camshaft flats will be parallel with the camshaft cover rail (1).

> ✳✳ **WARNING**
>
> **Use an open-end wrench at the camshaft hex to prevent camshaft/engine rotation. DO NOT remove the camshaft position actuator bolt at this time.**

9. Loosen the camshaft position actuator bolt.

➡**Ensure that the tips of the EN 46108 are fully engaged into the timing chain (3 and 4).**

Fig. 35 Camshaft flats shown

10. Install the EN 46108 (1 and 2) in order to retain the timing chain.

11. Firmly tighten the EN 46108 nuts.

> ✳✳ **WARNING**
>
> **Ensure that the camshaft timing chain and the camshaft position actuators are marked for proper assembly.**

12. Mark the timing chain and the respective locations on the camshaft position actuators (1-4).

13. Remove the camshaft position actuator bolt.

14. Observe the markings on the bearing caps. Each bearing cap is marked in order to identify its location.

15. The markings have the following meanings:

- The raised feature must always be oriented toward the center of the cylinder head.
- The I indicates the intake camshaft.
- The E indicates the exhaust camshaft
- The number indicates the journal position from the front of the engine

16. Remove the camshaft bearing cap bolts.

17. Remove the camshaft bearing caps.

18. Remove the camshafts.

19. Remove the rocker arms.

20. Remove lifters.

21. Replace the camshaft bearing caps and bolts.

To install:

> ✳✳ **WARNING**
>
> **Ensure that the marks on the camshaft position actuator and the timing chain (1—4) are aligned.**

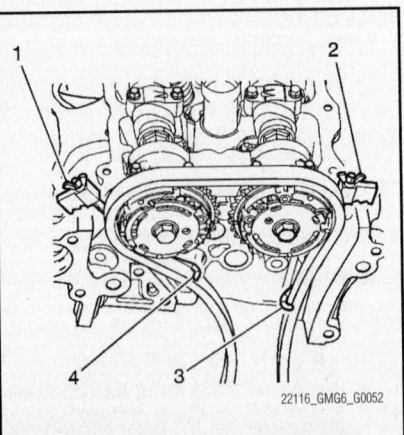

Fig. 36 Timing chain and gear holding tools EN 46108

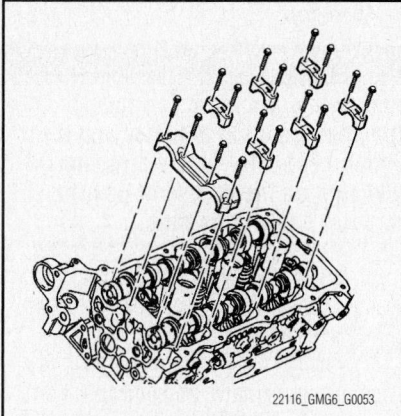

Fig. 37 Camshaft bearing cap removal—
3.6L engine

DO NOT tighten the camshaft position actuator bolt at this time.

22. Locate the camshafts to the cylinder head and assemble the camshaft actuators to the camshafts.

23. Ensure that the crankshaft is in the stage one timing drive assembly position using the EN 46111.

24. Ensure that the camshaft sealing rings (1) are in place in the camshaft grooves. Camshaft sealing rings must be in place below the surface of the camshaft journal in order to avoid being pinched between the cylinder head and the camshaft caps.

➡Ensure each valve lifter is filled with clean engine oil and the valve lifter does not tip over (plunger down) before the installation of the valve lifters. The loss of oil in the valve lifter lower pressure chamber or the dry stroking/cycling of the valve lifter plunger will allow air to travel into the high pressure chamber of the valve

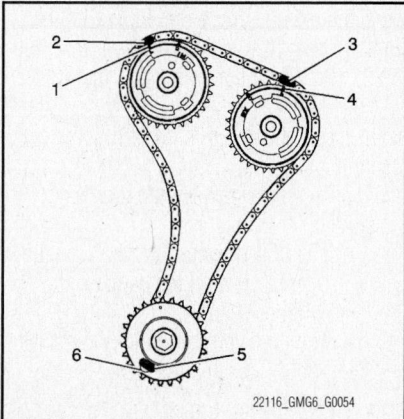

Fig. 38 Timing chain (1—4) alignment marks

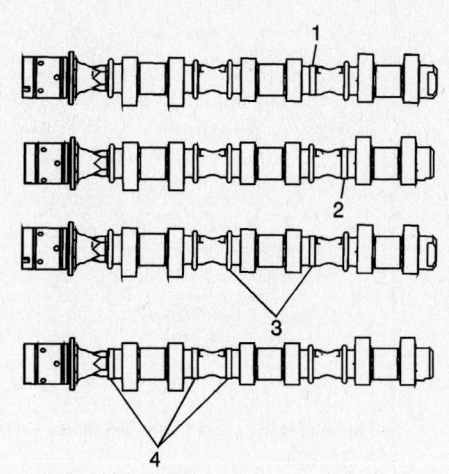

1. The number 4 identification ring for the left intake camshaft is machined off (1) - Third Design, Camshaft Timing Drive System.

2. The number 5 identification ring for the left exhaust camshaft is machined off (2) - Third Design and Fourth, except High Output, Camshaft Timing Drive System.

3. The number 3 and 4 identification rings for the left intake camshaft is machined off (3) - Fourth Design, Camshaft Timing Drive System.

4. The number 1, 2 and 3 identification rings for the left exhaust camshaft is machined off (4) - Fourth Design High Output, Camshaft Timing Drive System.

Fig. 39 Camshaft design identification—3.6L engine

lifter. Air in the high pressure chamber of the valve lifter may not be purged causing extensive engine component damage.

25. Install valve lifters.
26. Install rocker arms.
27. Apply a liberal amount of lubricant to the camshaft journals and the left cylinder head camshaft carriers.

28. Place the left intake and left exhaust camshafts in position in the left cylinder head.

29. Position the camshaft lobes in a neutral position with the flats on the back of the camshafts up and parallel (1) with the left cylinder head camshaft cover rail.

30. Observe the markings on the left cylinder head camshaft bearing caps. Each bearing cap is marked in order to identify its location.

31. The markings have the following meanings:

• The raised feature must always be oriented toward the center of the cylinder head.
• The I indicates the intake camshaft.
• The E indicates the exhaust camshaft
• The number indicates the journal position from the front of the engine

32. Apply a liberal amount of lubricant to the camshaft bearing caps.

33. Install the camshaft bearing thrust cap in the first journal of the left cylinder head.

34. Install the remaining bearing caps with their orientation mark toward the center of the cylinder head.

35. Hand start all the camshaft bearing cap bolts.

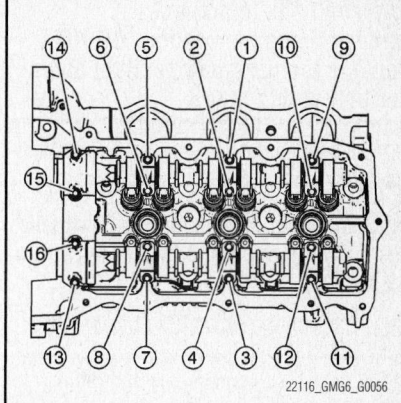

Fig. 40 Left camshaft bearing cap bolt tightening sequence—3.6L engine

36. Tighten the bearing cap bolts by following the next few steps:

a. Tighten the camshaft bearing cap bolts in sequence to 89 inch lbs.(10 Nm).

b. Loosen the center intake camshaft bearing cap bolts 1, 2 and the center exhaust camshaft bearing cap bolts.

c. Retighten the center camshaft bearing cap bolts 1, 2, 3, and 4.

d. Retighten the camshaft bearing cap bolts to 89 inch lbs.(10 Nm).

37. Install and tighten the camshaft position actuators.

38. Install the intake camshaft position actuator solenoid.

39. Install the camshaft sensors.
40. Install the crankshaft balancer.
41. Install the camshaft cover.
42. Install the lower intake manifold.
43. Connect the negative battery cable.
44. Drain crankcase and install recommended motor oil.

45. Start the vehicle, check for leaks and repair if necessary.

Right Camshaft & Lifters

See Figures 41 through 45.

1. Disconnect the negative battery cable.

2. Remove the lower intake manifold.

3. Remove the camshaft cover.

4. Remove the camshaft sensors.

5. Remove the intake camshaft position actuator solenoid.

6. Rotate the crankshaft with the EN 46111 until the camshafts are in a neutral (low tension) position. The camshaft flats will be parallel with the camshaft cover rail.

> ✳✳ **WARNING**
>
> **Use an open-end wrench at the camshaft hex to prevent camshaft/engine rotation. DO NOT remove the camshaft position actuator bolt at this time.**

7. Loosen the camshaft position actuator bolt.

➡ **Ensure that the tips of the EN 46108 are fully engaged into the timing chain (3 and 4).**

8. Install the EN 46108 (1 and 2) in order to retain the timing chain.

9. Firmly tighten the EN 46108 nuts.

> ✳✳ **WARNING**
>
> **Ensure that the camshaft timing chain and the camshaft position actuators are marked for proper assembly.**

10. Mark the timing chain and the respective locations on camshaft position actuators (15-18).

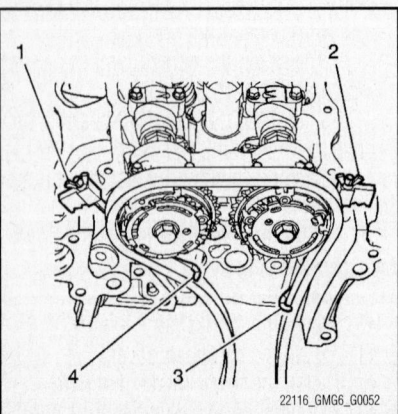

Fig. 41 Timing chain and gear holding tools EN 46108

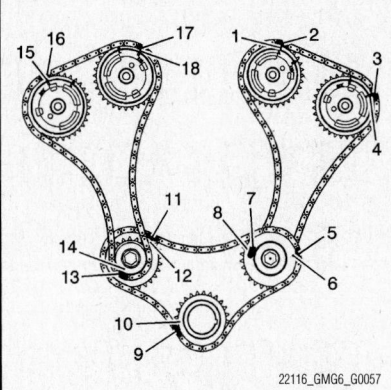

Fig. 42 Timing chain alignment marks — 3.6L engine

11. Remove the camshaft position actuator bolt.

12. Observe the markings on the right cylinder head camshaft bearing caps. Each bearing cap is marked in order to identify its location.

13. The markings have the following meanings:

- The raised feature must always be oriented toward the center of the cylinder head.
- The I indicates the intake camshaft.
- The E indicates the exhaust camshaft
- The number indicates the journal position from the front of the engine

14. Remove the camshaft bearing cap bolts.

15. Remove the camshaft bearing caps.

16. Remove the camshafts.

17. Remove the rocker arms.

18. Remove lifters.

19. Replace the camshaft bearing caps and bolts.

Fig. 43 Bearing cap markings view

To install:

> ✳✳ **WARNING**
>
> **Ensure that the marks on the camshaft position actuator and the timing chain (1—4) are aligned. DO NOT tighten the camshaft position actuator bolt at this time.**

20. Locate the camshafts to the cylinder head and assemble the camshaft actuators to the camshafts.

21. Ensure that the crankshaft is in the stage one timing drive assembly position using the EN 46111.

22. Ensure that the camshaft sealing rings (1) are in place in the camshaft grooves. Camshaft sealing rings must be in place below the surface of the camshaft journal in order to avoid being pinched between the cylinder head and the camshaft caps.

➡ **Ensure each valve lifter is filled with clean engine oil and the valve lifter does not tip over (plunger down) before the installation of the valve lifters. The loss of oil in the valve lifter lower pressure chamber or the dry stroking/cycling of the valve lifter plunger will allow air to travel into the high pressure chamber of the valve lifter. Air in the high pressure chamber of the valve lifter may not be purged causing extensive engine component damage.**

23. Install valve lifters.

24. Install rocker arms.

25. Apply a liberal amount of lubricant to the camshaft journals and the right cylinder head camshaft carriers.

26. Place the right intake and right exhaust camshafts in position in the right cylinder head.

27. Position the camshaft lobes in a neutral position with the flats on the back of the camshafts up and parallel (1) with the right cylinder head camshaft cover rail.

28. Observe the markings on the right cylinder head camshaft bearing caps. Each bearing cap is marked in order to identify its location.

29. The markings have the following meanings:

- The raised feature must always be oriented toward the center of the cylinder head.
- The I indicates the intake camshaft.
- The E indicates the exhaust camshaft
- The number indicates the journal position from the front of the engine

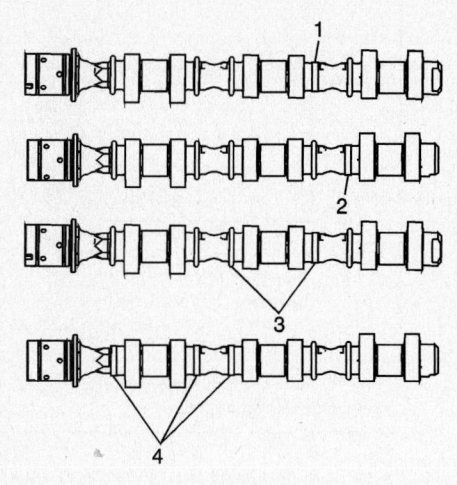

1. The number 4 identification ring for the left intake camshaft is machined off (1) - Third Design, Camshaft Timing Drive System.

2. The number 5 identification ring for the left exhaust camshaft is machined off (2) - Third Design and Fourth, except High Output, Camshaft Timing Drive System.

3. The number 3 and 4 identification rings for the left intake camshaft is machined off (3) - Fourth Design, Camshaft Timing Drive System.

4. The number 1, 2 and 3 identification rings for the left exhaust camshaft is machined off (4) - Fourth Design High Output, Camshaft Timing Drive System.

22116_GMG6_G0055

Fig. 44 Camshaft design identification—3.6L engine

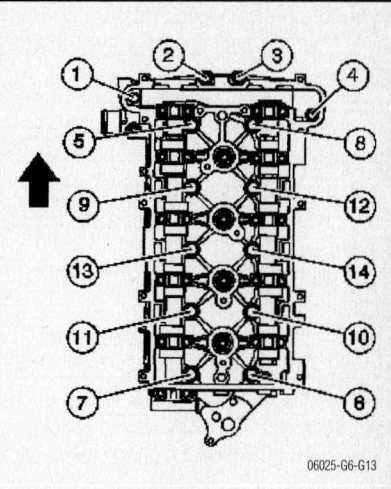

06025-G6-G13

Fig. 46 Cylinder head bolt removal sequence—2.4L engine

30. Apply a liberal amount of lubricant to the camshaft bearing caps.

31. Install the camshaft bearing thrust cap in the first journal of the right cylinder head.

32. Install the remaining bearing caps with their orientation mark toward the center of the cylinder head.

33. Hand start all the camshaft bearing cap bolts.

34. Tighten the bearing cap bolts by following the next few steps:

    a. Tighten the camshaft bearing cap bolts in sequence to 89 inch lbs.(10 Nm).

    b. Loosen the center intake camshaft bearing cap bolts (1, 2) and the center exhaust camshaft bearing cap bolts (3, 4).

    c. Retighten the center camshaft bearing cap bolts 1, 2, 3, and 4.

    d. Retighten the camshaft bearing cap bolts to 89 inch lbs.(10 Nm).

35. Install and tighten the camshaft position actuators.

36. Install the intake camshaft position actuator solenoid.

37. Install the camshaft sensors.

38. Install the crankshaft balancer.

39. Install the camshaft cover.

40. Install the lower intake manifold.

41. Connect the negative battery cable.

42. Drain crankcase and install recommended motor oil.

43. Start the vehicle, check for leaks and repair if necessary.

CYLINDER HEAD

REMOVAL & INSTALLATION

2.4L Engine

See Figures 46 and 47.

1. Before servicing the vehicle, refer to the precautions in the beginning of this section.

2. Relieve the fuel system pressure.

3. Drain the cooling system.

4. Remove or disconnect the following:

- Intake manifold.
- Exhaust manifold
- Timing chain
- Valve cover.
- Cylinder head bolts in the sequence shown.

To install:

5. Clean the gasket surfaces and the bolt holes.

6. Install the cylinder head gasket.

7. Install the cylinder head.

8. Lightly apply clean engine oil to the threads and the bottom side flange of the head bolts and allow the oil to drain before installing.

9. Install new cylinder head bolts.

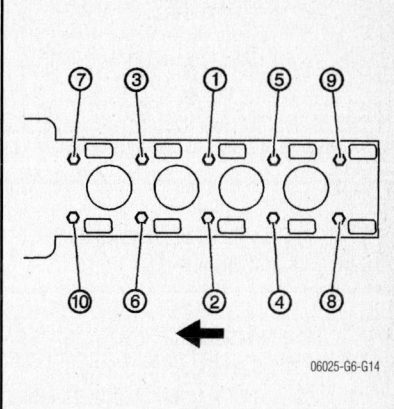

06025-G6-G14

Fig. 47 Cylinder head bolt tightening sequence—2.4L engine

10. Install and tighten the cylinder head bolts in the sequence shown to 22 ft. lbs. (30 Nm), plus an additional 155 degrees.

11. Install and tighten the 4 front cylinder head bolts and tighten to 26 ft. lbs. (35 Nm).

12. Install the timing chain.

13. Install the exhaust manifold.

14. Install the valve cover.

15. Install the intake manifold.

16. Connect the negative battery cable.

17. Fill and bleed the cooling system.

18. Start the vehicle, check for leaks and repair if necessary.

3.5L Engine

See Figure 48.

1. Before servicing the vehicle, refer to the precautions in the beginning of this section.

2. Relieve the fuel system pressure.

3. Drain the engine oil.

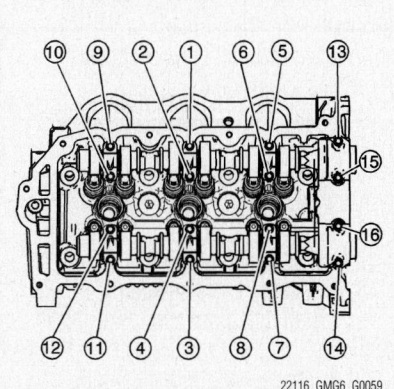

22116_GMG6_G0059

Fig. 45 Right camshaft bearing cap bolt tightening sequence—3.6L engine

4. Drain the cooling system.

5. Remove the upper and lower intake manifolds.

6. Remove the valve covers.

7. Remove the valve rocker arms and the pushrods.

8. Remove the exhaust manifolds.

9. Remove the spark plug wires and spark plugs.

10. On the left side, remove the oil dipstick and tube.

11. On the right side, remove the fuel line bracket and alternator.

12. On both sides, remove the cylinder head bolts and the heads.

13. Clean the gasket mating surfaces.

To install:

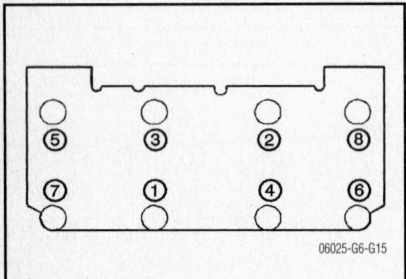

Fig. 48 Cylinder head bolt tightening sequence—3.5L engine

14. Using new head gaskets, install the cylinder heads over the locator pins.

15. Install new cylinder head bolts and tighten in sequence to 44 ft. lbs. (60 Nm), plus an additional 95 degrees.

16. On the right side, install the fuel line bracket and alternator.

17. On the left side, install the oil dipstick and tube.

18. Install the spark plug wires and spark plugs.

19. Install the exhaust manifolds.

20. Install the valve rocker arms and the pushrods.

21. Install the valve covers.

22. Install the upper and lower intake manifolds.

23. Connect the negative battery cable.

24. Fill the engine with clean oil.

25. Fill and bleed the cooling system.

26. Connect the negative battery cable.

27. Start the engine and check for leaks and repair if necessary.

3.6L Engine

Left

See Figure 49.

1. Before servicing the vehicle, refer to the precautions in the beginning of this section.

2. Relieve the fuel system pressure.

3. Drain the cooling system.

4. Drain engine oil.

5. Remove the upper and lower intake manifolds.

6. Remove the valve covers.

7. Remove the spark plugs in order to ease crankshaft/engine rotation.

8. Remove the engine front cover.

9. Remove the right bank secondary camshaft drive chain.

10. Remove the primary camshaft drive chain.

11. Remove the left bank secondary camshaft drive chain tensioner.

12. Remove the left bank secondary camshaft drive chain shoe.

13. Remove the left bank secondary camshaft drive chain guide.

14. Remove the left bank camshaft intermediate drive chain idler.

15. Remove the left bank secondary camshaft drive chain.

16. Remove the oil level indicator

17. Disconnect the coolant temperature sensor electrical connector.

18. Remove the wiring harness ground from the cylinder head.

19. Remove the catalytic converter.

20. Remove the two front M8 left cylinder head bolts.

21. Remove the left cylinder head bolts.

22. Remove the cylinder head with the exhaust manifold.

23. Remove and discard the cylinder head gasket.

24. Clean and inspect the cylinder head and the engine block sealing surfaces.

To install:

25. Ensure the cylinder head locating pins are securely mounted in the cylinder block deck face.

26. Install a new left cylinder head gasket using the deck face locating pins for retention.

27. Carefully install and align the left cylinder head with the deck face locating pins.

❊❊ WARNING

DO NOT allow oil on the cylinder head bolt bosses or reuse the old M11 cylinder head bolts.

28. Install new M11 cylinder head bolts.

29. Tighten the M11 cylinder head bolts a first pass in sequence to 33 ft. lbs. (45 Nm).

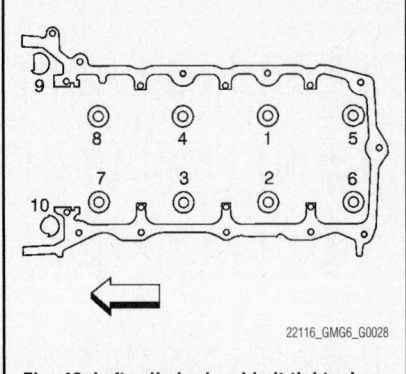

22116_GMG6_G0028

Fig. 49 Left cylinder head bolt tightening sequence—3.6L engine

30. Tighten the M11 cylinder head bolts a second pass in sequence an additional 120 degrees using a angel meter.

31. Install the 2 front M8 left cylinder head bolts.

32. Tighten the M8 cylinder head bolts a first pass to 11ft. lbs. (15 Nm).

33. Tighten the M8 cylinder head bolts a second pass in sequence an additional 60 degrees using a angel meter.

34. Install the catalytic converter to the exhaust manifold.

35. Connect the wiring harness electrical connector located at the side of the cylinder head.

36. Install the wiring harness ground to the cylinder head and tighten mounting bolt to 89 inch. lbs. (10 Nm).

37. Install the coolant temperature sensor electrical connector.

38. Install the oil level indicator with new seal.

39. Install the left bank secondary camshaft drive chain

40. Install the left bank camshaft intermediate drive chain idler.

41. Install the left bank secondary camshaft drive chain guide.

42. Install the left bank secondary camshaft drive chain shoe.

43. Install the left bank secondary camshaft drive chain tensioner.

44. Install the primary camshaft drive chain.

45. Install the right bank secondary camshaft drive chain.

46. Install the engine front cover.

47. Install the spark plugs.

48. Install the valve covers.

49. Install the upper and lower intake manifolds.

50. Fill the engine with clean oil.

51. Fill and bleed the cooling system.

52. Start the engine and check for leaks and repair if necessary.

Right

See Figure 50.

1. Before servicing the vehicle, refer to the precautions in the beginning of this section.
2. Remove the hood.
3. Relieve the fuel system pressure.
4. Drain the cooling system.
5. Drain engine oil.
6. Remove the upper and lower intake manifolds.
7. Remove the valve covers.
8. Remove the spark plugs in order to ease crankshaft/engine rotation.
9. Remove the engine front cover.
10. Remove the right bank secondary camshaft drive chain tensioner.
11. Remove the right bank secondary camshaft drive chain shoe
12. Remove the right bank secondary camshaft drive chain guide.
13. Remove the right bank secondary camshaft drive chain.
14. Remove the right cylinder head bolts.
15. With the aid of an assistant, remove the cylinder head with the exhaust manifold.
16. Remove and discard the cylinder head gasket.
17. Clean and inspect the cylinder head and the engine block sealing surfaces.

To install:

➡**Ensure the cylinder head locating pins are securely mounted in the cylinder block deck face.**

18. Install a new right cylinder head gasket using the deck face locating pins for retention.
19. Align the right cylinder head with the deck face locating pins.
20. With the aid of an assistant, carefully install the cylinder head with the exhaust manifold to the engine.

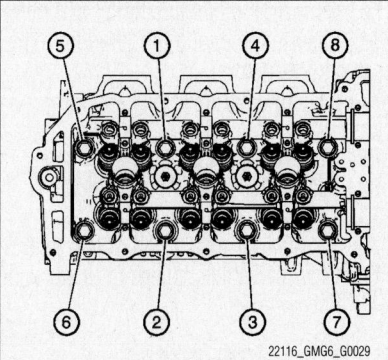

Fig. 50 Right cylinder head bolt tightening sequence—3.6L engine

22116_GMG6_G0029

⁕⁕ **WARNING**

DO NOT allow oil on the cylinder head bolt bosses or reuse the old M11 cylinder head bolts.

21. Tighten the M11 cylinder head bolts a first pass in sequence to 33 ft. lbs. (45 Nm).
22. Tighten the M11 cylinder head bolts a second pass in sequence an additional 120 degrees using a angel meter.
23. Install the right bank secondary camshaft drive chain
24. Install the right bank camshaft intermediate drive chain idler.
25. Install the right bank secondary camshaft drive chain guide.
26. Install the right bank secondary camshaft drive chain shoe.
27. Install the right bank secondary camshaft drive chain tensioner.
28. Install the engine front cover.
29. Install the spark plugs.
30. Install the valve covers.
31. Install the upper and lower intake manifolds.
32. Fill the engine with clean oil.
33. Fill and bleed the cooling system.
34. Start the engine and check for leaks and repair if necessary.

3.9L Engine

See Figures 51 through 53.

1. Relieve the fuel system pressure.
2. Drain the engine oil.
3. Drain the cooling system.
4. Remove the upper and lower intake manifolds.
5. Remove the valve covers.
6. Remove the valve rocker arms and pushrods.
7. Remove the exhaust manifolds.
8. Remove the spark plug wires and spark plugs.
9. On the right side, remove the fuel line bracket and the alternator.
10. On the left side, remove the oil dipstick and tube.
11. On both sides, remove and discard the cylinder head bolts and head.

To install:

12. Clean the gasket mating surfaces.
13. Install the cylinder head locator dowel pins, if necessary.
14. Inspect the cylinder head locator dowel pins for proper installation.
15. Install a new cylinder head gasket, noting the identification marks for each side.
16. Install the cylinder head onto the locator pins and the engine.

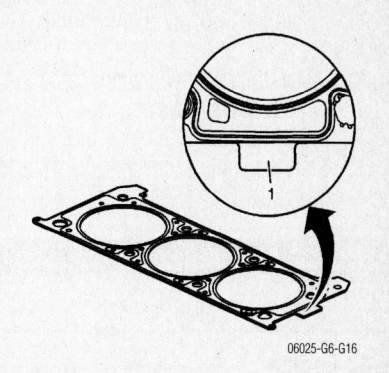

Fig. 51 Right side cylinder head gasket identification—3.9L engine

06025-G6-G16

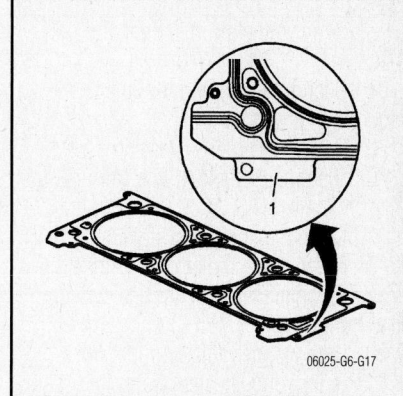

Fig. 52 Left side cylinder head gasket identification—3.9L engine

06025-G6-G17

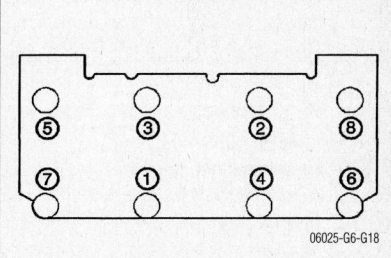

Fig. 53 Cylinder head bolt tightening sequence—3.9L engine

06025-G6-G18

17. Install new cylinder head bolts finger tight.
18. Tighten the cylinder head bolts in sequence to 44 ft. lbs. (60 Nm), plus an additional 95 degrees.
19. On the left side, install the oil dipstick and tube.
20. On the right side, install the fuel line bracket and the alternator.
21. Install the spark plug wires and spark plugs.
22. Install the exhaust manifolds.
23. Install the valve rocker arms and pushrods.

24. Install the valve covers.
25. Install the upper and lower intake manifolds.
26. Install the negative battery cable.
27. Fill the cooling system.
28. Fill the engine with clean oil.
29. Start the vehicle, check for leaks and repair if necessary.

ENGINE ASSEMBLY

REMOVAL & INSTALLATION

2.4L Engine

1. Place the wheels in the straight ahead position.
2. Disconnect the negative battery cable.
3. Remove the air inlet duct and resonator.
4. Secure the cooling module to the upper body structure.
5. Relieve the fuel system pressure.
6. Disconnect the fuel line from the fuel rail.
7. Drain the cooling system.
8. Remove the radiator inlet hose.
9. Remove the surge tank to cylinder head hose.
10. Remove the radiator outlet hose.
11. Remove the heater hoses.
12. Disconnect the following harness connectors:
    - Electronic throttle control
    - Manifold Absolute Pressure (MAP) sensor
    - Crankshaft Position (CKP) sensor
    - Oil pressure sensor
    - Purge solenoid
    - Ignition coils
    - Heated oxygen sensor
    - Vehicle Speed Sensor (VSS)
    - Engine Coolant Temperature (ECT) sensor
    - Back-up light switch
    - Camshaft position actuator solenoid control valves
    - Fuel rail
13. Raise and support the vehicle.
14. Remove the drive belt.
15. Remove the AC compressor bolts and set the compressor aside.
16. Disconnect the starter and alternator connectors.
17. Disconnect the front exhaust pipe from the exhaust manifold.
18. Lower the vehicle.
19. Disconnect the transmission harness connectors.
20. Disconnect the transmission shift cable from the transmission.
21. Use blocks of wood to support the powertrain assembly between the frame and the powertrain.
22. Remove the engine mount.
23. Remove the side transmission mount bracket bolts.
24. Raise the vehicle.
25. Disconnect the stabilizer links from the stabilizer bar.
26. Disconnect the outer tie rod ends from the steering knuckles.
27. Disconnect the intermediate shaft from the steering gear.
28. Disconnect the lower control arms from the steering knuckles.
29. Disconnect the drive axles from the transaxle and support with wire or bungee cords.
30. Use a paint pen or magic marker in order to mark the frame to body position.
31. Lower the vehicle to about 3 feet off the ground in order to position the lift table under the frame.
32. Use wood blocks as necessary between the lift table and the frame to support the assembly.
33. Remove the front frame bolts and then the rear frame bolts.
34. Slowly raise the vehicle off of the frame and powertrain.
35. Attach an engine lift hoist to the engine lift hooks.
36. Remove the starter.
37. Remove the torque converter-to-flywheel bolts.
38. Remove the transaxle to engine bolts.
39. Separate the engine from the transaxle.
40. Remove the following components:
    - Exhaust manifold
    - Engine mount bracket.
    - Engine block heater
    - Thermostat housing and feed pipe
    - Alternator
    - Fuel rail
    - Drive belt tensioner.
41. Install the engine to a suitable engine stand.

To install:

42. Attach a lifting device to the lifting hooks.
43. Install the following components:
    - Exhaust manifold
    - Engine mount bracket.
    - Engine block heater
    - Thermostat housing and feed pipe
    - Alternator
    - Fuel rail
    - Drive belt tensioner.
44. Lower the engine into the vehicle and install the engine to the transaxle bolts and tighten to 55 ft. lbs. (75 Nm).
45. Install the torque converter bolts and tighten to 46 ft. lbs. (62 Nm).
46. Install the starter.
47. Remove the engine lift from the engine.
48. Lower vehicle slowly over frame and powertrain.
49. Hand start all the frame bolts while aligning the frame to the paint marks.
50. Tighten the frame bolts to 74 ft. lbs. (100 Nm) plus an additional 180 degrees.
51. Remove the lift table.
52. Connect the drive axles to the transaxle.
53. Connect the lower control arm to the steering knuckle.
54. Connect the intermediate steering shaft to the steering gear.
55. Connect the outer tie rod ends to the steering knuckles.
56. Connect the stabilizer links to the stabilizer bar.
57. Install the side transmission mount bracket bolts and tighten to 37 ft. lbs. (50 Nm).
58. Install the engine mounts and tighten to 37 ft. lbs. (50 Nm).
59. Remove the wood blocks between the powertrain and frame.
60. Connect the transmission shift cable to the transmission.
61. Connect the transmission harness connector.
62. Install the catalytic converter to the exhaust manifold and tighten to 22 ft. lbs. (30 Nm).
63. Lower the vehicle.
64. Install the alternator and starter connections.
65. Install the AC compressor to the engine.
66. Install the engine drive belt.
67. Connect all electrical connectors disconnect previously.
68. Install the heater hoses.
69. Install the radiator outlet hose.
70. Connect the fuel line to the fuel rail.
71. Release the cooling module from the upper body structure.
72. Install the air inlet duct and resonator.
73. Connect the negative battery cable.
74. Fill and bleed the cooling system.
75. Fill the engine with clean oil.
76. Fill the transaxle to the proper level.
77. Start the vehicle, check for leaks and repair if necessary.

3.5L Engine (LX9—LZ4)

1. Drain the cooling system.
2. Drain the engine oil.
3. Drain the transaxle fluid.

4. Properly relieve the fuel system pressure.

5. Remove the intake manifold cover.

6. Remove the air cleaner assembly.

7. Remove the hood.

8. Remove the engine mount strut.

9. Remove the drive belt.

10. Disconnect the following electrical connectors:

- Knock Sensor (KS)
- Camshaft Position Sensor (CPS)
- Crankshaft Position (CKP) sensor
- Heated oxygen sensor
- Manifold Absolute Pressure (MAP) sensor
- EGR valve
- EVAP canister purge solenoid
- Electronic throttle control
- Ignition coils
- Body wiring harness-to-engine harness

11. Raise and support the vehicle.

12. Remove the catalytic converters.

13. Remove the engine wiring harness grounds from the transaxle.

14. Remove the engine mount lower nuts.

15. Remove the torque converter covers.

16. Remove the starter.

17. Remove the Air Conditioning (A/C) compressor. DO NOT discharge the A/C system. Support the compressor.

18. Remove the torque converter bolts.

19. Remove the transaxle brace.

20. Remove the 6 lower transaxle-to-engine bolts and the stud.

21. Remove the radiator outlet hose from the engine.

22. Lower the vehicle and support the transaxle.

23. Remove the heater outlet and inlet hoses from the engine.

24. Remove the vacuum hoses from the upper intake manifold.

25. Remove the brake booster vacuum hose from the upper intake manifold.

26. Remove the fuel lines from the fuel rail.

27. Remove the radiator inlet hose from the engine.

28. Install an engine lifting device to the engine.

29. Remove the upper transaxle-to-engine bolts and the stud.

30. Remove the engine from the vehicle.

31. Remove the flywheel.

32. Install the engine to the engine stand.

To install:

33. Remove the engine from the engine stand.

34. Install the flywheel.

35. Install the engine to the vehicle.

36. Install the upper transaxle-to-engine bolts and the stud and tighten to 55 ft. lbs. (75 Nm).

37. Remove the engine lifting device.

38. Install the radiator inlet hose to the engine.

39. Install the fuel lines to the fuel rail.

40. Install the brake booster vacuum hose to the upper intake manifold.

41. Install the vacuum hoses to the upper intake manifold.

42. Install the heater inlet and outlet hoses to the engine.

43. Raise the vehicle and remove the transaxle support.

44. Install the radiator outlet hose to the engine.

45. Install the lower transaxle-to-engine bolt and the stud and tighten to 55 ft. lbs. (75 Nm).

46. Install the transaxle brace and tighten to 53 ft. lbs. (72 Nm).

47. Install the torque converter bolts.

48. Install the A/C compressor.

49. Install the starter motor.

50. Install the torque converter covers.

51. Install the engine mount lower nuts and tighten to 32 ft. lbs.

52. Install the engine wiring harness grounds to the transaxle.

53. Install the engine wiring harness ground nut to the transaxle stud.

54. Install the catalytic converters.

55. Lower the vehicle.

56. Connect the electrical connectors disconnected previously.

57. Install the engine mount lower nuts and tighten to 32 ft. lbs. (43 Nm).

58. Install the engine wiring harness grounds to the transaxle.

59. Install the engine wiring harness ground nut to the transaxle stud.

60. Install the catalytic converters.

61. Lower the vehicle.

62. Connect the negative battery cable.

63. Fill and bleed the cooling system.

64. Fill the engine with clean oil.

65. Fill the transaxle to the proper level.

66. Start the vehicle, check for leaks and repair if necessary.

3.6L Engine

1. Disconnect the negative battery cable.

2. Remove the intake manifold cover.

3. Drain the cooling system.

4. Drain the engine oil.

5. Remove the air cleaner assembly.

6. Remove the hood.

7. Remove the engine mount strut.

8. Remove the drive belt.

9. Disconnect the front knock sensor (KS).

10. Disconnect the rear KS (1) and the crank sensor.

11. Re-position the plastic wire loom/shield on each valve cover, then disconnect the camshaft position (CMP) sensors.

12. Disconnect the Manifold Absolute Pressure (MAP) sensor.

13. Disconnect the evaporative emission (EVAP) canister purge solenoid.

14. Disconnect the front and rear ignition coils.

15. Disconnect the A/C compressor.

16. Disconnect the coolant temperature sensor.

17. Disconnect the following electrical connectors:

- The heated oxygen sensor (HO2S)
- The exhaust gas recirculation (EGR) valve
- The electronic throttle control
- The body wiring harness-to-engine harness

18. Raise and support the vehicle.

19. Remove the catalytic converters.

20. Remove the engine wiring harness grounds from the transaxle.

21. Remove the engine mount lower bolts .

22. Remove the torque converter covers.

23. Remove the starter motor.

24. Remove the Air Conditioning (A/C) compressor. DO NOT discharge the A/C system. Support the compressor and set aside.

25. Remove the power steering pump and position aside.

26. Remove the torque converter bolts.

27. Remove the engine mount bracket.

28. Remove the transaxle to oil pan brace bolts and brace.

29. Remove the lower transaxle-to-engine bolt and the stud.

30. Remove the radiator outlet hose from the engine.

31. Lower the vehicle and support the transaxle.

32. Remove the engine coolant thermostat housing from the engine.

33. Remove the vacuum hoses from the upper intake manifold.

34. Remove the brake booster vacuum hose from the upper intake manifold.

35. Remove the fuel lines from the fuel rail.

36. Remove the battery ground from the rear of engine.

37. Remove the radiator inlet hose from the engine

38. Install the engine lifting device to the engine.

39. Remove the upper transaxle-to-engine bolts and the stud.

40. Remove the engine from the vehicle.

41. Remove the flywheel.

42. Install the engine to the engine stand.

To install:

43. Remove the engine from the engine stand.

44. Install the flywheel and tighten the bolts in a star pattern to 52 ft. lbs (71 Nm).

45. Install the engine to the vehicle

46. Install the upper transaxle-to-engine bolts and the stud. Tighten to 55ft. lbs. (75 Nm).

47. Remove the engine lifting device.

48. Install the radiator inlet hose to the engine.

49. Install the battery ground to the rear of engine.

50. Install the fuel lines to the fuel rail.

51. Install the brake booster vacuum hose to the upper intake manifold.

52. Install the vacuum hoses to the upper intake manifold.

53. Install the engine coolant thermostat housing to the engine. Tighten mounting bolts to 18 ft. lbs. (25 Nm).

54. Raise the vehicle and remove the transaxle support.

55. Install the radiator outlet hose to the engine.

56. Install the lower transaxle-to-engine bolt and the stud. Tighten to 55ft. lbs. (75 Nm).

57. Position the transaxle to oil pan brace, install and tighten the bolts to 37 ft. lbs. (50 Nm).

58. Install the engine mount bracket. Tighten the Upper and lower bracket bolts to 37 ft. lbs. (50 Nm).

59. Install the torque converter bolts.

60. Install the power steering pump. Tighten engine mount adapter bolt to 43 ft. lbs. (58 Nm). Tighten pump bolt to 37 ft. lbs. (50 Nm).

61. Install the A/C compressor. Tighten A/C mounting bolts to 37 ft. lbs. (50 Nm).

62. Install starter motor, tighten mounting bolts to 37 ft. lbs. (50 Nm).

63. Install the torque converter covers.

64. Install the engine mount lower bolts and tighten to 37 ft. lbs. (50 Nm).

65. Install the engine wiring harness grounds to the transaxle.

66. Install the engine wiring harness ground nut to the transaxle stud. Tighten to 26 ft. lbs. (35 Nm).

67. Install the catalytic converters. Tighten converter to manifold bolts to 33ft.

lbs. (45 Nm). Tighten left and right converter joining bolts to 18 ft. lbs. (25 Nm).

68. Lower the vehicle.

69. Connect the following electrical connectors:

- The body wiring harness-to-engine harness
- The electronic throttle control
- The EGR valve
- The HO2S
- Coolant temperature sensor
- A/C compressor
- Front and rear ignition coils
- EVAP canister purge solenoid
- MAP sensor

70. Connect the CMP sensors, then reposition the plastic wire loom/shield on each valve cover.

71. Connect the rear KS

72. Connect the front KS and the crank sensor.

73. Install the drive belt.

74. Install the engine mount strut. Tighten the bolt to 81 ft. lbs. (110 Nm).

75. Install the hood and mounting bolts, tighten to 89 inch. lbs. (10 Nm).

76. Install the air cleaner assembly.

77. Connect the negative battery cable.

78. Fill the crankcase with engine oil.

79. Fill and bleed cooling system.

80. Perform a CKP system variation learn procedure.

81. Install the intake manifold cover

82. Start the vehicle, check for leaks and repair if necessary.

3.9L Engine

1. Disconnect the negative battery cable.

2. Drain the engine coolant.

3. Drain the engine oil.

4. Remove the air cleaner assembly.

5. Remove the hood.

6. Remove the intake manifold cover.

7. Remove the engine mount strut.

8. Remove the drive belt.

9. Remove the power steering pump and disconnect the power steering lines, if equipped.

10. Remove the oil pressure sensor heat shield nuts and shield.

11. Disconnect the oil pressure sensor connector.

12. Disconnect the knock sensor connector.

13. Disconnect the air conditioning compressor electrical connector.

14. Lower the vehicle.

15. Disconnect the EVAP canister purge solenoid connector.

16. Disconnect the electronic throttle control connector.

17. Remove the connector position assurance retainer.

18. Disconnect the heated oxygen sensor electrical connector.

19. Disconnect the Manifold Absolute Pressure (MAP) sensor connector.

20. Disconnect the ignition control module connector.

21. Disconnect the inlet manifold valve connector.

22. Disconnect the fuel injector inline connector.

23. Disconnect the camshaft phaser sensor connector.

24. Disconnect the rear upper HO2S electrical connector.

25. Disconnect the Crankshaft Position (CKP) sensor connector.

26. Disconnect the engine harness connector from the body harness connector.

27. Disconnect the body harness electrical connector from the powertrain control module (PCM).

28. Disconnect the engine harness electrical connectors from the PCM.

29. Disconnect the engine harness electrical connector from the transmission control module (TCM).

30. Remove the engine harness attachments from the transmission stud.

31. Remove the catalytic converters.

32. Remove the engine mount.

33. Remove the torque converter cover.

34. Remove the starter.

35. Remove the torque converter bolts.

36. Unbolt and reposition the A/C compressor of to the side. DO NOT discharge the A/C system.

37. Remove the transaxle brace.

38. Remove the lower transaxle-to-engine bolt and stud.

39. Reposition the radiator outlet hose clamp at the thermostat housing.

40. Remove the radiator outlet hose from the thermostat housing.

41. Lower the vehicle and support the transaxle.

42. Reposition the radiator surge tank hose clamp at the surge tank pipe.

43. Remove the radiator surge tank hose from the surge tank pipe.

44. Reposition the brake booster vacuum hose clamp at the intake manifold.

45. Remove the brake booster vacuum hose from the intake manifold.

46. Reposition the heater inlet and outlet hose clamps at the engine.

47. Remove the heater hoses.

48. Disconnect the fuel feed line from the fuel rail.

49. Disconnect the EVAP purge line from the canister purge solenoid.

50. Reposition the radiator inlet hose clamp at the engine.

51. Remove the radiator inlet hose from the engine.

52. Install a engine lifting device to the engine.

53. Remove the remaining transaxle-to-engine bolts/studs.

54. Remove the engine from the vehicle.

55. Remove the flywheel.

56. Install the engine to the engine stand.

To install:

57. Remove the engine from the engine stand.

58. Install the flywheel and tighten the bolts to 52 ft. lbs .(70 Nm).

59. Install the engine to the vehicle.

60. Install the transaxle-to-engine bolts/studs and tighten to 55 ft. lbs. (75 Nm).

61. Remove the engine lifting device from the engine.

62. Install the radiator inlet hose to the engine.

63. Position the radiator inlet hose clamp at the engine.

64. Connect the EVAP purge line to the canister purge solenoid.

65. Connect the fuel feed line to the fuel rail.

66. Install the heater hoses.

67. Install the brake booster vacuum hose to the intake manifold.

68. Install the radiator surge tank hose to the surge tank pipe.

69. Raise and support the vehicle.

70. Install the radiator outlet hose to the thermostat housing.

71. Install the lower transaxle-to-engine bolt and stud and tighten to 55 ft. lbs. (75 Nm).

72. Install the transaxle brace and tighten to 53 ft. lbs. (72 Nm).

73. Position the A/C compressor and tighten to 37 ft. lbs. (50 Nm).

74. Install the torque converter bolts and tighten to 37 ft. lbs. (50 Nm).

75. Install the starter.

76. Install the torque converter cover.

77. Install the engine mount and tighten to 37 ft. lbs. (50 Nm).

78. Install the catalytic converters.

79. Install the engine harness attachments to the transmission stud.

80. Connect the engine harness electrical connector to the TCM and PCM.

81. Connect the engine harness connector to the body harness connector and PCM.

82. Connect the CKP sensor connector.

83. Connect the knock sensor connector.

84. Connect the rear upper HO2S connector.

85. Install the CPA retainer.

86. Connect the camshaft phaser sensor connector.

87. Connect the fuel injector inline connector.

88. Connect the inlet manifold valve connector.

89. Connect the ignition control module connector.

90. Connect the MAP sensor connector.

91. Connect the HO2S connector.

92. Install the CPA retainer.

93. Connect the ETC connector.

94. Connect the EVAP canister purge solenoid connector.

95. Raise and support the vehicle.

96. Connect the A/C compressor electrical connector.

97. Connect the knock sensor connector.

98. Connect the oil pressure sensor connector.

99. Install the oil pressure sensor heat shield and nuts.

100. Lower the vehicle.

101. Connect the power steering lines and install the power steering pump, if equipped.

102. Install the drive belt.

103. Install the engine mount strut.

104. Install the intake manifold cover.

105. Install the hood.

106. Install the air cleaner assembly.

107. Fill the engine with oil.

108. Fill the cooling system.

109. Connect the negative battery cable.

110. Start the engine and check for leaks.

EXHAUST MANIFOLD

REMOVAL & INSTALLATION

2.4L Engine

See Figure 54.

1. Remove the exhaust manifold heat shield.

2. Remove the block heater, if equipped.

3. Remove the oxygen sensor.

4. Remove the exhaust manifold.

To install:

5. Clean the gasket mating surface and install a new exhaust manifold gasket.

6. Install new exhaust manifold studs and tighten to 89 inch lbs. (10 Nm).

7. Install the exhaust manifold and finger tighten the bolts.

8. Tighten the bolts in sequence to 10 ft. lbs. (14 Nm).

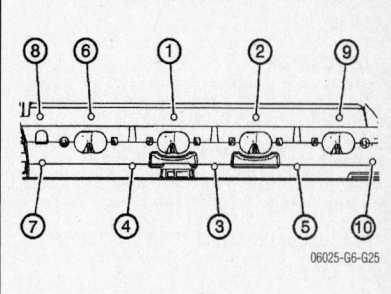

Fig. 54 Exhaust manifold tightening sequence—2.4L engine

9. Coat the threads of the oxygen sensor with anti-seize.

10. Install the oxygen sensor and tighten to 31 ft. lbs. (42 Nm).

11. Install the exhaust manifold heat shield.

3.5L Engine

Left

See Figure 55.

1. Remove the air intake duct.

2. Remove the Connector Position Assurance (CPA) retainer.

3. Disconnect the Heated Oxygen Sensor (HO2S) electrical connector.

4. Remove the HO2S using an approved tool.

5. Remove the exhaust manifold heat shield bolts and shield.

6. Remove the upper exhaust manifold nuts.

7. Raise and support the vehicle.

8. Remove the front catalytic converter.

9. Remove the lower exhaust manifold nuts.

10. Remove the exhaust manifold.

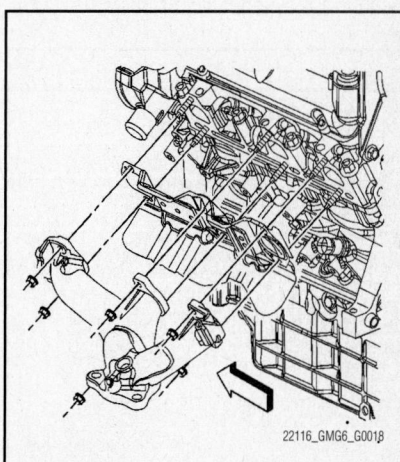

Fig. 55 Left exhaust manifold—3.5L engine

11. Remove and discard the exhaust manifold gasket.

To install:

12. Install a new exhaust manifold gasket onto the cylinder head studs.
13. Install the exhaust manifold.
14. Install the exhaust manifold nuts and tighten to 12 ft. lbs. (16 Nm).
15. Install new gasket and converter nuts, tighten to 23 ft. lbs. (31 Nm).

Right

See Figure 56.

1. Remove the generator.
2. Remove the Connector Position Assurance (CPA) retainer.
3. Disconnect the Heated Oxygen Sensor (HO2S) electrical connector.

※※ WARNING

The HO2S uses a permanently attached pigtail and connector. This pigtail should not be removed from the sensor. Damage or removal of the pigtail or connector will affect proper operation of the sensor.

4. Remove the HO2S using approved tool.
5. Remove the exhaust gas recirculation (EGR) pipe bolts (3). Reposition the pipe slightly.
6. Remove the upper exhaust manifold nuts.
7. Remove the rear catalytic converter.
8. Remove the lower exhaust manifold nuts.
9. Remove the exhaust manifold.
10. Remove and discard the exhaust manifold gasket.

To install:

11. Install a new exhaust manifold gasket onto the cylinder head studs.

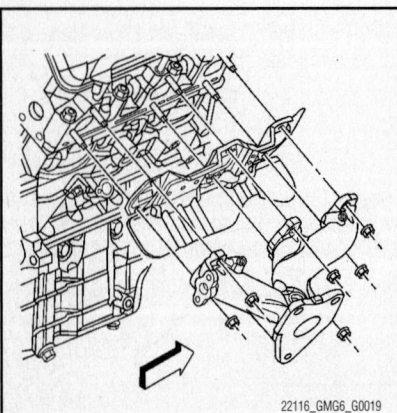

Fig. 56 Right exhaust manifold—3.5L engine

12. Install the exhaust manifold.
13. Install the exhaust manifold nuts and tighten to 12 ft. lbs.(16 Nm).
14. Install the rear catalytic converter.
15. Install new gasket and converter nuts, tighten to 23 ft. lbs. (31 Nm).

3.6L Engine

Left

See Figure 57.

1. Remove the exhaust manifold heat shield.
2. Remove the oil level indicator.
3. Remove the catalytic converter to exhaust manifold nuts.
4. Remove the exhaust manifold bolts.
5. Remove the exhaust manifold and gasket. Discard the gasket.

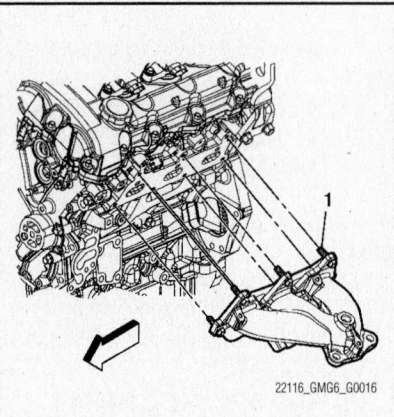

Fig. 57 Left exhaust manifold—3.6L engine

To install:

6. Install one exhaust manifold bolt to the exhaust manifold.
7. Install the new exhaust manifold gasket onto the cylinder head and bolt.
8. Install the exhaust manifold (with gasket) to the catalytic converter and the cylinder head.
9. Install the remaining exhaust manifold bolts and tighten to 15 ft. lbs. (20 Nm).
10. Install the catalytic converter to exhaust manifold nuts and tighten to 33 ft. lbs. (45 Nm).
11. Install the oil level indicator with new tube seal, and tighten mounting bolt to 89 inch. lbs. (10 Nm).
12. Install the exhaust manifold heat shield.

Right

See Figure 58.

1. Raise and safely support the vehicle.

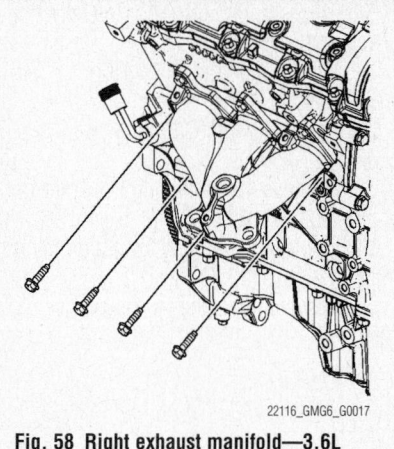

Fig. 58 Right exhaust manifold—3.6L engine

2. Remove the catalytic converter.
3. Remove the exhaust manifold lower bolts.
4. Lower the vehicle half way.
5. Remove the exhaust manifold upper bolts.
6. Remove the exhaust manifold.
7. Remove and discard the exhaust manifold gasket.

To install:

8. Install one upper exhaust manifold bolt to the exhaust manifold.
9. Place the new exhaust manifold gasket onto the bolt.
10. Position and install the exhaust manifold (with gasket) to the cylinder head.
11. Loosely install the remaining upper exhaust manifold bolts.
12. Raise and support the vehicle.
13. Loosely install the lower exhaust manifold bolts.
14. Tighten the exhaust manifold bolts 15 ft. lbs. (20 Nm).
15. Install the catalytic converter and tighten the mounting nuts to 33 Ft. Lbs. (45 Nm).

3.9L Engine

Left

See Figure 59.

1. Remove the air cleaner outlet duct.
2. Remove the Connector Position Assurance (CPA) retainer.
3. Disconnect the heated oxygen sensor (HO2S) electrical connector.
4. Remove the HO2S clip from the oil level indicator tube bracket.

※※ WARNING

The HO2S uses a permanently attached pigtail and connector. This

pigtail should not be removed from the sensor. Damage or removal of the pigtail or connector will affect proper operation of the sensor.

5. Remove the HO2S using approved tool.

6. Remove the exhaust manifold heat shield bolts.

7. Remove the exhaust manifold heat shield.

8. Remove the upper exhaust manifold bolts.

9. Raise and support the vehicle.

10. Remove the left catalytic converter.

11. Remove the lower exhaust manifold bolts.

12. Remove the exhaust manifold.

13. Remove and discard the exhaust manifold gasket.

To install:

14. Install a NEW exhaust manifold gasket onto the cylinder head studs.

15. Install the exhaust manifold.

16. Install the exhaust manifold bolts and tighten to 15 ft. lbs. (20 Nm).

17. Install the left catalytic converter.

18. Lower the vehicle.

19. Install the exhaust manifold heat shield and mounting bolts, tighten to 89 inch. lbs. (10 Nm).

➡Whenever the oxygen sensor is removed, coat the threads with nickel-based anti-seize compound.

20. Install the HO2S using approved tool and tighten to 31 ft. lbs. (42 Nm).

21. Connect the HO2S electrical connector.

22. Install the CPA retainer.

23. Install the HO2S clip to the oil level indicator tube bracket.

24. Install the air cleaner outlet duct.

Right (6-Speed M/T)

See Figure 60.

1. Remove the generator.

2. Remove the connector position assurance (CPA) retainer (5).

3. Disconnect the engine harness electrical connector (4) heated oxygen sensor (HO2S) electrical connector (4).

4. Remove the HO2S clip (3) from the oil level indicator tube bracket.

✳✳ WARNING

The HO2S uses a permanently attached pigtail and connector. This pigtail should not be removed from the sensor. Damage or removal of the pigtail or connector will affect proper operation of the sensor.

5. Remove the HO2S using approved tool.

6. Remove the exhaust manifold shield bolts.

7. Remove the exhaust manifold shield.

8. Remove the upper exhaust manifold bolts.

9. Remove the right catalytic converter.

10. Remove the lower exhaust manifold bolt.

11. Remove the exhaust manifold.

12. Remove and discard the exhaust manifold gasket.

To install:

13. Install a new exhaust manifold gasket onto the cylinder head studs.

14. Install the exhaust manifold.

15. Install the exhaust manifold bolts and tighten to 15 ft. lbs. (20 Nm).

16. Install the right catalytic converter.

17. Install the exhaust manifold shield.

18. Install the exhaust manifold shield bolts and tighten to 89 inch. lbs. (10 Nm).

➡Whenever the oxygen sensor is removed, coat the threads with nickel-based anti-seize compound.

19. Install the HO2S using approved tool and tighten to 31 ft. lbs. (42 Nm).

20. Connect the engine harness electrical connector to the HO2S electrical connector.

21. Install the CPA retainer.

22. Install the HO2S clip to the oil level indicator tube bracket.

23. Install the generator.

INTAKE MANIFOLD

REMOVAL & INSTALLATION

2.4L Engine

See Figure 61.

1. Properly relieve the fuel system pressure.

2. Drain the cooling system.

3. Remove the throttle body.

4. Remove the fuel rail.

5. Remove the evaporative emission (EVAP) canister purge solenoid valve tube.

6. Reposition the brake booster vacuum hose clamp at the intake manifold.

7. Remove the brake booster hose from the intake manifold.

8. Remove the oil level indicator tube bolt.

9. Disconnect the engine harness electrical connector from the fuel injector inline electrical connector.

10. Remove the fuel injector inline connector clip from the intake manifold.

11. Disconnect the engine harness electrical connector from the knock sensor harness.

12. Remove the knock sensor connector clip from the oil level indicator tube.

13. Remove the intake manifold bolts and nuts.

14. Remove the intake manifold.

➡The intake manifold gasket is reusable. Only replace the gasket if damage has occurred.

15. Remove the intake manifold gasket, if necessary.

To install:

16. Install the intake manifold gasket, if necessary.

17. Install the intake manifold.

18. Install the intake manifold bolts and nuts and tighten to 89 inch lbs. (10 Nm).

19. Connect the engine harness electrical connector to the knock sensor harness.

20. Install the knock sensor connector clip to the oil level indicator tube.

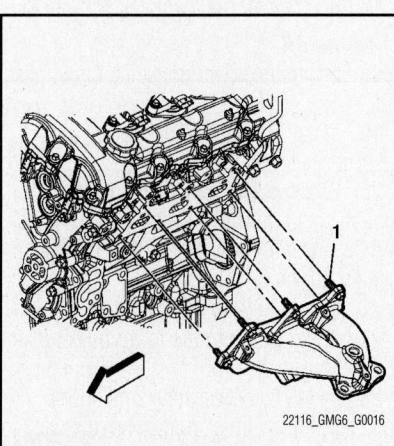

22116_GMG6_G0016

Fig. 59 Left exhaust manifold—3.9L engine

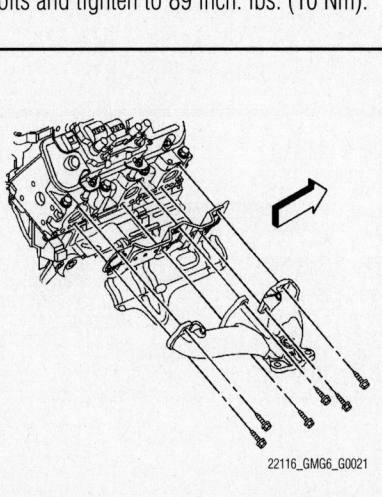

22116_GMG6_G0021

Fig. 60 Right exhaust manifold—3.9L engine

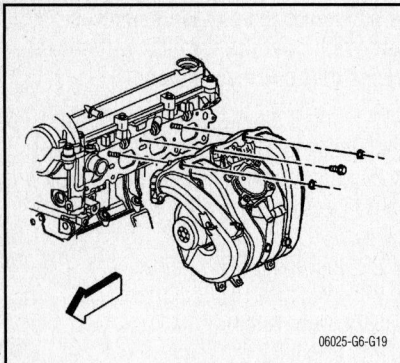

Fig. 61 Intake manifold mounting—2.4L engine

06025-G6-G19

21. Connect the engine harness electrical connector to the fuel injector inline electrical connector.

22. Install the fuel injector inline connector clip to the intake manifold.

23. Install the oil level indicator tube bolt.

24. Install the brake booster hose to the intake manifold.

25. Position the brake booster vacuum hose clamp at the intake manifold.

26. Install the EVAP canister purge solenoid valve tube.

27. Install the fuel rail.

28. Install the throttle body.

29. Connect the negative battery cable

30. Fill and bleed the cooling system.

31. Start the vehicle, check for leaks and repair if necessary.

3.5L Engine

Upper Manifold

See Figure 62.

1. Release the fuel system pressure.

2. Drain the cooling system.

3. Remove the intake manifold cover.

4. Remove the vacuum hoses from the following:

    a. Evaporative emissions (EVAP) canister purge valve

    b. Manifold vacuum source

    c. Brake booster

    d. Heater and Air Conditioning (A/C) source

5. Disconnect the electrical connectors from the following:

    a. Exhaust Gas Recirculation (EGR) valve

    b. Mass Air Flow (MAF) sensor

    c. Intake Air Temperature (IAT) sensor

    d. Electronic throttle control

    e. EVAP canister purge valve

6. Remove the air cleaner intake duct.

7. Remove the left side spark plug wires from the spark plugs.

8. Remove the following wiring harnesses from the retainers:

    a. Camshaft position (CMP) sensor wiring harness

    b. Left side spark plug wire harness

    c. Engine wiring harness

9. Remove the ignition coil bracket with the coils.

10. Remove the EVAP canister purge solenoid valve.

11. Remove the Manifold Absolute Pressure (MAP) sensor and the bracket.

12. Remove the EGR valve.

13. Remove the upper intake manifold bolts and the stud.

14. Remove the upper intake manifold.

15. Remove the upper intake manifold gaskets.

To install:

16. Install the throttle body.

17. Install the upper intake manifold gaskets.

18. Install the upper intake manifold.

19. Install the right upper intake manifold bolts and the stud and tighten to 18 ft. lbs. (25 Nm).

20. Install the EGR valve.

21. Install the MAP sensor bracket and the sensor.

22. Install the EVAP canister purge solenoid valve.

23. Install the ignition coil bracket with the coils.

24. Install the following wiring harnesses to the retainers:

    a. Engine wiring harness

    b. Left side spark plug wire harness

    c. CMP sensor wiring harness

25. Install the left side spark plug wires to the spark plugs.

26. Install the air cleaner intake duct.

27. Connect the electrical connectors to the following:

    a. EVAP canister purge valve

    b. Electronic throttle control

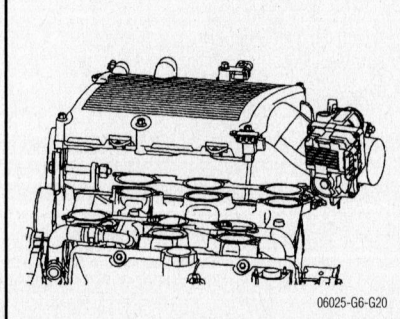

Fig. 62 Upper intake manifold mounting—3.5L engine

06025-G6-G20

    c. IAT sensor

    d. MAF sensor

    e. EGR valve

28. Install the vacuum hoses to the following: Heater and A/C source, brake booster, manifold vacuum, and EVAP canister purge valve.

29. Connect the negative battery cable.

30. Fill the cooling system.

31. Install the intake manifold cover.

Lower Manifold

See Figure 63.

1. Release the fuel system pressure.

2. Drain the cooling system.

3. Remove the upper intake manifold.

4. Remove the valve covers.

5. Disconnect the engine coolant temperature (ECT) wiring harness.

6. Disconnect and remove the fuel injector and manifold air pressure (MAP) wiring harness.

7. Remove the fuel injector rail.

8. Disconnect the heater inlet pipe with heater hose from the lower intake manifold and reposition.

9. Disconnect the radiator inlet hose from the engine.

10. Remove the thermostat housing and thermostat.

11. Remove the lower intake manifold bolts.

12. Remove the lower intake manifold.

13. Remove the valve rocker arms and pushrods.

14. Remove the lower intake manifold gaskets and seals.

15. Clean the lower intake manifold gasket and seal surfaces on the cylinder heads and the engine block.

16. Clean the gasket and seal surfaces on the lower intake manifold with degreaser.

17. Remove all the loose RTV sealer.

To install:

18. Install the lower intake manifold gaskets.

19. Install the valve rocker arms and pushrods.

20. With gaskets and seals in place apply a small drop 8-10 mm (0.31-0.39 in) of RTV sealer to the 4 corners of the intake manifold to block joints.

21. Install the lower intake manifold.

22. Apply sealer to the lower intake manifold bolt threads.

23. Install the lower intake manifold bolts and tighten in sequence as follows:

    a. Tighten the bolts in sequence to 115 inch lbs. (13 Nm),

    b. Tighten bolts (1, 2, 3, and 4) in

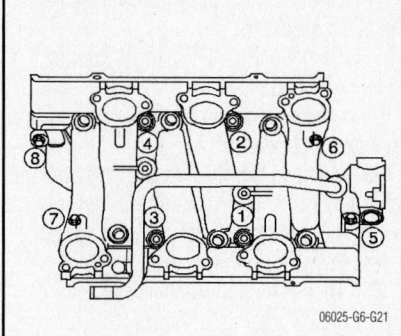

Fig. 63 Lower intake manifold tightening sequence—3.5L engine

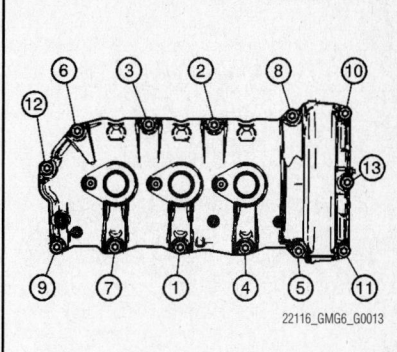

Fig. 64 Upper intake manifold—3.6L engine and mounting bolts shown

sequence to 15 ft. lbs. (20 Nm on the final pass.

   c. Tighten bolts (5, 6, 7, and 8) in sequence to 18 ft. lbs. (25 Nm (18 lb ft) on the final pass.

24. Install the heater inlet pipe and tighten to 18 ft. lbs. (25 Nm).

25. Install the thermostat and housing.

26. Install the ECT sensor.

27. Connect the thermostat bypass hose to the thermostat bypass pipe and lower intake manifold pipe.

28. Connect the radiator inlet hose to the engine.

29. Connect the heater inlet pipe and heater hose to the lower intake manifold.

30. Install the power steering pump to the front engine cover.

31. Install the fuel injector rail.

32. Connect the fuel feed pipe to the fuel injector rail.

33. Connect the fuel injector and MAP wiring harness.

34. Connect the ECT wiring harness.

35. Install the valve rocker arm covers.

36. Install the upper intake manifold.

37. Connect the negative battery cable.

3.6L Engine

Upper Manifold

See Figure 64.

1. Remove the fuel injector sight shield.

2. Remove the air cleaner outlet duct.

3. Disconnect the fuel feed line quick connect fitting from the fuel rail.

4. Remove the fuel feed pipe line nut and remove the fuel feed line clip from the stud.

5. Reposition the fuel feed line out of the way.

6. Remove the coolant air bleed hose/pipe clip bolt from the upper intake manifold.

7. Reposition the coolant air bleed hose clamp at the water outlet.

8. Remove the coolant air bleed hose from the water outlet.

9. Remove the coolant air bleed hose/pipe clip from the upper intake manifold stud and reposition out of the way.

10. Reposition the brake booster vacuum hose clamp at the upper intake manifold.

11. Remove the brake booster vacuum hose from the upper intake manifold.

12. Disconnect the engine wiring harness electrical connector from the Manifold Absolute Pressure (MAP) sensor.

13. Disconnect the engine wiring harness electrical connector from the electronic throttle control (ETC).

14. Disconnect the engine wiring harness electrical connector from the intake manifold tuning valve.

15. Disconnect the engine wiring harness electrical connector from the evaporative emission (EVAP) canister purge solenoid.

16. Disconnect the positive crankcase ventilation (PCV) tube from the upper intake manifold and reposition aside.

17. Disconnect the EVAP canister purge solenoid tube quick connect fitting at the upper intake manifold and reposition aside.

18. Remove the fuel rail to bracket bolt.

19. Remove the fuel rail wiring harness electrical connector bolt and reposition the harness out of the way.

20. Remove the upper intake bolts.

21. Remove the upper intake manifold and gaskets. Discard gaskets.

22. If replacing the upper intake manifold complete the following steps:
- Remove the MAP sensor.
- Remove the throttle body.
- Remove the EVAP canister purge solenoid valve.
- Remove the intake manifold tuning valve.

To install:

23. If the upper intake manifold was replaced complete the following steps:
- Install the MAP sensor.
- Install the throttle body.
- Install the EVAP canister purge solenoid valve.
- Install the intake manifold tuning valve.

24. Place NEW upper intake manifold gaskets onto the lower intake manifold.

25. Place the upper intake manifold onto the lower intake manifold.

26. Install the upper intake bolts and tighten to 17 ft. lbs. (23 Nm).

27. Position the fuel rail wiring harness, install the fuel rail wiring harness electrical

connector bolt and tighten bolt to 89 inch. lbs. (10 Nm).

28. Install the fuel rail to bracket bolt, tighten bolt to 89 inch. lbs. (10 Nm).

29. Position and install the EVAP canister purge solenoid tube quick connect fitting to the upper intake manifold.

30. Position and install the PCV tube to the upper intake manifold.

31. Connect the engine wiring harness electrical connector to the EVAP canister purge solenoid.

32. Connect the engine wiring harness electrical connector to the intake manifold tuning valve.

33. Connect the engine wiring harness electrical connector to the ETC.

34. Connect the engine wiring harness electrical connector to the MAP sensor.

35. Install the brake booster vacuum hose to the upper intake manifold.

36. Position the brake booster vacuum hose clamp at the upper intake manifold.

37. Position and install the coolant air bleed hose/pipe clip to the upper intake manifold stud.

38. Install the coolant air bleed hose to the water outlet.

39. Position the coolant air bleed hose clamp at the water outlet.

40. Install the coolant air bleed hose/pipe clip bolt to the upper intake manifold, tighten bolt to 89 inch. lbs. (10 Nm).

41. Position the fuel feed line and install the fuel feed line clip to the stud.

42. Install the fuel feed line nut and tighten to 89 inch. (10 Nm).

43. Connect the fuel feed line quick connect fitting to the fuel rail.

44. Install the air cleaner outlet duct.

45. Install the fuel injector sight shield.

Lower Manifold

See Figure 65.

Fig. 65 Lower intake manifold and related parts—3.6L engine

1. Release the fuel system pressure.
2. Remove the fuel injector sight shield.
3. Disconnect the engine wiring harness electrical connector from the fuel injector wiring harness electrical connector.
4. Disconnect the fuel feed pipe quick connect fitting from the fuel rail.
5. Remove the upper intake manifold.
6. Use compressed air in order to remove any debris from the around the area where the fuel injectors enter the lower intake manifold.
7. Remove the fuel rail bolts.

➡**Remove the fuel rail assembly carefully in order to prevent damage to the injector electrical connector terminals and the injector spray tips. Support the fuel rail after the fuel rail is removed in order to avoid damaging the fuel rail components. Cap the fittings and plug the holes when servicing the fuel system in order to prevent dirt and other contaminants from entering open pipes and passages.**

8. Remove the fuel rail with fuel injectors from the lower intake manifold.
9. Remove the lower intake manifold bolts.
10. Remove the lower intake manifold and gasket. Discard the gasket.
11. Clean and inspect the intake manifold and sealing surfaces.

To install:
12. Place a NEW lower intake manifold gasket onto the cylinder heads.
13. Place the lower intake manifold onto the cylinder heads.
14. Install the lower intake manifold bolts and tighten to 17 ft. lbs. (23 Nm).
15. Install the fuel injectors and fuel rail. Tighten fuel rail mounting bolts to 89 inch. lbs. (10 Nm).
16. Install upper intake manifold, fuel

line quick connect fitting, electrical harness and shield.

3.9L Engine

Upper Manifold
See Figures 66 and 67.

1. Drain the cooling system.
2. Relieve the fuel system pressure.
3. Remove the intake manifold cover.
4. Disconnect the fuel feed pipe quick connect fitting from the fuel rail.
5. Disconnect the evaporative (EVAP) emission pipe from the purge solenoid.
6. Open the retaining clip, and remove the fuel and EVAP pipes from the clip.
7. Remove the positive crankcase ventilation (PCV) air tubes.
8. Reposition the brake booster vacuum hose clamp at the intake manifold.
9. Remove the vacuum hose from the intake manifold.
10. Reposition the radiator surge tank inlet hose clamp.
11. Remove the radiator surge tank inlet hose from the inlet pipe.
12. Remove the oil fill neck.
13. Remove the radiator surge tank inlet pipe bolts.
14. Remove the radiator surge tank inlet pipe.
15. Disconnect the Manifold Absolute Pressure (MAP) sensor electrical connector.
16. Disconnect the evaporative emission (EVAP) canister purge solenoid electrical connector.
17. Disconnect the electronic throttle control (ETC) electrical connector.
18. Disconnect the inlet manifold valve electrical connector>
19. Remove the air cleaner outlet duct.
20. Disconnect the left side spark plug wires from the spark plugs.
21. Disconnect the left side spark plug wires from the ignition coil.
22. Disengage the spark plug wire retainer clips from the intake manifold bracket and the heater inlet/outlet pipe.
23. Remove the left side spark plug wires.
24. Remove the heater inlet and outlet pipe nuts from the throttle body studs.
25. Remove the inlet and outlet pipe from the studs.
26. Remove the 2 ignition coil bolts.
27. Remove the generator upper bolt, ball stud and rear brace.
28. Remove the upper intake manifold bolts and stud.
29. Separate and remove the upper intake manifold from the lower intake manifold.

30. Remove the upper to lower intake manifold gaskets.
31. Remove the inlet manifold tuning valve bolts and valve.
32. Remove the throttle body bolts/studs and throttle body.
33. Remove the MAP sensor bracket and sensor.
34. Remove the EVAP canister purge solenoid valve bolt and valve.
35. Clean the upper intake to lower intake gasket mating surfaces.
36. Inspect the intake manifold tuning valve seal for damage. The tuning valve blade attachment to the motor should be tight, with no looseness or slack present, Replace as necessary.
37. Apply lubricant to the nose of the tuning valve blade.

To install:
38. Inspect the EVAP canister purge solenoid valve seal for damage, replace as necessary.
39. Install the EVAP canister purge solenoid valve and tighten to 12 ft. lbs. (16 Nm).
40. Install the MAP sensor and bracket.
41. Apply threadlock to the throttle body bolts/studs threads and install the throttle body.
42. Install the inlet manifold tuning valve and tighten to 89 inch lbs. (10 Nm).
43. Install new upper-to-lower intake manifold gaskets.
44. Apply threadlock to the upper intake manifold bolts/stud threads.
45. Install the upper intake manifold and tighten the bolts to 18 ft. lbs. (25 Nm).
46. Install the alternator.
47. Install the ignition coils.
48. Install the heater inlet and outlet pipes to the throttle body studs.
49. Install the left side spark plug wires.

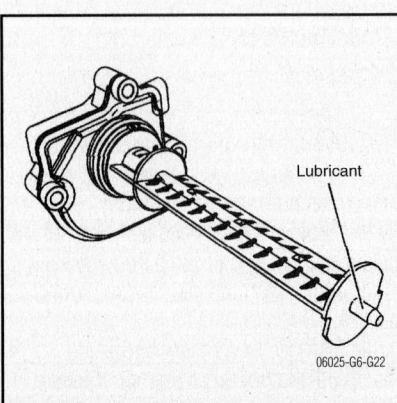

Fig. 66 Applying lubricant to intake manifold tuning blade—3.9L engine

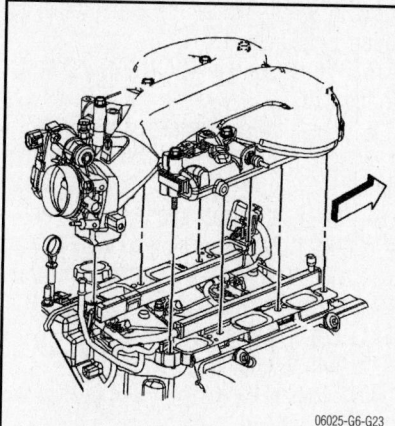

**Fig. 67 Upper intake manifold mounting—
3.9L engine**

50. Connect the left side spark plug
wires to the spark plugs.

51. Connect the left side spark plug
wires to the ignition coil.

52. Engage the spark plug wire retainer
clips to the intake manifold bracket and the
heater inlet/outlet pipe.

53. Install the air cleaner outlet duct.

54. Connect the inlet manifold valve
electrical connector.

55. Connect the electronic throttle control (ETC) electrical connector.

56. Connect the evaporative emission
(EVAP) canister purge solenoid electrical
connector.

57. Connect the Manifold Absolute Pressure (MAP) sensor electrical connector.

58. Install the radiator surge tank inlet
pipe.

59. Install the radiator surge tank inlet
pipe bolts.

60. Install the oil fill neck.

61. Install the radiator surge tank inlet
hose to the inlet pipe.

62. Position the radiator surge tank inlet
hose clamp.

63. Install the vacuum hose to the intake
manifold.

64. Position the brake booster vacuum
hose clamp at the intake manifold.

65. Install the positive crankcase ventilation (PCV) air tubes.

66. Install the fuel and EVAP pipes to the
retaining clip.

67. Connect the evaporative (EVAP)
emission pipe to the purge solenoid.

68. Connect the fuel feed pipe quick
connect fitting to the fuel rail.

69. Remove the intake manifold cover.

70. Fill the cooling system.

Lower Manifold

See Figure 68.

1. Drain the cooling system.
2. Relieve the fuel system pressure.
3. Remove the coolant crossover pipe.
4. Remove the upper intake manifold.
5. Remove the valve covers.
6. Disconnect the engine coolant temperature electrical connector.
7. Disconnect the fuel feed line from
the fuel rail.
8. Disconnect the fuel injector inline
connector.
9. Remove the fuel injector harness
connector bracket bolt from the intake manifold.
10. Disconnect the Camshaft Position
(CMP) sensor electrical connector.
11. Remove the fuel rail.
12. Remove the lower intake manifold.
13. Loosen the valve rocker arm bolts.

➡ **Place the valve train components in
a rack in order to ensure that the components are installed in the same location from which they were removed.**

14. Remove the valve rocker arms.
15. Remove the push rods.

➡ **The intake push rods measure 5.81
inches (147.51mm). The exhaust push
rods measure 6.1 inches (154.87mm).**

16. Remove the lower intake manifold
gaskets and seals.
17. Clean the lower intake manifold gasket and seal surfaces on the cylinder heads
and the engine block.
18. Clean the gasket and seal surfaces
on the lower intake manifold with
degreaser.
19. Remove all the loose RTV sealer.

To install:

➡ **Do not use RTV sealer under the
lower intake manifold gaskets.**

20. Install the lower intake manifold gaskets and seals.
21. Coat the ends of the push rods using
suitable prelube.
22. Install the push rods in their original
location.
23. Coat the rocker arm friction surfaces
using suitable prelube.
24. Install the valve rocker arms in their
original positions.
25. Install the valve rocker arm bolts and
tighten to 25 ft. lbs. (34 Nm).
26. With new gaskets and seals in place,
apply a small drop of RTV sealer to the 4
corners of the intake manifold to engine
block joints.
27. Install the lower intake manifold.
28. Apply sealer to the lower intake manifold bolt threads.

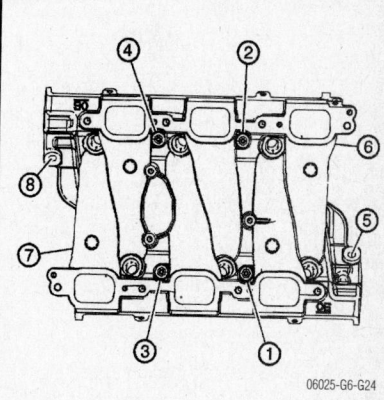

**Fig. 68 Lower intake manifold tightening
sequence—3.9L engine**

29. Tighten the bolts in sequence as follows:
    a. Tighten bolts 1, 2, 3, and 4 in
sequence to 12 ft. lbs. (16 Nm).
    b. Tighten bolts 5, 6, 7 and 8 in
sequence to 18 ft. lbs. (25 Nm).
30. Inspect the fuel rail, fuel injectors
and fuel injector O-rings for damage and
replace as necessary.
31. Lubricate the fuel injector O-rings.
32. Install the injector nozzles into the
lower intake manifold injector bores.
33. Press on the injector rail using the
palms of both hands until the injector are
fully seated.
34. Install the fuel injector rail bolts and
tighten to 89 inch lbs. (10 Nm).
35. Connect the CMP sensor electrical
connector.
36. Position the fuel injector harness
connector bracket to the intake manifold.
37. Install the fuel injector harness connector bracket bolt.
38. Connect the fuel injector inline connector.
39. Connect the fuel feed line to the fuel
rail.
40. Connect the ECT electrical connector.
41. Install the valve covers.
42. Install the upper intake manifold.
43. Install the coolant crossover pipe.
44. Fill the cooling system.

OIL PAN

REMOVAL & INSTALLATION

2.4L Engine

See Figure 69.

1. Raise and support the vehicle safely.
2. Drain the engine oil.
3. Disconnect the negative battery
cable.

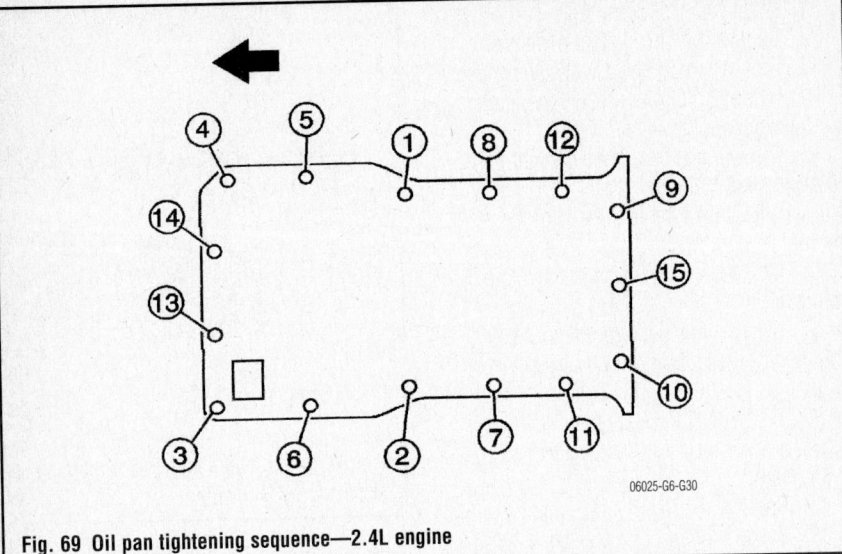

Fig. 69 Oil pan tightening sequence—2.4L engine

4. Remove the engine drive belt.

5. Remove the lower AC compressor bolt.

6. Remove the oil pan bolts and the oil pan.

To install:

7. Ensure that the oil pan and the sealing surface on the lower crankcase are free of all oil and debris.

8. Apply a bead of sealant around the perimeter of the oil pan and the oil suction port opening.

9. Install the oil pan.

10. Tighten the bolts in sequence to 18 ft. lbs. (25 Nm).

11. Install the lower AC compressor bolt.

12. Install the engine drive belt.

13. Lower the vehicle.

14. Fill the engine oil to the proper level.

15. Start the vehicle, check for leaks and repair if necessary.

3.5L and 3.9L Engines

1. Disconnect the negative battery cable.

2. Raise and support the vehicle.

3. Drain the crankcase.

4. Remove the right front tire and wheel.

5. Remove the right front splash shield.

6. Remove the oil filter and filter adapter.

7. Remove the catalytic converter.

8. Remove the wheel speed sensor harness from the right suspension support.

9. Remove the right front ball joint, bolt, and nut. Separate the ball joint from the steering knuckle.

10. Remove lower closeout panel.

11. Remove the Air Conditioning (A/C) compressor bolts and position the compressor aside.

12. Remove the braces that support the engine to the transmission.

13. Disconnect the oil level sensor.

14. Remove the retainers that secure the brake line to the frame.

15. Support the engine with a tall jack stand and a block of wood.

16. Remove the right side engine mount nuts and bolts.

17. Loosen the left side cradle bolts.

18. Remove the cradle bolts from the right front and the right rear.

19. Remove the starter.

20. Remove the oil pan side bolts.

21. Remove the oil pan bolts and oil pan.

To install:

22. Apply sealer to both sides of the crankshaft rear main bearing cap. Press the sealer into the gap using a putty knife.

23. Install a new oil pan gasket.

24. Position the oil pan to the engine, install the bolts and tighten to 18 ft. lbs. (25 Nm).

25. Install the oil pan side bolts and tighten to 37 ft. lbs. (50 Nm).

26. Install the starter.

27. Install the flywheel inspection cover.

28. Install the cradle bolts to the right front and the right rear.

29. Tighten the left side cradle bolts to 74 ft. lbs. (100 Nm), plus an additional 90 degrees.

30. Install the right side engine mount and tighten to 37 ft. lbs. (50 Nm).

31. Remove the support from the engine.

32. Install the retainers that secure the brake line to the frame.

33. Connect the oil level sensor electrical connector.

34. Install the braces that support the engine to the transmission.

35. Position and install the A/C compressor bolts.

36. Install lower closeout panel.

37. Install the right front ball joint, bolt, and nut.

38. Install the wheel speed sensor harness to the right suspension support.

39. Install the right front splash shield.

40. Install the right front tire and wheel.

41. Lower the vehicle.

42. Fill the engine with clean oil.

43. Start the vehicle and check for leaks.

3.6L Engine

See Figures 70 through 72.

1. Disconnect the negative battery cable.

2. Install the engine support fixture.

3. Remove the right side engine mount.

4. Raise and support the vehicle.

5. Drain the engine oil and remove the oil filter.

6. Remove the catalytic converter.

7. Remove the Air Conditioning (A/C) compressor.

8. Remove the oil pan bolts.

9. Remove the oil pan.

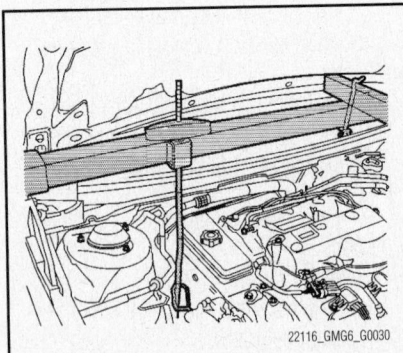

Fig. 70 Engine support systems shown on 3.6L engine

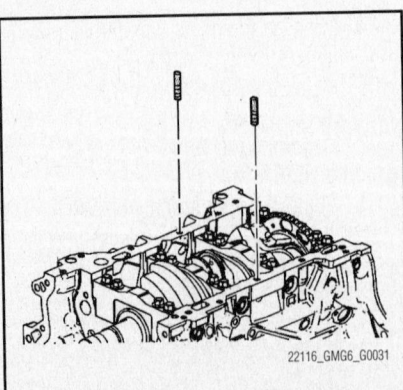

Fig. 71 Guide pins shown—3.6L engine

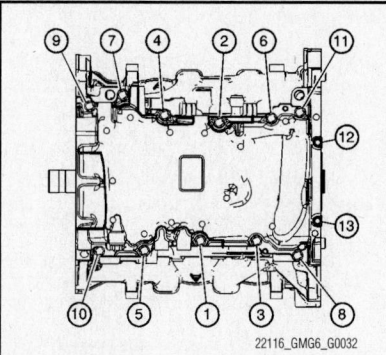

Fig. 72 Oil pan tightening sequence—3.6L engine

10. Clean the oil pan and the engine block gasket surface.

To install:

11. Install the 0.315 inch. (8 mm) guide pins into the center oil pan rail bolt hole on each side of the engine block.

12. Place a 0.118 inch. (3 mm) bead of RTV sealant on the block pan rail and the crankshaft rear oil seal housing.

13. Position the oil pan onto the block using guide pins.

14. Remove the guides from the engine block.

15. Loosely install the oil pan bolts.

16. Tighten the oil pan bolts in sequence shown.

   a. Tighten the 8 mm bolts (1—11) to 17 ft. lbs. (23 Nm).

   b. Tighten the 6 mm bolts (12, 13) to 89 inch. lbs. (10 Nm).

17. Install the Air Conditioning (A/C) compressor.

18. Install the catalytic converter.

19. Lower the vehicle.

20. Refill the engine oil.

21. Install the right side engine mount.

22. Remove the engine support fixture.

23. Connect the battery negative cable.

OIL PUMP

REMOVAL & INSTALLATION

2.4L Engine

➡ **The oil pump is mounted into the engine front cover.**

1. Relieve the fuel system pressure.

2. Drain the engine oil.

3. Remove the engine front cover.

4. Remove the oil pump cover.

5. Remove the oil pump from the inside of the front cover.

To install:

6. Coat the oil pump gears with oil and fit the pump to the cover.

7. Install the oil pump cover.

8. Install the engine front cover.

9. Fill the engine with clean oil.

10. Start the vehicle, check for leaks and repair if necessary.

3.5L and 3.9L Engines

1. Remove the oil pan.

2. Remove the oil pump bolt.

3. Remove the oil pump and the oil pump drive shaft.

To install:

4. Install the oil pump drive shaft and the oil pump.

5. Install the oil pump bolt and tighten to 30 ft. lbs. (40 Nm).

6. Install the oil pan.

7. Fill the engine with clean oil.

8. Start the vehicle, check for leaks and repair if necessary.

3.6L Engine

See Figure 73.

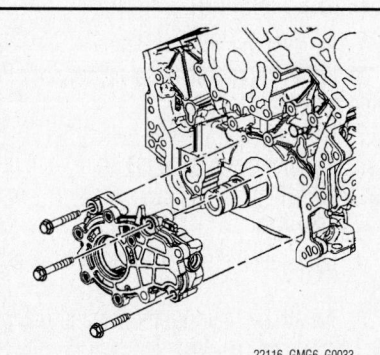

Fig. 73 Oil pump mounting view—3.6L engine

1. Remove the primary timing chain.

2. Remove the oil pump bolts and the oil pump.

To install:

3. Align the oil pump generator with the crankshaft flats and install the oil pump to the engine block.

4. Align the pump body with the mounting holes in the cylinder block.

5. Install the oil pump bolts and tighten to 17 ft. lbs. (23 Nm).

6. Install the primary timing chain.

INSPECTION

2.4L Engine

1. Disassemble the pressure relief valve.

2. Remove the oil pump gerotor cover and bolts.

3. Clean all of the parts in cleaning solvent. Remove varnish, sludge and dirt.

4. Inspect the oil pump for wear and scoring.

5. Replace the front cover and oil pump assembly if it is out of specification or damaged.

3.5L and 3.9L Engines

1. Clean all parts of sludge, oil, and varnish by soaking in cleaning solvent.

2. Inspect for foreign material and determine the source of the foreign material.

3. Inspect the pump housing and cover for cracks, scoring or damaged threads.

4. Do not attempt to repair the pump housing. Replace the pump housing.

5. Inspect the oil pump gears for scoring or excessive wear.

6. Inspect the idler shaft for looseness or scoring. If loose or damaged, replace the oil pump.

7. Inspect the drive gear shaft for looseness or scoring.

8. Inspect the pressure regulator valve for scoring or sticking burrs.

9. Inspect the pressure regulator valve spring for loss of tension or bending.

10. Inspect the suction pipe and screen assembly for looseness, broken wire mesh or screen.

11. Measure the oil pump gear lash. Install the gears, and measure in several places. If lash is more than 0.0037-0.0077 in. (0.094-0.195mm), replace the pump.

12. Measure the oil pump housing gear pocket. If depth is more than 1.202-1.204 in (30.53-30.59mm), or diameter is more than 1.503-1.505 in. (38.176-38.226mm), replace the pump.

13. Measure the oil pump gear diameter. If diameter is more than 1.498-1.500 in (38.05-38.10mm), replace the pump.

3.6L Engine

See Figure 74.

1. Clean the oil pump components with non-corrosive solvent.

2. Dry the oil pump components with compressed air.

3. Inspect the oil pump housing for the following:

  • Damage, scoring, or debris on the housing surface for the driven gear (1)

  • Damage to the oil pump mounting bosses (2)

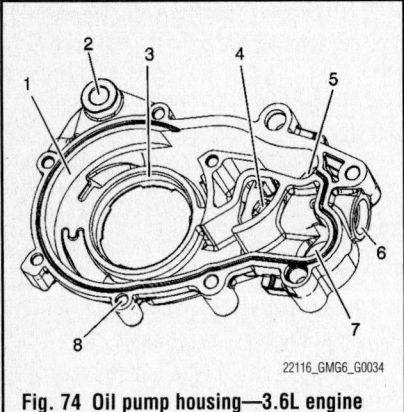

Fig. 74 Oil pump housing—3.6L engine

- Damage, scoring, or debris on the housing surface for the drive gear (3)
- Damage, scoring, or debris in the oil pump relief valve port (4)
- Damage, scoring, or debris in the oil pump intake port (5)
- Damage, scoring, or debris in the oil pump relief valve bore (6)
- Damage, scoring, or debris in the oil pump output port (7)
- Damage to the threads in the oil pump housing for the oil pump cover bolts (8)

4. Inspect the oil pump cover for the following conditions:

- Damage to the oil pump cover mounting bosses
- Damage, scoring, or debris in the oil pump cover oil passages
- Damage to the sealing surface between the oil pump cover and the oil pump housing

5. Inspect the inner drive gear for damage. If inner diameter damage is found, ensure the crankshaft is also inspected.

6. Inspect the outer driven gear for damage.

7. Inspect the oil pump relief valve components for debris or damage.

8. Inspect the primary camshaft drive chain lower guide for damage

9. If debris or damage is present within the oil pump, further inspection of all of the engine components is necessary.

PISTON AND RING

POSITIONING

See Figure 75.

Install the piston rings so the oil control ring end gaps are staggered 90 degrees, and the compression ring end gaps are staggered al least 1 inch (25mm).

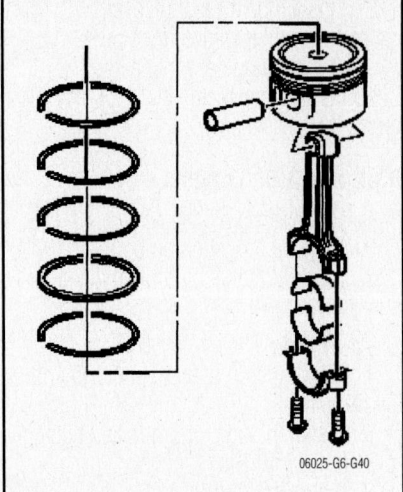

Fig. 75 Piston ring gap positioning—G6 engine

REAR MAIN SEAL

REMOVAL & INSTALLATION

2.4L, 3.5L and 3.9L Engines

1. Remove the transmission.
2. Hold the crankshaft balancer and remove the flywheel.
3. Carefully pry the seal out of the retainer without damaging the crankshaft or the seal retainer.

To install:

4. Lubricate the seal with clean engine oil.
5. Install the seal into the retainer using the appropriate seal installer.
6. Install the flywheel and tighten the bolts to 39 ft. lbs. (53 Nm) plus an additional 25 degrees on 2.5L, or 52 ft. lbs. (71 Nm) on 3.5L and 3.9L.
7. Install the transmission.

3.6L Engine

See Figures 76 through 78.

1. Remove the transaxle.
2. Secure flywheel with holding tool EN 46106.
3. Remove the engine flywheel bolts and flywheel.
4. Remove the oil pan.
5. Remove the crankshaft rear oil seal housing bolts.
6. Use the pry points located at the edge of the crankshaft rear oil seal housing to separate the RTV sealant.
7. Remove and discard the crankshaft rear oil seal housing.

To install:

8. Install the 0.236 inch (6 mm). guides pins from the EN 46109 into the 2 crank-

Fig. 76 Rear oil seal installation tools EN 47839 and J 42183

shaft rear oil seal housing corner bolt holes of the engine block.

9. Install the EN-47839 with the J 42183 (1, 2) onto the rear of the crankshaft flange.

10. Place a 0.118 inch. (3 mm) bead of RTV sealant, to the **NEW** crankshaft rear oil seal housing as shown (1).

11. Install the crankshaft rear oil seal housing to the engine block.

➡ **DO NOT allow any engine oil on the area where the crankshaft rear oil seal housing is to be installed.**

12. Remove the EN 46109 0.236 inch. (6 mm) guides from the engine block.

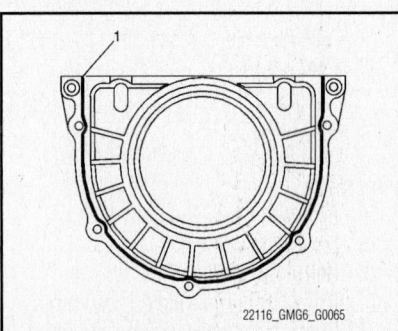

Fig. 77 Crankshaft rear oil seal housing shown with a 0.118 inch. (3 mm) bead of RTV sealant

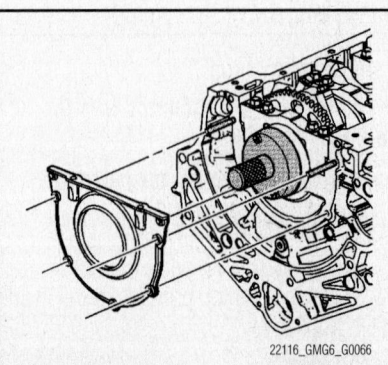

Fig. 78 Crankshaft rear oil seal housing installation

13. Install the crankshaft rear oil seal housing bolts and tighten to 89 inch. lbs. (10 Nm).

14. Remove the EN-47839 and J 42183 from the crankshaft flange.

15. Install the oil pan.

16. Place the engine flywheel in position on the crankshaft.

17. Install 2 new bolts in location at the top and bottom of the engine flywheel bolt pattern allowing the engine flywheel to hang in position

18. Install the remaining new engine flywheel bolts.

19. Tighten the new engine flywheel bolts to 22 ft. lbs. (30 Nm).

20. Tighten the new engine flywheel bolts an additional 45 degrees using a angle meter.

21. Install the transaxle.

22. Check transaxle fluid level and add if needed.

TIMING CHAIN, SPROCKETS, FRONT COVER AND SEAL

REMOVAL & INSTALLATION

2.4L Engine

See Figures 79 through 83.

1. Relieve the fuel system pressure.
2. Raise and support the vehicle safely.
3. Remove the drive belts.

➡**If only the crankshaft front seal is being replaced, go to steps 9, 10 and 11.**

4. Drain the cooling system.
5. Drain the engine oil.
6. Remove the no. 1 cylinder spark plug.
7. Rotate the crankshaft in the engine rotational direction clockwise, until the no. 1 piston is at TDC on the compression stroke.
8. Remove the camshaft cover.
9. Hold the crankshaft from turning and remove and discard the crankshaft balancer bolt.
10. Remove the crankshaft balancer.
11. If only the front seal is being replaced, use a flat-bladed too and pry the oil seal from the front cover. Press in a new seal with a seal installer. Install the crankshaft balancer using a new bolt and tighten to 74 ft. lbs. (100 Nm) plus an additional 125 degrees.
12. Remove the drive belt tensioner.
13. Remove the engine front cover-to-water pump bolt.
14. Remove the remaining engine front cover bolts.

15. Remove the engine front cover.
16. Remove the upper timing chain guide bolts and guide.
17. Remove the timing chain tensioner.
18. Install a 24 mm wrench on the hex on the exhaust camshaft in order to hold the camshaft.
19. Remove and discard the exhaust camshaft actuator bolt.
20. Remove the exhaust camshaft actuator from the camshaft and timing chain.
21. Remove the timing chain tensioner guide bolt and guide.
22. Remove the fixed timing chain guide access plug.
23. Remove the fixed timing chain guide bolts and guide.
24. Install a 24 mm wrench on the hex on the intake camshaft in order to hold the camshaft.
25. Remove and discard the intake camshaft actuator bolt.
26. Remove the intake camshaft actuator, and the timing chain through the top of the cylinder head.
27. Remove the timing chain crankshaft sprocket.
28. Remove the balance shaft drive chain tensioner bolts and tensioner.
29. Remove the adjustable balance shaft chain guide bolt and guide.
30. Remove the small balance shaft drive chain guide bolts and guide.
31. Remove the upper balance shaft drive chain guide bolts and guide.
32. Remove the balance shaft drive chain.
33. Remove the balance shaft drive sprocket.

To install:

34. Be sure all sealing surfaces are clean and prepared for assembly.

✳✳ CAUTION

If the balance shafts are not properly timed to the engine, the engine may vibrate or make noise.

35. Install the balance shaft drive chain (1) with the colored link lined up with the marks on the balance shaft sprockets and the balance shaft drive sprocket. There are three colored links on the chain. Two are chrome and one is copper. Use the following steps in order to line up the links with the sprockets.

a. Place the copper link (5) so that it lines up with the timing mark (2) on the intake side balance shaft sprocket.

b. Working clockwise around the chain, place the chrome link (4) in line

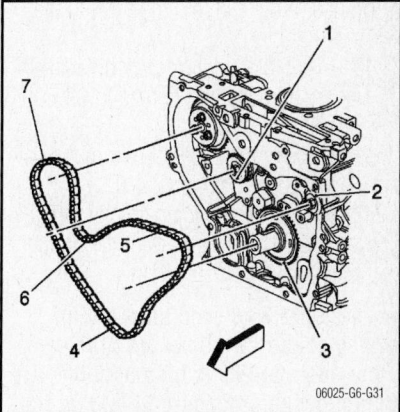

Fig. 79 Installing balance shaft timing chain—2.4L engine

06025-G6-G31

with the timing mark (3) on the balance shaft drive sprocket. (approximately 6 o'clock position on the sprocket).

c. Place the chain (7) on the water pump drive sprocket. The alignment is not critical.

d. Align the last chrome link (6) with the timing mark (1) on the exhaust side balance shaft drive sprocket.

36. Install the upper balance shaft drive chain guide and bolts and tighten to 11 ft. lbs. (15 Nm).

37. Install the small balance shaft drive chain guide and bolts and tighten to 11 ft. lbs. (15 Nm).

38. Install the adjustable balance shaft chain guide and bolt and tighten to 89 inch lbs. (10 Nm).

39. Reset the timing chain tensioner by performing the following steps:.

a. Rotate the tensioner plunger 90 degrees in its bore and compress the plunger.

b. Rotate the tensioner back to the original 12 o' clock position and insert a paper clip through the hole in the

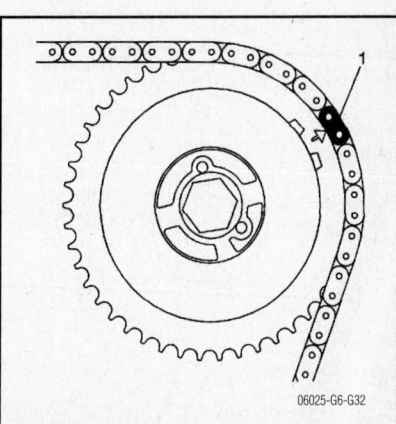

Fig. 80 Aligning timing chain link with the intake camshaft actuator—2.4L engine

06025-G6-G32

plunger body and into the hose in the tensioner plunger.

40. Install the balance shaft drive chain tensioner and bolts and tighten to 89 inch lbs. (10 Nm).

41. Remove the paper clip from the balance shaft drive chain tensioner.

42. Install the timing chain crankshaft sprocket to the crankshaft with the timing mark in the 5 o'clock position,

➡ There are 3 colored links on the timing chain. Two links are pink in color and one link is blue in color. Use the following procedure to line up the links with the sprockets. Orient the chain so that the colored links are visible.

43. Assemble the intake camshaft actuator to the timing chain with the timing mark lined up with the blue colored link (1). Install and hand tighten a new intake camshaft actuator bolt.

44. Lower the timing chain through the opening in the cylinder head. Use care to

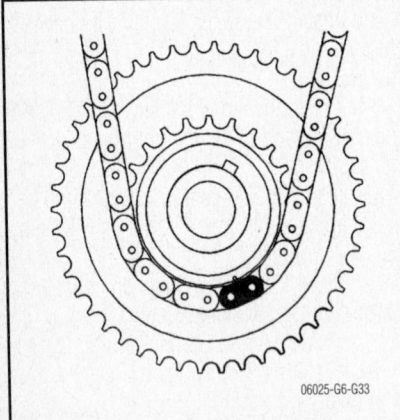

Fig. 81 Aligning timing chain link with the crankshaft sprocket—2.4L engine

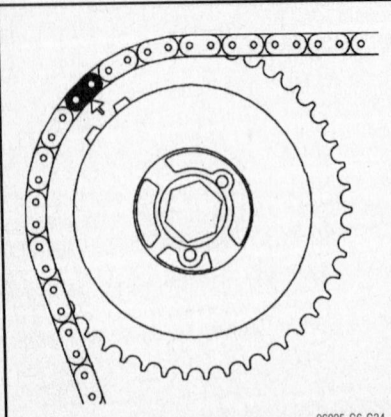

Fig. 82 Aligning timing chain link with the exhaust camshaft actuator—2.4L engine

ensure that the chain goes around both sides of the cylinder block bosses.

45. Route the timing chain around the crankshaft sprocket and line up the first pink link with the timing mark on the crankshaft sprocket, in approximately the 5 o'clock position.

46. Install the adjustable timing chain guide through the opening in the cylinder head. Install the adjustable timing chain bolt and tighten to 89 inch lbs. (10 Nm).

47. Install the exhaust camshaft actuator and a new bolt loosely onto the exhaust camshaft.

48. Align the timing mark on the actuator with the last pink colored link. Tighten the bolt finger tight.

49. If the camshaft is 180 degrees out of time, use a 24-mm wrench, first turn the intake camshaft until the alignment feature on the back of the camshaft actuator seats in the notch in the front of the intake camshaft.

50. Turn the crankshaft 45 degrees in either direction.

51. Turn the intake cam to the appropriate location.

52. Turn the crankshaft back to TDC.

53. When the actuator seats on the cam, tighten the actuator bolt hand tight.

54. Verify that all of the colored links and the appropriate timing marks are still aligned. If they are not, repeat the portion of the procedure necessary to align the timing marks.

55. Install the fixed timing chain guide and bolts and tighten to 89 inch lbs. (10 Nm).

56. Install the upper timing chain guide and bolts and tighten to 89 inch lbs. (10 Nm).

57. Install a 24 mm wrench onto the hex on the intake camshaft. Using a torque wrench, tighten the camshaft actuator bolt to 63 ft. lbs. (85 Nm), plus an additional 30 degrees.

58. Install a 24 mm wrench onto the hex on the exhaust camshaft. Using a torque wrench, tighten the camshaft actuator bolt to 63 ft. lbs. (85 Nm), plus an additional 30 degrees.

59. Remove the old oil from the timing chain tensioner.

60. Inspect the timing chain tensioner. If the timing tensioner, O-ring seal, or washer is damaged, replace the timing chain tensioner.

61. Measure the timing chain tensioner assembly from end to end. A new tensioner should be supplied in the fully compressed non-active state. A tensioner in the compressed state will measure 2.83 inch

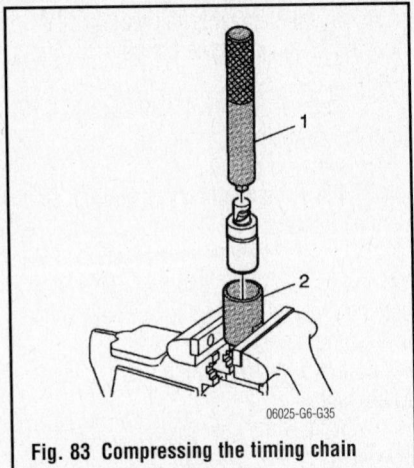

Fig. 83 Compressing the timing chain tensioner—2.4L engine

(72mm) from end to end. A tensioner in the active state will measure 3.35 inch (85mm) from end to end.

62. If the timing chain tensioner is not in the compressed state, perform the following steps:

a. Remove the piston assembly from the body of the timing chain tensioner by pulling it out.

b. Install the J 45027-2 (2) into a vise.

c. Install the notch end of the piston assembly into the J 45027-2 (2).

d. Using the J 45027-1 (1), turn the ratchet cylinder into the piston.

63. Install the compressed piston assembly back into the timing chain tensioner body until the assembly stops at the bottom of the bore. Do not compress the piston assembly against the bottom of the bore. If the piston assembly is compressed against the bottom of the bore, the assembly will activate the tensioner, which will then need to be reset again.

64. At this point the tensioner should measure approximately 2.83 inch (72mm) from end to end.

65. Ensure that all dirt and debris are removed from the timing chain tensioner threaded hole in the cylinder head.

66. Install the timing chain tensioner and tighten to 66 ft. lbs. (75 Nm).

67. The timing chain tensioner is released by compressing the tensioner 0.079 inch (2mm) which will release the locking mechanism in the ratchet. To release the timing chain tensioner, use a suitable tool with a rubber tip on the end. Feed the tool down through the cam drive chest to rest on the cam chain. Then give a sharp jolt diagonally downwards to release the tensioner.

68. Apply sealant to the threads and install the timing chain guide bolt access hole plug and tighten to 59 ft. lbs. (80 Nm).

69. Position and install the engine front cover.

70. Install the engine front cover-to-water pump bolt and tighten to 18 ft. lbs. (25 Nm).

71. Install the engine front cover bolts and tighten to 18 ft. lbs. (25 Nm).

72. Install the drive belt tensioner bolt and tighten to 33 ft. lbs. (45 Nm).

73. Install the crankshaft balancer using a new bolt and tighten to 74 ft. lbs. (100 Nm) plus an additional 125 degrees.

74. Install the camshaft cover.

75. Install the no. 1 cylinder spark plug.

76. Fill the engine oil.

77. Install the drive belts.

78. Connect the negative battery cable.

79. Fill and bleed the cooling system.

80. Start the vehicle, check for leaks and repair if necessary.

3.5L Engine

See Figures 84 through 86.

➡ **If only the crankshaft front seal is being replaced, perform steps 1 through 18.**

1. Properly relieve the fuel system pressure.

2. Drain the engine oil and cooling system.

3. Disconnect the negative battery cable.

4. Remove the drive belt.

5. Raise and support the vehicle.

6. Remove the right front tire and wheel.

7. Remove the right engine splash shield.

8. Install the jack stands to the frame.

9. Loosen the left frame bolts and remove the right side frame bolts.

10. Using the jack stands, lower the right side of the frame to access the crankshaft balancer.

11. Remove the torque converter covers.

12. Remove the oil pan.

13. Lock flywheel to prevent rotation.

14. Remove the crankshaft balancer bolt and the washer.

15. Remove the crankshaft balancer using a 3-jaw puller.

16. Remove the crankshaft key from the keyway.

17. Pry out the oil seal using a large screwdriver or the equivalent.

18. If only the oil seal is being replaced, lubricate the new oil seal using clean engine oil. Insert the oil seal into the front cover with the lip facing the engine and seat the seal. Install the crankshaft key into the keyway. Install the crankshaft balancer and

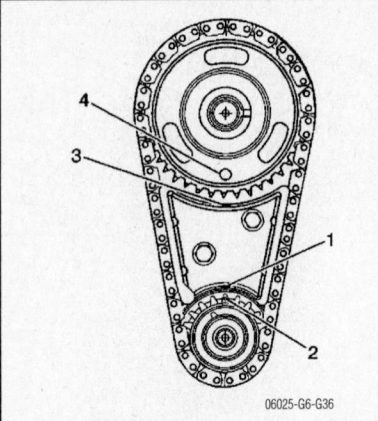

Fig. 84 Aligning the timing chain marks—3.5L engine

06025-G6-G36

tighten the bolt to 118 ft. lbs. (160 Nm). Reverse the removal procedure.

19. Remove the thermostat bypass pipe from the engine front cover.

20. Remove the radiator outlet hose from the engine front cover.

21. Remove the water pump from the engine front cover.

22. Remove the CKP sensor wiring harness bracket.

23. Remove the engine front cover bolts.

24. Remove the engine front cover.

25. Remove the engine front cover gasket.

26. Clean and inspect the engine front cover.

27. If replacing the engine front cover, remove the drive belt shield bolt and the drive belt shield and the water pump.

28. Rotate the crankshaft until the timing marks in the following locations are aligned: The camshaft alignment pin (4) to the timing chain dampener (3). The timing chain dampener (1) to the crankshaft sprocket (2).

29. Remove the camshaft sprocket bolt.

30. Remove the camshaft sprocket with the timing chain.

31. Remove the crankshaft sprocket.

32. Remove the timing chain dampener bolts and dampener.

33. If necessary, remove the camshaft thrust plate.

34. Clean and inspect the timing chain and the gears.

To install:

35. If removed, install the camshaft thrust plate and tighten to 89 inch lbs. (10 Nm).

36. Install the crankshaft sprocket.

37. Apply engine oil supplement to the sprocket thrust surface.

38. Install the timing chain dampener

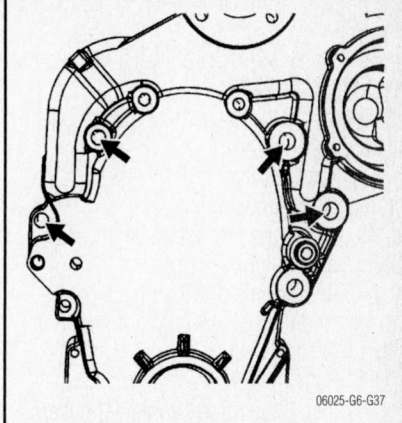

Fig. 85 Engine front cover sealant locations—3.5L engine

06025-G6-G37

and tighten the bolts to 15 ft. lbs. (21 Nm).

39. Install the timing chain onto the camshaft gear.

40. Hold the camshaft sprocket with the chain hanging down, and install the chain to the crankshaft gear.

41. Align the chain and sprocket timing marks.

42. Install the camshaft sprocket bolt and tighten to 103 ft. lbs. (140 Nm) to draw the sprocket onto the camshaft.

43. Coat the crankshaft and camshaft sprocket with engine oil.

44. If removed install the water pump and drive belt shield to the front cover.

45. Apply sealant to both sides of the lower tabs of the engine front cover gasket.

46. Install the engine front cover gasket.

47. Install the front cover.

48. Apply sealant to the bolt hole locations shown.

49. Install the engine front cover bolts and tighten the small engine front cover bolts (1) to 20 ft. lbs. (27 Nm). Tighten the

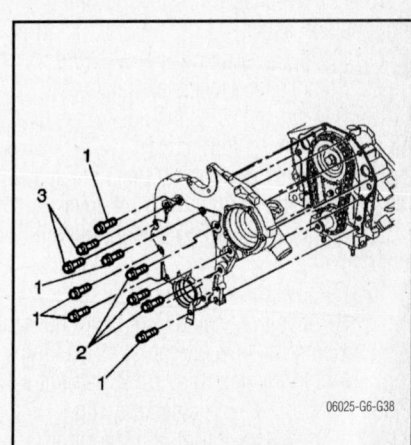

Fig. 86 Engine front cover bolt identification—3.5L engine

06025-G6-G38

large engine front cover bolts (2, 3) to 41 ft. lbs. (55 Nm).

50. Install the radiator outlet hose to the engine front cover.

51. Install the thermostat bypass pipe to the engine front cover.

52. Apply sealant to the keyway of the crankshaft balancer.

53. Install the crankshaft balancer using Balancer Installer J-29113.

54. Install the crankshaft balancer washer and the bolt and tighten to 118 ft. lbs. (160 Nm).

55. Remove the lock from the flywheel.

56. Install the torque converter covers.

57. Raise the frame to the original position.

58. Install and tighten the frame bolts to 73 ft. lbs. (100 Nm), plus an additional 180 degrees.

59. Install the oil pan.

60. Install the right engine splash shield.

61. Install the right front tire and wheel.

62. Lower the vehicle.

63. Install the drive belt.

64. Fill the engine with clean oil.

65. Fill and bleed the cooling system.

66. Start the engine and check for proper operation.

3.6L Engine

See Figures 87 through 98.

1. Relieve the fuel system pressure.

2. Raise and support the vehicle safely.

3. Remove the drive belts.

4. Remove the spark plugs in order to ease crankshaft/engine rotation.

5. Remove the lower intake manifold.

6. Remove the camshaft covers.

7. Drain the engine coolant.

8. Remove the drive belt tensioner.

9. Remove the water pump.

10. Remove the power steering pump and position aside.

11. Install the engine support fixture.

12. Remove the crankshaft balancer.

13. Remove the camshaft position actuator valves from the front cover.

14. Remove the camshaft position actuator solenoid valves from the front cover.

15. Remove the engine coolant thermostat housing.

16. Remove the engine oil pan.

17. Remove the engine front cover bolts.

18. Using the special camshaft locking tool EN 46111, rotate the crankshaft until the left cylinder head camshafts align with the EN 46105-2 tool and the right cylinder head camshafts align with the EN 46105-1.

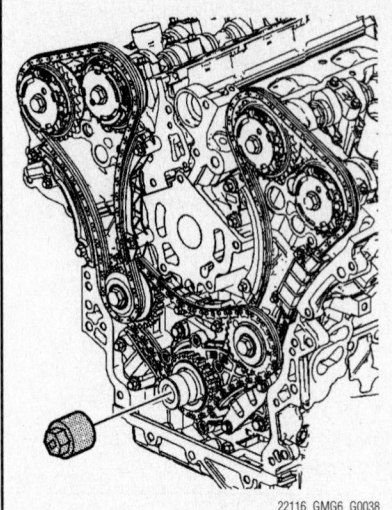

Fig. 87 Rotating crankshaft with tool EN 46111for camshaft alignment—3.6L engine

19. Install the EN 46105—1 to the right camshafts.

20. Install the EN 46105—2 to the left camshafts.

21. Remove the right secondary camshaft drive chain from the right camshaft position actuators and the right camshaft intermediate drive chain idler sprocket.

22. Remove the primary camshaft drive chain.

23. Remove the left secondary camshaft drive chain tensioner bolts.

24. Remove the left secondary camshaft drive chain tensioner.

25. Remove and discard the left secondary camshaft drive chain tensioner gasket.

➡Inspect the left secondary camshaft drive chain tensioner mounting surface on the left cylinder head for burrs or any defects that would degrade the

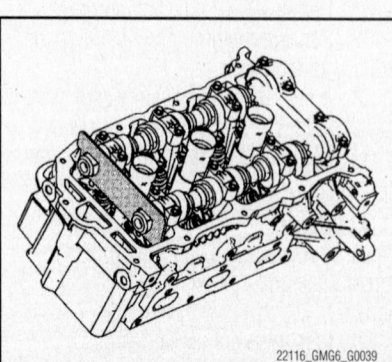

Fig. 88 Right camshaft alignment shown with tool EN 46105—1 left similar

sealing of the new left secondary camshaft drive chain tensioner gasket.

26. Remove the left secondary camshaft drive chain shoe bolt.

27. Remove the left secondary camshaft drive chain shoe.

28. Remove the left secondary camshaft drive chain guide bolts.

29. Remove the left secondary camshaft drive chain guide.

30. Remove the left camshaft intermediate drive chain idler bolt

31. Remove the left camshaft intermediate drive chain idler.

32. Remove the left secondary camshaft drive chain from the left camshaft position actuators and the left camshaft intermediate drive chain idler sprocket.

33. Clean and inspect all of the camshaft timing drive components.

To install:

✳✳ WARNING

All camshafts must be locked in place before installation of any camshaft drive chains.

34. Ensure that the EN 46105—1 is fully seated onto the camshafts.

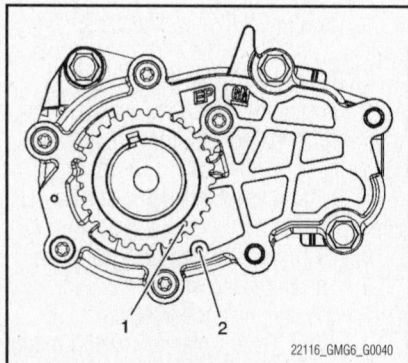

Fig. 89 Crankshaft sprocket (1) and oil pump (2) alignment marks

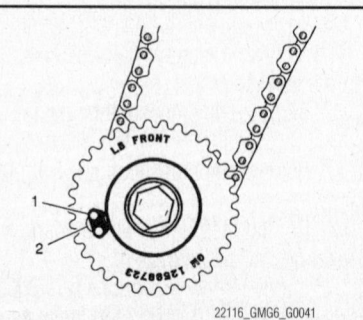

Fig. 90 Left camshaft intermediate drive chain idler outer sprocket and chain alignment.

35. Ensure the crankshaft is in the stage one timing position with the crankshaft sprocket timing mark (1) aligned to the stage one timing mark on the oil pump cover (2) using the EN-48589.

36. Install the left secondary camshaft drive chain.

37. Place the left secondary camshaft drive chain around the inner sprocket of the left camshaft intermediate drive chain idler with the timing camshaft drive chain link (1) aligned to the alignment access hole (2) made in the left camshaft intermediate drive chain idler outer sprocket.

38. Wrap the secondary camshaft drive chain around both left actuator drive sprockets.

39. Ensure there are 10 links (1) between the timing camshaft drive chain links for the camshaft position actuator sprockets.

40. Align the left exhaust camshaft position actuator sprocket alignment circle mark (2) with the timing camshaft drive chain link (1).

41. Align the left intake camshaft position actuator sprocket alignment circle mark (1) with the timing camshaft drive chain link (2).

42. Ensure that the left camshaft intermediate drive chain idler is being installed.

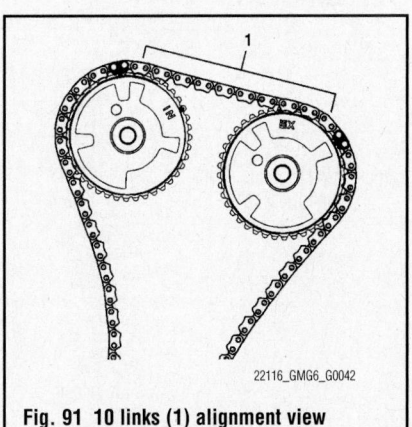

Fig. 91 10 links (1) alignment view

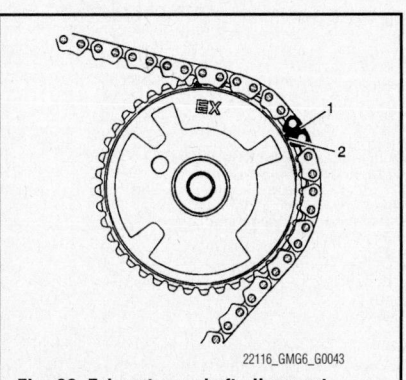

Fig. 92 Exhaust camshaft alignment marks

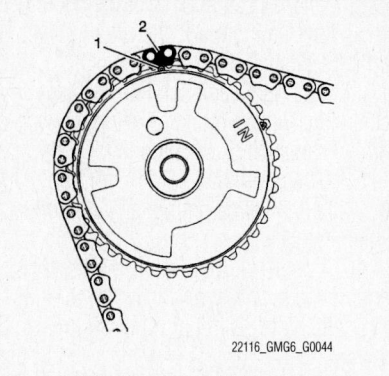

Fig. 93 Intake camshaft alignment marks

The recessed hub and the larger sprocket of the left camshaft intermediate drive chain idler is installed outward. The raised hub and the smaller sprocket of the left camshaft intermediate drive chain idler is installed towards the block.

43. Place the left camshaft intermediate drive chain idler to the cylinder block.

44. Install the camshaft intermediate drive chain idler bolt and tighten to 43 ft. lbs. (58 Nm).

45. Position the left secondary camshaft drive chain guide.

46. Install the secondary camshaft drive chain guide bolts and tighten to 17 ft. lbs. (23 Nm).

47. Position the left secondary camshaft drive chain shoe.

48. Install the secondary camshaft drive chain shoe bolt and tighten to 17 ft. lbs. (23 Nm).

49. Using the J 45027 , reset the left secondary camshaft drive chain tensioner plunger.

50. Install the plunger into the left secondary camshaft drive chain tensioner body.

51. Compress the plunger into the body and lock the left secondary camshaft drive chain tensioner by inserting the EN 46112 into the access hole in the side of the left secondary camshaft drive chain tensioner body.

52. Slowly release pressure on the left secondary camshaft drive chain tensioner. The left secondary camshaft drive chain tensioner should remain compressed.

53. Install a NEW left secondary camshaft drive chain tensioner gasket to the left secondary camshaft drive chain tensioner.

54. Install the left secondary camshaft drive chain tensioner bolts through the left secondary camshaft drive chain tensioner and gasket.

55. Ensure the left secondary camshaft drive chain tensioner mounting surface on the left cylinder head does not have any burrs or defects that would degrade the sealing of the NEW left secondary camshaft drive chain tensioner gasket.

56. Place the left secondary camshaft drive chain tensioner into position and loosely install the bolts to the block.

57. Verify the proper placement of the left secondary camshaft drive chain tensioner gasket tab.

58. Tighten the left secondary camshaft drive chain tensioner bolts in two steps:

   a. Tighten tensioner bolts to 44 inch. lbs. (5 Nm).

   b. Tighten tensioner bots an additional 17 ft. lbs.(23 Nm).

59. Release the left secondary camshaft drive chain tensioner by pulling out the EN 46112 pin and unlocking the tensioner plunger.

60. Verify the left secondary camshaft drive chain timing mark alignments.

❊❊ **WARNING**

Ensure that the crankshaft is in the stage one timing drive assembly position.

61. Install the primary camshaft drive chain.

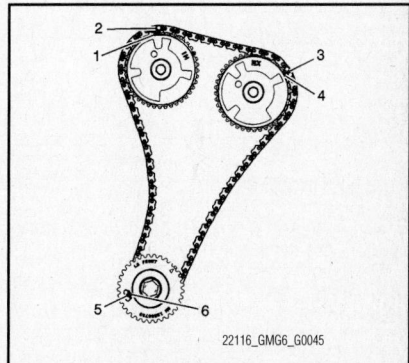

Fig. 94 Left secondary camshaft drive chain timing mark alignments (1—6)

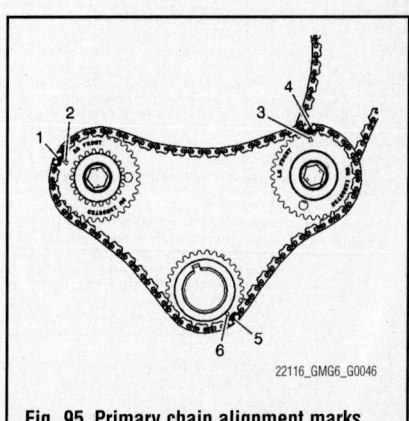

Fig. 95 Primary chain alignment marks

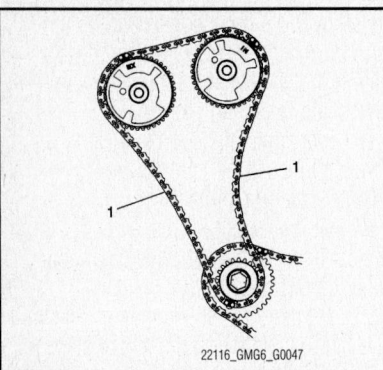

Fig. 96 Secondary drive chain alignment marks

62. Wrap the primary camshaft drive chain around the large sprockets of each camshaft intermediate drive chain idler and the crankshaft sprocket.

63. The left camshaft intermediate drive chain idler timing mark (1) will align with a timing camshaft drive chain link (2)

64. The right camshaft intermediate drive chain idler timing mark (2) will align with a timing camshaft drive chain link (1).

65. The crankshaft sprocket timing mark (2) will align with a timing camshaft drive chain link (1).

66. Ensure all the timing marks (2, 3, and 6) are properly aligned with the timing camshaft drive chain links (1, 4, and 5).

67. Ensure that the crankshaft is in the stage 2 timing drive assembly position (1).

68. Install the right secondary camshaft drive chain.

69. Place the secondary camshaft drive chain around the right camshaft intermediate drive chain idler outer sprocket, aligning the timing camshaft drive chain link (1) with the alignment access hole (2) made in the right camshaft intermediate drive chain idler inner sprocket.

70. Wrap the secondary camshaft drive chain around both right actuator drive sprockets.

71. Ensure there are 10 links (1) between the timing camshaft drive chain links for the camshaft position actuator sprockets

72. Align the right exhaust camshaft position actuator sprocket alignment triangle mark (1) with the timing camshaft drive chain link (2).

73. Align the right intake camshaft position actuator sprocket alignment triangle mark (2) with the timing camshaft drive chain link (1).

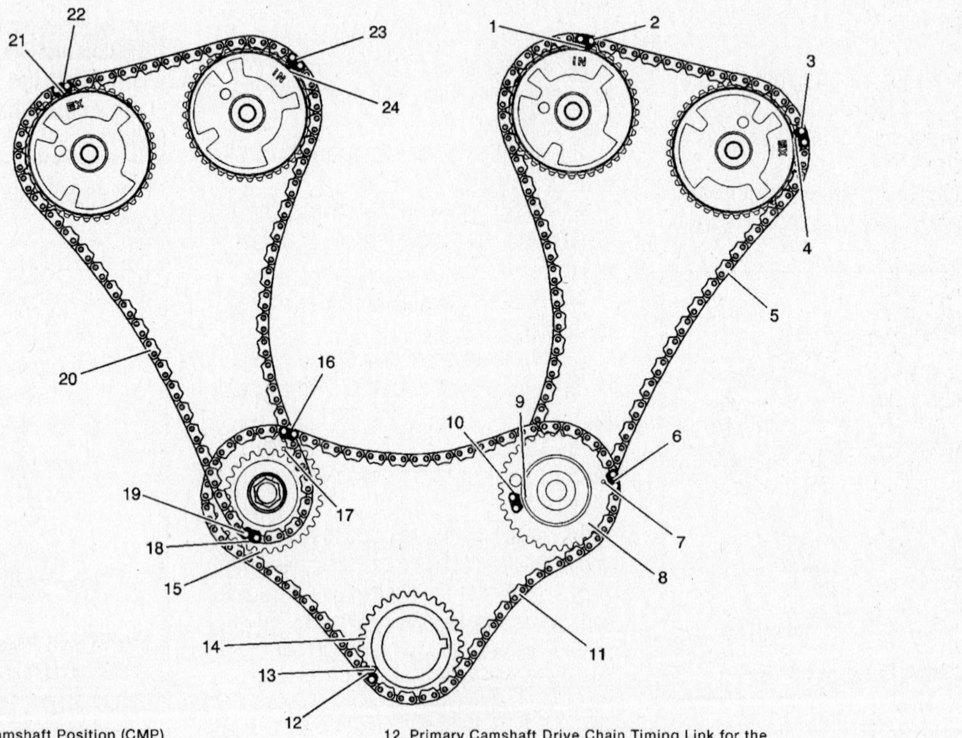

1. Left Intake Camshaft Position (CMP) Actuator Timing Mark - Circle
2. Left Intake Secondary Camshaft Timing Drive Chain Timing Link
3. Left Exhaust Secondary Camshaft Timing Drive Chain Timing Link
4. Left Exhaust Camshaft Position (CMP) Actuator Timing Mark - Circle
5. Left Secondary Camshaft Timing Drive Chain
6. Primary Camshaft Drive Chain Timing Link for the Left Primary Camshaft Intermediate Drive Chain Sprocket
7. Left Primary Camshaft Intermediate Drive Chain Sprocket Timing Mark for the Primary Camshaft Drive Chain
8. Left Primary Camshaft Intermediate Drive Chain Sprocket
9. Left Secondary Camshaft Timing Drive Chain Timing Link for the Left Primary Camshaft Intermediate Drive Chain Sprocket
10. Left Primary Camshaft Intermediate Drive Chain Sprocket Timing Window
11. Primary Camshaft Drive Chain
12. Primary Camshaft Drive Chain Timing Link for the Crankshaft Sprocket
13. Crankshaft Sprocket Timing Mark
14. Crankshaft Sprocket
15. Right Primary Camshaft Intermediate Drive Chain Sprocket
16. Primary Camshaft Drive Chain Timing Link for the Right Primary Camshaft Intermediate Drive Chain Sprocket
17. Right Primary Camshaft Intermediate Drive Chain Sprocket Timing Mark for the Primary Camshaft Drive Chain
18. Right Primary Camshaft Intermediate Drive Chain Sprocket Timing Mark/Window for the Right Secondary Camshaft Timing Drive Chain
19. Right Secondary Camshaft Timing Drive Chain Timing Link for the Right Primary Camshaft Intermediate Drive Chain Sprocket
20. Right Secondary Camshaft Timing Drive Chain
21. Right Exhaust Camshaft Position (CMP) Actuator Timing Mark - Triangle
22. Right Exhaust Secondary Camshaft Timing Drive Chain Timing Link
23. Right Intake Secondary Camshaft Timing Drive Chain Timing Link
24. Right Intake Camshaft Position (CMP) Actuator Timing Mark - Triangle

Fig. 97 Timing drive chain alignment diagram (Fourth Design)—3.6L engine

74. There will be 22 links (1) between the right camshaft intermediate drive chain idler timing camshaft drive chain link and each right camshaft position actuator sprocket timing camshaft drive chain link.

75. Install the 0.315 inch. (8 mm) guide pins from the EN 46109 into the cylinder block.

76. Install the engine front cover to cylinder block seal.

77. Place a 3 mm (0.118 in) bead of RTV sealant, or equivalent, on the engine front cover.

78. Place the engine front cover onto the guide pins EN 46109 and slide into position.

79. Remove the EN 46109 guide pins.

80. Hand start all the front cover bolts.

81. Tighten the engine front cover bolts in sequence to 17 ft. lbs. (23 Nm).

82. Install the engine oil pan.

83. Install the engine coolant thermostat housing.

84. Remove the engine mount bracket.

85. Install the camshaft position actuator solenoid valves from the front cover.

86. Install the camshaft position actuator valves from the front cover.

87. Install the crankshaft balancer.

88. Install the power steering pump and position aside.

89. Install the water pump.

90. Install the drive belt tensioner.

91. Install drive belt.

92. Install the camshaft covers.

93. Install the lower intake manifold.

94. Refill crankcase with recommended motor oil.

95. Fill and bleed the cooling system.

96. Start the engine and check for proper operation.

3.9L Engine

See Figure 99.

➡If only the crankshaft front seal is being replaced, perform steps 1 through 18.

1. Properly relieve the fuel system pressure.

2. Drain the engine oil and cooling system.

3. Disconnect the negative battery cable.

4. Remove the drive belt and drive belt tensioner.

5. Raise and support the vehicle.

6. Remove the right front tire and wheel.

7. Remove the right engine splash shield.

8. Install the jack stands to the frame.

9. Loosen the left frame bolts and remove the right side frame bolts.

10. Using the jack stands, lower the right side of the frame to access the crankshaft balancer.

11. Remove the torque converter covers.

12. Remove the oil pan.

13. Lock flywheel to prevent rotation.

14. Remove the crankshaft balancer bolt and the washer.

15. Remove the crankshaft balancer using a 3-jaw puller.

16. Remove the crankshaft key from the keyway.

17. Pry out the oil seal using a large screwdriver or the equivalent.

18. If only the oil seal is being replaced, lubricate the new oil seal using clean engine oil. Insert the oil seal into the front cover with the lip facing the engine and seat the seal. Install the crankshaft key into the keyway. Install the crankshaft balancer and tighten the bolt to 52 ft. lbs. (70 Nm), plus an additional 70 degrees. Reverse the removal procedure.

19. Remove the intake manifold cover.

20. Remove the air cleaner assembly.

21. Remove the engine mount strut bracket.

22. Disconnect the camshaft position actuator magnet electrical connector.

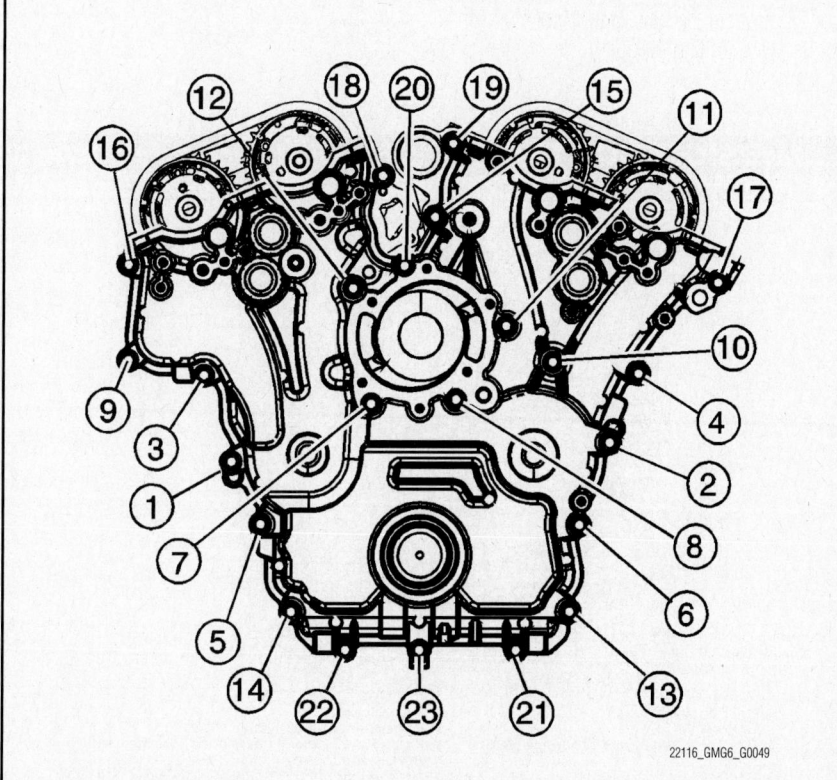

22116_GMG6_G0049

Fig. 98 Engine front cover tightening sequence—3.6L engine

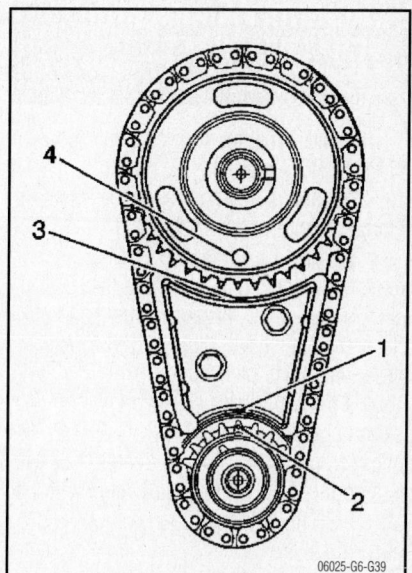

06025-G6-G39

Fig. 99 Aligning the timing chain marks—3.9L engine

23. Remove the crankshaft position actuator magnet.

24. Remove the thermostat housing.

25. Remove the water pump.

26. Remove the engine front cover bolts.

27. Remove the engine front cover and gasket.

28. Align the crankshaft timing mark (1) to the timing mark on the bottom of the timing chain tensioner (2). Align the timing mark on the camshaft gear (3) with the timing mark on top of the timing chain tensioner (4).

29. Remove the camshaft sprocket bolts.

30. Remove the timing chain, camshaft, and crankshaft sprockets.

31. Remove the timing chain tensioner.

32. Remove and discard the camshaft position actuator filter from the end of the camshaft.

To install:

33. Install a new camshaft position actuator filter to the end of the camshaft.

34. Install the crankshaft sprocket.

35. Apply prelube to the crankshaft sprocket thrust surface.

36. Install the timing chain tensioner and tighten the bolts to 15 ft. lbs. (20 Nm).

37. Using Tensioner Compressor EN-47719, fully collapse the tensioner, and place the tensioner retaining pin into the retaining hole.

38. Align the timing marks and hold the camshaft sprocket with the timing chain hanging down and install the timing chain to the crankshaft gear.

39. Align the dowel in the camshaft sprocket with the dowel hole in the camshaft.

40. Draw the camshaft sprocket onto the camshaft using the mounting bolts and tighten to 12 ft. lbs. (16 Nm).

41. Remove the retaining pin from the timing chain tensioner in order to make the tensioner active.

42. Coat the crankshaft and camshaft sprockets with clean engine oil.

43. Install the engine front cover gasket.

44. Install the engine front cover and tighten the bolts to 18 ft. lbs. (25 Nm).

45. Install the water pump.

46. Install the thermostat housing.

47. Install the crankshaft position actuator magnet.

48. Install the camshaft position actuator magnet O-ring seal and magnet.

49. Install the camshaft position actuator magnet bolts and tighten to 89 inch lbs. (10 Nm).

50. Connect the camshaft position actuator magnet electrical connector.

51. Install the engine mount strut bracket and tighten to 18 ft. lbs. (25 Nm).

52. Install the air cleaner assembly.

53. Install the intake manifold cover.

54. Lubricate the new crankshaft front oil seal using clean engine oil.

55. Insert the oil seal into the front cover with the lip facing the engine and seat the seal.

56. Install the crankshaft key into the keyway.

57. Install the crankshaft balancer and tighten the bolt to 52 ft. lbs. (70 Nm), plus an additional 70 degrees.

58. Unlock the flywheel.

59. Install the torque converter covers.

60. Install the oil pan.

61. Raise the frame into the original position.

62. Install and tighten the right and left side frame bolts to 74 ft. lbs. (100 Nm) plus an additional 90 degrees.

63. Install the right engine splash shield.

64. Install the right front tire and wheel.

65. Lower the vehicle.

66. Install the drive belt tensioner and drive belt.

67. Fill the engine with clean oil.

68. Fill and bleed the cooling system.

69. Start the engine and check for proper operation.

VALVE LASH

ADJUSTMENT

Hydraulic lash adjusters are used on all engines and no adjustment is necessary.

ENGINE PERFORMANCE & EMISSION CONTROL

MALFUNCTION INDICATOR LIGHT (MIL) RESET PROCEDURES

Here are 3 methods for clearing codes from the PCM memory:

• Use the Scan Tool (also clears Freeze Frame & Failure Records)

• If battery power to the PCM is removed (battery cable or PCM fuse), all current data (DTC, Freeze Frame, Fail Records, Statistical Filters and I/M Readiness Flags) will be cleared

• If the fault that caused a DTC to set has been corrected, the PCM will begin to count warm—up cycles. Once it has counted 40 warm—up cycles with no further faults detected, the DTC is cleared

COMPONENT LOCATIONS

See Figures 100 through 111.

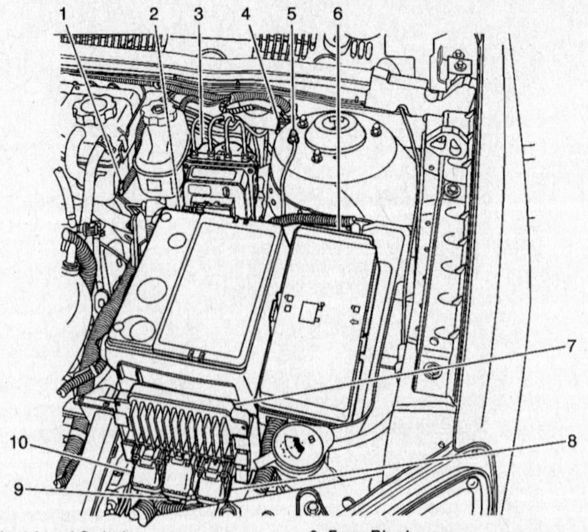

1. Coolant Level Switch
2. Battery
3. Electronic Brake Control Module (EBCM)
4. C101
5. G103
6. Fuse Block
7. Powertrain Control Module (PCM)
8. Powertrain Control Module (PCM), Connector 3
9. Powertrain Control Module (PCM), Connector 2
10. Powertrain Control Module (PCM), Connector 1

22116_GMG6_G0098

Fig. 100 Left rear of engine compartment—Pontiac G6

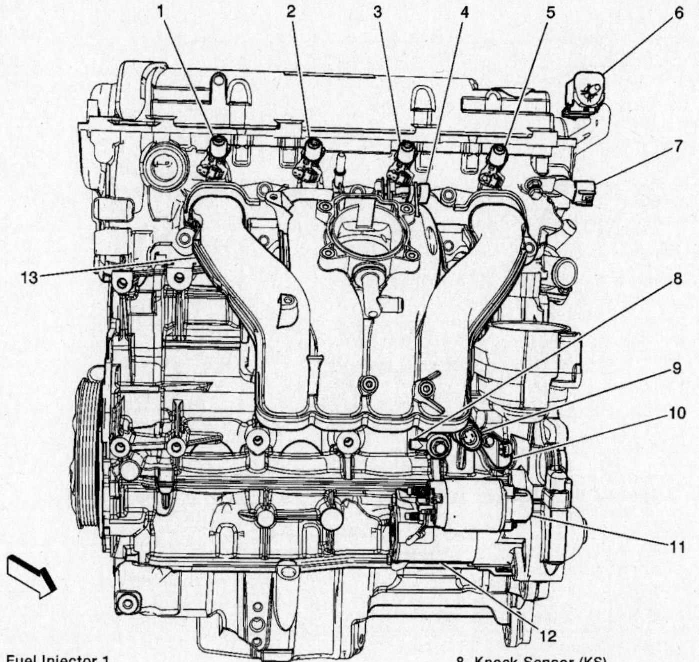

1. Fuel Injector 1
2. Fuel Injector 2
3. Fuel Injector 3
4. Manifold Absolute Pressure (MAP) Sensor
5. Fuel Injector 4
6. Evaporative Emission (EVAP) Canister Purge Solenoid Valve
7. Camshaft Position (CMP) Sensor - Intake
8. Knock Sensor (KS)
9. Engine Oil Pressure (EOP) Switch
10. Crankshaft Position (CKP) Sensor
11. Starter Solenoid
12. Starter
13. Intake Manifold

22116_GMG6_G0101

Fig. 101 Front view of 2.4L engine

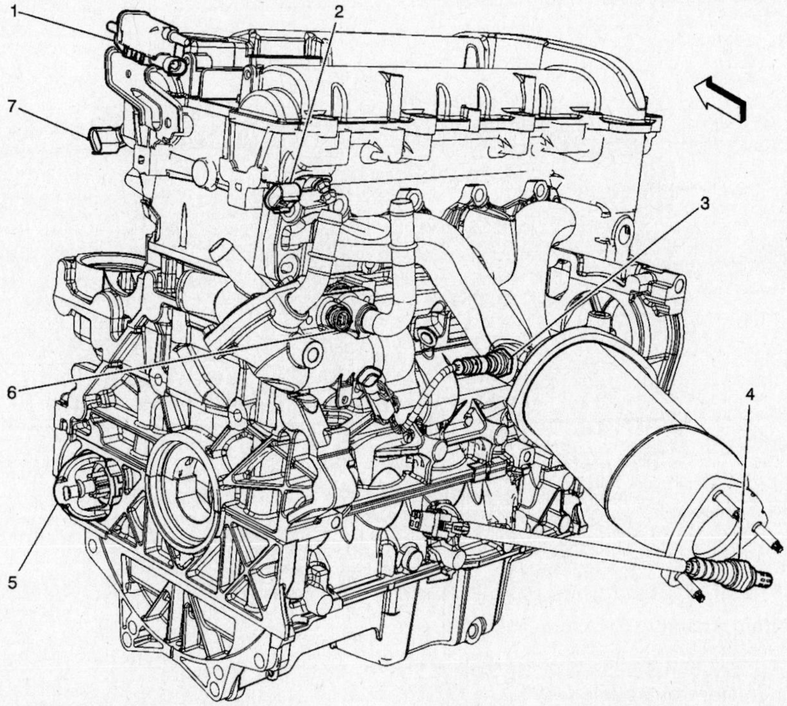

1. Evaporative Emission (EVAP) Canister Purge Solenoid Valve
2. Camshaft Position (CMP) Sensor - Exhaust
3. Heated Oxygen Sensor (HO2S) 1
4. Heated Oxygen Sensor (HO2S) 2
5. Starter
6. Engine Coolant Temperature (ECT) Sensor
7. Camshaft Position (CMP) Sensor - Intake

22116_GMG6_G0102

Fig. 102 Rear view of 2.4L engine

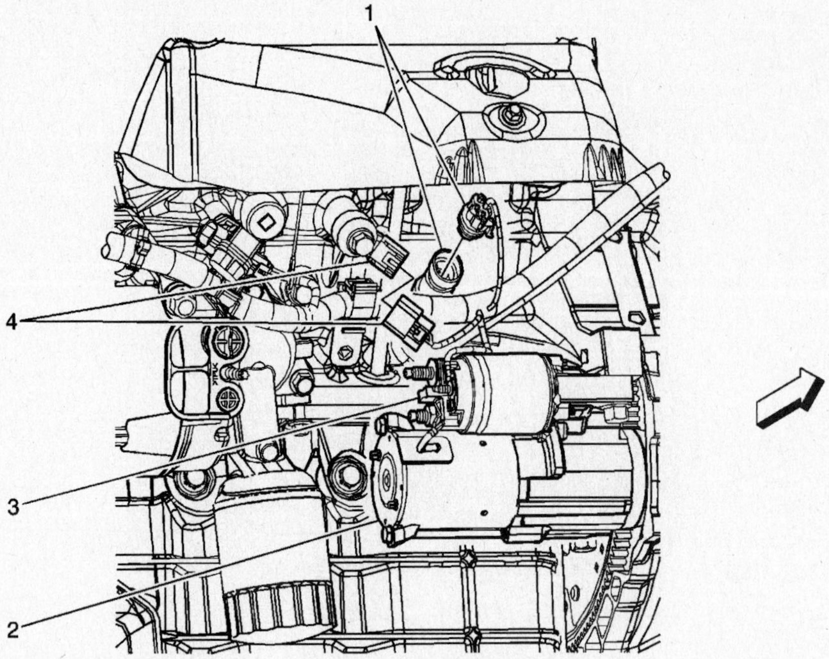

1. Engine Oil Pressure (EOP) Switch
2. Starter
3. Starter Solenoid
4. Knock Sensor (KS)

22116_GMG6_G0099

Fig. 103 Lower left front view of the 3.5L engine

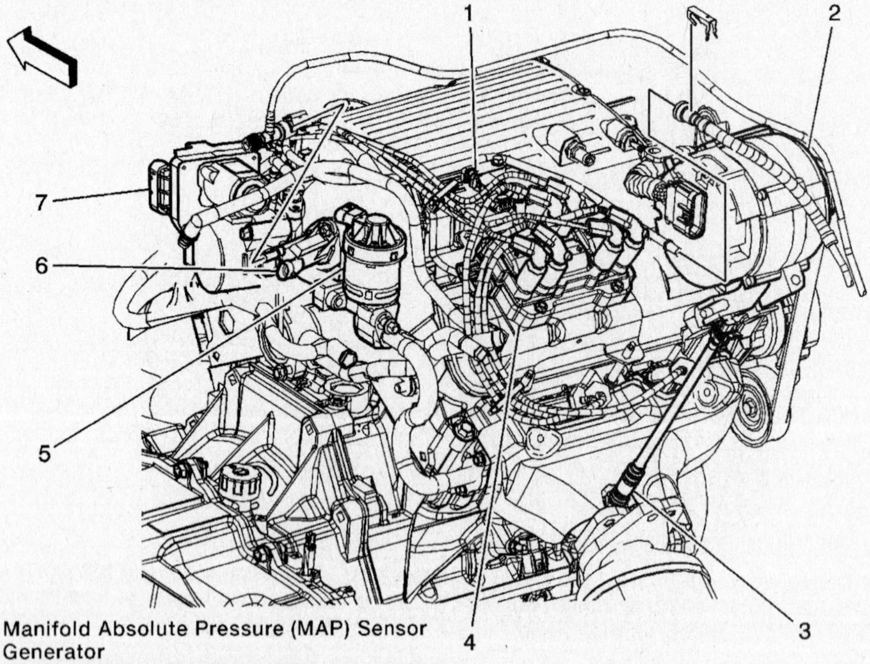

1. Manifold Absolute Pressure (MAP) Sensor
2. Generator
3. Heated Oxygen Sensor (HO2S) Bank 1 Sensor 1
4. Ignition Control Module (ICM)
5. Exhaust Gas Recirculation (EGR) Valve
7. Throttle Actuator Control (TAC) Module
6. Evaporative Emission (EVAP) Canister Purge Solenoid

22116_GMG6_G0100

Fig. 104 Top rear view of the 3.5L engine

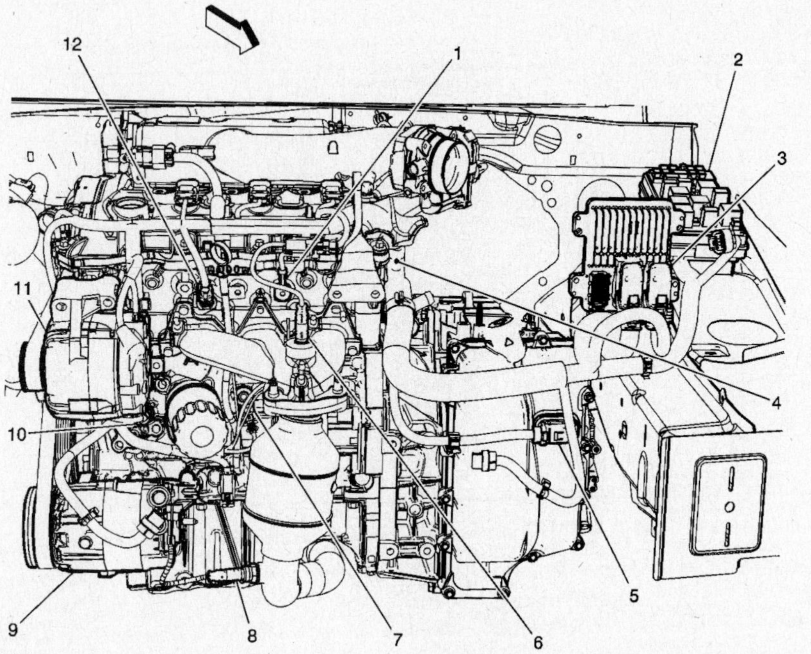

1. G113
2. Fuse Block
3. Engine Control Module (ECM)
4. S199
5. Transmission Control Module (TCM)
6. Heated Oxygen Sensor (HO2S) Bank 2 Sensor 1
7. Knock Sensor 2
8. Heated Oxygen Sensor (HO2S) Bank 2 Sensor 2
9. A/C Compressor
10. Engine Oil Pressure (EOP) Sensor
11. Generator
12. Engine Coolant Temperature (ECT) Sensor

22116_GMG6_G0103

Fig. 105 Front view of 3.6L engine

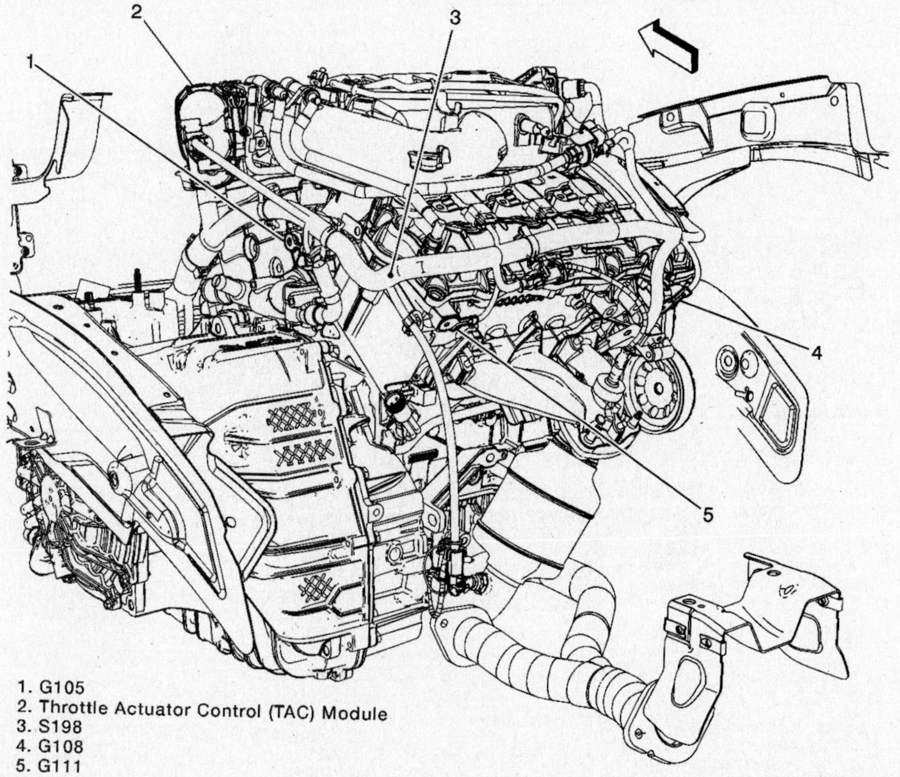

1. G105
2. Throttle Actuator Control (TAC) Module
3. S198
4. G108
5. G111

22116_GMG6_G0104

Fig. 106 Rear view of 3.6L engine

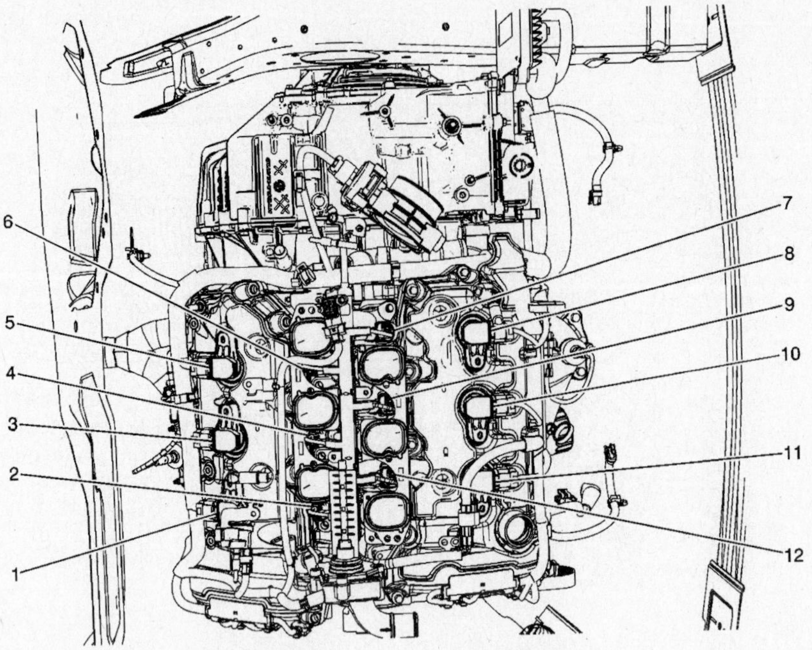

1. Ignition Coil 1
2. Fuel Injector 1
3. Ignition Coil 3
4. Fuel Injector 3
5. Ignition Coil 5
6. Fuel Injector 5
7. Fuel Injector 6
8. Ignition Coil 6
9. Fuel Injector 4
10. Ignition Coil 4
11. Ignition Coil 2
12. Fuel Injector 2

22116_GMG6_G0105

Fig. 107 Top view of the 3.6L engine

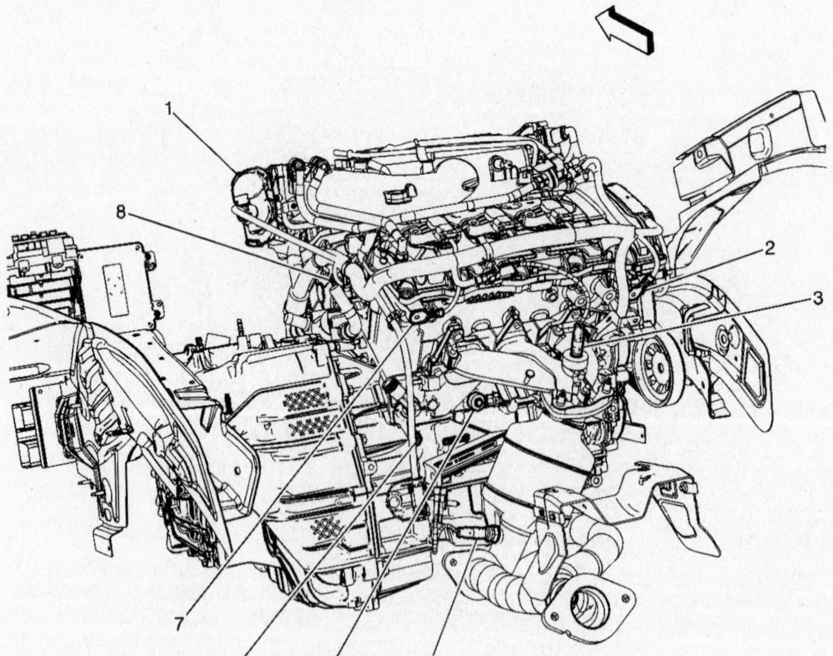

1. Throttle Actuator Control (TAC) Module
2. G108
3. Heated Oxygen Sensor (HO2S) Bank 1 Sensor 1
4. Heated Oxygen Sensor (HO2S) Bank 1 Sensor 2
5. Knock Sensor 1
6. Crankshaft Position (CKP) Sensor
7. G111
8. G105

22116_GMG6_G0106

Fig. 108 Rear view of 3.6L engine

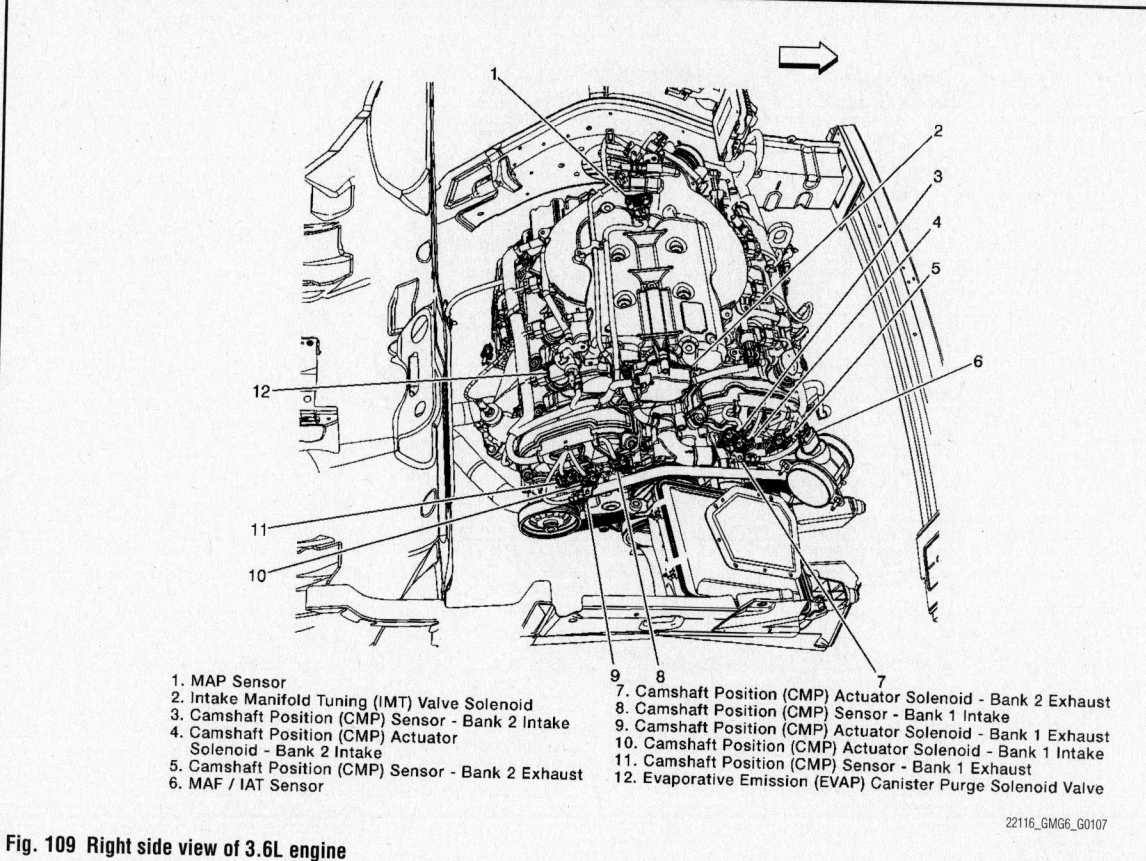

1. MAP Sensor
2. Intake Manifold Tuning (IMT) Valve Solenoid
3. Camshaft Position (CMP) Sensor - Bank 2 Intake
4. Camshaft Position (CMP) Actuator
   Solenoid - Bank 2 Intake
5. Camshaft Position (CMP) Sensor - Bank 2 Exhaust
6. MAF / IAT Sensor

7. Camshaft Position (CMP) Actuator Solenoid - Bank 2 Exhaust
8. Camshaft Position (CMP) Sensor - Bank 1 Intake
9. Camshaft Position (CMP) Actuator Solenoid - Bank 1 Exhaust
10. Camshaft Position (CMP) Actuator Solenoid - Bank 1 Intake
11. Camshaft Position (CMP) Sensor - Bank 1 Exhaust
12. Evaporative Emission (EVAP) Canister Purge Solenoid Valve

22116_GMG6_G0107

Fig. 109 Right side view of 3.6L engine

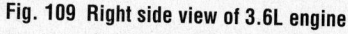

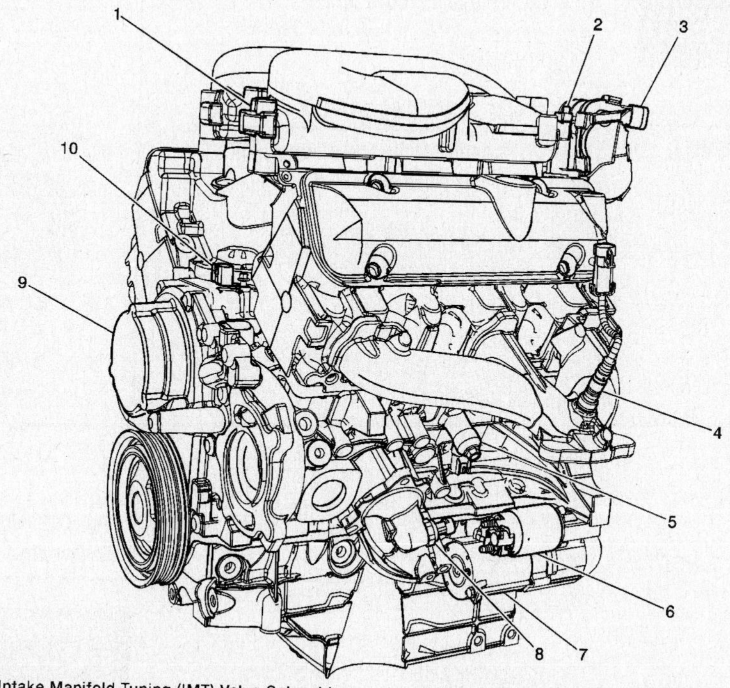

1. Intake Manifold Tuning (IMT) Valve Solenoid
2. Evaporative Emission (EVAP) Canister
   Purge Solenoid Valve
3. Throttle Actuator Control (TAC) Module
4. Heated Oxygen Sensor (HO2S) Bank 1 Sensor 1
5. Knock Sensor (KS) 2

6. Starter Solenoid
7. Starter
8. Engine Oil Pressure (EOP) Sensor
9. Camshaft Position (CMP) Actuator Solenoid
10. Camshaft Position (CMP) Sensor

22116_GMG6_G0108

Fig. 110 Front view of 3.9L engine

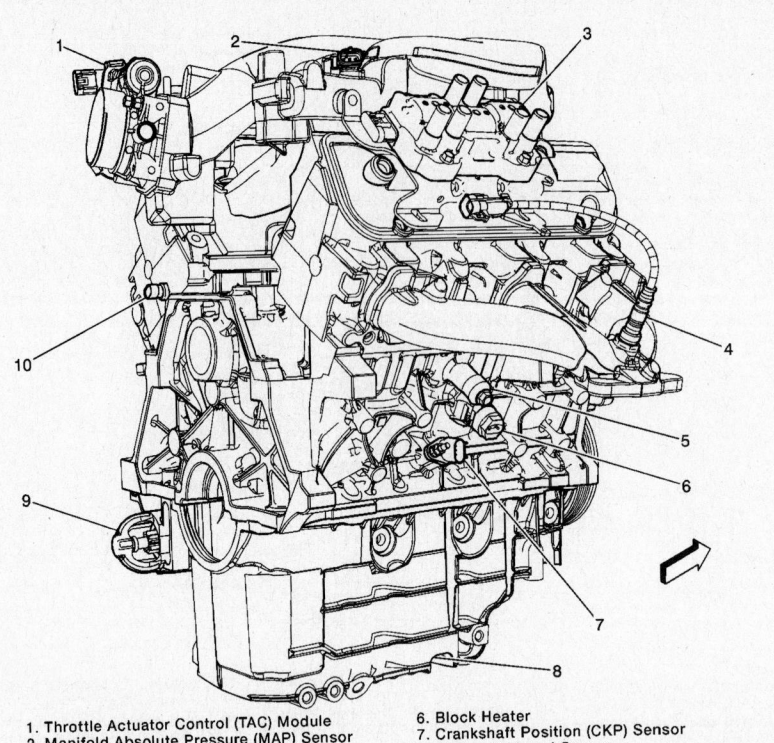

1. Throttle Actuator Control (TAC) Module
2. Manifold Absolute Pressure (MAP) Sensor
3. Ignition Control Module (ICM)
4. Heated Oxygen Sensor (HO2S) Bank 2 Sensor 1
5. Knock Sensor (KS) 2
6. Block Heater
7. Crankshaft Position (CKP) Sensor
8. Engine Oil Level Sensor
9. Starter
10. Engine Coolant Temperature (ECT) Sensor

22116_GMG6_G0109

Fig. 111 Rear view of 3.9L engine

ACCELERATOR PEDAL POSITION (APP) SENSOR

LOCATION

The Accelerator Pedal Position (APP) Sensor is located inside the vehicle. It is mounted at the top of the accelerator pedal and is part of the assembly.

OPERATION

The accelerator pedal contains 2 individual Accelerator Pedal Position (APP) sensors within the assembly. The APP sensors 1 and 2 are potentiometer type sensors each with 3 circuits:

- A 5-volt reference circuit
- A low reference circuit
- A signal circuit

The APP sensors are used to determine the pedal angle. The engine control module (ECM) provides each APP sensor a 5-volt reference circuit and a low reference circuit. The APP sensors provide the ECM with signal voltage proportional to the pedal movement. The APP sensor 1 signal voltage at rest position is less than 1 volt and increases to more than 4 volts as the pedal is actuated. The APP sensor 2 signal voltage at rest

position is less than 0.6 volt and increases to more than 2 volts as the pedal is actuated.

REMOVAL & INSTALLATION

1. Disconnect the Accelerator Pedal Position (APP) sensor electrical connector.
2. Remove the APP sensor bolts.
3. Remove the APP sensor.

To install:

4. Install the APP sensor
5. Install the APP bolts and tighten to 89 inch. lbs. (10 Nm).
6. Connect the APP sensor electrical connector.
7. Confirm that the APP sensor connector locking clip is fully secured.

TESTING

See Figure 112.

1. Disconnect the Accelerator Pedal Position (APP) electrical connector.
2. With digital multimeter check pin C for 5 volt reference signal.
3. With digital multimeter check pin F for 5 volt reference signal.
4. If 5 volt reference signal is not present, repair circuit in question.

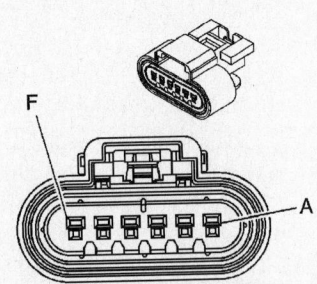

A. Low Reference
B. APP Sensor 2 Signal
C. 5-Volt Reference 1
D. Low Reference
E. APP Sensor 1 Signal
F. 5-Volt Reference 2

22116_GMG6_G0110

Fig. 112 Accelerator Pedal Position (APP) Sensor electrical connector

CAMSHAFT POSITION (CMP) SENSOR

LOCATION

2.4L Engine

There are two Camshaft Position Sensors (CMP) on the 2.4L engine. They are located to the rear of the engine cylinder head. The exhaust (CMP) sensor is located just below the canister purge valve and the intake sensor is on opposite side of cylinder head.

3.5L Engine

The 3.5L engine Camshaft Position Sensor is located just behind the top of the timing cover. In front of the intake manifold.

3.6L Engine

See Figure 113.

The 3.6L engine has four Camshaft Position sensors two on each Cylinder head. They are mounted to the left and right of the two (CMP) actuator solenoid valves.

3.9L Engine

The Camshaft Position actuator magnet (CMP) is located on the front of the engine above crank pulley and below power steering pump pulley.

OPERATION

The camshaft position (CMP) sensor is triggered by a notched reluctor wheel built onto the camshaft sprocket. The CMP sensor provides four signal pulses every camshaft revolution. Each notch, or feature of the reluctor wheel is of a different size which is used to identify the compression stroke of each cylinder and to enable sequential fuel injection. The ECM uses the CMP sensor output signal to determine the

camshaft relative position to the crankshaft position.

The CMP sensor is connected to the engine control module (ECM) by the following circuits:

- A 5-volt reference circuit
- A low reference circuit
- A signal circuit

REMOVAL & INSTALLATION

2.4L Engine

Exhaust Sensor

1. Disconnect the exhaust camshaft position (CMP) sensor electrical connector.
2. Remove the CMP sensor bolt. Intake CMP shown, exhaust CMP similar.
3. Remove the CMP sensor.

To install:

➡ **Inspect the CMP sensor for damage, replace as necessary.**

4. Lubricate the CMP sensor O-ring seal with clean engine oil.
5. Install the CMP sensor. Intake CMP shown, exhaust CMP similar.
6. Install the CMP sensor bolt and tighten to 89 inch. (10 Nm).
7. Connect the exhaust CMP sensor electrical connector.

Intake Sensor

1. Remove the intake manifold cover.
2. Disconnect the intake camshaft position (CMP) sensor electrical connector (1).
3. Remove the CMP sensor bolt.
4. Remove the CMP sensor.

To install:

5. Lubricate the CMP sensor O-ring seal with clean engine oil.
6. Install the CMP sensor.
7. Install the CMP sensor bolt and tighten to 89 inch. (10 Nm).
8. Connect the intake CMP sensor electrical connector.
9. Install the intake manifold cover.

3.5L Engine

1. Disconnect the Camshaft Position (CMP) sensor electrical connector.
2. Remove the CMP sensor bolt.
3. Remove the CMP sensor.
4. Inspect the sensor O-ring for wear, cracks, or leakage if the sensor is not being replaced.

To install:

5. Lubricate the O-ring with clean engine oil and replace the O-ring if damaged.
6. Install the CMP sensor.

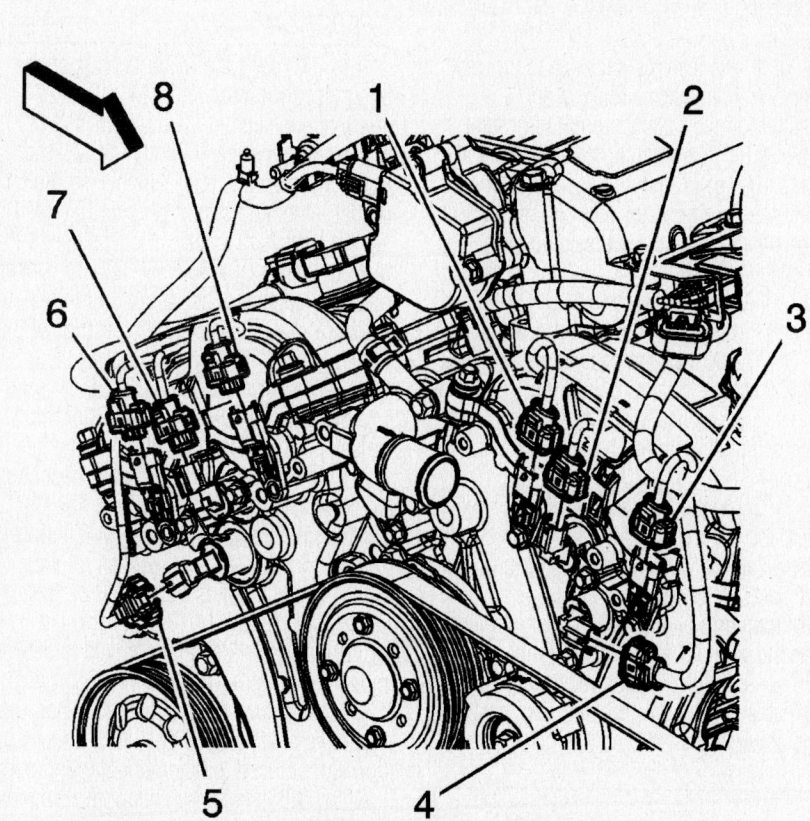

1. Bank 2 left (CMP) sensor (Intake)
2. Bank 2 left (CMP) actuator sensor (Intake)
3. Bank 2 left (CMP) sensor (Exhaust)
4. Bank 2 left (CMP) actuator sensor (Exhaust)
5. Bank 1 right (CMP) actuator sensor (Exhaust)
6. Bank 1 right (CMP) sensor (exhaust)
7. Bank 1 right (CMP) actuator sensor (Intake)
8. Bank 1 right (CMP) sensor (Intake)

22116_GMG6_G0138

Fig. 113 Camshaft Position (CMP) sensors and actuator sensors location view—3.6L engine

7. Install the CMP sensor bolt and tighten to 89 inch. lbs. (10 Nm).

8. Connect the CMP sensor electrical connector.

3.6L Engine

Bank 2 Left Side CMP Sensors

1. Remove the air cleaner assembly.

2. Disconnect the engine wiring harness electrical connector from the bank 2 exhaust or intake Camshaft Position (CMP) sensor.

3. Remove the CMP sensor bolt.

4. Remove the CMP sensor.

To install:

5. Install the CMP sensor.

6. Install the CMP sensor bolt and tighten to 89 inch. lbs. (10 Nm).

7. Connect the engine wiring harness electrical connector to the bank 2 exhaust or intake CMP sensor.

8. Install the air cleaner assembly.

Bank 1 Right Side CMP Sensors

1. Remove the air cleaner assembly.

2. Disconnect the engine wiring harness electrical connector from the bank 1 exhaust or intake camshaft position (CMP) sensor.

3. Remove the CMP sensor bolt.

4. Remove the CMP sensor.

To install:

5. Install the CMP sensor.

6. Install the CMP sensor bolt and tighten to 89 inch. lbs. (10 Nm).

7. Connect the engine wiring harness electrical connector to the bank 1 exhaust or intake CMP sensor.

8. Install the air cleaner assembly.

3.9L Engine

1. Remove the intake manifold cover.

2. Remove the air cleaner assembly.

3. Remove the engine mount strut bracket.

4. Remove the engine mount bracket, if equipped with a convertible top.

5. Disconnect the camshaft position actuator magnet electrical connector.

6. Remove the camshaft position actuator magnet bolts.

7. Remove the camshaft position actuator magnet and O-ring seal.

To install:

8. Install the camshaft position actuator magnet O-ring seal and magnet.

9. Install the camshaft position actuator magnet bolts and tighten to 89 inch. lbs. (10 Nm).

10. Connect the camshaft position actuator magnet electrical connector.

11. Install the engine mount bracket, if equipped with a convertible top.

12. Install the engine mount strut bracket.

13. Install the air cleaner assembly.

14. Install the intake manifold cover.

TESTING

See Figure 114.

1. Ignition OFF, disconnect the affected CMP sensor connector.

2. Test for less than 1 ohm of resistance between ECM side of the low reference circuit and ground.

a. If greater than the specified value, test the low reference circuit for an open/high resistance. If the circuit tests normal, replace the ECM.

3. Ignition ON, test for 4.8–5.2 volts between the ECM side of the 5 volt reference circuit and ground.

a. If less than the specified range, test the 5 volt reference circuit for an open/high resistance or short to ground. If the circuit tests normal, replace the ECM.

b. If greater than the specified range, test the 5 volt reference circuit for a short to voltage. If the circuit tests normal, replace the ECM.

4. Ignition ON, test for 4.8–5.2 volts between the signal circuit and ground.

a. If less than the specified range, test the affected signal circuit for an open/high resistance or short to ground. If the circuit tests normal, replace the ECM.

b. If greater than the specified range, test the affected signal circuit for a short to voltage. If the circuit tests normal, replace the ECM.

5. Ignition ON, using a jumper wire connected to ground, momentarily touch the CMP sensor signal circuit repeatedly. The applicable CMP active counter parameter should increment.

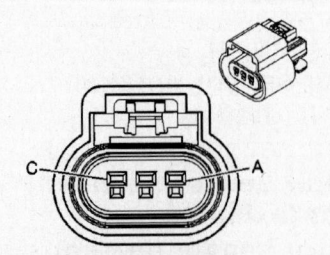

A. 5-Volt Reference 1
B. Low Reference
C. CMP Sensor Signal

22116_GMG6_G0111

Fig. 114 Camshaft Position (CMP) Sensor electrical connector

a. If the CMP active counter does not increment, replace the ECM.

6. If the circuits test normal, replace the CMP sensor.

CRANKSHAFT POSITION (CKP) SENSOR

LOCATION

2.4L Engine

The Crankshaft Position (CKP) sensor is mounted to the rear of the engine block, and above the starter motor.

3.5L, 3.6L and 3.9L Engines

The Crankshaft Position (CKP) sensor is located under right exhaust manifold in the engine block.

OPERATION

The CKP sensor circuits consist of an engine control module (ECM) supplied 5-volt reference circuit, low reference circuit and an output signal circuit. The CKP sensor is an internally magnetic biased digital output integrated circuit sensing device. The sensor detects magnetic flux changes of the teeth and slots of a 58-tooth reluctor wheel on the crankshaft. Each tooth on the reluctor wheel is spaced at 60-tooth spacing, with 2 missing teeth for the reference gap. The CKP sensor produces an ON/OFF DC voltage of varying frequency, with 58 output pulses per crankshaft revolution. The frequency of the CKP sensor output depends on the velocity of the crankshaft. The CKP sensor sends a digital signal, which represents an image of the crankshaft reluctor wheel, to the ECM as each tooth on the wheel rotates past the CKP sensor. The ECM uses each CKP signal pulse to determine crankshaft speed and decodes the crankshaft reluctor wheel reference gap to identify crankshaft position. This information is then used to determine the optimum ignition and injection points of the engine. The ECM also uses CKP sensor output information to determine the camshaft relative position to the crankshaft, to control camshaft phasing, and to detect cylinder misfire.

REMOVAL & INSTALLATION

2.4L Engine

1. Disconnect the negative battery cable.

2. Disconnect the CKP sensor electrical connector.

3. Remove the oil level indicator tube.

4. Remove the positive battery cable nut from the starter solenoid.

5. Remove the positive battery cable from the starter solenoid.

6. Remove Starter motor.

7. Remove the CKP sensor bolt

8. Remove the CKP sensor.

To install:

9. Lubricate the CKP sensor O-ring seal with clean engine oil.

10. Install the CKP sensor.

11. Install the CKP sensor bolt and tighten to 89 inch. lbs. (10 Nm).

12. Ensure that the engine harness terminal is still installed on the starter solenoid.

13. Install starter motor.

14. Install the positive battery cable to the starter solenoid.

15. Install the positive battery cable nut to the starter solenoid and tighten to 89 inch. lbs. (10 Nm).

16. Connect the CKP sensor electrical connector (3).

17. Install the oil level indicator tube.

18. Connect the negative battery cable.

3.5L Engine

1. Raise and support the vehicle.

2. Disconnect the CKP sensor electrical connector.

3. Remove the CKP sensor bolt.

4. Remove the CKP sensor.

➡**Inspect for wear, cracks, or leakage if the sensor is not being replaced.**

To install:

5. Lubricate the O-ring with clean engine oil before installation and replace the O-ring if necessary.

6. Install the CKP sensor.

7. Install the CKP sensor bolt and tighten to 97 inch. lbs. (11 Nm).

8. Connect the CKP sensor electrical connector.

9. Lower the vehicle.

10. Perform the CKP system variation learn procedure.

3.6L Engine

1. Remove the exhaust manifold lower heat shield.

2. Disconnect the engine wiring harness electrical connector from the CKP.

3. Remove the crankshaft sensor bolt.

4. Remove the crankshaft sensor.

To install:

5. Install the crankshaft position sensor.

6. Install the crankshaft position sensor bolt and tighten to 89 inch. lbs. (10 Nm).

7. Connect the engine wiring harness electrical connector (2) to the CKP sensor.

8. Install the exhaust manifold lower heat shield.

3.9L Engine

1. Raise and support the vehicle.

2. Disconnect the CKP sensor electrical connector.

3. Remove the CKP sensor stud.

4. Remove the CKP sensor.

To install:

5. Lubricate the CKP sensor O-ring with clean engine oil.

6. Install the CKP sensor.

7. Install the CKP sensor stud and tighten to 89 inch. lbs. (10 Nm).

8. Connect the CKP sensor electrical connector.

9. Lower the vehicle.

TESTING

See Figure 115.

1. Disconnect the CKP sensor connector.

2. Test for less than 1 ohm of resistance between low reference circuit and ground.

a. If greater than the specified value, test the low reference circuit for an open/high resistance. If the circuit tests normal, replace the ECM.

3. Ignition ON, test for 4.8–5.2 volts between the 5 volt reference circuit and ground.

a. If less than the specified range, test the 5 volt reference circuit for an open/high resistance or short to ground. If the circuit tests normal, replace the ECM.

b. If greater than the specified range, test the 5volt reference circuit for a short to voltage. If the circuit tests normal, replace the ECM.

4. Ignition ON, test for 4.8–5.2 volts between the signal circuit and ground.

a. If less than the specified range, test the signal circuit for an open/high resistance or short to ground. If the circuit tests normal, replace the ECM.

b. If greater than the specified range, test the signal circuit for a short to voltage. If the circuit tests normal, replace the ECM.

5. Ignition ON, using a jumper wire connected to ground, momentarily touch the CKP sensor signal circuit repeatedly. The CKP Active Counter parameter should increment

a. If the CKP Active Counter parameter does not increment, replace the ECM.

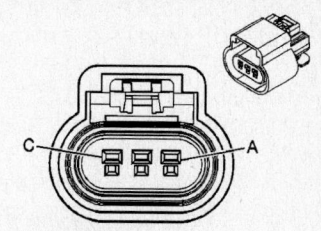

A. 5-Volt Reference 2
B. Low Reference
C. Medium Resolution Engine
Speed Signal

22116_GMG6_G0112

Fig. 115 Crankshaft Position (CKP) Sensor electrical connector

ELECTRONIC CONTROL MODULE (ECM)

LOCATION

The Engine Control Module (ECM) is located on the left side of engine compartment. It is mounted on the front of the battery box.

OPERATION

The Engine Control Module (ECM) can supply 5 volts or 12 volts to the various sensors or switches. This is done through pull-up resistors to the regulated power supplies within the ECM. In some cases, even an ordinary shop voltmeter will not give an accurate reading because the resistance is too low. Therefore, a DMM with at least 10 mega ohms input impedance is required in order to ensure accurate voltage readings.

The ECM controls the output circuits by controlling the ground or the power feed circuit through the transistors or a device called an output driver module.

REMOVAL & INSTALLATION

Turn the ignition OFF when installing or removing the Engine Control Module (ECM) connectors and disconnecting or reconnecting the power to the control module (battery cable, Powertrain Control Module (PCM)/ engine control module (ECM)/transaxle control module (TCM) pigtail, control module fuse, jumper cables, etc.) in order to prevent internal control module damage.

Control module damage may result when the metal case contacts battery voltage. DO NOT contact the control module metal case with battery voltage when servicing a control module, using battery booster cables, or when charging the vehicle battery.

In order to prevent any possible electrostatic discharge damage to the control module, do not touch the connector pins or the soldered components on the circuit board.

Remove any debris from around the control module connector surfaces before servicing the control module. Inspect the control module connector gaskets when diagnosing or replacing the control module. Ensure that the gaskets are installed correctly. The gaskets prevent contaminant intrusion into the control module.

The replacement control module must be programmed. It is necessary to record the remaining engine oil life. If the replacement module is not programmed with the remaining engine oil life, the engine oil life will default to 100 percent. If the replacement module is not programmed with the remaining engine oil life, the engine oil will need to be changed at 5 000 km (3,000 mi) from the last engine oil change.

1. Using a scan tool, retrieve the percentage of remaining engine oil. Record the remaining engine oil life.

2. Record the preset radio stations.

3. Turn the ignition OFF.

4. Disconnect the negative battery cable.

5. Disconnect the engine control module (ECM) harness connectors.

6. Release the retaining tab located in the battery box lower half using a small screwdriver or other suitable tool.

7. Remove the ECM by lifting upward after releasing the tab.

To install:

8. Slide the ECM into the bracket on the front of the battery box.

9. Push down on the ECM until the retaining tab snaps into place.

10. Connect the ECM harness connectors.

11. Connect the negative battery cable tighten to 13 ft. lbs. (17 Nm).

12. Reset the clock and preset radio stations.

13. If a NEW ECM was installed, the ECM must be programmed.

TESTING

See Figures 116 through 123.

1. Test the voltage and ground circuits to the control module for the following:
- A short
- High resistance
- An open

2. If all circuits test normal, suspect the ECM.

➡ **The replacement control module must be programmed.**

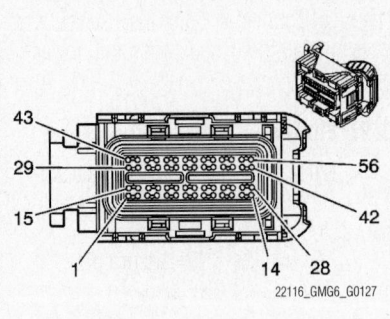

Fig. 116 Engine Control Module (ECM) connector C1 2.4L and 3.6L engines

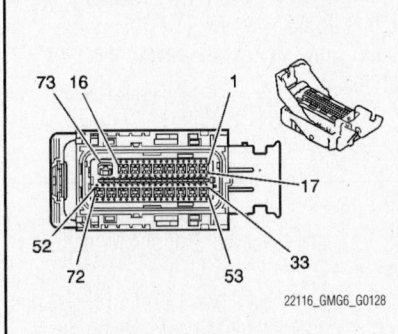

Fig. 117 Engine Control Module (ECM) connector C2 2.4L and 3.6L engines

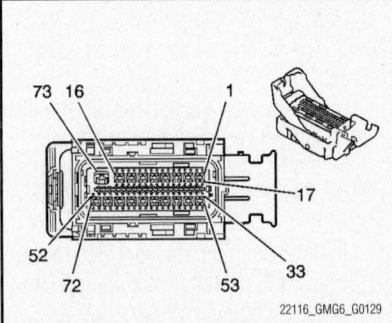

Fig. 118 Engine Control Module (ECM) connector C3 2.4L and 3.6L engines

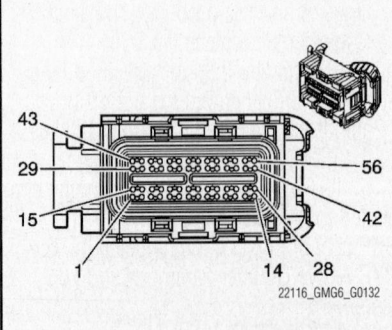

Fig. 119 Engine Control Module (ECM) connector C1 3.5L (LX9) engine 2005–06

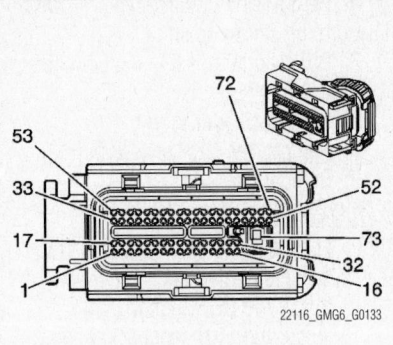

Fig. 120 Engine Control Module (ECM) connector C2 3.5L (LX9) engine 2005–06

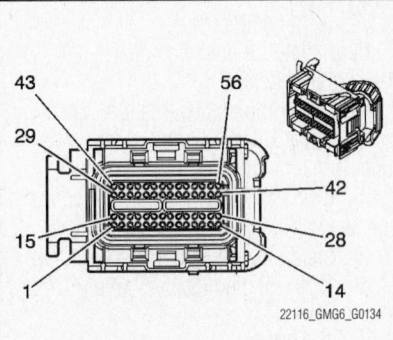

Fig. 121 Engine Control Module (ECM) connector C3 3.5L (LX9) engine 2005–06

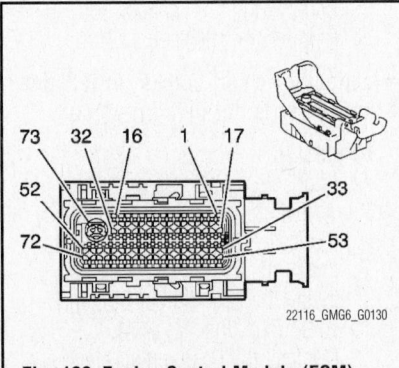

Fig. 122 Engine Control Module (ECM) connector C1 3.5L (LZ4) engine

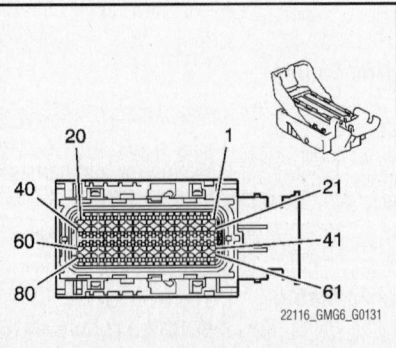

Fig. 123 Engine Control Module (ECM) connector C2 3.5L (LZ4) engine

ENGINE COOLANT TEMPERATURE (ECT) SENSOR

LOCATION

2.4L Engine

The Engine Coolant Temperature (ECT) sensor is located just to the left of the exhaust manifold in the thermostat housing.

3.5L Engine

The Engine Coolant Temperature (ECT) sensor is located below right exhaust manifold and above transaxle.

3.6L Engine

The Engine Coolant Temperature (ECT) sensor is located above right exhaust manifold in cylinder head. It is below and just to the right of the oil fill cap.

3.9L Engine

The Engine Coolant Temperature (ECT) sensor is located on the left cylinder head at the rear. It is just above the transaxle mounting bolts.

OPERATION

The ECM supplies a 5 volt signal to the engine coolant temperature sensor through a resistor in the ECM and measures the voltage. The voltage will be high when the engine is cold, and low when the engine is hot. By measuring the voltage, the ECM calculates the engine coolant temperature. Engine coolant temperature affects most systems the ECM controls.

REMOVAL & INSTALLATION

2.4L Engine

1. Partially drain the cooling system.
2. Disconnect the engine coolant temperature (ECT) sensor electrical connector.
3. Remove the ECT sensor.

To install:

➡Use a tap in order to remove any sealant residue in the sensor hole in the thermostat housing. Clean any sealant residue from the old sensor (if reusing) and apply the room temperature vulcanizing (RTV) sealant to the threads.

4. Apply sealant to the threads of the ECT sensor.
5. Install the ECT sensor and tighten to 15 ft. lbs. (20 Nm).
6. Connect the ECT sensor electrical connector.

7. Fill and bleed the cooling system as needed.

3.5L Engine

1. Partially drain the cooling system.
2. Disconnect the engine coolant temperature (ECT) sensor electrical connector.
3. Remove the ECT sensor.

➡Replacement components must be the correct part number for the application. Components requiring the use of the thread locking compound, lubricants, corrosion inhibitors, or sealants are identified in the service procedure. Some replacement components may come with these coatings already applied. Do not use these coatings on components unless specified. These coatings can affect the final torque, which may affect the operation of the component. Use the correct torque specification when installing components in order to avoid damage.

To install:

4. Coat the threads with sealer.
5. Install the ECT sensor and tighten to 15 ft. lbs. (20 Nm).
6. Connect the ECT electrical connector.
7. Fill and bleed the cooling system as needed.

3.6L Engine

1. Disconnect the engine wiring harness electrical connector (1) from the engine coolant temperature (ECT) sensor.
2. Remove the ECT sensor.

To install:

3. Install the ECT sensor and tighten to 16 ft. lbs. (22 Nm).
4. Connect the engine wiring harness electrical connector (1) to the ECT sensor.
5. Fill and bleed the cooling system as needed.

3.9L Engine

1. Drain the cooling system.
2. Remove the intake manifold cover, if necessary.
3. Disconnect the engine coolant temperature (ECT) sensor electrical connector.
4. Remove the ECT sensor.

➡Replacement components must be the correct part number for the application. Components requiring the use of the thread locking compound, lubricants, corrosion inhibitors, or sealants are identified in the service procedure. Some replacement components may come with these coatings already

applied. Do not use these coatings on components unless specified. These coatings can affect the final torque, which may affect the operation of the component. Use the correct torque specification when installing components in order to avoid damage.

To install:

5. Coat the threads of the ECT sensor with sealer.
6. Install the ECT sensor and tighten to 15 ft. lbs. (20 Nm).
7. Connect the ECT electrical connector.
8. Install the intake manifold cover, if necessary.
9. Fill and bleed the cooling system as needed.

TESTING

See Figures 124 and 125.

1. Ignition OFF, disconnect the harness connector at the ECT sensor.
2. Ignition OFF for 90 seconds, test for less than 5 ohms of resistance between the low reference circuit terminal A and ground.
   a. If greater than the specified range, test the low reference circuit for an open/high resistance. If the circuit tests normal, replace the ECM.
3. Ignition ON, verify the scan tool ECT parameter is less than -39°C (-38°F).
   a. If greater than the specified range, test the signal circuit terminal B for a short to ground. If the circuit tests normal, replace the ECM.
4. Install a 3-amp fused jumper wire between the signal circuit terminal B and the low reference circuit terminal A. Verify the scan tool ECT parameter is greater than 149°C (300°F).
5. If less than the specified range, test the signal circuit for a short to voltage or an open/high resistance. If the circuit tests normal, replace the ECM.

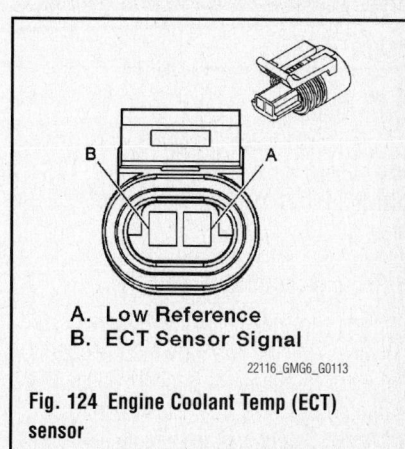

A. Low Reference
B. ECT Sensor Signal

22116_GMG6_G0113

Fig. 124 Engine Coolant Temp (ECT) sensor

Temperature Versus Resistance

°C	°F	OHMS
	Temperature vs Resistance Values (Approximate)	
150	302	47
140	284	60
130	266	77
120	248	100
110	230	132
100	212	177
90	194	241
80	176	332
70	158	467
60	140	667
50	122	973
45	113	1188
40	104	1459
35	95	1802
30	86	2238
25	77	2796
20	68	3520
15	59	4450
10	50	5670
5	41	7280
0	32	9420
-5	23	12300
-10	14	16180
-15	5	21450
-20	-4	28680
-30	-22	52700
-40	-40	100700

22116_GMG6_G0135

Fig. 125 Temperature versus resistance table

6. If all circuits test normal, test or replace the ECT sensor.

7. Measure and record the resistance of the ECT sensor at various ambient temperatures, then compare those measurements to the temperature versus resistance table.

HEATED OXYGEN SENSOR (HO2S)

LOCATION

2.4L Engine

The Front Heated Oxygen Sensor (HO2S) is mounted in the exhaust manifold. The rear (HO2S) is mounted in the front exhaust pipe.

3.5L, 3.6L and 3.9L Engine

The Front Heated Oxygen Sensor (HO2S)s left and right are mounted in the exhaust manifold. Bank 1 sensor 1 is mounted in the right exhaust manifold and bank 2 sensor 2 in the left manifold.

The rear Heated Oxygen Sensor (HO2S)s are mounted just behind the catalytic converters. Bank 1 sensor 2 is mounted behind right converter assembly and bank 2 sensor 2 behind left assembly.

OPERATION

The fuel control Heated Oxygen Sensors (Bank 1 HO2S 1 and Bank 2 HO2S 1) are mounted in the exhaust manifolds where they can monitor the oxygen content of the exhaust gas stream. The oxygen present in the exhaust gas reacts with the sensor to produce a voltage output. This voltage should constantly fluctuate from approximately 100mV (high oxygen content - lean mixture) to 900mV (low oxygen content - rich mixture). The heated oxygen sensor voltage can be monitored with a scan tool. By monitoring the voltage output of the oxygen sensor, the ECM can calculate what fuel mixture command to send the injectors (lean mixture-low HO2S voltage = rich command, rich mixture-high HO2S voltage = lean command).

REMOVAL & INSTALLATION

2.4L Engine

➡The oxygen sensor uses a permanently attached pigtail and connector. Do not remove the pigtail from the oxygen sensor. Damage to or removal of the pigtail connector could affect proper operation of the oxygen sensor. The use of excessive force may damage the threads in the exhaust manifold/pipe.

✳✳ WARNING

The HO2S may be difficult to remove when the engine temperature is less than 48°C (120°F).

1. Raise and support the vehicle.
2. Remove the Connector Position Assurance (CPA) retainer.
3. Disconnect the HO2S electrical connector.
4. For the front sensor remove the HO2S electrical connector clip from the thermostat housing.
5. Using the J 39194 or equivalent, remove the HO2S.

To install:

➡A special anti-seize compound is used on the HO2S threads. The compound consists of a liquid graphite and glass beads. The graphite will burn away but the glass beads will remain, making the sensor easier to remove. New or service sensors already have the compound applied to the threads. If the sensor is removed and is to be reinstalled, the threads must be coated with an anti-seize compound before reinstallation.

6. If reinstalling the old HO2S, coat the threads with anti-seize compound.
7. Using the J 39194 or equivalent, install the HO2S.
8. Tighten the HO2S to 30 ft. lbs. (41 Nm).
9. Connect the HO2S electrical connector.
10. For the front sensor install the HO2S electrical connector clip to the thermostat housing.
11. Install the CPA retainer.
12. Lower the vehicle.

When replacing the HO2S perform the following:
• A code clear with a scan tool, regardless of whether or not a DTC is set
• HO2S heater resistance learn reset with a scan tool, where available

Perform the above in order to reset the HO2S resistance learned value and avoid possible HO2S failure.

3.5L, 3.6L and 3.9L Engine

➡The oxygen sensor uses a permanently attached pigtail and connector. Do not remove the pigtail from the oxygen sensor. Damage to or removal of the pigtail connector could affect proper operation of the oxygen sensor. The use of excessive force may damage the threads in the exhaust manifold/pipe.

✳✳ WARNING

The HO2S may be difficult to remove when the engine temperature is less than 48°C (120°F).

1. Raise and support the vehicle.
2. Remove the Connector Position Assurance (CPA) retainer.
3. Disconnect the HO2S electrical connector.
4. Using the J 39194 or equivalent, remove the HO2S.

To install:

➡A special anti-seize compound is used on the HO2S threads. The compound consists of a liquid graphite and glass beads. The graphite will burn away but the glass beads will remain, making the sensor easier to remove. New or service sensors already have the compound applied to the threads. If the sensor is removed and is to be reinstalled, the threads must be coated with an anti-seize compound before reinstallation.

5. If reinstalling the old HO2S, coat the threads with anti-seize compound.
6. Using the J 39194 or equivalent, install the HO2S.
7. Tighten the HO2S to 31 ft. lbs. (42 Nm).
8. Connect the HO2S electrical connector.
9. Install the CPA retainer.
10. Lower the vehicle.
When replacing the HO2S perform the following:
• A code clear with a scan tool, regardless of whether or not a DTC is set
• HO2S heater resistance learn reset with a scan tool, where available
Perform the above in order to reset the HO2S resistance learned value and avoid possible HO2S failure.

TESTING

See Figures 126 through 131.

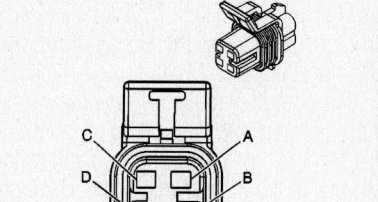
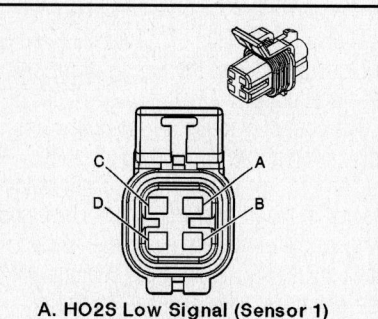

A. HO2S Low Signal (Sensor 1)
B. HO2S High Signal (Sensor 1)
C. HO2S Heater Low Control (Sensor 1)
D. Ignition 1 Voltage

22116_GMG6_G0118

Fig. 126 Front heated Oxygen Sensor (HO2S) 2.4L engine electrical connector (Sensor 1)

A. HO2S Low Signal (Sensor 2)
B. HO2S High Signal (Sensor 2)
C. HO2S Heater Low Control (Sensor 1)
D. Ignition 1 Voltage

22116_GMG6_G0119

Fig. 127 Rear heated oxygen sensor (HO2S) 2.4L engine electrical connector (Sensor 2)

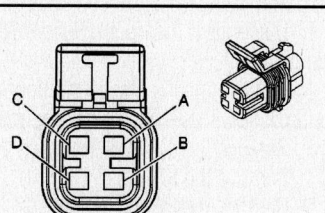

A. HO2S Low Signal (Bank 1 Sensor 1)
B. HO2S High Signal (Bank 1 Sensor 1)
C. HO2S Heater Low Control [- Bank 1 Sensor 1]
D. Ignition 1 Voltage

22116_GMG6_G0114

Fig. 128 Front heated Oxygen Sensor (HO2S) All V6 engines electrical connector (Bank 1 Sensor 1)

A. HO2S Low Signal (Bank 1 Sensor 2)
B. HO2S High Signal (Bank 1 Sensor 2)
C. HO2S Heater Low Control [Bank 2 Sensor 1]
D. Ignition 1 Voltage

22116_GMG6_G0115

Fig. 129 Rear heated oxygen sensor (HO2S) V6 All engines electrical connector (Bank 1 Sensor 2)

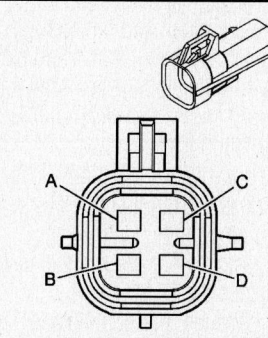
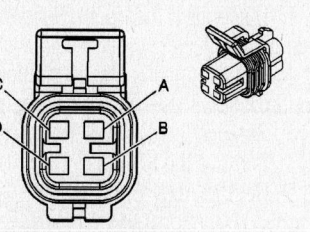

A. HO2S Low Reference (Bank 2 Sensor 1)
B. HO2S Reference Voltage (Bank 2 Sensor 1)
C. HO2S Heater Low Signal (Bank 2 Sensor 1)
D. Ignition 1 Voltage

22116_GMG6_G0116

Fig. 130 Front heated Oxygen Sensor (HO2S) V6 All engines electrical connector (Bank 2 Sensor 1)

1. Ignition OFF, disconnect the scan tool and wait 60 seconds to ensure all modules are powered down.
2. Ignition OFF, disconnect the harness connector at the appropriate HO2S.
3. Ignition OFF, measure for less than 5 ohms resistance between the appropriate HO2S low signal circuit terminal A and ground.
 a. If more than the specified range, test the appropriate HO2S low signal circuit for an open/high resistance. If the circuit tests normal, replace the ECM.
4. Ignition ON, verify the appropriate scan tool HO2S parameter is approximately 450 mV.
 a. If more than the specified value, test the appropriate HO2S high signal circuit for a short to voltage. If the circuit tests normal, replace the ECM.
 b. If less than the specified value, test the appropriate HO2S high signal circuit

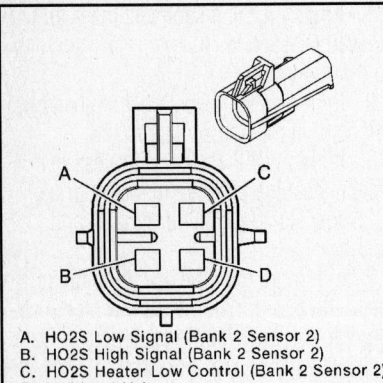

A. HO2S Low Signal (Bank 2 Sensor 2)
B. HO2S High Signal (Bank 2 Sensor 2)
C. HO2S Heater Low Control (Bank 2 Sensor 2)
D. Ignition 1 Voltage

22116_GMG6_G0117

Fig. 131 Rear heated oxygen sensor (HO2S) V6 All engines electrical connector (Bank 2 Sensor 2)

for a short to ground. If the circuit tests normal, replace the ECM.

5. Ignition ON, install a 3A fused jumper wire at the HO2S high signal circuit terminal B. Toggle the jumper wire between the HO2S low signal circuit terminal A and battery voltage. Verify the appropriate scan tool HO2S parameter toggles between 0 mV and approximately 1,000 mV

a. If the appropriate scan tool HO2S parameter does not toggle correctly, test the HO2S high signal circuit for an open/high resistance. If the circuits test normal, replace the ECM.

6. If all circuits test normal, replace the appropriate HO2S.

KNOCK SENSOR (KS)

LOCATION

2.4L Engine

The Knock Sensor (KS) is mounted in the engine block above the starter motor.

3.5L, 3.6L and 3.9L Engine

The 3.5L, 3.6L and 3.9L engine has 2 Knock Sensors (KS) that are located on both sides of engine block.

OPERATION

The Knock Sensor (KS) system enables the control module to control the ignition timing for the best possible performance while protecting the engine from potentially damaging levels of detonation. The control module uses the KS system to test for abnormal engine noise that may indicate detonation, also known as spark knock.

The KS system uses one or 2 flat response 2-wire sensors. The sensor uses piezo-electric crystal technology that pro-

duces an AC voltage signal of varying amplitude and frequency based on the engine vibration or noise level. The amplitude and frequency are dependent upon the level of knock that the KS detects. The control module receives the KS signal through the signal circuit.

The control module learns a minimum noise level, or background noise, at idle from the KS and uses calibrated values for the rest of the RPM range. The control module uses the minimum noise level to calculate a noise channel. normal KS signal will ride within the noise channel. As engine speed and load change, the noise channel upper and lower parameters will change to accommodate the normal KS signal, keeping the signal within the channel. In order to determine which cylinders are knocking, the control module only uses KS signal information when each cylinder is near top dead center (TDC) of the firing stroke. If knock is present, the signal will range outside of the noise channel.

If the control module has determined that knock is present, it will retard the ignition timing to attempt to eliminate the knock. The control module will always try to work back to a zero compensation level, or no spark retard. An abnormal KS signal will stay outside of the noise channel or will not be present. KS diagnostics are calibrated to detect faults with the KS circuitry inside the control module, the KS wiring, or the KS voltage output. Some diagnostics are also calibrated to detect constant noise from an outside influence such as a loose/damaged component or excessive engine mechanical noise.

REMOVAL & INSTALLATION

2.4L Engine

1. Disconnect the Knock Sensor (KS) electrical connector.
2. Remove the KS electrical connector clip from the oil level indicator tube bracket.
3. Remove the oil level indicator tube.
4. Remove the KS bolt.
5. Remove the KS.

To install:

➡**Rotate the pigtail 90 degrees from vertical before securing the fastener.**

6. Install the KS.
7. Install the KS bolt and tighten to 18 ft. lbs. (25 Nm).
8. Connect the KS electrical connector.
9. Install the oil level indicator tube.
10. Install the KS electrical connector clip to the oil level indicator tube bracket.

3.5L Engine

1. Raise and support the vehicle.
2. Disconnect the engine wiring harness electrical connector from the Knock Sensor (KS).
3. Remove the knock sensor bolt and sensor.

To install:

4. Position the knock sensor to the engine block and install the knock sensor bolt. Tighten the bolt to 18 ft. lbs. (25 Nm).
5. Connect the engine wiring harness electrical connector to the knock sensor.
6. Lower the vehicle

3.6L Engine

1. Remove the exhaust manifold lower heat shield. Bank 1 knock sensor only.
2. Disconnect the engine wiring harness electrical connector from the knock sensor.
3. Loosen the knock sensor bolt and remove the knock sensor.

To install:

4. Position the knock sensor and tighten the knock sensor bolt to 17 ft. (23 Nm).
5. Connect the engine wiring harness electrical connector to the bank 1 knock sensor.
6. Install the exhaust manifold lower heat shield. Bank 1 knock sensor only.

3.9L Engine

1. Raise and support the vehicle.
2. Disconnect the knock sensor electrical connector.
3. Loosen and remove the knock sensor.

To install:

4. Install and tighten the knock sensor and tighten the bolt to 18 ft. lbs. (25 Nm).
5. Connect the knock sensor electrical connector.
6. Lower the vehicle.

TESTING

See Figures 132 through 134.

1. Connect the Digital Multimeter (DMM) from the Knock Sensor (KS) signal circuit terminal A to the KS signal circuit terminal B on the sensor side of the KS harness connector.
2. Set the DMM to the 400 mV AC hertz scale and wait for the DMM to stabilize at 0 Hz.
3. Tap on the engine block with a non-metallic object near the KS while observing the signal indicated on the DMM.
4. The DMM should display a fluctuat-

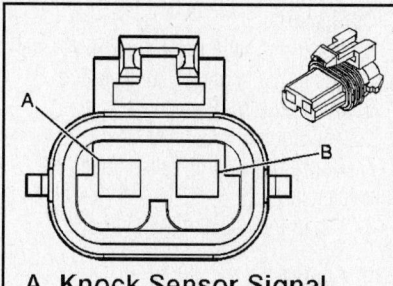

A. Knock Sensor Signal
B. Knock Sensor Signal B

22116_GMG6_G0120

Fig. 132 Knock sensor electrical connector 2.4L engine

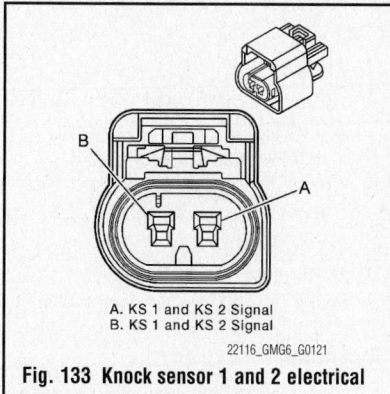

A. KS 1 and KS 2 Signal
B. KS 1 and KS 2 Signal

22116_GMG6_G0121

Fig. 133 Knock sensor 1 and 2 electrical connector 3.5L–3.9L engines

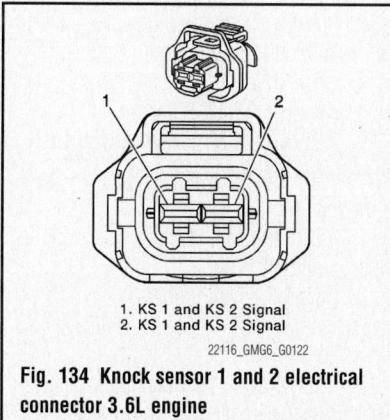

1. KS 1 and KS 2 Signal
2. KS 1 and KS 2 Signal

22116_GMG6_G0122

Fig. 134 Knock sensor 1 and 2 electrical connector 3.6L engine

ing frequency while tapping on the engine block.

5. If the DMM does not display a fluctuating frequency suspect faulty knock sensor.

MASS AIR FLOW (MAF) SENSOR

LOCATION

2.4L Engine

The Mass Air Flow (MAF) sensor/Intake Air Temperature (IAT) sensor is located at the end of the air cleaner box inlet tube.

3.5L & 3.9L Engines

The Mass Air Flow (MAF) sensor/Intake Air Temperature (IAT) sensor is located in the air cleaner intake duct fresh air tube.

3.6L Engine

The Mass Air Flow (MAF) sensor/Intake Air Temperature (IAT) sensor is located between air cleaner box and the fresh air intake tube.

OPERATION

The Mass Air Flow (MAF) sensor is integrated with the Intake Air Temperature (IAT) sensor. The MAF sensor is an air flow meter that measures the amount of air entering the engine. The engine control module (ECM) uses the MAF sensor signal to provide the correct fuel delivery for all engine speeds and loads. A small quantity of air entering the engine indicates a deceleration or idle condition. A large quantity of air entering the engine indicates an acceleration or high load condition. The MAF/IAT sensor has an ignition 1 voltage circuit, a ground circuit, a MAF sensor signal circuit, and IAT sensor signal circuit, and a low reference circuit.

The ECM applies 5 volts to the MAF sensor on the MAF sensor signal circuit. The sensor uses the voltage to produce a frequency based on the inlet air flow through the sensor bore. The frequency varies in a range of near 2,000 Hertz at idle to near 10,000 Hertz at maximum engine load.

REMOVAL & INSTALLATION

2.4L Engine

1. Disconnect the Mass Air Flow (MAF) / Intake Air Temperature (IAT) sensor electrical connector.
2. Using a tamper proof TORX®, remove the MAF/IAT sensor screws.
3. Remove the MAF/IAT sensor.

To install:

4. Install the MAF/IAT sensor.
5. Using a tamper proof TORX®, install the MAF/IAT sensor screws and tighten to 5 inch. lbs. (6 Nm).
6. Connect the MAF/IAT sensor electrical connector.

3.5L & 3.9L Engines

1. Remove the Positive Crankcase Ventilation (PCV) fresh air tube from the air cleaner intake duct.
2. Disconnect the Mass Air Flow (MAF) sensor electrical connector.
3. Loosen the clamps and remove the air cleaner intake duct with the MAF sensor

from the throttle body and the air cleaner housing cover.
4. Loosen the clamp and remove the MAF sensor from the air cleaner intake duct.

To install:

5. Install the MAF sensor to the air cleaner intake duct.
6. Tighten the clamp to 18 inch. lbs. (2 Nm),
7. Connect the MAF sensor electrical connector.
8. Install the PCV fresh air tube to the air cleaner intake duct.
9. Start and idle the engine.
10. Inspect the air intake duct for leaks.

3.6L Engine

1. Remove the air cleaner outlet duct.
2. Disconnect the engine wiring harness electrical connector from the Mass Airflow (MAF) / Intake Air Temperature (IAT) sensor.
3. Remove the MAF / IAT sensor screws.
4. Remove the MAF / IAT sensor.
5. Remove and discard the MAF / IAT sensor seal.

To install:

6. Install a new MAF / IAT sensor seal.
7. Install the MAF / IAT sensor.
8. Install the MAF / IAT sensor screws.
9. Tighten the mounting screws to 35 inch. lbs. (4 Nm).
10. Connect the engine wiring harness electrical connector to the MAF/IAT sensor.
11. Install the air cleaner outlet duct.

TESTING

See Figures 135 and 136.

1. Verify the integrity of the entire air induction system by inspecting for the following conditions:
   - Any damaged components
   - Loose or improper installation
   - An air flow restriction
   - Any vacuum leaks
   - Water intrusion
   - In cold climates, inspect for any snow or ice buildup
2. Ignition OFF, disconnect the MAF/IAT harness connector at the MAF/IAT sensor.
3. Ignition OFF for 90 seconds, test for less than 5.0 ohms of resistance between the ground circuit terminal C and ground.
   a. If greater than the specified range, test the ground circuit for an open/high resistance.
4. Ignition ON, verify that a test lamp illuminates between the ignition circuit terminal B and ground.

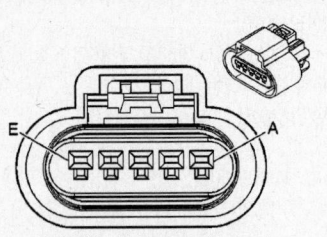

A. MAF Sensor Signal
B. Ground
C. Ignition 1 Voltage
D. Low Reference
E. IAT Sensor Signal

22116_GMG6_G0124

Fig. 135 Mass Air Flow (MAF) Sensor 2.4L engine electrical connector

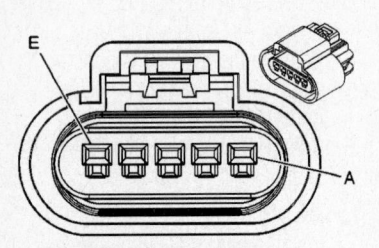

A. MAF Sensor Signal
B. Ignition 1 Voltage
C. Ground
D. IAT Sensor Signal
E. Low Reference

22116_GMG6_G0123

Fig. 136 Mass Air Flow (MAF) Sensor 3.5L, 3.6L, 3.9L engines electrical connector

a. If the test lamp does not illuminate, test the ignition circuit for a short to ground or an open/high resistance.

5. Ignition ON, test for 4.8-5.2 volts between the signal circuit terminal A and ground.

a. If less than the specified range, test the signal circuit for a short to ground or an open/high resistance. If the circuit tests normal, replace the ECM.

b. If greater than the specified range, test the signal circuit for a short to voltage. If the circuit tests normal, replace the ECM.

MANIFOLD ABSOLUTE PRESSURE (MAP) SENSOR

LOCATION

2.4L Engine

The Manifold Absolute Pressure (MAP) sensor is mounted to the intake manifold just below throttle body.

3.5L Engine

The Manifold Absolute Pressure (MAP) sensor is mounted to the intake manifold in front of ignition control module.

3.6L Engine

The Manifold Absolute Pressure (MAP) sensor is mounted to the intake manifold to the rear of throttle body.

The Manifold Absolute Pressure (MAP) sensor is mounted in the lower intake manifold in the center, just below the upper intake manifold

OPERATION

The MAP sensor has a 5-volt reference circuit, a low reference circuit, and a signal circuit. The control module supplies 5 volts to the MAP sensor on a 5-volt reference circuit, and provides a ground on a low reference circuit. The MAP sensor provides a voltage signal to the control module on a signal circuit relative to the intake manifold pressure changes.

REMOVAL & INSTALLATION

2.4L Engine

1. Remove the air cleaner outlet.
2. Disconnect the Electronic Throttle Control (ETC) electrical connector.
3. Remove the throttle body bolts.
4. Remove the throttle body from the intake manifold.
5. Disconnect the Manifold Absolute Pressure (MAP) sensor electrical connector.
6. Remove the MAP sensor and the MAP sensor port seal if it is still retained in the intake manifold.

To install:

7. Install the MAP sensor with the port seal into the intake manifold.
8. Connect the MAP sensor electrical connector.
9. Inspect the throttle body gasket and replace if necessary.
10. Position the throttle body to the intake manifold.
11. Install the throttle body bolts and tighten to 89 inch. lbs. (10 Nm).

3.5L Engine

1. Remove the intake manifold cover.
2. Disconnect the Manifold Absolute Pressure (MAP) sensor electrical connector.
3. Remove the MAP sensor attaching screw.
4. Remove the MAP sensor and MAP sensor seal from the upper intake manifold.

To install:

5. Install the MAP sensor and MAP sensor seal into the upper intake manifold.
6. Install the MAP sensor attaching screw and tighten to 57 inch. lbs. (6.5 Nm).
7. Connect the MAP sensor electrical connector.
8. Install the intake manifold cover.

3.6L Engine

1. Remove the fuel injector sight shield.
2. Disconnect the engine wiring harness electrical connector from the Manifold Absolute Pressure (MAP) sensor.
3. Remove the MAP sensor bolt and sensor.

To install:

4. Lubricate the MAP sensor O-ring seal with clean engine oil.
5. Install the MAP sensor and bolt.
6. Tighten the mounting bolt to 89 inch. lbs. (10 Nm).
7. Connect the engine wiring harness electrical connector to the MAP sensor.
8. Install the fuel injector sight shield.

3.9L Engine

1. Remove the intake manifold cover.
2. Disconnect the Manifold Absolute Pressure (MAP) sensor electrical connector.
3. Remove the spark plug wire clip from the intake manifold bracket, if necessary.
4. Remove the MAP sensor bolt.
5. Remove the MAP sensor.
6. Remove the MAP sensor seal from the upper intake manifold.

To install:

7. Install the MAP sensor seal into the upper intake manifold.
8. Install the MAP sensor.
9. Install the MAP sensor bolt and tighten to 89 inch. lbs. (10 Nm).
10. If required, install the spark plug wire clip to the intake manifold bracket.
11. Connect the MAP sensor electrical connector.
12. Install the intake manifold cover.

TESTING

See Figures 137 and 138.

1. Ignition OFF, disconnect the harness connector at the MAP sensor.
2. Ignition OFF for 90 seconds, test for less than 5 ohms of resistance between the low reference circuit terminal 2 and ground.

a. If greater than the specified range, test the low reference circuit for an open/high resistance. If the circuit tests normal, replace the ECM.

3. Ignition ON, test for 4.8-5.2 volts between the 5-volt reference circuit terminal 1 and ground.

   a. If less than the specified range, test the 5-volt reference circuit for a short to ground or an open/high resistance. If the circuit tests normal, replace the ECM.

   b. If greater than the specified range, test the 5-volt reference circuit for a short to voltage. If the circuit tests normal, replace the ECM.

4. Verify the scan tool MAP Sensor parameter is less than 2 kPa.

   a. If greater than the specified range, test the signal circuit terminal 3 for a short to voltage. If the circuit tests normal, replace the ECM.

5. Install a 3A fused jumper wire between the signal circuit terminal 3 and the 5-volt reference circuit terminal 1. Verify the scan tool MAP parameter is greater than 126 kPa.

   a. If less than the specified range, test the signal circuit for short to ground or an open/high resistance. If the circuit tests normal, replace the ECM.

6. If all circuits test normal, test or replace the MAP sensor.

To test (MAP) sensor observe the following procedure:

- Ignition OFF, remove the MAP sensor.
- Install a 3A fused jumper wire between the 5-volt reference circuit terminal 1 and the corresponding terminal of the MAP sensor.
- Install a jumper wire between the low reference circuit terminal 2 of the MAP sensor and ground.
- Install a jumper wire at terminal 3 of the MAP sensor.
- Connect a DMM between the jumper wire from terminal 3 of the MAP sensor and ground.
- Ignition ON, with a vacuum pump slowly apply vacuum to the sensor while

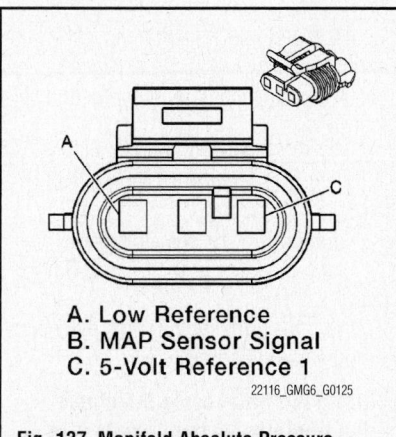

A. Low Reference
B. MAP Sensor Signal
C. 5-Volt Reference 1

22116_GMG6_G0125

Fig. 137 Manifold Absolute Pressure (MAP) Sensor 2.4L, 3.5L, 3.9L engines electrical connector

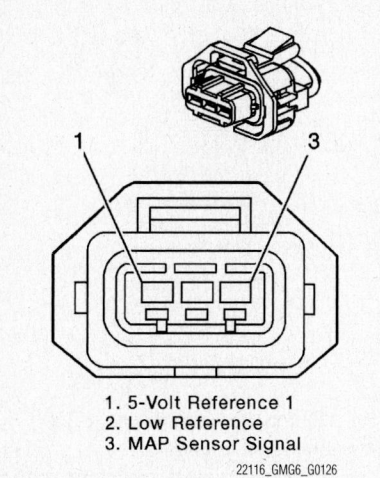

1. 5-Volt Reference 1
2. Low Reference
3. MAP Sensor Signal

22116_GMG6_G0126

Fig. 138 Manifold Absolute Pressure (MAP) Sensor 3.6L engine electrical connector

observing the voltage on the DMM. The voltage should vary between 0-5.2 volts, without any spikes or dropouts.

- If the voltage reading is erratic, replace the MAP sensor.

THROTTLE POSITION SENSOR (TPS)

LOCATION

The TP sensors 1 and 2 are located within the throttle body assembly.

OPERATION

The Throttle Actuator Control (TAC) system uses two Throttle Position (TP) sensors to monitor the throttle position. The TP sensors 1 and 2 are located within the throttle body assembly. Each sensor has the following circuits:

- A 5-volt reference circuit
- A low reference circuit
- A signal circuit

Two processors are also used to monitor the TAC system data. Both processors are located within the engine control module (ECM). Each signal circuit provides both processors with a signal voltage proportional to throttle plate movement. Both processors monitor each other's data to verify that the indicated TP calculation is correct.

REMOVAL & INSTALLATION

2.4L Engine

➡Do not use solvent of any type when cleaning the gasket surfaces on the intake manifold and the throttle body assembly, as damage to the gasket surfaces and throttle body assembly

may result. Use care in cleaning the gasket surfaces on the intake manifold and the throttle body assembly, as sharp tools may damage the gasket surfaces.

1. Remove the air cleaner outlet.
2. Disconnect the Electronic Throttle Control (ETC) electrical connector.
3. Remove the throttle body bolts.
4. Remove the throttle body from the intake manifold.

To install:

➡Inspect the throttle body gasket and replace if necessary.

5. Position the throttle body to the intake manifold.
6. Install the throttle body bolts and tighten to 89 inch. lbs. (10 Nm).
7. Connect the ETC electrical connector.
8. Install the air cleaner outlet.

3.5L Engine

1. Remove the air cleaner outlet duct.
2. Disconnect the Electronic Throttle Control (ETC) electrical connector.
3. Remove the heater pipe nut at the throttle body.
4. Remove the nuts and the bolts from the throttle body.
5. Remove the throttle body assembly.
6. Remove the throttle body gasket.

➡Do not use solvent of any type when cleaning the gasket surfaces on the intake manifold and the throttle body assembly, as damage to the gasket surfaces and throttle body assembly may result. Use care in cleaning the gasket surfaces on the intake manifold and the throttle body assembly, as sharp tools may damage the gasket surfaces.

7. Clean and inspect the throttle body gasket mating surfaces.

To install:

8. Install a new gasket, if necessary.
9. Install the throttle body assembly.
10. Install the throttle body nuts and the bolts, tighten to 89 inch. lbs.(10 Nm).
11. Install the heater pipe nut to the throttle body and tighten to 18 ft. lbs. (25 Nm).
12. Connect the ETC electrical connector.
13. Install the air cleaner outlet duct.
14. Perform the Throttle Learn Procedure

3.6L Engine

1. Remove the air cleaner outlet duct.
2. Disconnect the engine wiring harness electrical connector (2) from the Electronic Throttle Control (ETC).

3. Remove the throttle body bolts.

4. Remove the throttle body and gasket. Discard the gasket.

To install:

5. Position a new throttle body gasket to the upper intake manifold.

6. Position the throttle body to the upper intake manifold.

7. Install the throttle body bolts and tighten to 89 inch. lbs. (10 Nm).

8. Connect the engine wiring harness electrical connector to the ETC.

9. Install the air cleaner outlet duct.

10. Perform the Throttle Learn Procedure.

3.9L Engine

➡Do not use solvent of any type when cleaning the gasket surfaces on the intake manifold and the throttle body assembly, as damage to the gasket surfaces and throttle body assembly may result. Use care in cleaning the gasket surfaces on the intake manifold and the throttle body assembly, as sharp tools may damage the gasket surfaces.

1. Remove the intake manifold cover.

2. Remove the air cleaner outlet duct

3. Disconnect the Electronic Throttle Control (ETC) electrical connector.

4. Remove the heater inlet and outlet pipe nuts.

5. Remove the heater inlet and outlet pipe bracket from the throttle body studs. Reposition the pipes.

6. Remove the throttle body bolts/studs.

7. Remove the throttle body.

8. Remove the throttle body gasket.

To install:

9. Install a new gasket, if necessary.

10. Install the throttle body.

11. Install the throttle body bolts and studs.

12. Tighten the bolts and studs, tighten to 89 inch. lbs. (10 Nm).

13. Position the heater inlet and outlet pipes and install the pipe bracket to the throttle body studs.

14. Install the heater inlet and outlet pipe nuts and tighten to 89inch. lbs. (10 Nm).

15. Connect the ETC electrical connector.

16. Install the air cleaner outlet duct.

17. Install the intake manifold cover.

18. Perform the Throttle Learn Procedure.

TESTING

See Figures 139 and 140.

1. Ignition OFF, disconnect the harness connector at the throttle body.

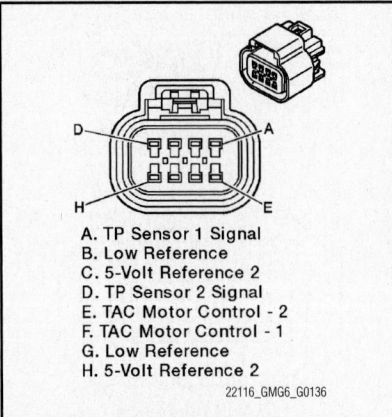

A. TP Sensor 1 Signal
B. Low Reference
C. 5-Volt Reference 2
D. TP Sensor 2 Signal
E. TAC Motor Control - 2
F. TAC Motor Control - 1
G. Low Reference
H. 5-Volt Reference 2

22116_GMG6_G0136

Fig. 139 Throttle Actuator Control (TAC) connector—2.4L engine

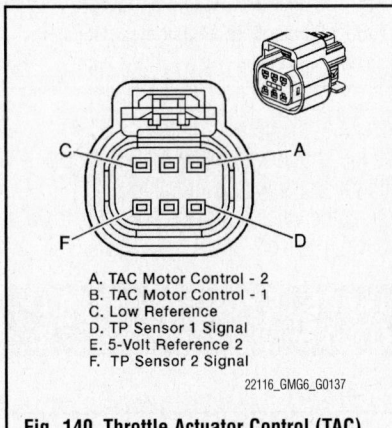

A. TAC Motor Control - 2
B. TAC Motor Control - 1
C. Low Reference
D. TP Sensor 1 Signal
E. 5-Volt Reference 2
F. TP Sensor 2 Signal

22116_GMG6_G0137

Fig. 140 Throttle Actuator Control (TAC) connector—3.5L, 3.6L and 3.9L engines

2. Ignition OFF for 90 seconds, test for less than 5 ohms of resistance between the low reference circuit terminal C and ground.

a. If greater than 5 ohms, test the low reference circuit for an open/high resistance. If the circuit tests normal, replace the ECM.

3. Ignition ON, test for 4.8-5.2 volts between 5-volt reference circuit terminal E and ground.

a. If less than 4.8 volts, test 5-volt reference circuit for a short to ground or an open / high resistance. If the circuit tests normal, replace the ECM.

b. If greater than 5.2 volts, test the 5-volt reference circuit for a short to voltage. If the circuit tests normal, replace the ECM.

4. Verify the scan tool TP sensor 1 voltage is less than 0.1 volt.

a. If greater than 0.1 volt, test the signal circuit terminal D for a short to voltage. If the circuit tests normal, replace the ECM.

5. Verify the scan tool TP sensor 2 voltage is greater than 4.8 volts.

a. If less than 4.8 volts, test the signal circuit for a short to ground. If the circuit tests normal, replace the ECM.

6. Install a 3A fused jumper wire between the signal circuit terminal D and the 5-volt reference circuit terminal E of the TP sensor 1. Verify the TP sensor 1 voltage is greater than 4.8 volts.

a. If less than 4.8 volts, test the TP sensor 1 signal circuit for a short to ground or an open/high resistance. If the circuit tests normal, replace the ECM.

7. Install a 3A fused jumper wire between the signal circuit terminal F and the low reference circuit terminal C of the TP sensor 2. Verify that the TP sensor 2 voltage is less than 0.1 volt

a. If greater than 1.0 volt, test the TP sensor 2 signal circuit for a short to voltage or an open/high resistance. If the circuit tests normal, replace the ECM.

8. Ignition OFF for 90 seconds, disconnect the harness connector at the ECM.

9. Test for less than 5 ohms of resistance on all TP sensor circuits between the following terminals:

a. ECM C2 signal circuit terminal 65 to TP terminal D

b. ECM C2 signal circuit terminal 63 to TP terminal F

c. ECM C2 5-volt reference circuit terminal 3 to terminal E

10. If greater than 5 ohms, repair the affected circuit for open/high resistance.

11. Test for infinite resistance between TP sensor 1 signal circuit terminal D and TP sensor signal circuit terminal F.

a. If less than infinite resistance, repair the short between TP sensor 1 signal circuit and TP sensor 2 signal circuit.

12. If all circuits test normal, replace the throttle body.

THROTTLE LEARN PROCEDURE

➡Do NOT perform this procedure if DTCs are set.

1. Start and idle the engine in PARK for 3 minutes.

2. With a scan tool, monitor desired and actual RPM.

3. The ECM will start to learn the new idle cells and Desired RPM should start to decrease.

4. Ignition OFF for 60 seconds.

5. Start and idle the engine in PARK for 3 minutes.

6. After the 3 minute run time the engine should be idling normal.

➡During the drive cycle the check engine light may come on with idle speed DTCs. If idle speed codes are set, clear codes so the ECM can continue to learn.

- If the engine idle speed has not been learned the vehicle will need to be driven at speeds above 70 km/h (44 mph) with several decelerations and extended idles.

7. After the drive cycle, the engine should be idling normally.

- If the engine idle speed has not been learned, turn OFF the ignition for 60 seconds and repeat step 6.

8. Once the engine speed has returned to normal, clear DTCs.

VARIABLE CAMSHAFT TIMING OIL CONTROL SOLENOID

LOCATION

2.4L Engine

The Camshaft Position (CMP) actuator sensors are located under the intake manifold cover in front of the ignition coil module for cylinder 1.

3.6L Engine

See Figure 141.

The Camshaft Position (CMP) actuator sensors are located between the Camshaft Position (CMP) sensors. The exhaust (CMP) actuator sensor on each head is the only one that does not point upward.

OPERATION

The Camshaft Position (CMP) actuator system is used on both the intake and exhaust camshafts. The CMP actuator system is used for a variety of engine performance enhancements. These enhancements include lower emission output through exhaust gas recirculation (EGR) control, a wider engine torque range, improved gas mileage, and improved engine idle stability. The CMP actuator system accomplishes this by controlling the amount of intake and exhaust valve overlap.

The camshaft position (CMP) actuator system is controlled by the control module. The control module sends a pulse width modulated 12-volt signal to each CMP actuator solenoid to control the amount of engine oil flow to a camshaft actuator passage. There are 2 different passages for oil to flow through, a passage for camshaft advance and a passage for camshaft retard. The camshaft actuator is attached to each camshaft and is hydraulically operated to change the angle of each camshaft relative to crankshaft position (CKP). Engine oil pressure (EOP), viscosity, temperature, and engine oil level can affect camshaft actuator performance.

The control module calculates the optimum camshaft position through the following inputs:

- Engine speed
- Manifold absolute pressure (MAP)
- Throttle position indicated angle
- CKP
- CMP
- Engine load
- Barometric pressure (BARO)

REMOVAL & INSTALLATION

2.4L Engine

1. Remove the intake manifold cover.
2. Disconnect the engine harness electrical connectors from the Camshaft Position (CMP) actuator solenoid valves.
3. Remove the exhaust CMP actuator solenoid valve bolt and valve, if required.
4. Remove the intake (2) CMP actuator solenoid valve bolt and valve, if required.
5. Inspect the solenoid valve O-ring seals for damage, replace as necessary.

To install:

6. Lubricate the solenoid valve O-ring seals with clean engine oil.
7. Install the intake CMP actuator solenoid valves and bolts, tighten to 89 inch. lbs. (10 Nm).
8. Connect the engine harness electrical connector to the appropriate CMP actuator solenoid valves.
9. Install the intake manifold cover.

3.6L Engine

Right Side

1. Remove the air cleaner assembly.
2. For Intake actuator sensor remove the Air Conditioning (A/C) line push pin retainer and reposition the line out of the way.
3. Disconnect the engine wiring harness electrical connector from the bank 1 exhaust camshaft position (CMP) actuator solenoid valve.
4. Remove the CMP actuator solenoid valve bolt.
5. Remove the CMP actuator solenoid valve.
6. Inspect the CMP actuator solenoid valve seal and replace as necessary.

To install:

7. Inspect the CMP actuator solenoid valve seal for damage. Replace the seal if necessary.
8. Install the CMP actuator solenoid valve.
9. Install the CMP actuator solenoid valve bolt and tighten to 89 inch. lbs. (10 Nm).
10. Connect the engine wiring harness electrical connector to the bank 1 exhaust CMP actuator solenoid valve.
11. For Intake actuator sensor install the

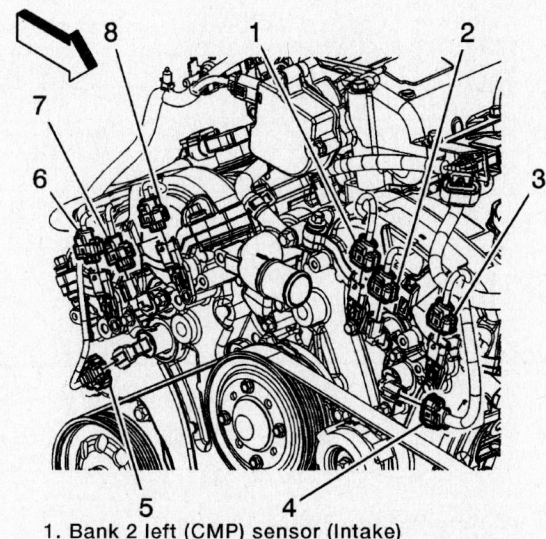

1. Bank 2 left (CMP) sensor (Intake)
2. Bank 2 left (CMP) actuator sensor (Intake)
3. Bank 2 left (CMP) sensor (Exhaust)
4. Bank 2 left (CMP) actuator sensor (Exhaust)
5. Bank 1 right (CMP) actuator sensor (Exhaust)
6. Bank 1 right (CMP) sensor (exhaust)
7. Bank 1 right (CMP) actuator sensor (Intake)
8. Bank 1 right (CMP) sensor (Intake)

22116_GMG6_G0138

Fig. 141 Camshaft Position (CMP) sensors and actuator sensors location view—3.6L engine

Air Conditioning (A/C) line and push pin retainer.

12. Install the air cleaner assembly.

Left Side

1. Remove the engine mount strut bracket.

2. Disconnect the engine wiring harness electrical connector from the bank 2 intake camshaft position (CMP) actuator solenoid valve.

3. Remove the CMP actuator solenoid valve bolt.

4. Remove the CMP actuator solenoid valve.

5. Inspect the CMP actuator solenoid valve seal for damage and replace as necessary.

To install:

6. Inspect the CMP actuator solenoid valve seal for damage. Replace the seal if necessary.

7. Install the CMP actuator solenoid valve.

8. Install the CMP actuator solenoid valve bolt and tighten to 89 inch. lbs. (10 Nm).

9. Connect the engine wiring harness electrical connector to the bank 2 intake CMP actuator solenoid valve.

10. Install the engine mount strut bracket.

TESTING

See Figure 142.

1. Ignition OFF, disconnect the CMP actuator solenoid harness connector at the CMP actuator solenoid

➡**Ensure component is tested at 20°C (68°F).**

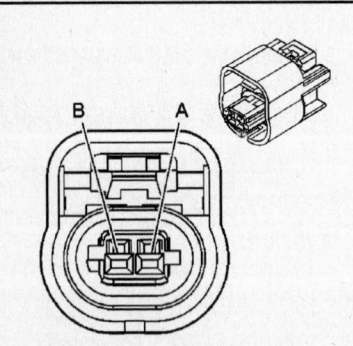

A. CMP Actuator Solenoid Control Intake
B. Low Reference

22116_GMG6_G0139

Fig. 142 Camshaft Position (CMP) actuator sensors intake connector view Exhaust similar

2. Test for 4.6–7.5 ohms of resistance between the high control terminal A and the low reference terminal B of the CMP actuator solenoid.

3. If the resistance is not within the specified range, replace the CMP actuator solenoid.

VEHICLE SPEED SENSOR (VSS)

LOCATION

See Figures 143 through 145.

Refer to the accompanying illustrations for Vehicle Speed Sensor (VSS) locations.

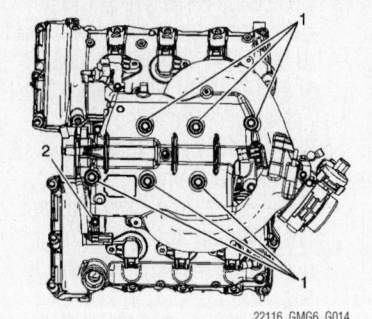

22116_GMG6_G014

Fig. 144 Vehicle Speed Sensor (VSS) location view 6T70–6T75 automatic transmissions

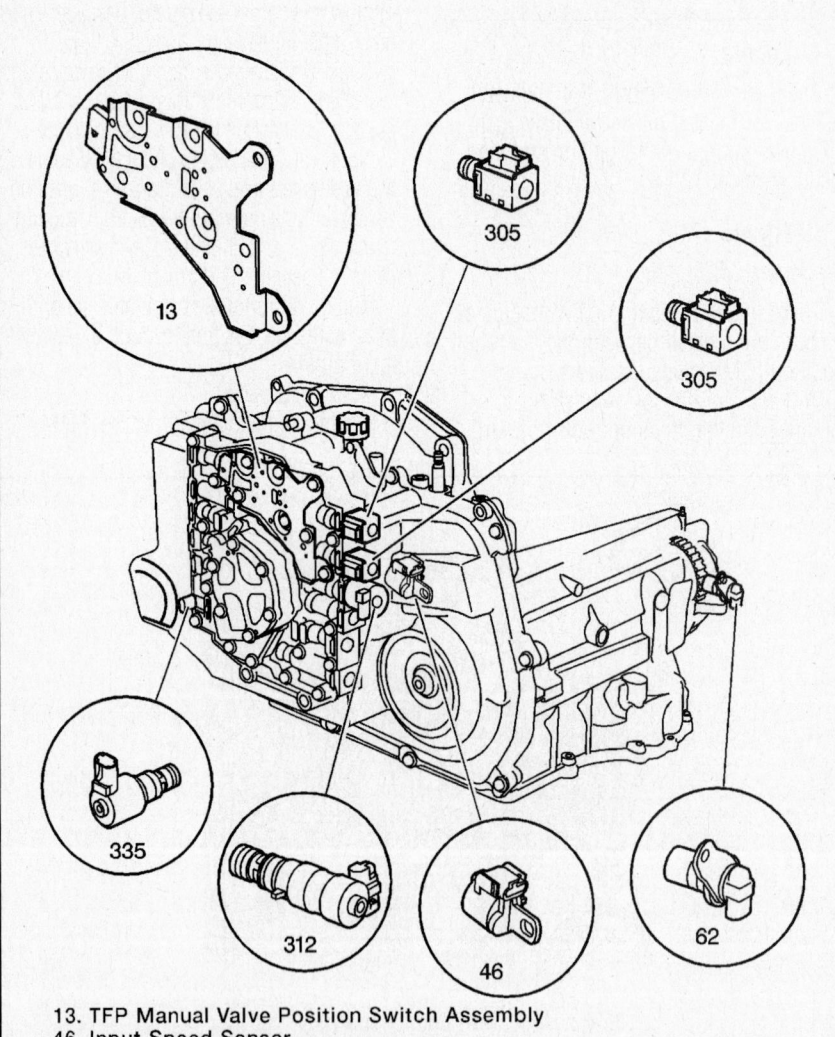

13. TFP Manual Valve Position Switch Assembly
46. Input Speed Sensor
62. Output Speed Sensor
305. 1-2 and 2-3 Shift Solenoid Valves
312. Pressure Control Solenoid
355. TCC Control PWM Solenoid

22116_GMG6_G0141

Fig. 143 Vehicle Speed Sensor (VSS) location view 4T45–E and 4T46–E automatic transmissions

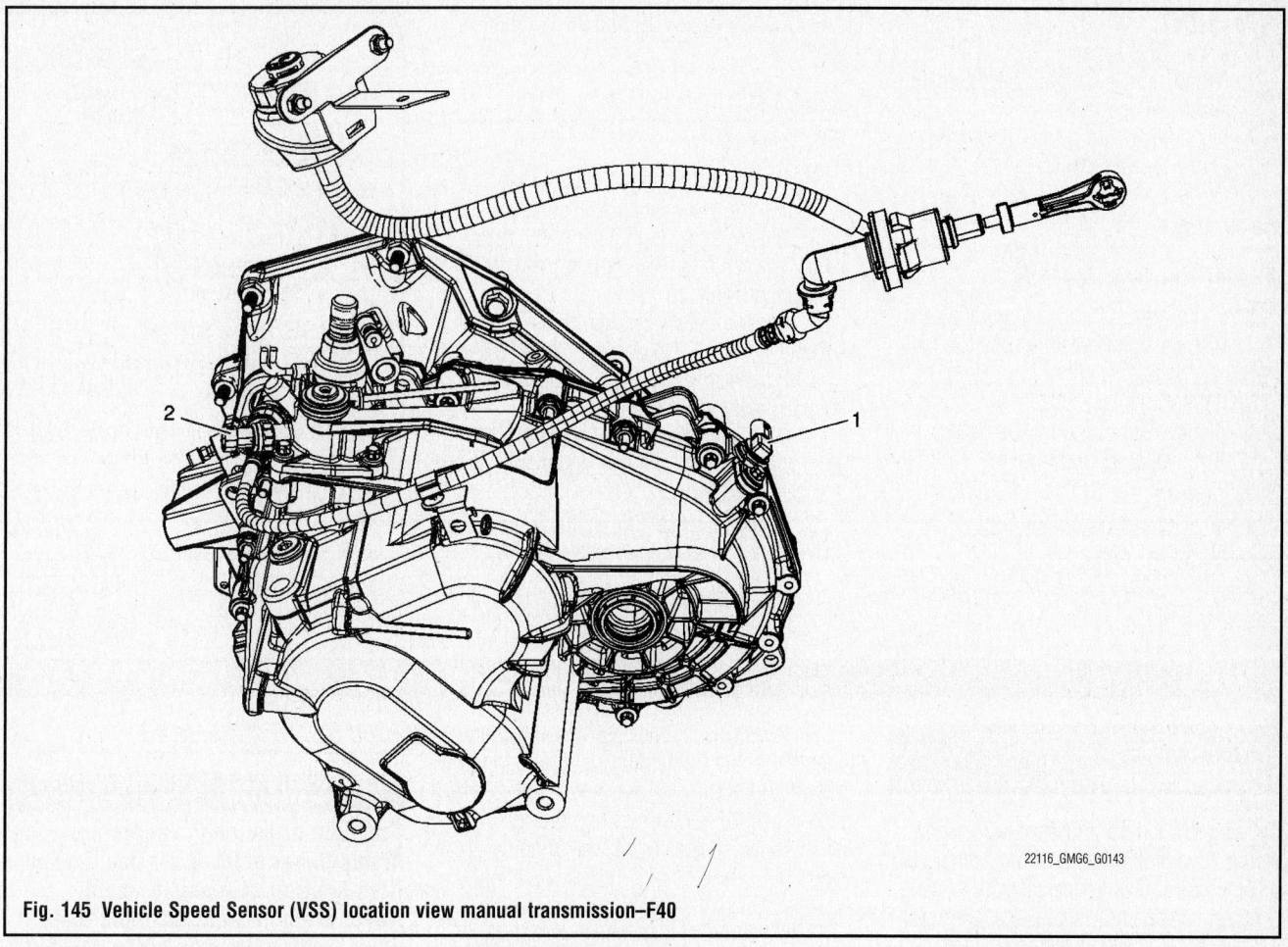

Fig. 145 Vehicle Speed Sensor (VSS) location view manual transmission–F40

22116_GMG6_G0143

OPERATION

The Vehicle Speed Sensor (VSS) is a magnetic inductive pickup that relays vehicle speed information to the TCM. The TCM uses this information in order to control shift timing, line pressure, and TCC apply and release.

The VSS mounts in the case extension at the vehicle speed sensor reluctor wheel, which is pressed onto the final drive carrier assembly. An air gap of 0.011–0.062 inch. (0.27–1.57 mm) occurs between the sensor and the teeth on the vehicle speed sensor reluctor wheel as the final drive carrier assembly rotates.

The sensor consists of a permanent magnet surrounded by a coil of wire. As the vehicle speed sensor reluctor wheel on the final drive carrier assembly rotates, an AC signal is produced by the VSS. This AC signal consists of a voltage and frequency that changes based on vehicle speed. The TCM uses the frequency portion of this signal to determine vehicle speed. Higher vehicle speeds induce a higher frequency and a higher voltage measurement at the sensor. The voltage portion of the signal is used in diagnostic procedures.

REMOVAL & INSTALLATION

4T45–E

1. Position the vehicle on a hoist and raise the vehicle.
2. Disconnect the Vehicle Speed Sensor (VSS) electrical connector.
3. Remove the VSS electrical harness retainer from the VSS stud.
4. Remove the VSS stud.
5. Remove the output VSS from the transmission case.
6. Remove the O-ring from the VSS.

To install:

7. Install the O-ring onto the VSS.
8. Install the output VSS into the transmission case.
9. Install the VSS stud and tighten to 8 ft. lbs. (11 Nm).
10. Install the VSS electrical harness retainer to the VSS stud.
11. Connect the VSS electrical connector.
12. Lower the vehicle.

4T65–E

1. Raise and support the vehicle.
2. Remove the right front tire and wheel.

3. Disconnect the Vehicle Speed Sensor (VSS) electrical connector.
4. Remove the VSS bolt.
5. Remove the VSS from the extension case.
6. Remove the O-ring from the VSS.

To install:

7. Install the O-ring to the VSS
8. Install the VSS.
9. Install the VSS bolt and tighten to 106 inch. lbs. (12 Nm).
10. Connect the VSS electrical connector.
11. Install the right front tire and wheel.
12. Lower the vehicle.

6T70–6T75

➡**The Vehicle Speed Sensor (VSS) is also referred to as the Output Speed Sensor (OSS).**

1. Raise and support the vehicle.
2. Remove the control valve body cover.
3. Disconnect the Output Speed Sensor (OSS) electrical connector.
4. Remove output shaft speed sensor.

To install:

5. Install OSS sensor.

6. Reconnect the Output Speed Sensor (OSS) electrical connector.

7. Install the control valve body cover.

8. Lower the vehicle.

9. Check transmission fluid level and add as needed.

Manual Transmission—F40

1. Remove the air cleaner outlet duct.

2. Disconnect the vehicle speed sensor electrical connector.

3. Remove the VSS bolt.

4. Remove the VSS from the case.

5. Remove the O-ring from the VSS.

To install:

6. Install the O-ring to the VSS

7. Install the VSS.

8. Install the VSS bolt and tighten to 13 inch. lbs. (18 Nm).

9. Connect the VSS electrical connector.

TESTING

See Figure 146.

1. Disconnect Vehicle Speed Sensor (VSS) electrical connector from sensor.

2. With a digital mutimeter check resistance between pin A VSS low signal and pin B VSS high signal.

3. Sensor resistance should measure between 1,650–2,200 ohms at 20°C 68°F.

4. If resistance reading is not as stated suspect faulty VSS sensor.

5. With a digital mutimeter check voltage between pin A VSS low signal and pin B VSS high signal.

6. Safely lift wheels off of the ground and run in gear to check voltage readings.

7. Check for output voltage this will vary with vehicle speed from a minimum of 0.5

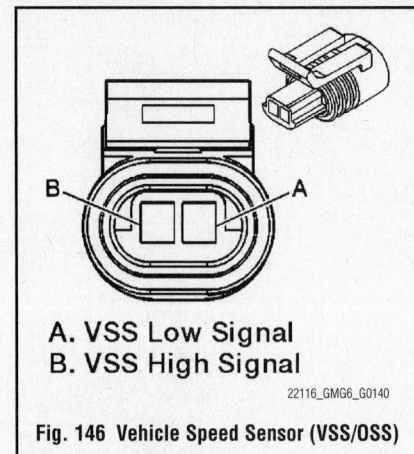

A. VSS Low Signal
B. VSS High Signal

22116_GMG6_G0140

Fig. 146 Vehicle Speed Sensor (VSS/OSS)

volts AC at 100 RPM to 200 volts at 6,000 RPM.

8. If no voltage reading is present suspect internal transmission problem or faulty VSS sensor.

FUEL   GASOLINE FUEL INJECTION SYSTEM

FUEL SYSTEM SERVICE PRECAUTIONS

Safety is the most important factor when performing not only fuel system maintenance but any type of maintenance. Failure to conduct maintenance and repairs in a safe manner may result in serious personal injury or death. Maintenance and testing of the vehicle's fuel system components can be accomplished safely and effectively by adhering to the following rules and guidelines.

• To avoid the possibility of fire and personal injury, always disconnect the negative battery cable unless the repair or test procedure requires that battery voltage be applied.

• Always relieve the fuel system pressure prior to disconnecting any fuel system component (injector, fuel rail, pressure regulator, etc.), fitting or fuel line connection. Exercise extreme caution whenever relieving fuel system pressure to avoid exposing skin, face and eyes to fuel spray. Please be advised that fuel under pressure may penetrate the skin or any part of the body that it contacts.

• Always place a shop towel or cloth around the fitting or connection prior to loosening to absorb any excess fuel due to spillage. Ensure that all fuel spillage (should it occur) is quickly removed from engine surfaces. Ensure that all fuel soaked cloths or towels are deposited into a suitable waste container.

• Always keep a dry chemical (Class B) fire extinguisher near the work area.

• Do not allow fuel spray or fuel vapors to come into contact with a spark or open flame.

• Always use a back-up wrench when loosening and tightening fuel line connection fittings. This will prevent unnecessary stress and torsion to fuel line piping.

• Always replace worn fuel fitting O-rings with new Do not substitute fuel hose or equivalent where fuel pipe is installed.

Before servicing the vehicle, make sure to also refer to the precautions in the beginning of this section as well.

RELIEVING FUEL SYSTEM PRESSURE

1. Loosen the fuel fill cap in order to relieve the tank pressure. Do not tighten at this time.

2. Raise and support the vehicle.

3. Disconnect the fuel pump electrical connector.

4. Lower the vehicle.

5. Start and run the engine until the fuel supply remaining in the fuel pipes is consumed. Engage the starter for 3.0 seconds in order to assure relief of any remaining pressure.

6. Disconnect the negative battery cable.

7. Connect the fuel pump electrical connector.

8. Lower the vehicle.

FUEL FILTER

REMOVAL & INSTALLATION

The fuel filter is integral with the fuel pump module assembly. See Fuel Pump Module.

FUEL SYSTEM CLEANING

> ✳✳ **CAUTION**
>
> **Gasoline or gasoline vapors are highly flammable. A fire could occur if an ignition source is present. Never drain or store gasoline or diesel fuel in an open container, due to the possibility of fire or explosion. Have a dry chemical (Class B) fire extinguisher nearby.**

1. Remove the fuel tank.

2. Remove the fuel pump module assembly.

3. Inspect the fuel pump module strainer.

> ✳✳ **CAUTION**
>
> **When flushing the fuel tank, handle the fuel and water mixture as a hazardous material. Handle the fuel and water in accordance with all applicable local, state, and federal laws and regulations**

4. Flush the fuel tank with hot water.

5. Pour the water out of the fuel sender assembly opening in the fuel tank. Rock the fuel tank in order to be sure that the removal of the water from the fuel tank is complete.

6. Allow the tank to dry completely before reassembly.

7. Disconnect the fuel feed pipe at the engine fuel rail.

➡**Only use oil-free compressed air to blow out the fuel pipes.**

8. Clean the fuel pipes by applying air pressure in the opposite direction of the fuel flow.

9. Connect the fuel feed pipe to the engine fuel rail.

10. Install the fuel pump module assembly.

11. Install the fuel tank.

FUEL INJECTORS

REMOVAL & INSTALLATION

2.4L Engine

❊❊ **CAUTION**

Gasoline or gasoline vapors are highly flammable. A fire could occur if an ignition source is present. Never drain or store gasoline or diesel fuel in an open container, due to the possibility of fire or explosion. Have a dry chemical (Class B) fire extinguisher nearby.

1. Before servicing the vehicle, refer to the precautions in the beginning of this section.

2. Relieve the fuel system pressure

3. Remove the air cleaner outlet duct.

4. Disconnect the fuel feed line quick connect fitting from the fuel rail.

5. Disconnect the Electronic Throttle Control (ETC) electrical connector.

6. Remove the 2 engine harness clips from the fuel rail tabs.

7. Remove the fuel injector wiring harness electrical connector clip from the intake manifold tab.

8. Disconnect the engine harness electrical connector from the fuel injector harness wiring electrical connector.

9. Remove the fuel rail bolts.

10. Pull the fuel rail back and upward in order to release the fuel injectors from the cylinder head ports.

11. Remove the fuel rail.

12. Remove the fuel injector retainer.

13. Remove the fuel injector from the fuel rail.

14. Remove and discard the fuel injector O-rings

To install:

15. Lubricate the new O-rings with clean engine oil and install the O-rings on the injector(s).

16. Install the fuel injector to the fuel rail.

17. Install the fuel injector retainer.

18. Install the fuel injector wiring harness clips to the fuel rail.

19. Connect the fuel injector wiring harness electrical connectors to the fuel injectors.

20. Lubricate the new fuel injector tip insulators with clean engine oil.

21. Install the new fuel injector tip insulators to the cylinder head.

22. With the fuel injectors positioned downward, lower the fuel injectors into the cylinder head ports.

23. Carefully push down on the fuel rail in order to insert the injectors into the cylinder head ports.

24. Install the fuel rail bolts and tighten to 89 inch lbs. (10 Nm).

25. Connect the engine harness electrical connector to the fuel injector wiring harness electrical connector.

26. Install the fuel injector wiring harness electrical connector clip to the intake manifold tab.

27. Install the 2 engine harness clips to the fuel rail tabs.

28. Connect the ETC electrical connector.

29. Connect the fuel feed line quick connect fitting to the fuel rail.

30. Install the air cleaner outlet duct.

31. Connect the negative battery cable.

32. Start the vehicle, check for leaks and repair if necessary.

3.5L and 3.9L Engines

❊❊ **CAUTION**

Gasoline or gasoline vapors are highly flammable. A fire could occur if an ignition source is present. Never drain or store gasoline or diesel fuel in an open container, due to the possibility of fire or explosion. Have a dry chemical (Class B) fire extinguisher nearby.

1. Before servicing the vehicle, refer to the precautions in the beginning of this section.

2. Relieve the fuel system pressure.

3. Remove the engine fuel feed pipe from the fuel rail.

4. Remove the upper intake manifold.

5. Disconnect the main injector harness electrical connector.

6. Disconnect the main fuel injector electrical harness connector.

7. On 3.9L, disconnect the CMP sensor electrical connector.

8. On all engines, depress the lock tabs and disconnect the fuel injector electrical connectors.

9. Remove the fuel injector electrical wiring harness from the fuel rail.

10. Remove the fuel rail assembly.

11. Remove the fuel injector O-ring seal from the spray tip end of each injector.

12. Remove and discard O-rings if damaged.

13. Remove the fuel injector retainer.

14. Remove the fuel injector from the fuel rail.

15. Remove and discard the fuel injector O-rings

To install:

16. Lubricate the new O-rings with clean engine oil and install the O-rings on the injector(s).

17. Install the fuel rail assembly into the intake manifold. Tilt the fuel rail assembly slightly to install the injectors.

18. Install the fuel rail bolts and tighten to 89 inch lbs. (10 Nm).

19. Install the fuel injector electrical wiring harness to the fuel rail.

20. Connect the fuel injector electrical connectors.

21. Push the slide locks into position.

22. Connect the main fuel injector electrical harness connector.

23. On 3.9L, connect the CMP sensor electrical connector.

24. Install the fuel feed pipe to the fuel rail.

25. Install the upper intake manifold.

26. Connect the negative battery cable.

27. Start the vehicle, check for leaks and repair if necessary.

3.6L Engine

See Figure 147.

❊❊ **CAUTION**

Gasoline or gasoline vapors are highly flammable. A fire could occur if an ignition source is present. Never drain or store gasoline or diesel fuel in an open container, due to the possibility of fire or explosion. Have a dry chemical (Class B) fire extinguisher nearby.

1. Before servicing the vehicle, refer to the precautions in the beginning of this section.

2. Remove the fuel injector sight shield.

3. Disconnect the engine wiring harness electrical connector from the fuel injector wiring harness electrical connector

4. Disconnect the fuel feed pipe quick connect fitting from the fuel rail. Use fuel line disconnect tool set J 37008—A or equivalent.

5. Remove the upper intake manifold.

❊❊ CAUTION

Wear safety glasses when using compressed air in order to prevent eye injury.

6. Use compressed air in order to remove any debris from the around the area where the fuel injectors enter the lower intake manifold.

7. Remove the fuel rail bolts.

➡Remove the fuel rail assembly carefully in order to prevent damage to the injector electrical connector terminals and the injector spray tips. Support the fuel rail after the fuel rail is removed in order to avoid damaging the fuel rail components. Cap the fittings and plug the holes when servicing the fuel system in order to prevent dirt and other contaminants from entering open pipes and passages.

8. Remove the fuel rail with fuel injectors from the lower intake manifold.

9. Lift up the fuel injector electrical connector retainer.

10. Push in the fuel injector electrical connector tab in order to disconnect the connector from the injector.

11. Remove the fuel injector retainer clip.

12. Remove the fuel injector.

13. Remove and discard the fuel injector seals.

To install:

14. Install new fuel injector seals.

15. Install the fuel injector.

16. Install the fuel injector retainer clip.

17. Install the fuel injector electrical connector.

18. Push down on the fuel injector electrical connector retainer, securing the electrical connector.

19. Install the fuel rail with fuel injectors to the lower intake manifold.

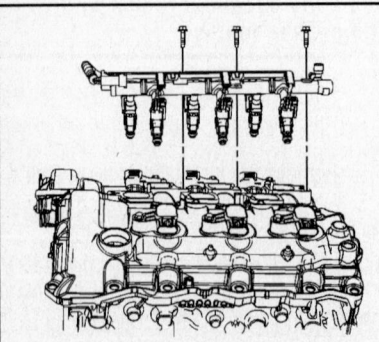

Fig. 147 Fuel rail and injector installation—3.6L engine

22116_GMG6_G0068

20. Install the fuel rail bolts and tighten to 89 inch. lbs. (10 Nm).

21. Install the upper intake manifold.

22. Connect the fuel feed pipe quick connect fitting to the fuel rail.

23. Connect the engine wiring harness electrical connector to the fuel injector wiring harness electrical connector.

24. Install the fuel injector sight shield.

FUEL PUMP

REMOVAL & INSTALLATION

❊❊ CAUTION

Gasoline or gasoline vapors are highly flammable. A fire could occur if an ignition source is present. Never drain or store gasoline or diesel fuel in an open container, due to the possibility of fire or explosion. Have a dry chemical (Class B) fire extinguisher nearby.

1. Before servicing the vehicle, refer to the precautions in the beginning of this section.

2. Release the fuel system pressure.

3. Remove the fuel tank.

4. Disconnect the fuel pressure sensor and sender electrical connections.

5. Disconnect the EVAP vapor line quick connect fittings.

6. Disengage the fuel feed line from the retaining features built into the fuel tank.

7. Use Fuel Lock Ring Remover J-45722 and a long breaker-bar in order to unlock the fuel lock ring.

8. Raise the fuel pump assembly out of the tank far enough to access the vapor line quick connect fitting on the underside of the cover.

9. Disconnect the vapor line quick connect fitting.

10. Remove the fuel pump assembly from the fuel tank.

➡Some lock rings were manufactured with "DO NOT REUSE" stamped into them. These lock rings may be reused if they are not damaged or warped.

11. Place the lock ring on a flat surface. Measure the clearance between the lock ring and the flat surface using a feeler gage at 7 points. If warpage is less than 0.016 inch (0.41mm), the lock ring does not require replacement. If warpage is more than specified, replace the lock ring.

To install:

12. Install a new o-ring seal onto the fuel pump.

13. Install the pump into the fuel tank far enough to connect the vapor line quick connect fitting on the underside of the cover.

14. Connect the vapor line quick connect fitting.

15. Align the cover paddle or anti-rotation feature with the corresponding feature in the top of the fuel tank.

16. Slowly apply pressure to the top of the spring loaded sender cover until the sender aligns flush with the surface of the tank.

17. Use the remover tool in order to install the fuel sender lock ring. Turn the fuel lock ring in a clockwise direction.

18. Turn the lock ring until the ring seats on the second detent.

19. Engage the fuel feed line to the retaining features built into the fuel tank.

20. Connect the EVAP vapor line quick connect fittings.

21. Connect the fuel pressure sensor and sender electrical connections.

22. Install the fuel tank.

23. Lower the vehicle.

24. Refill the tank.

25. Connect the negative battery cable.

26. Start the vehicle, check for leaks and repair if necessary.

FUEL TANK

REMOVAL & INSTALLATION

❊❊ CAUTION

Gasoline or gasoline vapors are highly flammable. A fire could occur if an ignition source is present. Never drain or store gasoline or diesel fuel in an open container, due to the possibility of fire or explosion. Have a dry chemical (Class B) fire extinguisher nearby.

❊❊ WARNING

Clean the fuel and Evaporative Emission (EVAP) connections and surrounding areas prior to disconnecting the lines in order the avoid possible system contamination.

1. Relieve the fuel system pressure.

2. Drain the fuel tank.

3. Raise and support the vehicle.

4. Disconnect the fuel tank fuel pump module wiring harness electrical connector from body wiring harness electrical connector.

5. Remove the body wiring harness electrical connector clip from the EVAP canister.

6. Disconnect the body wiring harness

electrical connector from the rear antilock brake system (ABS) wiring harness electrical connector.

7. Remove the rear ABS wiring harness electrical connector clip from the EVAP canister.

8. Disconnect the fuel tank fuel feed pipe quick connect fitting from the chassis fuel feed pipe.

9. Disconnect the fuel tank EVAP pipe quick connect fitting (2) from the chassis EVAP pipe (4).

10. Cap the chassis fuel and EVAP pipes in order to prevent possible fuel and/or EVAP system contamination.

11. Loosen the fuel fill pipe hose clamp at the fuel tank.

12. Separate the fuel fill pipe hose from the fuel tank.

13. Disconnect the EVAP canister vent solenoid tube quick connect fitting.

14. Disconnect the vapor recirculation line quick connect fitting.

15. Place a jack stand under the muffler assembly.

16. With the aid of an assistant, separate the muffler insulators from the underbody hangers.

17. Slowly lower the muffler assembly allowing it to rest on the jack stand. If this is not possible, remove the muffler assembly

18. Have assistants support either side of the fuel tank.

19. Remove fuel tank strap bolts and straps.

20. Place a suitable adjustable jack under the fuel tank, and have the assistants rest the fuel tank on the adjustable jack.

21. If applicable, in order to clear the muffler assembly, slowly lower the right side of the fuel tank.

22. Once the tank is clear of the right frame rail, lower the fuel tank down and remove forward toward the right side of the vehicle.

To install:

23. Have assistants support either side of the fuel tank.

24. If applicable, begin to install the right side of the fuel tank over the muffler assembly.

25. If applicable, raise the right side of the fuel tank into position inboard of the right frame rail. Use care in feeding the fuel feed, EVAP line wiring harness over the muffler assembly.

26. If applicable and the muffler assembly was removed, have assistants raise the fuel tank into position.

27. Install fuel tank straps and bolts and tighten to 15 ft. lbs. (20 Nm).

28. Raise the muffler assembly into position if applicable, otherwise install the muffler assembly.

29. With the aid of an assistant, install the muffler insulators to the underbody hangers.

30. Remove the jack stand from under the muffler assembly.

31. Install the fuel fill pipe hose to the fuel tank.

32. Connect the vapor recirculation line quick connect fitting.

33. Connect the EVAP canister vent solenoid tube quick connect fitting.

34. Tighten the fuel fill pipe hose clamp at the fuel tank to 35 inch. lbs. (4 Nm).

35. Remove the caps from the fuel and EVAP pipes.

36. Connect the fuel tank EVAP pipe quick connect fitting to the chassis EVAP pipe.

37. Connect the fuel tank fuel feed pipe quick connect fitting to the chassis fuel feed pipe.

38. Install the rear ABS wiring harness electrical connector clip to the EVAP canister.

39. Connect the body wiring harness electrical connector to the rear ABS wiring harness electrical connector.

40. Install the body wiring harness electrical connector clip to the underbody.

41. Connect the fuel tank fuel pump module wiring harness electrical connector (1) to the body wiring harness electrical connector.

42. Lower the vehicle

43. Refill the fuel tank.

44. Tighten the fuel fill cap.

45. Inspect for leaks as follows:

a. Turn ON the ignition, with the engine OFF for 10 seconds

b. Turn OFF the ignition for 10 seconds.

c. Turn ON the ignition, with the engine OFF.

d. Inspect for fuel leaks.

IDLE SPEED

ADJUSTMENT

Idle speed is maintained by the Powertrain Control Module (PCM). No adjustment is necessary or possible.

THROTTLE BODY

REMOVAL & INSTALLATION

2.4L and 3.5L Engines

1. Remove the air cleaner outlet.

2. Disconnect the electronic throttle control (ETC) electrical connector.

3. Remove the heater pipe nut at the throttle body, if equipped.

4. Remove the throttle body bolts.

5. Remove the throttle body from the intake manifold.

To install:

6. Inspect the throttle body gasket and replace if necessary.

7. Position the throttle body to the intake manifold.

8. Install the throttle body bolts and tighten to 89 inch lbs. (10 Nm).

9. Install the heater pipe nut at the throttle body, if equipped.

10. Connect the ETC electrical connector.

11. Install the air cleaner outlet.

3.6L Engine

See Figure 148.

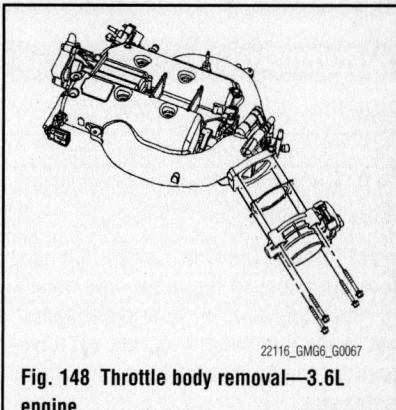

22116_GMG6_G0067

Fig. 148 Throttle body removal—3.6L engine

1. Remove the air cleaner outlet duct.

2. Disconnect the engine wiring harness electrical connector from the Electronic Throttle Control (ETC).

3. Remove the throttle body bolts.

4. Remove the throttle body and gasket. Discard the gasket

To install:

5. Position a NEW throttle body gasket to the upper intake manifold.

6. Position the throttle body to the upper intake manifold.

7. Install the throttle body bolts and tighten to 89 inch. lbs. (10 Nm).

8. Connect the engine wiring harness electrical connector (2) to the ETC.

9. Install the air cleaner outlet duct.

10. Perform the Throttle Learn Procedure.

3.9L Engine

1. Remove the intake manifold cover.

2. Remove the air cleaner outlet duct.

3. Disconnect the electronic throttle control (ETC) electrical connector.

4. Remove the heater inlet and outlet pipe nuts.

5. Remove the heater inlet and outlet pipe bracket from the throttle body studs.

6. Reposition the pipes.

7. Remove the throttle body bolts/studs.

8. Remove the throttle body.

9. Remove the throttle body gasket.

To install:

10. Install a new gasket, if necessary.

11. Install the throttle body.

12. Install the throttle body bolts/studs and tighten to 89 inch lbs. (10 Nm).

13. Position the heater inlet and outlet pipes and install the pipe bracket to the throttle body studs.

14. Install the heater inlet and outlet pipe nuts and tighten to 89 inch lbs. (10 Nm).

15. Connect the ETC electrical connector.

16. Install the air cleaner outlet duct.

17. Install the intake manifold cover.

THROTTLE LEARN PROCEDURE

➡**Do NOT perform this procedure if DTCs are set.**

1. Start and idle the engine in PARK for 3 minutes.

2. With a scan tool, monitor desired and actual RPM.

3. The ECM will start to learn the new idle cells and Desired RPM should start to decrease.

4. Ignition OFF for 60 seconds.

5. Start and idle the engine in PARK for 3 minutes.

6. After the 3 minute run time the engine should be idling normal.

➡**During the drive cycle the check engine light may come on with idle speed DTCs. If idle speed codes are set, clear codes so the ECM can continue to learn.**

7. If the engine idle speed has not been learned the vehicle will need to be driven at speeds above 70 km/h (44 mph) with several decelerations and extended idles.

8. After the drive cycle, the engine should be idling normally.

➡**If the engine idle speed has not been learned, turn OFF the ignition for 60 seconds and repeat step 6.**

9. Once the engine speed has returned to normal, clear DTCs.

HEATING & AIR CONDITIONING SYSTEM

BLOWER MOTOR

REMOVAL & INSTALLATION

1. Remove the right closeout panel.

2. Remove the blower motor wire harness connector.

➡**Cut through the case as straight as possible because the motor cup must be replaced. In order to prevent damage to the component, do not cut any deeper than necessary to remove the motor cup.**

3. Cut out the blower motor using a utility knife in the narrow groove of the lower case.

4. Remove the blower motor.

5. Remove the blower motor nuts.

6. Remove the blower motor from the blower motor cup.

To install:

7. Install the new blower motor to the blower motor cup.

8. Install the blower motor nuts and tighten to 21 inch. lbs. (2.4 Nm).

9. Install the motor blower seal to the blower motor service ring.

10. Install the blower motor.

11. Install the blower motor attachment ring.

12. Install the blower motor screws.

13. Install the blower motor wire harness connector.

14. Install the right closeout panel.

HEATER CORE

REMOVAL & INSTALLATION

See Figures 149 through 151.

1. Place the front wheels in the straight ahead position.

2. Disable the air bag system.

3. Disconnect the negative battery cable.

4. Drain the engine coolant.

5. Disconnect the heater hoses at the heater core.

6. Recover the air conditioning refrigerant.

7. Remove the hose at the thermal expansion valve and plug the hose.

8. Disconnect the HVAC module to front of dash plate bolts.

9. Remove the right and left side console trim panels.

10. Remove the front floor console.

11. Remove the left closeout panel.

12. Remove both instrument panel outer trim panels.

13. Remove the instrument panel-to-body wire harness and antenna left connectors.

14. Remove the instrument panel-to-wire harness right side connectors.

15. Remove the knee bolster.

16. Remove the upper steering column trim cover.

17. On the back side of the steering wheel are 4 openings for removing the driver inflator module. Place the steering wheel so that 2 of the openings are on top.

18. Install Driver Air Bag Removal tool J-44298 into 2 of the holes so it is fully inserted.

19. Pull the handle toward the back of the steering wheel, releasing the 2 spring-loaded fasteners at the same time.

20. Turn the steering wheel and open the tool.

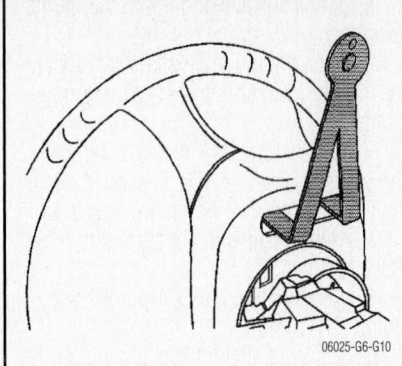

06025-G6-G10

Fig. 149 Installing driver air bag removal tool—G6

21. Place the tool and repeat the same steps for the other 2 openings.

22. Pull the driver inflator module gently away from the steering wheel.

23. Remove the connector position assurance (CPA) and the electrical connector for the driver inflator module.

24. Remove the horn grounded lead from the steering wheel.

25. Remove the inflatable restraint module.

26. Disconnect the steering wheel control electrical connector.

27. Remove the steering wheel nut.

28. Remove the steering wheel using a puller.

29. Remove the controls and the control harness from the steering wheel.

30. Remove the steering column trim covers.

31. Disconnect the restraint module coil connectors and remove the coil.

32. Remove the multifunction turn signal and housing.

33. Remove the steering column knee bolster.

34. Remove the steering column shaft pinch bolt from the intermediate steering shaft.

➡**Install tie straps between the rake bracket assembly and the neck of the assist mechanism housing to prevent jacket assembly pull-apart. The steering column rake lever MUST be in the LOCK (FULL UP) position during steering column removal and installation to ensure that the rake lever bracket remains rigid. Install a tie strap around the lever and the jacket assembly to keep the lever in the LOCK position. Do not bend the steering column energy absorbing straps located on the upper steering column mounting bracket.**

35. Disconnect the steering column electrical connectors and open the steering column wire harness retainer clip.

36. Without disconnecting the adjustable brake pedal cable, remove the accelerator pedal.

37. Position the adjustable brake pedal cable aside.

38. Remove the accelerator pedal bracket from the cowl.

39. Remove the upper and lower steering column mounting bolts.

40. Remove the steering column.

41. Remove the brake pedal assembly.

42. Remove the body control module (BCM).

43. Remove the center support bracket floor bolts.

44. Remove the automatic transmission shifter assembly.

45. Remove both windshield pillar garnish moldings.

46. Remove the instrument panel upper trim panel.

47. Remove the instrument panel-to-body bolts on both sides.

48. Remove the right and left floor heater ducts at the center floor heater duct.

49. Remove the instrument panel.

50. Remove the recirculation actuator wire harness connector.

51. Remove the air temperature actuator wire harness connector.

52. Remove the mode actuator wire harness connector.

53. Remove the blower motor wire harness connector.

54. Remove the blower motor resistor wire harness connector.

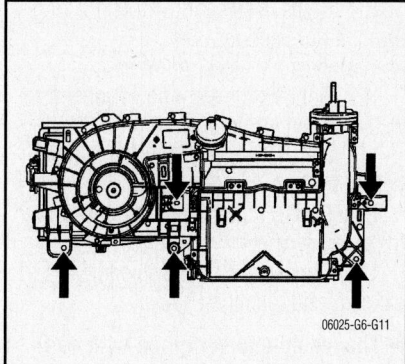

06025-G6-G11

Fig. 150 HVAC assembly mounting—G6

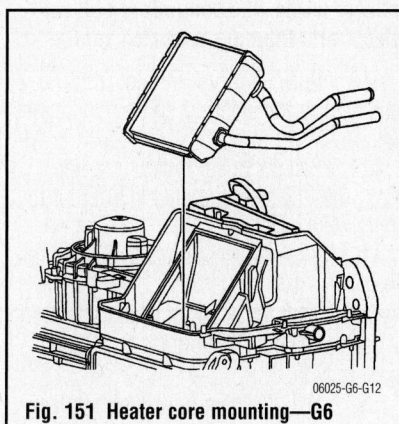

06025-G6-G12

Fig. 151 Heater core mounting—G6

55. Remove the left hand side window defogger outlet duct.

56. Remove the lower floor duct push-in fastener.

57. Remove the HVAC module assembly mounting bolts and the HVAC module.

58. Remove the upper and lower center floor air outlet ducts

59. Drill out the heater core cover heat stakes.

60. Remove the heater core cover.

61. Remove the heater core.

To install:

62. Install the heater core.

63. Install the heater core cover.

64. Install the upper and lower center floor air outlet ducts.

65. Install the HVAC module and tighten the bolts to 44 inch lbs. (5 Nm).

66. Install the lower floor duct push-in fastener.

67. Install the left hand side window defogger outlet duct.

68. Install the blower motor resistor wire harness connector.

69. Install the blower motor wire harness connector.

70. Install the mode actuator wire harness connector.

71. Install the air temperature actuator wire harness connector.

72. Install the recirculation actuator wire harness connector.

73. Install a new HVAC module drain seal and dash seal.

74. Install the instrument panel assembly.

75. Install the left and right floor heater ducts at the center floor heater duct.

76. Install the instrument panel-to-body bolts on both sides and tighten to 19 ft. Lbs. (26 Nm).

77. Install the I/P upper trim panel.

78. Install both windshield pillar garnish moldings.

79. Install the shifter assembly on automatic transmissions.

80. Install the center support bracket floor bolts and tighten to 89 inch lbs. (10 Nm).

81. Install the BCM.

82. Install the brake pedal assembly.

83. Tighten the 3 brake pedal assembly to I/P carrier bolts to 18 ft. lbs. (25 Nm).

84. Install the 2 brake pedal assembly to cowl mounting nuts and tighten to 11 ft. lbs. (15 Nm).

85. Connect the brake pedal pushrod retaining clip, the wave washers and the brake booster pushrod to the brake pedal pin.

86. On electric power steering models, install the motor/module assembly to the steering column.

87. Position the steering column in the vehicle.

88. Slide the lower end of the steering column shaft into the intermediate steering shaft,

89. Loosely install the lower steering column mounting bolt . Loosely install the upper steering column mounting bolts.

➡**Do not bend the steering column energy absorbing straps located on the upper steering column mounting bracket during installation.**

90. Align the energy absorbing straps with the bolt holes in the steering column. Loosely install the upper steering column bolts.

91. Tighten the steering column fasteners in the following sequence:

a. Tighten the lower bolt to 18 ft. lbs. (25 Nm).

b. Tighten the left side upper bolt to 18 ft. lbs. (25 Nm).

c. Tighten the right side upper bolt to 18 ft. lbs. (25 Nm).

92. Connect the steering column electrical connectors and close the wire harness retainer clip on the steering column.

93. Install the adjustable accelerator bracket to the vehicle.

94. Install the 3 adjustable accelerator bracket nuts and tighten to 89 inch lbs. (10 Nm).

➡ **Ensure that the adjustable accelerator pedal and adjustable brake pedal are synchronized in the full rearward position.**

95. Install a new adjustable brake pedal cable.

96. Install the accelerator pedal to the vehicle.

97. Install the steering column knee bolster.

98. Install the multifunction turn signal switch housing.

99. Install the multifunction turn signal.

100. Aim the wheels straight ahead.

101. Align the block tooth and the centering mark on the race and upper shaft assembly at the 12 o'clock position.

102. Slide the new SIR coil onto the steering shaft assembly.

103. Connect the SIR harness.

104. Remove and discard the centering tab from the new SIR coil.

105. Install the steering column trim covers.

106. Install the controls and the control harness to the steering wheel.

107. Route the steering column wiring through the steering wheel.

108. Install the steering wheel.

109. Connect the steering wheel control electrical connector.

110. Install the steering wheel nut and tighten to 24 ft. lbs. (32 Nm).

111. Connect the horn ground lead onto the steering wheel.

112. Connect the inflator module electrical connector and the CPA.

➡ **This vehicle is equipped with dual stage frontal air bags. Match the right color connector to the right color opening in the module. Route the driver inflator wires, the redundant control wires, and the horn wires correctly.**

113. Align the driver inflator module fasteners to the steering column fastener holes.

114. Push the driver inflator module firmly into the steering column in order to engage the fasteners.

115. Install the steering column trim covers.

116. Install the crush bracket to the front of dash plate nuts and tighten to 89 inch lbs. (10 Nm).

117. Install the steering column to the I/P wire harness connector.

118. Install the knee bolster.

119. Install the I/P to the body wire harness RH connectors.

120. Install the I/P to the body wire harness and antenna LH connectors.

121. Install both I/P outer trim panels.

122. Install the left closeout panel.

123. Install the console.

124. Install the left and right console trim panels

125. Install the right console trim panel.

126. Install the HVAC module to the MOD plate bolts and tighten to 35 inch lbs. (4 Nm).

127. Unplug the A/C components.

128. Install new sealing washers.

129. Install the liquid and suction lines at the TXV.

130. Evacuate and charge the refrigerant system.

131. Leak test the fittings.

132. Install the heater hoses at the heater core.

133. Fill the coolant.

134. Connect the negative battery cable.

135. Enable the SIR system.

136. Perform the power steering control module programming. See STEERING and SUSPERNSION.

137. Perform the brake pedal position sensor calibration. See BRAKES.

STEERING

POWER STEERING GEAR

REMOVAL & INSTALLATION

Hydraulic Steering Models

See Figure 152.

1. Raise and support the vehicle safely and remove the front wheels.

2. Remove the tie rod ends from the steering knuckle.

3. Remove the intermediate shaft to steering gear pinch bolt. Discard the bolt.

4. Disconnect the intermediate shaft from the steering gear.

5. Lower the vehicle.

6. Remove the intermediate shaft pinch bolt at the steering column shaft. Discard the pinch bolt.

7. Slide the intermediate shaft off the steering column shaft.

8. To unseat the intermediate shaft seal from the dash, squeeze the 4 tabs on the seal individually, then pull toward the inside of the vehicle.

9. Remove the intermediate shaft/seal from the vehicle.

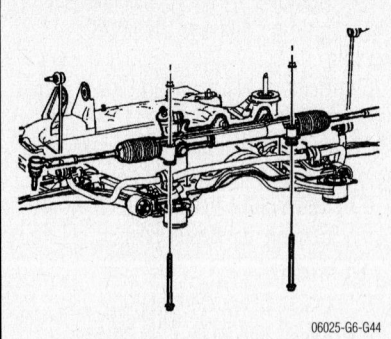

06025-G6-G44

Fig. 152 Hydraulic power steering gear mounting—G6

10. Remove the power steering hoses from the from the power steering gear and cap the openings.

11. Remove the power steering gear bolts from the gear.

12. Remove the power steering gear through the left wheel opening.

To install:

13. Position the power steering gear to the vehicle.

14. Install the power steering gear bolts and tighten to 81 ft. lbs. (110 Nm).

15. Install the power steering hoses to the steering gear.

16. Install the intermediate shaft/seal through the front of dash.

➡ **To ensure seal is properly seated, inspect the 4 tabs on the seal from the engine side of the seal. Do not twist or squeeze the seal during installation.**

17. Seat the intermediate shaft seal by pushing forward from the inside of the vehicle, until all four tabs of the seal are fully seated.

18. Connect the intermediate shaft to the steering column shaft.

19. Install the new steering column pinch bolt to the intermediate shaft and tighten to 46 ft. lbs. (62 Nm).

20. Connect the intermediate shaft to the steering gear shaft.

21. Install a new steering gear pinch bolt to the intermediate shaft and tighten to 36 ft. lbs. (49 Nm).

22. Install the tie rod ends to the steering knuckle.

23. Install the wheels.

24. Lower the vehicle.

25. Bleed the air from the power steering system.

26. Check the front wheel alignment.

Electronic Steering Models

See Figure 153.

1. Raise and support the vehicle safely and remove the front wheels.

2. Remove the intermediate shaft to steering gear pinch bolt. Discard the bolt.

3. Disconnect the intermediate shaft from the steering gear. Note the alignment for installation.

4. Disconnect the outer tie rod end from the steering knuckle.

5. Remove the steering gear-to-frame bolts.

6. Remove the steering gear through the left side of the vehicle. Rotate the gear 90 degrees in order to clear the rear transmission mount.

7. If replacing the steering gear, remove the outer tie rod ends.

To install:

8. Install the outer tie rod ends to the steering gear, if removed.

9. Install the steering gear to the vehicle. Rotate the gear as necessary to clear the rear transmission mount.

10. Install the steering gear-to-frame bolts and tighten to 52 ft. lbs. (70 Nm), plus an additional 90 degrees.

11. Connect the intermediate steering shaft to the steering gear using the alignment mark.

12. Install the intermediate steering shaft to steering gear pinch bolt and tighten to 36 ft. lbs. (49 Nm).

13. Connect the outer tie rod ends to the steering knuckle.

14. Install the wheels.

15. Lower the vehicle.

16. Check the front wheel alignment.

ELECTRONIC STEERING MOTOR

REMOVAL & INSTALLATION

See Figure 154 and 155.

1. Disconnect the sensor wire harness (6) from the motor/module assembly (5).

➡ **If replacing the motor/module assembly, you will need the sensor wire harness strap clip (7) for the new motor/module assembly installation. If replacing the steering column, a new sensor wire harness strap clip (7) will come with the column service kit. Keep the existing wire strap clip attached to the steering column sensor wire harness (6).**

2. Use needle nose pliers to remove the wire strap clip (7) from the motor/module assembly (5).

3. Use an M6x1 head bit to remove the 2 motor/module assembly TORX® screws (2). Discard the screws.

➡ **Once the motor/module assembly has been removed, inspect the steering column assist mechanism input shaft (3) for the rotor isolator bumper (4). If present, remove and insert back into the rotor isolator (8) in the motor/**

module assembly (5). **The assist mechanism housing must be free of any type of debris. Remove any loose debris from the steering column assist mechanism housing, but do NOT remove the remaining grease on the steering column assist mechanism input shaft (3).**

4. Grasp the motor/module assembly (5) by the motor housing and remove it from the steering column (1) by pulling with an even tension.

To install:

➡ **Before installing the motor/module assembly (2), verify the rotor isolator bumper (1) is installed into the rotor isolator (3) in the motor/module assembly (2).**

5. Fit the motor/module assembly rotor isolator over the steering column assist mechanism input shaft.

6. Use an M6x1 TORX® head bit to attach the motor/module assembly (2) to the steering column with the 2 new TORX® bolts (1).

7. Tighten the steering column bolts to 80 inch lbs. (9 Nm).

8. Connect the sensor wire harness (3) to the motor/module assembly (2).

9. Install the sensor wire harness strap clip (4) into the motor/module assembly (2).

10. Perform the control module setup procedure.

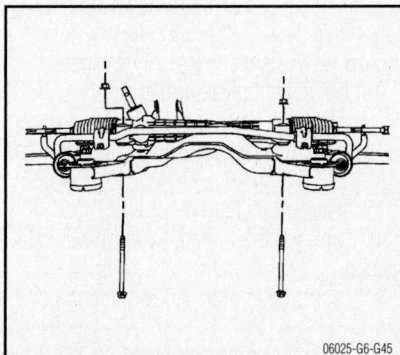

Fig. 153 Electronic power steering gear mounting—G6

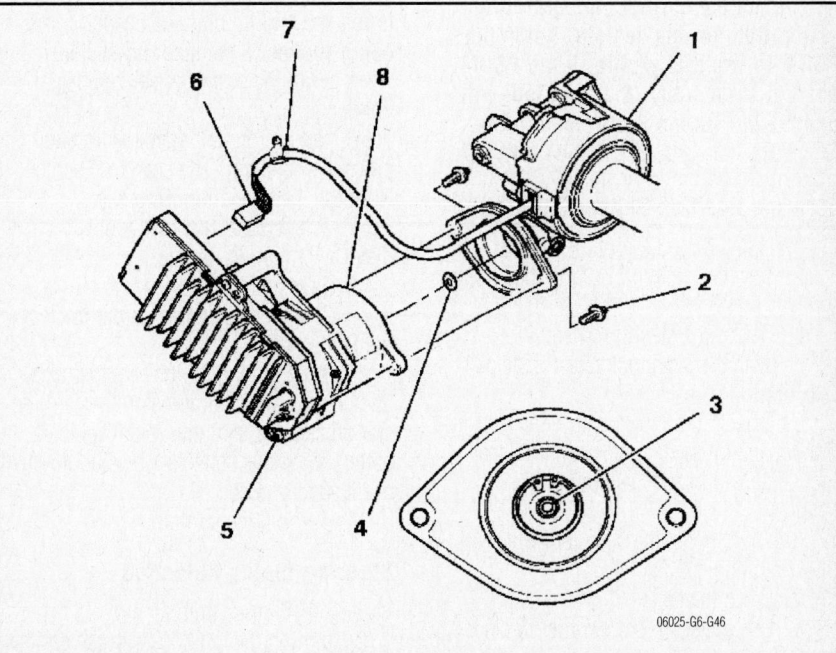

Fig. 154 Electronic steering motor mounting. Refer to the procedure for component identification—G6

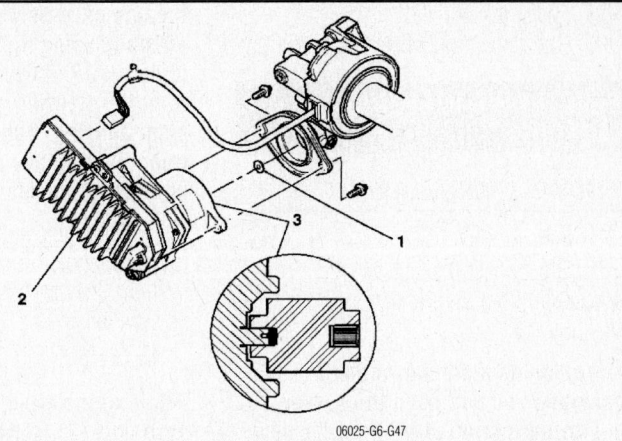

Fig. 155 Electronic steering rotor isolator installation. Refer to the procedure for component identification—G6

06025-G6-G47

REMOVAL & INSTALLATION

Control Module Setup

After replacing the power steering motor and module assembly the following 3 procedures must be performed. After replacing the steering column assembly only the steering position sensor and the torque sensor calibration procedures must be performed. The steering position sensor and torque sensor calibration procedures should also be performed after a suspension alignment.

➡ The power steering control module (PSCM) must be setup using the service programming system (SPS). There are 8 different tuning profile calibrations stored in the PSCM. The SPS will select the correct tuning profile calibration for this vehicle. Setup the PSCM to use that profile. If the PSCM has not been setup, the scan tool will display the Tuning Profile is 0 in the EPS data list, and DTC C0551 will set.

Steering Position Sensor Calibration

1. Install the scan tool.
2. Turn on the ignition, with the engine off.
3. Center the steering wheel.
4. With the scan tool select Special Functions.
5. Select Steering Position Sensor Calibration and press the Enter key. The scan tool screen will flash Calibration in Progress.
6. When done, the scan tool will display Calibration Complete.
7. Press the exit key.
8. Use the scan tool in order to clear the DTCs.
9. When done, the scan tool will display Calibration Complete.

10. Press the exit key.
11. Use the scan tool in order to clear the DTCs.
12. After turning off the ignition, allow 25 seconds of wait time before performing any procedures that require the vehicles battery to be disconnected, or module memory loss may occur.
13. Turn off the ignition.

Torque Sensor Calibration

1. Install the scan tool.
2. Turn on the ignition, with the engine off.
3. Center the steering wheel.
4. After centering the steering wheel, remove hands and other objects from the steering wheel and ensure the suspension is relaxed and no bias, or uneven force is being applied to the steering system.
5. With the scan tool select Special Functions.
6. Select Torque Sensor Calibration and press the Enter key. The scan tool screen will flash Calibration in Progress.
7. When done, the scan tool will display Calibration Complete.
8. Press the exit key
9. Use the scan tool in order to clear the DTCs
10. After turning off the ignition, allow 25 seconds of wait time before performing any procedures that require the vehicles battery to be disconnected, or module memory loss may occur.
11. Turn off the ignition.

Steering Tuning Selection

1. Install the scan tool.
2. Turn on the ignition, with the engine off.
3. With the scan tool select Special Functions

4. Select Steering Tuning Selection and press the enter key. The scan tool screen will flash Selection in Progress.
5. When done the scan tool will display Selection Complete.
6. Press the exit key.
7. Use the scan tool in order to clear the DTCs.
8. After turning OFF the ignition, allow 25 seconds of wait time before performing any procedures that require the vehicles battery to be disconnected, or module memory loss may occur.
9. Turn off the ignition.

POWER STEERING PUMP

REMOVAL & INSTALLATION

1. Remove the drive belt.
2. Remove the power steering pump pulley.
3. Remove the intake manifold cover.
4. Use an appropriate tool to remove the power steering fluid from the reservoir before removing the hoses from the pump.
5. Remove the hoses from the pump.
6. Remove the pump.

To install:

7. Install the pump.
8. Install the hoses from the pump.
9. Install the intake manifold cover.
10. Install the power steering pump pulley.
11. Install the drive belt.
12. File and bleed the power steering system.

BLEEDING

1. Remove the pump reservoir cap.
2. Fill the pump reservoir with fluid to the FULL COLD level.
3. Attach a vacuum pump and adapter to the pump reservoir filler neck.
4. Apply a vacuum of 20 in Hg (68 kPa) maximum.
5. Wait 5 minutes. Typical vacuum drop is 2-3 in Hg (7-10 kPa). If the vacuum does not remain steady, check the pump, lines and o-ring seals for leaks.
6. Remove the vacuum tools.
7. Reinstall the pump reservoir cap.
8. Start the engine. Allow the engine to idle.
9. Turn off the engine.
10. Verify the fluid level and fill as needed.
11. Start the engine. Allow the engine to idle.
12. Turn the steering wheel 180-360 degrees in both directions 5 times.
13. Switch the ignition off.

SUSPENSION   **FRONT SUSPENSION**

FRONT SUSPENSION FRAME

REMOVAL & INSTALLATION

1. Install an engine support fixture.
2. Raise the vehicle on a hoist.
3. Remove the tire and wheel.
4. Remove the front fender liner.
5. Disconnect the ABS sensor from the wheel speed sensor and frame.
6. Remove the tie rod ends from the steering knuckles.
7. Remove both stabilizer links from the stabilizer bar.
8. Remove the power steering gear mounting bolts and secure the gear out of the way using mechanic's wire or equivalent, being sure not to overextend the intermediate shaft.
9. Remove the front, rear, left and right transmission mount bolts or nuts from the frame.
10. Remove the brake lines from the retainers on the frame.
11. Lower the vehicle until the frame contacts Engine Support Stand J-39580,
12. Remove the rear reinforcement bolts.
13. Remove the front and rear frame bolts.
14. Remove the frame reinforcements.
15. Raise the vehicle off of the frame.

To install:

16. Lower the vehicle on to the frame.
17. Install the frame reinforcements.
18. Install the front and bolts and tighten to 73 ft. lbs. (100 Nm) plus 180 degrees.
19. Install the reinforcement bolts and tighten to 37 ft. lbs. (50 Nm).
20. Raise the vehicle.
21. Install the brake lines to the retainers on the frame.
22. Install the front and mission mount bracket nuts and tighten to 66 ft. lbs. (90 Nm).
23. Install the left and right transmission mount bracket bolts and tighten to 37 (50 Nm).
24. Install the power steering gear.
25. Install both stabilizer links to the stabilizer bar.
26. Install the tie rod ends to the steering knuckles.
27. Install the lower ball joints to the steering knuckles.
28. Connect the ABS sensor to the wheel speed sensor and frame.
29. Install the front fender liner.
30. Install the tire and wheel.
31. Remove the engine support fixture.
32. Bleed the power steering system

LOWER CONTROL ARM

REMOVAL & INSTALLATION

See Figure 156.

1. Raise and support the vehicle.
2. Remove the wheel.

⁂ WARNING

DO NOT re-use the lower ball joint bolt. Discard and use new only.

3. Remove the lower ball joint to knuckle nut and bolt.
4. Separate the lower control arm from the knuckle.
5. If removing the left lower control arm, refer to the following:
   - For vehicles equipped with the 4T45-E transmission, remove the left side transmission mount.
   - For vehicles equipped with the 4T65-E transmission, remove the left side transmission mount.
   - For vehicles equipped with the 6T70/6T75 transmission, remove the left side transmission mount.
6. If removing the right lower control arm, refer to the following:
   - For vehicles equipped with the 3.5L engine, remove the right engine mount.
   - For vehicles equipped with the 3.6L engine, remove the right engine mount.
   - For vehicles equipped with the 3.9L engine, remove the right engine mount.
7. Remove the front lower control arm bolt.
8. Remove the rear lower control arm bushing nuts and bolts.
9. Remove the control arm from the cradle

To install:

10. Position the lower control arm in the cradle.
11. Install and hand tighten the rear lower control arm bushing nuts and bolts.
12. Install and hand tighten the front lower control arm bolt.
13. Install the ball joint to knuckle bolt and nut.
14. Tighten the ball joint bolt and nut to 37 ft. lbs. (50 Nm). Reverse the nut 3/4 of a turn. Tighten to 37 ft. lbs. (50 Nm) plus 30 degrees.
15. Load the front suspension with the

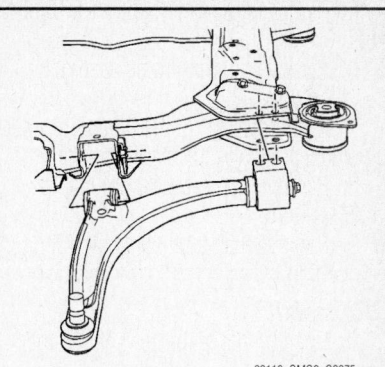

22116_GMG6_G0075

Fig. 156 Front lower control arm mounting to cradle—G6

proper jack stand before tightening bolts to the following specifications:
- Tighten the lower control arm bolt to 37 ft. lbs. (50 Nm). plus 90 degrees.
- Tighten the rear bushing to frame bolts to 37 ft. lbs. (50 Nm). plus 90 degrees.
16. Remove the jack stand.
17. If installing the left lower control arm, refer to the following:
   - For vehicles equipped with the 4T45-E transmission, remove the left side transmission mount
   - For vehicles equipped with the 4T65-E transmission, remove the left side transmission mount.
   - For vehicles equipped with the 6T70/6T75 transmission, remove the left side transmission mount.
18. If installing the right lower control arm, refer to the following:
   - For vehicles equipped with the 3.5L engine, remove the right engine mount.
   - For vehicles equipped with the 3.6L engine, remove the right engine mount.
   - For vehicles equipped with the 3.9L engine, remove the right engine mount.
19. Install the tire and wheel.
20. Verify wheel alignment.
21. Remove the support and lower the vehicle.

STABILIZER BAR

REMOVAL & INSTALLATION

1. Raise and support the vehicle.
2. Remove the wheels.
3. Disconnect the stabilizer links from the stabilizer shaft.

4. Using a suitable jack stand, support the rear of the frame assembly.

5. Remove the frame support-to-body bolts.

6. Remove the rear frame assembly mounting bolts.

7. Lower the rear of the cradle in order to gain clearance to the stabilizer shaft.

8. Remove the stabilizer bar clamps and insulators.

9. Remove the stabilizer shaft through the opening between the frame and body.

To install:

10. Position the stabilizer shaft to the frame.

11. Install the stabilizer bar clamps and insulators and tighten to 18 ft. lbs. (25 Nm).

12. Raise the rear of the cradle.

13. Install the frame support brackets. Loosely install the bracket and frame-to-body bolts.

14. Tighten the rear frame to body bolt-to-74 ft. lbs. (100 Nm).

15. Tighten the frame support bracket-to-body bolt 74 ft. lbs. (100).

16. Tighten all the bolts 90 degrees plus an additional 15 degrees.

17. Remove the jack stand.

18. Connect the stabilizer link to the stabilizer bar and tighten to 48 ft. lbs. (65 Nm).

19. Lower the vehicle.

STABILIZER LINK

REMOVAL & INSTALLATION

1. Raise and support the vehicle.

2. Remove the front tire and wheel assembly.

3. Disconnect the stabilizer link from the stabilizer shaft.

4. Disconnect the stabilizer link from the strut assembly and remove from the vehicle.

To install:

5. Connect the stabilizer link to the strut assembly.

6. Tighten the stabilizer link nut to 48 ft. lbs. (65 Nm).

7. Connect the stabilizer link to the stabilizer shaft.

8. Tighten the stabilizer link nut to 48 ft. lbs. (65 Nm).

9. Install the front tire and wheel assembly.

10. Lower the vehicle.

STEERING KNUCKLE

REMOVAL & INSTALLATION

1. Raise and support the vehicle.

2. Remove the wheels.

3. Remove the brake caliper and rotor.

4. Remove the wheel hub/ bearing assembly.

5. Remove the outer tie rod-to-knuckle nut.

6. Separate the tie rod from the steering knuckle.

7. Remove the lower control arm.

8. Remove the strut-to-steering knuckle nuts and bolts.

9. Remove the steering knuckle.

To install:

10. Install the steering knuckle to the strut assembly and the ABS harness bracket. Tighten the bolts and nuts to 89 ft. lbs. (120 Nm).

11. Guide the axle through the steering knuckle.

12. Install the lower control arm.

13. Install the outer tie rod to the steering knuckle and tighten the nut to 15 ft. lbs. (20 Nm), plus an additional 180 degrees.

14. Verify the torque is 37 ft. lbs. (50 Nm).

15. Install the wheel bearing, brake rotor, brake caliper and front wheels.

16. Lower the vehicle.

17. Road test the vehicle in order to verify alignment.

STRUT & COIL SPRING

REMOVAL & INSTALLATION

1. Raise and support the vehicle safely.

2. Remove the front wheel.

3. Disconnect the stabilizer link from the strut.

4. Remove the strut-to-steering knuckle nuts.

5. Reposition the wheel speed sensor/ABS harness and bracket.

6. Remove the strut-to-steering knuckle bolts.

7. Remove the upper strut cap-to-body nuts.

8. In order to prevent damage to the CV joint boot, place a shop towel over the CV joint.

9. Remove the strut from the vehicle.

10. Place the strut assembly into a spring compressor.

11. Adjust the compressing arms to contact the coils farthest away from the center of the spring.

12. Compress the spring to remove the spring tension from the upper strut mount.

13. Remove the strut shaft nut, while holding the strut shaft.

14. Lower the strut from the spring and the compressor.

15. Remove the upper strut mount assembly and mount bearing. Inspect for damage and replace as necessary.

16. Remove the upper spring seat and insulator from the spring and the compressor. Inspect for damage and replace as necessary.

17. Using the compressor, remove the spring tension in order to remove the spring. Inspect for damage and replace as necessary.

18. Remove the dust shield and jounce bumper assembly from the strut shaft. Inspect for damage and replace as necessary.

19. Remove the lower spring seat insulator. Inspect for damage and replace as necessary.

To install:

20. Install the spring into the compressor. Make sure the spring is level.

21. Compress the spring evenly.

22. Install the lower spring seat insulator.

23. Extend the strut shaft to the upper limit of its travel.

24. Insert the jounce bumper into the dust shield.

25. Slide the dust shield assembly onto the strut shaft.

26. Load the strut through the coil spring and the compressor.

27. Firmly align the lower spring coil in the spring seat pocket.

28. Place the upper spring insulator and spring seat onto the top of the coil spring.

29. Place the bearing and strut mount on the top of the spring seat.

30. Install the upper strut shaft nut and tighten to 52 ft. lbs. (70 Nm).

31. Using the compressor, remove spring tension.

32. Remove the strut assembly from the compressor.

33. Position the strut to the vehicles strut tower, using the alignment pin as a guide.

34. Install the upper strut cap-to-body nuts and tighten to 18 ft. lbs. (25 Nm).

35. Install the strut-to-steering knuckle bolts leaving the nuts off.

36. Place the wheel speed sensor harness and bracket to the bolt end.

37. Install the strut to steering knuckle nuts and tighten to 89 ft. lbs. (120 Nm).

38. Connect the stabilizer link to the strut and tighten to 48 ft. lbs. (65 Nm).

39. Install the front wheel.

40. Lower the vehicle.

WHEEL HUB AND BEARING

REMOVAL & INSTALLATION

1. Raise and support the vehicle.
2. Remove the wheel.
3. Remove the wheel drive shaft nut.
4. Remove the brake caliper and wire aside.
5. Remove the brake rotor.
6. Disconnect the electrical connector from the wheel speed sensor.
7. Remove the wheel speed sensor connector from the bracket by depressing the locking tabs.

8. Remove the 3 hub and bearing assembly bolts.
9. Install Wheel Hub Removal tool J-42129 to the hub and bearing assembly in order to remove the hub and bearing assembly from the wheel drive shaft.
10. Remove the hub and bearing assembly from the steering knuckle.

To install:

11. Install the hub and bearing assembly to the steering knuckle.
12. Install the 3 hub and bearing assembly bolts and tighten to 85 ft. lbs. (115 Nm).

13. Install the wheel speed sensor connector into the bracket until the locking tabs click into place.
14. Connect the electrical connector to the wheel speed sensor.
15. Install the axle nut to the wheel drive shaft and hand tighten.
16. Install the brake rotor.
17. Use a screw driver or similar tool to stop the rotation of the brake rotor.
18. Tighten the wheel drive shaft nut to 159 ft. lbs. (215 Nm).
19. Install the brake caliper.
20. Install the tire and wheel.

SUSPENSION

REAR SUSPENSION

COIL SPRING

REMOVAL & INSTALLATION

2005—06 Models

1. Raise and support the vehicle.
2. Remove the wheel and tire.
3. Use an OTC 204-167 compressor and OTC 204-167-01 adapter shoes or equivalent on-vehicle spring compressor to compress the coil spring.
4. Using a suitable jack stand, support the lower control arm.
5. Remove the lower control arm-to-knuckle bolt, nut, and inboard fastener.
6. Use the jack stand in order to lower the lower control arm with the coil spring attached.
7. Remove the coil spring from the lower control arm.
8. Inspect the coil spring insulators for damage and replace as necessary.

To install:

9. Position the spring on the lower control arm.
10. Use the jack stand to raise the lower control arm into position.
11. Install the lower control arm-to-knuckle bolt, nut, and inboard fastener. And tighten the bolt and nut to 44 ft. lbs. (60 Nm), plus an additional 60 degrees.
12. Remove the spring compressor.
13. Remove the jack stand.
14. Install the rear tire and wheel.
15. Lower the vehicle.

2007 Models

See Figure 157.

1. Raise and support the vehicle.
2. Remove the rear tire and wheel assembly.
3. Using a suitable jack stand, support the lower control arm.

4. Remove the lower control arm to knuckle bolt and nut.

✳✳ CAUTION

To prevent personal injury and/or component damage, use the proper tools to support the lower control arm when removing the coil spring. The coil spring is under extreme pressure and can become a projectile should the spring separate from the lower control arm before all of the tension is relieved.

5. Use the jack stand to swing the lower control arm downward with the coil spring attached.
6. Remove the coil spring from the lower control arm.

To install:

➡ **Be sure that the coil spring upper and lower insulators are properly seated prior to installation of the coil spring.**

7. Position the coil spring onto the lower control arm.

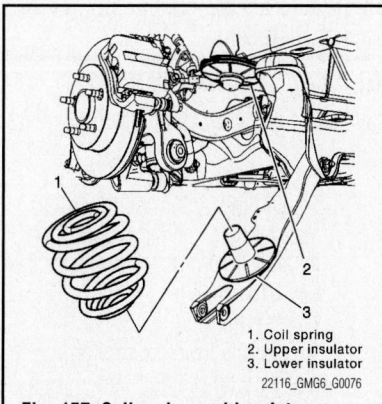

1. Coil spring
2. Upper insulator
3. Lower insulator

22116_GMG6_G0076

Fig. 157 Coil spring and insulators Pontiac—G6

8. Use the jack stand to raise the lower control arm upward into position.
9. Install the lower control arm to knuckle bolt and nut. Tighten to 81 ft. lbs. (110 Nm).
10. Remove the jack stand from under the vehicle.
11. Install the rear tire and wheel assembly.
12. Lower the vehicle.
13. Check the rear wheel alignment.

KNUCKLE

REMOVAL & INSTALLATION

1. Raise and support the vehicle.
2. Remove the wheels.
3. Remove the brake caliper and rotor.
4. Remove the wheel hub/ bearing assembly.
5. Using a suitable jack, raise the knuckle in order to relieve tension from the shock.
6. Remove the lower shock-to-knuckle bolt.
7. Remove the coil spring.
8. Remove the toe link.
9. Remove the upper control arm-to-knuckle bolt and nut.
10. Remove the trailing arm-to-knuckle bolts.
11. Remove the stabilizer shaft link-to-knuckle bolt.
12. Remove the knuckle from the vehicle.

To install:

13. Install the trailing arm-to-knuckle bolts and tighten to 133 ft. lbs. (180 Nm).
14. Install the upper control arm-to-knuckle bolt and nut and tighten to 81 ft. lbs. (110 Nm), plus 70 degrees.
15. Install the toe link.
16. Install the coil spring.

17. Install the lower shock absorber-to-knuckle bolt and tighten to 133 ft. lbs. (180 Nm).

18. Install the stabilizer link to the knuckle and tighten to 37 ft. lbs. (50 Nm).

19. Install the rear wheel bearing and brake components.

20. Install the tire and wheel.

21. Lower the vehicle.

LOWER CONTROL ARM

REMOVAL & INSTALLATION

See Figure 158.

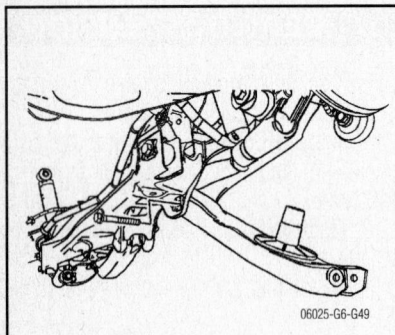

Fig. 158 Rear lower control arm mounting—G6

1. Raise and support the vehicle.
2. Remove the wheel.
3. Remove the rear spring.
4. Remove the lower control arm-to-support assembly bolt and nut.
5. Remove the lower control arm from the vehicle.
6. Remove the lower control arm spring insulators. Inspect the lower spring insulator for damage and replace as necessary.

To install:

7. Install the lower control arm spring insulators.
8. Position the lower control arm to the support assembly.
9. Install the lower control arm-to-support assembly bolt and nut and tighten to 81 ft. lbs. (110 Nm).
10. Install the rear spring.
11. Install the tire and wheel.
12. Lower the vehicle.
13. Check the rear alignment.

CONTROL ARM BUSHING REPLACEMENT

1. Remove the lower control arm-to-rear bushing bolt.
2. Note the position of the bushing during removal. Remove the bushing off the lower control arm.

3. Install the bushing on the lower control arm as previously noted.
4. Using Loctite on the bolt threads, install the lower control arm-to-bushing bolt.
5. Hold the rear bushing inner sleeve when tightening the rear bushings to control arm bolt. Tighten the bolt to 32 ft. lbs. (44 Nm).

REAR SUPPORT ASSEMBLY

REMOVAL & INSTALLATION

See Figure 159.

1. Raise and support the vehicle.
2. Remove the rear tire and wheel assemblies
3. Remove the muffler.
4. Remove the rear axle tie rod bracket braces. **Convertible Models**
5. Remove the knuckles.
6. If the vehicle is equipped with ABS, disconnect the ABS wiring harness from the clips on the support assembly and upper control arms.
7. Position a suitable jack stand under the support assembly.

➡**When replacing complete module assembly, mark fastener location of axle bracket (LH/RH) to body rail.**

8. Remove the support assembly to body bolts.

➡**Mark location of support assembly to body rails with a dab of paint.**

9. With the aid of an assistant, remove the support assembly from the vehicle.

✲✲ CAUTION

If a transfer of components is necessary, it is recommended that the fasteners be loosely installed, then all the suspension component fasteners be torqued after the support is in the vehicle and all the suspension components installed.

10. If a new rear support is being installed, a transfer of components is necessary:

- Upper control arms
- Tighten the upper control arm to rear support nut and bolt to 44 ft. lbs. (60 Nm) plus 60 degrees rotation.
- Lower control arms
- Tighten the lower control arm to rear support nut and bolt to 81 ft. lbs. (110 Nm).
- Stabilizer bar and insulators

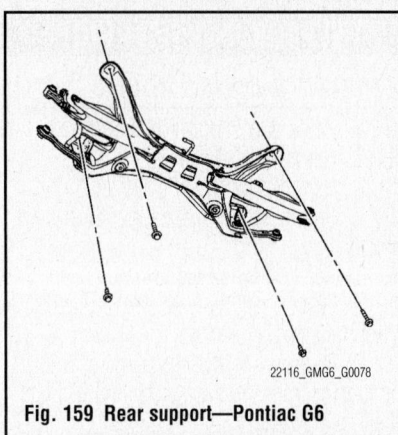

22116_GMG6_G0078

Fig. 159 Rear support—Pontiac G6

- Tighten the stabilizer shaft insulator bolts to 26 ft. lbs. (35 Nm).
- Toe link to support bolt and nut
- Tighten toe link to support bolt and nut to 81 ft. lbs. (110 Nm).

➡**Position the support assembly to the body rails by location of paint marks during removal.**

11. With the aid of an assistant, raise and position the support assembly to the vehicle.
12. Install the support assembly to body bolts. Tighten the bolts to 74 ft. lbs. (100 Nm) plus 30 degrees.
13. Remove the jack stand from under the vehicle.
14. If the vehicle is equipped with ABS, route the ABS wiring harness, connect it to the clips on the support assembly and upper control arms.
15. Install the knuckles.
16. Install the rear axle tie rod bracket braces. **Convertible Models**
17. Install the muffler.
18. Install the rear frame brace. **Convertible Models**
19. Install the rear tire and wheel assemblies.
20. Lower the vehicle.
21. Adjust the rear alignment.

SHOCK ABSORBER

REMOVAL & INSTALLATION

1. Raise and support the vehicle.
2. Remove the rear wheel.
3. Using a suitable jack stand, raise the rear knuckle to release the spring tension.
4. Remove the lower shock bolt.
5. Remove the upper shock nuts and remove the shock absorber.

To install:

6. Install the shock in the vehicle.
7. Install the shock absorber-to-body bolts and tighten to 18 ft. lbs. (25 Nm).

8. Install the shock absorber-to-knuckle bolt and tighten to 133 ft. lbs. (180 Nm).

9. Remove the jack stand from the rear knuckle.

10. Install the tire and wheel.

11. Lower the vehicle.

TESTING

1. Test drive vehicle.

2. Inspect each shock absorber for external fluid leakage.

3. Use your hands in order to lift up and push down each corner of the vehicle 3 times.

4. Remove your hands from the vehicle.

5. Replace any shock that exceeds more than two bounces.

STABILIZER BAR

REMOVAL & INSTALLATION

2005—06 Models

1. Raise and support the vehicle.

2. Remove the wheels.

3. Remove the muffler assembly.

4. Disconnect the fuel pump module electrical connector from the underbody wiring harness.

5. Disconnect the evaporative emissions (EVAP) vent valve solenoid harness electrical connector from the underbody wiring harness.

6. Suitably support the gas tank.

7. Remove the front fuel tank strap bolts.

8. Remove the fuel tank heat shield.

9. Lower the fuel tank as necessary for access.

10. Place a index mark on the rear camber adjusting bolts.

11. Suitably support the rear control arms.

12. Remove the right and left toe links.

13. Remove the stabilizer shaft bracket bolts.

14. Remove the stabilizer shaft insulators from the stabilizer shaft.

15. Remove the stabilizer link-to-knuckle bolts.

16. Remove the stabilizer shaft.

To install:

17. Position the stabilizer shaft.

18. Install the stabilizer shaft insulators and shaft brackets.

19. Install the stabilizer shaft bracket bolts and tighten to 26 ft. lbs. (35 Nm).

20. Install the stabilizer shaft links-to-knuckle bolts and tighten to 37 ft. lbs. (50 Nm).

21. Install the right and left toe links.

Line up the index marks on the camber bolts.

22. Tighten the toe link bolts to 81 ft. lbs. (110 Nm) plus 70 degrees.

23. Remove the supports from the rear control arms.

24. Raise the fuel tank into position.

25. Install the fuel tank heat shield.

26. Install the front fuel tank strap bolts and tighten to 15 ft. lbs. (20 Nm).

27. Remove support from the fuel tank.

28. Connect the evaporative emissions (EVAP) vent valve solenoid harness electrical connector to the underbody wiring harness.

29. Connect the fuel pump module electrical connector to the underbody wiring harness.

30. Install the muffler assembly.

31. Install the rear tire and wheel.

32. Lower the vehicle.

2007 Models

1. Raise and support the vehicle.

2. Scribe a line on the rear camber adjust bolts (both left and right).

3. Remove the rear axle toe link.

4. Remove the rear axle tie rod bracket brace.

5. Remove the muffler.

6. Remove the stabilizer shaft bracket bolts.

7. Remove the stabilizer shaft insulators from the stabilizer shaft.

8. Remove the stabilizer link to knuckle bolts.

9. Remove the stabilizer shaft.

To install:

10. Install the stabilizer shaft insulators.

11. Install the stabilizer shaft brackets.

12. Tighten the stabilizer shaft insulator bracket retaining bolts to 26 ft. lbs. (35 Nm).

13. Install the stabilizer shaft links to knuckle bolts and tighten to 41ft. lbs. (55 Nm).

14. Install the rear axle toe link.

15. Install the rear axle tie rod bracket brace.

16. Install the muffler.

17. Lower the vehicle.

TOE LINK

REMOVAL & INSTALLATION

See Figure 160.

1. Raise and support the vehicle.

2. Remove the tire and wheel.

3. Remove the toe link to steering knuckle bolt.

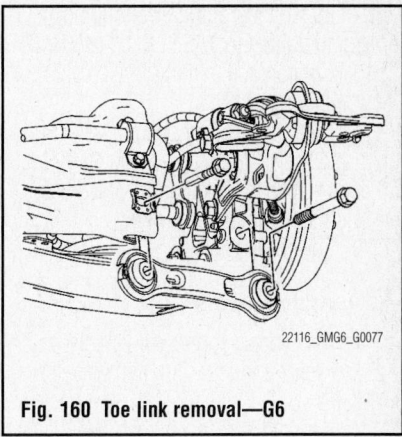

Fig. 160 Toe link removal—G6

4. Remove the toe link to support assembly bolt and nut.

5. Remove the toe link from the rear support assembly and vehicle.

To install:

6. Install the toe link into the support assembly

7. Loosely install the toe assembly bolt and nut.

8. Install the toe link to steering knuckle.

9. Tighten the bolt and nut to 81 ft. lbs. (110 Nm) plus 70 degrees.

10. Tighten the toe assembly bolt and nut to 81 ft. lbs. (110 Nm) plus 70 degrees.

11. Install the tire and wheel.

12. Lower the vehicle.

13. Adjust the rear toe.

TRAILING ARM

REMOVAL & INSTALLATION

Sedan & Coupe Models

1. Raise and support the vehicle.

2. Remove the wheels.

3. Remove the trailing arm bracket-to-body bolts.

4. Remove the trailing arm-to-knuckle through bolt.

5. Disconnect the parking brake cable from the trailing arm.

6. Remove the trailing arm.

7. Remove the trailing arm-to-bracket bolt and nut.

8. Remove the trailing arm from the bracket.

To install:

9. Assemble the trailing arm and bracket.

10. Tighten the trailing arm-to-bracket through bolt to 44 ft. lbs. (60 Nm) plus 60 degrees.

11. Position the trailing arm to the vehicle.

12. Install the trailing arm to knuckle bolts and tighten to 133 ft. lbs. (180 Nm).

13. Connect the parking brake cable to the trailing arm.

14. Install the trailing arm bracket-to-body bolts and tighten to 66 ft. lbs. (90 Nm) plus 30 degrees plus an additional 15 degrees.

15. Install the tire and wheel.

16. Lower the vehicle.

Convertible Models

1. Raise and support the vehicle.

2. Remove the rear tire and wheel assembly.

3. Remove the rear frame brace.

4. Remove the rear axle tie rod bracket brace.

5. Remove the 2 trailing arm bracket to body bolts.

6. Remove the rear parking brake cable routing bolt from the trailing arm.

7. Remove the 3 trailing arm to knuckle through bolts.

8. Lower the trailing arm to gain access to the trailing arm to bracket bolt and nut.

9. Remove the trailing arm to bracket bolt and nut.

10. Separate the trailing arm from the bracket and remove the trailing arm from the vehicle.

To install:

11. Position the trailing arm to the bracket, install the bolt and nut.

12. Tighten the trailing arm to bracket through bolt and nut to 44 ft. lbs. (60 Nm) plus 60 degrees.

13. Position the trailing arm to the vehicle.

14. Install the 3 trailing arm to knuckle bolts.

15. Tighten the 3 trailing arm to knuckle bolts to 133 ft. lbs. (180 Nm).

16. Install the rear parking brake cable routing bolt to the trailing arm.

17. Tighten the routing bolt to 89 inch. lbs. (10 Nm).

18. Install the 2 trailing arm bracket to body bolts.

19. Tighten the bracket to body bolts to 66 ft. lbs. (90 Nm) plus 30 degrees plus an additional 15 degrees.

20. Install the rear axle tie rod bracket brace.

21. Install the rear frame brace.

22. Install the rear tire and wheel assembly.

23. Lower the vehicle

UPPER CONTROL ARM

REMOVAL & INSTALLATION

1. Raise and support the vehicle.

2. Remove the wheel.

3. Disconnect the ABS harness connector and route the harness aside.

4. Remove the upper control arm to support assembly bolt.

5. Remove the upper control arm-to-knuckle bolt and nut.

6. Remove the upper control arm from the vehicle through the wheel well opening.

To install:

7. Position the upper control arm to the support assembly and knuckle.

8. Install the upper control arm-to-knuckle bolt and nut and hand tighten only.

9. Install the upper control arm-to-support assembly bolt.

10. Tighten the upper control arm-to-support assembly bolt to 44 ft. lbs. (60 Nm) plus 60 degrees.

11. Tighten the upper control arm-to-knuckle bolt to 81 ft. lbs. (110 Nm) plus 70 degrees.

12. Connect the ABS harness connector. Route the harness as previously noted.

13. Install the tire and wheel.

14. Lower the vehicle.

WHEEL HUB AND BEARING

REMOVAL & INSTALLATION

See Figure 161.

1. Raise and support the vehicle.

2. Remove the wheel.

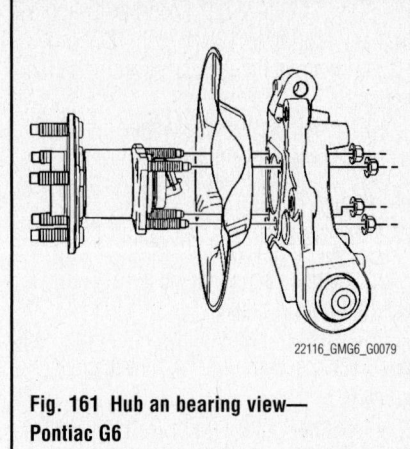

22116_GMG6_G0079

Fig. 161 Hub an bearing view— Pontiac G6

3. Remove the brake caliper and rotor.

4. Disconnect the electrical connector from the wheel speed sensor.

5. Remove the stabilizer link bolt at the knuckle and position the stabilizer link out of the way in order to provide access to the wheel bearing/hub nuts.

6. Remove the 4 wheel bearing/hub assembly nuts.

7. Remove the wheel bearing/hub assembly from the knuckle.

To install:

8. Install the wheel bearing/hub assembly to the knuckle.

9. Install the 4 wheel bearing/hub assembly nuts and tighten to 47 ft. lbs. (63 Nm).

10. Connect the stabilizer link bolt at the knuckle.

11. Connect the electrical connector to the wheel speed sensor.

12. Install the brake rotor and caliper.

13. Install the tire and wheel.

14. Lower the vehicle.

ADJUSTMENT

No adjustment is possible or necessary. If bearing is loose replace hub and bearing assembly.

PONTIAC

13

GTO

SPECIFICATIONS AND MAINTENANCE CHARTS

VEHICLE AND ENGINE IDENTIFICATION CHART

		Engine						Model Year	
Code	Liters	Cu. In.	Cyl.	Fuel Sys.	Engine Type	Eng. Mfg.		Code	Year
U	6.0	364	8	SEFI	OHV	General Motors		5	2005
SEFI: Sequential Multi-port Fuel Injection								6	2006

22116_GGTO_C0001

GENERAL ENGINE SPECIFICATIONS

Year	Engine Displacement Liters	Engine VIN	Net Horsepower @ rpm	Net Torque @ rpm (ft. lbs.)	Bore x Stroke (in.)	Compression Ratio	Oil Pressure @ rpm
2005	6.0	U	400@5200	400@4000	4.00x3.62	10.9:1	24@4000
2006	6.0	U	400@5200	400@4000	4.00x3.62	10.9:1	24@4000

22116_GGTO_C0002

GASOLINE ENGINE TUNE-UP SPECIFICATIONS

Year	Engine Displacement Liters	Engine VIN	Spark Plugs Gap (in.)	Ignition Timing (deg.) MT	AT	Fuel Pump (psi)	Idle Speed (rpm) MT	AT	Valve Clearance In.	Ex.
2005	6.0	U	0.040	①	①	55-64	①	①	HYD	HYD
2006	6.0	U	0.040	①	①	55-64	①	①	HYD	HYD

NOTE: The Vehicle Emission Control Information label often reflects specification changes changes made during production.

The label figures must be used if they differ from those in this chart.

HYD: Hydraulic

① Controlled by the Powertrain Control Module (PCM) and cannot be manually adjusted.

22116_GGTO_C0003

CAPACITIES

Year	Model	Engine Displacement Liters	Engine ID/VIN	Engine Oil with Filter (qts.)	Transmission (pts.)			Drive Axle		Fuel Tank (gal.)	Cooling System (qts.)
					4-Spd	6-Spd	Auto.	Front (pts.)	Rear (pts.)		
2005	GTO	6.0	U	6.2	—	8.5	8.7	—	①	18.5	11.6
2006	GTO	6.0	U	6.2	—	8.5	8.7	—	①	18.5	11.6

NOTE: All capacities are approximate. Add fluid gradually and check to be sure a proper fluid level is obtained.

① 1.7 qts. plus 1 oz. friction modifier

22116_GGTO_C0004

VALVE SPECIFICATIONS

Year	Engine VIN	Engine Displacement Liters	Seat Angle (deg.)	Face Angle (deg.)	Spring Test Pressure (lbs. @ in.)	Spring Installed Height (in.)	Stem-to-Guide Clearance (in.)		Stem Diameter (in.)	
							Intake	Exhaust	Intake	Exhaust
2005	U	6.0	46	45	220@1.32	1.800	0.0010-0.0026	0.0010-0.0026	0.3131-0.3140	0.3131-0.3140
2006	U	6.0	46	45	220@1.32	1.800	0.0010-0.0026	0.0010-0.0026	0.3131-0.3140	0.3131-0.3140

22116_GGTO_C0005

CRANKSHAFT AND CONNECTING ROD SPECIFICATIONS
All measurements are given in inches.

Year	Engine Displ. Liters	Engine VIN	Crankshaft				Connecting Rod		
			Main Brg. Journal Dia.	Main Brg. Oil Clearance	Shaft End-play	Thrust on No.	Journal Diameter	Oil Clearance	Side Clearance
2005	6.0	U	2.5587-2.5593	0.0008-0.0021	0.0015-0.0078	NA	2.0991-2.0999	0.0009-0.0025	0.0043-0.0200
2006	6.0	U	2.5587-2.5593	0.0008-0.0021	0.0015-0.0078	NA	2.0991-2.0999	0.0009-0.0025	0.0043-0.0200

22116_GGTO_C0006

PISTON AND RING SPECIFICATIONS

All measurements are given in inches.

Year	Engine Displ. Liters	Engine VIN	Piston Clearance	Ring Gap			Ring Side Clearance		
				Top Comp.	Bottom Comp.	Oil Control	Top Comp.	Bottom Comp.	Oil Control
2005	6.0	U	0.0009-0.0012	0.0078-0.0161	0.0145-0.0271	0.0086-0.0311	0.0012-0.0040	0.0014-0.0031	0.0005-0.0079
2006	6.0	U	0.0009-0.0012	0.0078-0.0161	0.0145-0.0271	0.0086-0.0311	0.0012-0.0040	0.0014-0.0031	0.0005-0.0079

22116_GGTO_C0007

TORQUE SPECIFICATIONS

All readings in ft. lbs.

Year	Engine VIN	Engine Displacement Liters	Cylinder Head Bolts	Main Bearing Bolts	Rod Bearing Bolts	Crankshaft Damper Bolts	Flywheel Bolts	Manifold		Spark Plugs	Oil Pan Drain Plug
								Intake	Exhaust		
2005	U	6.0	①	②	③	④	⑤	⑥	⑦	11	18
2006	U	6.0	①	②	③	④	⑤	⑥	⑦	11	18

① Step 1: M11 bolts 22 ft. lbs.
   Step 2: M11 bolts plus 90 degrees
   Step 3: M11 bolts plus 70 degrees
   Step 4: M8 bolts 22 ft. lbs.

② Step 1: M10 bolts 15 ft. lbs.
   Step 2: M10 bolts plus 80 degrees
   Step 3: M10 studs 15 ft. lbs.
   Step 4: M10 studs plus 51 degrees
   Step 5: M8 bolts 18 ft. lbs.

③ Step 1: 15 ft. lbs.
   Step 2: plus 75 degrees

④ Step 1: 37 ft. lbs.
   Step 2: plus 140 degrees

⑤ Step 1: 15 ft. lbs.
   Step 2: 37 ft. lbs.
   Step 3: 74 15 ft. lbs.

⑥ Step 1: 44 INCH lbs.
   Step 2: 89 INCH lbs.

⑦ Step 1: 11 ft. lbs.
   Step 2: 18 ft. lbs.

22116_GGTO_C0008

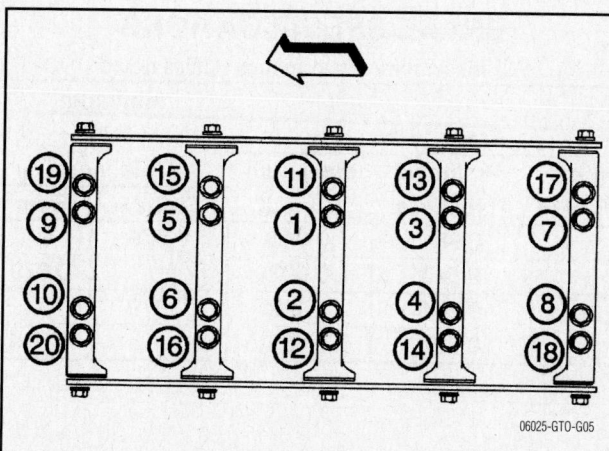

06025-GTO-G05

Fig. 1 Main bearing cap bolt tightening sequence—6.0L (VIN U) engines

WHEEL ALIGNMENT

Year	Model			Caster Range (+/-Deg.)	Caster Preferred Setting (Deg.)	Camber Range (+/-Deg.)	Camber Preferred Setting (Deg.)	Toe-in (Deg.)
2005	GTO	Front	Left	0.80	+7.7	0.60	-0.20	-0.17+/-0.17
			Right	0.80	+7.7	0.60	-0.20	-0.17+/-0.17
		Rear		—	—	0.58	-1.05	-0.40+/-0.34
2006	GTO	Front	Left	0.80	+7.7	0.60	-0.20	-0.17+/-0.17
			Right	0.80	+7.7	0.60	-0.20	-0.17+/-0.17
		Rear		—	—	0.58	-1.05	-0.40+/-0.34

22116_GGTO_C0009

TIRE AND WHEEL SPECIFICATIONS

Year	Model	OEM Tires Standard	OEM Tires Optional	Tire Pressures (psi) Front	Tire Pressures (psi) Rear	Wheel Size	Wheel Lug Nut Torque (Ft. Lbs.)
2005	GTO	P245/50R16	—	35	35	①	②
2006	GTO	P245/50R16	—	35	35	①	②

OEM: Original Equipment Manufacturer

PSI: Pounds Per Square Inch

STD: Standard

OPT: Optional

① Not available

② Step 1: 50 ft. lbs.

    Step 2: 100 ft. lbs.

22116_GGTO_C0010

BRAKE SPECIFICATIONS

All measurements in inches unless noted

Year	Model		Brake Disc Original Thickness	Brake Disc Minimum Thickness	Brake Disc Maximum Runout	Minimum Lining Thickness Front	Minimum Lining Thickness Rear	Brake Caliper Bracket Bolts (ft. lbs.)	Brake Caliper Mounting Bolts (ft. lbs.)
2005	GTO	F	①	0.984	0.002	0.079	—	②	24
		R	①	0.547	0.002	—	0.079	63	24
2006	GTO	F	①	0.984	0.002	0.079	—	②	24
		R	①	0.547	0.002	—	0.079	63	24

① Not available

② 63 ft. lbs., plus an additional 45 degrees

22116_GGTO_C0011

PRECAUTIONS

Before servicing any vehicle, please be sure to read all of the following precautions, which deal with personal safety, prevention of component damage, and important points to take into consideration when servicing a motor vehicle:

• Never open, service or drain the radiator or cooling system when the engine is hot; serious burns can occur from the steam and hot coolant.

• Observe all applicable safety precautions when working around fuel. Whenever servicing the fuel system, always work in a well-ventilated area. Do not allow fuel spray or vapors to come in contact with a spark, open flame, or excessive heat (a hot drop light, for example). Keep a dry chemical fire extinguisher near the work area. Always keep fuel in a container specifically designed for fuel storage; also, always properly seal fuel containers to avoid the possibility of fire or explosion. Refer to the additional fuel system precautions later in this section.

• Fuel injection systems often remain pressurized, even after the engine has been turned **OFF**. The fuel system pressure must be relieved before disconnecting any fuel lines. Failure to do so may result in fire and/or personal injury.

• Brake fluid often contains polyglycol ethers and polyglycols. Avoid contact with the eyes and wash your hands thoroughly after handling brake fluid. If you do get brake fluid in your eyes, flush your eyes with clean, running water for 15 minutes. If eye irritation persists, or if you have taken

brake fluid internally, IMMEDIATELY seek medical assistance.

• The EPA warns that prolonged contact with used engine oil may cause a number of skin disorders, including cancer. You should make every effort to minimize your exposure to used engine oil. Protective gloves should be worn when changing oil. Wash your hands and any other exposed skin areas as soon as possible after exposure to used engine oil. Soap and water, or waterless hand cleaner should be used.

• All new vehicles are now equipped with an air bag system, often referred to as a Supplemental Restraint System (SRS) or Supplemental Inflatable Restraint (SIR) system. The system must be disabled before performing service on or around system components, steering column, instrument panel components, wiring and sensors. Failure to follow safety and disabling procedures could result in accidental air bag deployment, possible personal injury and unnecessary system repairs.

• Always wear safety goggles when working with, or around, the air bag system. When carrying a non-deployed air bag, be sure the bag and trim cover are pointed away from your body. When placing a non-deployed air bag on a work surface, always face the bag and trim cover upward, away from the surface. This will reduce the motion of the module if it is accidentally deployed. Refer to the additional air bag system precautions later in this section.

• Clean, high quality brake fluid from a sealed container is essential to the safe and

proper operation of the brake system. You should always buy the correct type of brake fluid for your vehicle. If the brake fluid becomes contaminated, completely flush the system with new fluid. Never reuse any brake fluid. Any brake fluid that is removed from the system should be discarded. Also, do not allow any brake fluid to come in contact with a painted surface; it will damage the paint.

• Never operate the engine without the proper amount and type of engine oil; doing so WILL result in severe engine damage.

• Timing belt maintenance is extremely important. Many models utilize an interference-type, non-freewheeling engine. If the timing belt breaks, the valves in the cylinder head may strike the pistons, causing potentially serious (also time-consuming and expensive) engine damage. Refer to the maintenance interval charts for the recommended replacement interval for the timing belt, and to the timing belt section for belt replacement and inspection.

• Disconnecting the negative battery cable on some vehicles may interfere with the functions of the on-board computer system(s) and may require the computer to undergo a relearning process once the negative battery cable is reconnected.

• When servicing drum brakes, only disassemble and assemble one side at a time, leaving the remaining side intact for reference.

• Only an MVAC-trained, EPA-certified automotive technician should service the air conditioning system or its components.

BRAKES

ANTI-LOCK BRAKE SYSTEM (ABS)

GENERAL INFORMATION

PRECAUTIONS

• Certain components within the ABS system are not intended to be serviced or repaired individually.

• Do not use rubber hoses or other parts not specifically specified for and ABS system. When using repair kits, replace all parts included in the kit. Partial or incorrect repair may lead to functional problems and require the replacement of components.

• Lubricate rubber parts with clean, fresh brake fluid to ease assembly. Do not

use shop air to clean parts; damage to rubber components may result.

• Use only DOT 3 brake fluid from an unopened container.

• If any hydraulic component or line is removed or replaced, it may be necessary to bleed the entire system.

• A clean repair area is essential. Always clean the reservoir and cap thoroughly before removing the cap. The slightest amount of dirt in the fluid may plug an orifice and impair the system function. Perform repairs after components have been thoroughly cleaned; use only denatured alcohol

to clean components. Do not allow ABS components to come into contact with any substance containing mineral oil; this includes used shop rags.

• The Anti-Lock control unit is a microprocessor similar to other computer units in the vehicle. Ensure that the ignition switch is **OFF** before removing or installing controller harnesses. Avoid static electricity discharge at or near the controller.

• If any arc welding is to be done on the vehicle, the control unit should be unplugged before welding operations begin.

❋❋ CAUTION

Dust and dirt accumulating on brake parts during normal use may contain asbestos fibers from production or aftermarket brake linings. Breathing excessive concentrations of asbestos fibers can cause serious bodily harm. Exercise care when servicing brake parts. Do not sand or grind brake lining unless equipment used is designed to contain the dust residue. Do not clean brake parts with compressed air or by dry brushing. Cleaning should be done by dampening the brake components with a fine mist of water, then wiping the brake components clean with a dampened cloth. Dispose of cloth and all residue containing asbestos fibers in an impermeable container with the appropriate label. Follow practices prescribed by the Occupational Safety and Health Administration (OSHA) and the Environmental Protection Agency (EPA) for the handling, processing, and disposing of dust or debris that may contain asbestos fibers.

BRAKE CALIPER

REMOVAL & INSTALLATION

See Figure 2.

1. Use a siphon in order to remove half of the brake fluid from the reservoir.
2. Raise and support the vehicle.
3. Remove the tire and wheel.
4. Remove the caliper bolts.
5. Remove the caliper and the bracket from the brake rotor.

To install:

6. Ensure the mounting surfaces on the shield and on the caliper bracket are clean.
7. Ensure the caliper pistons are fully seated in the cylinder bores.
8. Position the caliper and the bracket over the rotor.
9. Install the caliper bolts and tighten to 63 ft. lbs. (85 Nm), plus an additional 45 degrees.
10. Install the tire and wheel assembly.
11. Lower the vehicle.
12. With the engine off, gradually apply and release the brake pedal several times in order to position the caliper pistons and the brake pads.

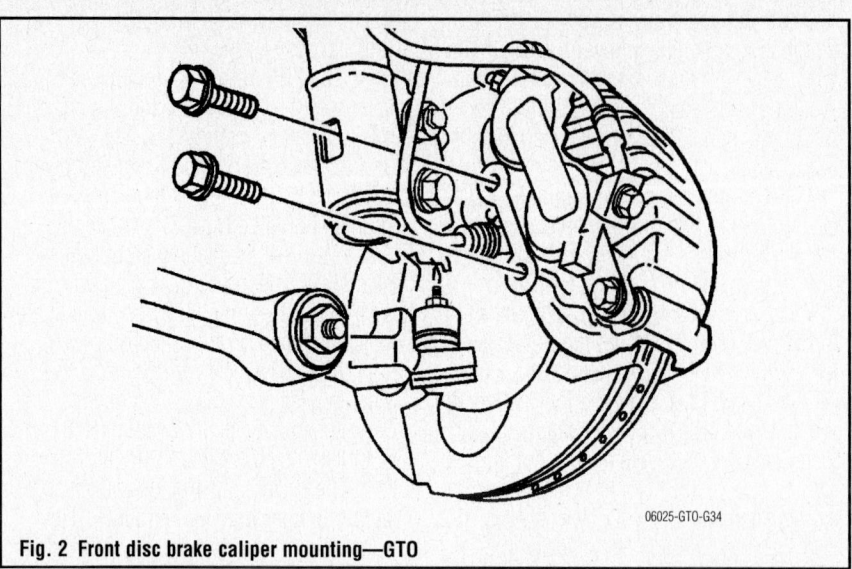

Fig. 2 Front disc brake caliper mounting—GTO

06025-GTO-G34

13. Fill the master cylinder reservoir.
14. Road test the vehicle and check for proper brake system operation.

DISC BRAKE PADS

REMOVAL AND INSTALLATION

1. Use a siphon in order to remove half of the brake fluid from the master cylinder reservoir.
2. Raise and support the vehicle.
3. Remove the tire and wheel.
4. Install a large C-clamp over the brake caliper. Position 1 end of the clamp on the head of the brake hose fitting. Position the other end of the clamp against the outer pad.
5. Install a second C-clamp over the brake caliper. Position 1 end of the clamp against the caliper body adjacent to the brake hose fitting. Position the other end of the clamp against the outer pad.
6. Tighten the 2 clamps in order to compress the 2 caliper pistons into the bores.
7. Remove the clamps.
8. Use a wrench in order to prevent the lower guide pin from turning.
9. Remove and discard the lower guide pin bolt.
10. Rotate the caliper assembly up and support the caliper with heavy mechanic's wire, or equivalent. Verify there is no tension on the brake hose.
11. Remove the 2 brake pads and the 2 spring clips, if equipped.

To install:

12. Use a large C-clamp and a wood block to push the caliper pistons back into their bores.
13. Clean the surfaces of the 2 pistons which contact the inner brake pad.
14. Clean the surface of the caliper which contacts the outer brake pad.
15. Install the inner brake pad to the bracket.
16. Install the outer brake pad to the caliper.
17. Position a leg of the steel spring onto the top of the inner pad.
18. Install the 2 spring clips, if equipped.
19. Rotate the caliper down over the brake rotor.
20. Ensure the outer spring clip engages the middle flange of the caliper housing.
21. Use a wrench in order to prevent the guide pin from rotating.
22. Install a new guide pin bolt and tighten to 24 ft. lbs. (32 Nm).
23. Install the wheel and tire assembly.
24. Lower the vehicle.
25. With the engine off, gradually apply and release the brake pedal several times in order to position the caliper piston.
26. Apply pressure to the brake pedal for at least 5 seconds in order to position the brake pads.
27. Fill the master cylinder fluid reservoir
28. If the disc brake calipers were replaced or repaired, be sure to bleed the system.
29. Road test the vehicle and check the brake system for proper operation.

BRAKES   **REAR DISC BRAKES**

Dust and dirt accumulating on brake parts during normal use may contain asbestos fibers from production or aftermarket brake linings. Breathing excessive concentrations of asbestos fibers can cause serious bodily harm. Exercise care when servicing brake parts. Do not sand or grind brake lining unless equipment used is designed to contain the dust residue. Do not clean brake parts with compressed air or by dry brushing. Cleaning should be done by dampening the brake components with a fine mist of water, then wiping the brake components clean with a dampened cloth. Dispose of cloth and all residue containing asbestos fibers in an impermeable container with the appropriate label. Follow practices prescribed by the Occupational Safety and Health Administration (OSHA) and the Environmental Protection Agency (EPA) for the handling, processing, and disposing of dust or debris that may contain asbestos fibers.

BRAKE CALIPER

REMOVAL & INSTALLATION

See Figure 3.

1. Use a siphon in order to remove half of the brake fluid from the reservoir.
2. Raise and support the vehicle.
3. Remove the tire and wheel.
4. Remove the caliper bolts.
5. Remove the caliper and the bracket from the brake rotor.

To install:

6. Ensure the mounting surfaces on the shield and on the caliper bracket are clean.
7. Ensure the caliper pistons are fully seated in the cylinder bores.
8. Position the caliper and the bracket over the rotor.
9. Install the caliper bolts and tighten to 63 ft. lbs. (85 Nm), plus an additional 45 degrees.

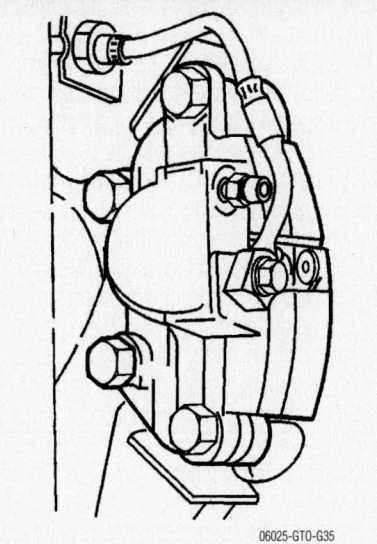

06025-GTO-G35

Fig. 3 Rear disc brake caliper mounting— GTO

10. Install the tire and wheel assembly.
11. Lower the vehicle.
12. With the engine off, gradually apply and release the brake pedal several times in order to position the caliper pistons and the brake pads.
13. Fill the master cylinder reservoir.
14. Road test the vehicle and check for proper brake system operation.

DISC BRAKE PADS

REMOVAL AND INSTALLATION

1. Use a siphon in order to remove half of the brake fluid from the master cylinder reservoir.
2. Raise and support the vehicle.
3. Remove the tire and wheel.
4. Install a large C-clamp over the brake caliper. Position 1 end of the clamp on the head of the brake hose fitting. Position the other end of the clamp against the outer pad.
5. Install a second C-clamp over the brake caliper. Position 1 end of the clamp against the caliper body adjacent to the brake hose fitting. Position the other end of the clamp against the outer pad.
6. Tighten the 2 clamps in order to

compress the 2 caliper pistons into the bores.
7. Remove the clamps.
8. Use a wrench in order to prevent the lower guide pin from turning.
9. Remove and discard the lower guide pin bolt.
10. Rotate the caliper assembly up and support the caliper with heavy mechanic's wire, or equivalent. Verify there is no tension on the brake hose.
11. Remove the 2 brake pads and the 2 spring clips, if equipped.

To install:

12. Use a large C-clamp and a wood block to push the caliper pistons back into their bores.
13. Clean the surfaces of the 2 pistons which contact the inner brake pad.
14. Clean the surface of the caliper which contacts the outer brake pad.
15. Install the inner brake pad to the bracket.
16. Install the outer brake pad to the caliper.
17. Position a leg of the steel spring onto the top of the inner pad.
18. Install the 2 spring clips, if equipped.
19. Rotate the caliper down over the brake rotor.
20. Ensure the outer spring clip engages the middle flange of the caliper housing.
21. Use a wrench in order to prevent the guide pin from rotating.
22. Install a new guide pin bolt and tighten to 24 ft. lbs. (32 Nm).
23. Install the wheel and tire assembly.
24. Lower the vehicle.
25. With the engine off, gradually apply and release the brake pedal several times in order to position the caliper piston.
26. Apply pressure to the brake pedal for at least 5 seconds in order to position the brake pads.
27. Fill the master cylinder fluid reservoir
28. If the disc brake calipers were replaced or repaired, be sure to bleed the system.
29. Road test the vehicle and check the brake system for proper operation.

CHASSIS ELECTRICAL — AIR BAG (SUPPLEMENTAL RESTRAINT SYSTEM)

GENERAL INFORMATION

✳✳ CAUTION

These vehicles are equipped with an air bag system. The system must be disarmed before performing service on, or around, system components, the steering column, instrument panel components, wiring and sensors. Failure to follow the safety precautions and the disarming procedure could result in accidental air bag deployment, possible injury and unnecessary system repairs.

SERVICE PRECAUTIONS

Disconnect and isolate the battery negative cable before beginning any airbag system component diagnosis, testing, removal, or installation procedures. Allow system capacitor to discharge for two minutes before beginning any component service. This will disable the airbag system. Failure to disable the airbag system may result in accidental airbag deployment, personal injury, or death.

Do not place an intact undeployed airbag face down on a solid surface. The airbag will propel into the air if accidentally deployed and may result in personal injury or death.

When carrying or handling an undeployed airbag, the trim side (face) of the airbag should be pointing towards the body to minimize possibility of injury if accidental deployment occurs. Failure to do this may result in personal injury or death.

Replace airbag system components with OEM replacement parts. Substitute parts may appear interchangeable, but internal differences may result in inferior occupant protection. Failure to do so may result in occupant personal injury or death.

Wear safety glasses, rubber gloves, and long sleeved clothing when cleaning powder residue from vehicle after an airbag deployment. Powder residue emitted from a deployed airbag can cause skin irritation. Flush affected area with cool water if irritation is experienced. If nasal or throat irritation is experienced, exit the vehicle for fresh air until the irritation ceases. If irritation continues, see a physician.

Do not use a replacement airbag that is not in the original packaging. This may result in improper deployment, personal injury, or death.

The factory installed fasteners, screws and bolts used to fasten airbag components have a special coating and are specifically designed for the airbag system. Do not use substitute fasteners. Use only original equipment fasteners listed in the parts catalog when fastener replacement is required.

During, and following, any child restraint anchor service, due to impact event or vehicle repair, carefully inspect all mounting hardware, tether straps, and anchors for proper installation, operation, or damage. If a child restraint anchor is found damaged in any way, the anchor must be replaced. Failure to do this may result in personal injury or death.

Deployed and non-deployed airbags may or may not have live pyrotechnic material within the airbag inflator.

Do not dispose of driver/passenger/curtain airbags or seat belt tensioners unless you are sure of complete deployment. Refer to the Hazardous Substance Control System for proper disposal.

Dispose of deployed airbags and tensioners consistent with state, provincial, local, and federal regulations.

After any airbag component testing or service, do not connect the battery negative cable. Personal injury or death may result if the system test is not performed first.

If the vehicle is equipped with the Occupant Classification System (OCS), do not connect the battery negative cable before performing the OCS Verification Test using the scan tool and the appropriate diagnostic information. Personal injury or death may result if the system test is not performed properly.

Never replace both the Occupant Restraint Controller (ORC) and the Occupant Classification Module (OCM) at the same time. If both require replacement, replace one, then perform the Airbag System test before replacing the other.

Both the ORC and the OCM store Occupant Classification System (OCS) calibration data, which they transfer to one another when one of them is replaced. If both are replaced at the same time, an irreversible fault will be set in both modules and the OCS may malfunction and cause personal injury or death.

If equipped with OCS, the Seat Weight Sensor is a sensitive, calibrated unit and must be handled carefully. Do not drop or handle roughly. If dropped or damaged, replace with another sensor. Failure to do so may result in occupant injury or death.

If equipped with OCS, the front passenger seat must be handled carefully as well. When removing the seat, be careful when setting on floor not to drop. If dropped, the sensor may be inoperative, could result in occupant injury, or possibly death.

If equipped with OCS, when the passenger front seat is on the floor, no one should sit in the front passenger seat. This uneven force may damage the sensing ability of the seat weight sensors. If sat on and damaged, the sensor may be inoperative, could result in occupant injury, or possibly death.

DISARMING THE SYSTEM

Air Bag Fuse

1. Place the front wheels in the straight ahead position.
2. Turn the ignition OFF.
3. Remove the SRS fuse in the instrument panel fuse block.
4. Wait one minute before proceeding to any work procedure.

Negative Battery Cable

1. Place the front wheels in the straight ahead position.
2. Turn the ignition OFF.
3. Disconnect the negative battery cable.
4. Wait one minute before proceeding to any work procedure.

ARMING THE SYSTEM

Air Bag Fuse

1. Turn the ignition OFF.
2. Install the SRS fuse.
3. Turn the ignition ON.
4. The AIR BAG indicator will flash and then turn off.
5. If the indicator does not flash and then turn off, perform a Diagnostic System check.

Negative Battery Cable

1. Turn the ignition OFF.
2. Connect the negative battery cable.
3. Turn the ignition ON.
4. The AIR BAG indicator will flash and then turn off.
5. If the indicator does not flash and then turn off, perform a Diagnostic System check.

DRIVETRAIN

AUTOMATIC TRANSMISSION ASSEMBLY

REMOVAL & INSTALLATION

1. Disconnect the negative battery cable.
2. Drain the transmission fluid.
3. Remove the transmission fluid filler tube.
4. Raise and suitably support the vehicle.
5. Remove the catalytic converter assembly from the vehicle.
6. Remove the starter motor.
7. Disconnect the selector lever linkage from the transmission.
8. Remove the propeller shaft.
9. Support the rear of the vehicle with a suitable jack.
10. Remove the torque converter covers.
11. Remove the torque converter bolts, then discard the bolts.
12. Remove the transmission crossmember from the vehicle.
13. Lower the tail section of the transmission slightly.
14. Disconnect the transmission oil cooler pipes from the transmission.
15. Remove the wiring harness clamp bolt attaching the clamp to the transmission.
16. Disconnect the transmission 20-way electrical connector. Compress both tabs on the connector and pull straight up; do not pry the connector.
17. Disconnect the vehicle speed sensor electrical connector.
18. Support the transmission using a transmission jack.
19. Remove the transmission bolts.
20. Separate the transmission from the engine.
21. Attach torque converter holding strap J-21366 to the transmission.
22. Lower the transmission from the vehicle.

To install:

23. Raise the transmission up to the vehicle.
24. Remove the holding strap from the transmission.
25. Align and install the transmission to the engine.
26. Install the transmission bolts and tighten to 28 ft. lbs. (38 Nm).
27. Connect the vehicle speed sensor electrical connector.
28. Connect the 20-way electrical connector.
29. Install the wiring harness clamp bolt attaching the clamp to the transmission.

30. Connect the transmission oil cooler pipes to the transmission.
31. Align the torque converter and flywheel mating marks, then install the new transmission torque converter bolts and tighten to 48 ft. lbs. (65 Nm).
32. Install the transmission crossmember support and tighten the bolts to 43 ft. lbs. (58 Nm).
33. Install and adjust the selector lever linkage.
34. Remove the transmission jack.
35. Install the propeller shaft.
36. Install the starter motor from the engine.
37. Install the catalytic converter assembly on the vehicle.
38. Remove the jack supporting the rear of the vehicle.
39. Lower the vehicle.
40. Install the transmission fluid filler tube.
41. Flush the transmission oil cooler, oil cooler pipes and the hoses.
42. Connect the negative battery cable.
43. Fill the transmission to the proper level with DEXRON® III transmission fluid.
44. Start the engine. Check for leaks and proper operation.

MANUAL TRANSMISSION ASSEMBLY

REMOVAL & INSTALLATION

See Figure 4.

1. Disconnect the negative battery cable.

2. From inside the vehicle, remove the shift lever assembly.
3. Drain the oil from the transmission.
4. Support the rear of the vehicle with safety stands.
5. Remove the catalytic converters.
6. Remove the propeller shaft.
7. Remove the starter motor.
8. Remove the clip from the transmission.
9. Disconnect the backup lamp switch electrical connector
10. Disconnect the skip shift solenoid, reverse lockout solenoid and VSS sensor electrical connectors.
11. Remove the push in retainer and wiring harness bracket.
12. Support the engine with safety stands.
13. Remove the left and right transmission close out covers.
14. Remove the retaining clip, then disconnect the clutch hydraulic line from the slave cylinder connector.
15. Remove the transmission crossmember support.
16. Support the transmission with a transmission jack.
17. Slowly lower the transmission to access the transmission bolts.

➡**Leave the 2 clutch housing to engine block retaining bolts located at the 10 and 2 o'clock positions tight at this time.**

18. Remove the lower 6 transmission retaining bolts.

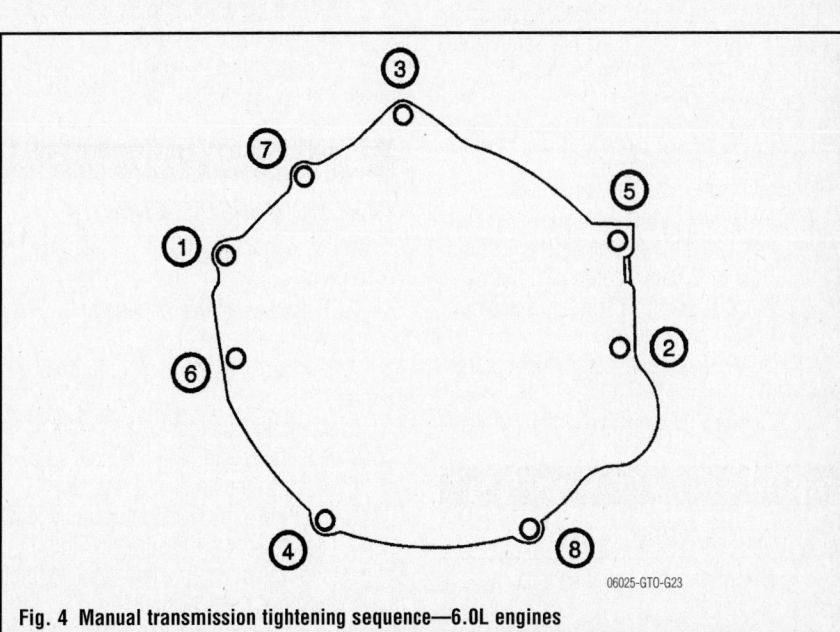

Fig. 4 Manual transmission tightening sequence—6.0L engines

06025-GTO-G23

19. Remove the 2 remaining transmission retaining bolts.

20. Pull the transmission rearward to just clear the locating dowels, then rotate the transmission 90 degrees to the right to gain clearance from the vehicle floor pan.

21. When the transmission input shaft clears the clutch pressure plate, lower the transmission from the vehicle.

To install:

22. Place the transmission in the 3rd gear position.

23. With the transmission positioned 90 degrees to the right side, position the transmission in the vehicle up to the locating dowels on the engine.

24. Slowly raise the transmission until in place.

25. Install the transmission to the vehicle, then rotate the transmission to the upright position.

26. Install the transmission bolts.

27. Tighten the transmission retaining bolts in sequence to 37 ft. lbs. (50 Nm).

28. Install the transmission crossmember support and tighten the bolts to 43 ft. lbs. (58 Nm).

29. Remove the transmission jack from the transmission.

30. Install the left and right transmission close out covers.

31. Connect the clutch actuator cylinder pipe to the clutch master cylinder hose.

32. Push together the clutch hydraulic hose fittings, then install the retaining clip.

33. Check the clutch hydraulic hoses for kinks or twists.

34. Remove the engine safety stands.

35. Install the wiring harness bracket and push in retainer.

36. Connect the VSS, reverse lockout solenoid and skip shift solenoid connectors.

37. Connect the backup lamp switch electrical connector.

38. Install the clip to the transmission.

39. Install the starter motor.

40. Install the catalytic converters.

41. Install the propeller shaft.

42. Remove the rear axle safety stands.

43. Refill the transmission with fluid.

44. Bleed the clutch hydraulic system.

45. Lower the vehicle.

46. Install the transmission shift control assembly.

47. Connect the negative battery cable.

CLUTCH

REMOVAL & INSTALLATION

1. Disconnect the negative battery cable.

2. Remove the transmission.

3. Remove the clutch pressure plate bolts.

4. Remove the clutch pressure plate and driven disc from the dowel pins on the flywheel.

5. Install the clutch pressure plate and driven plate to the dowel pins on the flywheel.

6. Install the clutch pressure plate bolts finger tight.

7. Install a suitable clutch alignment arbor in order to align the clutch driven plate to the clutch pilot bearing.

8. Tighten the clutch pressure plate bolts in star pattern to 37 ft. lbs. (50 Nm).

9. Install the manual transmission.

10. Connect the negative battery cable.

BLEEDING

1. Ensure the reservoir is filled to the fill line with new hydraulic clutch fluid.

2. Press the clutch pedal all the way down to the floor.

3. Open the bleeder on the actuator cylinder to purge the air.

4. Close the bleeder and release the clutch pedal.

5. Repeat steps 2, 3 and 4 until all air is out of the clutch system.

6. Check and refill the reservoir as needed while bleeding.

7. After bleeding, pump the clutch pedal several times. If the clutch engagement is not satisfactory, repeat the bleed procedure.

8. If the previous procedures are unsuccessful, perform the following steps.

   a. Pump the clutch pedal very fast for 30 seconds.

   b. Stop pumping and let the air escape into the reservoir.

   c. Repeat this procedure as necessary.

AXLE SHAFT

REMOVAL & INSTALLATION

1. Place the transmission in neutral (M/T) or Park (A/T).

2. Raise the vehicle on a hoist.

3. Remove the wheel.

4. Support the axle shaft until it is removed.

5. Mark the relationship of the inner constant velocity joint and the inner axle.

6. Remove the bolts and retaining plates from the inner constant velocity joint.

7. Remove the bolts and retaining plates from the outer constant velocity joint.

8. Remove the axle shaft.

To install:

9. Align the marks on the inner constant velocity joint and the inner axle.

10. Install the inner mount bolts and retainer plates and tighten to 37 ft. lbs. (50 Nm), plus an additional 68 degrees of torque.

11. Install the outer constant velocity joint mount bolts and tighten to 37 ft. lbs. (50 Nm).

12. Remove the support stand.

13. Lower the vehicle.

CONSTANT VELOCITY JOINT

OVERHAUL

Inner and Outer Joint

See Figure 5.

1. Place the wheel axle shaft horizontally in a bench vise.

2. Using a side cutter or other suitable tool, remove the large and small boot retaining clamps from the constant velocity joint boot and discard the clamp.

3. Remove the dust shield and end cap from the constant velocity joint by tapping with hammer and punch.

4. Slide the boot toward the center of the drive shaft.

5. Remove the constant velocity joint retainer clip from the drive shaft.

6. Support the inner race when removing the constant velocity joint.

7. Press the drive shaft from the constant velocity joint.

8. Remove the constant velocity joint boot from the drive shaft.

9. Tilt the cage and inner race and remove one ball.

10. Repeat the process to remove the remaining five balls.

11. Remove the inner race and cage.

12. Thoroughly clean the constant velocity (CV) joint components

13. Inspect the constant velocity joint components for pitting, galling, excessive play between ball and cage, damage or cracking of the cage or cracking, galling, or chips of the races.

14. If damaged, replace the constant velocity joint.

15. Thoroughly clean and inspect the drive shaft boot for tears, cracking and deterioration.

16. If the drive shaft seal is damaged, replace the boot.

17. Install the inner race and cage into the outer race ensuring the inner race step is opposite of the outer race groove.

18. Align the thick sections with the

outer race with the narrow sections on the inner race

19. Tilt the cage and inner race and fit one ball.

20. Repeat the process for the other five balls.

21. Check the plunge of the inner parts. If there is no movement, the constant velocity joint has been assembled incorrectly. Reassemble the constant velocity joint.

22. Remove the old sealing bead from the dust shields, end caps, and the constant velocity joint.

23. Install the large boot clamp over the drive shaft boot.

24. Install the dust shield onto the drive shaft boot.

25. Using crimping pliers, crimp the large clamp ensuring the crimp is positioned between 2 bolt holes.

26. Install a new small boot retaining clamp onto the wheel driveshaft.

27. Install the boot onto the driveshaft.

28. Press the constant velocity joint onto the drive shaft with the step on the inner race facing the shoulder on the driveshaft.

29. Install the constant velocity retaining clip.

30. Pack one tube of grease into the inner side of the constant velocity joint and the boot.

31. Pack a half tube of grease into the outside of the constant velocity joint.

32. Apply an 8 mm bead of RTV sealant to the inside of the end cap and the dust shield. Allow to cure.

33. Install the dust shield and end cap by gently tapping with a hammer and punch. Ensure the bolt holes are aligned.

34. Position the small boot retaining clamp onto the neck of the boot.

35. Position the boot and small retaining clamp into the boot groove on the drive shaft.

36. Using a small screwdriver, pry up the small end of the boot to equalize the air pressure.

37. Measure the distance (a) between the edge of the boot and the edge of the last axle shaft groove closing edge. The length should be 3.19 inch (81mm).

38. Using crimping pliers crimp the small end clamp.

39. Remove the wheel drive shaft from the bench vise.

REAR INNER DRIVE AXLE SHAFT AND SEAL

REMOVAL & INSTALLATION

1. Raise and support the vehicle.
2. Remove the rear wheel.
3. Remove the axle shaft.
4. Place a drain pan under the axle.
5. Remove the inner axle using a slide hammer and puller plate.
6. Remove the axle shaft seal with a seal removal tool.

To install:

7. Clean the axle seal housing.
8. Lubricate the seal bore and the seal lip with lithium grease.

9. Install the seal using an installer until the seal is fully seated in the bore.
10. Install the inner axle shaft.
11. Remove the drain pan.
12. Install the axle shaft.
13. Install the wheel.

PINION FLANGE AND SEAL

REMOVAL & INSTALLATION

1. Place the transmission in neutral.
2. Raise the vehicle on a hoist.
3. Remove both mufflers.
4. Index mark the driveshaft, then disconnect driveshaft and position it out of the way.
5. Use an inch lb. torque wrench and measure the amount of torque required to maintain pinion rotation through several revolutions.
6. Hold the pinion flange from turning, then remove the pinion nut.
7. Index mark the pinion flange, then use a puller and remove the flange.
8. Remove the pinion seal.

To install:

9. Inspect the pinion shaft seal surface for nicks and burrs. If damaged, replace the pinion flange.
10. Clean the threads on the pinion shaft and pinion nut.
11. Coat the pinion shaft splines and seal with gear oil.
12. Using a pinion seal installer, install the new pinion shaft seal until the seal is flush with the differential housing.
13. Install the pinion flange on to the pinion shaft aligning the punch marks.
14. Apply thread locking compound onto the threads of the pinion shaft.
15. Align the index marks and install the pinion flange.
16. Install new pinion flange nut loosely.
17. Rotate the pinion flange occasionally while tightening the flange nut to make sure the pinion bearings seat correctly.
18. Take frequent bearing preload torque readings.
19. The pinion bearing preload specification is 2–4 inch lbs. (0.2–0.43 Nm).
20. Connect the driveshaft and install new bolts.
21. Install both mufflers.
22. Fill the differential with gear lubricant and check for leaks.

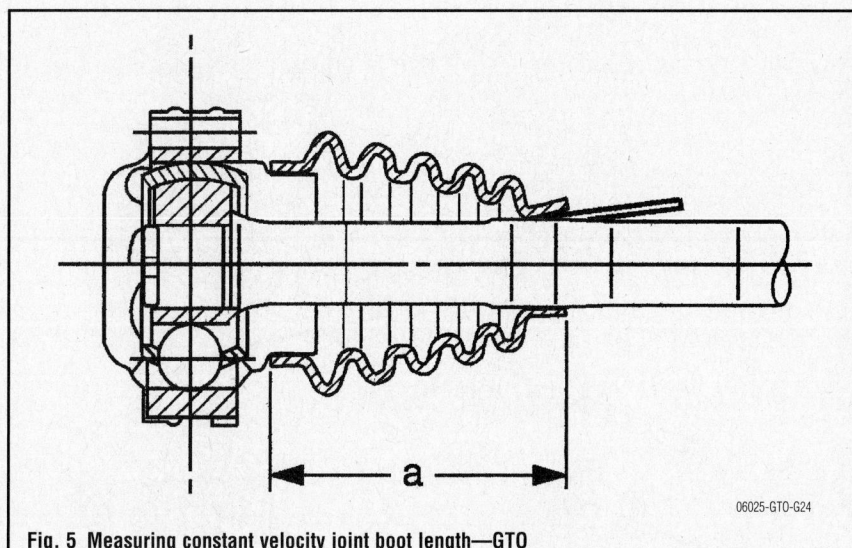

06025-GTO-G24

Fig. 5 Measuring constant velocity joint boot length—GTO

ENGINE COOLING

WATER PUMP

REMOVAL & INSTALLATION

See Figure 6.

1. Disconnect the negative battery cable.

2. Drain the engine cooling system.

3. Disconnect the Mass Air Flow (MAF) sensor electrical connector.

4. Disconnect the Intake Air Temperature (IAT) sensor electrical connector.

5. Loosen two intake duct clamps and remove the duct.

6. Remove the accessory drive belt.

7. Disconnect the heater hoses from the water pump.

8. Remove the drive belt tensioner.

9. Remove the 6 attaching bolts and remove the water pump. Clean and inspect the gasket mating surfaces.

To install:

10. Install the water pump. Use a new gasket and tighten the bolts in 2 steps 11 ft. lbs. (15 Nm), then 18 ft. lbs. (25 Nm).

11. Install the drive belt tensioner.

12. Connect the heater hoses to the water pump.

13. Install the accessory drive belt.

14. Install the MAF and IAT connectors.

15. Install the intake duct and the clamps.

16. Refill the cooling system.

17. Connect the negative battery cable.

18. Start the engine and check for coolant leaks.

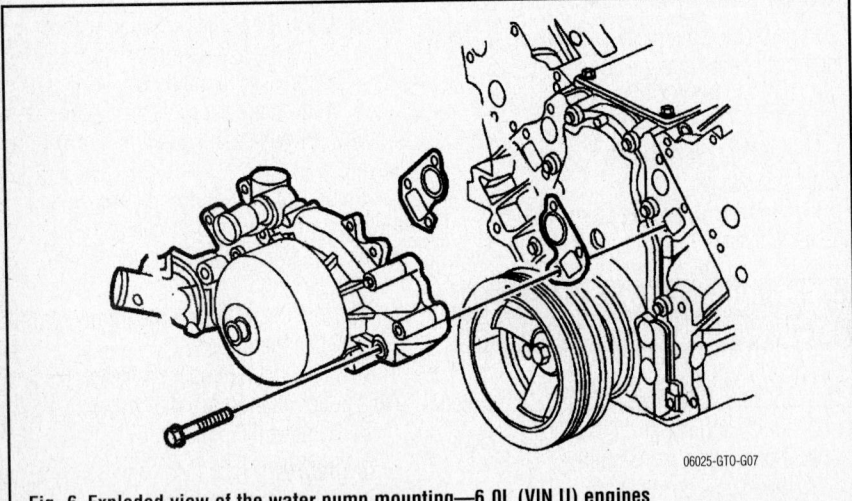

Fig. 6 Exploded view of the water pump mounting—6.0L (VIN U) engines

06025-GTO-G07

ENGINE ELECTRICAL

ALTERNATOR

REMOVAL & INSTALLATION

See Figure 7.

1. Disconnect the negative battery cable.

2. Remove the accessory drive belt.

3. Raise and support the vehicle.

4. Disconnect the positive alternator cable.

5. Remove the alternator rear mounting bracket.

6. Disconnect the oil cooler lines from the retainer.

7. Disconnect the alternator electrical connectors.

8. Remove the alternator front mounting bracket.

9. Remove the alternator from the vehicle.

To install:

10. Position the alternator onto engine. Tighten the front mounting bolts to 37 ft. lbs. (50 Nm).

11. Connect the alternator electrical connectors.

12. Connect the oil cooler lines to the retainer.

13. Install the alternator rear mounting bracket and tighten the bolt to 18 ft. lbs. (25 Nm).

14. Connect the positive alternator cable.

CHARGING SYSTEM

15. Lower the vehicle.

16. Install the accessory drive belt.

17. Connect the negative battery cable.

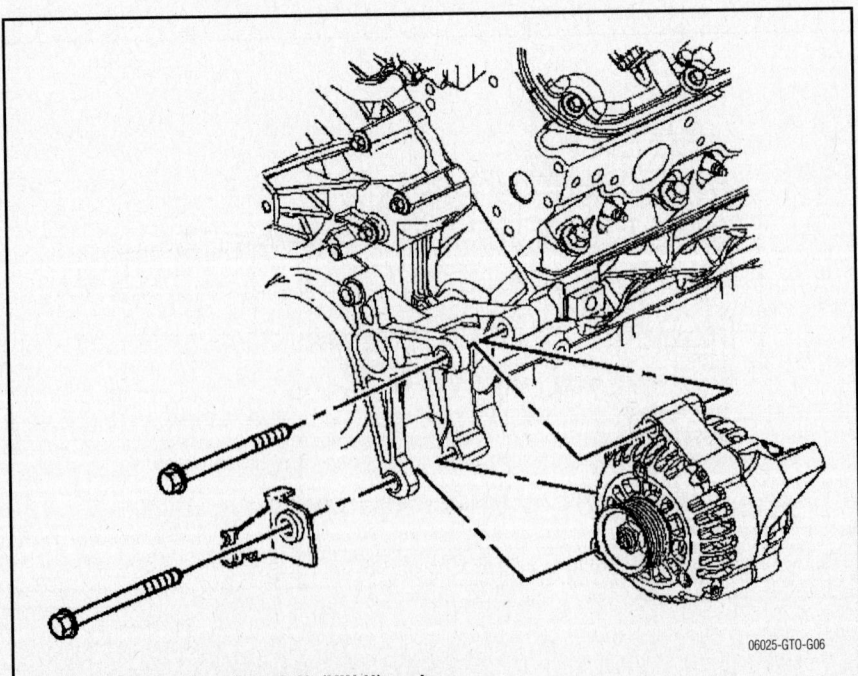

Fig. 7 Alternator mounting—6.0L (VIN U) engines

06025-GTO-G06

ENGINE ELECTRICAL · IGNITION SYSTEM

FIRING ORDER

See Figure 8.

IGNITION TIMING

ADJUSTMENT

The ignition timing is controlled by the Powertrain Control Module (PCM). No adjustment is necessary.

SPARK PLUGS

REMOVAL & INSTALLATION

1. Disconnect the spark plug wires.
2. Remove the spark plugs.
3. To install, install the spark plugs and tighten to 11 ft. lbs. (15 Nm).
4. Connect the spark plug wires.

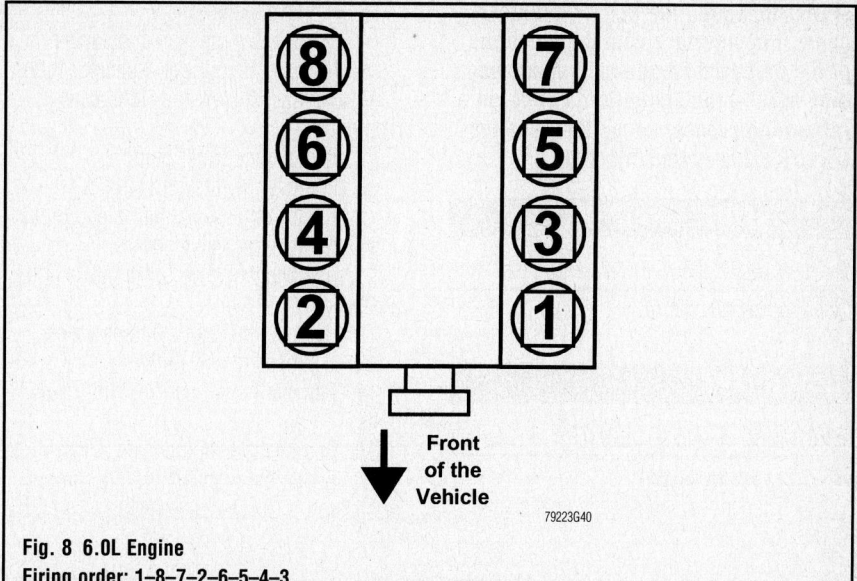

Fig. 8 6.0L Engine
Firing order: 1–8–7–2–6–5–4–3
Distributorless ignition system

Front of the Vehicle

79223G40

ENGINE ELECTRICAL · STARTING SYSTEM

STARTER

REMOVAL & INSTALLATION

See Figure 9.

1. Disconnect the negative battery cable.
2. Raise and support the vehicle.
3. Remove the left side catalytic converter.
4. Disconnect starter electrical connections.
5. Remove starter bolts.
6. Remove the starter.

To install:

7. Place the starter in position and attach the electrical connections.
8. Install starter. Tighten the bolts to 37 ft. lbs. (50 Nm).
9. Install the left side catalytic converter.
10. Connect starter electrical connections.
11. Connect the negative battery cable.

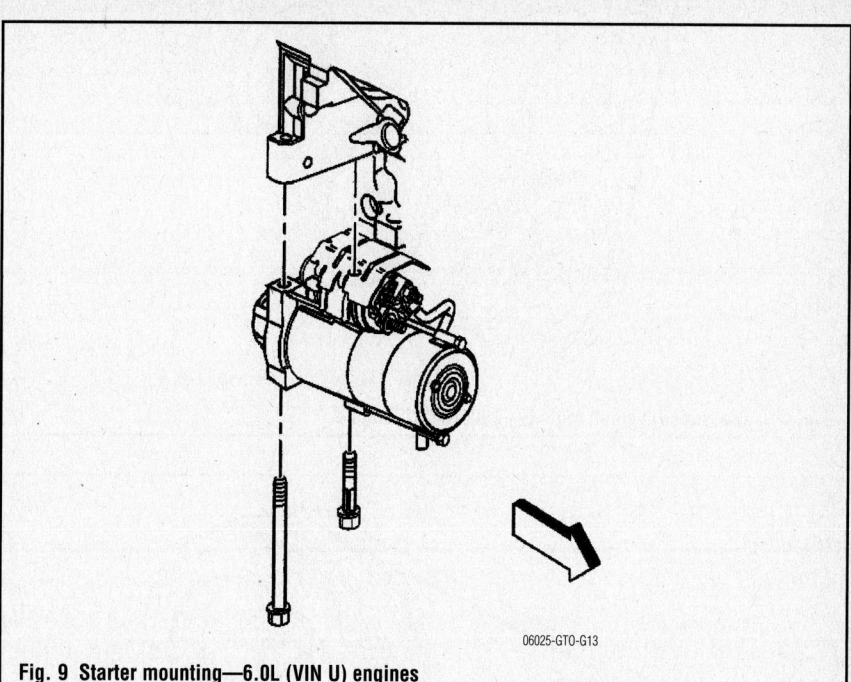

Fig. 9 Starter mounting—6.0L (VIN U) engines

06025-GTO-G13

ENGINE MECHANICAL

➡Disconnecting the negative battery cable may interfere with the functions of the on board computer systems and may require the computer to undergo a relearning process, once the negative battery cable is reconnected.

ACCESSORY DRIVE BELTS

ACCESSORY BELT ROUTING

See Figures 10 and 11.

CAMSHAFT

REMOVAL & INSTALLATION

1. Drain the cooling system.
2. Disconnect the negative battery cable.
3. Remove the engine.
4. Remove the crankshaft balancer.
5. Remove the oil level indicator tube.
6. Remove the left and right exhaust manifolds.
7. Remove the water pump.
8. Remove the intake manifold.
9. Remove the coolant air bleed pipe.
10. Remove the valve covers.
11. Remove the valve rocker arms and push rods.
12. Remove the right cylinder heads.
13. Remove the valve lifters.
14. Remove the oil pan-to-front cover bolts.
15. Remove the engine front cover.
16. Rotate the crankshaft until number one piston is at top dead center of compression stroke. In this position, cylinder number one rocker arms will be off lobe lift, and the crankshaft sprocket key will be at the 1:30 position. If viewing from the rear of the engine, the additional crankshaft pilot hole, non-threaded, will be in the 10:30 position. The engine firing order is 1, 8, 7, 2, 6, 5, 4, 3. Cylinders 1, 3, 5 and 7 are left bank. Cylinders 2, 4, 6, and 8 are right bank.
17. Remove the camshaft sensor.
18. Remove the camshaft retainer.
19. Install 3 M8-1.25 x 100 mm bolts in the camshaft front bolt holes.
20. Using the bolts as a handle, carefully rotate and pull the camshaft out of the engine block.
21. Remove the bolts from the front of the camshaft.
22. If the camshaft bearings need to be replaced, remove the oil pan-to rear cover bolts.
23. Remove the rear cover bolts.
24. Remove the rear cover and gasket. Discard the gasket.
25. Remove the camshaft bearings.

To install:
26. Install the camshaft bearings, if replaced.
27. Install the rear cover using a new gasket.
28. Install the oil pan-to-rear cover bolts.
29. Lubricate the camshaft journals and the bearings with clean engine oil.
30. Install 3 M8-1.25 x 100 mm bolts into the camshaft front bolt holes.
31. Using the bolts as a handle, carefully install the camshaft into the engine block.
32. Remove the 3 bolts from the front of the camshaft.
33. Install the camshaft retainer and the bolts and tighten to 18 ft. lbs. (25 Nm).
34. Inspect the camshaft sensor O-ring seal. If the O-ring seal is not cut or damaged, it may be used again.
35. Lubricate the O-ring seal with clean engine oil.
36. Install the camshaft sensor and tighten the bolts to 18 ft. lbs. (25 Nm).
37. Align the camshaft sprocket alignment mark in the 6 o'clock position.
38. Install the camshaft sprocket and timing chain.
39. Install the camshaft sprocket bolts and tighten to 26 ft. lbs. (35 Nm).
40. Install the engine front cover.
41. Install the valve lifters.
42. Install the cylinder heads.

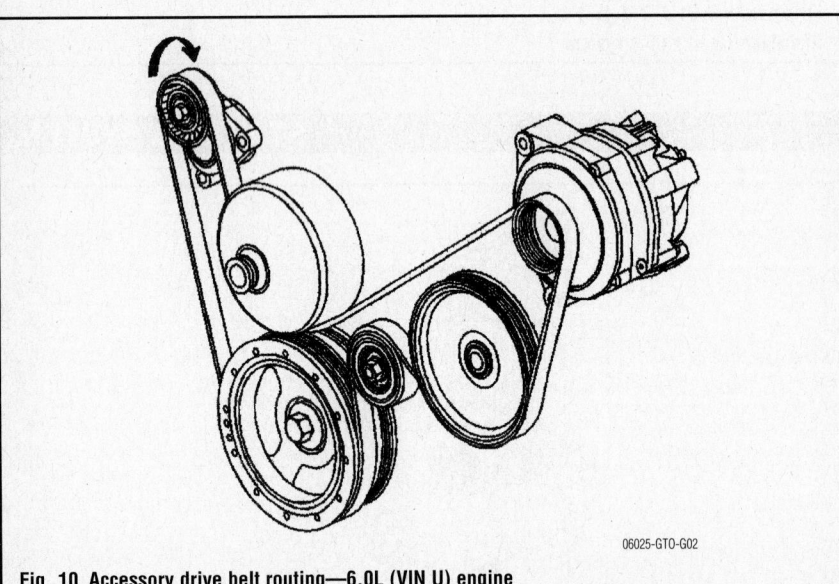

Fig. 10 Accessory drive belt routing—6.0L (VIN U) engine

06025-GTO-G02

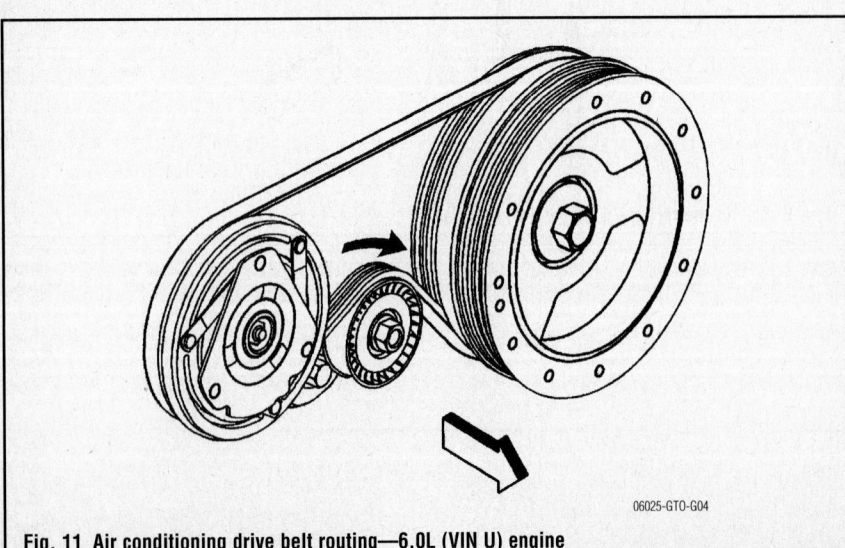

Fig. 11 Air conditioning drive belt routing—6.0L (VIN U) engine

06025-GTO-G04

43. Install the valve rocker arms and push rods.
44. Install the valve covers.
45. Install the coolant air bleed pipe.
46. Install the intake manifold.
47. Install the water pump.
48. Install the exhaust manifolds.
49. Install the oil level indicator tube.
50. Install the crankshaft balancer.
51. Install the engine assembly.
52. Connect the negative battery cable.
53. Start the engine and check for leaks.

CYLINDER HEAD

REMOVAL & INSTALLATION

Left Side

See Figure 12.

1. Disconnect the negative battery cable from the battery.
2. Remove the front suspension support brace.
3. Drain the cooling system.
4. Relieve the fuel system pressure.
5. Drain the engine oil.
6. Remove the fuel rail covers.
7. Disconnect the air intake sensor connector from the air intake sensor.
8. Loosen the hose clamps securing the intake duct and remove the intake duct.
9. Disconnect the fuel line from the fuel rail.
10. Disconnect the purge line from the purge valve.
11. Disconnect the spark plug wires from the ignition coils.
12. Disconnect the ignition coil wire harness main electrical connector.
13. Remove the ignition coil bracket bolts and screw from the rocker arm cover.
14. Remove the ignition coil bracket from the rocker arm cover.
15. Remove the valve cover.
16. Remove the valve rocker arm bolts and the rocker arms.
17. Remove the valve rocker arm pivot support.
18. Remove the pushrods.
19. Remove the engine coolant air bleed pipe.
20. Remove the two power steering pump bolts and power steering pump from the cylinder head.
21. Remove the exhaust manifold.
22. Remove the engine wiring harness ground bolts from the rear of the cylinder head. Reposition the ground wires.
23. Remove the cylinder head and discard the bolts.

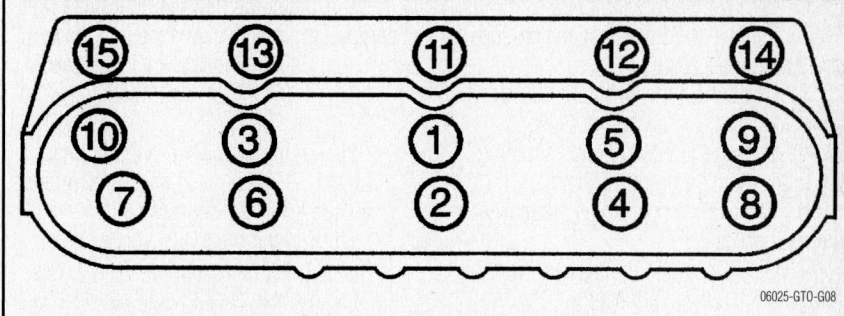

Fig. 12 Left side cylinder head bolt tightening sequence—6.0L (VIN U) engines

24. Remove the cylinder head gasket and discard.
25. Clean and inspect the cylinder head.

To install:
26. Install the new cylinder head gasket on the locating pins and install the cylinder head.

➥**The cylinder head bolts are a torque-to-yield design and cannot be reused.**

27. Tighten the new cylinder head bolts on 5.7L engines in sequence as follows:
    a. Tighten the M11 cylinder head bolts (1-10) a first pass in sequence to 22 ft. lbs. (30 Nm).
    b. Tighten the M11 cylinder head bolts (1-10) a second pass in sequence an additional 90 degrees.
    c. Tighten the M11 cylinder head bolts (1-8) an additional 90 degrees and the M11 cylinder head bolts (9 and 10) an additional 50 degrees.
    d. Tighten the M8 cylinder head bolts (11-15) to 22 ft. lbs. (30 Nm). Begin with the center bolt (11) and alternating side-to-side, work outward tightening all of the bolts.
28. Tighten the new cylinder head bolts on 6.0L engines in sequence as follows:
    a. Tighten the M11 cylinder head bolts (1-10) a first pass in sequence to 22 ft. lbs. (30 Nm).
    b. Tighten the M11 cylinder head bolts (1-10) a second pass in sequence an additional 90 degrees.
    c. Tighten the M11 cylinder head bolts (1-10) an additional 70 degrees.
    d. Tighten the M8 cylinder head bolts (11-15) to 22 ft. lbs. (30 Nm). Begin with the center bolt (11) and alternating side-to-side, work outward tightening all of the bolts.
29. Install the engine wiring harness ground bolts from the rear of the cylinder head. Reposition the ground wires.
30. Install the exhaust manifold.
31. Install the two power steering pump bolts and power steering pump to the cylin-

der head and tighten the bolts to 21 ft. lbs. (28 Nm).
32. Install the engine coolant air bleed pipe.
33. Install the pushrods.
34. Install the valve rocker arm pivot support.
35. Install the valve rocker arm bolts and the rocker arms.
36. Install a NEW cover gasket into the valve cover.
37. Install the valve cover and tighten the bolts to 106 inch lbs. (12 Nm).
38. Install the ignition coils, wire harness, and bolts onto the mounting bracket and tighten to 106 inch lbs. (12 Nm).
39. Install the ignition coils and bracket assembly and bolts onto the rocker cover and tighten to 106 inch lbs.
40. Install the crankcase ventilation hose.
41. Connect the ignition coil wire harness main electrical connector.
42. Connect the spark plug wires to the ignition coils.
43. Connect the purge line to the purge valve.
44. Connect the fuel line to the fuel rail.
45. Install the intake duct and hose clamps.
46. Connect the air intake sensor connector to the air intake sensor.
47. Install the fuel rail covers.
48. Fill the engine with oil.
49. Fill the cooling system.
50. Install the front suspension support brace.
51. Connect the negative battery cable.
52. Start the engine and check for leaks.

Right Side

See Figure 13.

1. Disconnect the negative battery cable from the battery.
2. Drain the cooling system.
3. Relieve the fuel system pressure.
4. Drain the engine oil.
5. Remove the heater hoses.

6. Remove the fuel rail covers.

7. Remove the front suspension support brace if necessary.

8. Disconnect the air intake sensor connector from the air intake sensor.

9. Loosen the hose clamps securing the intake duct and remove the duct.

10. Remove the spark plug wires from the ignition coils.

11. Disconnect the ignition coil wire harness main electrical connector.

12. Remove the ignition coil bracket from the rocker arm cover.

13. Remove the valve cover.

14. Remove the valve rocker arms and pushrods.

15. Remove the engine coolant air bleed pipe.

16. Remove the exhaust manifold.

17. Remove the cylinder head and discard the bolts.

18. Remove the cylinder head gasket and discard.

19. Clean and inspect the cylinder head.

To install:

20. Install the new cylinder head gasket on the locating pins and install the cylinder head.

➡**The cylinder head bolts are a torque-to-yield design and cannot be reused.**

21. Tighten the new cylinder head bolts on 5.7L engines in sequence as follows:

a. Tighten the M11 cylinder head bolts (1-10) a first pass in sequence to 22 ft. lbs. (30 Nm).

b. Tighten the M11 cylinder head bolts (1-10) a second pass in sequence an additional 90 degrees.

c. Tighten the M11 cylinder head bolts (1-8) an additional 90 degrees and the M11 cylinder head bolts (9 and 10) an additional 50 degrees.

d. Tighten the M8 cylinder head bolts (11-15) to 22 ft. lbs. (30 Nm). Begin with the center bolt (11) and alternating side-to-side, work outward tightening all of the bolts.

22. Tighten the new cylinder head bolts on 6.0L engines in sequence as follows:

a. Tighten the M11 cylinder head bolts (1-10) a first pass in sequence to 22 ft. lbs. (30 Nm).

b. Tighten the M11 cylinder head bolts (1-10) a second pass in sequence an additional 90 degrees.

c. Tighten the M11 cylinder head bolts (1-10) an additional 70 degrees.

d. Tighten the M8 cylinder head bolts (11-15) to 22 ft. lbs. (30 Nm). Begin with the center bolt (11) and alternating side-to-side, work outward tightening all of the bolts.

23. Install the exhaust manifold.

24. Install the engine coolant air bleed pipe.

25. Install the valve rocker arms and pushrods.

26. Install the valve cover and tighten the bolts to 106 inch lbs. (12 Nm).

27. Install the ignition coils, wire harness, and bolts onto the mounting bracket and tighten to 106 inch lbs. (12 Nm).

28. Install the ignition coils and bracket assembly and bolts onto the rocker cover and tighten to 106 inch lbs.

29. Install the spark plug wires to the ignition coils.

30. Install the intake duct and hose clamps securing the intake duct.

31. Connect the air intake sensor connector to the air intake sensor.

32. Install the front suspension support brace if removed.

33. Install the fuel rail covers.

34. Install the heater hoses.

35. Fill the engine with oil.

36. Fill the cooling system.

37. Connect the negative battery cable.

38. Start the engine and check for leaks.

ENGINE ASSEMBLY

REMOVAL & INSTALLATION

1. Discharge and recover the air conditioning refrigerant.

2. Drain the engine cooling system.

3. Drain the engine oil and remove the oil filter.

4. Disconnect the negative battery cable.

5. Relieve the fuel system pressure.

6. Remove the hood.

7. Remove the front suspension support brace.

8. Remove the fuel rail covers.

9. Disconnect the air intake sensor connector

10. Remove the intake duct.

11. Remove the radiator.

12. Disconnect the heater hoses from the water pump.

13. Remove the heater and radiator hoses from the water pump.

14. Separate the A/C compressor and condenser hose from the compressor.

15. Remove the ground lead screw from the block and left hand engine mount.

16. Remove the battery harness ground terminals from the ABS/TCS control module.

17. Disconnect the positive battery lead and lay the harness on the engine.

18. Disconnect the A/C harness connector.

19. Disconnect the wiring harness retaining clips from the engine compartment.

20. Disconnect the connector from the theft deterrent horn.

21. Remove the coolant surge tank.

22. Remove the PCM harness connector cover.

23. Loosen the connector retaining screws at each PCM connector, then remove the connectors from the PCM.

24. Disconnect the PCM wiring harness retaining clip.

25. Remove the engine wiring harness retaining clip from the power steering pipe bracket.

26. Remove the Powertrain Interface Module (PIM) and the Throttle Relaxer Module (TRM) as an assembly.

27. Disconnect the powertrain to main wiring harness connector.

28. Remove the harness to dash panel grommet and feed the harness and connectors out into the engine bay.

29. Place the powertrain wiring harness on top of the engine.

30. Lift the throttle cable up at the throttle body mounting bracket, then remove the cable from the throttle body cam lever. Set the throttle cable aside.

31. Disconnect the fuel line from the fuel rail.

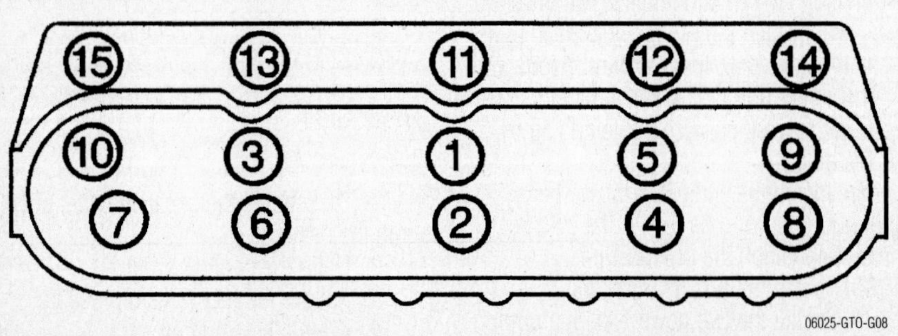

06025-GTO-G08

Fig. 13 Right side cylinder head bolt tightening sequence—6.0L (VIN U) engines

32. Disconnect the purge line from the purge valve.

33. Loosen the hose clamp on the return hose at the power steering reservoir.

34. Place a suitable container under the reservoir and remove the hose and drain the reservoir fluid.

35. Remove the high pressure line flare nut and O-ring from the pump outlet fitting at the rear of the power steering pump.

36. Disconnect the brake booster vacuum hose and heater control vacuum hose from the rear of the intake manifold.

37. Remove the four bolts securing the undertray to the crossmember.

38. Remove the tray from the crossmember.

39. Remove the 2 bolts securing the power steering high pressure line brackets to the oil pan.

40. Remove both exhaust manifolds.

41. Remove the transmission.

42. Remove the right and left engine mount to engine bracket nuts.

43. Attach a suitable lifting chain and hooks to the 2 engine lifting brackets.

44. Using a suitable lifting crane, slightly raise the engine to clear the engine mount stud.

45. Slowly lift the engine out of the vehicle.

To install:

46. Lower the engine into the vehicle and crossmember using a suitable hoist and lifting brackets.

47. Install left and right engine mount nuts and tighten the nuts to 59 ft. lbs. (80 Nm).

48. Remove the lifting brackets.

49. Install the transmission.

50. Install the exhaust manifolds.

51. Install the power steering high pressure line brackets to the oil pan and tighten to 18 ft. lbs. (25 Nm).

52. Install the tray to the crossmember.

53. Connect the brake booster vacuum hose and heater control vacuum hose to the rear of the intake manifold.

54. Install the high pressure line flare nut and O-ring to the pump outlet fitting at the rear of the power steering pump.

55. Install the hose to the reservoir fluid. Secure the hose with the hose clamp

56. Connect the fuel line to the fuel rail.

57. Connect the purge line to the purge valve.

58. Install the cable to the throttle body cam lever then install the throttle cable to the throttle body mounting bracket.

59. Install the cable to the retaining clip.

60. Feed the harness and connectors

into the passenger compartment and install the dash panel grommet.

61. Connect the powertrain to main wiring harness connector.

62. Install harness straps to retain the wiring harness.

63. Install the Powertrain Interface Module (PIM) and the Throttle Relaxer Module (TRM).

64. Install the engine wiring harness retaining clip to the power steering pipe bracket.

65. Connect the PCM wiring harness retaining clip.

66. Connect the connectors to the PCM.

67. Install the PCM harness connector cover.

68. Install the coolant surge tank.

69. Connect the connector to the theft deterrent horn.

70. Connect the wiring harness retaining clips to the engine compartment.

71. Connect the A/C wiring harness connector.

72. Connect the positive lead terminal to the battery.

73. Install the nut securing the battery harness ground terminals to the ABS/TCS control module bracket stud.

74. Install the ground lead screw to the engine block and left hand engine mount.

75. Install new O-rings onto the A/C compressor hose block fitting and install the A/C compressor and condenser hose to the A/C compressor.

76. Install the heater hoses to the water pump. Secure with the clamps.

77. Install the radiator hoses to the water pump. Secure with the clamps.

78. Install the radiator.

79. Install the intake duct and secure the intake duct with the hose clamps.

80. Connect the air intake sensor connector to the air intake sensor.

81. Install the fuel rail covers.

82. Install the front suspension support brace.

83. Install the hood.

84. Recharge the A/C system.

✳✳ WARNING

Be sure to check engine to see that all electrical connectors, hoses and cables are properly connected and secure.

85. Install new oil filter and fill engine with fresh oil.

86. Connect the negative battery cable.

87. Fill the cooling system.

88. Recharge the A/C system.

89. Start the engine and check for leaks.

ENGINE VALLEY COVER

REMOVAL & INSTALLATION

1. Remove the intake manifold.

2. Remove the oil pressure switch.

3. Remove the 11 valley cover bolts.

4. Remove the valley cover and gasket.

5. Remove and discard the o-rings on the bottom side of the cover.

To install:

6. Install new o-rings to the bottom of the cover.

7. Install a new gasket and the cover.

8. Install the bolts and tighten to 18 ft. lbs. (25 Nm).

9. Install the oil pressure switch.

10. Install the intake manifold.

EXHAUST MANIFOLD

REMOVAL & INSTALLATION

1. Disconnect the negative battery cable.

2. Remove the spark plug wires from the spark plugs.

3. Remove the exhaust pipe from the manifold.

4. Remove the heat shield.

5. Remove the exhaust manifold.

To install:

6. Apply threadlock to the manifold bolts.

7. Install the manifold and tighten the bolts from the center out first to 12 ft. lbs. (15 Nm), and then to 18 ft. lbs. (25 Nm).

8. Install the heat shield.

9. Connect the exhaust pipe.

10. Connect the spark plug wires.

11. Connect the negative battery cable.

INTAKE MANIFOLD

REMOVAL & INSTALLATION

See Figure 14.

➡️**The intake manifold, throttle body, fuel injection rail, and fuel injectors may be removed as an assembly. If not servicing the individual components, remove the manifold as a complete assembly.**

1. Relieve the fuel system pressure.

2. Disconnect the negative battery cable.

3. Drain the cooling system.

4. Remove the front suspension support brace.

5. Remove the fuel rail covers.

6. Disconnect the air intake sensor connector from the air intake sensor.

7. Loosen the hose clamps securing the intake duct and remove the duct.

8. Disconnect the fuel line from the fuel rail.

9. Disconnect the purge line from the purge valve.

10. Disconnect the connector from the Intake Air Control (IAC) motor.

11. Disconnect the connector from the Throttle Position (TP) sensor at the throttle body.

12. Lift the throttle cable up at the throttle body mounting bracket, then remove the cable from the throttle body cam lever.

13. Position the throttle cable aside.

14. Disconnect the fuel injector connectors from all the fuel injectors.

15. Remove the locks from the right and left side ignition coil main connectors and disconnect the connectors.

16. Disconnect the EVAP canister purge solenoid valve electrical connector.

17. Remove the harness securing clips from the fuel rail brackets and position the harnesses aside.

18. Disconnect the Manifold Absolute Pressure (MAP) sensor connector.

19. Disconnect the knock sensor connector.

20. Disconnect the oil pressure sensor connector.

21. Remove the fresh air hose from the rocker cover and the throttle body.

22. Remove the foul air hose from the throttle body and restricting orifice external connector.

23. Remove the engine coolant vent hose from the throttle body and vent pipe

24. Remove the coolant vent outlet hose from the throttle body and left-hand radiator tank.

25. Remove the EVAP canister purge

tube from the throttle body and EVAP canister purge solenoid valve.

26. Remove the EVAP canister purge solenoid valve and bracket from the intake manifold.

27. Remove the intake manifold bolts and fuel rail stop bracket.

28. Remove the intake manifold and discard the gaskets.

To install:

29. Install the intake manifold. Use new gaskets and apply threadlock to the manifold bolts.

30. Install the fuel rail stop bracket.

31. Tighten the manifold bolts, in sequence first to 44 inch lbs. (5 Nm), then to 89 inch lbs. (10 Nm).

32. Install the EVAP canister purge solenoid valve and bracket to the intake manifold.

33. Install the EVAP canister purge tube to the throttle body and EVAP canister purge solenoid valve.

34. Install the engine coolant vent hose to the throttle body and vent pipe.

35. Install the coolant vent outlet hose to the throttle body and left-hand radiator tank.

36. Install the fresh air hose to the rocker cover and the throttle body.

37. Install the foul air hose to the throttle body and restricting orifice external connector.

38. Connect the MAP sensor connector.

39. Connect the knock sensor connector.

40. Connect the oil pressure sensor connector.

41. Connect the fuel injector connectors to all the fuel injectors.

42. Install the locks to the right and left side ignition coil main connectors and connect the connectors.

43. Connect the EVAP canister purge solenoid valve electrical connector.

44. Install the harness securing clips to the fuel rail brackets.

45. Install the cable to the throttle body cam lever then install the throttle cable to the throttle body mounting bracket.

46. Install the cable to the retaining clip.

47. Connect the connector to IAC motor.

48. Connect the connector to the TP sensor at the throttle body.

49. Connect the fuel line to the fuel rail.

50. Connect the purge line to the purge valve.

51. Install the intake duct and secure with the hose clamps.

52. Connect the air intake sensor connector to the air intake sensor.

53. Install the fuel rail covers.

54. Install the front suspension support brace.

55. Fill the cooling system.

56. Connect the negative battery cable.

57. Start the engine and check for leaks.

OIL PAN

REMOVAL & INSTALLATION

➡ **The original oil pan gasket is retained and aligned to the oil pan by rivets. When installing a new gasket, it is not necessary to install new oil pan gasket rivets.**

1. Drain the engine oil.

2. Disconnect the negative battery cable.

3. Remove the engine.

4. Remove the left and right closeout covers from the lower engine block.

5. Remove the oil pan bolts and the oil pan.

6. Drill out the oil pan rivets.

7. Remove the gasket and discard it and the rivets.

To install:

➡ **The alignment of the structural oil pan is critical. The rear bolt hole locations of the oil pan provide mounting points for the transmission housing. To ensure the rigidity of the powertrain and correct transmission alignment, it is important that the rear of the block and the rear of the oil pan are flush, or even. The rear of the oil pan must NEVER protrude beyond the engine block and transmission housing plane.**

8. Apply a 5 mm (0.2 in) bead of sealant, 20 mm (0.8 in) long to the engine block. Apply the sealant directly onto the tabs of the front cover gasket that protrude

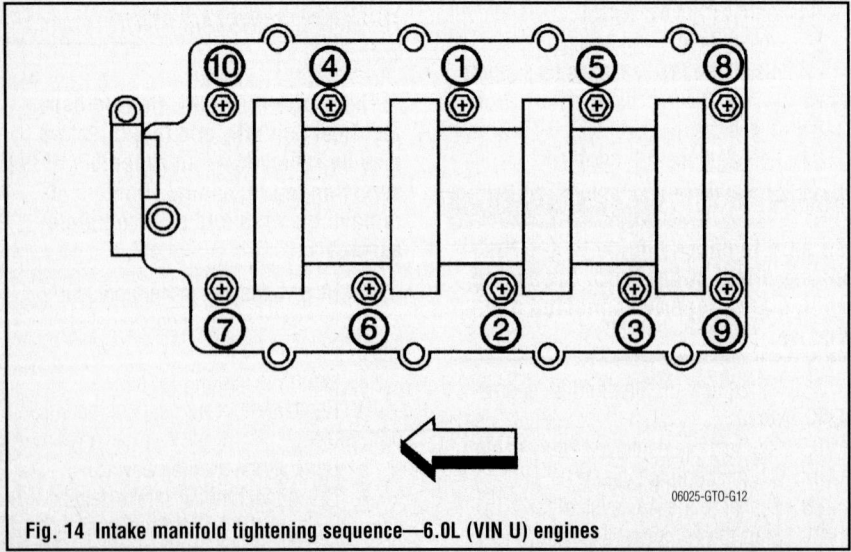

Fig. 14 Intake manifold tightening sequence—6.0L (VIN U) engines

06025-GTO-G12

into the oil pan surface. Apply a bead of sealant at the crankshaft rear seal retainer plate-to-cylinder block surface and the engine front cover-to-cylinder block surface.

9. Install the gasket onto the oil pan. Install the oil pan bolts to the pan and through the gasket.

10. Install the oil pan, gasket and bolts to the engine block.

11. Tighten bolts finger tight. Do not overtighten.

12. Place a straight edge across the rear of the engine block and the rear of the oil pan at the transmission housing mounting surfaces.

13. Align the oil pan until the rear of engine block and rear of oil pan are flush or even.

14. Tighten the oil pan-to-block and oil pan-to-front cover bolts to 18 ft. lbs. (25 Nm).

15. Tighten the oil pan-to-rear cover bolts to 106 inch lbs. (12 Nm).

16. Place a straight edge across the rear of the engine block and rear of oil pan at the transmission housing mounting surfaces.

17. Insert a feeler gage between the straight edge and the oil pan transmission housing mounting surface and check to make sure that there is no more than a 0.25 mm (0.01 in) gap between the pan and straight edge.

18. If the oil pan alignment is not within specifications, remove the oil pan and repeat the above procedure.

19. Install the left and right closeout covers to the lower engine block.

20. Install the engine.

21. Connect the negative battery cable.

22. Fill the engine with oil.

23. Start the engine and check for leaks.

OIL PUMP

REMOVAL & INSTALLATION

See Figure 15.

1. Drain the cooling system and the engine oil.

2. Disconnect the negative battery cable.

3. Disconnect the radiator hoses.

4. Remove the water pump.

5. Remove the radiator.

6. Remove the air conditioning (A/C) drive belt.

7. Remove the starter motor.

8. Remove the right transmission cover and bolt.

9. Lock the flywheel from turning.

10. Remove the crankshaft pulley bolt and the crankshaft damper using a puller.

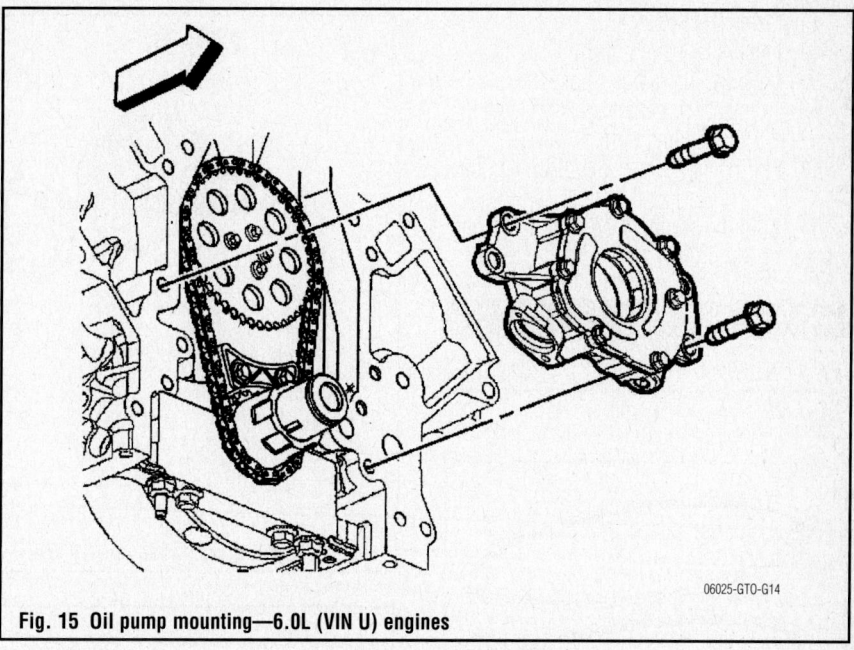

Fig. 15 Oil pump mounting—6.0L (VIN U) engines

06025-GTO-G14

11. Carefully pry out the front seal.

12. Remove the drive belt idler pulley bolt and pulley.

13. Remove the oil pan-to-front cover bolts.

14. Remove the front cover bolts.

15. Remove the front cover and gasket.

16. Discard the front cover gasket.

17. Remove the oil pan.

18. Remove the oil pump screen and discard the o-ring.

19. Remove the crankshaft oil deflector nuts.

20. Remove the crankshaft oil deflector.

21. Remove the oil pump.

To install:

➡**Inspect the oil pump and engine block oil gallery passages. These surfaces must be clear and free of debris and restrictions.**

22. Align the splined surfaces of the crankshaft sprocket and the oil pump drive gear and install the oil pump.

23. Install the oil pump onto the crankshaft sprocket until the pump housing contacts the face of the engine block.

24. Tighten the bolts to 18 ft. lbs. (25 Nm).

25. Install the crankshaft oil deflector.

26. Lubricate a NEW oil pump screen O-ring seal with clean engine oil.

27. Install the NEW O-ring seal onto the oil pump screen.

➡**Push the oil pump screen tube completely into the oil pump prior to tightening the bolt. Do not allow the bolt to pull the tube into the pump. Align the**

oil pump screen mounting brackets with the correct crankshaft bearing cap studs.

28. Install the oil pump screen and tighten the bolt to 106 inch lbs. (12 Nm).

29. Install the oil deflector and tighten the bolts to 18 ft. lbs. (25 Nm).

30. Install the oil pan.

31. Apply a 5 mm (0.20 in) bead of sealant 20 mm (0.80 in) long to the oil pan-to-engine block junction.

32. Install a new front cover gasket.

33. Install the front cover.

34. Install the crankshaft balancer bolt until snug.

35. Install the front cover bolts until snug.

36. Install the oil pan-to-front cover bolts until snug.

37. Install the drive belt idler pulley and tighten the bolt to 37 ft. lbs. (50 Nm).

38. Remove the crankshaft balancer bolt.

39. Use tool J-41665 and install the crankshaft balancer.

40. Install the used crankshaft balancer bolt and tighten to 240 ft. lbs. to position the balancer.

41. Remove the used bolt.

42. Check that the nose of the crankshaft is recessed at least 0.094-0.176 inch (2.40-4.48) into the balancer bore.

43. Install a new crankshaft balancer bolt and tighten first to 37 ft. lbs. (50 Nm) and then an additional 140 degrees.

44. Unlock the flywheel.

45. Install the right transmission cover and bolt.

46. Install the starter motor.

47. Install the air conditioning (A/C) drive belt.

48. Install the radiator.
49. Install the water pump.
50. Connect the radiator hoses.
51. Connect the negative battery cable.
52. Fill the cooling system.
53. Fill the crankcase with clean engine oil.
54. Start the engine. Check for leaks and proper operation.

PISTON AND RING

POSITIONING

See Figure 16.

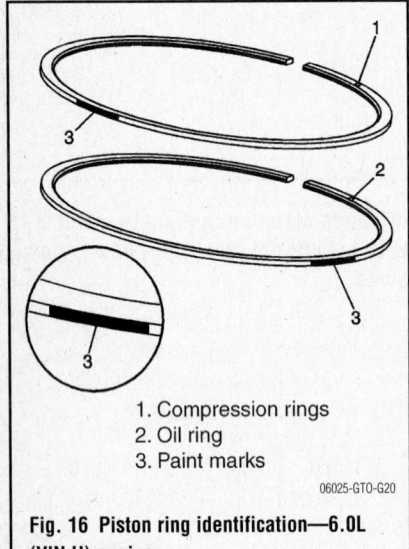

1. Compression rings
2. Oil ring
3. Paint marks

06025-GTO-G20

Fig. 16 Piston ring identification—6.0L (VIN U) engines

Position the oil control ring end gaps a minimum of 25 mm (1.0 in) from each other. Position the compression ring end gaps 180 degrees opposite each other.

REAR MAIN SEAL

REMOVAL & INSTALLATION

See Figures 17 and 18.

1. Disconnect the negative battery cable.
2. Remove the transmission.
3. Remove the flywheel.
4. Carefully pry the oil seal from the rear cover.

To install:

5. Lubricate the outside diameter of the oil seal with clean engine oil.
6. Lubricate the rear cover oil seal bore with clean engine oil.
7. Install the J-41479 cone (2) and bolts onto the rear of the crankshaft and tighten until snug.
8. Install the rear oil seal onto the

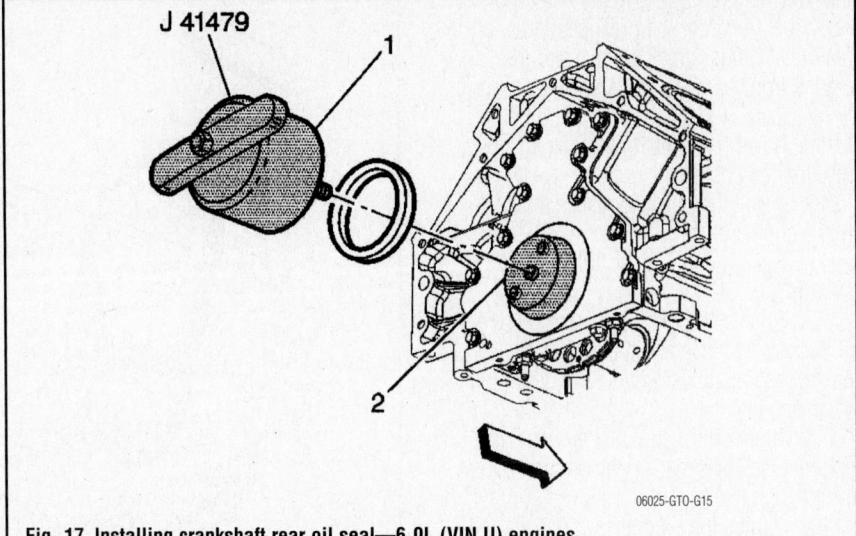

Fig. 17 Installing crankshaft rear oil seal—6.0L (VIN U) engines

tapered cone and push the seal to the rear cover bore.

9. Thread the J-41479 threaded rod into the tapered cone until the tool (1) contacts the oil seal.
10. Align the oil seal onto the tool (1).
11. Rotate the handle of the tool (1) clockwise until the seal enters the rear cover and bottoms into the cover bore.
12. Remove the tool.
13. Apply threadlock to the flywheel bolts.
14. Install the flywheel and tighten the bolts in sequence as follows:
   a. First step to 15 ft. lbs. (20 Nm).
   b. Second step to 37 ft. lbs. (50 Nm).
   c. Final step to 74 ft. lbs. (100 Nm).
15. Install the transmission.
16. Connect the negative battery cable.

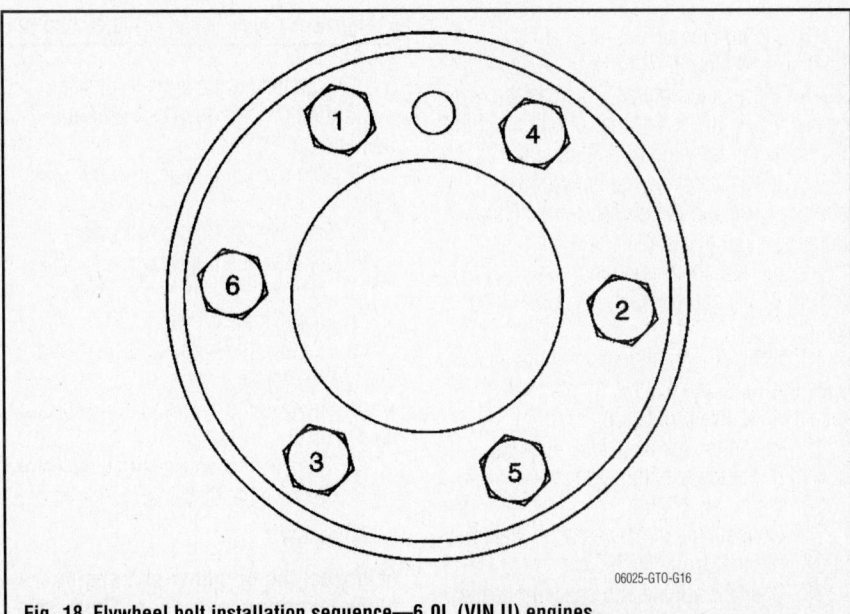

Fig. 18 Flywheel bolt installation sequence—6.0L (VIN U) engines

ROCKER ARMS

REMOVAL & INSTALLATION

See Figures 19 and 20.

➡**Place valve rocker arms, valve pushrods, and pivot support, in a rack so that they can be installed in the same location from which they were removed.**

1. Disconnect the negative battery cable.
2. Remove the valve covers. See the procedure under Cylinder Head.
3. Remove the valve rocker arm bolts.
4. Remove the valve rocker arms.
5. Remove the valve rocker arm pivot support.
6. Remove the push rods.

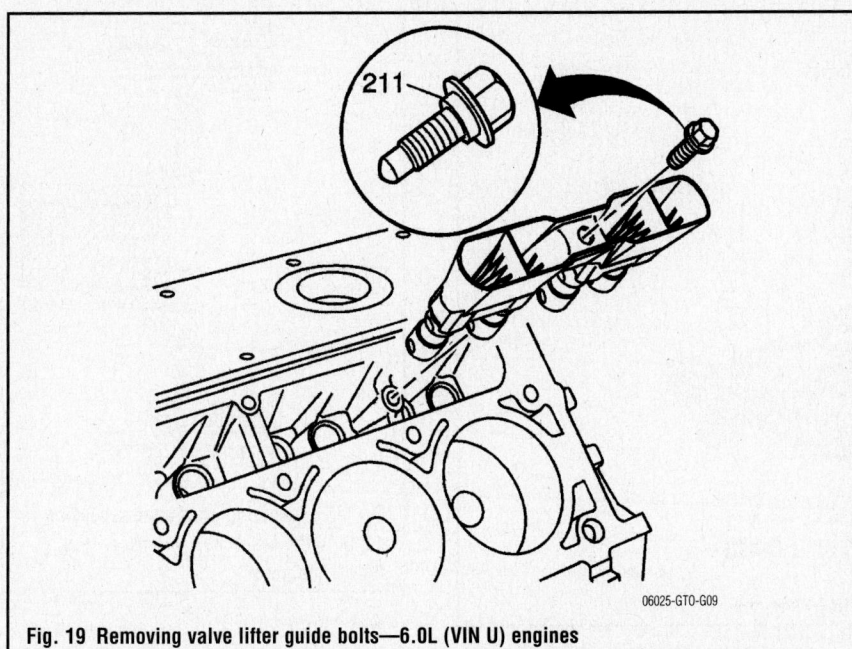

Fig. 19 Removing valve lifter guide bolts—6.0L (VIN U) engines

7. Remove the valve lifter guide bolts (211).

8. Remove the valve lifters and guide.

9. Remove the valve lifters from the guide.

10. Organize or mark the components so that they can be installed in the same location from which they were removed.

To install:

➡️**If the camshaft is being replaced, the valve lifters must also be replaced.**

11. Lubricate the valve lifters and engine block valve lifter bores with clean engine oil.

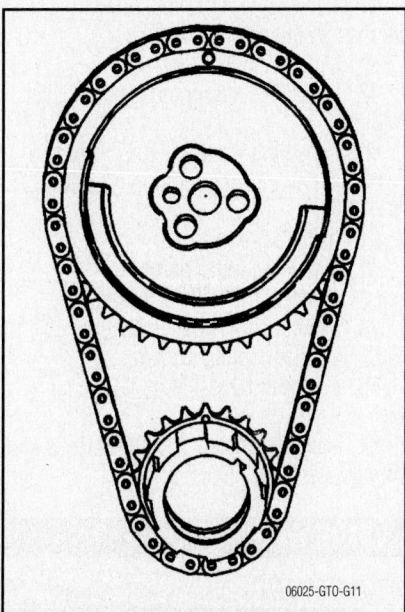

Fig. 20 Positioning crankshaft sprocket keyway at the 1:30 position—6.0L (VIN U) engine

12. Insert the valve lifters into the lifter guides. Align the flat area on the top of the lifter with the flat area in the lifter guide bore. Push the lifter completely into the guide bore

13. Install the valve lifters and guide assembly to the engine block.

14. Install the valve lifter guide bolt and tighten to 89 inch lbs. (10 Nm).

15. Lubricate the valve rocker arms and pushrods with clean engine oil.

16. Lubricate the flange of the valve rocker arm bolts with clean engine oil. Lubricate the flange or washer surface of the bolt that will contact the valve rocker arm.

17. Install the valve rocker arm pivot support.

18. Install the pushrods ensuring that they seat properly to the ends of the rocker arms.

19. Install the rocker arms and bolts but do not tighten.

20. Rotate the crankshaft until number one piston is at top dead center of compression stroke. In this position, cylinder number one rocker arms will be off lobe lift, and the crankshaft sprocket key will be at the 1:30 position. If viewing from the rear of the engine, the additional crankshaft pilot hole, non-threaded, will be in the 10:30 position. The engine firing order is 1, 8, 7, 2, 6, 5, 4, 3. Cylinders 1, 3, 5 and 7 are left bank. Cylinders 2, 4, 6, and 8 are right bank.

21. With the engine in the number one firing position, tighten the following valve rocker arm bolts as follows:

   a. Tighten exhaust valve rocker arm bolts 1, 2, 7, and 8 to 22 ft. lbs. (30 Nm).

   b. Tighten intake valve rocker arm bolts 1, 3, 4, and 5 to 22 ft. lbs. (30 Nm).

22. Rotate the crankshaft 360 degrees and tighten the following valve rocker arm bolts as follows:

   a. Tighten exhaust valve rocker arm bolts 3, 4, 5, and 6 to 22 ft. lbs. (30 Nm).

   b. Tighten intake valve rocker arm bolts 2, 6, 7, and 8 to 22 ft. lbs. (30 Nm).

23. Install the valve covers.

24. Connect the negative battery cable.

25. Start the engine and check for proper operation.

TIMING CHAIN, SPROCKETS, FRONT COVER AND SEAL

REMOVAL & INSTALLATION

See Figures 21 through 23.

1. Drain the cooling system and the engine oil.

2. Disconnect the negative battery cable.

3. Disconnect the radiator hoses.

4. Remove the water pump.

5. Remove the radiator.

6. Remove the air conditioning (A/C) drive belt.

7. Remove the starter motor.

8. Remove the right transmission cover and bolt.

9. Lock the flywheel from turning.

10. Remove the crankshaft pulley bolt and the crankshaft damper using a puller.

11. Carefully pry out the front seal.

12. Remove the drive belt idler pulley bolt and pulley.

13. Remove the oil pan-to-front cover bolts.

14. Remove the front cover bolts.

15. Remove the front cover and gasket.

16. Discard the front cover gasket.

17. Remove the oil pump.

18. Remove the camshaft sprocket bolts.

19. Remove the camshaft sprocket and timing chain.

20. Use tools J-8433, J-41816-2 and J-41558 and remove the crankshaft sprocket.

To install:

21. Install the crankshaft sprocket onto the front of the crankshaft. Align the crankshaft key with the crankshaft sprocket keyway.

22. Use tool J-41665 in order to install the crankshaft sprocket. Install the sprocket onto the crankshaft until fully seated against the crankshaft flange.

23. Rotate the crankshaft sprocket until the alignment mark is in the 12 o'clock position.

24. Install the camshaft sprocket and timing chain and locate the camshaft

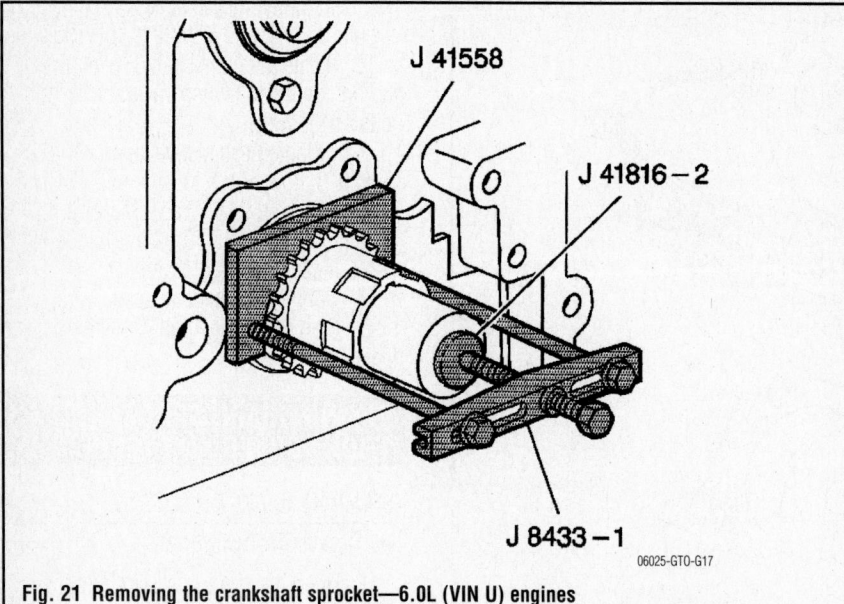

Fig. 21 Removing the crankshaft sprocket—6.0L (VIN U) engines

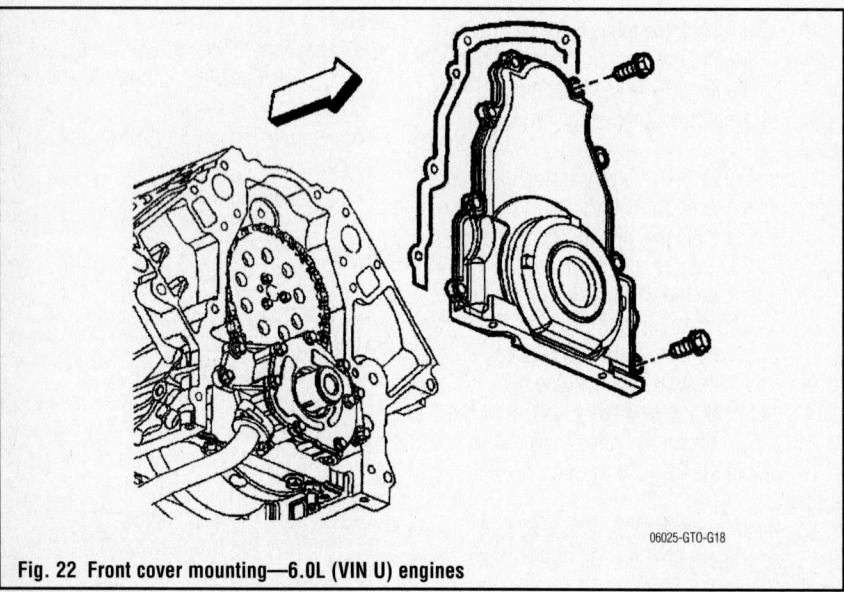

Fig. 22 Front cover mounting—6.0L (VIN U) engines

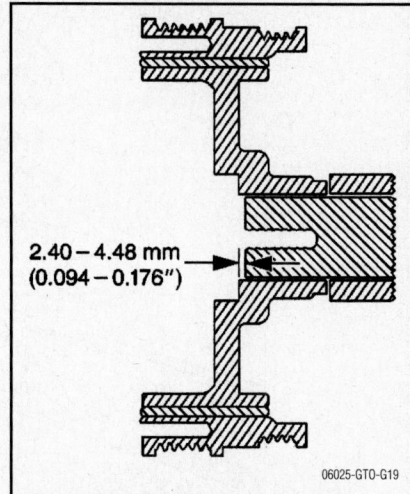

Fig. 23 Measuring crankshaft recession depth in the crankshaft balancer—6.0L (VIN U) engines

sprocket locating pin with the camshaft sprocket alignment hole.

➡**The camshaft and the crankshaft sprocket alignment marks MUST be aligned correctly. Locate the camshaft sprocket alignment mark in the 6 o'clock position.**

25. Rotate the crankshaft until number one piston is at top dead center of compression stroke.

26. Install the camshaft sprocket bolts and tighten to 26 ft. lbs. (35 Nm).

27. Install the oil pump.

28. Apply a 5 mm (0.20 in) bead of sealant 20 mm (0.80 in) long to the oil pan-to-engine block junction.

29. Install a new front cover gasket.

30. Install the front cover and hand tighten the bolts.

31. Install Front Cover Alignment tool no. J-41480 to the lower engine block.

32. Install Front Cover Alignment tool no. J-41476 to the oil seal opening.

33. Install the crankshaft balancer bolt until snug.

34. Install the front cover bolts and tighten to 18 ft. lbs. (25 Nm).

35. Remove the tools and ensure the front cover-to-oil pan surface is flush.

36. Install the oil pan-to-front cover bolts until snug.

37. Lubricate the outer edge of the front oil seal and seal bore with clean engine oil.

38. Use tool J-41478 and install the oil seal into the cover bore.

39. Remove the tool. Inspect the oil seal for proper installation. The oil seal should be installed evenly and completely into the front cover bore.

40. Install the drive belt idler pulley and tighten the bolt to 37 ft. lbs. (50 Nm).

41. Remove the crankshaft balancer bolt.

42. Use tool J-41665 and install the crankshaft balancer.

43. Install the used crankshaft balancer bolt and tighten to 240 ft. lbs. to position the balancer.

44. Remove the used bolt.

45. Check that the nose of the crankshaft is recessed at least 0.094-0.176 inch (2.40-4.48) into the balancer bore.

46. Install a new crankshaft balancer bolt and tighten first to 37 ft. lbs. (50 Nm) and then an additional 140 degrees.

47. Unlock the flywheel.

48. Install the right transmission cover and bolt.

49. Install the starter motor.

50. Install the air conditioning (A/C) drive belt.

51. Install the radiator.

52. Install the water pump.

53. Connect the radiator hoses.

54. Connect the negative battery cable.

55. Fill the cooling system.

56. Fill the crankcase with clean engine oil.

57. Start the engine. Check for leaks and proper operation.

VALVE LASH

ADJUSTMENT

The 6.0L engine is equipped with hydraulic lash adjusters. Valve clearance is not adjustable.

FUEL SYSTEM SERVICE PRECAUTIONS

Safety is the most important factor when performing not only fuel system maintenance, but any type of maintenance. Failure to conduct maintenance and repairs in a safe manner may result in serious personal injury or death. Work on a vehicle's fuel system components can be accomplished safely and effectively by adhering to the following rules and guidelines.

• To avoid the possibility of fire and personal injury, always disconnect the negative battery cable unless the repair or test procedure requires that battery voltage be applied.

• Always relieve the fuel system pressure prior to disconnecting any fuel system component (injector, fuel rail, pressure regulator, etc.) fitting or fuel line connection. Exercise extreme caution whenever relieving fuel system pressure to avoid exposing skin, face and eyes to fuel spray. Please be advised that fuel under pressure may penetrate the skin or any part of the body that it contacts.

• Always place a shop towel or cloth around the fitting or connection prior to loosening to absorb any excess fuel due to spillage. Ensure that all fuel spillage is quickly removed from engine surfaces. Ensure that all fuel-soaked cloths or towels are deposited into a flame-proof waste container with a lid.

• Always keep a dry chemical (Class B) fire extinguisher near the work area.

• Do not allow fuel spray or fuel vapors to come into contact with a spark or open flame.

• Always use a second wrench when loosening or tightening fuel line connection fittings. This will prevent unnecessary stress and torsion on fuel piping. Always follow the proper torque specifications.

• Always replace worn fuel fitting O-rings with new ones. Do not substitute fuel hose where rigid pipe is installed.

FUEL SYSTEM PRESSURE

RELIEVING

1. Disconnect the negative battery cable in order to avoid possible fuel discharge if an accidental attempt is made to start the engine. Loosen the fuel filler cap in order to relieve the fuel tank vapor pressure.

2. Remove the left fuel rail cover.

3. Connect the J 34730-1A fuel pressure gauge to the fuel pressure connection. Wrap a shop towel around the fitting while connecting the gauge in order to avoid spillage.

4. Install the bleed hose of the gauge into an approved container.

5. Open the valve on the gauge to bleed the system pressure. The fuel connections are now safe for servicing.

6. Drain any fuel remaining in the gauge into an approved container.

FUEL FILTER AND FUEL PUMP

REMOVAL & INSTALLATION

1. Relieve the fuel system pressure.

2. Disconnect the negative battery cable.

3. Drain the fuel tank.

4. Remove the fuel tank.

5. Disconnect the electrical connections from the fuel pump module.

6. Using the lock ring removal tool J45722 and a half-inch breaker bar, remove the fuel pump cover retainer lock ring by turning in a counter-clockwise direction.

7. Partially lift the modular fuel pump and sender assembly away from the fuel tank, taking care not to damage the fuel level sender assembly.

8. Disconnect the fuel tank EVAP vapor line quick connector from the underside of the modular fuel pump and sender assembly cover.

9. Insert hand into the fuel tank opening and disconnect the fuel feed line quick connector.

10. Remove the modular fuel pump and sender assembly and discard the gasket.

11. Remove the fuel strainer assembly.

12. Clamp the protruding end of the modular fuel pump in a soft-jawed vise to support the fuel filter and pump assembly in place.

13. Insert a pair of medium sized flat bladed screwdrivers through each of the service holes in the fuel filter assembly.

14. Firmly slide the blade between the fuel pump end cap and the internal fuel filter clips that hold the fuel pump in place.

15. Push the screwdrivers in far enough so that the internal fuel filter clips are deflected just free of each of the fuel pump end cap retainer shoulders.

16. Hold the screwdrivers in place with one hand, and move the fuel filter assembly in an upward direction to separate it from the fuel pump.

17. Remove the fuel pump.

To install:

18. Install the fuel pump.

19. Ensure the washer is firmly installed along the fuel pump end cap post and firmly pressed up against the suction filter molding.

20. Using hands only, locate the fuel pump in its correct orientation into the fuel filter.

21. Push the fuel pump firmly into place and lock the fuel pump into the fuel filter.

22. Install the fuel strainer assembly.

23. Before installation into the fuel tank, check the fuel sender float position.

24. Stand the assembly upright on a flat surface. Measure the distance between the middle of the fuel sender float and the flat surface. If required, the float position should be corrected, through careful adjustment of the float arm. The float should have a position of 0.27–0.55 inch (7–14mm).

25. Clean any dirt and foreign materials from the fuel tank seal recess and position a new seal in the recess.

26. Install the modular fuel pump and sender assembly into the fuel tank, taking care not to damage the fuel level sender float and arm in the process.

27. Insert hand into the fuel tank opening and connect the fuel feed line quick connector.

28. Connect the fuel tank EVAP vapor line quick connector from the underside of the modular fuel pump and sender assembly cover.

29. Ensure the locator in the cover engages in the slot in the tank opening.

30. Install the cover retainer lock ring. Use the half-inch breaker bar with special tool J45722 and rotate the retainer in a clockwise direction until the tangs are engaged.

31. Install the fuel tank pressure sensor connector, the fuel pump connector and the EVAP vapor hose quick connector to the modular fuel pump and sender assembly cover.

32. Install the fuel tank assembly.

33. Add fuel (10 gallons minimum) to the tank.

34. Install the gas cap.

35. Connect the negative battery cable.

36. Start the engine and check for leaks.

FUEL RAIL AND INJECTOR

REMOVAL & INSTALLATION

See Figure 24.

1. Relieve the fuel system pressure.
2. Disconnect the negative battery cable.
3. Disconnect the fuel feed hose from the fuel rail.
4. Disconnect the accelerator cable from the throttle body.
5. Move the accelerator cable aside.
6. Disconnect the electrical connectors from the fuel injectors. Identify the connectors to their corresponding injectors to ensure correct sequential injector firing order after reassembly.
7. Disconnect the electrical harness from the fuel rail brackets.
8. Remove the fuel rail attaching bolts.
9. Remove the fuel rail assembly.
10. Remove the injector lower O-ring seal from the spray tip end of each injector.
11. Discard the O-ring seals.
12. On both sides, remove the fuel injectors from the fuel rail.

To install:

13. Install the injectors to the fuel rail.
14. Lubricate the new lower injector O-ring seals with clean engine oil.
15. Install the new O-ring seals on the spray tip end of each injector.
16. Install the fuel rail assembly to the intake manifold.
17. Apply a 0.5 mm (0.020 in) of threadlock or equivalent to the threads of the fuel rail bolts.

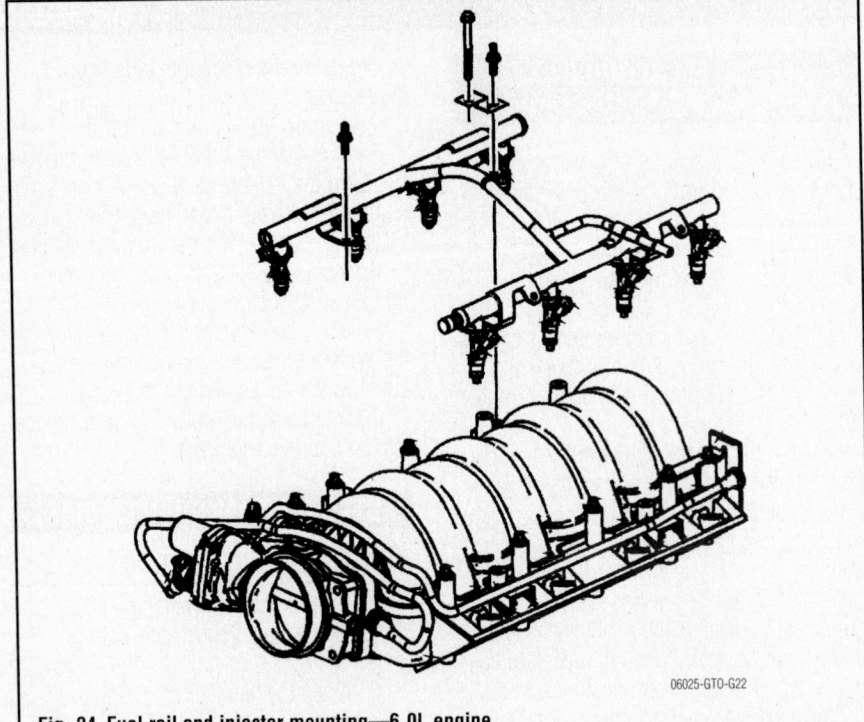

06025-GTO-G22

Fig. 24 Fuel rail and injector mounting—6.0L engine

18. Install the fuel rail attaching bolts and tighten to 89 inch lbs. (10 Nm).
19. Connect the injector electrical connectors.
20. Connect the electrical harness to the fuel rail brackets.
21. Connect the accelerator cable to the throttle body and the accelerator cable bracket, if the vehicle does not have traction control.
22. Connect the fuel feed hose to the fuel rail fuel pipe.
23. Tighten the fuel filler cap.

24. Connect the negative battery cable.
25. Turn ON the ignition for 2 seconds. Turn OFF the ignition for 10 seconds.
26. Turn ON the ignition. Inspect for fuel leaks

IDLE SPEED

ADJUSTMENT

Idle speed is controlled by the Powertrain Control Module and no adjustment is possible.

HEATING & AIR CONDITIONING SYSTEM

HEATER CORE

REMOVAL AND INSTALLATION

1. Disable the air bag system.
2. Disconnect the negative battery cable.
3. Recover the A/C refrigerant, if equipped.
4. Drain the cooling system.
5. Remove the floor console.
6. Remove the closeout insulator panels.
7. Remove the instrument panel compartment door.
8. Remove the instrument panel compartment lamp.
9. Remove the instrument panel compartment lamp switch.

10. Remove the instrument panel lower trim retainer panel.
11. Remove the instrument panel center trim.
12. Remove the instrument panel lower extension.
13. Remove the HVAC manual controls.
14. Remove the radio housing bracket.
15. Remove the instrument cluster.
16. Remove the headlamp switch.
17. Remove the driver information center switch.
18. Remove the instrument panel outer covers.
19. Remove the windshield defroster grilles.
20. Remove the daytime running lamp control module.

21. Remove the instrument panel speakers.
22. Remove the cruise control and wiper washer switches.
23. Place the steering wheel in the straight ahead position
24. Rotate the steering wheel 90 degrees to access 2 of the 4 holes in the rear of the steering column.
25. Using locating tool EL-46844, relieve the tension on the 2 spring loaded retaining clips. When the tension is released the steering wheel module will away from the wheel.
26. Rotate the steering wheel 180 degrees and repeat the procedure on the other 2 access holes.
27. Disconnect the air bag module connector.

28. Remove the air bag.

29. Lock the steering wheel with it in the straight ahead position.

30. Remove the steering column trim covers.

31. Disconnect the horn connector.

32. Match mark the steering wheel-to-steering column position and remove the steering wheel bolt.

33. Remove the steering wheel.

34. Remove the 2 inner screws attaching the instrument panel inflatable restraint and instrument panel passenger's bracket and brace assembly to the instrument panel inflatable restraint bracket.

35. Remove the 12 lower screws and 5 upper screws from the instrument panel pad, and remove the pad.

36. From the rear side of the instrument panel pad, remove the 4 screws attaching the instrument panel inflatable restraint opening trim cover to the instrument panel inflatable restraint bracket.

37. While pushing on the trim cover, detach the 4 tabs and remove the trim cover.

38. From the rear of the instrument pad, remove the 4 screws, attaching the instrument panel inflatable restraint bracket to the pad assembly.

39. Remove the 6 screws, and remove the bracket from the pad assembly.

40. Disconnect the instrument panel passenger air bag module connector, the module retaining nuts and bolts and the passenger air bag module.

41. Remove the right side HVAC duct from the HVAC unit.

42. Remove the lower radio bracket.

43. Remove the instrument panel right end and center support bracket.

44. Remove the radio antenna lead from the three retaining clips on the HVAC unit.

45. Mark and remove the heater hoses from the heater core pipes.

46. Disconnect the water valve vacuum hose.

47. Disconnect the vacuum supply hose from the check valve.

48. Remove the Thermal Expansion Valve (TXV).

49. Remove the fuel line retaining bracket and nut from the HVAC mounting stud.

50. Remove the HVAC unit mounting stud and screws.

51. Remove the HVAC unit from the vehicle.

52. Remove the two heater core pipe clamp screws.

53. Remove the two heater core pipe clamps.

54. Remove the heater core retaining strap mounting screw.

55. Remove the heater core retaining strap.

56. Remove the heater pipe bracket mounting screws.

57. Remove the heater pipe bracket

58. Remove the heater core from the HVAC module.

59. Remove the heater pipe retaining screws.

60. Remove the heater pipe retaining clamps.

61. Remove the heater pipes from the heater core.

62. Remove and discard the O-rings.

To install:

63. Install new O-rings on the heater pipes.

64. Install the heater pipes to the heater core.

65. Secure the heater pipes with the retaining clamps and screws.

66. Install the heater core to the HVAC module.

67. Install the heater pipe bracket.

68. Secure the heater pipe bracket with the mounting screws

69. Install the heater core retaining strap.

70. Secure the heater core retaining strap with the mounting screw.

71. Install the two heater core pipe clamps.

72. Secure the two heater core pipe clamps with the screws.

73. Install the HVAC module assembly.

74. Install the screws from inside the vehicle and the engine compartment which secure the HVAC module assembly to the dash.

75. Install the fuel line retaining bracket and nut to the HVAC mounting stud.

76. Install the Thermal Expansion Valve (TXV).

77. Connect the vacuum supply hose to the check valve.

78. Connect the water valve vacuum hose.

79. Install the heater hoses to the heater core pipes.

80. Install the radio antenna lead to the three retaining clips on the HVAC unit.

81. Install the instrument panel center support bracket.

82. Install the instrument panel right end bracket.

83. Install the lower radio bracket.

84. Install the right side HVAC duct to the HVAC unit.

85. Install the inflatable restraint I/P module and retaining nuts and tighten to 33 ft. lbs. (45 Nm).

86. Install the I/P module retaining bolts and tighten to 84 inch lbs. (10 Nm).

87. Connect the I/P module connector.

88. Place the passenger restraint bracket in position ensuring the lower screw hole tabs are positioned in the pad assembly.

89. Install the 6 screws attaching the bracket to the pad assembly.

90. Install the 4 screws, attaching the instrument panel inflatable restraint bracket to the pad assembly.

91. Locate the trim cover in the pad assembly opening, and align the trim cover with the 4 tabs.

92. Install the 4 screws attaching the instrument panel inflatable restraint trim cover to the inflatable restraint bracket.

93. Install the instrument panel pad to the vehicle and tighten the upper screws to 80 inch lbs. (9 Nm).

94. Install the 12 lower instrument pad screws and tighten to 18 inch lbs. (2 Nm).

95. Install the 2 inner screws attaching the instrument panel inflatable restraint and instrument panel passenger's bracket and brace assembly to the instrument panel inflatable restraint bracket.

96. If replacing the steering wheel, copy the match marks from the old steering wheel to the new steering wheel.

97. Verify the front tires have not moved since the removal of the steering wheel.

98. Verify the green indexing tab on the SIR coil is aligned with the window in the coil casing. The green tab indicates the coil is locked in the centralized position.

99. Align the match marks on the steering wheel and on the steering shaft.

100. Install the steering wheel to the steering shaft.

101. Clean the threads on the steering wheel bolt and on the steering shaft and apply Loctite® 242 or the equivalent to the steering wheel bolt.

102. Install the bolt to the steering wheel and tighten to 33 ft. lbs. (45 Nm).

103. Connect the horn connector.

104. Connect the driver air bag wiring harness connectors.

105. Connect the air bag electrical connector.

106. Install the air bag module. Align the module to the 4 retaining clips on the steering wheel and press the steering wheel module toward the steering wheel until the retaining clips lock.

107. Install the steering column trim covers.

108. Install the wiper washer and cruise control switches.

109. Install the instrument panel speakers.

110. Install the daytime running lamp control module.
111. Install the windshield defroster grilles.
112. Install the instrument panel outer covers.
113. Install the instrument cluster.
114. Install the driver information center switch.
115. Install the headlamp switch.

116. Install the radio housing bracket.
117. Install the HVAC manual controls.
118. Install the instrument panel lower extension.
119. Install the instrument panel center trim.
120. Install the instrument panel lower trim retainer panel.
121. Install the instrument panel compartment lamp switch and light.

122. Install the instrument panel compartment door.
123. Install the closeout insulator panels.
124. Install the floor console.
125. Enable the air bag system.
126. Connect the negative battery cable.
127. Fill the cooling system.
128. Recharge the A/C system.
129. Start the engine and check for leaks.

STEERING

POWER RACK AND PINION STEERING GEAR

REMOVAL & INSTALLATION

1. Lock the steering column with the steering wheel in the straight ahead position.
2. Disconnect the negative battery cable.
3. Place a drain pan under the vehicle in order to collect the fluid from the power steering system.
4. Remove front wheels.
5. Remove the pressure and return pipes from the steering gear.
6. Remove and discard the nut that retains the steering shaft coupling to the steering gear pinion.

7. Remove the bolt from the coupling.
8. Separate the retainer from the coupling.
9. Separate the coupling from the pinion.
10. Remove the 2 outer tie rod ends.
11. Remove the 2 nuts and the 2 bolts that retain the steering gear to the front frame.
12. Remove the steering gear.

To install:

13. Slide the steering gear pinion into the steering shaft coupling.
14. Install the steering gear to the front frame and tighten the bolts to 44 ft. lbs. (60 Nm), plus an additional 45 degrees.
15. Ensure the O-rings on the pipes and the hoses are in excellent condition.
16. Install the pressure and return pipes

to the steering gear and tighten to 15 lbs. (20 Nm).
17. Position the steering shaft coupling on the steering gear pinion.
18. Install the retainer on the coupling.
19. Install the bolt to the coupling. Install a NEW nut to the bolt and tighten to 20 ft. lbs. (27 Nm).
20. Install the 2 outer tie rod ends.
21. Install the front tire and wheel assemblies.
22. Remove the drain pan.
23. Lower the vehicle.
24. Connect the negative battery cable.
25. Fill the power steering system with the proper type and quantity of fluid.
26. Check the front end alignment and adjust as necessary.

SUSPENSION   FRONT SUSPENSION

COIL SPRING AND STRUT

REMOVAL & INSTALLATION

See Figure 25.

1. Raise and support the vehicle.
2. Remove the front wheel.
3. Hold the stabilizer bar link upper stud with a wrench, then remove the upper nut, washer, insulator and retainer.
4. Disconnect the speed sensor harness, insulator and connector.
5. Separate the brake hose from the strut bracket.
6. Position a jack and a block of wood below the control arm ball joint and raise the jack to support the control arm.
7. Remove the lower strut attaching nuts, washers and bolts.
8. Separate the strut from the knuckle.
9. Remove the strut upper mounting nut and bumper stop.
10. Lower the strut.
11. Remove the stabilizer link from the strut bracket.
12. Remove the strut/spring assembly.

13. Use a spring compressor to compress the spring.
14. Remove the strut mount nut and washers.
15. Remove the strut bearing from the upper spring seat.
16. Remove the strut shield strap, upper spring seat, insulator and bumper.
17. Release the spring compressor.
18. Remove the spring.
19. Remove and discard the strut shield clamp.
20. Remove the dust shield and filter.

To install:

21. Hold the strut rod and housing and pull the strut rod out to its maximum length.
22. Install the dust shield and ensure the filter is seated in the housing.
23. Check that the distance between the bottom of the dust shield and the bottom of the lower spring seat is 1.20–2.0 inch (30–50mm).
24. Install a new clamp to hold the dust shield.
25. Install the coil spring to the housing.

26. Compress the spring using a spring compressor.
27. Install the bumper.
28. Install the upper insulator with the step on the insulator to the straight projecting end of the spring.
29. Install the upper spring seat so the double notch in the upper flange of the seat in on the inboard side of the strut.
30. Pull the strut rod out to its maximum length.
31. Install the strut bearing so the narrow outer section faces toward the upper spring seat collar.
32. Install the lower washer so the cupped side faces upward.
33. Install the upper washer so the cupped side faces downward.
34. Install the strut mount nut and tighten to 58 ft. lbs. (78 Nm).
35. Install the dust shield to the upper spring shield so the shield fits over the lower flange of the spring seat collar.
36. Install a new dust shield strap.
37. Remove the spring compressor.

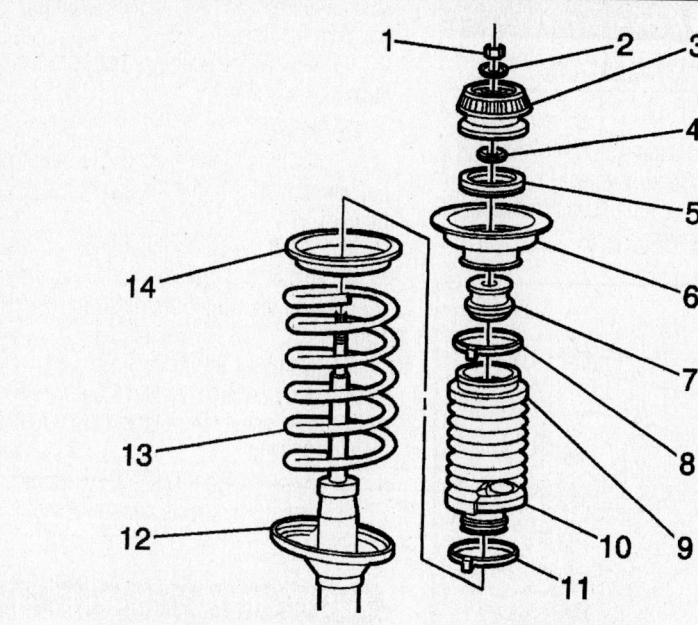

1. Nut
2. Washer
3. Mount
4. Washer
5. Strut bearing
6. Upper spring seat
7. Strut bumper
8. Shield clamp
9. Dust shield
10. Filter
11. Shield clamp
12. Lower spring seat
13. Spring
14. Upper insulator

06025-GTO-G25

Fig. 25 Exploded view of front strut and coil spring assembly—GTO

38. Install the stabilizer link to the strut bracket.

39. Position the strut in the strut tower.

40. Install the bumper stop, and new strut nut but do not tighten.

41. Install the lower strut to the steering knuckle and tighten the new bolts and nuts to 63 ft. lbs. (85 Nm).

42. Hold the end of the strut rod and tighten the upper nut to 41 ft. lbs. (55 Nm).

43. Install the strut cap.

44. Remove the jack

45. Attach the brake hose to the strut bracket.

46. Connect the speed sensor harness, insulator and connector.

47. Hold the stabilizer bar link upper stud with a wrench and install the washer, insulator, retainer, and upper nut and tighten to 12 ft. lbs. (16 Nm).

48. Install the front wheel.

49. Lower the vehicle and bounce the suspension 3 times to stabilize the suspension.

50. Check the wheel alignment.

51. Tighten the lower strut nuts to 74 ft. lbs. (100 Nm), plus an additional 90 degrees.

FRONT SUSPENSION FRAME

REMOVAL & INSTALLATION

1. Raise and support the vehicle.
2. Remove the front wheels.
3. Remove the power steering gear.
4. Remove the lower control arms and control arm rods and insulators.
5. Remove the hood.
6. Using an engine crane, support and raise the engine.
7. Remove the engine mount brackets from the frame.
8. Support the front frame with a jack.
9. Remove the 4 attaching bolts and remove the frame.

To install:

10. Install the frame to the side members.

11. Install the silver bolts to the rear of the frame and the black bolts to the front and tighten to 92 ft. lbs. (125 Nm).

12. Install the engine mount brackets and tighten to 37 ft. lbs. (50 Nm).

13. Lower the engine.

14. Install the hood.

15. Install the lower control arms and control arm rods and insulators.

16. Install the power steering gear.
17. Install the front wheels.
18. Lower the vehicle.

LOWER CONTROL ARM ROD

REMOVAL & INSTALLATION

1. Raise and support the vehicle.

2. Remove the front tire and wheel assembly.

3. Loosen the nut that retains the front lower control arm rod to the front lower control arm rod insulating bushing assembly.

4. Remove and discard the nut that retains the rod to the front lower control arm.

5. Remove the washer from the rod.

6. Remove the 4 nuts that retain the insulating bushing to the front frame.

7. Pull the insulating bushing away from the front frame.

8. Remove the rod and the rod retainer from the lower control arm.

9. Remove the rod retainer from the rod.

10. Pull the rod through the hole in the front frame. Remove the rod and the insulating bushing as an assembly.

11. Place the rod in a soft jaw vise.

12. Remove and discard the nut that retains the rod to the insulating bushing.

13. Remove the insulating bushing from the rod.

14. If a washer is on the rod, remove washer.

To install:

➡The front of the rod has more distance between the shoulder and the end of the threads. The washer for the front of the rod is for reducing caster.

15. If equipped, install the washer to the front of the rod.

16. Install the rod, rear end first, through the hole in the frame.

17. Install the rod retainer to the rod with the convex side toward the control arm.

18. Install the rod to the control arm.

19. Install the washer to the rear of the rod.

20. Install the new nut in order to retain the rod to the control arm.

21. Install the insulating bushing assembly over the front of the rod.

22. Install the insulating bushing to the studs on the frame.

23. Install the 4 nuts in order to retain the insulating bushing to the frame and tighten to 17 ft. lbs. (23 Nm).

24. Install the new nut in order to retain

the rod to the insulating bushing but do not tighten.

25. Install the front tire and wheel assembly.

26. Lower the vehicle.

27. With the weight of the vehicle on the tire and wheel assemblies, push down on the front bumper 3 times in order to stabilize the suspension.

28. Tighten the nut that retains the rod to the insulating bushing to 109 ft. lbs. (148 Nm).

29. Tighten the nut that retains the rod to the control arm to 76 ft. lbs. (103 Nm).

30. Check the wheel alignment.

LOWER CONTROL ARM

REMOVAL & INSTALLATION

1. Raise and support the vehicle.

2. Remove the tire and wheel assembly.

3. Turn the wheel to gain access to the ball joint stud.

4. Remove the ball joint stud nut and separate the stud from the steering knuckle.

5. Push the control arm away from the knuckle.

6. Remove the control arm rod nut and washer.

7. Remove the control arm-to-frame nut and discard.

8. Remove the control arm-to-frame bolt and remove the control arm from the rod.

To install:

9. Install the retainer on the control arm rod.

10. Install the control arm to the rod.

11. Install the control arm and bolt to the frame but do not tighten.

12. Install a new nut and washer to the rod but do not tighten.

13. Place a jack and a block of wood under the control arm and install the ball joint stud to the knuckle.

14. Raise the jack to seat the stud.

15. Install a new nut to the stud and tighten to 55 ft. lbs. (60 Nm).

16. Remove the jack.

17. Lower the vehicle.

18. With the weight of the vehicle on the tires, bounce the front bumper 3 times.

19. Tighten the control arm-to-frame nut to 72 ft. lbs. (98 Nm).

20. Tighten the control arm-to-control arm nut to 76 ft. lbs. (103 Nm).

21. Check the wheel alignment.

STABILIZER BAR

REMOVAL & INSTALLATION

See Figure 26.

1. Raise and support the vehicle.

2. Remove the front wheels.

3. Lower the front suspension frame. See Front Suspension Frame.

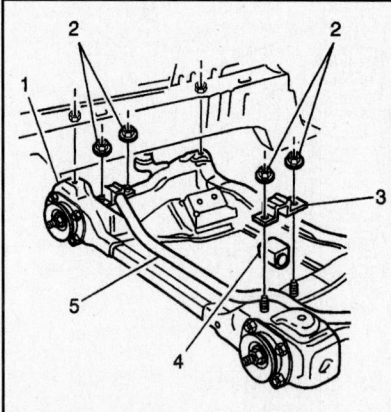

1. Suspension frame
2. Nuts
3. Insulator brackets
4. Insulator
5. Stabilizer bar

06025-GTO-G27

Fig. 26 Front stabilizer bar mounting to the front suspension frame—GTO

4. Remove the stabilizer bar nuts, brackets and insulators.

5. Use a wrench to hold the link lower studs, then remove the nuts and stabilizer bar from the links.

6. Remove the stabilizer bar from the suspension frame.

To install:

7. Install the insulators to the stabilizer bar with the slots in the insulators facing forward.

8. Install the bar to the frame.

9. Install the brackets to the insulators and tighten the nuts to 20 ft. lbs. (27 Nm).

10. Install the bar to the links.

11. Use a wrench to hold the link lower studs, then install the nuts and tighten to 37 ft. lbs. (50 Nm).

12. Raise the front suspension frame.

13. Install the wheels and lower the vehicle.

WHEEL HUB AND BEARING

REMOVAL & INSTALLATION

See Figure 27.

1. Raise and support the vehicle.

2. Remove the front wheel.

3. Remove the brake caliper and rotor.

4. Turn the steering wheel to the left or right, depending upon which is being serviced.

5. Disconnect the wheel speed sensor.

6. Remove the strut-to-knuckle bolts.

7. Remove 3 Allen bolts and remove the hub from the knuckle.

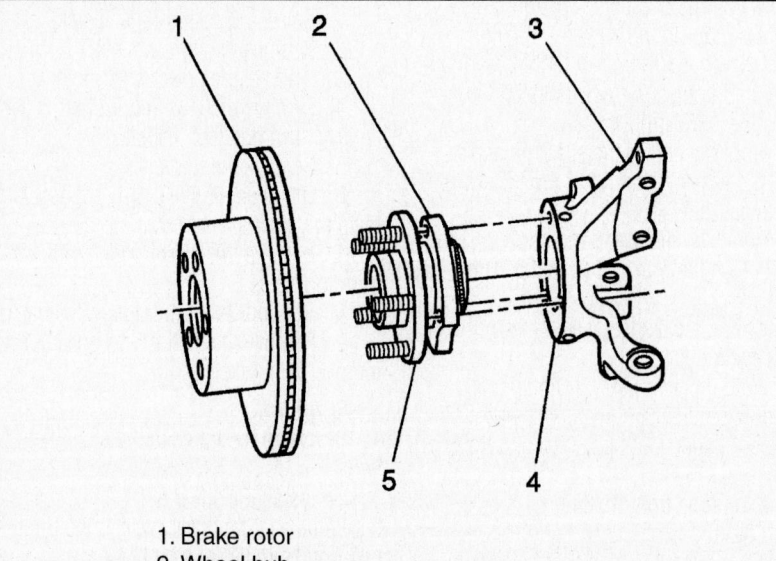

1. Brake rotor
2. Wheel hub
3. Steering knuckle

06025-GTO-G29

Fig. 27 Exploded view of front wheel hub and steering knuckle—GTO

To install:

8. Clean the steering knuckle/wheel hub mating surfaces.

9. Align the wheel speed sensor connection on the hub with the hole in the knuckle.

10. Install the hub to the knuckle.

11. Install the 3 Allen bolts to the hub and tighten to 80 ft. lbs. (108 Nm).

12. Connect the wheel speed sensor connector.

13. Install the knuckle to the strut and tighten the new bolts, washers and nuts to 64 ft. lbs. (85 Nm), then to 74 ft. lbs. (100 Nm), plus an additional 90 degrees.

14. Install the brake rotor and caliper.

15. Install the wheel.

16. Lower the vehicle.

SUSPENSION

COIL SPRING

REMOVAL & INSTALLATION

See Figure 28.

1. Raise and support the vehicle.

2. Remove the tire and wheel assembly.

3. Prevent the wheel hub from turning.

4. Remove the bolts and the retaining plates that retain the outer constant velocity joint to the drive shaft flange.

5. Separate the wheel drive shaft from the drive shaft flange and wire aside.

6. Loosen the nut that retains the stabilizer shaft to the shaft link.

7. Remove the nut and the bolt that retain the stabilizer shaft link to the lower control arm.

8. Loosen the nut that retains the outer adjustment link to the control arm. Position the top of the nut with the top of the outer adjustment link stud.

9. Use a tie-rod puller to separate the stud from the control arm.

10. Remove and discard the nut from the stud.

11. Position the adjustment link assembly away from the control arm.

12. Position a jack with a block of wood under the control arm.

13. Raise the jack slightly in order to reduce the spring load on the control arm.

14. Remove the bolt and washer from the shock absorber.

15. Separate the shock absorber from the control arm.

16. Lower the jack and the control arm.

17. Push down gently on the control arm and remove the spring and the 2 insulators.

18. Remove the insulators from the spring.

To install:

19. Install the lower insulator (3) to the control arm.

20. Install the upper insulator (1) to the spring (2).

21. Push down gently on the control arm. Install the spring and the upper insulator to the lower insulator.

22. Adjust the position of jack in order to align the control arm and the shock absorber.

➡ **Do not tighten the bolt yet. The weight of the vehicle must be on the tire and wheel assemblies before tightening the suspension fasteners.**

23. Install the washer and the bolt in order to retain the shock absorber to the control arm.

➡ **Do not tighten the nut or the bolt yet.**

24. Install the nut and the bolt in order to retain the stabilizer shaft link to the control arm.

➡ **Do not tighten the nut yet.**

25. Install the outer adjustment link stud and a NEW nut to the control arm.

26. Remove the jack and the wood from the control arm.

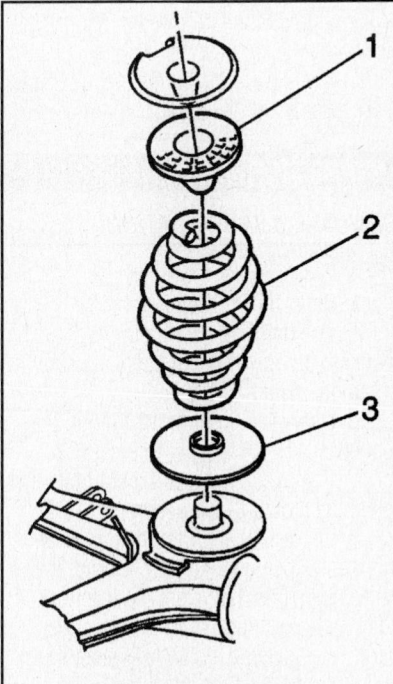

1. Upper insulator
2. Spring
3. Lower insulator

06025-GTO-G26

Fig. 28 Exploded view of the rear coil spring assembly—GTO

27. Lock the wheel hub from turning.

28. Install the retainers and the bolts in order to retain the outer constant velocity joint to the drive shaft flange and tighten to 37 ft. lbs. (50 Nm), plus an additional 68 degrees.

29. Remove the wire supporting the wheel drive shaft .

30. Install the driveshaft.

31. Install the tire and wheel assembly.

32. Lower the vehicle.

33. With the weight of the vehicle on the tire and wheel assemblies, bounce the rear of the vehicle several times in order to stabilize the rear suspension.

34. Tighten the stabilizer shaft link nuts to 72 ft. lbs. (98 Nm).

35. Tighten the shock absorber-to-control arm bolt and tighten to 85 ft. lbs. (115 Nm).

36. Tighten the outer adjustment link-to-control arm to 46 ft. lbs. (63 Nm).

37. Check the wheel alignment.

LOWER CONTROL ARM

REMOVAL & INSTALLATION

1. Raise and support the vehicle.

2. Remove the tire and wheel assembly.

3. Loosen the nut that retains the stabilizer shaft to the shaft link.

4. Remove the nut and the bolt that retain the stabilizer shaft link to the lower control arm.

5. Loosen the nut that retains the outer adjustment link to the control arm. Position the top of the nut with the top of the outer adjustment link stud.

6. Separate the stud from the control arm.

7. Remove and discard the nut from the stud.

8. Position the adjustment link assembly away from the control arm.

9. Remove the clip from the brake hose.

10. Pull the brake pipe and hose forward from the bracket.

11. Lift the brake pipe up through the slot in the bracket in order to separate the brake pipe and hose from the control arm.

12. Loosen the brake pipe flare nut.

13. Remove the clip from the backing plate bracket.

14. Remove the brake pipe from the brake hose.

15. Plug the brake hose in order to minimize fluid loss and contamination.

16. Remove the brake pipe from the backing plate bracket.

17. Plug the brake pipe.

18. Remove the 2 bolts and the brake caliper and bracket assembly from the control arm.

19. Remove the rear parking brake cable.

20. If necessary for sufficient access, remove the propeller shaft.

21. Mark the position of the brake rotor to the hub.

22. Remove the brake rotor from the hub.

23. Lock the wheel hub from turning.

24. Separate the axle shaft from the drive shaft flange and wire it aside.

25. Position a jack with a block of wood under the control arm.

26. Raise the jack slightly in order to reduce the spring load on the control arm.

27. Remove the coil spring.

28. Pull the differential carrier breather hose out of the hole in the vehicle underbody rear suspension support.

29. Disconnect the wheel speed sensor connectors from the body harness.

30. Use paint or a scribe in order to mark the outline of the differential carrier assembly mount on the body.

31. Use a jack to support the mount.

32. Remove and discard the 4 bolts that retain the mount to the body.

33. Lower the mount and the rear suspension support in order to access the control arm fasteners.

34. Remove and discard the 2 nuts that retain the control arm to the rear suspension support.

35. Remove the 2 bolts and the control arm.

To install:

36. Install the control arm and the 2 bolts to the rear suspension support, but do not tighten.

37. Install the 2 new nuts to the control arm.

38. Position a jack with a block of wood under the control arm.

39. Install the rotor to the hub.

40. Install the brake caliper and tighten to 63 ft. lbs. (85 Nm).

41. Install the coil spring.

42. Install the lower shock absorber bolt but do not tighten.

43. Install the nut and the bolt in order to retain the stabilizer shaft link to the lower control arm, but do not tighten.

44. Install the outer adjustment link stud and a nut to the control arm.

45. Remove the jack and the wood from the control arm.

46. Lock the wheel hub from turning.

47. Install the retainers and the bolts to retain the outer constant velocity joint to the drive shaft flange and tighten to 37 ft. lbs. (50 Nm) plus an additional 68 degrees.

48. Raise the jack and the differential carrier assembly mount.

49. Align the mount with the match marks.

50. Install the new bolts that retain the mount to the body and tighten to 26 ft. lbs. (35 Nm), plus an additional 68 degrees.

51. Lower and remove the jack from under the vehicle.

52. Install the rear parking brake cable.

53. Install the brake hose and pipe.

54. Install the drive shaft, if removed.

55. Install the tire and wheel assembly.

56. Lower the vehicle.

57. With the weight of the vehicle on the tire and wheel assemblies, bounce the rear of the vehicle several times in order to stabilize the rear suspension.

58. Tighten the nuts that retain the control arm to the rear suspension support to 74 ft. lbs. (100 Nm).

59. Tighten the stabilizer shaft link nuts to 72 ft. lbs. (98 Nm).

60. Tighten the lower shock bolt to 85 ft. lbs. (115 Nm).

61. Tighten the nut that retains the outer adjustment link to the control arm to 46 ft. lbs. (63 Nm).

62. Check the wheel alignment.

SHOCK ABSORBER

REMOVAL & INSTALLATION

1. Raise and support the vehicle.

2. Remove the bolt and the washer from the shock absorber.

3. Separate the shock absorber from the control arm.

4. Lower the vehicle to the appropriate height for accessing the rear compartment.

5. In the rear compartment, remove the rear center trim panel carpet.

6. If necessary in order to remove the right rear shock absorber, remove the fuel filler tube.

7. Remove the cap from the shock absorber.

8. Remove the upper mounting nut.

9. Remove the upper mounting upper washer.

10. Remove the upper mounting upper bushing.

11. Remove the shock absorber from the vehicle.

12. If necessary, remove the upper mounting lower bushing.

13. If necessary, remove the upper mounting lower washer.

14. Remove the shock absorber.

To install:

15. If removed, install the upper mounting lower washer to the shock absorber.

16. If removed, install the upper mounting lower bushing to the shock absorber.

17. Install the shock absorber to the vehicle.

18. Install the upper mounting upper bushing.

19. Install the upper mounting upper washer.

20. Install the upper mounting nut and tighten to 10 ft. lbs. (14 Nm).

21. Install the cap to the shock absorber.

22. Install the shock, washer and the bolt to the control arm.

23. Lower the vehicle.

24. With the weight of the vehicle on the tire and wheel assemblies, bounce the rear of the vehicle several times in order to stabilize the rear suspension.

25. Tighten the bolt to 85 ft. lbs. (115 Nm).

26. If removed, install the fuel filler tube.

27. Reinstall the carpet.

STABILIZER BAR

REMOVAL & INSTALLATION

See Figure 29.

1. Raise the vehicle on a hoist.

2. Use paint or a scribe in order to mark the outline of the differential carrier assembly mount on the body.

3. Use a jack in order to support the mount.

4. Remove and discard the 4 bolts that retain the mount to the body.

5. Lower the jack with the mount and the rear suspension support in order to access the bolts that retain the stabilizer shaft insulator brackets to the support.

6. Remove the 2 stabilizer shaft link bolts from the control arms.

7. Remove the stabilizer shaft links from the control arms.

8. Remove the bolts that retain the stabilizer shaft insulator brackets to the rear suspension support.

9. Use a flat blade tool as a lever in order to remove the brackets from the rear suspension support.

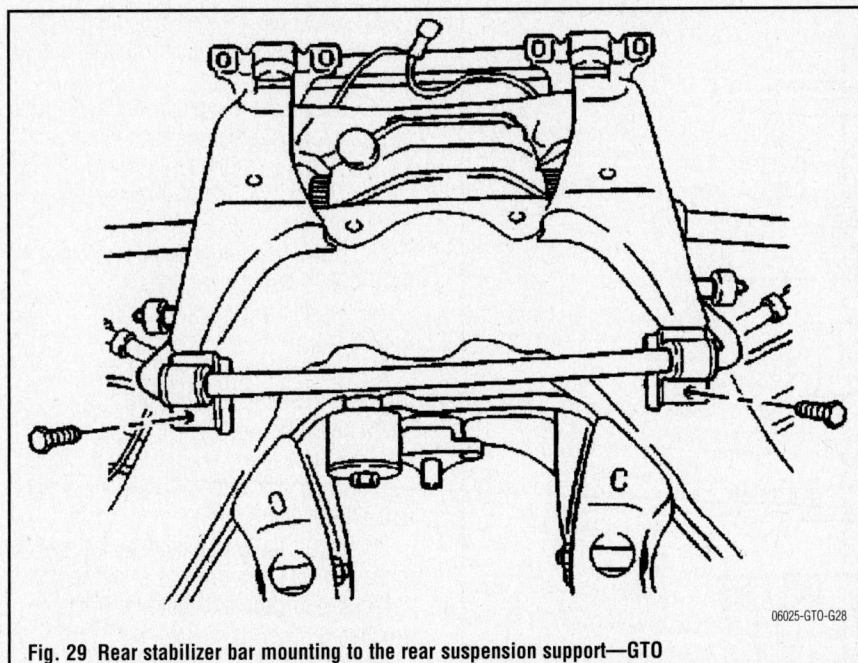

Fig. 29 Rear stabilizer bar mounting to the rear suspension support—GTO

10. Remove the stabilizer shaft assembly from the vehicle.

11. If necessary, remove the following components from the stabilizer shaft:

    a. The 2 stabilizer shaft link nuts.

    b. The 2 stabilizer shaft links.

    c. The 2 stabilizer shaft insulator brackets.

    d. The 2 stabilizer shaft insulators.

To install:

12. Install the components to the stabilizer bar, if removed.

13. Position the stabilizer shaft on the rear suspension support.

14. Install the insulator brackets to the slots on the rear suspension support.

15. Install the bolts to the stabilizer shaft insulator brackets and tighten to 16 ft. lbs. (22 Nm).

16. Raise the rear suspension support.

17. Install the stabilizer shaft link to the lower control arm.

18. Install the stabilizer shaft link bolts and the nuts to the lower control arm, but do not tighten.

19. Raise the jack with the differential carrier assembly mount and the rear suspension support.

20. Align the mount with the match marks.

21. Install 4 new bolts in order to retain the mount to the body, but do not tighten.

22. Install Crossmember Centering Tool no. CH-46839 to the underbody. The tool locates into 19 mm diameter body datum holes positioned forward of the rear suspension support.

23. With the aid of an assistant, position the rear suspension support. The locating pins of the tool engage the alignment holes in the rear suspension support.

24. Tighten the bolts that retain the differential mount to the body to 26 ft. lbs. (35 Nm), plus an additional 60 degrees.

25. Remove the centering tool.

26. Remove the jack from the vehicle.

27. Lower the vehicle.

28. With the weight of the vehicle on the tire and wheel assemblies, bounce the rear of the vehicle several times in order to stabilize the suspension.

29. Tighten the stabilizer shaft link nuts and the bolts to 72 ft. lbs. (98 Nm).

WHEEL HUB AND BEARING

REMOVAL & INSTALLATION

See Figures 30 through 33.

1. Raise and support the vehicle.

2. Remove the lower control arm.

3. Install the special Wheel Hub remover tool as shown, with the holes in the drive shaft flange. Use the outer CV joint bolts to hold the tool in place.

4. Remove and discard the hub nut retainer and hub nut.

5. Lubricate the threads of the J-42094-3 with Extreme Press Lubricant 1/4 Ounce Tube no. J-23444-A.

6. Install the J-42094-3 to the J-42094-4.

7. Lubricate the ball end of the J-42094-5.

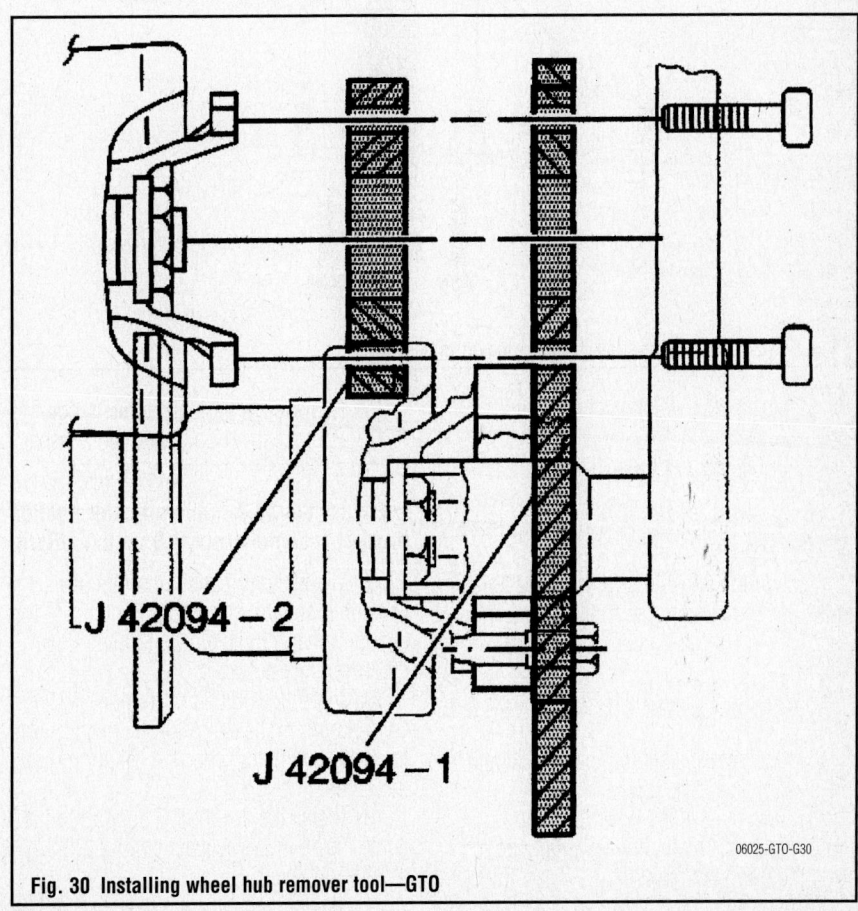

Fig. 30 Installing wheel hub remover tool—GTO

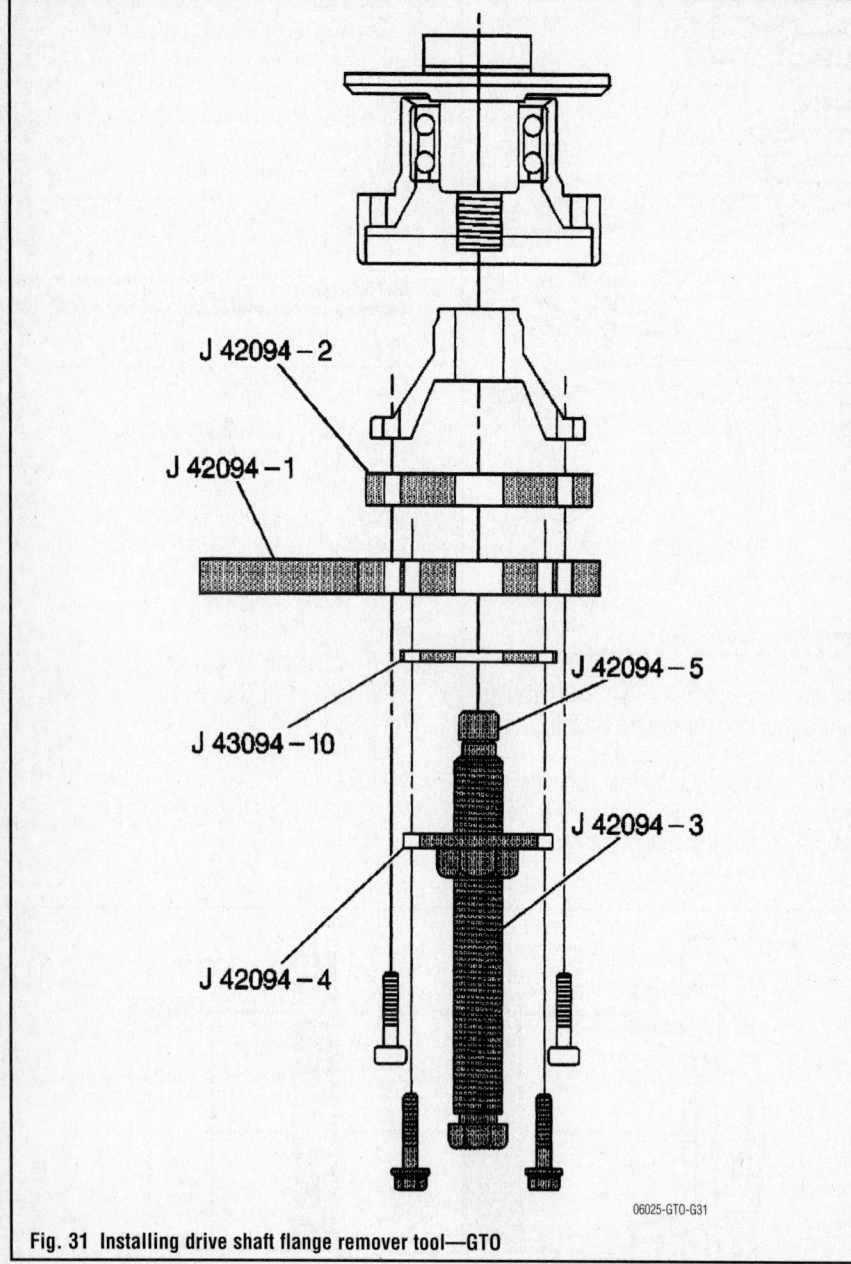

J 42094 – 2

J 42094 – 1

J 42094 – 5

J 43094 – 10

J 42094 – 3

J 42094 – 4

06025-GTO-G31

Fig. 31 Installing drive shaft flange remover tool—GTO

8. Install the J-42094-5 to the end of the J-42094-3.

9. Install the J-42094-10 to the J-42094-4.

10. Install the J-42094-4 and the 3 bolts to the J-42094-1.

11. Adjust the position of the J-42094-3 in the J-42094-4 in order to allow the J-42094-4 to be in full contact with the J-42094-1.

12. Ensure the J-42094-1 is secure in a vise.

13. Use an assistant to hold and support the control arm assembly.

14. Turn the J-42094-3 in order to remove the rear wheel drive shaft flange from the hub assembly.

15. Remove the tools from the flange.

16. Remove the 4 bolts and the 2 washers from the brake backing plate shield.

➡ **Ensure the park brake adjuster anchor bracket assembly remains on the shield.**

17. Clean the threads in control arm. From the inboard side, clean the threads for the control arm to shield bolt holes. Repair the threads if necessary.

18. Install 2 J-42094-7 supports to the control arm, in the 2 shallowest control arm to shield bolt holes, near the caliper mounting holes.

19. Install the J-42094-7 support to the control arm, in the deepest control arm to shield bolt hole.

20. Install the J-42094-7 support to the control arm, in the remaining control arm to shield bolt hole.

21. Ensure the 4 supports are in the correct positions in order to attach to the flat surface of the J-42094-1.

22. Attach the J-42094-1 to the 4 supports.

23. Install the 4 nuts in order to retain the J-42094-1 to the supports.

24. Install the J-42094-3 to the J-42094-4.

25. Lubricate the ball end of the J-42094-5 with press lubricant.

26. Install the J-42094-5 to the end of the J-42094-3.

27. Install the J-42094-4 and the 3 bolts to the J-42094-1.

28. Adjust the position of the J-42094-3 in the J-42094-4 in order to allow the J-42094-4 to be in full contact with the J-42094-1.

29. Ensure the J-42094-1 is secure in a vise.

30. Use an assistant to hold and support the control arm assembly.

31. Turn the J-42094-3 in order to press out the rear wheel hub.

32. Remove the hub and the bearing outside inner race from the control arm.

33. Turn the J-42094-3 away from the bearing.

34. Remove the shield and the park brake anchor bracket as an assembly from the control arm.

35. If you are NOT replacing the hub, remove the bearing outside inner race from the hub. Use the J-22912-01, or equivalent, and a press in order to remove the race from the hub.

36. Use snap ring pliers in order to remove the retainer from the wheel bearing in the control arm.

37. Turn the J-42094-3 in order to press out the bearing from the control arm.

38. Discard the wheel bearing.

39. Clean the bearing bore in the control arm.

To install:

40. Apply lithium lubricant, to the bearing bore in the control arm and the outside of the outer races of a new wheel bearing.

41. Remove the bolts retaining the J-42094-4 to the J-42094-1.

42. Remove the J-42094-4.

43. Remove the J-42094-3.

44. Install the J-42094-10 to the flanged end of the J-42094-4.

➡ **Do not install the J-42094-4 to the bolts on the J-42094-1.**

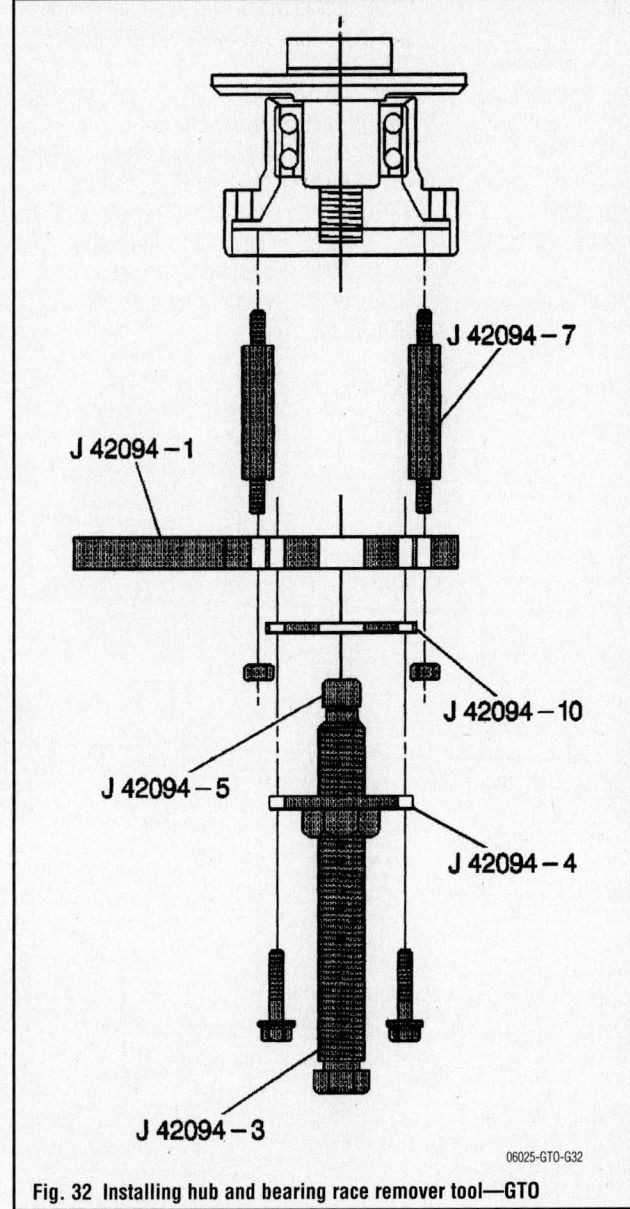

Fig. 32 Installing hub and bearing race remover tool—GTO

06025-GTO-G32

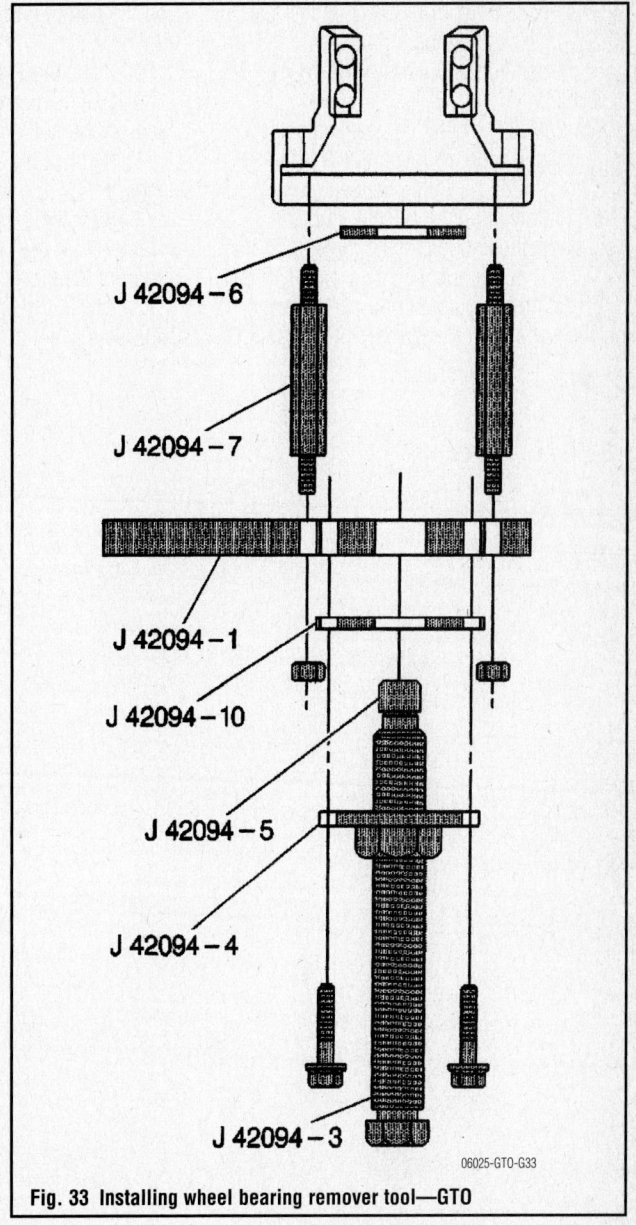

Fig. 33 Installing wheel bearing remover tool—GTO

06025-GTO-G33

45. Install the J-42094-10 and the J-42094-4 to the J-42094-1.

46. Install the J-42094-3 to the J-42094-1.

47. Install a new wheel bearing to the J-42094-8.

48. Position the wheel bearing on the wheel bearing bore in the control arm.

49. Engage a minimum of 8 threads of the J-42094-3 with the J-42094-8.

50. Use a breaker bar in order to hold the J-42094-3.

51. Rotate the J-42094-4 in order to press the wheel bearing into the control arm. Ensure the wheel bearing is seated properly in the control arm.

52. Remove the J-42094-8 from the bearing.

53. Use snap ring pliers in order to install the bearing retainer to the control arm.

54. Remove the tools from the control arm.

55. Install the rear disc brake backing plate shield and the parking brake anchor bracket assembly to the control arm.

56. Install the 2 Torx® bolts and washers to the shield and tighten to 55 ft. lbs. (75 Nm).

57. Install the 2 bolts to the anchor bracket and tighten to 65 ft. lbs. (88 Nm).

58. Use a hydraulic press in order to

install the hub to the wheel bearing. Use a bearing driver collar and press plates in order to support the outside end of the hub. Ensure the weight of the hub is on the outside end of the hub and not on the wheel studs.

59. Position the control arm and the bearing on the hub.

60. Use an assistant to hold and support the control arm assembly.

61. Place the J-42094-9 on the bearing inside inner race.

62. Use the press in order to install the hub to the bearing.

63. Remove the J-42094-9 from the bearing.

64. Position the J-42094-2 on the rear wheel drive shaft flange.

65. Position the J-42094-1-B on the J-42094-2.

66. Install the outer constant velocity joint bolts in order to retain the J-42094-2 and the J-42094-1 to the flange.

67. Apply lithium lubricant, to the splines on the flange and the threads on the inside end of the hub.

68. With the outside end of the hub on the collar and the press plates, position the flange on the inside end of the hub.

69. Place the J-42094-9 on the flange.

70. Use the press in order to install the flange to the hub and bearing assembly.

71. Remove the J-42094-9 from the flange.

72. With the J-42094-2 and the J-42094-1 on the flange, remove the control arm from the press.

73. Use a vise in order to hold the J-42094-1.

74. Install a new hub nut to the inside end of the hub and tighten to 221 ft. lbs. (300 Nm).

75. Remove the J-42094-1 and the control arm assembly from the vise.

76. Remove the bolts from the J-42094-1.

77. Remove the J-42094-2 and the J-42094-1 from the control arm assembly.

78. Install the new hub nut retainer.

79. Stake the retainer to the nut.

80. Install the control arm to the vehicle.

SATURN

Ion

SPECIFICATIONS AND MAINTENANCE CHARTS

ENGINE AND VEHICLE IDENTIFICATION

	Engine							Model Year	
Code ①	Liters (cc)	Cu. In.	Cyl.	Fuel Sys.	Engine Type	Eng. Mfg.		Code ②	Year
P	2.0 (1998)	112	4	SFI	DOHC	Saturn		5	2005
F	2.2 (2199)	112	4	SFI	DOHC	Saturn		6	2006
B	2.4 (2399)	146	4	SFI	DOHC	Saturn		7	2007

MFI: Multi-point Fuel Injection

SFI: Sequential Fuel Injection

DOHC: Double Overhead Camshafts

SOHC: Single Overhead Camshaft

① 8th digit of VIN

② 10th digit of VIN

22116_IION_C0001

GENERAL ENGINE SPECIFICATIONS

Year	Model	Engine Displacement Liters (cc)	Engine ID/VIN	Fuel System Type	Net Horsepower @ rpm	Net Torque @ rpm (ft. lbs.)	Bore x Stroke (in.)	Com- pression Ratio	Oil Pressure @ rpm
2005	ION	2.2 (2199)	P	SFI	105@5600	200@4400	3.38x3.38	9.5:1	50-80@1000
		2.0 (1988)	F	SFI	137@5800	147@4400	3.38x3.50	9.5:1	50-80@1000
2006	ION	2.2 (2199)	P	SFI	105@5600	200@4400	3.38x3.38	9.5:1	50-80@1000
		2.0 (1988)	F	SFI	175@6200	164@4800	3.46x3.46	9.5:1	50-80@1000
		2.4 (2399)	B	SFI	137@5800	147@4400	3.38x3.50	10.1:1	50-80@1000
2007	ION	2.2 (2199)	P	SFI	105@5600	200@4400	3.38x3.38	9.5:1	50-80@1000
		2.0 (1988)	F	SFI	137@5800	147@4400	3.38x3.50	9.5:1	50-80@1000
		2.4 (2399)	B	SFI	137@5800	147@4400	3.38x3.50	10.1:1	50-80@1000

MFI: Multi-port Fuel Injection

SFI: Sequential Fuel Injection

22116_IION_C0002

ENGINE TUNE-UP SPECIFICATIONS

Year	Engine Displacement Liters	Engine ID/VIN	Spark Plug Gap (in.)	Ignition Timing (deg.) MT	Ignition Timing (deg.) AT	Fuel Pump (psi) ①	Idle Speed (rpm) MT ②	Idle Speed (rpm) AT ②	Valve Clearance In.	Valve Clearance Ex.
2005	2.0	P	0.040	③	③	50-60	④	④	HYD	HYD
	2.2	F	0.045	③	③	55-65	④	④	HYD	HYD
2006	2.0	P	0.040	③	③	50-60	④	④	HYD	HYD
	2.2	F	0.045	③	③	55-65	④	④	HYD	HYD
	2.4	B	0.043	③	③	55-60	④	④	HYD	HYD
2007	2.0	P	0.040	③	③	50-60	④	④	HYD	HYD
	2.2	F	0.045	③	③	55-65	④	④	HYD	HYD
	2.4	B	0.043	③	③	55-60	④	④	HYD	HYD

NOTE: The Vehicle Emission Control Information label often reflects specification changes made during production.

The label figures must be used if they differ from those in this chart.

HYD: Hydraulic

① Pressure measured at idle

② Idle speed measured with manual transmission in Neutral; automatic transmission in D (drive)

③ Engines equipped with Distributorless Ignition System (DIS). Ignition timing is not adjustable

④ Refer to the Vehicle Emission Control Information label

22116_IION_C0004

CAPACITIES

Year	Model	Engine Displacement Liters	Engine ID/VIN	Engine Oil with Filter (qts.)	Transaxle (pts.) Manual	Transaxle (pts.) Auto. ①	Fuel Tank (gal.)
2005	ION	2.0	P	4.0	②	③	13.5
		2.2	F	4.0	②	③	13.5
2006	ION	2.0	P	4.0	②	③	13.5
		2.2	F	4.0	②	③	13.5
		2.4	B	5.0	②	③	13.5
2007	ION	2.0	P	4.0	②	③	13.5
		2.2	F	4.0	②	③	13.5
		2.4	B	5.0	②	③	13.5

NOTE: All capacities are approximate. Add fluid gradually and ensure a proper fluid level is obtained.

① Specification is for overhaul. 8.4 pts. with fluid and filter change

② Manual Getrag 5-speed: 1.8 quarts

Manual MU3: 2.0 quarts

③ Automatic 4T40-E/4T45-E:

Complete overhaul: 9.5 quarts

Drain and refill: 6.9 quarts

Dry: 12.9 quarts

22116_IION_C0003

FLUID SPECIFICATIONS

Year	Model	Engine Displacement Liters (VIN)	Engine Oil	Auto. Trans.	Drive Axle	Power Steering Fluid	Brake Master Cylinder
2005	ION	2.0 (P)	5W-30	②	—	—	DOT 3
		2.2 (F)	5W-30	②	—	—	DOT 3
2006	ION	2.0 (P)	5W-30	②	—	—	DOT 3
		2.2 (F)	5W-30	②	—	—	DOT 3
		2.4 (B)	①	②	—	—	DOT 3
2007	ION	2.0 (P)	5W-30	②	—	—	DOT 3
		2.2 (F)	5W-30	②	—	—	DOT 3
		2.4 (B)	①	②	—	—	DOT 3

DOT: Department Of Transpotation

① Mobil 1 5W-30 oil meeting GM Standard GM4718M

② DEXRON®-VI Automatic Transmission Fluid

③ DEXRON®-VI Automatic Transmission Fluid

22116_IION_C0010

VALVE SPECIFICATIONS

Year	Engine Displ. Liters	Engine ID/VIN	Seat Angle (deg.)	Face Angle (deg.)	Spring Test Pressure (lbs. @ in.)	Spring Free-Length (in.)	Stem-to-Guide Clearance (in.) Intake	Stem-to-Guide Clearance (in.) Exhaust	Stem Diameter (in.) Intake	Stem Diameter (in.) Exhaust
2005	2.0	P	44.5-45.4	45-45.5	①	1.6100	0.0012	0.0020	0.2344	0.2337
					②		0.0022	0.0026	0.2355	0.2343
	2.2	F	44.5-45.4	45-45.5	①	1.6100	0.0012	0.0020	0.2344	0.2337
					②		0.0022	0.0026	0.2355	0.2343
2006	2.0	P	44.5-45.4	45-45.5	①	1.6100	0.0012	0.0020	0.2344	0.2337
					②		0.0022	0.0026	0.2355	0.2343
	2.2	F	44.5-45.4	45-45.5	①	1.6100	0.0012	0.0020	0.2344	0.2337
					②		0.0022	0.0026	0.2355	0.2343
	2.4	B	44.5-45.4	45-45.5	①	1.6100	0.0012	0.0020	0.2344	0.2337
					②		0.0022	0.0026	0.2355	0.2343
2007	2.0	P	44.5-45.4	45-45.5	①	1.6100	0.0012	0.0020	0.2344	0.2337
					②		0.0022	0.0026	0.2355	0.2343
	2.2	F	44.5-45.4	45-45.5	①	1.6100	0.0012	0.0020	0.2344	0.2337
					②		0.0022	0.0026	0.2355	0.2343
	2.4	B	44.5-45.4	45-45.5	①	1.6100	0.0012	0.0020	0.2344	0.2337
					②		0.0022	0.0026	0.2355	0.2343

① Valve spring load closed: 245-271 N

② Valve spring load open: 525-575 N

22116_IION_C0005

CRANKSHAFT AND CONNECTING ROD SPECIFICATIONS

All measurements are given in inches.

Year	Engine Displacement Liters	Engine ID/VIN	Crankshaft				Connecting Rod		
			Main Brg. Journal Dia.	Main Brg. Oil Clearance	Shaft End-play	Thrust on No.	Journal Diameter	Oil Clearance	Side Clearance
2005	2.0	P	2.2045-2.2050	0.0012 0.0026	0.0012-0.0150	3	1.9291-1.9297	0.0001-0.0027	0.0028-0.0146
	2.2	F	2.2045-2.2050	0.0012 0.0026	0.0012-0.0150	3	1.9291-1.9297	0.0001-0.0027	0.0028-0.0146
2006	2.0	P	2.2045-2.2050	0.0012 0.0026	0.0012-0.0150	3	1.9291-1.9297	0.0001-0.0027	0.0028-0.0146
	2.2	F	2.2045-2.2050	0.0012 0.0026	0.0012-0.0150	3	1.9291-1.9297	0.0001-0.0027	0.0028-0.0146
	2.4	B	2.2045-2.2050	0.0012 0.0026	0.0012-0.0150	3	1.9291-1.9297	0.0001-0.0027	0.0028-0.0146
2007	2.0	P	2.2045-2.2050	0.0012 0.0026	0.0012-0.0150	3	1.9291-1.9297	0.0001-0.0027	0.0028-0.0146
	2.2	F	2.2045-2.2050	0.0012 0.0026	0.0012-0.0150	3	1.9291-1.9297	0.0001-0.0027	0.0028-0.0146
	2.4	B	2.2045-2.2050	0.0012 0.0026	0.0012-0.0150	3	1.9291-1.9297	0.0001-0.0027	0.0028-0.0146

22116_IION_C0006

PISTON AND RING SPECIFICATIONS

All measurements are given in inches.

Year	Engine Displacement Liters	Engine ID/VIN	Piston Clearance	Ring Gap			Ring Side Clearance	
				Top Compression	Bottom Compression	Oil Control	Top Compression	Bottom Compression
2005	2.0	P	0.0004-0.0016	0.008-0.016	0.0014 0.0022	0.0010 0.0030	0.0015-0.0031	0.0012-0.0027
	2.2	F	0.0004-0.0016	0.008-0.016	0.0014 0.0022	0.0010 0.0030	0.0015-0.0031	0.0012-0.0027
2006	2.0	P	0.0004-0.0016	0.008-0.016	0.0014 0.0022	0.0010 0.0030	0.0015-0.0031	0.0012-0.0027
	2.2	F	0.0004-0.0016	0.008-0.016	0.0014 0.0022	0.0010 0.0030	0.0015-0.0031	0.0012-0.0027
	2.4	B	0.0004-0.0016	0.008-0.016	0.0014 0.0022	0.0010 0.0030	0.0015-0.0031	0.0012-0.0027
2007	2.0	P	0.0004-0.0016	0.008-0.016	0.0014 0.0022	0.0010 0.0030	0.0015-0.0031	0.0012-0.0027
	2.2	F	0.0004-0.0016	0.008-0.016	0.0014 0.0022	0.0010 0.0030	0.0015-0.0031	0.0012-0.0027
	2.4	B	0.0004-0.0016	0.008-0.016	0.0014 0.0022	0.0010 0.0030	0.0015-0.0031	0.0012-0.0027

① Piston No. 2 and 3: 0.0002-0.0017
Piston No. 1, 4: 0.0003-0.0021

22116_IION_C0007

TORQUE SPECIFICATIONS
All readings in ft. lbs.

Year	Engine Displacement Liters	Engine ID/VIN	Cylinder Head Bolts	Main Bearing Bolts	Rod Bearing Bolts	Crankshaft Damper Bolts	Flywheel Bolts	Manifold Intake	Manifold Exhaust	Spark Plugs	Oil Pan Drain Plug
2005	2.0	P	①	②	③	④	⑤	⑥	⑦	15	18
	2.2	F	①	⑧	③	④	⑤	⑥	⑦	15	18
2006	2.0	P	①	②	③	④	⑤	⑥	⑦	15	18
	2.2	F	①	⑧	③	④	⑤	⑥	⑦	15	18
	2.4	B	①	⑧	③	④	⑤	⑥	⑦	15	18
2007	2.0	P	①	②	③	④	⑤	⑥	⑦	15	18
	2.2	F	①	⑧	③	④	⑤	⑥	⑦	15	18
	2.4	B	①	⑧	③	④	⑤	⑥	⑦	15	18

① Step 1: 22 ft. lbs.
  Step 2: 155 degrees

② 15 ft. lbs. Plus 70 degrees

③ 18 ft. lbs. Plus 100 degrees

④ 74 ft. lbs. Plus 125 degrees

⑤ Flexplate specification: 39 ft. lbs. Plus 25 degrees

⑥ Intake manifold to head nut and bolt: 89 inch lbs.
  Intake manifold to head stud: 53 inch lbs.

⑦ Exhaust manifold to head nut: 124 inch lbs.
  Exhaust manifold to head stud: 89 inch lbs.

⑧ 15 ft. lbs. Plus 70 degrees Plus 20 degrees

22116_IION_C0008

WHEEL ALIGNMENT

Year	Model		Caster Range (+/-Deg.)	Caster Preferred Setting (Deg.)	Camber Range (+/-Deg.)	Camber Preferred Setting (Deg.)	Toe-in (in.)
2005	ION	F	0.75	3.25	0.75	1.00	0.10 +/- 0.20
		R	—	—	0.75	-1.40	0.06 +/- 0.35
2006	ION	F	0.75	3.25	0.75	1.00	0.10 +/- 0.20
		R	—	—	0.75	-1.40	0.06 +/- 0.35
2007	ION	F	0.75	3.25	0.75	1.00	0.10 +/- 0.20
		R	—	—	0.75	-1.40	0.06 +/- 0.35

22116_IION_C0011

TIRE, WHEEL AND BALL JOINT SPECIFICATIONS

Year	Model	OEM Tires Standard	OEM Tires Optional	Tire Pressures (psi) Front	Tire Pressures (psi) Rear	Wheel Size	Ball Joint Inspection	Lug Nut (ft. lbs.)
2005	ION	①	①	①	①	①	①	138
2006	ION	①	①	①	①	①	①	138
2007	ION	①	①	①	①	①	①	138

OEM: Original Equipment Manufacturer

① For tire size and information, check the label located inside the glove compartment door.

22116_IION_C0012

BRAKE SPECIFICATIONS

All measurements in inches unless noted

Year	Model		Brake Disc Original Thickness	Brake Disc Minimum Thickness	Brake Disc Maximum Runout	Brake Drum Diameter Original Inside Diameter	Brake Drum Diameter Max. Wear Limit	Brake Drum Diameter Maximum Machine Diameter	Minimum Lining Thickness	Brake Caliper Bracket Bolt (ft. lbs.)	Brake Caliper Mounting Bolt (ft. lbs.)
2005	ION	F	①	②	0.002	—	—	—	0.039	85	25
		R	—	—	—	9.06	9.09	9.08	0.020	85	25
2006	ION	F	①	②	0.002	—	—	—	0.039	85	25
		R	—	—	—	9.06	9.09	9.08	0.020	85	25
2007	ION	F	①	②	0.002	—	—	—	0.039	85	25
		R	—	—	—	9.06	9.09	9.08	0.020	85	25

F: Front

R: Rear

① Front brakes J41/JM4: 0.933 inch

  Front brakes JL9: 0.551 inch

② Front brakes

  Front brakes JL9: 0.465 inch

SCHEDULED MAINTENANCE INTERVALS
SATURN—ION

TO BE SERVICED	TYPE OF SERVICE	VEHICLE MILEAGE INTERVAL (x1000)												
		3	6	9	12	15	18	21	24	27	30	33	36	39
Engine oil & filter ①	R		✓		✓		✓		✓		✓		✓	
Lubricate chassis, suspension and steering linkage	S/I		✓		✓		✓		✓		✓		✓	
Lubricate transaxle shift linkage and parking brake cable guides	S/I		✓		✓		✓		✓		✓		✓	
Lubricate underbody contact points & linkage	S/I		✓		✓		✓		✓		✓		✓	
Driveshaft boots, suspension bushings & ball joint seals	S/I		✓				✓		✓		✓		✓	
Exhaust system & throttle linkage	S/I		✓		✓		✓		✓		✓		✓	
Rotate tires	S/I		✓		✓		✓				✓			
Brake hoses & brake lining	S/I		✓				✓				✓			
Accessory drive belt(s)	S/I						✓						✓	
Engine coolant level, hoses & clamps	S/I						✓						✓	
Air filter element	R										✓			
Engine coolant	R												✓	
Manual transaxle oil	R		✓											
Spark plugs ②	R										✓			
Automatic transaxle fluid & filter	S/I										✓			
Ignition cables & fuel systems	S/I										✓			
Vacuum line/hose	S/I										✓			
Fuel filter ③	R													

S/I: Service or Inspect

R: Replace

① Newer models are equipped with an engine life oil system. The engine oil life system calculates when to change your engine oil and filter based on veh

Anytime your oil is changed, reset the system so it can calculate when the next oil change is required. If a situation occurs where you change

your oil prior to the CHG OIL message being turned on, reset the system as follows:

Press and release the trip/reset button until the OIL LIFE message is displayed.

Then press and hold the trip/reset button until a chime sounds five times, and RESET is displayed in the message center. When the system is reset,

the odometer will again be displayed in the message center. Turn the key to the lock position.

If the CHG OIL message comes back on when you start your vehicle, the engine oil life system has not reset. Repeat the procedure.

Your vehicle has a unique oil filter element. When installing the filler cap do not exceed 18 ft. lbs. Inspect the condition of the O-ring and replace if dan

② Platinum tip spark plugs: replace every 100,000 miles

③ Replace every 60,000 miles

FREQUENT OPERATION MAINTENANCE (SEVERE SERVICE)

If a vehicle is operated under any of the following conditions it is considered severe service:

- Extremely dusty areas

- 50% or more of the vehicle operation is in 32°C (90°F) or higher temps, or constant operation in temps below 0°C (32°F)

- Prolonged idling (vehicle operation in stop and go traffic)

- Frequent short running periods (engine does not warm to normal operating temperatures)

- Police, taxi, delivery usage or trailer towing usage

- Engine oil & oil filter: change every 3000 miles

PRECAUTIONS

Before servicing any vehicle, please be sure to read all of the following precautions, which deal with personal safety, prevention of component damage, and important points to take into consideration when servicing a motor vehicle:

• Never open, service or drain the radiator or cooling system when the engine is hot; serious burns can occur from the steam and hot coolant.

• Observe all applicable safety precautions when working around fuel. Whenever servicing the fuel system, always work in a well-ventilated area. Do not allow fuel spray or vapors to come in contact with a spark, open flame, or excessive heat (a hot drop light, for example). Keep a dry chemical fire extinguisher near the work area. Always keep fuel in a container specifically designed for fuel storage; also, always properly seal fuel containers to avoid the possibility of fire or explosion. Refer to the additional fuel system precautions later in this section.

• Fuel injection systems often remain pressurized, even after the engine has been turned **OFF**. The fuel system pressure must be relieved before disconnecting any fuel lines. Failure to do so may result in fire and/or personal injury.

• Brake fluid often contains polyglycol ethers and polyglycols. Avoid contact with the eyes and wash your hands thoroughly after handling brake fluid. If you do get brake fluid in your eyes, flush your eyes with clean, running water for 15 minutes. If eye irritation persists, or if you have taken brake fluid internally, IMMEDIATELY seek medical assistance.

• The EPA warns that prolonged contact with used engine oil may cause a number of skin disorders, including cancer. You should make every effort to minimize your exposure to used engine oil. Protective gloves should be worn when changing oil. Wash your hands and any other exposed skin areas as soon as possible after exposure to used engine oil. Soap and water, or waterless hand cleaner should be used.

• All new vehicles are now equipped with an air bag system, often referred to as a Supplemental Restraint System (SRS) or Supplemental Inflatable Restraint (SIR) system. The system must be disabled before performing service on or around system components, steering column, instrument panel components, wiring and sensors. Failure to follow safety and disabling procedures could result in accidental air bag deployment, possible personal injury and unnecessary system repairs.

• Always wear safety goggles when working with, or around, the air bag system. When carrying a non-deployed air bag, be sure the bag and trim cover are pointed away from your body. When placing a non-deployed air bag on a work surface, always face the bag and trim cover upward, away from the surface. This will reduce the motion of the module if it is accidentally deployed. Refer to the additional air bag system precautions later in this section.

• Clean, high quality brake fluid from a sealed container is essential to the safe and proper operation of the brake system. You should always buy the correct type of brake fluid for your vehicle. If the brake fluid becomes contaminated, completely flush the system with new fluid. Never reuse any brake fluid. Any brake fluid that is removed from the system should be discarded. Also, do not allow any brake fluid to come in contact with a painted surface; it will damage the paint.

• Never operate the engine without the proper amount and type of engine oil; doing so WILL result in severe engine damage.

• Timing belt maintenance is extremely important. Many models utilize an interference-type, non-freewheeling engine. If the timing belt breaks, the valves in the cylinder head may strike the pistons, causing potentially serious (also time-consuming and expensive) engine damage. Refer to the maintenance interval charts for the recommended replacement interval for the timing belt, and to the timing belt section for belt replacement and inspection.

• Disconnecting the negative battery cable on some vehicles may interfere with the functions of the on-board computer system(s) and may require the computer to undergo a relearning process once the negative battery cable is reconnected.

• When servicing drum brakes, only disassemble and assemble one side at a time, leaving the remaining side intact for reference.

• Only an MVAC-trained, EPA-certified automotive technician should service the air conditioning system or its components.

BRAKES

GENERAL INFORMATION

PRECAUTIONS

• Certain components within the ABS system are not intended to be serviced or repaired individually.

• Do not use rubber hoses or other parts not specifically specified for and ABS system. When using repair kits, replace all parts included in the kit. Partial or incorrect repair may lead to functional problems and require the replacement of components.

• Lubricate rubber parts with clean, fresh brake fluid to ease assembly. Do not use shop air to clean parts; damage to rubber components may result.

• Use only DOT 3 brake fluid from an unopened container.

• If any hydraulic component or line is removed or replaced, it may be necessary to bleed the entire system.

• A clean repair area is essential. Always clean the reservoir and cap thoroughly before removing the cap. The slightest amount of dirt in the fluid may plug an orifice and impair the system function. Perform repairs after components have been thoroughly cleaned; use only denatured alcohol to clean components. Do not allow ABS components to come into contact with any substance containing mineral oil; this includes used shop rags.

• The Anti-Lock control unit is a microprocessor similar to other computer units in the vehicle. Ensure that the ignition switch is **OFF** before removing or installing controller

ANTI-LOCK BRAKE SYSTEM (ABS)

harnesses. Avoid static electricity discharge at or near the controller.

• If any arc welding is to be done on the vehicle, the control unit should be unplugged before welding operations begin.

WHEEL SPEED SENSORS

REMOVAL & INSTALLATION

See Figure 1.

1. As an added safety precaution, you may wish to disable the air bag(s), if equipped.

2. Disconnect the negative battery cable.

3. Raise the front of the vehicle and support it safely using jackstands.

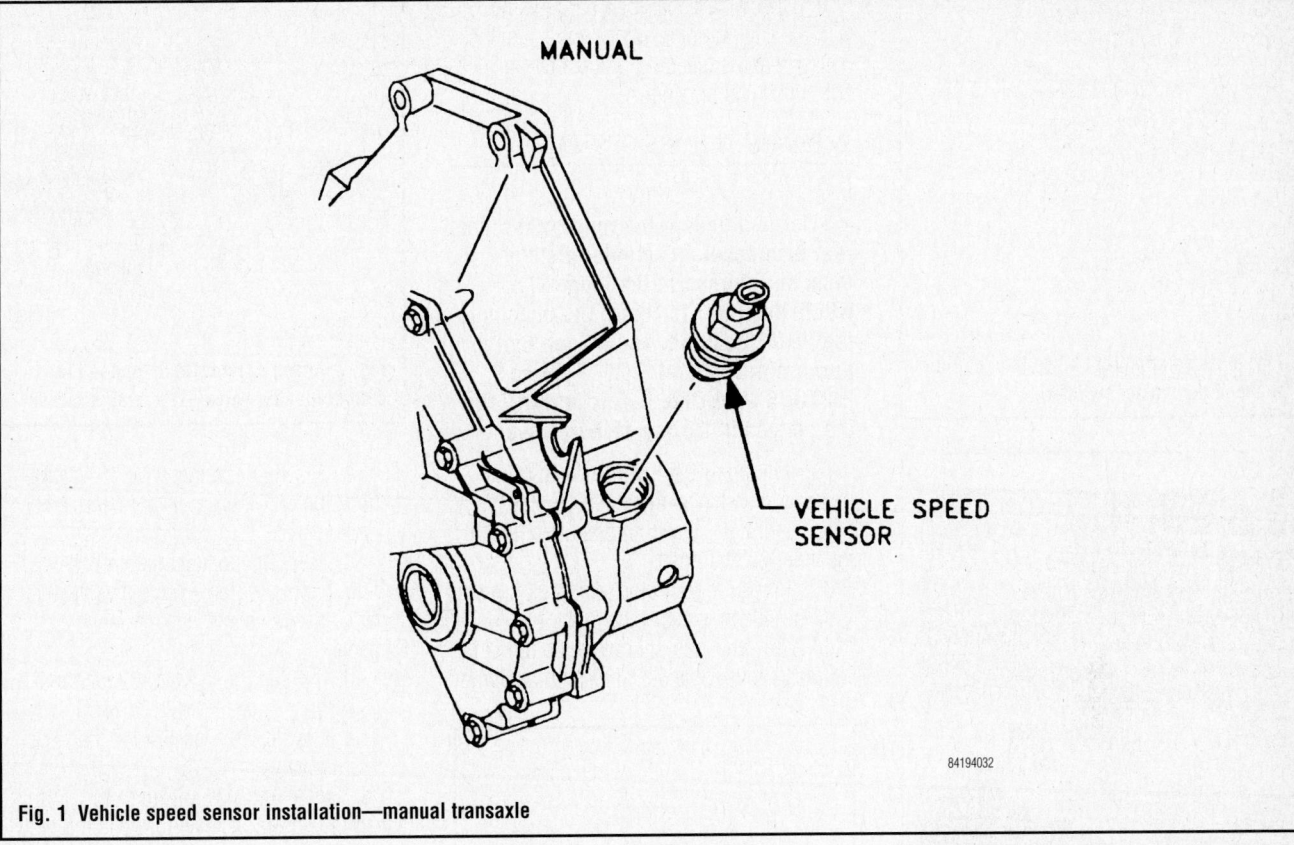

MANUAL

VEHICLE SPEED SENSOR

84194032

Fig. 1 Vehicle speed sensor installation—manual transaxle

4. Unplug the electrical connector from the sensor.

5. Unscrew and remove the sensor from the transaxle housing.

To install:

6. Install the VSS to the transaxle.

7. Attach the sensor electrical connector.

8. Lower the vehicle and connect the negative battery cable.

9. If necessary, enable the air bag(s).

BRAKES   BLEEDING THE BRAKE SYSTEM

BLEEDING PROCEDURE

BLEEDING PROCEDURE

See Figures 2 through 4.

The brake system bleeding procedure differs for ABS and non-ABS vehicles. The following procedure pertains only to non-ABS vehicles. For details on bleeding ABS equipped vehicles, refer to the ABS procedures later in this section.

✳✳ WARNING

Make sure the master cylinder contains clean DOT 3 brake fluid at all times during the procedure.

1. The master cylinder must be bled first if it is suspected of containing air. Bleed the master cylinder as follows:

   a. Position a container under the master cylinder to catch the brake fluid.

   b. Loosen the left front brake line (front upper port) at the master cylinder and allow the fluid to flow from the front port.

   c. Connect the line and tighten to 24 ft. lbs. (32 Nm).

   d. Have an assistant depress the brake pedal slowly one time and hold it down, while you loosen the front line to expel air from the master cylinder. Tighten the line, then release the brake pedal. Repeat until all air is removed from the master cylinder.

   e. Tighten the brake line to 24 ft. lbs. (32 Nm) when finished.

   f. Repeat these steps for the right front brake line (rear upper port) at the master cylinder.

✳✳ WARNING

Do not allow brake fluid to spill on or come in contact with the vehicle's finish, as it will remove the paint. In case of a spill, immediately flush the area with water.

2. If a single line or fitting was the only hydraulic line disconnected, then only the caliper(s) or wheel cylinder(s) affected by that line must be bled. If the master cylinder required bleeding, then all calipers and wheel cylinders must be bled in the proper sequence:

   a. Right rear

   b. Left front

   c. Left rear

   d. Right front

3. Bleed the individual calipers or wheel cylinders as follows:

   a. Place a suitable wrench over the bleeder screw and attach a clear plastic hose over the screw end.

   b. Submerge the other end in a transparent container of brake fluid.

   c. Loosen the bleed screw, then have an assistant apply the brake pedal slowly and hold it down. Close the bleed screw, then release the brake pedal. Repeat the sequence until all air is expelled from the caliper or cylinder.

   d. When finished, tighten the bleed screw to 97 inch lbs. (11 Nm) for the front, or 66 inch lbs. (7.5 Nm) for the rear.

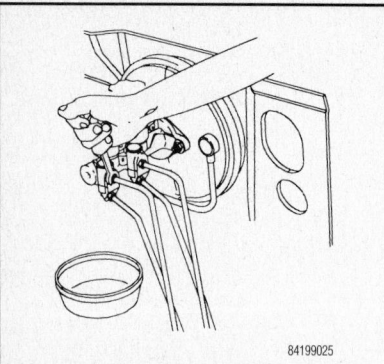

Fig. 2 Loosen the front brake line in order to bleed the master cylinder

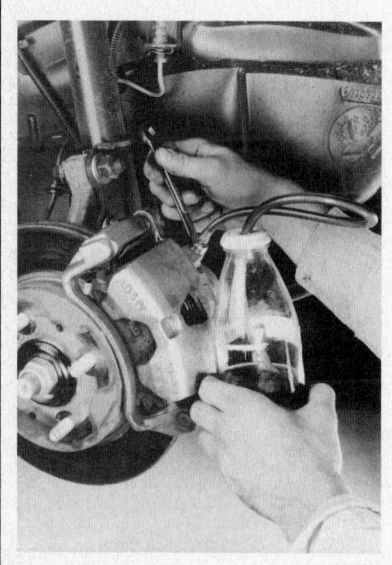

Fig. 3 Connect a bleed hose from the bleed valve on the front caliper to a jar of brake fluid

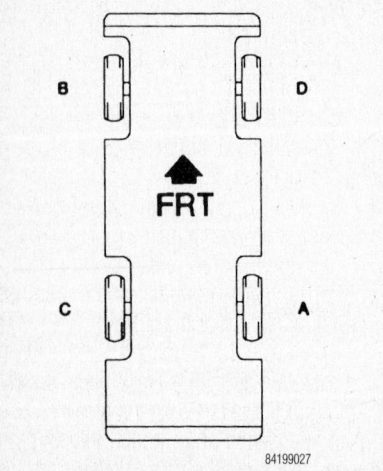

Fig. 4 Always follow the lettered sequence when bleeding the hydraulic brake system

4. Check the pedal for a hard feeling with the engine not running. If the pedal is soft, repeat the bleeding procedure until a firm pedal is obtained.

BLEEDING THE ABS SYSTEM

See Figures 5 through 7.

➡**Prior to bleeding the rear brakes, the rear displacement cylinder pistons must be returned to the topmost or HOME position. To return the pistons to the HOME position, use a Scan tool to perform the special test, "RUN ABS PISTONS UP-HOME." This test will run the pistons to the top of their travel.**

1. Fill the master cylinder with clean brake fluid and keep the reservoir at least ½ full during the bleeding operation. Install the fluid reservoir cap.

2. Prime the control assembly as follows:

a. Attach a clear tube to the rear bleeder valve and submerge the tube in a transparent container of clean brake fluid.

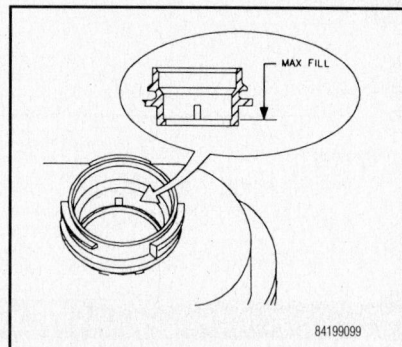

Fig. 5 On all Saturns, the brake fluid reservoir fill line is at the base of the fill neck

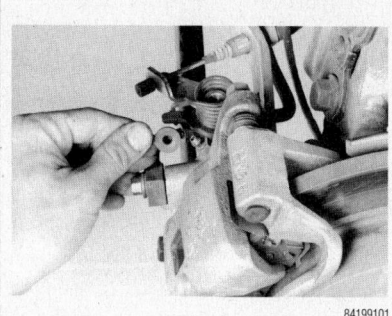

Fig. 7 Attach a transparent tube to the caliper bleeder valve—rear brakes shown

b. Slowly open the valve ½–¾ of a turn, then have an assistant depress the brake pedal.

c. Hold the brake pedal until fluid begins to flow from the valve, then close the valve and release the pedal.

d. Tighten the valve to 62 inch lbs. (7 Nm).

e. Repeat the procedure at the front bleeder valve.

3. Once fluid flows from both control assembly valves, it may not be completely purged of air. To assure that the unit is free of air, bleed the calipers to remove air from the system's lowest points, then return and bleed the control assembly one last time.

4. Be sure to bleed the calipers in the proper order:

a. Right rear
b. Left rear
c. Right front
d. Left front

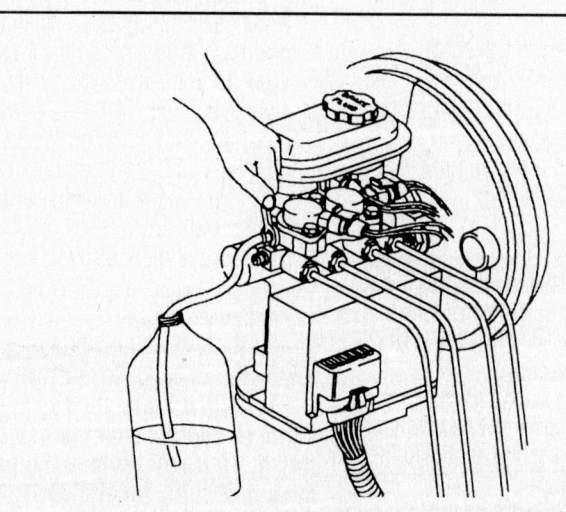

Fig. 6 Run a transparent tube from the ABS control assembly's front bleeder screw to a transparent container partially filled with clean brake fluid

➡**If, when performing the bleeding procedure on the rear calipers, brake fluid does not come out of the bleeder, the rear displacement pistons may not be at the HOME or topmost position.**

5. Bleed each caliper, in the proper order, as follows:

a. Attach a clear tube to the caliper bleeder valve and submerge the other end of the tube in a transparent container of clean brake fluid.

b. Open the valve ½–¾of a turn, then have an assistant slowly depress the brake pedal and hold.

c. Watch for air bubbles as the fluid begins to flow from the valve, then close the valve and release the pedal.

d. Wait 5 seconds and repeat until the pedal feels firm and no air is present in the brake line.

e. Tighten the valve to 97 inch lbs. (11 Nm) for the calipers and 66 inch lbs. (7.5 Nm) for the wheel cylinders.

6. Bleed the control assembly from the 2 valves in the same fashion as the calipers are bled. Tighten the bleeder valves to 62 inch lbs. (7 Nm) when finished.

7. Check the pedal for excessive travel both with the engine **OFF**and with the engine running. If pedal feel is firm, proceed to Step 11.

8. If the pedal feel is not firm, use a Scan tool to run the ABS motor up and down 2 times, making sure the pistons are run up to the HOME position.

9. Start the engine and let it run for 2 seconds after the ABS light goes out, then turn the engine **OFF**. Repeat this ignition cycle 9 more times.

10. Re-bleed the entire system.

11. With the engine running and brake applied, check the system for leaks.

12. Road test the vehicle and make several normal, non-ABS stops. Then, make 1–2 ABS stops from a higher speed (about 50 mph/80 kmh).

13. After road testing the vehicle, it is recommended that the entire system be bled and inspected one final time.

BRAKES   FRONT DISC BRAKES

✳✳ CAUTION

Dust and dirt accumulating on brake parts during normal use may contain asbestos fibers from production or aftermarket brake linings. Breathing excessive concentrations of asbestos fibers can cause serious bodily harm. Exercise care when servicing brake parts. Do not sand or grind brake lining unless equipment used is designed to contain the dust residue. Do not clean brake parts with compressed air or by dry brushing. Cleaning should be done by dampening the brake components with a fine mist of water, then wiping the brake components clean with a dampened cloth. Dispose of cloth and all residue containing asbestos fibers in an impermeable container with the appropriate label. Follow practices prescribed by the Occupational Safety and Health Administration (OSHA) and the Environmental Protection Agency (EPA) for the handling, processing, and disposing of dust or debris that may contain asbestos fibers.

BRAKE CALIPER

REMOVAL & INSTALLATION

1. Remove or disconnect the following:
   • Front wheel. Hand-tighten the lug nuts on the studs to prevent the rotor from falling off.
2. Install a C–clamp over the body of the caliper with the clamp ends against the rear of the caliper body and against the outboard pad. Tighten the clamp until the caliper piston is compressed enough to allow the caliper to be removed.
   • Brake hose from the caliper and discard the 2 copper washers. Plug the openings to prevent system contamination or excessive fluid loss.
   • Caliper bolts
   • Caliper from the bracket
   • Pin boots from the caliper support and inspect for damage

To install:

3. Install or connect the following:
   • Brake pads and clips to the caliper bracket, if removed
4. Lubricate the pin boots and guide pins with silicone grease.
   • Pin boots, if removed
   • Caliper onto the bracket and over the brake pads
   • Caliper bolts through the caliper and torque to 27 ft. lbs. (34 Nm)

➡**Make sure the brake line is properly routed with loop to the rear and that the hose is not twisted.**

   • Brake hose using 2 new copper washers. Torque the fitting bolt to 35 ft. lbs. (50 Nm).
5. Properly bleed the hydraulic brake system.
   • Wheel

DISC BRAKE PADS

REMOVAL & INSTALLATION

1. Before servicing the vehicle, refer to the Precautions Section.

2. Use a turkey baster or similar device to remove fluid from the master cylinder until it is about ½full.

3. Remove or disconnect the following:
   • Front wheel. Hand-tighten the lug nuts on the studs to prevent the rotor from falling off.

4. Install a C–clamp over the body of the caliper with the clamp ends against the rear of the caliper body and against the outboard pad. Tighten the clamp until the caliper piston is compressed enough to allow the caliper to be removed.
   • Caliper lower bolt
   • 2 brake pads and the pad clips from the caliper support. Discard the old pad clips.

5. Check the caliper pins, pin boots and the piston boot for deterioration or damage.

To install:

6. Install or connect the following:
   • Brake pads and clips to the caliper bracket

7. Lubricate the pin boots and guide pins with silicone grease.
   • Pin boots, if removed
   • Caliper over the brake pads
   • Caliper lower bolt through the caliper and torque to 27 ft. lbs. (34 Nm)

➡**Make sure the brake line is properly routed with loop to the rear and that the hose is not twisted.**

   • Wheel

8. Prior to operating the vehicle, depress the brake pedal a few times until the brake pads are seated against the rotor.

✳✳ CAUTION

Dust and dirt accumulating on brake parts during normal use may contain asbestos fibers from production or aftermarket brake linings. Breathing excessive concentrations of asbestos fibers can cause serious bodily harm. Exercise care when servicing brake parts. Do not sand or grind brake lining unless equipment used is designed to contain the dust residue. Do not clean brake parts with compressed air or by dry brushing. Cleaning should be done by dampening the brake components with a fine mist of water, then wiping the brake components clean with a dampened cloth. Dispose of cloth and all residue containing asbestos fibers in an impermeable container with the appropriate label. Follow practices prescribed by the Occupational Safety and Health Administration (OSHA) and the Environmental Protection Agency (EPA) for the handling, processing, and disposing of dust or debris that may contain asbestos fibers.

BRAKE CALIPER

REMOVAL & INSTALLATION

See Figures 8 and 9.

1. Inspect the fluid level in the brake master cylinder auxiliary reservoir.

2. If the brake fluid level is midway between the maximum-full point and the minimum allowable level, no brake fluid needs to be removed from the reservoir before proceeding.

3. If the brake fluid level is higher than midway between the maximum-full point and the minimum allowable level, remove brake fluid to the midway point before proceeding.

4. Release the park brake lever boot from the floor console by applying light pressure inward on the sides of the boot retainer, and pull the boot back.

5. Release the tension from the park brake cables. With the park brake lever in the released position, using ONLY HAND TOOLS, loosen the adjusting nut (1) completely to the end of the front cable threaded rod.

6. Raise and support the vehicle.

7. Remove the tire and wheel assembly.

8. Install and firmly hand tighten 2 wheel nuts to opposite wheel studs in order to retain the rotor to the hub.

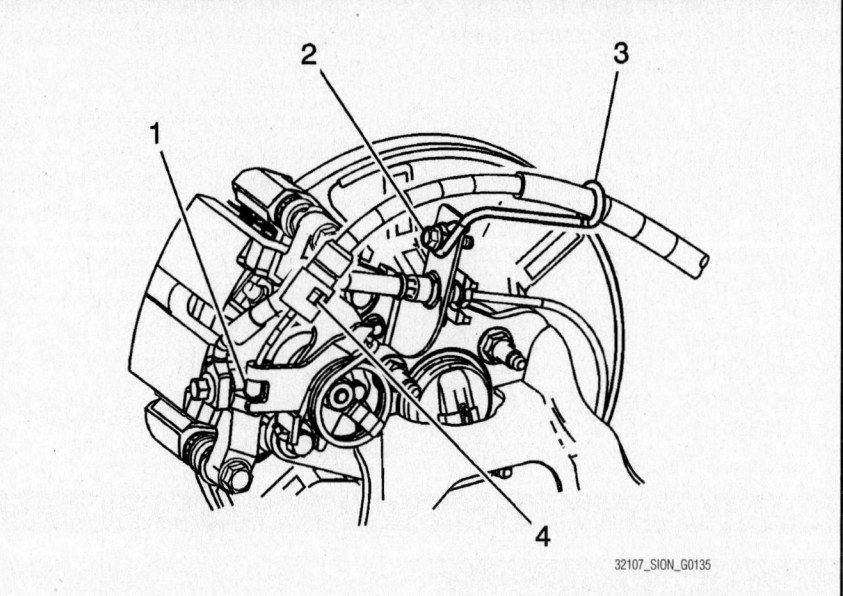

Fig. 8 Release the retaining tabs securing the park brake cable to the bracket on the caliper.

32107_SION_G0135

9. Release the park brake cable end from the lever on the caliper.

10. Release the retaining tabs securing the park brake cable to the bracket on the caliper.

11. Install a large C-clamp, over the body of the brake caliper with the C-clamp ends against the rear of the caliper body and against the outer brake pad.

➡ When using a large C-clamp to compress a caliper piston into a caliper bore of a caliper equipped with an integral park brake mechanism, do not exceed more than 1 mm (0.039 in) of piston travel. Exceeding this amount of piston travel will cause damage to the internal adjusting mechanism and/or the integral park brake mechanism.

12. Tighten the C-clamp just enough to compress the caliper piston 0.039 in (1 mm) of travel only.

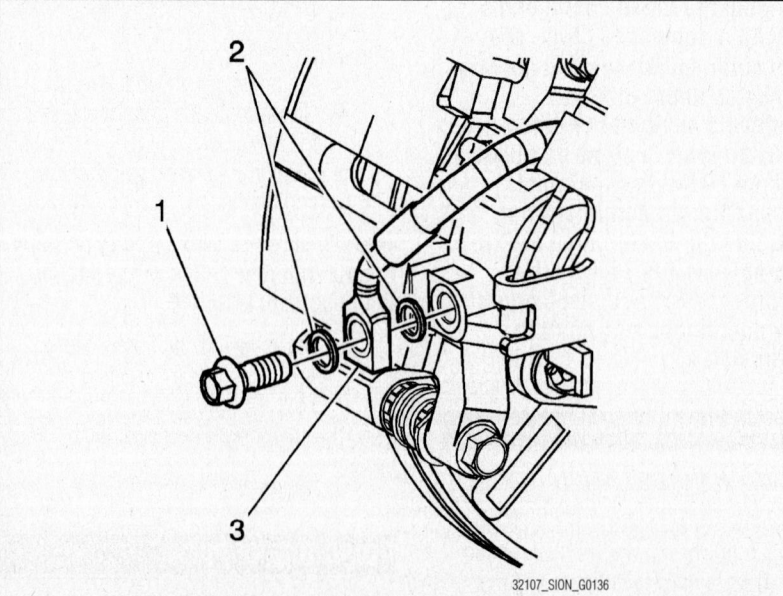

32107_SION_G0136

Fig. 9 Remove the brake hose-to-caliper bolt (1) from the brake caliper, the brake hose (2) from the brake caliper, and the two copper brake hose gaskets (3)

13. Remove the C-clamp from the caliper.

14. Remove the brake hose-to-caliper bolt from the brake caliper.

15. Remove the brake hose from the brake caliper.

16. Remove and discard the 2 copper brake hose gaskets. These gaskets may be stuck to the brake caliper and/or the brake hose end.

17. Cap or plug the opening in the brake caliper and the brake hose to prevent fluid loss and contamination.

18. While using a wrench on the flats of the caliper guide pins, remove the brake caliper guide pin bolts.

19. Remove the brake caliper from the caliper bracket.

20. Inspect the brake caliper guide pins for freedom of movement, and inspect the condition of the guide pin boots. Move the guide pins inboard and outboard within the bracket bores, without disengaging the slides from the boots, and observe for the following:

- Restricted caliper guide pin movement
- Looseness in the brake caliper mounting bracket
- Seized or binding caliper guide pins
- Split or torn boots

21. If any of the conditions listed are found, the brake caliper guide pins and/or boots require replacement.

To install:

22. Install the brake caliper to the caliper bracket.

23. While using a wrench on the flats of the caliper guide pins, install the brake caliper guide pin bolts and tighten the bolts to 25 ft. lbs. (34 Nm).

24. Press the park brake cable end fitting into the bracket on the caliper to secure the retaining tabs.

25. Secure the park brake cable end to the lever on the caliper.

26. Remove the caps or plugs from the brake caliper opening and the brake hose.

➡**Do not reuse the copper brake hose gaskets.**

27. Install NEW copper brake hose gaskets to the brake hose-to-caliper bolt and to the brake hose.

28. Install the brake hose and the brake hose-to-brake caliper bolt to the caliper, and tighten the bolt to 35 ft. lbs. (48 Nm).

29. Bleed the hydraulic brake system.

30. Remove the wheel nuts retaining the brake rotor to the wheel hub.

31. Install the tire and wheel assembly.

32. Lower the vehicle.

33. With the engine **OFF**, gradually apply the brake pedal to approximately two-thirds of its travel distance.

34. Slowly release the brake pedal.

35. Wait 15 seconds, then gradually apply the brake pedal approximately 2/3 of its travel distance again until a firm brake pedal apply is obtained. This will properly seat the brake caliper pistons and brake pads.

36. Adjust the park brake cable tension.

37. Position the park brake lever boot to the floor console and press the boot retainer into place to secure

DISC BRAKE PADS

REMOVAL & INSTALLATION

See Figures 10 and 11.

1. Inspect the fluid level in the brake master cylinder auxiliary reservoir.

2. If the brake fluid level is midway between the maximum-full point and the minimum allowable level, no brake fluid needs to be removed from the reservoir before proceeding.

3. If the brake fluid level is higher than midway between the maximum-full point and the minimum allowable level, remove brake fluid to the midway point before proceeding.

4. Raise and support the vehicle.

5. Remove the tire and wheel assembly.

6. Install and firmly hand tighten 2 wheel nuts to opposite wheel studs in order to retain the rotor to the hub.

7. Install a large C-clamp, over the body of the brake caliper with the C-clamp ends against the rear of the caliper body and against the outer brake pad.

➡**When using a large C-clamp to compress a caliper piston into a caliper bore of a caliper equipped with an integral park brake mechanism, do not exceed more than 1 mm (0.039 in) of piston travel. Exceeding this amount of piston travel will cause damage to the internal adjusting mechanism and/or the integral park brake mechanism.**

8. Tighten the C-clamp just enough to compress the caliper piston 0.039 inches (1 mm) of travel only.

9. Remove the C-clamp from the caliper.

10. While using a wrench on the flats of the caliper guide pins, remove the brake caliper guide pin bolts.

➡**Support the brake caliper with heavy mechanic's wire, or equivalent, whenever it is separated from its mount and the hydraulic flexible brake hose is still connected. Failure to support the caliper in this manner will cause the flexible brake hose to bear the weight of the caliper, which may cause damage to the brake hose and in turn may cause a brake fluid leak.**

11. Without disconnecting the hydraulic brake flexible hose, remove the caliper from the mounting bracket and secure the caliper with heavy mechanics wire, or equivalent.

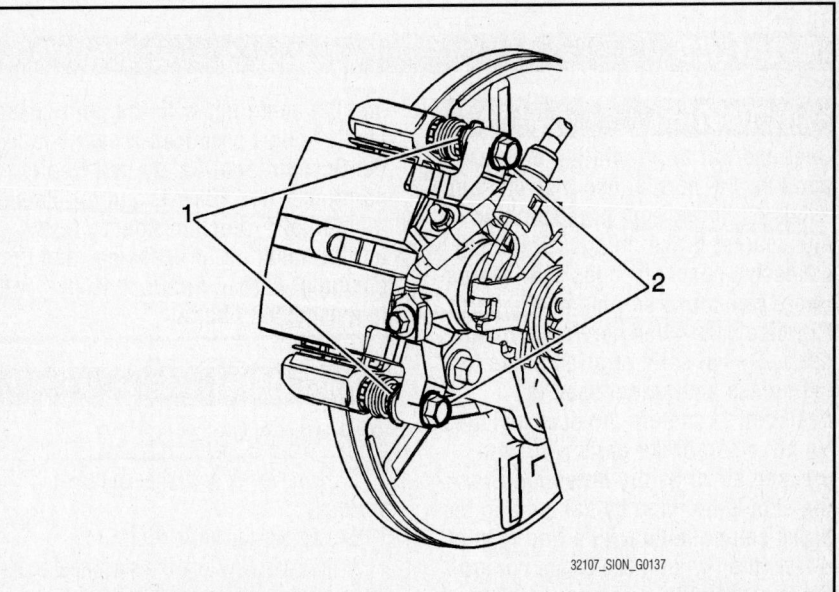

32107_SION_G0137

Fig. 10 While using a wrench on the flats of the caliper guide pins (1), remove the brake caliper guide pin bolts (2)

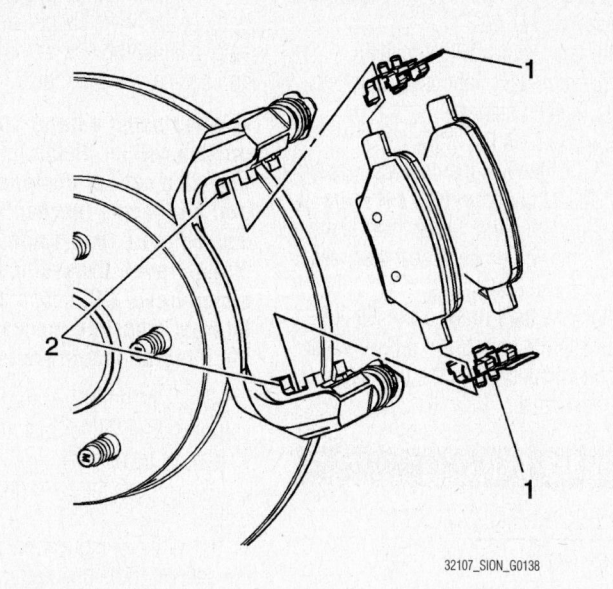

Fig. 11 Remove the brake pads from the caliper mounting bracket

12. Remove the brake pads from the caliper mounting bracket.

13. Remove the brake pad retainers from the caliper bracket.

14. Thoroughly clean the brake pad hardware mating surfaces of the caliper bracket (2), of any debris and corrosion.

15. Inspect the brake caliper guide pins for freedom of movement, and inspect the condition of the guide pin boots. Move the guide pins inboard and outboard within the bracket bores, without disengaging the slides from the boots, and observe for the following:

- Restricted caliper guide pin movement
- Looseness in the brake caliper mounting bracket
- Seized or binding caliper guide pins
- Split or torn boots

16. If any of the conditions listed are found, the brake caliper guide pins and/or boots require replacement.

17. Using a spanner wrench type caliper piston installer, fully retract the piston into the caliper bore.

To install:

18. Apply a very thin coating of high temperature silicone brake lubricant to the pad hardware mating surfaces of the caliper bracket (2) only.

19. Install the brake pad retainers (1) to the brake caliper bracket.

➡The wear sensor equipped disc brake pad must be mounted inboard of the rotor with the leading edge of the sensor facing the brake rotor during forward wheel rotation, or at the bottom of the pad when installed in vehicle position.

20. Install the brake pads to the caliper bracket.

21. Remove the support, and install the caliper into position over the disc brake pads and to the caliper mounting bracket.

22. While using a wrench on the flats of the caliper guide pins, install the brake caliper guide pin bolts, and tighten the bolts to 25 ft. lbs. (34 Nm).

23. Remove the wheel nuts retaining the brake rotor to the hub.

24. Install the tire and wheel assembly.

25. Lower the vehicle.

26. With the engine **OFF**, gradually apply the brake pedal approximately two-thirds of its travel distance.

27. Slowly release the brake pedal.

28. Wait 15 seconds, then gradually apply the brake pedal approximately two-thirds of its travel distance again until a firm brake pedal apply is obtained. This will properly seat the brake caliper pistons and brake pads.

29. Fill the master cylinder auxiliary reservoir to the proper level.

30. Burnish the pads and rotors.

BRAKES

✳✳ CAUTION

Dust and dirt accumulating on brake parts during normal use may contain asbestos fibers from production or aftermarket brake linings. Breathing excessive concentrations of asbestos fibers can cause serious bodily harm. Exercise care when servicing brake parts. Do not sand or grind brake lining unless equipment used is designed to contain the dust residue. Do not clean brake parts with compressed air or by dry brushing. Cleaning should be done by dampening the brake components with a fine mist of water, then wiping the brake components clean with a dampened cloth. Dispose of cloth and all residue containing asbestos fibers in an impermeable container with the appropriate label. Follow practices prescribed by the Occupational Safety and Health Administration (OSHA) and the Environmental Protection Agency (EPA) for the handling, processing, and disposing of dust or debris that may contain asbestos fibers.

BRAKE DRUM

REMOVAL & INSTALLATION

1. Remove the rear wheel and tire assembly.

2. Remove the brake drum.

3. If necessary, turn the starwheel of the brake adjuster assembly to loosen the brake shoes and allow for drum removal.

4. Remove the drum.

REAR DRUM BRAKES

To install:

5. Install brake drum over brake shoes and onto hub.

6. Install tire and wheel assembly. Torque to the proper specification.

7. Adjust brakes following the proper procedure.

8. Road test for braking operation.

BRAKE SHOES

REMOVAL & INSTALLATION

1. Before servicing the vehicle, refer to the Precautions Section.

2. Remove or disconnect the following:

- Wheels and brake drums
- Adjuster spring using a universal brake spring remover. Do not over extend the springs or they will

damaged and will need to be replaced.

- Brake adjuster lever from the pivot
- Spread the top of the shoes apart using brake shoe spanner and spring removal tool J 38400
- Adjuster assembly
- Lightly pull the universal spring end out of the shoe web hole using the hook end of J 38400. Hold the universal spring while removing the trailing shoe.
- Park brake cable from the lever
- Lightly pull the universal spring end out of the shoe web hole using the hook end of J 38400. Hold the universal spring while removing the leading shoe.

3. Inspect the wheel cylinder for signs of leakage and for cut or damaged boots. Do not attempt to repair a damaged cylinder, the assembly must be replaced.

To install:

4. Lubricate the adjuster assembly, the 6 backing plate raised shoe contact pads, the brake lever pin and surfaces which contact brake shoe webs with brake lubricant.

5. Install or connect the following:
- Position the hook end of tool J 38400 under the universal spring

and lightly pull the spring end out while installing the leading shoe. Make sure the spring is properly engaged in the shoe web hole.

- Park brake cable to the lever
- Position the hook end of tool J 38400 under the universal spring and lightly pull the spring end out while installing the trailing shoe. Make sure the spring is properly engaged in the shoe web hole.
- Spread the top of the shoes apart using tool J 38400
- Adjuster assembly
- Adjuster actuator lever to the shoe and adjuster assembly. Make sure the lever is engaged properly between the adjuster and the shoe.
- Adjuster spring. Make sure the loop end of the spring engages properly to the tab on the actuator lever

6. Release the parking brake.

7. Pull the parking lever boot away from the console after applying light pressure inwards on the boot retainer, this will allow access to the cable adjusting nut.

8. Release the tension on the cable. Make sure to use hand tools only when adjusting the nut.

9. Using a suitable drum clearance gauge, measure the inner diameter of the brake drum and adjust the outside diameter of the brake shoes using the adjuster screw to 0.025 inch (0.50mm) less than the inner diameter of the drum.

10. Repeat the procedure for the opposite brake shoes and install the brake drums.

11. Adjust the parking park and install the lever boot.

12. If the wheel cylinders have been replaced, bleed the hydraulic brake system.

13. Install the rear wheels.

ADJUSTMENT

The Saturn features a self-adjuster mechanism that is part of the brake assembly and compensates for normal brake lining wear. No external adjustment is necessary or possible.

When the brake shoes or components of the brake assembly are replaced, the inside diameter of the drum should be measured using a brake shoe clearance gauge. The outer diameter of the brake shoes should then be given the base setting of 0.020 in. (0.5mm) less than the drum's inner diameter. The automatic adjuster will take care of all adjustments from that point.

BRAKES | **PARKING BRAKE**

PARKING BRAKE CABLES

ADJUSTMENT

Disc Brakes

See Figure 12.

➡ **The park brake cable adjusting nut is a nylon lock type. Use ONLY HAND TOOLS whenever tightening or loosening the adjusting nut.**

1. Apply and fully release the park brake several times. Verify that the park brake lever releases completely.

2. Turn **ON** the ignition. Verify the red BRAKE warning lamp is not illuminated.

3. If the red BRAKE warning lamp is illuminated, verify the following:
- The park brake lever is in the fully released position and against the stop
- There is no slack in the park brake cables

4. Turn **OFF** the ignition.

5. Release the park brake lever boot from the floor console by applying light

pressure inward on the sides of the boot retainer, and pull the boot back.

6. With the park brake lever in the released position, loosen the adjusting nut (1) enough to completely relieve tension on the front cable.

7. Raise and support the vehicle. Raise the vehicle just enough to observe the rear calipers and rotate the rear tire and wheel assemblies

8. With all tension relieved from the park brake cables, rotate the rear tire and wheel assemblies, or the rear brake rotors if the wheels have been removed. Observe the amount of effort required for rotation, and the amount of drag if present.

9. Tighten the park brake cable adjusting nut until all slack is taken out of the front cable.

10. Further tighten the adjusting nut until one of the park brake levers on the rear calipers is just lifted off the stop on the caliper housing.

11. Slowly back off the adjusting nut until the park brake lever just rests on the stop.

12. Back off the adjusting nut 1 full turn.

13. Fully apply and release the park brake lever 3-5 times.

14. Raise the park brake lever 3 detent positions and attempt to rotate the rear tire and wheel assemblies, or the rear brake rotors.

15. If rotating the tire and wheel assemblies, they should be difficult to rotate, but should not be locked.

16. If rotating the brake rotors, they should be locked

17. Raise the park brake lever 1 additional detent position and attempt to rotate the rear tire and wheel assemblies, or the rear brake rotors. The tire and wheel assemblies, or the rear brake rotors should be locked.

18. Fully release the park brake lever.

19. Verify the park brake is released by rotating the rear tire and wheel assemblies, or the rear brake rotors. The rotors should rotate freely and exhibit no brake shoe drag from the park brake system.

20. With the lever released, if the rotors required more effort to rotate, or exhibited more drag than noted previously when all cable tension was relieved, check the park

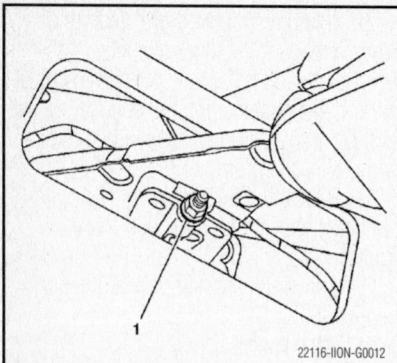

Fig. 12 Parking brake cable adjustment nut (1)

brake levers on the rear calipers. The levers should be on the stops.

21. If the levers are not against the stops, loosen the adjusting nut just until the levers rest against the stops, then repeat steps 14 through 18.

22. If the rotors still do not rotate freely, with the park lever fully released, park brake adjustment is not the cause of any drag in the brake system.

23. Lower the vehicle.

24. Position the park brake lever boot to the floor console and press the boot retainer into place to secure.

25. Release the park brake lever.

Drum Brakes

1. Apply and fully release the park brake several times. Verify that the park brake lever releases completely.

2. Turn **ON** the ignition. Verify the red BRAKE warning lamp is not illuminated.

3. If the red BRAKE warning lamp is illuminated, verify the following:
   - The park brake lever is in the fully released position and against the stop
   - There is no slack in the park brake cables

4. Turn **OFF** the ignition.

5. Release the park brake lever boot from the floor console by applying light pressure inward on the sides of the boot retainer, and pull the boot back.

6. With the park brake lever in the released position, loosen the adjusting nut enough to completely relieve tension on the front cable.

7. Raise and support the vehicle. Raise the vehicle just enough to allow rear tire and wheel assembly removal and rear drum adjustment.

8. Remove the rear tire and wheel assemblies.

9. Adjust the rear drum brakes.

10. Ensure there is no brake shoe drag after adjustment by rotating the brake drums. If drag exists, re-center the brake shoes and perform the brake shoe adjustment again.

11. Install 2 wheel nuts to the wheel studs and firmly hand tighten in order to retain the brake drums.

12. Raise the park brake lever 6 detent positions.

13. Tighten the park brake cable adjusting nut to 35 inch lbs.(3.9 Nm).

14. Attempt to rotate the rear brake drums. There should be no rotation forward or rearward.

15. Fully release the park brake lever.

16. Verify the park brake is released by rotating the rear brake drums. The drums should rotate freely and exhibit no brake shoe drag.

17. If the drums do not rotate freely, repeat the park brake cable adjustment procedure.

18. Raise the park brake lever 3 detent positions and attempt to rotate the rear brake drums: One of the brake drums should not rotate forward or rearward. The other brake drum should not rotate forward or rearward, or should require substantial effort to rotate.

Raise the park brake lever 1 additional detent position and attempt to rotate the rear brake drums.

19. Verify that the left and right brake drums cannot be rotated.

20. Remove the wheel nuts retaining the brake drums.

21. Install the rear tire and wheel assemblies.

22. Lower the vehicle.

23. Position the park brake lever boot to the floor console and press the boot retainer into place to secure.

24. Release the park brake lever.

CHASSIS ELECTRICAL

AIR BAG (SUPPLEMENTAL RESTRAINT SYSTEM)

GENERAL INFORMATION

✳✳ CAUTION

These vehicles are equipped with an air bag system. The system must be disarmed before performing service on, or around, system components, the steering column, instrument panel components, wiring and sensors. Failure to follow the safety precautions and the disarming procedure could result in accidental air bag deployment, possible injury and unnecessary system repairs.

SERVICE PRECAUTIONS

Disconnect and isolate the battery negative cable before beginning any airbag system component diagnosis, testing, removal, or installation procedures. Allow system capacitor to discharge for two minutes

before beginning any component service. This will disable the airbag system. Failure to disable the airbag system may result in accidental airbag deployment, personal injury, or death.

Do not place an intact undeployed airbag face down on a solid surface. The airbag will propel into the air if accidentally deployed and may result in personal injury or death.

When carrying or handling an undeployed airbag, the trim side (face) of the airbag should be pointing towards the body to minimize possibility of injury if accidental deployment occurs. Failure to do this may result in personal injury or death.

Replace airbag system components with OEM replacement parts. Substitute parts may appear interchangeable, but internal differences may result in inferior occupant protection. Failure to do so may result in occupant personal injury or death.

Wear safety glasses, rubber gloves, and long sleeved clothing when cleaning powder residue from vehicle after an airbag deployment. Powder residue emitted from a deployed airbag can cause skin irritation. Flush affected area with cool water if irritation is experienced. If nasal or throat irritation is experienced, exit the vehicle for fresh air until the irritation ceases. If irritation continues, see a physician.

Do not use a replacement airbag that is not in the original packaging. This may result in improper deployment, personal injury, or death.

The factory installed fasteners, screws and bolts used to fasten airbag components have a special coating and are specifically designed for the airbag system. Do not use substitute fasteners. Use only original equipment fasteners listed in the parts catalog when fastener replacement is required.

During, and following, any child restraint anchor service, due to impact event or vehicle repair, carefully inspect all mounting hardware, tether straps, and anchors for proper installation, operation, or damage. If a child restraint anchor is found damaged in any way, the anchor must be replaced. Failure to do this may result in personal injury or death.

Deployed and non-deployed airbags may or may not have live pyrotechnic material within the airbag inflator.

Do not dispose of driver/passenger/curtain airbags or seat belt tensioners unless you are sure of complete deployment. Refer to the Hazardous Substance Control System for proper disposal.

Dispose of deployed airbags and tensioners consistent with state, provincial, local, and federal regulations.

After any airbag component testing or service, do not connect the battery negative cable. Personal injury or death may result if the system test is not performed first.

If the vehicle is equipped with the Occupant Classification System (OCS), do not connect the battery negative cable before performing the OCS Verification Test using the scan tool and the appropriate diagnostic information. Personal injury or death may result if the system test is not performed properly.

Never replace both the Occupant Restraint Controller (ORC) and the Occupant Classification Module (OCM) at the same time. If both require replacement, replace one, then perform the Airbag System test before replacing the other.

Both the ORC and the OCM store Occupant Classification System (OCS) calibration data, which they transfer to one another when one of them is replaced. If both are replaced at the same time, an irreversible fault will be set in both modules and the OCS may malfunction and cause personal injury or death.

If equipped with OCS, the Seat Weight Sensor is a sensitive, calibrated unit and must be handled carefully. Do not drop or handle roughly. If dropped or damaged, replace with another sensor. Failure to do so may result in occupant injury or death.

If equipped with OCS, the front passenger seat must be handled carefully as well. When removing the seat, be careful when setting on floor not to drop. If dropped, the sensor may be inoperative, could result in occupant injury, or possibly death.

If equipped with OCS, when the passenger front seat is on the floor, no one should sit in the front passenger seat. This uneven force may damage the sensing ability of the seat weight sensors. If sat on and damaged, the sensor may be inoperative, could result in occupant injury, or possibly death.

DISARMING THE SYSTEM

1. Before servicing the vehicle, refer to the Precautions Section.
2. Align the steering wheel so the vehicle wheels are pointing in the straight-ahead position.
3. Turn the ignition switch to the **LOCK-**position.
4. Remove the SIR or AIR BAG fuse from the fuse block.
5. To disable the roof rail module left and seat belt pre-tensioner (left front), remove the garnish molding from the upper lock pillar. Remove the Connector Position Assurance (CPA) device from the roof rail module. Disconnect the roof rail module from the vehicle harness. Lower the headliner and remove the CPA from the seat belt pre-tensioner connector and disconnect the pre-tensioner connector.

ARMING THE SYSTEM

After the repairs, enable the system as follows:
1. Turn the ignition switch to the **LOCK-**position and remove the key.
2. Connect the pre-tensioner and install the CPA.
3. Install the headliner.
4. Connect the roof rail module and install the CPA.
5. Install the garnish molding.
6. Reinstall the Supplemental Inflatable Restraint (SIR) or AIR BAG fuse.
7. Turn the ignition switch to the **RUN-**position.
8. Verify the SIR indicator light flashes 7 times, if not, inspect the system for malfunction.

DRIVETRAIN

AUTOMATIC TRANSAXLE ASSEMBLY

REMOVAL & INSTALLATION

1. Before servicing the vehicle, refer to the precautions section.
2. Disconnect the negative battery cable.
3. Disconnect the air inlet duct hose from the intake plenum.
4. Disconnect the transaxle wiring harness from the transaxle and the PNP switch.
5. Remove the upper transmission to engine bolts and stud.
6. Install an engine support fixture.
7. Remove the front wheel assemblies.
8. Remove the both front fender liners.
9. Remove the steering gear mounting bolts and secure the steering gear with mechanics wire.
10. Disconnect the wheel speed sensor wires from the both front wheels and unclip from the frame.
11. Separate the ball joints from the steering knuckles.
12. Remove the frame as follows:
    a. Secure the radiator and condenser assembly to the radiator support.
    b. Remove the front transaxle mount to cradle through bolt.
    c. Remove the rear transaxle mount to frame bolts.
    d. Remove both stabilizer link to stabilizer shaft nuts.
    e. Remove both tie rod to steering knuckle nuts.
    f. Separate the outer tie rods from the steering knuckles.
    g. Remove the intermediate steering shaft to steering gear pinch bolt and discard.

➡**DO NOT rotate the intermediate shaft once separated from the gear. Possible damage or a malfunction could occur.**

    h. Disconnect the intermediate steering shaft from the steering gear.
    i. Remove both lower control arm ball stud to steering knuckle pinch bolts.

➡**Do not free the ball stud by using a pickle fork or a wedge-type tool. Damage to the seal or bushing may result.**

    j. Lower the lower control arms in order to disengage the steering knuckle. If necessary, use ball joint removal tool J 43631.
    k. Mark the frame to body position with a paint pen or permanent marker.
    l. Lower the vehicle to about 3 feet off the ground in order to place a hydraulic lift table under the frame.
    m. Use two 2 x 4 pieces of wood between the lift table and the frame and lift the table to the frame.
    n. Slowly remove the frame bolts using the following sequence:
    • Front frame bolts
    • Rear frame bolts
    o. Slowly lower the lift table to the floor.

13. Remove the 2 bolts from the transmission brace.

14. Disconnect the shift cable from the shift linkage.

15. Disconnect the cable from the bracket.

16. Remove the flywheel inspection cover.

17. Remove the starter

18. Mark the relationship of the flywheel to the torque converter for reassembly.

19. Use the flywheel holding tool to prevent the crankshaft from rotating.

20. Remove the torque converter to flywheel bolts.

21. Remove the transmission cooler lines by removing the nut holding the bracket to the transaxle case.

22. Disconnect the VSS wiring harness from the sensor.

23. Disconnect the wheel drive shafts from the transaxle.

24. Remove the body to transmission mount bolts.

25. Lower the transmission with the engine support fixture enough to remove the transmission.

26. Raise the vehicle.

27. Remove the oil pan to drain the transmission.

28. Support the transmission with a suitable jack.

29. Remove the transaxle to engine nut.

30. Separate the engine and the transaxle.

31. Remove the transaxle from the vehicle.

To install:

32. Position the transaxle in the vehicle.

➡**Use the correct fastener in the correct location. Replacement fasteners must be the correct part number for that application. Fasteners requiring replacement or fasteners requiring the use of thread locking compound or sealant are identified in the service procedure. Do not use paints, lubricants, or corrosion inhibitors on fasteners or fastener joint surfaces unless specified. These coatings affect fastener torque and joint clamping force and may damage the fastener. Use the correct tightening sequence and specifications when installing fasteners in order to avoid damage to parts and systems.**

33. Install the lower transmission to engine bolts and nuts. Tighten to 66 ft. lbs. (90 Nm).

34. Connect the transaxle cooler pipes to the transaxle. Tighten to 71 inch lbs. (8 Nm).

35. Use a flywheel holding tool to prevent the crankshaft from rotating.

36. Install the torque converter to flywheel bolts. Tighten to 46 ft. lbs. (62 Nm).

37. Install the wheel drive shafts to the transaxle.

38. Connect the wiring harness to the VSS.

39. Install the starter.

40. Install the flywheel inspection cover bolts.

41. Use the engine support fixture to raise the engine and transmission assembly.

42. Install the transaxle mount to body bolts. Tighten to 66 ft. lbs. (90 Nm).

43. Install the frame as follows:

   a. With the frame on the lift table, raise the frame to the vehicle.

   b. Hand start all the frame bolts while aligning the frame to the paint marks.

   c. Tighten the frame bolts. Tighten the bolts 74 ft. lbs. (100 Nm) plus an additional 180.

44. Lower and remove the hydraulic table.

   a. Connect the lower control arm to the steering knuckle.

➡**The torque sequence must be followed in the order that is listed.**

   b. Install the ball joint pinch bolt and nut. Tighten the nut to 37 ft. lbs. (50 Nm), back of the nut ¾ turn then retighten the nut to 37 ft. lbs. (50 Nm) plus an additional 30 degree turn.

➡**The front and rear transmission mounts must be allowed to settle with the through bolts loosened.**

   c. Hand start the front transaxle mount through bolt.

   d. Loosen the rear transmission mount through bolt.

   e. Tighten the rear transaxle mount to frame bolts to 37 ft. lbs. (50 Nm)

   f. Tighten the rear transaxle mount through bolts to 74 ft. lbs. (100 Nm), then tighten the front transaxle mount through bolts to 74 ft. lbs. (100 Nm).

   g. Install the outer tie rods to the steering knuckles. Install new outer tie rod to the knuckle nuts and tighten to 15 ft. lbs. (20 Nm) plus an additional 180 degree turn.

   h. Connect the stabilizer links to the stabilizer shaft. Tighten to 81 ft. lbs. (100 Nm).

   i. Connect the intermediate shaft to the steering gear. Install a new intermediate shaft pinch bolt and tighten to 25 ft. lbs. (34 Nm).

   j. Install the splash shields.

   k. Install the front wheels.

45. Route and clip the wheel speed sensor wiring into the proper position on both sides.

46. Install the steering gear to the front suspension crossmember.

47. Install the steering gear bolts to the front suspension crossmember. Tighten to 81 ft. lbs. (100 Nm).

48. Install the transmission to engine brace bolts. Tighten to 53 ft. lbs. (72 Nm).

49. Install the upper transmission to engine bolts and stud. Tighten to 66 ft. lbs. (90 Nm).

50. Install the engine wiring harness grounds to the transaxle to engine mount stud and nut.

51. Remove the engine support fixture

52. Install the shift linkage to the transmission.

53. Connect the electrical connectors to the PNP switch and transaxle.

54. Connect the air duct hose to the intake plenum.

55. Connect the negative battery cable.

56. Fill the transmission to the proper level.

MANUAL TRANSAXLE ASSEMBLY

REMOVAL & INSTALLATION

Getrag 5-Speed

See Figure 13.

1. Before servicing the vehicle, refer to the precautions section.

2. Drain the transaxle fluid.

3. Remove or disconnect the following:

   - Negative battery cable
   - Positive battery post from the under right hand hood junction block
   - Positive cables from the under right hand hood junction block
   - Surge tank inlet hose from the surge tank
   - Under right hand hood junction block bracket nuts and bolt
   - Front wiring harness from the junction block bracket
   - Move the junction block aside
   - Clutch hose from the actuator cylinder

4. Install an engine support fixture.

5. Secure the cooling module to the upper body structure.

   - Upper transmission-to-mount bolts
   - Upper transmission-to-engine bolt

6. Remove the front frame as follows:

   a. Mark the frame-to-body position.

b. Lower the vehicle until it is 3 feet off the ground so that a lift table may be placed in position. As necessary, use blocks of wood between the frame and table to support the assembly.

c. Slowly remove the front frame bolts, the partially unscrew the bolts until 1 ½inch of the bolt shank is exposed.

d. Slowly lower the table to the floor

7. Remove or disconnect the following:
- Drive shafts from the transmission and support with wire
- Starter
- Shift cable from the transmission as follows:

e. Apply the parking brake.

f. Shift the transmission to **Neutral**.

g. Remove the console.

h. Lift up the cable retainers.

i. Disconnect the cable ends from the shifter assembly.

j. Disconnect the cable ends from the transmission shift levers, make sure to mark the cable locations prior to removal, this will aid during assembly.

8. Remove or disconnect the following:
- Back-up lamp switch and Vehicle Speed Sensor connections

9. Use the engine support fixture to lower the powertrain assembly to allow clearance between the side rail and powertrain.

10. Attach a transmission jack and remove the transmission-to-engine bolts.

11. Remove the transmission.

To install:

➡ **The number 3 bolt position does not require a bolt. Refer to the accompanying illustration for bolt locations.**

12. Use the transmission jack to align the transmission, install the transmission-to-engine bolts and torque to 55 ft. lbs. (75 Nm).

13. Install or connect the following:
- Back-up lamp switch and Vehicle Speed Sensor connections

14. Connect the shift cable to the transmission as follows:

a. Connect the cable ends to the transmission shift levers as noted during removal.

b. Connect the cable ends to the shifter assembly.

c. Push the shifter neutral lock clip. Move the shifter slightly to center the clip and make sure the transmission is in **Neutral**.

d. Press down on the locking tabs.

e. Pull the shifter neutral lock into its original position.

f. Install the console.

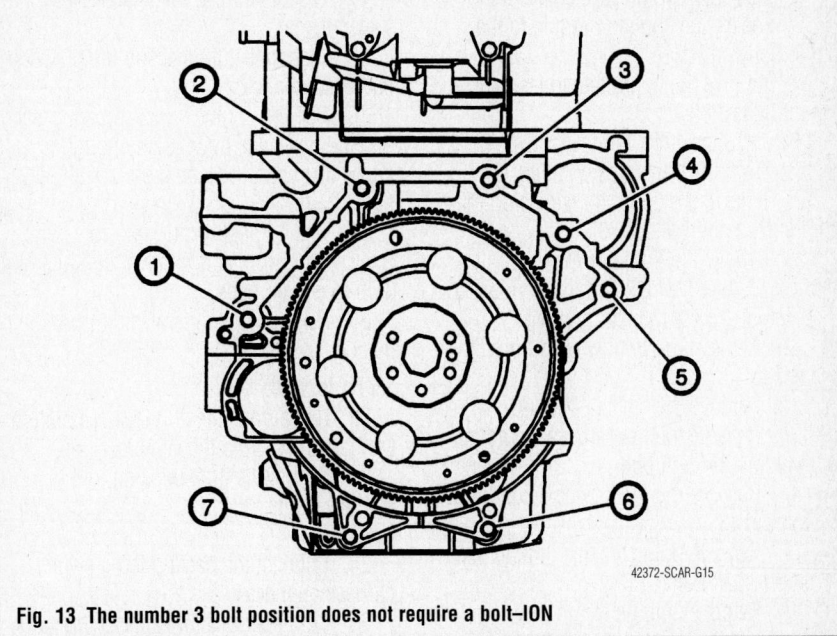

Fig. 13 The number 3 bolt position does not require a bolt–ION

42372-SCAR-G15

15. Install or connect the following:
- Starter
- Drive shafts

16. Use the engine support fixture to raise the powertrain assembly into position.

17. Install the side transmission mount as follows:

a. Place the mount in position and tighten the mount-to-rail bolts to 25 ft. lbs. (34 Nm).

18. Use a jack to align the mount when it is in position.

a. Install and hand tighten the mount-to-transmission bolts. Do not pry the transmission or mount to align the holes. Hand start the bolts in the following sequence; rear bolt, middle and then front bolt. Using the same sequence, tighten the bolts to 33 ft. lbs. (45 Nm).

19. Install or connect the following:
- Under right hand hood fuse block
- Surge tank inlet hose
- Front wiring harness to the junction block
- Positive battery cables to the junction block bracket
- Positive battery post to the junction block bracket
- Junction block bracket bolt and tighten to 18 ft. lbs. (25 Nm) and the nuts to 89 inch lbs. (10 Nm)

20. Install the front frame as follows:

a. Slowly raise the table to the into position and align the frame to the marks made during removal.

b. Hand tighten the frame bolts

c. Tighten the frame bolts to 74 ft. lbs.

(100 Nm) plus an additional torque of 180 degrees using a torque angle meter.

21. Remove the engine support fixture.

22. Install or connect the following:
- Top engine-to-transmission bolt and tighten to 55 ft. lbs. (75 Nm)
- Clutch hose to the actuator cylinder and bleed the hydraulic clutch system.
- Cooling module
- Negative battery cable.

23. Fill the transmission to the proper level.

24. Warm the engine and check the transmission fluid. Check and adjust vehicle alignment, as necessary.

MU–3

1. Before servicing the vehicle, refer to the precautions section.

2. Disconnect the negative battery cable.

3. Remove the cover from the under right hand hood electrical center.

4. Release the forward lamp harness retainer from the ABS modulator bracket, or the proportioning valve bracket, to allow the under right hand hood electrical center to be repositioned adequately.

5. Remove the under right hand hood electrical center bracket from the vehicle and reposition the electrical center to access the bracket .

6. Release the wiring harness retainers above the brake booster, to allow the electrical center to be repositioned adequately.

7. Disconnect the hydraulic clutch hose from the clutch actuator cylinder and the clutch master cylinder.

8. Install an engine support fixture.

9. Secure the cooling module to the upper body structure.

10. Remove the upper transmission to mount bolts.

11. Disconnect the wiring harness retainer from the transmission stud.

12. Remove the upper transmission to engine stud and bolt.

13. Remove the frame as follows:

a. Secure the radiator and condenser assembly to the radiator support.

b. Remove the front wheels from the vehicle.

c. Remove the splash shields.

d. Remove the front transaxle mount to cradle through bolt.

e. Remove the rear transaxle mount to frame bolts.

f. Remove both stabilizer link to stabilizer shaft nuts.

g. Remove both tie rod to steering knuckle nuts.

h. Separate the outer tie rods from the steering knuckles.

i. Remove the intermediate steering shaft to steering gear pinch bolt and discard.

➡**DO NOT rotate the intermediate shaft once separated from the gear. Possible damage or a malfunction could occur.**

j. Disconnect the intermediate steering shaft from the steering gear.

k. Remove both lower control arm ball stud to steering knuckle pinch bolts.

➡**Do not free the ball stud by using a pickle fork or a wedge-type tool. Damage to the seal or bushing may result.**

l. Lower the lower control arms in order to disengage the steering knuckle. If necessary, use ball joint removal tool J 43631.

m. Mark the frame to body position with a paint pen or permanent marker.

n. Lower the vehicle to about 3 feet off the ground in order to place a hydraulic lift table under the frame.

o. Use two 2 x 4 pieces of wood between the lift table and the frame and lift the table to the frame.

p. Slowly remove the frame bolts using the following sequence:

- Front frame bolts
- Rear frame bolts

q. Slowly lower the lift table to the floor.

14. Drain the transaxle fluid.

15. Disconnect the drive axle and intermediate shaft from the transmission and secure out of the way.

16. Remove the starter.

17. Disconnect the shift cables from the transmission.

18. Disconnect the backup lamp switch harness connector.

19. Use the engine support fixture rear hook to lower the powertrain enough to allow clearance between the side rail and powertrain.

20. Use a transmission jack to secure the transmission, and remove the transmission to engine bolts.

21. Remove the transmission from the vehicle.

To install:

22. Use a transmission jack to position the transmission to the vehicle.

23. Secure the transmission to the engine. Tighten the bolts to 55 ft. lbs. (75 Nm).

24. Connect the backup lamp switch harness connector.

25. Connect the shift cable to the transmission.

26. Install the starter.

27. Connect the drive axle and intermediate shaft to the transmission.

28. Use the engine support fixture in order to raise the powertrain assembly.

29. Install the left transmission mount. Tighten the bolts to 20 ft. lbs. (27 Nm).

30. Install the frame as follows:

a. With the frame on the lift table, raise the frame to the vehicle.

b. Hand start all the frame bolts while aligning the frame to the paint marks.

c. Tighten the frame bolts. Tighten the bolts 74 ft. lbs. (100 Nm) plus an additional 180.

31. Lower and remove the hydraulic table.

a. Connect the lower control arm to the steering knuckle.

➡**The torque sequence must be followed in the order that is listed.**

b. Install the ball joint pinch bolt and nut. Tighten the nut to 37 ft. lbs. (50 Nm), back of the nut ¾ turn then retighten the nut to 37 ft. lbs. (50 Nm) plus an additional 30 degree turn.

➡**The front and rear transmission mounts must be allowed to settle with the through bolts loosened.**

c. Hand start the front transaxle mount through bolt.

d. Loosen the rear transmission mount through bolt.

e. Tighten the rear transaxle mount to frame bolts to 37 ft. lbs. (50 Nm)

f. Tighten the rear transaxle mount through bolts to 74 ft. lbs. (100 Nm),

then tighten the front transaxle mount through bolts to 74 ft. lbs. (100 Nm).

g. Install the outer tie rods to the steering knuckles. Install new outer tie rod to the knuckle nuts and tighten to 15 ft. lbs. (20 Nm) plus an additional 180 degree turn.

h. Connect the stabilizer links to the stabilizer shaft. Tighten to 81 ft. lbs. (100 Nm).

i. Connect the intermediate shaft to the steering gear. Install a new intermediate shaft pinch bolt and tighten to 25 ft. lbs. (34 Nm).

j. Install the splash shields.

k. Install the front wheels.

32. Remove the engine support fixture.

33. Install the top engine to transmission bolt. Tighten the bolts to 55 ft. lbs. (75 Nm).

34. Install the top engine to transmission stud. Tighten to 55 ft. lbs. (75 Nm).

35. Connect the wiring harness retainer to the transmission stud.

36. Connect the hydraulic clutch hose to the clutch actuator cylinder.

37. Bleed the clutch hydraulic system.

38. Install the under right hand hood electrical center bracket to the vehicle and install the electrical center (1) into position on the bracket .

39. Secure the forward lamp harness retainer to the ABS modulator bracket, or the proportioning valve bracket .

40. Connect the electrical connector to the brake fluid level sensor, then press forward on the Connector Position Assurance (CPA) tab of the connector to secure.

41. Install the cover to the under right hand hood electrical center.

42. Release the cooling module from the upper body structure.

43. Connect the negative battery cable.

44. Fill the transmission to the proper level.

CLUTCH DRIVEN DISC & PRESSURE PLATE

REMOVAL & INSTALLATION

See Figures 14 through 21.

1. Properly disable the SIR system, if equipped, and disconnect the negative battery cable.

2. Remove the transaxle from the vehicle.

3. Unsnap the release fork from the ball stud, then remove the fork and bearing from the vehicle. Slide the bearing from the fork. The bearing should be checked for excessive play and for minimal bearing drag.

It should be replaced if no/little drag or excessive play is found.

➡**The release bearing is packed with grease and should not be washed with solvent.**

4. Using a feeler gauge, measure the distance between the pressure plate and flywheel surfaces in order to determine clutch face thickness. Replace the clutch disc if it is not within specification, 0.205–0.287 in. (5.2–7.3mm).

5. Remove the pressure plate-to-flywheel bolts in a progressive crisscross pattern to prevent warping the cover, then remove the pressure plate and clutch disc.

6. Inspect the pressure plate, as follows:

   a. Check for excessive wear, chatter marks, cracks overheating (indicated by a blue discoloration). Black random spots on the friction surface of the pressure plate is normal.

   b. Check the plate for warpage using a straightedge and a feeler gauge; the maximum allowable warpage is 0.006 in. (0.15mm).

   c. Replace the plate, if necessary.

7. Inspect the clutch disc, as follows:

   a. Check the disc face for oil or burnt spots.

   b. Check the disc for loose damper springs, hub or rivets.

   c. Replace the disc, if necessary.

8. Check the flywheel, as follows:

   a. Check the ring gear for wear or damage.

   b. Check the friction surface for excessive wear, chatter marks, cracks or over heating (indicated by a blue discoloration). Black random spots on the friction surface of the pressure plate is normal.

   c. Check flywheel thickness; the minimum allowable is 1.102 in. (28mm).

   d. Measure flywheel run-out using a dial indicator, positioned for at least 2 flywheel revolutions. Push the crankshaft forward to take up thrust bearing clearance. Maximum flywheel run-out is 0.006 in. (0.15mm).

   e. Check the flywheel for warpage using a straightedge and a feeler gauge; the maximum allowable warpage is 0.006 in. (0.15mm).

   f. Replace the flywheel, if necessary.

9. If necessary, remove the flywheel retaining bolts and remove the flywheel from the crankshaft.

To install:

10. If removed, install the flywheel and tighten the bolts in a crisscross sequence to 59 ft. lbs. (80 Nm).

11. Install the clutch disc and pressure plate with the yellow dot on the pressure plate aligned as close as possible to the mark on the flywheel. The clutch disc is labeled FLYWHEEL SIDE in order to help correctly position the disc. Start the pressure plate bolts.

12. Install clutch alignment tool SA9145T or equivalent in the clutch disc, and push in until it bottoms out in the crankshaft.

13. Tighten the pressure plate bolts using multiple passes, in sequence, to 18 ft. lbs. (25 Nm) and remove the alignment tool.

14. Lubricate the fork pivot point with high temperature grease and install the release bearing to the fork. Do not lubricate the release bearing or bearing quill.

15. Snap the release bearing and fork onto the ball stud.

16. Lubricate the splines of the input shaft lightly with a high temperature grease.

17. Install the transaxle assembly.

18. Connect the negative battery cable and, if equipped, properly enable the SIR system.

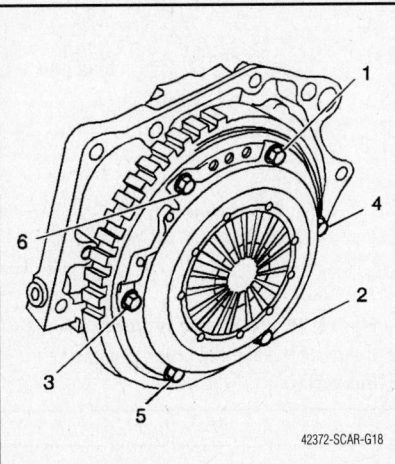

Fig. 14 Tighten the pressure plate bolts in sequence—ION

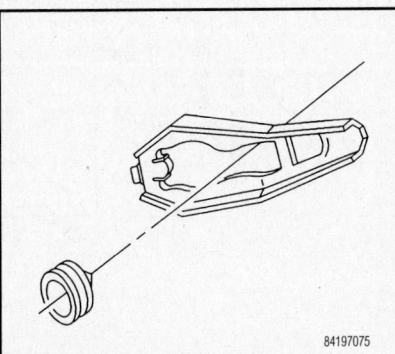

Fig. 15 Slide the bearing from the release fork

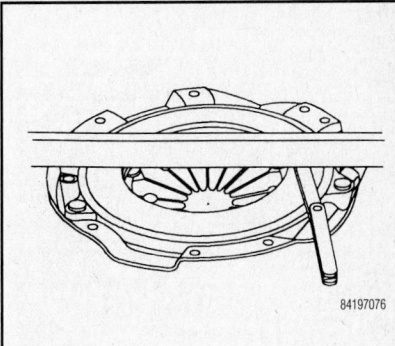

Fig. 16 Check the pressure plate for warpage

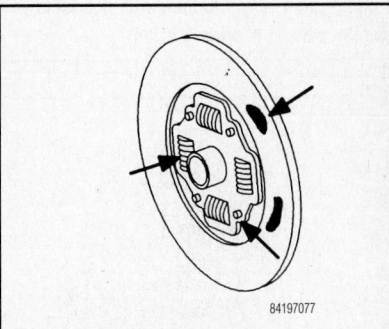

Fig. 17 Check the clutch disc for oil or burnt spots and check for loose springs, hub or rivets

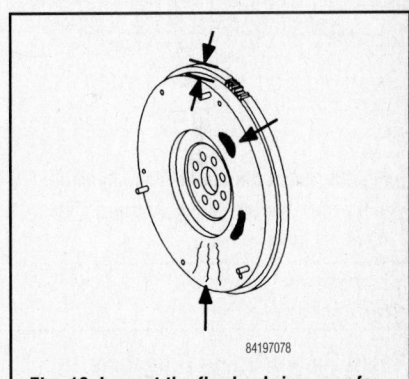

Fig. 18 Inspect the flywheel ring gear for damage and the contact surface for wear

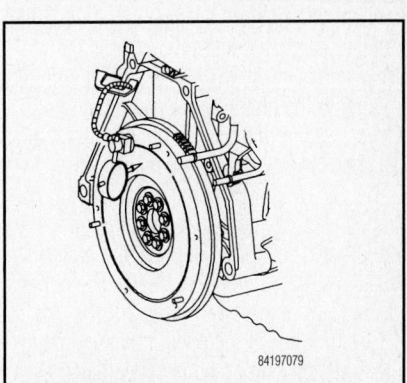

Fig. 19 Measure flywheel run-out using a dial indicator

Fig. 20 If removed, install the flywheel and tighten the mounting bolts in a criss-cross pattern to specifications

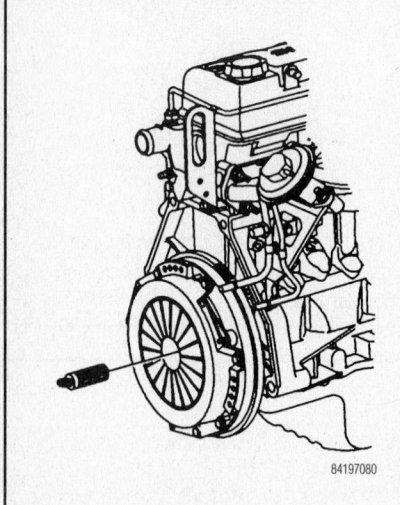

Fig. 21 Install a proper clutch alignment tool before tightening the pressure plate retaining bolts

ADJUSTMENTS

Pedal Height/Travel Diagnosis

See Figures 22 through 24.

The hydraulic clutch system is self-adjusting; therefore, no manual clutch pedal adjustments are necessary or possible. However, because the pedal travel is directly related to the clutch fork travel, the operating condition of the hydraulic system may be checked using clutch pedal travel.

1. Use a straightedge horizontally positioned from the center of the clutch pedal to the driver's seat, then depress the clutch pedal and measure pedal travel. The clutch pedal travel should be 5.3–6.2 in. (135–156mm). If the pedal travel is insufficient, look for an obvious cause, such as carpet or a floor mat blocking the pedal or a faulty/damaged pedal.

2. Through the access hole on the side of the transaxle (immediately to the right of the slave cylinder), use a caliper or depth gauge to measure travel of the clutch fork with the pedal in the full up and full down positions. Subtract the full down measurement from the full up figure to determine fork travel.

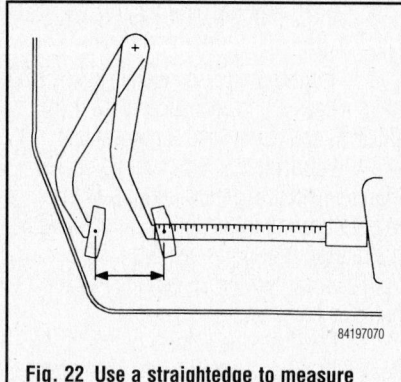

Fig. 22 Use a straightedge to measure pedal travel

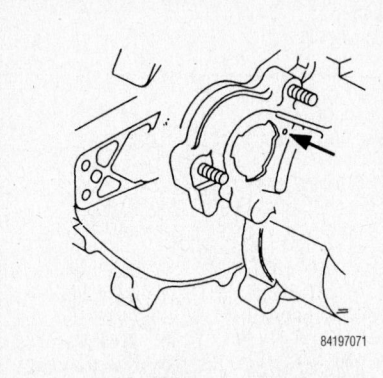

Fig. 23 An access hole is provided in the transaxle housing, in order to measure fork travel

➡ **If no caliper or depth gauge is available, use a round wire rod in the access hole and mark the pedal up/down positions. Then measure the distance between the 2 marks to determine fork travel.**

3. Compare the fork and pedal travel measurements using the chart.

4. If fork travel is less than the minimum allowable, check the following. (Conditions a, b and e require replacement of the master/slave cylinder assembly:

　　a. Fluid leaks in the hydraulic system.

　　b. Air in the system.

　　c. Improper installation of the master/slave cylinder.

　　d. Damaged master or slave cylinder.

　　e. Damage to the front of the dashboard.

5. If fork travel is acceptable and the hydraulics are working properly, check for a bent fork or damaged pressure plate, which may cause the improper pedal travel.

CLUTCH MASTER CYLINDER

REMOVAL & INSTALLATION

See Figures 25 through 27.

1. Remove the clutch pedal retainer from the front of the clutch pedal assembly.

2. Pull the clutch pedal upward in order to disengage the clutch master cylinder pushrod from the clutch pedal.

3. Remove the Under right hand hood Electrical Center (UBEC).

4. Place a shop towel under the clutch master cylinder in order to catch any fluid loss.

5. Disconnect the clutch damper from the clutch master cylinder.

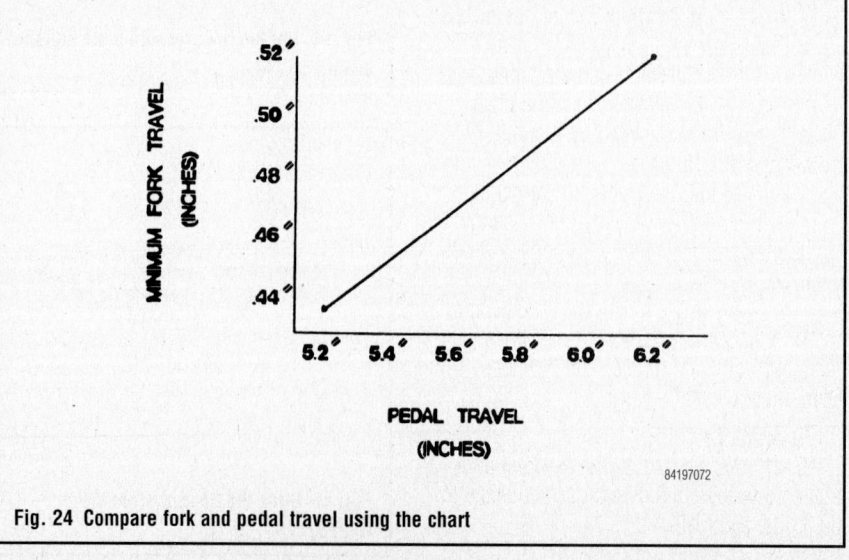

Fig. 24 Compare fork and pedal travel using the chart

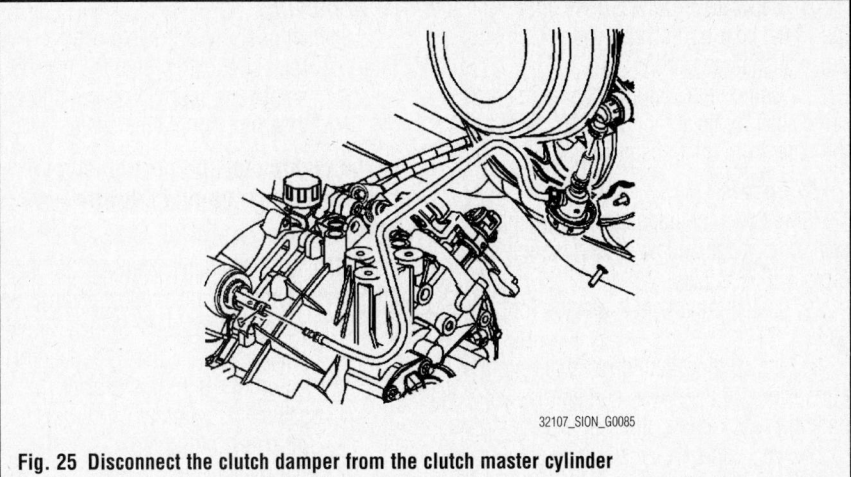

Fig. 25 Disconnect the clutch damper from the clutch master cylinder

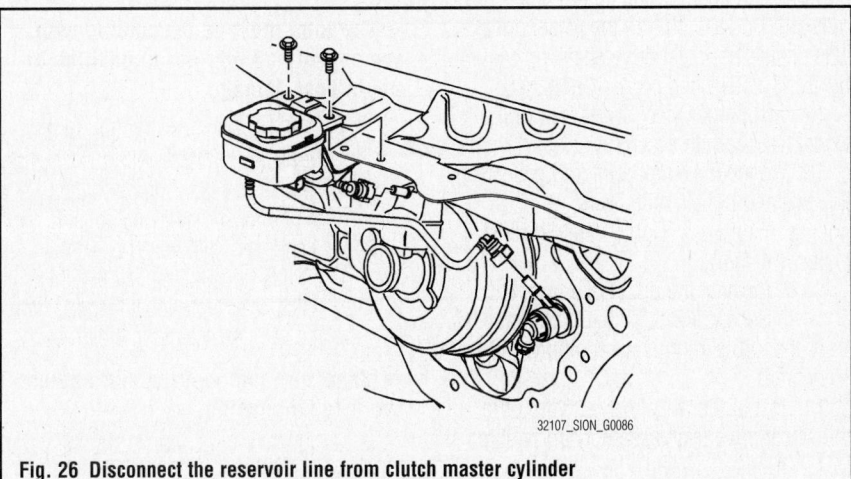

Fig. 26 Disconnect the reservoir line from clutch master cylinder

6. Disconnect the reservoir line from clutch master cylinder.

7. Cap the reservoir and hydraulic lines in order to prevent fluid loss and contamination.

8. Rotate the clutch master cylinder one quarter turn clockwise and remove the cylinder from the vehicle.

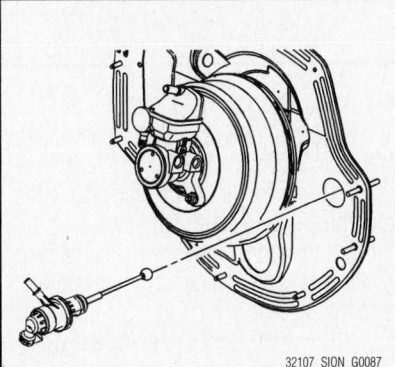

Fig. 27 Rotate the clutch master cylinder one quarter turn clockwise and remove the cylinder from the vehicle

To install:

➡️**While installing, ensure that the clutch master cylinder pushrod is aligned with the clutch pedal.**

9. Install the clutch master cylinder while rotating quarter turn counterclockwise.

10. Uncap the reservoir and hydraulic lines.

11. Connect the clutch damper to the clutch master cylinder.

12. Install the reservoir line in the clutch master cylinder.

13. Remove the shop towel and discard in a suitable container.

14. Install the UBEC.

15. Connect the clutch master cylinder pushrod to the clutch pedal.

16. Install the clutch pedal retainer.

17. Bleed the clutch hydraulic system.

CLUTCH SLAVE CYLINDER

REMOVAL & INSTALLATION

See Figure 28.

Fig. 28 Removal and installation of the slave cylinder

1. Remove the transaxle.

2. Remove the hydraulic line from the slave cylinder.

3. Remove the hydraulic line from the slave cylinder.

To install:

4. Install the slave cylinder. Use LOC-TITE 592® P/N 21485278 thread sealant on the screws.

5. Tighten the slave cylinder fasteners to 89 inch lbs. (10 Nm).

6. Connect the hydraulic line to the slave cylinder.

7. Bleed the slave cylinder. Refer to Clutch Slave Cylinder Bleeding.

8. Install the transaxle.

CLUTCH HYDRAULIC SYSTEM BLEEDING

BLEEDING PROCEDURE

Vacuum Bleeding

This procedure outlines how to bleed the hydraulic clutch with the transaxle in the vehicle. Only **DOT 3** brake fluid should be added to the system.

1. Before servicing the vehicle, refer to the Precautions Section.

2. Bleed the system as follows:

a. Remove the reservoir cap and fill the reservoir with new brake fluid.

b. Install a metal Mityvac® too J 3555 Tool and adapter J43485.

c. Hold J 43485 in position and apply 15–20 hg (51–68 kPa) of vacuum.

d. Remove the adapter and refill the reservoir.

e. Depress the clutch pedal and cycle it for 30 seconds.

f. Lift the pedal up to the stop position and hold for 30 seconds.

g. Repeat steps A through F until all air is removed.

h. Place the transmission in Neutral.

i. Start the engine and pump the clutch pedal until firm.

j. Pump the brake pedal until firm.

k. Add any additional fluid if needed.

Manual Bleeding

This procedure outlines how to bleed the hydraulic clutch with the transaxle in the vehicle. Only **DOT 3** brake fluid should be added to the system.

1. Before servicing the vehicle, refer to the Precautions Section.

2. Remove the reservoir cap and fill the reservoir with new brake fluid.

3. Attach a transparent hose over the clutch bleeder screw nipple and submerge the opposite end of the hose in a container of brake fluid.

4. Depress the clutch pedal quickly to the fully depressed position.

5. Push the clip in order to move the clutch line into the bleed position.

6. Move the clutch line into normal position making sure the clip returns.

7. Lift the clutch pedal to the up position and hold for 5 seconds.

8. Bleed the system until no air bubbles are seen in the hose.

9. Check the clutch pedal for a spongy feel. If the pedal feels soft, repeat the bleeding procedure.

10. Remove the bleeder tools and top off the fluid level if necessary.

FRONT HALFSHAFT

REMOVAL & INSTALLATION

1. Before servicing the vehicle, refer to the precautions section.

2. Remove the wheel assembly.

3. Remove the wheel drive shaft nut by inserting a drift or a flat-bladed tool into the caliper and the rotor to prevent the rotor from turning.

4. Carefully loosen the wheel drive shaft splines from the wheel bearing/hub assembly using a wood block and a hammer. The nut can be partially reinstalled to protect the threads.

➡**Be sure that the wheel speed sensor wiring harness is repositioned away from the ball joint after disconnecting the electrical connector from the sensor.**

5. Disconnect the ball joint from the steering knuckle.

6. Separate the wheel drive shaft from the wheel bearing/hub assembly, then support the shaft assembly.

7. Using slide hammer SA 9173G and drive shaft removal tool J 45341, remove the shaft from the transmission.

To install:

8. Inspect the transaxle output shaft seal for damage and/or contamination and replace if necessary.

9. Install the a Seal Protector Tool SA91112T.

10. Install the wheel drive shaft into the transaxle until the drive shaft splines are past the seal, remove the seal protector tool.

11. Verify that the wheel drive shaft is properly engaged by grasping the inner tri-pod housing and pull the inner housing outward. Do NOT pull on the wheel drive axle shaft. The wheel drive shaft will remain firmly in place when properly engaged.

12. Install the wheel drive shaft to the wheel bearing/hub assembly.

13. Connect the ball joint to the steering knuckle and tighten as follows:

a. First Pass: Tighten the nut to 37 ft. lbs. (50 Nm).

b. Reverse the nut ¾ of a turn.

c. Second Pass: Tighten the nut to 37 ft. lbs. (50 Nm) plus an additional 30 degrees.

14. Install the wheel drive shaft nut to the wheel drive shaft assembly and tighten to 155 ft. lbs. (210 Nm).

15. Install the wheel assembly.

16. Inspect the transaxle fluid level and wheel alignment.

CV-JOINTS OVERIGHT HANDAUL

Inner

1. Before servicing the vehicle, refer to the Precautions Section.

2. Remove or disconnect the following:

- Front wheel
- Halfshaft
- Small boot clamp ring using a side cutter and discard
- Earless clamp and discard
- Large CV-joint boot clamp using a side cutter and discard
- CV-joint boot by sliding it away from the tri-pod joint
- Tri-pod housing from the tri-pod spider
- Inboard spacer ring slide it rearward on the shaft
- Outboard retaining ring
- Tri-pod joint spider assembly
- Inboard spacer ring and CV-joint boot

To install:

3. Install or connect the following:

- Small boot clamp onto the neck of the inboard boot but do not tighten
- Inboard boot onto the shaft

➡**The clamp must be positioned correctly during crimping to ensure a correct seal.**

4. Use boot clamp installer SA9203C to tighten the clamp making sure the end gap on the clamp does not exceed 0.118 inch (3mm)

- Spider assembly past the retaining ring groove until it is seated against the shoulder
- Spider retaining ring
- ½ kit grease into the boot
- ½ kit grease into the tri-pod housing

➡**The joint must be assembled with the convoluted retainer in position to avoid boot damage.**

- Tri-lobal housing bushing making sure it is flush with the housing
- New large seal clamp onto the CV-joint boot and slide the housing over the tri-pod joint spider assembly
- CV-joint boot/clamp, slide it into place, over the trilobal tri-pod bushing with the seal lip in the groove

➡**Make sure the boot lies flat against the trilobal bushing.**

5. Position the CV-joint boot so it measures 4.9 in. (125mm)

6. Using a boot clamp installer SA9161C tighten the large clamp.

7. Install the halfshaft and the front wheel.

Outer

1. Before servicing the vehicle, refer to the Precautions Section.

2. Remove or disconnect the following:

- Axle shaft from the vehicle
- Large CV boot retaining clamp
- Small CV boot retaining clamp
- CV boot from the joint
- Axle shaft retaining ring
- Outer joint from the axle shaft
- CV boot

3. Disassemble the chrome alloy balls from the CV-joint cage as follows:

a. Position a brass drift against the CV-joint cage and tap it with a hammer to tilt the cage.

b. Remove the 1st chrome alloy ball from the cage.

c. Tilt the cage in the opposite direction.

d. Remove the opposite chrome alloy ball.

e. Repeat the procedure until all 6 balls are removed.

4. Disassemble the CV-joint cage and inner race as follows:

a. Pivot the cage and race 90 degrees to the center line of the outer race.

b. Align the cage windows with outer race lands.

c. Remove the cage from the outer race.

d. Rotate the inner race upward and remove it from the cage.

To install:

5. Lubricate the parts with a light coat of grease.

6. Assemble the CV-joint cage and inner race, as follows:

a. Rotate the inner race 90 degrees to the cage centerline.

b. Align the cage windows with inner race lands.

c. Insert the inner race into the cage by rotating the inner race downward.

d. Insert the cage/inner race into the outer race.

7. Assemble the chrome alloy balls into the CV-joint cage, as follows:

a. Position a brass drift against the CV-joint cage and tap it with a hammer to tilt the cage.

b. Insert the 1st chrome alloy ball into the cage.

c. Tilt the cage in the opposite direction.

d. Insert the opposite chrome alloy ball.

e. Repeat the procedure until all 6 balls are inserted.

8. Install ½of the grease provided, into the CV-joint.

9. Install or connect the following:

- Small CV boot retaining ring
- CV boot on the halfshaft
- New retaining ring on the half-shaft
- Large ring clamp on the CV boot
- Outer joint onto the axle shaft
- Retaining ring into the outer race

10. Install the remaining grease into the CV boot.

11. Position the CV boot and the small boot clamp.

12. Crimp the small boot clamp making sure not exceed an end gap of 0.118 inch (3mm).

13. Position and crimp in place the large boot clamp making sure not exceed an end gap of 0.118 inch (3mm)

14. Install the halfshaft in the vehicle.

CV-BOOTS INSPECTION

The CV (Constant Velocity) boots should be checked for damage each time the oil is changed and any other time the vehicle is raised for service. These boots keep water, grime, dirt and other damaging matter from entering the CV-joints. Any of these could cause early CV-joint failure, which can be expensive to repair. Heavy grease thrown around the inside of the front wheel(s) and on the brake caliper can be an indication of a torn boot. Thoroughly check the boots for missing clamps and tears. If the boot is damaged, it should be replaced immediately. Please refer to Section 7 for procedures.

REAR AXLE

REMOVAL & INSTALLATION

See Figure 29.

1. Raise and support the vehicle.
2. Remove the rear wheels.
3. Disconnect the left and right rear brake pipes from the rear brake hoses at the axle.
4. Disconnect the brake hoses from the axle brake hose bracket. Plug the brake pipes and hoses in order to prevent additional brake fluid loss.
5. Disconnect both rear parking brake cables at the rear brake.
6. If applicable, disconnect the ABS harness connectors and disconnect from the axle.
7. Support the rear axle with a hydraulic lift table.
8. Remove the lower shock bolts.
9. Lower the hydraulic lift table and remove the rear coil springs.
10. Disconnect the park brake cables from the cable brackets.
11. Remove the wheel bearing/hub retaining nuts from both sides.
12. Remove the wheel bearing/hubs, with the brakes and backing plate as an assembly.
13. Remove all rear axle bushing bracket bolts.
14. Use the hydraulic lift table to lower the rear axle from the vehicle.
15. Remove the rear axle bushing through bolts and the park brake cable brackets.
16. Remove the rear coil spring lower seat from the axle.

To install:

17. Install the rear coil spring lower insulators to the axle.
18. Install the axle brackets to the axle

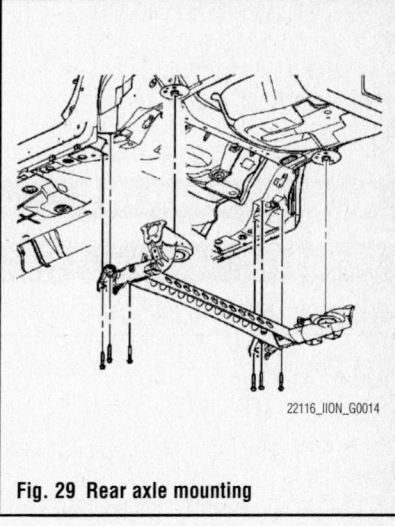

22116_IION_G0014

Fig. 29 Rear axle mounting

bushings, with the alignment slot on the outboard side.

➡**The axle bushing through bolts must be installed with the bolt head facing inboard.**

19. Loosely install the bushing bolts and nuts.
20. Place the axle on the hydraulic lift table and raise the axle into position.
21. Hand tighten the axle bracket to body bolts just enough to hold the brackets flush to the body.

➡**The axle through bolts must be tightened with the axle at the correct trim height and prior to torquing the axle bracket to body bolts.**

22. Using the lift table, raise the axle to the proper trim height specification by measuring the vertical distance between the bottom edge of the upper spring seat and the bottom of the notch in the lower spring seat. Tighten the axle bushing through bolts to 66 ft. lbs. (90 Nm) plus 45 degrees
23. Insert two 12 mm diameter pins through the axle brackets into the underbody.
24. Align the left and right side axle brackets and snug down the bolts.
25. Tighten all the bracket to body bolts to 66 ft. lbs. (90 Nm) plus 45 degrees
26. Install the wheel bearing/hubs, with the brakes and backing plate assemblies.
27. Install the bearing/hub nuts and tighten to 37 ft. lbs. (50 Nm) plus 30 degrees
28. Connect the brake hoses to the rear axle brackets.
29. Connect the brake pipes to the brake hoses at the axle.

30. Tighten the brake pipe fittings to 14 ft. lbs. (19 Nm).
31. Install the rear coil springs.
32. Install the lower shock bolts.

33. Lower and remove the hydraulic lift table.
34. If applicable, connect the ABS sensor harness connector and harness to axle retainer.

35. Connect the park brake cables to the axle brackets and rear brakes.
36. Bleed the brake system.
37. Install the rear wheels.
38. Lower the vehicle.

ENGINE COOLING

ENGINE FAN

REMOVAL & INSTALLATION

2.0L Engine

See Figures 30 through 33.

1. Disconnect the cooling fan electrical connectors.
2. Disconnect the fan relays from the shroud.
3. Raise and support the vehicle.
4. Remove the cooling fan assembly from the radiator by pushing up on the fan shroud to unsnap the retaining features. Position the cooling fan assembly away from the radiator.
5. Remove the air dam push-in retainers.

6. Remove the air dam.
7. Remove the right engine splash shield to radiator mount push-in retainer.
8. Remove the left engine splash shield to radiator mount push-in retainer.
9. Remove the charge air cooler radiator.
10. Remove the lower radiator mount, brackets, and bolts. Support the radiator and condenser.
11. Tilt the radiator and condenser forward in the vehicle.
12. Remove the cooling fan assembly from the vehicle.

To install:

13. Install the cooling fan assembly into the vehicle.
14. Restore the radiator and condenser to the original position.
15. Install the charge air cooler radiator.
16. Verify that the upper radiator mounts are installed in the vehicle.
17. Raise the radiator and condenser into position. Verify that the upper radiator mount pins align with the upper radiator mounts.
18. Install the lower radiator mounts, brackets, and bolts, and tighten the bolts to 18 ft. lbs. (25 Nm).
19. Install the right engine splash shield to radiator mount push-in retainer.
20. Install the left engine splash shield to radiator mount push-in retainer.
21. Install the air dam and the push-in retainers.
22. Align the cooling fan shroud retaining features to the radiator. Pull down on the cooling fan assembly to snap the shroud onto the radiator.
23. Lower the vehicle.
24. Connect the cooling fan electrical connectors.
25. Connect the fan relays to the fan shroud.

2.2L and 2.4L Engines

See Figures 34 through 36.

1. Disconnect the cooling fan electrical connector.

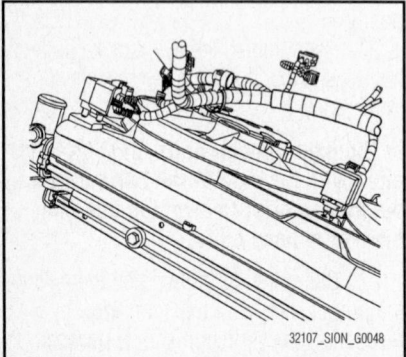

Fig. 30 Disconnect the fan relays from the shroud

32107_SION_G0048

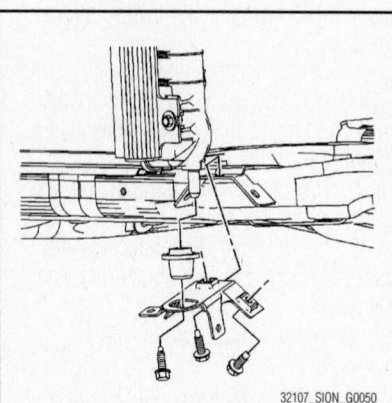

Fig. 32 Remove the lower radiator mount, brackets, and bolts. Support the radiator and condenser

32107_SION_G0050

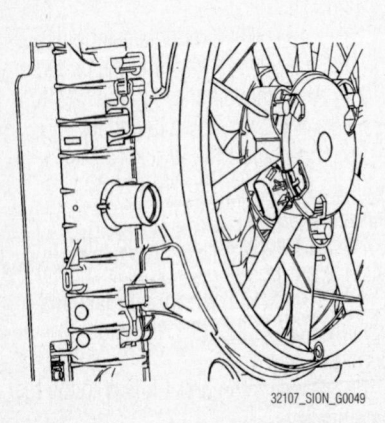

32107_SION_G0049

Fig. 31 Remove the cooling fan assembly from the radiator

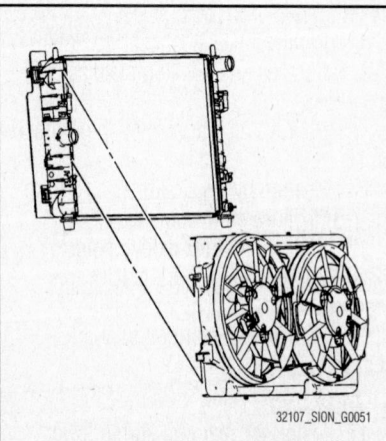

32107_SION_G0051

Fig. 33 Remove the cooling fan assembly from the vehicle

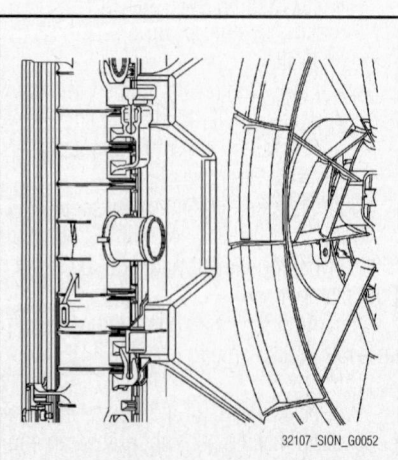

32107_SION_G0052

Fig. 34 Remove the cooling fan assembly from the radiator

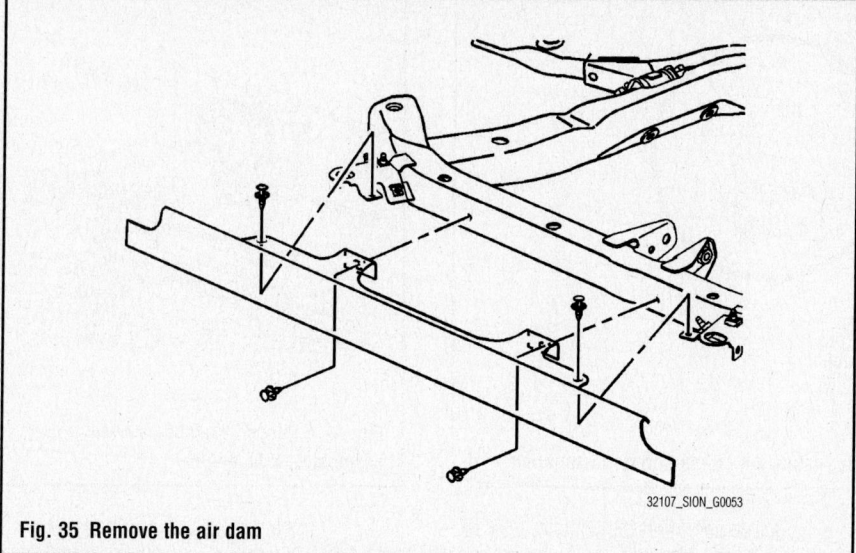

Fig. 35 Remove the air dam

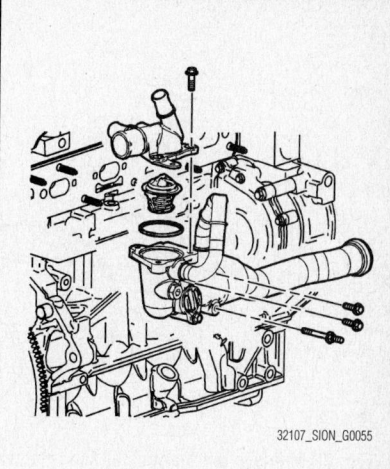

Fig. 37 An exploded-view of the removal and installation of the thermostat

2. Remove the cooling fan wire from the fan shroud.

3. Raise and support the vehicle.

4. Remove the cooling fan assembly from the radiator by pushing up on the fan shroud to unsnap the retaining features. Position the cooling fan assembly away from the radiator.

5. Remove the air dam push-in retainers.

6. Remove the air dam.

7. Remove the right engine splash shield to radiator mount push-in retainer.

8. Remove the left engine splash shield to radiator mount push-in retainer.

9. Remove the lower radiator mount, brackets, and bolts. Support the radiator and condenser.

10. Tilt the radiator and condenser forward in the vehicle. Remove the cooling fan assembly from the vehicle.

To install:

11. Tilt the radiator and condenser forward in the vehicle. Install the cooling fan assembly into the vehicle.

12. Verify that the upper radiator mounts are installed in the vehicle.

13. Raise the radiator and condenser into position. Verify that the upper radiator mount pins align with the upper radiator mounts.

14. Install the lower radiator mounts, brackets, and bolts, and tighten the bolts to 18 ft. lbs. (25 Nm).

15. Install the right engine splash shield to radiator mount push-in retainer.

16. Install the left engine splash shield to radiator mount push-in retainer.

17. Install the air dam and the push-in retainers.

18. Align the cooling fan shroud retaining features to the radiator. Pull down on the cooling fan assembly to snap the shroud onto the radiator.

19. Lower the vehicle.

20. Connect the cooling fan electrical connector.

21. Install the cooling fan wire to the fan shroud.

THERMOSTAT

REMOVAL & INSTALLATION

2.0L Engine

See Figure 37.

1. Drain the cooling system.

2. Remove the hoses from the thermostat housing cap.

3. Remove the thermostat housing cap and bolts.

4. Remove the thermostat.

To install:

5. Install the thermostat.

6. Install the thermostat housing cap bolts and cap, and tighten the bolt to 18 inch lbs. (10 Nm).

7. Install the hoses to the thermostat housing cap.

8. Fill the cooling system

2.2L Engine

See Figures 38 and 39.

1. Drain the cooling system.

2. Remove the bolts that secure the thermostat housing to the water pump feed pipe.

3. Remove the feed pipe.

4. Remove the thermostat and retaining sleeve, noting the orientation for installation.

To install:

5. Install the thermostat and retaining sleeve with the dimple placed into the housing slot.

➥**Lubricate the O-ring with soapy water or coolant before installing the O-ring in the water pump.**

6. Install the feed pipe that connects the thermostat housing to the water pump.

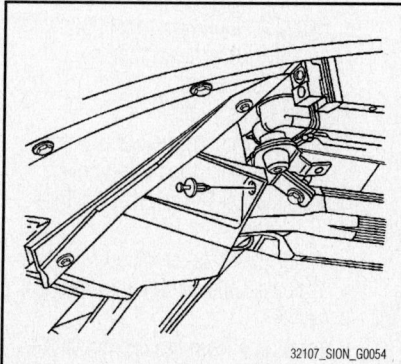

Fig. 36 Remove the right engine splash shield to radiator mount push-in retainer

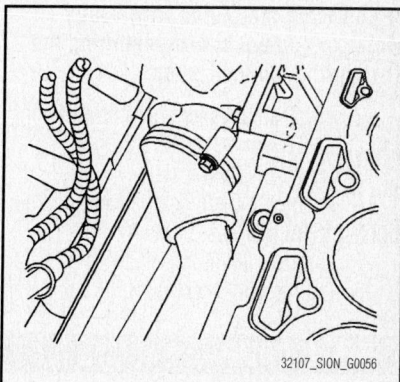

Fig. 38 Remove the bolts that secure the thermostat housing to the water pump feed pipe

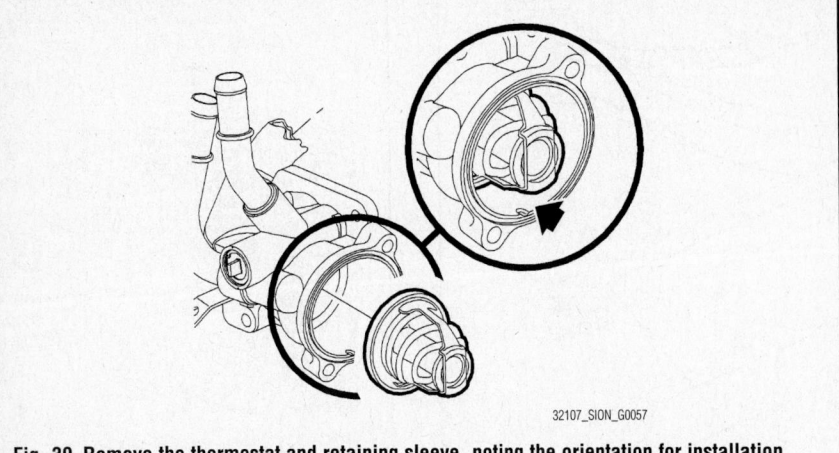

Fig. 39 Remove the thermostat and retaining sleeve, noting the orientation for installation

32107_SION_G0057

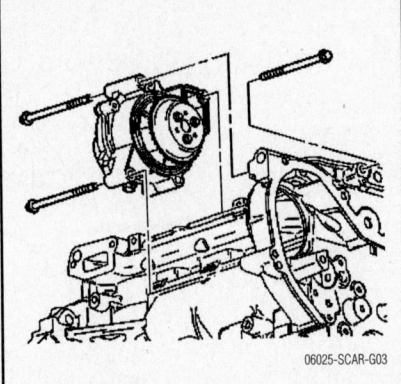

06025-SCAR-G03

Fig. 41 Exploded view of the water pump assembly—2.0L engine

7. Install the bolt that secures the water pump feed pipe, and tighten the bolt to 18 inch lbs. (10 Nm).

8. Fill the cooling system.

2.4L Engine

1. Drain the cooling system.
2. Remove the intake manifold cover
3. Reposition the radiator outlet hose clamp (1) at the thermostat cover.
4. Remove the radiator outlet hose from the thermostat cover
5. Reposition the radiator surge tank outlet hose clamp (1) at the thermostat cover.
6. Remove the radiator surge tank outlet hose from the thermostat cover
7. Reposition the radiator outlet hose clamp (1) at the thermostat cover.
8. Remove the radiator outlet hose from the thermostat cover
9. Remove the thermostat cover bolts and cover.
10. Remove the thermostat.
11. Remove and discard the thermostat cover O-ring seal.

To install:

➡**Lubricate the O-ring with soapy water or coolant before installing the O-ring in the water pump.**

12. Install a NEW thermostat cover O-ring seal.
13. Install the thermostat.
14. Install the thermostat cover bolts and tighten to 89 inch lbs. (10 Nm).
15. Connect all the hoses.
16. Fill the cooling system.

WATER PUMP

REMOVAL & INSTALLATION

2.0L Engine

See Figures 40 and 41.

1. Before servicing the vehicle, refer to the precautions section.
2. Drain the cooling system.
3. Remove the thermostat housing cap and bolts.
4. Remove the thermostat.
5. Remove the Oxygen (O2s) sensor clip.
6. Remove the thermostat housing and water feed pipe retaining bolts.

➡**Twist the water feed pipe while pulling to remove it from the water pump cover.**

7. Remove the thermostat housing and water feed pipe from the water pump cover.
8. Remove the water pump retaining bolts. Be sure to remove the bolt that goes through the front of the engine block.
9. Remove the water pump assembly.

To install:

10. Install the water pump assembly.
11. Install the water pump bolts and finger tighten the bolts.

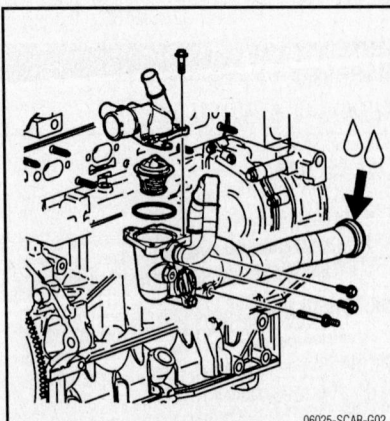

06025-SCAR-G02

Fig. 40 Exploded view of the thermostat housing and water feed pipe assembly—2.0L engine

12. Tighten the water pump bolts to 18 ft. lbs. (25 Nm).
13. Apply sealant P/N 12378521 to the water pump drain plug.
14. Install the water pump drain plug, if necessary and tighten to 15 ft. lbs. (20 Nm).
15. Install the water feed tube.
16. Lubricate the water feed tube O-ring with anti-freeze.
17. Install the water feed tube by twisting and pushing toward the water pump. Take care not to tear or damage the O-ring.
18. Install the thermostat housing to block bolts.
19. Install the thermostat.
20. Install the thermostat housing cap and bolts.
21. Fill the cooling system.
22. Start the vehicle and check for leaks, repair if necessary.

2.2L Engine

1. Before servicing the vehicle, refer to the precautions section.
2. Drain the cooling system.
3. Remove or disconnect the following:
   - Negative battery cable
   - Exhaust manifold, if equipped with an automatic transmission
   - Right front wheel
   - Front fender liner
   - Access plate on the water pump sprocket from the timing cover
4. Install a Water Pump Holding Tool J43651.
   - Water pump-to-block bolt
   - Water pump-to-engine front cover bolts
   - Feed pipe from the thermostat to the water pump
   - Water pump-to-block bolts
   - Water pump

To install:

5. Install or connect the following:
- Water pump
- Water pump-to-block bolts and tighten to 15 ft. lbs. (20 Nm)
- Feed pipe from the thermostat to the water pump
- Water pump-to-engine front cover bolts and tighten to 15 ft. lbs. (20 Nm)
- Water pump-to-block bolt and tighten to 15 ft. lbs. (20 Nm)
- Water pump sprocket and torque the bolts to 89 inch lbs. (10 Nm)
- Water pump sprocket access plate
- Front fender liner
- Right front wheel
- Exhaust manifold, if equipped with an automatic transmission
- Negative battery cable

6. Fill the cooling system.

7. Start the vehicle and check for leaks, repair if necessary.

2.4L Engine

See Figure 42.

1. Before servicing the vehicle, refer to the precautions section.

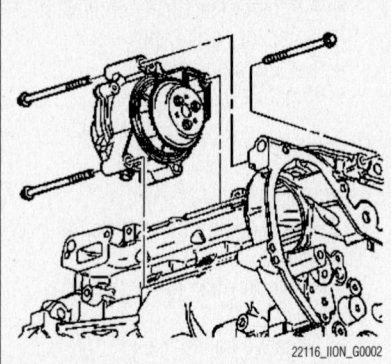

Fig. 42 Water pump mounting—2.4L engine shown

2. Drain the cooling system.

3. Remove the engine coolant temperature sensor.

4. Remove the thermostat and water feed pipe retaining bolts.

➡**Twist the water feed pipe while pulling to remove it from the water pump cover.**

5. Remove the thermostat at housing and water feed pipe from the water pump cover.

6. Remove the water pump retaining bolts. Be sure to remove the bolt that goes through the front of the engine block.

7. Remove the water pump assembly

To install:

8. Install the water pump assembly.

9. Install the water pump bolts and finger tighten the bolts.

10. Tighten the water pump bolts to 18 ft. lbs. (25 Nm).

11. Apply sealant P/N 12378521 to the water pump drain plug.

12. Install the water pump drain plug, if necessary and tighten to 15 ft. lbs. (20 Nm).

13. Install the water feed tube.

14. Lubricate the water feed tube O-ring with anti-freeze.

15. Install the water feed tube by twisting and pushing toward the water pump. Take care not to tear or damage the O-ring.

16. Install the thermostat housing to block bolts.

17. Install the thermostat.

18. Install the thermostat housing cap and bolts.

19. Fill the cooling system.

20. Start the vehicle and check for leaks, repair if necessary.

ENGINE ELECTRICAL

ALTERNATOR

REMOVAL & INSTALLATION

See Figure 43.

1. Before servicing the vehicle, refer to the precautions section.

2. Disconnect the negative battery cable.

3. Remove the drive belt.

CHARGING SYSTEM

4. Remove the supercharger.

5. Disconnect the alternator connectors.

6. Remove the alternator bolts.

7. Remove the alternator from the vehicle.

To install:

8. Before servicing the vehicle, refer to the precautions section.

9. Install the alternator on the engine.

10. Install the alternator bolts. Tighten to 18 ft. lbs. (25 Nm).

11. Connect the positive battery harness to the alternator battery terminal. Tighten the nut to 15 ft. lbs. (25 Nm).

12. Connect the alternator harness connectors.

13. Install the supercharger.

14. Install the drive belt.

15. Connect the negative battery cable.

2.2L Engine

See Figure 44.

1. Before servicing the vehicle, refer to the Precautions Section.

2. Remove or disconnect the following:
- Negative battery cable
- Throttle body air duct
- Accessory drive belt
- Alternator electrical connectors

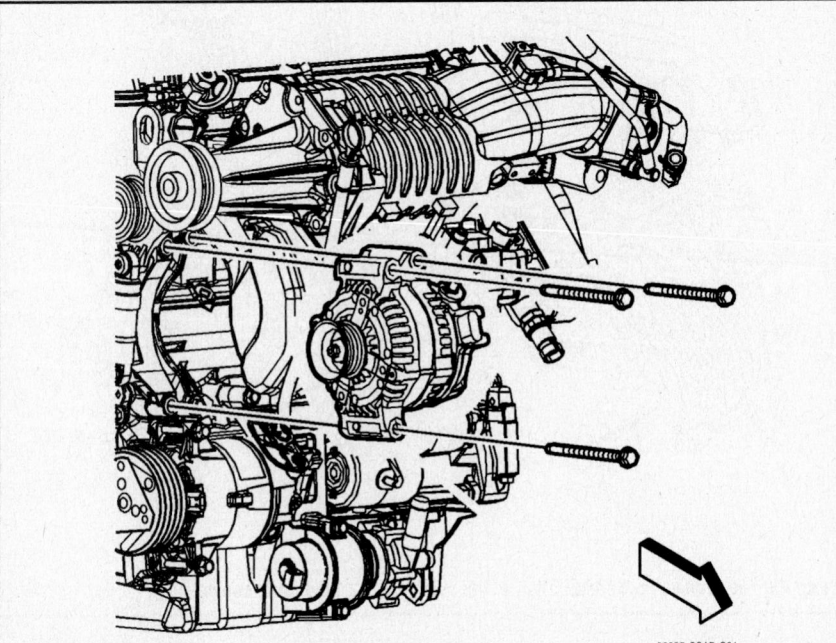

Fig. 43 Exploded view of the alternator mounting—2.0L engine

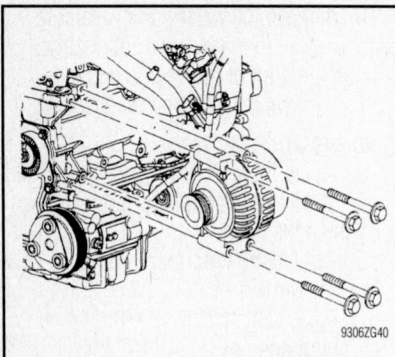

Fig. 44 Exploded view of the alternator–2.2L engine

- Alternator bolts
- Alternator

To install:

3. Install or connect the following:
   - Alternator and torque the bolts to 15 ft. lbs. (20 Nm)

- Alternator electrical connectors
- Accessory drive belt
- Throttle body air duct
- Negative battery cable

2.4L Engine
See Figure 45.

1. Before servicing the vehicle, refer to the Precautions Section.
2. Remove or disconnect the following:
   - Negative battery cable
   - Accessory drive belt
   - Air duct
   - Alternator electrical connectors
   - Alternator bolts
   - Alternator

To install:

3. Install or connect the following:
   - Alternator and torque the bolts to 16 ft. lbs. (22 Nm)

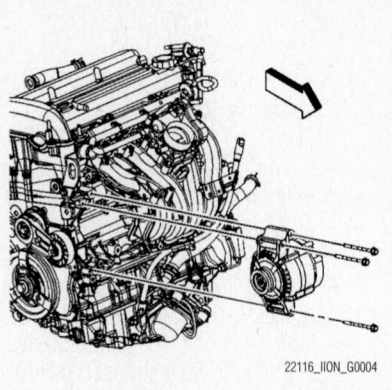

Fig. 45 Exploded view of the alternator mounting–2.4L engine

- Alternator electrical connectors
- Accessory drive belt
- Throttle body air duct
- Negative battery cable

ENGINE ELECTRICAL

IGNITION SYSTEM

FIRING ORDER

See Figure 47.

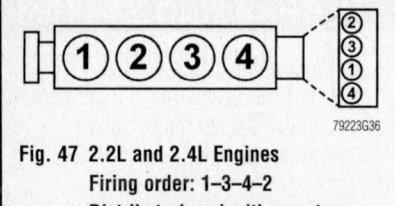

**Fig. 47 2.2L and 2.4L Engines
Firing order: 1–3–4–2
Distributorless ignition system**

IGNITION COIL

REMOVAL & INSTALLATION

2.0L Engine
See Figure 48.

1. Disconnect the ignition coil connectors from the ignition coils.
2. Remove the retaining bolts from the ignition coils.
3. Remove the ignition coils from the engine.

To install:

➡**Make sure that the ignition coil seals are properly seated to the valve cover.**

4. Install the ignition coil.
5. Install the ignition coil retaining bolts, and tighten the ignition coil retaining bolts to 89 inch lbs. (10 Nm).
6. Replace the ignition coil connectors.

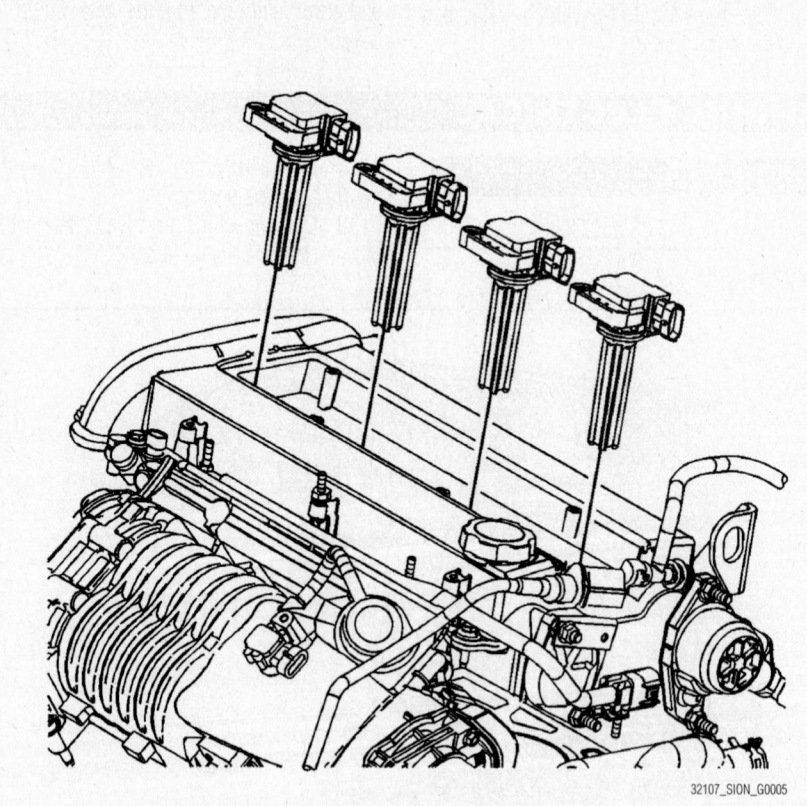

Fig. 48 The removal and installation of the coil pack—2.0L engine shown

2.4L Engine
See Figure 49.

1. Remove the intake manifold cover.
2. Disconnect the ignition coil connectors from the ignition coils.

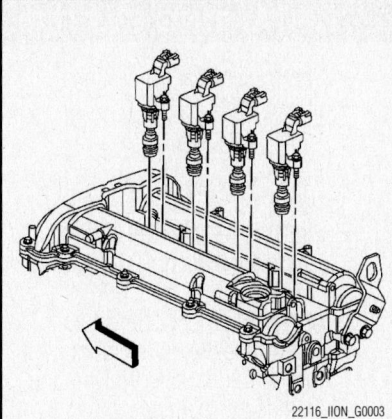

Fig. 49 The removal and installation of the coil pack—2.4L engine shown

3. Remove the retaining bolts from the ignition coils.

4. Remove the ignition coils from the engine.

To install:

➡**Make sure that the ignition coil seals are properly seated to the valve cover.**

5. Install the ignition coil.

6. Install the ignition coil retaining bolts, and tighten the ignition coil retaining bolts to 89 inch lbs. (10 Nm).

7. Replace the ignition coil connectors.

8. Install the intake manifold cover.

IGNITION TIMING

ADJUSTMENT

The ignition timing is controlled by the Powertrain Control Module (PCM). No adjustment is necessary or possible.

SPARK PLUGS

REMOVAL & INSTALLATION

1. Disconnect the negative battery cable and, if the vehicle has been run recently, allow the engine to thoroughly cool.

2. Carefully twist the spark plug wire boot to loosen it, then pull upward and remove the boot from the plug. Be sure to pull on the boot and not on the wire, otherwise the connector located inside the boot may become separated.

3. Using compressed air, blow any water or debris from the spark plug well to assure that no harmful contaminants are allowed to enter the combustion chamber when the spark plug is removed. If compressed air is not available, use a rag or a brush to clean the area.

➡**Remove the spark plugs when the engine is cold, if possible, to prevent damage to the threads. If removal of the plugs is difficult, apply a few drops of penetrating oil or silicone spray to the area around the base of the plug, and allow it a few minutes to work.**

4. Using a spark plug socket that is equipped with a rubber insert to properly hold the plug, turn the spark plug counterclockwise to loosen and remove the spark plug from the bore.

❋❋ WARNING

Be sure not to use a flexible extension on the socket. Use of a flexible extension may allow a shear force to be applied to the plug. A shear force could break the plug off in the cylinder head, leading to costly and frustrating repairs.

To install:

5. Inspect the spark plug boot for tears or damage. If a damaged boot is found, the spark plug wire must be replaced.

6. Using a wire feeler gauge, check and adjust the spark plug gap. When using a gauge, the proper size should pass between the electrodes with a slight drag. The next larger size should not be able to pass while the next smaller size should pass freely.

7. Carefully thread the plug into the bore by hand. If resistance is felt before the plug is almost completely threaded, back the plug out and begin threading again. In small, hard to reach areas, an old spark plug wire and boot could be used as a threading tool. The boot will hold the plug while you twist the end of the wire and the wire is supple enough to twist before it would allow the plug to crossthread.

❋❋ WARNING

Do not use the spark plug socket to thread the plugs. Always carefully thread the plug by hand or using an old plug wire to prevent the possibility of crossthreading and damaging the cylinder head bore.

8. Carefully tighten the spark plug. If the plug you are installing is equipped with a crush washer, seat the plug, then tighten about ¼ turn to crush the washer. If you are installing a tapered seat plug, tighten the plug to specifications provided by the vehicle or plug manufacturer.

9. Apply a small amount of silicone dielectric compound to the end of the spark plug lead or inside the spark plug boot to prevent sticking, then install the boot to the spark plug and push until it clicks into place. The click may be felt or heard, then gently pull back on the boot to assure proper contact.

ENGINE ELECTRICAL

STARTER

REMOVAL & INSTALLATION

2.0L Engine

1. Before servicing the vehicle, refer to the precautions section.
2. Disconnect the negative battery cable.
3. Remove the intercooler pump outer bracket.
4. Disconnect the electrical connectors from the starter.
5. Remove the starter bolts.
6. Remove the starter.

To install:

7. Install the starter.
8. Install the starter bolts and tighten to 37 ft. lbs. (50 Nm).

9. Connect the electrical connectors to the starter.
10. Install the intercooler pump outer bracket and tighten to 15 ft. lbs. (20 Nm).
11. Connect the negative battery cable

2.2L and 2.4L Engines

1. Before servicing the vehicle, refer to the precautions section.
2. Remove or disconnect the following:
   • Negative battery cable

➡ Spray the starter solenoid electrical connectors with penetrating oil before removal.

STARTING SYSTEM

   • Starter electrical connections
   • Starter bolts
   • Starter assembly

To install:

3. Install or connect the following:
   • Starter to the flywheel housing and torque the bolts to 30 ft. lbs. (40 Nm)
   • Starter electrical connectors and torque the solenoid ignition wire to 44 inch lbs. (5 Nm) and the positive battery cable to 13 ft. lbs. (17 Nm) and the S terminal connector to 27 inch lbs. (3 Nm).
   • Negative battery cable

ENGINE MECHANICAL

➡ Disconnecting the negative battery cable may interfere with the functions of the on board computer systems and may require the computer to undergo a relearning process, once the negative battery cable is reconnected.

ACCESSORY DRIVE BELTS

ACCESSORY BELT ROUTING

See Figures 50 and 51.

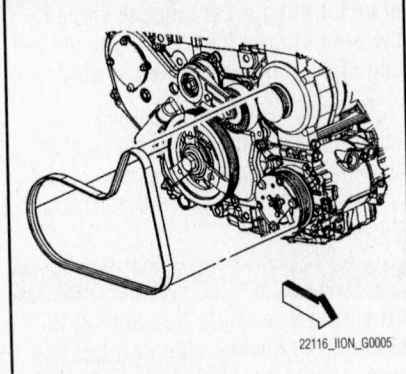

Fig. 51 Serpentine drive belt routing—2.4L Saturn engines

INSPECTION

See Figures 52 through 56.

Inspect the drive belt for signs of glazing or cracking. A glazed belt will be perfectly smooth from slippage, while a good belt will have a slight texture of fabric visible. Cracks will usually start at the inner edge of the belt and run outward. All worn or damaged drive belts should be replaced immediately.

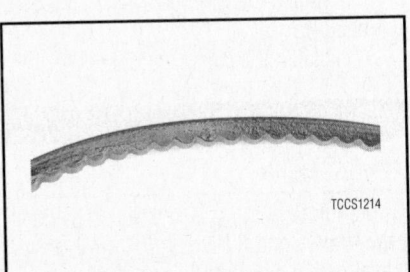

Fig. 53 An example of a healthy drive belt

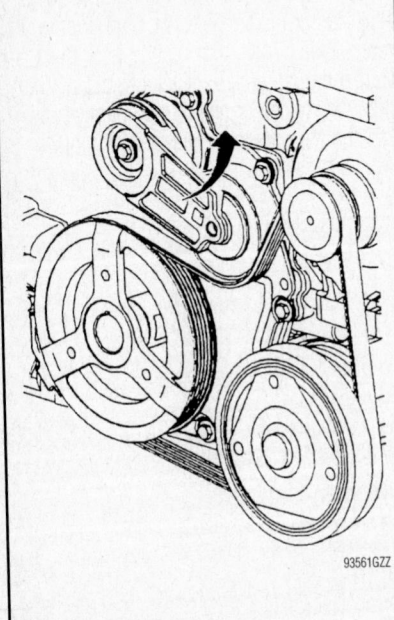

Fig. 50 Serpentine drive belt routing—2.2L Saturn engines

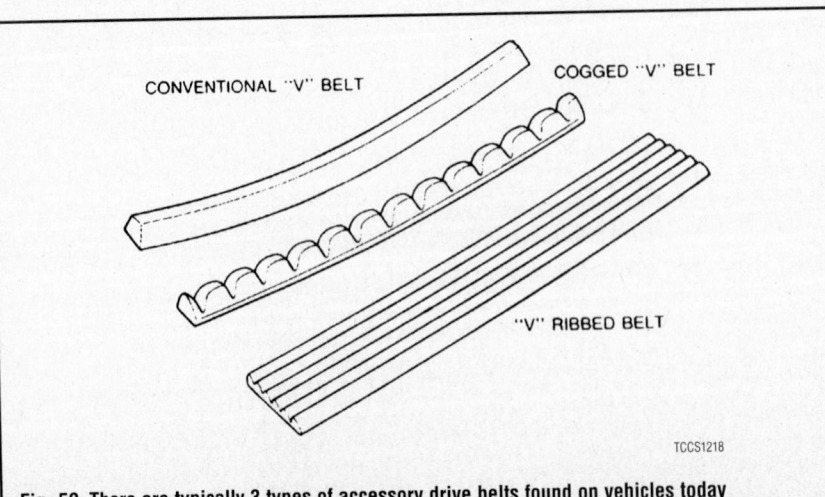

Fig. 52 There are typically 3 types of accessory drive belts found on vehicles today

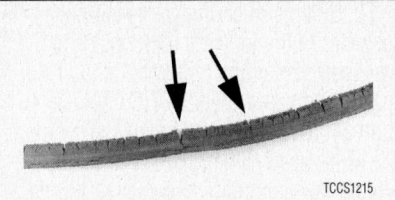

Fig. 54 Deep cracks in this belt will cause flex, building up heat that will eventually lead to belt failure

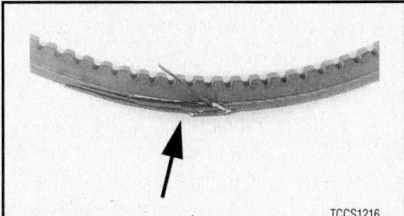

Fig. 55 The cover of this belt is worn, exposing the critical reinforcing cords to excessive wear

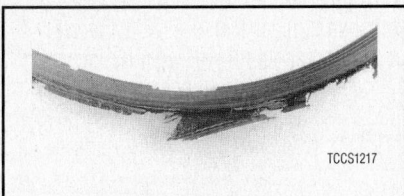

Fig. 56 Installing too wide a belt can result in serious belt wear and/or breakage

ADJUSTMENT

Belt Tension

See Figures 57 and 58.

The belt is automatically adjusted using a spring loaded tensioner. If belt slippage is suspected or unusual belt noises occurs, the following procedure should be used to determine if the tensioner or belt is at fault.

1. Start the engine and allow it to warm up to normal operating temperature with all accessories (such as the A/C) turned **ON**; this should take approximately 10 minutes. If the vehicle is equipped with power steering, turn the steering wheel to the left and right several times during warm-up to make sure a proper load is placed on the belt.

2. Turn the engine and accessories **OFF**.

3. Using a 14mm or ⁹⁄₁₆in. wrench, depress the tensioner arm until the belt becomes loosened, then slowly allow the tensioner to return to position and apply tension to the belt. Do not allow the tensioner to snap against the belt.

4. Inspect the markings located on the tensioner arm. If the marks on the arm fall outside the operating range, the drive belt must be replaced.

➡**Inspection of the belt using a tension gauge must be performed with the upper engine mount removed.**

5. Using tool SA9181-NE or an equivalent calibrated belt tension gauge, measure and note the tension readings at the 2 points located centrally between 2 belt pulleys as shown in the illustration. The dotted lines represent other possible paths which your belt may follow, depending on the engine and accessories with which your vehicle is equipped.

6. Repeat the measurements from the previous step 2 more times, then calculate the average result for each test location. The readings should be 50–65 lbs. (22.7–29.2 kg) for new belts or a minimum of 45 lbs. (20.4 kg) for used belts. If the readings are out of this range or do not meet the minimum and the drive belt passed the test in Step 4, the drive belt tensioner must be replaced.

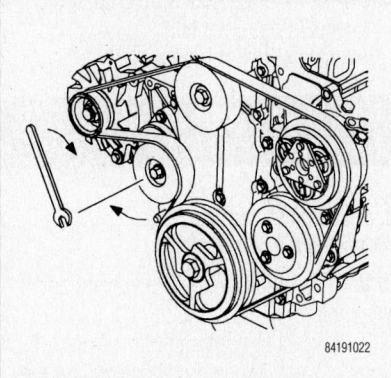

Fig. 57 Use a 14mm or ⁹⁄₁₆in. wrench to depress the tensioner arm until the belt becomes loose

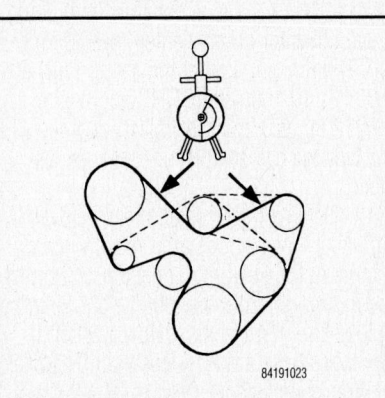

Fig. 58 Read the belt tension at 2 points centrally located between the indicated pulleys

Belt Alignment

See Figure 59.

1. Measure the distance from the front machined surface of the cylinder block to the inboard edge of the belt at the location as shown.

2. The distance should be 1.102–1.220 in. (28–31mm).

3. If the distance does not fall within the specification, check the following:
- Check that the belt is properly located within the pulley grooves.
- Check the drive belt for wear at the edges and, if necessary, replace a worn belt.
- Make sure the belt pulleys are not bent or damaged.
- Make sure the accessory assemblies have proper shaft and bearing end-play.
- Check the pulley hubs for proper installation on their shafts.

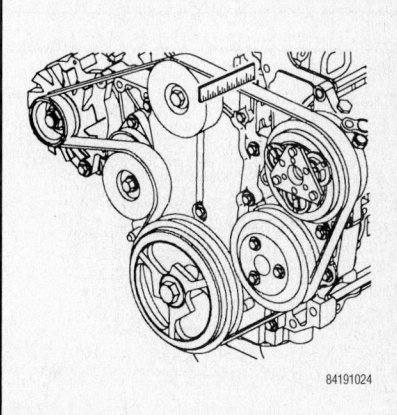

Fig. 59 Measuring serpentine drive belt alignment

REMOVAL & INSTALLATION

2.0L Engine

See Figures 60 and 61.

➡**The drive belt tensioner is a hydraulic tensioner with high initial torque. Release slowly to ensure proper operation.**

➡**Depending on the tolerances of the open end portion of different manufactures wrenches, ensure that care is taken so the wrench does not slip off of the lug.**

1. Install a tight fitting 15 mm open end wrench to the drive belt tensioner lug on the rear of the tensioner.

2. Very slowly push down and towards the back of the vehicle in order to slowly compress the drive belt tensioner.

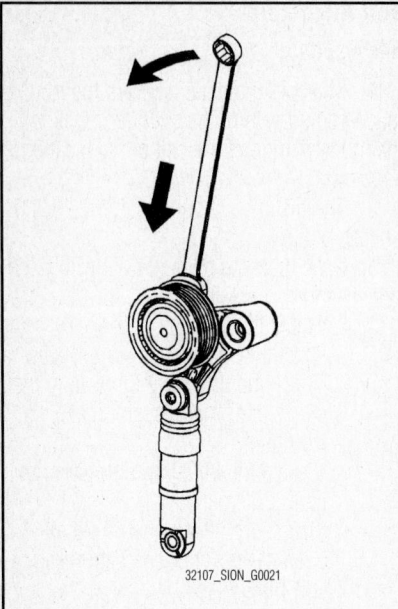

Fig. 60 Install a tight fitting 15 mm open end wrench to the drive belt tensioner lug on the rear of the tensioner.

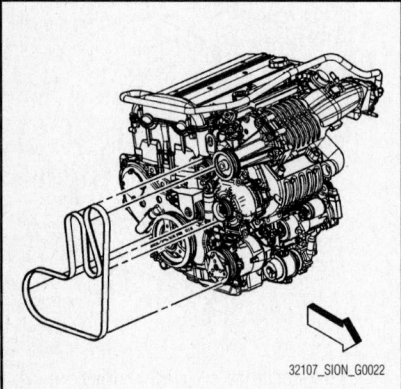

Fig. 61 Remove the drive belt from over the drive belt tensioner.

3. Remove the drive belt from over the drive belt tensioner.

4. Very slowly, allow the drive belt tensioner to return to the extended position.

5. Remove the drive belt from around the supercharger and alternator pulleys.

6. Remove the right front fender liner.

7. Remove the drive belt from under the idler pulley and around the air conditioning (A/C) compressor and crankshaft balancer.

8. From through the wheel house opening, remove the drive belt.

To install:

9. From through the wheel house opening, install the drive belt.

10. Route the drive belt around the A/C compressor and crankshaft balancer and under the idler pulley.

11. Install the right front fender liner.

12. Route the drive belt around the supercharger and alternator pulleys.

13. Ensure that the drive belt is still properly seated in the pulley grooves.

14. Very slowly push down and towards the back of the vehicle in order to slowly compress the drive belt tensioner.

15. Install the drive belt over the drive belt tensioner.

16. Very slowly, allow the drive belt tensioner to return to the extended position until tension is applied to the drive belt.

17. Remove the 15 mm open end wrench from the drive belt tensioner lug on the rear of the tensioner.

2.2L and 2.4L Engines

1. Remove the front fender liner.

2. Use the special tool J44811 in order to rotate the drive belt tensioner counterclockwise to release the spring tension.

3. Remove the drive belt.

To install:

4. Use the special tool J44811 in order to rotate the drive belt tensioner counterclockwise to release the spring tension.

5. Install the drive belt.

6. Install the front fender liner.

CAMSHAFT AND VALVE LIFTERS

INSPECTION

See Figures 62 through 65.

1. Clean the camshaft in solvent and allow it to dry.

2. Inspect the camshaft for obvious signs of wear: scores, nicks or pits on the journals or lobes. Light scuffs or nicks can be removed with an oil stone.

3. Position the camshaft in V-blocks with the front and rear journals riding on the blocks. Check if the camshaft is bent using a dial indicator on the center bearing journal. The run-out limit at the center journal is 0.004 in. (0.1mm) for DOHC engines or 0.0028 in. (0.07mm) for SOHC engines. Replace the camshaft if run-out is excessive.

4. Using a micrometer, measure the camshaft lobes across their maximum and minimum lobe height dimensions. Subtract the lobe width from the lobe height to arrive at lobe rise. Replace a SOHC camshaft if any lobes have a rise of less than 0.252 in. (6.4mm). Replace a DOHC camshaft if any intake rise is less than 0.351 in. (8.91mm), or any exhaust rise is less than 0.339 in. (8.61mm).

5. Using a micrometer, measure the diameter of the journals and replace any camshaft containing a journal that is less than the minimum. For SOHC engines, journal diameter should be greater than 1.747 in. (44.375mm). DOHC engines should have a minimum camshaft journal diameter of 1.139 in. (28.925mm).

6. Measure the diameter of the camshaft bearings. For the DOHC engine, temporarily install the bearing caps to the cylinder head in order to take the measurement. Bore diameter must be less than 1.753 in. (44.513mm) for SOHC engines or 1.144 in. (29.05mm) for DOHC engines, or the cylinder head must be replaced.

7. Subtract the journal diameter measurements from their respective bore diameter measurements to calculate oil clearance. Replace the camshaft and/or cylinder head if clearance is more than 0.0054 in. (0.138mm) for SOHC engines or 0.005 in. (0.125mm) for DOHC engines.

8. Position a precision straightedge across the bottom of the cylinder head camshaft contact surfaces. Use a feeler gauge to inspect for warpage; replace a cylinder head with warpage of more than 0.0025 in. (0.064mm) for SOHC engines or 0.003 in. (0.075mm) for DOHC engines.

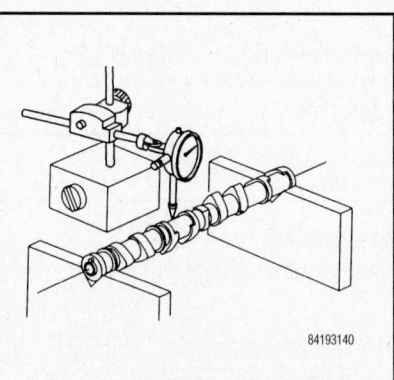

Fig. 62 Use a dial indicator to measure camshaft run-out at the center journal

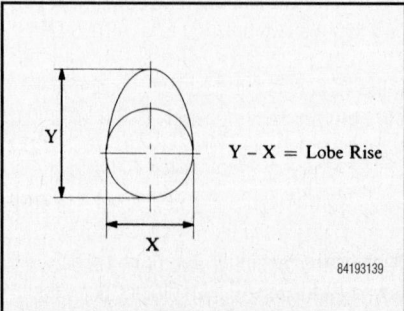

$Y - X = \text{Lobe Rise}$

Fig. 63 Subtract the lobe width from the height to determine lobe rise

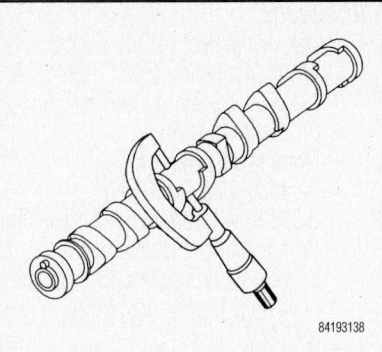

Fig. 64 Measure camshaft journal diameter using a micrometer

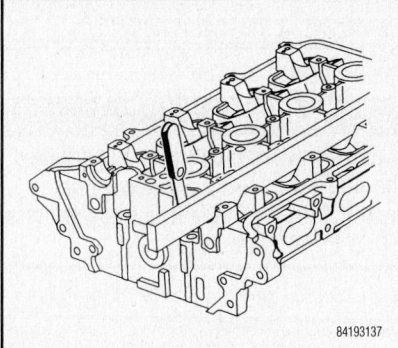

Fig. 65 Measuring camshaft contact surface warpage—DOHC engine shown

REMOVAL & INSTALLATION

2.0L Engine

1. Before servicing the vehicle, refer to the precautions section.

2. Disconnect the negative battery cable.

3. Remove the ignition coils.

4. Remove the ground strap and stud.

5. Disconnect the Positive Crankcase Ventilation (PCV) hose from the cam cover.

6. Disconnect the fuel feed pipe from the fuel rail.

7. Remove the camshaft cover bolts.

8. Remove the camshaft cover.

9. Remove the upper timing chain guide.

10. Install camshaft sprocket holding tool J 43655.

11. Remove both the intake and exhaust camshaft sprocket bolts and discard.

12. Slide the camshaft sprockets forward.

13. Mark the caps to ensure they are installed in the original position.

➡**Remove each bolt on each cap one turn at a time until there is no spring tension on the camshaft.**

14. Remove the caps.

15. Remove the camshaft.

16. Remove the camshaft roller followers.

17. Remove the hydraulic lash adjusters.

To install:

18. Lubricate the valve tips.

19. Install the hydraulic lash adjusters.

20. Install the camshaft roller followers.

21. Ensure that the alignment notches are aligned with the camshaft sprocket.

22. Install the intake camshaft.

23. Install the camshaft caps.

24. Tighten the caps in increments of 3 turns until they are seated, then tighten to 89 inch lbs. (10 Nm).

25. Apply 0.138 inch (3.55mm) of Permatex Anaerobic Gasket maker® 51813 to the rear camshaft bearing cap. Install the cap and tighten the bolts to 18 ft. lbs. (25 Nm).

26. Install camshaft sprockets onto the camshafts.

27. Hand tighten NEW camshaft sprocket bolts.

28. Remove camshaft sprocket holding tool J43655

29. Tighten the camshaft sprocket bolts and tighten to 63 ft. lbs. (85 Nm) plus an additional 30 degrees

30. Install the upper timing chain guide and tighten to 89 inch lbs. (10 Nm).

31. Install the camshaft cover and bolts and tighten to 89 inch lbs. (10 Nm).

32. Install the ground strap to the camshaft cover and tighten to 89 inch lbs. (10 Nm).

33. Install the ignition coils .

34. Connect the fuel feed pipe to the fuel rail.

35. Install the fuel pipe bracket and tighten to 89 inch lbs. (10 Nm).

36. Connect the PCV hose to the cam cover

37. Connect the negative battery cable.

2.2L and 2.4L Engines

See Figures 66 through 69.

1. Before servicing the vehicle, refer to the precautions section.

2. Remove or disconnect the following:
- Negative battery cable
- Air cleaner assembly
- Accelerator cable from the throttle body and bracket
- Accelerator bracket bolts and the bracket
- Positive Crankcase Ventilation (PCV) hose
- Fuel line bracket
- Ignition Coil Module (ICM) connector
- ICM screws and the ICM
- Ignition coil housing bolts and the housing
- Ground strap stud from the camshaft cover
- Ground strap
- Camshaft cover bolts
- Camshaft cover
- Upper timing chain guide

3. Install camshaft sprocket holding tool J43655 as illustrated.
- Intake and exhaust camshaft sprocket bolts and discard the bolts

4. Slide the sprockets forward and mark the camshaft bearing caps to ensure they are installed in their correct positions.

5. Remove each bearing cap bolt one turn at a time until there is no tension.

6. Remove the bearing cap and the camshaft
- Roller followers
- Lash adjusters

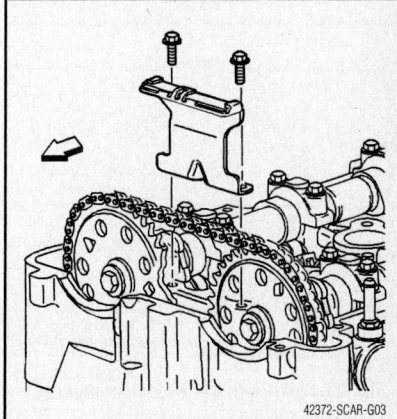

Fig. 66 Remove the upper timing chain guide—ION

Fig. 67 Install camshaft sprocket holding tool J43655–ION

To install:

7. Lubricate the valve tips.
8. Install or connect the following:
   - Lash adjusters
   - Roller followers
9. Make sure the alignment notches are aligned with the camshaft sprocket as illustrated.
   - Camshaft
   - Bearing caps except the rear camshaft cap
10. Tighten the caps in increments of 3 turns until they are seated, then tighten to 89 inch lbs. (10 Nm).
11. Apply 0.197 inch (5mm) of Permatex Anaerobic Gasket maker® 51813 to the rear camshaft bearing cap. Install the cap and tighten the bolts to 18 ft. lbs. (25 Nm).
   - Camshaft sprockets and hand tighten the bolts
12. Remove camshaft sprocket holding tool J43655
   - Camshaft sprocket bolts to 63 ft. lbs. (85 Nm) plus an additional 30 degrees

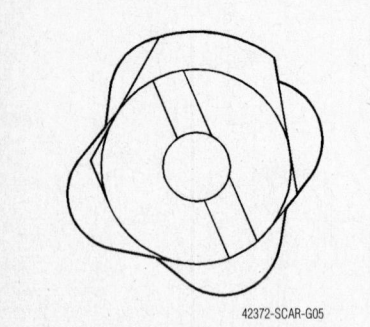

Fig. 68 Make sure the alignment notches are aligned with the camshaft sprocket—ION

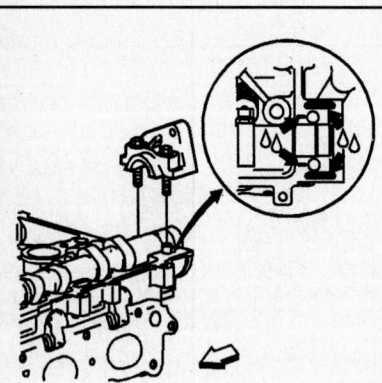

Fig. 69 Apply 0.197 inch (5mm) on 2.2L engines or 0.138 inch (3.55mm) of anaerobic Gasket maker to the rear camshaft bearing cap—ION

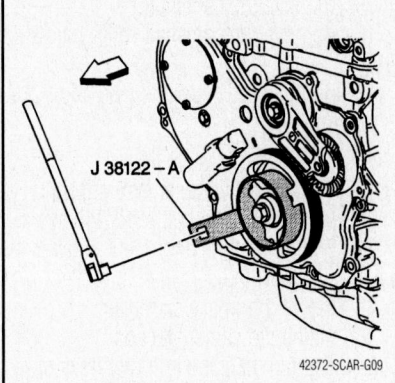

Fig. 70 Using harmonic balancer holder J 38122-A to prevent the crankshaft from rotating—ION models engine

13. Install or connect the following:
   - Upper timing chain guide and tighten to 89 inch lbs. (10 Nm)
   - Camshaft cover
   - Camshaft cover bolts and tighten to 89 inch lbs. (10 Nm)
   - Ground strap
   - Ground strap stud to the camshaft cover and tighten to 89 inch lbs. (10 Nm)
   - Ignition coil housing and tighten the bolts to 89 inch lbs. (10 Nm)
   - ICM and tighten the screws to 13 inch lbs. (1.5 Nm)
   - ICM connector
   - Fuel line bracket
   - PCV hose
   - Accelerator bracket and tighten the bolts to 89 inch lbs. (10 Nm)
   - Accelerator cable to the throttle body and bracket
   - Air cleaner assembly
   - Negative battery cable

CRANKSHAFT FRONT SEAL

REMOVAL & INSTALLATION

See Figure 70.

1. Before servicing the vehicle, refer to the Precautions Section.
2. Remove or disconnect the following:
   - Negative battery cable
   - Drive belt
   - Using harmonic balancer holder J 38122-A to prevent the crankshaft from rotating and remove the balancer bolt and discard
   - Crankshaft balancer
   - Front seal using a suitable prytool

To install:

3. Install or connect the following:
   - Front seal using driver J 35268-A to drive the seal into the position on the front cover
   - Crankshaft balancer
   - Balancer bolt and using tool J 38122-A to prevent the crankshaft from rotating, install a new balancer bolt and tighten to 74 ft. lbs. (100 Nm) plus an additional 75 degrees
   - Drive belt
   - Negative battery cable

CYLINDER HEAD

REMOVAL & INSTALLATION

See Figures 71 through 73.

✲✲ WARNING

Only remove the cylinder head when the engine is cold. Warpage may result if the cylinder head is removed while the engine is hot.

1. Before servicing the vehicle, refer to the Precautions Section.
2. Drain the cooling system.
3. Drain the engine oil.
4. Properly relieve the fuel system pressure.
5. Remove or disconnect the following:
   - Negative battery cable
   - Intake manifold
   - Exhaust manifold
   - Timing chain
   - Cylinder head bolts using the proper sequence
   - Cylinder head

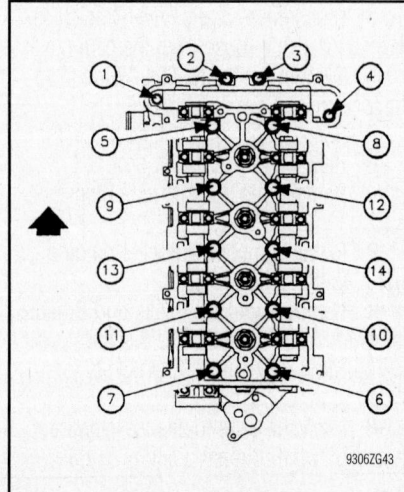

Fig. 71 Cylinder head bolt loosening sequence

To install:

➡**Set the crankshaft to 60 degrees Before Top Dead Center (BTDC) or after Top Dead Center (TDC) to prevent contact between the pistons and valves.**

6. Install or connect the following:
- New cylinder head gasket
- Cylinder head and align it on the dowels
- New cylinder head bolts and torque them in sequence to 22 ft. lbs. (30 Nm) plus 155 degrees
- Front 4 cylinder head bolts coated with Loctite® and torque them to 26 ft. lbs. (35 Nm)
- Timing chain
- Exhaust manifold
- Intake manifold
- Negative battery cable
7. Fill the engine with clean oil.
8. Fill the cooling system.

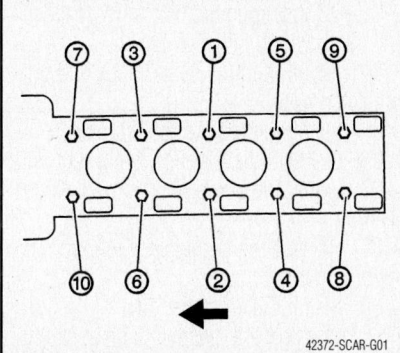

Fig. 72 Cylinder head bolt tightening sequence

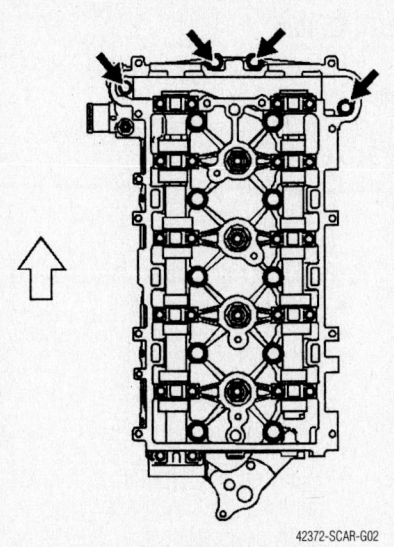

Fig. 73 Location of the 4 front cylinder head bolts

9. Prime the fuel system by cycling the ignition **ON** for 5 seconds and **OFF** for 10 seconds a few times without cranking the engine.

10. Start the engine, check for leaks, and repair if necessary.

ENGINE ASSEMBLY

REMOVAL & INSTALLATION

2.0L Engine

1. Before servicing the vehicle, refer to the precautions section.
2. With the tires in the straight forward position, remove the key from the ignition.
3. Disconnect the negative battery cable.
4. Remove the air outlet duct .
5. Secure the cooling module to the upper body structure.
6. Relieve the fuel system pressure.
7. Disconnect the fuel line from the fuel rail.
8. Remove the supercharger.
9. Drain the cooling system.
10. Remove the radiator inlet hose.
11. Remove the surge tank to cylinder head pipe.
12. Remove the radiator outlet hose.
13. Remove the inlet and outlet heater hoses.
14. Disconnect the following harness connectors:
- Tmap sensor
- Electronic Temperature Control (ETC) sensor
- Manifold Absolute Pressure (MAP) sensor
- Barometric Pressure (BARO) sensor
- Crankshaft Position (CKP) sensor
- Oil pressure sensor
- Purge solenoid
- Ignition coil modules
- Oxygen (O2s) sensor
- Vehicle speed sensor
- Engine temperature sensor
- Boost solenoid
- Back up lamp switch
15. Remove the drive belt.
16. Disconnect the charge air cooler hoses.
17. Recover the refrigerant.
18. Disconnect the compressor and condenser hose assembly from the compressor.
19. Remove the AC compressor bolts and set the compressor aside.
20. Disconnect the starter harness connectors.
21. Disconnect the alternator harness connectors.

22. Drain the engine oil.
23. Disconnect the front exhaust pipe from the exhaust manifold.
24. Disconnect the transmission shift cable from the transmission.
25. Use blocks of wood to support the powertrain assembly between the frame and the powertrain.
26. Remove the engine mount.
27. Remove the left transmission mount as follows:
   a. Remove the right hand hood electrical center bracket from the vehicle and reposition the electrical center.
   b. Support the transmission with a floor jack. Use a piece of wood between the jack and the transmission.
   c. Remove the transmission mount-to-transmission bracket bolts.
   d. Remove the transmission mount to mid-rail bolts.
   e. Using a floor jack, slowly lower the transmission enough to remove the transmission mount from the vehicle
28. Disconnect the stabilizer links from the stabilizer bar.
29. Disconnect the outer tie rod ends from the steering knuckles.

➡**In order to prevent possible SIR system deployment, do not attempt to rotate the steering shaft.**

30. Disconnect the intermediate shaft from the steering gear.
31. Disconnect the lower control arms from the steering knuckles.
32. Disconnect the drive axles from the steering knuckle.
33. Use a paint pen or magic marker in order to mark the frame to body position.
34. Lower the vehicle to about 3 feet off the ground in order to position the lift table under the frame.
35. Use wood blocks as necessary between the lift table and the frame to support the assembly.
36. Slowly remove the frame bolts using the following sequence:
   a. Remove the front frame bolts.
   b. Partially unscrew the rear frame bolts until 1.5 inches of bolt shank is exposed.
   c. Slowly lower the table to the floor.
   d. Attach the engine lift hoist to the engine lift hooks.
37. Remove the starter.
38. Remove the transmission to engine bolts.
39. Separate the engine from the transmission.

40. Remove the clutch pressure plate and disk.

41. Remove the following components:
- Exhaust manifold
- Exhaust manifold studs
- Engine mount bracket
- Fuel rail
- Thermostat housing and feed pipe
- Alternator

42. Remove the engine from the engine lift.

To install:

43. Attach the engine lift hoist to the engine lift hooks.

44. Install the exhaust manifold

45. Install the engine mount bracket as follows:

46. Install the intermediate bracket to the engine.

47. Hand tighten the engine mount intermediate bracket bolts with the long bolts in the forward and front lower holes and the short bolt in the rear upper hole.

48. Tighten the intermediate bracket bolts to 74 ft. lbs. (100 Nm).

49. Install the fuel rail.

50. Install the idler pulley.

51. Install the drive belt tensioner.

52. Install the thermostat housing and feed pipe.

53. Install the alternator.

54. Install the flywheel.

55. Install the clutch and pressure plate if equipped.

56. Install the A/C compressor.

57. Align the engine to the transmission. Tighten the transmission to engine bolts to 55 ft. lbs. (75 Nm).

58. Install the starter.

59. Remove the engine lift from the engine.

60. Raise and position the frame and powertrain assembly to the vehicle.

61. Hand start all the frame bolts while aligning the frame to the paint marks.

62. Tighten the frame bolts to 74 ft. lbs. (100 Nm) plus an additional 100 degree turn.

63. Remove the lift table.

64. Connect the drive axles to the steering knuckles. Tighten the nut to 155 ft. lbs. (210 Nm).

65. Connect the lower control arm to the steering knuckle and tighten the retainer as follows:

a. Install the ball stud pinch bolt and nut.

b. First Pass: Tighten the nut to 37 ft. lbs. (50 Nm), the back off ¾ turn.

c. Second Pass: Tighten the nut to 37 ft. lbs. (50 Nm plus an additional 30 degrees.

66. Connect the intermediate steering shaft to the steering gear. Tighten the bolt to 25 ft. lbs. (35 Nm).

67. Connect the outer tie rod ends to the steering knuckles. Tighten the nut to 44 ft. lbs. (60 Nm).

68. Connect the stabilizer links to the stabilizer bar. Tighten the retainers to 81 ft. lbs. (110 Nm).

69. Install the left transmission mount as follows:

a. Install the transmission mount to the mid-rail.

b. Install the transmission mount to mid-rail bolts and tighten to 20 ft. lbs. (27 Nm).

70. Using a floor jack, raise the transmission until it contacts the transmission mount.

➡ **The transmission mount to transmission bolts must be hand started. Do not pry the transmission or mount to align the holes.**

71. Hand start the transmission mount to bracket bolts using the following sequence:
- Rear bolt
- Middle bolt
- Front bolt

c. Using the previous sequence, tighten the transmission mount bolts to 37 ft. lbs. (50 Nm).

d. Install the right hand hood electrical center bracket to the vehicle and install the electrical center into position on the bracket

72. Install the engine mount as follows:

a. Place the engine mount onto the midrail and hand start the nuts.

b. Tighten the engine mount to midrail nuts to 74 ft. lbs. (100 Nm).

➡ **The engine mount to intermediate bracket bolts must be hand started. Do not pry the engine mount to align the holes.**

c. Hand start the engine mount to intermediate bracket bolts.

d. Tighten the engine mount to intermediate bracket bolts, starting with the center bolt to 37 ft. lbs. (50 Nm).

73. Remove the wood blocks between the powertrain and frame.

74. Connect the transmission shift cable to the transmission.

75. Connect the exhaust takedown pipe to the exhaust manifold and tighten the nuts to 22 ft. lbs. (30 Nm).

76. Connect the alternator harness connectors. Tighten to 15 ft. lbs. (20 Nm).

77. Connect the starter harness connectors.

78. Install the compressor and condenser hose assembly to the compressor.

79. Evacuate and charge the refrigerant system.

80. Install the supercharger.

81. Install the engine drive belt.

82. Connect the charge air cooler hoses.

83. Connect the following harness connectors:
- Tmap sensor
- Electronic Temperature Control (ETC) sensor
- Manifold Absolute Pressure (MAP) sensor
- Barometric Pressure (BARO) sensor
- Crankshaft Position (CKP) sensor
- Oil pressure sensor
- Purge solenoid
- Ignition coil modules
- O_2s sensor
- Vehicle speed sensor
- Engine temperature sensor
- Boost solenoid
- Back up lamp switch

84. Install the inlet heater hose and outlet heater hose.

85. Install the radiator outlet hose.

86. Connect the fuel line to the fuel rail.

87. Install the surge tank to the cylinder head pipe.

88. Release the cooling module from the upper body structure.

89. Install the air outlet duct .

90. Connect the negative battery cable.

91. Fill the engine with engine oil to the proper level.

92. Fill the cooling system.

93. Road test the vehicle.

2.2L Engine

1. Before servicing the vehicle, refer to the precautions section.

2. Properly relieve the fuel system pressure.

3. Drain the engine coolant.

4. Drain the engine oil.

5. Drain the power steering fluid.

6. Remove or disconnect the following:
- Negative battery cable
- Air cleaner and intake duct assembly

7. Secure the cooling module to the upper body.
- Throttle cable
- Fuel feed and return lines from the rail
- Radiator upper hose
- Surge tank-to-cylinder head hose
- Radiator lower hose
- Inlet and outlet heater hoses

8. Disconnect the following electrical connections:
- Intake Air Control (IAC)
- Throttle Position Sensor (TPS)
- Manifold Absolute Pressure (MAP) sensor
- Crankshaft Position (CKP) sensor
- Oil pressure sensor
- Purge solenoid
- Ignition coil and module
- Oxygen Sensor (O$_2$S)
- Vehicle Speed Sensor (VSS)
- Engine temperature sensor
- Back–up lamp switch

9. Remove or disconnect the following:
- Drive belt
- A/C compressor bolts and set the compressor aside without disconnecting the lines
- Starter and alternator wiring
- Front exhaust pipe from the manifold
- Transmission harness connectors
- Transmission shift cable

10. Use suitable blocks of wood to support the powertrain assembly between the assembly and the frame.

11. Support the engine with a jack using a piece of wood between the jack and the engine to avoid damage.
- Engine mount, nuts and bolts.

12. Remove the side transmission mount on models with a manual transmission as follows:
  a. Remove the under hood electrical tray.
  b. Disconnect the wiring harness from the tray bracket.
  c. Lift the electrical center up and swing it back out of the way.
  d. Remove the mount-to-transmission bolts and mount-to-rail bolts.
  e. Remove the mount.

13. Remove the side transmission mount on models with a automatic 5-speed transmission as follows:
  a. Support the transmission with a jack.
  b. Remove the front and rear transmission mount through bolts.
  c. Remove the under hood electrical center cover.
  d. Disconnect the engine control module harness connector.
  e. Disconnect the positive battery cable from the under hood electrical center.
  f. Make sure the surge tank hose is disconnected.
  g. Remove the electrical center tray.
  h. Disconnect the harness from the tray bracket.

  i. Lift the electrical center up and swing it back out of the way.
  j. Remove the mount-to-transmission bolts and mount-to-rail bolts.
  k. Remove the mount.

14. Remove the side transmission mount on models with a automatic 5-speed continuously variable transmission as follows:
  a. Remove the engine cradle.
  b. Remove the under hood electrical center cover.
  c. Disconnect the engine control module harness connector.
  d. Disconnect the positive battery cable from the under hood electrical center.
  e. Make sure the surge tank hose is disconnected.
  f. Remove the electrical center tray.
  g. Disconnect the harness from the tray bracket.
  h. Lift the electrical center up and swing it back out of the way.
  i. Install an engine support fixture. If not already removed, remove the engine mount.
  j. Disconnect the upper transmission cooler line from the radiator.
  k. Remove the mount-to-transmission bolts

➡ **Make sure the A/C clutch does not contact the inner metal rail of the vehicle.**

  l. Lower and tilt the powertrain assembly down approximately 4 inches.
  m. Remove the mount-to-rail bolts.
  n. Remove the mount.

15. Remove or disconnect the following:
- Stabilizer link from the stabilizer bar
- Outer tie rod ends from knuckles

✳✳ CAUTION

To prevent air bag system deployment, do not attempt to rotate the steering shaft.

- Intermediate shaft from the steering gear
- Lower control arms from the knuckles
- Half shafts from the knuckles

16. Remove the front frame as follows:
  a. Mark the frame-to-body position.
  b. Lower the vehicle until it is 3 feet off the ground so that a lift table may be placed in position. As necessary, use blocks of wood between the frame and table to support the assembly.
  c. Slowly remove the front frame bolts, the partially unscrew the bolts until 1 ½ inch of the bolt shank is exposed.

  d. Slowly lower the table to the floor
17. Attach the engine hooks to a hoist.
18. Remove or disconnect the following:
- Starter
- Torque converter-to-flywheel bolts, if equipped
- Engine-to-transmission bolts and the engine from the transmission.

To install:

19. Install or connect the following:
- Engine to the transmission and tighten the bolts to 55 ft. lbs. (75 Nm)
- Torque converter-to-flywheel bolts, if equipped and tighten the bolts to 46 ft. lbs. (62 Nm)
- Starter

20. Install the front frame as follows:
  a. Slowly raise the table to the into position and align the frame to the marks made during removal.
  b. Hand tighten the frame bolts
  c. Tighten the frame bolts to 74 ft. lbs. (100 Nm) plus an additional torque of 180 degrees using a torque angle meter.
  d. Remove the lift table.

21. Install or connect the following:
- Half shafts to the knuckles
- Lower control arms to the knuckles

✳✳ CAUTION

To prevent air bag system deployment, do not attempt to rotate the steering shaft.

- Intermediate shaft to the steering gear
- Outer tie rod ends to knuckles
- Stabilizer link to the stabilizer bar

22. Install the side transmission mount on models with a manual transmission as follows:
  a. Place the mount in position and tighten the mount-to-rail bolts to 25 ft. lbs. (34 Nm).

23. Use a jack to align the mount when it is in position.
  a. Install and hand tighten the mount-to-transmission bolts. Do not pry the transmission or mount to align the holes. Hand start the bolts in the following sequence; rear bolt, middle and then front bolt. Using the same sequence, tighten the bolts to 33 ft. lbs. (45 Nm).
  b. Place the electrical center in position.
  c. Connect the wiring harness to the tray bracket.
  d. Install the under hood electrical tray.

24. Install the side transmission mount on models with a automatic 5-speed transmission as follows:

  a. Place the mount in position and tighten the mount-to-rail bolts to 25 ft. lbs. (34 Nm).

25. Use a jack to align the mount when it is in position.

  a. Install and hand tighten the mount-to-transmission bolts. Do not pry the transmission or mount to align the holes. Hand start the bolts in the following sequence; rear bolt, middle and then front bolt. Using the same sequence, tighten the bolts to 33 ft. lbs. (45 Nm).

  b. Place the electrical center in position.

  c. Connect the wiring harness to the tray bracket.

  d. Install the under hood electrical tray.

  e. Connect the positive battery cable to the under hood electrical center.

  f. Connect the engine control module harness connector.

  g. Install the under hood electrical center cover.

  h. Install the front and rear transmission mount through bolts. Tighten to 74 ft. lbs. (100 Nm).

26. Install the side transmission mount on models with a automatic 5-speed continuously variable transmission as follows:

  a. Place the mount in position and tighten the mount-to-rail bolts to 25 ft. lbs. (34 Nm).

27. Use a jack raise the engine back into position and to align the mount when it is in position.

  a. Install and hand tighten the mount-to-transmission bolts. Do not pry the transmission or mount to align the holes. Hand start the bolts in the following sequence; rear bolt, middle and then front bolt. Using the same sequence, tighten the bolts to 33 ft. lbs. (45 Nm).

  b. If installed, install the engine mount and remove the engine support fixture.

  c. Connect the upper transmission cooler line to the radiator.

  d. Place the electrical center in position.

  e. Connect the wiring harness to the tray bracket.

  f. Install the under hood electrical tray.

  g. Connect the positive battery cable to the under hood electrical center.

  h. Connect the engine control module harness connector.

  i. Install the under hood electrical center cover.

  j. Install the front and rear transmission mount through bolts. Tighten to 74 ft. lbs. (100 Nm).

➡The engine mount bolts must be hand started. Do not pry on the engine mount to align the holes.

28. Install or connect the following:
  • Engine mount nuts and bolts. Tighten the nuts to 74 ft. lbs. (100 Nm) and the bolts to 37 ft. lbs. (50 Nm).

29. Remove the blocks of wood used to support the powertrain assembly between the assembly and the frame.
  • Transmission shift cable
  • Transmission harness connectors
  • Front exhaust pipe to the manifold
  • Starter and alternator wiring
  • A/C compressor
  • Drive belt

30. Connect the following electrical connections:
  • Back–up lamp switch
  • Engine temperature sensor
  • VSS
  • O_2S
  • Ignition coil and module
  • Purge solenoid
  • Oil pressure sensor
  • CKP
  • MAP sensor
  • TPS
  • IAC

31. Install or connect the following:
  • Inlet and outlet heater hoses
  • Radiator lower hose
  • Surge tank-to-cylinder head hose
  • Radiator upper hose
  • Fuel feed and return lines to the rail
  • Throttle cable
  • Cooling module
  • Air cleaner and intake duct assembly
  • Negative battery cable

32. Fill the engine with coolant.

33. Fill the engine with new oil.

34. Prime the fuel system by cycling the ignition **ON** for 5 seconds and **OFF** for 10 seconds a few times without cranking the engine.

35. Start the engine, check for leaks, and repair if necessary.

2.4L Engine

See Figure 74.

1. Ensure that the tires are in the straight forward position, remove the key from the ignition.

2. Before servicing the vehicle, refer to the precautions section.

3. Properly relieve the fuel system pressure.

4. Drain the engine coolant.

5. Drain the engine oil.

6. Drain the power steering fluid.

7. Disconnect the negative battery cable.

8. Disconnect the fuel feed line quick connect fitting from the fuel rail.

9. Disconnect the evaporative emission (EVAP) line quick connect fitting from the EVAP purge solenoid.

10. Remove the fuel line clips from the engine brackets.

11. Secure the cooling module to the upper body structure.

12. Remove the engine drive belt.

13. Disconnect the cooling fan electrical connector

14. Reposition the radiator inlet hose clamp at the engine.

15. Remove the radiator inlet hose from the engine

16. If the vehicle is equipped with engine oil cooler perform the following:

  a. Reposition the radiator outlet hose clamp at the water outlet.

  b. Reposition the radiator outlet hose clamp at the oil cooler.

  c. Remove the radiator outlet hose from the water outlet.

  d. Remove the radiator outlet hose from the oil cooler

17. If the vehicle is not equipped with an engine oil cooler, reposition the surge tank outlet hose clamp at the surge tank.

18. Remove the surge tank outlet hose from the surge tank

19. Reposition the radiator outlet hose clamp at the thermostat cover.

20. Remove the radiator outlet hose from the thermostat cover

21. Reposition the heater inlet and outlet hose clamps at the thermostat housing.

22. Reposition the brake booster vacuum hose clamp at the intake manifold.

23. Remove the brake booster vacuum hose from the intake manifold. Reposition the hose

24. Remove the heater inlet and outlet hoses from the thermostat housing.

25. Disconnect the Throttle actuator control (TAC), Manifold absolute pressure (MAP) sensor, Fuel injector harness and alternator connectors.

26. Disconnect the engine harness clip from the oil level indicator tube.

27. Disconnect the engine harness clips from the intake manifold.

28. Disconnect the ignition coils electrical connectors.

29. Disconnect the intake and exhaust camshaft position actuator electrical connectors.

30. Remove the engine harness clips from the camshaft cover.

31. Remove the negative battery cable ground nut.

32. Remove the engine harness ground terminal from the stud.

33. Remove the negative battery cable ground terminal from the stud.

34. Remove the stud.

35. Remove the engine harness ground terminals.

36. Disconnect Oil pressure sensor, Crankshaft position (CKP) sensor and Knock sensor (KS) the connectors.

37. Disconnect the EVAP purge solenoid electrical connector.

38. Remove the engine harness clip from the purge solenoid bracket.

39. Remove the engine harness ground bolt.

40. Reposition the engine harness ground terminal.

41. Disconnect the engine harness electrical connector from the air conditioning (A/C) pressure switch.

42. Disconnect the engine harness electrical connector (2) from A/C compressor.

43. Unbolt and reposition the AC compressor aside.

44. Raise and suitably support the vehicle.

45. Remove the transaxle fluid cooler bracket nut.

46. Remove the transaxle fluid cooler lines from the transaxle.

47. Remove the engine harness clip nut from the engine stud.

48. Remove the engine harness clip from the stud.

49. If equipped with an automatic transaxle, disconnect the engine harness electrical connector from the vehicle speed sensor (VSS).

50. Remove the engine harness clip from the speed sensor.

51. Remove the positive battery cable lead nut from the starter solenoid.

52. Remove the positive battery cable terminal from the starter.

53. Remove the engine harness to starter solenoid "S" terminal nut.

54. Remove the engine harness lead terminals from the starter solenoid.

55. Lower the vehicle.

56. Reposition the engine harness boot.

57. Remove the alternator nut.

58. Remove the engine harness lead terminal from the alternator.

59. If equipped with an automatic transaxle, disconnect the engine harness from the transaxle.

60. If equipped with an automatic transaxle, perform the following:

a. Disconnect the engine harness electrical connector from the engine coolant temperature (ECT) sensor.

b. Remove the heater oxygen sensor (HO2S) connector position assurance (CPA) retainers.

c. Disconnect the engine harness electrical connectors from the heater oxygen sensors (HO2S).

d. Remove the HO2S connector clips from the thermostat housing and engine bracket.

e. Disconnect the engine harness electrical connector from the park neutral position switch.

61. If equipped with a manual transaxle, perform the following:

a. Disconnect the engine harness electrical connector from the VSS.

b. Disconnect the engine harness electrical connector from the back up lamp switch.

c. Remove the HO2S CPA retainers.

d. Disconnect the engine harness electrical connectors from the HO2S.

e. Remove the HO2S clips from the engine brackets.

f. Gather all engine harness branches and reposition the harness off to the side, out of the way.

62. If equipped with an automatic transaxle, perform the following:

a. Disconnect the range selector lever cable from the transaxle lever.

b. Remove the range selector lever cable from the transaxle bracket.

63. If equipped with a manual transaxle, perform the following:

a. Disconnect the range selector and shift lever cables from the transaxle levers.

b. Remove the range selector and shift lever cables from the transaxle bracket.

c. Remove the catalytic converter.

d. Lower the vehicle.

64. Insert blocks of wood between the powertrain and the frame, in order to support the powertrain.

65. Remove the engine mount.

66. Remove the transaxle mount to transaxle bolts.

67. Raise the vehicle.

68. Disconnect the stabilizer links from the stabilizer bar.

69. Disconnect the outer tie rod ends from the steering knuckles.

70. Disconnect the intermediate shaft from the steering gear.

71. Disconnect the lower control arms from the steering knuckles.

72. Using a paint pen or magic marker, mark the frame to body position.

73. Lower the vehicle to about 3 feet off the ground.

74. Position an engine lift table under the frame.

75. Place wood blocks on top of the lift table between the table and the frame.

76. Lower the vehicle until the frame is resting on the blocks of wood.

77. Slowly loosen/remove the front then rear frame bolts

78. Slowly raise the vehicle away from the powertrain assembly.

79. Slide the lift table out from under the vehicle.

80. Attach the engine lift hoist to the engine lift hooks.

To install:

81. Remove the engine lift hoist from the engine lift hooks.

82. Slide the lift table under the vehicle.

83. Slowly lower the vehicle until it aligns with the alignment marks made during the removal.

84. Tighten the frame bolts to 74 ft. lbs. (100 Nm) plus 180 degrees.

85. Raise the vehicle until the lift table can be removed from under the vehicle.

86. Remove the lift table.

87. Install the transaxle fluid cooler lines to the transaxle and tighten the bracket nut to 62 inch lbs. (7 Nm).

88. Connect the lower control arms to the steering knuckles.

89. Connect the intermediate shaft to the steering gear.

90. Connect the outer tie rod ends to the steering knuckles.

91. Connect the stabilizer links to the stabilizer bar.

92. Lower the vehicle.

93. Install the transaxle mount to transaxle bolts and tighten to 33 ft. lbs. (45 Nm).

94. Install the engine mount. Tighten the bolts to 74 ft. lbs. (100 Nm) in the sequence illustrated and the bracket bolts in the sequence illustrated to 37 ft. lbs. (50 Nm).

95. Remove the blocks of wood from between the powertrain and the frame.

96. Install the catalytic converter.

97. Lower the vehicle.

➡**Ensure that the black cable is installed in the top notch of the transaxle bracket and the white cable in installed in the bottom notch of the transaxle bracket.**

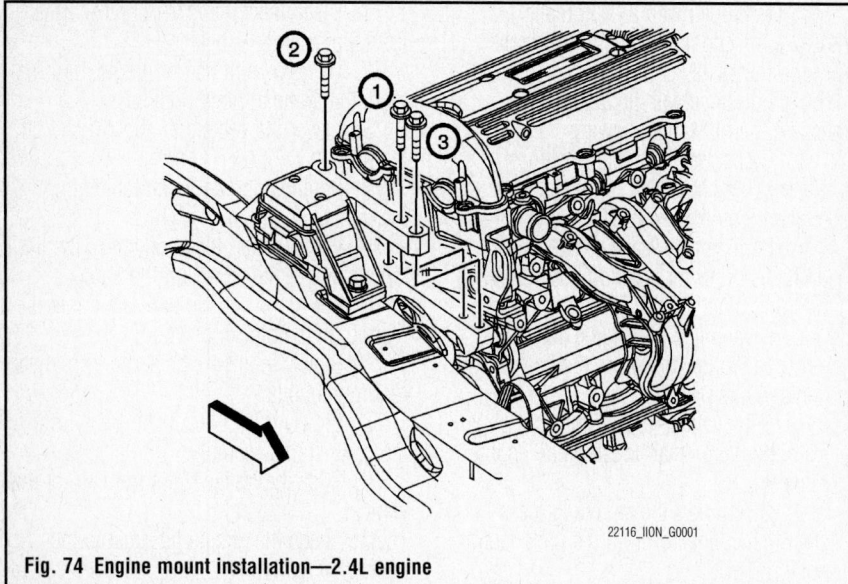

Fig. 74 Engine mount installation—2.4L engine

22116_IION_G0001

98. If equipped with a manual transaxle, install the range selector and shift lever cables to the transaxle bracket and connect the range selector and shift lever cables to the transaxle levers.

99. If equipped with an automatic transaxle, install the range selector lever cable to the transaxle bracket and connect the range selector lever cable to the transaxle lever.

100. Gather all engine harness branches and position the harness over the engine.

101. If equipped with a manual transaxle perform the following:

    a. Install the HO2S clips to the engine brackets.

    b. Connect the engine harness electrical connectors to the HO2S.

    c. Install the HO2S CPA retainers.

    d. Connect the engine harness electrical connector to the back up lamp switch.

    e. Connect the engine harness electrical connector to the VSS.

102. If equipped with an automatic transaxle perform the following:

    a. Connect the engine harness electrical connector to the park neutral position switch.

    b. Install the engine harness clips to the thermostat housing and engine brackets.

    c. Connect the engine harness electrical connectors to the HO2S.

    d. Install the HO2S CPA retainers.

    e. Connect the ECT sensor electrical connector.

103. If equipped with an automatic transaxle, connect the engine harness to the transaxle.

104. Install the engine harness lead terminal to the alternator.

105. Install the alternator nut and tighten to 20 ft. lbs. (27 Nm).

106. Position the engine harness boot.

107. Raise the vehicle.

108. Install the engine harness lead terminal to the starter solenoid.

109. Install the engine harness to starter solenoid "S" terminal nut.

110. Install the positive battery cable terminal to the starter.

111. Install the positive/negative battery cable lead nut to the starter solenoid. Tighten the nut to 13 ft. lbs. (13 ft. lbs. (17 Nm).

112. Install the engine harness clip to the speed sensor.

113. Connect the engine harness electrical connector to the VSS.

114. Install the engine harness clip to the stud.

115. Install the engine harness clip nut to the engine stud. Tighten to 37 ft. lbs. (50 Nm).

116. Lower the vehicle.

117. Reposition and install the A/C compressor. Tighten to 37 ft. lbs. (50 Nm).

118. Connect the engine harness electrical connector to the A/C compressor.

119. Connect the engine harness electrical connector to the A/C pressure switch.

120. Position the engine harness ground terminal to the engine block.

121. Install the engine harness ground bolt and tighten to 18 ft. lbs. (25 Nm).

122. Connect the EVAP purge solenoid electrical connector2).

123. Install the engine harness clip to the EVAP purge solenoid bracket. Connect the KS, CKP and oil pressure connectors.

124. Position the engine harness ground terminals. Install the stud and tighten to 18 ft. lbs. (25 Nm).

125. Install the negative battery cable ground terminal to the stud.

126. Install the engine harness ground terminal to the stud.

127. Install the negative battery cable ground nut.

128. Install the engine harness clip to the camshaft cover.

129. Connect the intake and exhaust camshaft position actuator electrical connectors.

130. Connect the ignition coils electrical connectors.

131. Connect the engine harness clips to the intake manifold.

132. Connect the engine harness clip to the oil level indicator tube.

133. Connect all remaining electrical connectors and hoses.

134. If the vehicle is not equipped with engine oil cooler perform the following:

    a. Install the surge tank outlet hose to the surge tank.

    b. Position the surge tank outlet hose clamp at the surge tank.

    c. Install the radiator outlet hose to the thermostat cover.

    d. Position the radiator outlet hose clamp at the thermostat cover.

135. If the vehicle is equipped with engine oil cooler perform the following:

    a. Install the radiator outlet hose to the oil cooler.

    b. Install the radiator outlet hose to the water outlet.

    c. Position the radiator outlet hose clamp at the oil cooler.

    d. Position the radiator outlet hose clamp at the water outlet.

136. Install the radiator inlet hose to the engine.

137. Position the radiator inlet hose clamp at the engine.

138. Connect the cooling fan electrical connector.

139. Install the engine drive belt.

140. Unfasten the cooling module from the upper body structure.

141. Fill the cooling system.

142. Check and fill the transaxle fluid as needed.

143. Connect the EVAP line quick connect fitting to the EVAP purge solenoid.

144. Connect the fuel feed line quick connect fitting to the fuel rail.

145. Install the fuel line clips to the engine brackets.

146. Fill the engine with oil.

147. Connect the negative battery cable.

148. Road test the vehicle.

EXHAUST MANIFOLD

REMOVAL & INSTALLATION

See Figures 75 through 77.

1. Before servicing the vehicle, refer to the precautions section.
2. Remove or disconnect the following:
   - Negative battery cable
   - Exhaust manifold heat shield
   - Oxygen Sensor (O$_2$S) from the manifold

➡**Do not bend the flex coupling more than 3 degrees in any direction to avoid damage.**

   - Pipe-to-manifold nuts, pull down and back on the pipe in order to separate the pipe from the manifold

   - Exhaust pipe from the manifold
   - Exhaust manifold-to-head nuts
   - Exhaust manifold

To install:

3. Install or connect the following:
   - Exhaust manifold with a new gasket and torque the bolts in the sequence illustrated, to 115 inch lbs. (13 Nm)
   - New manifold-to-flex pipe gasket, and place the pipe in position. Tighten the nuts to 32 ft. lbs. (43 Nm) on 2.2L engines or 37 ft. lbs. (50 Nm) on 2.0L engines.
   - O$_2$S
   - Exhaust manifold heat shield and torque the bolts to 18 ft. lbs. (25 Nm)
   - Negative battery cable

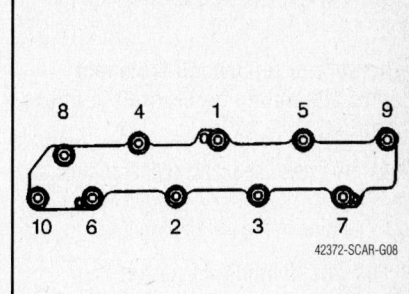

Fig. 77 Tighten the exhaust manifold nuts in the sequence shown—2.2L ION models

4. Start the vehicle and check for leaks, repair if necessary.

INTAKE MANIFOLD

REMOVAL & INSTALLATION

2.0L Engine

1. Before servicing the vehicle, refer to the precautions section.
2. Disconnect the negative battery cable.
3. Remove the supercharger.
4. Remove the alternator.
5. Drain the charged air cooling system.
6. Disconnect the charged air cooling system inlet and outlet hoses.
7. Remove the charged air coolant pump.
8. Remove the cooling fan assembly.
9. Remove the AC compressor bolts and reposition the compressor to access the oil level indicator tube.

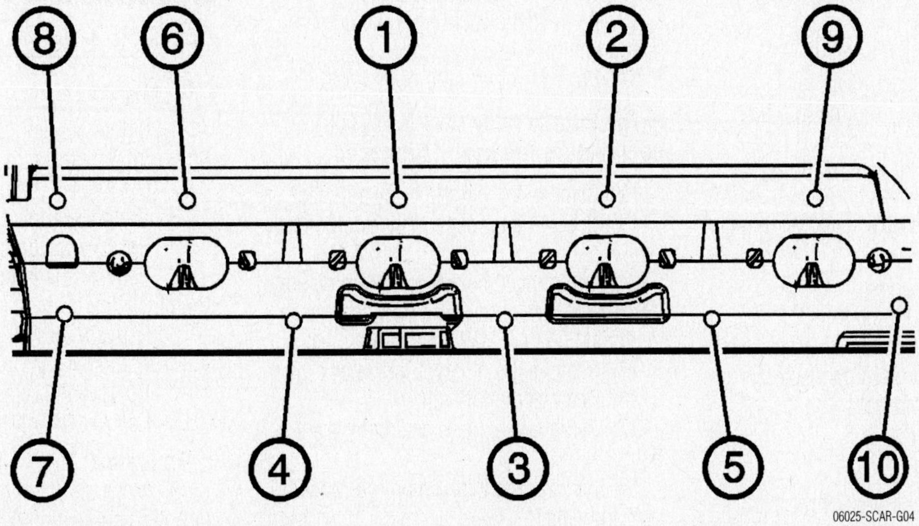

Fig. 75 Remove the exhaust manifold and gasket—ION models

Fig. 76 Tighten the exhaust manifold nuts in the sequence shown—2.0L ION models

10. Remove the oil level indicator tube bolt.

➡**Be sure to remove all fasteners before attempting to remove the intake manifold.**

11. Remove the intake manifold nuts and bolts.

12. Remove the intake manifold.

➡**The intake manifold gasket is reusable, only replace the gasket if damage has occurred.**

13. If applicable, remove the intake manifold gasket.

To install:

14. If applicable, install the intake manifold gasket.

15. Install the intake manifold.

16. Install the intake manifold nuts and bolts. Tighten to 89 inch lbs. (10 Nm).

17. Install the oil level indicator tube and bolt.

18. Reposition the AC compressor and install the bolts and tighten to 16 ft. lbs. (22 Nm).

19. Install the cooling fan assembly.

20. Install the charged air coolant pump.

21. Install the alternator.

22. Connect the charged air cooling system inlet and outlet hoses.

23. Fill the charged air cooling system.

24. Install the supercharger.

25. Connect the negative battery cable.

2.2L Engine

1. Before servicing the vehicle, refer to the precautions section.

2. Remove or disconnect the following:
   - Negative battery cable
   - Air cleaner assembly
   - Idle Air Control (IAC) valve electrical connectors
   - Throttle Position Sensor (TPS) electrical connectors
   - Vacuum hoses from the throttle body
   - Throttle control cable and bracket
   - Throttle body
   - Positive Crankcase Valve (PCV) hose
   - Purge solenoid tube
   - Brake booster hose
   - Oil dipstick tube bolt
   - Fuel rail
   - Knock Sensor (KS) connector
   - Intake manifold bolts and nuts
   - Intake manifold

To install:

3. Install or connect the following:
   - Intake manifold with a new gasket and torque the nuts to 89 inch lbs.

(10 Nm) starting from the center and working outward
   - Knock Sensor (KS) connector
   - Fuel rail
   - Oil dipstick tube bolt
   - Brake booster hose
   - Purge solenoid tube
   - PCV hose
   - Throttle body to the intake manifold and torque the bolts to 89 inch lbs. (10 Nm)
   - Throttle cable bracket and torque the bolts to 89 inch lbs. (10 Nm)
   - Throttle cable
   - IAC sensor electrical connector
   - TPS electrical connectors
   - Vacuum hoses from the throttle body
   - Air cleaner assembly
   - Negative battery cable

4. Start the engine, check for leaks, and repair if necessary.

2.4L Engine

1. Before servicing the vehicle, refer to the precautions section.

2. Remove the intake manifold cover.

3. Remove the air cleaner outlet duct.

4. Disconnect the engine harness electrical connector from the throttle actuator control (TAC).

5. Disconnect the engine harness electrical connector from the fuel injector harness.

6. Disconnect the engine harness clips from the intake manifold.

7. Disconnect the engine harness clip from the oil level indicator tube.

8. Disconnect the fuel injector electrical connector clip from the intake manifold.

9. Reposition the vacuum brake booster hose clamp at the intake manifold.

10. Remove the vacuum brake booster hose from the intake manifold.

11. Remove the throttle body bolts.

➡**The throttle body seal is reusable, only replace the seal if damaged.**

12. Remove the throttle body and seal.

13. Remove and inspect the throttle body seal.

14. Disconnect the evaporative emission (EVAP) canister purge tube from the intake manifold and the EVAP solenoid.

15. Remove the oil level indicator tube.

16. Remove the fuel rail.

17. Remove the intake manifold lower bolts.

18. Remove the intake manifold upper bolt and nuts.

19. Remove the intake manifold.

➡**The intake manifold gasket is reusable, only replace the gasket if damage has occurred.**

20. Remove and inspect the intake manifold gasket.

To install:

21. Install a NEW intake manifold gasket if necessary, otherwise install the old gasket.

22. Install the intake manifold.

23. Install the intake manifold upper bolt and nuts.

24. Install the intake manifold lower bolts and tighten to 89 in. lbs. (10 Nm).

25. Install the fuel rail.

26. Install the oil level indicator tube.

27. Connect the EVAP canister purge tube to the intake manifold and the EVAP solenoid

28. Install a NEW throttle body seal if necessary, otherwise install the old seal.

29. Position the throttle body and tighten to 89 in. lbs. (10 Nm).

30. Install the vacuum brake booster hose to the intake manifold.

31. Position the vacuum brake booster hose clamp at the intake manifold.

32. Connect the engine harness clips to the intake manifold.

33. Connect the engine harness clip to the oil level indicator tube.

34. Connect the fuel injector electrical connector clip to the intake manifold.

35. Connect the engine harness electrical connector to the fuel injector harness.

36. Connect the engine harness electrical connector to the TAC.

37. Install the air cleaner outlet duct.

38. Install the intake manifold cover.

OIL PAN

REMOVAL & INSTALLATION

2.0L Engine

1. Before servicing the vehicle, refer to the precautions section.

2. Disconnect the negative battery cable.

3. Drain the engine oil.

4. Remove the engine drive belt.

5. Remove the intercooler pump bracket bolts from the oil pan.

6. Remove the lower AC compressor bolt from the oil pan.

7. Remove the oil pan bolts.

8. Remove the oil pan.

To install:

9. Make sure that the oil pan and mounting surface on the lower crankcase are free of all oil and debris.

10. Apply a 0.138 inch (3.5 mm) bead of RTV sealer around the perimeter of the oil pan and the oil suction port opening.

11. Install the oil pan.

12. Install the oil pan bolts and tighten in sequence to 18 ft. lbs. (25 Nm).

13. Install the AC compressor bolts.

14. Install the intercooler pump bracket bolts and tighten to 18 ft. lbs. (25 Nm).

15. Install the engine drive belt.

16. Fill the engine oil to the proper level.

17. Connect the negative battery cable.

2.2L Engine

1. Before servicing the vehicle, refer to the precautions section.

2. Drain the engine oil.

3. Remove or disconnect the following:
- Negative battery cable
- Drive belt
- Lower A/C compressor bolt
- Oil pan bolts

4. Using a flat-bladed tool, pry the oil pan from the engine block.

To install:

5. Apply a 0.08 in. (2mm) bead of RTV sealer to the pan flange. Be sure the RTV is applied to the inner side of the flange.

6. Install or connect the following:
- Oil pan and torque the bolts in the proper sequence to 18 ft. lbs. (25 Nm)
- Lower A/C compressor bolt
- Drive belt
- Negative battery cable

7. Fill the engine with clean oil.

8. Start the vehicle and check for leaks, repair if necessary.

2.4L Engine

See Figure 78.

1. Before servicing the vehicle, refer to the precautions section.

2. Drain the engine oil.

3. Remove or disconnect the following:
- Negative battery cable
- Drive belt
- Lower A/C compressor bolt
- Oil pan to transaxle bolts
- Oil pan bolts

4. Using a flat-bladed tool, pry the oil pan from the engine block.

To install:

5. Apply a 0.08 in. (2mm) bead of RTV sealer to the pan flange. Be sure the RTV is applied to the inner side of the flange.

6. Install or connect the following:
- Oil pan
- Oil pan to transaxle bolts and tighten to 55 ft. lbs. (75 Nm)

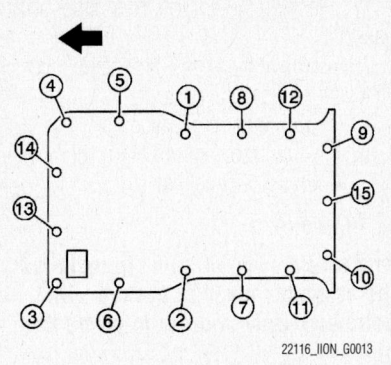

Fig. 78 Oil pan bolt torque sequence

- Oil pan bolts in the proper sequence to 18 ft. lbs. (25 Nm)
- Lower A/C compressor bolt
- Drive belt
- Negative battery cable

7. Fill the engine with clean oil.

8. Start the vehicle and check for leaks, repair if necessary.

OIL PUMP

REMOVAL & INSTALLATION

2.0L Engine

1. Before servicing the vehicle, refer to the precautions section.

2. Disconnect the negative battery cable.

3. Remove the drive belt.

4. Remove the accessory drive belt tensioner bolts.

5. Remove the accessory drive belt tensioner.

6. Remove the idler pulley bolts.

7. Remove the idler pulley.

8. Remove the alternator bracket and lift hook assembly bolts.

9. Remove the alternator bracket and lift hook assembly.

10. Remove the engine front cover bolts.

11. Remove the long water pump bolt.

12. Remove the engine front cover and gaskets.

13. Remove the crankshaft front cover oil seal with an appropriate tool.

14. Disassemble the pressure relief valve.

15. Remove the oil pump gerotor cover and bolts.

16. Clean all of the parts in cleaning solvent. Remove varnish, sludge and dirt.

17. Inspect the oil pump for wear and scoring.

To install:

18. Lubricate all oil pump parts with engine oil.

19. Install the inner gear into the outer gear.

➡ **If gears are improperly installed in the front cover, the gerotor cover will not bolt on.**

20. Install the gears together into the front cover with the hub of the center gear facing the front cover.

21. Install the oil pump gerotor cover and bolts. Tighten to 53 inch lbs. (6 Nm).

22. Install the pressure relief valve piston.

23. Install the pressure relief valve spring. Tighten the pressure relief valve plug to 30 ft. lbs. (40 Nm).

24. Install the engine front cover with a new gasket.

➡ **Use the correct fastener in the correct location. Replacement fasteners must be the correct part number for that application. Fasteners requiring replacement or fasteners requiring the use of thread locking compound or sealant are identified in the service procedure. Do not use paints, lubricants, or corrosion inhibitors on fasteners or fastener joint surfaces unless specified. These coatings affect fastener torque and joint clamping force and may damage the fastener. Use the correct tightening sequence and specifications when installing fasteners in order to avoid damage to parts and systems.**

25. Install the long water pump bolt. Tighten to 18 ft. lbs. (25 Nm).

26. Install the engine front cover bolts. Tighten to 18 ft. lbs. (25 Nm).

27. Install the alternator bracket and lift hook assembly. Tighten the bolts to 31 ft. lbs. (42 Nm).

28. Install the idler pulley. Tighten the bolts to 16 ft. lbs. (22 Nm).

29. Install the accessory drive belt tensioner. Tighten the bolts to 24 ft. lbs. (32 Nm).

30. Install the drive belt.

31. Connect the negative battery cable.

2.2L Engine

1. Before servicing the vehicle, refer to the precautions section.

2. Drain the engine oil.

3. Remove or disconnect the following:
- Negative battery cable
- Air cleaner assembly
- Right front wheel and splash shield
- Accessory drive belt
- Crankshaft damper pulley
- Belt tensioner

4. Install an engine support fixture.
- Right front engine mount
- Front cover bolts and the 13mm bolt under the water pump
- Front cover
- Oil pump cover plate
- Drive rotor and driven rotor
- Pressure relief valve

To install:

5. Install or connect the following:
- New relief valve into the cover bore, if removed. Coat the valve with clean engine oil and tap it into the bore. Torque the plug to 30 ft. lbs. (40 Nm).

➡Whenever the oil pump is installed, the assembly must be packed with petroleum jelly in order to prime the pump.

- Drive and driven rotors into the pump with the chamfer toward the front oil seal
- Oil pump body cover using new bolts and torque the bolts to 53 inch lbs. (6 Nm)
- Front cover with a new oil seal and torque the perimeter and center bolts to 19 ft. lbs. (25 Nm) and the lower center bolt to 89 inch lbs. (10 Nm)
- Right side engine mount and torque the bolts to 41 ft. lbs. (55 Nm)

6. Remove the engine support fixture.
- Drive belt tensioner and torque the bolts 37 ft. lbs. (50 Nm)
- Crankshaft damper pulley and torque the bolt to 74 ft. lbs. (100 Nm) plus 75 degrees
- Accessory drive belt
- Right front splash shield and wheel
- Air cleaner assembly
- Negative battery cable

7. Fill the engine with clean oil and replace the oil filter.

8. Start the vehicle and check for leaks, repair if necessary.

2.4L Engine

1. Before servicing the vehicle, refer to the precautions section.

2. Drain the engine oil.

3. Remove the accessory drive belt tensioner bolt.

4. Remove the accessory drive belt tensioner.

5. Remove the engine front cover bolts.

6. Remove the long water pump bolt.

7. Remove the engine front cover and gaskets.

8. Remove the crankshaft front cover oil seal with an appropriate tool.
- Oil pump cover plate
- Drive rotor and driven rotor
- Pressure relief valve

To install:

➡Whenever the oil pump is installed, the assembly must be packed with petroleum jelly in order to prime the pump.

- Drive and driven rotors into the pump with the chamfer toward the front oil seal
- Oil pump body cover using new bolts and torque the bolts to 53 inch lbs. (6 Nm)

9. Install the engine front cover with a new gasket.

10. Install the long water pump bolt. Tighten to 18 ft. lbs. (25 Nm).

11. Install the engine front cover bolts. Tighten to 18 ft. lbs. (25 Nm).

12. Install the accessory drive belt tensioner. Tighten to 33 ft. lbs. (45 Nm).

13. Fill the engine with clean oil and replace the oil filter.

14. Start the vehicle and check for leaks, repair if necessary.

INSPECTION

See Figures 79 through 81.

1. With the timing chain front cover and the oil pump body cover removed, use a feeler gauge to measure the clearance between the driven rotor and pump body. Clearance should not exceed 0.011 in. (0.277mm).

2. Use a feeler gauge to measure the clearance between the both rotor tips. Clearance should not exceed 0.006 in. (0.150mm).

3. Using Plastigage® or a feeler gauge, temporarily install the pump cover and measure the rotor-to-cover clearance. Clearance should not exceed 0.005 in. (0.128mm).

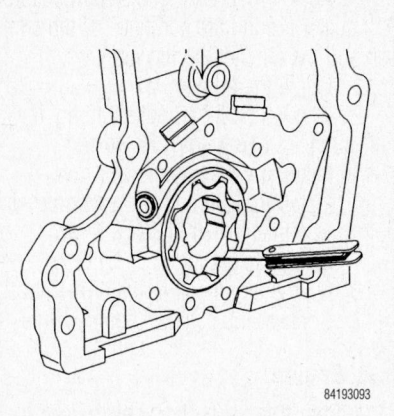

84193093

Fig. 80 Use a feeler gauge to measure the clearance between both rotor tips

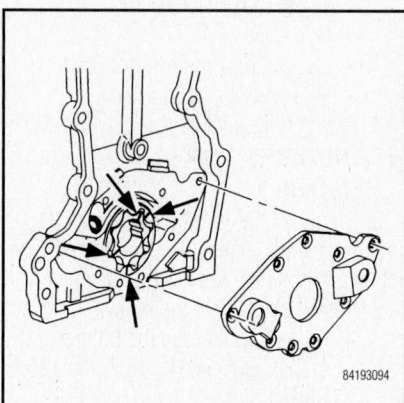

84193094

Fig. 81 Temporarily install the pump cover and measure the rotor-to-cover clearance

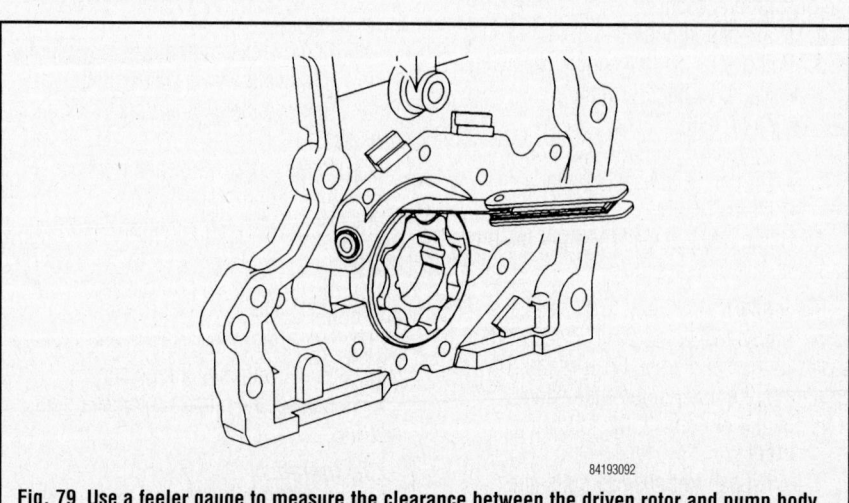

84193092

Fig. 79 Use a feeler gauge to measure the clearance between the driven rotor and pump body

4. If necessary, replace the pump components and/or the front cover assembly.

PISTON AND RING

POSITIONING

See Figure 82.

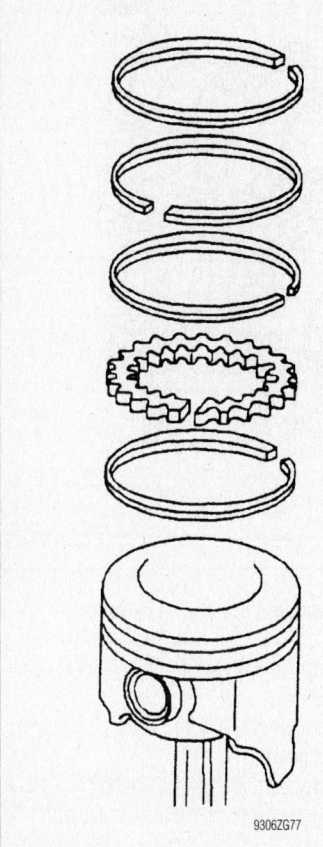

Fig. 82 Piston ring positioning—2.0L and 2.2L engines

REAR MAIN SEAL

REMOVAL & INSTALLATION

1. Before servicing the vehicle, refer to the Precautions Section.
2. Remove or disconnect the following:
- Negative battery cable
- Transaxle
- Clutch/pressure plate assembly, if equipped with a manual transaxle
- Flywheel
- Rear main bearing seal by prying it from the engine

➡Be careful not to damage or scratch the seal mounting surfaces.

To install:

3. Lubricate the new rear main bearing seal with engine oil.

4. Install or connect the following:
- New rear main seal using a Rear Main Bearing Oil Seal Installer Tool J42067 until it is flush with the block
- Flywheel
- Clutch/pressure plate assembly, if equipped with a manual transaxle
- Transaxle
- Negative battery cable
5. Start the engine and check for leaks, repair if necessary.

SUPERCHARGER

REMOVAL & INSTALLATION

2.0L Engine

See Figure 83.

1. Before servicing the vehicle, refer to the precautions section.
2. Disconnect the negative battery cable.
3. Remove the drive belt.
4. Remove the Evaporative Emission (EVAP) tube and EVAP valve.
5. Remove the throttle body and gasket.
6. Remove the Supercharger Inlet Pressure (SCIP) sensor.
7. Disconnect the vacuum brake booster hose.
8. Remove the intercooler fill neck bracket bolts.
9. Remove the supercharger.
10. Remove the gasket if damaged.

To install:

11. Install the supercharger gasket.
12. Install the supercharger and bolts. Tighten the bolts to 18 ft. lbs. (25 Nm).
13. Install the intercooler fill neck bracket bolts and tighten to 89 inch lbs. (10 Nm).
14. Connect the vacuum brake booster hose.
15. Install the SCIP sensor and bolt and tighten to 89 inch lbs. (10 Nm).
16. Install the throttle body.
17. Install the EVAP tube and EVAP valve.
18. Install the drive belt.
19. Connect the negative battery cable.

TIMING CHAIN, SPROCKETS, FRONT COVER AND SEAL

REMOVAL & INSTALLATION

2.0L Engine

See Figures 84 through 95.

1. Before servicing the vehicle, refer to the precautions section.

Fig. 83 The removal and installation of the supercharger—2.0L Engine

2. Disconnect the negative battery cable.

3. Remove the camshaft cover.

4. Remove the engine front cover as follows:

5. Remove the drive belt.

6. Using harmonic balancer holder J 38122-A to prevent the crankshaft from rotating and remove the balancer bolt and discard

7. Remove the crankshaft balancer.

8. Remove the drive belt tensioner.

9. Remove the idler pulley.

10. Remove the engine front cover to water pump bolt.

11. Remove the remaining engine front cover bolts.

12. Remove the engine front cover.

13. If the engine front cover gasket is damaged, remove the front engine mount.

14. Remove the front engine mount bracket

➡**To rotate the camshaft, use a 24 mm open-end wrench on the camshaft flats. Camshaft should be rotated in a clockwise direction only, facing camshaft sprockets from the passenger side of the vehicle.**

15. Locate the No. 1 piston to approximately 60 degrees before top dead center (diamond shaped hole on intake camshaft sprocket at 12 o'clock position). Remove the spark plugs. This will ease the rotation effort.

16. Remove the timing chain tensioner.

17. Remove the fixed timing chain guide access plug.

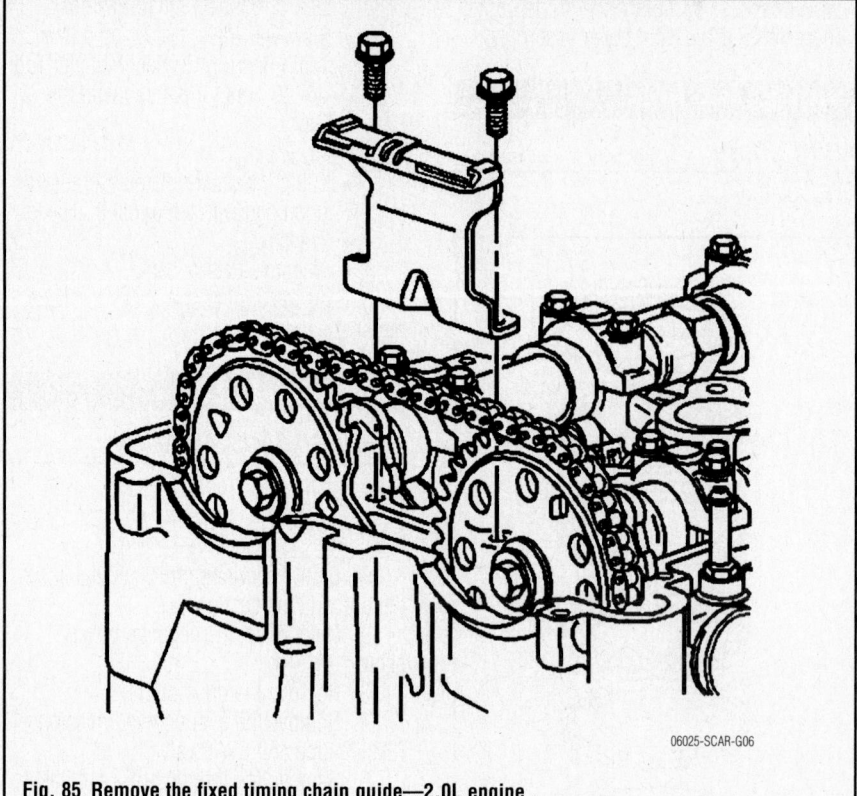

06025-SCAR-G06

Fig. 85 Remove the fixed timing chain guide—2.0L engine

18. Remove the fixed timing chain guide.

19. Remove the upper timing chain guide.

20. Use a 24 mm wrench to hold the camshafts from turning.

21. Remove the exhaust camshaft sprocket bolt and discard.

22. Remove the exhaust camshaft sprocket.

23. Remove the timing chain tensioner guide.

24. Remove the intake camshaft sprocket bolt and discard.

25. Remove the intake camshaft sprocket.

06025-SCAR-G05

Fig. 84 Locate the No. 1 piston to approximately 60 degrees before top dead center (diamond shaped hole on intake camshaft sprocket at 12 o'clock position)—2.0L engine

26. Remove the timing chain through the top of the cylinder head.

27. Remove the crankshaft sprocket.

28. Remove the oil nozzle and bolt.

29. Remove the balance shaft drive chain tensioner.

30. Remove the adjustable balance shaft chain guide.

31. Remove the small balance shaft drive chain guide.

32. Remove the upper balance shaft drive chain guide.

➡**It may ease removal of the balance shaft drive chain to get all of the slack in the chain between the crankshaft and water pump sprockets.**

33. Remove the balance shaft drive chain.

To install:

➡**If the balance shafts are not properly timed to the engine, the engine may vibrate and make noise.**

34. Install the upper balance shaft chain guide. Tighten the upper balance shaft chain guide bolts to 133 inch lbs. (15 Nm).

35. Install the balance shaft drive chain with the colored links lined up on with the marks on the balance shaft drive sprockets and the crankshaft sprocket. Use the following procedure to line up the links with the sprockets: Orient the chain so that the copper colored and chrome links are visible.

36. Place the uniquely colored link (1) so that it lines up with the timing mark on the intake side balance shaft sprocket.

37. Working clockwise around the chain, place the first matching colored link (2) in line with the timing mark on the crankshaft drive sprocket. (approximately 5 o'clock position on the crank sprocket).

38. Place the chain (3) on the water pump drive sprocket (alignment is not critical).

39. Align the last matching colored link (4) with the timing mark on the exhaust side balance shaft drive sprocket.

40. Install the small balance shaft chain guide. Tighten the balance shaft chain guide bolts to 89 inch lbs. (10 Nm).

41. Install the adjustable balance shaft drive chain guide. Tighten the chain guide bolts to 89 inch lbs. (10 Nm).

42. Turn the tensioner plunger 90 degrees in its bore and compress the plunger until a paper clip can be inserted through the hole in the plunger body and into hole in the tensioner plunger.

43. Install the timing chain tensioner. Tighten the chain tensioner bolts to 89 inch lbs. (10 Nm).

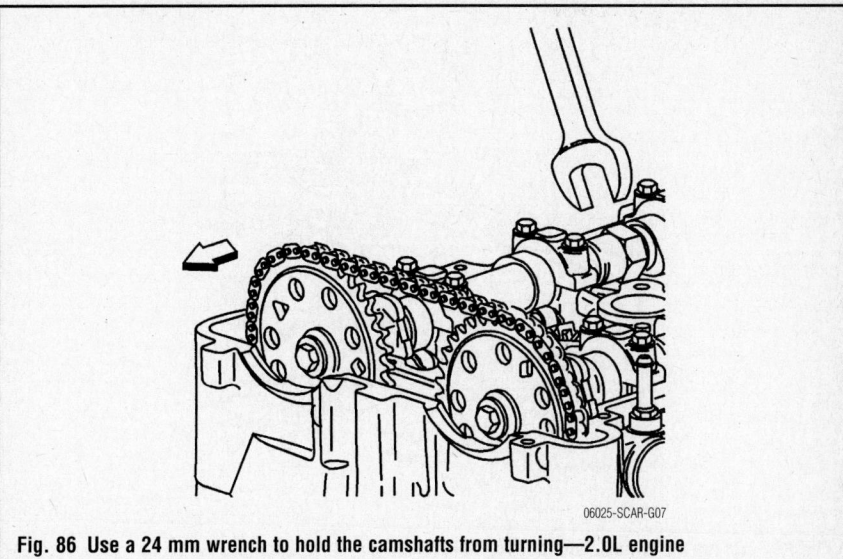

06025-SCAR-G07

Fig. 86 Use a 24 mm wrench to hold the camshafts from turning—2.0L engine

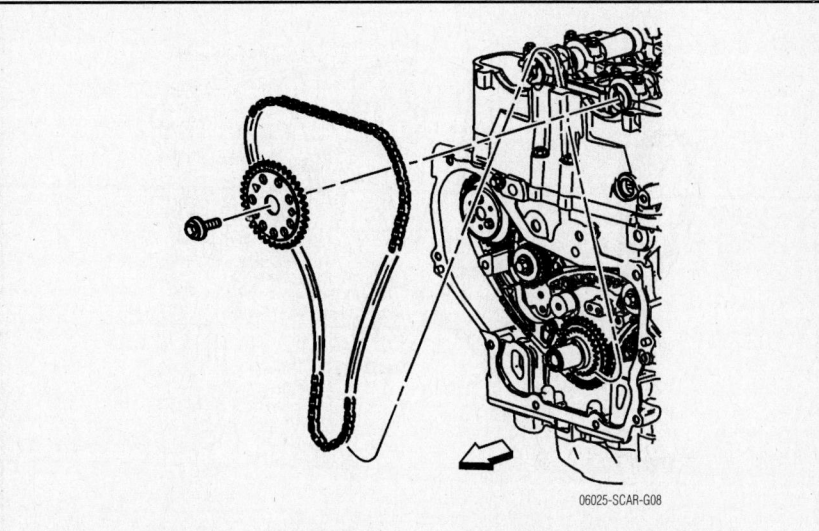

06025-SCAR-G08

Fig. 87 Remove the timing chain through the top of the cylinder head—2.0L engine

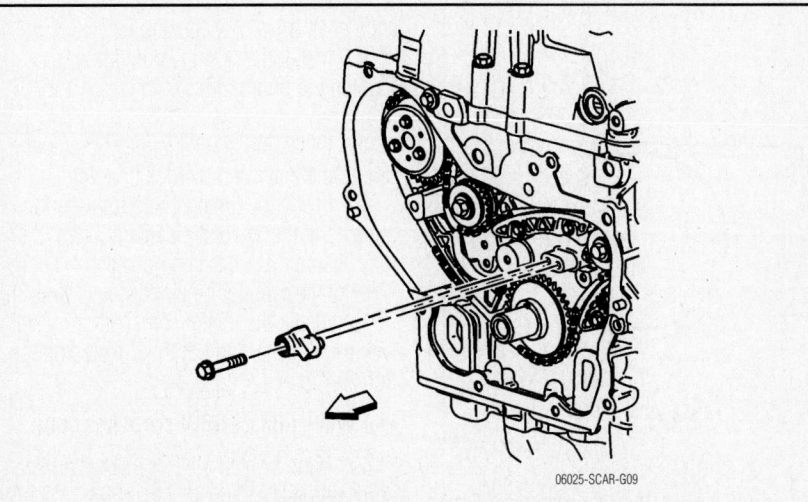

06025-SCAR-G09

Fig. 88 Remove the timing chain through the top of the cylinder head oil nozzle and bolt—2.0L engine

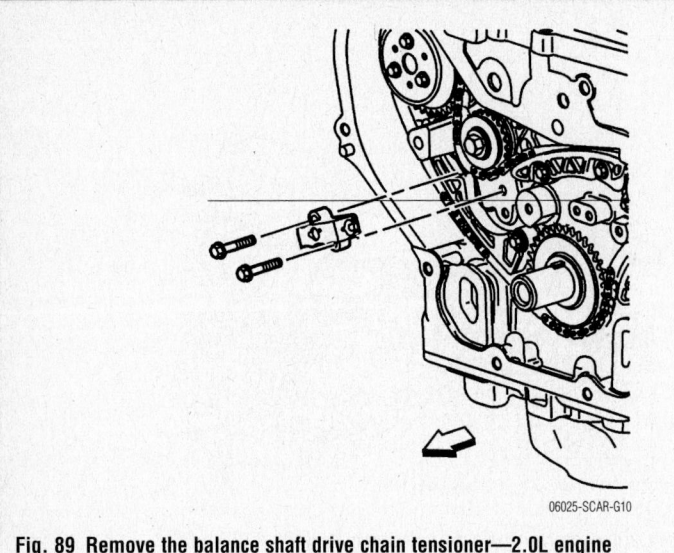

Fig. 89 Remove the balance shaft drive chain tensioner—2.0L engine

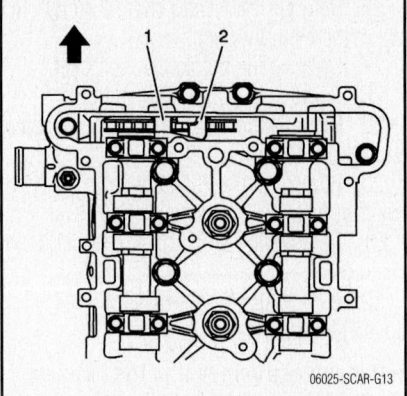

Fig. 92 Lower the timing chain through the opening in the top of the cylinder head. Carefully ensure that the chain goes around both sides of the cylinder block bosses (1 and 2)—2.0L engine

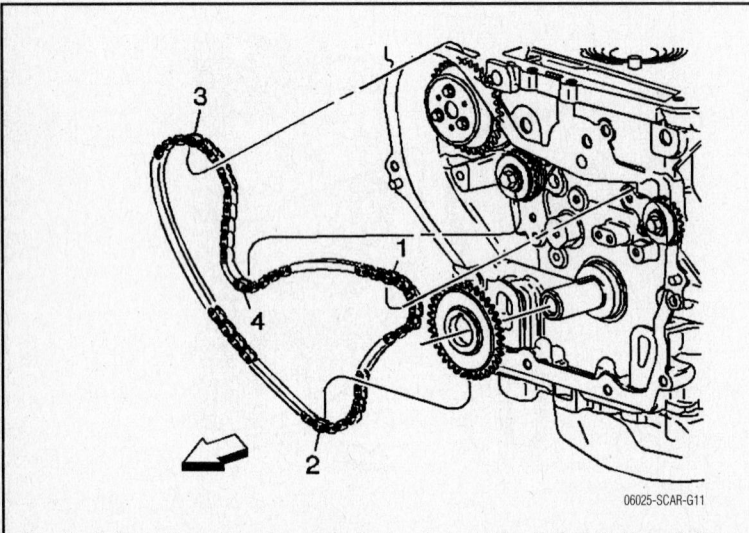

Fig. 90 Refer to the text for the proper timing chain routing for installation—2.0L engine

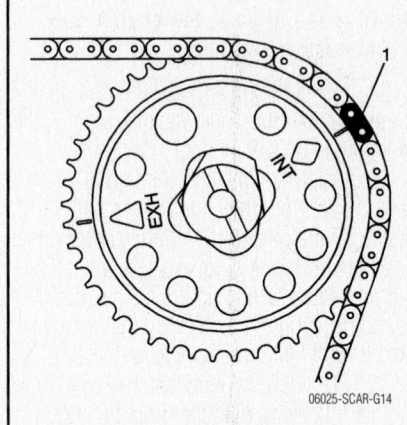

Fig. 93 Install the intake camshaft sprocket with the INT diamond at the 2 o'clock position—2.0L engine

Fig. 91 Install the crankshaft sprocket with timing mark at the 5 o'clock position—2.0L engine

44. Remove the paper clip from the balance shaft drive chain tensioner.

45. Install the oil nozzle and bolt. Tighten the oil nozzle bolt to 89 inch lbs. (10 Nm).

46. Install the crankshaft sprocket with timing mark at the 5 o'clock position.

47. Lower the timing chain through the opening in the top of the cylinder head. Carefully ensure that the chain goes around both sides of the cylinder block bosses (1 and 2).

48. Install the intake camshaft sprocket with the INT diamond at the 2 o'clock position.

➡**Always install NEW sprocket bolts.**

49. Hand tighten a NEW intake camshaft sprocket bolt.

50. Route the timing chain around the crankshaft sprocket with the matching colored link aligning with the timing mark.

51. Route the timing chain around the intake camshaft sprocket with the uniquely colored link (1) aligning with the INT diamond.

52. Install the timing chain tensioner guide through the opening in the top of the cylinder head. Tighten the timing chain tensioner guide bolt to 89 inch lbs. (10 Nm).

53. Install the exhaust camshaft sprocket with the timing chain matching colored link (3) at EXH triangle aligned at the 10 o'clock position.

54. Use a 24 mm wrench to rotate the camshaft slightly, until exhaust sprocket aligns with the camshaft.

➡**Always install NEW sprocket bolts.**

55. Hand tighten the NEW exhaust camshaft sprocket bolt.

56. Install the fixed timing chain guide

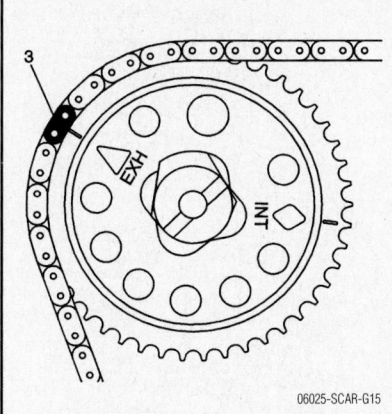

Fig. 94 Install the exhaust camshaft sprocket with the timing chain matching colored link (3) at EXH triangle aligned at the 10 o'clock position—2.0L engine

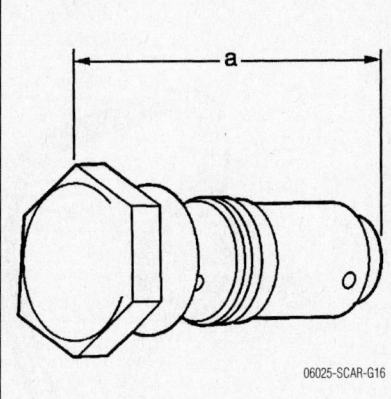

Fig. 95 Measure the timing chain tensioner assembly from end to end. Refer to the text for measurement specifications—2.0L engine

and tighten the fixed timing chain bolts to 133 inch lbs. (15 Nm)

57. Apply sealant, GM P/N 12378521 to the threads and install the timing chain guide bolt access hole plug. Tighten the chain guide plug to 59 ft. lbs. (90 Nm).

58. Install the timing chain upper guide. Tighten the timing chain upper guide bolts to 89 inch lbs. (10 Nm).

59. Inspect the timing chain tensioner. If the timing chain tensioner, O-ring seal, or washer is damaged, replace the timing chain tensioner.

60. Measure the timing chain tensioner assembly from end to end. A new tensioner should be supplied in the fully compressed non-active state. A tensioner in the compressed state will measure 2.83 inch (72 mm) (a) from end to end. A tensioner in the active state will measure 3.35 inch (85 mm) from end to end.

61. If the timing chain tensioner is not in the compressed state, perform the following steps:

   a. Remove the piston assembly from the body of the timing chain tensioner by pulling it out.

   b. Install tensioner tool J 45027-2 into a vise.

62. Install the notch end of the piston assembly into tensioner tool J 45027-2.

63. Using tool J 45027-1, turn the ratchet cylinder into the piston.

64. Inspect the bore of the tensioner body for dirt, debris, and damage. If any damage appears, replace the tensioner. Clean dirt or debris out with a lint-free cloth.

65. Install the compressed piston assembly back into the timing chain ten-

sioner body until it stops at the bottom of the bore. Do not compress the piston assembly against the bottom of the bore. If the piston assembly is compressed against the bottom of the bore, it will activate the tensioner, which will then need to be reset again.

66. At this point the tensioner should measure approximately 2.83 inch (72 mm) from end to end. If the tensioner does not read 2.83 inch (72 mm) from end to end repeat the compression steps.

67. Install the timing chain tensioner. Tighten the timing chain tensioner to 55 ft. lbs. (75 Nm).

68. Use a suitable tool with a rubber tip on the end. Feed the tool down through the camshaft drive chain to rest on the timing chain. Then give a sharp jolt diagonally downwards to release the tensioner.

69. Use a 24 mm wrench to hold the camshaft. Tighten the NEW camshaft bolts to 63 ft. Lbs. (85 Nm) plus an additional 30 degrees.

70. Install the camshaft cover.

71. If removed install a new engine front cover gasket.

72. Install the front engine mount bracket as follows:

   a. Install the intermediate bracket to the engine.

   b. Hand tighten the engine mount intermediate bracket bolts. Position the long bolts in the forward and front lower holes and the short bolt in the rear upper hole.

   c. Tighten the intermediate bracket bolts to 74 ft. lbs. (100 Nm).

73. Install the front engine mount as follows:

   a. Place the engine mount onto the midrail and hand start the nuts.

   b. Tighten the engine mount to midrail nuts to 74 ft. lbs. (100 Nm).

➡ **The engine mount to intermediate bracket bolts must be hand started. Do not pry the engine mount to align the holes.**

74. Hand start the engine mount to intermediate bracket bolts.

75. Tighten the engine mount to intermediate bracket bolts, starting with the center bolt. Tighten the bolts to 37 ft. lbs. (50 Nm).

76. Install the engine front cover.

77. Install the engine front cover bolts. Tighten the engine front cover bolts to 18 ft. lbs. (25 Nm).

78. Install the water pump bolt. Tighten the water pump bolt to 18 ft. lbs. (25 Nm).

79. Install the idler pulley. Tighten the bolts to 18 ft. lbs. (25 Nm).

80. Install the drive belt tensioner. Tighten the drive belt tensioner bolts to 33 ft. lbs. (45 Nm).

81. Install the crankshaft balancer.

82. Install a NEW crankshaft balancer bolt.

83. Using tool J 38122-A to prevent the crankshaft from rotating, install a new balancer bolt and tighten to 74 ft. lbs. (100 Nm) plus an additional 75 degrees

84. Install the engine drive belt.

85. Connect the negative battery cable.

2.2L Engine

See Figures 96 through 103.

1. Before servicing the vehicle, refer to the precautions section.

2. Drain the engine oil.

3. Remove or disconnect the following:
   • Negative battery cable
   • Air cleaner assembly
   • Accelerator cable from the throttle body and bracket
   • Accelerator bracket bolts and the bracket
   • Positive Crankcase Ventilation (PCV) hose
   • Fuel line bracket
   • Ignition Coil Module (ICM) connector
   • ICM screws and the ICM
   • Ignition coil housing bolts and the housing
   • Ground strap stud from the camshaft cover
   • Ground strap
   • Camshaft cover bolts
   • Camshaft cover
   • Accessory drive belt

- Using harmonic balancer holder J 38122-A to prevent the crankshaft from rotating and remove the balancer bolt and discard
- Crankshaft balancer
- Belt tensioner

4. Remove the front engine mount as follows:

   a. Support the engine with a jack and a piece of wood.

   b. Remove the mount-to-intermediate bracket bolts

   c. Remove the mount-to-midrail nuts

   d. Remove the mount.

- Front cover bolts and the 13mm bolt under the water pump
- Front cover

➡ **The timing chain has 2 matching colored links and 1 unique colored link.**

5. Rotate the engine until the crankshaft sprocket mark aligns with the matching colored link at the 5 o' clock position.

6. Make sure the timing chain to the intake camshaft sprocket alignment copper link to the "INT" diamond timing mark on the camshaft sprocket.

7. Make sure the "EXH" triangle on the exhaust camshaft sprocket is aligned with the colored link.

8. Remove or disconnect the following:
- Timing chain tensioner
- Fixed timing chain guide access plug and the guide
- Upper timing chain guide
- Exhaust camshaft sprocket
- Timing chain tensioner guide
- Intake camshaft sprocket
- Timing chain through the top of the cylinder head
- Timing chain sprocket from the crankshaft
- Balance shaft drive chain tensioner
- Adjustable timing chain guide
- Small balance shaft drive chain guide
- Upper balance shaft drive chain guide

➡ **To make it easier to remove the balance shaft chain, get all the slack in the chain between the crankshaft and the water pump sprockets.**

- Balance shaft drive chain

To install:

➡ **If the balance shafts are not properly aligned engine noise will occur.**

9. Install or connect the following:
- Upper balance shaft chain guide and tighten the bolts to 89 inch lbs. (10 Nm)

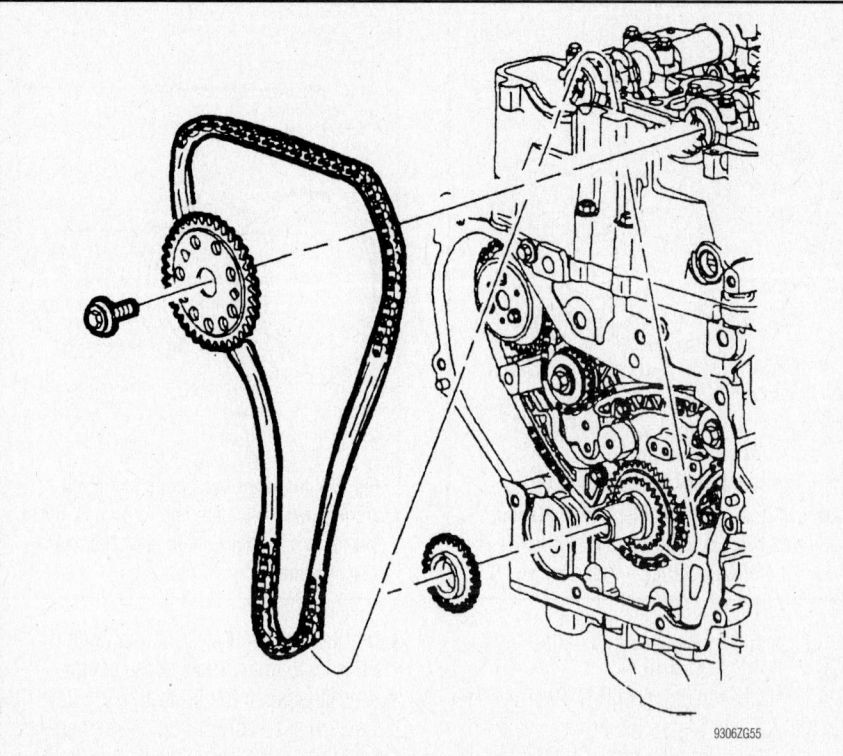

Fig. 96 Remove the timing chain through the top of the cylinder head–ION with 2.2L engine

10. Install the balance shaft chain with the colored links lined up on the marks on the balance shaft drive sprockets and crankshaft sprocket. Use the following to align the links with the sprockets while referring to the accompanying illustration for link location:

   e. Place the chain so that the copper colored and chrome links can be clearly seen

   f. Place link 1 (see illustration) so that it aligns with the timing mark on the intake side balance shaft sprocket.

   g. Working in a clockwise direction around the chain, place the link 2 (see illustration) in line with the timing mark on the crankshaft sprocket, this will be approximately at the 5 o'clock position.

   h. Place link 3 (see illustration) on the water pump sprocket (alignment is not critical).

   i. Align link 4 (see illustration) with the timing mark on the exhaust side balance shaft sprocket.

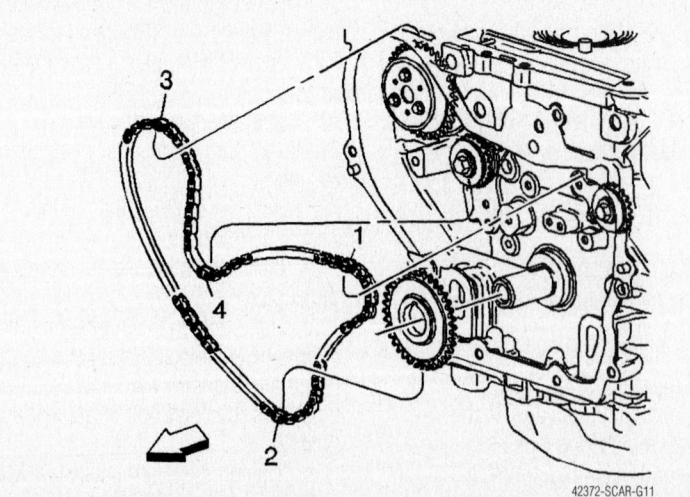

Fig. 97 Install the balance shaft chain with the colored links lined up on the marks on the balance shaft drive sprockets and crankshaft sprocket –ION with 2.2L engine

j. Install the small balance shaft chain guide and tighten the bolts to 89 inch lbs. (10 Nm).

k. Install the adjustable balance shaft drive chain guide and tighten the bolts to 89 inch lbs. (10 Nm).

l. Turn the tensioner plunger 90 degrees in its bore and compress the plunger until a paper clip can be inserted through the hole in the plunger body and the hole in the plunger.

m. Install the timing chain tensioner and tighten the bolts to 89 inch lbs. (10 Nm).

n. Remove the clip from the balance shaft tensioner.

11. Inspect the chain guides for wear and damage. Replace the guides if wear exceeds 0.045 inch (1.12mm). Inspect the timing chain shoe. Replace the shoe if wear exceeds 0.045 inch (1.12mm).

12. Install or connect the following:
- Timing chain sprocket to the crankshaft. Rotate the crankshaft so that the mark on the sprocket is at the 5 o'clock position.

13. Lower the timing chain through the opening in the cylinder head. make sure the chain goes around both sides of the cylinder block bosses (see illustration).

- Intake camshaft sprocket with the "INT" diamond at the 2 o'clock position and hand-tighten a new intake camshaft sprocket bolt
- Timing chain around the crankshaft sprocket and align the silver link to the timing mark
- Timing chain to the intake camshaft sprocket alignment copper link to the "INT" diamond timing mark on the camshaft sprocket
- Timing chain tensioner guide and torque the bolt to 89 inch lbs. (10 Nm)
- Exhaust camshaft sprocket loosely on the camshaft with the timing mark on the sprocket aligned with the silver link (3) on the chain at the 10 o'clock position and hand-tighten the new bolt at this time

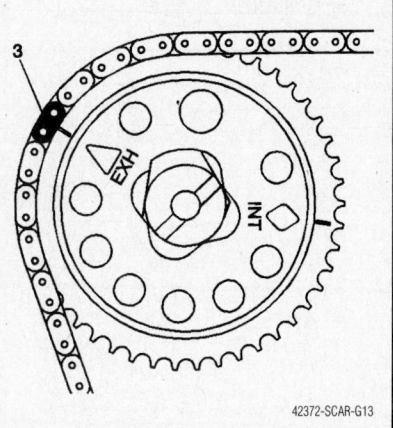

Fig. 99 Align the timing mark on the exhaust camshaft sprocket with the silver link (3) on the chain—ION with 2.2L engine

14. Align the camshaft sprocket to camshaft and tighten the bolt using the following procedure:

a. Make certain that the sprocket timing mark is at the 5 o'clock position.

b. Rotate the intake camshaft using a 24mm wrench on flats of the camshaft until the sprocket to camshaft alignment notch seats.

c. When seated properly hand-tighten the bolt.

d. Rotate the exhaust camshaft using a 24mm wrench on flats of the camshaft until the sprocket to camshaft alignment notch seats.

e. When seated properly hand-tighten the bolt.

15. Verify that all colored links are aligned with the proper marks on the camshaft and crankshaft sprockets.

16. Install or connect the following:
- Fixed timing chain guide and tighten the bolt to 89 inch lbs. (10 Nm)
- Apply Saturn compound 21485277 to the fixed timing chain guide bolt access plug threads, install the bolt and torque it to 30 ft. lbs. (40 Nm)
- Upper timing chain guide and torque the bolts to 89 inch lbs. (10 Nm)

17. Inspect the timing chain tensioner. If the tensioner O–ring or washer is damaged the tensioner must be replaced.

18. If replacing the tensioner, measure the tensioner assembly from end-to-end. A new tensioner should be in the fully compressed non-active state. A tensioner in the non-active state should measure 2.83 inches (72mm) from end-to-end. The tensioner in the active state will measure 3.35 inches (85mm) from end-to-end.

19. If the tensioner is not in the compressed state, perform the following steps:

a. Pull the piston assembly from the tensioner body.

b. Install tensioner tool J 45027-2 into a vise.

c. Install the notch end of the piston assembly into J 45027-2.

d. Using tool J 45027-1, turn the ratchet cylinder into the pump.

e. Inspect the bore of the tensioner body for damage or dirt. If any damage is present, replace the tensioner.

f. Install the compressed piston assembly back into the tensioner body until it bottoms out in the bore. Do not compress the piston against the bottom of the bore. If the piston is compressed in the bore it will activate the tensioner and the piston will have to be reset.

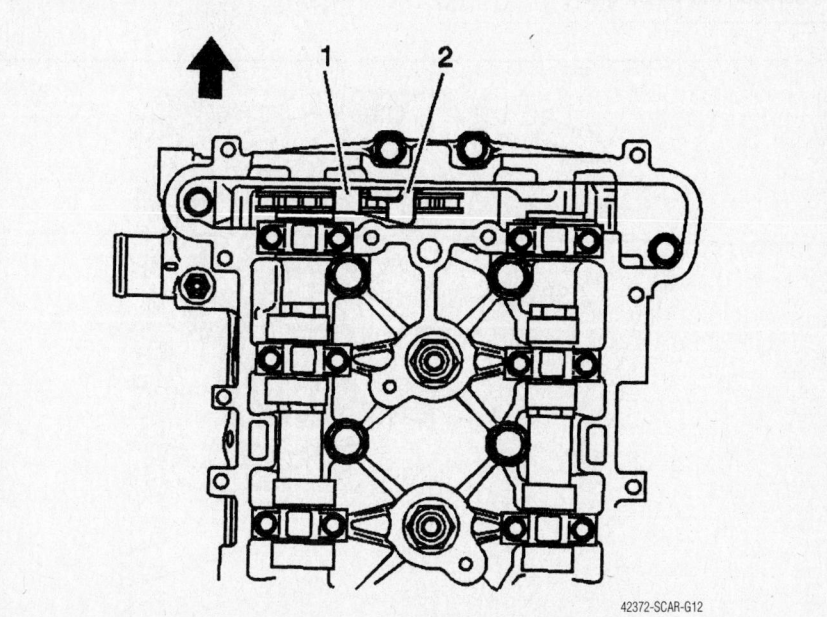

Fig. 98 Lower the timing chain through the opening in the cylinder head. make sure the chain goes around both sides of the cylinder block bosses—ION with 2.2L engine

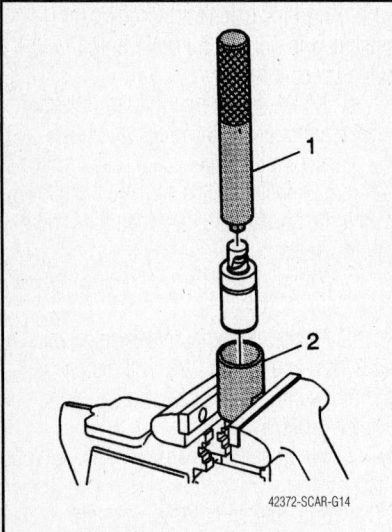

Fig. 100 Resetting the timing chain tensioner piston—ION with 2.2L engine

g. Check that the tensioner measures 2.83 inches (72mm) from end-to-end. If this measurement is incorrect, reset the piston.

h. Install the tensioner assembly and tighten to 55 ft. lbs. (75 Nm)

i. Using a suitable tool with a rubber tip on the end, feed the tool down through the camshaft drive chant to rest on the timing chain. Give a sharp jolt diagonally downwards to release the tensioner.

20. Install or connect the following:

• Intake and exhaust camshaft sprocket bolts and torque them to 63 ft. lbs. (85 Nm) plus 30 degrees. Use a 24mm wrench as a back-up when tightening the bolts.
• Sealing ring and tensioner assembly and torque the tensioner bolts to 44 ft. lbs. (60 Nm)
• Camshaft cover
• Camshaft cover bolts and tighten to 89 inch lbs. (10 Nm)
• Ground strap
• Ground strap stud to the camshaft cover and tighten to 89 inch lbs. (10 Nm)
• Ignition coil housing and tighten the bolts to 89 inch lbs. (10 Nm)
• ICM and tighten the screws to 13 inch lbs. (1.5 Nm)
• ICM connector
• Fuel line bracket
• PCV hose
• Accelerator bracket and tighten the bolts to 89 inch lbs. (10 Nm)
• Accelerator cable to the throttle body and bracket
• Front cover gasket

21. Install the front engine mount as follows:

a. Install the mount.

b. Install the mount-to-midrail nuts and torque them to 74 ft. lbs. (100 Nm).

c. Install the mount-to-intermediate bracket bolts and torque to 37 ft. lbs. (50 Nm). Never pry the mount to align the holes, raise or lower the jack for alignment purposes.

d. Remove the jack.

22. Install or connect the following:

• Front cover and torque the bolts to 18 ft. lbs. (25 Nm) and the water pump bolt to 15 ft. lbs. (20 Nm)
• Drive belt tensioner and torque the fasteners to 33 ft. lbs. (45 Nm)
• Crankshaft balancer

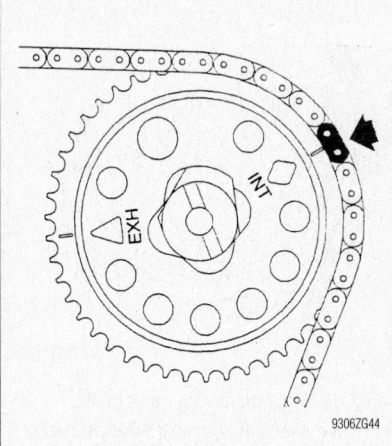

Fig. 101 Align the copper link on the timing chain with the INT diamond timing mark—ION with 2.2L engine

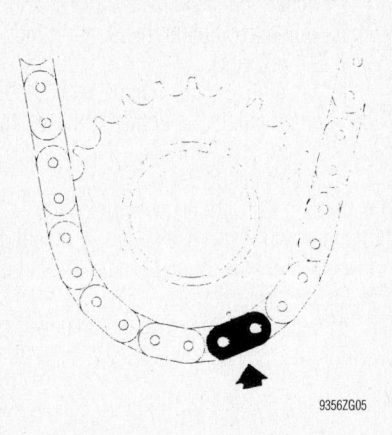

Fig. 103 Route the timing chain around the crankshaft sprocket and align the silver link to the timing mark (5 o'clock position)—ION with 2.2L engines

• Balancer bolt and using tool J 38122-A to prevent the crankshaft from rotating, install a new balancer bolt and tighten to 74 ft. lbs. (100 Nm) plus an additional 75 degrees
• Drive belt
• Negative battery cable

23. Fill the engine with clean oil.

24. Start the vehicle and check for leaks, repair if necessary.

2.4L Engine

See Figures 104 through 122.

1. Before servicing the vehicle, refer to the precautions section.

2. Drain the engine oil.

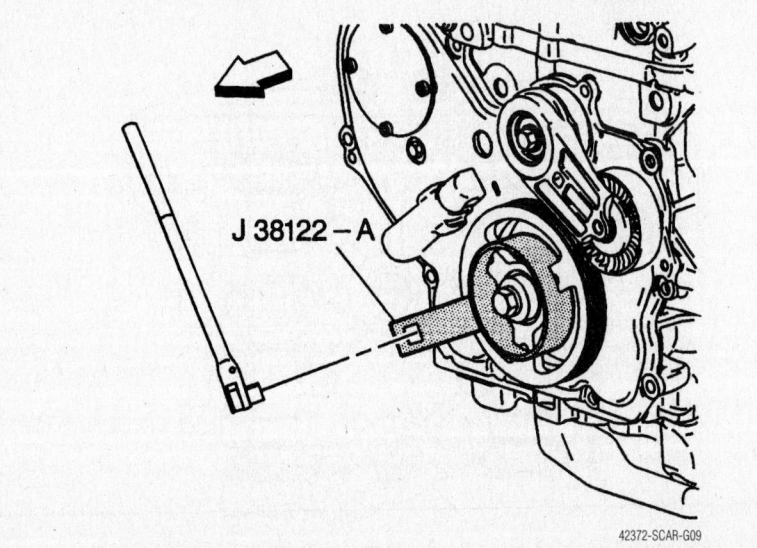

Fig. 102 Make sure the "EXH" triangle on the exhaust camshaft sprocket is aligned with the colored link Installing the balancer bolt using the special tool—ION with 2.2L engine

3. Remove the no. 1 cylinder spark plug.

4. Rotate the crankshaft in the engine rotational direction clockwise, until the no. 1 piston is at Top Dead Center (TDC) on the compression stroke.

5. Remove the camshaft cover.

6. Remove the engine front cover as follows:

   a. Remove the drive belt tensioner.

   b. Remove the crankshaft balancer.

   c. Remove the air cleaner assembly.

   d. Remove the windshield washer solvent reservoir.

   e. Install the engine support fixture.

   f. Remove the engine mount to bracket bolts.

   g. Remove the engine mount to side rail nuts.

   h. Remove the engine mount from the engine compartment.

   i. Remove the engine mount bracket to engine bolts.

   j. Remove the engine mount bracket.

   k. Remove the engine front cover to water pump bolt.

   l. Raise and suitably support the vehicle.

   m. Remove the engine front cover bolts.

   n. Remove the engine front cover.

   o. Remove and discard the engine front cover gasket.

7. Remove the upper timing chain guide bolts and guide.

➡**The timing chain tensioner must be removed to unload chain tension before the timing chain is removed. If it is not, the timing chain will become cocked and it will be difficult to remove.**

8. Remove the timing chain tensioner.

9. Install a 24 mm wrench on the hex on the exhaust camshaft in order to hold the camshaft.

10. Remove and discard the exhaust camshaft actuator bolt.

11. Remove the exhaust camshaft actuator from the camshaft and timing chain.

12. Remove the timing chain tensioner guide bolt and guide.

13. Remove the fixed timing chain guide access plug.

14. Remove the fixed timing chain guide bolts and guide.

15. Install a 24 mm wrench on the hex on the intake camshaft in order to hold the camshaft.

16. Remove and discard the intake camshaft actuator bolt.

17. Remove the intake camshaft actuator, and the timing chain through the top of the cylinder head.

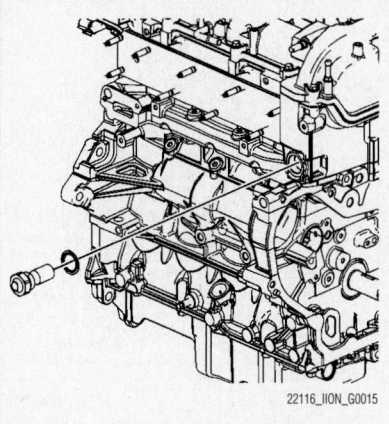

Fig. 104 The timing chain tensioner must be removed to unload chain tension before the timing chain is removed—2.4L engine

22116_IION_G0015

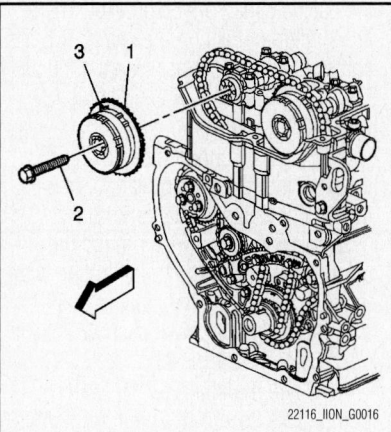

Fig. 105 Exhaust camshaft actuator assembly—2.4L engine

22116_IION_G0016

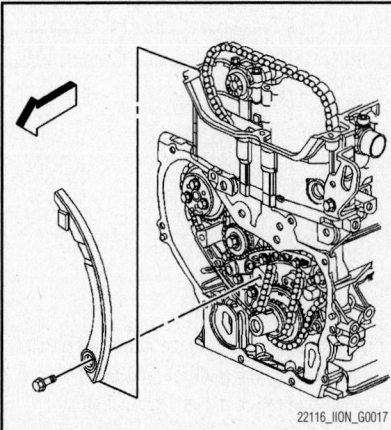

Fig. 106 Remove the timing chain tensioner guide—2.4L engine

22116_IION_G0017

18. Remove the timing chain crankshaft sprocket.

19. If replacing the balance shaft timing chain and sprocket, perform the following:

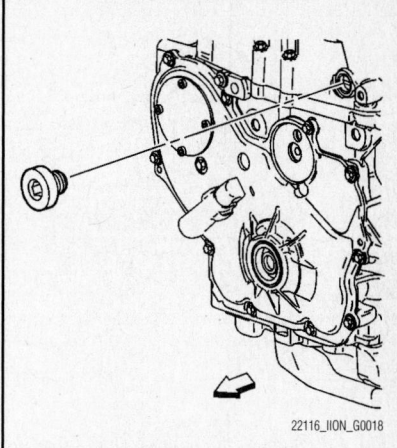

Fig. 107 Remove the fixed timing chain guide access plug—2.4L engine

22116_IION_G0018

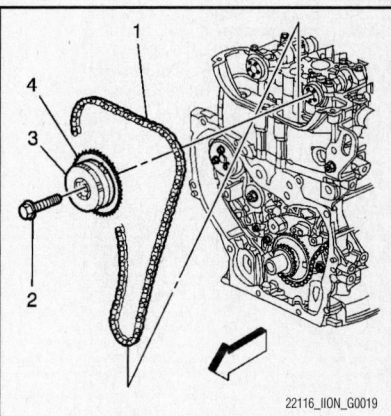

Fig. 108 Remove the intake camshaft actuator, and the timing chain through the top of the cylinder head—2.4L engine

22116_IION_G0019

   a. Remove the balance shaft drive chain tensioner bolts and tensioner.

   b. Remove the adjustable balance shaft chain guide bolt and guide.

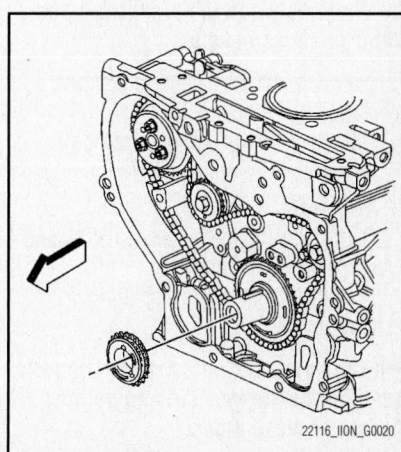

Fig. 109 Remove the timing chain crankshaft sprocket—2.4L engine

22116_IION_G0020

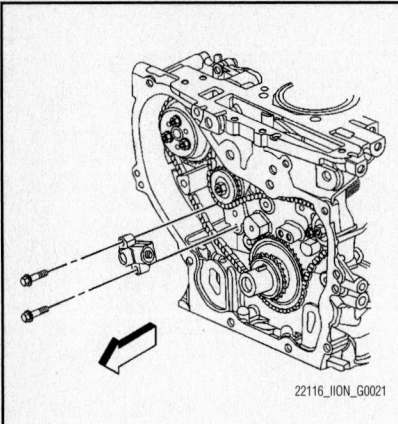

Fig. 110 Remove the balance shaft drive chain tensioner–2.4L engine

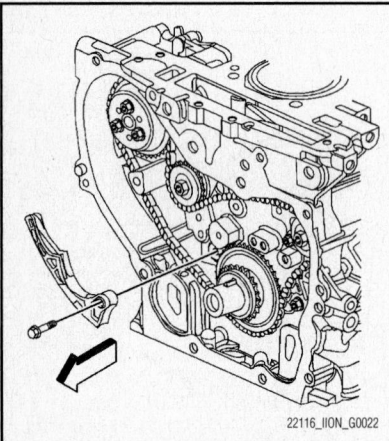

Fig. 111 Remove the adjustable balance shaft chain guide–2.4L engine

c. Remove the small balance shaft drive chain guide bolts and guide.

d. Remove the upper balance shaft drive chain guide bolts and guide.

➡ **It may ease removal of the balance shaft drive chain to get all the slack in the chain between the crankshaft and water pump sprockets.**

a. Remove the balance shaft drive chain.

b. Remove the balance shaft drive sprocket.

To install:

20. If replacing the balance shaft timing chain, perform the following:

a. Install the balance shaft drive sprocket.

➡ **If the balance shafts are not properly timed to the engine, the engine may vibrate or make noise.**

b. Install the balance shaft drive chain with the colored link lined up with the

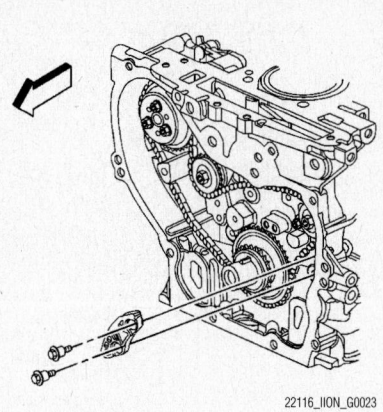

Fig. 112 Remove the small balance shaft drive chain guide–2.4L engine

marks on the balance shaft sprockets and the balance shaft drive sprocket. There are 3 colored links on the chain. Two are chrome and 1 is copper. Use the following steps in order to line up the links with the sprockets.

c. Place the copper link so that it lines up with the timing mark on the intake side balance shaft sprocket.

d. Working clockwise around the chain, place the chrome link in line with the timing mark on the balance shaft drive sprocket. (approximately 6 o'clock position on the sprocket).

e. Place the chain on the water pump drive sprocket. The alignment is not critical.

f. Align the last chrome link with the timing mark on the exhaust side balance shaft drive sprocket.

g. Install the upper balance shaft

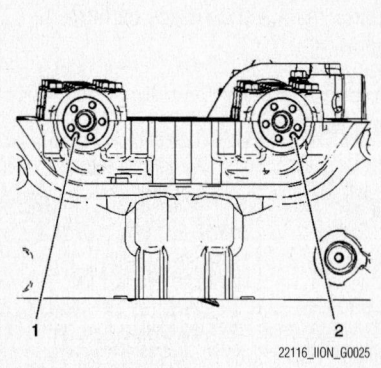

Fig. 113 Ensure the intake camshaft notch is in the 5 o'clock position and the exhaust camshaft notch is in the 7 o'clock position. The number 1 piston should be at TDC, crankshaft key at 12 o'clock–2.4L engine

drive chain guide and bolts. Tighten to 11 ft. lbs. (15 Nm).

h. Install the small balance shaft drive chain guide and bolts. Tighten to 11 ft. lbs. (15 Nm).

i. Install the adjustable balance shaft chain guide and bolt. Tighten to 89 in. lbs. (10 Nm).

21. Reset the timing chain tensioner as follows:

a. Rotate the tensioner plunger 90 degrees in its bore and compress the plunger.

b. Rotate the tensioner back to the original 12 o'clock position and insert a paper clip through the hole in the plunger body and into the hose in the tensioner plunger.

c. Install the balance shaft drive chain tensioner and bolts. Tighten to 89 in. lbs. (10 Nm).

d. Remove the paper clip from the balance shaft drive chain tensioner.

22. Ensure the intake camshaft notch is in the 5 o'clock position and the exhaust camshaft notch is in the 7 o'clock position. The number 1 piston should be at TDC, crankshaft key at 12 o'clock.

23. Install the timing chain drive sprocket to the crankshaft with the timing mark in the 5 o'clock position and the front of the sprocket facing out.

➡ **There are 3 colored links on the timing chain. Two links are of matching color, and 1 link is of a unique color. Use the following procedure to line up the links with the actuators. Orient the chain so that the colored links are visible. Always use new actuator bolts.**

Fig. 114 Install the timing chain drive sprocket to the crankshaft with the timing mark in the 5 o'clock position and the front of the sprocket facing out–2.4L engine

ENGINE PERFORMANCE & EMISSION CONTROL

COMPONENT LOCATIONS

See Figures 123 through 132.

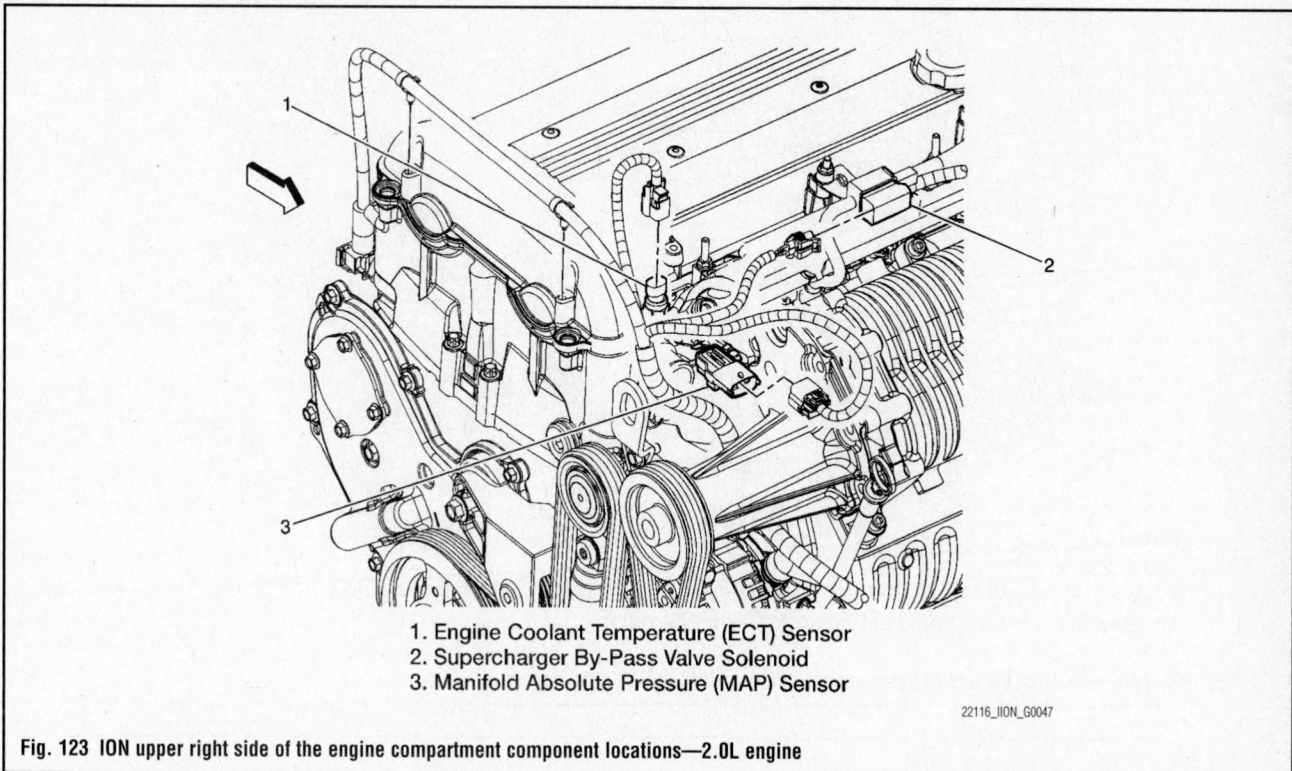

1. Engine Coolant Temperature (ECT) Sensor
2. Supercharger By-Pass Valve Solenoid
3. Manifold Absolute Pressure (MAP) Sensor

22116_IION_G0047

Fig. 123 ION upper right side of the engine compartment component locations—2.0L engine

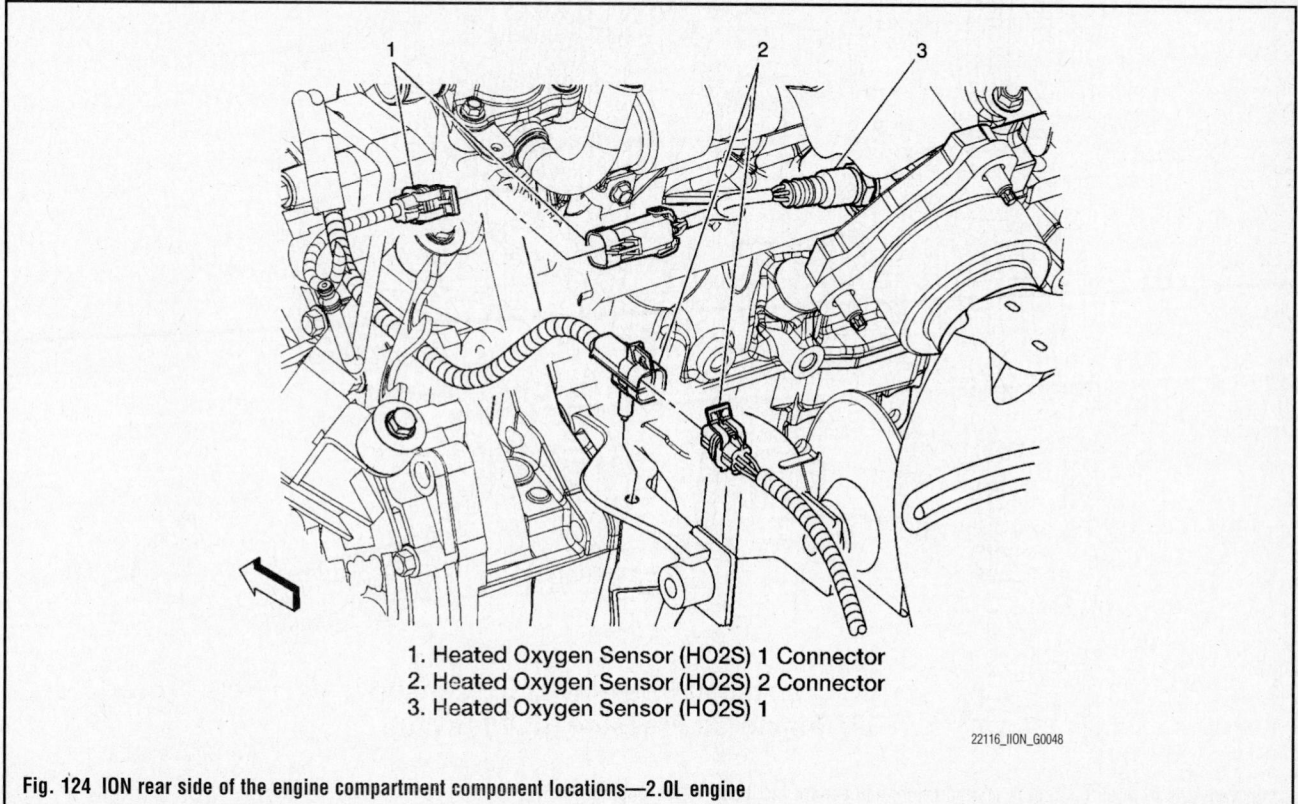

1. Heated Oxygen Sensor (HO2S) 1 Connector
2. Heated Oxygen Sensor (HO2S) 2 Connector
3. Heated Oxygen Sensor (HO2S) 1

22116_IION_G0048

Fig. 124 ION rear side of the engine compartment component locations—2.0L engine

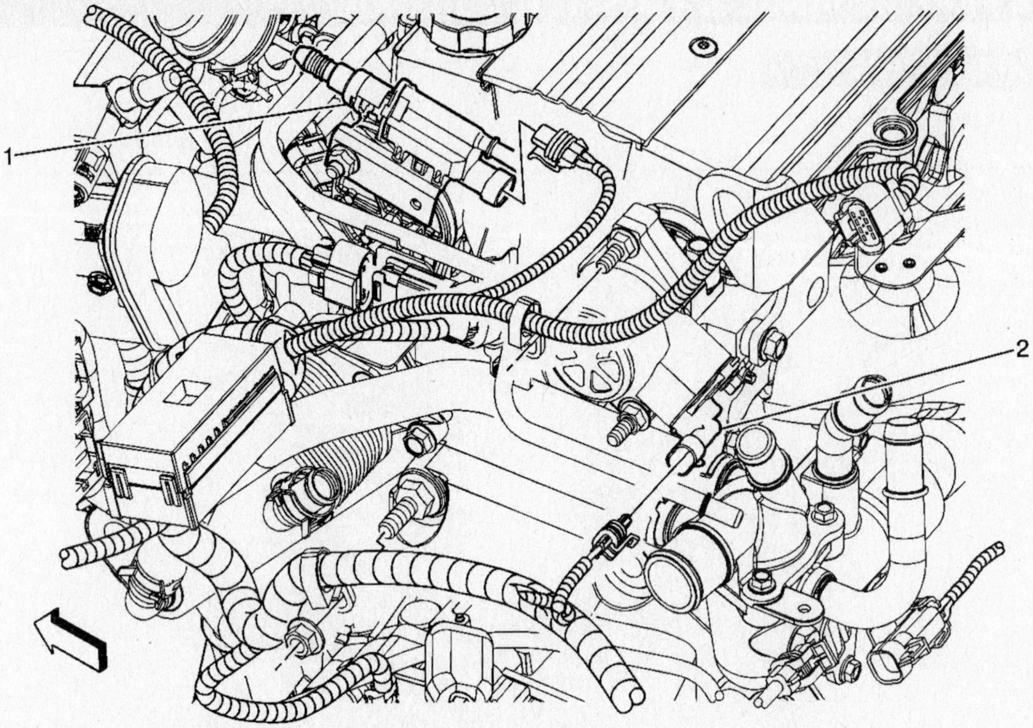

1. Evaporative Emission (EVAP) Canister Purge Solenoid
2. Camshaft Position (CMP) Sensor

22116_IION_G0049

Fig. 125 ION upper left side of the engine compartment component locations—2.0L engine

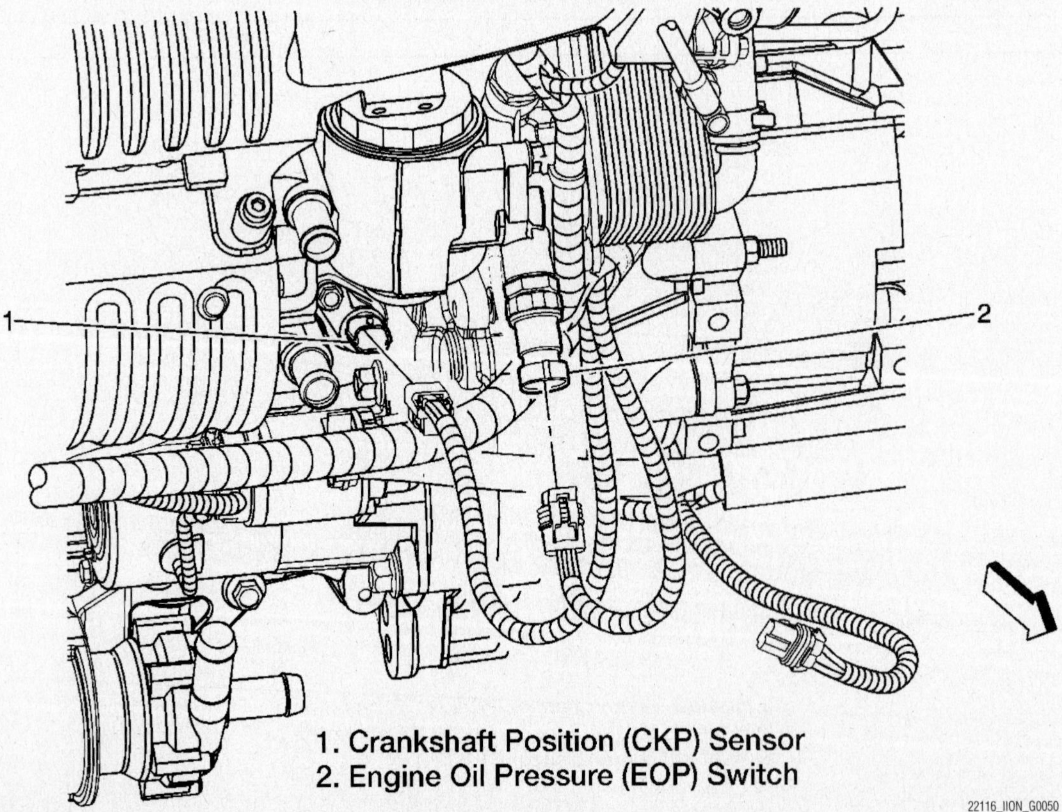

1. Crankshaft Position (CKP) Sensor
2. Engine Oil Pressure (EOP) Switch

22116_IION_G0050

Fig. 126 ION front of the engine compartment component locations—2.0L engine

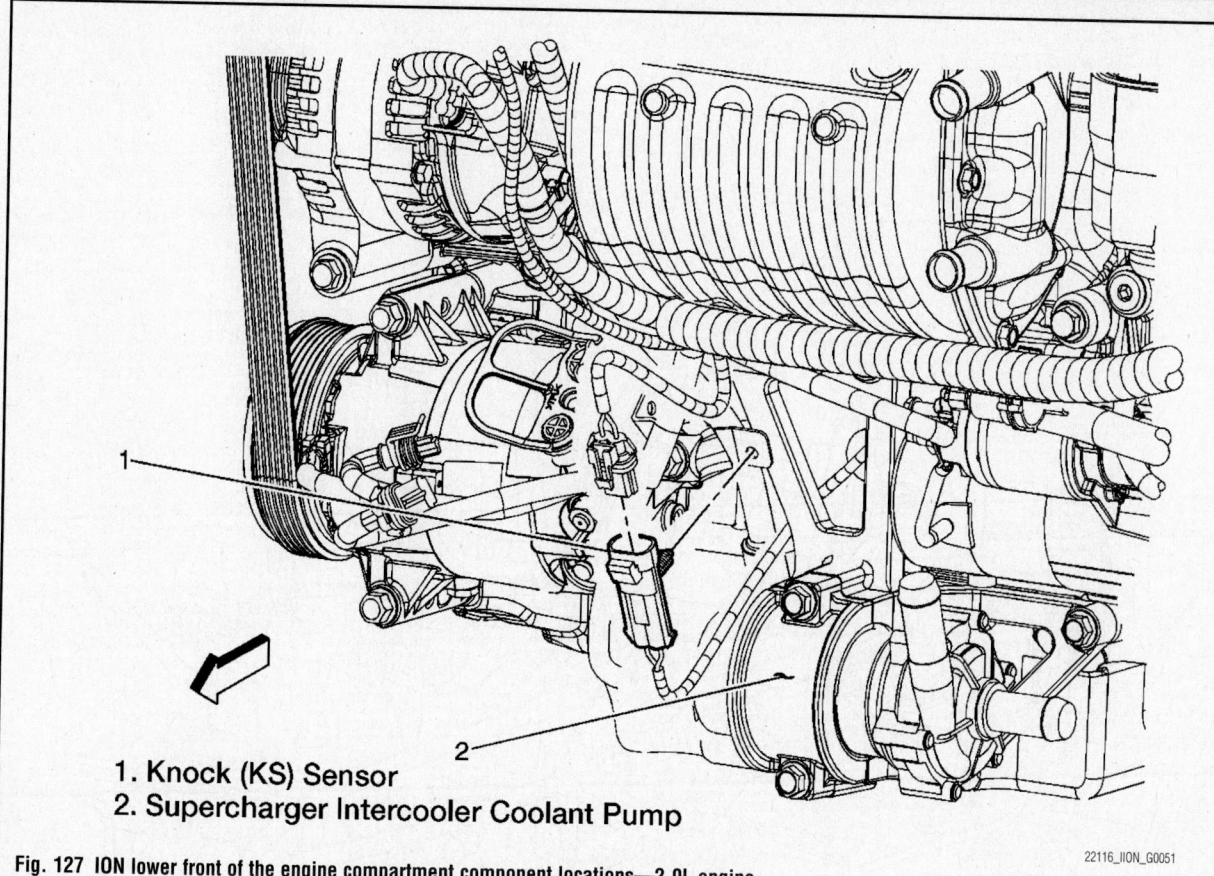

1. Knock (KS) Sensor
2. Supercharger Intercooler Coolant Pump

Fig. 127 ION lower front of the engine compartment component locations—2.0L engine

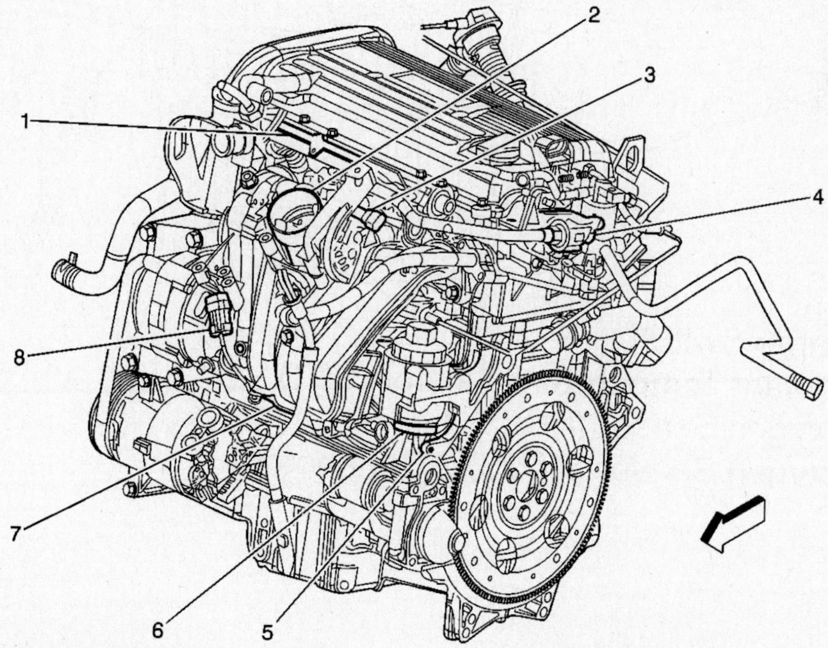

22116_IION_G0051

1. Fuel Injectors Rail
2. Throttle Body
3. Manifold Absolute Pressure (MAP) Sensor
4. Evaporative Emissions (EVAP)
   Canister Purge Solenoid Valve

5. G105 (2.0L Similar)
6. Crankshaft Position (CKP) Sensor
7. Knock Sensor (KS)
8. C150

Fig. 128 ION front left side of the engine compartment component locations—2.2L engine

22116_IION_G0052

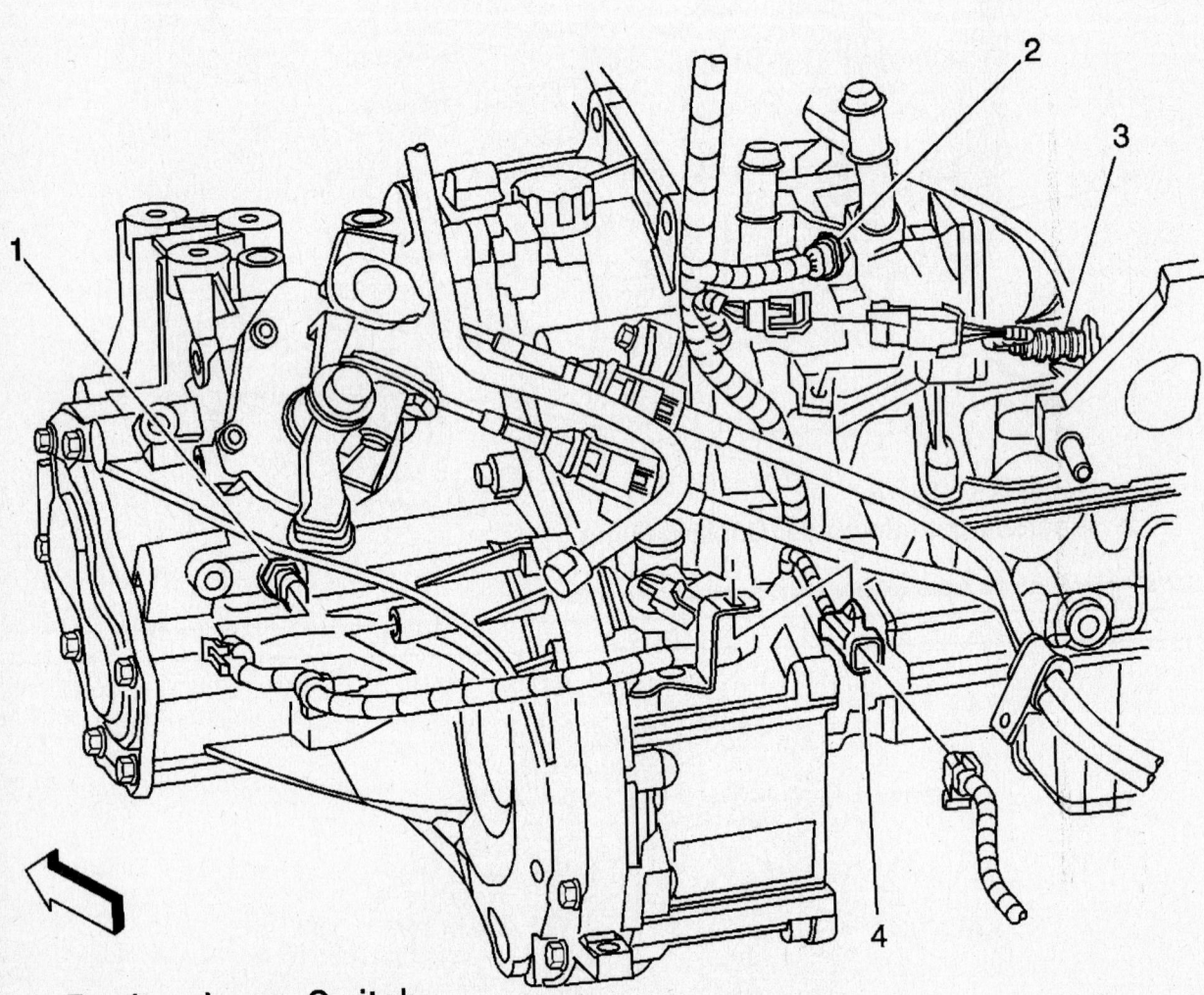

1. Backup Lamp Switch
2. Engine Coolant Temperature Sensor (ECT)
3. Heated Oxygen Sensor (HO2S) 1
4. Heated Oxygen Sensor (HO2S) 2 Connector

22116_IION_G0053

Fig. 129 ION rear side of the engine compartment component locations—2.2L engine

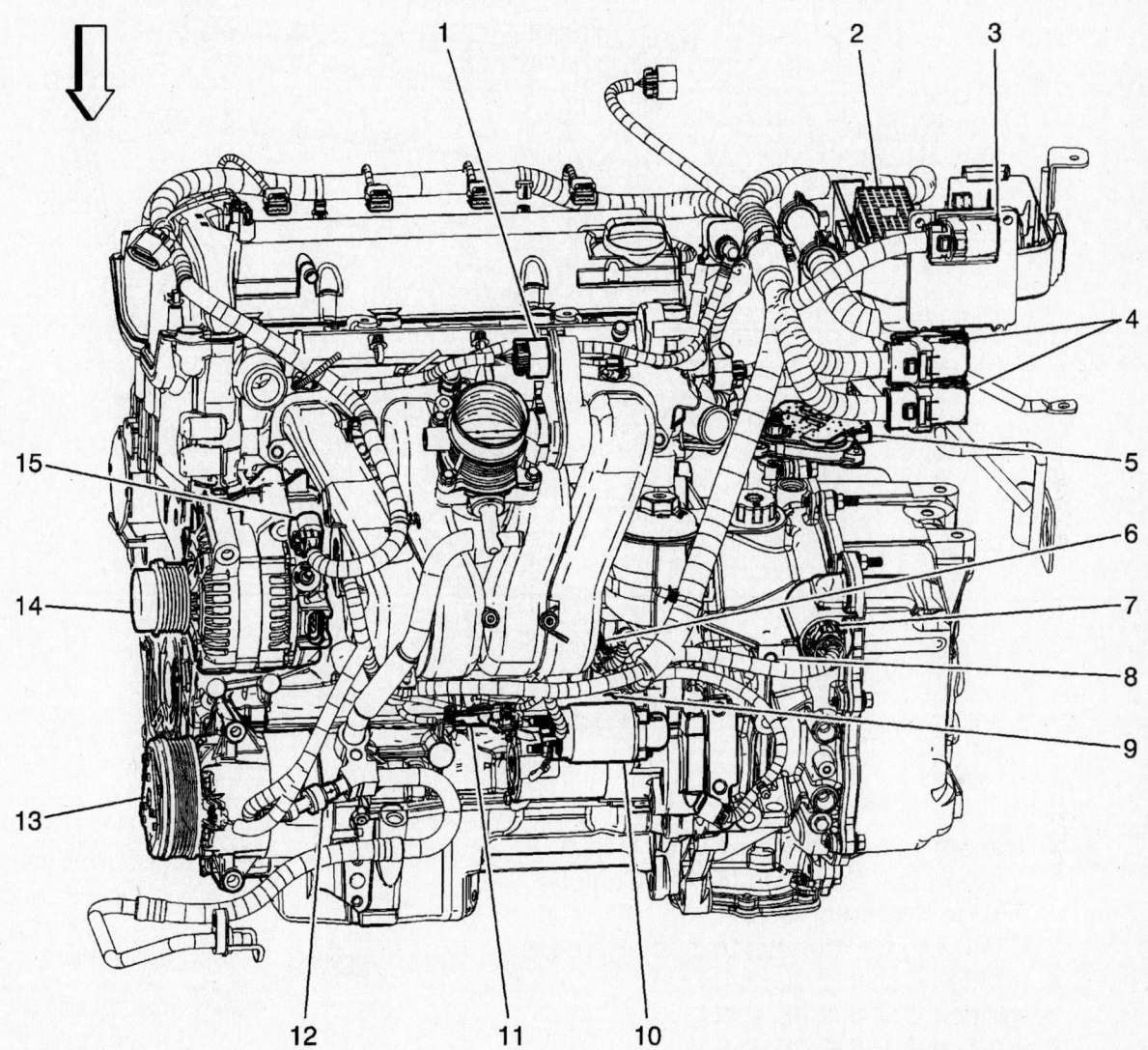

1. Throttle Body
2. Fuse Block Underhood C1
3. Transmission Control Module (TCM)
4. Engine Control Module (ECM)
5. Park/Neutral Position (PNP) Switch
6. Engine Oil Pressure (EOP) Switch
7. C100 Engine Harness to Transmission Harness
8. G105
9. Crankshaft Position (CKP) Sensor
10. Starter Motor
11. Knock Sensor Pigtail Connector
12. A/C High Pressure Switch
13. A/C Compressor
14. Alternator
15. C150 Engine Harness to Fuel Injector Harness

22116_IION_G0054

Fig. 130 ION front of the engine compartment component locations on models with an automatic transaxle—2.4L engine

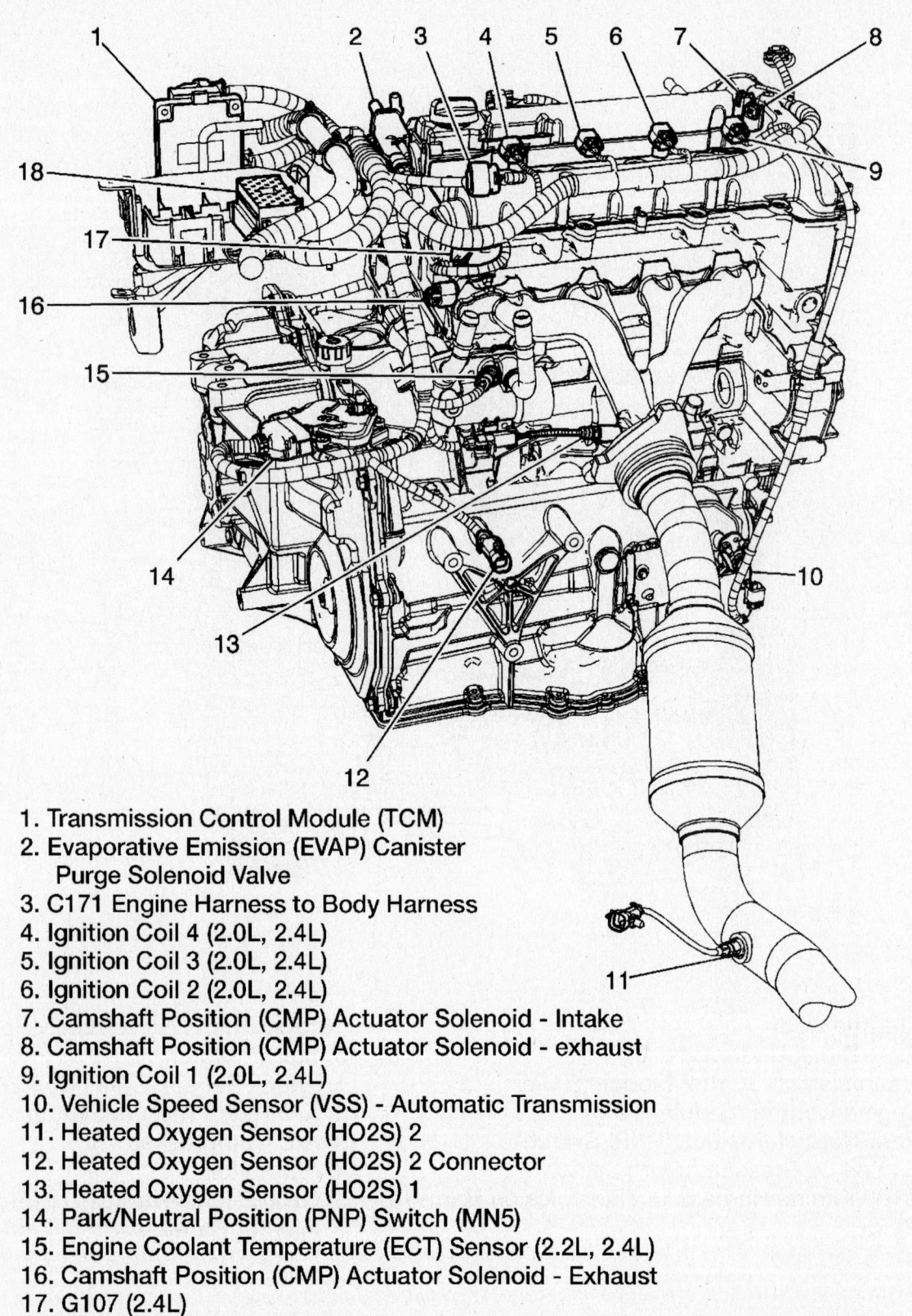

1. Transmission Control Module (TCM)
2. Evaporative Emission (EVAP) Canister Purge Solenoid Valve
3. C171 Engine Harness to Body Harness
4. Ignition Coil 4 (2.0L, 2.4L)
5. Ignition Coil 3 (2.0L, 2.4L)
6. Ignition Coil 2 (2.0L, 2.4L)
7. Camshaft Position (CMP) Actuator Solenoid - Intake
8. Camshaft Position (CMP) Actuator Solenoid - exhaust
9. Ignition Coil 1 (2.0L, 2.4L)
10. Vehicle Speed Sensor (VSS) - Automatic Transmission
11. Heated Oxygen Sensor (HO2S) 2
12. Heated Oxygen Sensor (HO2S) 2 Connector
13. Heated Oxygen Sensor (HO2S) 1
14. Park/Neutral Position (PNP) Switch (MN5)
15. Engine Coolant Temperature (ECT) Sensor (2.2L, 2.4L)
16. Camshaft Position (CMP) Actuator Solenoid - Exhaust
17. G107 (2.4L)
18. Fuse Block - Underhood C1

22116_IION_G0055

Fig. 131 ION rear of the engine compartment component locations—2.4L engine

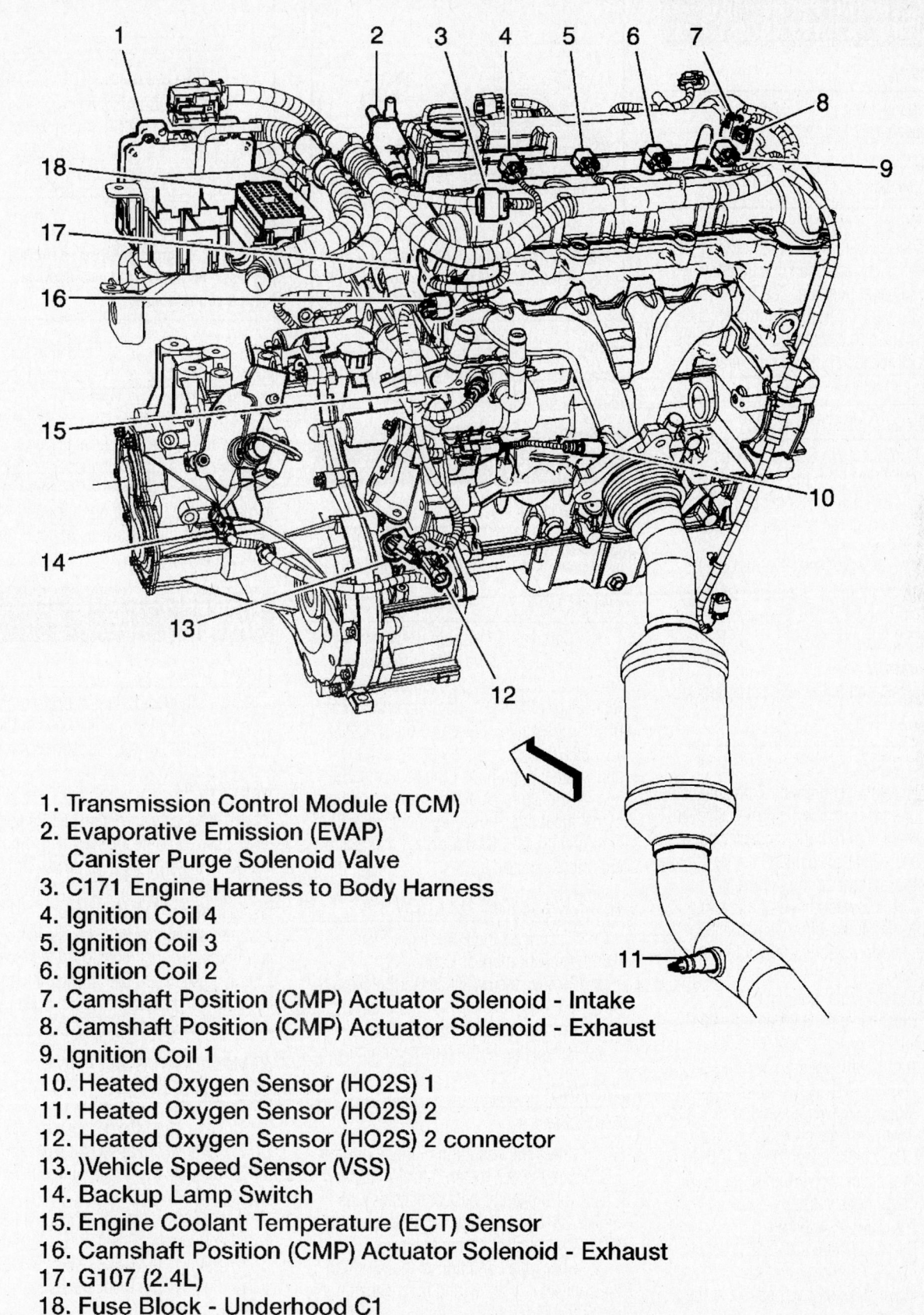

1. Transmission Control Module (TCM)
2. Evaporative Emission (EVAP)
   Canister Purge Solenoid Valve
3. C171 Engine Harness to Body Harness
4. Ignition Coil 4
5. Ignition Coil 3
6. Ignition Coil 2
7. Camshaft Position (CMP) Actuator Solenoid - Intake
8. Camshaft Position (CMP) Actuator Solenoid - Exhaust
9. Ignition Coil 1
10. Heated Oxygen Sensor (HO2S) 1
11. Heated Oxygen Sensor (HO2S) 2
12. Heated Oxygen Sensor (HO2S) 2 connector
13.)Vehicle Speed Sensor (VSS)
14. Backup Lamp Switch
15. Engine Coolant Temperature (ECT) Sensor
16. Camshaft Position (CMP) Actuator Solenoid - Exhaust
17. G107 (2.4L)
18. Fuse Block - Underhood C1

22116_IION_G0056

Fig. 132 ION rear of the engine compartment component locations on models with a manual transaxle—2.4L engine

ACCELERATOR PEDAL POSITION (APP) SENSOR

LOCATION

The Accelerator Pedal Position (APP) sensor assembly is attached to the pedal assembly.

OPERATION

The sensor is made up of the two individual sensors within a single housing. Each sensor has a unique functionality to determine pedal position. The APP system along with the Powertrain Control Module (PCM) is used to calculate and control the amount of acceleration and deceleration through fuel injector control.

REMOVAL & INSTALLATION

1. Disconnect the Connector Position Assurance (CPA) from the Accelerator Pedal Position (APP) sensor connector.
2. Disconnect the APP sensor harness connector.
3. Remove the APP assembly attachment bolts from the brake pedal assembly.
4. Remove the APP assembly from the vehicle

To install:

5. Installation is the reverse of removal.

TESTING

See Figure 133.

1. Check the condition of the connector. Make sure the connector is firmly attached. Check for broken or bent connector pins. Repair any connector damage before continuing with troubleshooting the issue.
2. Check the condition of the wiring to the connector. If the wiring is damaged, repair the wiring before continuing with any further tests.
3. Turn OFF the ignition.
4. Disconnect the accelerator pedal connector.
5. Turn ON the ignition, with the engine OFF.
6. Measure the voltage of the APP sensor 2 5-volt reference circuit to a good ground. The reading should be 4.8–5.2 volts. If not check the wiring for an open, short or high resistance.
7. Turn OFF the ignition.
8. Disconnect the accelerator pedal connector
9. Make sure that the pedal is at the rest position.
10. Measure the resistance from the 5-volt reference of the accelerator pedal assembly to the accelerator pedal position

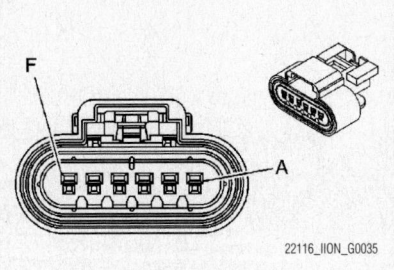

Fig. 133 Accelerator Pedal Position (APP) sensor terminals; (A) 5 volt reference (F) 5 volt reference

(APP) sensor 2 signal of the accelerator pedal assembly. If the resistance is less than 450 ohms, replace the sensor.

BAROMETRIC PRESSURE (BARO) SENSOR

LOCATION

The Barometric Pressure (BARO) sensor is located on the top left side of the engine.

OPERATION

The Barometric Pressure (BARO) sensor measures the pressure of the atmosphere. This pressure is affected by altitude and weather conditions. A diaphragm within the BARO sensor is displaced by the pressure changes that occur from varying altitudes and weather conditions. The sensor translates this diaphragm action into the voltage signal input that is used by the powertrain control module (PCM) for diagnostics and emissions control.

REMOVAL & INSTALLATION

1. Disconnect the Barometric Pressure (BARO) sensor harness connector.
2. Remove the BARO sensor bracket and bolt.
3. Remove the BARO sensor.
4. Installation is the reverse of removal.

TESTING

See Figure 134.

1. Check the condition of the connector. Make sure the connector is firmly attached. Check for broken or bent connector pins. Repair any connector damage before continuing with troubleshooting the issue.
2. Check the condition of the wiring to the connector. If the wiring is damaged, repair the wiring before continuing with any further tests.
3. Connect a jumper wire between the 5-volt reference circuit of the BARO sensor

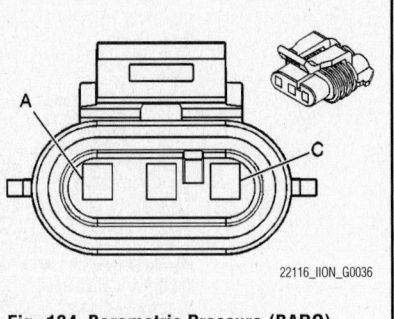

Fig. 134 Barometric Pressure (BARO) sensor terminals; (A) Low reference, (C) 5 volt reference

and the signal circuit of the BARO sensor at the harness connector. The reading should be approximately 4.8 volts.

4. Turn OFF the ignition for 90 seconds to allow the control modules to power down.
5. Measure the resistance from the low reference circuit of the BARO sensor at the harness connector to a good ground with a multimeter. If the resistance is not 5 ohms, replace the sensor.

CAMSHAFT POSITION (CMP) SENSOR

LOCATION

Refer to the Component Location illustrations for the location of the Camshaft Position (CMP) sensor for your vehicles engine.

OPERATION

The PCM uses the Camshaft Position (CMP) sensor to determine the position of the No. 1 piston during its power stroke. This signal is used by the PCM to calculate fuel injection mode of operation.

If the cam signal is lost while the engine is running, the fuel injection system will shift to a calculated fuel injected mode based on the last fuel injection pulse, and the engine will continue to run.

REMOVAL & INSTALLATION

See Figure 135.

1. Disconnect the negative battery cable.
2. Remove the drive belt tensioner.
3. Remove the underhood junction block.
4. Disconnect the electrical connector from the Camshaft Position (CMP) sensor.
5. Remove the CMP sensor studs.
6. Remove the CMP sensor.

To install:

7. Rotate the crankshaft until number 4 piston is at Top Dead Center (TDC) on the compression stroke.

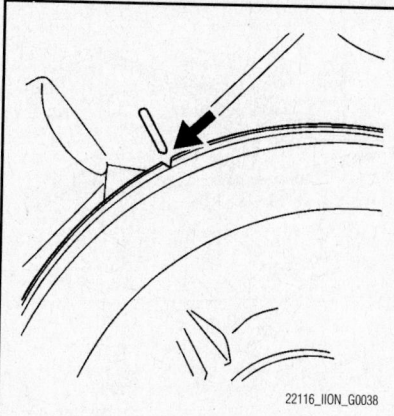

Fig. 135 Rotate the crankshaft until number 4 piston is at Top Dead Center (TDC) on the compression stroke before installing the new Camshaft Position (CMP) sensor

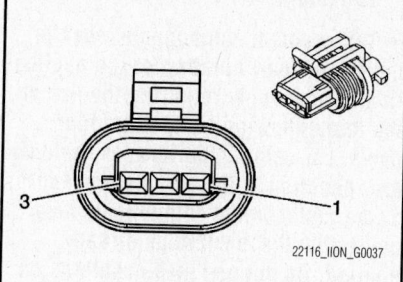

Fig. 136 Camshaft Position (CMP) sensor terminals; (1) 5 volt reference, (3) Low reference

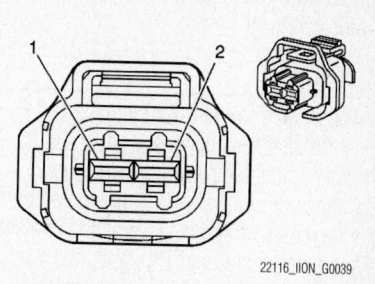

Fig. 137 Crankshaft Position (CKP) sensor terminals; (1) Low reference, (2) CKP sensor signal

8. Install the NEW camshaft position sensor housing seal.

9. Align the timing mark on the housing with the timing mark on the hex shaft.

10. Install the camshaft position sensor housing.

11. Install the camshaft position sensor housing studs and tighten to 16 ft. lbs. (22 Nm).

12. Install the underhood junction block.

13. Install the drive belt tensioner.

14. Connect the negative battery cable.

TESTING

See Figure 136.

1. Check the condition of the connector. Make sure the connector is firmly attached. Check for broken or bent connector pins. Repair any connector damage before continuing with troubleshooting the issue.

2. Check the condition of the wiring to the connector. If the wiring is damaged, repair the wiring before continuing with any further tests.

3. Visually inspect the CMP sensor reluctor ring for damage, repair as needed.

4. Measure the voltage from the 5-volt reference circuit of the CMP sensor to a good ground. The voltage should be 5 volts. If not check the wiring for an open or short.

5. Measure the resistance of the low reference circuit of the CMP sensor. The resistance should be 5 ohms. If the resistance is not as specified, check the low reference circuit of the CMP sensor for an open or high resistance.

6. Measure the resistance of the 5-volt reference circuit of the CMP sensor The resistance should be 5 ohms. If the resistance is not as specified, check the 5-volt reference circuit of the CMP sensor for an open or high resistance.

7. If there are no issues with the wiring and connectors, replace the sensor.

CRANKSHAFT POSITION (CKP) SENSOR

LOCATION

Refer to the Component Location illustrations for the location of the Crankshaft Position (CKP) sensor for your vehicles engine.

OPERATION

The Crankshaft Position (CKP) sensor senses the crank angle (piston position) of each cylinder and converts it into a pulse signal. The PCM receives this signal and then computes the engine speed and controls the fuel injector timing and ignition timing based on this input.

REMOVAL & INSTALLATION

1. Disconnect the crankshaft position (CKP) sensor electrical connector.

2. Remove the CKP sensor bolt.

3. Remove the CKP sensor

4. Installation is the reverse of removal.

TESTING

See Figure 137.

1. Check the condition of the connector. Make sure the connector is firmly attached. Check for broken or bent connector pins. Repair any connector damage before continuing with troubleshooting the issue.

2. Check the condition of the wiring to the connector. If the wiring is damaged, repair the wiring before continuing with any further tests.

3. Remove the CKP sensor.

4. Inspect the CKP sensor for the following:

• Physical damage
• Excessive play or looseness

• Improper installation
• Foreign material passing between the CKP sensor and the reluctor wheel
• Electromagnetic interference in the CKP sensor circuits

5. Inspect the CKP reluctor wheel for the following:

• Physical damage
• Excessive play or looseness
• Improper installation

6. Turn OFF the ignition.

7. Disconnect the harness connector of the powertrain control module (PCM).

8. Measure the resistance between the signal circuit and the low reference circuit of the crankshaft position (CKP) sensor. The resistance should be 600–1000 ohms.

9. Measure the resistance between the signal circuit of the CKP sensor and a good ground. The reading should be infinity.

10. Disconnect the harness connector of the CKP sensor.

11. Measure the resistance of the signal circuit of the CKP sensor from the harness connector of the PCM to the harness connector of the CKP sensor. The resistance should be 5 ohms, if it is more, check for an open or high resistance in the signal circuit of the CKP sensor.

12. Turn ON the ignition, with the engine OFF.

13. Connect a test lamp between the signal circuit of the CKP sensor and a good ground. If the lamp illuminates, test the signal circuit for a short to ground or a short to voltage.

14. If there are no issues with the wiring and connectors, replace the sensor.

ENGINE COOLANT TEMPERATURE (ECT) SENSOR

LOCATION

Refer to the Component Location illustrations for the location of the Engine Coolant

Temperature (ECT) sensor for your vehicles engine.

OPERATION

The Engine Coolant Temperature (ECT) sensor resistance changes in response to engine coolant temperature. The sensor resistance decreases as the coolant temperature increases, and increases as the coolant temperature decreases. This provides a reference signal to the PCM, which indicates engine coolant temperature. The signal sent to the PCM by the ECT sensor helps the PCM to determine spark advance, EGR flow rate, air/fuel ratio, and engine temperature. The ECT is a two wire sensor, a 5–volt reference signal is sent to the sensor and the signal return is based upon the change in the measured resistance due to temperature.

REMOVAL & INSTALLATION

2.0L Engine

See Figure 138.

➡Use care when handling the coolant sensor. Damage to the coolant sensor will affect the operation of the fuel control system.

1. Turn **OFF** the ignition.
2. Drain the coolant system to below the Engine Coolant Temperature (ECT) sensor.
3. Disconnect the ECT sensor electrical connector.
4. Carefully remove the ECT sensor.

To install:

➡Replacement components must be the correct part number for the application. Components requiring the use of the thread locking compound, lubricants, corrosion inhibitors, or sealants are identified in the service procedure. Some replacement components may come with these coatings already applied. Do not use these coatings on components unless specified. These coatings can affect the final torque, which may affect the operation of the component. Use the correct torque specification when installing components in order to avoid damage.

➡Use care when handling the coolant sensor. Damage to the coolant sensor will affect the operation of the fuel control system.

5. If you are reinstalling the original sensor, or if you are installing a new sensor without a sealer, coat the threads with sealer Saturn P/N 21485278, or an equivalent.
6. Install the ECT sensor, and tighten the ECT sensor to 16 ft. lbs. (22 Nm).
7. Connect the ECT sensor electrical connector.
8. Refill the engine coolant system.

2.2L and 2.4L Engines

See Figure 139.

➡Use care when handling the coolant sensor. Damage to the coolant sensor

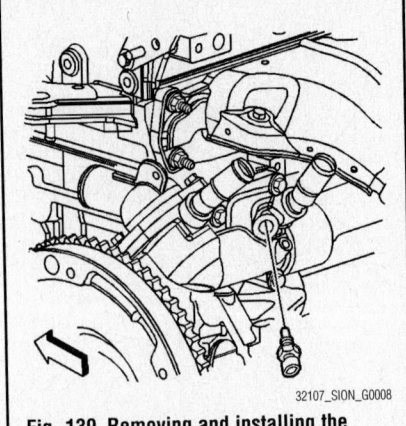

Fig. 139 Removing and installing the coolant temperature sensor

will affect the operation of the fuel control system.

1. Turn **OFF** the ignition.
2. Drain the coolant system to below the Engine Coolant Temperature (ECT) sensor.
3. Disconnect the ECT sensor electrical connector.
4. Carefully remove the ECT sensor.

To install:

➡Replacement components must be the correct part number for the application. Components requiring the use of the thread locking compound, lubricants, corrosion inhibitors, or sealants are identified in the service procedure. Some replacement components may come with these coatings already applied. Do not use these coatings on components unless specified. These coatings can affect the final torque, which may affect the operation of the component. Use the correct torque specification when installing components in order to avoid damage.

➡Use care when handling the coolant sensor. Damage to the coolant sensor will affect the operation of the fuel control system.

5. If you are reinstalling the original sensor, or if you are installing a new sensor without a sealer, coat the threads with sealer Saturn P/N 21485278, or an equivalent.
6. Install the ECT sensor, and tighten the ECT sensor to 89 inch lbs. (10 Nm).
7. Connect the ECT sensor electrical connector.
8. Refill the engine coolant system.

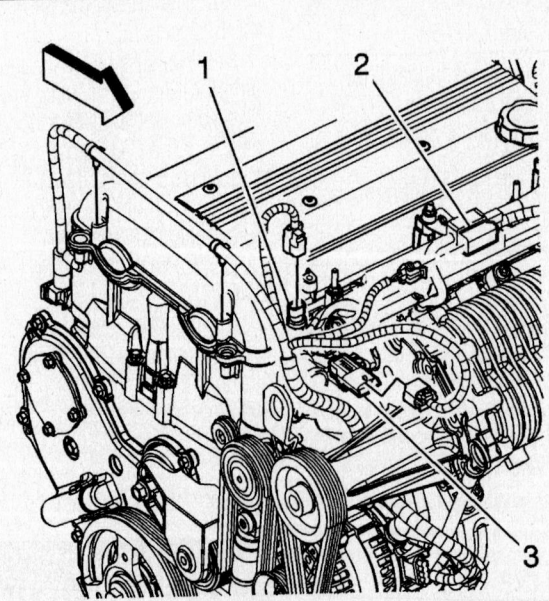

Fig. 138 Removing and installing the coolant temperature sensor

TESTING

See Figures 140 and 141.

1. Check the condition of the connector. Make sure the connector is firmly attached. Check for broken or bent connector pins. Repair any connector damage before continuing with troubleshooting the issue.

2. Check the condition of the wiring to the connector. If the wiring is damaged, repair the wiring before continuing with any further tests.

➡ **The sensor is threaded into the coolant passage in the back of the cylinder head.**

3. Unplug the connector from the sensor and use the chart to check the sensor resistance with an ohmmeter. This can also work if the sensor is removed and immersed in a container of water.

4. Remove the coolant temperature sensor.

5. Place the sensor in a container of water with a temperature approximately 20 degrees C (68 degrees F).

6. Using an ohmmeter, check resistance between the terminals. The resistance should be 3520 ohms.

7. Raise the temperature of the container of water to approximately 80 degrees C (176 degrees F).

8. Using an ohmmeter, check resistance between the terminals. The resistance should be 332 ohms.

9. If the resistance is not as specified, replace the sensor.

Temperature Versus Resistance

°C	°F	OHMS
	Temperature vs Resistance Values (Approximate)	
150	302	47
140	284	60
130	266	77
120	248	100
110	230	132
100	212	177
90	194	241
80	176	332
70	158	467
60	140	667
50	122	973
45	113	1188
40	104	1459
35	95	1802
30	86	2238
25	77	2796
20	68	3520
15	59	4450
10	50	5670
5	41	7280
0	32	9420
-5	23	12300
-10	14	16180
-15	5	21450
-20	-4	28680
-30	-22	52700
-40	-40	100700

22116_IION_G0041

Fig. 141 Temperature versus resistance chart

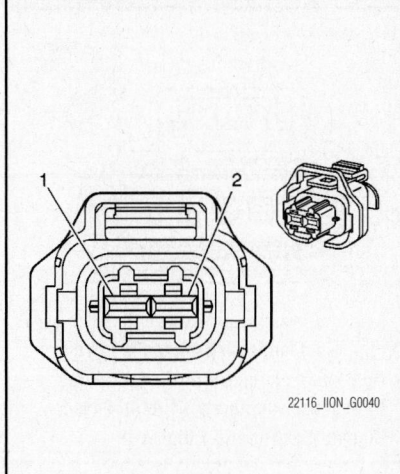

22116_IION_G0040

Fig. 140 Engine Coolant Temperature (ECT) sensor terminals; (1) Low reference, (2) ECT sensor signal

HEATED OXYGEN (HO2S) SENSOR

LOCATION

Refer to the Component Location illustrations for the location of the Heated Oxygen (HO2S) sensor for your vehicles engine.

OPERATION

The Heated Oxygen Sensor (HO2S) is a device which produces an electrical voltage when exposed to the oxygen present in the exhaust gases. The oxygen sensors are electrically heated internally for faster switching when the engine is started cold. The oxygen sensor produces a voltage within 0 and 1 volt. When there is a large amount of oxygen present (lean mixture), the sensor produces a low voltage (less than 0.4v). When there is a lesser amount present (rich mixture) it produces a higher voltage (0.6–1.0v). The stoichiometric or correct fuel to air ratio will read between 0.4 and 0.6v. By monitoring the oxygen content and converting it to electrical voltage, the sensor acts as a rich–lean switch. The voltage is transmitted to the PCM.

Two sensors per bank are used, one before the catalyst and one after. This is done for a catalyst efficiency monitor that is a part of the diagnostic system of the engine controls. The one before the catalyst measures the exhaust emissions right out of the engine, and sends the signal to the PCM about the state of the mixture as previously talked about. The second sensor reports the difference in the emissions after the exhaust gases have gone through the catalyst. This sensor reports to the PCM the amount of emissions reduction the catalyst is performing.

The oxygen sensor will not work until a predetermined temperature is reached, until this time the PCM is running in what is known as open loop operation. Open loop means that the PCM has not yet begun to correct the air–to–fuel ratio by reading the oxygen sensor. After the engine comes to operating temperature, the PCM will monitor the oxygen sensor and correct the air/fuel ratio from the sensor's readings. This is what is known as closed loop operation.

REMOVAL & INSTALLATION

1. Remove the heat shield.
2. Note the routing of the Heated Oxygen Sensor (HO2S) electrical harness.
3. Disconnect the HO2S electrical connector.
4. Using a suitable Oxygen sensor socket remove the sensor.

To install:

➡A special anti-seize compound is used on the HO2S threads. The compound consists of a liquid graphite and glass beads. The graphite will burn away but the glass beads will remain, making the sensor easier to remove. New or service sensors already have the compound applied to the threads. If the sensor is removed and is to be reinstalled, the threads must be coated with an anti-seize compound before reinstallation.

5. If reinstalling the old HO2S, coat the threads with anti-seize compound.
6. Carefully install the HO2S to the pipe. Tighten the sensor to 22 ft. lbs. (30 Nm) on the sensor located at exhaust manifold, or 30 ft. lbs. (41 Nm) for the rear oxygen sensor.
7. Attach the sensor electrical connections.

TESTING

See Figures 142 and 143.

1. Turn the ignition OFF. Disconnect the harness connector at the appropriate HO2S.
2. Turn the ignition ON, verify that a test lamp illuminates between the appropriate HO2S heater voltage supply circuit terminal D and ground. If the test lamp does not illuminate, test the HO2S heater voltage supply circuit for a short to ground or an open/high resistance. If the circuit tests normal and the HO2S heater voltage supply circuit fuse is open, test all components connected to the fuse and replace as necessary.
3. Turn the ignition ON, verify that a test lamp does not illuminate between the appropriate HO2S heater low control circuit terminal C and the HO2S heater voltage supply circuit terminal D. If the lamp illuminates, test the HO2S heater low control circuit for a short to ground. If the circuit tests normal, replace the PCM.
4. With the engine running, leave the test lamp connected from the previous step. The lamp should flash or be ON steady. If the test lamp is not on steady or flashing, test the HO2S heater low control circuit for a short to voltage or an open/high resistance. If the circuit tests normal, replace the PCM.

5. Turn the ignition off, install a 30A fused jumper wire between the appropriate HO2S heater low control circuit terminal C and the HO2S heater voltage supply circuit terminal D. Engine running, verify the appropriate scan tool Heater parameter is less than 0.1A. If more than the specified range, test the HO2S heater voltage supply and HO2S heater low control circuits for more than 1 ohm of resistance. If the circuits test normal, replace the PCM. If the PCM and all circuits test normal, replace the appropriate HO2S.

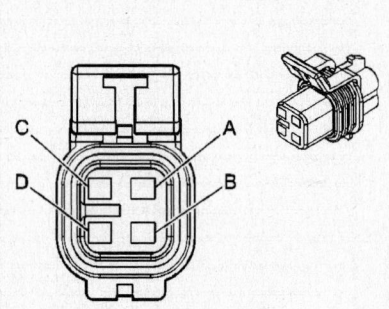

(A) Low signal sensor 1
(B) High signal sensor 1
(C) Heater Low Control Sensor 1
(D) Ignition 1 Voltage

22116_IION_G0042

Fig. 142 Upstream (manifold) Heated Oxygen Sensor (HO2S) sensor terminals

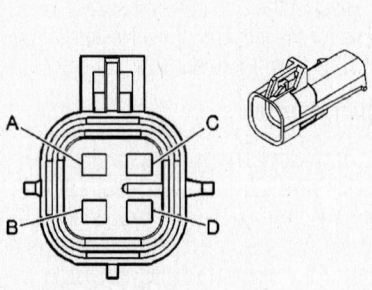

(A) Low signal sensor 2
(B) High signal sensor 2
(C) Heater Low Control Sensor 2
(D) Ignition 1 Voltage

22116_IION_G0043

Fig. 143 Downstream (exhaust pipe) Heated Oxygen Sensor (HO2S) sensor terminals

MANIFOLD ABSOLUTE PRESSURE/INTAKE AIR TEMPERATURE (MAP/IAT) SENSOR

LOCATION

The Manifold Absolute Pressure/Intake Air Temperature (MAP/IAT) sensor is attached to the air cleaner assembly.

OPERATION

The Manifold Absolute Pressure (MAP) and the Intake Air Temperature (IAT) sensor 2 are an integrated sensor. The IAT sensor is a variable resistor that measures the temperature of the air entering the engine intake manifold. The powertrain control module (PCM) supplies 5 volts to the IAT sensor 2 signal circuit and a ground for the IAT sensor 2 low reference circuit. When the sensor is cold the resistance is greater. This results in a greater voltage on the signal circuit that is interpreted by the PCM as a colder IAT. As the sensor becomes warmer the resistance decreases. This results in a lesser voltage on the IAT signal circuit that is interpreted by the PCM as a warmer IAT.

REMOVAL & INSTALLATION

1. Disconnect the MAP/IAT sensor harness connector.
2. Remove the IAT sensor bolt.
3. While twisting the IAT sensor, pull the sensor from the engine.
4. Installation is the reverse of removal.

TESTING

See Figure 144.

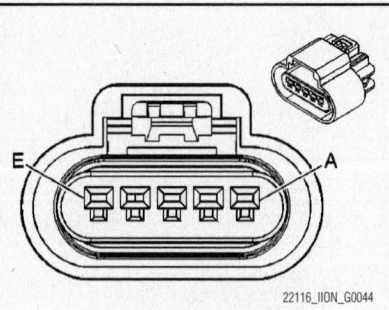

22116_IION_G0044

Fig. 144 Manifold Absolute Pressure (MAP) and the Intake Air Temperature (IAT) sensor terminals; (A) MAF Sensor Signal, (E) IAT Sensor Signal

1. Turn OFF the ignition.
2. Remove the IAT sensor.
3. Place the sensor on a work surface away from any heat source.

4. Allow the sensor to reach the ambient air temperature for 30-60 minutes.

5. Observe and record the ambient air temperature of the vehicle environment using an accurate thermometer.

6. Measure the resistance of the IAT sensor 2 and record the value.

7. Compare the resistance measurement of the IAT sensor to the ambient air temperature on the Temperature vs. Resistance chart illustration. If not within specification, replace the sensor.

KNOCK SENSOR (KS)

LOCATION

Refer to the Component Location illustrations for the location of the Knock Sensor (KS) for your vehicles engine.

OPERATION

The knock sensor system enables the PCM to control ignition timing for best performance while protecting the engine from detonation.

The KS system uses one or 2 flat response 2–wire sensors. The sensor uses piezo–electric crystal technology that produces an AC voltage signal of varying amplitude and frequency based on the engine vibration or noise level. The control module receives the KS signal through a signal circuit. The KS ground is supplied by the control module through a low reference circuit. The control module learns a minimum noise level, or background noise, at idle from the KS and uses calibrated values for the rest of the RPM range.

In order to determine which cylinders are knocking, the control module only uses KS signal information when each cylinder is near Top Dead Center (TDC) of the firing stroke. If knock is present, the signal will range outside of the noise channel. If the control module has determined that knock is present, it will retard the ignition timing to attempt to eliminate the knock. The control module will always try to work back to a zero compensation level, or no spark retard.

REMOVAL & INSTALLATION

1. Remove the starter.
2. Disconnect the knock sensor (KS) harness connector.
3. Remove the KS retaining bolt.
4. Remove the KS.
5. Installation is the reverse of removal.

TESTING

See Figure 145.

1. Turn OFF the ignition.
2. Disconnect the knock sensor (KS).

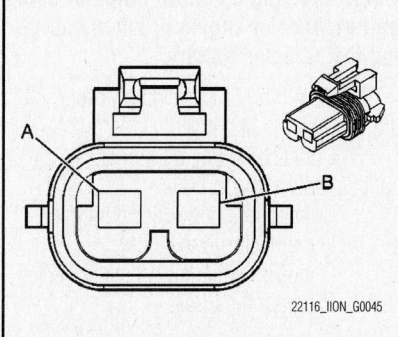

Fig. 145 Knock (KS) sensor terminals; (A) KS Sensor Signal, (B) KS Sensor Signal

3. Measure the resistance from the KS signal circuit terminal A on the sensor side of the KS harness connector to a good ground.

4. Measure the resistance from the KS signal circuit terminal B on the sensor side of the KS harness connector to a good ground. If the circuits display an open for both circuits, test for an intermittent and for a poor connection at the KS.

5. Turn ON the ignition, with the engine OFF.

6. On the Powertrain Control Module (PCM) side of the KS harness connector, measure the DC voltage from the KS signal circuit terminal A to a good ground..

7. On the PCM side of the KS harness connector, measure the DC voltage from the KS signal circuit terminal B to a good ground.

8. If the voltage more than the 4.2 volts, test the KS signal circuit for a short to voltage.

9. If there are no issues with the wiring and connectors, replace the sensor.

ENGINE CONTROL MODULE (ECM)/POWERTRAIN CONTROL MODULE (PCM)

The 2.0L Engine uses a Powertrain Control Module (PCM), while the 2.2L and 2.4L engines use an Engine Control Module (ECM).

LOCATION

The ECM/PCM is located in the engine compartment.

OPERATION

The Powertrain Control Module (PCM) performs many functions on your vehicle. The module accepts information from various sensors and computes the required fuel flow rate necessary to maintain the correct amount of air/fuel ratio throughout the entire engine operational range and controls the shifting of the transmission.

Based on the information that is received and programmed into the PCM's memory, the PCM generates output signals to control relays, actuators and solenoids. The module automatically senses and compensates for any changes in altitude when driving your vehicle.

REMOVAL & INSTALLATION

2.0L Engine

1. Using a scan tool, retrieve the percentage of remaining engine oil. Record the remaining engine oil life.
2. Disconnect the negative battery cable.
3. Disconnect the 3 powertrain control module (PCM) harness connectors from the PCM, noting proper orientation.

➡**Control module damage may result when the metal case contacts battery voltage. DO NOT contact the control module metal case with battery voltage when servicing a control module, using battery booster cables or when charging the vehicles battery.**

4. Use the retaining tab to release the PCM from the underhood junction block bracket.

To install:

➡**Control module damage may result when the metal case contacts battery voltage. DO NOT contact the control module metal case with battery voltage when servicing a control module, using battery booster cables or when charging the vehicles battery.**

5. Use the retaining tab to secure the PCM, when installing the PCM to the underhood junction block bracket.
6. Connect the PCM harness connectors to the PCM.
7. Connect the negative battery cable.
8. Program the PCM.

2.2L Engine

1. Using a scan tool, retrieve the percentage of remaining engine oil. Record the remaining engine oil life.
2. Disconnect the negative battery cable.
3. Remove the engine control module cover.
4. Disconnect the body wiring harness electrical connector from the ECM.
5. Disconnect the engine wiring harness electrical connector from the ECM.

➡Control module damage may result when the metal case contacts battery voltage. DO NOT contact the control module metal case with battery voltage when servicing a control module, using battery booster cables or when charging the vehicles battery.

6. Release the retaining tab in order to release the ECM from the underhood junction block bracket.

To install:

➡Control module damage may result when the metal case contacts battery voltage. DO NOT contact the control module metal case with battery voltage when servicing a control module, using battery booster cables or when charging the vehicles battery.

7. Install the ECM, securing the ECM to the underhood junction block bracket retaining tab.

8. Connect the engine wiring harness electrical connector to the ECM.

9. Connect the small ECM harness connector to the ECM.

10. Connect the negative battery cable.

11. Connect the body wiring harness electrical connector to the ECM.

12. Install the engine control module cover.

13. Connect the negative battery cable.

14. Program the ECM.

2.4L Engine

1. Using a scan tool, retrieve the percentage of remaining engine oil. Record the remaining engine oil life.

2. Disconnect the negative battery cable.

3. Disconnect the body wiring harness electrical connector from the engine control module (ECM).

4. Disconnect the engine harness electrical connectors from the ECM.

➡Control module damage may result when the metal case contacts battery voltage. DO NOT contact the control module metal case with battery voltage when servicing a control module, using battery booster cables or when charging the vehicles battery.

5. Disengage the side retaining tab in order to release the ECM from the bracket.

To install:

➡Control module damage may result when the metal case contacts battery voltage. DO NOT contact the control module metal case with battery voltage

when servicing a control module, using battery booster cables or when charging the vehicles battery.

6. Install the ECM to the bracket until the ECM snaps into place.

7. Connect the engine harness electrical connectors to the ECM.

8. Connect the body wiring harness electrical connector to the ECM.

9. Connect the negative battery cable.

10. Program the ECM.

THROTTLE POSITION SENSOR (TPS)

LOCATION

1. The Throttle Position (TP) sensors are located within the throttle body assembly and if defective the throttle body assembly must be replaced.

OPERATION

1. Each sensor has the following components:
   - A 5-volt reference circuit
   - A low reference circuit
   - A signal circuit

This provides the powertrain control module (PCM) with a signal voltage proportional to throttle plate movement. TP sensor 1 signal voltage at closed throttle is near the 5-volt reference and decreases as the throttle plate is opened. TP sensor 2 signal voltage at closed throttle is near the low reference and increases as the throttle plate is opened. When TP sensor 1 signal voltage is not within the predicted range, this DTC sets.

REMOVAL & INSTALLATION

2.0L Engine

See Figure 146.

➡Do not use solvent of any type when cleaning the gasket surfaces on the intake manifold and the throttle body assembly, as damage to the gasket surfaces and throttle body assembly may result. Use care in cleaning the gasket surfaces on the intake manifold and the throttle body assembly, as sharp tools may damage the gasket surfaces.

➡Do not use any solvent that contains Methyl Ethyl Ketone (MEK). This solvent may damage fuel system components.

1. Remove the air cleaner outlet duct.

2. Disconnect the evaporative emission (EVAP) purge line.

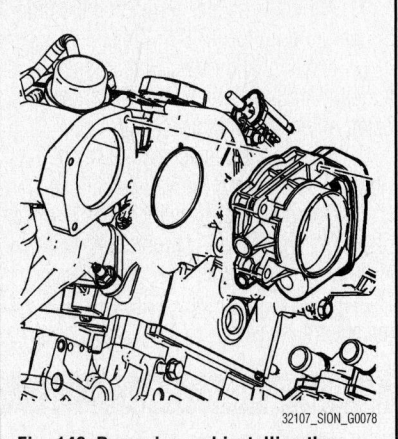

Fig. 146 Removing and installing the throttle body

32107_SION_G0078

3. Disconnect the throttle body control harness connector.

4. Remove the throttle body attaching bolts .

5. Remove the throttle body and gasket from the supercharger.

To install:

6. Inspect the throttle body gasket and replace if necessary.

7. Install the throttle body to the supercharger.

8. Install the throttle body attaching bolts, and tighten the throttle body attaching bolts to 89 inch lbs.(10 Nm).

9. Connect the throttle body control harness connector .

10. Connect the EVAP purge line.

11. Install the air cleaner outlet duct.

2.2L Engine

See Figures 147 and 148.

➡Do not use solvent of any type when cleaning the gasket surfaces on the intake manifold and the throttle body assembly, as damage to the gasket surfaces and throttle body assembly may result. Use care in cleaning the gasket surfaces on the intake manifold and the throttle body assembly, as sharp tools may damage the gasket surfaces.

➡Do not use any solvent that contains Methyl Ethyl Ketone (MEK). This solvent may damage fuel system components.

1. Remove the air cleaner resonator.

2. Disconnect the Idle Air Control (IAC) valve harness connector.

3. Disconnect the Throttle Position (TP) sensor harness connector.

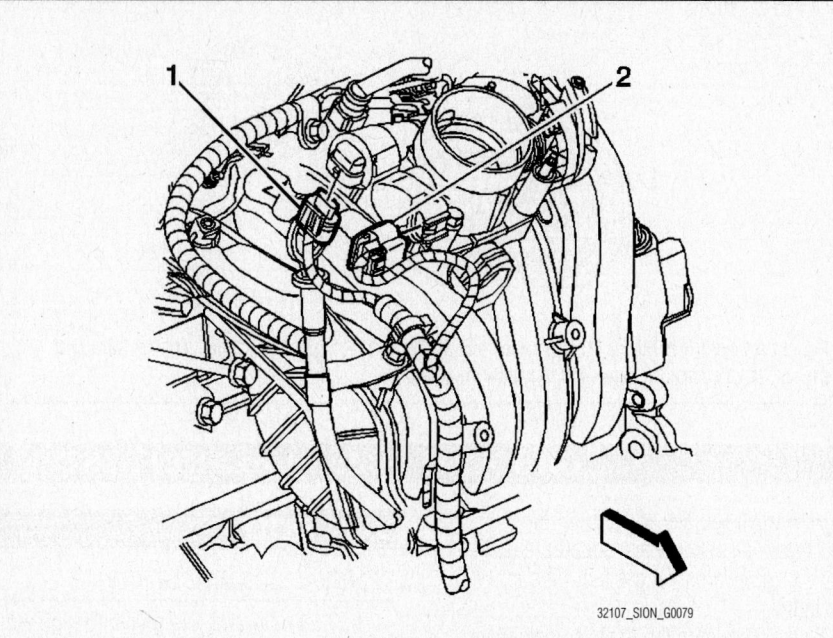

Fig. 147 Disconnect the Idle Air Control (IAC) and the Throttle Position (TP) sensor harness connectors

32107_SION_G0079

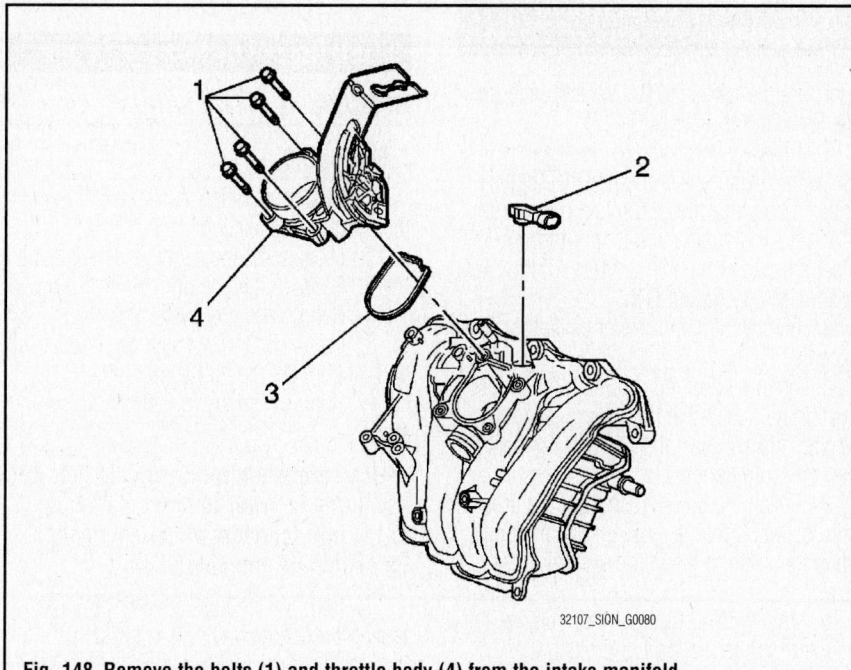

Fig. 148 Remove the bolts (1) and throttle body (4) from the intake manifold

32107_SION_G0080

4. Disconnect the vacuum hoses at the throttle body.

5. Remove the throttle body attaching bolts.

6. Remove the throttle body from the intake manifold.

To install:

7. Inspect the throttle body gasket and replace if necessary.

8. Install the throttle body to the intake manifold.

➡**Use the correct fastener in the correct location. Replacement fasteners must be the correct part number for that application. Fasteners requiring replacement or fasteners requiring the use of thread locking compound or sealant are identified in the service procedure. Do not use paints, lubricants, or corrosion inhibitors on fasteners or fastener joint surfaces unless specified. These coatings affect**

fastener torque and joint clamping force and may damage the fastener. Use the correct tightening sequence and specifications when installing fasteners in order to avoid damage to parts and systems.

9. Install the throttle body attaching bolts, and tighten the throttle body attaching bolts to 89 inch lbs.(10 Nm).

10. Connect the vacuum hoses to the throttle body.

11. Connect the TP sensor harness connector.

12. Connect the IAC valve harness connector.

13. Install the air cleaner resonator.

14. Test the accelerator movement by depressing the pedal to the floor and releasing the pedal.

2.4L Engine

1. Remove the air cleaner outlet duct.

2. Remove the intake manifold cover.

3. Disconnect the Throttle Actuator Control (TAC) electrical connector.

4. Remove the throttle body bolts.

5. Remove the throttle body .

6. Inspect the throttle body gasket, and replace if necessary.

To install:

7. Install the throttle body. Tighten the bolts to 89 inch lbs. (10 Nm).

8. Connect the TAC electrical connector.

9. Install the intake manifold cover.

10. Install the air cleaner outlet duct.

THROTTLE BODY RELEARN PROCEDURE

1. Turn the ignition **OFF** for 10 seconds

2. Turn the Ignition **ON** with the engine **OFF**.

3. Make sure these engine operating parameters are met before proceeding

4. The ECT is between 43 to 212°F (6 to 100°C).

5. The IAT is greater than 43°F (6°C).

6. The ignition voltage is above 10 volts.

7. The accelerator pedal angle is less than 14 percent.

8. Leave the ignition **ON** for 1 minute with the engine **OFF**.

TESTING

See Figure 149.

1. Turn OFF the ignition.

2. Disconnect the throttle body harness connector.

3. Turn ON the ignition, with the engine OFF.

4. Measure the voltage from the 5 volt reference circuit of the TP sensor 1 to a good ground. The voltage should be 4.8–5 volts. If not check sensor 1 5-volt reference circuit for an open, short to ground of high resistance and repair as needed.

5. Connect a fused jumper wire between the 5 volt reference circuit and the signal circuit of TP sensor 1. The voltage should be 4.8–5 volts. If not check sensor 1 5 volt signal circuit for an open, short to ground of high resistance and repair as needed.

6. If the wiring circuits are not defective, replace the throttle body assembly.

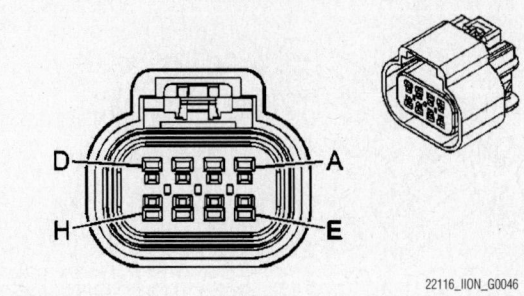

22116_IION_G0046

Fig. 149 Throttle Position (TPS) sensor terminals; (A) TP Sensor 1 Signal, (D) TP Sensor 2 Signal, (E) TAC Motor Control 1, (H) Low Reference

---

FUEL   GASOLINE FUEL INJECTION SYSTEM

FUEL SYSTEM SERVICE PRECAUTIONS

Safety is the most important factor when performing not only fuel system maintenance but any type of maintenance. Failure to conduct maintenance and repairs in a safe manner may result in serious personal injury or death. Maintenance and testing of the vehicle's fuel system components can be accomplished safely and effectively by adhering to the following rules and guidelines.

• To avoid the possibility of fire and personal injury, always disconnect the negative battery cable unless the repair or test procedure requires that battery voltage be applied.

• Always relieve the fuel system pressure prior to disconnecting any fuel system component (injector, fuel rail, pressure regulator, etc.), fitting or fuel line connection. Exercise extreme caution whenever relieving fuel system pressure to avoid exposing skin, face and eyes to fuel spray. Please be advised that fuel under pressure may penetrate the skin or any part of the body that it contacts.

• Always place a shop towel or cloth around the fitting or connection prior to loosening to absorb any excess fuel due to spillage. Ensure that all fuel spillage (should it occur) is quickly removed from engine surfaces. Ensure that all fuel soaked cloths or towels are deposited into a suitable waste container.

• Always keep a dry chemical (Class B) fire extinguisher near the work area.

• Do not allow fuel spray or fuel vapors to come into contact with a spark or open flame.

• Always use a back-up wrench when loosening and tightening fuel line connection fittings. This will prevent unnecessary stress and torsion to fuel line piping.

• Always replace worn fuel fitting O-rings with new Do not substitute fuel hose or equivalent where fuel pipe is installed.

Before servicing the vehicle, make sure to also refer to the precautions in the beginning of this section as well.

RELIEVING FUEL SYSTEM PRESSURE

1. Before servicing the vehicle, refer to the Precautions Section.
2. Unless battery voltage is necessary for testing, disconnect the negative battery cable. This will prevent the fuel pump from running and causing a fuel spill through the disconnected components if the ignition key is accidentally turned **ON**.
3. Remove the air cleaner assembly, for access.
4. Wrap a shop rag around the fuel test port fitting, located at the lower rear of the engine, then remove the cap and connect a fuel pressure gauge.
5. Install the bleed hose from the pressure gauge into an approved container and open the valve to bleed the system pressure.
6. After the pressure is bled, remove the gauge from the test port and recap it.
7. Install the air cleaner assembly.
8. After servicing the vehicle, connect the negative battery cable and prime the fuel system as follows:
   a. Turn the ignition **ON** for 5 seconds, then **OFF** for 10 seconds.
   b. Repeat the **ON/OFF** cycle 2 more times.
   c. Crank the engine until it starts.
   d. If the engine does not readily start, repeat sub-steps A–C.
9. Run the engine and check for leaks.

FUEL FILTER

REMOVAL & INSTALLATION

The fuel filter and fuel pressure regulator are one integral component of the new anti-return fuel injection system, and is located underneath the vehicle at the forward edge of the left side of the fuel tank.

FUEL INJECTORS

REMOVAL & INSTALLATION

2.0L Engine

1. Before servicing the vehicle, refer to the precautions section.
2. Disconnect the negative battery cable.
3. Remove the coolant overflow pipe.
4. Relieve the fuel system pressure.
5. Use a back up wrench on the fuel rail and disconnect the fuel supply pipe.
6. Remove the fuel rail attaching studs.

➡**Use care when removing the fuel rail assembly in order to prevent damage to the fuel injectors electrical connector terminals and spray tips.**

7. Remove the fuel rail using the following procedure:
   a. Pull the fuel rail back and upward to remove the fuel injectors from the cylinder head ports.
   b. Rotate the fuel rail in order to position the injectors downward.
   c. Remove the fuel rail.
8. Disconnect the fuel injector harness connectors.
9. Remove the fuel injector retainer clip.
10. Remove the fuel injectors from the fuel rail.
11. Visually inspect the fuel injector in order to determine if the upper O-ring was also removed. If the upper O-ring is not

removed, remove the O-ring from the fuel rail assembly.

12. Remove and discard the fuel injector O-rings.

To install:

➡**Always install new injector O-rings when servicing the fuel injectors. Lubricate the new injector O-rings with clean engine oil**

13. Install the O-rings on the fuel injector.

14. Install the fuel injector clip on the fuel injector.

➡**The fuel injector will click when the injector is installed correctly.**

15. Install the fuel injector in the fuel rail with the connector facing upward.

16. Connect the fuel injector harness connectors. Pull back to insure the connectors are locked in place.

➡**Install new lower O-rings when reusing fuel injectors. Lubricate the injector tip O-rings with clean engine oil prior to installing the injectors into the intake manifold.**

17. Install the fuel rail using the following procedure:

a. With the fuel injectors positioned downward, lower the fuel injectors into the cylinder head ports.

b. Align the injectors by rotating the fuel rail forward.

c. Carefully push the fuel injectors into the cylinder head ports.

d. Install the fuel rail attaching studs. Tighten the fuel rail studs to 89 inch lbs. (10 Nm).

18. Install the fuel supply pipe.

19. Using a backup wrench on the fuel rail tighten the fuel supply pipe to 10 ft .lbs. (14 Nm).

20. Install the coolant overflow pipe. Tighten the pipe bolt to 71 inch lbs. (8 Nm).

21. Connect the negative battery cable.

22. Inspect for fuel leaks using the following procedure:

a. Turn ON the ignition, with the engine OFF for 2 seconds.

b. Turn OFF the ignition for 10 seconds.

c. Turn ON the ignition.

d. Inspect for fuel leaks.

2.2L Engines

See Figure 150.

1. Before servicing the vehicle, refer to the Precautions Section.

2. Properly relieve the fuel system pressure.

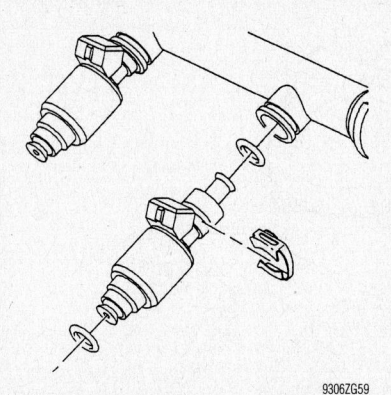

Fig. 150 Remove the retainer clip from the fuel injector—2.2L

3. Remove or disconnect the following:
- Negative battery cable
- Air intake tube
- Fuel pressure regulator hose
- Fuel feed line
- Throttle body
- Throttle control cable bracket
- Fuel injector electrical connectors
- Fuel rail
- Fuel injector retaining clip off the injector
- Fuel injector
- Fuel injector O-rings

To install:

4. Lubricate the new fuel injector O-ring with clean engine oil.

5. Install or connect the following:
- New O-ring seals on the fuel injector
- Retaining clip to the fuel injector
- Fuel injector to the fuel rail
- Fuel rail and torque the bolts to 89 inch lbs. (10 Nm)
- Fuel injector electrical connectors
- Throttle control cable bracket
- Throttle body and torque the bolts to 89 inch lbs. (10 Nm)
- Fuel feed line
- Fuel pressure regulator hose
- Air intake tube
- Negative battery cable

6. Start the vehicle and check for leaks, repair if necessary.

2.4L Engines

1. Before servicing the vehicle, refer to the Precautions Section.

2. Properly relieve the fuel system pressure.

3. Remove the air cleaner outlet duct.

4. Disconnect the fuel feed line quick connect fitting from the fuel rail.

5. Cap or plug the fuel line and the fuel rail to prevent contamination.

6. Disconnect the engine harness electrical connector from the fuel injector harness.

7. Remove the fuel injector harness connector clip from the intake manifold.

8. Disconnect the engine harness electrical connector from the Manifold Absolute Pressure (MAP) sensor.

9. Remove the fuel rail bolts.

➡**Use care when removing the fuel rail assembly in order to prevent damage to the fuel injector electrical connector terminals and spray tips.**

10. Pull the fuel rail back and upward to remove the fuel injectors from the cylinder head ports.

11. Remove the fuel rail.

12. Remove the fuel injectors.

To install:

➡**Install NEW lower O-rings when reusing fuel injectors. Lubricate the injector tip O-rings prior to installing the injectors into the intake manifold.**

13. Install the fuel injectors.

14. With the fuel injectors positioned downward, lower the fuel injectors into the cylinder head ports.

15. Carefully push the fuel injectors into the cylinder head ports.

16. Install the fuel rail bolts and tighten the bolts to 89 inch lbs. (10 Nm).

17. Connect the engine harness electrical connector to the MAP sensor.

18. Connect the engine harness electrical connector to the fuel injector harness.

19. Install the fuel injector harness connector clip to the intake manifold.

20. Remove the caps or plugs from the fuel line and the fuel rail.

21. Connect the fuel feed line quick connect fitting to the fuel rail.

22. Connect the negative battery cable.

23. Start the vehicle and check for leaks, repair if necessary.

24. Install the air cleaner outlet duct.

FUEL PUMP

REMOVAL & INSTALLATION

See Figure 151.

1. Before servicing the vehicle, refer to the Precautions Section.

2. Properly relieve the fuel system pressure.

3. Remove or disconnect the following:
- Negative battery cable
- Fuel tank
- Fuel lines from the fuel pump module cover

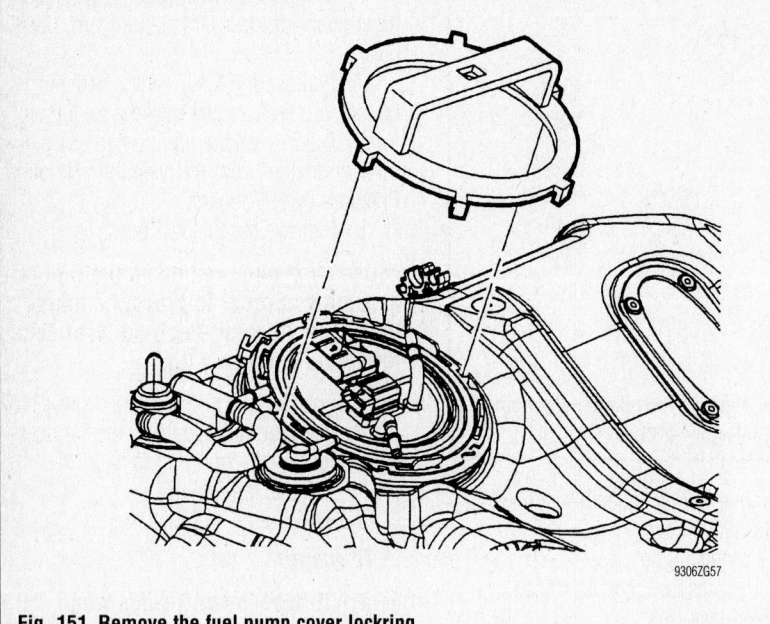

9306ZG57

Fig. 151 Remove the fuel pump cover lockring

- Fuel pump module retaining ring with a Sending Unit Wrench, J43827
- Pull the retaining clip toward the float arm and lift up
- Fuel pump straight up from the fuel tank
- Fuel pump tank seal and discard the seal
- Fuel feed line from the bottom of the fuel pump cover with Clamp Pliers J43914
- Fuel pump electrical connector

To install:
4. Install or connect the following:
- Fuel pump feed line to the cover
- Fuel pump electrical connector
- Fuel pump to the new seal
- Fuel pump cover lockring with Tool J-43827
- Fuel lines and wiring harness
- Fuel tank. Tighten the strap bolts to 18 ft. lbs. (25 Nm).
- Negative battery cable
5. Start the vehicle and check for leaks, repair if necessary.

FUEL TANK

REMOVAL & INSTALLATION

1. Relieve the fuel system pressure.
2. Drain the fuel tank.
3. Raise and support the vehicle.
4. Disconnect the fuel feed and return lines from the fuel filter.
5. Cap or plug the fuel tank feed and return pipes to prevent fuel loss and/or contamination. Disconnect the EVAP

purge pipe from the EVAP canister and fuel tank EVAP vapor pipe (3) from the EVAP canister
6. Cap or plug the EVAP purge and vapor pipes to prevent contamination.
7. Loosen the fuel filler hose clamp at the fuel tank.
8. Disconnect the fuel filler hose from the fuel tank.
9. Disconnect the fuel pump module harness electrical connector from the vehicle underbody connector.
10. Release the exhaust extension pipe insulators from the underbody hangers.
11. Release the muffler insulator from the underbody hanger and slowly lower the exhaust to rest on the rear axle beam.
12. Have an assistant support the fuel tank during fuel tank strap removal, and during tank removal.
13. Remove the left hand fuel tank strap bolts and the strap.
14. Remove the right hand tank strap bolts and the strap.
15. In order to clear the exhaust extension pipe, slowly lower the right hand side of the fuel tank. Use care in feeding the fuel feed and return pipes, the EVAP vapor pipe, and the fuel pump module electrical harness to clear the axle.
16. Once the tank is clear of the right hand frame rail, remove the fuel tank down and toward the right hand side of the vehicle.
17. If the fuel tank only is to be replaced, remove the fuel pump module assembly from the fuel tank. Refer to

To install:
18. If fuel tank replacement was necessary, install the fuel pump module assembly to the fuel tank.
19. Have an assistant support the fuel tank during fuel tank and fuel tank strap installation.
20. Begin to install the left hand side of the fuel tank over the exhaust pipe.
21. Raise the right hand side of the fuel tank into position inboard of the right hand frame rail.
22. Use care in feeding the fuel feed and return pipes, the EVAP vapor pipe, and the fuel pump module electrical harness over the rear axle.
23. Install the right hand fuel tank strap and strap bolts.
24. Install the left hand fuel tank strap and strap bolts. Tighten the bolts to 18 ft. lbs. (25 Nm).
25. Install the remaining components in the reverse order of removal.
26. Turn the ignition on for 2 seconds and off for 2 seconds. Turn the ignition off for 10 seconds. Turn the ignition on but do not start the engine. Start the engine and check for leaks.

IDLE SPEED

ADJUSTMENT

Idle speed is maintained by the Powertrain Control Module (PCM). No adjustment is necessary or possible.

THROTTLE BODY

REMOVAL & INSTALLATION

2.0L Engine
See Figure 146.

➡**Do not use solvent of any type when cleaning the gasket surfaces on the intake manifold and the throttle body assembly, as damage to the gasket surfaces and throttle body assembly may result. Use care in cleaning the gasket surfaces on the intake manifold and the throttle body assembly, as sharp tools may damage the gasket surfaces.**

➡**Do not use any solvent that contains Methyl Ethyl Ketone (MEK). This solvent may damage fuel system components.**

1. Remove the air cleaner outlet duct.
2. Disconnect the evaporative emission (EVAP) purge line.
3. Disconnect the throttle body control harness connector.

4. Remove the throttle body attaching bolts .

5. Remove the throttle body and gasket from the supercharger.

To install:

6. Inspect the throttle body gasket and replace if necessary.

7. Install the throttle body to the supercharger.

8. Install the throttle body attaching bolts, and tighten the throttle body attaching bolts to 89 inch lbs.(10 Nm).

9. Connect the throttle body control harness connector .

10. Connect the EVAP purge line.

11. Install the air cleaner outlet duct.

2.2L Engine

See Figure 147 and 148.

➡**Do not use solvent of any type when cleaning the gasket surfaces on the intake manifold and the throttle body assembly, as damage to the gasket surfaces and throttle body assembly may result. Use care in cleaning the gasket surfaces on the intake manifold and the throttle body assembly, as sharp tools may damage the gasket surfaces.**

➡**Do not use any solvent that contains Methyl Ethyl Ketone (MEK). This solvent may damage fuel system components.**

1. Remove the air cleaner resonator.

2. Disconnect the Idle Air Control (IAC) valve harness connector.

3. Disconnect the Throttle Position (TP) sensor harness connector.

4. Disconnect the vacuum hoses at the throttle body.

5. Remove the throttle body attaching bolts.

6. Remove the throttle body from the intake manifold.

To install:

7. Inspect the throttle body gasket and replace if necessary.

8. Install the throttle body to the intake manifold.

➡**Use the correct fastener in the correct location. Replacement fasteners must be the correct part number for that application. Fasteners requiring replacement or fasteners requiring the use of thread locking compound or sealant are identified in the service procedure. Do not use paints, lubricants, or corrosion inhibitors on fasteners or fastener joint surfaces unless specified. These coatings affect fastener torque and joint clamping force and may damage the fastener. Use the correct tightening sequence and specifications when installing fasteners in order to avoid damage to parts and systems.**

9. Install the throttle body attaching bolts, and tighten the throttle body attaching bolts to 89 inch lbs.(10 Nm).

10. Connect the vacuum hoses to the throttle body.

11. Connect the TP sensor harness connector.

12. Connect the IAC valve harness connector.

13. Install the air cleaner resonator.

14. Test the accelerator movement by depressing the pedal to the floor and releasing the pedal.

2.4L Engine

1. Remove the air cleaner outlet duct.

2. Remove the intake manifold cover.

3. Disconnect the Throttle Actuator Control (TAC) electrical connector.

4. Remove the throttle body bolts.

5. Remove the throttle body .

6. Inspect the throttle body gasket, and replace if necessary.

To install:

7. Install the throttle body. Tighten the bolts to 89 inch lbs. (10 Nm).

8. Connect the TAC electrical connector.

9. Install the intake manifold cover.

10. Install the air cleaner outlet duct.

THROTTLE BODY RELEARN PROCEDURE

1. Turn the ignition **OFF** for 10 seconds

2. Turn the Ignition **ON** with the engine **OFF**.

3. Make sure these engine operating parameters are met before proceeding

4. The ECT is between 43 to 212°F (6 to 100°C).

5. The IAT is greater than 43°F (6°C).

6. The ignition voltage is above 10 volts.

7. The accelerator pedal angle is less than 14 percent.

8. Leave the ignition **ON** for 1 minute with the engine **OFF**.

HEATING & AIR CONDITIONING SYSTEM

BLOWER MOTOR

REMOVAL & INSTALLATION

See Figures 152 and 153.

1. Disconnect the blower motor electrical connector.

2. Remove the lower blower motor cover retaining screws.

3. Remove the lower blower motor cover.

4. Remove the blower motor nuts.

➡**Cut through the case as straight as possible because the motor cup must be replaced.**

5. In order to prevent damage to the component, do not cut any deeper than necessary to remove the motor cup.

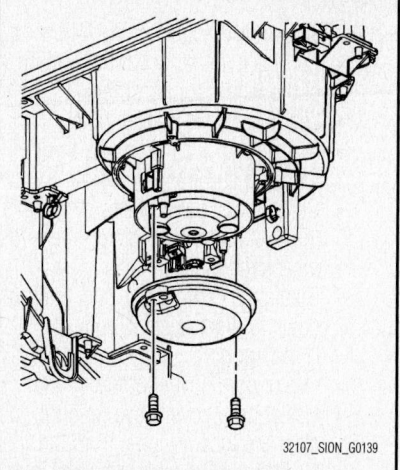

32107_SION_G0139

Fig. 152 Remove the lower blower motor cover

6. Remove the blower motor and cup from the lower case by cutting through the case between the circular ribs around the motor with a sharp utility knife.

7. Release the blower motor retaining tab and remove the motor from the cup.

To install:

8. Install the blower motor into the motor cup that was cut out of the lower case.

9. Install the blower motor nuts, and tighten the nuts to 21 inch lbs. (2.4 Nm).

10. Attach the service ring to the motor cup with the screws included in the kit, and tighten the screws to 15 inch lbs. (1.8 Nm).

11. Install the blower motor and service ring into the HVAC module using the screws included in the kit. Make certain the

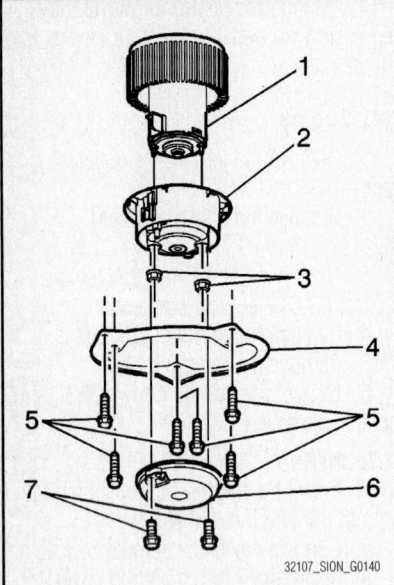

Fig. 153 Install the blower motor (1) into the motor cup (2) that was cut out of the lower case

32107_SION_G0140

blower motor electrical connector is pointing rearward in the vehicle, and tighten the screws to 15 inch lbs. (1.8 Nm).

12. Install the lower blower motor cover.

13. Install the lower blower motor cover retaining screws, and tighten the screws to 15 inch lbs. (1.8 Nm).

14. Connect the blower motor electrical connector.

HEATER CORE

REMOVAL & INSTALLATION

1. Before servicing the vehicle, refer to the Precautions Section.

2. Remove or disconnect the following:
- Surge tank cap
- Water pump drain bolt and drain the coolant from the pump. Once drained, close the bolt and torque to 88 inch lbs. (10 Nm).
- Heater outlet and inlet hose clamps
- Heater outlet and inlet hoses

3. Remove the Body Control Module (BCM) as follows:

a. Disconnect the negative battery cable.

b. Apply the parking brake and position the transmission into Neutral.

c. Remove the console shift lever bezel by lifting up around the edge carefully, if equipped with an automatic transmission.

d. Unsnap the shift boot from the console cup holder, if equipped with a manual transmission.

e. Lift the front console cup holder to disengage the retainers

f. Disconnect the cigar lighter connection.

g. Remove the cup holder, if equipped with a manual transmission, slide the boot through the cup holder.

h. Remove the console extension retainers from both sides by turning them counterclockwise.

i. Remove the console extensions by pulling the extension rearwards.

j. Remove the center extension screws, pull out the center extension to access any remaining fasteners and remove the extension.

k. Unsnap the parking brake boot.

l. If equipped with an armrest, remove the console compartment screws.

m. Lift up on the rear on the console to release the retainers.

n. Lift the console compartment and push the parking brake through the opening.

o. Slide the compartment over the parking brake lever.

p. Disconnect the rear power supply connector.

q. Remove the console screws and the console.

r. Remove the wiring harness rosebud from the right center support bracket.

s. Pull back the carpet from the right of the left Instrument Panel (IP) support bracket and remove the lower nuts.

t. Remove the center support bracket.

u. Disconnect the small then large harness connectors from the BCM.

v. Disconnect the small then large IP wiring harness connectors from the BCM.

w. Disconnect the Onstar® connector, if equipped.

x. Remove the BCM retainers and BCM.

4. Remove or disconnect the following:
- Pull back the carpet at the bottom of the left IP support bracket
- Left IP support bracket nuts
- Accelerator pedal from the front of the dash and position aside
- Center floor outlet ducts by raising the duct and then pushing them to disengage them
- Rotate the center floor duct and pull down to disconnect it from the HVAC module
- Heater core cover screws
- Heater core cover down enough to clear the locating pins from the HVAC module, slide the cover rearwards until the drain tube clears the front of the dash. Slide the cover

down, rearwards and to the right and remove it.
- Heater core

To install:

5. Inspect the heater core foam and if damaged use Kent Industries adhesive black foam 46480 to replace.

6. Install or connect the following:
- Heater core
- New drain tube seal on the drain tube

7. Spray the heater core seal and dash-mat with soapy water to ease installation.
- Heater core cover from the right side. Slide the cover up, forward and into position. Align the drain tube with the hole in the dash, raise the cover into position while aligning the holes with the locating pins on the HVAC module. Tighten the cover screws to 15 inch lbs. (1.8 Nm).
- Center floor ducts.
- Accelerator pedal
- Carpet at the bottom of the left IP support bracket
- Left IP center bracket nuts and tighten to 88 inch lbs. (10 Nm)

8. Install the BCM as follows:

a. Install the BCM and tighten the retainers to 88 inch lbs. (10 Nm).

b. Connect the small then large IP wiring harness connectors to the BCM.

c. Connect the small then large harness connectors to the BCM.

d. Connect the Onstar® connector, if equipped.

e. Pull back the carpet from the right of the left IP support bracket and the center support bracket. Tighten the nuts to 88 inch lbs. (10 Nm).

f. Connect the wiring harness rosebud to the right center support bracket.
- Install the front floor console over parking lever and shift lever. Push the console down on the carpet and tighten the screws to 22 inch lbs. (2.5 Nm).

g. Connect the rear power supply connector.

h. Slide the compartment over the parking brake lever.

i. Pull the parking brake boot through the opening.

j. Align the retainers with the console and push to engage.

k. If equipped with an armrest, install the console compartment screws and tighten the screws to 22 inch lbs. (2.5 Nm).

l. Snap the parking brake boot to the console.

m. Align the center extension to the IP and push the engage the retainers. Tighten the screws to 22 inch lbs. (2.5 Nm).

n. Install the cup holder, if equipped with a manual transmission, slide the boot through the cup holder.

o. Connect the cigar lighter connection.

p. Align the front console cup holder retainers and push to engage.

q. Snap the shift boot to the console

cup holder, if equipped with a manual transmission.

r. Install the console shift lever bezel by aligning the fingers on the lever bezel with the slots on the lever base and push to engage, if equipped with an automatic transmission.

s. Apply the parking brake and position the transmission into park.

t. Install the console extensions. Turn the retainers clockwise to secure.

9. Install or connect the following:
- Heater outlet and inlet hose clamps
- Heater outlet and inlet hoses
- Surge tank cap

10. Refill the cooling system.

11. Connect the negative battery cable.

12. Operate the engine to normal operating temperatures; then, check the climate control operation and check for leaks.

STEERING

POWER RACK & PINION STEERING GEAR

REMOVAL & INSTALLATION

1. Before servicing the vehicle, refer to the Precautions Section.

2. Turn the steering wheel to the straight ahead position, remove the key and lock the steering wheel.

3. Remove or disconnect the following:
- Negative battery cable
- Both front wheels

✳✳ WARNING

Do not rotate the intermediate shaft once it is disconnected from the gear as damage may occur.

- Intermediate shaft from the steering gear pinch bolt
- Shaft from the gear
- Tie rods from the knuckles
- Steering gear bolts
- Steering gear through the left side wheel opening

To install:

4. Install or connect the following:

- Steering gear through the left wheel opening
- Steering gear bolts to torque the fasteners to 81 ft. lbs. (110 Nm)
- Intermediate shaft to the steering gear and torque the new pinch bolt to 18 ft. lbs. (25 Nm)
- Tie rod ends to the steering knuckle and torque the nut to 15 ft. lbs. (20 Nm) plus an additional 180 degrees
- Wheels
- Negative battery cable

5. Check the alignment and adjust if necessary.

SUSPENSION

The front suspension consists of 4 major components: MacPherson struts, lower control arms, steering knuckle assemblies and the stabilizer or sway bar. Strut towers located in the wheel wells locate the upper ends of the MacPherson struts. The lower end of the strut is attached to the steering knuckle and the control arm. The control arm provides side-to-side stability, while body lean on turns is controlled by a sway bar that connects to both lower control arms. The strut assembly, which consists of a coil spring and a strut, provides both functions that a spring and a shock absorber would.

The front suspension components are lubricated for life and require no routine greasing or lubrication. However, they should be periodically checked for damage or wear.

COIL SPRING

REMOVAL & INSTALLATION

1. Before servicing the vehicle, refer to the Precautions Section.

2. Remove or disconnect the following:
- Strut from the vehicle

- Upper strut cap retainers and the cap
- Place the strut into a spring compressor. Fasten the assembly with a strut to steering knuckle bolt through the lower mounting hole
- Compress the spring enough to completely unload the upper strut mount
- Strut shaft nut while holding the shaft stationary with a Torx® socket
- Release the spring compressor and tilt the strut outward
- Upper strut mount assembly
- Spring

To install:

3. Install or connect the following:
- Strut into spring compressor
- Lower spring seat insulator
- Extend the strut shaft to its full travel
- Jounce bumper into the dust shield
- Dust shield assembly
- Spring to the strut and make certain that it is properly positioned in the seat and isolator
- Upper spring seat and insulator
- Bearing and strut mount

FRONT SUSPENSION

- Compress the spring while guiding the strut shaft through the upper strut mount assembly. Do not over compress the spring
- Strut shaft nut and torque to 52 ft. lbs. (70 Nm).

4. Release the spring compressor tool.
- Upper strut cap and retainers. Tighten the retainers to 124 inch lbs. (14 Nm).

5. Strut to the vehicle.

LOWER BALL JOINT

REMOVAL & INSTALLATION

1. Before servicing the vehicle, refer to the Precautions Section.

2. Remove or disconnect the following:
- Lower control arm from the vehicle
- Rivets retaining the ball joint to the control arm using a ½ in. (13mm) drill bit
- Ball joint from the control arm

To install:

3. Install or connect the following:
- Ball joint into the control arm

- Nuts and bolts (included with new ball joint kit) and torque them to 50 ft. lbs. (68 Nm)
- Control arm to the vehicle

INSPECTION

Raise and safely support the vehicle until the front wheel is clear of the floor. Try to rock the wheel up and down. If any play is felt, have an assistant rock the wheel while observing the lower ball joint. If any movement is seen between the steering knuckle and control arm, the ball joint is bad; if no movement is detected, the wheel play indicates wheel bearing wear.

LOWER CONTROL ARM

REMOVAL & INSTALLATION

1. Before servicing the vehicle, refer to the Precautions Section.
2. Remove or disconnect the following:
   - Wheel
   - Ball stud bolt
   - Separate the ball stud from the steering knuckle. Do not use a pickle fork as this may cause damage.
   - Rear frame bolt
   - Lower control arm-to-frame bolts
   - Lower control arm

To install:

3. Install or connect the following:
   - Control arm to the frame and loosely install the rear frame bolt

➡ **The control arm contains two fore/aft movement limiting brackets. Failure to install these brackets will affect handling.**

   - Ball joint stud to the steering knuckle
   - Fore/aft movement limiting brackets onto the control arm forward bushing
   - Control arm-to-frame-bolts and torque the bolts to 41 ft. lbs. (55 Nm)
   - Tighten the rear frame bolt to 74 ft. lbs. (100 Nm) plus an additional 180 degree turn
   - Ball joint pinch bolt and nut to 44 ft. lbs. (60 Nm) plus an additional 30 degree turn
   - Wheel
   - Check and adjust the alignment, if necessary.

LOWER CONTROL ARM BUSHING REPLACEMENT

See Figures 154 and 155.

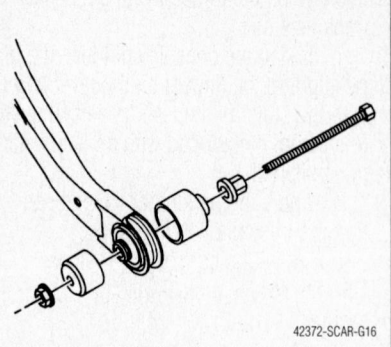

Fig. 154 Press out the front control arm front bushing—ION

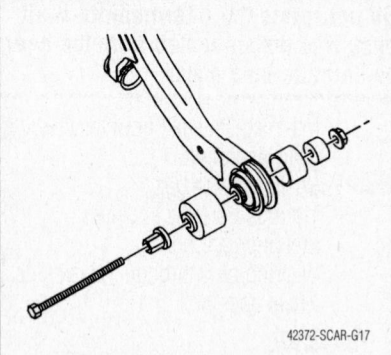

Fig. 155 Press in the front control arm rear bushing—ION

1. Before servicing the vehicle, refer to the Precautions Section.
2. Remove or disconnect the following:
   - Control arm

➡ **Make sure to note the depth and positioning of the old bushing prior to removal.**

3. Using bushing remover/installer KM-906B install KM-906-70, 906–42, 906-41 and 906-62 onto the bushing.
4. Hold the hex end of the threaded shaft while turning the large nut to pull the bushing through the arm.
5. Remove the tools and the bushing.

To install:

6. Install the new bushing into the tapered side of the arm.
7. Using bushing remover/installer KM-906B install KM-906-70, 906–42, 906-41 and 906-62 onto the bushing
8. Hold the hex end of the threaded shaft while turning the large nut to pull the bushing into the arm. Install the bushing to the same depth and positioning as the old one.
9. Remove the removal/installer tool.
10. Install the control arm.

MACPHERSON STRUT

REMOVAL & INSTALLATION

1. Before servicing the vehicle, refer to the Precautions Section.
2. If equipped with an Anti-lock Brake System (ABS), disconnect the negative battery cable, then raise and support the vehicle safely. Be sure the vehicle is at a height where under right hand hood access is still possible.
3. Remove or disconnect the following:
   - Front wheel
   - Stabilizer bar link to the strut assembly attaching nut and separate it from the strut
   - Loosen the steering knuckle to strut nuts
   - Wheel Speed Sensor (WSS) harness and bracket, if equipped
   - Strut cap and body nut
   - Place a rag over the CV-joint seal to protect it from damage, then remove the 2 steering knuckle-to-strut housing bolts
   - Steering knuckle to strut fasteners
   - Strut assembly from the vehicle

To install:

4. Install or connect the following:
   - Strut to the body and torque the new attaching nut to 81 ft. lbs. (110 Nm)
   - Strut to the steering knuckle bolts but leave the nuts off
   - WSS bracket and harness, if equipped
   - Strut to the steering knuckle nuts and torque to 89 ft. lbs. (120 Nm)
   - Stabilizer bar link to the strut and torque the fastener to 48 ft. lbs. (65 Nm)
   - Front wheel
   - Negative battery cable

5. Check and adjust the alignment as necessary.

OVERHAUL

1. Mount the strut in a bench vise, then attach a suitable spring compressor/holding fixture. Be sure that the strut component is firmly secured.
2. Compress the spring sufficiently to completely unload the upper strut mount.
3. Remove the strut shaft nut while holding the strut stationary with a Torx® head socket wrench.
4. Remove the upper mount assembly and inspect the rubber for cracks or deterioration. Rotate the support bearing by hand and check for smooth operation.
5. Remove the spring from the strut and inspect the spring for damage.

6. Remove the dust shield assembly and inspect for cracks or deterioration.

7. Remove the strut from the vise or applicable holding fixture and retract the strut shaft, checking for smooth, even resistance.

8. If replacing the coil spring, carefully release the spring compressor.

To assemble:

9. Secure the strut in the bench vise, or applicable holding fixture.

10. Extend the strut shaft to the limit of its travel.

11. Install the dust shield assembly onto the strut, then install the spring with the compressor tool installed.

12. Install the spring isolator and the strut mount to the top of the assembly.

13. Guide the strut shaft through the upper strut mount assembly. Compress the coil until the washer and shaft nut can be installed to the end of the shaft, but do not overcompress and damage the spring.

14. Tighten the shaft to the nut using a Torx®head socket wrench and a torque wrench, while holding the nut steady with an open end wrench. Tighten the fastener to 37 ft. lbs. (50 Nm).

15. Release the spring compressor tool and remove the strut from the fixture.

SHOCK ABSORBERS

REMOVAL & INSTALLATION

1. Before servicing the vehicle, refer to the Precautions Section.

2. Remove or disconnect the following:
   - Wheel

3. Support the rear axle with a jackstand positioned near the shock absorber being removed
   - Lower and upper shock absorber bolts
   - Shock

To install:

4. Install or connect the following:
   - Strut. Using new bolts, torque the upper bolt to 66 ft. lbs. (90 Nm) and the lower bolt to 81 ft. lbs. (110 Nm). Remove the jackstand.
   - Wheel

STABILIZER BAR

REMOVAL & INSTALLATION

See Figures 156 and 157.

1. Raise and support the vehicle.
2. Remove the front wheels.
3. Remove the rear transaxle mount.
4. Remove the steering gear.

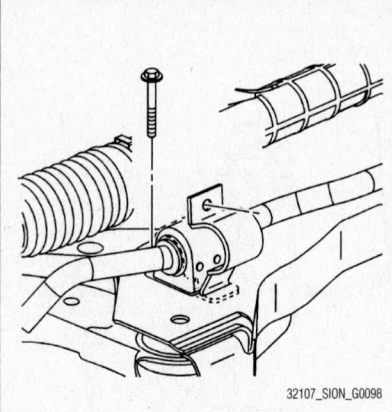

Fig. 156 Remove the stabilizer bar mounting clamp

Fig. 157 Remove the bushings from the stabilizer bar

5. Disconnect the stabilizer links from the stabilizer shaft.

6. Remove the stabilizer bar mounting clamp bolts and clamps from both sides of the vehicle.

7. Remove the bushings from the stabilizer bar.

8. Lift and rotate the stabilizer bar up and to the right.

9. Carefully remove the stabilizer bar from the right side of the vehicle.

To install:

10. Move the stabilizer bar into position from the right side of the vehicle.

11. Install the stabilizer bushings on the stabilizer bar with the cut line facing rearward.

12. Install the stabilizer bar clamps and bolts, and tighten the bolts to 37 ft. lbs. (50 Nm).

13. Connect the stabilizer links to the stabilizer shaft.

14. Install the steering gear.

15. Install the rear transaxle mount.
16. Install the front wheels.
17. Lower the vehicle.

STEERING KNUCKLE

REMOVAL & INSTALLATION

See Figures 158 through 160.

1. Raise and support the vehicle.
2. Remove the wheel bearing.
3. Remove the outer tie rod to knuckle nut.

4. Using the special tool SA91100C, separate the tie rod from the steering knuckle.

➡️**Do not free the ball stud by using a pickle fork or a wedge-type tool. Damage to the seal or bushing may result.**

5. Remove the lower control arm ball stud to steering knuckle pinch bolt and nut.

6. Lower the lower control arm to separate the ball stud from the steering knuckle. If necessary, use the special tool J43631 .

7. Remove the strut to steering knuckle nuts and bolts.

8. Remove the steering knuckle from the vehicle.

To install:

9. Position the steering knuckle onto the lower control arm ball stud, while guiding the axle through the knuckle.

10. Install the strut to knuckle bolts and nuts, and tighten the bolts and nuts to 89 ft. lbs. (120 Nm).

➡️**The torque sequence must be followed in the order that is listed.**

11. Install the lower control arm ball stud to steering knuckle pinch bolt and nut.

12. Tighten the pinch bolt and nut in the following sequence:
   - First Pass: Tighten the nut to 37 ft. lbs. (50 Nm).
   - Reverse nut three-quarters turn
   - Second Pass: Tighten the nut to 37 ft. lbs. (50 Nm) plus 30 degrees

13. Install the outer tie rod to the steering knuckle, and tighten the nut to 18 ft. lbs. (25 Nm) plus 90 degrees.

14. Install the wheel bearing, brake rotor, brake caliper and front wheels.

15. Lower the vehicle.

16. Road test the vehicle in order to verify alignment.

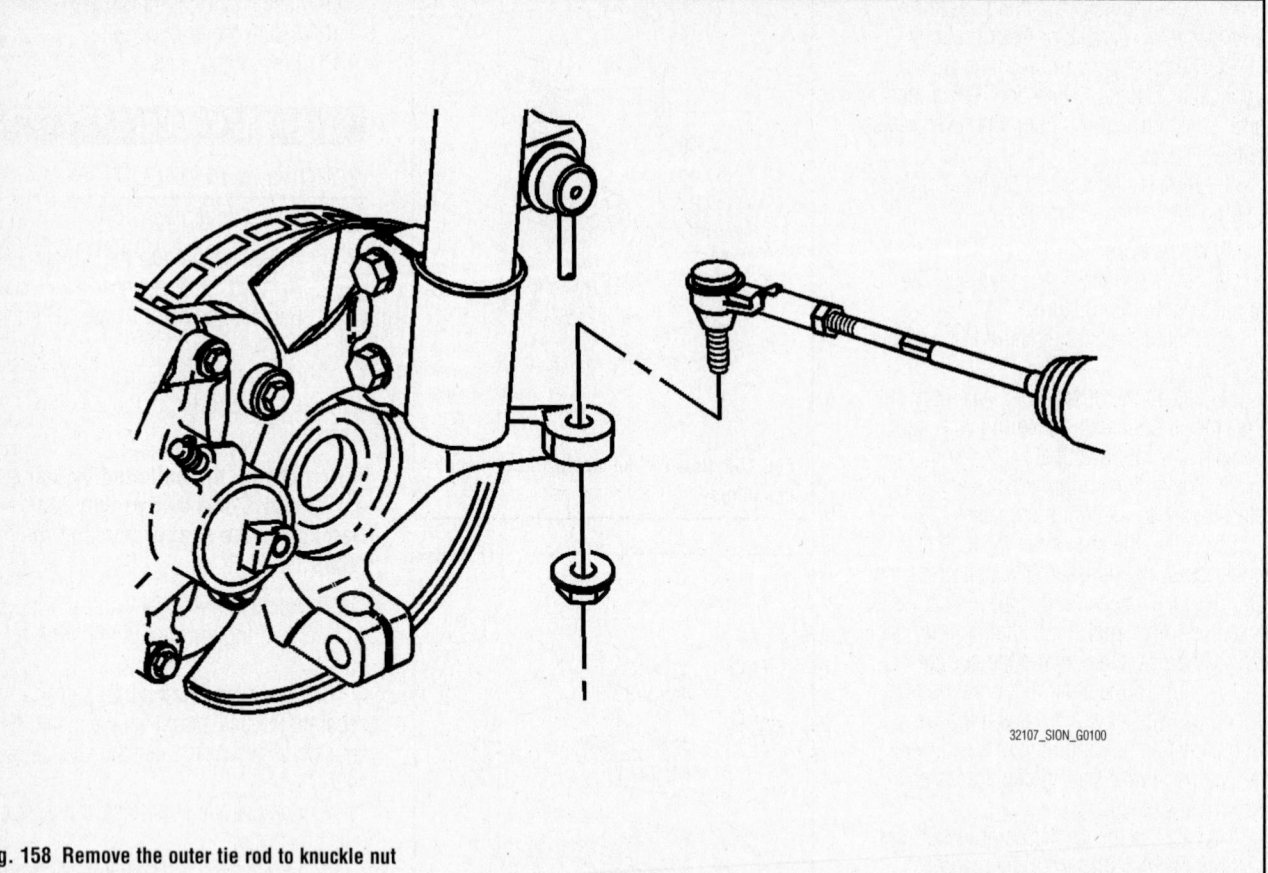

32107_SION_G0100

Fig. 158 Remove the outer tie rod to knuckle nut

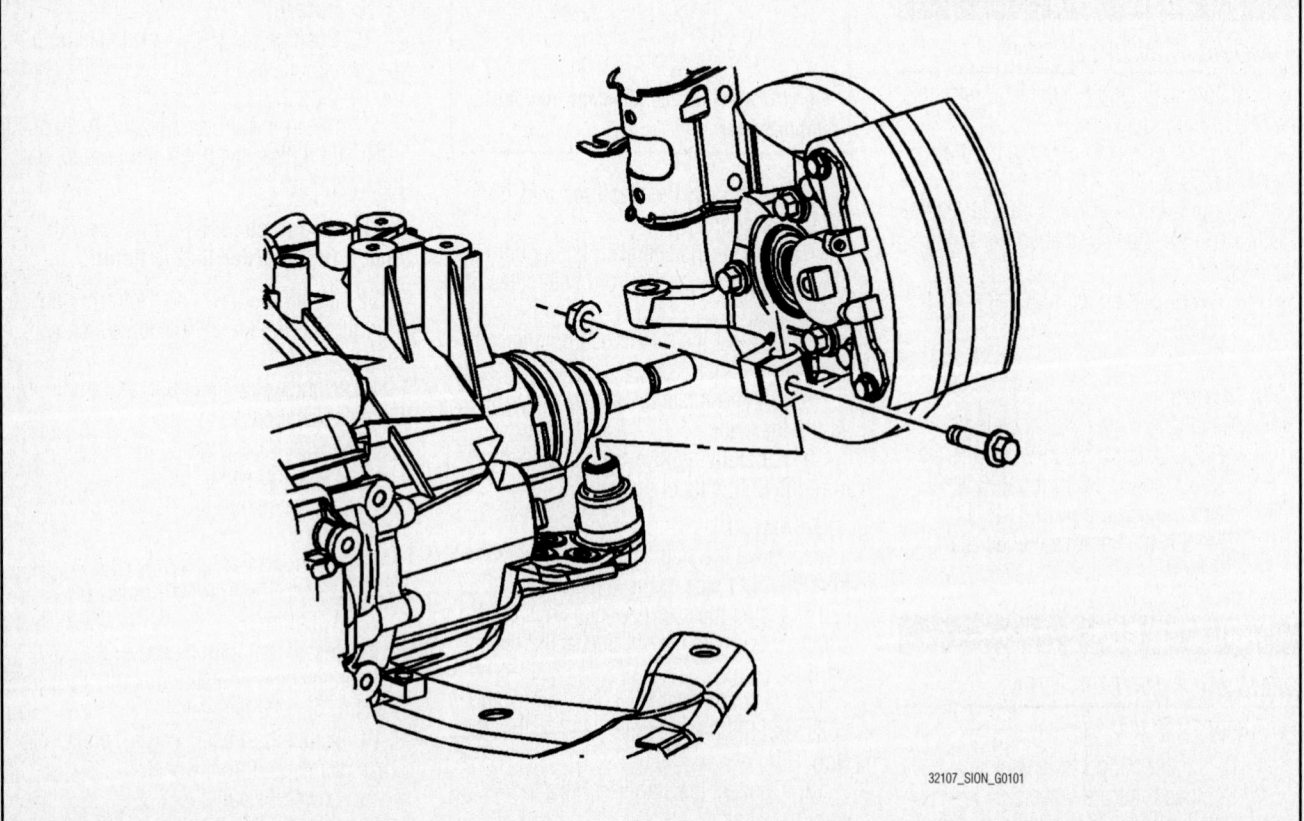

32107_SION_G0101

Fig. 159 Remove the lower control arm ball stud to steering knuckle pinch bolt and nut

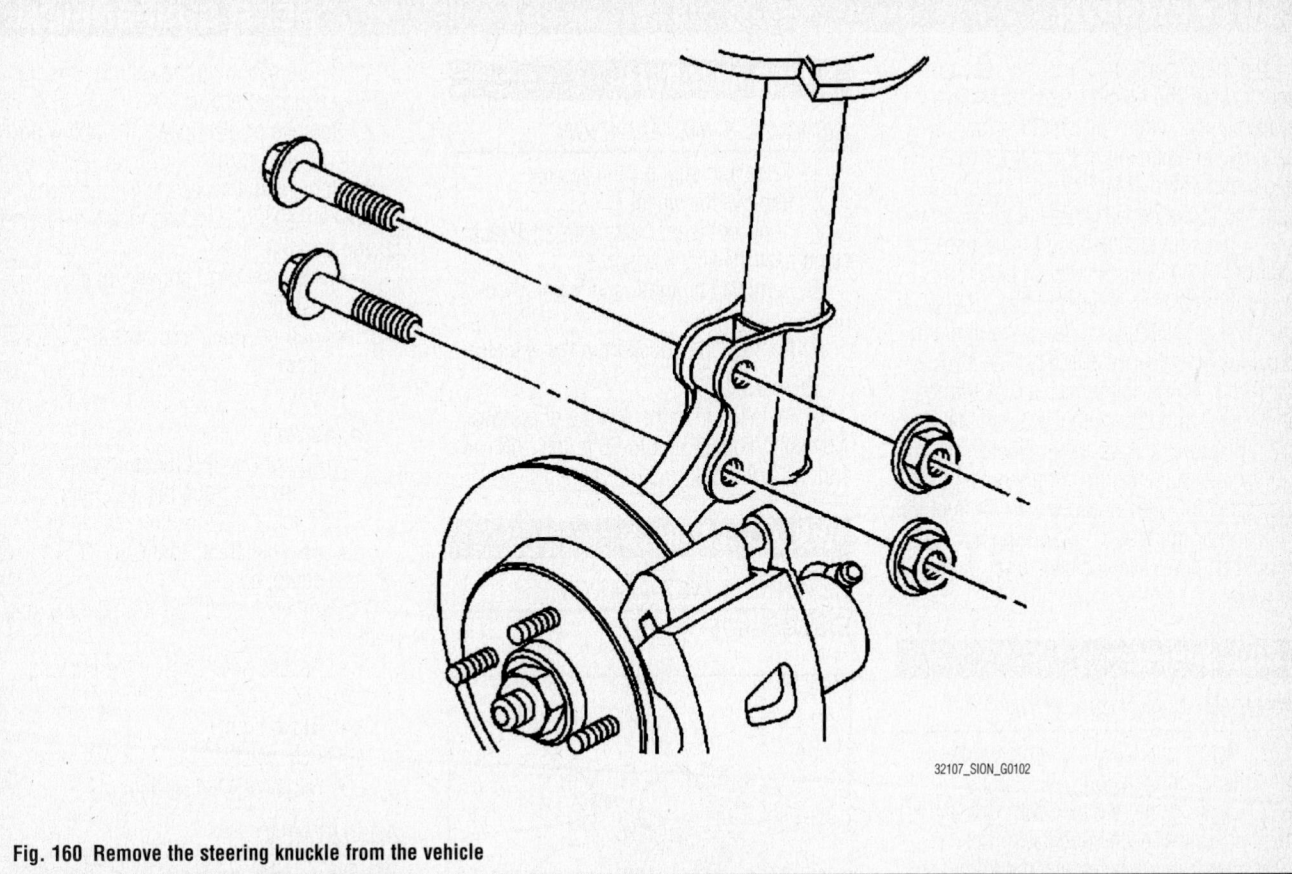

Fig. 160 Remove the steering knuckle from the vehicle

32107_SION_G0102

WHEEL BEARINGS

REMOVAL & INSTALLATION

1. Before servicing the vehicle, refer to the Precautions Section.

2. If equipped with an Antilock Braking System (ABS), disconnect the negative battery cable.

3. Loosen the front halfshaft nut, while an assistant depresses the brake pedal, then raise and support the vehicle safely.

4. Remove or disconnect the following:
- Wheel
- Axle to hub nut and discard it
- Brake caliper mounting bracket bolts and suspend the assembly from the strut spring with wire
- Brake rotor
- ABS sensor connector, if equipped
- ABS sensor jumper connector from the bracket on the strut, if equipped
- Bearing mounting bolts from the rear of the knuckle
- Bearing assembly and spacer. Make sure to note the positioning of the spacer before removal.

To install:

5. Install or connect the following:
- Bearing/hub assembly and spacer to the knuckle making sure to position the spacer as it was before removal. Tighten the bearing assembly-to-knuckle bolts evenly to draw the assembly into the knuckle and final tighten bolts to 85 ft. lbs. (115 Nm).
- ABS sensor jumper connector to the bracket on the strut, if equipped
- ABS sensor connector, if equipped
- Rotor
- Caliper mount bracket onto the knuckle and torque the bolts to 85 ft. lbs. (115 Nm)
- Caliper and tighten the bolts to 25 ft. lbs. (34 Nm)
- Negative battery cable

6. Depress the brake pedal and torque the axle to hub nut to 81 ft. lbs. (110 Nm)
- Wheel

7. Check and adjust the alignment

ADJUSTMENT

The wheel bearing are sealed at the factory and do not require any adjustment or maintenance.

SUSPENSION

The major components of the rear suspension are: the MacPherson struts, rear crossmember, knuckles, stabilizer bar (sway bar), lateral links and trailing arms. The upper ends of the MacPherson struts are attached to the body by fasteners. The lower end of the strut is attached to the crossmember through the knuckle, lateral links and trailing arm. The lateral links provide side-to-side stability, while the trailing arm provides front-to-rear stability. The strut assembly, which consists of a coil spring and a strut provides both functions that a spring and a shock absorber would.

The rear suspension components are lubricated for life and require no routine greasing or lubrication. However, they should be periodically checked for damage or wear.

COIL SPRING

REMOVAL & INSTALLATION

1. Before servicing the vehicle, refer to the Precautions Section.
2. Support the rear axle with jackstands positioned near each shock absorber.
3. Remove or disconnect the following:
   • Wheel
   • U–clips from the rear brake hose brackets at the axle
   • Lower shock bolts
4. Lower the jackstands slowly to remove rear spring tension and remove the spring.
   • Upper spring seat/jounce bumper from the spring while leaving the lower spring seat on the axle

To install:

✳✳ CAUTION

The rear springs are indexed with the colored tag towards the rear of the vehicle. No orientation for up or down is required.

5. Install or connect the following:
   • Upper spring seat/jounce bumper to the spring
   • Spring with the spring tag towards the rear of the vehicle and the lower coil is seated into the lower spring seat. Use the jackstands to raise the rear axle into position.
   • Lower shock absorber bolt and tighten to 81 ft. lbs. (110 Nm)
   • U–clips to the rear brake hose brackets at the axle
   • Wheel

SHOCK ABSORBER

REMOVAL & INSTALLATION

1. Raise and support the vehicle.
2. Remove the wheel
3. Support the rear axle with a tall jack stand near the shock absorber
4. Remove the upper and lower shock bolts.
5. Remove the shock from the vehicle

To install:

6. Installation is the reverse of removal. Tighten the upper bolt to 66 ft. lbs. (90 Nm) and the lower bolt to 81 ft. lbs. (110 Nm).

WHEEL BEARINGS

REMOVAL & INSTALLATION

See Figure 161.

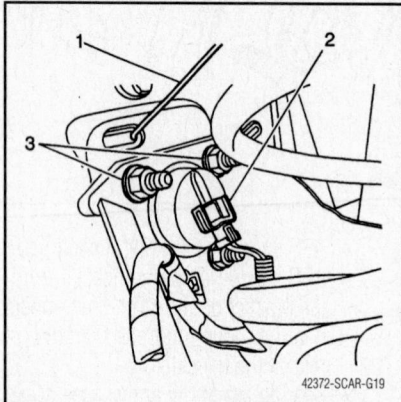

Fig. 161 Install a support (1) for the backing plate, disconnect the electrical connector (2) and remove the hub nuts (3)—ION

1. Before servicing the vehicle, refer to the Precautions Section.
2. Remove or disconnect the following:
   • Brake drum
3. Remove the access hole plug from the brake backing plate and install a support for the backing plate
   • ABS electrical connector, if equipped
   • Hub retaining arm nuts and discard them
   • Hub

To install:

4. Install or connect the following:
   • Hub and torque the new nuts to 37 ft. lbs. (50 Nm) plus 30 degrees
   • ABS electrical connector, if equipped
5. Remove the support from the backing plate.
   • Access hole plug on the backing plate
   • Brake drum
   • Rear wheel
   • Negative battery cable

ADJUSTMENT

See Figure 162.

The rear hub/bearing assembly is a sealed assembly, which requires no periodic maintenance and cannot be serviced. If the hub/bearing assembly becomes worn or damaged, the entire unit must be replaced.

REPACKING

All Saturn wheel bearing assemblies are an integral component of the wheel hub assembly. They are sealed at the factory and do not require any form of periodic lubrication.

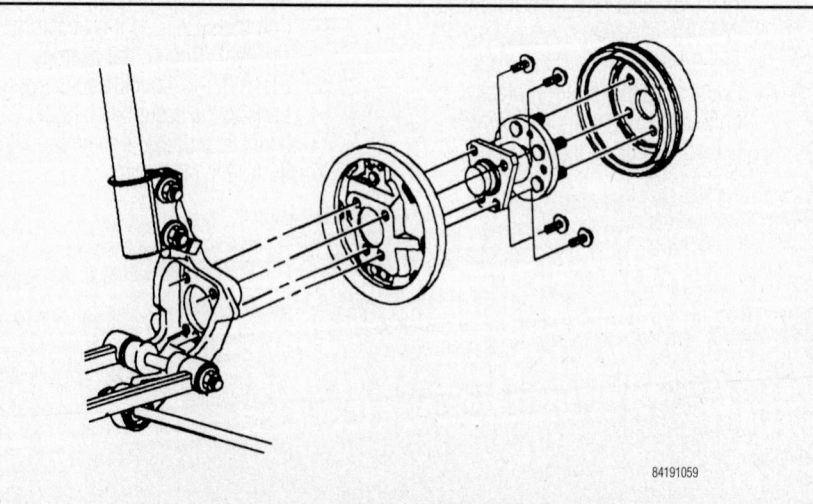

84191059

Fig. 162 Exploded view of the rear bearing/hub mounting—rear drum brake vehicles

BUICK

LaCrosse

15

SPECIFICATIONS AND MAINTENANCE CHARTS

ENGINE AND VEHICLE IDENTIFICATION

		Engine						Model Year	
Code ①	Liters (cc)	Cu. In.	Cyl.	Fuel Sys.	Engine Type	Eng. Mfg.		Code ②	Year
7	3.6 (3564)	217	6	MFI	DOHC	GM		6	2006
1	3.8 (3785)	231	6	MFI	OHV	GM		7	2007

MFI: Multi-point Fuel Injection

DOHC: Dual overhead camshafts

OHV: Overhead Valves

① 8th position of VIN

② 10th position of VIN

22116_LACR_C0001

GENERAL ENGINE SPECIFICATIONS

Year	Model	Engine Displacement Liters	Engine Series VIN	Net Horsepower @ rpm	Net Torque @ rpm (ft. lbs.)	Bore x Stroke (in.)	Compression Ratio	Oil Pressure @ rpm
2006	LaCrosse	3.6	7	240@6000	225@2000	3.70x3.37	10.2:1	20@2000
		3.8	1	200@5200	230@4000	3.80x3.40	9.4:1	60@1850
2007	LaCrosse	3.6	7	240@6000	225@2000	3.70x3.37	10.2:1	20@2000
		3.8	1	200@5200	230@4000	3.80x3.40	9.4:1	60@1850

22116_LACR_C0002

GASOLINE ENGINE TUNE-UP SPECIFICATIONS

Year	Engine Displacement Liters	Engine VIN	Spark Plug Gap (in.)	Ignition Timing (deg.)	Fuel Pump (psi)	Idle Speed (rpm)	Valve Clearance Intake	Valve Clearance Exhaust
2006	3.6	7	0.044	①	55-60	③	HYD	HYD
	3.8	1	0.060	①	41-47 ②	③	HYD	HYD
2007	3.6	7	0.044	①	55-60	③	HYD	HYD
	3.8	1	0.060	①	41-47 ②	③	HYD	HYD

NOTE: The Vehicle Emission Control Information label often reflects specification changes made during production.

The label figures must be used if they differ from those in this chart.

HYD: Hydraulic

① DIS Ignition System timing not adjustable

② Pressure at fuel pump

③ Idle speed maintained by ECM. There is no recommended adjustment procedure

22116_LACR_C0003

CAPACITIES

Year	Model	Engine Displacement Liters	Engine VIN	Engine Oil with Filter (qts.)	Transmission (pts.)*	Fuel Tank (gal.)	Cooling System (qts.)
2006	LaCrosse	3.6	7	5.5	14.8	17.5	11.0
		3.8	1	4.5	14.8	17.5	11.7
2007	LaCrosse	3.6	7	5.5	14.8	17.5	11.0
		3.8	1	4.5	14.8	17.5	11.7

NOTE: All capacities are approximate. Add fluid gradually and ensure a proper fluid level is obtained.

* Drain and refill

22116_LACR_C0004

FLUID SPECIFICATIONS

Year	Model	Engine Displacement Liters	Engine ID/VIN	Engine Oil	Auto. Trans.	Manual Trans.	Power Steering Fluid	Brake Master Cylinder
2006	LaCrosse	3.6	7	5W-30	Dexron VI	—	GM Part No. 89021184	DOT 3
		3.8	1	5W-30	Dexron VI	—	GM Part No. 89021184	DOT 3
2007	LaCrosse	3.6	7	5W-30	Dexron VI	—	GM Part No. 89021184	DOT 3
		3.8	1	5W-30	Dexron VI	—	GM Part No. 89021184	DOT 3

DOT: Department Of Transportation

22116_LACR_C0005

VALVE SPECIFICATIONS

Year	Engine Displacement Liters	Engine VIN	Seat Angle (deg.)	Face Angle (deg.)	Spring Test Pressure (lbs. @ in.)	Spring Installed Height (in.)	Stem-to-Guide Clearance (in.) Intake	Stem-to-Guide Clearance (in.) Exhaust	Stem Diameter (in.) Intake	Stem Diameter (in.) Exhaust
2006	3.6	7	45	44.25	134-149@ 0.9449	0.945-1.378	0.0010-0.0026	0.0014-0.0030	0.2344-0.2352	0.2341-0.2348
	3.8	1	45	46	228@ 1.277	1.690-1.750	0.0012-0.0028	0.0014-0.0029	0.3129-0.3136	0.3129-0.3136
2007	3.6	7	45	44.25	134-149@ 0.9449	0.945-1.378	0.0010-0.0026	0.0014-0.0030	0.2344-0.2352	0.2341-0.2348
	3.8	1	45	46	228@ 1.277	1.690-1.750	0.0012-0.0028	0.0014-0.0029	0.3129-0.3136	0.3129-0.3136

22116_LACR_C0006

CAMSHAFT AND BEARING SPECIFICATIONS CHART

All measurements are given in inches.

Year	Engine Displ. Liters	Engine ID/VIN	Journal Dia.	Brg. Oil Clearance	Shaft End-play	Runout	Journal Bore	Lobe Height Intake	Lobe Height Exhaust
2006	3.6	7	①	0.0016-0.0033	0.0018-0.0085	②	0.0016-0.0033	1.6687-1.6805	1.6703-1.6821
	3.8	1	1.8462-1.8448	0.0016-0.0047	NA	0.00025	NA	0.2580	0.2580
2007	3.6	7	①	0.0016-0.0033	0.0018-0.0085	②	0.0016-0.0033	1.6687-1.6805	1.6703-1.6821
	3.8	1	1.8462-1.8448	0.0016-0.0047	NA	0.00025	NA	0.2580	0.2580

NA: Not Available

① Front number 1 diameter: 1.754 - 1.3764 in.

  Middle and rear number 2-4 diameter: 1.0605 - 1.0614 in.

② Front and rear number 1 and 4 runout: 0.0010 in.

  Middle number 2 and 3 runout: 0.0020 in.

22116_LACR_C0007

CRANKSHAFT AND CONNECTING ROD SPECIFICATIONS

All measurements given in inches

Year	Engine Displacement Liters	Engine VIN	Crankshaft Main Brg. Journal Dia.	Crankshaft Main Brg. Oil Clearance	Crankshaft Shaft End-play	Crankshaft Thrust on No.	Connecting Rod Journal Diameter	Connecting Rod Oil Clearance	Connecting Rod Side Clearance
2006	3.6	7	2.6768-2.6775	0.0004-0.0024	0.0039-0.0130	3	2.2044-2.2050	0.0004-0.0028	0.0037-0.0140
	3.8	1	2.4988-2.4998	①	0.0030-0.0110	2	2.2487-2.2499	0.0005-0.0026	0.0040-0.0200
2007	3.6	7	2.6768-2.6775	0.0004-0.0024	0.0039-0.0130	3	2.2044-2.2050	0.0004-0.0028	0.0037-0.0140
	3.8	1	2.4988-2.4998	①	0.0030-0.0110	2	2.2487-2.2499	0.0005-0.0026	0.0040-0.0200

① Journal 1: 0.0007 - 0.0016

  Journals 2, 3, 4: 0.0009 - 0.0018

22116_LACR_C0008

PISTON AND RING SPECIFICATIONS
All measurements given in inches

Year	Engine Displacement Liters	Engine VIN	Piston Clearance	Ring Gap Top Compression	Ring Gap Bottom Compression	Ring Gap Oil Control	Ring Side Clearance Top Compression	Ring Side Clearance Bottom Compression	Ring Side Clearance Oil Control
2006	3.6	7	0.0010-0.0021	0.0059-0.0118	0.0110-0.0189	0.0059-0.0236	0.0012-0.0026	0.0006-0.0024	0.0012-0.0067
	3.8	1	①	0.0100-0.0180	0.0230-0.0330	0.0100-0.0300	0.0013-0.0031	0.0013-0.0031	0.0009-0.0079
2007	3.6	7	0.0010-0.0021	0.0059-0.0118	0.0110-0.0189	0.0059-0.0236	0.0012-0.0026	0.0006-0.0024	0.0012-0.0067
	3.8	1	①	0.0100-0.0180	0.0230-0.0330	0.0100-0.0300	0.0013-0.0031	0.0013-0.0031	0.0009-0.0079

① Piston-to-bore clearance (New): 0.0008 - 0.0018 in.
   Piston-to-bore clearance (Used): 0.0008 - 0.0039 in.

22116_LACR_C0009

TORQUE SPECIFICATIONS
All measurements given in ft. lbs. unless otherwise noted

Year	Engine Displacement Liters	Engine VIN	Cylinder Head Bolts	Main Bearing Bolts	Rod Bearing Bolts	Crankshaft Damper Bolts	Flywheel Bolts	Manifold Intake	Manifold Exhaust	Spark Plugs	Oil Pan Drain Plug
2006	3.6	7	①	②	③	④	⑤	⑥	⑦	13	18
	3.8	1	⑧	⑨	⑩	⑪	⑫	⑬	⑭	11	22
2007	3.6	7	①	②	③	④	⑤	⑥	⑦	13	18
	3.8	1	⑧	⑨	⑩	⑪	⑫	⑬	⑭	11	22

① M8 bolts:
  Step 1: 10 ft. lbs.
  Step2: plus 60 degrees
  M11 bolts:
  Step 1: 33 ft. lbs.
  Step 2: plus 120 degrees

② Inner:
  Step 1: 15 ft. lbs.
  Step 2: plus 80 degrees
  Outer:
  Step 1: 10 ft. lbs.
  Step 2: plus 110 degrees
  Side:
  Step 1: 22 ft. lbs.
  Step 2: plus 60 degrees

③ Step 1: 22 ft. lbs.
  Step 2: back off to zero
  Step 3: 18 ft. lbs.
  Step 4: plus 110 degrees

④ Step 1: 74 ft. lbs.
  Step 2: plus 150 degrees

⑤ Step 1: 22 ft. lbs.
  Step 2: plus 45 degrees

⑥ Intake manifold bolts: 17 ft. lbs.
  Tuning valve bolt: 89 in. lbs.

⑦ Exhaust manifold bolts: 15 ft. lbs.
  Heat shield bolt: 89 in. lbs.
  Studs: 53 in. lbs.

⑧ Step 1: Tighten all bolts to 37 ft. lbs.
  Step 2: Turn all bolts 120 degrees

⑨ Cap bolts: 30 ft. lbs. plus 110 degrees
  Side bolts: 11 ft. lbs. plus 45 degrees

⑩ 20 ft. lbs. plus 50 degrees

⑪ 111 ft. lbs. plus 76 degrees

⑫ 11 ft. lbs. plus 50 degrees

⑬ Upper manifold: 8 ft. lbs.
  Lower manifold: 11 ft. lbs.
  Upper manifold cover nut 27 in. lbs.

⑭ Exhaust manifold bolt/nut: 22 ft. lbs.
  Heat shield bolt & manifold stud: 89 in. lbs
  Heat shield nut: 18 ft. lbs.
  Manifold pipe stud nut: 24 ft. lbs.

22116_LACR_C0010

WHEEL ALIGNMENT SPECIFICATIONS

Year	Model		Caster Range (+/-Deg.)	Caster Preferred Setting (Deg.)	Camber Range (+/-Deg.)	Camber Preferred Setting (Deg.)	Toe-in (in.)
2006	LaCrosse	F	0.75	+3.40	0.75	-0.80	0.10 +/- 0.20
		R	—	—	0.50	-0.80	0.10 +/- 0.20
2007	LaCrosse	F	0.75	+3.40	0.75	-0.80	0.10 +/- 0.20
		R	—	—	0.50	-0.80	0.10 +/- 0.20

22116_LACR_C0011

TIRE, WHEEL AND BALL JOINT SPECIFICATIONS

Year	Model	OEM Tires Standard	OEM Tires Optional	Tire Pressures (psi) Front	Tire Pressures (psi) Rear	Wheel Size	Ball Joint Inspection	Lug Nut Torque (ft. lbs.)
2006	LaCrosse CX	P225/60R16	None	①	①	16 in.	0.125 in. ②	100
	LaCrosse CXL	P225/60R16	None	①	①	16 in.	0.125 in. ②	100
	LaCrosse CXS	P225/55R17	None	①	①	17 in.	0.125 in. ②	100
2007	LaCrosse CX	P225/60R16	None	①	①	16 in.	0.125 in. ②	100
	LaCrosse CXL	P225/60R16	None	①	①	16 in.	0.125 in. ②	100
	LaCrosse CXS	P225/55R17	None	①	①	17 in.	0.125 in. ②	100

OEM: Original Equipment Manufacturer

PSI: Pounds Per Square Inch

① See placard on vehicle

② Remove tension from the ball joint.

Measurement is maximum horizontal or vertical loose movement.

22116_LACR_C0012

BRAKE SPECIFICATIONS

All measurements given in inches unless otherwise noted

Year	Model		Brake Disc Original Thickness	Brake Disc Minimum Thickness	Brake Disc Maximum Runout	Minimum Lining Thickness	Caliper Bracket Bolts (ft. lbs.)	Caliper Mounting Bolts (ft. lbs.)
2006	LaCrosse	F	1.270	1.210	0.002	NA	133	70
		R	0.550	0.490	0.002	NA	89	25
2007	LaCrosse	F	1.270	1.210	0.002	NA	133	70
		R	0.550	0.490	0.002	NA	89	25

NA: Information not available

22116_LACR_C0013

MAINTENANCE I AND II SERVICE SCHEDULES
2006-07 Buick LaCrosse

When the CHANGE ENGINE OIL light appears, certain services and inspections are required.
Required services are described as Maintenance I and Maintenance II.
The first service on a vehicle should be Maintenance I, and the second service should be Maintenance II.

Alternate between the 2 thereafter. However, in some cases, Maintenance II may be required more often.
Maintenance I: Use Maintenance I if the CHANGE ENGINE OIL light comes on within 10 months since vehicle was purchased or, if Maintenance II was performed.
Maintenance II: Use Maintenance II if the previous service performed was Maintenance I. Always use Maintenance II whenever the CHANGE ENGINE OIL light comes on 10 months or more since the last service, or, if the CHANGE ENGINE OIL light has not come on at all for one year.

Service	Maintenance I	II
Change the engine oil and filter. Reset the oil life system.	✓	✓
Visually inspect the vehicle for leaks or damage. A fluid loss in the vehicle system could indicate a problem. Inspected, repair and add fluid to the system if necessary.	✓	✓
Inspect the engine air cleaner filter. If necessary, replace the filter.	--	✓
Rotate the tires. Inspect the tire inflation pressures and the tire wear.	✓	✓
Visually inspect the brake lines and hoses for proper hook-up, binding, leaks, cracks, chafing, etc. Inspect the disc brake pads for wear and the rotors for surface condition. Inspect the drum brake linings for wear or cracks. Inspect other brake parts, including drums, wheel cylinders, calipers, parking brake, etc. Inspect the parking brake adjustment.	✓	✓
Inspect the engine coolant and the windshield washer fluid levels. Add fluid as needed.	✓	✓
Inspect the suspension and steering components. Inspect the front and rear suspension and the steering system for damaged, loose or missing parts, or signs of wear. Inspect the power steering lines and the hoses for proper hook-up, binding, leaks, cracks, chafing, etc.	--	✓
Visually inspect the coolant hoses and replace the hoses if they are cracked, swollen or deteriorated. Inspect all pipes, fittings and clamps; replace with GM parts as needed. To help ensure proper operation, a pressure test of the cooling system and pressure cap and cleaning the outside of the radiator and air conditioning condenser is recommended at least once a year.	--	✓
Inspect the front and rear suspension and the steering system for damaged, loose or missing parts, or signs of wear. Inspect power steering lines and hoses for proper hook-up, binding, leaks, cracks, chafing, etc.	--	✓
Inspect the throttle system for interference or binding and for damaged or missing parts. Replace the parts as needed. Replace any components that have high effort or excessive wear. Do not lubricate the accelerator or the cruise control cables.	--	✓
Replace the passenger compartment air filter.	--	✓

To reset the CHANGE ENGINE OIL LIGHT:
1. Press the option button on the DIC until ENGINE OIL MONITOR appears on the DIC screen.
2. Press the set/reset button to reset the system. The next screen indicates that the CHANGE OIL SOON message message has been reset. If the vehicle has the uplevel DIC, when the gages button is pressed and the OIL LIFE REMAINING mode appears, it should read 100 percent OIL LIFE REMAINING
3. Turn the key to OFF.

Vehicles without Driver Information Center (DIC)
1. With the engine off, turn the ignition key to RUN.
2. Fully press and release the accelerator pedal slowly three times within five seconds.
3. Turn the key to OFF, then start the vehicle.

If the light or message comes back on when you start your vehicle, the oil life system has not reset. Repeat the procedure.

ADDITIONAL MAINTENANCE SERVICES
2006-07 Buick LaCrosse

TO BE SERVICED	SERVICE	VEHICLE MILEAGE INTERVAL (x1000)					
		25	50	75	100	125	150
Air cleaner filter	R	✓	✓	✓	✓	✓	✓
Accessory drive belt	I						✓
Auto. Trans. Fluid ①	R		✓		✓		✓
Cooling system hoses and clamps	S/I						✓
Engine coolant	R						✓
Fuel system	I	✓	✓	✓	✓	✓	✓
Exhaust system & heat shields	S/I	✓	✓	✓	✓	✓	✓
Spark plugs	R				✓		

R: Replace   S/I: Inspect and service, if necessary

① Replace if any of the following conditions are met:

   Heavy city traffic where the outside temperature regularly reaches 32°C (90°F) or higher

   Hilly or mountainous terrain

   Frequent trailer towing

   Taxi, police or delivery service

   Otherwise, change every 100,000 miles

22116_LACR_C0015

PRECAUTIONS

Before servicing any vehicle, please be sure to read all of the following precautions, which deal with personal safety, prevention of component damage, and important points to take into consideration when servicing a motor vehicle:

• Never open, service or drain the radiator or cooling system when the engine is hot; serious burns can occur from the steam and hot coolant.

• Observe all applicable safety precautions when working around fuel. Whenever servicing the fuel system, always work in a well-ventilated area. Do not allow fuel spray or vapors to come in contact with a spark, open flame, or excessive heat (a hot drop light, for example). Keep a dry chemical fire extinguisher near the work area. Always keep fuel in a container specifically designed for fuel storage; also, always properly seal fuel containers to avoid the possibility of fire or explosion. Refer to the additional fuel system precautions later in this section.

• Fuel injection systems often remain pressurized, even after the engine has been turned **OFF**. The fuel system pressure must be relieved before disconnecting any fuel lines. Failure to do so may result in fire and/or personal injury.

• Brake fluid often contains polyglycol ethers and polyglycols. Avoid contact with the eyes and wash your hands thoroughly after handling brake fluid. If you do get brake fluid in your eyes, flush your eyes with clean, running water for 15 minutes. If eye irritation persists, or if you have taken brake fluid internally, IMMEDIATELY seek medical assistance.

• The EPA warns that prolonged contact with used engine oil may cause a number of skin disorders, including cancer. You should make every effort to minimize your exposure to used engine oil. Protective gloves should be worn when changing oil. Wash your hands and any other exposed skin areas as soon as possible after exposure to used engine oil. Soap and water, or waterless hand cleaner should be used.

• All new vehicles are now equipped with an air bag system, often referred to as a Supplemental Restraint System (SRS) or Supplemental Inflatable Restraint (SIR) system. The system must be disabled before performing service on or around system components, steering column, instrument panel components, wiring and sensors. Failure to follow safety and disabling procedures could result in accidental air bag deployment, possible personal injury and unnecessary system repairs.

• Always wear safety goggles when working with, or around, the air bag system. When carrying a non-deployed air bag, be sure the bag and trim cover are pointed away from your body. When placing a non-deployed air bag on a work surface, always face the bag and trim cover upward, away from the surface. This will reduce the motion of the module if it is accidentally deployed. Refer to the additional air bag system precautions later in this section.

• Clean, high quality brake fluid from a sealed container is essential to the safe and proper operation of the brake system. You should always buy the correct type of brake fluid for your vehicle. If the brake fluid becomes contaminated, completely flush the system with new fluid. Never reuse any brake fluid. Any brake fluid that is removed from the system should be discarded. Also, do not allow any brake fluid to come in contact with a painted surface; it will damage the paint.

• Never operate the engine without the proper amount and type of engine oil; doing so WILL result in severe engine damage.

• Timing belt maintenance is extremely important. Many models utilize an interference-type, non-freewheeling engine. If the timing belt breaks, the valves in the cylinder head may strike the pistons, causing potentially serious (also time-consuming and expensive) engine damage. Refer to the maintenance interval charts for the recommended replacement interval for the timing belt, and to the timing belt section for belt replacement and inspection.

• Disconnecting the negative battery cable on some vehicles may interfere with the functions of the on-board computer system(s) and may require the computer to undergo a relearning process once the negative battery cable is reconnected.

• When servicing drum brakes, only disassemble and assemble one side at a time, leaving the remaining side intact for reference.

• Only an MVAC-trained, EPA-certified automotive technician should service the air conditioning system or its components.

BRAKES

GENERAL INFORMATION

PRECAUTIONS

• Certain components within the ABS system are not intended to be serviced or repaired individually.

• Do not use rubber hoses or other parts not specifically specified for and ABS system. When using repair kits, replace all parts included in the kit. Partial or incorrect repair may lead to functional problems and require the replacement of components.

• Lubricate rubber parts with clean, fresh brake fluid to ease assembly. Do not use shop air to clean parts; damage to rubber components may result.

• Use only DOT 3 brake fluid from an unopened container.

• If any hydraulic component or line is removed or replaced, it may be necessary to bleed the entire system.

• A clean repair area is essential. Always clean the reservoir and cap thoroughly before removing the cap. The slightest amount of dirt in the fluid may plug an orifice and impair the system function. Perform repairs after components have been thoroughly cleaned; use only denatured alcohol to clean components. Do not allow ABS components to come into contact with any substance containing mineral oil; this includes used shop rags.

• The Anti-Lock control unit is a microprocessor similar to other computer units in the vehicle. Ensure that the ignition switch

ANTI-LOCK BRAKE SYSTEM (ABS)

is **OFF** before removing or installing controller harnesses. Avoid static electricity discharge at or near the controller.

• If any arc welding is to be done on the vehicle, the control unit should be unplugged before welding operations begin.

SPEED SENSORS

REMOVAL & INSTALLATION

The front and rear wheel speed sensors and rings are integral with the hub and bearing assemblies. If a speed sensor or a ring needs replacement, replace the entire hub and bearing assembly. Do not service the harness pigtail individually because the harness pigtail is part of the sensor.

BLEEDING PROCEDURE

BLEEDING PROCEDURE

✳✳ WARNING

When adding fluid to the brake master cylinder reservoir, use only Delco Supreme 11®, GM P/N 12377967 (Canadian P/N 992667), or equivalent DOT-3 brake fluid from a clean, sealed brake fluid container. The use of any type of fluid other than the recommended type of brake fluid may cause contamination which could result in damage to the internal rubber seals and/or rubber linings of hydraulic brake system components.

1. Before servicing the vehicle, refer to the Precautions Section.

2. Place a clean shop cloth beneath the brake master cylinder to prevent brake fluid spills.

3. With the ignition OFF and the brakes cool, apply the brakes 3–5 times, or until the brake pedal effort increases significantly, in order to deplete the brake booster power reserve.

4. If you have performed a brake master cylinder bench bleeding on this vehicle, or if you disconnected the brake pipes from the master cylinder, you must perform the following steps:

    a. Ensure that the brake master cylinder reservoir is full to the maximum-fill level. If necessary, add Delco Supreme 11®, GM P/N 12377967 (Canadian P/N 992667), or equivalent DOT-3 brake fluid from a clean, sealed brake fluid container. If removal of the reservoir cap and diaphragm is necessary, clean the outside of the reservoir on and around the cap prior to removal.

    b. With the rear brake pipe installed securely to the master cylinder, loosen and separate the front brake pipe from the front port of the brake master cylinder.

    c. Allow a small amount of brake fluid to gravity bleed from the open port of the master cylinder.

    d. Reconnect the brake pipe to the master cylinder port and tighten securely.

    e. Have an assistant slowly depress the brake pedal fully and maintain steady pressure on the pedal.

    f. Loosen the same brake pipe to purge air from the open port of the master cylinder.

    g. Tighten the brake pipe, then have the assistant slowly release the brake pedal.

    h. Wait 15 seconds, then repeat steps 3-7 until all air is purged from the same port of the master cylinder.

    i. With the front brake pipe installed securely to the master cylinder, after all air has been purged from the front port of the master cylinder, loosen and separate the rear brake pipe from the master cylinder, then repeat steps 3-8.

    j. After completing the final master cylinder port bleeding procedure, ensure that both of the brake pipe to master cylinder fittings are properly tightened.

5. Fill the brake master cylinder reservoir with Delco Supreme 11®, GM P/N 12377967 (Canadian P/N 992667), or equivalent DOT-3 brake fluid from a clean, sealed brake fluid container. Ensure that the brake master cylinder reservoir remains at least half-full during this bleeding procedure. Add fluid as needed to maintain the proper level. Clean the outside of the reservoir on and around the reservoir cap prior to removing the cap and diaphragm.

6. Install a proper box-end wrench onto the RIGHT REAR wheel hydraulic circuit bleeder valve.

7. Install a transparent hose over the end of the bleeder valve.

8. Submerge the open end of the transparent hose into a transparent container partially filled with Delco Supreme 11®, GM P/N 12377967 (Canadian P/N 992667), or equivalent DOT-3 brake fluid from a clean, sealed brake fluid container.

9. Have an assistant slowly depress the brake pedal fully and maintain steady pressure on the pedal.

10. Loosen the bleeder valve to purge air from the wheel hydraulic circuit.

11. Tighten the bleeder valve, then, have the assistant slowly release the brake pedal.

12. Wait 15 seconds, then repeat steps 8-10 until all air is purged from the same wheel hydraulic circuit.

13. With the right rear wheel hydraulic circuit bleeder valve tightened securely, after all air has been purged from the right rear hydraulic circuit, install a proper box-end wrench onto the LEFT FRONT wheel hydraulic circuit bleeder valve.

14. Install a transparent hose over the end of the bleeder valve, then, repeat steps 7-11.

15. With the left front wheel hydraulic circuit bleeder valve tightened securely, after

all air has been purged from the left front hydraulic circuit, install a proper box-end wrench onto the LEFT REAR wheel hydraulic circuit bleeder valve.

16. Install a transparent hose over the end of the bleeder valve, then, repeat steps 7-11.

17. With the left rear wheel hydraulic circuit bleeder valve tightened securely, after all air has been purged from the left rear hydraulic circuit, install a proper box-end wrench onto the RIGHT FRONT wheel hydraulic circuit bleeder valve.

18. Install a transparent hose over the end of the bleeder valve, then, repeat steps 7-11.

19. After completing the final wheel hydraulic circuit bleeding procedure, ensure that each of the 4 wheel hydraulic circuit bleeder valves is properly tightened.

20. Fill the brake master cylinder reservoir to the maximum-fill level with Delco Supreme 11®, GM P/N 12377967 (Canadian P/N 992667), or equivalent DOT-3 brake fluid from a clean, sealed brake fluid container.

21. Slowly depress and release the brake pedal. Observe the feel of the brake pedal.

22. If the brake pedal feels spongy, repeat the bleeding procedure again. If the brake pedal still feels spongy after repeating the bleeding procedure, perform the following steps:

    a. Inspect the brake system for external leaks.

    b. Pressure bleed the hydraulic brake system in order to purge any air that may still be trapped in the system.

23. Turn the ignition key ON, with the engine OFF. Check to see if the brake system warning lamp remains illuminated.

BLEEDING THE ABS SYSTEM

Automated Bleed Procedure

➡**The Auto Bleed Procedure may be terminated at any time during the process by pressing the EXIT button. No further Scan Tool prompts pertaining to the Auto Bleed procedure will be given. After exiting the bleed procedure, relieve bleed pressure and disconnect bleed equipment per manufacturer's instructions. Failure to properly relieve pressure may result in spilled brake fluid causing damage to components and painted surfaces.**

1. Raise and support the vehicle.

2. Remove all 4 tire and wheel assemblies.

3. Inspect the brake system for leaks and visual damage.

4. Lower the vehicle.

5. Inspect the battery state of charge.

6. Install a scan tool.

7. Turn the ignition ON, with the engine OFF.

8. With the scan tool, establish communications with the ABS system. Select Special Functions. Select Automated Bleed from the Special Functions menu.

9. Raise and support the vehicle.

10. Following the directions given on the scan tool, pressure bleed the base brake system.

11. Follow the scan tool directions until the desired brake pedal height is achieved.

12. If the bleed procedure is aborted, a malfunction exists. Perform the following steps before resuming the bleed procedure:

a. If a DTC is detected, diagnose the appropriate DTC.

b. If the brake pedal feels spongy, perform the conventional brake bleed procedure again.

13. When the desired pedal height is achieved, press the brake pedal to inspect for firmness.

14. Lower the vehicle.

15. Remove the scan tool.

16. Install the tire and wheel assemblies.

17. Inspect the brake fluid level.

18. Road test the vehicle while inspecting that the pedal remains high and firm.

BRAKES

FRONT DISC BRAKES

✳✳ CAUTION

Dust and dirt accumulating on brake parts during normal use may contain asbestos fibers from production or aftermarket brake linings. Breathing excessive concentrations of asbestos fibers can cause serious bodily harm. Exercise care when servicing brake parts. Do not sand or grind brake lining unless equipment used is designed to contain the dust residue. Do not clean brake parts with compressed air or by dry brushing. Cleaning should be done by dampening the brake components with a fine mist of water, then wiping the brake components clean with a dampened cloth. Dispose of cloth and all residue containing asbestos fibers in an impermeable container with the appropriate label. Follow practices prescribed by the Occupational Safety and Health Administration (OSHA) and the Environmental Protection Agency (EPA) for the handling, processing, and disposing of dust or debris that may contain asbestos fibers.

BRAKE CALIPER

REMOVAL & INSTALLATION

See Figures 1 through 3.

1. Before servicing the vehicle, refer to the Precautions Section.

2. Inspect the fluid level in the brake master cylinder reservoir.

3. If the brake fluid level is midway between the maximum-full point and the minimum allowable level, then no brake fluid needs to be removed from the reservoir before proceeding. If the brake fluid level is higher than midway between the maximum-full point and the minimum allowable level, then remove brake fluid to the midway point before proceeding.

4. Raise and suitably support the vehicle.

5. Remove the front tire and the wheel assembly.

6. Hand tighten 2 wheel lug nuts to retain the rotor to the hub.

7. Install a large C-clamp over the top of the brake caliper and against the back of the outboard brake pad.

8. Tighten the C-clamp until the caliper piston is pushed into the caliper bore enough to slide the caliper off the rotor.

9. Remove the C-clamp from the caliper.

10. Remove the brake hose to caliper bolt from the caliper. Discard the 2 copper brake hose gaskets. These gaskets may be stuck to the brake caliper and/or the brake hose end.

11. Plug the opening in the front brake hose to prevent excessive brake fluid loss and contamination.

➡ Note the location of the caliper pin bolts. The leading caliper pin bolt, or top bolt, has a bushing as part of the assembly. The trailing caliper pin bolt, or bottom bolt, is a solid design.

12. Remove the caliper pin bolts. Note the location of the caliper pin bolts. The leading caliper pin, or top bolt, has a bushing as part of the assembly. The trailing caliper pin, or bottom bolt, is a solid design.

13. Remove the caliper from the rotor and the caliper bracket.

14. Inspect the caliper bolt boots in the caliper bracket for damage. Replace any damaged caliper bolt boots.

15. Inspect the caliper bolts for corrosion or damage. If corrosion or damage is found, use new caliper pin bolts when installing the caliper.

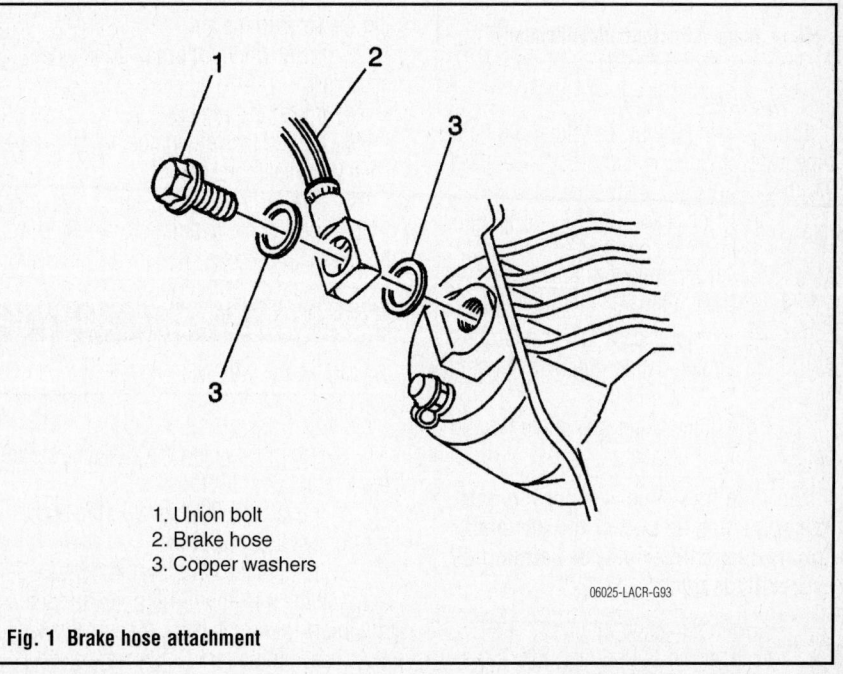

1. Union bolt
2. Brake hose
3. Copper washers

06025-LACR-G93

Fig. 1 Brake hose attachment

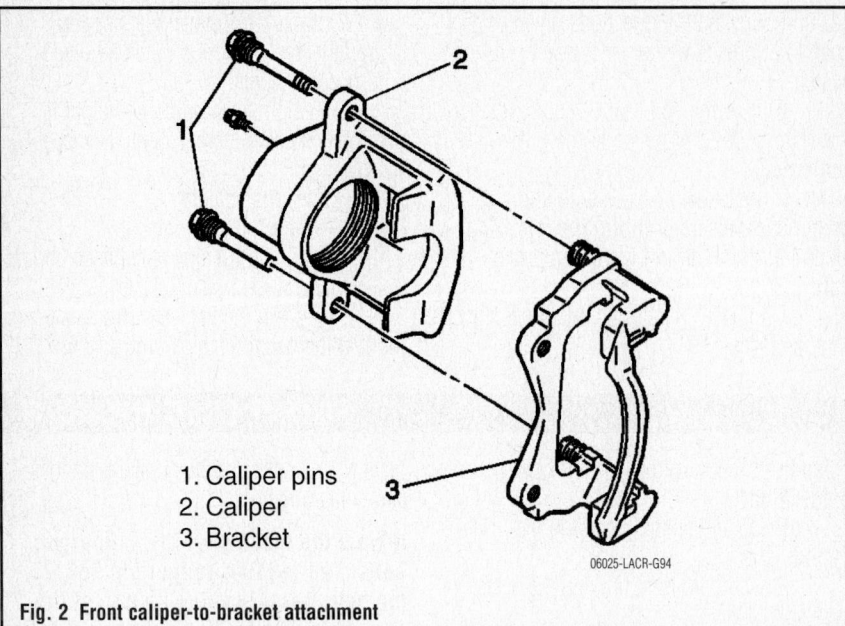

1. Caliper pins
2. Caliper
3. Bracket

06025-LACR-G94

Fig. 2 Front caliper-to-bracket attachment

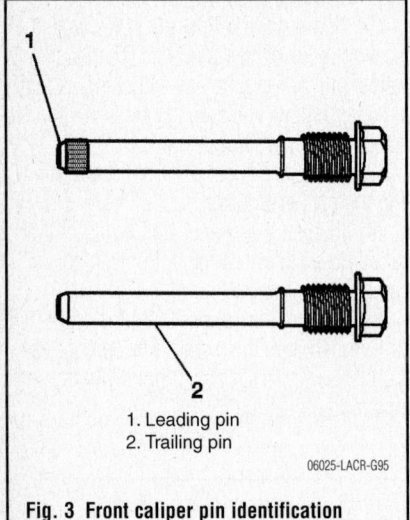

1. Leading pin
2. Trailing pin

06025-LACR-G95

Fig. 3 Front caliper pin identification

To install:

16. If reusing the brake caliper pin bolts, wipe away any debris and old lubricant with a with a clean shop cloth.

17. Apply lubricant, GM P/N 18047666, or equivalent, to the brake caliper pin bolts. Apply a thin layer to the pin bushing and to the caliper pin bolt shank. Ensure that there is not a buildup of excess lubricant at the end of the leading caliper pin, in front of the bushing.

18. Install the caliper over the rotor and onto the caliper bracket.

➡**The leading caliper pin, or top bolt, has a bushing as part of the assembly. The trailing caliper pin, or bottom bolt, is a solid design.**

19. Install the caliper pin bolts. The leading caliper pin bolt, or top bolt, has a

bushing as part of the assembly. The trailing caliper pin bolt, or bottom bolt, is a solid design. Ensure that the bolt boots fit securely in the groove of the caliper pin bolts. If the boots are damaged, they must be replaced. Tighten the bolts to 70 ft. lbs. (95 Nm).

➡**Install NEW copper brake hose gaskets.**

20. Assemble the brake hose bolt and the NEW copper brake hose gaskets to the brake hose.

21. Install the brake hose to caliper bolt to the brake caliper. Tighten the bolt to 40 ft. lbs. (54 Nm).

22. Remove the 2 wheel lug nuts retaining the rotor to the hub.

23. Install the front tire and the wheel assembly.

24. Lower the vehicle.

25. Fill the master cylinder to the proper level with clean brake fluid.

26. Bleed the brake system.

27. Inspect the hydraulic brake system for brake fluid leaks.

DISC BRAKE PADS

REMOVAL & INSTALLATION

See Figure 4.

1. Before servicing the vehicle, refer to the Precautions Section.

2. Inspect the fluid level in the brake master cylinder reservoir.

3. If the brake fluid level is midway between the maximum-full point and the minimum allowable level, then no brake fluid needs to be removed from the reser-

voir before proceeding. If the brake fluid level is higher than midway between the maximum-full point and the minimum allowable level, then remove brake fluid to the midway point before proceeding.

4. Raise and suitably support the vehicle.

5. Remove the tire and the wheel assembly.

6. Hand-tighten 2 wheel lug nuts in order to retain the rotor to the hub.

7. Install a large C-clamp over the top of the caliper housing and against the back of the outboard pad.

8. Slowly tighten the C-clamp until the piston pushes into the caliper bore enough to slide the caliper off the rotor.

9. Remove the C-clamp from the caliper.

10. Remove the lower caliper bolt (1).

❋❋ WARNING

Use care to avoid damaging pin boot when rotating caliper.

11. In order to access the pads, rotate the caliper upward and suitably support it.

12. Remove the pads (5) from the caliper bracket (3).

13. Remove the 2 retainer slides (4) from the caliper bracket (3).

14. Inspect all parts for cuts, tears, or deterioration. Replace any damaged parts.

15. Inspect the caliper bolts for corrosion or damage. If corrosion is found, use new caliper bolts when installing the caliper.

To install:

16. Using a C-clamp, bottom the piston into the caliper bore. Use an old brake pad or wooden block across the face of the piston. Do not damage the piston or the caliper boot.

17. Install the 2 retainers to the caliper bracket.

➡**The wear sensor is on the outside pad. The sensor is positioned at the leading or upward edge of the pad during forward wheel rotation.**

18. Install the pads to the caliper anchor bracket.

❋❋ WARNING

Use care to avoid damaging pin boot when rotating caliper.

19. Remove the support and reposition the caliper (2) back down over the front pads.

20. Lubricate the pin bolt and the inner diameter of the bolt boot with GM P/N

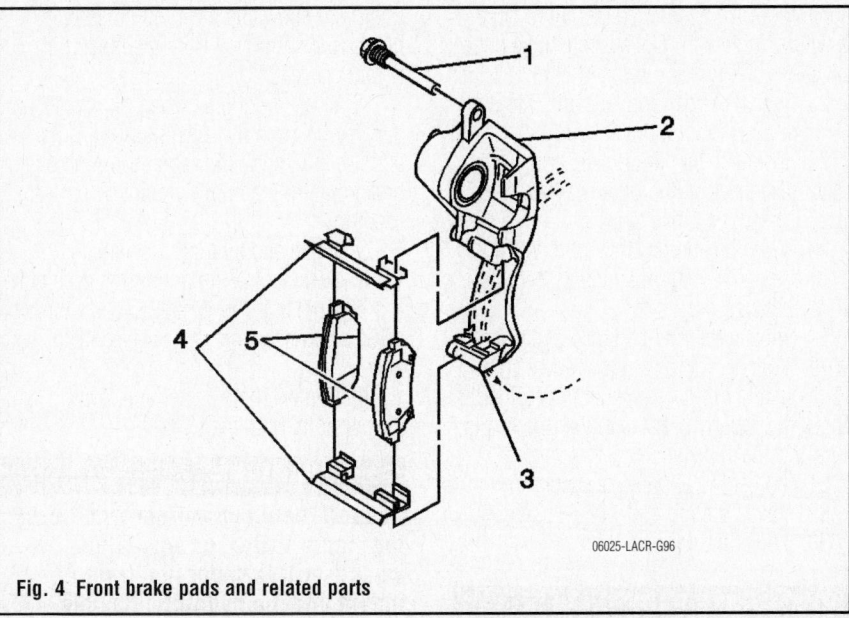

Fig. 4 Front brake pads and related parts

06025-LACR-G96

18047666, or equivalent. Do not lubricate the threads of the pin bolt.

21. Install the lower caliper bolt. Tighten the caliper bolts to 70 ft. lbs. (95 Nm).

22. Remove the 2 wheel lug nuts retaining the rotor to the hub.

23. Install the tire and the wheel assembly.

24. Lower the vehicle.

25. With the engine OFF, gradually apply the brake pedal to approximately ⅔ of its travel distance.

26. Slowly release the brake pedal.

27. Wait 15 seconds, then, repeat steps 10 and 11 until a firm brake pedal is obtained. This will properly seat the brake caliper pistons and brake pads.

28. Fill the brake master cylinder reservoir to the proper level.

29. Burnish the pads and rotors.

BRAKES

REAR DISC BRAKES

✷✷ CAUTION

Dust and dirt accumulating on brake parts during normal use may contain asbestos fibers from production or aftermarket brake linings. Breathing excessive concentrations of asbestos fibers can cause serious bodily harm. Exercise care when servicing brake parts. Do not sand or grind brake lining unless equipment used is designed to contain the dust residue. Do not clean brake parts with compressed air or by dry brushing. Cleaning should be done by dampening the brake components with a fine mist of water, then wiping the brake components clean with a dampened cloth. Dispose of cloth and all residue containing asbestos fibers in an impermeable container with the appropriate label. Follow practices prescribed by the Occupational Safety and Health Administration (OSHA) and the Environmental Protection Agency (EPA) for the handling, processing, and disposing of dust or debris that may contain asbestos fibers.

BRAKE CALIPER

REMOVAL & INSTALLATION

See Figures 5 and 6.

1. Before servicing the vehicle, refer to the Precautions Section.

2. Inspect the fluid level in the brake master cylinder reservoir.

3. If the brake fluid level is midway between the maximum-full point and the minimum allowable level, no brake fluid needs to be removed from the reservoir before proceeding.

4. If the brake fluid level is higher than midway between the maximum-full point and the minimum allowable level, remove brake fluid to the midway point before proceeding.

5. Raise and support the vehicle.

6. Remove the tire and wheel assembly.

7. Release tension from park brake system at the equalizer.

8. Disconnect the front and rear cables from one another at the connector clip.

9. Disconnect the park brake cable from the park brake lever on the brake caliper.

10. Remove the park brake cable from the caliper bracket.

11. Remove brake hose to caliper bolt.

12. Remove the brake hose from the brake caliper.

13. Remove and discard the 2 copper brake hose gaskets. These gaskets may be

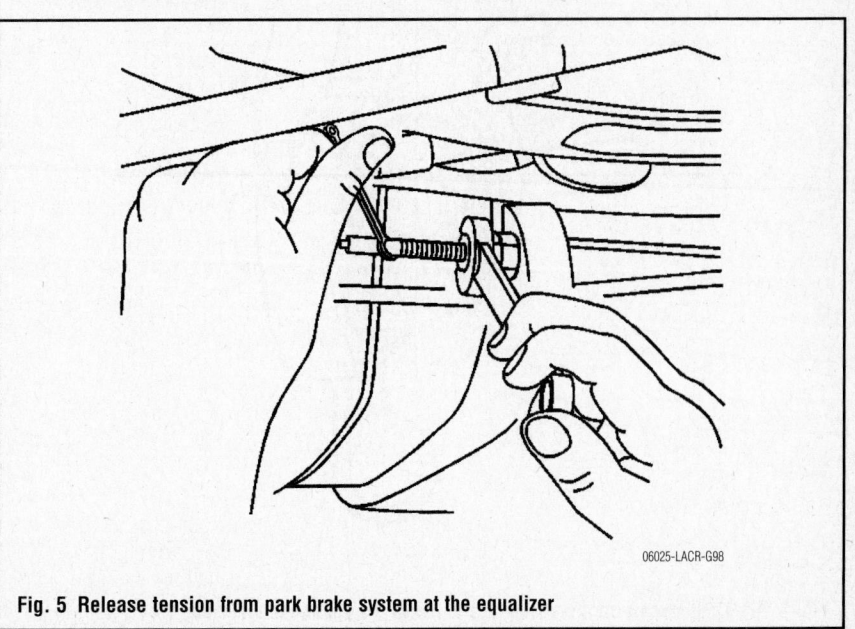

06025-LACR-G98

Fig. 5 Release tension from park brake system at the equalizer

stuck to the brake caliper and/or the brake hose end.

14. Plug the opening in the brake caliper and brake hose to prevent fluid loss and/or contamination.

15. Remove the brake caliper bolts.

16. Remove the brake caliper.

To install:

17. Align the indents on the piston face to match the pin on the brake pad.

18. Inspect the bracket bolt guide assembly.

19. Inspect the brake pad hardware and replace if necessary.

20. Install the brake caliper onto the caliper bracket insuring that the guide boots are not damaged.

21. Install the brake caliper bolts. Tighten the brake caliper bolts to 25 ft. lbs. (34 Nm).

22. Remove the plugs in the brake hose end.

➡ **Install NEW copper brake hose gaskets.**

23. Assemble the brake hose bolt and the NEW copper brake hose gaskets to the brake hose.

24. Install the brake hose to caliper bolt to the brake caliper. When installing the right rear brake hose to caliper, hold hose up while tightening. Tighten the brake hose to caliper bolt to 33 ft. lbs. (44 Nm).

25. Install the park brake cable into the park brake bracket on the caliper.

26. Connect the park brake cable to the park brake lever on the brake caliper.

27. Bleed the brake system.

28. With the engine OFF, gradually apply the brake pedal to approximately ⅔ of its travel distance.

29. Slowly release the brake pedal.

30. Wait 15 seconds, then repeat steps 12-13 until a firm brake pedal is obtained. This will properly seat the brake caliper pistons and brake pads.

31. Adjust the park brake system.

32. Install the tire and wheel assembly.

33. Lower the vehicle.

DISC BRAKE PADS

REMOVAL & INSTALLATION

See Figure 7.

1. Before servicing the vehicle, refer to the Precautions Section.

2. Inspect the fluid level in the brake master cylinder reservoir.

3. If the brake fluid level is midway between the maximum-full point and the minimum allowable level, no brake fluid needs to be removed from the reservoir before proceeding.

4. If the brake fluid level is higher than midway between the maximum-full point and the minimum allowable level, remove brake fluid to the midway point before proceeding.

5. Raise and support the vehicle.

6. Remove the tire and wheel assembly.

7. Unclamp the Wheel Speed Sensor (WSS) harness from the lower control arm.

8. Remove both upper and lower caliper bolts from the caliper.

⁎⁎ WARNING

Support the brake caliper with heavy mechanic's wire, or equivalent, whenever it is separated from its mount and the hydraulic flexible brake hose is still connected. Failure to support the caliper in this manner will cause the flexible brake hose to bear the weight of the caliper, which may cause damage to the brake hose and in turn may cause a brake fluid leak.

9. Pull the caliper straight off of the bracket and secure out of the way with heavy mechanic's wire. DO NOT disconnect the hydraulic brake flexible hose from the caliper.

10. Remove the inboard and outboard pads from the brake caliper bracket.

To install:

11. Inspect the brake caliper bracket guide boot assembly for condition.

12. Clean the brake pad hardware mating surfaces on the caliper bracket of any debris or corrosion.

13. Inspect the brake pad retainer clips for condition and replace, if necessary.

14. Inspect the piston boot for condition. Replace if damaged.

15. Retract the brake caliper piston into the brake caliper bore. Use a suitable spanner type wrench and turn the piston clockwise until it bottoms out fully in the brake caliper (Mac® Tools DBC 25 C 2500 MA Disc Brake Caliper Tool Set, or equivalent).

16. Align the indents on the piston face to match the pin on the back of the inboard brake pads.

17. Install the brake pad retainers into the brake caliper bracket.

18. Install the inboard and outboard brake pads into the brake caliper bracket insuring that the pad with the metallic wear

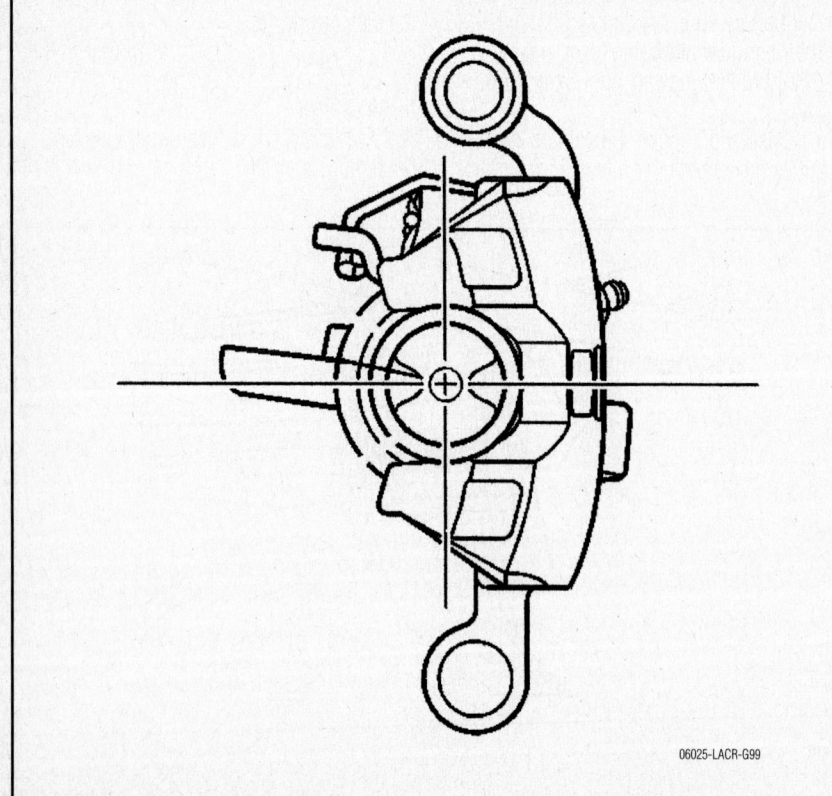

06025-LACR-G99

Fig. 6 Align the indents on the piston face to match the pin on the brake pad

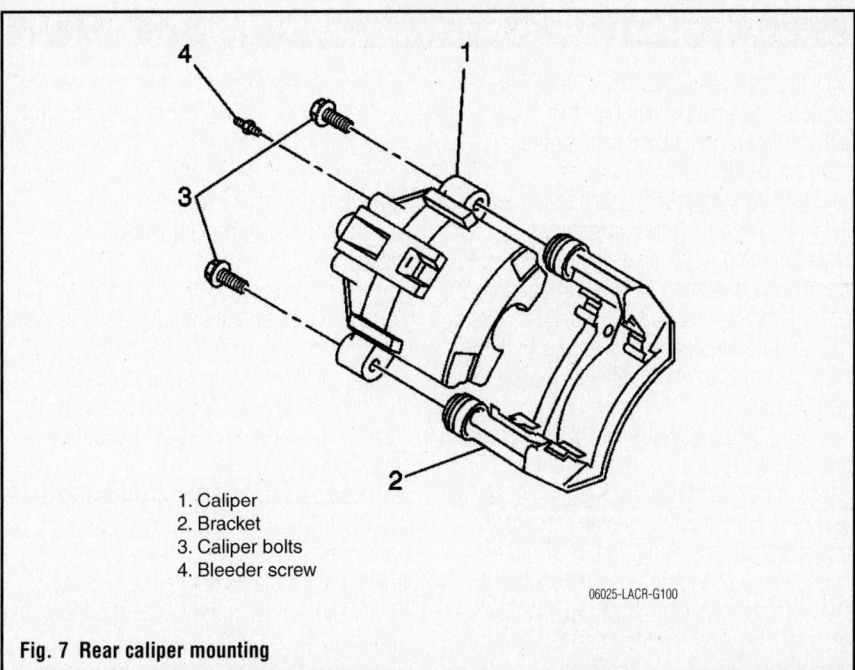

1. Caliper
2. Bracket
3. Caliper bolts
4. Bleeder screw

06025-LACR-G100

Fig. 7 Rear caliper mounting

sensor is placed on the inboard side of the bracket.

19. Slide the caliper onto the bracket insuring that the bracket guide boots are not damaged.

20. Insert the brake caliper bolts. Tighten the brake caliper bolts to 25 ft. lbs. (34 Nm).

21. Re-clamp the WSS harness onto the lower control arm.

22. Install the tire and wheel assembly.

23. Lower the vehicle.

24. With the engine OFF, gradually apply the brake pedal to approximately ⅔ of its travel distance.

25. Slowly release the brake pedal.

26. Wait 15 seconds, then repeat steps 10-11 until a firm brake pedal apply is obtained. This will properly seat the brake caliper pistons and brake pads.

27. Fill the brake master cylinder reservoir to the proper level.

BRAKES

PARKING BRAKE

PARKING BRAKE CABLES

ADJUSTMENT

Adjustment of manual adjustment park brake cable system is necessary whenever the rear brake cables have been disconnected. A need for park brake cable adjustment is indicated if the hydraulic brake system operates with good reserve, but a firm park brake pedal feel cannot be achieved with less than one full stroke of the park brake pedal.

1. Before servicing the vehicle, refer to the Precautions Section.

2. Apply and release the park brake four times.

3. Park brake light should be illuminated after park brake has been depressed slightly.

4. Check parking brake pedal assembly for full release by turning the ignition on and inspecting PARK BRAKE warning light. Light should be off. If PARK BRAKE warning light is on and park brake appears to be fully released, pull the pedal back by hand and continue with the adjustment procedure.

5. Raise the vehicle and suitably support.

6. Check park brake levers on rear calipers. Levers should be against the stops on the caliper housing. If levers are not against stops, check for binding in rear brake cables and position levers against stops.

7. Tighten park brake cable at equalizer until either the left or right lever begins to move off stop.

8. Loosen adjustment at equalizer until the lever which has moved off the stop, as in step 5, is again resting fully against stops. Loosen tension at equalizer until the cables feel slightly loose to the touch. Cables should not sag under their own weight.

9. Operate park brake several times to check adjustment. A firm pedal feel should be obtained by depressing the pedal less than one full stroke.

10. Inspect left and right caliper levers. Both levers must be resting on stops after adjustment of parking brake.

11. Check the operation of the park brake.

12. To achieve optimal performance ensure cables are not over-tensioned at the equalizer.

CHASSIS ELECTRICAL AIR BAG (SUPPLEMENTAL RESTRAINT SYSTEM)

GENERAL INFORMATION

✳✳ CAUTION

These vehicles are equipped with an air bag system. The system must be disarmed before performing service on, or around, system components, the steering column, instrument panel components, wiring and sensors. Failure to follow the safety precautions and the disarming procedure could result in accidental air bag deployment, possible injury and unnecessary system repairs.

SERVICE PRECAUTIONS

Disconnect and isolate the battery negative cable before beginning any airbag system component diagnosis, testing, removal, or installation procedures. Allow system capacitor to discharge for two minutes before beginning any component service. This will disable the airbag system. Failure to disable the airbag system may result in accidental airbag deployment, personal injury, or death.

Do not place an intact undeployed airbag face down on a solid surface. The airbag will propel into the air if accidentally deployed and may result in personal injury or death.

When carrying or handling an undeployed airbag, the trim side (face) of the airbag should be pointing towards the body to minimize possibility of injury if accidental deployment occurs. Failure to do this may result in personal injury or death.

Replace airbag system components with OEM replacement parts. Substitute parts may appear interchangeable, but internal differences may result in inferior occupant protection. Failure to do so may result in occupant personal injury or death.

Wear safety glasses, rubber gloves, and long sleeved clothing when cleaning powder residue from vehicle after an airbag deployment. Powder residue emitted from a deployed airbag can cause skin irritation. Flush affected area with cool water if irritation is experienced. If nasal or throat irritation is experienced, exit the vehicle for fresh air until the irritation ceases. If irritation continues, see a physician.

Do not use a replacement airbag that is not in the original packaging. This may result in improper deployment, personal injury, or death.

The factory installed fasteners, screws and bolts used to fasten airbag components have a special coating and are specifically designed for the airbag system. Do not use substitute fasteners. Use only original equipment fasteners listed in the parts catalog when fastener replacement is required.

During, and following, any child restraint anchor service, due to impact event or vehicle repair, carefully inspect all mounting hardware, tether straps, and anchors for proper installation, operation, or damage. If a child restraint anchor is found damaged in any way, the anchor must be replaced. Failure to do this may result in personal injury or death.

Deployed and non-deployed airbags may or may not have live pyrotechnic material within the airbag inflator.

Do not dispose of driver/passenger/curtain airbags or seat belt tensioners unless you are sure of complete deployment. Refer to the Hazardous Substance Control System for proper disposal.

Dispose of deployed airbags and tensioners consistent with state, provincial, local, and federal regulations.

After any airbag component testing or service, do not connect the battery negative cable. Personal injury or death may result if the system test is not performed first.

If the vehicle is equipped with the Occupant Classification System (OCS), do not connect the battery negative cable before performing the OCS Verification Test using the scan tool and the appropriate diagnostic information. Personal injury or death may result if the system test is not performed properly.

Never replace both the Occupant Restraint Controller (ORC) and the Occupant Classification Module (OCM) at the same time. If both require replacement, replace one, then perform the Airbag System test before replacing the other.

Both the ORC and the OCM store Occupant Classification System (OCS) calibration data, which they transfer to one another when one of them is replaced. If both are replaced at the same time, an irreversible fault will be set in both modules and the OCS may malfunction and cause personal injury or death.

If equipped with OCS, the Seat Weight Sensor is a sensitive, calibrated unit and must be handled carefully. Do not drop or handle roughly. If dropped or damaged, replace with another sensor. Failure to do so may result in occupant injury or death.

If equipped with OCS, the front passenger seat must be handled carefully as well. When removing the seat, be careful when setting on floor not to drop. If dropped, the sensor may be inoperative, could result in occupant injury, or possibly death.

If equipped with OCS, when the passenger front seat is on the floor, no one should sit in the front passenger seat. This uneven force may damage the sensing ability of the seat weight sensors. If sat on and damaged, the sensor may be inoperative, could result in occupant injury, or possibly death.

DISARMING THE SYSTEM

Zone 1

See Figures 8 and 9.

1. Before servicing the vehicle, refer to the Precautions Section.
2. Turn the steering wheel so that the vehicles wheels are pointing straight ahead.
3. Turn the ignition switch to the OFF position.
4. Remove the key from the ignition switch.
5. Open the hood and locate the underhood fuse center on right/passenger shock tower.

➡**With the SIR Fuse removed and the ignition ON, the AIR BAG indicator illuminates. This is normal operation, and does not indicate an SIR system malfunction.**

6. Lift the cover for the underhood fuse center.
7. Locate and remove the SIR Fuse from the underhood fuse center.
8. Remove the radiator upper air baffle and deflector and locate the left and/or right front end sensor also known as Electronic Frontal Sensor (EFS) that needs servicing.
9. Remove the Connector Position Assurance (CPA) from both front end sensors connector.
10. Remove both front end sensor connectors from each front end sensor.

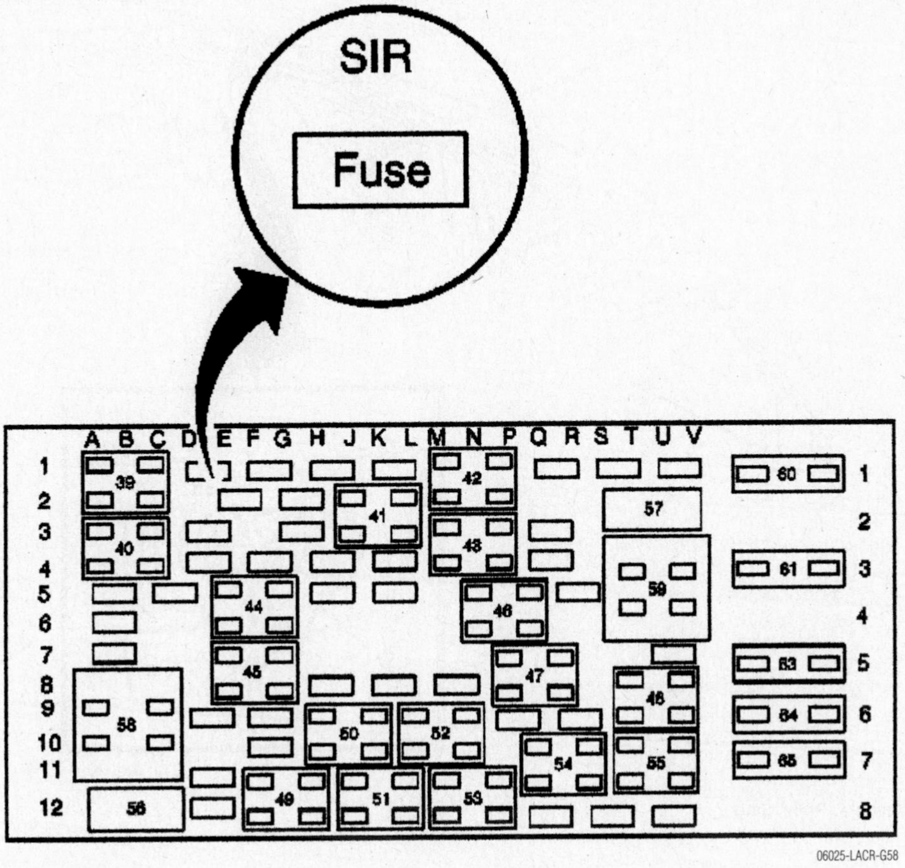

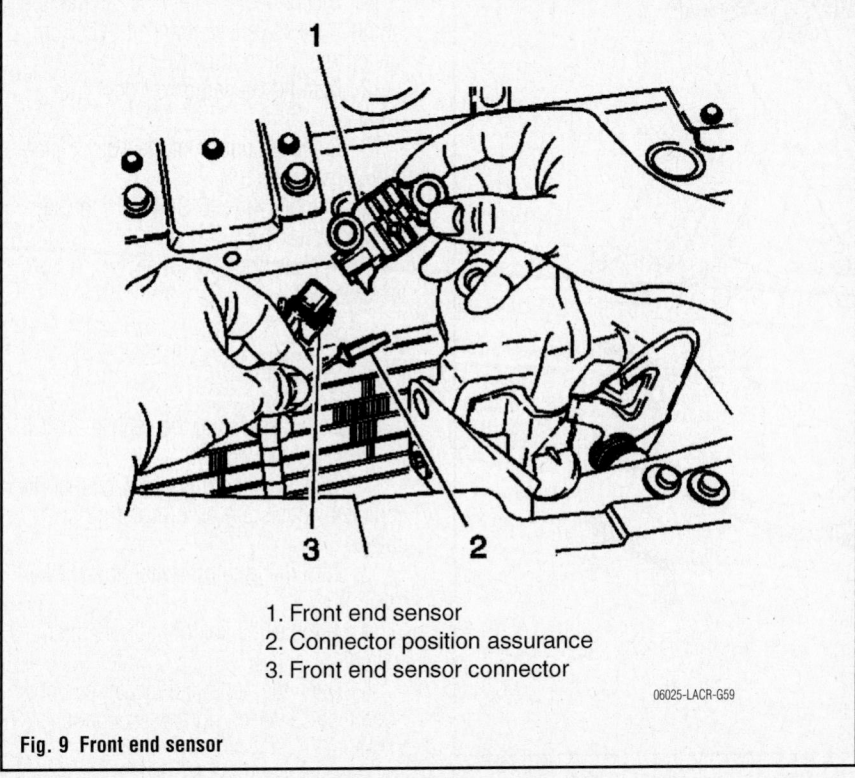

Fig. 8 SIR fuse

06025-LACR-G58

Fig. 9 Front end sensor

1. Front end sensor
2. Connector position assurance
3. Front end sensor connector

06025-LACR-G59

Zone 2

See Figures 10 and 11.

1. Before servicing the vehicle, refer to the Precautions Section.

2. Turn the steering wheel so that the vehicles wheels are pointing straight ahead.

3. Turn the ignition switch to the OFF position.

4. Remove the key from the ignition switch.

5. Open the hood and locate the under-hood fuse center on right/passenger shock tower.

➡**With the SIR Fuse removed and the ignition ON, the AIR BAG indicator illuminates. This is normal operation, and does not indicate an SIR system malfunction.**

6. Lift the cover for the underhood fuse center.

7. Locate and remove the SIR Fuse from the underhood fuse center.

8. When disabling the roof rail module go to step 8, if the Side impact Sensor (SIS) needs disabling then go to step 11.

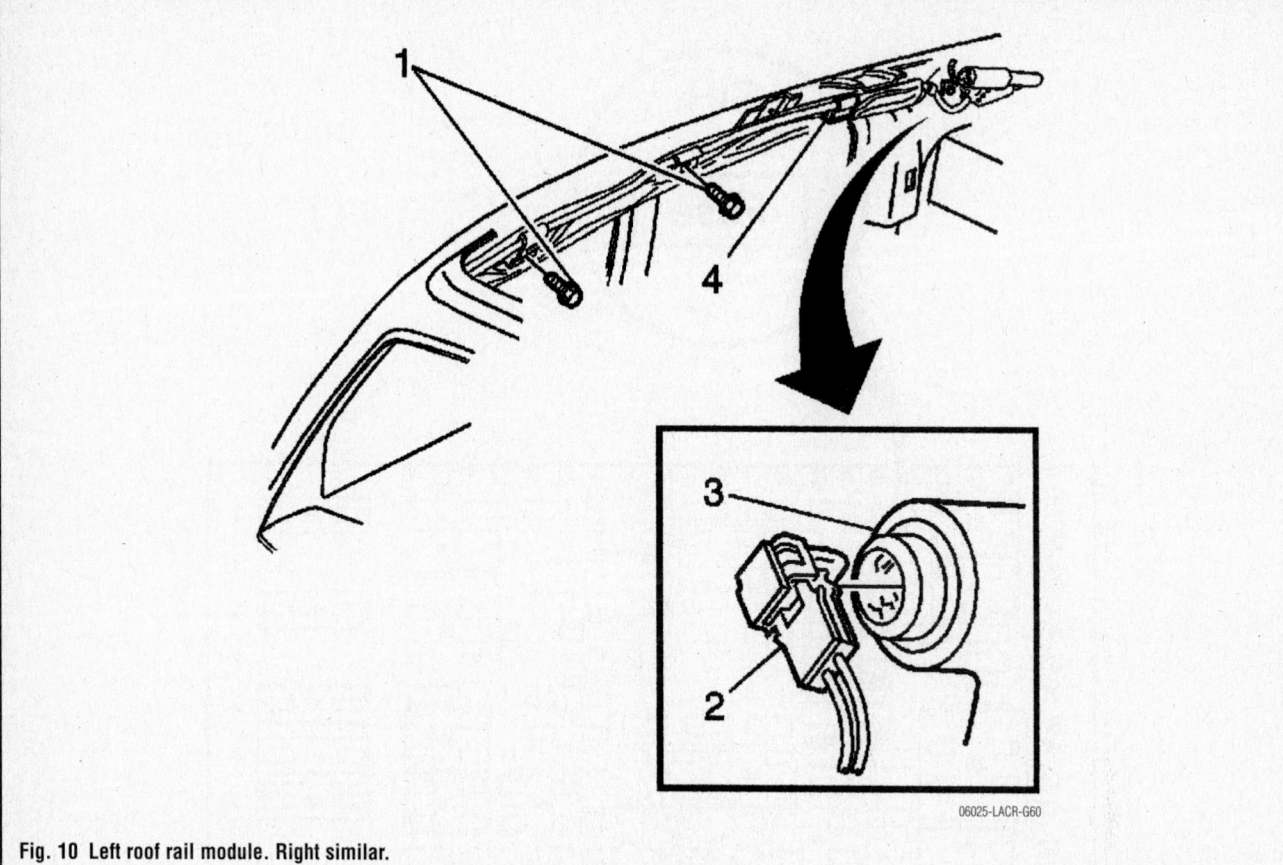

Fig. 10 Left roof rail module. Right similar.

06025-LACR-G60

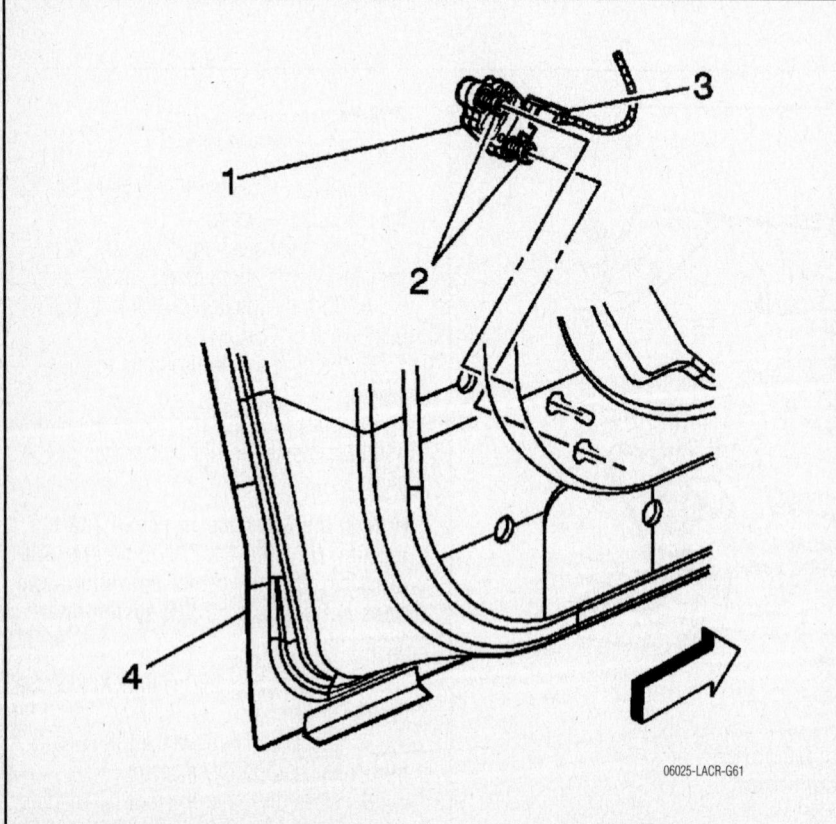

Fig. 11 Left side impact sensor. Right similar.

06025-LACR-G61

9. Remove the left rear panel.

10. Remove the Connector Position Assurance (CPA) from the left/driver roof rail module connector (2).

11. Disconnect the left roof rail module wiring harness yellow connector (2) from the left roof rail module (3).

12. Remove the left/driver door trim panel.

13. Remove enough of the water deflector to access the SIS.

14. Remove the SIS CPA from the left SIS connector (3).

15. Remove the SIS connector (3) from the SIS (1).

Zone 3

See Figure 12.

1. Before servicing the vehicle, refer to the Precautions Section.

2. Turn the steering wheel so that the vehicles wheels are pointing straight ahead.

3. Turn the ignition switch to the OFF position.

4. Remove the key from the ignition switch.

5. Open the hood and locate the underhood fuse center on right/passenger shock tower.

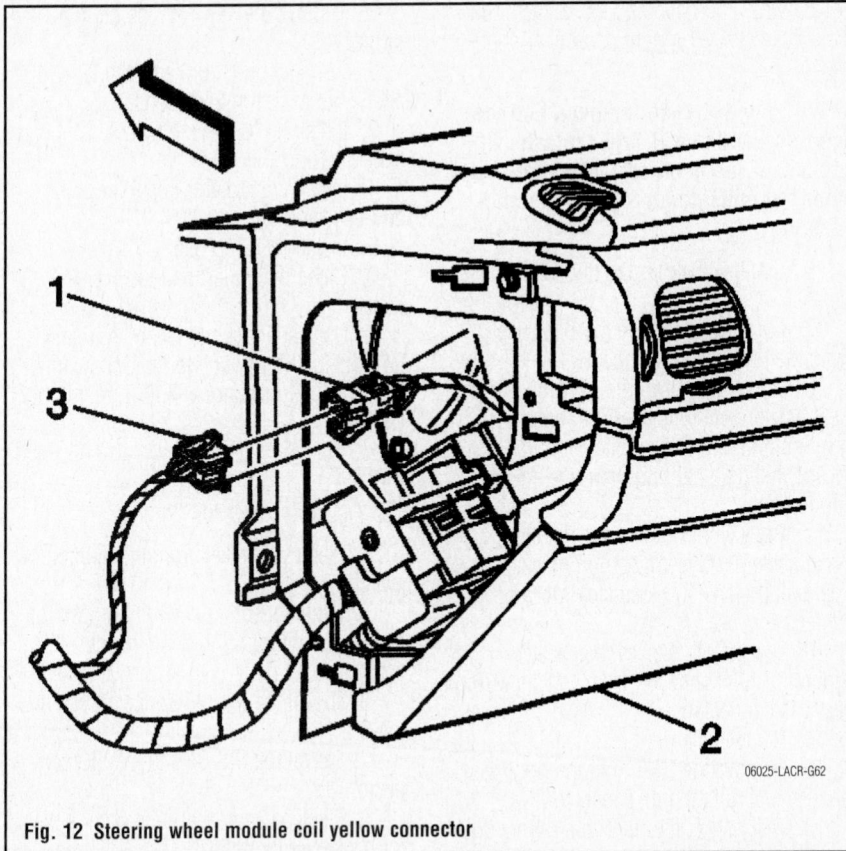

06025-LACR-G62

Fig. 12 Steering wheel module coil yellow connector

➡**With the SIR Fuse removed and the ignition ON, the AIR BAG indicator illuminates. This is normal operation, and does not indicate an SIR system malfunction.**

6. Lift the cover for the underhood fuse center.

7. Locate and remove the SIR fuse from the underhood fuse center.

8. Remove the left/driver sound insulator from the Instrument Panel (I/P) (2).

9. Remove the Connector Position Assurance (CPA) from the steering wheel module coil yellow connector (1).

10. Disconnect the steering wheel module coil yellow connector (1) from the vehicle harness yellow connector (3).

Zone 5

See Figure 13.

1. Before servicing the vehicle, refer to the Precautions Section.

2. Turn the steering wheel so that the vehicle wheels are pointing straight ahead.

3. Turn the ignition switch to the OFF position.

4. Remove the key from the ignition switch.

5. Open the hood and locate the underhood fuse center on right/passenger shock tower.

➡**With the SIR Fuse removed and the ignition ON, the AIR BAG indicator illuminates. This is normal operation, and does not indicate an SIR system malfunction.**

6. Lift the cover for the underhood fuse center.

7. Locate and remove the SIR fuse from the underhood fuse center.

8. Remove the right/passenger sound insulator from the Instrument Panel (I/P) (3).

9. Remove the Connector Position Assurance (CPA) from the I/P module yellow connector (1).

10. Disconnect the I/P module yellow connector (1) from the vehicle harness yellow connector (2).

Zone 6

1. Before servicing the vehicle, refer to the Precautions Section.

2. Turn the steering wheel so that the vehicles wheels are pointing straight ahead.

3. Turn the ignition switch to the OFF position.

4. Remove the key from the ignition switch.

5. Open the hood and locate the underhood fuse center on right/passenger shock tower.

➡**With the SIR Fuse removed and the ignition ON, the AIR BAG indicator illuminates. This is normal operation, and does not indicate an SIR system malfunction.**

6. Lift the cover for the underhood fuse center.

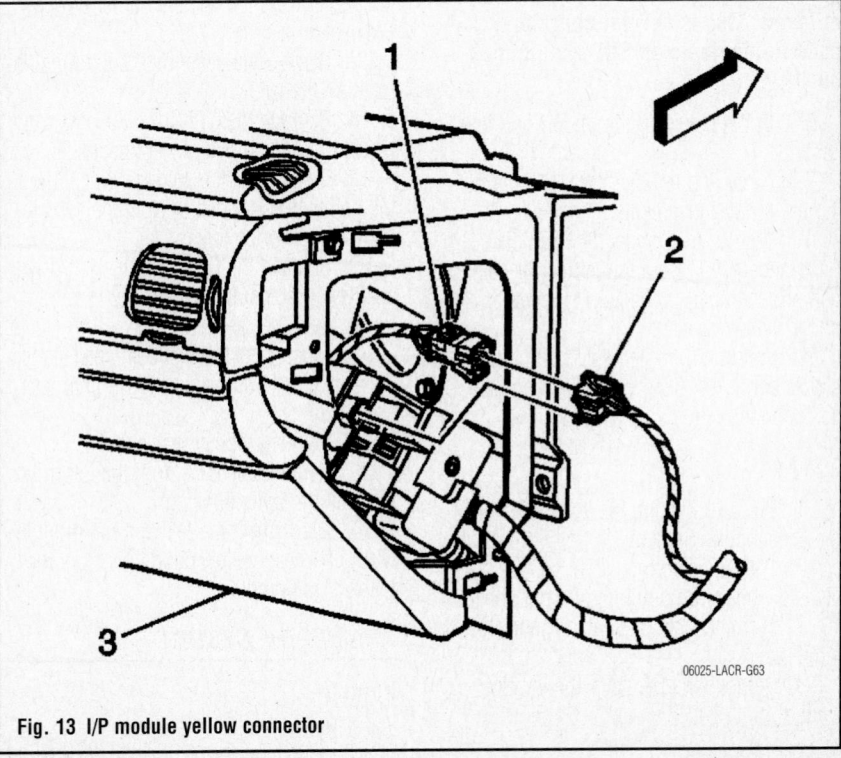

06025-LACR-G63

Fig. 13 I/P module yellow connector

7. Locate and remove the SIR Fuse from the underhood fuse center.

8. When disabling the roof rail module go to step 8, if the Side impact Sensor (SIS) needs disabling then go to step 11.

9. Remove the right rear panel.

10. Remove the Connector Position Assurance (CPA) from the right/passenger roof rail module connector.

11. Disconnect the right roof rail module wiring harness yellow connector from the right roof rail module.

12. Remove the right/passenger door trim panel.

13. Remove enough of the water deflector to access the SIS.

14. Remove the SIS CPA from the right SIS connector.

15. Remove the SIS connector from the SIS.

Zone 7

1. Before servicing the vehicle, refer to the Precautions Section.

2. Turn the steering wheel so that the vehicles wheels are pointing straight ahead.

3. Turn the ignition switch to the OFF position.

4. Remove the key from the ignition switch.

5. Open the hood and locate the underhood fuse center on right/passenger shock tower.

➡**With the SIR Fuse removed and the ignition ON, the AIR BAG indicator illuminates. This is normal operation, and does not indicate an SIR system malfunction.**

6. Lift the cover for the underhood fuse center.

7. Locate and remove the SIR Fuse from the underhood fuse center.

8. Remove the Connector Position Assurance (CPA) from the left/driver seat belt pretensioner connector (1) located under the driver seat.

9. Disconnect the left seat belt pretensioner connector from vehicle wiring harness connector (1).

Zone 9

1. Before servicing the vehicle, refer to the Precautions Section.

2. Turn the steering wheel so that the vehicle wheels are pointing straight ahead.

3. Turn the ignition switch to the OFF position.

4. Remove the key from the ignition switch.

5. Open the hood and locate the underhood fuse center on right/passenger shock tower.

➡**With the SIR Fuse removed and the ignition ON, the AIR BAG indicator illuminates. This is normal operation, and does not indicate an SIR system malfunction.**

6. Lift the cover for the underhood fuse center.

7. Locate and remove the SIR Fuse from the underhood fuse center.

8. When disabling the right/passenger seat belt pretensioner perform step 8, if the Sensing and Diagnostic Module (SDM) needs disabling then use entire procedure.

9. Remove the Connector Position Assurance (CPA) from the right/passenger seat belt pretensioner connector located under the passenger seat.

10. Disconnect the seat belt pretensioner—right connector from vehicle wiring harness connector.

11. Remove the right rear panel.

12. Remove the CPA from the right/passenger roof rail module connector.

13. Disconnect the right roof rail module wiring harness yellow connector from the right roof rail module.

14. Remove the right/passenger sound insulator from the Instrument Panel (I/P).

15. Remove the CPA from the I/P module yellow connector.

16. Disconnect the I/P module yellow connector from the vehicle harness yellow connector.

17. Remove the left/driver sound insulator from the I/P.

18. Remove the CPA from the steering wheel module coil yellow connector.

19. Disconnect the steering wheel module coil yellow connector from the vehicle harness yellow connector.

20. Remove the CPA from the left/driver seat belt pretensioner connector located under the driver seat.

21. Disconnect the seat belt pretensioner—left connector from vehicle wiring harness connector.

22. Remove the left rear panel.

23. Remove the CPA from the left/driver roof rail module connector.

24. Disconnect the left roof rail module wiring harness yellow connector from the left roof rail module.

ARMING THE SYSTEM

Zone 1

See Figures 8 and 9.

1. Remove the key from the ignition switch.

2. Connect both front end sensor connectors to each front end sensor.

3. Install both CPA's into each front end sensor connector.

4. Install the radiator upper air baffle and deflector.

5. Install the SIR Fuse.

6. Close the underhood fuse center cover.

7. Use caution while reaching in and turn the ignition switch to the ON position. The AIR BAG indicator will flash then turn OFF.

Zone 2

See Figures 10 and 11.

1. Remove the key from the ignition switch.

2. When enabling the SIS proceed to step 3, if the roof rail module needs enabling then go to step 7.

3. Install the left SIS connector (3) to the SIS (1).

4. Install the SIS CPA to the SIS connector (3).

5. Replace and secure the water deflector back over the SIS.

6. Install the left/driver door trim panel.

7. Connect the left roof rail module wiring harness yellow connector (2) to the left roof rail module (3).

8. Install the CPA to the left roof rail module connector (2).

9. Install the left rear panel.

10. Install the SIR Fuse.

11. Close the underhood fuse center cover.

12. Use caution while reaching in and turn the ignition switch to the ON position. The AIR BAG indicator will flash then turn OFF.

Zone 3

See Figure 12.

1. Remove the key from the ignition switch.

2. Connect the steering wheel module coil yellow connector (3) to the vehicle harness yellow connector (1).

3. Install the CPA to the steering wheel module coil yellow connector (1).

4. Install the left sound insulator to the I/P (2).

5. Install the SIR Fuse.

6. Close the underhood fuse center cover.

7. Use caution while reaching in and turn the ignition switch to the ON position. The AIR BAG indicator will flash then turn OFF.

Zone 5

See Figure 13.

1. Remove the key from the ignition switch.

2. Connect the I/P module yellow connector (1) to the vehicle harness yellow connector (2).

3. Install the CPA to the I/P module yellow connector (1).

4. Install the right sound insulator to the I/P (3).

5. Install the SIR Fuse.

6. Close the underhood fuse center cover.

7. Use caution while reaching in and turn the ignition switch to the ON position. The AIR BAG indicator will flash then turn OFF.

Zone 6

1. Remove the key from the ignition switch.

2. When enabling the SIS proceed to step 3, if the roof rail module needs enabling then go to step 7.

3. Install the right SIS connector to the SIS.

4. Install the SIS CPA to the SIS connector.

5. Replace and secure the water deflector back over the SIS.

6. Install the right/passenger door trim panel.

7. Connect the right roof rail module wiring harness yellow connector to the right roof rail module.

8. Install the CPA to the right roof rail module connector.

9. Install the right rear panel.

10. Install the SIR Fuse.

11. Close the underhood fuse center cover.

12. Use caution while reaching in and turn the ignition switch to the ON position. The AIR BAG indicator will flash then turn OFF.

Zone 7

1. Remove the key from the ignition switch.

2. Connect the left seat belt pretensioner connector to the vehicle wiring harness connector (1).

3. Install the CPA to the seat belt pretensioner connector (1).

4. Install the SIR Fuse.

5. Close the underhood fuse center cover.

6. Use caution while reaching in and turn the ignition switch to the ON position. The AIR BAG indicator will flash then turn OFF.

Zone 9

1. Remove the key from the ignition switch.

2. When enabling the right/passenger seat belt pretensioner proceed to step 3, if the SDM needs enabling then use entire procedure.

3. Connect the seat belt pretensioner–right connector to the vehicle wiring harness connector.

4. Install the CPA to the seat belt pretensioner connector.

5. Connect the right roof rail module wiring harness yellow connector to the right roof rail module.

6. Install the CPA to the right roof rail module connector.

7. Install the right rear panel.

8. Connect the I/P module yellow connector to the vehicle harness yellow connector.

9. Install the CPA to the I/P module yellow connector.

10. Install the right sound insulator to the I/P.

11. Connect the steering wheel module coil yellow connector to the vehicle harness yellow connector.

12. Install the CPA to the steering wheel module coil yellow connector.

13. Install the left sound insulator to the I/P.

14. Connect the seat belt pretensioner–left connector to the vehicle wiring harness connector.

15. Install the CPA to the seat belt pretensioner connector.

16. Connect the left roof rail module wiring harness yellow connector to the left roof rail module.

17. Install the CPA to the left roof rail module connector.

18. Install the left rear panel.

19. Install the SIR Fuse.

20. Close the underhood fuse center cover.

21. Use caution while reaching in and turn the ignition switch to the ON position. The AIR BAG indicator will flash then turn OFF.

CLOCKSPRING CENTERING

See Figures 14 through 18.

1. Before servicing the vehicle, refer to the Precautions Section.

✳✳ CAUTION

The new Supplemental Inflatable Restraint (SIR) coil assembly will be centered. Improper alignment of the SIR coil assembly may damage the

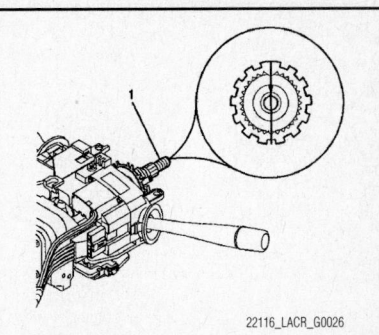

22116_LACR_G0026

Fig. 14 The block tooth (1) of the steering shaft assembly must be in the 12 o'clock position

unit, causing an inflatable restraint malfunction.

➡**If a double wire harness strap is installed onto the wire harness assembly and column, you must reuse the holder for the wire straps during installation.**

2. Remove the wire harness strap(s) where necessary.

3. Verify the following conditions before centering the SIR coil:

- The wheels on the vehicle are straight ahead
- The block tooth (1) of the steering shaft assembly is in the 12 o'clock position
- The ignition switch is in the LOCK position

4. Style 1: If the front (5) of the SIR coil has a centering window (4), and the back side (2) includes a spring service lock (1), perform the following steps:

a. Hold the SIR coil with the face up.

b. While depressing the spring service lock, rotate the coil hub clockwise until the coil ribbon stops.

c. Rotate the coil hub slowly, counter-clockwise, until the centering window

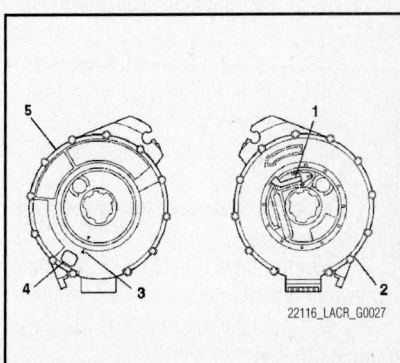

22116_LACR_G0027

Fig. 15 Supplemental Inflatable Restraint (SIR) coil assembly—Style 1

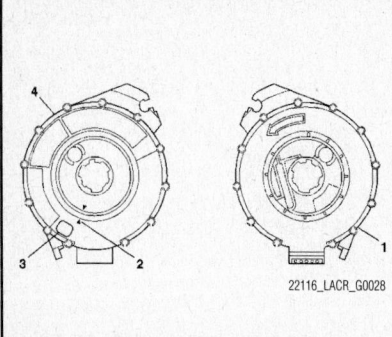

Fig. 16 Supplemental Inflatable Restraint (SIR) coil assembly—Style 2

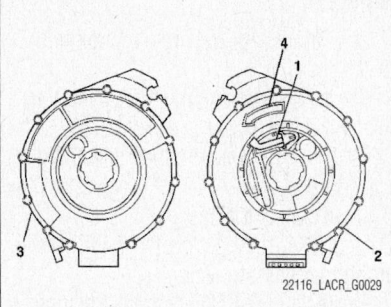

Fig. 17 Supplemental Inflatable Restraint (SIR) coil assembly—Style 3

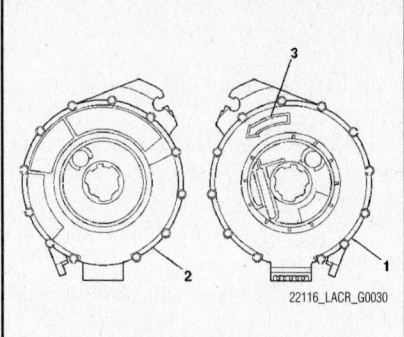

Fig. 18 Supplemental Inflatable Restraint (SIR) coil assembly—Style 4

appears yellow and both arrows (3) line up.

d. Release spring service lock between the locking tab. The SIR coil is now centered.

e. Align the centered SIR coil with the horn tower and slide onto the steering shaft assembly.

5. Style 2: If the front (4) of the SIR coil has a centering window (3), and the back side (1) includes NO spring service lock, perform the following steps:

a. Hold the SIR coil with the face up.

b. Rotate the coil hub clockwise until the coil ribbon stops.

c. Rotate the coil hub slowly, counterclockwise until the centering window appears yellow and both arrows (2) line up. This is the CENTER position.

d. While holding the coil hub in the CENTER position, align the SIR coil with

the horn tower and slide onto the steering shaft assembly.

6. Style 3: If the front side (3) of the SIR coil has NO centering window, but the back side (2) includes a spring service lock (1), perform the following steps:

a. Hold the SIR coil with the back side up.

b. While depressing the spring service lock, rotate the coil hub in the direction of the arrow (4) until the coil ribbon stops.

c. Still pressing the spring service lock, rotate the coil hub in the opposite direction 2 ½ revolutions.

d. Release the spring service lock between locking tabs. The SIR coil is now centered.

e. Align the centered SIR coil with the horn tower and slide onto the steering shaft assembly.

7. Style 4: If the front side (2) of the SIR

coil has NO centering window, and the back side (1) includes NO spring service lock, perform the following steps:

a. Hold the SIR coil with the face up.

b. Rotate the coil hub in the direction of the arrow until the coil ribbon stops.

c. Rotate the coil hub, slowly, counterclockwise, for 2 ½ revolutions. This is the CENTER position.

d. While maintaining the coil hub in the CENTER position, align the centered SIR coil with the horn tower and slide onto the steering shaft assembly.

8. If a double wire harness strap is installed onto the wire harness assembly and column, you must route the wires up against the steering column. One wire harness strap will surround one lead from the coil to the steering column. The other wire harness strap will surround all the leads to the steering column.

DRIVETRAIN

AUTOMATIC TRANSAXLE ASSEMBLY

REMOVAL & INSTALLATION

1. Before servicing the vehicle, refer to the Precautions Section.

2. Disconnect the negative battery cable.

3. Remove the air cleaner intake duct.

4. Disconnect the transaxle wiring harness electrical connector.

5. Remove the wiring harness ground nut from the transaxle.

6. Remove the wiring harness grounds from the transaxle.

7. Remove the wiring harness ground bolt from the transaxle.

8. Remove the wiring harness grounds from the transaxle.

9. Remove the wuiring harness bracket bolt and reposition the wiring harness.

10. Remove the range selector cable from the transaxle shift lever.

11. Remove the range selector retainer from the cable.

12. Remove the range selector cable from the transaxle.

13. Remove the upper transaxle bolts and the stud.

14. Install the engine support fixture. Refer to Engine Removal & Installation.

15. Raise and support the vehicle.

16. Remove the front wheels.

17. Remove the left and the right engine splash shields.

18. Remove the frame from the vehicle. Refer to Engine Removal & Installation.

19. Remove the starter motor.

20. Install flywheel holding tool J 37096 in order to gain access to the torque converter bolts and to prevent the flywheel from turning.

21. Remove the torque converter bolts.

22. Remove the oil cooler pipes from the transaxle.

➡**Position and secure the halfshafts out of the way.**

23. Remove the left and the right halfshafts from the transaxle.

24. Secure the drive shafts to the steering knuckles.

25. Disconnect the electrical connector from the vehicle speed sensor.

➡**Ensure that the transaxle jack is properly secured to the transaxle.**

26. Position a transaxle jack under the transaxle and secure the jack firmly to the transaxle.

27. Remove the transaxle brace.

28. Remove the lower transaxle bolt and the stud.

29. Remove the transaxle from the vehicle.

30. Transfer all necessary parts as needed.

To install:

➡**Ensure that the transaxle is secured properly to the transaxle jack.**

31. Position the transaxle onto a transaxle jack and secure the transaxle to the jack.

32. Install the transaxle into the vehicle.

33. Install the lower transaxle bolt and the stud. Tighten the bolt and the stud to 55 ft. lbs. (75 Nm).

34. Install the transaxle brace. Tighten the transaxle brace bolts to the transaxle to 32 ft. lbs. (43 Nm). Tighten the transaxle brace bolts to the engine to 46 ft. lbs. (63 Nm).

35. Prevent the flywheel from turning.

36. Install the torque converter bolts. Tighten the bolts to 46 ft. lbs. (63 Nm).

37. Install the halfshafts into the transaxle.

38. Install the oil cooler pipes to the transaxle.

39. Install the starter motor.

40. Remove the transaxle jack from the transaxle.

41. Install the frame to the vehicle.

42. Connect the electrical connector to the vehicle speed sensor.

43. Install the left and the right engine splash shield.

44. Install the front wheels.

45. Lower the vehicle.

46. Remove the engine support fixture.

47. Install the upper transaxle bolts and the stud. Tighten the bolts and the stud to 55 ft. lbs. (75 Nm).

48. Install the cable to the transaxle range selector cable bracket.

49. Install the A/T range selector cable retainer to the cable.

50. Install the transaxle range selector cable to the transaxle shift lever.

51. Reposition the wiring harness and install the wiring harness bracket and the bolt. Tighten the bolt to 18 ft. lbs. (25 Nm).

52. Install the wiring harness grounds to the transaxle.

53. Install the transaxle wiring harness ground bolt to the transaxle. Tighten the bolt to 18 ft. lbs. (25 Nm).

54. Install the wiring harness grounds to the transaxle.

55. Install the wiring harness ground nut to the transaxle. Tighten the nut to 33 ft. lbs. (45 Nm).

56. Connect the transaxle wiring harness electrical connector.

57. Install the air cleaner intake duct.

58. Connect the negative battery cable.

59. Fill the transaxle with transmission fluid.

60. Inspect the transaxle for fluid leaks.

➡**It is recommended that Transmission Adaptive Pressure (TAP) information be reset. Resetting the TAP values using a scan tool will erase all learned values in all cells. As a result, The ECM, PCM or TCM will need to relearn TAP values. Transaxle performance may be affected as new TAP values are learned.**

HALFSHAFTS

REMOVAL & INSTALLATION
See Figure 19.

✲✲ CAUTION

To prevent personal injury and/or component damage, do not allow the weight of the vehicle to load the front wheels, or attempt to operate the vehicle, when the halfshaft(s) or halfshaft nut(s) are removed. To do so may cause the inner bearing race to separate, resulting in damage to brake and suspension components and loss of vehicle control.

✲✲ WARNING

Wheel drive shaft boots, seals and clamps should be protected from sharp objects any time service is performed on or near the halfshaft(s). Damage to the boot(s), the seal(s) or the clamp(s) may cause lubricant to leak from the joint and lead to increased noise and possible failure of the halfshaft.

1. Before servicing the vehicle, refer to the Precautions Section.

2. Raise and suitably support the vehicle.

3. Remove the wheel and the tire.

4. Remove the control link.

5. Remove the front halfshaft nut. Insert a drift or a flat-bladed tool into the caliper and the rotor to prevent the rotor from turning.

6. Disconnect the outer tie rod assembly from the steering knuckle.

7. Separate the ball joint from the steering knuckle.

8. Separate the front halfshaft from the front halfshaft bearing using a slidehammer and adapter.

To install:

9. Install the front wheel drive axle into the transaxle.

10. Verify that the front halfshaft retaining ring is properly seated:

- Grasp the inner housing and pull the inner housing outward. Do not pull on the front wheel drive axle shaft.
- The front wheel drive axle will remain in place when the front half-

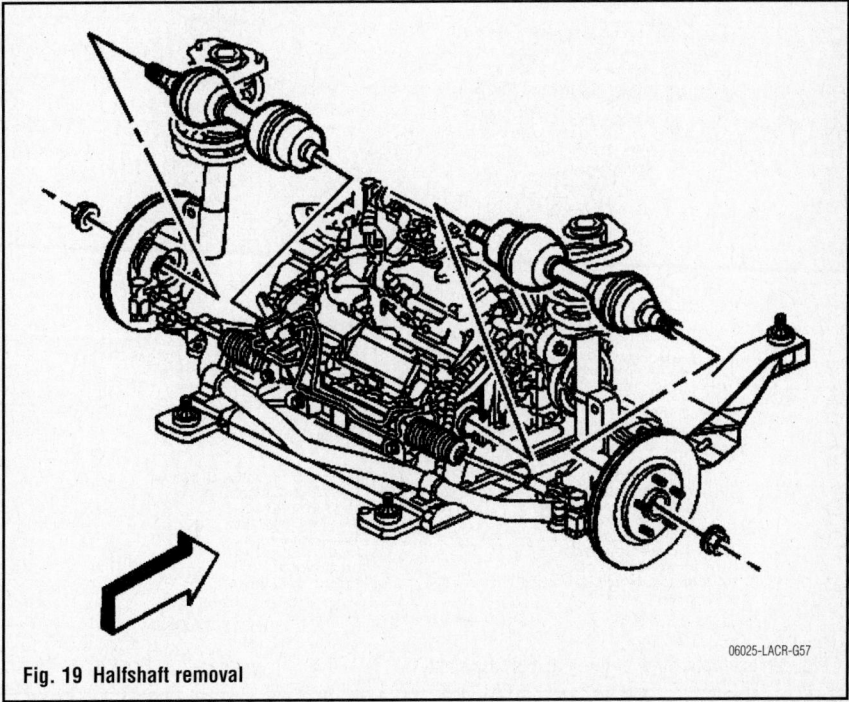

06025-LACR-G57

Fig. 19 Halfshaft removal

shaft retaining ring is properly seated.

11. Install the front wheel drive axle into the front halfshaft bearing.

12. Connect the ball joint to the steering knuckle.

13. Connect the outer tie rod assembly to the steering knuckle.

14. Install a new front halfshaft nut. Insert a drift or a flat-bladed tool into the caliper and the rotor to prevent the rotor from turning. Tighten the nut to 118 ft. lbs. (160 Nm).

15. Install the control link.

16. Install the wheel and the tire.

17. Lower the vehicle.

18. Inspect the transaxle fluid level.

19. Inspect the wheel alignment.

CV-JOINTS OVERHAUL

Inner (Tripod) Joint

See Figure 20.

1. Before servicing the vehicle, refer to the Precautions Section.

2. Raise and safely support the vehicle.

3. Remove or disconnect the following:

- Front wheel
- Halfshaft and place it in a vise
- Small CV-joint boot clamp, cut and discard it
- Large CV-joint boot clamp, cut and discard it
- CV-joint boot by sliding it away from the tripod joint
- Tripod housing from the tripod spider
- Inboard spacer ring and slide it rearward on the shaft
- Outboard retaining ring
- Tripod joint spider assembly
- Inboard spacer ring and discard it
- Tripod joint spider assembly by tapping it from the halfshaft with a brass drift

- Tripod spider retaining ring and discard it
- Trilobal tripod bushing from the housing
- CV-joint boot

4. Thoroughly clean and inspect all parts.

To install:

5. Install or connect the following:

- Small boot clamp
- CV-joint boot
- New inboard spacer ring. Slide it rearward on the shaft past the 2nd groove
- Tripod joint spider assembly onto the shaft until it passes the 2nd groove

6. Assemble the tripod spider assembly onto the halfshaft as follows:

  a. Position the tripod spider assembly onto the shop press plate.

  b. Position the halfshaft onto the tripod spider assembly, in the shop press.

  c. Press the halfshaft into the tripod spider assembly until the spider assembly passes the 2nd groove.

✳✳ WARNING

When assembling the tripod assembly onto the halfshaft, do not exceed 4,000 lbs. pressure.

7. Remove the halfshaft from the shop press and place it in vise.

8. Install or connect the following:

- New outboard retaining ring into the axle shaft groove
- Tripod joint spider assembly, slide it against the outboard retaining ring using a brass drift
- Inboard spacer ring, seat it in the groove

9. Use ½ of the grease supplied in the kit into the boot and the other ½ into the tripod housing.

- Trilobal tripod bushing flush with the tripod housing face
- New large seal clamp onto the CV-joint boot
- Tripod housing, slide it over the tripod joint spider assembly
- CV-joint boot/clamp, slide it into place, over the trilobal tripod bushing with the seal lip in the groove

➡**Make sure the boot lies flat against the trilobal bushing.**

10. Using the crimp tool, a torque wrench and a breaker bar, crimp the small CV-joint boot clamp to 100 ft. lbs. (136 Nm).

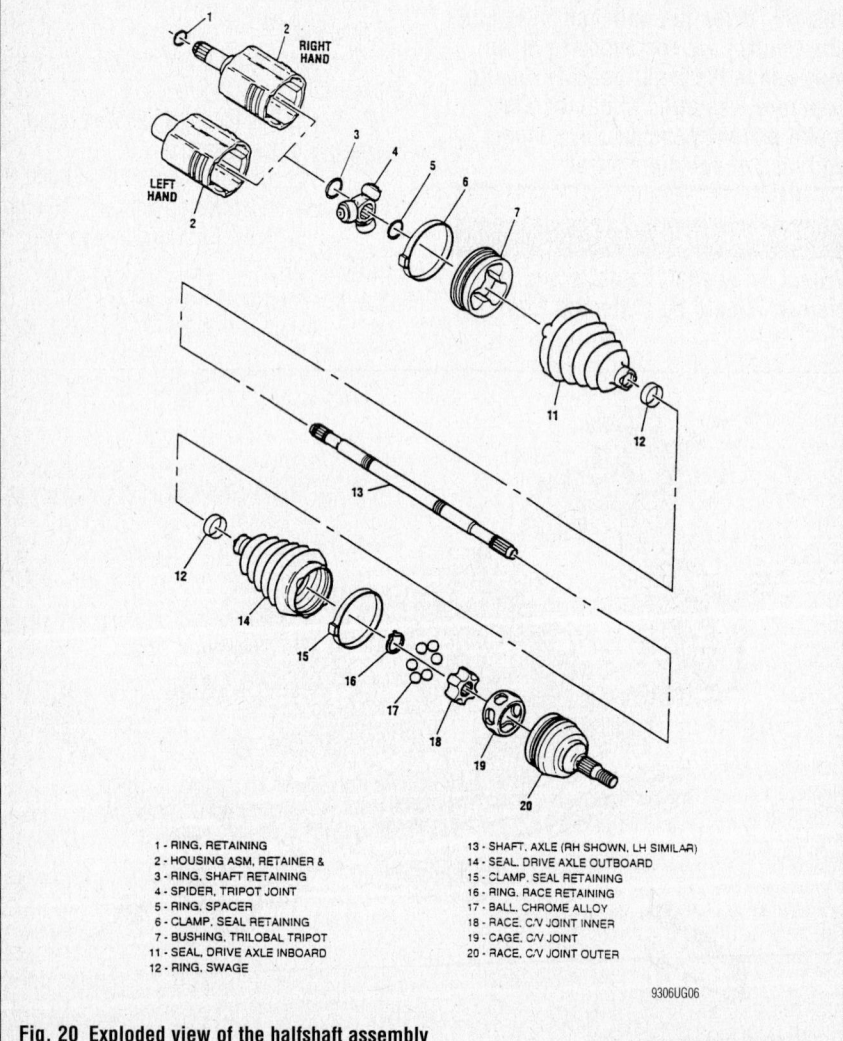

1 - RING, RETAINING
2 - HOUSING ASM, RETAINER &
3 - RING, SHAFT RETAINING
4 - SPIDER, TRIPOT JOINT
5 - RING, SPACER
6 - CLAMP, SEAL RETAINING
7 - BUSHING, TRILOBAL TRIPOT
11 - SEAL, DRIVE AXLE INBOARD
12 - RING, SWAGE

13 - SHAFT, AXLE (RH SHOWN, LH SIMILAR)
14 - SEAL, DRIVE AXLE OUTBOARD
15 - CLAMP, SEAL RETAINING
16 - RING, RACE RETAINING
17 - BALL, CHROME ALLOY
18 - RACE, C/V JOINT INNER
19 - CAGE, C/V JOINT
20 - RACE, C/V JOINT OUTER

9306UG06

Fig. 20 Exploded view of the halfshaft assembly

11. Using the crimp tool, latch the large CV-joint boot clamp.

12. Install the halfshaft and the front wheel.

Outer CV-Joint

See Figures 21 through 24.

1. Before servicing the vehicle, refer to the Precautions Section.

2. Remove or disconnect the following:

- Front wheel
- Halfshaft
- Swage ring using a hand grinder
- Large boot clamp
- CV-joint boot, slide it away from the CV-joint
- CV-joint assembly by spreading the inner race to axle shaft retaining ring ears using Snapring Pliers
- CV-joint boot from the axle shaft

3. Disassemble the chrome alloy balls from the CV-joint cage as follows:

a. Position a brass drift against the CV-joint cage and tap it with a hammer to tilt the cage.

b. Chrome alloy ball from the cage.

c. Tilt the cage in the opposite direction.

d. Remove the opposite chrome alloy ball.

e. Repeat the procedure until all 6 balls are removed.

4. Disassemble the CV-joint cage and inner race as follows:

a. Pivot the cage and race 90° to the center line of the outer race.

b. Align the cage windows with outer race lands.

c. Remove the cage from the outer race.

d. Rotate the inner race upward and remove it from the cage.

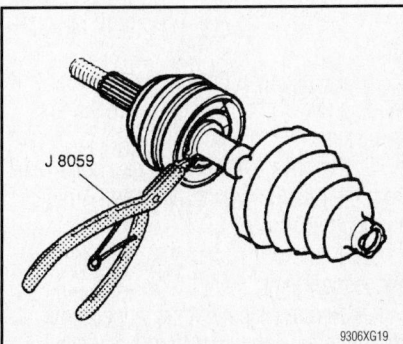

Fig. 21 Disconnecting the outer CV-joint from the axle shaft

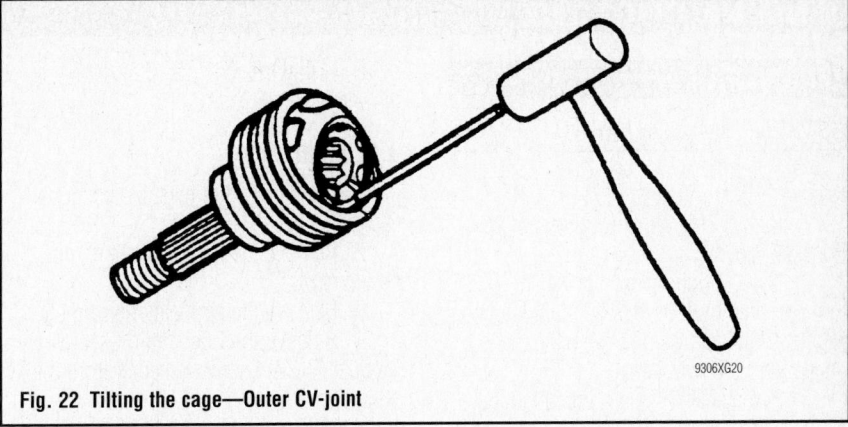

Fig. 22 Tilting the cage—Outer CV-joint

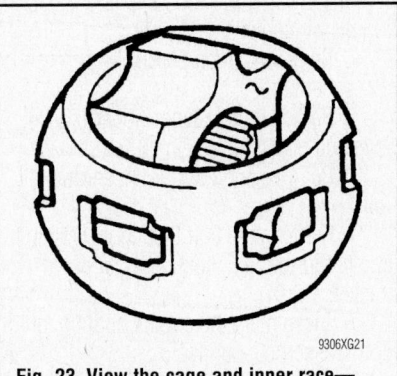

Fig. 23 View the cage and inner race— Outer CV-joint

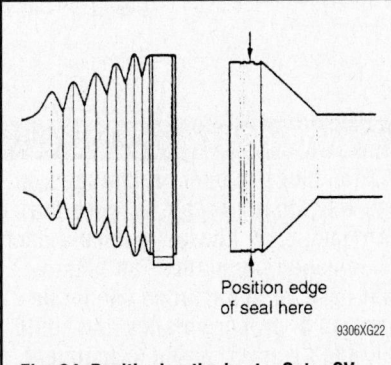

Fig. 24 Positioning the boot—Outer CV-joint

5. Thoroughly clean and inspect all parts.

To install:

6. Lubricate the parts with a light coat of grease.

7. Assemble the CV-joint cage and inner race, as follows:

a. Rotate the inner race 90° to the cage centerline.

b. Align the cage windows with inner race lands.

c. Insert the inner race into the cage by rotating the inner race downward.

d. Insert the cage/inner race into the outer race.

8. Assemble the chrome alloy balls into the CV-joint cage, as follows:

a. Position a brass drift against the CV-joint cage and tap it with a hammer to tilt the cage.

b. Insert the 1st chrome alloy ball into the cage.

c. Tilt the cage in the opposite direction.

d. Insert the opposite chrome alloy ball.

e. Repeat the procedure until all 6 balls are inserted.

9. Install or connect the following:

- Swage ring clamp
- CV-joint boot
- CV-joint onto the axle shaft until the retaining ring seats into the groove

10. Position the CV-joint boot seal into the axle shaft's joint seal groove and align the swage ring clamp on the boot.

11. Secure the swage ring clamp using appropriate crimping tool.

❄❄ WARNING

Make sure that there are no pinch points on the inboard seal.

12. Install or connect the following:

- ½ kit grease into the CV-joint boot
- ½ kit grease into the CV-joint
- New large seal clamp onto the CV-joint boot
- CV-joint boot/clamp, slide it into place, over the outer race with the seal lip in the groove

➡**Make sure the boot lies flat against the outer race.**

13. Using a Crimp tool, a torque wrench and a breaker bar, crimp the large CV-joint boot clamp to 130 ft. lbs. (176 Nm).

14. Install the halfshaft and the front wheel.

ENGINE COOLING

ENGINE FAN

REMOVAL & INSTALLATION

3.6L Engine

1. Remove the fan shroud assembly from the vehicle.
2. Using Cooling Fan Socket GE-47827 turn the fan motor drive plate in the clockwise until the fan motor drive plate disengages from the fan blade.
3. Remove and discard the fan blade.
4. Center punch each of the rivets from the rear of the motor.
5. Drill the head of the rivets from the fan motor using a 0.25 in. (6.35mm) drill bit.
6. Tap the rivets out of the fan shroud.
7. Remove the fan motor from the fan shroud.
8. Remove the tape covering the entry points from the fan motor.

To install:

9. Install the engine cooling fan motor to the fan shroud.
10. Position the fan motor to the fan shroud and insert the bolts from the front side.
11. Install the cooling fan motor bolts.
12. Install the cooling fan motor nuts and tighten to 53 inch lbs. (6 Nm).

✳✳ CAUTION

Failure to heat the fan hub in hot tap water before installation will result in cooling fan failure due to cracking. Allowing the heated fan to cool for more than one minute prior to installation will also result in failure due to cracking.

➡ Using hot tap water at a minimum of 49° Celsius 120 Fahrenheit, hold the new fan blade hub under the running water for a minimum of 60 seconds to hear the fan blade to the temperature of the water. Immediately after heating, position the fan blade on the fan motor drive plate.

13. Install the new engine cooling fan blade.
14. Using the special socket, turn the fan motor drive plate in the same direction of the arrow on the fan blade until the fan motor drive plate engages to the fan blade.
15. Rotate the cooling fan blade to ensure proper rotation.

16. Install the fan shroud assembly to the vehicle.

3.8L Engine

1. Disconnect the negative battery cable.
2. Remove the left and right engine mount struts.
3. Remove the air cleaner assembly.
4. Remove the Powertrain Control Module (PCM) harness retainer from the fan shroud.
5. Remove the transaxle oil cooler lines from the lower fan shroud clip and reposition the oil cooler lines aside.
6. Remove the fan shroud clip from the condenser tubes.
7. Remove the radiator upper bracket bolts and brackets.
8. Remove the cooling fan shroud bolts.
9. Remove the bolt that connects the fan shroud to the condenser hold down bracket.
10. Disconnect the engine cooling fan motors electrical connectors.
11. Remove the cooling fan electrical harness from the fan shroud clips.
12. Remove the cooling fan shroud.
13. Remove the engine cooling fan blade nut.
14. Remove the engine cooling fan blade.

✳✳ CAUTION

If a fan blade is bent or damaged in any way, do not repair or reuse the damaged part. Always replace a bent or damaged fan blade. Fan blades that have been damaged cannot be assured of proper balance and could fail and fly apart during subsequent use. This creates an extremely dangerous situation. The fan blades must remain in proper balance. You cannot assure fan blade balance once a fan blade has been bent or damaged. A fan blade that is not in proper balance could fail and fly apart during use, creating an extremely dangerous situation.

15. Inspect the cooling fan blades for bent or cracked blades, smoothness of the mating surfaces or burrs and other imperfections.
16. Remove the engine cooling fan motor bolts.
17. Remove the engine cooling fan motor.

To install:

18. Install the engine cooling fan motor.
19. Install the cooling fan motor bolts and tighten to 53 inch lbs. (6 Nm).
20. Install the engine cooling fan blade.
21. Install the engine cooling fan blade nut and tighten to 53 inch lbs. (6 Nm).
22. Ensure the lower edge of the fan shroud engages the clip at the bottom of the radiator.
23. Install the fan shroud.
24. Install the cooling fan shroud bolts and tighten to 53 inch lbs. (6 Nm).
25. Install the cooling fan electrical harness to the fan shroud clips.
26. Connect the engine cooling fan motors electrical connectors.
27. Install the fan shroud clip to the condenser tubes.
28. Install the bolt that connects the fan shroud to the condenser hold down bracket and tighten to 53 inch lbs. (6 Nm).
29. Install the radiator upper support brackets and bolts and tighten to 89 inch lbs. (10 Nm).
30. Install the transaxle oil cooler lines to the retainer at the bottom of the fan shroud.
31. Install the air cleaner assembly.
32. Install the PCM harness clip on to the fan shroud.
33. Install the engine mount struts.
34. Connect the negative battery cable.
35. Inspect the engine cooling fans for proper operation.

RADIATOR

REMOVAL & INSTALLATION

1. Disconnect the negative battery cable.
2. Remove the air cleaner assembly.
3. Drain the cooling system.
4. Remove the right and the left engine mount struts.
5. Remove the inlet hose from the radiator.
6. Remove the Powertrain Control Module (PCM) harness clip from the fan shroud.
7. Remove the transaxle oil cooler lines from the retainer clip at the bottom of the cooling fan shroud.
8. Remove the fan shroud clip from the condenser tubes.
9. Remove the bolt that connects the fan shroud to the condenser hold down bracket.
10. Remove the air deflectors from the top of the radiator.

11. Remove the cooling fan shroud bolts.

12. Remove the coolant reservoir hose from the radiator overflow neck.

13. Remove the radiator upper support brackets and bolts that connect to the fan shroud.

14. Disconnect the engine cooling fan motors electrical connectors.

15. Remove the cooling fan motors electrical harness from the fan shroud clips.

16. Remove the cooling fan shroud.

17. Remove the outlet hose from the radiator.

18. Disconnect the transaxle oil cooler pipes from the radiator.

19. Tilt the top of the radiator rearward.

20. Remove the condenser hold down bracket from the radiator.

21. Lift the condenser from the mounting tabs on the radiator and position the condenser aside.

22. Remove the radiator.

To install:

23. Install the radiator to the lower mounts.

➡**Verify that the condenser is fully seated in the radiator mounting tabs.**

24. Install the condenser to the mounting tabs on the radiator.

25. Install the condenser hold down bracket to the radiator and condenser.

26. Install the outlet hose to the radiator.

27. Connect the transaxle oil cooler pipes to the radiator.

➡**Ensure the lower edge of the fan shroud engages the clip at the bottom of the radiator.**

28. Install the cooling fan shroud.

29. Install the cooling fan motors electrical harness to the fan shroud clips.

30. Connect the engine cooling fan motors electrical connectors.

31. Install the fan shroud clip to the condenser tubes.

32. Install the cooling fan shroud bolts and tighten to 89 inch lbs. (10 Nm).

33. Install the radiator upper support brackets and bolts that connect to the fan shroud.

34. Install the air deflectors to the top of the radiator.

35. Install the bolt that connects the fan shroud to the condenser hold down bracket.

36. Install the PCM harness clip on to the fan shroud.

37. Install the inlet hose to the radiator.

38. Install the air cleaner assembly.

39. Install the coolant reservoir hose to the radiator overflow neck.

40. Install the right and the left engine mount struts.

41. Install the transaxle oil cooler lines to the retainer clip at the bottom of the cooling fan shroud.

42. Fill the cooling system.

43. Connect the negative battery cable.

44. Adjust the transaxle fluid level.

THERMOSTAT

REMOVAL & INSTALLATION

3.6L Engine

1. Remove the heater hoses.
2. Remove the throttle body.
3. Remove the radiator water pipe outlet.
4. Remove the thermostat and housing.

➡**The thermostat and housing are replaced as a complete unit.**

5. To install, reverse the removal procedure. Tighten the housing bolts to 15 ft. lbs. (20 Nm).

3.8L Engine

1. Remove the fuel injector sight shield.
2. Partially drain the cooling system.

3. Remove the radiator inlet hose from the water outlet housing.

4. Reposition the wiring harness from the water outlet housing stud.

5. Remove the water outlet housing bolt and the stud.

6. Remove the water outlet housing and the gasket.

7. Remove the thermostat.

8. Clean and Inspect the water outlet housing gasket mating surfaces.

To install:

9. Install the thermostat.

10. Install the gasket and the water outlet housing.

11. Install the water outlet housing bolt and the stud to the water outlet housing and tighten to 20 ft. lbs. (27 Nm).

12. Install the wiring harness to the water outlet housing stud.

13. Install the radiator inlet hose to the water outlet housing.

14. Fill the cooling system.

15. Install the fuel injector sight shield.

WATER PUMP

REMOVAL & INSTALLATION

3.6L Engine

See Figures 25 and 26.

06025-LACR-G11

Fig. 25 Use tool EN 46104 (1) in order to retain the water pump pulley

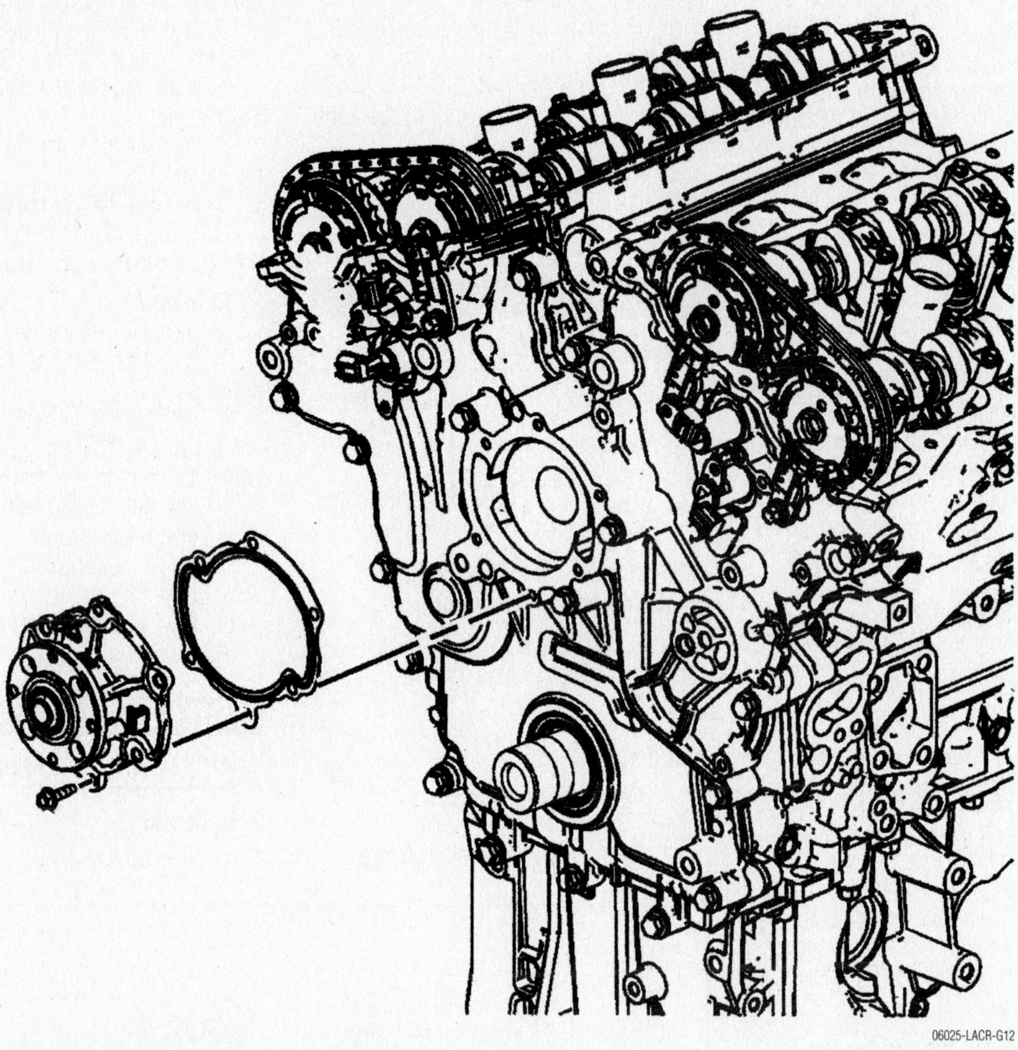

06025-LACR-G12

Fig. 26 Water pump—3.6L engine

1. Before servicing the vehicle, refer to the Precautions Section.

2. Drain the cooling system.

3. Remove the alternator drive belt.

4. Use tool EN 46104 in order to retain the water pump pulley.

5. Remove the water pump pulley bolts.

6. Remove the water pump pulley.

7. Remove the water pump bolts.

8. Remove the water pump.

9. Remove and DISCARD the water pump seal.

10. Carefully clean the water pump sealing surfaces.

To install:

11. Install a NEW water pump seal.

12. Install the water pump.

13. Install the water pump bolts. Tighten the water pump bolts to 89 inch lbs. (10 Nm).

14. Install the water pump pulley and the water pump pulley bolts.

15. Install the water pump pulley bolts. Tighten the water pump pulley bolts to 106 inch lbs. (12 Nm).

16. Install the alternator drive belt.

17. Fill the cooling system.

3.8L Engine

See Figure 27.

1. Before servicing the vehicle, refer to the Precautions Section.

2. Drain the cooling system.

3. Remove or disconnect the following:

- Negative battery cable
- Accessory drive belt
- Coolant hoses from the water pump
- Water pump pulley bolts

➡The long bolt can be removed by aligning the bolt head up with the hole in the frame rail.

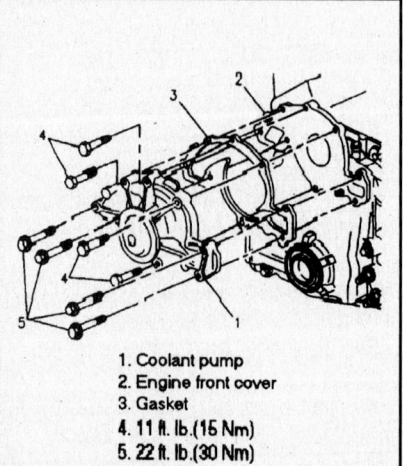

1. Coolant pump
2. Engine front cover
3. Gasket
4. 11 ft. lb. (15 Nm)
5. 22 ft. lb. (30 Nm)

7922UG01

Fig. 27 Exploded view of the water pump—3.8L engines

- Pulley
- Water pump bolts
- Water pump

To install:

4. Apply a thin bead of sealer around the outside edge of the water pump.

5. Install or connect the following:
- Water pump with new gasket. Torque the water pump short bolts to 11 ft. lbs. (15 Nm) and the long bolts to 22 ft. lbs. (30 Nm).
- Water pump pulley. Torque the bolts to 115 inch lbs. (13 Nm).

- Coolant hoses to the water pump
- Accessory drive belt

6. Refill and bleed the cooling system.

7. Run the engine and check for leaks.

8. Recheck the coolant level when the engine has cooled.

ENGINE ELECTRICAL

CHARGING SYSTEM

ALTERNATOR

REMOVAL & INSTALLATION

3.6L Engine

See Figures 28 and 29.

1. Before servicing the vehicle, refer to the Precautions Section.

2. Disconnect the battery ground (negative) cable from the battery.

3. Remove the bolt and the nut from the engine mount strut at the left engine mount strut bracket on the engine. Remove the bolt and the nut from the engine mount strut at the engine mount strut bracket on the upper radiator support.

4. Remove the engine mount strut.

5. Remove the bolt and the nut from the engine mount strut at the right engine mount strut bracket on the engine.

6. Remove the bolt and the nut from the engine mount strut at the engine mount strut bracket on the upper radiator support.

7. Remove the engine mount strut.

8. Remove the alternator B+ terminal nut and the battery cable from the alternator.

9. Disconnect the alternator electrical connector.

10. Remove the accessory drive belt from the alternator.

11. Remove the idler pulley.

12. Remove the alternator bolts.

13. Remove the alternator from the vehicle.

To install:

14. Install the alternator to the vehicle.

15. Install the alternator bolts. Tighten the alternator bolts to 37 ft. lbs. (50 Nm).

16. Install the idler pulley. Tighten the accessory drive belt idler pulley bolt to 37 ft. lbs. (50 Nm).

17. Install the accessory drive belt.

18. Connect the alternator electrical connector.

19. Install the battery cable and the alternator B+ terminal nut to the alternator. Tighten the alternator B+ terminal nut 15 ft. lbs. (20 Nm).

20. Install the engine mount strut.

21. Install the bolt and the nut to the engine mount strut at the engine mount strut bracket on the upper radiator support. HAND TIGHTEN ONLY.

22. Install the bolt and the nut to the engine mount strut at the right engine mount strut bracket on the engine. Tighten both engine mount strut nuts to 35 ft. lbs. (48 Nm).

23. Install the engine mount strut.

24. Install the bolt and the nut to the engine mount strut at the engine mount strut bracket on the upper radiator support. HAND TIGHTEN ONLY.

25. Install the bolt and the nut to the engine mount strut at the left engine mount strut bracket on the engine. Tighten bolt engine mount strut nuts to 35 ft. lbs. (48 Nm).

06025-LACR-G01

Fig. 28 Engine mount strut—3.6L engine

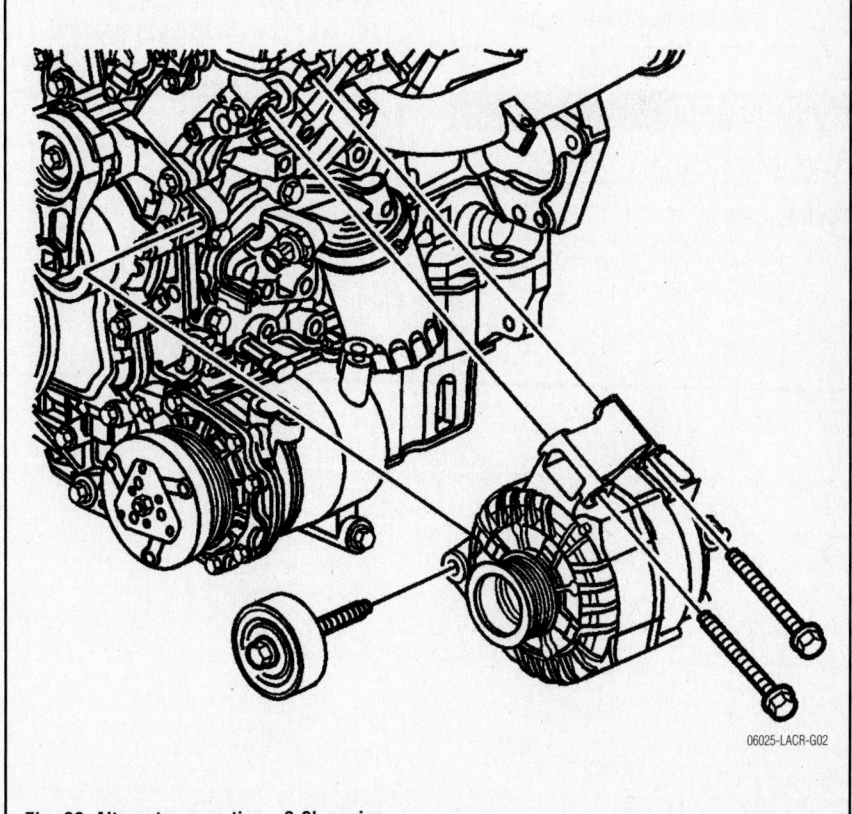

06025-LACR-G02

Fig. 29 Alternator mounting—3.6L engine

26. Connect the battery ground (negative) cable to the battery.

3.8L Engine

1. Before servicing the vehicle, refer to the Precautions Section.
2. Remove or disconnect the following:
   - Negative battery cable
   - Accessory drive belt

- Fuel injector sight shield
- Alternator brace
- Electrical connections
- Alternator bolts and the alternator

To install:
3. Install or connect the following:
   - Alternator and torque the bolts to 37 ft. lbs. (50 Nm)

- Electrical connections and torque the nut to 111 inch lbs. (13 Nm)
- Alternator brace. Torque the nut to 37 ft. lbs. (50 Nm) and the bolt to 22 ft. lbs. (30 Nm).
- Fuel injector sight shield
- Accessory drive belt
- Negative battery cable

ENGINE ELECTRICAL

FIRING ORDER

See Figure 30.

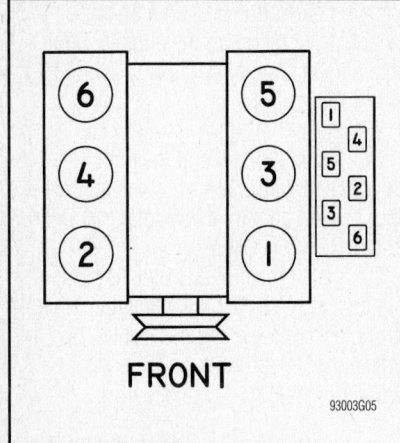

FRONT

93003G05

Fig. 30 3.8L Engine
Firing order: 1–6–5–4–3–2
Distributorless ignition system

IGNITION COIL

REMOVAL & INSTALLATION

3.6L Engine

1. Disconnect the negative battery cable.
2. Turn the ignition OFF.

3. On bank 1, remove the engine cover.
4. If replacing the ignition coil for cylinder 5 , remove and reposition the intake manifold as follows:
   a. Disconnect the air cleaner duct from the throttle body.
   b. Disconnect the positive Crankcase Ventilation (PCV) hose from the right bank camshaft cover.
   c. Remove the intake manifold bolts, brace bolts and brace.
   d. Remove the upper intake manifold bolts. Do not separate the manifolds.
5. On both banks, remove the ignition coil electrical connectors.
6. Remove the ignition coil bolts and the coils.

To install:
7. Install the ignition coils and tighten the bolts to 89 inch lbs. (10 Nm).
8. Install the ignition coil electrical connectors.
9. If necessary, install the intake manifold.
10. Install the engine cover.
11. Connect the negative battery cable.

3.8L Engine

1. Disconnect the negative battery cable.

IGNITION SYSTEM

2. Disconnect the spark plug wires from the ignition coil.
3. Remove the ignition coil screws.
4. Remove the ignition coil.

To install:
5. Install the ignition coils and tighten to 40 inch lbs. (5 Nm).
6. Connect the spark plug wires.
7. Connect the negative battery cable.

IGNITION TIMING

ADJUSTMENT

The ignition timing is not adjustable, and is set according to engine demand electronically. The Powertrain Control Module (PCM) controls the ignition timing for all driving conditions.

SPARK PLUGS

REMOVAL & INSTALLATION

1. Disconnect the spark plug wires.
2. On 3.6L engines, remove the ignition coils.
3. Remove the spark plugs.
4. To install, reverse the removal procedure. Tighten the spark plugs to 11 ft. lbs. (15 Nm).

STARTER

REMOVAL & INSTALLATION

3.6L Engine

See Figure 31.

1. Before servicing the vehicle, refer to the Precautions Section.
2. Disconnect the battery ground (negative) cable from the battery.
3. Raise and support the vehicle.
4. Remove the radiator air baffle.
5. Remove the starter motor BAT terminal nut and electrical leads.
6. Remove the starter motor bolts.
7. Remove the starter motor.

To install:

8. Install the starter motor.
9. Install the starter motor bolts. Tighten the starter motor bolts to 37 ft. lbs. (50 Nm).
10. Install the starter motor S terminal electrical connector.
11. Install the battery positive cable and the BAT terminal nut to the starter motor BAT terminal. Tighten the starter motor BAT terminal nut to 115 inch lbs. (13 Nm).
12. Install the radiator air baffle.
13. Lower the vehicle.
14. Install the battery ground (negative) cable to the battery.

3.8L Engine

See Figure 32.

1. Before servicing the vehicle, refer to the Precautions Section.
2. Remove or disconnect the following:
   - Negative battery cable
   - Flexplate inspection cover
   - Splash shield, if equipped
   - Electrical connectors
   - Transaxle cooler line clip from the transaxle, if necessary
   - Starter motor wiring
   - Starter motor bolts
   - Starter

To install:

3. Install or connect the following:
   - Starter and torque the bolts to 32 ft. lbs. (43 Nm)

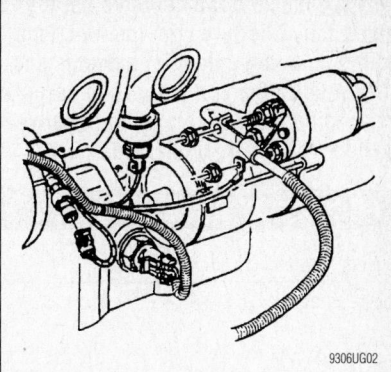

Fig. 32 Starter in place with wiring—3.8L engine

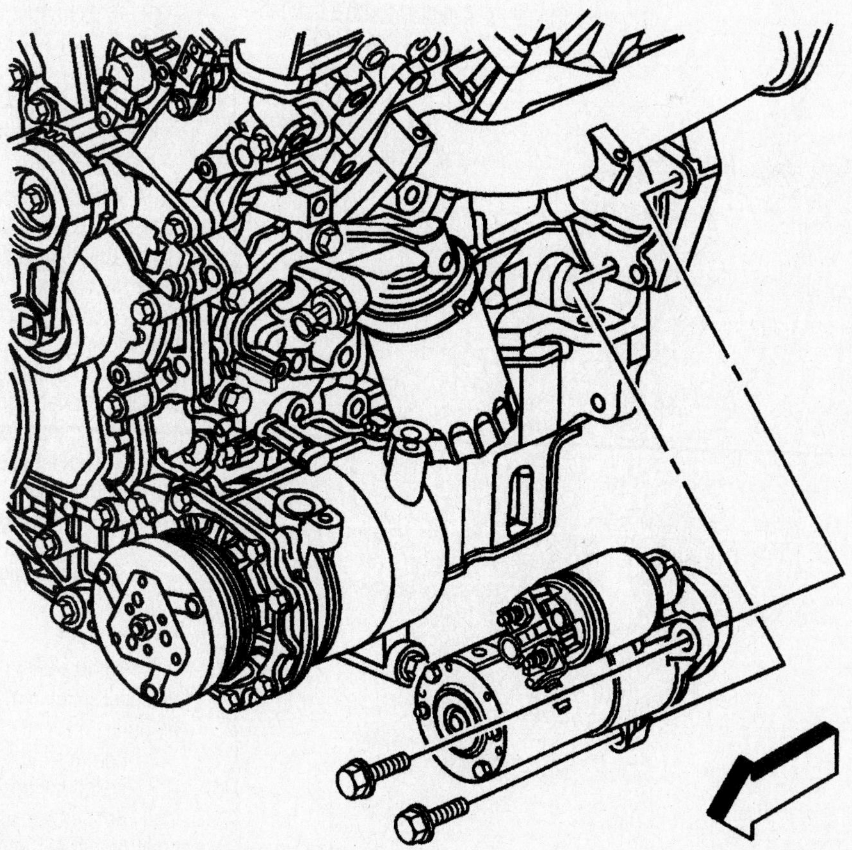

9306UG02

- Wiring and torque the "B" terminal nut to 89 inch lbs. (10 Nm) and the "S" terminal nut to 22 inch lbs. (3 Nm).
- Flexplate inspection cover and torque the bolts to 62 inch lbs. (7 Nm)
- Splash shield
- Negative battery cable

Fig. 31 Starter installation—3.6L engine

06025-LACR-G33

ENGINE MECHANICAL

➡ Disconnecting the negative battery cable may interfere with the functions of the on board computer systems and may require the computer to undergo a relearning process, once the negative battery cable is reconnected.

ACCESSORY DRIVE BELTS

ACCESSORY BELT ROUTING

See Figures 33 and 34.

INSPECTION

Inspect the accessory drive belt for signs of glazing or cracking. A glazed belt will be perfectly smooth from slippage, while a good belt will have a slight texture of fabric visible. Cracks will usually start at the inner edge of the belt and run outward. All worn or damaged accessory drive belts should be replaced immediately.

ADJUSTMENT

The accessory drive belt adjustment is maintained by an automatic tensioner.

REMOVAL & INSTALLATION

3.6L Engine

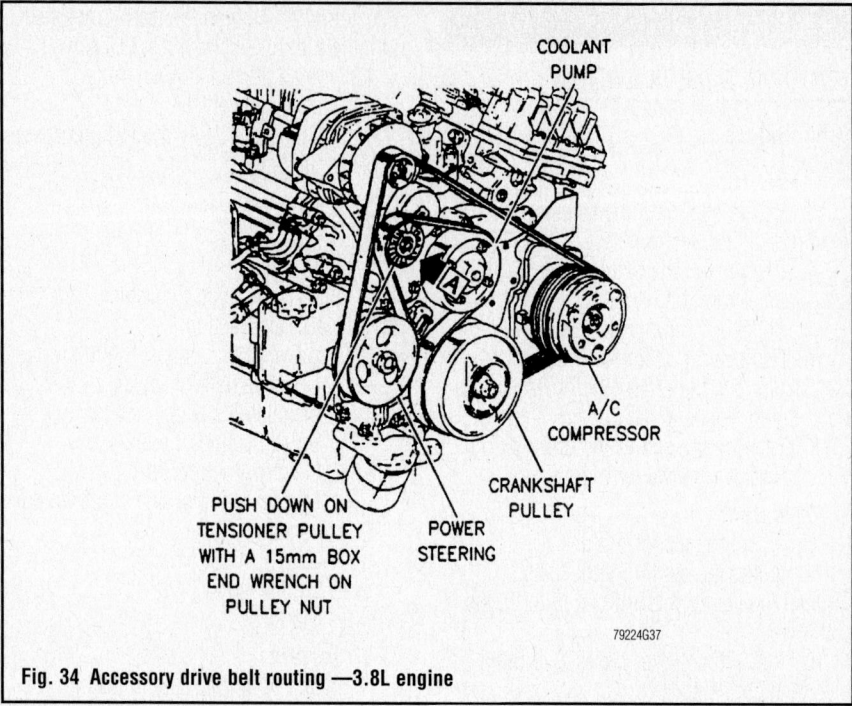

Fig. 34 Accessory drive belt routing —3.8L engine

1. Raise and support the vehicle.
2. Remove the right engine splash shield.
3. Rotate the accessory drive belt tensioner clockwise to release the accessory drive belt tension.
4. Remove the accessory drive belt from the alternator.
5. Slowly release the accessory drive belt tensioner.
6. Remove the accessory drive belt from the accessory drive pulleys.

To install:
7. Install the accessory drive belt to the accessory drive pulley.
8. Rotate the accessory drive belt tensioner clockwise.
9. Install the accessory drive belt to the alternator.
10. Ensure the accessory drive belt is properly aligned and seated into the grooves of the accessory drive pulleys.
11. Slowly release the accessory drive belt tensioner
12. Install the right engine splash shield.
13. Lower the vehicle.

3.8L Engine

1. Lift or rotate the accessory drive belt tensioner using a 15mm box end wrench on the pulley nut.
2. Remove the accessory drive belt.
3. Install the accessory drive belt
4. Rotate the accessory drive belt tensioner using a 15mm box end wrench on the pulley nut.

Fig. 33 Accessory drive belt routing —3.6L engine

BALANCE SHAFT

REMOVAL & INSTALLATION

3.8L Engine

See Figures 35 through 38.

1. Before servicing the vehicle, refer to the Precautions Section.
2. Remove the balance shaft driven gear bolt.
3. Remove the balance shaft driven gear.
4. Remove the balance shaft retainer bolts.

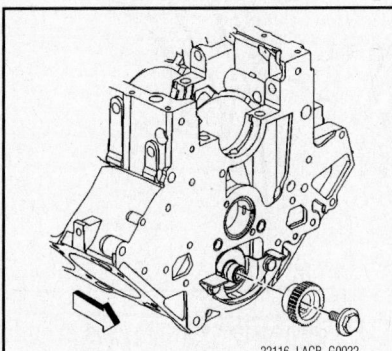

Fig. 35 Remove the balance shaft driven gear bolt—3.8L Engine

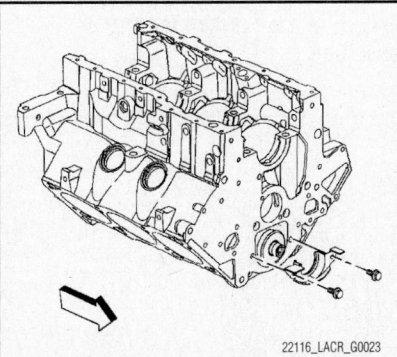

Fig. 36 Remove the balance shaft retainer bolts—3.8L Engine

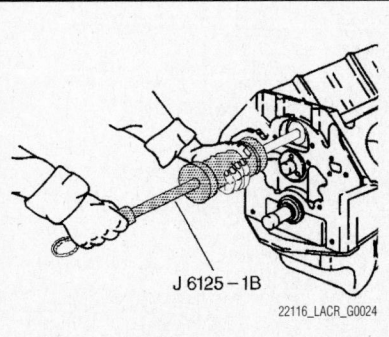

Fig. 37 Use J 6125-1B to remove the balance shaft—3.8L Engine

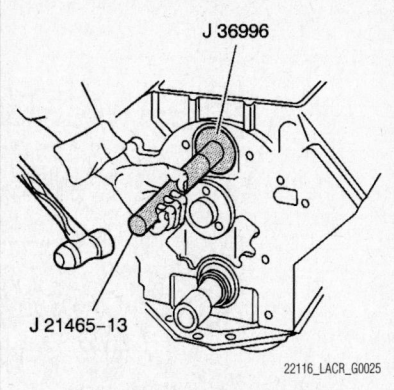

Fig. 38 Use J 21465-13 and J 36996 to install the balance shaft into the engine block—3.8L Engine

5. Remove the balance shaft retainer.
6. Use the slide hammer, J 6125-1B, to remove the balance shaft.

To install:

7. Use J 21465-13 and J 36996 to install the balance shaft into the engine block.
8. Install the balance shaft retainer.

➡️**Use the correct fastener in the correct location. Replacement fasteners must be the correct part number for that application. Fasteners requiring replacement or fasteners requiring the use of thread locking compound or sealant are identified in the service procedure. Do not use paints, lubricants, or corrosion inhibitors on fasteners or fastener joint surfaces unless specified. These coatings affect fastener torque and joint clamping force and may damage the fastener. Use the correct tightening sequence and specifications when installing fasteners in order to avoid damage to parts and systems.**

9. Install the balance shaft retainer bolts. Tighten the bolts to 22 ft. lbs. (30 Nm).
10. Install the balance shaft driven gear.
11. Install the balance shaft driven gear bolt. Tighten the bolt:
    a. Step 1: 16 ft. lbs. (22 Nm).
    b. Use J 45059 to tighten the bolt an additional 70°.
12. Using J 8001, measure the balance shaft end play. End play must not exceed 0.008 in. (0.028mm).
13. Using J 8001, measure the balance shaft radial play at the rear. Radial play must be between 0.0005–0.0047 in. (0.0127–0.119mm).
14. Install the balance shaft drive gear.
15. Install the camshaft sprocket.
16. Turn the camshaft so the timing mark on the camshaft sprocket is straight down.
17. Remove the camshaft sprocket and balance shaft drive gear.
18. Turn the balance shaft so the timing mark on the balance shaft driven gear points straight down.
19. Partially install the balance shaft drive gear so the gear teeth are not engaged.
20. Align the marks on the balance shaft driven gear and the balance shaft drive gear. Do this by turning the balance shaft.
21. Once the marks are aligned, fully seat the balance shaft drive gear and engage the gear teeth.
22. Turn the crankshaft so the number one piston is at Top Dead Center (TDC).
23. Install the timing chain and camshaft sprocket.
24. Using J 8001, measure the gear lash at four places. Measure every quarter turn. Gear lash must be between 0.002–0.005 in. (0.050–0.127mm).

CAMSHAFT AND VALVE LIFTERS

INSPECTION

1. Clean the camshafts with cleaning solvent.
2. Inspect the camshafts for scored journals, damaged lobes, damaged sprocket locator slots, and damaged threads.
3. Check the camshaft bearing journals for damage and binding.
4. If the journals are binding, check the cylinder head for damage.
5. Check the cylinder head for clogged oil passages.
6. Check the camshaft surface for abnormal wear and damage. Replace the camshaft, as required.
7. Measure the camshaft lobe surface and replace the camshaft if not within specification.
8. Measure the camshaft journal diameter and replace the camshaft if not within specification.
9. Measure the camshaft run out and replace the camshaft if not within specification.
10. Inspect the valve lash adjusters for excessive wear, clogged oil passages, damage, or collapsing and sponginess.

REMOVAL & INSTALLATION

3.6L Engine

Left Side

See Figures 39 through 47.

1. Before servicing the vehicle, refer to the Precautions Section.

2. Remove the upper intake manifold with the lower intake manifold.

3. Disconnect the ignition coil electrical connectors.

4. Remove the wiring harness from the side of the camshaft cover by sliding the conduit down and outboard.

5. Remove the wiring conduit retainers from the camshaft cover by rotating the wiring harness conduit retainers counter-clockwise.

➡It is not necessary to disconnect the engine front cover electrical connectors.

6. Remove the wiring harness from the front of the camshaft cover.

7. Reposition and secure the wiring harnesses away from the camshaft cover in order to provide clearance.

8. Remove the ignition coils.

9. Loosen the left engine strut bracket.

10. Loosen the left engine strut bracket to cylinder head bolts.

11. Remove the camshaft cover bolts and camshaft cover.

12. Remove and discard the camshaft cover seal and grommets. DO NOT reuse.

13. Remove the camshaft sensors.

➡Do not disconnect the power steering fluid lines/hoses from the reservoir.

14. Remove the power steering fluid reservoir bolts and reposition the power steering fluid reservoir in order to provide access.

15. Remove the Camshaft Position (CMP) actuator valve electrical connector.

16. Remove the camshaft position actuator solenoid.

17. Remove the crankshaft damper.

18. Rotate the crankshaft until the camshafts are in a neutral (low tension) position. The camshaft flats will be parallel with the camshaft cover rail

❄ WARNING

A wrench must be used on the hex of the camshaft when loosening or tightening in order to prevent component damage. Failure to prevent the torque reaction against the timing drive chain can lead to timing drive chain failure.

➡Use an open-end wrench at the camshaft hex to prevent camshaft/engine rotation. DO NOT remove the

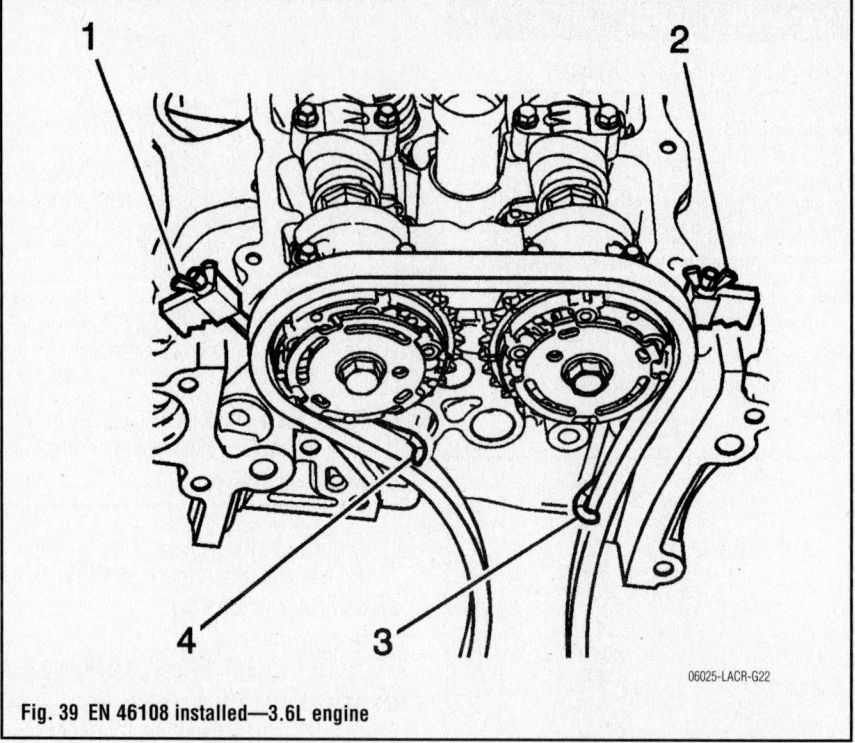

Fig. 39 EN 46108 installed—3.6L engine

camshaft position actuator bolt at this time.

19. Loosen the camshaft position actuator bolt.

➡Ensure that the tips of tool EN 46108 are fully engaged into the timing chain (3 and 4).

20. Install tool EN 46108 (1 and 2) in order to retain the timing chain. Firmly tighten the tool nuts.

➡Ensure that the camshaft timing chain and the camshaft position actuators are marked for proper assembly.

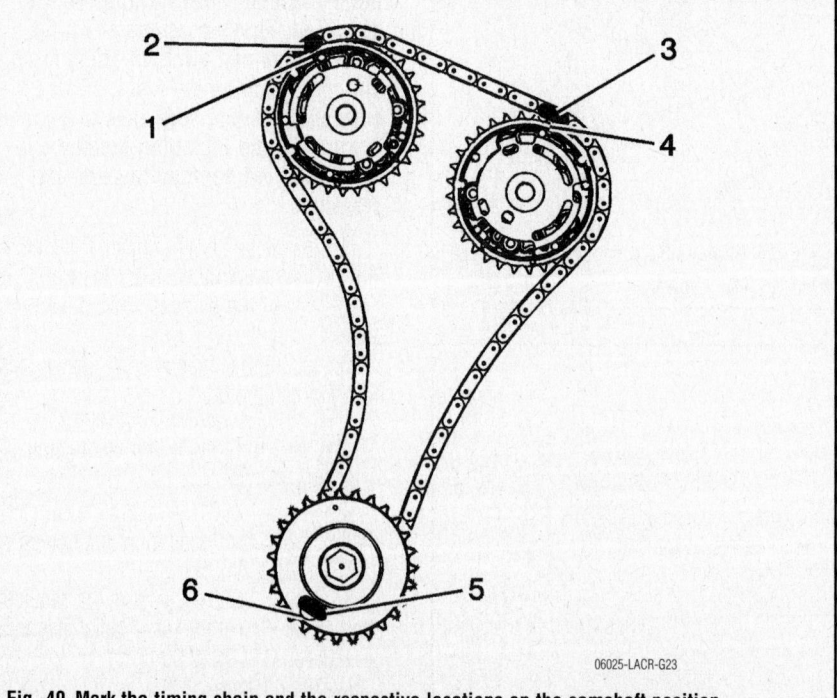

Fig. 40 Mark the timing chain and the respective locations on the camshaft position actuators—3.6L engine

21. Mark the timing chain and the respective locations on the camshaft position actuators.

22. Remove the camshaft position actuator bolt.

23. Remove the timing chain from the sprockets.

24. Position the camshaft lobes in a neutral position.

25. Observe the markings on the bearing caps. Each bearing cap is marked in order to identify its location. The markings have the following meanings:

- The raised feature must always be oriented toward the center of the cylinder head
- The E indicates the exhaust camshaft
- The I indicates the intake camshaft
- The number indicates the journal position from the front of the engine

26. Remove the camshaft bearing cap bolts.

27. Remove the camshaft bearing caps.

28. Remove the camshafts.

29. Replace the camshaft bearing caps and bolts.

To install:

➡ **Ensure that the marks on the camshaft position actuator and the timing chain (1-4) are aligned. DO NOT tighten the camshaft position actuator bolt at this time.**

30. Locate the camshafts to the cylinder head and assemble the camshaft actuators to the camshafts.

31. Ensure that the crankshaft is in the stage one timing drive assembly position. See the Timing Chain Removal & Installation procedure.

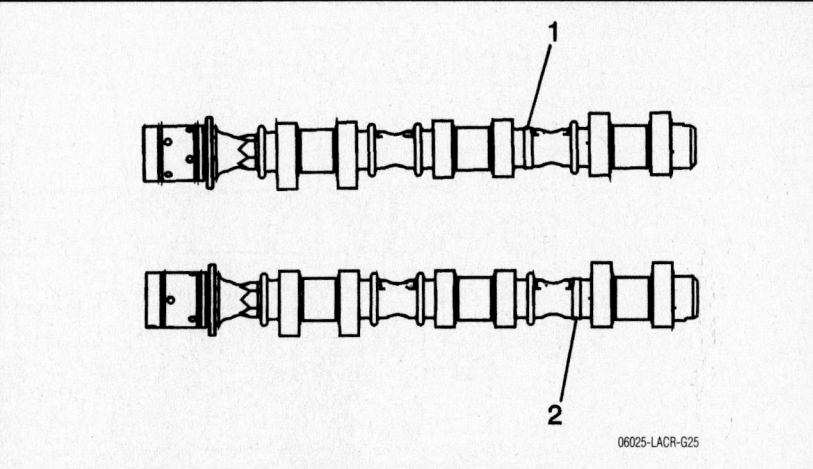

Fig. 42 Select the proper camshaft for the particular installation location—3.6L engine

32. Ensure that the camshaft sealing rings are in place in the camshaft grooves.

33. Select the proper camshaft for the particular installation location. The ring placement is defined as follows:

a. The number 4 identification ring for the left intake camshaft is machined off (1).

b. The number 5 identification ring for the left exhaust camshaft is machined off (2).

34. Apply a liberal amount of lubricant GM P/N 12345501 (Canadian P/N 992704), or equivalent, to the camshaft journals and the left cylinder head camshaft carriers.

35. Place the left intake and left exhaust camshafts in position in the left cylinder head.

36. Position the camshaft lobes in a neutral position with the flats on the back of the camshafts up and parallel (1) with the left cylinder head camshaft cover rail.

37. Observe the markings on the left cylinder head camshaft bearing caps. Each

bearing cap is marked in order to identify its location. The markings have the following meanings:

- The raised feature must always be oriented toward the center of the cylinder head.
- The E indicates the exhaust camshaft.
- The I indicates the intake camshaft.
- The number 2, 4, 6 indicates the cylinder position from the front of the engine.

38. Apply a liberal amount of lubricant GM P/N 12345501 (Canadian P/N 992704) or equivalent to the camshaft bearing caps.

39. Install the camshaft bearing thrust cap in the first journal of the left cylinder head.

40. Install the remaining bearing caps with their orientation mark toward the center of the cylinder head.

41. Hand start all the camshaft bearing cap bolts.

42. Tighten the camshaft bearing cap bolts in the sequence shown. Tighten the camshaft bearing cap bolts in sequence to 89 inch lbs. (10 Nm).

43. Loosen the center intake camshaft bearing cap bolts 1, 2 and the center exhaust camshaft bearing cap bolts 3, 4.

44. Retighten the center camshaft bearing cap bolts 1, 2, 3, 4. Retighten the camshaft bearing cap bolts to 89 inch lbs. (10 Nm).

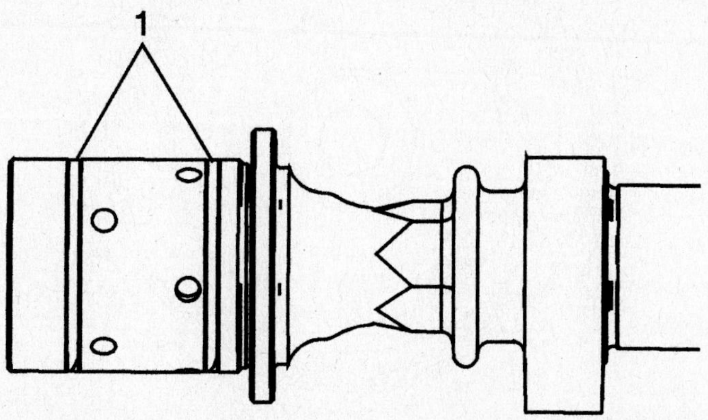

⚙ WARNING

Notice: A wrench must be used on the hex of the camshaft when loosening or tightening in order to prevent component damage. Failure to prevent the torque reaction against the timing drive chain can lead to timing drive chain failure.

Fig. 41 Ensure that the camshaft sealing rings (1) are in place in the camshaft grooves—3.6L engine

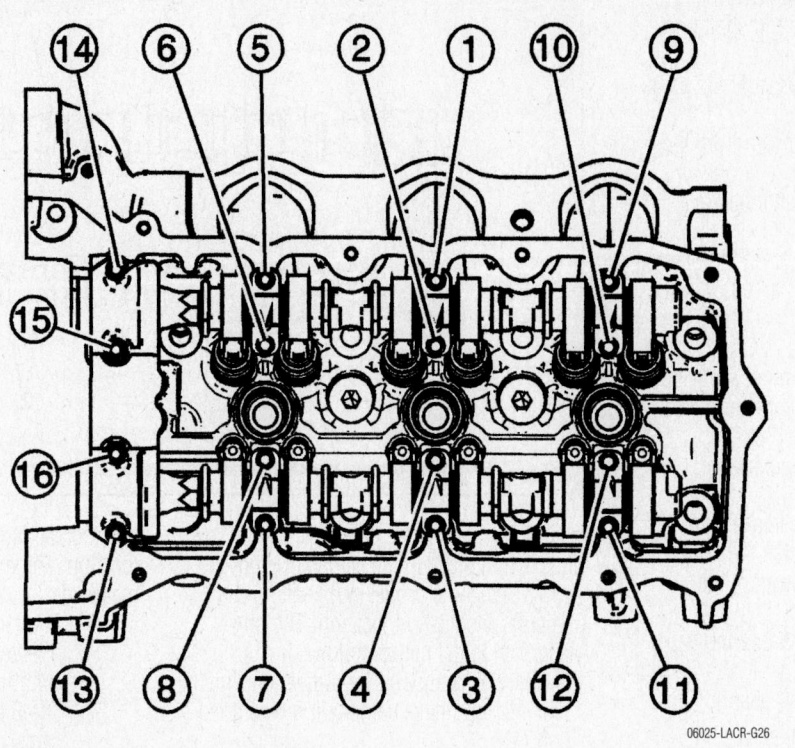

Fig. 43 Left side camshaft bearing torque sequence—3.6L engine

→ **Use an open-end wrench at the camshaft hex to prevent camshaft/engine rotation.**

45. Install and tighten the camshaft position actuators. Tighten the camshaft position actuator bolt to 43 ft. lbs. (58 Nm).

46. Install the CMP sensor.

47. Install the CMP sensor bolt. Tighten the CMP sensor bolt to 89 inch lbs. (10 Nm).

48. Install the CMP sensor electrical connector.

49. Install the power steering fluid reservoir. Tighten the M6 bolt to 80 inch lbs. (9 Nm). Tighten the M8 bolt to 18 ft. lbs. (25 Nm).

50. Install the CMP actuator valve.

51. Install the CMP actuator valve bolt. Tighten the CMP actuator valve bolt to 89 inch lbs. (10 Nm).

52. Install the CMP actuator valve electrical connector.

53. Install the camshaft sensors.

54. Install the crankshaft damper.

55. Install a NEW camshaft cover seal and NEW grommets.

56. Install a NEW camshaft cover seal and NEW grommets.

57. Install the camshaft cover.

58. Tighten the left engine strut bracket to cylinder head bolts. Tighten the left engine strut bracket to cylinder head bolts to 37 ft. lbs. (50 Nm).

59. Install the ignition coils.

60. Install the wiring harness to the front of the camshaft cover.

61. Install the wiring harness conduit retainers to the wiring harness conduit.

62. Install the wiring harness to the side of the camshaft cover.

63. Connect the ignition coil electrical connectors.

64. Install tool EN 46101 onto the spark plug tubes of the left cylinder head.

65. Install the camshaft cover bolt grommets prior to installing the camshaft cover bolts.

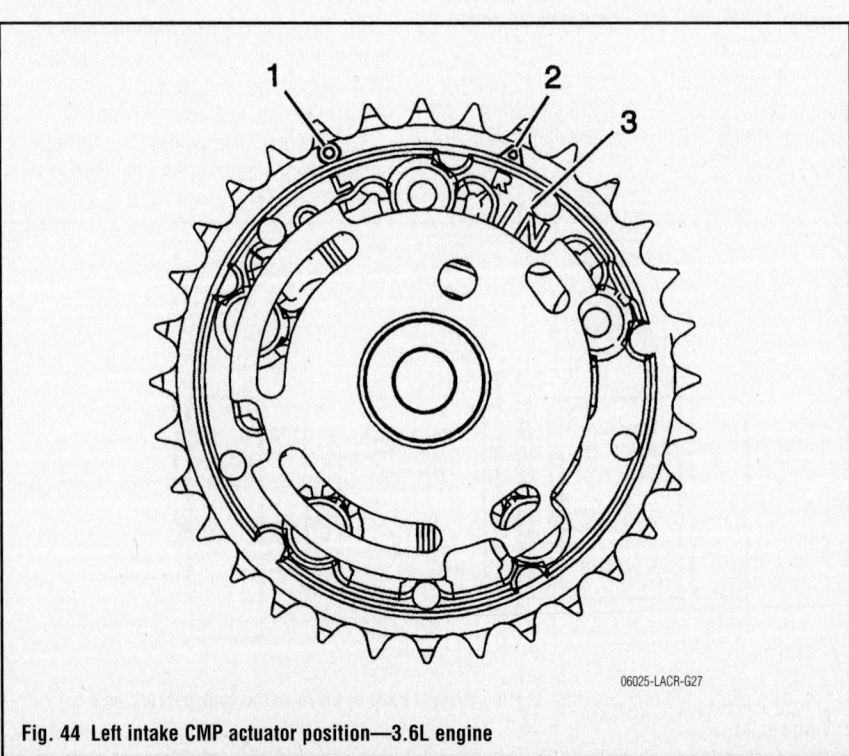

Fig. 44 Left intake CMP actuator position—3.6L engine

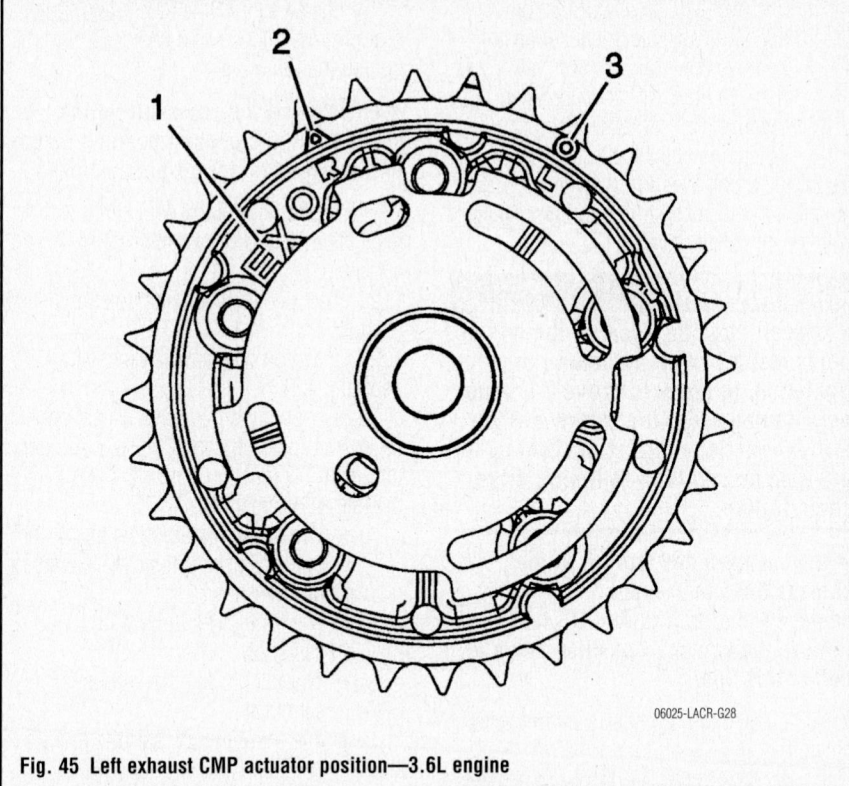

Fig. 45 Left exhaust CMP actuator position—3.6L engine

71. Remove the tool from the spark plug tubes of the left cylinder head.

72. Install the NEW spark plugs into the left cylinder head. Tighten the spark plugs to 15 ft. lbs. (20 Nm).

73. Install each ignition coil through the left camshaft cover into the spark plug tube taking care not to damage the spark plug and/or the seal in the left camshaft cover.

74. Install each ignition coil bolt. Tighten the ignition coil bolt to 89 inch lbs. (10 Nm).

75. Tighten the left engine strut bracket to cylinder head bolts. Tighten the left engine strut bracket to cylinder head bolts to 37 ft. lbs. (50 Nm).

76. Install the ignition coils.

77. Install the wiring harness to the front of the camshaft cover.

78. Install the wiring harness conduit retainers to the wiring harness conduit.

79. Install the wiring harness to the side of the camshaft cover.

80. Connect the ignition coil electrical connectors.

81. Install the upper intake manifold with the lower intake manifold.

Right Side
See Figures 48 through 50.

1. Before servicing the vehicle, refer to the Precautions Section.

2. Remove the upper intake manifold with the lower intake manifold.

66. Wipe the camshaft cover sealing surface on the left cylinder head with a clean, lint-free cloth.

67. Place a bead 8mm (0.3150 in.) in diameter by 4mm (0.1575 in.) in height of RTV sealant, GM P/N 12378521 (Canadian P/N 88901148) or equivalent, on the engine front cover split lines (1).

68. Place the left camshaft cover into position onto the left cylinder head.

69. Loosely install the left camshaft cover bolts.

70. Tighten the left camshaft cover bolts in the sequence shown. Tighten the left camshaft cover bolts in the sequence to 89 inch lbs. (10 Nm).

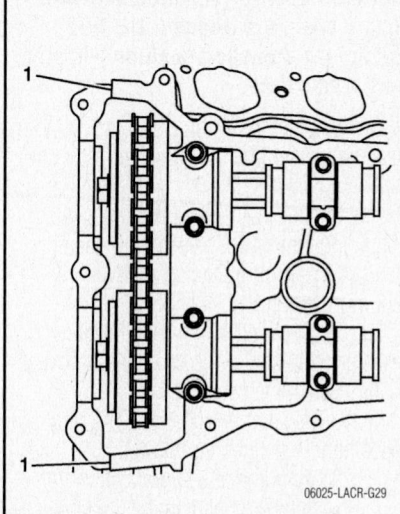

Fig. 46 Place a bead 8mm (0.3150 in.) in diameter by 4mm (0.1575 in.) in height of RTV sealant, GM P/N 12378521 (Canadian P/N 88901148) or equivalent, on the engine front cover split lines (1)—3.6L engine

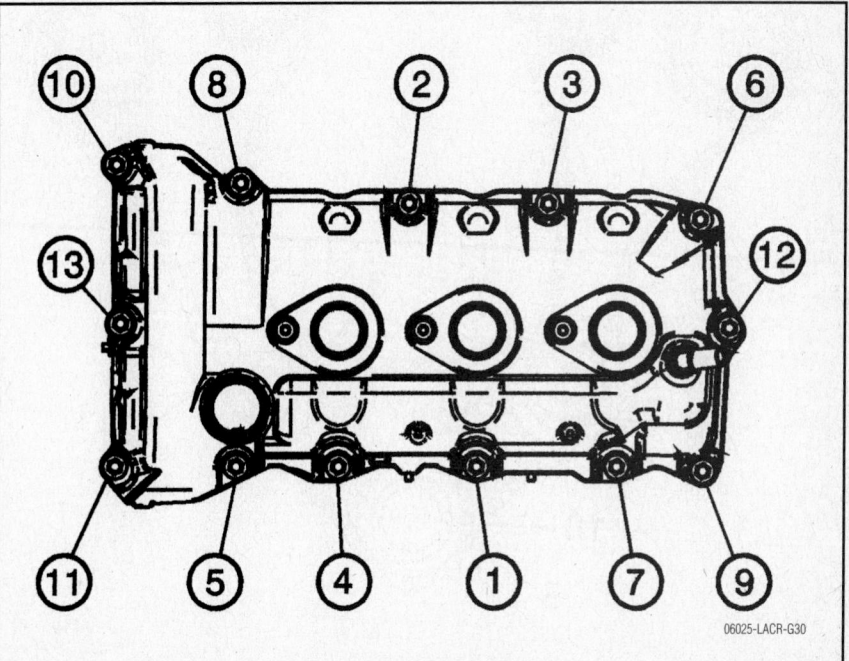

Fig. 47 Left side camshaft cover torque sequence—3.6L engine

3. Disconnect the ignition coil electrical connectors.

4. Remove the wiring harness from the side of the camshaft cover by sliding the conduit down and outboard.

5. Remove the wiring conduit retainers from the camshaft cover by rotating the wiring harness conduit retainers counter-clockwise.

➡ It is not necessary to disconnect the engine front cover electrical connectors.

6. Remove the wiring harness from the front of the camshaft cover.

7. Reposition and secure the wiring harnesses away from the camshaft cover in order to provide clearance.

8. Remove the ignition coils.

9. Remove the camshaft cover.

10. Remove and discard the camshaft cover seal and grommets.

11. Remove the camshaft sensors.

➡ Do not remove the Engine Control Module (ECM) from the ECM bracket. Do not remove the ECM redundant ground wire from the ECM.

12. Remove the ECM bracket bolts and reposition the ECM bracket in order to provide access.

13. Remove the Camshaft Position (CMP) actuator valve electrical connector.

14. Remove the CMP actuator valve bolt.

15. Remove the CMP actuator valve.

16. Remove the crankshaft damper.

17. Rotate the crankshaft until the camshafts are in a neutral (low tension) position. The camshaft flats will be parallel with the camshaft cover rail.

✳✳ WARNING

A wrench must be used on the hex of the camshaft when loosening or tightening in order to prevent component damage. Failure to prevent the torque reaction against the timing drive chain can lead to timing drive chain failure.

➡ Use an open-end wrench at the camshaft hex to prevent camshaft/engine rotation. DO NOT remove the camshaft position actuator bolt at this time.

18. Loosen the camshaft position actuator bolt.

➡ Ensure that the tips of tool EN 46108 are fully engaged into the timing chain (3 and 4).

19. Install tool EN 46108 (1 and 2) in order to retain the timing chain. Firmly tighten the tool nuts.

➡ Ensure that the camshaft timing chain and the camshaft position actuators are marked for proper assembly.

20. Mark the timing chain and the respective locations on camshaft position actuators.

21. Remove the camshaft position actuator bolt.

22. Position the camshaft lobes in a neutral position.

23. Observe the markings on the bearing caps. Each bearing cap is marked in order to identify its location. The markings have the following meanings:

- The raised feature must always be oriented toward the center of the cylinder head
- The I indicates the intake camshaft
- The E indicates the exhaust camshaft
- The number indicates the journal position from the front of the engine

24. Remove the camshaft bearing cap bolts.

25. Remove the camshaft bearing caps.

26. Remove the camshafts.

27. Replace the camshaft bearing caps and bolts.

To install:

➡ Ensure that the marks on the camshaft position actuators and the timing chain are aligned. DO NOT tighten the camshaft position actuator bolt at this time.

28. Locate the camshafts to the cylinder head and assemble the camshaft actuators to the camshafts.

29. Ensure that the crankshaft is in the stage one timing drive assembly position. Refer to the Timing Chain Removal & Installation procedure.

30. Ensure that the camshaft sealing rings are in place in the camshaft grooves.

31. Select the proper camshaft for the particular installation location. The ring placement is defined as follows:

a. The number 2 identification ring for the right exhaust camshaft is machined off (1).

b. The number 3 identification ring for the right intake camshaft is machined off (2).

32. Apply a liberal amount of lubricant GM P/N 12345501 (Canadian P/N 992704)

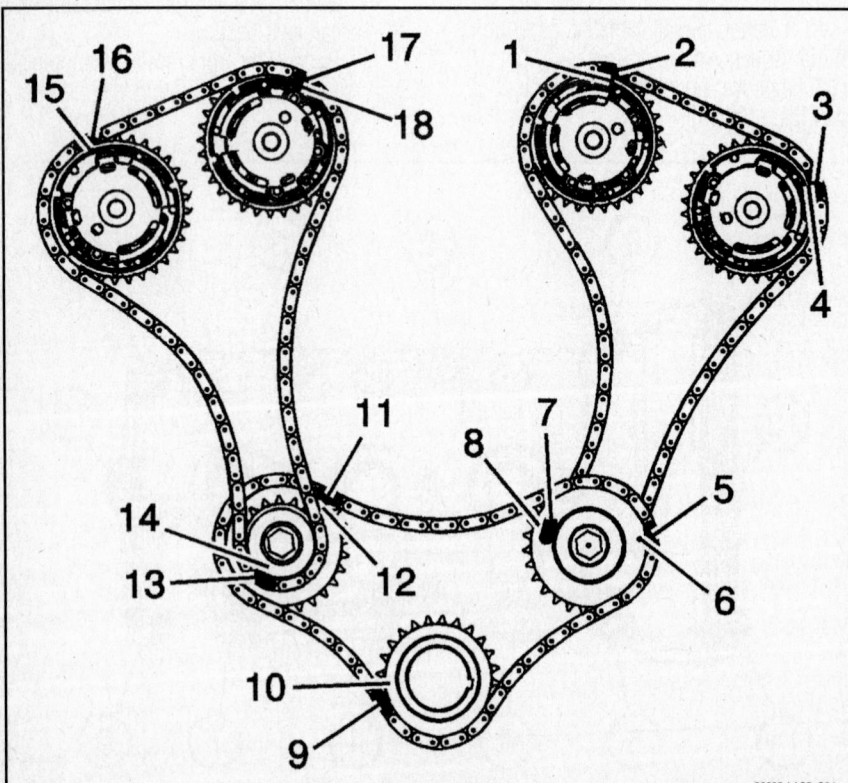

Fig. 48 Ensure that the camshaft timing chain and the camshaft position actuators are marked for proper assembly—3.6L engine right side

06025-LACR-G31

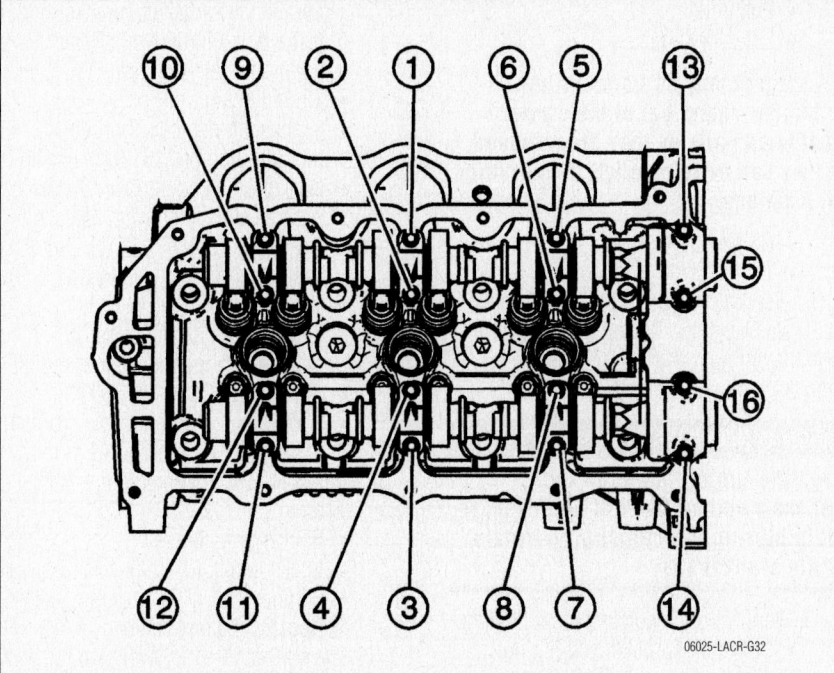

Fig. 49 Right side camshaft bearing cap torque sequence—3.6L engine

or equivalent to the camshaft journals and the right cylinder head camshaft carriers.

33. Place the right intake and right exhaust camshafts in position in the right cylinder head.

34. Position the camshaft lobes in a neutral position with the flats on the back of the camshafts up and parallel with the right cylinder head camshaft cover rail.

35. Observe the markings on the right cylinder head camshaft bearing caps. Each bearing cap is marked in order to identify its location. The markings have the following meanings:

- The raised feature must always be oriented toward the center of the cylinder head
- The I indicates the intake camshaft

- The E indicates the exhaust camshaft
- The number 1, 3, 5 indicates the cylinder position from the front of the engine

36. Apply a liberal amount of lubricant GM P/N 12345501 (Canadian P/N 992704) or equivalent to the camshaft bearing caps.

37. Install the camshaft bearing thrust caps in the first journal of the right cylinder head.

38. Install the remaining bearing caps with their orientation mark toward the center of the cylinder head.

39. Hand start all the camshaft bearing cap bolts.

40. Tighten the camshaft bearing cap bolts in the sequence shown. Tighten the camshaft bearing cap bolts in sequence to 89 inch lbs. (10 Nm).

41. Loosen the center intake camshaft bearing cap bolts (1, 2) and the center exhaust camshaft bearing cap bolts (3, 4).

42. Retighten the center camshaft bearing cap bolts (1, 2, 3, 4). Retighten the camshaft bearing cap bolts to 89 inch lbs. (10 Nm).

43. Install the crankshaft damper.

❋❋ WARNING

A wrench must be used on the hex of the camshaft when loosening or tightening in order to prevent component damage. Failure to prevent the torque reaction against the timing drive chain can lead to timing drive chain failure.

➡**Use an open-end wrench at the camshaft hex to prevent camshaft/engine rotation.**

44. Install the CMP actuator valve.

45. Install the CMP actuator valve bolt. Tighten the CMP actuator valve bolt to 89 inch lbs. (10 Nm).

46. Install the CMP actuator valve electrical connector.

47. Install the ECM bracket with the ECM.

48. Ensure the proper camshaft position actuator is installed. Observe the body of the camshaft position actuator for the "IN" or "EX" marking (3).

49. Ensure the proper timing mark is used. Observe the outer ring of the camshaft position actuator for the "R" and triangle marking (2). The marking is for alignment to the highlighted timing chain link on the right side of the engine.

50. Use an open wrench on the hex cast into the camshaft in order to prevent

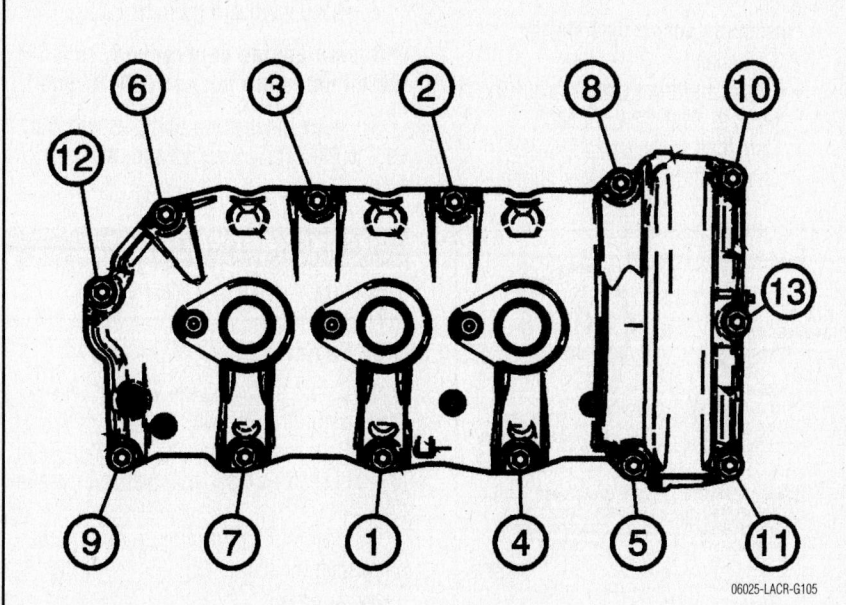

Fig. 50 Right side camshaft cover torque sequence—3.6L engine

camshaft rotation when tightening the camshaft position actuator bolt.

51. Install the right intake camshaft position actuator.

52. Install the camshaft position actuator bolt. Tighten the camshaft position actuator bolt to 43 ft. lbs. (58 Nm).

53. Install the intake camshaft position actuator solenoid.

54. Install the camshaft sensors.

55. Install a NEW camshaft cover seal and NEW grommets.

56. Install tool EN 46101 onto the spark plug tubes of the right cylinder head.

57. Install the camshaft cover bolt grommets prior to installing the camshaft cover bolts.

58. Wipe the camshaft cover sealing surface on the right cylinder head with a clean, lint-free cloth.

59. Place a bead 8mm (0.3150 in.) in diameter by 4mm (0.1575 in.) in height of RTV sealant, GM P/N 12378521 (Canadian P/N 88901148) or equivalent, on the engine front cover split lines (1).

60. Place the right camshaft cover into position onto the right cylinder head.

61. Loosely install the right camshaft cover bolts.

62. Tighten the right camshaft cover bolts in the sequence shown. Tighten the right camshaft cover bolts in the sequence to 89 inch lbs. (10 Nm).

63. Remove tool EN 46101 from the spark plug tubes of the right cylinder head.

64. Install the NEW spark plugs into the right cylinder head. Tighten the spark plugs to 15 ft. lbs. (20 Nm).

65. Install each ignition coil through the right camshaft cover into the spark plug tube taking care not to damage the spark plug and/or the seal in the right camshaft cover.

66. Install each ignition coil bolt. Tighten the ignition coil bolt to 89 inch lbs. (10 Nm).

67. Install the upper intake manifold with the lower intake manifold.

3.8L Engine

See Figure 51.

1. Before servicing the vehicle, refer to the Precautions Section.

2. Relieve the fuel system pressure.

3. Remove the engine and mount it on an engine stand.

4. Remove or disconnect the following:
- Negative battery cable
- Intake manifold
- Rocker arm covers
- Rocker arm assemblies
- Pushrods
- Lifters and guides

➡ **A magnet may be helpful when pulling the lifters out of their bores. Identify all parts as they are removed, so they can be reinstalled in their original locations.**

- Crankshaft damper
- Timing chain front cover

5. Set the engine to Top Dead Center (TDC) No. 1 cylinder (firing position) to align the timing marks, before disassembling the timing chain and sprockets.

❊❊ WARNING

Align the timing marks of the camshaft and crankshaft sprockets to avoid burring the camshaft journals by the crankshaft.

6. Remove or disconnect the following:
- Camshaft sprocket and timing chain
- Camshaft thrust plate
- Camshaft

❊❊ WARNING

If the camshaft was replaced the lifters must also be replaced. The old lifters have developed a wear pattern and will cause the new camshaft to wear prematurely.

To install:

7. Coat the camshaft lobes and bearings with camshaft break-in prelube prior to installation.

8. Install or connect the following:
- Camshaft
- Camshaft thrust plate. Torque the bolts to 10 ft. lbs. (14 Nm).
- Camshaft sprocket and timing chain with timing marks aligned.

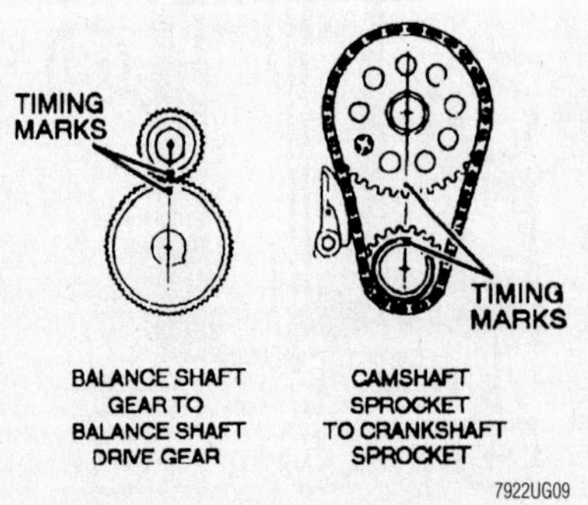

Fig. 51 The timing marks should face each other when the chain and gears are installed properly

Torque the camshaft sprocket bolt to 74 ft. lbs. (100 Nm) plus an additional 90° (¼) turn.
- Timing chain front cover
- Crankshaft damper. Torque the mounting bolt to 111 ft. lbs. (150 Nm). plus an additional 76° turn.

9. Coat the valve lifters with camshaft break-in prelube.

10. Install or connect the following:
- Valve lifters
- Lifter guides and lifter guide retainer. Torque the retainer mounting bolts to 22 ft. lbs. (30 Nm).
- Pushrods and rocker arms. Torque the rocker arm bolts to 11 ft. lbs. (15 Nm) plus an additional 90° turn.
- Rocker arm covers
- Intake manifold
- Engine
- Negative battery cable

11. Verify that all fluid levels are full and correct.

12. Start the engine and check for leaks. Check engine operation.

CAMSHAFT BEARING REPLACEMENT

3.8L Engine

1. Using Camshaft Bearing Remover/Installer J-33049, drive out the camshaft bearings.

2. Use the following procedure to install the camshaft bearings:

3. Assemble J 33049 according to the manufacturer's instructions.

4. Place the bearing on the tool.

➡ **Severe engine damage may result if the oil holes are not correctly aligned.**

5. Index the bearing oil holes with the engine block oil passages and drive in the bearings.

CRANKSHAFT FRONT SEAL

REMOVAL & INSTALLATION

3.6L Engine

1. Before servicing the vehicle, refer to the Precautions Section.

2. Remove the crankshaft damper. Refer to Crankshaft Damper, removal and installation.

3. Use J 45000 in order to remove the crankshaft oil seal.

To install:

➡ **Do not lubricate the crankshaft front oil seal or the crankshaft damper sealing surfaces.**

4. Use the J 29184, or equivalent, to install the crankshaft front oil seal.

5. Install the crankshaft damper. Refer to Crankshaft Damper, removal and installation.

3.8L Engine

1. Before servicing the vehicle, refer to the Precautions Section.

2. Remove the crankshaft damper. Refer to Crankshaft Damper, removal and installation.

✳✳ WARNING

Be careful not to damage the crankshaft.

3. Pry out the crankshaft front oil seal with a flat bladed tool such as a large screwdriver. Use care to avoid damaging the crankshaft front oil seal bore or the crankshaft front oil seal contact surfaces.

4. Inspect the crankshaft damper and engine front cover for scratches.

To install:

5. Install the crankshaft front oil seal in the engine front cover using the J 35354-A .

6. Tighten the bolt until the crankshaft front oil seal is seated in the engine front cover.

7. Remove the J 35354-A.

8. Install the crankshaft damper. Refer to Crankshaft Damper, removal and installation.

9. Inspect for leaks.

10. Perform the Crankshaft Position (CKP) system variation learn procedure.

CYLINDER HEAD

REMOVAL & INSTALLATION

3.6L Engine

Left Side

See Figure 52.

1. Before servicing the vehicle, refer to the Precautions Section.

2. Remove the engine/transaxle from the vehicle.

3. Remove the lower intake manifold.

4. Remove the alternator.

5. Remove the left bank secondary timing chain.

6. Remove the oil level indicator.

7. Remove the heat shield from the coolant temperature sensor and disconnect the coolant temperature sensor electrical connector.

➡**Do not remove the exhaust crossover pipe.**

8. Disconnect the exhaust crossover pipe from the left bank exhaust manifold.

9. Remove the two front M8 left cylinder head bolts.

10. Remove the left cylinder head bolts.

11. Remove the cylinder head with the exhaust manifold.

12. Remove and discard the cylinder head gasket.

13. Clean and inspect the cylinder head and the engine block sealing surfaces.

To install:

➡**Ensure that the crankshaft is in the stage one timing drive assembly position.**

14. Ensure the cylinder head locating pins are securely mounted in the cylinder block deck face.

15. Install a NEW left cylinder head gasket using the deck face locating pins for retention.

16. Align the left cylinder head with the deck face locating pins.

17. Place the left cylinder head in position on the deck face.

➡**DO NOT allow oil on the cylinder head bolt bosses.**

➡**DO NOT reuse the old M11 cylinder head bolts.**

18. Install new M11 cylinder head bolts.

a. Tighten the M11 cylinder head bolts a first pass in sequence to 33 ft. lbs. (45 Nm).

b. Tighten the M11 cylinder head bolts a second pass in sequence an additional 120°.

19. Install the 2 front M8 left cylinder head bolts.

a. Tighten the M8 cylinder head bolts a first pass to 11 ft. lbs. (15 Nm).

b. Tighten the M8 cylinder head bolts a second pass in sequence an additional 60°.

➡**Do not remove the exhaust crossover pipe.**

20. Connect the exhaust crossover pipe to the left bank exhaust manifold. Torque the fasteners to 18 ft. lbs. (25 Nm).

21. Install the lower intake manifold.

22. Install the oil level indicator.

23. Install the alternator.

24. Install the engine/transaxle assembly.

Right Side

See Figure 53.

1. Before servicing the vehicle, refer to the Precautions Section.

2. Remove the powertrain module from the vehicle.

3. Remove the lower intake manifold.

4. Remove the exhaust crossover pipe.

5. Remove the right bank secondary timing chain.

6. Remove the wiring harness ground from the rear of the cylinder head.

7. Remove the wiring harness ground from the front of the cylinder head.

8. Remove the wiring harness conduit upper bolt from the cylinder head and reposition the wiring harness to provide access.

9. Remove the right cylinder head bolts.

10. Remove the right cylinder head.

11. Remove and discard the cylinder head gasket.

12. Clean and inspect the cylinder head and the engine block sealing surfaces.

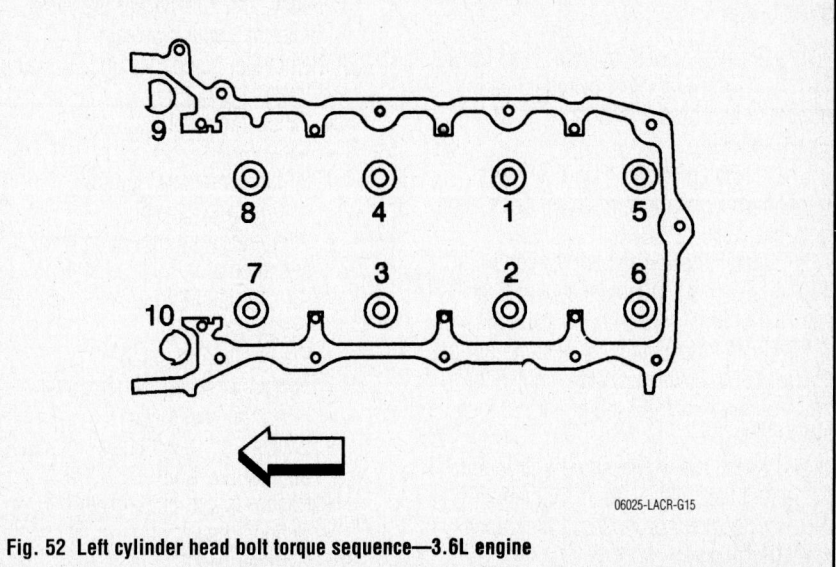

06025-LACR-G15

Fig. 52 Left cylinder head bolt torque sequence—3.6L engine

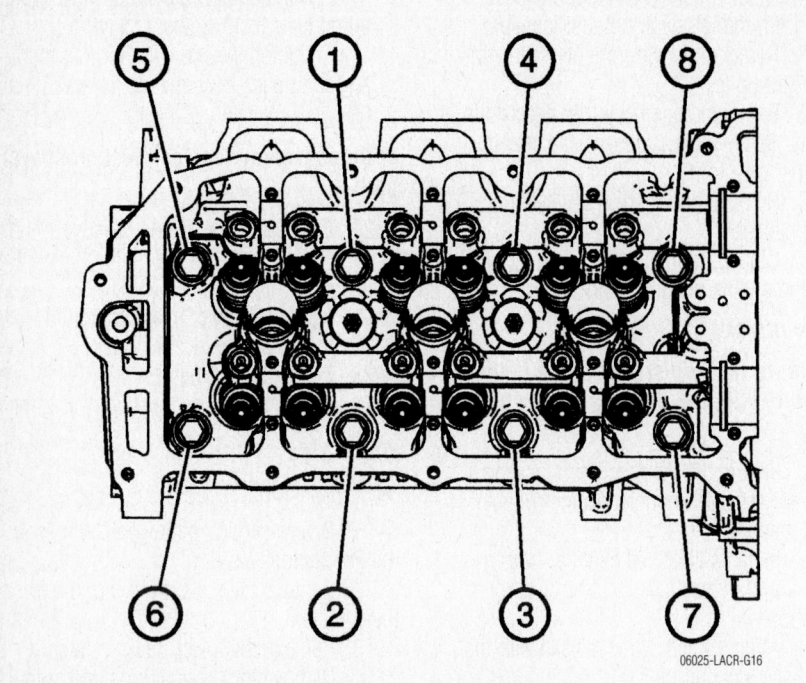

Fig. 53 Right cylinder head torque sequence—3.6L engine

06025-LACR-G16

To install:

13. Install a NEW cylinder head gasket.

➡**Ensure that the crankshaft is in the timing drive assembly position.**

14. Ensure the cylinder head locating pins are securely mounted in the cylinder block deck face.

15. Align the right cylinder head with the deck face locating pins.

16. Place the right cylinder head in position on the deck face.

➡**DO NOT allow oil on the cylinder head bolt bosses.**

➡**DO NOT reuse the old M11 cylinder head bolts.**

17. Install new M11 cylinder head bolts.

a. Tighten the M11 cylinder head bolts a first pass in sequence to 33 ft. lbs. (45 Nm).

b. Tighten the M11 cylinder head bolts a second pass in sequence an additional 120°.

18. Install the wiring harness conduit to the cylinder head. Tighten the wiring harness upper bolt to 89 inch lbs. (10 Nm).

19. Install the wiring harness ground to the front of the cylinder head. Tighten the cylinder head front ground bolt to 89 inch lbs. (10 Nm).

20. Install the wiring harness ground to the rear of the cylinder head. Tighten the cylinder head rear ground bolt to 89 inch lbs. (10 Nm).

21. Install the right bank secondary timing chain.

22. Install the exhaust crossover pipe. Torque the fasteners to 18 ft. lbs. (25 Nm).

23. Install the engine/transaxle assembly to the vehicle.

24. Install the lower intake manifold.

3.8L Engine

See Figure 54.

1. Before servicing the vehicle, refer to the Precautions Section.

2. Disconnect the negative battery cable.

3. Relieve the fuel system pressure.

4. Drain the cooling system.

5. Remove or disconnect the following:
- Intake manifold
- Exhaust manifold
- Valve covers
- Ignition wires and ignition coil/module assembly
- Alternator front mounting bracket and alternator
- Air conditioning bracket to cylinder head bolt
- Power steering pump
- Accessory drive belt tensioner
- Fuel pipe heat shield
- Rocker arm assemblies, note their original position
- Pushrods and guide plate
- Cylinder head bolts
- Cylinder head

To install:

6. Place the new cylinder head gasket on the engine block dowels with the note **THIS SIDE UP** facing the cylinder head and the arrow facing the front of the engine. Position the cylinder head on the engine block.

➡**The head gasket is identified by either a L or a R stamped on it next to the arrow.**

➡**This engine uses special torque to yield head bolts. The procedure must be followed carefully and new bolts must be used whenever the head is removed. Total bolt torque should not exceed 60 ft. lbs. (81 Nm).**

7. Install new cylinder head bolts and torque them in sequence as follows:
a. Step 1: 37 ft. lbs. (50 Nm).
b. Step 2: Plus 120°.

8. Install or connect the following:
- Pushrods and guide plate
- Rocker arm assemblies into their original location

➡**Apply a thread lock compound to the rocker arm pedestal bolts before assembly.**

- Valve covers
- Fuel pipe heat shield
- Accessory drive belt tensioner
- Power steering pump
- Air conditioning compressor bracket bolt. Torque it to 52 ft. lbs. (70 Nm).
- Alternator front mounting bracket, and alternator
- Ignition coil/module assembly and spark plug wires
- Exhaust manifold. Torque the bolts to 22 ft. lbs. (30 Nm).
- Intake manifold
- Negative battery cable

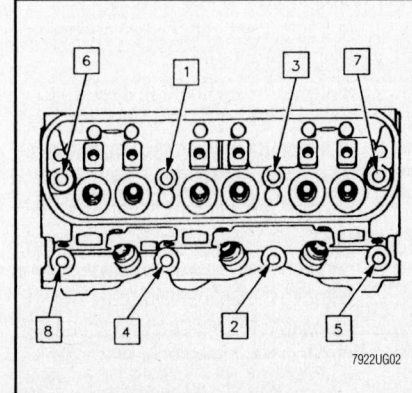

Fig. 54 Cylinder head bolt torque sequence—3.8L engine

7922UG02

9. Refill and bleed the cooling system.

10. Start the engine and check for leaks and proper operation.

ENGINE ASSEMBLY

REMOVAL & INSTALLATION

3.6L Engine

See Figures 55 through 61.

1. Before servicing the vehicle, refer to the Precautions Section.

2. Disconnect the battery negative cable.

3. Remove the throttle body air inlet duct.

➡**Do not disconnect the battery negative cable from the vehicle.**

4. Disconnect the battery negative cable from the engine block.

➡**Do not disconnect the battery positive cable from the vehicle, underhood electrical center or the battery.**

5. Disconnect the battery positive cable from the alternator and the starter.

6. Drain the cooling system.

7. Disconnect the radiator hoses from the engine.

8. Disconnect the heater hoses from the engine.

9. Remove the bolt and the nut from the engine mount strut at the left engine mount strut bracket on the engine. Remove the bolt and the nut from the engine mount strut at the engine mount strut bracket on the upper radiator support.

10. Remove the engine mount strut.

11. Remove the bolt and the nut from the engine mount strut at the right engine mount strut bracket on the engine.

12. Remove the bolt and the nut from the engine mount strut at the engine mount strut bracket on the upper radiator support.

13. Remove the engine mount strut.

➡**Relieve the fuel pressure. Refer to Relieving Fuel System Pressure.**

14. Disconnect the fuel pressure and Evaporative Emission (EVAP) pipes from the engine.

15. Remove the ECM chassis (outboard) side electrical connector from the ECM.

16. Remove the wiring harness ground from the transaxle.

17. Remove the vacuum brake booster hose from the intake manifold.

18. Evacuate the air conditioning system.

19. Remove the A/C compressor hose from the A/C compressor.

20. Relocate the compressor hose to the side.

21. Remove the transaxle electrical connector.

22. Raise and support the vehicle.

23. If you will be separating the engine from the transaxle, remove the torque converter bolts.

24. Drain the engine oil.

25. Remove the catalytic converter.

26. Remove the front tires and wheels.

27. Remove lower radiator air baffle.

28. Remove the engine splash shields.

29. Disconnect the Vehicle Speed Sensor (VSS) electrical connector and secure the wiring harness to the vehicle.

30. Remove the front wheel speed sensor wiring harnesses from the lower control arms and the frame.

31. Remove the tie rod ends from the steering knuckles.

32. Remove the lower ball joints from the knuckles.

33. Disconnect the drive axles from the transaxle.

34. Rotate the struts and reposition the drive axles toward the rear of the vehicle in order to provide clearance for the powertrain to be removed.

❋❋ CAUTION

Failure to disconnect the intermediate shaft from the rack and pinion steering gear stub shaft can result in damage to the steering gear and/or intermediate shaft. This damage may cause loss of steering control which could result in an accident and possible personal injury

35. Separate the intermediate steering shaft from the steering gear.

36. Remove the engine mount lower nuts.

37. Remove the transaxle mount lower nuts.

38. Position a powertrain lift table below the powertrain.

39. Lower the vehicle until the powertrain is supported by the powertrain lift table.

40. Remove the fuel injector sight shield.

41. Remove the engine mount struts.

42. One engine mount strut and nut can be reinstalled to the engine mount strut bracket on engine to be used as an attachment point for front engine attachment.

43. Disconnect the electrical harness clip at the UHJB and at coolant housing.

44. Disconnect the electrical connector at the Engine Control Module (ECM).

45. Remove the coolant recovery reservoir.

46. Remove the power steering reservoir and bracket.

47. Remove the attachment screw from the power steering pump reservoir to bracket.

48. Install the power steering reservoir bracket to powertrain. Tighten the power steering reservoir bracket bolts: M6 bolt to 80 inch lbs. (9 Nm) and M8 bolt to M8 Bolt to 18 ft. lbs. (25 Nm).

49. Install a J 28467-B and retention pin to each end of the J 28467-500 beam (2).

50. Position the J 28467-B to the left and right side inner fender rails in order to install the J 28467-500.

51. Install the radiator shelf tube J 28467-2A (2) on top of the strut tower tube J 28467-3 (1) above the engine front (right bank) lift bracket.

52. Install the round tube of the front support assembly J 28467-4A through the large hole in the radiator shelf tube J 28467-2A.

53. Locate the J 28467-4A front support assembly to the upper tie bar.

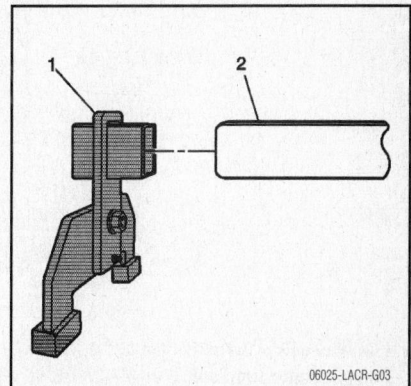

06025-LACR-G03

Fig. 55 Install a J 28467-B and retention pin to each end of the J 28467-500 beam (2)—3.6L engine

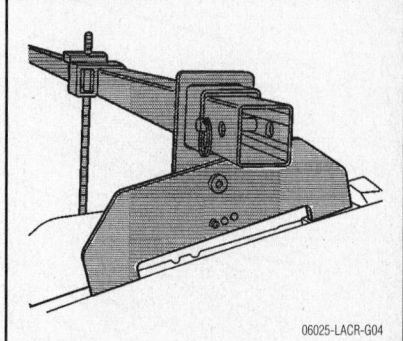

06025-LACR-G04

Fig. 56 Position the J 28467-B to the left and right side inner fender rails in order to install the J 28467-500—3.6L engine

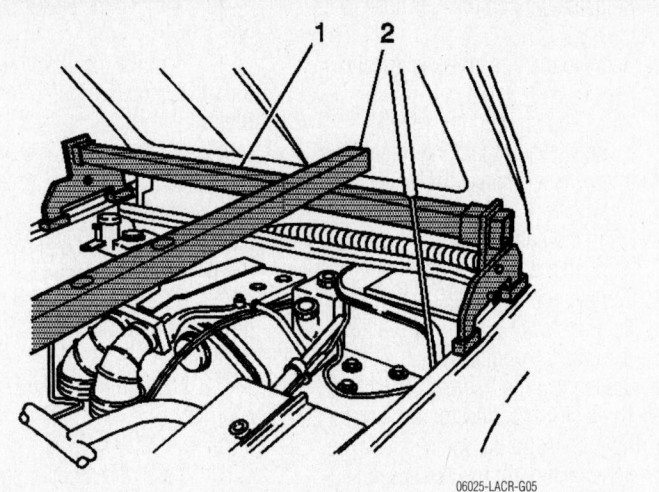

Fig. 57 Install the radiator shelf tube J 28467-2A (2) on top of the strut tower tube J 28467-3 (1) above the engine front (right bank) lift bracket—3.6L engine

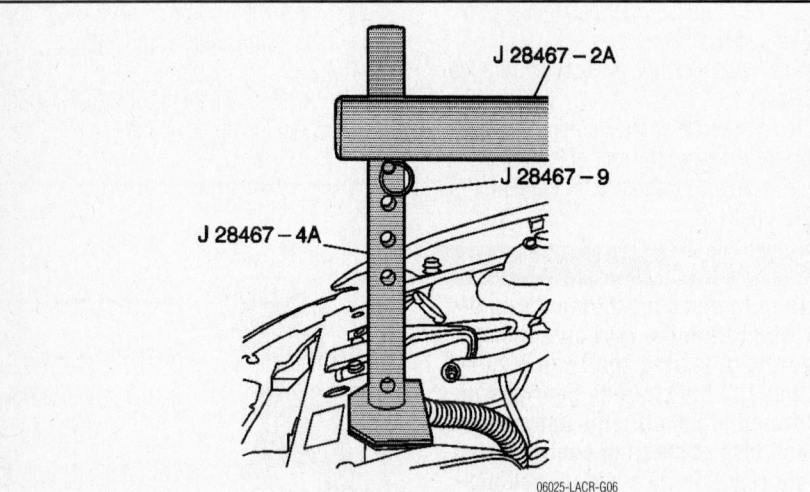

J 28467 — 2A

J 28467 — 9

J 28467 — 4A

Fig. 58 Install the round tube of the front support assembly J 28467-4A through the large hole in the radiator shelf tube J 28467-2A—3.6L engine

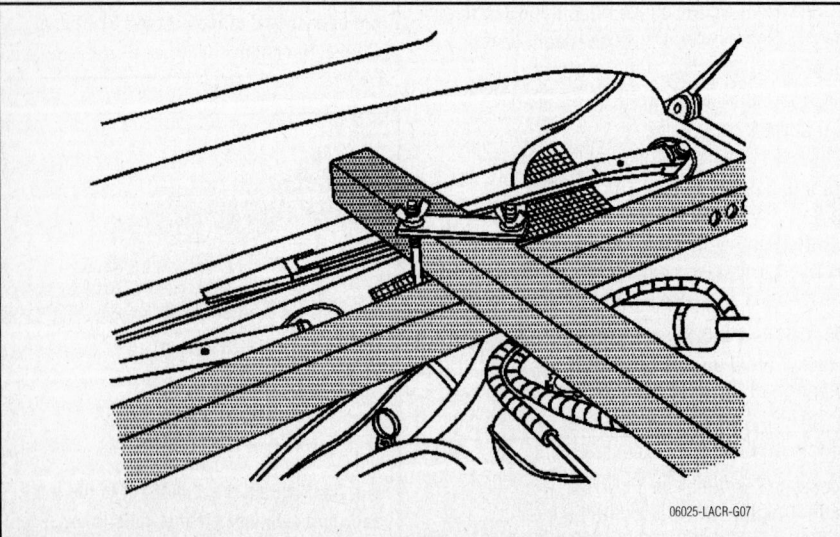

Fig. 59 Install the J 28467-1A cross bracket assembly—3.6L engine

54. Install the J 28467-9 7/16 in x 2.0 in quick-release pin through the top hole in the J 28467-4A front support assembly.

55. Install the J 28467-1A cross bracket assembly.

56. Assemble the following to create 2 lift hook assemblies as shown:
- J 28467-34
- J 28467-6A
- J 28467-7A

57. Install the 2 lift hook assemblies to the J 45057-2.

58. Install the LH engine mount strut nuts and bolts to the strut brackets.

59. Install the RH engine lift hook through the power steering reservoir bracket.

60. Gently tighten the J 28467-34 lift hook wing nuts to support powertrain.

61. Raise and support the vehicle.

62. Remove the front tires and wheels.

63. Remove and discard the two plastic braces from the front of the radiator lower air deflector. The plastic braces are directly below the front cradle bolts.

64. Remove the positive battery cable and the retainers from the frame and position aside.

65. Disconnect the power steering return hose from the frame.

66. Secure the power steering return hose.

67. Remove the control links and rotate the stabilizer shaft upward to gain access to the mounting bolts in the power steering gear.

68. Remove the mounting bolts from the power steering gear.

69. Secure the power steering gear.

70. Remove the nuts that secure the engine mount to the frame.

71. Remove the nuts which secure the transaxle mount to the frame.

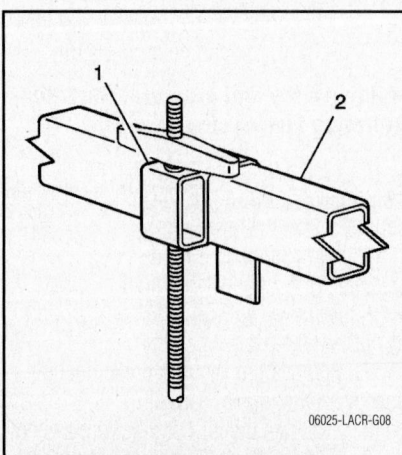

Fig. 60 Create 2 lift hook assemblies as shown—3.6L engine

06025-LACR-G09

Fig. 61 Install the 2 lift hook assemblies—3.6L engine

72. If applicable, disconnect the front wheel speed sensor harness connectors.

73. If applicable, disconnect the wheel speed sensor harness from the frame and lower control arms.

74. If applicable, remove the retainers at the front wheel speed harness from the frame and from the lower control arms.

75. Separate both of the lower ball joints from the steering knuckle.

76. Remove both front drivetrain reinforcements using the following procedure.

 a. Remove the drivetrain reinforcement to support brace bolts.

 b. Remove the drivetrain reinforcement to front cradle mounting stud nut.

 c. Remove the drivetrain reinforcement from the vehicle.

77. Lower the vehicle until the frame contacts the J 39580.

78. Remove the bolts which secure the front frame to the body.

79. Remove the bolts which secure the rear frame to the body.

80. Raise the vehicle in order to separate the frame from the body.

81. Carefully raise the vehicle or lower the powertrain table in order to remove the powertrain from the vehicle.

82. Remove the exhaust crossover pipe.

83. Remove the coolant inlet pipe.

84. Remove the power steering pressure pipe/hose from the pump.

85. Remove the power steering cooler lines from the reservoir.

86. Remove the accessory drive belt.

87. Disconnect the electrical harness clip at the underhood junction block and at the coolant reservoir.

88. Disconnect the Engine Control Module (ECM) wire harness from the ECM wire harness clip on the reservoir.

89. Disconnect the power steering hoses from the power steering reservoir.

90. Remove the power steering reservoir and bracket bolts, and remove the reservoir and bracket assembly from the vehicle.

91. Cap off the power steering reservoir and hoses to prevent contamination.

92. Remove the transaxle lower brace.

93. Remove the transaxle upper brace nut located behind the power steering pump.

94. Remove the engine to transaxle (bell housing) bolts.

95. Use 4 M1 0x1.5x40 GM P/N 11519182, or equivalent bolts to install the engine lift brackets to the left rear and right front cylinder heads. Tighten the lift bracket bolts to 48 ft. lbs. (65 Nm).

96. Use an engine hoist in order to separate the engine from the transaxle and the frame.

97. Install the engine to a suitable engine stand.

To install:

98. Use an engine hoist in order to remove the engine from the engine stand.

99. Install the engine to the transaxle and the frame at the powertrain lift table.

100. Remove the engine lift brackets.

101. Install the engine to transaxle (bell housing) bolts. Install the torque converter bolts. Tighten the bolts to 46 ft. lbs. (63 Nm). Install the transaxle bolts and the stud.

Tighten the bolts and the stud to 55 ft. lbs. (75 Nm).

102. Install the transaxle upper brace nut located behind the power steering pump.

103. Tighten the transaxle upper brace nut to 37 ft. lbs. (50 Nm).

104. Install the transaxle lower brace. Install the transaxle brace bolts to the transaxle. Tighten the transaxle brace bolts to the transaxle to 32 ft. lbs. (43 Nm).

105. Install the transaxle brace bolts to the engine. Tighten the transaxle brace bolts to the engine to 46 ft. lbs. (63 Nm).

106. Uncap the power steering reservoir and hoses .

107. Install the power steering reservoir and bracket to the vehicle. Tighten the M6 bolt to 80 inch lbs. (9 Nm). Tighten the M8 bolt to 18 ft. lbs. (25 Nm).

108. Connect the power steering reservoir hoses to the power steering reservoir.

109. Install the coolant recovery reservoir.

110. Connect the ECM wire harness to the ECM wire harness clip on the reservoir.

111. Connect the electrical harness clip at the underhood junction block and coolant reservoir.

112. Install the accessory drive belt.

113. Install the coolant inlet pipe.

114. Install the exhaust crossover pipe. Torque all fasteners to 18 ft. lbs. (44 Nm).

115. Carefully lower the vehicle or raise the powertrain table in order to install the powertrain to the vehicle.

116. Position the engine support table with the frame under the vehicle.

117. Lower the vehicle to the frame.

118. Loosely install the bolts to secure the rear frame to the body.

119. Loosely install the bolts to secure the front frame to the body.

120. Align the frame to the body by inserting two 0.74 by 8 in. (19 by 203mm) pins in the alignment holes on the right side of the frame.

121. Install the front and rear frame bolts. Tighten the front bolts to 107 ft. lbs. (145 Nm). Tighten the rear bolts to 118 ft. lbs. (160 Nm).

122. Install the drivetrain reinforcements using the following procedure:

 a. Position the drivetrain reinforcements to the font cradle mount stud to the support brace.

 b. Loosely install the drivetrain reinforcement to support brace bolts.

123. Install the drivetrain reinforcement to cradle mount nut. Tighten the drivetrain reinforcement brace nut to 37 ft. lbs. (50 Nm). Tighten the drivetrain reinforcement brace bolts to 18 ft. lbs. (25 Nm).

124. Connect both the lower ball joints to the steering knuckle.

125. Install the nuts that secure the engine mount to the frame. Tighten the engine mount upper nuts to 39 ft. lbs. (53 Nm).

126. Install the nuts which secure the transaxle mount to the frame. Tighten the transaxle mount lower nuts to 46 ft. lbs. (63 Nm). Tighten the transaxle mount upper nuts to 35 ft. lbs. (47 Nm).

127. Install the steering gear mounting bolts.

128. Install the control links.

129. If applicable, connect the wheel speed sensor wiring harness to the frame and lower control arm.

130. If applicable, connect the front wheel speed sensor connectors.

131. If applicable, install the front wheel speed harness retainers to the frame and to the lower control arm.

132. Install the positive battery cable and retainers to the frame.

133. Install the power steering cooler pipe.

134. Connect the fog lamp harness connectors.

135. Install the front tires and wheels.

136. Lower the vehicle.

137. Raise the vehicle and remove the powertrain lift table.

�֍֍ CAUTION

Failure to disconnect the intermediate shaft from the rack and pinion steering gear stub shaft can result in damage to the steering gear and/or intermediate shaft. This damage may cause loss of steering control which could result in an accident and possible personal injury

138. Install the intermediate steering shaft to the steering gear.

139. Rotate the struts and install the drive axles to the transaxle.

140. Install the lower ball joints to the knuckles.

141. Install the tie rod ends to the steering knuckles.

142. Install the front wheel speed sensor wiring harnesses to the lower control arms and the frame.

143. Connect the VSS electrical connector and secure the wiring harness to the vehicle.

144. Install the engine splash shields.

145. Install lower radiator air baffle.

146. Install the front tires and wheels.

147. Install the catalytic converter. Tighten the nuts to 44 ft. lbs. (60 Nm).

148. Install the torque converter bolts as necessary.

149. Lower the vehicle.

150. Fill the engine oil as necessary.

151. Install the transaxle electrical connector.

152. Install the A/C compressor hose to the A/C compressor. Tighten the nut to 13 ft. lbs. (17 Nm).

153. Recharge the air conditioning system.

154. Install the brake booster vacuum hose to the intake manifold.

155. Install the transaxle ground wire and the bolt. Tighten the transaxle ground bolt 55 ft. lbs. (75 Nm).

156. Install the ECM chassis (outboard) side electrical connector to the ECM.

157. Connect the fuel pressure and EVAP pipes to the engine.

158. Install the engine mount struts. Tighten engine mount strut nuts to 35 ft. lbs. (48 Nm).

159. Connect the heater hoses to the engine.

160. Connect the radiator hoses to the engine.

161. Fill the cooling system.

162. Connect the battery positive cable to the alternator and the starter.

163. Connect the battery negative cable to the engine block.

164. Install the throttle body air inlet duct.

165. Connect the battery negative cable to the battery.

166. Fill the power steering reservoir with power steering fluid.

167. Bleed the power steering system.

168. Inspect the system for leaks.

3.8L Engine

1. Before servicing the vehicle, refer to the Precautions Section.

2. Disconnect the negative battery cable.

3. Remove the hood.

4. Relieve the fuel system pressure.

5. Drain the coolant system and crankcase.

6. Remove or disconnect the following:
- Negative cable
- Fuel injector sight shield
- Vacuum brake booster hose from the vacuum connections
- Fuel feed and return lines from the fuel rail
- Evaporative emission canister purge valve
- Cruise control cable from the throttle body bracket and lever

- Electrical connector from the cruise control module
- Cruise control module from the mounting studs

➡**Always replace the accelerator control cable with a NEW cable whenever you remove the engine from the vehicle.**

- Accelerator control cable
- Accessory drive belt
- Bolt securing both the battery negative cable and the engine harness ground lead to the engine block

7. Disconnect the wiring harness connectors from the following components:
- A/C compressor clutch
- A/C pressure sensor
- Knock Sensor (KS)
- Engine coolant block heater
- Oil level sensor

8. Remove or disconnect the following:
- Wiring harness from the harness clip at the rear of the A/C compressor
- Torque converter cover
- Starter motor
- Bolts securing the flywheel to the torque converter

9. Disconnect then secure the following wiring harness electrical connectors to the cowl panel:
- Knock Sensor (KS) number 2 which can be found behind the right exhaust manifold
- Oil pressure sensor
- Vehicle Speed Sensor (VSS)

10. Remove or disconnect the following:
- Bolts securing the transaxle brace to the transaxle
- Nuts attaching the exhaust manifold pipe to the right exhaust manifold
- Exhaust manifold pipe from the right exhaust manifold studs, allowing it to rest on top of the power steering gear heat shield
- Exhaust manifold pipe gasket and discard the gasket
- Right wheelhouse extension
- Font A/C compressor mounting nuts
- Rear A/C compressor mounting bolt
- Compressor off of the mounting studs and rest on top of the engine frame
- Bolt securing the Powertrain Control Module (PCM) ground located at the left front cylinder head

11. Disconnect the wiring harness electrical connectors from the following components on the left side of the engine:

- Fuel injectors
- Ignition harness
- Boost control solenoid (VIN I only)
- Engine Coolant Temperature (ECT) sensor
- Throttle Position (TP) sensor
- Idle Air Control (IAC) valve
- Mass Air Flow (MAF) sensor

12. Disconnect the wiring harness connectors from the following components on the right side of the engine:
- Fuel injectors
- Exhaust Gas Recirculation (EGR) valve
- Manifold Absolute Pressure (MAP) sensor
- Heated Oxygen (O_2S) sensor
- AIR solenoid, if equipped
- Alternator

13. Remove or disconnect the following:
- Alternator
- Air cleaner intake duct

14. Attach an engine support fixture.
- Front power steering pump mounting bolts
- Side power steering pump mounting bolt and piston the power steering pump against the cowl, allowing it to rest on top of the transaxle housing
- Right engine mount bracket
- Right lower engine to transaxle mounting bolt
- Coolant and heater hoses

15. Use a block of wood between a floor jack and the transaxle, support the transaxle at the pan.

16. Remove the engine support fixture.

17. Attach an engine lift chain to the engine lift brackets and attach to an engine lift device.

18. Remove all remaining engine to transaxle bolts

19. Remove the engine from the vehicle.

To install:

20. Installation is the reverse of removal, please note the following torques:
- 5 upper engine to transaxle mounting bolts to 55 ft. lbs. (75 Nm)
- Right lower engine to transaxle mounting bolt to 55 ft. lbs. (75 Nm)
- Power steering pump bolts to 20 ft. lbs. (27 Nm)
- Bolt attaching the PCM ground to the left front cylinder head and tighten to 37 ft. lbs. (50 Nm)
- A/C compressor bolts 37 ft. lbs. (50 Nm)
- Transaxle brace bolts to 48 ft. lbs.(65 Nm)

- Flywheel to torque converter bolts to 46 ft. lbs. (63 Nm)

21. Refill the crankcase.

22. Refill and bleed the engine cooling system.

23. Start the engine and check for leaks.

24. Road test the vehicle and check operation.

EXHAUST MANIFOLD

REMOVAL & INSTALLATION

3.6L Engine

Left Side

See Figure 62.

1. Before servicing the vehicle, refer to the Precautions Section.

2. Remove the left torque strut bracket bolts.

3. Remove the left torque strut bracket.

4. Remove the left exhaust manifold heat shield bolts.

5. Remove the left exhaust manifold heat shield.

6. Remove the Engine Coolant Temperature (ECT) sensor.

7. Remove the exhaust manifold bolts from the left cylinder head.

8. Remove the left exhaust manifold.

9. Remove and discard the exhaust manifold gasket.

To install:

10. Position a NEW exhaust manifold gasket onto the left exhaust manifold.

11. Install the exhaust manifold bolts into the left exhaust manifold.

12. Place the left exhaust manifold, exhaust manifold gasket and bolts as an assembly in position on the left cylinder head.

13. Install the exhaust manifold bolts into the left cylinder head. Tighten the exhaust manifold bolts to 18 ft. lbs. (25 Nm).

14. Install the Engine Coolant Temperature (ECT) sensor. Tighten the ECT sensor to 16 ft. lbs. (22 Nm).

15. Install NEW O-rings on the crankshaft position sensor.

16. Place the left exhaust manifold heat shield in position.

17. Install the exhaust manifold heat shield bolts. Tighten the exhaust manifold heat shield bolts to 89 inch lbs. (10 Nm).

18. Install the left torque strut bracket.

19. Install the left torque strut bracket bolts. Tighten the left torque strut bracket bolts to 37 ft. lbs. (50 Nm).

Right Side

See Figure 63.

1. Before servicing the vehicle, refer to the Precautions Section.

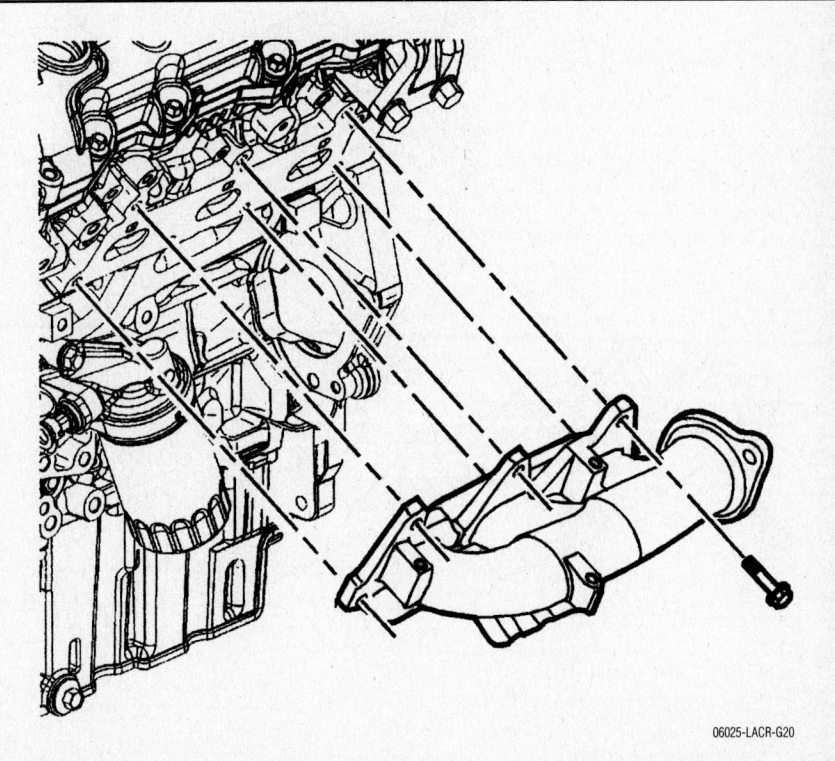

Fig. 62 Left side exhaust manifold—3.6L engine

06025-LACR-G20

2. Remove the right exhaust manifold heat shield bolts.

3. Remove the right exhaust manifold heat shield.

4. Remove the exhaust manifold bolts from the right cylinder head.

5. Remove the right exhaust manifold.

6. Remove and discard the exhaust manifold gasket.

To install:

7. Position a NEW exhaust manifold gasket onto the right exhaust manifold.

8. Install the exhaust manifold bolts into the right exhaust manifold.

9. Place the right exhaust manifold, exhaust manifold gasket and bolts as an assembly in position on the right cylinder head.

10. Install the exhaust manifold bolts into the right cylinder head. Tighten the exhaust manifold bolts to 18 ft. lbs. (25 Nm).

11. Place the right exhaust manifold heat shield in position.

12. Install the exhaust manifold heat shield bolts. Tighten the exhaust manifold heat shield bolts to 89 inch lbs. (10 Nm).

3.8L Engine

Left Side (Front) Manifold

See Figure 64.

1. Before servicing the vehicle, refer to the Precautions Section.

2. Remove or disconnect the following:
- Negative battery cable
- Spark plug wires
- Engine oil dipstick and tube
- Left side lift bracket, if necessary

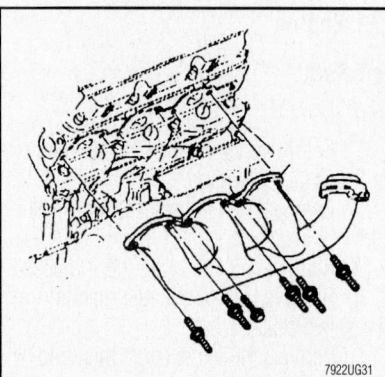

Fig. 64 Exploded view of the left exhaust manifold mounting—3.8L engine

- 2 bolts attaching the left exhaust manifold to the crossover pipe
- Exhaust manifold

To install:

3. Install or connect the following:
- Exhaust manifold with a new gasket. Torque the studs and bolts gradually and evenly to 22 ft. lbs. (30 Nm).
- 2 bolts attaching the left exhaust manifold to the crossover pipe. Torque the bolts to 15 ft. lbs. (20 Nm).
- Left side lift bracket, if removed
- Engine oil dipstick and tube. Torque the bolts to 15 ft. lbs. (20 Nm).
- Spark plug wires
- Negative battery cable

4. Run the engine and check for exhaust leaks.

Right Side (Rear) Manifold

1. Before servicing the vehicle, refer to the Precautions Section.

2. Remove or disconnect the following:
- Negative battery cable
- Fuel injector sight shield
- Air cleaner assembly
- Spark plug wires
- Brake booster heat shield
- Crossover pipe
- Engine harness from the right hand engine lift hook bracket
- Transaxle fluid dipstick and tube
- Oxygen (O_2S) sensor
- Exhaust Gas Recirculation (EGR) feed pipe bolt from the manifold
- Transaxle oil level tube and seal
- Exhaust manifold flange nuts
- Front exhaust pipe
- Engine lift bracket
- Exhaust manifold

To install:

3. Install or connect the following:
- Manifold to the cylinder head and crossover pipe using new gaskets
- Manifold mounting studs. Torque the studs and bolts to 22 ft. lbs. (30 Nm), beginning at the center and working outwards.
- Engine lift bracket
- Front exhaust pipe
- Front exhaust pipe to manifold nuts. Torque the nuts to 22 ft. lbs. (30 Nm).
- Transaxle dipstick tube seal and the tube
- EGR feed pipe to the manifold
- O_2S sensor
- Spark plug wires to the spark plugs

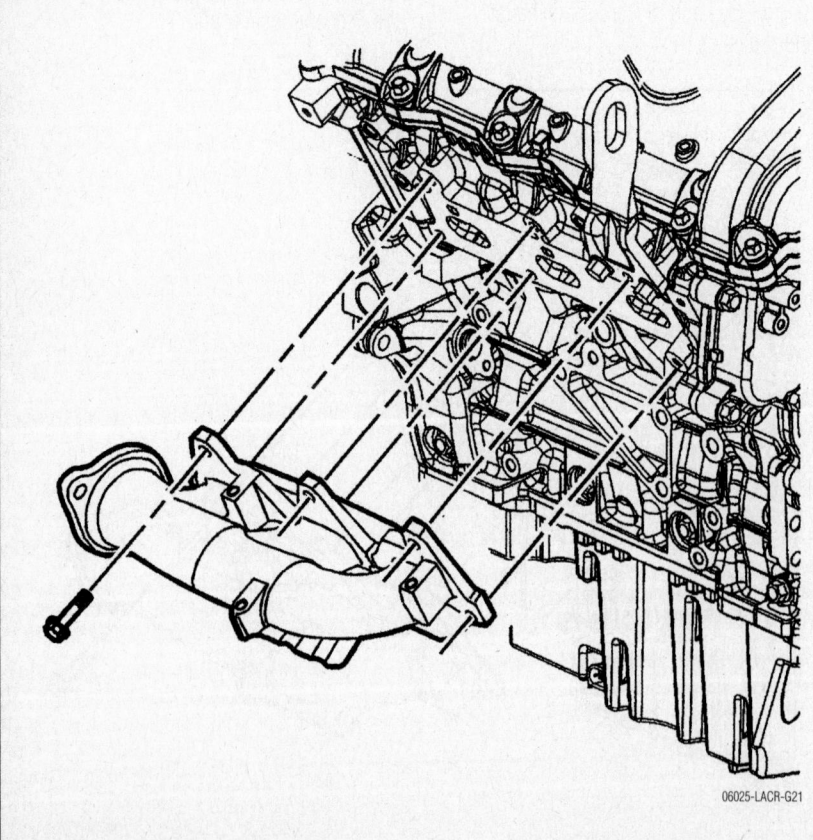

Fig. 63 Right side exhaust manifold—3.6L engine

- Engine harness to the right hand engine lift hook bracket
- Crossover pipe
- Brake booster heat shield
- Air cleaner assembly
- Fuel injector sight shield
- Negative battery cable

4. Run the engine and check for exhaust leaks.

INTAKE MANIFOLD

REMOVAL & INSTALLATION

3.6L Engine

Upper Manifold

See Figure 65.

1. Before servicing the vehicle, refer to the Precautions Section.
2. Turn the ignition OFF.
3. Remove the air inlet duct.
4. Relieve the fuel system pressure.
5. Remove the fuel pressure and Evaporative Emission (EVAP) hoses from the engine.
6. Remove the purge line from the purge line retainer.
7. Remove the fuel feed hose bracket bolt and reposition the fuel feed hose.

➡**Do not disconnect the Engine Control Module (ECM) electrical connectors. Do not remove the ECM from the ECM bracket.**

8. Remove the ECM bracket with the ECM and position it aside.
9. Disconnect the purge solenoid electrical connector.
10. Remove the wiring harness from the right side of the intake manifold.
11. Disconnect the fuel injector electrical connector.
12. Remove the fuel injector electrical connector from the fuel injector electrical connector bracket.
13. Remove the throttle body electrical connector.
14. Remove the brake booster vacuum hose and check valve from the brake booster.
15. Remove the electrical connector for the baro sensor.
16. Remove the positive Crankcase Ventilation (PCV) hose from the intake manifold.
17. Remove the intake manifold bolts.
18. Remove the upper intake manifold.
19. Remove and discard the upper intake manifold gasket.
20. Clean and inspect the intake manifold and the sealing surfaces.

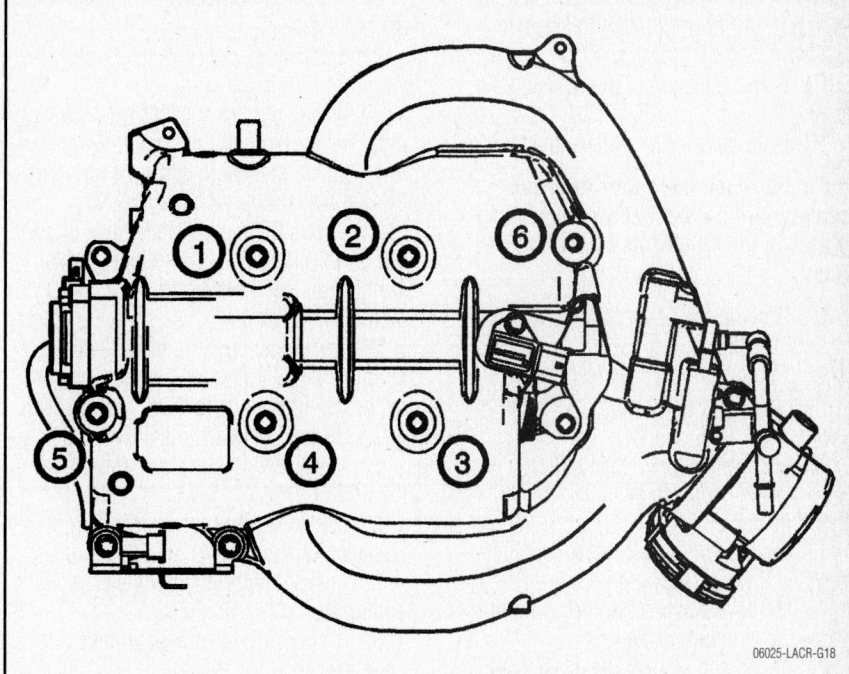

06025-LACR-G18

Fig. 65 Upper intake manifold bolt loosening/tightening sequence—3.6L engine

To install:

21. Install the intake manifold bolts. Tighten the intake manifold bolts in the order shown to 17 ft. lbs. (23 Nm).
22. Install the PCV hose to the intake manifold.
23. Install the brake booster vacuum hose and check valve to the brake booster.
24. Install the throttle body electrical connector.
25. Reconnect the electrical connector for the baro sensor.
26. Install the fuel injector electrical connector to the fuel injector electrical connector bracket.
27. Install the ECM bracket.
28. Connect the fuel injector electrical connector.
29. Install the wiring harness and bracket to the right side of the intake manifold. Tighten the wiring harness bracket bolts to 89 inch lbs. (10 Nm).
30. Connect the purge solenoid electrical connector.

❋❋ WARNING

In order to prevent any possible electrostatic discharge damage to the ECM, do not touch the connector pins.

31. Install the fuel feed hose bracket and the fuel feed hose bracket bolt. Tighten the fuel feed hose bracket bolt to 89 inch lbs. (10 Nm).

32. Install the purge line to the purge line retainer.
33. Install the fuel pressure and EVAP hoses to the engine.
34. Install the air inlet duct.

Lower Manifold

See Figure 66.

1. Before servicing the vehicle, refer to the Precautions Section.
2. Turn the ignition OFF.
3. Remove the air inlet duct.
4. Remove the fuel pressure and Evaporative Emission (EVAP) hoses from the engine.
5. Disconnect the BARO sensor electrical connector.

➡**Do not disconnect the Engine Control Module (ECM) electrical connectors.**

6. Remove the ECM bracket with the ECM and reposition aside.
7. Disconnect the purge solenoid electrical connector.
8. Disconnect the purge solenoid electrical connector.
9. Remove the wiring harness from the right side of the intake manifold.
10. Disconnect the fuel injector electrical connector.
11. Remove the throttle body electrical connector.
12. Remove the brake booster vacuum hose and check valve from the brake booster.

13. Remove the positive Crankcase Ventilation (PCV) hose from the intake manifold.

14. Remove the upper intake manifold bolts.

15. Remove the upper intake manifold.

➡ **Do not reuse the upper to lower intake manifold gasket and the intake manifold to cylinder head sealing gaskets.**

16. Remove the upper to lower intake manifold bolts.

17. Remove the fuel rail feed hose bracket bolts from the upper intake manifold.

18. Remove the fuel injector wiring harness bracket bolt from the upper intake manifold.

19. Remove the upper intake manifold from the lower intake manifold.

20. Remove and discard the upper to lower intake manifold gaskets.

21. Clean and inspect the intake manifold and the sealing surfaces.

To install:

➡ **Do not reuse the upper to lower intake manifold gasket and the intake manifold to cylinder head sealing gaskets.**

22. Install the NEW upper to lower intake manifold gaskets.

23. Install the upper intake manifold to the lower intake manifold.

24. Install the fuel injector wiring harness bracket bolts to the upper intake manifold. Tighten the fuel injector wiring harness bracket bolts to 89 inch lbs. (10 Nm).

25. Install the fuel rail feed hose bracket bolt to the upper intake manifold. Tighten the fuel rail feed hose bracket bolt to 89 inch lbs. (10 Nm).

26. Install the upper to lower intake manifold bolts. Tighten the upper to lower intake manifold bolts to 17 ft. lbs. (23 Nm).

27. Install the intake manifold.

28. Install the PCV hose to the intake manifold.

29. Install the brake booster vacuum hose and check valve to the brake booster.

30. Install the throttle body electrical connector.

31. Connect the fuel injector electrical connector.

32. Install the wiring harness to the right side of the intake manifold. Tighten the wiring harness bracket bolts to 89 inch lbs. (10 Nm).

33. Connect the purge solenoid electrical connector.

34. Install the ECM bracket with the ECM.

35. Connect the BARO sensor electrical connector.

36. Install the fuel pressure and EVAP hoses to the engine.

37. Install the air inlet duct.

3.8L Engine

See Figures 67 through 69.

1. Before servicing the vehicle, refer to the Precautions Section.

2. Disconnect the negative battery cable.

3. Drain the cooling system.

4. Relieve the fuel system pressure.

5. Remove or disconnect the following:
   - Fuel injector sight shield
   - Air inlet duct
   - Spark plug wires from the right side
   - Manifold Absolute Pressure (MAP) sensor
   - Vacuum lines from the intake manifold
   - Fuel lines
   - Fuel injector electrical connectors
   - Fuel regulator vacuum line
   - Fuel rail from the intake manifold
   - Exhaust Gas Recirculation (EGR) heat shield
   - Throttle cable bracket from the cylinder head mounting bracket and the throttle body cables
   - Throttle body support bracket
   - Upper intake plenum and gasket
   - Thermostat housing
   - Electrical connector from the Engine Coolant Temperature (ECT) sensor
   - Accessory drive belt tensioner assembly
   - EGR valve outlet pipe
   - Lower intake manifold

To install:

6. Install or connect the following:
   - Intake manifold using new manifold gaskets. Torque the bolts in sequence to 11 ft. lbs. (15 Nm); then, re-torque to 11 ft. lbs. (15 Nm).
   - EGR valve outlet pipe
   - Accessory drive belt tensioner assembly. Torque the tensioner bolts to 37 ft. lbs. (50 Nm).
   - Electrical connector to the ECT sensor
   - Thermostat housing
   - Upper intake plenum. Torque the intake plenum bolts to 88 inch. lbs. (10 Nm).
   - Throttle body support bracket

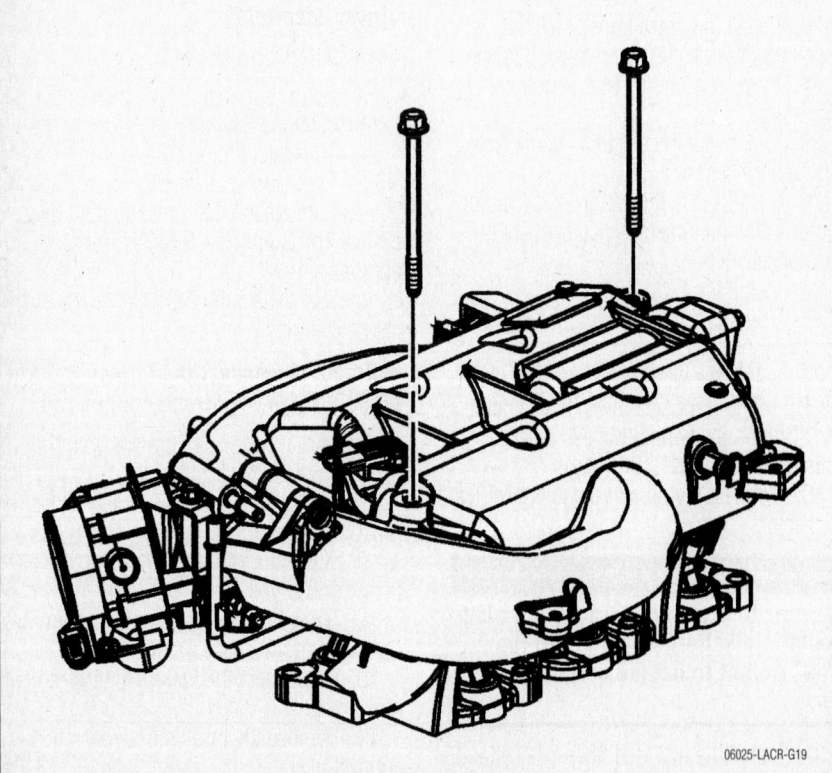

06025-LACR-G19

Fig. 66 Upper-to-lower manifold bolts—3.6L engine

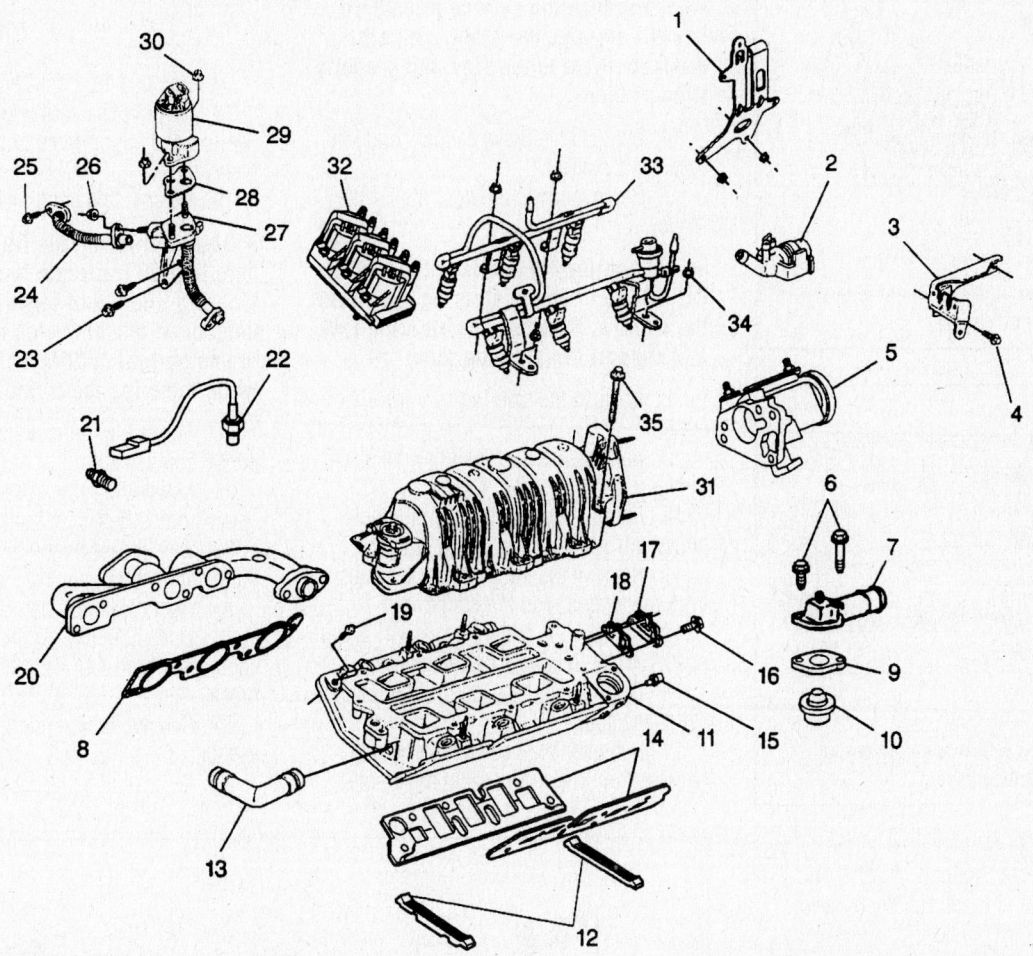

1. Fuel Injector Sight Shield Bracket
2. Vacuum Source Manifold
3. Accelerator Cable Control Bracket
4. Throttle Body Support Bolt
5. Throttle Body
6. Water Outlet Bolt
7. Water Outlet
8. Exhaust Manifold Gasket
9. Water Outlet Gasket
10. Thermostat
11. Lower Intake Manifold
12. Intake Manifold Seal
13. Heater Water Inlet Pipe
14. Lower Intake Manifold Gasket
15. Coolant Temperature Sensor
16. Engine Coolant Manifold Bolt
17. Engine Coolant Manifold
18. Engine Coolant Manifold Gasket
19. Lower Intake Manifold Bolt
20. Exhaust Manifold (Right)
21. Exhaust Manifold Bolt/Stud
22. Exhaust Oxygen Sensor
23. EGR Valve Adapter Bolt
24. EGR Valve Outlet Pipe
25. EGR Valve Outlet Pipe Bolt
26. EGR Valve Outlet Pipe Nut
27. EGR Valve Adapter
28. EGR Valve Gasket
29. EGR Valve
30. EGR Valve Nut
31. Upper Intake Manifold
32. ICM
33. Fuel Injection Rail
34. Fuel Injector Rail Nut
35. Upper Intake Manifold Bolt

9300UG02

Fig. 67 Exploded view of the intake manifold and related components—3.8L engine

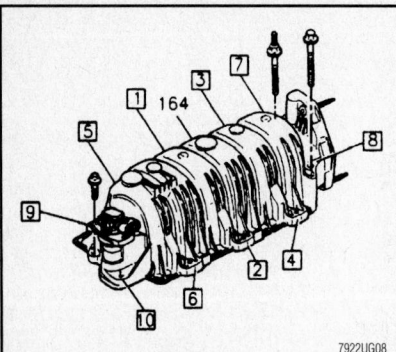

Fig. 68 Upper intake manifold torque sequence—3.8L engine

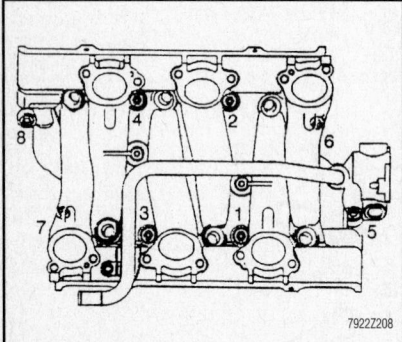

Fig. 69 Lower intake manifold torque sequence—3.8L engine

- Throttle cable bracket to the cylinder head mounting bracket and the cables to the throttle body lever
- EGR heat shield
- Fuel rail. Torque the fuel rail bolts to 88 inch. lbs. (10 Nm).
- Fuel lines
- Fuel regulator vacuum line
- Fuel injector electrical connectors
- Vacuum lines to the intake manifold
- MAP sensor
- Spark plug wires
- Fuel injector sight shield and air inlet duct
- Negative battery cable

7. Refill and bleed the cooling system.

8. Run the engine and check for leaks and proper engine operation.

OIL PAN

REMOVAL & INSTALLATION

3.6L Engine

See Figures 70 through 73.

1. Before servicing the vehicle, refer to the Precautions Section.

2. Remove the tires and wheels.

3. Remove the oil level indicator.

4. Remove the engine splash shields.

5. Drain the engine of oil.

➡ **In the following service procedure, DO NOT remove the brake calipers. Relocate them to the side and properly support them.**

6. Remove the brake calipers and relocate to the side.

7. Remove the retaining bolts for the struts.

➡ **In the following service procedure, DO NOT remove the steering rack from the vehicle. Relocate the steering rack and support the steering rack.**

8. Remove the steering rack from the cradle.

9. Remove the tie rods from the steering knuckle.

10. Remove the power steering cooler lines from the retainers on the cradle.

11. Remove the transaxle cooler lines from the retainers on the cradle.

12. Remove the battery cable wiring harness from the retainers on the cradle.

13. Disconnect the speed sensor electrical connectors.

14. Remove the speed sensor wiring harness from the retainers on the cradle.

15. Install the engine support fixture. See the procedure under Engine Removal & Installation.

16. Remove the right engine mount nuts.

17. Remove the transaxle mount bolts.

18. Remove the engine mount struts. See the procedure under Engine Removal & Installation.

19. Remove the cradle mounting bolts.

➡ **Before lowering the frame, make sure that all transaxle lines, power steering lines, and electrical harness have been disconnected and relocated to ensure that nothing will be damaged while lowering the frame.**

20. Lower the frame enough to remove the oil pan assembly.

21. Lower the frame. See the procedure under Engine Removal & Installation.

22. Disconnect the oil level senor electrical connector.

23. Remove the oil pan bolts.

24. Using the pry points on the oil pan, separate the oil pan from the engine block.

25. Remove the oil pan from the vehicle.

26. Disassemble the oil pan.

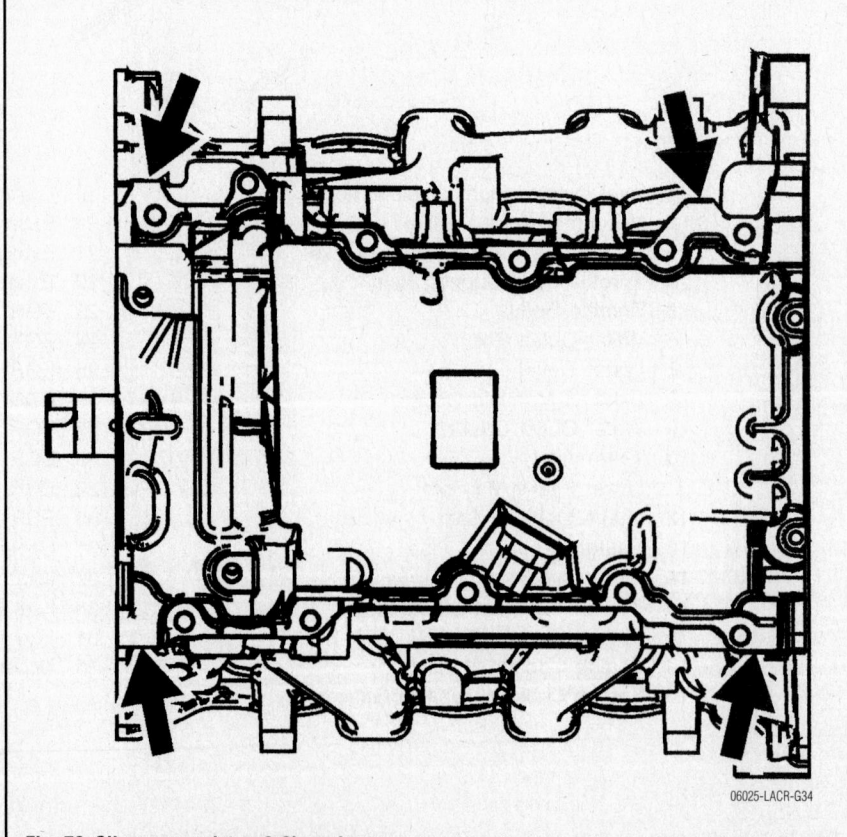

Fig. 70 Oil pan pry points—3.6L engine

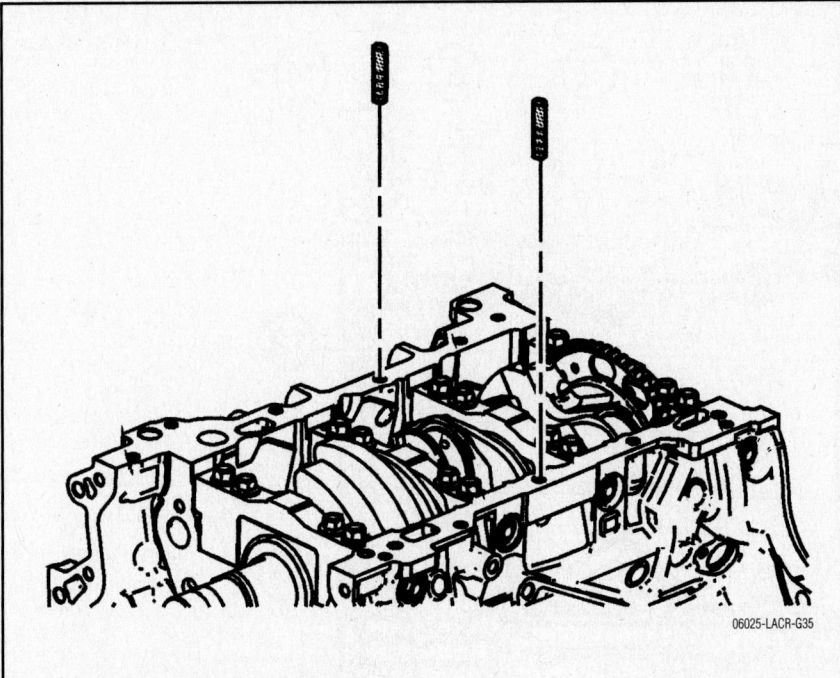

Fig. 71 Oil pan guide studs—3.6L engine

To install:

27. Install the 8mm (0.315 in.) guides from tool set EN 46109 into the center oil pan rail bolt hole on each side of the engine block.

28. Place a 3mm (0.118 in) bead (1) of RTV sealant, GM P/N 12378521 (Canadian P/N 88901148) or equivalent, on the block pan rail and the crankshaft rear oil seal housing.

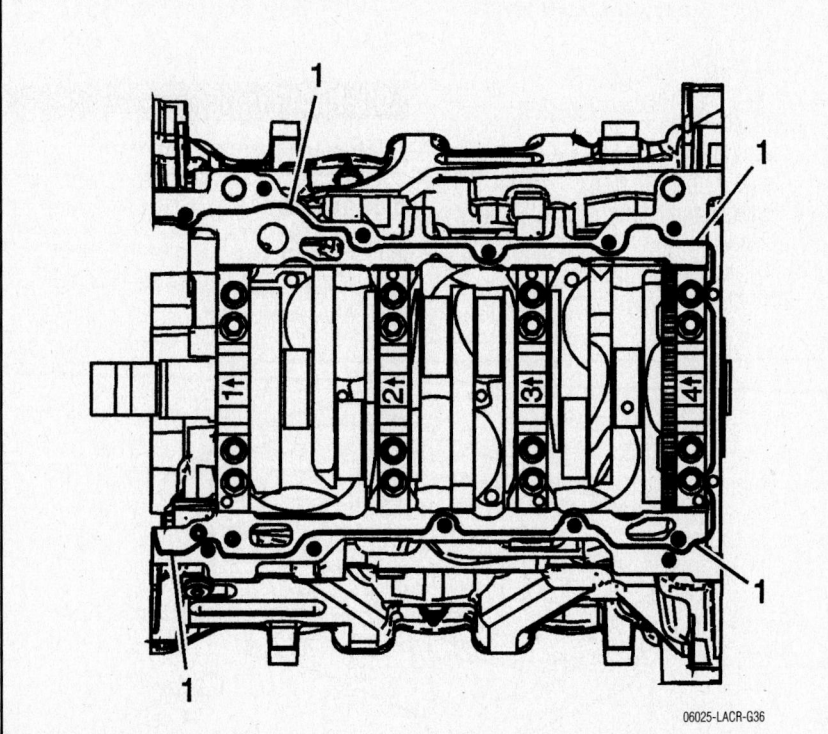

Fig. 72 Place a 3mm (0.118 in) bead (1) of RTV sealant, GM P/N 12378521 (Canadian P/N 88901148) or equivalent, on the block pan rail and the crankshaft rear oil seal housing—3.6L engine

29. Position the oil pan onto the block.
30. Remove the 8mm (0.315 in) guides from the engine block.
31. Loosely install the oil pan bolts.
32. Tighten the oil pan bolts in sequence shown.
   - Tighten the 8mm bolts (1–11) to 17 ft. lbs. (23 Nm).
   - Tighten the 6mm bolts (12, 13) to 89 inch lbs. (10 Nm).
33. Connect the oil level senor electrical connector.
34. Raise the frame. Refer to Engine Removal & Installation
35. Install the left engine mount strut.
36. Install the bolt and the nut to the engine mount strut at the engine mount strut bracket on the upper radiator support. HAND TIGHTEN ONLY.
37. Install the bolt and the nut to the engine mount strut at the left engine mount strut bracket on the engine. Tighten bolt engine mount strut nuts to 35 ft. lbs. (48 Nm).
38. Install the right engine mount strut.
39. Install the bolt and the nut to the engine mount strut at the engine mount strut bracket on the upper radiator support. HAND TIGHTEN ONLY.
40. Install the bolt and the nut to the engine mount strut at the right engine mount strut bracket on the engine. Tighten both engine mount strut nuts to 35 ft. lbs. (48 Nm).
41. Install the engine mount struts.
42. Install the transaxle mount bolts. Tighten the transaxle mount lower nuts to 46 ft. lbs. (63 Nm). Tighten the transaxle mount upper nuts to 35 ft. lbs. (47 Nm).
43. Install the right engine mount nuts. Tighten the engine mount upper nuts to 39 ft. lbs. (53 Nm).
44. Remove the engine support fixture. Refer to Engine Removal & Installation.
45. Install the battery cable wiring harness in the retainers on the cradle.
46. Install the speed sensor wiring harness in the retainers on the cradle.
47. Install the steering rack on the cradle.
48. Install the tie rods in the steering knuckle.
49. Install the retaining bolts for the struts.
50. Install the brakes calipers.
51. Install the engine splash shields.
52. Install the oil level indicator.
53. Install the tires and wheels.
54. Fill the engine with oil.

3.8L Engine

See Figure 74.

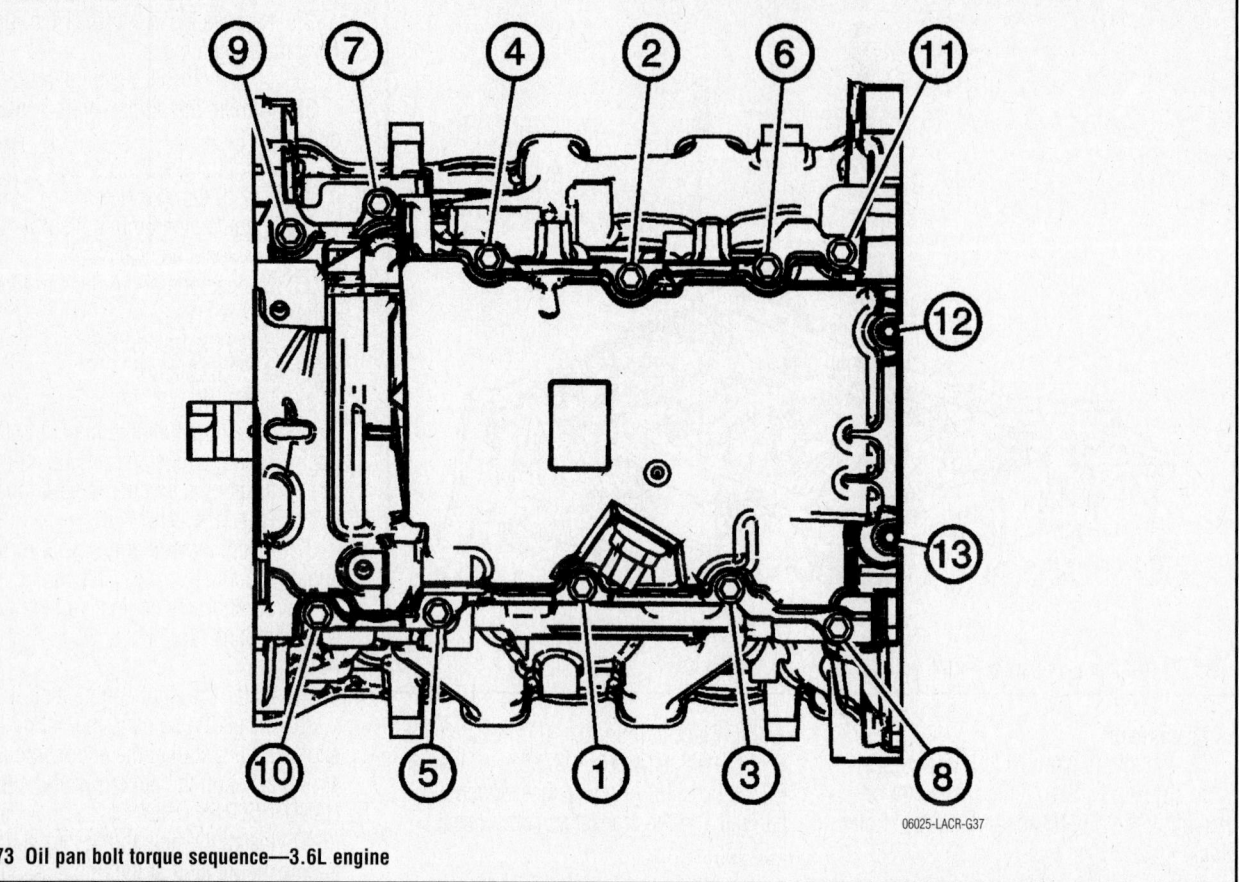

Fig. 73 Oil pan bolt torque sequence—3.6L engine

06025-LACR-G37

※※ **WARNING**

The oil level sensor, located in the oil pan, must be removed prior to removal of the oil pan. If the oil pan is removed first, damage to the oil level sensor may occur.

1. Before servicing the vehicle, refer to the Precautions Section.
2. Drain oil into an approved container.
3. Remove or disconnect the following:
   - Negative battery cable
   - Right engine mount bracket, if necessary
   - Flexplate cover
   - Oil level sensor
   - Oil filter
   - Torque axis mount bracket bolts, if necessary
   - Oil pan bolts
   - Oil pan
   - Oil pan gasket
4. Clean the oil pan and cylinder block mating surfaces.

To install:

5. Install or connect the following:
   - Oil pan with a new gasket and torque the bolts to 125 inch lbs. (14 Nm)
   - Torque axis mount bracket bolts, if removed
   - Oil filter
   - Flexplate cover
   - Oil level sensor
   - Oil drain plug and torque the plug to 30 ft. lbs. (40 Nm)
   - Right engine mount bracket, if necessary
   - Negative battery cable
6. Refill the crankcase.

7. Run the engine and check for leaks.

OIL PUMP

REMOVAL & INSTALLATION

3.6L Engine

See Figure 75.

1. Before servicing the vehicle, refer to the Precautions Section.

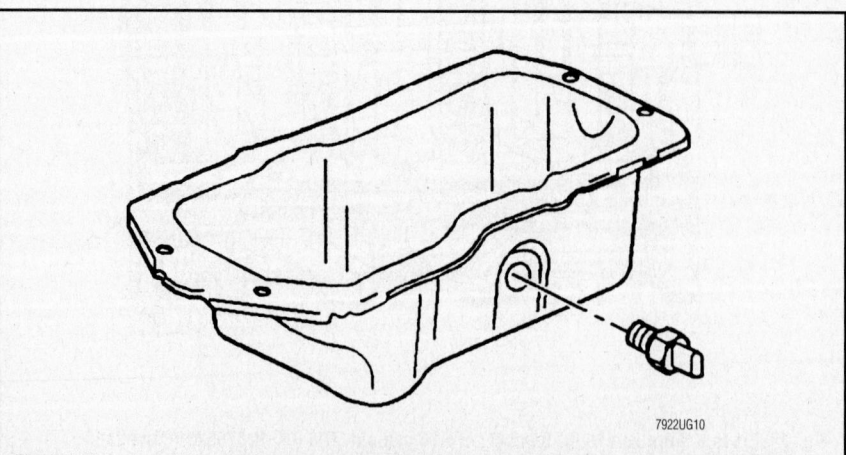

Fig. 74 If equipped, be sure to remove the oil level sensor before removing the pan—3.8L engine

7922UG10

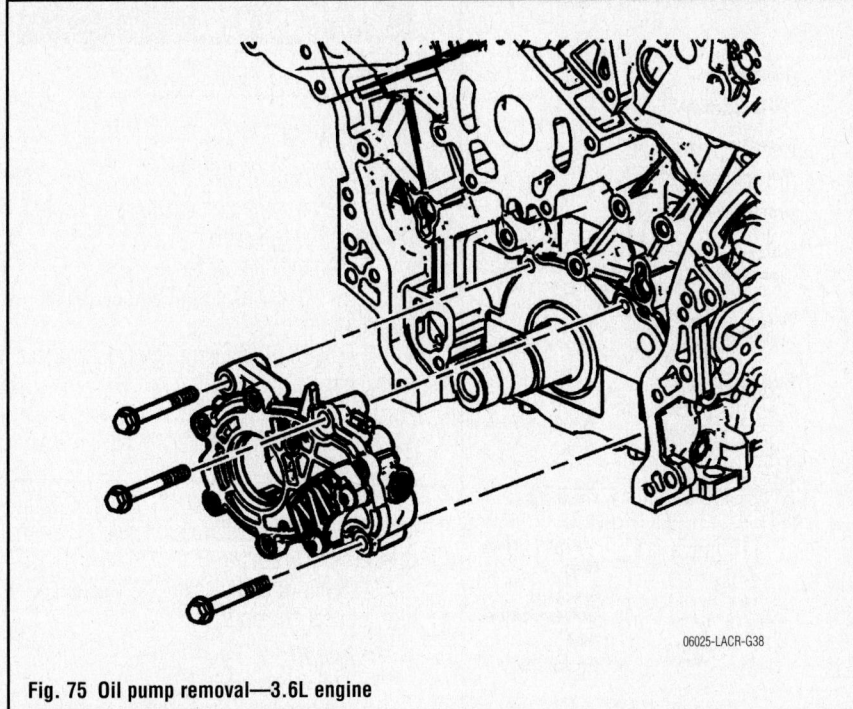

Fig. 75 Oil pump removal—3.6L engine

➡**Do not remove the left bank idler sprocket.**

2. Remove the primary timing chain.
3. Remove the crankshaft sprocket.

➡**There are no serviceable components within the oil pump. Disassemble the pump only to diagnose an oiling concern. A disassembled oil pump must not be reused. A disassembled oil pump must be replaced.**

4. Remove the oil pump bolts and the oil pump.

To install:
5. Align the oil pump gerotor with the crankshaft flats and install the oil pump to the engine block.
6. Align the pump body with the mounting holes in the cylinder block.
7. Install the oil pump bolts. Tighten the oil pump bolts to 17 ft. lbs. (23 Nm).
8. Install the crankshaft sprocket.
9. Install the primary timing chain.

3.8L Engine

See Figure 76.

1. Before servicing the vehicle, refer to the Precautions Section.
2. Support the engine using an engine support fixture.
3. Remove or disconnect the following:
   • Negative battery cable
   • Engine drive belts and tensioner assembly
   • Drive belt idler pulley and bracket

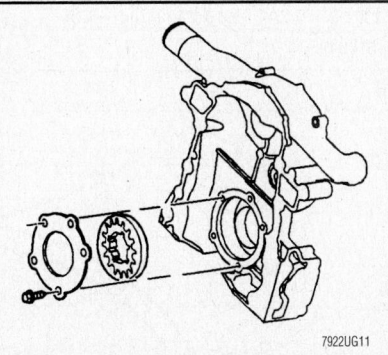

Fig. 76 The oil pump is located inside the front engine cover—3.8L engines

4. Remove or disconnect the following:
   • Torque axis mount bracket, if necessary
   • Engine front cover assembly
   • Oil filter adapter with pressure regulator valve and spring
   • Oil pump cover
   • Inner and outer pump gears

To install:
5. Lubricate the oil pump gears with petroleum jelly.
6. Install the gears into the oil pump housing.
7. Pack the gear cavity with petroleum jelly after the gears have been installed in the housing.
8. Install or connect the following:
   • Oil pump cover. Torque the screws to 97 inch lbs. (11 Nm).
   • Oil filter adapter with new gasket,

pressure regulator valve and spring. Torque the bolts to 11 ft. lbs. (15 Nm).
   • Front cover assembly
   • Tensioner assembly
   • Drive belt idler pulley and bracket, if removed
   • Drive belts
   • Torque axis mount bracket
   • Negative battery cable
9. Remove the engine support fixture.
10. Verify the correct engine oil level.
11. Start the vehicle and verify no leaks and proper oil pressure.

INSPECTION

3.6L Engine

The oil pump is not serviceable. If the oil pump fails, it must be replaced as a complete unit.

3.8L Engine

1. Use a suitable solvent to clean the oil pump.
2. Remove all old gasket material from the engine front cover and from the engine block.
3. Inspect the oil pump cover and the engine front cover for cracks, scoring, a porous or damaged casting, damaged threads or excessive wear.
4. Inspect the pressure regulator valve for scoring, burrs or foreign material or sticking in the bore.
5. Inspect the pressure regulator spring for loss of tension or bending. Replace the pressure regulator spring if damaged.
6. Inspect the oil pump gears for chipping, galling, scoring or excessive wear.
7. Measure the inner oil pump gear tip clearance. If the clearance for the inner oil pump gear tip is greater than 0.152mm (0.006 in) the oil pump must be replaced.
8. Measure the outer oil pump gear diameter clearance. If the outer oil pump gear diameter clearance is greater than 0.381mm (0.015 in) the oil pump must be replaced.
9. Measure the oil pump gear end clearance.
10. Measure the pressure regulator valve to bore clearance. If the pressure regulator valve to bore clearance is greater than 0.076mm (0.003 in) the oil pump must be replaced.

PISTON AND RING

POSITIONING

See Figures 77 through 81.

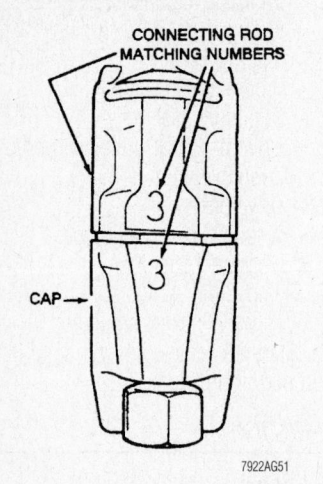

Fig. 77 Engine connecting rod and cap installation. Be sure to matchmark the cap and rod prior to disassembly, as shown.

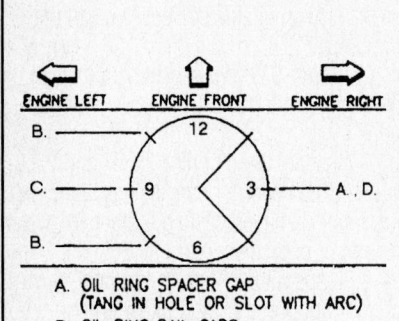

Fig. 78 Piston ring end–gap spacing— 3.8L engines

A. OIL RING SPACER GAP (TANG IN HOLE OR SLOT WITH ARC)
B. OIL RING RAIL GAPS
C. 2ND COMPRESSION RING GAP
D. TOP COMPRESSION RING GAP

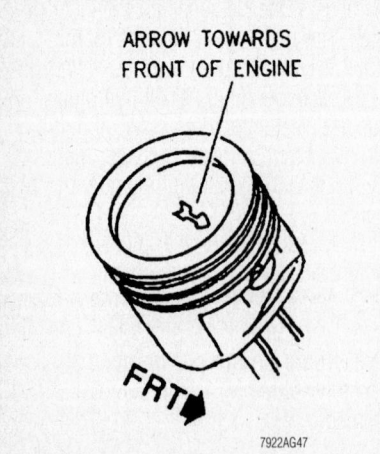

ARROW TOWARDS FRONT OF ENGINE

Fig. 79 Piston positioning. Often the arrow is replaced by a notch, which also must face toward the front of the engine— 3.8L engines

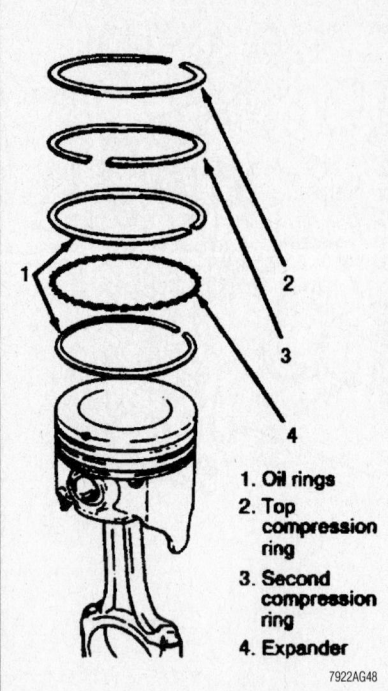

1. Oil rings
2. Top compression ring
3. Second compression ring
4. Expander

Fig. 80 Piston ring positioning—3.8L engines

REAR MAIN SEAL

REMOVAL & INSTALLATION

3.6L Engine

See Figures 82 through 84.

1. Before servicing the vehicle, refer to the Precautions Section.
2. Remove the transaxle.
3. Remove the engine flywheel bolts and discard.
4. Remove the engine flywheel from the crankshaft.
5. Remove the oil pan.
6. Remove the crankshaft rear oil seal housing bolts.
7. Using the pry points located at the edge of the crankshaft rear oil seal housing shear the RTV sealant.
8. Remove and discard the crankshaft rear oil seal housing.

To install:

9. Install the 6mm (0.236 in.) guides from kit EN 46109 into the 2 crankshaft rear oil seal housing corner bolt holes of the engine block.

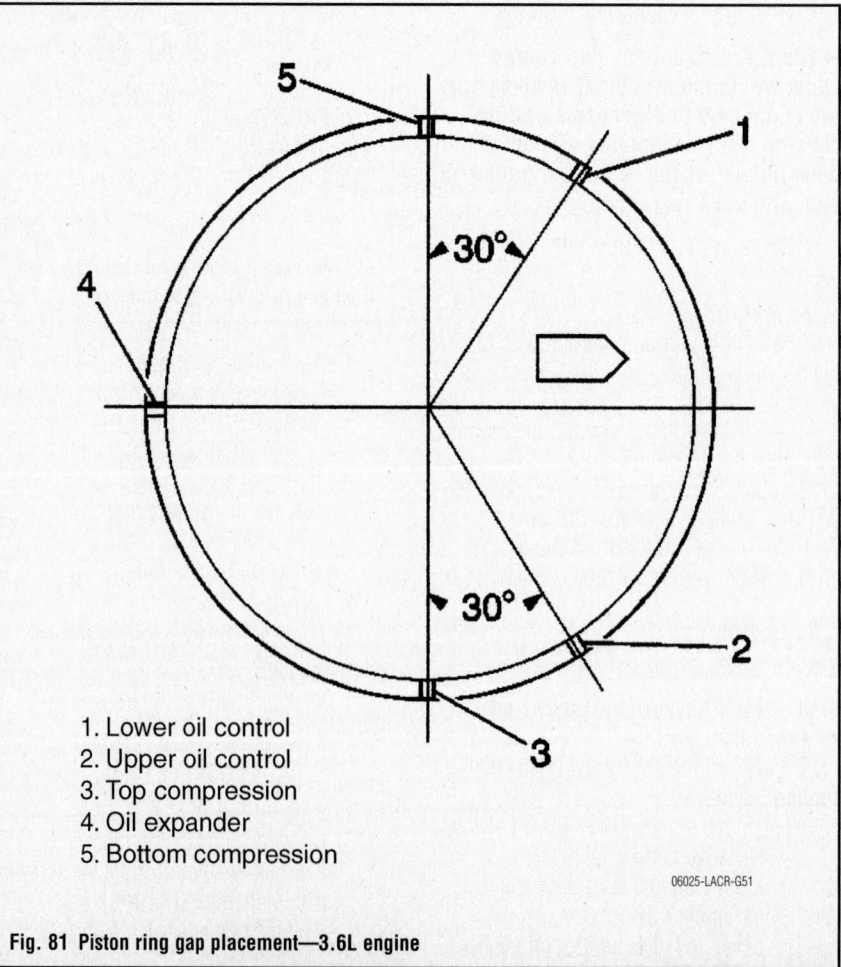

1. Lower oil control
2. Upper oil control
3. Top compression
4. Oil expander
5. Bottom compression

Fig. 81 Piston ring gap placement—3.6L engine

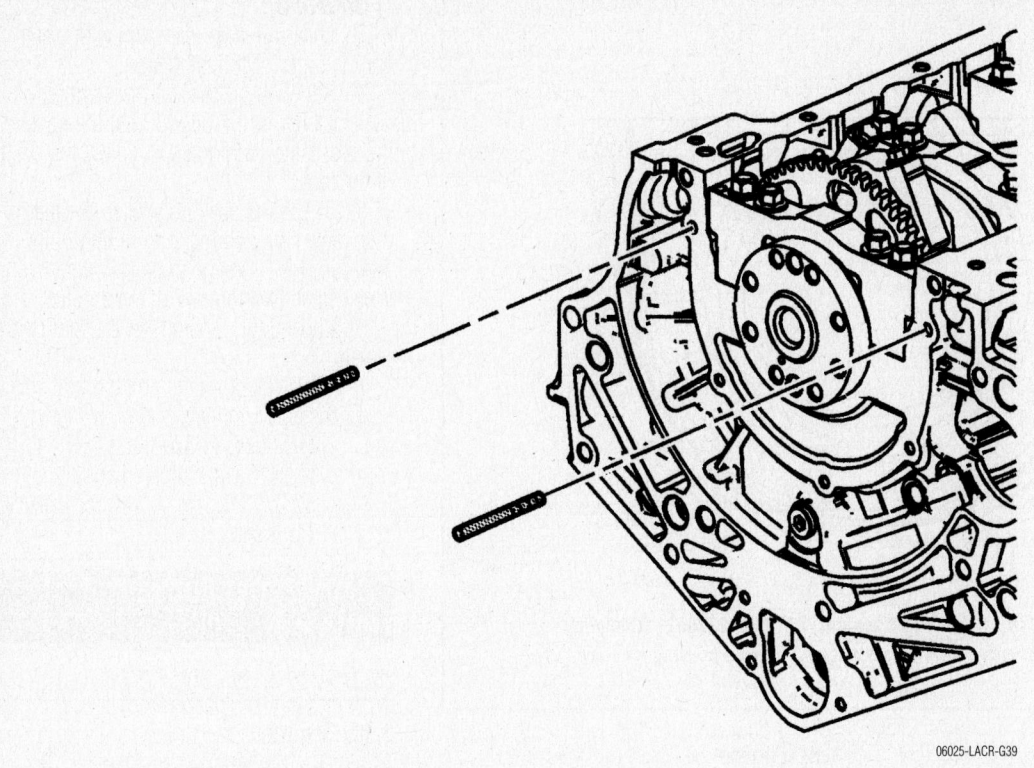

06025-LACR-G39

Fig. 82 Install the 6mm (0.236 in.) guides from kit EN 46109 into the 2 crankshaft rear oil seal housing corner bolt holes of the engine block—3.6L engine

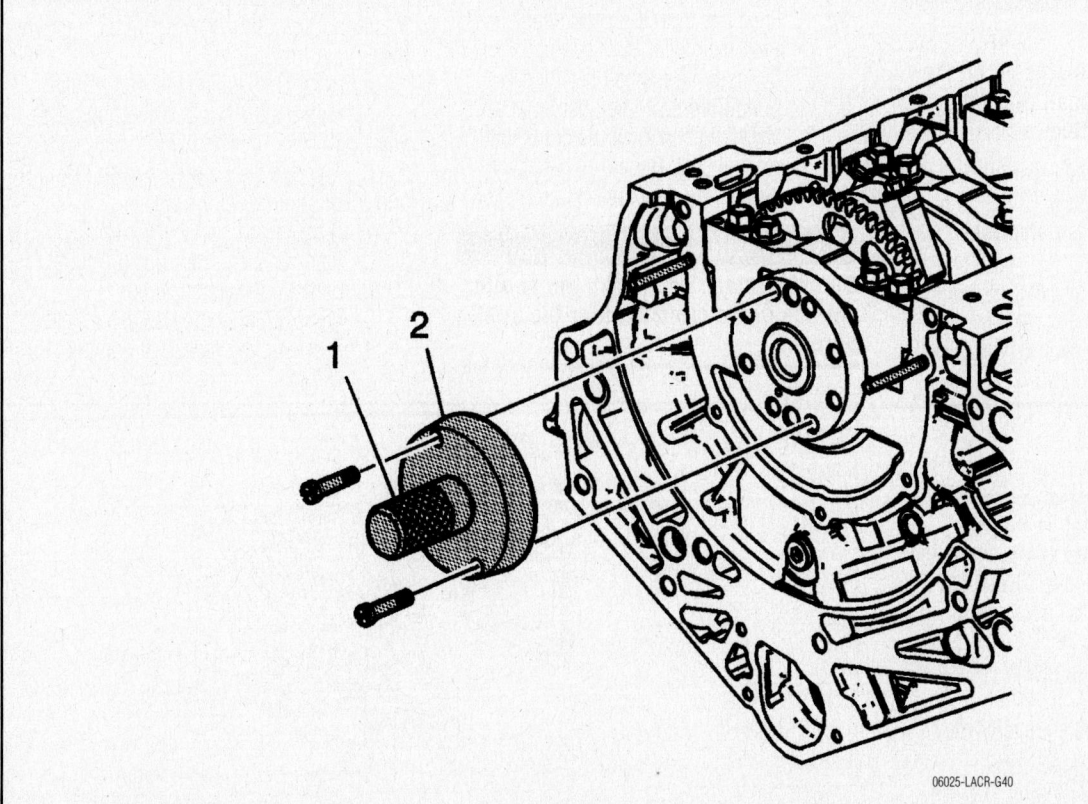

06025-LACR-G40

Fig. 83 Install seal tools EN-47839 with the J-42183 (1, 2) onto the rear of the crankshaft flange—3.6L engine

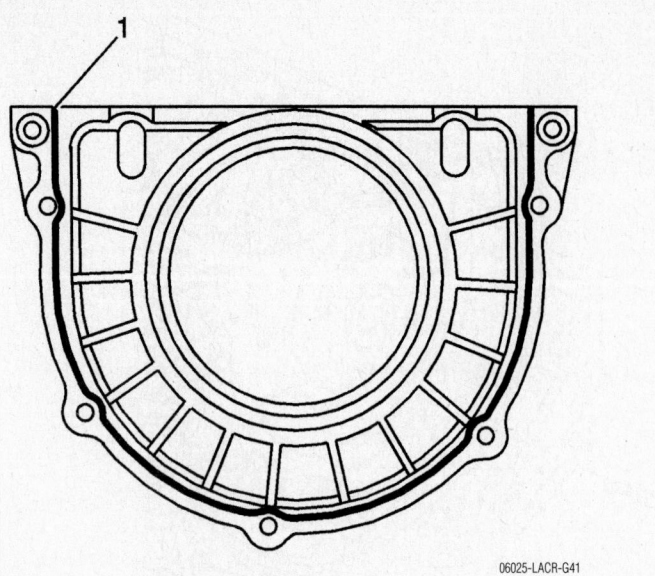

Fig. 84 Place a 3mm (0.118 in.) bead of RTV sealant, GM P/N 12378521 (Canadian P/N 88901148) or equivalent, to the NEW crankshaft rear oil seal housing as shown (1)— 3.6L engine

06025-LACR-G41

10. Install seal tools EN-47839 with the J-42183 (1, 2) onto the rear of the crankshaft flange.

11. Place a 3mm (0.118 in.) bead of RTV sealant, GM P/N 12378521 (Canadian P/N 88901148) or equivalent, to the NEW crankshaft rear oil seal housing as shown (1).

➡**DO NOT allow any engine oil on the area where the crankshaft rear oil seal housing is to be installed.**

12. Install the crankshaft rear oil seal housing to the engine block.

13. Remove the guides from the engine block.

14. Install the crankshaft rear oil seal housing bolts. Tighten the crankshaft rear oil seal housing bolts to 89 inch lbs. (10 Nm).

15. Remove the seal tool from the crankshaft flange.

16. Install the oil pan.

17. Place the engine flywheel in position on the crankshaft.

18. Install 2 NEW bolts in location at the top and bottom of the engine flywheel bolt pattern allowing the engine flywheel to hang in position.

19. Install the remaining NEW engine flywheel bolts.

- Tighten the NEW engine flywheel bolts to 22 ft. lbs. (30 Nm)
- Tighten the NEW engine flywheel bolts an additional 45°

20. Install the transaxle.

3.8L Engine

See Figure 85.

1. Before servicing the vehicle, refer to the Precautions Section.

2. Remove or disconnect the following:
- Transaxle assembly
- Flexplate from the crankshaft
- Rear main seal from engine block by inserting a small flat-bladed prytool through the dust lip at an angle, then pry out the crankshaft rear oil seal. Repeat as necessary around the seal until it is removed.

✲✲ WARNING

Do not damage or scratch the sealing surface of the crankshaft or the seal bore.

To install:

3. Lubricate new rear main with clean engine oil prior to installation.

4. Slide the oil seal on the mandrel of seal installer tool J-38196 until the back of the seal is seated squarely against the collar of the tool.

5. Attach the seal installer to the rear of the crankshaft with the 2 mounting bolts, then turn the T-handle until the oil seal is fully seated into the rear of the engine.

6. Loosen the T-handle of the tool completely.

7. Remove both bolts and the tool.

8. Install or connect the following:
- Flexplate. Torque the bolts to 11 ft. lbs. (15 Nm), plus an additional 50°.
- Transaxle

TIMING CHAIN COVER AND SEAL

REMOVAL & INSTALLATION

3.6L Engine

See Figures 86 through 90

1. Before servicing the vehicle, refer to the Precautions Section.

2. Disconnect the negative battery cable.

3. Remove the ECU module bracket. Position it out of the way. DO NOT remove the ECU or disconnect it.

4. Remove the alternator assembly.

5. Remove the coolant overflow reservoir.

6. Remove the power steering reservoir and position it out of the way.

7. Remove the camshaft covers.

8. Remove the upper radiator hose.

9. Remove the water pump.

10. Remove the engine splash shield.

11. Remove the crankshaft damper.

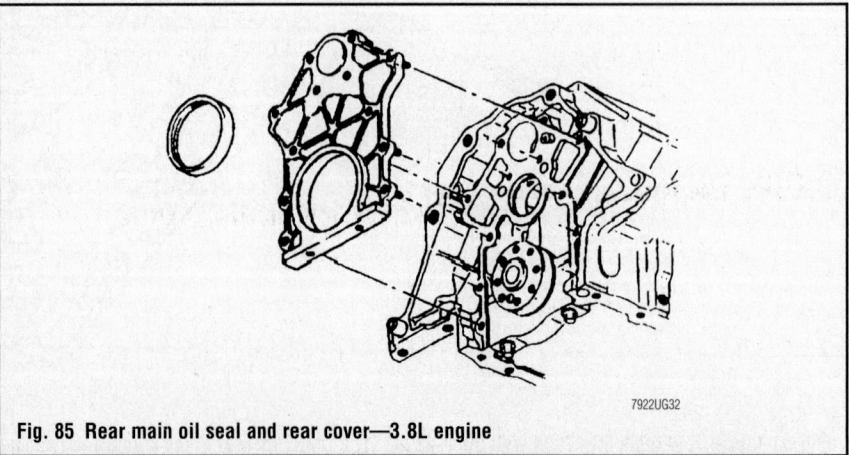

Fig. 85 Rear main oil seal and rear cover—3.8L engine

7922UG32

To install:

✳✳ WARNING

The oil pump is built into the front cover. When the cover is removed, oil drains from the pump. Since the pump "loses its prime" it may not establish oil pressure as soon as the engine starts. Therefore, it is important to remove the oil pump cover from the back of the timing chain front cover and pack the space around the oil pump gears completely full of petroleum jelly. If this is not done, the oil pump may not pump engine oil when the engine is started, resulting in severe engine damage.

5. Remove the screws and the oil pump cover from the back of the timing chain front cover. Pack the space around the oil pump gears completely full of petroleum jelly. There must be no air space left inside the pump.

6. Install or connect the following:
- Pump cover with new gaskets. Torque the screws to 97 inch lbs. (11 Nm).
- Timing chain front cover. Torque the front cover to engine bolts to 11 ft. lbs. (15 Nm) plus an additional 40°.
- Oil pan to front cover bolts. Torque the bolts to 125 inch lbs. (14 Nm).
- CKP sensor. Torque the bolts to 14–28 ft. lbs. (20–40 Nm).
- CKP sensor shield
- Crankshaft damper. Torque the bolt to 111 ft. lbs. (150 Nm) plus an additional 76° turn.
- Drive belt tensioner assembly
- Right inner fender access panel and the right front wheel

- Drive belt(s)
- Engine mount
- Coolant hoses
- Negative battery cable
7. Remove the engine support fixture.
8. Refill and bleed the cooling system.
9. Start the vehicle and check for leaks and proper engine operation.

TIMING CHAIN AND SPROCKETS

REMOVAL & INSTALLATION

3.6L Engine

See Figures 93 through 112.

1. Before servicing the vehicle, refer to the Precautions Section.

2. Remove the timing chain cover and seal. Refer to Timing Chain Cover and Seal, removal and installation.

3. Remove the right bank secondary camshaft drive chain tensioner:

   a. Remove the right secondary camshaft drive chain tensioner bolts.

   b. Remove the right secondary camshaft drive chain tensioner.

   c. Remove and discard the right secondary camshaft drive chain tensioner gasket.

   d. Inspect the right secondary camshaft drive chain tensioner mounting surface on the right cylinder head for burrs or any defects that would degrade the sealing of the NEW right secondary camshaft drive chain tensioner gasket.

4. Remove the right bank secondary camshaft drive chain shoe:

   a. Remove the right secondary camshaft drive chain shoe bolt.

   b. Remove the right secondary camshaft drive chain shoe.

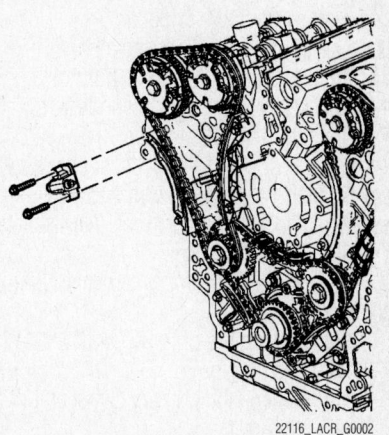

22116_LACR_G0002

Fig. 93 The right bank secondary camshaft drive chain tensioner—3.6L Engine

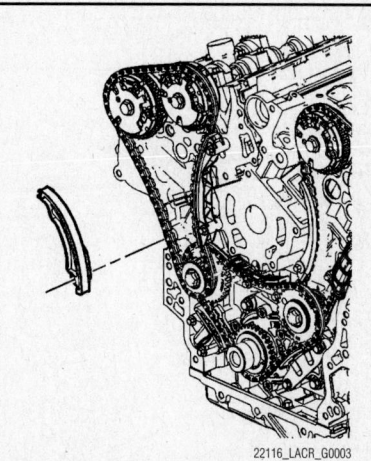

22116_LACR_G0003

Fig. 94 The right secondary camshaft drive chain shoe bolt and drive chain shoe—3.6L Engine

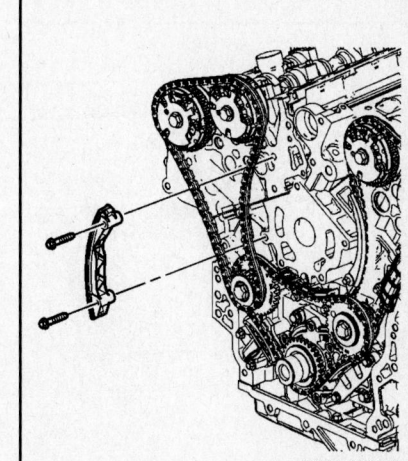

22116_LACR_G0004

Fig. 95 The right bank secondary camshaft drive chain guide—3.6L Engine

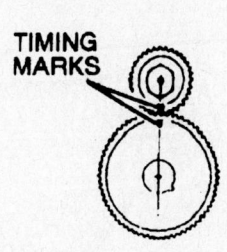
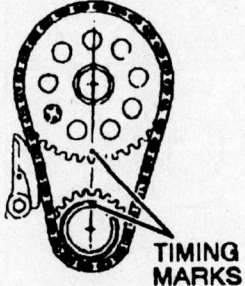

TIMING MARKS

BALANCE SHAFT GEAR TO BALANCE SHAFT DRIVE GEAR

TIMING MARKS

CAMSHAFT SPROCKET TO CRANKSHAFT SPROCKET

7922UG09

Fig. 92 Timing chain sprocket and balance shaft gear alignment—3.8L engines

5. Remove the right bank secondary camshaft drive chain guide:

a. Remove the right secondary camshaft drive chain guide bolts.

b. Remove the right secondary camshaft drive chain guide.

6. Remove the right secondary camshaft drive chain from the right camshaft position actuators and the right camshaft intermediate drive chain idler sprocket.

7. Remove the primary camshaft drive chain tensioner:

a. Remove the primary camshaft drive chain tensioner bolts.

b. Remove the primary camshaft drive chain tensioner.

c. Remove and discard the primary camshaft drive chain tensioner gasket.

d. Inspect the primary camshaft drive chain tensioner mounting surface on the engine block for burrs or any defects that would degrade the sealing of the NEW

primary camshaft drive chain tensioner gasket.

8. Remove the primary camshaft drive chain upper guide:

a. Remove the primary camshaft drive chain upper guide bolts.

b. Remove the primary camshaft drive chain upper guides.

To install:

➡**Ensure that the crankshaft is in the stage one timing drive assembly position.**

9. Install the primary camshaft drive chain:

a. Wrap the primary camshaft drive chain around the large sprockets of each camshaft intermediate drive chain idler and the crankshaft sprocket.

b. The left camshaft intermediate drive chain idler timing mark (1) will align with a timing camshaft drive chain link (2).

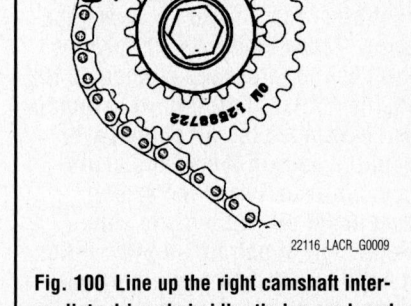

Fig. 100 Line up the right camshaft intermediate drive chain idler timing mark and the timing camshaft drive chain link—3.6L Engine

c. The right camshaft intermediate drive chain idler timing mark (2) will align with a timing camshaft drive chain link (1).

d. The crankshaft sprocket timing mark (2) will align with the timing camshaft drive chain link (1).

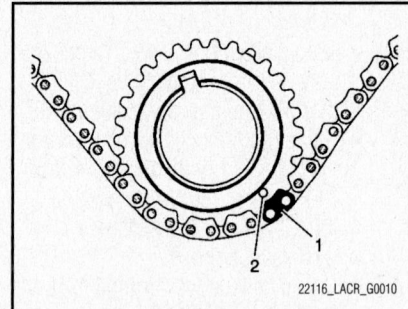

Fig. 101 The crankshaft sprocket timing mark will align with a timing camshaft drive chain link—3.6L Engine

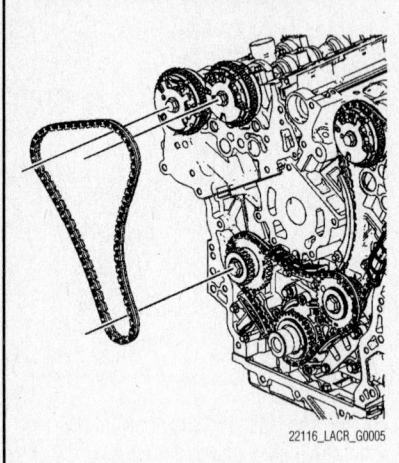

Fig. 96 The right bank secondary camshaft drive chain—3.6L Engine

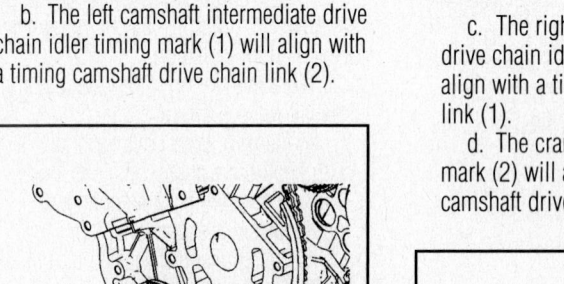

Fig. 98 The primary camshaft drive chain upper guide—3.6L Engine

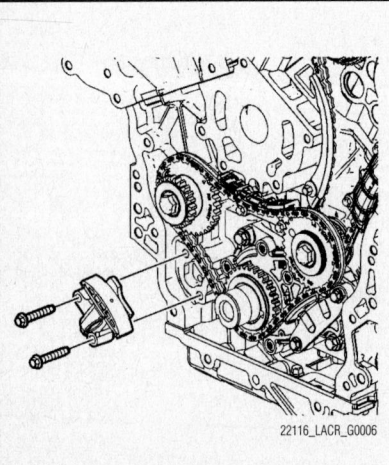

Fig. 97 The primary camshaft drive chain tensioner—3.6L Engine

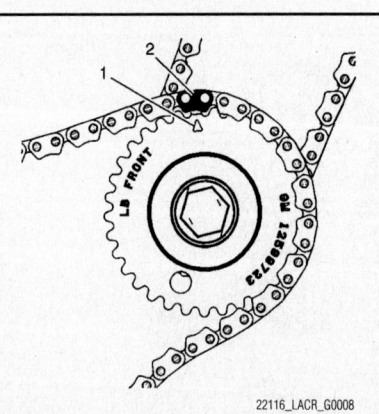

Fig. 99 Line up the left camshaft intermediate drive chain idler timing mark and the timing camshaft drive chain link—3.6L Engine

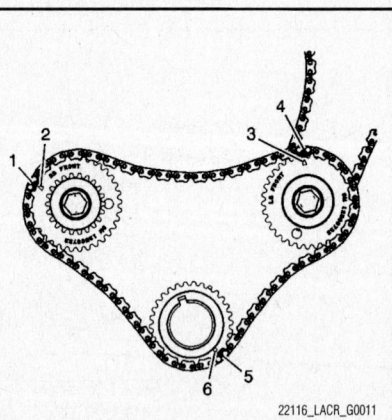

Fig. 102 Ensure all the timing marks are properly aligned with the timing camshaft drive chain links—3.6L Engine

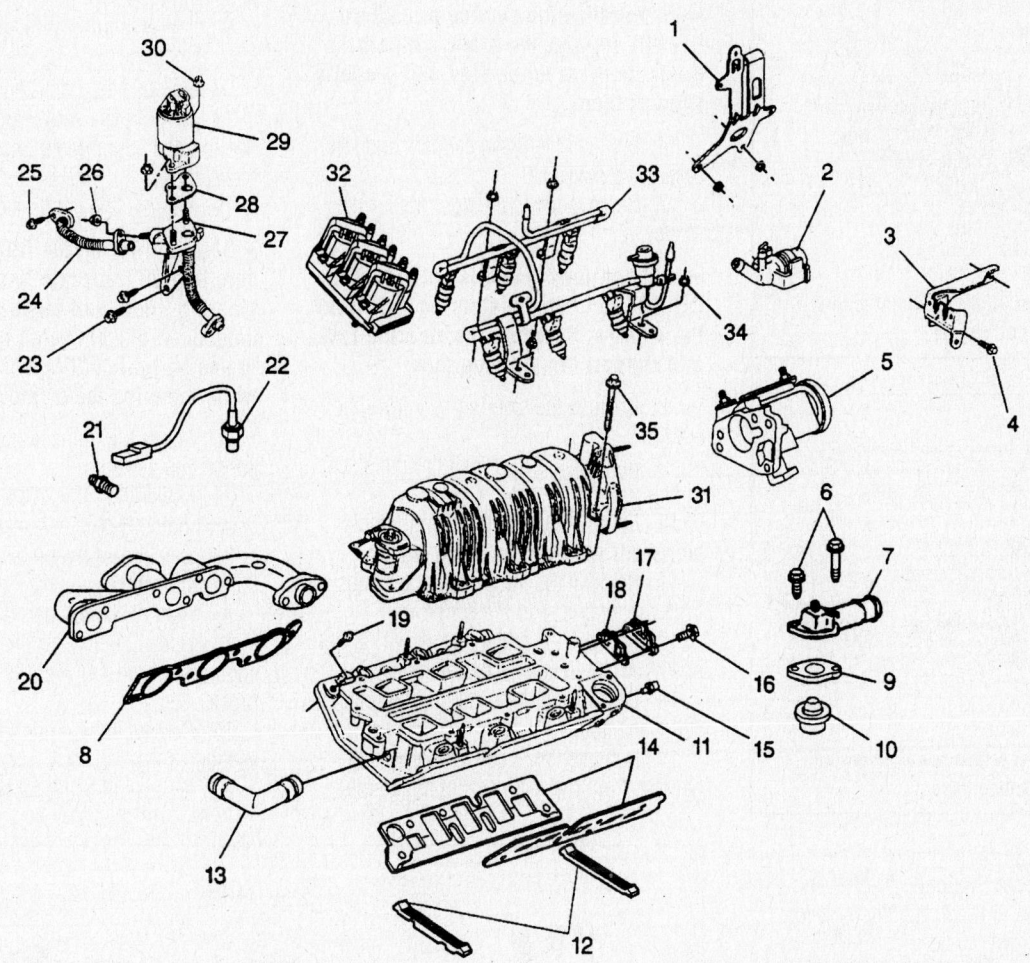

1 Fuel Injector Sight Shield Bracket	19 Lower Intake Manifold Bolt
2 Vacuum Source Manifold	20 Exhaust Manifold (Right)
3 Accelerator Cable Control Bracket	21 Exhaust Manifold Bolt/Stud
4 Throttle Body Support Bolt	22 Exhaust Oxygen Sensor
5 Throttle Body	23 EGR Valve Adapter Bolt
6 Water Outlet Bolt	24 EGR Valve Outlet Pipe
7 Water Outlet	25 EGR Valve Outlet Pipe Bolt
8 Exhaust Manifold Gasket	26 EGR Valve Outlet Pipe Nut
9 Water Outlet Gasket	27 EGR Valve Adapter
10 Thermostat	28 EGR Valve Gasket
11 Lower Intake Manifold	29 EGR Valve
12 Intake Manifold Seal	30 EGR Valve Nut
13 Heater Water Inlet Pipe	31 Upper Intake Manifold
14 Lower Intake Manifold Gasket	32 ICM
15 Coolant Temperature Sensor	33 Fuel Injection Rail
16 Engine Coolant Manifold Bolt	34 Fuel Injector Rail Nut
17 Engine Coolant Manifold	35 Upper Intake Manifold Bolt
18 Engine Coolant Manifold Gasket	

9300UG02

Fig. 67 Exploded view of the intake manifold and related components—3.8L engine

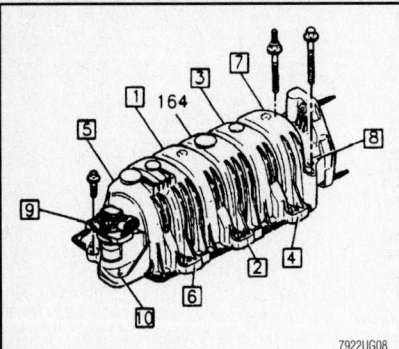

Fig. 68 Upper intake manifold torque sequence—3.8L engine

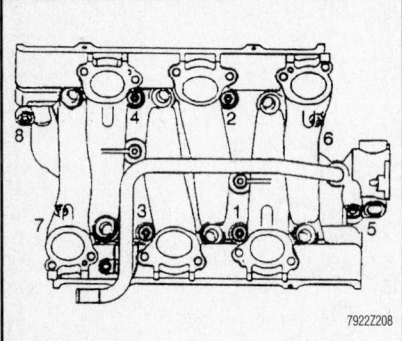

Fig. 69 Lower intake manifold torque sequence—3.8L engine

- Throttle cable bracket to the cylinder head mounting bracket and the cables to the throttle body lever
- EGR heat shield
- Fuel rail. Torque the fuel rail bolts to 88 inch. lbs. (10 Nm).
- Fuel lines
- Fuel regulator vacuum line
- Fuel injector electrical connectors
- Vacuum lines to the intake manifold
- MAP sensor
- Spark plug wires
- Fuel injector sight shield and air inlet duct
- Negative battery cable

7. Refill and bleed the cooling system.

8. Run the engine and check for leaks and proper engine operation.

OIL PAN

REMOVAL & INSTALLATION

3.6L Engine

See Figures 70 through 73.

1. Before servicing the vehicle, refer to the Precautions Section.
2. Remove the tires and wheels.
3. Remove the oil level indicator.

4. Remove the engine splash shields.
5. Drain the engine of oil.

➡In the following service procedure, DO NOT remove the brake calipers. Relocate them to the side and properly support them.

6. Remove the brake calipers and relocate to the side.
7. Remove the retaining bolts for the struts.

➡In the following service procedure, DO NOT remove the steering rack from the vehicle. Relocate the steering rack and support the steering rack.

8. Remove the steering rack from the cradle.
9. Remove the tie rods from the steering knuckle.
10. Remove the power steering cooler lines from the retainers on the cradle.
11. Remove the transaxle cooler lines from the retainers on the cradle.
12. Remove the battery cable wiring harness from the retainers on the cradle.
13. Disconnect the speed sensor electrical connectors.
14. Remove the speed sensor wiring harness from the retainers on the cradle.

15. Install the engine support fixture. See the procedure under Engine Removal & Installation.
16. Remove the right engine mount nuts.
17. Remove the transaxle mount bolts.
18. Remove the engine mount struts. See the procedure under Engine Removal & Installation.
19. Remove the cradle mounting bolts.

➡Before lowering the frame, make sure that all transaxle lines, power steering lines, and electrical harness have been disconnected and relocated to ensure that nothing will be damaged while lowering the frame.

20. Lower the frame enough to remove the oil pan assembly.
21. Lower the frame. See the procedure under Engine Removal & Installation.
22. Disconnect the oil level senor electrical connector.
23. Remove the oil pan bolts.
24. Using the pry points on the oil pan, separate the oil pan from the engine block.
25. Remove the oil pan from the vehicle.
26. Disassemble the oil pan.

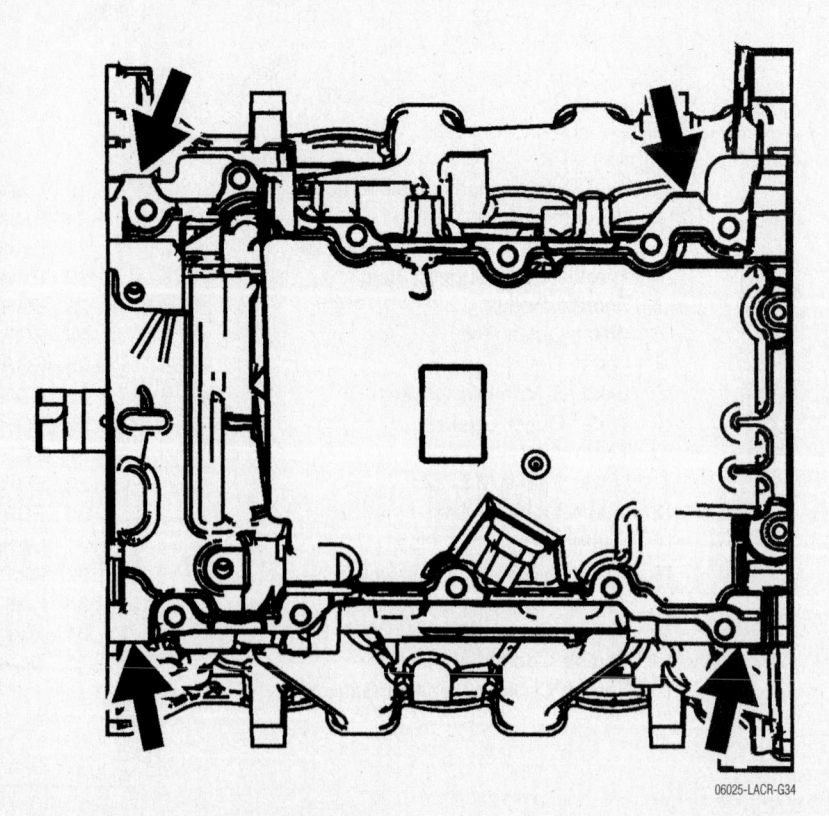

Fig. 70 Oil pan pry points—3.6L engine

e. Ensure all the timing marks (2, 3, 6) are properly aligned with the timing camshaft drive chain links (1, 4, 5).

10. Install the primary upper camshaft drive chain guide.

11. Install the upper primary camshaft drive chain guide bolts. Tighten bolts to 17 ft. lbs. (23 Nm).

12. Using the J 45027, reset the primary camshaft drive chain tensioner plunger.

13. Install the plunger into the primary camshaft drive chain tensioner body.

14. Compress the plunger into the body and lock the primary camshaft drive chain tensioner by inserting the EN 46112 into the access hole in the side of the primary camshaft drive chain tensioner body.

15. Slowly release pressure on the primary camshaft drive chain tensioner. The primary camshaft drive chain tensioner should remain compressed.

16. Install a NEW primary camshaft drive chain tensioner gasket to the primary camshaft drive chain tensioner.

17. Install the primary camshaft drive chain tensioner bolts through the primary camshaft drive chain tensioner and gasket.

18. Place the primary camshaft drive chain tensioner into position and loosely install the bolts to the block.

19. Tighten the primary camshaft drive chain tensioner bolts:
   a. Step 1: 44 inch lbs. (5 Nm).
   b. Step 2: 17 ft. lbs. (23 Nm).

20. Release the primary camshaft drive chain tensioner by pulling out the EN 46112 and unlocking the tensioner plunger.

21. Verify the primary and left secondary camshaft drive chain timing mark alignments (1-12).

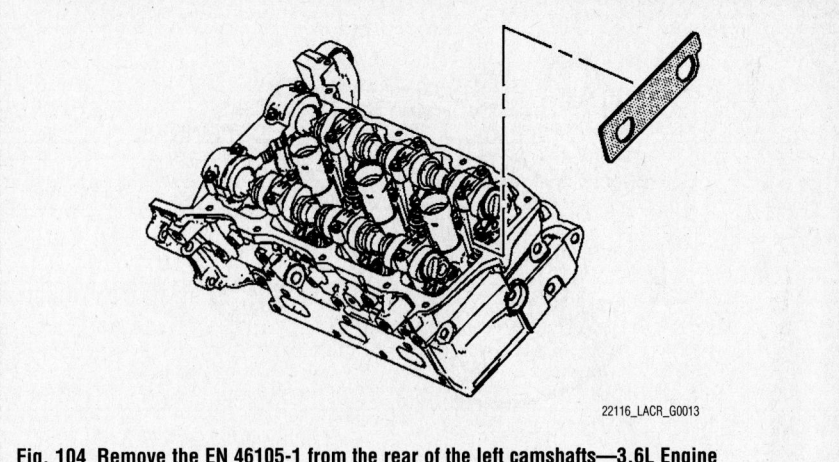

Fig. 104 Remove the EN 46105-1 from the rear of the left camshafts—3.6L Engine

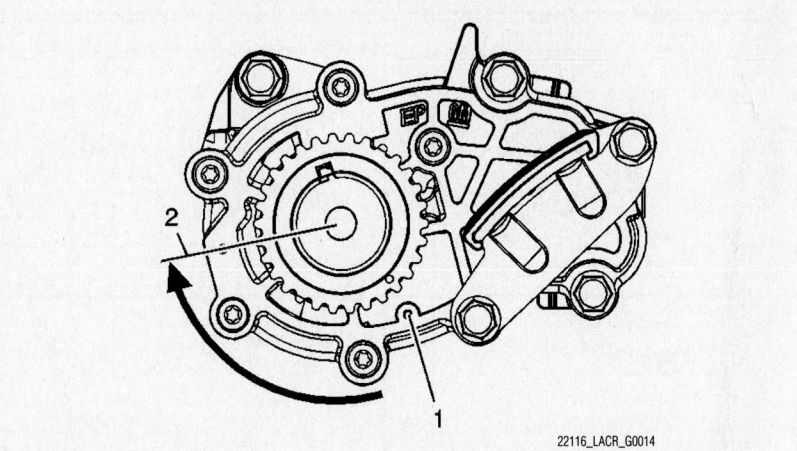

Fig. 105 Using the EN 46111, rotate the crankshaft and crankshaft sprocket from the stage 1 alignment position (1) to the stage 2 alignment position (2)—3.6L Engine

22. Remove the EN 46105-1 from the rear of the left camshafts.

23. Using the EN 46111, rotate the crankshaft and crankshaft sprocket from the stage 1 alignment position (1) to the stage 2 alignment position (2), 115 crankshaft degrees, in order to install the right secondary camshaft drive chain components.

24. Install the EN 46105-2 onto the rear of the left camshafts.

25. Install the EN 46105-1 onto the rear of the right camshafts.

26. Ensure that the crankshaft is in the stage 2 timing drive assembly position (2).

27. Install the right secondary camshaft drive chain.

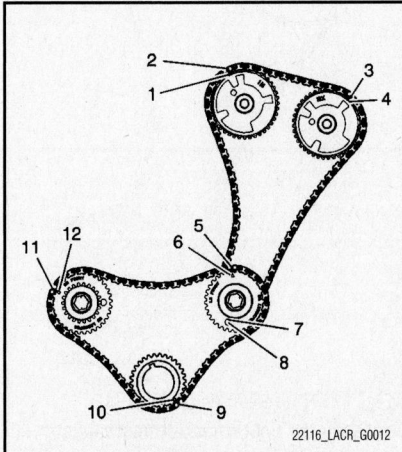

Fig. 103 Verify the primary and left secondary camshaft drive chain timing mark alignments—3.6L Engine

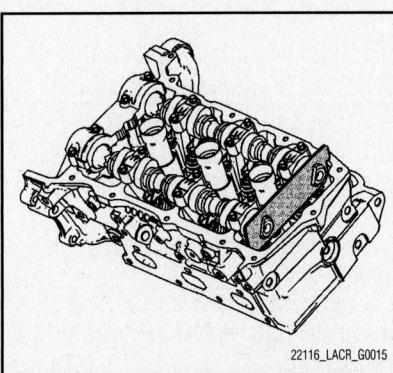

Fig. 106 Install the EN 46105-2 onto the rear of the left camshafts—3.6L Engine

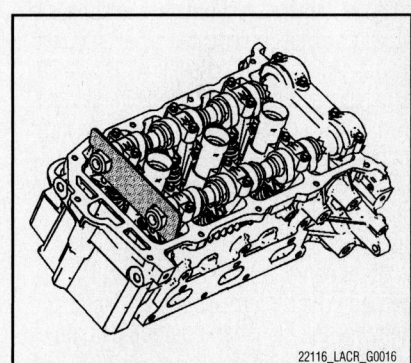

Fig. 107 Install the EN 46105-1 onto the rear of the right camshafts—3.6L Engine

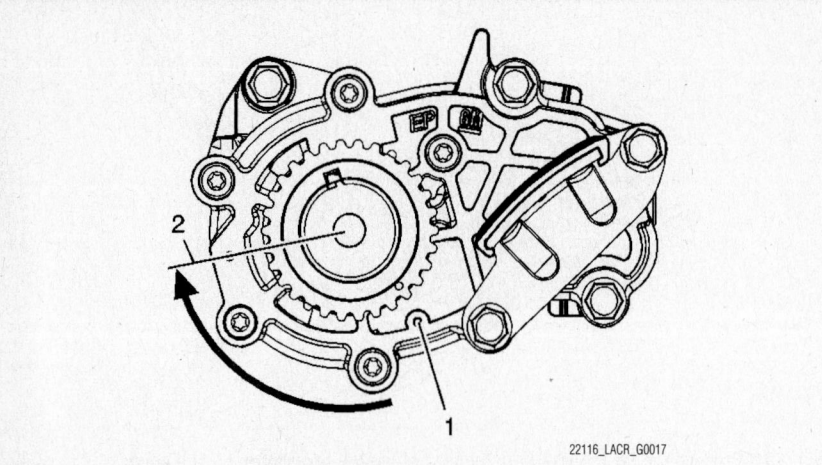

Fig. 108 Ensure that the crankshaft is in the stage 2 timing drive assembly position (2)—3.6L Engine

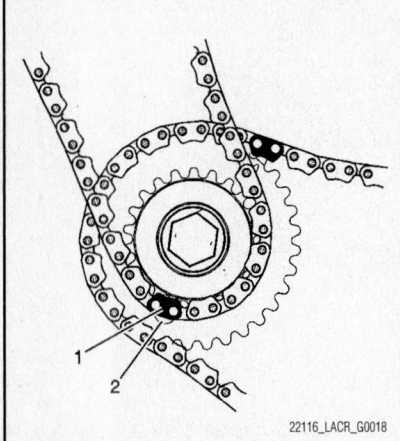

Fig. 109 Place the secondary camshaft drive chain around the right camshaft intermediate drive chain idler outer sprocket, aligning the timing camshaft drive chain link (1) with the alignment access hole (2) made in the right camshaft intermediate drive chain idler inner sprocket—3.6L Engine

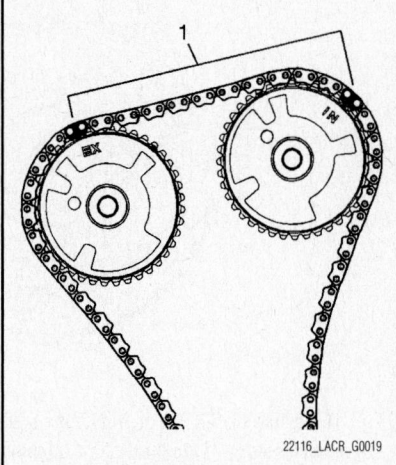

Fig. 110 Ensure there are 10 links (1) between the timing camshaft drive chain links for the camshaft position actuator sprockets—3.6L Engine

28. Place the secondary camshaft drive chain around the right camshaft intermediate drive chain idler outer sprocket, aligning the timing camshaft drive chain link (1) with the alignment access hole (2) made in the right camshaft intermediate drive chain idler inner sprocket.

29. Wrap the secondary camshaft drive chain around both right actuator drive sprockets.

30. Ensure there are 10 links (1) between the timing camshaft drive chain links for the camshaft position actuator sprockets.

31. Align the right exhaust camshaft position actuator sprocket alignment trian-gle mark with the timing camshaft drive chain link.

32. Align the right intake camshaft position actuator sprocket alignment triangle mark with the timing camshaft drive chain link.

33. Ensure that there are 22 links (1) between the right camshaft intermediate drive chain idler timing camshaft drive chain link and each right camshaft position actuator sprocket timing camshaft drive chain link.

34. Position the right secondary camshaft drive chain guide.

35. Install the secondary camshaft drive chain guide bolts. Tighten the bolts to 17 ft. lbs. (23 Nm).

36. Position the right secondary camshaft drive chain shoe.

37. Install the secondary camshaft drive chain shoe bolt. Tighten the bolt to 17 ft. lbs. (23 Nm).

38. Using the J 45027, reset the right secondary camshaft drive chain tensioner plunger.

39. Install the plunger into the right secondary camshaft drive chain tensioner body.

40. Compress the plunger into the body and lock the right secondary camshaft drive chain tensioner by inserting the EN 46112 into the access hole in the side of the right secondary camshaft drive chain tensioner body.

41. Slowly release pressure on the right secondary camshaft drive chain tensioner.

➡ **The right secondary camshaft drive chain tensioner should remain compressed.**

42. Install a NEW right secondary camshaft drive chain tensioner gasket to the right secondary camshaft drive chain tensioner.

43. Install the right secondary camshaft drive chain tensioner bolts through the right secondary camshaft drive chain tensioner and gasket.

➡ **Ensure the right secondary camshaft drive chain tensioner mounting surface on the right cylinder head does not have any burrs or defects that would degrade the sealing of the NEW right secondary camshaft drive chain tensioner gasket.**

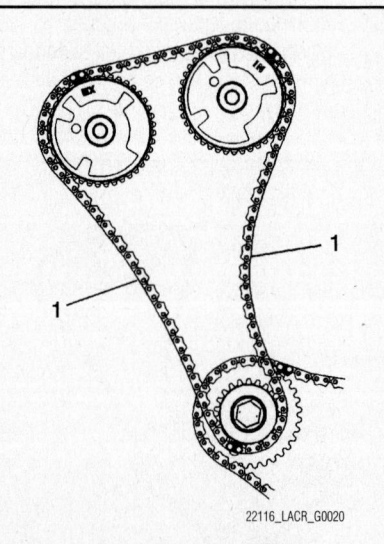

Fig. 111 There will be 22 links (1) between the right camshaft intermediate drive chain idler timing camshaft drive chain link and each right camshaft position actuator sprocket timing camshaft drive chain link—3.6L Engine

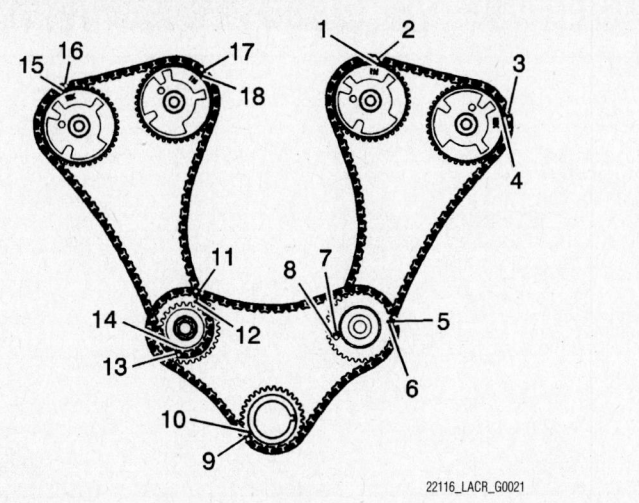

Fig. 112 Verify all primary and secondary camshaft drive chain timing mark alignments—3.6L Engine

22116_LACR_G0021

44. Place the right secondary camshaft drive chain tensioner into position and loosely install the bolts to the block.

45. Verify the proper placement of the right secondary camshaft drive chain tensioner gasket tab.

46. Tighten the right secondary camshaft drive chain tensioner bolts:

    a. Step 1: 44 inch lbs. (5 Nm).
    b. Step 2: 17 ft. lbs. (23 Nm).

47. Release the right camshaft drive chain tensioner by pulling out the EN 46112 and unlocking the tensioner plunger.

✳✳ WARNING

Ensure that all timing chain tensioners are completely released. A timing chain tensioner that is not properly released can lead to serious engine damage.

48. Verify all primary and secondary camshaft drive chain timing mark alignments (1-18).

49. Install the timing chain cover and seal. Refer to Timing Chain Cover and Seal, removal and installation.

3.8L Engine
See Figures 91 and 92.

1. Before servicing the vehicle, refer to the Precautions Section.
2. Drain the cooling system.
3. Support the engine.
4. Remove or disconnect the following:

- Negative battery cable
- Torque axis mount and bracket
- Drive belt
- Drive belt tensioner
- Crankshaft damper
- Crankshaft Position (CKP) sensor shield and the CKP sensor
- Oil pan to front cover bolts
- Timing chain front cover

5. Align the timing marks on the camshaft and crankshaft sprockets so they are as close together as possible.

- Timing chain damper
- Camshaft sprocket bolt, the camshaft sprocket and timing chain
- Crankshaft sprocket

✳✳ WARNING

Do not rotate the camshaft or crankshaft while the timing chain and sprockets are removed.

To install:
6. Install or connect the following:

- Timing chain and sprockets with the timing marks aligned
- Camshaft sprocket bolt. Torque the bolt to 74 ft. lbs. (100 Nm) plus an additional 90° turn.
- Timing chain damper. Torque the bolts to 16 ft. lbs. (22 Nm).

✳✳ WARNING

The oil pump is built into the front cover. When the cover is removed,

oil drains from the pump. Since the pump "loses its prime" it may not establish oil pressure as soon as the engine starts. Therefore, it is important to remove the oil pump cover from the back of the timing chain front cover and pack the space around the oil pump gears completely full of petroleum jelly. If this is not done, the oil pump may not pump engine oil when the engine is started, resulting in severe engine damage.

7. Remove the screws and the oil pump cover from the back of the timing chain front cover. Pack the space around the oil pump gears completely full of petroleum jelly. There must be no air space left inside the pump.

8. Install or connect the following:

- Pump cover with new gaskets. Torque the screws to 97 inch lbs. (11 Nm).
- Timing chain front cover. Torque the front cover to engine bolts to 11 ft. lbs. (15 Nm) plus an additional 40°.
- Oil pan to front cover bolts. Torque the bolts to 125 inch lbs. (14 Nm).
- CKP sensor. Torque the bolts to 14–28 ft. lbs. (20–40 Nm).
- CKP sensor shield
- Crankshaft damper. Torque the bolt to 111 ft. lbs. (150 Nm) plus an additional 76° turn.
- Drive belt tensioner assembly
- Right inner fender access panel and the right front wheel
- Drive belt(s)
- Engine mount
- Coolant hoses
- Negative battery cable

9. Remove the engine support fixture.
10. Refill and bleed the cooling system.
11. Start the vehicle and check for leaks and proper engine operation.

VALVE LASH

ADJUSTMENT

The valve clearance cannot be adjusted on these engines. The engine is equipped with hydraulic lifters, and adjustment is not necessary.

ENGINE PERFORMANCE & EMISSION CONTROL

MALFUNCTION INDICATOR LIGHT (MIL) RESET PROCEDURES

1. Proper operation of the Malfunction Indicator Lamp (MIL):
   - The MIL will illuminate with the ignition switch ON and the engine OFF
   - The MIL will turn OFF when the engine is started
   - The MIL will remain ON if the self-diagnostic system has detected a malfunction
   - The MIL may turn OFF if the malfunction is no longer present
   - If the MIL is illuminated and then the engine stalls, the MIL will remain illuminated as long as the ignition switch is ON
   - If the MIL is not illuminated and the engine stalls, the MIL will not illuminate until the ignition switch is cycled OFF, then ON

2. Resetting the MIL:
   - The control module turns OFF the Malfunction Indicator Lamp (MIL) after 3 consecutive ignition cycles that the diagnostic system runs and does not fail
   - A current Diagnostic Trouble Code (DTC) clears when the diagnostic cycle runs and passes
   - There may still be a history of DTC's stored in the system. These will clear after 40 consecutive warm–up cycles, if no failures are reported by any other related diagnostic system
   - Manual resetting of the MIL and any DTC stored in the system, requires the use of an OBD2 scan tool connected to the data link connector for communication with the vehicle. Follow the instructions of the scan tool for both retrieval and resetting of DTC's.

➡ If the error symptoms causing the MIL to illuminate have been corrected, the MIL will return to normal operation.

COMPONENT LOCATIONS

See Figures 113 through 122.

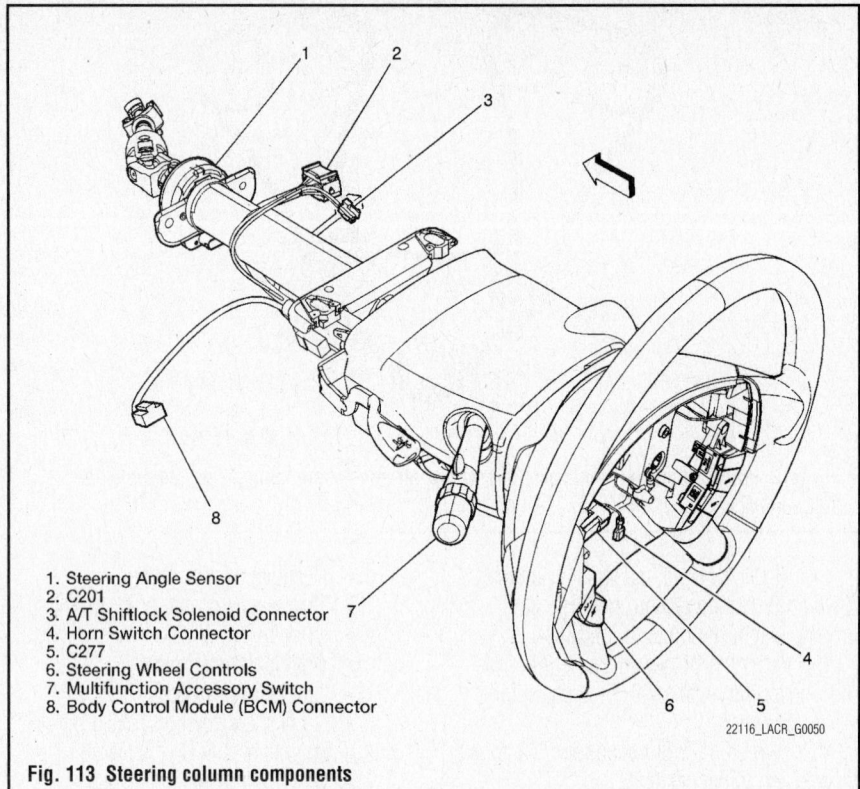

1. Steering Angle Sensor
2. C201
3. A/T Shiftlock Solenoid Connector
4. Horn Switch Connector
5. C277
6. Steering Wheel Controls
7. Multifunction Accessory Switch
8. Body Control Module (BCM) Connector

22116_LACR_G0050

Fig. 113 Steering column components

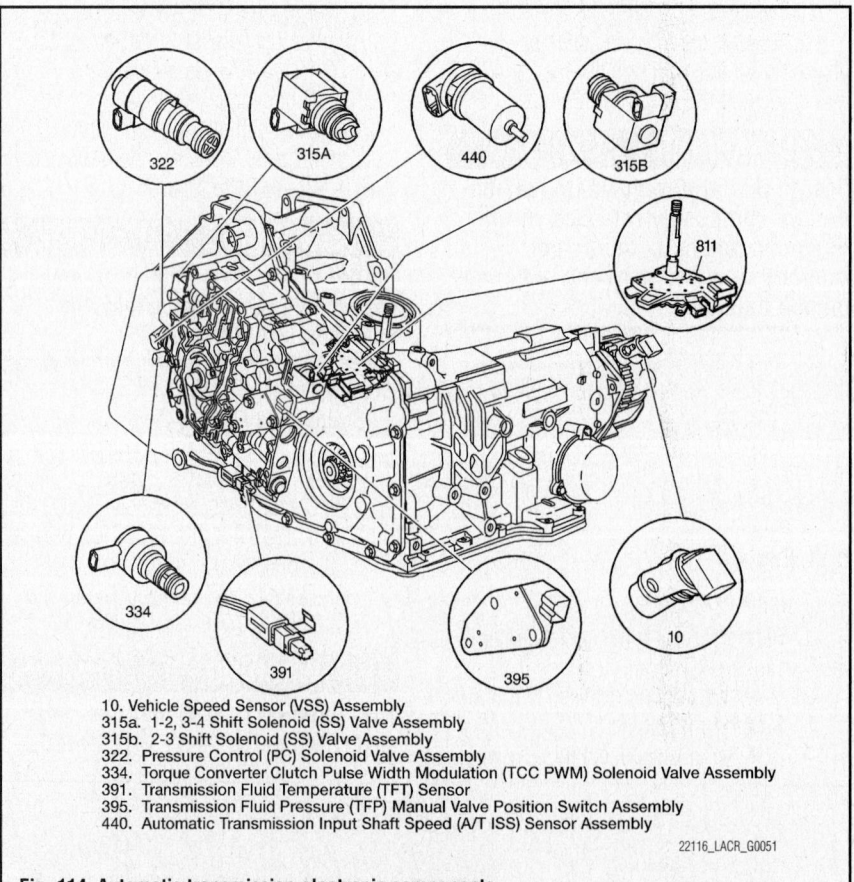

10. Vehicle Speed Sensor (VSS) Assembly
315a. 1-2, 3-4 Shift Solenoid (SS) Valve Assembly
315b. 2-3 Shift Solenoid (SS) Valve Assembly
322. Pressure Control (PC) Solenoid Valve Assembly
334. Torque Converter Clutch Pulse Width Modulation (TCC PWM) Solenoid Valve Assembly
391. Transmission Fluid Temperature (TFT) Sensor
395. Transmission Fluid Pressure (TFP) Manual Valve Position Switch Assembly
440. Automatic Transmission Input Shaft Speed (A/T ISS) Sensor Assembly

22116_LACR_G0051

Fig. 114 Automatic transmission electronic components

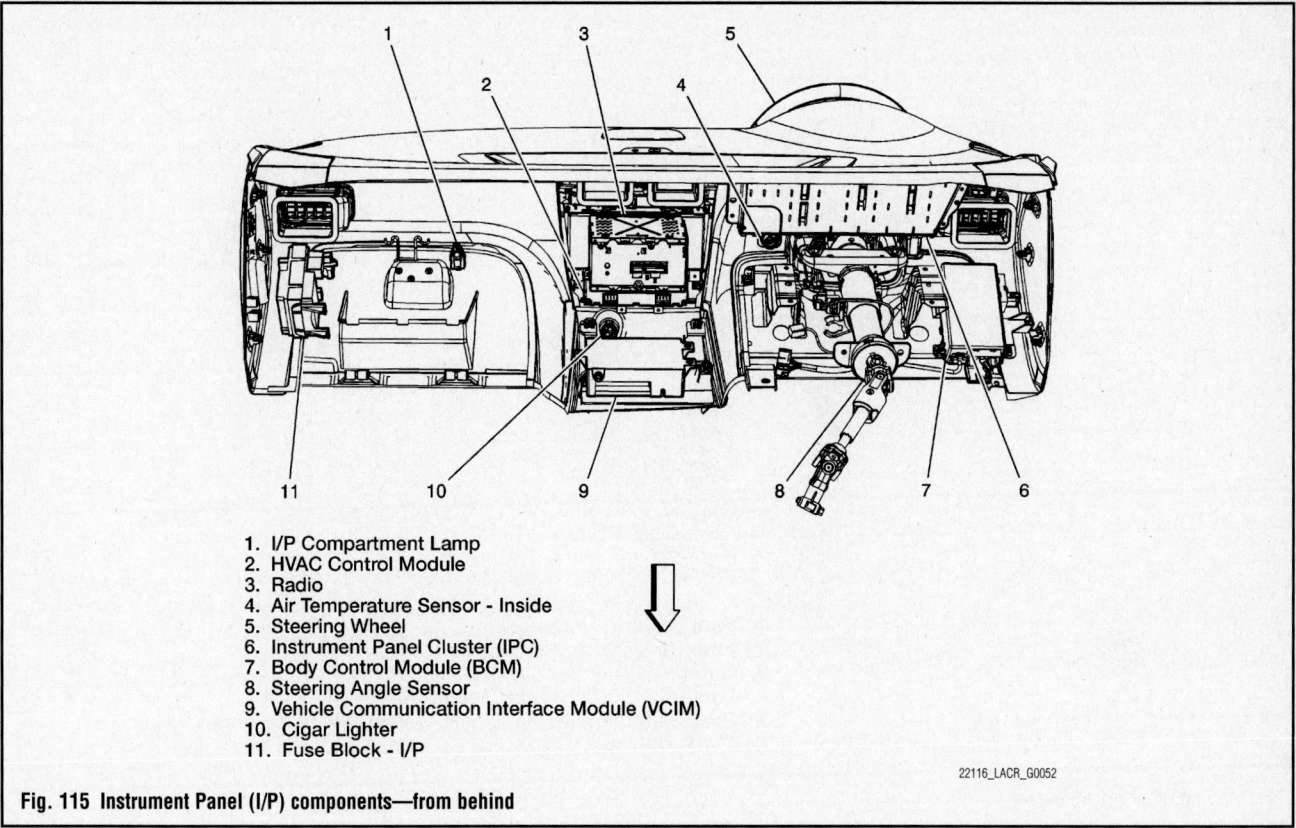

1. I/P Compartment Lamp
2. HVAC Control Module
3. Radio
4. Air Temperature Sensor - Inside
5. Steering Wheel
6. Instrument Panel Cluster (IPC)
7. Body Control Module (BCM)
8. Steering Angle Sensor
9. Vehicle Communication Interface Module (VCIM)
10. Cigar Lighter
11. Fuse Block - I/P

22116_LACR_G0052

Fig. 115 Instrument Panel (I/P) components—from behind

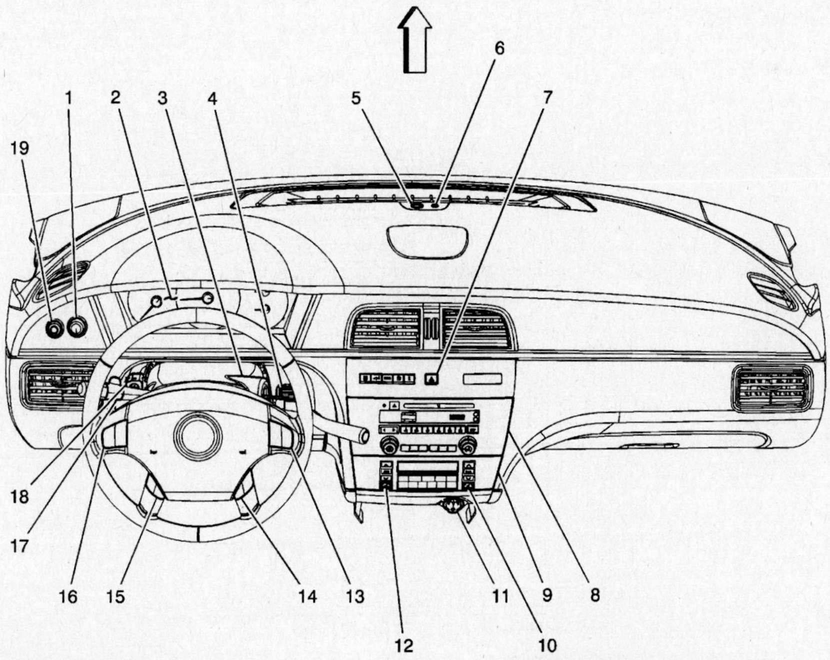

1. Lamp Switch Assembly - Fog Lamp
2. Instrument Panel Cluster (IPC)
3. Ignition Switch
4. Air Temperature Sensor - Inside
5. Sunload Sensor Assembly (CJ2) or Ambient Light Sensor (C67)
6. Theft LED
7. Driver Information Center(DIC)
8. Radio
9. HVAC Control Module
10. Heated Seat Switch - Front Passenger
11. Cigar Lighter
12. Heated Seat Switch - Driver
13. Steering Wheel Controls - Right
14. Cruise Control Switch
15. Voice Recorder / Cruise Switch Assembly
16. Steering Wheel Controls - Left
17. Turn Signal / Multifunction Switch
18. I/P Dimmer Switch
19. Lamp Switch Assembly - Interior Lamps

22116_LACR_G0053

Fig. 116 Instrument Panel (I/P) components—from front

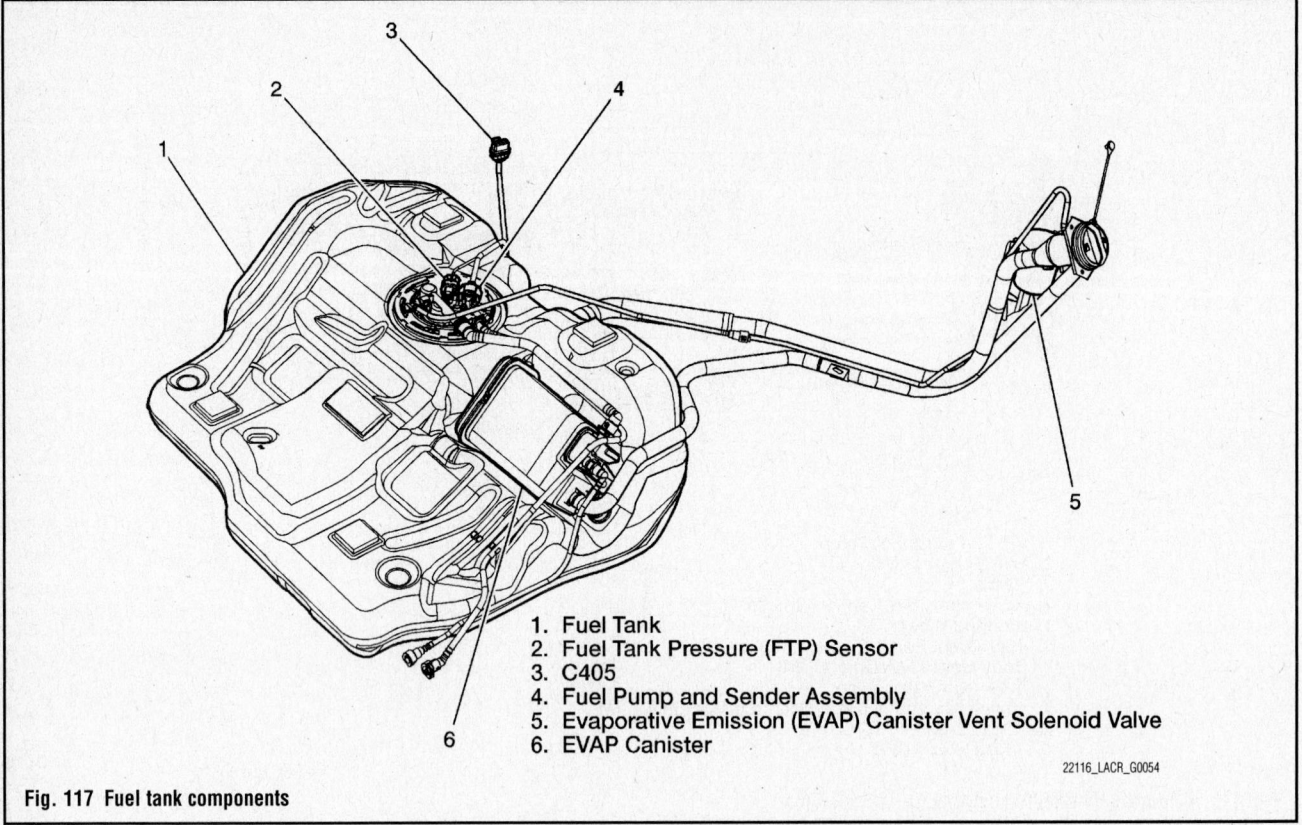

1. Fuel Tank
2. Fuel Tank Pressure (FTP) Sensor
3. C405
4. Fuel Pump and Sender Assembly
5. Evaporative Emission (EVAP) Canister Vent Solenoid Valve
6. EVAP Canister

22116_LACR_G0054

Fig. 117 Fuel tank components

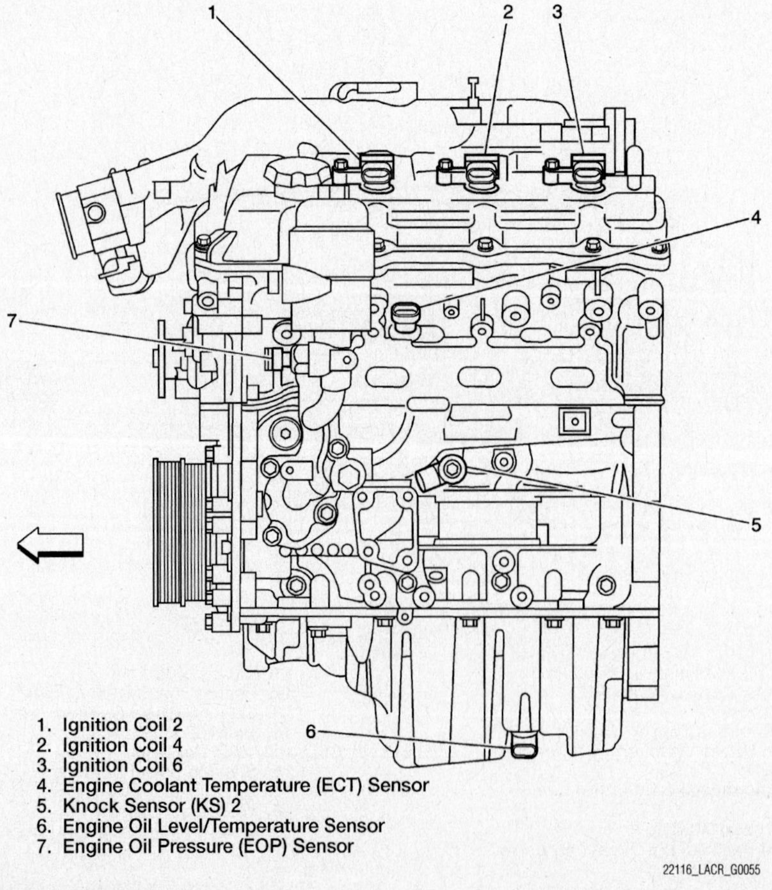

1. Ignition Coil 2
2. Ignition Coil 4
3. Ignition Coil 6
4. Engine Coolant Temperature (ECT) Sensor
5. Knock Sensor (KS) 2
6. Engine Oil Level/Temperature Sensor
7. Engine Oil Pressure (EOP) Sensor

22116_LACR_G0055

Fig. 118 Engine control components (front)—3.6L

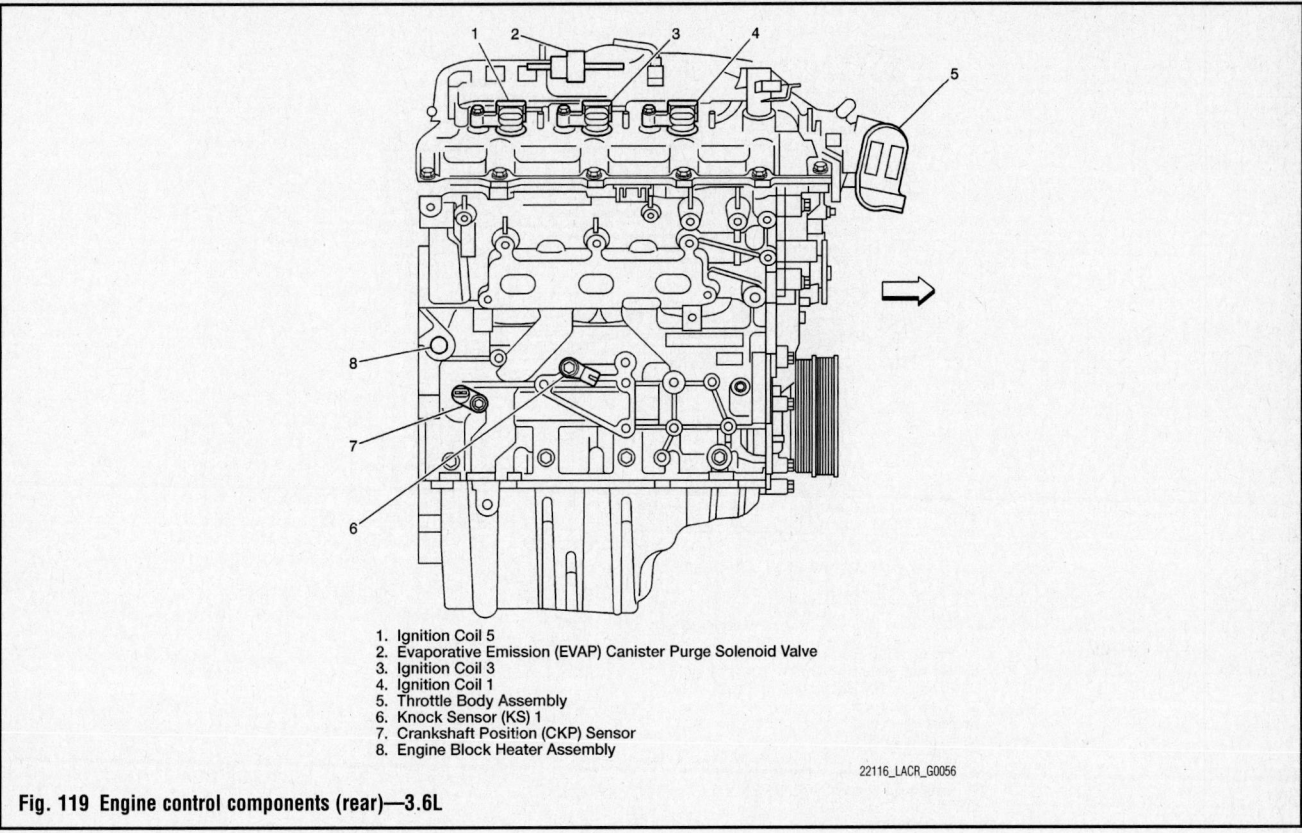

1. Ignition Coil 5
2. Evaporative Emission (EVAP) Canister Purge Solenoid Valve
3. Ignition Coil 3
4. Ignition Coil 1
5. Throttle Body Assembly
6. Knock Sensor (KS) 1
7. Crankshaft Position (CKP) Sensor
8. Engine Block Heater Assembly

22116_LACR_G0056

Fig. 119 Engine control components (rear)—3.6L

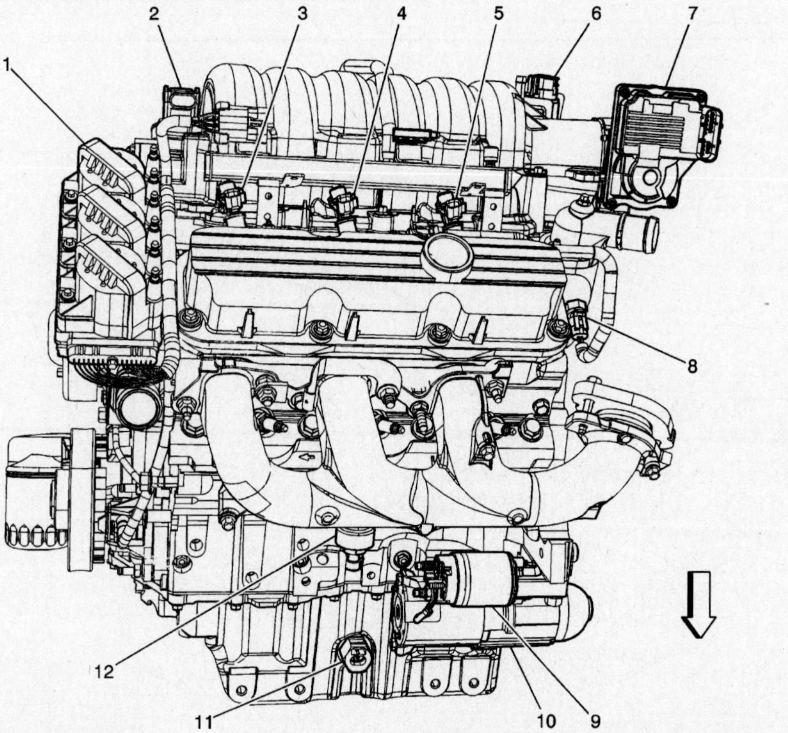

1. Ignition Coil Module
2. Manifold Absolute Pressure (MAP) Sensor
3. Fuel Injector 1
4. Fuel Injector 3
5. Fuel Injector 5
6. Exhaust Gas Recirculation (EGR) Valve
7. Throttle Actuator Control (TAC) Module
8. Engine Coolant Temperature (ECT) Sensor
9. Starter Solenoid
10. Starter
11. Engine Oil Level Switch
12. Knock Sensor (KS) 1

22116_LACR_G0057

Fig. 120 Engine control components (front)—3.8L

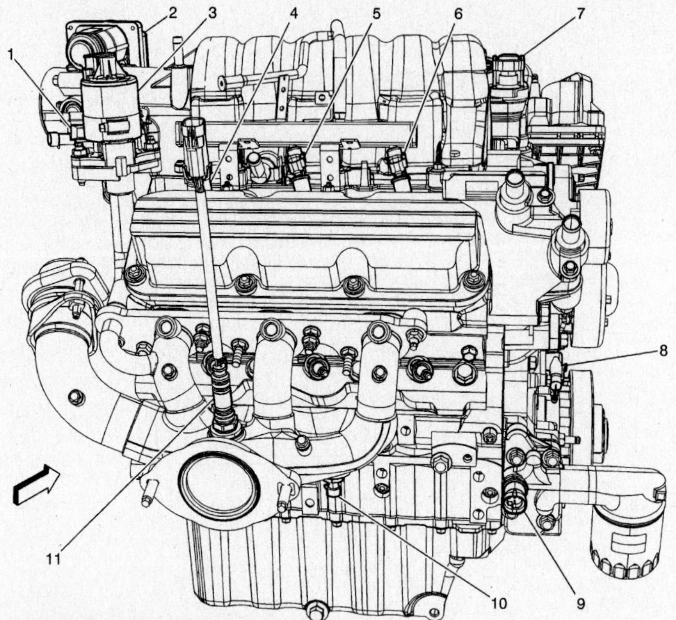

1. Evaporative Emission (EVAP) Canister Purge Solenoid Valve
2. Throttle Actuator Control (TAC) Module
3. Exhaust Gas Recirculation (EGR) Valve
4. Fuel Injector 6
5. Fuel Injector 4
6. Fuel Injector 2
7. Manifold Absolute Pressure (MAP) Sensor
8. Camshaft Position (CMP) Sensor
9. Engine Oil Pressure (EOP) Sensor
10. Knock Sensor (KS) 2

22116_LACR_G0058

Fig. 121 Engine control components (rear)—3.8L

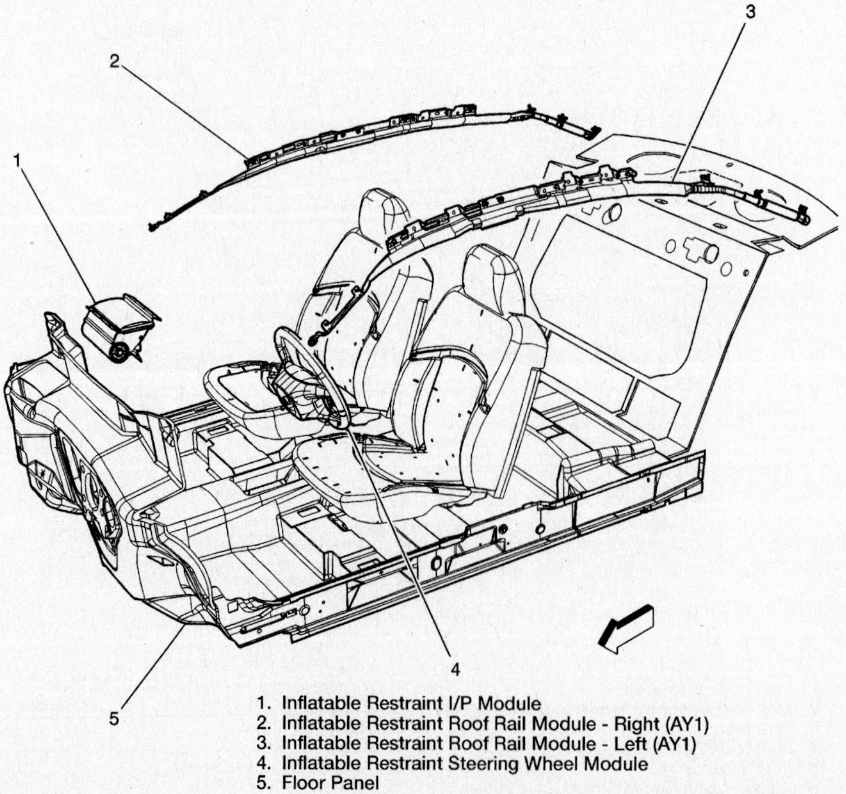

1. Inflatable Restraint I/P Module
2. Inflatable Restraint Roof Rail Module - Right (AY1)
3. Inflatable Restraint Roof Rail Module - Left (AY1)
4. Inflatable Restraint Steering Wheel Module
5. Floor Panel

22116_LACR_G0059

Fig. 122 Inflatable restraint air bag module components

ACCELERATOR PEDAL POSITION (APP) SENSOR

LOCATION

See Figures 123 and 124.

Refer to the accompanying illustrations for sensor location.

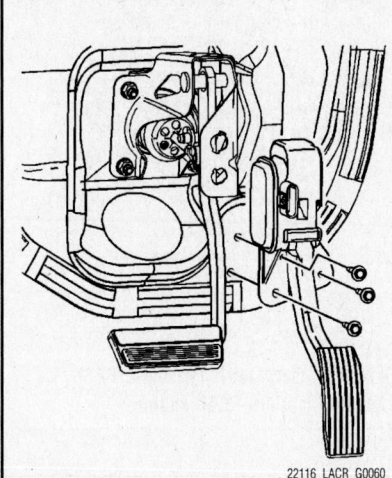

Fig. 123 Accelerator Pedal Position (APP) sensor location—3.6L engine

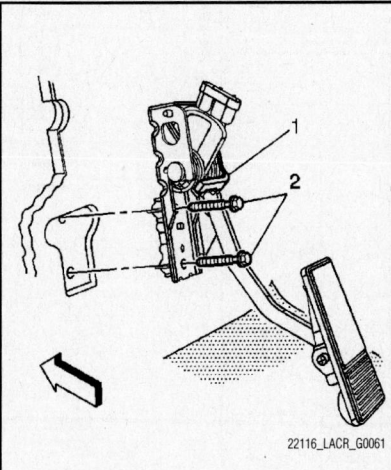

Fig. 124 Accelerator Pedal Position (APP) sensor location—3.8L engine

OPERATION

The accelerator pedal contains 2 individual Accelerator Pedal Position (APP) sensors within the assembly. The APP sensors 1 and 2 are potentiometer type sensors each with 3 circuits:

- A 5-volt reference circuit
- A low reference circuit
- A signal circuit

The APP sensors are used to determine the pedal angle. The Powertrain Control Module (PCM) provides each APP sensor with a 5-volt reference circuit and a low reference circuit. The APP sensors provide the PCM with signal voltage proportional to the pedal movement. The APP sensor 1 signal voltage at rest position is near the low reference and increases as the pedal is actuated. The APP sensor 2 signal voltage at rest position is near the 5-volt reference and decreases as the pedal is actuated.

REMOVAL & INSTALLATION

3.6L Engine

See Figure 123.

1. Turn the ignition OFF.
2. Remove the insulator panel from under the dashboard on the driver's side.

> ※※ **WARNING**
>
> **Handle the electronic throttle control components carefully. Use cleanliness in order to prevent damage. Do not drop or roughly handle the electronic throttle control components. Do not immerse the electronic throttle control components in cleaning solvents of any type.**

3. Disconnect the Accelerator Pedal Position (APP) sensor electrical connector from the accelerator pedal module.
4. Remove the APP sensor mounting bolts.
5. Remove the APP sensor from the vehicle.

To install:

6. Position the APP sensor to the mounting plate.
7. Install the APP sensor mounting bolts. Tighten the APP sensor mounting bolts to 89 inch lbs. (10 Nm).
8. Connect the APP sensor electrical connector.
9. Operate the accelerator pedal and observe the APP angles using a scan tool.

➡ **The accelerator pedal should operate freely, without binding between closed throttle and Wide Open Throttle (WOT).**

10. Install the insulator panel under the dashboard on the driver's side.

3.8L Engine

See Figure 124.

1. Remove the left Instrument Panel (I/P) sound insulator.
2. Disconnect the Accelerator Pedal Position (APP) sensor electrical connector.

3. Remove the accelerated pedal bolts (2).
4. Remove the accelerator pedal (1) from the vehicle.

To install:

5. Position the accelerator pedal (1) to the vehicle.
6. Install the accelerator pedal bolts (2). Tighten the bolts to 44 inch lbs. (5 Nm).
7. Connect APP sensor electrical connector.
8. Install the left I/P sound insulator.

TESTING

See Figures 125 and 126.

1. Before beginning vehicle diagnosis, the following preliminary inspections/tests must be performed:

- Ensure that the battery is fully charged
- Ensure that the battery cables are clean and tight
- Inspect for any open fuses
- Ensure that the grounds are clean, tight, and in the correct location
- Inspect the easily accessible systems or the visible system components for obvious damage or conditions that could cause the concern. This would include checking to ensure that all connections/connectors are fully seated and secured
- Inspect for aftermarket devices that could affect the operation of the system
- Search for applicable service bulletins

2. Install a scan tool. Verify that the scan tool powers up.
3. With the ignition ON, engine OFF, verify communication with all of the control modules on the vehicle.
4. With the ignition ON, observe the scan tool APP sensor 1 voltage parameter. The readings should be 1.0 volt at rest to just above 4.0 volts when fully depressed. Ensure there is a voltage change with accelerator pedal movement.
5. With the ignition ON, observe the scan tool APP sensor 2 voltage parameter. The readings should be 0.5 volts at rest to more than 2.0 volts with the accelerator pedal fully depressed. Ensure there is a voltage change with accelerator pedal movement.
6. Connect a fused jumper wire between the APP sensor 2 5-volt reference circuit and the APP sensor 2 signal circuit at the accelerator pedal harness connector.

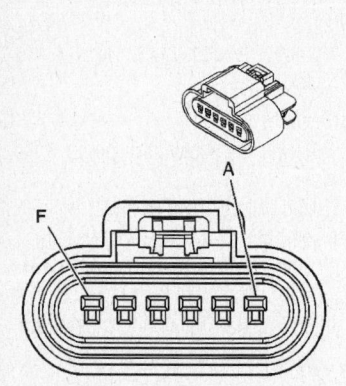

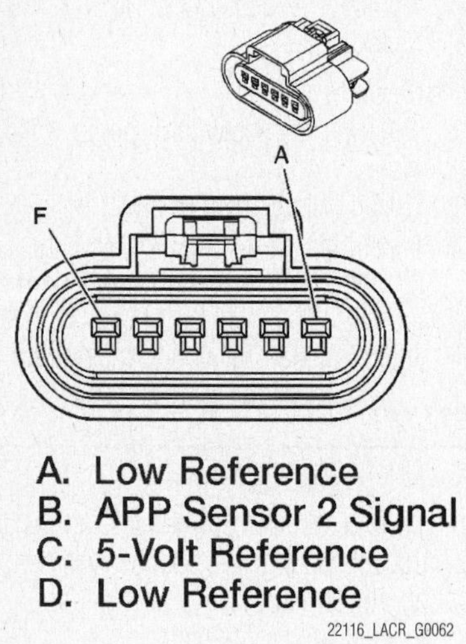

A. Low Reference
B. APP Sensor 2 Signal
C. 5-Volt Reference
D. Low Reference

22116_LACR_G0062

Fig. 125 Accelerator Pedal Position (APP) connector end view

7. Observe the APP sensor 2 voltage parameter with a scan tool. It should read 4.6–5.2 volts.

8. Turn OFF the ignition. Remove the fused jumper.

9. Turn ON the ignition, with the engine OFF.

10. Measure the voltage of the APP sensor 5-volt reference circuit with a DMM. It should read 4.6–5.2 volts.

11. If the reference voltage is below the acceptable range, check the low reference circuit for an open or high resistance interruption.

12. If all circuits are functioning properly and there is no voltage change when the accelerator pedal is moved, replace the APP.

BAROMETRIC PRESSURE (BARO) SENSOR

LOCATION

See Figures 127 and 128.

22116_LACR_G0064

Fig. 127 Barometric Pressure (BARO) sensor location—3.6L engine

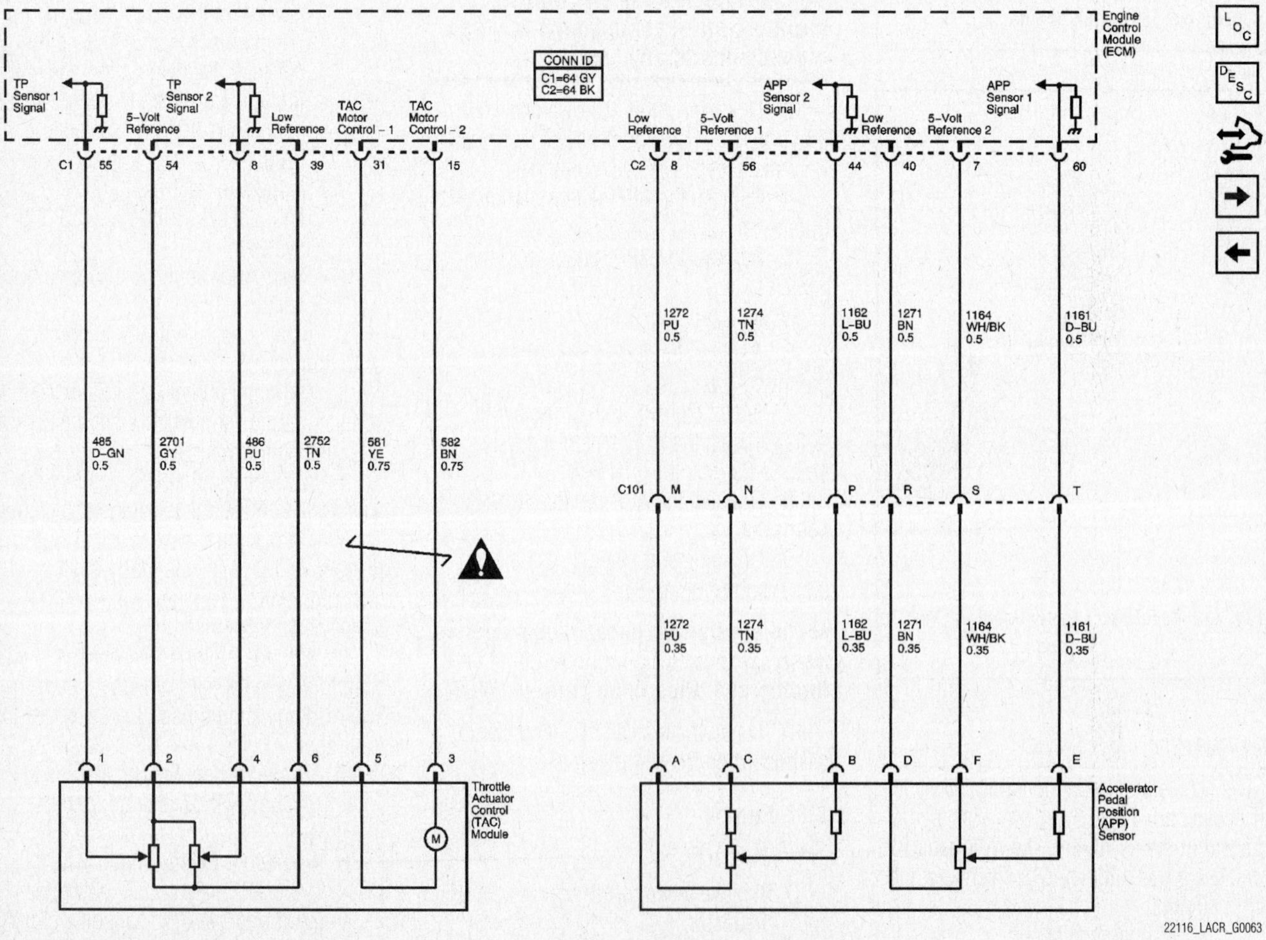

Fig. 126 Circuit schematics for electronic throttle controls—APP & TAC

22116_LACR_G0063

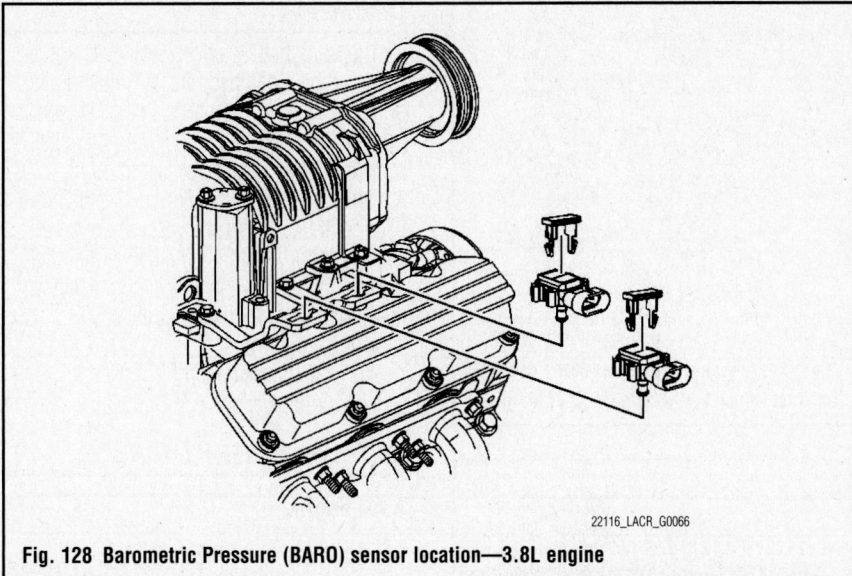

Fig. 128 Barometric Pressure (BARO) sensor location—3.8L engine

Refer to the accompanying illustrations for sensor location.

OPERATION

As a vehicle travels in different elevations, the barometric pressure changes. Based on the elevation above or below sea level, the pressure changes are compensated for through the vehicle electronics. As elevation increases, there is less overlying atmospheric mass, so that pressure decreases with increasing elevation.

The BARO sensor is a variable capacitance sensor used to determine altitude. The BARO signal affects injection timing and fuel quantity to optimize engine operation throughout all altitude conditions.

REMOVAL & INSTALLATION

3.6L Engine

See Figures 127 and 129.

1. Turn the ignition OFF.
2. Remove the Barometric Pressure (BARO) sensor electrical connector.
3. Remove the BARO sensor bolt.
4. Remove the BARO sensor.

To install:

5. Install the BARO sensor.
6. Install the BARO sensor bolt. Tighten the BARO sensor bolt to 89 inch lbs. (10 Nm).
7. Install the BARO sensor electrical connector.

3.8L Engine

See Figure 128.

1. Remove the fuel injector sight shield.
2. Disconnect the Barometric Pressure (BARO) sensor electrical connector.
3. Remove the BARO sensor retainer.
4. Remove the BARO sensor.

To install:

5. Install the BARO sensor.
6. Install the BARO sensor retainer.
7. Connect the BARO sensor electrical connector.
8. Install the fuel injector sight shield.

TESTING

1. Before beginning vehicle diagnosis, the following preliminary inspections/tests must be performed:
   - Ensure that the battery is fully charged
   - Ensure that the battery cables are clean and tight
   - Inspect for any open fuses
   - Ensure that the grounds are clean, tight, and in the correct location
   - Inspect the easily accessible systems or the visible system components for obvious damage or conditions that could cause the concern. This would include checking to ensure that all connections/connectors are fully seated and secured
   - Inspect for aftermarket devices that could affect the operation of the system
   - Search for applicable service bulletins

2. Install a scan tool. Verify that the scan tool powers up.
3. With the ignition ON, engine OFF, verify communication with all of the control modules on the vehicle.
4. Turn ON the ignition, with the engine OFF.
5. Observe the Barometric Pressure (BARO) sensor parameter on a scan tool while moving the related harness connectors at the BARO sensor and at the Engine Control Module (ECM).
   - The BARO parameter should remain steady and not change by more than 3 kPa
   - If the BARO parameter changes more than 3 kPa, check the integrity of the connectors and the immediate wiring
6. Turn OFF the ignition.
7. Disconnect the BARO sensor.
8. Turn ON the ignition, with the engine OFF.
9. Observe the BARO volts parameter with a scan tool.
   - The voltage should be within the range of 4.9–5.2 volts
10. Connect a fused jumper wire between the signal circuit of the BARO sensor and the ECM housing.

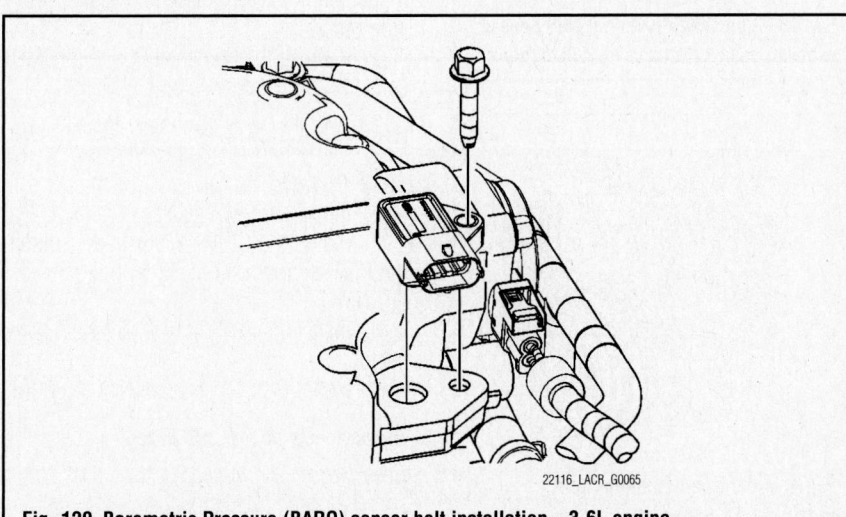

Fig. 129 Barometric Pressure (BARO) sensor bolt installation—3.6L engine

11. Observe the BARO volts parameter with a scan tool.
- The voltage should read 0.00 volts

12. Set up a Digital Multi-Meter (DMM) to test amperage on the 400 mA scale.

13. Measure the amperage between the 5-volt reference circuit of the BARO sensor and the ECM housing.
- The amperage should be no more than 80 mA

14. Turn OFF the ignition.

15. Remove the ECM fuse, or the PCM/ETC fuse, from the underhood electrical center.

✳✳ WARNING

Do NOT use a test lamp to test the continuity of the circuit. Damage to the control module may occur due to excessive current draw.

16. Measure the resistance between the low reference circuit of the BARO sensor and the ECM housing with a DMM.
- The resistance should not be more than 5 ohms

17. Test for shorted terminals and for poor connections at the BARO sensor.

18. If all circuits are functioning properly replace the BARO sensor.

CAMSHAFT POSITION (CMP) SENSOR

LOCATION

See Figures 130 through 134.

Refer to the accompanying illustrations for sensor location.

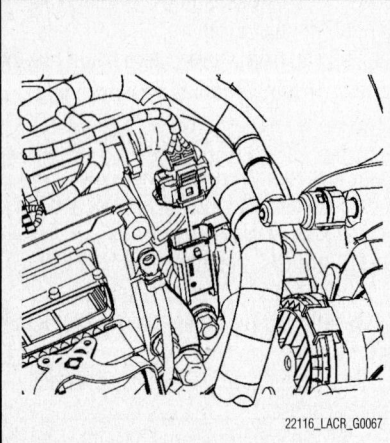

Fig. 130 Camshaft Position (CMP) sensor, intake, bank 1 (right side)—3.6L engine

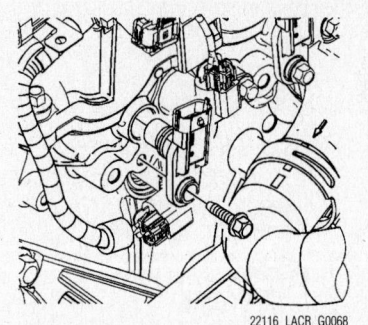

Fig. 131 Camshaft Position (CMP) sensor, exhaust, bank 1 (right side)—3.6L engine

Fig. 132 Camshaft Position (CMP) sensor, intake, bank 2 (left side)—3.6L engine

Fig. 133 Camshaft Position (CMP) sensor, exhaust, bank 2 (left side)—3.6L engine

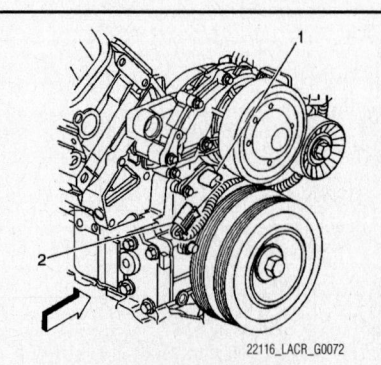

Fig. 134 Camshaft Position (CMP) sensor—3.8L engine

OPERATION

The Camshaft Position (CMP) sensor is triggered by a notched reluctor wheel built onto the camshaft sprocket. The CMP sensor provides four signal pulses every camshaft revolution. Each notch, or feature of the reluctor wheel, is of a different size which is used to identify the compression stroke of each cylinder and to enable sequential fuel injection. The CMP sensor is connected to the PCM by the following circuits:
- A 5-volt circuit
- A low reference circuit
- A signal circuit

REMOVAL & INSTALLATION

3.6L Engine

Intake—Bank 1 (Right Side)

See Figure 130.

1. Turn the ignition OFF.
2. Remove the Camshaft Position (CMP) sensor electrical connector.
3. Remove the CMP sensor bolt.
4. Remove the CMP sensor.

To install:
5. Install the CMP sensor.
6. Install the CMP sensor bolt. Tighten the CMP sensor bolt to 89 inch lbs. (10 Nm).
7. Install the CMP sensor electrical connector.

Exhaust—Bank 1 (Right Side)

See Figure 131.

1. Turn the ignition OFF.

➡**Do not remove the Engine Control Module (ECM) from the ECM bracket. Do not remove the ECM redundant ground wire from the ECM.**

2. Remove the ECM bracket bolts and reposition the ECM bracket in order to provide access.
3. Remove the Camshaft Position (CMP) sensor electrical connector.
4. Remove the CMP sensor bolt.
5. Remove the CMP sensor.

To install:
6. Install the CMP sensor.
7. Install the CMP sensor bolt. Tighten the CMP sensor bolt to 89 inch lbs. (10 Nm).
8. Install the CMP sensor electrical connector.
9. Install the ECM bracket with the ECM.

Intake—Bank 2 (Left Side)

See Figures 132 and 135.

1. Turn the ignition OFF.

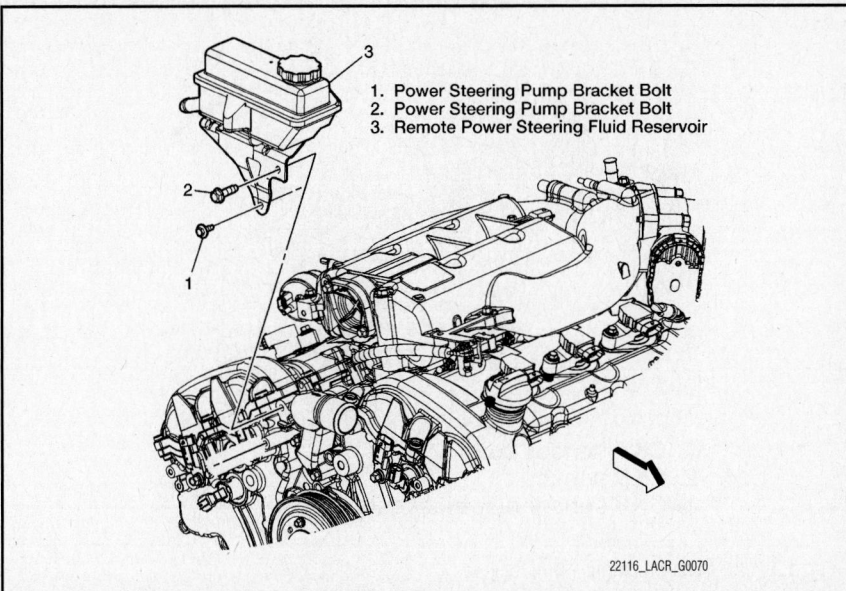

1. Power Steering Pump Bracket Bolt
2. Power Steering Pump Bracket Bolt
3. Remote Power Steering Fluid Reservoir

22116_LACR_G0070

Fig. 135 Move the Power Steering (PS) fluid reservoir in order to provide access—3.6L engine

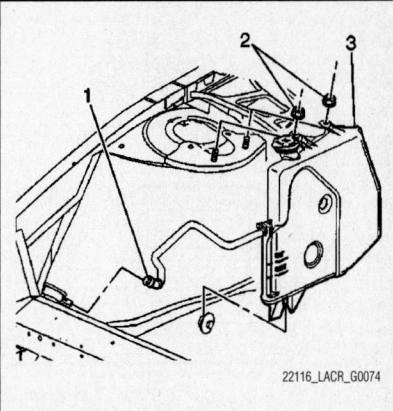

22116_LACR_G0074

Fig. 136 Remove the coolant recovery reservoir—3.8L engine

➡**Do not disconnect the power steering fluid lines/hoses from the reservoir.**

2. Remove the Power Steering (PS) fluid reservoir bolts and reposition the PS fluid reservoir in order to provide access.

3. Remove the Camshaft Position (CMP) sensor electrical connector.

4. Remove the CMP sensor bolt.

5. Remove the CMP sensor.

To install:

6. Install the CMP sensor.

7. Install the CMP sensor bolt. Tighten the CMP sensor bolt to 89 inch lbs. (10 Nm).

8. Install the CMP sensor electrical connector.

9. Install the PS fluid reservoir.

a. Tighten the PS pump bracket bolt (1) to 80 inch lbs. (9 Nm).

b. Tighten the PS pump bracket bolt (2) to 18 ft. lbs. (25 Nm).

Exhaust—Bank 2 (Left Side)

See Figures 133 and 135.

1. Turn the ignition OFF.

➡**Do not disconnect the power steering fluid lines/hoses from the reservoir.**

2. Remove the Power Steering (PS) fluid reservoir bolts and reposition the PS fluid reservoir in order to provide access.

3. Remove the Camshaft Position (CMP) sensor electrical connector.

4. Remove the CMP sensor bolt.

5. Remove the CMP sensor.

To install:

6. Install the CMP sensor.

7. Install the CMP sensor bolt. Tighten the CMP sensor bolt to 89 inch lbs. (10 Nm).

8. Install the CMP sensor electrical connector.

9. Install the PS fluid reservoir.

a. Tighten the PS pump bracket bolt (1) to 80 inch lbs. (9 Nm).

b. Tighten the PS pump bracket bolt (2) to 18 ft. lbs. (25 Nm).

3.8L Engine

See Figures 134 and 136.

1. Reposition the coolant reservoir hose clamp (1) aside at the radiator overflow fitting.

2. Remove the coolant reservoir hose from the radiator overflow fitting.

3. Disconnect the coolant reservoir hose support retainer from the electrical harness.

4. Remove the coolant reservoir nuts (2) from the shock tower studs.

5. Remove the coolant recovery reservoir (3) from the lower retainer and the shock tower studs.

6. Drain the coolant from the recovery reservoir into a clean container.

7. Remove the accessory drive belt. Refer to Accessory Drive Belt, removal and installation.

8. Disconnect the electrical connector (2) from the Camshaft Position (CMP) sensor (1).

9. Remove the CMP sensor bolt.

10. Remove the CMP sensor from the engine front cover.

To install:

11. Install the CMP sensor to the engine front cover.

12. Install the CMP sensor bolt. Tighten the bolt to 89 inch lbs. (10 Nm).

13. Connect the electrical connector (2) to the CMP sensor (1).

14. Install the accessory drive belt. Refer to Accessory Drive Belt, removal and installation.

15. Install the coolant recovery reservoir (3) to the lower retainer and the shock tower studs.

16. Install the nuts (2) to the shock tower studs. Tighten the nuts to 29 inch lbs. (3 Nm).

17. Lubricate the reservoir hose with clean water. Route the hose to the radiator overflow neck fitting.

➡**The hose end must be flush against the radiator filler neck. Seat the clamp squarely between the radiator filler neck and the flared end of the fitting.**

18. Install the coolant reservoir hose (1) to the radiator overflow fitting.

19. Connect the coolant reservoir hose support retainer to the electrical harness.

20. Position the coolant reservoir hose clamp to the radiator overflow fitting.

21. Fill the coolant recovery reservoir to the proper level.

TESTING

See Figures 137 and 138.

During normal operation the PCM controls all ignition functions. If either the Crankshaft Position (CKP) or Camshaft Position (CMP) sensor signal is lost, the engine will continue to run because the PCM will default to a limp home mode using the remaining sensor input. Diagnostic trouble codes are available to accurately diagnose the ignition system with an OBD2 scan tool.

1. Inspect the CMP sensor for correct installation. Remove the CMP sensor from the engine and inspect the sensor O-ring for damage. If the sensor is loose, incorrectly installed, or damaged, replace the CMP sensor.

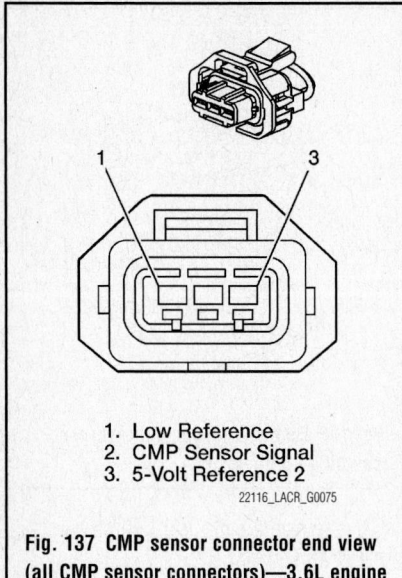

1. Low Reference
2. CMP Sensor Signal
3. 5-Volt Reference 2

22116_LACR_G0075

Fig. 137 CMP sensor connector end view (all CMP sensor connectors)—3.6L engine

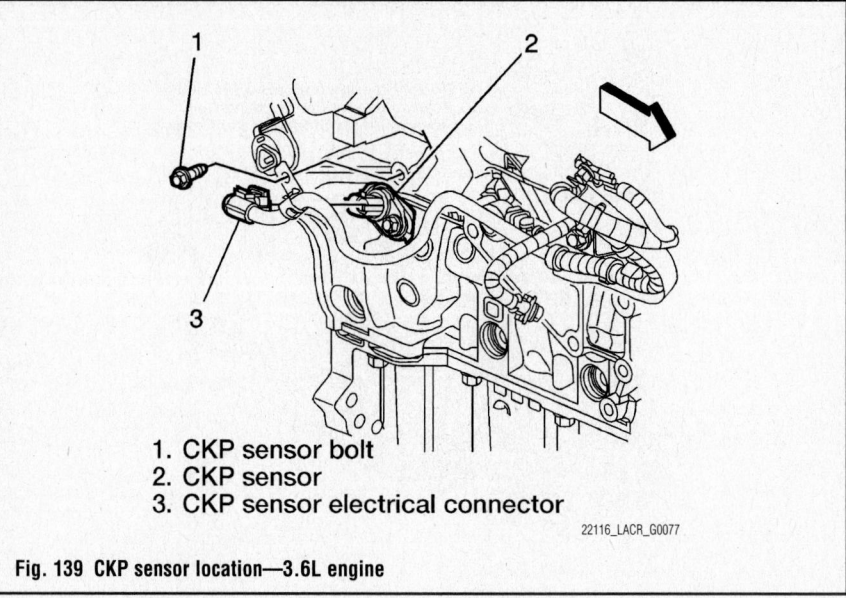

1. CKP sensor bolt
2. CKP sensor
3. CKP sensor electrical connector

22116_LACR_G0077

Fig. 139 CKP sensor location—3.6L engine

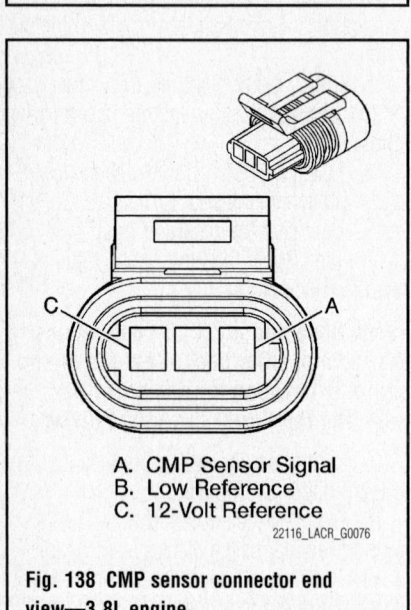

A. CMP Sensor Signal
B. Low Reference
C. 12-Volt Reference

22116_LACR_G0076

Fig. 138 CMP sensor connector end view—3.8L engine

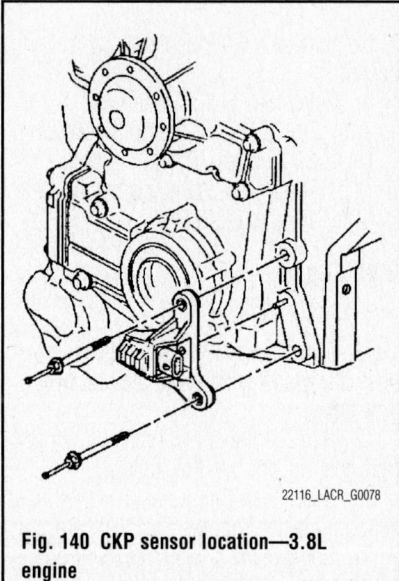

22116_LACR_G0078

Fig. 140 CKP sensor location—3.8L engine

2. Engage the CMP sensor harness connector to the CMP sensor.

3. Connect the scan tool to the diagnostic connector.

4. With the ignition ON, engine OFF observe the CMP active counter parameter on the scan tool.

5. Pass a flat steel object across the tip of the sensor repeatedly. The CMP active counter parameter should increment with each pass of the steel object.

6. If the parameter does not increment, replace the CMP sensor.

CRANKSHAFT POSITION (CKP) SENSOR

LOCATION

See Figures 139 and 140.

Refer to the accompanying illustrations for sensor location.

OPERATION

The Crankshaft Position (CKP) sensor is a permanent magnet generator known as a variable reluctance sensor. The CKP sensor produces an AC voltage of varying amplitude and frequency. The frequency depends on the velocity of the crankshaft. The AC output depends on the crankshaft position and the battery voltage. The CKP sensor works in conjunction with a reluctor wheel attached to the crankshaft. As each reluctor wheel tooth rotates past the CKP sensor, the resulting change in the magnetic field creates an ON/OFF pulse. The PCM processes the pulses to create a pattern that enables the PCM to determine the crankshaft position. The PCM can synchronize the ignition timing, the fuel injector timing, and the spark knock control based on the CKP sensor and the Camshaft Position (CMP) sensor inputs. The CKP sensor is also used to detect misfire and for tachometer display. The PCM learns the variations between different speed and load conditions to correctly detect misfires. The CKP sensor circuits consist of a signal circuit and a low reference circuit. The two wires are twisted together to prevent electromagnetic interference on the CKP sensor circuits.

REMOVAL & INSTALLATION

3.6L Engine

See Figure 139.

1. Turn the ignition OFF.
2. Raise and support the vehicle.
3. Reposition the wiring harness heat shield to obtain access.
4. Disconnect the Crankshaft Position (CKP) electrical connector (3).
5. Remove the crankshaft sensor bolt.
6. Remove the crankshaft sensor.

To install:

7. Install the crankshaft position sensor.
8. Install the crankshaft position sensor bolt. Tighten the crankshaft position sensor bolt to 89 inch lbs. (10 Nm).
9. Connect the CKP electrical connector (3).
10. Install the wiring harness heat shield to the oil level indicator tube.
11. Lower the vehicle.

3.8L Engine

See Figures 140 and 141.

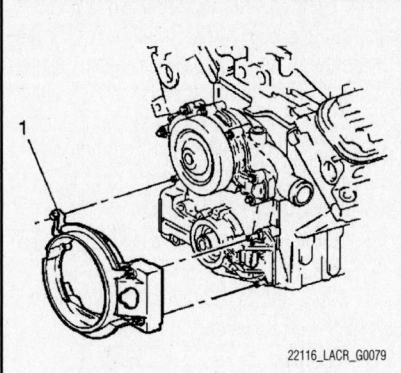

Fig. 141 Remove the CKP sensor shield—3.8L engine

1. Disconnect the negative battery cable.
2. Raise and support the vehicle.
3. Remove the crankshaft damper (harmonic balancer). Refer to Crankshaft Damper, removal and installation.
4. Disconnect the Crankshaft Position (CKP) sensor electrical connector.

❊❊ WARNING

Do not use a pry bar when removing the CKP sensor shield.

5. Remove the CKP sensor shield (1).
6. Remove the CKP sensor studs.
7. Remove the CKP sensor.

To install:

8. Install the CKP sensor.
9. Install the CKP sensor studs. Tighten the studs to 22 ft. lbs. (30 Nm).
10. Install the CKP sensor shield (1).
11. Connect the CKP sensor electrical connector.
12. Install the crankshaft damper. Refer to Crankshaft Damper, removal and installation.
13. Lower the vehicle.
14. Connect the negative battery cable.
15. Perform the CKP system Variation Learn Procedure. Refer to Crankshaft Position (CKP) Sensor, Testing, Variation Learn Procedure for CKP.

TESTING

See Figures 142 and 143.

During normal operation the PCM controls all ignition functions. If either the Crankshaft Position (CKP) or Camshaft Position (CMP) sensor signal is lost, the engine will continue to run because the PCM will default to a limp home mode using the remaining sensor input. Diagnostic trouble codes are available to accurately diagnose the ignition system with an OBD2 scan tool.

1. Inspect the CKP sensor for correct installation. Remove the CKP sensor from

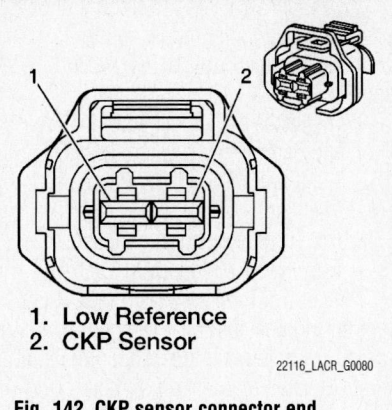

1. Low Reference
2. CKP Sensor

Fig. 142 CKP sensor connector end view—3.6L engine

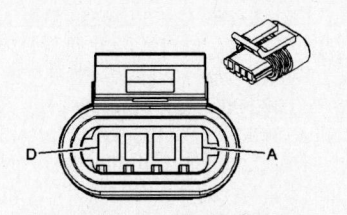

A. CKP Sensor 2 Signal
B. CKP Sensor 1 Signal
C. Low Reference
D. 12-Volt Reference

Fig. 143 CKP sensor connector end view—3.8L engine

the engine and inspect the sensor O–ring for damage. If the sensor is loose, incorrectly installed, or damaged, replace the CKP sensor.

2. Engage the CKP sensor harness connector to the CKP sensor.
3. Connect the scan tool to the diagnostic connector.
4. With the ignition ON, engine OFF observe the CKP active counter parameter on the scan tool.
5. Pass a flat steel object across the tip of the sensor repeatedly. The CKP active counter parameter should increment with each pass of the steel object.
6. If the parameter does not increment, replace the CKP sensor.

Variation Learn Procedure for CKP

The Crankshaft Position (CKP) system variation learn procedure is required when the following service procedures have been performed, regardless of whether DTC P0315 is set:
• Engine replacement
• Engine Control Module (ECM) replacement

• Crankshaft damper replacement
• Crankshaft replacement
• CKP sensor replacement
• Any engine repairs which disturb the crankshaft to CKP sensor relationship

The scan tool monitors certain component signals to determine if all the conditions are met to continue with the CKP system variation learn procedure. The scan tool only displays the condition that inhibits the procedure. The scan tool monitors the following components:
• CKP sensor activity. If there is a CKP sensor condition, refer to the applicable DTC that was set.
• Camshaft Position (CMP) signal activity. If there is a CMP signal condition, refer to the applicable DTC that was set.
• Engine Coolant Temperature (ECT). If the ECT is not warm enough, idle the engine until the ECT reaches the correct temperature.

1. Install a scan tool.
2. Monitor the ECM for DTC's with a scan tool. If other DTC's are set, except DTC P0315, refer to the applicable DTC information for that code.
3. With a scan tool, select the CKP system variation learn procedure and perform the following:
   a. Observe the fuel cut-off for the applicable engine.
   b. Block the drive wheels.
   c. Set the parking brake.
   d. Place the vehicle's transmission in Park or Neutral.
   e. Turn the Air Conditioning (A/C) **OFF**.
   f. Cycle the ignition from **OFF** to **ON**.
   g. Apply and hold the brake pedal for the duration of the procedure.
   h. Start and idle the engine.
   i. Accelerate to Wide Open Throttle (WOT). The engine should not accelerate beyond the calibrated fuel cut-off RPM value noted above. Release the throttle immediately if the value is exceeded.

➡️**While the learn procedure is in progress, release the throttle immediately when the engine starts to decelerate. The engine control is returned to the operator and the engine responds to throttle position after the learn procedure is complete.**

   j. Release the throttle when fuel cut-off occurs.
4. The scan tool displays Learn Status: Learned this Ignition.
   a. If the scan tool indicates that DTC P0315 ran and passed, the CKP variation learn procedure is complete.

b. If the scan tool indicates DTC P0315 failed or did not run, refer to DTC P0315 test procedures.

c. If any other DTC's are set, refer to a Diagnostic Trouble Code (DTC) list for the applicable DTC that was set.

5. Turn **OFF** the ignition for 30 seconds after the learn procedure is completed successfully in order to store the CKP system variation values in the PCM memory.

EGR VALVE POSITION (EVP) SENSOR

LOCATION

See Figure 144.

Refer to the accompanying illustration for sensor location.

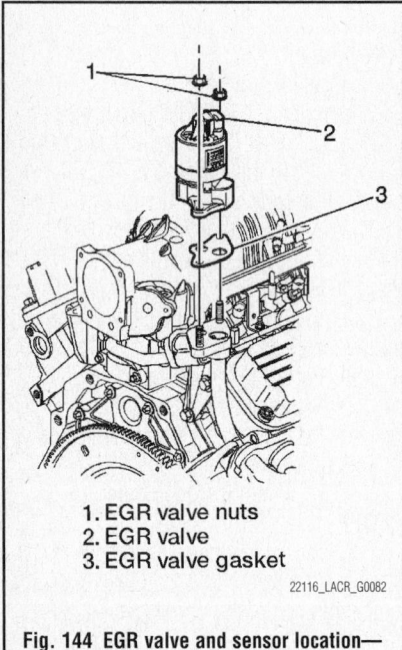

1. EGR valve nuts
2. EGR valve
3. EGR valve gasket

22116_LACR_G0082

Fig. 144 EGR valve and sensor location—3.8L engine

OPERATION

The Exhaust Gas Recirculation (EGR) system is used to reduce the amount of nitrogen oxide (NOx) emission levels caused by combustion temperatures exceeding 1,500°F (816°C). It does this by introducing small amounts of exhaust gas back into the combustion chamber. The exhaust gas absorbs a portion of the thermal energy produced by the combustion process and thus decreases combustion temperature. The EGR system will only operate under specific temperature, Barometric Pressure (BARO) and engine load conditions in order to prevent drivability concerns and to increase engine performance.

The PCM calculates the amount of EGR needed based on the following inputs:

• The Engine Coolant Temperature (ECT) sensor
• The Intake Air Temperature (IAT) sensor
• The Barometric Pressure (BARO)
• The Manifold Absolute Pressure (MAP) sensor
• The Throttle Position (TP) sensor
• The Mass Air Flow (MAF) sensor

The control module tests the EGR system during deceleration. The control module does this by momentarily commanding the EGR valve to open while monitoring the signal circuit of the Manifold Absolute Pressure (MAP) sensor. When the EGR valve is opened, the control module will expect to see a predetermined increase in MAP. If the expected increase in MAP is not detected, the control module records the amount of MAP difference that was detected and adjusts a calibrated fail counter towards a calibrated fail threshold level. The number of EGR flow test counts required to exceed the fail threshold may vary according to the amount of detected EGR flow error.

The EGR Valve Position (EVP) sensor is monitored by the control module. The 5-volt reference circuit, the low reference circuit, and the EVP signal circuit are used by the control module to determine the EGR valve position. The control module compares the EVP sensor parameter with the desired EGR position parameter when the valve is commanded open or closed.

The control module controls the EGR valve with a solid state device called a driver. The driver supplies the EGR solenoid with 12 volts that is Pulse Width Modulated (PWM) through the EGR solenoid high control circuit. A ground path is provided by the control module through the EGR solenoid low control circuit. The driver has the ability to detect an electrical malfunction on the EGR solenoid control circuits.

When the ignition switch is turned ON, the control module records the EGR learned minimum position. The control module compares the EGR learned minimum position parameter to the EVP parameter.

The control module will only allow one EGR flow test during an ignition cycle. To aid in verifying a repair, the control module will allow 9–16 EGR flow test counts during the first ignition cycle following a code clear event or a battery disconnect.

REMOVAL & INSTALLATION

3.8L Engine

See Figure 144.

The Exhaust Gas Recirculation (EGR) valve and the EGR Valve Position (EVP) sensor are integrated into the EGR valve assembly. The EVP is removed with the EGR valve.

1. Disconnect the Exhaust Gas Recirculation (EGR) valve electrical connector.
2. Remove the EGR valve nuts (1).
3. Remove the EGR valve (2).
4. Remove the gasket (3) from the EGR valve adapter.
5. Clean the EGR valve gasket mating surfaces.

To install:

6. Install a new EGR valve gasket (3).
7. Install the EGR valve (2).
8. Install the EGR valve nuts (1). Tighten the nuts to 18 ft. lbs. (25 Nm).
9. Connect the EGR valve electrical connector.

TESTING

See Figures 145 and 146.

1. With the ignition ON and the engine OFF, command the EGR from 0–90 percent. The Exhaust Gas Recirculation (EGR) position sensor parameter should remain within 3 percent of the desired EGR position parameter through the entire range.
2. With the ignition OFF, disconnect the EGR valve harness connector.
3. Turn the ignition ON, connect a test lamp between B and A. The test lamp should illuminate.

a. If the test lamp does not illuminate, test the EGR low control circuit for an open/high resistance.

b. If the circuit tests normal, replace the ECM.

4. Connect a test lamp between the EGR high control circuit (E) and a ground. Command the EGR valve from 0–90 percent and exit the EGR solenoid output control. The test lamp should turn ON when commanded between 10–90 percent and turn OFF when commanded to 0 percent.

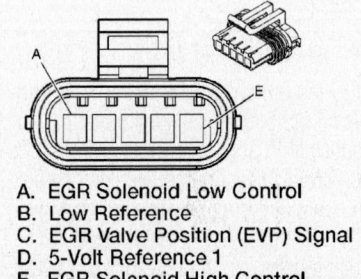

A. EGR Solenoid Low Control
B. Low Reference
C. EGR Valve Position (EVP) Signal
D. 5-Volt Reference 1
E. EGR Solenoid High Control

22116_LACR_G0083

Fig. 145 EGR connector end view—3.8L engine

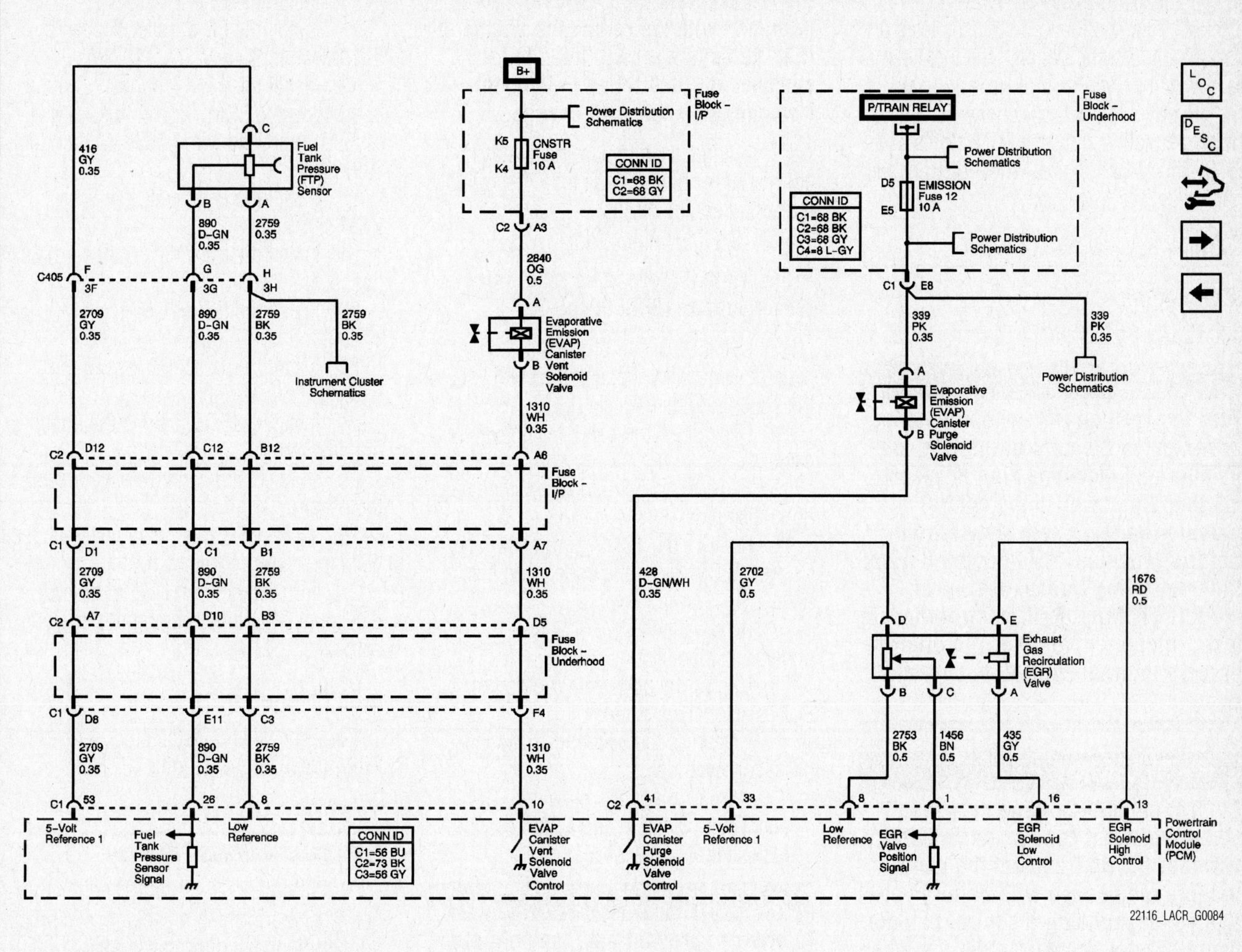

Fig. 146 EGR, EVAP, and FTP circuit schematics—3.8L engine

a. If the test lamp is ON when commanded to 0 percent, test the EGR high control circuit for a short to voltage.

b. If the circuit tests normal, replace the ECM.

c. If the test lamp is always OFF while commanding the EGR valve from 0-90 percent, test the EGR high control circuit for an open, high resistance, or a short to ground.

d. If the circuit tests normal, replace the ECM.

5. If all circuits test normal, replace the EGR valve.

ELECTRONIC CONTROL MODULE (ECM)

The Electronic Control Module (ECM) may also be referred to as the Engine Control Module (ECM).

LOCATION

See Figure 147.

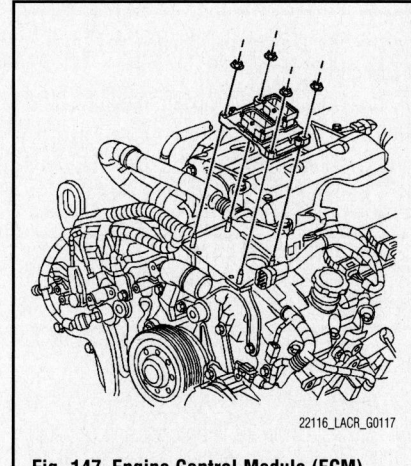

Fig. 147 Engine Control Module (ECM) location—3.6L engine

Refer to the accompanying illustration for ECM location.

OPERATION

The Engine Control Module (ECM) interacts with many emission related components and systems, and monitors the emission related components and systems for deterioration. OBD II diagnostics monitor the system performance and a Diagnostic Trouble Code (DTC) sets if the system performance degrades. The Malfunction Indicator Lamp (MIL) operation and the DTC storage are dictated by the DTC type. A DTC is ranked as a Type A or Type B if the DTC is emissions related. Type C is a non-emissions related DTC.

The ECM is in the engine compartment and is the control center of the engine controls system. The ECM controls the following components:

• The fuel injection system
• The ignition system
• The emission control systems
• The on-board diagnostics
• The A/C and fan systems
• The throttle actuation control (TAC) system

The ECM constantly monitors the information from various sensors and other inputs, and controls the systems that affect the vehicle performance and the emissions. The ECM also performs diagnostic tests on various parts of the system. The ECM can recognize operational problems and alert the driver via the MIL. When the ECM detects a malfunction, the ECM stores a DTC. The condition area is identified by the particular DTC that is set.

REMOVAL & INSTALLATION

3.6L Engine

See Figure 147.

> ✳✳ **WARNING**
>
> **Turn the ignition OFF when installing or removing the control module connectors and disconnecting or reconnecting the power to the control module (battery cable, Powertrain Control Module (PCM)/Engine Control Module (ECM)/Transaxle Control Module (TCM) pigtail, control module fuse, jumper cables, etc.) in order to prevent internal control module damage.**

> ✳✳ **WARNING**
>
> **Control module damage may result when the metal case contacts battery voltage. DO NOT contact the control module metal case with battery voltage when servicing a control module, using battery booster cables, or when charging the vehicle battery.**

> ✳✳ **WARNING**
>
> **In order to prevent any possible electrostatic discharge damage to the control module, do not touch the connector pins or the soldered components on the circuit board.**

➡ **Remove any debris from around the control module connector surfaces before servicing the control module. Inspect the control module connector gaskets when diagnosing or replacing the control module. Ensure that the gaskets are installed correctly. The gaskets prevent contaminant intrusion into the control module.**

➡ **The replacement control module must be programmed.**

➡ **It is necessary to record the remaining engine oil life. If the replacement module is not programmed with the remaining engine oil life, the engine oil life will default to 100 percent. If**

the replacement module is not programmed with the remaining engine oil life, the engine oil will need to be changed at 3,000 miles (5,000 km) from the last engine oil change.

1. Using a scan tool, retrieve the percentage of remaining engine oil. Record the remaining engine oil life.
2. Turn the ignition OFF.

➡ **Ensure that there is no main relay circuit voltage (ECM Fuse).**

3. Use a DVOM in order to measure the main relay circuit voltage at the ECM fuse in the underhood fuse block.
4. Disconnect the battery negative cable.
5. Remove the ECM fuse in the underhood fuse block.
6. Remove the TCM/Instrument Panel Cluster (IPC) fuse in the underhood fuse block.
7. Remove the ECM/TCM fuse in the underhood fuse block.
8. Unlock the body side (outboard) ECM electrical connector:
   a. Depress the ECM electrical connector lever lock.
   b. Simultaneously rotate the ECM connector clamp lever and depress the lock slide.

> ✳✳ **WARNING**
>
> **In order to prevent any possible electrostatic discharge damage to the ECM, do not touch the connector pins.**

9. Remove the body side (outboard) ECM connector.
10. Unlock and remove the engine side (inboard) ECM connector.
11. Remove the ECM redundant ground wire and bolt from the ECM.
12. Remove the ECM bolts.
13. Remove the ECM.
14. If necessary, perform the following steps:
   a. Remove the ECM bracket bolts.
   b. Remove the ECM bracket.

To install:

15. Install the ECM bracket, as necessary.
16. Install the ECM bracket bolts, as necessary. Tighten the ECM bracket bolts to 89 inch lbs. (10 Nm).

> ✳✳ **WARNING**
>
> **In order to prevent any possible electrostatic discharge damage to the ECM, do not touch the connector pins.**

17. Install the ECM.
18. Install the ECM bolts. Tighten the ECM bolts to 89 inch lbs. (10 Nm).
19. Install the ECM redundant ground and bolt to the ECM. Tighten the ECM redundant ground wire bolt to 44 inch lbs. (5 Nm).
20. Install the engine side (inboard) ECM connector.
21. Install the body side (outboard) ECM connector.
22. Install the ECM/TCM fuse in the underhood fuse block.
23. Install the TCM/IPC fuse in the underhood fuse block.
24. Install the ECM fuse in the underhood fuse block.
25. Connect the negative battery cable to the battery.
26. If a new ECM is being installed, the ECM must be programmed.
27. Turn the ignition OFF for at least 5 seconds after the programming event is complete.

3.8L Engine

For removal and installation, refer to Powertrain Control Module (PCM).

TESTING

See Figures 148 and 149.

1. Perform a careful underhood inspection when performing any diagnostic procedure or diagnosing the cause of an emission test failure. This can often lead to repairing a condition without further steps. Use the following guidelines when performing an inspection:
   a. Inspect all of the vacuum hoses for correct routing, pinches, cuts, or disconnects
   b. Inspect any hoses that are difficult to see
   c. Inspect all of the wires in the engine compartment for the following conditions:
   • Burned or chafed spots
   • Pinched wires
   • Contact with sharp edges
   • Contact with hot exhaust manifolds

The Engine Control Module (ECM) is programmed with test routines that test the operation of the various systems the ECM controls. Some tests monitor internal ECM functions. Many tests are run continuously. Other tests run only under specific conditions, referred to as conditions for running the Diagnostic Trouble Code (DTC). When the vehicle is operating within the conditions for running a particular test, the ECM monitors certain parameters and determines if the values are within an expected range. The parameters and values considered outside the range of normal operation are listed as conditions for setting the DTC. When the conditions for setting the DTC occur, the ECM executes the action taken when the DTC sets. Some DTC's alert the driver via the Malfunction Indicator Lamp (MIL) or a message. Other DTC's do not trigger a driver warning, but are stored in memory. The ECM also saves data and input parameters when most DTC's are set.

The DTC's are categorized by type. The DTC type is determined by the MIL operation and the manner in which the fault data is stored when a particular DTC fails. In some cases, there may be exceptions to this structure. Therefore, when diagnosing the system it is important to read the action taken when the DTC sets and the conditions for clearing the DTC.

Many intermittent open or shorted circuits come and go with harness and connector movement caused by vibration, engine torque, bumps, and rough pavement.

2. Test the wiring harness and connectors by performing the following:
- Move the related ECM connectors and wiring while monitoring the appropriate scan tool data
- With the engine running, move the related connectors and wiring while monitoring engine operation
- If harness or connector movement affects the data displayed, the component and system operation, or the engine operation, inspect and repair the harness or connections as necessary

3. Test the electrical connections and/or wiring by performing the following:
- Inspect for incorrect mating of the connector halves or terminals not fully seated in the connector body
- Inspect for improperly formed or damaged terminals. Test for incorrect terminal tension
- Inspect for poor terminal to wire connections including terminals crimped over insulation. This requires removing the terminal from the connector body
- Inspect for corrosion or water intrusion. Pierced or damaged insulation can allow moisture to enter the wiring. The conductor can corrode inside the insulation with little visible evidence. Look for swollen and stiff sections of wire in the suspect circuits
- Inspect for wires that are broken inside the insulation

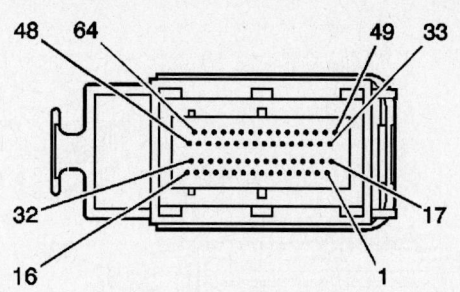

Pin	Wire Color	Circuit No.	Function
1	TN	407	Knock Sensor 2 Signal
2	--	--	Not Used
3	L-GN	5278	HO2S Input Pump Current Sensor 1
4	OG	5275	CMP Sensor Signal - Intake Bank 1
5	GY	605	5-Volt Reference 1
6	--	--	Not Used
7	TN	470	Low Reference
8	PU	486	TP Sensor 2 Signal
9	D-GN/WH	2124	Ignition Control 4
10	WH/BK	5039	CKP Sensor Signal
11	--	--	Not Used
12	OG/BK	5272	CMP Actuator Solenoid Control - Intake Bank 2
13	L-GN	5282	CMP Actuator Solenoid Control - Exhaust Bank 1
14	--	--	Not Used
15	BN	582	TAC Motor Control - 2
16	GY/WH	3113	HO2S Heater Low Control Sensor 1
17	GY	1716	Knock Sensor 1 Signal
18	--	--	Not Used
19	PU/WH	1665	HO2S High Signal
20	D-GN	5273	CMP Sensor Signal - Exhaust Bank 1
21	GY	23	Generator Field Duty Cycle Signal
22	--	--	Not Used
23	YE	410	ECT Sensor Signal
24	--	--	Not Used
25	L-BU/WH	2126	Ignition Control 6
26	OG/WH	2122	Ignition Control 2
27-28	--	--	Not Used
29	PU	5284	Actuator Solenoid Control - Intake Bank 1
30	WH/BK	5283	Actuator Solenoid Control - Exhaust Bank 2
31	YE	581	TAC Motor Control - 1
32	--	--	Not Used
33	D-BU	496	Knock Sensor 1 Signal
34	--	--	Not Used
35	WH	5279	HO2S Pump Current
36	PU	5274	CMP Sensor Signal - Exhaust Bank 2
37-38	--	--	Not Used
39	TN	2752	Low Reference
40	TN/BK	231	Engine Oil Pressure Switch Signal
41	D-GN	2125	Ignition Control 5
42	PU	2121	Ignition Control 1
43	OG	225	Generator Turn On Signal
44	--	--	Not Used
45	L-BU/BK	844	Fuel Injector 4 Control
46	PK/BK	1746	Fuel Injector 3 Control
47	TN/WH	845	Fuel Injector 5 Control
48	D-GN/WH	428	EVAP Canister Purge Solenoid Valve Control
49	GY/BK	1798	Ground
50	L-BU	1876	Knock Sensor 2 Signal
51	--	--	Not Used
52	TN	1664	HO2S Low Signal
53	YE	5276	CMP Sensor Signal Intake Bank 2
54	GY	2701	5-Volt Reference
55	D-GN	485	TP Sensor 1 Signal
56	L-GN/BK	5266	MAP Sensor Signal
57	GY	705	5-Volt Reference 2
58	L-BU	2123	Ignition Control 3
59	PU/WH	5024	Low Reference
60-61	--	--	Not Used
62	L-GN/BK	1745	Fuel Injector 2 Control
63	TN	1744	Fuel Injector 1 Control
64	YE/BK	846	Fuel Injector 6 Control

22116_LACR_G0118

Fig. 148 Engine Control Module (ECM) connector end view (C1)—3.6L engine

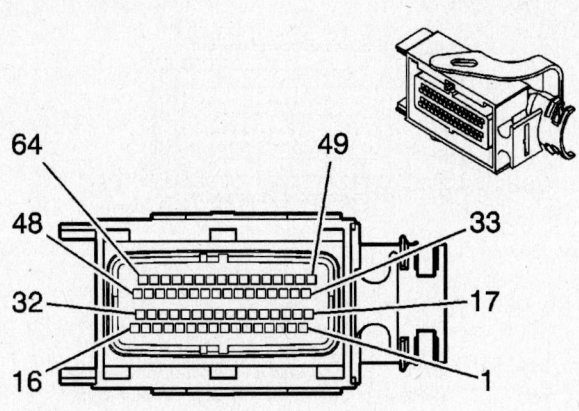

Pin	Wire Color	Circuit No.	Function
1	PK	39	Ignition 1 Voltage
2	BK/WH	3122	HO2S Heater Low Control Sensor 2
3	PK	439	Ignition 1 Voltage
4	D-BU	473	High Speed Cooling Fan Relay Control
5	WH	121	Engine Speed Signal
6	--	--	Not Used
7	WH/BK	1164	5-Volt Reference 2
8	PU	1272	Low Reference
9	RD/BK	380	A/C Refrigerant Pressure Sensor Signal
10	WH	17	Stop Lamp Switch Signal
11	TN	472	IAT Sensor Signal
12	D-GN	890	Fuel Tank Pressure Sensor Signal
13-14	--	--	Not Used
15	OG/BK	463	Requested Torque Signal
16	--	--	Not Used
17	PK	39	Ignition 1 Voltage
18	--	--	Not Used
19	D-GN/WH	465	Fuel Pump Relay Control
20	D-GN	335	Low Speed Cooling Fan Relay Control
21	--	--	Not Used
22	D-GN	389	Vehicle Speed Signal
23	D-BU	6105	High Speed GMLAN Serial Data Bus +
24	BN	5069	Main Relay Control
25	BK	2759	Low Reference
26	BK	2760	Low Reference
27-28	--	--	Not Used
29	PU	3120	HO2S High Signal
30-31	--	--	Not Used
32	OG/BK	1786	Park/Neutral Signal
33	WH	1310	EVAP Canister Vent Solenoid Control
34	--	--	Not Used
35	YE/BK	625	Starter Enable Relay Control
36	OG	540	Battery Positive Voltage
37	TN/BK	464	Delivered Torque Signal
38	--	--	Not Used
39	GY	2709	5-Volt Reference 2
40	BN	1271	Low Reference
41	--	--	Not Used
42	PU	1589	Fuel Level Sensor Signal
43	YE	492	MAF Sensor Signal
44	L-BU	1162	APP Sensor 2 Signal
45-47	--	--	Not Used
48	D-GN	1049	ECM Class 2 Serial Data
49	D-GN/WH	459	A/C Compressor Clutch Relay Control
50	BN/WH	419	MIL Control
51-54	--	--	Not Used
55	L-BU	6106	High Speed GMLAN Serial Data Bus -
56	TN	1274	5-Volt Reference 1
57	TN/WH	3121	HO2S Low Signal
58	BN	1141	Ignition 3 Voltage
59	GY	1884	Cruise Control Set/Coast and Resume/Accelerate Switch Signal
60	D-BU	1161	APP Sensor 1 Signal
61-64	--	--	Not Used

22116_LACR_G0119

Fig. 149 Engine Control Module (ECM) connector end view (C2)—3.6L engine

ENGINE COOLANT TEMPERATURE (ECT) SENSOR

LOCATION

See Figures 150 and 151.

Refer to the accompanying illustrations for sensor locations.

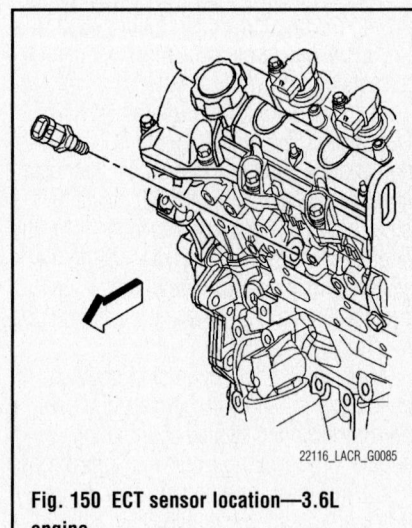

22116_LACR_G0085

Fig. 150 ECT sensor location—3.6L engine

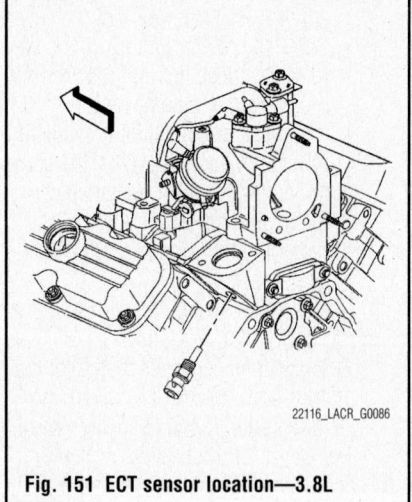

22116_LACR_G0086

Fig. 151 ECT sensor location—3.8L engine

OPERATION

The Engine Coolant Temperature (ECT) sensor is a thermistor device in which resistance changes with temperature. The electrical resistance of a thermistor decreases as the temperature increases, and resistance increases as the temperature decreases. The varying resistance affects the voltage drop across the sensor terminals and provides electrical signals to the PCM corresponding to temperature.

REMOVAL & INSTALLATION

3.6L Engine

See Figure 150.

✳✳ CAUTION

Allow sufficient time for the engine to cool before removing the Engine Coolant Temperature (ECT) sensor. A hot engine may cause excessive coolant loss or personal injury.

1. Turn the ignition OFF.
2. Partially drain the cooling system.
3. Remove the ECT sensor electrical connector.
4. Remove the ECT sensor.

To install:

5. Install the ECT sensor. Tighten the sensor to 16 ft. lbs. (22 Nm).
6. Install the ECT sensor electrical connector.
7. Inspect and fill the cooling system as necessary.

3.8L Engine

See Figure 151.

✳✳ WARNING

Use care when handling the coolant sensor. Damage to the coolant sensor will affect the operation of the fuel control system.

1. Partially drain the cooling system.
2. Disconnect the Engine Coolant Temperature (ECT) sensor electrical connector.
3. Remove the ECT sensor.

To install:

➡**Replacement components must be the correct part number for the application. Components requiring the use of the thread locking compound, lubricants, corrosion inhibitors, or sealants are identified in the service procedure. Some replacement components may come with these coatings already applied. Do not use these coatings on components unless specified. These coatings can affect the final torque, which may affect the operation of the component. Use the correct torque specification when installing components in order to avoid damage.**

4. Coat the threads with sealer GM P/N 12346004 (Canadian P/N 10953480) or equivalent.
5. Install the ECT sensor. Tighten the sensor to 18 ft. lbs. (25 Nm).

6. Connect the ECT sensor electrical connector.
7. Inspect and fill the cooling system as necessary.

TESTING

See Figures 152 and 153.

➡**If the PCM receives a high engine temperature signal from the Engine Coolant Temperature (ECT), it adjusts fueling rates to protect the engine from damage due to overheating.**

1. Turn OFF the ignition.
2. Inspect the cooling system surge tank for the proper coolant level.
3. If the ignition has been OFF for 8 hours or more, the ECT and the Intake Air

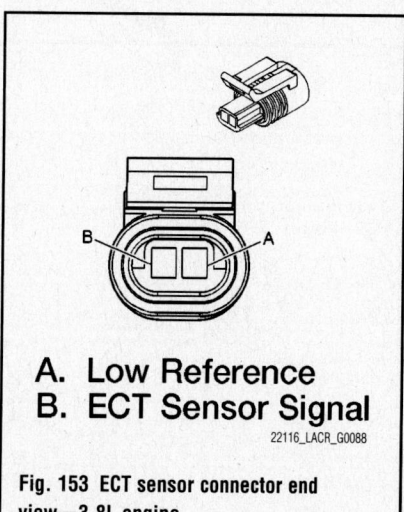

1. **ECT Sensor Signal**
2. **Low Reference**

22116_LACR_G0087

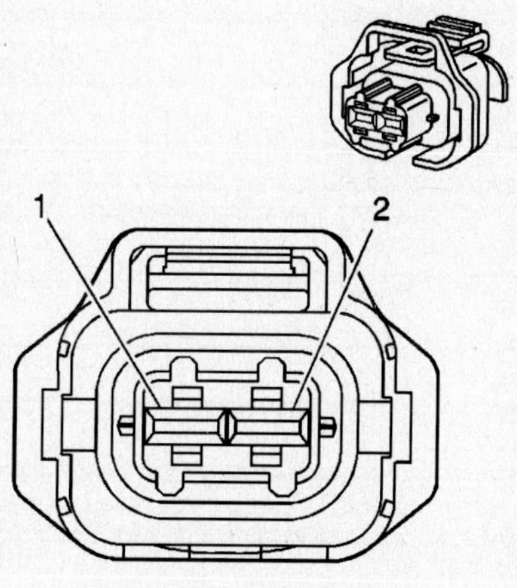

Fig. 152 ECT sensor connector end view—3.6L engines

A. **Low Reference**
B. **ECT Sensor Signal**

22116_LACR_G0088

Fig. 153 ECT sensor connector end view—3.8L engine

Temperature (IAT) should be within 27°F (15°C) of each other and also the ambient temperature.

4. Turn ON the ignition, with the engine OFF, and use a scan tool to observe the IAT and the ECT sensor parameters.
5. Use the scan tool to verify the proper operation of the engine cooling system fans.

➡**A critical analysis of the operation of the thermostat is important to the proper diagnosis of the ECT.**

6. Verify the proper heat range and the operation of the thermostat.

Circuit/System Testing

➡**All electrical components and accessories must be turned OFF and allowed to power down.**

1. With the ignition OFF, disconnect the harness connector at the ECT sensor.
2. Test for less than 5 ohms of resistance between the low reference circuit terminal and ground.
    a. If greater than the specified range, test the low reference circuit for an open/high resistance.
    b. If the circuit tests normal, replace the ECM.
3. With the ignition ON, verify the scan tool ECT parameter is less than a negative 38°F (negative 39°C).
    a. If greater than the specified range, test the signal circuit terminal for a short to ground.
    b. If the circuit tests normal, replace the ECM.
4. Install a 3-amp fused jumper wire between the signal circuit terminal and the low reference circuit terminal. Verify the scan tool ECT parameter is greater than 300°F (149°C).
    a. If less than the specified range, test the signal circuit for a short to voltage or an open/high resistance.
    b. If the circuit tests normal, replace the ECM.
5. If all circuits test normal, test or replace the ECT sensor.

ECT Component Testing

See Figure 154.

Measure and record the resistance of the ECT sensor at various temperatures, then compare those measurements to the following temperature verses resistance table.

Temperature Versus Resistance

Temperature C°/F°	Resistance Minimum Ohms	Resistance Maximum Ohms
Engine Coolant Temperature (ECT)		
-40/-40	40,490	50,136
-20/-4	14,096	16,827
-10/14	8,642	10,152
0/32	5,466	6,326
20/68	2,351	2,649
25/77	1,941	2,173
40/104	1,118	1,231
60/140	573	618
80/176	313	332
100/212	182	191
120/248	109	116
140/284	068	074

22116_LACR_G0089

Fig. 154 Temperature verses resistance table for ECT sensor

HEATED OXYGEN (HO2S) SENSOR

LOCATION

See Figures 155 through 158.

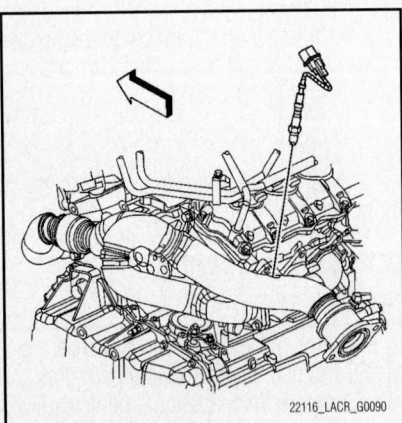

22116_LACR_G0090

Fig. 155 Location of the heated oxygen sensor 1—3.6L engine

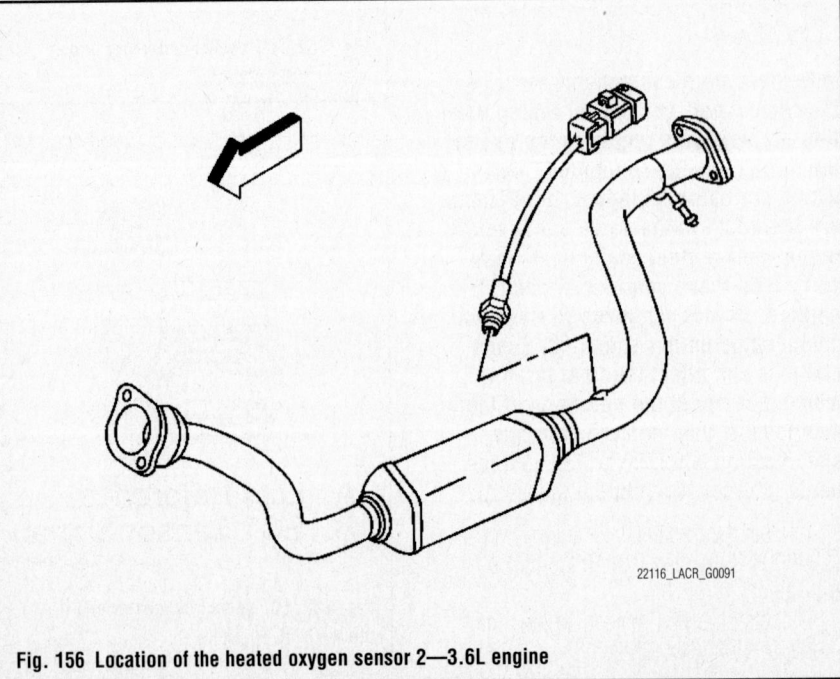

22116_LACR_G0091

Fig. 156 Location of the heated oxygen sensor 2—3.6L engine

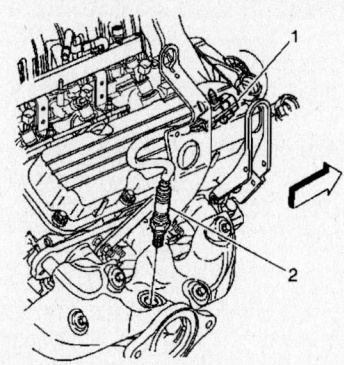

1. Heated Oxygen Sensor electrical connector
2. Heated Oxygen Sensor

22116_LACR_G0092

Fig. 157 Location of the heated oxygen sensor 1—3.8L engine

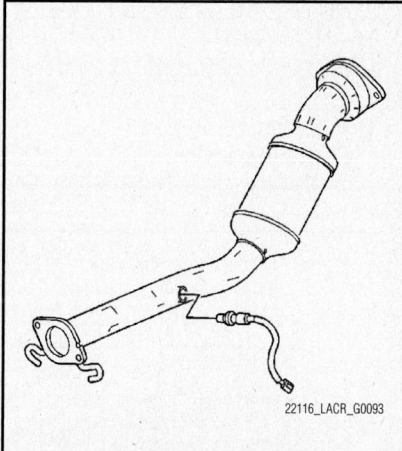

22116_LACR_G0093

Fig. 158 Location of the heated oxygen sensor 2—3.8L engine

Refer to the accompanying illustrations for sensor locations.

OPERATION

Heated oxygen sensors (HO2S) are used for fuel control and post catalyst monitoring. Each HO2S compares the oxygen content of the surrounding air with the oxygen content in the exhaust stream. The HO2S must reach operating temperature to provide an accurate voltage signal. A heating element inside the HO2S minimizes the time required for the sensor to reach operating temperature. Voltage is provided to the heater by the ignition 1 voltage circuit through a fuse. With the engine running, a ground is provided to the heater by the HO2S heater low control circuit through a low side driver within the Powertrain Control Module (PCM). The PCM commands the heater ON or OFF to maintain a specific HO2S operating temperature range. The PCM monitors the voltage on the HO2S heater low control circuit for heater fault diagnosis. If the PCM detects that the

HO2S heater low control circuit voltage is not within a specified range, a DTC is set.

REMOVAL & INSTALLATION

3.6L Engine

Heated Oxygen Sensor—1

See Figure 155.

> **✷✷ WARNING**
>
> **The Heated Oxygen Sensor (HO2S) uses a permanently attached pigtail and connector. Do not remove this pigtail from the HO2S. Damage or the removal of the pigtail or the connector could affect the proper operation of the sensor. Take care when handling the HO2S. Keep the in-line electrical connector, and the louvered end, free of grease, dirt, or other contaminants. Also avoid using cleaning solvents of any type. Do not drop the HO2S. Do not roughly handle the HO2S.**

1. Disconnect the HO2S electrical connector.

> **✷✷ WARNING**
>
> **The use of excessive force may damage the threads in the exhaust manifold/pipe.**

➡If the engine temperature is not above 120°F (48°C), the oxygen sensor may be difficult to remove.

2. Remove the HO2S.

To install:

➡A special anti-seize compound is used on the oxygen sensor threads. New service sensors should already have the compound applied to the

threads. Coat the threads of a reused sensor with anti-seize compound P/N 5613695 or equivalent.

3. Install the HO2S. Tighten the HO2S 1 to 31 ft. lbs. (42 Nm).
4. Connect the HO2S electrical connector.

Heated Oxygen Sensor—2

See Figure 156.

> **✷✷ WARNING**
>
> **The Heated Oxygen Sensor (HO2S) uses a permanently attached pigtail and connector. Do not remove this pigtail from the HO2S. Damage or the removal of the pigtail or the connector could affect the proper operation of the sensor. Take care when handling the HO2S. Keep the in-line electrical connector, and the louvered end, free of grease, dirt, or other contaminants. Also avoid using cleaning solvents of any type. Do not drop the HO2S. Do not roughly handle the HO2S.**

1. Raise and support the vehicle.
2. Disconnect the HO2S electrical connector.

> **✷✷ WARNING**
>
> **The use of excessive force may damage the threads in the exhaust manifold/pipe.**

➡If the engine temperature is not above 120°F (48°C), the oxygen sensor may be difficult to remove.

3. Remove the HO2S.

To install:

> **✷✷ WARNING**
>
> **Use the correct fastener in the correct location. Replacement fasteners must be the correct part number for that application. Fasteners requiring replacement or fasteners requiring the use of thread locking compound or sealant are identified in the service procedure. Do not use paints, lubricants, or corrosion inhibitors on fasteners or fastener joint surfaces unless specified. These coatings affect fastener torque and joint clamping force and may damage the fastener. Use the correct tightening sequence and specifications when installing fasteners in order to avoid damage to parts and systems.**

➡A special anti-seize compound is used on the oxygen sensor threads. New service sensors should already have the compound applied to the threads. Coat the threads of a reused sensor with anti-seize compound P/N 5613695 or equivalent.

4. Install the HO2S. Tighten the HO2S 2 to 31 ft. lbs. (42 Nm).

5. Connect the HO2S electrical connector.

6. Lower the vehicle.

3.8L Engine

Heated Oxygen Sensor—1

See Figure 157.

> **※※ WARNING**
>
> The Heated Oxygen Sensor (HO2S) uses a permanently attached pigtail and connector. Do not remove this pigtail from the HO2S. Damage to the pigtail or the connector could affect the proper operation of the sensor. Take care when handling the HO2S. Keep the in-line electrical connector, and the louvered end, free of grease, dirt, or other contaminants. Also avoid using cleaning solvents of any type. Do not drop the HO2S. Do not roughly handle the HO2S.

➡The oxygen sensor may be difficult to remove when the engine temperature is below 120°F (48°C). Excessive force may damage threads in the exhaust manifold or the exhaust pipe.

1. Remove the fuel injector sight shield.

2. Remove the HO2S retaining clip.

3. Disconnect the HO2S electrical connector (1).

4. Remove the HO2S electrical connector (1) from the fuel injector sight shield bracket.

5. Use the oxygen sensor wrench, J 39194, to remove the HO2S (2) from the right exhaust manifold.

To install:

➡A special anti-seize compound is used on the oxygen sensors threads. New service sensors should already have the compound applied to the threads. Coat the threads of a reused sensor with anti-seize compound GM P/N 12377953 or equivalent.

6. Install the HO2S (2) to the right exhaust manifold. Use the oxygen sensor

wrench, J 39194, to tighten the HO2S to 31 ft. lbs. (42 Nm).

7. Install the HO2S electrical connector (1) to the fuel injector sight shield bracket.

8. Connect the HO2S electrical connector (1).

9. Install the HO2S retaining clip.

10. Install the fuel injector sight shield.

Heated Oxygen Sensor—2

See Figure 158.

> **※※ WARNING**
>
> The Heated Oxygen Sensor (HO2S) uses a permanently attached pigtail and connector. Do not remove this pigtail from the HO2S. Damage to or the removal of the pigtail or the connector could affect the proper operation of the sensor. Take care when handling the HO2S. Keep the in-line electrical connector, and the louvered end, free of grease, dirt, or other contaminants. Also, avoid using cleaning solvents of any type. Do not drop the HO2S. Do not roughly handle the HO2S.

➡The oxygen sensor may be difficult to remove when the engine temperature is below 120°F (48°C). Excessive force may damage threads in the exhaust manifold or the exhaust pipe.

1. Raise and support the vehicle.

2. Remove the HO2S electrical connector retaining clip from the HO2S electrical harness connector.

3. Disconnect the HO2S electrical connector from the HO2S electrical harness connector.

4. Use the oxygen sensor wrench, J 39194, to remove the HO2S from the exhaust pipe.

To install:

➡A special anti-seize compound is used on the HO2S threads. New service sensors should already have the compound applied to the threads. Coat the threads of a reused sensor with anti-seize compound GM P/N 12377953 or equivalent.

5. Install the HO2S to the exhaust pipe. Use the oxygen sensor wrench, J 39194, to tighten the HO2S to 31 ft. lbs. (42 Nm).

6. Connect the HO2S electrical connector to the HO2S electrical harness connector.

7. Install the HO2S electrical connector retaining clip to the HO2S electrical harness connector.

8. Lower the vehicle.

TESTING

See Figures 159 through 163.

1. With an OBD2 scan tool connected to the datalink port:

a. Start the engine and allow it to reach normal operating temperature.

b. If the engine is at operating temperature when started, wait 15 seconds to allow the heated oxygen sensor (HO2S) heater current to stabilize.

c. Observe the affected HO2S heater parameter with a scan tool.

d. The HO2S heater parameter should be within the specified range: 0.5–2.0 Amps.

2. Replace the affected HO2S as necessary.

3. Probe for circuit voltage:

a. Turn engine OFF.

b. Disconnect the affected HO2S.

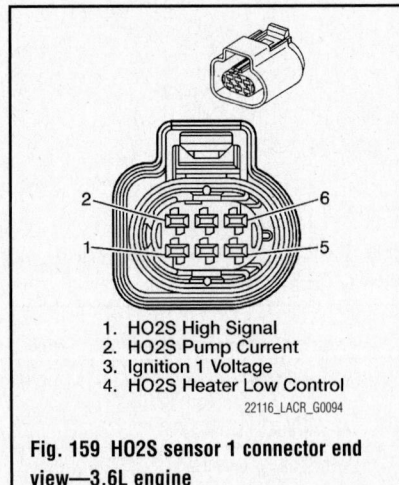

1. HO2S High Signal
2. HO2S Pump Current
3. Ignition 1 Voltage
4. HO2S Heater Low Control

22116_LACR_G0094

Fig. 159 HO2S sensor 1 connector end view—3.6L engine

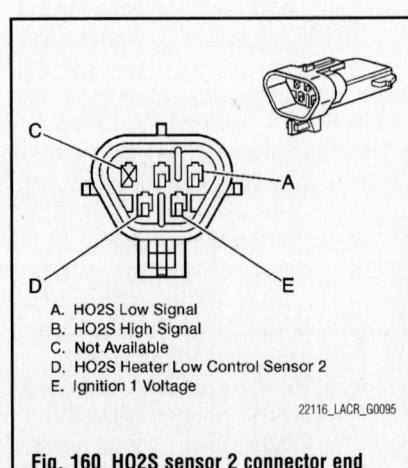

A. HO2S Low Signal
B. HO2S High Signal
C. Not Available
D. HO2S Heater Low Control Sensor 2
E. Ignition 1 Voltage

22116_LACR_G0095

Fig. 160 HO2S sensor 2 connector end view—3.6L engine

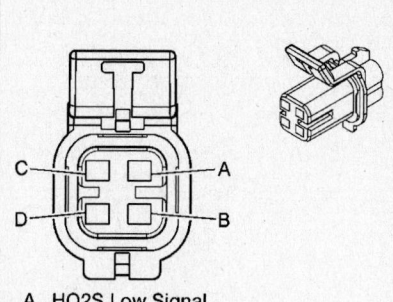

A. HO2S Low Signal
B. HO2S High Signal
C. HO2S Heater Low Control Sensor 1
D. Ignition 1 Voltage

22116_LACR_G0096

Fig. 161 HO2S sensor 1 connector end view (NU6)—3.8L engine

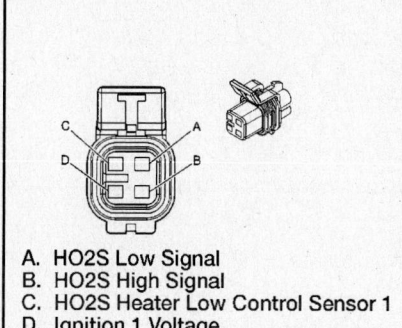

A. HO2S Low Signal
B. HO2S High Signal
C. HO2S Heater Low Control Sensor 1
D. Ignition 1 Voltage

22116_LACR_G0097

Fig. 162 HO2S sensor 1 connector end view (without NU6)—3.8L engine

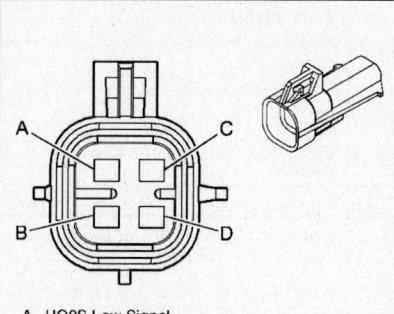

A. HO2S Low Signal
B. HO2S High Signal
C. HO2S Heater Low Control Sensor 2
D. Ignition 1 Voltage

22116_LACR_G0098

Fig. 163 HO2S sensor 2 connector end view—3.8L engine

c. Turn ON the ignition, with the engine OFF.

d. Probe the ignition 1 voltage circuit of the HO2S harness connector on the engine harness side with a test lamp that is connected to a good ground.

e. The test lamp should illuminate.

4. Test the ground circuit:

a. Turn OFF the ignition.

b. Probe the HO2S heater low control circuit of the HO2S harness connector on the engine harness side with a test lamp connected to battery voltage.

c. With the ignition still OFF, observe the test lamp.

d. The test lamp should illuminate.

5. If the ECM and all circuits test normal, replace the appropriate HO2S.

INTAKE AIR TEMPERATURE (IAT) SENSOR

LOCATION

See Figures 164 and 165.

Refer to the accompanying illustrations for sensor locations.

OPERATION

The Intake Air Temperature (IAT) sensor is a variable resistor that measures the temperature of the air entering the engine intake manifold. The Powertrain Control Module (PCM) supplies 5 volts to the IAT signal circuit and a ground for the IAT low reference circuit. When the sensor is cold, the resistance is greater. This results in a greater voltage on the signal circuit that is interpreted by the PCM as a colder IAT. As the sensor becomes warmer, the resistance decreases. This results in a lesser voltage on the IAT signal circuit that is interpreted by the PCM as a warmer IAT. If the PCM

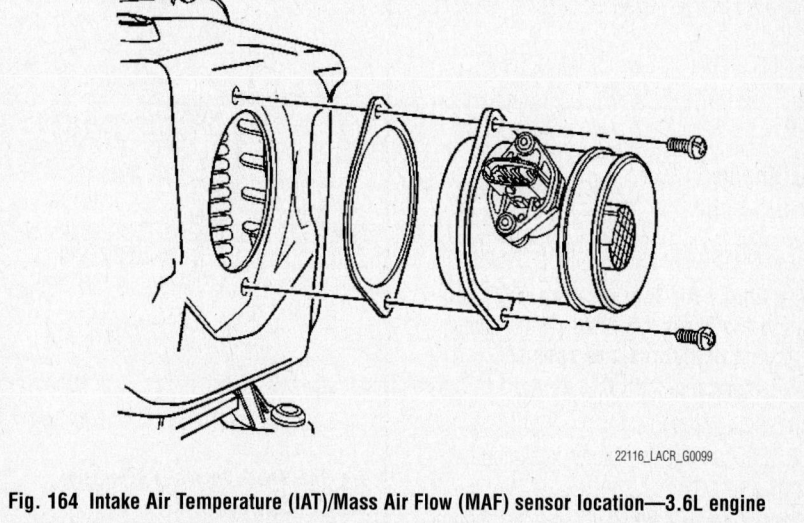

22116_LACR_G0099

Fig. 164 Intake Air Temperature (IAT)/Mass Air Flow (MAF) sensor location—3.6L engine

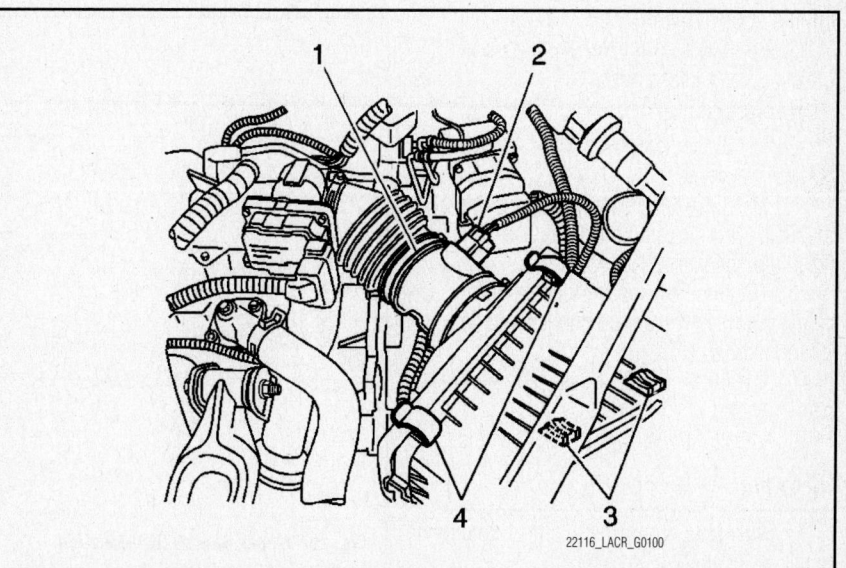

22116_LACR_G0100

Fig. 165 Intake Air Temperature (IAT)/Mass Air Flow (MAF) sensor location—3.8L engine

detects an IAT sensor signal voltage that is not within a calibrated range of the IAT sensor 1 signal voltage, a DTC is set.

REMOVAL & INSTALLATION

3.6L Engine

See Figure 164.

1. Turn the ignition OFF.
2. Remove the Intake Air Temperature (IAT)/Mass Air Flow (MAF) electrical connector.
3. Remove the air cleaner intake duct.
4. Remove the IAT/MAF sensor fasteners.
5. Remove the IAT/MAF sensor and the IAT/MAF sensor seal.

To install:

6. Install the new IAT/MAF sensor seal and the IAT/MAF sensor.
7. Install the IAT/MAF sensor screws. Tighten the IAT/MAF sensor screws to 35 inch lbs. (4 Nm).
8. Install the air cleaner intake duct.
9. Install the IAT/MAF electrical connector.

3.8L Engine

See Figure 165.

1. Remove the fuel injector sight shield.

➡**The Intake Air Temperature (IAT) sensor and the Mass Air Flow (MAF) sensor are combined as one sensor.**

2. Disconnect the MAF/IAT sensor electrical connector (2).
3. Loosen the air cleaner intake duct clamps.
4. Remove the air cleaner intake duct from the air cleaner housing cover and the throttle body assembly.
5. Remove the MAF/IAT sensor from the air cleaner intake duct.

To install:

6. Install the MAF/IAT sensor to the air cleaner intake duct.
7. Install the air cleaner intake duct to the air cleaner housing cover and the throttle body assembly.
8. Tighten the air cleaner intake duct clamp screws. Tighten the duct clamps to 27 inch lbs. (3 Nm).
9. Connect the MAF/IAT sensor electrical connector.
10. Install the fuel injector sight shield.

TESTING

1. Determine the ambient temperature by using an accurate thermometer.
2. If the ignition has been OFF for 8

hours or more, the Intake Air Temperature (IAT)/Mass Air Flow (MAF) sensor parameter and the Engine Coolant Temperature (ECT) sensor parameter should be within 27°F (15°C) of each other and also the ambient temperature.

3. Turn ON the ignition, and immediately observe the parameters. Compare those sensor parameters to each other and also to the ambient temperature, to determine if the IAT/MAF sensor parameter is skewed.
4. Replace the IAT/MAF sensor, if necessary.

KNOCK SENSOR (KS)

LOCATION

See Figures 166 through 169.

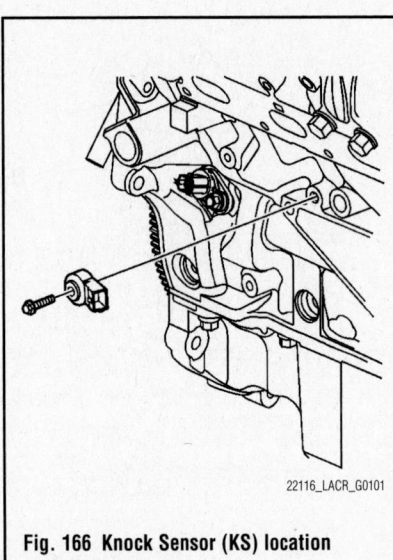

1. Knock Sensor (KS) location bank 1—3.6L engine

Fig. 166 Knock Sensor (KS) location bank 1—3.6L engine

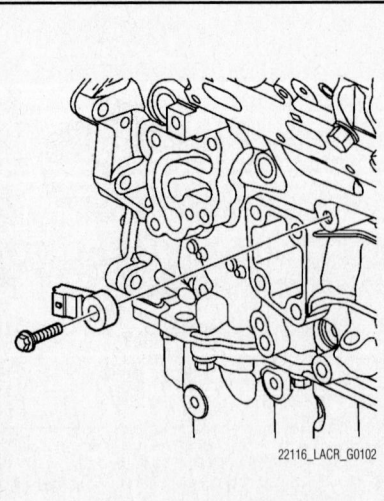

Fig. 167 Knock Sensor (KS) location bank 2—3.6L engine

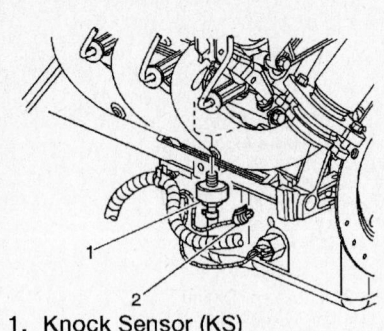

1. Knock Sensor (KS)
2. KS electrical connector

Fig. 168 Knock Sensor (KS) location bank 1—3.8L engine

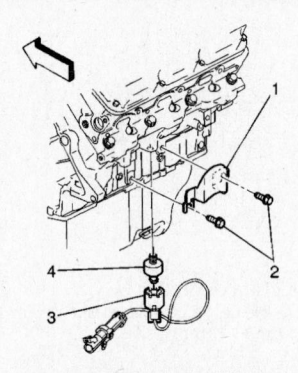

1. Knock Sensor (KS) heat shield
2. KS heat shield bolts
3. KS electrical connector
4. KS

Fig. 169 Knock Sensor (KS) location bank 2—3.8L engine

Refer to the accompanying illustrations for sensor locations.

OPERATION

The Knock Sensor (KS) system enables the control module to control the ignition timing for the best possible performance while protecting the engine from potentially damaging levels of detonation. The control module uses the KS system to test for abnormal engine noise that may indicate detonation, also known as spark knock.

This KS system uses one or two flat response two-wire sensors. The sensor uses piezo-electric crystal technology that produces an AC voltage signal of varying amplitude and frequency based on the engine vibration or noise level. The amplitude and frequency are dependent upon the level of knock that the KS detects. The control module receives the KS signal through a signal circuit. The KS ground is supplied by the control module through a low reference circuit.

The control module learns a minimum noise level, or background noise, at idle from the KS and uses calibrated values for the rest of the RPM range. The control module uses the minimum noise level to calculate a noise channel. A normal KS signal will ride within the noise channel. As engine speed and load change, the noise channel upper and lower parameters will change to accommodate the normal KS signal, keeping the signal within the channel. In order to determine which cylinders are knocking, the control module only uses KS signal information when each cylinder is near top dead center (TDC) of the firing stroke. If a knock is present, the signal will range outside of the noise channel.

If the control module has determined that a knock is present, it will retard the ignition timing to attempt to eliminate the knock. The control module will always try to work back to a zero compensation level, or no spark retard. An abnormal KS signal will stay outside of the noise channel or will not be present. KS diagnostics are calibrated to detect faults with the KS circuitry inside the control module, the KS wiring, and the KS voltage output. Some diagnostics are also calibrated to detect constant noise from an outside influence such as a loose/damaged component or excessive engine mechanical noise.

REMOVAL & INSTALLATION

3.6L Engine

Knock Sensor (KS)—Bank 1

See Figure 166.

1. Turn the ignition OFF.
2. Raise and support the vehicle.
3. Reposition the wiring harness heat shield to obtain access.
4. Remove the Knock Sensor (KS) electrical connector.
5. Remove the KS bolt.
6. Remove the KS.

To install:
7. Install the KS.
8. Install the KS bolt. Tighten the KS bolt to 17 ft. lbs. (23 Nm).
9. Install the KS electrical connector.
10. Install the wiring harness heat shield to the original position.
11. Lower the vehicle.

Knock Sensor (KS)—Bank 2

See Figures 167 and 170 through 173.

1. Turn the ignition OFF.
2. Raise and support the vehicle.

3. Remove the catalytic converter.
4. Remove the left engine splash shield.
5. Disconnect the intermediate steering shaft to the steering gear:
   a. Position the seal in order to provide access to the lower pinch bolt on the intermediate steering shaft.

✳✳ WARNING

The front wheels of the vehicle must be maintained in the straight ahead position and the steering column must be in the LOCK position before disconnecting the steering column or intermediate shaft. Failure to follow these procedures will cause improper alignment of some components during installation and result in damage to the SIR coil assembly.

   b. Remove the lower pinch bolt from the power steering gear stub shaft.
   c. Insert the steering column lock pin, J 42640, into the steering column access hole in order to lock the steering column. This will maintain the orientation.
   d. Disconnect the intermediate steering shaft from the power steering gear stub shaft. Note the shaft to gear alignment for installation.
6. Position jack under rear of frame.
7. Remove the bolts that secure the rear frame to the body.
8. Lower the frame to gain access to the crankshaft position sensor lower heat shield.
9. Remove the crankshaft position sen-

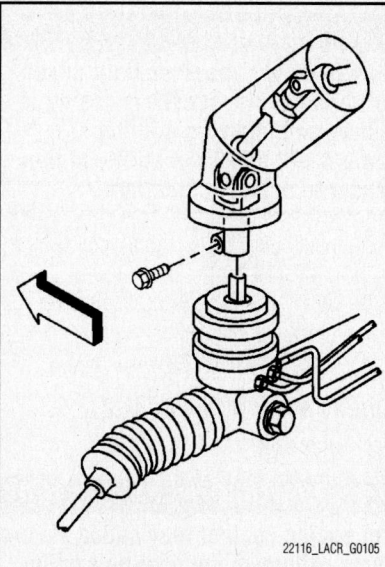

Fig. 170 Remove the lower pinch bolt from the power steering gear stub shaft— 3.6L engine

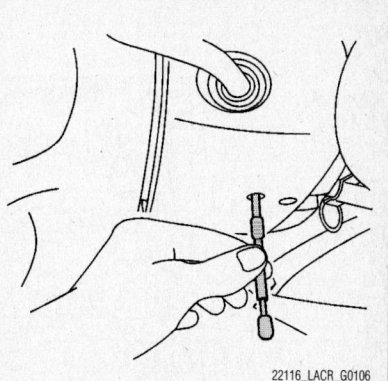

Fig. 171 Insert the steering column lock pin, J 42640, into the steering column access hole in order to lock the steering column—3.6L engine

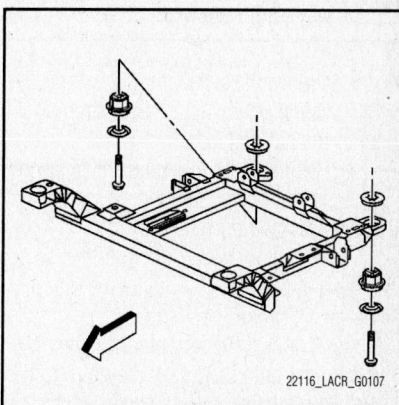

Fig. 172 Remove the bolts that secure the rear frame to the body—3.6L engine

sor lower heat shield bolts (1, 2) and position shield out of the way.
10. Remove the Knock Sensor (KS) electrical connector.
11. Remove the KS bolt.
12. Remove the KS.

To install:
13. Install the KS.
14. Install the KS bolt. Tighten the KS bolt to 17 ft. lbs. (23 Nm).
15. Install the KS electrical connector.
16. Install the crankshaft position sensor lower heat shield bolts.
   a. Tighten the crankshaft position sensor lower heat shield M6 bolt (1) to 89 inch lbs. (10 Nm).
   b. Tighten the crankshaft position sensor lower heat shield M10 bolt (2) to 37 ft. lbs. (50 Nm).
17. Raise the frame.
18. Install the bolts which secure the rear frame to the body.
19. Install the rear frame bolts. Tighten the bolts to 118 ft. lbs. (160 Nm).

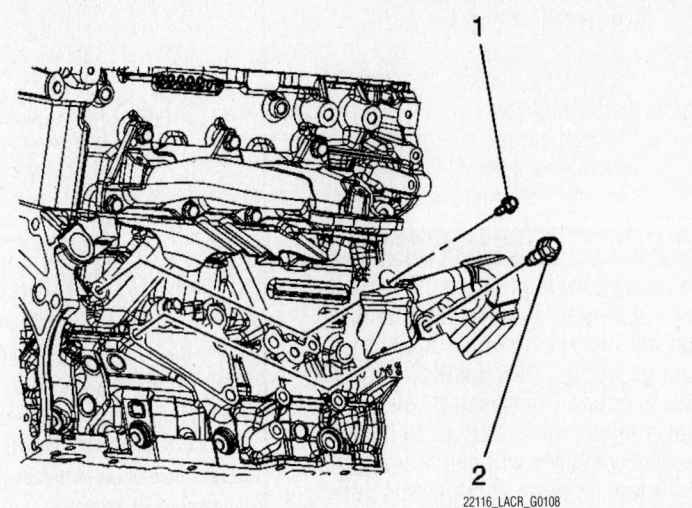

22116_LACR_G0108

Fig. 173 Remove the crankshaft position sensor lower heat shield bolts and position shield out of the way—3.6L engine

20. Remove the jack from under the frame.

21. Connect the intermediate steering shaft to the steering gear:

    a. Connect the intermediate steering shaft to the power steering gear stub shaft as noted during removal.

    b. Install the lower intermediate steering shaft pinch bolt. Tighten the pinch bolt to 35 ft. lbs. (48 Nm).

    c. Connect the intermediate steering shaft seal onto the power steering gear. Rotate the lower seal as necessary to gain maximum clearance.

22. Install the left engine splash shield.

23. Install the catalytic converter.

24. Lower the vehicle.

3.8L Engine

Knock Sensor (KS)—Bank 1

See Figure 168.

> **⁂ CAUTION**
>
> **Hot engine coolant may cause severe burns. Although the cooling system has been drained, coolant still remains in the engine water jacket. This coolant will drain with the removal of the knock sensor.**

1. Raise and support the vehicle.

2. Drain the cooling system.

3. Disconnect the Knock Sensor (KS) electrical connector (2).

4. Remove the KS (1).

To install:

> **⁂ WARNING**
>
> **Use the correct fastener in the correct location. Replacement fasteners**

must be the correct part number for that application. Fasteners requiring replacement or fasteners requiring the use of thread locking compound or sealant are identified in the service procedure. Do not use paints, lubricants, or corrosion inhibitors on fasteners or fastener joint surfaces unless specified. These coatings affect fastener torque and joint clamping force and may damage the fastener. Use the correct tightening sequence and specifications when installing fasteners in order to avoid damage to parts and systems.

> **⁂ WARNING**
>
> **DO NOT apply thread sealant to sensor threads. The sensor is coated at factory and applying additional sealant will affect the ability of the sensor to detect detonation.**

5. Install the KS (1). Tighten the sensor to 14 ft. lbs. (19 Nm).

6. Connect the KS electrical connector (2).

7. Lower the vehicle.

8. Fill the cooling system.

Knock Sensor (KS)—Bank 2

See Figure 169.

> **⁂ CAUTION**
>
> **Hot engine coolant may cause severe burns. Although the cooling system has been drained, coolant still remains in the engine water jacket. This coolant will drain with the removal of the knock sensor.**

1. Raise and support the vehicle.

2. Drain the cooling system.

3. Disconnect the Knock Sensor (KS) electrical connector (3) from the KS.

4. Remove the KS (4).

To install:

> **⁂ WARNING**
>
> **DO NOT apply thread sealant to sensor threads. The sensor is coated at factory and applying additional sealant will affect the sensors ability to detect detonation.**

5. Install the KS (4). Tighten the sensor to 14 ft. lbs. (19 Nm).

6. Connect the KS electrical connector.

7. Lower the vehicle.

8. Fill the cooling system.

TESTING

See Figures 174 through 177.

1. Inspect the Knock Sensor (KS) for physical damage. A KS that is dropped or damaged may cause a DTC to set.

2. Inspect the KS for proper installation. A KS that is loose or over-tightened may cause a DTC to set. The KS should be free of thread sealant other than the factory coating.

3. The KS mounting surface should be free of burrs, casting flash, and foreign material.

➡**If an engine mechanical noise can be heard, repair the condition before proceeding to test the KS.**

4. Test for an intermittent or poor connection at the affected KS.

5. With the ignition OFF, disconnect the affected KS.

    a. Measure the resistance for infinite ohms from the sensor signal terminal on the KS to a good ground with a Digital Multi-Meter (DMM).

    b. If resistance does not measure infinite ohms, replace the affected KS.

> **⁂ WARNING**
>
> **DO NOT tap on plastic engine components.**

6. Connect the DMM to the terminal of the affected KS. Set the DMM to the 400 Hz scale, let it stabilize at 0 Hz.

    a. Tap on engine block with a non-metallic object near the affected KS while observing the signal indicated on the DMM.

    b. If the DMM does not display a fluctuating frequency while tapping on the engine block, replace the affected KS.

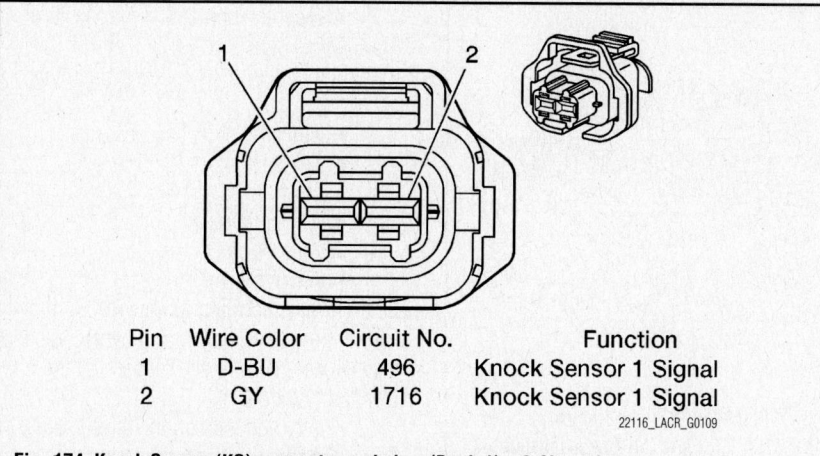

Pin	Wire Color	Circuit No.	Function
1	D-BU	496	Knock Sensor 1 Signal
2	GY	1716	Knock Sensor 1 Signal

22116_LACR_G0109

Fig. 174 Knock Sensor (KS) connector end view (Bank 1)—3.6L engine

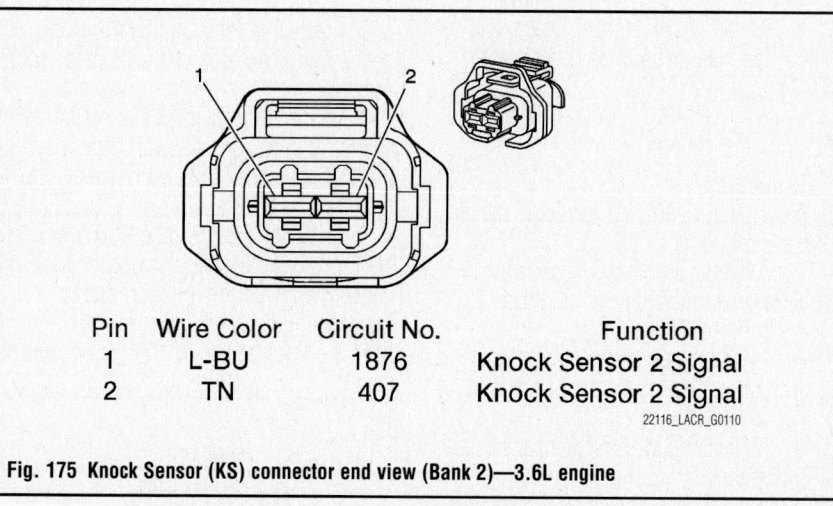

Pin	Wire Color	Circuit No.	Function
1	L-BU	1876	Knock Sensor 2 Signal
2	TN	407	Knock Sensor 2 Signal

22116_LACR_G0110

Fig. 175 Knock Sensor (KS) connector end view (Bank 2)—3.6L engine

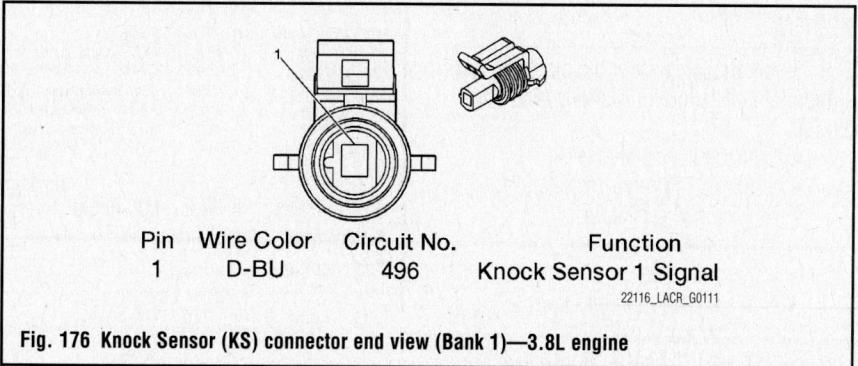

Pin	Wire Color	Circuit No.	Function
1	D-BU	496	Knock Sensor 1 Signal

22116_LACR_G0111

Fig. 176 Knock Sensor (KS) connector end view (Bank 1)—3.8L engine

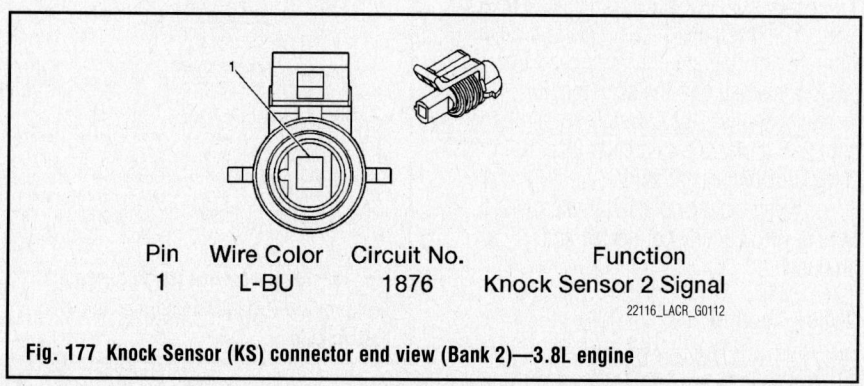

Pin	Wire Color	Circuit No.	Function
1	L-BU	1876	Knock Sensor 2 Signal

22116_LACR_G0112

Fig. 177 Knock Sensor (KS) connector end view (Bank 2)—3.8L engine

7. Turn the ignition ON, engine OFF. Set the DMM to the DC voltage scale. Measure for 4.2 volts from the KS signal circuit to a good ground with the DMM.

c. If over 4.2 volts, turn the ignition OFF, disconnect the control module and test the KS signal circuit for a short to voltage.

d. If under 4.2 volts, turn the ignition OFF, disconnect the control module test the KS signal circuit for an open, short to ground, or high resistance.

8. Test for intermittent or poor connections at the control module.

9. If all circuits test normal, replace the control module.

MASS AIR FLOW (MAF) SENSOR

LOCATION

See Figures 178 and 179.

Refer to the accompanying illustrations for sensor locations.

22116_LACR_G0099

Fig. 178 Intake Air Temperature (IAT)/Mass Air Flow (MAF) sensor location—3.6L engine

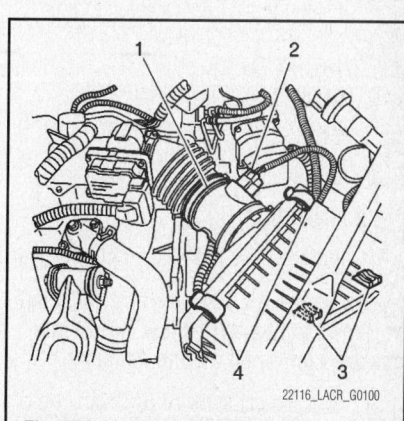

22116_LACR_G0100

Fig. 179 Intake Air Temperature (IAT)/Mass Air Flow (MAF) sensor location—3.8L engine

OPERATION

The Mass Air Flow (MAF) sensor is integrated with the Intake Air Temperature (IAT) sensor. The MAF sensor is an air flow meter that measures the amount of air entering the engine. The Engine Control Module (ECM) uses the MAF sensor signal to provide the correct fuel delivery for all engine speeds and loads. A small quantity of air entering the engine indicates a deceleration or idle condition. A large quantity of air entering the engine indicates an acceleration or high load condition.

The MAF/IAT sensor has the following circuits:

- An ignition 1 voltage circuit
- A ground circuit
- A MAF sensor signal circuit
- An IAT sensor signal circuit
- A low reference circuit

The ECM applies 5 volts to the MAF sensor on the MAF sensor signal circuit. The sensor uses the voltage to produce a frequency based on the inlet air flow through the sensor bore. The frequency varies in a range of near 1,700 Hertz at idle to near 9,500 Hertz at maximum engine load.

REMOVAL & INSTALLATION

3.6L Engine

See Figure 178.

1. Turn the ignition OFF.
2. Remove the Intake Air Temperature (IAT)/Mass Air Flow (MAF) electrical connector.
3. Remove the air cleaner intake duct.
4. Remove the IAT/MAF sensor fasteners.
5. Remove the IAT/MAF sensor and the IAT/MAF sensor seal.

To install:

6. Install the new IAT/MAF sensor seal and the IAT/MAF sensor.
7. Install the IAT/MAF sensor screws. Tighten the IAT/MAF sensor screws to 35 inch lbs. (4 Nm).
8. Install the air cleaner intake duct.
9. Install the IAT/MAF electrical connector.

3.8L Engine

See Figure 180.

1. Remove the fuel injector sight shield.

➡**The Intake Air Temperature (IAT) sensor and the Mass Air Flow (MAF) sensor are combined as one sensor.**

2. Disconnect the MAF/IAT sensor electrical connector (2).
3. Loosen the air cleaner intake duct clamps.

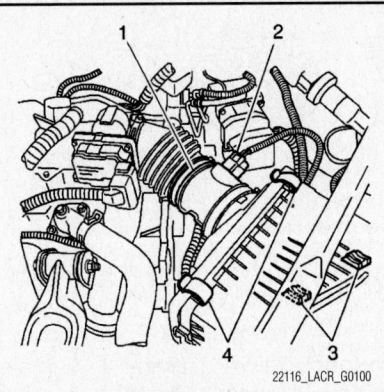

Fig. 180 Intake Air Temperature (IAT)/Mass Air Flow (MAF) sensor location—3.8L engine

22116_LACR_G0100

4. Remove the air cleaner intake duct from the air cleaner housing cover and the throttle body assembly.
5. Remove the MAF/IAT sensor from the air cleaner intake duct.

To install:

6. Install the MAF/IAT sensor to the air cleaner intake duct.
7. Install the air cleaner intake duct to the air cleaner housing cover and the throttle body assembly.
8. Tighten the air cleaner intake duct clamp screws. Tighten the duct clamps to 27 inch lbs. (3 Nm).
9. Connect the MAF/IAT sensor electrical connector.
10. Install the fuel injector sight shield.

TESTING

1. Verify the integrity of the air induction system by inspecting for the following conditions:

- Damaged components
- Loose or improper installation
- An air flow restriction
- Any vacuum leak
- Water intrusion

2. With the engine running, observe the scan tool MAF sensor parameter. The reading should be between 1,700–3,200 Hz depending on the Engine Coolant Temperature (ECT).
3. A Wide Open Throttle (WOT) acceleration from a stop should cause the MAF sensor parameter on the scan tool to increase rapidly. This increase should be from 2–6 g/s at idle to greater than 100 g/s at the time of the 1–2 shift.
4. Verify that any electrical aftermarket devices are properly connected and grounded.

Circuit Testing

See Figures 181 and 182.

1. Inspect the harness of the Mass Air Flow (MAF) sensor to verify that it is not routed too close to the following components:

- Any aftermarket accessories
- The secondary ignition wires or coils
- Any solenoids
- Any relays
- Any motors

2. A low minimum air rate through the sensor bore at idle or during deceleration may cause a DTC to set. Inspect for the following conditions:

- Any deposits on the throttle plate or in the throttle bore
- Any vacuum leak downstream of the MAF sensor

3. Inspect for any contamination or debris on the sensing elements of the MAF sensor.
4. Inspect the air induction system for any water intrusion. Any water that reaches the MAF sensor will skew the sensor and may cause a DTC to set.
5. A Wide Open Throttle (WOT) acceleration from a stop should cause the MAF sensor parameter on the scan tool to increase rapidly. This increase should be from 3–10 g/s at idle to 150 g/s or more at

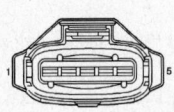

Pin	Wire Color	Circuit No.	Function
1	TN	472	IAT Sensor Signal
2	PK	339	Ignition 1 Voltage
3	BK	2760	Low Reference
4	GY	2709	5-Volt Reference 2
5	YE	492	MAF Sensor Signal

22116_LACR_G0113

Fig. 181 Mass Air Flow (MAF)/Intake Air Temperature (IAT) connector end view—3.6L engine

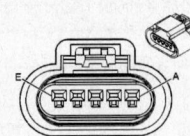

Pin	Wire Color	Circuit No.	Function
A	YE	492	MAF Sensor Signal
B	PK	339	Ignition 1 Voltage
C	BK/WH	451	Ground
D	TN	472	IAT Sensor Signal
E	BK	2760	Low Reference

22116_LACR_G0114

Fig. 182 Mass Air Flow (MAF)/Intake Air Temperature (IAT) connector end view—3.8L engine

the time of the 1 to 2 shift of the transmission. If the increase is not observed, inspect for a restriction in the induction system or the exhaust system.

6. Inspect for a skewed or stuck Engine Coolant Temperature (ECT) sensor.

7. Test for a high resistance of 15 ohms or more on the ignition 1 voltage circuit. This may cause a DTC to set. A high resistance may also cause a drivability concern before a DTC sets.

The Barometric Pressure (BARO) sensor that is used in order to calculate the predicted mass air flow value is initially based on the Manifold Absolute Pressure (MAP) sensor at key ON. When the engine is running, the BARO value is continually updated near WOT. A skewed MAP sensor will cause the calculated mass air flow value to be inaccurate and may result in a no start condition. The value shown for the MAP sensor parameter varies with the altitude. With the ignition ON and the engine OFF, 101 kPa is the approximate value near sea level. This value will decrease by approximately 3 kPa for every 1,000 feet (305 meters) of altitude.

➡**For the following tests, all electrical components and accessories must be turned OFF, and allowed to power down.**

8. With the ignition OFF, disconnect the MAF/IAT harness connector at the MAF/IAT sensor.

9. With the ignition ON, verify that a test lamp illuminates between the ignition circuit terminal and ground. If the test lamp does not illuminate, test the ignition circuit for a short to ground or an open/high resistance.

10. With the ignition ON, test for 4.8–5.2 volts between the signal circuit terminal and ground:

    a. If less than the specified range, test the signal circuit for a short to ground or an open/high resistance.

    b. If greater than the specified range, test the signal circuit for a short to voltage.

11. If all circuits test normal, replace the MAF sensor.

MANIFOLD ABSOLUTE PRESSURE (MAP) SENSOR

LOCATION

See Figure 183.

Refer to the accompanying illustration for sensor location.

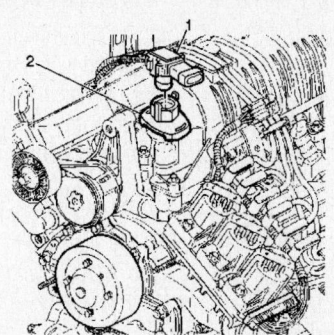

1. Manifold Absolute Pressure (MAP) sensor
2. Positive Crankcase Ventilation (PCV) valve cover

22116_LACR_G0115

Fig. 183 Manifold Absolute Pressure (MAP) sensor location—3.8L engine

OPERATION

The Manifold Absolute Pressure (MAP) sensor measures the pressure inside the intake manifold. Pressure in the intake manifold is affected by engine speed, throttle opening, air temperature, and Barometric Pressure (BARO). A diaphragm within the MAP sensor is displaced by the pressure changes that occur from the varying load and operating conditions of the engine. The sensor translates this action into electrical resistance. The MAP sensor wiring includes 3 circuits. The Engine Control Module (ECM) supplies a regulated 5 volts to the sensor on a 5 volt reference circuit. The ECM supplies a ground on a low reference circuit. The MAP sensor provides a signal voltage to the ECM, relative to the pressure changes, on the MAP sensor signal circuit. The ECM converts the signal voltage input to a pressure value.

Under normal operation the greatest pressure that can exist in the intake manifold is equal to BARO. This occurs when the vehicle is operated at Wide Open Throttle (WOT) or when the ignition is ON while the engine is OFF. Under these conditions, the ECM uses the MAP sensor to determine the current BARO. The least manifold pressure occurs when the vehicle is idling or decelerating. MAP can range from 10 kPa, when pressures are less, to as great as 104 kPa, depending on the current BARO. The ECM monitors the MAP sensor signal for pressure outside of the normal range.

REMOVAL & INSTALLATION

3.8L Engine

See Figure 183.

The Manifold Absolute Pressure (MAP) sensor is mounted to the Positive Crankcase Ventilation (PCV) valve cover.

1. Remove the fuel injector sight shield.

2. Disconnect the MAP sensor electrical connector.

3. Carefully release the locking tabs holding the MAP (1) sensor to the PCV valve cover (2) just enough to remove the MAP sensor.

4. Pull the MAP sensor straight out of PCV valve cover.

To install:

5. Ensure that the seal is installed on the MAP sensor and that the seal is not damaged.

6. Position and install the MAP sensor (1) to the PCV valve cover (2). Ensure that the locking tabs engage to hold the MAP sensor to the PCV valve cover.

7. Connect the MAP sensor electrical connector.

8. Install the fuel injector sight shield.

TESTING

See Figure 184.

Poor idle characteristics may be due to uncontrolled fueling caused by an open or high resistance in the Heated Oxygen Sensor (HO2S) 1 low signal circuit. Before replacing any component, ensure that this condition does not exist.

1. Start the engine.

2. Monitor the DTC information with the scan tool.

3. Turn the engine OFF.

4. If DTC P0641 or P0651 are set, correct these codes first.

5. Verify the integrity of the entire air induction system by inspecting for the following conditions:

- Any damage to, or hairline fractures of, the MAP sensor housing
- Disconnected, damaged, or incorrectly routed vacuum hoses

- Manifold Absolute Pressure (MAP) sensor disconnected from the vacuum source
- Restrictions in the MAP sensor vacuum source
- Intake manifold vacuum leaks
- Inspect for a properly functioning oxygen sensor

6. With the ignition ON, and the engine OFF, disconnect the MAP sensor.

7. Using a Digital Multi-Meter (DMM), measure the 5-volt reference circuit of the MAP sensor to a good ground. The reading should be 4.8–5.2 volts.

   a. If more than 5.2 volts, then test the circuit for a short to voltage. If the circuit tests normal, replace the control module.

   b. If less than 4.8 volts, then test the circuit for high resistance, an open, a short to ground, or an intermittent or poor connection at the control module. If the circuit tests normal, replace the control module.

8. Use a scan tool and observe the MAP sensor. It should read less than 12 kPa.

   a. If the MAP sensor is more than 12 kPa, test the MAP sensor signal circuit for a short to voltage.

   b. If the circuit tests normal, replace the control module.

9. Use a 3-Amp fused jumper wire and connect it between the MAP sensor 5-volt reference circuit and the MAP sensor signal circuit.

10. Use a scan tool and observe the MAP sensor. It should read more than 103 kPa.

   a. If the MAP sensor is less than 103 kPa, test the MAP sensor signal circuit for a short to ground, an open, high resistance.

   b. If the circuit tests normal, replace the control module.

11. Turn OFF the ignition and allow the control module to power down.

12. Remove the MAP sensor from the engine vacuum source, but leave the MAP sensor connected to the engine harness.

13. Connect the J 23738-A, or a similar vacuum pump, to the MAP sensor.

14. Turn ON the ignition, with the engine OFF.

15. Observe the MAP sensor pressure with the scan tool.

16. Apply vacuum to the MAP sensor with the J 23738-A in 1 inch Hg increments until 15 inches Hg is reached. Each 1 inch Hg should decrease MAP sensor pressure by 3–4 kPa. Monitor the MAP sensor pressure to see if the decrease in pressure is consistent.

   a. If decrease in pressure is not consistent then, test for intermittent and poor connections at the MAP sensor.

   b. If connections test OK, replace the MAP sensor.

17. Apply vacuum with the J 23738-A until 20 inches Hg is reached. Observe the MAP sensor pressure. It should read less than 34 kPa.

   a. If the pressure is more than 34 kPa, test for an intermittent or poor connection at the MAP sensor.

   b. If connections test OK, replace the MAP sensor.

18. With a DMM, measure the resistance between the low reference circuit of the MAP sensor and battery negative post. It should read less than 5 ohms.

   a. If the resistance is more than 5 ohms, test the low reference circuit for a high resistance.

   b. If the circuit tests normal, replace the control module.

POWERTRAIN CONTROL MODULE (PCM)

LOCATION

See Figure 185.

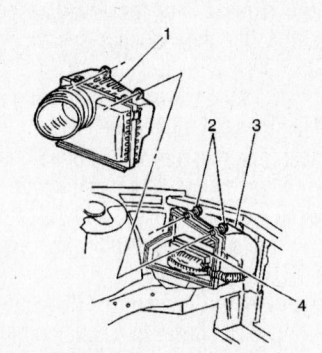

1. Air cleaner housing cover
2. Air cleaner housing cover screws
3. Air cleaner housing assembly
4. Powertrain Control Module (PCM)

22116_LACR_G0120

Fig. 185 Powertrain Control Module (PCM) location—3.8L engine

Refer to the accompanying illustration for PCM location.

OPERATION

The powertrain has electronic controls to reduce exhaust emissions while maintaining excellent drivability and fuel economy. The Powertrain Control Module (PCM) is the control center of this system. The PCM monitors numerous engine and vehicle functions. The PCM constantly looks at the information from various sensors and other inputs, and controls the systems that affect vehicle performance and emissions. The PCM also performs the diagnostic tests on various parts of the system. The PCM can recognize operational problems and alert the driver via the Malfunction Indicator Lamp (MIL). When the PCM detects a malfunction, the PCM stores a Diagnostic Trouble Code (DTC). The problem area is identified by the particular DTC that is set. The control module supplies a buffered voltage to various sensors and switches. Review the components and wiring diagrams in order to determine which systems are controlled by the PCM. The following are some of the functions that the PCM controls:

- The engine fueling
- The Ignition Control (IC)
- The Knock Sensor (KS) system
- The Evaporative Emissions (EVAP) system
- The Secondary Air Injection (AIR) system (if equipped)
- The Exhaust Gas Recirculation (EGR) system
- The automatic transmission functions
- The alternator

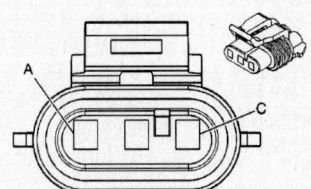

Pin	Wire Color	Circuit No.	Function
A	OG/BK	469	Low Reference
B	L-GN	432	MAP Sensor Signal
C	GY	2704	5-Volt Reference 2

22116_LACR_G0116

Fig. 184 Manifold Absolute Pressure (MAP) connector end view—3.8L engine

- The A/C clutch control
- The cooling fan control

REMOVAL & INSTALLATION

3.6L Engine

For removal and installation, refer to Electronic Control Module (ECM) which may also be referred to as the Engine Control Module (ECM).

3.8L Engine

See Figure 185.

➡**Service of the Powertrain Control Module (PCM) should normally consist of either replacement of the PCM or Electrically Erasable Programmable Read Only Memory (EEPROM) programming. If the diagnostic procedures call for the PCM to be replaced, the PCM should be inspected first to see if the correct part is being used. If the correct part is being used, remove the faulty PCM and install the new service PCM.**

❊❊ **WARNING**

Turn the ignition OFF when installing or removing the control module connectors and disconnecting or reconnecting the power to the control module (battery cable, PCM/Engine Control Module (ECM)/Transaxle Control Module (TCM) pigtail, control module fuse, jumper cables, etc.) in order to prevent internal control module damage.

❊❊ **WARNING**

Control module damage may result when the metal case contacts battery voltage. DO NOT contact the control module metal case with battery voltage when servicing a control module, using battery booster cables, or when charging the vehicle battery.

❊❊ **WARNING**

In order to prevent any possible electrostatic discharge damage to the control module, do not touch the connector pins or the soldered components on the circuit board.

➡**Remove any debris from around the control module connector surfaces before servicing the control module. Inspect the control module connector gaskets when diagnosing or replacing the control module. Ensure that the**

gaskets are installed correctly. The gaskets prevent contaminant intrusion into the control module.

➡**The new service PCM will not be programmed. You must program the new PCM. DTC P0602 indicates the EEPROM is not programmed or has malfunctioned.**

➡**It is necessary to record the remaining engine oil life. If the replacement module is not programmed with the remaining engine oil life, the engine oil life will default to 100 percent. If the replacement module is not programmed with the remaining engine oil life, the engine oil will need to be changed at 3,000 miles (5,000 km) from the last engine oil change.**

1. Using a scan tool, retrieve the percentage of remaining engine oil life. Record the remaining engine oil life.
2. Remove or disconnect the following:
   - The negative battery cable
   - The left front inner fender brace
   - The air cleaner intake duct
   - The air cleaner housing cover screws (2)
   - The air cleaner housing cover (1)
3. Without disconnecting the PCM electrical connectors, remove the PCM and the wiring harness from the air cleaner housing assembly (3).
4. Disconnect the PCM electrical connectors and remove the PCM (4).

To install:

5. Install or connect the following:
   - The PCM to the PCM electrical connectors (4). Tighten the connectors to 71 inch lbs. (8 Nm)
   - The PCM and the wiring harness to the air cleaner housing assembly (3)
   - The air cleaner housing cover (1)
   - The air cleaner housing cover screws (2). Tighten the screws to 35 inch lbs. (4 Nm)
   - The air cleaner intake duct
   - The left front inner fender brace
   - The negative battery cable
6. If a new PCM is being installed, the PCM must be programmed.

TESTING

The Powertrain Control Module (PCM) is programmed with test routines that test the operation of the various systems the PCM controls. Some tests monitor internal PCM functions. Many tests are run continuously. Other tests run only under specific conditions, referred to as conditions for

running the DTC. When the vehicle is operating within the conditions for running a particular test, the PCM monitors certain parameters and determines if the values are within an expected range. The parameters and values considered outside the range of normal operation are listed as conditions for setting the DTC. When the conditions for setting the DTC occur, the PCM executes the action taken when the DTC Sets. Some DTC's alert the driver via the Malfunction Indicator Lamp (MIL) or a message. Other DTC's do not trigger a driver warning, but are stored in memory. The PCM also saves data and input parameters when most DTC's are set. This data is stored in the freeze frame and/or failure records.

The DTC's are categorized by type. The DTC type is determined by the MIL operation and the manner in which the fault data is stored when a particular DTC fails. In some cases there may be exceptions to this structure. Therefore, when diagnosing the system it is important to read the action taken when the DTC sets and the conditions for clearing the DTC.

Many intermittent open or shorted circuits come and go with harness and connector movement caused by vibration, engine torque, bumps, and rough pavement.

1. Test the wiring harness and connectors by performing the following:
   - Move the related PCM connectors and wiring while monitoring the appropriate scan tool data
   - With the engine running, move the related connectors and wiring while monitoring engine operation
   - If harness or connector movement affects the data displayed, the component and system operation, or the engine operation, inspect and repair the harness or connections as necessary
2. Test the electrical connections and/or wiring by performing the following:
   - Inspect for incorrect mating of the connector halves, or terminals not fully seated in the connector body, backed-out
   - Inspect for improperly formed or damaged terminals. Test for incorrect terminal tension
   - Inspect for poor terminal to wire connections including terminals crimped over insulation. This requires removing the terminal from the connector body
   - Inspect for corrosion or water intrusion. Pierced or damaged insulation can allow moisture to enter the

wiring. The conductor can corrode inside the insulation with little visible evidence. Look for swollen and stiff sections of wire in the suspect circuits

- Inspect for wires that are broken inside the insulation

VARIABLE CAMSHAFT TIMING OIL CONTROL SOLENOID

LOCATION

See Figures 186 through 189.

Refer to the accompanying illustrations for solenoid locations.

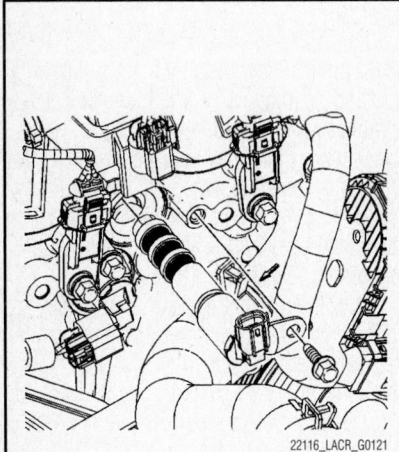

Fig. 186 Location of bank 1, intake, variable camshaft timing oil control solenoid—3.6L engine

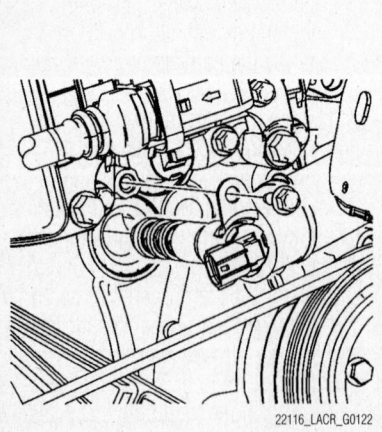

Fig. 187 Location of bank 1, exhaust, variable camshaft timing oil control solenoid—3.6L engine

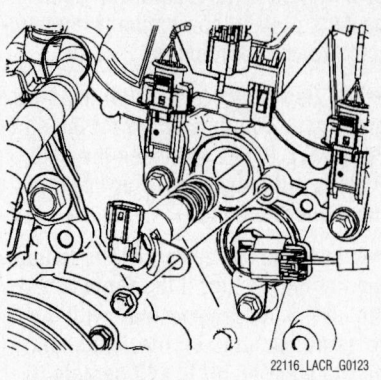

Fig. 188 Location of bank 2, intake, variable camshaft timing oil control solenoid—3.6L engine

Fig. 189 Location of bank 2, exhaust, variable camshaft timing oil control solenoid—3.6L engine

OPERATION

See Figure 190.

The variable camshaft timing oil control solenoid (also called the Camshaft Position (CMP) actuator) has an outer housing that is driven by an engine timing chain. Inside the assembly is a rotor with fixed vanes that is attached to the camshaft. Oil pressure that is applied to the fixed vanes will rotate a specific camshaft in relationship to the crankshaft. The movement of the intake camshafts will advance the intake valve timing up to a maximum of 50 crankshaft degrees. The movement of the exhaust camshafts will retard the exhaust valve timing up to a maximum of 50 crankshaft degrees. When oil pressure is applied to the return side of the vanes, the camshafts will return to 0 crankshaft degrees, or Top Dead Center (TDC). The CMP actuator solenoid valve directs the oil flow that controls the camshaft movement. The ECM commands the CMP solenoid to move the solenoid plunger and spool valve until oil flows from the advance passage (11). Oil flowing through the CMP actuator assembly from the CMP solenoid advance passage applies pressure to the advance side of the vanes in the CMP actuator assembly. When the camshaft position is retarded, the CMP actuator solenoid valve directs oil to flow into the CMP actuator assembly from the retard passage (3). The ECM can also command the CMP actuator solenoid valve to stop oil flow from both passages in order to hold the current camshaft position.

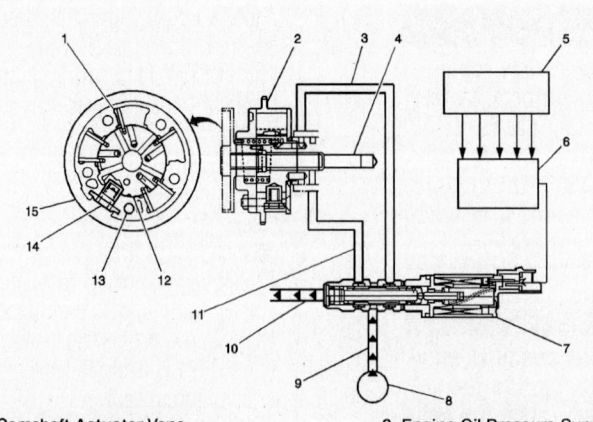

1. Camshaft Actuator Vane
2. Timing Chain Sprocket
3. Engine Oil Pressure-For retarding the camshaft
4. Camshaft
5. Input Signals from Engine Sensors
6. Engine Control Module ECM.
7. Camshaft Actuator Solenoid
8. Engine Oil Pump
9. Engine Oil Pressure Supply
10. Engine Oil Drain
11. Engine Oil Pressure-for advancing the camshaft
12. Camshaft Actuator Rotor
13. Camshaft Position Sensor Reluctor
14. Camshaft Actuator Lock Pin
15. Camshaft Actuator Housing

Fig. 190 Component view of variable camshaft timing oil control solenoid system—3.6L engine

The ECM operates the CMP actuator solenoid valve by Pulse Width Modulation (PWM) of the solenoid coil. The higher the PWM duty cycle, the larger the change in camshaft timing. The CMP actuator assembly also contains a lock pin (14) that prevents movement between the outer housing and the rotor vane assembly. The lock pin is released by oil pressure before any movement in the CMP actuator assembly takes place. The ECM is continuously comparing CMP sensor inputs with CKP sensor input in order to monitor camshaft position and detect any system malfunctions. If a condition exists in either the intake or exhaust camshaft actuator system, the opposite bank, intake or exhaust, camshaft actuator will default to 0 crankshaft degrees.

REMOVAL & INSTALLATION

3.6L Engine

Intake—Bank 1 (Right Side)

See Figure 186.

1. Turn the ignition OFF.

➡**Do not remove the Engine Control Module (ECM) from the ECM bracket.**

➡**Do not remove the ECM redundant ground wire from the ECM.**

2. Remove the ECM bracket bolts and reposition the ECM bracket in order to provide access.
3. Remove the Camshaft Position (CMP) actuator valve electrical connector. The CMP actuator valve is also referred to as the variable camshaft timing oil control solenoid.
4. Remove the CMP actuator valve bolt.
5. Remove the CMP actuator valve.

To install:
6. Install or connect the following:
   - The CMP actuator valve
   - The CMP actuator valve bolt. Tighten the CMP actuator valve bolt to 89 inch lbs. (10 Nm)
   - The CMP actuator valve electrical connector
   - The ECM bracket with the ECM

Exhaust—Bank 1 (Right Side)

See Figure 187.

1. Turn the ignition OFF.
2. Remove the Camshaft Position (CMP) actuator valve electrical connector. The CMP actuator valve is also referred to as the variable camshaft timing oil control solenoid.

3. Remove the CMP actuator valve bolt.
4. Remove the CMP actuator valve.

To install:
5. Inspect the CMP actuator valve seal for damage. Replace the seal if necessary.
6. Install the CMP actuator valve.
7. Install the CMP actuator valve bolt. Tighten the CMP actuator valve bolt to 89 inch lbs. (10 Nm).
8. Install the CMP valve electrical connector.

Intake—Bank 2 (Left Side)

See Figure 191.

1. Turn the ignition OFF.

➡**Do not disconnect the power steering fluid lines/hoses from the reservoir.**

2. Remove the power steering fluid reservoir bolts and reposition the power steering fluid reservoir in order to provide access.
3. Remove the Camshaft Position (CMP) actuator valve electrical connector. The CMP actuator valve is also referred to as the variable camshaft timing oil control solenoid.
4. Remove the CMP actuator valve bolt.
5. Remove the CMP actuator valve.

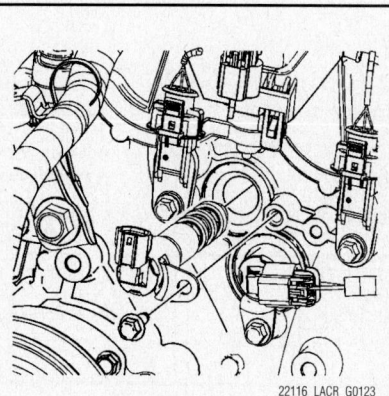

Fig. 191 Location of bank 2, intake, variable camshaft timing oil control solenoid—3.6L engine

To install:
6. Install or connect the following:
   - The CMP actuator valve.
   - The CMP actuator valve bolt. Tighten the CMP actuator valve bolt to 89 inch lbs. (10 Nm).
   - The CMP actuator valve electrical connector.
   - The power steering fluid reservoir.

Exhaust—Bank 2 (Left Side)

See Figure 192.

Fig. 192 Location of bank 2, exhaust, variable camshaft timing oil control solenoid—3.6L engine

1. Turn the ignition OFF.

➡**Do not disconnect the power steering fluid lines/hoses from the reservoir.**

2. Remove the power steering fluid reservoir bolts and reposition the power steering fluid reservoir in order to provide access.
3. Remove the Camshaft Position (CMP) actuator valve electrical connector. The CMP actuator valve is also referred to as the variable camshaft timing oil control solenoid.
4. Remove the CMP actuator valve bolt.
5. Remove the CMP actuator valve.

To install:
6. Install the CMP actuator valve.
7. Install the CMP actuator valve bolt. Tighten the CMP actuator valve bolt to 89 inch lbs. (10 Nm).
8. Install the CMP actuator valve electrical connector.
9. Install the power steering fluid reservoir.

TESTING

See Figure 194.

1. Ensure the vehicle has the proper oil viscosity.
2. Observe the engine oil level. The engine oil level should be within the operating range.
3. Allow the engine to reach operating temperature.
4. Increase the engine speed to 1,500 RPM.
5. Command each solenoid to 25 percent. The angle desired parameter should match the solenoid actual parameter.
6. If the condition is intermittent:
   a. With the engine running, move the related harnesses and connectors

b. Monitor the circuit status for the component with a scan tool.

c. If the circuit status parameter changes from OK, or indeterminate, to fault, there may be a condition with the circuit or a connection.

7. Turn OFF the ignition.

8. Disconnect the Camshaft Position (CMP) actuator solenoid to be tested. The CMP actuator valve is also referred to as the variable camshaft timing oil control solenoid.

9. Turn ON the ignition, with the engine OFF.

10. Probe the ignition 1 voltage circuit of the CMP actuator solenoid with a test lamp that is connected to the Engine Control Module (ECM) housing. The test lamp should illuminate.

11. Connect a test lamp between the control circuit of the CMP actuator solenoid and the ignition 1 voltage circuit of the CMP actuator solenoid.

12. Start the engine.

13. Command the appropriate CMP actuator solenoid from 0 to 40 and back to 0 degrees with a scan tool.

14. Exit the CMP actuator solenoid control function. The test lamp should turn ON when commanded with a scan tool.

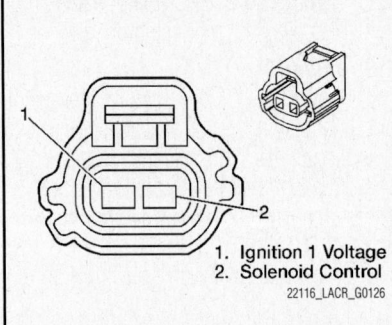

1. Ignition 1 Voltage
2. Solenoid Control

22116_LACR_G0126

Fig. 194 Connector end view of variable camshaft timing oil control solenoid (all)—3.6L engine

15. With the ignition ON and the engine OFF.

a. Measure the voltage from the control circuit of the solenoid to the ECM housing with a Digital Multi-Meter (DMM).

b. The voltage reading should be 2–3 volts.

VEHICLE SPEED SENSOR (VSS)

LOCATION

See Figure 195.

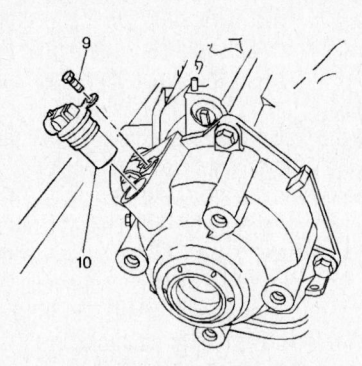

9. Vehicle Speed Sensor bolt
10. Vehicle Speed Sensor

22116_LACR_G0127

Fig. 195 Location of the Vehicle Speed Sensor (VSS) on automatic transaxle 4T65–E

Refer to the accompanying illustration for sensor location.

OPERATION

The Vehicle Speed Sensor (VSS) system is a pulse generator consisting of a speed sensor assembly, located in the case

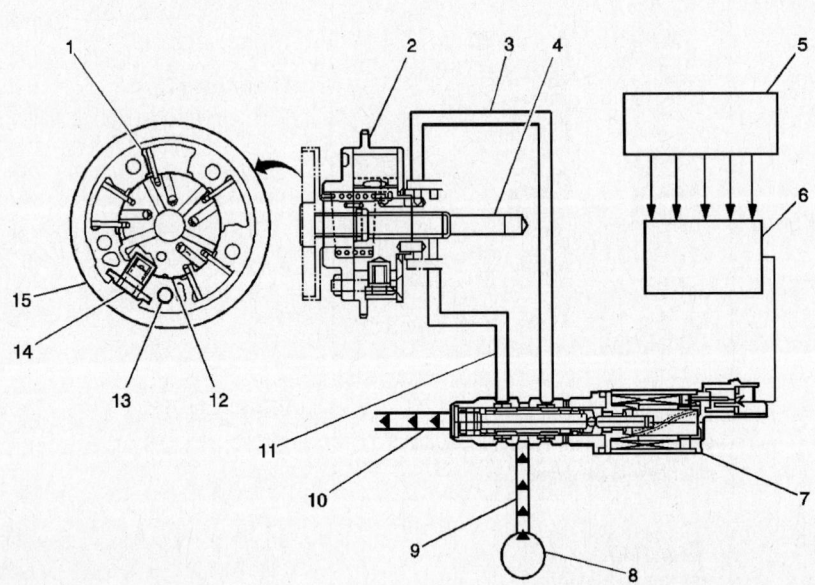

1. Camshaft Actuator Vane
2. Timing Chain Sprocket
3. Engine Oil Pressure-For retarding the camshaft
4. Camshaft
5. Input Signals from Engine Sensors
6. Engine Control Module ECM.
7. Camshaft Actuator Solenoid
8. Engine Oil Pump
9. Engine Oil Pressure Supply
10. Engine Oil Drain
11. Engine Oil Pressure-for advancing the camshaft
12. Camshaft Actuator Rotor
13. Camshaft Position Sensor Reluctor
14. Camshaft Actuator Lock Pin
15. Camshaft Actuator Housing

22116_LACR_G0125

Fig. 193 Component view of variable camshaft timing oil control solenoid system—3.6L engine

extension, and a toothed vehicle speed sensor reluctor wheel, which is pressed onto the final drive carrier assembly. As the vehicle drives forward, the vehicle speed sensor reluctor wheel rotates. This rotation produces a variable AC signal in the pickup coil that is proportional to vehicle speed. The Powertrain Control Module (PCM) uses this signal in order to calculate vehicle speed, shift timing, and gear ratios. If the PCM detects a low vehicle speed with a high engine speed while in a drive range, then a DTC is set.

REMOVAL & INSTALLATION

Automatic Transaxle 4T65–E

See Figure 195.

1. Raise and support the vehicle.
2. Remove the right front tire and wheel.
3. Disconnect the Vehicle Speed Sensor (VSS) electrical connector.
4. Remove the VSS bolt (9).
5. Remove the VSS (10) from the extension case.

6. Remove the O-ring from the VSS (10).

To install:

7. Install the O-ring to the VSS (10).
8. Install the VSS (10).
9. Install the VSS bolt (9). Tighten the bolt (9) to 106 inch lbs. (12 Nm).
10. Connect the VSS electrical connector.
11. Install the right front tire and wheel. Tighten the wheel lug nuts to 100 ft. lbs. (140 Nm).
12. Lower the vehicle.

TESTING

1. Ensure the Vehicle Speed Sensor (VSS) is correctly tightened to the transmission housing.
2. Install a scan tool.
3. Turn ON the ignition, with the engine OFF.

➡Before clearing the DTC, use the scan tool in order to record the Freeze Frame and Failure Records. Using the Clear Info function erases the Freeze Frame and Failure Records from the PCM. Record the DTC Freeze Frame and Failure Records, then clear the DTC(s).

❊❊ WARNING

Support the lower control arms in the normal horizontal position in order to avoid damage to the drive axles. Do not operate the vehicle in gear with the wheels hanging down at full travel.

4. Raise and support the drive wheels.
5. Start and idle the engine.
6. Place the transmission in DRIVE.
7. Monitor Transmission OSS on the scan tool.
8. With the drive wheels rotating, increase and decrease the throttle position.
9. The Transmission OSS RPM should increase when the wheel speed increases.

FUEL   GASOLINE FUEL INJECTION SYSTEM

FUEL SYSTEM SERVICE PRECAUTIONS

Safety is the most important factor when performing not only fuel system maintenance but any type of maintenance. Failure to conduct maintenance and repairs in a safe manner may result in serious personal injury or death. Maintenance and testing of the vehicle's fuel system components can be accomplished safely and effectively by adhering to the following rules and guidelines.

- To avoid the possibility of fire and personal injury, always disconnect the negative battery cable unless the repair or test procedure requires that battery voltage be applied.
- Always relieve the fuel system pressure prior to disconnecting any fuel system component (injector, fuel rail, pressure regulator, etc.), fitting or fuel line connection. Exercise extreme caution whenever relieving fuel system pressure to avoid exposing skin, face and eyes to fuel spray. Please be advised that fuel under pressure may penetrate the skin or any part of the body that it contacts.
- Always place a shop towel or cloth around the fitting or connection prior to loosening to absorb any excess fuel due to spillage. Ensure that all fuel spillage (should it occur) is quickly removed from

engine surfaces. Ensure that all fuel soaked cloths or towels are deposited into a suitable waste container.

- Always keep a dry chemical (Class B) fire extinguisher near the work area.
- Do not allow fuel spray or fuel vapors to come into contact with a spark or open flame.
- Always use a back-up wrench when loosening and tightening fuel line connection fittings. This will prevent unnecessary stress and torsion to fuel line piping.
- Always replace worn fuel fitting O-rings with new Do not substitute fuel hose or equivalent where fuel pipe is installed.

Before servicing the vehicle, make sure to also refer to the precautions in the beginning of this section as well.

RELIEVING FUEL SYSTEM PRESSURE

3.6L Engine

1. Before servicing the vehicle, refer to the Precautions Section.

❊❊ CAUTION

Remove the fuel tank cap and relieve the fuel system pressure before servicing the fuel system in order to reduce the risk of personal injury. After you relieve the fuel system pressure, a small amount of fuel may

be released when servicing the fuel lines, the fuel injection pump, or the connections. In order to reduce the risk of personal injury, cover the fuel system components with a shop towel before disconnection. This will catch any fuel that may leak out. Place the towel in an approved container when the disconnection is complete.

2. Turn the ignition OFF.
3. Remove the fuel pump fuse and the fuel pump relay.
4. Loosen the fuel filler cap to relieve the fuel tank vapor pressure.
5. Attempt to start the engine and allow the engine to run until it stops.
6. Remove the fuel pressure test port cap.

❊❊ CAUTION

Wrap a shop towel around the fuel pressure connection in order to reduce the risk of fire and personal injury. The towel will absorb any fuel leakage that occurs during the connection of the fuel pressure gage. Place the towel in an approved container when the connection of the fuel pressure gage is complete.

7. Wrap a shop towel around the fuel pressure test port and use a small flat-

bladed tool in order to depress (open) the fuel pressure test port valve.

8. Place the shop towel in an approved container.

9. Install the fuel pressure test port cap.

10. Tighten the fuel filler cap.

3.8L Engine

1. Before servicing the vehicle, refer to the Precautions Section.

2. Disconnect the negative battery cable to avoid possible fuel discharge if an accidental attempt is made to start the engine.

3. Remove the fuel tank cap to relieve tank pressure. Do not tighten until the service procedure has been completed.

4. Connect a fuel pressure gauge with bleed valve to the fuel pressure test port. Wrap a shop towel around the fitting while connecting the gauge to catch any spilled fuel.

5. Install the bleed hose into an approved container and open the valve to bleed off the fuel system pressure.

6. Drain any fuel remaining in the gauge into an approved container.

✳✳ CAUTION

There may still be residual fuel in the system, and a small amount of fuel may be released when servicing fuel lines or connections. In order to reduce the chance of personal injury, cover the fuel line fittings with a shop towel before disconnecting to catch any fuel that may leak out.

FUEL FILTER

REMOVAL & INSTALLATION

The fuel filter is located in the fuel tank and is not normally serviced. Vehicles with a 3.6L engine have a paper filter located in the fuel pump module. Vehicles with a 3.8L engine have an in tank fuel strainer and filter.

To service the fuel filter, refer to Fuel Pump, removal and installation.

FUEL INJECTORS

REMOVAL & INSTALLATION

3.6L Engine

See Figures 196 and 197.

1. Before servicing the vehicle, refer to the Precautions Section.

2. Relieve the fuel system pressure.

3. Remove the upper intake manifold.

4. Remove the fuel pipe retaining clip.

5. Disconnect the fuel feed pipe from the fuel injector rail.

✳✳ CAUTION

Wear safety glasses.

6. Use compressed air in order to remove debris from the area where the fuel injectors enter the intake manifold.

7. Remove the fuel rail bolts.

✳✳ WARNING

Remove the fuel rail assembly carefully in order to prevent damage to the injector electrical connector terminals and the injector spray tips. Support the fuel rail after the fuel rail is removed in order to avoid damaging the fuel rail components. Cap the fittings and plug the holes when servicing the fuel system in order to prevent dirt and other contaminants from entering open pipes and passages.

8. Remove the fuel rail with the fuel injectors.

9. Disengage the fuel injector electrical connector lock.

10. Disconnect the fuel injector electrical connector.

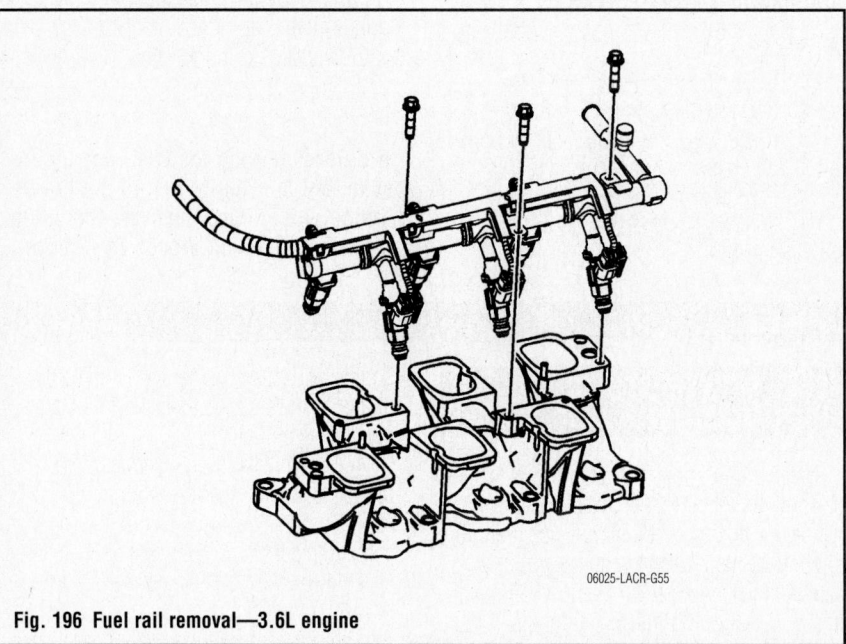

Fig. 196 Fuel rail removal—3.6L engine

06025-LACR-G55

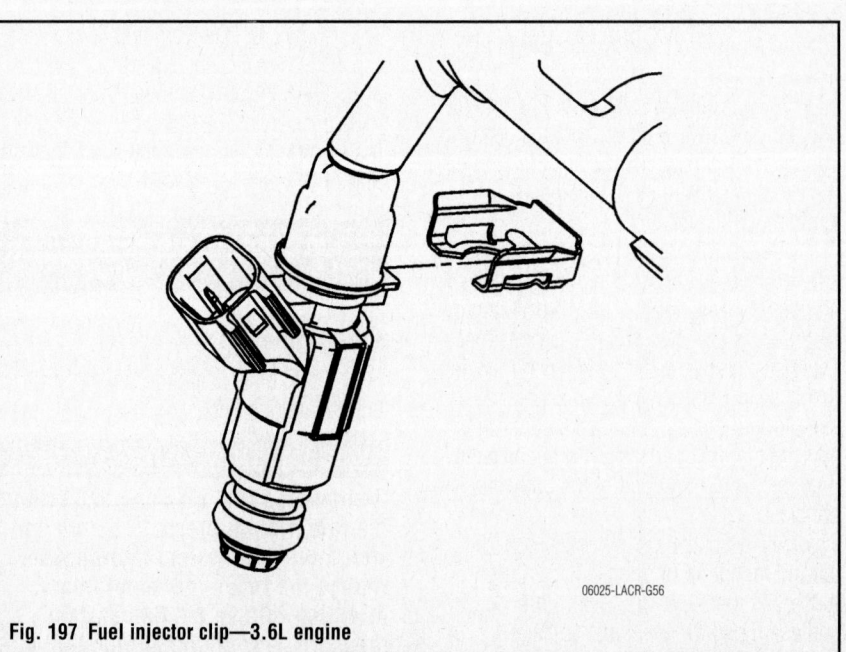

Fig. 197 Fuel injector clip—3.6L engine

06025-LACR-G56

11. Remove the fuel injector retainer clip.
12. Remove the fuel injector.
13. Remove and discard the fuel injector seals.

To install:

14. Install NEW fuel injector seals.
15. Install the fuel injector.
16. Install the fuel injector retainer clip.
17. Install the fuel injector electrical connector.
18. Engage the fuel injector electrical connector lock.
19. Install the fuel rail with the fuel injectors.
20. Install the fuel rail bolts. Tighten the fuel rail bolts to 89 inch lbs. (10 Nm).
21. Connect the fuel feed pipe to the fuel rail.
22. Install the fuel pipe retaining clip.
23. Install the upper intake manifold.

3.8L Engine

See Figure 198.

1. Before servicing the vehicle, refer to the Precautions Section.
2. Relieve the fuel system pressure.
3. Remove or disconnect the following:
   - Negative battery cable
   - Fuel lines
   - Fuel rail
   - Injector retaining clips
   - Fuel injector

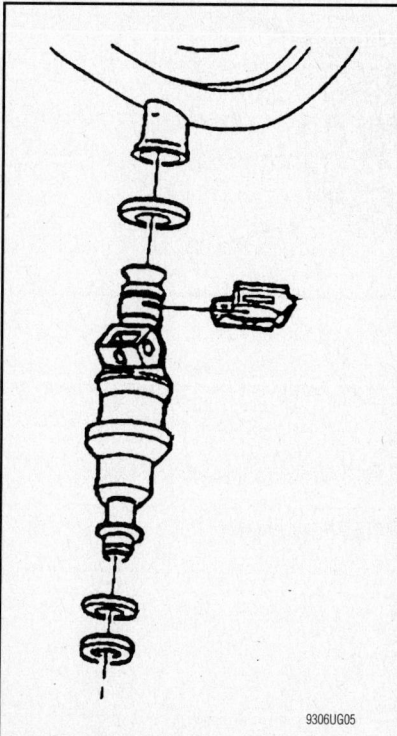

9306UG05

Fig. 198 Exploded view of the fuel injector assembly—3.8L engine

To install:

4. Install or connect the following:
   - Fuel injector with new O-rings, coat the o-rings with clean engine oil prior to installation
   - Injector retaining clips
   - Fuel rail and torque the bolts to 89 inch lbs. (10 Nm).
   - Fuel lines
   - Negative battery cable

FUEL PUMP

REMOVAL & INSTALLATION

3.6L Engine

See Figures 199 through 201.

➡ **Clean the fuel and Evaporative Emission (EVAP) connections and surrounding areas prior to disconnecting the lines in order to avoid possible system contamination.**

1. Before servicing the vehicle, refer to the Precautions Section.
2. Relieve the fuel system fuel pressure.
3. Drain the fuel tank.
4. Raise and support the vehicle.
5. Loosen the fuel fill hose clamp at the fuel tank.
6. Remove the fuel tank fill hose from the fuel tank.
7. Disconnect the EVAP vent solenoid hose on the tank from the EVAP vent valve solenoid hose.
8. Disconnect the EVAP vent pipe quick-connect fitting from the fill pipe EVAP vent pipe quick-connect fitting.
9. Disconnect the fuel feed, and the EVAP lines from the fuel tank lines.
10. Support the exhaust system.
11. Remove the rubber exhaust pipe hangers in order to allow the exhaust system to drop slightly.
12. Remove the fuel tank shield retainers.
13. Remove the fuel tank shield.

✳ WARNING

Do not bend the fuel tank straps as this may damage the straps.

14. Support the fuel tank with a suitable adjustable jack.
15. Remove the fuel tank strap bolts.
16. Using the jack lower the fuel tank.
17. Disconnect the fuel sender jumper harness electrical connector.
18. Remove the fuel tank and place the tank in a suitable work area.
19. Disconnect and remove the fuel pressure sensor and fuel sender jumper harness electrical connectors.

➡ **Note the routing of the lines for installation.**

20. Disconnect and remove the fuel feed line, and the EVAP lines.
21. Remove the EVAP canister.
22. Remove the insulator pads from the fuel tank. Note the location of the insulator pads for installation.
23. Disconnect the fuel sender module electrical connectors.

✳ WARNING

Do Not handle the fuel sender assembly by the fuel pipes. The amount of leverage generated by handling the fuel pipes could damage the joints.

24. Disconnect the fuel pipes from the fuel sender.

✳ WARNING

Avoid damaging the lockring. Use only J-45722 to prevent damage to the lockring.

✳ WARNING

Do Not handle the fuel sender assembly by the fuel pipes. The amount of leverage generated by handling the fuel pipes could damage the joints.

➡ **Do NOT use impact tools. Significant force will be required to release the lockring. The use of a hammer and screwdriver is not recommended. Secure the fuel tank in order to prevent fuel tank rotation.**

25. Use tool J 45722 and a long breaker-bar in order to unlock the fuel sender lockring. Turn the fuel sender lockring in a counterclockwise direction.
26. Remove the fuel sender lockring and the fuel sender from the fuel tank.
27. Remove and discard the fuel sender seal.
28. Remove the fuel level sensor from the fuel sender module.

➡ **Some lockring were manufactured with DO NOT REUSE stamped into them. These lockrings may be reused if they are not damaged or warped.**

➡ **Inspect the lockring for damage due to improper removal or installation procedures. If damage is found, install a NEW lockring.**

➡ **Check the lockring for flatness.**

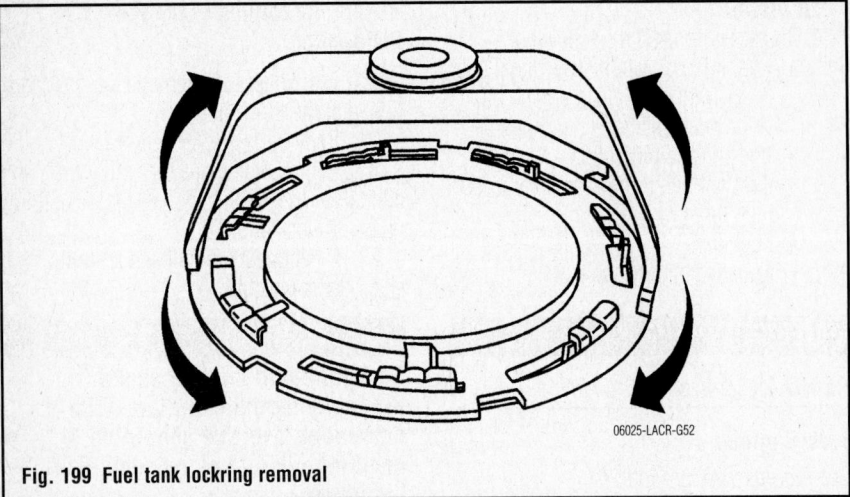

Fig. 199 Fuel tank lockring removal

34. Install the NEW fuel sender seal to the fuel tank seal groove.

35. Install the fuel sender and the fuel sender lockring.

➡ **Always replace the fuel sender seal when installing the fuel sender assembly. Replace the lockring if necessary. Do not apply any type of lubrication in the seal groove. Ensure the lockring is installed with the correct side facing upward. A correctly installed lockring will only turn in a clockwise direction.**

36. Use tool J 45722 in order to install the fuel sender lockring. Turn the fuel sender lockring in a clockwise direction.

29. Place the lockring on a flat surface. Measure the clearance between to lockring and the flat surface using a feeler gage at 7 points.

30. If the warpage is less than 0.41mm (0.016 in.), the lockring does not require replacement.

31. If the warpage is greater than 0.41mm (0.016 in.), the lockring must be replaced.

To install:

32. Install the fuel level sensor to the fuel sender module.

33. Clean the fuel sender sealing flange.

➡ **Always replace the fuel sender seal when installing the fuel sender assembly.**

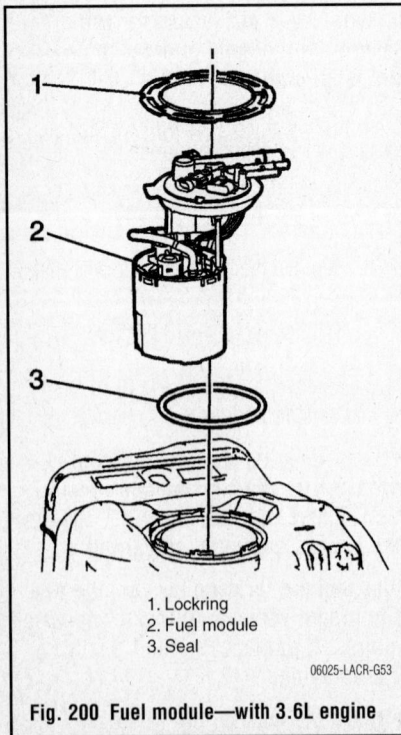

1. Lockring
2. Fuel module
3. Seal

06025-LACR-G53

Fig. 200 Fuel module—with 3.6L engine

1. Fill Limit Vent Valve (FLVV)
2. T-connector for vapor hose/pipes to vent/rollover valve and fill tube
3. Fuel Tank Pressure (FTP) sensor
4. FLVV outlet to Evaporative Emission (EVAP) canister
5. Fuel feed outlet
6. Fuel return inlet-not used
7. Fuel sender assembly connector
8. Fuel pump
9. Fuel pressure regulator
10. Fuel filter assembly
11. Fuel level sensor float

06025-LACR-G54

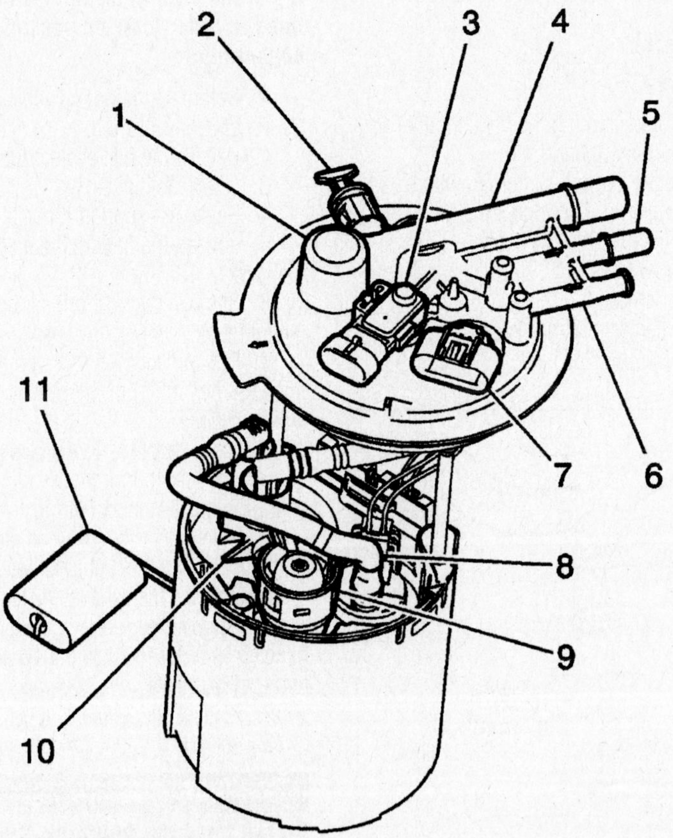

Fig. 201 Fuel module components—with 3.6L engine

37. Install the fuel pipes to the fuel sender.

38. Install the fuel sender sensor electrical connectors.

39. Install the insulator pads to the fuel tank.

40. Install the EVAP canister.

✳✳ WARNING

Do not attempt to straighten kinked nylon pipes. Replace any kinked nylon pipes in order to prevent damage to the vehicle. Do not attempt to repair sections of nylon pipes. Replace damaged nylon pipes. Replace the vapor pipes with original equipment or parts that meet GM specifications. Replace the vapor hoses with original equipment or parts meeting GM specifications. Use only reinforced fuel-resistant hose identified with the word Fluoroelastomer or GM 6163M on the hose.

41. Install and connect the fuel feed line, and the EVAP lines.

42. Install and connect the fuel pressure sensor and fuel sender jumper harness electrical connectors.

43. Install the fuel tank onto a suitable jack.

44. Partially raise the fuel tank until the electrical connection can be made.

45. Connect the fuel sender jumper harness electrical connector.

46. Completely raise the tank.

47. Install the fuel tank strap bolts. Tighten the bolts to 35 ft. lbs. (48 Nm).

48. Remove the jack from the fuel tank.

49. Position the fuel tank shield to the fuel tank.

50. Install the shield retainers.

51. Install the rubber exhaust pipe hangers.

52. Remove the support from the exhaust system.

53. Connect the fuel feed, and EVAP lines to the fuel tank lines.

54. Connect the EVAP vent pipe quick-connect fitting to the fill pipe EVAP vent pipe quick-connect fitting.

55. Connect the EVAP vent pipe quick-connect fitting to the fill pipe EVAP vent pipe quick-connect fitting.

56. Install the fuel tank fill hose onto the fuel tank. Install the hose over the orientation feature on the tank until fully seated to the tank.

57. Tighten the fuel fill hose clamp at the fuel tank. Tighten the clamp to 22 inch lbs. (3 Nm).

58. Lower the vehicle.

59. Add fuel and install the fuel fill cap.

60. Connect the negative battery cable.

61. Inspect the fuel system for leaks by performing the following steps:

  a. Turn ON the ignition for 2 seconds.

  b. Turn OFF the ignition for 10 seconds.

  c. Turn ON the ignition.

  d. Inspect for fuel leaks.

62. Install engine sight shield.

3.8L Engine

See Figures 202 and 203.

1. Before servicing the vehicle, refer to the Precautions Section.

2. Relieve the fuel system pressure.

3. Drain the fuel tank.

4. Remove or disconnect the following:
- Negative battery cable
- Spare tire and jack
- Trunk lining
- Fuel sender access panel
- Sender and quick connect fittings from the sender
- Electrical connector from the sender and position harness and hoses aside

✳✳ CAUTION

When removing the fuel sender from the tank, the reservoir bucket is full of fuel. Use caution in containing the fuel.

- Sender retaining ring
- Sender and take note of its position
- Fuel sender O-ring and discard it

➡**Note the direction the strainer is pointing.**

- Strainer from the pump by pulling it down and twisting

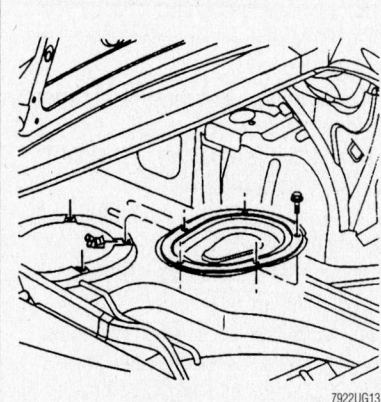

Fig. 202 The fuel pump service cover is located in the luggage compartment under the spare tire

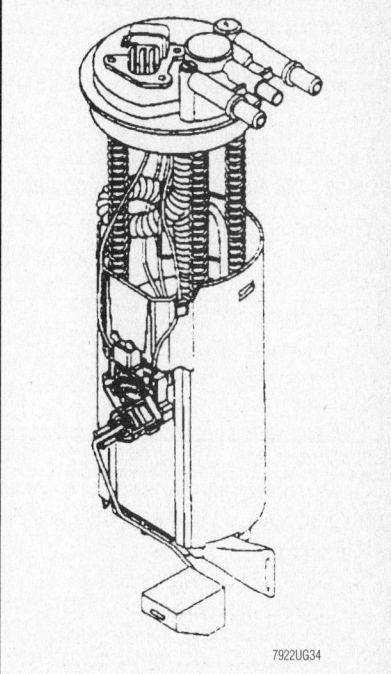

Fig. 203 Fuel pump and level sender assembly—3.8L engine

- Pump electrical wires and hoses
- Pump assembly out of the rubber connectors

To install:

5. Transfer any insulators and grommets from the old pump to the new one.

6. Connect the pump to the fuel hose and tilt the bottom of the pump into the mounting bracket.

7. Install or connect the following:
- New strainer on the pump so it points in the same direction as noted during removal
- Electrical connectors and fuel lines to the pump
- New O-ring on top of the fuel tank
- Fuel sender assembly into the tank
- Lockring
- Fuel line quick connectors
- Sender electrical connector
- Fuel sender access cover
- Trunk liner
- Spare tire and jack

8. Refill with fuel and check for leaks.

FUEL TANK

REMOVAL & INSTALLATION

3.6L Engine

1. Before servicing the vehicle, refer to the Precautions Section.

2. Disconnect the negative battery cable.

➡ Cap the fittings and plug the holes when servicing the fuel system in order to prevent dirt and other contaminants from entering the open pipes and passages.

➡ Always maintain cleanliness when servicing the fuel system components.

3. Relieve the fuel system fuel pressure. Refer to Relieving Fuel System Pressure.

4. Drain the fuel tank.

5. Raise and support the vehicle.

6. Loosen the fuel filler hose clamp at the fuel tank.

7. Remove the fuel tank filler hose from the fuel tank.

8. Disconnect the fuel feed, fuel return, and the Evaporative Emission (EVAP) pipes.

9. Support the exhaust system.

10. Remove the rubber exhaust pipe hangers in order to allow the exhaust system to drop slightly.

11. Separate the two halves of the EVAP fresh air hose at the splice.

12. Remove the fuel tank shield push pins.

13. Remove the fuel tank shield.

✳✳ WARNING

Do not bend the fuel tank straps as this may damage the straps.

14. Support the fuel tank with a suitable jack.

15. Remove the fuel tank strap bolts.

16. Using a suitable jack, lower the fuel tank.

17. Disconnect the fuel sender assembly electrical connectors.

18. Remove the fuel tank and place the tank in a suitable work area.

➡ Note the routing of the pipe assemblies and the retaining clips for installation.

19. Disconnect and remove the fuel feed, fuel return, and EVAP pipe assemblies and the insulator clips from the fuel tank.

20. Remove the EVAP canister from the fuel tank.

21. Remove the insulator pads from the fuel tank.

➡ Note the location of the insulator pads for installation.

To install:

22. Install the insulator pads to the fuel tank.

23. Install the EVAP canister to the fuel tank.

✳✳ WARNING

Do not attempt to straighten kinked nylon pipes. Replace any kinked nylon pipes in order to prevent damage to the vehicle. Do not attempt to repair sections of nylon pipes. Replace damaged nylon pipes. Replace the vapor pipes with original equipment or parts that meet GM specifications. Replace the vapor hoses with original equipment or parts meeting GM specifications. Use only reinforced fuel-resistant hose identified with the word Fluoroelastomer or GM 6163M on the hose.

24. Install and connect the fuel feed, fuel return, and EVAP pipe assemblies and the insulator clips to the fuel tank as noted during removal.

25. Place the fuel tank on a suitable jack.

26. Raise the fuel tank to its original position.

➡ Use the correct fastener in the correct location. Replacement fasteners must be the correct part number for that application. Fasteners requiring replacement or fasteners requiring the use of thread locking compound or sealant are identified in the service procedure. Do not use paints, lubricants, or corrosion inhibitors on fasteners or fastener joint surfaces unless specified. These coatings affect fastener torque and joint clamping force and may damage the fastener. Use the correct tightening sequence and specifications when installing fasteners in order to avoid damage to parts and systems.

27. Install the fuel tank strap bolts. Tighten the bolts to 35 ft. lbs. (48 Nm).

28. Remove the jack from the fuel tank.

29. Position the fuel tank shield to the fuel tank.

30. Install the push pins that retain the fuel tank shield to the fuel tank.

31. Install the two parts of the EVAP fresh air hose at the splice.

32. Raise the exhaust system to the original position.

33. Install the exhaust system to the exhaust pipe hangers.

34. Connect the fuel feed, fuel return, and Evaporative Emission (EVAP) pipes.

35. Install the fuel tank filler hose to the fuel tank.

36. Fully seat the filler hose on the fuel tank port.

37. Ensure that the clamp is properly located on the tank port between the bead and the tank. Tighten the hose clamp to 22 inch lbs. (3 Nm).

38. Lower the vehicle.

39. Add fuel and install the fuel fill cap.

40. Connect the negative battery cable.

41. Inspect the fuel system for leaks by performing the following steps:

a. Turn ON the ignition for 2 seconds.

b. Turn OFF the ignition for 10 seconds.

c. Turn ON the ignition.

d. Inspect for fuel leaks.

3.8L Engine

1. Before servicing the vehicle, refer to the Precautions Section.

2. Disconnect the negative battery cable.

➡ Clean the fuel and Evaporative Emission (EVAP) connections and surrounding areas prior to disconnecting the lines in order to avoid possible system contamination.

➡ Always maintain cleanliness when servicing the fuel system components.

3. Relieve the fuel system fuel pressure. Refer to Relieving Fuel System Pressure.

4. Drain the fuel tank.

5. Raise and support the vehicle.

6. Loosen the fuel fill hose clamp at the fuel tank.

7. Remove the fuel tank fill hose from the fuel tank.

8. Disconnect the EVAP vent solenoid hose on the tank from the EVAP vent valve solenoid hose.

9. Disconnect the EVAP vent pipe quick connect fitting from the fill pipe EVAP vent pipe quick connect fitting.

10. Disconnect the fuel feed and EVAP lines from the fuel tank lines.

11. Support the exhaust system.

12. Remove the rubber exhaust pipe hangers in order to allow the exhaust system to drop slightly.

13. Remove the fuel tank shield retainers.

14. Remove the fuel tank shield.

✳✳ WARNING

Do not bend the fuel tank straps as this may damage the straps.

15. Support the fuel tank with a suitable adjustable jack.

16. Remove the fuel tank strap bolts.

17. Using the jack lower the fuel tank.

18. Disconnect the fuel sender jumper harness electrical connector.

19. Remove the fuel tank and place the tank in a suitable work area.

20. Disconnect and remove the fuel pressure sensor and fuel sender jumper harness electrical connectors.

➡**Note the routing of the lines for installation.**

21. Disconnect and remove the fuel feed line and EVAP lines.

22. Remove the EVAP canister.

23. Remove the insulator pads from the fuel tank.

➡**Note the location of the insulator pads for installation.**

To install:

✲✲ WARNING

Do not attempt to straighten kinked nylon pipes. Replace any kinked nylon pipes in order to prevent damage to the vehicle. Do not attempt to repair sections of nylon pipes. Replace damaged nylon pipes. Replace the vapor pipes with original equipment or parts that meet GM specifications. Replace the vapor hoses with original equipment or parts meeting GM specifications. Use only reinforced fuel-resistant hose identified with the word Fluoroelastomer or GM 6163M on the hose.

24. Install the insulator pads to the fuel tank.

25. Install the EVAP canister.

26. Install and connect the fuel feed line and EVAP lines.

27. Install and connect the fuel pressure sensor and fuel sender jumper harness electrical connectors.

28. Place the fuel tank onto a suitable jack.

29. Partially raise the fuel tank until the electrical connections can be made.

30. Connect the fuel sender jumper harness electrical connector.

31. Completely raise the tank.

32. Install the fuel tank strap bolts. Tighten the bolts to 35 ft. lbs. (48 Nm).

33. Remove the jack from the fuel tank.

34. Position the fuel tank shield to the fuel tank.

35. Install the shield retainers.

36. Install the rubber exhaust pipe hangers.

37. Remove the support from the exhaust system.

38. Connect the fuel feed and EVAP lines to the fuel tank lines.

39. Connect the EVAP vent pipe quick connect fitting to the fill pipe EVAP vent pipe quick connect fitting.

40. Connect the EVAP vent solenoid hose on the tank to the EVAP vent valve solenoid hose.

41. Install the fuel tank fill hose onto the fuel tank. Install the hose over the orientation feature on the tank until fully seated to the tank.

42. Tighten the fuel fill hose clamp at the fuel tank. Tighten the clamp to 22 inch lbs. (3 Nm).

43. Lower the vehicle.

44. Add fuel and install the fuel fill cap.

45. Connect the negative battery cable.

46. Inspect the fuel system for leaks by performing the following steps:

 a. Turn ON the ignition for 2 seconds.

 b. Turn OFF the ignition for 10 seconds.

 c. Turn ON the ignition.

 d. Inspect for fuel leaks.

IDLE SPEED

ADJUSTMENT

Idle speed is maintained by the Powertrain Control Module (PCM). No adjustment is necessary or possible.

THROTTLE BODY

REMOVAL & INSTALLATION

3.6L Engine

1. Turn the ignition OFF.

2. Remove the air cleaner intake duct.

3. Remove the throttle body electrical connector.

4. Remove the throttle body bolts.

5. Remove the throttle body and gasket.

To install:

6. Clean the throttle body gasket mating surfaces.

7. Install the throttle body and NEW gasket.

8. Install the throttle body bolts and tighten to 89 inch lbs. (10 Nm).

9. Install the throttle body electrical connector.

10. Install the air cleaner intake duct.

11. Turn OFF the ignition for 30 seconds.

12. Turn ON the ignition, with the engine OFF for 60 seconds.

13. Turn OFF the ignition.

14. Turn ON the ignition, with the engine OFF.

15. Use the scan tool to clear all DTCs.

3.8L Engine

1. Turn the ignition OFF.

2. Partially drain the cooling system.

3. Remove the fuel injector sight shield.

4. Remove the air cleaner intake duct.

5. Disconnect the throttle body electrical connector.

6. Remove the throttle body nuts and the bolts.

7. Remove the throttle body assembly.

8. Clean the throttle body gasket mating surfaces.

To install:

9. Install the throttle body assembly.

10. Install the throttle body bolts and tighten to 89 inch lbs. (10 Nm).

11. Install the throttle body electrical connector.

12. Install the air cleaner intake duct.

13. Install the fuel injector sight shield.

14. Fill the cooling system.

HEATING & AIR CONDITIONING SYSTEM

BLOWER MOTOR

REMOVAL & INSTALLATION

1. Remove the right side instrument panel insulator.

2. Disconnect the blower motor electrical connector.

3. Remove the blower motor mounting screws.

4. Remove the blower motor.

To install:

5. Install the blower motor.

6. Install the blower motor screws and tighten.

7. Connect the blower motor electrical connector.

8. Install the right side instrument panel insulator.

HEATER CORE

REMOVAL & INSTALLATION

See Figures 204 and 205.

1. Before servicing the vehicle, refer to the Precautions Section.

2. Drain the coolant.

3. Position aside the heater hose inlet and outlet clamps at the heater core.

4. Disconnect the inlet and outlet heater hose from the heater core.

5. Remove the RH instrument panel closeout/insulator panel.

6. Remove the LH instrument panel closeout/insulator panel.

7. Remove the floor carpet.

8. Remove the center console, if equipped.

9. Remove the HVAC control.

➡The Vehicle Communication Interface Module (VCIM) has a specific set of unique numbers that tie the module to each vehicle. These numbers, the 10–digit station identification and the 11–digit electronic serial number, are used by the National Cellular Network and OnStar® to identify the specific vehicle. Because these numbers are tied to the vehicle identification number of the vehicle, you must never exchange these parts with those of another vehicle.

10. Remove the communication interface module screws.

11. Disconnect the mobile telephone antenna cable from the communication interface module by pulling outward on the square plastic housing.

12. Disconnect the electrical connectors.

13. Disconnect the navigation antenna coaxial antenna cable from the module.

14. Remove the communication interface module.

15. Remove the rear floor air outlet duct from the holes in the floor reinforcement.

16. Disconnect the rear floor air outlet duct from the heater core outlet cover.

17. Remove the rear floor air outlet duct.

18. Remove the heater core outlet cover screws.

19. Remove the heater core outlet cover heat stakes with a small chisel.

20. Remove the heater core outlet cover from the HVAC module assembly.

21. Remove the heater core cover screws.

22. Remove the heater core cover heat stakes with a small chisel.

23. Remove the heater core cover from the HVAC module assembly.

24. Remove the heater core from the HVAC module assembly.

25. Remove the heater core foam seal from the HVAC module assembly.

To install:

26. Install a new heater core foam seal to the HVAC module assembly.

27. Install the heater core to the HVAC module assembly.

28. From the inside of the heater core cover, drill the dimples adjacent to the heat stakes using a 7/32 in. (5.5mm) drill bit.

29. Install the heater core cover.

30. Install the heater core cover screws to the heater core cover. Tighten all the screws to 13 inch lbs. (2 Nm).

31. From the inside of the heater core outlet cover, drill the dimples adjacent to the heat stakes using a 7/32 in. (5.5mm) drill bit.

32. Install the heater core outlet cover.

33. Install the heater core outlet cover screws. Tighten the screws to 13 inch lbs. (2 Nm).

34. Connect the rear floor air outlet duct to the heater core outlet cover.

35. Install the rear floor air outlet duct to the holes in the floor reinforcement.

36. Install the HVAC module.

37. Install the center console.

✳✳ WARNING

Before you install the antenna cable connector of the Global Positioning System (GPS) to the Vehicle Communication Interface Module (VCM), align the connector properly in order to avoid damaging the connector.

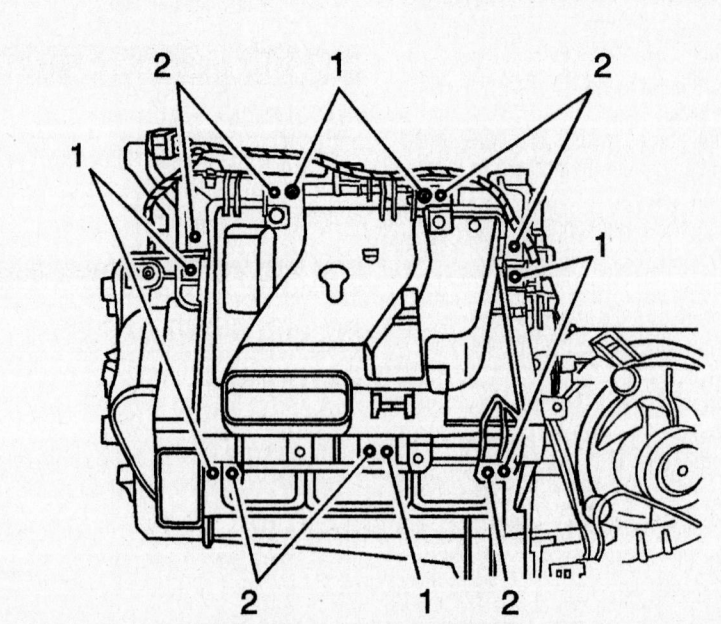

1. Outlet cover heat stakes
2. Heater core outlet cover screws

06025-LACR-G13

Fig. 204 HVAC core outlet side

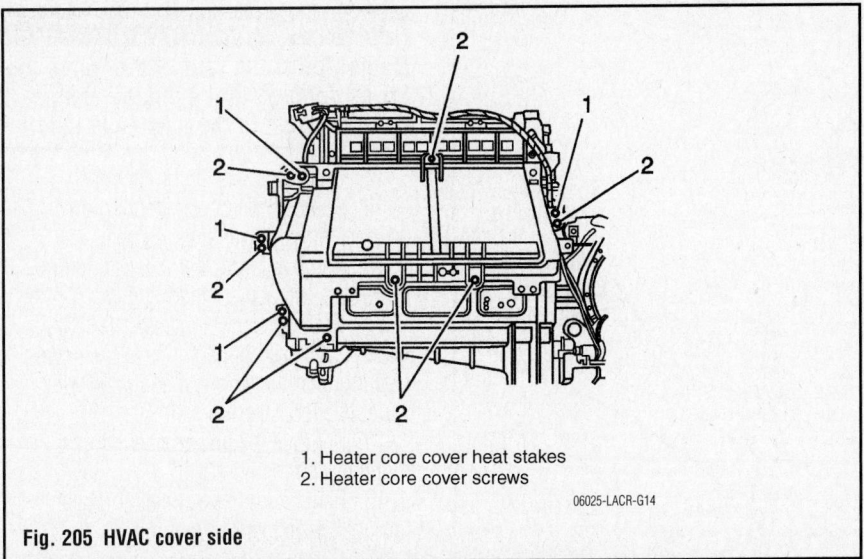

1. Heater core cover heat stakes
2. Heater core cover screws

06025-LACR-G14

Fig. 205 HVAC cover side

38. Connect the navigation antenna coaxial cable to the module.

39. Connect the electrical connectors.

40. Connect the mobile telephone antenna cable to the module by pushing inward on the square plastic housing.

41. Align the module to the vehicle antenna module bracket.

42. Install the communication interface module screws. Tighten the screws to 18 inch lbs. (2 Nm).

43. Install the floor carpet.

44. Install the RH instrument panel closeout/insulator panel.

45. Connect the inlet and outlet heater hose to the heater core.

46. Reposition the heater hose inlet and outlet clamps to the heater core.

47. Refill the coolant.

STEERING

POWER RACK & PINION STEERING GEAR

REMOVAL & INSTALLATION

See Figures 206 through 210.

1. Before servicing the vehicle, refer to the Precautions Section.

2. Raise and support the vehicle.

3. Place a drain pan under the vehicle.

4. Remove the tire and wheel assemblies.

✸✸ CAUTION

Failure to disconnect the intermediate shaft from the rack and pinion stub shaft can result in damage to the steering gear and/or intermediate shaft. This damage can cause loss of steering control which could result in personal injury.

✸✸ WARNING

Set steering shaft so the block tooth on the upper steering shaft is at the 12 o'clock position, the wheels on the vehicle are straight ahead and set the ignition switch to the LOCK position. Failure to follow these procedures could result in damage to the coil.

✸✸ WARNING

The wheels of the vehicle must be straight ahead and the steering column in the LOCK position before dis-

connecting the steering column or intermediate shaft from the steering gear. Failure to do so will cause the SIR coil assembly to become un-centered, which may cause damage to the coil assembly.

5. Remove the lower pinch bolt from the power steering gear stub shaft.

6. Insert tool J 42640 into the steering column access hole in order to lock the steering column. This will maintain the correct orientation.

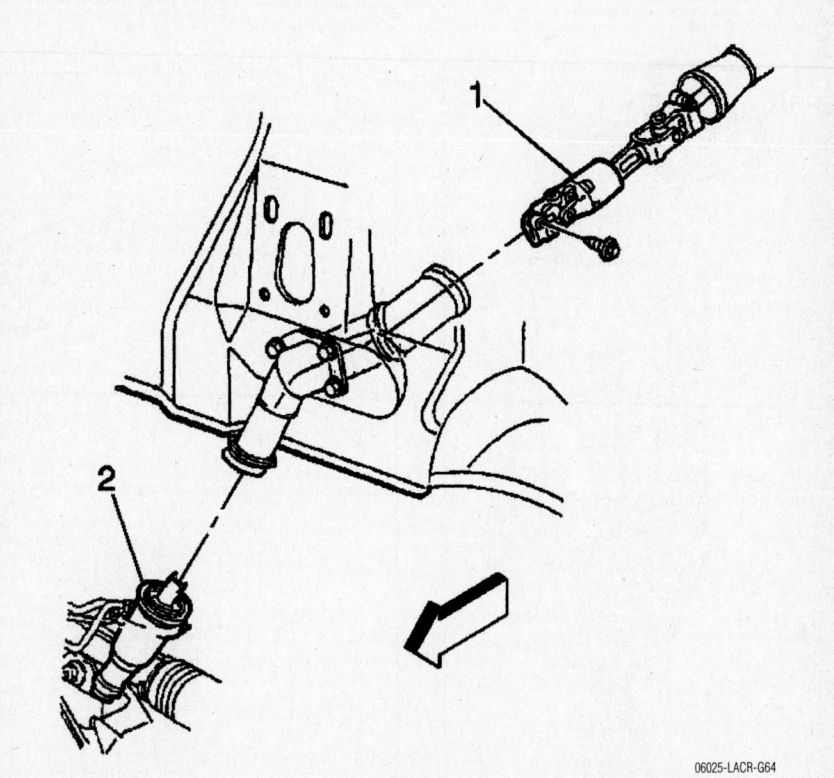

06025-LACR-G64

Fig. 206 Disconnect the intermediate steering shaft (1) from the power steering gear stub shaft (2)

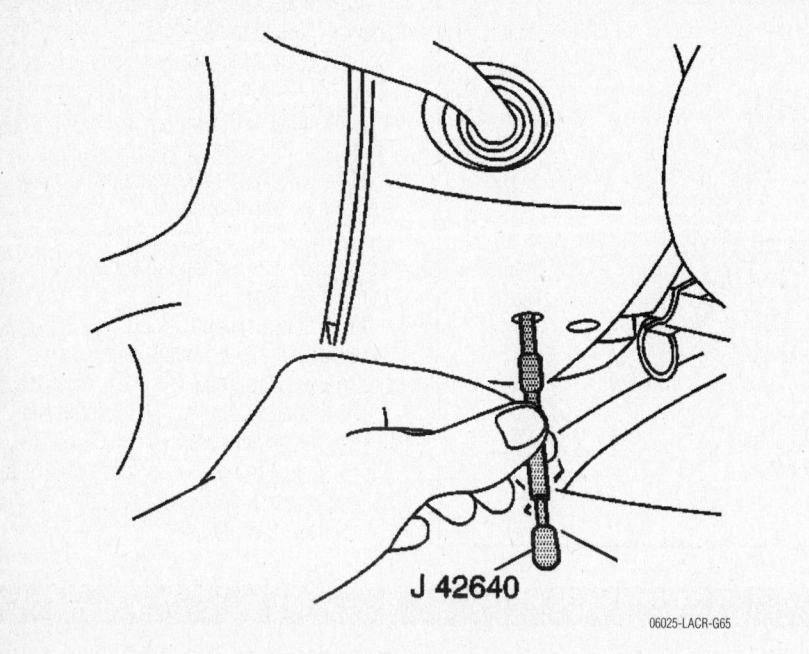

Fig. 207 Insert tool J 42640 into the steering column access hole in order to lock the steering column

7. Remove the intermediate steering shaft from the power steering gear stub shaft.

8. Remove both of the tie rod ends from the steering knuckles.

9. Support the rear of the frame using jackstands.

10. Remove the frame bolts from the rear of the frame. Refer to Engine Removal & Installation.

✳✳ WARNING

Do not lower the rear of the frame too far as damage to the engine components nearest to the cowl may result.

11. Lower the rear of the frame.

12. Remove the power steering pressure hose from the power steering gear.

13. Remove the power steering return hose from the power steering gear.

14. Remove the Magnasteer Variable Assist electrical connector from the power steering gear assembly, if equipped with variable effort steering.

15. Remove the power steering gear mounting bolts and nuts.

16. Remove the power steering gear through the left wheel opening.

To install:

17. Install the power steering gear through the left wheel opening.

18. Install the power steering gear mounting bolts and nuts. Tighten the power steering gear mounting bolts to 66 ft. lbs. (90 Nm).

19. Inspect the threads on the power steering pressure hose and the power steering return hose.

20. Inspect the O-ring seals on the power steering hoses.

21. Replace the seals if damaged, lubricate the seals before installation.

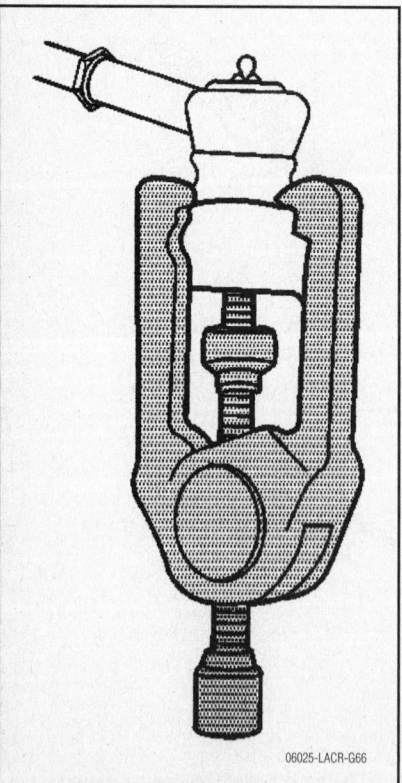

Fig. 208 Separating the tie rod end from the knuckle

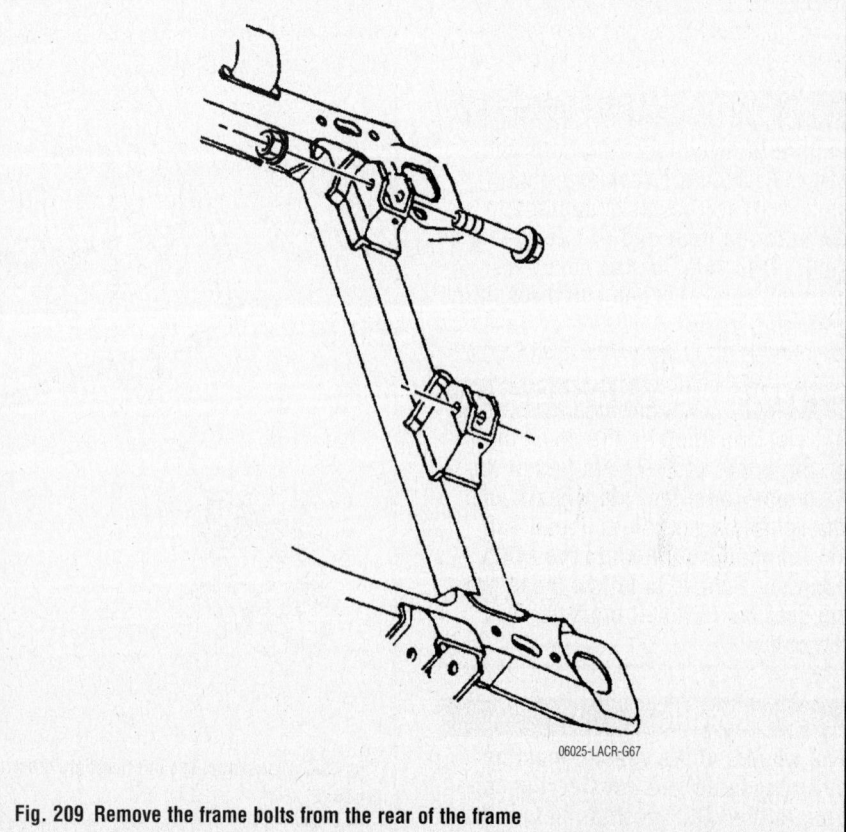

Fig. 209 Remove the frame bolts from the rear of the frame

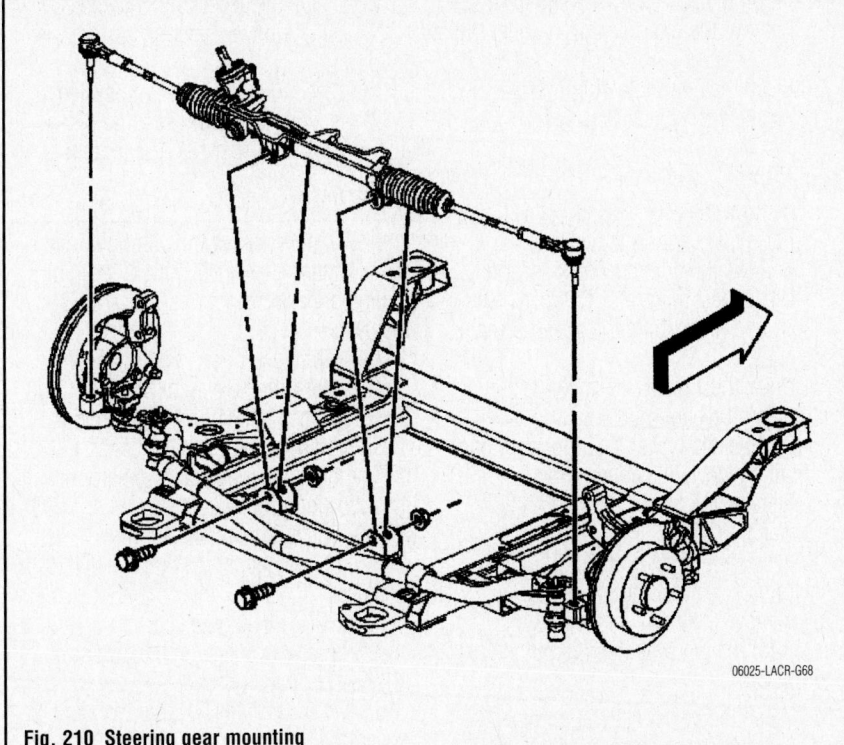

Fig. 210 Steering gear mounting

22. Install the clamp that holds the power steering hoses to the power steering gear.

23. Install the Magnasteer Variable Assist electrical connector to the power steering gear assembly, if equipped with variable effort steering.

24. Install the power steering pressure hose to the power steering gear. Tighten the power steering pressure hose to power steering gear. Tighten the pressure hose fittings to 20 ft. lbs. (27 Nm).

25. Install the power steering return hose to the power steering gear. Tighten the fitting to 20 ft. lbs. (27 Nm).

26. Raise the frame into position.

27. Install rear frame bolts. Tighten the rear bolts to 118 ft. lbs. (160 Nm).

28. Remove the jackstands.

29. Install the tie rod ends to the steering knuckles. Tighten the nut to 34 ft. lbs. (30 Nm) plus 120°. Inspect to ensure that 2½–4½ threads are visible above the nylon washer.

❋❋ WARNING

Set steering shaft so the block tooth on the upper steering shaft is at the 12 o'clock position, the wheels on the vehicle are straight ahead and set the ignition switch to the LOCK position. Failure to follow these procedures could result in damage to the coil.

➡**During the installation of the intermediate steering shaft, ensure the steering shaft is seated before you install the pinch bolt. The two mating shafts may disengage if the pinch bolt is inserted into the coupling before the steering shaft installation.**

30. Raise and support the vehicle.

31. Install the intermediate steering shaft to the power steering gear stub shaft.

32. Install the lower pinch bolt to the intermediate steering shaft at the power steering gear stub shaft. Tighten the pinch bolt to 35 ft. lbs. (48 Nm).

33. Install the intermediate steering shaft seal onto the power steering gear.

34. Install the tire and wheel assemblies.

35. Remove the drain pan from under the vehicle.

36. Lower the vehicle.

37. Remove tool J 42640 from the steering column.

38. Fill the power steering system with power steering fluid.

39. Bleed the power steering system:

❋❋ WARNING

When adding fluid or making a complete fluid change, always use the proper power steering fluid. Failure to use the proper fluid will cause hose and seal damage and fluid leaks.

➡**Use clean, new power steering fluid type only. See the Maintenance and Lubrication subsection for fluid specifications. Hoses touching the frame, body, or engine may cause system noise. Verify that the hoses do not touch any other part of the vehicle. Loose connections may not leak, but could allow air into the steering system. Verify that all hose connections are tight.**

➡**Maintain the fluid level throughout the bleed procedure**

e. Remove the pump reservoir cap.

f. Fill the pump reservoir with fluid to the FULL COLD level.

g. Attach a vacuum pump and adapter to the reservoir.

h. Apply a vacuum of 68 kPa (20 in Hg) maximum.

i. Wait 5 minutes. Typical vacuum drop is 7–10 kPa (2–3 in Hg).

j. Remove the vacuum pump and adapter.

k. Reinstall the pump reservoir cap.

l. Start the engine. Allow the engine to idle.

m. Turn OFF the engine.

n. Verify the fluid level. Repeat steps 8-10 until the fluid stabilizes.

➡**Do NOT turn the steering wheel to LOCK.**

o. Start the engine. Allow the engine to idle.

p. Turn the steering wheel 180–360° in both directions 5 times.

q. Turn OFF the ignition.

r. Verify the fluid level.

s. Remove the pump reservoir cap.

t. Attach a vacuum pump and adapter to the reservoir.

u. Apply a vacuum of 68 kPa (20 in. Hg) maximum.

v. Wait 5 minutes.

w. Remove the vacuum pump and adapter.

x. Verify the fluid level.

y. Reinstall the pump reservoir cap.

40. Inspect the power steering system for leaks.

41. Perform a front end alignment.

POWER STEERING PUMP

REMOVAL & INSTALLATION

3.6L Engine

1. Place a drain pan under the vehicle.
2. Remove the accessory drive belt.
3. Turn the steering wheel to the right

in order to allow clearance to remove the pump.

4. Raise and support the vehicle.

5. Remove the right front tire and wheel.

6. Disconnect the power steering pump inlet hose and pressure hose from the power steering pump.

7. Remove the power steering pump mounting bolts.

8. Remove the power steering pump from the engine.

9. Cap the power steering pump fittings and hoses to prevent contamination.

10. Remove the power steering pump pulley.

To install:

11. Install the power steering pump pulley.

12. Remove the caps from the power steering pump fittings and hoses.

13. Position the power steering pump on the engine.

14. Install the power steering pump mounting bolts. HAND TIGHTEN ONLY.

15. Tighten the front mounting bolt and then the rear to 37 ft. lbs. (50 Nm).

16. Clean the material from the power steering pressure hose and install a new seal.

17. Connect the power steering pressure hose to the power steering pump and tighten to 30 ft. lbs. (40 Nm).

18. Connect the power steering reservoir outlet hose to the power steering pump.

19. Install the right front tire and wheel.

20. Lower the vehicle.

21. Install the accessory drive belt.

22. Remove the drain pan from under the vehicle.

23. Bleed the power steering system.

24. Inspect the system for leaks.

3.8L Engine

1. Remove the accessory drive belt.

2. Raise and support the vehicle.

3. Remove the tire and wheel assembly.

4. Disconnect the power steering pressure hose and return from the power steering pump.

5. Disconnect the harness connector from the power steering pump.

6. Remove the power steering mounting bolts from the power steering pump.

7. Remove the power steering pump from the engine.

8. Remove the power steering pump pulley from the power steering pump.

9. Remove the power steering pump reservoir from the power steering pump.

To install:

10. Install the power steering pump reservoir to the power steering pump.

11. Install the power steering pump pulley to the power steering pump.

12. Position the power steering pump to the engine.

13. Install the power steering pump mounting bolts and tighten to 18 ft. lbs. (25 Nm).

14. Connect the power steering pressure hose to the power steering pump.

15. Install the harness connector to the power steering pump.

16. Install the accessory drive belt.

17. Fill the power steering system with fluid.

18. Bleed the power steering system.

19. Operate the power steering system and inspect for power steering system leaks.

BLEEDING

1. Fill pump reservoir with fluid to minimum system level, FULL COLD level, or middle of hash mark on cap stick fluid level indicator.

2. With hydro-boost, do not apply the brake pedal with the engine OFF. This will discharge the hydro-boost accumulator.

3. If equipped with hydro-boost, fully charge the hydro-boost accumulator using the following procedure:

    a. Start the engine.

    b. Firmly apply the brake pedal 10-15 times.

    c. Turn the engine OFF.

4. Raise the vehicle until the front wheels are off the ground.

5. Key on engine OFF, turn the steering wheel from stop to stop 12 times. Vehicles equipped with hydro-boost systems or longer length power steering hoses may require turns up to 15 to 20 stop to stops.

6. Verify power steering fluid level per operating specification.

7. Start the engine. Rotate steering wheel from left to right. Check for sign of cavitation or fluid aeration (pump noise/whining).

8. Verify the fluid level. Repeat the bleed procedure, if necessary.

SUSPENSION

CONTROL LINKS

REMOVAL & INSTALLATION

See Figure 211.

1. Before servicing the vehicle, refer to the Precautions Section.

2. Raise the vehicle and safely support the vehicle.

3. Remove the tire and wheel assembly.

4. Remove the control link bolt and nut.

5. Remove the control link from the vehicle.

To install:

6. Install the control link into the vehicle.

7. Install the control link bolt and nut. Tighten the nut to 17 ft. lbs. (23 Nm).

8. Install the tire and wheel assembly.

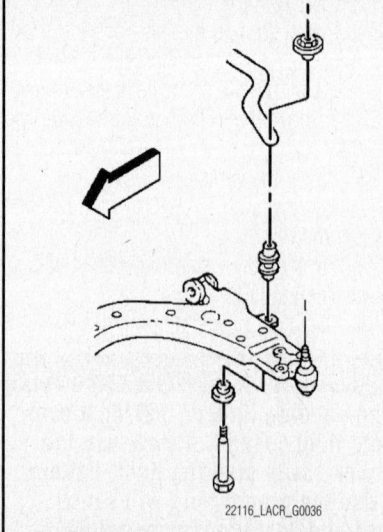

22116_LACR_G0036

Fig. 211 Expanded view of the control link components

FRONT SUSPENSION

Tighten the lug nut to 100 ft. lbs. (140 Nm) using a crisscross torque pattern.

9. Lower the vehicle.

LOWER BALL JOINT

REMOVAL & INSTALLATION

See Figures 212 and 213.

1. Before servicing the vehicle, refer to the Precautions Section.

2. Raise and support the vehicle.

3. Remove the tire and wheel.

4. Drill a pilot hole through the rivets.

5. Drill the remainder of the rivets.

6. Use a hammer and a chisel in order to remove the remainder of the rivet heads.

7. Remove the cotter pin from the ball stud.

8. Loosen the ball stud nut.

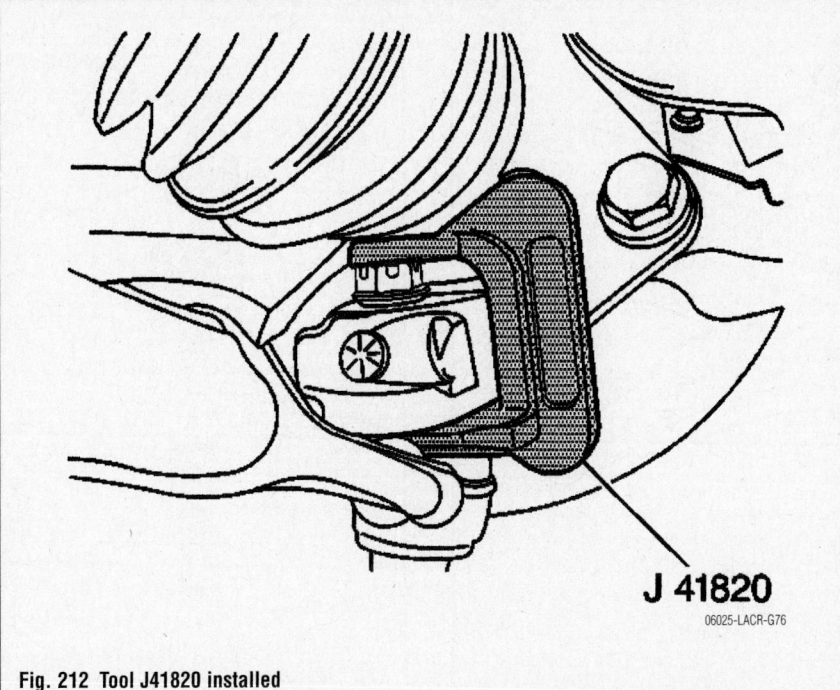

Fig. 212 Tool J41820 installed

9. Install a tool such as J 41820 over the ball stud and lower control arm.

10. Rotate the ball stud nut counterclockwise in order to separate the ball stud from the steering knuckle.

11. Remove the tool.

12. Remove the ball stud nut.

13. Remove the ball stud from the lower control arm.

To install:

14. Install the ball stud to the lower control arm.

15. Install the NEW ball stud bolts facing down, away from the ball stud.

16. Install the NEW ball stud nuts. Tighten the NEW ball stud nuts to 50 ft. lbs. (68 Nm).

17. Install the ball stud to the steering knuckle.

18. Install the ball stud castle nut. Tighten the nut to 15 ft. lbs. (20 Nm) plus an additional 120°.

19. Install a new cotter pin and bend the ends.

20. Install the tire and wheels.

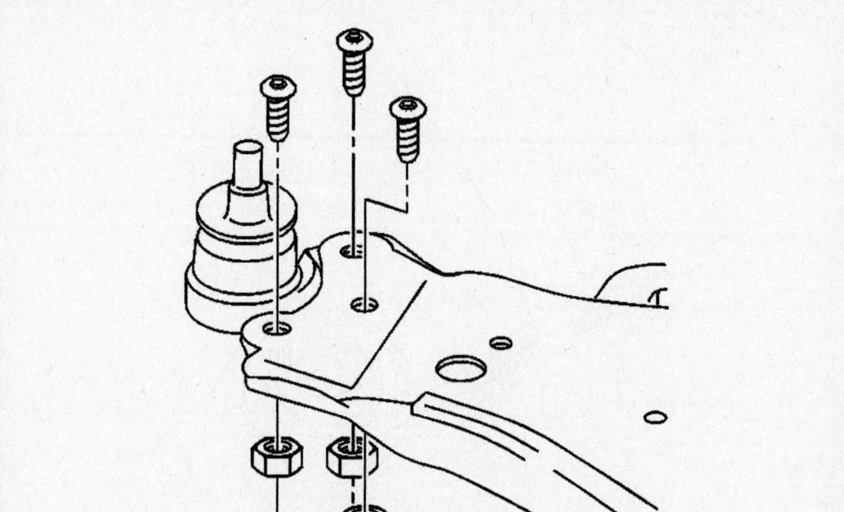

Fig. 213 Install the NEW ball stud bolts facing down, away from the ball stud

21. Lower the vehicle.

22. Check the wheel alignment.

LOWER CONTROL ARM

REMOVAL & INSTALLATION

See Figure 214.

1. Before servicing the vehicle, refer to the Precautions Section.

✶✶ WARNING

Use only the recommended tools for separating the ball joint from the knuckle. Do NOT hammer or pry the ball joint from the knuckle. Failure to use the recommended tools may cause damage to the ball joint and seal.

➡ **Use the ignition key in order to unlock the steering column.**

2. Turn the steering wheel in order to move the front of the applicable wheel to the outboard most position.

➡ **Use ONLY a frame-contact type vehicle lift or a floor jack at the recommended lift points. Do NOT use a suspension-contact type vehicle lift. Do NOT lift the vehicle by the lower control arms.**

3. Raise and support the vehicle.

4. Remove the tire and wheel.

5. If applicable, disconnect the ABS wheel speed sensor connector.

6. If applicable, disconnect the ABS wheel speed sensor jumper harness from the harness retainer clips.

7. Remove the cotter pin from the ball stud.

8. Loosen the ball stud nut.

9. Install tool J 41820 over the ball stud and lower control arm as shown.

10. Rotate the ball stud nut counterclockwise in order to separate the ball stud from the steering knuckle.

11. Remove the tool.

12. Remove the ball stud nut.

13. Remove the lower control arm bolts and nuts.

14. Remove the lower control arm.

To install:

15. Install the lower control arm.

16. Install the control arm bolts and nuts. Do not tighten at this time.

➡ **Align the ball stud cotter pin hole parallel to the knuckle in order to ease the cotter pin installation.**

17. Install the ball stud to the knuckle.

18. Install the ball stud castle nut.

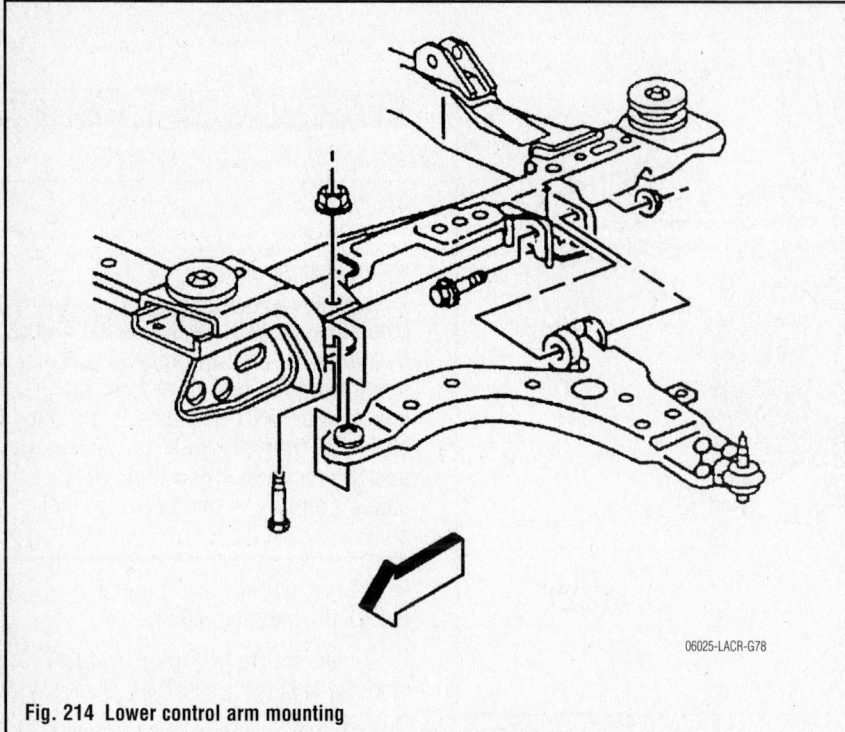

Fig. 214 Lower control arm mounting

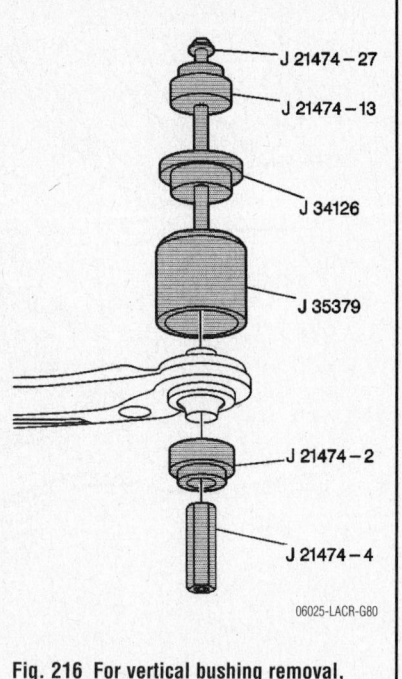

Fig. 216 For vertical bushing removal, assemble the tool as shown

Tighten the nut to 15 ft. lbs. (20 Nm) plus 120°.

➡**Do NOT loosen the ball stud nut in order to align the ball stud nut slots to the ball stud cotter pin hole.**

19. If necessary, tighten the ball stud castle nut in order to align the ball stud castle nut slot to the ball stud cotter pin hole.

➡**If applicable, ensure that the cotter pin ends do NOT contact the ABS wheel speed sensor, the ABS sensor connector or the drive axle.**

20. Install a NEW cotter pin and bend the ends as shown in either example.

21. If applicable, connect the ABS wheel speed sensor jumper harness to the harness retainer clips.

22. If applicable, connect the ABS wheel speed sensor connector.

➡**This is a prevailing torque type fastener. This fastener may be reused ONLY if the fastener and its counterpart are clean and free from rust and the fastener develops 27 inch lbs. (3 Nm) of torque against its counterpart prior to the fastener seating. If the fastener does not meet these criteria, REPLACE the fastener.**

23. Install the lower control arm nuts. Tighten the lower control arm nuts to 92 ft. lbs. (125 Nm).

24. Install the tire and wheel.

25. Lower the vehicle.

BUSHING REPLACEMENT

Vertical

See Figures 215 through 218.

1. Before servicing the vehicle, refer to the Precautions Section.

2. Remove the lower control arm.

3. Secure the lower control arm in a vice.

4. Mark the lower control arm along the flat edge of the bushing flange.

➡**Apply high pressure lubricant such as J 23444-A, or equivalent, to the threads of J 21474-27.**

5. Assemble the following bushing removal tools, or equivalent, as shown:
- J 21474-27
- J 21474-13
- J 34126
- J 35379
- J 21474-2
- J 21474-4

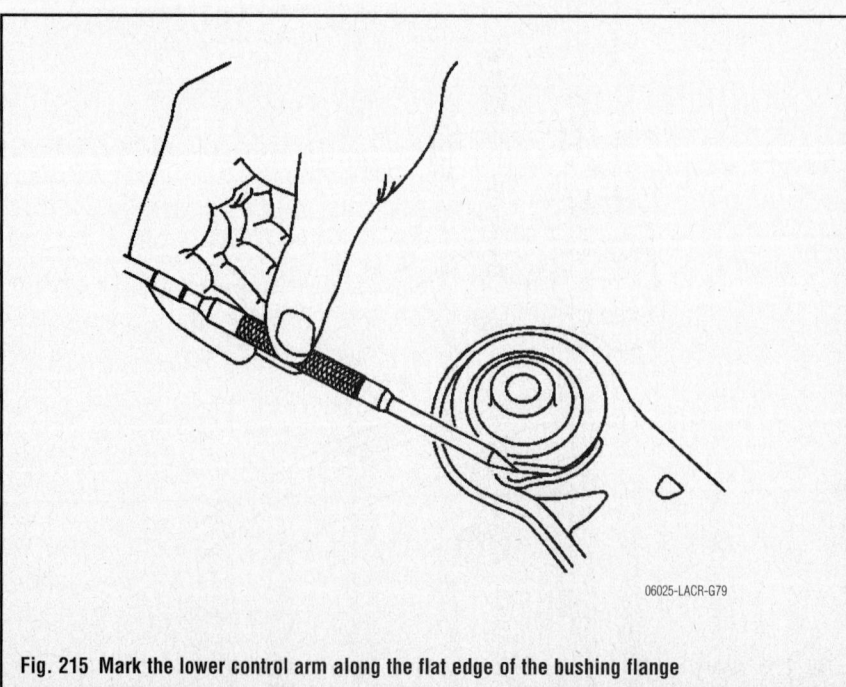

Fig. 215 Mark the lower control arm along the flat edge of the bushing flange

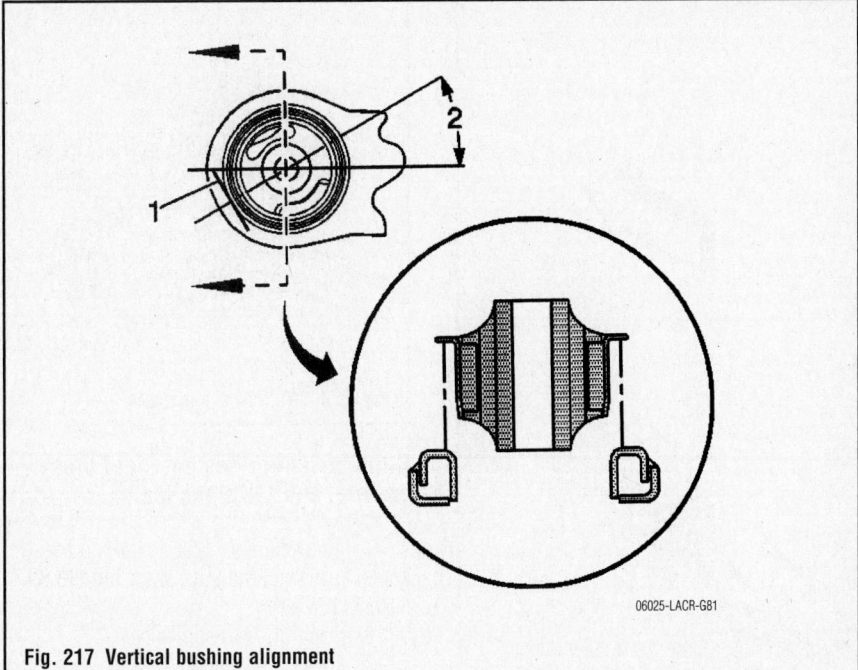

Fig. 217 Vertical bushing alignment

6. Tighten J 21474-4.

7. Disassemble the bushing removal tools.

To install:

➡ You MUST install the lower control arm vertical bushing in the same position in order to maintain the original vehicle ride, handling, and road feel.

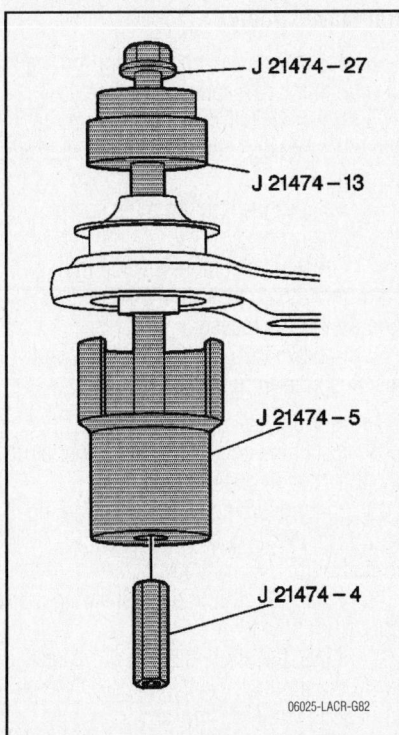

Fig. 218 For vertical bushing installation, assemble the tool as shown

8. Align the flat edge (1) of the bushing flange to the mark in the control arm. Ensure that the flat edge of the bushing flange is 30° (2) from the centerline of the lower control arm. Ensure that the thin slot in the bushing is facing outboard.

9. Insert the bushing into the control arm.

➡ Apply J 23444-A or equivalent to the threads of J 21474-27.

10. Assemble the following bushing installation tools as shown:
- J 21474-27
- J 21474-13
- J 21474-5
- J 21474-4

11. Tighten J 21474-4.

12. Disassemble the bushing installation tools.

13. Install the lower control arm.

Horizontal

See Figures 219 and 220.

1. Before servicing the vehicle, refer to the Precautions Section.

2. Remove the lower control arm.

3. Secure the lower control arm in a vise.

➡ Use a ½ x 20 in standard thread nut with the puller bolt.

4. Assemble the bushing removal tools as indicated:
- The nut (1)
- The J 21474-01 washer (2)
- The J 21474-01 bearing (3)

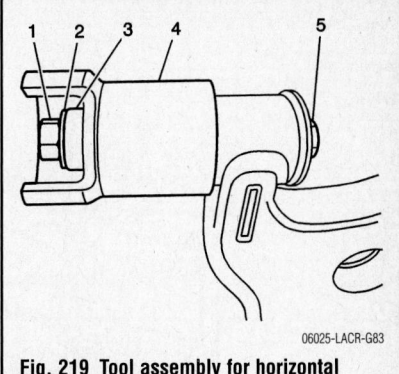

Fig. 219 Tool assembly for horizontal bushing removal

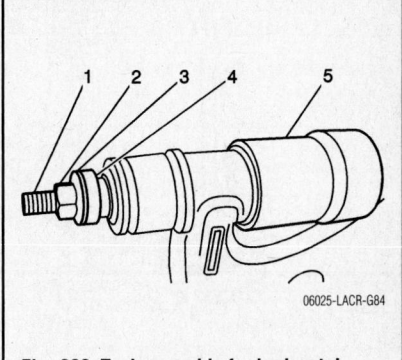

Fig. 220 Tool assembly for horizontal bushing installation

- The J 21474-5 (4)
- The J 21474-01 puller bolt (5)

5. Tighten the puller bolt (5) until the bushing is removed.

6. Disassemble the J 21474-01 and J 21474-5.

To install

7. Lubricate the bushing with liquid hand soap or equivalent.

➡ Use a ½ x 20 in standard thread nut with the puller bolt.

8. Assemble the following bushing installation tools as indicated:
- The nut (1)
- The J 21474-01 washer (2)
- The J 21474-01 bearing (3)
- The J 21474-5 (4)
- The J 21474-01 puller bolt (5)

9. Tighten the puller bolt (5) until the bushing is installed into the control arm.

10. Disassemble the J 21474-01 and J 21474-5 .

11. Remove the control arm from the vice.

12. Install the lower control arm.

MACPHERSON STRUT

REMOVAL & INSTALLATION

See Figures 221 through 223.

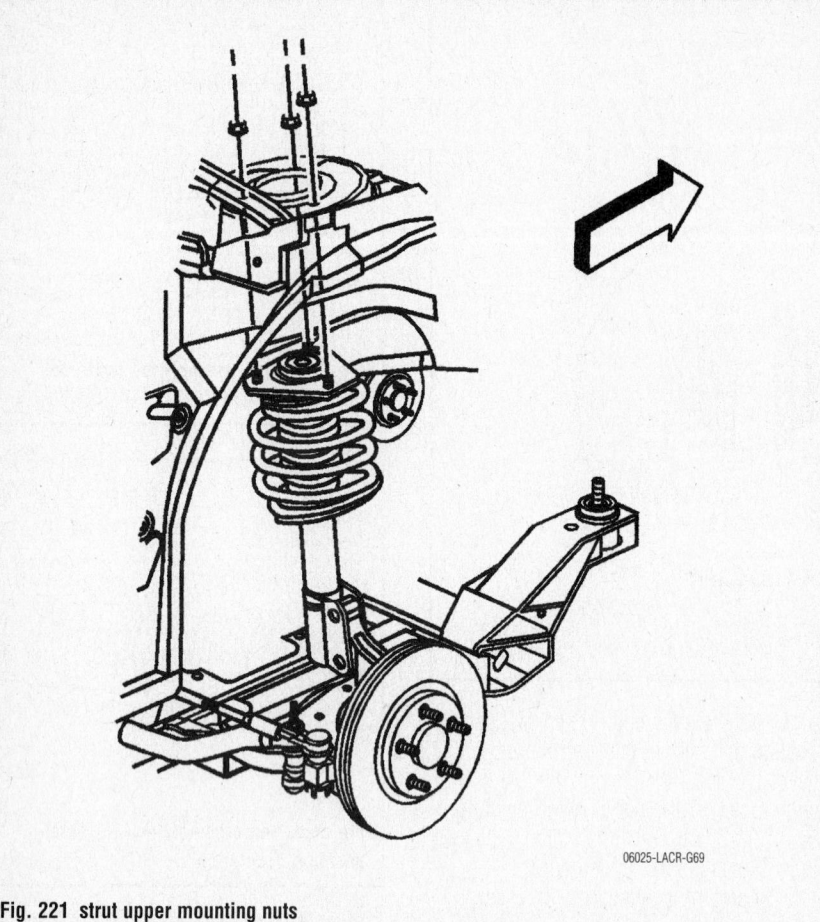

Fig. 221 strut upper mounting nuts

※※ WARNING

Care should be taken to avoid chipping or scratching the coating when handling the suspension coil spring. Damage to the coating can cause premature failure.

1. Remove the strut upper mounting nuts.

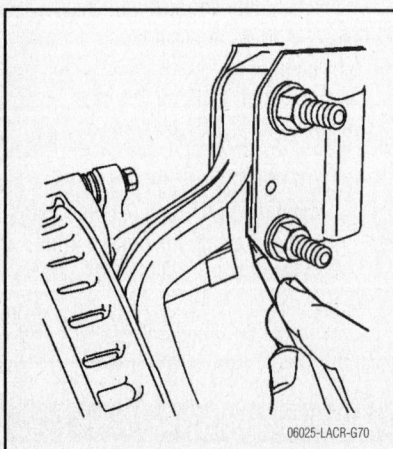

Fig. 222 Matchmark the strut to the knuckle

➡Lift the vehicle using ONLY a frame-contact vehicle lift. Do NOT lift the vehicle using a suspension-contact vehicle lift.

2. Before servicing the vehicle, refer to the Precautions Section.
3. Raise and support the vehicle.
4. Remove the tire and wheel.
5. Matchmark the strut to the knuckle.
6. Remove the strut lower bolts and nuts.
7. Remove the strut.

To install:

8. Install the strut.
9. Install the strut upper mounting nuts. Tighten the nuts to 24 ft. lbs. (33 Nm).
10. Install the strut lower bolts and nuts.

※※ WARNING

This is a prevailing torque type fastener. This fastener may be reused ONLY if the fastener and its counterpart are clean and free from rust and the fastener develops 27 inch lbs. (3 Nm) of torque/drag against its counterpart prior to the fastener seating.

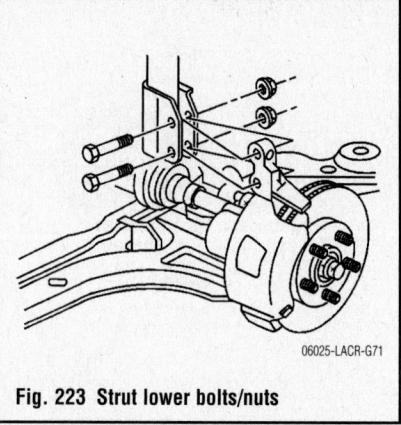

Fig. 223 Strut lower bolts/nuts

If the fastener does not meet these criteria, REPLACE the fastener.

11. Align the strut to the mark on the knuckle. Tighten the strut lower nuts to 89 ft. lbs. (120 Nm).
12. Install the tire and wheel.
13. Lower the vehicle.
14. Align the front wheels.

OVERHAUL

See Figures 224 and 225.

1. Before servicing the vehicle, refer to the Precautions Section.
2. Remove the strut from the vehicle.
3. Install the strut (2) in a strut compressor tool, such as J 45400 (1).

➡**The spring is compressed when the strut moves freely.**

4. Turn the spring compressor forcing screw until the coil spring is compressed.
5. Use a 45 TORX® socket in order to hold the strut shaft. Remove the upper strut mount nut.
6. Remove the strut from the compressor.
7. Loosen the compressor forcing screw until the upper strut mount and coil spring may be removed.
8. Remove the upper strut mount and the coil spring from the compressor.

To assemble:

9. Install the coil spring and upper strut mount in the compressor.
10. Turn the spring compressor forcing screw (1) until the coil spring is compressed.
11. Install the strut to the coil spring and upper strut mount.
12. Install the strut retaining nut. Install the strut mount nut. Tighten the strut mount nut to 55 ft. lbs. (75 Nm).
13. Remove the strut from the compressor.
14. Install the strut.

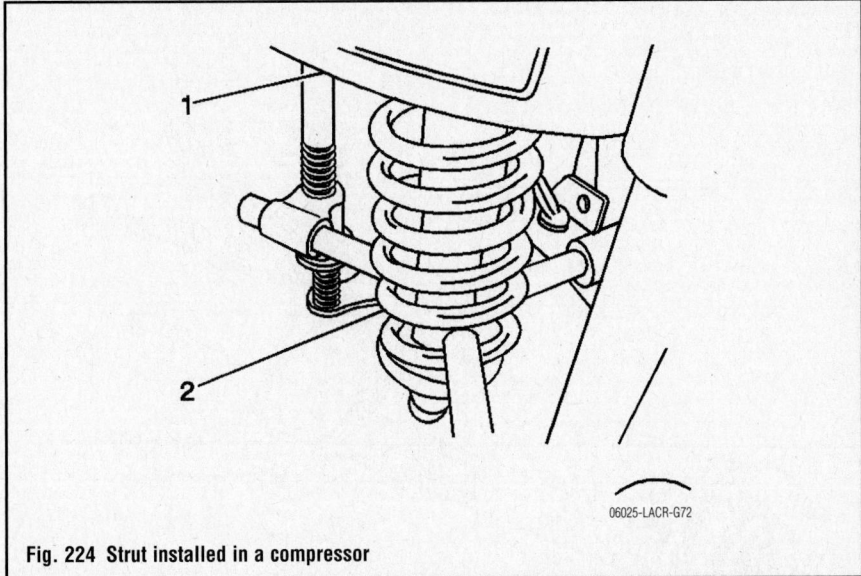

Fig. 224 Strut installed in a compressor

06025-LACR-G72

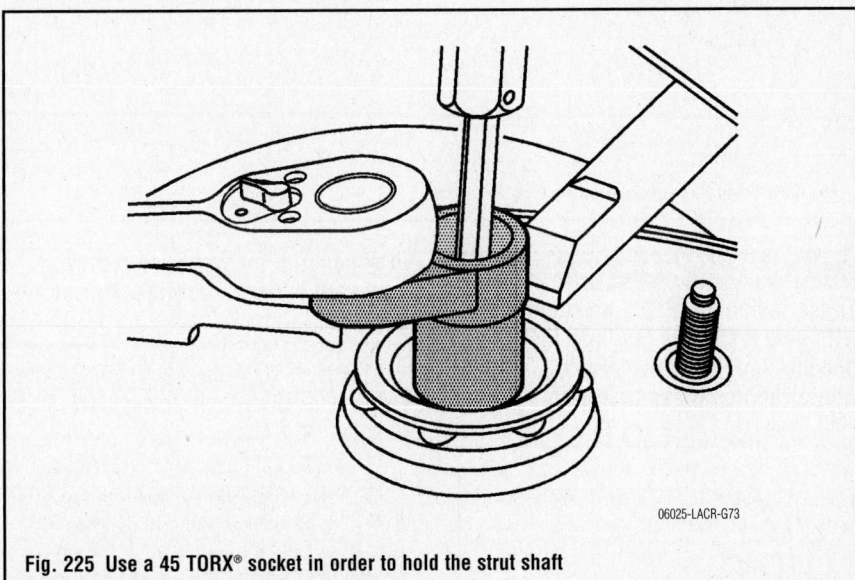

Fig. 225 Use a 45 TORX® socket in order to hold the strut shaft

06025-LACR-G73

STABILIZER BAR

REMOVAL & INSTALLATION

See Figures 226 and 227.

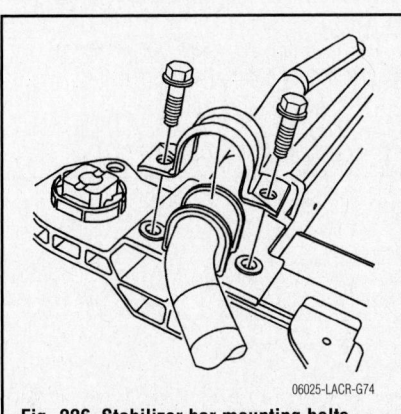

06025-LACR-G74

Fig. 226 Stabilizer bar mounting bolts

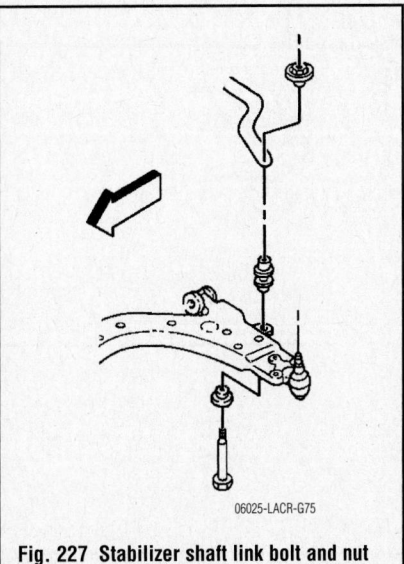

06025-LACR-G75

Fig. 227 Stabilizer shaft link bolt and nut

1. Before servicing the vehicle, refer to the Precautions Section.

2. Raise and support the vehicle.

3. Remove the tire and wheel assembly.

4. Remove the left and right side stabilizer shaft insulator clamp bolts.

5. Remove the left and right side stabilizer shaft insulator clamp.

6. Remove the left and right side stabilizer shaft insulators from the stabilizer shaft.

7. Remove the stabilizer shaft link (control link) bolt and nut.

8. Remove the control link from the vehicle.

To install:

9. Install the control link into the vehicle.

10. Install the control link bolt and nut. Tighten the control link nut to 17 ft. lbs. (23 Nm).

11. Install the left and right side stabilizer shaft insulators to the stabilizer shaft.

12. Install the left and right side stabilizer shaft insulator clamps.

13. Install the left and right side stabilizer shaft insulator clamp bolts. Tighten the bolts to 31 ft. lbs. (42 Nm).

14. Install the tire and wheel assembly.

15. Lower the vehicle.

STEERING KNUCKLE

REMOVAL & INSTALLATION

1. Before servicing the vehicle, refer to the Precautions Section.

2. Raise and support the vehicle.

3. Remove the bearing/hub assembly.

4. Disconnect the front lower control arm ball stud.

5. Disconnect the outer tie rod end from the steering knuckle.

6. Matchmark the strut to the knuckle.

7. Remove the bolts and nuts attaching the strut to the knuckle.

8. Remove the knuckle from the vehicle.

To install:

9. Install the knuckle to the vehicle.

10. Install the through bolts and nuts attaching the strut to the knuckle. Tighten the through bolts and nuts to 89 ft. lbs. (120 Nm).

11. Connect the outer tie rod to the steering knuckle.

12. Connect the front lower control arm ball stud to the knuckle.

13. Install the front wheel drive shaft bearing.

14. Lower the vehicle.

15. Inspect the front wheel alignment and adjust if necessary.

WHEEL HUB AND BEARINGS

REMOVAL & INSTALLATION

See Figures 228 and 229.

1. Before servicing the vehicle, refer to the Precautions Section.

2. Remove the tire and wheel.

3. Disconnect the wheel speed sensor electrical connector, if equipped.

4. Remove the wheel speed sensor electrical connector from the bracket, if equipped.

5. Remove the front halfshaft nut. Insert a drift or flat-bladed tool into the caliper and rotor to prevent from turning.

6. Remove the brake rotor.

7. Use 3 wheel nuts in order to attach a puller to the wheel bearing/hub.

8. Use the puller to push the halfshaft out of the wheel bearing/hub.

9. Remove and DISCARD the wheel bearing/hub bolts. Remove the puller from the hub.

➡**Ensure that the halfshaft outer seal/boot is not damaged.**

10. Remove the wheel bearing/hub and splash shield-noting the position of the shield for re-installation.

To install:

11. If necessary, remove the shipping bracket from the wheel bearing/hub.

12. Install the wheel bearing/hub with the splash shield as noted during removal.

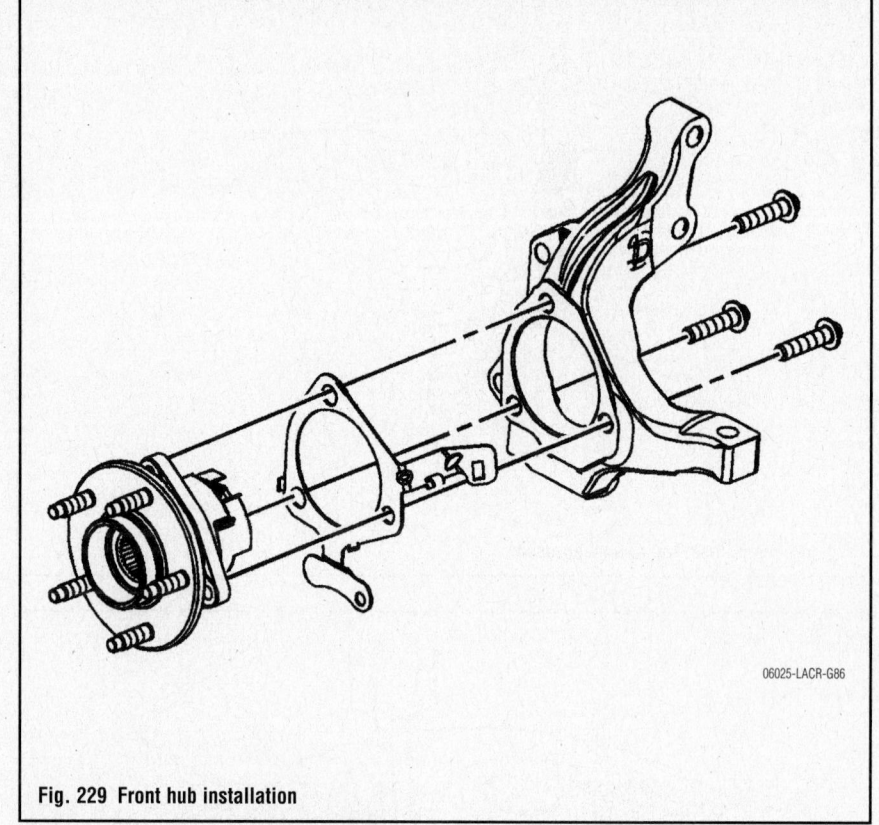

06025-LACR-G86

Fig. 229 Front hub installation

✳✳ CAUTION

These fasteners MUST be replaced with new fasteners anytime they become loose or are removed. Failure to replace these fasteners after they become loose or are removed may cause loss of vehicle control and personal injury.

---

13. Install NEW wheel bearing/hub bolts. Tighten the NEW wheel bearing/hub bolts to 96 ft. lbs. (130 Nm).

14. Install the brake rotor and caliper.

15. Install the front halfshaft nut. Insert a drift on a flat-bladed tool into caliper and rotor to prevent the rotor from turning. Tighten the front halfshaft nut to 118 ft. lbs. (160 Nm).

➡**Ensure that the connector clip engages the bracket properly.**

16. Install the wheel speed sensor electrical connector to the bracket, if equipped.

17. Connect the wheel speed sensor electrical connector, if equipped.

18. Install the tire and wheel.

ADJUSTMENT

No adjustment is possible.

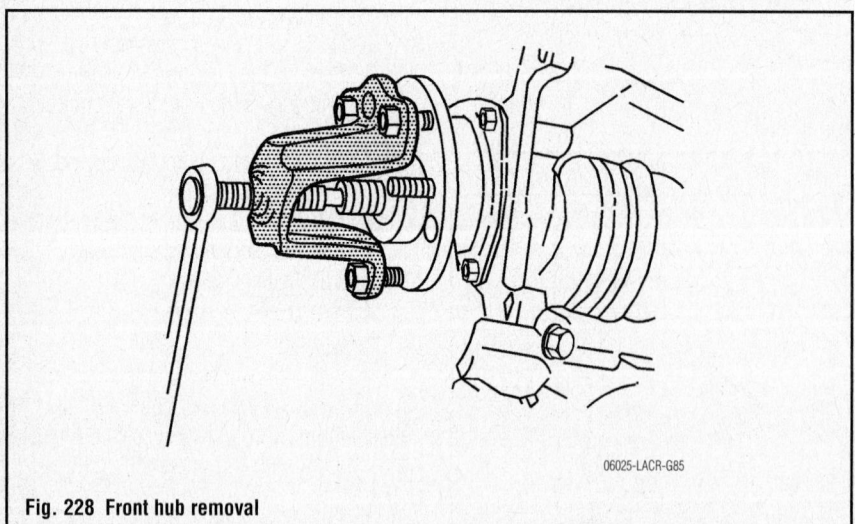

06025-LACR-G85

Fig. 228 Front hub removal

CONTROL ARMS/LINKS

REMOVAL & INSTALLATION

See Figures 230 and 231.

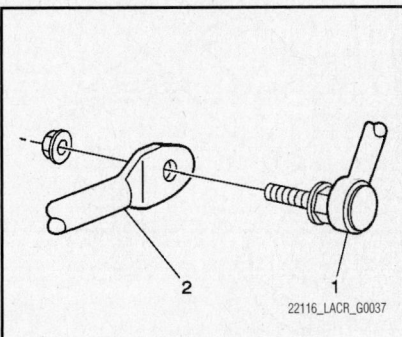

22116_LACR_G0037

Fig. 230 Remove the nut from the control link and the stabilizer shaft

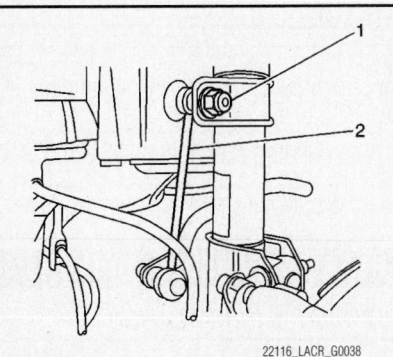

22116_LACR_G0038

Fig. 231 Remove the nut from the control link and the strut

1. Before servicing the vehicle, refer to the Precautions Section.
2. Raise and support the vehicle.
3. Remove the nut from the control link (1) and the stabilizer shaft (2).
4. Remove the nut (1) from the control link (2) and the strut.
5. Remove the control link (2) from the vehicle.

To install:

6. Install the control link to the vehicle.
7. Connect the control link to the stabilizer shaft.
8. Install the nut to the control link and the stabilizer shaft. Tighten the nut to 37 ft. lbs. (50 Nm).
9. Connect the control link to the strut.
10. Install the nut to the control link and the strut. Tighten the nut to 38 ft. lbs. (52 Nm).
11. Lower the vehicle.

KNUCKLE

REMOVAL & INSTALLATION

1. Before servicing the vehicle, refer to the Precautions Section.
2. Raise and suitably support the vehicle.
3. Remove the tire and wheel assembly.
4. Scribe the strut to the knuckle.
5. Remove the bearing/hub assembly.
6. Remove the rear wheel spindle rods from the knuckle.
7. Remove the trailing arm from the knuckle.
8. Remove the rear strut to knuckle bolts and the nuts.
9. Remove the knuckle from the vehicle.

To install:

10. Install the knuckle to the vehicle.
11. Hand start the strut to knuckle bolts and nuts. Do not tighten the nuts at this time.
12. Connect the rear suspension trailing arm to the knuckle.
13. Connect the rear wheel spindle rods to the knuckle.
14. Install the bearing/hub assembly.
15. Tighten the strut to knuckle bolts and nuts. Tighten bolts to 89 ft. lbs. (120 Nm).
16. Install the tire and wheel assembly.

17. Lower the vehicle.
18. Inspect the rear wheel alignment, adjust if necessary.

MACPHERSON STRUTS

REMOVAL & INSTALLATION

See Figure 232.

✳✳ WARNING

Care should be taken to avoid chipping or scratching the coating when handling the suspension coil spring. Damage to the coating can cause premature failure.

1. Before servicing the vehicle, refer to the Precautions Section.
2. Remove the strut to body mount nuts.
3. Raise and support the vehicle.
4. Remove the tire and wheel assembly.
5. Remove the control link from the strut.

✳✳ WARNING

The knuckle must be held in place after the strut to knuckle bolts have been removed. Failure to observe this may cause ball joint and/or wheel drive shaft damage.

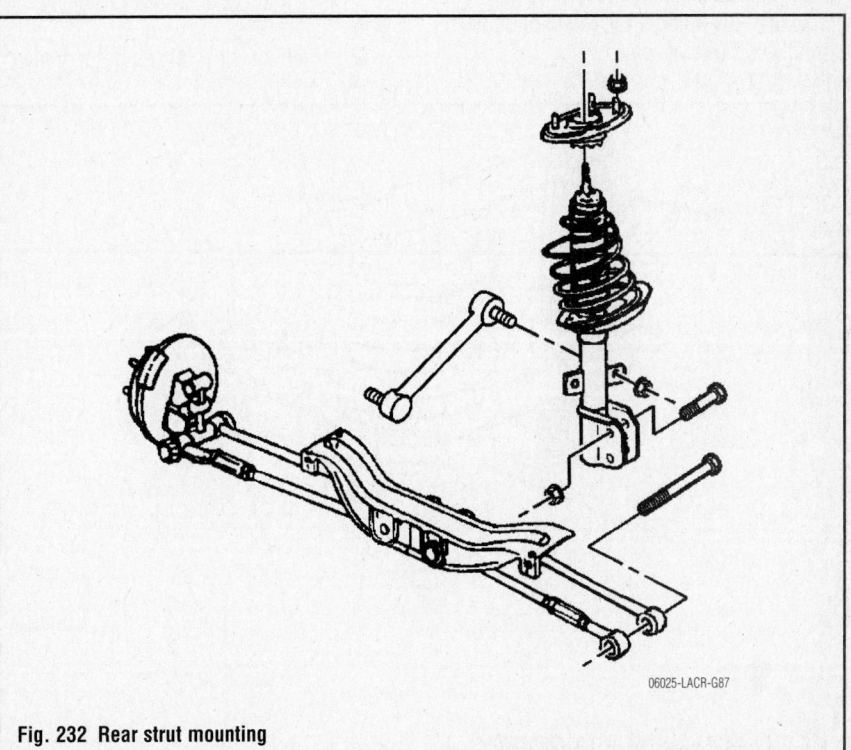

06025-LACR-G87

Fig. 232 Rear strut mounting

6. Remove the strut to knuckle bolts.

7. Remove the strut from the vehicle.

To install:

8. Install the strut into place.

9. Install the strut to knuckle bolts. Tighten the strut to knuckle bolts and nuts to 89 ft. lbs. (120 Nm).

10. Connect the control link to the strut.

11. Install the tire and wheel.

12. Install strut to body mount nuts. Tighten the strut to body mount nuts to 33 ft. lbs. (45 Nm).

13. Lower the vehicle.

14. Adjust the rear wheel alignment.

OVERHAUL

See Figures 233 and 234.

1. Before servicing the vehicle, refer to the Precautions Section.

2. Remove the strut from the vehicle.

3. Install the strut (2) in a strut compressor tool, such as J 45400 (1).

➡ **The spring is compressed when the strut moves freely.**

4. Turn the spring compressor forcing screw until the coil spring is compressed.

5. Use a 45 TORX® socket in order to hold the strut shaft. Remove the upper strut mount nut.

6. Remove the strut from the compressor.

7. Loosen the compressor forcing screw until the upper strut mount and coil spring may be removed.

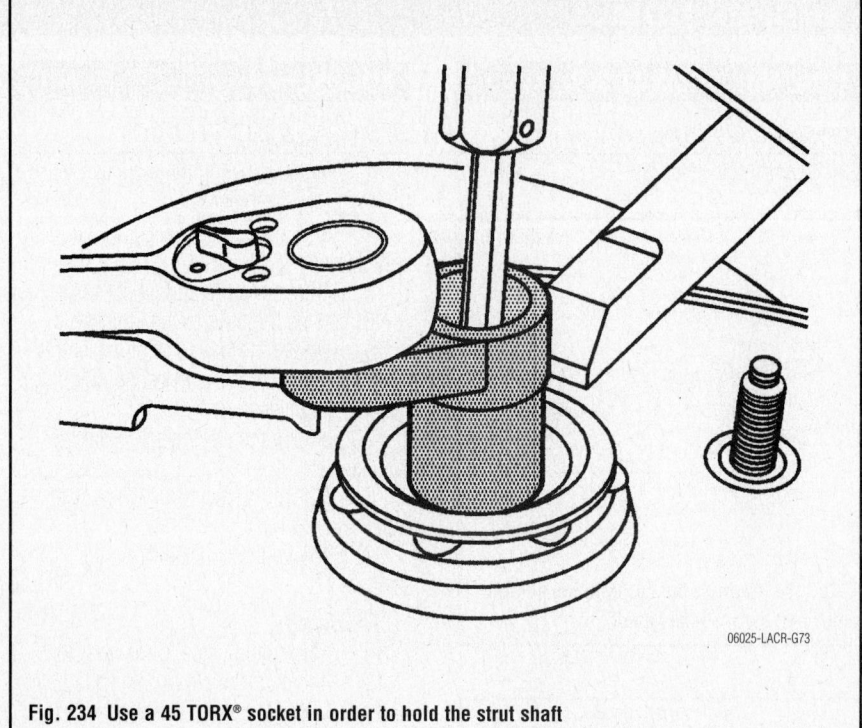

Fig. 234 Use a 45 TORX® socket in order to hold the strut shaft

06025-LACR-G73

8. Remove the upper strut mount and the coil spring from the compressor.

To assemble:

9. Install the coil spring and upper strut mount in the compressor.

10. Turn the spring compressor forcing screw (1) until the coil spring is compressed.

11. Install the strut to the coil spring and upper strut mount.

12. Install the strut retaining nut. Install the strut mount nut. Tighten the strut mount nut to 55 ft. lbs. (75 Nm).

13. Remove the strut from the compressor.

14. Install the strut.

REAR SUSPENSION SUPPORT

REMOVAL & INSTALLATION

See Figure 235.

1. Before servicing the vehicle, refer to the Precautions Section.

2. Raise and support the vehicle.

3. Remove the rear tires and wheels.

4. Remove the exhaust pipe.

5. Disconnect the brake lines from the rear suspension support.

6. Disconnect the parking brake cables and tensioner from the suspension support.

7. Remove the stabilizer shaft from the rear suspension support.

➡ **Support the rear suspension support with jack stands before removing the mounting bolts.**

8. Remove the rear wheel spindle rod bolts from the knuckle.

9. Remove the rear suspension support mounting bolts.

10. Remove the rear suspension support.

To install:

11. Position the rear suspension support in place.

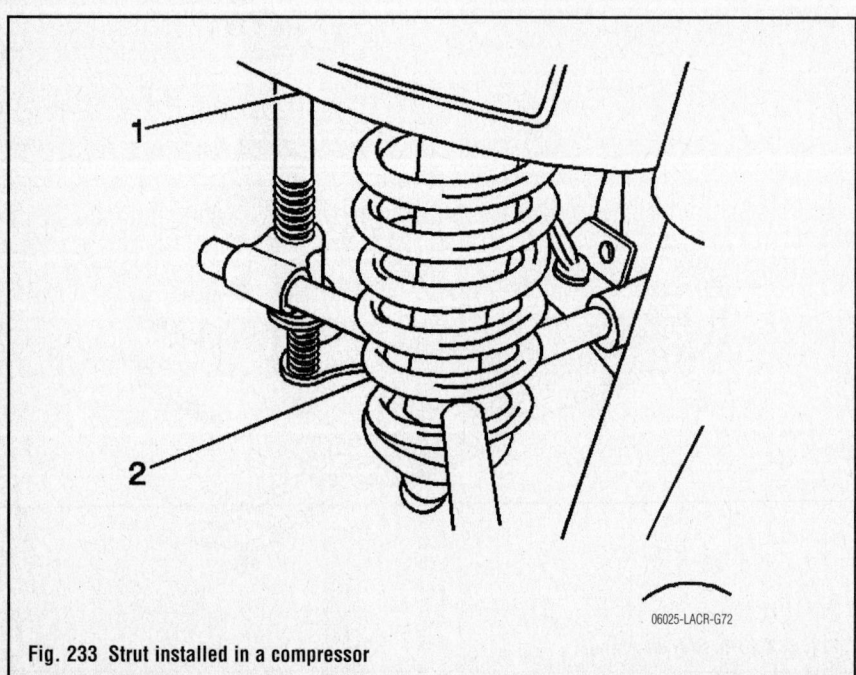

Fig. 233 Strut installed in a compressor

06025-LACR-G72

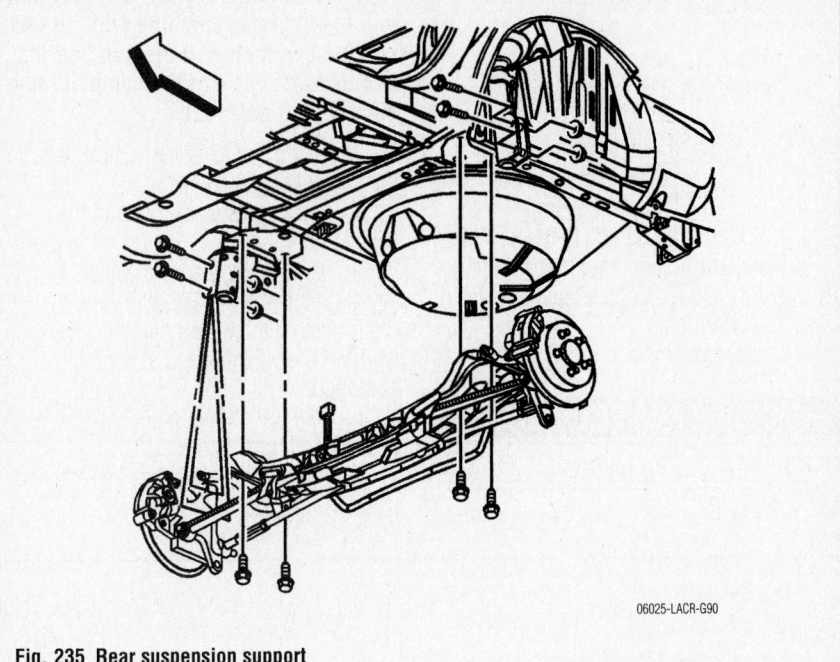

Fig. 235 Rear suspension support

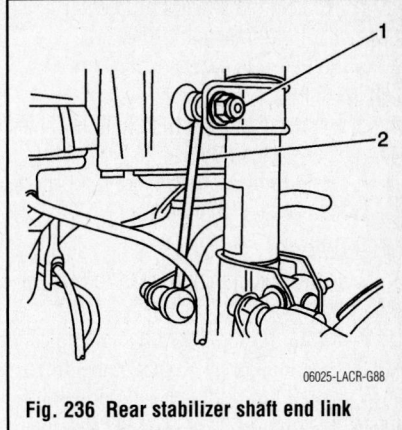

06025-LACR-G88

Fig. 236 Rear stabilizer shaft end link

12. Install 2 locating pins in the suspension support alignment holes, one on each side of the suspension support.

13. Install the rear suspension support mounting bolts. Tighten the bolts to 81 ft. lbs. (110 Nm).

14. Remove the locating pins from the suspension support alignment holes.

15. Position the rear wheel spindle rod to the knuckle. Install the retaining bolts and nuts to the knuckle. Tighten the bolts and nuts to 110 ft. lbs. (150 Nm).

16. Install the stabilizer shaft to the rear suspension support.

17. Connect the brake lines to the rear suspension support.

18. Install the parking brake cables and the tensioner.

19. Install the exhaust pipe.

20. Install the tires and wheels.

21. Lower the vehicle.

22. Adjust the rear wheel alignment.

SPINDLE ROD

REMOVAL & INSTALLATION

1. Before servicing the vehicle, refer to the Precautions Section.

2. Raise and support the vehicle.

3. Remove the tire and wheel assembly.

➡**Use a transaxle jack or suitable hoist stands to prop the rear suspension support.**

4. Lower the rear suspension support to gain clearance to the spindle rod to suspension support bolt.

5. Remove the bolt and nut from the spindle rod and the rear suspension support.

6. Remove the spindle rod to knuckle bolt and nut.

7. Remove the spindle rod from the vehicle.

To install:

8. Install the spindle rod to the vehicle.

9. Install the spindle rod to the knuckle.

10. Install the spindle rod to knuckle bolt and nut. Do not tighten at this time.

11. Install the spindle rod to the rear suspension support.

12. Install the bolt and nut to the rear suspension support. Tighten the bolt to 100 ft. lbs. (135 Nm).

13. Install the rear suspension support. Tighten the bolt to 110 ft. lbs. (150 Nm).

14. Install the tire and wheel assembly.

15. Lower the vehicle.

16. Adjust the wheel toe angle.

STABILIZER BAR

REMOVAL & INSTALLATION

See Figures 236 and 237.

1. Before servicing the vehicle, refer to the Precautions Section.

2. Raise and support the vehicle.

3. Remove the tires and wheels.

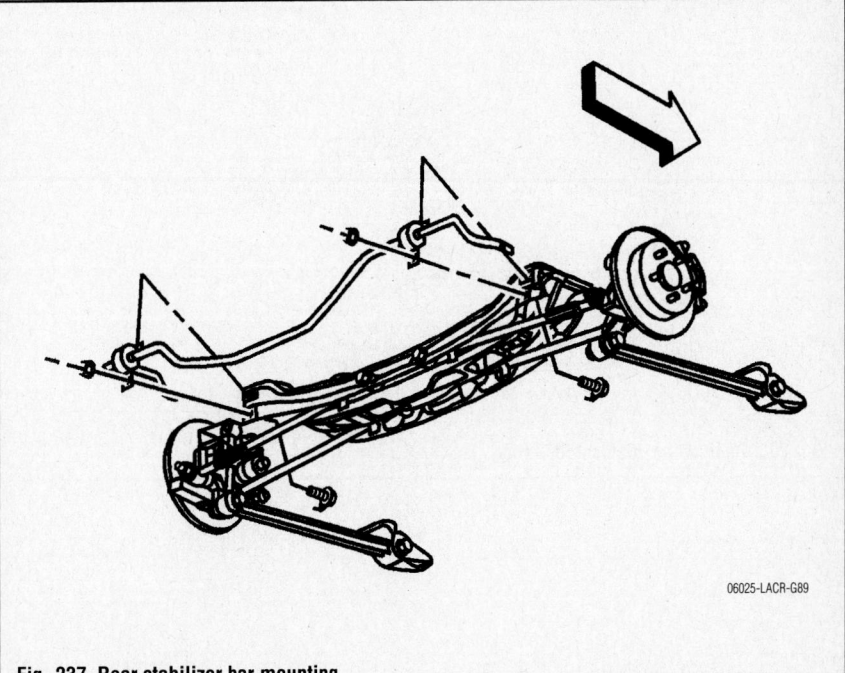

06025-LACR-G89

Fig. 237 Rear stabilizer bar mounting

4. Remove the left and right control link lower nuts from the control links.

5. Remove the clamp bolts from the stabilizer shaft.

6. Remove the stabilizer shaft from the rear suspension support.

7. Remove the control link nut (1) from the control link (2) and the strut.

To install:

8. Install the stabilizer shaft to the rear suspension support.

9. Install the stabilizer shaft clamps and bolts. Do not tighten the bolts at this time.

10. Install the right and left control link nuts to the control links. Tighten the control link nuts to 33 ft. lbs. (45 Nm). Tighten the stabilizer shaft insulator bracket nuts to 38 ft. lbs. (51 Nm). Install the control link nut to the control link and the strut. Tighten the nut to 38 ft. lbs. (51 Nm).

11. Install the tires and wheels.

12. Lower the vehicle.

TRAILING ARM

REMOVAL & INSTALLATION

See Figure 238.

1. Before servicing the vehicle, refer to the Precautions Section.

2. Raise and support the vehicle.

3. Remove the bolt and nut from the trailing arm and the knuckle.

4. Remove the nut and bolt from the trailing arm and the trailing arm bracket.

5. Remove the trailing arm from the vehicle.

To install:

6. Install the trailing arm to the trailing arm bracket.

7. Install the bolt and nut to the trailing arm and the trailing arm bracket. Tighten the bolt and nut to 77 ft. lbs. (105 Nm).

8. Install the trailing arm to the knuckle.

9. Install the bolt and nut to the trailing arm and the knuckle. Tighten the nut to 177 ft. lbs. (240 Nm).

10. Lower the vehicle.

WHEEL HUB AND BEARING

REMOVAL & INSTALLATION

See Figure 239.

➡The wheel bearing in the rear wheel hub is integrated into one unit. The hub is non-serviceable. If the hub/bearing is damaged, replace the complete hub and bearing assembly.

1. Before servicing the vehicle, refer to the Precautions Section.

2. Raise and suitably support the vehicle.

3. Remove the tires and wheels.

4. Remove the brake rotor.

5. Remove the ABS electrical connector from the wheel speed sensor, if equipped.

6. Remove the mounting bolts from the rear bearing/hub.

7. Remove the wheel bearing/hub and the backing plate.

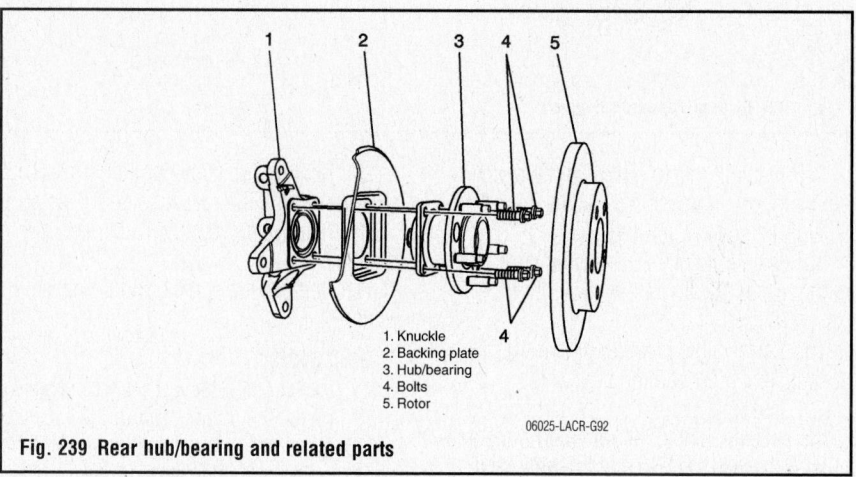

1. Knuckle
2. Backing plate
3. Hub/bearing
4. Bolts
5. Rotor

06025-LACR-G92

Fig. 239 Rear hub/bearing and related parts

To install:

8. Install the backing plate and the wheel bearing hub.

9. Install the wheel bearing/hub to knuckle bolts. Tighten the bolts to 55 ft. lbs. (75 Nm).

10. Install the ABS electrical connector to the wheel speed sensor, if equipped.

11. Install the brake rotor and caliper.

12. Install the tires and wheels.

13. Lower the vehicle.

ADJUSTMENT

All models use sealed wheel bearings that are pre-adjusted. If the bearing needs replacing, replace the rear wheel hub/bearing assembly.

1. Nut
2. Nut
3. Trailing arm
4. Nut
5. Washer
6. Bolt
7. Bolt
8. Knuckle
9. Stabilizer bar
10. Spindle rod
11. Suspension support
12. Bolt

06025-LACR-G91

Fig. 238 Rear suspension components

SPECIFICATIONS AND MAINTENANCE CHARTS

ENGINE AND VEHICLE IDENTIFICATION

	Engine							Model Year	
Code ①	Liters (cc)	Cu. In.	Cyl.	Fuel Sys.	Engine Type	Eng. Mfg.		Code ②	Year
K	3.8 (3785)	231	6	MFI	OHV	GM		6	2006
Y	4.6 (4572)	279	8	MFI	DOHC	GM		7	2007
								8	2008

MFI: Multi-point Fuel Injection

DOHC: Dual overhead camshafts

OHV: Overhead Valves

① 8th position of VIN

② 10th position of VIN

22116_LUCE_C0001

GENERAL ENGINE SPECIFICATIONS

Year	Model	Engine Displacement Liters	Engine Series VIN	Net Horsepower @ rpm	Net Torque @ rpm (ft. lbs.)	Bore x Stroke (in.)	Com- pression Ratio	Oil Pressure @ rpm
2006	Lucerne	3.8	K	200@5200	230@4000	3.80x3.40	9.4:1	60@1850
		4.6	Y	275@5600	300@4000	3.66x3.31	10.0:1	35@2000
2007	Lucerne	3.8	K	200@5200	230@4000	3.80x3.40	9.4:1	60@1850
		4.6	Y	275@5600	300@4000	3.66x3.31	10.0:1	35@2000
2008	Lucerne	3.8	K	200@5200	230@4000	3.80x3.40	9.4:1	60@1850
		4.6	Y	275@5600	300@4000	3.66x3.31	10.0:1	35@2000

22116_LUCE_C0002

GASOLINE ENGINE TUNE-UP SPECIFICATIONS

Year	Engine Displacement Liters	Engine VIN	Spark Plug Gap (in.)	Ignition Timing (deg.)	Fuel Pump (psi)	Idle Speed (rpm)	Valve Clearance	
							Intake	Exhaust
2006	3.8	K	0.060	①	41-47②	③	HYD	HYD
	4.6	Y	0.050	①	NA	③	HYD	HYD
2007	3.8	K	0.060	①	41-47②	③	HYD	HYD
	4.6	Y	0.050	①	NA	③	HYD	HYD
2008	3.8	K	0.060	①	41-47②	③	HYD	HYD
	4.6	Y	0.050	①	NA	③	HYD	HYD

NOTE: The Vehicle Emission Control Information label often reflects specification changes made during production.

The label figures must be used if they differ from those in this chart.

HYD: Hydraulic

① DIS Ignition System timing not adjustable

② Pressure at fuel pump

③ Idle speed maintained by ECM. There is no recommended adjustment procedure

22116_LUCE_C0003

CAPACITIES

Year	Model	Engine Displacement Liters	Engine VIN	Engine Oil with Filter (qts.)	Transmission (pts.)*	Fuel Tank (gal.)	Cooling System (qts.)
2006	Lucerne	3.8	K	4.5	14.8	18.5	11.0
		4.6	Y	7.5	14.8	18.5	13.0
2007	Lucerne	3.8	K	4.5	14.8	18.5	11.0
		4.6	Y	7.5	14.8	18.5	13.0
2008	Lucerne	3.8	K	4.5	14.8	18.5	11.0
		4.6	Y	7.5	14.8	18.5	13.0

NOTE: All capacities are approximate. Add fluid gradually and ensure a proper fluid level is obtained.

* Drain and refill

22116_LUCE_C0004

FLUID SPECIFICATIONS

Year	Model	Engine Displacement Liters	Engine ID/VIN	Engine Oil	Auto. Trans.	Manual Trans.	Power Steering Fluid	Brake Master Cylinder
2006	Lucerne	3.8	K	5W-30	Dexron VI	—	GM Part No. 89021184	DOT 3
		4.6	Y	5W-30	Dexron VI	—	GM Part No. 89021184	DOT 3
2007	Lucerne	3.8	K	5W-30	Dexron VI	—	GM Part No. 89021184	DOT 3
		4.6	Y	5W-30	Dexron VI	—	GM Part No. 89021184	DOT 3
2008	Lucerne	3.8	K	5W-30	Dexron VI	—	GM Part No. 89021184	DOT 3
		4.6	Y	5W-30	Dexron VI	—	GM Part No. 89021184	DOT 3

DOT: Department Of Transportation

22116_LUCE_C0005

VALVE SPECIFICATIONS

Year	Engine Displacement Liters	Engine VIN	Seat Angle (deg.)	Face Angle (deg.)	Spring Test Pressure (lbs. @ in.)	Spring Installed Height (in.)	Stem-to-Guide Clearance (in.) Intake	Stem-to-Guide Clearance (in.) Exhaust	Stem Diameter (in.) Intake	Stem Diameter (in.) Exhaust
2006	3.8	K	45	46	228@ 1.277	1.690-1.750	0.0012-0.0028	0.0014-0.0029	0.3129-0.3136	0.3129-0.3136
	4.6	Y	45.75	45	130-142@ 0.9646	1.378	0.0011-0.0027	0.0020-0.0039	0.2331-0.2339	0.2331-0.2339
2007	3.8	K	45	46	228@ 1.277	1.690-1.750	0.0012-0.0028	0.0014-0.0029	0.3129-0.3136	0.3129-0.3136
	4.6	Y	45.75	45	130-142@ 0.9646	1.378	0.0011-0.0027	0.0020-0.0039	0.2331-0.2339	0.2331-0.2339
2008	3.8	K	45	46	228@ 1.277	1.690-1.750	0.0012-0.0028	0.0014-0.0029	0.3129-0.3136	0.3129-0.3136
	4.6	Y	45.75	45	130-142@ 0.9646	1.378	0.0011-0.0027	0.0020-0.0039	0.2331-0.2339	0.2331-0.2339

22116_LUCE_C0006

CAMSHAFT AND BEARING SPECIFICATIONS CHART

All measurements are given in inches.

Year	Engine Displ. Liters	Engine ID/VIN	Journal Dia.	Brg. Oil Clearance	Shaft End-play	Runout	Journal Bore	Lobe Height	
								Intake	Exhaust
2006	3.8	K	1.8462-1.8448	0.0016-0.0047	NA	0.00025	NA	0.2580	0.2580
	4.6	Y	1.0610-1.0619	NA	0.0050-0.0087	0.0020	①	0.2421	0.2339
2007	3.8	K	1.8462-1.8448	0.0016-0.0047	NA	0.00025	NA	0.2580	0.2580
	4.6	Y	1.0610-1.0619	NA	0.0050-0.0087	0.0020	①	0.2421	0.2339
2008	3.8	K	1.8462-1.8448	0.0016-0.0047	NA	0.00025	NA	0.2580	0.2580
	4.6	Y	1.0610-1.0619	NA	0.0050-0.0087	0.0020	①	0.2421	0.2339

NA: Not Available

① Production: 0.0020 - 0.0030 in.

Service: 0.040-0.090 mm 0.0016-0.0035 in.

22116_LUCE_C0007

CRANKSHAFT AND CONNECTING ROD SPECIFICATIONS

All measurements given in inches

Year	Engine Displacement Liters	Engine VIN	Crankshaft				Connecting Rod		
			Main Brg. Journal Dia.	Main Brg. Oil Clearance	Shaft End-play	Thrust on No.	Journal Diameter	Oil Clearance	Side Clearance
2006	3.8	K	2.4988-2.4998	①	0.0030-0.0110	2	2.2487-2.2499	0.0005-0.0026	0.0040-0.0200
	4.6	Y	2.5335-2.5341	0.0006-0.0022	0.0020-0.0197	3	2.1239-2.1245	0.0010-0.0030	0.0079-0.0197
2007	3.8	K	2.4988-2.4998	①	0.0030-0.0110	2	2.2487-2.2499	0.0005-0.0026	0.0040-0.0200
	4.6	Y	2.5335-2.5341	0.0006-0.0022	0.0020-0.0197	3	2.1239-2.1245	0.0010-0.0030	0.0079-0.0197
2008	3.8	K	2.4988-2.4998	①	0.0030-0.0110	2	2.2487-2.2499	0.0005-0.0026	0.0040-0.0200
	4.6	Y	2.5335-2.5341	0.0006-0.0022	0.0020-0.0197	3	2.1239-2.1245	0.0010-0.0030	0.0079-0.0197

① Journal 1: 0.0007 - 0.0016

Journals 2, 3, 4: 0.0009 - 0.0018

22116_LUCE_C0008

PISTON AND RING SPECIFICATIONS

All measurements given in inches

Year	Engine Displacement Liters	Engine VIN	Piston Clearance	Ring Gap			Ring Side Clearance		
				Top Compression	Bottom Compression	Oil Control	Top Compression	Bottom Compression	Oil Control
2006	3.8	K	①	0.0100-0.0180	0.0230-0.0330	0.0100-0.0300	0.0013-0.0031	0.0013-0.0031	0.0009-0.0079
	4.6	Y	0.0008-0.0020	0.0098-0.0157	0.0020-0.0138	0.0098-0.0299	0.0016-0.0037	0.0016-0.0037	②
2007	3.8	K	①	0.0100-0.0180	0.0230-0.0330	0.0100-0.0300	0.0013-0.0031	0.0013-0.0031	0.0009-0.0079
	4.6	Y	0.0008-0.0020	0.0098-0.0157	0.0020-0.0138	0.0098-0.0299	0.0016-0.0037	0.0016-0.0037	②
2008	3.8	K	①	0.0100-0.0180	0.0230-0.0330	0.0100-0.0300	0.0013-0.0031	0.0013-0.0031	0.0009-0.0079
	4.6	Y	0.0008-0.0020	0.0098-0.0157	0.0020-0.0138	0.0098-0.0299	0.0016-0.0037	0.0016-0.0037	②

① Piston-to-bore clearance (New): 0.0008 - 0.0018 in.

Piston-to-bore clearance (Used): 0.0008 - 0.0039 in.

② None - side sealing

22116_LUCE_C0009

TORQUE SPECIFICATIONS

All measurements given in ft. lbs. unless otherwise noted

Year	Engine Displacement Liters	Engine VIN	Cylinder Head Bolts	Main Bearing Bolts	Rod Bearing Bolts	Crankshaft Damper Bolts	Flywheel Bolts	Manifold		Spark Plugs	Oil Pan Drain Plug
								Intake	Exhaust		
2006	3.8	K	①	②	③	④	⑤	⑥	⑦	11	22
	4.6	Y	⑧	⑨	⑩	⑪	⑫	7.5	18	11	15
2007	3.8	K	①	②	③	④	⑤	⑥	⑦	11	22
	4.6	Y	⑧	⑨	⑩	⑪	⑫	7.5	18	11	15
2008	3.8	K	①	②	③	④	⑤	⑥	⑦	11	22
	4.6	Y	⑧	⑨	⑩	⑪	⑫	7.5	18	11	15

① Step 1: Tighten all bolts to 37 ft. lbs.

Step 2: Turn all bolts 120 degrees

② Cap bolts: 30 ft. lbs. plus 110 degrees

Side bolts: 11 ft. lbs. plus 45 degrees

③ 20 ft. lbs. plus 50 degrees

④ 111 ft. lbs. plus 76 degrees

⑤ 11 ft. lbs. plus 50 degrees

⑥ Upper manifold: 8 ft. lbs.

Lower manifold: 11 ft. lbs.

Upper manifold cover nut 27 in. lbs.

⑦ Exhaust manifold bolt/nut: 22 ft. lbs.

Heat shield bolt & manifold stud: 89 in. lbs

Heat shield nut: 18 ft. lbs.

Manifold pipe stud nut: 24 ft. lbs.

⑧ M11 bolts:

Step 1: 30 ft. lbs.

Step 2: +70 degrees

Step 3: +60 degrees

Step 4: +45 degrees

Do not exceed 175 degrees total

M6 bolts: 106 inch lbs.

⑨ Lower crankcase

M10x1.5

Step 1: 15 ft. lbs.

Step 2: +65 degrees

M8x1.25: 22 ft. lbs.

⑩ Step 1: 22 ft. lbs.

Step 2: back off to zero

Step 3: 18 ft. lbs.

Step 4: +110 degrees

⑪ Step 1: 37 ft. lbs.

Step 2: +120 degrees

⑫ Step 1: 11 ft. lbs.

Step 2: +50 degrees

22116_LUCE_C0010

WHEEL ALIGNMENT SPECIFICATIONS

Year	Model		Caster Range (+/-Deg.)	Caster Preferred Setting (Deg.)	Camber Range (+/-Deg.)	Camber Preferred Setting (Deg.)	Toe-in (in.)
2006	Lucerne	F	0.75	+5.80	0.75	-0.00	0.20 +/- 0.20
		R	—	—	0.75	-0.05	0.10 +/- 0.20
2007	Lucerne	F	0.75	+5.80	0.75	-0.00	0.20 +/- 0.20
		R	—	—	0.75	-0.05	0.10 +/- 0.20

22116_LUCE_C0011

TIRE, WHEEL AND BALL JOINT SPECIFICATIONS

Year	Model	OEM Tires Standard	OEM Tires Optional	Tire Pressures (psi) Front	Tire Pressures (psi) Rear	Wheel Size	Ball Joint Inspection	Lug Nut Torque (ft. lbs.)
2006	Lucerne CX	P225/60R16	None	①	①	16 in.	0.063 in. ②	100
	Lucerne CXL	P235/55R17	None	①	①	17 in.	0.063 in. ②	100
	Lucerne CXS	P245/50R18	None	①	①	18 in.	0.063 in. ②	100
2007	Lucerne CX	P225/60R16	None	①	①	16 in.	0.063 in. ②	100
	Lucerne CXL	P235/55R17	None	①	①	17 in.	0.063 in. ②	100
	Lucerne CXS	P245/50R18	None	①	①	18 in.	0.063 in. ②	100
2008	Lucerne CX	P225/60R16	None	①	①	16 in.	0.063 in. ②	100
	Lucerne CXL	P235/55R17	None	①	①	17 in.	0.063 in. ②	100
	Lucerne CXS	P245/50R18	None	①	①	18 in.	0.063 in. ②	100

OEM: Original Equipment Manufacturer

PSI: Pounds Per Square Inch

① See placard on vehicle.

② Support the lower control arm with a floor stand. Gently lift or pry the suspension to induce ball joint movement.

22116_LUCE_C0012

BRAKE SPECIFICATIONS
All measurements given in inches unless otherwise noted

Year	Model		Brake Disc Original Thickness	Brake Disc Minimum Thickness	Brake Disc Maximum Runout	Minimum Lining Thickness	Caliper Bracket Bolts (ft. lbs.)	Caliper Mounting Bolts (ft. lbs.)
2006	Lucerne	F	1.181	1.126	0.002	NA	133	27
		R	0.472	0.413	0.002	NA	94	25
2007	Lucerne	F	1.181	1.126	0.002	NA	133	27
		R	0.472	0.413	0.002	NA	94	25
2008	Lucerne	F	1.181	1.126	0.002	NA	133	27
		R	0.472	0.413	0.002	NA	94	25

NA: Information not available

22116_LUCE_C0013

MAINTENANCE I AND II SERVICE SCHEDULES
2006-08 Buick Lucerne

When the CHANGE ENGINE OIL light appears, certain services and inspections are required.
Required services are described as Maintenance I and Maintenance II.
The first service on a vehicle should be Maintenance I, and the second service should be Maintenance II.

Alternate between the 2 thereafter. However, in some cases, Maintenance II may be required more often.
Maintenance I: Use Maintenance I if the CHANGE ENGINE OIL light comes on within 10 months since vehicle was purchased or, if Maintenance II was performed.
Maintenance II: Use Maintenance II if the previous service performed was Maintenance I. Always use Maintenance II whenever the CHANGE ENGINE OIL light comes on 10 months or more since the last service, or, if the CHANGE ENGINE OIL light has not come on at all for one year.

Service	Maintenance I	II
Change the engine oil and filter. Reset the oil life system.	✓	✓
Visually inspect the vehicle for leaks or damage. A fluid loss in the vehicle system could indicate a problem. Inspect, repair, and add fluid to the system if necessary.	✓	✓
Inspect the engine air cleaner filter. If necessary, replace the filter.	--	✓
Rotate the tires. Inspect the tire inflation pressures and the tire wear.	✓	✓
Visually inspect the brake lines and hoses for proper hook-up, binding, leaks, cracks, chafing, etc. Inspect the disc brake pads for wear and the rotors for surface condition. Inspect the drum brake linings for wear or cracks. Inspect other brake parts, including drums, wheel cylinders, calipers, parking brake, etc. Inspect the parking brake adjustment.	✓	✓
Inspect the engine coolant and the windshield washer fluid levels. Add fluid as needed.	✓	✓
Inspect the suspension and steering components. Inspect the front and rear suspension and the steering system for damaged, loose or missing parts, or signs of wear. Inspect the power steering lines and the hoses for proper hook-up, binding, leaks, cracks, chafing, etc.	--	✓
Visually inspect the coolant hoses and replace the hoses if they are cracked, swollen, or deteriorated. Inspect all pipes, fittings and clamps; replace with GM parts as needed. To help ensure proper operation, a pressure test of the cooling system and pressure cap and cleaning the outside of the radiator and air conditioning condenser is recommended at least once a year.	--	✓
Inspect the front and rear suspension and the steering system for damaged, loose, or missing parts, or signs of wear. Inspect power steering lines and hoses for proper hook-up, binding, leaks, cracks, chafing, etc.	--	✓
Inspect the throttle system for interference or binding and for damaged or missing parts. Replace the parts as needed. Replace any components that have high effort or excessive wear. Do not lubricate the accelerator or the cruise control cables.	--	✓
Replace the passenger compartment air filter.	--	✓

To reset the CHANGE ENGINE OIL LIGHT:
1. Press the option button on the DIC until ENGINE OIL MONITOR appears on the DIC screen.
2. Press the set/reset button to reset the system. The next screen indicates that the CHANGE OIL SOON message has been reset. If the vehicle has the uplevel DIC, when the gages button is pressed and the OIL LIFE REMAINING mode appears, it should read 100 percent OIL LIFE REMAINING.
3. Turn the key to OFF.

Vehicles without Driver Information Center (DIC)
1. With the engine off, turn the ignition key to RUN.
2. Fully press and release the accelerator pedal slowly three times within five seconds.
3. Turn the key to OFF, then start the vehicle.

If the light or message comes back on when you start your vehicle, the oil life system has not reset. Repeat the procedure.

22116_LUCE_C0014

ADDITIONAL MAINTENANCE SERVICES
2006-08 Buick Lucerne

TO BE SERVICED	SERVICE	VEHICLE MILEAGE INTERVAL (x1000)					
		25	50	75	100	125	150
Air cleaner filter	R	✓	✓	✓	✓	✓	✓
Accessory drive belt	I						✓
Auto. Trans. Fluid ①	R		✓		✓		✓
Cooling system hoses and clamps	S/I						✓
Engine coolant	R						✓
Fuel system	I	✓	✓	✓	✓	✓	✓
Exhaust system & heat shields	S/I	✓	✓	✓	✓	✓	✓
Spark plugs	R				✓		

R: Replace   S/I: Inspect and service, if necessary

① Replace if any of the following conditions are met:

    Heavy city traffic where the outside temperature regularly reaches 32°C (90°F) or higher

    Hilly or mountainous terrain

    Frequent trailer towing

    Taxi, police, or delivery service

    Otherwise, change every 100,000 miles

22116_LUCE_C0015

PRECAUTIONS

Before servicing any vehicle, please be sure to read all of the following precautions, which deal with personal safety, prevention of component damage, and important points to take into consideration when servicing a motor vehicle:

• Never open, service or drain the radiator or cooling system when the engine is hot; serious burns can occur from the steam and hot coolant.

• Observe all applicable safety precautions when working around fuel. Whenever servicing the fuel system, always work in a well-ventilated area. Do not allow fuel spray or vapors to come in contact with a spark, open flame, or excessive heat (a hot drop light, for example). Keep a dry chemical fire extinguisher near the work area. Always keep fuel in a container specifically designed for fuel storage; also, always properly seal fuel containers to avoid the possibility of fire or explosion. Refer to the additional fuel system precautions later in this section.

• Fuel injection systems often remain pressurized, even after the engine has been turned **OFF**. The fuel system pressure must be relieved before disconnecting any fuel lines. Failure to do so may result in fire and/or personal injury.

• Brake fluid often contains polyglycol ethers and polyglycols. Avoid contact with the eyes and wash your hands thoroughly after handling brake fluid. If you do get brake fluid in your eyes, flush your eyes with clean, running water for 15 minutes. If eye irritation persists, or if you have taken brake fluid internally, IMMEDIATELY seek medical assistance.

• The EPA warns that prolonged contact with used engine oil may cause a number of skin disorders, including cancer. You should make every effort to minimize your exposure to used engine oil. Protective gloves should be worn when changing oil. Wash your hands and any other exposed skin areas as soon as possible after exposure to used engine oil. Soap and water, or waterless hand cleaner should be used.

• All new vehicles are now equipped with an air bag system, often referred to as a Supplemental Restraint System (SRS) or Supplemental Inflatable Restraint (SIR) system. The system must be disabled before performing service on or around system components, steering column, instrument panel components, wiring and sensors. Failure to follow safety and disabling procedures could result in accidental air bag deployment, possible personal injury and unnecessary system repairs.

• Always wear safety goggles when working with, or around, the air bag system. When carrying a non-deployed air bag, be sure the bag and trim cover are pointed away from your body. When placing a non-deployed air bag on a work surface, always face the bag and trim cover upward, away from the surface. This will reduce the motion of the module if it is accidentally deployed. Refer to the additional air bag system precautions later in this section.

• Clean, high quality brake fluid from a sealed container is essential to the safe and proper operation of the brake system. You should always buy the correct type of brake fluid for your vehicle. If the brake fluid becomes contaminated, completely flush the system with new fluid. Never reuse any brake fluid. Any brake fluid that is removed from the system should be discarded. Also, do not allow any brake fluid to come in contact with a painted surface; it will damage the paint.

• Never operate the engine without the proper amount and type of engine oil; doing so WILL result in severe engine damage.

• Timing belt maintenance is extremely important. Many models utilize an interference-type, non-freewheeling engine. If the timing belt breaks, the valves in the cylinder head may strike the pistons, causing potentially serious (also time-consuming and expensive) engine damage. Refer to the maintenance interval charts for the recommended replacement interval for the timing belt, and to the timing belt section for belt replacement and inspection.

• Disconnecting the negative battery cable on some vehicles may interfere with the functions of the on-board computer system(s) and may require the computer to undergo a relearning process once the negative battery cable is reconnected.

• When servicing drum brakes, only disassemble and assemble one side at a time, leaving the remaining side intact for reference.

• Only an MVAC-trained, EPA-certified automotive technician should service the air conditioning system or its components.

BRAKES

GENERAL INFORMATION

PRECAUTIONS

• Certain components within the ABS system are not intended to be serviced or repaired individually.

• Do not use rubber hoses or other parts not specifically specified for and ABS system. When using repair kits, replace all parts included in the kit. Partial or incorrect repair may lead to functional problems and require the replacement of components.

• Lubricate rubber parts with clean, fresh brake fluid to ease assembly. Do not use shop air to clean parts; damage to rubber components may result.

• Use only DOT 3 brake fluid from an unopened container.

• If any hydraulic component or line is removed or replaced, it may be necessary to bleed the entire system.

• A clean repair area is essential. Always clean the reservoir and cap thoroughly before removing the cap. The slightest amount of dirt in the fluid may plug an orifice and impair the system function. Perform repairs after components have been thoroughly cleaned; use only denatured alcohol to clean components. Do not allow ABS components to come into contact with any substance containing mineral oil; this includes used shop rags.

ANTI-LOCK BRAKE SYSTEM (ABS)

• The Anti-Lock control unit is a microprocessor similar to other computer units in the vehicle. Ensure that the ignition switch is **OFF** before removing or installing controller harnesses. Avoid static electricity discharge at or near the controller.

• If any arc welding is to be done on the vehicle, the control unit should be unplugged before welding operations begin.

WHEEL SPEED SENSORS

This vehicle utilizes a Vehicle Speed Sensor (VSS) mounted to the transmission. Refer to Vehicle Speed Sensor.

BLEEDING PROCEDURE

BLEEDING PROCEDURE

✳✳ WARNING

When adding fluid to the brake master cylinder reservoir, use only Delco Supreme 11®, GM P/N 12377967 (Canadian P/N 992667), or equivalent DOT-3 brake fluid from a clean, sealed brake fluid container. The use of any type of fluid other than the recommended type of brake fluid may cause contamination which could result in damage to the internal rubber seals and/or rubber linings of hydraulic brake system components.

1. Before servicing the vehicle, refer to the Precautions Section.

2. Place a clean shop cloth beneath the brake master cylinder to prevent brake fluid spills.

3. With the ignition OFF and the brakes cool, apply the brakes 3–5 times, or until the brake pedal effort increases significantly, in order to deplete the brake booster power reserve.

4. If you have performed a brake master cylinder bench bleeding on this vehicle, or if you disconnected the brake pipes from the master cylinder, you must perform the following steps:

    a. Ensure that the brake master cylinder reservoir is full to the maximum-fill level. If necessary, add Delco Supreme 11®, GM P/N 12377967 (Canadian P/N 992667), or equivalent DOT-3 brake fluid from a clean, sealed brake fluid container. If removal of the reservoir cap and diaphragm is necessary, clean the outside of the reservoir on and around the cap prior to removal.

    b. With the rear brake pipe installed securely to the master cylinder, loosen and separate the front brake pipe from the front port of the brake master cylinder.

    c. Allow a small amount of brake fluid to gravity bleed from the open port of the master cylinder.

    d. Reconnect the brake pipe to the master cylinder port and tighten securely.

    e. Have an assistant slowly depress the brake pedal fully and maintain steady pressure on the pedal.

    f. Loosen the same brake pipe to purge air from the open port of the master cylinder.

    g. Tighten the brake pipe, then have the assistant slowly release the brake pedal.

    h. Wait 15 seconds, then repeat steps 3–7 until all air is purged from the same port of the master cylinder.

    i. With the front brake pipe installed securely to the master cylinder, after all air has been purged from the front port of the master cylinder, loosen and separate the rear brake pipe from the master cylinder, then repeat steps 3–8.

    j. After completing the final master cylinder port bleeding procedure, ensure that both of the brake pipe to master cylinder fittings are properly tightened.

5. Fill the brake master cylinder reservoir with Delco Supreme 11®, GM P/N 12377967 (Canadian P/N 992667), or equivalent DOT-3 brake fluid from a clean, sealed brake fluid container. Ensure that the brake master cylinder reservoir remains at least half-full during this bleeding procedure. Add fluid as needed to maintain the proper level. Clean the outside of the reservoir on and around the reservoir cap prior to removing the cap and diaphragm.

6. Install a proper box-end wrench onto the RIGHT REAR wheel hydraulic circuit bleeder valve.

7. Install a transparent hose over the end of the bleeder valve.

8. Submerge the open end of the transparent hose into a transparent container partially filled with Delco Supreme 11®, GM P/N 12377967 (Canadian P/N 992667), or equivalent DOT-3 brake fluid from a clean, sealed brake fluid container.

9. Have an assistant slowly depress the brake pedal fully and maintain steady pressure on the pedal.

10. Loosen the bleeder valve to purge air from the wheel hydraulic circuit.

11. Tighten the bleeder valve, then, have the assistant slowly release the brake pedal.

12. Wait 15 seconds, then repeat steps 8–10 until all air is purged from the same wheel hydraulic circuit.

13. With the right rear wheel hydraulic circuit bleeder valve tightened securely, after all air has been purged from the right rear hydraulic circuit, install a proper box-end wrench onto the LEFT FRONT wheel hydraulic circuit bleeder valve.

14. Install a transparent hose over the end of the bleeder valve, then, repeat steps 7–11.

15. With the left front wheel hydraulic circuit bleeder valve tightened securely, after all air has been purged from the left front hydraulic circuit, install a proper box-end wrench onto the LEFT REAR wheel hydraulic circuit bleeder valve.

16. Install a transparent hose over the end of the bleeder valve, then, repeat steps 7–11.

17. With the left rear wheel hydraulic circuit bleeder valve tightened securely, after all air has been purged from the left rear hydraulic circuit, install a proper box-end wrench onto the RIGHT FRONT wheel hydraulic circuit bleeder valve.

18. Install a transparent hose over the end of the bleeder valve, then, repeat steps 7–11.

19. After completing the final wheel hydraulic circuit bleeding procedure, ensure that each of the 4 wheel hydraulic circuit bleeder valves is properly tightened.

20. Fill the brake master cylinder reservoir to the maximum-fill level with Delco Supreme 11®, GM P/N 12377967 (Canadian P/N 992667), or equivalent DOT-3 brake fluid from a clean, sealed brake fluid container.

21. Slowly depress and release the brake pedal. Observe the feel of the brake pedal.

22. If the brake pedal feels spongy, repeat the bleeding procedure again. If the brake pedal still feels spongy after repeating the bleeding procedure, perform the following steps:

    a. Inspect the brake system for external leaks.

    b. Pressure bleed the hydraulic brake system in order to purge any air that may still be trapped in the system.

23. Turn the ignition key ON, with the engine OFF. Check to see if the brake system warning lamp remains illuminated.

BLEEDING THE ABS SYSTEM

➡ **The Auto Bleed Procedure may be terminated at any time during the process by pressing the EXIT button. No further Scan Tool prompts pertaining to the Auto Bleed procedure will be given. After exiting the bleed procedure, relieve bleed pressure and disconnect bleed equipment per manufacturer's instructions. Failure to properly relieve pressure may result in spilled brake fluid causing damage to components and painted surfaces.**

1. Raise and support the vehicle.

2. Remove all 4 tire and wheel assemblies.

3. Inspect the brake system for leaks and visual damage.

4. Lower the vehicle.

5. Inspect the battery state of charge.

6. Install a scan tool.

7. Turn the ignition ON, with the engine OFF.

8. With the scan tool, establish communications with the ABS system. Select Special Functions. Select Automated Bleed from the Special Functions menu.

9. Raise and support the vehicle.

10. Following the directions given on the scan tool, pressure bleed the base brake system.

11. Follow the scan tool directions until the desired brake pedal height is achieved.

12. If the bleed procedure is aborted, a malfunction exists. Perform the following steps before resuming the bleed procedure:

    a. If a DTC is detected, diagnose the appropriate DTC.

    b. If the brake pedal feels spongy, perform the conventional brake bleed procedure again.

13. When the desired pedal height is achieved, press the brake pedal to inspect for firmness.

14. Lower the vehicle.

15. Remove the scan tool.

16. Install the tire and wheel assemblies.

17. Inspect the brake fluid level.

18. Road test the vehicle while inspecting that the pedal remains high and firm.

BRAKES

✳✳ CAUTION

Dust and dirt accumulating on brake parts during normal use may contain asbestos fibers from production or aftermarket brake linings. Breathing excessive concentrations of asbestos fibers can cause serious bodily harm. Exercise care when servicing brake parts. Do not sand or grind brake lining unless equipment used is designed to contain the dust residue. Do not clean brake parts with compressed air or by dry brushing. Cleaning should be done by dampening the brake components with a fine mist of water, then wiping the brake components clean with a dampened cloth. Dispose of cloth and all residue containing asbestos fibers in an impermeable container with the appropriate label. Follow practices prescribed by the Occupational Safety and Health Administration (OSHA) and the Environmental Protection Agency (EPA) for the handling, processing, and disposing of dust or debris that may contain asbestos fibers.

BRAKE CALIPER

REMOVAL & INSTALLATION

3.8L Engine

See Figures 1 through 3.

1. Before servicing the vehicle, refer to the Precautions Section.

2. Inspect the fluid level in the brake master cylinder reservoir.

3. If the brake fluid level is midway between the maximum-full point and the minimum allowable level, then no brake fluid needs to be removed from the reservoir before proceeding. If the brake fluid level is higher than midway between the maximum-full point and the minimum allowable level, then remove brake fluid to the midway point before proceeding.

4. Raise and suitably support the vehicle.

5. Remove the front tire and the wheel assembly.

6. Hand tighten 2 wheel lug nuts to retain the rotor to the hub.

7. Install a large C-clamp over the top of the brake caliper and against the back of the outboard brake pad.

8. Tighten the C-clamp until the caliper piston is pushed into the caliper bore enough to slide the caliper off the rotor.

9. Remove the C-clamp from the caliper.

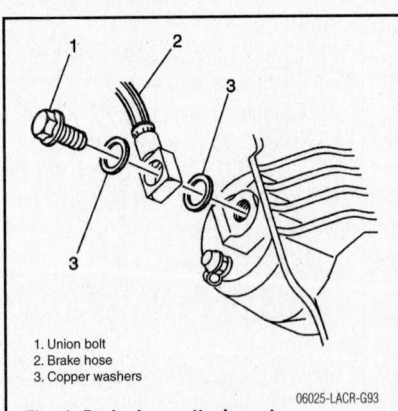

1. Union bolt
2. Brake hose
3. Copper washers

06025-LACR-G93

Fig. 1 Brake hose attachment

10. Remove the brake hose to caliper bolt from the caliper. Discard the 2 copper brake hose gaskets. These gaskets may be stuck to the brake caliper and/or the brake hose end.

11. Plug the opening in the front brake hose to prevent excessive brake fluid loss and contamination.

➡**Note the location of the caliper pin bolts. The leading caliper pin bolt, or top bolt, has a bushing as part of the assembly. The trailing caliper pin bolt, or bottom bolt, is a solid design.**

FRONT DISC BRAKES

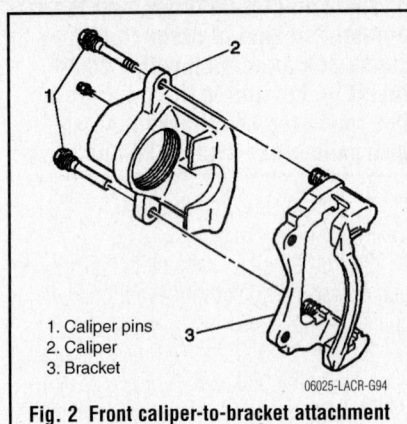

1. Caliper pins
2. Caliper
3. Bracket

06025-LACR-G94

Fig. 2 Front caliper-to-bracket attachment

12. Remove the caliper pin bolts. Note the location of the caliper pin bolts. The leading caliper pin, or top bolt, has a bushing as part of the assembly. The trailing caliper pin, or bottom bolt, is a solid design.

13. Remove the caliper from the rotor and the caliper bracket.

14. Inspect the caliper bolt boots in the caliper bracket for damage. Replace any damaged caliper bolt boots.

15. Inspect the caliper bolts for corrosion or damage. If corrosion or damage is found, use new caliper pin bolts when installing the caliper.

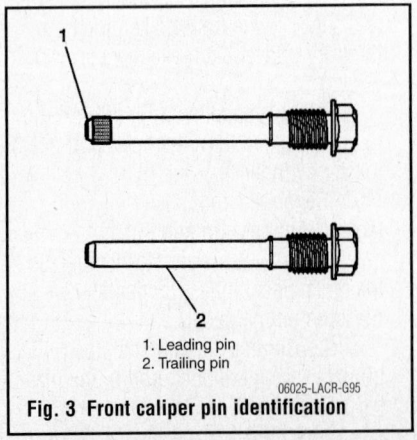

1. Leading pin
2. Trailing pin

06025-LACR-G95

Fig. 3 Front caliper pin identification

To install:

16. If reusing the brake caliper pin bolts, wipe away any debris and old lubricant with a with a clean shop cloth.

17. Apply lubricant, GM P/N 18047666, or equivalent, to the brake caliper pin bolts. Apply a thin layer to the pin bushing and to the caliper pin bolt shank. Ensure that there is not a buildup of excess lubricant at the end of the leading caliper pin, in front of the bushing.

18. Install the caliper over the rotor and onto the caliper bracket.

➡ **The leading caliper pin, or top bolt, has a bushing as part of the assembly. The trailing caliper pin, or bottom bolt, is a solid design.**

19. Install the caliper pin bolts. The leading caliper pin bolt, or top bolt, has a bushing as part of the assembly. The trailing caliper pin bolt, or bottom bolt, is a solid design. Ensure that the bolt boots fit securely in the groove of the caliper pin bolts. If the boots are damaged, they must be replaced. Tighten the bolts to 70 ft. lbs. (95 Nm).

➡ **Install NEW copper brake hose gaskets.**

20. Assemble the brake hose bolt and the NEW copper brake hose gaskets to the brake hose.

21. Install the brake hose to caliper bolt to the brake caliper. Tighten the bolt to 40 ft. lbs. (54 Nm).

22. Remove the 2 wheel lug nuts retaining the rotor to the hub.

23. Install the front tire and the wheel assembly.

24. Lower the vehicle.

25. Fill the master cylinder to the proper level with clean brake fluid.

26. Bleed the brake system.

27. Inspect the hydraulic brake system for brake fluid leaks.

4.6L Engine

See Figure 4.

1. Before servicing the vehicle, refer to the Precautions Section.

2. Inspect the fluid level in the brake master cylinder reservoir.

3. If the brake fluid level is midway between the maximum-full point and the minimum allowable level, no brake fluid needs to be removed from the reservoir before proceeding.

4. If the brake fluid level is higher than midway between the maximum-full point and the minimum allowable level, remove

brake fluid to the midway point before proceeding.

5. Raise and suitably support the vehicle.

6. Remove the tire and wheel assembly.

7. Install a large C-clamp over the body of the brake caliper with the C-clamp ends against the rear of the caliper body and against the outer brake pad.

8. Tighten the C-clamp until the caliper piston is compressed into the caliper bore enough to allow the caliper to slide past the brake rotor.

9. Remove the C-clamp from the caliper.

10. Remove the brake hose-to-caliper bolt attaching the brake hose to the brake caliper.

11. Remove the brake hose from the brake caliper.

12. Remove and discard the 2 copper brake hose gaskets. These gaskets may be stuck to the brake caliper and/or the brake hose end.

13. Plug the opening in the brake caliper and the brake hose to prevent fluid loss and contamination.

14. Remove the brake caliper pin bolts.

15. Remove the brake caliper from the brake caliper bracket.

To install:

➡ **Ensure that the caliper guide pin boots are fully seated to the caliper guide pin retaining seat of the caliper guide pin. Ensure that the caliper guide pin boots are fully seated to the caliper boot seal retaining seat of the brake caliper mounting bracket.**

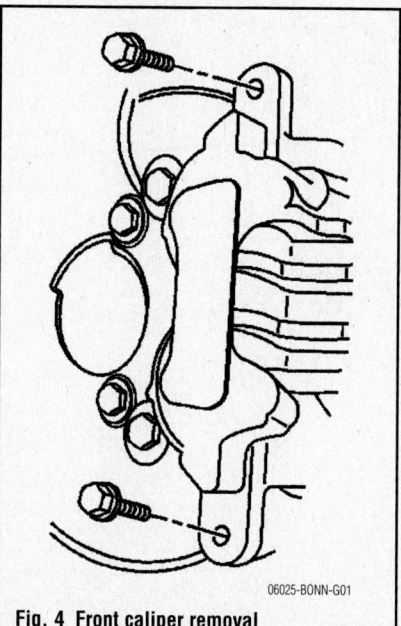

06025-BONN-G01

Fig. 4 Front caliper removal

16. Inspect the caliper guide pin boots for cuts, tears, or deterioration. If damaged, replace the slides and boots.

➡ **If reusing the brake caliper pin bolts, the threads of the caliper pin bolts and the threads of the caliper bracket mounting holes must be free of residue and debris prior to application of threadlocker in order to ensure proper adhesion and fastener retention.**

17. Prepare the bolts and the threaded holes for assembly: Thoroughly clean the residue from the bolt threads by using denatured alcohol or equivalent and allow to dry. Thoroughly clean the residue from the threaded holes by using denatured alcohol or equivalent and allow to dry.

18. Apply threadlocker GM P/N 12345493 (Canadian P/N 10953488) or equivalent, to ⅔ of the threaded length of the lower caliper bracket bolts. Ensure that there are no gaps in the threadlocker along the length of the filled area of the bolts.

19. Allow the threadlocker to cure approximately 10 minutes before installation.

20. Apply a thin coat of high temperature silicone brake lubricant to the brake caliper pin bolts.

21. Install the brake caliper pin bolts. Tighten the brake caliper pin bolts to 25 ft. lbs. (34 Nm).

22. Remove the plug from the brake caliper opening and the brake hose.

➡ **Install NEW copper brake hose gaskets.**

23. Assemble the NEW copper brake hose gaskets, and the brake caliper bolt to the brake hose.

24. Install the brake hose and the brake caliper bolt to the brake caliper. Tighten the brake hose to caliper bolt to 32 ft. lbs. (44 Nm).

25. Bleed the hydraulic brake system.

26. With the engine OFF, gradually apply the brake pedal to approximately ⅔ of its travel distance.

27. Slowly release the brake pedal.

28. Wait 15 seconds, then repeat steps 11 and 12 until a firm brake pedal apply is obtained. This will properly seat the brake caliper pistons and brake pads.

29. Install the tire and wheel assembly. Tighten the wheel lug nuts to 100 ft. lbs. (136 Nm).

30. Lower the vehicle.

DISC BRAKE PADS

REMOVAL & INSTALLATION

3.8L Engine

See Figure 5.

1. Before servicing the vehicle, refer to the Precautions Section.

2. Inspect the fluid level in the brake master cylinder reservoir.

3. If the brake fluid level is midway between the maximum-full point and the minimum allowable level, then no brake fluid needs to be removed from the reservoir before proceeding. If the brake fluid level is higher than midway between the maximum-full point and the minimum allowable level, then remove brake fluid to the midway point before proceeding.

4. Raise and suitably support the vehicle.

5. Remove the tire and the wheel assembly.

6. Hand-tighten 2 wheel lug nuts in order to retain the rotor to the hub.

7. Install a large C-clamp over the top of the caliper housing and against the back of the outboard pad.

8. Slowly tighten the C-clamp until the piston pushes into the caliper bore enough to slide the caliper off the rotor.

9. Remove the C-clamp from the caliper.

10. Remove the lower caliper bolt (1).

✳✳ WARNING

Use care to avoid damaging pin boot when rotating caliper.

11. In order to access the pads, rotate the caliper upward and suitably support it.

12. Remove the pads (5) from the caliper bracket (3).

13. Remove the 2 retainer slides (4) from the caliper bracket (3).

14. Inspect all parts for cuts, tears, or deterioration. Replace any damaged parts.

15. Inspect the caliper bolts for corrosion or damage. If corrosion is found, use new caliper bolts when installing the caliper.

To install:

16. Using a C-clamp, bottom the piston into the caliper bore. Use an old brake pad or wooden block across the face of the piston. Do not damage the piston or the caliper boot.

17. Install the 2 retainers to the caliper bracket.

➡ **The wear sensor is on the outside pad. The sensor is positioned at the leading or upward edge of the pad during forward wheel rotation.**

18. Install the pads to the caliper anchor bracket.

✳✳ WARNING

Use care to avoid damaging pin boot when rotating caliper.

19. Remove the support and reposition the caliper (2) back down over the front pads.

20. Lubricate the pin bolt and the inner diameter of the bolt boot with GM P/N 18047666, or equivalent. Do not lubricate the threads of the pin bolt.

21. Install the lower caliper bolt. Tighten the caliper bolts to 70 ft. lbs. (95 Nm).

22. Remove the 2 wheel lug nuts retaining the rotor to the hub.

23. Install the tire and the wheel assembly.

24. Lower the vehicle.

25. With the engine OFF, gradually apply the brake pedal to approximately ⅔ of its travel distance.

26. Slowly release the brake pedal.

27. Wait 15 seconds, then, repeat steps 10 and 11 until a firm brake pedal is obtained. This will properly seat the brake caliper pistons and brake pads.

28. Fill the brake master cylinder reservoir to the proper level.

29. Burnish the pads and rotors.

4.6L Engine

✳✳ CAUTION

Two different designs of the front brake rotors and front brake pads are used on this vehicle. Do NOT interchange first design and second design parts, or a loss of braking and personal injury could occur.

1. Inspect the fluid level in the brake master cylinder reservoir.

2. If the brake fluid level is midway between the maximum-full point and the minimum allowable level, no brake fluid needs to be removed from the reservoir before proceeding.

3. If the brake fluid level is higher than midway between the maximum-full point and the minimum allowable level, remove brake fluid to the midway point before proceeding.

4. Raise and suitably support the vehicle.

5. Remove the tire and wheel assembly.

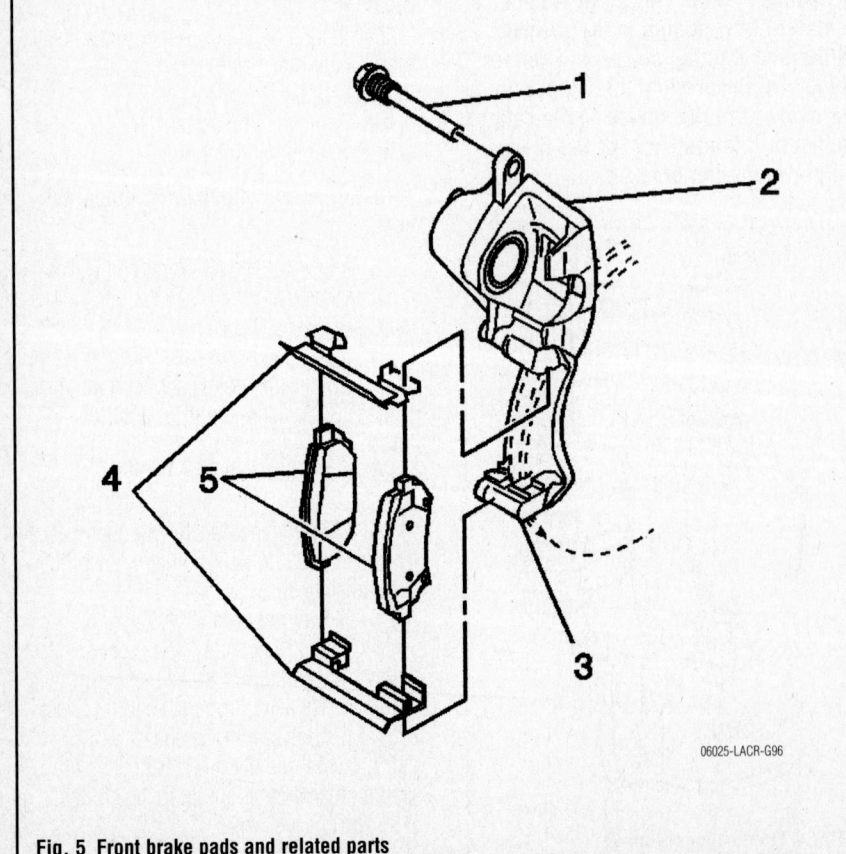

06025-LACR-G96

Fig. 5 Front brake pads and related parts

6. Install large C-clamp over the body of the brake caliper with the C-clamp ends against the rear of the caliper body and against the outboard brake pad.

7. Tighten the C-clamp evenly until the caliper pistons are compressed into the caliper bores enough to allow the caliper to slide past the brake rotor.

8. Remove the C-clamp from the caliper.

9. To loosen the brake caliper lower pin bolt, hold the brake caliper guide pin with a wrench.

10. Remove the brake caliper pin bolt.

※※ WARNING

Support the brake caliper with heavy mechanic's wire, or equivalent, whenever it is separated from its mount and the hydraulic flexible brake hose is still connected. Failure to support the caliper in this manner will cause the flexible brake hose to bear the weight of the caliper, which may cause damage to the brake hose and in turn may cause a brake fluid leak.

11. Pivot the brake caliper body upward and secure the caliper out of the way with heavy mechanic's wire or equivalent. Ensure that there is no tension on the hydraulic brake flexible hose. Do NOT disconnect the hydraulic brake flexible hose from the caliper.

12. Remove the brake pads from the caliper bracket.

13. Remove and inspect the brake pad retainers from the caliper bracket.

To install:

➡**Ensure that the caliper guide pin boots are fully seated to the caliper guide pin retaining seat of the caliper pin. Ensure that the caliper guide pin boots are fully seated to the caliper boot seal retaining seat of the brake caliper mounting bracket.**

14. Inspect the brake caliper guide pin bolts. If damaged or corroded replace the brake caliper guide bolts.

15. Inspect the brake caliper guide pins. If damaged, or corroded replace the brake caliper guide pin. Do not attempt to clean away any corrosion.

16. Inspect the brake caliper guide pin boots for cuts, tears, or deterioration. If damaged, replace the brake caliper guide pin boots.

17. Carefully pull outward on the caliper guide pin to ensure that the caliper guide pin retaining seat is fully seated to the caliper guide pin boot.

18. Inspect the brake caliper piston boot for deterioration, replace if damaged.

19. Install a large C-clamp over the body of the brake caliper, with the C-clamp ends against the rear of the caliper body and against an old inboard brake pad or a wood block installed against the caliper pistons.

20. Tighten the C-clamp evenly until the caliper pistons are compressed completely into the caliper bores.

21. Remove the C-clamp and the old brake pad or wood block from the caliper.

22. Install the brake pad retainers to the caliper bracket.

23. Install the brake pads to the caliper bracket.

24. Pivot the brake caliper downward, over the brake pads and into the caliper bracket.

➡**If reusing the lower caliper pin bolt, the threads of the lower caliper pin bolt and the threads of the caliper bracket mounting holes must be free of residue and debris prior to application of threadlocker in order to ensure proper adhesion and fastener retention.**

25. If reusing the caliper pin bolts prepare the bolt and the threaded hole for assembly: Thoroughly clean the residue from the bolt threads by using denatured alcohol or equivalent and allow to dry. Thoroughly clean the residue from the threaded holes by using denatured alcohol or equivalent and allow to dry.

26. Apply threadlocker GM P/N 12345493 (Canadian P/N 10953488), or equivalent to ⅔ of the threaded length of the lower caliper pin bolt. Ensure that there are no gaps in the threadlocker along the length of the filled area of the bolt.

27. Allow the threadlocker to cure approximately ten minutes before installation.

28. Apply a thin coat of Niglube® GM P/N 18046532 grease or equivalent, to the front brake caliper guide pin.

29. Install the lower brake caliper pin bolt. Hold the lower brake caliper guide pin with a wrench and tighten the lower brake caliper pin bolt to 25 ft. lbs. (34 Nm).

30. Install the tire and wheel assembly.

31. Lower the vehicle.

32. With the engine OFF, gradually apply the brake pedal to approximately ⅔ of its travel distance.

33. Slowly release the brake pedal.

34. Wait 15 seconds, then repeat steps 15 and 16 until a firm brake pedal apply is obtained; this will properly seat the brake caliper pistons and brake pads.

35. Fill the brake master cylinder reservoir to the proper level.

36. Burnish the pads and rotors.

✲✲ CAUTION

Dust and dirt accumulating on brake parts during normal use may contain asbestos fibers from production or aftermarket brake linings. Breathing excessive concentrations of asbestos fibers can cause serious bodily harm. Exercise care when servicing brake parts. Do not sand or grind brake lining unless equipment used is designed to contain the dust residue. Do not clean brake parts with compressed air or by dry brushing. Cleaning should be done by dampening the brake components with a fine mist of water, then wiping the brake components clean with a dampened cloth. Dispose of cloth and all residue containing asbestos fibers in an impermeable container with the appropriate label. Follow practices prescribed by the Occupational Safety and Health Administration (OSHA) and the Environmental Protection Agency (EPA) for the handling, processing, and disposing of dust or debris that may contain asbestos fibers.

BRAKE CALIPER

REMOVAL & INSTALLATION

Inspect the fluid level in the brake master cylinder reservoir. If the brake fluid level is midway between the maximum-full point and the minimum allowable level, no brake fluid needs to be removed from the reservoir before proceeding. If the brake fluid level is higher than midway between the maximum-full point and the minimum allowable level, remove brake fluid to the midway point before proceeding.

1. Raise the vehicle and suitably support.
2. Remove the tire and wheel assembly.
3. Pull down on the front park brake cable.
4. Remove the front park brake cable from the park brake cable connector.

✲✲ WARNING

When using a large C-clamp to compress a caliper piston into a caliper bore of a caliper equipped with an integral park brake mechanism, do not exceed more than 0.039 in. (1mm) of piston travel. Exceeding this amount of piston travel will

cause damage to the internal adjusting mechanism and/or the integral park brake mechanism.

5. Install a large C-clamp over the top of the brake caliper housing and against the back of the outboard brake pad. Compress the brake caliper piston into brake caliper bore to allow the piston enough clearance to slide the brake caliper off the brake rotor.
6. Remove the C-clamp.

➡ Be sure to plug the opening in the brake caliper and brake hose to prevent fluid loss and/or contamination.

7. Remove brake hose to caliper bolt attaching the brake hose to the brake caliper.
8. Remove the brake hose from the brake caliper.
9. Remove and discard the two copper brake hose gaskets. These gaskets may be stuck to the brake caliper and/or the brake hose end.
10. Remove the park brake cable bracket from the brake caliper. Leave the park brake cable attached to the cable bracket.
11. Disconnect the park brake cable from the park brake lever on the brake caliper.
12. Remove the lower brake caliper pin bolt.
13. Rotate the brake caliper up.
14. Remove the brake caliper from the upper brake caliper pin bolt.

To install:

15. If reusing the brake caliper retainers, clean the sleeves using denatured alcohol, or equivalent.
16. Lubricate the brake caliper pin bolts with a thin coat of high temperature silicone lube.
17. Install the brake caliper to the upper caliper pin bolt.
18. Rotate the brake caliper down over the brake pads into the brake caliper bracket.
19. Install the brake caliper pin bolts. Tighten the brake caliper pin bolts to 27 ft. lbs. (36 Nm).
20. Remove the plugs in the brake hose end.

➡ Install NEW copper brake hose gaskets.

21. Assemble the brake hose bolt and the NEW copper brake hose gaskets to the brake hose.
22. Install the brake hose to caliper bolt to the brake caliper. Tighten the brake hose to caliper bolt to 33 ft. lbs. (44 Nm).

23. Connect the park brake cable to the park brake lever on the brake caliper.
24. Install the park brake cable bracket to the brake caliper. Tighten the park brake cable bracket bolt to 32 ft. lbs. (43 Nm).
25. Install the front park brake cable to the park brake cable connector.
26. Bleed the brake system.
27. With the engine OFF, gradually apply the brake pedal to approximately ⅔ of its travel distance.
28. Slowly release the brake pedal.
29. Wait 15 seconds, then repeat until a firm brake pedal is obtained. This will properly seat the brake caliper pistons and brake pads.
30. Install the tire and wheel assembly. Tighten the wheel lug nuts to 100 ft. lbs. (136 Nm).
31. Lower the vehicle.

DISC BRAKE PADS

REMOVAL & INSTALLATION

See Figure 6.

Inspect the fluid level in the brake master cylinder reservoir. If the brake fluid level is midway between the maximum-full point and the minimum allowable level, no brake fluid needs to be removed from the reservoir before proceeding. If the brake fluid level is higher than midway between the maximum-full point and the minimum allowable level, remove brake fluid to the midway point before proceeding. Raise the vehicle and suitably support.

1. Remove the tire and wheel assembly.

➡ When using a large C-clamp to compress a caliper piston into a caliper bore of a caliper equipped with an integral park brake mechanism, do not exceed more than 0.039 in. (1mm) of piston travel. Exceeding this amount of piston travel will cause damage to the internal adjusting mechanism and/or the integral park brake mechanism.

2. Using a large C clamp, compress the brake caliper piston into the brake caliper bore to gain enough clearance to allow the brake caliper to pivot off the brake caliper bracket.
3. Compress the piston until resistance is felt.
4. Remove the park brake cable guide bolt from the lower control arm.
5. Remove the bottom brake caliper pin bolt.

➙Support the brake caliper with heavy mechanic's wire, or equivalent, whenever it is separated from its mount and the hydraulic flexible brake hose is still connected. Failure to support the caliper in this manner will cause the flexible brake hose to bear the weight of the caliper, which may cause damage to the brake hose and in turn may cause a brake fluid leak.

6. Pivot the brake caliper body upward and secure out of the way with heavy mechanic's wire. Do NOT disconnect the hydraulic brake flexible hose from the caliper.

7. Remove the inboard and outboard brake pads from the brake caliper bracket.

8. Remove and inspect the brake pad retainers.

To install:

9. Inspect the brake caliper bolt suspension boots for cuts, tears, or deterioration. If damaged, replace the brake caliper pin boots.

10. Inspect the brake caliper pin bolts for damage or corrosion. Replace if damaged or corroded. Do not attempt to clean away corrosion. Corrosion is typically caused by damaged pin boots.

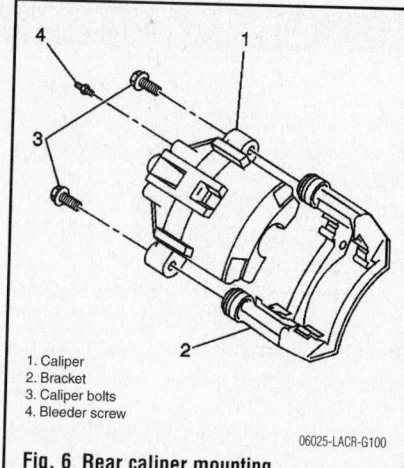

1. Caliper
2. Bracket
3. Caliper bolts
4. Bleeder screw

06025-LACR-G100

Fig. 6 Rear caliper mounting

11. Inspect the brake caliper piston boot for deterioration, repair or replace the brake caliper if damaged.

12. Retract the brake caliper piston into the brake caliper bore. Use a spanner type wrench to turn the piston clockwise until it bottoms in the brake caliper bore and align the piston.

13. Align the cutouts in the brake caliper piston to the alignment pins on the brake pads.

14. Apply a thin coat of high temperature silicone lube to the rear brake caliper bolts.

15. Install the brake pad retainers into the brake caliper bracket.

16. Install the inboard and outboard brake pads into the brake caliper bracket.

17. Pivot the brake caliper down over the brake pads and into the brake caliper racket.

18. Insert the lower brake caliper pin bolt. Tighten the brake caliper pin bolt to 27 ft. lbs. (36 Nm).

19. Install the park brake cable guide bolt to the lower control arm. Tighten the park brake cable guide bolt to 18 ft. lbs. (24 Nm).

20. Install the tire and wheel assembly. Tighten the wheel lug nuts to 100 ft. lbs. (136 Nm).

21. Lower the vehicle.

22. With the engine OFF, gradually apply the brake pedal to approximately ⅔ of its travel distance.

23. Slowly release the brake pedal.

24. Wait 15 seconds, then repeat until a firm brake pedal is obtained. This will properly seat the brake caliper pistons and brake pads.

25. Fill the brake master cylinder reservoir to the proper level.

26. Burnish the pads and rotors.

BRAKES

PARKING BRAKE CABLE

ADJUSTMENT

The plastic coated park brake cables do not require periodic lubrication. Coated park brake cables are used to reduce apply effort and increase corrosion protection. The cables are coated with a plastic material which slides against nylon seals inside the conduit end fittings.

The park brake lever has an indicator switch which closes when the park brake is set, thus illuminating the red BRAKE lamp.

The park brake lever/cable adjustment is automatic. Cycling the lever two to three times should result in properly adjusting the park brake after disabling it for service. The park brake application is completely independent of the hydraulic brake system. The park brake system is a mechanical system which operates the rear disc brakes through the calipers. The system is activated by depressing the park brake pedal, which applies the rear disc brakes via cables. When the park brake is set and the ignition switch is on, the BRAKE warning lamp on the instrument panel will be on. The park brake is released by pushing the pedal down

until a click is heard and then releasing. The pedal will click again and the BRAKE lamp in the instrument panel should go out when the park brake system is fully released.

Manual adjustment may be necessary when the rear brake cables have been disconnected. A need for park brake cable adjustment is indicated if the hydraulic brake system operates with good reserve, but a firm park brake pedal feel cannot be achieved with less than one full stroke of the park brake pedal.

1. Before servicing the vehicle, refer to the Precautions Section.

2. Apply and release the park brake four times.

3. The park brake light should be illuminated after park brake has been depressed slightly.

4. Check the parking brake pedal assembly for full release by turning the ignition on and inspecting the PARK BRAKE warning light. The light should be off. If the PARK BRAKE warning light is on and the park brake appears to be fully released, pull the pedal back by hand and continue with the adjustment procedure.

5. Raise the vehicle and suitably support.

PARKING BRAKE

6. Check the park brake levers on rear calipers. The levers should be against the stops on the caliper housing. If the levers are not against the stops, check for binding in the rear brake cables and position levers against stops.

7. Tighten the park brake cable at the equalizer until either the left or right lever begins to move off the stop.

8. Loosen the adjustment at the equalizer until the lever which has moved off the stop, as in step 5, is again resting fully against the stops. Loosen the tension at the equalizer until the cables feel slightly loose to the touch. The cables should not sag under their own weight.

9. Operate the park brake several times to check adjustment. A firm pedal feel should be obtained by depressing the pedal less than one full stroke.

10. Inspect the left and right caliper levers. Both levers must be resting on the stops after the adjustment of the parking brake.

11. Check the operation of the park brake.

12. To achieve optimal performance, ensure the cables are not over-tensioned at the equalizer.

GENERAL INFORMATION

✳✳ CAUTION

These vehicles are equipped with an air bag system. The system must be disarmed before performing service on, or around, system components, the steering column, instrument panel components, wiring and sensors. Failure to follow the safety precautions and the disarming procedure could result in accidental air bag deployment, possible injury and unnecessary system repairs.

SERVICE PRECAUTIONS

Disconnect and isolate the battery negative cable before beginning any airbag system component diagnosis, testing, removal, or installation procedures. Allow system capacitor to discharge for two minutes before beginning any component service. This will disable the airbag system. Failure to disable the airbag system may result in accidental airbag deployment, personal injury, or death.

Do not place an intact undeployed airbag face down on a solid surface. The airbag will propel into the air if accidentally deployed and may result in personal injury or death.

When carrying or handling an undeployed airbag, the trim side (face) of the airbag should be pointing towards the body to minimize possibility of injury if accidental deployment occurs. Failure to do this may result in personal injury or death.

Replace airbag system components with OEM replacement parts. Substitute parts may appear interchangeable, but internal differences may result in inferior occupant protection. Failure to do so may result in occupant personal injury or death.

Wear safety glasses, rubber gloves, and long sleeved clothing when cleaning powder residue from vehicle after an airbag deployment. Powder residue emitted from a deployed airbag can cause skin irritation. Flush affected area with cool water if irritation is experienced. If nasal or throat irritation is experienced, exit the vehicle for fresh air until the irritation ceases. If irritation continues, see a physician.

Do not use a replacement airbag that is not in the original packaging. This may result in improper deployment, personal injury, or death.

The factory installed fasteners, screws and bolts used to fasten airbag components have a special coating and are specifically designed for the airbag system. Do not use substitute fasteners. Use only original equipment fasteners listed in the parts catalog when fastener replacement is required.

During, and following, any child restraint anchor service, due to impact event or vehicle repair, carefully inspect all mounting hardware, tether straps, and anchors for proper installation, operation, or damage. If a child restraint anchor is found damaged in any way, the anchor must be replaced. Failure to do this may result in personal injury or death.

Deployed and non-deployed airbags may or may not have live pyrotechnic material within the airbag inflator.

Do not dispose of driver/passenger/curtain airbags or seat belt tensioners unless you are sure of complete deployment. Refer to the Hazardous Substance Control System for proper disposal.

Dispose of deployed airbags and tensioners consistent with state, provincial, local, and federal regulations.

After any airbag component testing or service, do not connect the battery negative cable. Personal injury or death may result if the system test is not performed first.

If the vehicle is equipped with the Occupant Classification System (OCS), do not connect the battery negative cable before performing the OCS Verification Test using the scan tool and the appropriate diagnostic information. Personal injury or death may result if the system test is not performed properly.

Never replace both the Occupant Restraint Controller (ORC) and the Occupant Classification Module (OCM) at the same time. If both require replacement, replace one, then perform the Airbag System test before replacing the other.

Both the ORC and the OCM store Occupant Classification System (OCS) calibration data, which they transfer to one another when one of them is replaced. If both are replaced at the same time, an irreversible fault will be set in both modules and the OCS may malfunction and cause personal injury or death.

If equipped with OCS, the Seat Weight Sensor is a sensitive, calibrated unit and must be handled carefully. Do not drop or handle roughly. If dropped or damaged, replace with another sensor. Failure to do so may result in occupant injury or death.

If equipped with OCS, the front passenger seat must be handled carefully as well. When removing the seat, be careful when setting on floor not to drop. If dropped, the sensor may be inoperative, could result in occupant injury, or possibly death.

If equipped with OCS, when the passenger front seat is on the floor, no one should sit in the front passenger seat. This uneven force may damage the sensing ability of the seat weight sensors. If sat on and damaged, the sensor may be inoperative, could result in occupant injury, or possibly death.

DISARMING THE SYSTEM

Zone 1

See Figures 7 and 8.

1. Before servicing the vehicle, refer to the Precautions Section.
2. Turn the steering wheel so that the vehicles wheels are pointing straight ahead.
3. Turn the ignition switch to the OFF position.
4. Remove the key from the ignition switch.
5. Open the hood and locate the underhood fuse center on right/passenger shock tower.

➡ **With the SIR Fuse removed and the ignition ON, the AIR BAG indicator illuminates. This is normal operation, and does not indicate an SIR system malfunction.**

6. Lift the cover for the underhood fuse center.
7. Locate and remove the SIR Fuse from the underhood fuse center.
8. Remove the radiator upper air baffle and deflector and locate the left and/or right front end sensor also known as Electronic Frontal Sensor (EFS) that needs servicing.
9. Remove the Connector Position Assurance (CPA) from both front end sensors connector.
10. Remove both front end sensor connectors from each front end sensor.

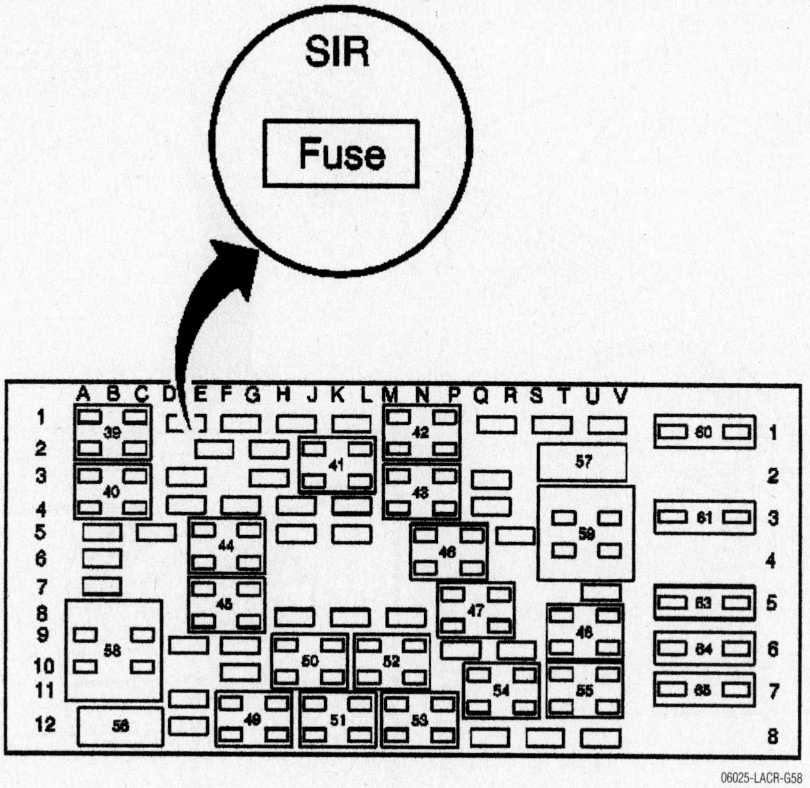

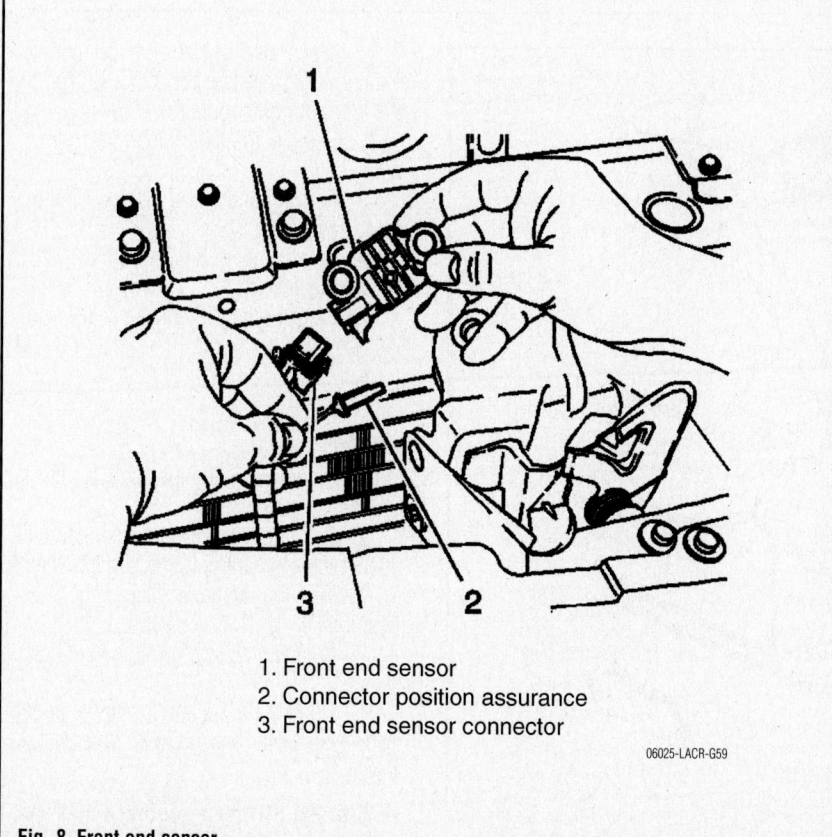

Fig. 7 SIR fuse

06025-LACR-G58

1. Front end sensor
2. Connector position assurance
3. Front end sensor connector

06025-LACR-G59

Fig. 8 Front end sensor

Zone 2

See Figures 9 and 10.

1. Before servicing the vehicle, refer to the Precautions Section.

2. Turn the steering wheel so that the vehicles wheels are pointing straight ahead.

3. Turn the ignition switch to the OFF position.

4. Remove the key from the ignition switch.

5. Open the hood and locate the underhood fuse center on right/passenger shock tower.

➡ **With the SIR Fuse removed and the ignition ON, the AIR BAG indicator illuminates. This is normal operation, and does not indicate an SIR system malfunction.**

6. Lift the cover for the underhood fuse center.

7. Locate and remove the SIR Fuse from the underhood fuse center.

8. When disabling the roof rail module go to step 8, if the Side impact Sensor (SIS) needs disabling then go to step 11.

9. Remove the left rear panel.

10. Remove the Connector Position Assurance (CPA) from the left/driver roof rail module connector (2).

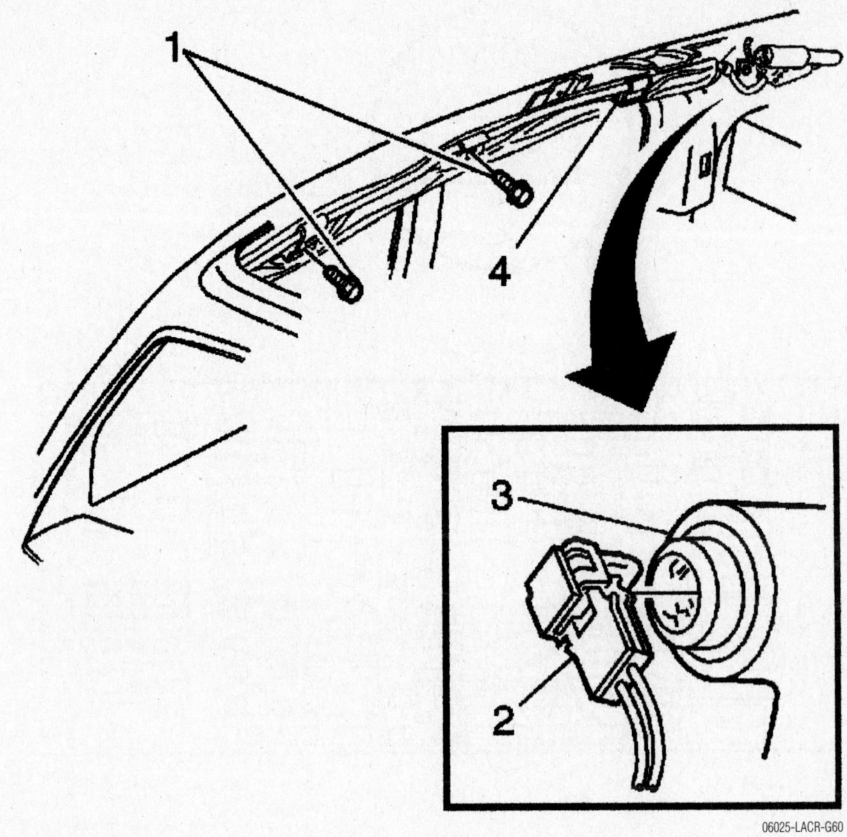

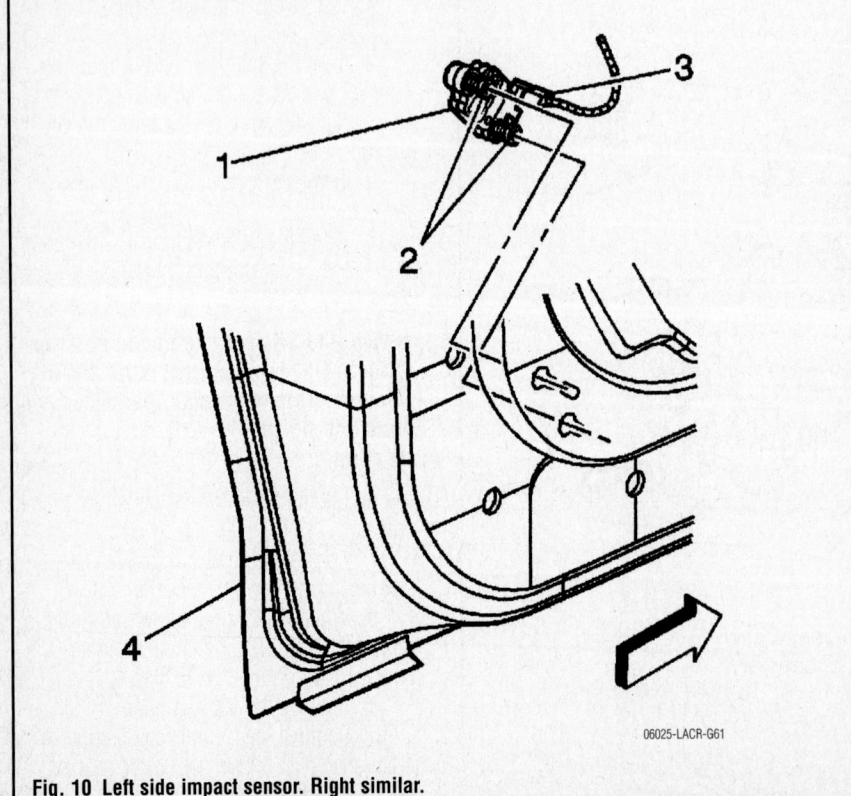

06025-LACR-G60

Fig. 9 Left roof rail module. Right similar.

06025-LACR-G61

Fig. 10 Left side impact sensor. Right similar.

11. Disconnect the left roof rail module wiring harness yellow connector (2) from the left roof rail module (3).

12. Remove the left/driver door trim panel.

13. Remove enough of the water deflector to access the SIS.

14. Remove the SIS CPA from the left SIS connector (3).

15. Remove the SIS connector (3) from the SIS (1).

Zone 3

See Figure 11.

1. Before servicing the vehicle, refer to the Precautions Section.

2. Turn the steering wheel so that the vehicles wheels are pointing straight ahead.

3. Turn the ignition switch to the OFF position.

4. Remove the key from the ignition switch.

5. Open the hood and locate the underhood fuse center on right/passenger shock tower.

➡ **With the SIR Fuse removed and the ignition ON, the AIR BAG indicator**

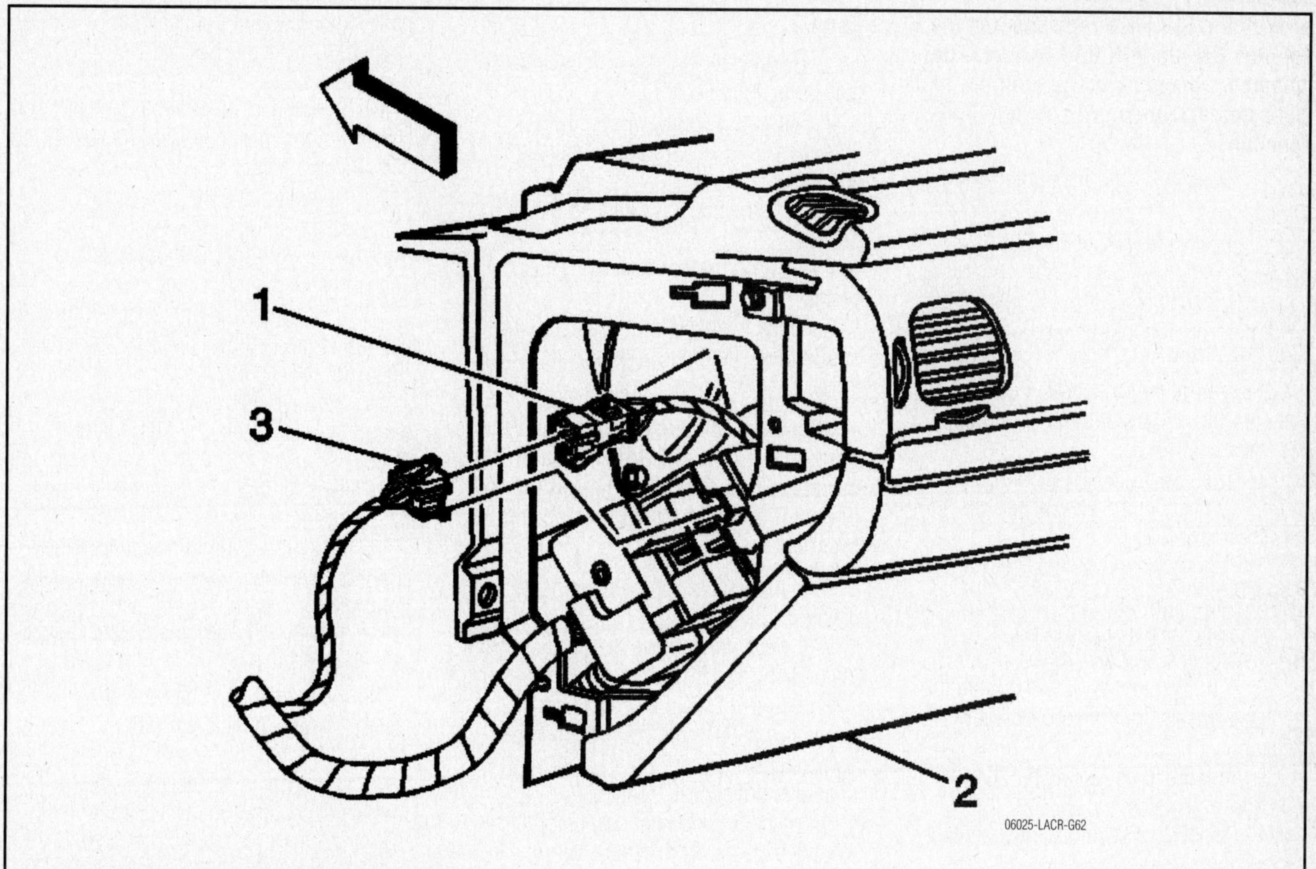

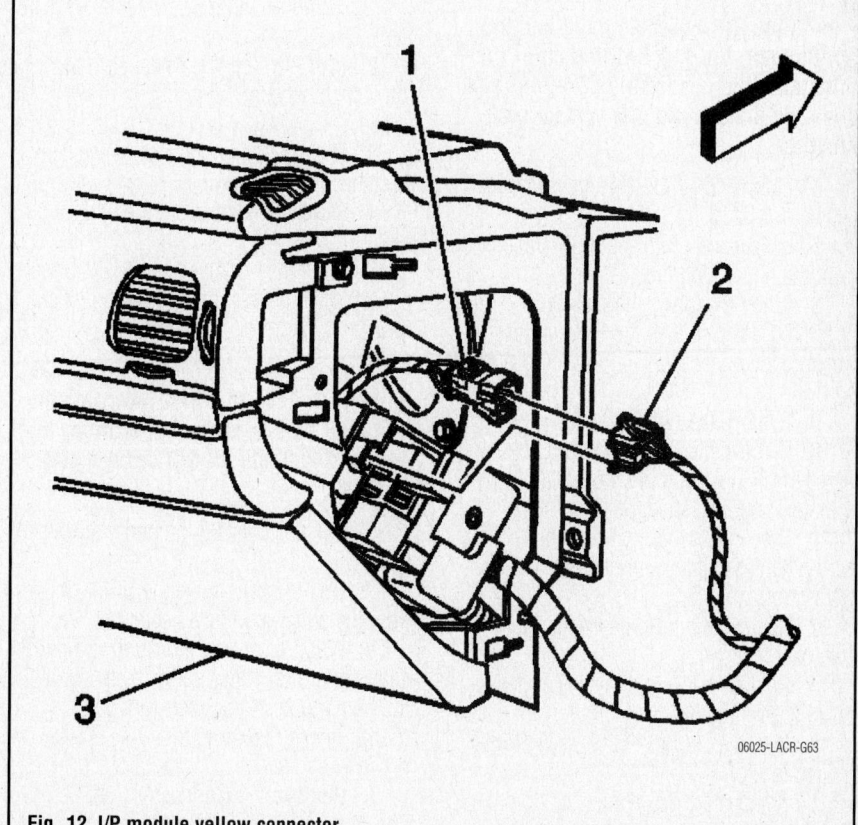

Fig. 11 Steering wheel module coil yellow connector

illuminates. This is normal operation, and does not indicate an SIR system malfunction.

6. Lift the cover for the underhood fuse center.

7. Locate and remove the SIR fuse from the underhood fuse center.

8. Remove the left/driver sound insulator from the Instrument Panel (I/P) (2).

9. Remove the Connector Position Assurance (CPA) from the steering wheel module coil yellow connector (1).

10. Disconnect the steering wheel module coil yellow connector (1) from the vehicle harness yellow connector (3).

Zone 5

See Figure 12.

1. Before servicing the vehicle, refer to the Precautions Section.

2. Turn the steering wheel so that the vehicle wheels are pointing straight ahead.

3. Turn the ignition switch to the OFF position.

4. Remove the key from the ignition switch.

5. Open the hood and locate the underhood fuse center on right/passenger shock tower.

Fig. 12 I/P module yellow connector

➡ **With the SIR Fuse removed and the ignition ON, the AIR BAG indicator illuminates. This is normal operation, and does not indicate an SIR system malfunction.**

6. Lift the cover for the underhood fuse center.

7. Locate and remove the SIR Fuse from the underhood fuse center.

8. Remove the right/passenger sound insulator from the Instrument Panel (I/P) (3).

9. Remove the Connector Position Assurance (CPA) from the I/P module yellow connector (1).

10. Disconnect the I/P module yellow connector (1) from the vehicle harness yellow connector (2).

Zone 6

1. Before servicing the vehicle, refer to the Precautions Section.

2. Turn the steering wheel so that the vehicles wheels are pointing straight ahead.

3. Turn the ignition switch to the OFF position.

4. Remove the key from the ignition switch.

5. Open the hood and locate the underhood fuse center on right/passenger shock tower.

➡ **With the SIR Fuse removed and the ignition ON, the AIR BAG indicator illuminates. This is normal operation, and does not indicate an SIR system malfunction.**

6. Lift the cover for the underhood fuse center.

7. Locate and remove the SIR Fuse from the underhood fuse center.

8. When disabling the roof rail module go to step 8, if the Side impact Sensor (SIS) needs disabling then go to step 11.

9. Remove the right rear panel.

10. Remove the Connector Position Assurance (CPA) from the right/passenger roof rail module connector.

11. Disconnect the right roof rail module wiring harness yellow connector from the right roof rail module.

12. Remove the right/passenger door trim panel.

13. Remove enough of the water deflector to access the SIS.

14. Remove the SIS CPA from the right SIS connector.

15. Remove the SIS connector from the SIS.

Zone 7

1. Before servicing the vehicle, refer to the Precautions Section.

2. Turn the steering wheel so that the vehicles wheels are pointing straight ahead.

3. Turn the ignition switch to the OFF position.

4. Remove the key from the ignition switch.

5. Open the hood and locate the underhood fuse center on right/passenger shock tower.

➡ **With the SIR Fuse removed and the ignition ON, the AIR BAG indicator illuminates. This is normal operation, and does not indicate an SIR system malfunction.**

6. Lift the cover for the underhood fuse center.

7. Locate and remove the SIR Fuse from the underhood fuse center.

8. Remove the Connector Position Assurance (CPA) from the left/driver seat belt pretensioner connector (1) located under the driver seat.

9. Disconnect the left seat belt pretensioner connector from vehicle wiring harness connector (1).

Zone 9

1. Before servicing the vehicle, refer to the Precautions Section.

2. Turn the steering wheel so that the vehicle wheels are pointing straight ahead.

3. Turn the ignition switch to the OFF position.

4. Remove the key from the ignition switch.

5. Open the hood and locate the underhood fuse center on right/passenger shock tower.

➡ **With the SIR Fuse removed and the ignition ON, the AIR BAG indicator illuminates. This is normal operation, and does not indicate an SIR system malfunction.**

6. Lift the cover for the underhood fuse center.

7. Locate and remove the SIR Fuse from the underhood fuse center.

8. When disabling the right/passenger seat belt pretensioner perform step 8, if the Sensing and Diagnostic Module (SDM) needs disabling then use entire procedure.

9. Remove the Connector Position Assurance (CPA) from the right/

passenger seat belt pretensioner connector located under the passenger seat.

10. Disconnect the seat belt pretensioner—right connector from vehicle wiring harness connector.

11. Remove the right rear panel.

12. Remove the CPA from the right/passenger roof rail module connector.

13. Disconnect the right roof rail module wiring harness yellow connector from the right roof rail module.

14. Remove the right/passenger sound insulator from the Instrument Panel (I/P).

15. Remove the CPA from the I/P module yellow connector.

16. Disconnect the I/P module yellow connector from the vehicle harness yellow connector.

17. Remove the left/driver sound insulator from the I/P.

18. Remove the CPA from the steering wheel module coil yellow connector.

19. Disconnect the steering wheel module coil yellow connector from the vehicle harness yellow connector.

20. Remove the CPA from the left/driver seat belt pretensioner connector located under the driver seat.

21. Disconnect the seat belt pretensioner—left connector from vehicle wiring harness connector.

22. Remove the left rear panel.

23. Remove the CPA from the left/driver roof rail module connector.

24. Disconnect the left roof rail module wiring harness yellow connector from the left roof rail module.

ARMING THE SYSTEM

Zone 1

See Figures 13 and 14.

1. Remove the key from the ignition switch.

2. Connect both front end sensor connectors to each front end sensor.

3. Install both CPA's into each front end sensor connector.

4. Install the radiator upper air baffle and deflector.

5. Install the SIR Fuse.

6. Close the underhood fuse center cover.

7. Use caution while reaching in and turn the ignition switch to the ON position. The AIR BAG indicator will flash then turn OFF.

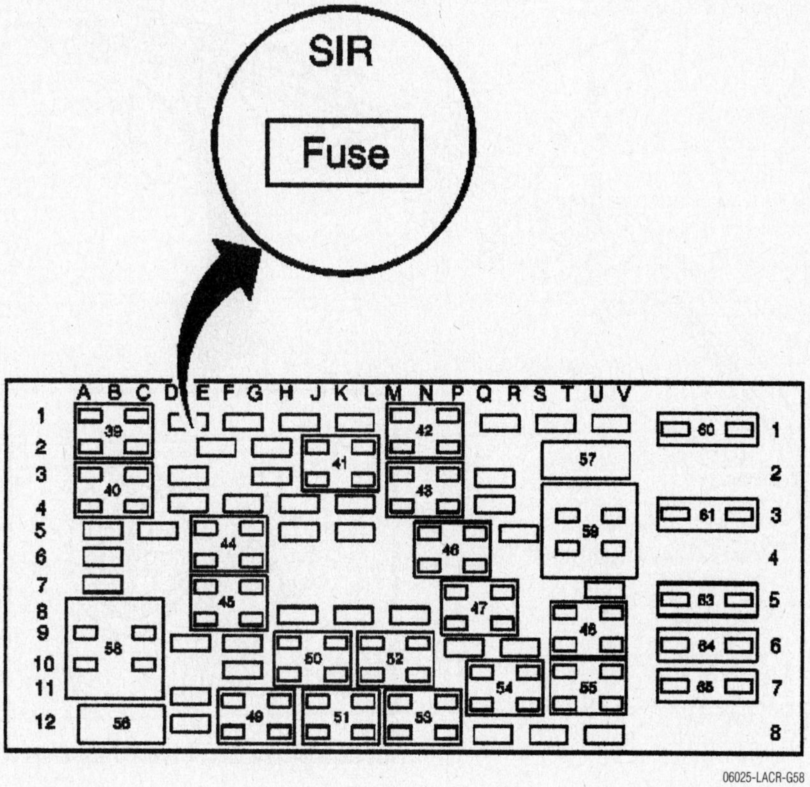

Fig. 13 SIR fuse

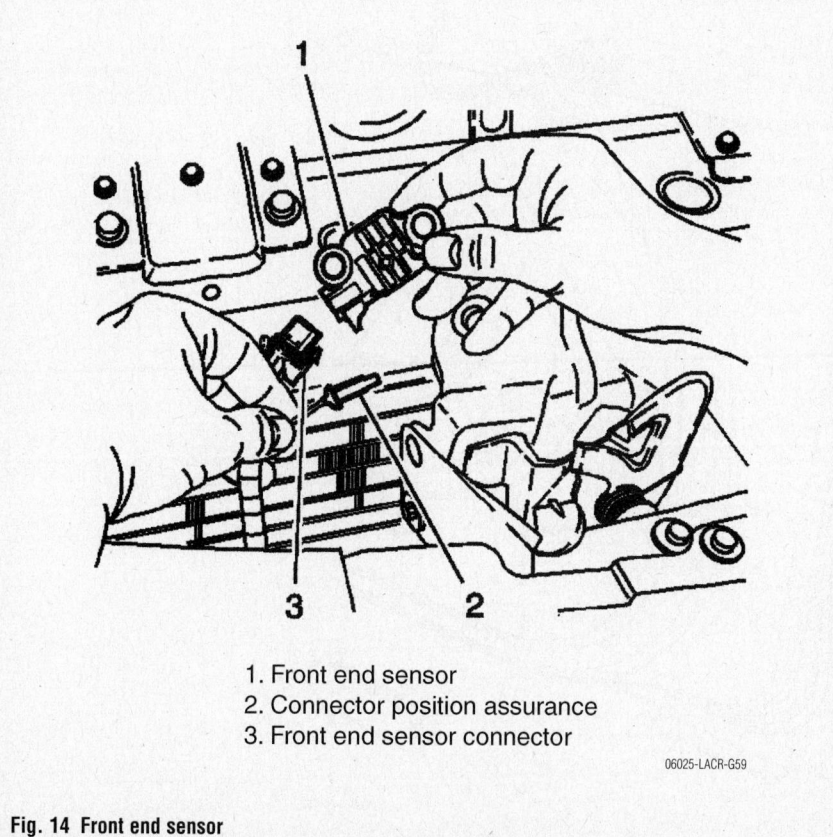

1. Front end sensor
2. Connector position assurance
3. Front end sensor connector

06025-LACR-G59

Fig. 14 Front end sensor

Zone 2

See Figures 15 and 16.

1. Remove the key from the ignition switch.

2. When enabling the SIS proceed to step 3, if the roof rail module needs enabling then go to step 7.

3. Install the left SIS connector (3) to the SIS (1).

4. Install the SIS CPA to the SIS connector (3).

5. Replace and secure the water deflector back over the SIS.

6. Install the left/driver door trim panel.

7. Connect the left roof rail module wiring harness yellow connector (2) to the left roof rail module (3).

8. Install the CPA to the left roof rail module connector (2).

9. Install the left rear panel.

10. Install the SIR Fuse.

11. Close the underhood fuse center cover.

12. Use caution while reaching in and turn the ignition switch to the ON position. The AIR BAG indicator will flash then turn OFF.

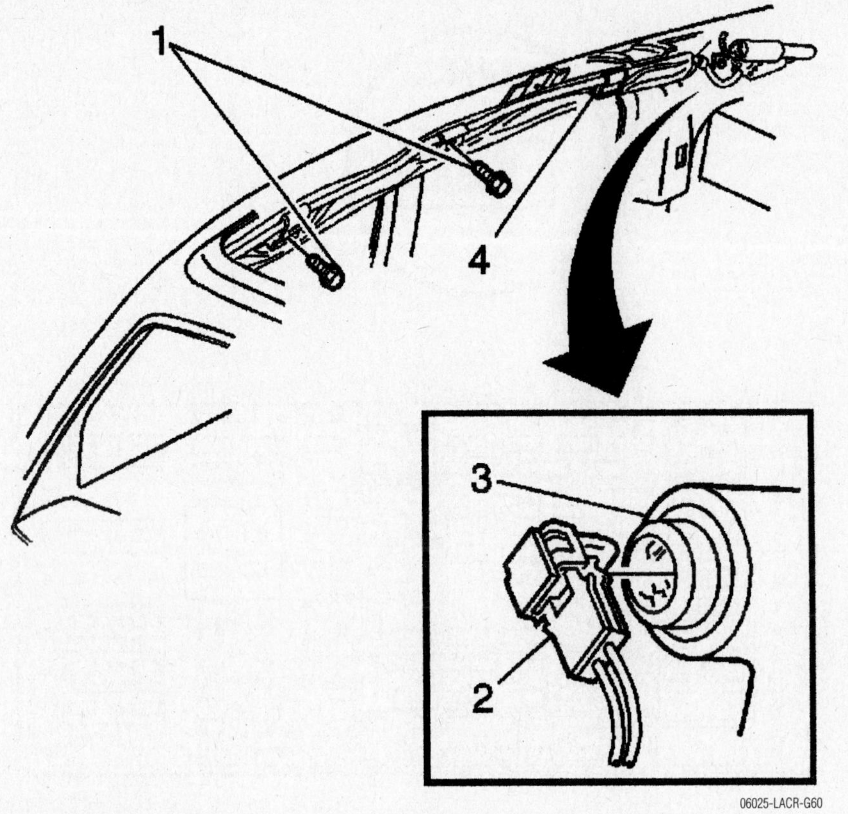

Fig. 15 Left roof rail module. Right similar.

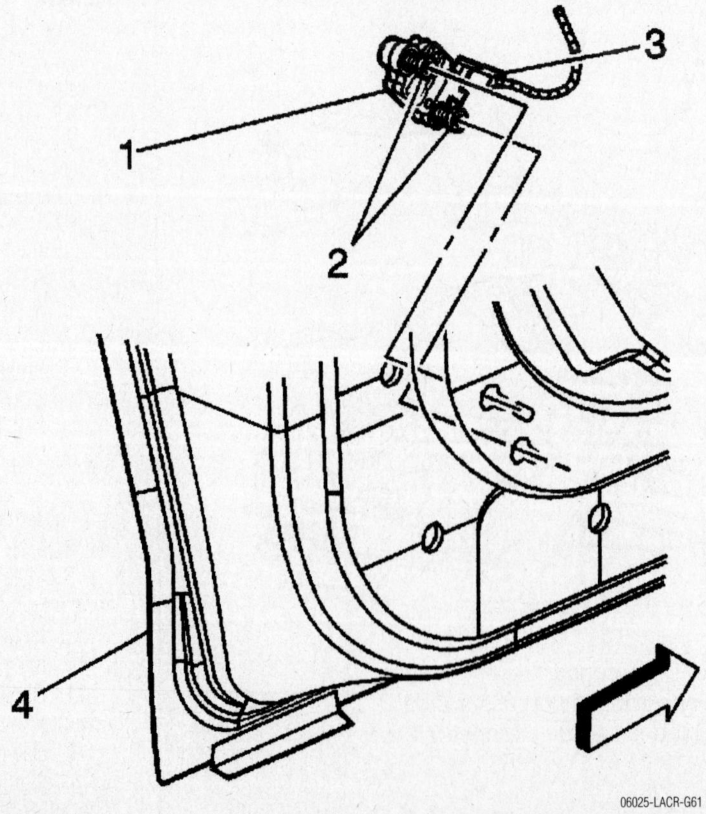

06025-LACR-G60

Fig. 16 Left side impact sensor. Right similar.

06025-LACR-G61

Zone 3

See Figure 17.

1. Remove the key from the ignition switch.

2. Connect the steering wheel module coil yellow connector (3) to the vehicle harness yellow connector (1).

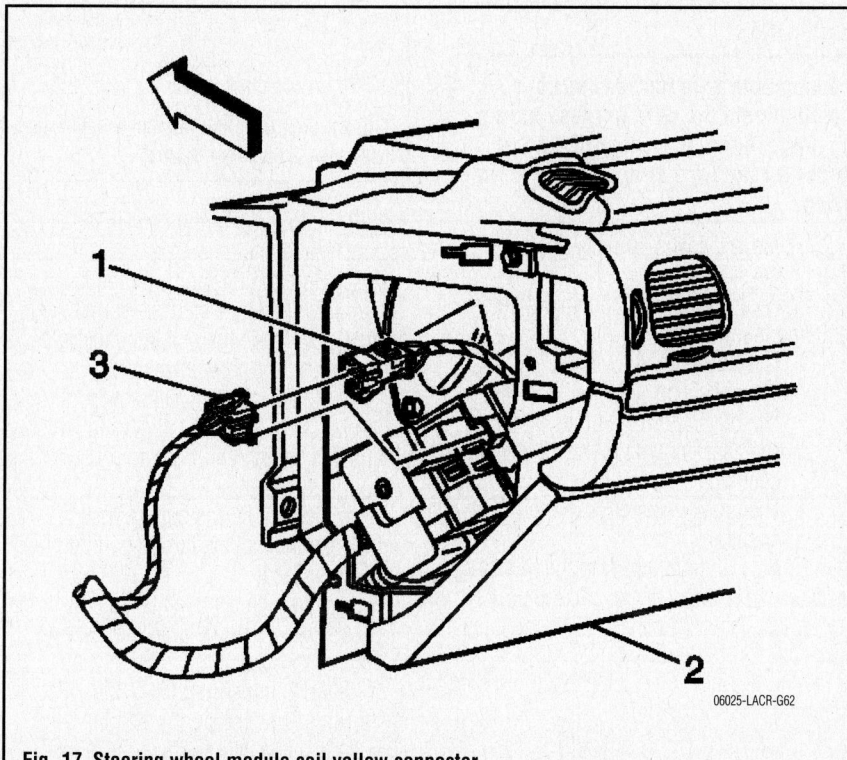

Fig. 17 Steering wheel module coil yellow connector

5. Install the SIR Fuse.

6. Close the underhood fuse center cover.

7. Use caution while reaching in and turn the ignition switch to the ON position. The AIR BAG indicator will flash then turn OFF.

3. Install the CPA to the steering wheel module coil yellow connector (1).

4. Install the left sound insulator to the I/P (2).

5. Install the SIR Fuse.

6. Close the underhood fuse center cover.

7. Use caution while reaching in and turn the ignition switch to the ON position. The AIR BAG indicator will flash then turn OFF.

Zone 5

See Figure 18.

1. Remove the key from the ignition switch.

2. Connect the I/P module yellow connector (1) to the vehicle harness yellow connector (2).

3. Install the CPA to the I/P module yellow connector (1).

4. Install the right sound insulator to the I/P (3).

Zone 6

1. Remove the key from the ignition switch.

2. When enabling the SIS proceed to step 3, if the roof rail module needs enabling then go to step 7.

3. Install the right SIS connector to the SIS.

4. Install the SIS CPA to the SIS connector.

5. Replace and secure the water deflector back over the SIS.

6. Install the right/passenger door trim panel.

7. Connect the right roof rail module wiring harness yellow connector to the right roof rail module.

8. Install the CPA to the right roof rail module connector.

9. Install the right rear panel.

10. Install the SIR Fuse.

11. Close the underhood fuse center cover.

12. Use caution while reaching in and turn the ignition switch to the ON position. The AIR BAG indicator will flash then turn OFF.

Zone 7

1. Remove the key from the ignition switch.

2. Connect the left seat belt pretensioner connector to the vehicle wiring harness connector (1).

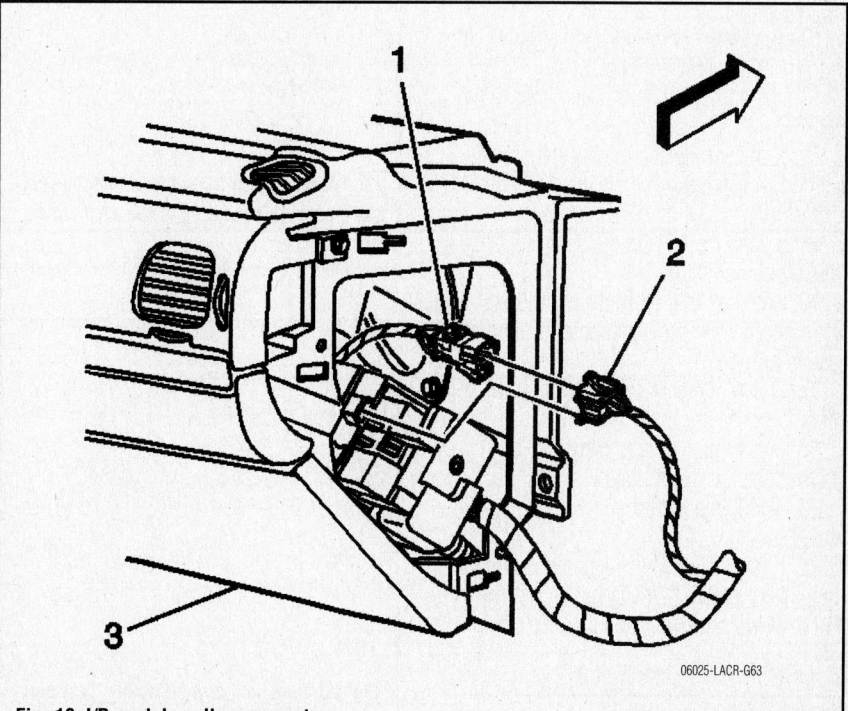

Fig. 18 I/P module yellow connector

3. Install the CPA to the seat belt pretensioner connector (1).

4. Install the SIR Fuse.

5. Close the underhood fuse center cover.

6. Use caution while reaching in and turn the ignition switch to the ON position. The AIR BAG indicator will flash then turn OFF.

Zone 9

1. Remove the key from the ignition switch.

2. When enabling the right/passenger seat belt pretensioner proceed to step 3, if the SDM needs enabling then use entire procedure.

3. Connect the seat belt pretensioner—right connector to the vehicle wiring harness connector.

4. Install the CPA to the seat belt pretensioner connector.

5. Connect the right roof rail module wiring harness yellow connector to the right roof rail module.

6. Install the CPA to the right roof rail module connector.

7. Install the right rear panel.

8. Connect the I/P module yellow connector to the vehicle harness yellow connector.

9. Install the CPA to the I/P module yellow connector.

10. Install the right sound insulator to the I/P.

11. Connect the steering wheel module coil yellow connector to the vehicle harness yellow connector.

12. Install the CPA to the steering wheel module coil yellow connector.

13. Install the left sound insulator to the I/P.

14. Connect the seat belt pretensioner—left connector to the vehicle wiring harness connector.

15. Install the CPA to the seat belt pretensioner connector.

16. Connect the left roof rail module wiring harness yellow connector to the left roof rail module.

17. Install the CPA to the left roof rail module connector.

18. Install the left rear panel.

19. Install the SIR Fuse.

20. Close the underhood fuse center cover.

21. Use caution while reaching in and turn the ignition switch to the ON position. The AIR BAG indicator will flash then turn OFF.

CLOCKSPRING CENTERING

See Figures 19 through 23.

1. Before servicing the vehicle, refer to the Precautions Section.

❋❋ CAUTION

The new Supplemental Inflatable Restraint (SIR) coil assembly will be centered. Improper alignment of the SIR coil assembly may damage the unit, causing an inflatable restraint malfunction.

➡**If a double wire harness strap is installed onto the wire harness assembly and column, you must reuse the holder for the wire straps during installation.**

2. Remove the wire harness strap(s) where necessary.

3. Verify the following conditions before centering the SIR coil:
- The wheels on the vehicle are straight ahead
- The block tooth (1) of the steering shaft assembly is in the 12 o'clock position
- The ignition switch is in the LOCK position

4. Style 1: If the front (5) of the SIR coil has a centering window (4), and the back

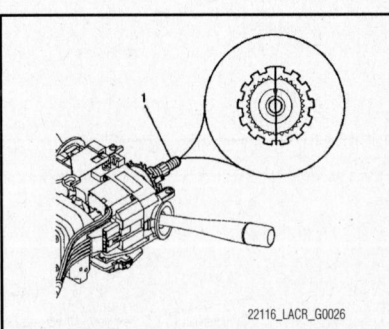

Fig. 19 The block tooth (1) of the steering shaft assembly must be in the 12 o'clock position

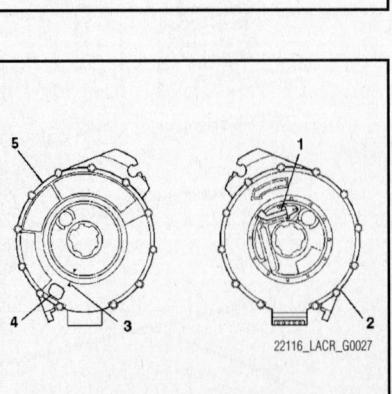

Fig. 20 Supplemental Inflatable Restraint (SIR) coil assembly—Style 1

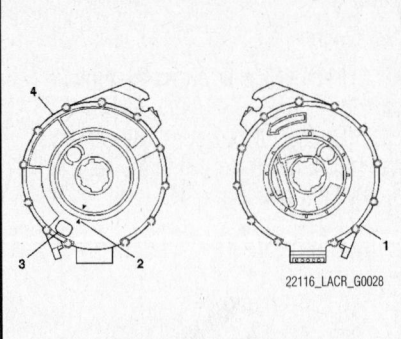

Fig. 21 Supplemental Inflatable Restraint (SIR) coil assembly—Style 2

side (2) includes a spring service lock (1), perform the following steps:

a. Hold the SIR coil with the face up.

b. While depressing the spring service lock, rotate the coil hub clockwise until the coil ribbon stops.

c. Rotate the coil hub slowly, counterclockwise, until the centering window appears yellow and both arrows (3) line up.

d. Release spring service lock between the locking tab. The SIR coil is now centered.

e. Align the centered SIR coil with the horn tower and slide onto the steering shaft assembly.

5. Style 2: If the front (4) of the SIR coil has a centering window (3), and the back side (1) includes NO spring service lock, perform the following steps:

a. Hold the SIR coil with the face up.

b. Rotate the coil hub clockwise until the coil ribbon stops.

c. Rotate the coil hub slowly, counterclockwise until the centering window appears yellow and both arrows (2) line up. This is the CENTER position.

d. While holding the coil hub in the CENTER position, align the SIR coil with

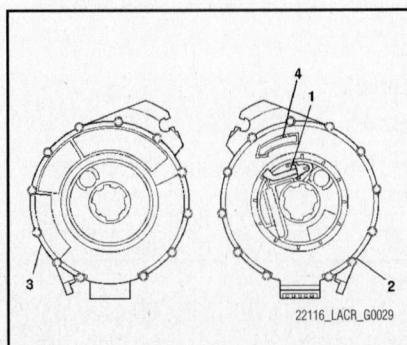

Fig. 22 Supplemental Inflatable Restraint (SIR) coil assembly—Style 3

the horn tower and slide onto the steering shaft assembly.

6. Style 3: If the front side (3) of the SIR coil has NO centering window, but the back side (2) includes a spring service lock (1), perform the following steps:

a. Hold the SIR coil with the back side up.

b. While depressing the spring service lock, rotate the coil hub in the direction of the arrow (4) until the coil ribbon stops.

c. Still pressing the spring service lock, rotate the coil hub in the opposite direction 2 ½ revolutions.

d. Release the spring service lock between locking tabs. The SIR coil is now centered.

e. Align the centered SIR coil with the horn tower and slide onto the steering shaft assembly.

7. Style 4: If the front side (2) of the SIR coil has NO centering window, and the back side (1) includes NO spring service lock, perform the following steps:

a. Hold the SIR coil with the face up.

b. Rotate the coil hub in the direction of the arrow until the coil ribbon stops.

c. Rotate the coil hub, slowly, counterclockwise, for 2 ½ revolutions. This is the CENTER position.

d. While maintaining the coil hub in the CENTER position, align the centered SIR coil with the horn tower and slide onto the steering shaft assembly.

8. If a double wire harness strap is installed onto the wire harness assembly and column, you must route the wires up against the steering column. One wire harness strap will surround one lead from the coil to the steering column. The other wire harness strap will surround all the leads to the steering column.

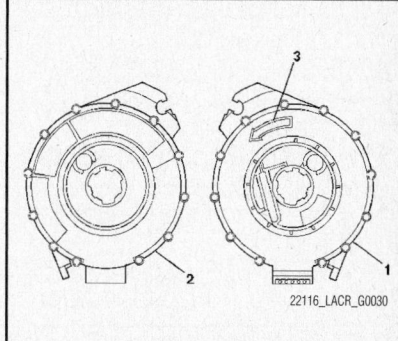

22116_LACR_G0030

Fig. 23 Supplemental Inflatable Restraint (SIR) coil assembly—Style 4

DRIVETRAIN

AUTOMATIC TRANSAXLE ASSEMBLY

REMOVAL & INSTALLATION
See Figure 24.

Tools Required:
*   J 41623-B Cooler Quick Connect Tool
*   J 42640 Steering Column Anti-Rotation Pin

❋❋ WARNING

The wheels of the vehicle must be straight ahead and the steering column in the LOCK position before disconnecting the steering column or intermediate shaft from the steering gear. Failure to do so will cause the SIR coil assembly to become uncentered, which may cause damage to the coil assembly.

1. Lock the steering column by installing J 42640 into the underside of the steering column.

2. Remove or disconnect the following:
*   The negative battery cable
*   The front compartment sight shield
*   The air cleaner assembly.
*   The range select cable terminal from the transaxle range select lever
*   The range selector cable bracket nuts
*   The range selector cable with bracket from the transmission case and position aside
*   The transaxle electrical connector C100

*   The wiring harness from the wiring harness retainer on the transaxle
*   The ground cable bolt from the transaxle

3. Install the engine support fixture.

4. Remove the upper engine to transaxle case bolts (2–5).

5. Raise and support the vehicle.

6. Remove or disconnect the following:
*   The front tire and wheel
*   The left front wheelhouse liner
*   The front air deflector
*   The stabilizer shaft links (control links)

7. Swing the stabilizer shaft downward in order to gain access to the power steering gear retaining bolts.

❋❋ WARNING

Failure to disconnect the intermediate shaft from the rack and pinion steering gear stub shaft can result in damage to the steering gear or to the

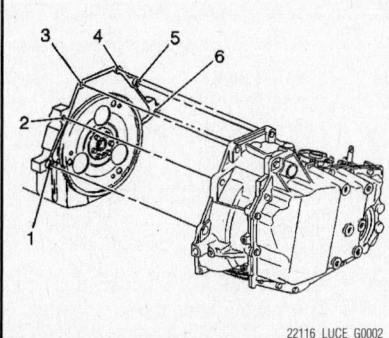

22116_LUCE_G0002

Fig. 24 Location of the upper engine to transaxle case bolts

intermediate shaft. This damage may cause loss of steering control, which could result in an accident and possible personal injury.

8. Remove the intermediate shaft lower pinch bolt.

9. Disconnect the intermediate shaft from the power steering gear.

10. Remove the power steering gear heat shield.

11. Remove the power steering gear mounting bolts.

12. Remove the power steering line retainers from the frame.

13. Secure the power steering gear to the exhaust manifold.

14. Remove the mounting bolts in order to allow removal of the brake pressure modulator valve from the bracket.

15. Remove the brake line retainers from the frame.

16. The following are exceptions while following the frame removal procedure:

a. Do not remove the front stabilizer shaft from the frame.

b. Do not remove the insulators from the frame.

c. Do not remove the control arms from the frame.

17. Remove or disconnect the following:
*   The front frame
*   The right and left drive axles from the transaxle. Refer to Halfshafts, removal & installation.
*   The transmission oil cooler hoses from the transaxle using the J 41623-B

- The transaxle fluid filler tube
- The torque converter cover

18. Mark the flywheel to converter relationship to ensure proper reassembly. Remove the flywheel to torque converter bolts.

19. Support the transaxle using an appropriate transaxle jack.

20. Remove or disconnect the following:
- The Vehicle Speed Sensor (VSS) electrical connector.
- The right engine to transaxle brace bolts
- The front transaxle to engine brace bolt
- The engine to transaxle case bolt (6) which is accessible through right wheel opening
- The remaining transaxle to engine bolt (1)
- The transaxle from vehicle using an appropriate transaxle jack
- The rear transaxle mount bracket from the transaxle
- The left transaxle mount bracket from the transaxle

21. Remove the automatic transaxle assembly.

To install:

22. Flush the transmission cooler and lines.

23. Install or connect the following:
- The left transaxle mount bracket to the transaxle
- The left transaxle bracket bolts. Tighten the bolts to 52 ft. lbs. (70 Nm)
- The rear transaxle mount bracket to the transaxle
- The rear transaxle mount bracket bolts. Tighten the bolts to 37 ft. lbs. (50 Nm)
- The transaxle into the vehicle and align the engine alignment dowels (1 and 5).
- The Install the transaxle case to engine bolts (1 and 6). Tighten the bolts to 55 ft. lbs. (75 Nm)
- The front transaxle to engine brace bolt. Tighten the bolt to 37 ft. lbs. (50 Nm)
- The right engine to transaxle brace bolts. Tighten the bolts to 37 ft. lbs. (50 Nm)
- The VSS electrical connector

24. Remove the transaxle jack.

➡ Align the mark made on the torque converter with the mark made on the flywheel made in the disassembly unless installing a new converter. Tighten all the torque converter to flywheel bolts twice.

25. Install or connect the following:
- The flywheel to torque converter bolts. Tighten the bolts to 47 ft. lbs. (63 Nm)
- The torque converter cover
- The transaxle fluid filler tube
- The transmission oil cooler hoses to the transaxle

✳✳ WARNING

Use care when installing the right side drive axle into the transaxle case. The splined shaft of the drive axle can easily damage the seal.

- The left and the right drive axle into the transaxle. Refer to Halfshafts, removal & installation
- The front frame assembly to the vehicle
- The left transaxle mount
- The brake pressure modulator valve into the bracket
- The brake pressure modulator valve mounting bolt. Tighten the bolt to 89 inch lbs. (10 Nm)
- The brake line retainers onto the frame
- The power steering gear mounting bolts. Tighten the bolts to 55 ft. lbs. (75 Nm)
- The power steering line retainers onto the frame
- The power steering gear heat shield

✳✳ CAUTION

When installing the intermediate shaft make sure that the shaft is seated prior to pinch bolt installation. If the pinch bolt is inserted into the coupling before shaft installation, the two mating shafts may disengage. Disengagement of the two mating shafts will cause loss of steering control which could result in personal injury.

- The intermediate shaft to the power steering gear
- The intermediate shaft lower pinch bolt. Tighten the bolt to 33 ft. lbs. (45 Nm)
- The stabilizer shaft links (control links)
- The air deflector extension
- The left front wheelhouse liner
- The front tire and wheel assembly. Tighten the wheel lug nuts to 100 ft. lbs. (136 Nm)

26. Lower the vehicle.

27. Install the upper transaxle case to engine bolts (2–5). Tighten the bolts to 55 ft. lbs. (75 Nm).

28. Remove the engine support fixture.

29. Install the range selector cable with bracket.

30. Install the range selector cable bracket nuts. Tighten the nuts to 18 ft. lbs. (25 Nm).

31. Install the range selector cable onto the range selector lever.

32. Check adjustment of the range selector cable. Re-adjust as needed.

33. Install or connect the following:
- The ground cable and bolt to transaxle. Tighten the bolt to 13 ft. lbs. (17 Nm)
- The transaxle electrical connector C100
- The wiring harness into the wiring harness retainer on the transaxle
- The air cleaner assembly
- The front compartment sight shield
- The negative battery cable

34. Remove the J 42640 from the steering column.

35. Fill the transaxle to the proper level.

36. Inspect for fluid leaks.

➡ It is recommended that Transmission Adaptive Pressure (TAP) information be reset. Resetting the TAP values using a scan tool will erase all learned values in all cells. As a result, The ECM, PCM or TCM will need to relearn TAP values. Transaxle performance may be affected as new TAP values are learned.

37. Clear Transmission Adaptive Pressures (TAPS).

38. Check the front end alignment.

39. Road test the vehicle and check for transaxle leaks.

HALFSHAFTS

REMOVAL & INSTALLATION
See Figure 25.

✳✳ CAUTION

To prevent personal injury and/or component damage, do not allow the weight of the vehicle to load the front wheels, or attempt to operate the vehicle, when the halfshaft(s) or halfshaft nut(s) are removed. To do so may cause the inner bearing race to separate, resulting in damage to brake and suspension components and loss of vehicle control.

Wheel drive shaft boots, seals and clamps should be protected from sharp objects any time service is performed on or near the halfshaft(s). Damage to the boot(s), the seal(s) or the clamp(s) may cause lubricant to leak from the joint and lead to increased noise and possible failure of the halfshaft.

1. Before servicing the vehicle, refer to the Precautions Section.
2. Raise and suitably support the vehicle.
3. Remove the wheel and the tire.
4. Remove the control link.
5. Remove the front halfshaft nut. Insert a drift or a flat-bladed tool into the caliper and the rotor to prevent the rotor from turning.
6. Disconnect the outer tie rod assembly from the steering knuckle.
7. Separate the ball joint from the steering knuckle.
8. Separate the front halfshaft from the front halfshaft bearing using a slidehammer and adapter.

To install

9. Install the front wheel drive axle into the transaxle.
10. Verify that the front halfshaft retaining ring is properly seated:
   • Grasp the inner housing and pull the inner housing outward. Do not

pull on the front wheel drive axle shaft.
   • The front wheel drive axle will remain in place when the front halfshaft retaining ring is properly seated.
11. Install the front wheel drive axle into the front halfshaft bearing.
12. Connect the ball joint to the steering knuckle.
13. Connect the outer tie rod assembly to the steering knuckle.
14. Install a new front halfshaft nut. Insert a drift or a flat-bladed tool into the caliper and the rotor to prevent the rotor from turning. Tighten the nut to 118 ft. lbs. (160 Nm).
15. Install the control link.
16. Install the wheel and the tire.
17. Lower the vehicle.
18. Inspect the transaxle fluid level.
19. Inspect the wheel alignment.

CV-JOINTS OVERHAUL

Inner (Tripod) Joint

See Figure 26.

1. Before servicing the vehicle, refer to the Precautions Section.
2. Raise and safely support the vehicle.
3. Remove or disconnect the following:
   • Front wheel
   • Halfshaft and place it in a vise
   • Small CV-joint boot clamp, cut and discard it

   • Large CV-joint boot clamp, cut and discard it
   • CV-joint boot by sliding it away from the tripod joint
   • Tripod housing from the tripod spider
   • Inboard spacer ring and slide it rearward on the shaft
   • Outboard retaining ring
   • Tripod joint spider assembly
   • Inboard spacer ring and discard it
   • Tripod joint spider assembly by tapping it from the halfshaft with a brass drift
   • Tripod spider retaining ring and discard it
   • Trilobal tripod bushing from the housing
   • CV-joint boot
4. Thoroughly clean and inspect all parts.

To install:

5. Install or connect the following:
   • Small boot clamp
   • CV-joint boot
   • New inboard spacer ring. Slide it rearward on the shaft past the 2nd groove
   • Tripod joint spider assembly onto the shaft until it passes the 2nd groove
6. Assemble the tripod spider assembly onto the halfshaft as follows:
   a. Position the tripod spider assembly onto the shop press plate.
   b. Position the halfshaft onto the tripod spider assembly, in the shop press.
   c. Press the halfshaft into the tripod spider assembly until the spider assembly passes the 2nd groove.

When assembling the tripod assembly onto the halfshaft, do not exceed 4,000 lbs. pressure.

7. Remove the halfshaft from the shop press and place it in vise.
8. Install or connect the following:
   • New outboard retaining ring into the axle shaft groove
   • Tripod joint spider assembly, slide it against the outboard retaining ring using a brass drift
   • Inboard spacer ring, seat it in the groove
9. Use ½ of the grease supplied in the kit into the boot and the other ½ into the tripod housing.
   • Trilobal tripod bushing flush with the tripod housing face

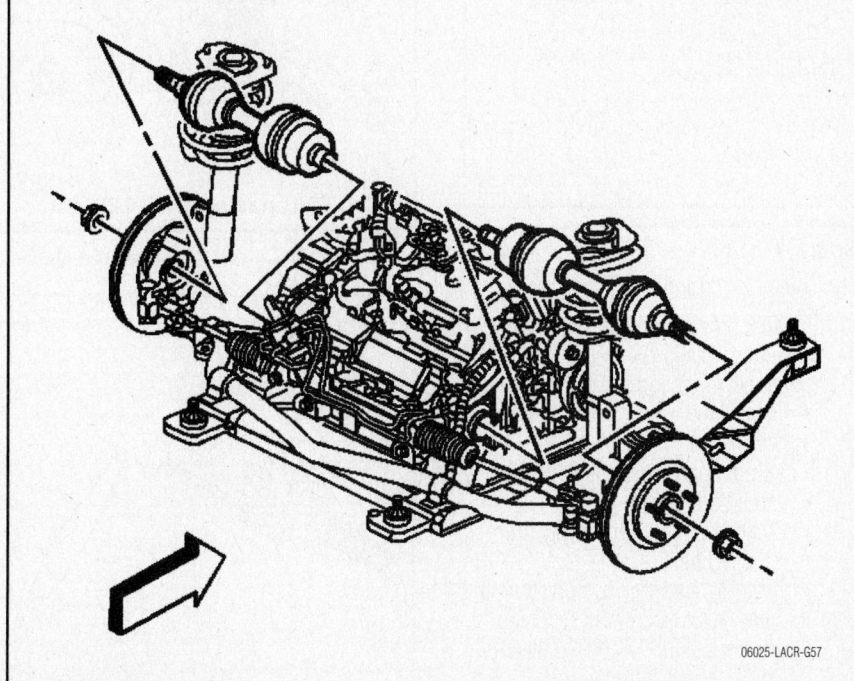

06025-LACR-G57

Fig. 25 Halfshaft removal

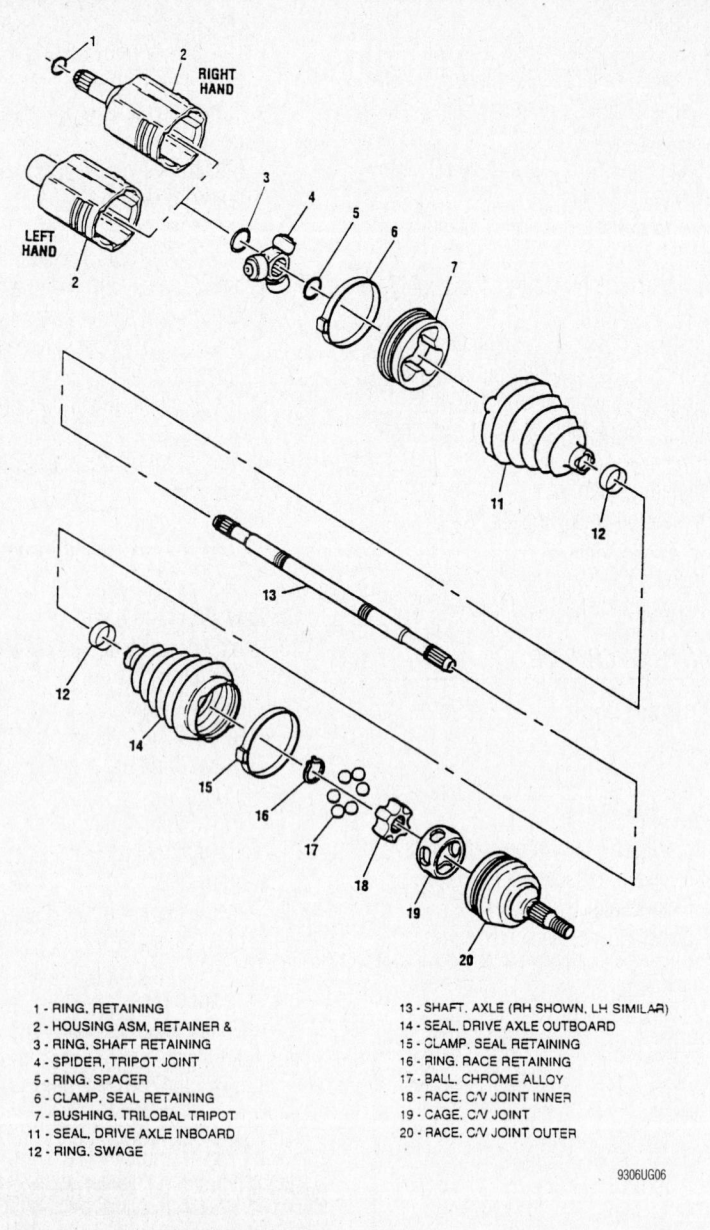

1 - RING, RETAINING
2 - HOUSING ASM, RETAINER &
3 - RING, SHAFT RETAINING
4 - SPIDER, TRIPOT JOINT
5 - RING, SPACER
6 - CLAMP, SEAL RETAINING
7 - BUSHING, TRILOBAL TRIPOT
11 - SEAL, DRIVE AXLE INBOARD
12 - RING, SWAGE

13 - SHAFT, AXLE (RH SHOWN, LH SIMILAR)
14 - SEAL, DRIVE AXLE OUTBOARD
15 - CLAMP, SEAL RETAINING
16 - RING, RACE RETAINING
17 - BALL, CHROME ALLOY
18 - RACE, C/V JOINT INNER
19 - CAGE, C/V JOINT
20 - RACE, C/V JOINT OUTER

9306UG06

Fig. 26 Exploded view of the halfshaft assembly

- New large seal clamp onto the CV-joint boot
- Tripod housing, slide it over the tripod joint spider assembly
- CV-joint boot/clamp, slide it into place, over the trilobal tripod bushing with the seal lip in the groove

➡**Make sure the boot lies flat against the trilobal bushing.**

10. Using the crimp tool, a torque wrench and a breaker bar, crimp the small CV-joint boot clamp to 100 ft. lbs. (136 Nm).

11. Using the crimp tool, latch the large CV-joint boot clamp.

12. Install the halfshaft and the front wheel.

Outer CV-Joint

See Figures 27 through 30.

1. Before servicing the vehicle, refer to the Precautions Section.

2. Remove or disconnect the following:
- Front wheel
- Halfshaft
- Swage ring using a hand grinder
- Large boot clamp
- CV-joint boot, slide it away from the CV-joint
- CV-joint assembly by spreading the inner race to axle shaft retaining ring ears using Snapring Pliers
- CV-joint boot from the axle shaft

3. Disassemble the chrome alloy balls from the CV-joint cage as follows:

a. Position a brass drift against the CV-joint cage and tap it with a hammer to tilt the cage.

b. Chrome alloy ball from the cage.

c. Tilt the cage in the opposite direction.

d. Remove the opposite chrome alloy ball.

e. Repeat the procedure until all 6 balls are removed.

4. Disassemble the CV-joint cage and inner race as follows:

a. Pivot the cage and race 90° to the center line of the outer race.

b. Align the cage windows with outer race lands.

c. Remove the cage from the outer race.

d. Rotate the inner race upward and remove it from the cage.

5. Thoroughly clean and inspect all parts.

To install:

6. Lubricate the parts with a light coat of grease.

7. Assemble the CV-joint cage and inner race, as follows:

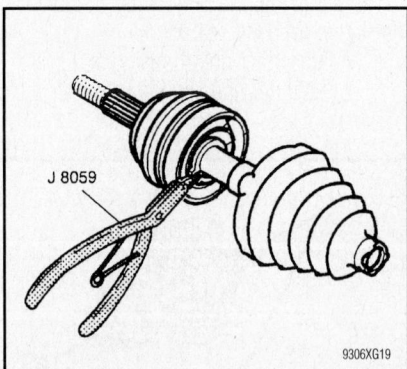

J 8059

9306XG19

Fig. 27 Disconnecting the outer CV-joint from the axle shaft

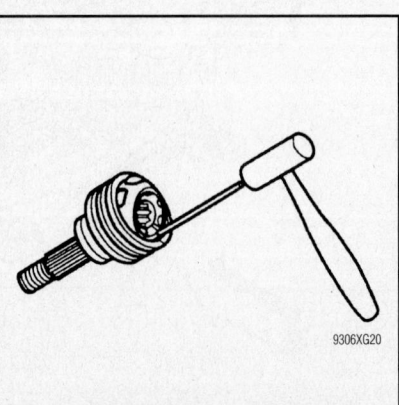

9306XG20

Fig. 28 Tilting the cage—Outer CV-joint

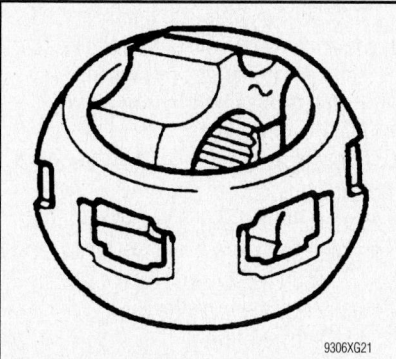

Fig. 29 View the cage and inner race—Outer CV-joint

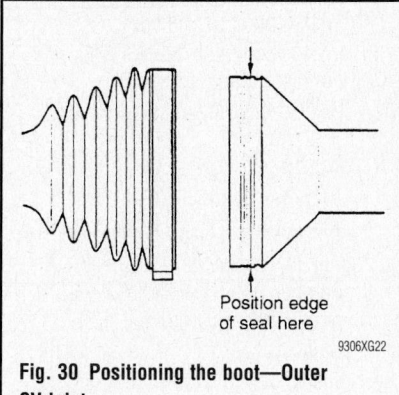

Position edge of seal here

Fig. 30 Positioning the boot—Outer CV-joint

a. Rotate the inner race 90° to the cage centerline.

b. Align the cage windows with inner race lands.

c. Insert the inner race into the cage by rotating the inner race downward.

d. Insert the cage/inner race into the outer race.

8. Assemble the chrome alloy balls into the CV-joint cage, as follows:

a. Position a brass drift against the CV-joint cage and tap it with a hammer to tilt the cage.

b. Insert the 1st chrome alloy ball into the cage.

c. Tilt the cage in the opposite direction.

d. Insert the opposite chrome alloy ball.

e. Repeat the procedure until all 6 balls are inserted.

9. Install or connect the following:
- Swage ring clamp
- CV-joint boot
- CV-joint onto the axle shaft until the retaining ring seats into the groove

10. Position the CV-joint boot seal into the axle shaft's joint seal groove and align the swage ring clamp on the boot.

11. Secure the swage ring clamp using appropriate crimping tool.

❈❈ WARNING

Make sure that there are no pinch points on the inboard seal.

12. Install or connect the following:
- ½ kit grease into the CV-joint boot
- ½ kit grease into the CV-joint
- New large seal clamp onto the CV-joint boot
- CV-joint boot/clamp, slide it into place, over the outer race with the seal lip in the groove

➡ **Make sure the boot lies flat against the outer race.**

13. Using a Crimp tool, a torque wrench and a breaker bar, crimp the large CV-joint boot clamp to 130 ft. lbs. (176 Nm).

14. Install the halfshaft and the front wheel.

CV-BOOTS INSPECTION

1. Before servicing the vehicle, refer to the Precautions Section.

2. Check the driveshaft boots for damage and deterioration.
- Raise front of vehicle
- Rotate axle and inspect for cracked or ripped CV boot material on inner and outer CV joints on both sides of vehicle
- Inspect for excessive grease deposits on or around the CV boot

3. Replace boot if damaged or deteriorated.

ENGINE COOLING

ENGINE FAN

REMOVAL & INSTALLATION

3.8L Engine

1. Disconnect the negative battery cable.

2. Remove the left and right engine mount struts.

3. Remove the air cleaner assembly.

4. Remove the Powertrain Control Module (PCM) harness retainer from the fan shroud.

5. Remove the transaxle oil cooler lines from the lower fan shroud clip and reposition the oil cooler lines aside.

6. Remove the fan shroud clip from the condenser tubes.

7. Remove the radiator upper bracket bolts and brackets.

8. Remove the cooling fan shroud bolts.

9. Remove the bolt that connects the fan shroud to the condenser hold down bracket.

10. Disconnect the engine cooling fan motors electrical connectors.

11. Remove the cooling fan electrical harness from the fan shroud clips.

12. Remove the cooling fan shroud.

13. Remove the engine cooling fan blade nut.

14. Remove the engine cooling fan blade.

❈❈ CAUTION

If a fan blade is bent or damaged in any way, do not repair or reuse the damaged part. Always replace a bent or damaged fan blade. Fan blades that have been damaged cannot be assured of proper balance and could fail and fly apart during subsequent use. This creates an extremely dangerous situation. The fan blades must remain in proper balance. You cannot assure fan blade balance once a fan blade has been bent or damaged. A fan blade that is not in proper balance could fail and fly apart during use, creating an extremely dangerous situation.

15. Inspect the cooling fan blades for bent or cracked blades, smoothness of the mating surfaces or burrs and other imperfections.

16. Remove the engine cooling fan motor bolts.

17. Remove the engine cooling fan motor.

To install:

18. Install the engine cooling fan motor.

19. Install the cooling fan motor bolts and tighten to 53 inch lbs. (6 Nm).

20. Install the engine cooling fan blade.

21. Install the engine cooling fan blade nut and tighten to 53 inch lbs. (6 Nm).

22. Ensure the lower edge of the fan shroud engages the clip at the bottom of the radiator.

23. Install the fan shroud.

24. Install the cooling fan shroud bolts and tighten to 53 inch lbs. (6 Nm).

25. Install the cooling fan electrical harness to the fan shroud clips.

26. Connect the engine cooling fan motors electrical connectors.

27. Install the fan shroud clip to the condenser tubes.

28. Install the bolt that connects the fan shroud to the condenser hold down bracket and tighten to 53 inch lbs. (6 Nm).

29. Install the radiator upper support brackets and bolts and tighten to 89 inch lbs. (10 Nm).

30. Install the transaxle oil cooler lines to the retainer at the bottom of the fan shroud.

31. Install the air cleaner assembly.

32. Install the PCM harness clip on to the fan shroud.

33. Install the engine mount struts.

34. Connect the negative battery cable.

35. Inspect the engine cooling fans for proper operation.

4.6L Engine

1. Disconnect the battery negative cable.

2. Remove the upper tie bar.

3. Drain the coolant.

4. Remove the engine oil cooler line bracket to fan shroud bolt.

5. Remove the engine oil cooler line bracket.

6. Remove the transaxle oil cooler pipe bracket to fan shroud bolt.

7. Remove the upper Transaxle Oil Cooler (TOC) line from the radiator.

8. Disconnect the wiring harness electrical connectors from the fan motors.

9. Reposition the hose clamp at the radiator outlet hose.

10. Remove the radiator outlet hose from the radiator.

11. Remove the 2 cooling fan mounting bolts.

12. Remove the lower TOC line from the radiator. Tilt the cooling fans toward the engine to access the TOC line nut.

13. Lift the fan assembly off the lower holding tabs.

14. Remove the fan assembly from the vehicle.

To install:

15. Install the fan assembly.

16. Insert the fan assembly into the lower radiator holding tabs.

17. Install the lower TOC line to the radiator. Tilt the cooling fans toward the engine

to access the TOC line. Tighten the fitting to 13 ft. lbs. (18 Nm).

18. Install the electric cooling fan mounting bolts and tighten to 80 inch lbs. (9 Nm).

19. Install the radiator outlet hose to the radiator.

20. Reposition the hose clamp at the radiator outlet hose.

21. Raise the vehicle.

22. Install the engine oil cooler bracket to the fan shroud.

23. Install the engine oil cooler bracket bolt and tighten to 89 inch lbs. (10 Nm).

24. Connect the wiring harness electrical connectors to the fan motors.

25. Install the upper TOC line to the radiator.

26. Install the transaxle oil cooler pipe bracket to fan shroud bolt and tighten to 89 inch lbs. (10 Nm).

27. Fill the cooling system.

28. Install the upper tie bar.

29. Connect the battery negative cable.

RADIATOR

REMOVAL & INSTALLATION

3.8L Engine

1. Drain the engine coolant.

2. Remove the upper radiator seal.

3. Remove the upper tie bar.

4. Disconnect the coolant overflow hose from the radiator.

5. Plug the coolant overflow hose.

6. Disconnect the upper and lower radiator hoses.

7. Remove the transaxle oil cooler pipe bracket bolt from the lower tie bar.

8. Remove the radiator cooling fan. Refer to Engine Fan, removal and installation.

9. Slide the plastic cap off the transaxle oil cooler pipe quick connect fittings.

10. Disconnect the upper and lower transaxle oil cooler pipes from the radiator.

11. Remove the A/C condenser mounting bolts.

12. Separate the condenser from the radiator.

13. Lift the radiator up and out of the vehicle.

To install:

14. Install the radiator to the vehicle. Place the bottom of the radiator in the lower pads.

15. Install the condenser to the radiator.

16. Install the A/C condenser mounting bolts and tighten to 115 inch lbs. (13 Nm).

17. Push the upper and lower transaxle oil cooler pipes into the radiator quick connect fittings, until a "click" is heard.

18. Tug gently on the cooler pipes to ensure proper retention.

19. Slide the plastic caps over the quick connect joints.

20. Install the radiator cooling fan. Refer to Engine Fan, removal and installation.

21. Install the transaxle oil cooler pipe bracket bolt to the lower tie bar and tighten to 89 inch lbs. (10 Nm).

22. Install the upper and lower radiator hoses.

23. Connect the coolant recovery hose to the radiator neck.

24. Install the upper tie bar.

25. Install the upper radiator seal.

26. Fill the cooling system.

27. Inspect the transmission oil level.

4.6L Engine

1. Drain the engine coolant.

2. Remove the radiator cooling fan. Refer to Engine Fan, removal and installation.

3. Remove the upper radiator seal.

4. remove the inlet radiator hose from the radiator.

5. Disconnect the lower engine oil cooler line from the radiator.

6. Disconnect the upper engine oil cooler line from the radiator.

7. Remove the headlamps.

8. Remove the condenser mounting bolts.

9. Lift the condenser upward slightly in order to release the lower feet from the lower mounting features located at the front of the radiator.

10. Lift the radiator up and out the vehicle.

To install:

11. Position the radiator alignment dowels to align with the insulators.

12. Position the condenser, aligning the lower feet to the lower mounting features located at the front of the radiator.

13. Install the condenser mounting bolts and tighten to 115 inch lbs. (13 Nm).

14. Install the headlamps.

15. Connect the lower engine oil cooler line to the radiator and tighten to 13 ft. lbs. (18 Nm).

16. Connect the upper engine oil cooler line to the radiator and tighten to 13 ft. lbs. (18 Nm).

17. Connect the inlet radiator hose to the radiator.

18. Install the upper radiator seal.

19. Install the radiator cooling fan. Refer to Engine Fan, removal and installation.

20. Fill the engine with coolant.

THERMOSTAT

REMOVAL & INSTALLATION

3.8L Engine

1. Remove the fuel injector sight shield.
2. Partially drain the cooling system.
3. Remove the radiator inlet hose from the water outlet housing.
4. Reposition the wiring harness from the water outlet housing stud.
5. Remove the water outlet housing bolt and the stud.
6. Remove the water outlet housing and the gasket.
7. Remove the thermostat.
8. Clean and Inspect the water outlet housing gasket mating surfaces.

To install:

9. Install the thermostat.
10. Install the gasket and the water outlet housing.
11. Install the water outlet housing bolt and the stud to the water outlet housing and tighten to 20 ft. lbs. (27 Nm).
12. Install the wiring harness to the water outlet housing stud.
13. Install the radiator inlet hose to the water outlet housing.
14. Fill the cooling system.
15. Install the fuel injector sight shield.

4.6L Engine

1. Partially drain the cooling system.
2. Remove the air cleaner assembly.
3. Remove the radiator outlet hose from the thermostat housing.
4. Remove the bolts securing the thermostat housing to the water pump inlet.
5. Remove the thermostat and the gasket from the water pump housing.

To install:

6. Install the thermostat and a new gasket into the water pump housing.
7. Install the thermostat housing.
8. Install the thermostat housing bolts and tighten to 89 inch lbs. (10 Nm).
9. Connect the radiator outlet hose to the thermostat housing.
10. Install the air cleaner assembly.
11. Fill the cooling system.

WATER PUMP

REMOVAL & INSTALLATION

3.8L Engine

See Figure 31.

1. Before servicing the vehicle, refer to the Precautions Section.

2. Drain the cooling system.
3. Remove or disconnect the following:
   * The negative battery cable
   * The accessory drive belt
   * The coolant hoses from the water pump
   * The water pump pulley bolts

➡ **The long bolt can be removed by aligning the bolt head up with the hole in the frame rail.**

   * The water pump pulley
   * The water pump bolts
   * The water pump

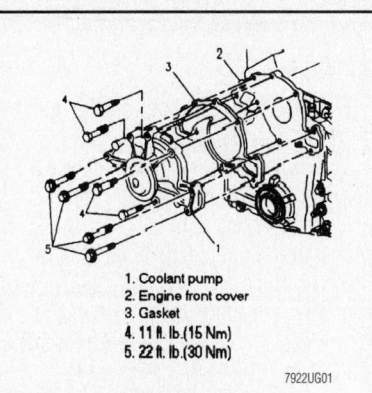

1. Coolant pump
2. Engine front cover
3. Gasket
4. 11 ft. lb. (15 Nm)
5. 22 ft. lb. (30 Nm)

7922UG01

Fig. 31 Exploded view of the water pump—3.8L engines

To install:

4. Apply a thin bead of sealer around the outside edge of the water pump.
5. Install or connect the following:
   * The water pump with a new gasket. Torque the water pump short bolts to 11 ft. lbs. (15 Nm) and the long bolts to 22 ft. lbs. (30 Nm).
   * The water pump pulley. Torque the bolts to 115 inch lbs. (13 Nm).
   * The coolant hoses to the water pump
   * The accessory drive belt
6. Refill and bleed the cooling system.
7. Run the engine and check for leaks.
8. Recheck the coolant level when the engine has cooled.

4.6L Engine

See Figures 32 and 33.

1. Drain the cooling system.
2. Remove or disconnect the following:
   * The upper filler panel
   * The air cleaner assembly
   * The secondary AIR injection control valve
   * The oil level indicator tube nut
   * The water pump belt shield fasteners

   * The water pump belt shield
   * The water pump drive belt
   * The radiator outlet hose from the thermostat housing
   * The water pump cover bolts
   * The water pump cover
   * The heater return hose

3. Position tool J 38816-A, or equivalent, to the water pump locking ears.
4. In order to ensure proper engagement of the tool to the water pump locking ears, fasten the support plate to the water housing crossover.
5. Using tool J 38816-A, or equivalent, turn the pump clockwise in order to remove the pump from the housing.
6. Remove the support plate from the water housing crossover.
7. Remove the water pump from the vehicle.
8. Remove the seal from the water crossover.
9. Clean the sealing surfaces of the water housing crossover and the pump cover.
10. Clean and inspect the water pump.

To install:

11. Insert the seal into the recessed portion of the water crossover.

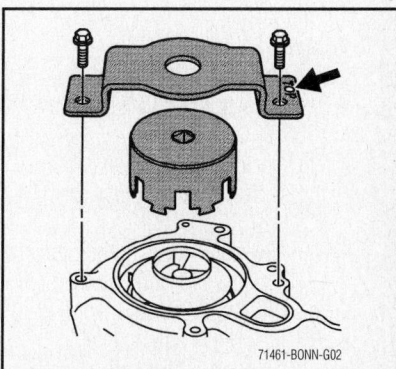

71461-BONN-G02

Fig. 32 Tool J 38816-A used on the water pump—4.6L engine

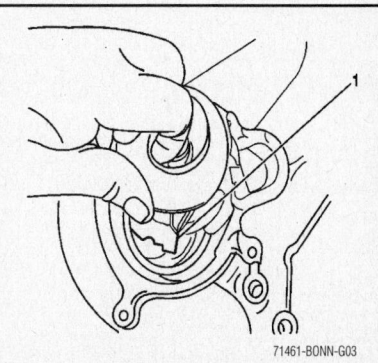

71461-BONN-G03

Fig. 33 The notched locking ear (1) must be in the 7 o'clock position

→**The notched locking ear (1) must be in the 7 o'clock position.**

12. Index the water pumps locking ears with the tangs in the water crossover.

13. Position tool J 38816-A, or equivalent, to the water pump locking ears.

14. Fasten the support plate to the water housing crossover, to ensure proper engagement of the tool to the water pump locking ears.

15. Turn tool J 38816-A, or equivalent, counterclockwise. Tighten the water pump to 74 ft. lbs. (100 Nm).

16. Remove the support plate from the water housing crossover.

17. Connect the water pump cover to the heater return hose.

18. Install the water pump cover to the water housing crossover.

19. Install the water pump cover bolts. Tighten the water pump cover bolts to 89 inch lbs. (10 Nm).

20. Connect the radiator outlet hose to the thermostat housing.

21. Install the water pump drive belt.

22. Place the water pump belt shield in position.

23. Install the water pump belt shield fasteners. Tighten the water pump belt shield fasteners to 89 inch lbs. (10 Nm).

24. Install the oil level indicator tube nut. Tighten the oil level indicator tube nut to 89 inch lbs. (10 Nm).

25. Install the secondary AIR injection control valve.

26. Install the air cleaner assembly.

27. Install the upper filler panel.

28. Fill the cooling system.

ENGINE ELECTRICAL

ALTERNATOR

REMOVAL & INSTALLATION

3.8L Engine

1. Before servicing the vehicle, refer to the Precautions Section.

2. Remove or disconnect the following:
   - The negative battery cable
   - The accessory drive belt
   - The fuel injector sight shield
   - The alternator brace
   - The electrical connections
   - The alternator bolts and the alternator

To install:

3. Install or connect the following:
   - The alternator and torque the bolts to 37 ft. lbs. (50 Nm)
   - The electrical connections and torque the nut to 111 inch lbs. (13 Nm)
   - The alternator brace. Torque the nut to 37 ft. lbs. (50 Nm) and the bolt to 22 ft. lbs. (30 Nm).
   - The fuel injector sight shield
   - The accessory drive belt
   - The negative battery cable

4.6L Engine

1. Before servicing the vehicle, refer to the Precautions Section.

2. Disconnect the battery negative cable.

3. Remove the drive belt.

4. Remove the engine cooling fans.

5. Disconnect the wiring harness connector from the alternator.

6. Reposition the protective boot from the alternator output BAT terminal for access.

7. Remove the alternator output BAT terminal nut and disconnect the positive lead from the alternator.

8. Loosen the lower alternator bolt.

9. Remove the alternator bolts from the alternator.

10. Remove the alternator from the vehicle.

To install:

11. Position the alternator to the A/C compressor and engine.

→**Use the correct fastener in the correct location. Replacement fasteners must be the correct part number for that application. Fasteners requiring replacement or fasteners requiring the**

CHARGING SYSTEM

use of thread locking compound or sealant are identified in the service procedure. Do not use paints, lubricants, or corrosion inhibitors on fasteners or fastener joint surfaces unless specified. These coatings affect fastener torque and joint clamping force and may damage the fastener. Use the correct tightening sequence and specifications when installing fasteners in order to avoid damage to parts and systems.**

12. Install the alternator mounting bolts. Tighten the alternator mounting bolts to 37 ft. lbs. (50 Nm).

13. Connect the wiring harness connector to the alternator.

14. Connect the battery positive lead and install the alternator output BAT terminal nut. Tighten the alternator output BAT terminal nut to 111 inch lbs. (13 Nm).

15. Press the protective boot on to the alternator output BAT terminal.

16. Install the engine cooling fans.

17. Install the drive belt.

18. Connect the battery negative cable.

FIRING ORDER

See Figures 34 and 35.

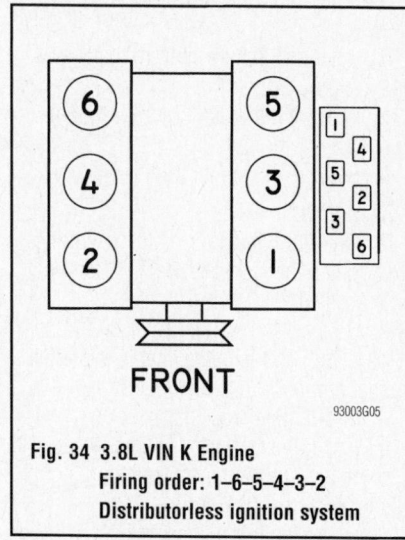

Fig. 34 3.8L VIN K Engine
Firing order: 1–6–5–4–3–2
Distributorless ignition system

93003G05

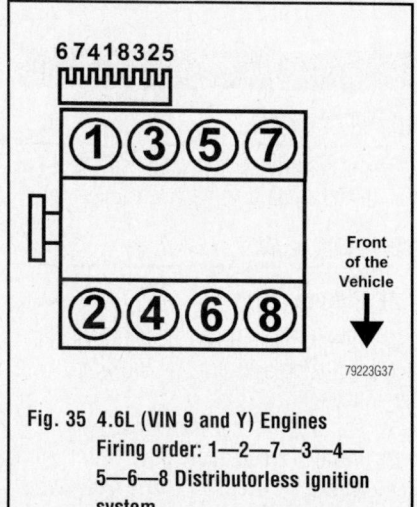

Fig. 35 4.6L (VIN 9 and Y) Engines
Firing order: 1—2—7—3—4—
5—6—8 Distributorless ignition
system

79223G37

IGNITION COIL

REMOVAL & INSTALLATION

3.8L Engine

1. Turn OFF the ignition.
2. Disconnect the spark plug wires from the coil assemblies.

3. Remove the screws securing the coil assemblies to the Ignition Control Module (ICM).
4. Remove the coils from the ICM.

To install:

5. Attach the coils to the ICM.
6. Install the ICM attaching screws and tighten to 40 inch lbs. (5 Nm).
7. Connect the spark plug wires to the coils assemblies.

4.6L Engine

1. Turn OFF the ignition.
2. Remove the fuel injector sight shield.
3. On bank 1, remove the ignition coil cover from the cam cover by lifting straight up, if equipped.
4. Disconnect the secondary Air Injection (AIR) vent solenoid electrical connector, if necessary, to gain access to the individual coil being serviced.
5. Remove the AIR check valve, if necessary, to gain access to the individual coil being serviced.
6. On bank 2, remove the upper filler panel, if necessary, to gain access to the individual coil being serviced. Remove the ignition coil cover from the cam cover by lifting straight up, if equipped.
7. On both banks, disconnect the ignition coil wiring harness electrical connector from the coil that needs to be replaced.
8. Remove the ignition coil retaining bolt.
9. Carefully remove the ignition coil.
10. If removal of all the coils are necessary, disconnect the main coil wiring harness at the cam cover.
11. Remove the coil assembly retaining bolts and studs.
12. Carefully remove the ignition coil assembly.

To install:

13. Carefully install the ignition coil assembly. Ensure that the spark plug seals are in position.
14. Install the ignition coil assembly retaining bolts and studs and tighten to 89 inch lbs. (10 Nm).

15. Connect the main coil wiring harness at the cam cover.
16. Install the ignition coil.
17. Install the ignition coil retaining bolt and tighten to 89 inch lbs. (10 Nm).
18. Reconnect the ignition coil electrical connector.
19. Install the ignition coil cover to the cam cover.
20. On bank 2, install the upper filler panel, if removed during disassembly.
21. On bank 1, install the AIR check valve.
22. Connect the AIR vent solenoid electrical connector.
23. On both banks, install the fuel injector sight shield.

IGNITION TIMING

ADJUSTMENT

The ignition timing is not adjustable, and is set according to engine demand electronically. The Powertrain Control Module (PCM) controls the ignition timing for all driving conditions.

SPARK PLUGS

REMOVAL & INSTALLATION

3.8L Engine

1. Disconnect the spark plug wires.
2. Use a spark plug socket and wrench to remove the spark plugs.
3. To install, reverse the removal procedure. Tighten the spark plugs to 11 ft. lbs. (15 Nm).

4.6L Engine

1. Remove the ignition coils. Refer to Ignition Coil, removal and installation.
2. Use a spark plug socket and wrench to remove the spark plugs.
3. To install, reverse the removal procedure. Tighten the spark plugs to 11 ft. lbs. (15 Nm).

ENGINE ELECTRICAL

STARTER

REMOVAL & INSTALLATION

3.8L Engine

See Figure 36.

1. Before servicing the vehicle, refer to the Precautions Section.
2. Remove or disconnect the following:
   - The negative battery cable
   - The flexplate inspection cover
   - The splash shield, if equipped
   - The electrical connectors
   - The transaxle cooler line clip from the transaxle, if necessary
   - The starter motor wiring
   - The starter motor bolts
   - The Starter

To install:

3. Install or connect the following:
   - The starter and torque the bolts to 32 ft. lbs. (43 Nm)
   - The wiring and torque the "B"

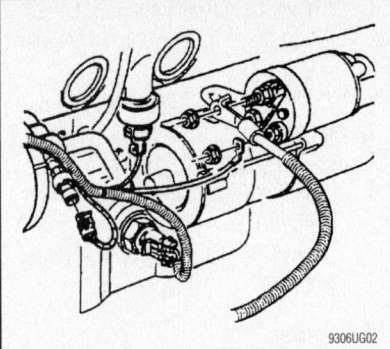

Fig. 36 Starter in place with wiring—3.8L engine

terminal nut to 89 inch lbs. (10 Nm) and the "S" terminal nut to 22 inch lbs. (3 Nm).
   - The flexplate inspection cover and torque the bolts to 62 inch lbs. (7 Nm)
   - The splash shield
   - The negative battery cable

STARTING SYSTEM

4.6L Engine

1. Disconnect the battery negative cable.
2. Remove the intake manifold.
3. Disconnect the BAT cable from the starter.
4. Disconnect the wire from the S terminal on the starter.
5. Remove the 2 starter motor mounting bolts.
6. Remove the starter motor.

To install:

7. Connect the starter motor S terminal wire. Tighten the starter solenoid S terminal nut to 35 inch lbs. (4 Nm).
8. Connect the starter motor BAT terminal wire. Tighten the battery cable to starter terminal nut to 89 inch lbs. (10 Nm).
9. Install the starter motor.
10. Install the starter motor mounting bolts. Tighten the starter motor mounting bolts to 22 ft. lbs. (30 Nm).
11. Install the intake manifold.
12. Connect the battery negative cable.

ENGINE MECHANICAL

➡ Disconnecting the negative battery cable may interfere with the functions of the on board computer systems and may require the computer to undergo a relearning process, once the negative battery cable is reconnected.

ACCESSORY DRIVE BELTS

ACCESSORY BELT ROUTING

See Figures 37 and 38.

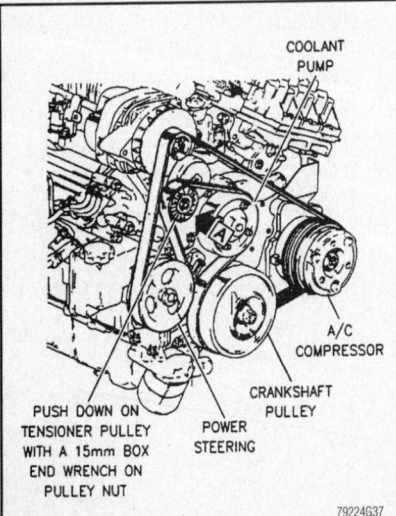

PUSH DOWN ON TENSIONER PULLEY WITH A 15mm BOX END WRENCH ON PULLEY NUT

COOLANT PUMP

A/C COMPRESSOR

CRANKSHAFT PULLEY

POWER STEERING

Fig. 37 Accessory drive belt routing—3.8L (VIN K) engine

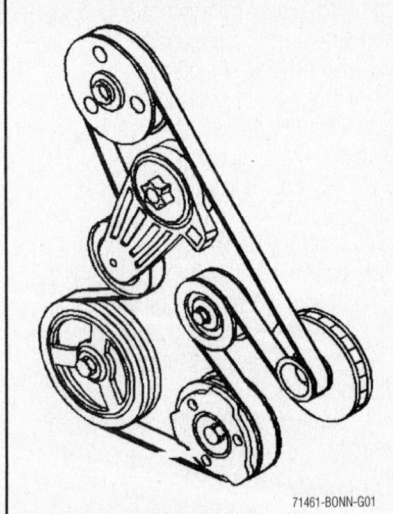

Fig. 38 Accessory drive belt routing—4.6L (VIN Y) engine

INSPECTION

Inspect the accessory drive belt for signs of glazing or cracking. A glazed belt will be perfectly smooth from slippage, while a good belt will have a slight texture of fabric visible. Cracks will usually start at the inner edge of the belt and run outward. All worn or damaged accessory drive belts should be replaced immediately.

ADJUSTMENT

The accessory drive belt adjustment is maintained by an automatic tensioner.

REMOVAL & INSTALLATION

3.8L Engine

1. Lift or rotate the accessory drive belt tensioner using a 15mm box end wrench on the pulley nut.
2. Remove the accessory drive belt.
3. Install the accessory drive belt.
4. Rotate the accessory drive belt tensioner using a 15mm box end wrench on the pulley nut.

4.6L Engine

See Figure 39.

1. Install a ½ inch extension onto the drive belt tensioner.
2. Push down on the extension to release tension.
3. Remove the drive belt from the power steering pump.
4. Slowly return the tensioner to the original position.
5. Remove the belt.

To install:

6. Thread the drive belt through all the pulleys except for the power steering pump and the drive belt tensioner.

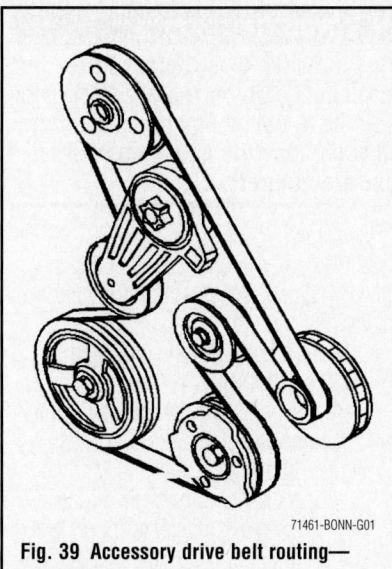

Fig. 39 Accessory drive belt routing—
4.6L (VIN Y) engine

7. Insert a ½ inch drive extension into the drive belt tensioner.

8. Push down on the tensioner and feed the belt around the tensioner wheel.

9. With the tension applied, complete the belt routing. Make sure the belt is properly seated in all pulleys.

10. Slowly return the tensioner back to its original position. This will apply tension to the drive belt.

11. After the installation, inspect the belt for the proper routing and the correct alignment.

12. Start the engine and check for proper belt and accessory operation.

BALANCE SHAFT

REMOVAL & INSTALLATION

3.8L Engine

See Figures 40 through 43.

1. Before servicing the vehicle, refer to the Precautions Section.

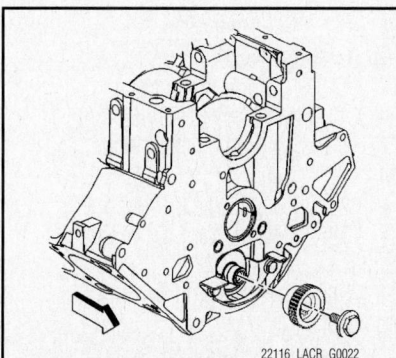

Fig. 40 Remove the balance shaft driven gear bolt—3.8L Engine

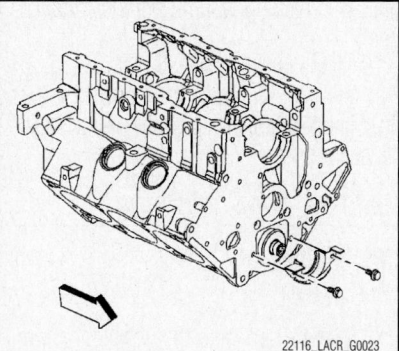

Fig. 41 Remove the balance shaft retainer bolts—3.8L Engine

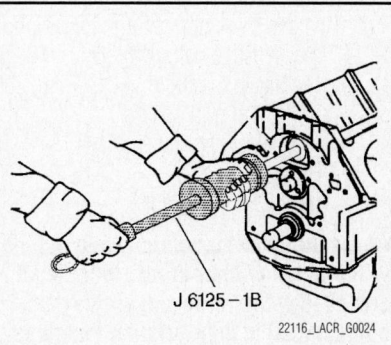

Fig. 42 Use J 6125-1B to remove the balance shaft—3.8L Engine

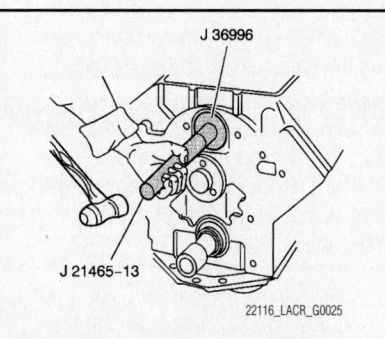

Fig. 43 Use J 21465-13 and J 36996 to install the balance shaft into the engine block—3.8L Engine

2. Remove the balance shaft driven gear bolt.

3. Remove the balance shaft driven gear.

4. Remove the balance shaft retainer bolts.

5. Remove the balance shaft retainer.

6. Use the slide hammer, J 6125-1B, to remove the balance shaft.

To install:

7. Use J 21465-13 and J 36996 to install the balance shaft into the engine block.

8. Install the balance shaft retainer.

→Use the correct fastener in the correct location. Replacement fasteners must be the correct part number for that application. Fasteners requiring replacement or fasteners requiring the use of thread locking compound or sealant are identified in the service procedure. Do not use paints, lubricants, or corrosion inhibitors on fasteners or fastener joint surfaces unless specified. These coatings affect fastener torque and joint clamping force and may damage the fastener. Use the correct tightening sequence and specifications when installing fasteners in order to avoid damage to parts and systems.

9. Install the balance shaft retainer bolts. Tighten the bolts to 22 ft. lbs. (30 Nm).

10. Install the balance shaft driven gear.

11. Install the balance shaft driven gear bolt. Tighten the bolt:

a. Step 1: 16 ft. lbs. (22 Nm).

b. Use J 45059 to tighten the bolt an additional 70°.

12. Using J 8001, measure the balance shaft end play. End play must not exceed 0.008 in. (0.028mm).

13. Using J 8001, measure the balance shaft radial play at the rear. Radial play must be between 0.0005–0.0047 in. (0.0127–0.119mm).

14. Install the balance shaft drive gear.

15. Install the camshaft sprocket.

16. Turn the camshaft so the timing mark on the camshaft sprocket is straight down.

17. Remove the camshaft sprocket and balance shaft drive gear.

18. Turn the balance shaft so the timing mark on the balance shaft driven gear points straight down.

19. Partially install the balance shaft drive gear so the gear teeth are not engaged.

20. Align the marks on the balance shaft driven gear and the balance shaft drive gear. Do this by turning the balance shaft.

21. Once the marks are aligned, fully seat the balance shaft drive gear and engage the gear teeth.

22. Turn the crankshaft so the number one piston is at Top Dead Center (TDC).

23. Install the timing chain and camshaft sprocket.

24. Using J 8001, measure the gear lash at four places. Measure every quarter turn. Gear lash must be between 0.002–0.005 in. (0.050–0.127mm).

CAMSHAFT AND VALVE LIFTERS

INSPECTION

3.8L Engine

1. Clean the camshaft in solvent.
2. Measure the camshaft journals with a micrometer. If the camshaft journals are not within specifications, replace the camshaft. The measurement should be 1.8462–1.8448 inch (47.655–46.858mm). If the measurement is not within specifications the engine camshaft must be replaced.
3. Measure the camshaft runout using a Magnetic Base Indicator Set J-7872.
4. Mount the camshaft in V-blocks between centers.
5. Check the intermediate camshaft journal.
6. If the camshaft journals are more than 0.0010 (0.025mm) out-of-round, then replace the engine camshaft.

4.6L Engine

1. Clean the camshaft in solvent.
2. Dry the camshaft with compressed air.
3. Cover the camshafts with a clean oil soaked towel in order to prevent corrosion.
4. Inspect the camshaft sprocket locating pin for damage or wear.
5. Inspect the threads for the camshaft sprocket bolt.
6. Inspect the camshaft lobes and journals for excessive scoring or pitting, discoloration from heat or deformation from excessive wear.
7. Inspect the left intake camshaft for the following additional conditions excessive wear on the camshaft seal surface or damage to the threads for the water pump pulley bolt.
8. If any of the above conditions exist on the camshaft, replace the camshaft.
9. Measure the camshaft journals for diameter and out-of-round using an outside micrometer.
10. If the diameter is smaller than 1.061 inches (26.948mm), replace the camshaft. If out-of-round exceeds 0.022 inch (0.0009mm), replace the camshaft.
11. Measure the camshaft runout. If runout exceeds 0.0020 inch, (0.050mm), replace the camshaft.
12. Measure the camshaft lobe wear using a dial indicator.
13. Place the indicator tip on the base circle of the camshaft lobe.
14. Place the dial at zero.
15. Rotate the camshaft until the indicator tip is at the highest point on the lobe. This reading is the lift of the camshaft lobe.
16. If the lift exceeds 0.2423 inch (6.154mm) for the intake lobe, or 0.2336 inch (5.944mm) for the exhaust lobe, replace the camshaft.

REMOVAL & INSTALLATION

3.8L Engine

See Figure 44.

1. Before servicing the vehicle, refer to the Precautions Section.
2. Relieve the fuel system pressure.
3. Remove the engine and mount it on an engine stand.
4. Remove or disconnect the following:
   - The negative battery cable
   - The intake manifold
   - The rocker arm covers
   - The rocker arm assemblies
   - The pushrods
   - The lifters and guides

➡A magnet may be helpful when pulling the lifters out of their bores. Identify all parts as they are removed, so they can be reinstalled in their original locations.

   - The crankshaft damper
   - The timing chain front cover
5. Set the engine to Top Dead Center (TDC) No. 1 cylinder (firing position) to align the timing marks, before disassembling the timing chain and sprockets.

✳✳ WARNING

Align the timing marks of the camshaft and crankshaft sprockets to avoid burring the camshaft journals by the crankshaft.

6. Remove or disconnect the following:
   - The camshaft sprocket and timing chain
   - The camshaft thrust plate
   - The camshaft

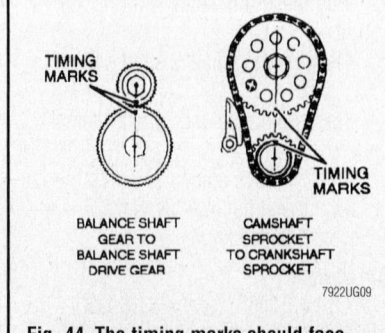

Fig. 44 The timing marks should face each other when the chain and gears are installed properly

✳✳ WARNING

If the camshaft was replaced the lifters must also be replaced. The old lifters have developed a wear pattern and will cause the new camshaft to wear prematurely.

To install:

7. Coat the camshaft lobes and bearings with camshaft break-in prelube prior to installation.
8. Install or connect the following:
   - The camshaft
   - The camshaft thrust plate. Torque the bolts to 10 ft. lbs. (14 Nm).
   - The camshaft sprocket and timing chain with timing marks aligned. Torque the camshaft sprocket bolt to 74 ft. lbs. (100 Nm) plus an additional 90° (¼) turn.
   - The timing chain front cover
   - The crankshaft damper. Torque the mounting bolt to 111 ft. lbs. (150 Nm). plus an additional 76° turn.
9. Coat the valve lifters with camshaft break-in prelube.
10. Install or connect the following:
    - The valve lifters
    - The lifter guides and lifter guide retainer. Torque the retainer mounting bolts to 22 ft. lbs. (30 Nm).
    - The pushrods and rocker arms. Torque the rocker arm bolts to 11 ft. lbs. (15 Nm) plus an additional 90° turn.
    - The rocker arm covers
    - The intake manifold
    - The engine
    - The negative battery cable
11. Verify that all fluid levels are full and correct.
12. Start the engine and check for leaks. Check engine operation.

4.6L Engine

Left Side

See Figures 45 through 55.

Tools Required
- J 45059 Torque Angle/Meter
- J 44212 Camshaft Holding Tool
- EN 46327 Timing Chain Retention Tool
- J 38185 Hose Clamp Pliers
- J 38823 Water Pump Drive Pulley Installer
- J 38825 Water Pump Drive Pulley Remover

1. Remove the fuel injector sight shield.
2. Partially drain the cooling system.
3. Position tool J 38185 to the clamp in

order to remove the radiator inlet hose from the water housing crossover.

4. Disconnect the PCV fresh air tube from the camshaft cover.

5. Remove the ignition coil cassette.

6. Remove the 4 spark plug boots.

7. Disconnect the cable harness clips at the front of the camshaft cover and position the cable harness aside.

8. Remove the secondary AIR valve bracket nut closest to the center of the engine.

9. Pry outward slightly on the secondary AIR valve bracket in order to gain clearance to remove the water pump drive belt shield nut.

10. Remove the water pump drive belt shield fasteners.

11. Remove the water pump drive belt shield.

12. Disconnect the water pump drive belt.

13. Loosen the 2 bolts attaching the water pump belt tensioner to the water crossover.

14. Remove the water pump belt tensioner .

15. Remove the plastic dust cap from the end of the intake camshaft.

16. Remove the water pump drive pulley from the intake camshaft using tool J 38825.

17. Remove the 3 camshaft seal retainer bolts.

➡**DO NOT reuse the camshaft seal.**

18. Remove the camshaft seal.

19. Remove the camshaft cover bolts.

20. Lift the camshaft drive end of the camshaft cover up.

21. Remove the camshaft cover reward to clear the water pump drive shaft.

22. Discard the camshaft cover perimeter seals and spark plug seals if there is any evidence of damage or if the seal comes out of the groove in the cover during removal.

23. Clean and inspect the camshaft cover.

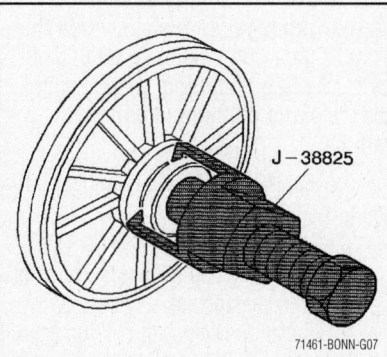

Fig. 45 Remove the water pump drive pulley from the intake camshaft using tool J 38825—4.6L engine

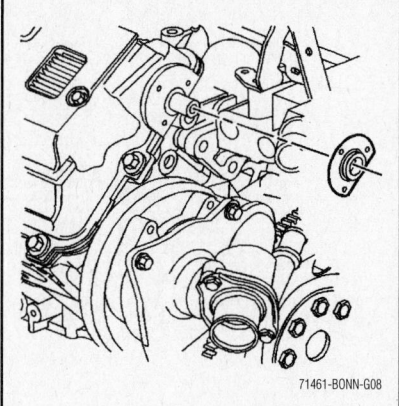

Fig. 46 Remove the camshaft seal—4.6L engine

24. Rotate the crankshaft to TDC of the no. 1 1 cylinders compression stroke, both camshaft sprocket drive pins should be at the top of their rotation.

✳✳ CAUTION

The camshaft holding tools must be installed on the camshafts to prevent camshaft rotation. When performing service to the valve train and/or timing components, valve spring pressure can cause the camshafts to rotate unexpectedly and can cause personal injury.

25. Install tool J 44212 over the camshafts.

26. Use a paint stick to create a mark on the timing chain link adjacent to each camshaft sprocket timing mark.

27. Install the timing chain retention tools using the procedure below:

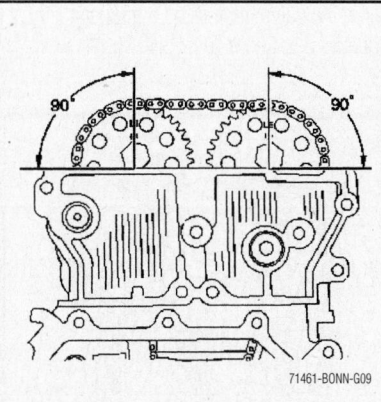

Fig. 47 Rotate the crankshaft to TDC of the no. 1 cylinders compression stroke, both camshaft sprocket drive pins should be at the top of their rotation—4.6L engine

Fig. 48 Install tool J 44212 over the camshafts—4.6L engine

Fig. 49 Use a paint stick to create a mark on the timing chain link adjacent to each camshaft sprocket timing mark—4.6L engine

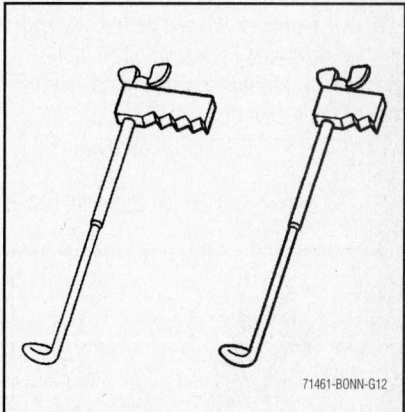

Fig. 50 Timing chain retention tools— 4.6L engine

a. Rotate the wing nut to the top of its travel.

b. Position the bottom retention tool on the cylinder head with the V-notch of the block adjacent to the left exhaust camshaft sprocket and chain.

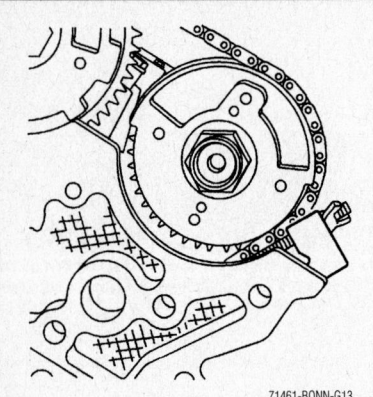

Fig. 51 Position the bottom retention tool on the cylinder head with the V-notch of the block adjacent to the left exhaust camshaft sprocket and chain—4.6L engine

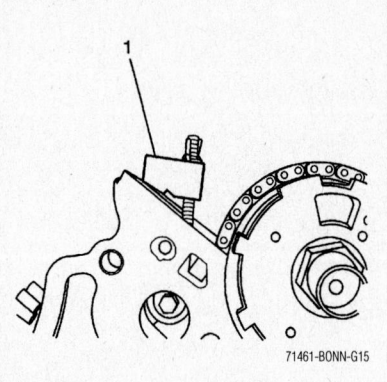

Fig. 53 Position the top retention tool on the cylinder head with the V-notch of the block adjacent to the left intake camshaft sprocket and chain—4.6L engine

c. Insert the hook end into a secondary timing chain link as shown.

d. Rotate the wing nut until it contacts the retention tool block. DO NOT tighten the wing nut at this time.

e. Rotate the wing nut to the top of its travel.

f. Position the top retention tool on the cylinder head with the V-notch of the block adjacent to the left intake camshaft sprocket and chain.

g. Insert the hook end into a secondary timing chain link as shown.

h. Rotate the wing nut until it contacts the retention tool block. Alternately tighten both wing nuts to retain the chain.

28. Use an open wrench on the hex cast into the camshafts in order to prevent the camshafts from rotating when removing the camshaft sprocket bolts.

29. Remove the camshaft sprocket bolts.

30. Remove the camshaft sprockets.

31. Alternately loosen the camshaft bearing cap bolts a few turns at a time until all valve spring pressure has been released.

32. Remove the camshaft bearing caps.

33. Remove tool J 44212 from the camshafts.

34. Remove the camshafts.

35. Remove the camshaft followers.

36. Clean and inspect the camshafts.

To install:

37. Apply a liberal amount of lubricant GM P/N 12345001 or equivalent to the roller pivot pocket and valve slot areas of the camshaft followers.

➡ **The follower must be positioned squarely on the valve tip so that the full width of the roller will completely contact the camshaft lobe. If the followers are being reused you must put them back in their original location.**

38. Place the camshaft followers in position on the valve tip and the Stationary Hydraulic Lash Adjusters (SHLA). The

rounded head of the follower goes on the SHLA, while the flat end goes on the valve tip.

39. Clean the camshaft carriers with a clean, lint-free cloth.

40. Apply a liberal amount of lubricant GM P/N 12345001 or equivalent to the camshaft carriers, camshaft lobes and the camshaft journals.

41. Place the camshaft in the camshaft carriers with the camshaft sprocket drive pins near the top of their rotation and the camshaft lobes in a neutral position. The camshafts can be identified by a stamping near the rear journal. For example: L-EXH is defined as Left bank Exhaust.

42. Observe the markings on the camshaft bearing caps. Each camshaft bearing cap is marked in order to identify its location. The markings have the following meanings:

- The arrow should point to the front of the engine.
- The number indicates the position from the front of the engine.
- The "E" indicates the exhaust camshaft.
- The "I" indicates the Intake camshaft.

43. Apply a liberal amount of lubricant GM P/N 12345001 or equivalent to the camshaft bearing caps.

44. Install the camshaft bearing caps according to the identification marks.

➡ **Use the correct fastener in the correct location. Replacement fasteners must be the correct part number for that application. Fasteners requiring replacement or fasteners requiring the use of thread locking compound or sealant are identified in the service procedure. Do not use paints, lubricants, or corrosion inhibitors on fasteners or fastener joint surfaces unless specified. These coatings affect fastener torque and joint clamping force and may damage the fastener. Use the correct tightening sequence and specifications when installing fasteners in order to avoid damage to parts and systems.**

45. Install the camshaft bearing cap bolts in sequence.

a. Alternately hand tighten the camshaft bearing cap bolts a few turns at a time until all caps are fully seated.

b. Tighten the camshaft bearing cap bolts to 44 inch lbs. (5 Nm).

c. Tighten the camshaft bearing cap bolts an additional 30° using tool J 36660-A.

46. Align the camshafts.

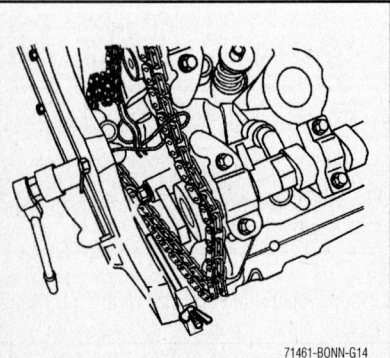

Fig. 52 Insert the hook end into a secondary timing chain link as shown—4.6L engine

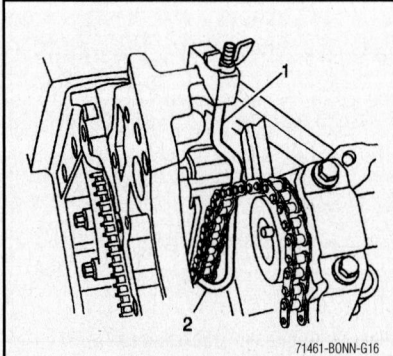

Fig. 54 Insert the hook end into a secondary timing chain link as shown—4.6L engine

The camshaft holding tools must be installed on the camshafts to prevent camshaft rotation. When performing service to the valve train and/or timing components, valve spring pressure can cause the camshafts to rotate unexpectedly and can cause personal injury.

47. Install tool J 44212 over the camshafts.

➡ **Ensure the camshaft sprockets properly engage the camshaft sprocket drive pins and camshafts.**

48. Slide the intake and exhaust camshaft sprockets off the pins of tool J 44213 and onto the pins of the camshafts.

49. Use an open wrench on the hex cast into the camshafts in order to prevent the camshafts from rotating when tightening the camshaft sprocket bolts.

50. Install the camshaft sprocket bolts. Tighten the camshaft sprocket bolts to 89 ft. lbs. (120 Nm).

51. Verify the camshaft sprocket alignment.

52. Remove tool J 44212 from the camshafts.

53. Install the camshaft cover seal as required.

➡ **Be careful to prevent the exposed section of the camshaft cover seal from being damaged by the edge of the cylinder head casting.**

54. Insert the intake camshaft end through the hole in the camshaft cover.

55. Work the camshaft cover into position by pivoting the cover down and to the left allowing the cover to clear the camshaft drive chain and then aligning the bolt holes.

56. Install the 9 camshaft cover bolts. Tighten the camshaft cover bolts to 89 inch lbs. (10 Nm).

57. Install the NEW seal as follows:

58. Lubricate the camshaft seal lips with engine oil.

59. Push the camshaft seal into position around the intake camshaft using the protective sleeve supplied with the seal.

60. Coat the bolt threads with sealant GM P/N 1052080 (Canadian P/N 10953480) or equivalent.

61. Install the camshaft seal bolts. Tighten the camshaft seal bolts to 27 inch lbs. (3 Nm).

62. Place the water pump drive pulley in position on the intake camshaft.

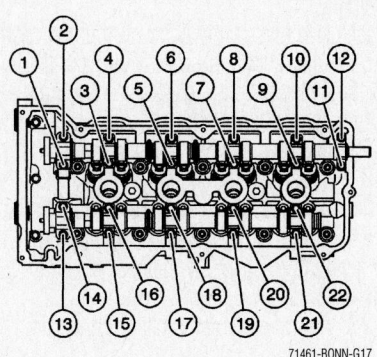

Fig. 55 Left side camshaft bearing cap torque sequence—4.6L engine

63. Install the water pump pulley using tool J 38823. During installation, the tool will bottom out on the camshaft at the proper depth.

64. Install the plastic dust cap into the end of the camshaft.

65. Position the water pump belt tensioner to the water crossover. Tighten the water pump belt tensioner bolts to 89 inch lbs. (10 Nm).

66. Connect the water pump drive belt.

67. Install the water pump drive belt shield.

68. Install the water pump drive belt shield fasteners. Tighten the water pump drive belt shield fasteners to 89 inch lbs. (10 Nm). Tighten the secondary AIR valve bracket nut to 80 inch lbs. (9 Nm).

69. Connect the cable harness clips to the cable harness at the front of the camshaft cover.

70. Install the spark plug boots onto the coil cassette. Ensure that the boots are fully seated against the cassette.

71. Install the ignition coil cassette.

72. Connect the PCV fresh air tube to the left camshaft cover.

73. Position tool J 38185 to the clamp in order to connect the radiator inlet hose to the water housing crossover.

74. Install the fuel injector sight shield.

75. Fill the cooling system.

Right Side

See Figures 56 through 59.

1. Remove the 2 nuts from the intake manifold sight shield.

2. Remove the sight shield from the engine.

3. Disconnect the PCV dirty air tube from the camshaft cover.

4. Disconnect the oxygen sensor wire.

5. Disconnect the vacuum tubes from the secondary AIR vent solenoid.

6. Disconnect the secondary AIR vent solenoid electrical connector.

7. Remove the secondary AIR control valve bracket.

8. Remove the nut securing the secondary AIR tube.

9. Remove the ignition coil cassette.

10. Remove the 4 spark plug boots.

11. Disconnect the cable harness clips at the front of the camshaft cover and position the cable harness aside.

12. Remove the 9 camshaft cover bolts.

13. Remove the camshaft cover.

14. Discard the camshaft cover perimeter seals and spark plug seals if there is any evidence of damage or if the seal comes out of the groove in the cover during removal.

15. Clean and inspect the camshaft cover.

16. Remove the camshaft position sensor.

17. Rotate the crankshaft to TDC of the no. 1 cylinders compression stroke, both camshaft sprocket drive pins should be at the top of their rotation.

The camshaft holding tools must be installed on the camshafts to prevent camshaft rotation. When performing service to the valve train and/or timing components, valve spring pressure can cause the camshafts to rotate unexpectedly and can cause personal injury.

18. Install tool J 44212 over the camshafts.

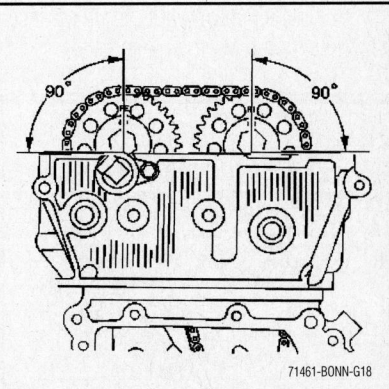

Fig. 56 Rotate the crankshaft to TDC of the no. 1 cylinders compression stroke, both right side camshaft sprocket drive pins should be at the top of their rotation—4.6L engine

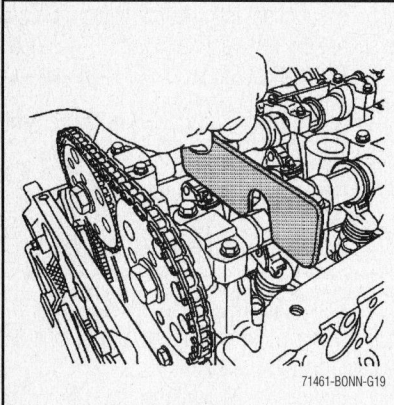

Fig. 57 Install tool J 44212 over the camshafts

19. Use a paint stick to create a mark on the timing chain link adjacent to each camshaft sprocket timing mark.

20. Install the using the procedure below:

a. Rotate the wing nut to the top of its travel.

b. Position the bottom retention tool on the cylinder head with the V-notch of the block adjacent to the right exhaust camshaft sprocket and chain.

c. Insert the hook end into a secondary timing chain link as shown.

d. Rotate the wing nut until it contacts the retention tool block. DO NOT tighten the wing nut at this time.

e. Rotate the wing nut to the top of its travel.

f. Position the top retention tool on the cylinder head with the V-notch of the block adjacent to the right intake camshaft sprocket and chain.

g. Insert the hook end into a secondary timing chain link as shown.

h. Rotate the wing nut until it contacts the retention tool block. Alternately

Fig. 58 Use a paint stick to create a mark on the timing chain link adjacent to each camshaft sprocket timing mark

tighten both wing nuts to retain the chain.

21. Use an open wrench on the hex cast into the camshafts in order to prevent the camshafts from rotating when removing the camshaft sprocket bolts.

22. Remove the camshaft sprocket bolts.

23. Alternately loosen the camshaft bearing cap bolts a few turns at a time until all valve spring pressure has been released.

24. Remove the camshaft bearing caps.

25. Remove tool J 44212 from the camshafts.

26. Remove the camshafts.

27. Remove the camshaft followers.

28. Clean and inspect the camshafts.

To install:

29. Apply a liberal amount of lubricant GM P/N 12345001 or equivalent to the roller pivot pocket and valve slot areas of the camshaft followers.

➡**The follower must be positioned squarely on the valve tip so that the full width of the roller will completely contact the camshaft lobe. If the followers are being reused you must put them back in their original location.**

30. Place the camshaft followers in position on the valve tip and the Stationary Hydraulic Lash Adjusters (SHLA). The rounded head of the follower goes on the SHLA, while the flat end goes on the valve tip.

31. Clean the camshaft carriers with a clean, lint-free cloth.

32. Apply a liberal amount of lubricant GM P/N 12345001 or equivalent to the camshaft carriers, camshaft lobes and the camshaft journals.

33. Place the camshaft in the camshaft carriers with the camshaft sprocket drive pins near the top of their rotation and the camshaft lobes in a neutral position. The camshafts can be identified by a stamping near the rear journal. For example: R-EXH is defined as Right Bank Exhaust.

34. Observe the markings on the camshaft bearing caps. Each camshaft bearing cap is marked in order to identify its location. The markings have the following meanings:

- The arrow should point to the front of the engine
- The number indicates the position from the front of the engine
- The **E** indicates the exhaust camshaft
- The **I** indicates the Intake camshaft

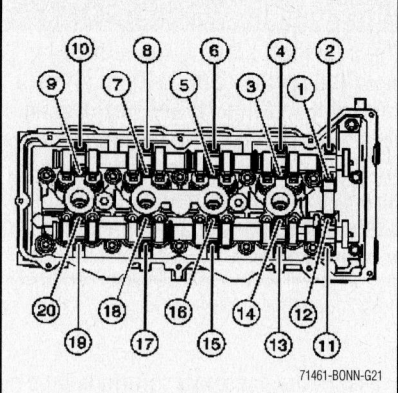

Fig. 59 Right side camshaft bearing cap torque sequence—4.6L engine

35. Apply a liberal amount of lubricant GM P/N 12345001 or equivalent to the camshaft bearing caps.

36. Install the camshaft bearing caps according to the identification marks.

37. Install the camshaft bearing cap bolts in sequence. Alternately hand tighten the camshaft bearing cap bolts a few turns at a time until all caps are fully seated.

a. Tighten the camshaft bearing cap bolts to 44 inch lbs. (5 Nm).

b. Tighten the camshaft bearing cap bolts an additional 30 degrees using tool J 36660-A.

38. Align the camshafts.

✳✳ CAUTION

The camshaft holding tools must be installed on the camshafts to prevent camshaft rotation. When performing service to the valve train and/or timing components, valve spring pressure can cause the camshafts to rotate unexpectedly and can cause personal injury.

39. Install tool J 44212 over the camshafts.

➡**Ensure the camshaft sprockets properly engage the camshaft sprocket drive pins and camshafts.**

40. Slide the intake and exhaust camshaft sprockets off the pins of tool J 44213 and onto the pins of the camshafts.

41. Use an open wrench on the hex cast into the camshafts in order to prevent the camshafts from rotating when tightening the camshaft sprocket bolts.

42. Install the camshaft sprocket bolts. Tighten the camshaft sprocket bolts to 89 ft. lbs. (120 Nm).

43. Verify the camshaft sprocket alignment.

44. Remove tool J 44212 from the camshafts.

45. Install the camshaft position sensor.

46. Install the camshaft cover seal as required.

➡**Be careful to prevent the exposed section of the camshaft cover seal from being damaged by the edge of the cylinder head casting.**

47. Install the camshaft cover.

48. Install the 9 camshaft cover bolts. Tighten the camshaft cover bolts to 89 inch lbs. (10 Nm).

49. Install the spark plug boots onto the coil cassette. Ensure that the boots are fully seated against the cassette.

50. Install the ignition coil cassette.

51. Install the secondary AIR control valve bracket.

52. Connect the cable harness clips to the cable harness at the front of the camshaft cover.

53. Connect the secondary AIR vent solenoid electrical connector.

54. Connect the vacuum tubes to the secondary AIR vent solenoid.

55. Connect the oxygen sensor wire.

56. Connect the PCV dirty air tube to the camshaft cover.

57. Position the intake manifold sight shield to the engine.

58. Install the 2 intake manifold sight shield nuts. Tighten the nuts to 27 inch lbs. (3 Nm).

CAMSHAFT BEARING REPLACEMENT

3.8L Engine

1. Assemble Camshaft Bearing Remover Tool J-33049.

2. Drive out the camshaft bearings.

To install:

3. Using the remover tool J-33049, place the bearing on the tool.

❋❋ **WARNING**

Severe engine damage may result if the oil holes are not correctly aligned.

4. Index the bearing oil holes with the engine block oil passages.

5. Install the bearings.

CRANKSHAFT DAMPER

REMOVAL & INSTALLATION

3.8L Engine

See Figures 60 and 61.

1. Before servicing the vehicle, refer to the Precautions Section.

2. Disconnect the negative battery cable.

3. Remove the accessory drive belt.

4. Raise and support the vehicle.

5. Remove the right front tire and wheel.

6. Remove the right engine splash shield retainers and the engine splash shield.

7. Remove the torque converter covers.

8. Use tool J 37096 to secure the flywheel in order to prevent the crankshaft from rotating.

9. Remove the crankshaft damper bolt and discard the damper bolt.

➡**Do not separate the crankshaft pulley from the crankshaft damper. Service the crankshaft pulley and the crankshaft damper as an assembly.**

10. Remove the crankshaft damper using tool J 38197-A.

To install:

11. Coat the engine front cover seal contact area on the crankshaft damper, and the seal surface with engine oil.

12. Install the crankshaft damper.

13. Prevent the crankshaft from rotating.

14. Install the new crankshaft damper bolt. Tighten the bolt to 111 ft. lbs. (150 Nm), plus 76°.

15. Install the torque converter covers.

16. Install the right engine splash shield and the engine splash shield retainers.

17. Install the right front tire and wheel.

18. Lower the vehicle.

19. Install the accessory drive belt.

➡**The following Crankshaft Position (CKP) System Variation Learn Procedure must be performed.**

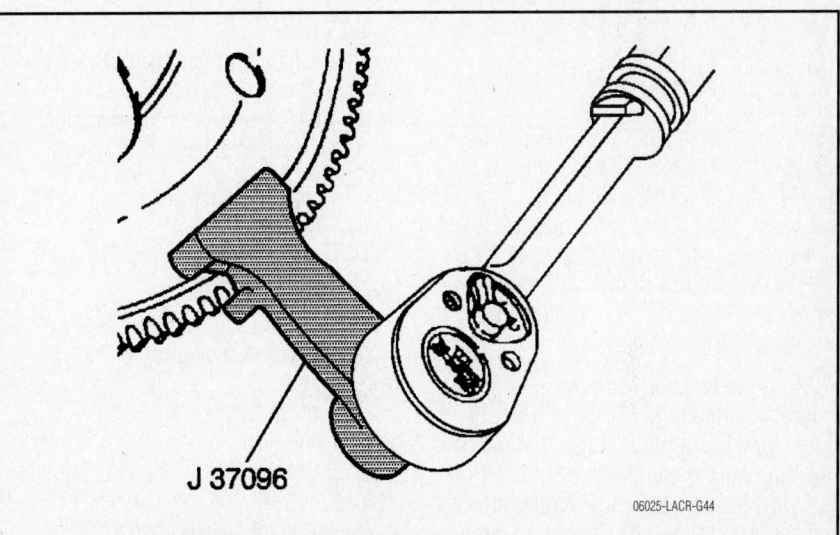

Fig. 60 Use tool J 37096 to secure the flywheel in order to prevent the crankshaft from rotating

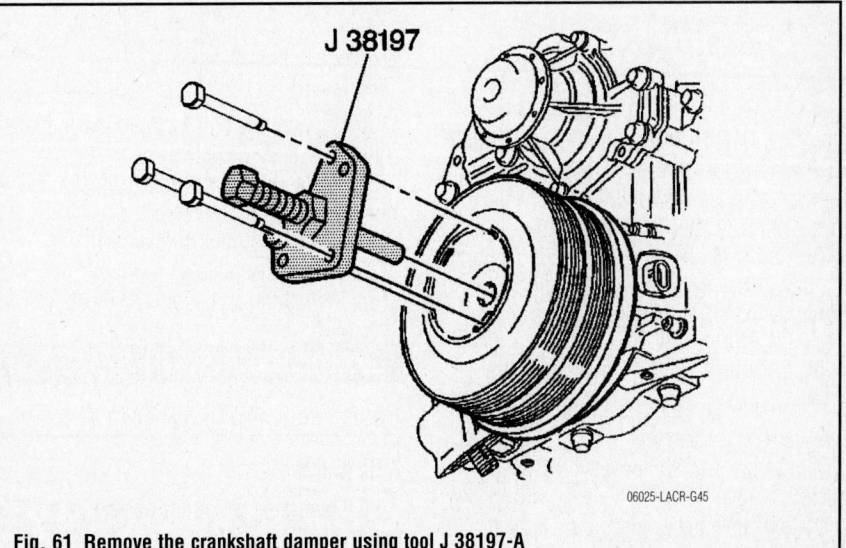

Fig. 61 Remove the crankshaft damper using tool J 38197-A

20. Install a scan tool.

21. Monitor the Powertrain Control Module (PCM) for DTC's with a scan tool.

22. Select the crankshaft position variation learn procedure with a scan tool.

23. The scan tool instructs you to perform the following:

 a. Accelerate to Wide Open Throttle (WOT).

 b. Release the throttle when fuel cut-off occurs.

 c. Observe the fuel cut-off specifications for the applicable engine.

 d. The engine should not accelerate beyond the calibrated RPM value.

 e. Release the throttle immediately if the value is exceeded.

 f. Block the drive wheels.

 g. Set the parking brake.

 h. DO NOT apply the brake pedal.

 i. Cycle the ignition from OFF to ON.

 j. Apply and hold the brake pedal.

 k. Start and idle the engine.

 l. Turn the A/C OFF.

 m. The vehicle must remain in Park or Neutral.

24. The scan tool monitors certain component signals to determine if all the conditions are met to continue with the procedure. The scan tool only displays the condition that inhibits the procedure.

25. Enable the crankshaft position system variation learn procedure with the scan tool and perform the following:

➡ **While the learn procedure is in progress, release the throttle immediately when the engine starts to decelerate. The engine control is returned to the operator and the engine responds to throttle position after the learn procedure is complete.**

26. Accelerate to WOT.

 a. Release when fuel cut-off occurs.

 b. Test in progress.

27. The scan tool displays Learn Status: Learned this ignition. If the scan tool indicates that DTC P0315 ran and passed, the CKP variation learn procedure is complete. If the scan tool indicates DTC P0315 failed or did not run, refer to DTC P0315.

28. Turn OFF the ignition for 30 seconds after the learn procedure is completed successfully.

4.6L Engine

1. Before servicing the vehicle, refer to the Precautions Section.

2. Disconnect the negative battery cable.

3. Remove the accessory drive belt.

4. Raise and support the vehicle.

5. Remove the right front wheel.

6. Remove the front fascia extension from the wheelhouse.

7. Remove the brace between the engine oil pan and the transaxle case.

8. Remove the torque converter cover.

9. Install Flywheel Holder J-44214.

10. Remove the crankshaft damper bolt.

11. Support the engine assembly with a suitable jack.

12. Remove the nut securing the right engine mount to the right engine mount bracket.

13. Lower the engine assembly to obtain clearance for the Damper (Balancer) Remover J-41816.

14. Place the remover pilot into the end of the crankshaft.

15. Remove the crankshaft damper using the J-41816.

16. Clean and inspect the crankshaft damper.

To install:

17. Position the crankshaft damper on the nose of the crankshaft.

18. Press the crankshaft damper in place using the Damper (Balancer) Installer J-41998-B.

19. Clean the crankshaft damper bolt threads.

20. Apply engine oil to the crankshaft damper bolt threads.

21. Install the crankshaft damper bolt.

22. Tighten the bolt to 37 ft. lbs. (50 Nm).

23. Tighten the crankshaft damper bolt an additional 120°.

24. Raise the engine assembly into position.

25. Install the nut securing the right engine mount to the right engine mount bracket and tighten to 59 ft. lbs. (80 Nm).

26. Remove the engine support jack.

27. Remove the flywheel lock.

28. Install the torque converter cover.

29. Install the oil pan to transaxle brace.

30. Tighten the oil pan to transaxle brace bolts to 37 ft. lbs. (50 Nm).

31. Install the front fascia extension to the wheelhouse.

32. Install the right front wheel.

33. Lower the vehicle.

34. Install the accessory drive belt.

CRANKSHAFT FRONT SEAL

REMOVAL & INSTALLATION

3.8L Engine

1. Before servicing the vehicle, refer to the Precautions Section.

2. Remove the crankshaft damper. Refer to Crankshaft Damper, removal and installation.

✳✳ WARNING

Be careful not to damage the crankshaft.

3. Pry out the crankshaft front oil seal with a flat bladed tool such as a large screwdriver. Use care to avoid damaging the crankshaft front oil seal bore or the crankshaft front oil seal contact surfaces.

4. Inspect the crankshaft damper and engine front cover for scratches.

To install:

5. Install the crankshaft front oil seal in the engine front cover using the J 35354-A .

6. Tighten the bolt until the crankshaft front oil seal is seated in the engine front cover.

7. Remove the J 35354-A.

8. Install the crankshaft damper. Refer to Crankshaft Damper, removal and installation.

9. Inspect for leaks.

10. Perform the Crankshaft Position (CKP) System Variation Learn Procedure.

4.6L Engine

Do not remove the crankshaft front oil seal. The crankshaft front oil seal is not serviced as an individual component. When replacing the crankshaft front oil seal, install a **NEW** engine front cover. In order to precisely align the crankshaft front oil seal to the crankshaft damper and crankshaft damper dust shield, the engine front cover and the crankshaft front oil seal are sold as an assembly.

CYLINDER HEAD

REMOVAL & INSTALLATION

3.8L Engine

See Figure 62.

1. Before servicing the vehicle, refer to the Precautions Section.

2. Disconnect the negative battery cable.

3. Relieve the fuel system pressure.

4. Drain the cooling system.

5. Remove or disconnect the following:
   - Intake manifold
   - Exhaust manifold
   - Valve covers
   - Ignition wires and ignition coil/module assembly
   - Alternator front mounting bracket and alternator

- Air conditioning bracket to cylinder head bolt
- Power steering pump
- Accessory drive belt tensioner
- Fuel pipe heat shield
- Rocker arm assemblies, note their original position
- Pushrods and guide plate
- Cylinder head bolts
- Cylinder head

To install:

6. Place the new cylinder head gasket on the engine block dowels with the note **THIS SIDE UP** facing the cylinder head and the arrow facing the front of the engine. Position the cylinder head on the engine block.

➡ **The head gasket is identified by either a L or a R stamped on it next to the arrow.**

➡ **This engine uses special torque to yield head bolts. The procedure must be followed carefully and new bolts must be used whenever the head is removed. Total bolt torque should not exceed 60 ft. lbs. (81 Nm).**

7. Install new cylinder head bolts and torque them in sequence as follows:
   a. Step 1: 37 ft. lbs. (50 Nm).
   b. Step 2: Plus 120°.
8. Install or connect the following:
   - Pushrods and guide plate
   - Rocker arm assemblies into their original location

➡ **Apply a thread lock compound to the rocker arm pedestal bolts before assembly.**

   - Valve covers
   - Fuel pipe heat shield
   - Accessory drive belt tensioner
   - Power steering pump
   - Air conditioning compressor bracket bolt. Torque it to 52 ft. lbs. (70 Nm).

- Alternator front mounting bracket, and alternator
- Ignition coil/module assembly and spark plug wires
- Exhaust manifold. Torque the bolts to 22 ft. lbs. (30 Nm).
- Intake manifold
- Negative battery cable

9. Refill and bleed the cooling system.
10. Start the engine and check for leaks and proper operation.

4.6L Engine

Left Side

See Figure 63.

1. Remove the following subassemblies:
   - The left exhaust manifold
   - The alternator
   - The water crossover
   - The intake manifold
   - The camshaft cover
   - The engine front cover
   - The left secondary camshaft drive chain
2. Remove the power steering return hose retaining bolt from the cylinder head.
3. Remove the 3 M6 external drive bolts from the front portion of the cylinder head.

➡ **DO NOT reuse the M11 cylinder head bolts.**

4. Remove and discard the ten M11 internal drive cylinder head bolts.
5. Remove the left cylinder head. Make sure that no dowel guide pins are stuck in the cylinder head.

➡ **You must clean the thread sealant material from the cylinder head bolt holes in the cylinder block. Failure to do so could cause false torque readings during reassembly.**

6. After removing the cylinder head, remove any remaining bolt thread sealant material from the threaded cylinder block holes.

➡ **DO NOT reuse the cylinder head gasket.**

7. Remove the left cylinder head gasket.
8. Remove all remaining gasket material from the cylinder head and cylinder block using tool J 28410.
9. Place the cylinder head on a flat, clean surface with the combustion chamber side face-up in order to prevent damage to the deck face.
10. Clean and inspect the cylinder head.

To install:

11. Make sure all the cylinder head locating pins are securely mounted in the cylinder block deck face.

➡ **Failure to remove all the old thread sealant material from the cylinder block could cause false torque readings.**

12. Make sure any old thread sealant material is removed from the cylinder head bolt holes in the cylinder block.
13. Install a new left cylinder head gasket using the deck face locating pins for retention.
14. Align the cylinder head with the deck face locating pins.
15. Place the cylinder head in position on the deck face.

➡ **DO NOT reuse the old M11 cylinder head bolts.**

16. Install new M11 cylinder head bolts in the cylinder head.
17. Install the M6 cylinder head bolts at the front of the cylinder head.
18. Tighten the left cylinder head bolts in the sequence shown:
   a. First Pass: Tighten the left cylinder head M11 cylinder head bolts to 30 ft. lbs. (40 Nm) in the sequence shown.
   b. Second Pass: Tighten the left cylinder head M11 cylinder head bolts an additional 70° in the sequence shown.
   c. Third Pass: Repeat the sequence turning each bolt another 60°.
   d. Final Pass: Repeat the sequence again turning each bolt a final 45°.

➡ **The total degrees of torque must not exceed 175°.**

19. Tighten the M6 bolts at the front of the cylinder head to 106 inch lbs. (12 Nm).
20. Install the power steering return hose retaining bolt to the cylinder head. Tighten

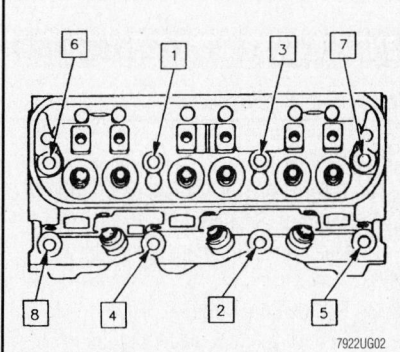

Fig. 62 Cylinder head bolt torque sequence—3.8L engine

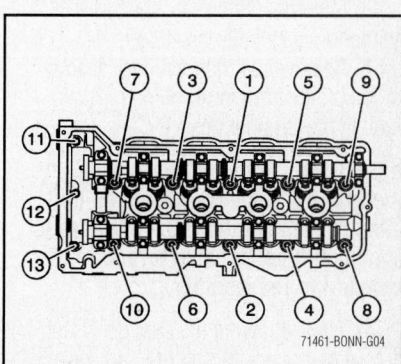

Fig. 63 Left cylinder head bolt torque sequence—4.6L engine

the power steering return hose retaining bolt to 37 ft. lbs. (50 Nm).

21. Install the following subassemblies:

- The left secondary camshaft drive chain
- The engine front cover
- The camshaft cover
- The intake manifold
- The water crossover
- The alternator
- The left exhaust manifold

Right Side

See Figure 64.

1. Remove the following subassemblies:

- The right exhaust manifold
- The water crossover
- The intake manifold
- The camshaft cover
- The engine front cover
- The right secondary camshaft drive chain

2. Disconnect the electrical connector from the Engine Coolant Temperature (ECT) sensor.

3. Remove the nut securing the coil cassette ground wire to the cylinder head.

4. Remove the bolt securing the exhaust crossover pipe to the cylinder head.

5. Raise and support the vehicle.

6. Remove the bolt securing the front transaxle brace to the cylinder head.

7. Loosen the bolts attaching the transaxle brace to the transaxle.

8. Remove the bolt securing the rear transaxle brace to the transaxle.

9. Lower the vehicle.

10. Remove the nuts securing the rear transaxle brace to the cylinder head.

11. Remove the rear transaxle brace.

12. Remove the 3 M6 external drive bolts from the front portion of the cylinder head.

➡**DO NOT reuse the M11 cylinder head bolts.**

13. Remove and discard the ten M11 internal drive cylinder head bolts.

14. Remove the right cylinder head. Make sure that no dowel guide pins are stuck in the cylinder head.

➡**You must clean the thread sealant material from the cylinder head bolt holes in the cylinder block. Failure to do so could cause false torque readings during reassembly.**

15. After removing the cylinder head, remove any remaining bolt thread sealant material from the threaded cylinder block holes.

➡**DO NOT reuse the cylinder head gasket.**

16. Remove the right cylinder head gasket.

17. Remove all remaining gasket material from the cylinder head and cylinder block.

18. Place the cylinder head on a flat, clean surface with the combustion chambers face-up in order to prevent damage to the deck face.

19. Clean and inspect the cylinder head.

To install:

20. Make sure all the cylinder head locating pins are securely mounted in the cylinder block deck face.

➡**Failure to remove all the old thread sealant material from the cylinder block could cause false torque readings.**

21. Make sure any old thread sealant material is removed from the cylinder head bolt holes in the cylinder block.

22. Install a new right cylinder head gasket using the deck face locating pins for retention.

23. Align the cylinder head with the deck face locating pins.

24. Place the cylinder head in position on the deck face.

➡**DO NOT reuse the old M11 cylinder head bolts.**

25. Install new M11 cylinder head bolts in the cylinder head.

26. Install the M6 cylinder head bolts at the front of the cylinder head.

27. Tighten the right cylinder head bolts in the sequence shown:

a. First Pass: Tighten the right cylinder head M11 cylinder head bolts to 30 ft. lbs. (40 Nm) in the sequence shown.

b. Second Pass: Tighten the right

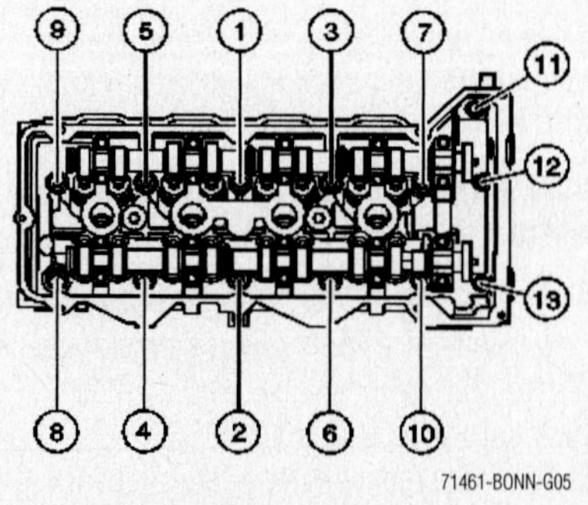

Fig. 64 Right cylinder head torque sequence—4.6L engine

71461-BONN-G05

cylinder head M11 cylinder head bolts an additional 70° in the sequence shown.

c. Third Pass: Repeat the sequence turning each bolt another 60°.

d. Final Pass: Repeat the sequence again turning each bolt a final 45°.

➡**The total degrees of torque must not exceed 175°.**

28. Tighten the M6 bolts at the front of the cylinder head to 106 inch lbs. (12 Nm).

29. Position the rear transaxle brace over the studs located at the rear of the right cylinder head.

30. Loosely install the nuts securing the rear transaxle brace to the cylinder head.

31. Raise and support the vehicle.

32. Install the bolt securing the rear transaxle brace to the transaxle. Tighten the rear transaxle brace bolt to 37 ft. lbs. (50 Nm).

33. Install the bolt securing the front transaxle brace to the cylinder head. Tighten the front transaxle brace bolts to 37 ft. lbs. (50 Nm).

34. Lower the vehicle.

35. Tighten the rear transaxle brace to the cylinder head nuts to 37 ft. lbs. (50 Nm).

36. Connect the electrical connector to the ECT sensor.

37. Install the bolt securing the exhaust crossover pipe to the cylinder head. Tighten the exhaust crossover pipe to cylinder head bolt to 18 ft. lbs. (25 Nm).

38. Install the nut securing the coil cassette ground wire to the cylinder head. Tighten the coil cassette ground wire nut to 13 ft. lbs. (17 Nm).

39. Install the following subassemblies:

- The right secondary camshaft drive chain
- The engine front cover
- The camshaft cover
- The intake manifold
- The water crossover
- The right exhaust manifold

ENGINE ASSEMBLY

REMOVAL & INSTALLATION

3.8L Engine

1. Before servicing the vehicle, refer to the Precautions Section.

2. Disconnect the negative battery cable.

3. Remove the hood.

4. Relieve the fuel system pressure.

5. Drain the coolant system and crankcase.

6. Remove or disconnect the following:
- The fuel injector sight shield
- The vacuum brake booster hose from the vacuum connections
- The fuel feed and return lines from the fuel rail
- The evaporative emission canister purge valve
- The cruise control cable from the throttle body bracket and lever
- The electrical connector from the cruise control module
- The cruise control module from the mounting studs

➥Always replace the accelerator control cable with a NEW cable whenever you remove the engine from the vehicle.

- The accelerator control cable
- The accessory drive belt
- The bolt securing both the battery negative cable and the engine harness ground lead to the engine block

7. Disconnect the wiring harness connectors from the following components:
- The A/C compressor clutch
- The A/C pressure sensor
- The Knock Sensor (KS)
- The engine coolant block heater
- The oil level sensor

8. Remove or disconnect the following:
- The wiring harness from the harness clip at the rear of the A/C compressor
- The torque converter cover
- The starter motor
- The bolts securing the flywheel to the torque converter

9. Disconnect then secure the following wiring harness electrical connectors to the cowl panel:
- The KS number 2 which can be found behind the right exhaust manifold
- The oil pressure sensor
- The Vehicle Speed Sensor (VSS)

10. Remove or disconnect the following:
- The bolts securing the transaxle brace to the transaxle
- The nuts attaching the exhaust manifold pipe to the right exhaust manifold
- The exhaust manifold pipe from the right exhaust manifold studs, allowing it to rest on top of the power steering gear heat shield
- The exhaust manifold pipe gasket and discard the gasket
- The right wheelhouse extension
- The font A/C compressor mounting nuts

- The rear A/C compressor mounting bolt
- The compressor off of the mounting studs and rest on top of the engine frame
- The bolt securing the Powertrain Control Module (PCM) ground located at the left front cylinder head

11. Disconnect the wiring harness electrical connectors from the following components on the left side of the engine:
- The fuel injectors
- The ignition harness
- The boost control solenoid (VIN 1 only)
- The Engine Coolant Temperature (ECT) sensor
- The Throttle Position (TP) sensor
- The Idle Air Control (IAC) valve
- The Mass Air Flow (MAF) sensor

12. Disconnect the wiring harness connectors from the following components on the right side of the engine:
- The fuel injectors
- The Exhaust Gas Recirculation (EGR) valve
- The Manifold Absolute Pressure (MAP) sensor
- The Heated Oxygen (HO$_2$S) sensor
- The AIR solenoid, if equipped
- The alternator

13. Remove or disconnect the following:
- The alternator
- The air cleaner intake duct

14. Attach an engine support fixture.

15. Remove or disconnect the following:
- The front power steering pump mounting bolts
- The side power steering pump mounting bolt and piston the power steering pump against the cowl, allowing it to rest on top of the transaxle housing
- The right engine mount bracket
- The right lower engine to transaxle mounting bolt
- The coolant and heater hoses

16. Use a block of wood between a floor jack and the transaxle, support the transaxle at the pan.

17. Remove the engine support fixture.

18. Attach an engine lift chain to the engine lift brackets and attach to an engine lift device.

19. Remove all remaining engine to transaxle bolts

20. Remove the engine from the vehicle.

To install:

21. Installation is the reverse of removal, please note the following torques:

- The 5 upper engine to transaxle mounting bolts to 55 ft. lbs. (75 Nm)
- The right lower engine to transaxle mounting bolt to 55 ft. lbs. (75 Nm)
- The power steering pump bolts to 20 ft. lbs. (27 Nm)
- The bolt attaching the PCM ground to the left front cylinder head and tighten to 37 ft. lbs. (50 Nm)
- The A/C compressor bolts to 37 ft. lbs. (50 Nm)
- The transaxle brace bolts to 48 ft. lbs.(65 Nm)
- The flywheel to torque converter bolts to 46 ft. lbs. (63 Nm)

22. Refill the crankcase.

23. Refill and bleed the engine cooling system.

24. Start the engine and check for leaks.

25. Road test the vehicle and check operation.

4.6L Engine

1. Recover the A/C refrigerant system.

2. Remove or disconnect the following:
- The battery negative cable
- The vacuum brake booster hose from the vacuum connection and position aside
- The fuel inlet and return quick-connect fittings at the fuel rail and secure to the air inlet grille
- The hose from the evaporative emission canister purge valve and secure to the air inlet grille
- The upper filler panel
- The air cleaner assembly
- The 2 nuts from the fuel injector sight shield
- The fuel injector sight shield from the engine
- The nut securing the battery positive cable to the remote positive terminal and secure to the top of the engine
- The secondary AIR relay from the relay bracket and secure to the top of the engine

3. Disconnect and secure the following wiring harness electrical connectors to the top of the engine:
- The Powertrain Control Module (PCM)
- The C101
- The engine electrical harness

4. Remove the bolt securing the engine ground cable from the right side body frame rail.

✳✳ WARNING

In order to avoid possible injury or vehicle damage, always replace the accelerator control cable with a NEW cable whenever you remove the engine from the vehicle. In order to avoid cruise control cable damage, position the cable out of the way while you remove or install the engine. Do not pry or lean against the cruise control cable and do not kink the cable. You must replace a damaged cable.

5. Push the lock release and remove the cruise control cable from the throttle body bracket and lever.

6. Remove the accelerator control cable from the throttle body. Push the lock release and remove the cruise control cable from the throttle body bracket and lever.

7. Remove the shift cable from the bracket and manual shift lever and position aside.

8. Drain the cooling system.

9. Position tool J 37097-A, or equivalent, to the clamp in order to remove the radiator inlet hose from the water housing crossover and position aside.

10. Position tool J 38185, or equivalent, to the clamp in order to remove the radiator outlet hose from the thermostat housing and position aside.

11. Disconnect the surge tank inlet hose from the water housing crossover.

12. Disconnect the surge tank outlet hose from the heater pipe.

13. Disconnect the heater hoses from the heater pipes.

✳✳ CAUTION

Brake fluid may irritate eyes and skin.

➡Record the location of the brake pipes to the Brake Pressure Modulator Valve (BPMV) for use as an aid during installation.

14. Remove the 2 master cylinder brake pipes from the BPMV.

15. Plug the open outlet ports to prevent fluid loss and contamination.

16. Remove the upper transaxle oil cooler pipe retaining bolt from the fan shroud.

17. Slide the plastic cap off the upper transaxle oil cooler pipe quick connect fitting.

18. Disconnect the upper transaxle oil cooler pipe from the radiator using tool, J 41623-B, or equivalent.

19. Disconnect the lower transaxle oil cooler pipe fitting from the radiator.

➡The wheels of the vehicle must be straight ahead and the steering column in the LOCK position before disconnecting the steering column or intermediate shaft from the steering gear. Failure to do so will cause the SIR coil assembly to become un-centered, which may cause damage to the coil assembly.

20. Lock the steering column by installing tool, J 42640, or equivalent, into underside of the steering column.

21. Remove the right and left side strut tower bolts.

22. Raise and support the vehicle.

23. Remove or disconnect the following:

- The rear exhaust manifold pipe
- The front wheels
- The front electronic brake pad wear sensor electrical connectors
- The front electronic brake pad wear sensor electrical leads from the strut brackets and secure to the body frame rails
- The front wheel speed sensor electrical leads from the body frame rail
- The road sensing suspension electrical connector at the body frame rail, if equipped
- The road sensing suspension electrical leads from the body frame rail , if equipped
- The electronic suspension position sensor links from the lower control arms, if equipped
- The front air deflector
- The front fascia extensions
- The secondary AIR inlet hose from the secondary AIR pump

24. Loosen the nuts securing the front brake pipe frame brackets to the body frame rails.

25. Disconnect the front brake pipes from the retainers at the body frame rails.

26. Carefully pull the front brake pipes away from the body frame rails.

27. Remove or disconnect the following:

- The 2 rear brake pipes at the rear of the engine frame. Plug the open outlet ports to prevent fluid loss and contamination
- The A/C pressure sensor
- The A/C discharge hose from the compressor and secure to the cooling fan assembly
- The A/C suction hose from the compressor and secure to the cooling fan assembly

✳✳ WARNING

Failure to disconnect the intermediate shaft from the rack and pinion stub shaft can result in damage to the steering gear and/or damage to the intermediate shaft. This damage may cause loss of steering control which could result in personal injury.

- The intermediate shaft pinch bolt
- The steering gear from the intermediate shaft
- The post Heated Oxygen Sensor (HO2S) at the sensor pigtail
- The engine oil cooler quick connect fittings from the engine oil filter adapter, with the oil pipes still attached, and position aside
- The brace between the engine oil pan and the transaxle case
- The torque converter cover

➡Mark the flywheel to torque converter relationship prior to removal of the bolts.

28. Remove the torque converter to the flywheel bolts.

29. Position tool J 39580, or equivalent powertrain support dolly, under the engine frame.

30. Lower the vehicle on to tool J 39580, or equivalent

➡If the powertrain support dolly is unavailable, support the powertrain with 4 suitable jackstands.

31. Place a block of wood between the front of the engine oil pan and the engine frame.

32. Remove the nut securing the right engine mount to the right engine mount bracket.

33. Remove the nut securing the left transaxle mount to the left transaxle mount bracket.

✳✳ CAUTION

To avoid any vehicle damage, serious personal injury or death when major components are removed from the vehicle and the vehicle is supported by a hoist, support the vehicle with jack stands at the opposite end from which the components are being removed.

34. Secure the front hoist pads to the vehicle. Remove the 6 frame to body mounting bolts.

➡**Ensure clearance is maintained between the engine/transaxle assembly and the following:**

- The A/C accumulator hose
- The A/C compressor hose
- The brake pipes
- The electronic brake pad wear sensor leads
- The heater hoses
- The radiator hoses
- The wheel speed sensor leads
- The wiring harnesses

35. Carefully raise the vehicle in order to clear the supported engine/transaxle assembly.

36. Drain the engine oil.

37. Remove or disconnect the following:

- The heater pipes
- The intermediate hose from the secondary AIR valve at bank 2
- The nut securing the intermediate hose to the secondary AIR valve at bank 1
- The nut securing the coil cassette ground wire to the right cylinder head
- The engine wiring harness from the engine
- The power steering hose from the power steering pump reservoir
- The power steering return hose retaining bolt from the cylinder head
- The power steering pressure hose from the power steering pump
- The nut securing the power steering pressure hose to the right engine mount bracket
- The 4 bolts securing the right engine mount bracket to the engine
- The right engine mount bracket
- The bolt securing the rear transaxle brace to the transaxle
- The Remove the nuts securing the rear transaxle brace to the stud located on the right cylinder head.
- The rear transaxle brace
- The bolts securing the front transaxle brace to the transaxle and right cylinder head
- The nuts securing the Vehicle Speed Sensor (VSS) heat shield to the transaxle
- The bolts securing the center transaxle brace to the engine and transaxle

38. Install tool J 42504, or equivalent, to the cylinder head.

39. Install an engine lift chain to the engine lift brackets and attach to an engine lift device.

40. Remove the nut securing the front engine mount to the engine frame.

41. Remove the bolts attaching the engine to the transaxle.

42. Raise the engine from the supported frame and transaxle assembly.

43. Remove the front engine mount bracket.

To install:

44. Install the front engine mount bracket.

45. Carefully position the engine to the supported frame and transaxle assembly, aligning the engine dowels to the transaxle cover.

46. Install the bolts attaching the engine to the transaxle. Tighten the engine to transaxle mounting bolts to 55 ft. lbs. (75 Nm).

47. Install the nut securing the front engine mount to the engine frame. Tighten the front engine mount nut to 52 ft. lbs. (70 Nm).

48. Place a block of wood between the front of the engine oil pan and the engine frame.

49. Remove the engine lift chain from the engine lift brackets.

50. Remove tool J 42504, or equivalent, from the cylinder head.

51. Install the 4 bolts securing the center transaxle brace to the engine and transaxle. Tighten the center transaxle brace bolts to 37 ft. lbs. (50 Nm).

52. Install the retaining nuts securing the VSS heat shield to the transaxle. Tighten the VSS heat shield nuts to 37 ft. lbs. (50 Nm).

53. Install the bolts securing the front transaxle brace to the transaxle and right cylinder head. Tighten the front transaxle brace bolts to 37 ft. lbs. (50 Nm).

54. Position the rear transaxle brace over the studs located at the rear of the right cylinder head.

55. Loosely install the nuts securing the rear transaxle brace to the cylinder head.

56. Install the bolt securing the rear transaxle brace to the transaxle. Tighten the rear transaxle brace bolt to 37 ft. lbs. (50 Nm). Tighten the rear transaxle brace nuts to 37 ft. lbs. (50 Nm).

57. Position the right engine mount bracket to the engine.

58. Install the 4 bolts securing the right engine mount bracket to the engine. Tighten the right engine mount bracket bolts to 37 ft. lbs. (50 Nm).

59. Install the nut securing the power steering pressure hose to the right engine mount bracket. Tighten the power steering pressure hose retaining nut to 80 inch lbs. (9 Nm).

60. Install the power steering pressure hose to the power steering pump. Tighten the power steering hose to power steering pump to 22 ft. lbs. (30 Nm).

61. Connect the power steering hose to the power steering pump reservoir.

62. Install the power steering return hose retaining bolt to the cylinder head. Tighten the power steering return hose retaining bolt to 37 ft. lbs. (50 Nm).

63. Connect the engine wiring harness to the engine.

64. Install the nut securing the coil cassette ground wire to the cylinder head. Tighten the coil cassette ground wire nut to 13 ft. lbs. (17 Nm).

65. Install the nut securing the intermediate hose to the secondary AIR valve at bank 1. Tighten the intermediate hose to secondary AIR valve nut to 80 inch lbs. (9 Nm).

66. Connect the intermediate hose to the secondary AIR valve at bank 2.

67. Install the heater pipes.

68. Position the engine/transaxle assembly under the vehicle.

➡**Ensure clearance is maintained between the engine/transaxle assembly and the following:**

- The A/C accumulator hose
- The A/C compressor hose
- The brake pipes
- The electronic brake pad wear sensor leads
- The heater hoses
- The radiator hoses
- The wheel speed sensor leads
- The wiring harnesses

69. Carefully lower the vehicle over the engine/transaxle assembly, aligning the struts to the strut towers.

70. Install the 6 frame mounting bolts retaining the frame to the vehicle.

71. Using dowel pins in the alignment holes, align the engine frame with the vehicle. Tighten the frame mounting bolts to 141 ft. lbs. (191 Nm).

72. Install the nut securing the right engine mount to the right engine mount bracket. Tighten the right engine mount nut to 59 ft. lbs. (80 Nm).

73. Remove the block of wood between the front of the engine oil pan and the engine frame.

74. Install the nut securing the left transaxle mount to the left transaxle mount bracket. Tighten the left transaxle mount nut to 59 ft. lbs. (80 Nm).

75. Raise and support the vehicle.

76. Remove tool J 39580, or equivalent powertrain support dolly, from under the engine frame.

➡**Line up the flywheel and converter, using the alignment marks made during disassembly.**

77. Install the bolts securing the flywheel to the torque converter. Tighten the flywheel to torque converter bolts to 44 ft. lbs. (60 Nm).

78. Install the torque converter cover.

79. Install the oil pan to transaxle brace. Tighten the oil pan to transaxle brace bolts to 37 ft. lbs. (50 Nm).

80. Install the engine oil cooler quick connect fittings to the engine oil filter adapter, if equipped.

81. Connect the post HO2S at the sensor pigtail.

✳✳ CAUTION

When installing the intermediate shaft make sure that the shaft is seated prior to pinch bolt installation. If the pinch bolt is inserted into the coupling before shaft installation, the two mating shafts may disengage. Disengagement of the two mating shafts will cause loss of steering control which could result in personal injury.

82. Install or connect the following:
- The intermediate shaft to the steering gear
- The intermediate shaft to the steering gear pinch bolt. Tighten the intermediate shaft to steering gear pinch bolt to 33 ft. lbs. (45 Nm)
- The A/C suction hose to the compressor. Tighten the A/C suction hose nut to 15 ft. lbs. (20 Nm)
- The A/C discharge hose to the compressor. Tighten the A/C discharge hose nut to 15 ft. lbs. (20 Nm)
- The A/C pressure sensor
- The 2 rear brake pipes at the rear of the engine frame. Tighten the brake pipes to 11 ft. lbs. (15 Nm)
- The front brake pipes to the retainers at the body frame rails
- The nuts securing the front brake pipe frame brackets to the body frame rails. Tighten the brake pipe frame bracket nuts to 11 ft. lbs. (15 Nm)
- The secondary AIR inlet hose to the secondary AIR pump
- The front fascia extensions
- The front air deflector
- The front wheel speed sensor electrical leads to the body frame rail
- The front electronic brake pad wear sensor electrical leads to the strut brackets

- The front electronic brake pad wear sensor electrical connectors
- The road sensing suspension electrical connector at the body frame rail, if equipped
- The road sensing suspension electrical leads to the body frame rail, if equipped
- The electronic suspension position sensor links to the lower control arms, if equipped
- The rear exhaust manifold pipe
- The front wheels

83. Lower the vehicle ONLY enough to allow the threaded holes in the strut to align with the holes in the strut towers.

84. Install the right and left side strut tower bolts. Tighten the strut tower bolts to 44 ft. lbs. (60 Nm).

85. Lower the vehicle.

86. Remove tool, J 42640, or equivalent, from the steering column.

87. Connect the lower transaxle oil cooler pipe fitting to the radiator.

➡**Ensure the lower transaxle oil cooler pipe is positioned upwards while tightening.**

88. Tighten the transaxle oil cooler pipe fitting to 26 ft. lbs. (35 Nm).

89. Install the upper transaxle oil cooler pipe retaining bolt to the fan shroud. Tighten the transaxle oil cooler pipe retaining bolt to 53 inch lbs. (6 Nm).

90. Push the upper transaxle oil cooler pipe into the radiator quick connect fitting, until a click is heard.

91. Tug gently on the cooler pipe to ensure proper retention.

92. Slide the plastic cap over the quick connect fitting.

93. Install the 2 master cylinder brake pipes to the BPMV using the location recorded during the removal procedure. Tighten the brake pipes to 11 ft. lbs. (15 Nm).

94. Connect the heater hoses to the heater pipes.

95. Connect the surge tank outlet hose to the heater pipe.

96. Connect the surge tank inlet hose to the water housing crossover.

97. Position tool J 38185, or equivalent, to the clamp in order to connect the radiator outlet hose to the thermostat housing.

98. Position tool J 37097-A, or equivalent, to the clamp in order to connect the radiator inlet hose to the engine.

99. Install the shift cable to the manual shift lever and the bracket.

✳✳ CAUTION

In order to avoid possible injury or vehicle damage, always replace the accelerator control cable with a NEW cable whenever you remove the engine from the vehicle. In order to avoid cruise control cable damage, position the cable out of the way while you remove or install the engine. Do not pry or lean against the cruise control cable and do not kink the cable. You must replace a damaged cable.

100. Install a NEW accelerator control cable to the throttle body.

101. Install the cruise control cable to the throttle body lever.

102. Slide the cruise control fully into the throttle body bracket until it snaps into place.

103. Install the bolt securing the engine ground cable to the right side body frame rail. Tighten the engine ground cable bolt to 37 ft. lbs. (50 Nm).

104. Connect the wiring harness electrical connectors to the following components:
- The PCM
- The C101
- The engine electrical harness

105. Install or connect the following:
- The nut securing the battery positive cable to the remote positive terminal. Tighten the battery positive cable to remote positive terminal nut to 106 inch lbs. (12 Nm)
- The secondary AIR relay to the relay bracket
- The air cleaner assembly
- The upper filler panel
- The hose to the evaporative emission canister purge valve
- The fuel inlet and return quick-connect fittings at the fuel rail
- The vacuum brake booster hose to the vacuum connection
- The fuel injector sight shield to the engine
- The 2 fuel injector sight shield nuts. Tighten the fuel injector sight shield nuts to 27 inch lbs. (3 Nm)
- The battery negative cable

106. Fill the engine with oil.

107. Fill the cooling system.

108. Bleed the hydraulic brake system.

109. Recharge the A/C refrigerant system.

110. Bleed the power steering system.

111. Measure the wheel alignment.

112. Complete the following procedure after the engine is installed in the vehicle:
   a. With the ignition OFF or discon-

nected, crank the engine several times. Listen for any unusual noises or evidence that any parts are binding.

b. Start the engine and listen for abnormal conditions.

c. Check the vehicle oil pressure gage or light and confirm that the engine has acceptable oil pressure.

d. Run the engine at approximately 1,000 RPM until the engine reaches normal operating temperature.

e. While the engine continues to idle raise and support the vehicle.

f. Inspect for oil, coolant and exhaust leaks while the engine is idling.

g. Lower the vehicle.

h. Perform the Crank Position (CKP) system variation learn procedure.

i. Perform a final inspection for the proper engine oil and coolant levels.

j. Road test the vehicle.

EXHAUST MANIFOLD

REMOVAL & INSTALLATION

3.8L Engine

Left Side (Front) Manifold

See Figure 65.

1. Before servicing the vehicle, refer to the Precautions Section.

2. Remove or disconnect the following:
   - Negative battery cable
   - Spark plug wires
   - Engine oil dipstick and tube
   - Left side lift bracket, if necessary
   - 2 bolts attaching the left exhaust manifold to the crossover pipe
   - Exhaust manifold

To install:

3. Install or connect the following:
   - Exhaust manifold with a new gasket. Torque the studs and bolts

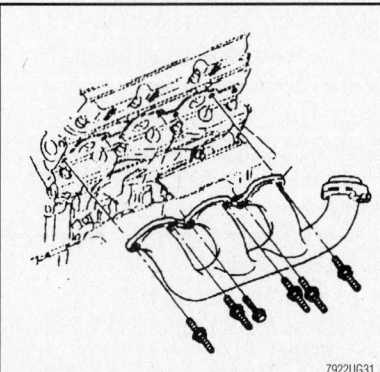

Fig. 65 Exploded view of the left exhaust manifold mounting—3.8L engine

gradually and evenly to 22 ft. lbs. (30 Nm).
   - 2 bolts attaching the left exhaust manifold to the crossover pipe. Torque the bolts to 15 ft. lbs. (20 Nm).
   - Left side lift bracket, if removed
   - Engine oil dipstick and tube. Torque the bolts to 15 ft. lbs. (20 Nm).
   - Spark plug wires
   - Negative battery cable

4. Run the engine and check for exhaust leaks.

Right Side (Rear) Manifold

1. Before servicing the vehicle, refer to the Precautions Section.

2. Remove or disconnect the following:
   - Negative battery cable
   - Fuel injector sight shield
   - Air cleaner assembly
   - Spark plug wires
   - Brake booster heat shield
   - Crossover pipe
   - Engine harness from the right hand engine lift hook bracket
   - Transaxle fluid dipstick and tube
   - Oxygen (O_2S) sensor
   - Exhaust Gas Recirculation (EGR) feed pipe bolt from the manifold
   - Transaxle oil level tube and seal
   - Exhaust manifold flange nuts
   - Front exhaust pipe
   - Engine lift bracket
   - Exhaust manifold

To install:

3. Install or connect the following:
   - Manifold to the cylinder head and crossover pipe using new gaskets
   - Manifold mounting studs. Torque the studs and bolts to 22 ft. lbs. (30 Nm), beginning at the center and working outwards.
   - Engine lift bracket
   - Front exhaust pipe
   - Front exhaust pipe to manifold nuts. Torque the nuts to 22 ft. lbs. (30 Nm).
   - Transaxle dipstick tube seal and the tube
   - EGR feed pipe to the manifold
   - O_2S sensor
   - Spark plug wires to the spark plugs
   - Engine harness to the right hand engine lift hook bracket
   - Crossover pipe
   - Brake booster heat shield
   - Air cleaner assembly
   - Fuel injector sight shield
   - Negative battery cable

4. Run the engine and check for exhaust leaks.

4.6L Engine

Left Side (Front) With Federal Emissions Tier 2

➡NC1 refers to vehicles with California Ultra Low Emission Vehicle package. NF7 refers to vehicles with Federal Emission package.

1. Remove the A.I.R. valve pipe nuts from the exhaust manifold.

2. Remove the A.I.R. valve bolt from the mounting bracket.

3. Remove the A.I.R. valve nuts from the mounting bracket.

4. Remove the A.I.R. valve.

➡DO NOT reuse the old A.I.R. valve pipe gasket.

5. Remove and discard the A.I.R. valve pipe gasket.

6. Remove the oxygen sensor and inspect the sensor for excessive deposits or damage.

7. Replace the oxygen sensor if necessary.

8. Remove the exhaust manifold to crossover pipe bolts.

9. Remove the exhaust manifold bolts.

10. Remove the exhaust manifold.

➡DO NOT reuse the exhaust manifold to crossover pipe gasket.

11. Remove and discard the exhaust manifold to crossover pipe gasket.

➡DO NOT reuse the exhaust manifold gasket.

12. Remove and discard the exhaust manifold gasket.

13. Disconnect the Exhaust Gas Recirculation (EGR) inlet tube nut from the exhaust crossover.

➡The EGR valve inlet pipe incorporates a crush seal connection at the water crossover. The EGR valve inlet pipe must be replaced if disconnected from the water crossover.

14. Remove the EGR inlet pipe bolt and flange from the water crossover.

15. Remove the EGR inlet tube and discard.

16. Remove the exhaust crossover stud and bolt.

17. Remove the exhaust crossover.

18. If equipped, remove the left coolant heater as follows:

a. Remove the coolant heater bolt.

b. Remove the coolant heater from the cylinder block.

To install:

19. If the engine is equipped with coolant heaters, install the left side heater as follows:

a. Place the coolant heater in position on the cylinder block.

b. Install the coolant heater bolt. Tighten the coolant heater bolt to 89 inch lbs. (10 Nm).

➡**DO NOT reuse the exhaust manifold gasket.**

20. With the manifold still on the bench, position a new manifold gasket in place on the manifold sealing surface.

21. Install 2 outer manifold bolts in the manifold to retain the gasket.

22. Install a new manifold to intermediate pipe flange gasket.

23. Using 2 hands, place the manifold in the intermediate pipe and onto the cylinder head.

24. Install new manifold flange bolts for maximum joint integrity. Hand tighten. Do not torque the flange bolts to specification until the engine is mounted in the vehicle.

25. Hand tighten the 2 outer manifold bolts.

26. Install the remaining manifold bolts. Tighten the exhaust manifold bolts to 18 ft. lbs. (25 Nm).

27. Coat the oxygen sensor threads with high temperature anti-seize, GM P/N 12377953 or equivalent.

28. Install the oxygen sensor. Tighten the oxygen sensor to 30 ft. lbs. (40 Nm).

➡**DO NOT reuse the old A.I.R. valve pipe gasket.**

29. Install the NEW A.I.R. valve pipe gasket.

30. Install the A.I.R. valve.

31. Install the A.I.R. valve nuts to the mounting bracket. Tighten the A.I.R. valve nuts to 80 inch lbs. (9 Nm).

32. Install the A.I.R. valve bolt through the mounting bracket. Tighten the A.I.R. valve bolt to 80 inch lbs. (9 Nm).

33. Install the A.I.R. valve pipe nuts to the exhaust manifold. Tighten the A.I.R. valve pipe nuts to 80 inch lbs. (9 Nm).

Left Side (Front) W/O Federal Emissions Tier 2

1. Remove the oxygen sensor and inspect the sensor for excessive deposits or damage.

2. Replace the oxygen sensor if necessary.

3. Remove the exhaust manifold to crossover pipe bolts.

4. Remove the exhaust manifold bolts.

5. Remove the exhaust manifold.

➡**DO NOT reuse the exhaust manifold to crossover pipe gasket.**

6. Remove and discard the exhaust manifold to crossover pipe gasket.

➡**DO NOT reuse the exhaust manifold gasket.**

7. Remove and discard the exhaust manifold gasket.

8. Disconnect the Exhaust Gas Recirculation (EGR) inlet tube nut from the exhaust crossover.

➡**The EGR valve inlet pipe incorporates a crush seal connection at the water crossover. The EGR valve inlet pipe must be replaced if disconnected from the water crossover.**

9. Remove the EGR inlet pipe bolt and flange from the water crossover.

10. Remove the EGR inlet tube and discard.

11. Remove the exhaust crossover stud and bolt.

12. Remove the exhaust crossover.

13. If equipped, remove the left coolant heater as follows:

a. Remove the coolant heater bolt.

b. Remove the coolant heater from the cylinder block.

To install:

14. If the engine is equipped with coolant heaters, install the left side heater as follows:

a. Place the coolant heater in position on the cylinder block.

b. Install the coolant heater bolt. Tighten the coolant heater bolt to 80 inch lbs. (9 Nm).

15. With the manifold still on the bench, position a new manifold gasket in place on the manifold sealing surface.

16. Install 2 outer manifold bolts in the manifold to retain the gasket.

17. Install a new manifold to intermediate pipe flange gasket.

18. Using 2 hands, place the manifold in the intermediate pipe and onto the cylinder head.

19. Install new manifold flange bolts for maximum joint integrity. Hand tighten. Do not torque the flange bolts to specification until the engine is mounted in the vehicle.

20. Hand tighten the 2 outer manifold bolts.

21. Install the remaining manifold bolts.

Tighten the exhaust manifold bolts to 18 ft. lbs. (25 Nm).

22. Coat the oxygen sensor threads with high temperature anti-seize, (GM P/N 12377953) or equivalent.

23. Install the oxygen sensor. Tighten the oxygen sensor to 30 ft. lbs. (40 Nm).

Right Side (Rear) With Federal Emissions Tier 2

1. Remove the A.I.R. valve pipe nuts from the exhaust manifold.

2. Remove the A.I.R. valve bolts from the mounting bracket.

3. Remove the A.I.R. valve.

➡**DO NOT reuse the A.I.R. valve pipe gasket.**

4. Remove and discard the A.I.R. valve pipe gasket.

5. Remove the oxygen sensor and inspect the sensor for excessive deposits or damage.

6. Replace the oxygen sensor if necessary.

➡**The stud must be reinstalled in the original location. The stud may remain attached to the nut when initially removed during exhaust manifold removal. In order to prevent exhaust leakage between the exhaust manifold and cylinder head the nut and stud combination must be reinstalled during exhaust manifold installation in the original location.**

7. Remove the right exhaust manifold retaining nuts.

➡**DO NOT reuse the exhaust manifold gasket.**

8. Remove the exhaust manifold and the gasket.

9. If equipped, remove the right coolant heater as follows:

a. Remove the coolant heater retaining bolt.

b. Remove coolant heater from the cylinder block.

To install:

10. If the engine is equipped with coolant heaters, install the right side heater as follows:

a. Place the coolant heater in position on the cylinder block.

b. Install the coolant heater bolt. Tighten the coolant heater bolt to 89 inch lbs. (10 Nm).

11. Position a new manifold gasket in place on the cylinder head studs.

12. Using two hands, position the manifold onto the cylinder head.

13. Install two outer manifold nuts to hold the manifold in place.

14. Install the remaining manifold nuts. Tighten the exhaust manifold nuts to 18 ft. lbs. (25 Nm).

15. Coat the oxygen sensor threads with high temperature anti-seize, GM P/N 12377953 or equivalent.

16. Install the oxygen sensor. Tighten the oxygen sensor to 30 ft. lbs. (40 Nm).

➡**DO NOT reuse the old A.I.R. valve pipe gasket.**

17. Install the NEW A.I.R. valve pipe gasket.

18. Install the A.I.R. valve.

19. Install the A.I.R. valve bolts through the mounting bracket. Tighten the A.I.R. valve bolts to 80 inch lbs. (9 Nm).

20. Install the A.I.R. valve pipe nuts to the exhaust manifold. Tighten the A.I.R. valve pipe nuts to 80 inch lbs. (9 Nm).

21. Place the exhaust intermediate pipe in position.

22. Install the intermediate pipe stud at the cylinder head and the bolt at the lower crankcase. Tighten the intermediate pipe-to-lower crankcase bolt to 18 ft. lbs. (25 Nm).

23. Tighten the intermediate pipe-to-cylinder head stud to 18 ft. lbs. (25 Nm).

➡**The EGR valve inlet pipe incorporates a crush seal connection at the water crossover. The EGR valve inlet pipe must be replaced if disconnected from the water crossover.**

24. Hand start the NEW EGR inlet tube to intermediate pipe nut to prevent cross-threading. Tighten the EGR inlet tube-to-intermediate pipe nut to 44 ft. lbs. (60 Nm).

25. Connect the EGR inlet pipe flange to the water crossover.

26. Install the EGR inlet pipe to water crossover flange bolt. Tighten the EGR inlet tube to water crossover bolt to 18 ft. lbs. (25 Nm).

Right Side (Rear) W/O Federal Emissions Tier 2

1. Remove the oxygen sensor and inspect the sensor for excessive deposits or damage.

2. Replace the oxygen sensor if necessary.

➡**The stud must be reinstalled in the original location. The stud may remain attached to the nut when initially removed during exhaust manifold removal. In order to prevent exhaust leakage between the exhaust manifold and cylinder head the nut and stud**

combination must be reinstalled during exhaust manifold installation in the original location.

3. Remove the right exhaust manifold retaining nuts.

➡**DO NOT reuse the exhaust manifold gasket.**

4. Remove the exhaust manifold and the gasket.

5. If equipped, remove the right coolant heater as follows:

   a. Remove the coolant heater retaining bolt.

   b. Remove coolant heater from the cylinder block.

To install:

6. If the engine is equipped with coolant heaters, install the right side heater as follows:

   a. Place the coolant heater in position on the cylinder block.

   b. Install the coolant heater bolt. Tighten the coolant heater bolt to 89 inch lbs. (10 Nm).

7. Position a new manifold gasket in place on the cylinder head studs.

8. Using two hands, position the manifold onto the cylinder head.

9. Install 2 outer manifold nuts to hold the manifold in place.

10. Install the remaining manifold nuts. Tighten the exhaust manifold nuts to 18 ft. lbs. (25 Nm).

11. Coat the oxygen sensor threads with high temperature anti-seize, GM P/N 12377953 or equivalent.

12. Install the oxygen sensor. Tighten the oxygen sensor to 30 ft. lbs. (40 Nm).

13. Place the exhaust intermediate pipe in position.

14. Install the intermediate pipe stud at the cylinder head and the bolt at the lower crankcase. Tighten the intermediate pipe-to-lower crankcase bolt to 25 ft. lbs. (35 Nm).

15. Tighten the intermediate pipe-to-cylinder head stud to 18 ft. lbs. (25 Nm).

➡**The EGR valve inlet pipe incorporates a crush seal connection at the water crossover. The EGR valve inlet pipe must be replaced if disconnected from the water crossover.**

16. Hand start the NEW EGR inlet tube to intermediate pipe nut to prevent cross-threading. Tighten the EGR inlet tube-to-intermediate pipe nut to 44 ft. lbs. (60 Nm).

17. Connect the EGR inlet pipe flange to the water crossover.

18. Install the EGR inlet pipe to water crossover flange bolt. Tighten the EGR inlet

tube to water crossover bolt to 18 ft. lbs. (25 Nm).

INTAKE MANIFOLD

REMOVAL & INSTALLATION

3.8L Engine

See Figures 66 through 68.

1. Before servicing the vehicle, refer to the Precautions Section.

2. Disconnect the negative battery cable.

3. Drain the cooling system.

4. Relieve the fuel system pressure.

5. Remove or disconnect the following:

   - Fuel injector sight shield
   - Air inlet duct
   - Spark plug wires from the right side
   - Manifold Absolute Pressure (MAP) sensor
   - Vacuum lines from the intake manifold
   - Fuel lines
   - Fuel injector electrical connectors
   - Fuel regulator vacuum line
   - Fuel rail from the intake manifold
   - Exhaust Gas Recirculation (EGR) heat shield
   - Throttle cable bracket from the cylinder head mounting bracket and the throttle body cables
   - Throttle body support bracket
   - Upper intake plenum and gasket
   - Thermostat housing
   - Electrical connector from the Engine Coolant Temperature (ECT) sensor
   - Accessory drive belt tensioner assembly
   - EGR valve outlet pipe
   - Lower intake manifold

To install:

6. Install or connect the following:

   - Intake manifold using new manifold gaskets. Torque the bolts in sequence to 11 ft. lbs. (15 Nm); then, re-torque to 11 ft. lbs. (15 Nm).
   - EGR valve outlet pipe
   - Accessory drive belt tensioner assembly. Torque the tensioner bolts to 37 ft. lbs. (50 Nm).
   - Electrical connector to the ECT sensor
   - Thermostat housing
   - Upper intake plenum. Torque the intake plenum bolts to 88 inch. lbs. (10 Nm).
   - Throttle body support bracket
   - Throttle cable bracket to the cylinder head mounting bracket and the cables to the throttle body lever
   - EGR heat shield

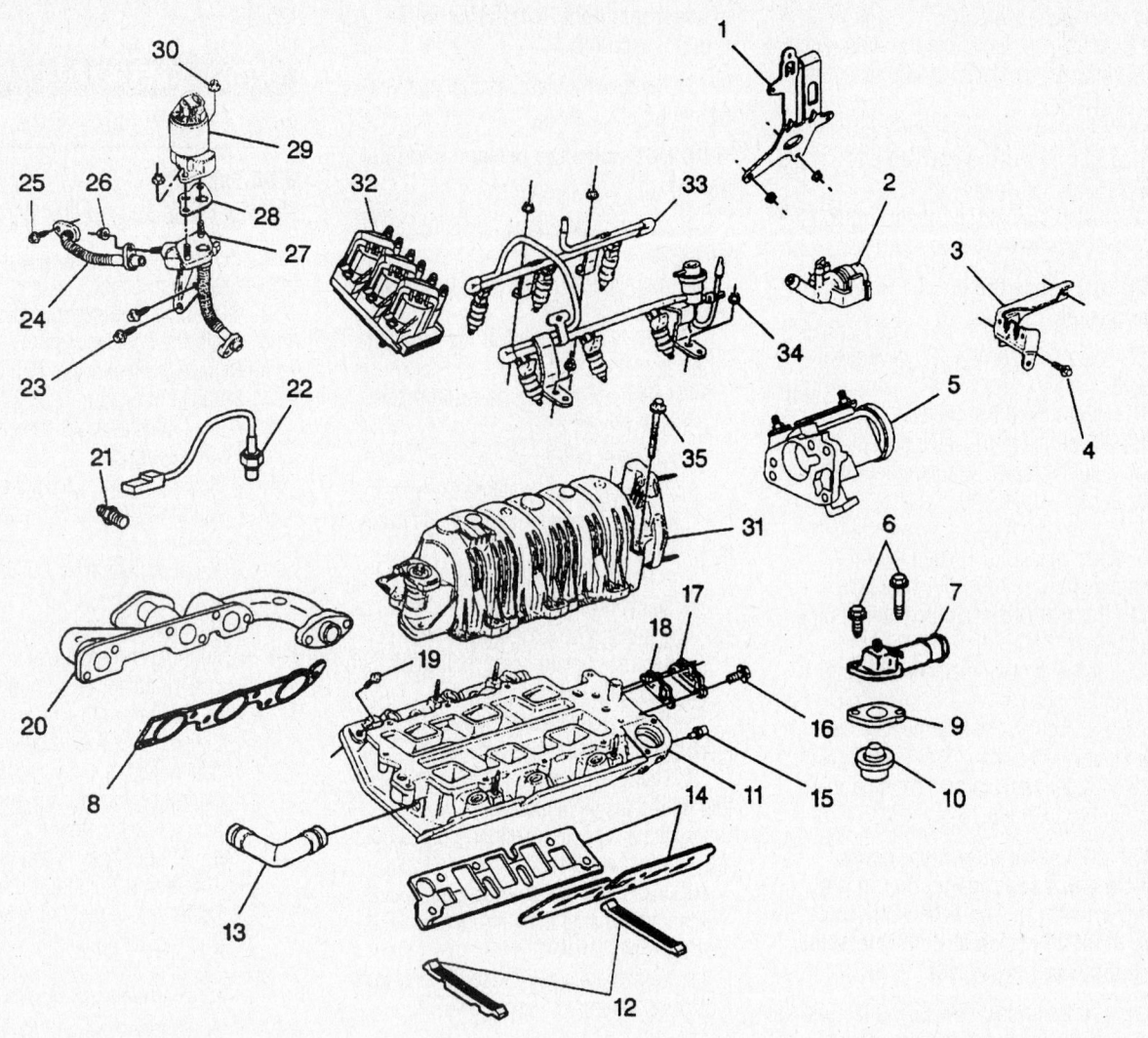

1 Fuel Injector Sight Shield Bracket
2 Vacuum Source Manifold
3 Accelerator Cable Control Bracket
4 Throttle Body Support Bolt
5 Throttle Body
6 Water Outlet Bolt
7 Water Outlet
8 Exhaust Manifold Gasket
9 Water Outlet Gasket
10 Thermostat
11 Lower Intake Manifold
12 Intake Manifold Seal
13 Heater Water Inlet Pipe
14 Lower Intake Manifold Gasket
15 Coolant Temperature Sensor
16 Engine Coolant Manifold Bolt
17 Engine Coolant Manifold
18 Engine Coolant Manifold Gasket

19 Lower Intake Manifold Bolt
20 Exhaust Manifold (Right)
21 Exhaust Manifold Bolt/Stud
22 Exhaust Oxygen Sensor
23 EGR Valve Adapter Bolt
24 EGR Valve Outlet Pipe
25 EGR Valve Outlet Pipe Bolt
26 EGR Valve Outlet Pipe Nut
27 EGR Valve Adapter
28 EGR Valve Gasket
29 EGR Valve
30 EGR Valve Nut
31 Upper Intake Manifold
32 ICM
33 Fuel Injection Rail
34 Fuel Injector Rail Nut
35 Upper Intake Manifold Bolt

9300UG02

Fig. 66 Exploded view of the intake manifold and related components—3.8L engine

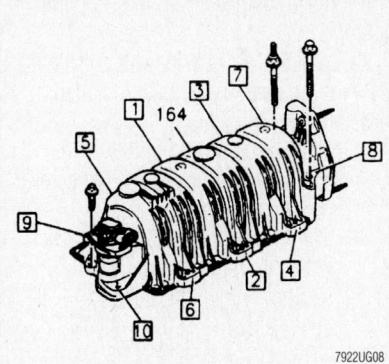

Fig. 67 Upper intake manifold torque sequence—3.8L engine

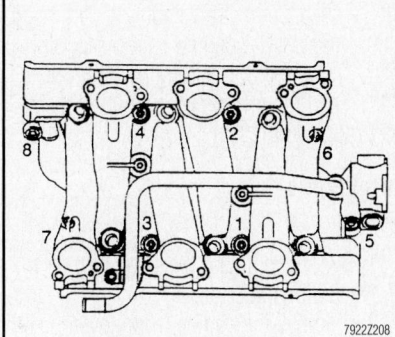

Fig. 68 Lower intake manifold torque sequence—3.8L engine

- Fuel rail. Torque the fuel rail bolts to 88 inch. lbs. (10 Nm).
- Fuel lines
- Fuel regulator vacuum line
- Fuel injector electrical connectors
- Vacuum lines to the intake manifold
- MAP sensor
- Spark plug wires
- Fuel injector sight shield and air inlet duct
- Negative battery cable

7. Refill and bleed the cooling system.

8. Run the engine and check for leaks and proper engine operation.

4.6L Engine

See Figure 69.

1. Before servicing the vehicle, refer to the Precautions Section.

2. Remove the brake booster hose from the throttle body.

3. Remove the fuel pressure regulator vacuum tube from the fuel pressure regulator and the water crossover.

4. Remove the Positive Crankcase Ventilation (PCV) fresh air feed tube from the camshaft cover and the throttle body.

5. Remove the PCV dirty air tube from the PCV orifice in the right camshaft cover and from the intake manifold.

6. Disconnect the fuel injector electrical connectors from the fuel injectors.

7. Remove the fuel injector wiring harness.

8. Remove the fuel rail bracket nut from the engine lift bracket.

9. Remove the fuel rail studs.

10. Lift and remove the fuel rail with injectors.

11. Loosen the plenum duct clamp in order to remove the intake manifold.

12. Remove the intake manifold bolts.

13. Remove the intake manifold.

To install:

14. Install the intake manifold, fitting the plenum duct over the intake manifold duct.

15. Loosely install the intake manifold bolts.

16. Tighten the intake manifold bolts in sequence. Tighten the intake manifold bolts to 89 inch lbs. (10 Nm).

17. Tighten the plenum duct clamp to the intake manifold. Tighten the plenum duct clamp to 24 inch lbs. (3 Nm).

18. Inspect the fuel injector O-rings. Ensure the fuel injector O-rings are not missing, misaligned or damaged. Replace the O-rings if necessary.

19. Lubricate the intake manifold fuel injector bores with light mineral oil (GM P/N 9981704), clean engine oil, or equivalent.

20. Install the fuel rail with fuel injectors as an assembly.

21. Install the fuel rail studs. Tighten the fuel rail studs to 80 inch lbs. (9 Nm).

22. Install the fuel rail bracket nut to the engine lift bracket. Tighten the fuel rail bracket nut to 89 inch lbs. (10 Nm).

23. Install the fuel injector wiring harness.

24. Connect the fuel injector electrical connectors to the fuel injectors.

25. Install the PCV dirty air tube to the PCV orifice in the right camshaft cover and to the intake manifold.

26. Install the PCV fresh air feed tube to the camshaft cover and the water crossover.

27. Install the fuel pressure regulator vacuum tube to the fuel pressure regulator and the throttle body.

28. Install the brake booster hose to the throttle body.

OIL PAN

REMOVAL & INSTALLATION

3.8L Engine

See Figure 70.

✳✳ WARNING

The oil level sensor, located in the oil pan, must be removed prior to removal of the oil pan. If the oil pan is removed first, damage to the oil level sensor may occur.

1. Before servicing the vehicle, refer to the Precautions Section.

2. Drain oil into an approved container.

3. Remove or disconnect the following:
- The negative battery cable
- The right engine mount bracket, if necessary
- The flexplate cover
- The oil level sensor
- The oil filter
- The torque axis mount bracket bolts, if necessary
- The oil pan bolts
- The oil pan
- The oil pan gasket

4. Clean the oil pan and cylinder block mating surfaces.

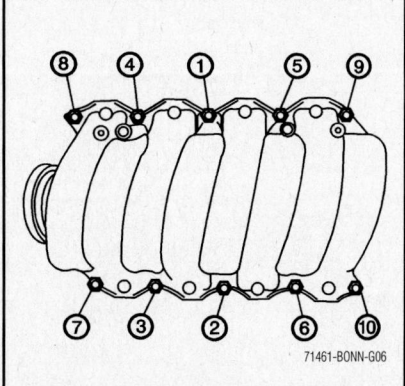

Fig. 69 Intake manifold torque sequence—4.6L engine

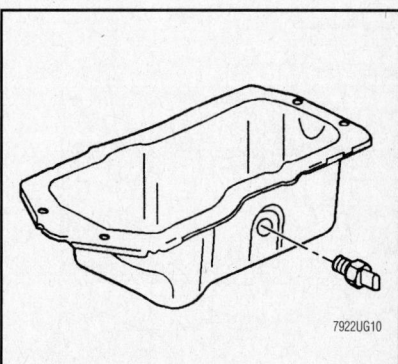

Fig. 70 If equipped, be sure to remove the oil level sensor before removing the pan—3.8L engine

To install:

5. Install or connect the following:
- The oil pan with a new gasket and torque the bolts to 125 inch lbs. (14 Nm)
- The torque axis mount bracket bolts, if removed
- The oil filter
- The flexplate cover
- The oil level sensor
- The oil drain plug and torque the plug to 30 ft. lbs. (40 Nm)
- The right engine mount bracket, if necessary
- The negative battery cable

6. Refill the crankcase.
7. Run the engine and check for leaks.

4.6L Engine

See Figure 71.

1. Before servicing the vehicle, refer to the Precautions Section.
2. Drain the engine oil.
3. Remove the front exhaust manifold pipe.
4. Disconnect the electrical connector from the engine oil level sensor.
5. Remove the engine oil level sensor from the oil pan.
6. Remove the oil pan bolts.

➡ **The oil pan gasket is reusable unless damaged. Do not remove the gasket from the oil pan groove unless replacement is required.**

7. Remove the oil pan.
8. Clean and inspect the oil pan.

To install:

9. If required, install a new oil pan seal using the following procedure:
   a. Clean any residual oil from the seal groove.

b. Work the seal into the pan groove in both directions around the pan.

10. Position the oil pan to the crankcase. Install the oil pan retaining bolts. Tighten the oil pan bolts to 89 inch lbs. (10 Nm) in the sequence shown.
11. Install the engine oil level sensor into the oil pan. Tighten the engine oil level sensor to 15 ft. lbs. (20 Nm).
12. Connect the electrical connector to the engine oil level sensor.
13. Install the front exhaust manifold pipe.
14. Fill the engine oil.
15. Inspect for oil leaks after engine start up.

OIL PUMP

REMOVAL & INSTALLATION

3.8L Engine

See Figure 72.

1. Before servicing the vehicle, refer to the Precautions Section.
2. Support the engine using an engine support fixture.
3. Remove or disconnect the following:
- Negative battery cable
- Engine drive belts and tensioner assembly
- Drive belt idler pulley and bracket
4. Remove or disconnect the following:
- Torque axis mount bracket, if necessary
- Engine front cover assembly
- Oil filter adapter with pressure regulator valve and spring
- Oil pump cover
- Inner and outer pump gears

To install:

5. Lubricate the oil pump gears with petroleum jelly.

6. Install the gears into the oil pump housing.
7. Pack the gear cavity with petroleum jelly after the gears have been installed in the housing.
8. Install or connect the following:
- Oil pump cover. Torque the screws to 97 inch lbs. (11 Nm).
- Oil filter adapter with new gasket, pressure regulator valve and spring. Torque the bolts to 11 ft. lbs. (15 Nm).
- Front cover assembly
- Tensioner assembly
- Drive belt idler pulley and bracket, if removed
- Drive belts
- Torque axis mount bracket
- Negative battery cable

9. Remove the engine support fixture.
10. Verify the correct engine oil level.
11. Start the vehicle and verify no leaks and proper oil pressure.

4.6L Engine

See Figure 73.

1. Before servicing the vehicle, refer to the Precautions Section.
2. Remove the engine front cover.
3. Remove the 3 oil pump assembly retaining bolts identified by the larger head size.
4. Slide the oil pump assembly off the nose of the crankshaft with the drive collar in place.
5. Clean and inspect the oil pump.

To install:

6. Install the oil pump drive spacer into the oil pump so that the drive flat engages the pump rotor.
7. Position the oil pump on the crankshaft.

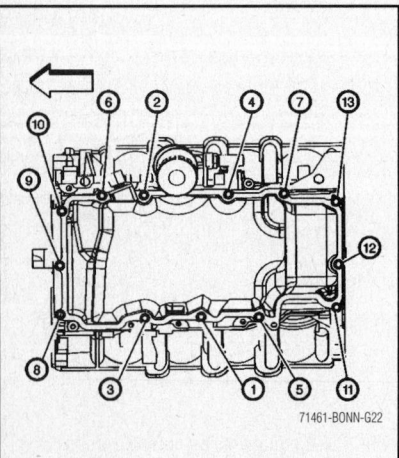

Fig. 71 Oil pan bolt torque sequence—4.6L engine

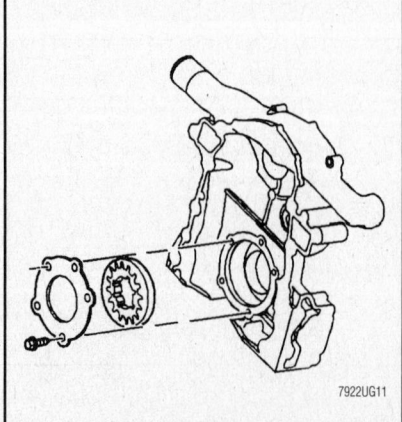

Fig. 72 The oil pump is located inside the front engine cover—3.8L engines

Fig. 73 Oil pump installation—4.6L engine

8. Install the retaining bolts.

9. Apply upward pressure on the pump while tightening the 3 retaining bolts. Tighten the bolts in the sequence shown:

    a. First Pass: Tighten the oil pump mounting bolts in sequence to 89 inch lbs. (10 Nm).

    b. Final Pass: Tighten the oil pump mounting bolts in sequence an additional 35°.

10. Install the engine front cover.

INSPECTION

3.8L Engine

1. Use a suitable solvent to clean the oil pump.

2. Remove all old gasket material from the engine front cover and from the engine block.

3. Inspect the oil pump cover and the engine front cover for cracks, scoring, a porous or damaged casting, damaged threads or excessive wear.

4. Inspect the pressure regulator valve for scoring, burrs or foreign material or sticking in the bore.

5. Inspect the pressure regulator spring for loss of tension or bending. Replace the pressure regulator spring if damaged.

6. Inspect the oil pump gears for chipping, galling, scoring, or excessive wear.

7. Measure the inner oil pump gear tip clearance. If the clearance for the inner oil pump gear tip is greater than 0.006 in. (0.152mm) the oil pump must be replaced.

8. Measure the outer oil pump gear diameter clearance. If the outer oil pump gear diameter clearance is greater than 0.015 in. (0.381mm) the oil pump must be replaced.

9. Measure the oil pump gear end clearance.

10. Measure the pressure regulator valve-to-bore clearance. If the pressure regulator valve-to-bore clearance is greater than 0.003 in. (0.076mm) the oil pump must be replaced.

4.6L Engine

➡The internal parts of the oil pump are not serviced separately. If wear or damage is noted, replace the entire pump assembly.

1. Clean the oil pump components with a non-corrosive solvent.

2. Inspect the housing and the cover for cracks, scoring, casting imperfections, and damaged threads.

3. Inspect the gerotor gears for chipping, galling, or wear.

4. Inspect the pressure relief valve for embedded particles and/or damage.

5. Replace as necessary.

PISTON AND RING

POSITIONING

See Figures 74 through 78.

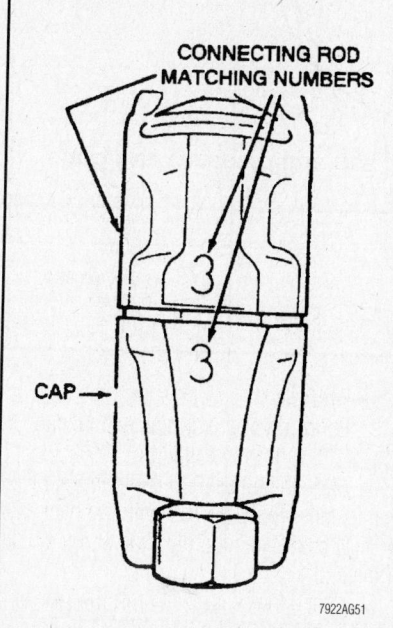

Fig. 74 Engine connecting rod and cap installation. Be sure to matchmark the cap and rod prior to disassembly, as shown.

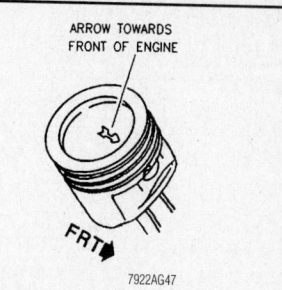

Fig. 76 Piston positioning. Often the arrow is replaced by a notch, which also must face toward the front of the engine—3.8L engine

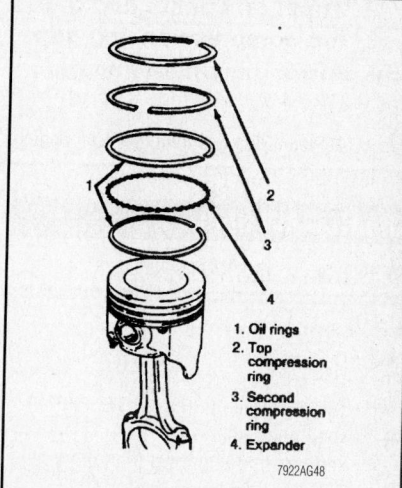

Fig. 77 Piston ring positioning—3.8L engine

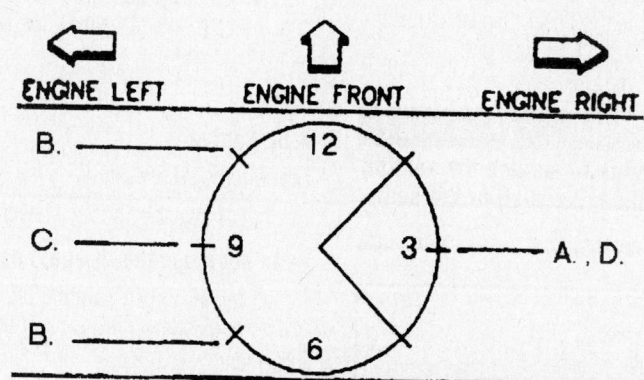

Fig. 75 Piston ring end-gap spacing—3.8L engine

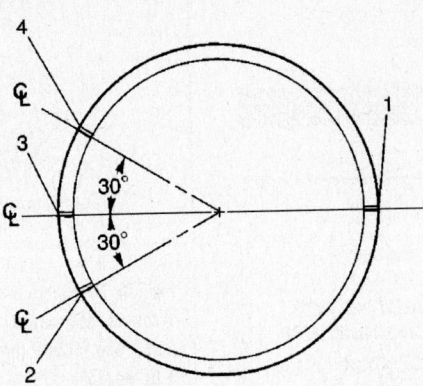

1. Oil control ring and expander, and 2nd compression ring gaps
2. Upper oil control ring gap
3. Top compression ring gap
4. Lower oil control ring gap

Fig. 78 Piston ring positioning—4.6L engine

REAR MAIN SEAL

REMOVAL & INSTALLATION

3.8L Engine

See Figure 79.

1. Before servicing the vehicle, refer to the Precautions Section.
2. Remove or disconnect the following:
   - The transaxle assembly
   - The flexplate from the crankshaft
   - The rear main seal from engine block by inserting a small flat-bladed prytool through the dust lip at an angle, then pry out the crankshaft rear oil seal. Repeat as necessary around the seal until it is removed.

✳✳ WARNING

Do not damage or scratch the sealing surface of the crankshaft or the seal bore.

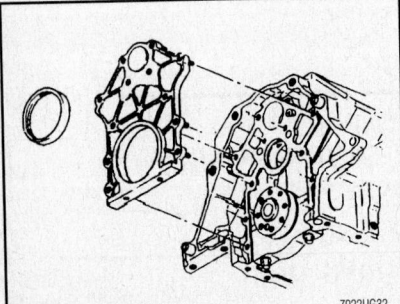

Fig. 79 Rear main oil seal and rear cover—3.8L engine

To install:

3. Lubricate new rear main with clean engine oil prior to installation.
4. Slide the oil seal on the mandrel of seal installer tool J-38196 until the back of the seal is seated squarely against the collar of the tool.
5. Attach the seal installer to the rear of the crankshaft with the 2 mounting bolts, then turn the T-handle until the oil seal is fully seated into the rear of the engine.
6. Loosen the T-handle of the tool completely.
7. Remove both bolts and the tool.
8. Install or connect the following:
   - The flexplate. Torque the bolts to 11 ft. lbs. (15 Nm), plus an additional 50°
   - The transaxle

4.6L Engine

See Figures 80 through 82.

1. Remove the transaxle assembly.

➡**Do not reuse the flywheel bolts.**

2. Remove the 8 mounting bolts.
3. Remove the flywheel and the reinforcement.
4. Place the tool J 42841 onto the crankshaft.
5. Install the tool J 42841 retaining bolts.
6. Using a drill motor, variable speed preferred, with a socket adapter, install eight 1.0 in. (25mm) self-drilling screws into the seal using the guide holes in the removal tool.

➡**When drilling, make sure you reduce the drill speed when the screw begins threading into the seal.**

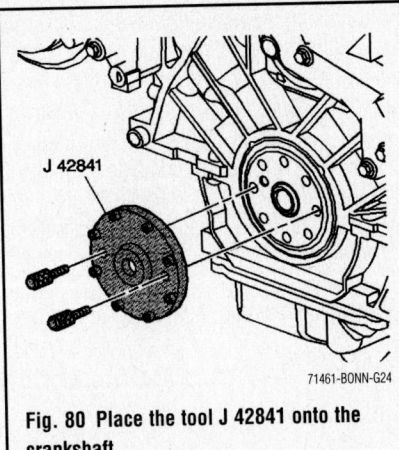

Fig. 80 Place the tool J 42841 onto the crankshaft

7. With all 8 removal screws installed, remove the tool J 42841 retaining bolts.
8. Install the center forcing screw.
9. Tighten the center screw on the tool J 42841 to pull the seal assembly off the end of the crankshaft.

To install:

✳✳ WARNING

Make sure the drain is clear before installing the new crankshaft rear oil seal. Failure to clear the drain could cause the crankshaft rear oil seal to leak.

10. Clean any debris from the crankshaft rear oil seal drain using wire or an unbound plastic tie-wrap.
11. Place a small amount of Gasket Maker, GM P/N 1052942 (Canadian P/N 10953466), or equivalent, at the crankcase split line across the end of the upper/lower crankcase seal.
12. Coat the outer diameter of the cylinder block crankshaft rear oil seal area with clean engine oil GM P/N 12345501 (Canadian P/N 992704), or equivalent.

➡**DO NOT allow any engine oil on the area where the crankshaft rear oil seal is to be pressed onto the crankshaft. The green coating is a sealant preapplied to the inner diameter of the crankshaft rear oil seal and must not be contaminated.**

13. Wipe the outer diameter of the flywheel flange clean with a lint-free cloth.
14. Lubricate the outer rubber surface of the crankshaft rear oil seal with clean engine oil GM P/N 12345501 (Canadian P/N 992704), or equivalent.
15. Loosen the center bolt of the tool J 45930 until the center hub protrudes approximately ½ in. (13mm) beyond the outer plate. It is not necessary to completely

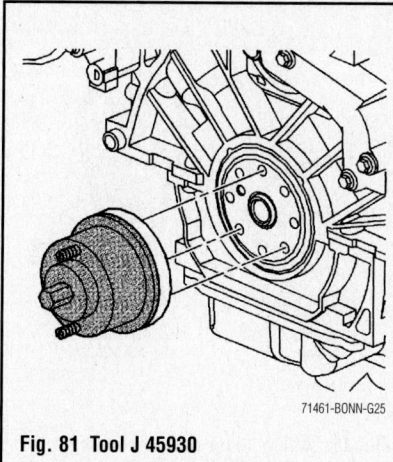

Fig. 81 Tool J 45930

unthread the center bolt and separate the 2 pieces of the tool J 45930.

16. Install the tool J 45930 to the rear of the crankshaft.

17. Thread the 2 mounting bolts into the crankshaft flange.

18. Tighten the bolts until the tool J 45930 is firmly mounted on the crankshaft.

19. Install the crankshaft rear oil seal by tightening the center bolt until the tool J 45930 bottoms against the crankcase.

20. Loosen the center bolt to release pressure on the crankcase.

21. Loosen the 2 mounting bolts.

22. Remove the tool J 45930 from the crankshaft flange.

23. Inspect to ensure the installation depth is equal around the crankshaft rear oil seal's circumference. If the depth is not equal reinstall the tool J 45930 and repeat the installation procedures.

24. Position the flywheel and the reinforcement to the crankshaft.

25. Apply sealant, GM P/N 12346004 (Canadian P/N 10953480) or equivalent, to the flywheel mounting bolts.

26. Install the 8 NEW mounting bolts.

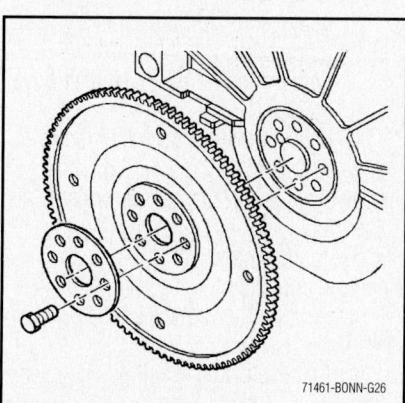

Fig. 82 Position the flywheel and the reinforcement to the crankshaft

a. First Pass: Tighten the flywheel mounting bolts to 11 ft. lbs. (15 Nm).

b. Final Pass: Tighten the flywheel mounting bolts an additional 50° using the tool J 36660-A .

27. Install the transaxle assembly.

TIMING CHAIN COVER AND SEAL

REMOVAL & INSTALLATION

3.8L Engine

See Figure 83.

1. Before servicing the vehicle, refer to the Precautions Section.

2. Drain the cooling system.

3. Support the engine.

4. Remove or disconnect the following:

- Negative battery cable
- Torque axis mount and bracket
- Drive belt
- Drive belt tensioner
- Crankshaft damper
- Crankshaft Position (CKP) sensor shield and the CKP sensor
- Oil pan to front cover bolts
- Timing chain front cover

To install:

❊❊ WARNING

The oil pump is built into the front cover. When the cover is removed, oil drains from the pump. Since the pump "loses its prime" it may not establish oil pressure as soon as the engine starts. Therefore, it is important to remove the oil pump cover from the back of the timing chain front cover and pack the space around the oil pump gears completely full of petroleum jelly. If this is not done, the oil pump may not pump engine oil when the engine is

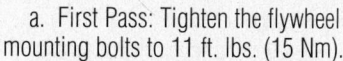

Fig. 83 Timing chain front cover—3.8L engines

started, resulting in severe engine damage.

5. Remove the screws and the oil pump cover from the back of the timing chain front cover. Pack the space around the oil pump gears completely full of petroleum jelly. There must be no air space left inside the pump.

6. Install or connect the following:

- Pump cover with new gaskets. Torque the screws to 97 inch lbs. (11 Nm).
- Timing chain front cover. Torque the front cover to engine bolts to 11 ft. lbs. (15 Nm) plus an additional 40°.
- Oil pan to front cover bolts. Torque the bolts to 125 inch lbs. (14 Nm).
- CKP sensor. Torque the bolts to 14–28 ft. lbs. (20–40 Nm).
- CKP sensor shield
- Crankshaft damper. Torque the bolt to 111 ft. lbs. (150 Nm) plus an additional 76°.
- Drive belt tensioner assembly
- Right inner fender access panel and the right front wheel
- Drive belt(s)
- Engine mount
- Coolant hoses
- Negative battery cable

7. Remove the engine support fixture.

8. Refill and bleed the cooling system.

9. Start the vehicle and check for leaks and proper engine operation.

4.6L Engine

See Figure 84.

1. Remove the front cover perimeter bolts.

2. Remove the front cover and the gasket. Ensure that you do not damage the sealing surface.

➡**Do not remove the crankshaft front oil seal.**

The crankshaft front oil seal is not serviced as an individual component. When replacing the crankshaft front oil seal, install a **NEW** engine front cover. In order to precisely align the crankshaft front oil seal to the crankshaft damper and crankshaft damper dust shield, the engine front cover and the crankshaft front oil seal are sold as an assembly.

To install:

3. Place a small amount of sealant GM P/N 12345739, (Canadian P/N 10953541), or equivalent at the split line of the upper and lower crankcases.

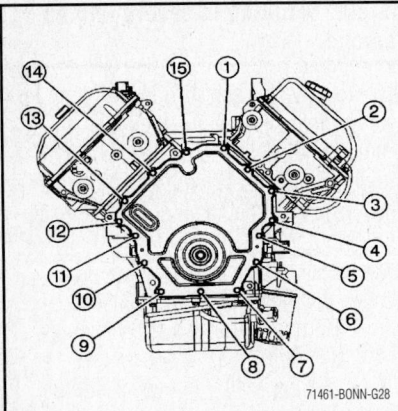

Fig. 84 Front cover torque sequence—4.6L engine

4. Place the front cover gasket over the crankcase dowel pins.

5. Place the front cover in position on the crankcase.

6. Install the front cover retaining bolts.

7. Tighten the front cover retaining bolts in the sequence shown. Tighten the front cover retaining bolts in proper sequence to 89 inch lbs. (10 Nm).

TIMING CHAIN AND SPROCKETS

REMOVAL & INSTALLATION

3.8L Engine

See Figures 83 and 85.

1. Before servicing the vehicle, refer to the Precautions Section.

2. Drain the cooling system.

3. Support the engine.

4. Remove or disconnect the following:
- The negative battery cable
- The torque axis mount and bracket
- The accessory drive belt
- The accessory drive belt tensioner
- The crankshaft damper
- The Crankshaft Position (CKP) sensor shield and the CKP sensor
- The oil pan to front cover bolts
- The timing chain front cover

5. Align the timing marks on the camshaft and crankshaft sprockets so they are as close together as possible.
- The timing chain damper
- The camshaft sprocket bolt, the camshaft sprocket and timing chain
- The crankshaft sprocket

✳✳ WARNING

Do not rotate the camshaft or crankshaft while the timing chain and sprockets are removed.

To install:

6. Install or connect the following:
- The timing chain and sprockets with the timing marks aligned
- The camshaft sprocket bolt. Torque the bolt to 74 ft. lbs. (100 Nm) plus an additional 90°.
- The timing chain damper. Torque the bolts to 16 ft. lbs. (22 Nm).

✳✳ WARNING

The oil pump is built into the front cover. When the cover is removed, oil drains from the pump. Since the pump "loses its prime" it may not establish oil pressure as soon as the engine starts. Therefore, it is important to remove the oil pump cover from the back of the timing chain front cover and pack the space around the oil pump gears completely full of petroleum jelly. If this is not done, the oil pump may not pump engine oil when the engine is started, resulting in severe engine damage.

7. Remove the screws and the oil pump cover from the back of the timing chain front cover. Pack the space around the oil pump gears completely full of petroleum jelly. There must be no air space left inside the pump.

8. Install or connect the following:
- The pump cover with new gaskets. Torque the screws to 97 inch lbs. (11 Nm).
- The timing chain front cover. Torque the front cover to engine bolts to 11 ft. lbs. (15 Nm) plus an additional 40°.
- The oil pan to front cover bolts. Torque the bolts to 125 inch lbs. (14 Nm).
- The CKP sensor. Torque the bolts to 14–28 ft. lbs. (20–40 Nm).
- The CKP sensor shield
- The crankshaft damper. Torque the bolt to 111 ft. lbs. (150 Nm) plus an additional 76°.
- The drive belt tensioner assembly
- The right inner fender access panel and the right front wheel
- The accessory drive belt(s)
- The engine mount
- The coolant hoses
- The negative battery cable

9. Remove the engine support fixture.

10. Refill and bleed the cooling system.

11. Start the vehicle and check for leaks and proper engine operation.

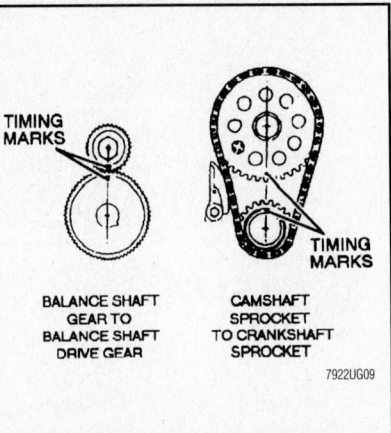

Fig. 85 Timing chain sprocket and balance shaft gear alignment—3.8L engines

4.6L Engine

See Figures 86 and 87.

1. Remove the front cover perimeter bolts.

2. Remove the front cover and the gasket. Ensure that you do not damage the sealing surface.

➡**Do not remove the crankshaft front oil seal.**

The crankshaft front oil seal is not serviced as an individual component. When replacing the crankshaft front oil seal, install a NEW engine front cover. In order to precisely align the crankshaft front oil seal to the crankshaft damper and crankshaft damper dust shield, the engine front cover and the crankshaft front oil seal are sold as an assembly.

3. Primary camshaft drive chain removal:

  a. Remove the camshaft intermediate drive shaft sprocket bolt.

  b. Remove the primary camshaft drive chain tensioner bolts.

  c. Remove the primary camshaft drive chain tensioner.

  d. Remove the primary camshaft drive chain guide bolts.

  e. Remove the primary camshaft drive chain guide.

  f. Remove the camshaft intermediate drive shaft sprocket, primary camshaft drive chain and crankshaft sprocket as an assembly.

4. Secondary camshaft drive chain removal—right side:

  a. Remove the camshaft position sensor bolt.

  b. Remove the camshaft position sensor.

  c. Remove and discard the camshaft position sensor O-ring.

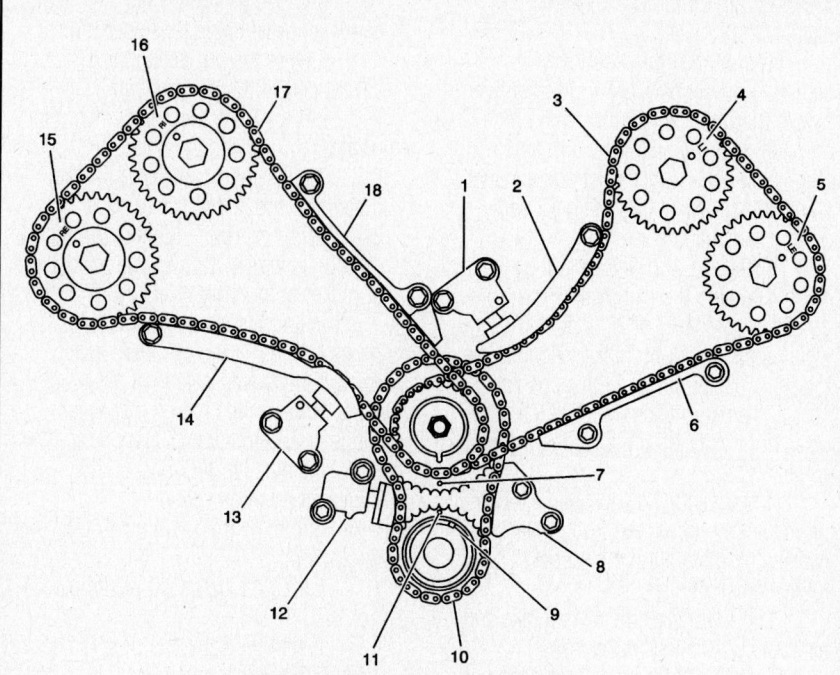

(1) Left Secondary Timing Chain Tensioner
(2) Left Secondary Timing Chain Shoe
(3) Left Secondary Timing Chain
(4) Left Intake Camshaft Sprocket Timing Mark
(5) Left Exhaust Camshaft Sprocket Timing Mark
(6) Left Secondary Timing Chain Guide
(7) Intermediate Sprocket Timing Mark
(8) Primary Timing Chain Guide
(9) Crankshaft Sprocket Pin Alignment Slot
(10) Primary Timing Chain
(11) Crankshaft Sprocket Timing Mark
(12) Primary Timing Chain Tensioner
(13) Right Secondary Timing Chain Tensioner
(14) Right Secondary Timing Chain Shoe
(15) Right Exhaust Camshaft Sprocket Timing Mark
(16) Right Intake Camshaft Sprocket Timing Mark
(17) Right Secondary Timing Chain
(18) Right Secondary Timing Chain Guide

71461-BONN-G27

Fig. 86 Correct alignment of the primary and secondary timing chains—4.6L engine

d. Remove the chain guide access plugs located in the cylinder heads. Ensure the O-ring seal is on each access plug.

e. Remove the right secondary drive chain tensioner bolts.

f. Remove the right secondary camshaft drive chain tensioner allowing it to expand as you remove it.

g. Remove the upper right secondary camshaft drive chain guide bolt.

h. Remove the camshaft sprocket bolts from the camshafts. Use an open wrench on the hex cast near the front of each camshaft to prevent engine rotation when loosening the camshaft sprocket bolts.

i. Lift the secondary camshaft drive chain from the camshaft sprocket teeth and slide the camshaft sprockets off of the camshafts.

j. Remove the right secondary camshaft drive chain.

k. Remove the right secondary camshaft drive chain shoe bolt.

l. Remove the right secondary camshaft drive chain shoe.

m. Remove the lower right secondary camshaft drive chain guide bolt.

n. Remove the right secondary camshaft drive chain guide.

5. Secondary camshaft drive chain removal—left side:

a. Remove the left secondary camshaft drive chain tensioner bolts.

b. Remove the left secondary camshaft drive chain tensioner allowing it to expand as you remove it.

c. Remove the upper left secondary camshaft drive chain guide bolt.

d. Remove the camshaft sprocket bolts from the camshafts. Use an open wrench on the hex cast near the front of each camshaft to prevent engine rotation when loosening the camshaft sprocket bolts.

e. Lift the secondary camshaft drive chain from the camshaft sprocket teeth and slide the camshaft sprockets off of the camshafts.

f. Remove the left secondary drive chain.

g. Remove the left secondary camshaft drive chain shoe bolt.

h. Remove the left secondary camshaft drive chain shoe.

i. Remove the lower left secondary camshaft drive chain guide bolt.

j. Remove the left secondary camshaft drive chain guide.

To install:

6. Secondary camshaft drive chain installation—left side:

a. Install the left secondary camshaft drive chain guide.

b. Loosely install the lower left secondary camshaft drive chain guide bolt.

c. Install the left secondary camshaft drive chain shoe.

d. Install the left secondary camshaft drive chain shoe bolt. Tighten the left secondary camshaft drive chain shoe bolt to 18 ft. lbs. (25 Nm).

e. Install the left secondary camshaft drive chain by sliding the chain down through the left cylinder head and placing the chain on the end of the camshafts.

f. Route the left secondary camshaft drive chain around the inner row of the intermediate drive chain sprocket teeth.

g. Install the left intake and exhaust camshaft sprockets into the left secondary camshaft drive chain.

h. Install the left intake and exhaust camshaft sprockets onto the camshafts. The camshaft sprocket notch marked "LI" which indicates left intake, engages the intake camshaft pin and the camshaft sprocket notch marked "LE" which indicates left exhaust, engages the exhaust camshaft pin.

i. If necessary, use an open wrench on the hex cast near the front of each camshaft to help align the sprocket notch to the camshaft pin.

j. Loosely install the left intake and exhaust camshaft sprocket bolts.

k. Ensure the perpendicular alignment of the left intake and exhaust camshaft sprocket notches and camshaft pins to the cylinder head.

l. Install tool J 44212 to the left cylinder head camshafts.

m. Install the upper left secondary camshaft drive chain guide bolt. Tighten BOTH the upper and lower left secondary camshaft drive chain guide bolts to 18 ft. lbs. (25 Nm).

n. Collapse the left secondary camshaft drive chain tensioner using the following procedure:

- Rotate the ratchet release lever counterclockwise and hold
- Collapse the left secondary camshaft drive chain tensioner shoe and hold
- Release the ratchet lever and slowly release the pressure on the shoe
- When the ratchet lever moves to the first detent a click should be heard and felt
- Insert a pin through the hole in the release lever in order to lock the left secondary camshaft drive chain tensioner shoe in the collapsed position

➡**Ensure the left secondary camshaft drive chain tensioner release lever is facing out.**

o. Install the left secondary camshaft drive chain tensioner.

p. Install the left secondary camshaft drive chain tensioner bolts. Tighten the left secondary camshaft drive chain tensioner bolts to 18 ft. lbs. (25 Nm).

q. Remove pin from left secondary camshaft drive chain tensioner lever.

7. Secondary camshaft dive chain installation—right side:

a. Install the right secondary camshaft drive chain guide.

b. Loosely install the lower right secondary camshaft drive chain guide bolt.

c. Install the right secondary camshaft drive chain shoe.

d. Install the right secondary camshaft drive chain shoe bolt. Tighten the right secondary camshaft drive chain shoe bolt to 18 ft. lbs. (25 Nm).

e. Install the right secondary camshaft drive chain by sliding the chain down through the right cylinder head and placing the chain on the end of the camshafts.

f. Route the right secondary camshaft drive chain around the outer row of the intermediate drive chain sprocket teeth.

g. Install the right intake and exhaust camshaft sprockets into the right secondary camshaft drive chain.

h. Install the right intake and exhaust camshafts onto the camshafts. The camshaft sprocket notch marked "RI" which indicates right intake, engages the intake camshaft pin and the camshaft sprocket notch marked "RE" which indicates right exhaust, engages the exhaust camshaft pin.

i. If necessary, use an open wrench on the hex cast near the front of each camshaft to help align the sprocket notch to the camshaft pin.

j. Loosely install the right intake and exhaust camshaft sprocket bolts.

k. Ensure the perpendicular alignment of the right intake and exhaust camshaft sprocket notches and camshaft pins to the cylinder head.

l. Install tool J 44212 to the right cylinder head camshafts.

m. Install the upper right secondary camshaft drive chain guide bolt. Tighten BOTH the upper and lower right secondary camshaft drive chain guide bolts to 18 ft. lbs. (25 Nm).

n. Collapse the right secondary camshaft drive chain tensioner using the following procedure:

- Rotate the ratchet release lever counter-clockwise and hold.
- Collapse the right secondary camshaft drive chain tensioner shoe and hold.
- Release the ratchet lever and slowly release the pressure on the shoe.
- When the ratchet lever moves to the first detent a click should be heard and felt.
- Insert a pin through the hole in the release lever in order to lock the right secondary camshaft drive chain tensioner shoe in the collapsed position.

➡**Ensure the right secondary camshaft drive chain tensioner release lever is facing out.**

o. Install the right secondary camshaft drive chain tensioner.

p. Install the right secondary camshaft drive chain tensioner bolts. Tighten the right secondary camshaft drive chain tensioner bolts to 18 ft. lbs. (25 Nm).

q. Remove pin from right secondary camshaft drive chain tensioner lever.

r. Ensure the correct alignment of all secondary timing components.

s. Ensure the correct alignment of all primary timing components.

t. Tighten ALL camshaft sprocket bolts. Use the hex cast into each camshaft to prevent engine rotation and provide leverage. Tighten ALL camshaft sprocket bolts to 90 ft. lbs. (120 Nm).

u. Install the chain guide access plugs located in the cylinder heads. Ensure the O-ring seal is on each access plug. Tighten the chain guide access plugs to 39 inch lbs. (5 Nm).

v. Install a NEW O-ring on the camshaft position sensor.

w. Lubricate the O-ring with clean engine oil.

x. Install the camshaft position sensor.

y. Install the camshaft position sensor bolt. Tighten the camshaft position sensor bolt to 89 inch lbs. (10 Nm).

8. Primary camshaft drive chain installation:

a. Install the primary camshaft drive chain on the camshaft intermediate drive shaft sprocket and crankshaft sprocket.

b. Align the timing marks of the camshaft intermediate drive shaft sprocket and crankshaft sprocket. Ensure the marks are aligned vertically.

c. Ensure the number one piston is at Top Dead Center (TDC) and the crankshaft pin is approximately at the one o'clock position using tool J 39946.

d. Install the primary camshaft drive chain, camshaft intermediate drive shaft sprocket and crankshaft sprocket as an assembly onto the camshaft intermediate drive shaft and the crankshaft.

e. Install the camshaft intermediate drive shaft sprocket bolt. Tighten the camshaft intermediate drive shaft sprocket bolt to 44 ft. lbs. (60 Nm).

f. Install the primary camshaft drive chain guide.

g. Install the primary camshaft drive chain guide bolts. Tighten the primary camshaft drive chain guide bolts to 18 ft. lbs. (25 Nm).

h. Collapse the primary camshaft drive chain tensioner using the following procedure:

- Rotate the ratchet release lever counterclockwise and hold
- Collapse the primary camshaft drive chain tensioner shoe and hold

- Release the ratchet lever and slowly release the pressure on the shoe
- When the ratchet lever moves to the first detent a click should be heard and felt
- Insert a pin through the hole in the release lever in order to lock the primary camshaft drive chain tensioner shoe in the collapsed position

➡**Ensure the primary camshaft drive chain tensioner release lever is facing out.**

i. Install the primary camshaft drive chain tensioner.

j. Install the primary camshaft drive chain tensioner bolts. Tighten the primary camshaft drive chain tensioner bolts to 18 ft. lbs. (25 Nm).

k. Remove the pin in the release lever locking the primary camshaft drive chain tensioner.

l. Ensure the timing marks are aligned vertically.

m. Place a small amount of sealant GM P/N 12345739, (Canadian P/N

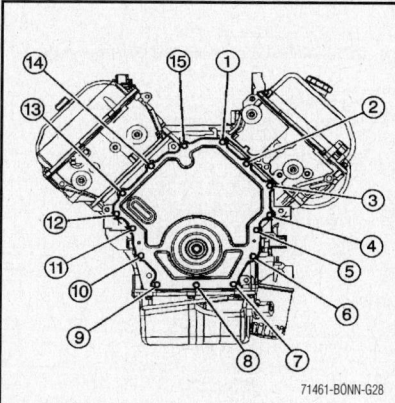

71461-BONN-G28

Fig. 87 Front cover torque sequence—4.6L engine

10953541), or equivalent at the split line of the upper and lower crankcases.

n. Place the front cover gasket over the crankcase dowel pins.

o. Place the front cover in position on the crankcase.

p. Install the front cover retaining bolts.

q. Tighten the front cover retaining bolts in the sequence shown. Tighten the front cover retaining bolts in proper sequence to 89 inch lbs. (10 Nm).

VALVE LASH

ADJUSTMENT

The valve clearance cannot be adjusted on these engines. The engine is equipped with hydraulic lifters, and adjustment is not necessary.

ENGINE PERFORMANCE & EMISSION CONTROL

COMPONENT LOCATIONS

See Figures 88 through 98.

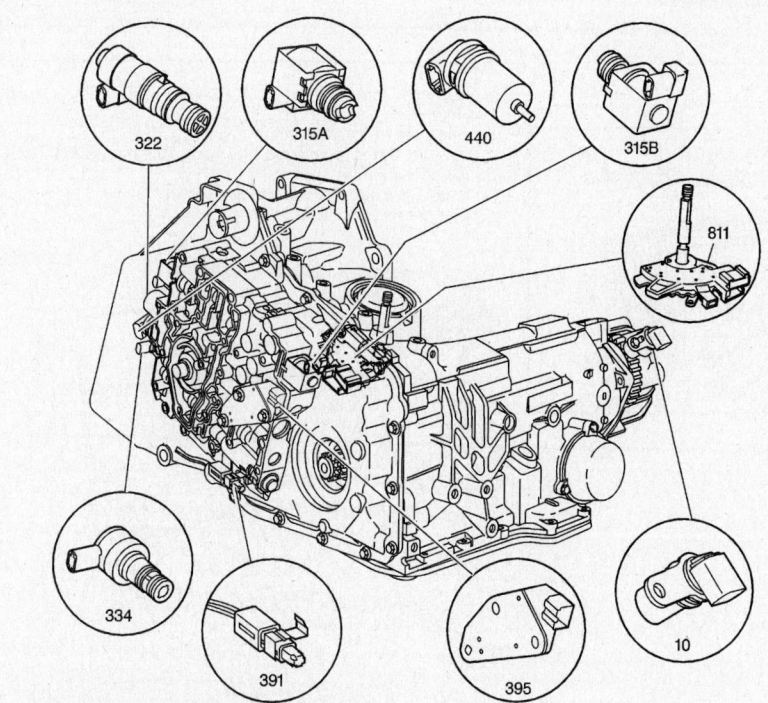

10. Vehicle Speed Sensor (VSS) Assembly
315a. 1-2, 3-4 Shift Solenoid (SS) Valve Assembly
315b. 2-3 Shift Solenoid (SS) Valve Assembly
322. Pressure Control (PC) Solenoid Valve Assembly
334. Torque Converter Clutch Pulse Width Modulation (TCC PWM) Solenoid Valve Assembly
391. Transmission Fluid Temperature (TFT) Sensor
395. Transmission Fluid Pressure (TFP) Manual Valve Position Switch Assembly
440. Automatic Transmission Input Shaft Speed (A/T ISS) Sensor Assembly
811. Lever Assembly-Manual Shaft Detent with Shift Position Switch - Internal Mode Switch (IMS)

22116_LUCE_G0025

Fig. 88 Automatic transmission electronic components

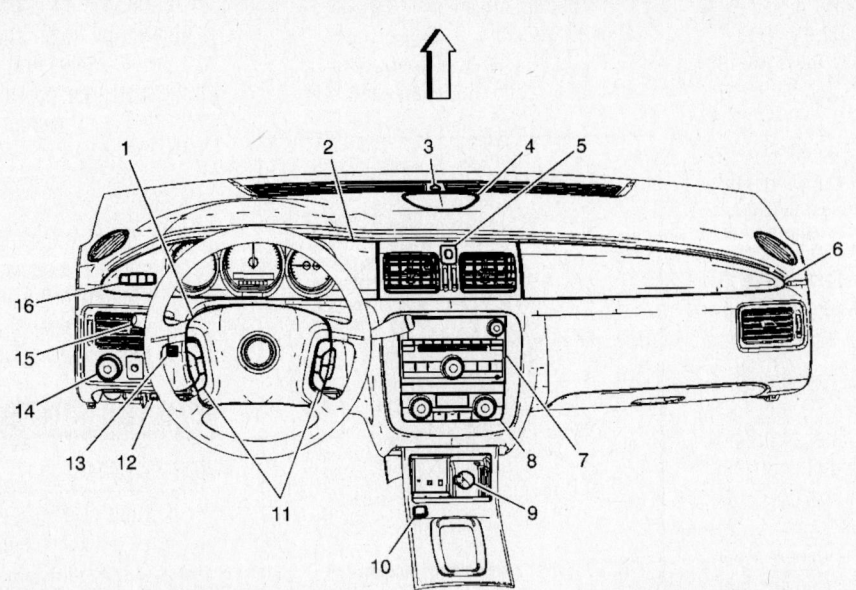

1. Inflatable Restraint Steering Wheel Module
2. Instrument Panel Cluster (IPC)
3. Sunload Twilight Sensor (CJ2)/Ambient Light Sensor (C67)
4. Speaker - Front Center (UQA)
5. Hazard Switch
6. Inflatable Restraint I/P Module
7. I/P Compartment Lamp
8. Radio
9. HVAC Control Module
10. Auxiliary Power Outlet - Console (A51)/Cigar Lighter (DT4/A51)

11. Traction Control Switch (A51)
12. Steering Wheel Controls
13. Data Link Connector (DLC)
14. Air Temperature Sensor - Inside (CJ2)
15. Headlamp Switch
16. Turn Signal/Multifunction Switch
17. Driver Information Display Switch

22116_LUCE_G0022

Fig. 89 Instrument Panel (I/P) components

1. Remote Control Door Lock Receiver (RCDLR)
2. Rear Park Assist Indicator (UD7)
3. Speaker - Right Rear
4. Vehicle Communication Interface Module (VCIM) (UE1)
5. Amplifier (UQA)
6. Rear Compartment Courtesy Lamp
7. Speaker - Left Rear

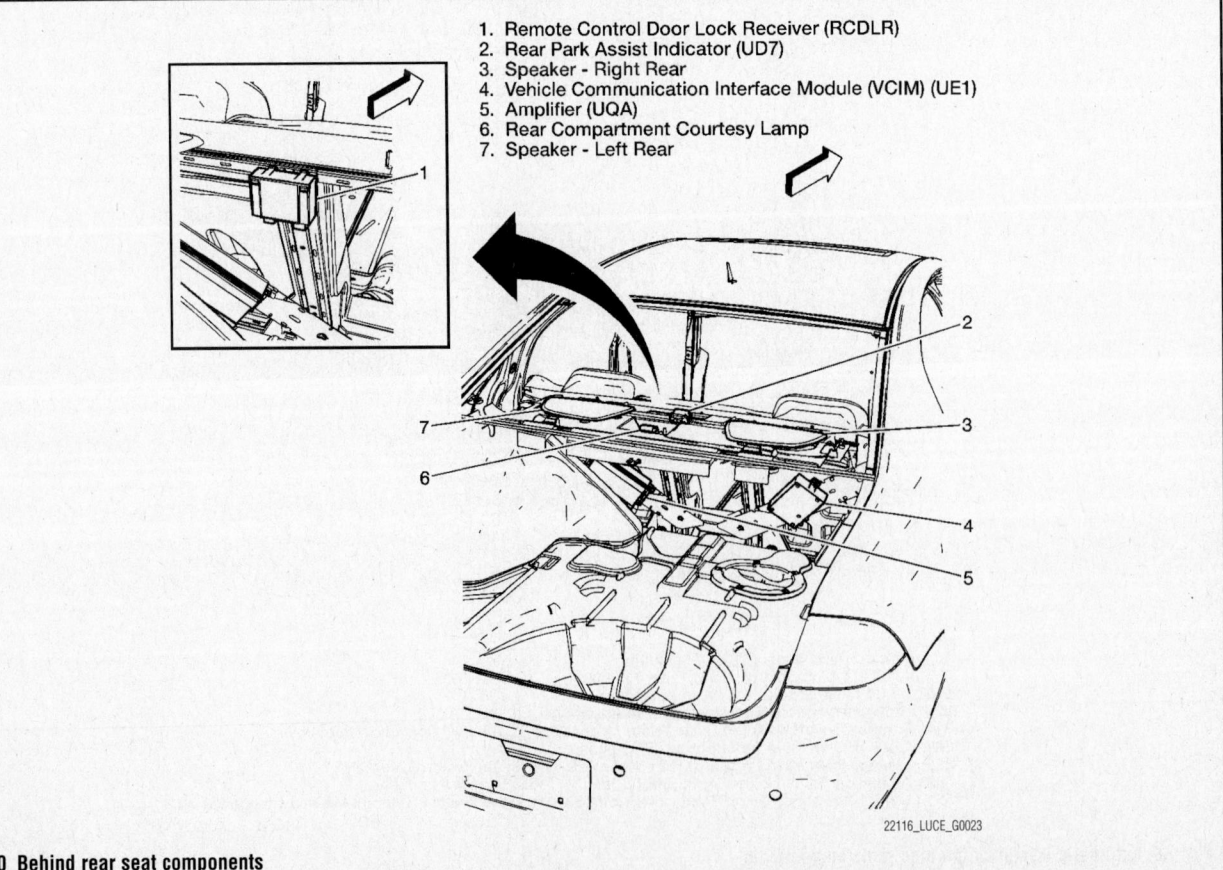

22116_LUCE_G0023

Fig. 90 Behind rear seat components

5
2
1
3
4
1. Steering Angle Sensor (JL4)
2. Electronic Brake Control Module (EBCM)
3. Variable Effort Steering Actuator (LD8/L37)
4. Power Steering Rack
5. Steering Column Assembly
22116_LUCE_G0024

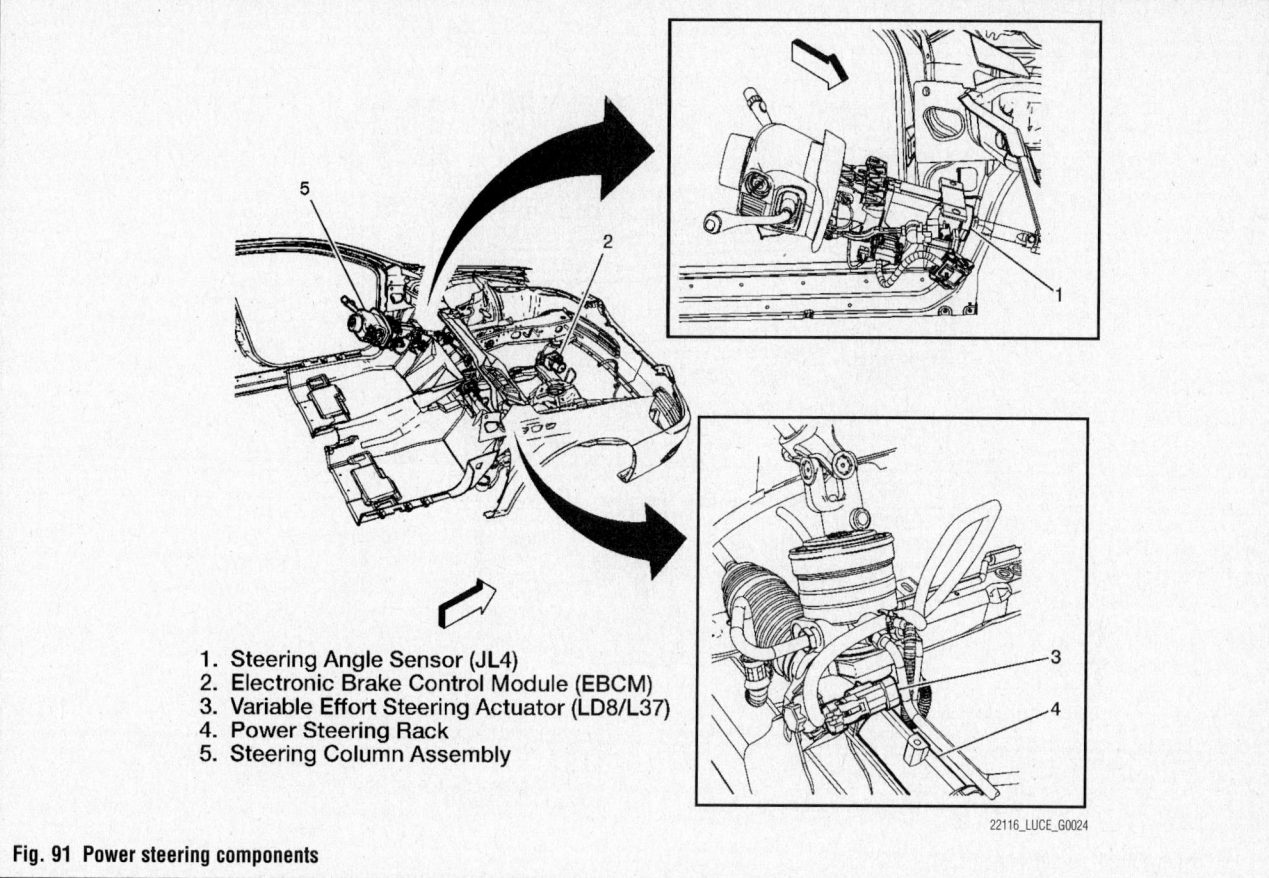

Fig. 91 Power steering components

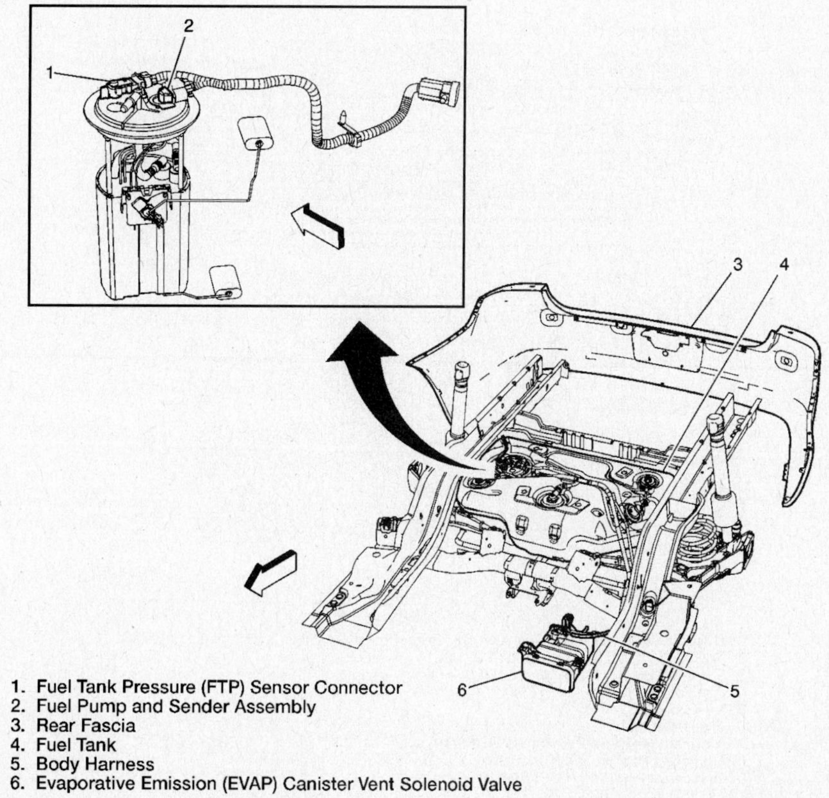

1
2
3
4
5
6
1. Fuel Tank Pressure (FTP) Sensor Connector
2. Fuel Pump and Sender Assembly
3. Rear Fascia
4. Fuel Tank
5. Body Harness
6. Evaporative Emission (EVAP) Canister Vent Solenoid Valve
22116_LUCE_G0027

Fig. 92 Fuel tank components

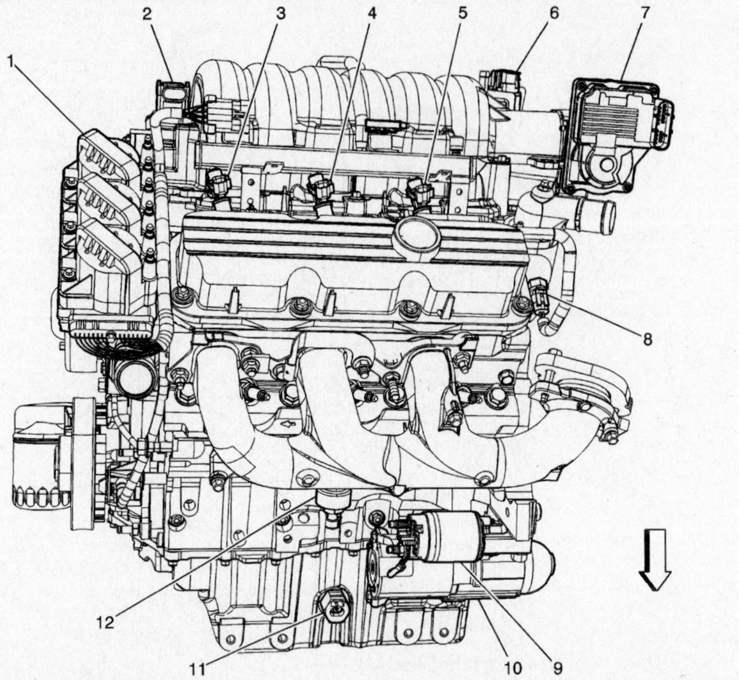

1. Ignition Coil Module
2. Manifold Absolute Pressure (MAP) Sensor
3. Fuel Injector 1
4. Fuel Injector 3
5. Fuel Injector 5
6. Exhaust Gas Recirculation (EGR) Valve
7. Throttle Actuator Control (TAC) Module
8. Engine Coolant Temperature (ECT) Sensor
9. Starter Solenoid
10. Starter
11. Engine Oil Level Switch
12. Knock Sensor (KS) 1

22116_LACR_G0057

Fig. 93 Engine control components (front)—3.8L

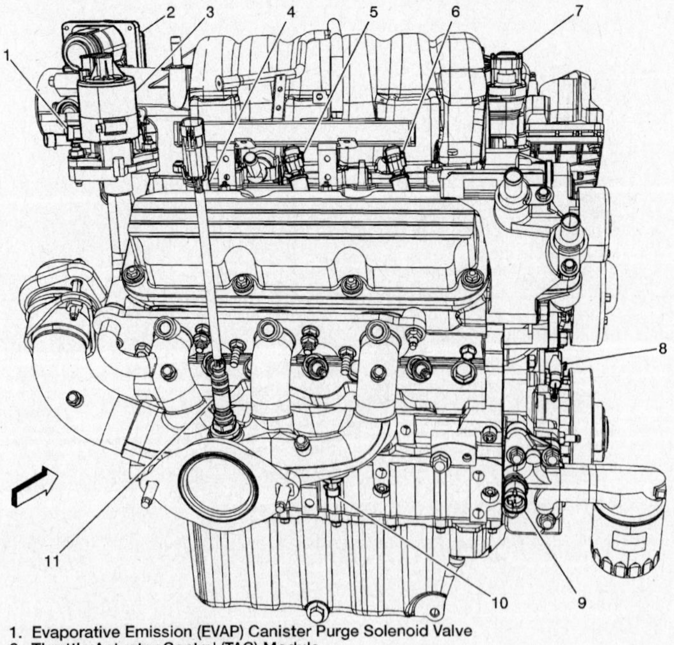

1. Evaporative Emission (EVAP) Canister Purge Solenoid Valve
2. Throttle Actuator Control (TAC) Module
3. Exhaust Gas Recirculation (EGR) Valve
4. Fuel Injector 6
5. Fuel Injector 4
6. Fuel Injector 2
7. Manifold Absolute Pressure (MAP) Sensor
8. Camshaft Position (CMP) Sensor
9. Engine Oil Pressure (EOP) Sensor
10. Knock Sensor (KS) 2

22116_LACR_G0058

Fig. 94 Engine control components (rear)—3.8L

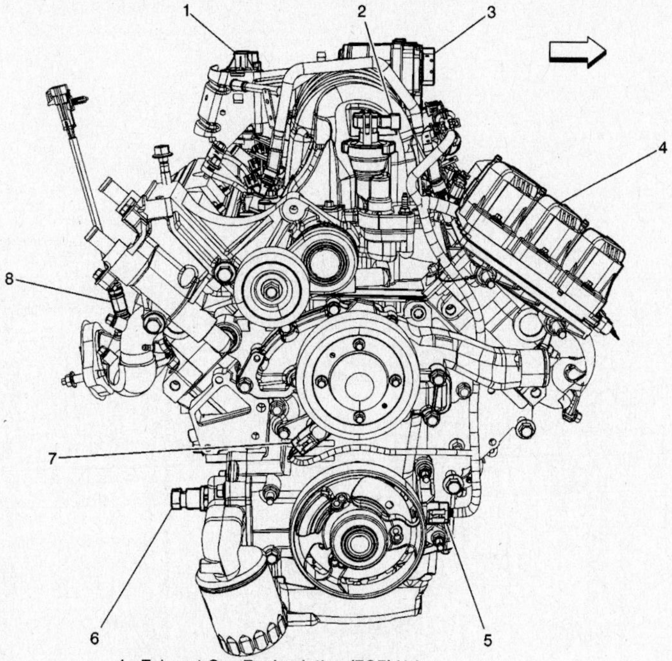

1. Exhaust Gas Recirculation (EGR) Valve
2. Manifold Absolute Pressure (MAP) Sensor
3. Throttle Actuator Control (TAC) Module
4. Ignition Coil / Module
5. Crankshaft Position (CKP) Sensor
6. Engine Oil Pressure (EOP) Sensor
7. Camshaft Position (CMP) Sensor
8. Heated Oxygen Sensor (HO2S) 1

22116_LUCE_G0026

Fig. 95 Engine control components (right side)—3.8L

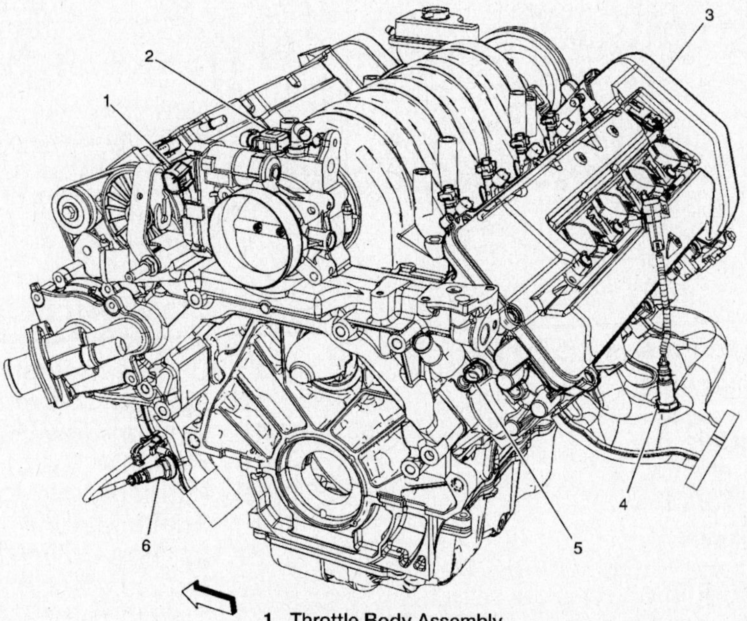

1. Throttle Body Assembly
2. Manifold Absolute Pressure (MAP) Sensor
3. Valve Cover
4. Heated Oxygen Sensor (HO2S) Bank 1 Sensor 1
5. Engine Coolant Temperature (ECT) Sensor
6. Heated Oxygen Sensor (HO2S) Bank 2 Sensor 2

22116_LUCE_G0028

Fig. 96 Engine control components (rear)—4.6L

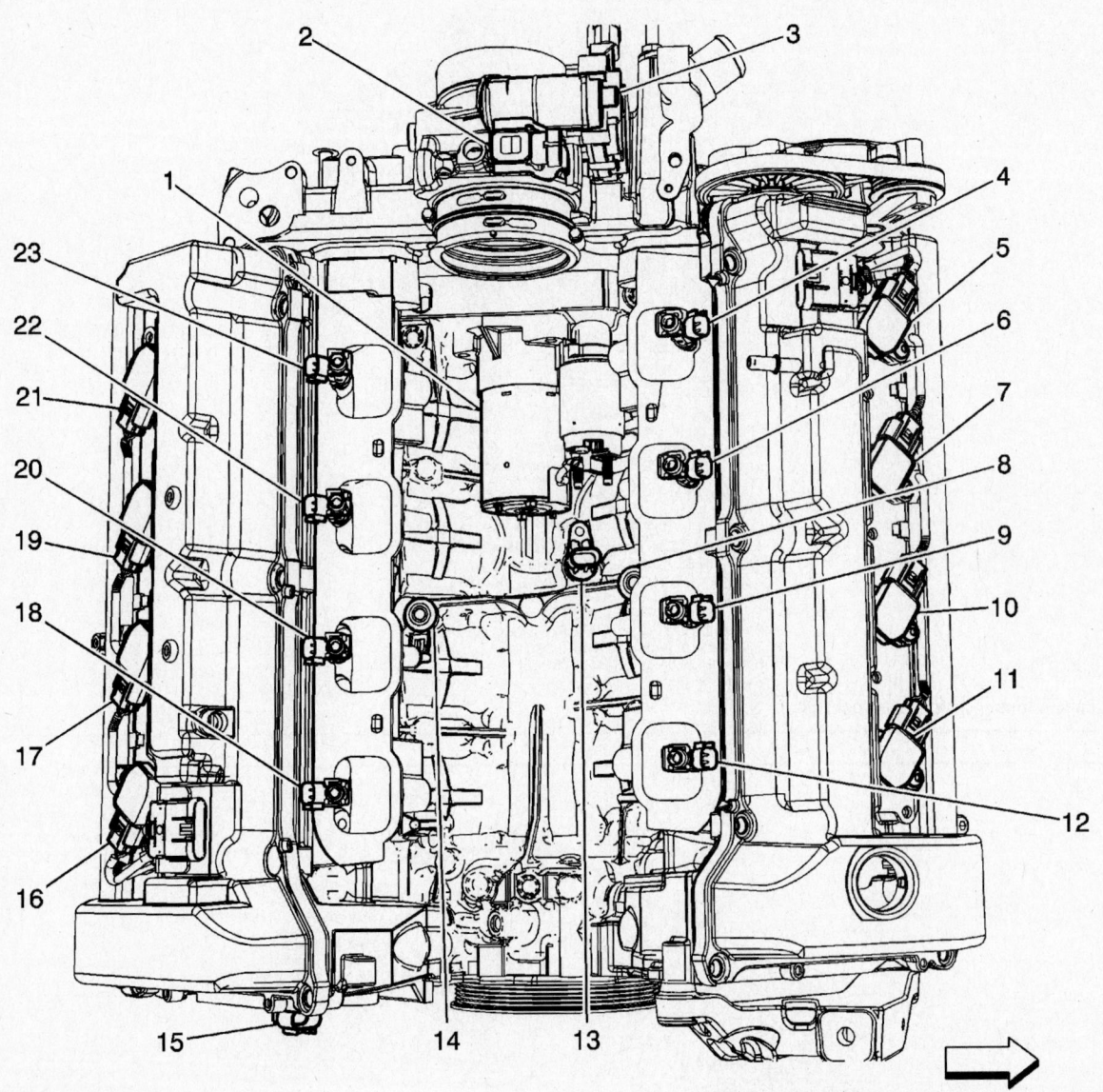

1. Starter
2. Manifold Absolute Pressure (MAP) Sensor
3. Throttle Body Assembly
4. Fuel Injector 8
5. Ignition Coil/Module 8
6. Fuel Injector 6
7. Ignition Coil/Module 6
8. Knock Sensor (KS) 2
9. Fuel Injector 4
10. Ignition Coil/Module 4
11. Ignition Coil/Module 2
12. Fuel Injector 2
13. Crankshaft Position (CKP) Sensor
14. Knock Sensor (KS) 1
15. Camshaft Position (CMP) Sensor
16. Ignition Coil/Module 1
17. Ignition Coil/Module 3
18. Fuel Injector 1
19. Ignition Coil/Module 5
20. Fuel Injector 3
21. Ignition Coil/Module 7
22. Fuel Injector 5
23. Fuel Injector 7

22116_LUCE_G0029

Fig. 97 Engine control components (top)—4.6L

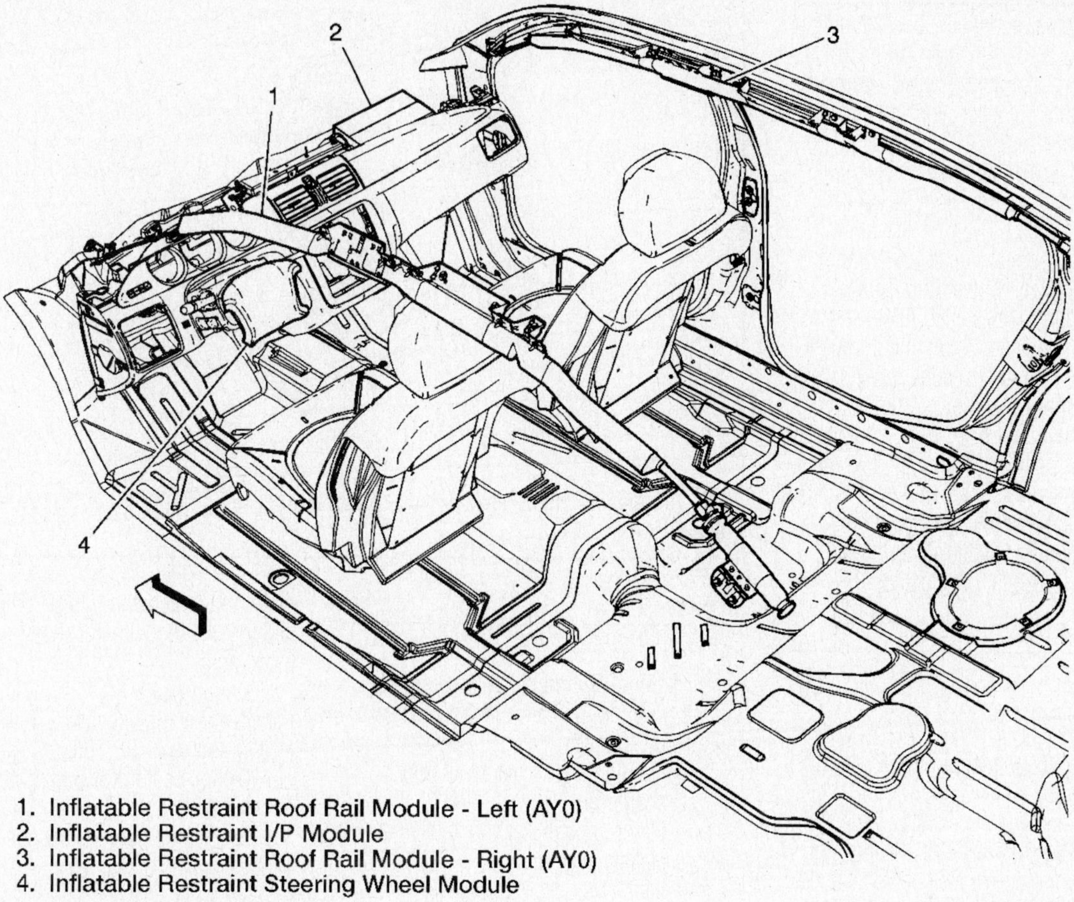

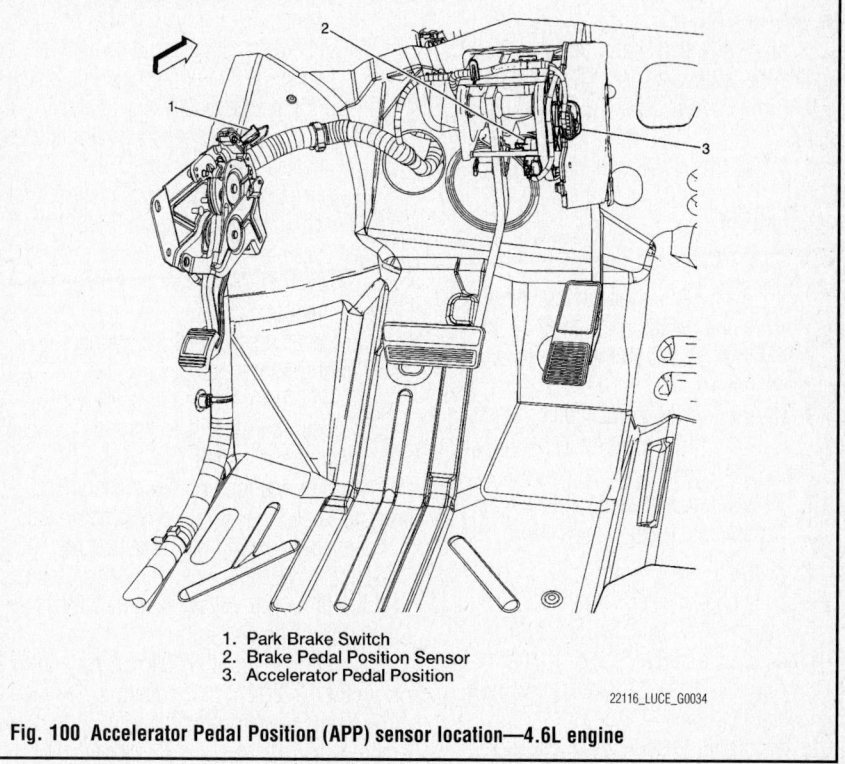

1. Inflatable Restraint Roof Rail Module - Left (AY0)
2. Inflatable Restraint I/P Module
3. Inflatable Restraint Roof Rail Module - Right (AY0)
4. Inflatable Restraint Steering Wheel Module

22116_LUCE_G0030

Fig. 98 Inflatable restraint air bag module components

ACCELERATOR PEDAL POSITION (APP) SENSOR

LOCATION

See Figures 99 and 100.

Refer to the accompanying illustrations for sensor locations.

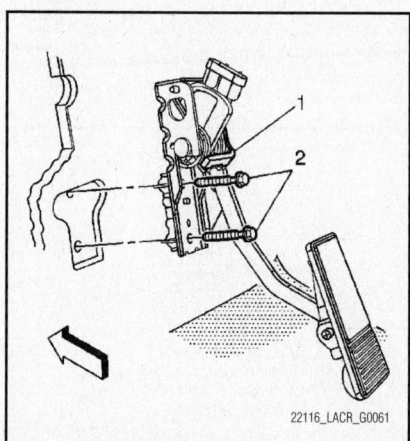

22116_LACR_G0061

Fig. 99 Accelerator Pedal Position (APP) sensor location—3.8L engine

1. Park Brake Switch
2. Brake Pedal Position Sensor
3. Accelerator Pedal Position

22116_LUCE_G0034

Fig. 100 Accelerator Pedal Position (APP) sensor location—4.6L engine

OPERATION

The accelerator pedal contains 2 individual Accelerator Pedal Position (APP) sensors within the assembly. The APP sensors 1 and 2 are potentiometer type sensors each with 3 circuits:

- A 5-volt reference circuit
- A low reference circuit
- A signal circuit

The APP sensors are used to determine the pedal angle. The Powertrain Control Module (PCM) provides each APP sensor with a 5-volt reference circuit and a low reference circuit. The APP sensors provide the PCM with signal voltage proportional to the pedal movement. The APP sensor 1 signal voltage at rest position is near the low reference and increases as the pedal is actuated. The APP sensor 2 signal voltage at rest position is near the 5-volt reference and decreases as the pedal is actuated.

REMOVAL & INSTALLATION

3.8L Engine

See Figure 99.

1. Remove the left Instrument Panel (I/P) sound insulator.
2. Disconnect the Accelerator Pedal Position (APP) sensor electrical connector.
3. Remove the accelerated pedal bolts (2).
4. Remove the accelerator pedal (1) from the vehicle.

To install:

5. Position the accelerator pedal (1) to the vehicle.
6. Install the accelerator pedal bolts (2). Tighten the bolts to 44 inch lbs. (5 Nm).
7. Connect APP sensor electrical connector.
8. Install the left I/P sound insulator.

4.6L Engine

See Figure 101.

1. Before servicing the vehicle, refer to the Precautions Section.
2. Remove the left Instrument Panel (I/P) sound insulator.
3. Disconnect the body harness electrical connector (1) from the Accelerator Pedal Position (APP) sensor.
4. Remove the accelerated pedal nuts.
5. Remove the accelerator pedal.

To install:

6. Install the accelerator pedal.
7. Install the accelerated pedal nuts. Tighten the nuts to 89 inch lbs. (10 Nm).
8. Connect the body harness electrical connector (1) to the APP sensor.
9. Install the left I/P sound insulator.

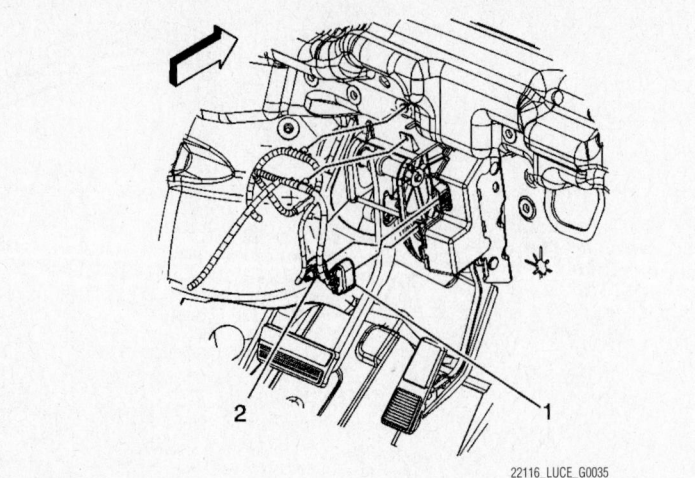

Fig. 101 Remove the Accelerator Pedal Position (APP) sensor electrical connector—4.6L engine

TESTING

See Figures 102 and 103.

1. Before beginning vehicle diagnosis, the following preliminary inspections/tests must be performed:

- Ensure that the battery is fully charged
- Ensure that the battery cables are clean and tight
- Inspect for any open fuses
- Ensure that the grounds are clean, tight, and in the correct location
- Inspect the easily accessible systems or the visible system components for obvious damage or conditions that could cause the concern. This would include checking to ensure that all connections/connectors are fully seated and secured
- Inspect for aftermarket devices that could affect the operation of the system
- Search for applicable service bulletins

2. Install a scan tool. Verify that the scan tool powers up.
3. With the ignition ON, engine OFF, verify communication with all of the control modules on the vehicle.
4. With the ignition ON, observe the scan tool APP sensor 1 voltage parameter. The readings should be 1.0 volt at rest to just above 4.0 volts when fully depressed. Ensure there is a voltage change with accelerator pedal movement.
5. With the ignition ON, observe the scan tool APP sensor 2 voltage parameter. The readings should be 0.5 volts at rest to more than 2.0 volts with the accelerator

pedal fully depressed. Ensure there is a voltage change with accelerator pedal movement.
6. Connect a fused jumper wire between the APP sensor 2 5-volt reference circuit and the APP sensor 2 signal circuit at the accelerator pedal harness connector.
7. Observe the APP sensor 2 voltage parameter with a scan tool. It should read 4.6–5.2 volts.
8. Turn OFF the ignition. Remove the fused jumper.
9. Turn ON the ignition, with the engine OFF.
10. Measure the voltage of the APP sensor 5-volt reference circuit with a DMM. It should read 4.6–5.2 volts.
11. If the reference voltage is below the acceptable range, check the low reference circuit for an open or high resistance interruption.
12. If all circuits are functioning properly and there is no voltage change when the accelerator pedal is moved, replace the APP.

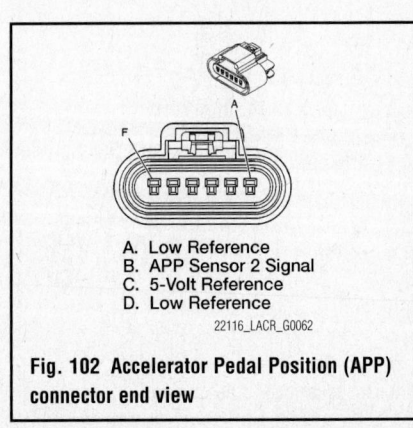

A. Low Reference
B. APP Sensor 2 Signal
C. 5-Volt Reference
D. Low Reference

22116_LACR_G0062

Fig. 102 Accelerator Pedal Position (APP) connector end view

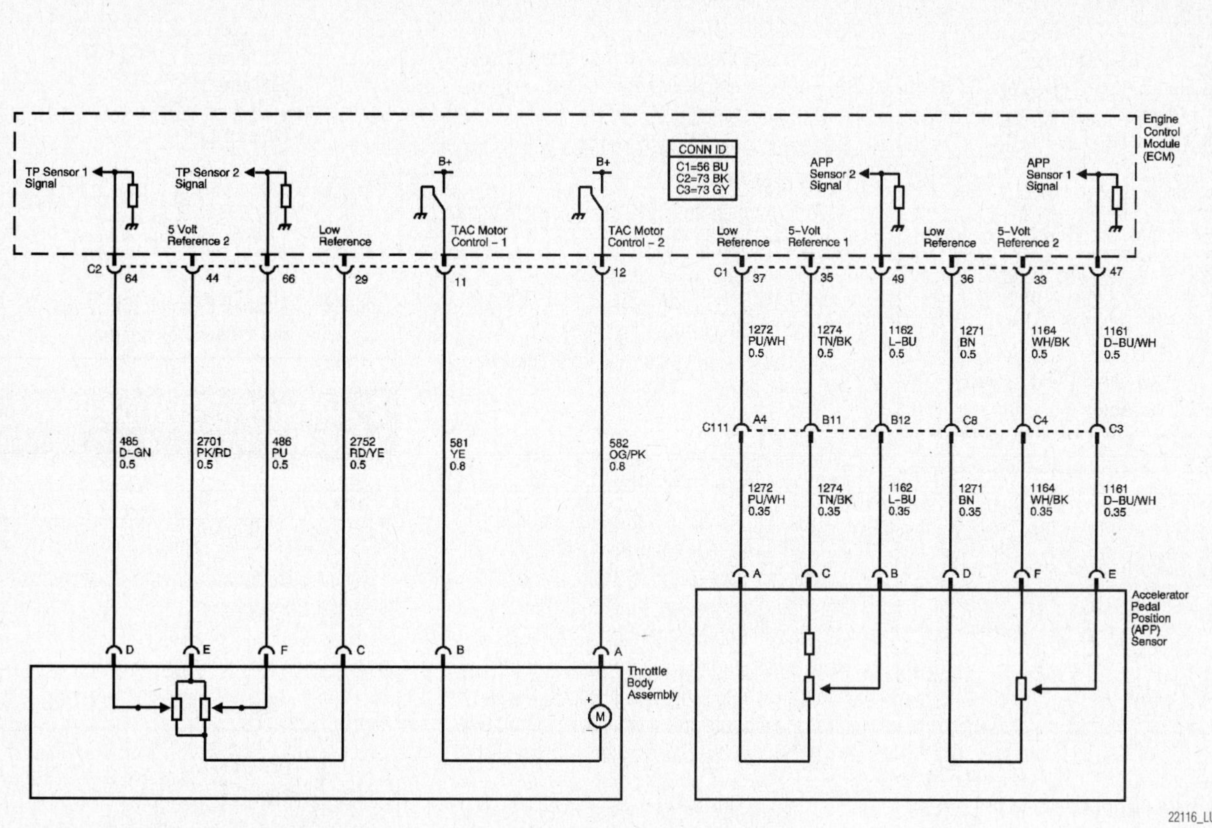

Fig. 103 Circuit schematics for Accelerator Pedal Position (APP) & Throttle Body Assembly

22116_LUCE_G0056

CAMSHAFT POSITION (CMP) SENSOR

LOCATION

See Figures 104 and 105.

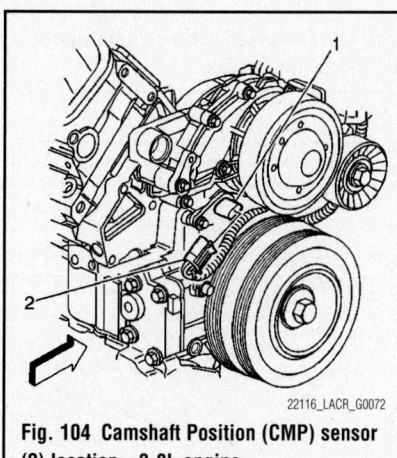

22116_LACR_G0072

Fig. 104 Camshaft Position (CMP) sensor (2) location—3.8L engine

Refer to the accompanying illustrations for sensor locations.

OPERATION

The Camshaft Position (CMP) sensor is triggered by a notched reluctor wheel built

22116_LUCE_G0036

Fig. 105 Camshaft Position (CMP) sensor location—4.6L engine

onto the camshaft sprocket. The CMP sensor provides four signal pulses every camshaft revolution. Each notch, or feature of the reluctor wheel, is of a different size which is used to identify the compression stroke of each cylinder and to enable sequential fuel injection. The CMP sensor is connected to the PCM by the following circuits:

- A 5-volt circuit
- A low reference circuit
- A signal circuit

REMOVAL & INSTALLATION

3.8L Engine

See Figures 104, 106 and 107.

1. Reposition the coolant reservoir hose clamp (1) aside at the radiator overflow fitting.
2. Remove the coolant reservoir hose from the radiator overflow fitting.
3. Disconnect the coolant reservoir hose support retainer from the electrical harness.
4. Remove the coolant reservoir nuts (2) from the shock tower studs.
5. Remove the coolant recovery reservoir (3) from the lower retainer and the shock tower studs.
6. Drain the coolant from the recovery reservoir into a clean container.
7. Remove the accessory drive belt. Refer to Accessory Drive Belt, removal and installation.
8. Disconnect the electrical connector (2) from the Camshaft Position (CMP) sensor (1).
9. Remove the CMP sensor bolt.
10. Remove the CMP sensor from the engine front cover.

To install:

11. Install the CMP sensor to the engine front cover.

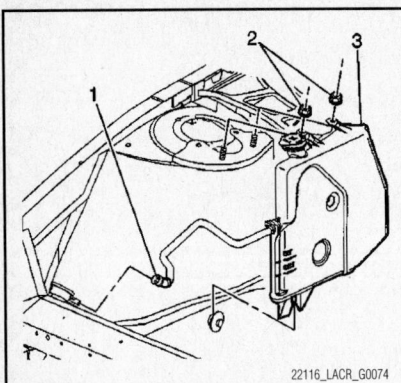

Fig. 106 Remove the coolant recovery reservoir—3.8L engine

Fig. 107 Camshaft Position (CMP) sensor bolt removal—3.8L engine

12. Install the CMP sensor bolt. Tighten the bolt to 89 inch lbs. (10 Nm).

13. Connect the electrical connector (2) to the CMP sensor (1).

14. Install the accessory drive belt. Refer to Accessory Drive Belt, removal and installation.

15. Install the coolant recovery reservoir (3) to the lower retainer and the shock tower studs.

16. Install the nuts (2) to the shock tower studs. Tighten the nuts to 29 inch lbs. (3 Nm).

17. Lubricate the reservoir hose with clean water. Route the hose to the radiator overflow neck fitting.

➡**The hose end must be flush against the radiator filler neck. Seat the clamp squarely between the radiator filler neck and the flared end of the fitting.**

18. Install the coolant reservoir hose (1) to the radiator overflow fitting.

19. Connect the coolant reservoir hose support retainer to the electrical harness.

20. Position the coolant reservoir hose clamp to the radiator overflow fitting.

21. Fill the coolant recovery reservoir to the proper level.

4.6L Engine

See Figure 105.

1. Before servicing the vehicle, refer to the Precautions Section.

2. Disconnect the electrical connector from the Camshaft Position (CMP) sensor.

3. Remove the CMP sensor bolt.

4. Remove the CMP sensor.

To install:

5. Lubricate the CMP sensor O-ring seal with clean engine oil.

6. Install the CMP sensor.

7. Install the CMP sensor bolt. Tighten the bolt to 89 inch lbs. (10 Nm).

8. Connect the electrical connector to the CMP sensor.

TESTING

See Figures 108 and 109.

During normal operation the PCM controls all ignition functions. If either the Crankshaft Position (CKP) or Camshaft Position (CMP) sensor signal is lost, the engine will continue to run because the PCM will default to a limp home mode using the remaining sensor input. Diagnostic trouble codes are available to accurately diagnose the ignition system with an OBD2 scan tool.

1. Inspect the CMP sensor for correct installation. Remove the CMP sensor from the engine and inspect the sensor O-ring for damage. If the sensor is loose, incorrectly installed, or damaged, replace the CMP sensor.

2. Engage the CMP sensor harness connector to the CMP sensor.

3. Connect the scan tool to the diagnostic connector.

4. With the ignition ON, engine OFF observe the CMP active counter parameter on the scan tool.

5. Pass a flat steel object across the tip of the sensor repeatedly. The CMP active counter parameter should increment with each pass of the steel object.

6. If the parameter does not increment, replace the CMP sensor.

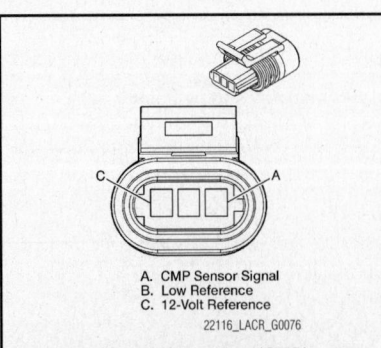

A. CMP Sensor Signal
B. Low Reference
C. 12-Volt Reference

Fig. 108 Camshaft Position (CMP) sensor connector end view—3.8L engine

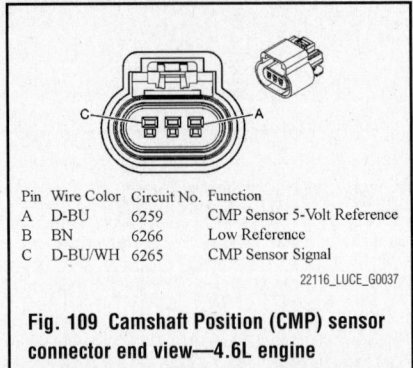

Pin	Wire Color	Circuit No.	Function
A	D-BU	6259	CMP Sensor 5-Volt Reference
B	BN	6266	Low Reference
C	D-BU/WH	6265	CMP Sensor Signal

Fig. 109 Camshaft Position (CMP) sensor connector end view—4.6L engine

CRANKSHAFT POSITION (CKP) SENSOR

LOCATION

See Figures 110 and 111.

Refer to the accompanying illustrations for sensor locations.

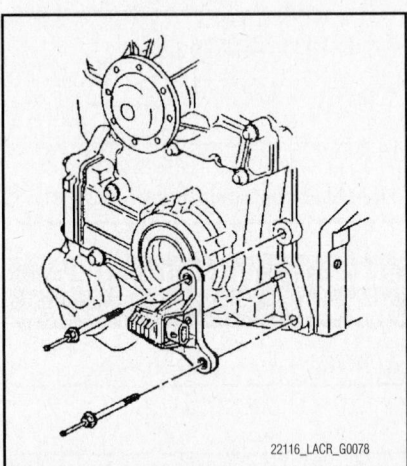

Fig. 110 Crankshaft Position (CKP) sensor location—3.8L engine

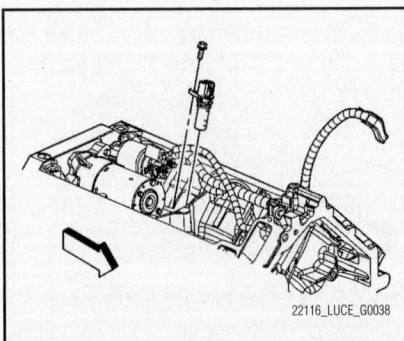

Fig. 111 Crankshaft Position (CKP) sensor location—4.6L engine

OPERATION

The Crankshaft Position (CKP) sensor is a permanent magnet generator known as a variable reluctance sensor. The CKP sensor produces an AC voltage of varying amplitude and frequency. The frequency depends on the velocity of the crankshaft. The AC output depends on the crankshaft position and the battery voltage. The CKP sensor works in conjunction with a reluctor wheel attached to the crankshaft. As each reluctor wheel tooth rotates past the CKP sensor, the resulting change in the magnetic field creates an ON/OFF pulse. The PCM processes the pulses to create a pattern that enables the PCM to determine the crankshaft position. The PCM can synchronize the ignition timing, the fuel injector timing, and the spark knock control based on the CKP sensor and the Camshaft Position (CMP) sensor inputs. The CKP sensor is also used to detect misfire and for tachometer display. The PCM learns the variations between different speed and load conditions to correctly detect misfires. The CKP sensor circuits consist of a signal circuit and a low reference circuit. The two wires are twisted together to prevent electromagnetic interference on the CKP sensor circuits.

REMOVAL & INSTALLATION

3.8L Engine

See Figure 110 and 112.

1. Disconnect the negative battery cable.
2. Raise and support the vehicle.
3. Remove the crankshaft damper (harmonic balancer). Refer to Crankshaft Damper, removal and installation.
4. Disconnect the Crankshaft Position (CKP) sensor electrical connector.

✳ WARNING

Do not use a pry bar when removing the CKP sensor shield.

5. Remove the CKP sensor shield (1).
6. Remove the CKP sensor studs.
7. Remove the CKP sensor.

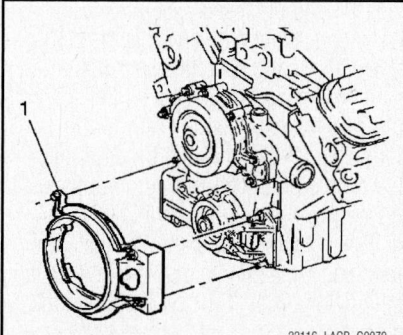

Fig. 112 Remove the CKP sensor shield—3.8L engine

To install:

8. Install the CKP sensor.
9. Install the CKP sensor studs. Tighten the studs to 22 ft. lbs. (30 Nm).
10. Install the CKP sensor shield (1).
11. Connect the CKP sensor electrical connector.
12. Install the crankshaft damper. Refer to Crankshaft Damper, removal and installation.
13. Lower the vehicle.
14. Connect the negative battery cable.
15. Perform the CKP system Variation Learn Procedure. Refer to Crankshaft Position (CKP) Sensor, Testing, Variation Learn Procedure for CKP.

4.6L Engine

See Figure 111.

1. Before servicing the vehicle, refer to the Precautions Section.
2. Remove the intake manifold. Refer to Intake Manifold, removal & installation.
3. Disconnect the Crankshaft Position (CKP) sensor wiring harness electrical connector from the CKP sensor.
4. Remove the CKP sensor bolt. (The cylinder heads are shown removed, for clarity).
5. Remove the CKP sensor.

To install:

6. Lubricate the crankshaft sensor O-ring seal with clean engine oil.
7. Install the CKP sensor.
8. Install the CKP sensor bolt. Tighten the bolt to 89 inch lbs. (10 Nm).
9. Connect the CKP sensor wiring harness electrical connector to the CKP sensor.
10. Install the intake manifold. Refer to Intake Manifold, removal & installation.
11. Perform the CKP System Variation Learn Procedure.

TESTING

See Figures 113 and 114.

During normal operation the PCM controls all ignition functions. If either the Crankshaft Position (CKP) or Camshaft Position (CMP) sensor signal is lost, the engine will continue to run because the PCM will default to a limp home mode using the remaining sensor input. Diagnostic trouble codes are available to accurately diagnose the ignition system with an OBD2 scan tool.

1. Inspect the CKP sensor for correct installation. Remove the CKP sensor from the engine and inspect the sensor O–ring for damage. If the sensor is loose, incorrectly installed, or damaged, replace the CKP sensor.

2. Engage the CKP sensor harness connector to the CKP sensor.
3. Connect the scan tool to the diagnostic connector.
4. With the ignition ON, engine OFF observe the CKP active counter parameter on the scan tool.
5. Pass a flat steel object across the tip of the sensor repeatedly. The CKP active counter parameter should increment with each pass of the steel object.
6. If the parameter does not increment, replace the CKP sensor.

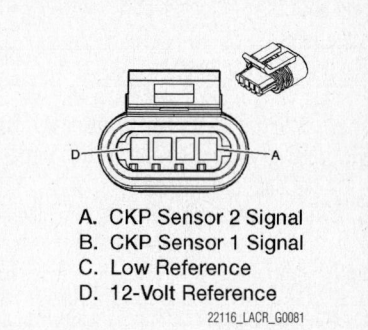

A. CKP Sensor 2 Signal
B. CKP Sensor 1 Signal
C. Low Reference
D. 12-Volt Reference

Fig. 113 CKP sensor connector end view—3.8L engine

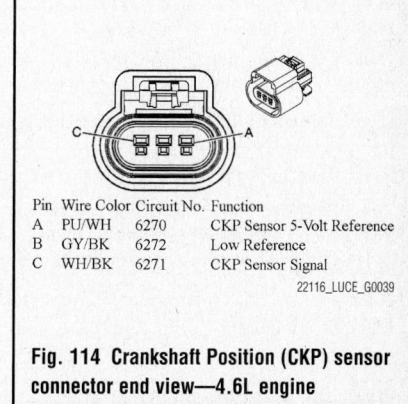

Pin	Wire Color	Circuit No.	Function
A	PU/WH	6270	CKP Sensor 5-Volt Reference
B	GY/BK	6272	Low Reference
C	WH/BK	6271	CKP Sensor Signal

Fig. 114 Crankshaft Position (CKP) sensor connector end view—4.6L engine

Variation Learn Procedure for CKP

The Crankshaft Position (CKP) system variation learn procedure is required when the following service procedures have been performed, regardless of whether DTC P0315 is set:

- Engine replacement
- Engine Control Module (ECM) replacement
- Crankshaft damper replacement
- Crankshaft replacement
- CKP sensor replacement
- Any engine repairs which disturb the crankshaft to CKP sensor relationship

The scan tool monitors certain component

signals to determine if all the conditions are met to continue with the CKP system variation learn procedure. The scan tool only displays the condition that inhibits the procedure. The scan tool monitors the following components:

• CKP sensor activity. If there is a CKP sensor condition, refer to the applicable DTC that was set.

• Camshaft Position (CMP) signal activity. If there is a CMP signal condition, refer to the applicable DTC that was set.

• Engine Coolant Temperature (ECT). If the ECT is not warm enough, idle the engine until the ECT reaches the correct temperature.

1. Install a scan tool.

2. Monitor the ECM for DTC's with a scan tool. If other DTC's are set, except DTC P0315, refer to the applicable DTC information for that code.

3. With a scan tool, select the CKP system variation learn procedure and perform the following:

a. Observe the fuel cut-off for the applicable engine.

b. Block the drive wheels.

c. Set the parking brake.

d. Place the vehicle's transmission in Park or Neutral.

e. Turn the Air Conditioning (A/C) **OFF**.

f. Cycle the ignition from **OFF** to **ON**.

g. Apply and hold the brake pedal for the duration of the procedure.

h. Start and idle the engine.

i. Accelerate to Wide Open Throttle (WOT). The engine should not accelerate beyond the calibrated fuel cut-off RPM value noted above. Release the throttle immediately if the value is exceeded.

➡ **While the learn procedure is in progress, release the throttle immediately when the engine starts to decelerate. The engine control is returned to the operator and the engine responds to throttle position after the learn procedure is complete.**

j. Release the throttle when fuel cut-off occurs.

4. The scan tool displays Learn Status: Learned this Ignition.

a. If the scan tool indicates that DTC P0315 ran and passed, the CKP variation learn procedure is complete.

b. If the scan tool indicates DTC P0315 failed or did not run, refer to DTC P0315 test procedures.

c. If any other DTC's are set, refer to a Diagnostic Trouble Code (DTC) list for the applicable DTC that was set.

5. Turn **OFF** the ignition for 30 seconds after the learn procedure is completed successfully in order to store the CKP system variation values in the PCM memory.

EGR VALVE POSITION (EVP) SENSOR

LOCATION

See Figures 115 and 116.

Refer to the accompanying illustrations for sensor locations.

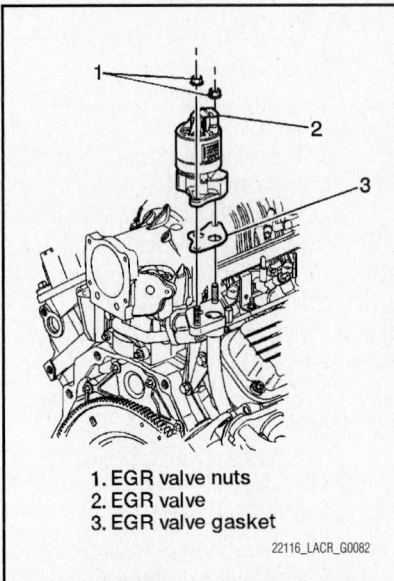

1. EGR valve nuts
2. EGR valve
3. EGR valve gasket

22116_LACR_G0082

Fig. 115 EGR valve and sensor location— 3.8L engine

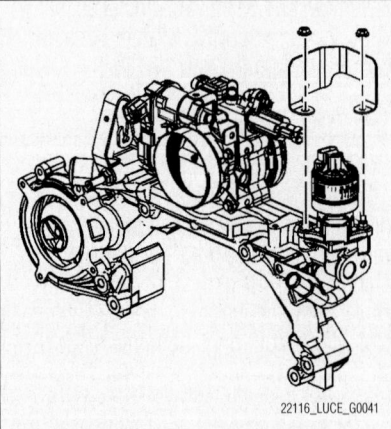

22116_LUCE_G0041

Fig. 116 EGR valve and sensor location— 4.6L engine

OPERATION

The Exhaust Gas Recirculation (EGR) system is used to reduce the amount of nitrogen oxide (NOx) emission levels caused by combustion temperatures exceeding 1,500°F (816°C). It does this by introducing small amounts of exhaust gas back into the combustion chamber. The exhaust gas absorbs a portion of the thermal energy produced by the combustion process and thus decreases combustion temperature. The EGR system will only operate under specific temperature, Barometric Pressure (BARO) and engine load conditions in order to prevent drivability concerns and to increase engine performance.

The PCM calculates the amount of EGR needed based on the following inputs:

• The Engine Coolant Temperature (ECT) sensor

• The Intake Air Temperature (IAT) sensor

• The Barometric Pressure (BARO)

• The Manifold Absolute Pressure (MAP) sensor

• The Throttle Position (TP) sensor

• The Mass Air Flow (MAF) sensor

The control module tests the EGR system during deceleration. The control module does this by momentarily commanding the EGR valve to open while monitoring the signal circuit of the Manifold Absolute Pressure (MAP) sensor. When the EGR valve is opened, the control module will expect to see a predetermined increase in MAP. If the expected increase in MAP is not detected, the control module records the amount of MAP difference that was detected and adjusts a calibrated fail counter towards a calibrated fail threshold level. The number of EGR flow test counts required to exceed the fail threshold may vary according to the amount of detected EGR flow error.

The EGR Valve Position (EVP) sensor is monitored by the control module. The 5-volt reference circuit, the low reference circuit, and the EVP signal circuit are used by the control module to determine the EGR valve position. The control module compares the EVP sensor parameter with the desired EGR position parameter when the valve is commanded open or closed.

The control module controls the EGR valve with a solid state device called a driver. The driver supplies the EGR solenoid with 12 volts that is Pulse Width Modulated (PWM) through the EGR solenoid high control circuit. A ground path is provided by the control module through the EGR solenoid low control circuit. The driver has the ability to detect an electrical malfunction on the EGR solenoid control circuits.

When the ignition switch is turned ON, the control module records the EGR learned minimum position. The control module compares the EGR learned minimum position parameter to the EVP parameter.

The control module will only allow one EGR flow test during an ignition cycle. To aid in verifying a repair, the control module will allow 9–16 EGR flow test counts during the first ignition cycle following a code clear event or a battery disconnect.

REMOVAL & INSTALLATION

3.8L Engine

See Figure 115.

The Exhaust Gas Recirculation (EGR) valve and the EGR Valve Position (EVP) sensor are integrated into the EGR valve assembly. The EVP is removed with the EGR valve.

1. Disconnect the Exhaust Gas Recirculation (EGR) valve electrical connector.
2. Remove the EGR valve nuts (1).
3. Remove the EGR valve (2).
4. Remove the gasket (3) from the EGR valve adapter.
5. Clean the EGR valve gasket mating surfaces.

To install:

6. Install a new EGR valve gasket (3).
7. Install the EGR valve (2).
8. Install the EGR valve nuts (1). Tighten the nuts to 18 ft. lbs. (25 Nm).
9. Connect the EGR valve electrical connector.

4.6L Engine

See Figure 116.

1. Before servicing the vehicle, refer to the Precautions Section.
2. Remove or disconnect the following:
   - The fuel injector sight shield, if necessary
   - The engine harness electrical connector from the Exhaust Gas Recirculation (EGR) valve
   - The EGR bracket shield nuts
   - The EGR bracket shield
   - The EGR valve bolts
   - The EGR valve
3. Remove and discard the EGR valve gasket.

➡Inspect the EGR passages in the water pump housing for deposits. Clean the EGR passages as needed.

4. Clean the EGR valve mounting surface.

To install:

5. Install or connect the following:
   - The NEW EGR gasket

- The EGR valve
- The EGR valve bolts. Tighten the bolts to 18 ft. lbs. (24 Nm)
- The EGR bracket shield
- The EGR bracket shield nuts. Tighten the nuts to 89 inch lbs. (10 Nm)
- The engine harness electrical connector to the EGR valve
- The fuel injector sight shield if necessary

TESTING

See Figures 117 through 119.

1. With the ignition ON and the engine OFF, command the EGR from 0–90 percent. The Exhaust Gas Recirculation (EGR) position sensor parameter should remain within 3 percent of the desired EGR position parameter through the entire range.
2. With the ignition OFF, disconnect the EGR valve harness connector.
3. Turn the ignition ON, connect a test lamp between B and A. The test lamp should illuminate.
   a. If the test lamp does not illuminate, test the EGR low control circuit for an open/high resistance.
   b. If the circuit tests normal, replace the ECM.
4. Connect a test lamp between the EGR high control circuit (E) and a ground. Command the EGR valve from 0–90 percent and exit the EGR solenoid output control. The test lamp should turn ON when commanded between 10–90 percent and turn OFF when commanded to 0 percent.
   a. If the test lamp is ON when commanded to 0 percent, test the EGR high control circuit for a short to voltage.

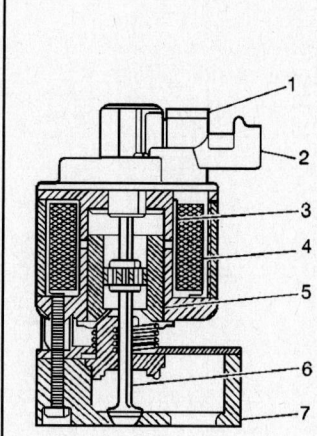

1. **Cap-Sensor**
2. **Sensor-EGR Pintle Position**
3. **Pole Piece-Primary**
4. **Bobbin and Coil Assembly**
5. **Sleeve-Armature**
6. **Valve-Pintle**
7. **Armature and Base Assembly**

22116_LUCE_G0040

Fig. 118 EGR linear valve cut-away view

b. If the circuit tests normal, replace the ECM.
   c. If the test lamp is always OFF while commanding the EGR valve from 0–90 percent, test the EGR high control circuit for an open, high resistance, or a short to ground.
   d. If the circuit tests normal, replace the ECM.
5. If all circuits test normal, replace the EGR valve.

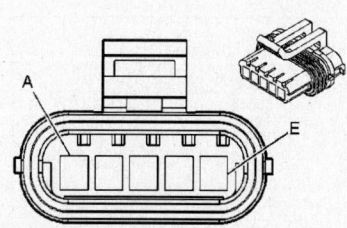

A. EGR Solenoid Low Control
B. Low Reference
C. EGR Valve Position (EVP) Signal
D. 5-Volt Reference 1
E. EGR Solenoid High Control

22116_LACR_G0083

Fig. 117 EGR connector end view—3.8L & 4.6L engines

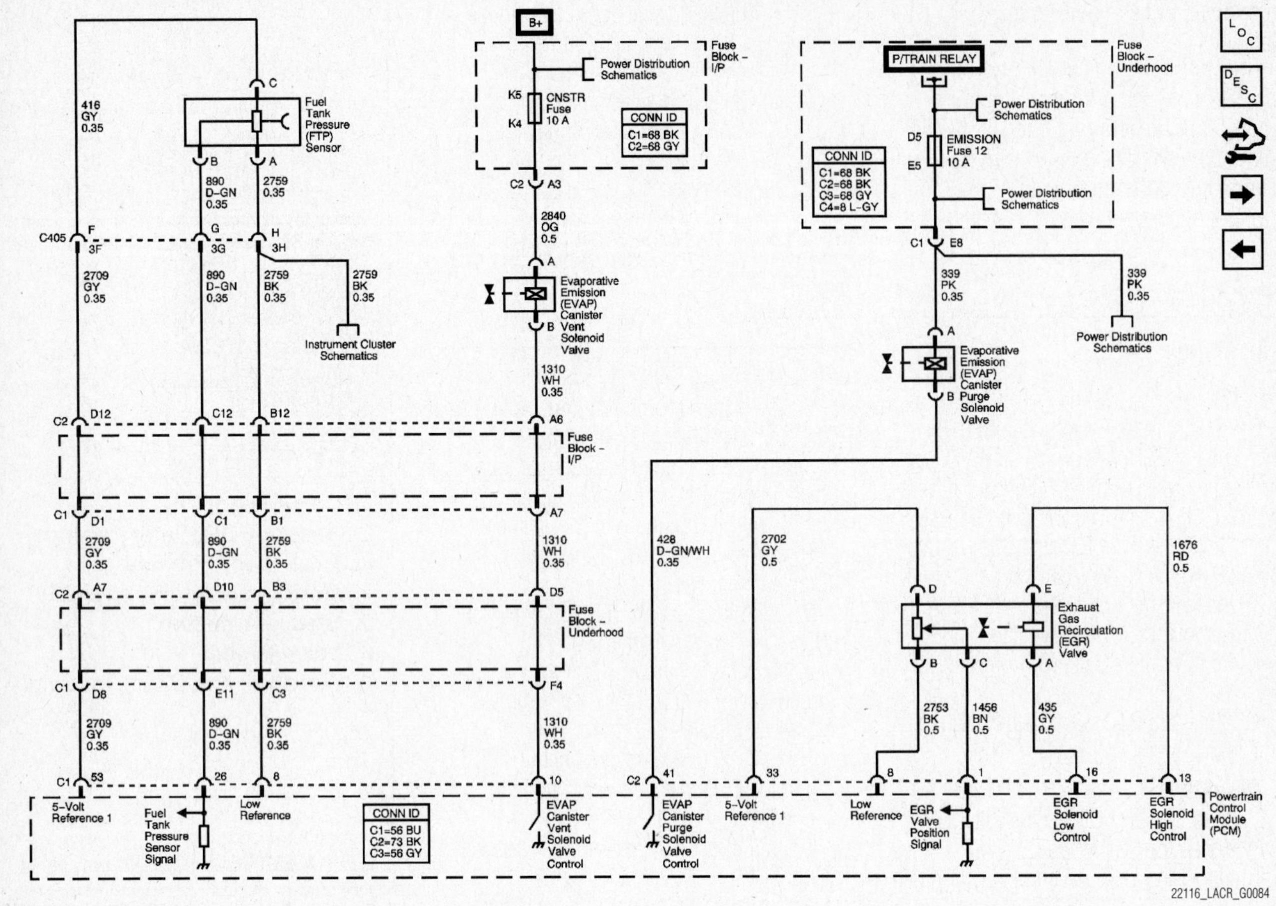

Fig. 119 EGR, EVAP, and FTP circuit schematics—3.8L engine

ELECTRONIC CONTROL MODULE (ECM)

The Electronic Control Module (ECM) may also be referred to as the Engine Control Module (ECM).

LOCATION

See Figure 120.

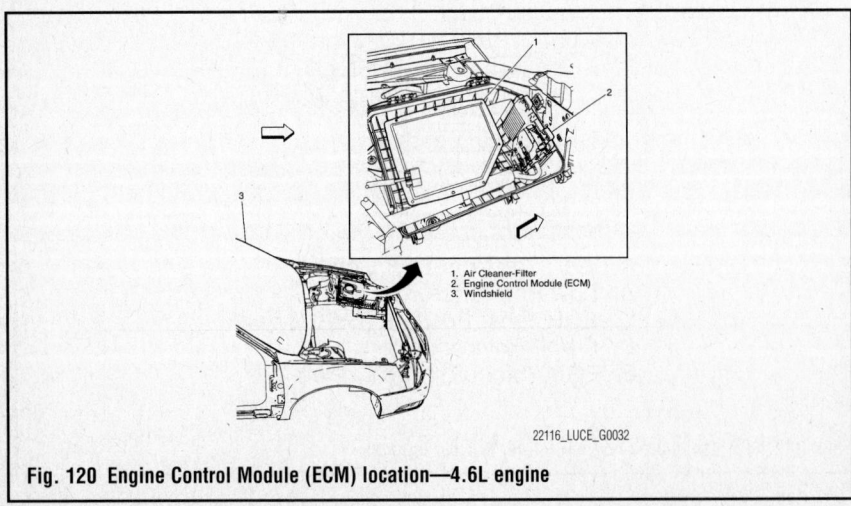

1. Air Cleaner-Filter
2. Engine Control Module (ECM)
3. Windshield

Fig. 120 Engine Control Module (ECM) location—4.6L engine

Refer to the accompanying illustration for ECM location.

OPERATION

The Engine Control Module (ECM) interacts with many emission related components and systems, and monitors the emission related components and systems for deterioration. OBD2 diagnostics monitor the system performance and a Diagnostic Trouble Code (DTC) sets if the system performance degrades. The Malfunction Indicator Lamp (MIL) operation and the DTC storage are dictated by the DTC type. A DTC is ranked as a Type A or Type B if the DTC is emissions related. Type C is a non-emissions related DTC.

The ECM is in the engine compartment and is the control center of the engine controls system. The ECM controls the following components:

- The fuel injection system
- The ignition system
- The emission control systems
- The on-board diagnostics
- The A/C and fan systems
- The throttle actuation control (TAC) system

The ECM constantly monitors the information from various sensors and other inputs, and controls the systems that affect the vehicle performance and the emissions. The ECM also performs diagnostic tests on various parts of the system. The ECM can recognize operational problems and alert the driver via the MIL. When the ECM detects a malfunction, the ECM stores a DTC. The condition area is identified by the particular DTC that is set.

REMOVAL & INSTALLATION

3.8L Engine

For removal and installation, refer to Powertrain Control Module (PCM).

4.6L Engine

> **⁜ WARNING**
>
> **Turn the ignition OFF when installing or removing the control module connectors and disconnecting or reconnecting the power to the control module (battery cable, Powertrain Control Module (PCM)/Engine Control Module (ECM)/Transaxle Control Module (TCM) pigtail, control module fuse, jumper cables, etc.) in order to prevent internal control module damage.**

> **⁜ WARNING**
>
> **Control module damage may result when the metal case contacts battery voltage. DO NOT contact the control module metal case with battery voltage when servicing a control module, using battery booster cables, or when charging the vehicle battery.**

> **⁜ WARNING**
>
> **In order to prevent any possible electrostatic discharge damage to the control module, do not touch the connector pins or the soldered components on the circuit board.**

➡**Remove any debris from around the control module connector surfaces before servicing the control module. Inspect the control module connector gaskets when diagnosing or replacing the control module. Ensure that the gaskets are installed correctly. The gaskets prevent contaminant intrusion into the control module.**

➡**The replacement control module must be programmed.**

➡**It is necessary to record the remaining engine oil life. If the replacement engine control module (ECM) is not programmed with the remaining engine oil life, the engine oil life will default to 100 percent. If the replacement ECM is not programmed with the remaining**

engine oil life, the engine oil will need to be changed at 3,000 miles (5,000 km) from the last oil change.

➡**It is necessary to record the remaining automatic transaxle fluid life. If the replacement ECM is not programmed with the remaining transaxle fluid life, the transaxle fluid life will default to 100 percent. If the replacement ECM is not programmed with the remaining transaxle fluid life, the transaxle fluid will need to be changed at 50,000 miles (83,000 km) from the last transaxle fluid change.**

1. Before servicing the vehicle, refer to the Precautions Section.
2. Disconnect the negative battery cable.
3. Using a scan tool, retrieve the percentage of remaining engine oil and automatic transaxle fluid life. Record the remaining engine oil and transaxle fluid life.
4. Ensure that the ignition is in the OFF position.
5. Disconnect the negative battery cable.
6. Disconnect the engine harness electrical connector from the Mass Air Flow/Intake Air Temperature (MAF/IAT) sensor.
7. Disconnect the Positive Crankcase Ventilation (PCV) fresh air tube quick connect fitting from the air duct.
8. Disconnect the secondary Air Injection (AIR) pump inlet tube quick connect fitting from the air cleaner upper housing.
9. Loosen the air cleaner outlet duct clamp at the throttle body.
10. Remove the air cleaner outlet duct from the throttle body.
11. Disengage the lower housing clips.
12. Disengage the upper housing front tabs from the lower housing.
13. Remove the air cleaner upper housing.
14. Disengage the engine harness electrical connector lever locks at the ECM.
15. Remove the engine harness electrical connectors from the ECM.
16. Remove the ECM from the air cleaner lower housing.

To install:
17. Inspect the following areas prior to installing the ECM:
   - Ensure there is no debris in the air filter/ECM housing assembly, or the MAF/IAT sensor inlet screen that may distort the air flow
   - Ensure there are no signs of damage to the air filter/ECM housing

assembly, or the intake air duct. If a problem is found, replace the components as necessary.
18. Install the ECM to the lower air cleaner housing.
19. Install the engine harness electrical connectors to the ECM.
20. Engage the engine harness electrical connector lever locks at the ECM.
21. Install the air cleaner upper housing.
22. Engage the upper housing front tabs to the lower housing.
23. Engage the lower housing clips.

➡**Properly install the air cleaner outlet duct to the throttle body. An improperly installed, distorted, or damaged air duct may cause a Diagnostic Trouble Code (DTC) to set.**

24. Install the air cleaner outlet duct to the throttle body.
25. Tighten the air cleaner outlet duct clamp at the throttle body. Tighten the clamp to 27 inch lbs. (3 Nm).
26. Connect the AIR pump inlet tube quick connect fitting to the air cleaner upper housing.
27. Connect the PCV fresh air tube quick connect fitting to the air duct.
28. Connect the engine harness electrical connector to the MAF/IAT sensor.
29. Connect the negative battery cable.
30. Program the ECM.

TESTING

1. Perform a careful underhood inspection when performing any diagnostic procedure or diagnosing the cause of an emission test failure. This can often lead to repairing a condition without further steps. Use the following guidelines when performing an inspection:
   a. Inspect all of the vacuum hoses for correct routing, pinches, cuts, or disconnects
   b. Inspect any hoses that are difficult to see
   c. Inspect all of the wires in the engine compartment for the following conditions:
   - Burned or chafed spots
   - Pinched wires
   - Contact with sharp edges
   - Contact with hot exhaust manifolds

The Electronic Control Module (ECM), also called the Engine Control Module (ECM), is programmed with test routines that test the operation of the various systems the ECM controls. Some tests monitor internal ECM functions. Many tests are run continuously. Other tests run only under specific conditions, referred to as conditions for running the Diagnostic Trouble Code (DTC). When the vehicle is operating within the conditions for running a particular test, the ECM monitors certain parameters and determines if the values are within an expected range. The parameters and values considered outside the range of normal operation are listed as conditions for setting the DTC. When the conditions for setting the DTC occur, the ECM executes the action taken when the DTC sets. Some DTC's alert the driver via the Malfunction Indicator Lamp (MIL) or a message. Other DTC's do not trigger a driver warning, but are stored in memory. The ECM also saves data and input parameters when most DTC's are set.

The DTC's are categorized by type. The DTC type is determined by the MIL operation and the manner in which the fault data is stored when a particular DTC fails. In some cases, there may be exceptions to this structure. Therefore, when diagnosing the system it is important to read the action taken when the DTC sets and the conditions for clearing the DTC.

Many intermittent open or shorted circuits come and go with harness and connector movement caused by vibration, engine torque, bumps, and rough pavement.

2. Test the wiring harness and connectors by performing the following:
- Move the related ECM connectors and wiring while monitoring the appropriate scan tool data
- With the engine running, move the related connectors and wiring while monitoring engine operation
- If harness or connector movement affects the data displayed, the component and system operation, or the engine operation, inspect and repair the harness or connections as necessary

3. Test the electrical connections and/or wiring by performing the following:
- Inspect for incorrect mating of the connector halves or terminals not fully seated in the connector body
- Inspect for improperly formed or damaged terminals. Test for incorrect terminal tension
- Inspect for poor terminal to wire connections including terminals crimped over insulation. This requires removing the terminal from the connector body
- Inspect for corrosion or water intrusion. Pierced or damaged insulation can allow moisture to enter the wiring. The conductor can corrode inside the insulation with little visible evidence. Look for swollen and

stiff sections of wire in the suspect circuits
- Inspect for wires that are broken inside the insulation

ENGINE COOLANT TEMPERATURE (ECT) SENSOR

LOCATION

See Figures 121 and 122.

Refer to the accompanying illustrations for sensor locations.

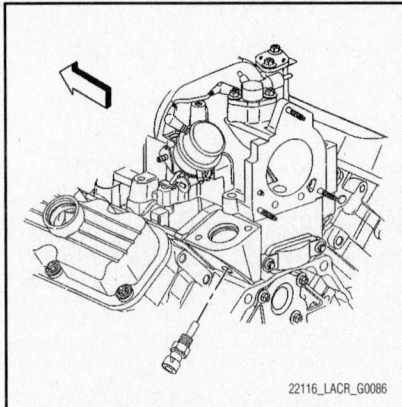

22116_LACR_G0086

Fig. 121 Engine Coolant Temperature (ECT) sensor location—3.8L engine

OPERATION

The ECT sensor is a thermistor device in which resistance changes with temperature. The electrical resistance of a thermistor decreases as the temperature increases, and resistance increases as the temperature decreases. The varying resistance affects the voltage drop across the sensor terminals and provides electrical signals to the PCM corresponding to temperature.

REMOVAL & INSTALLATION

3.8L Engine

See Figure 121.

> ✳✳ **WARNING**
>
> **Use care when handling the coolant sensor. Damage to the coolant sensor will affect the operation of the fuel control system.**

1. Partially drain the cooling system.
2. Disconnect the Engine Coolant Temperature (ECT) sensor electrical connector.
3. Remove the ECT sensor.

To install:

➡**Replacement components must be the correct part number for the application. Components requiring the use of the thread locking compound, lubricants, corrosion inhibitors, or sealants are identified in the service procedure. Some replacement components may come with these coatings already applied. Do not use these coatings on components unless specified. These coatings can affect the final torque, which may affect the operation of the component. Use the correct torque specification when installing components in order to avoid damage.**

4. Coat the threads with sealer GM P/N 12346004 (Canadian P/N 10953480) or equivalent.
5. Install the ECT sensor. Tighten the sensor to 18 ft. lbs. (25 Nm).
6. Connect the ECT sensor electrical connector.
7. Inspect and fill the cooling system as necessary.

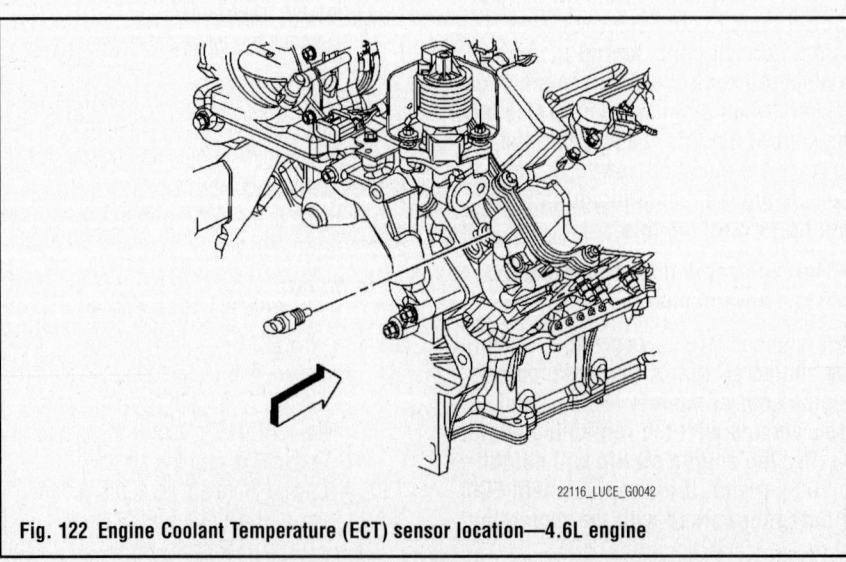

22116_LUCE_G0042

Fig. 122 Engine Coolant Temperature (ECT) sensor location—4.6L engine

4.6L Engine

See Figure 124.

✳✳ CAUTION

Allow sufficient time for the engine to cool before removing the Engine Coolant Temperature (ECT) sensor. A hot engine may cause excessive coolant loss and/or personal injury.

✳✳ WARNING

Use care when handling the ECT. Damage to the coolant sensor will affect the operation of the fuel control system.

1. Before servicing the vehicle, refer to the Precautions Section.
2. Remove the fuel injector sight shield.
3. Drain the cooling system.
4. Disconnect the engine harness electrical connector from the Engine Coolant Temperature (ECT) sensor.
5. Remove the ECT sensor.

To install:

✳✳ WARNING

Replacement components must be the correct part number for the application. Components requiring the use of the thread locking compound, lubricants, corrosion inhibitors, or sealants are identified in the service procedure. Some replacement components may come with these coatings already applied. Do not use these coatings on components unless specified. These coatings can affect the final torque, which may affect the operation of the component. Use the correct torque specification when installing components in order to avoid damage.

6. Apply sealant GM P/N 12346004 (Canadian P/N 10953480) or equivalent to the threads of the ECT sensor.
7. Install the ECT sensor. Tighten the sensor to 15 ft. lbs. (20 Nm).
8. Connect the engine harness electrical connector to the ECT sensor.
9. Fill the cooling system.
10. Install the fuel injector sight shield.
11. Inspect and fill the cooling system as necessary.

TESTING

See Figure 125.

➡**If the PCM receives a high engine temperature signal from the Engine Coolant Temperature (ECT), it adjusts fueling rates to protect the engine from damage due to overheating.**

1. Turn OFF the ignition.
2. Inspect the cooling system surge tank for the proper coolant level.
3. If the ignition has been OFF for 8 hours or more, the ECT and the Intake Air Temperature (IAT) should be within 27°F (15°C) of each other and also the ambient temperature.
4. Turn ON the ignition, with the engine OFF, and use a scan tool to observe the IAT and the ECT sensor parameters.
5. Use the scan tool to verify the proper operation of the engine cooling system fans.

➡**A critical analysis of the operation of the thermostat is important to the proper diagnosis of the ECT.**

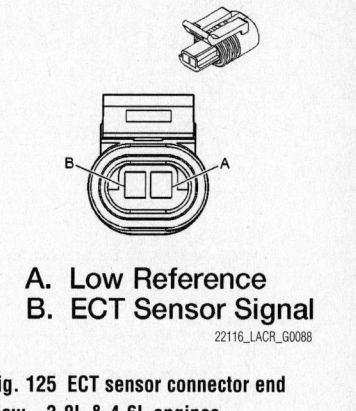

A. Low Reference
B. ECT Sensor Signal

22116_LACR_G0088

Fig. 125 ECT sensor connector end view—3.8L & 4.6L engines

6. Verify the proper heat range and the operation of the thermostat.

Circuit/System Testing

➡**All electrical components and accessories must be turned OFF and allowed to power down.**

1. With the ignition OFF, disconnect the harness connector at the ECT sensor.
2. Test for less than 5 ohms of resistance between the low reference circuit terminal and ground.
   a. If greater than the specified range, test the low reference circuit for an open/high resistance.
   b. If the circuit tests normal, replace the ECM.
3. With the ignition ON, verify the scan tool ECT parameter is less than a negative 38°F (negative 39°C).
   a. If greater than the specified range, test the signal circuit terminal for a short to ground.
   b. If the circuit tests normal, replace the ECM.
4. Install a 3-amp fused jumper wire between the signal circuit terminal and the low reference circuit terminal. Verify the scan tool ECT parameter is greater than 300°F (149°C).
   a. If less than the specified range, test the signal circuit for a short to voltage or an open/high resistance.
   b. If the circuit tests normal, replace the ECM.
5. If all circuits test normal, test or replace the ECT sensor.

ECT Component Testing

See Figure 126.

Measure and record the resistance of the ECT sensor at various temperatures, then compare those measurements to the following temperature verses resistance table.

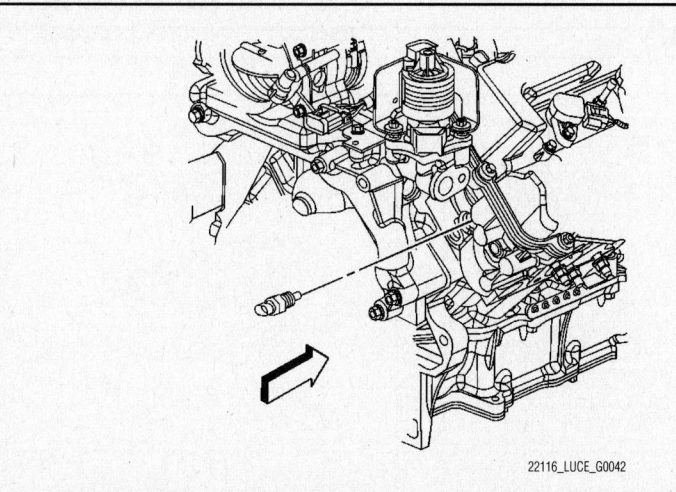

22116_LUCE_G0042

Fig. 124 Engine Coolant Temperature (ECT) sensor location—4.6L engine

Temperature Versus Resistance

Temperature C°/F°	Resistance Minimum Ohms	Resistance Maximum Ohms
Engine Coolant Temperature (ECT)		
-40/-40	40,490	50,136
-20/-4	14,096	16,827
-10/14	8,642	10,152
0/32	5,466	6,326
20/68	2,351	2,649
25/77	1,941	2,173
40/104	1,118	1,231
60/140	573	618
80/176	313	332
100/212	182	191
120/248	109	116
140/284	068	074

22116_LACR_G0089

Fig. 126 Temperature verses resistance table for ECT sensor

HEATED OXYGEN (HO2S) SENSOR

LOCATION

See Figures 127 through 131.

Refer to the accompanying illustrations for sensor locations.

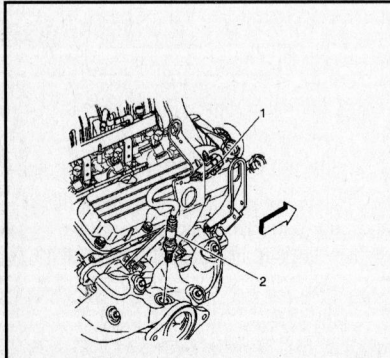

1. Heated Oxygen Sensor electrical connector
2. Heated Oxygen Sensor

22116_LACR_G0092

Fig. 127 Location of the heated oxygen sensor 1—3.8L engine

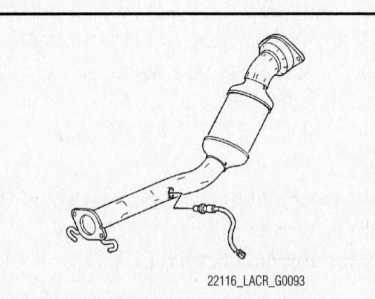

22116_LACR_G0093

Fig. 128 Location of the heated oxygen sensor 2—3.8L engine

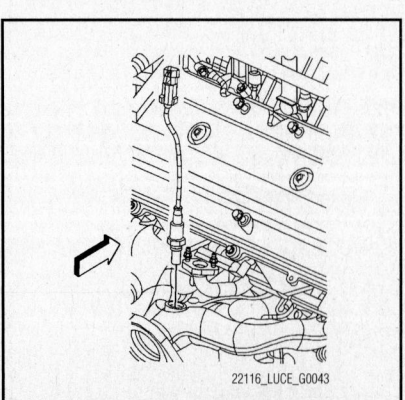

22116_LUCE_G0043

Fig. 129 Location of the heated oxygen sensor (bank 1, sensor 1)—4.6L engine

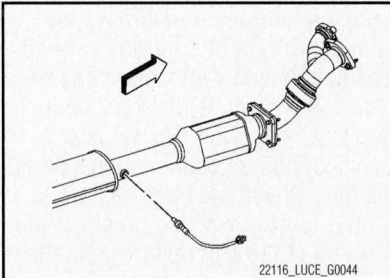

22116_LUCE_G0044

Fig. 130 Location of the heated oxygen sensor (bank 1, sensor 2)—4.6L engine

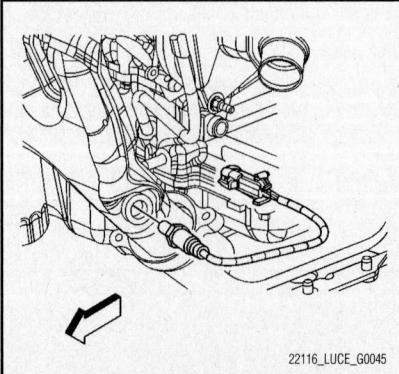

22116_LUCE_G0045

Fig. 131 Location of the heated oxygen sensor (bank 2, sensor 1)—4.6L engine

OPERATION

Heated Oxygen Sensors (HO2S) are used for fuel control and post catalyst monitoring. Each HO2S compares the oxygen content of the surrounding air with the oxygen content in the exhaust stream. The HO2S must reach operating temperature to provide an accurate voltage signal. A heating element inside the HO2S minimizes the time required for the sensor to reach operating temperature. Voltage is provided to the heater by the ignition 1 voltage circuit through a fuse. With the engine running, a ground is provided to the heater by the HO2S heater low control circuit through a low side driver within the Powertrain Control Module (PCM). The PCM commands the heater ON or OFF to maintain a specific HO2S operating temperature range. The PCM monitors the voltage on the HO2S heater low control circuit for heater fault diagnosis. If the PCM detects that the HO2S heater low control circuit voltage is not within a specified range, a DTC is set.

REMOVAL & INSTALLATION

3.8L Engine

Heated Oxygen Sensor—1

See Figure 127.

✳✳ WARNING

The Heated Oxygen Sensor (HO2S) uses a permanently attached pigtail and connector. Do not remove this pigtail from the HO2S. Damage to the pigtail or the connector could affect the proper operation of the sensor. Take care when handling the HO2S. Keep the in-line electrical connector, and the louvered end, free of grease, dirt, or other contaminants. Also avoid using cleaning solvents of any type. Do not drop the HO2S. Do not roughly handle the HO2S.

➡**The oxygen sensor may be difficult to remove when the engine temperature is below 120°F (48°C). Excessive force may damage threads in the exhaust manifold or the exhaust pipe.**

1. Remove the fuel injector sight shield.
2. Remove the HO2S retaining clip.
3. Disconnect the HO2S electrical connector (1).
4. Remove the HO2S electrical connector (1) from the fuel injector sight shield bracket.
5. Use the oxygen sensor wrench, J 39194, to remove the HO2S (2) from the right exhaust manifold.

To install:

➡**A special anti-seize compound is used on the oxygen sensors threads. New service sensors should already have the compound applied to the threads. Coat the threads of a reused sensor with anti-seize compound GM P/N 12377953 or equivalent.**

6. Install the HO2S (2) to the right exhaust manifold. Use the oxygen sensor wrench, J 39194, to tighten the HO2S to 31 ft. lbs. (42 Nm).
7. Install the HO2S electrical connector (1) to the fuel injector sight shield bracket.
8. Connect the HO2S electrical connector (1).
9. Install the HO2S retaining clip.
10. Install the fuel injector sight shield.

Heated Oxygen Sensor—2

See Figure 128.

✳✳ WARNING

The Heated Oxygen Sensor (HO2S) uses a permanently attached pigtail and connector. Do not remove this pigtail from the HO2S. Damage to or the removal of the pigtail or the connector could affect the proper operation of the sensor. Take care when handling the HO2S. Keep the in-line electrical connector, and the louvered end, free of grease, dirt, or other contaminants. Also, avoid using cleaning solvents of any type. Do not drop the HO2S. Do not roughly handle the HO2S.

➡**The oxygen sensor may be difficult to remove when the engine temperature is below 120°F (48°C). Excessive force may damage threads in the exhaust manifold or the exhaust pipe.**

1. Raise and support the vehicle.
2. Remove the HO2S electrical connector retaining clip from the HO2S electrical harness connector.
3. Disconnect the HO2S electrical connector from the HO2S electrical harness connector.
4. Use the oxygen sensor wrench, J 39194, to remove the HO2S from the exhaust pipe.

To install:

➡**A special anti-seize compound is used on the HO2S threads. New service sensors should already have the compound applied to the threads. Coat the threads of a reused sensor with anti-**

seize compound GM P/N 12377953 or equivalent.

5. Install the HO2S to the exhaust pipe. Use the oxygen sensor wrench, J 39194, to tighten the HO2S to 31 ft. lbs. (42 Nm).
6. Connect the HO2S electrical connector to the HO2S electrical harness connector.
7. Install the HO2S electrical connector retaining clip to the HO2S electrical harness connector.
8. Lower the vehicle.

4.6L Engine

Heated Oxygen Sensor—Bank 1, Sensor 1

See Figure 129 and 132.

✳✳ WARNING

Handle the oxygen sensors carefully in order to prevent damage to the component. Keep the electrical connector and the exhaust inlet end free of contaminants. Do not use cleaning solvents on the sensor. Do not drop or mishandle the sensor.

When replacing the Heated Oxygen Sensor (HO2S) perform the following in order to reset the HO2S resistance learned value and avoid possible HO2S failure:
- A code clear with a scan tool, regardless of whether or not a DTC is set
- A HO2S heater resistance learn reset with a scan tool, where available

➡**Remove the HO2S with the engine temperature above 120°F (48°C). Otherwise, the HO2S may be difficult to remove.**

1. Before servicing the vehicle, refer to the Precautions Section.
2. Remove the fuel injector sight shield.
3. Remove the Connector Position Assurance (CPA) retainer.
4. Disconnect the engine harness electrical connector from the HO2S.
5. Remove the HO2S clip from the secondary Air Injection (AIR) check valve hose bracket.
6. Raise and support the vehicle.
7. Support the rear of the frame with a tall screw type jack.
8. Remove the 4 rearward frame to body bolts (1) (left side shown, right side similar).
9. Lower the screw type jack approximately 1 ½ inches (4 cm) but not more than 3 inches (76mm), allowing the rear of the frame to lower.
10. Remove the HO2S.

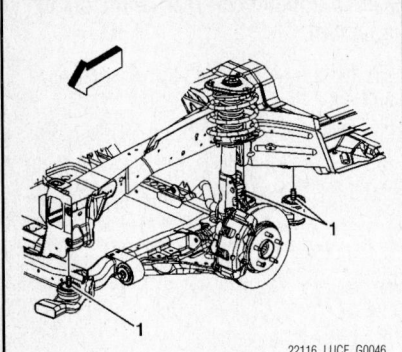

Fig. 132 Remove the 4 rearward frame to body bolts (left side shown, right side similar) (bank 1, sensor 1)—4.6L engine

22116_LUCE_G0046

To install:

➡A special anti-seize compound is used on the HO2S threads. The compound consists of liquid graphite and glass beads. The graphite tends to burn away, but the glass beads remain, making the sensor easier to remove. New, or service replacement sensors, already have the compound applied to the threads. If the sensor is removed from an exhaust components, and if for any reason the sensor is to be reinstalled, the threads must have anti-seize compound applied before the reinstallation.

11. If reusing the old HO2S, coat the threads with anti-seize compound, GM P/N 12377953 or equivalent.
12. Install the HO2S. Tighten the sensor to 30 ft. lbs. (41 Nm).
13. Raise the engine frame into position.
14. Install the 4 rearward frame to body bolts (1) (left side shown, right side similar). Tighten the bolts to 141 ft. lbs. (191 Nm).
15. Remove the screw type jack.
16. Install the HO2S clip to the AIR check valve hose bracket.
17. Connect the engine harness electrical connector to the HO2S.
18. Install the CPA retainer.
19. Install the fuel injector sight shield.

Heated Oxygen Sensor—Bank 1, Sensor 2

See Figure 130.

⚹⚹ WARNING

Handle the oxygen sensors carefully in order to prevent damage to the component. Keep the electrical connector and the exhaust inlet end free of contaminants. Do not use cleaning solvents on the sensor. Do not drop or mishandle the sensor.

When replacing the Heated Oxygen Sensor (HO2S) perform the following in order to reset the HO2S resistance learned value and avoid possible HO2S failure:
• A code clear with a scan tool, regardless of whether or not a DTC is set
• A HO2S heater resistance learn reset with a scan tool, where available

➡Remove the HO2S with the engine temperature above 120°F (48°C). Otherwise, the HO2S may be difficult to remove.

1. Before servicing the vehicle, refer to the Precautions Section.
2. Remove the oxygen sensor wiring harness heat shield.
3. Disconnect the engine harness electrical connector from the Heated Oxygen Sensor (HO2S).
4. Remove the HO2S.

To install:

➡A special anti-seize compound is used on the HO2S threads. The compound consists of liquid graphite and glass beads. The graphite tends to burn away, but the glass beads remain, making the sensor easier to remove. New, or service replacement sensors, already have the compound applied to the threads. If the sensor is removed from an exhaust components, and if for any reason the sensor is to be reinstalled, the threads must have anti-seize compound applied before the reinstallation.

5. If reusing the old HO2S, coat the threads with anti-seize compound, GM P/N 12377953 or equivalent.
6. Install the HO2S. Tighten the sensor to 30 ft. lbs. (41 Nm).
7. Connect the engine harness electrical connector to the HO2S.
8. Install the oxygen sensor wiring harness heat shield.

Heated Oxygen Sensor—Bank 2, Sensor 1

See Figure 131.

⚹⚹ WARNING

Handle the oxygen sensors carefully in order to prevent damage to the component. Keep the electrical connector and the exhaust inlet end free of contaminants. Do not use cleaning solvents on the sensor. Do not drop or mishandle the sensor.

When replacing the Heated Oxygen Sensor (HO2S) perform the following in order to reset the HO2S resistance learned value and avoid possible HO2S failure:
• A code clear with a scan tool, regardless of whether or not a DTC is set
• A HO2S heater resistance learn reset with a scan tool, where available

➡Remove the HO2S with the engine temperature above 120°F (48°C). Otherwise, the HO2S may be difficult to remove.

1. Before servicing the vehicle, refer to the Precautions Section.
2. Remove the front air deflector.
3. Remove the Connector Position Assurance (CPA) retainer.
4. Disconnect the engine harness electrical connector from the HO2S.
5. Remove the HO2S clip from the engine bracket.
6. Remove the HO2S.

To install:

➡A special anti-seize compound is used on the HO2S threads. The compound consists of liquid graphite and glass beads. The graphite tends to burn away, but the glass beads remain, making the sensor easier to remove. New, or service replacement sensors, already have the compound applied to the threads. If the sensor is removed from an exhaust components, and if for any reason the sensor is to be reinstalled, the threads must have anti-seize compound applied before the reinstallation.

7. If reusing the old HO2S, coat the threads with anti-seize compound, GM P/N 12377953 or equivalent.
8. Install the HO2S. Tighten the sensor to 30 ft. lbs. (41 Nm).
9. Connect the engine harness electrical connector to the HO2S.
10. Install the CPA retainer.
11. Install the HO2S clip to the engine bracket.
12. Install the front air deflector.

TESTING

See Figures 133 through 138.

1. With an OBD2 scan tool connected to the datalink port:
   a. Start the engine and allow it to reach normal operating temperature.
   b. If the engine is at operating

temperature when started, wait 15 seconds to allow the Heated Oxygen Sensor (HO2S) heater current to stabilize.

c. Observe the affected HO2S heater parameter with a scan tool.

d. The HO2S heater parameter should be within the specified range: 0.5–2.0 Amps.

2. Replace the affected HO2S as necessary.

3. Probe for circuit voltage:

a. Turn engine OFF.

b. Disconnect the affected HO2S.

c. Turn ON the ignition, with the engine OFF.

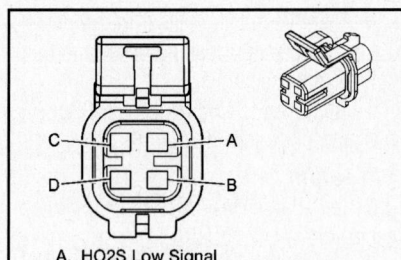

A. HO2S Low Signal
B. HO2S High Signal
C. HO2S Heater Low Control Sensor 1
D. Ignition 1 Voltage

22116_LACR_G0096

Fig. 133 HO2S sensor 1 connector end view (NU6)—3.8L engine

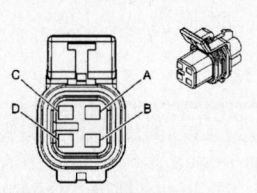

A. HO2S Low Signal
B. HO2S High Signal
C. HO2S Heater Low Control Sensor 1
D. Ignition 1 Voltage

22116_LACR_G0097

Fig. 134 HO2S sensor 1 connector end view (without NU6)—3.8L engine

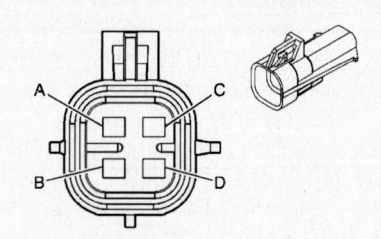

A. HO2S Low Signal
B. HO2S High Signal
C. HO2S Heater Low Control Sensor 2
D. Ignition 1 Voltage

22116_LACR_G0098

Fig. 135 HO2S sensor 2 connector end view—3.8L engine

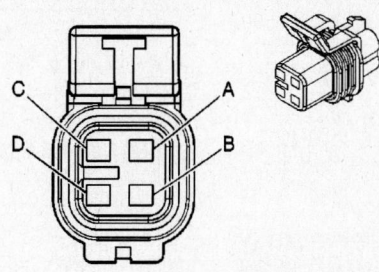

Pin	Wire Color	Circuit No.	Function
A	TN/OG	3111	HO2S Low Reference Bank 1 Sensor 1
B	D-GN	3110	HO2S Reference Voltage Bank 1 Sensor 1
C	WH	3113	HO2S Heater Low Control Bank 1 Sensor 1
D	PK/BK	5293	Powertrain Main Relay Fused Supply

22116_LUCE_G0047

Fig. 136 HO2S sensor connector end view (bank 1, sensor 1)—4.6L engine

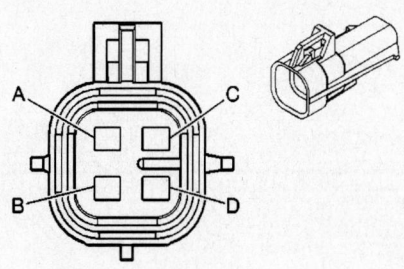

Pin	Wire Color	Circuit No.	Function
A	TN/PK	3121	HO2S 2 Low Reference
B	PK/OG	3120	HO2S 2 Reference Voltage
C	GY/WH	3122	HO2S 2 Heater Low Control
D	PK/BK	5294	Engine Main Relay Fused Control

22116_LUCE_G0048

Fig. 137 HO2S sensor connector end view (bank 1, sensor 2)—4.6L engine

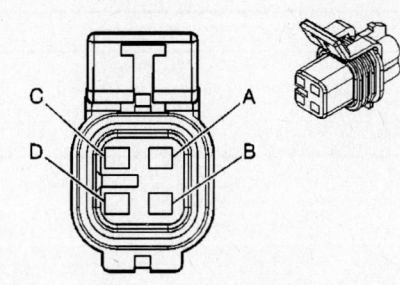

Pin	Wire Color	Circuit No.	Function
A	TN/WH	3211	HO2S Low Reference Bank 2 Sensor 1
B	PU/WH	3210	HO2S Reference Voltage Bank 2 Sensor 1
C	L-GN/WH	3112	HO2S Heater Low Control Bank 2 Sensor
D	PK/BK	5293	Powertrain Main Relay Fused Supply

22116_LUCE_G0049

Fig. 138 HO2S sensor connector end view (bank 2, sensor 1)—4.6L engine

d. Probe the ignition 1 voltage circuit of the HO2S harness connector on the engine harness side with a test lamp that is connected to a good ground.

e. The test lamp should illuminate.

4. Test the ground circuit:

a. Turn OFF the ignition.

b. Probe the HO2S heater low control

circuit of the HO2S harness connector on the engine harness side with a test lamp connected to battery voltage.

    c. With the ignition still OFF, observe the test lamp.

    d. The test lamp should illuminate.

5. If the ECM and all circuits test normal, replace the appropriate HO2S.

INTAKE AIR TEMPERATURE (IAT) SENSOR

LOCATION

See Figures 139 and 140.

Refer to the accompanying illustrations for sensor locations.

OPERATION

The Intake Air Temperature (IAT) sensor is a variable resistor that measures the temperature of the air entering the engine intake manifold. The Powertrain Control Module (PCM) supplies 5 volts to the IAT signal circuit and a ground for the IAT low reference circuit. When the sensor is cold, the resistance is greater. This results in a greater voltage on the signal circuit that is interpreted by the PCM as a colder IAT. As the sensor becomes warmer, the resistance decreases. This results in a lesser voltage on the IAT signal circuit that is interpreted by the PCM as a warmer IAT. If the PCM detects an IAT sensor signal voltage that is not within a calibrated range of the IAT sensor 1 signal voltage, a DTC is set.

REMOVAL & INSTALLATION

3.8L Engine

See Figure 139.

1. Remove the fuel injector sight shield.

➡**The Intake Air Temperature (IAT) sensor and the Mass Air Flow (MAF) sensor are combined as one sensor.**

2. Disconnect the MAF/IAT sensor electrical connector (2).

3. Loosen the air cleaner intake duct clamps.

4. Remove the air cleaner intake duct from the air cleaner housing cover and the throttle body assembly.

5. Remove the MAF/IAT sensor from the air cleaner intake duct.

To install:

6. Install the MAF/IAT sensor to the air cleaner intake duct.

7. Install the air cleaner intake duct to the air cleaner housing cover and the throttle body assembly.

8. Tighten the air cleaner intake duct clamp screws. Tighten the duct clamps to 27 inch lbs. (3 Nm).

9. Connect the MAF/IAT sensor electrical connector.

10. Install the fuel injector sight shield.

4.6L Engine

> ✳✳ **WARNING**
>
> **Handle the Intake Air Temperature (IAT)/Mass Air Flow (MAF) sensor carefully. Do not drop the sensor. Do not damage the screen located on the air inlet end of the sensor. Do not touch the sensing elements. Do not allow solvents and lubricants to come in contact with the sensing elements. Use a small amount of a soap-based solution in order to aid in the installation.**

1. Before servicing the vehicle, refer to the Precautions Section.

2. Disconnect the engine harness electrical connector from the Intake Air Temperature (IAT)/Mass Air Flow (MAF) sensor.

3. Loosen the air cleaner outlet duct clamp at the throttle body.

4. Loosen the air cleaner outlet duct clamp at the MAF/IAT sensor.

5. Remove the air cleaner outlet duct.

6. Remove the MAF/IAT sensor bolts.

7. Remove the MAF/IAT sensor.

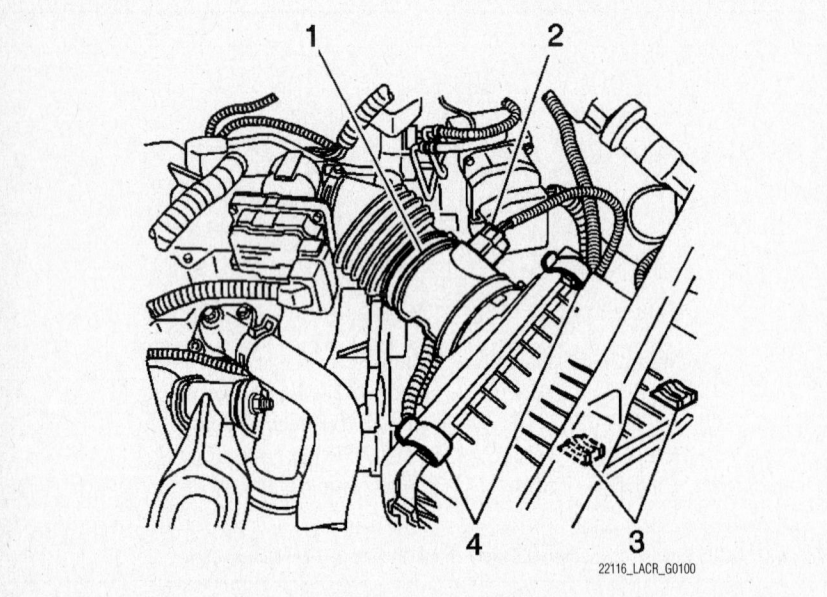

Fig. 139 Intake Air Temperature (IAT)/Mass Air Flow (MAF) sensor location—3.8L engine

22116_LACR_G0100

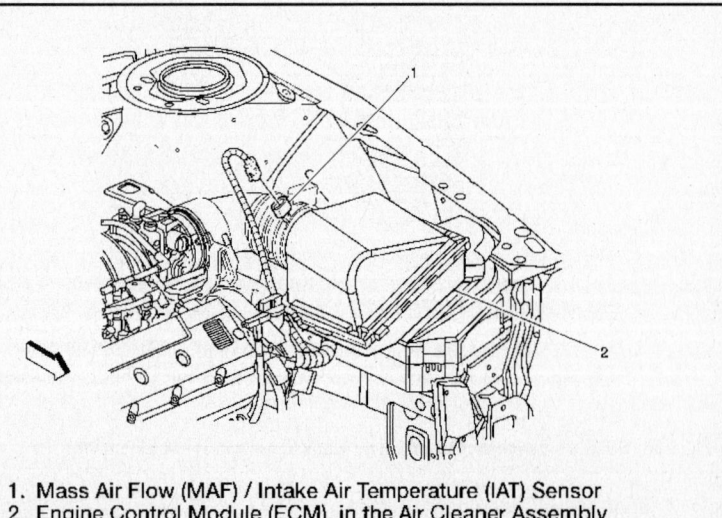

1. Mass Air Flow (MAF) / Intake Air Temperature (IAT) Sensor
2. Engine Control Module (ECM), in the Air Cleaner Assembly

22116_LUCE_G0031

Fig. 140 Intake Air Temperature (IAT)/Mass Air Flow (MAF) sensor location—4.6L engine

To install:

8. Install the MAF/IAT sensor.

9. Install the MAF/IAT sensor bolts. Tighten the bolts to 35 inch lbs. (4 Nm).

10. Install the air cleaner outlet duct.

11. Tighten the air cleaner outlet duct clamp at the MAF/IAT sensor. Tighten the clamp to 35 inch lbs. (4 Nm).

12. Tighten the air cleaner outlet duct clamp at the throttle body. Tighten the clamp to 35 inch lbs. (4 Nm).

13. Connect the engine harness electrical connector to the MAF/IAT sensor.

TESTING

1. Determine the ambient temperature by using an accurate thermometer.

2. If the ignition has been OFF for 8 hours or more, the Intake Air Temperature (IAT)/Mass Air Flow (MAF) sensor parameter and the Engine Coolant Temperature (ECT) sensor parameter should be within 27°F (15°C) of each other and also the ambient temperature.

3. Turn ON the ignition, and immediately observe the parameters. Compare those sensor parameters to each other and also to the ambient temperature, to determine if the IAT/MAF sensor parameter is skewed.

4. Replace the IAT/MAF sensor, if necessary.

KNOCK SENSOR (KS)

LOCATION

See Figures 141 through 143.

Refer to the accompanying illustrations for sensor locations.

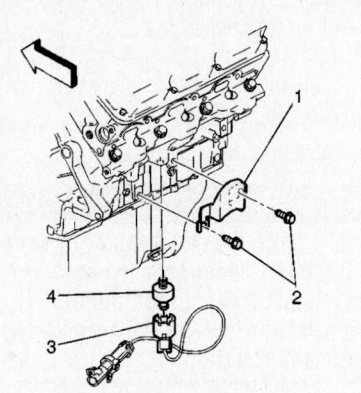

1. Knock Sensor (KS) heat shield
2. KS heat shield bolts
3. KS electrical connector
4. KS

22116_LACR_G0104

Fig. 142 Knock Sensor (KS) location bank 2—3.8L engine

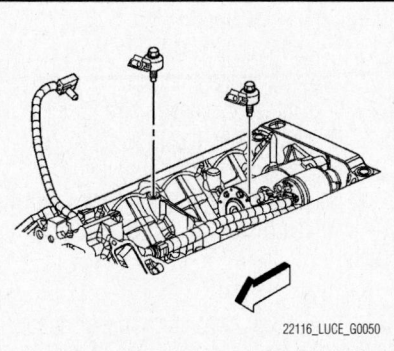

22116_LUCE_G0050

Fig. 143 Knock Sensor (KS) location bank 1 & 2—4.6L engine

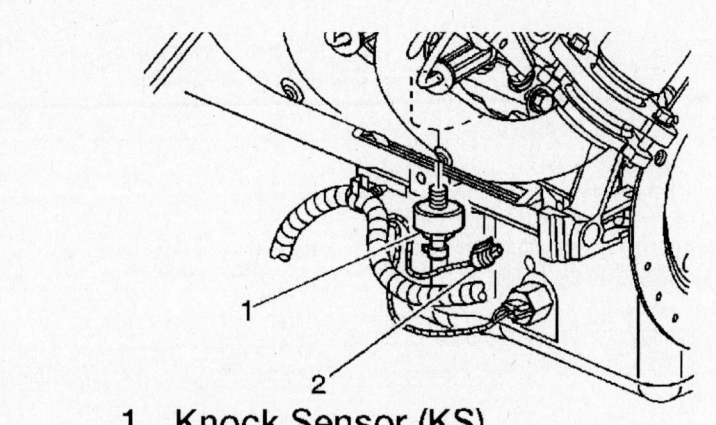

1. Knock Sensor (KS)
2. KS electrical connector

22116_LACR_G0103

Fig. 141 Knock Sensor (KS) location bank 1—3.8L engine

OPERATION

The Knock Sensor (KS) system enables the control module to control the ignition timing for the best possible performance while protecting the engine from potentially damaging levels of detonation. The control module uses the KS system to test for abnormal engine noise that may indicate detonation, also known as spark knock.

This KS system uses one or two flat response two-wire sensors. The sensor uses piezo-electric crystal technology that produces an AC voltage signal of varying amplitude and frequency based on the engine vibration or noise level. The amplitude and frequency are dependent upon the level of knock that the KS detects. The control module receives the KS signal through a signal circuit. The KS ground is supplied by the control module through a low reference circuit.

The control module learns a minimum noise level, or background noise, at idle from the KS and uses calibrated values for the rest of the RPM range. The control module uses the minimum noise level to calculate a noise channel. A normal KS signal will ride within the noise channel. As engine speed and load change, the noise channel upper and lower parameters will change to accommodate the normal KS signal, keeping the signal within the channel. In order to determine which cylinders are knocking, the control module only uses KS signal information when each cylinder is near Top Dead Center (TDC) of the firing stroke. If a knock is present, the signal will range outside of the noise channel.

If the control module has determined that a knock is present, it will retard the ignition timing to attempt to eliminate the knock. The control module will always try to work back to a zero compensation level, or no spark retard. An abnormal KS signal will stay outside of the noise channel or will not be present. KS diagnostics are calibrated to detect faults with the KS circuitry inside the control module, the KS wiring, and the KS voltage output. Some diagnostics are also calibrated to detect constant noise from an outside influence such as a loose/damaged component or excessive engine mechanical noise.

REMOVAL & INSTALLATION

3.8L Engine

Knock Sensor (KS)—Bank 1

See Figure 141.

✳✳ CAUTION

Hot engine coolant may cause severe burns. Although the cooling system has been drained, coolant still remains in the engine water jacket. This coolant will drain with the removal of the knock sensor.

1. Raise and support the vehicle.
2. Drain the cooling system.
3. Disconnect the Knock Sensor (KS) electrical connector (2).
4. Remove the KS (1).

To install:

✳✳ WARNING

Use the correct fastener in the correct location. Replacement fasteners must be the correct part number for that application. Fasteners requiring replacement or fasteners requiring the use of thread locking compound or sealant are identified in the service procedure. Do not use paints, lubricants, or corrosion inhibitors on fasteners or fastener joint surfaces unless specified. These coatings affect fastener torque and joint clamping force and may damage the fastener. Use the correct tightening sequence and specifications when installing fasteners in order to avoid damage to parts and systems.

✳✳ WARNING

DO NOT apply thread sealant to sensor threads. The sensor is coated at factory and applying additional sealant will affect the ability of the sensor to detect detonation.

5. Install the KS (1). Tighten the sensor to 14 ft. lbs. (19 Nm).
6. Connect the KS electrical connector (2).
7. Lower the vehicle.
8. Fill the cooling system.

Knock Sensor (KS)—Bank 2

See Figure 142.

✳✳ CAUTION

Hot engine coolant may cause severe burns. Although the cooling system has been drained, coolant still remains in the engine water jacket. This coolant will drain with the removal of the knock sensor.

1. Raise and support the vehicle.
2. Drain the cooling system.
3. Disconnect the Knock Sensor (KS) electrical connector (3) from the KS.
4. Remove the KS (4).

To install:

✳✳ WARNING

DO NOT apply thread sealant to sensor threads. The sensor is coated at factory and applying additional sealant will affect the sensors ability to detect detonation.

5. Install the KS (4). Tighten the sensor to 14 ft. lbs. (19 Nm).
6. Connect the KS electrical connector.
7. Lower the vehicle.
8. Fill the cooling system.

4.6L Engine

See Figure 143.

1. Before servicing the vehicle, refer to the Precautions Section.
2. Remove the intake manifold.
3. Disconnect the electrical connector from the right knock sensor, if required.
4. Disconnect the electrical connector from the left knock sensor, if required.
5. Remove the appropriate knock sensor. (The cylinder heads are shown removed for clarity).

To install:

6. Install the appropriate knock sensor. Tighten the sensor to 18 ft. lbs. (25 Nm).
7. Connect the electrical connector to the left knock sensor, if required.
8. Connect the electrical connector to the right knock sensor, if required.
9. Install the intake manifold.

TESTING

See Figures 144 through 147.

1. Inspect the Knock Sensor (KS) for physical damage. A KS that is dropped or damaged may cause a DTC to set.
2. Inspect the KS for proper installation. A KS that is loose or over-tightened may cause a DTC to set. The KS should be free of thread sealant other than the factory coating.
3. The KS mounting surface should be free of burrs, casting flash, and foreign material.

➡ If an engine mechanical noise can be heard, repair the condition before proceeding to test the KS.

4. Test for an intermittent or poor connection at the affected KS.

5. With the ignition OFF, disconnect the affected KS.
    a. Measure the resistance for infinite ohms from the sensor signal terminal on the KS to a good ground with a Digital Multi-Meter (DMM).
    b. If resistance does not measure infinite ohms, replace the affected KS.

✳✳ WARNING

DO NOT tap on plastic engine components.

6. Connect the DMM to the terminal of the affected KS. Set the DMM to the 400 Hz scale, let it stabilize at 0 Hz.
    a. Tap on engine block with a non-metallic object near the affected KS while observing the signal indicated on the DMM.
    b. If the DMM does not display a fluctuating frequency while tapping on the engine block, replace the affected KS.
7. Turn the ignition ON, engine OFF. Set the DMM to the DC voltage scale. Measure for 4.2 volts from the KS signal circuit to a good ground with the DMM.

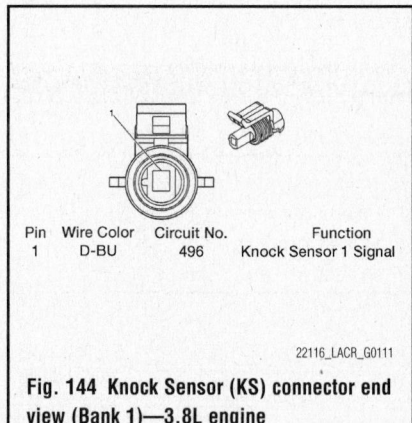

Pin	Wire Color	Circuit No.	Function
1	D-BU	496	Knock Sensor 1 Signal

22116_LACR_G0111

Fig. 144 Knock Sensor (KS) connector end view (Bank 1)—3.8L engine

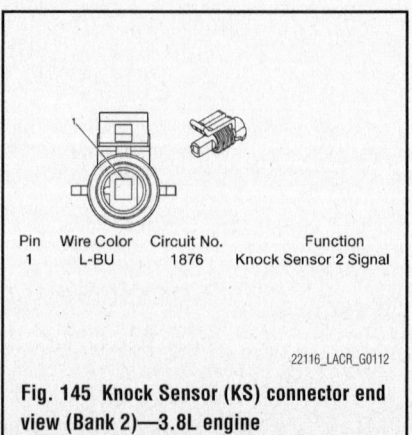

Pin	Wire Color	Circuit No.	Function
1	L-BU	1876	Knock Sensor 2 Signal

22116_LACR_G0112

Fig. 145 Knock Sensor (KS) connector end view (Bank 2)—3.8L engine

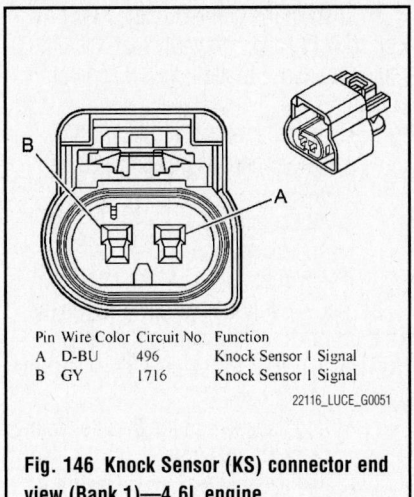

Pin Wire Color Circuit No. Function
A D-BU   496   Knock Sensor 1 Signal
B GY   1716   Knock Sensor 1 Signal

22116_LUCE_G0051

Fig. 146 Knock Sensor (KS) connector end view (Bank 1)—4.6L engine

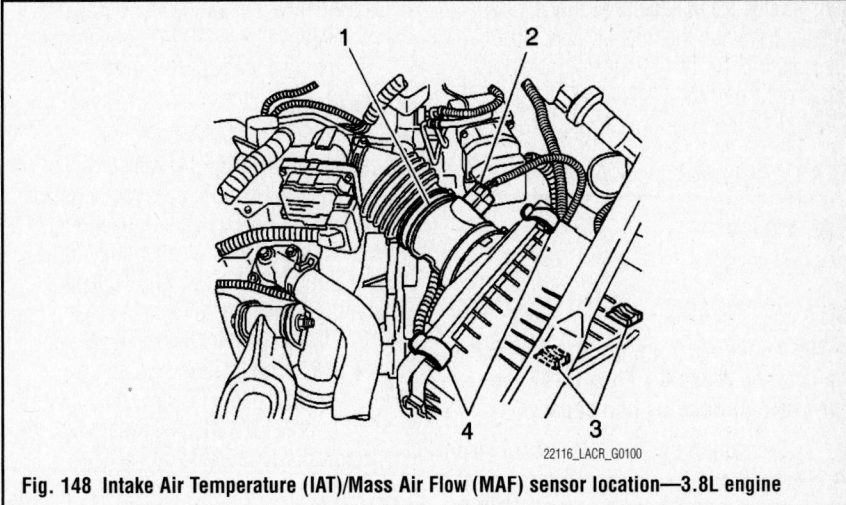

22116_LACR_G0100

Fig. 148 Intake Air Temperature (IAT)/Mass Air Flow (MAF) sensor location—3.8L engine

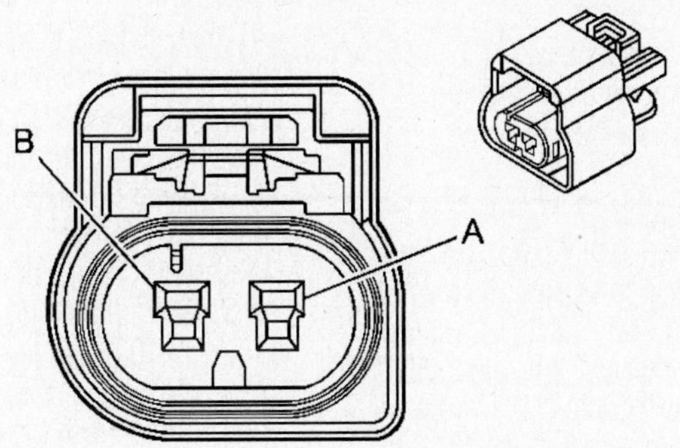

Pin Wire Color Circuit No. Function
A L-BU   1876   Knock Sensor 2 Signal
B GY   2303   Knock Sensor 2 Signal

22116_LUCE_G0052

Fig. 147 Knock Sensor (KS) connector end view (Bank 2)—4.6L engine

OPERATION

The Mass Air Flow (MAF) sensor is integrated with the Intake Air Temperature (IAT) sensor. The MAF sensor is an air flow meter that measures the amount of air entering the engine. The Engine Control Module (ECM) uses the MAF sensor signal to provide the correct fuel delivery for all engine speeds and loads. A small quantity of air entering the engine indicates a deceleration or idle condition. A large quantity of air entering the engine indicates an acceleration or high load condition. The MAF/IAT sensor has the following circuits:

- An ignition 1 voltage circuit
- A ground circuit
- A MAF sensor signal circuit
- An IAT sensor signal circuit
- A low reference circuit

The ECM applies 5 volts to the MAF sensor on the MAF sensor signal circuit. The

c. If over 4.2 volts, turn the ignition OFF, disconnect the control module and test the KS signal circuit for a short to voltage.

d. If under 4.2 volts, turn the ignition OFF, disconnect the control module test the KS signal circuit for an open, short to ground, or high resistance.

8. Test for intermittent or poor connections at the control module.

9. If all circuits test normal, replace the control module.

MASS AIR FLOW (MAF) SENSOR

LOCATION

See Figures 148 and 149.

Refer to the accompanying illustrations for sensor locations.

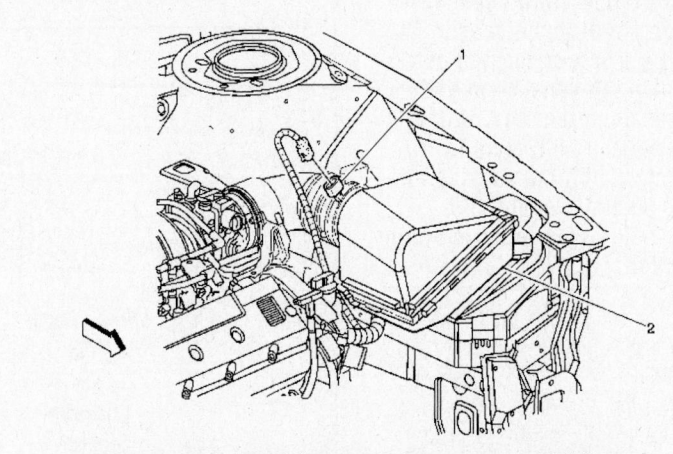

1. Mass Air Flow (MAF) / Intake Air Temperature (IAT) Sensor
2. Engine Control Module (ECM), in the Air Cleaner Assembly

22116_LUCE_G0051

Fig. 149 Intake Air Temperature (IAT)/Mass Air Flow (MAF) sensor location—4.6L engine

sensor uses the voltage to produce a frequency based on the inlet air flow through the sensor bore. The frequency varies in a range of near 1,700 Hertz at idle to near 9,500 Hertz at maximum engine load.

REMOVAL & INSTALLATION

3.8L Engine

See Figure 139.

1. Remove the fuel injector sight shield.

➡ **The Intake Air Temperature (IAT) sensor and the Mass Air Flow (MAF) sensor are combined as one sensor.**

2. Disconnect the MAF/IAT sensor electrical connector (2).
3. Loosen the air cleaner intake duct clamps.
4. Remove the air cleaner intake duct from the air cleaner housing cover and the throttle body assembly.
5. Remove the MAF/IAT sensor from the air cleaner intake duct.

To install:

6. Install the MAF/IAT sensor to the air cleaner intake duct.
7. Install the air cleaner intake duct to the air cleaner housing cover and the throttle body assembly.
8. Tighten the air cleaner intake duct clamp screws. Tighten the duct clamps to 27 inch lbs. (3 Nm).
9. Connect the MAF/IAT sensor electrical connector.
10. Install the fuel injector sight shield.

4.6L Engine

✴✴ WARNING

Handle the Intake Air Temperature (IAT)/Mass Air Flow (MAF) sensor carefully. Do not drop the sensor. Do not damage the screen located on the air inlet end of the sensor. Do not touch the sensing elements. Do not allow solvents and lubricants to come in contact with the sensing elements. Use a small amount of a soap-based solution in order to aid in the installation.

1. Before servicing the vehicle, refer to the Precautions Section.
2. Disconnect the engine harness electrical connector from the Intake Air Temperature (IAT)/Mass Air Flow (MAF) sensor.
3. Loosen the air cleaner outlet duct clamp at the throttle body.
4. Loosen the air cleaner outlet duct clamp at the MAF/IAT sensor.

5. Remove the air cleaner outlet duct.
6. Remove the MAF/IAT sensor bolts.
7. Remove the MAF/IAT sensor.

To install:

8. Install the MAF/IAT sensor.
9. Install the MAF/IAT sensor bolts. Tighten the bolts to 35 inch lbs. (4 Nm).
10. Install the air cleaner outlet duct.
11. Tighten the air cleaner outlet duct clamp at the MAF/IAT sensor. Tighten the clamp to 35 inch lbs. (4 Nm).
12. Tighten the air cleaner outlet duct clamp at the throttle body. Tighten the clamp to 35 inch lbs. (4 Nm).
13. Connect the engine harness electrical connector to the MAF/IAT sensor.

TESTING

1. Verify the integrity of the air induction system by inspecting for the following conditions:

- Damaged components
- Loose or improper installation
- An air flow restriction
- Any vacuum leak
- Water intrusion

2. With the engine running, observe the scan tool MAF sensor parameter. The reading should be between 1,700–3,200 Hz depending on the Engine Coolant Temperature (ECT).
3. A Wide Open Throttle (WOT) acceleration from a stop should cause the MAF sensor parameter on the scan tool to increase rapidly. This increase should be from 2–6 g/s at idle to greater than 100 g/s at the time of the 1–2 shift.
4. Verify that any electrical aftermarket devices are properly connected and grounded.

Circuit Testing

See Figures 150 and 151.

1. Inspect the harness of the Mass Air Flow (MAF) sensor to verify that it is not routed too close to the following components:

- Any aftermarket accessories
- The secondary ignition wires or coils
- Any solenoids
- Any relays
- Any motors

2. A low minimum air rate through the sensor bore at idle or during deceleration may cause a DTC to set. Inspect for the following conditions:

- Any deposits on the throttle plate or in the throttle bore
- Any vacuum leak downstream of the MAF sensor

3. Inspect for any contamination or debris on the sensing elements of the MAF sensor.
4. Inspect the air induction system for any water intrusion. Any water that reaches the MAF sensor will skew the sensor and may cause a DTC to set.
5. A Wide Open Throttle (WOT) acceleration from a stop should cause the MAF sensor parameter on the scan tool to increase rapidly. This increase should be from 3–10 g/s at idle to 150 g/s or more at the time of the 1 to 2 shift of the transmission. If the increase is not observed, inspect for a restriction in the induction system or the exhaust system.
6. Inspect for a skewed or stuck Engine Coolant Temperature (ECT) sensor.
7. Test for a high resistance of 15 ohms or more on the ignition 1 voltage circuit. This may cause a DTC to set. A high resistance

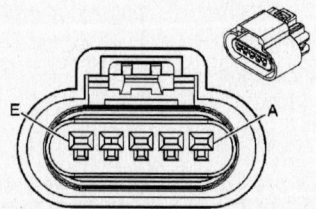

Pin	Wire Color	Circuit No.	Function
A	YE	492	MAF Sensor Signal
B	PK	339	Ignition 1 Voltage
C	BK/WH	451	Ground
D	TN	472	IAT Sensor Signal
E	BK	2760	Low Reference

22116_LACR_G0114

Fig. 150 Mass Air Flow (MAF)/Intake Air Temperature (IAT) connector end view—3.8L engine

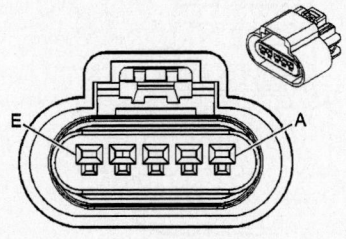

Pin	Wire Color	Circuit No.	Function
A	TN/YE	492	MAF Sensor Signal
B	PK/BK	5294	Engine Main Relay Fused Control
C	BK/WH	1551	Ground
D	TN	472	IAT Sensor Signal
E	TN/D-BU	2760	Low Reference

22116_LUCE_G0053

Fig. 151 Mass Air Flow (MAF)/Intake Air Temperature (IAT) connector end view—4.6L engine

may also cause a drivability concern before a DTC sets.

The Barometric Pressure (BARO) sensor that is used in order to calculate the predicted mass air flow value is initially based on the Manifold Absolute Pressure (MAP) sensor at key ON. When the engine is running, the BARO value is continually updated near WOT. A skewed MAP sensor will cause the calculated mass air flow value to be inaccurate and may result in a no start condition. The value shown for the MAP sensor parameter varies with the altitude. With the ignition ON and the engine OFF, 101 kPa is the approximate value near sea level. This value will decrease by approximately 3 kPa for every 1,000 feet (305 meters) of altitude.

➡**For the following tests, all electrical components and accessories must be turned OFF, and allowed to power down.**

8. With the ignition OFF, disconnect the MAF/IAT harness connector at the MAF/IAT sensor.

9. With the ignition ON, verify that a test lamp illuminates between the ignition circuit terminal and ground. If the test lamp does not illuminate, test the ignition circuit for a short to ground or an open/high resistance.

10. With the ignition ON, test for 4.8–5.2 volts between the signal circuit terminal and ground:

   a. If less than the specified range, test the signal circuit for a short to ground or an open/high resistance.

   b. If greater than the specified range, test the signal circuit for a short to voltage.

11. If all circuits test normal, replace the MAF sensor.

MANIFOLD ABSOLUTE PRESSURE (MAP) SENSOR

LOCATION

See Figures 152 and 153.

Refer to the accompanying illustrations for sensor locations.

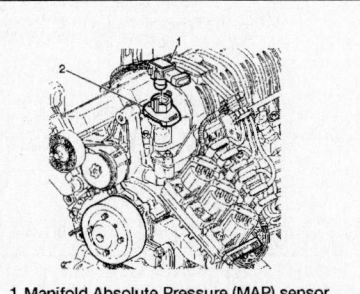

1. Manifold Absolute Pressure (MAP) sensor
2. Positive Crankcase Ventilation (PCV) valve cover

22116_LACR_G0115

Fig. 152 Manifold Absolute Pressure (MAP) sensor location—3.8L engine

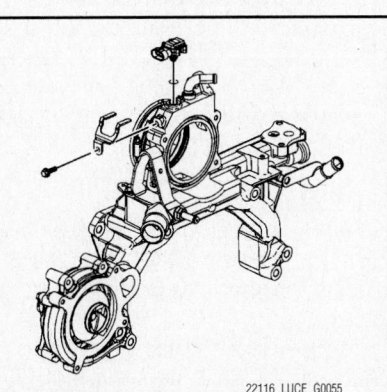

22116_LUCE_G0055

Fig. 153 Manifold Absolute Pressure (MAP) sensor location—4.6L engine

OPERATION

The Manifold Absolute Pressure (MAP) sensor measures the pressure inside the intake manifold. Pressure in the intake manifold is affected by engine speed, throttle opening, air temperature, and Barometric Pressure (BARO). A diaphragm within the MAP sensor is displaced by the pressure changes that occur from the varying load and operating conditions of the engine. The sensor translates this action into electrical resistance. The MAP sensor wiring includes 3 circuits. The Engine Control Module (ECM) supplies a regulated 5 volts to the sensor on a 5 volt reference circuit. The ECM supplies a ground on a low reference circuit. The MAP sensor provides a signal voltage to the ECM, relative to the pressure changes, on the MAP sensor signal circuit. The ECM converts the signal voltage input to a pressure value.

Under normal operation the greatest pressure that can exist in the intake manifold is equal to BARO. This occurs when the vehicle is operated at Wide Open Throttle (WOT) or when the ignition is ON while the engine is OFF. Under these conditions, the ECM uses the MAP sensor to determine the current BARO. The least manifold pressure occurs when the vehicle is idling or decelerating. MAP can range from 10 kPa, when pressures are less, to as great as 104 kPa, depending on the current BARO. The ECM monitors the MAP sensor signal for pressure outside of the normal range.

REMOVAL & INSTALLATION

3.8L Engine

See Figure 152.

The Manifold Absolute Pressure (MAP) sensor is mounted to the Positive Crankcase Ventilation (PCV) valve cover.

1. Remove the fuel injector sight shield.
2. Disconnect the MAP sensor electrical connector.
3. Carefully release the locking tabs holding the MAP (1) sensor to the PCV valve cover (2) just enough to remove the MAP sensor.
4. Pull the MAP sensor straight out of PCV valve cover.

To install:

5. Ensure that the seal is installed on the MAP sensor and that the seal is not damaged.
6. Position and install the MAP sensor (1) to the PCV valve cover (2). Ensure that the locking tabs engage to hold the MAP sensor to the PCV valve cover.
7. Connect the MAP sensor electrical connector.
8. Install the fuel injector sight shield.

4.6L Engine

See Figure 153.

1. Remove the fuel injector sight shield, if necessary.

2. Disconnect the engine harness electrical connector from the Manifold Absolute Pressure (MAP) sensor.

3. Remove the MAP sensor bracket bolt.

4. Remove the MAP sensor bracket.

5. Remove the MAP sensor.

To install:

6. Install the MAP sensor.

7. Install the MAP sensor bracket.

8. Install the MAP sensor bracket bolt. Tighten the bolt to 89 inch lbs. (10 Nm).

9. Connect the engine harness electrical connector to the MAP sensor.

10. Install the fuel injector sight shield, if necessary.

TESTING

See Figures 154 and 155.

Poor idle characteristics may be due to uncontrolled fueling caused by an open or high resistance in the Heated Oxygen Sensor (HO2S) 1 low signal circuit. Before replacing any component, ensure that this condition does not exist.

1. Start the engine.

2. Monitor the DTC information with the scan tool.

3. Turn the engine OFF.

4. If DTC P0641 or P0651 are set, correct these codes first.

5. Verify the integrity of the entire air induction system by inspecting for the following conditions:

- Any damage to, or hairline fractures of, the MAP sensor housing
- Disconnected, damaged, or incorrectly routed vacuum hoses
- Manifold Absolute Pressure (MAP) sensor disconnected from the vacuum source
- Restrictions in the MAP sensor vacuum source
- Intake manifold vacuum leaks
- Inspect for a properly functioning oxygen sensor

6. With the ignition ON, and the engine OFF, disconnect the MAP sensor.

7. Using a Digital Multi-Meter (DMM), measure the 5-volt reference circuit of the MAP sensor to a good ground. The reading should be 4.8–5.2 volts.

a. If more than 5.2 volts, then test the circuit for a short to voltage. If the circuit tests normal, replace the control module.

b. If less than 4.8 volts, then test the

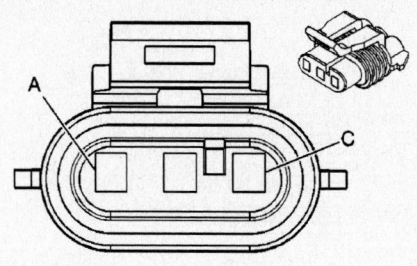

Pin	Wire Color	Circuit No.	Function
A	OG/BK	469	Low Reference
B	L-GN	432	MAP Sensor Signal
C	GY	2704	5-Volt Reference 2

22116_LACR_G0116

Fig. 154 Manifold Absolute Pressure (MAP) connector end view—3.8L engine

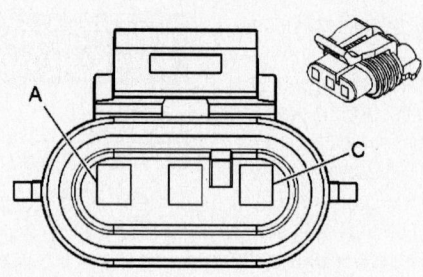

Pin	Wire Color	Circuit No.	Function
A	OG/BK	469	Low Reference
B	L-GN/BK	432	MAP Sensor Signal
C	GY/WH	2704	5-Volt Reference

22116_LUCE_G0054

Fig. 155 Manifold Absolute Pressure (MAP) connector end view—4.6L engine

circuit for high resistance, an open, a short to ground, or an intermittent or poor connection at the control module. If the circuit tests normal, replace the control module.

8. Use a scan tool and observe the MAP sensor. It should read less than 12 kPa.

a. If the MAP sensor is more than 12 kPa, test the MAP sensor signal circuit for a short to voltage.

b. If the circuit tests normal, replace the control module.

9. Use a 3-Amp fused jumper wire and connect it between the MAP sensor 5-volt reference circuit and the MAP sensor signal circuit.

10. Use a scan tool and observe the MAP sensor. It should read more than 103 kPa.

a. If the MAP sensor is less than 103

kPa, test the MAP sensor signal circuit for a short to ground, an open, high resistance.

b. If the circuit tests normal, replace the control module.

11. Turn OFF the ignition and allow the control module to power down.

12. Remove the MAP sensor from the engine vacuum source, but leave the MAP sensor connected to the engine harness.

13. Connect the J 23738-A, or a similar vacuum pump, to the MAP sensor.

14. Turn ON the ignition, with the engine OFF.

15. Observe the MAP sensor pressure with the scan tool.

16. Apply vacuum to the MAP sensor with the J 23738-A in 1 inch Hg increments until 15 inches Hg is reached. Each 1 inch Hg should decrease MAP sensor pressure by 3–4 kPa. Monitor the MAP sensor pres-

sure to see if the decrease in pressure is consistent.

 a. If decrease in pressure is not consistent then, test for intermittent and poor connections at the MAP sensor.

 b. If connections test OK, replace the MAP sensor.

17. Apply vacuum with the J 23738-A until 20 inches Hg is reached. Observe the MAP sensor pressure. It should read less than 34 kPa.

 a. If the pressure is more than 34 kPa, test for an intermittent or poor connection at the MAP sensor.

 b. If connections test OK, replace the MAP sensor.

18. With a DMM, measure the resistance between the low reference circuit of the MAP sensor and battery negative post. It should read less than 5 ohms.

 a. If the resistance is more than 5 ohms, test the low reference circuit for a high resistance.

 b. If the circuit tests normal, replace the control module.

POWERTRAIN CONTROL MODULE (PCM)

LOCATION

See Figure 156.

Refer to the accompanying illustration for PCM location.

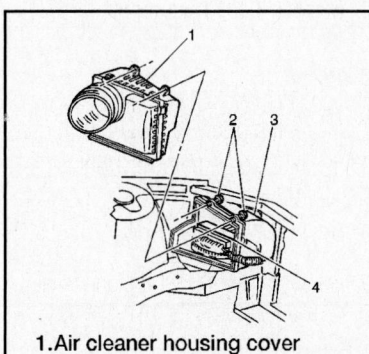

1. Air cleaner housing cover
2. Air cleaner housing cover screws
3. Air cleaner housing assembly
4. Powertrain Control Module (PCM)

22116_LACR_G0120

Fig. 156 Powertrain Control Module (PCM) location—3.8L engine

OPERATION

The powertrain has electronic controls to reduce exhaust emissions while maintaining excellent drivability and fuel economy. The Powertrain Control Module (PCM) is the control center of this system. The PCM monitors numerous engine and vehicle functions. The PCM constantly looks at the information from various sensors and other inputs, and controls the systems that affect vehicle performance and emissions. The PCM also performs the diagnostic tests on various parts of the system. The PCM can recognize operational problems and alert the driver via the Malfunction Indicator Lamp (MIL). When the PCM detects a malfunction, the PCM stores a Diagnostic Trouble Code (DTC). The problem area is identified by the particular DTC that is set. The control module supplies a buffered voltage to various sensors and switches. Review the components and wiring diagrams in order to determine which systems are controlled by the PCM. The following are some of the functions that the PCM controls:

- The engine fueling
- The Ignition Control (IC)
- The Knock Sensor (KS) system
- The Evaporative Emissions (EVAP) system
- The Secondary Air Injection (AIR) system (if equipped)
- The Exhaust Gas Recirculation (EGR) system
- The automatic transmission functions
- The alternator
- The A/C clutch control
- The cooling fan control

REMOVAL & INSTALLATION

3.8L Engine

See Figure 156.

➡ Service of the Powertrain Control Module (PCM) should normally consist of either replacement of the PCM or Electrically Erasable Programmable Read Only Memory (EEPROM) programming. If the diagnostic procedures call for the PCM to be replaced, the PCM should be inspected first to see if the correct part is being used. If the correct part is being used, remove the faulty PCM and install the new service PCM.

✳✳ WARNING

Turn the ignition OFF when installing or removing the control module connectors and disconnecting or reconnecting the power to the control module (battery cable, PCM/Engine Control Module (ECM)/Transaxle Control Module (TCM) pigtail, control module fuse, jumper cables, etc.) in order to prevent internal control module damage.

✳✳ WARNING

Control module damage may result when the metal case contacts battery voltage. DO NOT contact the control module metal case with battery voltage when servicing a control module, using battery booster cables, or when charging the vehicle battery.

✳✳ WARNING

In order to prevent any possible electrostatic discharge damage to the control module, do not touch the connector pins or the soldered components on the circuit board.

➡ Remove any debris from around the control module connector surfaces before servicing the control module. Inspect the control module connector gaskets when diagnosing or replacing the control module. Ensure that the gaskets are installed correctly. The gaskets prevent contaminant intrusion into the control module.

➡ The new service PCM will not be programmed. You must program the new PCM. DTC P0602 indicates the EEPROM is not programmed or has malfunctioned.

➡ It is necessary to record the remaining engine oil life. If the replacement module is not programmed with the remaining engine oil life, the engine oil life will default to 100 percent. If the replacement module is not programmed with the remaining engine oil life, the engine oil will need to be changed at 3,000 miles (5,000 km) from the last engine oil change.

1. Using a scan tool, retrieve the percentage of remaining engine oil life. Record the remaining engine oil life.

2. Remove or disconnect the following:

- The negative battery cable
- The left front inner fender brace
- The air cleaner intake duct
- The air cleaner housing cover screws (2)
- The air cleaner housing cover (1)

3. Without disconnecting the PCM electrical connectors, remove the PCM and the wiring harness from the air cleaner housing assembly (3).

4. Disconnect the PCM electrical connectors and remove the PCM (4).

To install:

5. Install or connect the following:

- The PCM to the PCM electrical

connectors (4). Tighten the connectors to 71 inch lbs. (8 Nm)
- The PCM and the wiring harness to the air cleaner housing assembly (3)
- The air cleaner housing cover (1)
- The air cleaner housing cover screws (2). Tighten the screws to 35 inch lbs. (4 Nm)
- The air cleaner intake duct
- The left front inner fender brace
- The negative battery cable

6. If a new PCM is being installed, the PCM must be programmed.

4.6L engine

For removal and installation, refer to Electronic Control Module (ECM) which may also be referred to as the Engine Control Module (ECM).

TESTING

The Powertrain Control Module (PCM) is programmed with test routines that test the operation of the various systems the PCM controls. Some tests monitor internal PCM functions. Many tests are run continuously. Other tests run only under specific conditions, referred to as conditions for running the DTC. When the vehicle is operating within the conditions for running a particular test, the PCM monitors certain parameters and determines if the values are within an expected range. The parameters and values considered outside the range of normal operation are listed as conditions for setting the DTC. When the conditions for setting the DTC occur, the PCM executes the action taken when the DTC Sets. Some DTC's alert the driver via the Malfunction Indicator Lamp (MIL) or a message. Other DTC's do not trigger a driver warning, but are stored in memory. The PCM also saves data and input parameters when most DTC's are set. This data is stored in the freeze frame and/or failure records.

The DTC's are categorized by type. The DTC type is determined by the MIL operation and the manner in which the fault data is stored when a particular DTC fails. In some cases there may be exceptions to this structure. Therefore, when diagnosing the system it is important to read the action taken when the DTC sets and the conditions for clearing the DTC.

Many intermittent open or shorted circuits come and go with harness and connector movement caused by vibration, engine torque, bumps, and rough pavement.

1. Test the wiring harness and connectors by performing the following:

- Move the related PCM connectors and wiring while monitoring the appropriate scan tool data
- With the engine running, move the related connectors and wiring while monitoring engine operation
- If harness or connector movement affects the data displayed, the component and system operation, or the engine operation, inspect and repair the harness or connections as necessary

2. Test the electrical connections and/or wiring by performing the following:

- Inspect for incorrect mating of the connector halves, or terminals not fully seated in the connector body, backed-out
- Inspect for improperly formed or damaged terminals. Test for incorrect terminal tension
- Inspect for poor terminal to wire connections including terminals crimped over insulation. This requires removing the terminal from the connector body
- Inspect for corrosion or water intrusion. Pierced or damaged insulation can allow moisture to enter the wiring. The conductor can corrode inside the insulation with little visible evidence. Look for swollen and stiff sections of wire in the suspect circuits
- Inspect for wires that are broken inside the insulation

VEHICLE SPEED SENSOR (VSS)

LOCATION

See Figure 157.

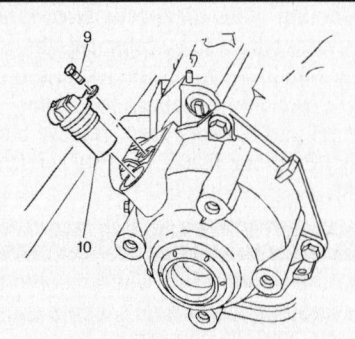

9. Vehicle Speed Sensor bolt
10. Vehicle Speed Sensor

22116_LACR_G0127

Fig. 157 Location of the Vehicle Speed Sensor (VSS) on automatic transaxle 4T65–E

Refer to the accompanying illustration for sensor location.

OPERATION

The Vehicle Speed Sensor (VSS) system is a pulse generator consisting of a speed sensor assembly, located in the case extension, and a toothed vehicle speed sensor reluctor wheel, which is pressed onto the final drive carrier assembly. As the vehicle drives forward, the vehicle speed sensor reluctor wheel rotates. This rotation produces a variable AC signal in the pickup coil that is proportional to vehicle speed. The Powertrain Control Module (PCM) uses this signal in order to calculate vehicle speed, shift timing, and gear ratios. If the PCM detects a low vehicle speed with a high engine speed while in a drive range, then a DTC is set.

REMOVAL & INSTALLATION

Automatic Transaxle 4T65–E

See Figure 157.

1. Raise and support the vehicle.
2. Remove the right front tire and wheel.
3. Disconnect the Vehicle Speed Sensor (VSS) electrical connector.
4. Remove the VSS bolt (9).
5. Remove the VSS (10) from the extension case.
6. Remove the O-ring from the VSS (10).

To install:

7. Install the O-ring to the VSS (10).
8. Install the VSS (10).
9. Install the VSS bolt (9). Tighten the bolt (9) to 106 inch lbs. (12 Nm).
10. Connect the VSS electrical connector.
11. Install the right front tire and wheel. Tighten the wheel lug nuts to 100 ft. lbs. (140 Nm).
12. Lower the vehicle.

TESTING

1. Ensure the Vehicle Speed Sensor (VSS) is correctly tightened to the transmission housing.
2. Install a scan tool.
3. Turn ON the ignition, with the engine OFF.

➡**Before clearing the DTC, use the scan tool in order to record the Freeze Frame and Failure Records. Using the Clear Info function erases the Freeze Frame and Failure Records from the**

PCM. Record the DTC Freeze Frame and Failure Records, then clear the DTC(s).

✳✳ WARNING

Support the lower control arms in the normal horizontal position in order to

avoid damage to the drive axles. Do not operate the vehicle in gear with the wheels hanging down at full travel.

4. Raise and support the drive wheels.
5. Start and idle the engine.

6. Place the transmission in DRIVE.
7. Monitor Transmission OSS on the scan tool.
8. With the drive wheels rotating, increase and decrease the throttle position.
9. The Transmission OSS RPM should increase when the wheel speed increases.

FUEL
GASOLINE FUEL INJECTION SYSTEM

FUEL SYSTEM SERVICE PRECAUTIONS

Safety is the most important factor when performing not only fuel system maintenance but any type of maintenance. Failure to conduct maintenance and repairs in a safe manner may result in serious personal injury or death. Maintenance and testing of the vehicle's fuel system components can be accomplished safely and effectively by adhering to the following rules and guidelines.

• To avoid the possibility of fire and personal injury, always disconnect the negative battery cable unless the repair or test procedure requires that battery voltage be applied.

• Always relieve the fuel system pressure prior to disconnecting any fuel system component (injector, fuel rail, pressure regulator, etc.), fitting or fuel line connection. Exercise extreme caution whenever relieving fuel system pressure to avoid exposing skin, face and eyes to fuel spray. Please be advised that fuel under pressure may penetrate the skin or any part of the body that it contacts.

• Always place a shop towel or cloth around the fitting or connection prior to loosening to absorb any excess fuel due to spillage. Ensure that all fuel spillage (should it occur) is quickly removed from engine surfaces. Ensure that all fuel soaked cloths or towels are deposited into a suitable waste container.

• Always keep a dry chemical (Class B) fire extinguisher near the work area.

• Do not allow fuel spray or fuel vapors to come into contact with a spark or open flame.

• Always use a back-up wrench when loosening and tightening fuel line connection fittings. This will prevent unnecessary stress and torsion to fuel line piping.

• Always replace worn fuel fitting O-rings with new Do not substitute fuel hose or equivalent where fuel pipe is installed.

Before servicing the vehicle, make sure to also refer to the precautions in the beginning of this section as well.

RELIEVING FUEL SYSTEM PRESSURE

1. Before servicing the vehicle, refer to the Precautions Section.
2. Disconnect the negative battery cable to avoid possible fuel discharge if an accidental attempt is made to start the engine.
3. Remove the fuel tank cap to relieve tank pressure. Do not tighten until the service procedure has been completed.
4. Connect a fuel pressure gauge with bleed valve to the fuel pressure test port. Wrap a shop towel around the fitting while connecting the gauge to catch any spilled fuel.
5. Install the bleed hose into an approved container and open the valve to bleed off the fuel system pressure.
6. Drain any fuel remaining in the gauge into an approved container.

✳✳ CAUTION

There may still be residual fuel in the system, and a small amount of fuel may be released when servicing fuel lines or connections. In order to reduce the chance of personal injury, cover the fuel line fittings with a shop towel before disconnecting to catch any fuel that may leak out.

FUEL FILTER

REMOVAL & INSTALLATION

A fuel strainer is attached to the lower end of the fuel sender. The fuel strainer is made of woven plastic. The functions of the fuel strainer are to filter contaminants and to wick fuel. The fuel strainer is self-cleaning and normally requires no maintenance. Fuel stoppage at this point indicates that the fuel tank contains an abnormal amount of sediment, water, or contamination.

To service this filter, remove the fuel pump. Refer to Fuel Pump, removal & installation.

FUEL INJECTORS

REMOVAL & INSTALLATION

3.8L Engine
See Figure 158.

1. Before servicing the vehicle, refer to the Precautions Section.
2. Relieve the fuel system pressure.
3. Remove or disconnect the following:
   • The negative battery cable
   • The fuel lines
   • The fuel rail
   • The injector retaining clips
   • The fuel injector

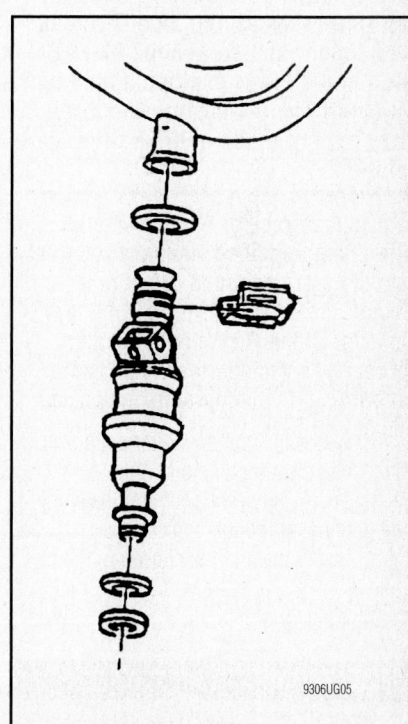

Fig. 158 Exploded view of the fuel injector assembly—3.8L engine

To install:
4. Install or connect the following:
   • The fuel injector with new O-rings, coat the O-rings with clean engine oil prior to installation
   • The injector retaining clips

- The fuel rail and torque the bolts to 89 inch lbs. (10 Nm)
- The fuel lines
- The negative battery cable

4.6L Engine

➡If the fuel injectors are leaking, the engine oil may be contaminated with fuel.

1. Remove the fuel rail.
2. Remove the fuel injector by pushing the locking tab on the fuel rail toward the center of the fuel rail.
3. Remove the fuel injector upper O-ring.
4. Remove the fuel injector lower O-ring.
5. Discard the injector O-ring seals.

To install:

✳✳ CAUTION

In order to reduce the risk of fire and personal injury that may result from a fuel leak, always install the fuel injector O-rings in the proper position. If the upper and lower O-rings are different colors (black and blue), be sure to install the blue O-ring in the upper position and the black O-ring in the lower position on the fuel injector. The O-rings are the same size but are made of different materials.

➡The fuel injector O-rings should always be replaced whenever the fuel injectors are serviced. Be sure to install the correct O-ring for the fuel injector. If the O-ring is not seated properly, a vacuum leak is possible and drivability complaints may occur.

6. Lubricate the new upper and lower O-rings with clean engine oil.
7. Install the new upper and lower injector O-rings on the fuel injector.
8. Install the fuel injector on to the fuel rail.
9. Install the fuel rail.

FUEL PUMP

REMOVAL & INSTALLATION

See Figures 159 and 160.

1. Before servicing the vehicle, refer to the Precautions Section.
2. Relieve the fuel system pressure.
3. Drain the fuel tank.
4. Remove or disconnect the following:
   - The negative battery cable
   - The spare tire and jack
   - The trunk lining

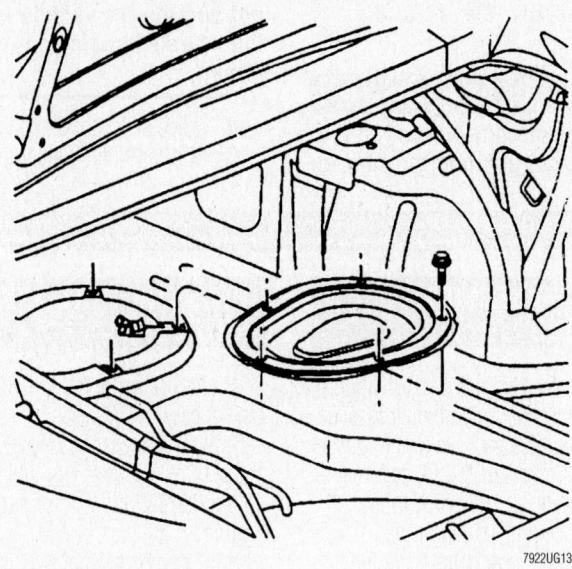

Fig. 159 The fuel pump service cover is located in the luggage compartment under the spare tire

- The fuel sender access panel
- The sender and quick connect fittings from the sender
- The electrical connector from the sender and position harness and hoses aside

✳✳ CAUTION

When removing the fuel sender from the tank, the reservoir bucket is full of fuel. Use caution in containing the fuel.

- The sender retaining ring
- The sender (take note of its position)
- The fuel sender O-ring and discard it

➡Take note of the direction that the strainer is pointing.

- The strainer from the pump by pulling it down and twisting
- The pump electrical wires and hoses
- The pump assembly out of the rubber connectors

To install:

5. Transfer any insulators and grommets from the old pump to the new one.
6. Connect the pump to the fuel hose and tilt the bottom of the pump into the mounting bracket.
7. Install or connect the following:
   - The new strainer on the pump so it points in the same direction as noted during removal

- The electrical connectors and fuel lines to the pump
- The new O-ring on top of the fuel tank
- The fuel sender assembly into the tank
- The lockring

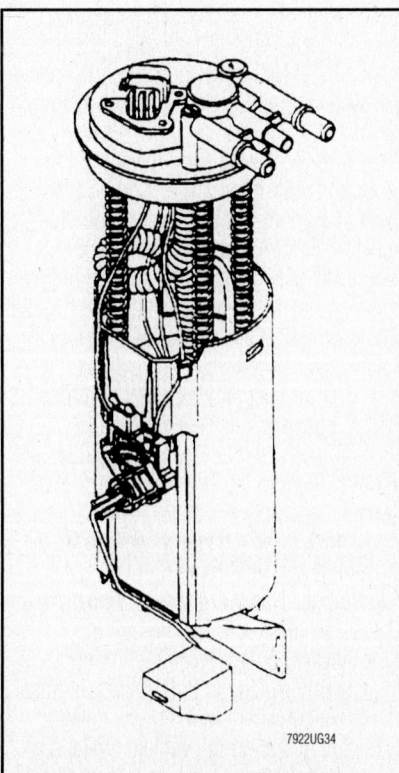

Fig. 160 Fuel pump and level sender assembly

- The fuel line quick connectors
- The sender electrical connector
- The fuel sender access cover
- The trunk liner
- The spare tire and jack

8. Refill with fuel and check for leaks.

FUEL TANK

REMOVAL & INSTALLATION

1. Before servicing the vehicle, refer to the Precautions Section.

2. Disconnect the negative battery cable.

➡**Clean the fuel and Evaporative Emission (EVAP) connections and surrounding areas prior to disconnecting the lines in order to avoid possible system contamination.**

➡**Always maintain cleanliness when servicing the fuel system components.**

3. Relieve the fuel system fuel pressure. Refer to Relieving Fuel System Pressure.

4. Drain the fuel tank.

5. Raise and support the vehicle.

6. Loosen the fuel fill hose clamp at the fuel tank.

7. Remove the fuel tank fill hose from the fuel tank.

8. Disconnect the EVAP vent solenoid hose on the tank from the EVAP vent valve solenoid hose.

9. Disconnect the EVAP vent pipe quick connect fitting from the fill pipe EVAP vent pipe quick connect fitting.

10. Disconnect the fuel feed and EVAP lines from the fuel tank lines.

11. Support the exhaust system.

12. Remove the rubber exhaust pipe hangers in order to allow the exhaust system to drop slightly.

13. Remove the fuel tank shield retainers.

14. Remove the fuel tank shield.

❋❋ WARNING

Do not bend the fuel tank straps as this may damage the straps.

15. Support the fuel tank with a suitable adjustable jack.

16. Remove the fuel tank strap bolts.

17. Using the jack lower the fuel tank.

18. Disconnect the fuel sender jumper harness electrical connector.

19. Remove the fuel tank and place the tank in a suitable work area.

20. Disconnect and remove the fuel pressure sensor and fuel sender jumper harness electrical connectors.

➡**Note the routing of the lines for installation.**

21. Disconnect and remove the fuel feed line and EVAP lines.

22. Remove the EVAP canister.

23. Remove the insulator pads from the fuel tank.

➡**Note the location of the insulator pads for installation.**

To install:

❋❋ WARNING

Do not attempt to straighten kinked nylon pipes. Replace any kinked nylon pipes in order to prevent damage to the vehicle. Do not attempt to repair sections of nylon pipes. Replace damaged nylon pipes. Replace the vapor pipes with original equipment or parts that meet GM specifications. Replace the vapor hoses with original equipment or parts meeting GM specifications. Use only reinforced fuel-resistant hose identified with the word Fluoroelastomer or GM 6163M on the hose.

24. Install the insulator pads to the fuel tank.

25. Install the EVAP canister.

26. Install and connect the fuel feed line and EVAP lines.

27. Install and connect the fuel pressure sensor and fuel sender jumper harness electrical connectors.

28. Place the fuel tank onto a suitable jack.

29. Partially raise the fuel tank until the electrical connections can be made.

30. Connect the fuel sender jumper harness electrical connector.

31. Completely raise the tank.

32. Install the fuel tank strap bolts. Tighten the bolts to 35 ft. lbs. (48 Nm).

33. Remove the jack from the fuel tank.

34. Position the fuel tank shield to the fuel tank.

35. Install the shield retainers.

36. Install the rubber exhaust pipe hangers.

37. Remove the support from the exhaust system.

38. Connect the fuel feed and EVAP lines to the fuel tank lines.

39. Connect the EVAP vent pipe quick connect fitting to the fill pipe EVAP vent pipe quick connect fitting.

40. Connect the EVAP vent solenoid hose on the tank to the EVAP vent valve solenoid hose.

41. Install the fuel tank fill hose onto the fuel tank. Install the hose over the orientation feature on the tank until fully seated to the tank.

42. Tighten the fuel fill hose clamp at the fuel tank. Tighten the clamp to 22 inch lbs. (3 Nm).

43. Lower the vehicle.

44. Add fuel and install the fuel fill cap.

45. Connect the negative battery cable.

46. Inspect the fuel system for leaks by performing the following steps:

a. Turn ON the ignition for 2 seconds.

b. Turn OFF the ignition for 10 seconds.

c. Turn ON the ignition.

d. Inspect for fuel leaks.

IDLE SPEED

ADJUSTMENT

Idle speed is maintained by the Powertrain Control Module (PCM). No adjustment is necessary or possible.

THROTTLE BODY

REMOVAL & INSTALLATION

3.8L Engine

1. Turn the ignition OFF.

2. Partially drain the cooling system.

3. Remove the fuel injector sight shield.

4. Remove the air cleaner intake duct.

5. Disconnect the throttle body electrical connector.

6. Remove the throttle body nuts and the bolts.

7. Remove the throttle body assembly.

8. Clean the throttle body gasket mating surfaces.

To install:

9. Install the throttle body assembly.

10. Install the throttle body bolts and tighten to 89 inch lbs. (10 Nm).

11. Install the throttle body electrical connector.

12. Install the air cleaner intake duct.

13. Install the fuel injector sight shield.

14. Fill the cooling system.

4.6L Engine

1. Relieve the fuel system pressure.

2. Remove the air cleaner intake duct.

3. Remove the PCV valve fresh air tube.

4. Remove the cruise control cable from the accelerator controls cable bracket.

5. Remove the accelerator cable from the accelerator controls cable bracket.

6. Remove the cruise control cable from the throttle body lever.

7. Remove the accelerator control cable from the throttle body lever.

8. Remove the Idle Air Control (IAC) valve electrical connector from the IAC valve.

9. Remove the Throttle Position (TP) sensor electrical connector from the TP sensor.

10. Remove the fuel feed and return lines from the retainer on the accelerator controls cable bracket.

11. Remove the transaxle shift cable clip from the accelerator controls cable bracket.

12. Remove the throttle body from the water crossover.

13. Remove the accelerator controls cable bracket from the throttle body.

To install:

➡ The outlet of the air cleaner assembly and the Mass Air Flow (MAF) sensor inlet duct must line up when completely installed. Misalignment may cause incorrect airflow readings resulting in Malfunction Indicator Light (MIL) illumination or a drivability concern. An improperly installed inlet duct assembly or air cleaner assembly may cause misalignment.

14. Install the accelerator cable bracket to the throttle body and tighten to 106 inch lbs. (12 Nm).

15. Position the new throttle body gasket on to the throttle body.

16. Install bolts from the throttle body to throttle body spacer and finger tighten 2 lower bolts.

17. Tighten all the bolts to 106 inch lbs. (12 Nm).

18. Install the IAC valve electrical connector to the IAC valve.

19. Install the TP sensor electrical connector to the TP sensor.

20. Install the accelerator control cable at the throttle body lever.

21. Install the cruise control cable at the throttle body lever.

22. Install the accelerator cable to the accelerator controls cable bracket.

23. Install the cruise control cable to accelerator controls cable bracket.

24. Install the transaxle shift cable clip to the accelerator controls cable bracket.

25. Install the fuel feed and return lines from the retainer on to the accelerator controls cable bracket.

26. Install the air cleaner intake duct clamp to the air cleaner intake air duct.

27. Install the PCV valve fresh air tube.

28. Install the fuel injector sight shield.

29. Connect the negative battery cable.

30. Perform the TP sensor learn procedure as follows:

  a. Turn ignition switch to the RUN/ON position.

  b. Wait 1 minute.

  c. Turn ignition switch to the LOCK/OFF position.

  d. Wait 15 seconds.

31. Perform the IAC valve learn procedure as follows:

  a. Start and idle the engine for 15 seconds.

  b. Turn the ignition switch to the LOCK/OFF position.

  c. Wait 15 seconds,

  d. Restart the engine and check for proper idle operation.

HEATING & AIR CONDITIONING SYSTEM

BLOWER MOTOR

REMOVAL & INSTALLATION

1. Remove the right side sound insulator in the passenger compartment.

2. Disconnect the electrical connector from the blower motor.

3. Disconnect the blower ventilation tube from the module.

4. Remove the blower motor screws.

5. Remove the blower motor from the housing.

6. Install the blower motor into the housing.

To install:

7. Install the blower motor screws and tighten to 9 inch lbs. (1 Nm).

8. Install the blower ventilation tube to the module.

9. Connect the blower motor electrical connector.

10. Install the right side sound insulator.

HEATER CORE

REMOVAL & INSTALLATION

See Figures 161 and 162.

1. Before servicing the vehicle, refer to the Precautions Section.

2. Drain the coolant.

3. Position aside the heater hose inlet and outlet clamps at the heater core.

4. Disconnect the inlet and outlet heater hose from the heater core.

5. Remove the RH instrument panel closeout/insulator panel.

6. Remove the LH instrument panel closeout/insulator panel.

7. Remove the floor carpet.

8. Remove the center console, if equipped.

9. Remove the HVAC control.

➡ The Vehicle Communication Interface Module (VCIM) has a specific set of unique numbers that tie the module to each vehicle. These numbers, the 10-digit station identification and the 11-digit electronic serial number, are used by the National Cellular Network and OnStar® to identify the specific vehicle. Because these numbers are tied to the Vehicle Identification Number (VIN) of the vehicle, you must never exchange these parts with those of another vehicle.

10. Remove the communication interface module screws.

11. Disconnect the mobile telephone antenna cable from the communication interface module by pulling outward on the square plastic housing.

12. Disconnect the electrical connectors.

13. Disconnect the navigation antenna coaxial antenna cable from the module.

14. Remove the communication interface module.

15. Remove the rear floor air outlet duct from the holes in the floor reinforcement.

16. Disconnect the rear floor air outlet duct from the heater core outlet cover.

17. Remove the rear floor air outlet duct.

18. Remove the heater core outlet cover screws.

19. Remove the heater core outlet cover heat stakes with a small chisel.

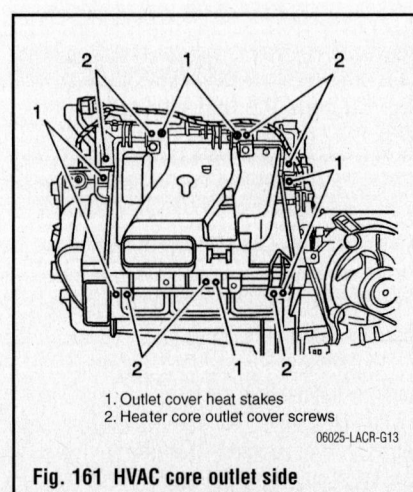

1. Outlet cover heat stakes
2. Heater core outlet cover screws

06025-LACR-G13

Fig. 161 HVAC core outlet side

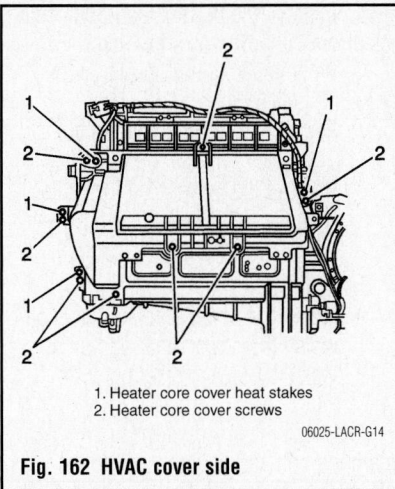

1. Heater core cover heat stakes
2. Heater core cover screws

06025-LACR-G14

Fig. 162 HVAC cover side

20. Remove the heater core outlet cover from the HVAC module assembly.
21. Remove the heater core cover screws.
22. Remove the heater core cover heat stakes with a small chisel.
23. Remove the heater core cover from the HVAC module assembly.
24. Remove the heater core from the HVAC module assembly.

25. Remove the heater core foam seal from the HVAC module assembly.

To install:
26. Install a new heater core foam seal to the HVAC module assembly.
27. Install the heater core to the HVAC module assembly.
28. Install the heater core cover.
29. Install the heater core cover screws to the heater core cover. Tighten all the screws to 13 inch lbs. (2 Nm).
30. Install the heater core outlet cover.
31. Install the heater core outlet cover screws. Tighten the screws to 13 inch lbs. (2 Nm).
32. Connect the rear floor air outlet duct to the heater core outlet cover.
33. Install the rear floor air outlet duct to the holes in the floor reinforcement.
34. Install the HVAC module.
35. Install the center console.

※ **WARNING**

Before you install the antenna cable connector of the Global Positioning

System (GPS) to the Vehicle Communication Interface Module (VCM), align the connector properly in order to avoid damaging the connector.

36. Connect the navigation antenna coaxial cable to the module.
37. Connect the electrical connectors.
38. Connect the mobile telephone antenna cable to the module by pushing inward on the square plastic housing.
39. Align the module to the vehicle antenna module bracket.
40. Install the communication interface module screws. Tighten the screws to 18 inch lbs. (2 Nm).
41. Install the floor carpet.
42. Install the RH instrument panel closeout/insulator panel.
43. Connect the inlet and outlet heater hose to the heater core.
44. Reposition the heater hose inlet and outlet clamps to the heater core.
45. Refill the coolant.

STEERING

POWER RACK & PINION STEERING GEAR

REMOVAL & INSTALLATION

Tools Required:
• J 24319-B Universal Steering Linkage Puller
• J 42640 Steering Column Anti-Rotation Pin
1. Before servicing the vehicle, refer to the Precautions Section.
2. Lock the steering column by installing J 42640 into the underside of the steering column.
3. Raise and support the vehicle.
4. Remove the tires and wheels.
5. Remove the power steering gear heat shield.

※ **CAUTION**

Failure to disconnect the intermediate shaft from the rack and pinion stub shaft can result in damage to the steering gear and/or intermediate shaft. This damage can cause loss of steering control which could result in personal injury.

※ **WARNING**

The wheels of the vehicle must be straight ahead and the steering col-

umn in the LOCK position before disconnecting the steering column or intermediate shaft from the steering gear. Failure to do so will cause the coil assembly in the steering column to become uncentered which will cause damage to the coil assembly.

6. Remove the intermediate shaft lower pinch bolt coupling.
7. Disconnect the intermediate shaft from the power steering gear.
8. Remove the outer tie rods retaining nuts.
9. Using the J 24319-B separate the outer tie rods from the steering knuckles.
10. Remove the power steering pressure and return hoses from the power steering gear.
11. If equipped, disconnect the variable effort steering electrical connector.
12. Remove the left stabilizer shaft insulator.
13. Disconnect the tie rod ends from the knuckles.
14. Remove the power steering gear mounting bolts.
15. Remove the power steering gear through the left wheel opening.

To install:
16. Transfer the outer tie rods if replacing the power steering gear.

17. Install the power steering gear through the left wheel opening.
18. Install the power steering gear mounting bolts. Tighten the power steering gear mounting bolts to 70 ft. lbs. (95 Nm).
19. Install the left stabilizer shaft insulator.
20. Install the power steering pressure and return hoses to the power steering gear. Tighten the power steering pressure and return hoses to 22 ft. lbs. (30 Nm).
21. If equipped, connect the variable effort steering electrical connector.
22. Install the outer tie rod to the steering knuckles.
23. Install the outer tie rod retaining nuts. Tighten the outer tie rod retaining nuts to 22 ft. lbs. (30 Nm), plus an additional 180°.
24. Connect the intermediate shaft to the power steering gear.
25. Install the intermediate shaft lower pinch bolt. Tighten the intermediate shaft lower pinch bolt to 37 ft. lbs. (47 Nm).
26. Install the power steering gear heat shield.
27. Install the tires and wheels. Tighten the wheel lug nuts to 100 ft. lbs. (136 Nm).
28. Lower the vehicle.
29. Remove the J 42640 from the steering column.
30. Bleed the power steering system:

✳✳ WARNING

When adding fluid or making a complete fluid change, always use the proper power steering fluid. Failure to use the proper fluid will cause hose and seal damage and fluid leaks.

➡Use clean, new power steering fluid type only. Hoses touching the frame, body, or engine may cause system noise. Verify that the hoses do not touch any other part of the vehicle. Loose connections may not leak, but could allow air into the steering system. Verify that all hose connections are tight.

➡Maintain the fluid level throughout the bleed procedure.

  e. Remove the pump reservoir cap.
  f. Fill the pump reservoir with fluid to the FULL COLD level.
  g. Attach a vacuum pump and adapter to the reservoir.
  h. Apply a vacuum of 68 kPa (20 in Hg) maximum.
  i. Wait 5 minutes. Typical vacuum drop is 7–10 kPa (2–3 in Hg).
  j. Remove the vacuum pump and adapter.
  k. Reinstall the pump reservoir cap.
  l. Start the engine. Allow the engine to idle.
  m. Turn OFF the engine.
  n. Verify the fluid level. Repeat steps 8–10 until the fluid stabilizes.

➡Do NOT turn the steering wheel to LOCK.

  o. Start the engine. Allow the engine to idle.
  p. Turn the steering wheel 180–360° in both directions 5 times.
  q. Turn OFF the ignition.
  r. Verify the fluid level.
  s. Remove the pump reservoir cap.
  t. Attach a vacuum pump and adapter to the reservoir.
  u. Apply a vacuum of 68 kPa (20 in. Hg) maximum.
  v. Wait 5 minutes.
  w. Remove the vacuum pump and adapter.
  x. Verify the fluid level.
  y. Reinstall the pump reservoir cap.

31. Inspect the power steering system for leaks.
32. Adjust the front toe as necessary.

POWER STEERING PUMP

REMOVAL & INSTALLATION

3.8L Engine

1. Before servicing the vehicle, refer to the Precautions Section.
2. Remove the accessory drive belt.
3. Raise and support the vehicle.
4. Remove the tire and wheel assembly.
5. Disconnect the power steering pressure hose and return from the power steering pump.
6. Disconnect the harness connector from the power steering pump.
7. Remove the power steering mounting bolts from the power steering pump.
8. Remove the power steering pump from the engine.
9. Remove the power steering pump pulley from the power steering pump.
10. Remove the power steering pump reservoir from the power steering pump.

To install:

11. Install the power steering pump reservoir to the power steering pump.
12. Install the power steering pump pulley to the power steering pump.
13. Position the power steering pump to the engine.
14. Install the power steering pump mounting bolts and tighten to 18 ft. lbs. (25 Nm).
15. Connect the power steering pressure hose to the power steering pump.
16. Install the harness connector to the power steering pump.
17. Install the accessory drive belt.
18. Fill the power steering system with fluid.
19. Bleed the power steering system.
20. Operate the power steering system and inspect for power steering system leaks.

4.6L Engine

1. Before servicing the vehicle, refer to the Precautions Section.
2. Remove the accessory drive belt.
3. Install a drain pan under the vehicle.
4. Disconnect the power steering return hose from the power steering reservoir.

5. Remove the power steering pressure hose from the power steering pump.
6. Remove the power steering pump mounting bolt.
7. Remove the power steering pump from the vehicle.
8. Remove the power steering pulley.
9. Remove the power steering reservoir.

To install:

10. Install the power steering reservoir.
11. Install the power steering pulley.
12. Install the power steering pump to the vehicle.
13. Install the power steering pump mounting bolt and tighten to 37 ft. lbs. (50 Nm).
14. Install the power steering pressure hose to the power steering pump and tighten to 20 ft. lbs. (27 Nm).
15. Install the power steering return hose to the power steering reservoir.
16. Remove the drain pan from under vehicle.
17. Install the drive belt.
18. Bleed the power steering system.

BLEEDING

1. Fill pump reservoir with fluid to minimum system level, FULL COLD level, or middle of hash mark on cap stick fluid level indicator.
2. With hydro-boost, do not apply the brake pedal with the engine OFF. This will discharge the hydro-boost accumulator.
3. If equipped with hydro-boost, fully charge the hydro-boost accumulator using the following procedure:
  a. Start the engine.
  b. Firmly apply the brake pedal 10–15 times.
  c. Turn the engine OFF.
4. Raise the vehicle until the front wheels are off the ground.
5. With the key ON engine OFF, turn the steering wheel from stop to stop 12 times. Vehicles equipped with hydro-boost systems, or longer length power steering hoses, may require turning up to 15–20 times from stop to stop.
6. Verify power steering fluid level per operating specification.
7. Start the engine. Rotate steering wheel from left to right. Check for signs of cavitation or fluid aeration (pump noise/whining).
8. Verify the fluid level. Repeat the bleed procedure, if necessary.

SUSPENSION   **FRONT SUSPENSION**

CONTROL LINKS

REMOVAL & INSTALLATION

See Figure 163.

1. Before servicing the vehicle, refer to the Precautions Section.
2. Raise the vehicle and safely support the vehicle.
3. Remove the tire and wheel assembly.
4. Remove the control link bolt and nut.
5. Remove the control link from the vehicle.

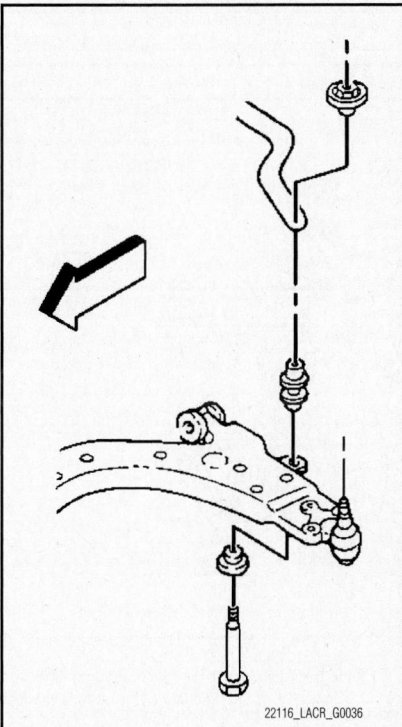

Fig. 163 Expanded view of the control link components

To install:

6. Install the control link into the vehicle.
7. Install the control link bolt and nut. Tighten the nut to 17 ft. lbs. (23 Nm).
8. Install the tire and wheel assembly. Tighten the lug nut to 100 ft. lbs. (1360 Nm) using a crisscross torque pattern.
9. Lower the vehicle.

LOWER BALL JOINT

REMOVAL & INSTALLATION

The lower ball joint is serviced as part of the lower control arm. Refer to Lower Control Arm, removal & installation.

LOWER CONTROL ARM

REMOVAL & INSTALLATION

See Figure 164.

Special tool required:
• J 39549 Ball Joint and Tie Rod End Separator

1. Before servicing the vehicle, refer to the Precautions Section.
2. Raise and support the vehicle.
3. Remove the front tire and wheel assembly.
4. Remove the front stabilizer shaft link (control link). Refer to Control Links, removal & installation.
5. Use the J 39549 to separate the ball joint from the control arm.

➡**Always replace the ball joint nut after it has been used.**

6. Remove the bolts from the control arm bracket.
7. Remove the bolt from the control arm.
8. Remove the control arm from the vehicle.

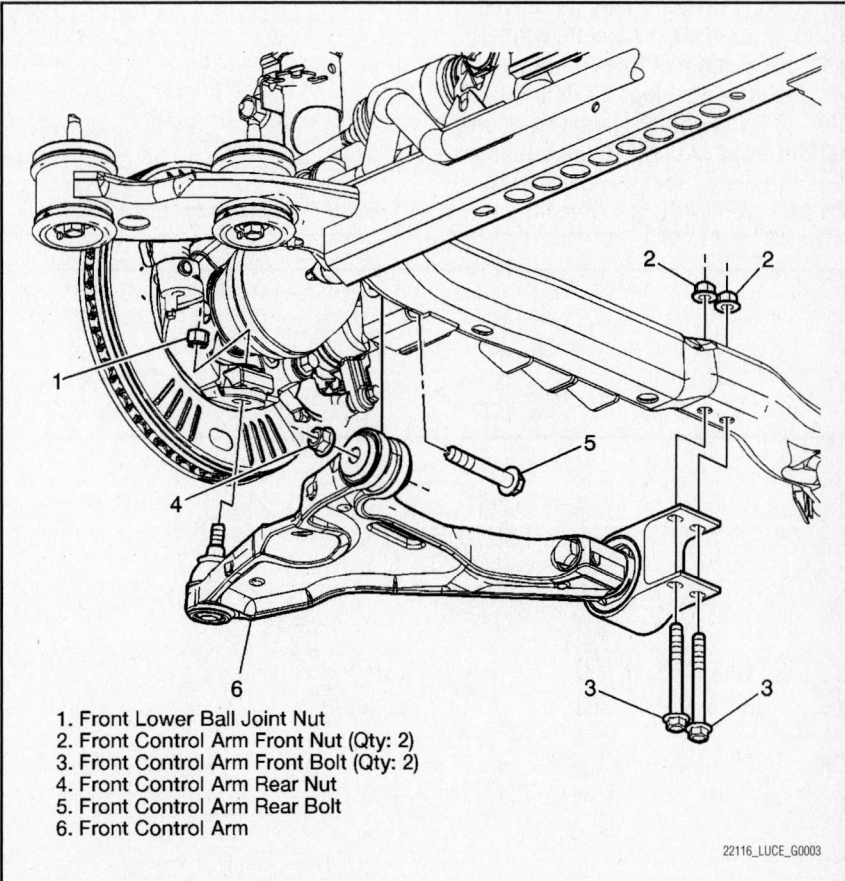

1. Front Lower Ball Joint Nut
2. Front Control Arm Front Nut (Qty: 2)
3. Front Control Arm Front Bolt (Qty: 2)
4. Front Control Arm Rear Nut
5. Front Control Arm Rear Bolt
6. Front Control Arm

Fig. 164 Exploded view of lower control arm

To install:

9. Installation is the reverse of the removal procedure.

➡**Do not tighten the control arm nut until the weight of the vehicle is supported by the control arm. The vehicle needs to be sitting at normal trim height.**

10. Tighten the front control arm rear nut to 116 ft. lbs. (157 Nm).
11. Tighten the front control arm front nuts to 111 ft. lbs. (150 Nm).
12. Tighten the lower ball joint nut in 2 steps:
   a. Step 1: tighten to 22 ft. lbs. (30 Nm).
   b. Step 2: tighten an additional 210°.
13. Tighten the wheel lug nuts to 100 ft. lbs. (136 Nm).

MACPHERSON STRUT

REMOVAL & INSTALLATION

See Figures 165 through 167.

✴ WARNING

Care should be taken to avoid chipping or scratching the coating when handling the suspension coil spring. Damage to the coating can cause premature failure.

1. Remove the strut upper mounting nuts.

➡ Lift the vehicle using ONLY a frame-contact vehicle lift. Do NOT lift the vehicle using a suspension-contact vehicle lift.

2. Before servicing the vehicle, refer to the Precautions Section.
3. Raise and support the vehicle.
4. Remove the tire and wheel.
5. Matchmark the strut to the knuckle.
6. Remove the strut lower bolts and nuts.
7. Remove the strut.

To install:

8. Install the strut.
9. Install the strut upper mounting nuts. Tighten the nuts to 24 ft. lbs. (33 Nm).
10. Install the strut lower bolts and nuts.

✴ WARNING

This is a prevailing torque type fastener. This fastener may be reused ONLY if the fastener and its counterpart are clean and free from rust and the fastener develops 27 inch lbs. (3 Nm) of torque/drag against its counterpart prior to the fastener seating. If the fastener does not meet these criteria, REPLACE the fastener.

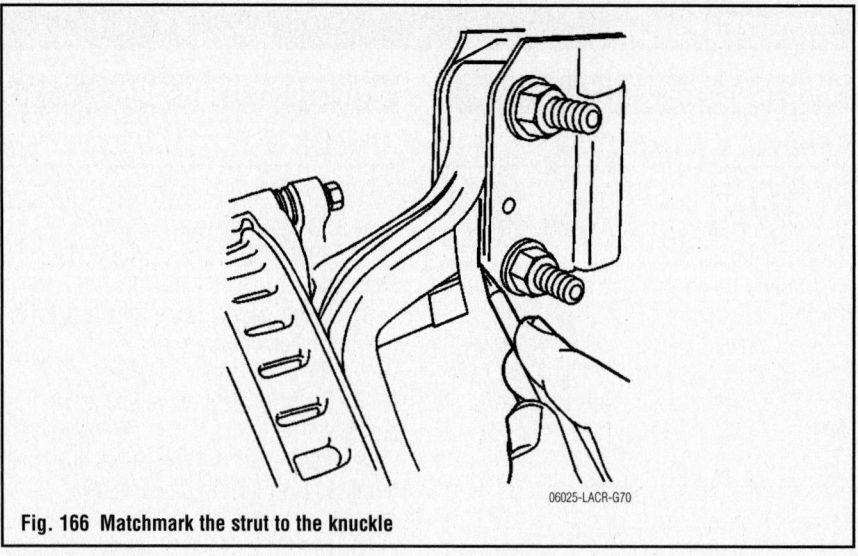

Fig. 166 Matchmark the strut to the knuckle

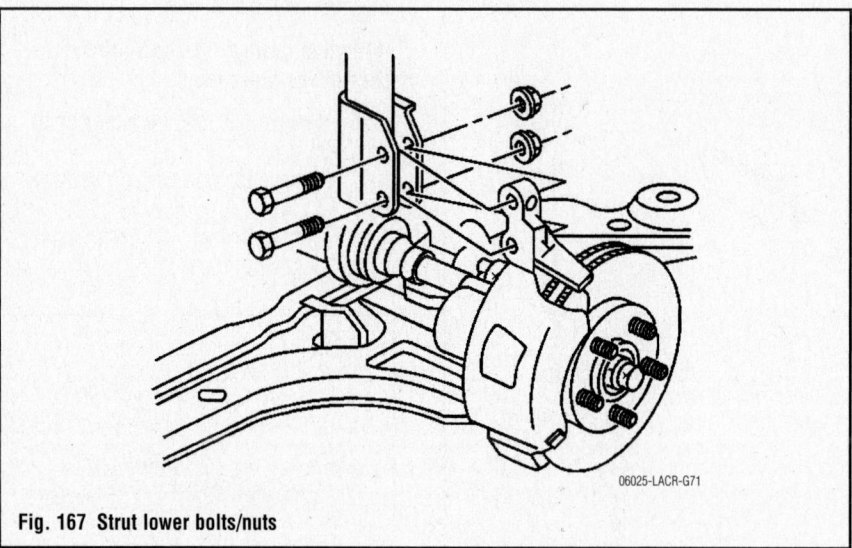

Fig. 167 Strut lower bolts/nuts

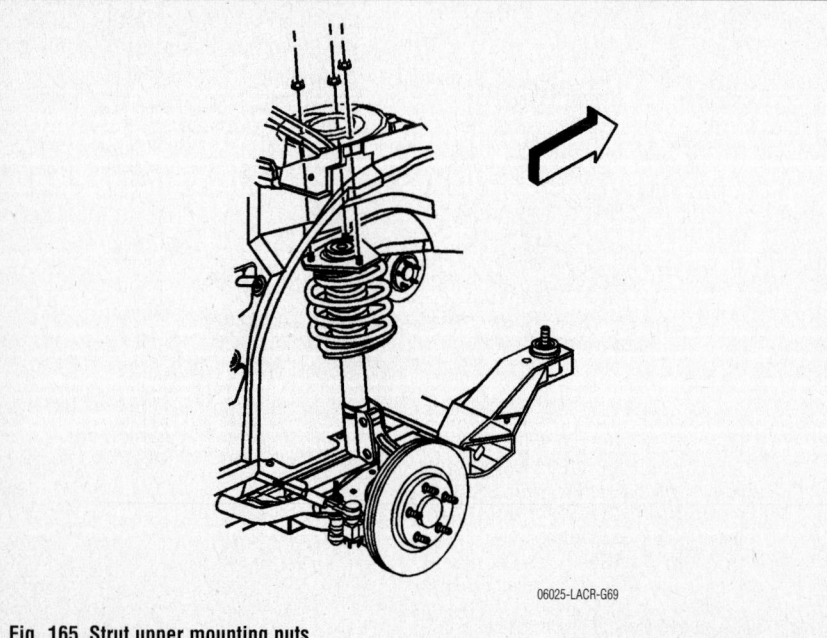

Fig. 165 Strut upper mounting nuts

11. Align the strut to the mark on the knuckle. Tighten the strut lower nuts to 89 ft. lbs. (120 Nm).
12. Install the tire and wheel.
13. Lower the vehicle.
14. Align the front wheels.

OVERHAUL

See Figures 168 and 169.

1. Before servicing the vehicle, refer to the Precautions Section.
2. Remove the strut from the vehicle.
3. Install the strut in a strut compressor tool, such as J 45400.

➡ The spring is compressed when the strut moves freely.

4. Turn the spring compressor forcing screw until the coil spring is compressed.
5. Use a 45 TORX® socket in order to hold the strut shaft. Remove the upper strut mount nut.

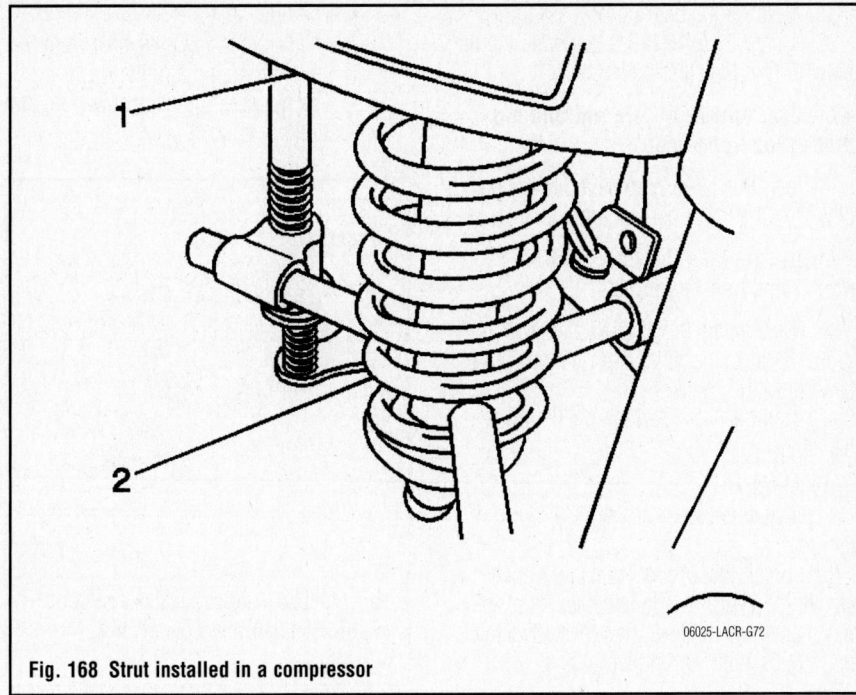

Fig. 168 Strut installed in a compressor

06025-LACR-G72

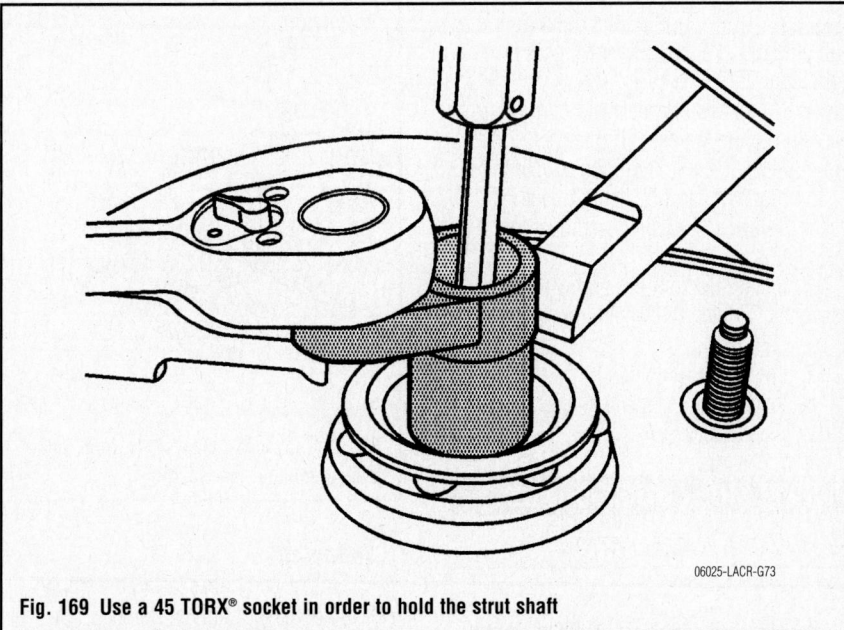

Fig. 169 Use a 45 TORX® socket in order to hold the strut shaft

06025-LACR-G73

6. Remove the strut from the compressor.

7. Loosen the compressor forcing screw until the upper strut mount and coil spring may be removed.

8. Remove the upper strut mount and the coil spring from the compressor.

To assemble;

9. Install the coil spring and upper strut mount in the compressor.

10. Turn the spring compressor forcing screw until the coil spring is compressed.

11. Install the strut to the coil spring and upper strut mount.

12. Install the strut retaining nut. Install the strut mount nut. Tighten the strut mount nut to 55 ft. lbs. (75 Nm).

13. Remove the strut from the compressor.

14. Install the strut.

STABILIZER BAR

REMOVAL & INSTALLATION

Front Stabilizer Bar

Tools Required:
• J 24319-B Universal Steering Linkage Puller

1. Before servicing the vehicle, refer to the Precautions Section.

2. Raise and support the vehicle.

3. Remove the front tires and wheels.

4. Remove the stabilizer shaft links (control links). Refer to Control Links, removal & installation.

5. Remove the stabilizer shaft insulators.

6. Remove the left outer tie rod retaining nut.

7. Use the J 24319-B in order to remove the left tie rod end from the steering knuckle.

8. Remove the exhaust manifold pipe.

9. Turn the left strut completely to the left. Guide the stabilizer shaft out the left side of the vehicle between the body and the strut.

10. Remove the stabilizer shaft from the vehicle.

To install:

11. Install the stabilizer shaft to the vehicle.

12. Install the exhaust manifold pipe.

13. Loosely install the following components:

a. The left and right stabilizer shaft insulators.

b. The stabilizer shaft insulator brackets.

c. The stabilizer shaft bracket bolts.

14. Install the stabilizer shaft links (control links). Refer to Control Links, removal & installation.

15. Install the left tie rod end to the steering knuckle.

✳✳ WARNING

Use the correct fastener in the correct location. Replacement fasteners must be the correct part number for that application. Fasteners requiring replacement or fasteners requiring the use of thread locking compound or sealant are identified in the service procedure. Do not use paints, lubricants, or corrosion inhibitors on fasteners or fastener joint surfaces unless specified. These coatings affect fastener torque and joint clamping force and may damage the fastener. Use the correct tightening sequence and specifications when installing fasteners in order to avoid damage to parts and systems.

16. Tighten the stabilizer shaft insulator bracket bolts to 37 ft. lbs. (50 Nm).

17. Tighten the outer tie rod end to steering knuckle retaining nut in 2 steps:

a. Step 1: tighten to 22 ft. lbs. (30 Nm).

b. Step 2: tighten an additional 200°.

18. Install the front tires and wheels. Tighten the wheel lug nuts to 100 ft. lbs. (136 Nm).

19. Lower the vehicle.

Rear Stabilizer Bar

1. Raise and support the vehicle.
2. Remove the stabilizer shaft links.
3. Remove the stabilizer shaft insulator bracket bolt.
4. Bend the open end of the stabilizer shaft insulator bracket clamp upward.
5. Remove the stabilizer shaft insulators.
6. Remove the stabilizer shaft.

To install:

7. Install the stabilizer shaft to the vehicle.
8. Install the stabilizer shaft insulators to the stabilizer shaft with the slits forward.
9. Bend the stabilizer shaft insulator brackets downward.

➡ Use the correct fastener in the correct location. Replacement fasteners must be the correct part number for that application. Fasteners requiring replacement or fasteners requiring the use of thread locking compound or sealant are identified in the service procedure. Do not use paints, lubricants, or corrosion inhibitors on fasteners or fastener joint surfaces unless specified. These coatings affect fastener torque and joint clamping force and may damage the fastener. Use the correct tightening sequence and specifications when installing fasteners in order to avoid damage to parts and systems.

10. Install the stabilizer shaft bracket retaining bolt. Tighten the stabilizer shaft bracket retaining bolts to 24 ft. lbs. (33 Nm).
11. Install the stabilizer shaft links.
12. Lower the vehicle.

STEERING KNUCKLE

REMOVAL & INSTALLATION

Tools Required:
- J 24319-B Steering Linkage and Tie Rod Puller
- J 39549 Ball Joint and Tie Rod End Separator

1. Before servicing the vehicle, refer to the Precautions Section.
2. Raise and support the vehicle.
3. Remove the front tire and wheel assembly.
4. Remove the brake rotor from the wheel hub/bearing.

5. Remove the bearing/hub assembly.
6. Use the J 24319-B to separate the tie rod end from the steering knuckle.

➡ **Always replace the tie rod end nut after it has been used.**

7. Use the J 39549 to separate the ball joint from the lower control arm.

➡ **Always replace the ball joint nut after it has been used.**

8. Matchmark the strut to the knuckle.
9. Remove the bolts and nuts attaching the strut to the knuckle.
10. Remove the steering knuckle from the vehicle.

To install:

11. Install the steering knuckle to the vehicle.
12. Install the through bolts and nuts attaching the strut to the knuckle. Align the matchmarks made during removal. Tighten the through bolts and nuts to 131 ft. lbs. (177 Nm).
13. Connect the outer tie rod to the steering knuckle. Tighten the outer tie rod end nuts to 22 ft. lbs. (30 Nm), plus an additional 200°.
14. Connect the front lower control arm ball stud to the knuckle. Tighten to 22 ft. lbs. (30 Nm), plus an additional 210°.
15. Install the front wheel drive shaft bearing. Refer to Halfshaft, removal and installation.
16. Install the front tire and wheel assembly. Tighten the wheel lug nuts to 100 ft. lbs. (136 Nm).
17. Lower the vehicle.
18. Inspect the front wheel alignment and adjust if necessary.

WHEEL HUB AND BEARINGS

REMOVAL & INSTALLATION

See Figures 170 and 171.

1. Before servicing the vehicle, refer to the Precautions Section.
2. Raise and support the vehicle.
3. Remove the front tire and wheel assembly.

➡ **Insert a drift punch through the caliper and into the rotor cooling fins to prevent the rotor from turning.**

4. Remove or disconnect the following:
- The halfshaft nut and washer
- The brake caliper
- The brake rotor
- The Anti-Lock Brake System (ABS) speed sensor
- The 3 hub/bearing assembly bolts

- The dust shield
- The hub/bearing assembly from the halfshaft, using a puller
- The hub/bearing assembly from the steering knuckle

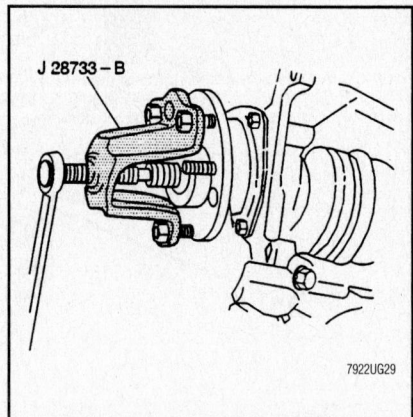

Fig. 170 Use a puller such as J 28733-B to press the halfshaft from the hub assembly

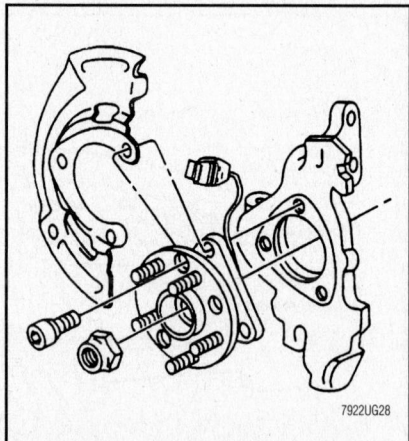

Fig. 171 Exploded view of the front hub and wheel bearing assembly

To install:

5. Install the hub/bearing assembly over the halfshaft splines. Be sure the splines engage smoothly.
6. Apply a light coating of grease to the steering knuckle bore.
7. Slide the hub assembly onto the halfshaft as far as possible. If the hub will not bottom out on the halfshaft, install the hub mounting bolts and use the halfshaft nut to draw the hub onto the halfshaft.
8. Once the hub is flush with the steering knuckle, remove the mounting bolts and install the dust shield.
9. Install the mounting bolts. Torque the bolts to 70 ft. lbs. (95 Nm).
10. Place the transaxle in **N**.
11. Install or connect the following:

- The ABS front wheel speed sensor connector, and clip to the dust shield
- The brake rotor
- The caliper

12. Torque the halfshaft nut to 118 ft. lbs. (160 Nm).

13. Install the front wheels. Tighten the wheel lug nuts to 100 ft. lbs. (136 Nm).

14. Road test the vehicle.

ADJUSTMENT

No adjustment is possible. The wheel bearings are not adjustable.

If a wheel bearing is out of specification, it must be replaced. Using a dial indicator, check for looseness. If play exceeds 0.005 inch (0.127mm), the bearing wear is excessive and the hub/bearing should be replaced.

SUSPENSION

COIL SPRING

REMOVAL & INSTALLATION

Tool Required:
- J 24319-B Universal Steering Linkage Puller

1. Before servicing the vehicle, refer to the Precautions Section.
2. Raise and support the vehicle.
3. Remove the tire and wheel.
4. Support the control arm with a suitable jack.
5. Remove the automatic level control sensor link from the control arm.
6. Remove the lower shock absorber retaining bolts.
7. Disconnect the stabilizer link from the control arm.
8. Remove the rear caliper pin bolts.
9. Using heavy wire, hang the rear brake caliper.
10. Remove the adjustment link retaining nut.
11. Using J 24319-B, separate the adjustment link from the lower control arm.
12. Slowly lower the lower control arm until it bottoms on the support assembly.
13. Using a pry bar, pry under the lower coil spring insulator and remove the coil spring with the insulator.
14. Remove the upper coil spring insulator by pulling downward.
15. Separate the lower control arm insulator from the coil spring.

To install:
16. Install the upper coil spring insulator to the body.
17. Install the lower coil spring insulator in the control arm.
18. Install the coil spring ensuring that the coil spring insulators are seated in the upper and lower control arms.

➡**Use the correct fastener in the correct location. Replacement fasteners must be the correct part number for that application. Fasteners requiring replacement or fasteners requiring the use of thread locking compound or sealant are identified in the service procedure. Do not use paints, lubri-**

cants, or corrosion inhibitors on fasteners or fastener joint surfaces unless specified. These coatings affect fastener torque and joint clamping force and may damage the fastener. Use the correct tightening sequence and specifications when installing fasteners in order to avoid damage to parts and systems.**

19. Raise the lower control arm and install the shock absorber retaining bolts in the lower control arm. Tighten the lower shock absorber retaining bolts to 18 ft. lbs. (25 Nm).
20. Attach the rear brake caliper to the bracket using the caliper guide pin bolts. Tighten the caliper guide pin bolts to 25 ft. lbs. (34 Nm).
21. Install the stabilizer link.
22. Install the adjustment link to the control arm. Tighten adjustment link retaining nut to 22 ft. lbs. (30 Nm), plus an additional 180°.
23. Connect the automatic level control sensor link to the control arm.
24. Install the tire and wheel. Tighten the wheel lug nuts to 100 ft. lbs. (136 Nm).
25. Lower the vehicle.

CONTROL ARMS/LINKS

REMOVAL & INSTALLATION

1. Before servicing the vehicle, refer to the Precautions Section.
2. Raise and support the vehicle.
3. Remove the control link (or stabilizer shaft link) bolts.
4. Remove the control link insulators and spacer.

To install:

➡**Use the correct fastener in the correct location. Replacement fasteners must be the correct part number for that application. Fasteners requiring replacement or fasteners requiring the use of thread locking compound or sealant are identified in the service procedure. Do not use paints, lubricants, or corrosion inhibitors on fasteners or fastener joint surfaces unless specified. These coatings affect fastener torque**

REAR SUSPENSION

and joint clamping force and may damage the fastener. Use the correct tightening sequence and specifications when installing fasteners in order to avoid damage to parts and systems.**

5. Loosely install the stabilizer link insulators, spacer, nut and bolt. Tighten the stabilizer shaft link nut to 11 ft. lbs. (15 Nm).
6. Lower the vehicle.

SHOCK ABSORBER

REMOVAL & INSTALLATION

1. Before servicing the vehicle, refer to the Precautions Section.
2. Raise and support the vehicle.
3. Remove the tire and wheel.
4. Support the control arm with a jack stand.
5. Disconnect the automatic level control air tube from the shock.
6. Remove the lower shock absorber retaining bolts.
7. Remove the trunk trim to gain access to the shock absorber upper mounting nuts.
8. Remove the upper shock absorber cover.
9. Remove the upper shock absorber retaining nuts.
10. Remove the upper shock absorber reinforcement.
11. Remove the shock from the vehicle.

To install:

➡**Use the correct fastener in the correct location. Replacement fasteners must be the correct part number for that application. Fasteners requiring replacement or fasteners requiring the use of thread locking compound or sealant are identified in the service procedure. Do not use paints, lubricants, or corrosion inhibitors on fasteners or fastener joint surfaces unless specified. These coatings affect fastener torque and joint clamping force and may damage the fastener. Use the correct tightening sequence and specifications when installing fasteners in order to avoid damage to parts and systems.**

12. Install the shock, reinforcement, and the retaining nuts. Tighten the upper shock absorber retaining nuts to 18 ft. lbs. (25 Nm).

13. Install the upper shock absorber cover.

14. Install the trunk trim.

15. Install the lower shock absorber retaining bolts. Tighten the lower shock absorber retaining bolts to 18 ft. lbs. (25 Nm).

16. Connect the automatic level control air tube to the shock.

17. Install the tire and wheel. Refer to Tire and Wheel Removal and Installation .

18. Lower the vehicle.

TESTING

1. Check the rubber parts for damage or deterioration.

2. Check for correct height and proper return of shock absorber to original height.

3. Check the shock absorber for abnormal resistance or unusual sounds.

4. Check for oil leakage around seals.

5. Replace if necessary.

WHEEL HUB AND BEARING

REMOVAL & INSTALLATION

See Figure 172.

1. Before servicing the vehicle, refer to the Precautions Section.

2. Raise and support the vehicle.

3. Remove or disconnect the following:
- The tire and wheel
- The brake rotor
- The wheel bearing/hub electrical connector
- The wheel bearing/hub retaining bolts
- The wheel bearing/hub from lower control arm
- The brake shield from the lower control arm

To install:

4. Clean the control arm face and the bore before installing the hub and the bearing.

5. Install or connect the following:
- The brake shield and the wheel bearing/hub to the control arm
- The wheel bearing/hub retaining bolts. Tighten the wheel bearing/hub bolts to 50 ft. lbs. (68 Nm)

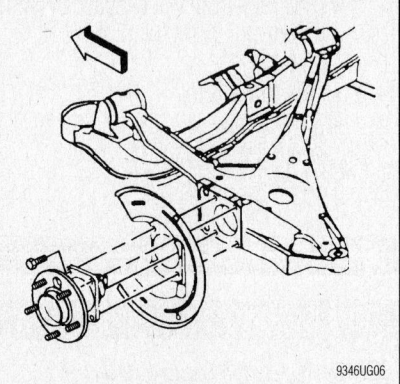

Fig. 172 Exploded view of the rear hub/wheel bearing assembly

- The wheel/hub electrical connector
- The brake rotor
- The tire and wheel. Tighten the wheel lug nuts to 100 ft. lbs. (136 Nm)

6. Lower the vehicle.

ADJUSTMENT

All models use sealed wheel bearings that are pre-adjusted. If the bearing needs replacing, replace the rear wheel hub/bearing assembly.

CHEVROLET

Malibu

17

SPECIFICATIONS AND MAINTENANCE CHARTS

ENGINE AND VEHICLE IDENTIFICATION

Code ①	Liters (cc)	Cu. In.	Cyl.	Fuel Sys.	Engine Type	Eng. Mfg.	Code ②	Year
			Engine				Model Year	
F	2.2 (2189)	134	4	SFI	DOHC	General Motors	5	2005
8	3.5 (3500)	214	6	SFI	OHV	General Motors	6	2006
1	3.9 (3900)	238	6	SFI	OHV	General Motors	7	2007
							8	2008

SFI: Sequential Fuel Injection

① 8th position of VIN

② 10th position of VIN

22116_MALI_C0001

GENERAL ENGINE SPECIFICATIONS

Year	Model	Engine Displacement Liters	Engine Series VIN	Net Horsepower @ rpm	Net Torque @ rpm (ft. lbs.)	Bore x Stroke (in.)	Compression Ratio	Oil Pressure @ rpm
2005	Malibu	2.2	F	145@5600	155@4000	3.50x3.31	10.0:1	50-80@1000
		3.5	8	200@5400	220@3200	3.70x3.31	9.8:1	30-45@1850
2006	Malibu	3.5	8	200@5400	220@3200	3.70x3.31	9.8:1	30-45@1850
		2.2	F	145@5600	155@4000	3.39x3.72	10.0:1	50-80@1000
		3.9	1	240@6000	241@2800	3.90x3.31	9.8:1	30-45@1850
2007	Malibu	3.5	8	200@5400	220@3200	3.70x3.31	9.8:1	30-45@1850
		2.2	F	145@5600	155@4000	3.39x3.72	10.0:1	50-80@1000
		3.9	1	240@6000	241@2800	3.90x3.31	9.8:1	30-45@1850
2008	Malibu	2.2	F	145@5600	155@4000	3.50x3.31	10.0:1	50-80@1000
		3.5	8	200@5400	220@3200	3.70x3.31	9.8:1	30-45@1850

22116_MALI_C0002

ENGINE TUNE-UP SPECIFICATIONS

Year	Engine Displacement Liters	Engine VIN	Spark Plug Gap (in.)	Ignition Timing (deg.)	Fuel Pump (psi)	Idle Speed (rpm)	Valve Clearance In.	Valve Clearance Ex.
2005	2.2	F	0.042	①	50-60	①	HYD	HYD
	3.5	8	0.060	①	50-60	①	HYD	HYD
2006	2.2	F	0.042	①	50-60	①	HYD	HYD
	3.5	8	0.060	①	50-60	①	HYD	HYD
	3.9	1	0.040	①	50-60	①	HYD	HYD
2007	2.2	F	0.045	①	50-60	①	HYD	HYD
	3.5	8	0.040	①	50-60	①	HYD	HYD
	3.9	1	0.040	①	50-60	①	HYD	HYD
2008	2.2	F	0.045	①	50-60	①	HYD	HYD
	3.5	8	0.040	①	50-60	①	HYD	HYD

NOTE: The Vehicle Emission Control Information label often reflects specification changes made during production.

HYD: Hydraulic

① Refer to Vehicle Emission Control Information label

The label figures must be used if they differ from those in this chart.

22116_MALI_C0003

CAPACITIES

Year	Model	Engine Displacement Liters	Engine VIN	Engine Oil with Filter (qts.)	Transmission (pts.) ① ②	Fuel Tank (gal.)	Cooling System (qts.)
2005	Malibu	2.2	F	5.0	19.0	16.1	6.9
	Malibu	3.5	8	4.0	19.0	16.1	10.1
2006	Malibu	2.2	F	5.0	19.0	16.1	6.9
	Malibu	3.5	8	4.0	19.0	16.1	10.1
	Malibu	3.9	1	4.0	19.0	16.1	13.1
2007	Malibu	2.2	F	5.0	19.0	16.1	6.9
	Malibu	3.5	8	4.0	19.0	16.1	10.1
	Malibu	3.9	1	4.0	19.0	16.1	13.1
2008	Malibu	2.2	F	5.0	19.0	16.1	6.9
	Malibu	3.5	8	4.0	19.0	16.1	10.1

NOTE: All capacities are approximate. Add fluid gradually and ensure a proper fluid level is obtained.

① 4T65-E Transaxle 20 pts.

② Complete fluid exchange

22116_MALI_C0005

FLUID SPECIFICATIONS

Year	Model	Engine Displacement Liters	Engine VIN	Engine Oil	Auto. Trans.	Drive Axle	Power Steering Fluid	Brake Master Cylinder	Engine Coolant
2005	Malibu	2.2	F	5W-30	DEXRON® III	NA	GM PS Fluid	DOT 3	DEX-COOL®
		3.5	8	5W-30	DEXRON® III	NA	GM PS Fluid	DOT 3	DEX-COOL®
2006	Malibu	2.2	F	5W-30	DEXRON® VI	NA	GM PS Fluid	DOT 3	DEX-COOL®
		3.5	8	5W-30	DEXRON® VI	NA	GM PS Fluid	DOT 3	DEX-COOL®
		3.9	1	5W-30	DEXRON® VI	NA	GM PS Fluid	DOT 3	DEX-COOL®
2007	Malibu	2.2	F	5W-30	DEXRON® VI	NA	GM PS Fluid	DOT 3	DEX-COOL®
		3.5	8	5W-30	DEXRON® VI	NA	GM PS Fluid	DOT 3	DEX-COOL®
		3.9	1	5W-30	DEXRON® VI	NA	GM PS Fluid	DOT 3	DEX-COOL®
2008	Malibu	2.2	F	5W-30	DEXRON® VI	NA	GM PS Fluid	DOT 3	DEX-COOL®
		3.5	8	5W-30	DEXRON® VI	NA	GM PS Fluid	DOT 3	DEX-COOL®

DOT: Department Of Transpotation

NA: Information not available

22116_MALI_C0004

VALVE SPECIFICATIONS

Year	Engine Displacement Liters	Engine VIN	Seat Angle (deg.)	Face Angle (deg.)	Spring Test Pressure (lbs. @ in.)	Spring Installed Height (in.)	Stem-to-Guide Clearance (in.)		Stem Diameter (in.)	
							Intake	Exhaust	Intake	Exhaust
2005	2.2	F	NA	NA	NA	NA	0.0012-0.0022	0.0020-0.0026	0.2344-0.2355	0.2337 0.2343
	3.5	8	46	45	234@1.299	1.740	0.0010-0.0027	0.0010-0.0027	NA	NA
2006	2.2	F	NA	NA	NA	NA	0.0012-0.0022	0.0020-0.0026	0.2344-0.2355	0.2337 0.2343
	3.5	8	46	45	234@1.299	1.740	0.0010-0.0027	0.0010-0.0027	NA	NA
	3.9	1	46	45	230@1.26	1.701	0.0010-0.0027	0.0010-0.0027	NA	NA
2007	2.2	F	NA	NA	NA	NA	0.0012-0.0022	0.0020-0.0026	0.2344-0.2355	0.2337 0.2343
	3.5	8	46	45	234@1.299	1.740	0.0010-0.0027	0.0010-0.0027	NA	NA
	3.9	1	46	45	230@1.26	1.701	0.0010-0.0027	0.0010-0.0027	NA	NA
2008	2.2	F	NA	NA	NA	NA	0.0012-0.0022	0.0020-0.0026	0.2344-0.2355	0.2337 0.2343
	3.5	8	46	45	234@1.299	1.740	0.0010-0.0027	0.0010-0.0027	NA	NA

NA: Information not available

22116_MALI_C0006

CAMSHAFT AND BEARING SPECIFICATIONS CHART

All measurements are given in inches.

Year	Engine Displ. Liters	Engine VIN	Journal Dia.	Brg. Oil Clearance	Shaft End-play	Runout	Journal Bore	Lobe Height	
								Intake	Exhaust
2005	2.2	F	1.0604-1.0614	1.8710-1.8720	0.0016-0.0057	0.001	NA	NA	NA
	3.5	8	1.8680-1.8690	1.8710-1.8720	—	0.001	NA	0.2727	0.2727
2006	2.2	F	1.0604-1.0614	1.8710-1.8720	0.0016-0.0057	0.001	NA	NA	NA
	3.5	8	1.8680-1.8690	1.8710-1.8720	—	0.001	NA	0.2727	0.2727
	3.9	1	1.0614-1.0620	—	0.0016-0.0035	0.0024	NA	1.6981-1.7020	1.6933-1.6972
2007	2.2	F	1.0604-1.0614	1.8710-1.8720	0.0016-0.0057	0.001	NA	NA	NA
	3.5	8	2.0240-2.0250	2.0280-2.0290	—	0.001	NA	0.2727	0.2727
	3.9	1	1.0614-1.0620	—	0.0016-0.0035	0.001	NA	1.6981-1.7020	1.6933-1.6972
2008	2.2	F	1.0604-1.0614	1.8710-1.8720	0.0016-0.0057	0.001	NA	NA	NA
	3.5	8	2.0240-2.0250	2.0280-2.0290	—	0.001	NA	0.2727	0.2727

NA: Not Available

22116_MALI_C0007

CRANKSHAFT AND CONNECTING ROD SPECIFICATIONS

All measurements are given in inches.

Year	Engine Displacement Liters	Engine VIN	Crankshaft				Connecting Rod		
			Main Brg. Journal Dia.	Main Brg. Oil Clearance	Shaft End-play	Thrust on No.	Journal Diameter	Oil Clearance	Side Clearance
2005	2.2	F	2.2045-2.2050	0.0012-0.0026	0.0012-0.0150	3	2.0519-2.0525	0.0011-0.0027	0.0028-0.0146
	3.5	8	2.6473-2.6483	0.0008-0.0025	0.0024-0.0083	3	2.2490-2.2500	0.0007-0.0170	0.0080-0.0090
2006	2.2	F	2.2045-2.2050	0.0012-0.0026	0.0012-0.0150	3	2.0519-2.0525	0.0011-0.0027	0.0028-0.0146
	3.5	8	2.6473-2.6483	0.0008-0.0025	0.0024-0.0083	3	2.2490-2.2500	0.0007-0.0170	0.0080-0.0090
	3.9	1	2.6473-2.6483	①	0.0024-0.0083	3	2.2488-2.2495	0.0007-0.0024	0.0078-0.0094
2007	2.2	F	2.2045-2.2050	0.0012-0.0026	0.0012-0.0150	3	2.0519-2.0525	0.0011-0.0027	0.0028-0.0146
	3.5	8	2.6473-2.6483	0.0008-0.0025	0.0024-0.0083	3	2.2490-2.2500	0.0007-0.0170	0.0080-0.0090
	3.9	1	2.6473-2.6483	①	0.0024-0.0083	3	2.2488-2.2495	0.0007-0.0024	0.0078-0.0094
2008	2.2	F	2.2045-2.2050	0.0012-0.0026	0.0012-0.0150	3	2.0519-2.0525	0.0011-0.0027	0.0028-0.0146
	3.5	8	2.6473-2.6483	0.0008-0.0025	0.0024-0.0083	3	2.2490-2.2500	0.0007-0.0170	0.0080-0.0090

① 0.0008-0.0025 except no. 3
0.0012-0.0030 on no. 3

22116_MALI_C0008

PISTON AND RING SPECIFICATIONS

All measurements are given in inches.

Year	Engine Displacement Liters	Engine VIN	Piston Clearance	Ring Gap			Ring Side Clearance		
				Top Compression	Bottom Compression	Oil Control	Top Compression	Bottom Compression	Oil Control
2005	2.2	F	0.0004-0.0016	0.008-0.016	0.014-0.022	0.010-0.030	0.0015-0.0031	0.0012-0.0027	0.0035-0.0042
	3.5	8	0.003 max	0.007-0.015	0.019-0.029	0.010-0.029	0.001-0.003	0.002-0.003	0.0040
2006	2.2	F	0.0004-0.0016	0.008-0.016	0.014-0.022	0.010-0.030	0.0015-0.0031	0.0012-0.0027	0.0035-0.0042
	3.5	8	0.003 max	0.007-0.015	0.098-0.029	0.010-0.029	0.001-0.003	0.002-0.003	0.0040
	3.9	1	0.0003-0.0018	0.0059-0.0118	0.0098-0.0177	0.0059-0.0255	0.0011-0.0025	0.0007-0.0021	0.0040
2007	2.2	F	0.0004-0.0016	0.008-0.016	0.014-0.022	0.010-0.030	0.0015-0.0031	0.0012-0.0027	0.0035-0.0042
	3.5	8	0.003 max	0.007-0.015	0.098-0.029	0.010-0.029	0.001-0.003	0.002-0.003	0.0040
	3.9	1	0.0003-0.0018	0.0059-0.0118	0.0098-0.0177	0.0059-0.0255	0.0011-0.0025	0.0007-0.0021	0.0040
2008	2.2	F	0.0004-0.0016	0.008-0.016	0.014-0.022	0.010-0.030	0.0015-0.0031	0.0012-0.0027	0.0035-0.0042
	3.5	8	0.003 max	0.007-0.015	0.019-0.029	0.010-0.029	0.001-0.003	0.002-0.003	0.0040

22116_MALI_C0009

TORQUE SPECIFICATIONS
All readings in ft. lbs.

Year	Engine Displacement Liters	Engine VIN	Cylinder Head Bolts	Main Bearing Bolts	Rod Bearing Bolts	Crankshaft Damper Bolts	Flywheel Bolts	Manifold		Spark Plug	Oil Pan Drain Plug
								Intake	Exhaust		
2005	2.2	F	①	②	③	④	⑤	10	10	15	18
	3.5	8	⑥	⑦	⑧	⑨	52	⑩	15	11	18
2006	2.2	F	①	②	③	④	⑤	10	10	15	18
	3.5	8	⑥	⑦	⑧	⑨	52	⑩	15	11	18
	3.9	1	⑥	⑦	⑧	⑨	52	⑩	15	11	18
2007	2.2	F	①	②	③	④	⑤	10	10	15	18
	3.5	8	⑥	⑦	⑧	⑨	52	⑩	15	11	18
	3.9	1	⑥	⑦	⑧	⑨	52	⑩	15	11	18
2008	2.2	F	①	②	③	④	⑤	10	10	15	18
	3.5	8	⑥	⑦	⑧	⑨	52	⑩	15	11	18

① Step 1: 22 ft. lbs.
Step 2: Plus 155 degrees

② Step 1: 15 ft. lbs.
Step 2: Plus 70 degrees

③ Step 1: 18 ft. lbs.
Step 2: Plus 100 degrees

④ Step 1: 74 ft. lbs.
Step 2: Plus 125 degrees

⑤ Step 1: 39 ft. lbs.
Step 2: Plus 25 degrees

⑥ Step 1: 44 ft. lbs.
Step 2: Plus 140 degrees

⑦ Step 1: 37 ft. lbs.
Step 2: Plus 77 degrees

⑧ Step 1: 18 ft. lbs.
Step 2: Plus 110 degrees

⑨ Step 1: 92 ft. lbs.
Step 2: Plus 130 degrees

⑩ Lower intake manifold bolts: 11 ft. lbs.
Upper intake manifold bolts: 18 ft. lbs.

22116_MALI_C0010

WHEEL ALIGNMENT

Year	Model		Caster		Camber		Toe-in (in.)
			Range (+/-Deg.)	Preferred Setting (Deg.)	Range (+/-Deg.)	Preferred Setting (Deg.)	
2005	Malibu	F	0.75	3.00	0.75	-0.4	0.20+/-0.20
		R	—	—	0.50	-0.8	0.20+/-0.20
2006	Malibu	F	0.75	3.00	0.75	-0.4	0.20+/-0.20
		R	—	—	0.50	-0.8	0.20+/-0.20
2007	Malibu	F	0.75	3.00	0.75	-0.4	0.20+/-0.20
		R	—	—	0.50	-0.8	0.20+/-0.20
2008	Malibu	F	0.75	3.00	0.75	-0.4	0.20+/-0.20
		R	—	—	0.50	-0.8	0.20+/-0.20

22116_MALI_C0011

TIRE, WHEEL AND BALL JOINT SPECIFICATIONS

Year	Model	OEM Tires		Tire Pressures (psi)		Wheel Size	Ball Joint Inspection	Wheel Lug Torque (ft. lbs.)
		Standard	Optional	Front	Rear			
2005	Malibu	P205/65R15	—	30	30	6.5J	①	100
	Malibu Classic	P205/65R15	—	29	26	6J	①	100
	Malibu LS	P205/65R15	—	30	30	6.5J	①	100
	Malibu LT	P215/60R16	—	30	30	6.5J	①	100
	Malibu Maxx LS	P215/60R16	—	30	30	6.5J	①	100
	Malibu Maxx LT	P215/60R16	—	30	30	6.5J	①	100
2006	Malibu LS	P205/65R15	—	30	30	6.5J	①	100
	Malibu LT	P215/60R16	—	30	30	6.5J	①	100
	Malibu LTZ	P225/50R17	—	30	30	7J	①	100
	Malibu Maxx LS	P215/60R16	—	30	30	6.5J	①	100
	Malibu Maxx LT	P215/60R16	—	30	30	6.5J	①	100
	Malibu Maxx LTZ	P225/50R17	—	30	30	7J	①	100
	Malibu SS	P225/50R18	—	30	30	7J	①	100
	Malibu Maxx SS	P225/50R18	—	30	30	7J	①	100
2007	Malibu LS	P205/65R15	—	30	30	6.5J	①	100
	Malibu LT	P215/60R16	—	30	30	6.5J	①	100
	Malibu LTZ	P225/50R17	—	30	30	7J	①	100
	Malibu Maxx LS	P215/60R16	—	30	30	6.5J	①	100
	Malibu Maxx LT	P215/60R16	—	30	30	6.5J	①	100
	Malibu Maxx LTZ	P225/50R17	—	30	30	7J	①	100
	Malibu SS	P225/50R18	—	30	30	7J	①	100
	Malibu Maxx SS	P225/50R18	—	30	30	7J	①	100
2008	Malibu LS	P205/65R15	—	30	30	6.5J	①	100
	Malibu LT	P215/60R16	—	30	30	6.5J	①	100
	Malibu LTZ	P225/50R17	—	30	30	7J	①	100
	Malibu Maxx LS	P215/60R16	—	30	30	6.5J	①	100
	Malibu Maxx LT	P215/60R16	—	30	30	6.5J	①	100
	Malibu Maxx LTZ	P225/50R17	—	30	30	7J	①	100
	Malibu SS	P225/50R18	—	30	30	7J	①	100
	Malibu Maxx SS	P225/50R18	—	30	30	7J	①	100

OEM: Original Equipment Manufacturer

PSI: Pounds Per Square Inch

① Replace if any measurable movement is found.

22116_MALI_C0012

BRAKE SPECIFICATIONS
All measurements in inches unless noted

Year	Model		Brake Disc Original Thickness	Brake Disc Minimum Thickness	Brake Disc Maximum Runout	Brake Drum Diameter Original Inside Diameter	Brake Drum Diameter Max. Wear Limit	Brake Drum Diameter Maximum Machine Diameter	Minimum Lining Thickness Front	Minimum Lining Thickness Rear	Brake Caliper Bracket Bolts (ft. lbs.)	Brake Caliper Mounting Bolts (ft. lbs.)
2005	Malibu	F	1.023	0.898	0.002	—	—	—	NA	—	85	26
		R	0.551	0.465	0.002	9.060	9.075	9.094	—	NA	85	26
2006	Malibu	F	1.023	0.898	0.002	—	—	—	NA	—	85	26
		R	0.551	0.465	0.002	9.060	9.075	9.094	—	NA	85	26
2007	Malibu	F	1.023	0.898	0.002	—	—	—	NA	—	85	26
		R	0.551	0.465	0.002	9.060	9.075	9.094	—	NA	85	26
2008	Malibu	F	1.023	0.898	0.002	—	—	—	NA	—	85	26
		R	0.551	0.465	0.002	—	—	—	—	NA	85	26

22116_MALI_C0013

MAINTENANCE I AND II SERVICE SCHEDULES
2005-08 Chevrolet Malibu/Malibu MAXX

When the CHANGE ENGINE OIL light appears, certain services and inspections are required.
Required services are described as Maintenance I and Maintenance II.
The first service on a vehicle should be Maintenance I, and the second service should be Maintenance II.
Alternate between the 2 thereafter. However, in some cases, Maintenance II may be required more often.
Maintenance I: Use Maintenance I if the CHANGE ENGINE OIL light comes on within 10 months since vehicle was purchased or, if Maintenance II was performed.
Maintenance II: Use Maintenance II if the previous service performed was Maintenance I. Always use Maintenance II whenever the CHANGE ENGINE OIL light comes on 10 months or more since the last service, or, if the CHANGE ENGINE OIL light has not come on at all for one year.

Service	Maintenance I	Maintenance II
Change the engine oil and filter. Reset the oil life system.	✓	✓
Visually inspect the vehicle for leaks or damage. A fluid loss in the vehicle system could indicate a problem. Inspected, repair and add fluid to the system if necessary.	✓	✓
Inspect the engine air cleaner filter. If necessary, replace the filter.	✓	✓
Rotate the tires. Inspect the tire inflation pressures and the tire wear.	✓	✓
Visually inspect the brake lines and hoses for proper hook-up, binding, leaks, cracks, chafing, etc. Inspect the disc brake pads for wear and the rotors for surface condition. Inspect the drum brake linings for wear or cracks. Inspect other brake parts, including drums, wheel cylinders, calipers, parking brake, etc. Inspect the parking brake adjustment.	✓	✓
Inspect the engine coolant and the windshield washer fluid levels. Add fluid as needed.	✓	✓
Inspect the suspension and steering components. Inspect the front and rear suspension and the steering system for damaged, loose or missing parts, or signs of wear. Inspect the power steering lines and the hoses for proper hook-up, binding, leaks, cracks,	--	✓
Visually inspect the coolant hoses and replace the hoses if they are cracked, swollen or deteriorated. Inspect all pipes, fittings and clamps; replace with GM parts as needed. To help ensure proper operation, a pressure test of the cooling system and pressure cap and cleaning the outside of the radiator and air conditioning condenser is recommended at least once a year.	--	✓
Inspect the front and rear suspension and the steering system for damaged, loose or missing parts, or signs of wear. Inspect power steering lines and hoses for proper hook-up, binding, leaks, cracks, chafing, etc.	--	✓
Inspect the throttle system for interference or binding and for damaged or missing parts. Replace the parts as needed. Replace any components that have high effort or excessive wear. Do not lubricate the accelerator or the cruise control cables.	--	✓
Replace the passenger compartment air filter.	--	✓

Reset the oil life system:
   1. Display OIL LIFE RESET on the DIC.
   2. Press and hold the ENTER button for at least one second. An ACKNOWLEDGED display message will appear for three seconds or until the next button is pressed. This will tell you the system has been reset.
   3. Turn the key to OFF.
If the Change Oil Soon message comes back on when you start your vehicle, the engine oil life system has not reset, repeat the procedure.

PRECAUTIONS

Before servicing any vehicle, please be sure to read all of the following precautions, which deal with personal safety, prevention of component damage, and important points to take into consideration when servicing a motor vehicle:

• Never open, service or drain the radiator or cooling system when the engine is hot; serious burns can occur from the steam and hot coolant.

• Observe all applicable safety precautions when working around fuel. Whenever servicing the fuel system, always work in a well-ventilated area. Do not allow fuel spray or vapors to come in contact with a spark, open flame, or excessive heat (a hot drop light, for example). Keep a dry chemical fire extinguisher near the work area. Always keep fuel in a container specifically designed for fuel storage; also, always properly seal fuel containers to avoid the possibility of fire or explosion. Refer to the additional fuel system precautions later in this section.

• Fuel injection systems often remain pressurized, even after the engine has been turned **OFF**. The fuel system pressure must be relieved before disconnecting any fuel lines. Failure to do so may result in fire and/or personal injury.

• Brake fluid often contains polyglycol ethers and polyglycols. Avoid contact with the eyes and wash your hands thoroughly after handling brake fluid. If you do get brake fluid in your eyes, flush your eyes with clean, running water for 15 minutes. If eye irritation persists, or if you have taken

brake fluid internally, IMMEDIATELY seek medical assistance.

• The EPA warns that prolonged contact with used engine oil may cause a number of skin disorders, including cancer. You should make every effort to minimize your exposure to used engine oil. Protective gloves should be worn when changing oil. Wash your hands and any other exposed skin areas as soon as possible after exposure to used engine oil. Soap and water, or waterless hand cleaner should be used.

• All new vehicles are now equipped with an air bag system, often referred to as a Supplemental Restraint System (SRS) or Supplemental Inflatable Restraint (SIR) system. The system must be disabled before performing service on or around system components, steering column, instrument panel components, wiring and sensors. Failure to follow safety and disabling procedures could result in accidental air bag deployment, possible personal injury and unnecessary system repairs.

• Always wear safety goggles when working with, or around, the air bag system. When carrying a non-deployed air bag, be sure the bag and trim cover are pointed away from your body. When placing a non-deployed air bag on a work surface, always face the bag and trim cover upward, away from the surface. This will reduce the motion of the module if it is accidentally deployed. Refer to the additional air bag system precautions later in this section.

• Clean, high quality brake fluid from a sealed container is essential to the safe and

proper operation of the brake system. You should always buy the correct type of brake fluid for your vehicle. If the brake fluid becomes contaminated, completely flush the system with new fluid. Never reuse any brake fluid. Any brake fluid that is removed from the system should be discarded. Also, do not allow any brake fluid to come in contact with a painted surface; it will damage the paint.

• Never operate the engine without the proper amount and type of engine oil; doing so WILL result in severe engine damage.

• Timing belt maintenance is extremely important. Many models utilize an interference-type, non-freewheeling engine. If the timing belt breaks, the valves in the cylinder head may strike the pistons, causing potentially serious (also time-consuming and expensive) engine damage. Refer to the maintenance interval charts for the recommended replacement interval for the timing belt, and to the timing belt section for belt replacement and inspection.

• Disconnecting the negative battery cable on some vehicles may interfere with the functions of the on-board computer system(s) and may require the computer to undergo a relearning process once the negative battery cable is reconnected.

• When servicing drum brakes, only disassemble and assemble one side at a time, leaving the remaining side intact for reference.

• Only an MVAC-trained, EPA-certified automotive technician should service the air conditioning system or its components.

BRAKES

ANTI-LOCK BRAKE SYSTEM (ABS)

GENERAL INFORMATION

When wheel slip is detected during a brake application, the ABS enters antilock mode. During antilock braking, hydraulic pressure in the individual wheel circuits is controlled to prevent any wheel from slipping. A separate hydraulic line and specific solenoid valves are provided for each wheel. The ABS can decrease, hold, or increase hydraulic pressure to each wheel brake. The ABS cannot, however, increase hydraulic pressure above the amount which is transmitted by the master cylinder during braking.

During antilock braking, a series of rapid pulsations is felt in the brake pedal. These pulsations are caused by the rapid changes in position of the individual solenoid valves

as the EBCM responds to wheel speed sensor inputs and attempts to prevent wheel slip. These pedal pulsations are present only during antilock braking and stop when normal braking is resumed or when the vehicle comes to a stop. A ticking or popping noise may also be heard as the solenoid valves cycle rapidly. During antilock braking on dry pavement, intermittent chirping noises may be heard as the tires approach slipping. These noises and pedal pulsations are considered normal during antilock operation.

Vehicles equipped with ABS may be stopped by applying normal force to the brake pedal. Brake pedal operation during normal braking is no different than that of previous non-ABS systems. Maintaining a constant force on the brake pedal provides

the shortest stopping distance while maintaining vehicle stability.

PRECAUTIONS

• Certain components within the ABS system are not intended to be serviced or repaired individually.

• Do not use rubber hoses or other parts not specifically specified for and ABS system. When using repair kits, replace all parts included in the kit. Partial or incorrect repair may lead to functional problems and require the replacement of components.

• Lubricate rubber parts with clean, fresh brake fluid to ease assembly. Do not use shop air to clean parts; damage to rubber components may result.

• Use only DOT 3 brake fluid from an unopened container.

- If any hydraulic component or line is removed or replaced, it may be necessary to bleed the entire system.
- A clean repair area is essential. Always clean the reservoir and cap thoroughly before removing the cap. The slightest amount of dirt in the fluid may plug an orifice and impair the system function. Perform repairs after components have been thoroughly cleaned; use only denatured alcohol to clean components. Do not allow ABS

components to come into contact with any substance containing mineral oil; this includes used shop rags.
- The Anti-Lock control unit is a microprocessor similar to other computer units in the vehicle. Ensure that the ignition switch is **OFF** before removing or installing controller harnesses. Avoid static electricity discharge at or near the controller.
- If any arc welding is to be done on the vehicle, the control unit should be

unplugged before welding operations begin.

WHEEL SPEED SENSORS

REMOVAL & INSTALLATION

The wheel speed sensors are integral to the hub and bearing assemblies. Refer to the Wheel Hub and Bearing procedures in the Suspension section.

BRAKES

BLEEDING THE BRAKE SYSTEM

BLEEDING PROCEDURE

BLEEDING PROCEDURE

Manual Procedure

➡**When adding fluid to the brake master cylinder reservoir, use only Delco Supreme 11®, GM P/N 12377967 (Canadian P/N 992667), or equivalent DOT-3 brake fluid from a clean, sealed brake fluid container. The use of any type of fluid other than the recommended type of brake fluid, may cause contamination which could result in damage to the internal rubber seals and/or rubber linings of hydraulic brake system components.**

1. Place a clean shop cloth beneath the brake master cylinder to prevent brake fluid spills. With the ignition **OFF** and the brakes cool, apply the brakes 3–5 times, or until the brake pedal effort increases significantly, in order to deplete the brake booster power reserve.
2. If you have performed a brake master cylinder bench bleeding on this vehicle, or if you disconnected the brake pipes from the master cylinder, you must perform the following steps:
   - Ensure that the brake master cylinder reservoir is full to the maximum-fill level. If necessary, add Delco Supreme 11®, GM P/N 12377967 (Canadian P/N 992667), or equivalent DOT-3 brake fluid from a clean, sealed brake fluid container. If removal of the reservoir cap and diaphragm is necessary, clean the outside of the reservoir on and around the cap prior to removal.
   - With the rear brake pipe installed securely to the master cylinder, loosen and separate the front brake pipe from the front port of the brake master cylinder.
   - Allow a small amount of brake fluid

to gravity bleed from the open port of the master cylinder.
   - Reconnect the brake pipe to the master cylinder port and tighten securely.
   - Have an assistant slowly depress the brake pedal fully and maintain steady pressure on the pedal.
   - Loosen the same brake pipe to purge air from the open port of the master cylinder.
   - Tighten the brake pipe, then have the assistant slowly release the brake pedal.
   - Wait 15 seconds, then repeat steps 3.3–3.7 until all air is purged from the same port of the master cylinder.
   - With the front brake pipe installed securely to the master cylinder, after all air has been purged from the front port of the master cylinder, loosen and separate the rear brake pipe from the master cylinder, then repeat steps 3.3–3.8.
   - After completing the final master cylinder port bleeding procedure, ensure that both of the brake pipe-to-master cylinder fittings are properly tightened.

3. Fill the brake master cylinder reservoir with Delco Supreme 11®, GM P/N 12377967 (Canadian P/N 992667), or equivalent DOT-3 brake fluid from a clean, sealed brake fluid container. Ensure that the brake master cylinder reservoir remains at least half-full during this bleeding procedure. Add fluid as needed to maintain the proper level. Clean the outside of the reservoir on and around the reservoir cap prior to removing the cap and diaphragm.
4. Install a proper box-end wrench onto the RIGHT REAR wheel hydraulic circuit bleeder valve.
5. Install a transparent hose over the end of the bleeder valve.

6. Submerge the open end of the transparent hose into a transparent container partially filled with Delco Supreme 11®, GM P/N 12377967 (Canadian P/N 992667), or equivalent DOT-3 brake fluid from a clean, sealed brake fluid container.
7. Have an assistant slowly depress the brake pedal fully and maintain steady pressure on the pedal.
8. Loosen the bleeder valve to purge air from the wheel hydraulic circuit.
9. Tighten the bleeder valve, then have the assistant slowly release the brake pedal.
10. Wait 15 seconds, then repeat steps 8–10 until all air is purged from the same wheel hydraulic circuit.
11. With the right rear wheel hydraulic circuit bleeder valve tightened securely, after all air has been purged from the right rear hydraulic circuit, install a proper box-end wrench onto the LEFT FRONT wheel hydraulic circuit bleeder valve.
12. Install a transparent hose over the end of the bleeder valve, then repeat steps 7–11.
13. With the left front wheel hydraulic circuit bleeder valve tightened securely, after all air has been purged from the left front hydraulic circuit, install a proper box-end wrench onto the LEFT REAR wheel hydraulic circuit bleeder valve.
14. Install a transparent hose over the end of the bleeder valve, then repeat steps 7–11.
15. With the left rear wheel hydraulic circuit bleeder valve tightened securely, after all air has been purged from the left rear hydraulic circuit, install a proper box-end wrench onto the RIGHT FRONT wheel hydraulic circuit bleeder valve.
16. Install a transparent hose over the end of the bleeder valve, then repeat steps 7–11.
17. After completing the final wheel hydraulic circuit bleeding procedure, ensure that each of the 4 wheel hydraulic circuit bleeder valves are properly tightened.

18. Fill the brake master cylinder reservoir to the maximum-fill level with Delco Supreme 11®, GM P/N 12377967 (Canadian P/N 992667), or equivalent DOT-3 brake fluid from a clean, sealed brake fluid container.

19. Slowly depress and release the brake pedal. Observe the feel of the brake pedal.

➡**If it is determined that air was inducted into the system upstream of the ABS modulator prior to servicing, the ABS Automated Bleed Procedure must be performed.**

20. If the brake pedal feels spongy, repeat the bleeding procedure again. If the brake pedal still feels spongy after repeating the bleeding procedure, perform the following steps:

21. Inspect the brake system for external leaks and pressure bleed the hydraulic brake system in order to purge any air that may still be trapped in the system.

22. Turn the ignition key **ON**, with the engine **OFF**. Check to see if the brake system warning lamp remains illuminated.

➡**DO NOT allow the vehicle to be driven until it is diagnosed and repaired.**

Pressure Procedure

➡ **When adding fluid to the brake master cylinder reservoir, use only Delco Supreme 11®, GM P/N 12377967 (Canadian P/N 992667), or equivalent DOT-3 brake fluid from a clean, sealed brake fluid container. The use of any type of fluid other than the recommended type of brake fluid, may cause contamination which could result in damage to the internal rubber seals and/or rubber linings of hydraulic brake system components.**

1. Place a clean shop cloth beneath the brake master cylinder to prevent brake fluid spills.

2. With the ignition **OFF** and the brakes cool, apply the brakes 3–5 times, or until the brake pedal effort increases significantly, in order to deplete the brake booster power reserve.

3. If you have performed a brake master cylinder bench bleeding on this vehicle, or if you disconnected the brake pipes from the master cylinder, you must perform the following steps:

- Ensure that the brake master cylinder reservoir is full to the maximum-fill level. If necessary, add Delco Supreme 11®, GM P/N 12377967 (Canadian P/N 992667), or equivalent DOT-3 brake fluid

from a clean, sealed brake fluid container. If removal of the reservoir cap and diaphragm is necessary, clean the outside of the reservoir on and around the cap prior to removal.

- With the rear brake pipe installed securely to the master cylinder, loosen and separate the front brake pipe from the front port of the brake master cylinder.

- Allow a small amount of brake fluid to gravity bleed from the open port of the master cylinder.

- Reconnect the brake pipe to the master cylinder port and tighten securely.

- Have an assistant slowly depress the brake pedal fully and maintain steady pressure on the pedal.

- Loosen the same brake pipe to purge air from the open port of the master cylinder.

- Tighten the brake pipe, then have the assistant slowly release the brake pedal.

- Wait 15 seconds, then repeat steps 3.3–3.7 until all air is purged from the same port of the master cylinder.

- With the front brake pipe installed securely to the master cylinder, after all air has been purged from the front port of the master cylinder, loosen and separate the rear brake pipe from the master cylinder, then repeat steps 3.3–3.8.

- After completing the final master cylinder port bleeding procedure, ensure that both of the brake pipe-to-master cylinder fittings are properly tightened.

4. Fill the brake master cylinder reservoir to the maximum-fill level with Delco Supreme 11®, GM P/N 12377967 (Canadian P/N 992667), or equivalent DOT-3 brake fluid from a clean, sealed brake fluid container. Clean the outside of the reservoir on and around the reservoir cap prior to removing the cap and diaphragm.

5. Install the J 35589-A to the brake master cylinder reservoir.

6. Check the brake fluid level in the J 29532 , or equivalent. Add Delco Supreme 11®, GM P/N 12377967 (Canadian P/N 992667), or equivalent DOT-3 brake fluid from a clean, sealed brake fluid container as necessary to bring the level to approximately the half-full point.

7. Connect the J 29532 , or equivalent, to the J 35589-A .

8. Charge the J 29532 , or equivalent, air tank to 25–30 psi (175–205 kPa).

9. Open the J 29532 , or equivalent, fluid tank valve to allow pressurized brake fluid to enter the brake system.

10. Wait approximately 30 seconds, then inspect the entire hydraulic brake system in order to ensure that there are no existing external brake fluid leaks. Any brake fluid leaks identified require repair prior to completing this procedure.

11. Install a proper box-end wrench onto the RIGHT REAR wheel hydraulic circuit bleeder valve.

12. Install a transparent hose over the end of the bleeder valve.

13. Submerge the open end of the transparent hose into a transparent container partially filled with Delco Supreme 11®, GM P/N 12377967 (Canadian P/N 992667), or equivalent DOT-3 brake fluid from a clean, sealed brake fluid container.

14. Loosen the bleeder valve to purge air from the wheel hydraulic circuit. Allow fluid to flow until air bubbles stop flowing from the bleeder, then tighten the bleeder valve.

15. With the right rear wheel hydraulic circuit bleeder valve tightened securely, after all air has been purged from the right rear hydraulic circuit, install a proper box-end wrench onto the LEFT FRONT wheel hydraulic circuit bleeder valve.

16. Install a transparent hose over the end of the bleeder valve, then repeat steps 13–14.

17. With the left front wheel hydraulic circuit bleeder valve tightened securely, after all air has been purged from the left front hydraulic circuit, install a proper box-end wrench onto the LEFT REAR wheel hydraulic circuit bleeder valve.

18. Install a transparent hose over the end of the bleeder valve, then repeat steps 13–14. With the left rear wheel hydraulic circuit bleeder valve tightened securely, after all air has been purged from the left rear hydraulic circuit, install a proper box-end wrench onto the RIGHT FRONT wheel hydraulic circuit bleeder valve

19. Install a transparent hose over the end of the bleeder valve, then repeat steps 13–14.

20. After completing the final wheel hydraulic circuit bleeding procedure, ensure that each of the 4 wheel hydraulic circuit bleeder valves are properly tightened.

21. Close the J 29532 , or equivalent, fluid tank valve, then disconnect the J 29532 , or equivalent, from the J 35589-A .

22. Remove the J 35589-A from the brake master cylinder reservoir.

23. Fill the brake master cylinder reservoir to the maximum-fill level with Delco

Supreme 11®, GM P/N 12377967 (Canadian P/N 992667), or equivalent DOT-3 brake fluid from a clean, sealed brake fluid container.

24. Slowly depress and release the brake pedal. Observe the feel of the brake pedal.

➡**If it is determined that air was inducted into the system upstream of the ABS modulator prior to servicing, the ABS Automated Bleed Procedure must be performed.**

25. If the brake pedal feels spongy, perform the following steps:

26. Inspect the brake system for external leaks.

27. Using a scan tool, perform the antilock brake system automated bleeding procedure to remove any air that may have been trapped in the BPMV.

28. Turn the ignition key **ON**, with the engine **OFF**. Check to see if the brake system warning lamp remains illuminated.

➡**DO NOT allow the vehicle to be driven until it is diagnosed and repaired.**

Master Cylinder Bench Bleeding Procedure

See Figure 1.

➡**When adding fluid to the brake master cylinder reservoir, use only Delco Supreme 11®, GM P/N 12377967 (Canadian P/N 992667), or equivalent DOT-3 brake fluid from a clean, sealed brake fluid container. The use of any type of fluid other than the recommended type of brake fluid, may cause contamination which could result in damage to the internal rubber seals and/or rubber linings of hydraulic brake system components.**

1. Secure the mounting flange of the brake master cylinder in a bench vise so that the rear of the primary piston is accessible.

2. Remove the master cylinder reservoir cap and diaphragm.

3. Install suitable fittings to the master cylinder ports that match the type of flare seat required and also provide for hose attachment.

4. Install transparent hoses to the fittings installed to the master cylinder ports, then route the hoses into the master cylinder reservoir.

5. Fill the master cylinder reservoir to at least the half-way point with Delco Supreme 11®, GM P/N 12377967 (Canadian P/N 992667), or equivalent DOT-3 brake fluid from a clean, sealed brake fluid container.

6. Ensure that the ends of the transparent hoses running into the master cylinder reservoir are fully submerged in the brake fluid.

7. Using a smooth, round-ended tool, depress and release the primary piston as far as it will travel, a depth of about 25 mm (1 in), several times. Observe the flow of fluid coming from the ports.

➡**As air is bled from the primary and secondary pistons, the effort required to depress the primary piston will increase and the amount of travel will decrease.**

8. Continue to depress and release the primary piston until fluid flows freely from the ports with no evidence of air bubbles.

9. Remove the transparent hoses from the master cylinder reservoir.

10. Install the master cylinder reservoir cap and diaphragm.

11. Remove the fittings with the transparent hoses from the master cylinder ports. Wrap the master cylinder with a clean shop cloth to prevent brake fluid spills.

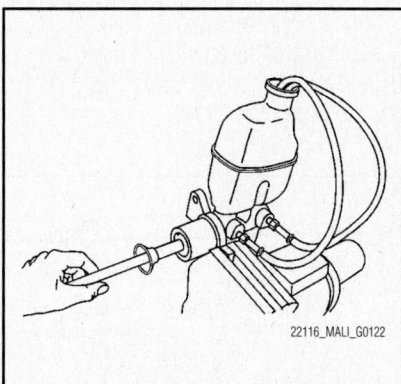

22116_MALI_G0122

Fig. 1 Master cylinder bench bleeding

12. Remove the master cylinder from the vise.

BLEEDING THE ABS SYSTEM

➡**The Auto Bleed Procedure may be terminated at any time during the process by pressing the EXIT button. No further Scan Tool prompts pertaining to the Auto Bleed procedure will be given. After exiting the bleed procedure, relieve bleed pressure and disconnect bleed equipment per manufacturer's instructions. Failure to properly relieve pressure may result in spilled brake fluid causing damage to components and painted surfaces.**

1. Raise the vehicle on a suitable support.

2. Remove all four tire and wheel assemblies.

3. Inspect the brake system for leaks and visual damage.

4. Inspect the battery state of charge.

5. Install a scan tool.

6. Turn **ON** the ignition, with the engine **OFF**.

7. With the scan tool, establish communications with the EBCM. Select special functions. Select automated bleed from the special functions menu.

8. Bleed the base brake system.

9. Follow the scan tool directions until the desired brake pedal height is achieved.

10. If the bleed procedure is aborted, a malfunction exists. Perform the following steps before resuming the bleed procedure:

- If a DTC is detected, refer to Diagnostic Trouble Code (DTC) List — Vehicle , to diagnose the appropriate DTC.
- If the brake pedal feels spongy, perform the conventional brake bleed procedure again.

11. When the desired pedal height is achieved, press the brake pedal in order to inspect for firmness.

12. Remove the scan tool.

13. Install the tire and wheel assemblies.

14. Inspect the brake fluid level.

15. Road test the vehicle while inspecting that the pedal remains high and firm.

BRAKES   **FRONT DISC BRAKES**

BRAKE CALIPER

REMOVAL & INSTALLATION

See Figures 2 through 4.

1. Raise and safely support the vehicle.
2. Remove the wheel and tire assembly.
3. Install a large C-clamp over the body of the brake caliper (2) with the C-clamp ends against the rear of the caliper body and against the outer brake pad.
4. Tighten the C-clamp until the caliper piston is compressed into the caliper bore enough to allow the caliper to slide past the brake rotor.
5. Remove the C-clamp from the caliper.
6. Remove the brake hose-to-caliper bolt from the brake caliper.
7. Remove the brake hose from the brake caliper.
8. Remove and discard the 2 copper brake hose gaskets. These gaskets may be stuck to the brake caliper and/or the brake hose end. Cap or plug the opening in the brake caliper and the brake hose to prevent fluid loss and contamination.
9. Remove the brake caliper guide pin bolts.

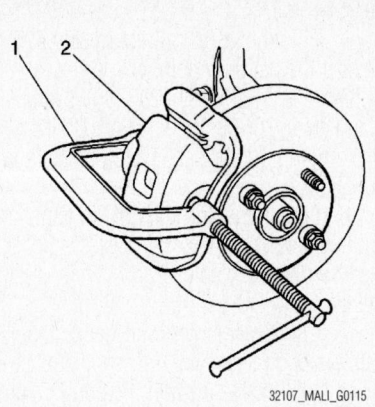

Fig. 2 Install a large C-clamp over the body of the brake caliper (2) with the C-clamp ends against the rear of the caliper body and against the outer brake pad

10. Remove the brake caliper from the caliper bracket.
11. Inspect the brake caliper guide pins for freedom of movement, and inspect the condition of the guide pin boots. Move the guide pins inboard and outboard within the bracket bores, without disengaging the slides from the boots, and observe for the following:
    - Restricted caliper guide pin movement
    - Looseness in the brake caliper mounting bracket
    - Seized or binding caliper guide pins
    - Split or torn boots
12. If any of the conditions listed are found, the brake caliper guide pins and/or boots require replacement.

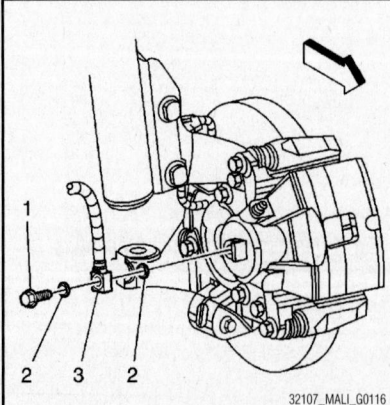

Fig. 3 Remove the brake hose-to-caliper bolt (1) from the brake caliper and the brake hose (3) from the brake caliper

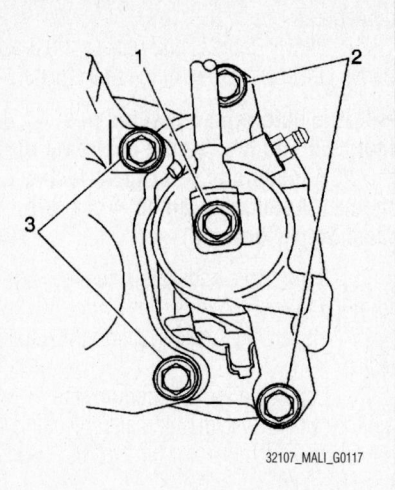

Fig. 4 Remove the brake caliper guide pin bolts

To install:

13. Install the brake caliper to the brake caliper bracket.
14. Install the brake caliper guide pin bolts, and tighten the bolts to 26 ft. lbs. (35 Nm).
15. Remove the caps or plugs from the brake caliper opening and the brake hose.

➡ **Do not reuse the copper brake hose gaskets.**

16. Install NEW copper brake hose gaskets to the brake hose-to-caliper bolt and to the brake hose.
17. Install the brake hose and the brake hose-to-brake caliper bolt to the brake caliper, and tighten the bolt to 37 ft. lbs. (50 Nm).
18. Bleed the hydraulic brake system.
19. Remove the wheel nuts retaining the brake rotor to the wheel hub.
20. Install the tire and wheel assembly.
21. Lower the vehicle.
22. With the engine **OFF**, gradually apply the brake pedal to approximately ⅔ of its travel distance.
23. Slowly release the brake pedal.
24. Wait 15 seconds, then repeat the steps until a firm brake pedal apply is obtained; this will properly seat the brake caliper piston and brake pads.

DISC BRAKE PADS

REMOVAL & INSTALLATION

See Figures 5 through 8.

1. Raise and safely support the vehicle.
2. Remove the wheel and tire assembly.

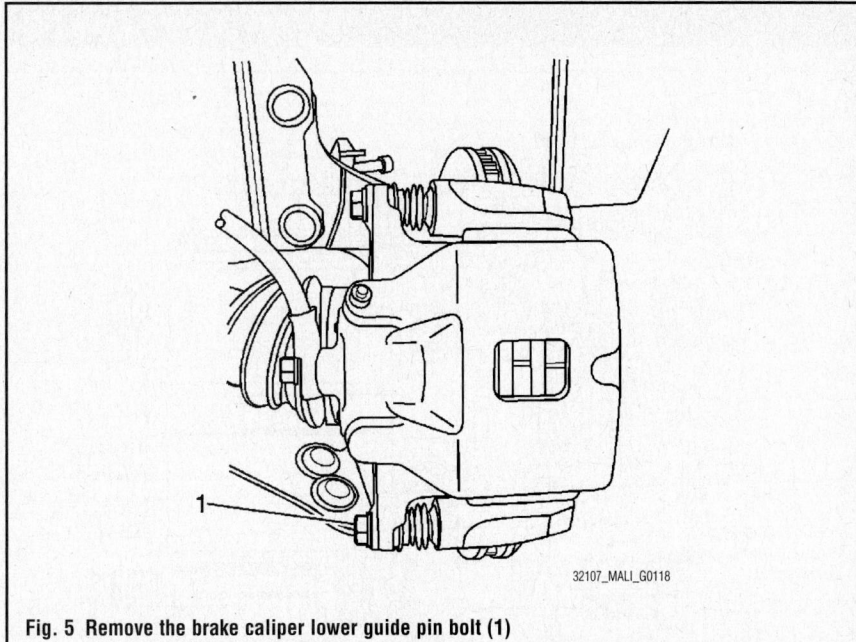

Fig. 5 Remove the brake caliper lower guide pin bolt (1)

3. Remove the brake caliper lower guide pin bolt.

4. Push the disc brake caliper piston into the caliper bore using an old inner disc brake pad and a disc brake piston installation tool.

➡ Support the brake caliper with heavy mechanic's wire, or equivalent, whenever it is separated from its mount and the hydraulic flexible brake hose is still connected. Failure to support the caliper in this manner will cause the flexible brake hose to bear the weight of the caliper, which may cause damage to the brake hose and in turn may cause a brake fluid leak.

5. Without disconnecting the hydraulic brake flexible hose, pivot the caliper upward and secure the caliper with heavy mechanics wire, or equivalent.

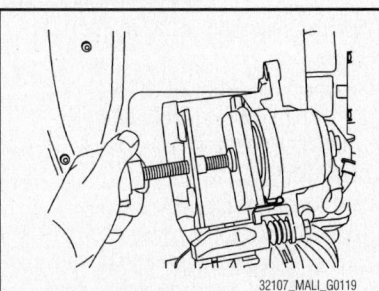

Fig. 6 Push the disc brake caliper piston into the caliper bore using an old inner disc brake pad and a disc brake piston installation tool

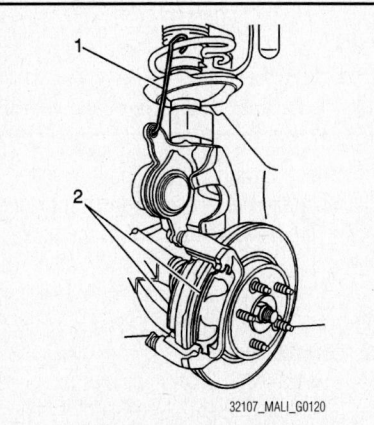

Fig. 7 Without disconnecting the hydraulic brake flexible hose, pivot the caliper upward and secure the caliper with heavy mechanics wire (1), or equivalent

6. Remove the brake pads from the caliper mounting bracket.

7. Remove the brake pad retainers from the caliper bracket.

8. Thoroughly clean the brake pad hardware mating surfaces of the caliper bracket, of any debris and corrosion.

9. Inspect the brake caliper guide pins for freedom of movement, and inspect the condition of the guide pin boots. Move the guide pins inboard and outboard within the bracket bores, without disengaging the slides from the boots, and observe for the following:
- Restricted caliper guide pin movement
- Looseness in the brake caliper mounting bracket

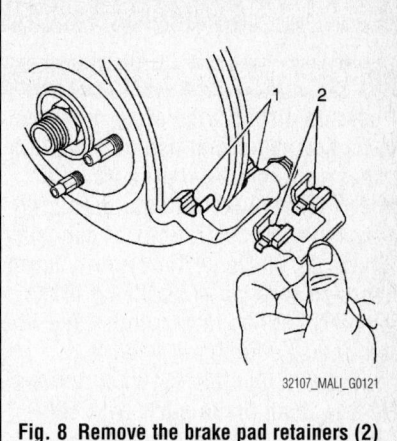

Fig. 8 Remove the brake pad retainers (2) from the caliper bracket (1)

- Seized or binding caliper guide pins
- Split or torn boots

10. If any of the conditions listed are found, the brake caliper guide pins and/or boots require replacement.

To install:
11. Ensure the brake pad hardware mating surfaces are clean.

12. Install the brake pad retainers to the brake caliper bracket.

➡ The wear sensor equipped disc brake pad must be mounted inboard of the rotor with the leading edge of the sensor facing the brake rotor during forward wheel rotation, or at the top of the pad when installed in vehicle position.

13. Install the brake pads to the caliper bracket.

14. Remove the support, and rotate the brake caliper into position over the disc brake pads and to the caliper mounting bracket.

15. Install the lower brake caliper guide pin bolt, and tighten the bolt to 26 ft. lbs. (35 Nm).

16. Remove the wheel nuts retaining the brake rotor to the hub.

17. Install the tire and wheel assembly.

18. Lower the vehicle.

19. With the engine **OFF**, gradually apply the brake pedal approximately ⅔ of its travel distance.

20. Slowly release the brake pedal.

21. Wait 15 seconds, then gradually apply the brake pedal approximately ⅔ of its travel distance again until a firm brake pedal apply is obtained. This will properly seat the brake caliper pistons and brake pads.

22. Fill the master cylinder auxiliary reservoir to the proper level.

23. Burnish the pads and rotors.

BRAKES

REAR DISC BRAKES

✳✳ CAUTION

Dust and dirt accumulating on brake parts during normal use may contain asbestos fibers from production or aftermarket brake linings. Breathing excessive concentrations of asbestos fibers can cause serious bodily harm. Exercise care when servicing brake parts. Do not sand or grind brake lining unless equipment used is designed to contain the dust residue. Do not clean brake parts with compressed air or by dry brushing. Cleaning should be done by dampening the brake components with a fine mist of water, then wiping the brake components clean with a dampened cloth. Dispose of cloth and all residue containing asbestos fibers in an impermeable container with the appropriate label. Follow practices prescribed by the Occupational Safety and Health Administration (OSHA) and the Environmental Protection Agency (EPA) for the handling, processing, and disposing of dust or debris that may contain asbestos fibers.

BRAKE CALIPER

REMOVAL & INSTALLATION

See Figures 9 through 11.

1. Raise and safely support the vehicle.
2. Remove the wheel and tire assembly.
3. Remove the brake hose to caliper bolt from the brake caliper.
4. Remove the brake hose from the brake caliper.

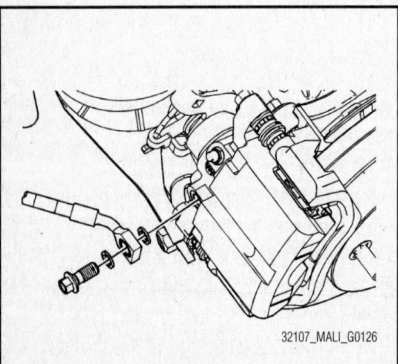

Fig. 9 Remove the brake hose to caliper bolt from the brake caliper

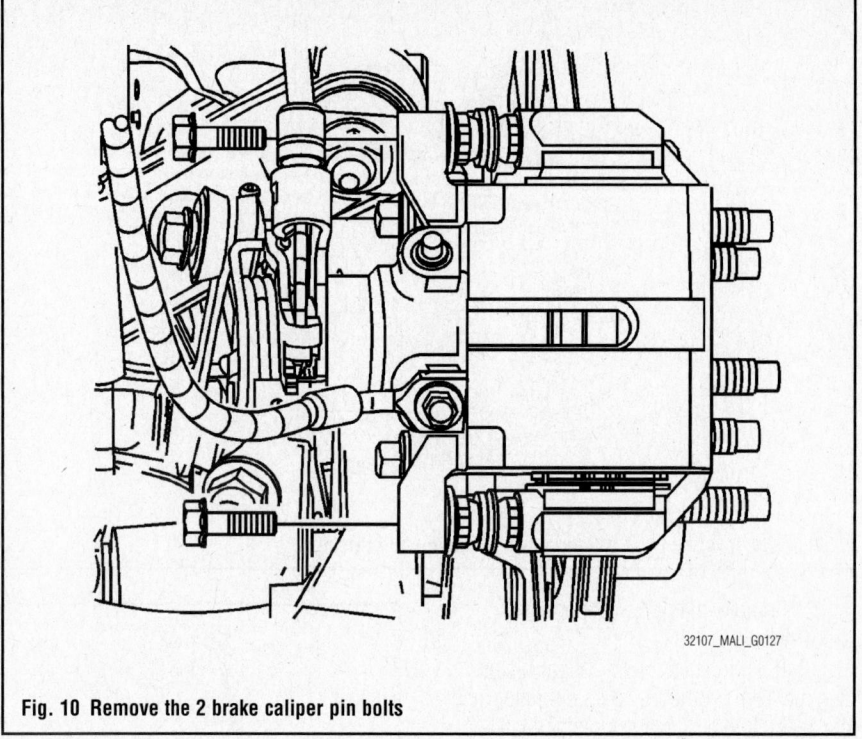

32107_MALI_G0127

Fig. 10 Remove the 2 brake caliper pin bolts

5. Remove and discard the 2 copper brake hose gaskets. These gaskets may be stuck to the brake caliper and/or the brake hose end.
6. Cap or plug the opening in the brake caliper and the brake hose to prevent fluid loss and contamination.
7. Remove the 2 brake caliper pin bolts.
8. Remove the park brake cable from the caliper.
9. Remove the brake caliper from the brake caliper bracket.

To install:

10. Inspect the caliper slide boots for cuts, tears, or deterioration. If damaged, replace the slides and boots.

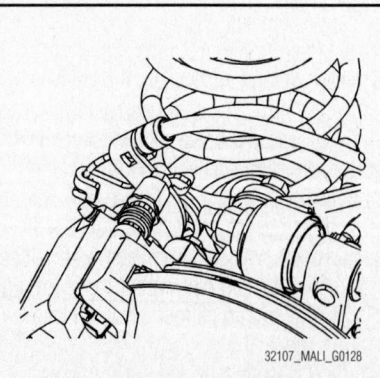

32107_MALI_G0128

Fig. 11 Remove the park brake cable from the caliper

11. Install the brake caliper to the brake caliper bracket.
12. Install the 2 brake caliper pin bolts, and tighten the brake caliper pin bolts to 26 ft. lbs. (35 Nm).
13. Install the park brake cable to the caliper.
14. Remove the caps or plugs from the brake caliper opening and the brake hose.

➡ **DO NOT reuse the copper brake hose gaskets.**

15. Install NEW copper brake hose gaskets to the brake hose-to-caliper bolt and to the brake hose.
16. Install the brake hose and the brake hose-to-caliper bolt to the brake caliper, and tighten the brake caliper bolt to 37 ft. lbs. (50 Nm).
17. Bleed the hydraulic brake system.
18. With the engine **OFF**, gradually apply the brake pedal to approximately ⅔ of its travel distance.
19. Slowly release the brake pedal.
20. Wait 15 seconds, then repeat steps 11 and 12 until a firm brake pedal apply is obtained; this will properly seat the brake caliper pistons and brake pads.
21. Install the tire and wheel assembly.
22. Lower the vehicle.
23. Apply and release the park brake pedal 4 times.

DISC BRAKE PADS

REMOVAL & INSTALLATION

See Figures 12 and 13.

1. Raise and safely support the vehicle.
2. Remove the wheel and tire assembly.
3. Remove the brake pads from the brake caliper mounting bracket.

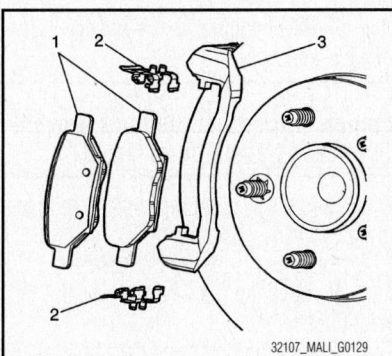

Fig. 12 Remove the brake pads (1) from the brake caliper mounting bracket (3)

4. Remove and the brake pad retainers from the brake caliper mounting bracket.

To install:

5. Inspect the following brake components for damage and corrosion:
   - Restricted caliper guide pin movement
   - Looseness in the brake caliper mounting bracket
   - Seized or binding caliper guide pins
   - Split or torn boots
6. Do not attempt to clean away any corrosion. If damaged or corroded replace the necessary components.
7. Inspect the brake caliper piston boot for deterioration, replace if damaged.
8. Use a piston installation tool in order to twist the brake caliper piston into the brake caliper bore.
9. Install the brake pad retainers to the brake caliper mounting bracket.
10. Install the brake pads to the brake caliper mounting bracket.
11. Pivot the brake caliper downward, over the brake pads and into the caliper bracket.
12. Install the brake caliper guide pin bolt to the brake caliper guide pin, and tighten the brake caliper guide pin bolt to 26 ft. lbs. (35 Nm).
13. Install the tire and wheel assembly.

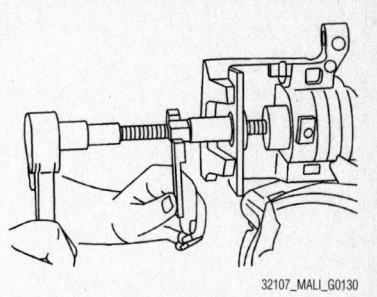

Fig. 13 Use a piston installation tool in order to twist the brake caliper piston into the brake caliper bore

14. Lower the vehicle.
15. With the engine **OFF**, gradually apply the brake pedal to approximately ⅔ of its travel distance.
16. Slowly release the brake pedal.
17. Wait 15 seconds, then repeat steps 15 and 16 until a firm brake pedal apply is obtained; this will properly seat the brake caliper pistons and brake pads.
18. Fill the brake master cylinder reservoir to the proper level.
19. Apply and release the park brake pedal 4 times.
20. Burnish the pads and rotors.

BRAKES

BRAKE DRUM

REMOVAL & INSTALLATION

2005–06 Models

See Figure 14.

✳ WARNING

Some models or aftermarket brake parts may contain asbestos fibers which can become airborne in dust. Breathing dust with asbestos fibers may cause serious bodily harm. Use a water-dampened cloth in order to remove any dust on brake parts. Equipment is available commercially in order to perform this washing function. These wet methods prevent fibers from becoming airborne.

1. Before servicing the vehicle, refer to the Precautions Section.
2. Check to ensure that the park brake is fully released.
3. Raise and support the vehicle.
4. Remove the tire and wheel assembly.

5. Remove the brake drum.
6. If the brake drum is to be reinstalled to the vehicle, use the J 41013 sanding disc in order to clean any rust or corrosion from the hub/flange mating surface of the brake drum.

To install:

7. If installing a new brake drum, use denatured alcohol or an equivalent approved brake cleaner and a clean shop towel to remove the protective coating from the friction surfaces
8. Adjust the drum brakes.

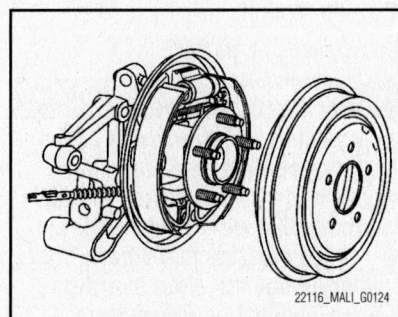

Fig. 14 Rear brake drum removal

REAR DRUM BRAKES

9. Install the brake drum.
10. Install the tire and wheel assembly.
11. Apply the brakes approximately three times in order to seat and center the brake shoes within the drum.
12. Lower the vehicle.

BRAKE SHOES

REMOVAL & INSTALLATION

2005–06 Models

See Figures 15 through 17.

✳ WARNING

Some models or aftermarket brake parts may contain asbestos fibers which can become airborne in dust. Breathing dust with asbestos fibers may cause serious bodily harm. Use a water-dampened cloth in order to remove any dust on brake parts. Equipment is available commercially in order to perform this washing function. These wet methods prevent fibers from becoming airborne.

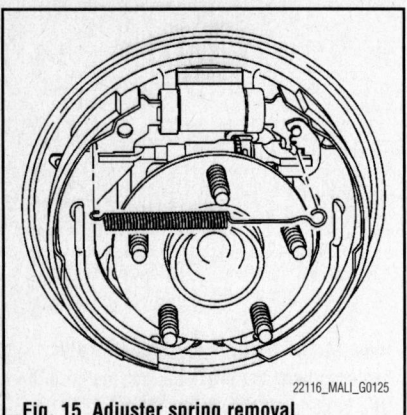

Fig. 15 Adjuster spring removal

1. Before servicing the vehicle, refer to the Precautions Section.

2. Raise and support the vehicle.

3. Remove the tire and wheel assembly.

4. Remove the brake drum.

5. Remove the adjuster spring.

6. Remove the adjuster actuator lever from the pivot.

7. Use the J 38400 to spread the top of the brake shoes to remove the adjuster assembly from the brake shoes.

8. Position the hook end of the J 38400 under the universal spring and lightly pull the universal spring end out of the shoe web hole. Hold the universal spring with the tool while removing the brake shoe.

9. Release the park brake cable from the park brake lever.

10. Position the hook end of the J 38400 under the universal spring and lightly pull the universal spring end out of the shoe web hole. Hold the universal spring with the tool while removing the brake shoe.

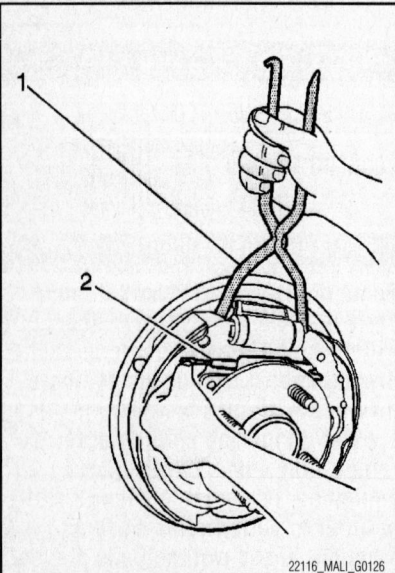

Fig. 16 J 38400 (1) used to spread the top of the brake shoes

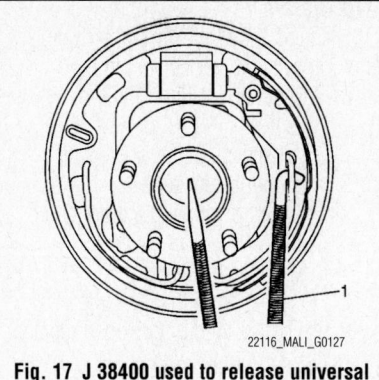

Fig. 17 J 38400 used to release universal spring

To install:

11. Apply a thin, light coat of high temperature silicone brake lubricant to the contact surfaces of the right and left brake backing plates.

12. Position the hook end of the J 38400 under the universal spring and lightly pull the universal spring end out while installing the trailing brake shoe. Ensure that the universal spring properly engages the brake shoe web hole.

13. Position the hook end of the J 38400 under the universal spring and lightly pull the universal spring end out while installing the trailing brake shoe. Ensure that the universal spring properly engages the brake shoe web hole.

14. Install the park brake cable to the park brake lever on the brake shoe.

15. Use the J 38400 to spread the top of the brake shoes to install the adjuster assembly.

16. Install the adjuster actuator lever to the pivot.

17. Install the adjuster spring.

18. Adjust the drum brake system.

19. Install the brake drum.

20. Install the tire and wheel assembly.

21. Lower the vehicle.

ADJUSTMENT

2005–06 Models

See Figures 18 through 20.

⁎⁎ WARNING

Some models or aftermarket brake parts may contain asbestos fibers which can become airborne in dust. Breathing dust with asbestos fibers may cause serious bodily harm. Use a water-dampened cloth in order to remove any dust on brake parts. Equipment is available commercially in order to perform this washing

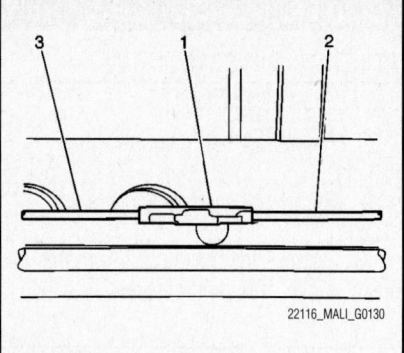

Fig. 18 Parking brake cables and connector

function. These wet methods prevent fibers from becoming airborne.

1. Before servicing the vehicle, refer to the Precautions Section.

2. Raise and support the vehicle.

3. Remove the rear tire and wheel assemblies.

4. Ensure that the park brake lever is in the fully released position.

5. Pull down on the front cable and disconnect the short cable leading to the drum backing plate from the cable connector. Do this step for both sides of the vehicle in order to ensure no cable drag is present.

6. Remove the rear brake drums.

7. Position the J 21177-A clearance gage to widest point of the brake drum inside diameter.

8. Firmly hand tighten the set screw on the J 21177-A.

9. Remove the J 21177-A from the brake drum and position it over the corresponding brake shoe assembly at its widest point.

10. While holding the J 21177-A in position, insert a 0.025 inch. (0.635 mm) feeler gage between one side of the J 21177-A, and the corresponding brake shoe.

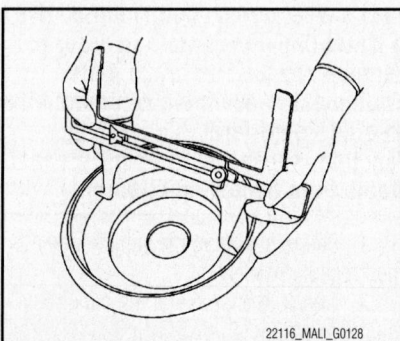

Fig. 19 Positioning the J 21177-A to the widest point of the brake drum inside diameter

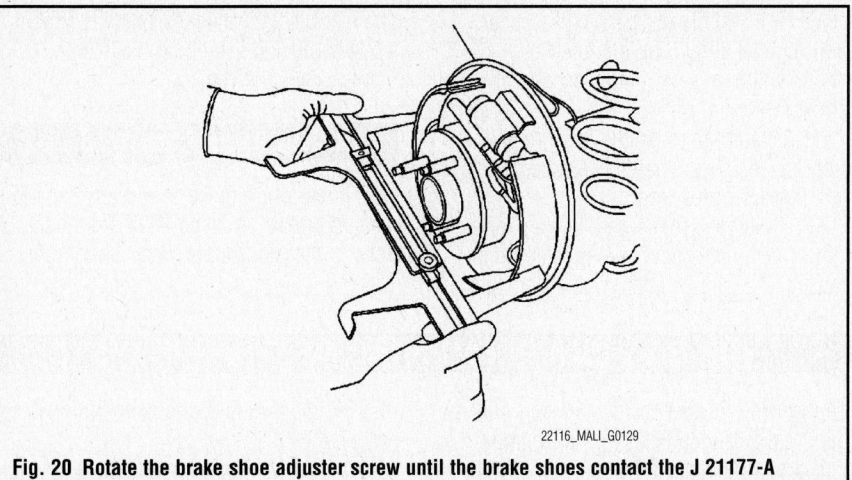

Fig. 20 Rotate the brake shoe adjuster screw until the brake shoes contact the J 21177-A

11. Rotate the brake shoe adjuster screw until the brake shoes contact the J 21177-A, and the feeler gage.

➡**Brake shoe-to-drum clearance: 0.025 inch. (0.635 mm)**

12. Repeat the above steps for the opposite brake drum and brake shoe assembly.

13. Install the brake drums.

14. Pull down on the front cable and connect the short cable leading to the drum backing plate to the cable connector. Repeat for opposite side.

15. Adjust the park brake.

16. Install the rear tire and wheel assemblies.

17. Lower the vehicle.

| BRAKES | | PARKING BRAKE |

PARKING BRAKE CABLES

ADJUSTMENT

2005–06 Models with Drum Brakes

➡**This vehicle utilizes a self-tensioning, or self-adjusting park brake cable system. The park brake system does not require adjustment under normal operating conditions. The tension on the park brake cables can be disabled and enabled when necessary during service of the drum brakes and/or the park brake system.**

✱✱ WARNING

Some models or aftermarket brake parts may contain asbestos fibers which can become airborne in dust. Breathing dust with asbestos fibers may cause serious bodily harm. Use a water-dampened cloth in order to remove any dust on brake parts. Equipment is available commercially in order to perform this washing function. These wet methods prevent fibers from becoming airborne.

1. Before servicing the vehicle, refer to the Precautions Section.

2. Apply and fully release the park brake several times. Verify that the park brake pedal releases completely.

3. Turn ON the ignition. Verify the red BRAKE warning lamp is not illuminated.

4. If the red BRAKE warning lamp is illuminated, verify the following:
   - The park brake pedal is in the fully released position and against the stop.

- There is no slack in the park brake cables.

5. If the red BRAKE warning lamp remained illuminated and there were no other visible causes, check hydraulic system.

6. Turn OFF the ignition.

7. Raise and support the vehicle just enough to allow the rear tires and wheel assembly removal and rear brake drum adjustment.

8. Remove the rear tire and wheel assemblies.

9. Adjust the rear drum brakes.

10. Ensure there is no brake shoe drag after adjustment by rotating the brake drums. If drag exists, re-center the brake shoes and perform the brake shoe adjustment again.

11. Install the rear tire and wheel assemblies.

12. Fully apply and release the park brake pedal 3–5 times in order for the cable tensioner to take up any slack in the park brake cables.

13. Fully apply the park brake pedal, a firm pedal should be obtained by depressing the pedal less than one full stroke.

14. Attempt to rotate the rear brake drums. There should be no rotation forward or rearward.

15. Fully release the park brake pedal.

16. Verify the park brake is released by rotating the rear brake drums. The drums should rotate freely and exhibit no brake shoe drag.

17. Lower the vehicle.

2005–08 Models with Rear Disc Brakes

➡**This vehicle utilizes a self-tensioning, or self-adjusting park brake cable**

system. The park brake system does not require adjustment under normal operating conditions. The tension on the park brake cables can be disabled and enabled when necessary during service of the disc brake and/or the park brake system.

✱✱ WARNING

Some models or aftermarket brake parts may contain asbestos fibers which can become airborne in dust. Breathing dust with asbestos fibers may cause serious bodily harm. Use a water-dampened cloth in order to remove any dust on brake parts. Equipment is available commercially in order to perform this washing function. These wet methods prevent fibers from becoming airborne.

1. Before servicing the vehicle, refer to the Precautions Section.

2. Apply and fully release the park brake several times. Verify that the park brake pedal releases completely.

3. Turn ON the ignition. Verify the red BRAKE warning lamp is not illuminated.

4. If the red BRAKE warning lamp is illuminated, verify the following:
   - The park brake pedal is in the fully released position and against the stop
   - There is no slack in the park brake cables.

5. If the red BRAKE warning lamp remained illuminated and there were no other visible causes, check hydraulic system.

6. Turn OFF the ignition.

7. Raise and support the vehicle.

8. With the park brake pedal fully released, check the park brake levers on the rear calipers. The levers should be against the stops on the caliper housings. If the levers are not against the stops, binding may exist. Repair as needed.

9. Fully apply and release the park brake pedal 3-5 times in order for the cable tensioner to take up any slack in the park brake cables.

10. Fully apply the park brake pedal, a firm pedal should be obtained by depressing the pedal less than one full stroke.

11. Attempt to rotate the rear tire and wheel assemblies. There should be no rotation forward or rearward.

12. Fully release the park brake pedal.

13. Verify the park brake is released by rotating the rear tire and wheel assemblies.

The rear tire and wheel assemblies should rotate freely and exhibit no brake drag.

14. Lower the vehicle.

PARKING BRAKE SHOES

The rear drum brake shoes serve as the parking brakes on some 2005–06 models. Refer to the procedures under Rear drum brakes.

CHASSIS ELECTRICAL

GENERAL INFORMATION

✳✳ CAUTION

These vehicles are equipped with an air bag system. The system must be disarmed before performing service on, or around, system components, the steering column, instrument panel components, wiring and sensors. Failure to follow the safety precautions and the disarming procedure could result in accidental air bag deployment, possible injury and unnecessary system repairs.

SERVICE PRECAUTIONS

Disconnect and isolate the battery negative cable before beginning any airbag system component diagnosis, testing, removal, or installation procedures. Allow system capacitor to discharge for two minutes before beginning any component service. This will disable the airbag system. Failure to disable the airbag system may result in accidental airbag deployment, personal injury, or death.

Do not place an intact undeployed airbag face down on a solid surface. The airbag will propel into the air if accidentally deployed and may result in personal injury or death.

When carrying or handling an undeployed airbag, the trim side (face) of the airbag should be pointing towards the body to minimize possibility of injury if accidental deployment occurs. Failure to do this may result in personal injury or death.

Replace airbag system components with OEM replacement parts. Substitute parts may appear interchangeable, but internal differences may result in inferior occupant protection. Failure to do so may result in occupant personal injury or death.

Wear safety glasses, rubber gloves, and long sleeved clothing when cleaning powder residue from vehicle after an airbag

AIR BAG (SUPPLEMENTAL RESTRAINT SYSTEM)

deployment. Powder residue emitted from a deployed airbag can cause skin irritation. Flush affected area with cool water if irritation is experienced. If nasal or throat irritation is experienced, exit the vehicle for fresh air until the irritation ceases. If irritation continues, see a physician.

Do not use a replacement airbag that is not in the original packaging. This may result in improper deployment, personal injury, or death.

The factory installed fasteners, screws and bolts used to fasten airbag components have a special coating and are specifically designed for the airbag system. Do not use substitute fasteners. Use only original equipment fasteners listed in the parts catalog when fastener replacement is required.

During, and following, any child restraint anchor service, due to impact event or vehicle repair, carefully inspect all mounting hardware, tether straps, and anchors for proper installation, operation, or damage. If a child restraint anchor is found damaged in any way, the anchor must be replaced. Failure to do this may result in personal injury or death.

Deployed and non-deployed airbags may or may not have live pyrotechnic material within the airbag inflator.

Do not dispose of driver/passenger/curtain airbags or seat belt tensioners unless you are sure of complete deployment. Refer to the Hazardous Substance Control System for proper disposal.

Dispose of deployed airbags and tensioners consistent with state, provincial, local, and federal regulations.

After any airbag component testing or service, do not connect the battery negative cable. Personal injury or death may result if the system test is not performed first.

If the vehicle is equipped with the Occupant Classification System (OCS), do not connect the battery negative cable before performing the OCS Verification Test using the scan tool and the appropriate diagnostic information. Personal injury or death may

result if the system test is not performed properly.

Never replace both the Occupant Restraint Controller (ORC) and the Occupant Classification Module (OCM) at the same time. If both require replacement, replace one, then perform the Airbag System test before replacing the other.

Both the ORC and the OCM store Occupant Classification System (OCS) calibration data, which they transfer to one another when one of them is replaced. If both are replaced at the same time, an irreversible fault will be set in both modules and the OCS may malfunction and cause personal injury or death.

If equipped with OCS, the Seat Weight Sensor is a sensitive, calibrated unit and must be handled carefully. Do not drop or handle roughly. If dropped or damaged, replace with another sensor. Failure to do so may result in occupant injury or death.

If equipped with OCS, the front passenger seat must be handled carefully as well. When removing the seat, be careful when setting on floor not to drop. If dropped, the sensor may be inoperative, could result in occupant injury, or possibly death.

If equipped with OCS, when the passenger front seat is on the floor, no one should sit in the front passenger seat. This uneven force may damage the sensing ability of the seat weight sensors. If sat on and damaged, the sensor may be inoperative, could result in occupant injury, or possibly death.

DISARMING THE SYSTEM

✳✳ CAUTION

The Supplemental Restraint System (SRS) must be disarmed before performing service procedures around the air bag or SRS wiring. Failure to do so may cause accidental deployment of the air bag, resulting in unnecessary SRS repairs and/or personal injury.

1. Disconnect the negative battery cable.
2. Turn the steering wheel so the vehicle's wheels are pointing straight-ahead.
3. Turn the ignition switch to the **LOCK** position.
4. Remove or disconnect the following:
   - Key
   - **AIR BAG** fuse from the fuse block
   - Left sound insulator
   - Connector retainer clip from the yellow 2-way connector at the base of the steering column
   - Connector retainer and yellow 2-way connector from the passenger air bag lead, if equipped with a passenger's side air bag

ARMING THE SYSTEM

1. Turn the ignition switch to the **LOCK** position and remove the key.
2. Install or connect the following:
   - Yellow 2-way connector at the base of steering column and the connector retainer clip
   - Yellow 2-way connector at the passenger air bag lead and secure it with the connector retainer clip, if equipped with a passenger's side air bag
   - Left sound insulator
   - **AIR BAG** fuse in the fuse block
3. Turn the ignition switch to the **RUN** position and verify that the **AIR BAG** warning lamp flashes 7 times, then turns **OFF**.
4. Connect the negative battery cable.

CLOCKSPRING CENTERING

See Figure 21.

1. Verify the following conditions before centering the Supplemental Inflatable Restraint (SIR) steering wheel module coil:
   - The wheels on the vehicle are straight ahead.
   - The block tooth and the centering mark of the steering shaft is in the 12 o'clock position.
2. If available, remove the yellow retaining tab from the SIR steering wheel module coil and save the tab for reassembly.
3. Hold the SIR steering wheel module coil face up by the casing.
4. Slowly turn the SIR steering wheel module coil hub (3) clockwise until the coil ribbon stops.

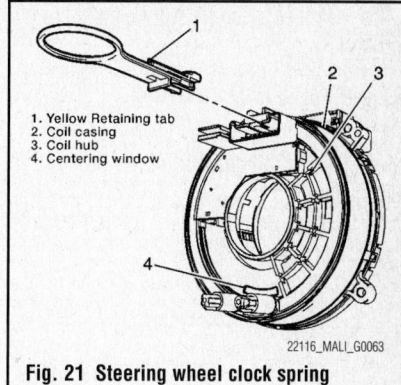

1. Yellow Retaining tab
2. Coil casing
3. Coil hub
4. Centering window

22116_MALI_G0063

Fig. 21 Steering wheel clock spring module

5. Slowly rotate the SIR steering wheel module coil hub (3) counterclockwise 2.5 revolutions until the centering window (4) turns yellow. This indicates the **CENTER** position.
6. If the retaining tab is not available, the use of tape to secure the SIR steering wheel module coil is recommended for installation to the steering column.
7. Slide the centered SIR steering wheel module coil onto the steering shaft.

DRIVETRAIN

AUTOMATIC TRANSAXLE ASSEMBLY

REMOVAL & INSTALLATION

4T40–E & 4T45–E Transaxles

2005–08 Models

1. Before servicing the vehicle, refer to the Precautions Section.
2. Drain the transmission fluid.
3. Remove the air intake duct from the throttle body and air cleaner assembly.
4. Remove the battery cover and disconnect the negative battery cable.
5. Disconnect the transaxle wiring harness from the transaxle and the Park/Neutral Position (PNP) switch.
6. Remove the shift cable bracket and shift cable from the lever.
7. Remove the transmission wiring harness from the retainer on the transmission.
8. Remove the upper transmission to engine bolts and stud.
9. Install the engine support fixture.
10. Support the radiator and condenser from above using the condenser tabs on each side.
11. Raise and support the vehicle.
12. Remove the front wheel and tire assemblies.
13. Remove the steering gear intermediate shaft .
14. Separate the control arm from the frame and the outer tie rod ends from the steering knuckles. Support the lower control arm with mechanics wire or a similar method.
15. Remove the frame.
16. Remove the 3 bolts from the transmission brace near the right axle shaft.
17. Remove the oil pan to bell housing bracket (3 bolts).
18. Remove the flywheel inspection cover.
19. Remove the starter.

➡**Mark the relationship of the flywheel to the torque converter for reassembly.**

20. Remove the torque converter to flywheel bolts.
21. Remove the transmission cooler lines by removing the nut holding the bracket to the transaxle case.
22. Disconnect the Vehicle Speed Sensor (VSS) wiring harness from the sensor.
23. Disconnect the rear 02 sensor harness from the bracket on the steering gear.
24. Disconnect the wheel drive shafts from the transaxle.
25. Remove the front transmission mount bracket from the transmission.
26. Use a transmission jack to support the transmission.
27. Remove the remaining bell housing bolts and studs and separate the transmission from the engine.
28. Lower the transmission with the transmission jack far enough to remove the transmission.
29. If the transmission is being replaced or installed in a holding fixture, remove the rear transmission mount bracket from transmission.
30. Remove the PNP switch from the transmission.

To install:

31. Install the PNP switch.
32. Install the Torque Converter Clutch (TCC) lock up clutch O—ring.
33. Install the torque converter.
34. Transfer the transaxle from the bench fixture to transmission jack.
35. Install the side cover transmission mount bracket to the transmission.
36. Install the rear transmission mount bracket to the transmission.
37. Position the transaxle in the vehicle.
38. Install the lower transmission to engine bolts and nuts and tighten to 66 ft. lbs. (90 Nm).
39. Install the front transmission mount bracket to the transmission.

40. Connect the wheel drive shafts to the transmission.

41. Connect the VSS wiring harness to the VSS.

42. Install the torque converter to flywheel bolts and tighten to 46 ft. lbs. (62 Nm).

43. Install the starter and tighten mounting bolts to 30 ft. lbs. (40 Nm). Tighten the cable to starter nut to 7 ft. lbs. (10 Nm).

44. Tighten solenoid S terminal nut to 4 ft. lbs. (5 Nm).

45. Install the flywheel inspection cover bolts and tighten to 89 inch. lbs. (10 Nm).

46. Connect the transaxle cooler pipes to the transaxle and tighten to 71 inch. lbs. (8 Nm).

47. Install the oil pan to bell housing bracket (3 bolts) and tighten to 53 ft. lbs. (72 Nm).

48. Install the 3 bolts to the transmission brace at final area and tighten to 53 ft. lbs. (72 Nm).

49. Remove the transmission jack.

50. Install the frame.

51. Install the engine splash shields.

52. Install the front wheel and tire assemblies.

53. Lower the vehicle.

54. Remove the radiator and condenser support, and the engine support fixture

55. Install the upper transmission to engine bolts and stud tighten to 66 ft. lbs. (90 Nm).

56. Install the shift cable bracket and shift cable to the lever.

57. Install the exhaust pipe upper bolts and heat shield.

58. Connect the electrical connectors to the PNP switch and transaxle.

59. Connect the negative battery cable.

60. Install the battery cover.

61. Install the air intake duct to the throttle body and air cleaner assembly.

62. Add approved Automatic Transmission Fluid (ATF) and verify the proper fluid level of transaxle.

63. Road test the vehicle.

4T65–E Transaxle

2006–07 Models

See Figure 22.

1. Before servicing the vehicle, refer to the Precautions Section.

2. Raise and support the vehicle.

3. Spray penetrating oil on the exposed threads of both lower ball joint bolt to facilitate their removal later in this procedure.

4. Lower the vehicle.

5. Remove the air cleaner outlet duct.

6. Disconnect the negative battery cable.

7. Disconnect the transaxle wiring harness from the transaxle and the Park Neutral Position (PNP) switch.

8. Remove the shift cable bracket and shift cable from the lever.

9. Remove the transmission wiring harness from the retainer on the transmission.

10. Remove the upper transmission to engine bolt and studs.

11. Install the engine support fixture.

12. Support the radiator and condenser from above using the condenser tabs on each side

13. Raise the vehicle.

14. Remove the front wheels and tires.

15. Remove the steering gear intermediate shaft .

16. Separate the control arm from the frame and the outer tie-rod end from the steering knuckles. Support the lower control arm with mechanic's wire.

17. Remove the frame.

18. Remove the bolts from the transmission brace near the right axle shaft.

19. Remove the oil pan to bellhousing bracket bolts.

20. Remove the flywheel inspection cover.

21. Remove the starter.

22. Mark the relationship of the flywheel to the torque converter for reassembly.

23. Remove the torque converter to flywheel bolts.

24. Remove the transmission oil cooler lines by removing the nut holding the bracket to the transaxle case.

25. Disconnect the Vehicle Speed Sensor (VSS) wiring harness from the sensor.

26. Disconnect the rear Heated Oxygen Sensor (HO2S) harness from the bracket on the steering gear.

27. Disconnect the wheel drive shafts from the transaxle.

28. Remove the front transmission mount from the transmission.

29. Use a transmission jack in order to support the transmission.

30. Remove the remaining bellhousing bolts and studs and separate the transmission from the engine.

31. Lower the transmission with the transmission jack far enough to remove the transmission.

32. If the transmission is being replace or installed in a holding fixture, remove the rear transmission mount from the transmission.

33. Remove the PNP switch from the transmission.

34. Remove the transaxle to engine bolts.

35. Separate the engine and the transaxle.

36. Remove the transaxle from the vehicle.

37. Remove the PNP switch.

38. Remove the shifter cable bracket.

39. Remove the lower transmission to engine stud.

40. Remove the left transmission mount bracket.

To install:

41. Install the PNP switch.

42. Install the Torque Converter Clutch (TCC) lock up clutch O-ring.

43. Install the torque converter.

44. Transfer the transaxle from the bench fixture to the transmission jack.

45. Install the left transmission mount bracket to the transmission.

46. Install the rear transmission mount to the transmission.

47. Position the transaxle in the vehicle.

48. Install the lower transmission to engine bolts and tighten to 66 ft. lbs. (90 Nm).

49. Install the front transmission mount to the transmission.

50. Install the wheel drive shafts to the transaxle.

51. Connect the wiring harness to the VSS.

52. Install the torque converter to flywheel bolts and tighten to 46 ft. lbs. (62 Nm).

53. Install the starter and tighten mounting bolts to 30 ft. lbs. (40 Nm). Tighten the cable to starter nut to 7 ft. lbs. (10 Nm).

54. Tighten solenoid S terminal nut to 4 ft. lbs. (5 Nm).

55. Install the flywheel inspection cover and tighten mounting bolts to 89 inch. lbs. (10 Nm).

56. Connect the transaxle oil cooler pipes to the transaxle and tighten to 71 inch. lbs. (8 Nm).

57. Install the oil pan to bellhousing bracket bolts and tighten to 53 ft. lbs. (72 Nm).

58. Install the bolts to the transmission brace at the final drive area and tighten.

59. Remove the transmission jack.

60. Install the frame.

61. Install the engine splash shields.

62. Install the front wheels and tires.

63. Lower the vehicle.

64. Remove the radiator and condenser support.

65. Remove the engine support fixture.

66. Install the upper transmission to engine bolt and studs. Tighten to 66 ft. lbs. (90 Nm).

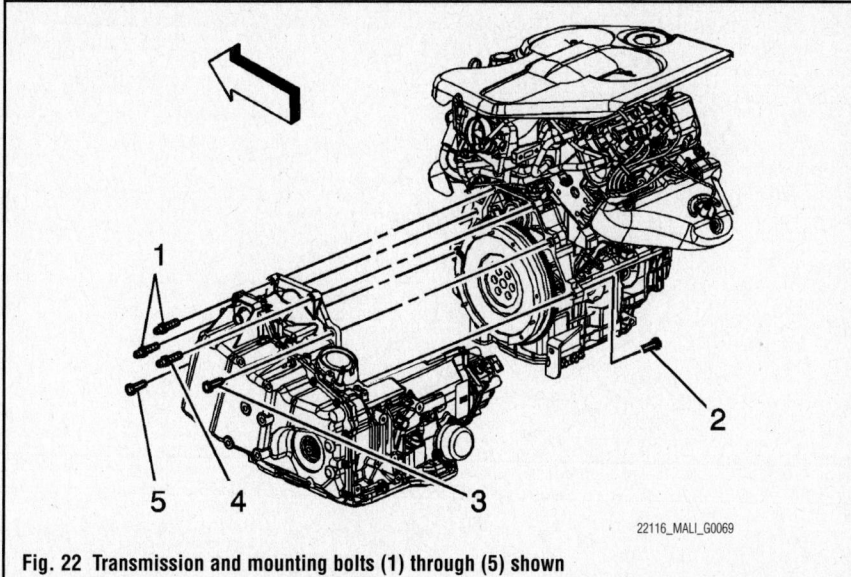

Fig. 22 Transmission and mounting bolts (1) through (5) shown

67. Install the shift cable bracket and shift cable to the lever.
68. Install the exhaust pipe upper bolts and heat shield.
69. Connect the electrical connectors to the PNP switch and transaxle.
70. Connect the negative battery cable.
71. Install the air cleaner outlet duct.

➡It is recommended that the Transmission Adaptive Pressure (TAP) information be reset. Resetting the TAP values using a scan tool will erase all learned values in all cells. As a result, the engine and or transmission control modules will need to relearn the TAP values. Transmission performance may be affected as new TAP values are learned.

72. Reset the TAP values.
73. Add approved Automatic Transmission Fluid (ATF) and verify the proper fluid level of the transaxle.
74. Road test the vehicle.

FRONT HALFSHAFTS

REMOVAL & INSTALLATION

See Figures 23 and 24.

1. Before servicing the vehicle, refer to the Precautions Section

➡Wheel drive shaft boots, seals and clamps should be protected from sharp objects any time service is performed on or near the wheel drive shaft(s). Damage to the boot(s), the seal(s) or the clamp(s) may cause lubricant to leak from the joint and lead to increased noise and possible failure of the wheel drive shaft.

2. Raise and suitably support the vehicle.
3. Remove the wheel and the tire.
4. Remove the front wheel drive shaft nut.
5. Remove the outer tie rod assembly from the steering knuckle.
6. Remove the ball joint from the steering knuckle
7. Using the J 42129 hub puller, remove the front wheel drive axle from the front wheel drive shaft bearing.
8. Using an approved axle removing tool, remove the wheel drive shaft from the vehicle.

To install:
9. Install the J 44394 seal protector into the differential output shaft seal.

⁂ WARNING

In order to prevent lubricant leaks, use care when installing the wheel drive shaft to the differential. Do not damage the oil seal. Replace the oil

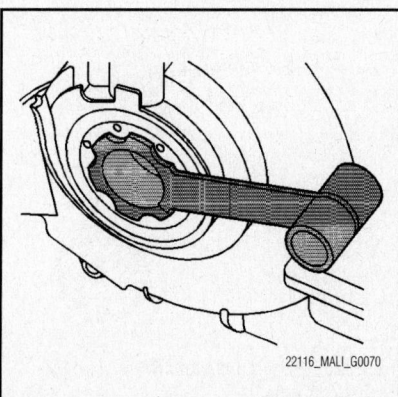

Fig. 23 Front wheel drive axle removal

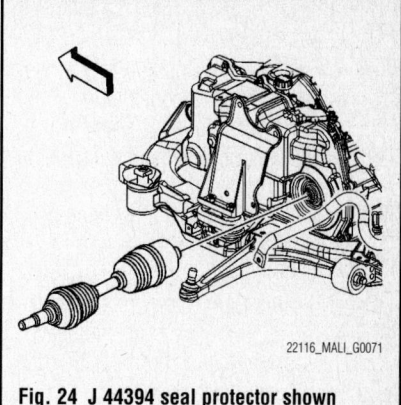

Fig. 24 J 44394 seal protector shown

seal if it becomes nicked, distorted, or otherwise damaged.

10. Carefully install the wheel drive shaft into the differential until the splines are past the J 44394.
11. Carefully remove the J 44394 from the differential output shaft seal.
12. Carefully continue installing the wheel drive shaft into the differential until the retaining ring is fully seated.
13. Verify the front wheel drive shaft retaining ring is properly seated:
   - Grasp the inner housing and pull the inner housing outward. Do not pull on the front wheel drive axle shaft.
   - The front wheel drive axle will remain in place when the front wheel drive shaft retaining ring is properly seated.
14. Install the front wheel drive shaft into the front wheel bearing.
15. Connect the ball joint to the steering knuckle.
16. Tighten the ball joint bolt and nut to 37 ft. lbs. (50 Nm). Reverse the nut 3/4 of a turn. Tighten to 37 ft. lbs. (50 Nm). plus 30°.
17. Connect the outer tie rod assembly to the steering knuckle. Tighten to 18 ft. lbs. (25 Nm) plus 90°.
18. Install a new wheel drive shaft nut. Insert a drift or a flat-bladed tool into the caliper and the rotor to prevent the rotor from turning.
19. Tighten the axle nut to 159 ft. lbs. (215 Nm).
20. Lower the vehicle.
21. Inspect the transaxle fluid level.

CV-JOINTS OVERHAUL

Outer CV-Joint

See Figures 25 through 27.

1. Before servicing the vehicle, refer to the Precautions Section.

2. Remove or disconnect the following:
- Front wheel
- Halfshaft and position it in a vise
- Large CV-joint boot clamp
- Small CV-joint boot clamp
- CV-joint boot and slide it back on the shaft
- Outer race from the halfshaft by spreading the outer race-to-half-shaft retaining ring
- Retaining ring from the halfshaft
- CV-joint boot from the halfshaft

3. Disassemble the chrome alloy balls from the CV-joint cage as follows:

a. Position a brass drift against the CV-joint cage and tap it with a hammer to tilt the cage.

b. Remove the 1st chrome alloy ball from the cage.

c. Tilt the cage in the opposite direction.

d. Remove the opposite chrome alloy ball.

e. Repeat the procedure until all 6 balls are removed.

4. Disassemble the CV-joint cage and inner race as follows:

a. Pivot the cage and race 90 degrees to the center line of the outer race.

b. Align the cage windows with outer race lands.

c. Remove the cage from the outer race.

d. Rotate the inner race upward and remove it from the cage.

To install:

5. Lubricate the parts with a light coat of grease.

6. Assemble the CV-joint cage and inner race, as follows:

a. Rotate the inner race 90 degrees to the cage centerline.

b. Align the cage windows with inner race lands.

c. Insert the inner race into the cage by rotating the inner race downward.

d. Insert the cage/inner race into the outer race.

7. Assemble the chrome alloy balls into the CV-joint cage, as follows:

a. Position a brass drift against the CV-joint cage and tap it with a hammer to tilt the cage.

b. Insert the 1st chrome alloy ball into the cage.

c. Tilt the cage in the opposite direction.

d. Insert the opposite chrome alloy ball.

e. Repeat the procedure until all 6 balls are inserted.

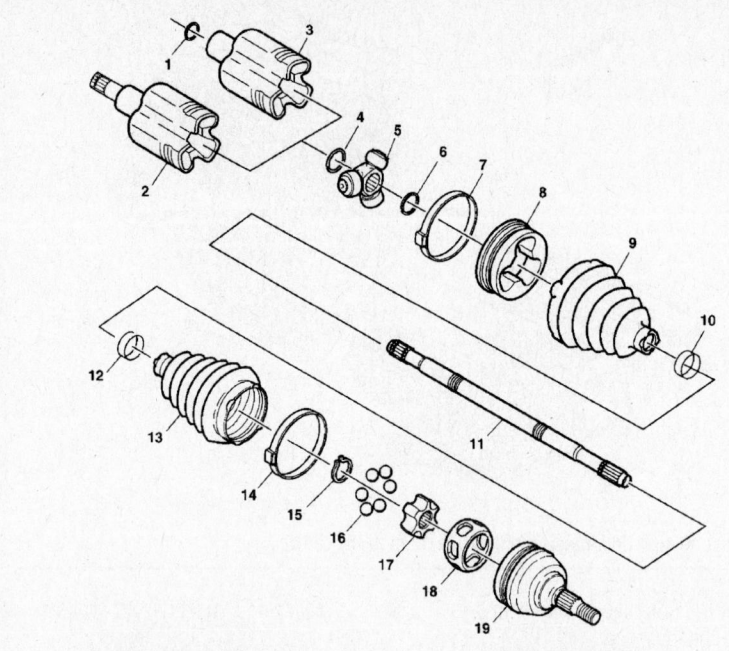

1. Retaining Ring
2. Housing Assembly
3. Retainer and Housing Assembly
4. Spacer Ring
5. Tripod Joint Spider Assembly
6. Spacer Ring (If Equipped)
7. Boot Retaining Clamp
8. Trilobal Tripod Bushing
9. Tripod Joint Boot
10. Swage Ring
11. Halfshaft Bar
12. Swage Ring
13. CV Joint Boot
14. Boot Retaining Clamp
15. Race Retaining Ring
16. Chrome Alloy Ball
17. CV Joint Inner Race
18. CV Joint Cage
19. CV Joint Outer Race

22116_MALI_G0072

Fig. 25 Exploded view of the halfshaft assemblies

8. Install ½ of the grease provided into the CV-joint.

9. Install or connect the following:
- Small ring clamp on the CV boot
- CV boot onto the halfshaft

10. Slide the small end of the CV-joint boot/clamp into place, with the seal lip in the halfshaft groove.

➡**Make sure the boot lies flat against the halfshaft.**

11. Using a Crimp tool, a torque wrench and a breaker bar, crimp the small CV-joint boot clamp to 100 ft. lbs. (136 Nm).

12. Install the remainder of the grease into the CV-joint boot.

13. Install or connect the following:
- New retaining ring on the halfshaft
- Outer race assembly onto the halfshaft until the ring engages the halfshaft groove
- Large ring clamp on the CV boot

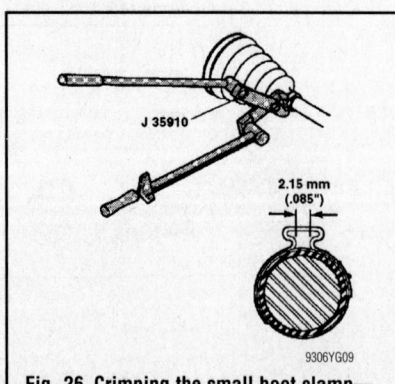

J 35910

2.15 mm (.085")

9306YG09

Fig. 26 Crimping the small boot clamp—Outer CV-joint

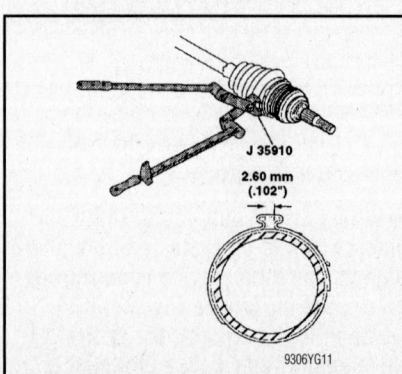

J 35910

2.60 mm (.102")

9306YG11

Fig. 27 Crimping the large boot clamp—Outer CV-joint

14. Using a Crimp tool, a torque wrench and a breaker bar, crimp the large CV-joint boot clamp to 130 ft. lbs. (176 Nm).

15. Install the halfshaft and the front wheel.

Inner (Tri-Pod) Joint

See Figure 28.

1. Before servicing the vehicle, refer to the Precautions Section.

2. Remove or disconnect the following:
   - Front wheel
   - Halfshaft and place it in a vise
   - Snapring from the stub shaft
   - Small CV-joint boot clamp
   - Large CV-joint boot clamp
   - CV-joint boot by sliding it away from the tri-pod joint

3. Install a Stub Shaft Removal Tool J-38868-A to the stub shaft snapring groove.

4. Using a slide hammer puller, pull the stub shaft from the tri-pod housing.

5. Remove or disconnect the following:
   - Tri-pod housing from the tri-pod spider
   - Inboard spacer ring slide it rearward on the shaft
   - Outboard retaining ring
   - Tri-pod joint spider assembly
   - Inboard spacer ring and discard it
   - CV-joint boot
   - Trilobal tri-pod bushing from the housing

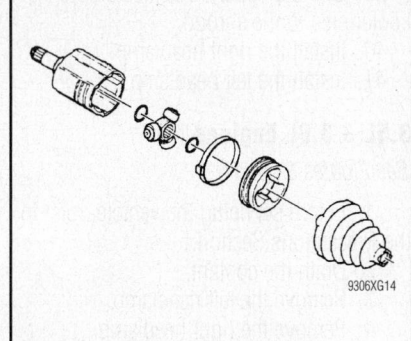

Fig. 28 Exploded view of the inner (tri-pod) joint

To install:

6. Install or connect the following:
   - New snapring onto the stub shaft
   - Small boot clamp
   - CV-joint boot

7. Using a Crimp tool, a torque wrench and a breaker bar, crimp the small CV-joint boot clamp to 100 ft. lbs. (136 Nm).

8. Install or connect the following:
   - Inboard spacer ring slide it rearward on the shaft beyond the second groove
   - Tri-pod joint spider assembly onto the shaft until it passes the 2nd groove
   - Outboard retaining ring into the axle shaft groove
   - Tri-pod joint spider assembly, slide it against the outboard retaining ring

- Inboard spacer ring, seat it in the groove
- ½ of the grease provided into the boot
- The remaining grease into the tri-pod housing
- Trilobal tri-pod bushing flush with the tri-pod housing face
- New large seal clamp onto the CV-joint boot
- Tri-pod housing, slide it over the tri-pod joint spider assembly
- CV-joint boot/clamp, slide it into place, over the trilobal tri-pod bushing with the seal lip in the groove

➡**Make sure the boot lies flat against the trilobal bushing.**

9. Using a Crimp tool, a torque wrench and a breaker bar, crimp the large CV-joint boot clamp to 130 ft. lbs. (176 Nm).

10. Check the clamp gap dimension; if it is not 0.085 in. (2.16mm), continue tightening the clamp until it is.

11. Install the halfshaft and the front wheel.

CV-BOOTS INSPECTION

1. Raise and support the vehicle.

2. Slowly turn drive wheels and inspect axles for the following:
   - Cracks or cuts on boots
   - Loose or missing clamps
   - Grease leaking from boot or clamp
   - Foreign material on axle or boot

3. Repair as needed.

ENGINE COOLING

ENGINE FAN

REMOVAL & INSTALLATION

2.2L Engine

See Figures 29 and 30.

1. Before servicing the vehicle, refer to the Precautions Section.

2. Remove the left headlamp.

3. Remove the right headlamp.

4. Unclip the upper transmission oil cooler pipe from the fan shroud. Do not disconnect transmission oil cooler pipe from transmission or radiator.

5. Loop a rope around each of the upper 2 tabs on the condenser and tie a rope around the upper tie bar.

6. Remove the upper radiator support bracket bolts.

7. Remove the upper radiator support brackets.

8. Pry upward on the fan shroud tabs at the radiator clips.

9. Raise the vehicle.

10. Remove the lower radiator air deflector retainers.

11. Remove the lower radiator air deflector.

12. Remove the right front fender liner.

13. Remove the right radiator air deflector retainers.

14. Remove the right radiator air deflector.

15. Remove the left radiator air deflector retainers.

16. Remove the left radiator air deflector.

17. Remove the lower radiator support bracket bolts.

18. Remove the lower radiator support brackets.

19. Remove the fan wire harness connectors.

20. Remove the fan shroud assembly.

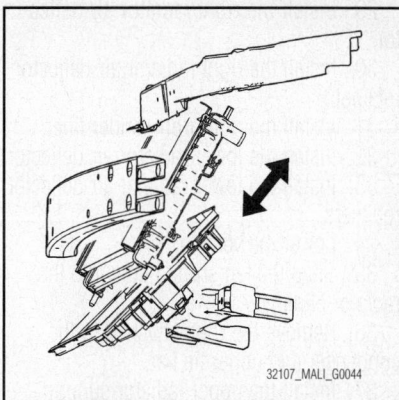

Fig. 29 Removal and installation of the fan

To install:

21. Install the fan shroud assembly.

22. Bend the radiator air side seals and insert the seals into the channel of the intake air splash shields.

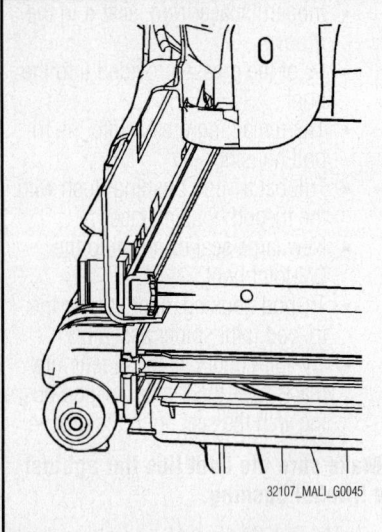

Fig. 30 Bend the radiator air side seals and insert the seals into the channel of the intake air splash shields

23. The radiator air side seals must be in the proper position for proper air flow.

24. Install the lower radiator support brackets.

25. Install the lower radiator support bracket bolts, and tighten the bolts to 44 ft. lbs. (60 Nm).

26. Install the fan wire harness connectors.

➡**Radiator air deflectors must be properly installed or reduced A/C and engine cooling system performance could occur.**

27. Install the left radiator air deflector.

28. Install the left radiator air deflector retainers.

29. Install the right radiator air deflector.

30. Install the right radiator air deflector retainers.

31. Install the right front fender liner.

32. Install the lower radiator air deflector.

33. Install the lower radiator air deflector retainers.

34. Lower the vehicle.

35. Snap the fan shroud tabs into the radiator clips.

36. Remove the rope attached to the condenser and upper tie bar.

37. Install the upper radiator support brackets.

➡**Do not allow the upper bracket to twist when tightening the screw or vibration may result.**

38. Install the upper radiator support bracket bolts, and tighten the bolts to 7 ft. lbs. (10 Nm).

39. Clip the upper transmission oil cooler pipe to the shroud.

40. Install the right headlamp.

41. Install the left headlamp.

3.5L & 3.9L Engines

See Figures 31 and 32.

1. Before servicing the vehicle, refer to the Precautions Section.

2. Drain the coolant.

3. Remove the left headlamp.

4. Remove the right headlamp.

5. Remove the upper transmission oil cooler pipe from the radiator.

6. Loop a rope around each of the upper 2 tabs of the condenser and tie a rope around the upper tie bar.

7. Remove the upper radiator support bracket bolts.

8. Remove the upper radiator support brackets.

9. Pry upward on the fan shroud tabs at the radiator clips.

10. Raise the vehicle.

11. Remove the lower radiator air deflector retainers.

12. Remove the lower radiator air deflector.

13. Remove the right front fender liner.

14. Remove the right radiator air deflector retainers.

15. Remove the right radiator air deflector.

16. Remove the left radiator air deflector retainers.

17. Remove the left radiator air deflector.

18. Reposition the radiator outlet hose clamp at the radiator using the special tool J38185.

19. Remove the radiator outlet hose from the radiator.

20. Remove the fan wire harness connectors.

21. Remove the lower radiator support bracket bolts.

22. Remove the lower radiator support brackets.

23. Place a drain pan under the transmission oil cooler pipes.

24. Remove the transmission oil cooler pipes attachment nut from the transmission.

25. Remove both transmission oil cooler pipes from the transmission.

26. Remove the transmission oil cooler pipe clip from the fan shroud.

27. Remove the lower transmission oil cooler pipe from the radiator.

28. Remove the transmission oil cooler pipes.

29. Remove the fan wire harness connectors.

30. Remove the fan shroud assembly.

To install:

31. Install the fan shroud assembly.

32. Install the transmission oil cooler pipes.

33. Install the lower transmission oil cooler pipe to the radiator.

34. Install the transmission oil cooler pipe clip to the fan shroud.

35. Install both transmission oil cooler pipes to the transmission.

36. Install the transmission oil cooler pipe attachment nut to the transmission, and tighten the nut to 62 lb inches (7 Nm).

37. Bend the radiator air side seals and insert the seals into the channel of the intake air splash shields.

38. The radiator air side seals must be in the proper position for proper air flow.

39. Install the lower radiator support brackets.

40. Install the lower radiator support bracket bolts, and tighten the bolts to 44 ft. lbs. (60 Nm).

41. Install the fan wire harness connectors.

42. Install the radiator outlet hose to the radiator.

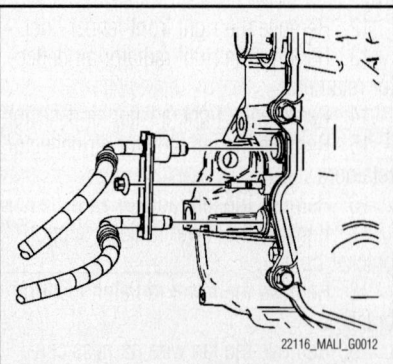

Fig. 31 Transmission oil cooler pipe and attachment nut

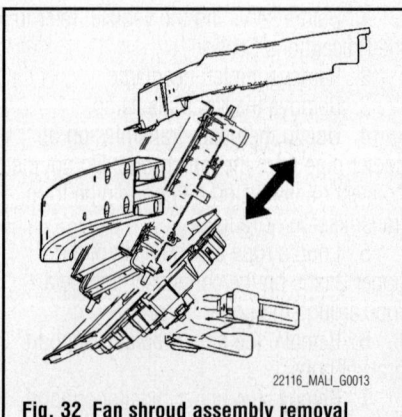

Fig. 32 Fan shroud assembly removal

43. Reposition the radiator outlet hose clamp at the radiator using the special tool J38185.

➡️**Radiator air deflectors must be properly installed or reduced A/C and engine cooling system performance could occur.**

44. Install the left radiator air deflector.
45. Install the left radiator air deflector retainers.
46. Install the right radiator air deflector.
47. Install the right radiator air deflector retainers.
48. Install the right front fender liner.
49. Install the lower radiator air deflector.
50. Install the lower radiator air deflector retainers.
51. Lower the vehicle.
52. Snap fan shroud tabs into the radiator clips.
53. Remove the rope attached to the condenser and upper tie bar.
54. Install the upper radiator support brackets.

➡️**Do not allow the upper bracket to twist when tightening the screw or vibration may result.**

55. Install the upper radiator support bracket bolts, and tighten the bolts to 89 lb inches (10 Nm).
56. Install the upper transmission oil cooler pipe to the radiator.
57. Install the right headlamp.
58. Install the left headlamp.
59. Fill the coolant.
60. Inspect the transmission fluid level.

RADIATOR

REMOVAL & INSTALLATION

2.2L Engine

See Figures 33 through 35.

1. Before servicing the vehicle, refer to the Precautions Section.
2. Drain the coolant.
3. Remove the left headlamp.
4. Remove the right headlamp.
5. Loop a rope around each of the 2 tabs of the condenser and tie the rope around the upper tie bar.
6. Remove the upper radiator support bracket bolts.
7. Remove the upper radiator support brackets.
8. Reposition the radiator outlet hose clamp at the radiator using the special tool J38185.

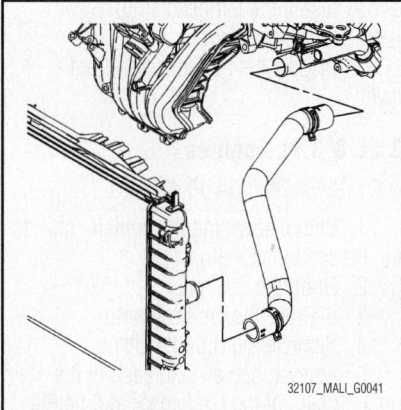

Fig. 33 Remove the radiator inlet hose from the radiator

9. Remove the radiator outlet hose from the radiator.
10. Reposition the radiator inlet hose clamp at the radiator using the special tool J38185.
11. Remove the radiator inlet hose from the radiator.
12. Raise the vehicle.
13. Remove the lower radiator air deflector retainers.
14. Remove the lower radiator air deflector.
15. Remove the right front fender liner.
16. Remove the right radiator air deflector retainers.
17. Remove the right radiator air deflector.
18. Remove the left radiator air deflector retainers.
19. Remove the left radiator air deflector.
20. Place a drain pan under the transmission oil cooler pipes.
21. Remove the transmission oil cooler pipes attachment nut from the transmission.
22. Remove the transmission oil cooler pipes from the transmission.
23. Remove the lower radiator support bracket bolts.

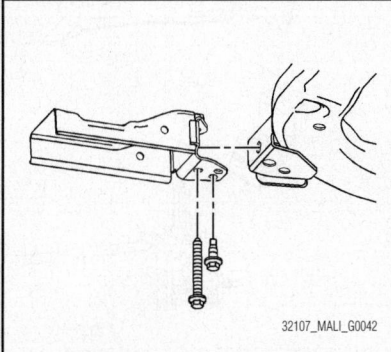

Fig. 34 Remove the lower radiator support brackets

24. Remove the lower radiator support brackets.
25. Remove the radiator lower mounts.
26. Remove and discard the condenser mounting bolts.
27. Push upward on the radiator and downward on the condenser to unsnap the condenser mounting tabs from the radiator clips.
28. Remove and discard the condenser mounting nuts from the radiator.
29. Remove the radiator air side seals.
30. Remove the radiator, cooling fan shroud and transmission oil cooler pipe assembly.
31. Remove the transmission oil cooler pipes from the radiator.
32. Pry upward on the fan shroud tabs at the radiator clips.
33. Remove the cooling fan and shroud assembly from the radiator.

To install:

34. Install the cooling fan and shroud assembly to the radiator.
35. Snap the fan shroud tabs into the radiator clips.
36. Install the transmission oil cooler pipes to the radiator.
37. Install the radiator, cooling fan shroud and transmission oil cooler pipe assembly.
38. Install the radiator air side seals onto the condenser mounting tabs on the radiator.

➡️**The bolt retaining the condenser to the radiator end tank is a special length and should be the only bolt used upon reinstallation. The use of a longer bolt will damage the radiator end tank.**

➡️**Replace the condenser mounting bolts and nuts.**

39. Install the condenser mounting nuts to the radiator.

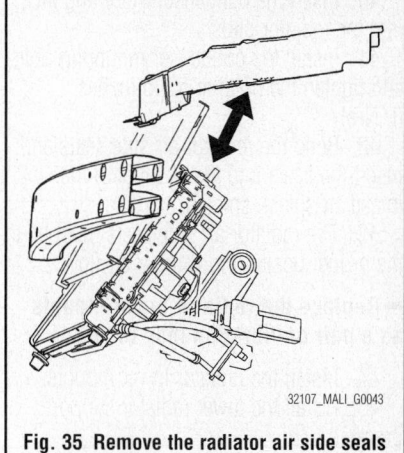

Fig. 35 Remove the radiator air side seals

40. Insert the condenser mounting tabs into the radiator clips.

41. Install the condenser mounting bolts, and tighten the bolts to 53 lb inches (6 Nm).

42. Bend the radiator air side seals and insert the seals into the channel of the intake air splash shields.

43. The radiator air side seals must be in the proper position for proper air flow.

➡ **Replace the radiator lower mounts as a pair or vibration may result.**

44. Install the radiator lower mounts.

45. Install the lower radiator support brackets.

46. Install the lower radiator support bracket bolts, and tighten the bolts to 44 ft. lbs. (60 Nm).

47. Install the transmission oil cooler pipes to the transmission.

48. Install the transmission oil cooler pipes attachment nut to the transmission, and tighten the nut to 62 lb inches (7 Nm).

➡ **Radiator air deflectors must be properly installed or reduced A/C and engine cooling system performance could occur.**

49. Install the left radiator air deflector.

50. Install the left radiator air deflector retainers.

51. Install the right radiator air deflector.

52. Install the right radiator air deflector retainers.

53. Install the right front fender liner.

54. Install the lower radiator air deflector.

55. Install the lower radiator air deflector retainers.

56. Lower the vehicle.

57. Install the radiator inlet hose to the radiator.

58. Reposition the radiator inlet hose clamp at the radiator using the special tool J38185.

59. Install the radiator outlet hose to the radiator.

60. Reposition the radiator outlet hose clamp at the radiator using the special tool J38185.

61. Remove the rope attached to the condenser and upper tie bar.

62. Install the upper radiator support brackets.

➡ **Do not allow the upper bracket to twist when tightening the screw or vibration may result.**

63. Install the upper radiator support bracket bolts, and tighten the bolts to 89 lb inches (10 Nm).

64. Install the right headlamp.

65. Install the left headlamp.

66. Fill the coolant.

67. Inspect the transmission fluid level.

3.5L & 3.9L Engines

See Figures 36 through 41.

1. Before servicing the vehicle, refer to the Precautions Section.

2. Drain the coolant.

3. Remove the left headlamp.

4. Remove the right headlamp.

5. Loop a rope around each of the upper 2 tabs of the condenser and tie the rope around the upper tie bar.

6. Remove the upper radiator support bracket bolts.

7. Remove the upper radiator support brackets.

8. Reposition the surge tank outlet hose clamp at the radiator using the special tool J38185.

9. Remove the surge tank outlet hose from the radiator.

10. Reposition the radiator inlet hose clamp at the radiator using the special tool J38185.

11. Remove the radiator inlet hose from the radiator.

12. Raise the vehicle.

13. Remove the lower radiator air deflector retainers.

14. Remove the lower radiator air deflector.

15. Remove the right front fender liner. Remove the right radiator air deflector retainers.

16. Remove the right radiator air deflector.

17. Remove the left radiator air deflector retainers.

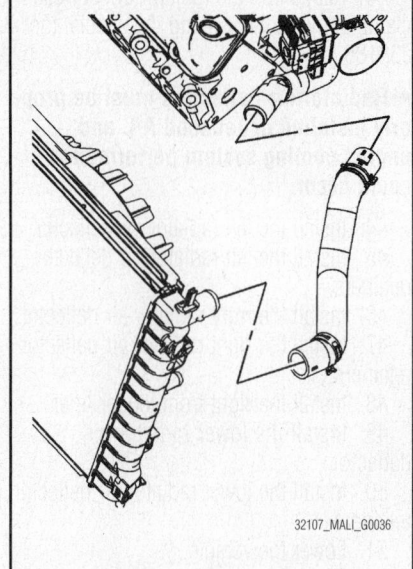

Fig. 37 Remove the radiator inlet hose from the radiator

18. Remove the left radiator air deflector.

19. Reposition the radiator outlet hose clamp at the radiator using the special tool J38185.

20. Remove the radiator outlet hose from the radiator.

21. Place a drain pan under the transmission oil cooler pipes.

22. Remove the transmission oil cooler pipe attachment nut from the transmission.

23. Remove the transmission oil cooler pipes from the transmission.

24. Remove the lower radiator support bracket bolts.

25. Remove the lower radiator support brackets.

26. Remove the radiator lower mounts.

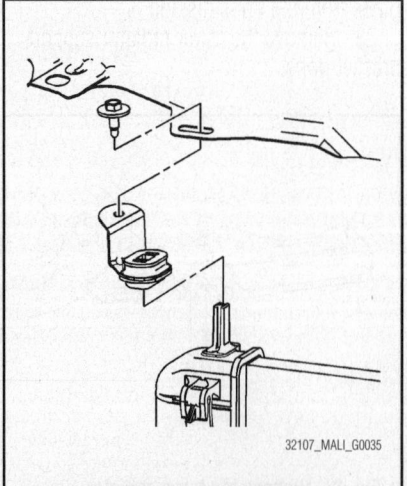

Fig. 36 Remove the upper radiator support bracket bolts

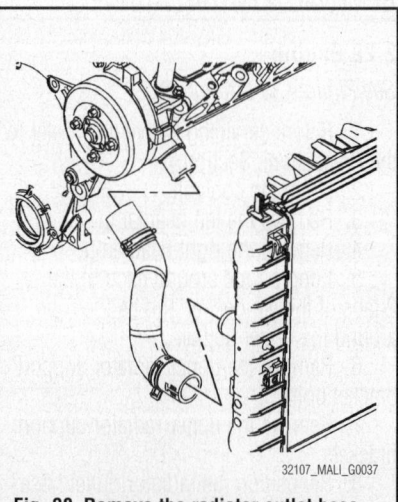

Fig. 38 Remove the radiator outlet hose from the radiator

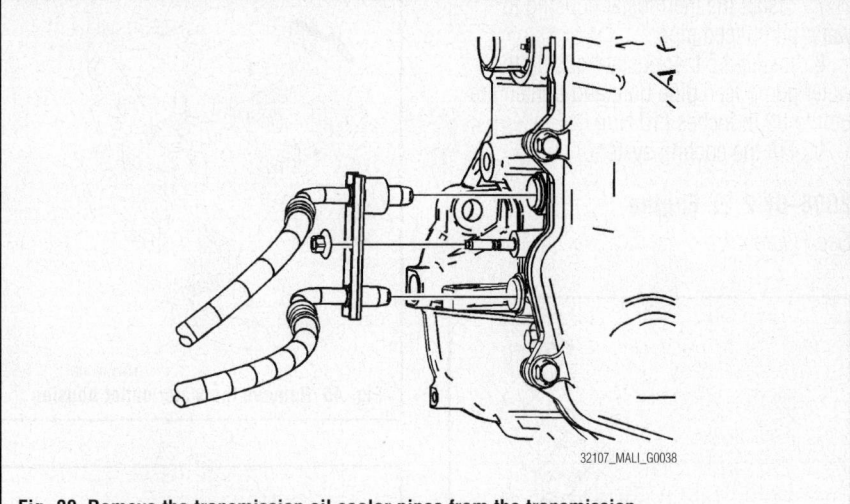

Fig. 39 Remove the transmission oil cooler pipes from the transmission

27. Remove and discard the condenser mounting bolts from the radiator.

28. Push upward on the radiator and downward on the condenser to unsnap the condenser mounting tabs from the radiator clips.

29. Remove and discard the condenser mounting nuts from the radiator.

30. Remove the radiator air side seals.

31. Remove the radiator, cooling fan shroud and transmission oil cooler pipe assembly.

32. Remove the transmission oil cooler pipes from the radiator.

33. Pry upward on the fan shroud tabs at the radiator clips.

34. Remove the cooling fan and shroud assembly.

To install:

35. Install the cooling fan and shroud assembly to the radiator.

36. Snap the fan shroud tabs into the radiator clips.

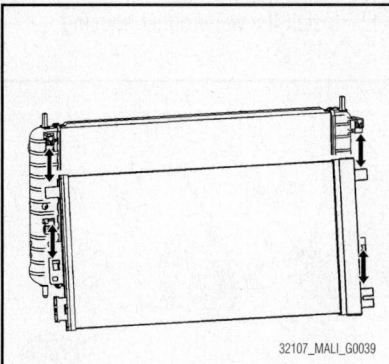

Fig. 40 Push upward on the radiator and downward on the condenser to unsnap the condenser mounting tabs from the radiator clips

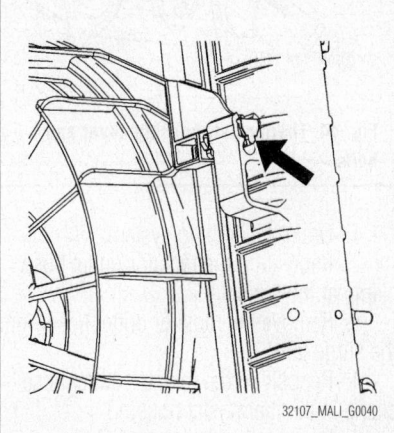

Fig. 41 Pry upward on the fan shroud tabs at the radiator clips

37. Install the transmission oil cooler pipes to the radiator. Install the radiator, cooling fan shroud and transmission oil cooler pipe assembly.

38. Install the radiator air side seals onto the condenser mounting tabs on the radiator.

➡ **The bolt retaining the condenser to the radiator end tank is a special length and should be the only bolt used upon reinstallation. The use of a longer bolt will damage the radiator end tank.**

➡ **Replace the condenser mounting bolts and nuts.**

39. Install the condenser mounting nuts to the radiator.

40. Insert the condenser mounting tabs into the radiator clips.

41. Install the condenser to the radiator bolts, and tighten the bolts to 53 lb inches (6 Nm).

42. Bend the radiator air side seals and

insert the seals into the channel of the intake air splash shields.

43. The radiator air side seals must be in the proper position for proper air flow.

➡ **Replace the radiator lower mounts as a pair or vibration may result.**

44. Install the radiator lower mounts.

45. Install the lower radiator support brackets.

46. Install the lower radiator support bracket bolts, and tighten the bolts to 44 ft. lbs. (60 Nm).

47. Install the transmission oil cooler pipes to the transmission.

48. Install the transmission oil cooler pipes attachment nut to the transmission, and tighten the nut to 62 lb inches (7 Nm).

49. Install the radiator outlet hose to the radiator.

50. Reposition the radiator outlet hose clamp at the radiator using the special tool J38185.

➡ **Radiator air deflectors must be properly installed or reduced A/C and engine cooling system performance could occur.**

51. Install the left radiator air deflector.

52. Install the left radiator air deflector retainers.

53. Install the right radiator air deflector.

54. Install the right radiator air deflector retainers.

55. Install the right front fender liner.

56. Install the lower radiator air deflector.

57. Install the lower radiator air deflector retainers.

58. Lower the vehicle.

59. Install the radiator inlet hose to the radiator.

60. Reposition the radiator inlet hose clamp at the radiator using the special tool J38185.

61. Install the surge tank outlet hose to the radiator.

62. Reposition the surge tank outlet hose clamp at the radiator using the special tool J38185 .

63. Remove the rope attached to the condenser and upper tie bar.

64. Install the upper radiator support brackets.

➡ **Do not allow the upper bracket to twist when tightening the screw or vibration may result.**

65. Install the upper radiator support bracket bolts, and tighten the bolts to 7 ft. lbs. (10 Nm).

66. Install the right headlamp.

67. Install the left headlamp.

68. Fill the coolant.
69. Inspect the transmission fluid level.

THERMOSTAT

REMOVAL & INSTALLATION

2005 2.2L Engine

See Figures 42 and 43.

1. Before servicing the vehicle, refer to the Precautions Section.
2. Drain the cooling system.
3. Remove the thermostat housing to water pump feed pipe bolts.
4. Remove the thermostat housing to water pump feed pipe.
5. Remove the thermostat and retaining sleeve, noting orientation for installation.

To install:
6. Install the thermostat and retaining sleeve with the dimple placed into the housing slot.

➡**Lubricate the O-rings with coolant only.**

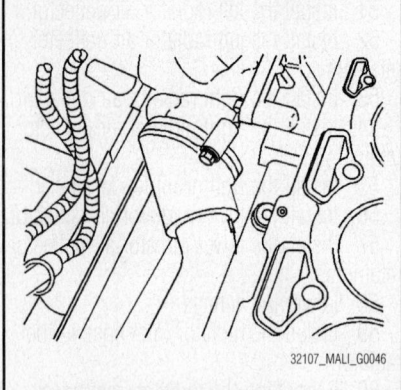

Fig. 42 Remove the thermostat housing to water pump feed pipe bolts

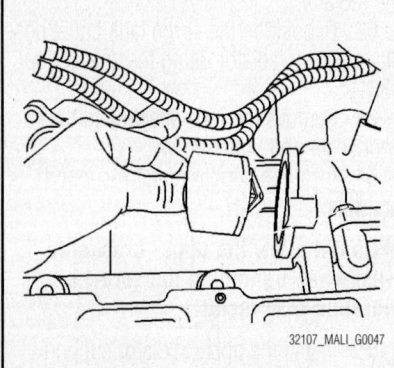

Fig. 43 Remove the thermostat and retaining sleeve

7. Install the thermostat housing to water pump feed pipe.
8. Install the thermostat housing to water pump feed pipe bolt, and tighten the bolt to 89 lb inches (10 Nm).
9. Fill the cooling system.

2006–08 2.2L Engine

See Figure 44.

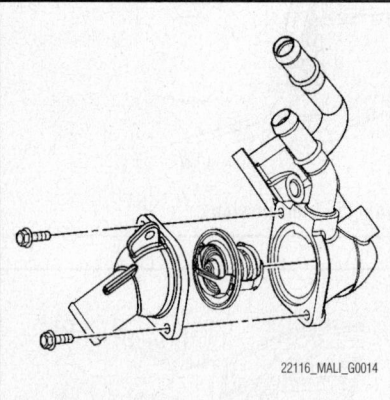

Fig. 44 Thermostat, housing cover and bolts

1. Drain the cooling system.
2. Reposition the radiator outlet hose clamp at the surge tank.
3. Remove the radiator outlet hose from the surge tank.
4. Reposition the radiator outlet hose clamp at the thermostat housing.
5. Remove the radiator outlet hose from the thermostat housing.
6. Remove the thermostat housing cover bolts and cover.
7. Remove the thermostat.
8. Remove and discard the thermostat housing O-ring seal.

To install:
9. Install a new thermostat housing cover O-ring seal.
10. Install the thermostat.
11. Install the thermostat housing cover bolts and tighten to 89 inch. lbs. (10 Nm).
12. Install the radiator outlet hose to the thermostat housing.
13. Position the radiator outlet hose clamp at the thermostat housing.

3.5L (LX9) Engine

See Figures 45 through 47.

1. Before servicing the vehicle, refer to the Precautions Section.
2. Remove the air cleaner intake duct.
3. Partially drain the cooling system.
4. Use the special tool J38185 in order

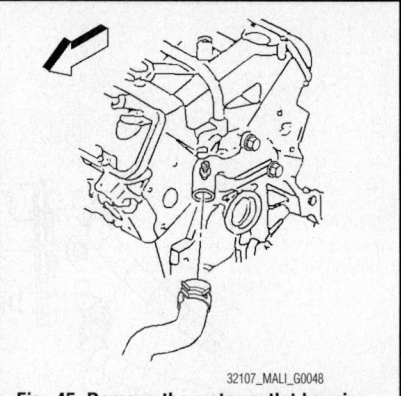

Fig. 45 Remove the water outlet housing

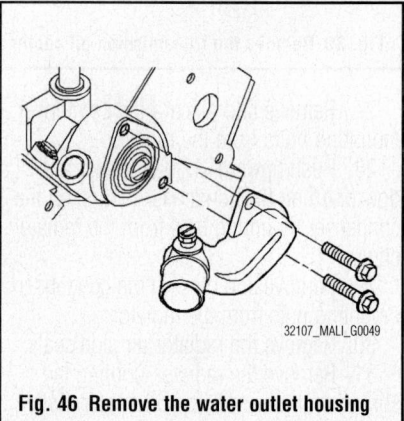

Fig. 46 Remove the water outlet housing

to reposition the hose clamp from the water outlet housing.
5. Remove the radiator inlet hose from the water outlet housing.
6. Remove the water outlet housing bolts.
7. Remove the water outlet housing.
8. Remove the thermostat.
9. Clean and inspect the water outlet housing gasket mating surfaces.

To install:
10. Install the thermostat.
11. Install the water outlet housing.

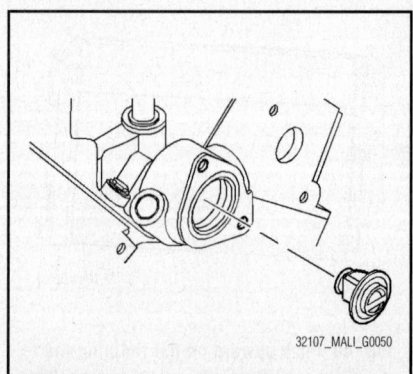

Fig. 47 Removal and installation of the thermostat

12. Install the water outlet housing bolts, and tighten the bolts to 18 ft. lbs. (25 Nm).

13. Install the radiator inlet hose to the water outlet housing.

14. Use the special tool J38185 in order to reposition and install the hose clamp to the water outlet housing.

15. Install the air cleaner intake duct.

16. Fill the cooling system.

3.5L (LZ4) & 3.9L (LZ9) Engines

See Figure 48.

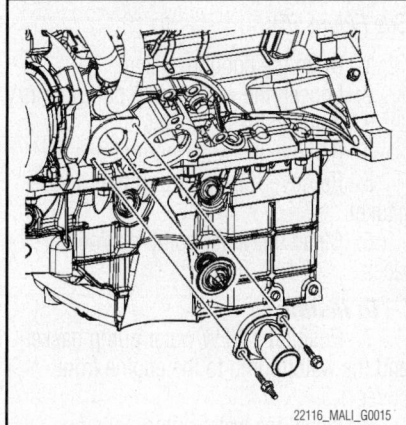

Fig. 48 Thermostat, housing and mounting bolts

1. Before servicing the vehicle, refer to the Precautions Section.

2. Drain the cooling system.

3. Remove the air cleaner outlet duct.

4. Reposition the radiator outlet hose clamp at the thermostat housing.

5. Remove the radiator outlet hose from the thermostat housing.

6. Remove the thermostat housing bolt and stud.

7. Remove the thermostat housing and gasket.

8. Remove the thermostat.

9. Clean the gasket surfaces.

To install:

10. Install a new thermostat.

11. Position a new gasket and the thermostat housing to the engine block.

12. Install the thermostat housing bolt and stud. Tighten the bolt and stud to 18 ft. lbs. (25 Nm).

13. Install the radiator outlet hose to the thermostat housing.

14. Position the radiator outlet hose clamp at the thermostat housing.

15. Install the air cleaner outlet duct.

16. Fill and bleed the cooling system.

17. Inspect the system for leaks.

WATER PUMP

REMOVAL & INSTALLATION

2.2L Engine

See Figures 49 through 53.

1. Before servicing the vehicle, refer to the Precautions Section.

2. Drain the cooling system.

➡**A drain plug is located at the bottom of the water pump assembly for additional coolant drainage from the engine block and water pump.**

3. Remove the thermostat housing.

4. Remove the coolant heater.

5. Remove the water pump access plate from the front cover.

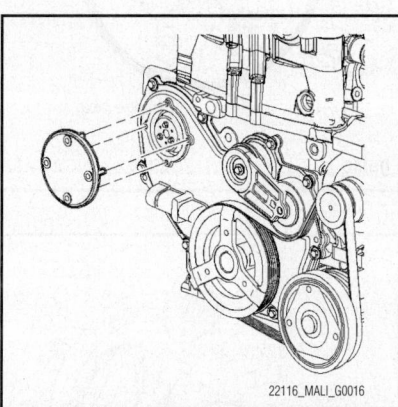

Fig. 49 Water pump access plate removal

✳✳ WARNING

The water pump holding tool supports the sprocket and chain during water pump service. The tool must be used or the balance shaft must be re-timed.

6. Install the J 43651 water pump holding tool into position.

7. Tighten the bolts on the water pump holding tool into the threads on the water pump sprocket.

8. Install the access cover bolts that were removed earlier to secure the water pump holding tool to the front cover assembly.

9. Remove the 3 inner water pump sprocket to water pump bolts through the holes in the water pump holding tool.

10. Remove the 2 water pump bolts.

➡**Be sure to remove both water pump bolts from the front of the engine block.**

11. Remove the rear 2 water pump bolts.

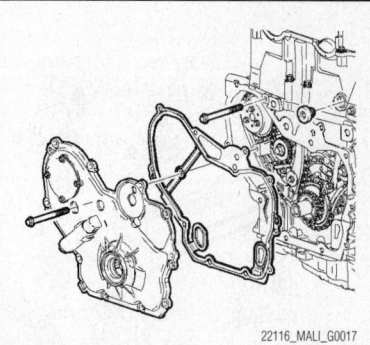

Fig. 50 Front water pump mounting bolts shown

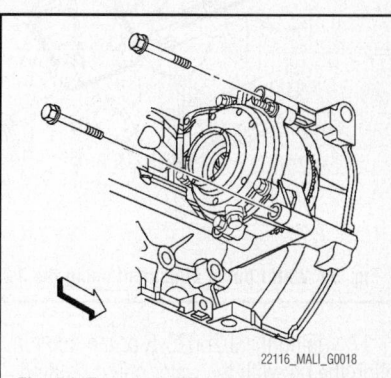

Fig. 51 Rear water pump mounting bolts shown

12. Remove the engine wiring harness clip nut from the water pump stud.

13. Remove the engine wiring harness clip from the stud.

14. Remove the water pump.

To install:

15. Apply sealant GM P/N 12378521 (Canadian P/N 88901148) or equivalent to the water pump drain plug.

16. Install the water pump drain plug and tighten to 15 ft. lbs. (20 Nm).

➡**A guide pin can be created to aid in water pump alignment. Use a M6 m x 6 mm stud.**

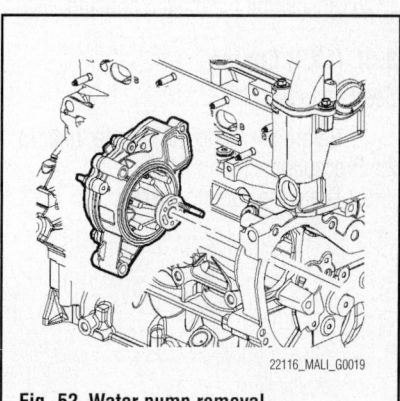

Fig. 52 Water pump removal

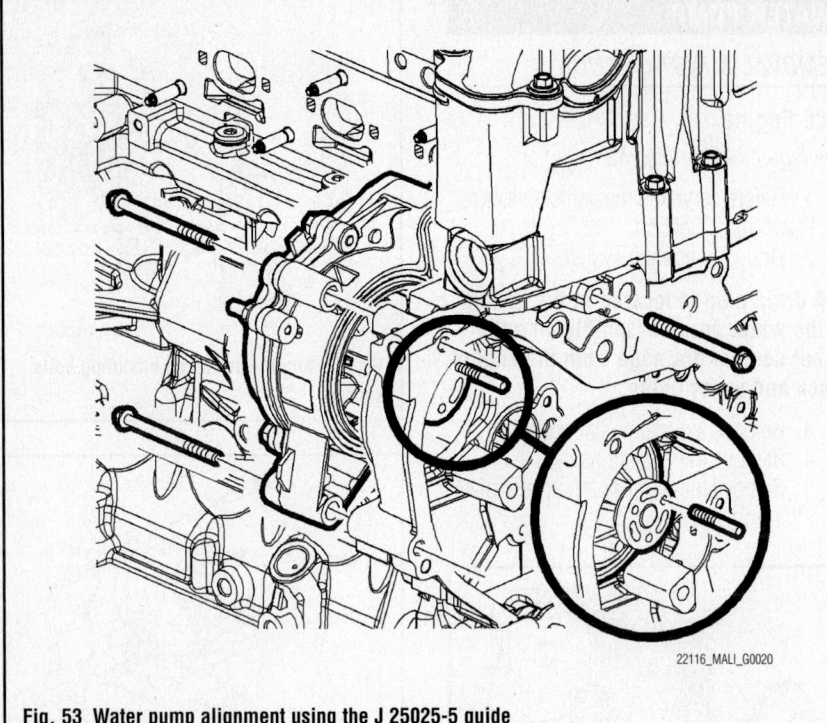

Fig. 53 Water pump alignment using the J 25025-5 guide

17. Using the J 25025-5 or a guide pin, align the pin with the water pump holding tool.

18. Position the water pump against the engine block and hand tighten the water pump bolts.

19. Install the inner water pump sprocket bolts. After 2 are snug, remove the guide pin and install the 3rd bolt.

20. Tighten the bolts to 18 ft. lbs. (25 Nm).

21. Tighten the water pump sprocket bolts last. Tighten the bolts to 89 inch. lbs. (10 Nm).

22. Remove the J 43651 water pump holding tool.

23. Install the coolant heater.

24. Install the water pump access plate and bolts and tighten to 89 inch. lbs. (10 Nm).

25. Install the thermostat housing.

3.5L (LX9) Engine

See Figure 54.

1. Before servicing the vehicle, refer to the Precautions Section.

2. Drain the cooling system.

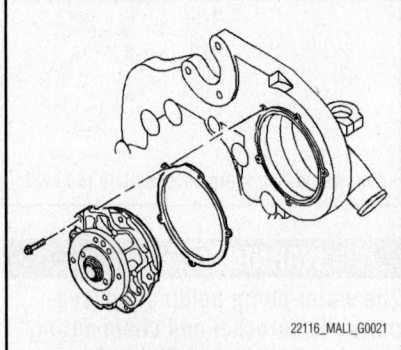

Fig. 54 Exploded view of water pump mounting 3.5L (LX9) engine

3. Remove or disconnect the following:
- Negative battery cable
- Water pump pulley bolts, loosen
- Accessory drive belt
- Water pump pulley
- Water pump bolts, pump and gasket

To install:

4. Apply a thin bead of sealer around the outside edge of the water pump along the gasket sealing area.

5. Install or connect the following:
- Water pump with a new gasket. Tighten the bolts to 89 inch lbs. (10 Nm).
- Water pump pulley and finger-tighten the bolts
- Accessory drive belt
- Water pump pulley bolts and torque to 18 ft. lbs. (24 Nm)
- Negative battery cable

6. Refill and bleed the cooling system.

7. Operate the engine and check for leaks.

3.5L (LZ4) & 3.9L (LZ9) Engines

See Figure 55.

1. Drain the cooling system.

2. Loosen the water pump pulley bolts.

3. Remove the drive belt.

4. Remove the water pump bolts.

5. Remove the water pump and gasket.

6. Clean the water pump mating surfaces.

To install:

7. Position a NEW water pump gasket and the water pump to the engine front cover.

8. Install the water pump bolts and tighten the bolts to 89 inch lbs. (10 Nm).

9. Install the water pump pulley and bolts

10. Install the drive belt.

11. Tighten water pump pulley bolts to 18 ft. lbs. (25 Nm).

12. Fill and bleed the cooling system.

13. Inspect for leaks.

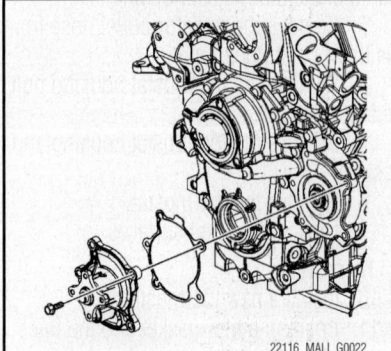

Fig. 55 Exploded view of water pump mounting 3.5L (LZ4) engine

ENGINE ELECTRICAL   CHARGING SYSTEM

ALTERNATOR

REMOVAL & INSTALLATION

2005–06 2.2L Engine

1. Before servicing the vehicle, refer to the Precautions Section.
2. Remove or disconnect the following:
   • Negative battery cable
   • Air intake assembly
   • Oil dipstick assembly mounting bolt
   • Accessory drive belt
   • Alternator electrical connectors
   • Alternator

To install:

3. Install or connect the following:
   • Alternator. Tighten bolts to 16 ft. lbs. (22 Nm)
   • Alternator electrical connections. Tighten nut to 15 ft. lbs. (20 Nm).
   • Accessory drive belt
   • Oil dipstick assembly mounting bolt
   • Air intake assembly
   • Negative battery cable

2007–08 2.2L Engine

See Figure 56.

1. Before servicing the vehicle, refer to the Precautions Section.
2. Disconnect negative battery cable.
3. Remove the air cleaner resonator.
4. Remove the drive belt.
5. Remove the radiator inlet hose.
6. Disconnect the engine wiring harness electrical connector from the alternator.
7. Reposition the engine wiring harness lead rubber boot.
8. Remove the engine wiring harness terminal lead to alternator nut.
9. Remove the engine wiring harness terminal from the alternator stud.
10. Remove the alternator r bolts.
11. Remove the alternator.

To install:

12. Position the alternator to the engine block.
13. Install the alternator bolts and tighten to 16 ft. lbs. (22 Nm).
14. Install the engine wing harness terminal to the alternator stud.
15. Install the engine wiring harness terminal lead to alternator nut and tighten to 15 ft. lbs.(20 Nm).
16. Position the engine wiring harness lead rubber boot.

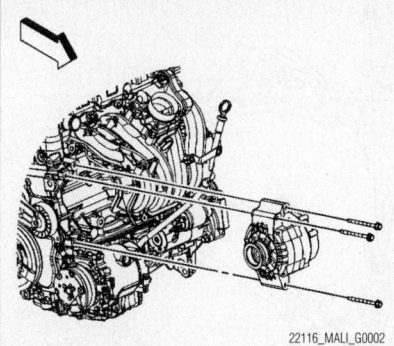

Fig. 56 2.2L Engine alternator and mounting bolts

22116_MALI_G0002

17. Connect the engine wiring harness electrical connector to the alternator.
18. Install the radiator inlet hose.
19. Install the drive belt.
20. Install the air cleaner resonator.
21. Connect negative battery cable.
22. Fill and bleed the cooling system.

3.5L Engines

See Figure 57.

1. Before servicing the vehicle, refer to the Precautions Section.
2. Remove or disconnect the following:
   • Negative battery cable
   • Accessory drive belt
   • Alternator electrical connectors
   • Power steering line clip
   • Alternator

To install:

3. Install or connect the following:
   • Alternator. Tighten the nuts to 22 ft.

lbs. (30 Nm) and the bolts to 37 ft. lbs. (50 Nm).
   • Alternator electrical connector. Tighten the nut to 15 ft. lbs. (20 Nm).
   • Power steering line clip. Tighten the nut to 44 inch. lbs. (5 Nm).
   • Accessory drive belt
   • Negative battery cable

3.9L Engines

See Figure 58.

1. Before servicing the vehicle, refer to the Precautions Section.
2. Disconnect the negative battery cable.
3. Remove the drive belt.
4. Disconnect the engine wiring harness electrical connector
5. Reposition the engine wiring harness terminal boot
6. Remove the engine wiring harness terminal lead to alternator nut
7. Remove the engine wiring harness terminal from the alternator stud.
8. Remove the power steering line clip nut.
9. Remove the power steering line clip from the alternator stud and reposition the lines out of the way.
10. Remove the alternator side bolt and stud.
11. Remove the alternator through bolt.
12. Remove the alternator.

To install:

13. Position the alternator to the coolant crossover.

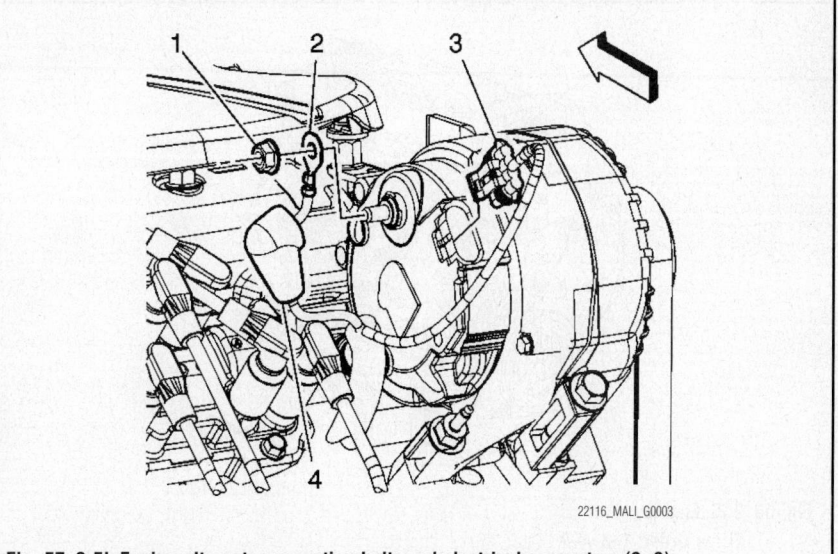

22116_MALI_G0003

Fig. 57 3.5L Engine alternator, mounting bolts and electrical connectors (2, 3)

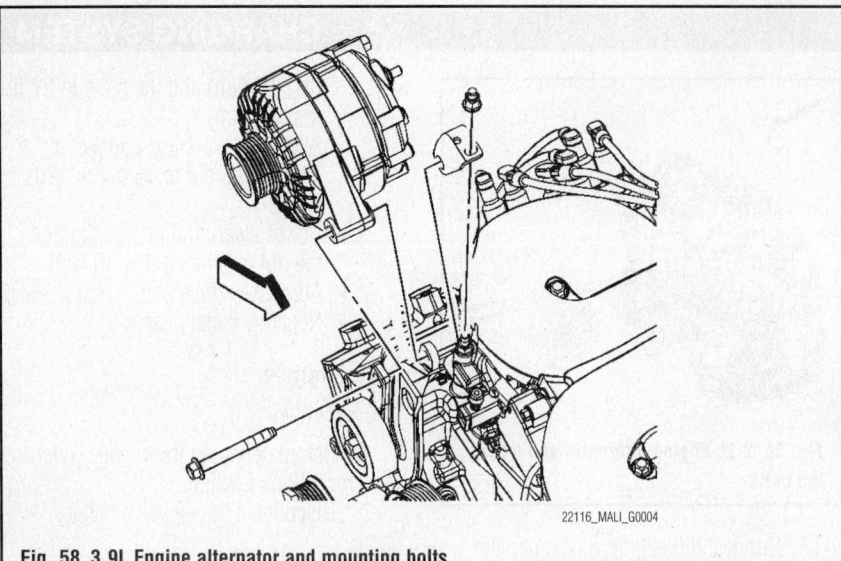

Fig. 58 3.9L Engine alternator and mounting bolts

14. Loosely install the alternator through bolt.

15. Loosely install the alternator side bolt and stud. Tighten to 37 ft. lbs. (50 Nm).

16. Position the power steering lines and install the power steering line clip to the generator stud.

17. Install the power steering line clip nut and tighten the nut to 44 inch. lbs. (5 Nm).

18. Install the engine wiring harness terminal to the alternator stud.

19. Install the engine wiring harness terminal lead to alternator nut. Tighten the nut to 15 ft. lbs. (20 Nm).

20. Position the engine wiring harness terminal boot.

21. Connect the engine wiring harness electrical connector.

22. Install the drive belt.

23. Connect the negative battery cable.

ENGINE ELECTRICAL

IGNITION SYSTEM

FIRING ORDER

See Figures 59 and 60.

IGNITION TIMING

ADJUSTMENT

The engines covered by this manual are equipped with distributorless ignitions, ignition timing is controlled by the Powertrain Control Module (PCM), as applicable. No adjustments are possible. If ignition timing is not within specification, there is a fault in the engine control system. Diagnose and repair the problem as necessary.

Fig. 60 3.5L & 3.9L Engines
Firing order: 1–2–3–4–5–6
Distributorless ignition system

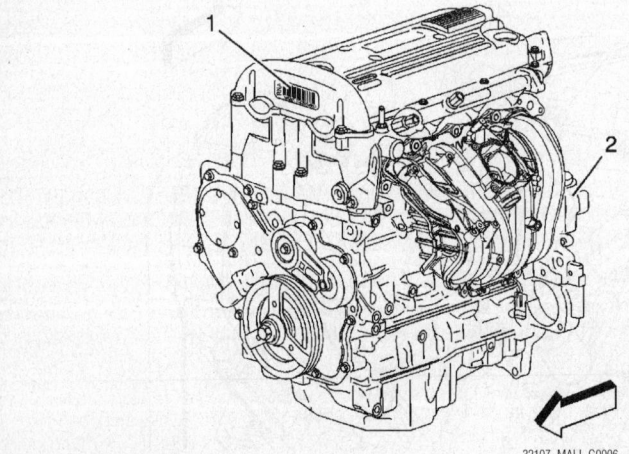

Fig. 59 2.2L Engine
Firing Order: 1–3–4–2
Distributorless ignition system

SPARK PLUGS

REMOVAL & INSTALLATION

2005–06 2.2L Engine

1. Observe the following service precautions:

• Allow the engine to cool before removing the spark plugs. Attempting to remove spark plugs from a hot engine can cause the spark plugs to seize. This can damage the cylinder head threads.

• Clean the spark plug recess area before removing the spark plug. Failure to do so can result in engine damage due to dirt or foreign material entering the cylinder head, or in contamination of the cylinder head threads. Contaminated threads may prevent proper seating of the new spark plug.

- Use only the spark plugs specified for use in the vehicle. Do not install spark plugs that are either hotter or colder than those specified for the vehicle. Installing spark plugs of another type can severely damage the engine.

2. Turn the ignition **OFF**.

3. Disconnect the Electronic Ignition (EI) module harness connector.

4. Remove the spark plugs using a ⅝ inch spark plug socket.

To install:

> ✳✳ **WARNING**
>
> **Do not coat spark plug threads with anti-seize compound. If anti-seize compound is used and spark plugs are over—torqued, damage to the cylinder head threads may result.**

5. Inspect the gap on the new spark plugs, re—gap the plugs as required. The spark plug gap specification is 42 inch. (1.0 mm).

6. Install the spark plugs and tighten to 15 ft. lbs. (20 Nm).

7. Apply dielectric compound to the spark plug boots and make sure no corrosion is present.

8. Install the ignition coil housing to cam cover and attachment bolts.

9. Tighten the ignition coil housing bolts to 89 inch. lbs. (10 Nm).

10. Connect the EI module harness connector. Push in until a click is heard and pull back to confirm a positive engagement.

2007–08 2.2L Engine

1. Observe the following service precautions:

- Allow the engine to cool before removing the spark plugs. Attempting to remove spark plugs from a hot engine can cause the spark plugs to seize. This can damage the cylinder head threads.
- Clean the spark plug recess area before removing the spark plug. Failure to do so can result in engine damage due to dirt or foreign material entering the cylinder head, or in contamination of the cylinder head threads. Contaminated threads may prevent

proper seating of the new spark plug.

- Use only the spark plugs specified for use in the vehicle. Do not install spark plugs that are either hotter or colder than those specified for the vehicle. Installing spark plugs of another type can severely damage the engine.

2. Disconnect the engine wiring harness electrical connectors from the ignition coils.

3. Remove the ignition coil bolts.

4. Remove the ignition coils.

5. Remove the spark plugs.

To install:

> ✳✳ **WARNING**
>
> **Do not coat spark plug threads with anti-seize compound. If anti-seize compound is used and spark plugs are over—torqued, damage to the cylinder head threads may result.**

6. Inspect the gap on the new spark plugs, re—gap the plugs as required. The spark plug gap specification is 45 inch. (1.1 mm).

7. Install the spark plugs and tighten to 15 ft. lbs. (20 Nm).

8. Install the ignition coils.

9. Install the ignition coil bolts and tighten to 89 inch lbs. (10 Nm).

10. Connect the engine wiring harness electrical connectors to the ignition coils.

3.5L Engine

1. Observe the following service precautions:

- Allow the engine to cool before removing the spark plugs. Attempting to remove spark plugs from a hot engine can cause the spark plugs to seize. This can damage the cylinder head threads.
- Clean the spark plug recess area before removing the spark plug. Failure to do so can result in engine damage due to dirt or foreign material entering the cylinder head, or in contamination of the cylinder head threads. Contaminated threads may prevent proper seating of the new spark plug.
- Use only the spark plugs specified for use in the vehicle. Do not install spark plugs that are either hotter or colder than those specified for the

vehicle. Installing spark plugs of another type can severely damage the engine.

2. Remove the intake manifold cover, if required.

3. Remove the air cleaner duct, if required.

4. Remove the left side spark plug wires from the spark plugs, if required.

5. Remove the right side spark plug wires from the spark plugs, if required.

6. Remove the spark plugs from the engine.

To install:

7. Inspect the gap on the new spark plugs, re—gap the plugs as required.

8. The spark plug gap specification is as follows:

- 2005–06 3.5L engines 60 inch. (1.52 mm).
- 2007–08 3.5L engines 40 inch. (1.02 mm).

9. Install the spark plugs and tighten to 15 ft. lbs. (20 Nm).

10. Install the right side spark plug wires to the spark plugs, if required.

11. Install the left side spark plug wires to the spark plugs, if required.

12. Install the air cleaner duct, if required.

13. Install the intake manifold cover, if required.

3.9L Engine

1. Observe the following service precautions:

- Allow the engine to cool before removing the spark plugs. Attempting to remove spark plugs from a hot engine can cause the spark plugs to seize. This can damage the cylinder head threads.
- Clean the spark plug recess area before removing the spark plug. Failure to do so can result in engine damage due to dirt or foreign material entering the cylinder head, or in contamination of the cylinder head threads. Contaminated threads may prevent proper seating of the new spark plug.
- Use only the spark plugs specified for use in the vehicle. Do not install spark plugs that are either hotter or colder than those specified for the vehicle. Installing spark plugs of another type can severely damage the engine.

2. Remove the intake manifold cover, if required.

3. Remove the air cleaner duct, if required.

4. Remove the left side spark plug wires from the spark plugs, if required.

5. Remove the right side spark plug wires from the spark plugs, if required.

6. Remove the spark plugs from the engine.

To install:

7. Inspect the gap on the new spark plugs, re—gap the plugs as required. The spark plug gap specification is 40 inch. (1.02 mm).

8. Install the spark plugs and tighten to 15 ft. lbs. (20 Nm).

9. Install the right side spark plug wires to the spark plugs, if required.

10. Install the left side spark plug wires to the spark plugs, if required.

11. Install the air cleaner duct, if required.

12. Install the intake manifold cover, if required.

ENGINE ELECTRICAL

STARTER

REMOVAL & INSTALLATION

2.2L Engine

1. Before servicing the vehicle, refer to the Precautions Section.

2. Remove or disconnect the following:
- Negative battery cable
- Starter motor electrical connections
- Starter motor mounting bolts
- Starter motor

To install:

3. Install or connect the following:
- Starter motor
- Starter motor mounting bolts. Tighten the mounting bolts for 2005–06 models to 30 ft. lbs. (40 Nm).
- Tighten the mounting bolts for 2007–08 models to 39 ft. lbs. (53 Nm).
- Starter motor electrical connections. Tighten the battery cable for 2005–06 models to 7 ft. lbs. (10 Nm). Tighten the solenoid cable to 4 ft. lbs. (5 Nm).
- Tighten the battery cable for 2007–08 models to 89 inch. lbs. (10 Nm). Tighten the solenoid cable to 27 inch. lbs. (3 Nm).
- Negative battery cable

3.5L Engine

1. Before servicing the vehicle, refer to the Precautions Section.

2. Remove or disconnect the following:
- Negative battery cable
- Flywheel inspection cover
- Starter motor electrical connections
- Starter motor mounting bolts
- Starter motor

To install:

3. Install or connect the following:
- Starter motor and mounting bolts. Tighten mounting bolts for 2005–06 models to 30 ft. lbs. (40 Nm).
- Tighten mounting bolts for 2007–08 models to 32 ft. lbs. (43 Nm).
- Starter motor electrical connections.

Tighten battery cable to 89 inch. lbs. (10 Nm). Tighten the solenoid cable to 27 inch lbs. (3 Nm).
- Flywheel inspection cover. Tighten mounting bolts to 89 inch. lbs. (10 Nm).
- Negative battery cable

3.9L Engine

See Figure 61.

1. Before servicing the vehicle, refer to the Precautions Section.

2. Disconnect the negative battery cable.

3. Raise and support the vehicle.

4. Remove the torque converter cover bolt.

5. Remove the torque converter cover.

6. Disconnect the engine wiring harness electrical connector from the starter motor.

7. Remove the positive battery cable nut from the starter solenoid.

8. Remove the positive battery cable and the engine wiring harness terminal from the starter solenoid.

9. Remove the starter motor bolts.

10. Remove the starter motor.

To install:

11. Install the starter motor.

12. Install the starter motor bolts and tighten to 32 inch. lbs. (42 Nm).

13. Install the engine wiring harness terminal and the positive battery cable to the starter solenoid.

14. Tighten the solenoid cable to 27 inch lbs. (3 Nm).

15. Install the positive battery cable nut to the starter solenoid. Tighten battery cable to 89 inch. lbs. (10 Nm).

16. Connect the engine wiring harness electrical connector to the starter motor.

17. Install the torque converter cover.

18. Install the torque converter cover bolt and tighten to 89 inch. lbs. (10 Nm).

19. Lower the vehicle.

20. Connect the negative battery cable.

SOLENOID REPLACEMENT

See Figures 62 and 63.

1. Before servicing the vehicle, refer to the Precautions Section.

2. Disconnect the negative battery cable.

3. Remove the starter motor from the vehicle and place on a clean work surface.

4. Disconnect the solenoid-to-starter lead wire.

5. Remove the solenoid mounting bolts and slide out the solenoid. Pull out the solenoid torsion spring, if so equipped. On some models, it may be

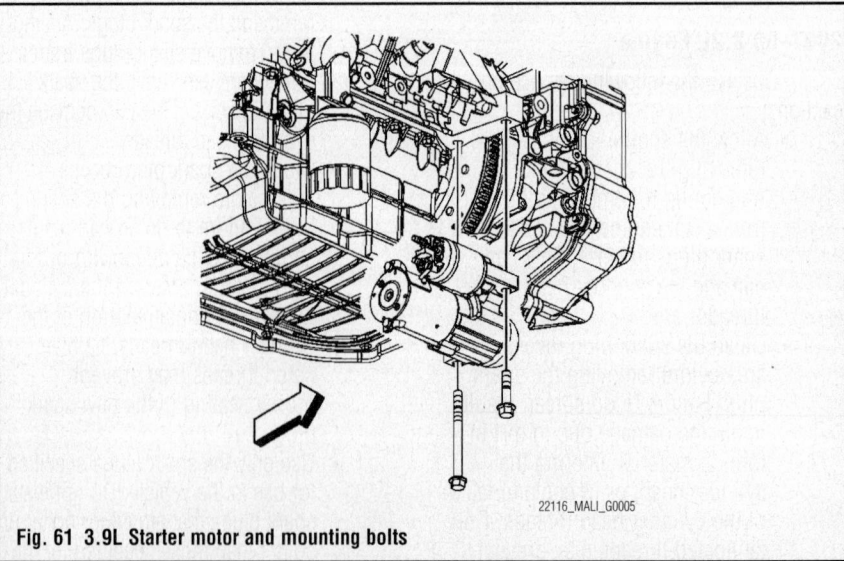

22116_MALI_G0005

Fig. 61 3.9L Starter motor and mounting bolts

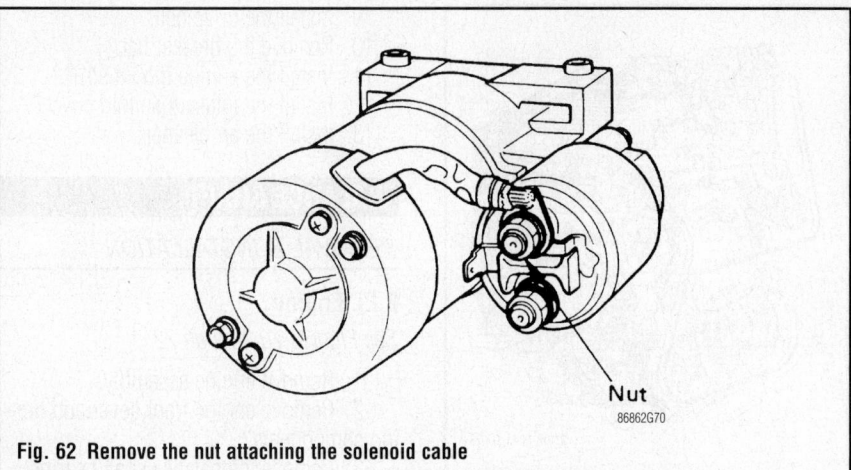

Fig. 62 Remove the nut attaching the solenoid cable

Nut

86862G70

necessary to remove the starter assembly through bolts from the yoke to remove the solenoid.

6. If equipped with shims between the solenoid and starter, remove and place aside.

To install:

7. Install the solenoid with any adjustment shims.

8. Torque the bolts to 15 ft. lbs. (20 Nm).

9. Connect the starter-to-solenoid electrical lead.

10. Install the starter through-bolts if removed.

11. Install the starter motor.

12. Check for proper operation.

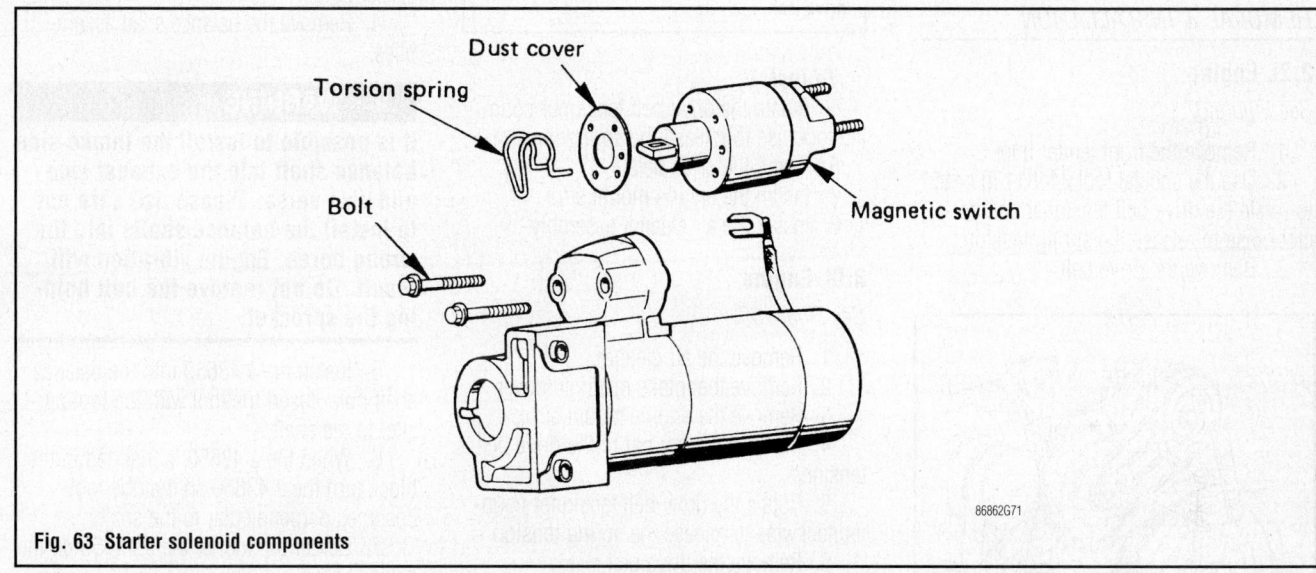

Dust cover

Torsion spring

Magnetic switch

Bolt

Fig. 63 Starter solenoid components

86862G71

ENGINE MECHANICAL

➡ Disconnecting the negative battery cable may interfere with the functions of the on board computer systems and may require the computer to undergo a relearning process, once the negative battery cable is reconnected.

ACCESSORY DRIVE BELTS

ACCESSORY BELT ROUTING

See Figures 64 through 66.

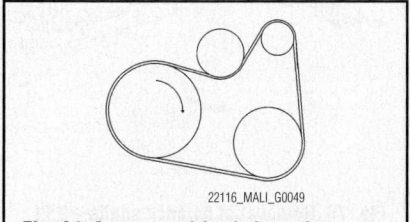

22116_MALI_G0049

Fig. 64 Accessory drive belt routing—2.2L VIN F (L61) engine

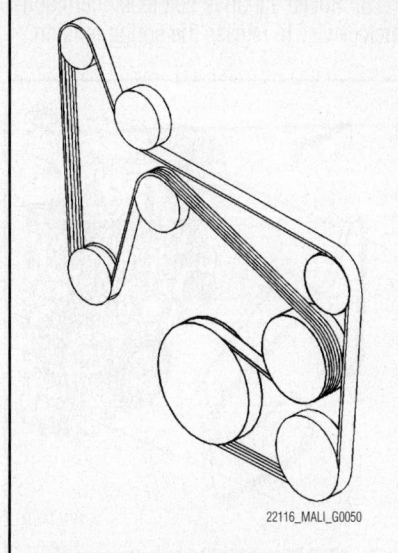

22116_MALI_G0050

Fig. 65 Accessory drive belt routing—3.5L VIN 8 (LZ4 & LX9) engine

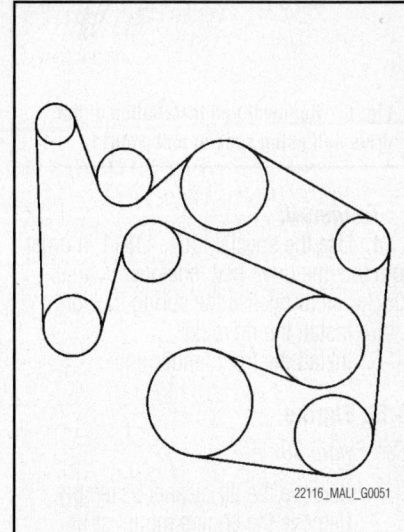

22116_MALI_G0051

Fig. 66 Accessory drive belt routing—3.9L VIN 1 (LZ9) engine

INSPECTION

Inspect the drive belt for signs of glazing or cracking. A glazed belt will be perfectly smooth from slippage, while a good belt will have a slight texture of fabric visible. Cracks will usually start at the inner edge of the belt and run outward. All worn or damaged drive belts should be replaced immediately.

ADJUSTMENT

All engines use an automatic drive belt tensioner. No adjustment is necessary. If the tensioner is at Maximum travel, the belt is most likely stretched or the incorrect belt was installed.

REMOVAL & INSTALLATION

2.2L Engine

See Figure 67.

1. Remove the front fender liner.
2. Use the special tool J44811 in order to rotate the drive belt tensioner counterclockwise to release the spring tension.
3. Remove the drive belt.

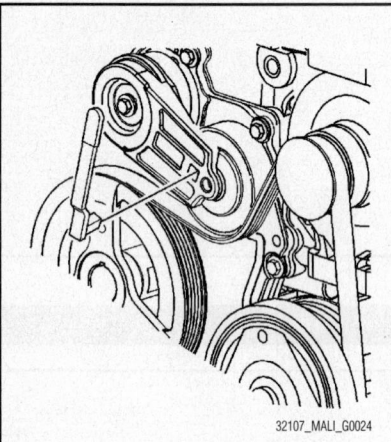

Fig. 67 Removal and installation of the drive belt using special tool J44811

To install:

4. Use the special tool J44811 in order to rotate the drive belt tensioner counterclockwise to release the spring tension.
5. Install the drive belt.
6. Install the front fender liner.

3.5L Engine

See Figure 68.

1. Remove the air cleaner assembly.
2. Remove the engine mount strut.
3. Rotate the drive belt tensioner counterclockwise to release the spring tension.
4. Remove the drive belt.

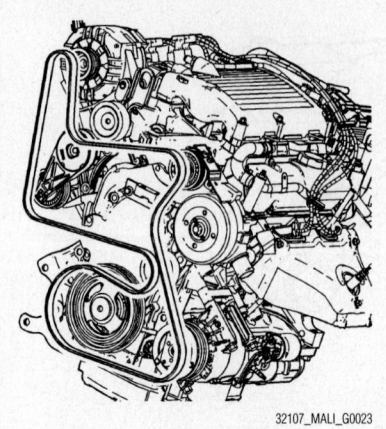

Fig. 68 Removal and installation of the drive belt

To install:

5. Rotate the drive belt tensioner counterclockwise to release the spring tension.
6. Install the drive belt.
7. Install the engine mount strut.
8. Install the air cleaner assembly.

3.9L Engine

See Figure 69.

1. Remove the air cleaner.
2. Remove the intake manifold cover.
3. Remove the engine mount strut.
4. Install a breaker bar to the drive belt tensioner.
5. Rotate the drive belt tensioner counterclockwise to release the spring tension.
6. Remove the drive belt.

To install:

7. Install a breaker bar to the drive belt tensioner.
8. Rotate the drive belt tensioner counterclockwise to release the spring tension.

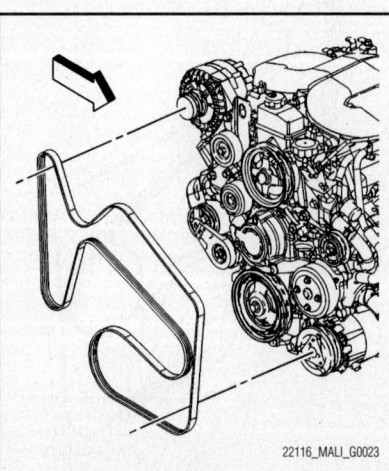

Fig. 69 3.9L engine Drive belt removal and installation

9. Install the drive belt.
10. Remove the breaker bar.
11. Install the engine mount strut.
12. Install the intake manifold cover.
13. Install the air cleaner.

BALANCE SHAFT

REMOVAL & INSTALLATION

2.2L Engine

See Figures 70 through 72.

1. Remove engine assembly.
2. Remove engine front cover and timing components.
3. Remove the balance shaft bearing carrier bolts.
4. Remove the balance shaft assemblies.

❋❋ WARNING

It is possible to install the intake side balance shaft into the exhaust side and vice versa. Please use care not to install the balance shafts into the wrong bores. Engine vibration will result. Do not remove the bolt holding the sprocket.

5. Install the J 43650 into the balance shaft hole. Insert the tool with the foot parallel to the shaft.
6. When the J 43650 is inserted in the block turn the J 43650 so that the foot becomes perpendicular to the shaft.
7. Center the foot of the J 43650 on the balance shaft bushing.
8. Once the J 43650 is centered on the balance shaft bushing, then insert the centering guide into the front balance shaft bore and tighten the nut with an appropriate wrench

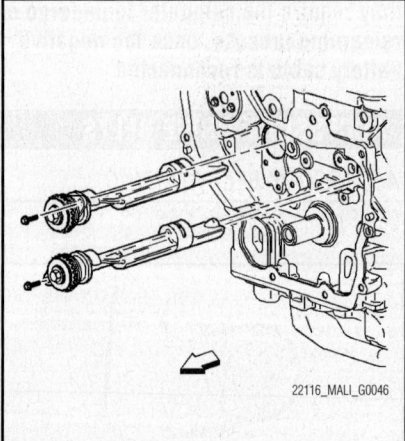

Fig. 70 Removal of balance shafts—2.2L engine

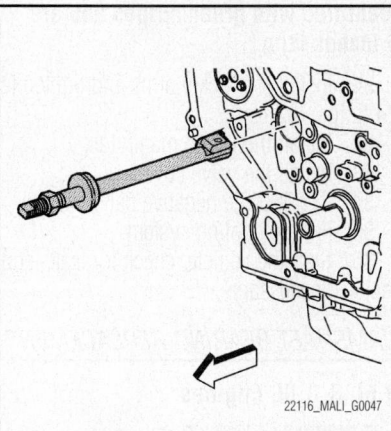

Fig. 71 J 43650— Balance shaft bushing removal tool

9. When the J 43650 is properly installed, before removing the bushing, the end of the tool should be 4.6 inch. (116 mm) from the block face.

10. If the J 43650 is less than approximately 4.5 inch. (114 mm) recheck the tool alignment.

11. Tighten the nut on the J 43650 until the tension releases. When the tension releases, remove the J 43650 and the balance shaft bushing.

To install:

12. Install the balance shaft bushing using the J 43650.

13. Seat the balance shaft bushing into the bore using the J 43650 and a wrench.

14. When the J 43650 is fully seated in the engine block, remove it with a wrench.

❋❋ WARNING

If the balance shafts are not properly timed to the engine, the engine may vibrate or make noise.

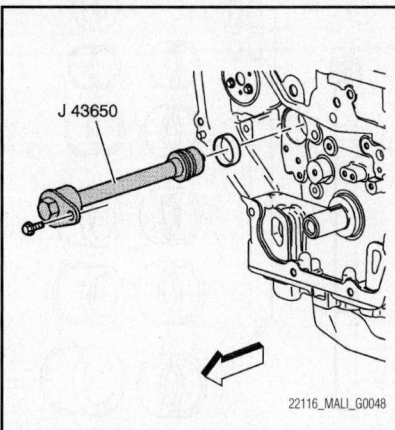

J 43650

Fig. 72 Balance shaft bushing installation—2.2L engine

15. Install the balance shaft assemblies to the engine using the following steps:
   a. Place the number one piston at top dead center (TDC).
   b. Lubricate the balance shaft lobes with engine oil.
   c. Install the balance shafts into their bores.

➡ **Use the correct fastener in the correct location. Replacement fasteners must be the correct part number for that application. Fasteners requiring replacement or fasteners requiring the use of thread locking compound or sealant are identified in the service procedure. Do not use paints, lubricants, or corrosion inhibitors on fasteners or fastener joint surfaces unless specified. These coatings affect fastener torque and joint clamping force and may damage the fastener. Use the correct tightening sequence and specifications when installing fasteners in order to avoid damage to parts and systems.**

16. Install the balance shaft retaining bolts.

17. Tighten the balance shaft retaining bolts to 89 inch. lbs. (10 Nm).

CAMSHAFT AND VALVE LIFTERS

INSPECTION

2.2L Engine

1. Inspect the camshaft journals and lobes for wear or scoring.

2. Inspect the camshaft sprocket alignment notch for damage.

3. Inspect the camshaft cover for damage or loose oil control baffles.

4. Clean the camshaft cover.

5. Wash the camshaft in solvent.

6. Oil the camshaft.

7. Inspect the camshaft cover for cracks or other signs of damage.

8. Check for valve tappet face wear.

9. Check for excessive valve tappet clearance.

3.5L & 3.9L Engines

1. Remove and discard the camshaft position actuator filter.

2. Clean the camshaft with cleaning solvent.

3. Inspect the camshaft for scored bearing journals, damaged lobes or damaged position sensor reluctor areas.

4. Measure the camshaft journals using a micrometer. If the camshaft journals are not within 1.868-1.869 in (47.443-47.468mm) on 3.5L or 2.024-2.025 in (51.415-51.440mm) on 3.9L, replace the camshaft.

5. Measure the camshaft run out. If run out exceeds 0.001 in (0.025mm), replace the camshaft.

6. Measure the camshaft lobe lift using a dial indicator. Lubricate the camshaft and set the camshaft on V-blocks. If lobe lift exceeds 0.2727 in (6.9263mm), replace the camshaft.

7. Install a new camshaft position actuator filter.

8. Check for valve tappet face wear.

9. Check for excessive valve tappet clearance.

REMOVAL & INSTALLATION

2.2L Engine

1. Before servicing the vehicle, refer to the Precautions Section.

2. Remove or disconnect the following:
   - Negative battery cable
   - Air intake assembly
   - PCV hose
   - Fuel line bracket
   - Ignition coil and module assembly
   - Ground strap and ground strap retaining stud from camshaft cover
   - Camshaft cover
   - Upper timing chain guide

3. Install Camshaft Sprocket Holding Tool J-43655 and remove both the intake and exhaust camshaft sprocket bolts.

4. Slide the camshaft sprockets forward.

5. Matchmark the caps and remove.

6. Remove the camshaft.

To install:

7. Install the camshaft.

8. Install the camshaft caps as follows:
   a. Apply a 0.13 inch (3.5mm) bead of GM P/N 12378521 sealant to the rear intake camshaft cap.
   b. Install camshaft caps and tighten bolts in increments of 3 turns until they are seated.
   c. Tighten cap bolts to 89 inch lbs. (10 Nm).
   d. Tighten intake camshaft rear cap bolts to 18 ft. lbs. (25 Nm).

9. Install the camshaft sprockets onto the camshafts and hand tighten new camshaft sprocket bolts.

10. Remove Camshaft Sprocket Holding Tool J-43655.

11. Tighten the camshaft sprocket bolts to 63 ft. lbs. (85 Nm) plus 30 degrees.

12. Install or connect the following:
- Upper timing chain guide. Tighten bolts to 89 inch lbs. (10 Nm).
- Camshaft cover. Tighten bolts to 89 inch lbs. (10 Nm).
- Ground strap
- Ignition coil and module assembly
- Fuel line bracket
- PCV hose
- Air intake assembly
- Negative battery cable

13. Start the engine and check for leaks.

3.5L Engines

1. Before servicing the vehicle, refer to the Precautions Section.
2. Relieve the fuel system pressure.

➡**When removing valve train components, marked them for installation in the same location they are removed from.**

3. Remove or disconnect the following:
- Rocker arm covers
- Intake manifold
- Rocker arms and push rods
- Lifter guide bolts and the guide
- Valve lifter(s) from the lifter bores
- Crankshaft balancer
- Front cover
- Timing chain and sprockets
- Oil pump driven gear bolt and gear
- Camshaft thrust plate
- Camshaft

To install:

4. Install or connect the following:
- Camshaft, lubricated with camshaft lubricant
- Camshaft thrust plate. Torque bolts to 89 inch lbs. (10 Nm).
- Oil pump driven gear. Torque the bolt to 27 ft. lbs. (36 Nm).
- Timing chain and sprocket. Torque the bolt to 103 ft. lbs. (140 Nm).
- Front cover. Torque the bolts to 35 ft. lbs. (47 Nm).
- Crankshaft balancer. Torque the bolt to 76 ft. lbs. (103 Nm).
- Valve lifters in their original locations
- Lifter guide. Torque the bolts to 89 inch lbs. (10 Nm).
- Pushrods, rocker arms, rocker balls and rocker arm nuts. Torque the rocker arm nuts to 89 inch lbs. (10 Nm) plus an additional 30 degrees.
- Intake manifold. Torque the upper and lower intake bolts to 115 inch lbs. (13 Nm).

- Rocker arm covers. Torque the bolts to 89 inch lbs. (10 Nm).
- Negative battery cable

5. Start the engine and verify no oil leaks.

3.9L Engines

1. Drain the engine oil and cooling system.
2. Relieve the fuel system pressure.
3. To remove the valve lifters, remove the valve covers.
4. Remove the intake manifolds.
5. Remove the rocker arm bolts.
6. Remove the rocker arms.
7. Remove the pushrods.
8. Remove the intake manifold oil splash shield.
9. Remove the lifter guide bolts.
10. Remove the valve lifter guides.
11. Remove the valve lifters.
12. Clean all gasket surfaces with degreaser.
13. Clean the valve train parts.
14. Inspect the valve lifters and the cam lobes for wear.
15. To remove the camshaft, remove the engine front cover, timing chain and sprockets.
16. Remove the camshaft position sensor.
17. Remove the camshaft thrust plate.
18. Install the camshaft sprocket bolt into the camshaft. Tighten finger tight only.
19. Carefully rotate and remove the camshaft from the engine block.

To install:

20. Coat the camshaft journals with clean engine oil.
21. Coat the camshaft lobes with pre-lube.
22. Install the camshaft sprocket bolt into the camshaft. Tighten finger tight only.
23. Carefully rotate and install the camshaft to the engine block.
24. Install the camshaft thrust plate and tighten to 89 inch lbs. (10 Nm).
25. Install the camshaft position sensor and tighten to 89 inch lbs. (10 Nm).
26. Install the timing chain, sprockets and front cover.
27. Coat the valve lifters with prelube and install them.
28. Install the valve lifter guides and tighten to 89 inch lbs. (10 Nm).
29. Install the intake manifold oil splash shield.
30. Install the pushrods in their original locations.

➡**The intake pushrods are identified with yellow stripes and are 5-3/4 inches long. Exhaust pushrods are**

identified with green stripes and are 6 inches long.

31. Install the rocker arms and tighten to 24 ft. lbs. (32 Nm).
32. Install the intake manifolds.
33. Install the valve covers.
34. Connect the negative battery cable.
35. Fill the cooling system.
36. Start the vehicle, check for leaks and repair if necessary.

CAMSHAFT BEARING REPLACEMENT

3.5L & 3.9L Engines

See Figures 73 through 75.

1. Select the expander assembly and driving washer.
2. Assemble the J 33049.
3. Drive out the camshaft bearings. Use the J 33049.

To install:

4. Assemble the J 33049 service set according to the manufacturer's instructions.

✳✳ WARNING

Severe engine damage may result if the oil holes are not correctly aligned.

5. Install the camshaft bearings in the following order:
- Index the camshaft bearing oil holes with the engine block oil passages.

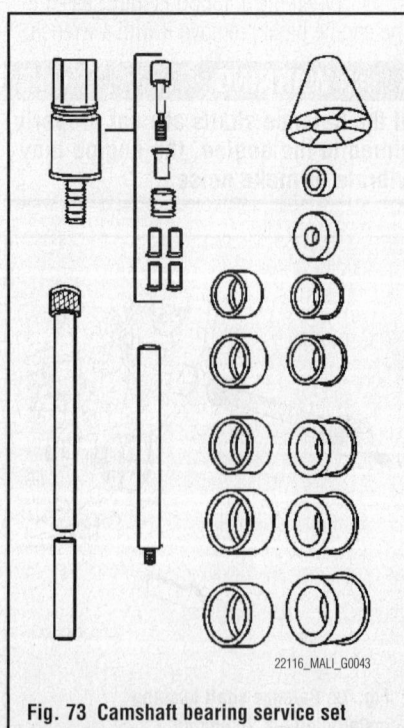

22116_MALI_G0043

Fig. 73 Camshaft bearing service set J 33049

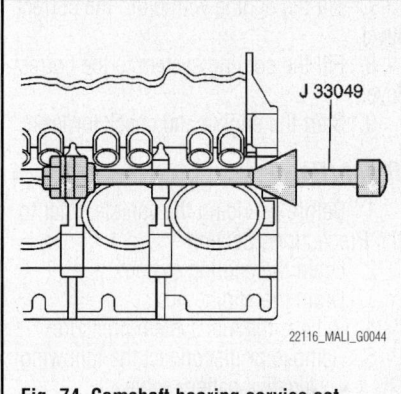

Fig. 74 Camshaft bearing service set J 33049 installed for bearing installation

- Place the bearing on the J 33049.
- Install the third camshaft bearing.
- Install the second camshaft bearing.
- Install the outer camshaft bearings.

6. Apply sealer GM P/N 12377901 (Canadian P/N 10953504) or the equivalent to the camshaft rear bearing hole plug.

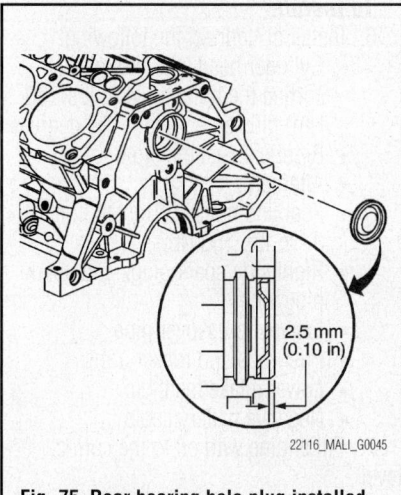

Fig. 75 Rear bearing hole plug installed to 0.10 inch. (2.5 mm).

7. Install the camshaft rear bearing hole plug.

CYLINDER HEAD

REMOVAL & INSTALLATION

2.2L Engine

See Figures 76 through 78.

1. Before servicing the vehicle, refer to the Precautions Section.
2. Drain the cooling system.
3. Relieve the fuel system pressure.
4. Remove or disconnect the following:
   - Intake manifold
   - Exhaust manifold

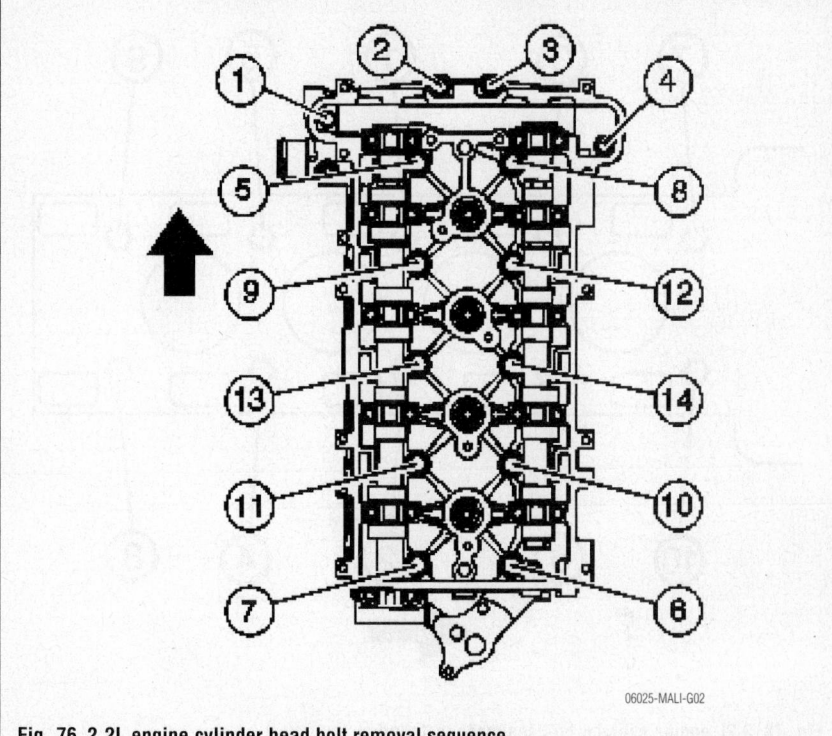

Fig. 76 2.2L engine cylinder head bolt removal sequence.

- Timing chain
- Cylinder head bolts in sequence
- Cylinder head

To install:

5. Install the cylinder head using new gaskets. Tighten the bolts in sequence to 22 ft. lbs. (30 Nm) plus 155 degrees.

6. Using new bolts, install the front cylinder head bolts. Tighten to 26 ft. lbs. (35 Nm).

7. Install or connect the following:
   - Timing chain
   - Exhaust manifold
   - Intake manifold

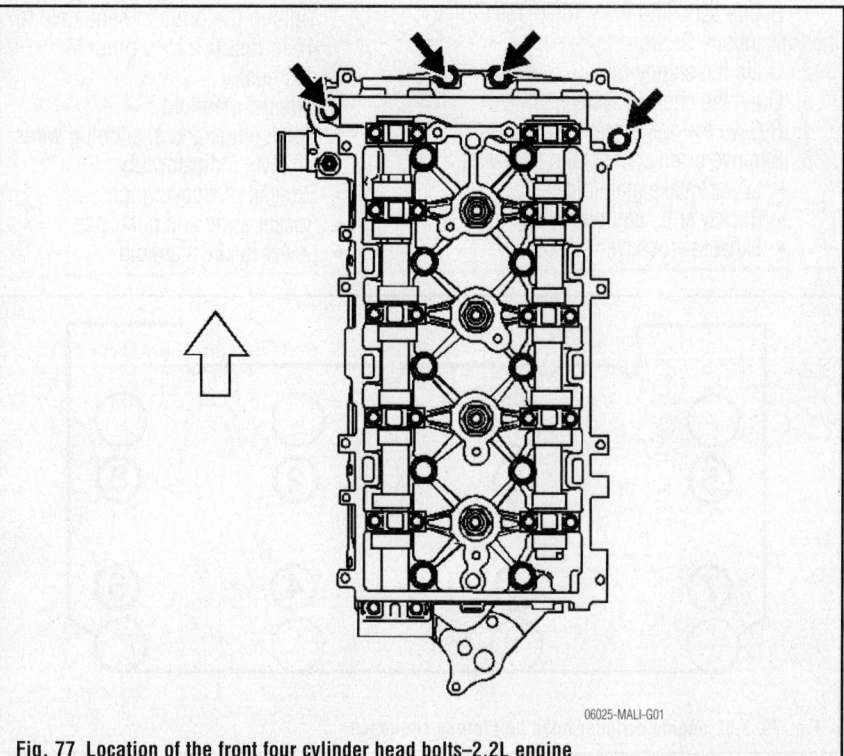

Fig. 77 Location of the front four cylinder head bolts–2.2L engine

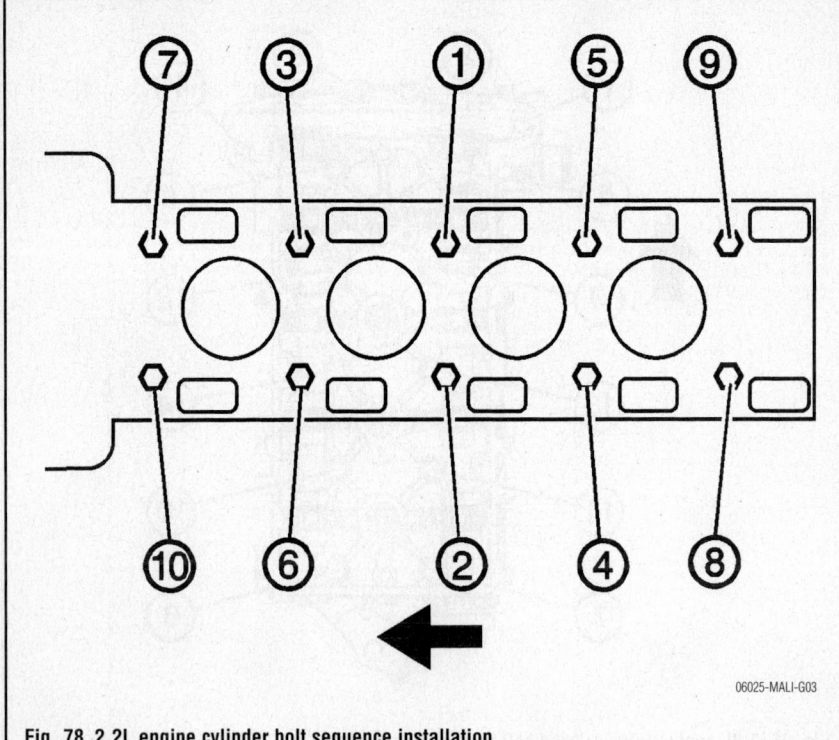

Fig. 78 2.2L engine cylinder bolt sequence installation.

8. Fill the cooling system to the correct level.

9. Start the engine and check for leaks.

3.5L Engine

Left (Front)

See Figure 79.

1. Before servicing the vehicle, refer to the Precautions Section.
2. Drain the engine oil.
3. Drain the cooling system.
4. Relieve the fuel system pressure.
5. Remove or disconnect the following:
   • Lower intake manifold
   • Rocker arms and pushrods
   • Exhaust crossover pipe
   • Oil level indicator tube
   • Spark plug wires and spark plugs
   • Exhaust manifold
   • Cylinder head bolts
   • Cylinder head

To install:

6. Install or connect the following:
   • Cylinder head using new gasket. Tighten the bolts in sequence to 44 ft. lbs. (60 Nm) plus 95 degrees.
   • Exhaust manifold
   • Spark plugs and spark plug wires
   • Oil level indicator tube
   • Exhaust crossover pipe
   • Rocker arms and pushrods
   • Lower intake manifold

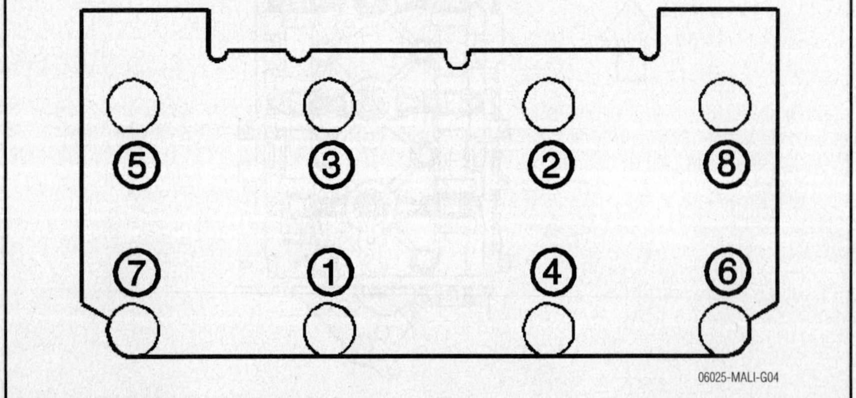

Fig. 79 3.5L engine cylinder head bolt torque sequence

7. Fill the engine with oil to the correct level.

8. Fill the cooling system to the correct level.

9. Start the engine and check for leaks.

Right (Rear)

1. Before servicing the vehicle, refer to the Precautions Section.
2. Drain the cooling system.
3. Drain the engine oil.
4. Relieve the fuel system pressure.
5. Remove or disconnect the following:
   • Negative battery cable
   • Lower intake manifold
   • Rocker arms and pushrods
   • Exhaust crossover pipe
   • Right side spark plug wires and spark plugs
   • Fuel line bracket
   • Alternator
   • Right exhaust manifold
   • Cylinder head bolts, in reverse order of the torque sequence
   • Cylinder head

To install:

6. Install or connect the following:
   • Cylinder head with new gasket. Torque the bolts to 44 ft. lbs. (60 Nm) plus an additional 95 degrees.
   • Right exhaust manifold
   • Alternator
   • Fuel line bracket. Tighten bolt to 37 ft. lbs. (50 Nm).
   • Right side spark plugs and spark plug wires
   • Exhaust crossover pipe
   • Pushrods and rocker arms
   • Lower intake manifold
   • Negative battery cable

7. Fill engine with oil to the correct level.

8. Fill the cooling system to the correct level.

9. Start the engine and check for leaks.

3.9L Engine

Left (Front)

See Figures 80 and 81.

1. Before servicing the vehicle, refer to the Precautions Section.
2. Drain the engine oil.
3. Drain the cooling system.
4. Lower the vehicle.
5. Remove the upper and lower intake manifolds.
6. Remove the valve rocker arms and the pushrods.
7. Remove the exhaust manifold.
8. Remove the oil level indicator tube.

9. Remove the left spark plugs.

10. Remove and discard the cylinder head bolts.

11. Remove the cylinder head.

12. Remove and discard the cylinder head gasket.

13. Remove the cylinder head locator dowel pins, if necessary.

14. Clean and inspect the cylinder head.

✻✻ WARNING

Head gaskets are specific for right hand and left hand applications, and also must be installed with the correct side facing up. Note the markings on the head gaskets for proper installation. Failure to do so may lead to engine damage.

15. Install the cylinder head locator dowel pins, if previously removed

16. Inspect the cylinder head locator dowel pins for proper installation.

17. Install a new cylinder head gasket.

18. Install the cylinder head onto the locator pins and the engine.

✻✻ WARNING

This component uses torque-to-yield bolts. When servicing this component

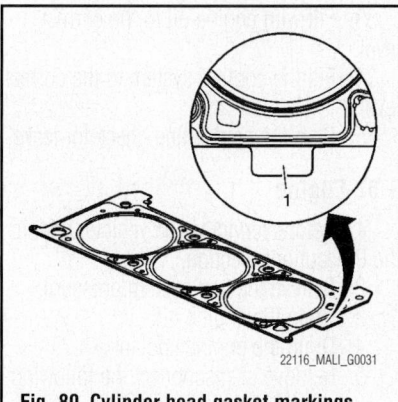

22116_MALI_G0031

Fig. 80 Cylinder head gasket markings shown

do not reuse the bolts, New torque-to-yield bolts must be installed. Reusing used torque-to-yield bolts will not provide proper bolt torque and clamp load. Failure to install NEW torque-to-yield bolts may lead to engine damage.

19. Install new cylinder head bolts finger tight.

20. Tighten the cylinder head bolts in sequence to 44 ft. lbs. (60 Nm). plus an additional 140 degrees using the J 45059 angle meter.

21. Install the left spark plugs.

22. Install the oil level indicator tube.

23. Install the exhaust manifold.

24. Install the valve rocker arms and the pushrods.

25. Install the lower intake manifold.

26. Fill the engine with oil.

27. Fill and bleed the cooling system.

28. Start the engine and check for leaks.

Right (Rear)

See Figure 81.

1. Before servicing the vehicle, refer to the Precautions Section.

2. Raise the vehicle.

3. Drain the cooling system.

4. Drain the engine oil.

5. Lower the vehicle.

6. Remove the upper and lower intake manifold.

7. Remove the valve rocker arms and pushrods.

8. Remove the exhaust manifold.

9. Remove the right spark plugs.

10. Remove the fuel line bracket bolt and stud.

11. Remove the fuel line bracket.

12. Remove the alternator.

13. Remove and discard the cylinder head bolts.

14. Remove the cylinder head.

15. Remove and discard the cylinder head gasket.

16. Remove the cylinder head locator dowel pins, if necessary.

✻✻ WARNING

Head gaskets are specific for right hand and left hand applications, and also must be installed with the correct side facing up. Note the markings on the head gaskets for proper installation. Failure to do so may lead to engine damage.

17. Clean and inspect the cylinder head.

To install:

18. Install the cylinder head locator dowel pins, if previously removed

19. Install a new cylinder head gasket.

20. Install the cylinder head onto the locator pins and the engine.

✻✻ WARNING

This component uses torque-to-yield bolts. When servicing this component do not reuse the bolts, New torque-to-yield bolts must be installed. Reusing used torque-to-yield bolts will not provide proper bolt torque and clamp load. Failure to install NEW torque-to-yield bolts may lead to engine damage.

21. Install new cylinder head bolts finger tight.

22. Tighten the cylinder head bolts in sequence to 44 ft. lbs. (60 Nm). plus an additional 140 degrees using the J 45059 angle meter.

23. Install the alternator.

24. Position the fuel line bracket to the cylinder head and tighten to 37 ft. lbs. (50 Nm).

25. Install the right spark plugs.

26. Install the exhaust manifold.

27. Install the valve rocker arms and pushrods.

28. Install the lower intake manifold.

29. Fill the engine with oil.

30. Fill and bleed the cooling system.

31. Start the engine and check for leaks.

ENGINE ASSEMBLY

REMOVAL & INSTALLATION

2.2L Engine

1. Before servicing the vehicle, refer to the Precautions Section.

2. Relieve the fuel system pressure.

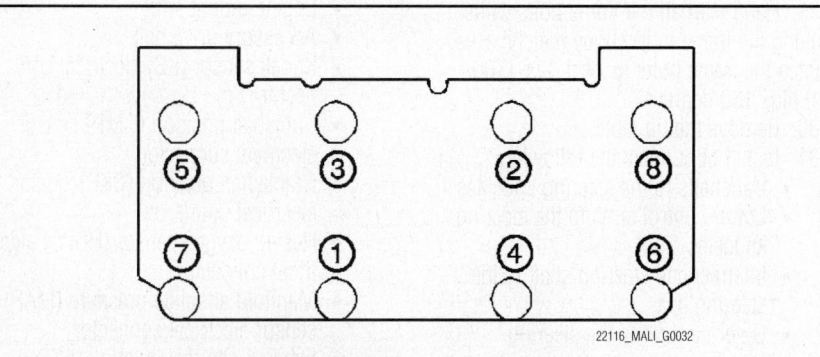

22116_MALI_G0032

Fig. 81 Cylinder head bolt tightening sequence—3.9L engine

3. Drain the engine oil.

4. Drain the engine coolant.

5. With the tires in the straight forward position, remove the key from the ignition.

6. Secure the cooling module to the upper body structure.

7. Remove or disconnect the following:
- Negative battery cable
- Air intake assembly
- Fuel lines from the fuel rail
- Coolant hoses
- Heater hoses
- Throttle control electrical connector
- MAP sensor electrical connector
- Crankshaft sensor electrical connector
- Oil pressure electrical connector
- Purge solenoid electrical connector
- Ignition coil electrical connector
- O2 sensor electrical connector
- Vehicle speed sensor (VSS) electrical connector
- Coolant temperature sensor electrical connector
- Back-up lamp switch electrical connector

8. Raise and support the vehicle.

9. Remove or disconnect the following:
- Accessory drive belt
- A/C compressor mounting bolts and set compress aside
- Starter electrical connectors
- Alternator electrical connector
- Front exhaust down pipe from the exhaust manifold
- Transmission harness connectors
- Transmission shift cable from the transmission

10. Support the powertrain assembly between the frame and the powertrain using a block of wood or suitable equivalent.

11. Remove or disconnect the following:
- Engine mount
- Side transmission mount, if equipped with automatic transmission
- Stabilizer links
- Outer tie rods from steering knuckles
- Intermediate shaft from the steering gear

❋❋ WARNING

In order to prevent possible SIR system deployment, do not attempt to rotate the steering shaft.

- Lower control arms from the steering knuckles
- Halfshafts from the steering knuckles

12. Matchmark the frame to body position.

13. Position a lift table under the frame to support the frame assembly.

14. Slowly remove the front frame bolts.

15. Partially unscrew the rear frame bolts until 1.5 inches of bolt shank is exposed.

16. Slowly lower the lift table.

17. Attach an engine lift hoist to the engine.

18. Remove the starter.

19. Remove the torque converter to flywheel bolts, if equipped.

20. Remove the transmission to engine bolts.

21. Separate the engine from the transmission.

22. Remove the clutch pressure plate and disc, if equipped.

23. Remove or disconnect the following:
- Exhaust manifold and studs
- Catalytic converter assembly
- Engine mount bracket
- Engine block heater, if equipped
- Thermostat housing and feed pipe
- Alternator

To install:

24. If removed, install or connect the following:
- Exhaust manifold
- Engine mount bracket
- Fuel rail
- Engine block heater, if equipped
- Thermostat housing and feed pipe
- Alternator
- Flywheel
- Clutch pressure plate and disc, if equipped

25. Align the engine to the transmission. Tighten to the engine-to-transmission bolts to 55 ft. lbs. (75 Nm).

26. Install the torque converter bolts, if equipped. Tighten bolts to 46 ft. lbs. (62 Nm).

27. Install the starter.

28. Reinstall the powertrain assembly to the frame assembly. Raise and position the frame/powertrain assembly to the vehicle.

29. Hand start all the frame bolts while aligning the frame to the body matchmarks. Tighten the frame bolts to 74 ft. lbs. (100 Nm) plus 180 degrees.

30. Remove the lift table.

31. Install or connect the following:
- Halfshafts to the steering knuckles
- Lower control arms to the steering knuckles
- Intermediate steering shaft to the steering gear
- Outer tie rods to the steering knuckles
- Stabilizer links

- Side transmission mount, if equipped with automatic transmission
- Engine mount
- Transmission shift cable to the transmission
- Transmission wiring harness connector
- Front exhaust down pipe to the exhaust manifold. Tighten nuts to 22 ft. lbs. (30 Nm).
- Alternator electrical connectors
- Starter harness connectors
- A/C compressor
- Accessory drive belt
- Throttle control electrical connector
- MAP sensor electrical connector
- Oil pressure electrical connector
- Purge solenoid electrical connector
- Ignition coil electrical connector
- O2 sensor electrical connector
- VSS electrical connector
- Coolant temperature sensor electrical connector
- Heater hoses
- Coolant hoses
- Fuel line to fuel rail
- Air intake assembly
- Negative battery cable

32. Release the cooling module from the upper body structure.

33. Fill with engine oil to the correct level.

34. Fill the cooling system to the correct level.

35. Start the engine and check for leaks.

3.5L Engine

1. Before servicing the vehicle, refer to the Precautions Section.

2. Relieve the fuel system pressure.

3. Drain the engine oil.

4. Drain the engine coolant.

5. Remove or disconnect the following:
- Negative battery cable
- Air intake assembly
- Hood
- Engine mount strut
- Accessory drive belt
- Knock sensor (KS) electrical connector
- Camshaft position (CMP) sensor electrical connector
- Crankshaft position (CKP) sensor electrical connector
- Heated oxygen sensor (HO2S) electrical connector
- Manifold absolute pressure (MAP) sensor electrical connector
- Exhaust gas recirculation (EGR) valve electrical connector

- Evaporative emission (EVAP) canister purge solenoid electrical connector
- Throttle control electrical connector
- Ignition coil electrical connector
- Body wiring harness

6. Raise and support the vehicle.

7. Remove or disconnect the following:
- Catalytic converters
- Engine wiring harness grounds
- Engine mount lower nuts
- Torque converter covers
- Starter
- A/C compressor mounting bolts and support the compress aside
- Torque converter bolts
- Transmission support brace
- Lower transmission-to-engine bolt
- Radiator hoses

8. Lower the vehicle and support the transmission.

9. Remove or disconnect the following:
- Heater hoses
- Vacuum hoses from upper intake manifold
- Fuel lines from the fuel rail

10. Install a suitable engine lifting device to the engine.

11. Remove the remaining transmission-to-engine bolts.

12. Remove the engine from the vehicle.

To install:

13. Install the engine to the transmission. Tighten the upper bolts to 55 ft. lbs. (75 Nm).

14. Remove the engine lifting device.

15. Install or connect the following:
- Radiator hoses
- Fuel lines to the fuel rail
- Brake booster vacuum hose to the upper intake manifold
- Heater hoses
- Lower transmission bolt and tighten to 55 ft. lbs. (75 Nm)
- Transmission support brace. Tighten bolts to 53 ft. lbs. (72 Nm)
- Torque converter bolts
- A/C compressor mounting bolts
- Starter
- Torque converter covers
- Engine mount lower nuts. Tighten nuts to 32 ft. lbs. (43 Nm).
- Engine wiring grounds. Tighten nut to 26 ft. lbs. (35 Nm).
- Catalytic converters
- Body wiring harness
- Ignition coil electrical connector
- Throttle control electrical connector

- EVAP canister purge solenoid electrical connector
- EGR valve electrical connector
- MAP sensor electrical connector
- HO2S electrical connector
- CKP sensor electrical connector
- CMP sensor electrical connector
- KS electrical connector
- Accessory drive belt
- Engine mount strut
- Hood
- Air intake assembly
- Negative battery cable

16. Fill the engine with oil to the correct level.

17. Fill the cooling system to the correct level.

18. Start the engine and check for leaks.

3.9L Engine

1. Before servicing the vehicle, refer to the Precautions Section.

2. Relieve the fuel system pressure.

3. Disconnect the negative battery cable.

4. Remove the air cleaner assembly.

5. Remove the hood.

6. Remove the intake manifold cover.

7. Remove the engine mount strut.

8. Remove the drive belt.

9. Drain the cooling system.

10. Drain the engine oil.

11. Remove the starter motor.

12. Remove the oil pressure sensor heat shield nuts and shield.

13. Disconnect the engine wiring harness electrical connector from the oil pressure sensor.

14. Disconnect the engine wiring harness electrical connector from the knock sensor.

15. Remove the engine wiring harness clip from the Air Conditioning (A/C) compressor bracket.

16. Remove the engine wiring harness clip bolt.

17. Separate the engine wiring harness clip from the engine boss

18. Disconnect the engine wiring harness electrical connector from the A/C compressor.

19. Disconnect the engine wiring harness electrical connector from the oil level sensor.

20. Remove the engine wiring harness clips from the transaxle bracket.

21. Remove the engine wiring harness clip from the transaxle bracket.

22. Remove the Connector Position Assurance (CPA) retainer.

23. Disconnect the lower front Heated Oxygen Sensor (HO2S) electrical connector from the engine wiring harness electrical connector.

24. Remove the engine wiring harness electrical connector from the thermostat housing stud.

25. Disconnect the lower rear HO2S electrical connector.

26. Remove the engine wiring harness electrical connector rosebud from the transaxle mount.

27. Disconnect the Knock Sensor (KS) and Crankshaft Position (CKP) sensor.

28. Lower the vehicle.

29. Remove all wiring harness clips.

30. Using the J 25034—C, remove power steering pump pulley.

31. Remove power steering pump.

32. Disconnect the Evaporative Emission (EVAP) canister purge solenoid.

33. Disconnect the Electronic Throttle Control (ETC).

34. Disconnect the Heated Oxygen Sensor (HO2S).

35. Disconnect the Manifold Absolute Pressure (MAP) sensor and the ignition control module.

36. Disconnect the alternator electrical connectors.

37. Disconnect the inlet manifold valve and the fuel injector inline electrical connector.

38. Disconnect the electrical connector from the camshaft phaser.

39. Disconnect the engine wiring harness electrical connectors from the body wiring harness electrical connector.

40. Disconnect the engine wiring harness electrical connectors from the Powertrain Control Module (PCM).

41. Disconnect the engine harness electrical connector from the Transmission Control Module (TCM).

42. Disconnect the vehicle speed sensor and transaxle wiring harness.

43. Remove engine wiring harness bolts and ground connections.

44. Remove battery cable ground terminal.

45. Reposition all of the harnesses out of the way.

46. Remove the catalytic converters.

47. Remove the engine mount.

48. Remove the torque converter cover.

49. Remove the flexplate to torque converter bolts.

50. Unbolt and reposition the A/C compressor to the side. DO NOT discharge the A/C system.

51. Remove the transaxle brace to oil pan bolts.

52. Remove the transaxle brace to transaxle bolts and remove the brace.

53. Remove the radiator outlet hose from the thermostat housing.

54. Lower the vehicle and support the transaxle.

55. Reposition the radiator surge tank hose clamp at the surge tank pipe.

56. Remove the radiator surge tank hose from the surge tank pipe.

57. Remove the brake booster vacuum hose from the intake manifold.

58. Remove the heater outlet and inlet hoses from the engine.

59. Disconnect the fuel feed line from the fuel rail.

60. Disconnect the EVAP purge line from the canister purge solenoid.

61. Remove the radiator inlet hose from the engine.

62. Install an engine lifting device to the engine.

63. Remove all the transaxle-to-engine bolts and studs.

64. Separate the engine from the transaxle and remove the engine from the vehicle.

To install:

65. Install the engine to the vehicle and install the engine to the transaxle.

66. Install the transaxle-to-engine bolts and studs.

67. Install the remaining transaxle-to-engine bolts and studs and tighten to 55 ft. lbs. (75 Nm).

68. Install the radiator inlet hose and tighten clamp.

69. Connect the EVAP purge line to the canister purge solenoid.

70. Connect the fuel feed line from the fuel rail.

71. Install the heater outlet and inlet hoses and tighten clamps.

72. Install the brake booster vacuum hose to the intake manifold.

73. Install the radiator surge tank hose to the surge tank pipe and tighten clamp.

74. Remove the support from the transaxle and raise the vehicle.

75. Install the radiator outlet hose to the thermostat housing.

76. Snug all the transaxle brace to engine block bolts and oil pan lower bolts.

77. Tighten the bolts to 37 ft. lbs. (50 Nm).

78. Install A/C compressor and tighten to 37 ft. lbs. (50 Nm).

79. Install the flexplate to torque converter bolts and tighten to 46 ft. lbs. (62 Nm).

80. Install the torque converter cover.

81. Install the engine mount and tighten the frame nuts to 37 ft. lbs. (50 Nm).

82. Install the catalytic converters and tighten to 23 ft. lbs. (31 Nm).

83. Position the branches of the engine wiring harness over the engine.

84. Install the battery cable ground terminal and the engine harness ground terminal to the transaxle stud.

85. Tighten the harness retaining nut to 18 ft. lbs. (25 Nm).

86. Install the engine wiring harness ground bolt and tighten to 18 ft. lbs. (25 Nm).

87. Install and tighten all additional harness mounting bolts and tighten to 18 ft. lbs. (25 Nm).

88. Connect the engine wiring harness electrical connector to the transaxle and the vehicle speed sensor.

89. Reconnect the PCM and TCM electrical connectors.

90. Connect all the engine wiring harness electrical connectors to the body wiring harness electrical connectors.

91. Install all wiring harness clips and any remaining wiring harness bolts.

92. Reconnect the camshaft phaser, fuel injector inline electrical connector and the inlet manifold valve.

93. Reconnect the alternator electrical connectors and tighten stud nut to 15 ft. (20 Nm).

94. Reconnect the rear upper HO2S electrical connector, ignition control module and the MAP sensor.

95. Reconnect the front HO2S electrical connector, the ETC and the EVAP canister purge solenoid.

96. Install the power steering pump and tighten mounting bolts to 18 ft. lbs. (25 Nm).

97. Using the J 25033—C, install power steering pump pulley.

98. Install the engine wiring harness clip to the power steer pump bracket.

99. Raise the vehicle.

100. Reconnect the CKP sensor and the KS sensor.

101. Install the engine wiring harness electrical connector rosebud to the transaxle mount.

102. Connect the lower rear HO2S electrical connector.

103. Install the engine wiring harness electrical connector to the thermostat housing stud.

104. Connect the lower front HO2S electrical connector.

105. Install the entire remaining engine wiring harness clips to the transaxle.

106. Reconnect the oil level sensor

and the A/C compressor electrical connectors.

107. Install the engine wiring harness clip to the engine boss.

108. Reconnect to the knock sensor and oil pressure sensor electrical connectors.

109. Install the oil pressure sensor heat shield tighten the mounting nuts to 89 inch. lbs. (10 Nm).

110. Install the starter motor and tighten mounting bolts to 32 ft. lbs. (43 Nm).

111. Tighten the solenoid mounting nut to 89 inch. lbs. (10 Nm).

112. Install the drive belt.

113. Install the engine mount strut and tighten bots to 37 ft. lbs. (50 Nm).

114. Install the intake manifold cover.

115. Install the air cleaner assembly.

116. Install the hood and tighten bolts to 89 inch. lbs. (10 Nm).

117. Fill the cooling system.

118. Refill crankcase with engine oil.

119. Connect the negative battery cable.

120. Perform the CKP system variation learn procedure.

121. Check for leaks and recheck all fluid levels.

EXHAUST MANIFOLD

REMOVAL & INSTALLATION

2.2L Engine

See Figure 82.

1. Before servicing the vehicle, refer to the Precautions Section.

2. Drain the cooling system.

3. Remove or disconnect the following:
- Negative battery cable
- Exhaust manifold heat shield
- Block heater, if equipped
- Oxygen sensor
- Exhaust manifold retaining nuts
- Exhaust manifold and catalytic converter assembly

To install:

4. Install or connect the following:
- New manifold studs if necessary. Tighten to 89 inch lbs. (10 Nm).
- Exhaust manifold gasket
- Exhaust manifold and catalytic converter assembly. Tighten new nuts to 124 inch lbs. (14 Nm)
- Oxygen sensor. Tighten to 22 ft. lbs. (30 Nm)
- Block heater, if equipped
- Exhaust manifold heat shield
- Negative battery cable

5. Refill the cooling system to the correct level.

6. Start the engine and check for leaks.

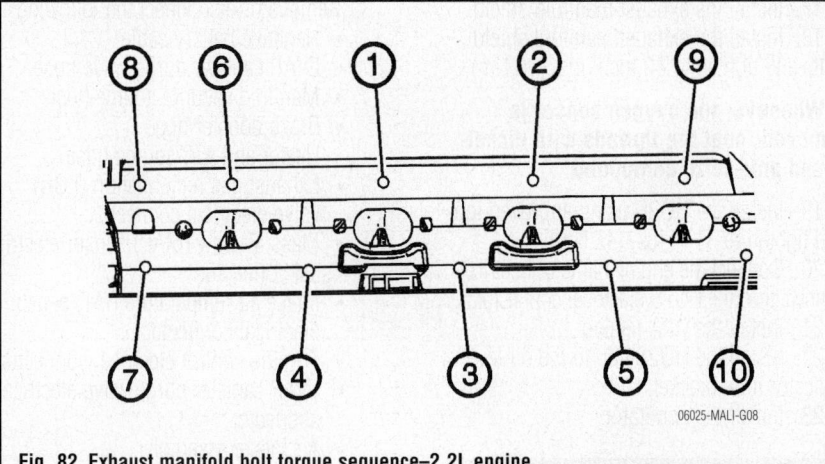

Fig. 82 Exhaust manifold bolt torque sequence–2.2L engine

3.5L Engine

Left Side

See Figure 83.

1. Before servicing the vehicle, refer to the Precautions Section.
2. Remove or disconnect the following:
   - Negative battery cable
   - Heated oxygen (HO2S) sensor
   - Spark plugs
   - Exhaust manifold heat shield
   - Exhaust manifold

To install:

3. Install new exhaust manifold if necessary. Tighten to 13 ft. lbs. (18 Nm).
4. Install or connect the following:
   - Exhaust manifold gasket
   - Exhaust manifold. Tighten nuts in sequence to 12 ft. lbs. (16 Nm).
   - Exhaust manifold heat shield
   - Spark plugs
   - HO2S sensor
   - Negative battery cable

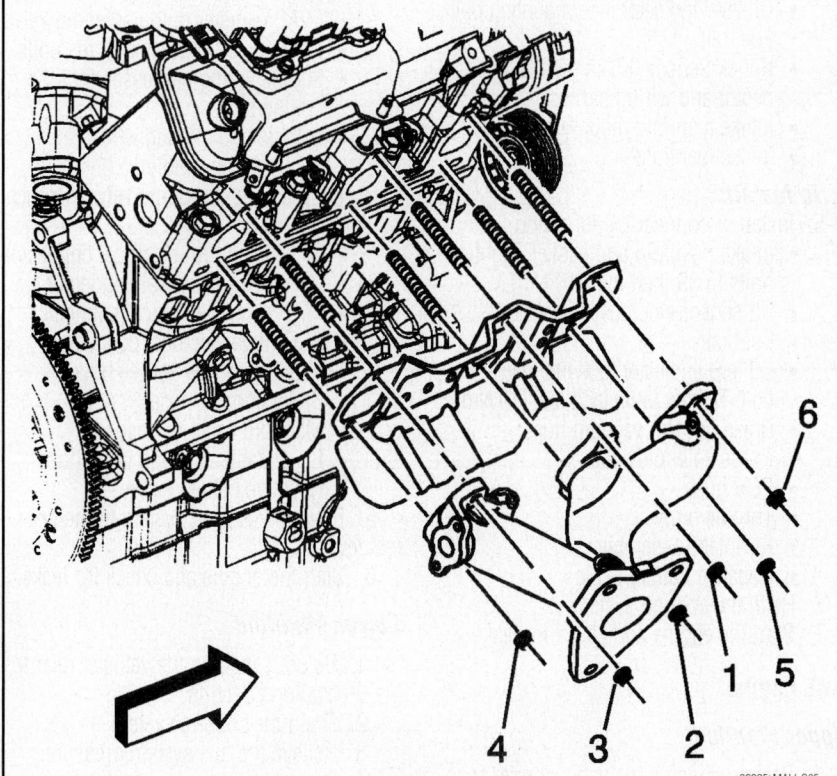

Fig. 83 Exploded view of the left-hand exhaust manifold and tightening sequence–3.5L engine

Right Side

1. Before servicing the vehicle, refer to the Precautions Section.
2. Remove or disconnect the following:
   - Negative battery cable
   - Heated oxygen (HO2S) sensor
   - Spark plugs
   - Exhaust gas circulation (EGR) pipe
   - Exhaust manifold heat shield
   - Exhaust manifold and gasket

To install:

3. Install or connect the following:
   - New exhaust manifold studs, if necessary. Tighten to 13 ft. lbs. (18 Nm).
   - Exhaust manifold and gasket. Tighten nuts in sequence to 12 ft. lbs. (16 Nm).
   - Exhaust manifold heat shield. Tighten bolts to 89 inch lbs. (10 Nm).
   - EGR pipe
   - Spark plugs
   - HO2S sensor
   - Negative battery cable

3.9L Engine

Left Side

1. Remove the air cleaner outlet duct.
2. Remove the Connector Position Assurance (CPA) retainer.
3. Disconnect the heated oxygen sensor (HO2S) electrical connector.
4. Remove the HO2S clip from the oil level indicator tube bracket.

> **✳✳ WARNING**
>
> **The HO2S uses a permanently attached pigtail and connector. This pigtail should not be removed from the sensor. Damage or removal of the pigtail or connector will affect proper operation of the sensor.**

5. Remove the HO2S using approved tool.
6. Remove the exhaust manifold heat shield bolts.
7. Remove the exhaust manifold heat shield.
8. Remove the upper exhaust manifold bolts.
9. Raise and support the vehicle.
10. Remove the left catalytic converter.
11. Remove the lower exhaust manifold bolts.
12. Remove the exhaust manifold.
13. Remove and discard the exhaust manifold gasket.

To install:

14. Install a NEW exhaust manifold gasket onto the cylinder head studs.
15. Install the exhaust manifold.
16. Install the exhaust manifold bolts and tighten to 15 ft. lbs. (20 Nm).
17. Install the left catalytic converter.
18. Lower the vehicle.
19. Install the exhaust manifold heat shield and mounting bolts, tighten to 89 inch. lbs. (10 Nm).

➡**Whenever the oxygen sensor is removed, coat the threads with nickel-based anti-seize compound.**

20. Install the HO2S using approved tool and tighten to 31 ft. lbs. (42 Nm).
21. Connect the HO2S electrical connector.
22. Install the CPA retainer.
23. Install the HO2S clip to the oil level indicator tube bracket.
24. Install the air cleaner outlet duct.

Right Side

1. Remove the generator.
2. Remove the connector position assurance (CPA) retainer.
3. Disconnect the engine harness electrical connector heated oxygen sensor (HO2S) electrical connector (4).
4. Remove the HO2S clip from the oil level indicator tube bracket.

❋❋ WARNING

The HO2S uses a permanently attached pigtail and connector. This pigtail should not be removed from the sensor. Damage or removal of the pigtail or connector will affect proper operation of the sensor.

5. Remove the HO2S using approved tool.
6. Remove the exhaust manifold shield bolts.
7. Remove the exhaust manifold shield.
8. Remove the upper exhaust manifold bolts.
9. Remove the right catalytic converter.
10. Remove the lower exhaust manifold bolt.
11. Remove the exhaust manifold.
12. Remove and discard the exhaust manifold gasket.

To install:

13. Install a new exhaust manifold gasket onto the cylinder head studs.
14. Install the exhaust manifold.
15. Install the exhaust manifold bolts and tighten to 15 ft. lbs. (20 Nm).
16. Install the right catalytic converter.

17. Install the exhaust manifold shield.
18. Install the exhaust manifold shield bolts and tighten to 89 inch. lbs. (10 Nm).

➡**Whenever the oxygen sensor is removed, coat the threads with nickel-based anti-seize compound.**

19. Install the HO2S using approved tool and tighten to 31 ft. lbs. (42 Nm).
20. Connect the engine harness electrical connector to the HO2S electrical connector.
21. Install the CPA retainer.
22. Install the HO2S clip to the oil level indicator tube bracket.
23. Install the generator.

INTAKE MANIFOLD

REMOVAL & INSTALLATION

2.2L Engine

1. Before servicing the vehicle, refer to the Precautions Section.
2. Drain the cooling system.
3. Relieve the fuel system pressure.
4. Remove or disconnect the following:
   - Negative battery cable
   - Air intake assembly
   - Throttle body
   - PCV hose
   - Purge solenoid tube
   - Brake booster vacuum hose
   - Oil level indicator tube mounting bolt
   - Fuel rail
   - Knock Sensor (KS) electrical connector and wiring harness
   - Intake manifold mounting bolts
   - Intake manifold

To install:

5. Install or connect the following:
   - Intake manifold and gasket. Tighten bolts to 89 inch lbs. (10 Nm).
   - KS sensor electrical connector
   - Fuel rail
   - Oil level indicator tube mounting bolt. Tighten to 89 inch lbs. (10 Nm).
   - Brake booster vacuum hose
   - Purge solenoid rube
   - PCV hose
   - Throttle body
   - Air intake assembly
   - Negative battery cable
6. Refill the cooling system.
7. Start the engine and check for leaks.

3.5L Engine

Upper Manifold

1. Before servicing the vehicle, refer to the Precautions Section.
2. Drain the cooling system.

3. Remove or disconnect the following:
   - Negative battery cable
   - EVAP canister purge valve hose
   - Manifold vacuum source hose
   - Brake booster hose
   - Heater and A/C source hose
   - Exhaust gas recirculation (EGR) valve electrical connector
   - Mass air flow (MAP) sensor electrical connector
   - Intake air temperature (IAT) sensor electrical connector
   - Throttle control electrical connector
   - EVAP canister purge valve electrical connector
   - Air intake assembly
   - Left side spark plug wires
   - Engine wiring harnesses from their retainers
   - Ignition coil bracket with the coils
   - EVAP canister purge solenoid valve
   - MAP sensor
   - EGR valve
   - Upper intake manifold mounting bolts
   - Upper intake manifold

To install:

4. Install or connect the following:
   - Intake manifold with gaskets. Tighten bolts to 18 ft. lbs. (25 Nm)
   - EGR valve
   - MAP sensor
   - EVAP canister purge solenoid valve
   - Ignition coil bracket with the coils
   - Engine wiring harnesses into the retainers
   - Left side spark plug wires
   - Air intake assembly
   - EVAP canister purge valve electrical connector
   - Throttle control electrical connector
   - IAT sensor electrical connector
   - MAP sensor electrical connector
   - EGR valve electrical connector
   - Heater and A/C source hose
   - Brake booster hose
   - Manifold vacuum hose
   - EVAP canister purge valve hose
   - Negative battery cable
5. Refill the cooling system to the correct level.
6. Start the engine and check for leaks.

Lower Manifold

1. Before servicing the vehicle, refer to the Precautions Section.
2. Drain the cooling system.
3. Relieve the fuel system pressure.
4. Remove or disconnect the following:
   - Negative battery cable
   - Upper intake manifold

- Valve covers
- Engine coolant temperature (ECT) wiring harness
- Fuel injector wiring harness
- Manifold air pressure (MAP) wiring harness
- Fuel rail
- Heater inlet pipe with heater hose from the lower manifold and place aside
- Upper radiator hose
- Thermostat housing inlet pipe
- Thermostat
- Lower intake manifold mounting bolts
- Lower intake manifold
- Rocker arms and pushrods
- Lower intake manifold gaskets

To install:

5. Install the lower intake manifold gaskets.

6. Install the rocker arms and pushrods.

7. With the gaskets in place, apply a small drop of RTV sealant to the four corners of the manifold-to-engine block joints.

8. Install the lower intake manifold. Tighten bolts to as follows:

   a. Step 1: Apply GM P/N 12345382 sealer or equivalent to the bolt threads.

   b. Step 2: Tighten all bolts 115 inch lbs. (13 Nm).

   c. Step 3: Tighten bolts 1-4 in sequence to 15 ft. lbs. (20 Nm).

   d. Step 4: Tighten bolts 5-8 in sequence to 18 ft. lbs. (25 Nm).

9. Install or connect the following:

- Heater inlet pipe
- Thermostat
- Thermostat housing inlet pipe
- Upper radiator hose
- Heater inlet pipe and heater hose
- Fuel rail
- MAP wiring harness
- Fuel injector and MAP wiring harness
- ECT wiring harness
- Valve covers
- Upper intake manifold
- Negative battery cable

10. Refill the cooling system to the correct level.

11. Start the engine and check for leaks.

3.9L Engine

Upper Manifold

See Figure 84.

1. Before servicing the vehicle, refer to the Precautions Section.

2. Remove the intake manifold cover.

3. Relieve the fuel system pressure.

4. Disconnect the fuel feed pipe quick connect fitting from the fuel rail.

5. Disconnect the Evaporative Emission (EVAP) pipe from the purge solenoid.

6. Open the retaining clip and remove the fuel and EVAP pipes from the clip.

7. Drain the cooling system.

8. Remove the Positive Crankcase Ventilation (PCV) fresh air tube.

9. Remove the PCV foul air tube.

10. Reposition the brake booster vacuum hose clamp at the intake manifold.

11. Remove the vacuum hose from the intake manifold.

12. Remove the radiator surge tank inlet hose from the inlet pipe.

13. Remove the radiator surge tank inlet pipe bolts.

14. Remove the radiator surge tank inlet pipe.

15. Disconnect the Manifold Absolute Pressure (MAP) sensor electrical connector.

16. Disconnect the evaporative emission EVAP canister purge solenoid electrical connector.

17. Disconnect the Electronic Throttle Control (ETC) electrical connector.

18. Disconnect the inlet manifold valve electrical connector.

19. Remove the air cleaner outlet duct.

20. Disconnect the left side spark plug wires from the spark plugs.

21. Disconnect the left side spark plug wires from the ignition coil.

22. Disengage the spark plug wire retainer clips from the intake manifold bracket and the heater inlet and outlet pipe.

23. Remove the left side spark plug wires.

24. Remove the heater inlet and outlet pipe nuts from the throttle body studs.

25. Remove the inlet and outlet pipe from the studs.

26. Remove the 2 ignition coil bolts.

27. Remove the alternator upper bolt.

28. Remove the alternator ball stud.

29. Remove the alternator rear brace.

30. Remove the upper intake manifold bolts and stud.

31. Separate and remove the upper intake manifold from the lower intake manifold.

32. Remove the upper to lower intake manifold gaskets.

To install:

33. Install the new upper to lower intake manifold gaskets.

34. Set the upper intake manifold onto the lower intake manifold.

35. Apply threadlock to the upper intake manifold bolts and stud threads.

36. Install the upper intake manifold bolts and stud. Tighten to 18 ft. lbs. (25 Nm).

37. Install the alternator rear brace.

38. Install the alternator ball stud and tighten to 15 ft. lbs. (20 Nm).

39. Install the alternator upper bolt and tighten to 37 ft. lbs. (50 Nm).

40. Install the 2 ignition coil bolts. Tighten to 18 ft. lbs. (25 Nm).

41. Install the inlet and outlet pipe to the studs.

42. Install the heater inlet and outlet pipe nuts to the throttle body studs. Tighten the nuts to 89 inch. lbs. (10 Nm).

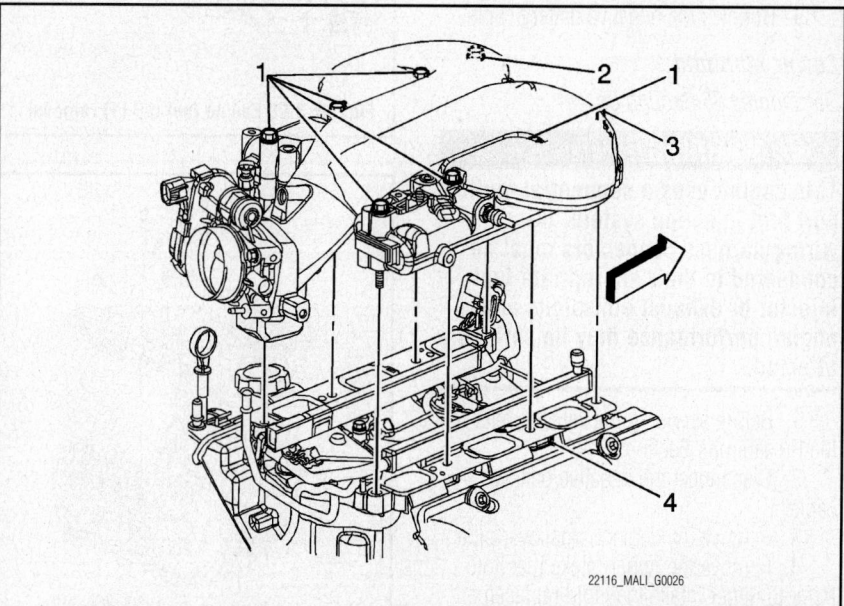

22116_MALI_G0026

Fig. 84 3.9L Engine upper intake manifold bolts (1, 2), stud (3) and (4) lower intake manifold

43. Install the left side spark plug wires.

44. Connect the left side spark plug wires to the spark plugs.

45. Connect the left side spark plug wires to the ignition coil.

46. Engage the spark plug wire retainer clips to the intake manifold bracket and the heater inlet/outlet pipe.

47. Install the air cleaner outlet duct.

48. Connect the inlet manifold valve electrical connector.

49. Connect the EVAP canister purge solenoid electrical connector

50. Connect the ETC electrical connector

51. Connect the MAP sensor electrical connector.

52. Install the radiator surge tank inlet pipe.

53. Install the radiator surge tank inlet pipe bolts. Tighten the bolts to 89 inch. lbs. (10 Nm).

54. Install the radiator surge tank inlet hose to the inlet pipe.

55. Position the radiator surge tank inlet hose clamp.

56. Install the brake booster vacuum hose to the intake manifold.

57. Position the vacuum hose clamp at the intake manifold.

58. Install the PCV foul air tube.

59. Install the PCV fresh air tube.

60. Install the fuel and EVAP pipes to the retainer clip and close the clip.

61. Connect the fuel feed pipe quick connect fitting to the fuel rail.

62. Connect the EVAP emission pipe to the purge solenoid.

63. Fill and bleed the cooling system.

64. Install the intake manifold cover.

65. Connect the negative battery cable.

Lower Manifold

See Figures 85 through 88.

✳✳ WARNING

This engine uses a sequential multi-port fuel injection system. Injector wiring harness connectors must be connected to their appropriate fuel injector or exhaust emissions and engine performance may be seriously affected.

1. Before servicing the vehicle, refer to the Precautions Section.

2. Disconnect the negative battery cable.

3. Remove the coolant crossover pipe.

4. Remove the upper intake manifold. Refer to upper intake manifold replacement.

5. Remove the left valve rocker arm cover.

6. Remove the right valve rocker arm cover.

7. Disconnect the Engine Coolant Temperature (ECT) electrical connector.

8. Disconnect the fuel feed line from the fuel rail.

9. Disconnect the fuel injector inline connector.

10. Remove the fuel injector harness connector bracket bolt from the intake manifold.

11. Disconnect the Camshaft Position (CMP) sensor electrical connector.

12. Remove the fuel injector rail bolts.

13. Remove the fuel rail.

14. Remove the lower intake manifold bolts.

15. Remove the lower intake manifold.

16. Loosen the valve rocker arm bolts.

➡**Place the valve train components in a rack in order to ensure that the components are installed in the same location from which they were removed.**

17. Remove the valve rocker arms.

18. Remove the push rods.

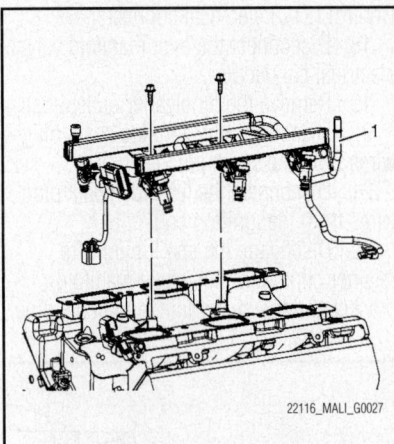

Fig. 85 3.9L Engine fuel rail (1) removal

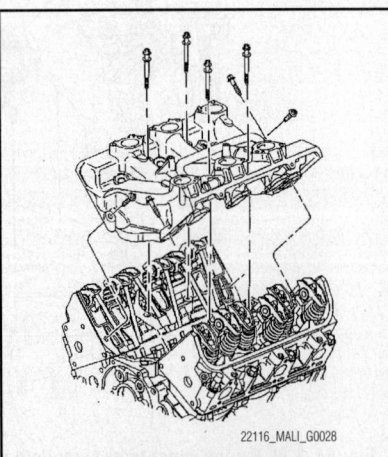

Fig. 86 3.9L Lower intake removal

19. Take note of the following:
- The intake push rods measure 5.81 inch. (147.51 mm).
- The exhaust push rods measure 6.1 inch. (154.87 mm).

20. Remove the lower intake manifold gaskets and seals.

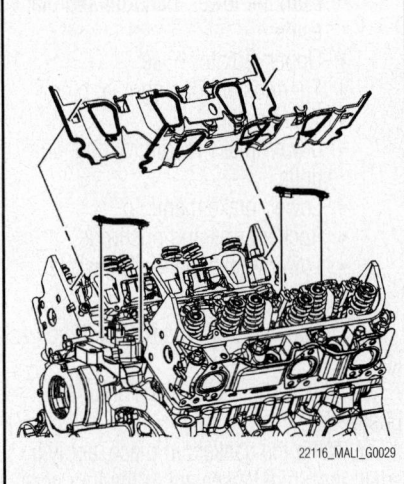

Fig. 87 3.9L Engine lower intake manifold gaskets and seals

21. Clean the lower intake manifold gasket and seal surfaces on the cylinder heads and the engine block.

22. Clean the gasket and seal surfaces on the lower intake manifold with degreaser.

23. Remove all the loose room temperature vulcanizing sealer (RTV).

To install:

✳✳ WARNING

RTV sealer is NOT to be placed under the lower intake manifold gaskets.

24. Install the lower intake manifold gaskets and seals.

25. Coat the ends of the push rods using prelube.

26. Install the push rods in their original location.

27. Take note of the following:
- The intake push rods measure 5.81 inch. (147.51 mm).
- The exhaust push rods measure 6.1 inch. (154.87 mm).

28. Coat the rocker arm friction surfaces using prelube.

➡**Shims (P/N 88894006) may be required under the valve rocker arm pedestals if reconditioning has been performed on the cylinder head or its components.**

29. Install the valve rocker arms in their original positions.

30. Install the valve rocker arm bolts and tighten to 25 ft. lbs. (34 Nm).

31. With the new gaskets and seals in place, apply a small drop, 0.031–0.39 inch. (8–10 mm) of RTV sealer to the 4 corners of the intake manifold to engine block joints.

32. Install the lower intake manifold.

➡ **Maximum gasket performance is achieved when using new fasteners, which contain a thread-locking patch. If the fasteners are not replaced, a thread locking chemical must be applied to the fastener threads. Failure to replace the fasteners or apply a thread-locking chemical may reduce gasket sealing capability.**

33. Apply sealer to the lower intake manifold bolt threads.

34. Install the lower intake manifold bolts.

35. Tighten the lower intake manifold bolts in the sequence shown.

➡ **Failure to tighten vertical bolts before the diagonal bolts may cause an oil leak.**

36. Tighten the lower intake manifold bolts as follows:
- Tighten the bolts (1, 2, 3, and 4) in sequence to 12 ft. lbs. (16 Nm).
- Tighten the bolts (5, 6, 7, and 8) in sequence to 18 ft. lbs. (25 Nm).

37. Inspect the fuel rail, fuel injectors and fuel injector O-rings for damage and replace as necessary.

38. Lubricate the fuel injector O-rings using lubricant.

39. Install the injector nozzles into the lower intake manifold injector bores.

40. Press on the injector rail using the palms of both hands until the injector is fully seated.

41. Install the fuel injector rail bolts and tighten to 89 inch. lbs. (10 Nm).

42. Connect the CMP sensor electrical connector.

43. Position the fuel injector harness connector bracket to the intake manifold.

44. Install the fuel injector harness connector bracket bolt and tighten to 71 inch. lbs. (8 Nm).

45. Connect the fuel injector inline connector.

46. Connect the fuel feed line to the fuel rail.

47. Connect the ECT electrical connector.

48. Install the right valve rocker arm cover.

49. Install the left valve rocker arm cover.

50. Install the upper intake manifold. Refer to upper intake manifold replacement.

51. Install the coolant crossover pipe.

52. Fill and bleed the cooling system.

53. Install the intake manifold cover.

54. Connect the negative battery cable.

OIL PAN

REMOVAL & INSTALLATION

2.2L Engine

See Figure 89.

1. Before servicing the vehicle, refer to the Precautions Section.
2. Drain the engine oil.
3. Remove or disconnect the following:
- Negative battery cable
- Accessory drive belt
- Lower A/C compressor mounting bolt

- Oil pan mounting bolts
- Oil pan

To install:

4. Apply a 0.13 inch (3.5mm) bead of the GM P/N 12378521 sealant around the perimeter of the oil pan and oil suction port opening.

5. Install or connect the following:
- Oil pan. Tighten the bolts in sequence to 18 ft. lbs. (25 Nm).
- Lower A/C compressor mounting bolt. Tighten the bolt to 37 ft. lbs. (50 Nm).
- Accessory drive belt
- Negative battery cable

6. Fill the engine with oil to the correct level.

3.5L Engine

1. Before servicing the vehicle, refer to the Precautions Section.
2. Drain the engine oil.
3. Remove or disconnect the following:
- Negative battery cable
- Right front wheel
- Inner fender splash shield
- Oil filter and oil filter adapter
- Catalytic converter
- ABS wheel speed sensor
- Right front ball joint from the steering knuckle
- Lower closeout panel
- A/C compress mounting bolts and position compress aside
- Engine-to-transmission support braces
- Oil level sensor

4. Support the engine using a jack

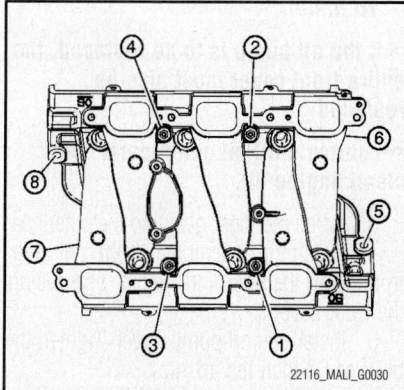

Fig. 88 3.9L Engine lower intake manifold tightening sequence

22116_MALI_G0030

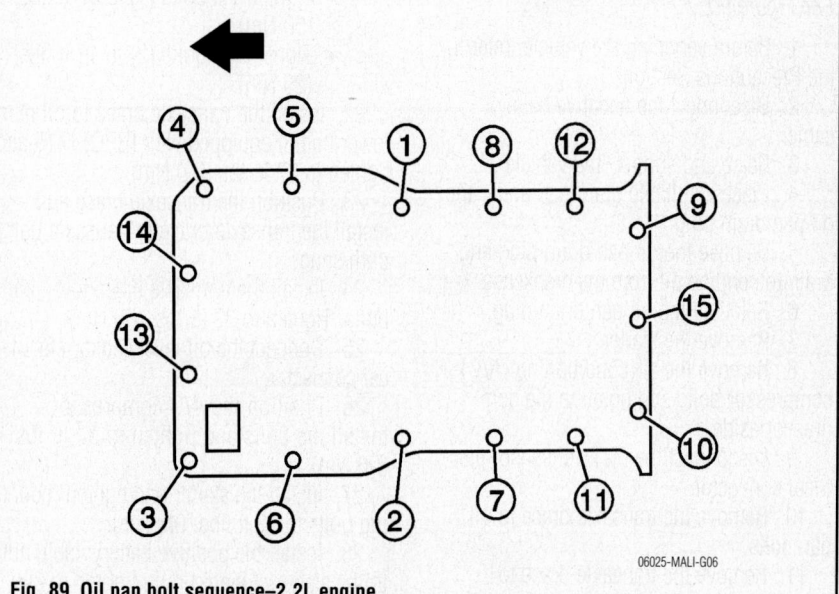

Fig. 89 Oil pan bolt sequence–2.2L engine

06025-MALI-G06

stand or equivalent and remove the right side engine mounting bolts.

5. Loosen the left side cradle bolts.
6. Remove the cradle bolts from the right front and right rear.
7. Remove the starter motor.
8. Remove the oil pan mounting bolts.
9. Remove the oil pan.

To install:

10. Install or connect the following:
   • Oil pan with a new gasket.

➡**Apply silicone sealant on the tabs that insert into the gasket groove on the outer surface of the mean bearing cap.**

   • Oil pan bolts. Tighten the bolts to 18 ft. lbs. (25 Nm) and the side bolts to 37 ft. lbs. (50 Nm).
   • Starter motor
   • Flywheel inspection cover
   • A/C compressor. Tighten the bolts to 37 ft. lbs. (50 Nm).
   • Engine cradle bolts. Tighten the bolts to 37 ft. lbs. (50 Nm).
   • Ball joint to the steering knuckle
   • ABS wheel speed sensor
   • Engine-to-transmission support braces
   • Catalytic converter
   • Oil filter adapter and oil filter
   • Inner fender splash shield
   • Right front wheel
   • Lower closeout panel
   • Negative battery cable

11. Fill the engine with oil to the correct level.
12. Start the engine and check for leaks.

3.9L Engine

See Figure 90.

1. Before servicing the vehicle, refer to the Precautions Section.
2. Disconnect the negative battery cable.
3. Raise and support the vehicle.
4. Place a suitable drain pan under the oil pan drain plug.
5. Remove the oil pan drain plug and drain the engine oil from the crankcase.
6. Reinstall the oil pan drain plug.
7. Remove the starter.
8. Remove the air conditioning (A/C) compressor bolts and position the compressor aside.
9. Disconnect the oil level sensor electrical connector.
10. Remove the transaxle brace to oil pan bolts.
11. Remove the transaxle brace to transaxle bolt and remove the brace.

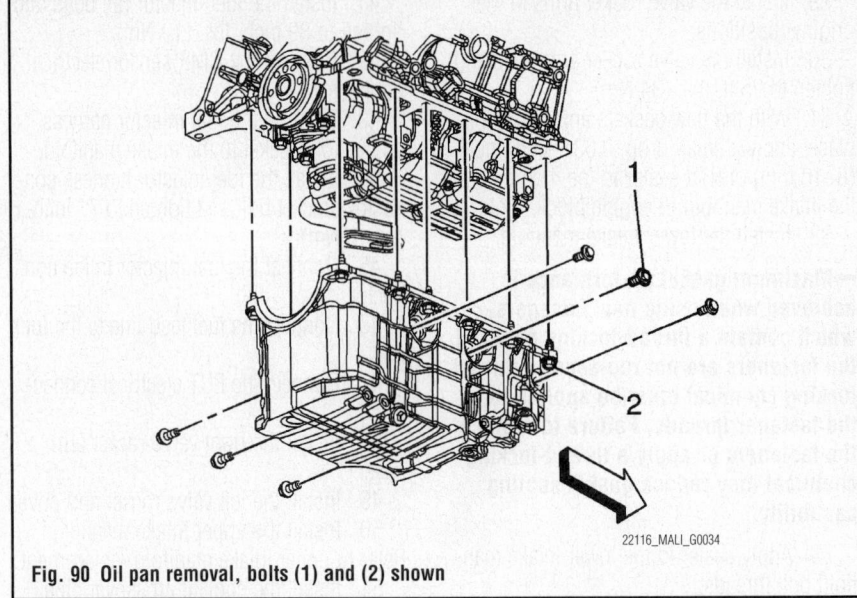

Fig. 90 Oil pan removal, bolts (1) and (2) shown

12. Remove the transaxle brace to oil pan lower bolt, if equipped with regular production option (RPO) M15.
13. Remove the oil pan bolts.
14. Remove the oil pan.
15. Remove and discard the oil pan gasket.
16. Clean the oil pan sealing surfaces.

To install:

17. Apply sealer to both sides of the crankshaft rear main bearing cap. Press the sealer into the gap using a putty knife.
18. Apply sealer to both sides of the front cover and block mating area.
19. Install a new oil pan gasket.
20. Position the oil pan to the engine.
21. Install the oil pan bolts and note the following:
   • Tighten the bolts (1) to 37 ft. lbs. (50 Nm).
   • Tighten the bolts (2) to 18 ft. lbs. (25 Nm).
22. Install the transaxle brace to oil pan lower bolt, if equipped with (RPO) M15 and tighten to 37 ft. lbs. (50 Nm).
23. Position the transaxle brace and install the transaxle brace to transaxle bolt until snug.
24. Install the transaxle brace to oil pan bolts. Tighten to 37 ft. lbs. (50 Nm).
25. Connect the oil level sensor electrical connector.
26. Position the A/C compressor install the bolts and tighten to 37 ft. lbs. (50 Nm).
27. Install the starter and tighten mounting bolts to 32 ft. lbs. (43 Nm).
28. Install the positive battery cable nut to the starter solenoid. And tighten to 89 inch. lbs. (10 Nm).

29. Tighten the oil pan drain plug to 19 ft. lbs. (26 Nm).
30. Lower the vehicle.
31. Fill the crankcase.
32. Connect the negative battery cable.

OIL PUMP

REMOVAL & INSTALLATION

2.2L Engine

See Figure 91.

1. Before servicing the vehicle, refer to the Precautions Section.

➡**The oil pump is part of the engine front cover assembly.**

2. Remove or disconnect the following:
   • Front cover
   • Pressure relief valve from front cover
   • Oil pump cover
   • Oil pump

To install:

➡**If the oil pump is to be replaced, the entire front cover must also be replaced.**

➡**Lubricate all oil pump parts with clean engine oil.**

3. Install the inner gear into the outer gear.
4. Install the assembly together into the front cover the hub of the center gear facing the front cover.
5. Install the oil pump cover. Tighten the bolts to 53 inch lbs. (6 Nm).
6. Install the pressure relief valve. Tighten the plug to 30 ft. lbs. (40 Nm).
7. Install the front cover.

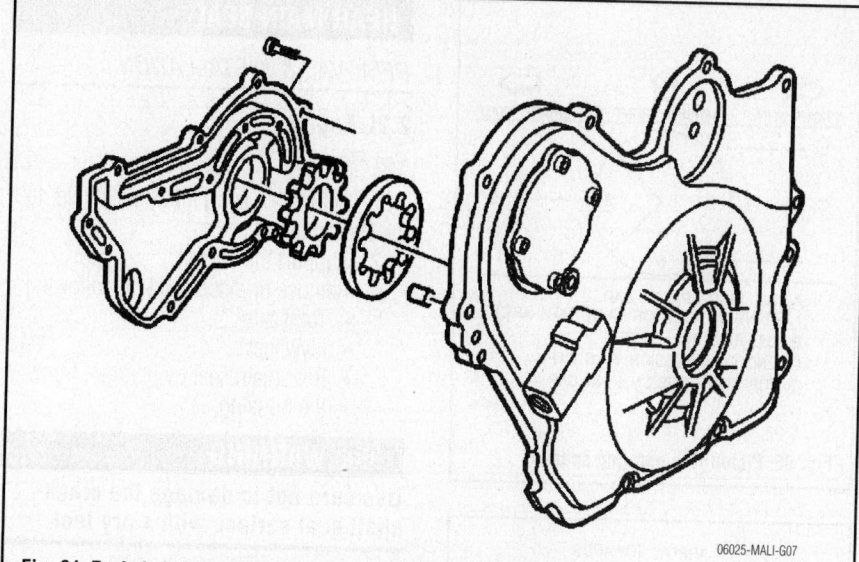

Fig. 91 Exploded view of the oil pump assembly–2.2L engine

06025-MALI-G07

3.5L Engine

1. Before servicing the vehicle, refer to the Precautions Section.
2. Raise the vehicle.
3. Drain the engine oil.
4. Remove or disconnect the following:

- Negative battery cable
- Oil pan
- Oil pump bolt
- Oil pump and the oil pump drive shaft

To install:

➡**Rotate the oil pump drive shaft as necessary to mate with the oil pump drive unit.**

5. Install the oil pump drive shaft and oil pump.
6. Tighten the oil pump bolt to 30 ft. lbs (41 Nm).
7. Install the oil pan.
8. Connect the negative battery cable.
9. Lower vehicle.
10. Fill the engine with oil to the correct level.
11. Start the engine and check for leaks.

3.9L Engine

See Figure 92.

1. Before servicing the vehicle, refer to the Precautions Section.
2. Raise the vehicle.
3. Drain the engine oil.
4. Remove the oil pan.
5. Remove the oil pump bolt.
6. Remove the oil pump and the oil pump drive shaft.

➡**Rotate the oil pump drive shaft as necessary in order to obtain the engagement with the oil pump drive unit.**

7. Install the oil pump drive shaft and the oil pump.
8. Install the oil pump bolt and tighten to 30 ft. lbs. (41 Nm).
9. Install the oil pan.
10. Lower vehicle.
11. Fill the engine with oil to the correct level.
12. Start the engine and check for leaks.

INSPECTION

1. Clean all parts of sludge, oil, and varnish by soaking in cleaning solvent.

2. Inspect for foreign material and determine the source of the foreign material.
3. Inspect the pump housing and cover for the following conditions:

- Cracks or casting imperfections
- Scoring
- Damaged threads

4. Do not attempt to repair the pump housing. Replace the pump housing.
5. Inspect the oil pump gears for the following conditions:

- Scoring
- Excessive wear

6. Inspect the idler shaft for looseness or scoring. If loose or damaged, replace the oil pump.
7. Inspect the drive gear shaft for looseness or scoring.
8. Inspect the pressure regulator valve for the following conditions:

- Scoring
- Sticking Burrs may be removed using a fine oil stone

9. Inspect the pressure regulator valve spring for the following conditions:

- Loss of tension
- Bending

10. Inspect the suction pipe and screen assembly for the following conditions:

- Looseness If the suction pipe is loose, bent or has been removed, replace the pump body cover and suction pipe.
- Broken wire mesh or screen

11. Measure the oil pump gear lash. Install the gears, and measure in several places.
12. Measure the oil pump housing gear pocket.

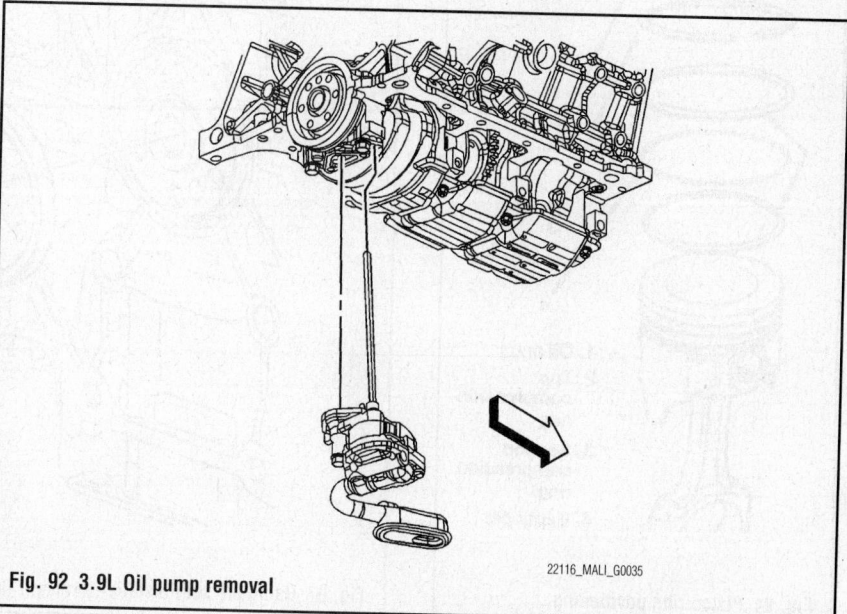

Fig. 92 3.9L Oil pump removal

22116_MALI_G0035

13. Measure the oil pump gears .

➡**When deciding pump serviceability based on end clearance, consider depth of the wear pattern in the pump cover.**

14. Measure the oil pump gear side clearance.

PISTON AND RING

POSITIONING

See Figures 93 through 96.

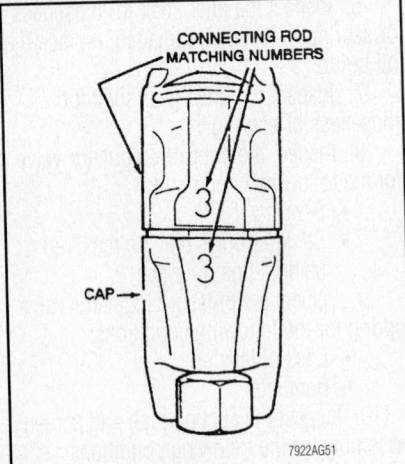

Fig. 93 Connecting rod and cap installation. Be sure to matchmark the cap and rod prior to disassembly, as shown

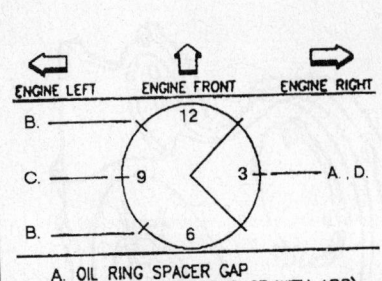

A. OIL RING SPACER GAP
   (TANG IN HOLE OR SLOT WITH ARC)
B. OIL RING RAIL GAPS
C. 2ND COMPRESSION RING GAP
D. TOP COMPRESSION RING GAP

Fig. 95 Piston ring end-gap spacing

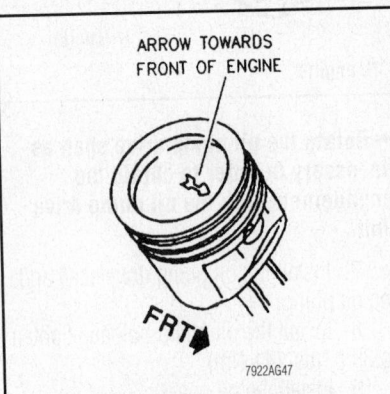

Fig. 96 Piston positioning. Often the arrow is replaced by a notch, which also must face toward the front of the engine

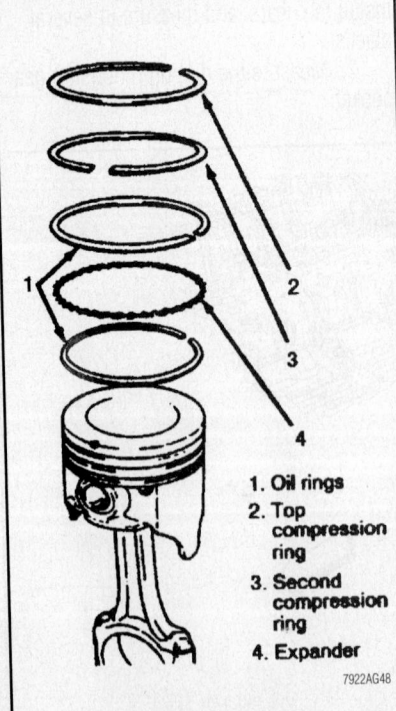

1. Oil rings
2. Top compression ring
3. Second compression ring
4. Expander

Fig. 94 Piston ring positioning

REAR MAIN SEAL

REMOVAL & INSTALLATION

2.2L Engine

See Figure 97.

1. Before servicing the vehicle, refer to the Precautions Section.
2. Support the engine.
3. Remove or disconnect the following:
   - Transaxle
   - Flywheel
   - Rear main seal by prying it from the housing

✲✲ WARNING

Use care not to damage the crankshaft seal surface with a pry tool.

To install:

4. Lubricate the seal bore and new seal with engine oil.
5. Install the new seal by performing the following procedure:

   a. Slide the new seal over the mandrel until the dust lip bottoms squarely against the tool collar.

   b. Align the dowel pin of the tool with the dowel pin hole in the crankshaft and attach the tool to the crankshaft. Tighten the attaching screws to 24–60 inch lbs. (2.7–6.8 Nm).

   c. Tighten the T-handle of the tool to push the seal into the bore. Continue

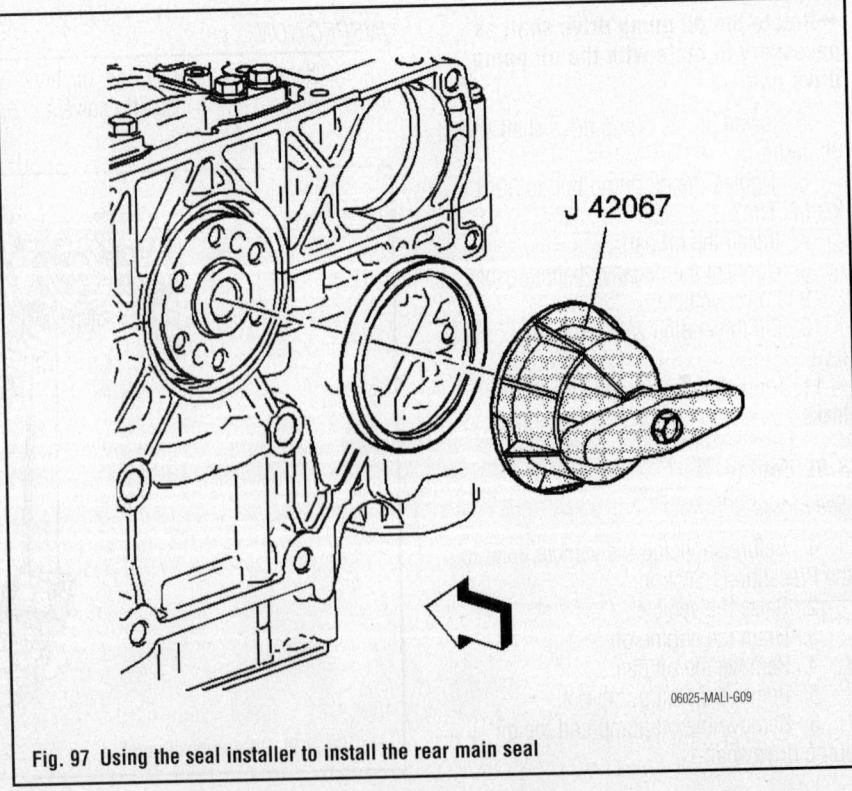

J 42067

Fig. 97 Using the seal installer to install the rear main seal

until the tool collar is flush against the block.

d. Loosen the T-handle completely. Remove the attaching screws and the tool.

➡**Check to see that the seal is squarely seated in the bore.**

6. Install or connect the following:
   • Flywheel. Tighten flywheel bolts to 39 ft. lbs. (53Nm).
   • Transaxle
7. Start the engine and check for leaks.

3.5L & 3.9L Engines

See Figures 98 through 103.

1. Before servicing the vehicle, refer to the Precautions Section.

➡**Before replacement of the new design crankshaft rear main oil seal, ensure the Positive Crankcase Ventilation (PCV) system is operating correctly.**

2. Support the engine.
3. Remove the transaxle.
4. Remove the engine flywheel.
5. The EN—48672 has a unique design to allow the technician to easily remove the rear main seal without nicking the crankshaft sealing surface when removing the seal. Before proceeding with removal, review the illustration to become familiar with the components.
6. Install the removal plate and both threaded adjustment pins and jam nuts into the back of the crankshaft flange and secure the plate with adjustment pins and jam nuts.

7. Install the number 2 self drill screws 38 mm (1.5 in) long, 8 needed and tighten the screws down flush to the plate.
8. Before installing the force screw, apply a small amount of the extreme pressure lubricant J 23444-A, provided in the tool kit.
9. Install the force screw and back off both jam nuts. Continue to turn the force screw into the removal plate in order to remove the seal from the crankshaft.
10. Once the seal is removed from the crankshaft, remove and save all 8 screws. Discard the old seal.

To install:

✴✴ WARNING

Do not remove the protective sleeve from the seal. The sleeve assures the seal is installed correctly and protects the seal from damage. If removed, the EN—48108 installation tool will not work.

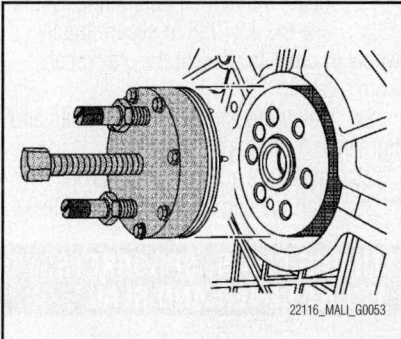

Fig. 99 Rear main oil seal removal with tool EN—48672 shown

➡**Clean the crankshaft sealing surface with a clean, lint free towel. Inspect lead-in edge of crankshaft for burrs/sharp edges that could damage the rear main oil seal. Remove burrs/sharp edges with crocus cloth before proceeding.**

✴✴ WARNING

Do not remove protective nylon sleeve prior to installation. The rear main oil seal installation tool is designed to install the rear main seal with the protective sleeve in place. Never apply or use any oil, lubricants or sealing compounds on the crankshaft rear main oil seal.

A new design crankshaft rear main oil seal and installation tool, EN—48108, has been released. This seal incorporates features that improve high mileage durability. Replace the crankshaft rear main oil seal with the new design rear main oil seal, GM P/N 12592195 (Canadian P/N 12592195).

11. The EN—48108 has a unique design to allow the technician to easily install the rear main seal squarely to the correct depth and direction. Before proceeding with installation, review the illustration to become familiar with the components.
12. Align the mandrel dowel pin to the dowel pin hole in the crankshaft.
13. Using a large flat-blade screwdriver, tighten the 2 mandrel screws to the crankshaft. Ensure the mandrel is snug to the crankshaft hub.
14. Install the rear main seal, with the

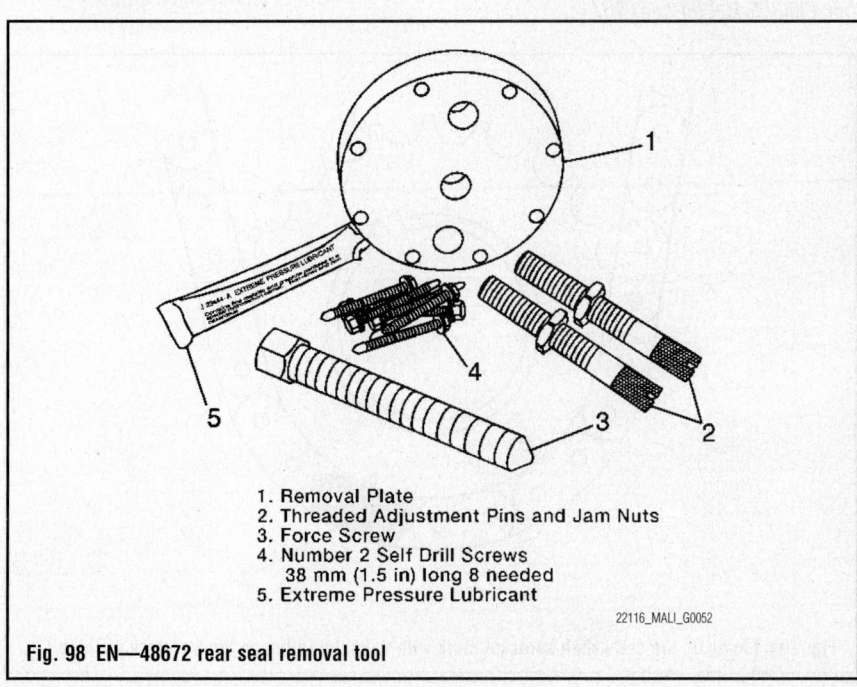

1. Removal Plate
2. Threaded Adjustment Pins and Jam Nuts
3. Force Screw
4. Number 2 Self Drill Screws 38 mm (1.5 in) long 8 needed
5. Extreme Pressure Lubricant

Fig. 98 EN—48672 rear seal removal tool

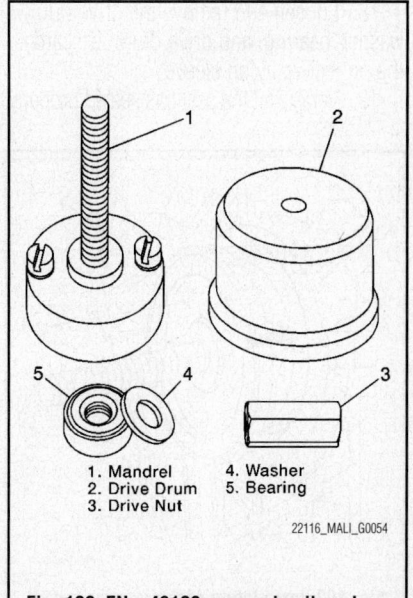

1. Mandrel
2. Drive Drum
3. Drive Nut
4. Washer
5. Bearing

Fig. 100 EN—48108 rear main oil seal Installation tool

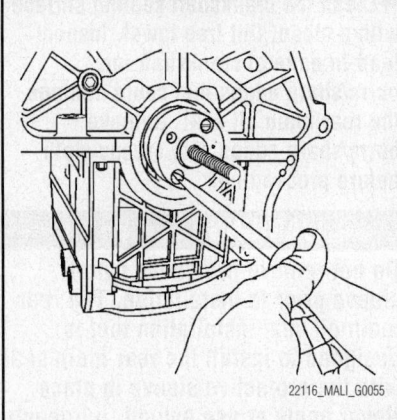

Fig. 101 Tightening the 2 mandrel screws to the crankshaft

protective nylon sleeve attached, onto the mandrel. The seal, if properly installed, will center on a step that protrudes from the center of the mandrel. As an error proof, the seal will fit only 1 way onto the mandrel.

➡**Before installing the outer drive drum, bearing, washer, and drive nut onto the threaded shaft, apply a small amount of the extreme pressure lubricant J 23444—A, provided in the tool kit.**

15. Install the outer drive drum onto the mandrel.

16. Install the bearing, washer, and drive nut onto the threaded shaft.

17. Using a wrench, turn the drive nut on the mandrel, which will push the seal into the engine block bore. Turn the wrench until the drive drum is snug and flush against the engine block.

18. Loosen and remove the drive nut, washer, bearing, and drive drum. Discard the protective nylon sleeve.

19. Verify that the seal has seated properly.

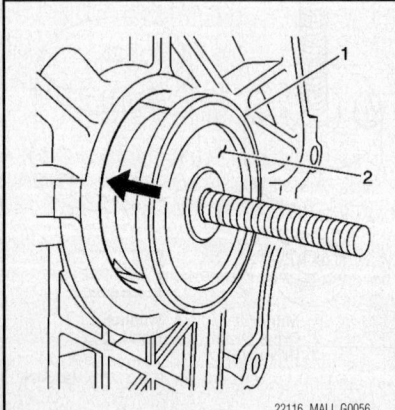

Fig. 102 Installation of the rear main seal onto the mandrel

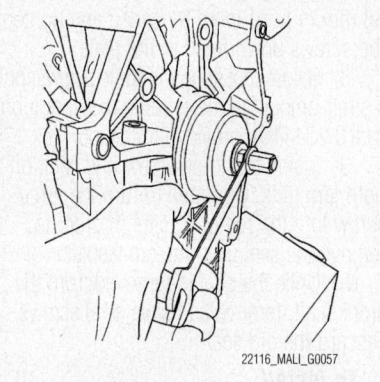

Fig. 103 Installation of rear main seal until the drive drum is flush against the engine block

20. Use a flat-blade screwdriver in order to remove the 2 attachment screws from the mandrel and remove the mandrel from the crankshaft hub.

21. Position the flywheel to the crankshaft.

22. Install the flywheel bolts finger tight.

23. Use the J 37096 to secure the flywheel in order to prevent the crankshaft from rotating.

24. Install the engine flywheel bolts and tighten to 52 ft. lbs. (70 Nm).

25. Install the automatic transaxle.

26. Start the engine and check for leaks.

TIMING CHAIN, SPROCKETS, FRONT COVER AND SEAL

REMOVAL & INSTALLATION

2.2L Engine

See Figures 104 through 107.

1. Before servicing the vehicle, refer to the Precautions Section.

2. Drain the cooling system.

3. Drain the engine oil.

4. Remove or disconnect the following:

- Negative battery cable
- PCV hose
- Fuel line bracket
- Ignition coil and module assembly
- Ground strap from camshaft cover
- Camshaft cover
- Front fender liner
- Accessory drive belt
- Crankshaft balancer pulley
- Accessory drive belt tensioner
- Front cover-to-water pump bolt
- Remaining front cover bolts
- Front cover

➡**The timing chain has 2 matching colored links and 1 uniquely colored link.**

5. Rotate the engine until the crankshaft sprocket mark aligns with the matching colored link (2) at the 5 o'clock position.

6. Confirm that the INT diamond on the intake camshaft sprocket is aligned with the uniquely colored link at (1) the 2 o'clock position.

7. Confirm that the EXH triangle on the exhaust camshaft sprocket is aligned with the matching colored link (3).

8. Remove or disconnect the following:

- Timing chain tensioner
- Fixed timing chain guide access plug
- Fixed timing chain guide
- Upper timing chain guide

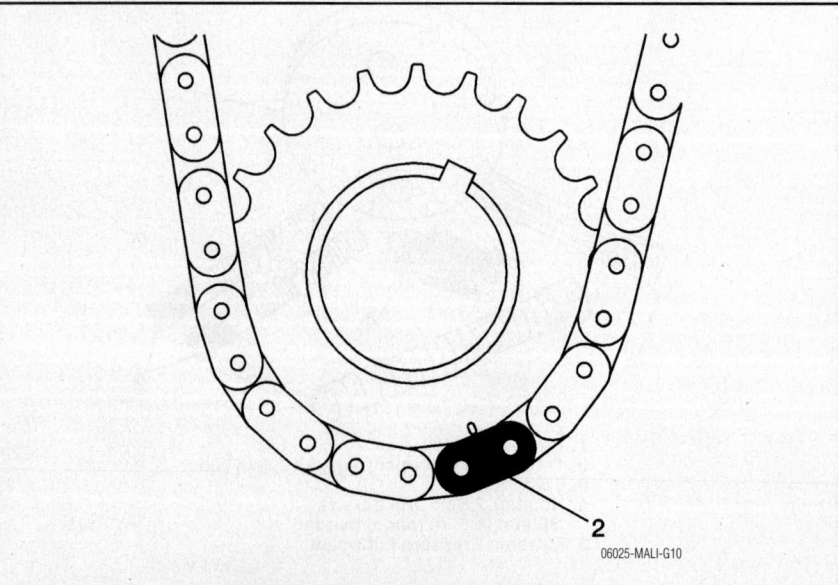

Fig. 104 Lining up the crankshaft sprocket mark with the colored link in the 5 o'clock position (2).

→Use a 24 mm wrench to hold the camshafts to prevent them from turning.

- Exhaust camshaft sprocket
- Timing chain tensioner guide
- Intake camshaft sprocket
- Timing chain through the top of the cylinder head
- Crankshaft sprocket

To install:

9. Install the crankshaft sprocket with the timing mark in the 5 o'clock position.

10. Assemble the intake camshaft sprocket to the timing chain with the timing mark lined up with the uniquely colored link (1). Hand tighten a new intake camshaft sprocket bolt.

11. Lower the timing chain through the opening in the cylinder head.

12. Route the timing chain around the crankshaft sprocket and line up the first marching colored link (2) with the timing mark on the crankshaft sprocket.

13. Install the exhaust camshaft sprocket with a new bolt loosely onto the exhaust camshaft.

14. Align the timing mark on the sprocket with the last matching colored (3).

15. If necessary, align the camshaft as follows:

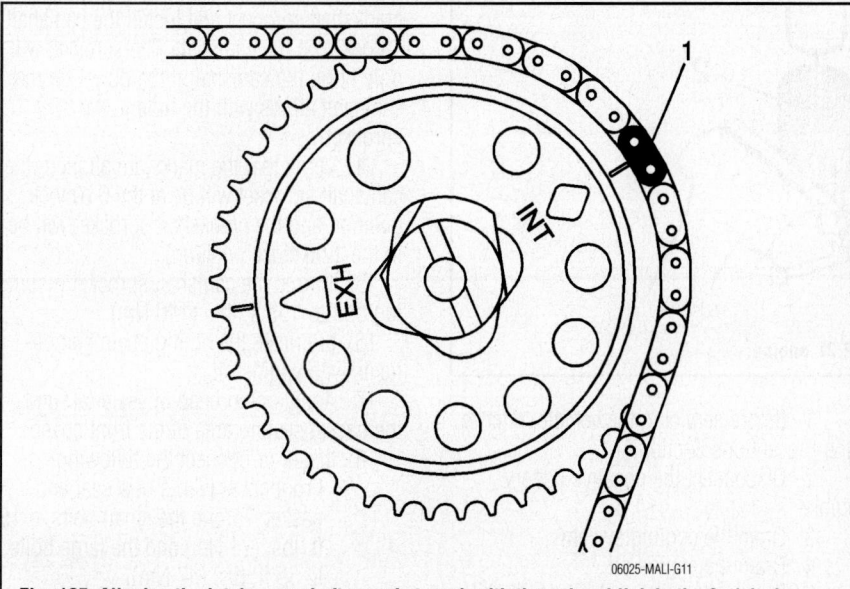

Fig. 105 Aligning the intake camshaft sprocket mark with the colored link in the 2 o'clock position (1).

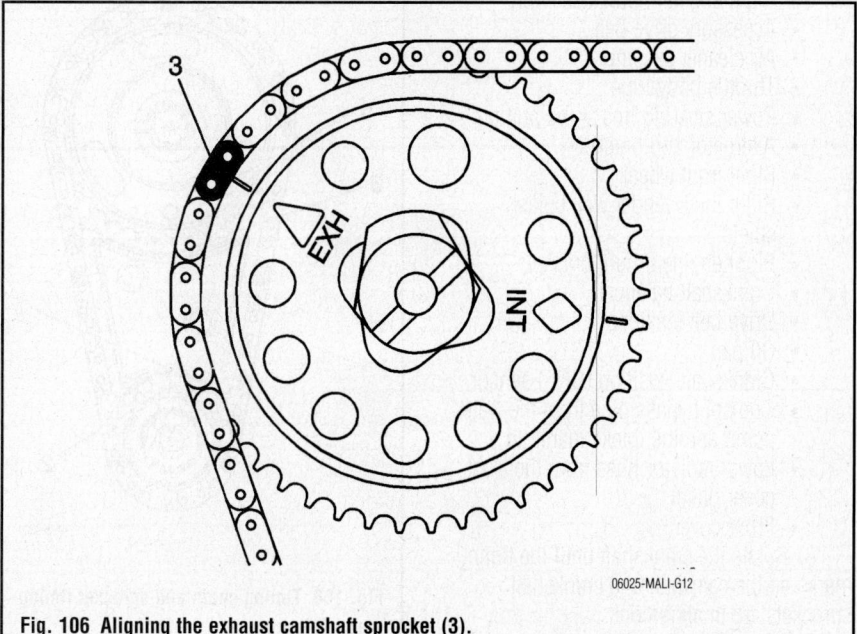

Fig. 106 Aligning the exhaust camshaft sprocket (3).

a. Using a 24 mm wrench, first turn the intake camshaft until the alignment feature on the back of the camshaft sprocket seats in the notch in the front of the intake camshaft.

b. Turn the crankshaft 45 degrees in either direction.

c. Turn the intake camshaft to the appropriate location.

d. Turn the crankshaft back to top dead center (TDC).

16. When the sprocket seats in on the camshaft, tighten the sprocket bolt hand tight.

17. Verify all of the colored links and the appropriate timing marks are still aligned.

18. Install the fixed timing chain guide. Tighten the bolts to 133 inch lbs. (15 Nm).

19. Install the upper timing chain guide. Tighten the bolts to 89 inch lbs. (10 Nm).

20. Using a 24 mm wrench to hold the camshafts, tighten the camshaft sprocket bolts 63 ft. lbs. (85 Nm) plus 30 degrees.

21. Measure the timing chain tensioner from end to end. A new tensioner should be supplied in the fully compressed non-active state. A tensioner in the compressed state will measure 2.83 inches (72 mm) front end to end. A tensioner in the active state will measure 3.35 inches (85 mm) from end to end.

22. If the timing chain tensioner is not in the compressed state, perform the following steps:

a. Remove the piston assembly from the body of the timing chain tensioner by pulling it out.

b. Install the bottom half of the Tensioner tool J-45027-2 into a vise.

c. Install the notch end of the piston assembly into the bottom half of the tensioner tool.

d. Using the top half of the Tensioner tool J-45027-1, turn the ratchet cylinder into the piston.

e. Install the compressed piston assembly back into the timing chain tensioner body until it stops at the bottom of the bore. Do not compress the piston assembly against the bottom of the bore.

23. Install the timing chain tensioner assembly. Tighten to 66 ft. lbs. (75 Nm).

24. Release the timing chain tensioner by compressing it approximately 0.08 inches (2mm). Feed a rubber-tipped tool down through the cam drive chest to reset on the cam chain. Give the tool a sharp jolt diagonally downwards to release the tensioner.

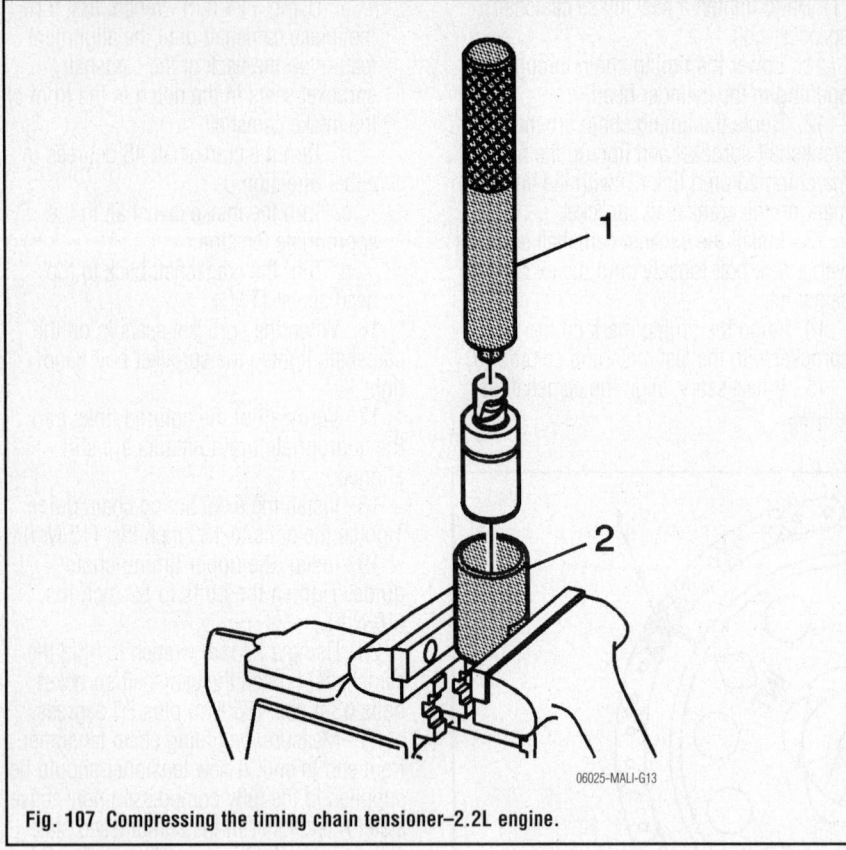

Fig. 107 Compressing the timing chain tensioner–2.2L engine.

25. Install the timing chain oiling nozzle.

26. Install the timing chain guide bolt access hold plug with silicone sealant on the threads. Tighten the plug to 59 ft. lbs. (90 Nm).

27. Install or connect the following:
- Camshaft cover. Tighten the bolts to 89 inch lbs. (10 Nm).
- Front cover with new gasket. Tighten the bolts to 18 ft. lbs. (25 Nm).
- Accessory drive belt tensioner. Tighten the bolts to 33 ft. lbs. (45 Nm).
- Crankshaft balancer pulley using a new bolt. Tighten the bolt to 74 ft. lbs. (100 Nm) plus 75 degrees.
- Accessory drive belt
- Front fender liner
- Ground strap to camshaft cover
- Ignition coil and module assembly
- Fuel line bracket
- Air intake assembly
- Negative battery cable

28. Refill the cooling system to the correct level.

29. Refill the engine with oil to the correct level.

30. Start the engine and check for leaks.

3.5L Engines

See Figure 108.

1. Before servicing the vehicle, refer to the Precautions Section.

2. Disconnect the negative battery cable.

3. Drain the cooling system.

4. Drain the engine oil.

5. Recover the A/C system refrigerant.

6. Install an engine support fixture.

7. Remove or disconnect the following:
- Right engine mount assembly
- Accessory drive belt
- Air cleaner assembly
- Throttle body tube
- Power steering line at the pump
- Alternator and bracket
- Right front wheel
- Right inner fender well splash shield
- Right engine mount bracket
- Crankshaft balancer
- Drive belt tensioner
- Oil pan
- Crankshaft Position (CKP) sensor
- Coolant bypass pipe from the water pump and the intake manifold
- Lower radiator hose from the front cover outlet
- Front cover

8. Rotate the crankshaft until the timing marks on the camshaft and crankshaft sprockets are in alignment.

9. Remove or disconnect the following:

- Camshaft sprocket and timing chain
- Crankshaft sprocket
- Timing chain damper

To install:

10. Install or connect the following:
- Timing chain damper. Torque the bolts to 15 ft. lbs. (21 Nm).
- Crankshaft sprocket

11. Be sure the crankshaft sprocket timing mark is pointing straight up.

12. Install the timing chain over the camshaft sprocket and hold the sprocket in such a way, that the timing mark is pointing down, and the timing chain is hanging down off the sprocket.

13. Loop the timing chain under the crankshaft sprocket and install the camshaft sprocket on the camshaft. The sprocket will only fit on the camshaft if the dowel on the camshaft aligns with the hole in the sprocket.

14. Verify that the marks are aligned (the camshaft sprocket will be at the 6 o'clock position and the crankshaft sprocket will be in the 12 o'clock position).

15. Torque the camshaft sprocket mounting bolt to 103 ft. lbs. (140 Nm).

16. Lubricate the timing chain components with engine oil.

17. Apply a thin bead of sealer around the gasket sealing area of the front cover.

18. Install or connect the following:
- Front cover with a new seal and gasket. Torque the small bolts to 15 ft. lbs. (21 Nm) and the large bolts to 35 ft. lbs. (47 Nm).

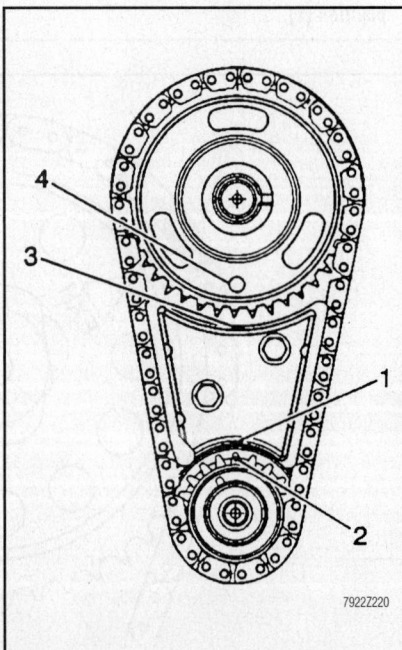

Fig. 108 Timing chain and sprocket timing mark alignment

- Radiator hose to the coolant outlet
- Coolant bypass pipe to the water pump and intake manifold
- CKP sensor
- Oil pan. Torque the bolts to 18 ft. lbs. (24 Nm) and the side bolts to 37 ft. lbs. (50 Nm).
- Crankshaft balancer. Torque the bolt to 76 ft. lbs. (103 Nm).
- Accessory drive belt tensioner. Torque the bolt to 40 ft. lbs. (54 Nm).
- Right engine mount bracket. Torque the bolts to 96 ft. lbs. (130 Nm).
- Right inner fender well splash shield
- Wheel

19. Remove the engine support fixture.
20. Install or connect the following:
- Alternator. Torque the front bolt to 37 ft. lbs. (50 Nm) and the rear bolt to 18 ft. lbs. (24 Nm).
- Power steering line
- Throttle body tube
- Air cleaner assembly
- Accessory drive belt
- Negative battery cable

21. Refill the cooling system.
22. Check the engine oil level.

➡**An oil and filter change is recommended.**

23. Start the engine and verify that there are no leaks.

3.9L Engines

See Figures 109 through 113.

1. Before servicing the vehicle, refer to the Precautions Section.
2. Drain the cooling system.
3. Remove the drive belt tensioner.
4. Remove the oil pan.
5. Remove the crankshaft balancer.
6. Remove the crankshaft position actuator magnet.
7. Remove the thermostat housing.
8. Remove the water pump.
9. Remove the engine front cover bolts.
10. Remove the engine front cover.
11. Align the crankshaft timing mark (1) to the timing mark on the bottom of the timing chain tensioner (2).
12. Align the timing mark on the camshaft gear (3) with the timing mark on top of the timing chain tensioner (4).
13. Remove the camshaft sprocket bolts.
14. Remove the timing chain, camshaft, and crankshaft sprockets.
15. Remove the timing chain tensioner bolts.
16. Remove the timing chain tensioner.

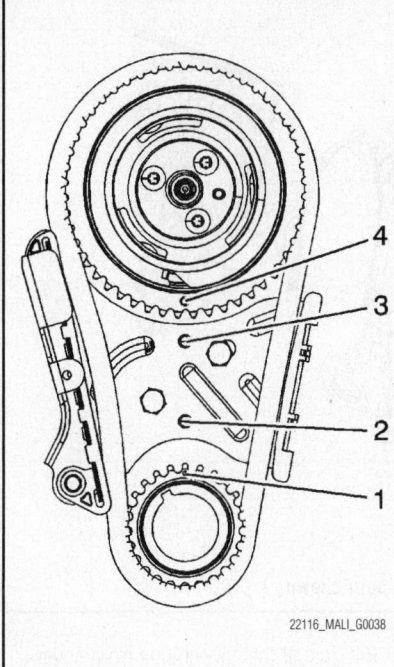

Fig. 109 3.9L Engine timing mark alignment shown

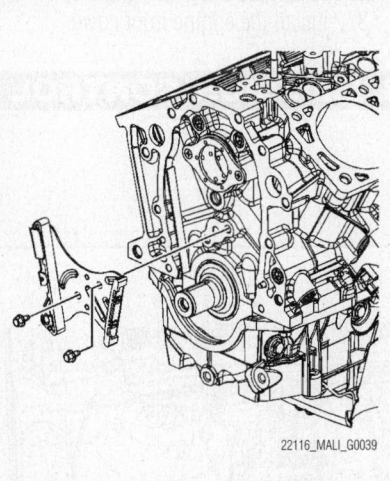

Fig. 110 3.9L Engine timing chain tensioner removal

17. Remove and discard the camshaft position actuator filter from the end of the camshaft.

➡**Always install a NEW camshaft position actuator filter anytime the camshaft position actuator is removed.**

To install:

18. Install a new camshaft position actuator filter (1) to the end of the camshaft.
19. Install the crankshaft sprocket.
20. Apply prelube to the crankshaft sprocket thrust surface.
21. Install the timing chain tensioner.

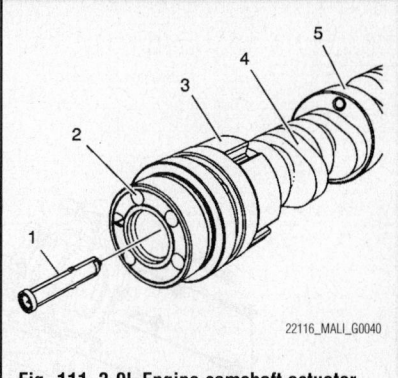

Fig. 111 3.9L Engine camshaft actuator filter (1)

22. Install the timing chain tensioner bolts and tighten to 15 ft. lbs. (21 Nm).
23. Using the EN-47719, fully collapse the tensioner, and place the tensioner retaining pin into the retaining hole (1).
24. Align the crankshaft timing mark (1) to the timing mark on the bottom of the timing chain tensioner (2).
25. Hold the camshaft sprocket with the timing chain hanging down and install the timing chain to the crankshaft gear.
26. Align the timing mark on the camshaft gear (3) with the timing mark on top of the timing chain tensioner (4).
27. Align the dowel in the camshaft sprocket with the dowel hole in the camshaft.
28. Draw the camshaft sprocket onto the camshaft using the mounting bolts and tighten to 12 ft. lbs. (16 Nm).
29. Remove the retaining pin from the timing chain tensioner in order to make the tensioner active.
30. Coat the crankshaft and camshaft sprockets with clean engine oil.

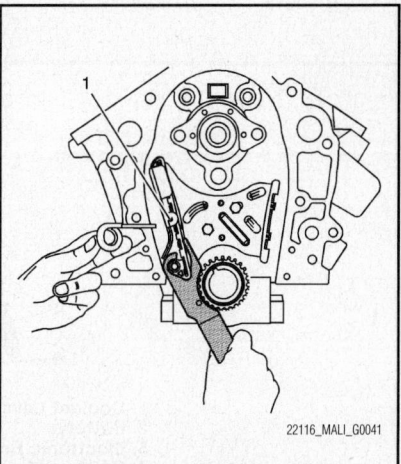

Fig. 112 Using the EN-47719, to fully collapse the tensioner and installing retainer pin

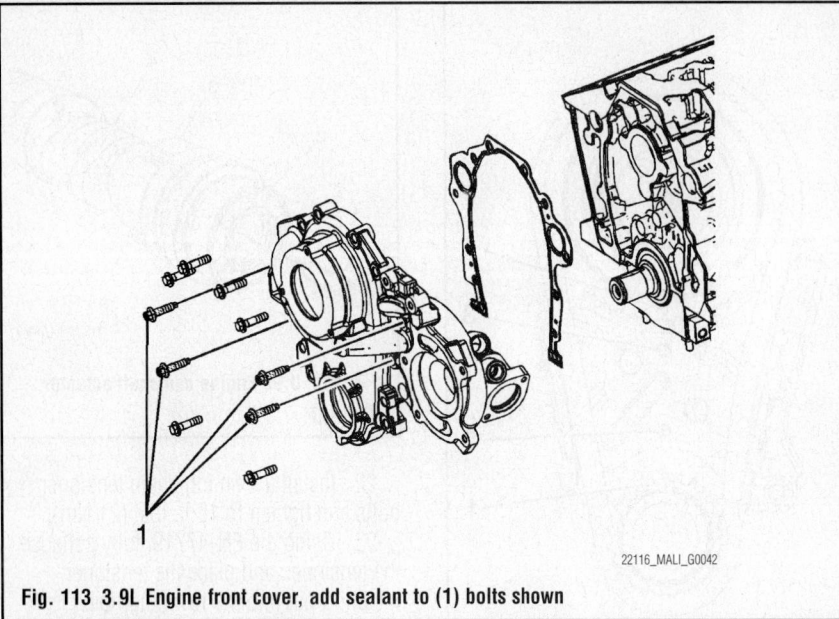

Fig. 113 3.9L Engine front cover, add sealant to (1) bolts shown

31. Pry out the crankshaft front oil seal from the cover using a suitable tool.

32. Lubricate the NEW oil seal with clean engine oil.

33. Install the crankshaft front oil seal using J 35468 and a suitable tool.

34. Install the new engine front cover gasket.

35. Install the engine front cover.

36. Add sealant to the bolts (1) in the locations pointed out in the graphic.

37. Install the engine front cover.

38. Install the engine front cover bolts and tighten to 18 ft. lbs. (25 Nm).

39. Install the water pump.

40. Install the thermostat housing.

41. Install the crankshaft position actuator magnet.

42. Install the crankshaft balancer.

43. Install the oil pan.

44. Install the drive belt tensioner.

45. Fill and bleed the cooling system.

➡ **An oil and filter change is recommended.**

46. Check the engine oil level.

47. Start the engine and verify that there are no leaks.

VALVE LASH

ADJUSTMENT

All of the engines are equipped with hydraulic valve lifters that do not require periodic valve lash adjustment. Adjustment to zero lash is maintained automatically by hydraulic pressure in the lifters. Also, the rocker arm retaining nuts are tightened to a specific torque value (refer to the rocker arm procedure) to provide proper rocker arm placement.

ENGINE PERFORMANCE & EMISSION CONTROL

COMPONENT LOCATIONS

See Figures 114 through 126.

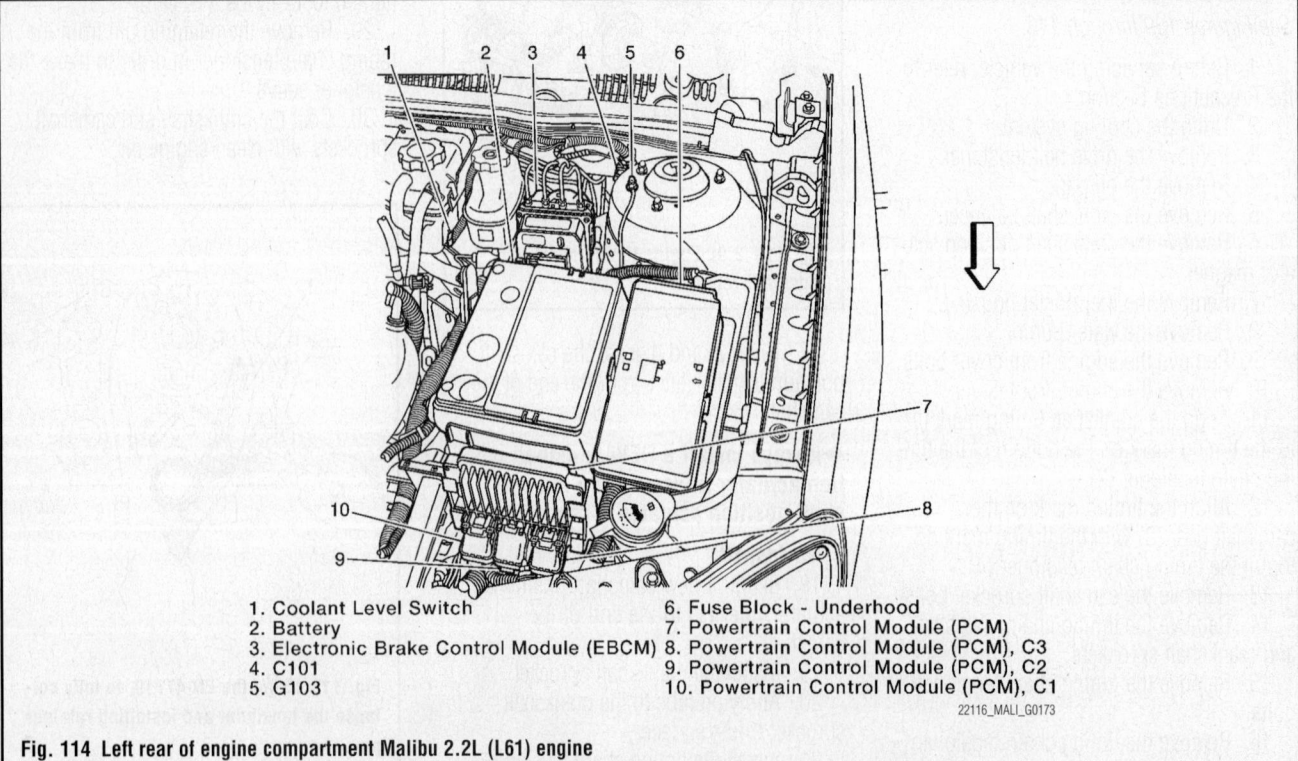

1. Coolant Level Switch
2. Battery
3. Electronic Brake Control Module (EBCM)
4. C101
5. G103
6. Fuse Block - Underhood
7. Powertrain Control Module (PCM)
8. Powertrain Control Module (PCM), C3
9. Powertrain Control Module (PCM), C2
10. Powertrain Control Module (PCM), C1

Fig. 114 Left rear of engine compartment Malibu 2.2L (L61) engine

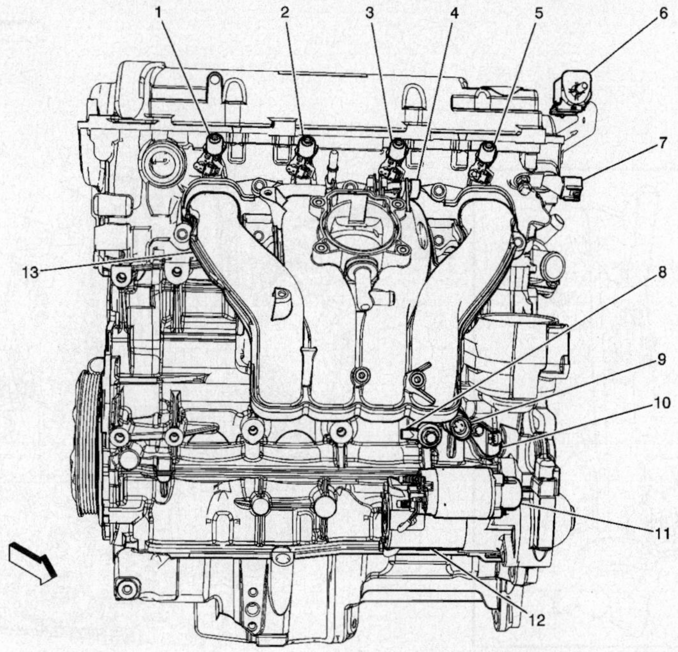

1. Fuel Injector 1
2. Fuel Injector 2
3. Fuel Injector 3
4. Manifold Absolute Pressure (MAP) Sensor
5. Fuel Injector 4
6. Evaporative Emission (EVAP) Canister Purge Solenoid
7. Camshaft Position (CMP) Sensor - Intake
8. Knock Sensor (KS)
9. Engine Oil Pressure (EOP) Switch
10. Crankshaft Position (CKP) Sensor
11. Starter Solenoid
12. Starter

22116_MALI_G0174

Fig. 115 Front of engine Malibu 2.2L (L61) engine

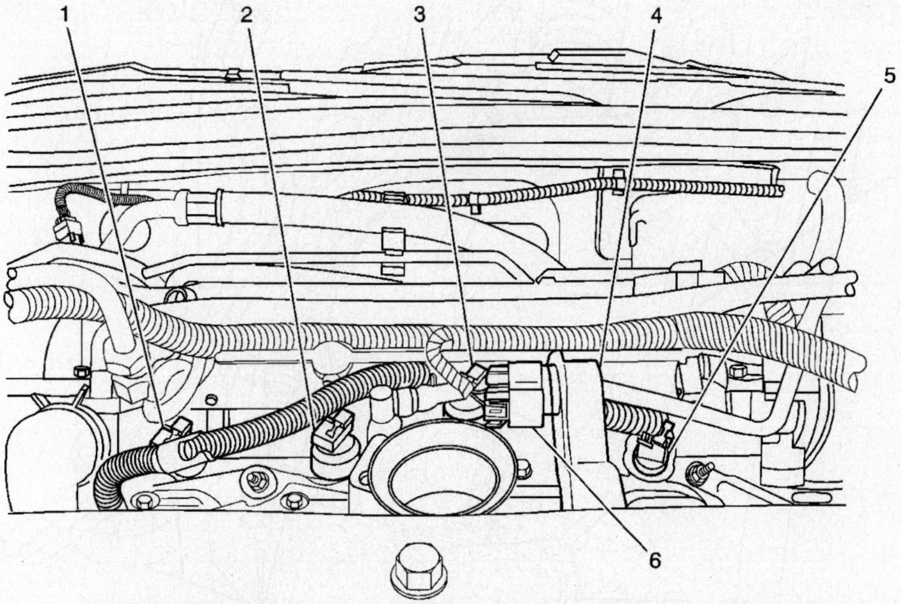

1. Fuel Injector 1
2. Fuel Injector 2
3. Fuel Injector 3
4. Throttle Actuator Control (TAC) Module
5. Fuel Injector 4
6. Manifold Absolute Pressure (MAP) Sensor

22116_MALI_G0175

Fig. 116 Top front of engine Malibu 2.2L (L61) engine

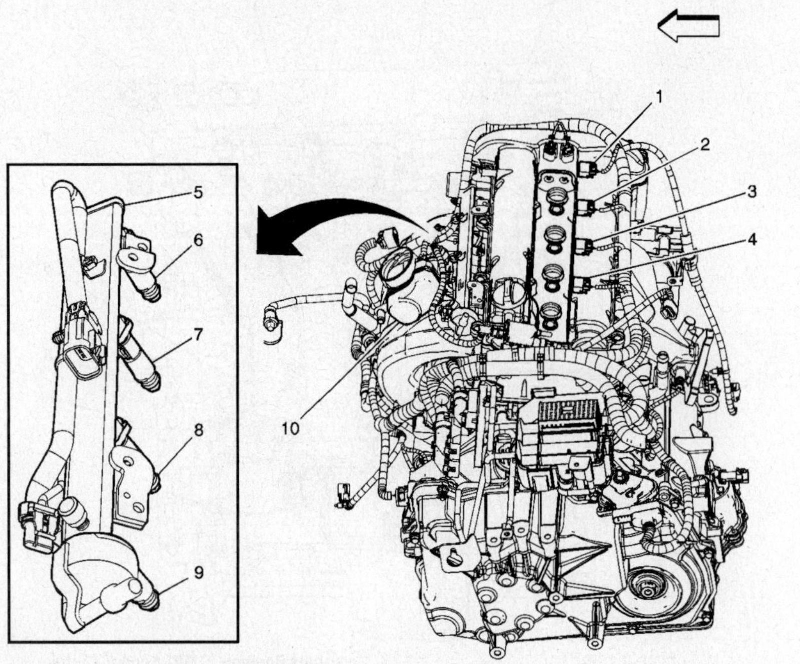

1. Ignition Coil Module 1
2. Ignition Coil Module 2
3. Ignition Coil Module 3
4. Ignition Coil Module 4
5. Fuel Rail

6. Fuel Injector 1
7. Fuel Injector 2
8. Fuel Injector 3
9. Fuel Injector 4
10. Throttle Actuator Control (TAC) Module

22116_MALI_G0176

Fig. 117 Left side of engine Malibu 2.2L (L61) engine

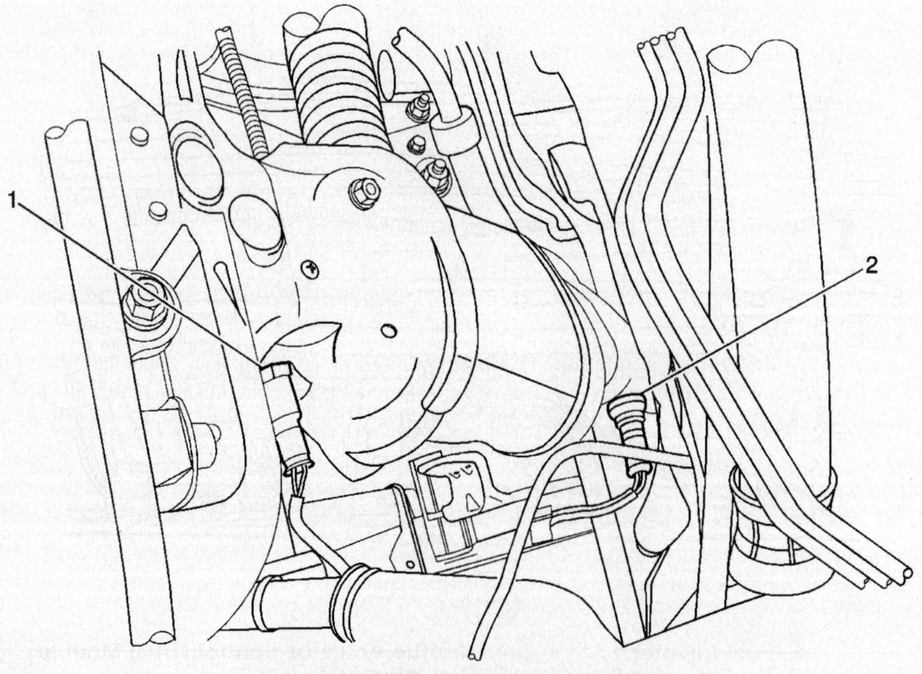

1. Heated Oxygen Sensor (HO2S) 1
2. Heated Oxygen Sensor (HO2S) 2

22116_MALI_G0177

Fig. 118 Rear of engine Malibu 2.2L (L61) engine

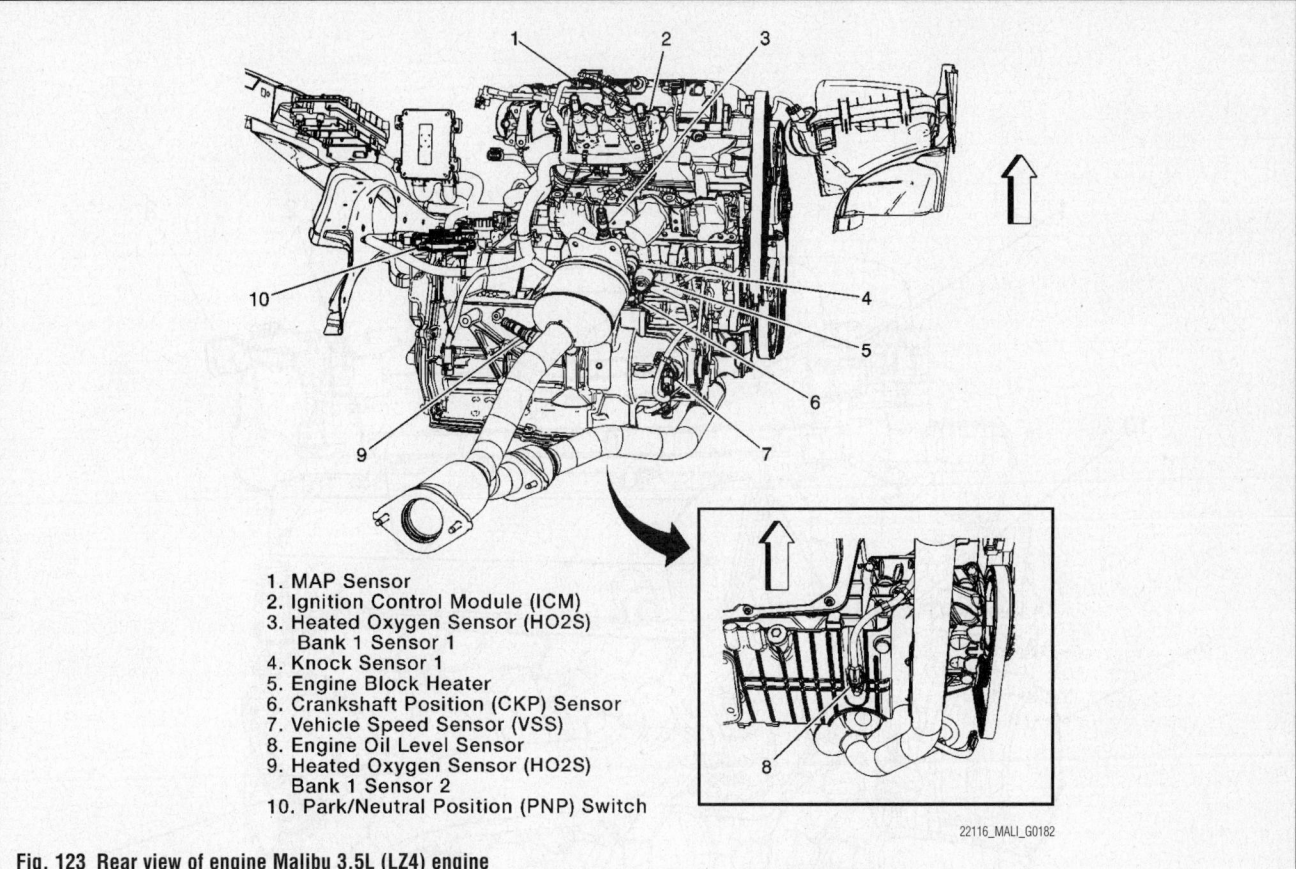

1. MAP Sensor
2. Ignition Control Module (ICM)
3. Heated Oxygen Sensor (HO2S)
   Bank 1 Sensor 1
4. Knock Sensor 1
5. Engine Block Heater
6. Crankshaft Position (CKP) Sensor
7. Vehicle Speed Sensor (VSS)
8. Engine Oil Level Sensor
9. Heated Oxygen Sensor (HO2S)
   Bank 1 Sensor 2
10. Park/Neutral Position (PNP) Switch

22116_MALI_G0182

Fig. 123 Rear view of engine Malibu 3.5L (LZ4) engine

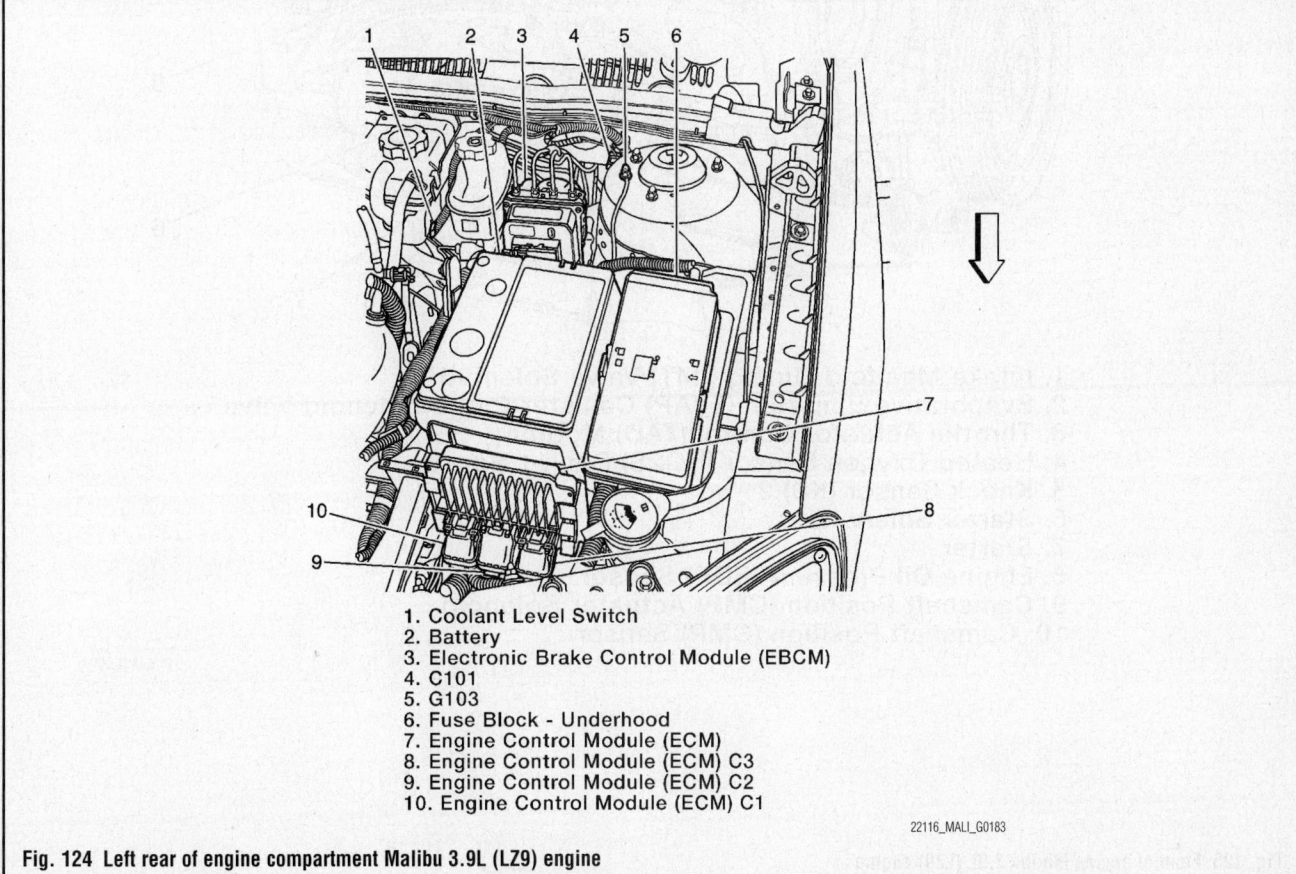

1. Coolant Level Switch
2. Battery
3. Electronic Brake Control Module (EBCM)
4. C101
5. G103
6. Fuse Block - Underhood
7. Engine Control Module (ECM)
8. Engine Control Module (ECM) C3
9. Engine Control Module (ECM) C2
10. Engine Control Module (ECM) C1

22116_MALI_G0183

Fig. 124 Left rear of engine compartment Malibu 3.9L (LZ9) engine

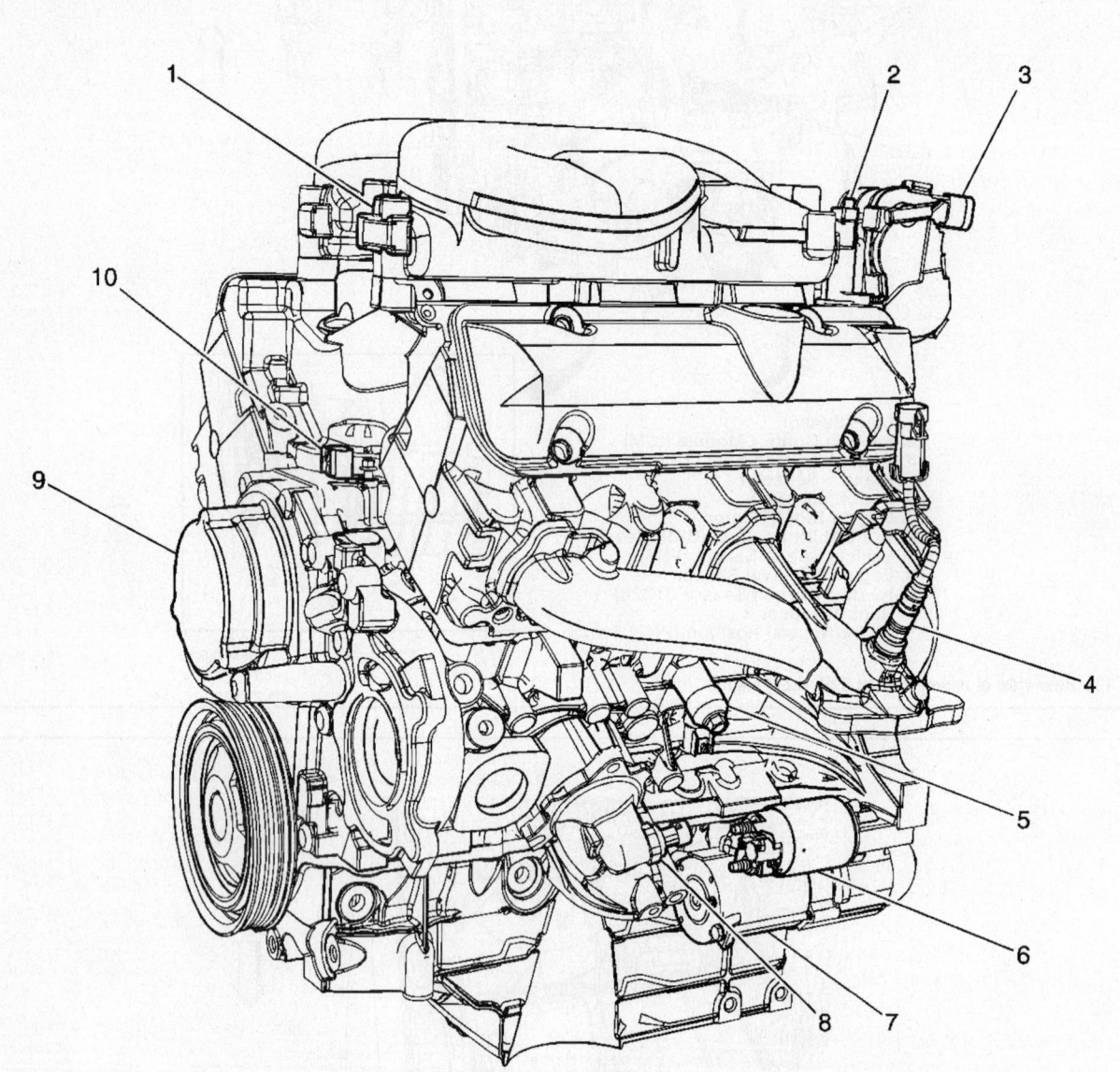

1. Intake Manifold Tuning (IMT) Valve Solenoid
2. Evaporative Emission (EVAP) Canister Purge Solenoid Valve
3. Throttle Actuator Control (TAC) Module
4. Heated Oxygen Sensor (HO2S) Bank 1 Sensor 1
5. Knock Sensor (KS) 2
6. Starter Solenoid
7. Starter
8. Engine Oil Pressure (EOP) Sensor
9. Camshaft Position (CMP) Actuator Solenoid
10. Camshaft Position (CMP) Sensor

22116_MALI_G0184

Fig. 125 Front of engine Malibu 3.9L (LZ9) engine

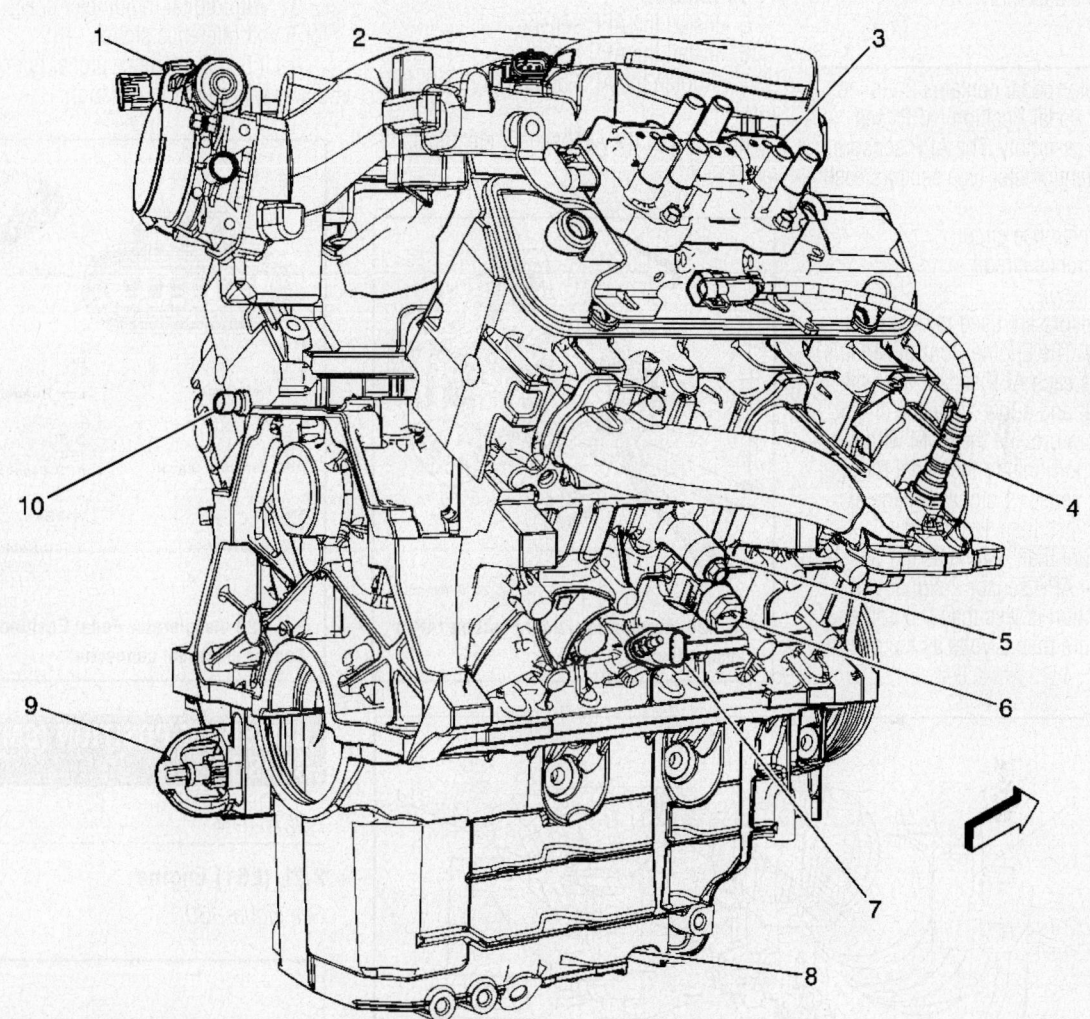

1. Throttle Actuator Control (TAC) Module
2. Manifold Absolute Pressure (MAP) Sensor
3. Ignition Control Module (ICM)
4. Heated Oxygen Sensor (HO2S) Bank 2 Sensor 1
5. Knock Sensor (KS) 2
6. Block Heater
7. Crankshaft Position (CKP) Sensor
8. Engine Oil Level Sensor
9. Starter
10. Engine Coolant Temperature (ECT) Sensor

22116_MALI_G0185

Fig. 126 Rear of engine Malibu 3.9L (LZ9) engine

ACCELERATOR PEDAL POSITION (APP) SENSOR

LOCATION

See Figure 127.

The Accelerator Pedal Position (APP) Sensor is located inside the vehicle. It is mounted at the top of the accelerator pedal and is part of the assembly.

OPERATION

The accelerator pedal contains 2 individual Accelerator Pedal Position (APP) sensors within the assembly. The APP sensors 1 and 2 are potentiometer type sensors each with 3 circuits:

- A 5-volt reference circuit
- A low reference circuit
- A signal circuit

The APP sensors are used to determine the pedal angle. The Engine Control Module (ECM) provides each APP sensor a 5-volt reference circuit and a low reference circuit. The APP sensors provide the ECM with signal voltage proportional to the pedal movement. The APP sensor 1 signal voltage at rest position is less than 1 volt and increases to more than 4 volts as the pedal is actuated. The APP sensor 2 signal voltage at rest position is less than 0.6 volt and increases to more than 2 volts as the pedal is actuated.

REMOVAL & INSTALLATION

See Figure 128.

1. Before servicing the vehicle, refer to the Precautions Section.
2. Disconnect the accelerator pedal position (APP) sensor electrical connector.
3. Remove the APP sensor bolts .
4. Remove the APP sensor.

To install:

5. Install the APP sensor.
6. Install the APP bolts.
7. Tighten the APP bolts to 89 inch. lbs. (10 Nm).
8. Connect the APP sensor electrical connector.

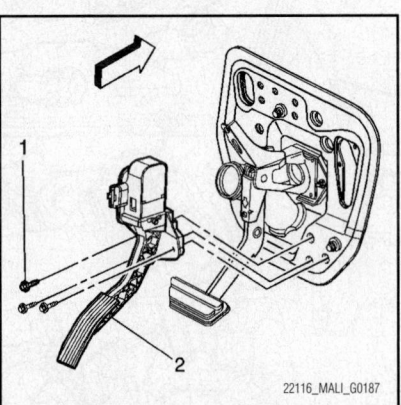

22116_MALI_G0187

Fig. 128 Accelerator Pedal Position (APP) sensor removal

9. Confirm that the APP sensor connector locking clip is fully secured.

TESTING

See Figure 129.

1. Disconnect the Accelerator Pedal Position (APP) electrical connector.
2. With digital multimeter check pin C for 5 volt reference signal.
3. With digital multimeter check pin F for 5 volt reference signal.
4. If 5 volt reference signal is not present, repair circuit in question.

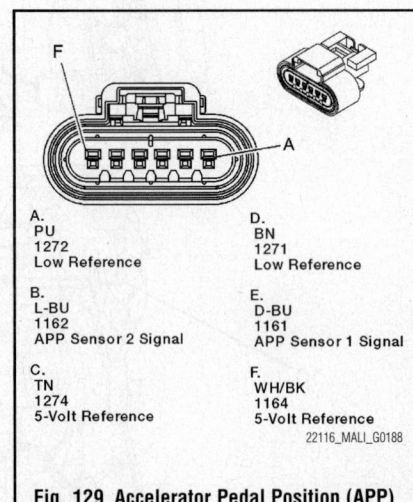

A.
PU
1272
Low Reference

B.
L-BU
1162
APP Sensor 2 Signal

C.
TN
1274
5-Volt Reference

D.
BN
1271
Low Reference

E.
D-BU
1161
APP Sensor 1 Signal

F.
WH/BK
1164
5-Volt Reference

22116_MALI_G0188

Fig. 129 Accelerator Pedal Position (APP) Sensor electrical connector

CAMSHAFT POSITION (CMP) SENSOR

LOCATION

2.2L (L61) Engine

See Figure 130.

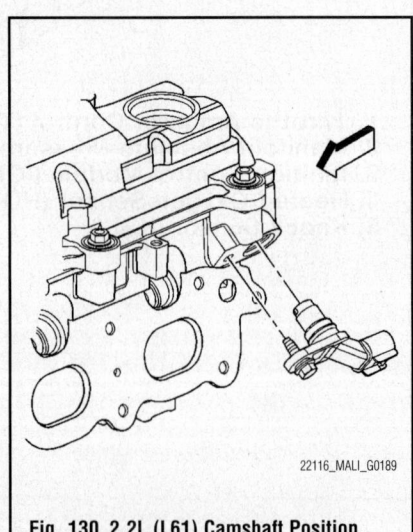

22116_MALI_G0189

Fig. 130 2.2L (L61) Camshaft Position (CMP) sensor view

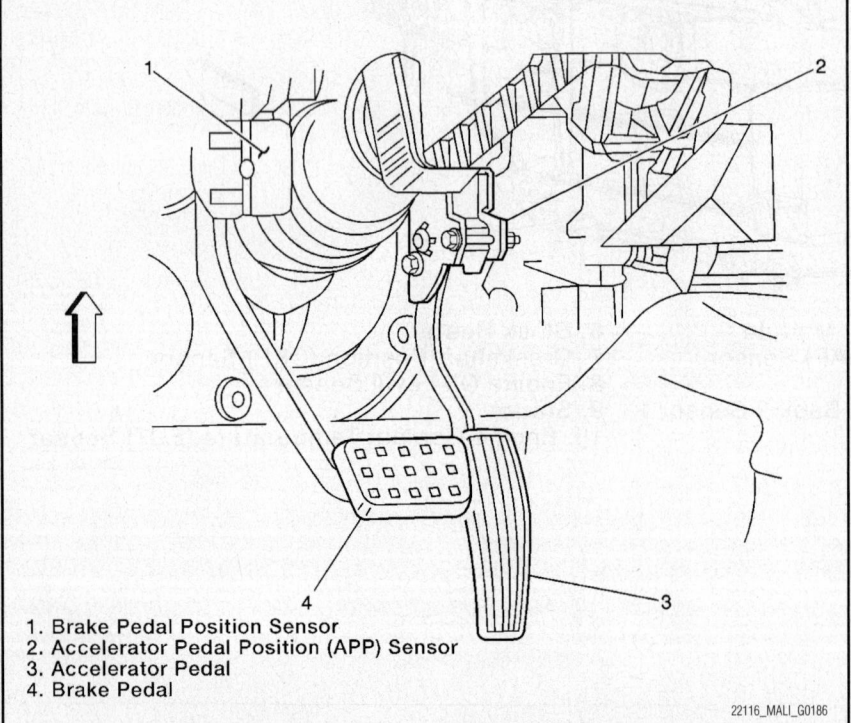

1. Brake Pedal Position Sensor
2. Accelerator Pedal Position (APP) Sensor
3. Accelerator Pedal
4. Brake Pedal

22116_MALI_G0186

Fig. 127 Accelerator Pedal Position (APP) sensor location view

The Camshaft Position (CMP) sensor is located to the right of the intake manifold at the rear of the cylinder head and sits just below the Evaporative Emission (EVAP) Canister Purge Solenoid.

3.5L (LZ4) Engine

See Figure 131.

The 3.5L (LZ4) engine Camshaft Position (CMP) Sensor is located just behind the top of the timing cover, in front of the intake manifold.

22116_MALI_G0190

Fig. 131 3.5L (LZ4) engine Camshaft Position (CMP) Sensor view—3.5L (LZ4) and 3.9L (LZ9) engines

3.9L (LZ9) Engine

See Figure 131.

The 3.9L (LZ9) engine Camshaft Position (CMP) Sensor is located just behind the top of the timing cover, in front of the intake manifold.

OPERATION

The Camshaft Position (CMP) sensor is triggered by a notched reluctor wheel built onto the camshaft sprocket. The CMP sensor provides four signal pulses every camshaft revolution. Each notch, or feature of the reluctor wheel is of a different size which is used to identify the compression stroke of each cylinder and to enable sequential fuel injection. The ECM uses the CMP sensor output signal to determine the camshaft relative position to the crankshaft position.

The CMP sensor is connected to the Engine Control Module (ECM) by the following circuits:
- A 5-volt reference circuit
- A low reference circuit
- A signal circuit

The 4X Camshaft Position (CMP) sensor circuits consist of an Engine Control Module (ECM) supplied 5-volt reference circuit, low reference circuit, and an out-put signal circuit. The CMP sensor is an internally magnetic biased digital output integrated circuit sensing device. The sensor detects magnetic flux changes of the teeth and slots of a 4-tooth reluctor wheel attached to the camshaft. As each reluctor wheel tooth rotates past the CMP sensor, the resulting change in the magnetic field is used by the sensor electronics to produce a digital output pulse. The sensor returns a digital ON/OFF DC voltage pulse of varying frequency, with 4 varying width output pulses per camshaft revolution that represent an image of the camshaft reluctor wheel. The frequency of the CMP sensor output depends on the velocity of the camshaft. The ECM decodes the narrow and wide tooth pattern to identify camshaft position. This information is then used to determine the optimum ignition and injection points of the engine. The ECM also uses the CMP sensor output information to determine the camshaft relative position to the crankshaft, to control camshaft phasing, and for limp-home operation.

REMOVAL & INSTALLATION

2.2L (L61) Engine

1. Before servicing the vehicle, refer to the Precautions Section.
2. Disconnect the engine wiring harness electrical connector from the intake Camshaft Position (CMP) sensor.
3. Remove the CMP sensor bolt.
4. Remove the CMP sensor.

To install:

➥**Inspect the CMP sensor for damage, replace as necessary.**

5. Lubricate the CMP sensor O-ring seal with clean engine oil.
6. Install the CMP sensor.
7. Install the CMP sensor bolt.
8. Tighten the CMP sensor bolt to 89 inch. lbs. (10 Nm).
9. Connect the engine wiring harness electrical connector (1) to the intake CMP sensor.

3.5L (LZ4) Engine

1. Before servicing the vehicle, refer to the Precautions Section.
2. Remove the intake manifold cover. if required.
3. Remove the power steering pump, if required.
4. Disconnect the fuel injector wiring harness electrical connector from the camshaft position (CMP) sensor.

5. Remove the CMP sensor bolt.
6. Remove the CMP sensor.
7. Inspect the sensor O-ring for wear, cracks, or leakage if the sensor is not being replaced.

To install:

8. Replace the O-ring if damaged, lubricate the NEW O-ring with clean engine oil.
9. Install the CMP sensor.
10. Install the CMP sensor bolt.
11. Tighten the CMP sensor bolts to 89 inch. lbs. (10 Nm).
12. Connect the fuel injector wiring harness electrical connector to the CMP sensor.
13. Install the power steering pump, if required.
14. Install the intake manifold cover. if required.

3.9L (LZ9) Engine

1. Before servicing the vehicle, refer to the Precautions Section.
2. Remove the power steering pump
3. Disconnect the camshaft position (CMP) sensor electrical connector.
4. Remove the CMP sensor bolt.
5. Remove the CMP sensor.
6. Inspect the sensor O-ring for wear, cracks, or leakage if the sensor is not being replaced.

To install:

7. Replace the O-ring if damaged, lubricate the NEW O-ring with clean engine oil.
8. Install the CMP sensor.
9. Install the CMP sensor bolt.
10. Tighten the CMP sensor bolts to 89 inch. lbs. (10 Nm).
11. Connect the CMP sensor electrical connector.
12. Install the power steering pump.

TESTING

See Figures 132 and 133.

Test the Camshaft Position (CMP) sensor circuit as follows:
1. Ignition OFF, disconnect the appropriate CMP sensor wire harness connector.
2. Test for less than 1 ohm of resistance between the low reference circuit terminal B and ground.
3. If greater than the specified value, test the low reference circuit for an open/high resistance. If the circuit tests normal, replace the ECM
4. Ignition ON, test for 4.8-5.2 volts between the 5-volt reference circuit terminal A and ground.

5. If less than the specified range, test the 5-volt reference circuit for an open/high resistance or short to ground. If the circuit tests normal, replace the ECM

6. If greater than the specified range, test the 5-volt reference circuit for a short to voltage. If the circuit tests normal, replace the ECM.

7. Ignition ON, test for 4.8-5.2 volts between the signal circuit terminal C and ground.

8. If less than the specified range, test the signal circuit for an open/high resistance or short to ground. If the circuit tests normal, replace the ECM.

9. If greater than the specified range, test the signal circuit for a short to voltage. If the circuit tests normal, replace the ECM.

10. Ignition OFF, connect a fused jumper wire to the CMP signal circuit terminal C.

11. Ignition ON, momentarily touch the other end of the fused jumper wire to the battery negative post. The CMP active counter parameter on the scan tool should increment.

12. If the CMP active counter increments, replace the CMP sensor.

13. If the CMP active counter does not increment, replace the ECM.

Test the Camshaft Position (CMP) sensor as follows:

14. Inspect the Camshaft Position (CMP) sensor for correct installation. Remove the CMP sensor from the engine and inspect the sensor and the O-ring for damage.

15. If the sensor is loose, incorrectly installed, or damaged, repair or replace the CMP sensor.

16. Connect the CMP sensor connector

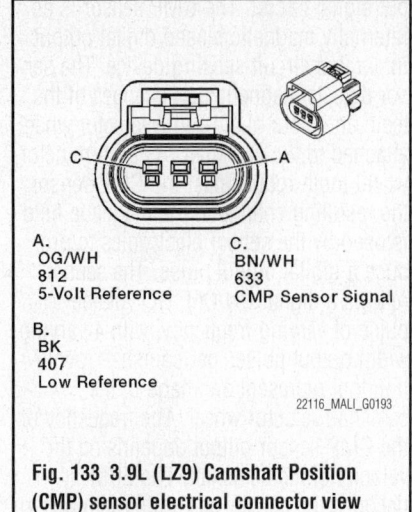

A.
OG/WH
812
5-Volt Reference

C.
BN/WH
633
CMP Sensor Signal

B.
BK
407
Low Reference

22116_MALI_G0193

Fig. 133 3.9L (LZ9) Camshaft Position (CMP) sensor electrical connector view

to the CMP sensor. Turn ON the ignition, with the engine OFF.

17. Ignition ON, and engine OFF. Observe the CMP Active Counter parameter on the scan tool. Pass a steel object by the tip of the sensor repeatedly. The CMP Active Counter parameter should increment.

18. If the parameter does not increment, replace the CMP sensor.

CRANKSHAFT POSITION (CKP) SENSOR

LOCATION

2.2L (L61) Engine
See Figure 134.

The Crankshaft Position (CKP) sensor is located at the rear of the engine block below the oil filter housing. The starter motor must be removed for sensor replacement.

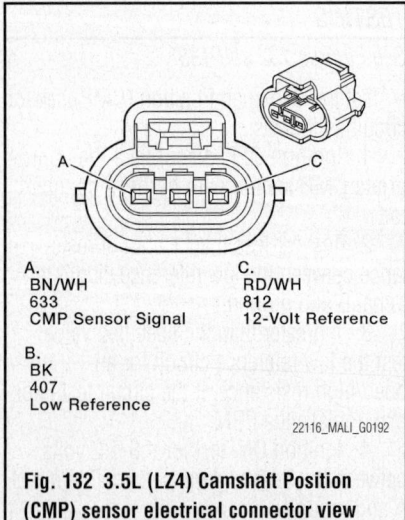

A.
BN/WH
633
CMP Sensor Signal

C.
RD/WH
812
12-Volt Reference

B.
BK
407
Low Reference

22116_MALI_G0192

Fig. 132 3.5L (LZ4) Camshaft Position (CMP) sensor electrical connector view

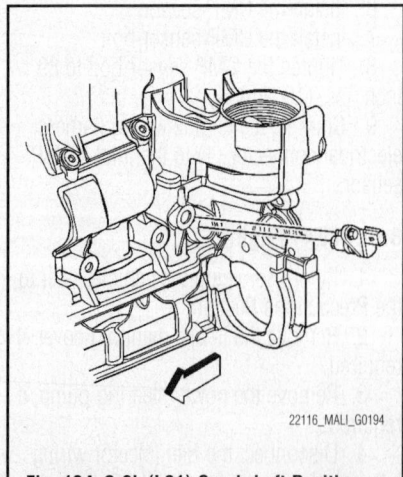

22116_MALI_G0194

Fig. 134 2.2L (L61) Crankshaft Position (CKP) sensor view

3.5L (LZ4) & 3.9L (LZ9) Engines
See Figure 135.

The Crankshaft Position (CKP) sensor is located on the right side of the engine, above the transaxle and just below the exhaust manifold.

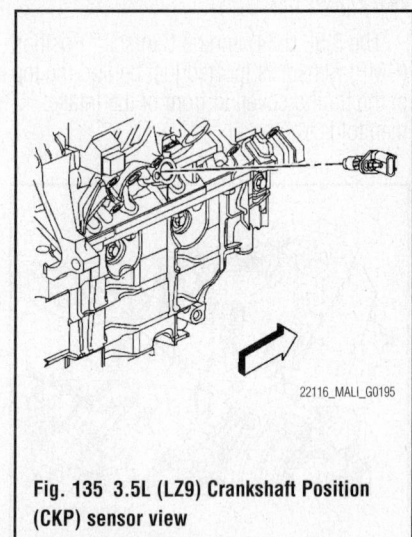

22116_MALI_G0195

Fig. 135 3.5L (LZ9) Crankshaft Position (CKP) sensor view

OPERATION

The Crankshaft Position (CKP) sensor circuits consist of an Engine Control Module (ECM) supplied 5-volt reference circuit, low reference circuit and an output signal circuit. The CKP sensor is an internally magnetic biased digital output integrated circuit sensing device. The sensor detects magnetic flux changes of the teeth and slots of a 58-tooth reluctor wheel on the crankshaft. Each tooth on the reluctor wheel is spaced at 60-tooth spacing, with 2 missing teeth for the reference gap. The CKP sensor produces an ON/OFF DC voltage of varying frequency, with 58 output pulses per crankshaft revolution. The frequency of the CKP sensor output depends on the velocity of the crankshaft. The CKP sensor sends a digital signal, which represents an image of the crankshaft reluctor wheel, to the ECM as each tooth on the wheel rotates past the CKP sensor. The ECM uses each CKP signal pulse to determine crankshaft speed and decodes the crankshaft reluctor wheel reference gap to identify crankshaft position. This information is then used to determine the optimum ignition and injection points of the engine. The ECM also uses CKP sensor output information to determine the camshaft relative position to the crankshaft, to control camshaft phasing, and to detect cylinder misfire.

REMOVAL & INSTALLATION

2.2L (L61) Engine

1. Before servicing the vehicle, refer to the Precautions Section.
2. Remove the starter motor.
3. Disconnect the engine wiring harness electrical connector from the crankshaft position (CKP) sensor.
4. Remove the CKP sensor bolt.
5. Remove the CKP sensor.

To install:

6. Lubricate the new CKP sensor O-ring seal with clean engine
7. Install the CKP sensor.
8. Tighten the CKP sensor bolt to 89 inch. lbs. (10 Nm).
9. Connect the engine wiring harness electrical connector to the CKP sensor.
10. Install the starter motor.

3.5L (LZ4) & 3.9L (LZ9) Engines

1. Before servicing the vehicle, refer to the Precautions Section.
2. Raise and support the vehicle
3. Disconnect the engine wiring harness electrical connector from the Crankshaft Position (CKP) sensor.
4. Remove the CKP sensor stud
5. Remove the CKP sensor.

To install:

6. Lubricate the CKP sensor O-ring with clean engine oil.
7. Install the CKP sensor.
8. Install the CKP sensor stud.
9. Tighten the stud to 89 inch. lbs. (10 Nm).
10. Connect the engine wiring harness electrical connector to the CKP sensor.
11. Lower the vehicle.
12. Perform the CKP system variation learn procedure.

TESTING

See Figures 136 and 137.

Test the Crankshaft Position (CKP) sensor circuit as follows:

1. Disconnect the CKP sensor connector.
2. Test for less than 1 ohm of resistance between low reference circuit and ground.
3. If greater than the specified value, test the low reference circuit for an open/high resistance. If the circuit tests normal, replace the ECM.
4. Ignition ON, test for 4.8-5.2 volts between the 5-volt reference circuit and ground.
5. If less than the specified range, test

the 5-volt reference circuit for an open/high resistance or short to ground. If the circuit tests normal, replace the ECM.

6. If greater than the specified value, test the 5-volt reference circuit for a short to voltage. If the circuit tests normal, replace the ECM.
7. Ignition ON, test for 4.8-5.2 volts between the signal circuit and ground.
8. If less than the specified range, test signal circuit for an open/high resistance or short to ground. If the circuit tests normal, replace the ECM.
9. If greater than the specified range, test signal circuit for a short to voltage. If the circuit tests normal, replace the ECM.
10. Ignition ON, using a jumper wire connected to ground, momentarily touch the CKP sensor signal circuit repeatedly. The CKP Active Counter parameter should increment.
11. If the CKP Active Counter parameter does not increment, replace the ECM.

Test the Crankshaft Position (CKP) sensor as follows:

12. Inspect the CKP sensor for looseness and correct installation. Remove the CKP sensor from the engine and inspect the sensor and the O-ring for damage.
13. If the sensor is loose, incorrectly installed, or damaged; repair or replace the CKP sensor.
14. Connect the CKP Sensor connector to the CKP Sensor; turn ON the ignition, with the engine OFF.
15. Observe the CKP Active Counter parameter on the scan tool; pass a steel object by the tip of the sensor repeatedly. The CKP Active Counter parameter should increment.
16. If the parameter does not increment, replace the CKP sensor.

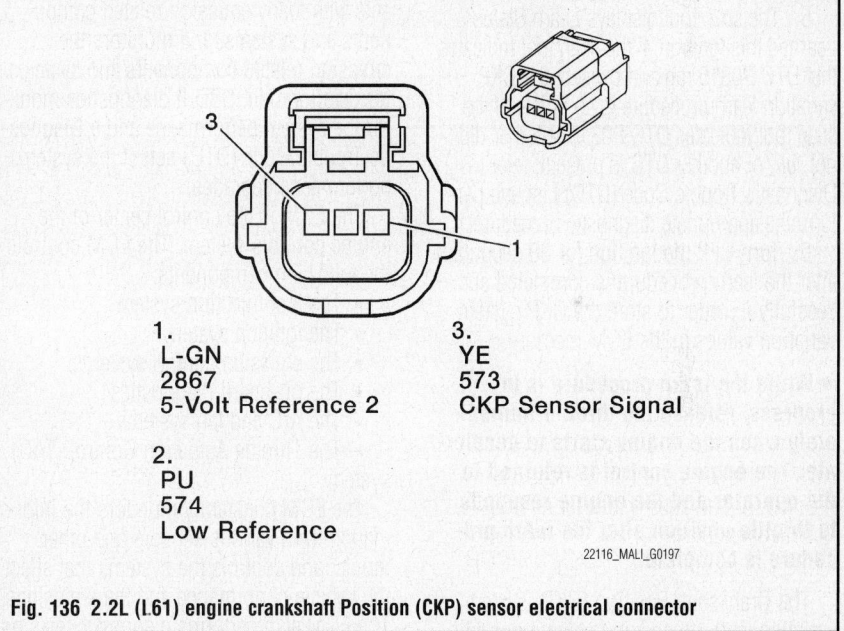

1.
L-GN
2867
5-Volt Reference 2

2.
PU
574
Low Reference

3.
YE
573
CKP Sensor Signal

22116_MALI_G0197

Fig. 136 2.2L (L61) engine crankshaft Position (CKP) sensor electrical connector

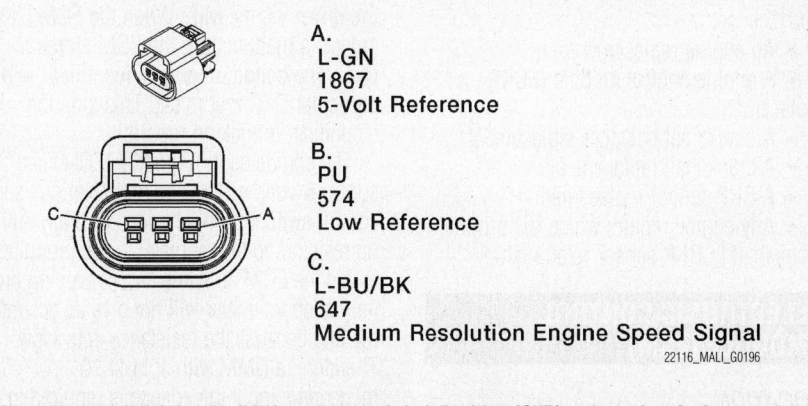

A.
L-GN
1867
5-Volt Reference

B.
PU
574
Low Reference

C.
L-BU/BK
647
Medium Resolution Engine Speed Signal

22116_MALI_G0196

Fig. 137 3.5L (LZ4) & 3.9L (LZ9) engine crankshaft Position (CKP) sensor electrical connector

CRANKSHAFT POSITION SYSTEM VARIATION LEARN PROCEDURE

1. Install a scan tool.

2. Monitor the ECM for DTCs with a scan tool. If other DTCs are set, except DTC P0315, refer to Diagnostic Trouble Code (DTC) List for the applicable DTC that set.

3. With a scan tool, select the CKP System Variation Learn Procedure and perform the following:

  a. Block drive wheels.

  b. Set parking brake.

  c. DO NOT apply brake pedal.

  d. Cycle ignition from OFF to ON.

  e. Apply and hold brake pedal for the duration of the procedure.

  f. Start and idle engine

  g. Turn the air conditioning (A/C) OFF.

  h. The vehicle must remain in Park or Neutral.

4. Accelerate to wide open throttle (WOT) and release when the fuel cut-off occurs.

5. The scan tool displays Learn Status: Learned this Ignition. If the scan tool indicates that DTC P0315 ran and passed, the CKP variation learn procedure is complete. If the scan tool indicates DTC P0315 failed or did not run, or another DTC is present, refer to Diagnostic Trouble Code (DTC) List and perform the appropriate diagnostic procedure.

6. Turn OFF the ignition for 30 seconds after the learn procedure is completed successfully in order to store the CKP system variation values in the ECM memory.

➡ **While the learn procedure is in progress, release the throttle immediately when the engine starts to decelerate. The engine control is returned to the operator and the engine responds to throttle position after the learn procedure is complete.**

The Crankshaft Position (CKP) system variation learn procedure is also required when the following service procedures have been performed, regardless of whether DTC P0315 is set:

• An engine replacement

• A engine control module (ECM) replacement

• A crankshaft balancer replacement

• A crankshaft replacement

• A CKP sensor replacement

• Any engine repairs which disturb the crankshaft to CKP sensor relationship.

ELECTRONIC CONTROL MODULE (ECM)

LOCATION

See Figure 138.

The Engine Control Module (ECM) is located in the engine compartment. It is mounted on the front of the battery box.

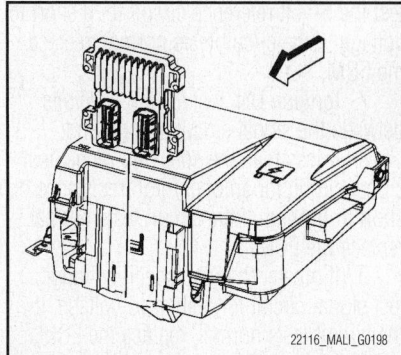

22116_MALI_G0198

Fig. 138 Engine Control Module (ECM) location

OPERATION

The Engine Control Module (ECM) interacts with many emission related components and systems, and monitors the emission related components and systems for deterioration. OBD II diagnostics monitor the system performance and a Diagnostic Trouble Code (DTC) sets if the system performance degrades.

The ECM is the control center of the engine controls system. The ECM controls the following components:

• The fuel injection system

• The ignition system

• The emission control systems

• The on-board diagnostics

• The A/C and fan systems

• The Throttle Actuation Control (TAC) system

The ECM constantly monitors the information from various sensors and other inputs, and controls the systems that affect the vehicle performance and the emissions. The ECM also performs diagnostic tests on various parts of the system. The ECM can recognize operational problems and alert the driver via the MIL. When the ECM detects a malfunction, the ECM stores a DTC. The condition area is identified by the particular DTC that is set. This aids the technician in making repairs.

The engine control module (ECM) can supply 5 volts or 12 volts to the various sensors or switches. This is done through pull-up resistors to the regulated power supplies within the ECM. In some cases, even an ordinary shop voltmeter will not give an accurate reading because the resistance is too low. Therefore, a DMM with at least 10 megaohms input impedance is required in order to ensure accurate voltage readings.

REMOVAL & INSTALLATION

✳✳ WARNING

Turn the ignition OFF when installing or removing the control module connectors and disconnecting or reconnecting the power to the control module (battery cable, Powertrain Control Module (PCM)/Engine Control Module (ECM)/Transaxle Control Module (TCM) pigtail, control module fuse, jumper cables, etc.) in order to prevent internal control module damage.

➡ **The replacement control module must be programmed.**

1. Using a scan tool, retrieve the percentage of remaining engine oil. Record the remaining engine oil life.

2. Record the preset radio stations.

3. Turn the ignition **OFF**.

4. Disconnect the negative battery cable.

5. Disconnect the engine wiring harness electrical connector from the ECM.

6. Disconnect the body wiring harness electrical connector from the ECM.

7. Release the retaining tab located on the battery tray using a small screwdriver or other suitable tool.

8. Remove the ECM by lifting upward after releasing the tab.

To install:

9. Slide the ECM into the bracket on the battery tray.

10. Push down on the ECM until the retaining tab snaps into place.

11. Connect the body wiring harness electrical connector to the ECM.

12. Connect the engine wiring harness electrical connector to the ECM.

13. Connect the negative battery cable.

14. Reset the clock and preset radio stations.

15. If a new ECM was installed, the ECM must be programmed.

TESTING

See Figures 139 through 144.

1. Observe the DTCs with the scan tool.

2. If DTC P0602 is set, attempt to program the Engine Control Module (ECM) before replacing the ECM.

3. If DTC P0602 resets, replace the ECM.

4. Test the voltage and ground circuits to the control module for the following:

• A short

• An open

• High resistance

• If all circuits test normal, replace the ECM.

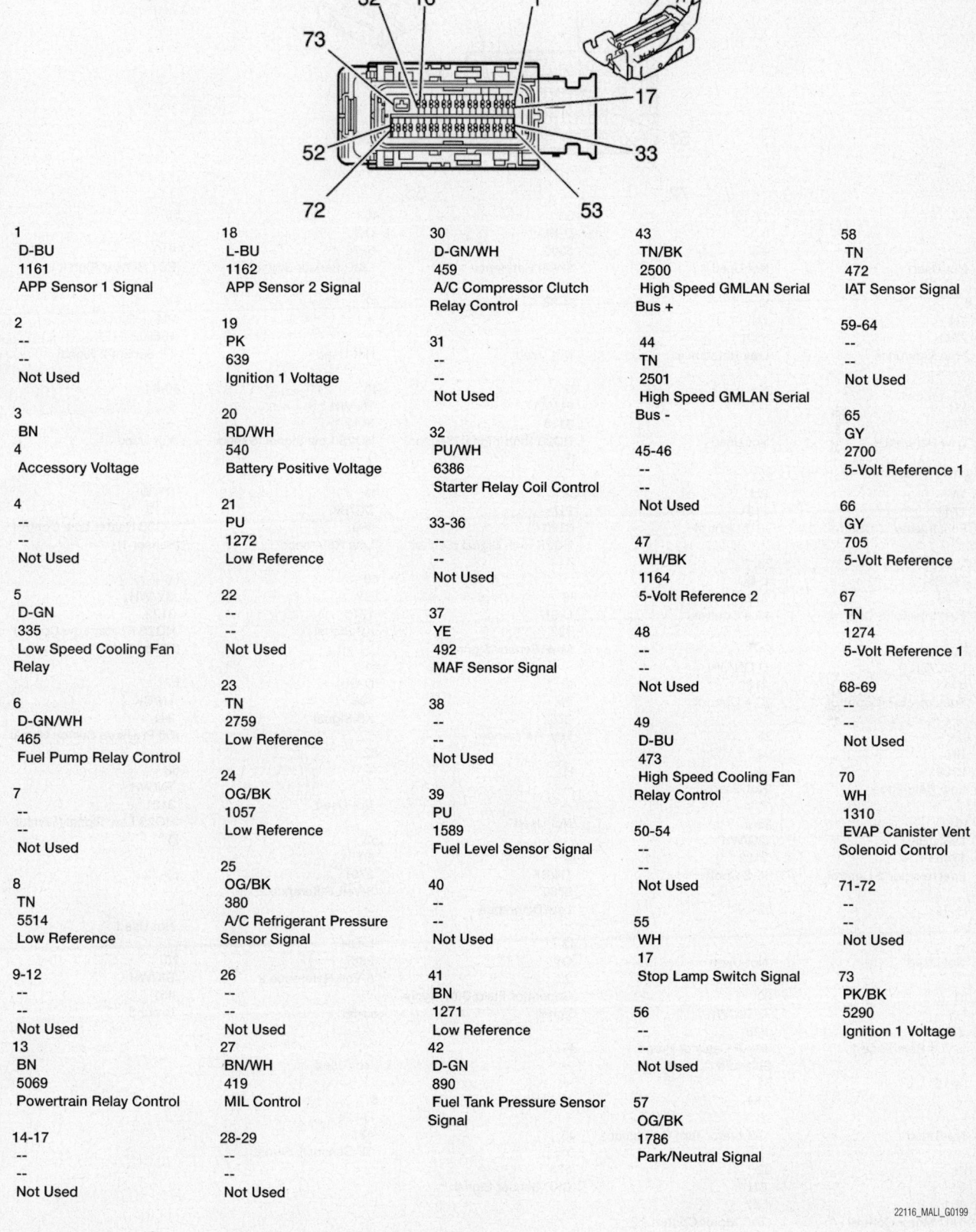

1
D-BU
1161
APP Sensor 1 Signal

2
--
--
Not Used

3
BN
4
Accessory Voltage

4
--
--
Not Used

5
D-GN
335
Low Speed Cooling Fan Relay

6
D-GN/WH
465
Fuel Pump Relay Control

7
--
--
Not Used

8
TN
5514
Low Reference

9-12
--
--
Not Used

13
BN
5069
Powertrain Relay Control

14-17
--
--
Not Used

18
L-BU
1162
APP Sensor 2 Signal

19
PK
639
Ignition 1 Voltage

20
RD/WH
540
Battery Positive Voltage

21
PU
1272
Low Reference

22
--
--
Not Used

23
TN
2759
Low Reference

24
OG/BK
1057
Low Reference

25
OG/BK
380
A/C Refrigerant Pressure Sensor Signal

26
--
--
Not Used

27
BN/WH
419
MIL Control

28-29
--
--
Not Used

30
D-GN/WH
459
A/C Compressor Clutch Relay Control

31
--
--
Not Used

32
PU/WH
6386
Starter Relay Coil Control

33-36
--
--
Not Used

37
YE
492
MAF Sensor Signal

38
--
--
Not Used

39
PU
1589
Fuel Level Sensor Signal

40
--
--
Not Used

41
BN
1271
Low Reference

42
D-GN
890
Fuel Tank Pressure Sensor Signal

43
TN/BK
2500
High Speed GMLAN Serial Bus +

44
TN
2501
High Speed GMLAN Serial Bus -

45-46
--
--
Not Used

47
WH/BK
1164
5-Volt Reference 2

48
--
--
Not Used

49
D-BU
473
High Speed Cooling Fan Relay Control

50-54
--
--
Not Used

55
WH
17
Stop Lamp Switch Signal

56
--
--
Not Used

57
OG/BK
1786
Park/Neutral Signal

58
TN
472
IAT Sensor Signal

59-64
--
--
Not Used

65
GY
2700
5-Volt Reference 1

66
GY
705
5-Volt Reference

67
TN
1274
5-Volt Reference 1

68-69
--
--
Not Used

70
WH
1310
EVAP Canister Vent Solenoid Control

71-72
--
--
Not Used

73
PK/BK
5290
Ignition 1 Voltage

22116_MALI_G0199

Fig. 139 2.2L (L61) Engine Control Module (ECM) electrical connector (C1)

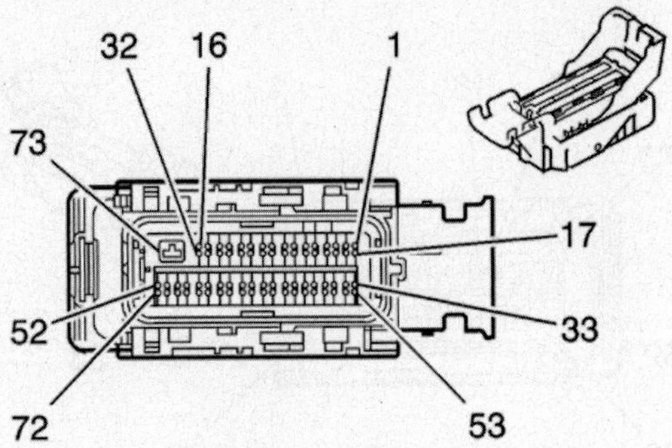

1-3	17-19	33	46	58
--	--	D-BU	OG	YE
--	--	5300	5275	410
Not Used	Not Used	5-Volt Reference 1	CMP Sensor Signal	ECT Sensor Signal
4	20	34-36	47	59
TN	TN	--	--	PU
2761	5301	--	--	486
Low Reference	Low Reference	Not Used	Not Used	TP Sensor 2 Signal
5	21	37	48	60-64
PU	--	PU/WH	TN/WH	--
574	--	3110	3111	--
Low Reference	Not Used	HO2S High Signal (Sensor 1)	HO2S Low Signal (Sensor 1)	Not Used
6	22	38	49	65
TN	PU	PU	OG/BK	GY/WH
1744	2121	3120	469	3113
Fuel Injector 1 Control	IC 1 Control	HO2S High Signal (Sensor 2)	Low Reference	HO2S Heater Low Control (Sensor 1)
7	23	39	50	66
PK/BK	L-BU	L-GN	GY	GY/WH
1746	2123	432	1716	3122
Fuel Injector 3 Control	IC 3 Control	MAP Sensor Signal	KS Signal	HO2S Heater Low Control (Sensor 2)
8	24	40	51	67
L-BU/BK	D-GN/WH	TN	D-BU	TN/BK
844	2124	2752	496	231
Fuel Injector 4 Control	IC 4 Control	Low Reference	KS Signal	Oil Pressure Switch Signal
9	25	41	52	68
BN	--	--	--	TN/WH
2129	--	--	--	3121
Low Reference	Not Used	Not Used	Not Used	HO2S Low Signal (Sensor 2)
10	26	42	53	69-72
L-GN/BK	OG/WH	TN/BK	GY	--
1745	2122	2760	2701	--
Fuel Injector 2 Control	IC 2 Control	Low Reference	5-Volt Reference 2	Not Used
11-12	27-29	43	54	73
--	--	GY	L-GN	BK/WH
--	--	23	2867	451
Not Used	Not Used	Generator Field Duty Cycle Signal	5-Volt Reference 2	Ground
13	30	44	55-56	
GY	D-GN/WH	--	--	
2704	428	--	--	
5-Volt Reference 1	EVAP Canister Purge Solenoid Control	Not Used	Not Used	
14-15	31	45	57	
--	OG	YE	D-GN	
--	225	573	485	
Not Used	Generator Turn On Signal	CKP Sensor Signal	TP Sensor 1 Signal	
16	32			
YE	BN			
581	582			
TAC Motor Control - 1	TAC Motor Control - 2			

22116_MALI_G0200

Fig. 140 2.2L (L61) Engine Control Module (ECM) electrical connector (C2)

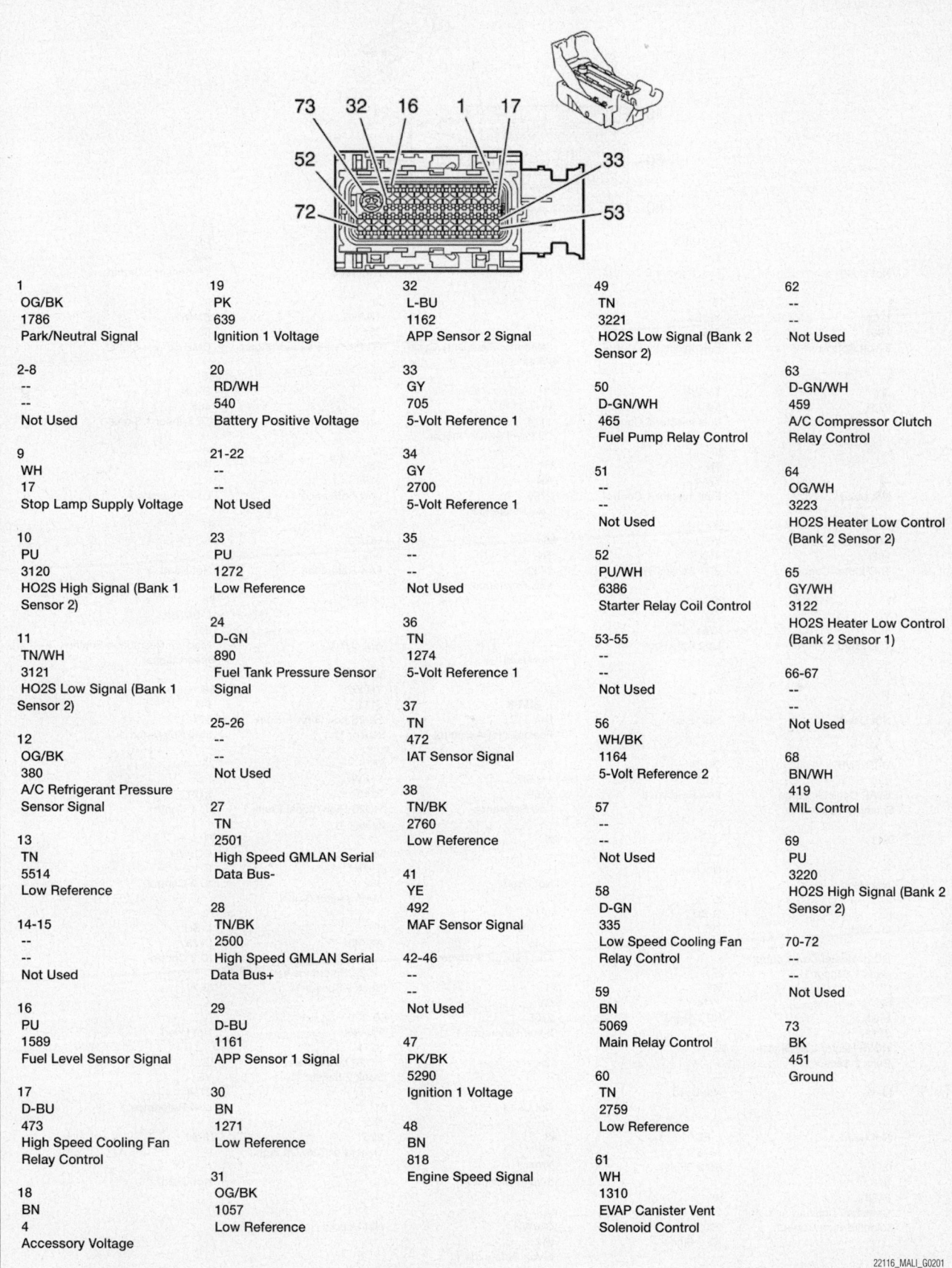

1
OG/BK
1786
Park/Neutral Signal

2-8
--
--
Not Used

9
WH
17
Stop Lamp Supply Voltage

10
PU
3120
HO2S High Signal (Bank 1
Sensor 2)

11
TN/WH
3121
HO2S Low Signal (Bank 1
Sensor 2)

12
OG/BK
380
A/C Refrigerant Pressure
Sensor Signal

13
TN
5514
Low Reference

14-15
--
--
Not Used

16
PU
1589
Fuel Level Sensor Signal

17
D-BU
473
High Speed Cooling Fan
Relay Control

18
BN
4
Accessory Voltage

19
PK
639
Ignition 1 Voltage

20
RD/WH
540
Battery Positive Voltage

21-22
--
--
Not Used

23
PU
1272
Low Reference

24
D-GN
890
Fuel Tank Pressure Sensor
Signal

25-26
--
--
Not Used

27
TN
2501
High Speed GMLAN Serial
Data Bus-

28
TN/BK
2500
High Speed GMLAN Serial
Data Bus+

29
D-BU
1161
APP Sensor 1 Signal

30
BN
1271
Low Reference

31
OG/BK
1057
Low Reference

32
L-BU
1162
APP Sensor 2 Signal

33
GY
705
5-Volt Reference 1

34
GY
2700
5-Volt Reference 1

35
--
--
Not Used

36
TN
1274
5-Volt Reference 1

37
TN
472
IAT Sensor Signal

38
TN/BK
2760
Low Reference

41
YE
492
MAF Sensor Signal

42-46
--
--
Not Used

47
PK/BK
5290
Ignition 1 Voltage

48
BN
818
Engine Speed Signal

49
TN
3221
HO2S Low Signal (Bank 2
Sensor 2)

50
D-GN/WH
465
Fuel Pump Relay Control

51
--
--
Not Used

52
PU/WH
6386
Starter Relay Coil Control

53-55
--
--
Not Used

56
WH/BK
1164
5-Volt Reference 2

57
--
--
Not Used

58
D-GN
335
Low Speed Cooling Fan
Relay Control

59
BN
5069
Main Relay Control

60
TN
2759
Low Reference

61
WH
1310
EVAP Canister Vent
Solenoid Control

62
--
--
Not Used

63
D-GN/WH
459
A/C Compressor Clutch
Relay Control

64
OG/WH
3223
HO2S Heater Low Control
(Bank 2 Sensor 2)

65
GY/WH
3122
HO2S Heater Low Control
(Bank 2 Sensor 1)

66-67
--
--
Not Used

68
BN/WH
419
MIL Control

69
PU
3220
HO2S High Signal (Bank 2
Sensor 2)

70-72
--
--
Not Used

73
BK
451
Ground

22116_MALI_G0201

Fig. 141 3.5L (LZ4) Engine Control Module (ECM) electrical connector (C1)

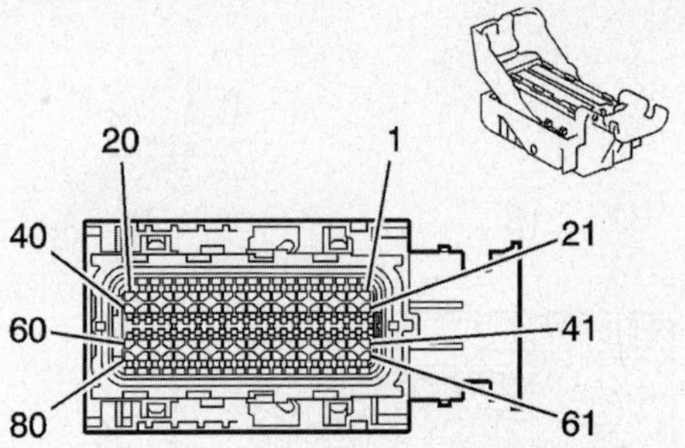

1
--
1745
Not Used

2
L-GN
1867
5-Volt Reference 2

3
GY
2701
5-Volt Reference 2

4
--
--
Not Used

5
BN
582
TAC Motor Control - 2

6
YE
581
TAC Motor Control - 1

7
--
--
Not Used

8
D-GN/WH
428
EVAP Canister Purge
Solenoid Control

9-11
--
--
Not Used

12
GY/WH
3113
HO2S Heater Low Control
(Bank 1 Sensor 1)

13
L-GN
3212
HO2S Heater Low Signal
(Bank 2 Sensor 1)

14-15
--
--
Not Used

16
BN
2198
Camshaft Position Actuator
Solenoid High Control

17
L-GN/BK
1745
Fuel Injector 2 Control

18
YE/BK
846
Fuel Injector 6 Control

19
TN/WH
845
Fuel Injector 5 Control

20
TN
1744
Fuel Injector 1 Control

21
YE
410
ECT Sensor Signal

22
TN
2761
Low Reference

23
--
--
Not Used

24
OG/BK
1175
Low Reference

25
--
--
Not Used

26
D-BU
496
KS 1 Signal

27
GY
1716
KS 1 Signal

28
--
--
Not Used

29
L-BU
1876
KS 2 Signal

30
GY
2303
KS 2 Signal

31
--
--
Not Used

32
GY
23
Generator Field Duty Cycle
Signal

33
BN
1174
Oil Level Switch Signal

34
BK
2755
Low Reference

35
TN
2752
Low Reference

36
--
--
Not Used

37
L-BU/BK
844
Fuel Injector 4 Control

38
TN/BK
2760
Low Reference

39
--
--
Not Used

40
PK/BK
1746
Fuel Injector 3 Control

41
GY
2705
5-Volt Reference 1

42
--
--
Not Used

43
GY
2704
5-Volt Reference 1

44
OG/WH
812
5-Volt Reference 1

45-49
--
--
Not Used

50
TN/WH
331
Oil Pressure Sensor Signal

51
--
--
Not Used

52
TN
2199
Low Reference

53
OG/BK
469
Low Reference

54-55
--
--
Not Used

56
TN/WH
3111
HO2S Low Signal (Bank 1
Sensor 1)

57
PU/WH
3110
HO2S High Signal (Bank 1
Sensor 1)

58
L-GN
432
MAP Sensor Signal

59
PU/WH
3210
HO2S Reference Voltage
(Bank 2 Sensor 1)

60
TN/WH
3211
HO2S Low Reference
(Bank 2 Sensor 1)

61
OG
225
Generator Turn On Signal

62
--
--
Not Used

63
PU
486
TP Sensor 2 Signal

64
BN/WH
633
CMP Sensor Signal

65
D-GN
485
TP Sensor 1 Signal

66
PK/BK
632
Low Reference

67
--
--
Not Used

68
L-BU/BK
647
Medium Resolution Engine
Speed Signal

69
PU
574
Low Reference

70
PU
2121
IC 1 Control

71
OG/WH
2122
IC 2 Control

72
L-BU
2123
IC 3 Control

73-77
--
--
Not Used

78
YE
2174
Low Reference

79-80
--
--
Not Used

22116_MALI_G0202

Fig. 142 3.5L (LZ4) Engine Control Module (ECM) electrical connector (C2)

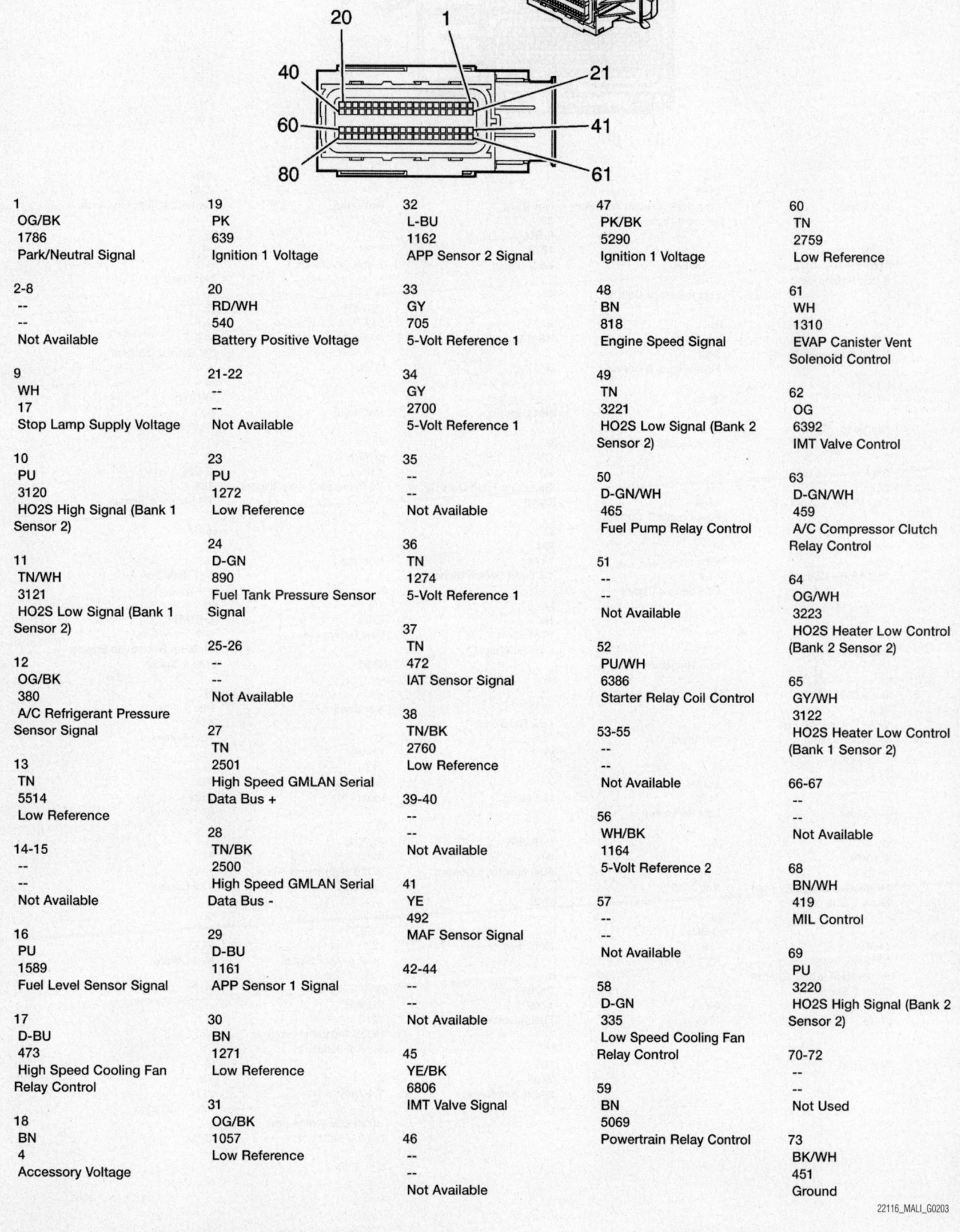

1
OG/BK
1786
Park/Neutral Signal

2-8
--
--
Not Available

9
WH
17
Stop Lamp Supply Voltage

10
PU
3120
HO2S High Signal (Bank 1 Sensor 2)

11
TN/WH
3121
HO2S Low Signal (Bank 1 Sensor 2)

12
OG/BK
380
A/C Refrigerant Pressure Sensor Signal

13
TN
5514
Low Reference

14-15
--
--
Not Available

16
PU
1589
Fuel Level Sensor Signal

17
D-BU
473
High Speed Cooling Fan Relay Control

18
BN
4
Accessory Voltage

19
PK
639
Ignition 1 Voltage

20
RD/WH
540
Battery Positive Voltage

21-22
--
--
Not Available

23
PU
1272
Low Reference

24
D-GN
890
Fuel Tank Pressure Sensor Signal

25-26
--
--
Not Available

27
TN
2501
High Speed GMLAN Serial Data Bus +

28
TN/BK
2500
High Speed GMLAN Serial Data Bus -

29
D-BU
1161
APP Sensor 1 Signal

30
BN
1271
Low Reference

31
OG/BK
1057
Low Reference

32
L-BU
1162
APP Sensor 2 Signal

33
GY
705
5-Volt Reference 1

34
GY
2700
5-Volt Reference 1

35
--
--
Not Available

36
TN
1274
5-Volt Reference 1

37
TN
472
IAT Sensor Signal

38
TN/BK
2760
Low Reference

39-40
--
--
Not Available

41
YE
492
MAF Sensor Signal

42-44
--
--
Not Available

45
YE/BK
6806
IMT Valve Signal

46
--
--
Not Available

47
PK/BK
5290
Ignition 1 Voltage

48
BN
818
Engine Speed Signal

49
TN
3221
HO2S Low Signal (Bank 2 Sensor 2)

50
D-GN/WH
465
Fuel Pump Relay Control

51
--
--
Not Available

52
PU/WH
6386
Starter Relay Coil Control

53-55
--
--
Not Available

56
WH/BK
1164
5-Volt Reference 2

57
--
--
Not Available

58
D-GN
335
Low Speed Cooling Fan Relay Control

59
BN
5069
Powertrain Relay Control

60
TN
2759
Low Reference

61
WH
1310
EVAP Canister Vent Solenoid Control

62
OG
6392
IMT Valve Control

63
D-GN/WH
459
A/C Compressor Clutch Relay Control

64
OG/WH
3223
HO2S Heater Low Control (Bank 2 Sensor 2)

65
GY/WH
3122
HO2S Heater Low Control (Bank 1 Sensor 2)

66-67
--
--
Not Available

68
BN/WH
419
MIL Control

69
PU
3220
HO2S High Signal (Bank 2 Sensor 2)

70-72
--
--
Not Used

73
BK/WH
451
Ground

22116_MALI_G0203

Fig. 143 3.9L (LZ9) Engine Control Module (ECM) electrical connector (C1)

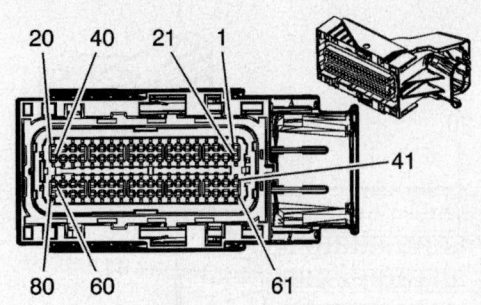

1

2
L-GN
1867
5-Volt Reference 2

3
GY
2701
5-Volt Reference 2

4
--
--
Not Used

5
BN
582
TAC Motor Control - 2

6
YE
581
TAC Motor Control - 1

7
--
--
Not Used

8
D-GN/WH
482
EVAP Canister Purge
Solenoid Control

9-11
--
--
Not Used

12
GY/WH
3113
HO2S Heater Low Control
(Bank 1 Sensor 1)

13
L-GN
3212
HO2S Heater Low Control
(Bank 2 Sensor 1)

14-15
--
--
Not Used

16
BN
2198
Camshaft Position Actuator
Solenoid High Control

17
L-GN/BK
1745
Fuel Injector 2 Control

18
YE/BK
846
Fuel Injector 6 Control

19
TN/WH
845
Fuel Injector 5 Control

20
TN
1744
Fuel Injector 1 Control

21
YE
410
ECT Sensor Signal

22
TN
2761
Low Reference

23
--
--
Not Used

24
OG/BK
1175
Low Reference

25
--
--
Not Used

26
D-BU
496
KS 1 Signal

27
GY
1716
KS 1 Signal

28
--
--
Not Used

29
L-BU
1876
KS 2 Signal

30
GY
2303
KS 2 Signal

31
--
--
Not Used

32
GY
23
Generator Field Duty Cycle
Signal

33
BN
1174
Oil Level Switch Signal

34
BK
2755
Low Reference

35
TN
2752
Low Reference

36
--
--
Not Used

37
L-BU/BK
844
Fuel Injector 4 Control

38-39
--
--
Not Used

40
PK/BK
1746
Fuel Injector 3 Control

41
GY
2705
5-Volt Reference 1

42
--
--
Not Used

43
GY
2704
5-Volt Reference 1

44
OG/WH
812
5-Volt Reference 1

45-49
--
--
Not Used

50
TN/WH
331
Oil Pressure Sensor Signal

51
--
--
Not Used

52
TN
2199
Low Reference

53-55
--
--
Not Used

56
TN/WH
3111
HO2S Low Signal (Bank 1
Sensor 1)

57
PU/WH
3110
HO2S High Signal (Bank 1
Sensor 1)

58
L-GN
432
MAP Sensor Signal

59
PU/WH
3210
HO2S Reference Voltage
(Bank 2 Sensor 1)

60
TN/WH
3211
HO2S Low Reference
(Bank 2 Sensor 1)

61
OG
225
Generator Turn On Signal

62
--
--
Not Used

63
PU
486
TP Sensor 2 Signal

64
BN/WH
633
CMP Sensor Signal

65
D-GN
485
TP Sensor 1 Signal

66-67
--
--
Not Used

68
L-BU/BK
647
Medium Resolution Engine
Speed Signal

69
PU
574
Low Reference

70
PU
2121
IC 1 Control

71
PU
2122
IC 2 Control

72
PU
2123
IC 3 Control

73-77
--
--
Not Used

78
YE
2174
Low Reference

79-80
--
--
Not Used

22116_MALI_G0204

Fig. 144 3.9L (LZ9) Engine Control Module (ECM) electrical connector (C2)

ENGINE COOLANT TEMPERATURE (ECT) SENSOR

LOCATION

2.2L (L61) Engine

The Engine Coolant Temperature (ECT) sensor is located just to the left of the exhaust manifold in the thermostat housing between the two coolant pipes.

3.5L (LZ4) & 3.9L (LZ9) Engine

The Engine Coolant Temperature (ECT) sensor is located on the left cylinder head at the rear. It is just above the transaxle mounting bolts.

OPERATION

The ECM supplies a 5 volt signal to the engine coolant temperature sensor through a resistor in the ECM and measures the voltage. The voltage will be high when the engine is cold, and low when the engine is hot. By measuring the voltage, the ECM calculates the engine coolant temperature. Engine coolant temperature affects most systems the ECM controls.

REMOVAL & INSTALLATION

2.2L (L61) Engine

See Figure 145.

1. Before servicing the vehicle, refer to the Precautions Section.
2. Partially drain the cooling system.
3. Disconnect the engine wiring harness electrical connector from the Engine Coolant Temperature (ECT) sensor.
4. Remove the ECT sensor.

To install:

5. Apply sealant to the threads of the ECT sensor.
6. Install the ECT sensor.

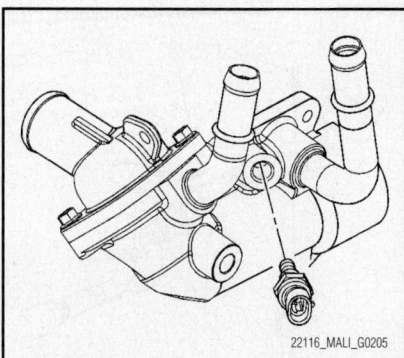

Fig. 145 Engine Coolant Temperature (ECT) sensor removal

7. Tighten the ECT sensor to 15 ft. lbs. (20 Nm).
8. Connect the engine wiring harness electrical connector to the ECT sensor.
9. Fill and bleed the cooling system as needed.

3.5L (LZ4) & 3.9L (LZ9) Engine

1. Drain the cooling system.
2. Remove the intake manifold cover, if necessary.
3. Disconnect the Engine Coolant Temperature (ECT) sensor electrical connector.
4. Remove the ECT sensor.

➡**Replacement components must be the correct part number for the application. Components requiring the use of the thread locking compound, lubricants, corrosion inhibitors, or sealants are identified in the service procedure. Some replacement components may come with these coatings already applied. Do not use these coatings on components unless specified. These coatings can affect the final torque, which may affect the operation of the component. Use the correct torque specification when installing components in order to avoid damage.**

To install:

5. Coat the threads of the ECT sensor with sealer.
6. Install the ECT sensor and tighten to 15 ft. lbs. (20 Nm).
7. Connect the ECT electrical connector.
8. Install the intake manifold cover, if necessary.
9. Fill and bleed the cooling system as needed.

TESTING

See Figures 146 through 148.

Test the Engine Coolant Temperature (ECT) sensor circuit as follows:

1. Ignition OFF, disconnect the harness connector at the Engine Coolant Temperature (ECT) sensor.
2. Ignition OFF for 90 seconds, test for less than 5 ohms of resistance between the low reference circuit terminal A and ground.
3. If greater than the specified range, test the low reference circuit for an open/high resistance. If the circuit tests normal, replace the ECM.
4. Ignition ON, verify the scan tool ECT parameter is less than -39°C (-38°F).
5. If greater than the specified range,

test the signal circuit terminal B for a short to ground. If the circuit tests normal, replace the ECM.

6. Install a 3-amp fused jumper wire between the signal circuit terminal B and the low reference circuit terminal A. Verify the scan tool ECT parameter is greater than 149°C (300°F).
7. If less than the specified range, test the signal circuit for a short to voltage or an open/high resistance. If the circuit tests normal, replace the ECM.
8. If all circuits test normal, test or replace the ECT sensor.

Check the Engine Coolant Temperature (ECT) sensor as follows:

9. Measure and record the resistance of the ECT sensor at various ambient temperatures, then compare those measurements to the temperature versus resistance table.

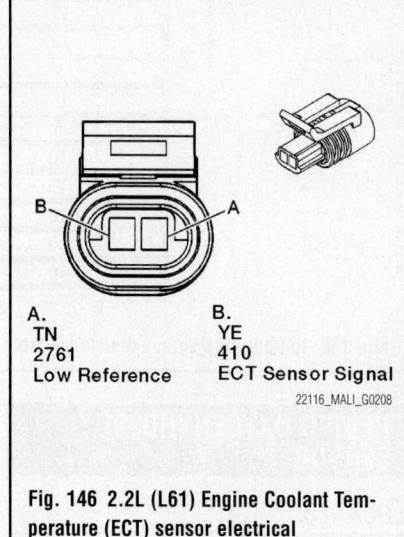

A.
TN
2761
Low Reference

B.
YE
410
ECT Sensor Signal

22116_MALI_G0208

Fig. 146 2.2L (L61) Engine Coolant Temperature (ECT) sensor electrical

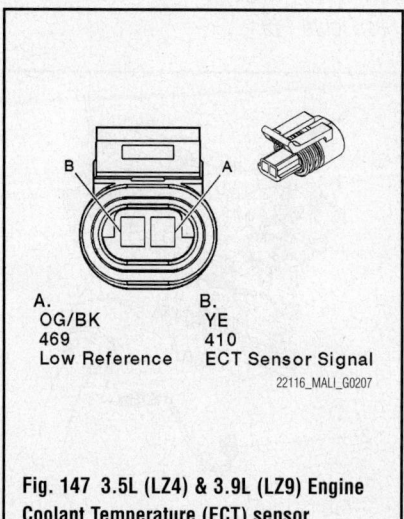

A.
OG/BK
469
Low Reference

B.
YE
410
ECT Sensor Signal

22116_MALI_G0207

Fig. 147 3.5L (LZ4) & 3.9L (LZ9) Engine Coolant Temperature (ECT) sensor electrical connector

Temperature Versus Resistance

°C	°F	OHMS
Temperature vs Resistance Values (Approximate)		
150	302	47
140	284	60
130	266	77
120	248	100
110	230	132
100	212	177
90	194	241
80	176	332
70	158	467
60	140	667
50	122	973
45	113	1188
40	104	1459
35	95	1802
30	86	2238
25	77	2796
20	68	3520
15	59	4450
10	50	5670
5	41	7280
0	32	9420
-5	23	12300
-10	14	16180
-15	5	21450
-20	-4	28680
-30	-22	52700
-40	-40	100700

22116_MALI_G0206

Fig. 148 Temperature versus resistance table

HEATED OXYGEN (HO2S) SENSOR

LOCATION

2.2L (L61) Engine

See Figure 149.

The front Heated Oxygen Sensor (HO2S) is mounted in the exhaust manifold. The rear Heated Oxygen Sensor (HO2S) is mounted in the front exhaust pipe after the catalytic converter.

3.5L (LZ4) & 3.9L (LZ9) Engine

Front Sensors

See Figure 150.

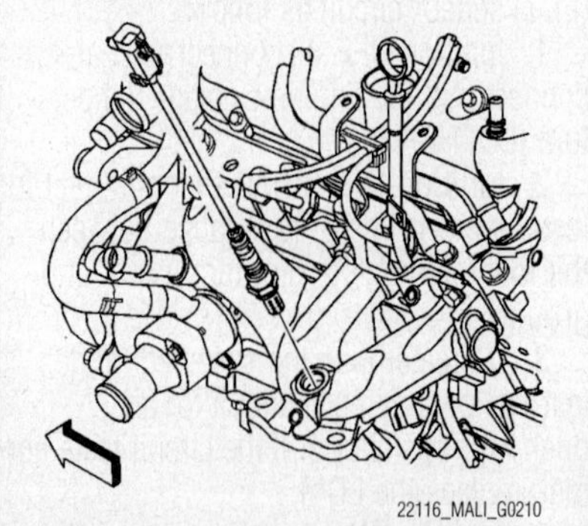

The front Heated Oxygen Sensor (HO2S) Sensors left and right are mounted in the exhaust manifold. Bank 1 sensor 1 is mounted in the right exhaust manifold and bank 2 sensor 2 in the left manifold.

Rear Sensors

See Figure 151.

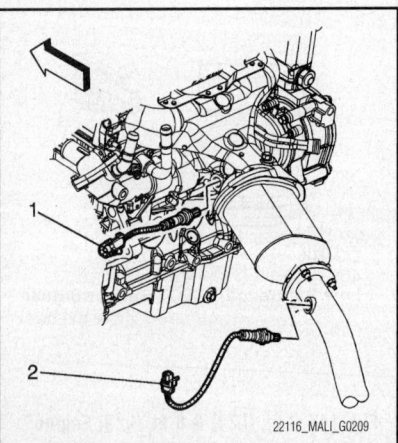

Fig. 149 Front (1) and rear (2) Heated Oxygen Sensor (HO2S) location

Fig. 150 Front Heated Oxygen (HO2S) Sensors left side shown right similar

22116_MALI_G0210

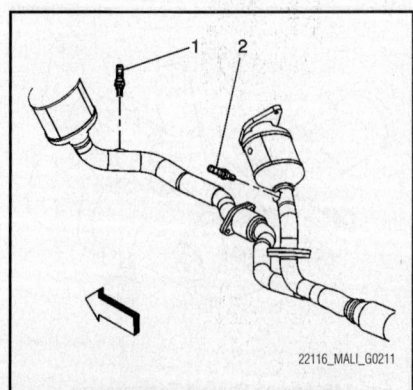

22116_MALI_G0211

Fig. 151 Rear Heated Oxygen (HO2S) Sensors (1, 2)

The rear Heated Oxygen (HO2S) Sensors are mounted just behind the catalytic converters. Bank 1 sensor 2 is mounted behind right converter assembly and bank 2 sensor 2 behind left assembly.

OPERATION

Heated Oxygen Sensors (HO2S) are used for fuel control and post catalyst monitoring. Each HO2S compares the oxygen content of the surrounding air with the oxygen content in the exhaust stream. The HO2S must reach operating temperature to provide an accurate voltage signal. Heating elements inside the HO2S minimize the time required for the sensors to reach operating temperature. The engine control module (ECM) supplies the HO2S with a reference, or bias, voltage of about 450 mV. When the engine is first started, the ECM operates in Open Loop, ignoring the HO2S voltage signal. Once the HO2S reaches operating temperature and Closed Loop is achieved, the HO2S generates a voltage within a range of 0-1,000 mV that fluctuates above and below bias voltage. High HO2S voltage indicates a rich exhaust stream. Low HO2S voltage indicates a lean exhaust stream.

REMOVAL & INSTALLATION

2.2L (L61) Engine

Front Sensor 1

✵✵ WARNING

The in-line connector and louvered end must be kept clear of grease, dirt or other contaminants. Avoid using cleaning solvents of any type. DO NOT drop or roughly handle the heated oxygen sensor (HO2S).

1. Before servicing the vehicle, refer to the Precautions Section.
2. Remove the Connector Position Assurance (CPA) retainer.
3. Disconnect the engine wiring harness electrical connector from the HO2S electrical connector.
4. Remove the HO2S electrical connector rosebud clip from the thermostat housing tab.
5. Remove the HO2S.

➡**A special anti-seize compound is used on the HO2S threads. The compound consists of a liquid graphite and glass beads. The graphite will burn away, but the glass beads will remain, making the sensor easier to remove. New or service sensors will have the compound applied to the threads. If a** sensor is removed and is to be reinstalled, the threads must have an antiseize compound applied before installation.

6. If reinstalling the old HO2S, coat the threads with anti-seize compound.
7. Install the HO2S and tighten to 31 ft. lbs. (42 Nm).
8. Connect the engine wiring harness electrical connector to the HO2S electrical connector.
9. Install the CPA retainer.
10. Install the HO2S electrical connector rosebud clip to the thermostat housing tab.

Rear Sensor 2

➡**The HO2S may be difficult to remove when the engine temperature is less than 48°C (120°F).**

1. Before servicing the vehicle, refer to the Precautions Section.
2. Raise and support the vehicle.
3. Remove the Connector Position Assurance (CPA) retainer.
4. Disconnect the engine wiring harness electrical connector from the HO2S electrical connector.
5. Using the J 39194, remove the HO2S.

To install:

➡**A special anti-seize compound is used on the HO2S threads. The compound consists of a liquid graphite and glass beads. The graphite will burn away but the glass beads will remain, making the sensor easier to remove. New or service sensors already have the compound applied to the threads. If the sensor is removed and is to be reinstalled, the threads must be coated with an anti-seize compound before reinstallation.**

6. If reinstalling the old HO2S, coat the threads with anti-seize compound.
7. Using the J 39194, install the HO2S. Tighten to 31 ft. lbs. (42 Nm).
8. Connect the engine wiring harness electrical connector (2) to the HO2S electrical connector.
9. Install the CPA retainer.
10. Lower the vehicle.

3.5L (LZ4) & 3.9L (LZ9) Engines

Bank 1 Sensor 1

1. Before servicing the vehicle, refer to the Precautions Section.
2. Remove the intake manifold cover.

3. Remove the Connector Position Assurance (CPA) retainer.
4. Disconnect the engine wiring harness electrical connector from the heated oxygen sensor (HO2S) electrical connector.
5. Remove the HO2S electrical connector rosebud clip from the ignition coil bracket.

➡**The oxygen sensor may be difficult to remove when the engine temperature is below 48°C (120°F). Excessive force may damage threads in the exhaust manifold or the exhaust pipe.**

6. Remove the HO2S using the J 39194-B.

To install:

➡**A special anti-seize compound is used on the HO2S threads. The compound consists of graphite suspended in fluid and glass beads. The graphite will burn away, but the glass beads will remain, making the sensor easier to remove. New or service sensors will already have the compound applied to the threads. If a sensor is removed from an engine and is to be reinstalled, the threads must have anti-seize compound applied before the reinstallation.**

7. Coat the threads of the HO2S with anti-seize compound.
8. Install and tighten the HO2S to 31 ft. lbs. (42 Nm).
9. Connect the engine wiring harness electrical connector to the HO2S electrical connector.
10. Install the CPA retainer.
11. Install the HO2S electrical connector rosebud clip to the ignition coil bracket.
12. Install the intake manifold cover.

Bank 1 Sensor 2

1. Before servicing the vehicle, refer to the Precautions Section.
2. Raise and support the vehicle.
3. Remove the Connector Position Assurance (CPA) retainer.
4. Disconnect the engine heated oxygen sensor (HO2S) electrical connector from the engine wiring harness electrical connector.
5. Remove the HO2S using the J 39194-B.

To install:

6. Coat the threads of the HO2S with anti-seize compound.
7. Install and tighten the HO2S to 31 ft. lbs. (42 Nm).

8. Connect the engine HO2S electrical connector to the engine wiring harness electrical connector.

9. Install the CPA retainer.

10. Lower the vehicle.

Bank 2 Sensor 1

1. Before servicing the vehicle, refer to the Precautions Section.

2. Remove the Connector Position Assurance (CPA) retainer.

3. Disconnect the engine wiring harness electrical connector from the heated oxygen sensor (HO2S) electrical connector.

4. Remove the HO2S rosebud clip from the oil level indicator tube tab.

➡**The oxygen sensor may be difficult to remove when the engine temperature is below 48°C (120°F). Excessive force may damage threads in the exhaust manifold or the exhaust pipe.**

5. Remove the HO2S using the J 39194-B.

To install:

6. Coat the threads of the HO2S with anti-seize compound.

7. Install and tighten the HO2S to 31 ft. lbs. (42 Nm).

8. Connect the engine HO2S electrical connector to the engine wiring harness electrical connector.

9. Install the CPA retainer.

10. Lower the vehicle.

Bank 2 Sensor 2

1. Before servicing the vehicle, refer to the Precautions Section.

2. Raise and support the vehicle.

3. Remove the Connector Position Assurance (CPA) retainer.

4. Disconnect the engine heated oxygen sensor (HO2S) electrical connector from the engine wiring harness electrical connector.

5. Remove the HO2S using the J 39194-B.

To install:

6. Coat the threads of the HO2S with anti-seize compound.

7. Install and tighten the HO2S to 31 ft. lbs. (42 Nm).

8. Connect the engine HO2S electrical connector to the engine wiring harness electrical connector.

9. Install the CPA retainer.

10. Lower the vehicle.

TESTING

See Figures 152 through 156.

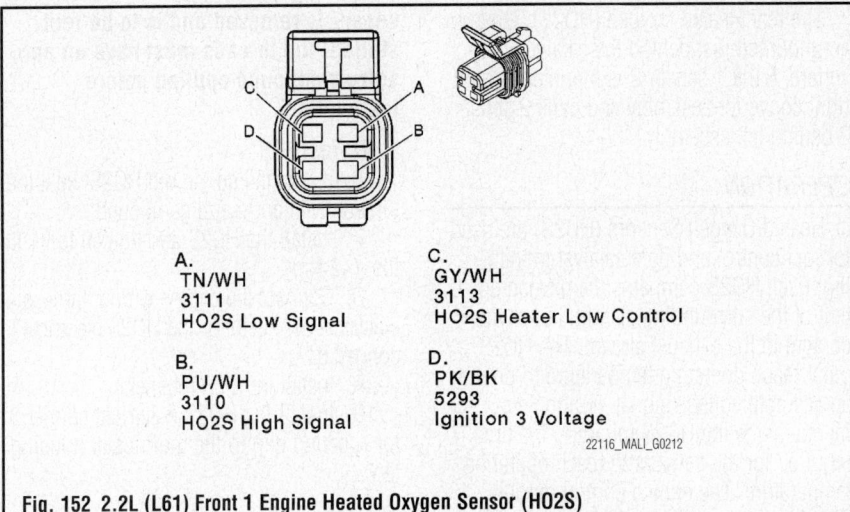

A.
TN/WH
3111
HO2S Low Signal

B.
PU/WH
3110
HO2S High Signal

C.
GY/WH
3113
HO2S Heater Low Control

D.
PK/BK
5293
Ignition 3 Voltage

22116_MALI_G0212

Fig. 152 2.2L (L61) Front 1 Engine Heated Oxygen Sensor (HO2S)

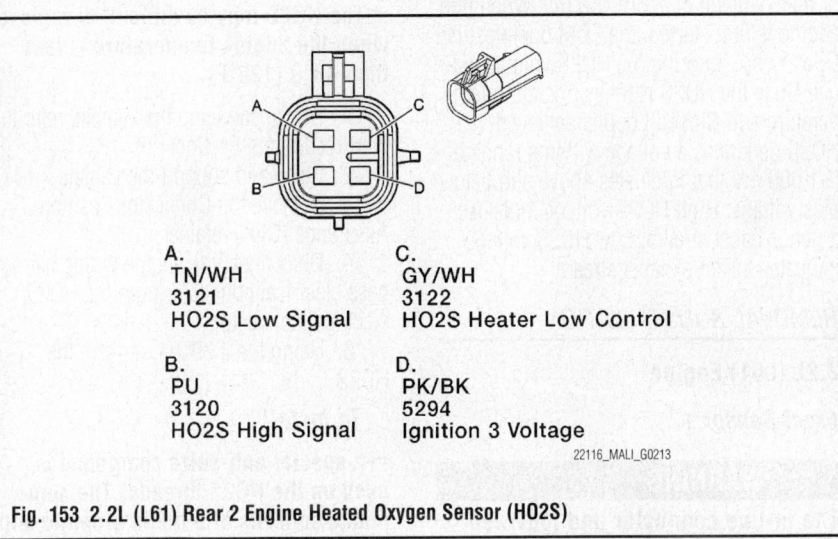

A.
TN/WH
3121
HO2S Low Signal

B.
PU
3120
HO2S High Signal

C.
GY/WH
3122
HO2S Heater Low Control

D.
PK/BK
5294
Ignition 3 Voltage

22116_MALI_G0213

Fig. 153 2.2L (L61) Rear 2 Engine Heated Oxygen Sensor (HO2S)

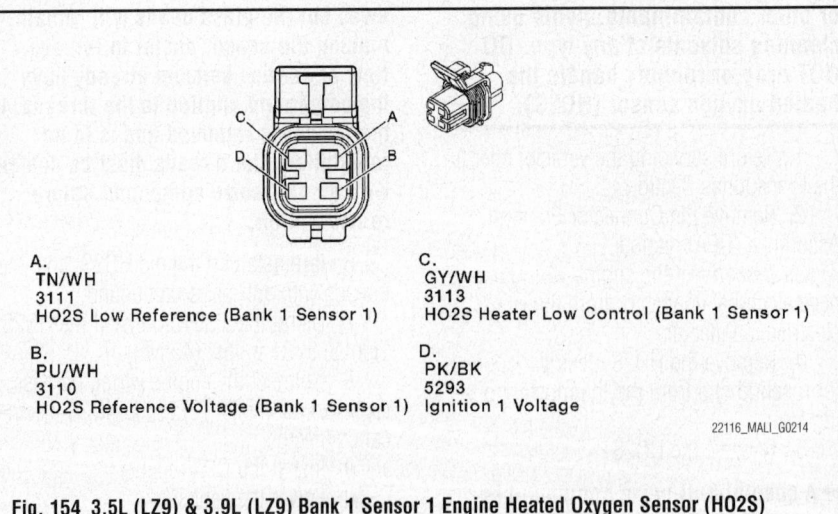

A.
TN/WH
3111
HO2S Low Reference (Bank 1 Sensor 1)

B.
PU/WH
3110
HO2S Reference Voltage (Bank 1 Sensor 1)

C.
GY/WH
3113
HO2S Heater Low Control (Bank 1 Sensor 1)

D.
PK/BK
5293
Ignition 1 Voltage

22116_MALI_G0214

Fig. 154 3.5L (LZ9) & 3.9L (LZ9) Bank 1 Sensor 1 Engine Heated Oxygen Sensor (HO2S)

1. Ignition OFF, disconnect the scan tool and wait 60 seconds to ensure all modules are powered down.

2. Ignition OFF, disconnect the harness connector at the appropriate HO2S.

3. Ignition OFF, measure for less than 5 ohms resistance between the appropriate HO2S low signal circuit terminal A and ground.

4. If more than the specified range, test

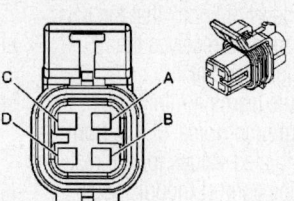

A.
TN/WH
3211
HO2S Low Reference (Bank 2 Sensor 1)

C.
L-GN
3212
HO2S Heater Low Control (Bank 2 Sensor 1)

B.
PU/WH
3210
HO2S Reference Voltage (Bank 2 Sensor 1)

D.
PK/BK
5293
Ignition 1 Voltage

22116_MALI_G0215

Fig. 155 3.5L (LZ9) & 3.9L (LZ9) Bank 2 Sensor 1 Engine Heated Oxygen Sensor (HO2S)

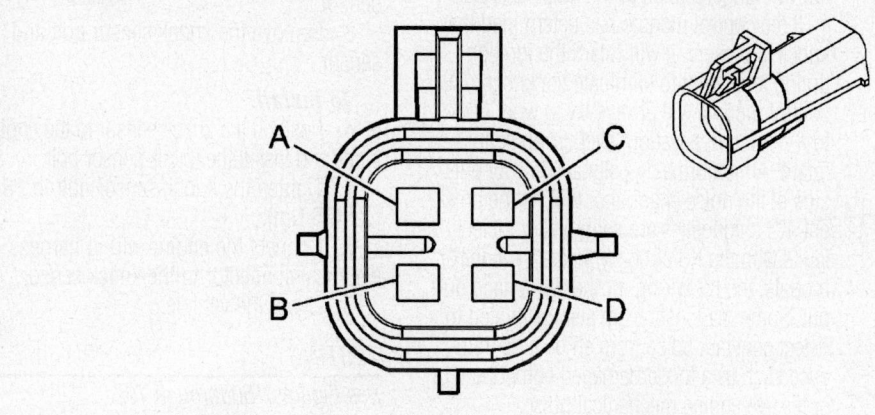

A.
TN
3221
HO2S Low Signal (Bank 2 Sensor 2)

C.
OG/WH
3223
HO2S Heater Low Control (Bank 2 Sensor 2)

B.
PU
3220
HO2S High Signal (Bank 2 Sensor 2)

D.
PK/BK
5294
Ignition 1 Voltage

22116_MALI_G0216

Fig. 156 3.5L (LZ9) & 3.9L (LZ9) Bank 2 Sensor 2 Engine Heated Oxygen Sensor (HO2S)

the appropriate HO2S low signal circuit for an open/high resistance. If the circuit tests normal, replace the ECM.

5. Ignition ON, verify the appropriate scan tool HO2S parameter is approximately 450 mV.

6. If more than the specified value, test the appropriate HO2S high signal circuit for a short to voltage. If the circuit tests normal, replace the ECM.

7. If less than the specified value, test the appropriate HO2S high signal circuit for a short to ground. If the circuit tests normal, replace the ECM.

8. Ignition ON, install a 3A fused jumper wire at the HO2S high signal circuit terminal B. Toggle the jumper wire between the HO2S low signal circuit

terminal A and battery voltage. Verify the appropriate scan tool HO2S parameter toggles between 0 mV and approximately 1,000 mV

9. If the appropriate scan tool HO2S parameter does not toggle correctly, test the HO2S high signal circuit for an open/high resistance. If the circuits test normal, replace the ECM.

10. If all circuits test normal, replace the appropriate HO2S.

KNOCK SENSOR (KS)

LOCATION

2.2L (L61) Engine

See Figure 157.

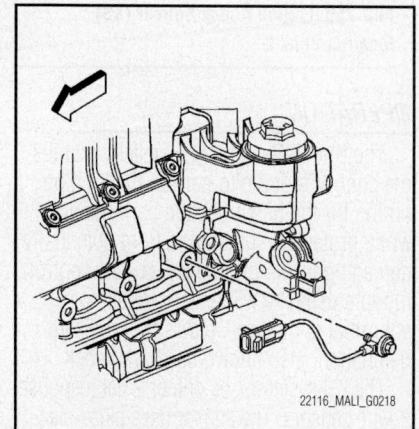

22116_MALI_G0218

Fig. 157 2.2L (L61) Engine Knock Sensor (KS) location

The Knock Sensor (KS) is located on the engine block just below and to the front of the oil filter housing.

3.5L (LZ4) & 3.9L (LZ9) Engines

See Figures 158 and 159.

The 3.5L (LZ4), and 3.9L (LZ9) engine has 2 Knock sensors that are located on both sides of the engine block.

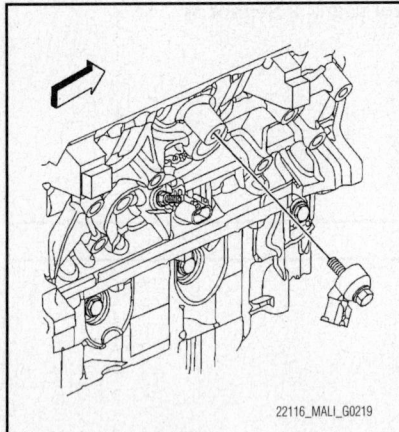

Fig. 158 Engine Knock Sensor (KS) location Bank 1

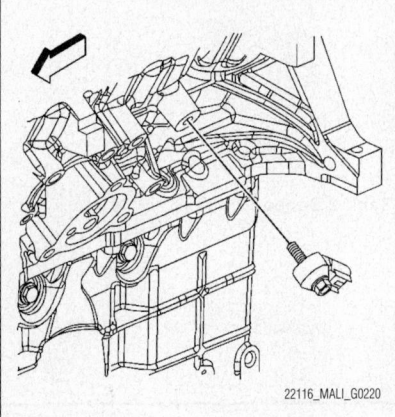

Fig. 159 Engine Knock Sensor (KS) location Bank 2

OPERATION

The Knock Sensor (KS) system enables the control module to control the ignition timing for the best possible performance while protecting the engine from potentially damaging levels of detonation. The control module uses the KS system to test for abnormal engine noise that may indicate detonation, also known as spark knock.

The KS system uses one or 2 flat response 2-wire sensors. The sensor uses piezo-electric crystal technology that produces an AC voltage signal of varying amplitude and frequency based on the engine vibration or noise level. The amplitude and frequency are dependent upon the level of knock that the KS detects. The control module receives the KS signal through the signal circuit.

The control module learns a minimum noise level, or background noise, at idle from the KS and uses calibrated values for the rest of the RPM range. The control module uses the minimum noise level to calculate a noise channel. normal KS signal will ride within the noise channel. As engine speed and load change, the noise channel upper and lower parameters will change to accommodate the normal KS signal, keeping the signal within the channel. In order to determine which cylinders are knocking, the control module only uses KS signal information when each cylinder is near Top Dead Center (TDC) of the firing stroke. If knock is present, the signal will range outside of the noise channel.

If the control module has determined that knock is present, it will retard the ignition timing to attempt to eliminate the knock. The control module will always try to work back to a zero compensation level, or no spark retard. An abnormal KS signal will stay outside of the noise channel or will not be present. KS diagnostics are calibrated to detect faults with the KS circuitry inside the control module, the KS wiring, or the KS voltage output. Some diagnostics are also calibrated to detect constant noise from an outside influence such as a loose/damaged component or excessive engine mechanical noise.

REMOVAL & INSTALLATION

2.2L (L61) Engine

1. Disconnect the Knock Sensor (KS) electrical connector.
2. Remove the KS electrical connector clip from the oil level indicator tube bracket.
3. Remove the oil level indicator tube.
4. Remove the KS bolt.
5. Remove the KS.

To install:

➡**Rotate the pigtail 90 degrees from vertical before securing the fastener.**

6. Install the KS.
7. Install the KS bolt and tighten to 18 ft. lbs. (25 Nm).
8. Connect the KS electrical connector.
9. Install the oil level indicator tube.
10. Install the KS electrical connector clip to the oil level indicator tube bracket.

3.5L (LZ4) & 3.9L (LZ9) Engines

Bank 1

1. Before servicing the vehicle, refer to the Precautions Section.

2. Raise and support the vehicle.
3. Disconnect the engine wiring harness electrical connector from the knock sensor.
4. Remove the knock sensor bolt and sensor.

To install:

5. Position the knock sensor to the engine block and install the knock sensor bolt.
6. Tighten the knock sensor bolt to 18 ft. lbs. (25 Nm).
7. Connect the engine wiring harness electrical connector to the knock sensor.
8. Lower the vehicle.

Bank 2

1. Before servicing the vehicle, refer to the Precautions Section.
2. Disconnect the engine wiring harness electrical connector from the knock sensor.
3. Remove the knock sensor bolt and sensor.

To install:

4. Position the knock sensor to the engine block and install the knock sensor bolt.
5. Tighten the knock sensor bolt to 18 ft. lbs. (25 Nm).
6. Connect the engine wiring harness electrical connector to the knock sensor.
7. Lower the vehicle.

TESTING

See Figures 160 through 162.

1. Connect the Digital Multimeter (DMM) from the Knock Sensor (KS) signal circuit terminal A to the KS signal circuit terminal B on the sensor side of the KS harness connector.
2. Set the DMM to the 400 mV AC hertz scale and wait for the DMM to stabilize at 0 Hz.
3. Tap on the engine block with a non-metallic object near the KS while observing the signal indicated on the DMM.

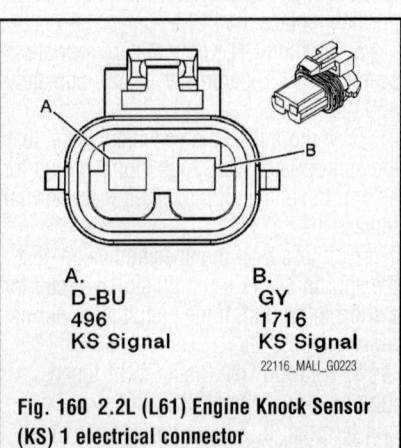

A.	B.
D-BU	GY
496	1716
KS Signal	KS Signal

Fig. 160 2.2L (L61) Engine Knock Sensor (KS) 1 electrical connector

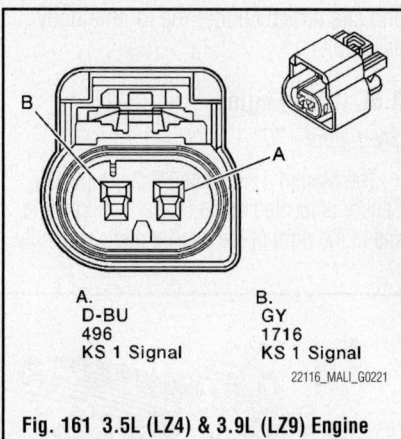

A.
D-BU
496
KS 1 Signal

B.
GY
1716
KS 1 Signal

22116_MALI_G0221

Fig. 161 3.5L (LZ4) & 3.9L (LZ9) Engine Knock Sensor (KS) 1 electrical connector

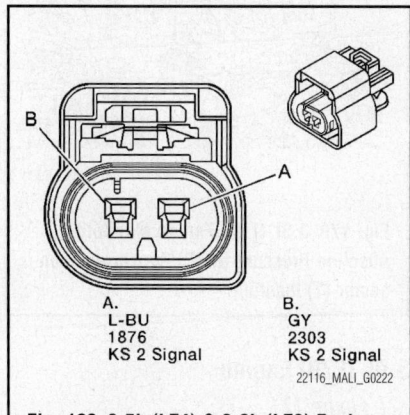

A.
L-BU
1876
KS 2 Signal

B.
GY
2303
KS 2 Signal

22116_MALI_G0222

Fig. 162 3.5L (LZ4) & 3.9L (LZ9) Engine Knock Sensor (KS) 2 electrical connector

4. The DMM should display a fluctuating frequency while tapping on the engine block.

5. If the DMM does not display a fluctuating frequency suspect faulty knock sensor.

MASS AIR FLOW (MAF) SENSOR

LOCATION

2.2L (L61) Engine

See Figure 163.

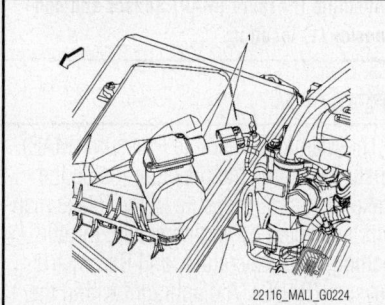

22116_MALI_G0224

Fig. 163 2.2L (L61) Engine Mass Air Flow (MAF) sensor location

The Mass Air Flow (MAF) sensor is located on the top of the air filter housing.

3.5L (LZ4) & 3.9L (LZ9) Engines

See Figure 164.

The Mass Air Flow (MAF)/Intake Air Temperature (IAT) sensor is located in the air cleaner intake duct fresh air tube.

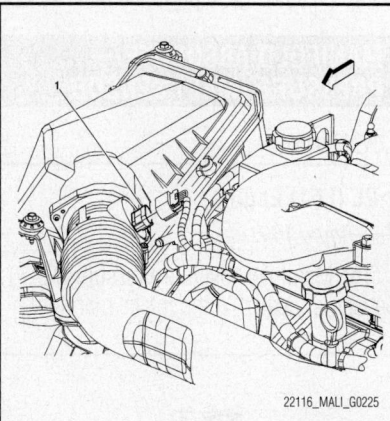

22116_MALI_G0225

Fig. 164 3.5L (LZ4) & 3.9L (LZ9) Mass Air Flow (MAF)/Intake Air Temperature (IAT) sensor location

OPERATION

The Mass Air Flow (MAF) sensor is integrated with the Intake Air Temperature (IAT) sensor. The MAF sensor is an air flow meter that measures the amount of air entering the engine. The engine control module (ECM) uses the MAF sensor signal to provide the correct fuel delivery for all engine speeds and loads. A small quantity of air entering the engine indicates a deceleration or idle condition. A large quantity of air entering the engine indicates an acceleration or high load condition. The MAF/IAT sensor has an ignition 1 voltage circuit, a ground circuit, a MAF sensor signal circuit, and IAT sensor signal circuit, and a low reference circuit.

The ECM applies 5 volts to the MAF sensor on the MAF sensor signal circuit. The sensor uses the voltage to produce a frequency based on the inlet air flow through the sensor bore. The frequency varies in a range of near 2,000 Hertz at idle to near 10,000 Hertz at maximum engine load.

REMOVAL & INSTALLATION

2.2L (L61) Engine

See Figure 165.

1. Before servicing the vehicle, refer to the Precautions Section.

2. Disconnect the engine wiring harness

22116_MALI_G0227

Fig. 165 Mass Air Flow (MAF) sensor removal

electrical connector from the Mass Air Flow (MAF) sensor.

3. Remove the MAF sensor screws.

4. Remove the MAF sensor from the air cleaner cover.

To install:

5. Install the MAF sensor and screws to the air cleaner cover.

6. Tighten the mounting screws to 5 inch. lbs. (0.6 Nm).

7. Connect the engine wiring harness electrical connector to the MAF sensor.

3.5L (LZ4) & 3.9L (LZ9) Engines

See Figure 166.

1. Before servicing the vehicle, refer to the Precautions Section.

2. Remove the air cleaner outlet duct.

3. Disconnect the engine wiring harness electrical connector from the Mass Air Flow (MAF)/Intake Air Temperature (IAT) sensor.

4. Remove the MAF/IAT sensor screws (1).

5. Remove the MAF/IAT sensor (2).

6. Remove and discard the MAF/IAT sensor O-ring seal.

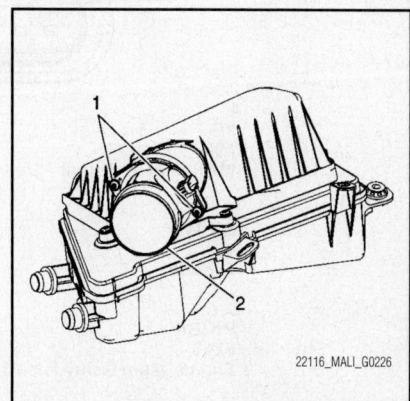

22116_MALI_G0226

Fig. 166 Mass Air Flow (MAF)/Intake Air Temperature (IAT) sensor removal

To install:

7. Install the new MAF/IAT sensor O-ring seal.

8. Install the MAF/IAT sensor screws and tighten to 44 inch. lbs. (1.5 Nm).

9. Connect the engine wiring harness electrical connector to the MAF/IAT sensor.

10. Install the air cleaner outlet duct.

TESTING

See Figures 167 and 168.

To determine if the ECM can properly process the MAF sensor frequency signal, connect the J 38522 variable signal generator to the vehicle as follows:

- Turn OFF the ignition
- Connect the battery voltage supply, and ground the black lead.
- Connect the red lead to the signal circuit terminal A.

- Set the duty cycle switch to Normal.
- Set the Frequency switch to 5 K.
- Set the signal switch to 5 volts.
- Start the engine.
- Observe the MAF Sensor parameter for the correct range of 4,950–5,025 Hz.

1. If the MAF Sensor parameter is not within the specified range, replace the ECM.

2. If the MAF Sensor parameter is within the specified range, replace the MAF sensor.

MANIFOLD ABSOLUTE PRESSURE (MAP) SENSOR

LOCATION

2.2L (L61) Engine

See Figure 169.

The Manifold Absolute Pressure (MAP) Sensor is located in the intake manifold

and sits directly under the throttle body assembly.

3.5L (LZ4) Engine

See Figure 170.

The Manifold Absolute Pressure (MAP) Sensor is located in the intake manifold and sits to the right of the throttle body assembly.

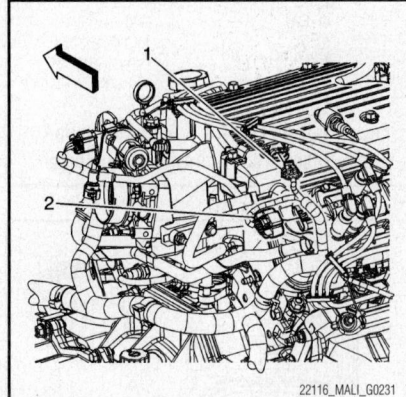

22116_MALI_G0231

Fig. 170 3.5L (LZ4) Engine Manifold Absolute Pressure (MAP) Sensor and connector (1) location

3.9L (LZ9) Engine

See Figure 171.

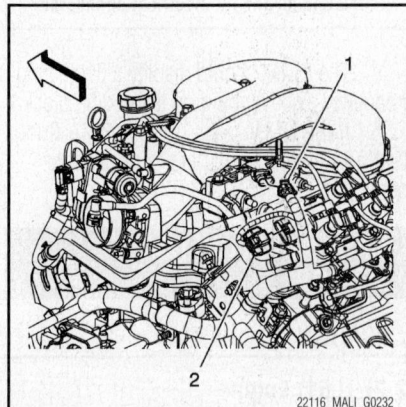

22116_MALI_G0232

Fig. 171 3.9L (LZ9) Engine Manifold Absolute Pressure (MAP) Sensor and connector (1) location

OPERATION

The Manifold Absolute Pressure (MAP) sensor measures the pressure inside the intake manifold. Pressure in the intake manifold is affected by engine speed, throttle opening, air temperature, and Barometric Pressure (BARO). A diaphragm within the MAP sensor is displaced by the pressure changes that occur from the varying load

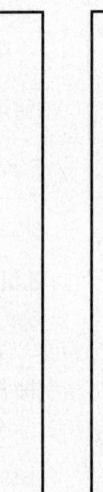

22116_MALI_G0229

Fig. 167 Variable signal generator J 38522 shown

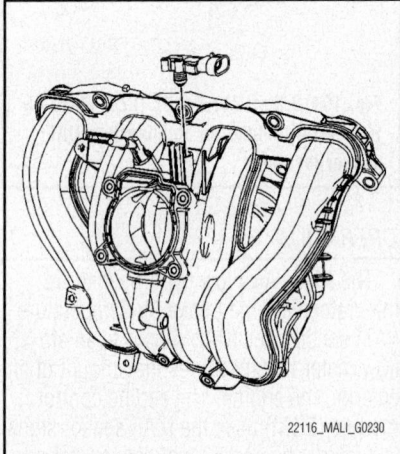

22116_MALI_G0230

Fig. 169 2.2L (L61) Engine Manifold Absolute Pressure (MAP) Sensor location

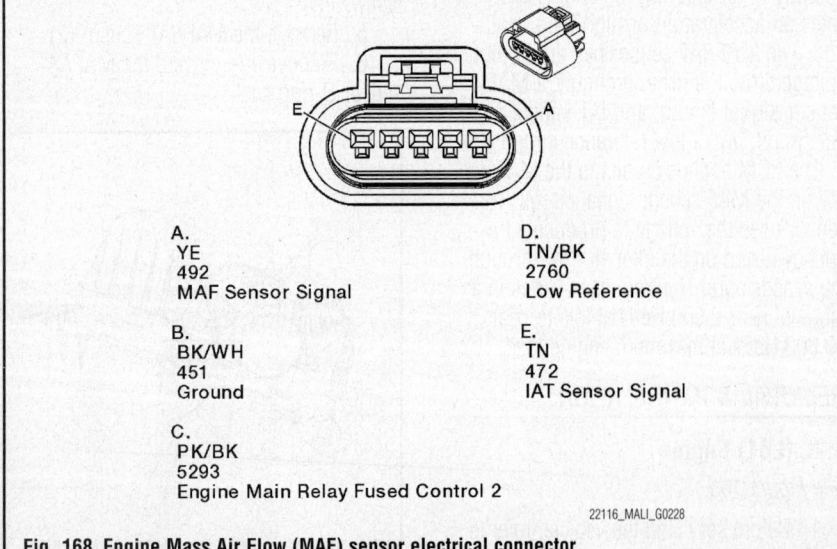

A.
YE
492
MAF Sensor Signal

B.
BK/WH
451
Ground

C.
PK/BK
5293
Engine Main Relay Fused Control 2

D.
TN/BK
2760
Low Reference

E.
TN
472
IAT Sensor Signal

22116_MALI_G0228

Fig. 168 Engine Mass Air Flow (MAF) sensor electrical connector

and operating conditions of the engine. The sensor translates this action into electrical resistance. The MAP sensor wiring includes 3 circuits. The engine control module (ECM) supplies a regulated 5 volts to the sensor on a 5-volt reference circuit. The ECM supplies a ground on a low reference circuit. The MAP sensor provides a signal voltage to the ECM, relative to the pressure changes, on the MAP sensor signal circuit. The ECM converts the signal voltage input to a pressure value.

Under normal operation the greatest pressure that can exist in the intake manifold is equal to BARO. This occurs when the vehicle is operated at Wide-Open Throttle (WOT) or when the ignition is on while the engine is off. Under these conditions, the ECM uses the MAP sensor to determine the current BARO. The least manifold pressures occur when the vehicle is idling or decelerating. MAP can range from 10 kPa, when pressures are less, to as great as 104 kPa, depending on the current BARO. The ECM monitors the MAP sensor signal for pressure outside of the normal range.

REMOVAL & INSTALLATION

2.2L (L61) Engine

1. Before servicing the vehicle, refer to the Precautions Section.
2. Remove the throttle body.
3. Disconnect the engine wiring harness electrical connector from the Manifold Absolute Pressure (MAP) sensor.
4. Remove the MAP sensor and the MAP sensor port seal if it is still retained in the intake manifold.

To install:

5. Install the MAP sensor with the port seal into the intake manifold.
6. Connect the engine wiring harness electrical connector to the MAP sensor.
7. Install the throttle body.

3.5L (LZ4) Engine

1. Before servicing the vehicle, refer to the Precautions Section.
2. Remove the intake manifold cover.
3. Disconnect the engine wiring harness electrical connector from the Manifold Absolute Pressure (MAP) sensor.
4. Remove the spark plug wire clip from the MAP sensor bracket, if necessary.
5. Remove the upper intake manifold bolt.
6. Remove the MAP sensor bracket.
7. Remove the MAP sensor and seal from the upper intake manifold. Discard the seal.

To install:

8. Lubricate the new MAP sensor seal with clean engine oil.
9. Install the MAP sensor into the upper intake manifold.
10. Place the MAP sensor bracket into position.
11. Install the upper intake manifold bolt and tighten to 18 ft. lbs. (25 Nm).
12. Install the spark plug wire clip to the MAP sensor bracket, if necessary.
13. Connect the engine wiring harness electrical connector to the MAP sensor.
14. Install the intake manifold cover.

3.9L (LZ9) Engine

1. Before servicing the vehicle, refer to the Precautions Section.
2. Remove the intake manifold cover.
3. Disconnect the Manifold Absolute Pressure (MAP) sensor electrical connector.
4. Remove the spark plug wire clip from the intake manifold bracket, if necessary.
5. Remove the MAP sensor bolt.
6. Remove the MAP sensor.
7. Remove the MAP sensor seal from the upper intake manifold.

To install:

8. Install the MAP sensor seal into the upper intake manifold.
9. Install the MAP sensor.
10. Install the MAP sensor bolt and tighten to 89 inch lbs. (10 Nm).
11. If required, install the spark plug wire clip to the intake manifold bracket.
12. Connect the MAP sensor electrical connector.
13. Install the intake manifold cover.

TESTING

See Figure 172.

Check the Manifold Absolute Pressure (MAP) sensor circuit as follows:
1. Ignition OFF, disconnect the MAP harness connector at the MAP sensor.
2. Ignition OFF, test for less than 5 ohms of resistance between the low reference circuit terminal 2 and ground.
3. If greater than the specified range, test the low reference circuit for an open/high resistance. If the circuit tests normal, replace the ECM.
4. Ignition ON, test for 4.8-5.2 volts between the 5—volt reference circuit terminal 1 and ground.
5. If less than the specified range, test the 5—volt reference circuit for a short to ground or an open/high resistance. If the circuit tests normal, replace the ECM.

6. If greater than the specified range, test the 5—volt reference circuit for a short to voltage. If the circuit tests normal, replace the ECM.
7. Verify the scan tool MAP Sensor parameter is less than 1 kPa.
8. If greater than the specified range, test the signal circuit terminal 3 for a short to voltage. If the circuit tests normal, replace the ECM.
9. Install a 3A fused jumper wire between the signal circuit terminal 3 and the 5-volt reference circuit terminal 1. Verify the scan tool MAP Sensor parameter is greater than 126 kPa.
10. If less than the specified range, test the signal circuit terminal 3 for a short to ground or an open/high resistance. If the circuit tests normal, replace the ECM.
11. If all circuits test normal, test or replace the MAP sensor.

Check the Manifold Absolute Pressure (MAP) sensor as follows:
12. Turn ON the ignition, with the engine OFF, and remove the MAP sensor.
13. Install a 3A fused jumper wire between the 5—volt reference circuit terminal 1 and the corresponding terminal of the MAP sensor.
14. Install a jumper wire between the low reference circuit terminal 2 of the MAP sensor and ground.
15. Install a jumper wire at terminal 3 of the MAP sensor.
16. Connect a Digital Multi-Meter (DMM) between the jumper wire from terminal 3 of the MAP sensor and ground.
17. Install the J 35555 Vacuum tester to the MAP sensor vacuum port. Slowly apply vacuum to the sensor while observing the voltage on the DMM. The voltage should

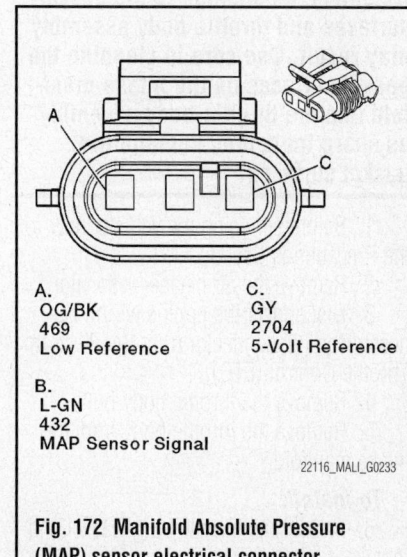

A.
OG/BK
469
Low Reference

B.
L-GN
432
MAP Sensor Signal

C.
GY
2704
5-Volt Reference

22116_MALI_G0233

Fig. 172 Manifold Absolute Pressure (MAP) sensor electrical connector

vary between 0—5.2 volts, without any spikes or dropouts

18. If the voltage is not within the specified range or is erratic, replace the MAP sensor.

THROTTLE POSITION SENSOR (TPS)

LOCATION

The Throttle Position (TP) sensors 1 and 2 are located within the throttle body assembly.

OPERATION

The throttle actuator control (TAC) system uses two throttle position (TP) sensors to monitor the throttle position. The TP sensors 1 and 2 are located within the throttle body assembly. Each sensor has the following circuits:

- A 5-volt reference circuit
- A low reference circuit
- A signal circuit

Two processors are also used to monitor the TAC system data. Both processors are located within the Engine Control Module (ECM). Each signal circuit provides both processors with a signal voltage proportional to throttle plate movement. Both processors monitor each other's data to verify that the indicated TP calculation is correct.

REMOVAL & INSTALLATION

2.2L (L61) Engine

See Figure 173.

❊❊ WARNING

Do not use solvent of any type when cleaning the gasket surfaces on the intake manifold and the throttle body assembly, as damage to the gasket surfaces and throttle body assembly may result. Use care in cleaning the gasket surfaces on the intake manifold and the throttle body assembly, as sharp tools may damage the gasket surfaces.

1. Before servicing the vehicle, refer to the Precautions Section.
2. Remove the air cleaner resonator.
3. Disconnect the engine wiring harness electrical connector from the Electronic Throttle Control (ETC).
4. Remove the throttle body bolts.
5. Remove the throttle body from the intake manifold.

To install:

6. Inspect the throttle body gasket and replace if necessary.

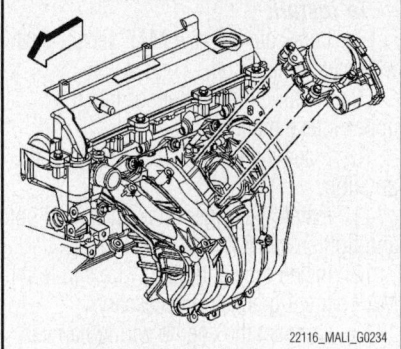

Fig. 173 2.2L (L61) Throttle body assembly

7. Position the throttle body to the intake manifold.
8. Install the throttle body bolts and tighten to 89 inch. lbs. (10 Nm).
9. Connect the engine wiring harness electrical connector to the ETC.
10. Install the air cleaner resonator.

3.5L (LZ4) & 3.9L (LZ9) Engines

See Figure 174.

❊❊ WARNING

Do not use solvent of any type when cleaning the gasket surfaces on the intake manifold and the throttle body assembly, as damage to the gasket surfaces and throttle body assembly may result. Use care in cleaning the gasket surfaces on the intake manifold and the throttle body assembly, as sharp tools may damage the gasket surfaces.

1. Before servicing the vehicle, refer to the Precautions Section.
2. Remove the intake manifold cover.
3. Remove the air cleaner outlet duct.
4. Disconnect the engine wiring harness electrical connector from the Electronic Throttle Control (ETC).
5. Remove the heater inlet and outlet pipe nuts.
6. Remove the heater inlet and outlet pipe bracket from the throttle body studs. Reposition the pipes.
7. Remove the throttle body bolts and nuts.
8. Remove the throttle body.
9. Remove and discard the throttle body gasket.

To install:

10. Install a new throttle body gasket.
11. Install the throttle body.
12. Install the throttle body bolts and nuts.
13. Tighten the nuts and bolts to 89 inch. lbs. (10 Nm).

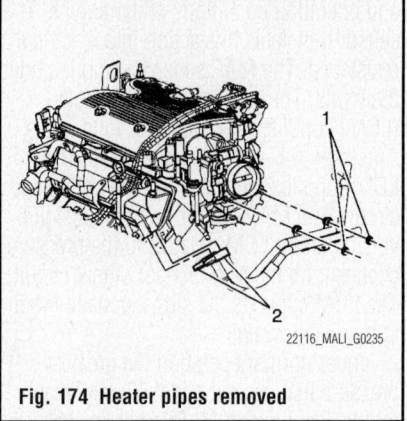

Fig. 174 Heater pipes removed

14. Reposition the heater inlet and outlet pipes and install the pipe bracket to the throttle body studs.
15. Install the heater inlet and outlet pipe nuts and tighten to 89 inch. lbs.
16. Connect the engine wiring harness electrical connector to the ETC.
17. Install the air cleaner outlet duct
18. Install the intake manifold cover.
19. Perform the Throttle Learn Procedure.

TESTING

See Figure 175.

Check the Throttle Position (TP) sensor circuits as follows:

1. Ignition OFF, disconnect the harness connector at the throttle body.
2. Ignition OFF for 90 seconds, test for less than 5 ohms of resistance between the low reference circuit terminal C and ground.

   a. If greater than 5 ohms, test the low reference circuit for an open/high resistance. If the circuit tests normal, replace the ECM.

3. Ignition ON, test for 4.8–5.2 volts between 5–volt reference circuit terminal E and ground.

   a. If less than 4.8 volts, test 5–volt reference circuit for a short to ground or an open / high resistance. If the circuit tests normal, replace the ECM.

   b. If greater than 5.2 volts, test the 5-volt reference circuit for a short to voltage. If the circuit tests normal, replace the ECM.

4. Verify the scan tool TP sensor 1 voltage is less than 0.1 volt.

   a. If greater than 0.1 volt, test the signal circuit terminal D for a short to voltage. If the circuit tests normal, replace the ECM.

5. Verify the scan tool TP sensor 2 voltage is greater than 4.8 volts.

   a. If less than 4.8 volts, test the signal circuit for a short to ground. If the circuit tests normal, replace the ECM.

6. Install a 3A fused jumper wire between the signal circuit terminal D and the 5–volt reference circuit terminal E of the TP sensor 1. Verify the TP sensor 1 voltage is greater than 4.8 volts.

   a. If less than 4.8 volts, test the TP sensor 1 signal circuit for a short to ground or an open/high resistance. If the circuit tests normal, replace the ECM.

7. Install a 3A fused jumper wire between the signal circuit terminal F and the low reference circuit terminal C of the TP sensor 2. Verify that the TP sensor 2 voltage is less than 0.1 volt

   a. If greater than 1.0 volt, test the TP sensor 2 signal circuit for a short to voltage or an open/high resistance. If the circuit tests normal, replace the ECM.

8. Ignition OFF for 90 seconds, disconnect the harness connector at the ECM.

9. Test for less than 5 ohms of resistance on all TP sensor circuits between the following terminals:

   a. ECM C2 signal circuit terminal 65 to TP terminal D

   b. ECM C2 signal circuit terminal 63 to TP terminal F

   c. ECM C2 5–volt reference circuit terminal 3 to terminal E

10. If greater than 5 ohms, repair the affected circuit for open/high resistance.

11. Test for infinite resistance between TP sensor 1 signal circuit terminal D and TP sensor signal circuit terminal F.

   a. If less than infinite resistance, repair the short between TP sensor 1 signal circuit and TP sensor 2 signal circuit.

12. If all circuits test normal, replace the throttle body.

THROTTLE LEARN PROCEDURE

➡**Do NOT perform this procedure if DTCs are set.**

1. Start and idle the engine in PARK for 3 minutes.

2. With a scan tool, monitor desired and actual RPM.

3. The ECM will start to learn the new idle cells and Desired RPM should start to decrease.

4. Ignition OFF for 60 seconds.

5. Start and idle the engine in PARK for 3 minutes.

6. After the 3 minute run time the engine should be idling normal.

➡**During the drive cycle the check engine light may come on with idle speed DTCs. If idle speed codes are set, clear codes so the ECM can continue to learn.**

- If the engine idle speed has not been learned the vehicle will need to be driven at speeds above 70 km/h (44 mph) with several decelerations and extended idles.

7. After the drive cycle, the engine should be idling normally.\

- If the engine idle speed has not been learned, turn OFF the ignition for 60 seconds and repeat step 6.

8. Once the engine speed has returned to normal, clear DTCs.

VEHICLE SPEED SENSOR (VSS)

LOCATION

See Figure 176.

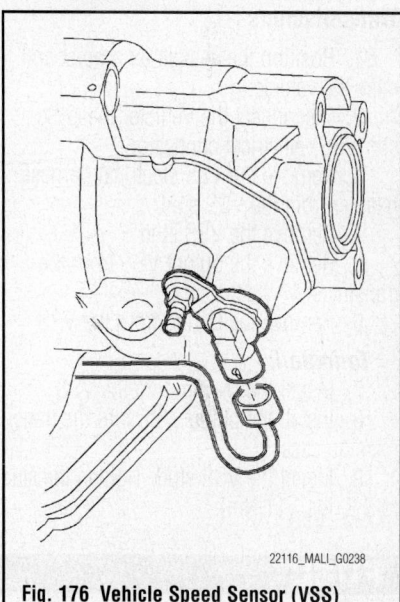

22116_MALI_G0238

Fig. 176 Vehicle Speed Sensor (VSS) location View

The Vehicle Speed Sensor (VSS), also referred to as Output Speed Sensor (OSS), is mounted in the end of the transmission tail shaft.

OPERATION

The Vehicle Speed Sensor (VSS) is a magnetic inductive pickup that relays vehicle speed information to the TCM. The TCM uses this information in order to control shift timing, line pressure, and TCC apply and release.

The VSS mounts in the case extension at the vehicle speed sensor reluctor wheel, which is pressed onto the final drive carrier assembly. An air gap of 0.011–0.062 inch.

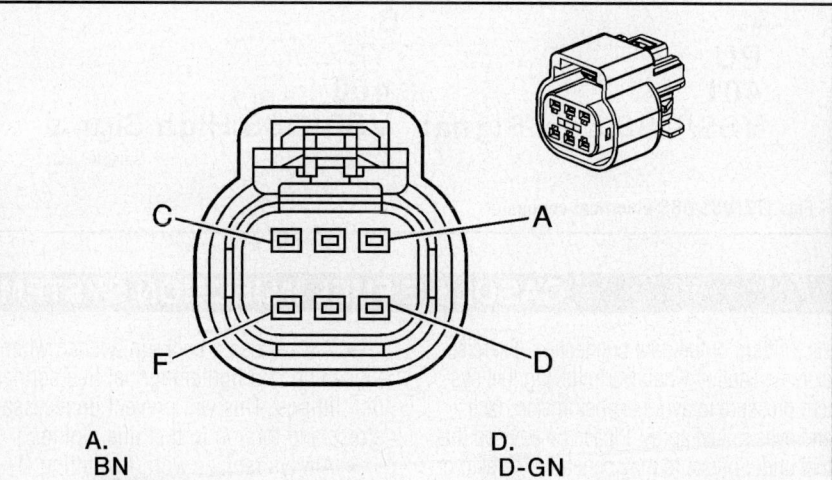

A.
BN
582
TAC Motor Control - 2

B.
YE
581
TAC Motor Control - 1

C.
TN
2752
Low Reference

D.
D-GN
485
TP Sensor 1 Signal

E.
GY
2701
5-Volt Reference 2

F.
PU
486
TP Sensor 2 Signal

22116_MALI_G0236

Fig. 175 Throttle Actuator Control electrical connector

(0.27–1.57 mm) occurs between the sensor and the teeth on the vehicle speed sensor reluctor wheel as the final drive carrier assembly rotates.

The sensor consists of a permanent magnet surrounded by a coil of wire. As the vehicle speed sensor reluctor wheel on the final drive carrier assembly rotates, an AC signal is produced by the VSS. This AC signal consists of a voltage and frequency that changes based on vehicle speed. The TCM uses the frequency portion of this signal to determine vehicle speed. Higher vehicle speeds induce a higher frequency and a higher voltage measurement at the sensor. The voltage portion of the signal is used in diagnostic procedures.

REMOVAL & INSTALLATION

4T40—E/4T45—E and 4T65—E Transmissions

1. Position the vehicle on a hoist and raise the vehicle.
2. Disconnect the Vehicle Speed Sensor (VSS) electrical connector
3. Remove the VSS electrical harness retainer from the VSS stud.
4. Remove the VSS stud.
5. Remove the output VSS from the transmission case.
6. Remove the O-ring from the VSS.

To install:

7. Install the O-ring onto the VSS.
8. Install the output VSS into the transmission case.
9. Install the VSS stud. Tighten the stud to 8 ft. lbs. (11 Nm).

10. Install the VSS electrical harness retainer to the VSS stud.
11. Connect the VSS electrical connector.
12. Lower the vehicle.

TESTING

See Figure 177.

Check the Vehicle Speed Sensor/Output Speed Sensor (VSS/OSS) as follows:
1. Disconnect Vehicle Speed Sensor (VSS) electrical connector from sensor.
2. With a digital multimeter check resistance between pin A VSS low signal and pin B VSS/OSS high signal.

3. Sensor resistance should measure between 1,650–2,200 ohms at 20°C 68°F.
4. If resistance reading is not as stated suspect faulty VSS/OSS sensor.
5. With a digital multimeter check voltage between pin A VSS low signal and pin B VSS/OSS high signal.
6. Safely lift wheels off of the ground and run in gear to check voltage readings.
7. Check for output voltage this will vary with vehicle speed from a minimum of 0.5 volts AC at 100 RPM to 200 volts at 6,000 RPM.
8. If no voltage reading is present suspect internal transmission problem or faulty VSS/OSS sensor.

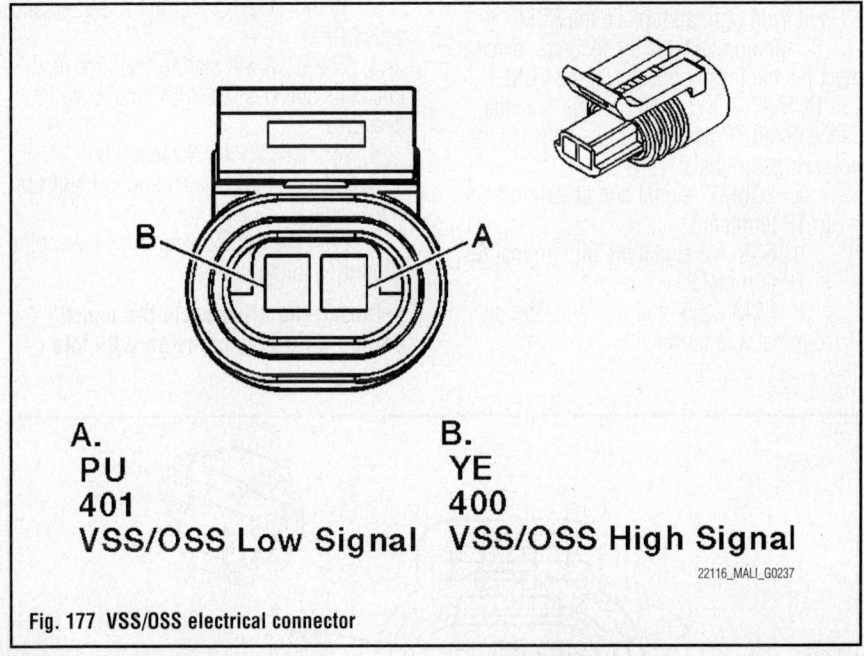

A.
PU
401
VSS/OSS Low Signal

B.
YE
400
VSS/OSS High Signal

22116_MALI_G0237

Fig. 177 VSS/OSS electrical connector

FUEL
GASOLINE FUEL INJECTION SYSTEM

FUEL SYSTEM SERVICE PRECAUTIONS

Safety is the most important factor when performing not only fuel system maintenance but any type of maintenance. Failure to conduct maintenance and repairs in a safe manner may result in serious personal injury or death. Maintenance and testing of the vehicle's fuel system components can be accomplished safely and effectively by adhering to the following rules and guidelines.
• To avoid the possibility of fire and personal injury, always disconnect the negative battery cable unless the repair or test procedure requires that battery voltage be applied.
• Always relieve the fuel system pressure prior to disconnecting any fuel system component (injector, fuel rail, pressure regulator,

etc.), fitting or fuel line connection. Exercise extreme caution whenever relieving fuel system pressure to avoid exposing skin, face and eyes to fuel spray. Please be advised that fuel under pressure may penetrate the skin or any part of the body that it contacts.
• Always place a shop towel or cloth around the fitting or connection prior to loosening to absorb any excess fuel due to spillage. Ensure that all fuel spillage (should it occur) is quickly removed from engine surfaces. Ensure that all fuel soaked cloths or towels are deposited into a suitable waste container.
• Always keep a dry chemical (Class B) fire extinguisher near the work area.
• Do not allow fuel spray or fuel vapors to come into contact with a spark or open flame.

• Always use a back-up wrench when loosening and tightening fuel line connection fittings. This will prevent unnecessary stress and torsion to fuel line piping.
• Always replace worn fuel fitting O-rings with new Do not substitute fuel hose or equivalent where fuel pipe is installed.

Before servicing the vehicle, make sure to also refer to the precautions in the beginning of this section as well.

RELIEVING FUEL SYSTEM PRESSURE

RELIEVING

✸✸ CAUTION

Remove the fuel tank cap and relieve the fuel system pressure before ser-

vicing the fuel system in order to reduce the risk of personal injury. After you relieve the fuel system pressure, a small amount of fuel may be released when servicing the fuel lines, the fuel injection pump, or the connections. In order to reduce the risk of personal injury, cover the fuel system components with a shop towel before disconnection. This will catch any fuel that may leak out. Place the towel in an approved container when the disconnection is complete.

1. If the fuel system requires repair, prevent fuel spillage by removing the fuel pump fuse or fuel pump module electrical connector.

2. Loosen the fuel fill cap in order to relieve the fuel tank vapor pressure.

3. Remove the engine cover, if required.

4. Remove the fuel rail service port cap.

5. Wrap a shop towel around the fuel rail service port and using a small flat-bladed tool, depress (open) the fuel rail test port valve.

6. Remove the shop towel from around the fuel rail service port, and place in an approved gasoline container.

7. Install the fuel rail service port cap.

8. Install the engine cover, if required.

9. Tighten the fuel fill cap.

FUEL FILTER

REMOVAL & INSTALLATION

The fuel strainer attaches to the lower end of the fuel pump module. The fuel strainer is made of woven plastic. The functions of the fuel strainer are to filter contaminants and to wick fuel. The fuel strainer normally requires no maintenance. Fuel stoppage at this point indicates that the fuel tank contains an abnormal amount of sediment or contamination.

FUEL INJECTORS

REMOVAL & INSTALLATION

2.2L Engine

1. Before servicing the vehicle, refer to the Precautions Section.

2. Relieve the fuel system pressure.

3. Remove or disconnect the following:
- Negative battery cable
- Air intake assembly

- Vacuum hose from the fuel pressure regulator
- Fuel supply and return hoses
- Fuel injector harness connectors
- Fuel rail mounting studs
- Fuel rail
- Fuel injectors

To install:

4. Install or connect the following:
- Fuel injectors with new O-rings
- Fuel rail attaching studs. Tighten studs to 89 inch lbs. (10 Nm).
- Fuel injector harness connectors
- Fuel supply and return hoses
- Vacuum pipe to the fuel pressure regulator
- Air intake assembly
- Negative battery cable

5. Pressurize the fuel system and check for leaks.

3.5L Engine

1. Before servicing the vehicle, refer to the Precautions Section.

2. Relieve the fuel system pressure.

3. Remove or disconnect the following:
- Negative battery cable
- Fuel supply hose from fuel rail
- Upper intake manifold
- Main injector harness electrical connector
- Fuel injector electrical connectors
- Injector wiring harness from the fuel rail
- Fuel injector retaining clip
- Fuel injectors

To install:

4. Install or connect the following:
- Fuel injectors with new O-rings
- Fuel injector retaining clip
- Fuel rail assembly. Tighten the bolts to 89 inch lbs. (10 Nm).
- Injector wiring harness to the fuel rail
- Fuel injector electrical connectors
- Main fuel injector harness electrical connector
- Upper intake manifold
- Fuel supply hose to the fuel rail
- Negative battery cable

3.9L Engine

See Figures 178 and 179.

1. Before servicing the vehicle, refer to the Precautions Section.

2. Relieve the fuel system pressure.

➡An 8-digit identification number is stamped on the fuel rail. Refer to this number if servicing or part replacement is required.

In order to reduce the risk of fire and personal injury that may result from a fuel leak, always install the fuel injector O—rings in the proper position. If the upper and lower O—rings are different colors (black and brown), be sure to install the black O—ring in the upper position and the brown O-ring in the lower position on the fuel injector. The O—rings are the same size but are made of different materials.

3. Disconnect the fuel feed pipe from the fuel rail.

4. Disconnect any remaining electrical connectors.

5. Remove the upper intake manifold.

6. Remove the fuel injector harness connector bracket bolt from the intake manifold.

7. Disconnect the Camshaft Position (CMP) sensor electrical connector.

8. Remove the fuel rail bolts.

9. Remove the fuel rail.

10. Remove and discard the O—rings from the spray tip end of each injector.

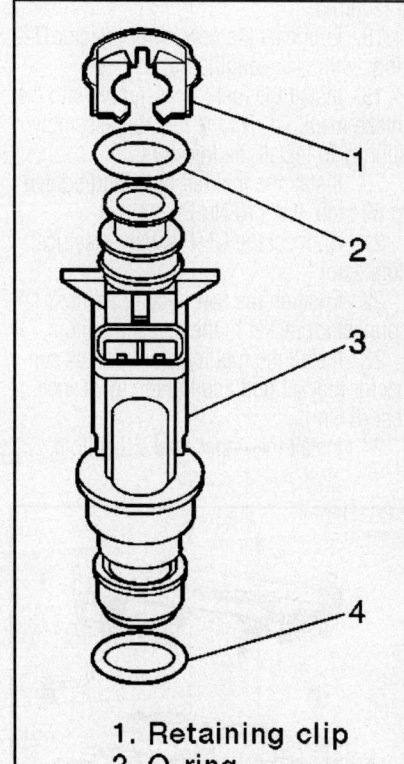

1. Retaining clip
2. O-ring
3. Fuel injector
4. O-ring

22116_MALI_G0059

Fig. 178 Fuel injector

Use care in removing the fuel injectors in order to prevent damage to the fuel injector electrical connector pins or the fuel injector nozzles. Do not immerse the fuel injector in any type of cleaner. The fuel injector is an electrical component and may be damaged by this cleaning method.

11. Remove the fuel injector retaining clip, if required.

12. Remove the fuel injector from the fuel rail, if required.

13. Remove and discard the fuel injector upper O—ring.

To install:

➡ **DO NOT reuse the fuel injector O-ring seals. Install new O—ring seals during assembly.**

14. Lubricate the new injector O—rings with clean engine oil.

15. Install the new fuel injector upper O—ring.

16. Install the fuel injector to the fuel rail, if required.

17. Install the fuel injector retaining clip, if required.

18. Lubricate the new lower injector O—rings with clean engine oil.

19. Install the fuel rail assembly into the intake manifold. Tilt the fuel rail assembly slightly to install the injectors.

20. Install the fuel rail bolts and tighten to 89 inch. lbs. (10 Nm).

21. Connect the CMP sensor electrical connector.

22. Position the fuel injector harness connector bracket to the intake manifold.

23. Install the fuel injector harness connector bracket bolt and tighten to 71 inch. lbs. (8 Nm).

24. Install the upper intake manifold.

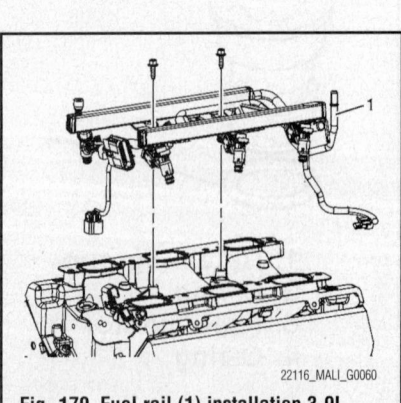

Fig. 179 Fuel rail (1) installation 3.9L engine

25. Connect any remaining electrical connectors.

26. Connect the fuel feed pipe to the fuel rail.

27. Inspect for fuel leaks with the following procedure:
   - Turn **ON** the ignition for 2 seconds.
   - Turn **OFF** the ignition for 10 seconds.
   - Turn **ON** the ignition.
   - Inspect for fuel leaks.

FUEL PUMP

REMOVAL & INSTALLATION

See Figure 180.

1. Before servicing the vehicle, refer to the Precautions Section.

2. Remove the fuel tank.

3. Disconnect the fuel tank fuel pump module wiring harness electrical connectors from the fuel pressure sensor and the module.

4. Disconnect the fuel tank fuel pump module wiring harness electrical connector from the EVAP canister vent solenoid.

5. Remove the EVAP emission canister vent pipe from the retaining features built into the fuel tank.

6. Reposition the EVAP emission canister vent pipe enough in order to install the J 45722.

7. Install the J 45722 to the fuel pump module lock ring.

➡ **Avoid damaging the lock ring. Use only J-45722 to prevent damage to the lock ring. Do NOT use impact tools. Significant force will be required to release the lock ring. The use of a hammer and screwdriver is not recommended.**

Do Not handle the fuel sender assembly by the fuel pipes. The

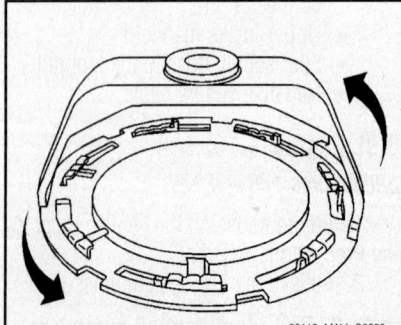

Fig. 180 Installation of the J-45722 to the fuel pump module lock ring.

amount of leverage generated by handling the fuel pipes could damage the joints.

8. Using the J-45722 and a long breaker-bar, rotate the lock ring in a counterclockwise direction in order to unlock the lock ring.

9. Remove the J-45722 from the fuel pump module lock ring.

10. Lift the fuel pump module up slightly in order to disconnect the fuel tank vent pipe quick connect fitting from the module cover.

11. Raise the fuel pump module up from the fuel tank. Tilt the module in order to allow the fuel level sensor arm and float to clear the module opening.

12. Remove the fuel pump module.

13. Remove and discard the fuel pump module seal.

14. Clean the fuel pump module sealing surfaces.

To install:

➡ **Some lock rings were manufactured with DO NOT REUSE stamped into them. These lock rings may be reused if they are not damaged or warped. Inspect the lock ring for damage due to improper removal or installation procedures. If damage is found, install a new fuel pump module.**

15. Clean any contamination from the male pipe ends of the fuel pump module.

16. Place a new fuel tank module seal onto the fuel tank.

17. Insert the fuel pump module into the fuel tank allowing the sensor arm and float to clear the module opening.

18. Lower the module down into the fuel tank until the fuel tank vent pipe quick connect fitting can be connected.

19. Connect the fuel tank vent pipe quick connect fitting at the module cover.

20. Press the fuel tank module downward.

21. Reposition the EVAP emission canister vent line enough to install the J-45722.

22. Install the J-45722 to the fuel pump module lock ring.

➡ **Ensure that the lock ring is installed with the correct side facing upward. A correctly installed lock ring will only turn in a clockwise direction.**

23. Using the J-45722 and a long breaker-bar, rotate the lock ring in a clockwise direction in order the lock the lock ring.

24. Remove the J-45722 from the fuel pump module lock ring.

25. Install the EVAP emission canister vent pipe to the retaining features built into the fuel tank.

26. Connect the fuel tank fuel pump module wiring harness electrical connector to the EVAP canister vent solenoid.

27. Connect the fuel tank fuel pump module wiring harness electrical connectors to the fuel pressure sensor and the module.

28. Install the fuel tank.

THROTTLE BODY

REMOVAL & INSTALLATION

2.2L Engine

See Figure 181.

1. Before servicing the vehicle, refer to the Precautions Section.

➡**Do not use solvent of any type when cleaning the gasket surfaces on the intake manifold and the throttle body assembly, as damage to the gasket surfaces and throttle body assembly may result. Use care in cleaning the gasket surfaces on the intake manifold and the throttle body assembly, as sharp tools may damage the gasket surfaces.**

➡**Do not use any solvent that contains Methyl Ethyl Ketone Peroxide (MEKP). This solvent may damage fuel system components.**

2. Remove the air cleaner resonator.
3. Disconnect the throttle body harness connector.
4. Remove the throttle body attaching bolts.
5. Remove the throttle body from the intake manifold.

To install:

6. Inspect the throttle body gasket and replace if necessary.
7. Install the throttle body to the intake manifold.

➡**Use the correct fastener in the correct location. Replacement fasteners must be the correct part number for that application. Fasteners requiring replacement or fasteners requiring the use of thread locking compound or sealant are identified in the service procedure. Do not use paints, lubricants, or corrosion inhibitors on fasteners or fastener joint surfaces unless specified. These coatings affect fastener torque and joint clamping force and may damage the fastener. Use the correct tightening sequence and speci-**

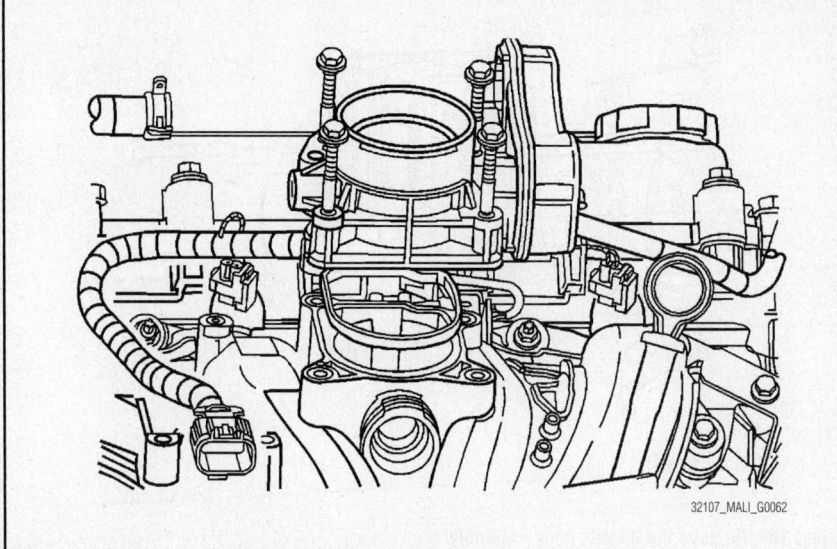

Fig. 181 Removal and installation of the throttle body

fications when installing fasteners in order to avoid damage to parts and systems.**

8. Install the throttle body attaching bolts, and tighten the throttle body attaching bolts to 89 lb inches (10 Nm).
9. Connect the throttle body harness connector.
10. Install the air cleaner resonator.

3.5L Engine

See Figures 182 and 183.

1. Before servicing the vehicle, refer to the Precautions Section.
2. Remove the air cleaner intake duct.
3. Disconnect the Electronic Throttle Control (ETC) electrical connector.

4. Remove the heater pipe nut at the throttle body.
5. Remove the nuts and the bolts from the throttle body.
6. Remove the throttle body assembly.
7. Remove the throttle body gasket.

➡**Do not use solvent of any type when cleaning the gasket surfaces on the intake manifold and the throttle body assembly, as damage to the gasket surfaces and throttle body assembly may result. Use care in cleaning the gasket surfaces on the intake manifold and the throttle body assembly, as sharp tools may damage the gasket surfaces.**

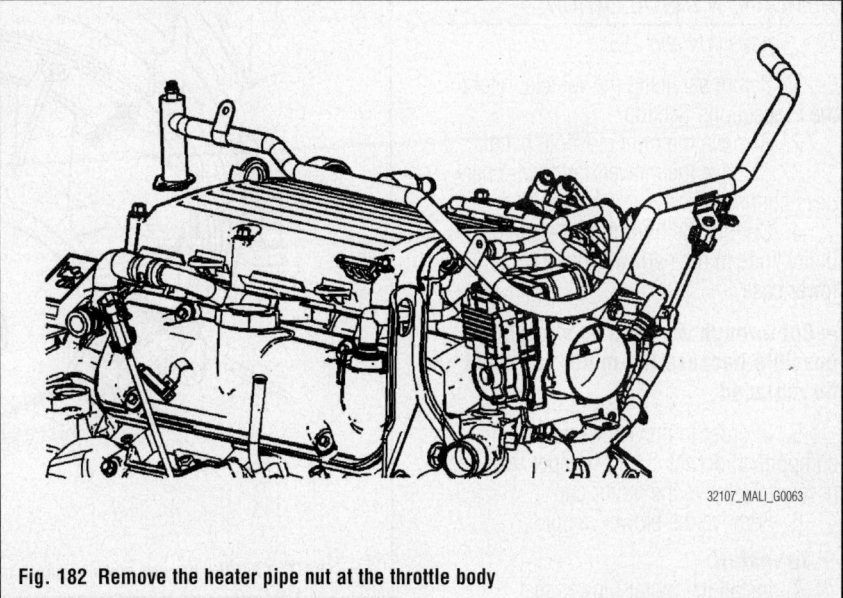

Fig. 182 Remove the heater pipe nut at the throttle body

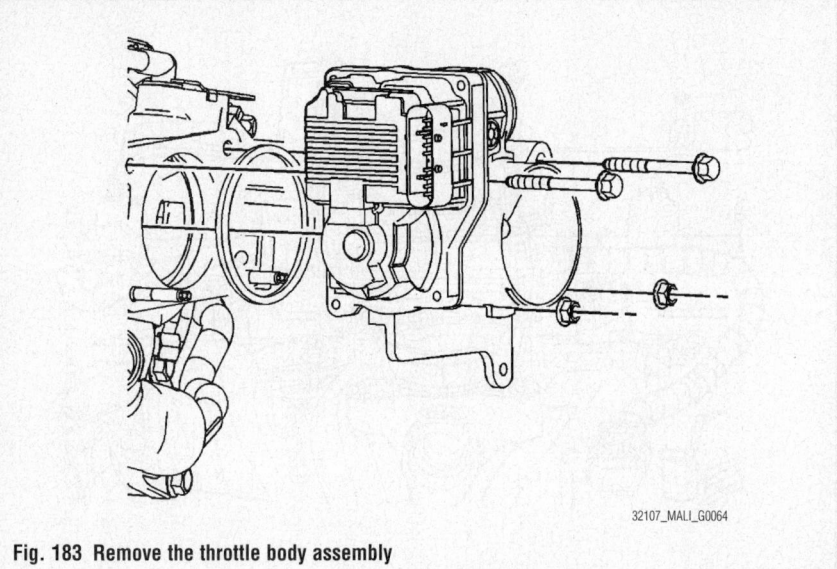

Fig. 183 Remove the throttle body assembly

8. Clean and inspect the throttle body gasket mating surfaces.

To install:

9. Install a new gasket, if necessary.
10. Install the throttle body assembly.
11. Install the throttle body nuts and the bolts, and tighten the nuts and the bolts to 89 lb inches (10 Nm).
12. Install the heater pipe nut to the throttle body, and tighten the nut to 18 ft. lbs. (25 Nm).
13. Connect the ETC electrical connector.
14. Install the air cleaner intake duct.

3.9L Engine

➡ Do not use solvent of any type when cleaning the gasket surfaces on the intake manifold and the throttle body assembly, as damage to the gasket surfaces and throttle body assembly may result. Use care in cleaning the gasket surfaces on the intake manifold and the throttle body assembly, as sharp tools may damage the gasket surfaces.

1. Before servicing the vehicle, refer to the Precautions Section.

2. Remove the intake manifold cover.
3. Remove the air cleaner outlet duct.
4. Disconnect the Electronic Throttle Control (ETC) electrical connector.
5. Remove the heater inlet and outlet pipe nuts.
6. Remove the heater inlet and outlet pipe bracket from the throttle body studs. Reposition the pipes.
7. Remove the throttle body bolts/studs.
8. Remove the throttle body.
9. Remove the throttle body gasket.

To install:

10. Install a new gasket, if necessary.
11. Install the throttle body.
12. Install the throttle body bolts and studs tighten to 89 inch. lbs. (10 Nm).
13. Position the heater inlet and outlet pipes and install the pipe bracket to the throttle body studs.
14. Install the heater inlet and outlet pipe nuts and tighten to 89 inch. lbs. (10 Nm).
15. Connect the ETC electrical connector.
16. Install the air cleaner outlet duct.
17. Install the intake manifold cover.

IDLE SPEED

ADJUSTMENT

Idle speed is maintained by the Powertrain Control Module (PCM). No adjustment is necessary or possible.

HEATING & AIR CONDITIONING SYSTEM

BLOWER MOTOR

REMOVAL & INSTALLATION

See Figures 184 and 185.

1. Before servicing the vehicle, refer to the Precautions Section.
2. Remove the right closeout panel.
3. Remove the blower motor wire harness connector.
4. Cut out the blower motor using a utility knife in the narrow groove of the lower case.

➡ Cut through the case as straight as possible because the motor cup must be replaced.

5. In order to prevent damage to the component, do not cut any deeper than necessary to remove the motor cup.
6. Remove the blower motor.

To install:

7. Install the motor blower seal.

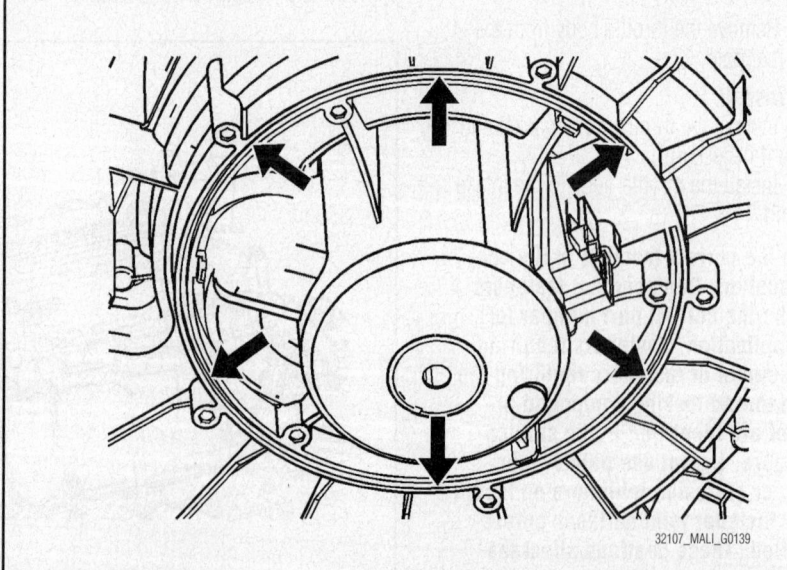

Fig. 184 Cut out the blower motor using a utility knife in the narrow groove of the lower case

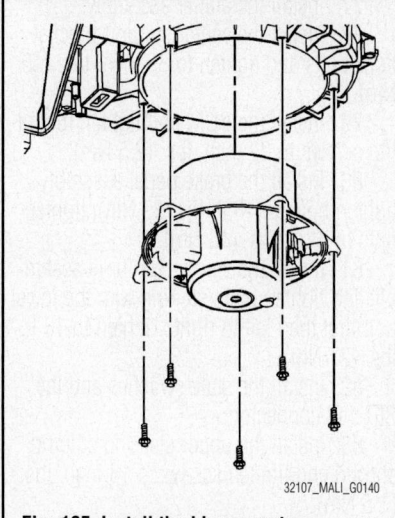

Fig. 185 Install the blower motor

8. Install the blower motor.

9. Install the blower motor attachment ring if reusing the blower motor.

10. Tighten the blower motor screws, and tighten the screws to 13 lb inches (1.5 Nm).

11. Install the blower motor wire harness connector.

12. Install the right closeout panel.

HEATER CORE

REMOVAL & INSTALLATION

See Figures 186 through 191.

1. Before servicing the vehicle, refer to the Precautions Section.

2. Disable the Supplemental Inflatable Restraint (SIR) system.

3. Disconnect the negative battery cable.

4. Drain the coolant.

5. Remove the inlet heater hose at the heater core.

6. Remove the outlet heater hose at the heater core.

7. Recover the refrigerant.

➡**Cap all A/C components immediately to prevent system contamination.**

8. Remove the suction hose at the Thermostatic Expansion Valve (TXV).

9. Remove the liquid line at the TXV.

10. Remove and discard the sealing washers.

11. Disconnect the HVAC module to front of dash plate bolts.

12. Remove the right console trim panel.

13. Remove the left console trim panel.

14. Remove the console.

15. Remove the left closeout panel.

16. Remove both Instrument Panel (I/P) outer trim panels.

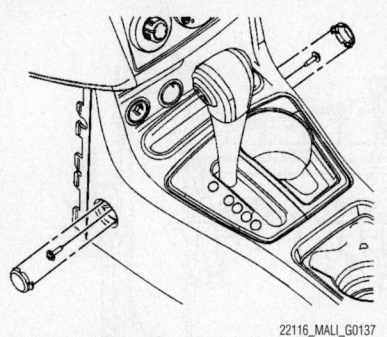

Fig. 186 Console front mounting screw location

17. Remove the I/P to the body wire harness and antenna LH connectors.

18. Remove the I/P to the wire harness RH connectors.

19. Remove the knee bolster.

20. Remove the accelerator pedal.

21. Remove the steering column to the I/P wire harness connector.

22. Remove the crush bracket to the front of dash plate nuts.

23. Remove the upper steering column shroud from the lower shroud.

24. Remove the stalk switches and the SIR coil connectors.

25. Position the steering wheel in full forward telescoping position.

26. Position the front seat in the full rearward position.

27. Remove the steering column mounting bolts.

28. Lower the steering column to the floor.

29. Remove the brake pedal assembly.

30. Remove the Body Control Module (BCM).

31. Remove the center support bracket floor bolts.

32. Remove the shifter assembly.

33. Remove both windshield pillar garnish moldings.

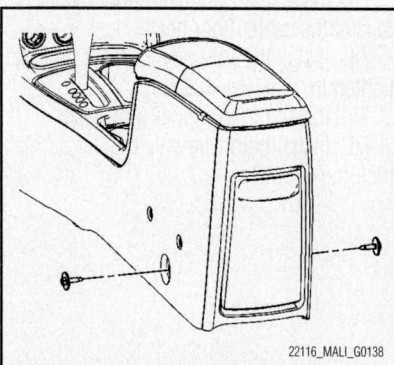

Fig. 187 Console front mounting screw location

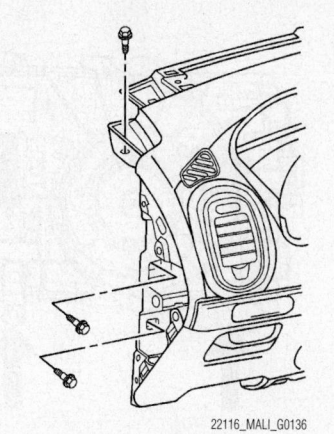

Fig. 188 Instrument panel body LH bolts shown

34. Remove the I/P upper trim panel.

35. Remove the I/P body LH bolts.

36. Remove the I/P body RH bolts.

37. Remove the right hand floor heater duct at the center floor heater duct.

38. Remove the left hand floor heater duct at the center floor heater duct.

39. Remove the I/P assembly.

40. Remove the recirculation actuator wire harness connector.

41. Remove the air temperature actuator wire harness connector.

42. Remove the mode actuator wire harness connector.

43. Remove the blower motor wire harness connector.

44. Remove the blower motor resistor wire harness connector.

45. Remove the left hand side window defogger outlet duct.

46. Remove the lower floor duct push-in fastener.

47. Remove the HVAC module assembly mounting bolts.

48. Remove the HVAC module assembly.

49. Remove the lower center floor air outlet duct

50. Remove the upper center floor air outlet duct screws.

51. Remove the upper center floor air outlet duct

52. Drill out the heater core cover heat stakes.

53. Remove the heater core cover screws.

54. Remove the heater core cover.

55. Remove the heater core.

To install:

56. Install heater core.

57. Install the heater core cover.

58. Install heater core screws and tighten to 13 inch. lbs. (1.5 Nm).

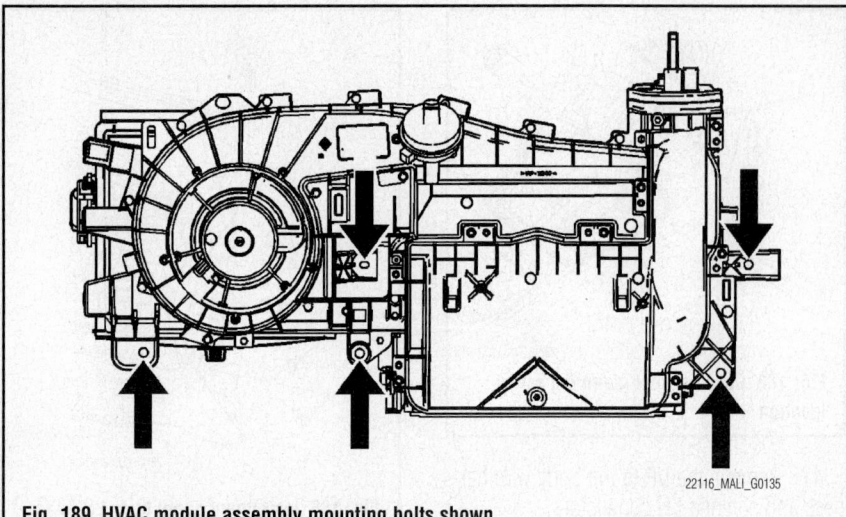

Fig. 189 HVAC module assembly mounting bolts shown

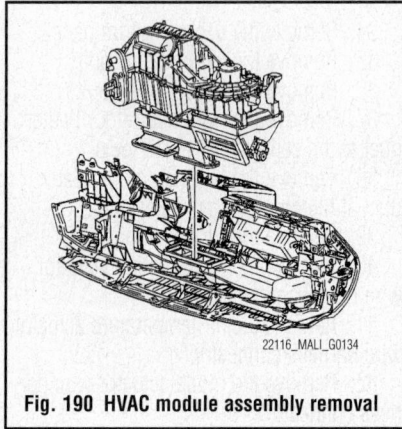

Fig. 190 HVAC module assembly removal

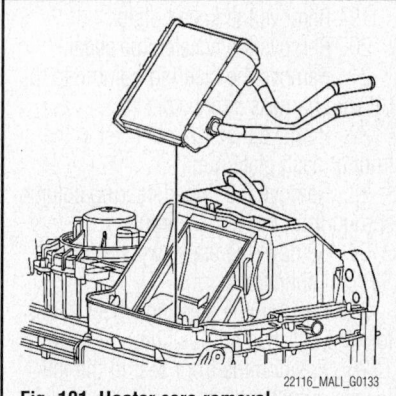

Fig. 191 Heater core removal

59. Install the upper center floor air outlet duct.

60. Install the upper center floor air outlet duct screws and tighten to 13 inch. lbs. (1.5 Nm).

61. Install the lower center floor air outlet duct.

62. Install the HVAC module assembly.

63. Install the HVAC module assembly mounting bolts and tighten to 44 inch. lbs. (5 Nm).

64. Install the lower floor duct push-in fastener.

65. Install the left hand side window defogger outlet duct.

66. Install the blower motor resistor wire harness connector.

67. Install the blower motor wire harness connector.

68. Install the mode actuator wire harness connector.

69. Install the air temperature actuator wire harness connector.

70. Install the recirculation actuator wire harness connector.

71. Install the I/P assembly.

72. Install the left hand floor heater duct at the center floor heater duct.

73. Install the right hand floor heater duct at the center floor heater duct.

74. Install the I/P body RH/LH bolts and tighten to 19 ft. lbs. (26 Nm).

75. Install the I/P upper trim panel.

76. Install both windshield pillar garnish moldings.

77. Install the shifter assembly.

78. Install the center support bracket floor bolts and tighten to 89 inch. lbs. (10 Nm).

79. Install the BCM and tighten mounting screws to 22 inch. lbs. (2.5 Nm).

80. Install the brake pedal assembly tighten bolts to 18 ft. lbs. 25 Nm), tighten nuts to 11 ft. lbs. (15 Nm).

81. Install the steering column assembly and tighten bolts starting with the lower bolt first then left to right. Tighten to 18 ft. lbs. (27 Nm).

82. Install the stalk switches and the SIR coil connectors.

83. Install the upper steering column shroud and tighten screws to 13 inch. lbs. (1.5 Nm).

84. Install the crush bracket to the front of dash plate nuts and tighten to 89 inch. lbs. (10 Nm).

85. Install the steering column to the I/P wire harness connector.

86. Install the accelerator pedal.

87. Install the knee bolster.

88. Install the I/P to the body wire harness RH connectors.

89. Install the I/P to the body wire harness and antenna LH connectors.

90. Install both I/P outer trim panels.

91. Install the left closeout panel.

92. Install the console and tighten mounting bolts and screws to 10 inch. lbs. (1 Nm).

93. Install the left and right console trim panel

94. Install the HVAC module to front of dash plate bolts and tighten to 35 inch. lbs. (4 Nm).

95. Install new sealing washers.

96. Install the liquid line and the suction hose at the TXV.

97. Tighten the liquid line and suction hose nut to 15 ft. lbs. (20 Nm).

98. Evacuate and charge the refrigerant system.

99. Install the outlet and inlet heater hoses at the heater core, tighten the clamps.

100. Fill and bleed the cooling system.

101. Enable the SIR system.

102. Connect the negative battery cable.

STEERING

POWER RACK & PINION STEERING GEAR

REMOVAL & INSTALLATION

Electronic Power Steering

See Figures 192 and 193.

1. Before servicing the vehicle, refer to the Precautions Section.
2. Turn the steering wheel to the straight forward position and remove the key from the ignition.
3. Disable the Supplemental Inflatable Restraint (SIR) system.
4. Disconnect the negative battery cable.
5. Raise and support the vehicle.
6. Remove the front tires and wheels.

7. Remove the intermediate shaft to steering gear pinch bolt. Discard the bolt.

➡ **Do not rotate the intermediate shaft once separated from the steering gear.**

8. Disconnect the intermediate shaft from the steering gear. Note the alignment for installation.
9. Remove the transmission rear mount bolt if needed.
10. Remove the steering gear to frame bolts.
11. Remove the steering gear through the left side of the vehicle. Rotate the gear 90 degrees in order to clear the rear transmission mount.
12. If replacing the steering gear, remove the outer tie rod ends.

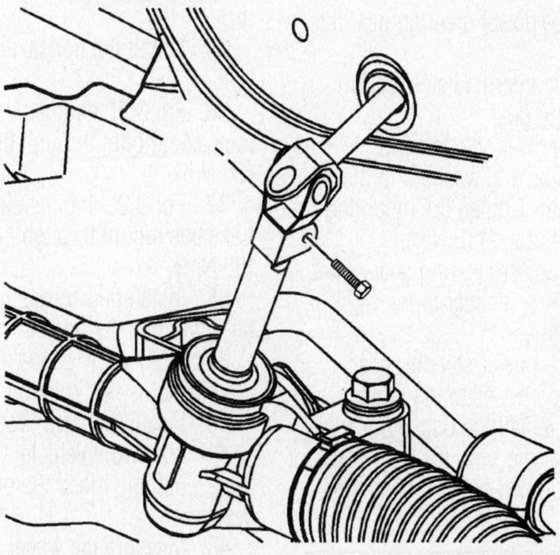

To install:

13. Install the outer tie rod ends to the steering gear.
14. Install the steering gear to the vehicle. Rotate the gear as necessary to clear the rear transmission mount.
15. Install the steering gear to frame bolts, and tighten the bolts to 52 ft. lbs. (70 Nm) plus an additional 90 degrees.
16. Install transmission mount bolt if previously removed. Tighten to 66 ft. lbs.(90 Nm).
17. Connect the intermediate steering shaft to the steering gear as noted during removal.
18. Install the new intermediate steering shaft to steering gear pinch bolt, and tighten the bolt to 36 ft. lbs. (49 Nm).
19. Connect the outer tie rod ends to the steering knuckle.
20. Install the front tires and wheels.
21. Lower the vehicle.
22. Connect the negative battery cable.
23. Enable SIR System.
24. Check the vehicle for alignment

Hydraulic Power Steering

See Figures 194 through 196.

1. Before servicing the vehicle, refer to the Precautions Section.
2. Turn the steering wheel to the straight forward position and remove the key from the ignition.
3. Disable the Supplemental Inflatable Restraint (SIR) system.
4. Disconnect the negative battery cable.
5. Remove the front tires and wheels.
6. Remove the tie rod end castle nuts.
7. Using the J 24319—B, separate the tie rod ends from the steering knuckles.
8. Remove the intermediate shaft to steering gear pinch bolt. Discard the bolt.

❊❊ WARNING

Secure the steering wheel in the straight forward position before separating the intermediate shaft from the steering gear, or damage to the SIR coil will occur.

9. Separate the intermediate shaft from the steering gear.
10. Loosen the transaxle mount through bolt.
11. Disconnect the heated oxygen sensor (HO2S) electrical connector.
12. Disconnect the HO2S sensor harness from the transmission mount bracket.

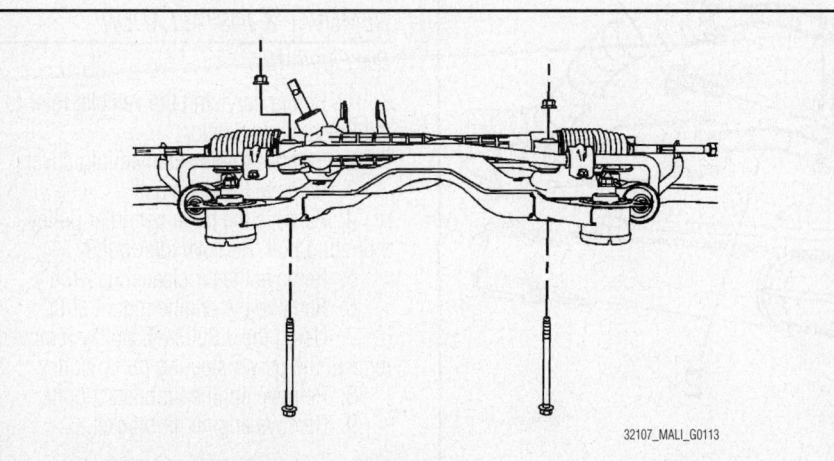

32107_MALI_G0112

Fig. 192 Remove the intermediate shaft to steering gear pinch bolt

32107_MALI_G0113

Fig. 193 Remove the steering gear to frame bolts

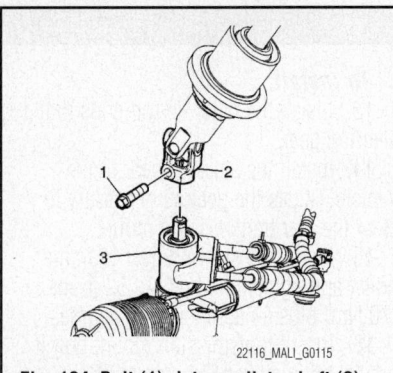

Fig. 194 Bolt (1), intermediate shaft (2), steering gear (3)

13. Remove the 3 transaxle mount to transaxle bolts.

14. Remove the 3 transaxle bracket to frame nuts.

15. Position the transaxle bracket and rear mount aside.

16. Remove the bolt and disconnect the power steering gear inlet and outlet

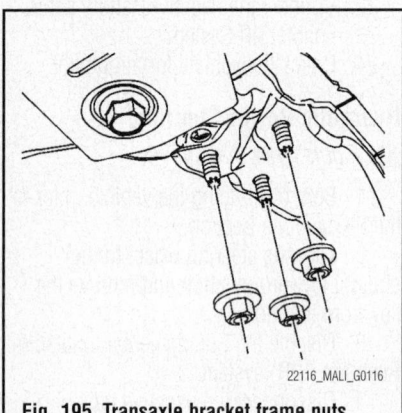

Fig. 195 Transaxle bracket frame nuts

pipe/hoses from the power steering gear. Cap off the pipe/hoses and position aside.

17. Remove the power steering gear outlet pipe routing pin style retainer from the right rear side of the frame.

18. Remove the power steering gear mounting bolts, nuts, and washers from the gear.

➡**The power steering gear will need to be rotated while it is removed through the left wheel opening.**

19. Remove the power steering gear through the left wheel opening.

20. If the power steering gear is to be replaced, transfer the outer tie rod ends to the new steering gear.

To install:

➡**The power steering gear will need to be rotated while it is installed through the left wheel opening.**

21. Position the power steering gear into the vehicle.

22. Connect the intermediate steering shaft to the steering gear.

23. Install the power steering gear mounting bolts, nuts and washers to the power steering gear. Tighten the mounting bolts, nuts to 81 ft. lbs. (110 Nm).

24. Install the power steering gear outlet pipe routing pin style retainer to the right rear side of the frame.

25. Connect the power steering gear inlet and outlet pipe/hoses to the power steering gear and install the bolt. Prior to tightening the retaining bolt, rotate the outlet pipe clockwise/down so it touches the

inlet pipe. Verify the hoses are still touching after the retaining bolt is tight.

26. Tighten the pipe/hose to power steering gear bolt to 20 ft. lbs. (27 Nm).

27. Install the new intermediate steering shaft to steering gear pinch bolt and tighten to 36 ft. lbs. (49 Nm).

28. Position the transaxle bracket and rear mount back to their original position.

29. Install the 3 transaxle bracket to frame nuts and tighten to 37 ft. lbs. (50 Nm).

30. Install the 3 transaxle mount to transaxle bolts.

31. For 3.5L engines tighten the transaxle mount bolts to 66 ft. lbs. (90 Nm).

32. For 3.9L engines tighten the transaxle mount bolts to 37 ft. lbs. (50 Nm).

33. Connect the HO2S sensor harness to the transmission mount bracket.

34. Connect the HO2S electrical connector.

35. Install the transaxle mount through bolt.

36. For 3.5L engines tighten the transaxle mount through bolt to 66 ft. lbs. (90 Nm).

37. For 3.9L engines tighten the transaxle mount through bolt to 37 ft. lbs. (50 Nm).

38. Install new torque castle nuts to the tie rod end ball studs.

39. Tighten the castle nuts to 18 ft. lbs. (25 Nm) plus 90° rotation.

40. Install the front tires and wheels.

41. Lower the vehicle.

42. Fill and bleed the power steering system.

43. Measure the wheel alignment and adjust as necessary.

POWER STEERING PUMP

REMOVAL & INSTALLATION

See Figure 197.

1. Before servicing the vehicle, refer to the Precautions Section.

2. Remove the intake manifold cover.

3. Remove the drive belt.

4. Remove the drive belt idler pulley mounting bolt. Remove idler pulley.

5. Remove the air cleaner assembly.

6. Remove the engine mount strut.

7. Using the J 25034-C pulley remover, remove the power steering pump pulley.

8. Remove engine lift bracket bolts.

9. Remove engine lift bracket.

➡**Use an appropriate tool to remove the power steering fluid from the reser-**

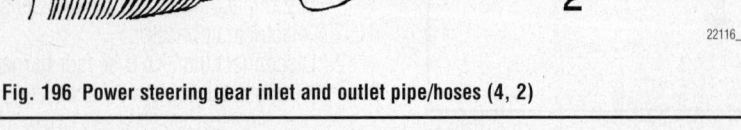

Fig. 196 Power steering gear inlet and outlet pipe/hoses (4, 2)

voir before removing the hoses from the pump.

10. Remove the power steering gear inlet pressure hose.

11. Remove the power steering return hose.

12. Remove the power steering pump mounting bolts.

13. Remove the power steering pump.

To install:

14. Install the power steering pump.

15. Install the power steering pump mounting bolts and tighten to 18 ft. lbs. (25 Nm).

16. Install and tighten the power steering return hose.

17. Install the power steering gear inlet pressure hose. Use a new O-ring seal for installation.

18. Tighten the power steering gear inlet pressure hose fitting to 20 ft. lbs. (27 Nm).

19. Install the engine lift bracket and bolts, tighten the bolts to 37 ft. lbs. (50 Nm).

20. Using the J 25033-C pulley installer, install the power steering pump pulley.

21. Install the engine mount strut.

22. Install the air cleaner assembly.

23. Install the drive belt idler pulley and tighten the bolt to 37 ft. lbs. (50 Nm).

24. Install the drive belt.

25. Install the intake manifold cover.

POWER STEERING ASSIST MOTOR

REMOVAL & INSTALLATION

See Figure 198.

1. Before servicing the vehicle, refer to the Precautions Section.

2. Remove the knee bolster.

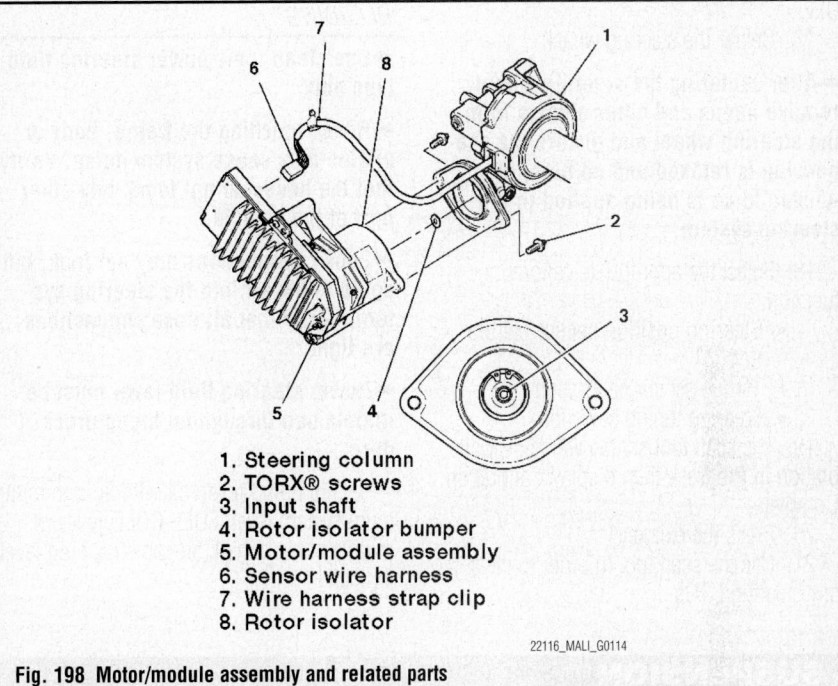

1. Steering column
2. TORX® screws
3. Input shaft
4. Rotor isolator bumper
5. Motor/module assembly
6. Sensor wire harness
7. Wire harness strap clip
8. Rotor isolator

22116_MALI_G0114

Fig. 198 Motor/module assembly and related parts

3. Disconnect the sensor wire harness from the motor/module assembly.

4. Use needle nose pliers to remove the wire strap clip from the motor/module assembly.

5. If replacing the motor/module assembly, remove the wire strap clip from the sensor wire harness.

6. If replacing the steering column, keep the wire harness strap clip attached to the sensor wire harness.

7. Use a M6x1 head bit to remove the 2 motor/module assembly TORX® screws. Discard the screws.

➡ **Once the motor/module assembly has been removed, inspect the steering column assist mechanism input shaft for the rotor isolator bumper. If present, remove and insert back into the rotor isolator in the motor/module assembly.**

8. Grasp the motor/module assembly by the motor housing and remove it from the steering column by pulling with an even tension.

To install:

9. Fit the motor/module assembly rotor isolator over the steering column assist mechanism input shaft.

10. Use a M6x1 TORX® head bit to attach the motor/module assembly to the steering column with the 2 new TORX® bolts. Tighten to 80 inch. lbs. (90 Nm).

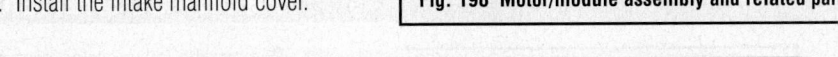

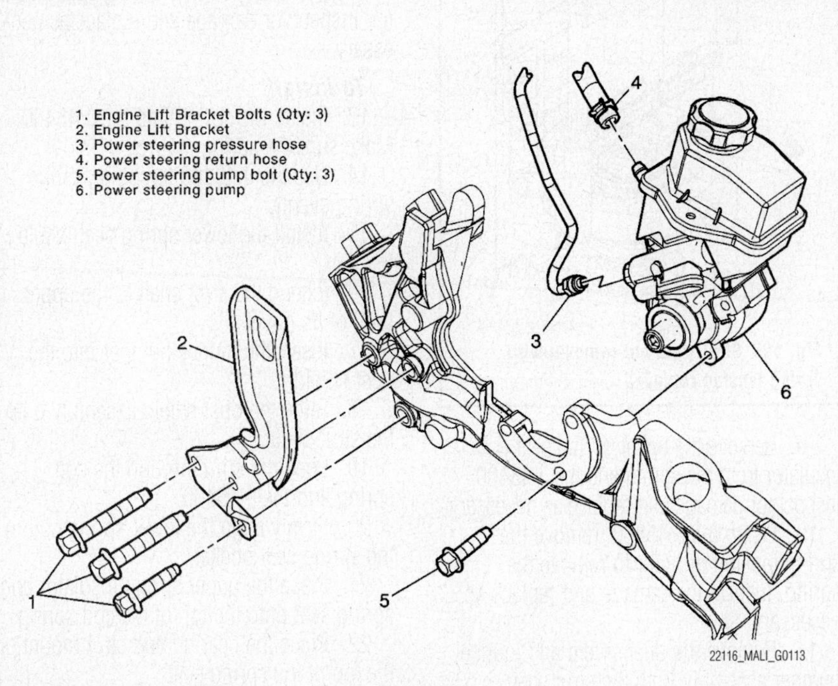

1. Engine Lift Bracket Bolts (Qty: 3)
2. Engine Lift Bracket
3. Power steering pressure hose
4. Power steering return hose
5. Power steering pump bolt (Qty: 3)
6. Power steering pump

22116_MALI_G0113

Fig. 197 Power steering pump and related parts

11. Connect the sensor wire harness to the motor/module assembly.

12. Install the sensor wire harness strap clip into the motor/module assembly.

13. Install the knee bolster.

14. Perform the control module setup.

15. Install an approved scan tool, select special functions.

16. Turn ON the ignition, with the engine OFF.

17. Center the steering wheel.

➡After centering the steering wheel, remove hands and other objects from the steering wheel and ensure the suspension is relaxed and no bias, or uneven force is being applied to the steering system.

18. Select the appropriate calibration function:
- Steering position sensor calibration
- Torque sensor calibration
- Steering tuning selection

19. The scan tool screen will flash Calibration in Progress then display Calibration Complete.

20. Press the exit key.

21. Use the scan tool in order to clear any steering DTCs

➡After turning OFF the ignition, allow 25 seconds of wait time before performing any procedures that require the vehicles battery to be disconnected, or module memory loss may occur.

22. Turn OFF the ignition.

23. Inspect all of the steering column components for correct operation.

BLEEDING

➡Use clean, new power steering fluid type only

➡Hoses touching the frame, body or engine may cause system noise. Verify that the hoses do not touch any other part of the vehicle.

➡Loose connections may not leak, but could allow air into the steering system. Verify that all hose connections are tight.

➡Power steering fluid level must be maintained throughout bleed procedure.

1. Fill pump reservoir with fluid to minimum system level, FULL COLD level, or middle of hash mark on cap stick fluid level indicator.

➡With hydro-boost only, the oil level will appear falsely high if the hydro-boost accumulator is not fully charged. Do not apply the brake pedal with the engine OFF. This will discharge the hydro-boost accumulator.

2. If equipped with hydro-boost, fully charge the hydro-boost accumulator using the following procedure:
- Start the engine.
- Firmly apply the brake pedal 10-15 times.
- Turn the engine OFF.

3. Raise the vehicle until the front wheels are off the ground.

4. Key on engine OFF, turn the steering wheel from stop to stop 12 times.

5. Vehicles equipped with hydro-boost systems or longer length power steering hoses may require turns up to 15 to 20 stop to stops.

6. Verify power steering fluid level per operating specification..

7. Start the engine. Rotate steering wheel from left to right. Check for sign of cavitation or fluid aeration (pump noise/whining).

8. Verify the fluid level. Repeat the bleed procedure, if necessary.

SUSPENSION

COIL SPRING

REMOVAL & INSTALLATION

See Figures 199 through 201.

1. Before servicing the vehicle, refer to the Precautions Section.

2. Remove the strut assembly.

3. Place the strut assembly into the J 45400.

4. Adjust the compressing arms to contact the coils farthest away from the center of the spring.

5. Using the J 45400, compress the spring to remove the spring tension from the upper strut mount.

➡Before removing the strut shaft nut, support the strut to prevent the strut from falling.

6. Remove the strut shaft nut, while holding the strut shaft.

7. Lower the strut from the spring and the J 45400.

8. Remove the upper strut mount assembly and mount bearing. Inspect for damage and replace as necessary.

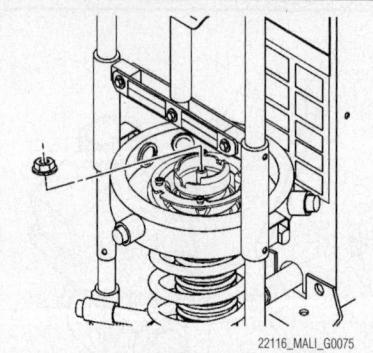

22116_MALI_G0075

Fig. 199 Strut shaft nut removal with spring tension removed

9. Remove the upper spring seat and insulator from the spring and the J 45400. Inspect for damage and replace as necessary.

10. Using the J 45400, remove the spring tension in order to remove the spring. Inspect for damage and replace as necessary.

11. Remove the dust shield and jounce bumper assembly from the strut shaft. Inspect for damage and replace as necessary

FRONT SUSPENSION

12. Remove the lower spring seat insulator. Inspect for damage and replace as necessary.

To install:

13. Install the spring into the J 45400. Make sure the spring is level.

14. Use the J 45400 to compress the spring evenly.

15. Install the lower spring seat insulator.

16. Extend the strut shaft to the upper limit of its travel.

17. Insert the jounce bumper into the dust shield.

18. Slide the dust shield assembly onto the strut shaft.

19. Load the strut through the coil spring and the J 45400.

20. Firmly align the lower spring coil in the spring seat pocket.

21. Place the upper spring insulator and spring seat onto the top of the coil spring.

22. Place the bearing and strut mount on the top of the spring seat

23. Install the upper strut shaft nut and tighten to 52 ft. lbs. (70 Nm).

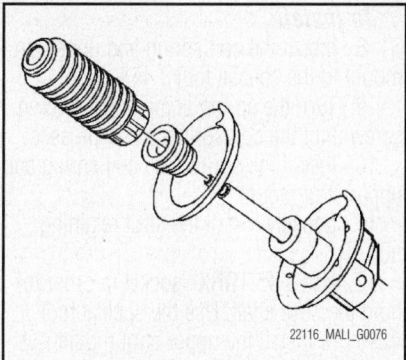

Fig. 200 Spring seat, jounce bumper and dust shield

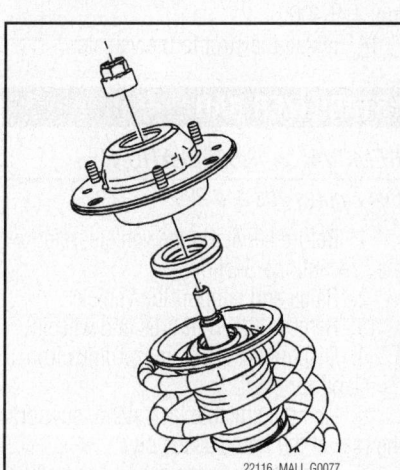

Fig. 201 Spring insulator, spring seat, bearing and strut mount

24. Using the J 45400, remove the spring tension.

25. Remove the strut assembly from the J 45400.

26. Install the strut assembly.

CONTROL LINKS

REMOVAL & INSTALLATION

See Figures 202 and 203.

1. Before servicing the vehicle, refer to the Precautions Section.

2. Raise and support the vehicle.

3. Remove the front wheel.

4. Disconnect the stabilizer control link from the stabilizer shaft.

5. Disconnect the stabilizer control link from the strut assembly and remove from the vehicle.

To install:

6. Connect the stabilizer control link to the strut assembly.

7. Connect the stabilizer control link to the stabilizer shaft.

8. Tighten stabilizer control link nuts to 48 ft. lbs. (65 Nm).

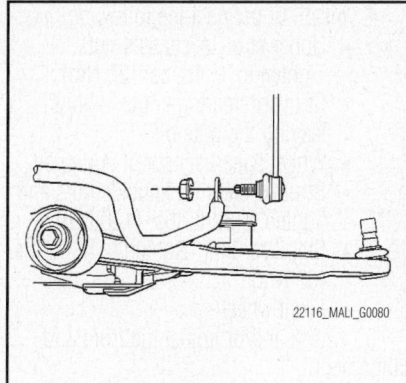

Fig. 202 Control link lower view

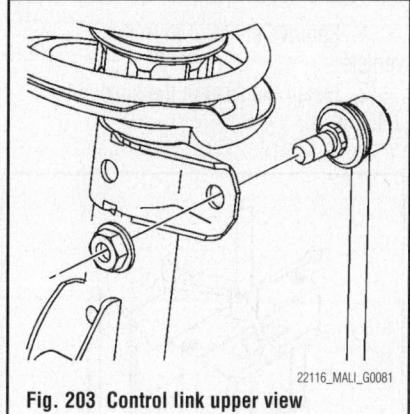

Fig. 203 Control link upper view

9. Install the front wheel.
10. Lower the vehicle.

LOWER CONTROL ARM

REMOVAL & INSTALLATION

See Figure 204.

1. Before servicing the vehicle, refer to the Precautions Section.

2. Remove the front wheel.

3. If equipped with a 3.5L engine:

   a. If removing the left lower control arm, remove the side transmission mount.

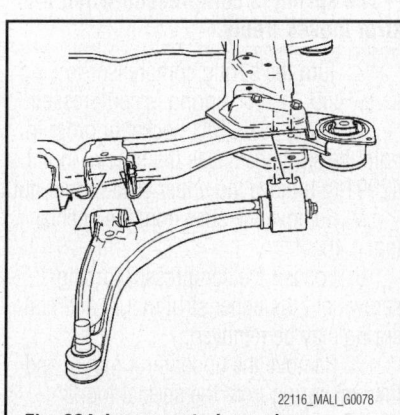

Fig. 204 Lower control arm view

b. If removing the right lower control arm, remove the engine mount.

4. Remove or disconnect the following:
   - Lower control arm front bushing-to-frame bolt
   - Lower control arm rear bushing-to-frame bolts
   - Lower control arm-to-steering knuckle pinch bolt, noting its original position.
   - Ball stud from the steering knuckle
   - Control arm

To install:

5. Position the lower control arm to the frame assembly and steering knuckle.

6. Install or connect the following:

7. Install a new lower control arm-to-steering knuckle pinch bolt to its original position. Hand tighten only.

8. Install the lower control arm front bushing-to-frame bolt. Hand tighten only.

9. Install the lower control arm rear bushing-to-frame bolt.

10. Tighten components as follows:

   a. Tighten the ball stud-to-steering knuckle pinch bolt to 37 ft. lbs. (50 Nm). Reverse the nut ¾ of a turn and tighten to 37 ft. lbs. (50 Nm) plus 60 degrees.

   b. Tighten the bolts with the front suspension loaded using a jack stand.

   c. Tighten the front bushing bolt to 37 ft. lbs. (50 Nm).

   d. Tighten the rear bushing bolt to 37 ft. lbs. (50 Nm).

11. If equipped with a 3.5L engine:

   a. Install the side transmission mount if removed. Tighten bolt to 37 ft. lbs. (50 Nm).

   b. Install the engine mount if removed. Tighten bolt to 37 ft. lbs. (50 Nm).

12. Install the front wheel.

CONTROL ARM BUSHING REPLACEMENT

See Figure 205.

1. Before servicing the vehicle, refer to the Precautions Section.

2. Raise and support the vehicle.

3. Remove the tire and wheel.

4. Remove the lower control arm.

5. Remove the lower control arm to rear bushing bolt.

6. Note the position of the bushing during removal. Remove the bushing off the lower control arm.

7. Install the bushing on the lower control arm as previously noted.

8. Using Loctite® 234 or equivalent on the bolt threads, install the lower control arm to bushing bolt.

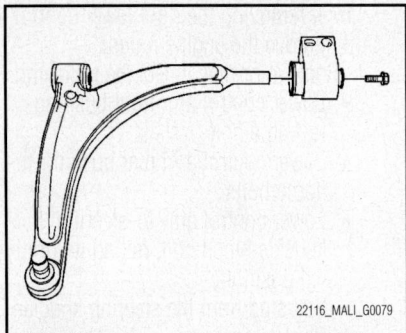

Fig. 205 Lower control arm rear bushing removal

9. Hold the rear bushing inner sleeve when tightening the rear bushings to control arm bolt. Tighten the bolt to 32 ft. lbs. (44 Nm).
10. Install the lower control arm.
11. Install the tire and wheel.
12. Lower the vehicle.

MACPHERSON STRUT

REMOVAL & INSTALLATION

See Figure 206.

1. Before servicing the vehicle, refer to the Precautions Section.
2. Remove or disconnect the following:
   • Front wheel
   • Stabilizer link from the strut
   • Strut-to-steering knuckle nuts
   • Wheel speed sensor, if equipped
   • Strut-to-steering knuckle bolts
   • Upper strut-to-chassis nuts
   • Strut

To install:
3. Position the strut in the strut tower, using the alignment pin as a guide.

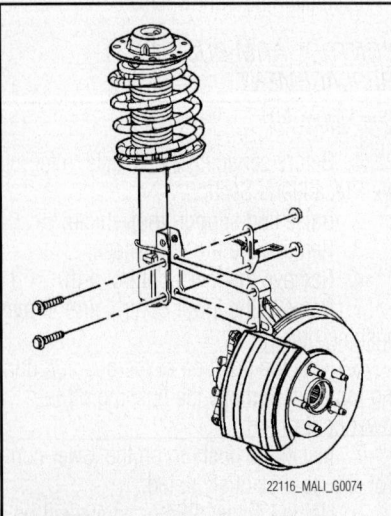

Fig. 206 Strut, steering knuckle nuts and bolts

4. Install or connect the following:
   • Upper strut-to-chassis nuts. Tighten to 18 ft. lbs. (25 Nm).
   • Strut-to-steering knuckle bolts, leaving the nuts off
   • Wheel speed sensor, if equipped
   • Strut-to-steering knuckle nuts and tighten to 89 ft. lbs. (120 Nm)
   • Stabilizer link. Tighten to 48 ft. lbs. (65 Nm)
   • Front wheel
5. Check and/or adjust the front end alignment.

OVERHAUL

See Figure 207.

1. Remove the strut from the vehicle.
2. Install the strut in the special tool J 45400.

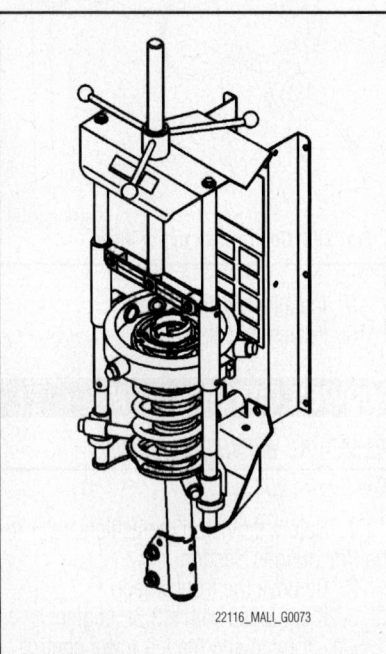

Fig. 207 Strut in the special tool J 45400

➡ **The spring is compressed when the strut moves freely.**

3. Turn the spring compressor forcing screw until the coil spring is compressed.
4. Use a 45 TORX® socket in order to hold the strut shaft. Use the special tool J 42991 to remove the upper strut mount nut
5. Remove the strut from the special tool J 45400 .
6. Loosen the compressor forcing screw until the upper strut mount and coil spring may be removed.
7. Remove the upper strut mount and the coil spring from the special tool J 45400 .

To install:
8. Install the coil spring and upper strut mount to the special tool J 45400.
9. Turn the spring compressor forcing screw until the coil spring is compressed.
10. Install the strut to the coil spring and upper strut mount.
11. Loosely install the strut retaining nut.
12. Use a 45 TORX® socket in order to hold the strut shaft. Use the special tool J 42991 to install the upper strut mount nut and tighten the strut mount nut to 63 ft. lbs. (85 Nm).
13. Remove the strut from the special tool J 45400.
14. Install the strut to the vehicle.

STABILIZER BAR

REMOVAL & INSTALLATION

See Figures 208 and 209.

1. Before servicing the vehicle, refer to the Precautions Section.
2. Raise and support the vehicle.
3. Remove the front tires and wheels.
4. Disconnect the stabilizer links from the stabilizer shaft.
5. Using a suitable jack stand, support the rear of the frame assembly.
6. Remove the frame support to body bolts.
7. Remove the rear frame assembly mounting bolts.
8. Lower the rear of the cradle in order to gain clearance to the stabilizer shaft.
9. Remove the stabilizer bar clamps and insulators.
10. Remove the stabilizer shaft through the opening between the frame and body.

To install:
11. Position the stabilizer shaft to the frame.
12. Install the stabilizer bar clamps and insulators.
13. Raise the rear of the cradle.
14. Install the frame support brackets. Loosely install the bracket and frame to body bolts.

➡ **The frame and frame support bolts require a minimum of 81 ft. lbs. (110 Nm).**

15. Tighten the frame and bracket support bolts, and tighten the rear frame to body bolt to 74 ft. lbs. (100 Nm).
16. Tighten the frame support bracket to body bolt to 74 ft. lbs. (100 Nm).
17. Tighten all the bolts 90 degrees plus an additional 15 degrees.
18. Remove the jack stand.

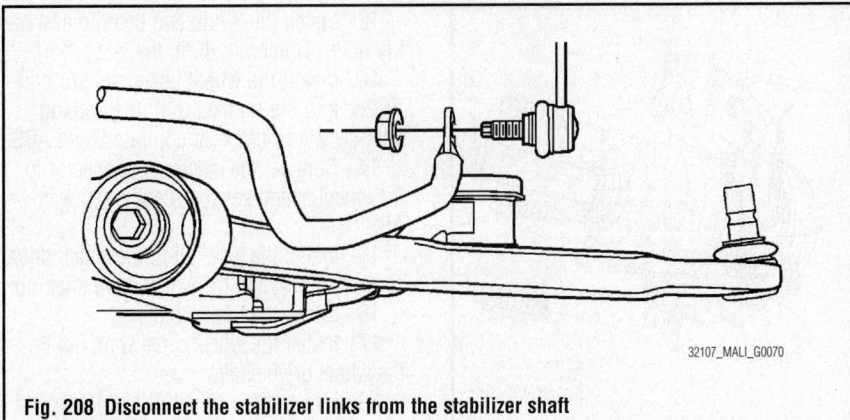

Fig. 208 Disconnect the stabilizer links from the stabilizer shaft

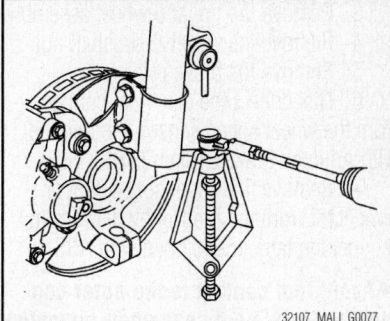

Fig. 211 Using the special tool J24319-B, separate the tie rod from the steering knuckle

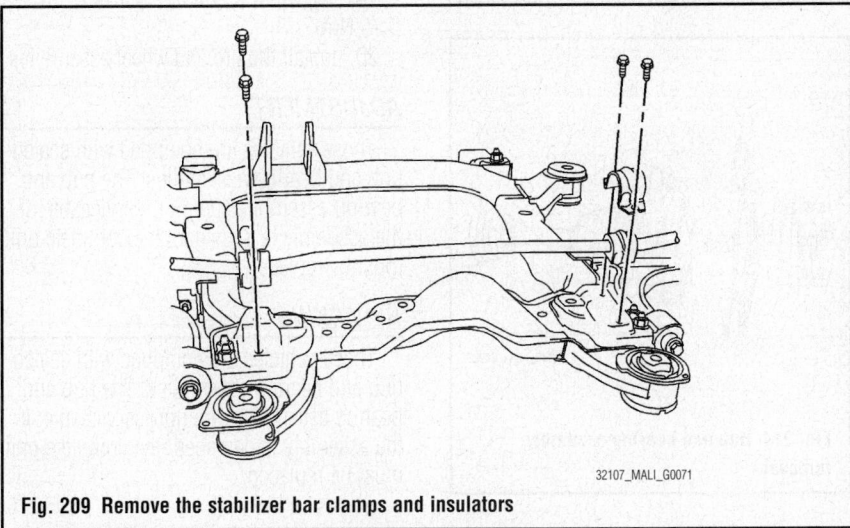

Fig. 209 Remove the stabilizer bar clamps and insulators

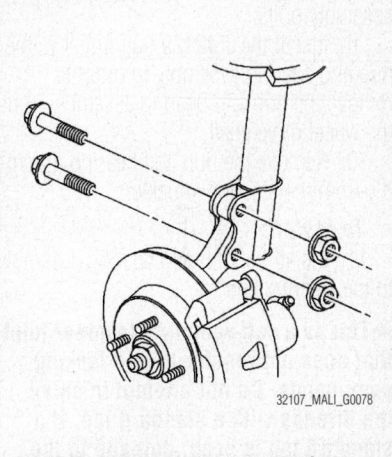

Fig. 212 Remove the strut to steering knuckle nuts and bolts

19. Connect the stabilizer link to the stabilizer bar.
20. Lower the vehicle.

STEERING KNUCKLE

REMOVAL & INSTALLATION

See Figures 210 through 212.

1. Before servicing the vehicle, refer to the Precautions Section.

2. Raise and support the vehicle.
3. Remove the wheel bearing.
4. Remove the outer tie rod to knuckle nut.
5. Using the special tool J24319-B, separate the tie rod from the steering knuckle.
6. Remove the lower control arm.
7. Remove the strut to steering knuckle nuts and bolts.
8. Remove the steering knuckle from the vehicle.

To install:

9. Install the steering knuckle to the strut assembly and if applicable the ABS harness bracket. Tighten the bolts and nuts to 89 ft. lbs. (120 Nm).
10. Guide the axle through the steering knuckle.
11. Install the lower control arm.
12. Install the outer tie rod to the steering knuckle, and tighten the nut to 15 ft. lbs. (20 Nm). Turn the nut an additional 180 degrees and verify the torque to 37 ft. lbs. (50 Nm).
13. Install the wheel bearing, brake rotor, brake caliper and front wheels.
14. Lower the vehicle.
15. Road test the vehicle in order to verify alignment.

WHEEL HUB AND BEARING

REMOVAL & INSTALLATION

See Figures 213 and 214.

1. Before servicing the vehicle, refer to the Precautions Section.
2. Raise the vehicle.

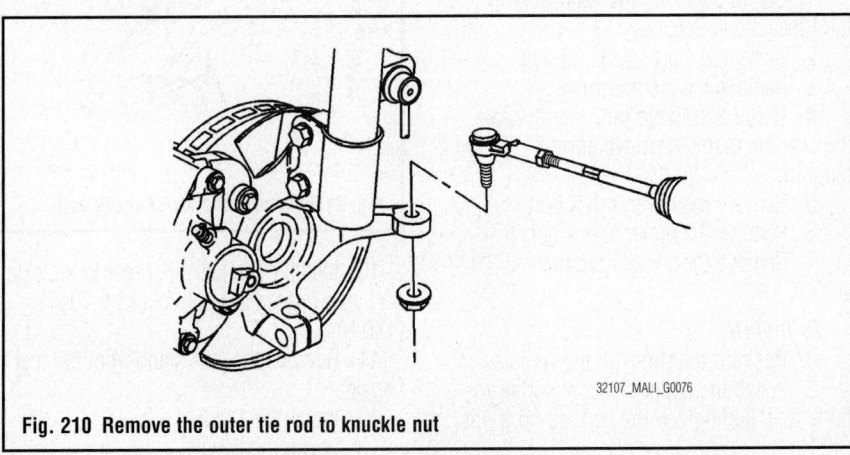

Fig. 210 Remove the outer tie rod to knuckle nut

3. Remove the tire and wheel assembly.

4. Remove the wheel drive shaft nut.

5. Remove the brake rotor.

6. Disconnect the electrical connector from the wheel speed sensor, if equipped with Antilock Brake System (ABS).

7. Remove the wheel speed sensor connector from the bracket by depressing the locking tabs, if equipped with ABS.

➡ **Avoid tool contact to the outer constant velocity boot seal when removing the wheel bearing mounting bolts. Failure to observe this notice may result in damage to the CV boot.**

8. Remove the 3 hub and bearing assembly bolts.

9. Install the J 42129 hub puller to the hub and bearing assembly in order to remove the hub and bearing assembly from the wheel drive shaft.

10. Remove the hub and bearing assembly from the steering knuckle.

To install:

11. Install the hub and bearing assembly to the steering knuckle.

➡ **This is a self-retaining fastener joint that does not require thread locking compounds. Do not attempt to clean the threads with a standard tap. If a standard tap is used, damage to the joint threads will occur.**

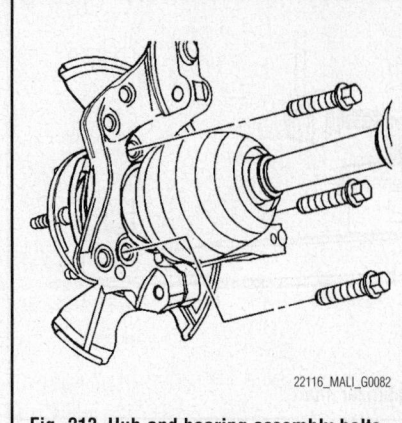

Fig. 213 Hub and bearing assembly bolts

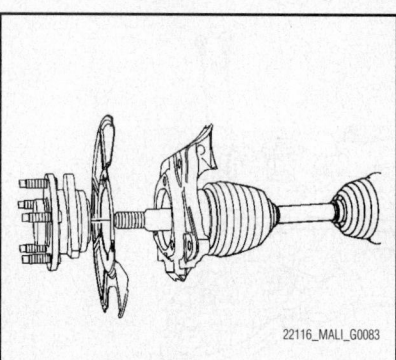

Fig. 214 Hub and bearing assembly removal

12. Install the 3 hub and bearing assembly bolts. Tighten to 85 ft. lbs. (115 Nm).

13. Install the wheel speed sensor connector into the bracket until the locking tabs click into place, if equipped with ABS.

14. Connect the electrical connector to the wheel speed sensor, if equipped with ABS.

15. Install the axle nut to the wheel drive shaft, hand tighten the wheel drive shaft nut.

16. Install the brake rotor.

17. Install the wheel drive shaft nut to the wheel drive shaft.

18. Use a screw driver or similar tool to stop the rotation of the brake rotor

19. Tighten the axle nut to 159 ft. lbs. (215 Nm).

20. Install the tire and wheel assemblies.

ADJUSTMENT

These vehicles are equipped with sealed hub and bearing assemblies. The hub and bearing assemblies are non-serviceable. If the assembly is damaged, the complete unit must be replaced.

REPACKING

These vehicles are equipped with sealed hub and bearing assemblies. The hub and bearing assemblies are non-serviceable. If the assembly is damaged, the complete unit must be replaced.

SUSPENSION

COIL SPRING

REMOVAL & INSTALLATION

1. Before servicing the vehicle, refer to the Precautions Section.

2. Raise and support the vehicle.

3. Remove the wheel.

4. Install a spring compressor and compress the coil spring.

5. Using a jack stand or suitable equivalent, support the lower control arm.

6. Remove the lower control arm-to-knuckle bolt.

7. Lower the control arm and remove the coil spring.

8. Inspect the coil spring insulators for damage and replace as necessary.

To install:

9. Position the coil spring onto the lower control arm.

10. Use the jack stand to raise the lower control arm into position.

11. Install the lower control arm-to-knuckle bolt and tighten to 44 ft. lbs. (60 Nm) plus 60 degrees.

12. Remove the spring compressor.

13. Remove the jack stand.

14. Install the wheel.

15. Lower the vehicle.

SHOCK ABSORBER

REMOVAL & INSTALLATION

See Figures 215 and 216.

1. Before servicing the vehicle, refer to the Precautions Section.

2. Raise and support the vehicle.

3. Remove the tire and wheel. .

4. Using a suitable jack stand, raise the rear knuckle to remove spring tension.

5. Remove the lower shock bolt.

6. Remove the upper shock bolt.

7. Remove the shock from the vehicle.

To install:

8. Position the shock in the vehicle.

9. Install the upper shock absorber to body bolt, and tighten the bolts to 66 ft. lbs. (90 Nm).

REAR SUSPENSION

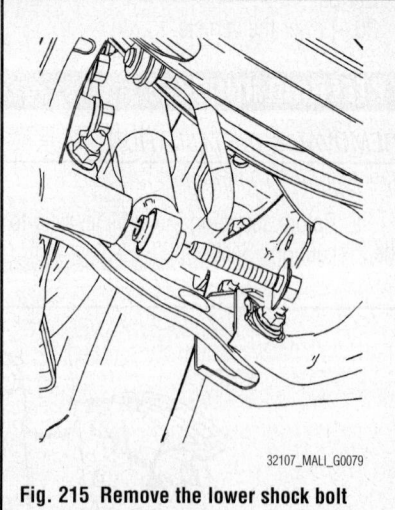

Fig. 215 Remove the lower shock bolt

10. Install the shock absorber to knuckle bolt, and tighten the bolt to 133 ft. lbs. (180 Nm).

11. Remove the jack stand from the rear knuckle.

12. Install the tire and wheel.

13. Lower the vehicle.

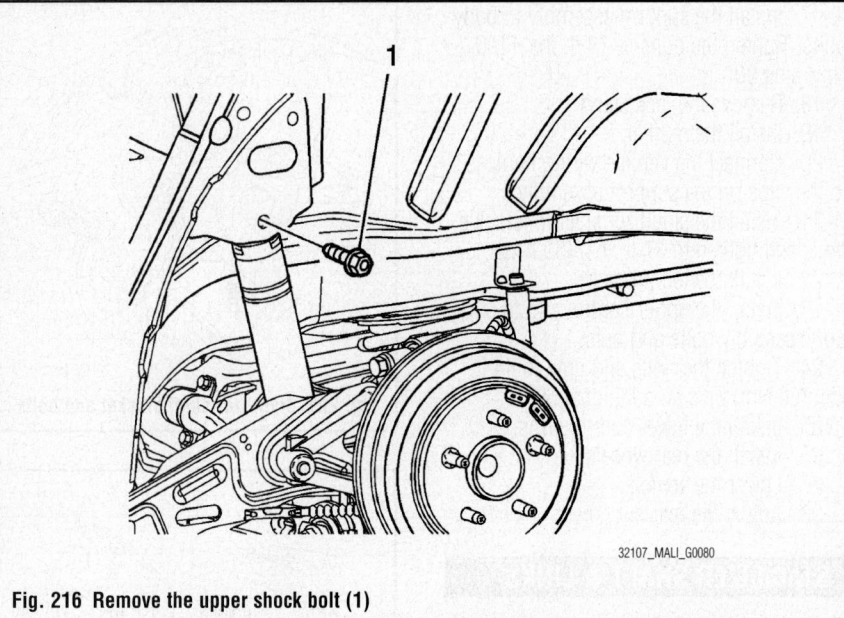

Fig. 216 Remove the upper shock bolt (1)

TESTING

1. Test drive vehicle.
2. Inspect each shock absorber for external fluid leakage.
3. Use your hands in order to lift up and push down each corner of the vehicle 3 times.
4. Remove your hands from the vehicle.
5. Replace any shock that exceeds more than two bounces.

KNUCKLE

REMOVAL & INSTALLATION

See Figures 217 and 218.

1. Before servicing the vehicle, refer to the Precautions Section.
2. Raise and support the vehicle.
3. Remove the tire and wheel.
4. Remove the rear wheel bearing.
5. Using a suitable jack, raise the knuckle in order to relieve tension from the shock.

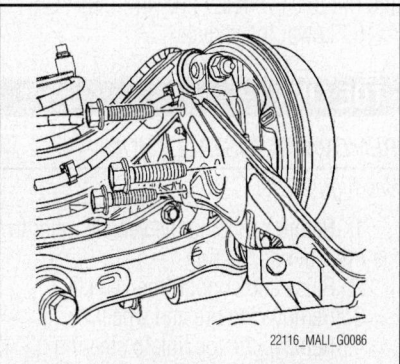

Fig. 217 Trailing arm to knuckle bolts removal

6. Remove the lower shock to knuckle bolt.
7. Remove the coil spring.
8. Remove the toe link.
9. Remove the upper control arm to knuckle bolt and nut
10. Remove the trailing arm to knuckle bolts.
11. Remove the stabilizer shaft link to knuckle bolt.
12. Remove the knuckle from the vehicle.

To install:

13. Install the trailing arm to knuckle bolts and tighten to 133 ft. lbs. 180 Nm).
14. Install the upper control arm to knuckle bolt and nut.
15. Tighten the bolt and nut to 81 ft. lbs. (110 Nm) plus 70°.
16. Install the toe link. Tighten the bolt and nut to 81 ft. lbs. (110 Nm) plus 70°.
17. Install the coil spring.

Fig. 218 Upper control arm to knuckle bolt

18. Install the lower shock absorber to knuckle bolt and tighten to 133 ft. lbs. (180 Nm)
19. Install the stabilizer link to the knuckle and tighten to 41 ft. lbs. (55 Nm).
20. Install the rear wheel bearing and brake components.
21. Install the tire and wheel.
22. Lower the vehicle.

LOWER CONTROL ARM

REMOVAL & INSTALLATION

See Figure 219.

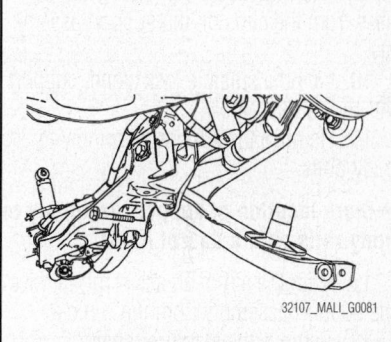

Fig. 219 Removal and installation of the lower control arm

1. Before servicing the vehicle, refer to the Precautions Section.
2. Raise and support the vehicle.
3. Remove the tire and wheel.
4. Remove the rear spring.
5. Remove the lower control arm to support assembly bolt and nut.
6. Remove the lower control arm from the vehicle.
7. Remove the lower control arm spring insulators. Inspect the lower spring insulator for damage and replace as necessary.

To install:

8. Install the lower control arm spring insulators.
9. Position the lower control arm to the support assembly.
10. Install the lower control arm to support assembly bolt and nut, and tighten the nut and bolt to 81 ft. lbs. (110 Nm).
11. Install the rear spring.
12. Install the tire and wheel.
13. Lower the vehicle.
14. Check the rear alignment.

REAR SUPPORT ASSEMBLY

REMOVAL & INSTALLATION

See Figure 220.

1. Before servicing the vehicle, refer to the Precautions Section.
2. Raise and support the vehicle.
3. Remove the rear wheels.
4. Remove the muffler.
5. Remove the lower control arms.

➡ **When replacing complete module assembly, mark fastener location of axle bracket (LH/RH) to body rail.**

6. Remove the upper control arm to support assembly bolts and nuts.
7. Remove the toe links.
8. Remove the stabilizer shaft to knuckle bolts.
9. Disconnect the vehicle wiring harness from the clips on the support assembly.
10. Using a suitable jack stand, support the support assembly.
11. Remove the support assembly to body bolts.

➡ **Mark location of support assembly to body rails with a dab of paint.**

12. With the aid of an assistant, remove the support assembly from the vehicle.
13. Remove the stabilizer shaft.

To install:
14. Install the stabilizer shaft.
15. With the aid of an assistant, position the support assembly to the vehicle.
16. Using a suitable jack stand, support the support assembly.

17. Install the support assembly to body bolts. Tighten the bolts to 74 ft. lbs. (100 Nm) plus 30°.
18. Remove the jack stand.
19. Install the muffler.
20. Connect the vehicle wiring harness to the clips on the support assembly.
21. Install the stabilizer shaft to knuckle bolts and tighten to 37 ft. lbs. (50 Nm).
22. Install the toe links.
23. Install the upper control arm to support assembly bolts and nuts.
24. Tighten the bolts and nuts to 44 ft. lbs. (60 Nm) plus an additional 60°.
25. Install the lower control arms.
26. Install the rear wheels.
27. Lower the vehicle.
28. Adjust the rear alignment.

STABILIZER SHAFT & LINKS

REMOVAL & INSTALLATION

See Figures 221 and 222.

1. Before servicing the vehicle, refer to the Precautions Section.
2. Raise and support the vehicle.
3. Scribe a line on the rear camber adjust bolts (both left and right).
4. Remove the toe link.
5. Remove the stabilizer shaft bracket bolts.
6. Remove the stabilizer shaft insulators from the stabilizer shaft.

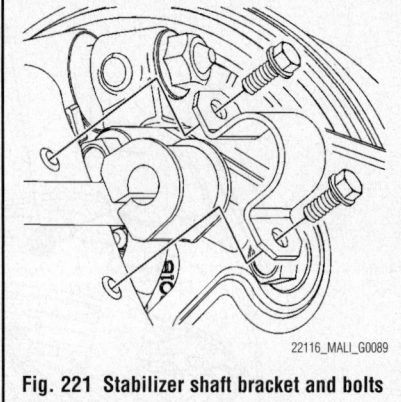
Fig. 221 Stabilizer shaft bracket and bolts

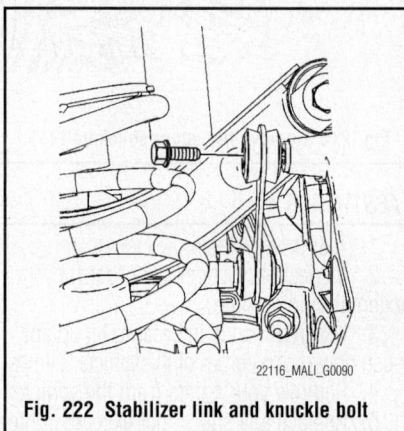
Fig. 222 Stabilizer link and knuckle bolt

7. Remove the stabilizer link to knuckle bolts.
8. Remove the stabilizer shaft.

To install:
9. Install the stabilizer shaft
10. Install the stabilizer shaft insulators.
11. Install the stabilizer shaft brackets.
12. Install the stabilizer shaft bracket bolts and tighten to 26 ft. lbs. (35 Nm).
13. Install the stabilizer shaft links to knuckle bolts and tighten to 41 ft. lbs. (55 Nm).
14. Install the toe link. Tighten the bolt and nut to 81 ft. lbs. (110 Nm) plus 70°.
15. Lower the vehicle.

TOE LINK

REMOVAL & INSTALLATION

See Figure 223.

1. Before servicing the vehicle, refer to the Precautions Section.
2. Raise and support the vehicle.
3. Remove the tire and wheel.
4. Remove the toe link to steering knuckle bolt.
5. Remove the toe link to support assembly bolt and nut.

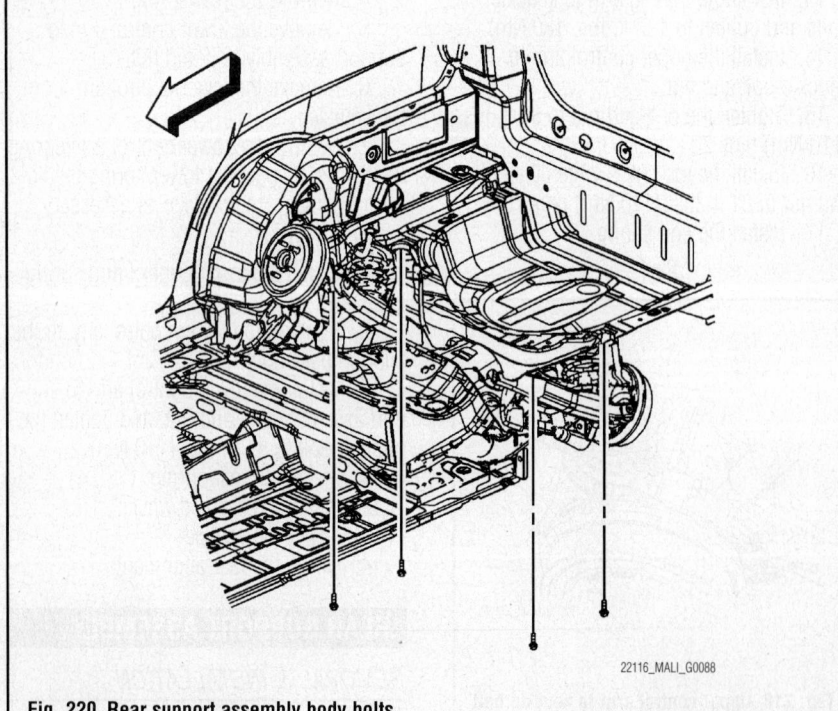
Fig. 220 Rear support assembly body bolts

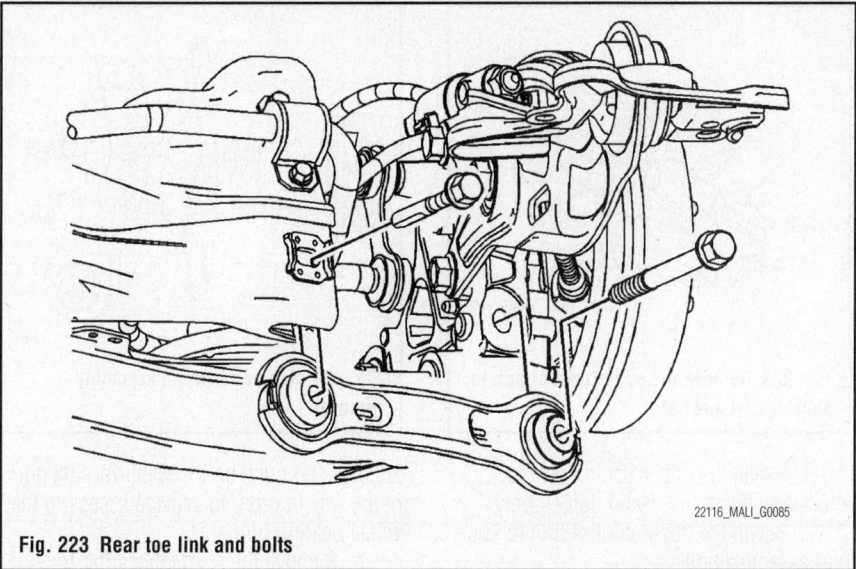

Fig. 223 Rear toe link and bolts

6. Remove the toe link from the rear support assembly and vehicle.

To install:

7. Install the toe link into the support assembly

8. Loosely install the toe assembly bolt and nut.

9. Install the toe link to steering knuckle and tighten as follows:
- Tighten the bolt and nut to 81 ft. lbs. (110 Nm) plus 70°.
- Tighten the toe assembly bolt and nut to 81 ft. lbs. (110 Nm) plus 70°.

10. Install the tire and wheel.

11. Lower the vehicle.

12. Adjust the rear toe.

TRAILING ARMS

REMOVAL & INSTALLATION

See Figures 224 through 226.

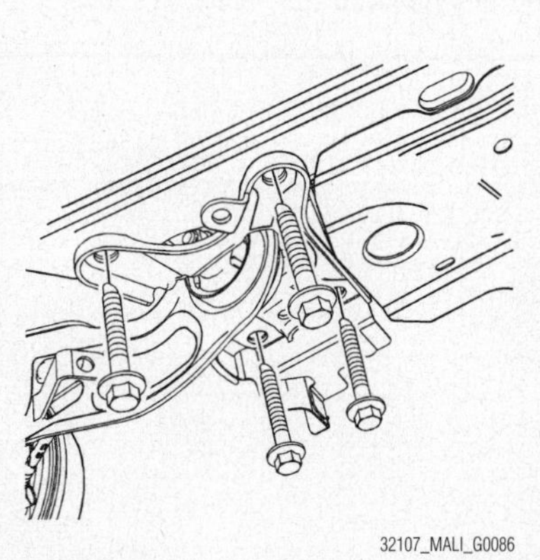

1. Before servicing the vehicle, refer to the Precautions Section.

2. Raise and support the vehicle.

3. Remove the tire and wheel.

4. Remove the trailing arm bracket to body bolts.

5. Remove the trailing arm to knuckle through bolt.

6. Disconnect the parking brake cable from the trailing arm.

7. Remove the trailing arm from the vehicle.

8. Remove the trailing arm to bracket bolt and nut.

9. Remove the trailing arm from the bracket.

To install:

10. Assemble the trailing arm and bracket, and tighten the trailing arm to bracket through bolt to 44 ft. lbs. (60 Nm) plus 60 degrees.

11. Position the trailing arm to the vehicle.

12. Install the trailing arm to knuckle bolts, and tighten the bolts to 133 ft. lbs. (180 Nm).

13. Connect the parking brake cable to the trailing arm.

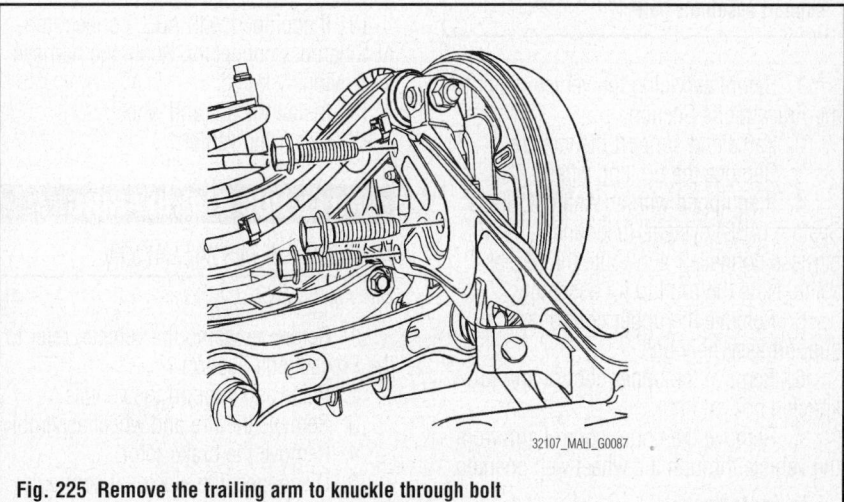

Fig. 225 Remove the trailing arm to knuckle through bolt

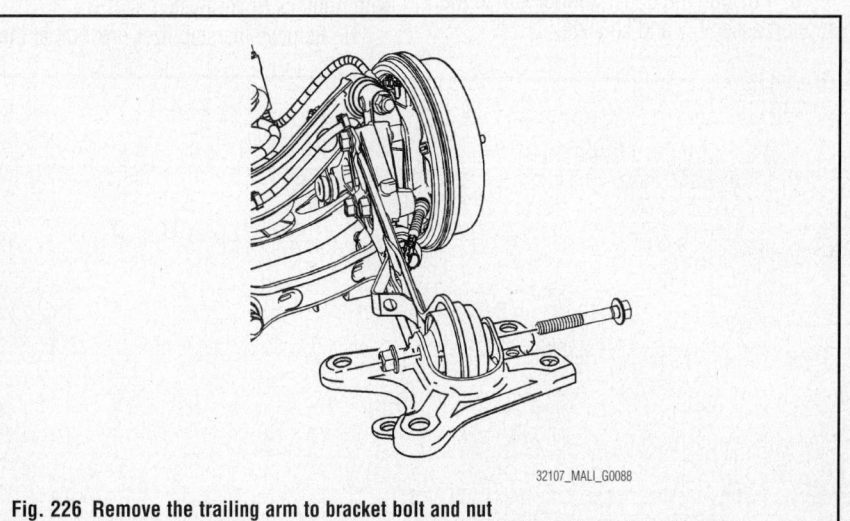

Fig. 224 Remove the trailing arm bracket to body bolts

Fig. 226 Remove the trailing arm to bracket bolt and nut

14. Install the trailing arm bracket to body bolts, and tighten the bracket to body bolts to 66 ft. lbs. (90 Nm) plus 30 degrees plus an additional 15 degrees.

15. Install the tire and wheel.

16. Lower the vehicle.

UPPER CONTROL ARM

REMOVAL & INSTALLATION

See Figures 227 and 228.

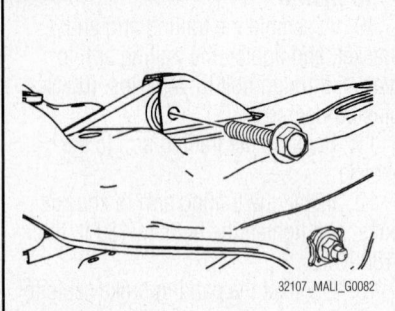

Fig. 227 Remove the upper control arm to support assembly bolt

1. Before servicing the vehicle, refer to the Precautions Section.

2. Raise and support the vehicle.

3. Remove the tire and wheel.

4. If equipped with an Antilock Brake System (ABS) system, disconnect the ABS harness connector and route the harness aside. Note the routing for assembly.

5. Remove the upper control arm to support assembly bolt.

6. Remove the upper control arm to knuckle bolt and nut.

7. Remove the upper control arm from the vehicle through the wheel well opening.

To install:

8. Position the upper control arm to the support assembly and knuckle.

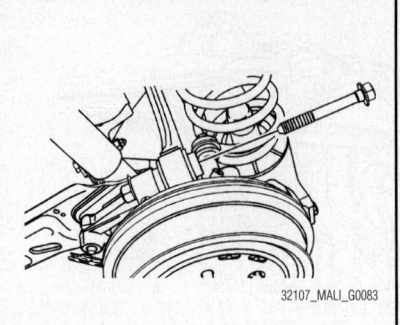

Fig. 228 Remove the upper control arm to knuckle bolt and nut

9. Install the upper control arm to knuckle bolt and nut. Hand tighten only.

10. Install the upper control arm to support assembly bolt.

11. Tighten the upper control arm to support assembly bolt to 44 ft. lbs. (60 Nm) plus 60 degrees.

12. Tighten the upper control arm to knuckle bolt to 81 ft. lbs. (110 Nm) plus 70 degrees.

13. If equipped with ABS, connect the ABS harness connector. Route the harness as previously noted.

14. Install the tire and wheel.

15. Lower the vehicle.

WHEEL HUB AND BEARING

REMOVAL & INSTALLATION

See Figure 229.

1. Before servicing the vehicle, refer to the Precautions Section.

2. Raise and support the vehicle.

3. Remove the tire and wheel assembly.

4. Remove the brake rotor.

5. Disconnect the electrical connector from the wheel speed sensor, if equipped with Antilock Brake System (ABS).

6. Remove the stabilizer link bolt at the

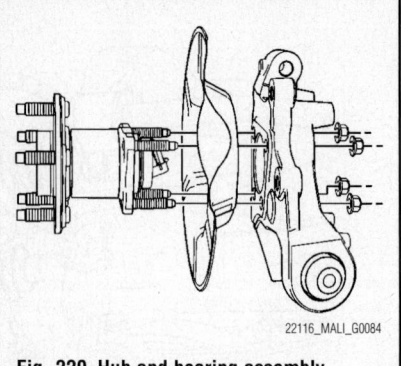

Fig. 229 Hub and bearing assembly removal

knuckle and position the stabilizer link out of the way in order to provide access to the wheel bearing hub nuts.

7. Remove the 4 wheel bearing hub assembly nuts.

8. Remove the wheel bearing hub assembly from the knuckle.

To install:

9. Install the wheel bearing hub assembly to the knuckle.

10. Install the 4 wheel bearing hub assembly nuts and tighten to 47 ft. lbs. (63 Nm).

11. Connect the stabilizer link bolt at the knuckle and tighten to 41 ft. lbs. (55 Nm).

12. Connect the electrical connector to the wheel speed sensor, if equipped with ABS.

13. Install the brake rotor.

14. Install the tire and wheel assembly.

15. Lower the vehicle.

ADJUSTMENT

These vehicles are equipped with sealed hub and bearing assemblies. The hub and bearing assemblies are non-serviceable. If the assembly is damaged, the complete unit must be replaced.

BUICK, CHEVROLET, PONTIAC AND SATURN

Montana • Relay • Terraza • Uplander

18

SPECIFICATIONS AND MAINTENANCE CHARTS

ENGINE AND VEHICLE IDENTIFICATION

	Engine						Model Year	
Code ①	Liters (cc)	Cu. In.	Cyl.	Fuel Sys.	Engine Type	Eng. Mfg.	Code ②	Year
L	3.5 (3497)	214	6	SFI	DOHC	CPC	5	2005
1	3.9 (3884)	238	6	SFI	DOHC	CPC	6	2006
W	3.9 (3884)	238	6	SFI (FFV)	DOHC	CPC	7	2007

CPC: Chevrolet/Pontiac/Canada

SFI: Sequential Fuel Injection

FFV: Flexible Fuel Vehicle

① 8th position of VIN

② 10th position of VIN

22116_TERR_C0001

GENERAL ENGINE SPECIFICATIONS

All measurements are given in inches.

Year	Model	Engine Displacement Liters (cc)	Engine Series VIN	Net Horsepower @ rpm	Net Torque @ rpm (ft. lbs.)	Bore x Stroke (in.)	Compression Ratio	Oil Pressure @ rpm
2005	Montana SV6	3.5 (3497)	L	200@5200	200@5200	3.70x3.31	9.8:1	30-45@1850
	Terraza	3.5 (3497)	L	200@5200	200@5200	3.70x3.31	9.8:1	30-45@1850
	Relay	3.5 (3497)	L	200@5200	200@5200	3.70x3.31	9.8:1	30-45@1850
	Uplander	3.5 (3497)	L	200@5200	220@4400	3.70x3.31	9.8:1	30-45@1850
2006	Montana SV6	3.5 (3497)	L	200@5200	200@5200	3.70x3.31	9.8:1	30-45@1850
	Montana SV6 AWD	3.5 (3497)	L	196@5600	213@3200	3.70x3.31	9.8:1	30-45@1850
	Montana SV6	3.9 (3884)	1	240@6000	240@4800	3.90x3.31	9.8:1	30-45@1850
	Terraza	3.5 (3497)	L	200@5200	200@5200	3.70x3.31	9.8:1	30-45@1850
	Terraza AWD	3.5 (3497)	L	196@5600	213@3200	3.70x3.31	9.8:1	30-45@1850
	Terraza	3.9 (3884)	1	240@6000	240@4800	3.90x3.31	9.8:1	30-45@1850
	Relay	3.5 (3497)	L	200@5200	200@5200	3.70x3.31	9.8:1	30-45@1850
	Relay AWD	3.5 (3497)	L	196@5600	213@3200	3.70x3.31	9.8:1	30-45@1850
	Relay 3	3.9 (3884)	1	240@6000	240@4800	3.90x3.31	9.8:1	30-45@1850
	Uplander	3.5 (3497)	L	201@5600	216@4000	3.70x3.31	9.8:1	30-45@1850
	Uplander AWD	3.5 (3497)	L	196@5600	213@3200	3.70x3.31	9.8:1	30-45@1850
	Uplander 2LT/3LT	3.9 (3884)	1	240@6000	240@4800	3.90x3.31	9.8:1	30-45@1850
2007	Terraza	3.9 (3884)	1/W	240@6000	240@4800	3.90x3.31	9.8:1	30-45@1850
	Relay	3.9 (3884)	1/W	240@6000	240@4800	3.90x3.31	9.8:1	30-45@1850
	Uplander	3.9 (3884)	1/W	240@6000	240@4800	3.90x3.31	9.8:1	30-45@1850

22116_TERR_C0002

GASOLINE ENGINE TUNE-UP SPECIFICATIONS

Year	Engine Displacement Liters	Engine VIN	Spark Plug Gap (in.)	Ignition Timing (deg) AT	Fuel Pump (psi)	Idle Speed (rpm) AT	Valve Clearance In.	Valve Clearance Ex.
2005	3.5	L	0.060	①	50-60	②	HYD	HYD
2006	3.5	L	0.060	①	50-60	②	HYD	HYD
	3.9	1	0.040	①	NA	②	HYD	HYD
2007	3.9	1/W	0.040	①	NA	②	HYD	HYD

NOTE: The Vehicle Emission Control Information label often reflects specification changes made during production.

The label figures must be used if they differ from those in this chart.

HYD: Hydraulic

① Ignition timing is preset and cannot be adjusted

② Idle speed is maintained by the PCM

22116_TERR_C0003

CAPACITIES

Year	Model	Engine Displacement Liters	Engine VIN	Engine Oil with Filter (qts.)	Transmission (pts.) * AWD	Transmission (pts.) * 2WD	Transfer Case (pts.)	Drive Axle Rear (pts.)	Fuel Tank (gal.)	Cooling System (qts.)
2005	Montana SV6	3.5	L	4	27.6	26.8	NA	4.2	20 ①	②
	Terraza	3.5	L	4	27.6	26.8	NA	4.2	20 ①	②
	Relay	3.5	L	4	27.6	26.8	NA	4.2	20 ①	②
	Uplander	3.5	L	4	27.6	26.8	NA	4.2	20 ①	②
2006	Montana SV6	3.5	L	4	27.6	26.8	NA	4.2	20 ①	②
	Montana SV6	3.9	1	4	NA	26.8	NA	4.2	20 ①	③
	Terraza	3.5	L	4	27.6	26.8	NA	4.2	25.1	②
	Terraza	3.9	1	4	NA	26.8	NA	4.2	25.1	③
	Relay	3.5	L	4	27.6	26.8	NA	4.2	25.1	②
	Relay 3	3.9	1	4	NA	26.8	NA	4.2	25.1	③
	Uplander	3.5	L	4	27.6	26.8	NA	4.2	20 ①	②
	Uplander 2LT/3LT	3.9	1	4	NA	26.8	NA	4.2	20 ①	③
2007	Terraza	3.9	1/W	4	NA	26.8	NA	NA	25.1	③
	Relay	3.9	1/W	4	NA	26.8	NA	NA	25.1	③
	Uplander	3.9	1/W	4	NA	26.8	NA	NA	20 ①	③

NOTE: All capacities are approximate. Add fluid gradually and check to be sure a proper fluid level is obtained.

NA: Not available

* Dry fill.

① Extended: 25.1 gal.

② Without rear A/C: 11.3 qts.
   With rear A/C: 12.8 qts.

③ Without rear A/C: 10.8 qts.
   With rear A/C: 12.1 qts.

22116_TERR_C0004

FLUID SPECIFICATIONS

Year	Model	Engine Displacement Liters	Engine ID/VIN	Engine Oil	Auto. Trans.	Drive Axle	Power Steering Fluid	Brake Master Cylinder ①
2005	Montana SV6	3.5	L	5W-30	DEXRON® III	VERSATRAK Fluid	GM PS Fluid	Delco® Supreme 11
	Terraza	3.5	L	5W-30	DEXRON® III	VERSATRAK Fluid	GM PS Fluid	Delco® Supreme 11
	Relay	3.5	L	5W-30	DEXRON® III	VERSATRAK Fluid	GM PS Fluid	Delco® Supreme 11
	Uplander	3.5	L	5W-30	DEXRON® III	VERSATRAK Fluid	GM PS Fluid	Delco® Supreme 11
2006	Montana SV6	3.5	L	5W-30	DEXRON® VI	VERSATRAK Fluid	GM PS Fluid	Delco® Supreme 11
	Montana SV6	3.9	1	5W-30	DEXRON® VI	VERSATRAK Fluid	GM PS Fluid	Delco® Supreme 11
	Terraza	3.5	L	5W-30	DEXRON® VI	VERSATRAK Fluid	GM PS Fluid	Delco® Supreme 11
	Terraza	3.9	1	5W-30	DEXRON® VI	VERSATRAK Fluid	GM PS Fluid	Delco® Supreme 11
	Relay	3.5	L	5W-30	DEXRON® VI	VERSATRAK Fluid	GM PS Fluid	Delco® Supreme 11
	Relay 3	3.9	1	5W-30	DEXRON® VI	VERSATRAK Fluid	GM PS Fluid	Delco® Supreme 11
	Uplander	3.5	L	5W-30	DEXRON® VI	VERSATRAK Fluid	GM PS Fluid	Delco® Supreme 11
	Uplander 2LT/3LT	3.9	1	5W-30	DEXRON® VI	VERSATRAK Fluid	GM PS Fluid	Delco® Supreme 11
2007	Terraza	3.9	1/W	5W-30	DEXRON® VI	VERSATRAK Fluid	GM PS Fluid	Delco® Supreme 11
	Relay	3.9	1/W	5W-30	DEXRON® VI	VERSATRAK Fluid	GM PS Fluid	Delco® Supreme 11
	Uplander	3.9	1/W	5W-30	DEXRON® VI	VERSATRAK Fluid	GM PS Fluid	Delco® Supreme 11

DOT: Department Of Transpotation

① Equivalent DOT 3 may be substituted

22116_TERR_C0005

VALVE SPECIFICATIONS

Year	Engine Displacement Liters	Engine ID/VIN	Seat Angle (deg.)	Face Angle (deg.)	Spring Test Pressure (lbs. @ in.)	Spring Installed Height (in.)	Stem-to-Guide Clearance (in.)		Stem Diameter (in.)	
							Intake	Exhaust	Intake	Exhaust
2005	3.5	L	46	45	234@1.299	1.740	0.0010-0.0027	0.0010-0.0027	NA	NA
2006	3.5	L	46	45	234@1.299	1.740	0.0010-0.0027	0.0010-0.0027	NA	NA
	3.9	1	46	45	234@1.299	1.740	0.0010-0.0027	0.0010-0.0027	NA	NA
2007	3.9	1/W	46	45	230@1.260	1.701	0.0010-0.0027	0.0010-0.0027	NA	NA

NA: Not Available

22116_TERR_C0008

CAMSHAFT AND BEARING SPECIFICATIONS CHART

All measurements are given in inches.

Year	Engine Displacement Liters	Engine VIN	Journal Diameter	Brg. Oil Clearance	Shaft End-play	Runout	Journal Bore	Lobe Lift	
								Intake	Exhaust
2005	3.5	L	1.8680-1.8690	NA	NA	0.0001	1.8710-1.8720	0.2727	0.2727
2006	3.5	L	1.8680-1.8690	NA	NA	0.0001	1.8710-1.8720	0.2727	0.2727
	3.9	1	2.0240-2.0250	NA	NA	0.0010	2.0280-2.0290	0.2727	0.2727
2007	3.9	1/W	2.0240-2.0250	NA	NA	0.0010	2.0280-2.0290	0.2727	0.2727

NA: Not Available

22116_TERR_C0007

CRANKSHAFT AND CONNECTING ROD SPECIFICATIONS

All measurements are given in inches.

Year	Engine Displacement Liters	Engine VIN	Crankshaft				Connecting Rod		
			Main Brg. Journal Dia.	Main Brg. Oil Clearance	Shaft End-play	Thrust on No.	Journal Diameter	Oil Clearance	Side Clearance
2005	3.5	L	2.6473-2.6483	0.0008-0.0025	0.0024-0.0083	3	2.2490-2.2500	0.0007-0.0170	0.0080-0.0090
2005	3.5	L	2.6473-2.6483	0.0008-0.0025	0.0024-0.0083	3	2.2490-2.2500	0.0007-0.0170	0.0080-0.0090
	3.9	1	NA	①	0.0024-0.0083	3	2.2480-2.2490	0.0007-0.0024	0.0080-0.0090
2007	3.9	1/W	NA	①	0.0024-0.0083	3	2.2480-2.2490	0.0007-0.0024	0.0080-0.0090

Not Available

① Except no. 3: 0.0008 - 0.0025 in.
   No. 3: 0.0012 - 0.0030 in.

22116_TERR_C0006

PISTON AND RING SPECIFICATIONS

All measurements are given in inches.

| Year | Engine Displ. Liters | Engine VIN | Piston Clearance | Ring Gap | | | Ring Side Clearance | | |
				Top Compression	Bottom Compression	Oil Control	Top Compression	Bottom Compression	Oil Control
2005	3.5	L	0.0011-0.0110	0.0070-0.0150	0.0190-0.0290	0.010-0.029	0.0010-0.0030	0.0020-0.0030	0.0040
2006	3.5	L	0.0011-0.0110	0.0070-0.0150	0.0190-0.0290	0.010-0.029	0.0010-0.0030	0.0020-0.0030	0.0040
	3.9	1	0.0003-0.0018	0.0060-0.0110	0.0090-0.0170	0.006-0.025	0.0010-0.002	0.0007-0.0020	0.0040
2007	3.9	1/W	0.0003-0.0018	0.0060-0.0110	0.0090-0.0170	0.006-0.025	0.0010-0.0020	0.0007-0.0020	0.0040

22116_TERR_C0009

TORQUE SPECIFICATIONS

All readings in ft. lbs.

| Year | Engine Displacement Liters | Engine VIN | Cylinder Head Bolts | Main Bearing Bolts | Rod Bearing Bolts | Crankshaft Damper Bolts | Flywheel Bolts | Manifold | | Spark Plugs | Oil Pan Drain Plug |
								Intake	Exhaust		
2005	3.5	L	①	②	③	118	52	④	13	11	18
2006	3.5	L	①	②	③	118	52	④	13	11	18
	3.9	1	①	②	③	⑤	52	④	15	11	18
2007	3.9	1/W	①	②	③	⑤	52	④	15	11	18

① 1st pass: 44 ft. lbs.
2nd pass: Plus 95 degrees

② 1st pass: 37 ft. lbs.
2nd pass: plus 77 degrees

③ 1st pass: 18 ft. lbs.
2nd pass: plus 110 degrees

④ 1st pass: 115 in. lbs.
2nd pass: Center bolts 15 ft. lbs.
2nd pass: Corner bolts 18 ft. lbs.

⑤ 1st pass: 92 ft. lbs.
2nd pass: plus 130 degrees

22116_TERR_C0010

WHEEL ALIGNMENT

| Year | All Models | | Caster | | Camber | | Toe-in (Deg.) |
			Range (+/-Deg.)	Preferred Setting (Deg.)	Range (+/-Deg.)	Preferred Setting (Deg.)	
2005	Twist Axle	Front	0.75	2.70	0.75	-0.65	0+/-0.20
		Rear	--	--	0.50	-1.00	0+/-0.30
	IRS	Front	0.75	2.70	0.75	-0.65	0+/-0.20
		Rear	--	--	0.50	-1.00	0+/-0.30
2006	Twist Axle	Front	0.75	2.70	0.75	-0.65	0+/-0.20
		Rear	--	--	0.50	-1.00	0+/-0.30
	IRS	Front	0.75	2.70	0.75	-0.65	0+/-0.20
		Rear	--	--	0.50	-1.00	0+/-0.30
2007	Twist Axle	Front	0.75	2.70	0.75	-0.65	0+/-0.20
		Rear	--	--	0.50	-1.00	0+/-0.30
	IRS	Front	0.75	2.70	0.75	-0.65	0+/-0.20
		Rear	--	--	0.50	-1.00	0+/-0.30

(IRS) - Independent Rear Suspension

(--) No adjustment provided

22116_TERR_C0011

TIRE, WHEEL AND BALL JOINT SPECIFICATIONS

| Year | Model | OEM Tires | | Tire Pressures (psi) | | Wheel Size | Ball Joint Inspection | Wheel Lug Nut Torque (Ft. Lbs.) |
		Standard	Optional	Front	Rear			
2005	All	P225/60R17	None	①	①	NA	②	100
2006	All	P225/60R17	None	①	①	NA	②	100
2007	All	P225/60R17	None	①	①	NA	②	100

NA: Not Available

OEM: Original Equipment Manufacturer

PSI: Pounds Per Square Inch

STD: Standard

OPT: Optional

① A tire and loading Information label is attached to the vehicle's center pillar (B-pillar), below the driver's door latch. This label shows your vehicle's original equipment tires and the correct inflation pressures for your tires when they are cold. The recommended cold tire inflation pressure, shown on the label, is the minimum amount of air pressure needed to support your vehicle's maximum load carrying capacity.

② Horizontal and vertical play, unloaded: 0.125 in. max.

22116_TERR_C0013

BRAKE SPECIFICATIONS
All measurements in inches unless noted

| Year | Model | | Brake Disc | | | Minimum Lining Thickness | Brake Caliper | |
			Original Thickness	Minimum Thickness	Maximum Runout		Bracket Bolts (ft. lbs.)	Mounting Bolts (ft. lbs.)
2005	All	F	1.270	1.210	0.002	NA	137	40
		R	0.472	0.413	0.002	NA	96	25
2006	All	F	1.270	1.210	0.002	NA	137	40
		R	0.472	0.413	0.002	NA	96	25
2007	All	F	1.270	1.210	0.002	NA	137	40
		R	0.472	0.413	0.002	NA	96	25

22116_TERR_C0012

MAINTENANCE I AND II SERVICE SCHEDULES
2005-07 Buick Terraza, Chevrolet Uplander, Pontiac Montana SV6, Saturn Relay

When the CHANGE ENGINE OIL light appears, certain services and inspections are required. Services are described below. Generally, it is recommended that the first service be Maintenance I, second service be Maintenance II, and that services are then alternated from Maintenance I and Maintenance II thereafter. In some cases, Maintenance II may be Required services are described as Maintenance I and Maintenance II.

The first service of a vehicle should be Maintance I, and the second service should be Maintenance II.

Alternate between the 2 services thereafter. However, in some cases, Maintenance II may be required more often.

Maintenance I: Use Maintenance I if the CHANGE ENGINE OIL light comes on within 10 months since the vehicle was purcahses or, if Maintenance II was performed.

Maintenance II: Use Maintenance II if the previous service performed was Maintenance I. Always used Maintenance II whenever the CHANGE ENGINE OIL light comes on 10 months or more since the last service, or, if the CHANGE ENGINE OIL light has not come on at all for one year.

Service	Maintenance I	Maintenance II
Change engine oil and filter. Reset oil life system.	✓	✓
Visually check for any leaks or damage. A fluid loss in the vehicle system could indicate a problem. Inspect, repair and add fluid to the system, if necessary.	✓	✓
Inspect engine air cleaner filter. If necessary, replace filter.	—	✓
Rotate tires and check inflation pressures and wear.	✓	✓
Visually inspect brake lines and hoses for proper hook-up, binding, leaks, cracks, chafing, etc. Inspect the disc brake pads for wear and the rotors for surface condition. Inspect the drum brake lings for wear or cracks. Inspect other brake parts, including drums, wheel cylinders, calipers, parking brake, etc. Inspect parking brake adjustment.	✓	✓
Check engine coolant and windshield washer fluid levels and add fluid as needed.	✓	✓
Inspect the suspension and steering components. Inspect the front and rear suspension systems and steering system for damaged, loose, or missing parts, or signs of wear. Inspect the power steering lines and the hoses for proper hook-up, binding, leaks, cracks, chafing, etc.	—	✓
Inspect the coolant hoses and replace the hoses if they are crackes, swollen or deteriorated. Inspect all pipes, fittings and clamps; replace with OEM parts as needed. To help ensure proper operation, a pressure test of the cooling system and pressure cap, and cleaning the outside of the radiator and A/C condesnser is recommended at least once a year.	—	✓
Inspect wiper blades for wear or cracking		✓
Inspect restraint system components.	—	✓
Lubricate all key lock cylinders, latch assemblies and hinges		✓
Inspect the transmission and transaxle fluid level and add fluid as needed.	—	✓
Replace passenger compartment air filter.		✓
Inspect throttle system	—	✓

To reset the CHANGE ENGINE OIL LIGHT:

1. Press the up or down arrow to scroll the DIC to show OIL LIFE.

2. Once the XXX% ENGINE OIL LIFE menu item is highlighted, press and hold the RESET button until the percentage shows 100%. If the percentage does not return to 100% or if the CHANGE ENGINE OIL SOON message comes back on when the vehicle is started, the engine oil life system was not properly reset. Repeat the procedure.

22116_TERR_C0014

ADDITIONAL MAINTENANCE SERVICES
2005-07 Buick Terraza, Chevrolet Uplander, Pontiac Montana SV6, Saturn Relay

TO BE SERVICED	TYPE OF SERVICE	VEHICLE MILEAGE INTERVAL (x1000)					
		25	50	75	100	125	150
Air cleaner filter	R		✓		✓		✓
Accessory drive belt	I						✓
Auto. Trans. Fluid ①	R		✓		✓		✓
Cooling system hoses and clamps	S/I						✓
Transfer case fluid	R		✓		✓		✓
Throttle body	I	✓	✓	✓	✓	✓	✓
Engine coolant	R						✓
Fuel system	I	✓	✓	✓	✓	✓	✓
Exhaust system & heat shields	S/I	✓	✓	✓	✓	✓	✓
Spark plugs	R				✓		

R: Replace

S/I: Inspect and service, if necessary

① Replace if any of the following condition are met:

Heavy city traffic where the outside temperature regularly reaches 90oF (32oC) or higher.

Hilly or mountainous terrain

Frequent trailer towing

Taxi, police or delivery service

Otherwise, change every 100,000 miles

22116_TERR_C0015

PRECAUTIONS

Before servicing any vehicle, please be sure to read all of the following precautions, which deal with personal safety, prevention of component damage, and important points to take into consideration when servicing a motor vehicle:

• Never open, service or drain the radiator or cooling system when the engine is hot; serious burns can occur from the steam and hot coolant.

• Observe all applicable safety precautions when working around fuel. Whenever servicing the fuel system, always work in a well-ventilated area. Do not allow fuel spray or vapors to come in contact with a spark, open flame, or excessive heat (a hot drop light, for example). Keep a dry chemical fire extinguisher near the work area. Always keep fuel in a container specifically designed for fuel storage; also, always properly seal fuel containers to avoid the possibility of fire or explosion. Refer to the additional fuel system precautions later in this section.

• Fuel injection systems often remain pressurized, even after the engine has been turned **OFF**. The fuel system pressure must be relieved before disconnecting any fuel lines. Failure to do so may result in fire and/or personal injury.

• Brake fluid often contains polyglycol ethers and polyglycols. Avoid contact with the eyes and wash your hands thoroughly after handling brake fluid. If you do get brake fluid in your eyes, flush your eyes with clean, running water for 15 minutes. If eye irritation persists, or if you have taken brake fluid internally, IMMEDIATELY seek medical assistance.

• The EPA warns that prolonged contact with used engine oil may cause a number of skin disorders, including cancer. You should make every effort to minimize your exposure to used engine oil. Protective gloves should be worn when changing oil. Wash your hands and any other exposed skin areas as soon as possible after exposure to used engine oil. Soap and water, or waterless hand cleaner should be used.

• All new vehicles are now equipped with an air bag system, often referred to as a Supplemental Restraint System (SRS) or Supplemental Inflatable Restraint (SIR) system. The system must be disabled before performing service on or around system components, steering column, instrument panel components, wiring and sensors. Failure to follow safety and disabling procedures could result in accidental air bag deployment, possible personal injury and unnecessary system repairs.

• Always wear safety goggles when working with, or around, the air bag system. When carrying a non-deployed air bag, be sure the bag and trim cover are pointed away from your body. When placing a non-deployed air bag on a work surface, always face the bag and trim cover upward, away from the surface. This will reduce the motion of the module if it is accidentally deployed. Refer to the additional air bag system precautions later in this section.

• Clean, high quality brake fluid from a sealed container is essential to the safe and proper operation of the brake system. You should always buy the correct type of brake fluid for your vehicle. If the brake fluid becomes contaminated, completely flush the system with new fluid. Never reuse any brake fluid. Any brake fluid that is removed from the system should be discarded. Also, do not allow any brake fluid to come in contact with a painted surface; it will damage the paint.

• Never operate the engine without the proper amount and type of engine oil; doing so WILL result in severe engine damage.

• Timing belt maintenance is extremely important. Many models utilize an interference-type, non-freewheeling engine. If the timing belt breaks, the valves in the cylinder head may strike the pistons, causing potentially serious (also time-consuming and expensive) engine damage. Refer to the maintenance interval charts for the recommended replacement interval for the timing belt, and to the timing belt section for belt replacement and inspection.

• Disconnecting the negative battery cable on some vehicles may interfere with the functions of the on-board computer system(s) and may require the computer to undergo a relearning process once the negative battery cable is reconnected.

• When servicing drum brakes, only disassemble and assemble one side at a time, leaving the remaining side intact for reference.

• Only an MVAC-trained, EPA-certified automotive technician should service the air conditioning system or its components.

BRAKES

GENERAL INFORMATION

PRECAUTIONS

• Certain components within the ABS system are not intended to be serviced or repaired individually.

• Do not use rubber hoses or other parts not specifically specified for and ABS system. When using repair kits, replace all parts included in the kit. Partial or incorrect repair may lead to functional problems and require the replacement of components.

• Lubricate rubber parts with clean, fresh brake fluid to ease assembly. Do not use shop air to clean parts; damage to rubber components may result.

• Use only DOT 3 brake fluid from an unopened container.

• If any hydraulic component or line is removed or replaced, it may be necessary to bleed the entire system.

• A clean repair area is essential. Always clean the reservoir and cap thoroughly before removing the cap. The slightest amount of dirt in the fluid may plug an orifice and impair the system function. Perform repairs after components have been thoroughly cleaned; use only denatured alcohol to clean components. Do not allow ABS components to come into contact with any substance containing mineral oil; this includes used shop rags.

• The Anti-Lock control unit is a microprocessor similar to other computer units in the vehicle. Ensure that the ignition switch is **OFF** before removing or installing con-

ANTI-LOCK BRAKE SYSTEM (ABS)

troller harnesses. Avoid static electricity discharge at or near the controller.

• If any arc welding is to be done on the vehicle, the control unit should be unplugged before welding operations begin.

SPEED SENSORS

REMOVAL & INSTALLATION

The wheel speed sensors and rings are integral with the hub and bearing assemblies. If a speed sensor or a ring needs replacement, replace the entire hub and bearing assembly. Do not service the harness pigtail individually because the harness pigtail is part of the sensor.

BRAKES   **BLEEDING THE BRAKE SYSTEM**

BLEEDING PROCEDURE

BLEEDING PROCEDURE

1. Place a clean shop cloth beneath the brake master cylinder to catch brake fluid spills.

2. With the ignition OFF and the brakes cool, apply the brakes 3-5 times, or until the brake pedal effort increases significantly, in order to deplete the brake booster power reserve.

3. If you have performed a brake master cylinder bench bleeding on this vehicle, or if you disconnected the brake pipes from the master cylinder, or if you have disconnected the brake pipes from the proportioning valve assembly or the brake modulator assembly, you must perform the following steps to bleed air at the ports of the hydraulic component:

a. Ensure that the brake master cylinder reservoir is full to the maximum-fill level. If necessary, add Delco Supreme 11, or equivalent DOT 3 brake fluid from a clean, sealed brake fluid container. If removal of the reservoir cap and diaphragm is necessary, clean the outside of the reservoir on and around the cap prior to removal.

b. With the brake pipes installed securely to the master cylinder, proportioning valve assembly, or brake modulator assembly, loosen and separate one of the brake pipes from the port of the component. For the proportioning valve assembly or the brake modulator assembly, perform these steps in the sequence of system flow; begin with the fluid feed pipes from the master cylinder.

c. Allow a small amount of brake fluid to gravity bleed from the open port of the component.

d. Connect the brake pipe to the component and tighten securely.

e. Have an assistant slowly press the brake pedal fully and maintain steady pressure on the pedal.

f. Loosen the same brake pipe to purge air from the open port of the component.

g. Tighten the brake pipe, then have the assistant slowly release the brake pedal.

h. Wait 15 seconds, then repeat the steps until all air is purged from the same port of the component.

i. With the brake pipe installed securely to the master cylinder, proportioning valve assembly, or brake modula-

tor assembly, after all air has been purged from the first port of the component that was bled, loosen and separate the next brake pipe from the component, then repeat the steps until each of the ports on the component has been bled.

j. After completing the final component port bleeding procedure, ensure that each of the brake pipe-to-component fittings are properly tightened.

4. Fill the brake master cylinder reservoir with Delco Supreme 11 or equivalent DOT 3 brake fluid from a clean, sealed brake fluid container. Ensure that the brake master cylinder reservoir remains at least half-full during this bleeding procedure. Add fluid as needed to maintain the proper level. Clean the outside of the reservoir on and around the reservoir cap prior to removing the cap and diaphragm.

5. Install a proper box-end wrench onto the RIGHT REAR wheel hydraulic circuit bleeder valve.

6. Install a transparent hose over the end of the bleeder valve.

7. Submerge the open end of the transparent hose into a transparent container partially filled with brake fluid from a clean, sealed brake fluid container.

8. Have an assistant slowly press the brake pedal fully and maintain steady pressure on the pedal.

9. Loosen the bleeder valve to purge air from the wheel hydraulic circuit.

10. Tighten the bleeder valve, then have the assistant slowly release the brake pedal.

11. Wait 15 seconds, then repeat the until all air is purged from the same wheel hydraulic circuit.

12. With the right rear wheel hydraulic circuit bleeder valve tightened securely, after all air has been purged from the right rear hydraulic circuit, install a proper box-end wrench onto the LEFT FRONT wheel hydraulic circuit bleeder valve.

13. Install a transparent hose over the end of the bleeder valve, then repeat the procedure.

14. With the left front wheel hydraulic circuit bleeder valve tightened securely, after all air has been purged from the left front hydraulic circuit, install a proper box-end wrench onto the LEFT REAR wheel hydraulic circuit bleeder valve.

15. Install a transparent hose over the end of the bleeder valve, then repeat the procedure.

16. With the left rear wheel hydraulic circuit bleeder valve tightened securely, after

all air has been purged from the left rear hydraulic circuit, install a proper box-end wrench onto the RIGHT FRONT wheel hydraulic circuit bleeder valve.

17. Install a transparent hose over the end of the bleeder valve, then repeat the procedure.

18. After completing the final wheel hydraulic circuit bleeding procedure, ensure that each of the 4 wheel hydraulic circuit bleeder valves are properly tightened.

19. Fill the brake master cylinder reservoir to the maximum-fill level with Delco Supreme 11, or equivalent DOT 3 brake fluid from a clean, sealed brake fluid container.

20. Slowly press and release the brake pedal. Observe the feel of the brake pedal.

21. If the brake pedal feels spongy, repeat the bleeding procedure again. If the brake pedal still feels spongy after repeating the bleeding procedure, perform the following steps:

a. Inspect the brake system for external leaks.

b. Pressure bleed the hydraulic brake system in order to purge any air that may still be trapped in the system.

c. Turn the ignition key ON, with the engine OFF. Check to see if the brake system warning lamp remains illuminated.

22. If the brake light is on, DO NOT allow the vehicle to be driven until it is diagnosed and repaired.

BLEEDING THE ABS SYSTEM

1. Raise and vehicle on a suitable support.

2. Turn the ignition switch to OFF position.

3. Remove all 4 tires, if necessary.

4. Connect the pressure bleeding tool according to the manufacturer's instructions.

5. Turn the ignition switch to RUN position, engine off.

6. Connect a scan tool and establish communications with the ABS system.

7. Pressurize the bleeding tool to 206-241 kPa (30-35 psi).

8. With the pressure bleeding tool at 206-241 kPa (30-35 psi), and all bleeder screws in closed position, select Automated Bleed Procedure on the scan tool and follow the instructions.

9. The first part of the automated bleed procedure will cycle the pump and front release valves for one minute. After the cycling has stopped the scan tool will

enter a "cool down" mode and display a 3 minute timer. The auto bleed will not continue until this timer expires, and cannot be overridden.

10. During the next step, the scan tool will request the technician to open one of the bleeder screws. The scan tool will then cycle the respective release valve and pump motor for 1 minute.

11. The scan tool will repeat the step for the remaining bleeder screws.

12. With the bleeder tool still attached to the vehicle and maintaining 241 kPa (35 psi), the scan tool will instruct the technician to independently open each bleeder screw for approximately 20 seconds. This should allow any remaining air to be purged from the brake lines.

13. When the automated bleed procedure is completed the scan tool will display the appropriate message.

14. Install all 4 tires, if necessary.

15. Remove pressure from the pressure bleeding tool and then disconnect the tool from the vehicle.

16. Depress the brake pedal to gage pedal height and feel. Repeat the steps until the pedal is acceptable.

17. Remove the scan tool from the DLC connector.

18. Lower the vehicle.

19. Inspect the brake fluid level in master cylinder.

20. Road test the vehicle while ensuring the brake pedal remains high and firm.

BRAKES

✳✳ CAUTION

Dust and dirt accumulating on brake parts during normal use may contain asbestos fibers from production or aftermarket brake linings. Breathing excessive concentrations of asbestos fibers can cause serious bodily harm. Exercise care when servicing brake parts. Do not sand or grind brake lining unless equipment used is designed to contain the dust residue. Do not clean brake parts with compressed air or by dry brushing. Cleaning should be done by dampening the brake components with a fine mist of water, then wiping the brake components clean with a dampened cloth. Dispose of cloth and all residue containing asbestos fibers in an impermeable container with the appropriate label. Follow practices prescribed by the Occupational Safety and Health Administration (OSHA) and the Environmental Protection Agency (EPA) for the handling, processing, and disposing of dust or debris that may contain asbestos fibers.

BRAKE CALIPER

REMOVAL & INSTALLATION
See Figure 1.

1. Before servicing the vehicle, refer to the Precautions Section.

➡Inspect the fluid level in the brake master cylinder reservoir. If the brake fluid level is midway between the maximum-full point and the minimum allowable level, then no brake fluid needs to be removed from the reservoir before proceeding. If the brake fluid level is higher than midway between the maximum full point and the minimum allowable level, then remove brake fluid to the midway point before proceeding.

2. Remove the wheel, marking the location of the wheel to the hub prior to removal. Mark the individual location of all retainers as they are removed.

3. Install two wheel lug nuts to retain the rotor to the hub

4. Install a large C-clamp over the top of the brake caliper and against the back of the outboard brake pad

5. Tighten the C-clamp until the caliper piston is pushed into the caliper bore enough to slide the caliper off the rotor

6. Remove or disconnect the following:
- Brake hose bolt
- Brake hose from the brake caliper
- Discard the two copper brake hose gaskets. These gaskets may be stuck to the brake caliper and/or the brake hose end
- Plug the openings in the brake caliper and the brake hose in order to prevent brake fluid loss and contamination.
- Clean off any dirt or corrosion on the brake caliper near the brake hose fitting
- Brake caliper bolts
- Brake caliper from the brake caliper bracket

➡Inspect the brake caliper pin boots, if the caliper pin boots are damaged, inspect the caliper pins for corrosion or damage. If corrosion is found on the brake caliper pin shaft, replace the brake caliper pin and the brake caliper pin boot. Do not attempt to polish away the corrosion.

To install:

7. Ensure that the caliper bolt boots are properly installed.

8. Install or connect the following:
- Caliper to the caliper bracket

FRONT DISC BRAKES

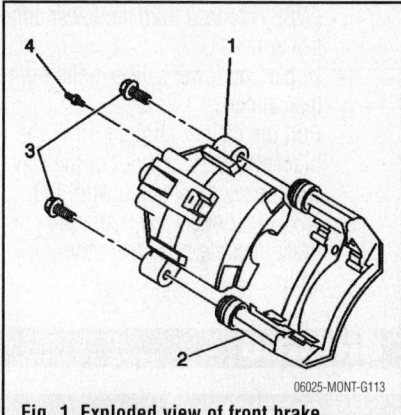

06025-MONT-G113

Fig. 1 Exploded view of front brake caliper assembly

- Caliper bolts and tighten the bolts to 40 ft. lbs. (54 Nm)

✳✳ WARNING

Install NEW copper brake hose gaskets

- Brake hose bolt and the NEW copper brake hose gaskets to the brake hose
- Brake hose bolt to the brake caliper and tighten the bolt to 40 ft. lbs. (54 Nm)

9. Install the tire and wheel assembly. Tighten the lug nuts to 100 ft. lbs. (140 Nm) in a criss—cross pattern, after aligning the wheel hub with the reference mark and holes as shown in appropriate illustration.

10. Refill the master cylinder to the correct level. Bleed the brake system.

DISC BRAKE PADS

REMOVAL & INSTALLATION

1. Before servicing the vehicle, refer to the Precautions Section.

➡Inspect the fluid level in the brake master cylinder reservoir. If the brake fluid level is midway between the maximum-full point and the minimum allowable level, then no brake fluid needs to be removed from the reservoir before proceeding. If the brake fluid level is higher than midway between the maximum full point and the minimum allowable level, then remove brake fluid to the midway point before proceeding.

2. Remove the wheel, marking the location of the wheel to the hub prior to removal. Mark the individual location of all retainers as they are removed.

3. Remove or disconnect the following:

- Unclamp the wheel speed sensor (WSS) harness from the lower control arm
- Upper and lower caliper bolts from the caliper
- Pull the caliper straight off of the bracket and secure out of the way with heavy mechanics wire. DO NOT disconnect the hydraulic brake flexible hose from the caliper

- Inboard and outboard pads from the brake caliper bracket

To install:

4. Clean the brake pad hardware mating surfaces on the caliper bracket of any debris or corrosion.

5. Inspect the brake pad retainer clips and replace, if necessary.

6. Inspect the piston boot. Replace if damaged.

7. Retract the brake caliper piston into the brake caliper bore. Use a suitable spanner type wrench and turn the piston clockwise until it bottoms out fully in the brake caliper.

8. Align the indents on the piston face to match the pin on the back of the inboard brake pads.

9. Install or connect the following:

- Brake pad retainers into the brake caliper bracket
- Inboard and outboard brake pads into the brake caliper bracket insuring that the pad with the metallic wear sensor is placed

on the inboard side of the bracket
- Slide the caliper onto the bracket insuring that the bracket guide boots are not damaged
- Brake caliper bolts and tighten the bolts to 25 ft. lbs. (34 Nm)
- WSS harness onto the lower control arm

10. Install the tire and wheel assembly. Tighten the lug nuts to 100 ft. lbs. (140 Nm) in a criss—cross pattern, after aligning the wheel hub with the reference mark and holes as shown in appropriate illustration.

11. Lower the vehicle.

12. With the engine OFF, gradually apply the brake pedal to approximately ⅔ of its travel distance. Slowly release the brake pedal.

13. Wait 15 seconds, then repeat steps until a firm brake pedal apply is obtained. This will properly seat the brake caliper pistons and brake pads.

14. Fill the brake master cylinder reservoir to the proper level.

BRAKES

BRAKE CALIPER

REMOVAL & INSTALLATION
See Figures 2 and 3.

1. Before servicing the vehicle, refer to the Precautions Section.

➡Inspect the fluid level in the brake master cylinder reservoir. If the brake fluid level is midway between the maximum-full point and the minimum allowable level, then no brake fluid needs to be removed from the reservoir before proceeding. If the brake fluid level is higher than midway between the maximum full point and the minimum allowable level, then remove brake fluid to the midway point before proceeding.

2. Remove the tire and wheel assembly

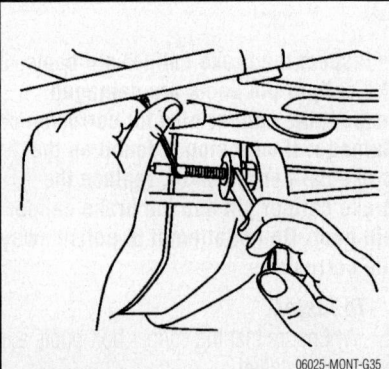

Fig. 2 Showing the park brake system equalizer

06025-MONT-G35

REAR DISC BRAKES

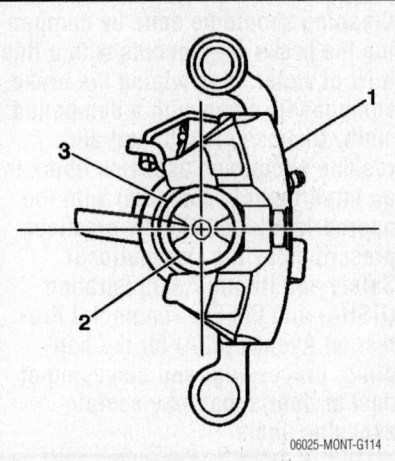

06025-MONT-G114

Fig. 3 Aligning indents on piston face during caliper installation

3. Release tension from the park brake system at the equalizer

4. Remove or disconnect the following:

- Front and rear cables from one another at the connector clip
- Park brake cable from the park brake lever on the brake caliper
- Park brake cable from the caliper bracket
- Brake hose to caliper bolt
- Brake hose from the brake caliper
- Discard the 2 copper brake hose gaskets. These gaskets may be

stuck to the brake caliper and/or the brake hose end
- Plug the opening in the brake caliper and brake hose to prevent fluid loss and/or contamination
- Brake caliper bolts
- Brake caliper

To install:

5. Align the indents on the piston face to match the pin on the brake pad.

6. Inspect the bracket bolt guide assembly.

7. Inspect the brake pad hardware and replace, if necessary.

8. Install or connect the following:
- Brake caliper onto the caliper bracket ensuring that the guide boots are not damaged
- Brake caliper bolts and tighten the brake caliper bolts to 25 ft. lbs. (34 Nm)

➡**Install NEW copper brake hose gaskets.**

- Brake hose bolt and the NEW copper brake hose gaskets to the brake hose
- Brake hose to caliper bolt to the brake caliper. When installing the rear brake hose to caliper, hold the hose up while tightening. Tighten the brake hose to caliper bolt to 30 ft. lbs. (40 Nm)
- Park brake cable into the park brake bracket on the caliper
- Park brake cable to the park brake lever on the brake caliper

9. Bleed the brake system.

10. With the engine OFF, gradually apply the brake pedal to approximately ⅔ of its travel distance. Slowly release the brake pedal.

11. Wait 15 seconds, then repeat steps until a firm brake pedal is obtained. This

will properly seat the brake caliper pistons and brake pads.

12. Adjust the park brake system.

13. Install the tire and wheel assembly.

14. Lower the vehicle.

DISC BRAKE PADS

REMOVAL & INSTALLATION

1. Before servicing the vehicle, refer to the Precautions Section.

➡**Inspect the fluid level in the brake master cylinder reservoir. If the brake fluid level is midway between the maximum-full point and the minimum allowable level, then no brake fluid needs to be removed from the reservoir before proceeding. If the brake fluid level is higher than midway between the maximum full point and the minimum allowable level, then remove brake fluid to the midway point before proceeding.**

2. Remove the wheel, marking the location of the wheel to the hub prior to removal. Mark the individual location of all retainers as they are removed.

3. Remove or disconnect the following:
- Unclamp the wheel speed sensor (WSS) harness from the lower control arm
- Upper and lower caliper bolts from the caliper
- Pull the caliper straight off of the bracket and secure out of the way with heavy mechanics wire. DO NOT disconnect the hydraulic brake flexible hose from the caliper
- Inboard and outboard pads from the brake caliper bracket

To install:

4. Clean the brake pad hardware mating

surfaces on the caliper bracket of any debris or corrosion.

5. Inspect the brake pad retainer clips and replace, if necessary.

6. Inspect the piston boot. Replace if damaged.

7. Retract the brake caliper piston into the brake caliper bore. Use a suitable spanner type wrench and turn the piston clockwise until it bottoms out fully in the brake caliper.

8. Align the indents on the piston face to match the pin on the back of the inboard brake pads.

9. Install or connect the following:
- Brake pad retainers into the brake caliper bracket
- Inboard and outboard brake pads into the brake caliper bracket insuring that the pad with the metallic wear sensor is placed on the inboard side of the bracket
- Slide the caliper onto the bracket insuring that the bracket guide boots are not damaged
- Brake caliper bolts and tighten the bolts to 25 ft. lbs. (34 Nm)
- WSS harness onto the lower control arm

10. Install the tire and wheel assembly. Tighten the lug nuts to 100 ft. lbs. (140 Nm) in a criss—cross pattern, after aligning the wheel hub with the reference mark and holes as shown in appropriate illustration.

11. Lower the vehicle.

12. With the engine OFF, gradually apply the brake pedal to approximately ⅔ of its travel distance. Slowly release the brake pedal.

13. Wait 15 seconds, then repeat steps until a firm brake pedal apply is obtained. This will properly seat the brake caliper pistons and brake pads.

14. Fill the brake master cylinder reservoir to the proper level.

BRAKES

PARKING BRAKE

PARKING BRAKE CABLES

ADJUSTMENT

1. Apply and fully release the parking brake six times.
2. Verify that the parking brake pedal releases completely.
3. Turn ON the ignition. Verify that the BRAKE indicator lamp is OFF.
4. If the BRAKE indicator lamp is ON, ensure that the parking brake pedal is in release mode and fully returned to stop. Remove the slack in the front parking brake cable by pulling downward on the cable.
5. Raise and suitably support the vehicle.
6. Relieve tension on the park brake system at the park brake equalizer.
7. Adjust the parking brake by turning the nut at the equalizer while spinning both rear wheels. When either rear wheel starts to drag, back off the nut one full turn.
8. Lower the vehicle to curb height.
9. Apply the parking brake, then inspect for rotation of the rear wheels. If the rear wheels rotate during this inspection, readjust the parking brake.
10. Release the parking brake. Verify that the wheels rotate freely.
11. Lower the vehicle.

CHASSIS ELECTRICAL

AIR BAG (SUPPLEMENTAL RESTRAINT SYSTEM)

GENERAL INFORMATION

✳✳ CAUTION

These vehicles are equipped with an air bag system. The system must be disarmed before performing service on, or around, system components, the steering column, instrument panel components, wiring and sensors. Failure to follow the safety precautions and the disarming procedure could result in accidental air bag deployment, possible injury and unnecessary system repairs.

SERVICE PRECAUTIONS

Disconnect and isolate the battery negative cable before beginning any airbag system component diagnosis, testing, removal, or installation procedures. Allow system capacitor to discharge for two minutes before beginning any component service. This will disable the airbag system. Failure to disable the airbag system may result in accidental airbag deployment, personal injury, or death.

Do not place an intact undeployed airbag face down on a solid surface. The airbag will propel into the air if accidentally deployed and may result in personal injury or death.

When carrying or handling an undeployed airbag, the trim side (face) of the airbag should be pointing towards the body to minimize possibility of injury if accidental deployment occurs. Failure to do this may result in personal injury or death.

Replace airbag system components with OEM replacement parts. Substitute parts may appear interchangeable, but internal differences may result in inferior occupant protection. Failure to do so may result in occupant personal injury or death.

Wear safety glasses, rubber gloves, and long sleeved clothing when cleaning powder residue from vehicle after an airbag deployment. Powder residue emitted from a deployed airbag can cause skin irritation. Flush affected area with cool water if irritation is experienced. If nasal or throat irritation is experienced, exit the vehicle for fresh air until the irritation ceases. If irritation continues, see a physician.

Do not use a replacement airbag that is not in the original packaging. This may result in improper deployment, personal injury, or death.

The factory installed fasteners, screws and bolts used to fasten airbag components have a special coating and are specifically designed for the airbag system. Do not use substitute fasteners. Use only original equipment fasteners listed in the parts catalog when fastener replacement is required.

During, and following, any child restraint anchor service, due to impact event or vehicle repair, carefully inspect all mounting hardware, tether straps, and anchors for proper installation, operation, or damage. If a child restraint anchor is found damaged in any way, the anchor must be replaced. Failure to do this may result in personal injury or death.

Deployed and non-deployed airbags may or may not have live pyrotechnic material within the airbag inflator.

Do not dispose of driver/passenger/curtain airbags or seat belt tensioners unless you are sure of complete deployment. Refer to the Hazardous Substance Control System for proper disposal.

Dispose of deployed airbags and tensioners consistent with state, provincial, local, and federal regulations.

After any airbag component testing or service, do not connect the battery negative cable. Personal injury or death may result if the system test is not performed first.

If the vehicle is equipped with the Occupant Classification System (OCS), do not connect the battery negative cable before performing the OCS Verification Test using the scan tool and the appropriate diagnostic information. Personal injury or death may result if the system test is not performed properly.

Never replace both the Occupant Restraint Controller (ORC) and the Occupant Classification Module (OCM) at the same time. If both require replacement, replace one, then perform the Airbag System test before replacing the other.

Both the ORC and the OCM store Occupant Classification System (OCS) calibration data, which they transfer to one another when one of them is replaced. If both are replaced at the same time, an irreversible fault will be set in both modules and the OCS may malfunction and cause personal injury or death.

If equipped with OCS, the Seat Weight Sensor is a sensitive, calibrated unit and must be handled carefully. Do not drop or handle roughly. If dropped or damaged, replace with another sensor. Failure to do so may result in occupant injury or death.

If equipped with OCS, the front passenger seat must be handled carefully as well. When removing the seat, be careful when setting on floor not to drop. If dropped, the sensor may be inoperative, could result in occupant injury, or possibly death.

If equipped with OCS, when the passenger front seat is on the floor, no one should sit in the front passenger seat. This uneven force may damage the sensing ability of the seat weight sensors. If sat on and damaged, the sensor may be inoperative, could result in occupant injury, or possibly death.

SIR DISABLING AND ENABLING ZONES

See Figures 4 and 5.

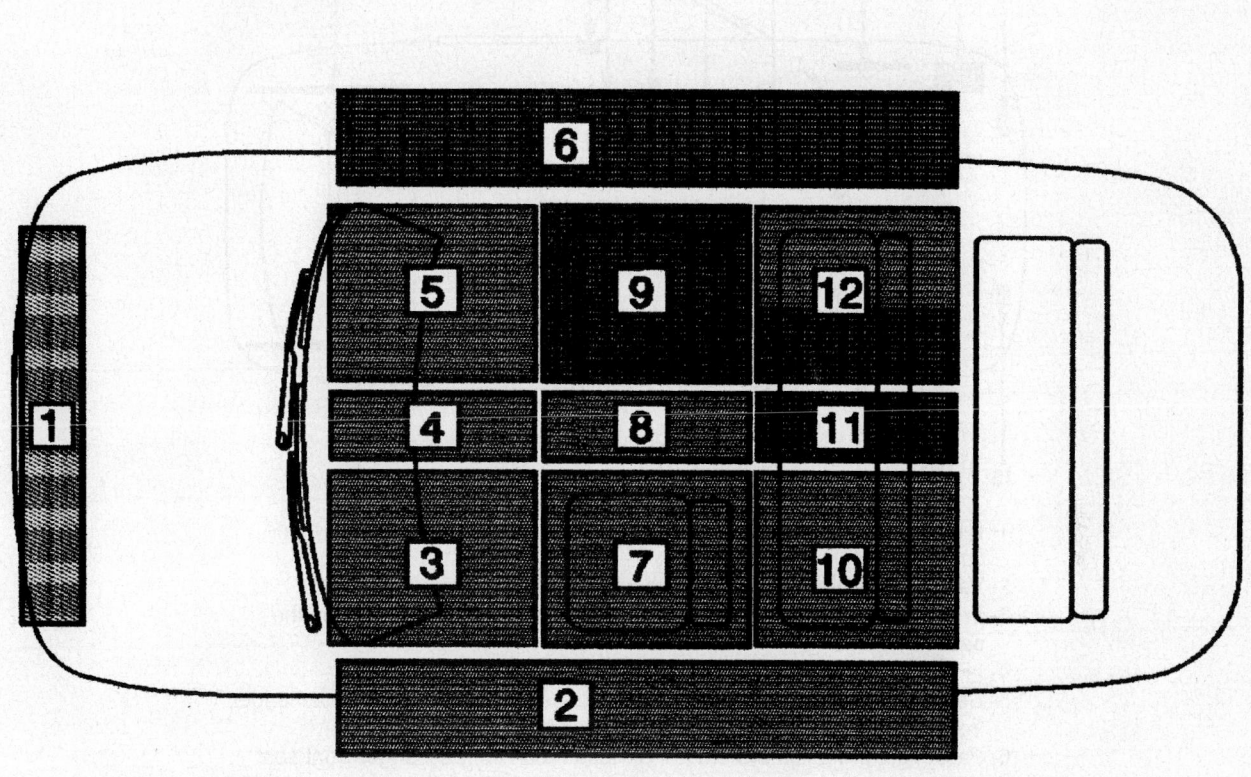

Zone	Description
1	Left and right front end
2	Driver/left side impact sensor (SIS) and seat belt retractor pretensioner
3	Inflatable restraint steering wheel module and coil
4	Not used
5	Inflatable restraint instrument panel (I/P) module
6	Passenger/right side impact module
7	Driver seat with LF side impact module
8	Not used
9	Passenger seat with RF side impact module, passenger presence system (PPS), and inflatable restraint sensing and diagnostic module (SDM)
10-12	Not used

06025-MONT-G36

Fig. 4 Identifying the SIR System Zones

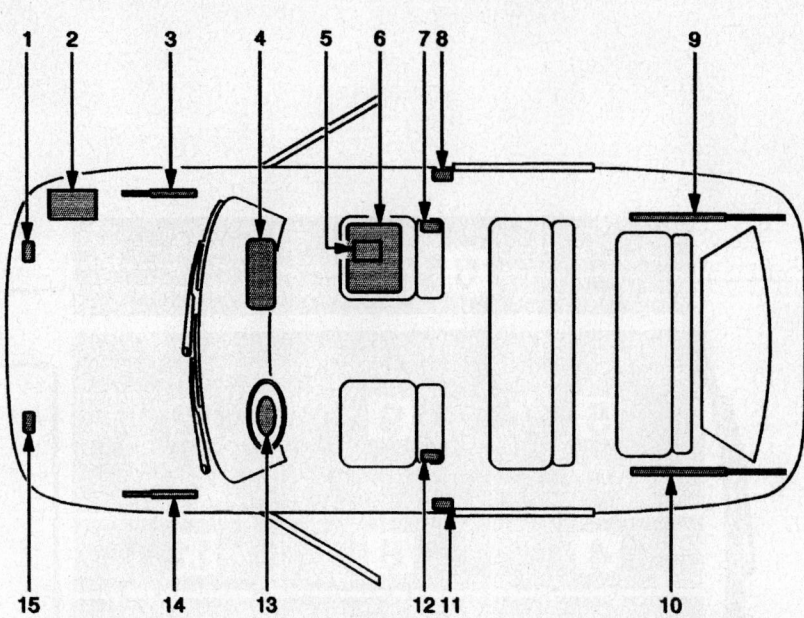

1- Right front end sensor - located on the front of the vehicle in the engine compartment

2- Vehicle battery- located under the hood on the right side

3- Front hood assist rod- a gas shock located under the front hood on the passenger side

4- I/P air bag- located at the top right under the instrument panel

5- Sensing and diagnostic module (SDM)- located underneath the passenger front seat

6- Passenger presence system (PPS)- located on the passenger front seat underneath the seat bottom trim

7- RF side impact air bag- located on the seat back of the passenger front seat

8- Right seat belt retractor pretensioner and right side impact sensor (SIS)- the right SIS is located above the right seat belt retractor pretensioner under the center pillar trim near the bottom on passenger side of vehicle

9- Rear compartment lid assist rod- a gas shock is located under the rear trunk lid on the passenger side

10- Rear compartment lid assist rod- a gas shock is locate under the rear trunk lid on the driver side

11- Left seat belt retractor pretensioner and left side impact sensor (SIS)- the left sis is located above the left seat belt retractor pretensioner under the center pillar trim near the bottom on the driver side of vehicle

12- LF side impact air bag- located on the seat back of the driver front seat

13- Steering wheel air bag- located on the steering wheel

14- Front hood assist rod- a gas shock located under the front hood on the driver side

15- Left front end sensor- located on the front of the vehicle in the engine compartment

06025-MONT-G37

Fig. 5 Identifying components and their locations in the SIR System

---

✷✷ CAUTION

Before disabling the SIR system, refer to SIR Service Precautions.

The supplemental inflatable restraint (SIR) system has been divided into

Disabling and Enabling Zones. When performing service on or near SIR components or SIR wiring, it may be necessary to disable the SIR components in that zone. It may be necessary to disable more than one zone depending on the

location of other SIR components and the area being serviced. See the illustration to identify the specific zone or zones in which service will be performed. After identifying the zone or zones, proceed to the disabling and enabling procedures for that particular zone or zones.

DISARMING

Zone 1

See Figure 6.

> **✱✱ CAUTION**
>
> **Before disabling the SIR system, refer to SIR Service Precautions.**

1. Turn the steering wheel so that the vehicle's wheels are pointing straight ahead.
2. Turn OFF the ignition.
3. Remove the key from the ignition switch.
4. Open the hood and locate the underhood fuse center.
5. Lift the cover for the underhood fuse center.

> **✱✱ WARNING**
>
> **With the Air Bag Fuse removed and the ignition ON, the AIR BAG indicator illuminates. This is normal operation, and does not indicate an SIR System malfunction.**

6. Locate and remove the air bag fuse from the underhood fuse center.
7. Open the front hood and locate both right and left front-end sensors (1), also known as the electronic front sensor (EFS).
8. Remove both connector position assurances (CPAs) from the right and left front-end sensor.
9. Disconnect both front-end sensor wiring harness connectors from the left and right front-end sensor (1).
10. Open the front hood and locate both right and left front-end sensors, also known as the electronic front sensor (EFS).
11. Remove both connector position assurances (CPAs) from the right and left front-end sensor.

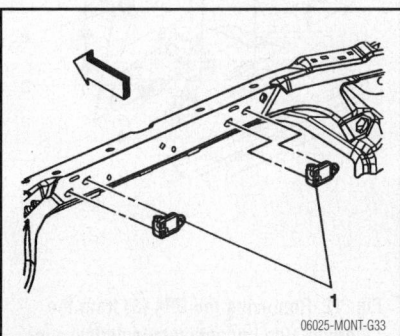

Fig. 6 Showing the location of the electronic front sensors—Zone 1

12. Disconnect both front-end sensor wiring harness connectors from the left and right front-end sensor.

Zone 2

See Figures 7 and 8.

> **✱✱ CAUTION**
>
> **Before disabling the SIR system, refer to SIR Service Precautions.**

1. Turn the steering wheel so that the vehicle's wheels are pointing straight ahead.
2. Turn OFF the ignition.
3. Remove the key from the ignition switch.
4. Open the hood and locate the underhood fuse center.
5. Lift the cover for the underhood fuse center.
6. Locate and remove the air bag fuse from the underhood fuse center.

> **✱✱ CAUTION**
>
> **With the Air Bag Fuse removed and the ignition ON, the AIR BAG indicator illuminates. This is normal opera-**

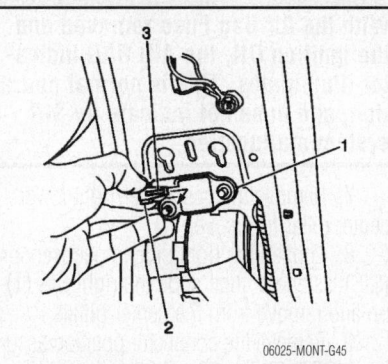

Fig. 7 Removing the left side impact sensor from the driver's side pillar—Zone 2

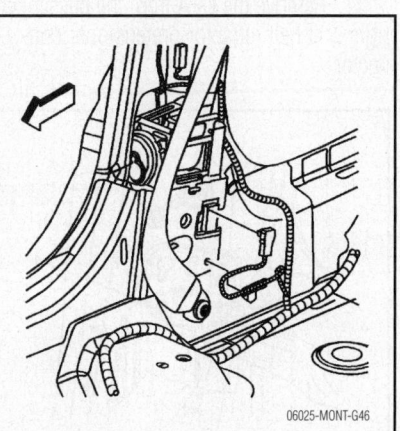

Fig. 8 Removing the CPA from the seat belt retractor/pretensioner—Zone 2, Zone 6 and Zone 9

tion, and does not indicate an SIR System malfunction.

7. Remove the driver/left lower center pillar trim cover.
8. Loosen the left side impact sensor (SIS) fasteners, then slide the left SIS (1) up and remove the sensor from the center pillar.
9. Remove the connector position assurance (CPA) (3) from the SIS connector (2).
10. Disconnect the SIS wiring harness connector (2) from the SIS (1).
11. Remove the CPA from the driver/left seat belt retractor pretensioner connector.
12. Remove the vehicle wiring harness connector from the left seat belt retractor pretensioner.

Zone 3

See Figure 9.

> **✱✱ CAUTION**
>
> **Before disabling the SIR system, refer to SIR Service Precautions.**

1. Turn the steering wheel so that the vehicle's wheels are pointing straight ahead.
2. Turn OFF the ignition.
3. Remove the key from the ignition switch.
4. Open the hood and locate the underhood fuse center.
5. Lift the cover for the underhood fuse center.
6. Locate and remove the air bag fuse from the underhood fuse center.

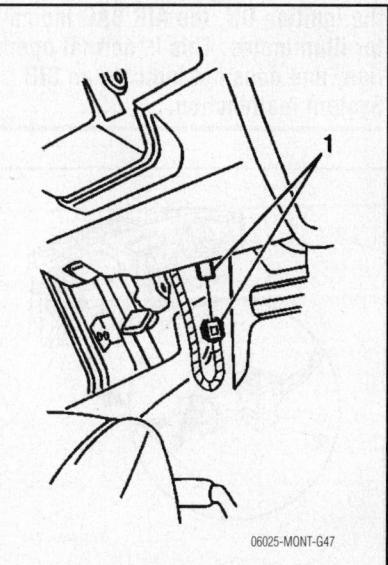

Fig. 9 Removing the CPA from the steering wheel module coil yellow connector—Zone 3 and Zone 9

※※ CAUTION

With the Air Bag Fuse removed and the ignition ON, the AIR BAG indicator illuminates. This is normal operation, and does not indicate an SIR System malfunction.

7. Remove the driver/left instrument panel (I/P) insulator panel.

8. Remove the connector position assurance (CPA) from the steering wheel module coil yellow connector (1) located at the base of the steering column.

9. Disconnect the steering wheel module coil connector (1).

➡**Zone 4 not used on these vehicles.**

Zone 5

See Figure 10.

※※ CAUTION

Before disabling the SIR system, refer to SIR Service Precautions.

1. Turn the steering wheel so that the vehicle's wheels are pointing straight ahead.

2. Turn OFF the ignition.

3. Remove the key from the ignition switch.

4. Open the hood and locate the underhood fuse center.

5. Lift the cover for the underhood fuse center.

6. Locate and remove the air bag fuse from the underhood fuse center.

※※ CAUTION

With the Air Bag Fuse removed and the ignition ON, the AIR BAG indicator illuminates. This is normal operation, and does not indicate an SIR System malfunction.

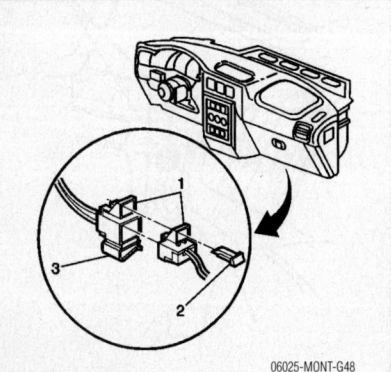

Fig. 10 Removing the CPA from the instrument panel module yellow connector—Zone 5

7. Remove the passenger/right instrument panel (I/P) insulator panel.

8. Remove the connector position assurance (CPA) (2) from the I/P module yellow connector (1).

9. Disconnect the I/P module connector (1).

Zone 6

See Figure 11.

※※ CAUTION

Before disabling the SIR system, refer to SIR Service Precautions.

1. Turn the steering wheel so that the vehicle's wheels are pointing straight ahead.

2. Turn OFF the ignition.

3. Remove the key from the ignition switch.

4. Open the hood and locate the underhood fuse center.

5. Lift the cover for the underhood fuse center.

6. Locate and remove the air bag fuse from the underhood fuse center.

※※ CAUTION

With the Air Bag Fuse removed and the ignition ON, the AIR BAG indicator illuminates. This is normal operation, and does not indicate an SIR system malfunction.

7. Remove the passenger/right lower center pillar trim cover.

8. Loosen the right side impact sensor (SIS) fasteners, then slide the right SIS (1) up and remove from the center pillar.

9. Remove the connector position assurance (CPA) (3) from the SIS connector (2).

10. Disconnect the SIS wiring harness connector (2) from the SIS (1).

11. Remove the CPA from the passenger/right seat belt retractor pretensioner connector.

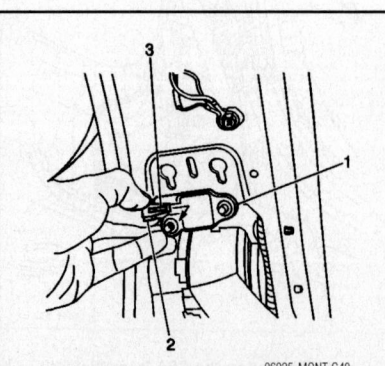

Fig. 11 Removing the right side impact sensor from the center pillar—Zone 6

12. Remove the vehicle wiring harness connector from the right seat belt retractor pretensioner.

Zone 7

See Figure 12.

※※ CAUTION

Before disabling the SIR system, refer to SIR Service Precautions.

1. Turn the steering wheel so that the vehicle's wheels are pointing straight ahead.

2. Turn OFF the ignition.

3. Remove the key from the ignition switch.

4. Open the hood and locate the underhood fuse center.

5. Lift the cover for the underhood fuse center.

※※ CAUTION

With the Air Bag Fuse removed and the ignition ON, the AIR BAG indicator illuminates. This is normal operation, and does not indicate an SIR system malfunction.

6. Locate and remove the air bag fuse from the underhood fuse center

7. Remove the connector position assurance (CPA) (3) from the LF/driver side impact module yellow connector (3), which is located under the driver seat.

8. Disconnect the vehicle harness connector (4) from the LF side impact module connector (1).

➡**Zone 8 not used with these vehicles.**

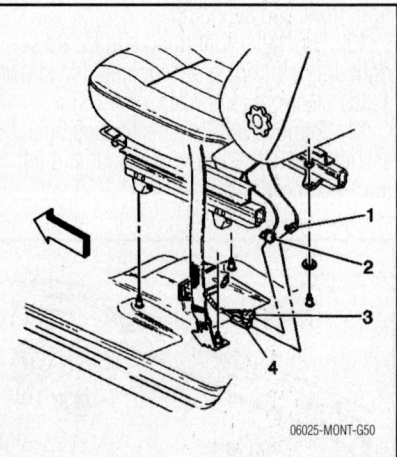

Fig. 12 Removing the CPA (3) from the LF/driver side impact module yellow connector (3) under the driver seat—Zone 7 and Zone 9

Zone 9

See Figure 10.

✳✳ CAUTION

Before disabling the SIR system, refer to SIR Service Precautions.

1. Turn the steering wheel so that the vehicle's wheels are pointing straight ahead.
2. Turn OFF the ignition.
3. Remove the key from the ignition switch.
4. Open the hood and locate the underhood fuse center.
5. Lift the cover for the underhood fuse center.

✳✳ CAUTION

With the Air Bag Fuse removed and the ignition ON, the AIR BAG indicator illuminates. This is normal operation, and does not indicate an SIR system malfunction.

6. Locate and remove the air bag fuse from the underhood fuse center.
7. When disabling only the side impact module - RF proceed to step 21. If the entire SIR system needs to be disabled, then go to step 7.
8. Remove the driver/left lower center pillar trim cover.
9. Remove the connector position assurance (CPA) from the driver/left seat belt retractor pretensioner connector.
10. Remove the vehicle wiring harness connector from the left seat belt retractor pretensioner.
11. Remove the driver/left instrument panel (I/P) insulator panel.
12. Remove the CPA from the steering wheel module coil yellow connector, located at the base of the steering column.
13. Disconnect the steering wheel module coil connector.
14. Remove the CPA (3) from the LF/driver side impact module yellow connector (3), which is located under the driver seat.
15. Disconnect the vehicle harness connector (4) from the LF side impact module connector (1).
16. Remove the passenger/right instrument panel (I/P) insulator panel.
17. Remove the CPA (2) from the I/P module yellow connector (1).
18. Disconnect the I/P module connector (1).
19. Remove the passenger/right lower center pillar trim cover.

20. Remove the CPA from the right seat belt retractor pretensioner connector.
21. Remove the vehicle wiring harness connector from the right seat belt retractor pretensioner.
22. Remove the CPA (3) from the RF/passenger side impact module yellow connector (3), which is located under the passenger seat.
23. Disconnect the vehicle harness connector (4) from the RF side impact module connector (1).

ARMING

Zone 1

1. Remove the key from the ignition.
2. Connect both front end sensor wiring harness connectors to the left and right front end sensor (1).
3. Install the CPAs to the left and right front end sensor connector.
4. Install the Air Bag Fuse.
5. Install the cover for the underhood fuse center.
6. Use caution while reaching in and turning the ignition switch to the ON position. The AIR BAG indicator will flash, then turn OFF.
7. Perform the Diagnostic System Checks. Ensure the Air Bag indicator operates properly.

Zone 2

1. Remove the key from the ignition.
2. Connect the vehicle wiring harness connector to the left seat belt retractor pretensioner.
3. Install the CPA to the left seat belt retractor pretensioner connector.
4. Connect the left SIS wiring harness connector (2) to the left SIS (1).
5. Install the CPA (3) to the SIS connector (1).
6. Position the SIS (1) back inside the center pillar and slide back into place and tighten the SIS fasteners.
7. Install the left lower center pillar trim cover.
8. Install the Air Bag Fuse.
9. Install the cover for the underhood fuse center.
10. Use caution while reaching in and turning the ignition switch to the ON position. The AIR BAG indicator will flash, then turn OFF.
11. Perform the Diagnostic System Check, if the AIR BAG warning indicator does not operate as described.

Zone 3

1. Remove the key from the ignition.

2. Connect the steering wheel module coil yellow connector (1).
3. Install the CPA to the steering wheel module coil connector (1) located at the base of the steering column.
4. Install the left I/P insulator panel.
5. Install the Air Bag Fuse.
6. Install the cover for the underhood fuse center.
7. Use caution while reaching in and turning the ignition switch to the ON position. The AIR BAG indicator will flash, then turn OFF.
8. Perform the Diagnostic System Check, if the AIR BAG warning indicator does not operate as described.

Zone 5

1. Remove the key from the ignition.
2. Connect the I/P module yellow connector (1).
3. Install the CPA (2) to the I/P module connector (1).
4. Install the right I/P insulator panel.
5. Install the Air Bag Fuse.
6. Install the cover for the underhood fuse center.
7. Use caution while reaching in and turning the ignition switch to the ON position. The AIR BAG indicator will flash, then turn OFF.
8. Perform the Diagnostic System Check, if the AIR BAG warning indicator does not operate as described.

Zone 6

1. Remove the key from the ignition.
2. Connect the vehicle wiring harness connector to the right seat belt retractor pretensioner.
3. Install the CPA to the right seat belt retractor pretensioner connector.
4. Connect the right SIS wiring harness connector (2) to the right SIS (1).
5. Install the CPA (3) to the SIS connector (1).
6. Position SIS (1) back inside the center pillar and slide back into place and tighten the SIS fasteners.
7. Install the right lower center pillar trim cover.
8. Install the Air Bag Fuse.
9. Install the cover for the underhood fuse center.
10. Use caution while reaching in and turning the ignition switch to the ON position. The AIR BAG indicator will flash, then turn OFF.
11. Perform the Diagnostic System Check, if the AIR BAG warning indicator does not operate as described.

Zone 7

1. Remove the key from the ignition.
2. Connect the vehicle harness connector (4) to the LF side impact module yellow connector (1).
3. Install the CPA to the LF side impact module connector (1).
4. Install the Air Bag Fuse.
5. Install the cover for the underhood fuse center.
6. Use caution while reaching in and turning the ignition switch to the ON position. The AIR BAG indicator will flash, then turn OFF.
7. Perform the Diagnostic System Check, if the AIR BAG warning indicator does not operate as described.

Zone 9

1. Remove the key from the ignition.
2. When enabling the side impact module - RF proceed to step 17. If the entire SIR system needs to be enabled, then go to step 3.
3. Connect the vehicle wiring harness connector to the left seat belt retractor pretensioner.
4. Install the CPA to the left seat belt retractor pretensioner connector.
5. Install the left lower center pillar trim cover.
6. Connect the steering wheel module coil yellow connector (1).

7. Install the CPA to the steering wheel module coil connector (1), located at the base of the steering column.
8. Install the left I/P insulator panel.
9. Connect the vehicle harness connector (4) to the LF side impact module yellow connector (1).
10. Install the CPA to the LF side impact module connector (1).
11. Connect the I/P module yellow connector (1).
12. Install the CPA (2) to the I/P module connector (1).
13. Install the right I/P insulator panel.
14. Connect the vehicle wiring harness connector to the right seat belt retractor pretensioner.
15. Install the CPA to the right seat belt retractor pretensioner connector.
16. Install the right lower center pillar trim cover.
17. Connect the vehicle harness connector (4) to the RF side impact module yellow connector (1).
18. Install the CPA to the RF side impact module connector (1).
19. Install the Air Bag Fuse.
20. Install the cover for the underhood fuse center.
21. Use caution while reaching in and turning the ignition switch to the ON position. The AIR BAG indicator will flash, then turn OFF.

22. Perform the Diagnostic System Check, if the AIR BAG warning indicator does not operate as described.

DIAGNOSTIC SYSTEM CHECKS

1. Ensure that the battery, and the vehicle primary power and ground systems are functioning correctly.
2. With scan tool attached, check for proper communication. Lack of communication may be due to a particular malfunction of a serial data circuit. Further scan tool or communications diagnosis may be required.
3. With the scan tool, check that all indicated engine electronic modules are operating in the incorrect power mode, based on key position. If not, this may cause other vehicle symptoms and/or DTCs to set.
4. With the scan tool, check for any Power Mode Mismatch and correct the condition before checking for module DTCs or symptoms.
5. Ensure that all data link communication DTCs are diagnosed before system level DTCs.
6. Ensure that all electronic control unit (ECU) internal DTCs are diagnosed before other system level DTCs.
7. Ensure that all device voltage DTCs are diagnosed before other system level DTCs.

DRIVETRAIN

AUTOMATIC TRANSAXLE ASSEMBLY

REMOVAL & INSTALLATION

See Figure 13.

1. Before servicing the vehicle, refer to the Precautions Section.
2. Remove or disconnect the following:
   - Negative battery cable
   - Position aside coolant recovery bottle
   - Air cleaner assembly
   - Automatic transmission range selector cable from the manual shaft
   - Automatic transmission range selector cable bracket
   - Wiring harness connector from the transaxle
   - Wiring harness retainer from the side cover
   - The top 4 bell housing bolts and stud

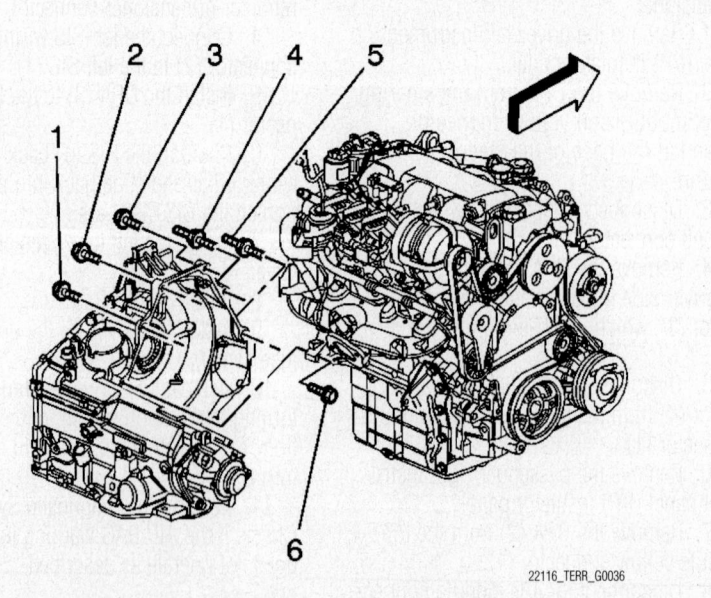

22116_TERR_G0036

Fig. 13 Remove the top four bell housing bolts and stud (4)

3. Install the engine support fixture.
  • Front tires and wheels

➡**When removing the wheel, mark the location of the wheel to the hub prior to removal. Mark the individual location of all retainers as they are removed.**

  • Front fender liner enough to gain access to the front frame bolts
  • Both outer tie rod ends from the steering knuckles
  • Stabilizer shaft
  • Propeller shaft, if equipped with all wheel drive (AWD).

➡**It is NOT necessary to remove the catalytic converter pipe on FWD models.**

  • Catalytic converter pipe, if equipped with AWD
  • Power steering gear heat shield
  • Power steering gear bolts and suspend steering gear from the frame
  • Front engine splash shield
  • Power steering cooler pipe from the frame, use mechanics wire to secure the power steering cooler line out of the way
  • Front wheel speed sensor connectors
  • Front wheel speed sensor wiring harnesses from the lower control arms
  • Lower ball joints from the steering knuckles
  • Engine mount nuts
  • Transaxle mount nuts

4. Lower the vehicle. until the frame contacts the J 39580, or equivalent
  • Frame front bolts
  • Frame rear bolts
  • Frame strap bolts and straps
  • Raise the vehicle in order to separate the frame from the vehicle
  • Torque converter inspection cover
  • Torque converter bolts
  • Vehicle speed sensor
  • Right and left axle shafts from the transmission
  • Transmission cooler lines
  • Position the transmission jack under the transaxle
  • Transaxle brace
  • Lower transaxle bolt and stud
  • Transaxle from the vehicle

To install:
5. Install or connect the following:
  • Align the transaxle filler tube to the transmission and Install the transaxle into the vehicle.

  • Lower transaxle bolt and stud and tighten the bolt and stud to 55 ft. lbs. (75 Nm)
  • Transaxle brace
  • Transmission cooler lines
  • Right and left axle shafts into the transaxle
  • Vehicle speed sensor
  • Torque converter bolts and tighten the bolts to 46 ft. lbs. (63 Nm)
  • Torque converter inspection cover
  • Position the transaxle table with the frame under the vehicle

✳✳ WARNING

Ensure that the power steering cooler line does not become trapped by the engine mount during this step

6. Lower the vehicle. until the frame is close to the vehicle
  • Adjust the utility straps as necessary in order to align the powertrain mounts with the frame

✳✳ WARNING

Ensure that the alignment pins remain installed during the frame installation.

  • Insert two 19mm (0.75 inch) diameter X 203mm (8.0 inches) long guide pins or drill bits into the frame right side alignment holes in order to align the frame
  • Frame front bolts and tighten the bolts to 96 ft. lbs. (130 Nm)
  • Frame straps and bolts and tighten the bolts to 37 ft. lbs. (50 Nm)
  • Frame rear bolts and tighten the bolts to 177 ft. lbs. (240 Nm)
  • Remove the alignment pins from the frame
  • Transaxle mount nuts
  • Engine mount nuts
  • Wheel speed sensor wiring harnesses to the lower control arms
  • Wheel speed sensor electrical connectors.
  • Lower ball joints to the steering knuckles
  • Power steering cooler pipe to the frame
  • Front engine splash shield
  • Power steering gear to the frame
  • Power steering gear bolts
  • Power steering gear heat shield
  • Propeller shaft, if equipped with AWD
  • Catalytic converter pipe, if equipped with AWD
  • Stabilizer shaft

  • Both tie rod ends to the steering knuckles
  • Front fender liner
  • Frame
  • Remove the engine support fixture.
  • Upper transaxle bolts and stud and tighten the bolts and stud to 55 ft. lbs. (75 Nm)
  • Wiring harness to the transaxle
  • Transmission range selector cable bracket
  • Transmission range selector cable on the manual shaft
  • Air cleaner assembly
  • Coolant recovery bottle

7. Install the tire and wheel assembly. Tighten the lug nuts to 100 ft. lbs. (140 Nm) in a criss—cross pattern, after aligning the wheel hub with the reference mark and holes as shown in appropriate illustration.

✳✳ WARNING

Do NOT overfill the transaxle. The overfilling of the transaxle causes foaming, loss of fluid, shift complaints, and possible damage to the transaxle. Adjust the fluid level.

➡**It is recommended the ate transmission adaptive pressure (TAP) information be reset. Resetting the TAP values using a scan tool will erase all learned values in all cells. As a result the ECM, PCM, or TCM will need to relearn TAP values. Transmission performance may be affected as new TAP values are learned.**

8. Reset the TAP values.
9. Refill the transmission with the proper amount and type of fluid.
10. Connect the negative battery cable. Start the vehicle and allow to warm while checking for leaks.
11. Road test the vehicle to check for shift quality.

TRANSFER CASE ASSEMBLY

REMOVAL & INSTALLATION
See Figures 14 through 18.

1. Before servicing the vehicle, refer to the Precautions Section.
2. Disconnect the negative battery cable.

➡**Transmission oil circulates between the transmission and the transfer case. In situations where transmission failures circulate debris into the transfer case, the transfer case must be disassembled, cleaned, and inspected for damage.**

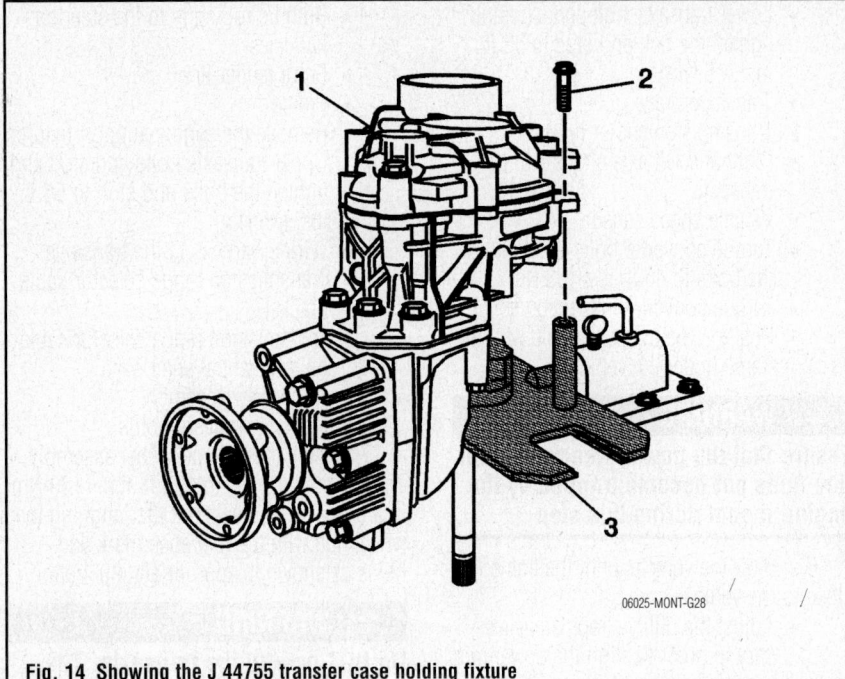

Fig. 14 Showing the J 44755 transfer case holding fixture

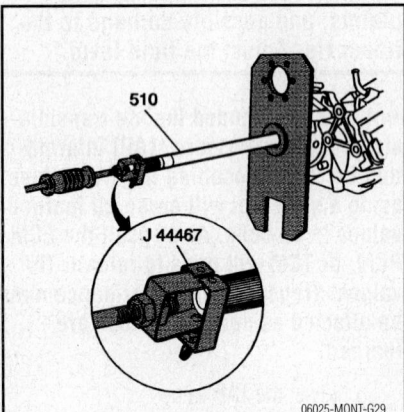

Fig. 15 Indicating the J 44467 output shaft remover

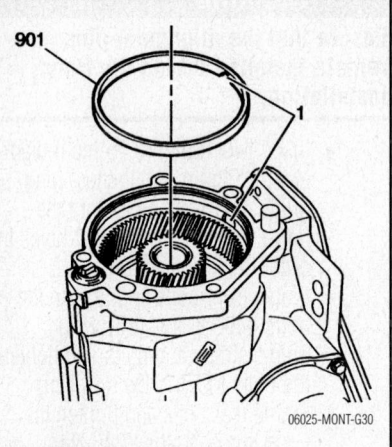

Fig. 16 Removing the oil dam

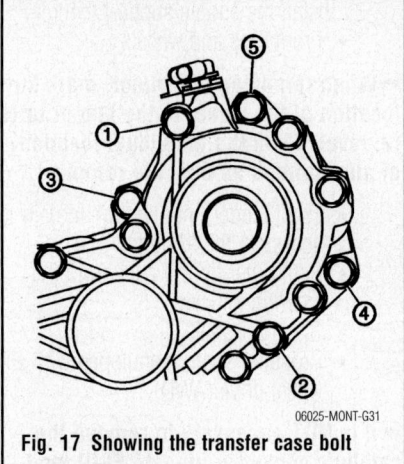

Fig. 17 Showing the transfer case bolt torque sequence

3. Raise and safely support the vehicle.

4. Drain the transfer case oil.

5. Drain the transmission fluid.

6. Remove or disconnect the following:
- Propeller shaft
- Vehicle speed sensor electrical connector
- Vent tube from the transfer case

✱✱ WARNING

Removal and installation of the transfer case while the transmission is in vehicle may cause improper positioning of the park gear thrust bearing. If the transfer case fasteners are tightened while the park gear thrust bearing is out of position, the park gear thrust bearing, transmis-

sion, and/or the transfer case will be damaged.

- Transfer case with the transaxle

7. Install the transaxle to the transmission support fixture.

8. Remove and discard the left output shaft retaining ring.

9. Rotate the transaxle 90 degrees so that the transmission side cover is facing down.

10. Remove the transfer case side brace bolts, and the transfer case side brace.

11. Remove the transfer case bolts.

✱✱ WARNING

During removal of the transfer case/output shaft, do not use excessive force or damage to the bushings may occur.

12. Remove the transfer case with the output shaft from the transaxle.

13. Install the transfer case assembly to the J 44755, or equivalent.

14. Install the retaining bolts and tighten the bolts to 37 ft. lbs. (50 Nm).

15. Attach the J 6125-1B, or equivalent slide hammer to the J 44467.

16. Install the J 44467 into the snap ring groove on the output shaft (510) and tighten securely.

17. Use the J 6125-1B and the J 44467 to remove the output shaft.

18. Remove the output shaft from the transfer case.

19. Remove the transfer case seal from the transfer case.

20. Remove the oil dam (901) from the transaxle.

To install:

➡**If you are replacing anything other than gaskets or seals, the transmission to transfer case end play check must be performed.**

21. Install or connect the following:
- New transfer case seal

✱✱ WARNING

The oil dam must be installed with the notch aligned to the oil passage in the transaxle case.

- Oil dam to the transaxle

22. Rotate the transaxle 90 degrees, then position the transfer case to the transaxle.

23. Install and tighten the transfer case bolts in the following sequence:
- Transfer case bolts (1) and (2) and tighten the bolts to 26 ft. lbs. (35 Nm), then rotate the bolts 160 degrees

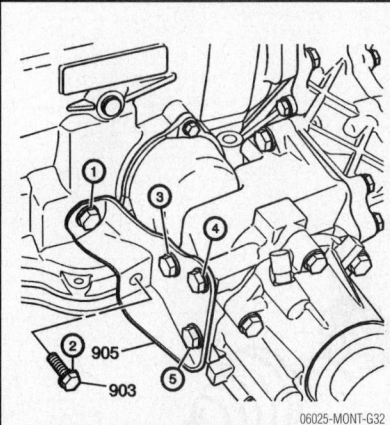

Fig. 18 Showing the transfer case side bolts torque sequence

- Transfer case bolt (3) and tighten the bolt to 26 ft. lbs. (35 Nm), then rotate the bolts 70 degrees
- Transfer case bolts (4) and (5) and tighten the bolts to 30 ft. lbs. (40Nm)

24. Install the transfer case side brace .
25. Install and tighten the remaining transfer case bolts in the following sequence:
- Tighten the transfer case side brace bolts in the order shown. Tighten transfer case side brace bolts to 24 ft. lbs. (32 Nm)
- Transfer case lower brace to transaxle bolt and tighten the bolt to 42 ft. lbs. (56 Nm)
- Transfer case lower brace to transfer case bolts and tighten the bolts to 24 ft. lbs. (32 Nm)

26. Install or connect the following:
- Output shaft to the transmission
- New output shaft retaining ring
- Transaxle with the transfer case
- Vent hose and the clamp to the transfer case
- Vehicle speed sensor electrical connector
- Propeller shaft

27. Fill the transfer case with the specified synthetic gear oil.
28. Install the transfer case lower brace.
29. Lower the vehicle.
30. Inspect and adjust the transmission fluid level.
31. Connect the negative battery cable.

FRONT AXLE SHAFT, BEARING & SEAL

REMOVAL & INSTALLATION

Wheel Bearing & Hub

See Figure 19.

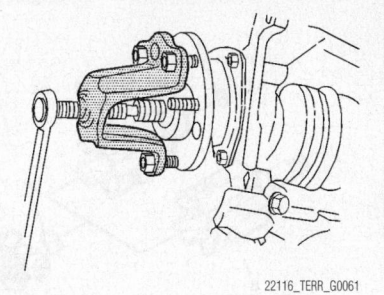

Fig. 19 Remove the front hub spindle remover to push the halfshaft out of the wheel bearing.

1. Before servicing the vehicle, refer to the Precautions Section.
2. Raise and safely support the vehicle.
3. Remove the wheel, marking the location of the wheel to the hub prior to removal. Mark the individual location of all retainers as they are removed.
4. Remove or disconnect the following:
- Wheel speed sensor electrical connector.
- Wheel speed sensor electrical connector from the bracket.
- Brake caliper bracket with the brake caliper.
- Brake rotor. For additional information, refer to the following section, "Rotor, Removal & Installation."
- Halfshaft nut

5. Use 3 wheel nuts and attach the bearing/hub tool, J 28733-B, to the hub. Push the halfshaft out of the wheel bearing/hub.
6. Remove and discard the wheel bearing/hub bolts.
7. Remove and examine the wheel bearing/hub.

To install:

※※ CAUTION

The fasteners MUST be replaced with new fasteners anytime they become loose or are removed. Failure to replace these fasteners after they become loose or are removed may cause loss of vehicle control and personal injury.

➡Use the correct fastener in the correct location. Replacement fasteners must be the correct part number for that application. Fasteners requiring replacement or fasteners requiring the use of thread locking compound or sealant are identified in the service procedure. Do not use paints, lubricants, or corrosion inhibitors on fasteners or fastener joint surfaces unless specified. These coatings affect fastener torque and joint clamping force and may damage the fastener. Use the correct tightening sequence and specifications when installing fasteners in order to avoid damage to parts and systems.

8. Install or connect the following:
- Wheel bearing/hub
- NEW wheel bearing/hub bolts and tighten the bolts to 96 ft. lbs. (130 Nm)
- Halfshaft nut
- Brake rotor
- Brake caliper bracket with the brake caliper

➡Ensure that the connector clip engages the bracket properly.

- Wheel speed sensor electrical connector

9. Install the tire and wheel assembly. Tighten the lug nuts to 100 ft. lbs. (140 Nm) in a criss—cross pattern, after aligning the wheel hub with the reference mark and holes as shown in appropriate illustration.
10. Lower the vehicle.

FRONT HALFSHAFTS

REMOVAL & INSTALLATION

See Figures 20 through 23.

1. Raise and safely support the vehicle.
2. Remove the wheel, marking the location of the wheel to the hub prior to removal. Mark the individual location of all retainers as they are removed.
3. Remove the engine splash shield.
4. Insert a drift or punch (1) through the brake caliper and into the brake rotor in

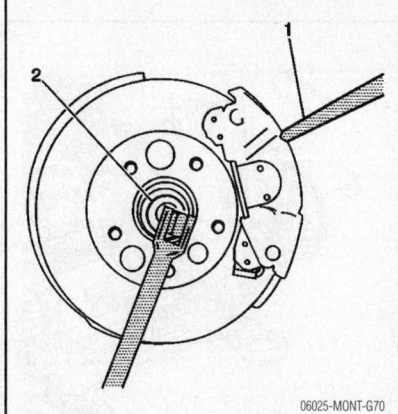

Fig. 20 Using drift through brake caliper to hold wheel hub and bearing from turning

order to prevent the wheel hub and bearing from turning.

5. Remove the halfshaft spindle nut (2).

6. Remove the stabilizer shaft link.

7. Disconnect the outer tie rod end from the steering knuckle; do NOT loosen the tie rod end jam nut.

8. Disconnect the electrical connector from the wheel speed sensor and reposition the wiring harness away from the ball joint.

9. Disconnect the lower ball joint from the steering knuckle.

10. Install the puller/remover J 42129 onto the wheel hub and secure with wheel nuts.

✳✳ CAUTION

Be sure to support the halfshaft until it is fully removed from the vehicle.

11. Using the puller/remover tool, disengage the halfshaft from the wheel hub and bearing.

12. Assemble the special slide hammer and tool attachments (J 33008-A, J 29794, J 2619-O1) and disengage the halfshaft from the transaxle.

13. Remove the halfshaft from the vehicle

To install:

14. Install the halfshaft to the transaxle

➡**Verify that the wheel halfshaft is properly engaged to the transaxle by grasping the inner tripot housing and pulling outward. Do not pull on the halfshaft bar. The wheel halfshaft will remain firmly in place when properly engaged.**

15. Install or connect the following:
- Halfshaft to the hub and bearing
- Ball joint to the steering knuckle. See Lower Control Arm

Fig. 21 Removing/installing the front halfshaft

06025-MONT-G76

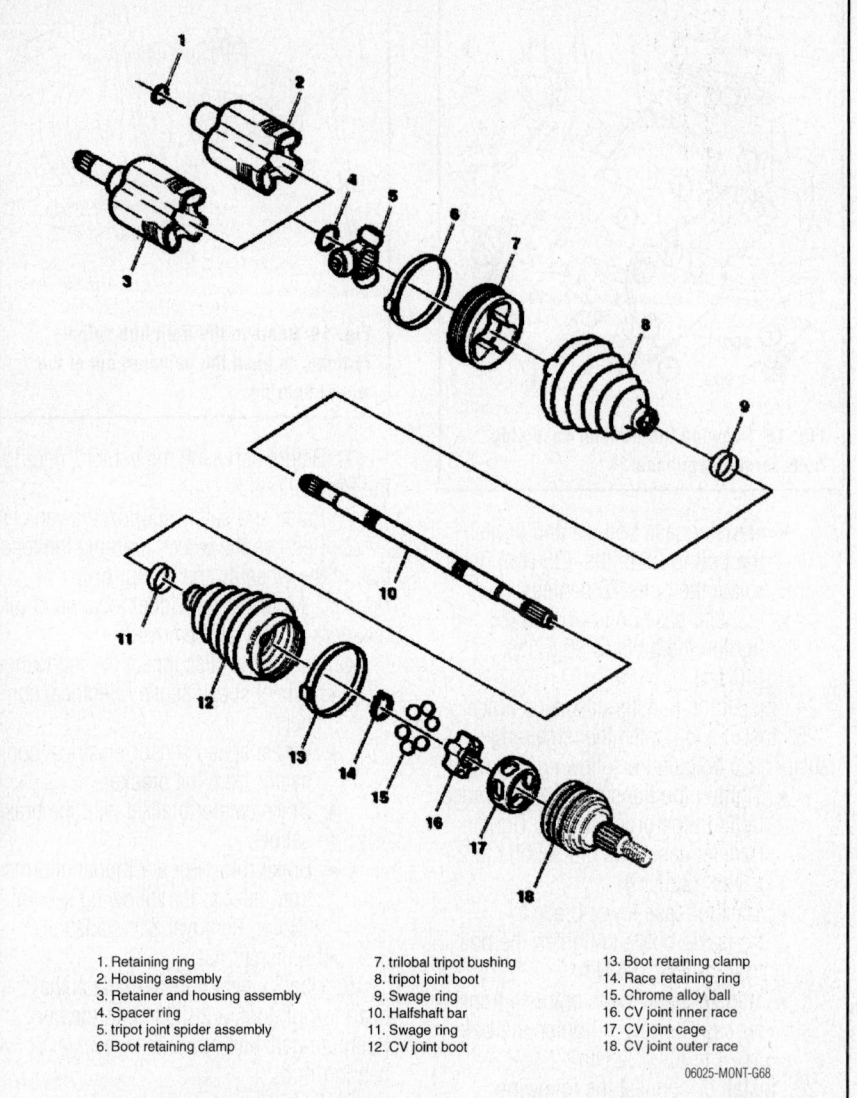

1. Retaining ring	7. trilobal tripot bushing	13. Boot retaining clamp
2. Housing assembly	8. tripot joint boot	14. Race retaining ring
3. Retainer and housing assembly	9. Swage ring	15. Chrome alloy ball
4. Spacer ring	10. Halfshaft bar	16. CV joint inner race
5. tripot joint spider assembly	11. Swage ring	17. CV joint cage
6. Boot retaining clamp	12. CV joint boot	18. CV joint outer race

06025-MONT-G68

Fig. 22 Exploded view of the front halfshaft assembly

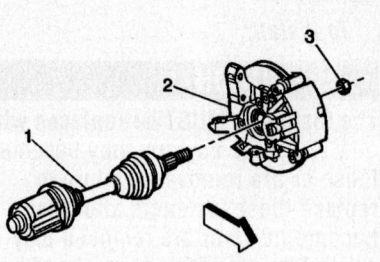

06025-MONT-G77

Fig. 23 Installing the hub and bearing (2) to the halfshaft (1), with retaining nut (3)

- Wheel speed sensor electrical connector
- Stabilizer shaft link. See Stabilizer Bar under FRONT SUSPENSION.

➡**Insert a drift or punch through the brake caliper and into the brake rotor**

in order to prevent the hub and bearing from turning.

- Install the nut to the halfshaft spindle and tighten the nut to 118 ft. lbs. (160 Nm)
- Outer tie rod end to the steering knuckle. See Tie Rod Ends
- Engine splash shield

16. Install the tire and wheel assembly. Tighten the lug nuts to 100 ft. lbs. (140 Nm) in a criss—cross pattern, after aligning the wheel hub with the reference mark and holes as shown in appropriate illustration.

17. Lower the vehicle.

CV-JOINTS OVERHAUL

See Figures 24 through 31.

1. Before servicing the vehicle, refer to the Precautions Section.

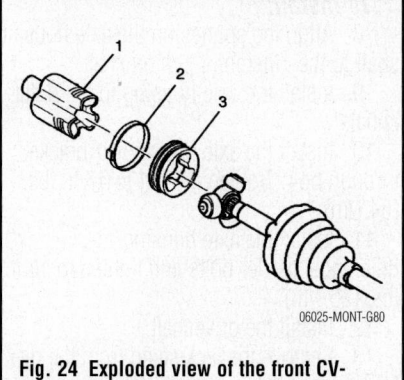

Fig. 24 Exploded view of the front CV-Joint assembly

✳✳ CAUTION

Do not cut through the wheel drive shaft inboard seal during service. Cutting through the seal may damage the sealing surface of the housing and the tripot bushing. Damage to the sealing surface may lead to water and dirt intrusion and premature wear of the constant velocity joint.

2. Disconnect the swage ring from the halfshaft bar using a hand grinder to cut through the ring, taking care not to damage the halfshaft bar.

3. Remove the large seal retaining clamp (2) from the tripot joint with side cutters. Discard the large seal retaining clamp.

4. Separate the inboard seal from the tri-lobal tripot bushing (3) at the large diameter.

5. Slide the seal away from the joint along the halfshaft bar.

6. Remove the housing (1) from the tripot joint spider and the halfshaft bar (2).

7. Spread the spacer ring (1) using J 8059 (or equivalent).

8. Remove the spacer ring (1), spider assembly (2), spacer ring (3) (if equipped) using J 8059, and tripot boot (4). Discard the boot and rings.

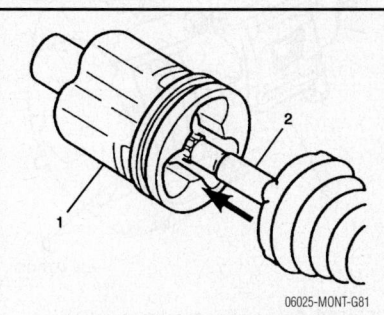

Fig. 25 Removing the housing (1) from the tripot joint spider (CV joint) and the halfshaft bar (2)

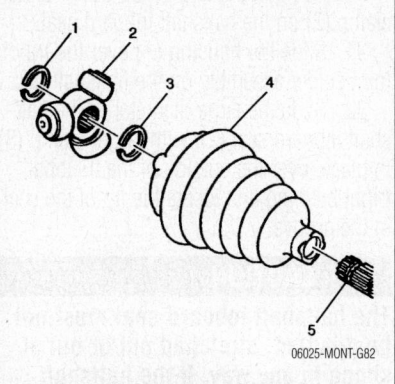

Fig. 26 Disassembling the CV joint components: spacer ring (1), spider assembly (2), spacer ring (3), tripot boot (4), halfshaft bar (5)

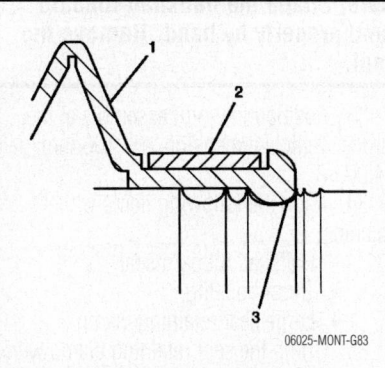

Fig. 27 Assembling the CV joint components: joint seal (1), swage ring (2), joint seal groove (3)

9. Clean the halfshaft bar (5). Use a wire brush in order to remove any rust in the boot mounting area (grooves).

10. Inspect the needle rollers, needle bearings, and trunnion. Check the tripot housing for unusual wear, cracks, or other damage. Replace any damaged parts with the appropriate kit.

To install:

11. Place the new small swage ring or eared clamp (2) onto the small end of the joint seal (1). Slide the joint seal (1) and the small swage ring or eared clamp (2) onto the halfshaft bar.

12. Position the small end of the joint seal (1) into the joint seal groove (3) on the halfshaft bar.

13. For swage ring installation, mount J 41048 in a vise and proceed as follows:

14. Position the inboard end (1) of the halfshaft assembly in tool J 41048.

15. Align the top of the seal neck on the bottom die using the indicator.

16. Place the top half of the J 41048 on the lower half.

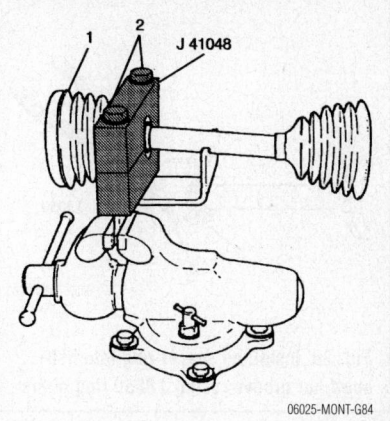

Fig. 28 Installing the swage ring, using a J 41048 holding tool. Position inboard end (1) into tool, assemble J 41048, tighten tool bolts (2) and align components

✳✳ CAUTION

Before proceeding, ensure there are no pinch points on the halfshaft inboard seal. This could cause damage to the halfshaft inboard seal.

17. Insert the bolts (2).
18. Tighten the bolts by hand until snug.
19. Align the following items:
   • Halfshaft inboard seal (1)
   • Halfshaft bar
   Swage ring (2)

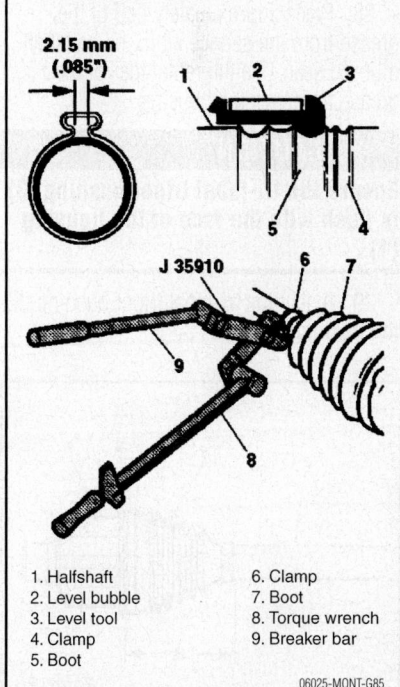

1. Halfshaft
2. Level bubble
3. Level tool
4. Clamp
5. Boot
6. Clamp
7. Boot
8. Torque wrench
9. Breaker bar

06025-MONT-G85

Fig. 29 Assembling the eared clamp with special tool J 35910 to properly crimp clamp

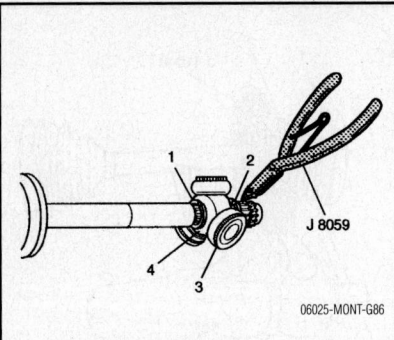

Fig. 30 Installing spacer ring into half-shaft bar groove, using J 8059 ring pliers

20. Tighten each bolt of the clamping tool (J 41048) 180 degrees at a time using a ratchet wrench.

21. Alternate between each bolt until both sides are bottomed.

22. For eared clamp installation, mount the halfshaft into a vise.

23. Slide the tripot seal (7) to the corresponding groove on the halfshaft bar.

24. Crimp the eared clamp (6) using J 35910, a torque wrench (8), and a breaker bar (9).

25. If equipped, install the spacer ring (2) into the groove of the halfshaft bar using J 8059.

26. Slide the tripot joint spider assembly (4) as far as it will go on the halfshaft bar.

27. Install the spacer ring (2) into the groove of the halfshaft bar J 8059.

28. Place approximately half of the grease from the service kit in the halfshaft inboard seal. Use the remainder of the grease to repack the housing.

✳✳ CAUTION

Ensure the tri-lobal tripot bushing (3) is flush with the face of the housing (1).

29. Install the tri-lobal tripot bushing (3) to housing (1).

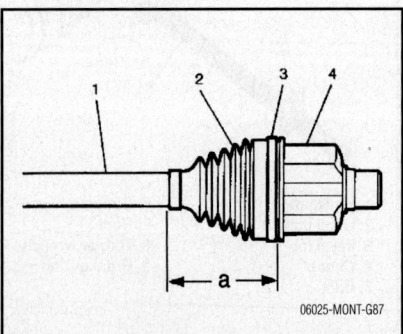

Fig. 31 Installing joint assembly to proper dimension ("a")

30. Position the larger new seal retaining clamp (2) on the halfshaft inboard seal.

31. Slide the housing (1) over the tripot joint spider assembly on the halfshaft bar.

32. Slide the large diameter of the half-shaft inboard seal (2), with larger clamp (3) in place, over the outside of the tri-lobal tripot bushing and locate the lip of the seal in the groove.

✳✳ CAUTION

The halfshaft inboard seal must not be dimpled, stretched out or out of shape in any way. If the halfshaft inboard seal is not shaped correctly, carefully insert a thin flat blunt tool, no sharp edges, between the large seal opening and the tri-lobal tripot bushing in order to equalize the pressure. Shape the halfshaft inboard seal properly by hand. Remove the tool.

33. Position the joint assembly at the proper vehicle dimension, a = 106 mm (4.00 in).

34. Align the following items while latching:
- Halfshaft inboard seal
- Tripot housing
- Large seal retaining clamp

35. Crimp the seal retaining clamp with J 35910 to 130 ft. lbs. (176 Nm). Add the breaker bar and the torque wrench to J 35910 if necessary.

36. Check the gap dimension (a) on the clamp ear. If the gap dimension is larger than shown, continue tightening until the gap dimension of 0.102 inch (2.6mm) is reached.

37. Fully stroke the joint several times to disperse the grease.

REAR AXLE HOUSING

REMOVAL & INSTALLATION

1. Raise and safely support the vehicle.

2. Position a jack stand under the front of the rear differential and firmly secure the differential to the jack.

3. Remove the front driveshaft.

4. Remove the axle housing-to-bracket through bolt and nut.

5. Remove the axle housing-to-differential bolts.

6. Pull the axle housing toward the front of the vehicle in order to disengage the axle housing from the differential pinion shaft.

7. Remove the axle housing from the differential.

To install:

8. Align the splines on the axle housing shaft to the differential pinion shaft.

9. Install the axle housing to the differential.

10. Install the axle housing-to-bracket through bolt. Tighten the nut to 47 ft. lbs. (64 Nm).

11. Install the axle housing-to-differential carrier bolts and tighten to 18 ft. lbs. (25 Nm).

12. Install the driveshaft.

13. Remove the jack stand from the differential and lower the vehicle.

REAR AXLE SHAFT, BEARING & SEAL

REMOVAL & INSTALLATION

See Figures 32 through 34.

1. Apply the parking brake.
2. Raise and safely support the vehicle.
3. Remove the tire and wheel assembly.

➡**When removing the wheel, mark the location of the wheel to the hub prior to removal. Mark the individual location of all retainers as they are removed.**

➡**The halfshaft nut must not be reused. Replace the halfshaft nut with new nut whenever it is removed.**

4. Remove the halfshaft nut and discard it.

5. Release the parking brake.

6. Remove and support the brake caliper bracket as follows:

a. Remove the brake caliper from the mounting bracket and support the brake caliper (2) with heavy mechanics wire (1), or equivalent.

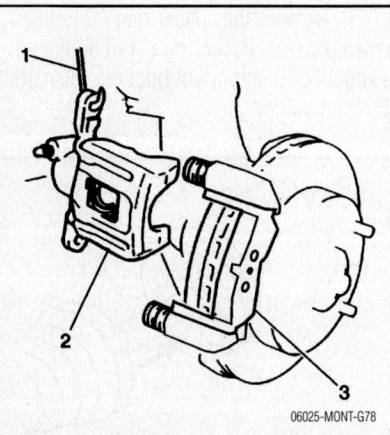

Fig. 32 Suspending the brake caliper bracket (2) out of the way on mechanic's wire (1) after detaching it from the brake caliper (3)

✳✳ CAUTION

Do NOT disconnect the hydraulic brake flexible hose from the caliper.

   b. Remove the brake pads from the brake caliper bracket (3).

   c. Remove the brake pad retainers from the brake caliper bracket (3).

   7. Remove the nut securing the park brake cable routing bracket, if necessary.

   8. Remove the bolt retaining the rear tie rod end from the rear suspension knuckle; do NOT loosen the tie rod end jam nut.

   9. Loosen, but do not remove, the bolts securing the park brake cable bracket to the suspension knuckle.

   10. Detach the wheel speed sensor electrical connector.

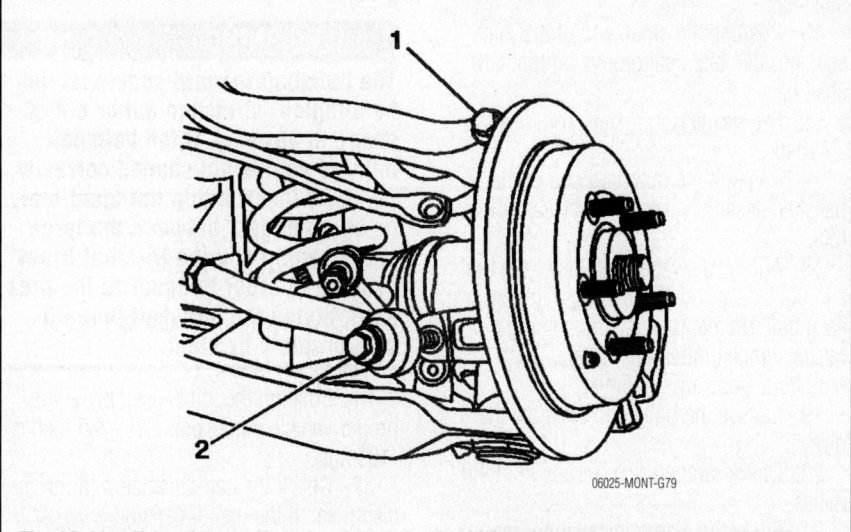

Fig. 33 Identifying the rear tie rod end retaining bolt (2) and the upper control arm bolt (1)

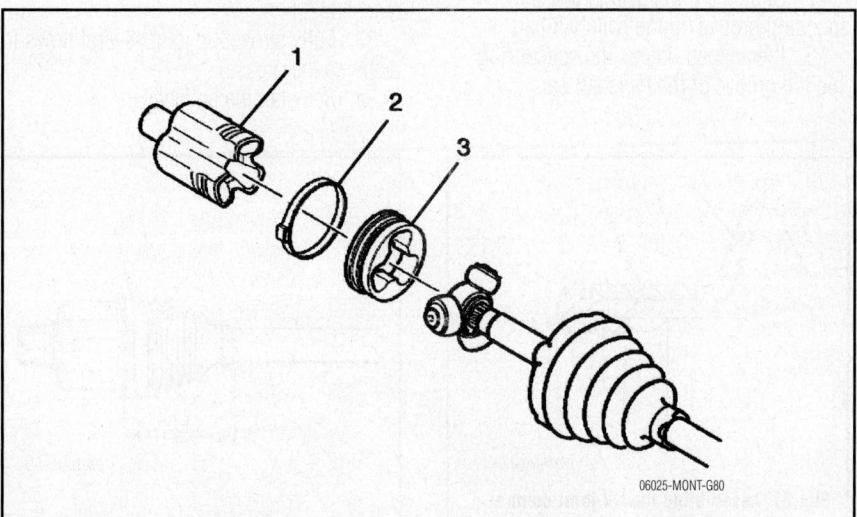

Fig. 34 Separating the halfshaft from the wheel hub and bearing, using the special puller (J-42129)

   11. Install the puller, J-42129, onto the wheel hub and secure with wheel nuts.

   12. Begin to disengage the halfshaft from the wheel hub and bearing.

   13. Reposition the suspension knuckle toward the rear of the vehicle.

   14. Remove the special puller from the wheel hub.

   15. Remove the halfshaft from the rear axle differential and remove the halfshaft from the vehicle, using special removal tool assembly (J 33008-A, J 29794, and J 2619-01).

✳✳ WARNING

The differential output shaft oil seal must be replaced when removing the rear halfshaft.

   16. Remove the rear halfshaft oil seal.

To install:

   17. Position the halfshaft to the differential output shaft.

✳✳ WARNING

Do not damage the differential output shaft oil seal.

   18. Carefully align and guide the halfshaft onto the differential output shaft.

   19. Install the halfshaft fully onto the differential output shaft using light force.

   20. Verify that the halfshaft is fully seated on the differential output shaft retaining ring by grasping the inner tripot housing and pulling outward. Do not pull on the halfshaft bar. The halfshaft will remain firmly in place when properly engaged.

   21. Align and carefully guide the halfshaft into the hub and bearing but do not seat fully.

   22. Position the suspension knuckle to the upper control arm.

   23. Install or connect the following:

- Bolt and nut to the upper control arm/suspension knuckle assembly and tighten the bolt to 63 ft. lbs. (85Nm)
- Secure the park brake cable bracket.
- Rear tie rod to the rear suspension knuckle
- Tie rod to knuckle bolt and tighten the bolt to 63 ft. lbs. (85 Nm)
- Brake caliper bracket
- Wheel speed sensor electrical connector
- Park brake cable routing bracket, if removed
- Park brake cable routing bracket nut, if removed. Tighten the nut to 89 inch lbs. (10 Nm)
- Set the park brake
- NEW halfshaft spindle nut

   24. Slowly tighten the nut in order to draw the halfshaft spindle into the wheel hub and bearing and tighten the halfshaft spindle nut to 192 ft. lbs. (260 Nm).

   25. Install the tire and wheel assembly.

   26. Lower the vehicle.

   27. Release the parking brake.

REAR CV-JOINTS

OVERHAUL

See Figures 35 through 38.

   1. Remove the small seal clamp from the wheel drive shaft bar using side cutters and discard the clamp.

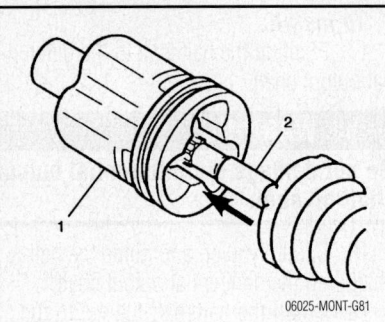

Fig. 35 Removing the housing (1) from the tripot joint spider (CV joint) and the halfshaft bar (2)

✷✷ CAUTION

Do not cut into the wheel drive shaft tri-lobal tripot bushing.

2. Remove the large seal clamp from the tripot joint with side cutters and discard the clamp.

3. Separate the wheel drive shaft inboard seal from the tri-lobal tripot bushing.

4. Slide the seal away from the joint along the wheel drive shaft bar.

5. Remove the housing (1) from the tripot joint spider and the wheel drive shaft bar (2).

6. Remove the guide (3) from the spring.

7. Remove the spring (4) from the tripot housing.

✷✷ CAUTION

The correct 60 degree offset relationship between the inner and outer tripot spiders must be maintained. Accurately reference mark the tripot spider position on the wheel drive shaft bar before disassembly.

8. Reference mark the position of the tripot spider (1) on the wheel drive shaft bar (2).

9. Using a brass drift and hammer, carefully tap around the tripot spider face in order to compress the barrel retaining ring on the wheel drive shaft bar.

10. Remove the tripot spider from the wheel drive shaft bar.

11. Remove and discard the barrel retaining ring from the wheel drive shaft bar.

12. Remove the joint seal from the wheel drive shaft bar.

13. Inspect the following parts for damage or wear:
- Wheel drive shaft inboard seal
- Tripot joint spider assembly
- Housing
- Tri-lobal tripot bushing

To install:

14. Place the new small swage ring or eared clamp onto the small end of the joint seal. Slide the joint seal and the small swage ring or eared clamp onto the halfshaft bar.

15. Position the small end of the joint seal into the joint seal groove on the halfshaft bar.

16. For swage ring installation, use the J 41048.

17. Position the outboard end of the halfshaft assembly into the J 41048 holding tool.

18. Align the swage ring. Insert the bolts and tighten by hand until snug. Tighten each bolt 180 degrees at a time using a ratchet wrench. Alternate between each bolt until both sides are bottomed.

19. Loosen the bolts and separate the dies.

20. Check swaged ring for any lip deformities.

21. For eared clamp installation, mount the halfshaft into a vise.

22. Slide the tripot seal to the corresponding groove on the halfshaft bar.

23. If equipped, install the spacer ring into the groove of the halfshaft bar.

24. Slide the tripot joint spider assembly as far as it will go on the halfshaft bar.

25. Install the spacer ring into the groove of the halfshaft bar.

26. Place approximately half of the grease from the service kit in the halfshaft inboard seal. Use the remainder of the grease to repack the housing.

➡ **Ensure the tri-lobal tripot bushing is flush with the face of the housing.**

27. Install the tri-lobal tripot bushing to housing.

28. Position the larger new seal retaining clamp on the halfshaft inboard seal.

29. Slide the housing over the tripot joint spider assembly on the halfshaft bar.

30. Slide the large diameter of the halfshaft inboard seal, with larger clamp in place, over the outside of the tri-lobal tripot bushing and locate the lip of the seal in the groove.

✷✷ WARNING

The halfshaft inboard seal must not be dimpled, stretched out or out of shape in any way. If the halfshaft inboard seal is not shaped correctly, carefully insert a thin flat blunt tool, no sharp edges, between the large seal opening and the tri-lobal tripot bushing in order to equalize the pressure. Shape the halfshaft inboard seal properly by hand.

31. Position the joint assembly at the proper vehicle dimension ("a" - 4.0 inches (106mm).

32. Check the gap dimension (a) on the clamp ear. If the gap dimension is larger than shown, continue tightening until the gap dimension of 0.102 inch (2.6mm) is reached.

33. Fully stroke the joint several times to disperse the grease.

34. Reinstall the halfshaft.

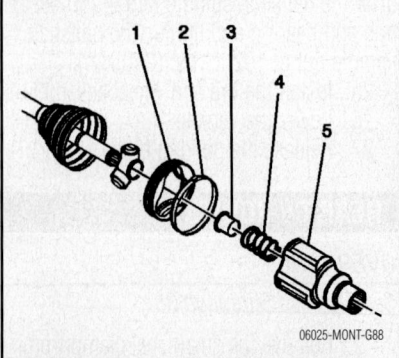

Fig. 36 Exploded view of the rear (tripot) joint assembly

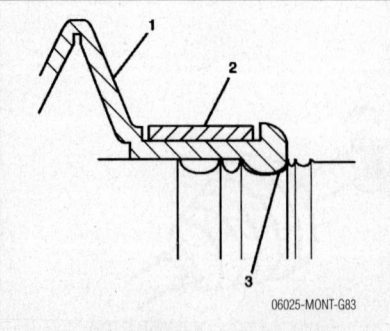

Fig. 37 Assembling the CV joint components: joint seal (1), swage ring (2), joint seal groove (3)

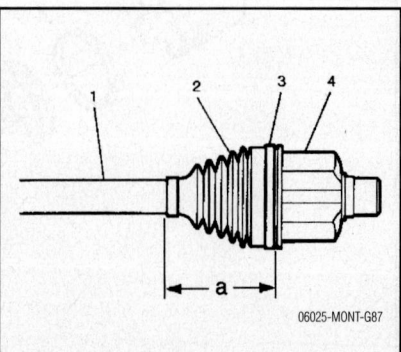

Fig. 38 Installing joint assembly to proper dimension ("a")

REAR DIFFERENTIAL CARRIER

REMOVAL & INSTALLATION

1. Before servicing the vehicle, refer to the Precautions Section.
2. Set the parking brake.
3. Drain the rear differential.
4. Remove or disconnect the following:
   • Right rear tire and wheel assembly

➡**When removing the wheel, mark the location of the wheel to the hub prior to removal. Mark the individual location of all retainers as they are removed.**

   • Electrical connector from the clutch pump check valve
   • Right rear halfshaft
   • Front propeller shaft
   • Place an adjustable support beneath the torque tube
   • Loosen, but do not remove the torque tube to bracket through bolt and nut
   • Bolts from the torque tube bracket
   • Differential carrier to cradle mounting bolts, nuts, washers, and mounts from the differential

✴✴ WARNING

During the removal of the halfshaft, the differential output shaft may become disengaged from the differential. If this occurs, firmly grasp and separate the output shaft from the halfshaft. Align the splines on the output shaft to the differential and reposition the output shaft to the differential.

   • While simultaneously moving the differential assembly to the right side of the vehicle, disengage the left halfshaft from the differential.
   • Rear differential and axle housing as an assembly
   • Axle housing from the differential

To install:

5. Install the axle housing to the differential.
6. Install the rear differential and axle housing assembly to the suspension cradle; at the same time, guide the left halfshaft onto the differential output shaft while positioning the differential assembly to the suspension cradle.
7. Place an adjustable support under the torque tube.
8. Ensure that the left halfshaft is fully engaged to the differential output shaft.
9. Install the differential carrier mounts, washers, bolts, and nuts to the differential.

Tighten the differential carrier to cradle mounting bolts to 37 ft. lbs. (50 Nm).
10. Torque tube bracket to body bolts to 41 ft. lbs. (55 Nm). Tighten the torque tube to bracket through bolt and nut to 47 ft. lbs. (64 Nm).
11. Install the front propeller shaft.
12. Install the right rear halfshaft.
13. Install the right rear tire and wheel assembly.
14. Fill the axle with synthetic gear oil.
15. Inspect the differential oil level to ensure it is even with, but not lower than, 6mm (0.25 in) below the opening of the fill hole.
16. Attach the electrical connector to the clutch pump check valve.
17. Lower the vehicle.

REAR PINION SEAL

REMOVAL & INSTALLATION

See Figure 39.

1. Before servicing the vehicle, refer to the Precautions Section.

2. Raise and safely support the vehicle.
3. Position a jack stand under the rear differential and firmly secure the differential to the jack.
4. Remove the front propeller shaft.
5. Remove the torque tube to bracket through bolt and nut.
6. Remove the torque tube to differential bolts.
7. Pull the torque tube toward the front of the vehicle in order to disengage the torque tube from the differential pinion shaft.
8. Remove the torque tube from the differential.
9. Remove the drive pinion housing oil seal and discard.

➡**The internal components of the torque tube assembly cannot be serviced separately. If corrosion exists that cannot be polished off, or there is excessive scoring or wear, the torque tube must be replaced as a complete assembly.**

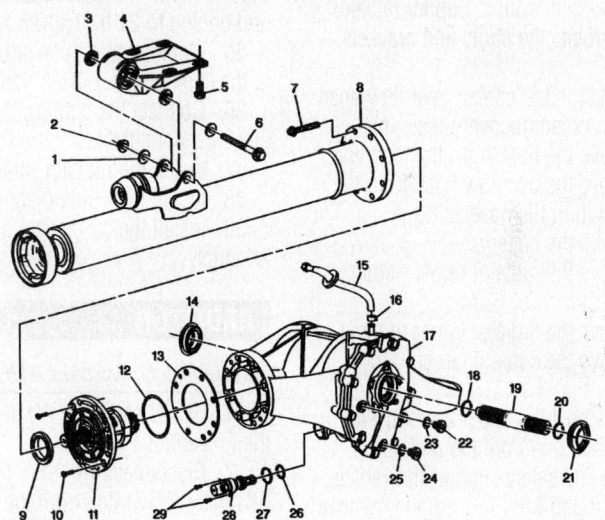

1. Washer
2. Nut
3. Spacer
4. Bracket
5. Bolt
6. Bolt
7. Bolt
8. Torque tube assembly
9. Oil seal
10. Bolt
11. Pinion and housing assembly
12. O-Ring
13. Shim
14. Oil seal (right)
15. Vent hose assembly
16. Clamp
17. Differential assembly
18. Snap ring
19. Axle shaft
20. Snap ring
21. Oil seal (left)
22. Fill plug
23. Gasket
24. Drain plug
25. Gasket
26. O-Ring
27. O-Ring
28. Clutch pump check valve
29. Bolts

06025-MONT-G89

Fig. 39 Exploded view of differential assembly, showing pinion components

10. Inspect the sealing surface of the propeller shaft contained inside the torque tube, polish corrosion off with a crocus cloth.

To install:

11. Lubricate the new pinion housing assembly oil seal with synthetic gear oil.

12. Use the seal installer, J 44915, in order to install a new oil seal to the drive pinion housing.

13. Install the torque tube assembly.

14. Inspect the differential carrier lubricant level.

15. Align the splines on the torque tube shaft to the differential pinion shaft.

16. Install the torque tube to the differential.

17. Install the torque tube to bracket through bolt and tighten the torque tube to

bracket through bolt nut to 47 ft. lbs. (64 Nm).

18. Install the torque tube-to-differential carrier bolts and tighten the bolts to 18 ft. lbs. (25 Nm).

19. Install the front propeller shaft.

20. Remove the jack stand from under the rear differential.

21. Lower the vehicle.

ENGINE COOLING

ENGINE FAN

REMOVAL & INSTALLATION

1. Before servicing the vehicle, refer to the Precautions Section.

2. Remove the air cleaner and duct assembly.

3. Remove right side diagonal brace.

4. Remove radiator inlet hose.

5. Disconnect the cooling fan harness electrical connector.

6. Loosen the engine mount strut nuts at the engine side.

7. Remove the engine mount strut bracket brace bolts from the upper radiator support and rotate the struts and brackets rearward.

8. Reposition the coolant overflow hose clamp at the coolant recovery reservoir.

9. Remove the hose from the reservoir.

10. Remove the overflow hose from the retainers. Position the hose aside.

11. Remove the battery.

12. Remove the radiator upper mount bolts.

13. Remove the radiator upper mounts.

14. Remove the cooling fan shroud bolts.

15. Disconnect the upper transmission oil cooler (TOC) line from the radiator.

16. Raise and safely support the vehicle.

17. If equipped with 3.9L engine, remove the radiator air baffle.

18. Disconnect the TOC lines from the fan shroud retainer clip.

19. Lower the vehicle.

20. Remove the cooling fan shroud and fans.

To install:

21. Install the cooling fan shroud and fans.

22. Raise and safely support the vehicle.

23. Connect the TOC lines to the fan shroud retainer clip.

24. If equipped with 3.9L engine, install the radiator air baffle.

25. Connect the upper TOC line to the radiator.

26. Install the cooling fan shroud bolts.

27. Install the radiator upper mounts.

28. Install the radiator upper mount bolts and tighten to 89 inch lbs. (10 Nm).

29. Install the battery.

30. Position the hose. Install the overflow hose to the retainers.

31. Install the hose to the reservoir.

32. Position the coolant overflow hose clamp at the coolant recovery reservoir.

33. Position the engine mount struts brackets flush with the upper radiator support.

34. Install the engine mount strut bracket brace bolts to the upper radiator support and tighten to 21 ft. lbs. (28 Nm).

35. Tighten the engine strut mount nuts at the engine side to 35 ft. lbs. (48 Nm).

36. Connect the cooling fan harness electrical connector.

37. Install the radiator inlet hose.

38. Install right side diagonal brace.

39. Install the air cleaner and duct assembly.

RADIATOR

REMOVAL & INSTALLATION

1. Before servicing the vehicle, refer to the Precautions Section.

2. Disconnect the lower transmission oil cooler (TOC) line from the radiator.

3. Remove the cooling fans and shroud.

4. Remove the radiator inlet hose.

5. Remove the radiator outlet hose.

6. Remove the bolt that secures the radiator to the condenser.

7. Remove the condenser tube clip screw.

8. Tilt the radiator and condenser inward toward the engine and remove the radiator.

To install:

9. Install the radiator.

10. Install the condenser tube clip screw.

11. Install the bolt that secures the radiator to the condenser.

12. Install the radiator hoses.

13. Install the cooling fan and shroud.

14. Connect the lower transmission oil cooler (TOC) line to the radiator.

15. Refill the cooling system.

16. Inspect the transmission fluid level.

THERMOSTAT

REMOVAL & INSTALLATION

3.5L Engine

1. Before servicing the vehicle, refer to the Precautions Section.

2. Remove the air cleaner intake duct.

3. Partially drain the cooling system.

4. Remove the radiator inlet hose from the thermostat housing.

5. Remove the thermostat housing bolts.

6. Remove the thermostat.

7. Clean and inspect the thermostat housing gasket mating surfaces.

To install:

8. Install the thermostat.

9. Install the thermostat housing.

10. Install the thermostat housing bolts and tighten to 18 ft. lbs. (25 Nm).

11. Install the radiator inlet hose to the thermostat housing.

12. Install the air cleaner intake duct.

13. Fill the cooling system.

14. Start the engine and check for leaks.

3.9L Engine

See Figure 40.

1. Before servicing the vehicle, refer to the Precautions Section.

2. Drain the cooling system.

3. Release the tension on the hose clamp at the thermostat housing and remove coolant hose.

4. Remove the thermostat housing mounting bolts and remove the thermostat housing.

5. Remove the thermostat.

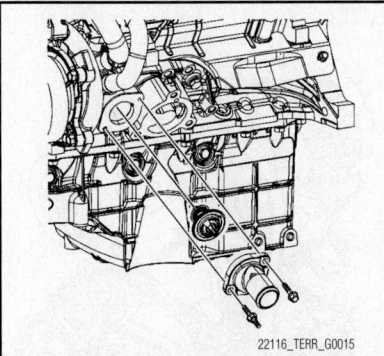

Fig. 40 Remove the thermostat housing to access the thermostat—3.9L engine shown

22116_TERR_G0015

To install:

6. Install the thermostat.

7. Install the thermostat housing and tighten the bolts to 18 ft. lbs. (25 Nm).

8. Install the coolant hose to the thermostat housing and install the hose clamp.

9. Refill the cooling system to the correct level.

10. Start the engine and check for leaks.

WATER PUMP

REMOVAL & INSTALLATION

See Figures 41 through 43.

1. Before servicing the vehicle, refer to the Precautions Section.

2. Disconnect the negative battery cable.

3. Drain the engine cooling system.

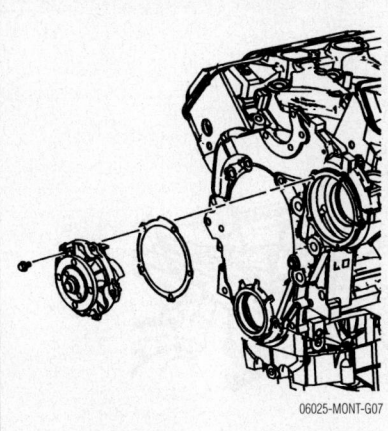

06025-MONT-G07

Fig. 41 Showing the water pump and gasket on the 3.5L engine

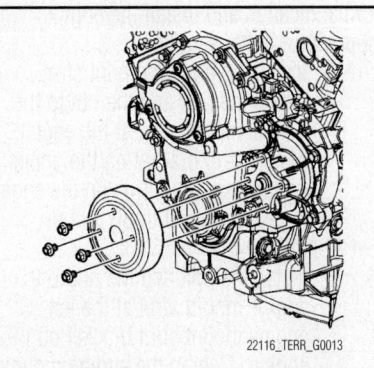

22116_TERR_G0013

Fig. 42 Remove the water pump pulley bolts and pulley—3.9L engine shown

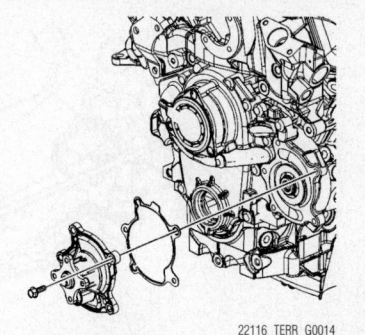

22116_TERR_G0014

Fig. 43 Water pump and gasket mounting on the 3.9L engine

4. Relieve the belt tension and remove the accessory drive belt.

5. Remove or disconnect the following:
   - Water pump pulley
   - Water pump bolts
   - Water pump and gasket

To install:

6. Clean the gasket mating surfaces.

7. Install or connect the following:
   - Water pump using a new gasket. Tighten the water pump bolts to 89 inch lbs. (10 Nm)
   - Water pump pulley and tighten the bolts to 18 ft. lbs. (25 Nm).
   - Drive belt
   - Negative battery cable

8. Refill the engine cooling system.

9. Run the engine and check for leaks.

ENGINE ELECTRICAL   CHARGING SYSTEM

ALTERNATOR

REMOVAL & INSTALLATION

3.5L and 3.9L Engines

See Figures 44 through 51.

1. Before servicing the vehicle, refer to the Precautions Section.

2. Disconnect the negative battery cable.

3. Disconnect the windshield wiper transmission link in front of the wiper motor and position out of the way as follows:

   a. Remove the driver side and passenger side wiper arms.

   b. Remove the air inlet grille panel by removing the retaining screws after the wiper arms are removed.

   c. Lower the washer container into the engine compartment.

   d. Disconnect the electrical connector (2) from the wiper motor (1).

   e. Remove the 4 bolts, in sequence as shown, from the wiper module (5). Care-

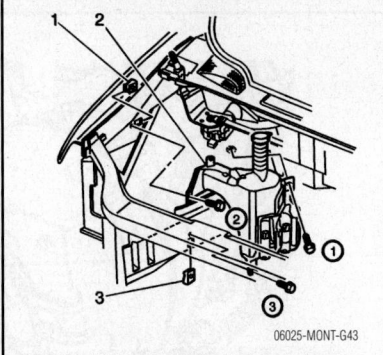

06025-MONT-G43

Fig. 44 Disconnect washer container to lower it into the engine compartment

fully guide the wiper modules out of the way to access the alternator.

4. Rotate the engine forward as follows:

   a. Remove the throttle body air inlet duct.

   b. Set the park brake.

   c. Shift the transaxle into Neutral.

   d. Remove the engine mount strut

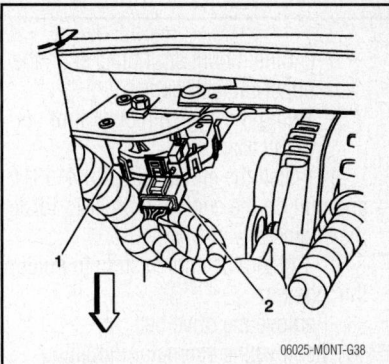

06025-MONT-G38

Fig. 45 Detaching the electrical connector from the wiper/washer motor

bolts. Swing the engine mount struts aside as follows:

   - Remove the bolt and the nut from the engine mount strut at the left engine mount strut bracket on the engine.
   - Remove the bolt and the nut from the engine mount strut at the

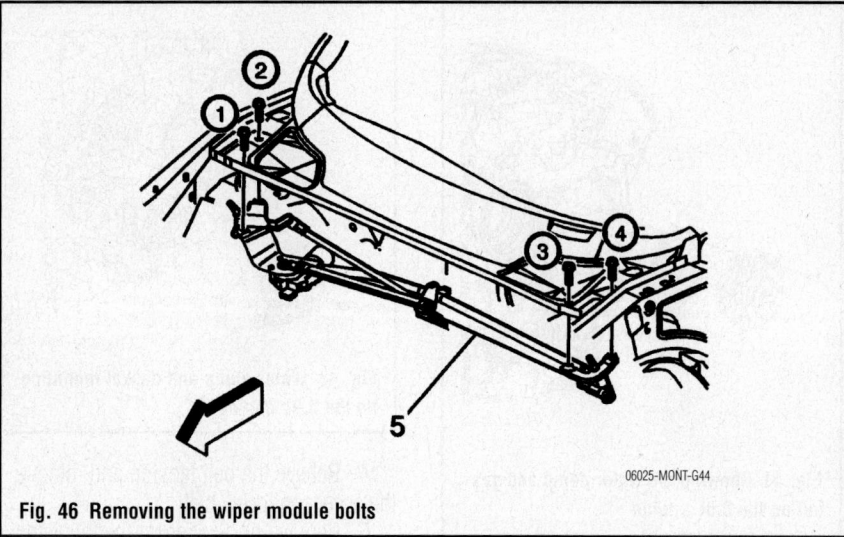

Fig. 46 Removing the wiper module bolts

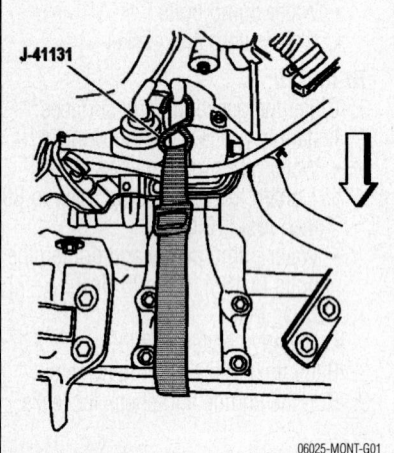

Fig. 47 Identifying the J 41131 engine strap

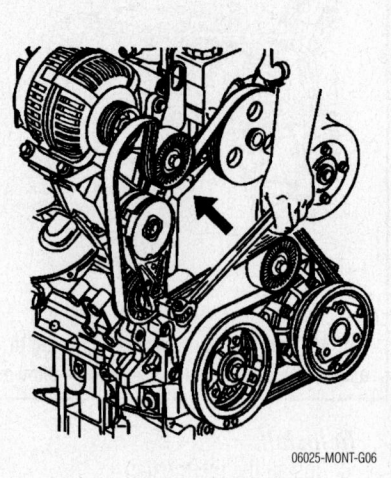

Fig. 49 Removing the drive belt from the 3.5L engine

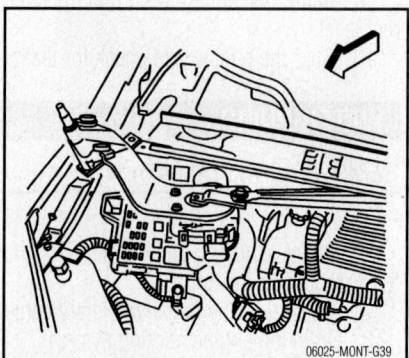

Fig. 50 Moving the wiper transmission module aside

normal location and install the engine mount strut bolts, as follows:

- Install the engine mount strut.
- Install the bolt and the nut to the engine mount strut at the engine mount strut bracket on the upper radiator support. Tighten the engine mount strut bolt to 36 ft. lbs. (48 Nm).
- Install the bolt and the nut to the engine mount strut at the left engine mount strut bracket on the engine. Tighten the engine mount strut bolt and nut to 36 ft. lbs. (48 Nm).

12. Connect the windshield wiper transmission as follows:

  a. Position the wiper module to the engine mount strut bracket on the upper radiator support.

- Swing the engine mount strut out of the way.

  e. Install the engine strap (J 41131) and pull on the engine in order to rotate the engine forward.

  f. Tighten the engine strap to hold in this position.

5. Remove the drive belt.

6. Remove the alternator mounting bolts and the alternator.

To install:

7. Install the alternator into position.

8. Install the mounting bolts and torque the bolts 37 ft. lbs. (50 Nm) and the nuts to 22 ft. lbs. (15 Nm).

9. Reattach the alternator wiring connectors.

10. Install the alternator drive belt and ensure proper position and tension.

11. Position the engine back into the

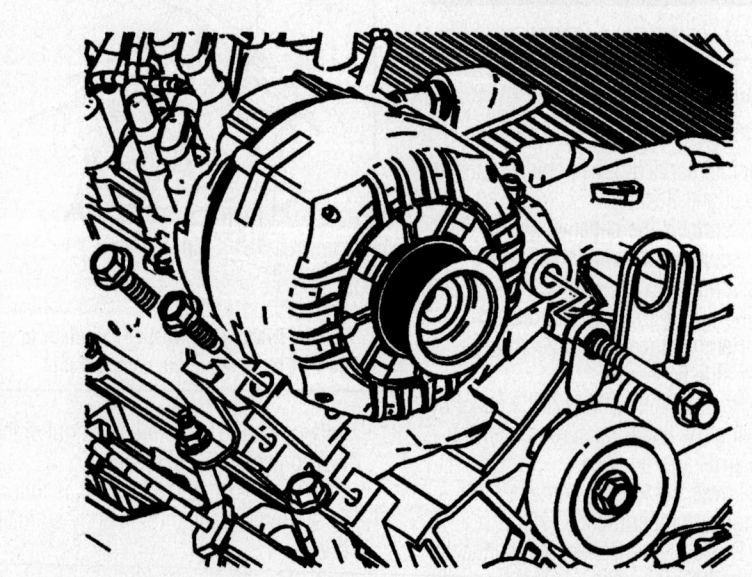

Fig. 48 Indicating the alternator mounting bolts

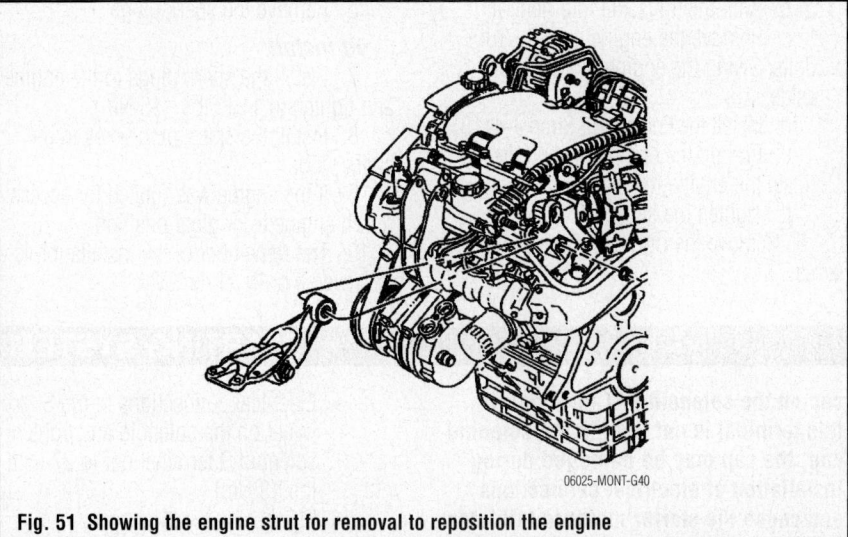

Fig. 51 Showing the engine strut for removal to reposition the engine

06025-MONT-G40

lower plenum in the driver side fender flange opening first.

b. Rotate the module into the opening at the passenger side plenum.

c. Ensure the rear center mount is secure into the sheet metal flange at the rear of the module.

d. Install the wiper module bolts. Tighten the bolts in sequence, as shown, to 10 Nm (89 inch lbs.).

e. Connect the electrical connector to the motor.

f. Install the air inlet grille panel.

g. Install the driver side wiper arm and the passenger side wiper arm.

h. Secure the washer container.

i. Close the hood. Inspect the wiper system for proper operation.

13. Connect the negative battery cable.

ENGINE ELECTRICAL

IGNITION COIL

REMOVAL & INSTALLATION

The ignition coils are part of the ignition coil module assembly. This procedure covers removal and installation of the ignition coil module.

3.5L Engine

1. Before servicing the vehicle, refer to the Precautions Section.

2. Disconnect the brake booster vacuum hose from the intake manifold.

3. Note the position of the spark plug wires for the installation and disconnect the spark plug wires from the ignition coil and module assembly.

4. Remove the 4 screws securing the ignition coil and module assembly to the bracket.

5. Remove the ignition coil and module assembly.

To install:

6. Install the ignition coil and module assembly to the bracket.

7. Install the ignition coil and module assembly screws and tighten to 40 inch lbs. (4.5 Nm).

8. Connect the spark plug wires as noted during the removal.

9. Connect the brake booster vacuum hose to the intake manifold.

3.9L Engine

1. Before servicing the vehicle, refer to the Precautions Section.

2. Remove the intake manifold cover.

3. Disconnect the brake booster vacuum hose from the intake manifold.

4. Disconnect the manifold absolute pressure (MAP) sensor electrical connector.

5. Disconnect the ignition coil electrical connector.

6. Disconnect the left side spark plug wires from the ignition coil.

7. Disconnect the right side spark plug wires from the ignition coil.

8. Remove the upper left coil mount bracket bolt.

9. Raise and safely support the vehicle.

10. Disconnect the wire retainers on the ignition coil bracket.

11. Remove the remaining bolt and two nuts on the coil bracket.

12. Lower the vehicle.

13. Remove the ignition coil bracket assembly.

To install:

14. Install the ignition coil.

15. Raise and safely support the vehicle.

16. Install the upper right coil mount bolt.

17. Install the coil mount nuts and tighten to 15 ft. lbs. (20 Nm).

18. Lower the vehicle.

19. Install the upper left coil mount bolt and tighten to 15 ft. lbs. (20 Nm).

20. Connect the right and left side spark plug wires to the ignition coil.

21. Connect the ignition coil electrical connector.

22. Connect the MAP sensor electrical connector.

23. Connect the brake booster to the intake manifold.

24. Install the intake manifold cover.

IGNITION SYSTEM

IGNITION TIMING

ADJUSTMENT

The ignition timing is controlled by the Powertrain Control Module (PCM). No adjustment is necessary or possible.

SPARK PLUGS

REMOVAL & INSTALLATION

3.5L Engine

1. Replacing the engine left bank spark plugs requires, rotating the engine for access as follows:

a. Remove the throttle body air inlet duct.

b. Set the park brake.

c. Shift the transaxle into Neutral.

d. Remove the engine mount strut bolts. Swing the engine mount struts aside.

e. Install the Engine Tilt Strap J-41131.

f. Pull on the engine in order to rotate the engine forward.

g. Tighten the strap.

2. Remove the spark plug wires from the spark plugs.

3. Remove the spark plugs from the engine.

To install:

4. Install the spark plugs to the engine and tighten to 11 ft. lbs. (15 Nm). If installing the spark plugs into a new cylinder head, tighten to 15 ft. lbs. (20 Nm).

5. Install the spark plug wires to the spark plugs.

6. If the engine was rotated for access, return engine to original position.

3.9L Engine

1. Remove the air intake assembly.
2. Remove the intake manifold.
3. Remove the left side spark plug wires.
4. Rotate the engine for access as follows:
    a. Set the parking brake.

    b. Shift the transaxle into neutral.
    c. Remove the engine mount strut bolts. Swing the engine mount struts aside.
    d. Install the Engine Tilt Strap J-41131.
    e. Pull on the engine in order to rotate the engine forward.
    f. Tighten the strap.
5. Remove the right side spark plug wires.

6. Remove the spark plugs.

To install:

7. Install the spark plugs to the engine and tighten to 11 ft. lbs. (15 Nm).
8. Install the spark plug wires to the spark plugs.
9. If the engine was rotated for access, return engine to original position.
10. The remainder of the installation is the reverse order of removal.

ENGINE ELECTRICAL

STARTER

REMOVAL & INSTALLATION

See Figure 52.

1. Before servicing the vehicle, refer to the Precautions Section.
2. Remove or disconnect the following:
   - Negative battery cable
   - Radiator air baffle, for clearance if necessary
   - Flywheel inspection cover bolts
   - Flywheel inspection cover
   - Electrical connections from the starter motor
   - Starter motor mounting bolts
   - Starter motor

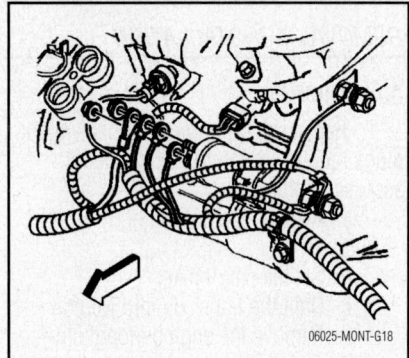

Fig. 52 Showing the starter motor location and electrical connections

06025-MONT-G18

To install:

3. Install or connect the following:

➡️**Before installing the starter motor to the engine, tighten the nut next to the**

cap on the solenoid BAT terminal. If this terminal is not tight in the solenoid cap, the cap may be damaged during installation of electrical connections and cause the starter motor to fail later.

- Starter motor
- Starter motor mounting bolts and tighten the bolts to 30 ft. lbs. (40 Nm)
- Electrical connection to the battery terminal on the solenoid and tighten the battery terminal nut to 13 ft. lbs. (17 Nm)

STARTING SYSTEM

- Electrical connections to the S terminal on the solenoid and tighten solenoid S terminal nut to 27 inch lbs. (3 Nm)
- Flywheel inspection cover
- Flywheel inspection cover bolts
- Radiator air baffle, if removed
4. Connect the negative battery cable

SOLENOID REPLACEMENT

See Figure 53.

The starter motor solenoid is located on the starter motor.

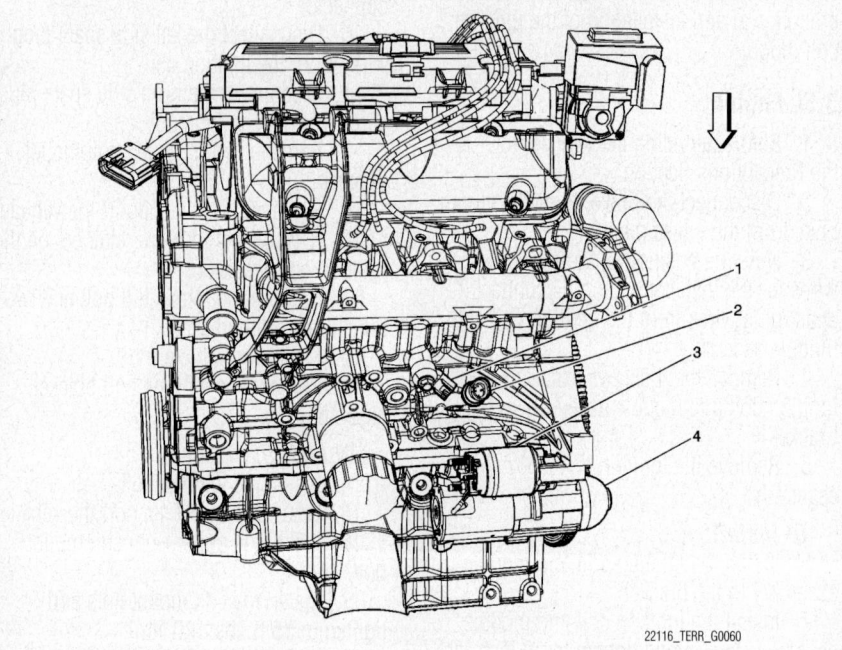

22116_TERR_G0060

Fig. 53 The starter motor solenoid (3) is located on the starter motor (4).

ENGINE MECHANICAL

➡ **Disconnecting the negative battery cable may interfere with the functions of the on board computer systems and may require the computer to undergo a relearning process, once the negative battery cable is reconnected.**

ACCESSORY DRIVE BELTS

ACCESSORY BELT ROUTING

See Figures 54 and 55.

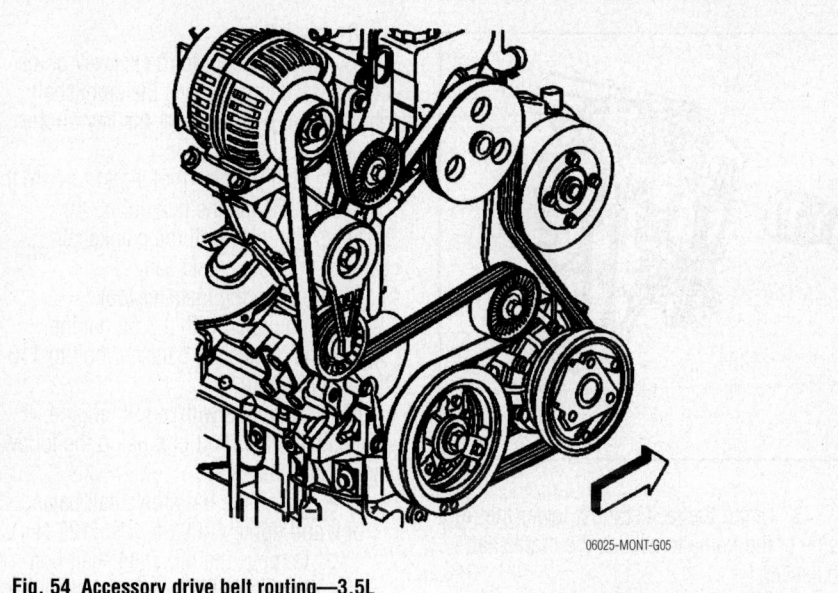

Fig. 54 Accessory drive belt routing—3.5L

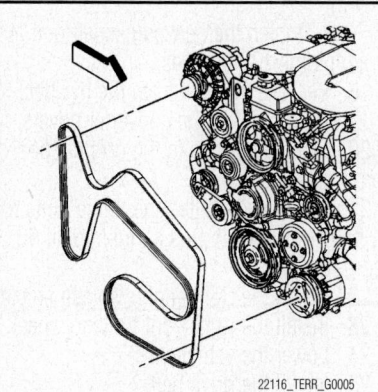

Fig. 55 Accessory drive belt routing—3.9L

INSPECTION

Inspect the drive belt for signs of glazing or cracking. A glazed belt will be perfectly smooth from slippage, while a good belt will have a slight texture of fabric visible. Cracks will usually start at the inner edge of the belt and run outward. All worn or damaged drive belts should be replaced immediately.

ADJUSTMENT

These engines are equipped with an automatic tensioner and do not need manual adjustment.

REMOVAL & INSTALLATION

1. Before servicing the vehicle, refer to the Precautions Section.
2. Rotate the drive belt tensioner counterclockwise to release the spring tension.
3. Remove the drive belt.
4. To install, reverse the removal procedure. Make sure the belt is properly seated.

CAMSHAFT AND VALVE LIFTERS

INSPECTION

1. Clean the camshaft with cleaning solvent.
2. Inspect the camshaft for scored bearing journals, damaged lobes or damaged position sensor reluctor areas.
3. Measure the camshaft journals using a micrometer. If the camshaft journals are not within: 1.868-1.869 in (47.443-47.468mm) for the 3.5L engine or 2.024-2.025 in (51.415-51.440mm), replace the camshaft.
4. Measure the camshaft runout. If runout exceeds 0.001 in (0.025mm), replace the camshaft.

5. Measure the camshaft lobe lift using a dial indicator. Lubricate the camshaft and set the camshaft on V-blocks. If lobe lift exceeds 0.2727 in (6.9263mm), replace the camshaft.

REMOVAL & INSTALLATION

See Figures 56 through 58.

1. Before servicing the vehicle, refer to the Precautions Section.
2. Properly relieve the fuel system pressure.
3. Disconnect the negative battery cable.
4. Drain the engine cooling system and the engine oil.
5. Remove the intake manifold. For additional information, refer to the following section, "Intake Manifold, Removal & Installation."
6. Remove the rocker arms and pushrods. For additional information, refer to the following section, "Rocker Arms, Removal & Installation."
7. Remove the timing chain cover. For additional information, refer to the following section, "Timing Chain Cover and Seal, Removal & Installation."
8. Remove the timing chain. For additional information, refer to the following section, "Timing Chain, Removal & Installation."
9. Remove the camshaft position sensor.
10. Remove the camshaft thrust plate.
11. Install the camshaft sprocket bolt into the camshaft. Tighten the bolt finger tight.
12. Carefully rotate and remove the camshaft from the engine block.

To install:

13. Coat the camshaft journals with clean engine oil.
14. Coat the camshaft lobes with prelube.

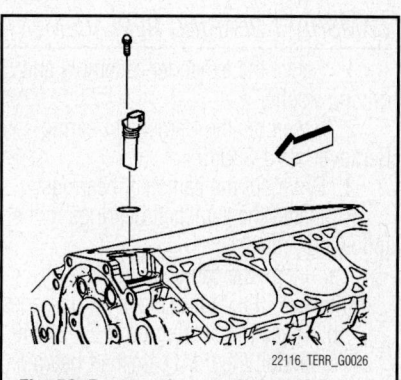

Fig. 56 Remove the camshaft position sensor

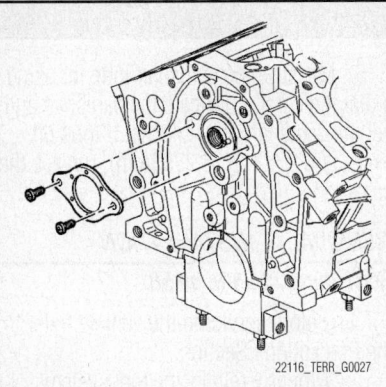

Fig. 57 Remove the camshaft thrust plate.

22116_TERR_G0027

22116_TERR_G0021

Fig. 60 Use Special Too J-29113 to install the crankshaft damper onto the crankshaft.

CRANKSHAFT DAMPER

REMOVAL & INSTALLATION

See Figures 59 and 60.

1. Before servicing the vehicle, refer to the Precautions Section.
2. Remove the drive belt.
3. Raise and safely support the vehicle.
4. Remove the right front tire and wheel.
5. Remove the right engine splash shield.
6. Install the jack stands to the frame.
7. Loosen the left frame bolts and remove the right side frame bolts.

![Showing camshaft mounting in block]

06025-MONT-G59

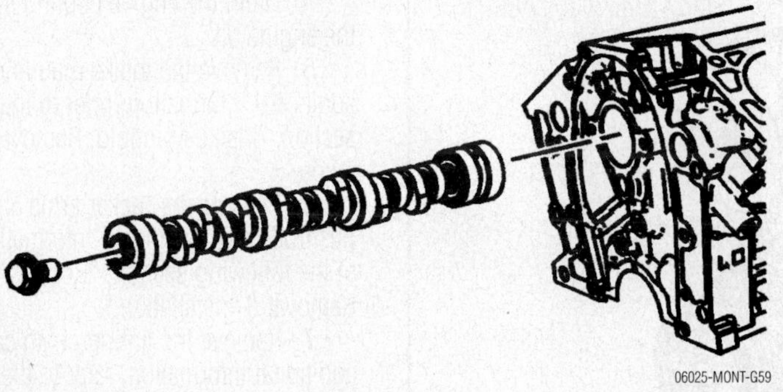

Fig. 58 Showing camshaft mounting in block

15. With the sprocket bolt still installed finger tight, carefully rotate the camshaft while installing the camshaft into the camshaft bearings.

16. Install the camshaft thrust plate and tighten the bolts to 89 inch lbs. (10 Nm).

17. Install the camshaft position sensor and tighten the bolt to 89 inch lbs. (10 Nm).

18. The remainder of the installation is the reverse order of removal.

19. Refill the cooling system to the correct level.

20. Refill the engine with oil to the correct level.

21. Start the engine and check for leaks.

CAMSHAFT BEARING REPLACEMENT

1. Select the expander assembly and driving washer.

2. Assemble the Camshaft Bearing Remover set J-33049

3. Drive out the camshaft bearings.

4. Install the camshaft bearings in the following order:

   a. Index the camshaft bearing oil holes with the engine block oil passages.

   b. Place the bearing on the J-33049.

   c. Install the third camshaft bearing.

   d. Install the second camshaft bearing.

   e. Install the outer camshaft bearings.

8. Using the jack stands, lower the right side of the frame to access the crankshaft balancer.

9. Remove the torque converter covers.

10. Install the Flywheel Lock J-37096 to the flywheel to prevent flywheel rotation.

11. Remove the crankshaft balancer bolt and the washer.

12. Remove the crankshaft balancer using a 3 jaw puller.

![Remove the crankshaft damper using a Special Tool J-41816]

22116_TERR_G0020

Fig. 59 Remove the crankshaft damper using a Special Tool J-41816 or equivalent 3-jaw puller.

To install:

13. Apply sealant to the keyway of the crankshaft damper. Place the crankshaft damper into position over the key on the crankshaft.

14. Install Special Tool J-29113 onto the crankshaft. Rotate the hex nut on the Installer Tool to install the crankshaft damper onto the crankshaft.

15. Remove the installer tool.

16. If equipped with a 3.5L engine, tighten the crankshaft balancer bolt to 118 ft. lbs. (160 Nm).

17. If equipped with a 3.9L engine, tighten the crankshaft bolt using the following procedure:

   a. Install the old crankshaft balancer bolt and tighten to 92 ft. lbs. (125 Nm).

   b. Remove the old crankshaft bolt.

   c. Install a NEW crankshaft balancer bolt. Tighten the bolt to 92 ft. lbs. (125 Nm).

   d. Tighten the new crankshaft bolt an additional 130 degrees.

18. Remove the lock from the flywheel.

19. Install the torque converter covers.

20. Raise the frame to the original position.

21. Install and tighten the frame bolts to 74 ft. lbs. (100 Nm) plus an additional 90 degrees.

22. Install the right engine splash shield.

23. Install the right front tire and wheel.

24. Lower the vehicle.

25. Install the drive belt.

CRANKSHAFT FRONT SEAL

REMOVAL & INSTALLATION

See Figures 61 and 62.

1. Before servicing the vehicle, refer to the Precautions Section.

2. Remove the crankshaft damper. For additional information, refer to the following section, "Crankshaft Damper, Removal & Installation."

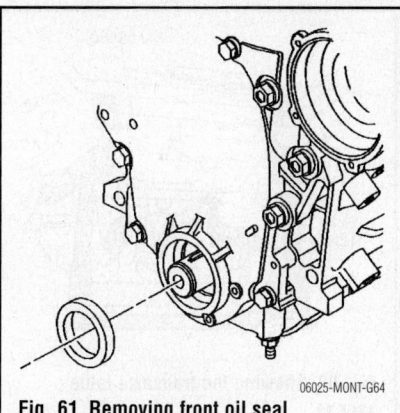

Fig. 61 Removing front oil seal

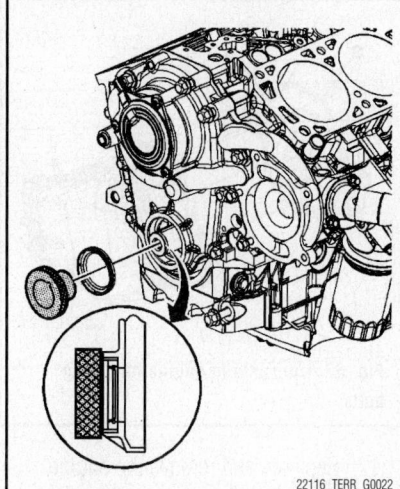

Fig. 62 Install the front seal with Special Tool J-35468.

3. Pry out the crankshaft front oil seal using a suitable pry tool. Use care not to damage the front cover or crankshaft.

To install:

4. Lubricate the new oil seal with clean engine oil.

5. Align Special Tool J-35468 and the crankshaft front oil seal with the engine front cover and crankshaft.

6. Tap the oil seal into position and remove the installer tool.

7. Install the crankshaft balancer.

8. Start the engine and check for leaks.

CYLINDER HEAD

REMOVAL & INSTALLATION

3.5L Engine

See Figures 63 and 64.

1. Before servicing the vehicle, refer to the Precautions Section.

2. Drain the cooling system.

3. Drain the engine oil.

4. Remove the lower intake manifold. For additional information, refer to the following section, "Intake Manifold, Removal & Installation."

5. Remove the valve rocker arms and the pushrods. For additional information, refer to the following section, "Rocker Arms, Removal & Installation."

6. Remove the exhaust crossover pipe. For additional information, refer to the following section, "Exhaust Manifold, Removal & Installation."

7. For the left cylinder head, remove the oil level indicator tube.

8. Remove the spark plug wires from the spark plugs.

9. Remove the spark plugs.

10. For the right side cylinder head, remove the alternator. For additional information, refer to the following section, "Alternator, Removal & Installation."

11. Remove the appropriate side exhaust manifold. For additional information, refer to the following section, "Exhaust Manifold, Removal & Installation."

12. Remove the cylinder head bolts and discard.

13. Remove the cylinder head.

14. Remove the cylinder head gasket.

15. Clean and inspect the cylinder head and the gasket mating surfaces.

To install:

16. Install a new cylinder head gasket over the alignment pins.

17. Install the cylinder head over the locator pins and the gasket.

18. Install the new cylinder head bolts. Tighten the bolts, in the sequence shown, to 44 ft. lbs. (60 Nm).

19. Use the angle tool, J 45059, or suitable angle measuring device, to rotate the bolts in sequence an additional 95 degrees.

20. Install the exhaust manifold. For additional information, refer to the following section, "Exhaust Manifold, Removal & Installation."

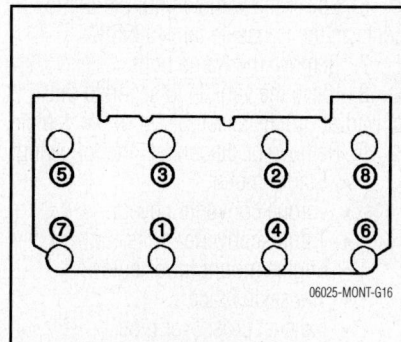

Fig. 63 Cylinder head bolt torque sequence—3.5L and 3.9L engines

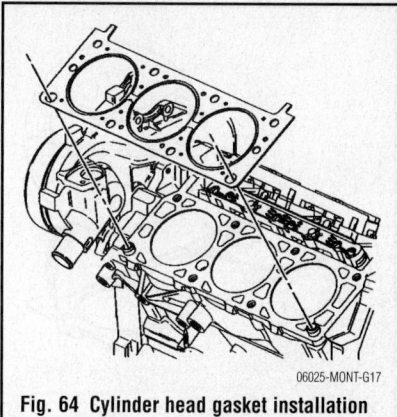

Fig. 64 Cylinder head gasket installation

21. Install the spark plugs. Torque the spark plugs to 15 ft. lbs. (20 Nm), if using a new cylinder head, or to 11 ft. lbs. (15 Nm), if using an existing head.

22. For the right side cylinder head, install the alternator. For additional information, refer to the following section, "Alternator, Removal & Installation."

23. Install the spark plug wires to the spark plugs.

24. For the left side cylinder head, install the oil level indicator tube.

25. Install the exhaust crossover pipe. For additional information, refer to the following section, "Exhaust Manifold, Removal & Installation."

26. Install the valve rocker arms and pushrods. For additional information, refer to the following section, "Rocker Arms, Removal & Installation."

27. Install the lower intake manifold. For additional information, refer to the following section, "Intake Manifold, Removal & Installation."

28. Fill the crankcase with engine oil.

29. Fill the cooling system.

30. Start the engine and inspect for leaks.

3.9L Engine

See Figure 65.

1. Before servicing the vehicle, refer to the Precautions Section.

2. Drain the engine oil.

3. Drain the cooling system.

4. Remove the lower intake manifold. For additional information, refer to the following section, "Intake Manifold, Removal & Installation."

5. Remove the exhaust crossover pipe. For additional information, refer to the following section, "Exhaust Manifold, Removal & Installation."

6. If removing the left side cylinder head, remove the oil dipstick tube.

7. Remove the spark plugs.

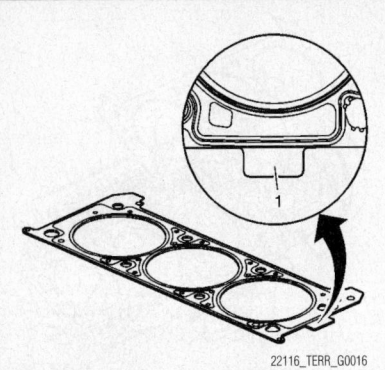

22116_TERR_G0016

Fig. 65 Head gaskets are specific for right hand and left hand applications, and also must be installed with the correct side facing up. Note the markings (1) on the head gaskets for proper installation.

8. Remove the and discard the cylinder head bolts.

9. Remove the cylinder head.

To install:

10. Clean and inspect the cylinder head and the gasket mating surfaces.

11. Install the spark plugs to the cylinder head.

12. Install a new cylinder head gasket.

13. Install the cylinder head on to the locator pins on the engine block. Install the cylinder head bolts finger tight.

14. Tighten the bolts, in the sequence shown, to 44 ft. lbs. (60 Nm).

15. Use the angle tool, J 45059, or suitable angle measuring device, to rotate the bolts in sequence an additional 95 degrees.

16. Install the oil dipstick tube, if removed.

17. Install the exhaust crossover pipe. For additional information, refer to the following section, "Exhaust Manifold, Removal & Installation."

18. Install the lower intake manifold. For additional information, refer to the following section, "Intake Manifold, Removal & Installation."

19. Refill the engine with oil to the correct level.

20. Refill the cooling system to the correct level.

21. Start the engine and check for leaks.

ENGINE ASSEMBLY

REMOVAL & INSTALLATION

3.5L Engine

See Figures 66 and 67.

1. Before servicing the vehicle, refer to the Precautions Section.

2. Disconnect the battery cables and properly relieve the fuel system pressure.

3. Drain the engine cooling system and the engine oil into separate drain pans.

4. Remove the wheel, marking the location of the wheel to the hub prior to removal. Mark the individual location of all retainers as they are removed.

5. Remove or disconnect the following:
- Negative battery cable
- Radiator and heater hoses
- Vacuum hoses from upper intake manifold
- Fuel lines from the fuel rail
- Electrical connectors
- Engine wiring harness grounds from the transaxle
- Engine mount strut
- Raise and support the vehicle
- Rear driveshaft (AWD only)
- Catalytic converter
- Lower radiator baffle assembly
- Engine splash shields
- Stabilizer shaft links from the lower control arms
- Tie rod ends from the steering knuckles
- Lower ball joints from the steering knuckles
- A/C compressor bolts and position compressor aside, support the compressor

➡ **DO NOT discharge the A/C system**

- Drive axles from the transaxle, secure the drive axles
- Intermediate shaft pinch bolt from the steering gear

✷✷ CAUTION

Failure to disconnect the intermediate shaft from the rack and pinion steering gear stub shaft can result in damage to the steering gear and/or intermediate shaft.

6. Lower the vehicle until the frame contacts the transaxle table J39580.

7. Remove the frame bolts.

8. Raise the vehicle to separate the powertrain/frame assembly from the vehicle.

9. Remove or disconnect the following:
- Starter motor
- Torque converter covers
- Torque converter bolts
- Engine mount lower nuts
- Transaxle brace
- Exhaust crossover pipe

10. Install engine hoist to engine.

11. Remove the transaxle to engine bolts (3, 4, 5, 6) and the studs (1, 2)

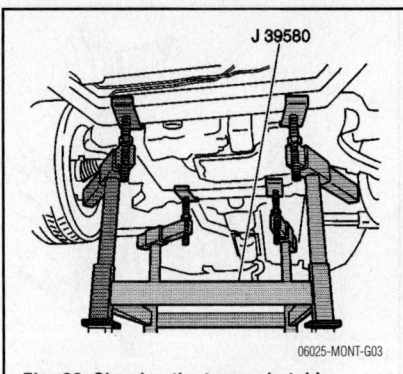

06025-MONT-G03

Fig. 66 Showing the transaxle table J39580

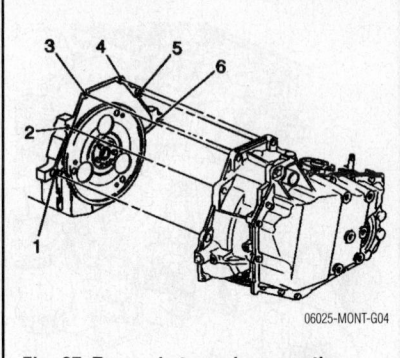

06025-MONT-G04

Fig. 67 Transaxle to engine mounting bolts

12. Separate and remove the engine from the transaxle/frame

13. Remove the flywheel.

14. Remove the drive belt.

To install:

15. Install or connect the following:
- Drive belt
- Flywheel
- Engine to the transaxle/frame
- Transaxle to engine bolts and tighten the bolts to 55 ft. lbs. (75 Nm)

16. Remove the engine hoist from engine.

17. Install or connect the following:
- Exhaust crossover pipe
- Transaxle brace
- Engine mount lower nuts and tighten to 32 ft. lbs. (43 Nm)
- Torque converter bolts
- Torque converter covers
- Starter motor

18. Position the transaxle table with the powertrain/frame under the vehicle.

19. Lower the vehicle until the frame contacts the transaxle table.

20. Install NEW frame bolts.

21. Raise and safely support the vehicle.

22. Remove the transaxle table.

23. Install or connect the following:

- Intermediate shaft pinch bolt to the steering gear
- Drive axles to transaxle
- A/C compressor to engine and install bolts
- Lower ball joints to steering knuckles
- Stabilizer shaft links to lower control arms
- Engine splash shields
- Lower radiator baffle assembly
- Catalytic converter
- Rear driveshaft (AWD only)
- Lower vehicle
- Fill engine with oil
- Engine mount strut
- Electrical connectors
- Engine wiring harness ground nut to transaxle stud and tighten to 18 ft. lbs. (2 Nm)
- Fuels lines to fuel rail
- Vacuum hoses to upper intake manifold
- Radiator and heater hoses

24. Install the tire and wheel assembly. Tighten the lug nuts to 100 ft. lbs. (140 Nm) in a criss—cross pattern, after aligning the wheel hub with the reference mark and holes as shown in appropriate illustration.

25. Check all powertrain fluid levels and add, as necessary. Be sure to properly fill the engine crankcase with clean engine oil.

26. Connect the battery cables and properly fill the engine cooling system.

27. Start and run the engine, then check for leaks.

3.9L Engine

See Figure 68.

1. Before servicing the vehicle, refer to the Precautions Section.

2. Lock the steering column by installing the J 42640 into the underside of the steering column.

3. Drain the cooling system.

4. Drain the engine oil.

5. Pull up on the intake manifold cover in order to disengage it from the studs.

6. Disconnect the battery cables.

7. Disconnect the battery current sensor, auxiliary ground cable on the inner fender and positive battery feed at the junction box.

8. Remove the lower radiator air baffle.

9. Remove the coolant recovery reservoir hose from the crossover.

10. Remove the coolant reservoir.

11. Remove the left side diagonal brace.

12. Unsnap and remove the junction block cover.

13. Remove the air intake assembly.

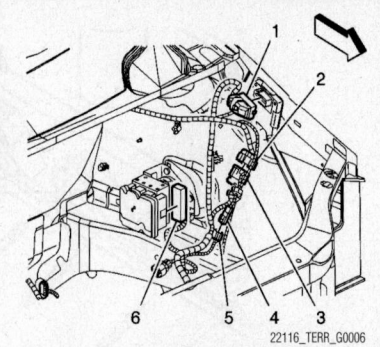

Fig. 68 Disconnect the various engine wiring harness connectors—3.9L engine

14. Remove the engine control module (ECM) from the air cleaner cover.

15. Disconnect the engine harness electrical connector (1) from the transaxle control module (TCM).

16. Disconnect the engine harness electrical connector (3) from the instrument panel (I/P) harness electrical connector (2).

17. Disconnect the engine harness electrical connector (5) from the I/P harness electrical connector (4).

18. Disconnect the engine harness electrical connector (6) from the ABS module.

19. Disconnect the engine harness clip from the air conditioning (A/C) line.

20. Remove the underhood junction box.

21. Disconnect the engine harness electrical connector from the mass air flow (MAF)/intake air temperature (IAT) sensor.

22. Disconnect the positive crankcase ventilation (PCV) fresh air tube quick connect fitting from the air cleaner outlet duct.

23. Remove the air cleaner outlet duct from the throttle body and MAF/IAT sensor.

24. Gather the outer branches of the engine harness and lay them on top of the engine.

25. Disconnect the radiator hoses.

26. Disconnect the heater hoses from the inlet and outlet pipes.

27. Remove the brake booster vacuum hose from the upper intake manifold fitting.

28. Disconnect the fuel supply hose and evaporative emission (EVAP) line.

29. Remove the engine mount struts.

30. Raise and safely support the vehicle. Remove the front wheels and tires.

31. If equipped with AWD, remove rear propeller shaft.

32. Disconnect the left and right wheel speed sensor electrical connectors.

33. Remove the drive belt.

34. Disconnect the engine harness electrical connectors from the A/C compressor.

35. Remove the A/C compressor and

reposition and support the A/C compressor out of the way.

➡**Leave the refrigerant lines connected and it is not necessary to evacuate the A/C system prior to repositioning the A/C compressor.**

36. Remove the catalytic converter.

37. Remove the engine splash shield.

38. If equipped with FWD, remove the stabilizer shaft link lower nuts.

39. Remove the stabilizer shaft links from the stabilizer shaft.

40. Remove the tie rod end nuts at the steering knuckles.

41. Using Special Tool J 24319-B, separate the outer tie rod ends from the steering knuckle.

✳✳ WARNING

Do not attempt to free the ball stud by using a pickle fork or wedge type tool, because seal or bushing damage could result. Use the proper tool to separate all ball joints.

✳✳ CAUTION

Use only the recommended tools for separating the ball joint from the knuckle. Do NOT hammer or pry the ball joint from the knuckle. Failure to use the recommended tools may cause damage to the ball joint and seal.

42. Using the J 33008-A , J 29794 , and the J 2619-01 disengage the halfshafts from the transaxle. Secure the halfshafts to the steering knuckle/struts.

43. Reposition the intermediate steering shaft seal in order to provide access to the intermediate steering shaft pinch bolt. Remove the intermediate steering shaft pinch bolt.

44. Disconnect the intermediate steering shaft from the power steering gear.

45. Place transaxle table J 39580 under the frame and lower the vehicle until the frame contacts transaxle table.

46. Remove the front and rear frame bolts, frame rear strap bolts and frame rear straps.

47. Raise the vehicle in order to separate the drivetrain/frame assembly from the vehicle.

48. Remove or disconnect the following:
- Starter motor
- Torque converter covers
- Torque converter bolts
- Engine mount lower nuts
- Transaxle brace
- Exhaust crossover pipe

49. Install a suitable engine hoist to the engine.

50. Remove the transaxle to engine bolts.

51. Separate and remove the engine from the transaxle/frame

52. Installation is the reverse order of removal.

EXHAUST MANIFOLD

REMOVAL & INSTALLATION

3.5L Engine

See Figures 69 and 70.

1. Before servicing the vehicle, refer to the Precautions Section.

2. Remove the negative battery cable.

3. Remove the spark plug wires.

4. Remove the spark plugs.

5. For right side exhaust manifold, remove the following:
   • EGR pipe from the exhaust manifold
   • Heated oxygen sensor

6. Remove the exhaust manifold heat shield bolts.

7. Remove the exhaust manifold heat shields.

8. Remove the exhaust manifold nuts.

9. Remove the exhaust manifold and gasket.

To install:

10. Install the exhaust manifold studs. Tighten the exhaust manifold studs to 13 ft. lbs. (18 Nm).

11. Install the exhaust manifold gasket.

12. Install the exhaust manifold.

13. Install the exhaust manifold nuts.

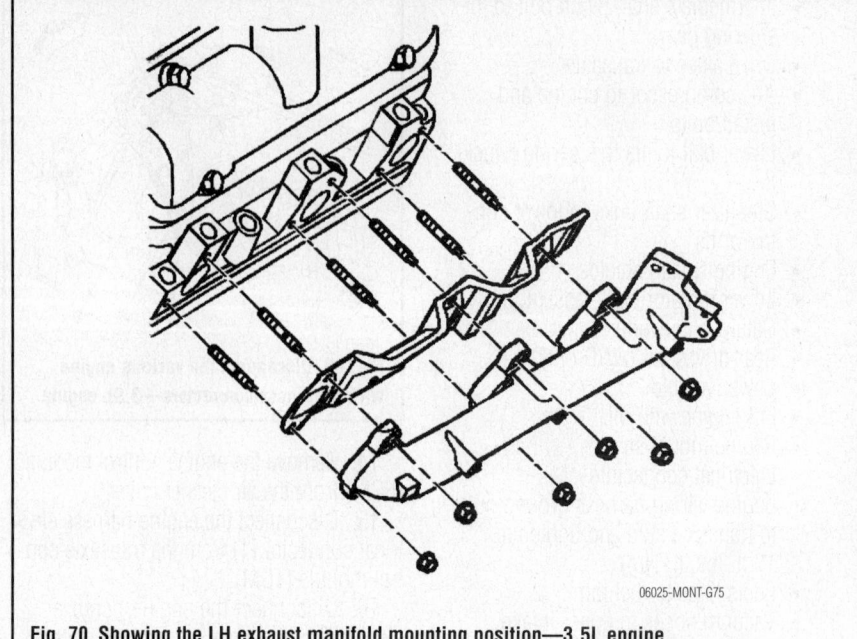

06025-MONT-G75

Fig. 70 Showing the LH exhaust manifold mounting position—3.5L engine

Tighten the exhaust manifold nuts working from the center out to 12 ft. lbs. (16 Nm).

14. Install the right side spark plugs. Tighten the spark plugs to 11 ft. lbs. (15 Nm).

15. Install the spark plug wires onto the spark plugs.

16. Install the lower exhaust manifold heat shield.

17. Install the upper exhaust manifold heat shield.

18. Install the exhaust manifold heat shield bolts. Tighten the exhaust manifold heat shield bolts to 89 inch lbs. (10 Nm).

19. For right exhaust manifold, coat the threads of the heated oxygen sensor with anti-seize compound.

20. Install the heated oxygen sensor.

Tighten the heated oxygen sensor to 31 ft. lbs. (42 Nm).

21. Install the spark plug wires.

22. Reconnect the negative battery cable.

3.9L Engine

Left Side

See Figures 71 and 72.

1. Before servicing the vehicle, refer to the Precautions Section.

2. Disconnect the negative battery cable.

3. Remove the air intake assembly.

4. Remove the upper radiator hose.

5. Disconnect the heater hoses from the heater pipes.

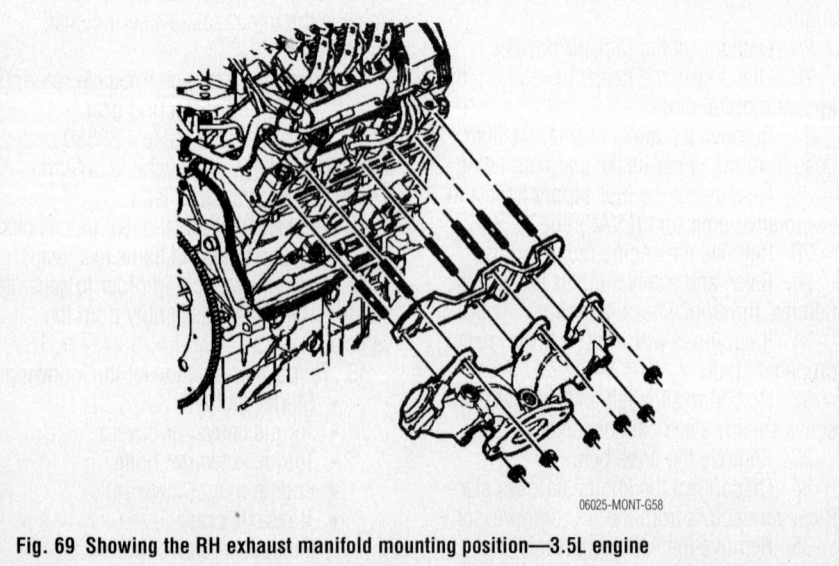

06025-MONT-G58

Fig. 69 Showing the RH exhaust manifold mounting position—3.5L engine

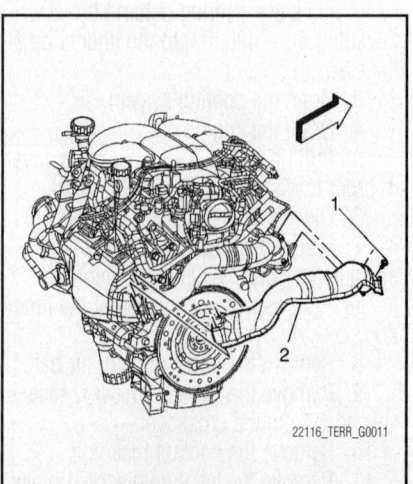

22116_TERR_G0011

Fig. 71 Remove the heat shield bolts (1) and remove the exhaust crossover heat shield (2)—3.9L engine

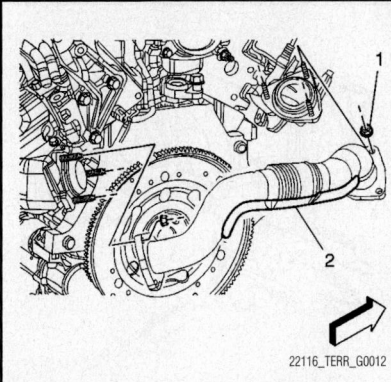

Fig. 72 Remove the mounting nuts (1) to remove the exhaust crossover pipe (2)—3.9L engine

6. Remove the nuts that hold the heater pipes to the throttle body and position the heater pipes aside.

7. Remove the exhaust crossover heat shield.

8. Remove the exhaust crossover pipe nuts and remove the crossover pipe.

9. Remove the exhaust manifold heat shield.

10. Remove the exhaust manifold mounting bolts.

11. Remove the exhaust manifold and gasket.

To install:

12. Position a new exhaust manifold gasket on the cylinder head and install the exhaust manifold.

13. Install the exhaust manifold bolts and tighten to 15 ft. lbs. (20 Nm).

14. Install the exhaust manifold heat shield. Tighten the bolts to 89 inch lbs. (10 Nm).

15. Install the exhaust crossover pipe and tighten the nuts to 15 ft. lbs. (20 Nm).

16. Position the heater pipes back to their original position and connect the heater hoses.

17. Install the nuts holding the heater pipes to the throttle body.

18. Install the exhaust crossover heat shield and tighten the bolts to 89 inch lbs. (10 Nm).

19. Install the upper radiator hose.

20. Install the air intake assembly.

21. Connect the negative battery cable.

Right Side

1. Before servicing the vehicle, refer to the Precautions Section.

2. Disconnect the negative battery cable.

3. Remove the air intake assembly.

4. Remove the alternator.

5. Remove the ignition coil.

6. Disconnect the engine wiring harness connector from the heated oxygen sensor (HO2S).

7. Remove the HO2S.

8. Remove the nuts that hold the heater pipes to the throttle body and position the heater pipes aside.

9. Remove the exhaust crossover heat shield.

10. Remove the exhaust crossover pipe nuts and remove the crossover pipe.

11. Remove the catalytic converter.

12. Remove the exhaust manifold heat shield.

13. Remove the exhaust manifold mounting bolts.

14. Remove the exhaust manifold and gasket.

To install:

15. Position a new exhaust manifold gasket on the cylinder head and install the exhaust manifold.

16. Install the exhaust manifold bolts and tighten to 15 ft. lbs. (20 Nm).

17. Install the exhaust manifold heat shield. Tighten the bolts to 89 inch lbs. (10 Nm).

18. Install the catalytic converter.

19. Install the exhaust crossover pipe and tighten the nuts to 15 ft. lbs. (20 Nm).

20. Install the exhaust crossover heat shield and tighten the bolts to 89 inch lbs. (10 Nm).

21. Position the heater pipes back to their original position and connect the heater hoses.

22. Install the nuts holding the heater pipes to the throttle body.

23. Install the HO2S and tighten to 31 ft. lbs. (42 Nm). Connect the HO2S electrical connector.

24. Install the ignition coil.

25. Install the alternator.

26. Install the air intake assembly.

27. Connect the negative battery.

INTAKE MANIFOLD

REMOVAL & INSTALLATION

3.5L Engines

Upper Manifold

See Figures 73 through 76.

1. Before servicing the vehicle, refer to the Precautions Section.

2. Drain the cooling system

3. Remove or disconnect the following:
   • Negative battery cable
   • Vacuum hose to EVAP canister purge valve

• Vacuum hose to brake booster
• EGR electrical connector
• Mass air flow sensor electrical connector
• Throttle control valve electrical connector
• EVAP canister purge valve electrical connector
• Air cleaner intake duct
• Left side spark plug wires
• Camshaft position sensor (CMP) wiring harness from retainer
• Left side spark plug wire harness from retainer
• Engine wiring harness from retainer
• Ignition coil bracket and coils
• EVAP canister purge solenoid valve
• Manifold absolute pressure (MAP) sensor and bracket

4. Remove the EGR valve as follows:

   a. Disconnect the electrical connector (1) from the exhaust gas recirculation (EGR) valve (2), as shown.

   b. Raise and safely support the vehicle.

   c. Remove the transaxle filler tube retaining fasteners to the transaxle case and position the filler tube out-of-the-way.

   d. Lower the vehicle.

   e. Remove the EGR pipe bolt and carefully pull the pipe assembly back.

   f. Remove the EGR valve bolts.

   g. Remove EGR valve.

   h. Remove the EGR valve gasket.

   i. Clean and inspect the EGR valve gasket mating surfaces.

5. Remove the upper intake manifold bolts and the stud.

6. Remove the alternator bracket after removing the alternator and drive belt tensioner.

7. Remove the upper intake manifold and gasket.

8. If replacing the upper intake manifold, transfer the throttle body.

9. If necessary to transfer the throttle body, remove it as follows:

   a. Disconnect the electronic throttle control (ETC) electrical connector (1) from the throttle body (2).

   b. Remove the heater pipe nut at the throttle body.

   c. Remove only the heater inlet pipe.

   d. Remove the nuts and the bolts from the throttle body.

   e. Remove the throttle body assembly.

   f. Remove the throttle body gasket.

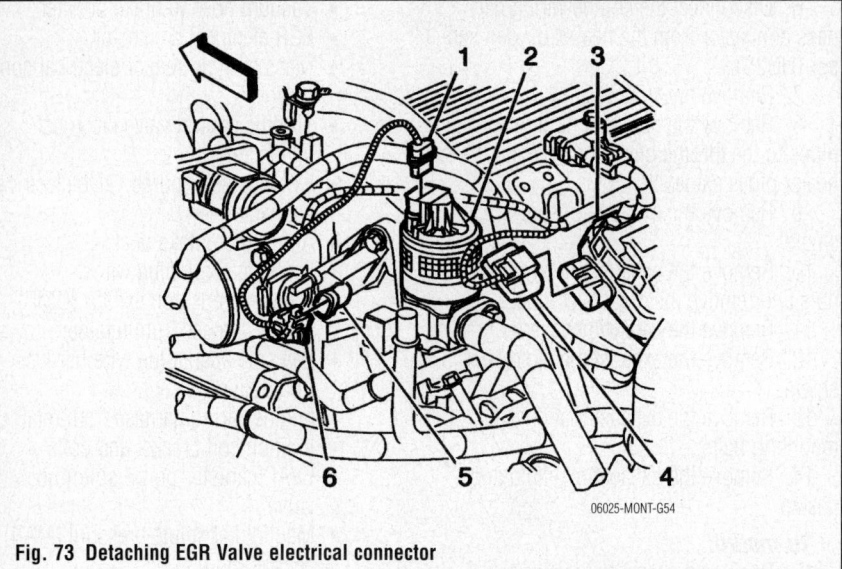

Fig. 73 Detaching EGR Valve electrical connector

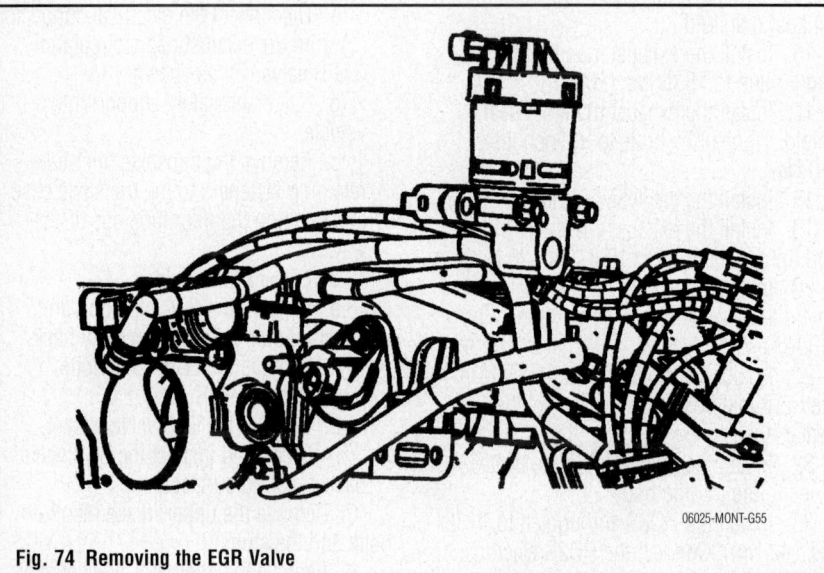

Fig. 74 Removing the EGR Valve

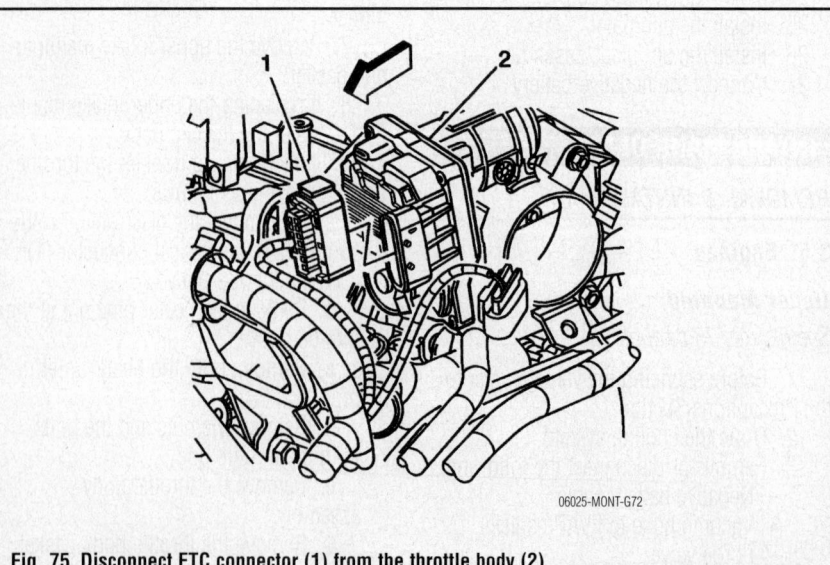

Fig. 75 Disconnect ETC connector (1) from the throttle body (2)

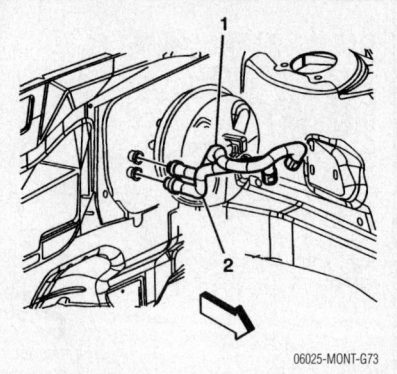

Fig. 76 Remove the heater inlet pipe (1) only

✶✶ CAUTION

Do not use solvent of any type when cleaning the gasket surfaces on the intake manifold and the throttle body assembly, as damage to the gasket surfaces and throttle body assembly may result. Use care in cleaning the gasket surfaces on the intake manifold and the throttle body assembly, as sharp tools may damage the gasket surfaces.

g. Clean and inspect the throttle body gasket mating surfaces.

To install:

10. If removed, install the throttle body to the upper intake manifold, as follows:

a. Install a new gasket, if necessary.

b. Install the throttle body assembly.

c. Install the throttle body nuts and the bolts. Tighten the nuts and the bolts to 89 inch lbs. (10 Nm).

d. Install the heater inlet pipe.

e. Install the heater pipe nut to the throttle body. Tighten the nut to 18 ft. lbs. (25 Nm).

f. Connect the ETC electrical connector (1) to the throttle body (2).

11. Install or connect the following:

- Intake manifold with new gasket
- Apply threadlock (GM P/N 12345382, or equivalent) to the intake manifold bolts
- Upper intake manifold bolts and the stud; tighten the bolts to 18 ft. lbs. (25 Nm)
- Generator bracket. Torque bracket bolts to 37 ft. lbs. (50 Nm).

12. Install the EGR valve as follows:

a. Install a new EGR valve gasket.

b. Install the EGR valve.

c. Install the EGR valve bolts. Tighten the bolt to 22 ft. lbs. (30 Nm).

d. Install the EGR pipe to the EGR valve.

e. Install the EGR pipe. Tighten the bolt to 18 ft. lbs. (25 Nm).

f. Connect the electrical connector (1) to the EGR valve (2).

g. Raise and safely support the vehicle.

h. Position the transaxle filler tube to the normal installed position and install the filler tube to transaxle case fasteners. Tighten the fasteners to 115 ft. lbs. (130 Nm).

i. Lower the vehicle.

13. Install or connect the following:
- MAP sensor bracket and sensor; tighten retaining bolt to 89 inch lbs. (10 Nm)
- EVAP canister purge solenoid valve; tighten bracket bolt to 89 inch lbs. (10 Nm)
- Ignition coil bracket and coils; tighten bolts to 40 inch lbs. (4.5 Nm)
- Camshaft position sensor (CMP) wiring harness to retainer
- Left side spark plug wire harness to retainer
- Engine wiring harness to retainer
- Left side spark plug wires
- Air cleaner intake duct
- EGR electrical connector
- Mass air flow sensor electrical connector
- Throttle control valve electrical connector
- EVAP canister purge valve electrical connector
- Vacuum hose to EVAP canister purge valve
- Vacuum hose to brake booster
- Negative battery cable

14. Fill the cooling system.

15. Start the engine and check for leaks.

Lower Manifold

See Figures 77 through 79.

> ✳✳ **CAUTION**
>
> **This engine uses a sequential multi-port fuel injection system. Injector wiring harness connectors must be connected to the appropriate fuel injector.**

1. Before servicing the vehicle, refer to the Precautions Section.

2. Drain the cooling system.

3. Remove or disconnect the following:

- Upper intake manifold; see Upper Manifold
- Both rocker arm covers; see Rocker Arms/Covers
- Engine coolant temperature (ECT) wiring harness
- Fuel injector and manifold air pressure (MAP) wiring harness

4. Remove the fuel injector rail after removing 2 retaining bolts.

5. Remove the heater inlet pipe, with heater hose, from the lower intake manifold and reposition aside.

6. Remove the radiator inlet hose from the engine.

7. Remove or disconnect the following:

- Water outlet
- Thermostat
- Lower intake manifold bolts

Fig. 77 Removing/installing the fuel rail assembly

06025-MONT-G74

- Lower intake manifold
- Valve rocker arms and pushrods

> ✳✳ **CAUTION**
>
> **Keep components separated in order to reinstall in the same location.**

- Lower intake manifold gaskets and seals

To install:

8. Install or connect the following:
- Lower intake manifold gaskets
- Valve rocker arms and pushrods

➡ The intake pushrods are identified with yellow stripes and are 5–3\w inches long. Exhaust pushrods are identified with green stripes and are n inches long.

➡ With gaskets and seals in place apply a small drop of RTV sealer or equivalent, to the 4 corners of the intake manifold to block joints (1).

- Lower intake manifold

➡ Maximum gasket performance is achieved when using new fasteners that contain a thread locking patch. If the fasteners are not replaced, a thread locking chemical must be applied to the fastener threads. Failure to replace the fasteners or apply a thread-locking chemical MAY reduce gasket sealing capability.

> ✳✳ **CAUTION**
>
> **Failure to tighten vertical bolts before the diagonal bolts may cause an oil leak**

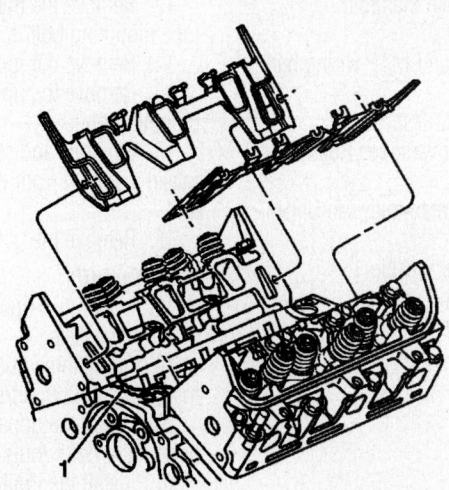

06025-MONT-G57

Fig. 78 Removing lower intake manifold and gaskets

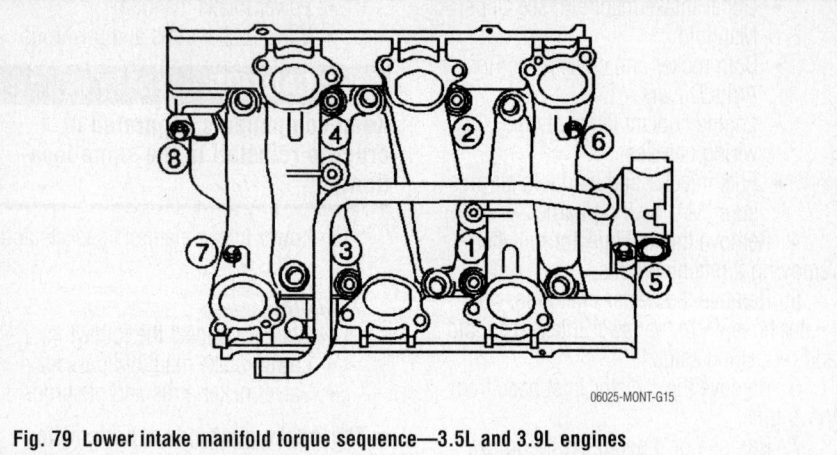

Fig. 79 Lower intake manifold torque sequence—3.5L and 3.9L engines

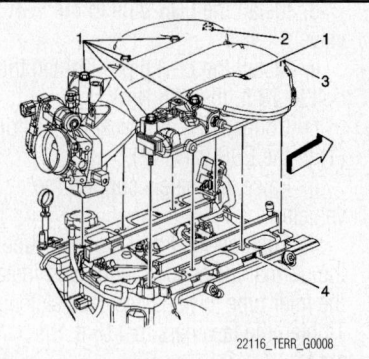

Fig. 80 Remove the upper intake manifold bolts (1, 2) and stud (3) to remove—3.9L Engine

9. Install and tighten the new lower intake manifold bolts in sequence as follows:

a. Tighten the lower intake manifold bolts in sequence to 115 inch lbs. (13 Nm) on the first pass.

b. Tighten the lower intake manifold bolts (1, 2, 3, and 4) in sequence to 15 ft. lbs. (20 Nm) on the final pass.

c. Tighten the lower intake manifold bolts (5, 6, 7, and 8) in sequence to 18 ft. lbs. (25 Nm) on the final pass.

10. Install the heater inlet pipe and nut; tighten the heater inlet pipe nut to 18 ft. lbs. (25 Nm).

11. Install or connect the following:
- Thermostat
- Water outlet bolts
- ECT sensor, tighten the ECT sensor to 15 ft. lbs. (20 Nm)
- Thermostat bypass hose to the thermostat bypass pipe and lower intake manifold pipe
- Radiator inlet hose to the engine
- Heater inlet pipe and heater hose to the lower intake manifold
- Fuel injector rail
- Fuel injector and MAP wiring harness
- ECT wiring harness
- Rocker arm covers; see Rocker Arms/Covers.
- Upper intake manifold; see Upper Manifold.
- Negative battery cable

12. Refill the cooling system.

13. Start and run the engine to check for leaks.

3.9L Engine

Upper Manifold

See Figure 80.

1. Before servicing the vehicle, refer to the Precautions Section.

2. Disconnect the negative battery cable.

3. Drain the cooling system.

4. Remove the intake manifold cover.

5. Remove the positive crankcase ventilation (PCV) fresh air tube and foul air tube.

6. Reposition the brake booster vacuum hose clamp at the intake manifold.

7. Remove the vacuum hose from the intake manifold.

8. Disconnect the engine wiring harness from the following electrical connectors:
- Manifold absolute pressure (MAP) sensor
- Evaporative emission (EVAP) canister purge solenoid
- Electronic throttle control (ETC)
- Intake manifold tuning valve

9. Remove the air intake assembly.

10. Remove the left side spark plug wires.

11. Remove the heater pipe mounting nuts from the manifold.

12. Remove the alternator bracket from the manifold.

13. Remove the transmission dipstick tube mounting bolt in the manifold.

14. Remove the ignition coils.

15. Remove the upper intake manifold mounting bolts.

16. Separate and remove the upper intake manifold from the lower intake manifold.

17. Remove the gaskets.

To install:

18. Install new upper-to-lower intake manifold gaskets.

19. Apply threadlocker to the upper intake manifold bolts/stud threads.

20. Install the upper intake manifold and tighten the bolts /nuts to 18 ft. lbs. (25 Nm).

21. Install the ignition coils.

22. Reposition the transmission dipstick tube and install the mounting bolt.

23. Install the alternator bracket to the manifold.

24. Reattach the heater pipes to the mounts on the intake manifold and tighten the nuts to 89 inch lbs. (10 Nm).

25. Install the left side spark plug wires.

26. Install the air intake assembly.

27. Connect the wiring harness to the following electrical connectors:
- Intake manifold tuning valve
- ETC
- EVAP purge solenoid
- MAP sensor

28. Install the PCV foul air and fresh air tube.

29. Install the intake manifold cover.

30. Refill the cooling system to the correct level.

31. Connect the negative battery cable.

32. Start the engine and check for leaks.

Lower Manifold

See Figures 81 and 82.

1. Before servicing the vehicle, refer to the Precautions Section.

2. Disconnect the negative battery cable.

3. Drain the cooling system,

4. Remove the coolant crossover pipe as follows:

a. Remove the intake manifold cover.

b. Remove the alternator.

c. Remove the accessory drive belt and idler pulleys.

d. Remove the power steering pump.

e. Remove the coolant recovery reservoir inlet hose from the coolant crossover.

f. Remove the radiator inlet hose from the crossover pipe.

g. Remove the thermal bypass hose from the crossover pipe.

h. Remove the bolts holding the heater pipe and wiring harness at the

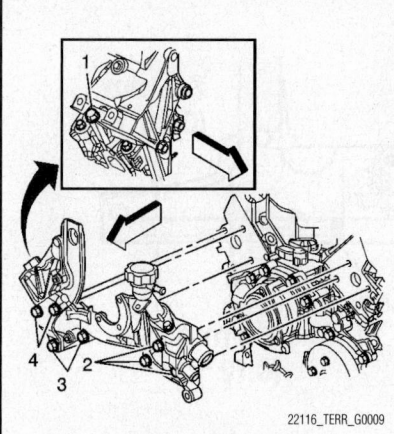

Fig. 81 Remove the crossover pipe mounting bolts (1-4) to remove the crossover pipe—3.9L engine

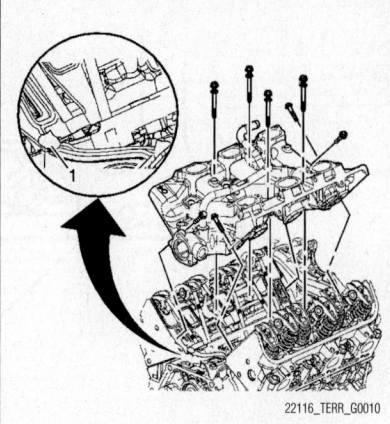

Fig. 82 Apply a small drop of RTV to the corners where the intake manifold meets the engine block—3.9L engine

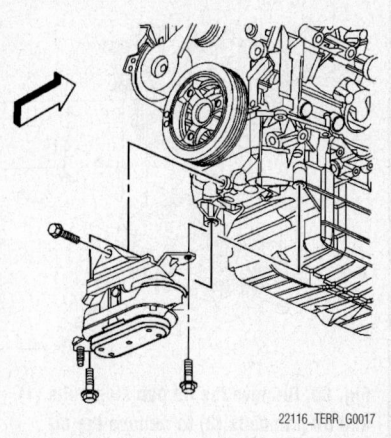

Fig. 83 With the engine assembly supported, remove the front engine mount to access the oil pan—3.9L engine

coolant crossover pipe and position the heater pipe aside.

  i. Remove the crossover pipe mounting bolts and remove the crossover pipe.

5. Remove the upper intake manifold. For additional information, please refer to following section, "Intake manifold, Removal & Installation, Upper Manifold."

6. Remove the valve covers.

7. Disconnect the engine coolant temperature sensor electrical connector.

8. Remove the fuel rail. For additional information, please refer to following section, "Fuel Rail, Removal & Installation."

9. Remove the lower intake manifold mounting bolts.

10. Remove the lower intake manifold.

11. Remove the lower intake manifold gaskets and seals.

To install:

12. Clean the gasket and seal surfaces on the cylinder head, engine block and lower intake manifold.

13. Remove all loose RTV from the sealing surfaces.

14. Install new lower intake manifold gaskets and seals.

✳✳ CAUTION

RTV sealer is not be placed under the lower intake manifold gaskets.

15. Apply a small drop of RTV sealer to the four corners of the intake manifold-to-engine block joints.

16. Install the lower intake manifold and tighten the bolts as follows:

  a. Tighten bolts 1-4 in sequence to 12 ft. lbs. (16 Nm).

  b. Tighten bolts 5-8 in sequence to 18 ft. lbs. (25 Nm).

17. Install the fuel rail.

18. Install the valve covers.

19. Install the upper intake manifold.

20. Install the coolant crossover pipe and tighten the mounting bolts to 37 ft. lbs. (50 Nm).

21. The remainder of the installation is the reverse order of removal.

22. Refill the cooling system to the correct level.

23. Start the engine and check for leaks.

OIL PAN

REMOVAL & INSTALLATION

See Figures 85 through 87.

1. Before servicing the vehicle, refer to the Precautions Section.

2. Install the engine support fixture J-45057 to the engine to properly support the engine.

3. Raise and safely support the vehicle.

4. Remove the right front wheel.

5. Remove the right front splash shield.

6. Drain the engine oil.

7. Remove the lower ball joint nut and separate the lower control arm from the wheel knuckle. Refer to the following section for additional information, "Lower Control Arm, Removal & Installation."

8. Remove the A/C compressor mounting bolts and position aside.

9. Remove the transaxle brace bolts and transaxle braces.

10. Remove the starter motor.

11. Disconnect the oil level sensor electrical connector.

12. Remove the front engine mount.

13. Place a suitable floor jack under the frame.

14. Loosen (but do not remove) the left side frame bolts and remove the right side frame bolts.

15. Lower the right side of the frame enough to remove the oil pan.

16. Remove the oil pan mounting bolts, oil pan and gasket.

To install:

17. Clean the oil pan flanges, oil pan rail, front cover, rear main bearing cap and threaded holes of any old sealant material.

18. Apply sealant GM P/N 12378521, (Canadian P/N 88901148) or the equivalent, to both sides of the crankshaft rear main bearing cap. Press the sealant into the gaps using a putty knife.

19. Apply sealer GM P/N 12378521, (Canadian P/N 88901148) or the equivalent, to both sides of the front cover mating area.

20. Install the oil pan gasket.

21. Install the oil pan. Tighten the oil pan bolts to 18 ft. lbs. (25 Nm). Tighten the oil pan side bolts to 37 ft. lbs. (50 Nm).

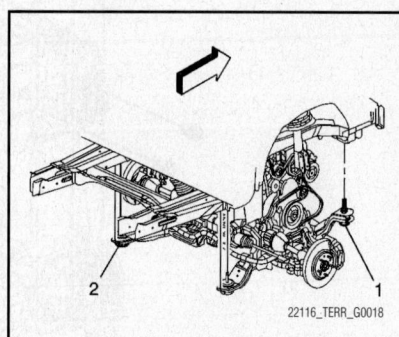

Fig. 84 Remove the right side frame bolts (1) and loosen the left side frame bolts and lower the frame to access the oil pan—3.9L engine

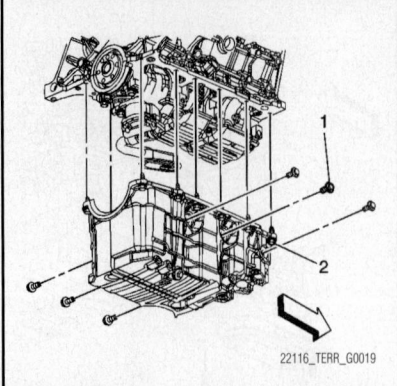

Fig. 85 Remove the oil pan side bolts (1) and oil pan bolts (2) to remove the oil pan—3.9L engine

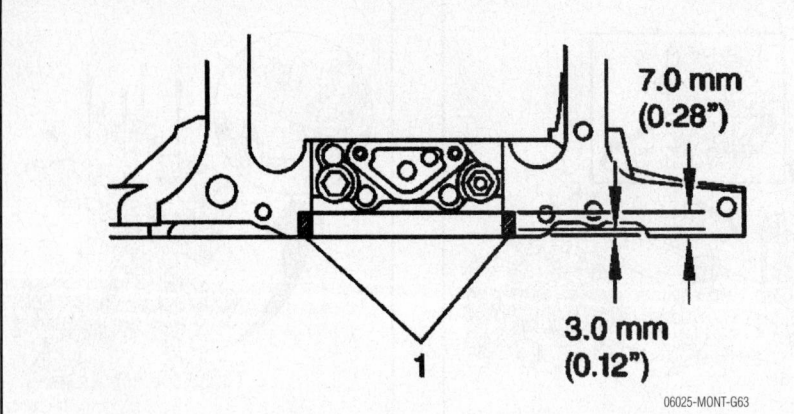

Fig. 87 Applying sealant to rear main bearing cap

22. Using a suitable jack, raise the right side of the frame and tighten the frame bolts as follows:

    a. Front frame bolts to 96 ft. lbs. (130 Nm).

    b. Rear frame bolts to 177 ft. lbs. (240 Nm).

23. Remove the jack and install the front engine mount. Tighten the nuts to 37 ft. lbs. (50 Nm).

24. Connect the oil level sensor electrical connector.

25. Install the starter motor.

26. Install the transaxle braces and tighten the bolts to 32 ft. lbs. (43 Nm).

27. Install the A/C compressor and tighten the mounting bolts to 37 ft. lbs. (50 Nm).

28. Connect the lower control arm to the steering knuckle, tighten the nuts to 40 ft. lbs. (55 Nm) and install a new cotter pin.

29. Install the right front splash shield.

30. Install the front wheel.

31. Remove the engine support fixture.

32. Refill the engine with oil to the correct level.

33. Start the engine and check for leaks.

OIL PUMP

REMOVAL & INSTALLATION

See Figure 88.

1. Before servicing the vehicle, refer to the Precautions Section.

2. Drain the engine oil.

3. Remove the oil pan and gasket. For additional information, refer to the following section, "Oil Pan, Removal & Installation."

4. Remove the oil pump bolt.

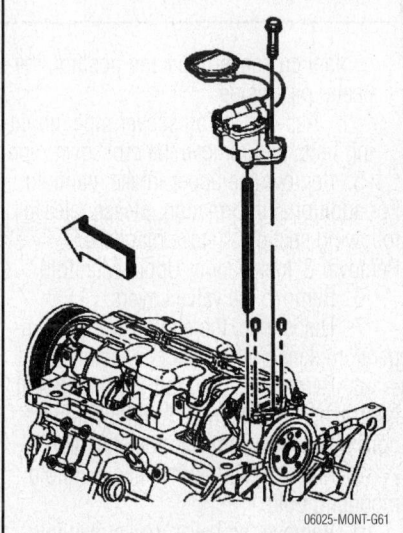

Fig. 88 Showing oil pump mounting location

5. Remove the oil pump and oil pump drive shaft.

To install:

✳✳ CAUTION

Do not reuse the oil pump driveshaft retainer. During assembly, install a NEW oil pump driveshaft retainer.

6. Install the oil pump.

7. Position the oil pump onto the pins.

8. Install the oil pump bolt attaching the oil pump to the rear crankshaft bearing cap. Tighten the oil pump bolt to 30 ft. lbs. (41 Nm).

9. Install the oil pan gasket and oil pan.

10. Refill the engine with oil to the correct level.

11. Start the engine and check for leaks.

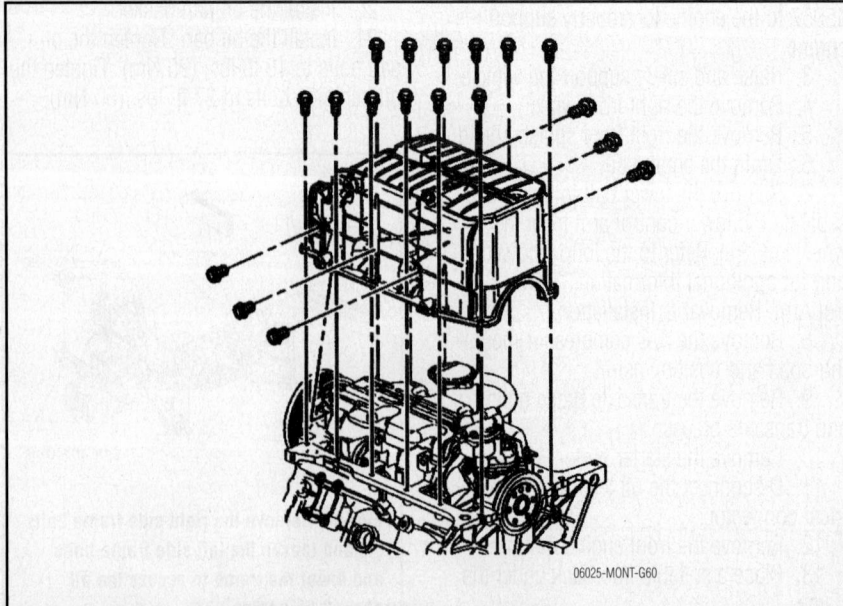

Fig. 86 Showing oil pan mounting bolt locations—3.5L engine

INSPECTION

1. Clean all parts of sludge, oil, and varnish by soaking in cleaning solvent.

2. Inspect for foreign material and determine the source of the foreign material.

3. Inspect the pump housing and cover for cracks, scoring or damaged threads.

4. Do not attempt to repair the pump housing. Replace the pump housing.

5. Inspect the oil pump gears for scoring or excessive wear.

6. Inspect the idler shaft for looseness or scoring. If loose or damaged, replace the oil pump.

7. Inspect the drive gear shaft for looseness or scoring.

8. Inspect the pressure regulator valve for scoring or sticking burrs.

9. Inspect the pressure regulator valve spring for loss of tension or bending.

10. Inspect the suction pipe and screen assembly for looseness, broken wire mesh or screen.

11. Measure the oil pump gear lash. Install the gears, and measure in several places. If lash is more than 0.0037-0.0077 in. (0.094-0.195mm), replace the pump.

12. Measure the oil pump housing gear pocket. If depth is more than 1.202-1.204 in (30.53-30.59mm), or diameter is more than 1.503-1.505 in. (38.176-38.226mm), replace the pump.

13. Measure the oil pump gear diameter. If diameter is more than 1.498-1.500 in (38.05-38.10mm), replace the pump.

PISTON AND RING

POSITIONING
See Figure 89.

REAR MAIN SEAL

REMOVAL & INSTALLATION
See Figure 90.

1. Before servicing the vehicle, refer to the Precautions Section.

2. Remove or disconnect the following:
- Negative battery cable
- Transmission assembly
- Flywheel
- Crankshaft seal by prying it from out oil seal housing

➡ **Be careful not to damage the crankshaft seal surface with the prying tool.**

To install:

✳ CAUTION

Note the direction of the rear oil seal. The new design seal is a reverse style as opposed to what has been used in the past. "THIS SIDE OUT" has been stamped into the seal.

➡ **Do not apply or use any oil lubrication on the crankshaft rear oil seal or the seal installer. Do not touch the sealing lip of the oil seal once the protective sleeve is removed. Doing so will damage or deform the seal. Clean the crankshaft sealing surface with a clean, lint free towel. Inspect the edge of crankshaft for burrs or sharp edges that could damage the rear main oil seal. Remove burrs or sharp edges with a crocus cloth.**

3. Install the new rear seal by using a seal installer.

4. Install or connect the following:

- Flywheel
- Transmission assembly
- Negative battery cable

5. Start the engine and check for leaks.

TIMING CHAIN COVER AND SEAL

REMOVAL & INSTALLATION

3.5L Engine
See Figure 91.

1. Before servicing the vehicle, refer to the Precautions Section.

2. Disconnect the negative battery cable.

3. Drain the cooling system.

4. Drain the engine oil.

5. Remove the accessory drive belt.

6. Remove the drive belt tensioner by accessing it through the wheelhouse opening.

7. Remove the oil pan. For additional information, refer to the following section, "Oil Pan, Removal & Installation."

8. Remove the crankshaft damper. For additional information, refer to the following section, "Crankshaft Damper, Removal & Installation."

9. Remove the thermostat bypass pipe from the timing chain cover.

10. Remove the radiator output hose from the timing chain cover.

11. Remove the water pump. For additional information, refer to the following section, "Water Pump, Removal & Installation."

12. Remove the power steering pump. For additional information, refer to the following section, "Power Steering Pump, Removal & Installation."

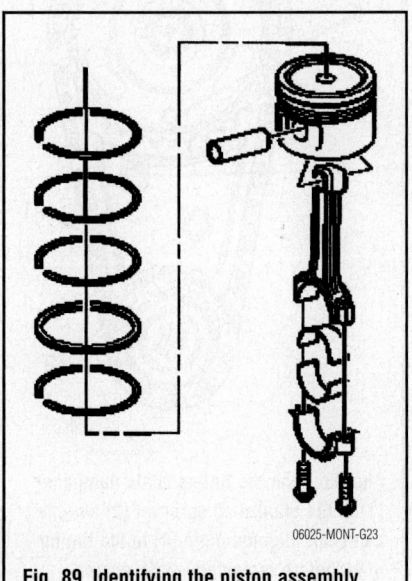

06025-MONT-G23

Fig. 89 Identifying the piston assembly

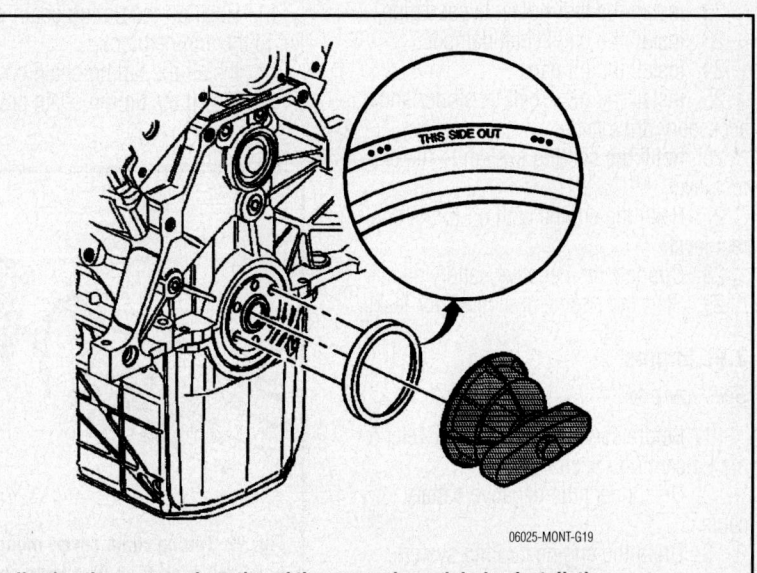

06025-MONT-G19

Fig. 90 Indicating the proper orientation of the rear main seal during installation

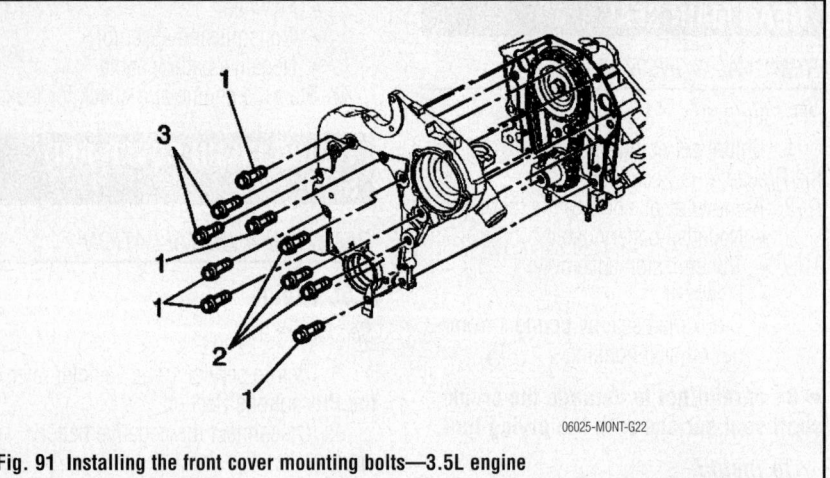

Fig. 91 Installing the front cover mounting bolts—3.5L engine

13. Remove the timing chain cover bolts.
14. Remove the timing chain cover and gasket.

To install:

→If you are replacing the timing chain cover, transfer the drive belt shield bolt and drive belt shield to the new cover.

15. Apply sealer GM P/N 12346004, or equivalent, to both sides of the lower tabs of the engine front cover gasket. Apply the sealer no less than 5.0 mm (0.20 in) wide.
16. Install the timing chain cover.
17. Install the timing chain cover bolts (1). Tighten the timing chain cover bolts to 20 ft. lbs. (27 Nm).
18. Install the timing chain cover bolts (2,3). Tighten the timing chain cover bolts to 41 ft. lbs. (55 Nm).
19. Install the power steering pump.
20. Install the water pump.
21. Install the radiator output hose to the timing chain cover.
22. Install the thermostat bypass pipe.
23. Install the crankshaft damper.
24. Install the oil pan.
25. Install the drive belt tensioner and accessory drive belt.
26. Refill the cooling system to the correct level.
27. Refill the engine with oil to the correct level.
28. Connect the negative battery cable.
29. Start the engine and check for leaks.

3.9L Engine

See Figure 92.

1. Before servicing the vehicle, refer to the Precautions Section.
2. Disconnect the negative battery cable.
3. Drain the engine cooling system.
4. Drain the engine oil

5. Remove the accessory drive belt.
6. Remove the drive belt tensioner by accessing it through the wheelhouse opening.
7. Remove the oil pan. For additional information, refer to the following section, "Oil Pan, Removal & Installation."
8. Remove the crankshaft damper. For additional information, refer to the following section, "Crankshaft Damper, Removal & Installation."
9. Remove the thermostat housing. For additional information, refer to the following section, "Thermostat, Removal & Installation."
10. Remove the water pump. For additional information, refer to the following section, "Water Pump, Removal & Installation."
11. Remove the timing chain cover bolts.
12. Remove the timing chain cover and gasket.

To install:

13. Position the timing chain cover gasket to the engine block.
14. Install the timing chain cover.
15. Install the timing chain cover bolts.

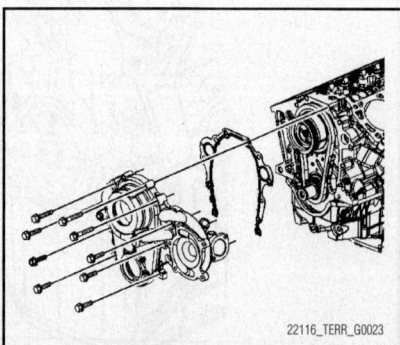

Fig. 92 Timing chain cover, mounting bolts and gasket—3.9L engine shown

Apply sealant to the bolts that pass through the water jacket.

✳✳ CAUTION

Failure to properly seal the bolts may result in coolant leaking from the bolt holes passing through the water jacket.

16. Tighten the timing chain cover bolts to 18 ft. lbs. (25 Nm).
17. Install the water pump.
18. Install the thermostat housing.
19. Install the crankshaft damper.
20. Install the oil pan.
21. Install the drive belt tensioner and accessory drive belt.
22. Refill the cooling system to the correct level.
23. Refill the engine with oil to the correct level.
24. Start the engine and check for leaks.

TIMING CHAIN AND SPROCKETS

REMOVAL & INSTALLATION

3.5L Engine

See Figures 93 and 94.

1. Before servicing the vehicle, refer to the Precautions Section.
2. Remove the timing chain cover. For additional information, refer to the following

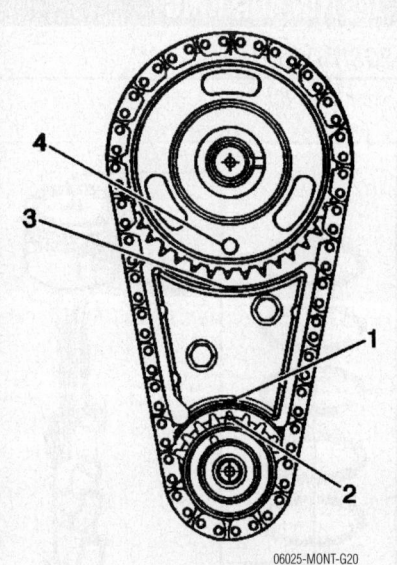

Fig. 93 Align the timing chain dampener (1) to the crankshaft sprocket (2) and the camshaft alignment pin (4) to the timing mark before removing—3.5L engine

section, "Timing Chain Cover and Seal, Removal & Installation."

3. Rotate the crankshaft until the timing marks are aligned.

4. Remove the camshaft sprocket bolt.

5. Remove the camshaft sprocket with the timing chain.

6. Remove the crankshaft sprocket.

7. Remove the timing chain dampener bolts and timing chain dampener.

8. If necessary, remove the camshaft thrust plate.

To install:

9. Clean and inspect the timing chain and gears.

10. If removed, install the camshaft thrust plate and tighten the bolts to 89 inch lbs. (10 Nm).

11. Install the crankshaft sprocket. Apply engine oil supplement (EOS) to the sprocket thrust surface.

12. Install the timing chain dampener and tighten to the bolts to 15 ft. lbs. (21 Nm).

13. Install the timing chain onto the camshaft gear. Hold the camshaft sprocket with the chain hanging down, and install the chain to the crankshaft gear.

14. Align the crankshaft timing mark (2) to the timing mark on the bottom of the timing chain dampener (1).

15. Align the timing mark on the camshaft gear, center line of the locator hole (4), with the timing mark on the top of the chain dampener (3).

16. Align the dowel in the camshaft with the dowel hole in the camshaft sprocket (1).

17. Install the camshaft sprocket bolt and tighten to 103 ft. lbs. (140 Nm).

18. Coat the crankshaft and camshaft sprocket with clean engine oil.

19. Install the timing chain cover.

20. Start the engine and check for leaks.

3.9L Engine

See Figures 95 and 96.

1. Before servicing the vehicle, refer to the Precautions Section.

2. Remove the timing chain cover. For additional information, refer to the following section, "Timing Chain Cover and Seal, Removal & Installation."

3. Align the crankshaft timing mark (1) to the timing mark on the bottom of the timing chain tensioner (2).

4. Align the timing mark on the camshaft gear (3) with the timing mark on top of the timing chain tensioner (4).

5. Remove the camshaft sprocket bolts.

6. Remove the timing chain, camshaft sprocket and crankshaft sprocket.

7. Remove the timing chain tensioner.

To install:

8. Clean and inspect the timing chain and gears.

9. Install the crankshaft sprocket. Apply engine oil supplement (EOS) to the sprocket thrust surface.

10. Install the timing chain tensioner and tighten the bolts to 15 ft. lbs. (21 Nm).

11. Using Special Tool EN-47719, fully collapse the tensioner, and place the tensioner retaining pin into the retaining hole.

12. Align the crankshaft timing mark (1) to the timing mark on the bottom of the timing chain tensioner (2).

13. Hold the camshaft sprocket with the

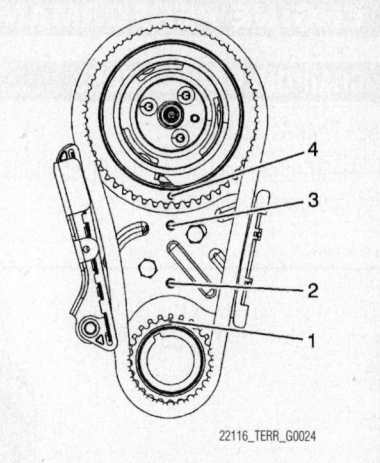

Fig. 95 Align the timing marks before removing the timing chain—3.9L engine

timing chain hanging down and install the timing chain to the crankshaft gear.

14. Align the timing mark on the camshaft gear (3) with the timing mark on top of the timing chain tensioner (4).

15. Align the down in the camshaft sprocket with the dowel hole in the camshaft.

16. Draw the camshaft sprocket onto the camshaft using the mounting bots. Tighten bolts to 12 ft. lbs. (16 Nm).

17. Remove the retaining pin from the timing chain tensioner in order to make the tensioner active.

18. Coat the crankshaft and camshaft sprockets with clean engine oil.

19. Install the timing chain cover.

20. Start the engine and check for leaks.

VALVE LASH

ADJUSTMENT

Hydraulic lash adjusters are used and no adjustment is necessary.

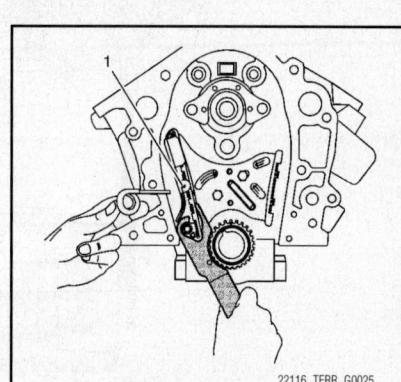

Fig. 96 Use the Special Tool to collapse the tensioner and place the retaining pin into the retaining hole (1)—3.9L engine

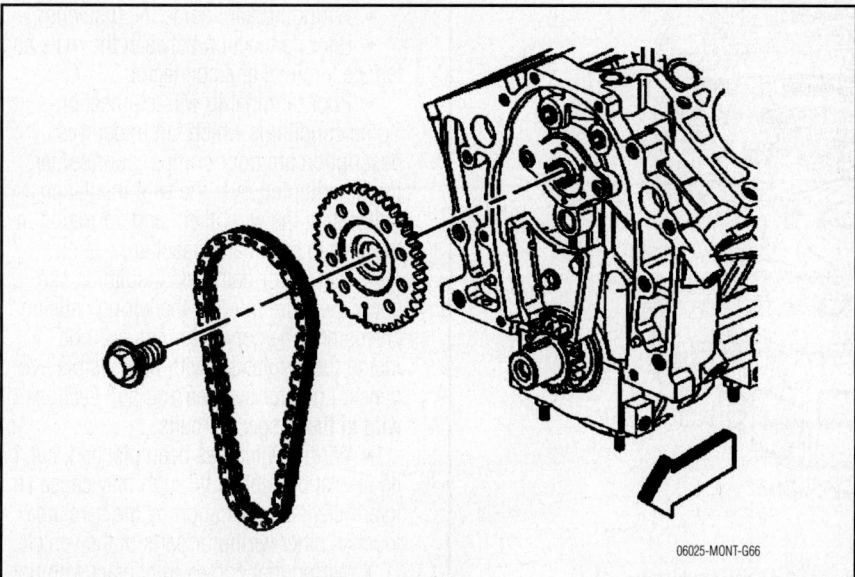

Fig. 94 Removing camshaft sprocket and timing chain

ENGINE PERFORMANCE & EMISSION CONTROL

COMPONENT LOCATIONS

See Figures 97 and 98.

Refer to the accompanying illustrations for component locations.

GENERAL TESTING

It is important to test terminal contact at the component and any inline connectors before replacing a suspect component. Mating terminals must be inspected to ensure good terminal contact. A poor connection between the male and female terminal at a connector may be the result of contamination or deformation.

Contamination may be caused by the connector halves being improperly connected. A missing or damaged connector seal, damage to the connector itself, or exposing the terminals to moisture and dirt can also cause contamination. Contamination, usually in the underhood or underbody connectors, leads to terminal corrosion, causing an open circuit or intermittently open circuit.

Deformation is caused by probing the mating side of a connector terminal without the proper adapter. Always use the appropriate test kit when probing connectors. Other causes of terminal deformation are improperly joining the connector halves, or repeatedly separating and joining the connector halves. Deformation, usually to the female terminal contact tang, can result in poor terminal contact causing an open or intermittently open circuit.

When the condition is not currently present, but is indicated in DTC history, the cause may be intermittent. An intermittent may also be the cause when there is a customer complaint, but the symptom cannot be duplicated. Refer to the Symptom Table of the system that is suspect of causing the condition before trying to locate an intermittent condition.

Most intermittent conditions are caused by faulty electrical connections or wiring. Inspect for the following items:
- Wiring broken inside the insulation
- Poor connection between the male and female terminal at a connector
- Poor terminal to wire connection— Some conditions which fall under this description are poor crimps, poor solder joints, crimping over the wire insulation rather than the wire itself, and corrosion in the wire to terminal contact area, etc.
- Pierced or damaged insulation can allow moisture to enter the wiring causing corrosion. The conductor can corrode inside the insulation, with little visible evidence. Look for swollen and stiff sections of wire in the suspect circuits.
- Wiring which has been pinched, cut, or its insulation rubbed through may cause an intermittent open or short as the bare area touches other wiring or parts of the vehicle.
- Wiring that comes in contact with hot or exhaust components

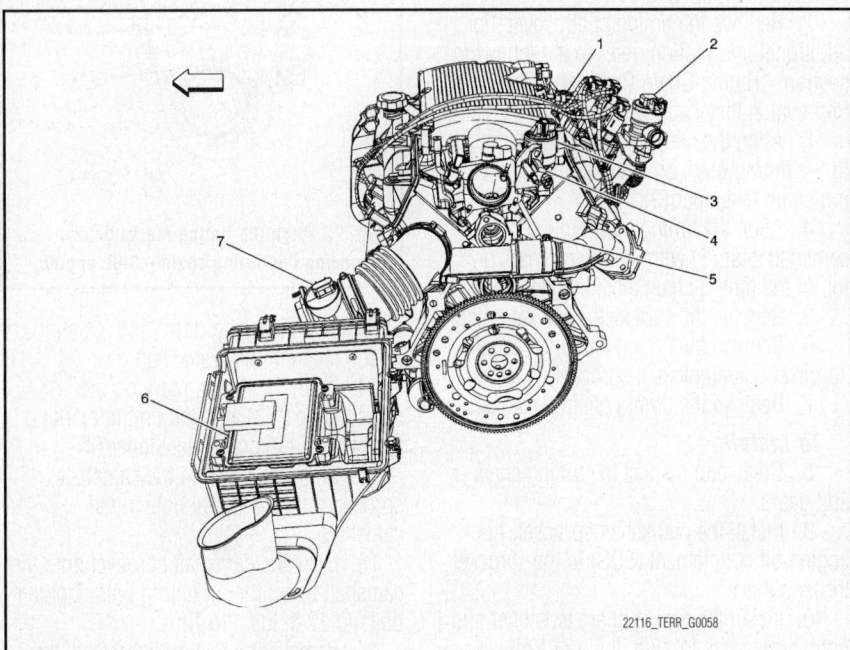

22116_TERR_G0058

Fig. 97 Location of the MAP sensor (1), EGR Valve (3), ECT sensor (5), PCM (6) and MAF/IAT Sensor (7)

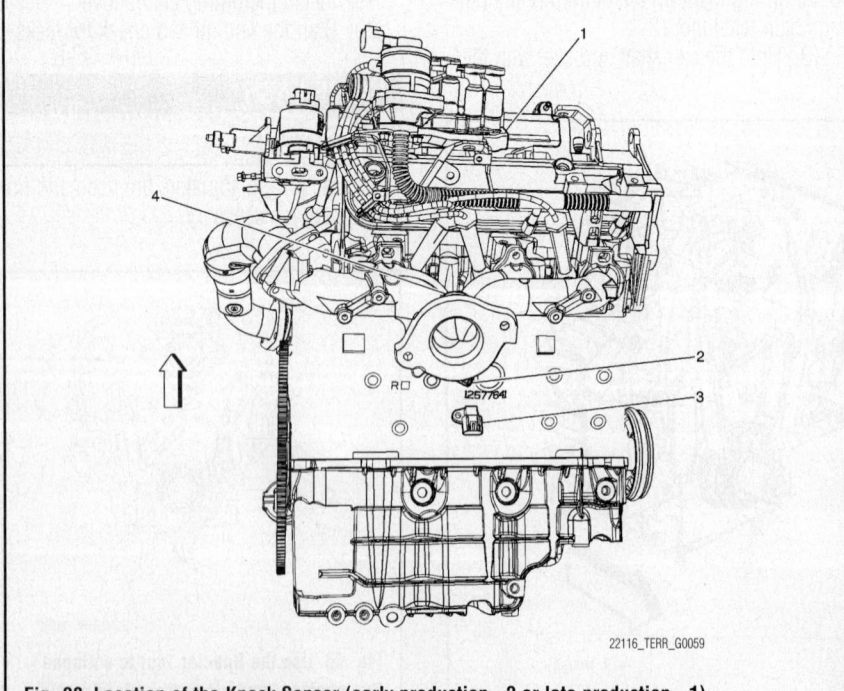

22116_TERR_G0059

Fig. 98 Location of the Knock Sensor (early production - 2 or late production - 1), CKP Sensor (3) and HO2S Sensor 1 (4)

Test all control module voltage supply circuits. Many vehicles have multiple circuits supplying voltage to a control module. Other components in the system may have separate voltage supply circuits that may also need to be tested. Inspect connections at the module/component connectors, fuses, and any intermediate connections between the voltage source and the module/component. A test lamp or a Digital Multimeter may indicate that voltage is present, but neither tests the ability of the circuit to carry sufficient current. Ensure that the circuit can carry the current necessary to operate the component.

Test all control module ground and system ground circuits. The control module may have multiple ground circuits. Other components in the system may have separate grounds that may also need to be tested. Inspect grounds for clean and tight connections at the grounding point. Inspect the connections at the component and in splice packs, where applicable. Ensure that the circuit can carry the current necessary to operate the component.

ACCELERATOR PEDAL POSITION (APP) SENSOR

LOCATION

See Figure 99.

Refer to the accompanying illustration for sensor location.

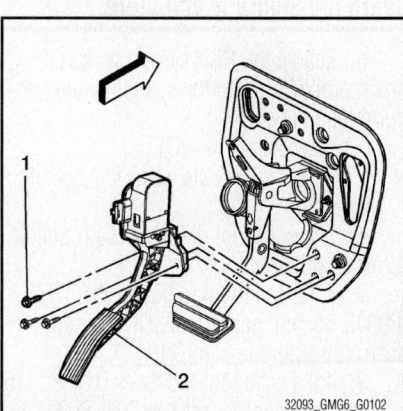

Fig. 99 Showing APP sensor on accelerator pedal assembly

OPERATION

The accelerator pedal contains 2 individual Accelerator Pedal Position (APP) sensors within the assembly. The APP sensors 1 and 2 are potentiometer type sensors each with 3 circuits:
- 5-volt reference circuit
- low reference circuit
- signal circuit

The APP sensors are used to determine the pedal angle. The powertrain control module (PCM) provides each APP sensor with a 5-volt reference circuit and a low reference circuit. The APP sensors provide the PCM with signal voltage proportional to the pedal movement. Both APP sensor signal voltages are low at rest position and increase as the pedal is applied.

REMOVAL & INSTALLATION

1. Remove lower instrument panel insulator panel.
2. Remove the electrical connector position assurance clip.
3. Disconnect the accelerator pedal position sensor electrical connector.
4. Remove the accelerator mounting bolts (1) from the accelerator bracket.
5. Remove the accelerator assembly (2) from the vehicle.
6. To install, reverse removal procedure. Tighten the accelerator pedal nuts to 89 inch lbs. (10 Nm).

CAMSHAFT POSITION (CMP) SENSOR

LOCATION

See Figures 100 and 101.

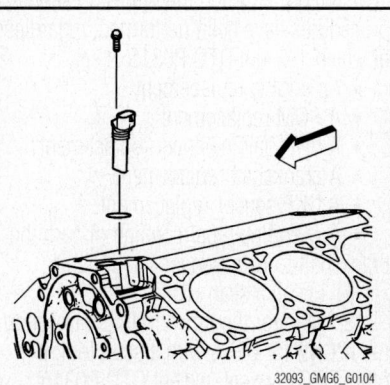

Fig. 100 CMP sensor location on 3.5L engine

Fig. 101 CMP sensor location on 3.9L engine

Refer to the accompanying illustrations for sensor locations.

OPERATION

The Camshaft Position (CMP) sensor signal is a digital ON/OFF pulse output once per revolution of the camshaft. The CMP sensor does not directly affect the operation of the ignition system. The CMP sensor information is used by the powertrain control module (PCM) to determine the position of the valve train relative to the crankshaft position. By monitoring the CMP and crankshaft position (CKP) signals, the PCM can accurately time the operation of the fuel injectors. The PCM supplies the sensor with a 12-volt reference circuit, a low reference circuit, and a signal circuit.

REMOVAL & INSTALLATION

1. Remove the power steering pump.
2. Disconnect the Camshaft Position (CMP) sensor electrical connector.
3. Remove the CMP sensor bolt.
4. Remove the CMP sensor.
5. Inspect the CMP sensor O-rings for wear, cracks, or leakage if the sensor is being reused. Replace the O-rings if damaged.

To install:
6. Lubricate the O-ring with clean engine oil and replace if damaged.
7. Install the CMP sensor.
8. Tighten the retaining bolt to 89 inch lbs. (10 Nm).
9. Connect the sensor electrical connector.
10. Install the power steering pump.,

CRANKSHAFT POSITION (CKP) SENSOR

LOCATION

See Figure 102.

Refer to the accompanying illustration for sensor location.

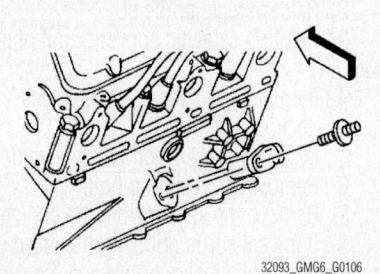

Fig. 102 CKP sensor location on 3.5L engine showing sensor and mounting nut, 3.9L engine similar

OPERATION

The Crankshaft Position (CKP) sensor is a 3-wire sensor based on the magneto resistive principle. A magneto resistive sensor uses 2 magnetic pickups between a permanent magnet. As an element such as a reluctor wheel passes the magnets, the resulting change in the magnetic field is used by the sensor electronics to produce a digital output pulse. The CKP sensor returns a digital ON/OFF pulse 24 times per crankshaft revolution. The pulse width encoding pattern is used to synchronize the coil firing sequence with the crankshaft position. The CKP sensor is used for ignition timing, fuel injector timing, misfire diagnostics, and tachometer display. The powertrain control module (PCM) supplies a 12-volt reference, a low reference, and a medium resolution engine speed signal circuit to the CKP sensor.

The crankshaft reluctor wheel is mounted in the middle of the crankshaft. The wheel is comprised of three 120-degree segments. Each segment represents a pair of cylinders at top dead center (TDC), and is further divided into six 20-degree segments. Within each 20-degree segment is a notch of 2 different sizes. Each 120-degree segment has a unique pattern of notches. This is known as pulse width encoding. This pulse width encoding pattern allows the PCM to quickly recognize which pair of cylinders are at TDC. The reluctor wheel is also a dual track, or mirror image, design. This means there is an additional wheel pressed against the first wheel with a gap of equal size to each notch of the mating wheel. When one sensing element of the CKP sensor is reading a notch, the other is reading a set of teeth. The resulting signals are then converted into a digital square wave output by the circuitry within the CKP sensor.

REMOVAL & INSTALLATION

3.5L Engine

1. Remove the negative battery cable.
2. Raise vehicle on hoist.
3. Position catalytic converter out of the way.
4. If equipped, disconnect the block heater electrical connector.
5. Disconnect the electrical connector.
6. Remove the retaining bolt.
7. Remove the sensor from the engine.
8. If the sensor is not being replaced inspect for wear, cracks, or leakage. Replace the O-ring if necessary.
9. Lubricate the new O-ring with clean engine oil before installing.

To install:

10. Install the sensor into the block.
11. Reinstall the retainer bolt to hold sensor to block face. Tighten the bolt to 97 inch lbs. (11 Nm).
12. Connect the electrical connector.
13. Connect the block heater electrical connector, if equipped.
14. Reposition and properly install the catalytic converter.
15. Lower the vehicle. Reconnect the negative battery cable.

3.9L Engine

1. Remove the exhaust manifold.
2. Disconnect the sensor electrical connector.
3. Remove the CKP sensor bolt.
4. Remove the CKP sensor.

To install:

5. Lubricate the CKP sensor O-ring with clean engine oil.
6. Install the CKP sensor.
7. Install the CKP sensor stud and tighten to 89 inch lbs. (10 Nm).
8. Connect the sensor electrical connector.
9. Install the exhaust manifold.

Crankshaft Variation Learn Procedure

The CKP system variation learn procedure is also required when the following service procedures have been performed, regardless of whether or not DTC P0315 is set:

- An engine replacement
- A PCM replacement
- A harmonic balancer replacement
- A crankshaft replacement
- A CKP sensor replacement
- Any engine repairs which disturb the crankshaft to CKP sensor relationship
  1. Install a scan tool.
  2. Monitor the powertrain control module (PCM) for DTCs with a scan tool. If other DTCs are set, except DTC P0315, refer to Diagnostic Trouble Code (DTC) List.
  3. Select the crankshaft position variation learn procedure with a scan tool.
  4. The scan tool instructs you to perform the following:
     - Accelerate to wide open throttle (WOT)
     - Observe fuel cut-off for applicable engine
     - Release throttle when fuel cut-off occurs
     - Engine should not accelerate beyond calibrated RPM value
     - Release throttle immediately if value is exceeded
     - Block drive wheels

- Set parking brake
- DO NOT apply brake pedal
- Cycle ignition from OFF to ON
- Apply and hold brake pedal
- Start and idle engine
- Turn the A/C OFF

➡️Vehicle must remain in Park or Neutral. The scan tool monitors certain component signals to determine if all the conditions are met to continue with the procedure. The scan tool only displays the condition that inhibits the procedure. The scan tool monitors the following components:

- Crankshaft position (CKP) sensors activity—If there is a CKP sensor condition, refer to the applicable DTC
- Camshaft position (CMP) signal activity—If there is a CMP signal condition, refer to the applicable DTC
- Engine coolant temperature (ECT)—If the engine coolant temperature is not warm enough, idle the engine until the engine coolant temperature reaches the correct temperature

✷✷ CAUTION

While the learn procedure is in progress, release the throttle immediately when the engine starts to decelerate. The engine control is returned to the operator and the engine responds to throttle position after the learn procedure is complete.

5. Enable the CKP system variation learn procedure with the scan tool and perform the following:
   a. Accelerate to WOT.
   b. Release throttle when fuel cut-off occurs.
6. The scan tool displays Learn Status: Learned this ignition.
7. If the scan tool indicates that DTC P0315 ran and passed, the CKP variation learn procedure is complete.
8. If the scan tool indicates DTC P0315 failed or did not run, refer to DTC P0315 in Diagnostic Trouble Codes List.
9. If any other DTCs set, refer to Diagnostic Trouble Code (DTC) List .
10. Turn OFF the ignition for 30 seconds after the learn procedure is completed successfully.

EGR VALVE POSITION (EVP) SENSOR

LOCATION

See Figure 103.

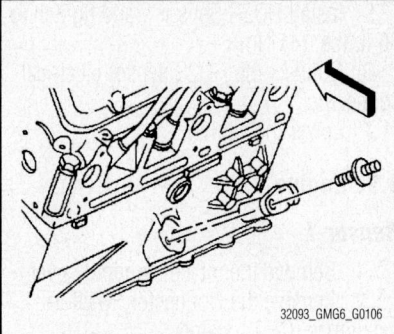

Fig. 103 Showing the EGR Solenoid Valve location on 3.5L engine

Refer to the accompanying illustration for locations.

OPERATION

The Exhaust Gas Recirculation (EGR) system is used to reduce the amount of nitrogen oxide (NOx) emission levels caused by combustion temperatures exceeding 816°C (1,500°F). It does this by introducing small amounts of exhaust gas back into the combustion chamber. The exhaust gas absorbs a portion of the thermal energy produced by the combustion process and thus decreases combustion temperature.

The exhaust gas recirculation (EGR) valve is controlled by a high side driver within the powertrain control module (PCM). This high side driver uses a 12-volt pulse width modulated (PWM) signal. The ground path for the EGR valve is completed by turning in a separate driver within the PCM.

REMOVAL & INSTALLATION

1. Remove the air cleaner inlet duct.
2. Disconnect the EGR valve electrical connector.
3. Loosen and reposition the transmission dipstick and tube.
4. Remove the exhaust gas recirculation (EGR) pipe.
5. Remove the EGR valve bolts.
6. Remove the EGR valve.
7. Remove the EGR valve gasket.
8. Clean the EGR valve mating surface.

To install:

9. Install the EGR valve with a new gasket to the intake manifold.
10. Install the EGR valve bolts.
11. Tighten the bolts to 22 ft. lbs. (30 Nm).
12. Install the EGR pipe.
13. Reposition and install the transmission fill tube and dipstick.

14. Connect the EGR valve electrical connector.
15. Install the air cleaner inlet duct.

ELECTRONIC CONTROL MODULE (ECM)

The ECM and PCM references are interchangeable for the 3.5L and 3.9L engines. Refer to the following section for additional information, "Powertrain Control Module (PCM)."

ENGINE COOLANT TEMPERATURE (ECT) SENSOR

LOCATION

See Figure 104.

Refer to the accompanying illustration and the removal and installation procedure for sensor location.

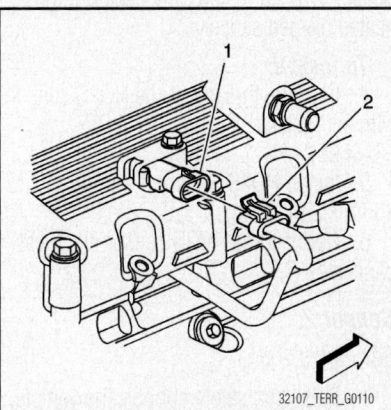

Fig. 104 Indicating the ECT sensor location on 3.5L engine

REMOVAL & INSTALLATION

✳✳ CAUTION

Use care when handling the coolant sensor. Damage to the coolant sensor will affect the operation of the fuel control system

3.5L Engine

See Figure 105.

1. Engine coolant must be drained below the level of the Engine Coolant Temperature (ECT) sensor.
2. Remove the air intake duct.
3. Disconnect the ECT sensor harness connector.
4. Remove the ECT sensor.

To install:

5. Tap out the sensor mounting hole to

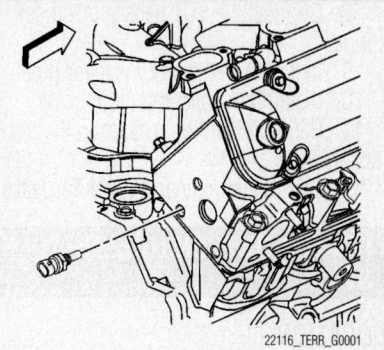

Fig. 105 Removing the coolant temperature sensor from the engine–3.5L engine

remove any thread sealant residue. If the old sensor is to be reused, clean the threads of all sealant residue.

6. Apply thread sealant to sensor threads.
7. Install the ECT sensor and tighten to 17 ft. lbs. (23 Nm).
8. Connect the ECT sensor harness connector. Push in the connector until a click is heard, then pull back to confirm a positive engagement.
9. Fill engine coolant to proper level.
10. Install the air intake duct.
11. Start the engine and check for leaks.

3.9L Engine

See Figure 106.

1. Engine coolant must be drained below the level of the Engine Coolant Temperature (ECT) sensor.
2. Remove the intake manifold cover.
3. Remove the exhaust crossover pipe.
4. Disconnect the ECT sensor harness connector.
5. Remove the ECT sensor.

To install:

6. Apply thread sealant to sensor threads.
7. Install the ECT sensor and tighten to 15 ft. lbs. (20 Nm).

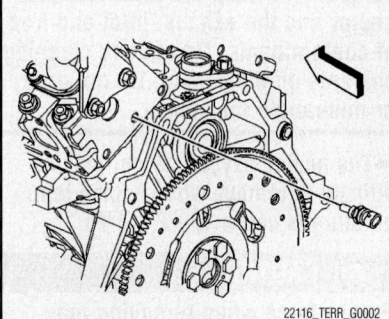

Fig. 106 Removing the coolant temperature sensor from the engine–3.9L engine

8. Connect the ECT sensor electrical connector.

9. Install the exhaust crossover pipe.

10. Install the intake manifold cover.

11. Refill the cooling system to the correct level.

12. Start the engine and check for leaks.

HEATED OXYGEN (HO2S) SENSOR

LOCATION

See Figure 107.

Refer to the accompanying illustration for sensor location.

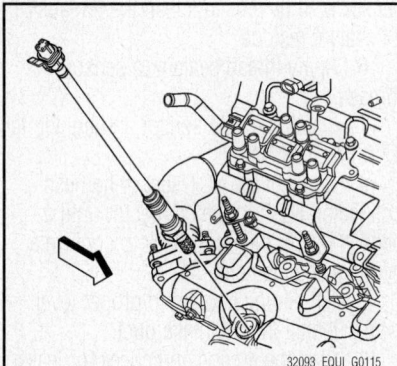

Fig. 107 Showing the locations of the HO2S 1 (Sensor 1) on 3.5L engine

FIGREMOVAL & INSTALLATION

> **✳✳ CAUTION**
>
> **Do not remove the pigtail from either the Heated Oxygen Sensor (HO2S) or the Oxygen Sensor (O2S). Removing the pigtail or the connector will affect sensor operation.**

> **✳✳ CAUTION**
>
> **Handle the oxygen sensors carefully in order to prevent damage to the component. Keep the electrical connector and the exhaust inlet end free of contaminants. Do not use cleaning solvents on the sensor. Do not drop or mishandle the sensor.**

➡The heated oxygen sensor may be difficult to remove when engine temperature is below 120°F (48°C).

> **✳✳ CAUTION**
>
> **Excess force when removing may damage the threads in the exhaust manifold or exhaust pipe.**

➡A special anti-seize compound is used on the heated oxygen sensor threads. The compound consists of graphite suspended in fluid and glass beads. The graphite will burn away, but the glass beads will remain, making the sensor easier to remove. New or service sensors will already have the compound applied to the threads. If a sensor is removed from an engine and if for any reason is to be reinstalled, the threads must have anti-seize compound applied before reinstallation.

3.5L Engine

Sensor 1

1. Disconnect the HO2S Sensor 1 electrical connector.

2. Remove the HO2S Sensor 1 from the exhaust manifold.

3. Use Special Tool J-39194-B Oxygen Sensor Wrench to carefully back out the heated oxygen sensor.

To install:

4. Coat the threads of the HO2S sensor with anti-seize compound (GM P/N 5613695).

5. Install HO2S Sensor 1 and tighten to 30 ft. lbs. (41 Nm).

6. Connect the HO2S sensor electrical connector.

Sensor 2

See Figure 108.

1. Raise and safely support the vehicle.

2. Disconnect the HO2S Sensor 2 electrical connector.

3. Use Special Tool J-39194-B Oxygen Sensor Wrench to carefully back out the heated oxygen sensor.

To install:

4. Coat the threads of the HO2S sensor with anti-seize compound (GM P/N 5613695).

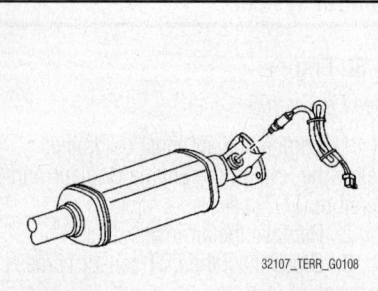

Fig. 108 Removing HO2S 2 (Sensor 2) from exhaust pipe location on 3.5L engine

5. Install HO2S Sensor 2 and tighten to 30 ft. lbs. (41 Nm).

6. Connect the HO2S sensor electrical connector.

7. Lower the vehicle.

3.9L Engine

Sensor 1

1. Remove the intake manifold cover.

2. Remove the Connector Position Assurance (CPA) retainer.

3. Disconnect the engine harness electrical connector from the HO2S 1 connector.

4. Raise and safely support the vehicle.

5. Remove the HO2S 1 electrical connector from the ignition coil bracket.

6. Remove the HO2S from the exhaust manifold.

To install:

7. If you are re-installing the old sensor, coat the threads with anti-seize compound (GM P/N 12377953).

8. Install the HO2S to the exhaust manifold and tighten to 31 ft. lbs. (42 Nm).

9. Connect the engine harness electrical connector to the HO2S connector.

10. Install the CPA retainer.

11. Install the HO2S electrical connector to the ignition coil bracket.

12. Lower the vehicle.

13. Install the intake manifold cover.

Sensor 2

1. Raise and safely support the vehicle.

2. Remove the connector position assurance (CPA) retainer.

3. Disconnect the engine harness electrical connector from the HO2S 2 connector.

4. Remove the HO2S from the catalytic converter.

To install:

5. If you are re-installing the old sensor, coat the threads with anti-seize compound (GM P/N 12377953).

6. Install the HO2S to the catalytic converter and tighten to 31 ft. lbs. (42 Nm).

7. Connect the engine harness electrical connector to the HO2S connector.

8. Install the CPA retainer.

9. Lower the vehicle.

INTAKE AIR TEMPERATURE (IAT) SENSOR

LOCATION

See Figure 109.

Refer to the accompanying illustration for sensor location.

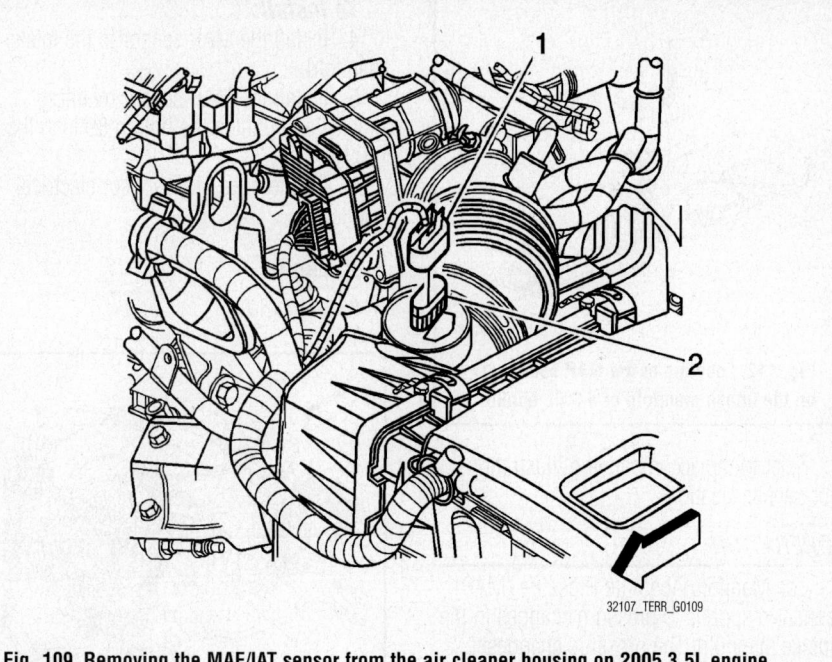

Fig. 109 Removing the MAF/IAT sensor from the air cleaner housing on 2005 3.5L engine

32107_TERR_G0109

FREMOVAL & INSTALLATION

1. Disconnect the Mass Airflow (MAF) sensor electrical connector (1).
2. Loosen the clamps and remove the air cleaner intake duct.
3. Remove the MAF/IAT sensor from the air filter housing.
4. Installation is the reverse of the removal procedure.

KNOCK SENSOR (KS)

LOCATION

See Figure 110.

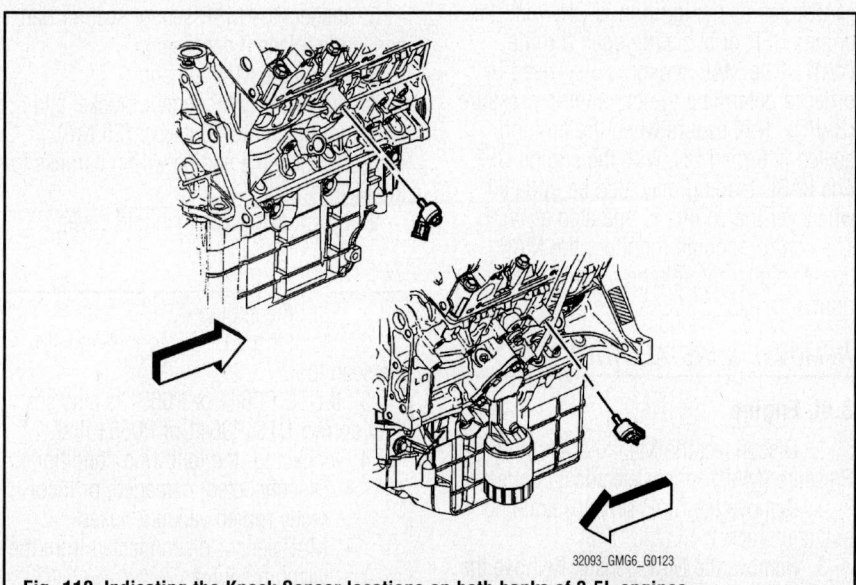

32093_GMG6_G0123

Fig. 110 Indicating the Knock Sensor locations on both banks of 3.5L engines, 3.9L engine similar

Refer to the accompanying illustration for sensor location.

OPERATION

The Knock Sensor (KS) system enables the control module to control the ignition timing for the best possible performance while protecting the engine from potentially damaging levels of detonation. The control module uses the KS system to test for abnormal engine noise that may indicate detonation, also known as spark knock.

This KS system uses one or two flat response two-wire sensors. The sensor uses piezo-electric crystal technology that produces an AC voltage signal of varying amplitude and frequency based on the engine vibration or noise level. The amplitude and frequency are dependent upon the level of knock that the KS detects. The control module receives the KS signal through a signal circuit. The KS ground is supplied by the control module through a low reference circuit.

The control module learns a minimum noise level, or background noise, at idle from the KS and uses calibrated values for the rest of the RPM range. The control module uses the minimum noise level to calculate a noise channel. A normal KS signal will ride within the noise channel. As engine speed and load change, the noise channel upper and lower parameters will change to accommodate the normal KS signal, keeping the signal within the channel. In order to determine which cylinders are knocking, the control module only uses KS signal information when each cylinder is near top dead center (TDC) of the firing stroke. If knock is present, the signal will range outside of the noise channel.

If the control module has determined that knock is present, it will retard the ignition timing to attempt to eliminate the knock. The control module will always try to work back to a zero compensation level, or no spark retard. An abnormal KS signal will stay outside of the noise channel or will not be present. KS diagnostics are calibrated to detect faults with the KS circuitry inside the control module, the KS wiring, or the KS voltage output. Some diagnostics are also calibrated to detect constant noise from an outside influence such as a loose/damaged component or excessive engine mechanical noise.

REMOVAL & INSTALLATION

3.5L Engine

1. Raise and safely support the vehicle.
2. Disconnect the knock sensor wiring harness electrical connector.
3. Remove the knock sensor.

To install:

❋❋ CAUTION

DO NOT apply thread sealant to the sensor threads. The sensor threads are coated at the factory. Applying additional sealant affects the sensors ability to detect detonation.

4. Install the knock sensor and tighten to 18 ft. lbs. (25 Nm).

5. Connect the knock sensor wiring harness.

6. Lower the vehicle.

3.9L Engine

1. Raise and safely support the vehicle.

2. Remove the radiator air baffle, if removing the knock sensor from Bank 1.

3. Remove the right front wheel and engine splash shield, if removing the knock sensor from Bank 2.

4. Disconnect the wiring harness from the knock sensor.

5. Loosen and remove the knock sensor.

To install:

> ✸✸ **CAUTION**
>
> **DO NOT apply thread sealant to the sensor threads. The sensor threads are coated at the factory. Applying additional sealant affects the sensors ability to detect detonation.**

6. Install the knock sensor and tighten to 18 ft. lbs. (25 Nm).

7. The remainder of the installation is the reverse order of removal.

MASS AIR FLOW (MAF) SENSOR

The MAF sensor and intake air temperature sensor are integrated as a single component. Refer to the following section for additional information, "Intake Air Temperature (IAT) Sensor, Operation."

MANIFOLD ABSOLUTE PRESSURE (MAP) SENSOR

LOCATION

See Figures 111 and 112.

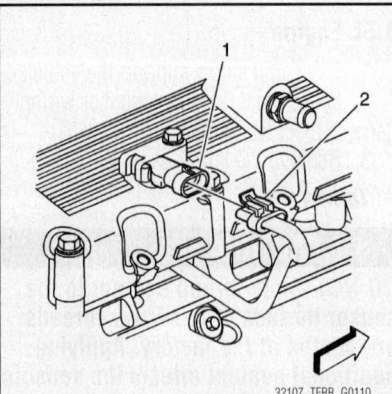

Fig. 111 Removing the MAP sensor (1) from the intake manifold location on 3.5L engine

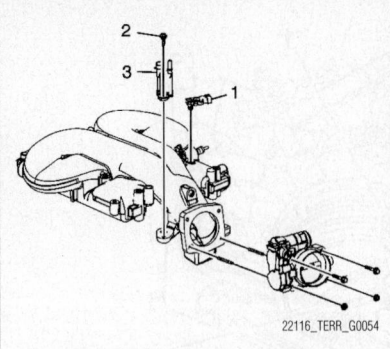

Fig. 112 Location of the MAP sensor (1) on the intake manifold of a 3.9L engine

Refer to the accompanying illustrations for sensor locations.

OPERATION

The Manifold Absolute Pressure (MAP) sensor responds to pressure changes in the intake manifold. The pressure changes occur based on the engine load. The MAP sensor has the following circuits:

- 5-volt reference circuit
- Low reference circuit
- MAP sensor signal circuit

The control module supplies 5 volts to the MAP sensor on the 5-volt reference circuit. The control module also provides a ground on the low reference circuit. The MAP sensor provides a signal to the control module on the MAP sensor signal circuit which is relative to the pressure changes in the manifold. The control module should detect a low signal voltage at a low MAP, such as during an idle or a deceleration. The control module should detect a high signal voltage at a high MAP, such as the ignition is ON, with the engine OFF, or at a wide open throttle (WOT). The MAP sensor is also used in order to determine the barometric pressure (BARO). This occurs when the ignition switch is turned ON, with the engine OFF. The BARO reading may also be updated whenever the engine is operated at WOT. The control module monitors the MAP sensor signal for voltage outside of the normal range.

REMOVAL & INSTALLATION

3.5L Engine

1. Disconnect the Manifold Absolute Pressure (MAP) sensor electrical connector.

2. Remove the MAP sensor retraining bolt and bracket.

3. Remove the MAP sensor. Remove the MAP sensor port seal if it is still retained in the intake manifold.

To install:

4. Install the MAP sensor to the intake manifold.

5. Install the MAP sensor retaining bracket and tighten the bolt to 89 inch lbs. (10 Nm).

6. Connect the MAP sensor electrical connector.

3.9L Engine

See Figure 113.

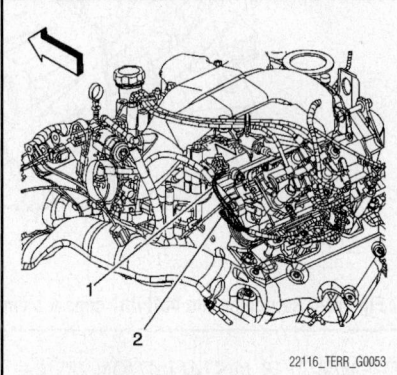

Fig. 113 Disconnect the engine wiring harness (1) from the MAP sensor—3.9L engine

1. Remove the intake manifold cover.

2. Disconnect the engine harness electrical connector from the Manifold Absolute Pressure (MAP) sensor.

3. Remove the MAP sensor bracket bolts and bracket.

4. Remove the MAP sensor from the intake manifold.

To install:

5. Inspect the MAP sensor seal for damage, and replace if necessary.

6. Install the MAP sensor.

7. Install the MAP sensor bracket and bolts and tighten to 18 ft. lbs. (25 Nm).

8. Connect the engine wiring harness to the MAP sensor.

9. Install the intake manifold cover.

TESTING

1. Start the engine.

2. Monitor the DTC information with the scan tool.

3. If DTC P0641 or P0651 is also set then correct DTC P0641 or P0651 first.

4. Inspect for the following conditions:

- Disconnected, damaged, or incorrectly routed vacuum hoses
- MAP sensor disconnected from the vacuum source
- Restrictions in the MAP sensor vacuum source

- Intake manifold vacuum leaks
- Inspect for a properly functioning oxygen sensor—refer to Scan Tool Data List .

5. With the ignition ON, and the engine OFF, disconnect the MAP sensor.

6. Measure for 4.8-5.2 volts from the 5-volt reference circuit of the MAP sensor to a good ground, with a DMM.

  a. If more than 5.2 volts, then test the circuit for a short to voltage or faulty control module.

  b. If less than 4.8 volts, then test the circuit for high resistance, an open, a short to ground, or an intermittent and poor connection or at the control module, or a faulty control module.

7. Use a scan tool and observe the MAP sensor for less than 12 kPa.

- If the MAP sensor is more than 12 kPa then test the MAP sensor signal circuit for a short to voltage or a faulty control module.

8. Use a 3-amp fused jumper wire and connect it between the MAP sensor 5-volt reference circuit and the MAP sensor signal circuit.

9. Use a scan tool and observe the MAP sensor for more than 103 kPa.

- If the MAP sensor is less than 103 kPa, then test the MAP sensor signal circuit for a short to ground, an open, high resistance, or a faulty control module.

10. Turn OFF the ignition and allow the control module to power down.

11. Remove the MAP sensor from the engine vacuum source. Leave the MAP sensor connected to the engine harness.

12. Connect a J 23738-A Mityvac to the MAP sensor.

13. Turn ON the ignition, with the engine OFF.

14. Observe the MAP sensor pressure with the scan tool.

15. Apply vacuum to the MAP sensor with the J 23738-A in 1 inch Hg increments until 15 inches Hg is reached. Each 1 inch Hg should decrease MAP sensor pressure by 3-4 kPa. Monitor the MAP sensor pressure to see if the decrease in pressure is consistent.

- If the decrease in pressure is not consistent then, test for intermittent and poor connections at the MAP sensor. If connections test OK, replace the MAP sensor

16. Apply vacuum with the J 23738-A until 20 inches Hg is reached. Observe the MAP sensor pressure for less than 34 kPa. \

- If it is more than 34 kPa, test for an intermittent and for a poor connection at the MAP sensor. If connec-

tions test OK, replace the MAP sensor.

17. With a DMM measure for less than 5 ohms of resistance between the low reference circuit of the MAP sensor and battery negative post.

- If the resistance is more than 5 ohms, then test the low reference circuit for a high resistance or a faulty control module.

POWERTRAIN CONTROL MODULE (PCM)

LOCATION

See Figure 114.

Refer to the accompanying illustration for PCM location.

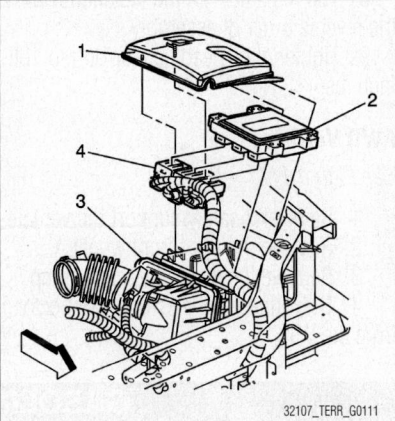

Fig. 114 Removing the powertrain control module (2) from under the air cleaner housing cover (1)

OPERATION

The Powertrain Control Module (PCM) constantly looks at the information from various sensors and other inputs and controls systems that affect vehicle performance and emissions. The PCM also performs diagnostic tests on various parts of the system. The PCM can recognize operational problems and alert the driver via the malfunction indicator lamp (MIL). When the PCM detects a malfunction, the PCM stores a diagnostic trouble code (DTC). The problem area is identified by the particular DTC that is set. The control module supplies a buffered voltage to various sensors and switches. The input and output devices in the PCM include analog-to-digital converters, signal buffers, counters, and output drivers. The output drivers are electronic switches that complete a ground or voltage circuit when turned on. Most PCM controlled components are operated via output

drivers. The PCM monitors these driver circuits for proper operation and, in most cases, can set a DTC corresponding to the controlled device if a problem is detected.

REMOVAL & INSTALLATION

See Figure 114.

1. Using a scan tool, retrieve the percentage of remaining engine oil and the remaining automatic transmission fluid life. Record the remaining engine oil and the remaining automatic transmission fluid life.

2. Disconnect the negative battery cable.

3. Remove the left sheet metal diagonal brace.

4. Remove the air cleaner assembly cover and lift the PCM from the air cleaner assembly.

5. Disconnect the engine harness electrical connectors from the PCM.

6. Remove the PCM.

To install:

7. Install the PCM electrical connectors.

8. Install the PCM into the air cleaner assembly.

9. Install the air cleaner assembly cover.

10. Install the left sheet metal diagonal brace.

11. Connect the negative battery cable.

12. Reprogram the PCM if a new PCM was installed.

THROTTLE POSITION SENSOR (TPS)

LOCATION

There are two individual throttle position sensors located with the throttle body assembly.

OPERATION

The TP sensors are used to determine the throttle plate angle. The TP sensors provide the powertrain control module (PCM) with a signal voltage proportional to throttle plate movement. Both TP sensor signal voltages are low at closed throttle and increase as the throttle opens.

REMOVAL & INSTALLATION

The throttle position sensors are not serviceable as individual parts. The throttle body must be replaced.

VEHICLE SPEED SENSOR (VSS)

LOCATION

See Figures 115 and 116.

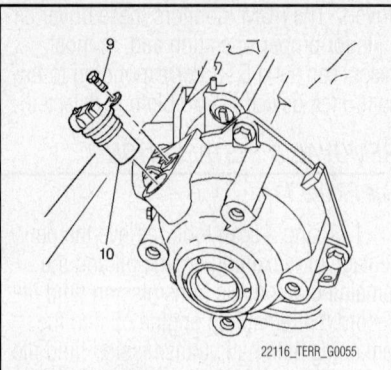

Fig. 115 Location of the VSS in the transaxle extension case—FWD vehicles

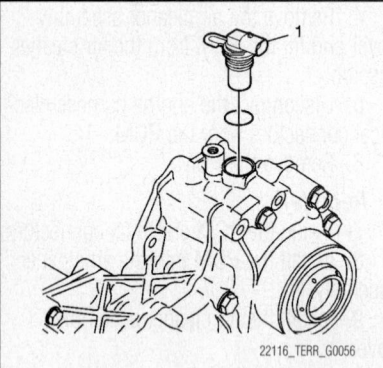

Fig. 116 Location of the VSS in the transfer case housing—AWD vehicles

The Vehicle Speed Sensor (VSS) is located in the transaxle extension case of FWD vehicle or in the transfer case housing of AWD vehicles.

REMOVAL & INSTALLATION

FWD Vehicles

1. Raise and safely support the vehicle.
2. Remove the right front wheel.
3. Remove the right engine splash shield.
4. Disconnect the Vehicle Speed Sensor (VSS) wiring harness.
5. Remove the VSS bolt.
6. Remove the VSS from the extension case.

To install:

7. Inspect the VSS O-ring for cuts or damage. Replace if necessary.
8. The remainder of the installation is the reverse order of assembly.
9. Tighten the speed sensor bolt to 106 inch lbs. (12 Nm).

AWD Vehicles

See Figure 117.

1. Raise and safely support the vehicle.
2. Remove the right front wheel.
3. Remove the power steering pump.
4. Disconnect the electrical connector from the VSS.

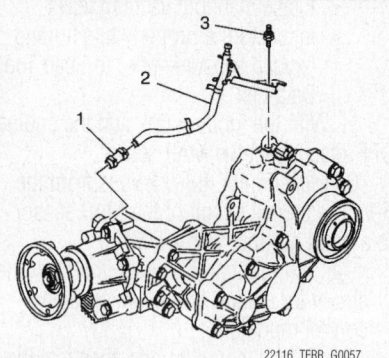

Fig. 117 Remove the speed sensor/vent hose bolt (3) and reposition the pinion housing vent hose (2) to access the VSS—AWD vehicles.

5. Remove the speed sensor/vent hose bolt from the transfer case.
6. Reposition the pinion housing vent hose and mounting bracket away from the speed sensor bolt boss.
7. Remove the VSS.

To install:

8. Inspect the VSS O-ring for cuts or damage. Replace if necessary.
9. The remainder of the installation is the reverse order of assembly.
10. Tighten the speed sensor bolt to 22 ft. lbs. (30 Nm).

FUEL | GASOLINE FUEL INJECTION SYSTEM

FUEL SYSTEM SERVICE PRECAUTIONS

Safety is the most important factor when performing not only fuel system maintenance but any type of maintenance. Failure to conduct maintenance and repairs in a safe manner may result in serious personal injury or death. Maintenance and testing of the vehicle's fuel system components can be accomplished safely and effectively by adhering to the following rules and guidelines.

• To avoid the possibility of fire and personal injury, always disconnect the negative battery cable unless the repair or test procedure requires that battery voltage be applied.

• Always relieve the fuel system pressure prior to disconnecting any fuel system component (injector, fuel rail, pressure regulator, etc.), fitting or fuel line connection. Exercise extreme caution whenever relieving fuel system pressure to avoid exposing skin, face and eyes to fuel spray. Please be advised that fuel under pressure may

penetrate the skin or any part of the body that it contacts.

• Always place a shop towel or cloth around the fitting or connection prior to loosening to absorb any excess fuel due to spillage. Ensure that all fuel spillage (should it occur) is quickly removed from engine surfaces. Ensure that all fuel soaked cloths or towels are deposited into a suitable waste container.

• Always keep a dry chemical (Class B) fire extinguisher near the work area.

• Do not allow fuel spray or fuel vapors to come into contact with a spark or open flame.

• Always use a back-up wrench when loosening and tightening fuel line connection fittings. This will prevent unnecessary stress and torsion to fuel line piping.

• Always replace worn fuel fitting O-rings with new Do not substitute fuel hose or equivalent where fuel pipe is installed.

Before servicing the vehicle, make sure to also refer to the precautions in the beginning of this section as well.

RELIEVING FUEL SYSTEM PRESSURE

The fuel systems operate under high fuel pressures. It is very important that the pressure be properly relieved prior to servicing the system or any of its components.

3.5L Engine

1. Before servicing the vehicle, refer to the Precautions Section.
2. Loosen the fuel filler cap in order to relieve the tank pressure. Do not tighten at this time.
3. Raise the vehicle.
4. Disconnect the fuel pump electrical connector.
5. Lower the vehicle.
6. Start and run the engine until the fuel supply remaining in the fuel pipes is consumed. Engage the starter for 3.0 seconds in order to assure relief of any remaining pressure.
7. Raise the vehicle.
8. Connect the fuel pump electrical connector.

9. Lower the vehicle.

10. Disconnect the negative battery cable in order to avoid possible fuel discharge if an accidental attempt is made to start the engine.

11. When fuel service is finished, tighten the fuel filler cap and connect the negative battery cable.

3.9L Engine

See Figure 118.

1. Disconnect the negative battery cable.

2. Install Special Tool J-34730-1A Fuel Pressure Gauge to the fuel line as follows:

　a. Remove the intake manifold cover.

　b. Remove the fuel rail pressure fitting cap.

　c. Connect the fuel pressure gauge to the fuel pressure valve. Wrap a shop towel around the fitting to avoid an fuel spillage.

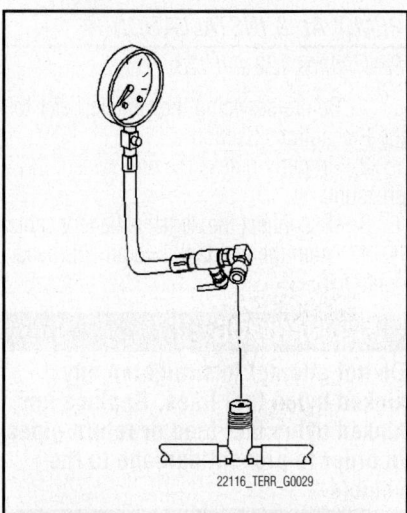

Fig. 118 Install a fuel pressure gauge to relieve the fuel pressure—3.9L Engine

3. Loosen the fuel fill cap in order to relieve the fuel tank vapor pressure.

4. Install the drain hose of the fuel pressure into an approved container and open the valve to relieve the fuel system pressure.

5. Drain any remaining fuel in the gauge into the approved container.

6. Once the fuel pressure has been relieved, remove the fuel pressure gauge.

7. When fuel service is finished, tighten the fuel filler cap and connect the negative battery cable.

FUEL FILTER

REMOVAL & INSTALLATION

The fuel filter is an integral part of the fuel pump/sender. The fuel filter attaches to

the lower end of the fuel sender. The fuel strainer is self-cleaning and normally requires no maintenance.

FUEL INJECTORS

REMOVAL & INSTALLATION

3.5L Engine

See Figures 119 and 120.

1. Before servicing the vehicle, refer to the Precautions Section.

2. Relieve the fuel system pressure. Refer to the fuel system relief procedure in this section.

> ❋❋ **CAUTION**
>
> In order to reduce the risk of fire and personal injury that may result from a fuel leak, always install the fuel injector O-rings in the proper position. If the upper and lower O-rings are different colors (black and brown), be sure to install the black O-ring in the upper position and the brown O-ring in the lower position on the fuel injector. The O-rings are the same size but are made of different materials.

3. Clean all engine fuel pipe connections and areas surrounding the engine fuel pipe connections before disconnecting the engine fuel pipe connections to avoid possible contamination of the fuel system.

4. Remove or disconnect the following:
- Fuel feed pipe retaining clip
- Fuel feed pipe from the fuel rail
- Evaporative emission (EVAP) pipe from the EVAP canister purge solenoid valve
- Upper intake manifold
- Fuel injector harness from the fuel rail
- Coolant temperature sensor and camshaft position sensor electrical connectors
- Main fuel injector electrical connector
- Fuel rail retaining bolts
- Fuel rail assembly

> ❋❋ **WARNING**
>
> Use care in removing the fuel injectors in order to prevent damage to the fuel injector electrical connector pins or the fuel injector nozzles. Do not immerse the fuel injector in any type of cleaner. The fuel injector is

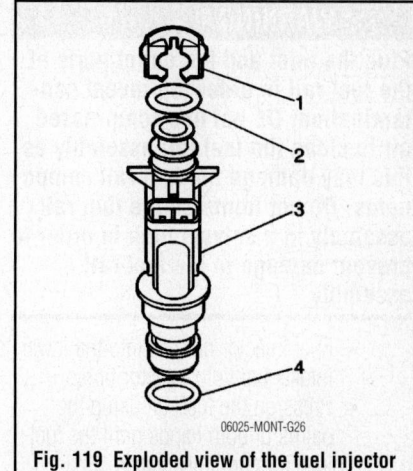

Fig. 119 Exploded view of the fuel injector

an electrical component and may be damaged by this cleaning method.

> ❋❋ **WARNING**
>
> If the fuel injectors are found to be leaking, the engine oil may be contaminated with fuel.

- Fuel injector retaining clip
- Fuel injector from the fuel rail
- Fuel injector upper O-ring
- Fuel injector lower O-ring

To install:

➥Be sure to use the correct part number when ordering replacement fuel injectors. The fuel injector assembly is stamped with a part number identification

5. Lubricate the new injector O-ring seats with engine oil.

6. Install or connect the following:
- Fuel injector upper O-ring
- Fuel injector lower O-ring
- Fuel injector to the fuel rail
- Fuel injector retaining clip

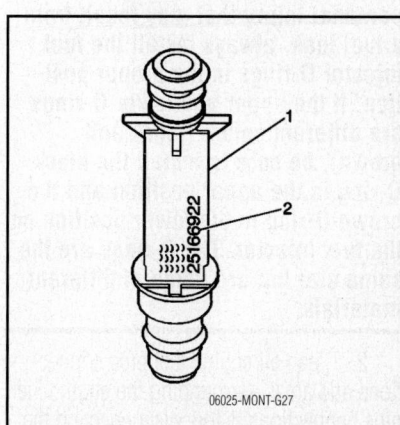

Fig. 120 Indicating the fuel injector ID number

※※ WARNING

Plug the inlet and the outlet ports of the fuel rail in order to prevent contamination. Do not use compressed air to clean the fuel rail assembly as this may damage the fuel rail components. Do not immerse the fuel rail assembly in a solvent bath in order to prevent damage to the fuel rail assembly.

- Fuel injector nozzles into the lower intake manifold injector bores
- Press on the fuel rail using the palms of both hands until the fuel injectors are fully seated
- Install the fuel rail attaching bolts and tighten the bolt to 89 inch lbs. (10Nm)
- Injector electrical harness to the fuel rail
- Fuel injector electrical connectors
- Coolant temperature sensor and camshaft position sensor electrical connectors
- Main fuel injector electrical harness connector
- Engine fuel feed pipe to the fuel rail
- EVAP pipe to the EVAP canister purge solenoid valve
- Upper intake manifold
- Negative battery cable

7. Turn the ignition **ON** for 2 seconds and then turn it **OFF** for 10 seconds. Again turn the ignition **ON** and check for leaks.

3.9L Engine

See Figure 121.

1. Relieve the fuel system pressure. Refer to the fuel system relief procedure in this section.

※※ CAUTION

In order to reduce the risk of fire and personal injury that may result from a fuel leak, always install the fuel injector O-rings in the proper position. If the upper and lower O-rings are different colors (black and brown), be sure to install the black O-ring in the upper position and the brown O-ring in the lower position on the fuel injector. The O-rings are the same size but are made of different materials.

2. Clean all engine fuel pipe connections and areas surrounding the engine fuel pipe connections before disconnecting the engine fuel pipe connections to avoid possible contamination of the fuel system.

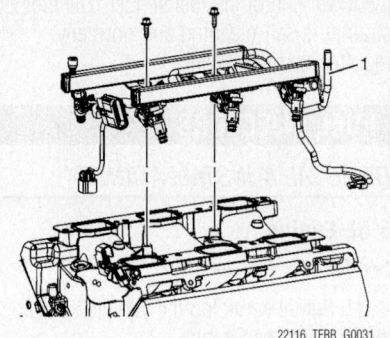

Fig. 121 Fuel rail mounting—3.9L engine shown

3. Disconnect the fuel supply pipe from the fuel rail.
4. Disconnect any remaining electrical connectors.
5. Remove the upper intake manifold.
6. Remove the fuel injector harness connector bracket bolt from the intake manifold.
7. Disconnect the camshaft position (CMP) sensor electrical connector.
8. Remove the fuel rail mounting bolts.
9. Remove the fuel rail.
10. Remove the and discard the O-rings from the spray tip end of each injector.
11. Remove the fuel injector retaining clip.
12. Remove the fuel injector from the fuel rail.
13. Remove and discard the fuel injector upper O-ring.

To install:

➡Be sure to use the correct part number when ordering replacement fuel injectors. The fuel injector assembly is stamped with a part number identification

14. Lubricate the new injector O-ring seats with engine oil.
15. Install the new fuel injector upper O-ring.
16. Install each fuel injector to the fuel rail.
17. Install each fuel injector retaining clip.

※※ WARNING

Plug the inlet and the outlet ports of the fuel rail in order to prevent contamination. Do not use compressed air to clean the fuel rail assembly as this may damage the fuel rail components. Do not immerse the fuel rail assembly in a solvent bath in order to prevent damage to the fuel rail assembly.

18. Lubricate the new lower injector O-ring with clean engine oil.
19. Install the fuel rail assembly into the

intake manifold. Tilt the fuel rail assembly slightly to install the injectors.
20. Install the fuel rail mounting bolts and tighten to 89 inch lbs. (10 Nm).
21. Connect the CMP sensor electrical connector.
22. Position the fuel injector harness connector bracket to the intake manifold.
23. Install the fuel injector harness connector bracket bolt. Tighten to the bolt to 71 inch lbs. (8 Nm).
24. Install the upper intake manifold.
25. Connect any remaining electrical connectors.
26. Connect the fuel supply pipe to the fuel rail.
27. Connect the negative battery cable.
28. Turn the ignition **ON** for 2 seconds and then turn it **OFF** for 10 seconds. Again turn the ignition **ON** and check for leaks.

FUEL PUMP/SENDER

REMOVAL & INSTALLATION

See Figures 122 and 123.

1. Before servicing the vehicle, refer to the Precautions Section.
2. Properly relieve the fuel system pressure.
3. Disconnect the negative battery cable.
4. Drain the fuel tank into an approved container.

※※ WARNING

Do not attempt to straighten any kinked nylon fuel lines. Replace any kinked nylon fuel feed or return pipes in order to prevent damage to the vehicle.

※※ WARNING

Do not attempt to repair sections of nylon fuel pipes. If the nylon fuel pipes are damaged, replace the pipes.

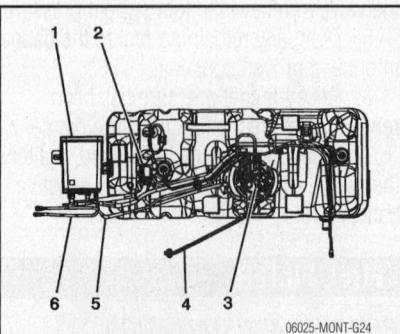

Fig. 122 Showing the fuel tank assembly and related components

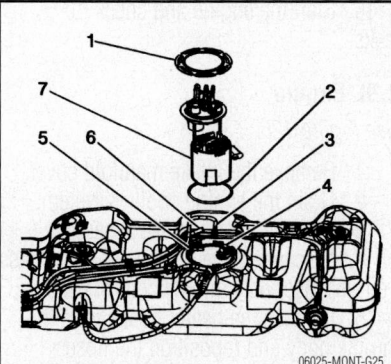

Fig. 123 Identifying the fuel sender assembly

5. Raise the vehicle.

6. Disconnect the fuel supply pipe (5) quick-connect fitting.

7. Disconnect the evaporative emission (EVAP) purge pipe (6) quick connect fitting at the EVAP canister.

8. Loosen the fuel tank filler pipe hose clamp.

9. Disconnect the fuel tank filler from the fuel tank.

10. Disconnect the vapor recirculation pipe from the filler tube.

11. Remove the fuel tank shield.

12. With the aid of an assistant, support the fuel tank.

13. Remove the fuel tank strap attaching bolts.

14. Disconnect the fuel sender and the fuel tank pressure (FTP) sensor electrical connectors at the body pass through.

15. Remove the fuel tank from the vehicle.

16. Remove the fuel sender assembly (3).

17. Disconnect the fuel sender electrical connections (3).

18. Clean all of the fuel pipe connections, all of the hose connections, and all of the areas surrounding the connections before disconnecting the connections in order to avoid possible contamination of the fuel system.

19. Disconnect the fuel supply pipe quick-connect fitting (4) at the fuel sender assembly.

20. Disconnect the evaporative emission (EVAP) pipe quick-connect fittings (5, 6) at the fuel sender assembly.

❋❋ CAUTION

Do NOT use impact tools. Significant force will be required to release the lock ring. The use of a hammer and screwdriver is not recommended. Secure the fuel tank in order to prevent fuel tank rotation.

21. Use the J 45722 fuel sender lock nut

wrench or equivalent, and a long breaker bar in order to unlock the fuel sender lock ring. Turn the fuel sender lock ring in a counterclockwise direction.

❋❋ CAUTION

Drain the fuel from the fuel sender assembly into an approved container in order to reduce the risk of fire and personal injury. Never store the fuel in an open container.

22. Remove the fuel sender assembly (2) and the seal (7) from the fuel tank.

23. Discard the fuel sender assembly seal.

24. Clean the fuel sender assembly sealing surfaces.

➡ **Some lock ring were manufactured with DO NOT REUSE stamped into them. These lock rings may be reused if they are not damaged or warped. Inspect the lock ring for damage due to improper removal or installation procedures. If damage is found, install a NEW lock ring.**

➡ **Check the lock ring for flatness. Place the lock ring on a flat surface. Measure the clearance between to lock ring and the flat surface using a feeler gage. If the warpage is less than 0.41mm (0.016 in), the lock ring does not require replacement. If the warpage is greater than 0.41mm (0.016 in), the lock ring must be replaced.**

To install:

❋❋ CAUTION

In order to reduce the risk of fire and personal injury that may result from a fuel leak, always replace the fuel sender gasket when reinstalling the fuel sender assembly.

25. Position the new fuel sender assembly seal on the fuel tank.

❋❋ WARNING

Care should be taken not to fold over or twist the fuel pump strainer when installing the fuel sender assembly, as this will restrict fuel flow. Also, ensure that the fuel pump strainer does not block full travel of float arm.

26. Install the fuel sender assembly into the fuel tank.

❋❋ WARNING

Always replace the fuel sender seal when installing the fuel sender

assembly. **Do not apply any type of lubrication in the seal groove.**

27. Ensure the lock ring is installed with the correct side facing upward. A correctly installed lock ring will only turn in a clockwise direction.

28. Use the J 45722 fuel sender lock nut wrench or equivalent, in order to install the fuel sender lock ring. Turn the fuel sender lock ring in a clockwise direction.

29. Connect the fuel supply pipe quick-connect fitting (4) at the fuel sender assembly.

30. Connect the EVAP quick-connect fittings at the fuel sender assembly.

31. Connect the fuel sender electrical connections.

32. With the aid of an assistant, position and support the fuel tank.

33. Connect the fuel sender and the FTP sensor electrical connectors at the body pass through.

34. Install the fuel tank retaining strap attaching bolts and tighten the bolts to 35 ft. lbs. (47.5 Nm).

35. Install the fuel tank shield.

36. Connect the vapor recirculation pipe to the fuel fill pipe.

37. Connect the fuel tank filler pipe to the fuel tank.

38. Connect the fuel feed pipe quick connect fitting.

39. Connect the EVAP purge pipe quick connect fitting at the EVAP canister.

40. Lower the vehicle.

41. Fill the tank with gasoline.

42. Connect the negative battery cable.

43. Turn the ignition **ON** for 2 seconds and then turn it **OFF** for 10 seconds. Again turn the ignition **ON** and check for leaks.

44. Check for fuel leaks.

FUEL TANK

REMOVAL & INSTALLATION

See Figures 124 and 125.

1. Relieve the fuel system pressure. Refer to the fuel system relief procedure in this section.

2. Using an air operated pump, drain as much fuel through the fuel fill pipe as possible.

3. Raise and safely support the vehicle.

4. Disconnect the fuel supply pipe quick-connect fitting from the tank.

5. Disconnect the evaporative emission (EVAP) purge pipe quick-connect fitting at the EVAP canister.

6. Loosen the fuel tank filler pipe hose clamp and disconnect the fuel tank filler from the fuel tank.

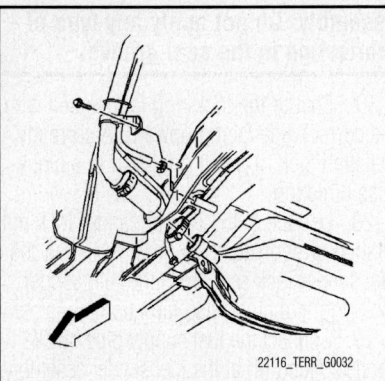

Fig. 124 Loosen the fuel filler hose clamp to disconnect the filler pipe from the fuel tank.

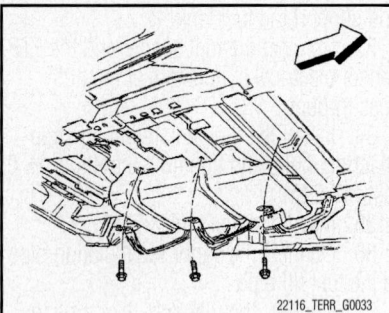

Fig. 125 Remove the tank retaining strap bolts to remove the tank—Long Wheelbase model shown.

7. Disconnect the vapor recirculation pipe from the filler tube.

8. Remove the fuel tank shield.

9. Support the fuel tank with the aid of an assistant.

10. Remove the fuel tank strap mounting bolts.

11. Disconnect the fuel sender and fuel tank pressure sensor electrical connections.

12. Lower and remove the fuel tank from the vehicle.

13. If the fuel tank is being replaced, the following components must be transferred over to the new tank:

- Fuel feed pipe
- EVAP canister vent solenoid
- EVAP pipe assembly
- Fuel pump assembly. For additional information, refer to the following section, "Fuel Pump/Sender, Removal & Installation."

To install:

14. With the aid of an assistant, move the fuel tank into position and safely support it.

15. Connect the fuel sender and fuel tank pressure sensor electrical connections.

16. Install the fuel tank retaining strap bolts and tighten to 35 ft. lbs. (47.5 Nm).

17. Install the fuel tank shield.

18. Connect the vapor recirculation pipe to the fuel filler pipe.

19. Connect the fuel tank filler pipe to the fuel tank. Tighten the hose clamp to 22 inch lbs. (2.5 Nm).

20. Connect the fuel feed pipe quick-connect fitting.

21. Connect the EVAP purge pipe quick-connect fitting at the EVAP canister.

22. Lower the vehicle and add fuel.

23. Connect the negative battery cable.

24. Turn the ignition **ON** for 2 seconds and then turn it **OFF** for 10 seconds. Again turn the ignition **ON** and check for leaks.

IDLE SPEED

ADJUSTMENT

Idle speed is maintained by the Powertrain Control Module (PCM). No adjustment is necessary or possible.

THROTTLE BODY

REMOVAL & INSTALLATION

3.5L Engine

1. Remove the air cleaner intake duct.

2. Disconnect the electronic throttle control (ETC) electrical connector (1) from the throttle body.

3. Remove the heater pipe nut at the throttle body.

4. Remove only the heater inlet pipe.

5. Remove the nuts and the bolts from the throttle body.

6. Remove the throttle body assembly.

7. Remove the throttle body gasket.

8. Clean and inspect the throttle body gasket mating surfaces.

To install:

9. Install a new gasket, if necessary.

10. Install the throttle body assembly.

11. Install the throttle body nuts and the bolts and tighten to 89 inch lbs. (10 Nm).

12. Install the heater inlet pipe.

13. Install the heater pipe nut to the throttle body and tighten to 89 inch lbs. (10 Nm).

14. Connect the ETC electrical connector to the throttle body.

15. Install the air cleaner intake duct.

16. Start the engine and check for leaks.

3.9L Engine

See Figure 126.

1. Remove the intake manifold cover.

2. Drain the engine cooling system.

3. Remove the air intake assembly.

4. Disconnect the engine wiring harness from the electronic throttle control (ETC).

5. Remove the heater hoses from the throttle body and reposition the hoses aside.

6. Remove the throttle body mounting bolts and nuts.

7. Remove the throttle body assembly and gasket.

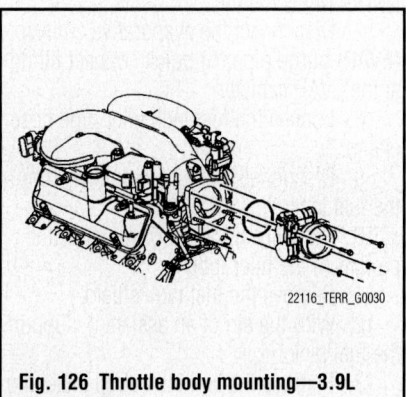

Fig. 126 Throttle body mounting—3.9L engine shown

To install:

❋❋ WARNING

Do not reuse the throttle body gasket. Install a NEW gasket during assembly.

8. Install a new throttle gasket by aligning the locating tab of the gasket with the notch in the manifold.

9. Position the throttle body to the intake manifold. Tighten the bolts and nuts to 89 inch lbs. (10 Nm).

10. Reconnect the heater hoses to the throttle body. Tighten the pipe clamp nuts to 89 inch lbs. (10 Nm).

11. Connect the engine wiring harness to the ETC.

12. Install the air intake assembly.

13. Install the intake manifold cover.

14. Refill the engine coolant to the correct level.

15. Start the engine and check for leaks.

HEATING & AIR CONDITIONING SYSTEM

BLOWER MOTOR

REMOVAL & INSTALLATION

See Figure 127.

1. Remove the right side instrument panel (I/P) insulator.
2. Disconnect the blower motor electrical connector.
3. Remove the blower motor screws.
4. Remove the blower motor

To install:

5. Install the blower motor.
6. Install the blower motor screws.
7. Connect the blower motor electrical connector.
8. Install the right side I/P insulator.

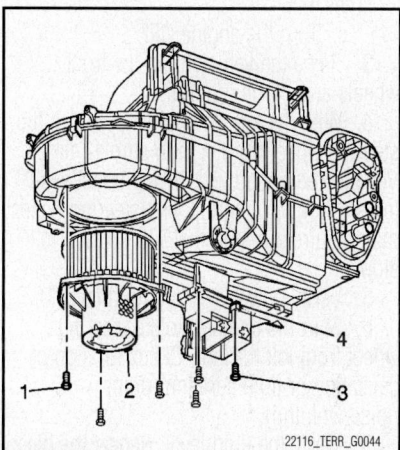

Fig. 127 Remove the mounting screws (1) to remove the blower motor.

22116_TERR_G0044

HEATER CORE

REMOVAL & INSTALLATION

See Figures 128 and 129.

1. Before servicing the vehicle, refer to the Precautions Section.
2. Drain the engine cooling system.
3. Remove or disconnect the following:
   • Heater hoses from the heater core

➡ **Cap off the heater core inlet and outlet pipes to prevent coolant spilling inside the vehicle**

   • Floor air outlet duct, if necessary

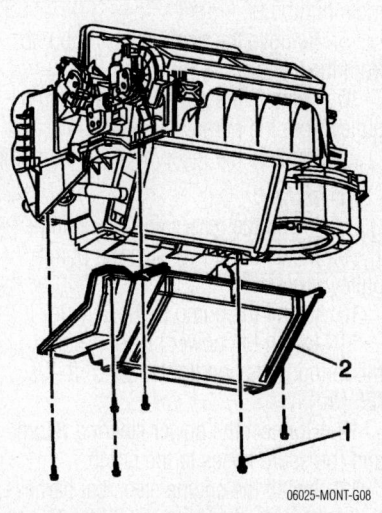

Fig. 128 Showing the heater core cover screws

06025-MONT-G08

   • Heater core cover screws and cover
   • Heater core pipe clamp screw
   • Heater core

To install:

4. Install or connect the following:
   • Heater core
   • Heater core pipe clamp screw
   • Heater core cover and screws
   • Floor air outlet duct, if removed
   • Heater hoses and clamps
5. Refill the cooling system to the correct level.
6. Run the engine to normal operating temperatures; then, check the climate control operation and check for leaks.

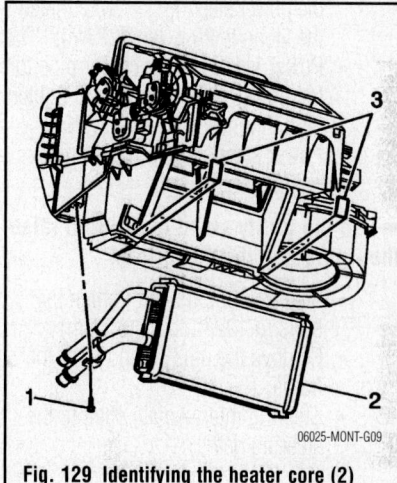

Fig. 129 Identifying the heater core (2)

06025-MONT-G09

STEERING

POWER STEERING GEAR

REMOVAL & INSTALLATION

See Figure 130.

1. Before servicing the vehicle, refer to the Precautions Section.
2. Raise and safely support the vehicle.
3. Remove or disconnect the following:
   • Stabilizer shaft
   • Tie rod ends from the steering knuckles
   • Steering intermediate shaft from the steering gear
   • Rear frame bolts, use a utility stand in order to support the frame

✳ WARNING

Do not lower the rear of the frame too far as damage to the engine components nearest to the cowl may result.

   • Use the utility stand in order to lower the frame and the powertrain
   • Power steering gear heat shield
   • Power steering gear cooler pipe from the steering gear
   • Power steering gear pressure hose from the power steering gear
   • Power steering gear bolts and nuts
   • Power steering gear through the vehicle left side wheel opening

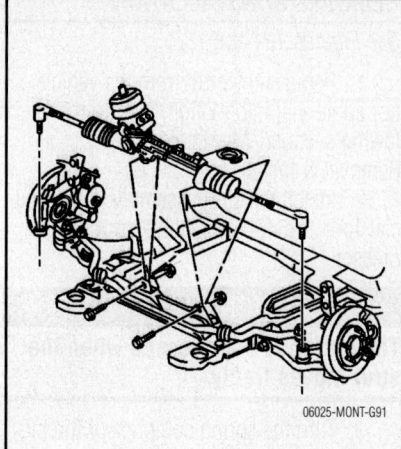

Fig. 130 Installed position of the power steering gear

06025-MONT-G91

To install:

4. Install or connect the following:
   - Power steering gear through the vehicle left side wheel opening to the frame
   - Power steering gear bolts

➡ This is a prevailing torque type fastener. This fastener may be reused ONLY if: The fastener and its counterpart are clean and free from rust. The fastener develops 18 inch lbs. (2 Nm) of torque/drag against its counterpart prior to the fastener seating. If the fastener does not meet these criteria, REPLACE the fastener.

   - Power steering gear nuts and tighten nuts to 44 ft. lbs. (60 Nm) plus 60 degrees
   - Power steering gear heat shield
   - Power steering gear pressure hose to the power steering gear and tighten the fitting to 20 ft. lbs. (27 Nm)
   - Power steering gear cooler pipe to the power steering gear and tighten the fitting to 20 ft. lbs. (27 Nm)
   - Power steering gear cooler pipe retaining clip

➡ Use the utility stand in order to raise the frame and the powertrain.

   - Rear frame bolts and tighten the bolts to 122 ft. lbs. (165 Nm)
   - Remove the utility stand from the frame
   - Steering intermediate shaft to the steering gear
   - Tie rod ends to the steering knuckles
   - Stabilizer shaft
5. Lower the vehicle.
6. Fill the power steering system.
7. Bleed the power steering system.

POWER STEERING PUMP

REMOVAL & INSTALLATION

1. Remove the accessory drive belt from the pump.
2. Disconnect the power steering return and pressure hoses from the pump.
3. Remove the engine electrical harness from the reservoir retainers.
4. Remove the power steering pump mounting bolts.
5. Remove the power steering pump from the vehicle.
6. Remove the power steering pump pulley from the pump.
7. Remove the reservoir from the pump.

To install:

8. Install the reservoir to the pump.
9. Install the power steering pump pulley.
10. Install the pump to the vehicle.
11. Install the power steering pump mounting bolts and tighten to 18 ft. lbs. (25 Nm).
12. Connect the power steering return and [pressure hoses to the pump.
13. Install the engine electrical harness to the reservoir retainers.
14. Install the drive belt.
15. Bleed the power steering system.

BLEEDING

1. Fill pump reservoir with fluid to minimum system level, FULL COLD level, or middle of hash mark on cap stick fluid level indicator.

➡ With hydro-boost only, the oil level will appear falsely high if the hydroboost accumulator is not fully charged. Do not apply the brake pedal with the engine OFF. This will discharge the hydro-boost accumulator.

2. If equipped with hydro-boost, fully charge the hydro-boost accumulator using the following procedure:
   a. Start the engine.
   b. Firmly apply the brake pedal 10-15 times.
   c. Turn the engine OFF.
3. Raise the vehicle until the front wheels are off the ground.
4. With the key on engine OFF, turn the steering wheel from stop to stop 12 times. Vehicles equipped with hydro-boost systems or longer length power steering hoses may require turns up to 15 to 20 stop to stops.
5. Verify power steering fluid level.
6. Start the engine. Rotate steering wheel from left to right. Check for sign of cavitation or fluid aeration (pump noise/whining).
7. Verify the fluid level. Repeat the bleed procedure, if necessary.

SUSPENSION

FRONT SUSPENSION

COIL SPRING

REMOVAL & INSTALLATION

See Figures 131 and 132.

1. Remove the strut from the vehicle. For additional information, refer to the following section, "MacPherson Strut, Removal & Installation."
2. Install the strut assembly in the Special Tool J-45400 or suitable spring compressor.

✳ CAUTION

The spring is compressed when the strut moves freely.

3. Turn the spring compressor forcing screw until the coil spring is compressed.
4. Use a 45 TORX® socket in order to hold the strut shaft. Use the J-42991 to remove the upper strut mount nut.

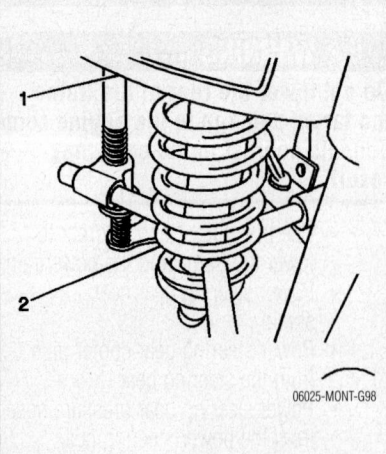

Fig. 131 Showing strut (2) installed in J-45400 coil spring retaining/compressing device (1).

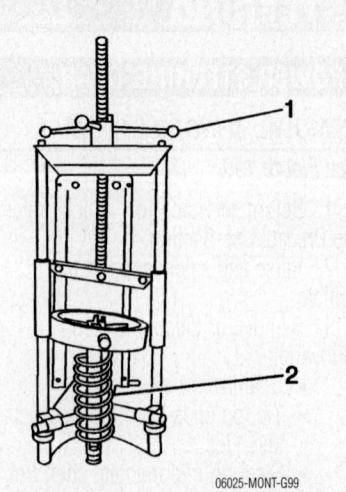

Fig. 132 Turning the forcing screw (1) until the upper strut mount and coil spring (2) can be removed.

5. Remove the strut from the spring compressor.

6. Loosen the compressor forcing screw until the upper strut mount and coil spring may be removed.

7. Remove the upper strut mount and the coil spring from the spring compressor.

To install:

8. Install the coil spring and upper strut mount to the spring compressor.

9. Turn the spring compressor forcing screw until the coil spring is compressed.

10. Install the strut to the coil spring and upper strut mount.

11. Loosely install the strut retaining nut.

12. Use a 45 TORX® socket in order to hold the strut shaft. Install the upper strut mount nut and tighten the nut to 63 ft. lbs. (85 Nm).

13. Remove the strut from the spring compressor.

14. Install the strut to the vehicle. For additional information, refer to the following section, "MacPherson Strut, Removal & Installation."

LOWER BALL JOINT

REMOVAL & INSTALLATION

See Figure 133.

1. Before servicing the vehicle, refer to the Precautions Section.

2. Remove the lower control arm. See Lower Control Arm.

3. Secure the lower control arm in a vice.

4. Drill or grind off the ball stud rivet heads.

5. Use a hammer and a drift punch in order to remove the rivets.

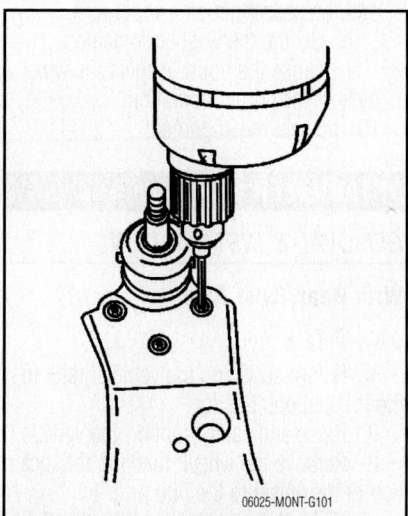

06025-MONT-G101

Fig. 133 Drilling rivets to remove lower ball joint

6. Remove the ball stud from the lower control arm.

To install:

7. Install the ball stud to the lower control arm.

8. Install the NEW ball stud bolts facing down, away from the ball stud.

➡This is a prevailing torque type fastener. This fastener may be reused ONLY if: The fastener and its counterpart are clean and free from rust. The fastener develops 18 inch lbs. (2 Nm) of torque/drag against its counterpart prior to the fastener seating. If the fastener does not meet these criteria, REPLACE the fastener.

9. Install NEW ball stud nuts, tighten the ball stud nuts to 50 ft. lbs. (68 Nm).

10. Install the lower control arm.

LOWER CONTROL ARM

REMOVAL & INSTALLATION

See Figures 134 and 135.

1. Before servicing the vehicle, refer to the Precautions Section.

2. Raise and safely support the vehicle.

3. Remove the wheel, marking the location of the wheel to the hub prior to removal. Mark the individual location of all retainers as they are removed.

4. Detach the ABS wheel speed sensor connector.

5. Remove the ABS wheel speed sensor jumper harness from the harness retainer clips.

6. Remove the stabilizer shaft link.

7. Remove the cotter pin from the ball stud and loosen the ball stud nut.

8. Install Special Tool J-41820 ball joint separator tool over the ball stud and lower control arm as shown.

9. Rotate the ball stud nut counter-

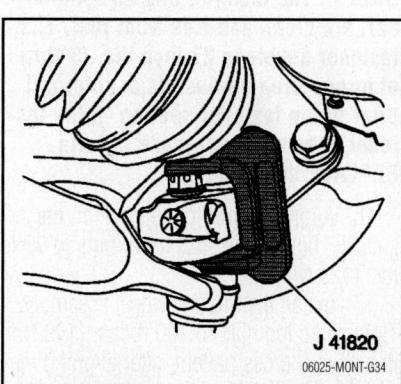

J 41820

06025-MONT-G34

Fig. 134 Using Special Tool J-41820 Ball Joint Separator

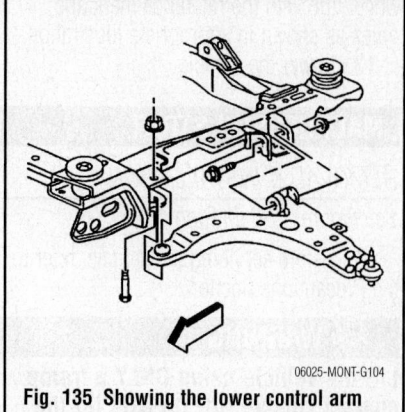

06025-MONT-G104

Fig. 135 Showing the lower control arm

clockwise in order to separate the ball stud from the steering knuckle.

10. Remove the lower control arm bolts and nuts, and then the lower control arm.

To install:

11. Install or connect the following:
- Lower control arm
- Control arm bolts and nuts
- Ball stud to the knuckle
- Ball stud castle nut, tighten the ball stud castle nut to 22 ft. lbs. (30 Nm), plus 135 degrees

➡Do NOT loosen the ball stud nut in order to align the ball stud nut slots to the ball stud cotter pin hole. If necessary, tighten the ball stud castle nut in order to align the ball stud castle nut slot to the ball stud cotter pin hole. Ensure that the cotter pin ends do NOT contact the ABS wheel speed sensor, the ABS sensor connector or the drive axle.

- NEW cotter pin and bend the ends
- Stabilizer shaft link
- ABS wheel speed sensor jumper harness to the harness retainer clips
- ABS wheel speed sensor connector

➡This is a prevailing torque type fastener. This fastener may be reused ONLY if: The fastener and its counterpart are clean and free from rust. The fastener develops 18 inch lbs. (2 Nm) of torque/drag against its counterpart prior to the fastener seating. If the fastener does not meet these criteria, REPLACE the fastener.

- Lower control arm nuts, tighten the lower control arm nuts to 71 ft. lbs. (96 Nm)

12. Install the tire and wheel assembly. Tighten the lug nuts to 100 ft. lbs. (140 Nm) in a criss—cross pattern, after aligning the

wheel hub with the reference mark and holes as shown in appropriate illustration.

13. Lower the vehicle

MACPHERSON STRUT

REMOVAL & INSTALLATION

See Figures 136 through 138.

1. Before servicing the vehicle, refer to the Precautions Section.

❋ WARNING

Lift the vehicle using ONLY a frame contact vehicle lift. Do NOT lift the vehicle using a suspension contact vehicle lift.

2. Raise and safely support the vehicle.

3. Remove the wiper module as follows:

   a. Open and support the hood.

   b. Remove the driver side wiper arm

   c. Remove the passenger side wiper arm.

   d. Remove the air inlet grille panel.

   e. Lower the washer container into the engine compartment.

   f. Disconnect the electrical connector from the wiper motor.

   g. Remove the 4 bolts from the wiper module.

   h. Carefully guide the passenger side module out first from the opening in the front plenum.

   i. Pull the module from the drive side fender flange opening.

   j. Remove the module from the vehicle.

4. Remove the tire and wheel assembly, marking the location to the hub assembly. Mark the location of each hub retainer before removal.

5. Lower the vehicle.

6. Remove the strut upper nuts.

7. Raise the vehicle.

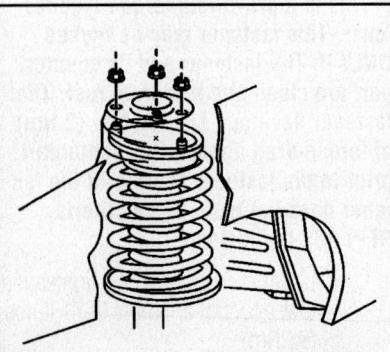

Fig. 136 Removing the strut assembly upper nuts

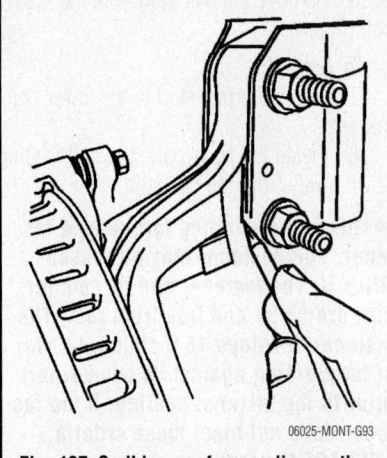

Fig. 137 Scribing a reference line on the knuckle-to-strut position

8. Scribe the strut to the knuckle position for installation reference.

9. Remove the strut lower clamp retaining bolts and nuts.

10. Remove the strut assembly from the vehicle.

To install:

➥**Care should be taken to avoid chipping or scratching the coating when handling the suspension coil spring. Damage to the coating can cause premature failure.**

11. Install the strut assembly into position in the vehicle. Ensure the upper studs align with the mounting holes and the lower clamp retaining portion aligns with steering knuckle holes.

12. Lower the vehicle to

13. Install the strut upper nuts; tighten the strut upper nuts to 30 ft. lbs. (41 Nm)

14. Raise the vehicle.

15. Install the strut lower bolts and nuts.

➥**This is a prevailing torque type fastener. This fastener may be reused ONLY if: The fastener and its counterpart are clean and free from rust. The fastener develops 27 inch lbs. (3 Nm) of torque/drag against its counterpart prior to the fastener seating. If the fastener does not meet these criteria, REPLACE the fastener.**

16. Align the strut to the mark on the knuckle; tighten the strut lower nuts to 90 ft. lbs. (123 Nm).

17. Install the tire and wheel assembly. Tighten the lug nuts to 100 ft. lbs. (140 Nm) in a criss—cross pattern, after aligning the wheel hub with the reference mark and holes as shown.

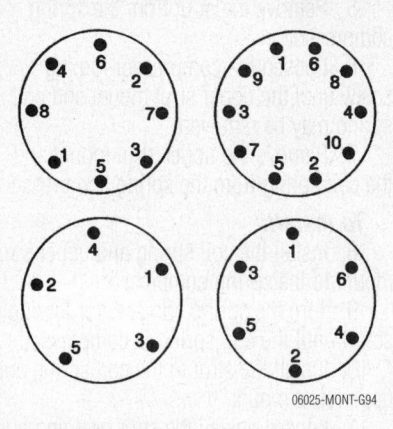

Fig. 138 Showing wheel hub hole patterns, for proper alignment and installation

❋ CAUTION

Be sure to use the correct fastener in the proper location, according to the illustration provided.

18. Install the wiper motor module as follows:

   a. Position the wiper module to the lower plenum in the driver side fender flange opening first.

   b. Rotate the module into the opening at the passenger side plenum.

   c. Ensure the rear center mount is secure into the sheet metal flange at the rear of the module.

   d. Install the wiper module bolts. Tighten the bolts in sequence, as shown, to 10 Nm (89 inch lbs.).

   e. Connect the electrical connector to the motor.

   f. Install the air inlet grille panel.

   g. Install the driver side wiper arm and the passenger side wiper arm.

   h. Secure the washer container.

   i. Close the hood. Inspect the wiper system for proper operation.

19. Inspect the alignment.

STABILIZER BAR

REMOVAL & INSTALLATION

With Rear Twist Axle

See Figure 139.

1. Before servicing the vehicle, refer to the Precautions Section.

2. Raise and safely support the vehicle.

3. Remove the wheel, marking the location of the wheel to the hub prior to removal. Mark the individual location of all retainers as they are removed.

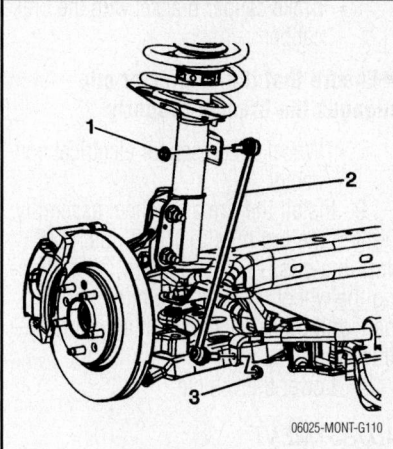

Fig. 139 Identifying front stabilizer bar components: upper nut (1); shaft bar (link) (2); lower nut (3)

4. Remove the left and right stabilizer shaft link lower nut (3).

5. Remove the stabilizer bar (link) (2) from the suspension strut and stabilizer shaft.

To install:

6. Install the stabilizer link (2) to the suspension strut and stabilizer shaft.

7. Install the stabilizer shaft link nuts. Tighten the nut to 33 ft. lbs. (45 Nm).

8. Install the tire and wheel assembly. Tighten the lug nuts to 100 ft. lbs. (140 Nm) in a criss—cross pattern, after aligning the wheel hub with the reference mark and holes as shown in appropriate illustration.

9. Lower the vehicle.

With Independent Rear Suspension

See Figure 140.

1. Before servicing the vehicle, refer to the Precautions Section.

2. Raise and safely support the vehicle.

3. Remove the wheel, marking the location of the wheel to the hub prior to removal. Mark the individual location of all retainers as they are removed.

4. Remove or disconnect the following:
- Left and right stabilizer shaft links
- Left and right stabilizer shaft insulators and brackets
- Stabilizer shaft from the left side of the vehicle

To install:

5. Install or connect the following:
- Stabilizer shaft from the left side of the vehicle
- Stabilizer shaft link bolt and nut, tighten the stabilizer shaft link nut to 14 ft. lbs. (19 Nm)
- Left and right stabilizer shaft insulators and brackets
- Left front wheel

6. Lower the vehicle.

STEERING KNUCKLE

REMOVAL & INSTALLATION

See Figure 141.

1. Before servicing the vehicle, refer to the Precautions Section.

2. Raise and safely support the vehicle.

3. Remove the wheel, marking the location of the wheel to the hub prior to removal. Mark the individual location of all retainers as they are removed.

4. Remove or disconnect the following:
- Front halfshaft bearing. For additional information, refer to the following section, "Wheel Hub and Bearing, Removal & Installation."
- Lower ball joint. For additional information, refer to the following section, "Lower Ball Joint, Removal & Installation."

- Outer tie rod end from the steering knuckle

5. Scribe the strut to the knuckle for reinstallation reference

6. Remove the bolts connecting the strut to the knuckle.

7. Remove the steering knuckle

To install:

8. Install or connect the following:
- Steering knuckle
- Bolts which connect the strut to the knuckle, tighten the strut to knuckle bolts to 83 ft. lbs. (112 Nm)
- Outer tie rod to the steering knuckle
- Front lower control arm ball stud to knuckle; tighten to 22 ft. lbs. (30 Nm), plus 135 degrees.
- Front halfshaft bearing. See Wheel Hub/Bearing Assembly.

9. Install the tire and wheel assembly. Tighten the lug nuts to 100 ft. lbs. (140 Nm) in a criss—cross pattern, after aligning the wheel hub with the reference mark and holes as shown in appropriate illustration.

10. Lower the vehicle

WHEEL HUB AND BEARINGS

REMOVAL & INSTALLATION

See Figures 142 and 143.

1. Before servicing the vehicle, refer to the Precautions Section.

2. Raise and safely support the vehicle.

3. Remove the wheel, marking the location of the wheel to the hub prior to removal. Mark the individual location of all retainers as they are removed.

4. Remove or disconnect the following:
- Wheel speed sensor electrical connector.
- Wheel speed sensor electrical connector from the bracket.

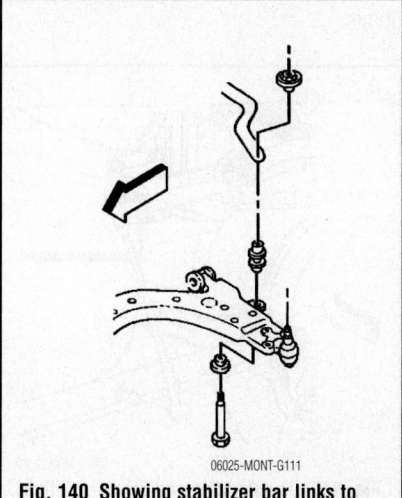

Fig. 140 Showing stabilizer bar links to control arm

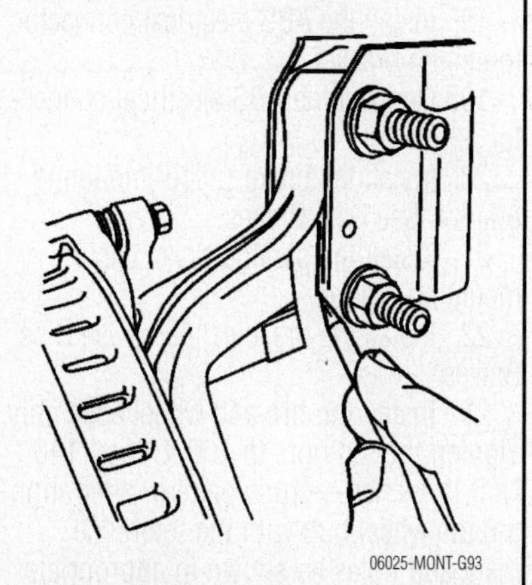

Fig. 141 Scribing a reference line on the knuckle-to-strut position

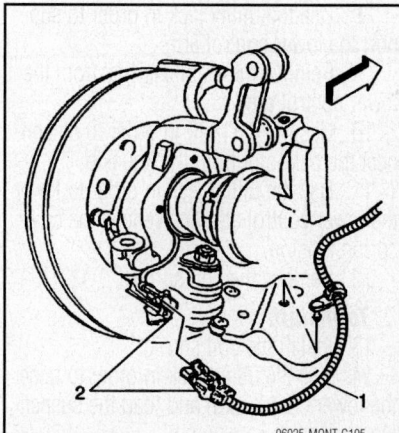

Fig. 142 Removing electrical connector from wheel speed sensor

- Brake caliper bracket with the brake caliper.
- Brake rotor. For additional information, refer to the following section, "Rotor, Removal & Installation."
- Halfshaft nut

5. Use 3 wheel nuts and attach the bearing/hub tool, J 28733-B, to the hub. Push the halfshaft out of the wheel bearing/hub.

6. Remove and discard the wheel bearing/hub bolts.

7. Remove and examine the wheel bearing/hub.

To install:

8. Install or connect the following:
- Wheel bearing/hub
- NEW wheel bearing/hub bolts

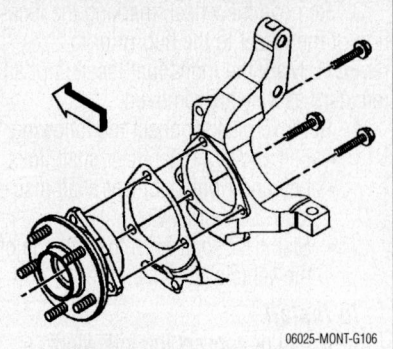

Fig. 143 Exploded view of the wheel bearing/hub assembly

and tighten the bolts to 96 ft. lbs. (130 Nm)
- Halfshaft nut
- Brake rotor

- Brake caliper bracket with the brake caliper

➡**Ensure that the connector clip engages the bracket properly.**

- Wheel speed sensor electrical connector

9. Install the tire and wheel assembly. Tighten the lug nuts to 100 ft. lbs. (140 Nm) in a criss—cross pattern, after aligning the wheel hub with the reference mark and holes as shown in appropriate illustration.

10. Lower the vehicle.

ADJUSTMENT

The wheel hub and bearing assembly cannot be adjusted. If runout is excessive, the hub assembly must be replaced.

SUSPENSION

REAR SUSPENSION

COIL SPRING

REMOVAL & INSTALLATION

With Independent Suspension

See Figure 144.

1. Raise and safely support the vehicle.

2. Remove the wheel and tire assemblies, making location reference marks on wheel to hub and on each retainer for reinstallation reference.

3. Remove the brake calipers. See Disc Brakes.

4. Remove the parking brake cable mounting bracket. See Parking Brake.

5. Remove the brake caliper mounting bracket. See Disc Brakes.

6. Disconnect the ABS electrical connector from the wheel speed sensor.

7. Remove the ABS electrical connector mounting bracket.

8. Use the utility jack in order to support the lower control arm.

9. Remove the stabilizer link from the lower control arm.

10. Use the J 41820 in order to disconnect the ball joint from the knuckle.

11. Use the utility jack in order to lower the lower control arm and relieve the coil spring tension.

12. Remove the coil spring.

To install:

13. Install the coil spring.

14. Use the utility jack in order to raise the lower control arm and load the suspension.

15. Use the J 41820 in order to connect the ball joint to the knuckle.

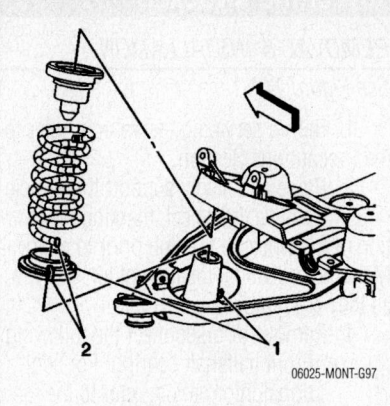

Fig. 144 Showing coil spring position, showing spring alignment marks (1, 2)

16. Install the stabilizer link to the lower control arm.

17. Use the utility jack in order to support the lower control arm.

18. Install the ABS electrical connector mounting bracket.

19. Connect the ABS electrical connector.

20. Install the brake caliper mounting bracket. See Disc Brakes.

21. Install the parking brake cable mounting bracket.

22. Install the brake calipers. See Disc Brakes.

23. Install the tire and wheel assembly. Tighten the lug nuts to 100 ft. lbs. (140 Nm) in a criss—cross pattern, after aligning the wheel hub with the reference mark and holes as shown in appropriate illustration.

24. Lower the vehicle.

With All Wheel Drive

See Figures 144 and 145.

1. Raise and safely support the vehicle.

2. Remove the wheel and tire assemblies, making location reference marks on wheel to hub and on each retainer for reinstallation reference.

3. Remove the brake caliper and support the brake caliper. Do not disconnect the brake hose. See Disc Brakes.

4. Disconnect the tie rod from the knuckle. See Tie Rods.

5. Use a utility stand in order to support the lower control arm.

6. Disconnect the height sensor link from the lower control arm, as shown.

7. Disconnect the shock absorber from the lower control arm. See Shocks/Struts.

8. Use the J 41820 in order to disconnect the ball joint from the knuckle. See Ball Joints.

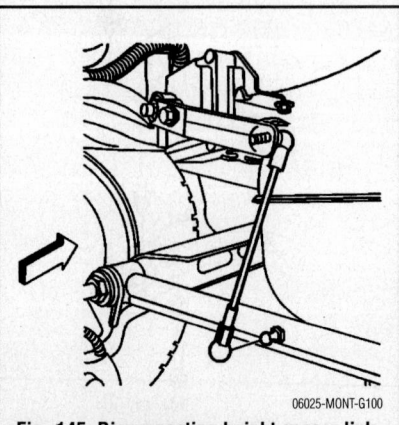

Fig. 145 Disconnecting height sensor link from the lower control arm

9. Remove the lower ball joint nut.

10. Use the utility stand in order to lower the control arm and relieve the coil spring tension.

11. Carefully remove the coil spring and jounce bumper.

12. Remove the spring insulator (2).

13. Remove the lower control arm.

To install:

14. Install the spring jounce bumper to the spring.

15. Index and install the spring insulator to the spring (2).

16. Index and install the spring insulator with the spring and the jounce bumper to the lower control arm (1).

17. Use the utility stand in order to raise the lower control arm.

18. Install the lower ball joint to the knuckle.

19. Install the lower ball joint nut. Tighten the ball joint nut to 26 ft. lbs. (35 Nm), plus 130 degrees.

20. Connect the shock absorber to the lower control arm. See Shocks/Struts.

21. Connect the height sensor link to the lower control arm.

22. Connect the tie rod to the knuckle. See Tie Rods.

23. Install the brake caliper. See Disc Brakes.

24. Install the tire and wheel assembly. Tighten the lug nuts to 100 ft. lbs. (140 Nm) in a criss—cross pattern, after aligning the wheel hub with the reference mark and holes as shown in appropriate illustration.

25. Lower the vehicle.

KNUCKLE

REMOVAL & INSTALLATION
See Figure 146.

1. Before servicing the vehicle, refer to the Precautions Section.

2. Raise and safely support the vehicle.

3. Remove the wheel, marking the location of the wheel to the hub prior to removal. Mark the individual location of all retainers as they are removed.

4. Remove or disconnect the following:
- Brake caliper and support the bake caliper. Do not disconnect the bake hose. See Disc Brakes.
- Brake caliper bracket
- Brake rotor. See Disc Brakes.
- Tie rod from the knuckle
- Stabilizer shaft link at the lower control arm
- Halfshaft from the wheel bearing/hub. See Wheel Hub/Bearing Assembly.

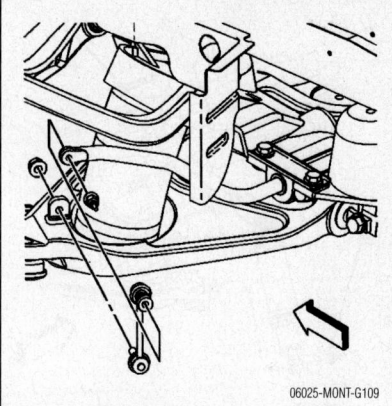

Fig. 146 Removing stabilizer shaft link from lower control arm

06025-MONT-G109

- Park brake cable and the park brake cable bracket aside
- Wheel bearing and the backing plate
- Use a utility stand in order to support the lower control arm
- Height sensor link from the lower control arm as necessary. See Lower Control Arm.
- Shock absorber from the lower control arm. See Shocks/Struts.
- Upper control arm from the knuckle. See Upper Control Arm.

5. Using the J 41820 separator, disconnect the lower ball joint from the knuckle.

6. Remove the knuckle from vehicle.

7. Detach the wheel speed sensor connector bracket from the knuckle.

To install:

8. Install or connect the following:
- Wheel speed sensor connector bracket to the knuckle; tighten the bolt and nut to 106 inch lbs. (12 Nm)
- Knuckle to the vehicle
- Lower ball joint to the knuckle; tighten the ball joint nut to 26 ft. lbs. (35 Nm) plus 130 degrees
- Upper control arm to the knuckle. Tighten to 74 ft. lbs. (100 Nm).
- Shock absorber to the lower control arm. Tighten to 63 ft. lbs. (85 Nm) without IRS or to 66 ft. lbs. (90 Nm) with IRS.
- Height sensor link to the lower control arm as necessary. See Lower Control Arm.
- Backing plate and the wheel bearing; tighten bolts to 96 ft. lbs. (130 Nm) with IRS or to 59 ft. lbs. (80 Nm) on new bolts for models without IRS
- Halfshaft to the wheel bearing/hub; tighten halfshaft nut to 192 ft. lbs. (260 Nm)

- Stabilizer shaft link to the lower control arm; tighten nuts to 30 ft. lbs. (40 Nm)
- Tie rod to the knuckle; with IRS, tighten tie rod nut to 59 ft. lbs. (80 Nm) and bolt to 66 ft. lbs. (90 Nm); with twist axle, tighten tie rod bolt to body to 100 ft. lbs. (135 Nm) and tie rod bolt to axle to 92 ft. lbs. (125 Nm)
- Brake rotor. See Disc Brakes
- Brake caliper bracket
- Brake caliper. See Disc Brakes

9. Install the tire and wheel assembly. Tighten the lug nuts to 100 ft. lbs. (140 Nm) in a criss—cross pattern, after aligning the wheel hub with the reference mark and holes as shown in appropriate illustration.

LOWER CONTROL ARM

REMOVAL & INSTALLATION
See Figure 147.

1. Raise and safely support the vehicle.

2. Rear the rear wheel.

3. Remove the disc brake caliper and support the brake caliper. Do not disconnect the brake hose. For additional information, refer to the following section, "Brake Caliper, Removal & Installation."

4. Use a suitable jack to support the lower control arm.

5. Disconnect the height sensor link from the lower control arm, if equipped.

6. Disconnect the speed sensor harness from the lower control arm.

7. Disconnect the speed sensor connector.

8. Remove the speed sensor connecting mounting bracket.

9. Remove the stabilizer link from the lower control arm.

10. Disconnect the lower shock absorber from the lower control arm.

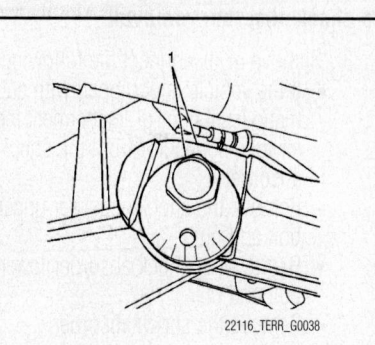

22116_TERR_G0038

Fig. 147 Matchmark the lower control arm at the indicator (1) before removing—Rear suspension

11. Use Special Tool J-41820 Ball Joint Separator to disconnect the ball joint from the knuckle and remove the lower ball joint nut.

12. Using the jack, slowly lower the control arm to relieve the tension on the coil spring and remove the jack.

13. Remove the coil spring.

14. Matchmark the lower control arm at the cam indicator.

15. Remove the lower control arm-to-crossmember mounting bolts to remove the lower control arm.

To install:

16. Install the lower control arm to the crossmember. Tighten the mounting bolts to 37 ft. lbs. (50 Nm).

17. Install the cam bolt and washer to the lower control arm. Align the cam indicator with the mark previously made on the lower control arm.

18. Install the cam nut and tighten to 107 ft. lbs. (145 Nm).

19. Install the rear coil spring assembly to the control. Using a suitable jack, slowly raise the lower control arm.

20. Install the lower ball joint to the wheel knuckle and tighten the nut to 26 ft. lbs. (35 Nm) plus an additional 130°.

21. Install the stabilizer link to the lower control arm.

22. The remainder of the installation is the reverse order of removal.

SHOCK ABSORBER

REMOVAL & INSTALLATION

See Figures 148 and 149.

1. Before servicing the vehicle, refer to the Precautions Section.

2. Support the rear axle.

➡ **On independent rear suspension vehicles, use a utility stand to slightly raise the rear suspension at the shock absorber to compress the coil spring and relieve some spring tension prior to shock absorber removal.**

3. Remove or disconnect the following:
- If the vehicle is equipped with automatic level control, disconnect the air tube connector from the shock absorber
- Remove the shock absorber upper bolt and nut
- Remove the shock absorber lower bolt and nut
- Remove the shock absorber

To install:

4. Install the shock absorber.

5. Install the shock absorber bolts and

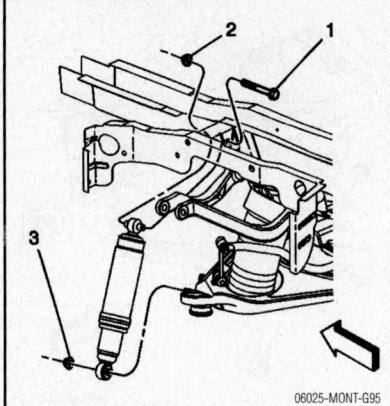

Fig. 148 Removing the rear shock absorber on vehicles with independent rear suspension, showing upper nut and bolt (1, 2) and lower nut (3)

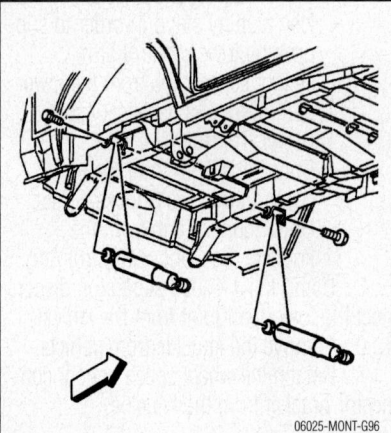

Fig. 149 Showing the rear shock absorber on vehicles with twist axle rear suspension

nuts and tighten the shock absorber bolts and nuts to 63 ft. lbs. (85 Nm).

6. If the vehicle is equipped with automatic level control, install the air tube connector to the shock absorber.

7. Remove the support from the rear axle.

8. Lower the vehicle.

STABILIZER BAR

REMOVAL & INSTALLATION

See Figure 150.

1. Before servicing the vehicle, refer to the Precautions Section.

2. Raise and safely support the vehicle.

3. Remove or disconnect the following:

4. Install the tire and wheel assembly. Tighten the lug nuts to 100 ft. lbs. (140 Nm) in a criss—cross pattern, after aligning the wheel hub with the reference mark and holes as shown in appropriate illustration.

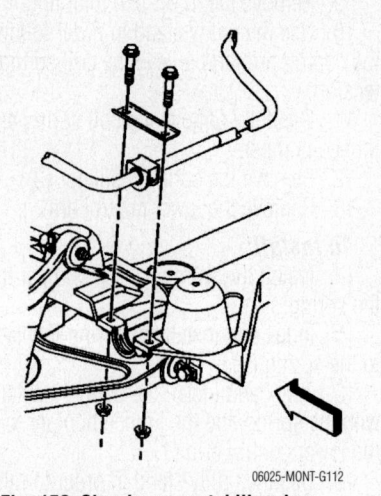

Fig. 150 Showing rear stabilizer bar removal

- Load level sensor
- Clamp holding the right park brake cable to the stabilizer shaft
- Left and right side stabilizer shaft insulators and brackets
- Left and right stabilizer shaft links
- Spare tire from the spare tire hoist
- Stabilizer shaft

To install:

5. Install or connect the following:
- Stabilizer shaft
- Spare tire to the spare tire hoist
- Left and right stabilizer shaft links
- Left and right stabilizer shaft insulators and brackets
- Clamp holding the right park brake cable to the stabilizer shaft
- Load level sensor

6. Install the tire and wheel assembly. Tighten the lug nuts to 100 ft. lbs. (140 Nm) in a criss—cross pattern, after aligning the wheel hub with the reference mark and holes as shown in appropriate illustration.

7. Lower the vehicle.

STABILIZER LINK

REMOVAL & INSTALLATION

See Figure 151.

1. Raise and safely support the vehicle.

2. Use a wrench in order hold the stabilizer shaft link and remove the link nuts.

3. Remove the stabilizer link.

To install:

4. Install the stabilizer link.

➡ **Use the correct fastener in the correct location. Replacement fasteners must be the correct part number for that application. Use the correct**

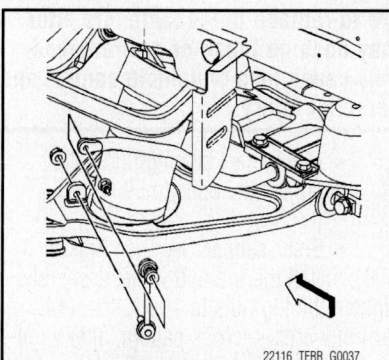

Fig. 151 Remove the mounting nuts to remove the rear stabilizer links.

tightening sequence and specifications when installing fasteners in order to avoid damage to parts and systems.

5. Install the stabilizer link nuts and tighten to 30 ft. lbs. (40 Nm).
6. Lower the vehicle.

UPPER CONTROL ARM

REMOVAL & INSTALLATION

See Figures 152 and 153.

1. Before servicing the vehicle, refer to the Precautions Section.
2. Raise and safely support the vehicle.
3. Remove the wheel and tire assemblies, making location reference marks on wheel to hub and on each retainer for reinstallation reference.
4. Remove the disc brake caliper and support the brake caliper. Do not disconnect the brake hose. For additional information, refer to the following section, "Brake Caliper, Removal & Installation."
5. Detach the park brake cable from the park brake actuator and the park brake cable bracket. For additional information, refer to the following section, "Parking Brake Cables."
6. Use a suitable jack stand in order to support the lower control arm.
7. Disconnect the height sensor link from the lower control arm, if equipped.
8. Remove the shock absorber from the lower control arm. For additional information, refer to the following section, "Shock Absorber, Removal & Installation."
9. Remove the upper control arm to knuckle nut and bolt.
10. Use two jack stands in order to support the crossmember.
11. Remove the crossmember to underbody bolts.
12. Slowly lower the crossmember until

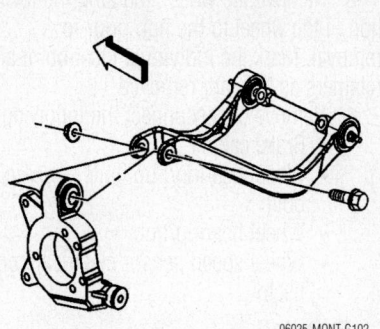

Fig. 152 Removing nut and bolt retaining upper control arm to knuckle

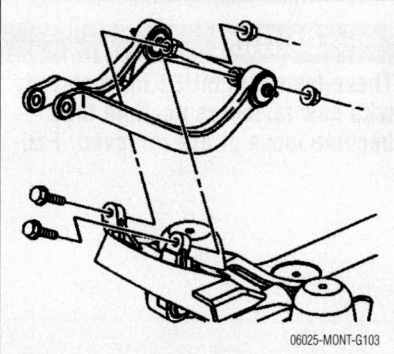

Fig. 153 Removing nut and bolt retaining upper control arm to crossmember

there is enough clearance to remove the upper control arm.

13. Remove the upper control arm to crossmember bolts and nuts.
14. Remove the upper control arm.

To install:

15. Install the upper control arm into position.
16. Install the bolts and the nuts which secure the upper control arm to the crossmember. Tighten the nuts to 55 ft. lbs. (75 Nm).
17. Use 2 utility stands in order to raise the crossmember. Install and tighten the crossmember to underbody bolts to 96 ft. lbs. (130 Nm).
18. Install or connect the following:
   • Upper control arm to the knuckle, tighten the nut which secures the upper control arm to 74 ft. lbs. (100 Nm)
   • Shock absorber to the lower control arm
   • Height sensor link to the lower control arm as necessary
   • Park brake cable to the park brake actuator and the park brake cable bracket
   • Brake caliper
19. Install the tire and wheel assembly.

Tighten the lug nuts to 100 ft. lbs. (140 Nm) in a criss—cross pattern, after aligning the wheel hub with the reference mark and holes as shown in appropriate illustration.

20. Lower the vehicle.

WHEEL BEARINGS

REMOVAL & INSTALLATION

With Independent Suspension

See Figure 154.

1. Before servicing the vehicle, refer to the Precautions Section.
2. Raise and safely support the vehicle.
3. Remove the wheel, marking the location of the wheel to the hub prior to removal. Mark the individual location of all retainers as they are removed.
4. Remove or disconnect the following:
   • Knuckle. See Steering Knuckle
   • Wheel bearing/hub assembly knuckle bolts
   • Wheel bearing/hub assembly from the knuckle

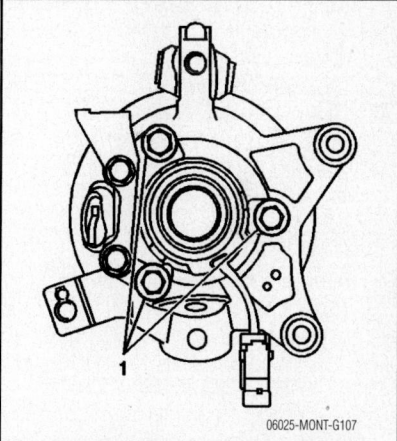

Fig. 154 Identifying wheel bearing/hub-to-knuckle retaining bolts

To install:

5. Install or connect the following:
   • Wheel bearing/hub assembly on to the knuckle
   • Bolts into the wheel bearing/hub assembly, tighten the wheel bearing/hub bolts to 96 ft. lbs. (130 Nm)
6. Install the tire and wheel assembly. Tighten the lug nuts to 100 ft. lbs. (140 Nm) in a criss—cross pattern, after aligning the wheel hub with the reference mark and holes as shown in appropriate illustration.
7. Lower the vehicle.

Without Independent Suspension

See Figure 155.

1. Before servicing the vehicle, refer to the Precautions Section.
2. Raise and safely support the vehicle.

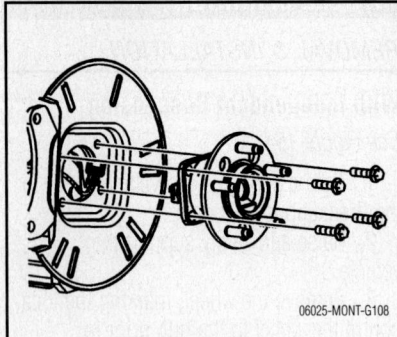

06025-MONT-G108

Fig. 155 Showing mounting view of rear bearing/hub assembly mounting

3. Remove the wheel, marking the location of the wheel to the hub prior to removal. Mark the individual location of all retainers as they are removed.
4. Remove or disconnect the following:
   - Brake caliper
   - Wheel bearing/hub bolts, discard bolts
   - Wheel bearing/hub
   - Wheel speed sensor electrical connector

To install:

5. Install or connect the following:
   - Wheel speed sensor electrical connector
   - Wheel bearing/hub

✳✳ CAUTION

These fasteners MUST be replaced with new fasteners anytime they become loose or are removed. Failure to replace these fasteners after they become loose or are removed may cause loss of vehicle control and personal injury.

   - NEW wheel bearing/hub bolts, tighten the bolts to 59 ft. lbs. (80 Nm)
   - Brake caliper. See Disc Brakes
6. Install the tire and wheel assembly. Tighten the lug nuts to 100 ft. lbs. (140 Nm) in a criss—cross pattern, after aligning the wheel hub with the reference mark and holes as shown in appropriate illustration.
7. Lower the vehicle.

ADJUSTMENT

The wheel hub and bearing assembly cannot be adjusted. If runout is excessive, the hub assembly must be replaced.

SPECIFICATIONS AND MAINTENANCE CHARTS

ENGINE AND VEHICLE IDENTIFICATION

			Engine					Model Year	
Code ①	Liters (cc)	Cu. In.	Cyl.	Fuel Sys.	Engine Type	Eng. Mfg.		Code ②	Year
L	3.4 (3350)	214	6	SFI	OHV	CPC		5	2005
L	3.5 (3448)	214	6	SFI	OHV	CPC		6	2006
7	3.6 (3556)	217	6	SFI	DOHC	CPC		7	2007

SFI: Sequential Fuel Injection

OHV: Overhead Valves

DOHC: Dual overhead camshafts

CPC: Chevrolet/Pontiac/Canada

① 8th position of VIN

② 10th position of VIN

22116_REND_C0001

GENERAL ENGINE SPECIFICATIONS

All measurements are given in inches.

Year	Model	Engine Displacement Liters	Engine Series VIN	Net Horsepower @ rpm	Net Torque @ rpm (ft. lbs.)	Bore x Stroke (in.)	Com- pression Ratio	Oil Pressure @ rpm
2005	Rendevous	3.4	E	185@5200	210@4000	3.62x3.31	9.6:1	15@1100
		3.6	7	245@6000	235@3200	3.70x3.37	10.2:1	20@2000
2006	Rendevous	3.5	L	200@5400	220@3200	3.70x3.31	9.8:1	30-45@1850
		3.6	7	245@6000	235@3200	3.70x3.37	10.2:1	20@2000
2007	Rendevous	3.5	L	200@5400	220@3200	3.70x3.31	9.8:1	30-45@1850

22116_REND_C0002

ENGINE TUNE-UP SPECIFICATIONS

Year	Engine Displacement Liters	Engine VIN	Spark Plug Gap (in.)	Ignition Timing (deg.)	Fuel Pump (psi)	Idle Speed (rpm)	Valve Clearance	
							Intake	Exhaust
2005	3.4	E	0.060	①	41-47	②	HYD	HYD
	3.6	7	0.044	①	55-60	②	HYD	HYD
2006	3.5	L	0.060	①	56-62	②	HYD	HYD
	3.6	7	0.044	①	55-60	②	HYD	HYD
2007	3.5	L	0.060	①	56-62	②	HYD	HYD

NA: Information not available

NOTE: The Vehicle Emissions Control Information label often reflects specification changes made during production.

The label figures must be used if they differ from those in the chart.

HYD: Hydraulic

① Refer to underhood label for exact setting.

② Idle speed is maintained by the PCM.

22116_REND_C0003

CAPACITIES

Year	Model	Engine Displacement Liters	Engine VIN	Engine Oil with Filter (qts.)	Transmission (pts.)	Transfer Case (pts.)	Rear Axle (pts.)	Fuel Tank (gal.)	Cooling System (qts.)
2005	Rendevous	3.4	E	4.0	①	0.6	4.2	18.0	9.6
		3.6	7	5.5	①	0.6	4.2	18.0	9.6
2006	Rendevous	3.5	L	4.0	①	0.6	4.2	18.0	9.6
		3.6	7	5.5	①	0.6	4.2	18.0	9.6
2007	Rendevous	3.5	L	4.0	①	0.6	4.2	18.0	9.6

NOTE: All capacities are approximate. Add fluid gradually and check to be sure a proper fluid level is obtained.

① Front wheel drive:

  Drain and refill: 7.4 quarts

  Complete overhaul: 10 quarts

  All wheel drive:

  Drain and refill: 7.8 quarts

  Complete overhaul: 10.4 quarts

22116_REND_C0004

VALVE SPECIFICATIONS

Year	Engine Displacement Liters	Engine VIN	Seat Angle (deg.)	Face Angle (deg.)	Spring Test Pressure (lbs. @ in.)	Spring Installed Height (in.)	Stem-to-Guide Clearance (in.) Intake	Stem-to-Guide Clearance (in.) Exhaust	Stem Diameter (in.) Intake	Stem Diameter (in.) Exhaust
2005	3.4	E	46	45	230@1.26	1.70	0.0010-0.0027	0.0010-0.0027	NA	NA
	3.6	7	44.25	45	134-149@0.9449	1.38	0.0010-0.0026	0.0014-0.0030	0.2344-0.2352	0.2341-0.2348
2006	3.5	L	46	45	234@1.299	1.74	0.0010-0.0027	0.0010-0.0027	NA	NA
	3.6	7	44.25	45	134-149@0.9449	1.38	0.0010-0.0026	0.0014-0.0030	0.2344-0.2352	0.2341-0.2348
2007	3.5	L	46	45	234@1.299	1.74	0.0010-0.0027	0.0010-0.0027	NA	NA

NA: Information not Available

22116_REND_C0005

CRANKSHAFT AND CONNECTING ROD SPECIFICATIONS

All measurements are given in inches.

| Year | Engine Displacement Liters | Engine VIN | Crankshaft | | | | Connecting Rod | | |
			Main Brg. Journal Dia.	Main Brg. Oil Clearance	Shaft End-play	Thrust on No.	Journal Diameter	Oil Clearance	Side Clearance
2005	3.4	E	2.6473-2.6483	0.0008-0.0023	0.0024-0.0083	3	1.9987-1.9994	0.0007-0.0024	0.007-0.017
	3.6	7	2.6768-2.6775	0.0004-0.0024	0.0039-0.0130	3	2.2044-2.2050	0.0004-0.0028	0.0037-0.0140
2006	3.5	L	2.6473-2.6483	0.0008-0.0025	0.0024-0.0083	3	2.2490-2.2500	0.0007-0.0017	0.008-0.009
	3.6	7	2.6768-2.6775	0.0004-0.0024	0.0039-0.0130	3	2.2044-2.2050	0.0004-0.0028	0.0037-0.0140
2007	3.5	L	2.6473-2.6483	0.0008-0.0025	0.0024-0.0083	3	2.2490-2.2500	0.0007-0.0017	0.008-0.009

22116_REND_C0006

PISTON AND RING SPECIFICATIONS

All measurements are given in inches.

| Year | Engine Displ. Liters | Engine VIN | Piston Clearance | Ring Gap | | | Ring Side Clearance | | |
				Top Compression	Bottom Compression	Oil Control	Top Compression	Bottom Compression	Oil Control
2005	3.4	E	0.0036 Max	0.006-0.014	0.0188-0.029	0.0098-0.0303	0.0020-0.0033	0.0020-0.0031	0.0028-0.0037
	3.6	7	0.0010-0.0021	0.0059-0.0118	0.0110-0.0189	0.0059-0.0236	0.0012-0.0026	0.0006-0.0024	0.0012-0.0067
2006	3.5	L	0.0030 Max	0.007-0.015	0.019-0.029	0.010-0.029	0.001-0.0030	0.0020-0.0030	0.0040 Max
	3.6	7	0.0010-0.0021	0.0059-0.0118	0.0110-0.0189	0.0059-0.0236	0.0012-0.0026	0.0006-0.0024	0.0012-0.0067
2007	3.5	L	0.0030 Max	0.007-0.015	0.019-0.0291	0.010-0.0290	0.001-0.0030	0.0020-0.0030	0.0040 Max

NA: Information not available

22116_REND_C0007

TORQUE SPECIFICATIONS
All readings in ft. lbs.

Year	Engine Displacement Liters	Engine VIN	Cylinder Head Bolts	Main Bearing Bolts	Rod Bearing Bolts	Crankshaft Damper Bolts	Flywheel Bolts	Manifold Intake*	Manifold Exhaust	Spark Plugs	Oil Pan Drain Plug
2005	3.4	E	①	②	③	④	52	⑤	12	15	18
	3.6	7	⑥	⑦	⑧	⑨	⑩	17	15	13	18
2006	3.5	L	①	②	⑪	⑫	52	⑬	12	11	18
	3.6	7	⑥	⑦	⑧	⑨	⑩	17	15	13	18
2007	3.5	L	①	②	⑪	⑫	52	⑬	12	11	18

* Lower

① 44 ft. lbs. Plus 95 degrees

② 37 ft. lbs. plus 77 degrees

③ 15 ft. lbs. plus 75 degrees

④ 52 ft. lbs. plus 72 degrees

⑤ Center bolts:
Step 1: 62 inch lbs.
Step 2: 115 inch lbs.
Corner bolts:
Step 1: 115 inch lbs.
Step 2: 18 ft. lbs.
Step 2: 115 inch lbs.

⑥ M8 bolts:
Step 1: 10 ft. lbs.
Step 2: plus 60 degrees
M11 bolts:
Step 1: 33 ft. lbs.
Step2: plus 120 degress

⑦ Inner
Step 1: 15 ft. lbs.
Step 2: plus 80 degrees
Outer:
Step 1: 10 ft. lbs.
Step 2: plus 110 degrees
Side
Step 1: 22 ft. lbs.
Step 2: plus 60 degrees

⑧ Step 1: 22 ft. lbs.
Step 2: back off to 0
Step 3: 18 ft. lbs.
Step 4: plus 110 degrees

⑨ Step 1: 74 ft. lbs.
Step 2: plus 150 degrees

⑩ Step 1: 22 ft. lbs.
Step 2: plus 45 degrees

⑪ 18 ft. lbs. Plus 110 degrees

⑫ 92 ft. lbs. Plus 130 degrees

⑬ Lower Center bolts: 15 ft. lbs.
Lower Corner bolts: 18 ft. lbs.
Upper Bolts: 18ft.lbs.

22116_REND_C0008

WHEEL ALIGNMENT

Year	Model		Caster Range (+/-Deg.)	Caster Preferred Setting (Deg.)	Camber Range (+/-Deg.)	Camber Preferred Setting (Deg.)	Toe-in (in.)
2005	FWD	F	0.75	2.40	0.50	-0.65	0+/-0.20
		R	—	—	0.50	0	0 +/-0.30
	AWD and I.R.S.	F	0.75	2.40	0.75	-0.65	0+/-0.20
		R	—	—	0.60	-0.30	0 +/-0.20
2006	FWD	F	0.75	2.40	0.75	-0.65	0+/-0.20
		R	—	—	0.60	-0.30	0 +/-0.20
	AWD and I.R.S.	F	0.75	2.40	0.75	-0.65	0+/-0.20
		R	—	—	0.60	-0.30	0 +/-0.20
2007	All	F	0.75	2.40	0.75	-0.65	0+/-0.20
		R	—	—	0.60	-0.30	0 +/-0.20

NOTE: All alignment figures based on nominal ride height and standard tires

22116_REND_C0009

TIRE, WHEEL AND BALL JOINT SPECIFICATIONS

| Year | Model | OEM Tires | | Tire Pressures (psi) | | Wheel Size | Ball Joint Inspection | Lug Nut Torque (ft. lbs.) |
		Standard	Optional	Front	Rear			
2005	All	P225/60R17	N/A	①	①	6-JJ	U ②	100
							L: 0.090 in.	
2006	All	P255/60R17	N/A	std: 35	std.: 35	6-JJ	U ②	100
				opt: 32	opt.: 32		L: 0.090 in.	
2007	All	P225/60R17	N/A	std: 35	std.: 35	6-JJ	U ②	100
				opt: 32	opt.: 32		L: 0.090 in.	

OEM: Original Equipment Manufacturer

PSI: Pounds Per Square Inch

STD: Standard

OPT: Optional

L: Lower

U: Upper

① See placard on vehicle.

② Replace if any movement is noted or if stud can be moved by hand

22116_REND_C0010

BRAKE SPECIFICATIONS

All measurements in inches unless noted

| Year | Model | | Brake Disc | | | Brake Drum Diameter | | | Minimum Lining Thickness | | Brake Caliper | |
			Original Thickness	Minimum Thickness	Maximum Runout	Original Inside Diameter	Max. Wear Limit	Maximum Machine Diameter	Front	Rear	Bracket Bolts (ft. lbs.)	Mounting Bolts (ft. lbs.)
2005	Rendevous	F	1.181	1.063	0.002	—	—	—	NA	—	137	26
		R	0.43	0.350	0.002	—	9.902	9.882	—	NA	96	33
2006	Rendevous	F	1.181	1.063	0.002	—	—	—	NA	—	137	26
		R	0.430	0.350	0.002	—	—	—	—	—	92	33
2007	Rendevous	F	1.181	1.063	0.002	—	—	—	NA	—	137	26
		R	0.430	0.350	0.002	—	—	—	—	—	92	33

NA: Information not available

22116_REND_C0011

SCHEDULED MAINTENANCE INTERVALS
2005-07 BUICK RENDEZVOUS

TO BE SERVICED	TYPE OF SERVICE	VEHICLE MILEAGE INTERVAL (x1000)															
		5	10	15	20	25	30	35	40	45	50	55	60	65	70	75	80
Accessory drive belt	I/R	Every 150,000 miles															
Air cleaner filter	R					✓					✓					✓	
Air distributor air filter	R		✓		✓		✓		✓		✓		✓		✓		✓
Brake system	I	✓	✓	✓	✓	✓	✓	✓	✓	✓	✓	✓	✓	✓	✓	✓	✓
Engine coolant	R	Every 150,000 miles															
Engine oil & filter	S/I	✓	✓	✓	✓	✓	✓	✓	✓	✓	✓	✓	✓	✓	✓	✓	✓
Exhaust system	I					✓					✓					✓	
Fuel tank, cap & lines	I					✓					✓					✓	
Transmission fluid	R										✓						
Rotate tires	S/I	✓	✓	✓	✓	✓	✓	✓	✓	✓	✓	✓	✓	✓	✓	✓	✓
Spark plug wires	S/I	Every 100,000 miles															
Spark plugs	R	Every 100,000 miles															

R: Replace   I: Inspect   S: Service

22116_REND_C0013

PRECAUTIONS

Before servicing any vehicle, please be sure to read all of the following precautions, which deal with personal safety, prevention of component damage, and important points to take into consideration when servicing a motor vehicle:

• Never open, service or drain the radiator or cooling system when the engine is hot; serious burns can occur from the steam and hot coolant.

• Observe all applicable safety precautions when working around fuel. Whenever servicing the fuel system, always work in a well-ventilated area. Do not allow fuel spray or vapors to come in contact with a spark, open flame, or excessive heat (a hot drop light, for example). Keep a dry chemical fire extinguisher near the work area. Always keep fuel in a container specifically designed for fuel storage; also, always properly seal fuel containers to avoid the possibility of fire or explosion. Refer to the additional fuel system precautions later in this section.

• Fuel injection systems often remain pressurized, even after the engine has been turned **OFF**. The fuel system pressure must be relieved before disconnecting any fuel lines. Failure to do so may result in fire and/or personal injury.

• Brake fluid often contains polyglycol ethers and polyglycols. Avoid contact with the eyes and wash your hands thoroughly after handling brake fluid. If you do get brake fluid in your eyes, flush your eyes with clean, running water for 15 minutes. If eye irritation persists, or if you have taken brake fluid internally, IMMEDIATELY seek medical assistance.

• The EPA warns that prolonged contact with used engine oil may cause a number of skin disorders, including cancer. You should make every effort to minimize your exposure to used engine oil. Protective gloves should be worn when changing oil. Wash your hands and any other exposed skin areas as soon as possible after exposure to used engine oil. Soap and water, or waterless hand cleaner should be used.

• All new vehicles are now equipped with an air bag system, often referred to as a Supplemental Restraint System (SRS) or Supplemental Inflatable Restraint (SIR) system. The system must be disabled before performing service on or around system components, steering column, instrument panel components, wiring and sensors. Failure to follow safety and disabling procedures could result in accidental air bag deployment, possible personal injury and unnecessary system repairs.

• Always wear safety goggles when working with, or around, the air bag system. When carrying a non-deployed air bag, be sure the bag and trim cover are pointed away from your body. When placing a non-deployed air bag on a work surface, always face the bag and trim cover upward, away from the surface. This will reduce the motion of the module if it is accidentally deployed. Refer to the additional air bag system precautions later in this section.

• Clean, high quality brake fluid from a sealed container is essential to the safe and proper operation of the brake system. You should always buy the correct type of brake fluid for your vehicle. If the brake fluid becomes contaminated, completely flush the system with new fluid. Never reuse any brake fluid. Any brake fluid that is removed from the system should be discarded. Also, do not allow any brake fluid to come in contact with a painted surface; it will damage the paint.

• Never operate the engine without the proper amount and type of engine oil; doing so WILL result in severe engine damage.

• Timing belt maintenance is extremely important. Many models utilize an interference-type, non-freewheeling engine. If the timing belt breaks, the valves in the cylinder head may strike the pistons, causing potentially serious (also time-consuming and expensive) engine damage. Refer to the maintenance interval charts for the recommended replacement interval for the timing belt, and to the timing belt section for belt replacement and inspection.

• Disconnecting the negative battery cable on some vehicles may interfere with the functions of the on-board computer system(s) and may require the computer to undergo a relearning process once the negative battery cable is reconnected.

• When servicing drum brakes, only disassemble and assemble one side at a time, leaving the remaining side intact for reference.

• Only an MVAC-trained, EPA-certified automotive technician should service the air conditioning system or its components.

BRAKES

ANTI-LOCK BRAKE SYSTEM (ABS)

GENERAL INFORMATION

When wheel slip is detected during a brake application, the ABS enters antilock mode. During antilock braking, hydraulic pressure in the individual wheel circuits is controlled to prevent any wheel from slipping. A separate hydraulic line and specific solenoid valves are provided for each wheel. The ABS can decrease, hold, or increase hydraulic pressure to each wheel brake. The ABS cannot, however, increase hydraulic pressure above the amount which is transmitted by the master cylinder during braking.

During antilock braking, a series of rapid pulsations is felt in the brake pedal. These pulsations are caused by the rapid changes in position of the individual solenoid valves as the EBCM responds to wheel speed sensor inputs and attempts to prevent wheel slip. These pedal pulsations are present only during antilock braking and stop when normal braking is resumed or when the vehicle comes to a stop. A ticking or popping noise may also be heard as the solenoid valves cycle rapidly. During antilock braking on dry pavement, intermittent chirping noises may be heard as the tires approach slipping. These noises and pedal pulsations are considered normal during antilock operation.

Vehicles equipped with ABS may be stopped by applying normal force to the brake pedal. Brake pedal operation during normal braking is no different than that of previous non-ABS systems. Maintaining a constant force on the brake pedal provides the shortest stopping distance while maintaining vehicle stability.

PRECAUTIONS

• Certain components within the ABS system are not intended to be serviced or repaired individually.

• Do not use rubber hoses or other parts not specifically specified for and ABS system. When using repair kits, replace all parts included in the kit. Partial or incorrect repair may lead to functional problems and require the replacement of components.

• Lubricate rubber parts with clean, fresh brake fluid to ease assembly. Do not

use shop air to clean parts; damage to rubber components may result.
- Use only DOT 3 brake fluid from an unopened container.
- If any hydraulic component or line is removed or replaced, it may be necessary to bleed the entire system.
- A clean repair area is essential. Always clean the reservoir and cap thoroughly before removing the cap. The slightest amount of dirt in the fluid may plug an orifice and impair the system function. Perform repairs after components have been thoroughly cleaned; use only denatured alcohol to clean components. Do not allow ABS components to come into contact with any substance containing mineral oil; this includes used shop rags.
- The Anti-Lock control unit is a microprocessor similar to other computer units in the vehicle. Ensure that the ignition switch is **OFF** before removing or installing controller harnesses. Avoid static electricity discharge at or near the controller.
- If any arc welding is to be done on the vehicle, the control unit should be unplugged before welding operations begin.

DIAGNOSIS & TESTING

1. Begin the system diagnosis with a Diagnostic System Check—Vehicle. The Diagnostic System Check will provide the following information:
- The identification of the control modules which command the system
- The ability of the control modules to communicate through the serial data circuit
- The identification of any stored Diagnostic Trouble Codes (DTCs) and their status
2. The use of the Diagnostic System Check will identify the correct procedure for diagnosing the system and where the procedure is located.

SPEED SENSORS

REMOVAL & INSTALLATION

Front

See Figure 1.

➡The front wheel speed sensors and rings are integral with the hub and bearing assemblies. If a speed sensor or a ring needs replacement, replace the entire hub and bearing assembly. Do not service the harness pigtail indi-

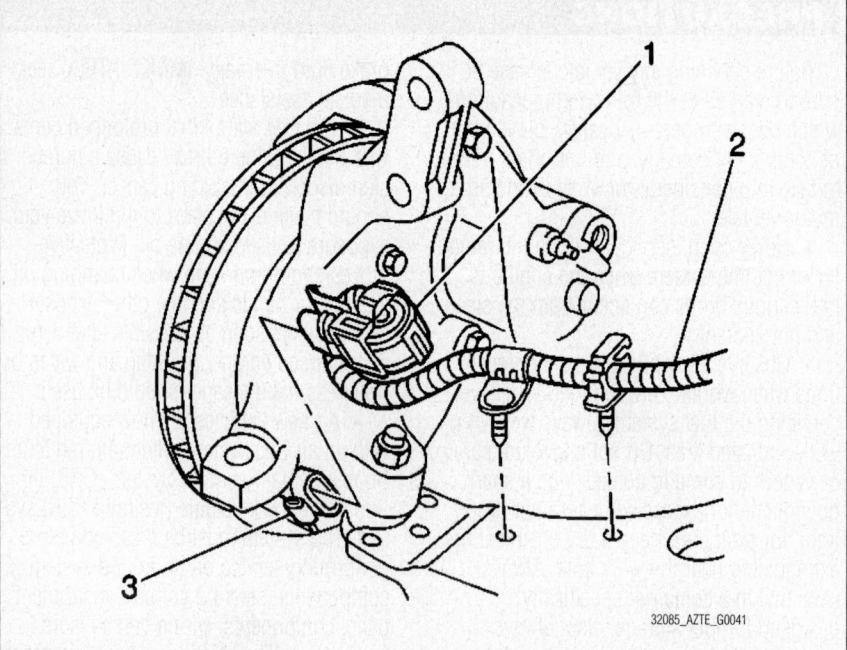

Fig. 1 Remove the front wheel speed sensor jumper harness electrical connector (1) from the front wheel speed sensor connector (3).

32085_AZTE_G0041

vidually because the harness pigtail is part of the sensor.

1. Raise and support the vehicle on a suitable hoist.
2. Remove the front tire and wheel assembly.
3. Remove the front wheel speed sensor jumper harness electrical connector from the front wheel speed sensor connector.
4. Remove the hub and bearing assembly.

To install:

5. Install the hub and bearing assembly to the vehicle.
6. Install the front wheel speed sensor jumper harness electrical connector to front wheel speed sensor connector.
7. Install the wheel and tire assembly.
8. Lower the vehicle.
9. Turn the ignition switch to the **RUN** position with the engine off.

Rear

➡The rear wheel speed sensors and rings are integral with the hub and bearing assemblies. If a speed sensor or a ring needs replacement, replace the entire hub and bearing assembly.

1. Raise and support the vehicle on a suitable hoist.
2. Remove the rear tire and wheel assembly.

3. Remove the rear wheel speed sensor electrical connector located next to the rear strut.
4. Remove the hub and bearing assembly.

To install:

5. Install the hub and bearing assembly to the vehicle.
6. Install the rear wheel speed sensor electrical connector.
7. Install the wheel and tire assembly.
8. Lower the vehicle.
9. Turn the ignition switch to the **RUN** position with the engine off.

ELECTRONIC BRAKE CONTROL MODULE (EBCM)/ELECTRONIC BRAKE TRACTION CONTROL MODULE (EBTCM)

REMOVAL & INSTALLATION

See Figure 2.

➡Always connect or disconnect the wiring harness connector from the EBCM/EBTCM with the ignition switch in the OFF position. Failure to observe this precaution could result in damage to the EBCM/EBTCM.

1. Turn the ignition switch to the **OFF** position.
2. Remove the air cleaner housing from the engine compartment.

3. Disconnect the Electronic Brake Control Module (EBCM) harness connector.

4. Brush off any dirt/debris that has accumulated on the assembly.

5. Disconnect the pump motor connector at the bottom of the EBCM.

6. Do not damage the seal by prying the EBCM from the brake pressure modulator valve (BPMV).

7. Do not damage the solenoid valves while removing the EBCM from the BPMV.

8. Remove the six EBCM-to-BPMV screws.

9. Separate the EBCM from the BPMV by gently pulling apart until separated.

To install:

➡**Use only new wave springs and screws supplied with the new EBCM.**

10. Clean the BPMV surface with alcohol using a clean towel.

11. Install the EBCM to the BPMV.

12. Install the six screws that attach the EBCM to the BPMV.

13. Tighten the top four mounting

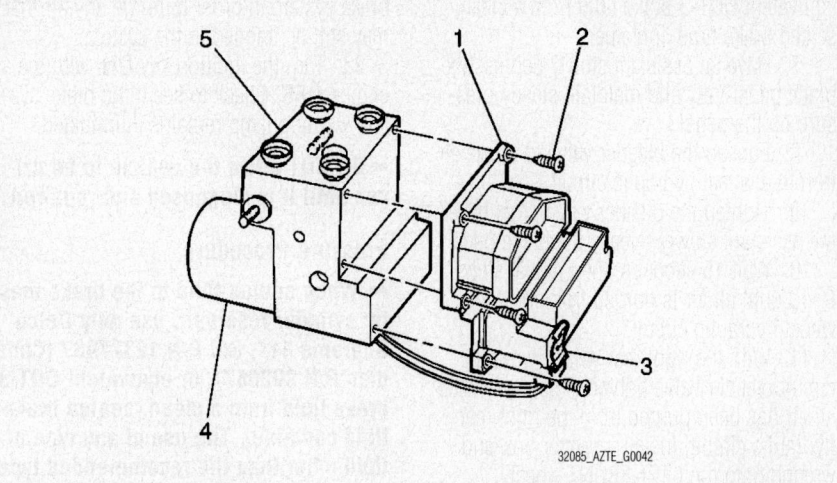

Fig. 2 Remove the 6 EBCM to BPMV screws and separate the EBCM from the BPMV by gently pulling apart until separated

32085_AZTE_G0042

screws to 44 inch lbs. (5 Nm). Tighten screws in an X pattern

14. Tighten the bottom two mounting screws to 44 inch lbs. (5 Nm).

15. Connect the pump motor connector to the bottom of the EBCM

16. Connect the EBCM harness connector and depress the locking tab to secure.

17. Install the air cleaner housing.

18. Turn the ignition switch to the **RUN** position, do not start engine.

BRAKES
BLEEDING THE BRAKE SYSTEM

BLEEDING PROCEDURE

BLEEDING PROCEDURE

Manual Procedure

➡**When adding fluid to the brake master cylinder reservoir, use only Delco Supreme 11®, GM P/N 12377967 (Canadian P/N 992667), or equivalent DOT-3 brake fluid from a clean, sealed brake fluid container. The use of any type of fluid other than the recommended type of brake fluid, may cause contamination which could result in damage to the internal rubber seals and/or rubber linings of hydraulic brake system components.**

1. Place a clean shop cloth beneath the brake master cylinder to prevent brake fluid spills. With the ignition **OFF** and the brakes cool, apply the brakes 3–5 times, or until the brake pedal effort increases significantly, in order to deplete the brake booster power reserve.

2. If you have performed a brake master cylinder bench bleeding on this vehicle, or if you disconnected the brake pipes from the master cylinder, you must perform the following steps:

- Ensure that the brake master cylinder

reservoir is full to the maximum-fill level. If necessary, add Delco Supreme 11®, GM P/N 12377967 (Canadian P/N 992667), or equivalent DOT-3 brake fluid from a clean, sealed brake fluid container. If removal of the reservoir cap and diaphragm is necessary, clean the outside of the reservoir on and around the cap prior to removal.

- With the rear brake pipe installed securely to the master cylinder, loosen and separate the front brake pipe from the front port of the brake master cylinder.

- Allow a small amount of brake fluid to gravity bleed from the open port of the master cylinder.

- Reconnect the brake pipe to the master cylinder port and tighten securely.

- Have an assistant slowly depress the brake pedal fully and maintain steady pressure on the pedal.

- Loosen the same brake pipe to purge air from the open port of the master cylinder.

- Tighten the brake pipe, then have the assistant slowly release the brake pedal.

- Wait 15 seconds, then repeat steps 3.3–3.7 until all air is purged from

the same port of the master cylinder.

- With the front brake pipe installed securely to the master cylinder, after all air has been purged from the front port of the master cylinder, loosen and separate the rear brake pipe from the master cylinder, then repeat steps 3.3–3.8.

- After completing the final master cylinder port bleeding procedure, ensure that both of the brake pipe-to-master cylinder fittings are properly tightened.

3. Fill the brake master cylinder reservoir with Delco Supreme 11®, GM P/N 12377967 (Canadian P/N 992667), or equivalent DOT-3 brake fluid from a clean, sealed brake fluid container. Ensure that the brake master cylinder reservoir remains at least half-full during this bleeding procedure. Add fluid as needed to maintain the proper level. Clean the outside of the reservoir on and around the reservoir cap prior to removing the cap and diaphragm.

4. Install a proper box-end wrench onto the RIGHT REAR wheel hydraulic circuit bleeder valve.

5. Install a transparent hose over the end of the bleeder valve.

6. Submerge the open end of the transparent hose into a transparent container partially filled with Delco Supreme 11®, GM P/N 12377967 (Canadian P/N 992667), or

equivalent DOT-3 brake fluid from a clean, sealed brake fluid container.

7. Have an assistant slowly depress the brake pedal fully and maintain steady pressure on the pedal.

8. Loosen the bleeder valve to purge air from the wheel hydraulic circuit.

9. Tighten the bleeder valve, then have the assistant slowly release the brake pedal.

10. Wait 15 seconds, then repeat steps 8–10 until all air is purged from the same wheel hydraulic circuit.

11. With the right rear wheel hydraulic circuit bleeder valve tightened securely, after all air has been purged from the right rear hydraulic circuit, install a proper box-end wrench onto the LEFT FRONT wheel hydraulic circuit bleeder valve.

12. Install a transparent hose over the end of the bleeder valve, then repeat steps 7–11.

13. With the left front wheel hydraulic circuit bleeder valve tightened securely, after all air has been purged from the left front hydraulic circuit, install a proper box-end wrench onto the LEFT REAR wheel hydraulic circuit bleeder valve.

14. Install a transparent hose over the end of the bleeder valve, then repeat steps 7–11.

15. With the left rear wheel hydraulic circuit bleeder valve tightened securely, after all air has been purged from the left rear hydraulic circuit, install a proper box-end wrench onto the RIGHT FRONT wheel hydraulic circuit bleeder valve.

16. Install a transparent hose over the end of the bleeder valve, then repeat steps 7–11.

17. After completing the final wheel hydraulic circuit bleeding procedure, ensure that each of the 4 wheel hydraulic circuit bleeder valves are properly tightened.

18. Fill the brake master cylinder reservoir to the maximum-fill level with Delco Supreme 11®, GM P/N 12377967 (Canadian P/N 992667), or equivalent DOT-3 brake fluid from a clean, sealed brake fluid container.

19. Slowly depress and release the brake pedal. Observe the feel of the brake pedal.

➡**If it is determined that air was induced into the system upstream of the ABS modulator prior to servicing, the ABS Automated Bleed Procedure must be performed.**

20. If the brake pedal feels spongy, repeat the bleeding procedure again. If the brake pedal still feels spongy after repeating the bleeding procedure, perform the following steps:

21. Inspect the brake system for external leaks and pressure bleed the hydraulic

brake system in order to purge any air that may still be trapped in the system.

22. Turn the ignition key **ON**, with the engine **OFF**. Check to see if the brake system warning lamp remains illuminated.

➡**DO NOT allow the vehicle to be driven until it is diagnosed and repaired.**

Pressure Procedure

➡ **When adding fluid to the brake master cylinder reservoir, use only Delco Supreme 11®, GM P/N 12377967 (Canadian P/N 992667), or equivalent DOT-3 brake fluid from a clean, sealed brake fluid container. The use of any type of fluid other than the recommended type of brake fluid, may cause contamination which could result in damage to the internal rubber seals and/or rubber linings of hydraulic brake system components.**

1. Place a clean shop cloth beneath the brake master cylinder to prevent brake fluid spills.

2. With the ignition **OFF** and the brakes cool, apply the brakes 3–5 times, or until the brake pedal effort increases significantly, in order to deplete the brake booster power reserve.

3. If you have performed a brake master cylinder bench bleeding on this vehicle, or if you disconnected the brake pipes from the master cylinder, you must perform the following steps:

- Ensure that the brake master cylinder reservoir is full to the maximum-fill level. If necessary, add Delco Supreme 11®, GM P/N 12377967 (Canadian P/N 992667), or equivalent DOT-3 brake fluid from a clean, sealed brake fluid container. If removal of the reservoir cap and diaphragm is necessary, clean the outside of the reservoir on and around the cap prior to removal.
- With the rear brake pipe installed securely to the master cylinder, loosen and separate the front brake pipe from the front port of the brake master cylinder.
- Allow a small amount of brake fluid to gravity bleed from the open port of the master cylinder.
- Reconnect the brake pipe to the master cylinder port and tighten securely.
- Have an assistant slowly depress the brake pedal fully and maintain steady pressure on the pedal.

- Loosen the same brake pipe to purge air from the open port of the master cylinder.
- Tighten the brake pipe, then have the assistant slowly release the brake pedal.
- Wait 15 seconds, then repeat steps 3.3–3.7 until all air is purged from the same port of the master cylinder.
- With the front brake pipe installed securely to the master cylinder, after all air has been purged from the front port of the master cylinder, loosen and separate the rear brake pipe from the master cylinder, then repeat steps 3.3–3.8.
- After completing the final master cylinder port bleeding procedure, ensure that both of the brake pipe-to-master cylinder fittings are properly tightened.

4. Fill the brake master cylinder reservoir to the maximum-fill level with Delco Supreme 11®, GM P/N 12377967 (Canadian P/N 992667), or equivalent DOT-3 brake fluid from a clean, sealed brake fluid container. Clean the outside of the reservoir on and around the reservoir cap prior to removing the cap and diaphragm.

5. Install the J 35589-A to the brake master cylinder reservoir.

6. Check the brake fluid level in the J 29532 , or equivalent. Add Delco Supreme 11®, GM P/N 12377967 (Canadian P/N 992667), or equivalent DOT-3 brake fluid from a clean, sealed brake fluid container as necessary to bring the level to approximately the half-full point.

7. Connect the J 29532 , or equivalent, to the J 35589-A .

8. Charge the J 29532 , or equivalent, air tank to 25–30 psi (175–205 kPa).

9. Open the J 29532 , or equivalent, fluid tank valve to allow pressurized brake fluid to enter the brake system.

10. Wait approximately 30 seconds, then inspect the entire hydraulic brake system in order to ensure that there are no existing external brake fluid leaks. Any brake fluid leaks identified require repair prior to completing this procedure.

11. Install a proper box-end wrench onto the RIGHT REAR wheel hydraulic circuit bleeder valve.

12. Install a transparent hose over the end of the bleeder valve.

13. Submerge the open end of the transparent hose into a transparent container partially filled with Delco Supreme 11®, GM P/N 12377967 (Canadian P/N 992667), or equivalent DOT-3 brake fluid from a clean, sealed brake fluid container.

14. Loosen the bleeder valve to purge air from the wheel hydraulic circuit. Allow fluid to flow until air bubbles stop flowing from the bleeder, then tighten the bleeder valve.

15. With the right rear wheel hydraulic circuit bleeder valve tightened securely, after all air has been purged from the right rear hydraulic circuit, install a proper box-end wrench onto the LEFT FRONT wheel hydraulic circuit bleeder valve.

16. Install a transparent hose over the end of the bleeder valve, then repeat steps 13–14.

17. With the left front wheel hydraulic circuit bleeder valve tightened securely, after all air has been purged from the left front hydraulic circuit, install a proper box-end wrench onto the LEFT REAR wheel hydraulic circuit bleeder valve.

18. Install a transparent hose over the end of the bleeder valve, then repeat steps 13–14. With the left rear wheel hydraulic circuit bleeder valve tightened securely, after all air has been purged from the left rear hydraulic circuit, install a proper box-end wrench onto the RIGHT FRONT wheel hydraulic circuit bleeder valve

19. Install a transparent hose over the end of the bleeder valve, then repeat steps 13–14.

20. After completing the final wheel hydraulic circuit bleeding procedure, ensure that each of the 4 wheel hydraulic circuit bleeder valves are properly tightened.

21. Close the J 29532 , or equivalent, fluid tank valve, then disconnect the J 29532 , or equivalent, from the J 35589-A .

22. Remove the J 35589-A from the brake master cylinder reservoir.

23. Fill the brake master cylinder reservoir to the maximum-fill level with Delco Supreme 11®, GM P/N 12377967 (Canadian P/N 992667), or equivalent DOT-3 brake fluid from a clean, sealed brake fluid container.

24. Slowly depress and release the brake pedal. Observe the feel of the brake pedal.

➡**If it is determined that air was induced into the system upstream of the ABS modulator prior to servicing, the ABS Automated Bleed Procedure must be performed.**

25. If the brake pedal feels spongy, perform the following steps:

26. Inspect the brake system for external leaks.

27. Using a scan tool, perform the antilock brake system automated bleeding procedure to remove any air that may have been trapped in the BPMV.

28. Turn the ignition key **ON**, with the engine **OFF**. Check to see if the brake system warning lamp remains illuminated.

➡**DO NOT allow the vehicle to be driven until it is diagnosed and repaired.**

BLEEDING THE ABS SYSTEM

➡**In most circumstances a base brake bleed is all that is required for most component replacements (such as wheel cylinders, calipers, brake tubes, and master cylinder) except for Brake Pressure Modulator Valve (BPMV) replacement.**

➡**The following automated ABS bleed procedure is required when one of the following occur:**

- Manual bleeding at the wheel cylinders does not achieve the desired pedal height or feel.
- BPMV replacement
- Extreme loss of brake fluid has occurred.
- Air ingestion is suspected.

1. If none of the above conditions apply, use standard bleed procedures.

2. The auto bleed procedure is used on BOSH 5.3 equipped vehicles. This procedure uses a scan tool to cycle the system solenoid valves and run the pump in order to purge the air from the secondary circuits. These secondary circuits are normally closed off, and are only opened during system initialization at vehicle start up and during ABS operation. The automated bleed procedure opens these secondary circuits and allows any air trapped inside the BPMV to flow out toward the wheel cylinders or calipers where it can be purged out of the system.

3. Inspect the battery for full charge, repair the battery and charging system, as necessary.

4. Connect a scan tool to the data link connector (DLC) and select current and history DTCs. Repair any DTCs prior to performing the ABS bleed procedure. Inspect for visual damage and leaks and repair, as needed.

5. Raise and vehicle on a suitable support.

6. Turn the ignition switch to the **OFF** position.

7. Remove all 4 tires.

8. Connect the pressure bleeding tool according to the manufacturer's instructions.

9. Turn the ignition switch to **RUN** position, engine off.

10. Connect a scan tool and establish communications with the ABS system.

11. Pressurize the bleeding tool to 30–35 psi (206–241 kPa).

12. Performing the Automated Bleed Procedure

➡**The Auto Bleed Procedure may be terminated at any time during the process by pressing the EXIT button. No further Scan Tool prompts pertaining to the Auto Bleed procedure will be given. After exiting the bleed procedure, relieve bleed pressure and disconnect bleed equipment per manufacturer's instructions. Failure to properly relieve pressure may result in spilled brake fluid causing damage to components and painted surfaces.**

13. With the pressure bleeding tool at 30–35 psi (206–241 kPa), and all bleeder screws in closed position, select Automated Bleed Procedure on the scan tool and follow the instructions.

14. The first part of the automated bleed procedure will cycle the pump and front release valves for one minute. After the cycling has stopped the scan tool will enter a cool down mode and display a 3 minute timer. The auto bleed will not continue until this timer expires, and cannot be overridden.

15. During the next step, the scan tool will request the technician to open one of the bleeder screws. The scan tool will then cycle the respective release valve and pump motor for one minute.

16. The scan tool will repeat step 3 for the remaining bleeder screws.

17. With the bleeder tool still attached to the vehicle and maintaining 30–35 psi (206–241 kPa), the scan tool will instruct the technician to independently open each bleeder screw for approximately 20 seconds. This should allow any remaining air to be purged from the brake lines.

18. When the automated bleed procedure is completed the scan tool will display the appropriate message.

19. Install all 4 tires.

20. Remove pressure from the pressure bleeding tool and then disconnect the tool from the vehicle.

21. Depress the brake pedal to gage pedal height and feel. Repeat steps 1-8 until the pedal is acceptable.

22. Remove the scan tool from the DLC connector.

23. Lower the vehicle.

24. Inspect the brake fluid level in master cylinder.

25. Road test the vehicle while making sure the brake pedal remains high and firm.

26. If the vehicle is equipped with a traction control system (TCS), the scan tool will cycle both the ABS and the TCS solenoid valves. This bleed procedure is the same as above.

✳✳ CAUTION

Dust and dirt accumulating on brake parts during normal use may contain asbestos fibers from production or aftermarket brake linings. Breathing excessive concentrations of asbestos fibers can cause serious bodily harm. Exercise care when servicing brake parts. Do not sand or grind brake lining unless equipment used is designed to contain the dust residue. Do not clean brake parts with compressed air or by dry brushing. Cleaning should be done by dampening the brake components with a fine mist of water, then wiping the brake components clean with a dampened cloth. Dispose of cloth and all residue containing asbestos fibers in an impermeable container with the appropriate label. Follow practices prescribed by the Occupational Safety and Health Administration (OSHA) and the Environmental Protection Agency (EPA) for the handling, processing, and disposing of dust or debris that may contain asbestos fibers.

BRAKE CALIPER

REMOVAL & INSTALLATION

1. Before servicing the vehicle, refer to the Precautions Section.
2. Remove or disconnect the following:
   - Enough fluid from the master cylinder to place the level between Full and Minimum
   - Wheel
3. If the caliper is being repaired or replaced, remove the brake hose, cap the end, and discard the washers.
4. Remove the caliper bolts and lift the caliper off the bracket.
5. Brake pads

➡If any corrosion is found on the bolt shaft, replace the following:

- Bolt
- Bolt bushing
- Bolt boot

To install:

6. Make sure that the boots are properly installed. Bottom the caliper piston.
7. Install or connect the following:
   - Brake pads
   - Caliper. Do not lubricate the bolt threads. Lubricate the boots. Torque the bolts to 26 ft. lbs. (35 Nm).
   - Brake hose, using new washers. Torque the bolt to 40 ft. lbs. (54 Nm).
8. If the hose was disconnected, bleed the system.
9. Install the wheel.
10. Apply approximately 175 ft. lbs. of force to the brake pedal for 10 seconds

DISC BRAKE PADS

REMOVAL & INSTALLATION

See Figure 3.

1. Before servicing the vehicle, refer to the Precautions Section.
2. Remove the wheel.
3. Remove the lower caliper bolt.
4. Rotate the caliper up.
5. Remove the pads and pad retainers.

6. Remove enough fluid from the master cylinder to place the level between Full and Minimum
7. Bottom the piston.
8. Inspect the bolt boots and piston boot for tears or deterioration. Replace as necessary.

➡If any corrosion is found on the bolt shaft, replace the following:

- Bolt
- Bolt bushing
- Bolt boot

✳✳ WARNING

Never attempt to polish away the corrosion.

To install:

9. Install the pad retainers and pads. Make sure that the wear indicator is at the upper edge of the inner pad.
10. Rotate the caliper over the pads.
11. Apply a threadlocking compound meeting GM P/N 12345493 specs to the threads of the caliper bolt. Install the bolt and torque to 26 ft. lbs. (35 Nm).
12. Install the wheel.
13. Pump the brakes to seat the pads.

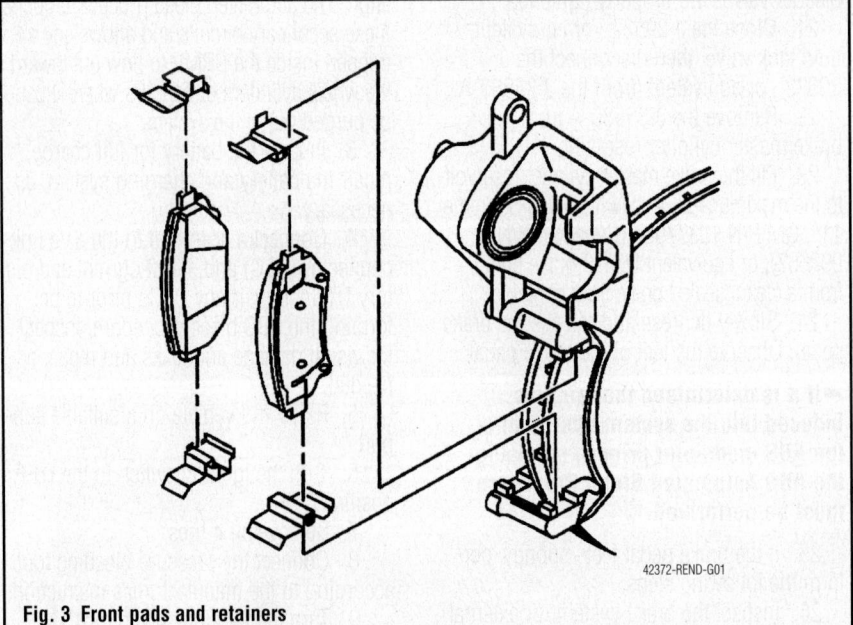

Fig. 3 Front pads and retainers

42372-REND-G01

BRAKES

REAR DISC BRAKES

BRAKE CALIPER

REMOVAL & INSTALLATION

1. Before servicing the vehicle, refer to the Precautions Section.
2. Remove or disconnect the following:
   • Enough fluid from the master cylinder to place the level between Full and Minimum
   • Wheel
3. If the caliper is being repaired or replaced, remove the brake hose, cap the end, and discard the washers.
4. Remove the caliper bolts and lift the caliper off the bracket.
5. Brake pads

➡**If any corrosion is found on the bolt shaft, replace the following:**

   • Bolt
   • Bolt bushing
   • Bolt boot

To install:

6. Make sure that the boots are properly installed. Bottom the caliper piston.
7. Install or connect the following:
   • Brake pads
   • Caliper. Do not lubricate the bolt threads. Lubricate the boots. Torque the bolts to 33 ft. lbs. (45 Nm).
   • Brake hose, using new washers. Torque the bolt to 40 ft. lbs. (54 Nm).
8. If the hose was disconnected, bleed the system.
9. Install the wheel.
10. Apply approximately 175 ft. lbs. of force to the brake pedal for 10 seconds.

DISC BRAKE PADS

REMOVAL & INSTALLATION

See Figure 4.

1. Before servicing the vehicle, refer to the Precautions Section.
2. Remove the wheel.
3. Remove the upper caliper bolt.
4. Rotate the caliper down.

5. Remove the pads and pad retainers.
6. Remove enough fluid from the master cylinder to place the level between Full and Minimum
7. Bottom the piston.
8. Inspect the bolt boots and piston boot for tears or deterioration. Replace as necessary.

➡**If any corrosion is found on the bolt shaft, replace the following:**

   • Bolt
   • Bolt bushing
   • Bolt boot

To install:

9. Install the pad retainers and pads. Make sure that the wear indicator is at the downward edge of the outer pad.
10. Rotate the caliper over the pads.
11. Install the bolt and torque to 33 ft. lbs. (45 Nm).
12. Install the wheel.
13. Pump the brakes to seat the pads.

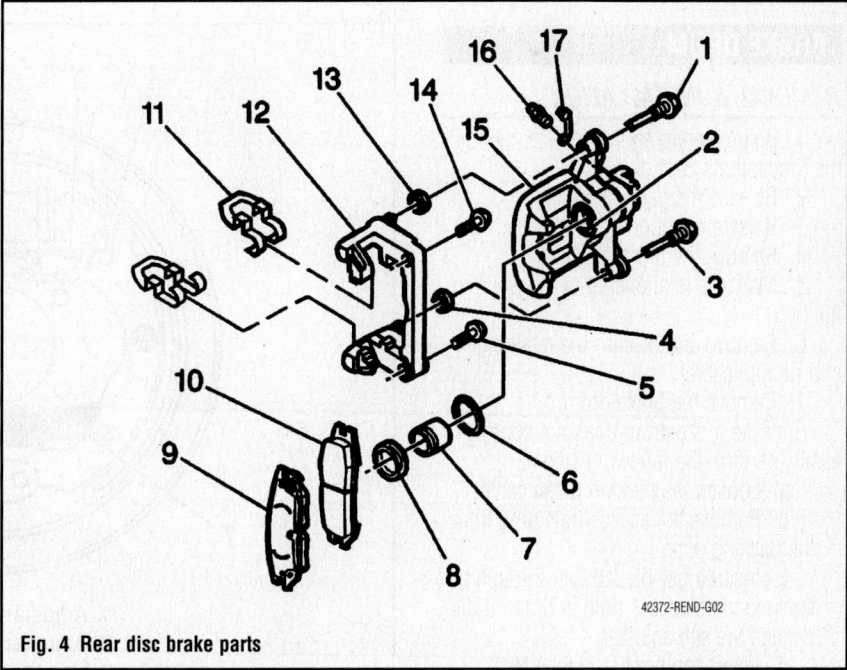

Fig. 4 Rear disc brake parts

42372-REND-G02

BRAKE DRUM

REMOVAL & INSTALLATION

1. Before servicing the vehicle, refer to the Precautions Section.
2. Release the parking brake.
3. Raise and support the vehicle.
4. Remove the tire and wheel.
5. Mark the relationship of the drum to the hub.
6. Remove and discard the retaining clip (if applicable).
7. Remove the brake drum.
8. If the brake drum does not come off easily, perform the following steps:
   a. Loosen the parking brake cable.
   b. Remove the access hole plug from the backing plate.
   c. Insert a flat-bladed tool through the backing plate access hole in order to disengage the self adjuster.
   d. Insert another flat-bladed tool through the same backing plate access hole in order to loosen the adjuster screw.
   e. Install the access hole plug in order to prevent dirt or contamination from entering the drum brake.
   f. Apply a small amount of penetrat-

ing oil around the brake drum center hole.
   g. Remove the brake drum.

To install:

➡**Align the marks on the brake drum and the hub made during the removal procedure.**

9. Install the brake drum.
10. Inspect the brake to shoe adjustment.
11. Install the tire and wheel.
12. Lower the vehicle.

BRAKE SHOES

REMOVAL & INSTALLATION
See Figure 5.

1. Before servicing the vehicle, refer to the Precautions Section.
2. Raise and support the vehicle.
3. Remove the brake drum.

➡**Do not over stretch the adjuster spring. Damage can occur if the spring is over stretched.**

4. Disengage the adjuster spring hook end from the tab on the adjuster actuator.

5. Remove the straight end of the adjuster spring from the brake shoe.
6. Remove the adjuster actuator from the brake shoe.
7. Remove the return spring from the brake shoes.
8. Remove the park brake cable from the park brake actuator lever.
9. Remove the brake shoe hold-down springs and retainers from the brake shoes.
10. Remove the adjuster from the brake shoes and the park brake actuator lever.
11. Remove the horseshoe clip retaining the park brake actuator lever to the brake shoe.
12. Remove the park brake actuator lever and wave washer from the brake shoe.
13. Clean all of the drum brake system components with denatured alcohol.
14. Inspect all of the drum brake system components.
15. Replace drum brake system components as necessary.
16. Inspect the wheel cylinder for the following conditions:
- Brake fluid leakage
- Worn or damaged dust boots

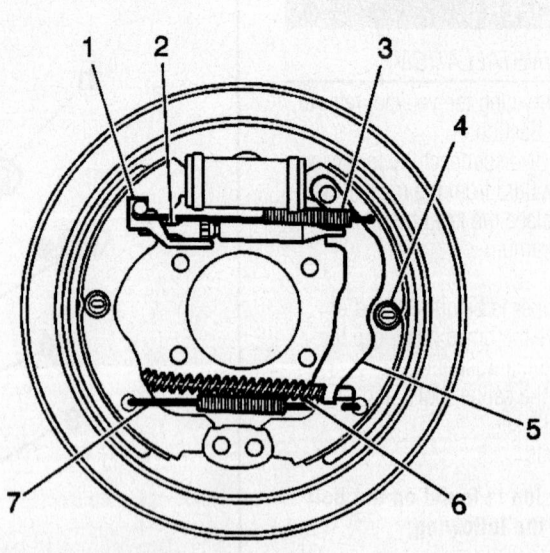

1. Adjuster actuator
2. Adjuster
3. Upper spring
4. Hold-down springs
5. Parking brake lever
6. Parking brake cable
7. Lower spring

06025-AZTEK-G01

Fig. 5 Drum brakes

17. Replace damaged or leaking wheel cylinders as necessary.

To install:

18. Apply GM P/N 1052196 (Canadian P/N 5264008) brake lubricant, or equivalent, to the following areas:
- The brake shoe contact points on the backing plate
- The adjuster screw threads
- The inside diameter of the adjuster socket

19. Install the park brake actuator lever and wave washer to the brake shoe.

20. Install the horseshoe clip to the park brake actuator lever pivot pin.

21. Install the brake shoes to the brake backing plate.

22. Install the brake shoe hold-down pins, springs and retainers to the brake shoes.

23. Install the park brake cable to the park brake actuator lever.

➡**Ensure that the adjuster engages the brake shoe and the park brake actuator properly.**

24. Install the adjuster screw to the brake shoe and the park brake actuator.

25. Apply GM P/N 1052196 (Canadian P/N 5264008) brake lubricant or equivalent to the adjuster actuator/brake shoe interface.

26. Install the adjuster actuator to the brake shoe.

➡**Do not over stretch the adjuster spring. Damage can occur if the spring is over stretched.**

27. Install the straight end of the adjuster spring to the brake shoe.

28. Install the adjuster spring hook end to the tab on the adjuster actuator.

29. Install the return spring to the brake shoes.

➡**Ensure that the adjuster operates properly.**

30. Move the park brake actuator lever in order to spread the brake shoes apart. The adjuster actuator lever should move downward, then upward as the park brake actuator lever is released, forcing the adjuster wheel to rotate. If the adjuster does not operate properly, remove then reinstall the adjuster.

31. Adjust the brake shoes.

32. Adjust the park brake cable.

33. Install the brake drum.

34. Lower the vehicle.

ADJUSTMENT

1. Raise and support the vehicle.

2. Remove the rear wheels and tires.

3. Relieve cable tension from the park brake system at the equalizer. there should be no tension on the park brake cables, so that the brake shoes are positioned only by the adjuster strut.

4. Remove the rear drums.

5. Set the J 21177-A so that the J 21177-A contacts the inside diameter of the drum at the widest point.

6. Position the J 21177-A over the shoes at the widest point.

7. Turn the adjuster nut until the shoes just contact the J 21177-A .

8. Repeat steps 2-7 for the other rear brake assembly.

9. Install the rear drums..

10. Install the rear wheels and tires.

11. Adjust the park brake cable system.

12. Lower the vehicle.

BRAKES

PARKING BRAKE

PARKING BRAKE CABLES

ADJUSTMENT

See Figures 6 and 7.

1. Before servicing the vehicle, refer to the Precautions Section.

2. Apply and fully release the parking brake six times.

3. Verify that the parking brake pedal releases completely.
   a. Turn ON the ignition. Verify that the BRAKE indicator lamp is off.
   b. If the BRAKE indicator lamp is on, ensure that the parking brake pedal is in release mode and fully returned to stop.
   c. Remove the slack in the front parking brake cable by pulling downward on the cable.

4. Raise and suitably support the vehicle.

5. Remove the rear wheels and tires.

6. Relieve tension on the park brake system at the park brake equalizer.

7. Remove both rear caliper bracket bolts.

❊❊ WARNING

Support the brake caliper with heavy mechanic's wire, or equivalent, whenever it is separated from its mount and the hydraulic flexible brake hose is still connected. Failure to support the caliper in this manner will cause the flexible brake hose to bear the weight of the caliper, which may cause damage to the brake hose and in turn may cause a brake fluid leak.

8. Remove brake caliper and bracket as one assembly. Do not disconnect the brake hose from the caliper.

9. Support the assembly with mechanic's wire, or equivalent.

10. Remove rear brake rotor.

11. Set the J 21177-A inside of the park brake drum at the widest point. Tighten the

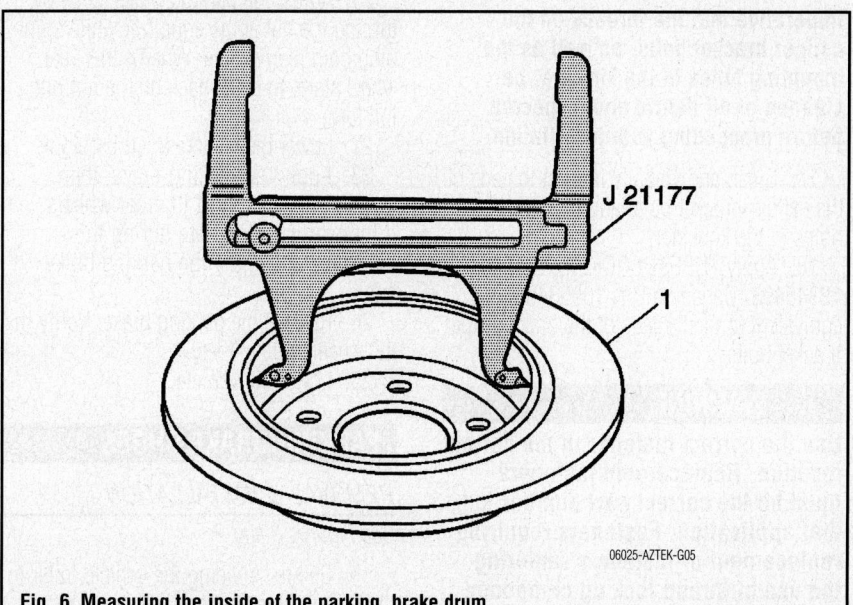

06025-AZTEK-G05

Fig. 6 Measuring the inside of the parking brake drum

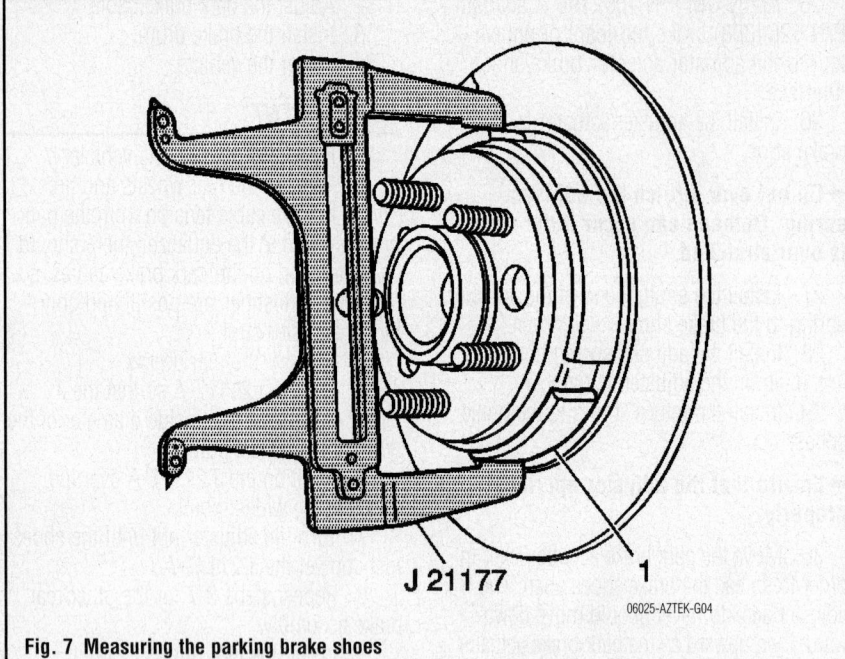

Fig. 7 Measuring the parking brake shoes

set screw on the tool to ensure the proper measurement when removing the tool from the drum.

12. Position the J 21177-A over the park brake shoe at the widest point.

13. Turn the adjuster on the actuator until the park brake shoe just contacts the J 21177-A.

14. Repeat these steps for the opposite side.

15. Install both rear brake rotors.

16. Install both rear brake calipers and brackets.

➡ To ensure that the proper clamp load will be present when installed. It is imperative that the threads on the caliper bracket bolts, as well as the mounting holes in the knuckle, be cleaned of all debris and inspected before proceeding with installation.

17. Clean and visually inspect threads of the caliper bracket bolts and mounting holes in the knuckle.

18. Apply THREADLOCKER, GM P/N 12345493 (Canadian P/N 10953488), or equivalent to the threads of the brake caliper bracket bolts.

✳✳ WARNING

Use the correct fastener in the correct location. Replacement fasteners must be the correct part number for that application. Fasteners requiring replacement or fasteners requiring the use of thread locking compound or sealant are identified in the service procedure. Do not use paints, lubricants, or corrosion inhibitors on fasteners or fastener joint surfaces unless specified. These coatings affect fastener torque and joint clamping force and may damage the fastener. Use the correct tightening sequence and specifications when installing fasteners in order to avoid damage to parts and systems.

19. Install the caliper bracket bolts. Tighten the brake caliper bracket bolts to 96 ft. lbs. (130 Nm).

20. Install the rear wheels and tires.

21. Adjust the parking brake cable by turning the nut at the equalizer while spinning both rear wheels. When either rear wheel starts to drag, back off the nut one full turn.

22. Lower the vehicle to curb height.

23. Apply the parking brake, then inspect for rotation of the rear wheels. If the rear wheels rotate during this inspection, readjust the parking brake cable.

24. Release the parking brake. Verify that the wheels rotate freely.

25. Lower the vehicle.

PARKING BRAKE SHOES

REMOVAL & INSTALLATION

See Figures 8 and 9.

1. Before servicing the vehicle, refer to the Precautions Section.

2. Raise and support the vehicle.

3. Remove the rear tire and wheel assemblies.

4. Relieve the park brake system tension at the equalizer assembly.

5. Remove the rear caliper bracket.

6. Remove the rear rotor.

7. Disconnect and remove the rear park brake cable from the bracket at the rear wheel.

8. Disconnect the park brake cable return spring from the park brake actuator and bracket at the rear wheel.

9. Remove the rear hub. The rear hub, backing plate, park brake cable bracket, and park brake actuator will be removed as an assembly.

10. Remove the 2 retainers and the park brake cable bracket from the park brake actuator. Position the rear hub aside.

11. Remove the park brake shoe and actuator from the backing plate.

12. Separate the park brake shoe from the actuator.

To install:

13. Assemble the park brake shoe to the actuator.

14. Install the park brake shoe and actuator onto the backing plate.

15. Position the park brake shoe, actuator, and backing plate over the rear hub.

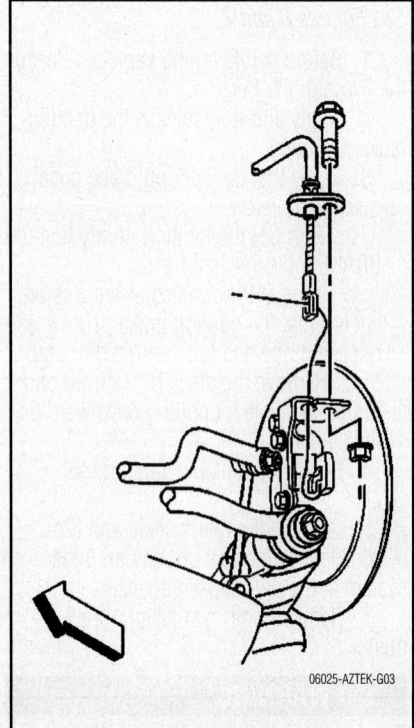

Fig. 8 Parking brake cable attachment—rear disc brakes

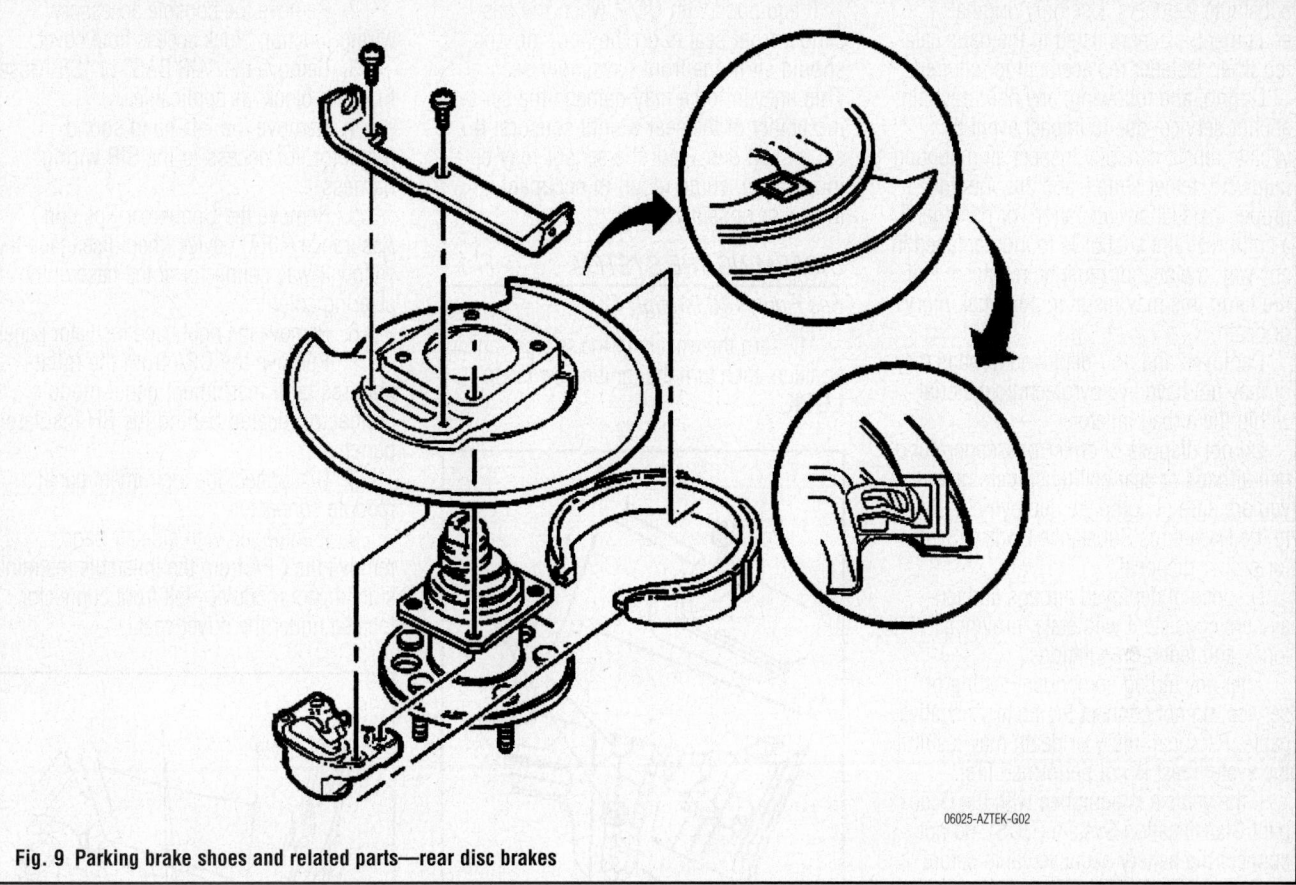

06025-AZTEK-G02

Fig. 9 Parking brake shoes and related parts—rear disc brakes

16. Install the park brake cable bracket and the two retainers.

17. Install the rear hub. The rear hub, backing plate, park brake cable bracket, and park brake actuator will be installed as an assembly.

18. Connect the rear park brake cable to the bracket at the rear wheel.

19. Connect the park brake cable return spring to the park brake actuator and bracket at the rear wheel.

20. Install the rear rotor.

21. Install the rear caliper bracket.

22. Install the rear tire and wheel assemblies.

23. Adjust the park brake system.

24. Lower the vehicle.

CHASSIS ELECTRICAL

AIR BAG (SUPPLEMENTAL RESTRAINT SYSTEM)

GENERAL INFORMATION

✳✳ CAUTION

These vehicles are equipped with an air bag system. The system must be disarmed before performing service on, or around, system components, the steering column, instrument panel components, wiring and sensors. Failure to follow the safety precautions and the disarming procedure could result in accidental air bag deployment, possible injury and unnecessary system repairs.

SERVICE PRECAUTIONS

Disconnect and isolate the battery negative cable before beginning any airbag system component diagnosis, testing, removal, or installation procedures. Allow system capacitor to discharge for two minutes before beginning any component service. This will disable the airbag system. Failure to disable the airbag system may result in accidental airbag deployment, personal injury, or death.

Do not place an intact undeployed airbag face down on a solid surface. The airbag will propel into the air if accidentally deployed and may result in personal injury or death.

When carrying or handling an undeployed airbag, the trim side (face) of the airbag should be pointing toward the body to minimize possibility of injury if accidental deployment occurs. Failure to do this may result in personal injury or death.

Replace airbag system components with OEM replacement parts. Substitute parts may appear interchangeable, but internal differences may result in inferior occupant protection. Failure to do so may result in occupant personal injury or death.

Wear safety glasses, rubber gloves, and long sleeved clothing when cleaning powder residue from vehicle after an airbag deployment. Powder residue emitted from a deployed airbag can cause skin irritation. Flush affected area with cool water if irritation is experienced. If nasal or throat irritation is experienced, exit the vehicle for fresh air until the irritation ceases. If irritation continues, see a physician.

Do not use a replacement airbag that is not in the original packaging. This may result in improper deployment, personal injury, or death.

The factory installed fasteners, screws and bolts used to fasten airbag components have a special coating and are specifically designed for the airbag system. Do not use substitute fasteners. Use only original equipment fasteners listed in the parts catalog when fastener replacement is required.

During, and following, any child restraint anchor service, due to impact event or vehicle repair, carefully inspect all mounting hardware, tether straps, and anchors for proper installation, operation, or damage. If a child restraint anchor is found damaged in any way, the anchor must be replaced. Failure to do this may result in personal injury or death.

Deployed and non-deployed airbags may or may not have live pyrotechnic material within the airbag inflator.

Do not dispose of driver/passenger/curtain airbags or seat belt tensioners unless you are sure of complete deployment. Refer to the Hazardous Substance Control System for proper disposal.

Dispose of deployed airbags and tensioners consistent with state, provincial, local, and federal regulations.

After any airbag component testing or service, do not connect the battery negative cable. Personal injury or death may result if the system test is not performed first.

If the vehicle is equipped with the Occupant Classification System (OCS), do not connect the battery negative cable before performing the OCS Verification Test using the scan tool and the appropriate diagnostic information. Personal injury or death may result if the system test is not performed properly.

Never replace both the Occupant Restraint Controller (ORC) and the Occupant Classification Module (OCM) at the same time. If both require replacement, replace one, then perform the Airbag System test before replacing the other.

Both the ORC and the OCM store Occupant Classification System (OCS) calibration data, which they transfer to one another when one of them is replaced. If both are replaced at the same time, an irreversible fault will be set in both modules and the OCS may malfunction and cause personal injury or death.

If equipped with OCS, the Seat Weight Sensor is a sensitive, calibrated unit and must be handled carefully. Do not drop or handle roughly. If dropped or damaged, replace with another sensor. Failure to do so may result in occupant injury or death.

If equipped with OCS, the front passenger seat must be handled carefully as well. When removing the seat, be careful when setting on floor not to drop. If dropped, the sensor may be inoperative, could result in occupant injury, or possibly death.

If equipped with OCS, when the passenger front seat is on the floor, no one should sit in the front passenger seat. This uneven force may damage the sensing ability of the seat weight sensors. If sat on and damaged, the sensor may be inoperative, could result in occupant injury, or possibly death.

DISARMING THE SYSTEM

See Figures 10 through 12.

1. Turn the wheels to the straight-ahead position, then turn the ignition switch to **LOCK**.

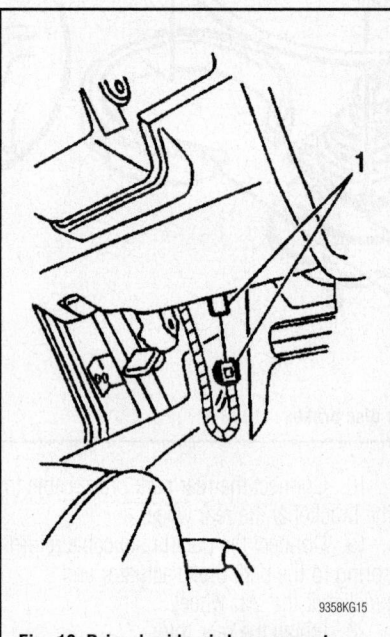

9358KG15

Fig. 10 Driver's side air bag connector location

2. Remove the console accessory wiring junction block access hole cover.

3. Remove the "AIR BAG" or "SIR" fuse from the block, as applicable.

4. Remove the left-hand sound insulator, for access to the SIR wiring harness.

5. Remove the Connector Position Assurance (CPA) device, then disengage the yellow 2-way connector at the base of the steering column.

6. Remove the right hand insulator panel.

7. Remove the CPA from the inflatable restraint instrument panel module connector located behind the RH insulator panel.

8. Disconnect the instrument panel module connector

9. If equipped with side air bags, remove the CPA from the inflatable restraint side impact module—left front connector located under the driver seat.

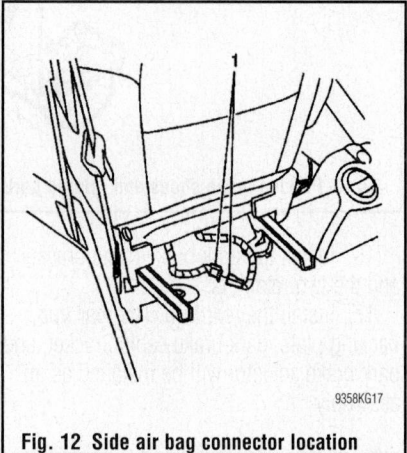

9358KG17

Fig. 12 Side air bag connector location

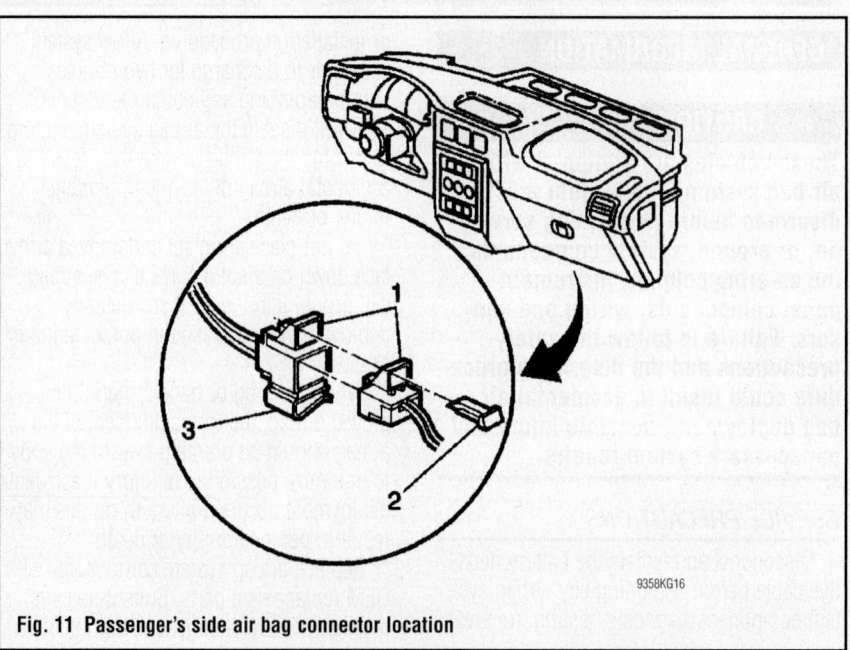

9358KG16

Fig. 11 Passenger's side air bag connector location

10. Disconnect the side impact module—left front connector.

11. Remove the CPA from the inflatable restraint side impact module—right front connector located under the front passenger seat.

12. Disconnect the side impact module—right front connector.

➡ **With the fuse removed, the AIR BAG or SIR light will illuminate if the ignition switch is turned ON at any time. This is normal and does not indicate a problem when the system is disarmed.**

ARMING THE SYSTEM

1. Be sure the ignition is in the **LOCK** position.

2. Connect the inflatable restraint side impact module—right front connector located under the front passenger seat.

3. Install the CPA to the side impact module—right front connector.

4. Connect the inflatable restraint side impact module—left front connector located under the driver seat.

5. Install the CPA to the side impact module—left front connector.

6. Engage the yellow SIR connector, then secure using the CPA device for both the drivers and passenger sides.

7. Install the sound insulator panel.

8. Install the SIR system fuse to the fuse block.

9. Turn the ignition switch to the **ON** position and verify that the AIR BAG indicator light flashes 7 times, then extinguishes. If it does not go out, troubleshoot the SIR system fault.

10. Install the instrument panel lower extension.

DRIVETRAIN

AUTOMATIC TRANSAXLE ASSEMBLY

REMOVAL & INSTALLATION

3.4L and 3.5L Engine

See Figure 13.

1. Install a suitable engine support fixture.

2. Remove or disconnect the following:
- Push pins from the coolant recovery bottle. Position the bottle aside.
- Air cleaner assembly
- Right side engine strut
- Transaxle range selector cable from the manual shaft
- Transaxle range selector cable bracket
- Wiring harness connectors from the transaxle
- Wiring harness bracket from the side cover
- Top four bell housing bolts
- Propeller shaft, if equipped
- Frame
- Transfer case lower brace
- Filler tube bracket retaining bolt
- Inspection cover
- Torque converter bolts
- Vehicle Speed Sensor (VSS) connector
- Right and left halfshafts from the transaxle
- Transmission cooler lines

3. Install a transmission jack under the transmission.
- Transfer case-to-engine mount bolts
- Lower transaxle bolts and stud
- Neutral safety switch connector
- Transaxle
- Transfer case from the transaxle

4. Flush the transaxle oil coolers, hoses and pipes.

To install:

5. Install or connect the following:
- Transfer case to the transaxle

6. Position the flex plate alignment hole to the seven O'clock position.

7. Align the transaxle filler tube to the transmission and install the transaxle into the vehicle.

8. Install or connect the following:
- Lower transaxle bolt and stud. Torque to 55 ft. lbs. (75 Nm).
- Wiring harness bracket to the side cover
- Neutral safety switch connector
- Transaxle brace
- Transmission cooler lines
- Right and left halfshafts
- VSS connector
- Transfer case lower brace. Torque bolts to 35 ft. lbs. (47 Nm).
- Torque converter bolts. Tighten the torque converter bolts to 46 ft. lbs. (63 Nm).
- Torque converter cover
- Filler tube bracket retaining bolt

➡ **Thoroughly clean and apply LOCTITE® DRI-LOC 201® (GM P/N 12345493, or equivalent) to the bolt threads prior to assembly.**

- Propeller shaft, if equipped. Ensure the special washer is in place on each pair of bolts. Tighten the bolts to 24 ft. lbs. (33 Nm).
- Front wheels

9. Lower vehicle and remove the engine support fixture
- Right side engine strut
- Upper transaxle bolts and stud. Torque to 55 ft. lbs. (75 Nm).
- Wiring harness the transaxle
- Range selector cable bracket
- Range selector cable on the manual shaft
- Air cleaner assembly
- Coolant recovery bottle.

10. Check and adjust the fluid level. Inspect for fluid leaks

3.6L Engine

1. Before servicing the vehicle, refer to the Precautions Section.

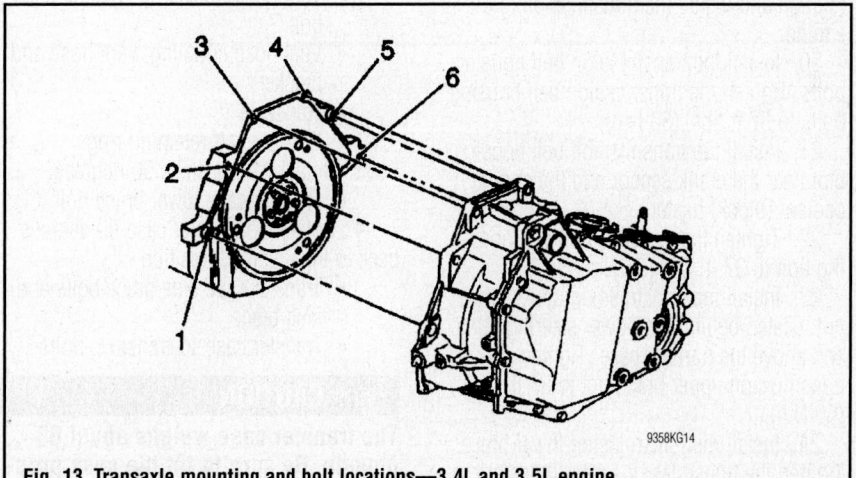

Fig. 13 Transaxle mounting and bolt locations—3.4L and 3.5L engine

9358KG14

➡Transmission oil circulates between the transmission assembly and the transfer case. In situations where transmission related failures circulate debris into the transfer case, the transfer case must be disassembled, cleaned, and inspected for damage.

2. Raise and support the vehicle.

3. Remove the transmission lower bell housing bolt located between the engine oil pan and the transmission oil pan.

4. Remove the powertrain (engine, transmission and frame) from the vehicle.

5. Remove the filler tube.

6. Remove the transmission bell housing bolts.

7. If the vehicle is equipped with all wheel drive (AWD), remove the transfer case brace.

8. Remove the coolant inlet pipe.

9. Remove the transmission mount with the transmission mount bracket.

10. Remove the starter motor.

11. Remove the torque converter bolts.

12. Remove the transmission lower brace.

13. Remove the transmission upper brace nut located behind the power steering pump and above the transfer case.

14. Remove the transmission bolt near the crank sensor and the engine coolant (block) heater.

15. Separate the transmission from the engine.

16. If the vehicle is equipped with AWD, remove the transfer case.

17. Flush the transaxle oil cooler and the transaxle oil cooler hoses.

To install:

18. If the vehicle is equipped with AWD, install the transfer case.

19. Use the dowel locator pins in order to align and install the transmission to the engine.

20. Install the transmission bell housing bolts. Tighten the transmission bell housing bolts to 37 ft. lbs. (50 Nm).

21. Install the transmission bell housing bolt near the crank sensor and the engine coolant (block) heater.

22. Tighten the transmission bell housing bolt to 37 ft. lbs. (50 Nm).

23. Install the transmission upper brace nut located behind the power steering pump and above the transfer case. Tighten the transmission upper brace nut to 37 ft. lbs. (50 Nm).

24. Install the transmission lower brace. Tighten the transmission upper brace nut to 37 ft. lbs. (50 Nm).

25. Install the torque converter bolts. Tighten the bolts to 47 ft. lbs. (63 Nm).

26. Install the starter motor.

27. Install the transmission mount with the transmission mount bracket. Start with the forward lower bolt and work clockwise to tighten the transaxle mount bracket bolts to 70 ft. lbs. (95 Nm).

28. Install the coolant inlet pipe.

29. If the vehicle is equipped with AWD, install the transfer case brace. Tighten the transfer case brace bolts to 37 ft. lbs. (50 Nm). Tighten the transfer case brace nuts to 37 ft. lbs. (50 Nm).

30. Install the filler tube.

31. Install the powertrain (engine, transmission and frame) to the vehicle.

32. Install the transmission lower bell housing bolt located between the engine oil pan and the transmission oil pan. Tighten the transmission bell housing bolt to 37 ft. lbs. (50 Nm).

33. Inspect and adjust the transaxle fluid level as needed.

TRANSFER CASE ASSEMBLY

REMOVAL & INSTALLATION

3.4L and 3.5L Engine

See Figures 14 through 16.

1. Before servicing the vehicle, refer to the Precautions Section.

2. Remove or disconnect the following:
- Propeller shaft
- Gear oil from the extension housing
- Transmission fluid from the case
- Speed sensor electrical connector
- Transfer case lower brace bolts and brace
- Clamp from the extension housing vent hose coupling
- Vent hose bracket-to-transfer case bolt
- Vent hose coupling, vent hose and bracket
- Transaxle
- Output shaft retaining ring

3. Rotate the transaxle 90 degrees.
- Transfer case lower brace bolt

4. Rotate the transfer case 90 degrees back to the installed position
- Transfer case side brace bolts and side brace
- Transfer case-to-transaxle bolts

❋❋ CAUTION

The transfer case weighs about 60 pounds. Be sure to lift the case properly, to avoid injury.

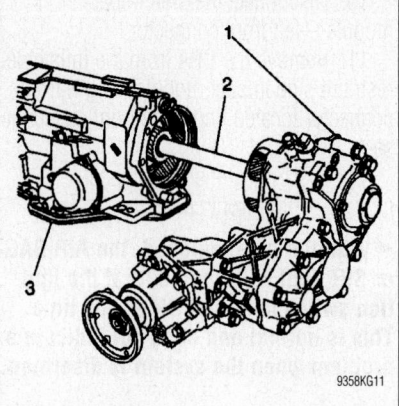

9358KG11

Fig. 14 Transfer case (1), output shaft (2) and transaxle (3)—3.4L and 3.5L engine

- Transfer case from the transaxle. Note that the output shaft withdraws from the transaxle with the transfer case.
- Output shaft
- Transfer case O-ring from the transfer case

To install:

5. Install or connect the following:
- O-ring seal to the transfer case

6. Rotate the transaxle so the bottom pan is facing the floor.
- Transfer case to the transaxle

7. Torque the transfer case bolts, in sequence, as follows:

a. Bolts 1 and 2: 26 ft. lbs. (35 Nm), plus an additional 160 degrees.

b. Bolt 3: 26 ft. lbs. (35 Nm), plus an additional 70 degrees.

c. Bolts 4 and 5: 30 ft. lbs. (40 Nm).

- Transfer case side brace. Tighten the bolts, in sequence, to 35 ft. lbs. (47 Nm).

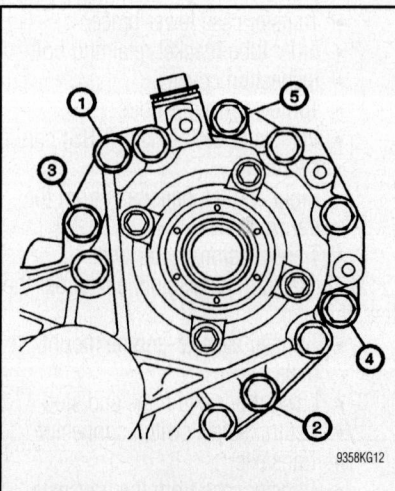

9358KG12

Fig. 15 Transfer case bolt tightening sequence—3.4L and 3.5L engine

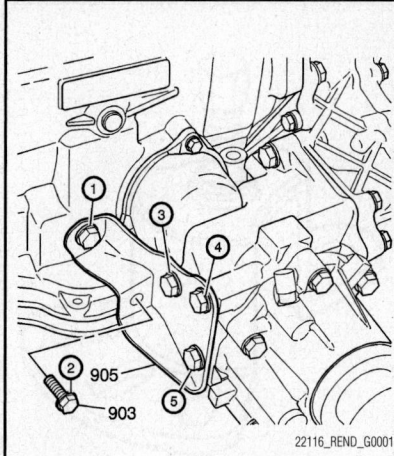

Fig. 16 Transfer case side brace bolt tightening sequence—3.4L and 3.5L engine

8. Rotate the transaxle 90 degrees.
- Transfer case lower brace-to-transaxle bolt. Torque the bolt to 35 ft. lbs. (47 Nm).
- Output shaft
- New output shaft retaining ring
- Transaxle
- Vent hose and coupling to the extension housing. Secure with the clamp.
- Vent hose bracket and bolt/stud. Tighten to 106 inch lbs. (10 Nm).
- Speed sensor electrical connector
- Propeller shaft
- Transfer case lower brace. Tighten the bolts to 35 ft. lbs. (47 Nm).
- Drain plugs and gaskets to the transfer case and extension housing. Torque the plugs to 24 ft. lbs. (32 Nm).

9. Check the transaxle fluid level.
10. Remove the extension housing fill plug and fill the housing with suitable gear oil. Install the plug and tighten to 24 ft. lbs. (32 Nm).

3.6L Engine

See Figures 17 and 18.

1. Before servicing the vehicle, refer to the Precautions Section.

➡Transmission oil circulates between the transmission assembly and the transfer case. In situations where transmission related failures circulate debris into the transfer case, the transfer case must be disassembled, cleaned, and inspected for damage.

2. Remove the drive shaft retaining ring.
3. Rotate the transaxle 90 degrees.

4. Remove the transfer case lower brace bolt.
5. Rotate the transaxle 90 degrees.
6. Remove the transfer case side brace bolts. Remove the side brace.
7. Remove the transfer case to case bolts.

✳✳ CAUTION

This component weighs approximately 60 lbs. Personal injury may result if you lift the component improperly.

➡During removal of the transfer case/output shaft, do not use excessive force or damage to the bushings may occur.

8. Remove the transfer case assembly from the transmission case.
9. Remove the transfer case lower brace bolts.
10. Remove the transfer case lower brace.
11. Remove the case extension seal from the transfer case.
12. Position the transaxle so that the case side cover is facing down.
13. Remove the oil dam from the transaxle.
14. Install the transfer case assembly onto a work stand.

To install:

15. Install the case extension seal.

➡The oil dam must be installed with the oil passage notch aligned to the passage in the case. Incorrect alignment will cause oil flow stoppage and damage to the transmission.

16. Line up the notch to the hole in the case and install the oil dam.
17. Install the transfer case lower brace.
18. Install the transfer case lower brace bolts. Hand tighten.

➡The park gear thrust bearing must be retained in the park gear when installing the transfer case to the transmission, or damage may occur.

➡When the transfer case is installed onto the transmission, there should be no gap between these parts. If a gap exists, check the park gear thrust bearing for proper retention to the park gear.

19. Install the transfer case assembly onto the transmission case.
20. Install the 5 transfer case to case bolts.

➡Do not use air powered tools in order to assemble or disassemble transmissions. Use hand tools in order to properly determine bolt tightness. Improper bolt torque can contribute to transmission repair conditions, and this information, which is vital to diagnosis, can only be detected when using hand tools.

➡Use the correct fastener in the correct location. Replacement fasteners must be the correct part number for that application. Fasteners requiring

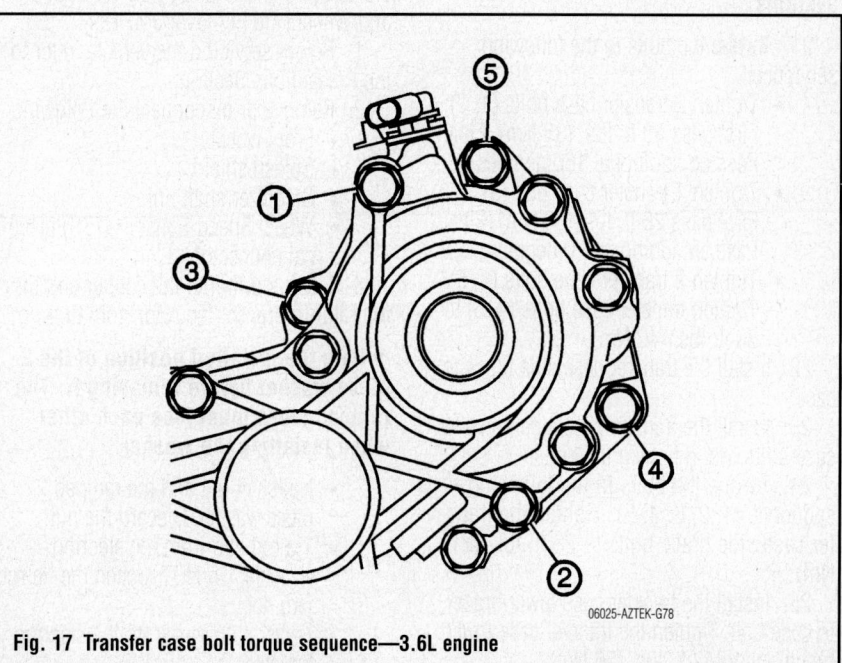

Fig. 17 Transfer case bolt torque sequence—3.6L engine

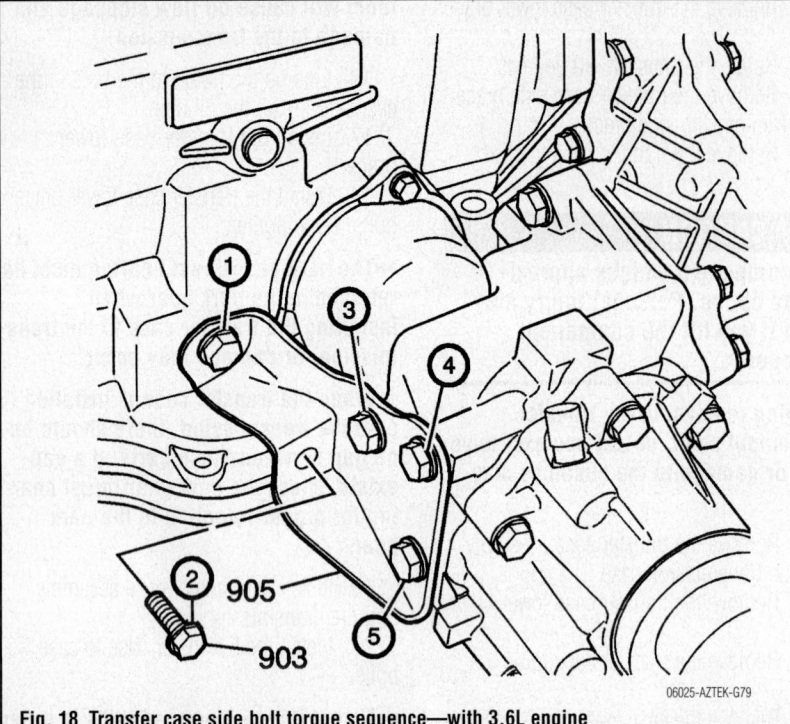

Fig. 18 Transfer case side bolt torque sequence—with 3.6L engine

06025-AZTEK-G79

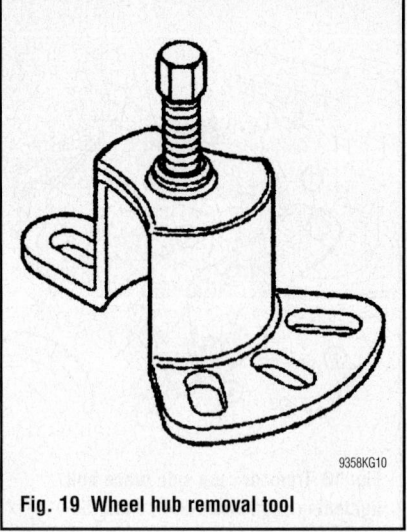

9358KG10

Fig. 19 Wheel hub removal tool

replacement or fasteners requiring the use of thread locking compound or sealant are identified in the service procedure. Do not use paints, lubricants, or corrosion inhibitors on fasteners or fastener joint surfaces unless specified. These coatings affect fastener torque and joint clamping force and may damage the fastener. Use the correct tightening sequence and specifications when installing fasteners in order to avoid damage to parts and systems.

21. Torque the bolts in the following sequence:

- Tighten 2 transfer case bolts (1, 2): First pass 26 ft. lbs. (35 Nm). Final Pass an additional 160 degrees
- Tighten 1 transfer case bolt (3): First pass 26 ft. lbs. (35 Nm). Final Pass an additional 70 degrees
- Tighten 2 transfer case bolts (4, 5): Tighten transfer case bolts (4, 5) to 30 ft. lbs. (40 Nm).

22. Install the transfer case side brace to case.

23. Install the transfer case side brace to case bolts. Hand tighten the bolts.

24. Torque the bolts in the following sequence (1, 2, 3, 4, 5). Tighten the transfer case side brace bolts to 23 ft. lbs. (31 Nm).

25. Install the transfer case lower brace to case bolt. Tighten the transfer case lower brace bolt to 42 ft. lbs. (56 Nm).

26. Tighten the transfer case lower brace to case bolts. Tighten the transfer case lower brace bolts to 23 ft. lbs. (31 Nm).

FRONT HALFSHAFT

REMOVAL & INSTALLATION

See Figures 19 through 21.

These procedures requires the use of the following special tools. Slide Hammer Tool No. J 2619-01, Axle Shaft Remover Extension J 29794, Axle Shaft Puller J 33008-A and Wheel Hub Remover J 42129.

1. Before servicing the vehicle, refer to the Precautions Section.

2. Remove or disconnect the following:

- Front wheel
- Splash shield
- Stabilizer shaft link
- Wheel Speed Sensor (WSS) electrical connector

3. Insert a drift into the caliper and into the rotor to prevent the rotor from turning.

➡Note the installed position of the 2-piece washer before removing it. The ramped sides must face each other when installing the washer.

- Halfshaft nut and the ramped 2-piece washer. Discard the nut.
- Tie rod end from the steering knuckle; Do NOT loosen the tie rod jam nut
- Lower ball joint from the steering knuckle

4. Install wheel hub removal tool (J 42129) onto the hub and secure with the lug nuts. Use the tool to disengage the halfshaft from the hub and bearing, then support the shaft.

5. Assemble the Slide Hammer Tool No. J 2619-01, Axle Shaft Remover Extension J 29794 and Axle Shaft Puller J 33008-A. Use the assembled tool to disengage the halfshaft from the transaxle.

6. Remove or disconnect the following:

- Halfshaft from the vehicle
- Halfshaft retaining ring and discard. On the right halfshaft, the retaining ring is on the splined shaft of the inner tripot housing. On the left halfshaft, the retaining ring is on the splined transmission output shaft.

To install:

7. Install or connect the following:

- New halfshaft retaining ring
- Halfshaft to the transaxle. Push the halfshaft into the transaxle until it is fully seated. Pull on the tri-pot joint

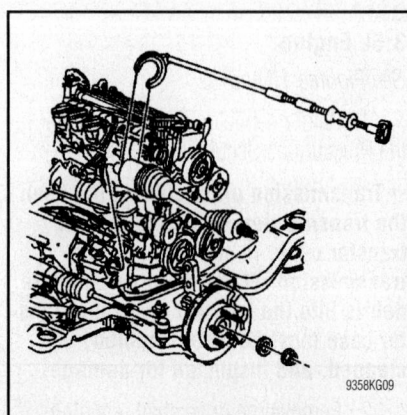

9358KG09

Fig. 20 Assemble the special tools to separate the halfshaft from the transaxle

to verify that the retaining ring is fully engaged.

✶✶ WARNING

Do not pull on the halfshaft bar.

- Halfshaft to the hub and bearing.
- Ball joint to the steering knuckle
- 2-piece washer. Make sure the ramped sides of the washer are facing each other.
- Drift through the caliper and into the rotor to prevent it from turning
- New halfshaft nut. Torque it to 192 ft. lbs. (260 Nm).
- Stabilizer shaft link. Torque the nut to 17 ft. lbs. (23 Nm).
- WSS electrical connector
- Splash shield
- Front wheel

8. Check the transaxle fluid level. Check and adjust the alignment as needed.

9. Road test the vehicle and check for any abnormal noise.

CV-JOINTS OVERHAUL

1. Before servicing the vehicle, refer to the Precautions Section.

2. Remove or disconnect the following:
- Halfshaft
- Large seal retaining clamp from the CV-joint and discard the clamp
- Swage ring by using a hand grinder to cut through it. Do not damage the axle shaft with the grinder
- Halfshaft outboard seal from the CV-joint outer race and slide the seal away from the joint
- CV-joint and boot from the half-shaft and discard the boot

3. Place a brass drift against the CV-joint cage and gently tap on it until it tilts.

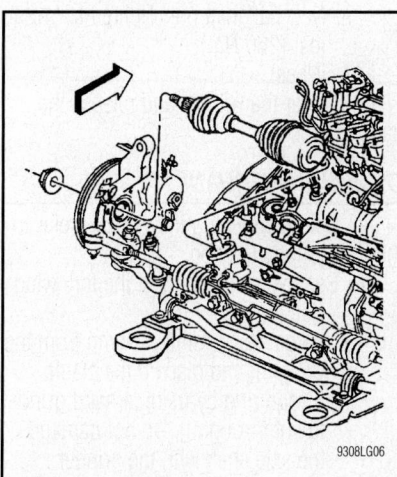

9308LG06

Fig. 21 Install the left side halfshaft

Remove the chrome alloy ball. Tilt the cage in the opposite direction and remove the ball. Continue to rotate the cage until all six alloy balls have been removed.

4. Pivot the cage and inner race 90 degrees to the center line of the of the outer race. Align the cage windows with the outer race lands. Lift the cage and the inner race out of the CV-joint.

5. Remove the inner race from the cage by rotating the race upward.

6. Clean the grease and contaminates with cleaning solvent from the inner/outer races; CV-joint cage and the alloy balls.

7. Remove any rust from the boot mounting area and clean the halfshaft bar.

To assemble:

8. Coat the inner and outer race grooves with grease and align the inner race with the windows of the cage.

9. Insert the inner race to the cage by rotating the race downward.

10. Insert the cage and inner race into the outer race.

11. Install the six alloy balls into the cage by tilting the cage. Repeat this process until all the balls are in place.

12. Pack the CV boot and joint with the grease supplied in the kit.

13. Install or connect the following:
- New boot clamp onto the boot
- CV boot on to the halfshaft bar and position the small end of the boot into the groove on the half-shaft bar. Secure the clamp to the boot with a Seal Clamp tool J 35910. Torque the clamp to 100 ft. lbs. (136 Nm).
- Swage ring over the large diameter of the boot by pinching the ring into an oval shape

➡ **Make certain that the retaining ring side of the inner race faces the half-shaft bar before installation.**

14. Slide the joint onto the halfshaft with the retaining snapring inside of the inner race. The race is properly seated when it snaps into place. Pull on the CV-joint to verify full engagement.

15. Install the large diameter of the boot with the large swage ring in place over the outside edge of the joint outer race.

16. Clamp the boot tightly to the outer race with the large swage ring by mounting Split Plate Swage Clamp tool J 36652 in a vise.

17. Position the outboard end of the halfshaft in the bottom of the tool.

18. Align the CV boot, joint and swage ring.

19. Install the top half of the tool and align the swage ring and clamp. Install the bolts to the top of the tool and tighten snugly. Tighten each bolt an additional 180 degrees. Alternate between the bolts until both sides of the top portion of the tool touch the bottom half.

20. Loosen the bolts and remove the split plate swage clamp tool.

21. Install the halfshaft.

22. Road test the vehicle and make certain there are no abnormal noises in the front end.

23. Check and adjust the alignment if necessary.

REAR AXLE HOUSING

REMOVAL & INSTALLATION

1. Before servicing the vehicle, refer to the Precautions Section.

2. Set the parking brake.

3. Drain the rear differential gear oil.

4. Remove or disconnect the following:
- Right rear tire and wheel
- Electrical connector from the clutch pump check valve
- Right rear halfshaft
- Front propeller shaft

5. Place an adjustable support beneath the torque tube.
- Torque tube-to-bracket through bolt and nut; loosen only
- Bolts from the torque tube bracket
- Differential carrier-to-cradle mounting bolts, nuts, washers, and mounts from the differential

➡ **During the removal of the wheel drive shaft, the differential output shaft may become disengaged from the differential. If this occurs, firmly grasp and separate the output shaft from the wheel drive shaft. Align the splines on the output shaft to the differential and reposition the output shaft to the differential.**

6. While simultaneously moving the differential assembly to the right side of the vehicle, disengage the left halfshaft from the differential.
- Rear differential and torque tube as an assembly
- Torque tube from the differential

To install:

7. Install or connect the following:
- Torque tube to the differential.
- Rear differential and torque tube assembly to the suspension cradle. Simultaneously guide the left wheel drive shaft onto the differential

output shaft while positioning the differential assembly to the suspension cradle.

8. Place an adjustable support under the torque tube. Ensure that the left wheel drive shaft is fully engaged to the differential output shaft.

- Differential carrier mounts, washers, bolts, and nuts to the differential. Torque the bolts to 37 ft. lbs. (50 Nm).
- Torque tube bracket-to-body bolts. Torque the torque tube bracket-to-body bolts to 41 ft. lbs. (55 Nm) and the torque tube-to-bracket through bolt and nut to 47 ft. lbs. (64 Nm).
- Front propeller shaft
- Right rear wheel halfshaft
- Tire and wheel assembly
- Differential drain plug and gasket. Tighten the drain plug to 22 ft. lbs. (30 Nm).

9. Fill the axle with synthetic gear oil. Check the differential oil level to ensure it is even with, to no lower than, 0.25 in. (6mm) below the opening of the fill hole.

- Differential fill plug and gasket. Tighten the fill plug to 22 ft. lbs. (30 Nm).
- Clutch pump check valve connector

10. Remove the adjustable support from the torque tube.

11. Operate the vehicle making tight left, then right turns in order to engage the All-Wheel-Drive (AWD) system and distribute the gear oil throughout the differential.

12. Fill the axle with synthetic gear oil. Check the differential oil level to ensure it is even with, to no lower than, 0.25 in. (6mm) below the opening of the fill hole.

REAR AXLE SHAFT, BEARING & SEAL

REMOVAL & INSTALLATION

1. Before servicing the vehicle, refer to the Precautions Section.
2. Remove or disconnect the following:
   - Rear tire and wheel assembly
   - Rear halfshaft
   - Differential output shaft oil seal. Do not damage the differential sealing surfaces.

To install:

3. Install or connect the following:
   - Left axle shaft oil seal, using the J 44809

➡Inspect the sealing surface of the wheel drive shaft inner tri-pot housing

to ensure it is free of corrosion. Use a crocus cloth in order to remove any light corrosion and clean the sealing surface with denatured alcohol, or equivalent.

4. Lubricate the wheel drive shaft sealing surface of the oil seal with synthetic gear oil.
   - Left wheel halfshaft
   - Tire and wheel assembly
5. Inspect the differential lubricant level.

REAR HALFSHAFT

REMOVAL & INSTALLATION

1. Before servicing the vehicle, refer to the Precautions Section.
2. Apply the parking brake.
3. Remove or disconnect the following:
   - Rear wheel
   - Halfshaft nut and discard
4. Release the parking brake.
   - Brake caliper bracket and support it with a piece of wire
   - Parking brake cable routing bracket nut, if necessary
   - Rear tie rod end-to-knuckle bolt; DO NOT loosen the tie rod end jam nut
   - Parking brake cable bracket-to-knuckle bolts; loosen only.
   - Wheel Speed Sensor (WSS) electrical connector
5. Install the Wheel Hub Removal Tool No. K 42129 onto the wheel hub and secure with wheel nuts. Begin to disengage the halfshaft from the hub and bearing.
   - Bolt and nut securing the upper control arm to the suspension knuckle
   - Halfshaft completely from the hub and bearing
6. Reposition the suspension knuckle toward the rear of the vehicle.
   - Tool from the wheel hub

➡Support the halfshaft until it is completely removed from the vehicle.

7. Assemble the Slide Hammer Tool No. J 2619-01, Axle Shaft Remover Extension J 29794 and Axle Shaft Puller J 33008-A. Install the Axle Shaft Puller evenly onto the rear beveled surface of the halfshaft inner joint housing.
   - Halfshaft from the rear axle differential using the assembled tools
   - Halfshaft from the vehicle

➡The differential output shaft oil seal must be replaced when removing the rear wheel drive shaft.

   - Halfshaft oil seal

To install:

> ✳✳ **WARNING**
>
> Support the wheel drive shaft until it is completely installed.

8. Install or connect the following:
   - Halfshaft to the differential output shaft. Carefully align and guide the halfshaft onto the differential output shaft.

> ✳✳ **WARNING**
>
> Be careful not to damage the differential output shaft oil seal.

   - Halfshaft fully onto the differential output shaft using light force. Make sure it is fully seated on the differential output shaft retaining ring by grasping the inner tripot housing and pulling outward. Do not pull on the wheel drive shaft bar. The halfshaft will remain firmly in place when properly engaged.

9. Begin to position the suspension knuckle to the halfshaft. Align and carefully guide the halfshaft into the hub and bearing but do not seat fully.
   - Suspension knuckle to the upper control arm
   - Bolt and nut to the upper control arm/suspension knuckle assembly. Torque the bolt to 63 ft. lbs. (85 Nm).
   - Parking brake cable bracket.
   - Tie rod to the knuckle. Tighten the bolt to 63 ft. lbs. (85 Nm).
   - Brake caliper bracket
   - WSS electrical connector
   - Parking brake cable routing bracket, if removed. Tighten the nuts to 89 inch lbs. (10 Nm).

10. Set the park brake.
   - New halfshaft nut. Tighten to 192 ft. lbs. (260 Nm).
   - Wheel

11. Lower the vehicle and release the parking brake.

CV-JOINT OVERHAUL

1. Before servicing the vehicle, refer to the Precautions Section.
2. Remove or disconnect the following:
   - Halfshaft
   - Large seal retaining clamp from the CV-joint and discard the clamp
   - Swage ring by using a hand grinder to cut through it. Do not damage the axle shaft with the grinder
   - Halfshaft outboard seal from the CV-joint outer race and slide the seal away from the joint

- CV-joint and boot from the half-shaft and discard the boot

3. Place a brass drift against the CV-joint cage and gently tap on it until it tilts. Remove the chrome alloy ball. Tilt the cage in the opposite direction and remove the ball. Continue to rotate the cage until all six alloy balls have been removed.

4. Pivot the cage and inner race 90 degrees to the center line of the of the outer race. Align the cage windows with the outer race lands. Lift the cage and the inner race out of the CV-joint.

5. Remove the inner race from the cage by rotating the race upward.

6. Clean the grease and contaminates with cleaning solvent from the inner/outer races; CV-joint cage and the alloy balls.

7. Remove any rust from the boot mounting area and clean the halfshaft bar.

To assemble:

8. Coat the inner and outer race grooves with grease and align the inner race with the windows of the cage.

9. Insert the inner race to the cage by rotating the race downward.

10. Insert the cage and inner race into the outer race.

11. Install the six alloy balls into the cage by tilting the cage. Repeat this process until all the balls are in place.

12. Pack the CV boot and joint with the grease supplied in the kit.

13. Install or connect the following:
- New boot clamp onto the boot
- CV boot on to the halfshaft bar and position the small end of the boot into the groove on the half-shaft bar. Secure the clamp to the boot with a Seal Clamp tool J 35910. Torque the clamp to 100 ft. lbs. (136 Nm).
- Swage ring over the large diameter of the boot by pinching the ring into an oval shape

➡**Make certain that the retaining ring side of the inner race faces the half-shaft bar before installation.**

14. Slide the joint onto the halfshaft with the retaining snapring inside of the inner race. The race is properly seated when it snaps into place. Pull on the CV-joint to verify full engagement.

15. Install the large diameter of the boot with the large swage ring in place over the outside edge of the joint outer race.

16. Clamp the boot tightly to the outer race with the large swage ring by mounting Split Plate Swage Clamp tool J 36652 in a vise.

17. Position the outboard end of the halfshaft in the bottom of the tool.

18. Align the CV boot, joint and swage ring.

19. Install the top half of the tool and align the swage ring and clamp. Install the bolts to the top of the tool and tighten snugly. Tighten each bolt an additional 180 degrees. Alternate between the bolts until both sides of the top portion of the tool touch the bottom half.

20. Loosen the bolts and remove the split plate swage clamp tool.

21. Install the halfshaft.

22. Road test the vehicle and make certain there are no abnormal noises in the front end.

23. Check and adjust the alignment if necessary.

REAR PINION SEAL

REMOVAL & INSTALLATION

See Figure 22.

1. Before servicing the vehicle, refer to the Precautions Section.

2. Drain the differential lubricant.

3. Remove or disconnect the following:
- Torque tube assembly.
- Drive pinion oil seal from the drive pinion housing and discard
- Pinion housing-to-differential bolts
- Drive pinion and housing assembly
- Drive pinion housing shim from the differential
- O-ring seal from the drive pinion housing and discard

To install:

4. Lubricate the O-ring seal with synthetic gear oil.

5. Install or connect the following:
- Oil seal to the drive pinion housing, using a seal installation tool
- O-ring seal to the drive pinion housing
- Drive pinion housing assembly and shim to the differential carrier
- Pinion housing-to-differential mounting bolts. Torque the bolts to 21 ft. lbs. (28 Nm).

6. Lubricate the sealing surfaces of the drive pinion oil seal with synthetic gear oil.

- Torque tube assembly.

7. Fill the differential with synthetic gear oil.

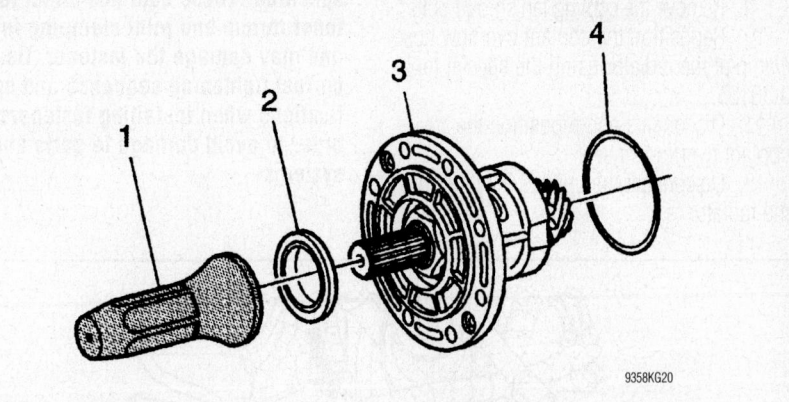

9358KG20

Fig. 22 View of the seal installer (1), drive pinion housing shim (2), differential (3) and O-ring (4)

ENGINE COOLING

ENGINE FAN

REMOVAL & INSTALLATION

See Figure 23.

> **✳✳ CAUTION**
>
> **An electric fan under the hood can start up even when the engine is not running and can injure you. Keep hands, clothing and tools away from any underhood electric fan.**

> **✳✳ CAUTION**
>
> **To help avoid personal injury or damage to the vehicle, a bent, cracked, or damaged fan blade or housing should always be replaced.**

1. Remove the air cleaner and duct assembly.
2. Remove the cooling fan harness electrical connector.
3. Remove right side diagonal brace.
4. Loosen the engine mount strut nuts.
5. Remove the engine mount strut bracket brace bolts from the upper radiator support and rotate the struts and brackets rearward.
6. Remove upper radiator hose.
7. Remove the radiator upper mount bolts.
8. Remove the radiator upper mounts.
9. Remove the cooling fan shroud bolts.
10. Reposition the coolant overflow hose clamp at the radiator using the special tool J 38185.
11. Disconnect and reposition the coolant overflow hose.
12. Disconnect the upper TOC line from the radiator.

13. Raise the vehicle.
14. Disconnect the TOC lines from the fan module retainer clip.
15. Lower the vehicle.
16. Disconnect the engine wiring harness retainers at the engine harness bracket.
17. Reposition the engine wiring harness. Remove the cooling fans with the cooling fan shroud.

To install:

18. Install the cooling fans with the cooling fan shroud.
19. Reposition the engine wiring harness.
20. Connect the engine wiring harness retainers at the engine harness bracket.
21. Raise the vehicle.
22. Connect the TOC lines to the fan module retainer clip.
23. Lower the vehicle.
24. Connect the upper TOC line to the radiator.

➡ **Use the correct fastener in the correct location. Replacement fasteners must be the correct part number for that application. Fasteners requiring replacement or fasteners requiring the use of thread locking compound or sealant are identified in the service procedure. Do not use paints, lubricants, or corrosion inhibitors on fasteners or fastener joint surfaces unless specified. These coatings affect fastener torque and joint clamping force and may damage the fastener. Use the correct tightening sequence and specifications when installing fasteners in order to avoid damage to parts and systems.**

25. Install the cooling fan shroud bolts and tighten them to 53 inch lbs. (6 Nm).
26. Install the radiator upper mounts.
27. Install the radiator upper mount bolts and tighten them to 88 inch lbs. (10 Nm).
28. Install the coolant overflow hose to the radiator.
29. Reposition the hose clamp to secure the coolant overflow hose using the special tool J 38185.
30. Install the upper radiator hose.
31. Position the engine mount struts brackets flush with the upper radiator support.
32. Install the engine mount strut bracket brace bolts to the upper radiator support and tighten them to 21 ft. lbs. (28 Nm).
33. Tighten the engine mount strut nuts to 35 ft. lbs. (48 Nm).
34. Install right side diagonal brace.
35. Install the cooling fan harness electrical connector.
36. Install the air cleaner and duct assembly.

RADIATOR

REMOVAL & INSTALLATION

1. Recover the refrigerant from the A/C system.
2. Drain the cooling system.
3. Remove the cooling fans with the cooling fan shroud.
4. Reposition the hose clamp at the water pump housing using the special tool J 38185
5. Disconnect the radiator outlet hose from the water pump housing.
6. Raise the vehicle.
7. Reposition the hose clamp at the radiator using special tool J 38185.
8. Disconnect the radiator outlet hose from the radiator.
9. Remove the radiator outlet hose.
10. Disconnect the lower TOC line from the radiator.
11. Lower the vehicle.
12. Remove the nut which secures the A/C discharge hose to the condenser block.
13. Disconnect the A/C discharge hose from the condenser block.
14. Remove and discard the sealing washer.

➡ **Cap or tape off the open A/C hose immediately to prevent system contamination.**

15. Cap or tape off the A/C discharge hose.

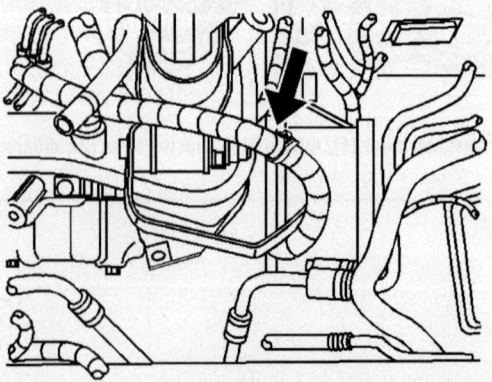

32085_AZTE_G0011

Fig. 23 Removal and installation of the wiring harness retainers (arrow)

16. Remove the bolt which secures the evaporator inlet tube to the condenser block.

17. Disconnect the evaporator inlet tube from the condenser block.

18. Cap or tape off the evaporator inlet tube.

19. Remove the radiator and condenser assembly.

20. Remove the condenser tube clip bolt.

21. Remove the condenser mounting bolts.

22. Remove the condenser from the radiator.

To install:

23. Install the condenser to the radiator.

➡Use the correct fastener in the correct location. Replacement fasteners must be the correct part number for that application. Fasteners requiring replacement or fasteners requiring the use of thread locking compound or sealant are identified in the service procedure. Do not use paints, lubricants, or corrosion inhibitors on fasteners or fastener joint surfaces unless specified. These coatings affect fastener torque and joint clamping force and may damage the fastener. Use the correct tightening sequence and specifications when installing fasteners in order to avoid damage to parts and systems.

24. Install the mounting bolts that secure the condenser to the radiator and tighten them to 53 inch lbs. (6 Nm).

25. Install the condenser tube clip bolt and tighten to 22 inch lbs. (2.5 Nm).

26. Install the radiator and condenser assembly.

27. Remove the cap or the tape from the evaporator inlet tube.

28. Install a new seal washer to the evaporator inlet tube.

29. Install the evaporator inlet tube and the bolt to the condenser block and tighten them to 12 ft. lbs. (16 Nm).

30. Remove the cap or the tape from the A/C discharge hose.

31. Install a new sealing washer to the A/C discharge hose.

32. Install the A/C discharge hose and the nut to the condenser block and tighten the nut to 12 ft. lbs. (16 Nm).

33. Raise the vehicle.

34. Connect the lower TOC line to the radiator.

35. Install the radiator outlet hose.

36. Connect the radiator outlet hose to the radiator.

37. Reposition the hose clamp at the

radiator to secure the hose using special tool J 38185.

38. Lower the vehicle.

39. Connect the radiator outlet hose to the water pump housing.

40. Reposition the hose clamp at the water pump housing to secure the hose using the special tool J 38185.

41. Install the cooling fans with the cooling fan shroud..

42. Fill the cooling system.

43. Evacuate and recharge the A/C system.

44. Leak test the fittings of the component using the special tool J 38185.

45. Inspect the transmission fluid level.

THERMOSTAT

REMOVAL & INSTALLATION

3.4L and 3.5L Engine

See Figures 24 and 25.

1. Remove the air cleaner and duct assembly.

2. Drain the coolant until the coolant level is below the thermostat.

3. Remove the crossover exhaust pipe.

4. Remove the radiator hose from the thermostat housing.

5. Remove the thermostat housing bolts and clean any sealer from the bolt threads.

6. Remove the thermostat housing and gasket.

7. Remove the thermostat.

8. Clean the mating surfaces.

To install:

9. Install the thermostat.

10. Install the thermostat housing and gasket.

➡Use the correct fastener in the correct location. Replacement fasteners must be the correct part number for that application. Fasteners requiring replacement or fasteners requiring the use of thread locking compound or

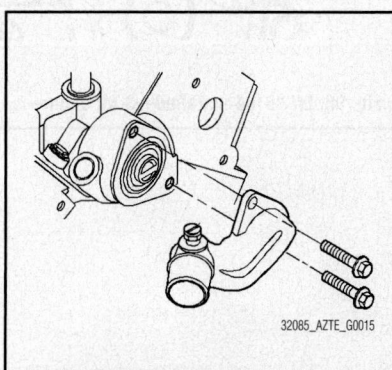

Fig. 24 Remove the housing bolts

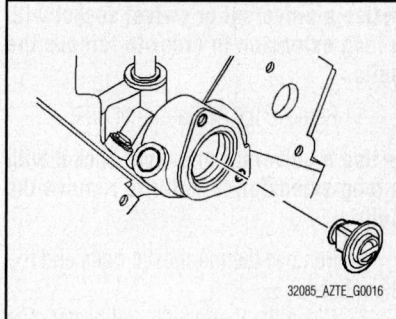

Fig. 25 The removal and installation of the thermostat

sealant are identified in the service procedure. Do not use paints, lubricants, or corrosion inhibitors on fasteners or fastener joint surfaces unless specified. These coatings affect fastener torque and joint clamping force and may damage the fastener. Use the correct tightening sequence and specifications when installing fasteners in order to avoid damage to parts and systems.

11. Install the thermostat housing bolts and tighten them to 18 ft. lbs. (25 Nm).

12. Install the radiator hose to the thermostat housing.

13. Install the crossover exhaust pipe.

14. Install the air cleaner and duct assembly.

15. Fill the cooling system.

3.6L Engine

See Figure 26.

1. Remove the air cleaner.

2. Remove the throttle body assembly.

3. Remove the heater pipes.

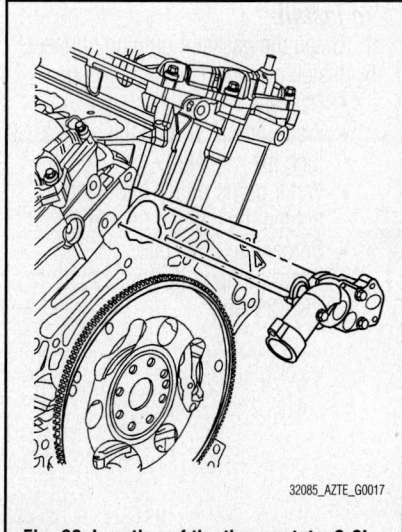

Fig. 26 Location of the thermostat—3.6L Engine

➡**Use a universal or swivel socket with a long extension in order to remove the bolts.**

4. Remove the coolant inlet pipe.

➡**Use a universal or swivel socket with a long extension in order to remove the bolts.**

5. Remove the thermostat bolts and the thermostat.

6. Clean the thermostat and heater pipe sealing surfaces.

To install:

7. Install a NEW thermostat gasket.

8. Install the thermostat and gasket.

9. Install the thermostat bolts and tighten them to 89 inch lbs. (10 Nm).

10. Install the coolant inlet pipe.

11. Install the heater pipes.

12. Install the throttle body assembly.

13. Install the air cleaner.

14. Fill the cooling system.

WATER PUMP

REMOVAL & INSTALLATION

3.4L and 3.5L Engine

See Figure 27.

1. Before servicing the vehicle, refer to the Precautions Section.

2. Drain the coolant from the engine.

3. Remove or disconnect the following:
   • Negative battery cable
   • Serpentine drive belt guard
   • Loosen the water pump pulley bolts
   • Serpentine drive belt
   • Water pump pulley
   • Water pump
   • Water pump gasket

To install:

4. Clean the gasket mounting surfaces.

5. Install or connect the following:
   • Gasket
   • Water pump. Torque the bolts to 89 inch lbs. (10 Nm).
   • Water pump pulley and hand-tighten the bolts at this time
   • Serpentine drive belt
   • Water pump pulley bolts to 18 ft. lbs. (25 Nm)

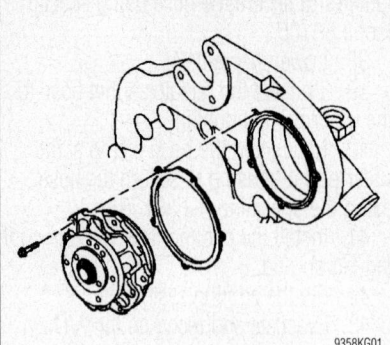

Fig. 27 Exploded view of the water pump—3.4L and 3.5L engine

   • Serpentine drive belt guard

6. Fill the cooling system.

7. Start the engine and check for leaks, repair if necessary.

8. Road test the vehicle and verify there is no air in the cooling system.

3.6L Engine

See Figure 28.

1. Before servicing the vehicle, refer to the Precautions Section.

2. Install the EN 46104 onto the water pump pulley.

3. Remove the water pump pulley bolts.

4. Remove the water pump pulley.

5. Remove the water pump bolts.

6. Remove the water pump from the front cover.

7. Remove the water pump gasket.

To install:

8. Ensure that the engine front cover and water pump are clear of old gasket material.

9. Place a new water pump gasket on the water pump.

10. Place the water pump in position on the front cover.

11. Install the water pump bolts. Tighten the water pump bolts to 89 inch lbs. (10 Nm).

12. Install the water pump pulley.

13. Loosely install the water pump pulley bolts.

14. Install the EN 46104 onto the water pump pulley. Tighten the water pump pulley bolts to 89 inch lbs. (10 Nm).

Fig. 28 EN 46104 installed—3.6L engine

ENGINE ELECTRICAL   **CHARGING SYSTEM**

ALTERNATOR

REMOVAL & INSTALLATION

3.4L and 3.5L Engine

1. Before servicing the vehicle, refer to the Precautions Section.
2. Remove or disconnect the following:
   - Negative battery cable
3. Rotate the engine forward.
   - Alternator terminal nut, lead and electrical connector
   - Serpentine belt
   - Front bolts and two rear bolts
   - Alternator from the bracket; position it above the drive axle
   - Serpentine belt tensioner
   - Bracket
   - Power steering pipes from the retainer
   - Fuel pressure test port cap from the injector rail

➡ **Do not disconnect the power steering pipes from the pump**

   - Power steering pump and reposition it to gain access to the alternator
   - Alternator

To install:

4. Install or connect the following:
   - Alternator
   - Electrical harness to the right fender well retainer
   - Power steering pump. Torque the bolts to 25 ft. lbs. (34 Nm).
   - Fuel pressure test port cap to the fuel rail
   - Power steering pipes to the retainer. Torque the fastener to 54 inch lbs. (6 Nm).
   - Alternator bracket. Torque the bolt to 37 ft. lbs. (50 Nm).
   - Serpentine belt tensioner
   - Alternator to the bracket. Torque the bolts to 37 ft. lbs. (50 Nm).
   - Serpentine belt
   - Alternator electrical connector, lead and nut. Torque the nut to 115 inch lbs. (13 Nm).
5. Rotate the engine to its original position.
   - Negative battery cable

6. Perform a charging system test and verify the proper operation of the system.

3.6L Engine

See Figure 29.

1. Before servicing the vehicle, refer to the Precautions Section.
2. Disconnect the battery ground (negative) cable from the battery
3. Remove the torque struts and rotate the engine in order to provide access to remove the alternator.
4. Remove the bolts and the nuts from the engine mount struts brackets on the engine.
5. Remove the bolt and the nut from the engine mount strut at the engine mount strut bracket on the upper radiator support.
6. Remove the engine mount strut.
7. Remove the alternator B+ terminal nut and the battery cable from the alternator.
8. Disconnect the alternator electrical connector.
9. Remove the drive belt from the alternator.
10. Remove the idler pulley.

11. Remove the alternator bolts.
12. Remove the alternator from the vehicle.

To install:

13. Install the alternator to the vehicle.
14. Install the alternator bolts. Tighten the alternator bolts to 37 ft. lbs. (50 Nm).
15. Install the idler pulley.
16. Install the drive belt.
17. Connect the alternator electrical connector.
18. Install the battery cable and the alternator B+ terminal nut to the alternator. Tighten the alternator B+ terminal nut 15 ft. lbs. (20 Nm).
19. Install the torque struts.
20. Install the bolt and the nut to the engine mount strut at the engine mount strut bracket on the upper radiator support. HAND TIGHTEN ONLY.
21. Install the bolt and the nut to the engine mount strut at the engine mount strut bracket on the engine.
22. Tighten engine mount strut nuts to 35 ft. lbs. (48 Nm).
23. Connect the battery ground (negative) cable to the battery.

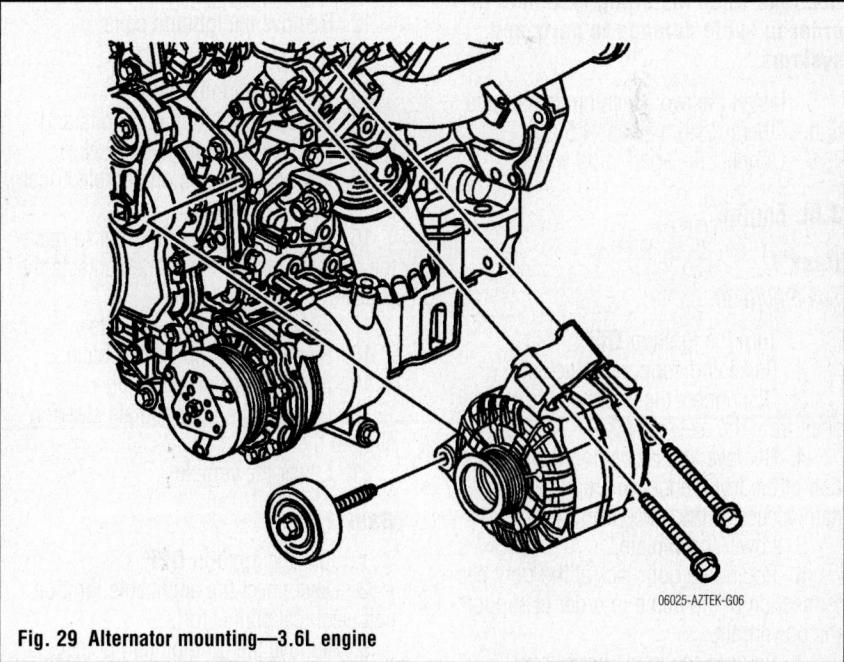

06025-AZTEK-G06

Fig. 29 Alternator mounting—3.6L engine

IGNITION COIL

REMOVAL & INSTALLATION

3.4L and 3.5L Engine

1. Disconnect the spark plug wires. Note the position from which the wires are removed.
2. Remove the 2 screws that secure the ignition coil to the ignition control module.
3. Remove the ignition coil.

To install:

4. Install the ignition coil.

➡Use the correct fastener in the correct location. Replacement fasteners must be the correct part number for that application. Fasteners requiring replacement or fasteners requiring the use of thread locking compound or sealant are identified in the service procedure. Do not use paints, lubricants, or corrosion inhibitors on fasteners or fastener joint surfaces unless specified. These coatings affect fastener torque and joint clamping force and may damage the fastener. Use the correct tightening sequence and specifications when installing fasteners in order to avoid damage to parts and systems.

5. Install the two attaching screws and tighten them to 40 lb-inch (4.5 Nm).
6. Connect the spark plug wires.

3.6L Engine

Bank 1

See Figure 30.

1. Turn the ignition **OFF**.
2. Raise and support the vehicle.
3. Disconnect the intermediate steering shaft from the steering gear.
4. Remove and reposition the front portion of the front fender liners in order to gain access to the frame front bolts.
5. Lower the vehicle.
6. Position a floor jack at the front center section of the frame in order to support the powertrain.
7. Remove the frame front bolts.

❈❈ WARNING

Do not lower the powertrain more than 4 inches (100mm)

8. Carefully lower the powertrain in order to provide access.

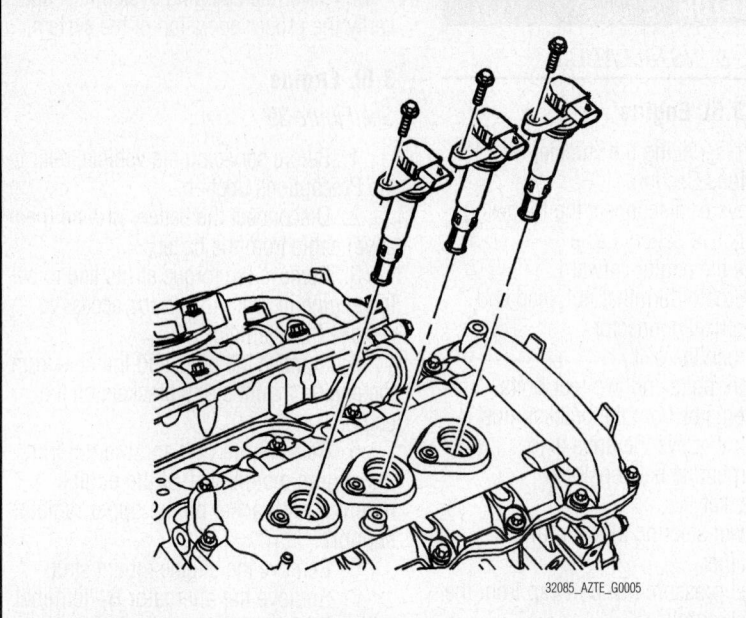

Fig. 30 Removal and installation of the ignition coils

9. Reposition the Evaporative emission (EVAP) purge hoses as necessary in order to provide access.
10. Disconnect the applicable ignition coil electrical connectors.
11. Remove the ignition coil bolts.
12. Remove the ignition coils.

To install:

13. Install the ignition coils.
14. Install the ignition coil bolts and tighten them to 89 lb-inches (10 Nm).
15. Connect the ignition coil electrical connectors.
16. Use the floor jack in order to raise the powertrain until the frame contacts the chassis.
17. Install the frame front bolts.
18. Raise and support the vehicle.
19. Install the front fender liners.
20. Connect the intermediate steering shaft to the steering gear.
21. Lower the vehicle.

Bank 2

1. Turn the ignition **OFF**.
2. Disconnect the applicable ignition coil electrical connector(s).
3. Remove the ignition coil bolt(s).
4. Remove the ignition coil(s).

To install:

5. Install the ignition coil(s).
6. Install the ignition coil bolts and tighten them to 89 lb-inches (10 Nm).
7. Connect the ignition coil electrical connector(s).

IGNITION TIMING

ADJUSTMENT

The ignition timing is controlled by the Powertrain Control Module (PCM). No adjustment is necessary or possible.

SPARK PLUGS

REMOVAL & INSTALLATION

3.4L and 3.5L Engine

➡Observe the following service precautions:

- Allow the engine to cool before removing the spark plugs. Attempting to remove spark plugs from a hot engine can cause the spark plugs to seize. This can damage the cylinder head threads.
- Clean the spark plug recess area before removing the spark plug. Failure to do so can result in engine damage due to dirt or foreign material entering the cylinder head, or in contamination of the cylinder head threads. Contaminated threads may prevent proper seating of the new spark plug.
- Use only the spark plugs specified for use in the vehicle. Do not install spark plugs that are either hotter or colder than those specified for the vehicle. Installing spark plugs of

another type can severely damage the engine.

1. Turn the ignition **OFF.**
2. Remove the intake manifold cover (3.5L).
3. Remove the spark plug wire(s) (2, 4, and 6) from the left side spark plug(s).
4. Remove the air cleaner outlet duct.
5. Set the park brake.
6. Shift the transaxle into neutral (N).
7. Remove the left and right engine mount struts.
8. Install the J 41131 rotation tool.
9. Pull on the engine in order to rotate the engine forward.
10. Tighten the J 41131 tool.
11. Remove the spark plug wire(s) (1, 3, and/or 5) from the right side spark plug(s).
12. Remove the spark plug(s) from the cylinder head.

To install:

➡It is important to check the gap of all new and reconditioned spark plugs before installation. Pre-set gaps may have changed during handling. Use a round wire feeler gauge to be sure of an accurate check, particularly on used plugs. Installing plugs with the wrong gap can cause poor engine performance and may even damage the engine.

13. Gap the spark plugs to 0.60 in (1.52mm).

➡Be sure plug threads smoothly into cylinder head and is fully seated. Use a thread chaser if necessary to clean threads in cylinder head. Cross-threading or failing to fully seat spark plug can cause overheating of plug, exhaust blow-by, or thread damage. Follow the recommended torque specifications carefully. Over or under-tightening can also cause severe damage to engine or spark plug.

➡Use the correct fastener in the correct location. Replacement fasteners must be the correct part number for that application. Fasteners requiring replacement or fasteners requiring the use of thread locking compound or sealant are identified in the service procedure. Do not use paints, lubricants, or corrosion inhibitors on fasteners or fastener joint surfaces unless specified. These coatings affect fastener torque and joint clamping force and may damage the fastener. Use the correct tightening sequence and specifications when installing fasteners in order to avoid damage to parts and systems.

14. Install the spark plug(s).
15. If the spark plugs are installed into a new cylinder head, tighten the spark plugs to 15 lb-ft (20 Nm). If the spark plugs are installed into an existing cylinder head, tighten the spark plugs to 11 lb-ft (15 Nm).
16. Install the spark plug wire(s) (1, 3, and 5) to the right side spark plug(s).
17. Carefully release the tension on the J 41131 tool.
18. Remove the J 41131 tool.
19. Install the left and right engine mount struts.
20. Install the spark plug wire(s) (2, 4, and/or 6) from the left side spark plug(s).
21. Install the intake manifold cover (3.5L).

3.6L Engine

1. Turn the ignition **OFF**.
2. Remove the ignition coil.

✳✳ CAUTION

Wear safety glasses when using compressed air in order to prevent eye injury.

➡Clean the spark plug recess area before removing the spark plug. Failure to do so could result in engine damage because of dirt or foreign material entering the cylinder head, or by the contamination of the cylinder head threads. The contaminated threads may prevent the proper seating of the new plug. Use a thread chaser to clean the threads of any contamination.

3. Use compressed air in order to remove debris from the spark plug cavity.

➡Notice: Allow the engine to cool before removing the spark plugs. Attempting to remove the spark plugs from a hot engine may cause the plug threads to seize, causing damage to cylinder head threads.

4. Remove the spark plug.

To install:

➡Use only the spark plugs specified for use in the vehicle. Do not install spark plugs that are either hotter or colder than those specified for the vehicle. Installing spark plugs of another type can severely damage the engine.

➡Check the gap of all new and reconditioned spark plugs before installation. The pre-set gaps may have changed during handling. Use a round feeler gage to ensure an accurate check. Installing the spark plugs with the wrong gap can cause poor engine performance and may even damage the engine.

5. Gap the spark plugs to 0.044 in (1.10 mm).

➡Be sure that the spark plug threads smoothly into the cylinder head and the spark plug is fully seated. Use a thread chaser, if necessary, to clean threads in the cylinder head. Cross-threading or failing to fully seat the spark plug can cause overheating of the plug, exhaust blow-by, or thread damage.

6. Install the spark plugs.
7. Tighten the spark plugs to 15 lb ft (20 Nm).
8. Install the ignition coil.

ENGINE ELECTRICAL   **STARTING SYSTEM**

STARTER

REMOVAL & INSTALLATION

3.4L and 3.5L Engine

See Figure 31.

1. Before servicing the vehicle, refer to the Precautions Section.
2. Remove or disconnect the following:
   - Negative battery cable
   - Radiator air baffle assembly
   - Electrical connections
   - Torque converter cover
   - Starter

To install:

3. Install or connect the following:
   - Starter. Torque the bolts to 35 ft. lbs. (47 Nm).
   - Torque converter cover
   - Solenoid "BAT" terminal. Torque the nut to 89 inch lbs. (10 Nm).
   - Solenoid "S" terminal. Torque the nut to 27 inch lbs. (3 Nm).

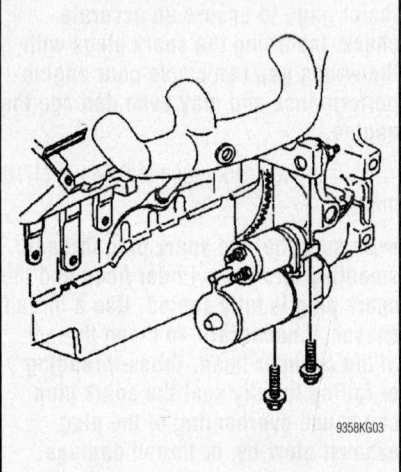

Fig. 31 Starter motor mounting—3.4L and 3.5L engine

- Radiator air baffle assembly
- Negative battery cable

4. Perform a charging system test and verify the starter is operating properly.

3.6L Engine

See Figure 32.

1. Before servicing the vehicle, refer to the Precautions Section.
2. Disconnect the battery ground (negative) cable from the battery.
3. Raise and support the vehicle.
4. Remove the radiator air baffle.
5. Remove the starter motor BAT terminal nut and electrical leads.
6. Remove the starter motor bolts.
7. Remove the starter motor.

To install:

8. Install the starter motor.

➡**Use the correct fastener in the correct location.**

9. Install the starter motor bolts. Tighten the starter motor bolts to 37 ft. lbs (50 Nm).
10. Install the starter motor S terminal electrical connector.
11. Install the battery positive cable and the BAT terminal nut to the starter motor BAT terminal. Tighten the starter motor BAT terminal nut to 115 inch lbs. (13 Nm).
12. Install radiator air baffle assembly.
13. Lower the vehicle.
14. Install the battery ground (negative) cable to the battery.

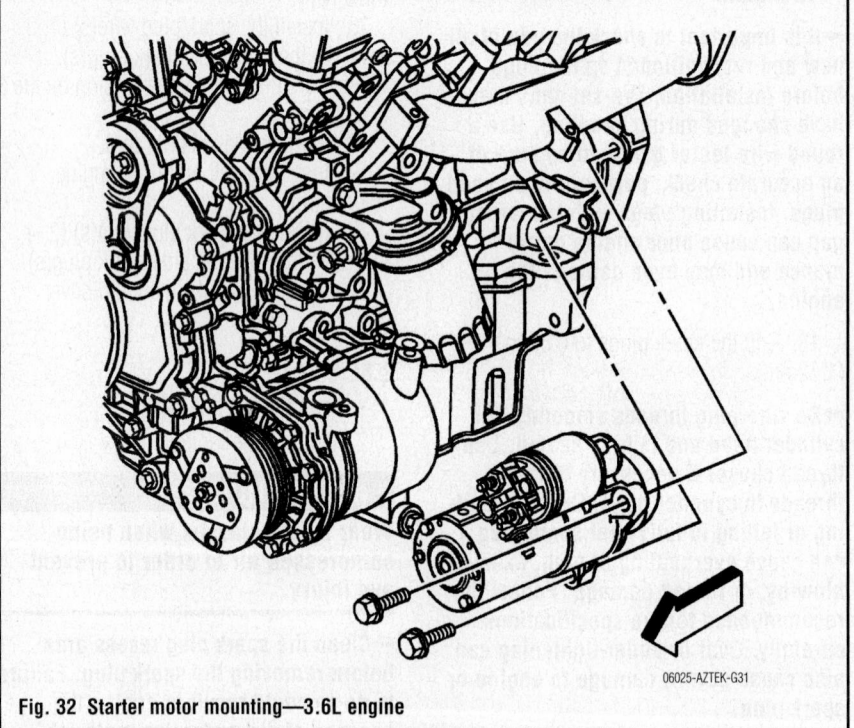

Fig. 32 Starter motor mounting—3.6L engine

ENGINE MECHANICAL

➡ **Disconnecting the negative battery cable may interfere with the functions of the on board computer systems and may require the computer to undergo a relearning process, once the negative battery cable is reconnected.**

ACCESSORY DRIVE BELTS

ACCESSORY BELT ROUTING

See Figures 33 and 34.

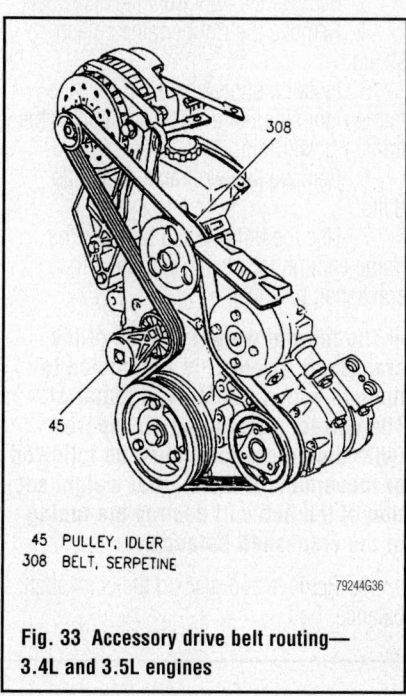

45 PULLEY, IDLER
308 BELT, SERPETINE

79244G36

Fig. 33 Accessory drive belt routing— 3.4L and 3.5L engines

INSPECTION

Inspect the drive belt for signs of glazing or cracking. A glazed belt will be perfectly smooth from slippage, while a good belt will have a slight texture of fabric visible. Cracks will usually start at the inner edge of the belt and run outward. All worn or damaged drive belts should be replaced immediately.

REMOVAL & INSTALLATION

3.4L and 3.5L Engine

See Figures 35 and 36.

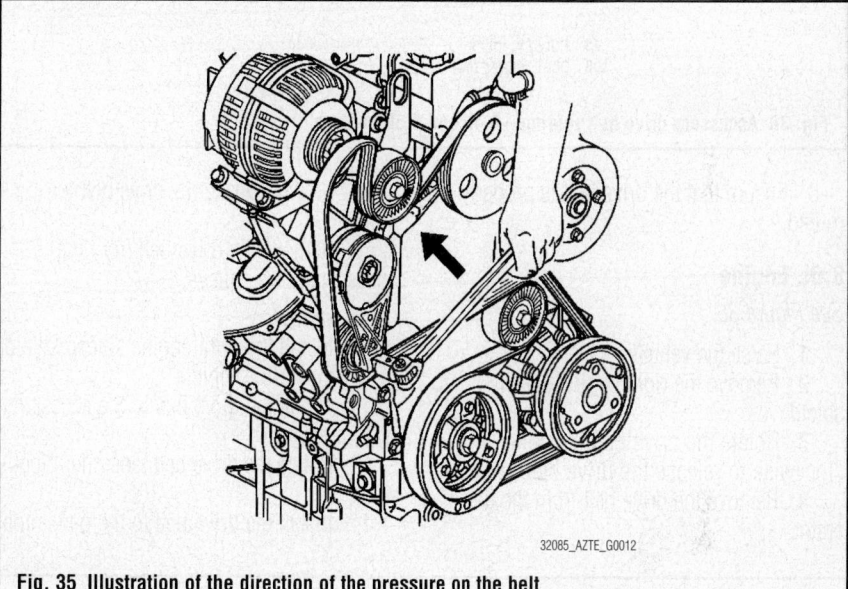

32085_AZTE_G0012

Fig. 35 Illustration of the direction of the pressure on the belt

1. Rotate the drive belt tensioner in order to release the pressure on the drive belt.
2. Remove the drive belt.

To install:

3. Install the drive belt to all of the pulleys except the generator pulley.
4. Rotate the drive belt tensioner in order to install the drive belt over the generator pulley.
5. Ensure that the drive belt is aligned into the proper grooves of the accessory drive belt pulleys.

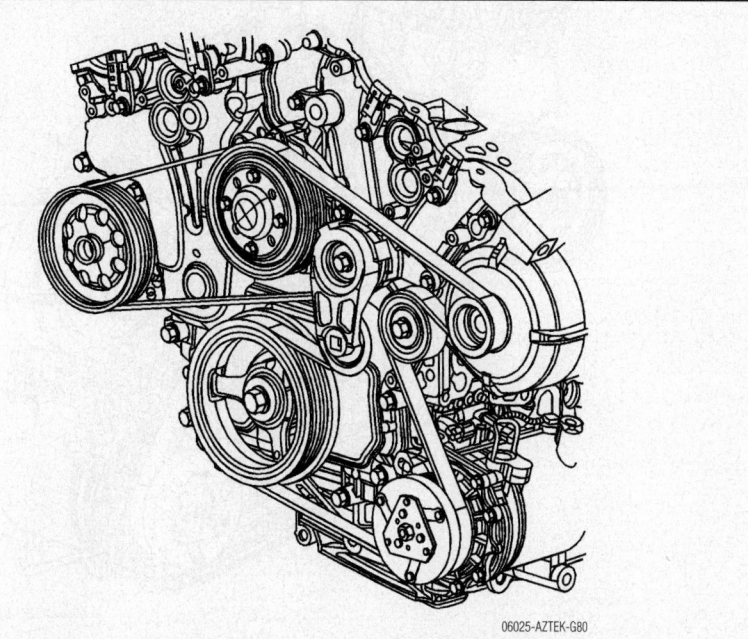

06025-AZTEK-G80

Fig. 34 Accessory drive belt routing—3.6L engines

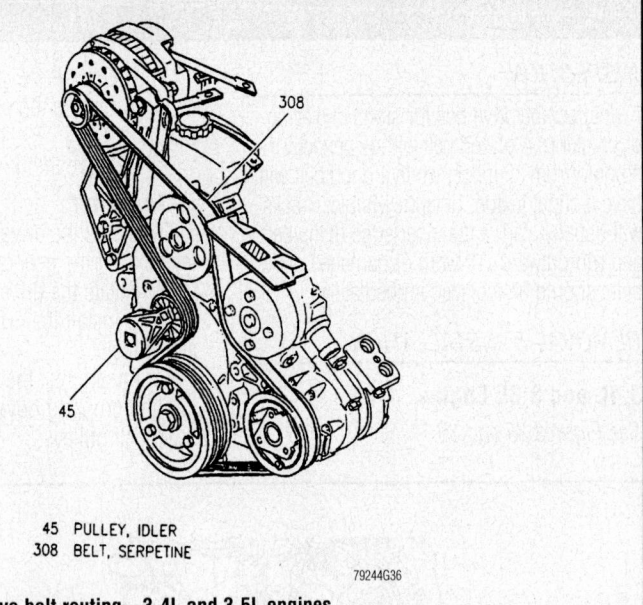

45 PULLEY, IDLER
308 BELT, SERPETINE

79244G36

Fig. 36 Accessory drive belt routing—3.4L and 3.5L engines

6. Ensure that the drive belt is properly routed.

3.6L Engine

See Figure 38.

1. Raise the vehicle.
2. Remove the right engine splash shield.
3. Rotate the drive belt tensioner clockwise to release the drive belt tension.
4. Remove the drive belt from the generator.

5. Slowly release the drive belt tensioner.
6. Remove the drive belt from the accessory drive pulleys.

To install:

7. Install the right engine splash shield.
8. Lower the vehicle.
9. Install the drive belt to the accessory drive pulley.
10. Rotate the drive belt tensioner clockwise.
11. Install the drive belt to the generator.

12. Ensure the drive belt is properly aligned and seated into the grooves of the accessory drive pulleys.
13. Slowly release the drive belt tensioner.

BALANCE SHAFT

REMOVAL & INSTALLATION

3.4L and 3.5L Engine

See Figures 39 and 40.

1. Remove the drive belt..
2. Raise and support the vehicle.
3. Remove the right front tire and wheel.
4. Remove the right engine splash shield.
5. Install a utility stand beneath the frame right side rail in order to support the frame / powertrain.
6. Remove the two frame right side bolts.
7. Use the utility stand to lower the frame enough to provide access to the crankshaft balancer.

➡**The inertial weight section of the crankshaft balancer is assembled to the hub with a rubber type material. The correct installation procedures (with the proper tool) must be followed or movement of the inertial weight section of the hub will destroy the tuning of the crankshaft balancer.**

8. Remove and discard the crankshaft balancer bolt.

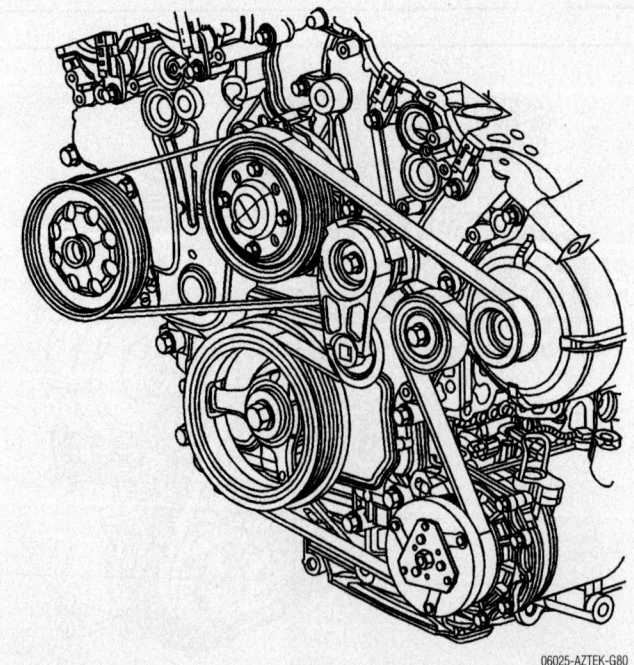

06025-AZTEK-G80

Fig. 38 Accessory drive belt routing—3.6L engines

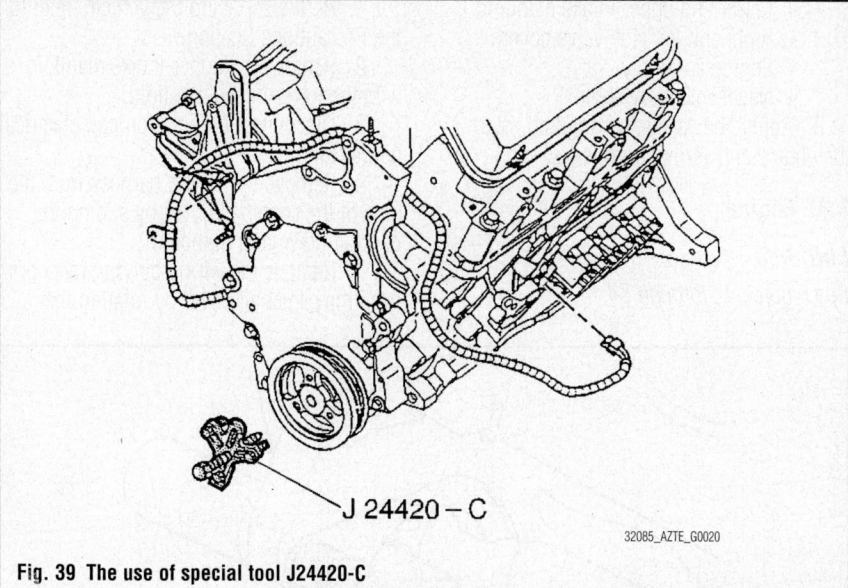

Fig. 39 The use of special tool J24420-C

32085_AZTE_G0020

9. Remove the crankshaft balancer using the J 24420-C .

10. Clean and inspect the crankshaft balancer.

To install:

11. Apply sealer GM P/N 12345739 or the equivalent to the keyway of the crankshaft balancer.

12. Install the crankshaft balancer into position over the key in the crankshaft.

13. Use the J 29113 in order to install the crankshaft balancer to the crankshaft.

14. Remove the J 29113 from the crankshaft balancer.

➡Use the correct fastener in the correct location. Replacement fasteners must be the correct part number for that application. Fasteners requiring replacement or fasteners requiring the use of thread locking compound or sealant are identified in the service procedure. Do not use paints, lubricants, or corrosion inhibitors on fasteners or fastener joint surfaces unless specified. These coatings affect fastener torque and joint clamping force and may damage the fastener. Use the correct tightening sequence and specifications when installing fasteners in order to avoid damage to parts and systems.

15. 3.4L Install the crankshaft balancer washer and the new crankshaft balancer bolt and tighten the bolt to 52 ft. lbs. (70 Nm).

16. Use a torque angle meter in order to rotate the bolt 72 degrees.

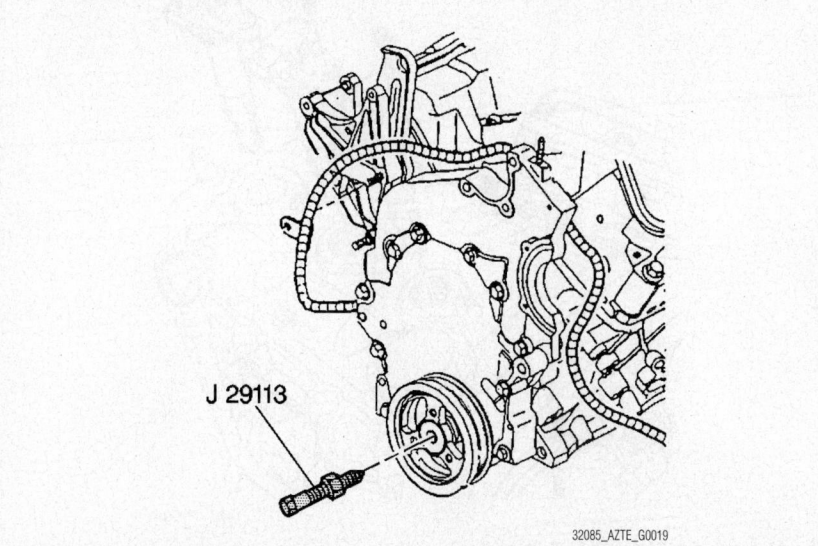

Fig. 40 The use of special tool J29113

32085_AZTE_G0019

17. 3.5L Install the crankshaft balancer washer and the new crankshaft balancer bolt and tighten the bolt to 92 ft. lbs. (125 Nm).

18. Use a torque angle meter in order to rotate the bolt 110 degrees.

19. Use the utility stand in order to raise the frame/powertrain.

20. Install the frame right side bolts.

21. Install the engine splash shield.

22. Install the right front tire and wheel.

23. Lower the vehicle.

24. Install the drive belt.

3.6L Engine

See Figure 41.

1. Remove the accessory drive belt.

2. Raise and support the vehicle.

3. Use the special tool J 41816-A in order to remove the crankshaft balancer.

4. Use a utility stand to support the right side of the frame and powertrain.

5. Remove the right side frame bolts.

6. Raise the vehicle or lower the frame and powertrain in order to gain access to the crankshaft balancer.

Fig. 41 The removal of the crankshaft balancer

32085_AZTE_G0021

To install:

7. Install the crankshaft balancer.

8. Install the accessory drive belt.

9. Lower the vehicle or raise the frame and powertrain in order to align the frame to the vehicle.

10. Install the frame right side bolts.

11. Remove the utility stand.

12. Lower the vehicle.

CAMSHAFT AND VALVE LIFTERS

REMOVAL & INSTALLATION

3.4L and 3.5L Engine

1. Before servicing the vehicle, refer to the Precautions Section.

2. Relieve the fuel system pressure.
3. Remove or disconnect the following:
   • Engine assembly

✳✳ WARNING

When removing valvetrain components they must be marked for installation in their original location. When the camshaft is being replaced, the valve lifters must also be replaced.

   • Right and left side valve covers
   • Upper and lower intake manifold
   • Rocker arm bolts, balls, rocker arms and pushrods
   • Oil splash shield
   • Lifter guide bolts and the guide
   • Valve lifter(s) from the bores
   • Crankshaft balancer and front cover
   • Timing chain and sprockets
   • Oil pump driven gear bolt and gear
   • Camshaft thrust plate
   • Camshaft, using a large screwdriver inserted in the bolt hole to carefully rotate and pull the camshaft out of the bearings

✳✳ WARNING

Avoid damaging the camshaft bearing surfaces.

To install:

4. Coat the camshaft with Prelube.
5. Install or connect the following:
   • Camshaft
   • Camshaft thrust plate. Tighten the bolts to 89 inch lbs. (10 Nm).
   • Oil pump driven gear. Tighten the bolt to 27 ft. lbs. (36 Nm).
   • Timing chain and sprocket
   • Camshaft thrust button and front cover
   • Crankshaft balancer
6. Lubricate the bearing surfaces with Molykote®.

➡**Installation of a new camshaft or a wear pattern on the old valve lifter will require the replacement of the camshaft and lifters together. If camshaft replacement is not necessary, be sure to install the used valve lifters in their original position.**

7. Install or connect the following:
   • Lifters in their original locations
   • Lifter guide. Tighten the guide bolts to 89 inch lbs. (10 Nm).
   • Oil splash shield
   • Pushrods, rocker arms, balls and bolts. Tighten the nuts to 89 inch lbs. (10 Nm) plus an additional 30 degree turn.

   • Lower and upper intake manifold
   • Right and left side valve covers
   • Engine assembly
   • Negative battery cable
8. Adjust the valves, as required. Start the engine and verify no oil leaks.

3.6L Engine

Left Side

See Figures 42 through 54.

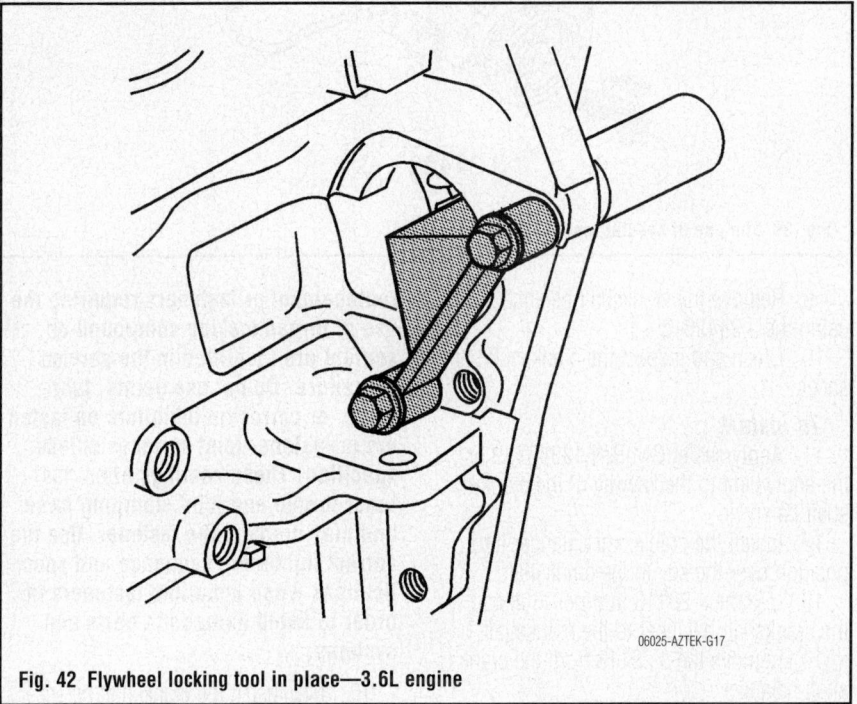

Fig. 42 Flywheel locking tool in place—3.6L engine

06025-AZTEK-G17

Fig. 43 Ignition coil removal—3.6L engine

06025-AZTEK-G14

1. Before servicing the vehicle, refer to the Precautions Section.
2. Remove the upper intake manifold with the lower intake manifold.
3. Disconnect the ignition coil electrical connectors.
4. Remove the wiring harness from the side of the camshaft cover by sliding the conduit down and outboard.
5. Remove the wiring conduit retainers from the camshaft cover by rotating the

wiring harness conduit retainers counter-clockwise.

➡️**It is not necessary to disconnect the engine front cover electrical connectors.**

6. Remove the wiring harness from the front of the camshaft cover.

7. Reposition and secure the wiring harnesses away from the camshaft cover in order to provide clearance.

8. Remove the ignition coils.

9. Loosen the left engine strut bracket.

10. Loosen the left engine strut bracket-to-cylinder head bolts.

11. Remove the camshaft cover bolts and camshaft cover.

12. Remove and discard the camshaft cover seal and grommets. DO NOT reuse.

13. Remove the camshaft sensors.

14. Remove the camshaft position actuator solenoid.

15. Remove the crankshaft balancer.

16. Rotate the crankshaft with the EN 46111 until the camshafts are in a neutral (low tension) position. The camshaft flats will be parallel with the camshaft cover rail.

✳️✳️ **WARNING**

A wrench must be used on the hex of the camshaft when loosening or tightening in order to prevent component damage. Failure to prevent the torque reaction against the timing drive chain can lead to timing drive chain failure.

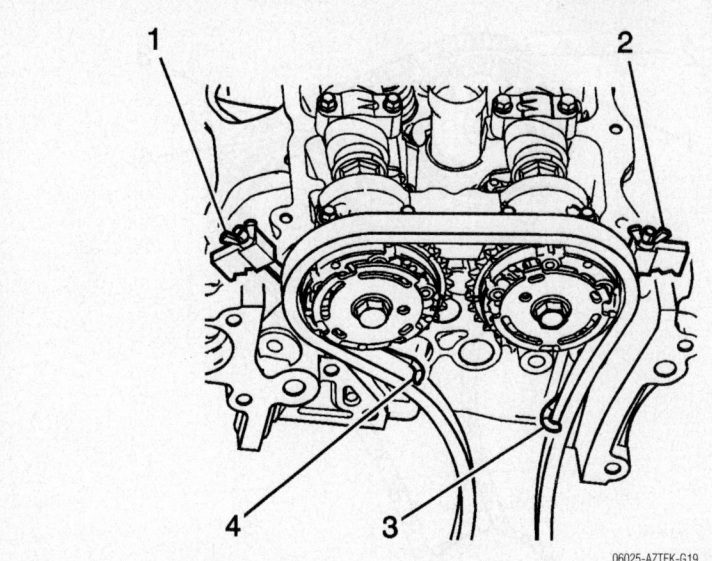

Fig. 45 Install the EN 46108 in order to retain the timing chain. Firmly tighten the EN 46108 nuts—3.6L engine

✳️✳️ **WARNING**

Use an open-end wrench at the camshaft hex to prevent camshaft/engine rotation. DO NOT remove the camshaft position actuator bolt at this time.

17. Loosen the camshaft position actuator bolt.

➡️**Ensure that the tips of the EN 46108 are fully engaged into the timing chain.**

18. Install the EN 46108 in order to retain the timing chain. Firmly tighten the EN 46108 nuts.

➡️**Ensure that the camshaft timing chain and the camshaft position actuators are marked for proper assembly.**

19. Mark the timing chain and the respective locations on the camshaft position actuators.

20. Remove the camshaft position actuator bolt.

21. Remove the EN 46105-2 from the left camshafts.

22. Position the camshaft lobes in a neutral position.

23. Observe the markings on the bearing caps. Each bearing cap is marked in order to identify its location. The markings have the following meanings:

- The raised feature must always be oriented toward the center of the cylinder head.
- The I indicates the intake camshaft.
- The E indicates the exhaust camshaft.
- The number indicates the journal position from the front of the engine.

24. Remove the camshaft bearing cap bolts.

25. Remove the camshaft bearing caps.

26. Remove the camshafts.

27. Replace the camshaft bearing caps and bolts.

28. Remove the valve rocker arms, camshaft followers, from the left cylinder head.

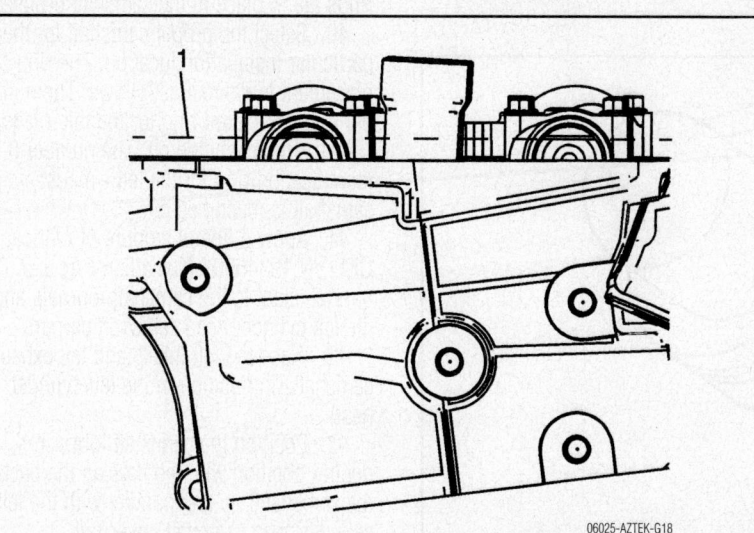

Fig. 44 Rotate the crankshaft with the EN 46111 until the camshafts are in a neutral (low tension) position. The camshaft flats will be parallel with the camshaft cover rail—3.6L engine

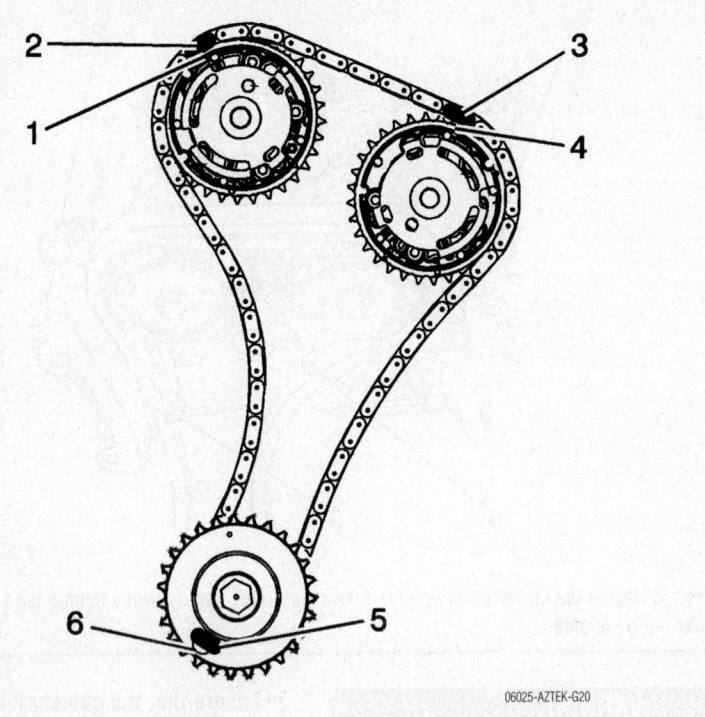

Fig. 46 Mark the timing chain and the respective locations on the camshaft position actuators—3.6L engine

06025-AZTEK-G20

29. Remove the valve lifters, stationary hydraulic lash adjuster, (SHLAs) from the left cylinder head.

To install:

30. Fill the stationary hydraulic lash adjuster (SHLA) with clean engine oil GM P/N 12378006 or equivalent. Take precautions to prevent scratching the pivot sphere area (1) of the SHLA.

31. Lubricate the SHLA bores in the cylinder head with clean engine oil GM P/N 12378006 or equivalent.

32. Install the SHLAs in the cylinder head.

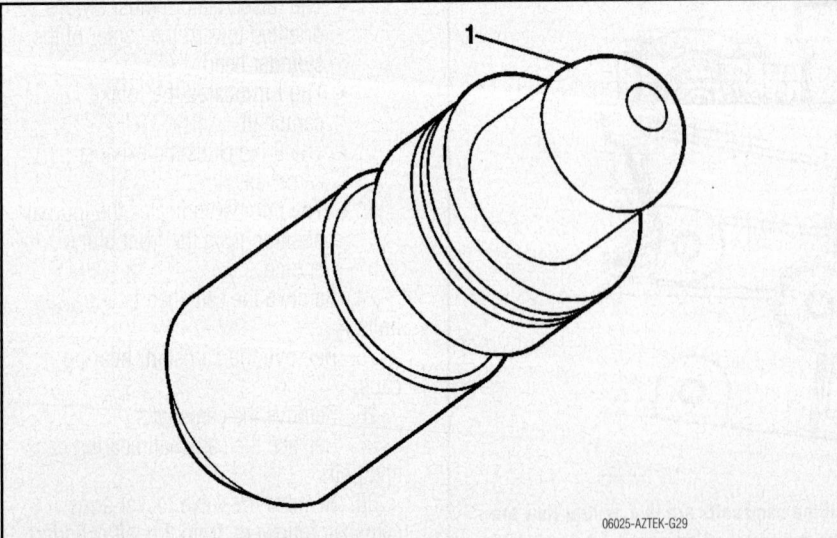

Fig. 47 Stationary hydraulic lash adjuster—3.6L engine

06025-AZTEK-G29

33. Apply a liberal amount of lubricant GM P/N 12345501 (Canadian P/N 992704) or equivalent to the SHLA pivot spheres.

34. Apply a liberal amount of lubricant GM P/N 12345501 (Canadian P/N 992704) or equivalent to the pivot pocket (1), roller (2) and valve slot (3) areas of the camshaft followers.

35. Place the camshaft followers in position on the valve tip and stationary hydraulic lash adjuster (SHLA). The rounded head end of the follower goes on the SHLA while the flat end goes on the valve tip.

36. Clean the camshaft journals and carriers with a clean, lint-free cloth.

➡ **Ensure that the marks on the camshaft position actuator and the timing chain are aligned. DO NOT tighten the camshaft position actuator bolt at this time.**

37. Locate the camshafts to the cylinder head and assemble the camshaft actuators to the camshafts.

38. Ensure that the crankshaft is in the stage one timing drive assembly position using the EN 46111.

39. Ensure that the camshaft sealing rings are in place in the camshaft grooves.

40. Select the proper camshaft for the particular installation location. The ring placement is defined as follows: The number 4 identification ring for the left intake camshaft is machined off. The number 5 identification ring for the left exhaust camshaft is machined off.

41. Apply a liberal amount of lubricant GM P/N 12345501 (Canadian P/N 992704) or equivalent to the camshaft journals and the left cylinder head camshaft carriers.

42. Place the left intake and left exhaust camshafts in position in the left cylinder head.

43. Position the camshaft lobes in a neutral position with the flats on the back of the camshafts up and parallel with the left cylinder head camshaft cover rail.

44. Observe the markings on the left cylinder head camshaft bearing caps. Each bearing cap is marked in order to identify its

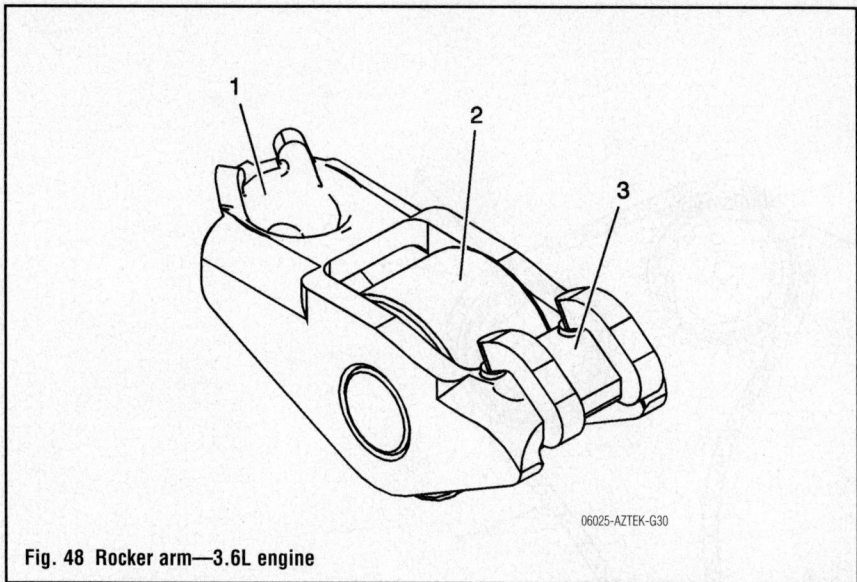

06025-AZTEK-G30

Fig. 48 Rocker arm—3.6L engine

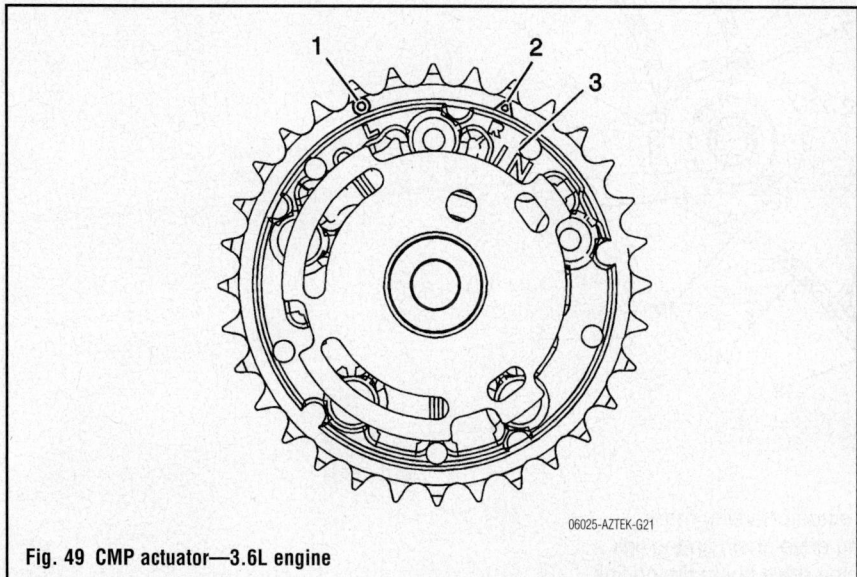

06025-AZTEK-G21

Fig. 49 CMP actuator—3.6L engine

location. The markings have the following meanings:

- The raised feature must always be oriented toward the center of the cylinder head.
- The I indicates the intake camshaft.
- The E indicates the exhaust camshaft.
- The number 2, 4, 6 indicates the cylinder position from the front of the engine.

45. Apply a liberal amount of lubricant GM P/N 12345501 (Canadian P/N 992704) or equivalent to the camshaft bearing caps.

46. Install the camshaft bearing thrust cap in the first journal of the left cylinder head.

47. Install the remaining bearing caps with their orientation mark toward the center of the cylinder head.

48. Hand start all the camshaft bearing cap bolts.

49. Tighten the camshaft bearing cap bolts in the sequence shown to 89 inch lbs. (10 Nm).

50. Loosen the center intake camshaft bearing cap bolts 1, 2 and the center exhaust camshaft bearing cap bolts 3, 4.

51. Retighten the center camshaft bearing cap bolts 1, 2, 3, 4 to 89 inch lbs. (10 Nm).

52. Remove the EN 46108.

✳✳ WARNING

Use an open-end wrench at the camshaft hex to prevent camshaft/engine rotation.

53. Observe the body of the camshaft position actuator for the "IN" marking. The marking is for an intake camshaft position actuator.

54. Ensure the proper timing mark is used. Observe the outer ring of the camshaft position actuator for the "L" and circle marking. The marking is for alignment to the highlighted timing chain link on the left side of the engine.

55. Use an open wrench on the hex cast into the camshaft in order to prevent camshaft rotation when tightening the camshaft position actuator bolt.

56. Install the left intake camshaft position actuator.

57. Install the camshaft position actuator bolt. Tighten the camshaft position actuator bolt to 43 ft. lbs. (58 Nm).

58. Observe the body of the camshaft position actuator for the "EX" marking. The marking is for an exhaust camshaft position actuator.

59. Ensure the proper timing mark is used. Observe the outer ring of the camshaft position actuator for the "L" and circle marking. The marking is for alignment to the highlighted timing chain link on the left side of the engine.

60. Use an open wrench on the hex cast into the camshaft in order to prevent camshaft rotation when tightening the camshaft position actuator bolt.

61. Install the left exhaust camshaft position actuator.

62. Install the camshaft position actuator bolt. Tighten the camshaft position actuator bolt to 43 ft. lbs. (58 Nm).

63. Install the CMP actuator valve.

64. Install the CMP actuator valve bolt. Tighten the CMP actuator valve bolt to 89 inch lbs. (10 Nm).

65. Install the camshaft sensors. Torque to 89 inch lbs. (10 Nm).

➡**The EN 46106 must be installed onto the flywheel.**

66. Use the J 41998-B, nut, bearing and washer to install the crankshaft balancer.

➡**Do not lubricate the crankshaft front oil seal or crankshaft balancer sealing surfaces. The crankshaft balancer is installed into a dry seal.**

67. Apply lubricant to the inside of the crankshaft balancer hub bore.

68. Place the crankshaft balancer in position on the crankshaft.

69. Thread the J 41998-B in the crankshaft. Ensure you engage at least 10 threads of the J 41998-B before pressing the crankshaft balancer in place.

70. Push the crankshaft balancer into

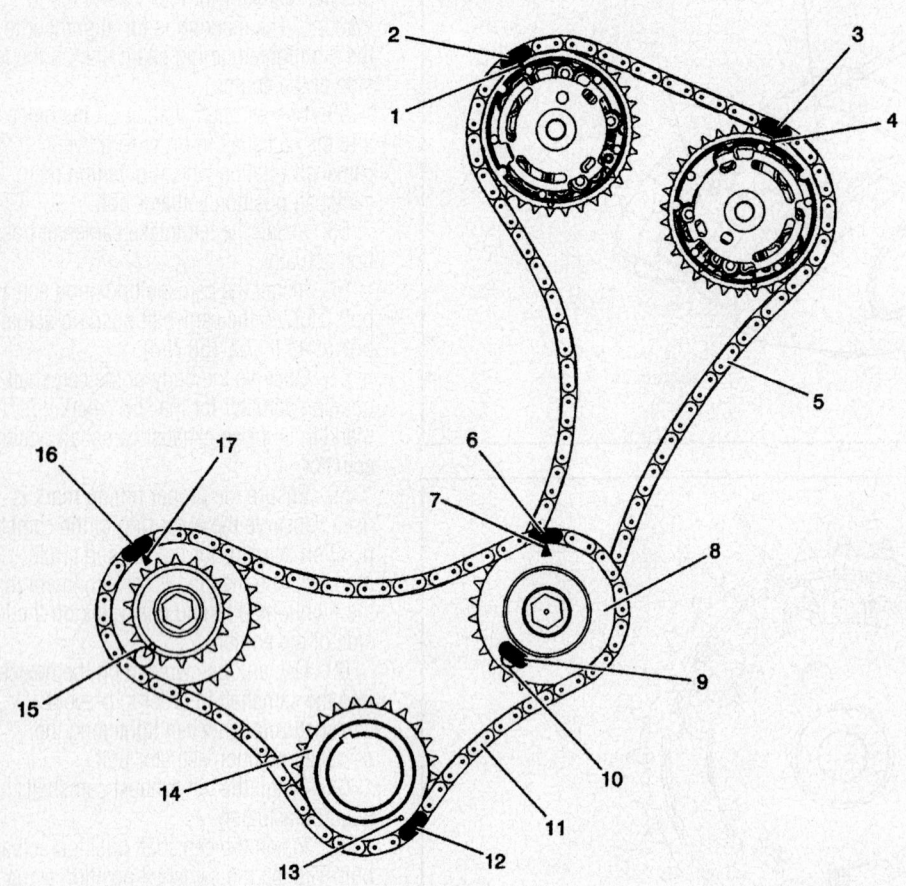

1. Left intake Camshaft Position (CMP) actuator timing mark
2. Left intake secondary camshaft timing drive chain timing link
3. Left exhaust secondary camshaft timing drive chain timing link
4. Left exhaust Camshaft Position (CMP) actuator timing mark
5. Left secondary camshaft timing drive chain
6. Primary camshaft drive chain timing link for the left primary camshaft intermediate drive chain sprocket
7. Left primary camshaft intermediate drive chain sprocket timing mark for the primary camshaft drive chain
8. Left primary camshaft intermediate drive chain sprocket
9. Left secondary camshaft timing drive chain timing link for the left primary camshaft intermediate drive chain sprocket
10. Left primary camshaft intermediate drive chain sprocket timing window for the left secondary camshaft timing drive chain timing link
11. Primary camshaft drive chain
12. Primary camshaft drive chain timing link for the crankshaft sprocket
13. Crankshaft sprocket timing mark
14. Crankshaft sprocket
15. Right primary camshaft intermediate drive chain sprocket
16. Primary camshaft drive chain timing link for the right primary camshaft intermediate drive chain sprocket
17. Right primary camshaft intermediate drive chain sprocket timing mark

06025-AZTEK-G22

Fig. 50 Ensure that the crankshaft is in the stage one timing drive assembly position using the EN 46111—3.6L engine

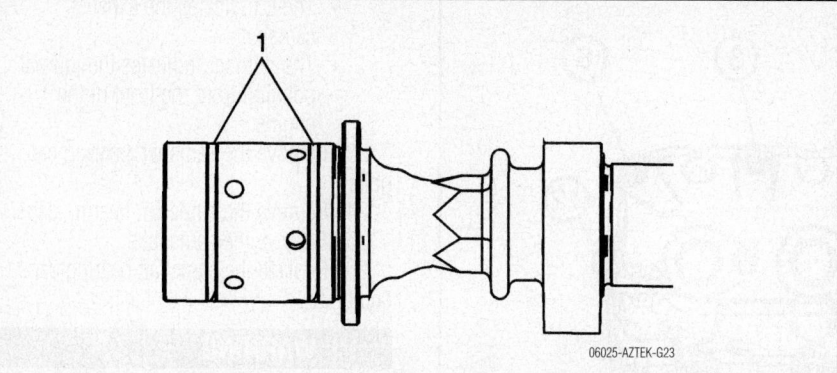

Fig. 51 Ensure that the camshaft sealing rings are in place in the camshaft grooves—3.6L engine

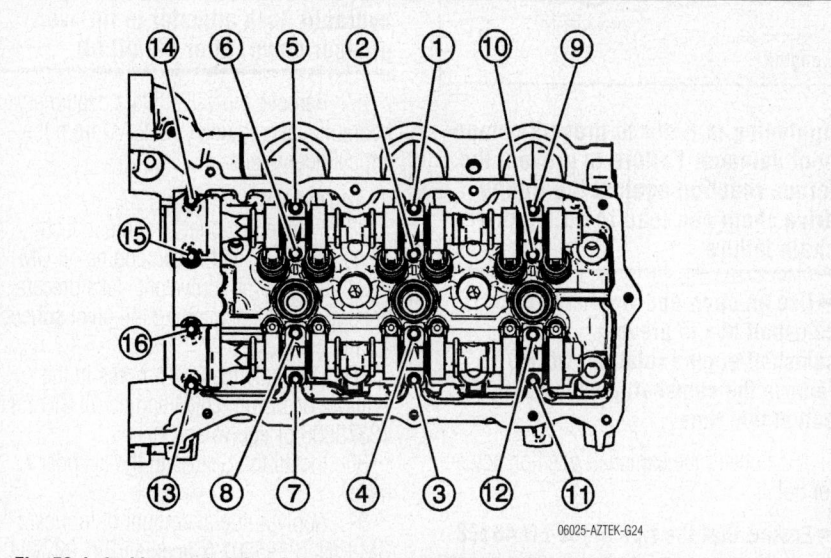

Fig. 52 Left side camshaft bearing cap torque sequence—3.6L engine

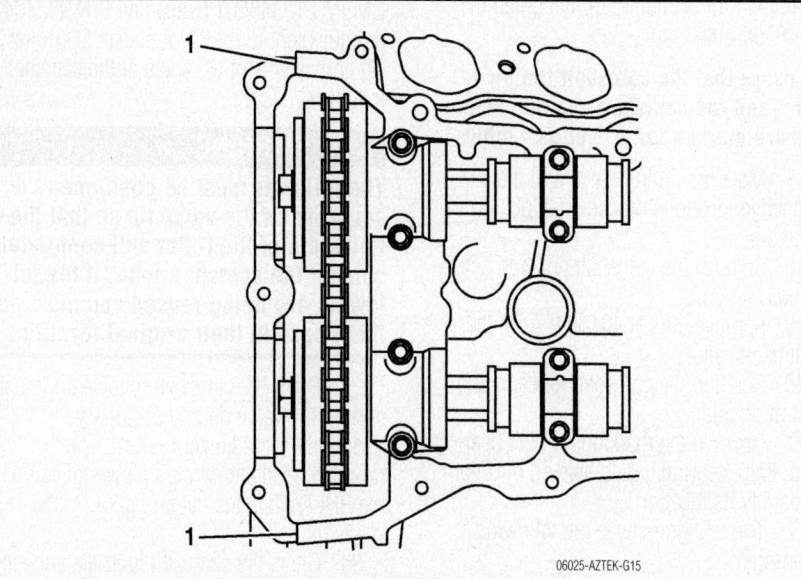

Fig. 53 Place a bead 8mm (0.3150 in.) in diameter by 4mm (0.1575 in.) of RTV sealant, GM P/N 12378521 (Canadian P/N 88901148) or equivalent, on the engine front cover split lines—3.6L engine

position by tightening the nut on the J 41998-B until the large washer bottoms out on the crankshaft end.

71. Remove the J 41998-B.

72. Install the crankshaft balancer bolt. Tighten the crankshaft balancer bolt to 74 ft. lbs. (100 Nm). Tighten the crankshaft balancer bolt an additional 150 degrees using the J 45059.

73. Remove the EN 46106.

74. Install a NEW camshaft cover seal and NEW grommets.

75. Remove the EN 46105-2 from the rear of the left camshafts.

76. Install the EN 46101 onto the spark plug tubes of the left cylinder head.

77. Install the camshaft cover bolt grommets prior to installing the camshaft cover bolts.

78. Wipe the camshaft cover sealing surface on the left cylinder head with a clean, lint-free cloth.

79. Place a bead 8mm (0.3150 in.) in diameter by 4mm (0.1575 in.) in height of RTV sealant, GM P/N 12378521 (Canadian P/N 88901148) or equivalent, on the engine front cover split lines.

80. Place the left camshaft cover into position onto the left cylinder head.

81. Loosely install the left camshaft cover bolts.

82. Tighten the left camshaft cover bolts in the sequence shown to 89 inch lbs. (10 Nm).

83. Remove the EN 46101 from the spark plug tubes of the left cylinder head.

84. Install the NEW spark plugs into the left cylinder head. Tighten the spark plugs to 15 ft. lbs. (20 Nm).

85. Install each ignition coil through the left camshaft cover into the spark plug tube taking care not to damage the spark plug and/or the seal in the left camshaft cover.

86. Install each ignition coil bolt. Tighten the ignition coil bolt to 89 inch lbs. (10 Nm).

87. Tighten the left engine strut bracket-to-cylinder head bolts to 37 ft. lbs. (50 Nm).

88. Install the ignition coils.

89. Install the wiring harness to the front of the camshaft cover.

90. Install the wiring harness conduit retainers to the wiring harness conduit.

91. Install the wiring harness to the side of the camshaft cover.

92. Connect the ignition coil electrical connectors.

93. Install the upper intake manifold with the lower intake manifold.

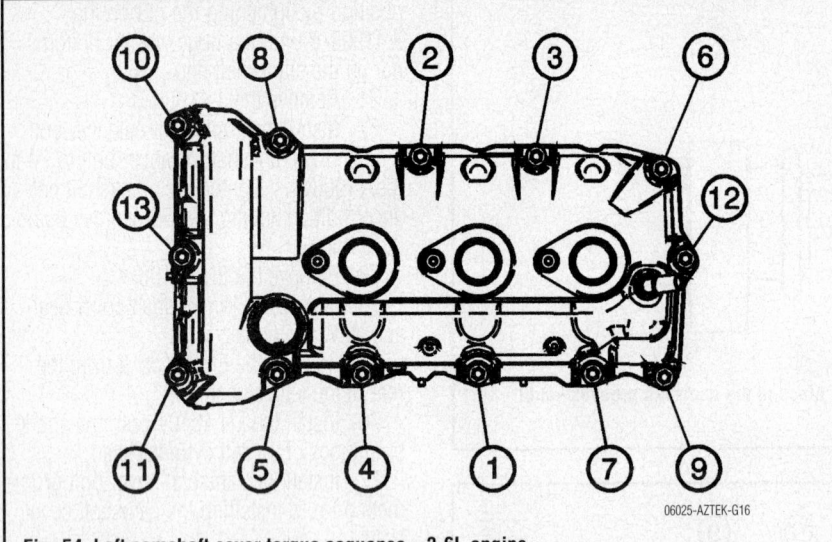

Fig. 54 Left camshaft cover torque sequence—3.6L engine

Right Side

See Figures 55 through 58.

1. Before servicing the vehicle, refer to the Precautions Section.

2. Remove the upper intake manifold with the lower intake manifold.

3. Disconnect the ignition coil electrical connectors.

4. Remove the wiring harness from the side of the camshaft cover by sliding the conduit down and outboard.

5. Remove the wiring conduit retainers from the camshaft cover by rotating the wiring harness conduit retainers counterclockwise.

➡ **It is not necessary to disconnect the engine front cover electrical connectors.**

6. Remove the wiring harness from the front of the camshaft cover.

7. Reposition and secure the wiring harnesses away from the camshaft cover in order to provide clearance.

8. Remove the ignition coils.

9. Remove the camshaft cover.

10. Remove and discard the camshaft cover seal and grommets.

11. Remove the camshaft sensors.

12. Remove the intake camshaft position actuator solenoid.

13. Remove the crankshaft balancer.

14. Rotate the crankshaft with the EN 46111 until the camshafts are in a neutral (low tension) position. The camshaft flats will be parallel with the camshaft cover rail.

✳✳ WARNING

A wrench must be used on the hex of the camshaft when loosening or

tightening in order to prevent component damage. Failure to prevent the torque reaction against the timing drive chain can lead to timing drive chain failure.

➡ **Use an open-end wrench at the camshaft hex to prevent camshaft/engine rotation. DO NOT remove the camshaft position actuator bolt at this time.**

15. Loosen the camshaft position actuator bolt.

➡ **Ensure that the tips of the EN 46108 are fully engaged into the timing chain.**

16. Install the EN 46108 in order to retain the timing chain. Firmly tighten the EN 46108 nuts.

➡ **Ensure that the camshaft timing chain and the camshaft position actuators are marked for proper assembly.**

17. Mark the timing chain and the respective locations on camshaft position actuators.

18. Remove the camshaft position actuator bolt.

19. Remove the EN 46105-1 from the right camshafts.

20. Position the camshaft lobes in a neutral position.

21. Observe the markings on the bearing caps. Each bearing cap is marked in order to identify its location.

22. The markings have the following meanings:
- The raised feature must always be oriented toward the center of the cylinder head.
- The I indicates the intake camshaft.

- The E indicates the exhaust camshaft.
- The number indicates the journal position from the front of the engine.

23. Remove the camshaft bearing cap bolts.

24. Remove the camshaft bearing caps.

25. Remove the camshafts.

26. Replace the camshaft bearing caps and bolts.

✳✳ WARNING

Do not stroke/cycle the stationary hydraulic lash adjuster plunger without oil in the lower pressure chamber. Do not allow the stationary hydraulic lash adjuster to tip over, plunger down, after the oil fill.

27. Remove the valve lifters, stationary hydraulic lash adjuster, (SHLAs) from the left cylinder head.

To install:

28. Fill the stationary hydraulic lash adjuster (SHLA) with clean engine oil GM P/N 12378006 or equivalent. Take precautions to prevent scratching the pivot sphere area (1) of the SHLA.

29. Lubricate the SHLA bores in the cylinder head with clean engine oil GM P/N 12378006 or equivalent.

30. Install the SHLAs in the cylinder head.

31. Apply a liberal amount of lubricant GM P/N 12345501 (Canadian P/N 992704) or equivalent to the SHLA pivot spheres.

32. Apply a liberal amount of lubricant GM P/N 12345501 (Canadian P/N 992704) or equivalent to the pivot pocket (1), roller (2) and valve slot (3) areas of the camshaft followers.

✳✳ WARNING

The follower must be positioned squarely on the valve tip so that the full width of the roller will completely contact the camshaft lobe. If the followers are being reused you must put them back in their original location.

33. Place the camshaft followers in position on the valve tip and stationary hydraulic lash adjuster (SHLA). The rounded head end of the follower goes on the SHLA while the flat end goes on the valve tip.

34. Clean the camshaft journals and carriers with a clean, lint-free cloth.

➡ **Ensure that the marks on the camshaft position actuators and the** timing chain (15-18) are aligned. DO NOT tighten the camshaft position actuator bolt at this time.

35. Locate the camshafts to the cylinder head and assemble the camshaft actuators to the camshafts.

36. Ensure that the crankshaft is in the stage one timing drive assembly position using the EN 46111.

37. Ensure that the camshaft sealing rings are in place in the camshaft grooves.

38. Select the proper camshaft for the particular installation location. The ring placement is defined as follows: The number 2 identification ring for the right exhaust camshaft is machined off. The number 3 identification ring for the right intake camshaft is machined off.

39. Apply a liberal amount of lubricant GM P/N 12345501 (Canadian P/N 992704) or equivalent to the camshaft journals and the right cylinder head camshaft carriers. Place the right intake and right exhaust camshafts in position in the right cylinder head.

40. Position the camshaft lobes in a neutral position with the flats on the back of the camshafts up and parallel with the right cylinder head camshaft cover rail. Observe the markings on the right cylinder head camshaft bearing caps. Each bearing cap is marked in order to identify its location. The markings have the following meanings:
- The raised feature must always be oriented toward the center of the cylinder head.
- The I indicates the intake camshaft.
- The E indicates the exhaust camshaft.

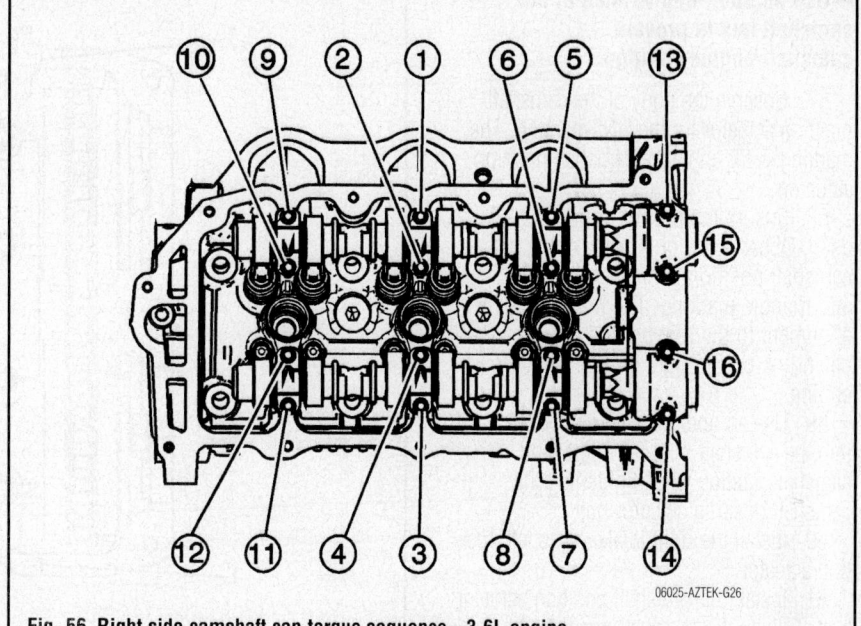

Fig. 56 Right side camshaft cap torque sequence—3.6L engine

- The number 1, 3, 5 indicates the cylinder position from the front of the engine.

41. Apply a liberal amount of lubricant GM P/N 12345501 (Canadian P/N 992704) or equivalent to the camshaft bearing caps.

42. Install the camshaft bearing thrust caps in the first journal of the right cylinder head.

43. Install the remaining bearing caps with their orientation mark toward the center of the cylinder head.

44. Hand start all the camshaft bearing cap bolts.

45. Tighten the camshaft bearing cap bolts in the sequence shown to 89 inch lbs. (10 Nm).

46. Loosen the center intake camshaft bearing cap bolts and the center exhaust camshaft bearing cap bolts.

47. Retighten the center camshaft bearing cap bolts to 89 inch lbs. (10 Nm).

48. Remove the EN 46108.

➡The EN 46106 must be installed onto the flywheel.

49. Use the J 41998-B, nut, bearing and washer to install the crankshaft balancer.

➡Do not lubricate the crankshaft front oil seal or crankshaft balancer sealing surfaces. The crankshaft balancer is installed into a dry seal.

50. Apply lubricant to the inside of the crankshaft balancer hub bore.

51. Place the crankshaft balancer in position on the crankshaft.

52. Thread the J 41998-B in the crankshaft. Ensure you engage at least 10 threads of the J 41998-B before pressing the crankshaft balancer in place.

53. Push the crankshaft balancer into position by tightening the nut on the J 41998-B until the large washer bottoms out on the crankshaft end.

54. Remove the J 41998-B.

55. Tighten the crankshaft balancer bolt to 74 ft. lbs. (100 Nm). Tighten the crankshaft balancer bolt an additional 150 degrees using the J 45059.

56. Remove the EN 46106.

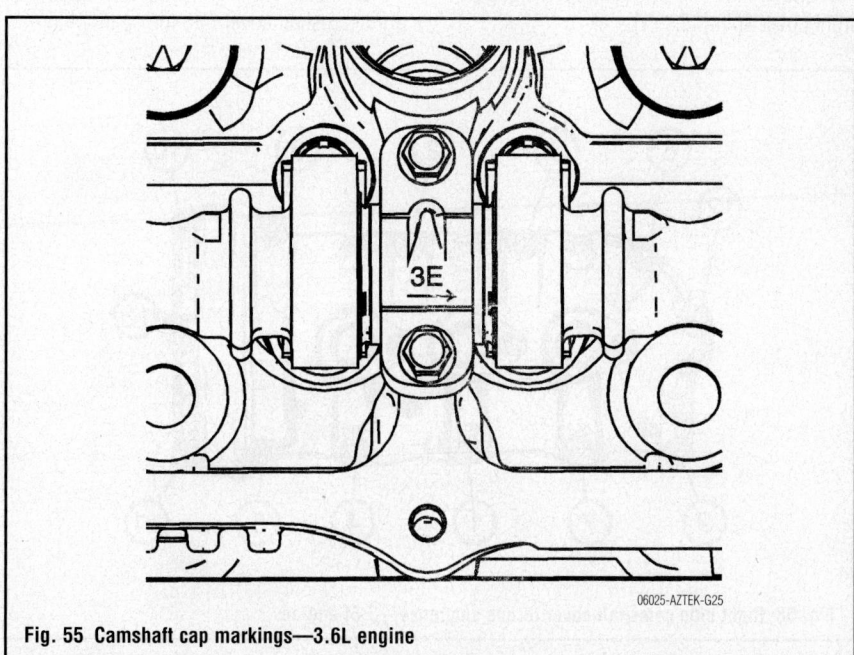

Fig. 55 Camshaft cap markings—3.6L engine

➡️**Use an open-end wrench at the camshaft hex to prevent camshaft/engine rotation.**

57. Observe the body of the camshaft position actuator for the "IN" marking. The marking is for an intake camshaft position actuator.

58. Ensure the proper timing mark is used. Observe the outer ring of the camshaft position actuator for the "R" and triangle marking. The marking is for alignment to the highlighted timing chain link on the right side of the engine.

59. Use an open wrench on the hex cast into the camshaft in order to prevent camshaft rotation when tightening the camshaft position actuator bolt.

60. Install the right intake camshaft position actuator.

61. Install the camshaft position actuator bolt. Tighten the camshaft position actuator bolt to 43 ft. lbs. (58 Nm).

62. Observe the body of the camshaft position actuator for the "EX" marking. The marking is for an exhaust camshaft position actuator.

63. Ensure the proper timing mark is used. Observe the outer ring of the camshaft position actuator for the "R" and triangle marking. The marking is for alignment to the highlighted timing chain link on the right side of the engine.

64. Use an open wrench on the hex cast into the camshaft in order to prevent camshaft rotation when tightening the camshaft position actuator bolt.

65. Install the right exhaust camshaft position actuator.

66. Install the camshaft position actuator bolt. Tighten the camshaft position actuator bolt to 43 ft. lbs. (58 Nm).

67. Install the CMP actuator valve.

68. Install the CMP actuator valve bolt. Tighten the CMP actuator valve bolt to 89 inch lbs. (10 Nm). Connect the CMP actuator valve electrical connector.

69. Install the power steering pressure hose bracket and nut as necessary.

70. Install the CMP sensor.

71. Install the CMP sensor bolt. Tighten the CMP sensor bolt to 89 inch lbs. (10 Nm).

72. Connect the CMP sensor electrical connector.

73. Install the power steering pressure hose as necessary.

74. Install a NEW camshaft cover seal and NEW grommets.

75. Remove the EN 46105-1 from the rear of the right camshafts.

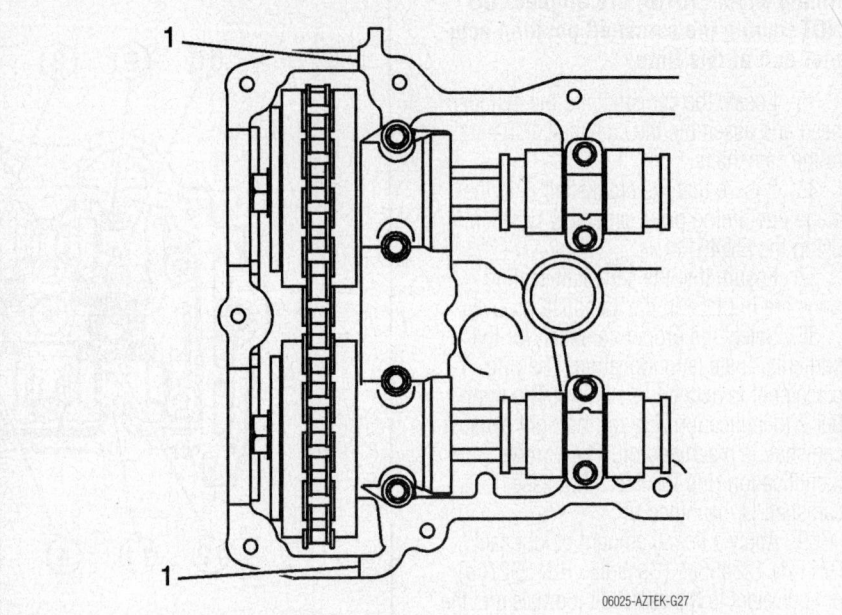

Fig. 57 Place a bead 8mm (0.3150 in) in diameter by 4mm (0.1575 in) in height of RTV sealant, GM P/N 12378521 (Canadian P/N 88901148) or equivalent, on the engine front cover split lines

76. Install the EN 46101 onto the spark plug tubes of the right cylinder head.

77. Install the camshaft cover bolt grommets prior to installing the camshaft cover bolts.

78. Wipe the camshaft cover sealing surface on the right cylinder head with a clean, lint-free cloth.

79. Place a bead 8mm (0.3150 in) in diameter by 4mm (0.1575 in) in height of RTV sealant, GM P/N 12378521 (Canadian P/N 88901148) or equivalent, on the engine front cover split lines (1).

80. Place the right camshaft cover into position onto the right cylinder head.

81. Loosely install the right camshaft cover bolts.

82. Tighten the right camshaft cover bolts in the sequence shown to 89 inch lbs. (10 Nm).

83. Remove the EN 46101 from the spark plug tubes of the right cylinder head.

84. Install the NEW spark plugs into the right cylinder head. Tighten the spark plugs to 15 ft. lbs. (20 Nm).

85. Install each ignition coil through the right camshaft cover into the spark plug

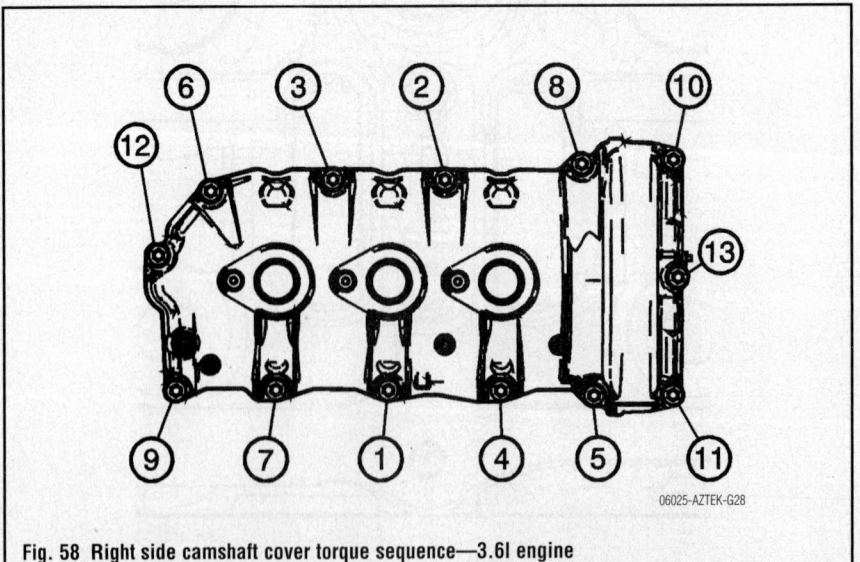

Fig. 58 Right side camshaft cover torque sequence—3.6l engine

tube taking care not to damage the spark plug and/or the seal in the right camshaft cover.

86. Install each ignition coil bolt. Tighten the ignition coil bolt to 89 inch lbs. (10 Nm).

87. Install the upper intake manifold with the lower intake manifold.

CAMSHAFT BEARING REPLACEMENT

See Figure 59.

1. Select the expander assembly and driving washer.

2. Assemble the special tool J 33049.

3. Drive out the camshaft bearings with special tool J 33049.

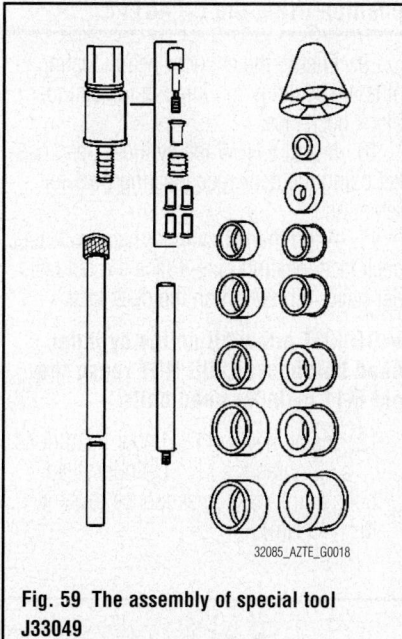

32085_AZTE_G0018

Fig. 59 The assembly of special tool J33049

To install:

4. Assemble special tool J 33049 according to the manufacturer's instructions.

5. Notice: Severe engine damage may result if the oil holes are not correctly aligned.

6. Install the camshaft bearings in the following order:

- Index the camshaft bearing oil holes with the engine block oil passages.
- Place the bearing on special tool J 33049.
- Install the third camshaft bearing.
- Install the second camshaft bearing.
- Install the outer camshaft bearings.

7. Apply sealer GM P/N 12377901 (Canadian P/N 10953504) or the equiva-

lent to the camshaft rear bearing hole plug.

8. Install the camshaft rear bearing hole plug.

CYLINDER HEAD

REMOVAL & INSTALLATION

3.4L and 3.5L Engine

This engine uses aluminum cylinder heads. Use care when working with light alloy parts. Valve guides are pressed in. Roller rocker arms are located on a pedestal in a slot in the cylinder head and are retained on individual threaded bolts.

The cylinder heads are retained by torque-to-yield bolts. A torque angle meter is required for proper torque during assembly. New replacement head bolts are recommended.

Before removing the cylinder head(s) from the engine and before disassembling the valve mechanism, perform a compression test and note the results. During disassembly, be sure that the valvetrain components are kept together and identified so that they can be installed in their original locations.

Left (Front) Side

See Figure 60.

1. Before servicing the vehicle, refer to the Precautions Section.

2. Relieve the fuel system pressure using the recommended procedure.

3. Drain the cooling system.

4. Drain the oil.

5. Remove or disconnect the following:

- Negative battery cable
- Upper intake manifold
- Lower intake manifold
- Valve rocker arms and pushrods
- Exhaust crossover pipe
- Thermostat bypass pipe
- Right side engine mount strut bracket
- Oil level indicator tube
- Left side spark plug wires and spark plugs
- Left side exhaust manifold
- Left side cylinder head and gasket

To install:

6. Clean all parts well. Clean all gasket surfaces. Carefully remove all varnish soot and carbon to the bare metal. DO NOT use a motorized wire brush on any gasket surface since the soft aluminum will be damaged. If necessary, the head can be disassembled for thorough inspection and reconditioning.

7. Inspect the cylinder head for cracks. Do not attempt to weld the cylinder head. If cracked, replace it. Check the cylinder head deck, intake and exhaust manifold mating surfaces for flatness. These surfaces may be reconditioned by milling. If the surfaces are warped more than 0.005 in. (0.127mm), the surface should be milled. If more than 0.010 in. (0.251mm) of metal must be removed from the head, the head should be replaced.

8. Clean the cylinder head bolts and the bolt holes. Check the head bolts for damaged threads or stretching. New replacement head bolts are recommended.

9. Install or connect the following:

- New cylinder head gasket which is marked which side is **UP**
- Cylinder head by aligning it with the dowel pins
- New cylinder head bolts coated with a sealant (such as GM 1052080). Torque the bolts in the proper sequence (1–8) to 44 ft. lbs. (60 Nm) for –05. Using a torque angle meter turn the bolts 95 degrees for –05, in the proper sequence.
- Left side exhaust manifold. Torque the bolts to 12 ft. lbs. (16 Nm).
- Spark plugs. Torque the plugs 11 ft. lbs. (15 Nm).
- Spark plug wires
- Oil level indicator tube. Torque the fastener to 18 ft. lbs. (25 Nm).
- Right side mount strut bracket. Torque the fastener to 37 ft. lbs. (50 Nm).
- Thermostat bypass pipe. Torque it to 18 ft. lbs. (25 Nm).
- Exhaust crossover pipe. Torque the fastener to 18 ft. lbs. (25 Nm).
- Valve rocker arms and pushrods. Torque the fastener to 89 inch lbs. (10 Nm). Using a torque angle meter torque the fastener an additional 30 degrees.
- Lower intake manifold. Torque the bolts to 115 inch lbs. (13 Nm).

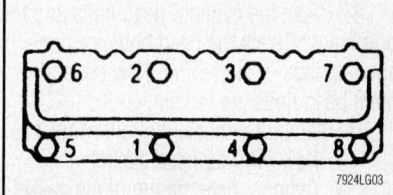

7924LG03

Fig. 60 Cylinder head bolt torque sequence—3.4L and 3.5L engine

- Upper intake manifold. Torque the bolts to 18 ft. lbs. (25 Nm).
- Negative battery cable
10. Refill the coolant system.
11. Change the oil filter and fill the engine with clean oil.
12. Turn the ignition to the **ON** position several times to pressurize the fuel system. Start the engine and inspect for any leaks, repair if necessary. Check and top off the fluid levels if required.

Right (Rear) Side

See Figure 60.

1. Before servicing the vehicle, refer to the Precautions Section.
2. Relieve the fuel system pressure using the recommended procedure.
3. Drain the coolant system.
4. Drain the oil from the engine.
5. Remove or disconnect the following:
- Negative battery cable
- Upper intake manifold
- Lower intake manifold
- Valve rocker arms and pushrods
- Exhaust crossover pipe
- Right side spark plug wires
- Right side exhaust manifold
- Right side cylinder head and gasket
- Right side spark plugs from the cylinder head

To install:

6. Clean all parts well. Clean all gasket surfaces. Carefully remove all varnish soot and carbon to the bare metal. DO NOT use a motorized wire brush on any gasket surface since the soft aluminum will be damaged. If necessary, the head can be disassembled for thorough inspection and reconditioning.
7. Inspect the cylinder head for cracks. Do not attempt to weld the cylinder head. If cracked, replace it. Check the cylinder head deck, intake and exhaust manifold mating surfaces for flatness. These surfaces may be reconditioned by milling. If the surfaces are "out of flat" by more than 0.005 inch, the surface should be milled. If more than 0.010 inch of metal must be removed from the head, the head should be replaced.
8. Clean the cylinder head bolts and the bolt holes. Check the head bolts for damaged threads or stretching. New replacement head bolts are recommended.
9. Install or connect the following:
- New cylinder head gasket
- Cylinder head on top of the gasket and make certain it is lined up properly with the dowel pins
- New cylinder head bolts coated

with a sealant (such as GM 1052080). Torque the bolts in the proper sequence (1-8) to 37 ft. lbs. (50 Nm). Using a torque angle meter turn the bolts 90 degrees in the proper sequence.
- Right side exhaust manifold. Torque the bolts to 12 ft. lbs. (16 Nm).
- Spark plugs. Torque the plugs 11 ft. lbs. (15 Nm).
- Spark plug wires
- Exhaust crossover pipe. Torque the fastener to 18 ft. lbs. (25 Nm).
- Valve rocker arms and pushrods. Torque the fastener to 89 inch lbs. (10 Nm). Using a torque angle meter torque the fastener an additional 30 degrees.
- Lower intake manifold. Torque the bolts to 115 inch lbs. (13 Nm).
- Upper intake manifold. Torque the bolts to 18 ft. lbs. (25 Nm).
- Negative battery cable
10. Refill the coolant system.
11. Change the oil filter and fill the engine with clean oil.
12. Start the vehicle and verify no leaks, abnormal noises and correct engine operation.
13. Check the fluid levels and top off if necessary.

3.6L Engine

Left Side

See Figures 61 and 62.

1. Before servicing the vehicle, refer to the Precautions Section.
2. Remove the upper and lower intake manifolds.
3. Remove the camshafts.
4. Remove the exhaust manifold.
5. Remove the two front M8 left cylinder head bolts.
6. Remove the left cylinder head bolts.
7. Remove the left cylinder head.
8. Remove and discard the left cylinder head gasket.

To install:

✳✳ WARNING

Ensure that the crankshaft is in the stage one timing drive assembly position using the EN 46111.

9. Ensure the cylinder head locating pins are securely mounted in the cylinder block deck face.
10. Install a NEW left cylinder head gasket using the deck face locating pins for retention.
11. Align the left cylinder head with the deck face locating pins. Place the left cylinder head in position on the deck face.

➡ **DO NOT allow oil on the cylinder head bolt bosses. DO NOT reuse the old M11 cylinder head bolts.**

12. Install new M11 cylinder head bolts.
   a. Tighten the M11 cylinder head bolts a first pass in sequence to 33 ft. lbs. (45 Nm).

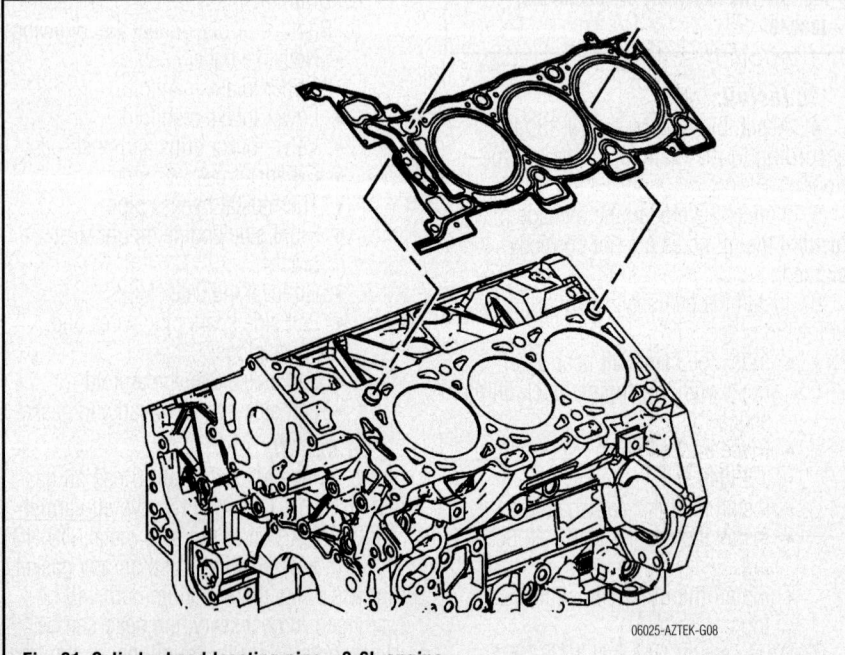

06025-AZTEK-G08

Fig. 61 Cylinder head locating pins—3.6L engine

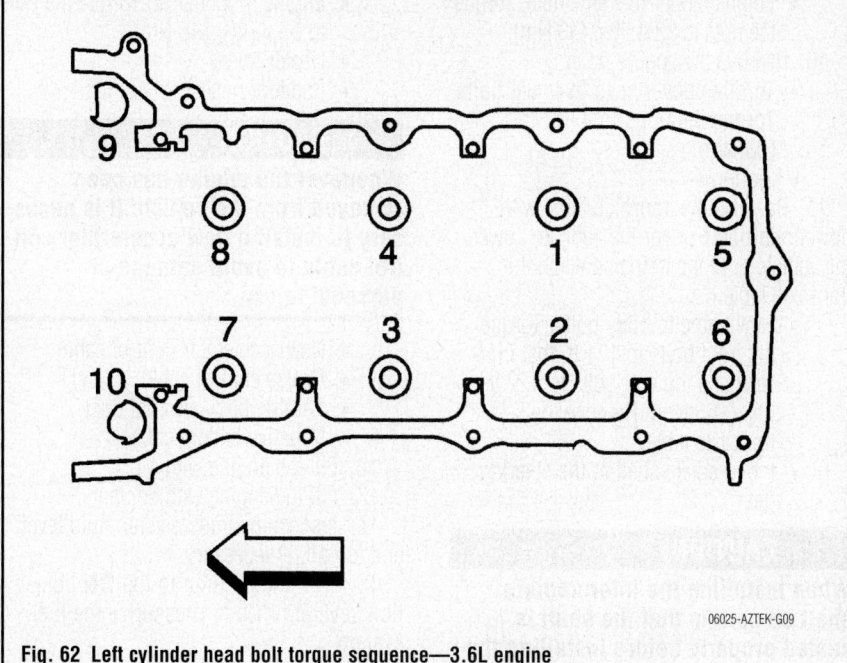

Fig. 62 Left cylinder head bolt torque sequence—3.6L engine

b. Tighten the M11 cylinder head bolts a second pass in sequence an additional 120 degrees.

13. Install the 2 front M8 left cylinder head bolts.

a. Tighten the M8 cylinder head bolts a first pass to 11 ft. lbs. (15 Nm).

b. Tighten the M8 cylinder head bolts a second pass in sequence an additional 60 degrees.

14. The remainder of installation is the reverse of removal.

Right Side

See Figure 63.

1. Before servicing the vehicle, refer to the Precautions Section.

2. Remove the upper and lower intake manifolds.

3. Remove the camshafts.

4. Remove the exhaust manifold.

5. Remove the right cylinder head bolts.

6. Remove the right cylinder head.

7. Remove and discard the right cylinder head gasket.

To install:

➡**Ensure that the crankshaft is in the timing drive assembly position using the EN 46111.**

8. Ensure the cylinder head locating pins are securely mounted in the cylinder block deck face.

9. Install a NEW right cylinder head gasket using the deck face locating pins for retention.

10. Align the right cylinder head with the deck face locating pins.

11. Place the right cylinder head in position on the deck face.

➡**DO NOT allow oil on the cylinder head bolt bosses. DO NOT reuse the old M11 cylinder head bolts.**

12. Install new M11 cylinder head bolts.

a. Tighten the M11 cylinder head bolts a first pass in sequence to 33 ft. lbs. (45 Nm).

b. Tighten the M11 cylinder head bolts a second pass in sequence an additional 120 degrees using the J 45059.

13. The remainder of installation is the reverse of removal.

ENGINE ASSEMBLY

REMOVAL & INSTALLATION

3.4L and 3.5L Engine

See Figure 64.

1. Before servicing the vehicle, refer to the Precautions Section.

2. Drain the cooling system.

3. Drain the engine oil.

4. Relieve the fuel system pressure.

5. Remove or disconnect the following:

- Negative battery cable
- Throttle body air inlet duct
- Cruise control cable
- Accelerator control cable
- Radiator hoses from the engine
- Heater hoses from the engine
- Engine mount struts
- Fuel lines from the fuel rail
- Engine wiring harness connectors
- Vacuum hoses
- Brake booster vacuum hose
- Automatic transaxle range selector cable
- Wiring harness grounds
- Catalytic converter three-way pipe from the right side exhaust manifold
- Rear propeller shaft, on AWD vehicles
- Front wheels

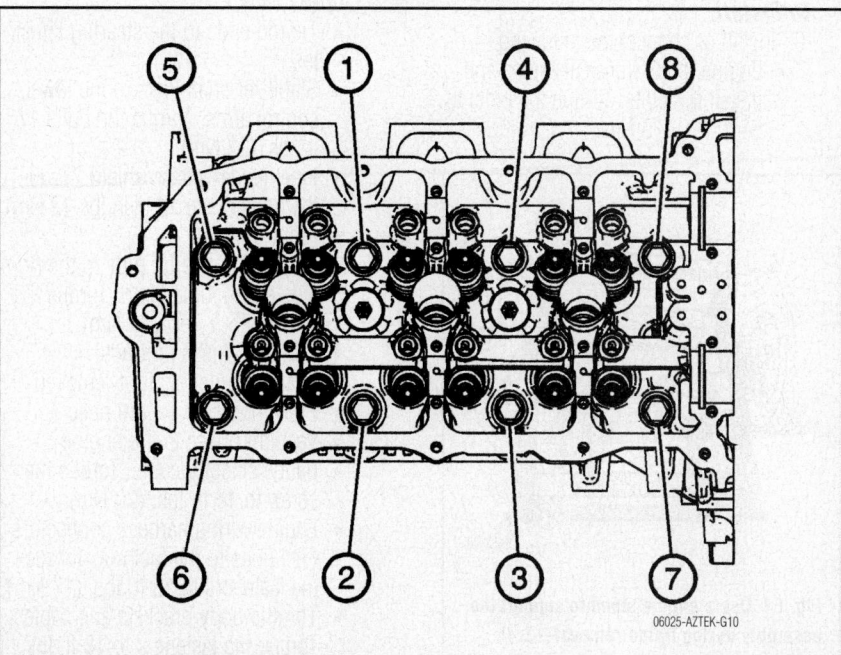

Fig. 63 Right side cylinder head bolt torque sequence—3.6L engine

- Lower radiator baffle
- Splash shields
- Stabilizer shaft links from the lower control arms
- Tie rod ends from the steering knuckles
- Lower ball joints from the steering knuckles
- Cooler lines and bracket from the transaxle
- A/C compressor bolts and position compressor aside
- Axles from the transaxle and secure them to the steering knuckle/struts

❋❋ **CAUTION**

Failure to remove the intermediate shaft from the steering gear may result in damage to the gear or intermediate shaft and may cause a loss of steering control.

- Intermediate shaft from the steering gear
6. Lower the vehicle until the frame is in contact with a suitable transaxle table/engine stand (such as J 39580). Make certain that an engine stand (such as J 39580) is aligned below the engine.
- Frame bolts
7. Raise the vehicle to separate the assembly from the vehicle.
- Starter
- Flywheel-to-torque converter bolts
8. Install a suitable engine hoist
- Engine to transaxle bolts and studs
- Engine from the transaxle and place it on the engine stand

To install:
9. Install or connect the following:
- Engine to the transaxle/frame and install the bolts. Torque the bolts to 55 ft. lbs. (75 Nm).

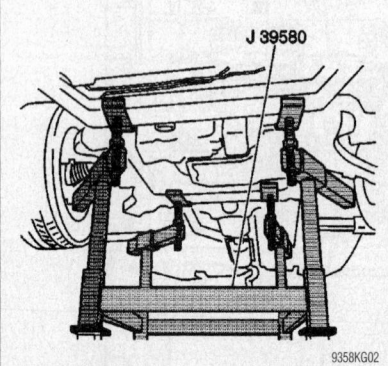

Fig. 64 Use a engine stand to support the assembly during frame removal—3.4L and 3.5L Engine

- Engine mount-to-frame nuts. Torque the nuts to 32 ft. lbs. (43 Nm).
10. Remove the engine hoist.
- Torque converter to flywheel bolts. Torque the bolts to 47 ft. lbs. (63 Nm).
- Starter
11. Position the transaxle table with powertrain/frame under the vehicle. Lower the vehicle until the frame contacts transaxle table.
- New frame to body bolts. Torque the front bolts to 111 ft. lbs. (150 Nm) and the rear bolts to 122 ft. lbs. (165 Nm). Remove the transaxle table.
- Intermediate shaft to the steering gear

❋❋ **CAUTION**

When installing the intermediate shaft be certain that the shaft is seated properly before installing the pinch bolt. If the pinch bolt is inserted into the coupling before the shaft, the mating surfaces disengage. Disengagement of the two shafts may lead to a loss of steering control.

- Pinch bolt at the intermediate shaft. Torque the bolt 35 ft. lbs. (48 Nm).
- Drive axles to the transaxle
- Cooler lines and bracket to the transaxle. Torque the fasteners to 17 ft. lbs. (23 Nm).
- Lower ball joints to the steering knuckles. Torque to 40 ft. lbs. (55 Nm).
- Tie rod ends to the steering knuckles
- Stabilizer shaft links to the lower control arms. Torque the bolts 17 ft. lbs. (23 Nm).
- Inner fender splash shield. Torque the fasteners to 18 inch lbs. (2 Nm).
- Front wheels
- Catalytic converter pipe to the right side exhaust manifold. Torque the nuts to 25 ft. lbs. (34 Nm).
- Wiring harness grounds
- Rear propeller shaft, if removed
- Brake booster vacuum hose
- Vacuum hoses to the engine
- Range selector cable. Torque the screw to 14 ft. lbs. (20 Nm).
- Engine wiring harness connectors
- Fuel lines to the fuel rail. Torque the fasteners to 13 ft. lbs. (17 Nm).
- Throttle body brackets and cables. Torque the fasteners to 18 ft. lbs. (25 Nm).

- Engine mount strut. Torque the bolt to 35 ft. lbs. (48 Nm).
- Heater hoses
- Radiator hoses

❋❋ **CAUTION**

Whenever the engine has been removed from the vehicle it is necessary to install a new accelerator control cable to avoid damage or personal injury.

- New accelerator control cable
- Cruise control cable
- Throttle body air inlet duct
- Negative battery cable
12. Fill the engine with oil.
13. Fill the engine with coolant.
14. Inspect the transmission fluid level and top off, if necessary.
15. Turn the ignition to the **ON** position several times to pressurize the fuel system.
16. Start the engine and inspect for leaks, repair if necessary.
17. Check and top off the fluid levels if required.

3.6L Engine

1. Before servicing the vehicle, refer to the Precautions Section.
2. Disconnect the battery negative cable.
3. Remove the throttle body air inlet duct.

➡**Do not disconnect the battery negative cable from the vehicle.**

4. Disconnect the battery negative cable from the engine block.

➡**Do not disconnect the battery positive cable from the vehicle, underhood electrical center or the battery.**

5. Disconnect the battery positive cable from the alternator and the starter.
6. Drain the cooling system.
7. Disconnect the radiator hoses from the engine.
8. Disconnect the heater hoses from the engine.
9. Remove the engine mount struts.

❋❋ **WARNING**

Relieve the fuel pressure.

10. Disconnect the fuel pressure and evaporative emission (EVAP) pipes from the engine.
11. Remove the ECM chassis (outboard) side electrical connector from the ECM.
12. Remove the wiring harness ground from the transmission.

13. Remove the vacuum brake booster hose from the intake manifold.

14. Properly evacuate the air conditioning system.

15. Disconnect the discharge hose from the condenser.

16. Disconnect the suction hose from the evaporator outlet tube.

17. Secure the discharge and suction hoses to the powertrain.

18. Remove the transmission electrical connector.

19. Raise and support the vehicle.

20. If you will be separating the engine from the transmission, remove the torque converter bolts.

21. Drain the engine oil.

22. If the vehicle is equipped with all wheel drive (AWD), remove rear propeller shaft.

23. Remove the catalytic converter.

24. Remove the front tires and wheels.

25. Remove lower radiator air baffle.

26. Remove the engine splash shields.

27. Disconnect the vehicle speed sensor (VSS) electrical connector and secure the wiring harness to the vehicle.

28. Remove the front wheel speed sensor wiring harnesses from the lower control arms and the frame.

29. Remove the tie rod ends from the steering knuckles.

30. Remove the lower ball joints from the knuckles.

31. Disconnect the drive axles from the transaxle.

32. Rotate the struts and reposition the drive axles toward the rear of the vehicle in order to provide clearance for the powertrain to be removed.

CAUTION

Failure to disconnect the intermediate shaft from the rack and pinion steering gear stub shaft can result in damage to the steering gear and/or intermediate shaft. This damage may cause loss of steering control which could result in an accident and possible personal injury

33. Separate the intermediate steering shaft from the steering gear.

34. Remove the engine mount lower nuts.

35. Remove the transmission mount lower nuts.

36. Position a powertrain lift table below the powertrain.

37. Lower the vehicle until the powertrain is supported by the powertrain lift table.

38. Remove the frame bolts.

39. Carefully raise the vehicle or lower the powertrain table in order to remove the powertrain from the vehicle.

40. Remove the exhaust crossover pipe.

41. Remove the coolant inlet pipe.

42. Perform the following steps if it is necessary to separate the engine from the transmission.

➡Do not disconnect the power steering pipes or drain the power steering fluid.

43. Remove the power steering pressure pipe/hose from the water outlet.

44. Remove the accessory drive belt.

45. Remove the power steering reservoir and reposition to provide access.

46. Remove and reposition the power steering pump with the power steering pipe/hose.

47. Remove the transfer case brace.

48. Remove the transmission lower brace.

49. Remove the transmission upper brace nut located behind the power steering pump.

50. Remove the engine to transmission (bell housing) bolts.

51. Use 4 M1 0x1.5x40 GM P/N 11519182, or equivalent bolts to install the EN 46114 engine lift brackets to the left rear and right front cylinder heads.

52. Tighten the lift bracket bolts to 48 ft. lbs. (65 Nm).

53. Use an engine hoist in order to separate the engine from the transmission and the frame.

54. Install the engine to a suitable engine stand.

To install:

➡Use an engine hoist in order to remove the engine from the engine stand.

55. Install the engine to the transmission and the frame at the powertrain lift table.

56. Remove the EN 46114 engine lift brackets.

57. Install the engine to transmission (bell housing) bolts.

58. Install the transmission upper brace nut located behind the power steering pump.

59. Tighten the transmission upper brace nut to 37 ft. lbs. (50 Nm).

60. Install the transmission lower brace.

61. Install the transfer case brace.

62. Install the power steering pump with the power steering pipe/hose.

63. Install the power steering reservoir and reposition to provide access.

64. Install the accessory drive belt.

65. Install the power steering pressure pipe/hose to the water outlet.

66. Install the coolant inlet pipe.

67. Install the exhaust crossover pipe.

68. Carefully lower the vehicle or raise the powertrain table in order to install the powertrain to the vehicle.

69. Install the frame bolts.

70. Raise the vehicle and remove the powertrain lift table.

71. Install the transmission mount lower nuts. Torque the bolt to 35 ft. lbs. (48 Nm).

72. Install the engine mount lower nuts.

CAUTION

Failure to disconnect the intermediate shaft from the rack and pinion steering gear stub shaft can result in damage to the steering gear and/or intermediate shaft. This damage may cause loss of steering control which could result in an accident and possible personal injury

73. Install the intermediate steering shaft to the steering gear.

74. Rotate the struts and install the drive axles to the transaxle.

75. Install the lower ball joints to the knuckles.

76. Install the tie rod ends to the steering knuckles.

77. Install the front wheel speed sensor wiring harnesses to the lower control arms and the frame.

78. Connect the VSS electrical connector and secure the wiring harness to the vehicle.

79. Install the engine splash shields.

80. Install lower radiator air baffle.

81. Install the front tires and wheels.

82. Install the catalytic converter.

83. If the vehicle is equipped with AWD, install rear propeller shaft.

84. Install the torque converter bolts as necessary.

85. Lower the vehicle.

86. Fill the engine oil as necessary.

87. Install the transmission electrical connector.

88. Connect the suction hose to the evaporator outlet pipe.

89. Connect the discharge hose to the condenser.

90. Recharge the air conditioning system.

91. Install the brake booster vacuum hose to the intake manifold.

92. Install the transmission ground wire and the bolt.

93. Tighten the transmission ground bolt 55 ft. lbs. (75 Nm).

94. Install the ECM chassis (outboard) side electrical connector to the ECM.

95. Connect the fuel pressure and EVAP pipes to the engine.

96. Install the engine mount struts.

97. Connect the heater hoses to the engine.

98. Connect the radiator hoses to the engine.

99. Fill the cooling system.

100. Connect the battery positive cable to the alternator and the starter.

101. Connect the battery negative cable to the engine block.

102. Install the throttle body air inlet duct.

103. Connect the battery negative cable to the battery.

EXHAUST MANIFOLD

REMOVAL & INSTALLATION

3.4L and 3.5L Engine

The exhaust manifolds are conventional iron castings. The left and right manifolds are connected by a crossover pipe. Use care with the exhaust manifold-to-cylinder head fasteners. The cylinder heads are aluminum.

Left (Front) Side

See Figures 65 and 66.

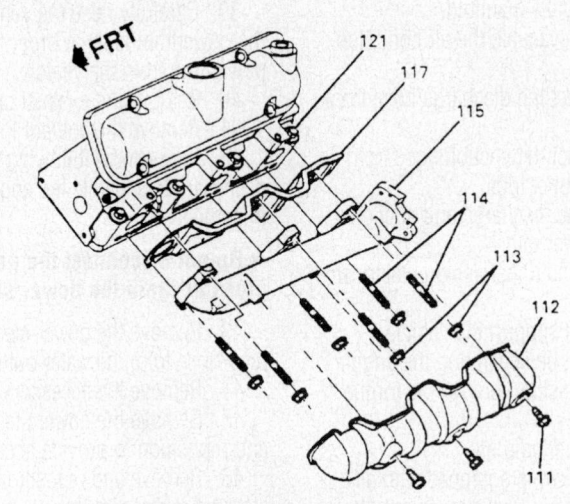

111 SCREW, LH EXHAUST MANIFOLD HEAT SHIELD
112 SHIELD LH EXHAUST MANIFOLD
113 NUT, LH EXHAUST MANIFOLD
114 STUD, LH EXHAUST MANIFOLD
115 MANIFOLD, LH EXHAUST
117 GASKET, LH EXHAUST MANIFOLD
121 HEAD, LH CYLINDER

Fig. 66 Left exhaust manifold mounting—3.4L and 3.5L engine

1. Before servicing the vehicle, refer to the Precautions Section.
2. Drain the cooling system.
3. Remove or disconnect the following:

- Negative battery cable
- Throttle body air inlet duct
- Right side engine mount strut bracket
- Radiator inlet hose
- Thermostat bypass pipe
- Exhaust crossover pipe heat shield
- Exhaust crossover pipe
- Left side exhaust manifold heat shield
- Left side exhaust manifold and discard the gasket

To install:

4. Clean the gasket mounting surfaces.
5. Install or connect the following:

- Left side exhaust manifold gasket
- Left side exhaust manifold. Torque the nuts to 12 ft. lbs. (16 Nm).
- Left side exhaust manifold heat shield. Torque the fasteners to 89 inch lbs. (10 Nm).
- Exhaust crossover pipe. Torque the bolts to 18 ft. lbs. (25 Nm).
- Exhaust crossover pipe heat shield. Torque the bolts to 89 inch lbs. (10 Nm).
- Thermostat bypass pipe. Torque the fastener to 18 ft. lbs. (25 Nm).
- Radiator inlet hose to the engine
- Right side engine mount strut bracket. Torque the bolts to 35 ft. lbs. (48 Nm).

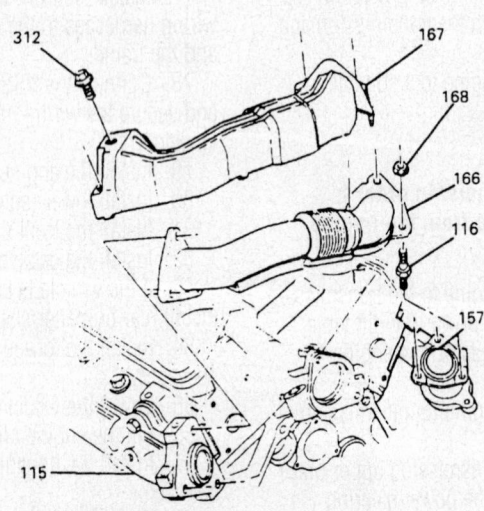

115 MANIFOLD, LEFT HAND EXHAUST
116 STUD, EXHAUST CROSSOVER
157 MANIFOLD, RIGHT HAND EXHAUST
166 CROSSOVER PIPE, EXHAUST
167 SHIELD, EXHAUST CROSSOVER UPPER HEAT
168 NUT, EXHAUST CROSSOVER
312 BOLT/SCREW, EXHAUST CROSSOVER UPPER HEAT SHIELD

Fig. 65 Exploded view of the exhaust crossover and heat shield mounting

- Throttle body air inlet duct
- Negative battery cable

6. Fill the cooling system

7. Start the vehicle and check for leaks, repair if necessary.

8. Check and top off all fluid levels if necessary.

Right (Rear) Side

See Figure 67.

1. Before servicing the vehicle, refer to the Precautions Section.

2. Remove or disconnect the following:
- Negative battery cable
- Throttle body air inlet duct
- Accelerator cable bracket from the throttle body
- Manifold Absolute Pressure (MAP) sensor
- Exhaust Gas Recirculation (EGR) valve

3. Rotate the engine for access.
- Ignition module
- Ignition coils and bracket
- Spark plug wires from the right bank spark plugs
- Heated Oxygen (HO$_2$) sensor electrical connector
- EVAP solenoid bracket
- Fasteners for the crossover pipe from the right bank exhaust manifold
- Catalytic converter

- Right side exhaust manifold heat shields
- Right side exhaust manifold
- Right side exhaust manifold gasket
- EGR valve pipe, if replacing the exhaust manifold
- HO$_2$ sensor, if replacing the exhaust manifold

To install:

4. Clean the gasket mounting surfaces.

5. Install or connect the following:
- HO$_2$ sensor, if removed. Torque the sensor to 31 ft. lbs. (42 Nm).
- EGR valve pipe, if removed. Torque the fastener to 18 ft. lbs. (25 Nm).
- Exhaust manifold gasket
- Exhaust manifold. Torque the bolts to 12 ft. lbs. (16 Nm).
- Both manifold heat shields. Torque the bolts to 89 inch lbs. (10 Nm).
- Catalytic converter. Torque the fasteners to 25 ft. lbs. (34 Nm).
- Exhaust manifold crossover pipe. Torque the bolts to 18 ft. lbs. (25 Nm).
- HO$_2$ sensor electrical connector
- EVAP solenoid bracket
- Plug wires to the spark plugs
- Ignition module
- Ignition coils and bracket. Torque the fastener to 18 ft. lbs. (25 Nm).

6. Rotate the engine to its original position.

7. Install or connect the following:
- EGR valve to the intake manifold
- MAP sensor
- Accelerator cable bracket to the throttle body. Torque the bolt to 89 inch lbs. (10 Nm).
- Throttle body air inlet duct
- Negative battery cable

8. Start the engine and inspect for leaks, repair if necessary.

3.6L Engine

Left Side

1. Before servicing the vehicle, refer to the Precautions Section.

2. Remove the left torque strut bracket bolts.

3. Remove the left torque strut bracket.

4. Remove the left exhaust manifold heat shield bolts.

5. Remove the left exhaust manifold heat shield.

6. Remove the engine coolant temperature (ECT) sensor.

7. Disconnect the exhaust pipes from the manifold.

8. Remove the exhaust manifold bolts from the left cylinder head.

9. Remove the left exhaust manifold.

10. Remove and discard the exhaust manifold gasket.

To install:

11. Position a NEW exhaust manifold gasket onto the left exhaust manifold.

12. Install the exhaust manifold bolts into the left exhaust manifold.

13. Place the left exhaust manifold, exhaust manifold gasket and bolts as an assembly in position on the left cylinder head.

14. Install the exhaust manifold bolts into the left cylinder head. Tighten the exhaust manifold bolts to 18 ft. lbs. (25 Nm).

15. Connect the exhaust pipes.

16. Install the engine coolant temperature (ECT) sensor. Tighten the ECT sensor to 16 ft. lbs. (22 Nm).

17. Install NEW O-rings on the crankshaft position sensor.

18. Place the left exhaust manifold heat shield in position.

19. Install the exhaust manifold heat shield bolts. Tighten the exhaust manifold heat shield bolts to 89 inch lbs. (10 Nm).

20. Install the left torque strut bracket.

21. Install the left torque strut bracket bolts. Tighten the left torque strut bracket bolts to 37 ft. lbs. (50 Nm).

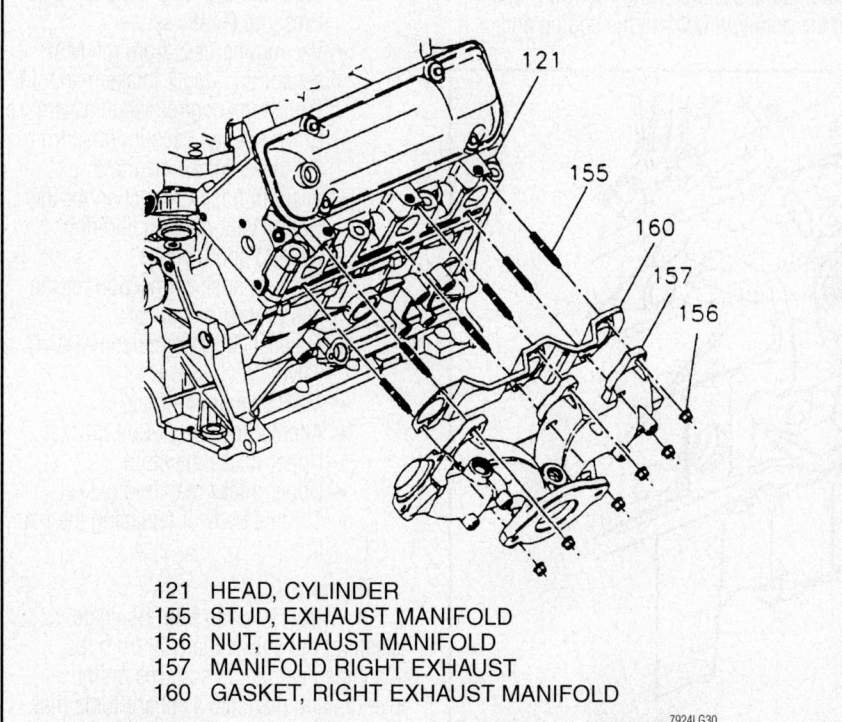

121	HEAD, CYLINDER
155	STUD, EXHAUST MANIFOLD
156	NUT, EXHAUST MANIFOLD
157	MANIFOLD RIGHT EXHAUST
160	GASKET, RIGHT EXHAUST MANIFOLD

7924LG30

Fig. 67 Exploded view of the right exhaust manifold mounting—3.4L and 3.5L engine

Right Side

See Figure 68.

1. Before servicing the vehicle, refer to the Precautions Section.

2. Remove the right exhaust manifold heat shield bolts.

3. Remove the right exhaust manifold heat shield.

4. Remove the exhaust manifold bolts from the right cylinder head.

5. Remove the right exhaust manifold.

6. Remove and discard the exhaust manifold gasket.

7. Remove the block heater cartridge, if equipped.

8. Remove the right knock sensor bolt.

9. Remove the right knock sensor.

10. Remove the crankshaft position sensor bolt.

11. Remove the crankshaft position sensor.

12. Remove and discard the crankshaft position sensor O-ring, if damaged.

To install:

13. Install a NEW O-ring on the crankshaft position sensor, if damaged.

14. Position the crankshaft position sensor into the cylinder block.

15. Install the crankshaft position sensor bolt. Tighten the crankshaft position sensor bolt to 89 inch lbs. (10 Nm).

16. Position the right knock sensor to the cylinder block as shown.

17. Install the knock sensor bolt. Tighten the knock sensor bolt to 17 ft. lbs. (23 Nm). Ensure proper knock sensor orientation.

18. Install the block heater cartridge, if equipped.

19. Position a NEW exhaust manifold gasket onto the right exhaust manifold.

20. Install the exhaust manifold bolts into the right exhaust manifold.

21. Place the right exhaust manifold, exhaust manifold gasket and bolts as an assembly in position on the right cylinder head.

22. Connect the exhaust pipes.

23. Install the exhaust manifold bolts into the right cylinder head. Tighten the exhaust manifold bolts to 18 ft. lbs. (25 Nm).

24. Place the right exhaust manifold heat shield in position.

25. Install the exhaust manifold heat shield bolts. Tighten the exhaust manifold heat shield bolts to 89 inch lbs. (10 Nm).

INTAKE MANIFOLD

REMOVAL & INSTALLATION

3.4L and 3.5L Engine

Upper

See Figure 69.

This engine uses a 2-piece intake manifold. The upper half (often called a plenum) mounts the throttle body. The lower half of the manifold bolts to the engine and contains the fuel injectors. Please note that this engine uses a sequential multi-port fuel injection system. Injector connectors must be connected to their appropriate fuel injector assembly or engine emissions and engine performance will be seriously affected. Identify and tag for identification all wiring connectors as well as vacuum and other components as required to assure correct assembly.

1. Before servicing the vehicle, refer to the Precautions Section.

2. Drain the engine coolant. Remove the coolant recovery bottle.

3. Relieve the fuel system pressure using the recommended procedure.

4. Remove or disconnect the following:

- Negative battery cable
- Throttle body air inlet duct
- Accelerator and cruise control cables and bracket from the throttle body
- Throttle Position (TP) sensor connector from the throttle body
- Idle Air Control (IAC) valve connector from the throttle body
- Left side spark plug wires
- Left side spark plug wire harness clip and harness
- Throttle body heater hoses
- Evaporative emissions (EVAP) canister purge solenoid valve vacuum hoses
- EVAP canister purge solenoid valve
- Ignition coil bracket and coils
- Wire harness for the Manifold Air Pressure (MAP) sensor
- Vacuum harness from the MAP sensor and upper intake manifold
- Emissions control vacuum harness
- Brake booster vacuum hose from the upper intake manifold
- Vacuum hose connection for the Heater Vent Air Conditioning (HVAC) source hose
- Vacuum hose connection for the fuel pressure regulator
- Exhaust Gas Recirculation (EGR) valve
- MAP sensor and bracket
- Alternator through-bolt bracket
- Upper intake manifold
- Upper intake manifold gasket
- Throttle body, if replacing the manifold

To install:

5. Clean all parts well. Use care in cleaning old gasket material from the machined aluminum surfaces on the plenum and manifold as sharp tools may damage sealing surfaces.

6. Clean the mating surfaces to the

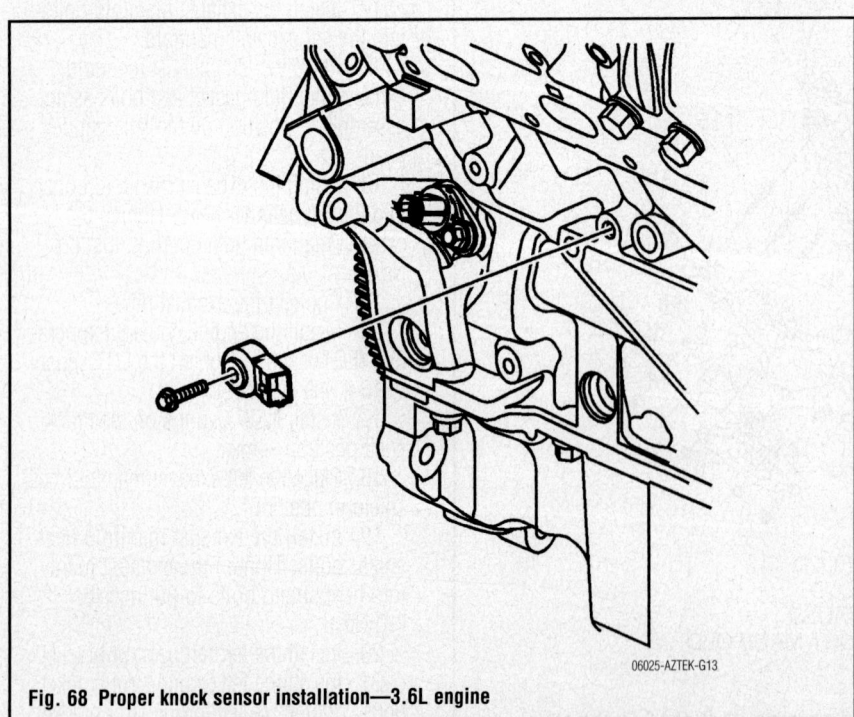

06025-AZTEK-G13

Fig. 68 Proper knock sensor installation—3.6L engine

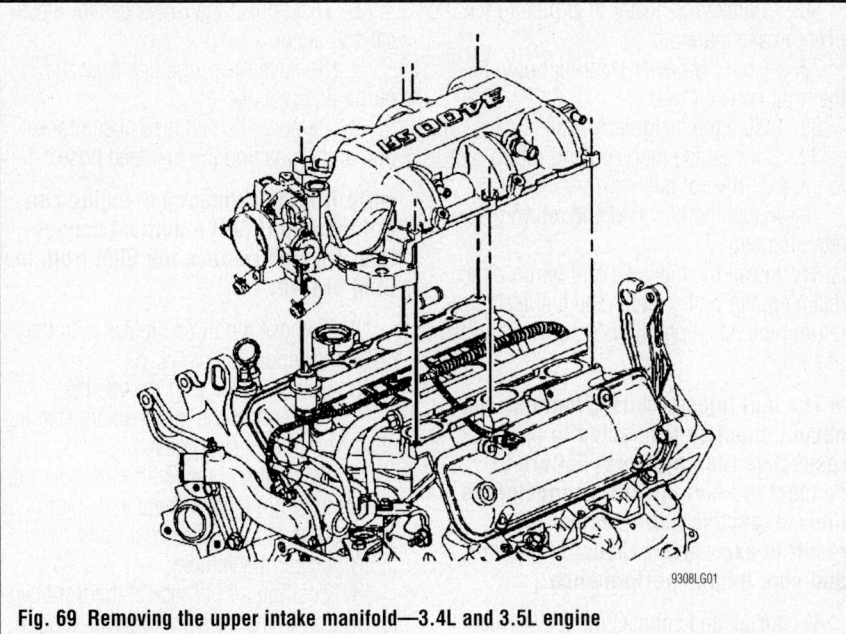

Fig. 69 Removing the upper intake manifold—3.4L and 3.5L engine

9308LG01

upper intake manifold and engine block. Remove any loose pieces of RTV sealer.

7. Install or connect the following:
- Throttle body to the upper intake manifold (if removed). Torque the bolts to 18 ft. lbs. (25 Nm).
- Upper intake manifold gasket
- Upper intake manifold
- MAP sensor and bracket. Torque the bolt to 44 inch lbs. (5 Nm).
- Upper intake manifold bolts. Torque the bolts to 18 ft. lbs. (25 Nm).
- EGR valve. Torque the fastener to 18 ft. lbs. (25 Nm).
- HVAC vacuum source hose to the upper intake manifold
- Fuel pressure regulator vacuum hose to the upper intake manifold
- Brake booster vacuum hose
- MAP sensor and bracket. Torque the bolt to 44 inch lbs. (5 Nm).
- Emissions control vacuum harness
- Vacuum hose for the MAP sensor and upper intake manifold
- Wiring harness to the MAP sensor
- Ignition coil bracket and coils. Torque the fasteners to 18 ft. lbs. (25 Nm).
- EVAP canister purge solenoid valve
- Vacuum hoses to the EVAP canister purge solenoid valve
- Throttle body heater hoses
- Left side spark plug wire harness clip
- Spark plugs wires
- TP sensor wire harness connector to the throttle body
- IAV valve wire harness connector to the throttle body

- Accelerator and cruise control cables and bracket to the throttle body. Torque the fasteners to 106 inch lbs. (12 Nm).
- Throttle body air inlet duct
- Negative battery cable

8. Fill the coolant system.
9. Fill the engine with new oil.
10. Turn the ignition to the **ON** position several times to pressurize the fuel system.
11. Start the engine and check for any leakage and repair if necessary.
12. Check and top off all fluid levels if needed.

Lower

See Figure 70.

1. Remove the upper intake manifold.
2. Remove the engine left side valve rocker arm cover.
3. Remove the engine right side valve rocker arm cover.
4. Disconnect the wiring harness from the engine coolant temperature (ECT) sensor.

➡️**Use masking tape or another appropriate method in order to identify each fuel injector wiring harness connector cylinder number.**

5. Disconnect and remove the fuel injector, manifold air pressure (MAP) and ECT wiring harness.
6. Remove the fuel feed and return pipe from the fuel injector rail.
7. Remove the fuel feed and return pipe retaining clip bolt.
8. Remove the fuel feed and return pipe retaining clip.

9. Remove the fuel injector rail bolts.
10. Remove the fuel injector rail with the fuel injectors.

➡️**Do NOT disconnect the power steering pipes or hoses from the power steering pump.**

11. Remove the power steering pump from the front engine cover and reposition.
12. Disconnect the heater inlet pipe with heater hose from the lower intake manifold and reposition.
13. Disconnect the inlet radiator hose from the engine.
14. Disconnect the thermostat bypass hose from the lower intake manifold pipe.
15. Remove the lower intake manifold bolts.
16. Remove the lower intake manifold.
17. Loosen the valve rocker arms and remove the push rods.
18. Remove the lower intake manifold gaskets and seals.
19. Clean the lower intake manifold gasket and seal surfaces on the cylinder heads and the engine block.
20. Clean and inspect the lower intake manifold.
21. If you are replacing the lower intake manifold, perform the following steps:
   a. Remove the ECT sensor.
   b. Remove the thermostat.

To install:

If you are replacing the lower intake manifold, perform the following steps.

22. Install the ECT sensor.
23. Install the thermostat.

➡️**All gasket-mating surfaces need to be free of oil, and foreign material. Use GM P/N 12346139 (Canadian P/N 10953463), or equivalent, to clean the surfaces.**

24. Install the lower intake manifold gaskets.
25. Install the push rods and tighten the valve rocker arms.
26. With the gaskets in place apply a small drop 8–10 mm (0.31–0.39 in.) of RTV sealer GM P/N 12346286 (Canadian P/N 10953472) or equivalent to the 4 corners of the intake manifold to block joint.
27. Connect the 2 small drops with a bead of RTV sealer that is between 8–10 mm (0.31–0.39 in.) wide and 3.0–5.0 mm (0.12–0.20 in.) thick.
28. Install the lower intake manifold.
29. Apply sealer GM P/N 12345382, (Canadian P/N 10953489) or the equivalent to the lower intake manifold bolt threads.

➡Maximum gasket performance is achieved when using new fasteners, which contain a thread-locking patch. If the fasteners are not replaced, a thread locking chemical must be applied to the fastener threads. Failure to replace the fasteners or apply a thread-locking chemical MAY reduce gasket sealing capability.

➡All lower intake manifold bolts need to be cleaned, free of any foreign material, and reused only if new bolts are unavailable. Use GM P/N 12345382 (Canadian P/N 10953489) or equivalent and apply to the old intake manifold bolt threads.

✳✳ WARNING

The manufacturer recommends the center bolts be fully torqued before the diagonal bolts to assure proper seal ability.

➡Lower intake manifold bolts in location 6 and 7 should be torqued to specification using a crow's foot type tool.

30. Install the lower intake manifold bolts.

31. Tighten the lower intake manifold bolts in sequence to 62 inch lbs. (7 Nm) on the first pass.

32. Tighten the lower intake manifold bolts (1, 2, 3, 4) in sequence to 15 ft. lbs. (20 Nm) on the final pass.

33. Tighten the lower intake manifold bolts (5, 6, 7, 8) in sequence to 18 ft. lbs. (25 Nm) on the final pass.

34. Connect the thermostat bypass hose to the lower intake manifold pipe.

35. Connect the inlet radiator hose to the engine.

36. Connect the heater inlet pipe to the lower intake manifold.

37. Install the power steering pump to the front engine cover.

38. Install the fuel injector rail.

39. Connect the fuel feed and return pipe to the fuel injector rail.

40. Install the fuel feed and return pipe retaining clip.

41. Install the fuel feed and return pipe retaining clip bolt. Tighten the fuel feed and return pipe retaining clip bolt to 71 inch lbs. (8 Nm).

➡The fuel injector wiring harness connectors must be connected to their respective fuel injectors. Failure to connect the fuel injector connectors to their respective fuel injectors may result in excessive exhaust emissions and poor engine performance.

42. Install and connect the fuel injector, MAP and ECT wiring harness.

43. Install the wiring harness to the ECT sensor.

44. Install the engine right side valve rocker arm cover.

45. Install the engine left side valve rocker arm cover.

46. Install the upper intake manifold.

3.6L Engine

Upper

See Figure 71.

1. Before servicing the vehicle, refer to the Precautions Section.

2. Turn the ignition **OFF**.

3. Remove the air inlet duct.

4. Relieve the fuel system pressure.

5. Disconnect the fuel pressure and evaporative emission (EVAP) hoses from the engine.

6. Disconnect the BARO sensor electrical connector.

7. Remove the purge line from the purge line retainer.

8. Remove the fuel feed hose bracket bolt and reposition the fuel feed hose.

➡Do NOT disconnect the engine control module (ECM) electrical connectors. Do NOT remove the ECM from the ECM bracket.

9. Remove the ECM bracket with the ECM and reposition aside.

10. Raise and support the vehicle.

11. Disconnect the intermediate steering shaft from the steering gear.

12. Remove and reposition the front portion of the front fender liners in order to gain access to the frame front bolts.

13. Lower the vehicle.

14. Position a floor jack at the front center section of the frame in order to support the powertrain.

15. Remove the frame front bolts.

16. Carefully lower the powertrain or raise the vehicle enough to provide access.

17. Disconnect the purge solenoid electrical connector.

18. Remove the wiring harness from the right side of the intake manifold.

19. Disconnect the fuel injector electrical connector.

20. Remove the fuel injector electrical connector from the fuel injector electrical connector bracket.

21. Disconnect the intake manifold runner control solenoid electrical connector.

22. Disconnect the throttle body electrical connector.

23. Remove the brake booster vacuum hose and check valve from the intake manifold.

24. Remove the positive crankcase ventilation (PCV) hose from the cylinder head and the intake manifold.

25. Remove the intake manifold bolts (1-6).

26. Remove the upper intake manifold.

27. Remove and discard the upper intake manifold gasket.

28. Disassemble the intake manifold if necessary.

29. Clean and inspect the intake manifold and the sealing surfaces.

To install:

30. Assemble the intake manifold if necessary.

31. Install the intake manifold.

32. Install the intake manifold bolts (1-6). Tighten the bolts in the order shown to 17 ft. lbs. (23 Nm).

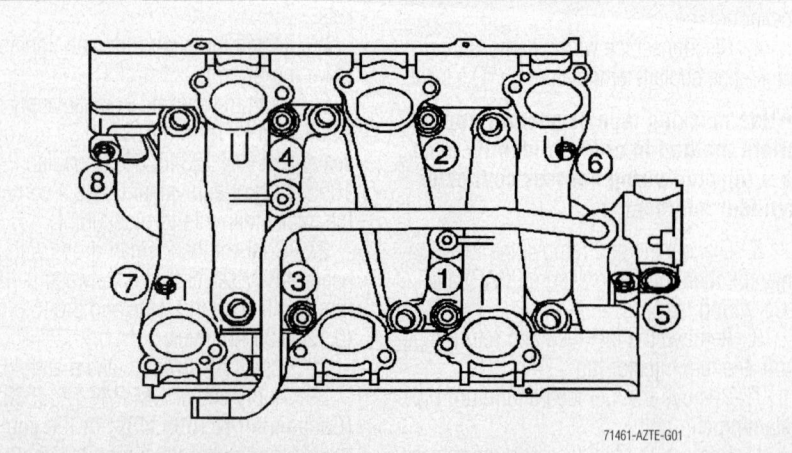

71461-AZTE-G01

Fig. 70 Lower intake manifold torque sequence—3.4L and 3.5L engine

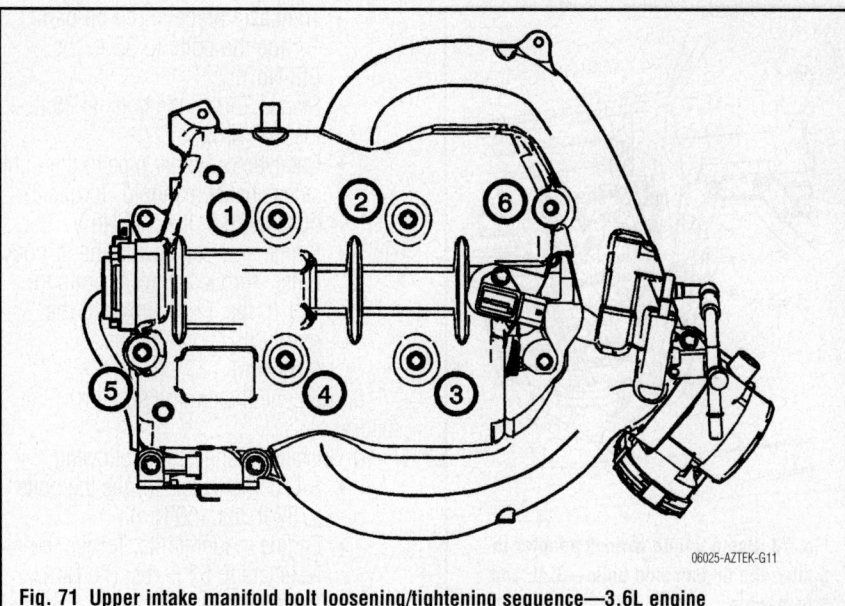

Fig. 71 Upper intake manifold bolt loosening/tightening sequence—3.6L engine

33. Install the PCV hose to the intake manifold and the cylinder head.

34. Install the brake booster vacuum hose and check valve to the brake booster.

35. Install the throttle body electrical connector.

36. Connect the intake manifold runner control solenoid electrical connector.

37. Install the fuel injector electrical connector to the fuel injector electrical connector bracket.

38. Install the fuel injector bracket.

39. Connect the fuel injector electrical connector.

40. Install the wiring harness and bracket to the right side of the intake manifold. Tighten the bracket bolts to 89 inch lbs. (10 Nm).

41. Connect the purge solenoid electrical connector.

42. Carefully raise the powertrain or lower the vehicle in order to install the frame bolts.

43. Install the frame front bolts. Torque to 114 ft. lbs. (155 Nm).

44. Remove the floor jack.

45. Raise and support the vehicle.

46. Install the front fender liners.

47. Connect the intermediate steering shaft to the steering gear.

48. Lower the vehicle.

49. Install the ECM bracket with the ECM.

50. Install the fuel feed hose bracket and the bracket bolt. Tighten the bracket bolt to 89 inch lbs. (10 Nm).

51. Connect the BARO sensor electrical connector.

52. Install the purge line to the purge line retainer.

53. Connect the fuel pressure and EVAP hoses to the engine.

54. Install the air inlet duct.

Lower

See Figure 72.

1. Before servicing the vehicle, refer to the Precautions Section.

2. Turn the ignition **OFF**.

3. Remove the air inlet duct.

4. Relieve the fuel pressure.

5. Disconnect the fuel pressure and evaporative emission (EVAP) hoses from the engine.

6. Disconnect the barometric pressure (BARO) sensor electrical connector.

➡Do NOT disconnect the engine control module (ECM) electrical connectors.

7. Remove the ECM bracket with the ECM and reposition aside.

8. Raise and support the vehicle.

9. Disconnect the intermediate steering shaft from the steering gear.

10. Remove and reposition the front portion of the front fender liners in order to gain access to the frame front bolts.

11. Lower the vehicle.

12. Position a floor jack at the front center section of the frame in order to support the powertrain.

13. Remove the frame front bolts.

14. Carefully lower the powertrain or raise the vehicle enough to provide access.

15. Disconnect the purge solenoid electrical connector.

16. Remove the wiring harness from the right side of the intake manifold.

17. Disconnect the fuel injector electrical connector.

18. Disconnect the intake manifold runner control solenoid electrical connector.

19. Remove the throttle body electrical connector.

20. Remove the brake booster vacuum hose from the intake manifold.

21. Remove the positive crankcase ventilation (PCV) hose from the intake manifold and the cylinder head.

22. Remove the intake manifold bolts (1-6).

23. Remove the intake manifold.

24. Disassemble the intake manifold as necessary.

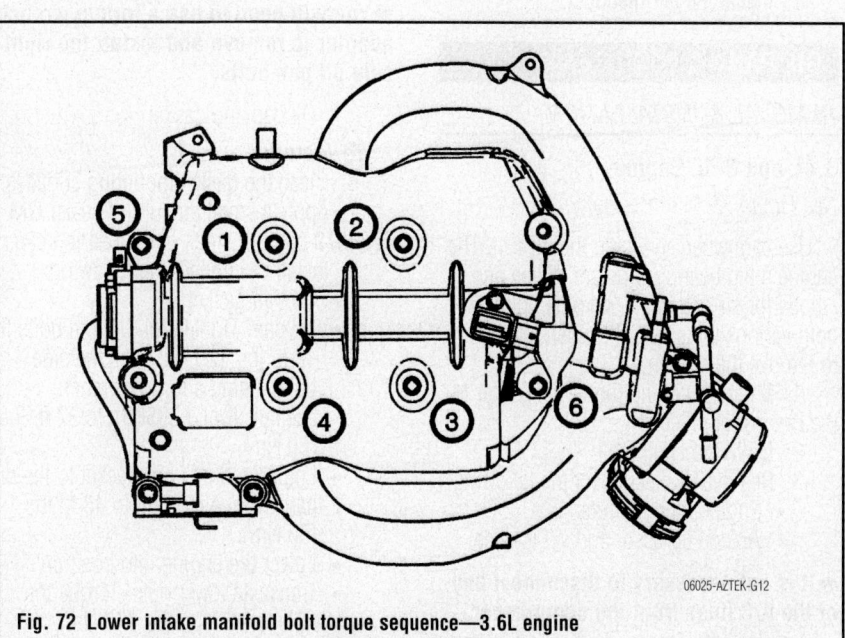

Fig. 72 Lower intake manifold bolt torque sequence—3.6L engine

25. Clean and inspect the intake manifold and the sealing surfaces.

To install:

26. Assemble the intake manifold as necessary.

27. Install the intake manifold. Tighten the bolts in the order shown to 17 ft. lbs. (23 Nm).

28. Install the PCV hose to the intake manifold and the cylinder head.

29. Install the brake booster vacuum hose to the intake manifold.

30. Connect the throttle body electrical connector.

31. Connect the intake manifold runner control solenoid electrical connector.

32. Connect the fuel injector electrical connector.

33. Install the wiring harness to the right side of the intake manifold. Tighten the bracket bolts to 89 inch lbs. (10 Nm).

34. Connect the purge solenoid electrical connector.

35. Carefully raise the powertrain or lower the vehicle in order to install the frame bolts.

36. Install the frame front bolts. Torque to 114 ft. lbs. (155 Nm).

37. Remove the floor jack.

38. Raise and support the vehicle.

39. Install the front fender liners.

40. Connect the intermediate steering shaft to the steering gear.

41. Lower the vehicle.

42. Install the ECM bracket with the ECM.

43. Connect the BARO sensor electrical connector.

44. Connect the fuel pressure and EVAP hoses to the engine.

45. Install the air inlet duct.

OIL PAN

REMOVAL & INSTALLATION

3.4L and 3.5L Engine

See Figure 73.

Use care when servicing the oil pan. The engine main bearing caps are drilled and tapped for structural oil pan side bolts. Do not overlook the side bolts when attempting to remove the oil pan.

1. Before servicing the vehicle, refer to the Precautions Section.

2. Drain the engine oil.

3. Remove or disconnect the following:
- Engine mount struts
- A/C compressor and set it aside

➡It is not necessary to disconnect any of the A/C lines from the compressor.

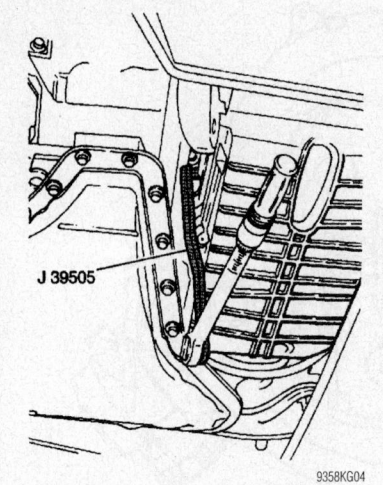

J 39505

9358KG04

Fig. 73 Use a torque wrench adapter to tighten the oil pan side bolts—3.4L and 3.5L engine

4. Install an engine support fixture.

5. Remove or disconnect the following:
- Catalytic converter pipe from the right side exhaust manifold
- Frame bolts and make certain that an engine stand (such as J 39580) is aligned below the engine, lower the frame
- Oil level sensor wiring harness connector
- Starter
- Transaxle brace from the oil pan
- Transaxle mount lower nuts
- Engine mount lower nuts and raise the engine with the support fixture
- Engine mount and bracket from the oil pan

➡You will need to use a torque wrench adapter to remove and install the right side oil pan bolts.

- Oil pan and gasket

To install:

6. Clean the gasket mounting surfaces.

7. Apply a small amount of sealer GM 1234579 on both sides of the bearing cap.

8. Install or connect the following:
- Oil pan gasket
- Oil pan. Tighten the bottom bolts to 18 ft. lbs. (25 Nm) and the side bolts, using a torque wrench adapter (tool J 39505), to 37 ft. lbs. (50 Nm).
- Engine mount and bracket to the oil pan. Torque the bolt to 43 ft. lbs. (58 Nm).
- Lower the engine into position
- Transaxle lower nuts. Torque the nuts to 90 inch lbs. (10 Nm).

- Transaxle brace to the oil pan. Torque the bolts to 32 ft. lbs. (43 Nm).
- Starter. Torque the bolts to 35 ft. lbs. (47 Nm).
- Catalytic converter pipe to the right side exhaust manifold. Torque the bolts to 26 ft. lbs. (35 Nm).
- Frame and use new frame to body bolts. Torque the front bolts to 111 ft. lbs. (150 Nm) and the rear bolts to 122 ft. lbs. (165 Nm).

9. Remove the engine support fixture.

10. Install or connect the following:
- A/C compressor. Torque the bolts to 37 ft. lbs. (50 Nm).
- Engine mount struts. Torque the fasteners to 52 ft. lbs. (70 Nm).
- Negative battery cable

11. Fill the engine with oil.

12. Start the vehicle and inspect for leaks, repair if necessary.

3.6L Engine

See Figures 74 through 78.

1. Before servicing the vehicle, refer to the Precautions Section.

2. Remove the engine, transaxle and sub-frame from the vehicle and install the engine on an engine stand.

3. Remove the A/C compressor with the hoses from the engine.

4. Remove the engine front cover.

5. Remove the oil pan bolts and, using the pry points, remove the pan.

To install:

6. Install 8mm (0.315 in) guides pins into the center oil pan rail bolt hole on each side of the engine block.

7. Place a 3mm (0.118 in) bead of RTV sealant, GM P/N 12378521 (Canadian P/N 88901148) or equivalent, on the block pan rail and the crankshaft rear oil seal housing.

8. Position the oil pan onto the block.

9. Remove the 8mm (0.315 in) guides from the engine block.

10. Loosely install the oil pan bolts.

11. Tighten the oil pan bolts in sequence shown. Tighten the 8mm bolts (1-11) to 17 ft. lbs. (23 Nm). Tighten the 6 mm bolts (12, 13) to 89 inch lbs. (10 Nm).

12. Install the engine front cover.

13. Place the A/C compressor in position to the cylinder block.

14. Loosely install the A/C compressor bolts.

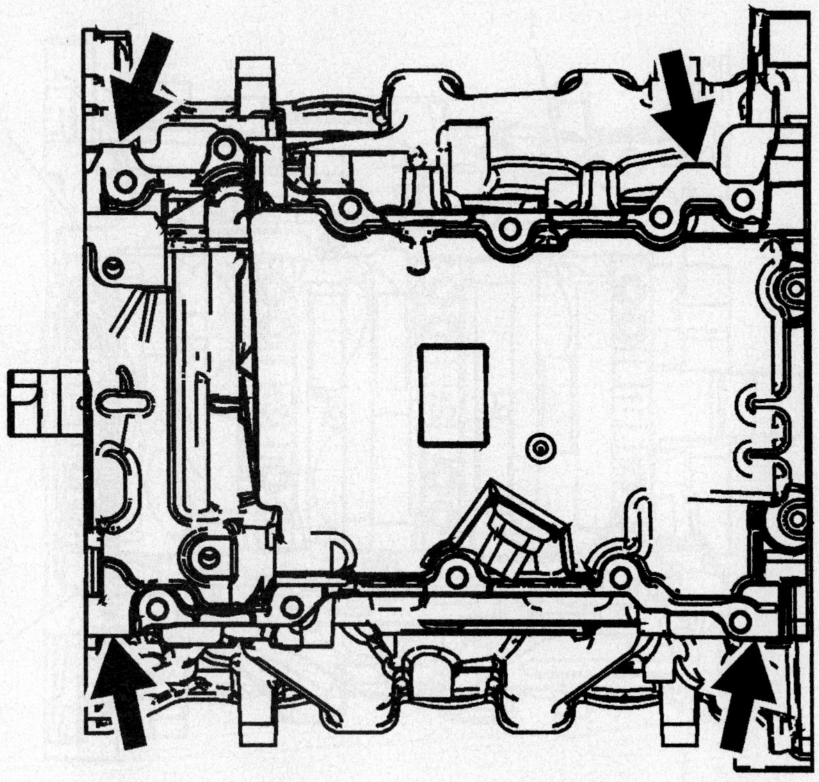

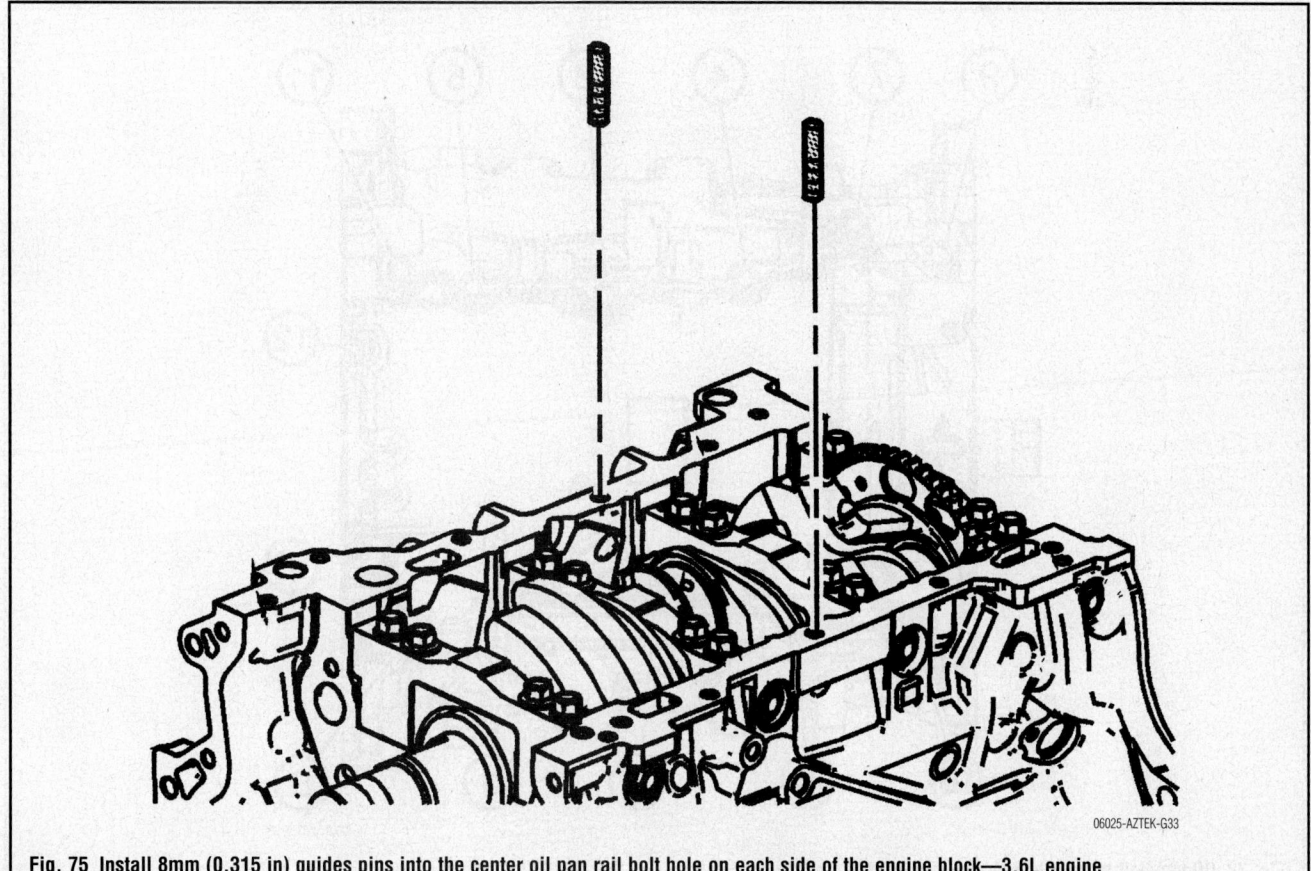

Fig. 74 Oil pan pry points—3.6L engine

06025-AZTEK-G32

06025-AZTEK-G33

Fig. 75 Install 8mm (0.315 in) guides pins into the center oil pan rail bolt hole on each side of the engine block—3.6L engine

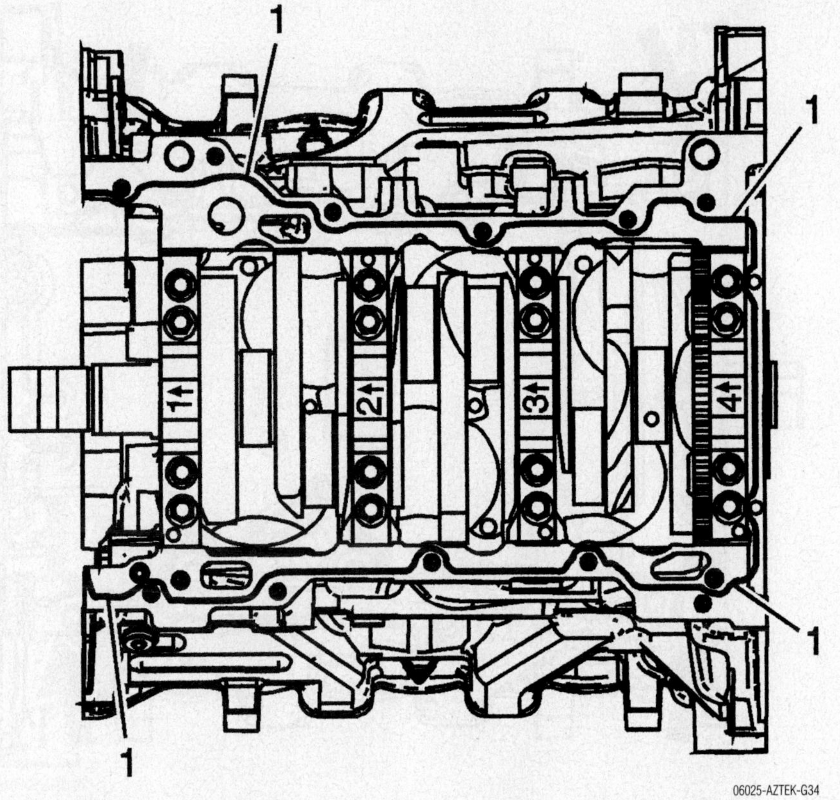
1
1
1
1
1↑
2↑
3↑
4↑
06025-AZTEK-G34

Fig. 76 Place a 3mm (0.118 in) bead of RTV sealant on the block pan rail and the crankshaft rear oil seal housing—3.6L engine

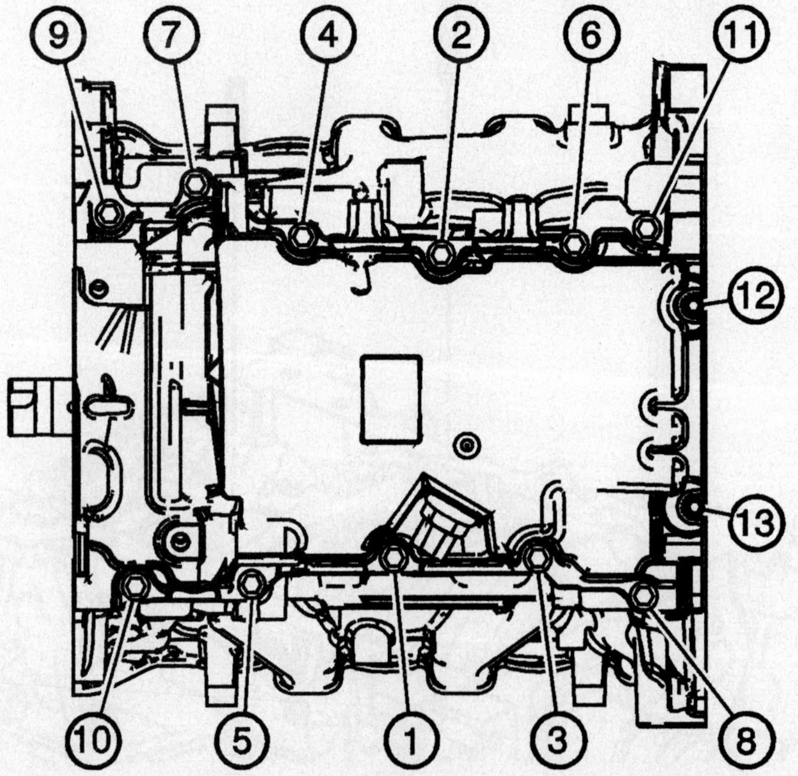
9
7
4
2
6
11
12
13
10
5
1
3
8
06025-AZTEK-G35

Fig. 77 Oil pan bolt torque sequence—3.6L engine

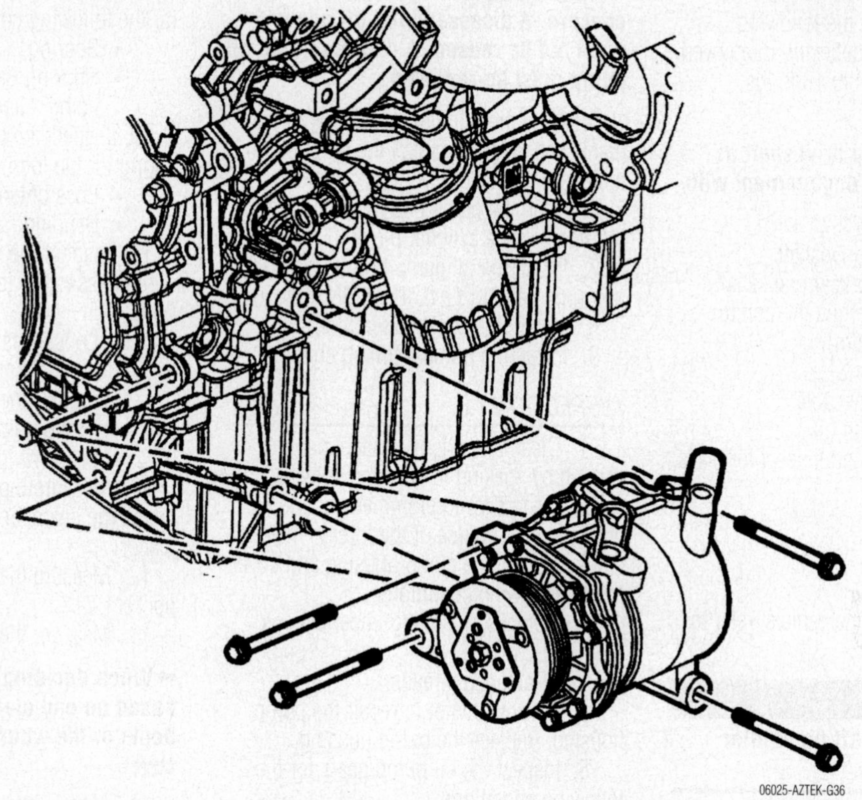

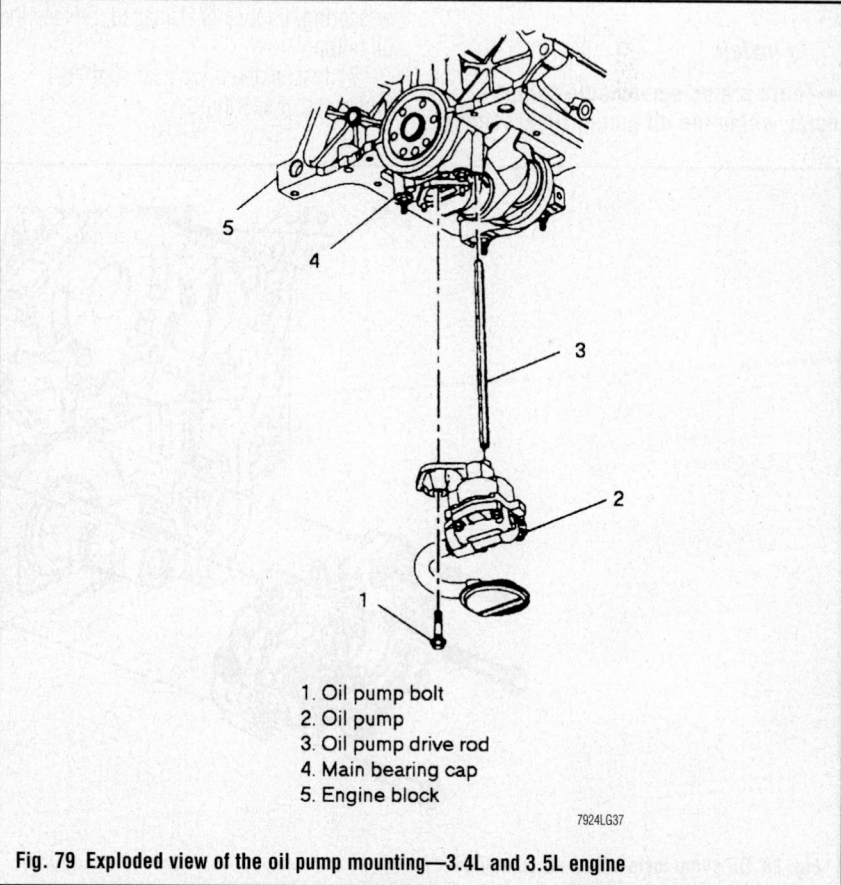

Fig. 78 Compressor mounting—3.6L engine

06025-AZTEK-G36

15. Tighten the A/C compressor front upper bolt to 37 ft. lbs. (50 Nm).

16. Tighten the A/C compressor rear upper bolt to 37 ft. lbs. (50 Nm).

17. Tighten the A/C compressor rear lower bolt to 37 ft. lbs. (50 Nm).

18. Tighten the A/C compressor front lower bolt to 16 ft. lbs. (22 Nm).

19. Install the engine to the transmission and frame and install the assembled unit in the vehicle.

OIL PUMP

REMOVAL & INSTALLATION

3.4L and 3.5L Engine

See Figure 79.

1. Before servicing the vehicle, refer to the Precautions Section.

2. Drain the engine oil.

3. Remove or disconnect the following:
   - Negative battery cable
   - Oil pan
   - Bolt attaching the oil pump to the rear crankshaft bearing cap
   - Oil pump and driveshaft
   - Crankshaft oil deflector nuts and deflector, if necessary

4. Inspect the oil pump and oil pump driveshaft.

1. Oil pump bolt
2. Oil pump
3. Oil pump drive rod
4. Main bearing cap
5. Engine block

7924LG37

Fig. 79 Exploded view of the oil pump mounting—3.4L and 3.5L engine

To install:

5. Install or connect the following:
- Crankshaft oil deflector, if removed. Torque the nuts to 18 ft. lbs. (25 Nm).

➡**Rotate the oil pump driveshaft as necessary for proper engagement with the oil pump drive.**

- Oil pump and driveshaft
- Oil pump to the rear crankshaft bearing cap. Torque the bolt to 30 ft. lbs. (41 Nm).
- Oil pan
- Negative battery cable

6. Fill the engine with oil.
7. Start the vehicle and inspect for leaks, repair if necessary.

3.6L Engine

See Figure 80.

1. Before servicing the vehicle, refer to the Precautions Section.

✳✳ WARNING

Do not remove the left bank idler sprocket.

2. Remove the primary timing chain.
3. Remove the crankshaft sprocket.
4. Remove the oil pump bolts and the oil pump.

To install:

➡**There are no serviceable components within the oil pump. Disassemble** the pump only to diagnose an oiling concern. A disassembled oil pump must not be reused. A disassembled oil pump must be replaced.

5. Align the oil pump gerotor with the crankshaft flats and install the oil pump to the engine block.
6. Align the pump body with the mounting holes in the cylinder block.
7. Install the oil pump bolts. Tighten the oil pump bolts to 17 ft. lbs. (23Nm).
8. Install the crankshaft sprocket.
9. Install the primary timing chain.

INSPECTION

1. Clean all parts of sludge, oil, and varnish by soaking in cleaning solvent.
2. Inspect for foreign material and determine the source of the foreign material.
3. Inspect the pump housing and cover for the following conditions:
- Cracks or casting imperfections
- Scoring
- Damaged threads
4. Do not attempt to repair the pump housing. Replace the pump housing.
5. Inspect the oil pump gears for the following conditions:
- Scoring
- Excessive wear
6. Inspect the idler shaft for looseness or scoring. If loose or damaged, replace the oil pump.
7. Inspect the drive gear shaft for looseness or scoring.

8. Inspect the pressure regulator valve for the following conditions:
- Scoring
- Sticking Burrs may be removed using a fine oil stone
9. Inspect the pressure regulator valve spring for the following conditions:
- Loss of tension
- Bending
10. Inspect the suction pipe and screen assembly for the following conditions:
- Looseness If the suction pipe is loose, bent or has been removed, replace the pump body cover and suction pipe.
- Broken wire mesh or screen
11. Measure the oil pump gear lash. Install the gears, and measure in several places.
12. Measure the oil pump housing gear pocket.
13. Measure the oil pump gears .

➡**When deciding pump serviceability based on end clearance, consider depth of the wear pattern in the pump cover.**

14. Measure the oil pump gear side clearance.

PISTON AND RING

POSITIONING

See Figures 81 through 84.

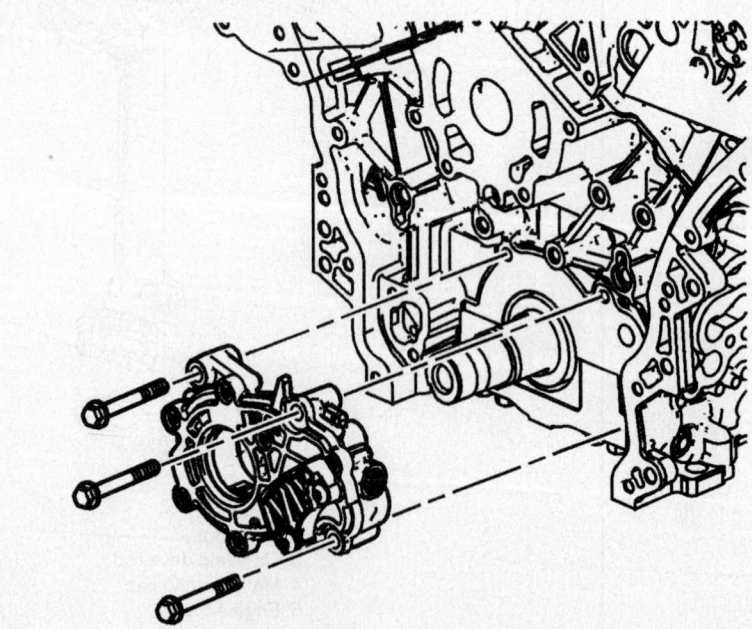

06025-AZTEK-G37

Fig. 80 Oil pump installation—3.6L engine

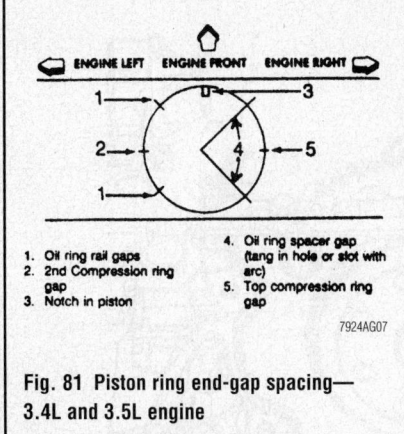

Fig. 81 Piston ring end-gap spacing— 3.4L and 3.5L engine

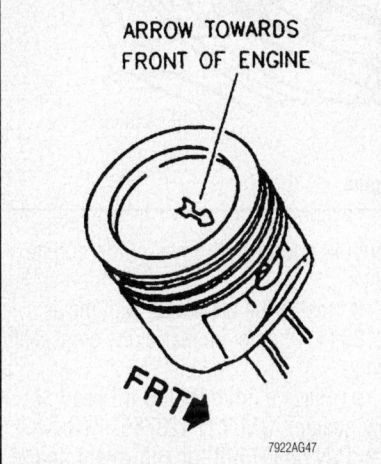

Fig. 82 Piston positioning. Often the arrow is replaced with a notch, which must face toward the front of the engine— 3.4L and 3.5L engine

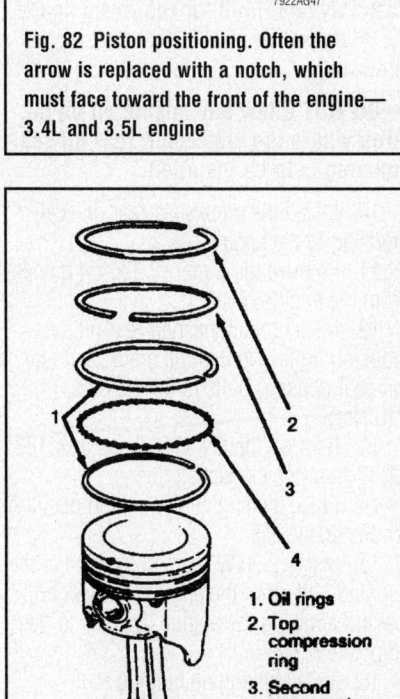

Fig. 83 Piston ring positioning—3.4L and 3.5L engine

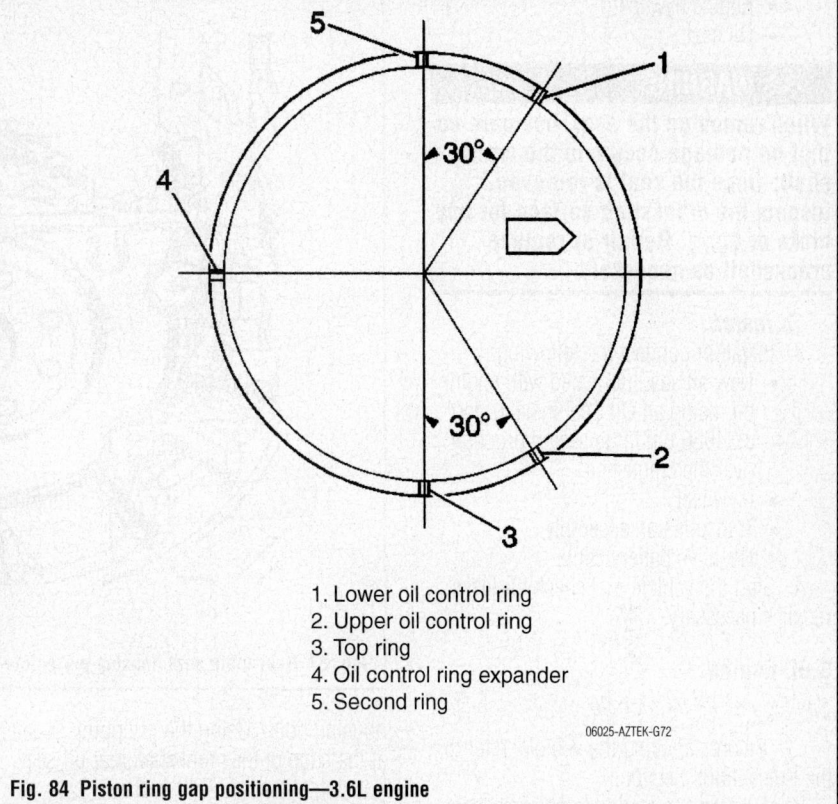

1. Lower oil control ring
2. Upper oil control ring
3. Top ring
4. Oil control ring expander
5. Second ring

Fig. 84 Piston ring gap positioning—3.6L engine

REAR MAIN SEAL

REMOVAL & INSTALLATION

3.4L and 3.5L Engine

See Figure 85.

The transaxle assembly must be removed to perform this service. This requires spe- cial tooling to support the engine assembly while the transaxle and sub-frame are low- ered from under the vehicle.

1. Before servicing the vehicle, refer to the Precautions Section.

2. Remove or disconnect the following:
• Negative battery cable
• Transmission assembly

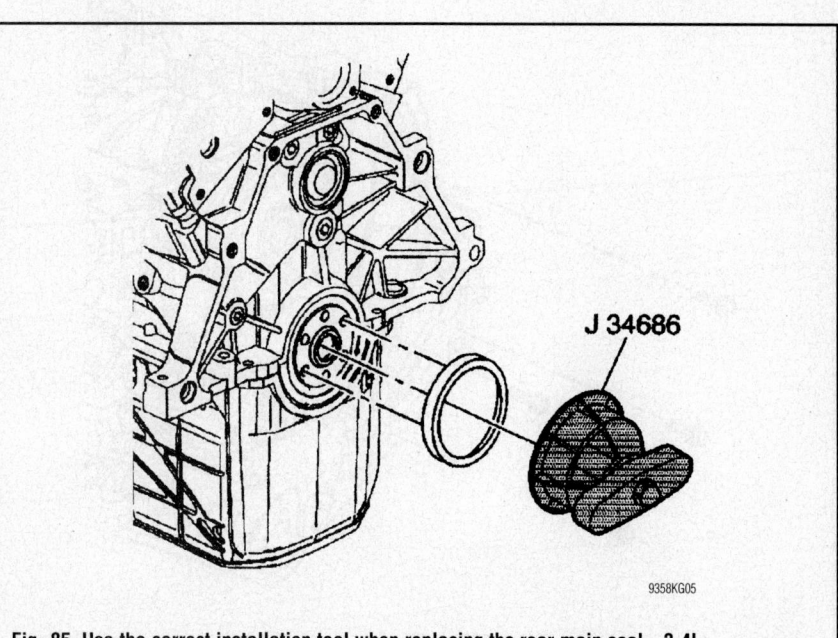

Fig. 85 Use the correct installation tool when replacing the rear main seal—3.4L and 3.5L engine

- Engine flywheel
- Oil seal

✳✳ WARNING

When removing the seal, use care so that no damage occurs to the crankshaft. Once the seal is removed, inspect the crankshaft surface for any nicks or burrs. Repair or replace crankshaft as necessary.

To install:

3. Install or connect the following:
- New oil seal lubricated with engine oil, using an Oil Seal Installer tool J 34686 until it is seated properly over the crankshaft
- Flywheel
- Transmission assembly
- Negative battery cable

4. Start the vehicle and check for leaks, repair if necessary.

3.6L Engine

See Figures 86 through 90.

1. Before servicing the vehicle, refer to the Precautions Section.
2. Remove the engine/transaxle assembly.
3. Separate the transaxle from the engine.
4. Remove the flywheel.
5. Remove the crankshaft rear oil seal

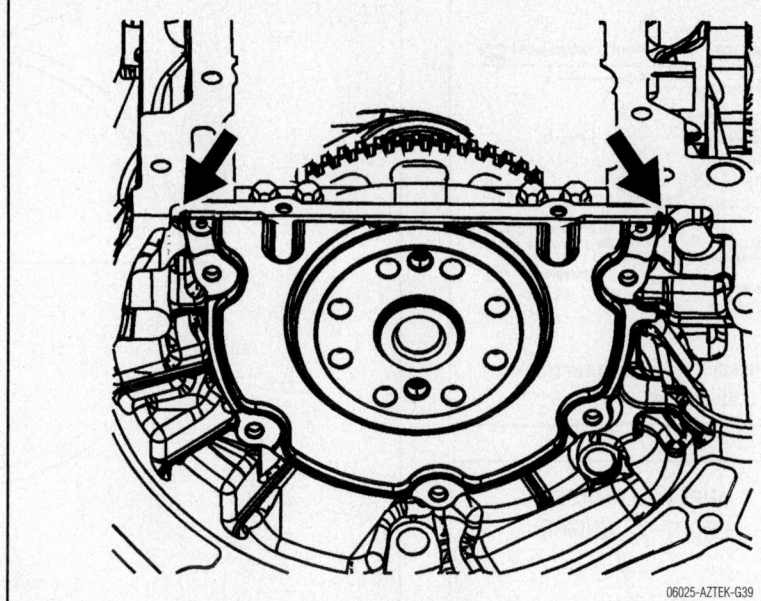

Fig. 87 Rear main seal housing pry points—3.6L engine

housing bolts. Using the pry points located at the edge of the crankshaft rear oil seal housing, shear the RTV sealant.

6. Remove and discard the crankshaft rear oil seal housing.

To install:

7. Install the 6 mm (0.236 in) guide pins into the 2 crankshaft rear oil seal

housing corner bolt holes of the engine block.

8. Install the EN-47839 with the J-42183 (1, 2) onto the rear of the crankshaft flange.

9. Place a 3mm (0.118 in) bead of RTV sealant, GM P/N 12378521 (Canadian P/N 88901148) or equivalent, to the NEW crankshaft rear oil seal housing as shown (1).

➡**DO NOT allow any engine oil on the area where the crankshaft rear oil seal housing is to be installed.**

10. Install the crankshaft rear oil seal housing to the engine block.
11. Remove the 6 mm (0.236 in) guides from the engine block.
12. Install the crankshaft rear oil seal housing bolts. Tighten the crankshaft rear oil seal housing bolts to 89 inch lbs. (10 Nm).
13. Remove the EN-47839 and J-42183 (1, 2) from the crankshaft flange.
14. Place the engine flywheel in position on the crankshaft.
15. Install 2 NEW bolts in location at the top and bottom of the engine flywheel bolt pattern allowing the engine flywheel to hang in position.
16. Install an engine holding tool.
17. Install the remaining NEW engine flywheel bolts. Tighten the NEW engine flywheel bolts to 22 ft. lbs. (30 Nm). Tighten the NEW engine flywheel bolts an additional 45 degrees.
18. Install the engine/transaxle.

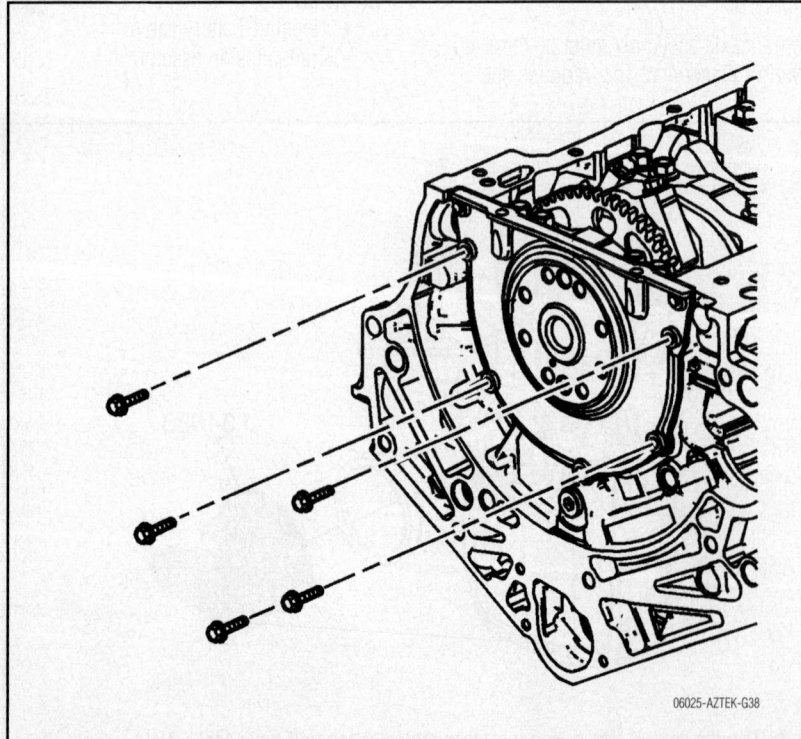

Fig. 86 Rear main seal housing bolts—3.6L engine

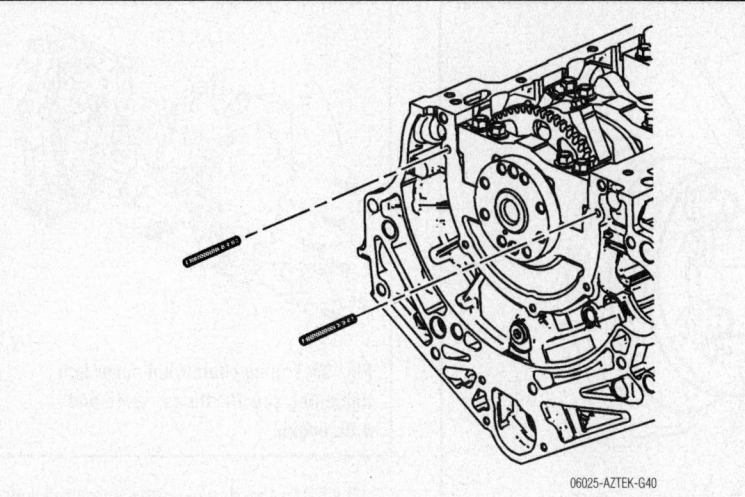

Fig. 88 Install the 6 mm (0.236 in) guide pins into the 2 crankshaft rear oil seal housing corner bolt holes of the engine block—3.6L engine

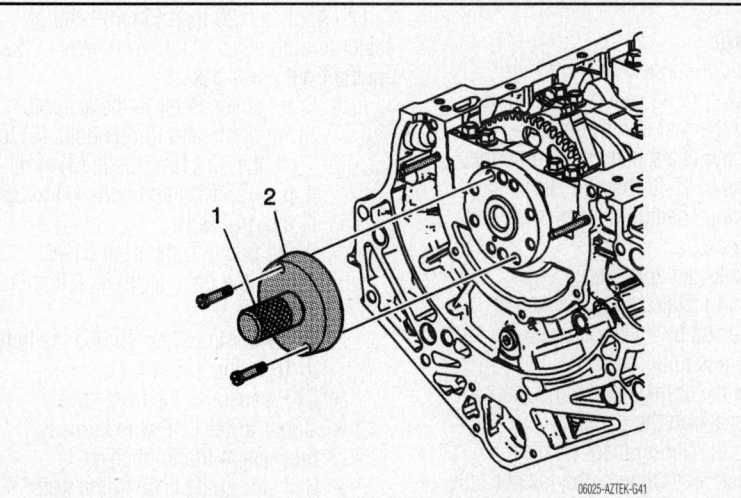

Fig. 89 Install the EN-47839 with the J-42183 (1, 2) onto the rear of the crankshaft flange—3.6L engine

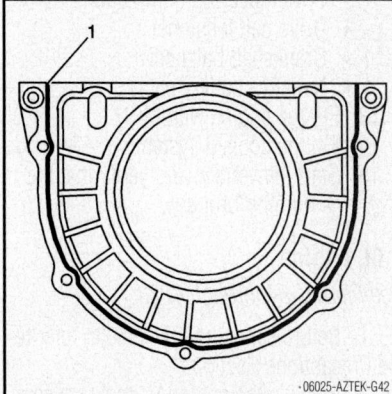

Fig. 90 Place a 3mm (0.118 in) bead of RTV sealant, GM P/N 12378521 (Canadian P/N 88901148) or equivalent, to the NEW crankshaft rear oil seal housing as shown (1)—3.6L engine

ROCKER ARMS/SHAFTS

REMOVAL & INSTALLATION

3.4L and 3.5L Engine

➡Valve train components which are to be reused must be installed in their original positions. If removed, be sure to tag or arrange all rocker arms and pushrods to assure proper installation.

1. Before servicing the vehicle, refer to the Precautions Section.
2. Remove or disconnect the following:
   - Negative battery cable
   - Rocker arm cover
   - Rocker arm bolts
   - Rocker arms

➡Place the valve train parts in order to ensure they are installed in the proper location. Intake pushrods are yellow and measure 5.68 inches (144.18mm). Exhaust pushrods are green and measure 6.0 inches (152.51mm). When removing the pushrods, make certain they do not fall into the lifter valley.

   - Pushrods

To install:

3. Inspect and replace components if worn or damaged. Clean all old thread locking material from the pedestal bolts.
4. Coat the bearing surface of the rocker arms, pushrods and rocker arm bolts with a prelube (such as GM 1052365). Make certain to install the components in their original position.
5. Install or connect the following:
   - 3.4L Intake valve pushrods are 5.75 inches (146.00mm) long
   - 3.5L Intake valve pushrods are 5.67 inches (144.2mm) long
   - Exhaust valve pushrods are 6.0 inches (152.51mm) long
   - Rocker arms. Torque bolts to 24 ft. lbs. (32 Nm).
   - Rocker arm cover. Torque the bolt to 89 inch lbs. (10 Nm).
   - Negative battery cable
6. Start the engine and verify the vehicle is running properly.

3.6L Engine

See the procedure under Camshaft Removal and Installation.

TIMING CHAIN, SPROCKETS, FRONT COVER AND SEAL

REMOVAL & INSTALLATION

3.4L and 3.5L Engine

See Figures 91 through 93.

1. Before servicing the vehicle, refer to the Precautions Section.
2. Drain the engine oil.
3. Drain the coolant.
4. Remove or disconnect the following:
   - Negative battery cable
   - Crankshaft balancer
   - Drive belt tensioner
   - Power steering pump and lines. Do not disconnect the lines from the pump.
   - Thermostat bypass pipe from the front cover
   - Radiator outlet hose from the water pump
   - Water pump pulley

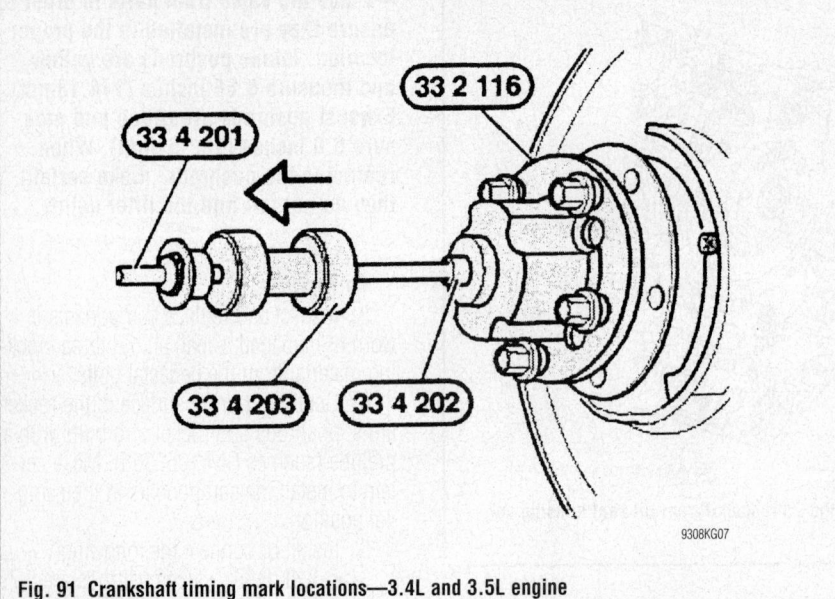

Fig. 91 Crankshaft timing mark locations—3.4L and 3.5L engine

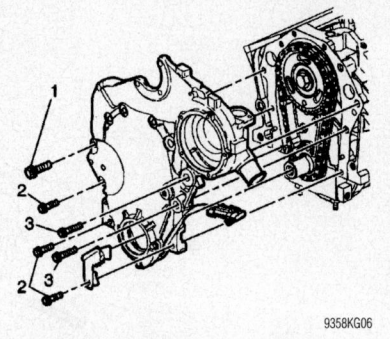

Fig. 93 Timing chain front cover bolt tightening specifications—3.4L and 3.5L engine

- Upper and lower Crankshaft Position (CKP) sensor wire harness bracket from the front cover
- CKP sensor from the front cover
- Front cover and gasket

5. Rotate the crankshaft until the timing marks are aligned in the following locations:
- Camshaft alignment pin (1)
- Timing chain damper (2) to the crankshaft sprocket (3)
- Crankshaft key (4)
- Timing chain damper (5) to the camshaft sprocket locator hole (6)

6. Remove or disconnect the following:
- Camshaft sprocket bolt
- Timing chain, timing chain sprockets and damper
- Front oil seal

To install:

7. Install or connect the following:
- New front oil seal by making certain the seal is fully seated
- Timing chain damper. Torque the bolts to 15 ft. lbs. (21 Nm).
- Timing chain to the camshaft sprocket
- Crankshaft sprocket
- Timing chain to the crankshaft sprocket by making certain the chain is fully seated

8. Align the crankshaft timing mark to the bottom mark on the damper.

9. Align the timing mark on the camshaft gear center line of the locator hole with the timing mark on the top of the damper.

10. Align the dowel in the camshaft with the dowel hole in the camshaft sprocket.

11. Install or connect the following:
- Camshaft sprocket bolt. Torque the bolt to 103 ft. lbs. (140 Nm).

12. Apply a 0.20 inch (5mm) bead of sealer to both sides of the lower tabs of the engine front cover gasket.
- Front cover. Refer to the accompanying figure and torque bolts (2) to 15 ft. lbs. (21 Nm), bolts (3) to 41 ft. lbs. (55 Nm) and bolts (1) to 35 ft. lbs. (47 Nm).
- Water pump to the front cover. Torque the bolts to 89 inch lbs. (10 Nm).
- Water pump pulley. Torque the bolt to 18 ft. lbs. (25 Nm).
- CKP sensor to the front cover
- Upper/lower CKP wire harness brackets to the front cover
- Radiator outlet hose to the water pump
- Thermostat bypass pipe to the front cover
- Power steering pump and lines
- Drive belt tensioner
- Crankshaft balancer
- Negative battery cable

13. Fill the engine with oil.
14. Fill the coolant system.
15. Start the vehicle and verify that the engine is running properly.

3.6L Engine

See Figures 94 through 123.

1. Before servicing the vehicle, refer to the Precautions Section.
2. Remove the engine/transaxle assembly.
3. Remove the alternator, power steering pump and A/C compressor.
4. Remove the crankshaft balancer.
5. Remove the camshaft position actuator valve bolts.

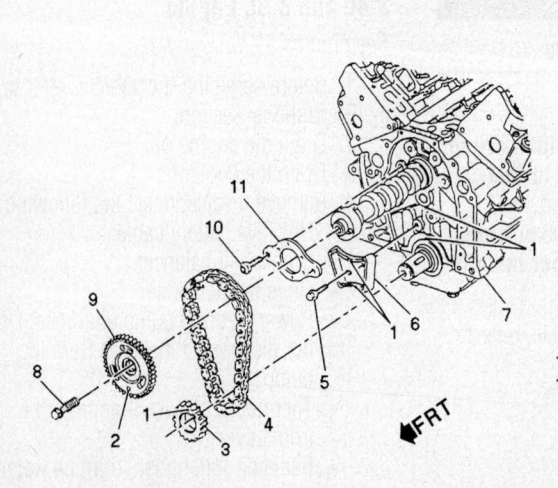

1. Timing alignment marks
2. Locator hole
3. Crankshaft sprocket
4. Timing chain
5. Timing chain dampener bolt
6. Timing chain dampener
7. Engine block
8. Camshaft sprocket bolt
9. Camshaft sprocket
10. Thrust plate bolt
11. Thrust plate

Fig. 92 Exploded view of the timing chain assembly—3.4L and 3.5L engine

6. Remove the camshaft position actuator valves from the front cover.

7. Remove the engine front cover bolts.

➡ **Do not pry between the engine front cover and the camshaft position sensors or the camshaft position actuators in order to shear the RTV. Use the pry points and a bolt in the jackscrew hole in order to remove the engine front cover. Damage to the camshaft position sensors or the camshaft position actuators may occur if the camshaft position sensors or the camshaft position actuators are used to pry against in order to remove the engine front cover.**

8. Loosely install a 10 x 1.5 mm bolt in the "jackscrew" hole (1).

9. Using the pry points (2) located at the edge of the front cover and the "jackscrew", shear the RTV sealant.

10. Remove the engine front cover.

11. Using tool EN 46111 , rotate the crankshaft until the left cylinder head camshafts align with tool EN 46105-2 and the right cylinder head camshafts align with tool EN 46105-1.

12. Install tool EN 46105-1 to the right camshafts.

13. Install tool EN 46105-2 to the left camshafts.

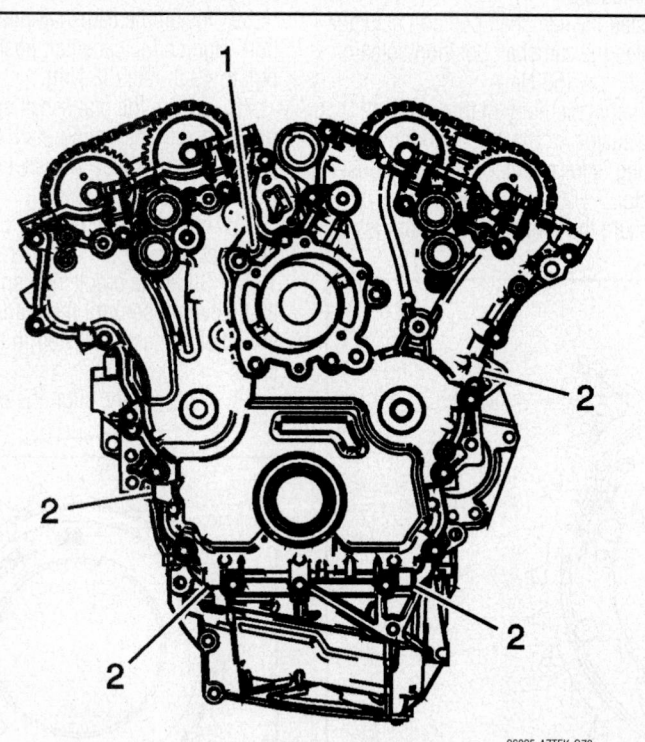

Fig. 94 Loosely install a 10 x 1.5 mm bolt in the "jackscrew" hole (1). Using the pry points (2) located at the edge of the front cover and the "jackscrew", shear the RTV sealant—3.6L engine

06025-AZTEK-G70

14. Remove the right secondary camshaft drive chain tensioner bolts.

15. Remove the right secondary camshaft drive chain tensioner.

16. Remove and discard the right secondary camshaft drive chain tensioner gasket.

17. Inspect the right secondary camshaft drive chain tensioner mounting surface on the right cylinder head for burrs or any defects that would degrade the sealing of the NEW right secondary camshaft drive chain tensioner gasket.

18. Remove the right secondary camshaft drive chain shoe bolt.

19. Remove the right secondary camshaft drive chain shoe.

20. Remove the right secondary camshaft drive chain guide bolts.

21. Remove the right secondary camshaft drive chain guide.

22. Remove the right secondary camshaft drive chain from the right camshaft position actuators and the right camshaft intermediate drive chain idler sprocket.

23. Remove the primary camshaft drive chain tensioner bolts.

24. Remove the primary camshaft drive chain tensioner.

25. Remove and discard the primary camshaft drive chain tensioner gasket.

26. Inspect the primary camshaft drive chain tensioner mounting surface on the engine block for burrs or any defects that would degrade the sealing of the NEW primary camshaft drive chain tensioner gasket.

27. Remove the primary camshaft drive chain upper guide bolts.

28. Remove the primary camshaft drive chain upper guide.

➡ **Do not remove the primary camshaft drive chain lower guide. The primary camshaft drive chain lower guide is not serviceable separately. If the primary camshaft drive chain lower guide must be replaced, the oil pump must be replaced.**

29. Remove the primary camshaft drive chain.

30. Remove the right camshaft intermediate drive chain idler bolt.

31. Remove the right camshaft intermediate drive chain idler.

32. Remove the left secondary camshaft drive chain tensioner bolts.

33. Remove the left secondary camshaft drive chain tensioner.

34. Remove and discard the left secondary camshaft drive chain tensioner gasket.

35. Inspect the left secondary camshaft drive chain tensioner mounting surface on the left cylinder head for burrs or any defects that would degrade the sealing of the NEW left secondary camshaft drive chain tensioner gasket.

36. Remove the left secondary camshaft drive chain shoe bolt.

37. Remove the left secondary camshaft drive chain shoe.

38. Remove the left secondary camshaft drive chain guide bolts.

39. Remove the left secondary camshaft drive chain guide.

40. Remove the left secondary camshaft drive chain from the left camshaft position actuators and the left camshaft intermediate drive chain idler sprocket.

41. Remove the left camshaft intermediate drive chain idler bolt.

42. Remove the left camshaft intermediate drive chain idler.

43. Remove the crankshaft sprocket from the nose of the crankshaft.

➡ **Use an open wrench on the hex cast into the camshaft in order to prevent engine rotation when loosening the camshaft position actuator bolt.**

44. Remove the left exhaust camshaft position actuator bolt.

45. Remove the left exhaust camshaft position actuator.

➡**A wrench must be used on the hex of the camshaft when loosening or tightening in order to prevent component damage. Failure to prevent the torque reaction against the timing drive chain can lead to timing drive chain failure.**

46. Use an open wrench on the hex cast into the camshaft in order to prevent engine rotation when loosening the camshaft position actuator bolt.

47. Remove the left intake camshaft position actuator bolt.

48. Remove the left intake camshaft position actuator.

➡**Use an open wrench on the hex cast into the camshaft in order to prevent engine rotation when loosening the camshaft position actuator bolt.**

49. Remove the right exhaust camshaft position actuator bolt.

50. Remove the right exhaust camshaft position actuator.

➡**Use an open wrench on the hex cast into the camshaft in order to prevent engine rotation when loosening the camshaft position actuator bolt.**

51. Remove the right intake camshaft position actuator bolt.

52. Remove the right intake camshaft position actuator.

To install:

53. Observe the body of the camshaft position actuator for the "IN" marking (3). The marking is for an intake camshaft position actuator.

54. Ensure the proper timing mark is used. Observe the outer ring of the camshaft position actuator for the "R" and triangle marking (2). The marking is for alignment to the highlighted timing chain link on the right side of the engine.

55. Use an open wrench on the hex cast into the camshaft in order to prevent camshaft rotation when tightening the camshaft position actuator bolt.

56. Install the right intake camshaft position actuator.

57. Install the camshaft position actuator bolt. Tighten the camshaft position actuator bolt to 43 ft. lbs. (58 Nm).

58. Observe the body of the camshaft position actuator for the "EX" marking (1). The marking is for an exhaust camshaft position actuator.

59. Ensure the proper timing mark is used. Observe the outer ring of the camshaft position actuator for the "R" and triangle marking (2). The marking is for alignment to the highlighted timing chain link on the right side of the engine.

➡**Use an open wrench on the hex cast into the camshaft in order to prevent camshaft rotation when tightening the camshaft position actuator bolt.**

60. Install the right exhaust camshaft position actuator.

61. Install the camshaft position actuator bolt. Tighten the camshaft position actuator bolt to 43 ft. lbs. (58 Nm).

62. Observe the body of the camshaft position actuator for the "IN" marking (3). The marking is for an intake camshaft position actuator.

63. Ensure the proper timing mark is

used. Observe the outer ring of the camshaft position actuator for the "L" and circle marking (1). The marking is for alignment to the highlighted timing chain link on the left side of the engine.

➡**Use an open wrench on the hex cast into the camshaft in order to prevent camshaft rotation when tightening the camshaft position actuator bolt.**

64. Install the left intake camshaft position actuator.

65. Install the camshaft position actuator bolt. Tighten the camshaft position actuator bolt to 43 ft. lbs. (58 Nm).

66. Observe the body of the camshaft position actuator for the "EX" marking (1). The marking is for an exhaust camshaft position actuator.

67. Ensure the proper timing mark is used. Observe the outer ring of the camshaft position actuator for the "L" and circle marking (3). The marking is for alignment to the highlighted timing chain link on the left side of the engine.

➡**Use an open wrench on the hex cast into the camshaft in order to prevent camshaft rotation when tightening the camshaft position actuator bolt.**

68. Install the left exhaust camshaft position actuator.

69. Install the camshaft position actuator bolt. Tighten the camshaft position actuator bolt to 43 ft. lbs. (58 Nm).

70. Ensure the crankshaft sprocket is installed with the timing mark (1) visible. Install the crankshaft sprocket on to the nose of the crankshaft.

71. Align the notch in the crankshaft sprocket with the pin in the crankshaft.

72. Slide the crankshaft sprocket on the crankshaft nose until the crankshaft sprocket contacts the step in the crankshaft.

73. If necessary, align the crankshaft

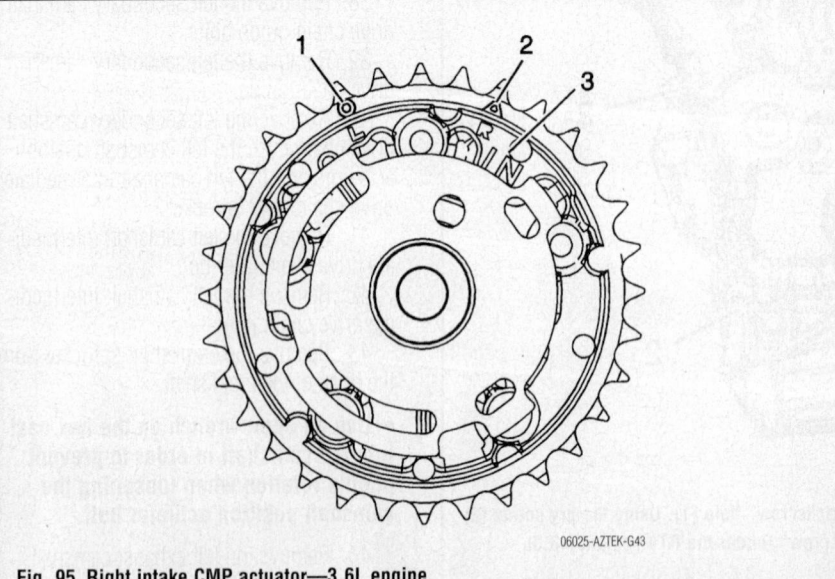

06025-AZTEK-G43

Fig. 95 Right intake CMP actuator—3.6L engine

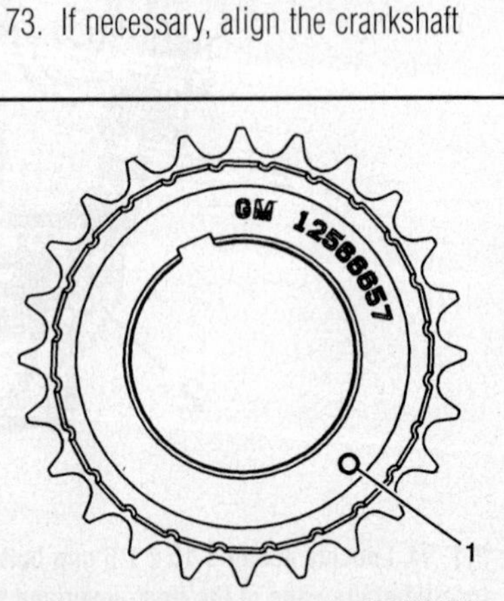

06025-AZTEK-G44

Fig. 96 Crankshaft sprocket—3.6L engine

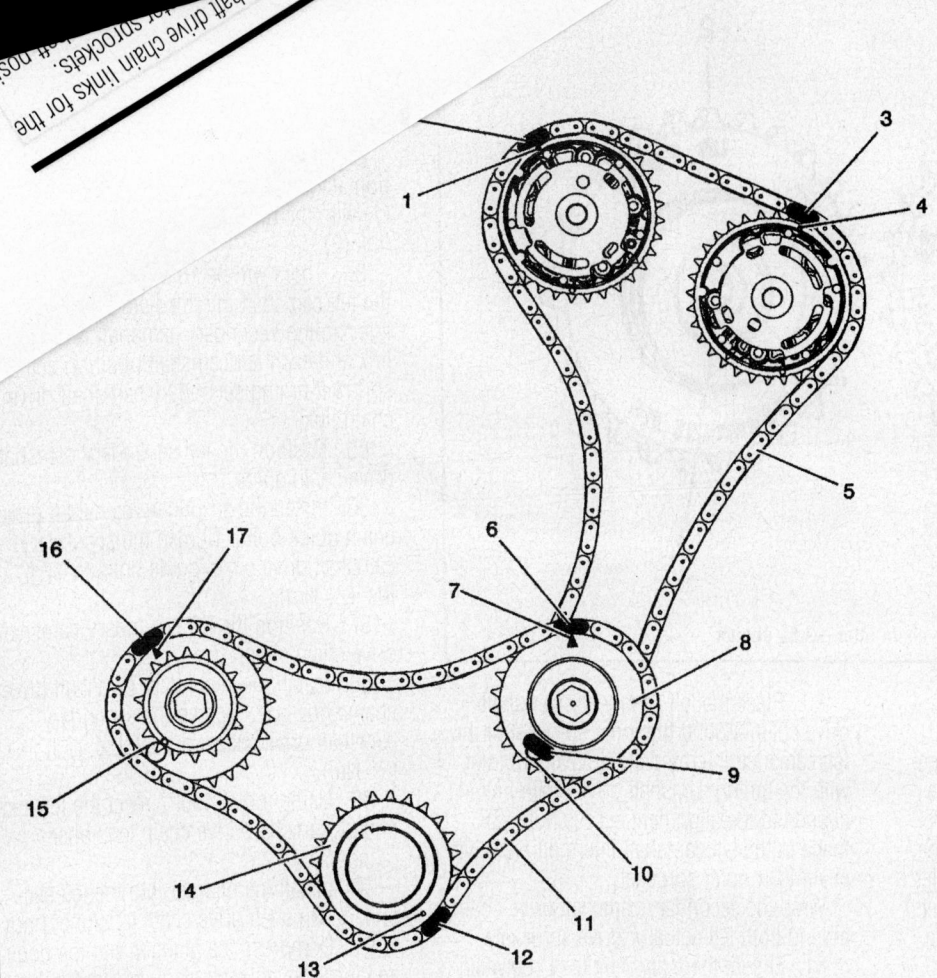

1. Left intake Camshaft Position (CMP) actuator timing mark
2. Left intake secondary camshaft timing drive chain timing link
3. Left exhaust secondary camshaft timing drive chain timing link
4. Left exhaust Camshaft Position (CMP) actuator timing mark
5. Left secondary camshaft timing drive chain
6. Primary camshaft drive chain timing link for the left primary camshaft intermediate drive chain sprocket
7. Left primary camshaft intermediate drive chain sprocket timing mark for the primary camshaft drive chain
8. Left primary camshaft intermediate drive chain sprocket
9. Left secondary camshaft timing drive chain timing link for the left primary camshaft intermediate drive chain sprocket
10. Left primary camshaft intermediate drive chain sprocket timing window for the left secondary camshaft timing drive chain timing link
11. Primary camshaft drive chain
12. Primary camshaft drive chain timing link for the crankshaft sprocket
13. Crankshaft sprocket timing mark
14. Crankshaft sprocket
15. Right primary camshaft intermediate drive chain sprocket
16. Primary camshaft drive chain timing link for the right primary camshaft intermediate drive chain sprocket
17. Right primary camshaft intermediate drive chain sprocket timing mark

06025-AZTEK-G22

Fig. 97 Ensure that the crankshaft is in the stage one timing drive assembly position using the EN 46111—3.6L engine

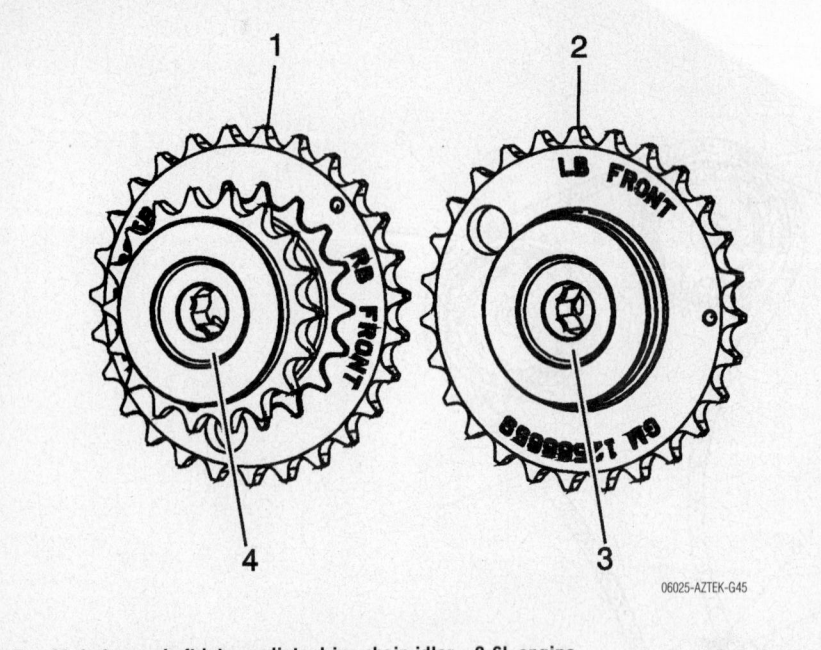

Fig. 98 Left camshaft intermediate drive chain idler—3.6L engine

sprocket to the stage one timing drive assembly position using tool EN 46111.

74. The recessed hub (3) and the larger sprocket of the left camshaft intermediate drive chain idler is installed outward. The raised hub and the smaller sprocket of the left camshaft intermediate drive chain idler is installed toward the block. Place the left camshaft intermediate drive chain idler to the cylinder block.

75. Install the camshaft intermediate drive chain idler bolt. Tighten the camshaft intermediate drive chain idler bolt to 43 ft. lbs. (58 Nm).

✳✳ WARNING

There should be no need to rotate the camshaft more than 10 degrees. Using the hex cast into the camshaft rotate the camshaft in order to install tool EN 46105.

76. Install tool EN 46105-1 onto the rear of the left camshafts.

✳✳ WARNING

All camshafts must be locked in place before installation of any camshaft drive chains.

77. Ensure that tool EN 46105-1 is fully seated onto the camshafts.

78. Ensure that the crankshaft is in the stage one timing drive assembly position using tool EN 46111.

79. Install the left secondary camshaft drive chain.

80. Place the left secondary camshaft drive chain around the inner sprocket of the left camshaft intermediate drive chain idler with the timing camshaft drive chain link (1) aligned to the alignment access hole (2) made in the left camshaft intermediate drive chain idler outer sprocket.

Wrap the secondary camshaft drive chain around both left actuator drive sprockets.

81. Ensure there are 7 links (1) between

the timing cam[...] camshaft position actua[...]

82. Align the left exhaust camshaft [posi]tion actuator sprocket alignment circle mark (2) with the timing camshaft drive chain link (1).

83. Align the left intake camshaft position actuator sprocket alignment circle mark (1) with the timing camshaft drive chain link (2).

84. There will be 18 links (1) between the left camshaft intermediate drive chain idler timing secondary camshaft drive chain link and each left camshaft position actuator sprocket timing secondary camshaft drive chain link.

85. Position the left secondary camshaft drive chain guide.

86. Install the secondary camshaft drive chain guide bolts. Tighten the secondary camshaft drive chain guide bolts to 17 ft. lbs. (23 Nm).

87. Position the left secondary camshaft drive chain shoe.

88. Install the secondary camshaft drive chain shoe bolt. Tighten the secondary camshaft drive chain shoe bolt to 17 ft. lbs. (23 Nm).

89. Using tool J 45027 reset the left secondary camshaft drive chain tensioner plunger.

90. Install the plunger into the left secondary camshaft drive chain tensioner body.

91. Compress the plunger into the body and lock the left secondary camshaft drive

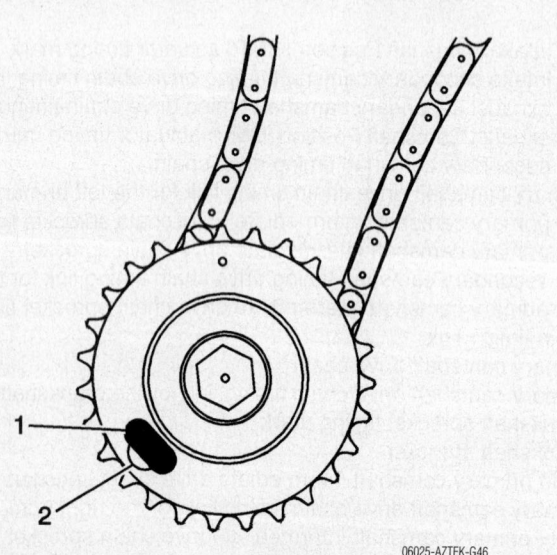

Fig. 99 Place the left secondary camshaft drive chain around the inner sprocket of the left camshaft intermediate drive chain idler with the timing camshaft drive chain link (1) aligned to the alignment access hole (2) made in the left camshaft intermediate drive chain idler outer sprocket—3.6L engine

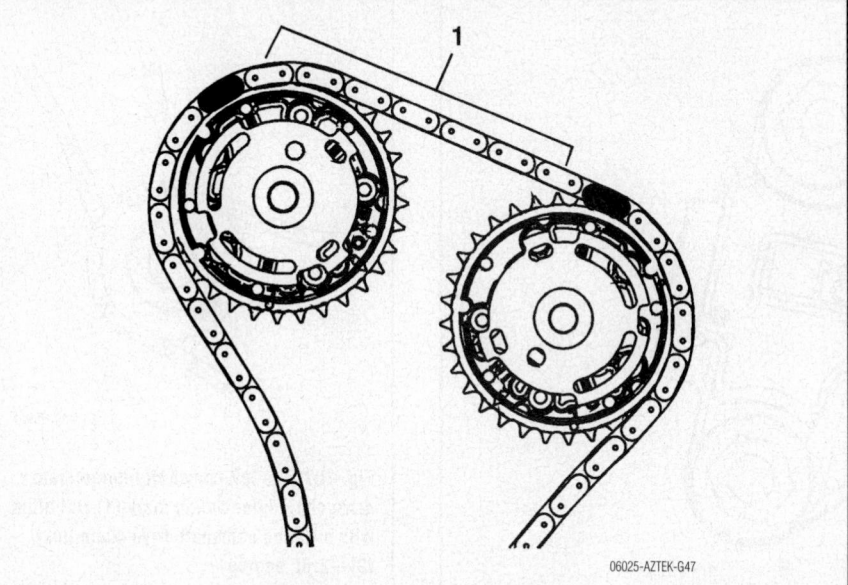

06025-AZTEK-G47

Fig. 100 Ensure there are 7 links (1) between the timing camshaft drive chain links for the camshaft position actuator sprockets—3.6L engine

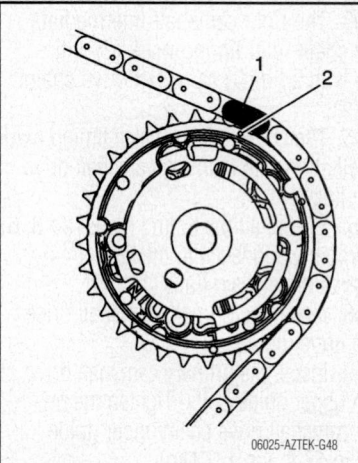

06025-AZTEK-G48

Fig. 101 Align the left exhaust camshaft position actuator sprocket alignment circle mark (2) with the timing camshaft drive chain link (1)—3.6L engine

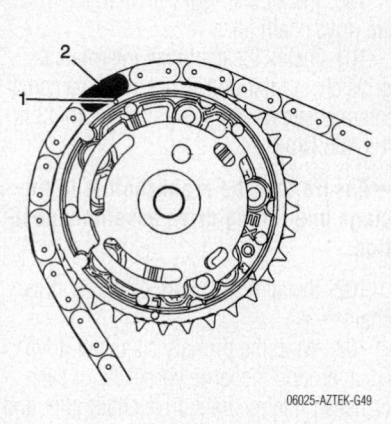

06025-AZTEK-G49

Fig. 102 Align the left intake camshaft position actuator sprocket alignment circle mark (1) with the timing camshaft drive chain link (2)—3.6L engine

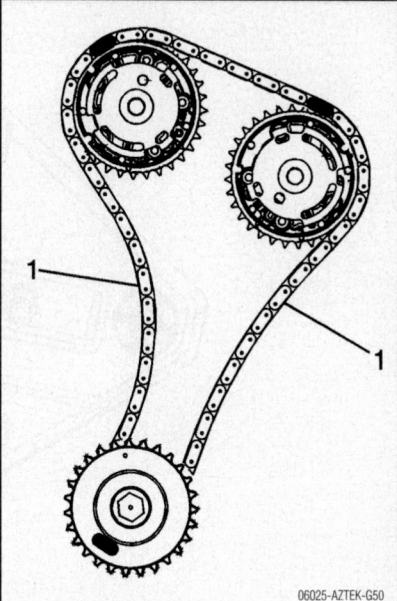

06025-AZTEK-G50

Fig. 103 There will be 18 links (1) between the left camshaft intermediate drive chain idler timing secondary camshaft drive chain link and each left camshaft position actuator sprocket timing secondary camshaft drive chain link—3.6L engine

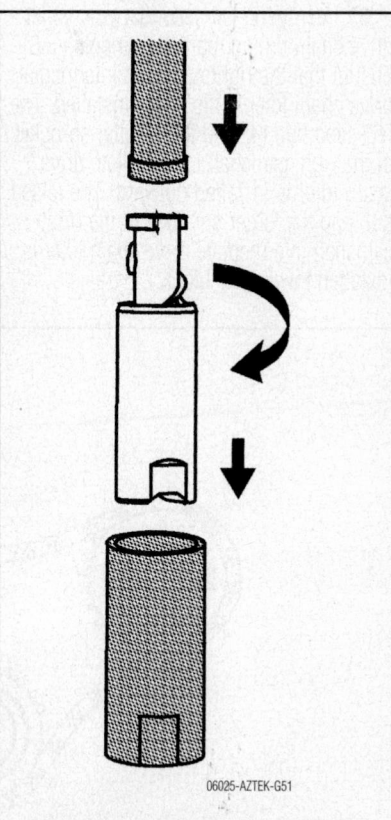

06025-AZTEK-G51

Fig. 104 Using tool J 45027 reset the left secondary camshaft drive chain tensioner plunger—3.6L engine

chain tensioner by inserting tool EN 46112 into the access hole in the side of the left secondary camshaft drive chain tensioner body.

92. Slowly release pressure on the left secondary camshaft drive chain tensioner. The left secondary camshaft drive chain tensioner should remain compressed.

93. Install a NEW left secondary camshaft drive chain tensioner gasket to the left secondary camshaft drive chain tensioner.

94. Install the left secondary camshaft drive chain tensioner bolts through the left secondary camshaft drive chain tensioner and gasket.

95. Ensure the left secondary camshaft drive chain tensioner mounting surface on the left cylinder head does not have any burrs or defects that would degrade the sealing of the NEW left secondary camshaft drive chain tensioner gasket.

96. Place the left secondary camshaft drive chain tensioner into position and loosely install the bolts to the block.

97. Verify the proper placement of the left secondary camshaft drive chain tensioner gasket tab (1).

- First Pass: Tighten the left secondary camshaft drive chain tensioner bolts to 44 inch lbs. (5 Nm).
- Final Pass: Tighten the left sec-

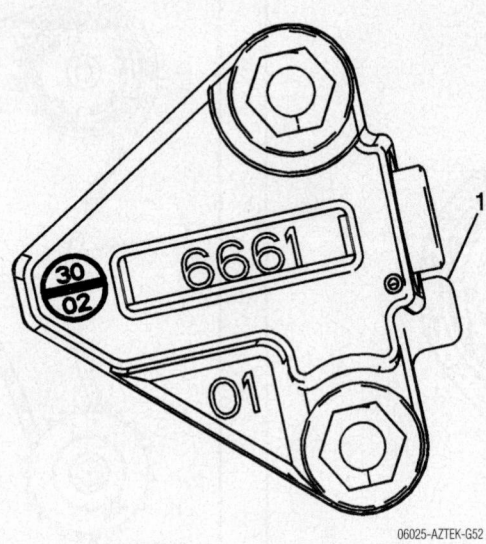

06025-AZTEK-G52

Fig. 105 Verify the proper placement of the left secondary camshaft drive chain tensioner gasket tab (1)—3.6L engine

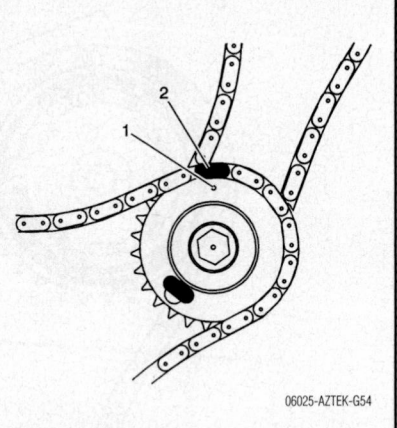

06025-AZTEK-G54

Fig. 107 The left camshaft intermediate drive chain idler timing mark (1) will align with a timing camshaft drive chain link (2)—3.6L engine

ondary camshaft drive chain tensioner bolts to 17 ft. lbs. (23 Nm).

98. Release the left secondary camshaft drive chain tensioner by pulling out tool EN 46112 and unlocking the tensioner plunger.

99. Verify the left secondary camshaft drive chain timing mark alignments (1-6). Ensure that the right camshaft intermediate drive chain idler (1) is being installed. The recessed hub (4) and the smaller sprocket of the right camshaft intermediate drive chain idler is installed outward. The raised hub and the larger sprocket of the right camshaft intermediate drive chain idler is installed toward the block.

100. Install the right camshaft intermediate drive chain idler.

101. Install the camshaft intermediate drive chain idler bolt. Tighten the camshaft intermediate drive chain idler bolt to 43 ft. lbs. (58 Nm).

➡**Ensure that the crankshaft is in the stage one timing drive assembly position.**

102. Install the primary camshaft drive chain.

103. Wrap the primary camshaft drive chain around the large sprockets of each camshaft intermediate drive chain idler and the crankshaft sprocket.

104. The left camshaft intermediate drive chain idler timing mark (1) will align with a timing camshaft drive chain link (2).

105. The right camshaft intermediate drive chain idler timing mark (2) will align with a timing camshaft drive chain link (1).

106. The crankshaft sprocket timing mark (2) will align with a timing camshaft drive chain link (1).

107. Ensure all the timing marks (2, 3, 6) are properly aligned with the timing camshaft drive chain links (1, 4, 5).

108. Install the primary camshaft drive chain upper guide.

109. Install the primary camshaft drive chain upper guide bolts. Tighten the primary camshaft drive chain upper guide bolts to 17 ft. lbs. (23 Nm).

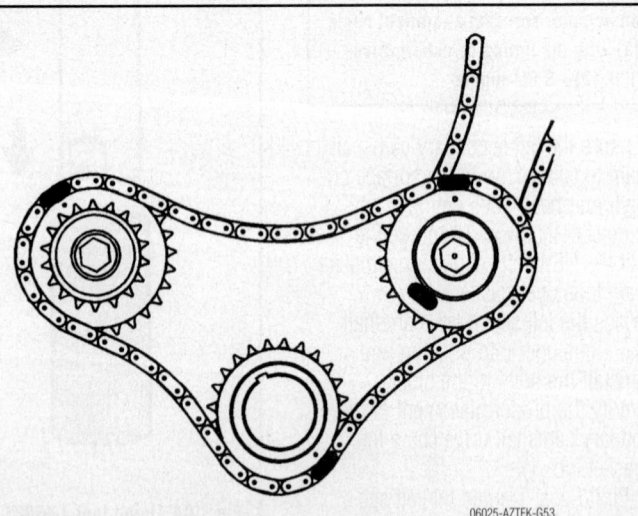

06025-AZTEK-G53

Fig. 106 Wrap the primary camshaft drive chain around the large sprockets of each camshaft intermediate drive chain idler and the crankshaft sprocket—3.6L engine

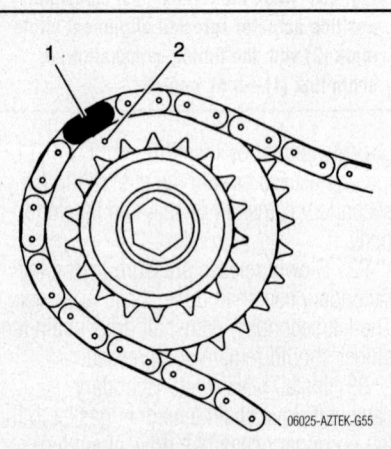

06025-AZTEK-G55

Fig. 108 The right camshaft intermediate drive chain idler timing mark (2) will align with a timing camshaft drive chain link (1)—3.6L engine

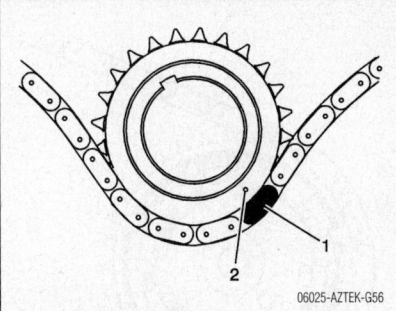

Fig. 109 The crankshaft sprocket timing mark (2) will align with a timing camshaft drive chain link (1)—3.6L engine

110. Using tool J 45027 reset the primary camshaft drive chain tensioner plunger.

111. Install the plunger into the primary camshaft drive chain tensioner body.

112. Compress the plunger into the body and lock the primary camshaft drive chain tensioner by inserting tool EN 46112 into the access hole in the side of the primary camshaft drive chain tensioner body.

113. Slowly release pressure on the primary camshaft drive chain tensioner. The primary camshaft drive chain tensioner should remain compressed.

114. Install a NEW primary camshaft drive chain tensioner gasket to the primary camshaft drive chain tensioner.

115. Install the primary camshaft drive chain tensioner bolts through the primary camshaft drive chain tensioner and gasket.

116. Ensure the primary camshaft drive chain tensioner mounting surface on the engine block does not have any burrs or defects that would degrade the sealing of the NEW primary camshaft drive chain tensioner gasket.

117. Place the primary camshaft drive chain tensioner into position and loosely install the bolts to the block.

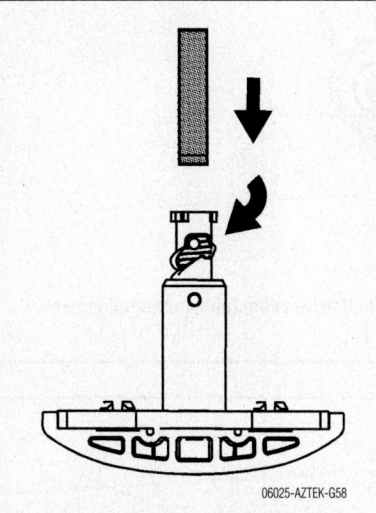

Fig. 111 Compress the plunger into the body and lock the primary camshaft drive chain tensioner by inserting tool EN 46112 into the access hole in the side of the primary camshaft drive chain tensioner body—3.6L engine

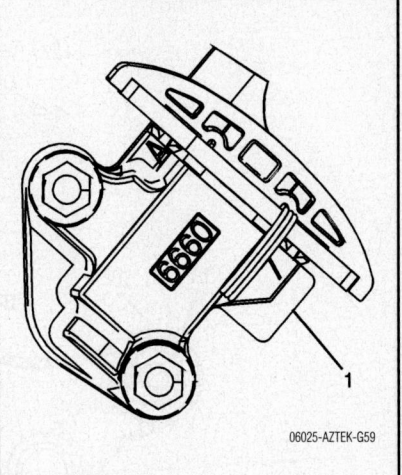

Fig. 112 Verify the proper placement of the primary camshaft drive chain tensioner gasket tab (1)—3.6L engine

118. Verify the proper placement of the primary camshaft drive chain tensioner gasket tab (1).

- First Pass: Tighten the primary camshaft drive chain tensioner bolts to 44 inch lbs. (5 Nm).
- Final Pass: Tighten the primary camshaft drive chain tensioner bolts to 17 ft. lbs. (23 Nm).

119. Release the primary camshaft drive chain tensioner by pulling out tool EN 46112 and unlocking the tensioner plunger.

120. Verify the primary and left secondary camshaft drive chain timing mark alignments (1-12).

121. Remove tool EN 46105-1 from the rear of the left camshafts.

122. Using tool EN 46111 rotate the crankshaft and crankshaft sprocket from the stage one alignment position (1) to the stage two alignment position (2), 115 crankshaft degrees, in order to install the right secondary camshaft drive chain components.

123. Install tool EN 46105-2 onto the rear of the left camshafts.

124. Install tool EN 46105-1 onto the rear of the right camshafts.

125. Ensure that the crankshaft is in the stage two timing drive assembly position.

126. Install the right secondary camshaft drive chain.

127. Place the secondary camshaft drive chain around the right camshaft intermediate drive chain idler outer sprocket, aligning the timing camshaft drive chain link (1) with the alignment access hole (2) made in the right camshaft intermediate drive chain idler inner sprocket.

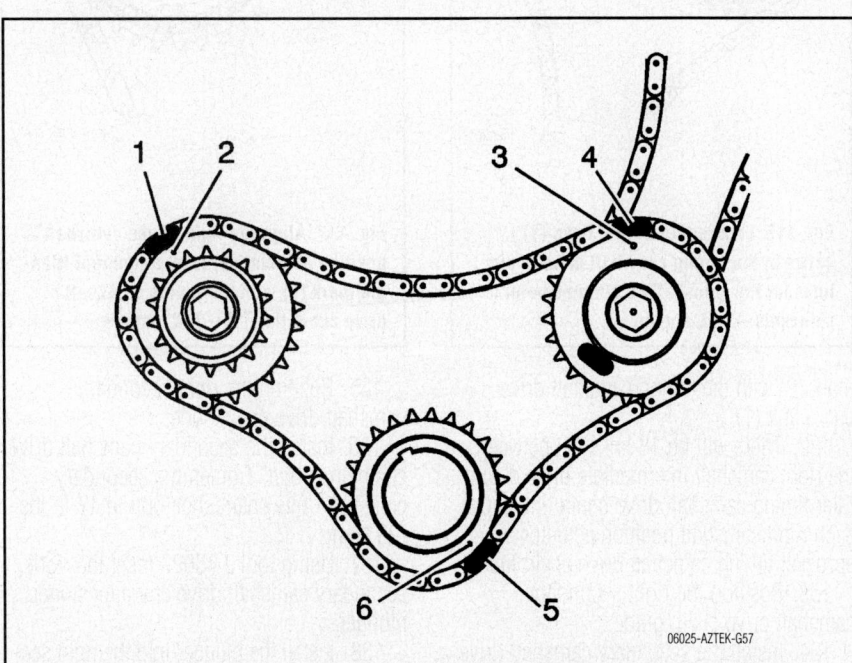

Fig. 110 Ensure all the timing marks (2, 3, 6) are properly aligned with the timing camshaft drive chain links (1, 4, 5)—3.6L engine

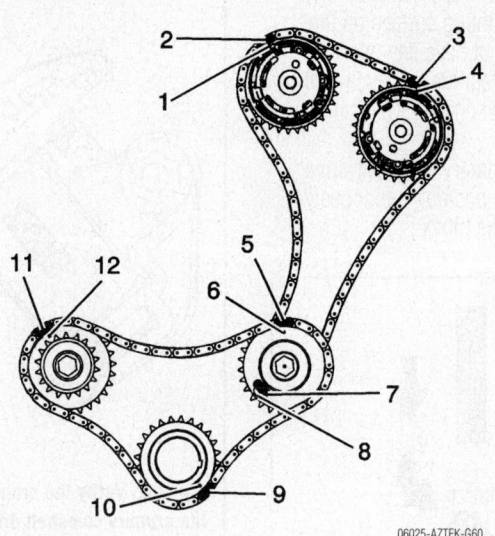

Fig. 113 Verify the primary and left secondary camshaft drive chain timing mark alignments (1-12)—3.6L engine

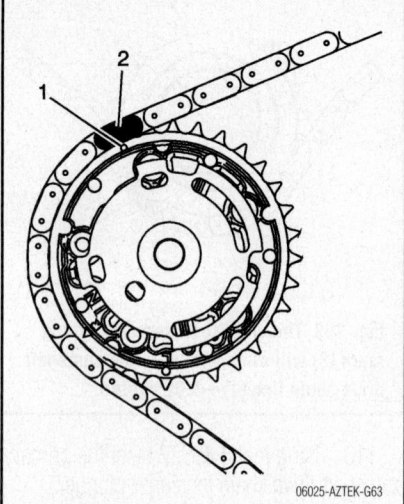

Fig. 116 Align the right exhaust camshaft position actuator sprocket alignment triangle mark (1) with the timing camshaft drive chain link (2)—3.6L engine

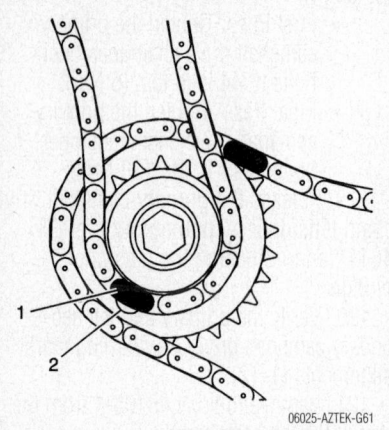

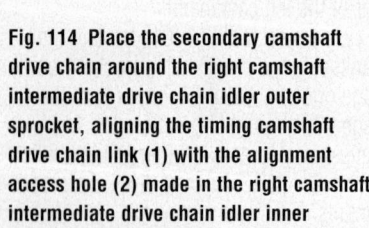

Fig. 114 Place the secondary camshaft drive chain around the right camshaft intermediate drive chain idler outer sprocket, aligning the timing camshaft drive chain link (1) with the alignment access hole (2) made in the right camshaft intermediate drive chain idler inner sprocket—3.6L engine

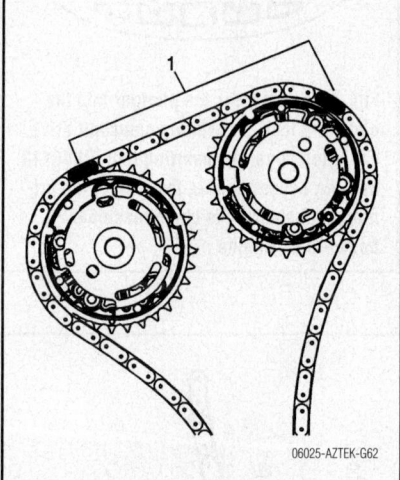

Fig. 115 Ensure there are 7 links (1) between the timing camshaft drive chain links for the camshaft position actuator sprockets—3.6L engine

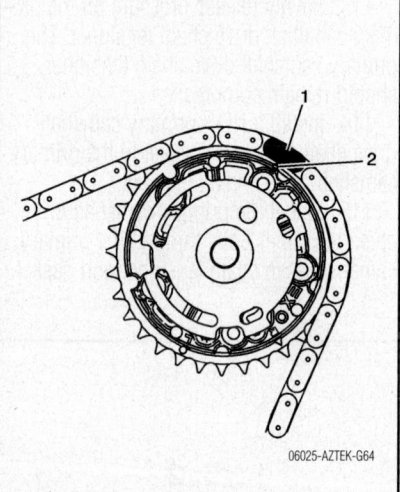

Fig. 117 Align the right intake camshaft position actuator sprocket alignment triangle mark (2) with the timing camshaft drive chain link (1)—3.6L engine

128. Wrap the secondary camshaft drive chain around both right actuator drive sprockets.

129. Ensure there are 7 links (1) between the timing camshaft drive chain links for the camshaft position actuator sprockets.

130. Align the right exhaust camshaft position actuator sprocket alignment triangle mark (1) with the timing camshaft drive chain link (2).

131. Align the right intake camshaft position actuator sprocket alignment triangle

mark (2) with the timing camshaft drive chain link (1).

132. There will be 18 links (1) between the right camshaft intermediate drive chain idler timing camshaft drive chain link and each right camshaft position actuator sprocket timing camshaft drive chain link.

133. Position the right secondary camshaft drive chain guide.

134. Install the secondary camshaft drive chain guide bolts. Tighten the secondary camshaft drive chain guide bolts to 17 ft. lbs. (23 Nm).

135. Position the right secondary camshaft drive chain shoe.

136. Install the secondary camshaft drive chain shoe bolt. Tighten the secondary camshaft drive chain shoe bolt to 17 ft. lbs. (23 Nm).

137. Using tool J 45027 reset the right secondary camshaft drive chain tensioner plunger.

138. Install the plunger into the right secondary camshaft drive chain tensioner body.

139. Compress the plunger into the body and lock the right secondary camshaft drive

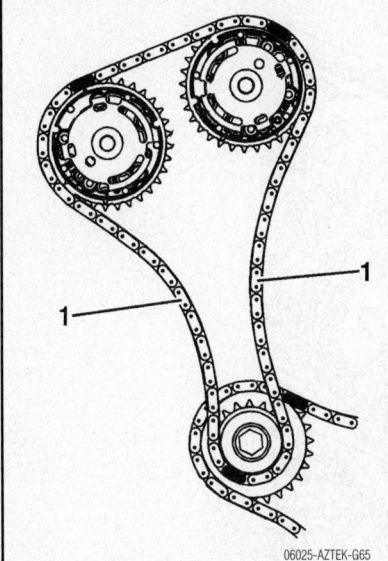

Fig. 118 There will be 18 links (1) between the right camshaft intermediate drive chain idler timing camshaft drive chain link and each right camshaft position actuator sprocket timing camshaft drive chain link—3.6L engine

06025-AZTEK-G65

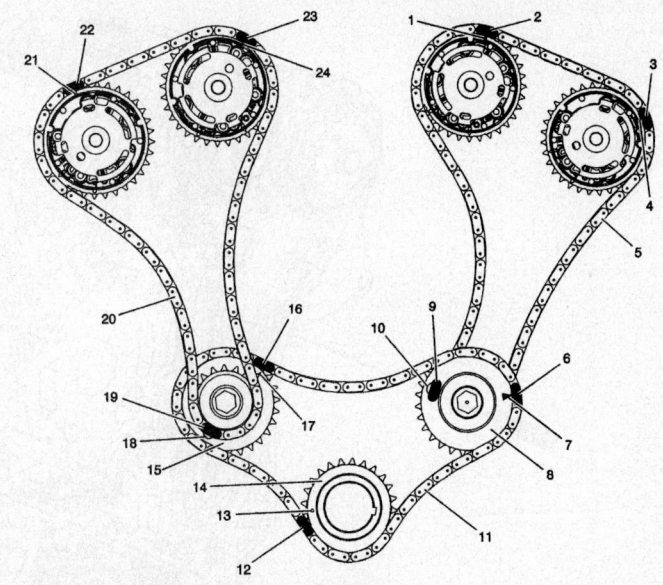

1. Left intake Camshaft Position (CMP) actuator timing mark
2. Left intake secondary camshaft timing drive chain timing link
3. Left exhaust secondary camshaft timing drive chain timing link
4. Left exhaust Camshaft Position (CMP) actuator timing mark
5. Left secondary camshaft timing drive chain
6. Primary camshaft drive chain timing link for the left primary camshaft intermediate drive chain sprocket
7. Left primary camshaft intermediate drive chain sprocket timing mark for the primary camshaft drive chain
8. Left primary camshaft intermediate drive chain sprocket
9. Left secondary camshaft timing drive chain timing link for the left primary camshaft intermediate drive chain sprocket
10. Left primary camshaft intermediate drive chain sprocket timing window
11. Primary camshaft drive chain
12. Primary camshaft drive chain timing link for the crankshaft sprocket
13. Crankshaft sprocket timing mark
14. Crankshaft sprocket
15. Right primary camshaft intermediate drive chain sprocket
16. Primary camshaft drive chain timing link for the right primary camshaft intermediate drive chain sprocket
17. Right primary camshaft intermediate drive chain sprocket timing mark for the primary camshaft drive chain
18. Right primary camshaft intermediate drive chain sprocket timing mark/window for the right secondary camshaft timing drive chain
19. Right secondary camshaft timing drive chain timing link for the right primary camshaft intermediate drive chain sprocket
20. Right secondary camshaft timing drive chain
21. Right exhaust Camshaft Position (CMP) actuator timing mark
22. Right exhaust secondary camshaft timing drive chain timing link
23. Right intake Camshaft Position (CMP) actuator timing mark
24. Right intake Camshaft Position (CMP) actuator timing mark

06025-AZTEK-G71

Fig. 119 Verify all primary and secondary camshaft drive chain timing mark alignments (1-18) Stage Two—3.6L engine

chain tensioner by inserting tool EN 46112 into the access hole in the side of the right secondary camshaft drive chain tensioner body.

140. Slowly release pressure on the right secondary camshaft drive chain tensioner. The right secondary camshaft drive chain tensioner should remain compressed.

141. Install a NEW right secondary camshaft drive chain tensioner gasket to the right secondary camshaft drive chain tensioner.

142. Install the right secondary camshaft drive chain tensioner bolts through the right secondary camshaft drive chain tensioner and gasket.

143. Ensure the right secondary camshaft drive chain tensioner mounting surface on the right cylinder head does not have any burrs or defects that would degrade the sealing of the NEW right secondary camshaft drive chain tensioner gasket.

144. Place the right secondary camshaft drive chain tensioner into position and loosely install the bolts to the block.

145. Verify the proper placement of the right secondary camshaft drive chain tensioner gasket tab (1).

- First Pass: Tighten the right secondary camshaft drive chain tensioner bolts to 44 inch lbs. (5 Nm).
- Final Pass: Tighten the right secondary camshaft drive chain tensioner bolts to 17 ft. lbs. (23 Nm).

146. Release the right camshaft drive chain tensioner by pulling out tool EN 46112 and unlocking the tensioner plunger.

147. Verify all primary and secondary camshaft drive chain timing mark alignments (1-18) Stage Two.

148. Install the 8mm (0.315 in) guide pins from tool EN 46109 into the cylinder block positions as shown.

149. Install the NEW engine front cover to cylinder block seal.

150. Place a 3mm (0.118 in) bead of RTV sealant, GM P/N 12378521 (Canadian P/N 88901148) or equivalent, on the engine front cover as shown (1).

151. Place the engine front cover onto tool EN 46109 and slide into position.

152. Remove tool EN 46109 from the cylinder block.

153. Hand start all the front cover bolts.

154. Tighten the engine front cover bolts in the sequence shown. Tighten the engine front cover bolts in sequence to 17 ft. lbs. (23 Nm).

155. Install NEW O-rings on the camshaft position sensor.

156. Place the camshaft position sensors in position on the front cover.

157. Install the camshaft position sensor bolts. Tighten the camshaft position sensor bolts to 89 inch lbs. (10 Nm).

158. Place the camshaft position actuator valves in position on the front cover.

159. Install the camshaft position actuator valve bolts. Tighten the camshaft position actuator valve bolts to 89 inch lbs. (10 Nm).

160. The EN 46106 must be installed onto the flywheel.

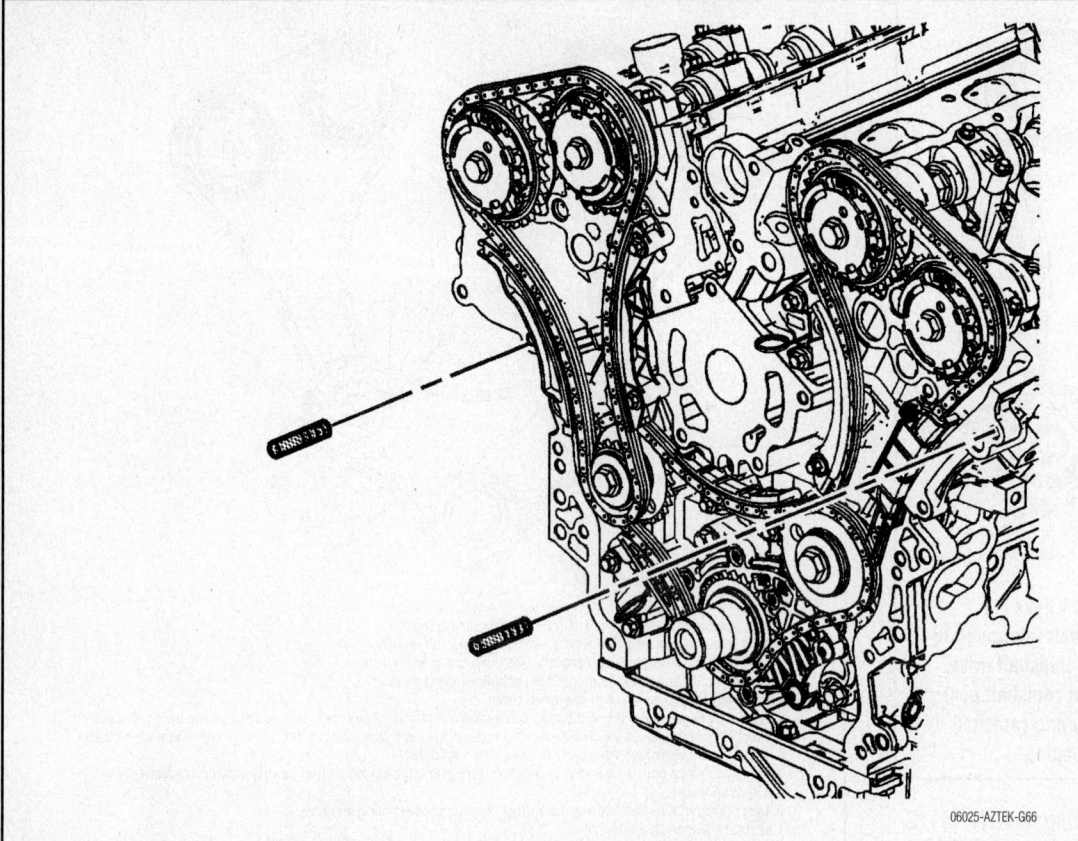

Fig. 120 Install the 8mm (0.315 in) guide pins from tool EN 46109 into the cylinder block positions as shown—3.6L engine

06025-AZTEK-G66

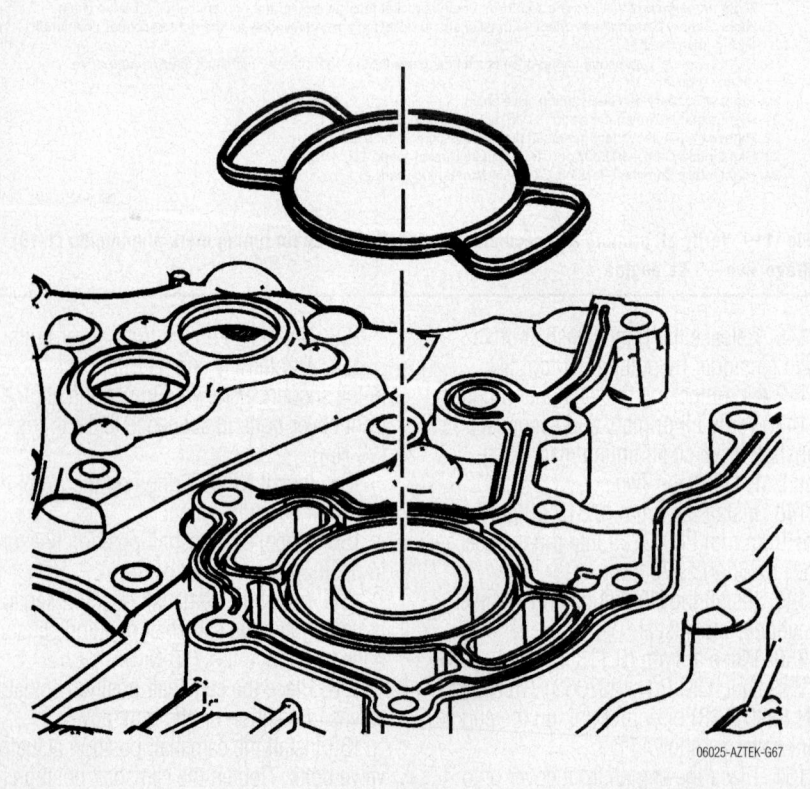

Fig. 121 Install the NEW engine front cover to cylinder block seal—3.6L engine

06025-AZTEK-G67

161. Use tool J 41998-B, nut, bearing and washer to install the crankshaft balancer.

➡ **Do not lubricate the crankshaft front oil seal or crankshaft balancer sealing surfaces. The crankshaft balancer is installed into a dry seal.**

162. Apply lubricant to the inside of the crankshaft balancer hub bore.

163. Place the crankshaft balancer in position on the crankshaft.

164. Thread tool J 41998-B in the crankshaft. Ensure you engage at least 10 threads of tool J 41998-B before pressing the crankshaft balancer in place.

165. Push the crankshaft balancer into position by tightening the nut on tool J 41998-B until the large washer bottoms out on the crankshaft end.

166. Remove tool J 41998-B.

167. Install the crankshaft balancer bolt.

168. Tighten the crankshaft balancer bolt. Tighten the crankshaft balancer bolt to 74 ft. lbs. (100 Nm).

169. Tighten the crankshaft balancer bolt an additional 150 degrees using tool J 45059.

170. Remove tool EN 46106.

171. The remainder of installation is the reverse of removal.

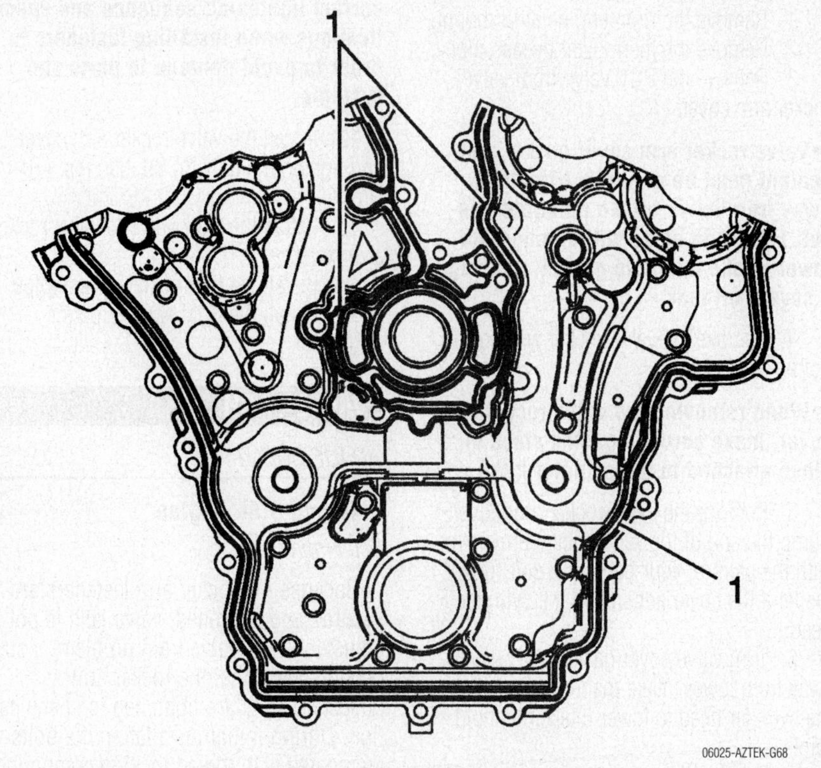

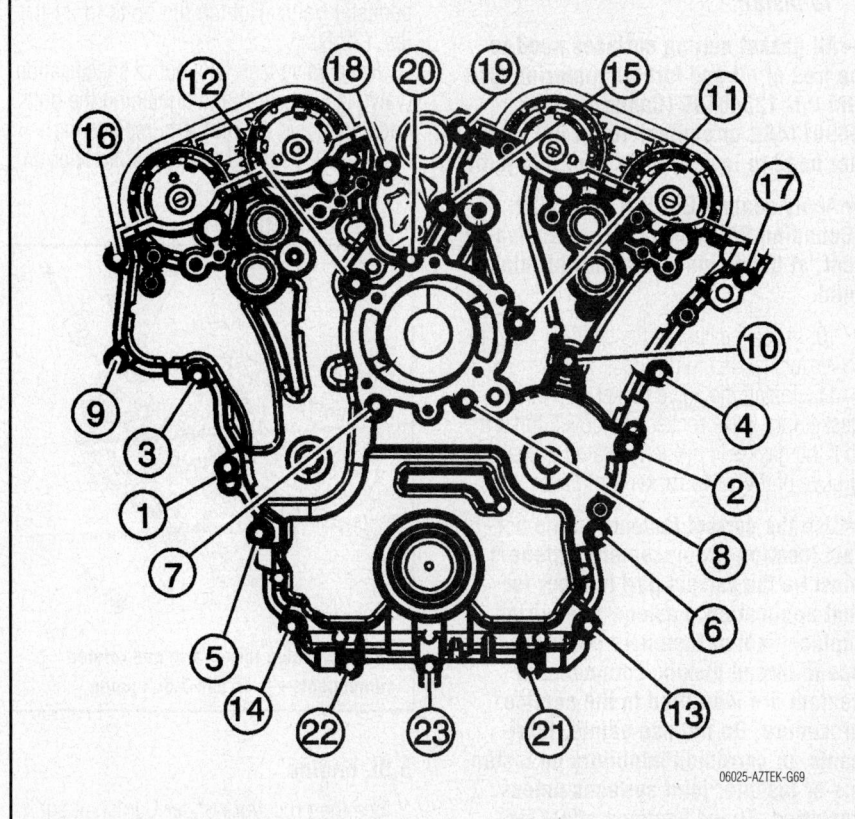

Fig. 122 Place a 3mm (0.118 in) bead of RTV sealant, GM P/N 12378521 (Canadian P/N 88901148) or equivalent, on the engine front cover as shown (1)—3.6L engine

Fig. 123 Tighten the engine front cover bolts in the sequence shown—3.6L engine

VALVE (ROCKER ARM) COVERS

REMOVAL & INSTALLATION

3.4L and 3.5L Engine

Right

See Figure 124.

1. Remove the drive belt.
2. Remove the generator.
3. Remove the generator bracket.
4. Disconnect the engine right side spark plug wires.
5. Disconnect the vacuum hoses from the Evaporative emissions (EVAP) canister purge solenoid valve.
6. Remove the EVAP canister purge solenoid valve.
7. Remove the ignition module bracket with the coils.
8. Remove the vacuum hose from the grommet in the engine right side valve rocker arm cover.

➡**Valve rocker arm cover gasket and sealant must be carefully trimmed away from lower intake manifold gasket. Failure to do so will damage the lower intake manifold gasket, causing a severe oil leak.**

9. Remove the valve rocker arm cover bolts.

➡**When removing the valve rocker arm cover, make sure the gasket stays in place attached to the cylinder head.**

10. Remove the valve rocker. Bump the end of the valve rocker arm cover with the

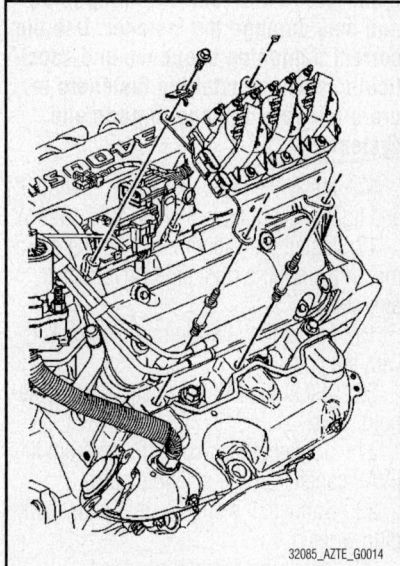

Fig. 124 Remove the ignition module bracket with the coils

palm of your hand or a soft rubber mallet if the cover adheres to the cylinder head.

11. Trim the valve cover gasket and sealant away from lower intake manifold gasket at the cylinder head to lower intake manifold joints.

12. Remove the valve cover gasket.

13. Clean the sealing surface on the cylinder head with degreaser.

14. Clean the valve rocker arm cover.

To install:

➡ All gasket mating surfaces need to be free of oil and foreign material. Use GM P/N 12346139 (Canadian P/N 10953463) or equivalent to clean surfaces. Important: Apply sealant GM P/N 12378521 (Canadian P/N 88901148), or equivalent, at the cylinder head to lower intake manifold joint.

15. Apply sealant at the cylinder head to lower intake manifold joint. Install the valve rocker arm cover gasket into the valve rocker arm cover. Ensure that the gasket is properly seated in the groove of the valve rocker arm cover.

16. Install valve rocker arm cover.

➡ Use the correct fastener in the correct location. Replacement fasteners must be the correct part number for that application. Fasteners requiring replacement or fasteners requiring the use of thread locking compound or sealant are identified in the service procedure. Do not use paints, lubricants, or corrosion inhibitors on fasteners or fastener joint surfaces unless specified. These coatings affect fastener torque and joint clamping force and may damage the fastener. Use the correct tightening sequence and specifications when installing fasteners in order to avoid damage to parts and systems.

17. Install the valve rocker arm cover bolts and tighten the bolts to 89 inch lbs. (10 Nm).

18. Install the vacuum hose to the grommet in the engine right side valve rocker arm cover.

19. Install the ignition module bracket with the coils.

20. Install the EVAP canister purge solenoid valve.

21. Connect the vacuum hoses from the EVAP canister purge solenoid valve.

22. Connect the engine right side spark plug wires.

23. Install the generator bracket.

24. Install the generator.

25. Install the drive belt.

Left

1. Remove the right engine strut mount.
2. Remove the thermostat bypass pipe.
3. Remove the PCV valve from valve rocker arm cover.

➡ Valve rocker arm cover gasket and sealant must be carefully trimmed away from lower intake manifold gasket. Failure to do so will damage the lower intake manifold gasket, causing a severe oil leak.

4. Remove the valve rocker arm cover bolts.

➡ When removing the valve rocker arm cover, make sure the gasket stays in place attached to the cylinder head.

5. Remove the valve rocker arm cover. Bump the end of the valve rocker arm cover with the palm of your hand or a soft rubber mallet if the cover adheres to the cylinder head.

6. Trim valve cover gasket and sealant away from lower intake manifold gasket at the cylinder head to lower intake manifold joints.

7. Remove the valve cover gasket.

8. Clean the sealing surface on the cylinder head with degreaser.

9. Clean the valve rocker arm cover.

To install:

➡ All gasket mating surfaces need to be free of oil and foreign material. Use GM P/N 12346139 (Canadian P/N 88901148), or equivalent, at the cylinder head to lower intake manifold joint.

➡ Apply sealant GM P/N 12378521 (Canadian P/N 88901148), or equivalent, at the cylinder head lower intake joint.

10. Apply sealant at the cylinder head to lower intake manifold joints.

11. Install the valve rocker arm cover gasket into valve rocker arm cover. Ensure that the gasket is properly seated in the groove of the valve rocker arm cover.

➡ Use the correct fastener in the correct location. Replacement fasteners must be the correct part number for that application. Fasteners requiring replacement or fasteners requiring the use of thread locking compound or sealant are identified in the service procedure. Do not use paints, lubricants, or corrosion inhibitors on fasteners or fastener joint surfaces unless specified. These coatings affect fastener torque and joint clamping force

and may damage the fastener. Use the correct tightening sequence and specifications when installing fasteners in order to avoid damage to parts and systems.

12. Install the valve rocker arm cover and tighten the bolts to 89 inch lbs. (10 Nm).

13. Install the PCV valve to valve rocker arm cover.

14. Install the thermostat bypass pipe.

15. Install the right engine mount strut.

VALVE LASH

ADJUSTMENT

3.4L and 3.5L Engine

See Figure 125.

Because the rocker arm fasteners are secured and tightened, valve lash is not adjustable. If a valve train problem is suspected, check that the rocker arm pedestals bolts are tightened to specification. During initial installation the bolts are coated with thread locking compound. If they are sufficiently loosened to cause valvetrain noise, they should be removed and thoroughly cleaned. Apply thread locking compound to the rocker arm pedestal bolts. Tighten the bolts to 24 ft. lbs. (32 Nm).

When valve lash falls out of specification (valve tap is heard) and tightening the bolts does not solve the problem, replace the rocker arm, pushrod and hydraulic lifter on the offending cylinder.

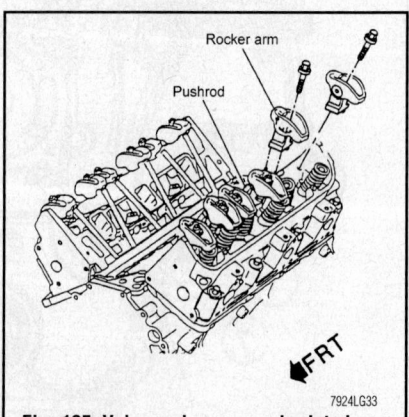

Fig. 125 Valve rocker arm and related components—3.4L and 3.5L engine

3.6L Engine

See the procedure under Camshaft and Lifters.

FUEL   **GASOLINE FUEL INJECTION SYSTEM**

FUEL SYSTEM SERVICE PRECAUTIONS

Safety is the most important factor when performing not only fuel system maintenance but any type of maintenance. Failure to conduct maintenance and repairs in a safe manner may result in serious personal injury or death. Maintenance and testing of the vehicle's fuel system components can be accomplished safely and effectively by adhering to the following rules and guidelines.

• To avoid the possibility of fire and personal injury, always disconnect the negative battery cable unless the repair or test procedure requires that battery voltage be applied.

• Always relieve the fuel system pressure prior to disconnecting any fuel system component (injector, fuel rail, pressure regulator, etc.), fitting or fuel line connection. Exercise extreme caution whenever relieving fuel system pressure to avoid exposing skin, face and eyes to fuel spray. Please be advised that fuel under pressure may penetrate the skin or any part of the body that it contacts.

• Always place a shop towel or cloth around the fitting or connection prior to loosening to absorb any excess fuel due to spillage. Ensure that all fuel spillage (should it occur) is quickly removed from engine surfaces. Ensure that all fuel soaked cloths or towels are deposited into a suitable waste container.

• Always keep a dry chemical (Class B) fire extinguisher near the work area.

• Do not allow fuel spray or fuel vapors to come into contact with a spark or open flame.

• Always use a back-up wrench when loosening and tightening fuel line connection fittings. This will prevent unnecessary stress and torsion to fuel line piping.

• Always replace worn fuel fitting O-rings with new Do not substitute fuel hose or equivalent where fuel pipe is installed.

Before servicing the vehicle, make sure to also refer to the precautions in the beginning of this section as well.

RELIEVING FUEL SYSTEM PRESSURE

RELIEVING

3.4L and 3.5L Engine

A Schrader valve is provided on these fuel systems to conveniently test or release the system pressure. A fuel pressure gauge

and adapter will be necessary to connect the gauge to the fitting. Most of the SFI systems utilize a service valve on one end of the fuel rail assembly.

1. Before servicing the vehicle, refer to the Precautions Section.
2. Disconnect the negative battery cable
3. Loosen the fuel filler cap to relieve tank vapor pressure.
4. Connect a fuel pressure gauge to the connector. Wrap a shop towel around the fittings to prevent spillage.
5. Install the bleed hose into an approved container and open the valve.
6. Drain any remaining fuel from the pressure gauge.
7. When fuel service is finished, tighten the fuel filler cap and connect the negative battery cable.

3.6L Engine

1. Before servicing the vehicle, refer to the Precautions Section.
2. Turn the ignition **OFF**.
3. Remove the fuel pump fuse and the fuel pump relay.
4. Loosen the fuel filler cap to relieve the fuel tank vapor pressure.
5. Attempt to start the engine and allow the engine to run until it stops.
6. Remove the fuel pressure test port cap.

> ✳✳ **CAUTION**
>
> **Wrap a shop towel around the fuel pressure connection in order to reduce the risk of fire and personal injury. The towel will absorb any fuel leakage that occurs during the connection of the fuel pressure gage. Place the towel in an approved container when the connection of the fuel pressure gage is complete.**

7. Wrap a shop towel around the fuel pressure test port and use a small flat-bladed tool in order to depress (open) the fuel pressure test port valve.
8. Place the shop towel in an approved container.
9. Install the fuel pressure test port cap.
10. Tighten the fuel filler cap.

FUEL FILTER

REMOVAL & INSTALLATION

3.4L and 3.5L Engine
See Figure 126.

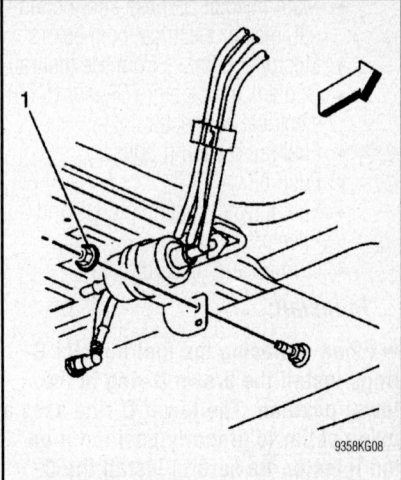

Fig. 126 The fuel filter is located on the frame rail near the tank—with 3.4L and 3.5L engine

9358KG08

1. Before servicing the vehicle, refer to the Precautions Section.
2. Relieve fuel system pressure.
3. Remove or disconnect the following:
   • Negative battery cable
   • Quick connect fittings at the inlet/outlet sides of the in-pipe fuel filter
   • Fuel filter mounting bracket nut
   • Fuel filter and drain any remaining fuel

To install:
4. Install or connect the following:
   • Fuel filter to the bracket
   • Fuel filter assembly to the side rail near the fuel tank. Torque the nut to 89 inch lbs. (10 Nm).
   • Inlet/outlet quick connectors to the fuel filter
   • Negative battery cable
5. Start the vehicle and checks for leaks, repair if necessary.

3.6L Engine

See the Fuel Pump procedure.

FUEL INJECTORS

REMOVAL & INSTALLATION

3.4L and 3.5L Engine
See Figure 127.

1. Before servicing the vehicle, refer to the Precautions Section.
2. Relieve the fuel system pressure.
3. Remove or disconnect the following:
   • Negative battery cable
   • Upper intake manifold

- Engine fuel feed pipe at the fuel rail
- Fuel return line from the regulator
- Main injector harness and individual injector electrical connectors
- Electrical harness from the fuel rail
- Coolant Temperature Sensor (CTS) electrical connector
- Fuel rail retaining bolts
- Fuel rail
- Fuel injector retaining clips and injectors
- O-rings and discard them

To install:

➡**When replacing the fuel injector O-rings install the brown O-ring in the lower position. The lower O-ring uses a nylon collar to properly position it on the injector. Be sure to install the O-ring backup or the sealing O-ring may move when the injector is installed to the fuel rail. If the sealing ring is not seated properly, a vacuum leak is possible thus causing drivability complaints.**

4. Install or connect the following:
- Upper O-ring to the fuel injector
- Lower O-ring backup to the injector
- Lower O-ring to the injector
- Fuel injector to the fuel rail
- Fuel rail into the intake manifold. Tilt the rail to install the injectors.
- Fuel rail retaining bolts. Torque the bolts to 89 inch lbs. (10 Nm).
- CTS electrical connector
- Injector electrical harness
- Injector electrical connectors. Make

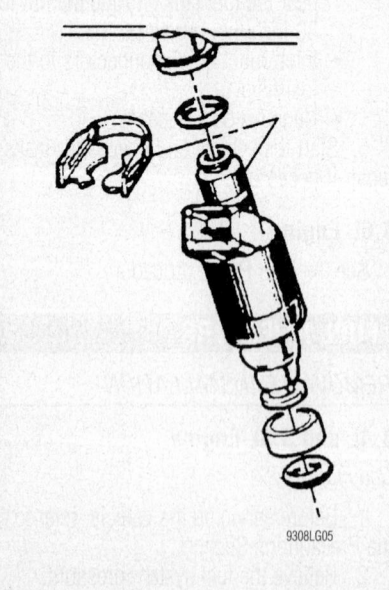

Fig. 127 Fuel injector—3.4L and 3.5L engine

sure to push the slide locks into position.
- Main injector harness connector
- Fuel feed and return pipe, using new O-rings
- Fuel feed pipe. Torque the nut to 89 inch lbs. (10 Nm).
- Fuel return pipe to the pressure regulator. Torque the nut to 13 ft. lbs. (17 Nm).
- Upper intake manifold
- Negative battery cable

5. Prime the fuel system as follows:
   a. Turn the ignition switch **ON** for two seconds.
   b. Turn the ignition switch **OFF** for 10 seconds.
   c. Turn the ignition switch **ON** and checks for leaks. Repair if necessary.

3.6L Engine

See Figures 128 through 130.

1. Before servicing the vehicle, refer to the Precautions Section.
2. Relieve the fuel system pressure.
3. Remove the upper intake manifold.
4. Remove the fuel pipe retaining clip.
5. Use compressed air in order to remove debris from the area where the fuel injectors enter the intake manifold.
6. Remove the fuel rail bolts.

➡**Remove the fuel rail assembly carefully in order to prevent damage to the injector electrical connector terminals and the injector spray tips. Support the fuel rail after the fuel rail is removed in order to avoid damaging the fuel rail components. Cap the fittings and plug the holes when servicing the fuel system in order to prevent dirt and other contaminants from entering open pipes and passages.**

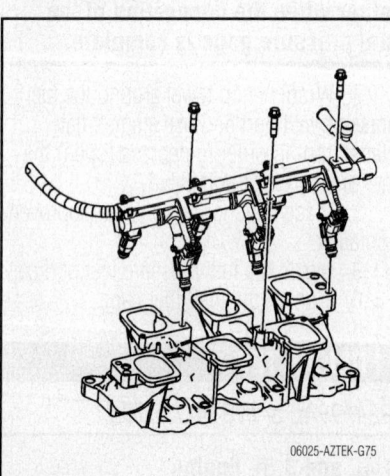

06025-AZTEK-G75

Fig. 128 Fuel rail removal—3.6L engine

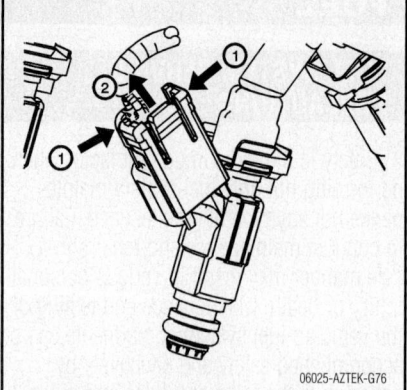

06025-AZTEK-G76

Fig. 129 Squeeze the tabs (1) and pull up (2) to disconnect the injector wiring—3.6L engine

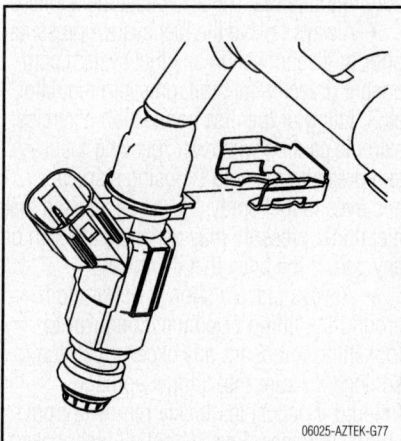

06025-AZTEK-G77

Fig. 130 Fuel injector retaining clip—3.6L engine

7. Remove the fuel rail with the fuel injectors.
8. Disengage the fuel injector electrical connector lock.
9. Disconnect the fuel injector electrical connector.
10. Remove the fuel injector retainer clip.
11. Remove the fuel injector.
12. Remove and discard the fuel injector seals.

To install:
13. Install NEW fuel injector seals.
14. Install the fuel injector.
15. Install the fuel injector retainer clip.
16. Install the fuel injector electrical connector.
17. Engage the fuel injector electrical connector lock.
18. Install the fuel rail with the fuel injectors.
19. Install the fuel rail bolts. Tighten the fuel rail bolts to 89 inch lbs. (10 Nm).
20. Install the upper intake manifold.

FUEL PUMP

REMOVAL & INSTALLATION

3.4L and 3.5L Engine

1. Before servicing the vehicle, refer to the Precautions Section.

2. Properly relieve the fuel system pressure.

3. Drain and remove the fuel tank from the vehicle

4. Remove or disconnect the following:
- Negative battery cable
- Fuel tank
- Fuel sender shield
- Quick connect fittings at the fuel pump
- Fuel Tank Pressure (FTP) electrical connector
- Fuel pump assembly lockring

✳✳ WARNING

Do NOT pick up the fuel pump by the fuel pipes. Doing this could cause the joints to be damaged.

- Fuel pump assembly from the fuel tank and discard the O-ring

To install:

5. Install or connect the following:
- New O-ring on the fuel tank
- Fuel pump into the fuel tank making certain not to fold or twist the strainer and that it does not interfere with the full travel of the float arm
- Fuel pump locking nut
- Quick connect fittings at the fuel pump
- FTP sensor electrical connector
- Fuel sender shield
- Fuel tank and fill the tank
- Negative battery cable

6. Prime the fuel system as follows:

a. Turn the ignition switch **ON** for two seconds.

b. Turn the ignition switch **OFF** for 10 seconds.

c. Turn the ignition switch **ON** and checks for leaks. Repair if necessary.

3.6L Engine

See Figures 131 and 132.

1. Before servicing the vehicle, refer to the Precautions Section.

2. Relieve the fuel system fuel pressure.

3. Drain the fuel tank.

4. Raise the vehicle.

5. Disconnect the fuel tank wiring harness connector.

6. Disconnect the fuel evaporative emission (EVAP) pipes.

7. Remove the EVAP canister bracket nut.

8. Loosen the fuel tank fill pipe hose clamp.

9. Disconnect the fuel tank fill pipe hose from the fuel tank.

10. Disconnect the EVAP vent pipe near the fill pipe hose.

➡**Do not bend the fuel tank straps. Bending the fuel tank straps may damage the straps.**

11. With the aid of an assistant or a transmission jack, support the fuel tank and remove the fuel tank strap attaching bolts.

12. Remove the fuel tank from the vehicle and place the fuel tank in a suitable work area.

13. Disconnect the fuel sender module electrical connectors.

➡**Do Not handle the fuel sender assembly by the fuel pipes. The amount of leverage generated by handling the fuel pipes could damage the joints.**

14. Disconnect the fuel pipes from the fuel sender.

➡**Avoid damaging the lock ring. Use only J-45722 to prevent damage to the lock ring.**

✳✳ WARNING

Do NOT use impact tools. Significant force will be required to release the lock ring. The use of a hammer and screwdriver is not recommended. Secure the fuel tank in order to prevent fuel tank rotation.

15. Use tool J 45722 and a long breaker-bar in order to unlock the fuel sender lock ring. Turn the lock ring in a counterclockwise direction.

16. Remove the fuel sender lock ring and the fuel sender from the fuel tank.

17. Remove and discard the fuel sender seal.

18. Remove the fuel level sensor from the fuel sender module.

➡**Some lock rings were manufactured with "DO NOT REUSE" stamped into them. These lock rings may be reused if they are not damaged or warped.**

➡**Inspect the lock ring for damage due to improper removal or installation procedures. If damage is found, install a NEW lock ring.**

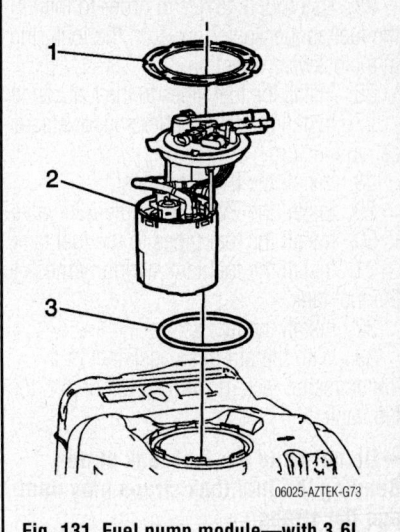

Fig. 131 Fuel pump module—with 3.6L engine

➡**Check the lock ring for flatness.**

19. Place the lock ring on a flat surface. Measure the clearance between the lock ring and the flat surface using a feeler gage at 7 points.

20. If warpage is less than 0.41 mm (0.016 in.), the lock ring does not require replacement. If warpage is greater than 0.41 mm (0.016 in.), the lock ring must be replaced.

To install:

21. Install the fuel level sensor to the fuel sender module.

22. Clean the fuel sender sealing flange.

➡**Always replace the fuel sender seal when installing the fuel sender assembly. Replace the lock ring if necessary. DO NOT apply any type of lubrication to the seal groove.**

23. Install the NEW fuel sender seal to the fuel tank seal groove.

24. Install the fuel sender and the fuel sender lock ring.

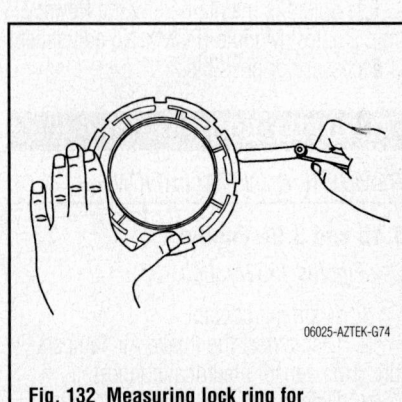

Fig. 132 Measuring lock ring for flatness—with 3.6L engine

25. Use tool J 45722 in order to install the fuel sender lock ring. Turn the lock ring in a clockwise direction.

26. Install the fuel pipes to the fuel sender.

27. Install the fuel sender sensor electrical connectors.

28. Install the EVAP canister.

29. Install the EVAP vent solenoid valve.

30. Install the fuel pipes to the fuel tank.

31. Install the fuel tank wiring harness to the fuel tank.

32. Install the fuel sender.

33. With the aid of an assistant or a transmission jack, position and support the fuel tank.

➡ **Do not bend the fuel tank straps. Bending the fuel tank straps may damage the straps.**

34. Install the fuel tank strap bolts. Tighten the fuel tank strap bolts to 35 ft. lbs. (47 Nm).

35. Install the EVAP canister bracket nut. Tighten the EVAP canister bracket nut to 53 inch lbs. (6 Nm).

36. Install the EVAP vent pipe near the fill pipe hose.

37. Install the fuel tank filler pipe hose to the fuel tank. Tighten the fuel tank filler pipe hose clamp to 22 inch lbs. (2.5 Nm).

38. Connect the fuel pipes.

39. Install the fuel tank wiring harness connector.

40. Lower the vehicle.

41. Add fuel as necessary and install the fuel tank filler pipe cap.

42. Inspect for fuel leaks. Perform the following steps:
- Turn **ON** the ignition for 2 seconds.
- Turn **OFF** the ignition for 10 seconds.
- Turn **ON** the ignition.
- Inspect for fuel leaks.

IDLE SPEED

ADJUSTMENT

Idle speed is maintained by the Powertrain Control Module (PCM). No adjustment is necessary or possible.

THROTTLE BODY

REMOVAL & INSTALLATION

3.4L and 3.5L Engine

See Figures 133 through 135.

1. Drain the coolant.

2. Disconnect the Intake Air Temperature (IAT) sensor electrical connector.

3. Disconnect the breather tube from the air intake tube.

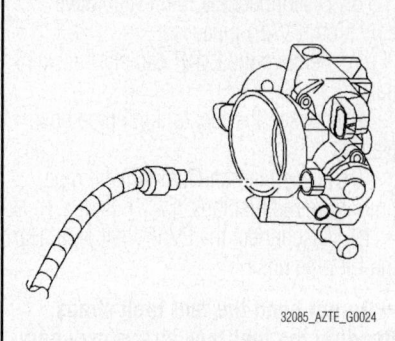

Fig. 133 Removal and installation of the throttle body sensor

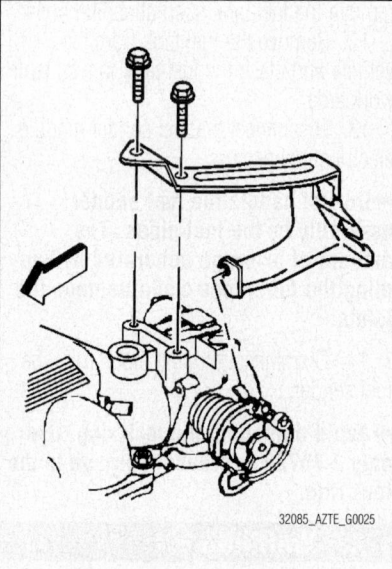

Fig. 134 Removal and installation of the accelerator control cable bracket

4. Remove the air intake tube.

5. Disconnect the Idle Air Control (IAC) valve electrical connector.

6. Disconnect the Throttle Position (TP) sensor electrical connector.

7. Remove the accelerator control cable bracket.

8. Disconnect the throttle body coolant bypass hoses.

9. Disconnect the heater pipe nut at the throttle body.

10. Remove the nuts and bolts holding the throttle body to the intake manifold.

11. Remove the throttle body assembly.

To install:

➡ **Do not use solvent of any type when cleaning the gasket surfaces on the intake manifold and the throttle body assembly, as damage to the gasket surfaces and throttle body assembly may result. Use care in cleaning the gasket surfaces on the intake manifold and the throttle body assembly, as sharp tools may damage the gasket surfaces.**

12. Clean the gasket surface on the intake manifold and the throttle body assembly.

13. Install a new gasket, if necessary.

14. Install the throttle body assembly.

➡ **Use the correct fastener in the correct location. Replacement fasteners must be the correct part number for that application. Fasteners requiring replacement or fasteners requiring the use of thread locking compound or**

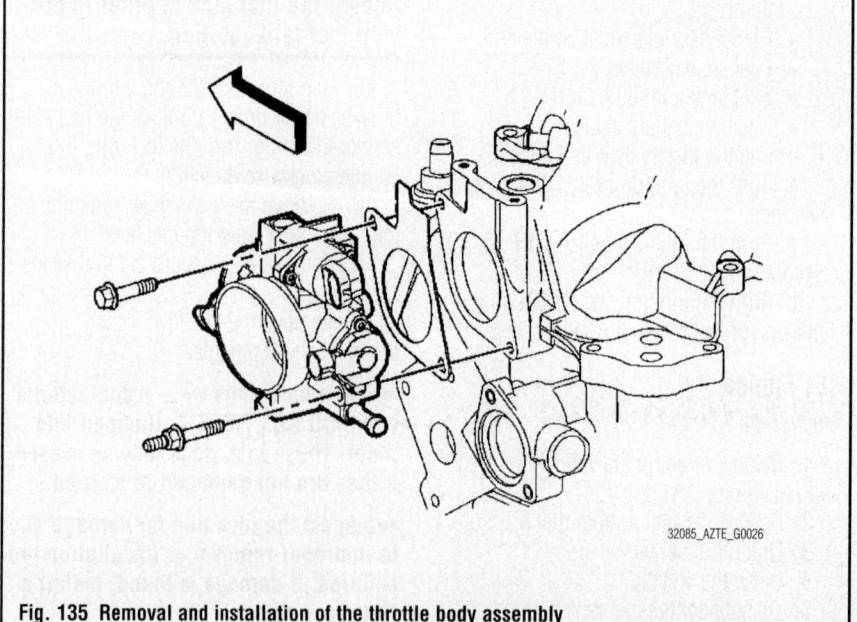

Fig. 135 Removal and installation of the throttle body assembly

sealant are identified in the service procedure. **Do not use paints, lubricants, or corrosion inhibitors on fasteners or fastener joint surfaces unless specified. These coatings affect fastener torque and joint clamping force and may damage the fastener. Use the correct tightening sequence and specifications when installing fasteners in order to avoid damage to parts and systems.**

15. Install the throttle body retaining nuts and bolts and tighten the throttle body retaining nuts and bolts to 89 inch lbs. (10 Nm).

16. Connect the throttle body coolant bypass hoses.

17. Connect the heater pipe nut at the throttle body.

18. Connect the Idle Air Control (IAC) valve electrical connector.

19. Connect the Throttle Position (TP) sensor electrical connector.

20. Install the accelerator controls cable bracket.

21. Install the air intake tube and tighten the clamps.

22. Connect the Intake Air Temperature (IAT) sensor electrical connector.

23. Connect the breather tube to the air intake tube.

24. Refill the coolant.

➡**The throttle should operate freely without binding between full closed and Wide Open Throttle (WOT).**

25. Inspect for complete throttle opening and closing positions by operating the accelerator pedal. Also inspect for poor carpet fit under the accelerator pedal.

3.6L Engine

See Figure 136.

1. Remove the air cleaner intake duct.

2. Remove the throttle body electrical connector.

3. Remove the throttle body bolts.

4. Remove the throttle body and gasket.

To install:

5. Carefully clean the throttle body mounting surfaces of any gasket and/or seal material.

6. Install the throttle body and new gasket.

7. Install the throttle body bolts and tighten to 89 inch lbs. (10 Nm).

8. Install the throttle body electrical connector.

9. Install the air cleaner intake duct.

10. Perform the idle learn procedure..

11. Use the scan tool to clear all DTCs.

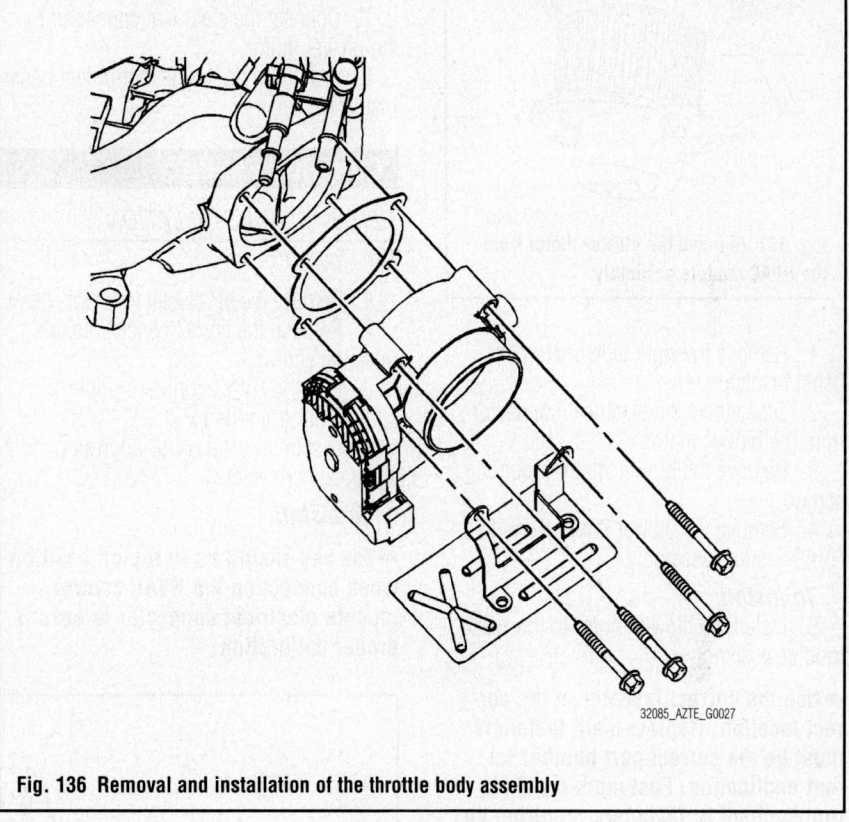

32085_AZTE_G0027

Fig. 136 Removal and installation of the throttle body assembly

HEATING & AIR CONDITIONING SYSTEM

BLOWER MOTOR

REMOVAL & INSTALLATION

See Figures 137 and 138.

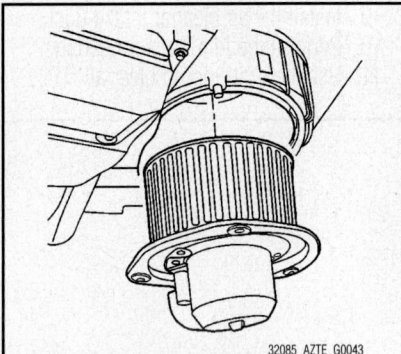

Fig. 137 Remove the blower motor from the HVAC module assembly

1. Remove the right side instrument panel insulator.
2. Disconnect the electrical connector from the blower motor.
3. Remove the blower motor mounting screws.
4. Remove the blower motor from the HVAC module assembly.

To install:

5. Install the blower motor to the HVAC module assembly.

➡️**Use the correct fastener in the correct location. Replacement fasteners must be the correct part number for that application. Fasteners requiring replacement or fasteners requiring the use of thread locking compound or sealant are identified in the service procedure. Do not use paints, lubricants, or corrosion inhibitors on fasteners or fastener joint surfaces unless**

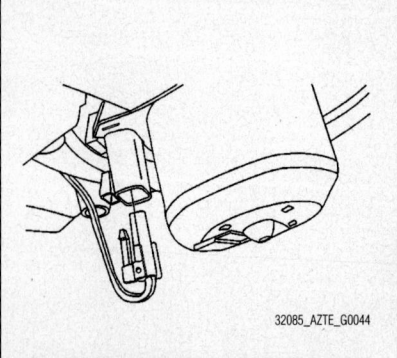

Fig. 138 Connect the electrical connector to the blower motor

specified. These coatings affect fastener torque and joint clamping force and may damage the fastener. Use the correct tightening sequence and specifications when installing fasteners in order to avoid damage to parts and systems.**

6. Install the blower motor mounting screws and tighten the screws to 16 inch lbs. (1.8 Nm).
7. Connect the electrical connector to the blower motor.
8. Install the right side instrument panel insulator.

CONTROL PANEL

REMOVAL & INSTALLATION

See Figure 139.

1. Remove the I/P cluster trim plate bezel.
2. Remove the HVAC control module retaining screws.
3. Pull the HVAC control module straight out from the I/P.
4. Disconnect the HVAC control module electrical connector.

To install:

➡️**The key should be in the off position when connecting the HVAC control module electrical connector to ensure proper calibration.**

5. Connect the HVAC control module electrical connector.
6. Install the HVAC control module into the I/P opening.

➡️**Use the correct fastener in the correct location. Replacement fasteners must be the correct part number for that application. Fasteners requiring replacement or fasteners requiring the use of thread locking compound or sealant are identified in the service procedure. Do not use paints, lubricants, or corrosion inhibitors on fasteners or fastener joint surfaces unless specified. These coatings affect fastener torque and joint clamping force and may damage the fastener. Use the correct tightening sequence and specifications when installing fasteners in order to avoid damage to parts and systems. Install the HVAC control module retaining screws and tighten the screws to 22 inch lbs. (2.5 Nm).**

7. Install the IP cluster trim plate bezel.

➡️**Do not adjust any controls on the HVAC control module while the HVAC control module is self-calibrating. If interrupted, improper HVAC performance will result.**

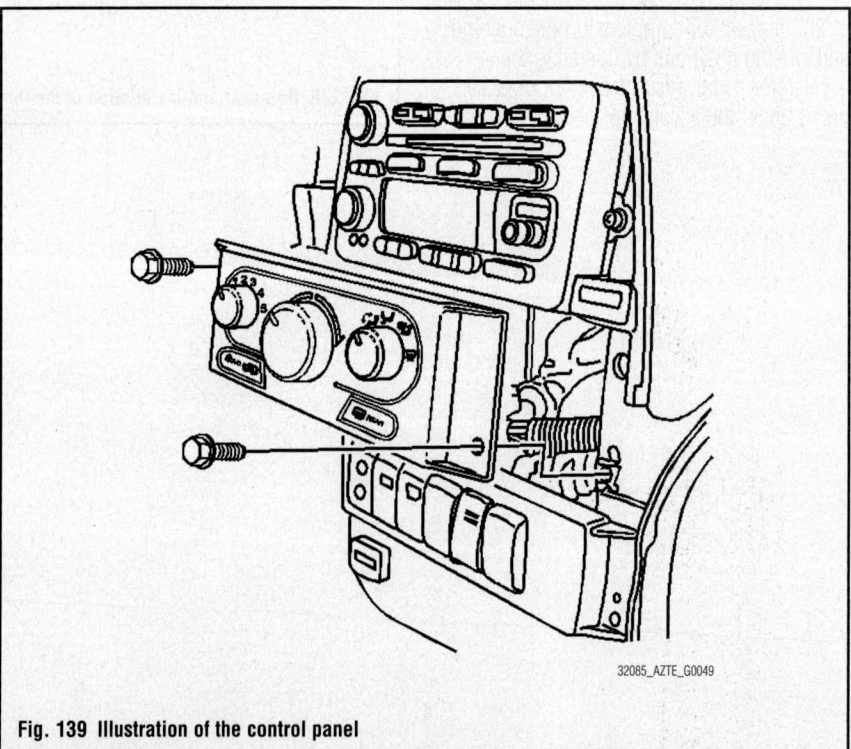

Fig. 139 Illustration of the control panel

8. The engine must be running for proper calibration to occur.

9. Start and allow the engine to run for a least one minute.

HEATER CORE

REMOVAL & INSTALLATION

1. Before servicing the vehicle, refer to the Precautions Section.
2. Drain the cooling system.
3. Remove or disconnect the following:
   - Wiper module
   - Brake booster vacuum hose
   - Air cleaner cover and intake tube
   - Throttle and cruise control cables, from the TBI bracket
   - Transmission filler tube
   - Hoses from the heater core
   - Right and left instrument panel insulators
   - Center floor air outlet
   - Heater outlet duct
   - Tie strap holding the instrument panel harness to the heater core cover
   - Heater core cover
   - Heater core retaining screw
   - Heater core

To install:

4. Install or connect the following:
   - Heater core
   - Heater core retaining screw
   - Heater core cover
   - Heater outlet duct
   - Tie strap holding the instrument panel harness to the heater core cover
   - Center floor air outlet
   - Right and left instrument panel insulators
   - Hoses to the heater core
   - Transmission filler tube
   - Throttle and cruise control cables
   - Air cleaner cover and intake tube
   - Brake booster vacuum hose
   - Wiper module

STEERING

POWER STEERING GEAR

REMOVAL & INSTALLATION

See Figures 140 and 141.

1. Before servicing the vehicle, refer to the Precautions Section.
2. Remove or disconnect the following:
   - Negative battery cable
   - Left front wheel
   - Stabilizer shaft
   - Tie rod ends from the steering knuckle
   - Intermediate shaft from the steering gear
3. Support the frame using a suitable utility stand.
   - Frame rear bolts and discard them
   - Power steering gear heat shield
   - Cooler pipe from the power steering gear
   - Pressure hose from the power steering gear
   - Power steering gear through the left wheel opening

To install:

4. Install or connect the following:
   - Power steering gear through the left wheel opening

✳✳ WARNING

This is a prevailing torque type fastener. This fastener may be reused ONLY if: The fastener and its counterpart are clean and free from rust. The fastener develops 18 inch lbs. (2 Nm) of torque (drag) against its counterpart prior to the fastener seating. If the fastener does not meet these criteria, REPLACE the fastener.

   - New power steering gear bolts/nuts. Torque them to 59 ft. lbs. (80 Nm).
   - Pressure hose and cooler pipe to the power steering gear. Torque the fasteners to 20 ft. lbs. (27 Nm).
   - Heat shield. Torque the bolts to 54 inch lbs. (6 Nm).
   - Utility stand to support the frame
   - New rear frame bolts. Torque them to 122 ft. lbs. (165 Nm).
5. Remove the utility stand.
6. Install or connect the following:
   - Intermediate shaft to the steering

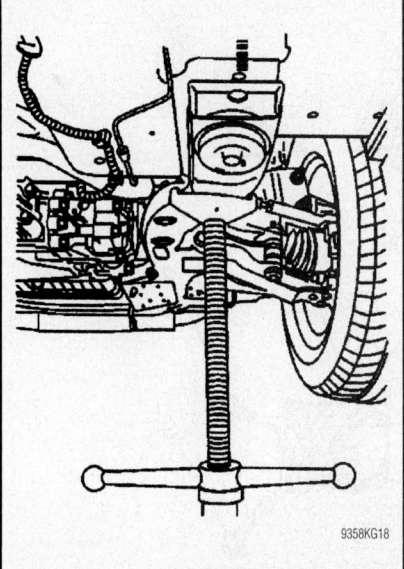

Fig. 140 Use a utility stand to support the frame

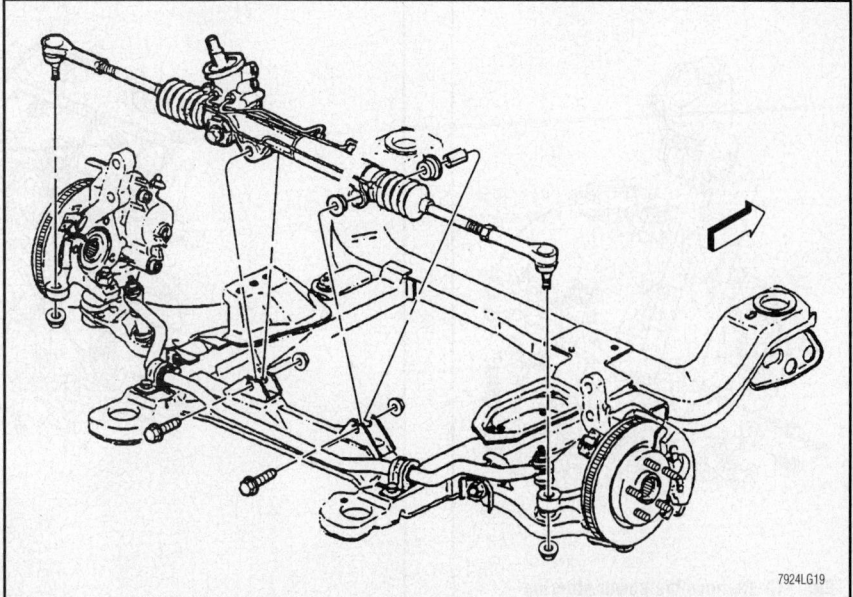

Fig. 141 The rack and pinion steering gear is bolted to the rear of the subframe

gear. Torque the bolt to 35 ft. lbs. (47 Nm).
- Tie rod ends to the steering knuckle
- Stabilizer shaft. Torque the bolt to 17 ft. lbs. (23 Nm).
- Left front wheel

7. Fill and bleed the power steering system and check for leaks.

8. Road test the vehicle and adjust the toe as necessary.

POWER STEERING PUMP

REMOVAL & INSTALLATION

3.4L and 3.5L Engine

See Figure 142.

1. Remove the wiring harness from the wiring harness retainer located on the power steering pump reservoir.

2. Remove the accessory drive belt from the power steering pump pulley.

3. Remove the power steering pressure hose from the power steering pump.

4. Remove the power steering return hose from the power steering pump.

5. Remove the power steering pump mounting bolts from the power steering pump.

6. Remove the power steering pump from the vehicle.

7. Cap off the power steering pump and hoses in order to prevent contamination.

8. Remove the power steering pump pulley from the pump.

9. Remove the power steering pump reservoir from the power steering pump.

To install:

10. Install the power steering pump reservoir to the power steering pump.

11. Install the power steering pump pulley to the power steering pump.

12. Uncap the power steering pump and hoses.

13. Position the power steering pump to the vehicle.

14. Install the power steering pump mounting bolts and tighten the power steering pump mounting bolts to 25 ft. lbs. (34 Nm).

15. Install the wiring harness to the wiring harness retainer located on the power steering pump reservoir.

16. Install the power steering return hose to the power steering pump.

17. Install the power steering pressure hose to the power steering pump.

18. Install the accessory drive belt.

19. Bleed the power steering system.

20. Inspect the system for leaks.

3.6L Engine

See Figure 143.

1. Turn the steering wheel in order to move the front of the right wheel to the outboard most position in order to allow clearance to remove the power steering pump.

2. Raise and support the vehicle.

3. Remove the front right wheel.

4. Remove the accessory drive belt from the power steering pump pulley.

5. Remove the right engine splash shield.

6. Remove the right front drive shaft.

7. Disconnect the power steering pump inlet hose from the power steering pump.

8. Disconnect the power steering pressure pipe/hose from the power steering pump.

9. Remove the power steering pump mounting bolts.

10. Remove the power steering pump from the vehicle.

11. Cap off the power steering pump and hoses in order to prevent contamination.

12. Remove the power steering pulley from the power steering pump.

To install:

13. Install the power steering pulley to the power steering pump.

14. Uncap off the power steering pump and hoses .

15. Position the power steering pump to the vehicle.

16. Install the power steering pump mounting bolts. HAND TIGHTEN ONLY.

17. Install the side power steering mounting bolt and tighten the side power steering mounting bolt to 37 ft. lbs. (50 Nm).

18. Install the rear power steering mounting bolt and tighten the rear power steering mount bolt to 37 ft. lbs. (50 Nm).

19. Connect the power steering pressure pipe/hose to the power steering pump and tighten the power steering pressure pipe/hose fitting to 20 ft. lbs. (27 Nm).

20. Connect the power steering reservoir inlet hose to the power steering pump.

21. Install the right front drive shaft.

22. Install the right engine splash shield.

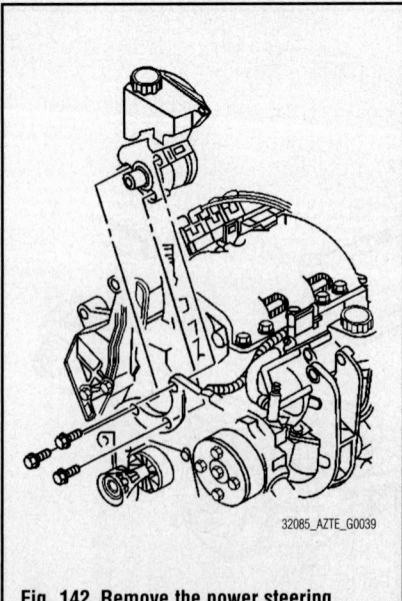

32085_AZTE_G0039

Fig. 142 Remove the power steering pump from the vehicle

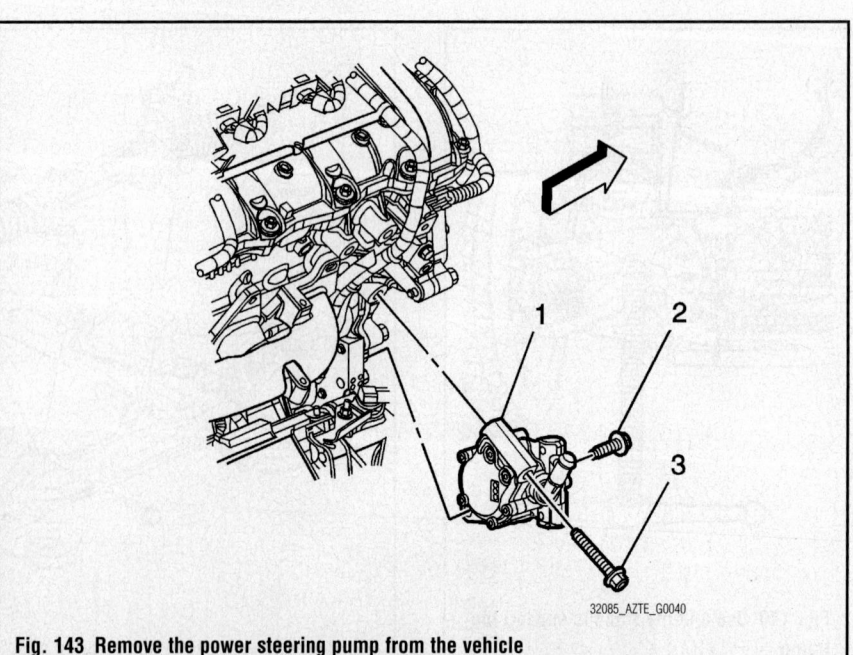

32085_AZTE_G0040

Fig. 143 Remove the power steering pump from the vehicle

23. Install the accessory drive belt to the power steering pump pulley.
24. Install the front right wheel.
25. Lower the vehicle.
26. Bleed the power steering system.
27. Inspect the system for leaks.

BLEEDING

➡ **Use clean, new power steering fluid type only**

➡ **Hoses touching the frame, body or engine may cause system noise. Verify that the hoses do not touch any other part of the vehicle.**

➡ **Loose connections may not leak, but could allow air into the steering system. Verify that all hose connections are tight.**

➡ **Power steering fluid level must be maintained throughout bleed procedure.**

1. Fill pump reservoir with fluid to minimum system level, FULL COLD level, or middle of hash mark on cap stick fluid level indicator.

➡ **With hydro-boost only, the oil level will appear falsely high if the hydro-boost accumulator is not fully charged. Do not apply the brake pedal with the engine OFF. This will discharge the hydro-boost accumulator.**

2. If equipped with hydro-boost, fully charge the hydro-boost accumulator using the following procedure:
   • Start the engine.
   • Firmly apply the brake pedal 10–15 times.
   • Turn the engine OFF.
3. Raise the vehicle until the front wheels are off the ground.
4. Key on engine OFF, turn the steering wheel from stop to stop 12 times.
5. Vehicles equipped with hydro-boost systems or longer length power steering hoses may require turns up to 15 to 20 stop to stops.
6. Verify power steering fluid level per operating specification..
7. Start the engine. Rotate steering wheel from left to right. Check for sign of cavitation or fluid aeration (pump noise/whining).
8. Verify the fluid level. Repeat the bleed procedure, if necessary.

SUSPENSION

FRONT SUSPENSION

COIL SPRING

REMOVAL & INSTALLATION

The service procedure for the front coil springs is covered under MacPherson Strut removal and installation.

LOWER BALL JOINT

REMOVAL & INSTALLATION

1. Raise and support the vehicle.
2. Remove the tires and wheels.
3. Remove the lower control arm.
4. Secure the lower control arm in a vice.
5. Drill out the rivet heads from the lower control arm.
6. Use a hammer and a drift punch in order to remove the rivets from the lower control arm.
7. Remove the ball joint from the lower control arm.

To install:
8. Install the ball joint to the lower control arm.
9. Install the new ball joint bolts facing downward, away from the ball stud.
10. Install the new ball joint retaining nuts and tighten the ball joint retaining nuts to 50 ft. lbs. (68 Nm).
11. Install the lower control arm.
12. Install the tire and wheels.
13. Lower the vehicle.
14. Align the front suspension.

LOWER CONTROL ARM

REMOVAL & INSTALLATION

⚠ WARNING

Use only the recommended tools for separating the ball joint from the knuckle. Do NOT hammer or pry the ball joint from the knuckle. Failure to use the recommended tools may cause damage to the ball joint and seal.

➡ **Use the ignition key in order to unlock the steering column.**

1. Turn the steering wheel in order to move the front of the applicable wheel to the outboard most position in order to allow for tool access to the lower control arm ball stud nut.

➡ **Use only a frame-contact type vehicle lift or a floor jack at the recommended lift points. Do NOT use a suspension-contact type vehicle lift. Do NOT lift the front of the vehicle by the lower control arms.**

2. Raise and support the vehicle.
3. Remove the tire and wheel.
4. Disconnect the wheel speed sensor wiring harness from the lower control arm.
5. Remove the stabilizer shaft link.
6. Remove the cotter pin from the ball stud.
7. Loosen the ball stud nut. Do not remove the ball stud nut.
8. Install tool J 41820 over the ball stud nut and the steering knuckle.
9. Rotate the ball stud nut counterclockwise in order to separate the ball stud from the steering knuckle.
10. Remove the lower control arm bolts and nuts.
11. Remove the lower control arm.

To install:
12. Install the lower control arm.
13. Install the control arm bolts and nuts. Hand tighten only.

➡ **Align the ball stud cotter pin hole parallel to the knuckle in order to ease the cotter pin installation.**

14. Install the ball stud to the knuckle.
15. Install the ball stud castle nut.
16. Tighten the ball stud castle nut to 22 ft. lbs. (30 Nm) plus 135 degrees.

➡ **Do not loosen the ball stud nut in order to align the ball stud nut slots to the ball stud cotter pin hole. If necessary, tighten the ball stud castle nut in order to align the ball stud castle nut slot to the ball stud cotter pin hole.**

➡ **Ensure that the cotter pin ends do not contact the ABS sensor connector or the drive axle.**

17. Install a new cotter pin and bend the ends as shown in either example.
18. Install the stabilizer shaft link.
19. Install the wheel speed sensor harness to the lower control arm.

➡ **This is a prevailing torque type fastener. This fastener may be reused only if: The fastener and its counterpart are clean and free from rust. The fastener develops 27 inch lbs. (3 Nm) of torque (drag) against its counterpart prior to the fastener seating. If the fastener does not meet these criteria, replace the fastener.**

20. Install the lower control arm nuts.
21. Tighten the lower control arm nuts to 72 ft. lbs. (98 Nm).
22. Install the tire and wheel.
23. Lower the vehicle.

CONTROL ARM BUSHING REPLACEMENT

See Figure 144.

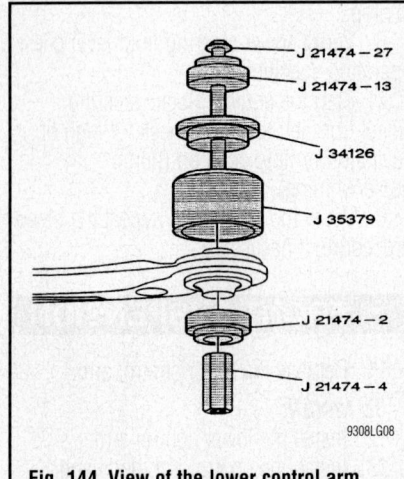

Fig. 144 View of the lower control arm bushing

1. Before servicing the vehicle, refer to the Precautions Section.
2. Remove the lower control arm and secure it in a vise and mark the control arm along the flat edge of the bushing flange.
3. Assemble the bushing removal tool.
4. Tighten the assembly until the bushing is removed.

To install:

5. Install the bushing into the control arm by align the flat edge of the bushing to the mark in the control arm.
6. Make certain that the flat edge of the bushing is 30 degrees from the centerline of the control arm and the thin slot in the bushing is facing outboard.
7. Fully seat the bushing in the control arm.
8. Install the lower control arm.
9. Road test the vehicle and adjust the alignment, if necessary.

MACPHERSON STRUT

REMOVAL & INSTALLATION

See Figure 145.

✳✳ CAUTION

Do not remove the top center nut from the strut assembly. This nut should only be removed when the strut assembly is out of the vehicle,

mounted in a holding fixture and the coil spring is in a compressed position using the proper coil spring compressor.

1. Before servicing the vehicle, refer to the Precautions Section.
2. Remove or disconnect the following:
   • Wiper module
   • Three upper strut nuts

➥**Use a frame contact lift to raise the vehicle. DO NOT use a suspension contact lift.**

   • Tire and wheel
   • Lower strut bolts and nuts after marking the position of the strut to the knuckle

➥**The strut to steering knuckle position must be marked so that the camber angle will not change. If the angle is change, the wheel alignment will also be affected.**

   • Strut
   • Nut from the top of the strut by placing the assembly in a Strut Compressor tool J 34013-B and Damper Rod Clamp J 34013-20. Turn the compressor forcing screw until the spring compresses slightly
   • Strut mount
   • Spring from the strut assembly

To install:

3. Install or connect the following:
   • Spring over the strut in the proper position
   • Strut mount
   • Compressor screw and start turning the screw clockwise until the strut

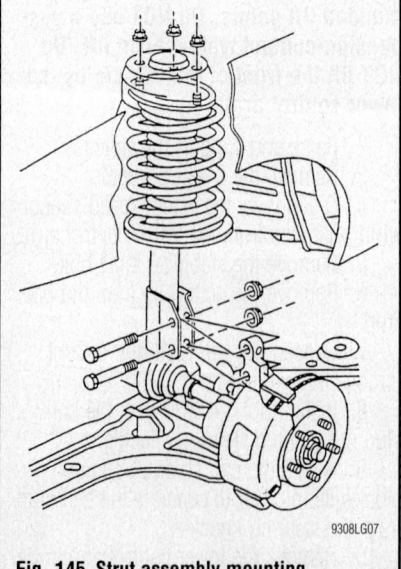

Fig. 145 Strut assembly mounting

shaft threads are visible through the top of the strut. Torque the nut to 63 ft. lbs. (85 Nm).
   • Strut and the upper nuts. Torque the nuts to 22 ft. lbs. (30 Nm).
   • Wiper module
   • Lower strut bolts and nuts by aligning the strut to the steering knuckle. Torque the nuts to 90 ft. lbs. (123 Nm).
   • Front wheel

4. Road test the vehicle and check the front end alignment and adjust as needed.

OVERHAUL

See Figure 146.

1. Remove the strut from the vehicle.
2. Install the strut in the special tool J 45400.

➥**The spring is compressed when the strut moves freely.**

3. Turn the spring compressor forcing screw until the coil spring is compressed.
4. Use a 45 Torx® socket in order to hold the strut shaft. Use the special tool J 42991 to remove the upper strut mount nut
5. Remove the strut from the special tool J 45400 .
6. Loosen the compressor forcing screw until the upper strut mount and coil spring may be removed.
7. Remove the upper strut mount and the coil spring from the special tool J 45400.

To Assemble:

8. Install the coil spring and upper strut mount to the special tool J 45400.
9. Turn the spring compressor forcing screw (1) until the coil spring is compressed.
10. Install the strut to the coil spring and upper strut mount.

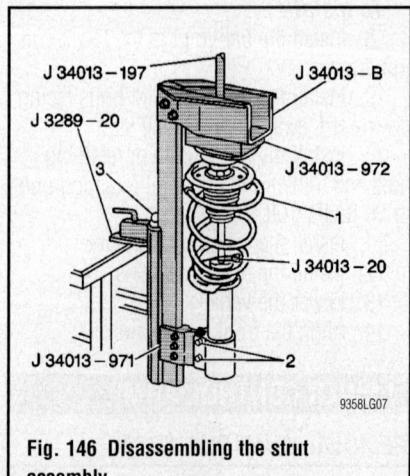

Fig. 146 Disassembling the strut assembly

11. Loosely install the strut retaining nut. Use a 45 Torx® socket in order to hold the strut shaft. Use the special tool J 42991 to install the upper strut mount nut and tighten the strut mount nut to 63 ft. lbs. (85 Nm).

12. Remove the strut from the special tool J 45400.

13. Install the strut to the vehicle.

STABILIZER BAR

REMOVAL & INSTALLATION

See Figure 147.

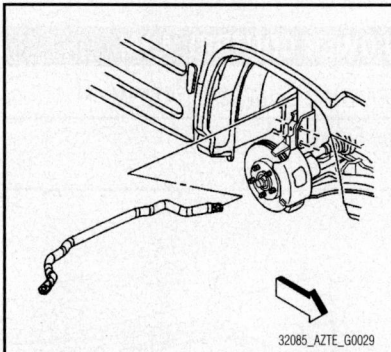

Fig. 147 Remove the stabilizer shaft from the right side of the vehicle

1. Raise and support the vehicle.
2. Remove the tires and wheels.
3. Remove the stabilizer shaft links.
4. Remove the left and right stabilizer shaft insulators and brackets.
5. Remove the stabilizer shaft from the right side of the vehicle.

To install:
6. Install the stabilizer shaft to the vehicle from the right side of the vehicle.
7. Install the stabilizer shaft insulators and brackets.
8. Install the left and right stabilizer shaft links.
9. Install the tires and wheels.
10. Lower the vehicle.

STEERING KNUCKLE

REMOVAL & INSTALLATION

See Figure 148.

1. Raise and suitably support the vehicle.
2. Remove the tire and wheel assembly.
3. Remove the front wheel drive shaft bearing.
4. Remove the front lower control arm ball stud.

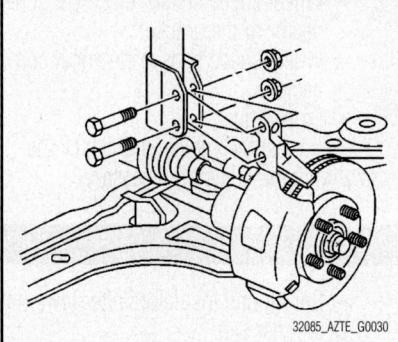

Fig. 148 Location of the bolts that connect the strut to the knuckle

5. Remove the outer tie rod end from the steering knuckle.
6. Remove the bolt retaining the ABS harness bracket to the steering knuckle.
7. Scribe the strut to the knuckle.
8. Remove the bolts connecting the strut to the knuckle.
9. Remove the knuckle from the vehicle.

To install:
10. Install the knuckle to the vehicle.
11. Install the bolts which connect the strut to the knuckle. Hand tighten only.
12. Connect the front lower control arm ball stud to knuckle.
13. Attach the ABS bracket to the steering knuckle and torque the bracket bolt to 7 ft. lbs. (10 Nm).
14. Install the outer tie rod to the steering knuckle.
15. Install the front wheel drive shaft bearing.
16. Install the tire and wheel assembly.
17. Lower the vehicle.
18. Measure and adjust the front alignment.

WHEEL BEARINGS

REMOVAL & INSTALLATION

See Figures 149 through 151.

1. Before servicing the vehicle, refer to the Precautions Section.
2. Remove or disconnect the following:
   - Front wheel
   - Wheel speed sensor electrical connector and the connector from the bracket
   - Brake caliper and bracket
   - Brake rotor
   - Halfshaft nut
3. Attach a front hub spindle removal tool to the wheel bearing/hub.
4. Push the halfshaft out of the wheel bearing hub assembly.

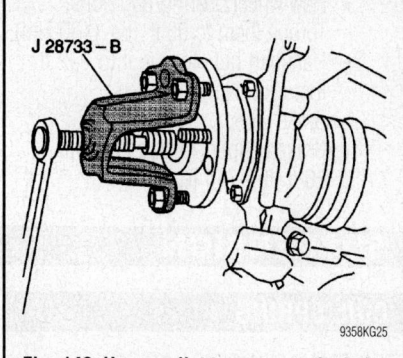

Fig. 149 Use a pullet to separate the hub from the halfshaft

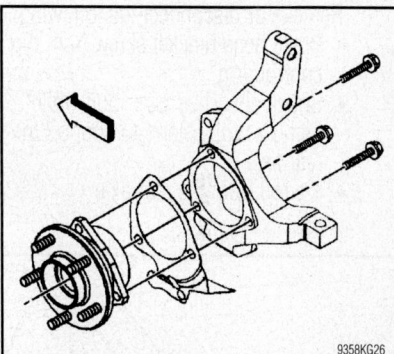

Fig. 150 Front hub and bearing assembly mounting

5. Remove or disconnect the following:
   - Wheel bearing/hub bolts and discard them
   - Wheel bearing/hub assembly

To install:
6. Install or connect the following:
   - Wheel bearing/hub assembly

❄❄ CAUTION

The wheel bearing/hub bolts must be replaced whenever they are loosened or removed.

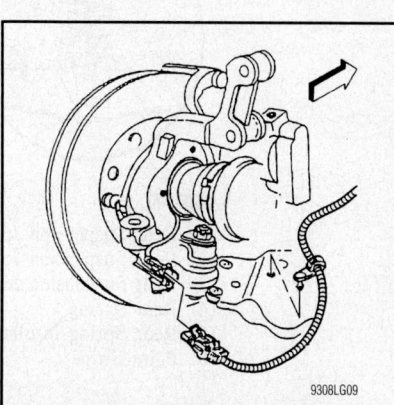

Fig. 151 View of the front steering assembly

- New wheel bearing/hub bolts. Torque them to 96 ft. lbs. (130 Nm).
- Halfshaft nut. Torque it to 192 ft. lbs. (260 Nm).
- Brake rotor
- Brake caliper. Torque the bolts to 26 ft. lbs. (35 Nm).

- Wheel speed sensor electrical connector to the bracket
- Wheel speed sensor electrical connector
- Front wheel

7. Road test the vehicle and check the front alignment, adjust if necessary.

ADJUSTMENT

Both front and rear wheel bearings are integral to the hub assembly and are not adjustable. If the bearings are found to be defective, the hub assembly must be replaced.

SUSPENSION

COIL SPRING

REMOVAL & INSTALLATION

1. Before servicing the vehicle, refer to the Precautions Section.
2. Remove or disconnect the following:
   - Brake hose bracket screw from the control arm
   - Shock absorber lower bolt while using a utility stand to support the rear axle
   - Tie rod from the rear axle

- Spring and insulators after lowering the rear axle

To install:

3. Install or connect the following:
   - Insulators and springs on the rear axle with the paint stripe is facing rearward
   - Rear axle tie rod after raising the rear axle into its proper position. Torque the nut to 92 ft. lbs. (125 Nm).
   - Shock absorbers to the rear axle.

REAR SUSPENSION

Torque the upper and lower nuts to 66 ft. lbs. (90 Nm).
   - Brake hose bracket to the control arm. Torque the bolt to 33 ft. lbs. (44 Nm).
4. Remove the axle supports.

LOWER CONTROL ARM

REMOVAL & INSTALLATION

See Figure 153.

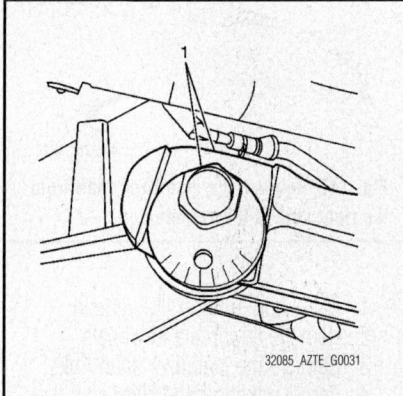

32085_AZTE_G0031

Fig. 153 Make a mark on the lower control arm at the cam indicator

1. Remove the coil spring.
2. Make a mark on the lower control arm at the cam indicator
3. Remove the lower control arm to crossmember mounting bolts
4. Remove the lower control arm.

To install:

5. Install the lower control arm to the crossmember.
6. Install the bolts and the nuts to the lower control arm and tighten the nuts to 37 ft. lbs. (50 Nm).
7. Install the cam bolt and the cam washer to the lower control arm.

➡**Align the cam indicator to the mark on the lower control arm.**

8. Install the cam nut to the lower control arm and tighten the cam nut to 107 ft. lbs. (145 Nm).
9. Install the coil spring.

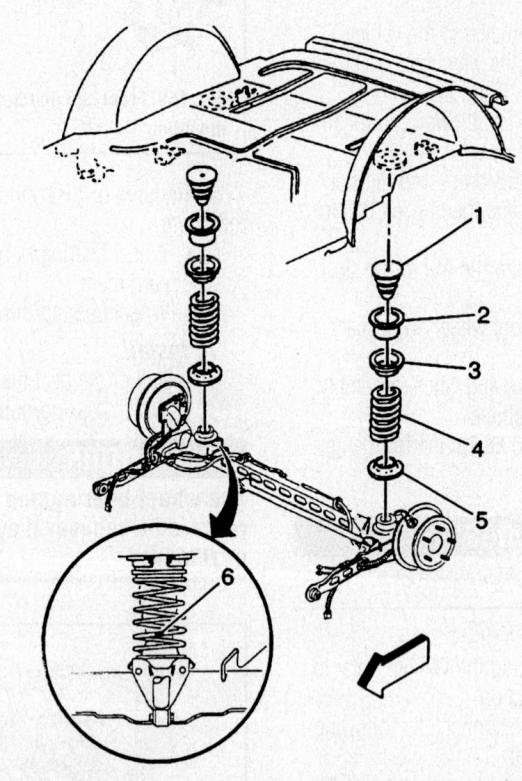

Legend

(1) Rear Suspension Jounce Bumper
(2) Rear Suspension Jounce Bumper Retainer
(3) Rear Suspension Insulator
(4) Rear Spring
(5) Rear Spring Insulator
(6) Paint Stripe

7924LG21

Fig. 152 Exploded view of the coil spring assembly

SHOCK ABSORBER

REMOVAL & INSTALLATION

See Figure 154.

1. Before servicing the vehicle, refer to the Precautions Section.
2. Raise and support the vehicle.
3. Support the rear axle using a utility stand to slightly compress the coil spring and relieve the shock absorber tension.
4. If the vehicle is equipped with automatic level control, disconnect the air tube connector from the shock absorber.
5. Remove or disconnect the following:
   - Shock absorber upper bolt and nut
   - Shock absorber lower bolt and/or nut, as applicable
   - Shock absorber from the brackets by compressing it slightly

To install:

6. Inspect the shock absorber, upper and lower mounting brackets and the frame mounting hole for cracks excessive wear and burrs.

7. Install or connect the following:
   - Shock absorber
   - Shock absorber bolts and nuts. Torque the nuts to 66 ft. lbs. (90 Nm).
   - Air tube connector to the shock absorber, if equipped with automatic level control
8. Remove the support from the rear axle.
9. Road test the vehicle.

UPPER CONTROL ARM

REMOVAL & INSTALLATION

1. Raise and support the vehicle.
2. Remove the rear wheel.
3. Remove the rear stabilizer link.
4. Remove the brake hose bracket-to-knuckle bolts.
5. Remove the brake hose bracket in order to disconnect the brake hose from the parking brake lever.
6. Use a utility stand in order to support the lower control arm.

7. Disconnect the height sensor link from the lower control arm as necessary.
8. Remove the upper control arm to knuckle nut and bolt.
9. Remove the upper control arm to crossmember bolts and nuts.
10. Remove the upper control arm.

To install:

11. Install the upper control arm.
12. Install the bolts and the nuts which secure the upper control arm to the crossmember and tighten the nuts to 55 ft. lbs. (75 Nm).
13. Install the upper control arm to the knuckle, and tighten the nut which secures the upper control arm to 74 ft. lbs. (100 Nm).
14. Connect the height sensor link to the lower control arm as necessary.
15. Remove the utility stand.
16. Install the brake hose bracket.
17. Install the brake hose bracket belts.
18. Install the rear stabilizer link and tighten the stabilizer link ball nut to 29 ft. lbs. (40 Nm).
19. Install the rear wheel.
20. Lower the vehicle.

WHEEL BEARINGS

REMOVAL & INSTALLATION

FWD Models

See Figure 155.

1. Before servicing the vehicle, refer to the Precautions Section.
2. Remove or disconnect the following:
   - Rear wheel
   - Brake drum
   - Wheel speed sensor
   - Bearing/hub assembly

To install:

3. Install or connect the following:
   - Bearing/hub to the axle beam. Torque the bolts to 63 ft. lbs.

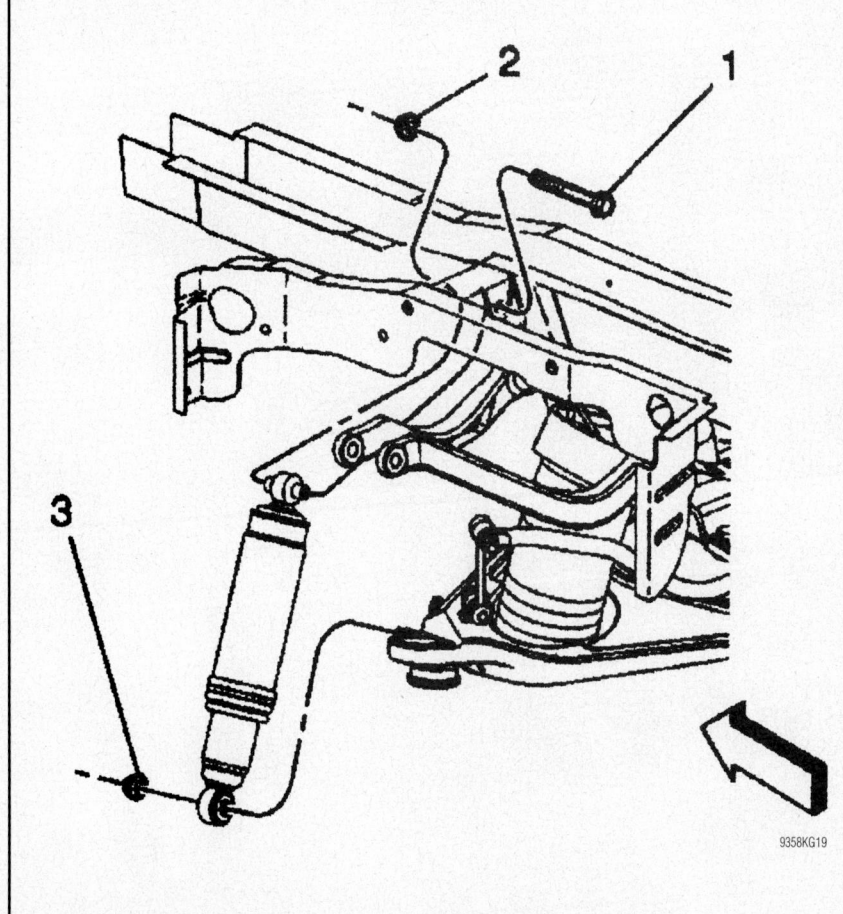

Fig. 154 Rear shock absorber mounting—AWD vehicle shown

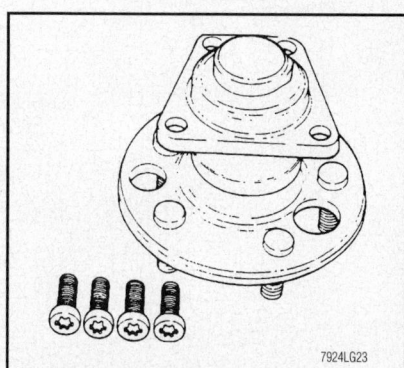

Fig. 155 The rear wheel hub is mounted with 4 Torx® head bolts

(85 Nm) for drum brakes; 96 ft. lbs. (130 Nm) with disc brakes.

- Wheel speed sensor electrical connector to the bearing/hub assembly
- Brake drum
- Rear wheel

AWD Models

1. Before servicing the vehicle, refer to the Precautions Section.
2. Remove or disconnect the following:

- Rear wheel
- Brake caliper and support it with a piece of wire
- Brake caliper bracket
- Rotor
- Wheel speed sensor connector from the sensor and bracket
- Halfshaft from the hub and bearing
- Bearing/hub bolts and bearing/hub

To install:

3. Install or connect the following:

- Bearing/hub. Tighten the bolts to 63 ft. lbs. (85 Nm) for drum brakes; 96 ft. lbs. (130 Nm) with disc brakes.
- Halfshaft
- Wheel speed sensor connector to the bracket and sensor
- Rotor
- Caliper bracket
- Caliper
- Tire and wheel

CHEVROLET AND GMC

Sierra • Sierra Classic • Silverado • Silverado Classic

SPECIFICATIONS AND MAINTENANCE CHARTS

ENGINE AND VEHICLE IDENTIFICATION

Engine								Model Year	
Code ①	Liters	Cu. In.	Cyl.	Fuel Sys.	Engine Type	Eng. Mfg.		Code ②	Year
X	4.3	262	6	MFI	OHV	CPC		5	2005
V	4.8	293	8	MFI	OHV	CPC		6	2006
C	4.8	293	8	MFI	OHV	CPC		7	2007
B	5.3	325	8	MFI	OHV	CPC			
T	5.3	325	8	MFI	OHV	CPC			
Z	5.3	325	8	MFI	OHV	CPC			
M	5.3	325	8	MFI	OHV	CPC			
0	5.3	325	8	MFI	OHV	CPC			
J	5.3	325	8	MFI	OHV	CPC			
3	5.3	325	8	MFI	OHV	CPC			
N	6.0	364	8	MFI	OHV	CPC			
U	6.0	364	8	MFI	OHV	CPC			
Y	6.0	364	8	MFI	OHV	CPC			
K	6.0	364	8	MFI	OHV	CPC			
8	6.2	376	8	MFI	OHV	CPC			
2	6.6	402	8	DSL	OHV	CPC			
D	6.6	402	8	DSL	OHV	CPC			
6	6.6	402	8	DSL	OHV	CPC			
G	8.1	496	8	MFI	OHV	CPC			

CPC: Chevrolet/Pontiac/Canada

DSL: Diesel

MFI: Multi-port Fuel Injection

① 8th position of VIN

② 10th position of VIN

22116_SIER_C0001

GENERAL ENGINE SPECIFICATIONS

All measurements are given in inches.

Year	Model	Engine Displacement Liters	Engine Series (ID/VIN)	Net Horsepower @ rpm	Net Torque @ rpm (ft. lbs.)	Bore x Stroke (in.)	Compression Ratio	Oil Pressure @ rpm
2005	Sierra	4.3	X	200@4600	260@2800	4.00x3.48	9.2:1	18@2000
		4.8	V	270@5200	285@4000	3.78x3.27	9.5:1	18@2000
		5.3	B	285@4000	360@4000	3.78x3.62	9.5:1	18@2000
		5.3	T	285@4000	360@4000	3.78x3.62	9.5:1	18@2000
		5.3	Z	285@4000	360@4000	3.78x3.62	9.5:1	18@2000
		6.0	N	300@4400	360@4000	4.00x3.62	9.4:1	18@2000
		6.0	U	300@4400	360@4000	4.00x3.62	9.4:1	18@2000
		6.6	2	300@3000	520@1800	4.00x3.90	17.5:1	57@3250
		8.1	G	340@4200	455@3200	4.25x4.37	9.1:1	10@2000
	Silverado	4.3	X	200@4600	260@2800	4.00x3.48	9.2:1	18@2000
		4.8	V	270@5200	285@4000	3.78x3.27	9.5:1	18@2000
		5.3	B	285@4000	360@4000	3.78x3.62	9.5:1	18@2000
		5.3	T	285@4000	360@4000	3.78x3.62	9.5:1	18@2000
		5.3	Z	285@4000	360@4000	3.78x3.62	9.5:1	18@2000
		6.0	N	300@4400	360@4000	4.00x3.62	9.4:1	18@2000
		6.0	U	300@4400	360@4000	4.00x3.62	9.4:1	18@2000
		6.6	2	300@3000	520@1800	4.00x3.90	17.5:1	57@3250
		8.1	G	340@4200	455@3200	4.25x4.37	9.1:1	10@2000
2006	Sierra	4.3	X	200@4600	260@2800	4.00x3.48	9.2:1	18@2000
		4.8	V	270@5200	285@4000	3.78x3.27	9.5:1	18@2000
		5.3	B	285@4000	360@4000	3.78x3.62	9.5:1	18@2000
		5.3	T	285@4000	360@4000	3.78x3.62	9.5:1	18@2000
		5.3	Z	285@4000	360@4000	3.78x3.62	9.5:1	18@2000
		6.0	N	300@4400	360@4000	4.00x3.62	9.4:1	18@2000
		6.0	U	300@4400	360@4000	4.00x3.62	9.4:1	18@2000
		6.6	2	300@3000	520@1800	4.00x3.90	17.5:1	57@3250
		6.6	D	300@3000	520@1800	4.00x3.90	17.5:1	57@3250
		8.1	G	340@4200	455@3200	4.25x4.37	9.1:1	10@2000
	Silverado	4.3	X	200@4600	260@2800	4.00x3.48	9.2:1	18@2000
		4.8	V	270@5200	285@4000	3.78x3.27	9.5:1	18@2000
		5.3	B	285@4000	360@4000	3.78x3.62	9.5:1	18@2000
		5.3	T	285@4000	360@4000	3.78x3.62	9.5:1	18@2000
		5.3	Z	285@4000	360@4000	3.78x3.62	9.5:1	18@2000
		6.0	N	300@4400	360@4000	4.00x3.62	9.4:1	18@2000
		6.0	U	300@4400	360@4000	4.00x3.62	9.4:1	18@2000
		6.6	2	300@3000	520@1800	4.00x3.90	17.5:1	57@3250
		6.6	D	300@3000	520@1800	4.00x3.90	17.5:1	57@3250
		8.1	G	340@4200	455@3200	4.25x4.37	9.1:1	10@2000
2007	Sierra Classic	4.3	X	200@4600	260@2800	4.00x3.48	9.2:1	18@2000
		4.8	V	270@5200	285@4000	3.78x3.27	9.5:1	18@2000
		5.3	B	285@4000	360@4000	3.78x3.62	9.5:1	18@2000
		5.3	T	285@4000	360@4000	3.78x3.62	9.5:1	18@2000
		5.3	Z	285@4000	360@4000	3.78x3.62	9.5:1	18@2000
		6.0	N	300@4400	360@4000	4.00x3.62	9.4:1	18@2000
		6.0	U	300@4400	360@4000	4.00x3.62	9.4:1	18@2000
		6.6	D	300@3000	520@1800	4.00x3.90	17.5:1	57@3250
		8.1	G	340@4200	455@3200	4.25x4.37	9.1:1	10@2000

22116_SIER_C0002

GENERAL ENGINE SPECIFICATIONS

All measurements are given in inches.

Year	Model	Engine Displacement Liters	Engine Series (ID/VIN)	Net Horsepower @ rpm	Net Torque @ rpm (ft. lbs.)	Bore x Stroke (in.)	Com- pression Ratio	Oil Pressure @ rpm
2007 cont.	Sierra	4.3	X	195@4600	260@2800	4.00x3.48	9.2:1	18@2000
		4.8	C	295@5600	305@4800	3.78x3.27	9.08:1	18@2000
		5.3	M	315@5200	338@4400	3.78x3.62	9.95:1	18@2000
		5.3	0	315@5200	338@4400	3.78x3.62	9.95:1	18@2000
		5.3	J	315@5200	338@4400	3.78x3.62	9.95:1	18@2000
		5.3	3	315@5200	338@4400	3.78x3.62	9.95:1	18@2000
		6.0	Y	367@5500	375@4300	4.00x3.62	9.67:1	18@2000
		6.0	K	353@5400	373@4400	4.00x3.62	9.67:1	18@2000
		6.2	8	403@5700	417@4300	4.06x3.62	10.5:1	18@2000
		6.6	6	365@3000	660@1600	4.00x3.90	16.8:1	42@1800
	Silverado Classic	4.3	X	200@4600	260@2800	4.00x3.48	9.2:1	18@2000
		4.8	V	270@5200	285@4000	3.78x3.27	9.5:1	18@2000
		5.3	B	285@4000	360@4000	3.78x3.62	9.5:1	18@2000
		5.3	T	285@4000	360@4000	3.78x3.62	9.5:1	18@2000
		5.3	Z	285@4000	360@4000	3.78x3.62	9.5:1	18@2000
		6.0	N	300@4400	360@4000	4.00x3.62	9.4:1	18@2000
		6.0	U	300@4400	360@4000	4.00x3.62	9.4:1	18@2000
		6.6	D	300@3000	520@1800	4.00x3.90	17.5:1	57@3250
		8.1	G	340@4200	455@3200	4.25x4.37	9.1:1	10@2000
	Silverado	4.3	X	195@4600	260@2800	4.00x3.48	9.2:1	18@2000
		4.8	C	295@5600	305@4800	3.78x3.27	9.08:1	18@2000
		5.3	M	315@5200	338@4400	3.78x3.62	9.95:1	18@2000
		5.3	0	315@5200	338@4400	3.78x3.62	9.95:1	18@2000
		5.3	J	315@5200	338@4400	3.78x3.62	9.95:1	18@2000
		5.3	3	315@5200	338@4400	3.78x3.62	9.95:1	18@2000
		6.0	Y	367@5500	375@4300	4.00x3.62	9.67:1	18@2000
		6.0	K	353@5400	373@4400	4.00x3.62	9.67:1	18@2000
		6.6	6	365@3000	660@1600	4.00x3.90	16.8:1	42@1800

22116_SIER_C0003

GASOLINE ENGINE TUNE-UP SPECIFICATIONS

Year	Engine Displacement Liters	Engine ID/VIN	Spark Plugs Gap (in.)	Ignition Timing (deg.) MT	Ignition Timing (deg.) AT	Fuel Pump (psi)	Idle Speed (rpm) MT	Idle Speed (rpm) AT	Valve Clearance In.	Valve Clearance Ex.
2005	4.3	X	0.060	①	①	55-62 ②	③	③	HYD	HYD
	4.8	V	0.060	①	①	55-62 ②	③	③	HYD	HYD
	5.3	B	0.060	①	①	55-62 ②	③	③	HYD	HYD
	5.3	T	0.060	①	①	55-62 ②	③	③	HYD	HYD
	5.3	Z	0.060	①	①	55-62 ②	③	③	HYD	HYD
	6.0	U	0.060	①	①	55-62 ②	③	③	HYD	HYD
	6.0	N	0.060	①	①	55-62 ②	③	③	HYD	HYD
	8.1	G	0.060	①	①	55-62 ②	③	③	HYD	HYD
2006	4.3	X	0.060	①	①	55-62 ②	③	③	HYD	HYD
	4.8	V	0.060	①	①	55-62 ②	③	③	HYD	HYD
	5.3	B	0.060	①	①	55-62 ②	③	③	HYD	HYD
	5.3	T	0.060	①	①	55-62 ②	③	③	HYD	HYD
	5.3	Z	0.060	①	①	55-62 ②	③	③	HYD	HYD
	6.0	U	0.060	①	①	55-62 ②	③	③	HYD	HYD
	6.0	N	0.060	①	①	55-62 ②	③	③	HYD	HYD
	8.1	G	0.060	①	①	55-62 ②	③	③	HYD	HYD
2007	4.3	X	0.060	①	①	50-60 ②	③	③	HYD	HYD
	4.8	V	0.060	①	①	55-62 ②	③	③	HYD	HYD
	4.8	C	0.040	①	①	50-60 ②	③	③	HYD	HYD
	5.3	B	0.060	①	①	55-62 ②	③	③	HYD	HYD
	5.3	T	0.060	①	①	55-62 ②	③	③	HYD	HYD
	5.3	Z	0.060	①	①	55-62 ②	③	③	HYD	HYD
	5.3	M	0.040	①	①	50-60 ②	③	③	HYD	HYD
	5.3	0	0.040	①	①	50-60 ②	③	③	HYD	HYD
	5.3	J	0.040	①	①	50-60 ②	③	③	HYD	HYD
	5.3	3	0.040	①	①	50-60 ②	③	③	HYD	HYD
	6.0	U	0.060	①	①	55-62 ②	③	③	HYD	HYD
	6.0	N	0.060	①	①	55-62 ②	③	③	HYD	HYD
	6.0	Y	0.040	①	①	50-60 ②	③	③	HYD	HYD
	6.0	K	0.040	①	①	50-60 ②	③	③	HYD	HYD
	6.2	8	0.040	①	①	50-60 ②	③	③	HYD	HYD
	8.1	G	0.060	①	①	55-62 ②	③	③	HYD	HYD

NOTE: The Vehicle Emission Control Information label often reflects specification changes made during production.

The label figures must be used if they differ from those in this chart.

HYD: Hydraulic

① Ignition timing is preset and cannot be adjusted

② With key ON and engine OFF

③ Idle speed is maintained by the Powertrain Control Module (PCM)

DIESEL ENGINE TUNE-UP SPECIFICATIONS

Year	Engine Displacement Liters	Engine ID/VIN	Valve Clearance		Intake Valve Opens (deg.)	Injection Pump Setting (deg.)	Injection Nozzle Pressure (psi)		Idle Speed (rpm)	Cranking Compression Pressure (psi)
			Intake (in.)	Exhaust (in.)			New	Used		
2005	6.6	2	HYD	HYD	①	①	NA	NA	①	300
2006	6.6	2	HYD	HYD	①	①	NA	NA	①	300
	6.6	D	HYD	HYD	①	①	NA	NA	①	300
2007	6.6	D	HYD	HYD	①	①	NA	NA	①	300
	6.6	6	HYD	HYD	①	①	NA	NA	①	NA

NOTE: The Vehicle Emission Control Information label often reflects specification changes made during production.

The label figures must be used if they differ from those in this chart.

HYD: Hydraulic

NA: Not Available

① Refer to Vehicle Emission Control Information label

22116_SIER_C0007

CAPACITIES

Year	Model	Engine Displacement Liters	Engine ID/VIN	Engine Oil with Filter (qts.)	Transmission (pts.) Man.	Transmission (pts.) Auto.	Transfer Case (pts.)	Drive Axle Front (pts.)	Drive Axle Rear (pts.)	Fuel Tank (gal.)	Cooling System (qts.)
2005	Sierra	4.3	X	4.5	①	②	4.0	③	④	⑤	⑥
		4.8	V	6.0	①	②	4.0	③	④	⑤	⑦
		5.3	B	6.0	①	②	4.0	③	④	⑤	⑦
		5.3	T	6.0	①	②	4.0	③	④	⑤	⑦
		5.3	Z	6.0	①	②	4.0	③	④	⑤	⑦
		6.0	N	6.0	①	②	4.8	③	④	⑤	⑧
		6.0	U	6.0	①	②	4.8	③	④	⑤	⑧
		6.6	2	10.0	①	②	4.8	③	④	⑤	⑨
		8.1	G	6.5	①	②	4.8	③	④	⑤	⑩
	Silverado	4.3	X	4.5	①	②	4.0	③	④	⑤	⑥
		4.8	V	6.0	①	②	4.8	③	④	⑤	⑦
		5.3	B	6.0	①	②	4.0	③	④	⑤	⑦
		5.3	T	6.0	①	②	4.0	③	④	⑤	⑦
		5.3	Z	6.0	①	②	4.0	③	④	⑤	⑦
		6.0	N	6.0	①	②	4.8	③	④	⑤	⑧
		6.0	U	6.0	①	②	4.8	③	④	⑤	⑧
		6.6	2	10.0	①	②	4.8	③	④	⑤	⑨
		8.1	G	6.5	①	②	4.8	③	④	⑤	⑩
2006	Sierra	4.3	X	4.5	①	②	4.0	③	④	⑤	⑥
		4.8	V	6.0	①	②	4.0	③	④	⑤	⑦
		5.3	B	6.0	①	②	4.0	③	④	⑤	⑦
		5.3	T	6.0	①	②	4.0	③	④	⑤	⑦
		5.3	Z	6.0	①	②	4.0	③	④	⑤	⑦
		6.0	N	6.0	①	②	4.8	③	④	⑤	⑧
		6.0	U	6.0	①	②	4.8	③	④	⑤	⑧
		6.6	2	10.0	①	②	4.8	③	④	⑤	⑨
		6.6	D	10.0	①	②	4.8	③	④	⑤	⑨
		8.1	G	6.5	①	②	4.8	③	④	⑤	⑩
	Silverado	4.3	X	4.5	①	②	4.0	③	④	⑤	⑥
		4.8	V	6.0	①	②	4.8	③	④	⑤	⑦
		5.3	B	6.0	①	②	4.0	③	④	⑤	⑦
		5.3	T	6.0	①	②	4.0	③	④	⑤	⑦
		5.3	Z	6.0	①	②	4.0	③	④	⑤	⑦
		6.0	N	6.0	①	②	4.8	③	④	⑤	⑧
		6.0	U	6.0	①	②	4.8	③	④	⑤	⑧
		6.6	2	10.0	①	②	4.8	③	④	⑤	⑨
		6.6	D	10.0	①	②	4.8	③	④	⑤	⑨
		8.1	G	6.5	①	②	4.8	③	④	⑤	⑩

22116_SIER_C0004

CAPACITIES

Year	Model	Engine Displacement Liters	Engine ID/VIN	Engine Oil with Filter (qts.)	Transmission (pts.) Man.	Transmission (pts.) Auto.	Transfer Case (pts.)	Drive Axle Front (pts.)	Drive Axle Rear (pts.)	Fuel Tank (gal.)	Cooling System (qts.)
2007	Sierra Classic	4.3	X	4.5	①	②	4.0	③	④	⑤	⑥
		4.8	V	6.0	①	②	4.0	③	④	⑤	⑦
		5.3	B	6.0	①	②	4.0	③	④	⑤	⑦
		5.3	T	6.0	①	②	4.0	③	④	⑤	⑦
		5.3	Z	6.0	①	②	4.0	③	④	⑤	⑦
		6.0	N	6.0	①	②	4.8	③	④	⑤	⑧
		6.0	U	6.0	①	②	4.8	③	④	⑤	⑧
		6.6	2	10.0	①	②	4.8	③	④	⑤	⑨
		8.1	G	6.5	①	②	4.8	③	④	⑤	⑩
	Sierra	4.3	X	4.5	NA	②	3.2	③	④	⑤	⑥
		4.8	C	6.0	NA	②	3.2	③	④	⑤	⑦
		5.3	M	6.0	NA	②	3.2	③	④	⑤	⑦
		5.3	0	6.0	NA	②	3.2	③	④	⑤	⑦
		5.3	J	6.0	NA	②	3.2	③	④	⑤	⑦
		5.3	3	6.0	NA	②	3.2	③	④	⑤	⑦
		6.0	Y	6.0	NA	②	3.2	③	④	⑤	⑧
		6.0	K	6.0	NA	②	3.2	③	④	⑤	⑧
		6.2	8	6.0	NA	②	3.2	③	④	⑤	NA
		6.6	6	10.0	NA	②	3.2	③	④	⑤	25.4
	Silverado Classic	4.3	X	4.5	①	②	4.0	③	④	⑤	⑥
		4.8	V	6.0	①	②	4.8	③	④	⑤	⑦
		5.3	B	6.0	①	②	4.0	③	④	⑤	⑦
		5.3	T	6.0	①	②	4.0	③	④	⑤	⑦
		5.3	Z	6.0	①	②	4.0	③	④	⑤	⑦
		6.0	N	6.0	①	②	4.8	③	④	⑤	⑧
		6.0	U	6.0	①	②	4.8	③	④	⑤	⑧
		6.6	2	10.0	①	②	4.8	③	④	⑤	⑨
		8.1	G	6.5	①	②	4.8	③	④	⑤	⑩
	Silverado	4.3	X	4.5	NA	②	3.2	③	④	⑤	⑥
		4.8	C	6.0	NA	②	3.2	③	④	⑤	⑦
		5.3	M	6.0	NA	②	3.2	③	④	⑤	⑦
		5.3	0	6.0	NA	②	3.2	③	④	⑤	⑦
		5.3	J	6.0	NA	②	3.2	③	④	⑤	⑦
		5.3	3	6.0	NA	②	3.2	③	④	⑤	⑦
		6.0	Y	6.0	NA	②	3.2	③	④	⑤	⑧
		6.0	K	6.0	NA	②	3.2	③	④	⑤	⑧
		6.6	6	10.0	NA	②	3.2	③	④	⑤	25.4

NOTE: All capacities are approximate. Add fluid gradually and check to be sure a proper fluid level is obtained.

NA: Not Available

① New Venture Gear 3500: 4.8 pts.
New Venture Gear 4500: 8.0 pts.
6-speed M/T: 12.6 pts.

② 4L60-E: 10 pts.
4L70-E: 10 pts.
4L80-E: 15.4 pts.
6L80-E: 12 pts.
6L90-E: 14.8 pts.
Allison: 14.8 pts.

③ 8.25 in ring gear: 3.5 pts.
9.25 ring gear: 3.7 pts.

④ 8.6 in. ring gear: 4.3 pts.
9.5 & 10.5 in. ring gear: 5.5 pts.
9.75 in. ring gear: 6.0 pts.
11.5 in. ring gear: 6.3 pts.

⑤ Short bed: 26 gals.
Long bed: 34 gals.
3500: Front 27 gals., Rear 23 gals.

⑥ With A/T non electric fan: 14.8 qts.
With A/T electric fan: 16.5 qts.
With M/T non-electric fan: 15.1 qts.
With M/T electric fan: 16.6 qts.

⑦ With A/T non electric fan: 15.2 qts.
With A/T electric fan: 16.8 qts.
With M/T non-electric fan: 15.5 qts.
With M/T electric fan: 17.0 qts.

⑧ With A/T: 16.4 qts.
With A/T electric fan: 16.8 qts.

⑨ With A/T: 20.3 qts.
With M/T: 20.7 qts.

⑩ With A/T: 26.9 qts.

22116_SIER_C0005

FLUID SPECIFICATIONS

Year	Model	Engine Displacement Liters	Engine ID/VIN	Engine Oil	Auto. Trans.	Drive Axle	Power Steering Fluid	Brake Master Cylinder
2005	Sierra	4.3	X	5W-30	Dexron VI	①	GM PS Fluid	DOT-3
		4.8	V	5W-30	Dexron VI	①	GM PS Fluid	DOT-3
		5.3	B	5W-30	Dexron VI	①	GM PS Fluid	DOT-3
		5.3	T	5W-30	Dexron VI	①	GM PS Fluid	DOT-3
		5.3	Z	5W-30	Dexron VI	①	GM PS Fluid	DOT-3
		6.0	N	5W-30	Dexron VI	①	GM PS Fluid	DOT-3
		6.0	U	5W-30	Dexron VI	①	GM PS Fluid	DOT-3
		6.6	2	15W-40	Dexron VI	①	GM PS Fluid	DOT-3
		8.1	G	5W-30	Dexron VI	①	GM PS Fluid	DOT-3
	Silverado	4.3	X	5W-30	Dexron VI	①	GM PS Fluid	DOT-3
		4.8	V	5W-30	Dexron VI	①	GM PS Fluid	DOT-3
		5.3	B	5W-30	Dexron VI	①	GM PS Fluid	DOT-3
		5.3	T	5W-30	Dexron VI	①	GM PS Fluid	DOT-3
		5.3	Z	5W-30	Dexron VI	①	GM PS Fluid	DOT-3
		6.0	N	5W-30	Dexron VI	①	GM PS Fluid	DOT-3
		6.0	U	5W-30	Dexron VI	①	GM PS Fluid	DOT-3
		6.6	2	15W-40	Dexron VI	①	GM PS Fluid	DOT-3
		8.1	G	5W-30	Dexron VI	①	GM PS Fluid	DOT-3
2006	Sierra	4.3	X	5W-30	Dexron VI	①	GM PS Fluid	DOT-3
		4.8	V	5W-30	Dexron VI	①	GM PS Fluid	DOT-3
		5.3	B	5W-30	Dexron VI	①	GM PS Fluid	DOT-3
		5.3	T	5W-30	Dexron VI	①	GM PS Fluid	DOT-3
		5.3	Z	5W-30	Dexron VI	①	GM PS Fluid	DOT-3
		6.0	N	5W-30	Dexron VI	①	GM PS Fluid	DOT-3
		6.0	U	5W-30	Dexron VI	①	GM PS Fluid	DOT-3
		6.6	2	15W-40	Dexron VI	①	GM PS Fluid	DOT-3
		6.6	D	15W-40	Dexron VI	①	GM PS Fluid	DOT-3
		8.1	G	5W-30	Dexron VI	①	GM PS Fluid	DOT-3
	Silverado	4.3	X	5W-30	Dexron VI	①	GM PS Fluid	DOT-3
		4.8	V	5W-30	Dexron VI	①	GM PS Fluid	DOT-3
		5.3	B	5W-30	Dexron VI	①	GM PS Fluid	DOT-3
		5.3	T	5W-30	Dexron VI	①	GM PS Fluid	DOT-3
		5.3	Z	5W-30	Dexron VI	①	GM PS Fluid	DOT-3
		6.0	N	5W-30	Dexron VI	①	GM PS Fluid	DOT-3
		6.0	U	5W-30	Dexron VI	①	GM PS Fluid	DOT-3
		6.6	2	15W-40	Dexron VI	①	GM PS Fluid	DOT-3
		6.6	D	15W-40	Dexron VI	①	GM PS Fluid	DOT-3
		8.1	G	5W-30	Dexron VI	①	GM PS Fluid	DOT-3
2007	Sierra Classic	4.3	X	5W-30	Dexron VI	①	GM PS Fluid	DOT-3
		4.8	V	5W-30	Dexron VI	①	GM PS Fluid	DOT-3
		5.3	B	5W-30	Dexron VI	①	GM PS Fluid	DOT-3
		5.3	T	5W-30	Dexron VI	①	GM PS Fluid	DOT-3
		5.3	Z	5W-30	Dexron VI	①	GM PS Fluid	DOT-3
		6.0	N	5W-30	Dexron VI	①	GM PS Fluid	DOT-3
		6.0	U	5W-30	Dexron VI	①	GM PS Fluid	DOT-3
		6.6	2	15W-40	Dexron VI	①	GM PS Fluid	DOT-3
		8.1	G	5W-30	Dexron VI	①	GM PS Fluid	DOT-3

FLUID SPECIFICATIONS

Year	Model	Engine Displacement Liters	Engine ID/VIN	Engine Oil	Auto. Trans.	Drive Axle	Power Steering Fluid	Brake Master Cylinder
2007 cont.	Sierra	4.3	X	5W-30	Dexron VI	①	GM PS Fluid	DOT-3
		4.8	C	5W-30	Dexron VI	①	GM PS Fluid	DOT-3
		5.3	M	5W-30	Dexron VI	①	GM PS Fluid	DOT-3
		5.3	0	5W-30	Dexron VI	①	GM PS Fluid	DOT-3
		5.3	J	5W-30	Dexron VI	①	GM PS Fluid	DOT-3
		5.3	3	5W-30	Dexron VI	①	GM PS Fluid	DOT-3
		6.0	Y	5W-30	Dexron VI	①	GM PS Fluid	DOT-3
		6.0	K	5W-30	Dexron VI	①	GM PS Fluid	DOT-3
		6.2	8	5W-30	Dexron VI	①	GM PS Fluid	DOT-3
		6.6	6	15W-40	Dexron VI	①	GM PS Fluid	DOT-3
	Silverado Classic	4.3	X	5W-30	Dexron VI	①	GM PS Fluid	DOT-3
		4.8	V	5W-30	Dexron VI	①	GM PS Fluid	DOT-3
		5.3	B	5W-30	Dexron VI	①	GM PS Fluid	DOT-3
		5.3	T	5W-30	Dexron VI	①	GM PS Fluid	DOT-3
		5.3	Z	5W-30	Dexron VI	①	GM PS Fluid	DOT-3
		6.0	N	5W-30	Dexron VI	①	GM PS Fluid	DOT-3
		6.0	U	5W-30	Dexron VI	①	GM PS Fluid	DOT-3
		6.6	2	15W-40	Dexron VI	①	GM PS Fluid	DOT-3
		8.1	G	5W-30	Dexron VI	①	GM PS Fluid	DOT-3
	Silverado	4.3	X	5W-30	Dexron VI	①	GM PS Fluid	DOT-3
		4.8	C	5W-30	Dexron VI	①	GM PS Fluid	DOT-3
		5.3	M	5W-30	Dexron VI	①	GM PS Fluid	DOT-3
		5.3	0	5W-30	Dexron VI	①	GM PS Fluid	DOT-3
		5.3	J	5W-30	Dexron VI	①	GM PS Fluid	DOT-3
		5.3	3	5W-30	Dexron VI	①	GM PS Fluid	DOT-3
		6.0	Y	5W-30	Dexron VI	①	GM PS Fluid	DOT-3
		6.0	K	5W-30	Dexron VI	①	GM PS Fluid	DOT-3
		6.6	6	15W-40	Dexron VI	①	GM PS Fluid	DOT-3

DOT: Department Of Transpotation

① Front axle 1500: 80W90

Front axle except 1500: 75W90

Rear axle: 75W90

22116_SIER_C0019

VALVE SPECIFICATIONS

Year	Engine Displacement Liters	Engine ID/VIN	Seat Angle (deg.)	Face Angle (deg.)	Spring Test Pressure (lbs. @ in.)	Spring Installed Height (in.)	Stem-to-Guide Clearance (in.)		Stem Diameter (in.)	
							Intake	Exhaust	Intake	Exhaust
2005	4.3	X	46	45	187-203@1.27	1.67-1.70	0.0010-0.0037	0.0010-0.0037	NA	NA
	4.8	V	46	45	220@1.32	1.80	0.0010-0.0026	0.0010-0.0026	0.3132-0.3140	0.3132-0.3140
	5.3	B	46	45	220@1.32	1.80	0.0010-0.0026	0.0010-0.0026	0.3130-0.3140	0.3130-0.3140
	5.3	T	46	45	220@1.32	1.80	0.0010-0.0026	0.0010-0.0026	0.3130-0.3140	0.3130-0.3140
	5.3	Z	46	45	220@1.32	1.80	0.0010-0.0026	0.0010-0.0026	0.3130-0.3140	0.3130-0.3140
	6.0	U	46	45	230@1.40	1.80	0.0010-0.0027	0.0010-0.0027	0.3130-0.3140	0.3130-0.3140
	6.0	N	46	45	230@140	1.80	0.0010-0.0026	0.0010-0.0026	0.3130-0.3140	0.3130-0.3140
	6.6	2	45	45	NA	1.61	0.0012-0.0025	0.0015-0.0028	0.2737-0.2744	0.2734-0.2741
	8.1	G	46	45	216-236@1.34	1.81-1.84	0.0010-0.0029	0.0012-0.0031	0.3715-0.3722	0.3713-0.3720
2006	4.3	X	46	45	187-203@1.27	1.67-1.70	0.0010-0.0037	0.0010-0.0037	NA	NA
	4.8	V	46	45	220@1.32	1.80	0.0010-0.0026	0.0010-0.0026	0.3132-0.3140	0.3132-0.3140
	5.3	B	46	45	220@1.32	1.80	0.0010-0.0026	0.0010-0.0026	0.3130-0.3140	0.3130-0.3140
	5.3	T	46	45	220@1.32	1.80	0.0010-0.0026	0.0010-0.0026	0.3130-0.3140	0.3130-0.3140
	5.3	Z	46	45	220@1.32	1.80	0.0010-0.0026	0.0010-0.0026	0.3130-0.3140	0.3130-0.3140
	6.0	U	46	45	230@1.40	1.80	0.0010-0.0027	0.0010-0.0027	0.3130-0.3140	0.3130-0.3140
	6.0	N	46	45	230@140	1.80	0.0010-0.0026	0.0010-0.0026	0.3130-0.3140	0.3130-0.3140
	6.6	2	45	45	NA	1.61	0.0012-0.0025	0.0015-0.0028	0.2737-0.2744	0.2734-0.2741
	6.6	D	NA	NA	NA	NA	NA	NA	NA	NA
	8.1	G	46	45	216-236@1.34	1.81-1.84	0.0010-0.0029	0.0012-0.0031	0.3715-0.3722	0.3713-0.3720
2007	4.3	X	46	45	187-203@1.27	1.67-1.70	0.0010-0.0037	0.0010-0.0037	NA	NA
	4.8	V	46	45	220@1.32	1.80	0.0010-0.0026	0.0010-0.0026	0.3132-0.3140	0.3132-0.3140
	4.8	C	46	45	220@1.32	1.80	0.0010-0.0026	0.0010-0.0026	0.3132-0.3140	0.3132-0.3140
	5.3	B	46	45	220@1.32	1.80	0.0010-0.0026	0.0010-0.0026	0.3130-0.3140	0.3130-0.3140
	5.3	T	46	45	220@1.32	1.80	0.0010-0.0026	0.0010-0.0026	0.3130-0.3140	0.3130-0.3140

22116_SIER_C0008

VALVE SPECIFICATIONS

Year	Engine Displacement Liters	Engine ID/VIN	Seat Angle (deg.)	Face Angle (deg.)	Spring Test Pressure (lbs. @ in.)	Spring Installed Height (in.)	Stem-to-Guide Clearance (in.)		Stem Diameter (in.)	
							Intake	Exhaust	Intake	Exhaust
2007 cont.	5.3	Z	46	45	220@1.32	1.80	0.0010-0.0026	0.0010-0.0026	0.3130-0.3140	0.3130-0.3140
	5.3	M	46	45	220@1.32	1.80	0.0010-0.0026	0.0010-0.0026	0.3130-0.3140	0.3130-0.3140
	5.3	0	46	45	220@1.32	1.80	0.0010-0.0026	0.0010-0.0026	0.3130-0.3140	0.3130-0.3140
	5.3	J	46	45	220@1.32	1.80	0.0010-0.0026	0.0010-0.0026	0.3130-0.3140	0.3130-0.3140
	5.3	3	46	45	220@1.32	1.80	0.0010-0.0026	0.0010-0.0026	0.3130-0.3140	0.3130-0.3140
	6.0	U	46	45	230@1.40	1.80	0.0010-0.0027	0.0010-0.0027	0.3130-0.3140	0.3130-0.3140
	6.0	N	46	45	230@140	1.80	0.0010-0.0026	0.0010-0.0026	0.3130-0.3140	0.3130-0.3140
	6.0	Y	46	45	220@1.32	1.80	0.0010-0.0026	0.0010-0.0026	0.3130-0.3140	0.3130-0.3140
	6.0	K	46	45	220@1.32	1.80	0.0010-0.0026	0.0010-0.0026	0.3130-0.3140	0.3130-0.3140
	6.2	8	46	45	220@1.32	1.80	0.0010-0.0026	0.0010-0.0026	0.3130-0.3140	0.3130-0.3140
	6.6	D	NA	NA	NA	NA	NA	NA	NA	NA
	6.6	6	NA	NA	NA	NA	NA	NA	NA	NA
	8.1	G	46	45	216-236@1.34	1.81-1.84	0.0010-0.0029	0.0012-0.0031	0.3715-0.3722	0.3713-0.3720

NA: Not Available

22116_SIER_C0009

CAMSHAFT AND BEARING SPECIFICATIONS CHART

All measurements are given in inches.

Year	Engine Displ. Liters	Engine ID/VIN	Journal Dia.	Brg. Oil Clearance	Shaft End-play	Runout	Journal Bore	Lobe Height Intake	Lobe Height Exhaust
2005	4.3	X	1.8677-1.8696	NA	0.0010-0.0090	0.0039	NA	0.2704	0.2793
	4.8	V	2.164-2.166	NA	0.001-0.012	0.002	①	0.283	0.283
	5.3	B	2.164-2.166	NA	0.001-0.012	0.002	①	0.283	0.283
	5.3	T	2.164-2.166	NA	0.001-0.012	0.002	①	0.268	0.274
	5.3	Z	2.164-2.166	NA	0.001-0.012	0.002	①	0.268	0.274
	6.0	N	2.164-2.166	NA	0.001-0.012	0.002	①	0.274	0.281
	6.0	U	2.164-2.166	NA	0.001-0.012	0.002	①	0.274	0.281
	6.6	2	2.3990-2.4001	NA	0.0079	0.002	NA	0.2863	0.2326
	8.1	G	1.9477-1.9497	NA	NA	0.002	NA	0.2726-0.2766	0.2745-0.2785
2006	4.3	X	1.8677-1.8696	NA	0.0010-0.0090	0.0039	NA	0.2704	0.2793
	4.8	V	2.164-2.166	NA	0.001-0.012	0.002	①	0.283	0.283
	5.3	B	2.164-2.166	NA	0.001-0.012	0.002	①	0.283	0.283
	5.3	T	2.164-2.166	NA	0.001-0.012	0.002	①	0.268	0.274
	5.3	Z	2.164-2.166	NA	0.001-0.012	0.002	①	0.268	0.274
	6.0	N	2.164-2.166	NA	0.001-0.012	0.002	①	0.274	0.281
	6.0	U	2.164-2.166	NA	0.001-0.012	0.002	①	0.274	0.281
	6.6	2	2.3990-2.4001	NA	0.0079	0.002	NA	0.2863	0.2326
	6.6	D	NA	NA	NA	NA	NA	NA	NA
	8.1	G	1.9477-1.9497	NA	NA	0.002	NA	0.2726-0.2766	0.2745-0.2785
2007	4.3	X	1.8677-1.8696	NA	0.0010-0.0090	0.0039	NA	0.2704	0.2793
	4.8	V	2.164-2.166	NA	0.001-0.012	0.002	①	0.283	0.283
	4.8	C	2.164-2.166	NA	0.001-0.012	0.002	②	0.283	0.283
	5.3	B	2.164-2.166	NA	0.001-0.012	0.002	①	0.283	0.283

22116_SIER_C0010

CAMSHAFT AND BEARING SPECIFICATIONS CHART
All measurements are given in inches.

Year	Engine Displ. Liters	Engine ID/VIN	Journal Dia.	Brg. Oil Clearance	Shaft End-play	Runout	Journal Bore	Lobe Height Intake	Lobe Height Exhaust
2007 cont.	5.3	T	2.164-2.166	NA	0.001-0.012	0.002	①	0.268	0.274
	5.3	Z	2.164-2.166	NA	0.001-0.012	0.002	①	0.268	0.274
	5.3	M	2.164-2.166	NA	0.001-0.012	0.002	②	③	③
	5.3	0	2.164-2.166	NA	0.001-0.012	0.002	②	③	③
	5.3	J	2.164-2.166	NA	0.001-0.012	0.002	②	③	③
	5.3	3	2.164-2.166	NA	0.001-0.012	0.002	②	③	③
	6.0	N	2.164-2.166	NA	0.001-0.012	0.002	①	0.274	0.281
	6.0	U	2.164-2.166	NA	0.001-0.012	0.002	①	0.274	0.281
	6.0	Y	2.164-2.166	NA	0.001-0.012	0.002	②	④	⑤
	6.0	K	2.164-2.166	NA	0.001-0.012	0.002	②	④	⑤
	6.2	8	2.164-2.166	NA	0.001-0.012	0.002	②	0.294	0.294
	6.6	D	NA	NA	NA	NA	NA	NA	NA
	6.6	6	NA	NA	NA	NA	NA	NA	NA
	8.1	G	1.9477-1.9497	NA	NA	0.002	NA	0.2726-0.2766	0.2745-0.2785

NA: Not Available

① Bore 1 and 5: 2.347-2.349
  Bore 2 and 4: 2.327-2.329
  Bore 3: 2.307-2.309

② Bore 1 and 5: 2.345-2.347
  Bore 2 and 4: 2.325-2.327
  Bore 3: 2.306-2.308

③ Active Fuel Management Cylinders: 0.289
  Non Active Fuel Management Cylinders: 0.283

④ Active Fuel Management Cylinders: 0.283
  Non Active Fuel Management Cylinders: 0.279

⑤ Active Fuel Management Cylinders: 0.287
  Non Active Fuel Management Cylinders: 0.282

22116_SIER_C0011

CRANKSHAFT AND CONNECTING ROD SPECIFICATIONS

All measurements are given in inches.

Year	Engine Displacement Liters	Engine ID/VIN	Crankshaft				Connecting Rod		
			Main Brg. Journal Dia.	Main Brg. Oil Clearance	Shaft End-play	Thrust on No.	Journal Diameter	Oil Clearance	Side Clearance
2005	4.3	X	①	②	0.0020-0.0078	4	2.2487-2.2497	0.0015-0.0031	0.0060-0.0173
	4.8	V	2.5580-2.5593	0.0008-0.0021	0.0015-0.0078	5	2.0990-2.1000	0.0009-0.0025	0.0043-0.0200
	5.3	B	2.5580-2.5590	0.0008-0.0021	0.0015-0.0078	5	2.0990-2.1000	0.0006-0.0030	0.0043-0.0200
	5.3	T	2.5580-2.5593	0.0008-0.0021	0.0015-0.0078	5	2.0987-2.0999	0.0009-0.0025	0.0043-0.0200
	5.3	Z	2.5580-2.5590	0.0008-0.0021	0.0015-0.0078	5	2.0991-2.0999	0.0009-0.0030	0.0043-0.2000
	6.0	N	2.5580-2.5590	0.0008-0.0021	0.0015-0.0078	5	2.0991-2.0999	0.0009-0.0025	0.0043-0.2000
	6.0	U	2.5580-2.5593	0.0008-0.0021	0.0015-0.0078	5	2.0990-2.1000	0.0009-0.0025	0.0043-0.0200
	6.6	2	3.1459-3.1466	0.0015-0.0028	0.0016-0.0081	NA	2.4764-2.4772	0.0014-0.0030	0.0122-0.0193
	8.1	G	2.7482-2.7489	③	0.0050-0.0138	NA	2.1990-2.1996	0.0013-0.0027	0.0151-0.0270
2006	4.3	X	①	②	0.0020-0.0078	4	2.2487-2.2497	0.0015-0.0031	0.0060-0.0173
	4.8	V	2.5580-2.5593	0.0008-0.0021	0.0015-0.0078	5	2.0990-2.1000	0.0009-0.0025	0.0043-0.0200
	5.3	B	2.5580-2.5590	0.0008-0.0021	0.0015-0.0078	5	2.0990-2.1000	0.0006-0.0030	0.0043-0.0200
	5.3	T	2.5580-2.5593	0.0008-0.0021	0.0015-0.0078	5	2.0987-2.0999	0.0009-0.0025	0.0043-0.0200
	5.3	Z	2.5580-2.5590	0.0008-0.0021	0.0015-0.0078	5	2.0991-2.0999	0.0009-0.0030	0.0043-0.2000
	6.0	N	2.5580-2.5590	0.0008-0.0021	0.0015-0.0078	5	2.0991-2.0999	0.0009-0.0025	0.0043-0.2000
	6.0	U	2.5580-2.5593	0.0008-0.0021	0.0015-0.0078	5	2.0990-2.1000	0.0009-0.0025	0.0043-0.0200
	6.6	2	3.1459-3.1466	0.0015-0.0028	0.0016-0.0081	NA	2.4764-2.4772	0.0014-0.0030	0.0122-0.0193
	6.6	D	NA	NA	NA	NA	NA	NA	NA
	8.1	G	2.7482-2.7489	③	0.0050-0.0138	NA	2.1990-2.1996	0.0013-0.0027	0.0151-0.0270
2007	4.3	X	①	②	0.0020-0.0078	4	2.2487-2.2497	0.0015-0.0031	0.0060-0.0173
	4.8	V	2.5580-2.5593	0.0008-0.0021	0.0015-0.0078	5	2.0990-2.1000	0.0009-0.0025	0.0043-0.0200
	4.8	C	2.5580-2.5593	0.0008-0.0021	0.0015-0.0078	5	2.0990-2.1000	0.0009-0.0025	0.0043-0.0200
	5.3	B	2.5580-2.5590	0.0008-0.0021	0.0015-0.0078	5	2.0990-2.1000	0.0006-0.0030	0.0043-0.0200
	5.3	T	2.5580-2.5593	0.0008-0.0021	0.0015-0.0078	5	2.0987-2.0999	0.0009-0.0025	0.0043-0.0200

CRANKSHAFT AND CONNECTING ROD SPECIFICATIONS

All measurements are given in inches.

Year	Engine Displacement Liters	Engine ID/VIN	Crankshaft				Connecting Rod		
			Main Brg. Journal Dia.	Main Brg. Oil Clearance	Shaft End-play	Thrust on No.	Journal Diameter	Oil Clearance	Side Clearance
2007 cont.	5.3	Z	2.5580-2.5590	0.0008-0.0021	0.0015-0.0078	5	2.0991-2.0999	0.0009-0.0030	0.0043-0.2000
	5.3	M	2.5580-2.5590	0.0008-0.0021	0.0015-0.0078	5	2.0990-2.1000	0.0006-0.0030	0.0043-0.0200
	5.3	0	2.5580-2.5593	0.0008-0.0021	0.0015-0.0078	5	2.0987-2.0999	0.0009-0.0025	0.0043-0.0200
	5.3	J	2.5580-2.5590	0.0008-0.0021	0.0015-0.0078	5	2.0991-2.0999	0.0009-0.0030	0.0043-0.2000
	5.3	3	2.5580-2.5590	0.0008-0.0021	0.0015-0.0078	5	2.0991-2.0999	0.0009-0.0030	0.0043-0.2000
	6.0	N	2.5580-2.5590	0.0008-0.0021	0.0015-0.0078	5	2.0991-2.0999	0.0009-0.0025	0.0043-0.2000
	6.0	U	2.5580-2.5593	0.0008-0.0021	0.0015-0.0078	5	2.0990-2.1000	0.0009-0.0025	0.0043-0.0200
	6.0	Y	2.5580-2.5590	0.0008-0.0021	0.0015-0.0078	5	2.0991-2.0999	0.0009-0.0025	0.0043-0.2000
	6.0	K	2.5580-2.5593	0.0008-0.0021	0.0015-0.0078	5	2.0990-2.1000	0.0009-0.0025	0.0043-0.0200
	6.2	8	2.5580-2.5593	0.0008-0.0021	0.0015-0.0078	5	2.0990-2.1000	0.0009-0.0025	0.0043-0.0200
	6.6	D	NA	NA	NA	NA	NA	NA	NA
	6.6	6	NA	NA	NA	NA	NA	NA	NA
	8.1	G	2.7482-2.7489	③	0.0050-0.0138	NA	2.1990-2.1996	0.0013-0.0027	0.0151-0.0270

NA - Not Available

① No. 1: 2.4488 in.-2.4495 in.

   Nos. 2, 3: 2.4485 in.-2.4494 in.

   No. 4: 2.4480 in.-2.4489 in.

② No. 1: 0.0008-0.0020 in.

   No. 2, 3, 4: 0.0011-0.00236 in.

③ No. 1, 2, 3, 4: 0.0008-0.0020 in.

   No. 5: 0.0014-0.0026 in.

PISTON AND RING SPECIFICATIONS

All measurements are given in inches.

Year	Engine Displacement Liters	Engine ID/VIN	Piston Clearance	Ring Gap			Ring Side Clearance		
				Top Compression	Bottom Compression	Oil Control	Top Compression	Bottom Compression	Oil Control
2005	4.3	X	0.0007-0.0024	0.010-0.020	0.015-0.031	0.0002 0.0035	0.0012 0.0033	0.0012 0.0033	0.0030-0.0079
	4.8	V	-0.0014 0.0006	0.0015-0.0033	0.015-0.0031	0.0005-0.0078	0.0090-0.0196	0.00173-0.0031	0.0070-0.0320
	5.3	B	-0.0014 0.0006	0.0090-0.0196	0.0173-0.030	0.007-0.032	0.0016-0.0033	0.0016-0.0031	0.0005-0.0078
	5.3	T	-0.0014 0.0006	0.0090-0.0196	0.0173-0.030	0.007-0.032	0.0016-0.0033	0.0016-0.0031	0.0005-0.0078
	5.3	Z	-0.0014 0.0006	0.0090-0.0196	0.0173-0.030	0.007-0.032	0.0016-0.0033	0.0016-0.0031	0.0005-0.0078
	6.0	N	-0.0009 0.0012	0.012-0.020	0.020-0.030	0.012-0.034	0.0014-0.0031	0.0013-0.0030	0.0005-0.0008
	6.0	U	-0.0009 0.0012	0.012-0.023	0.020-0.033	0.012-0.037	0.0015-0.0031	0.0015-0.0031	0.0006-0.0078
	6.6	2	NA	0.0118-0.018	0.0197-0.026	0.0059-0.014	0.0030-0.0067	0.0004-0.0012	0.0004-0.0012
	8.1	G	①	0.012-0.018	0.017-0.025	0.010-0.030	0.0012-0.0029	0.0012-0.0029	0.002-0.008
2006	4.3	X	0.0007-0.0024	0.010-0.020	0.015-0.031	0.0002 0.0035	0.0012 0.0033	0.0012 0.0033	0.0030-0.0079
	4.8	V	-0.0014 0.0006	0.0015-0.0033	0.015-0.0031	0.0005-0.0078	0.0090-0.0196	0.00173-0.0031	0.0070-0.0320
	5.3	B	-0.0014 0.0006	0.0090-0.0196	0.0173-0.030	0.007-0.032	0.0016-0.0033	0.0016-0.0031	0.0005-0.0078
	5.3	T	-0.0014 0.0006	0.0090-0.0196	0.0173-0.030	0.007-0.032	0.0016-0.0033	0.0016-0.0031	0.0005-0.0078
	5.3	Z	-0.0014 0.0006	0.0090-0.0196	0.0173-0.030	0.007-0.032	0.0016-0.0033	0.0016-0.0031	0.0005-0.0078
	6.0	N	-0.0009 0.0012	0.012-0.020	0.020-0.030	0.012-0.034	0.0014-0.0031	0.0013-0.0030	0.0005-0.0008
	6.0	U	-0.0009 0.0012	0.012-0.023	0.020-0.033	0.012-0.037	0.0015-0.0031	0.0015-0.0031	0.0006-0.0078
	6.6	2	NA	0.0118-0.018	0.0197-0.026	0.0059-0.014	0.0030-0.0067	0.0004-0.0012	0.0004-0.0012
	6.6	D	NA	NA	NA	NA	NA	NA	NA
	8.1	G	①	0.012-0.018	0.017-0.025	0.010-0.030	0.0012-0.0029	0.0012-0.0029	0.002-0.008
2007	4.3	X	0.0007-0.0024	0.010-0.020	0.015-0.031	0.0002 0.0035	0.0012 0.0033	0.0012 0.0033	0.0030-0.0079
	4.8	V	-0.0014 0.0006	0.0015-0.0033	0.015-0.0031	0.0005-0.0078	0.0090-0.0196	0.00173-0.0031	0.0070-0.0320
	4.8	C	-0.0014 0.0006	0.0015-0.0033	0.015-0.0031	0.0005-0.0078	0.0090-0.0196	0.00173-0.0031	0.0070-0.0320
	5.3	B	-0.0014 0.0006	0.0090-0.0196	0.0173-0.030	0.007-0.032	0.0016-0.0033	0.0016-0.0031	0.0005-0.0078

PISTON AND RING SPECIFICATIONS

All measurements are given in inches.

Year	Engine Displacement Liters	Engine ID/VIN	Piston Clearance	Ring Gap			Ring Side Clearance		
				Top Compression	Bottom Compression	Oil Control	Top Compression	Bottom Compression	Oil Control
2007 cont.	5.3	T	-0.0014 0.0006	0.0090- 0.0196	0.0173- 0.030	0.007- 0.032	0.0016- 0.0033	0.0016- 0.0031	0.0005- 0.0078
	5.3	Z	-0.0014 0.0006	0.0090- 0.0196	0.0173- 0.030	0.007- 0.032	0.0016- 0.0033	0.0016- 0.0031	0.0005- 0.0078
	5.3	M	-0.0014 0.0006	0.0090- 0.0196	0.0173- 0.030	0.007- 0.032	0.0016- 0.0033	0.0016- 0.0031	0.0005- 0.0078
	5.3	0	-0.0014 0.0006	0.0090- 0.0196	0.0173- 0.030	0.007- 0.032	0.0016- 0.0033	0.0016- 0.0031	0.0005- 0.0078
	5.3	J	-0.0014 0.0006	0.0090- 0.0196	0.0173- 0.030	0.007- 0.032	0.0016- 0.0033	0.0016- 0.0031	0.0005- 0.0078
	5.3	3	-0.0014 0.0006	0.0090- 0.0196	0.0173- 0.030	0.007- 0.032	0.0016- 0.0033	0.0016- 0.0031	0.0005- 0.0078
	6.0	N	-0.0009 0.0012	0.012- 0.020	0.020- 0.030	0.012- 0.034	0.0014- 0.0031	0.0013- 0.0030	0.0005- 0.0008
	6.0	U	-0.0009 0.0012	0.012- 0.023	0.020- 0.033	0.012- 0.037	0.0015- 0.0031	0.0015- 0.0031	0.0006- 0.0078
	6.0	Y	-0.0009 0.0012	0.008- 0.016	0.015- 0.027	0.009- 0.031	0.0012- 0.0040	0.0014- 0.0031	0.0005- 0.0079
	6.0	K	-0.0009 0.0012	0.008- 0.016	0.015- 0.027	0.009- 0.031	0.0012- 0.0040	0.0014- 0.0031	0.0005- 0.0079
	6.2	8	-0.0014 0.0006	0.009- 0.017	0.017- 0.027	0.007- 0.029	0.00157- 0.00335	0.0015- 0.0031	0.0005- 0.0078
	6.6	D	NA	NA	NA	NA	NA	NA	NA
	6.6	6	NA	NA	NA	NA	NA	NA	NA
	8.1	G	①	0.012- 0.018	0.017- 0.025	0.010- 0.030	0.0012- 0.0029	0.0012- 0.0029	0.002- 0.008

① Interference fit (coated piston)

TORQUE SPECIFICATIONS
All readings in ft. lbs.

Year	Engine Displacement Liters	Engine ID/VIN	Cylinder Head Bolts	Main Bearing Bolts	Rod Bearing Bolts	Crankshaft Damper Bolts	Flywheel Bolts	Manifold Intake *	Manifold Exhaust	Spark Plugs	Oil Pan Drain Plug
2005	4.3	X	①	77	②	70	74	③	④	11	18
	4.8	V	⑤	⑥	⑦	⑧	⑨	⑩	⑪	11	18
	5.3	B	⑤	⑥	⑦	⑧	⑨	⑩	⑪	11	18
	5.3	T	⑤	⑥	⑦	⑧	⑨	⑩	⑪	11	18
	5.3	Z	⑤	⑥	⑦	⑧	⑨	⑩	⑪	11	18
	6.0	N	⑤	⑥	⑦	⑧	⑨	⑩	⑪	11	18
	6.0	U	⑤	⑥	⑦	⑧	⑨	⑩	⑪	11	18
	6.6	2	⑫	⑬	⑭	⑮	⑯	15	25	—	62
	8.1	G	⑰	⑱	⑲	189	⑳	㉑	㉒	22	21
2006	4.3	X	①	77	②	70	74	③	④	11	18
	4.8	V	⑤	⑥	⑦	⑧	⑨	⑩	⑪	11	18
	5.3	B	⑤	⑥	⑦	⑧	⑨	⑩	⑪	11	18
	5.3	T	⑤	⑥	⑦	⑧	⑨	⑩	⑪	11	18
	5.3	Z	⑤	⑥	⑦	⑧	⑨	⑩	⑪	11	18
	6.0	N	⑤	⑥	⑦	⑧	⑨	⑩	⑪	11	18
	6.0	U	⑤	⑥	⑦	⑧	⑨	⑩	⑪	11	18
	6.6	2	⑫	⑬	⑭	⑮	⑯	15	25	—	62
	6.6	D	⑫	⑬	⑭	⑮	⑯	15	25	—	62
	8.1	G	⑰	⑱	⑲	189	⑳	㉑	㉒	22	21
2007	4.3	X	①	77	②	70	74	③	④	11	18
	4.8	V	⑤	⑥	⑦	⑧	⑨	⑩	⑪	11	18
	4.8	C	⑤	⑥	⑦	⑧	⑨	⑩	⑪	11	18
	5.3	B	⑤	⑥	⑦	⑧	⑨	⑩	⑪	11	18
	5.3	T	⑤	⑥	⑦	⑧	⑨	⑩	⑪	11	18
	5.3	Z	⑤	⑥	⑦	⑧	⑨	⑩	⑪	11	18
	5.3	M	⑤	⑥	⑦	⑧	⑨	⑩	⑪	11	18
	5.3	0	⑤	⑥	⑦	⑧	⑨	⑩	⑪	11	18
	5.3	J	⑤	⑥	⑦	⑧	⑨	⑩	⑪	11	18
	5.3	3	⑤	⑥	⑦	⑧	⑨	⑩	⑪	11	18
	6.0	N	⑤	⑥	⑦	⑧	⑨	⑩	⑪	11	18
	6.0	U	⑤	⑥	⑦	⑧	⑨	⑩	⑪	11	18
	6.0	Y	⑤	⑥	⑦	⑧	⑨	⑩	⑪	11	18
	6.0	K	⑤	⑥	⑦	⑧	⑨	⑩	⑪	11	18
	6.2	8	⑤	⑥	⑦	⑧	⑨	⑩	⑪	11	18
	6.6	D	⑫	⑬	⑭	⑮	⑯	15	25	—	62
	6.6	6	⑫	⑬	⑭	⑮	⑯	15	25	—	62
	8.1	G	⑰	⑱	⑲	189	⑳	㉑	㉒	22	21

* NOTE: Applies to Lower Manifold only.

① Step 1: 22 ft. lbs.
Step 2:
Short bolt: Plus 55 degrees
Medium bolt: Plus 65 degrees
Long bolt: Plus 75 degrees

② 20 ft. lbs. plus 70 degrees

③ Lower intake manifold:
Step 1: 27 inch lbs.
Step 2: 106 inch lbs.
Step 3: 11 ft. lbs.
Upper manifold bolts:
Step 1: 44 inch lbs.
Step 2: 88 inch lbs.

④ Tighten bolts to 12 ft. lbs.
Retorque to 22 ft. lbs.

⑤ M11 bolts Step 1: 22 ft. lbs.
M11 bolts Step 2: 90 degrees
M11 bolts Step 3: 70 degrees
M8 bolts: 22 ft. lbs.

⑥ Inner bolts:
Step 1: 15 ft. lbs.
Step 2: 80 degrees
Side Bolts: 18 ft. lbs.
Outer bolts:
Step 1: 15 ft. lbs.
Step 2: 51 degrees

⑦ Step 1: 15 ft. lbs.
Step 2: 85 degrees

⑧ Installation pass: 240 ft. lbs.
Step 1: Replace bolt with new bolt
Step 2: 37 ft. lbs.
Step 3: 140 degrees

⑨ Step 1: 15 ft. lbs.
Step 2: 37 ft. lbs.
Step 3: 74 ft. lbs.

⑩ Step 1: 44 inch lbs.
Step 2: 89 inch lbs.

⑪ Step 1: 11 ft. lbs.
Step 2: 18 ft. lbs.

⑫ M12 bolts: Step 1: 37 ft. lbs.
Step 2: 59 ft. lbs.
Step 3: Plus 60 degrees
Step 4: Plus 90 degrees

⑬ Step 1: 74 ft. lbs.
Step 2: Plus 90 degrees

⑭ Step 1: 47 ft. lbs.
Step 2: Plus 30 degrees
Step 3: Plus 30 degrees

⑮ 1st pass: 74 ft. lbs.
2nd pass: Plus 90 degrees

⑯ Step 1: 58 ft. lbs.
Step 2: Plus 60 degrees
Step 3: Plus 60 degrees

⑰ Step 1: 22 ft. lbs.
Step 2: 22 ft. lbs.,
Step 3: plus 120 degrees
Step 4:
Short bolt: Plus 60 degrees
Med. bolt: Plus 45 degrees
Long bolt: Plus 30 degrees

⑱ Inner bolts: 22 ft. lbs.,
plus 90 degrees
Outer studs: 22 ft. lbs.,
plus 80 degrees

⑲ 22 ft. lbs., plus 90 degrees

⑳ Step 1: 59 ft. lbs.
Step 2: 74 ft. lbs.

㉑ Steps 1 & 2: 44 inch lbs.
Step 3: 89 inch lbs.
Step 4: 106 inch lbs.

㉒ Center bolt: 26 ft. lbs.
Nut: 12 ft. lbs.
Stud: 15 ft. lbs.
plus 90 degrees
Outer studs: 22 ft. lbs.,
plus 80 degrees

WHEEL ALIGNMENT

Year	Series	Model	Caster Range (+/-Deg.)	Caster Preferred Setting (Deg.)	Camber Range (+/-Deg.)	Camber Preferred Setting (Deg.)	Toe-in (Deg.)
2005	Silverado/Sierra C15 Series w/ Reg.Ext./Crew Cab	2WD	1.00	L +3.75 R +4.00	0.50	+0.25	0.10+/-0.20
	Silverado/Sierra K15 Series Reg./Ext./Crew Cab	4WD	1.00	L +3.60 R +4.10	0.50	+0.25	0.10+/-0.20
	Silverado SS	2WD	1.00	L +4.10 R +5.10	0.50	+0.10	0.10+/-0.20
	C25 LD	2WD	1.00	L +4.50 R +4.75	1.00	+0.25	0.10+/-0.20
	C25HD/C35/K25 LD	2WD/4WD	1.00	L +4.25 R +4.75	1.00	+0.25	0.10+/-0.20
	K25HD/K35HD	4WD	1.00	L +4.00 R +4.75	1.00	+0.25	0.10+/-0.20
2006	Silverado/Sierra C15 Series w/ Reg.Ext./Crew Cab	2WD	1.00	L +3.75 R +4.00	0.50	+0.25	0.10+/-0.20
	Silverado/Sierra K15 Series Reg./Ext./Crew Cab	4WD	1.00	L +3.60 R +4.10	0.50	+0.25	0.10+/-0.20
	Silverado SS	2WD	1.00	L +4.10 R +5.10	0.50	+0.10	0.10+/-0.20
	C25 LD	2WD	1.00	L +4.50 R +4.75	1.00	+0.25	0.10+/-0.20
	C25HD/C35/K25 LD	2WD/4WD	1.00	L +4.25 R +4.75	1.00	+0.25	0.10+/-0.20
	K25HD/K35HD	4WD	1.00	L +4.00 R +4.75	1.00	+0.25	0.10+/-0.20
2007	Silverado/Sierra C15 Series w/ Reg.Ext./Crew Cab Classic	2WD	1.00	L +3.75 R +4.00	0.50	+0.25	0.10+/-0.20
	Silverado/Sierra K15 Series Reg./Ext./Crew Cab Classic	4WD	1.00	L +3.60 R +4.10	0.50	+0.25	0.10+/-0.20
	Silverado SS Classic	2WD	1.00	L +4.10 R +5.10	0.50	+0.10	0.10+/-0.20
	C25HD/C35HD Classic	2WD	1.00	L +4.25 R +4.75	1.00	+0.25	0.10+/-0.20
	K25HD/K35HD Classic	4WD	1.00	L +4.00 R +4.75	1.00	+0.25	0.10+/-0.20
	C/K 1500	2WD/4WD	NA	NA	0.60	-0.10	0.10+/-0.20
	C/K 2500	2WD/4WD	1.00	L +3.30 R +3.60	0.60	0.25	0.10+/-0.20
	C/K 3500	2WD/4WD	1.00	L +3.30 R +3.60	0.60	0.25	0.10+/-0.20

22116_SIER_C0020

TIRE, WHEEL AND BALL JOINT SPECIFICATIONS

Year	Model	OEM Tires Standard	OEM Tires Optional	Tire Pressures (psi) Front	Tire Pressures (psi) Rear	Wheel Size	Ball Joint Inspection	Lug Nut Torque (ft. lbs.)
2005	1500 2WD	P235/75R15	None	36	36	6-JJ	L ①	③
	1500 4WD	P245/75R16	None	36	36	7-JJ	L ①	③
	2500	LT225/75R16D	LT245/75R16C	36	36	7-JJ	L ①	③
			LT245/75R16E	36	36			
	3500 SRW	LT245/75R16E	None	36	36	7-JJ	0.125 in.②	③
	3500 DRW	LT225/75R16D	LT215/85R16D	36	36	7-JJ	0.125 in.②	③
2006	1500 2WD	P235/75R15	None	36	36	6-JJ	L ①	③
	1500 4WD	P245/75R16	None	36	36	7-JJ	L ①	③
	2500	LT225/75R16D	LT245/75R16C	36	36	7-JJ	L ①	③
			LT245/75R16E	36	36			
	3500 SRW	LT245/75R16E	None	36	36	7-JJ	0.125 in.②	③
	3500 DRW	LT225/75R16D	LT215/85R16D	36	36	7-JJ	0.125 in.②	③
2007	1500 2WD Classic	P235/75R15	None	36	36	6-JJ	L ①	③
	1500 4WD Classic	P245/75R16	None	36	36	7-JJ	L ①	③
	2500 Classic	LT225/75R16D	LT245/75R16C	36	36	7-JJ	L ①	③
			LT245/75R16E	36	36			
	3500 SRW Classic	LT245/75R16E	None	36	36	7-JJ	0.125 in.②	③
	3500 DRW Classic	LT225/75R16D	LT215/85R16D	36	36	7-JJ	0.125 in.②	③
	Denali	LT266/65R18	NA	④	④	NA	0.079	③
	1500 2WD	LT245/70R17	NA	④	④	NA	0.079	③
	1500 4WD	LT265/70R17	NA	④	④	NA	0.079	③
	2500	LT245/75R16	NA	④	④	NA	0.079	③
	2500 SLT	LT265/75R17	NA	④	④	NA	0.079	③
	3500 SRW	LT265/75R16	NA	④	④	NA	0.079	③
	3500 DRW	LT215/85R16	NA	④	④	NA	0.079	③

OEM: Original Equipment Manufacturer   OPT: Optional

PSI: Pounds Per Square Inch   L: Lower

STD: Standard   U: Upper

① Do not lift truck. Inspect the boss into which the grease fitting is threaded. Replace if the boss is flush or receded below the surface of the ball joint

② Applies to both upper and lower

③ Single wheels: 140 ft. lbs.

  Dual rear wheels: 175 ft. lbs.

④ Refer to the tire placard

22116_SIER_C0021

BRAKE SPECIFICATIONS
All measurements in inches unless noted

Year	Model		Brake Disc Original Thickness	Brake Disc Minimum Thickness	Brake Disc Maximum Runout	Brake Drum Diameter Original Inside Diameter	Brake Drum Diameter Max. Wear Limit	Brake Drum Diameter Max. Machine Diameter	Minimum Lining Thickness	Brake Caliper Bracket Bolts (ft. lbs.)	Brake Caliper Mounting Bolts (ft. lbs.)
2005	Sierra	F	①	②	0.005	—	—	—	—	③	④
		R	⑤	⑥	0.005	—	—	—	—	③	④
	Silverado	F	①	②	0.005	—	—	—	—	③	④
		R	⑤	⑥	0.005	—	—	—	—	③	④
2006	Sierra	F	①	②	0.005	—	—	—	—	③	④
		R	⑤	⑥	0.005	—	—	—	—	③	④
	Silverado	F	①	②	0.005	—	—	—	—	③	④
		R	⑤	⑥	0.005	—	—	—	—	③	④
2007	Sierra Classic	F	①	②	0.005	—	—	—	—	③	④
		R	⑤	⑥	0.005	—	—	—	—	③	④
	Sierra	F	⑦	⑧	0.005	—	—	—	—	⑨	⑩
		R	⑪	⑫	0.005	NA	11.673	NA	0.030	⑨	⑩
	Silverado Classic	F	①	②	0.005	—	—	—	—	③	④
		R	⑤	⑥	0.005	—	—	—	—	③	④
	Silverado	F	⑦	⑧	0.005	—	—	—	—	⑨	⑩
		R	⑪	⑫	0.005	NA	11.673	NA	0.030	⑨	⑩

NA: Not Available

① 6400/7000 GVW: 1.181
7200 GVW: 1.142
9900/12,300 GVW: 1.50
② 6400/7000 GVW: 1.100
7200 GVW: 1.100
9900/12,300 GVW: 1.46
③ Light Duty: 133 ft. lbs. front, 148 ft. lbs. rear
Med/heavy Duty: 221 ft. lbs. front and rear
④ Light Duty: 74 ft. lbs. front, 31 ft. lbs. rear
Med/heavy Duty: 80 ft. lbs. front and rear
⑤ 6400 GVW: 0.787
7200/12,300 GVW: 1.181
9900 GVW: 1.141
⑥ 6400 GVW: 0.784
7200/12,300 GVW: 1.142
9900 GVW: 1.102

⑦ Light Duty: 1.181
Med/heavy Duty: 1.496
⑧ Light Duty: 1.10
Med/heavy Duty: 1.437
⑨ Light Duty: 129 ft. lbs. front, 148 ft. lbs. rear
Med. Duty: 221 ft. lbs. Front, 148 ft. lbs. rear
Heavy Duty: 221 ft. lbs. front and rear
⑩ Light Duty: 74 ft. lbs. front, 28 ft. lbs. rear
Med/heavy Duty: 80 ft. lbs. front and rear
⑪ Light Duty: 0.787
Med/heavy Duty: 1.181
⑫ Light Duty: 0.709
Med. Duty: 1.083
Heavy Duty: 1.122

22116_SIER_C0022

MAINTENANCE I AND II SERVICE SCHEDULES
SIERRA AND SILVERADO

When the CHANGE ENGINE OIL light appears, certain services and inspections are required.
Required services are described as Maintenance I and Maintenance II.
The first service on a vehicle should be Maintenance I, and the second service should be Maintenance II.
Alternate between the 2 thereafter. However, in some cases, Maintenance II may be required more often.
Maintenance I: Use Maintenance I if the CHANGE ENGINE OIL light comes on within 10 months
since vehicle was purchased or, if Maintenance II was performed.
Maintenance II: Use Maintenance II if the previous service performed was Maintenance I.
Always use Maintenance II whenever the CHANGE ENGINE OIL light comes on 10 months or more since the last
service, or, if the CHANGE ENGINE OIL light has not come on at all for one year.

Service	Maintenance I	Maintenance
Change the engine oil and filter. Reset the oil life system.	✓	✓
Visually inspect the vehicle for leaks or damage. A fluid loss in the vehicle system could indicate a problem. Inspected, repair and add fluid to the system if necessary.	✓	✓
Inspect the engine air cleaner filter. If necessary, replace the filter.	✓	✓
Rotate the tires. Inspect the tire inflation pressures and the tire wear.	✓	✓
Visually inspect the brake lines and hoses for proper hook-up, binding, leaks, cracks, chafing, etc. Inspect the disc brake pads for wear and the rotors for surface condition. Inspect the drum brake linings for wear or cracks. Inspect other brake parts, including drums, wheel cylinders, calipers, parking brake, etc. Inspect the parking brake adjustment.	✓	✓
Inspect the engine coolant and the windshield washer fluid levels. Add fluid as needed.	✓	✓
Inspect the suspension and steering components. Inspect the front and rear suspension and the steering system for damaged, loose or missing parts, or signs of wear. Inspect the power steering lines and the hoses for proper hook-up, binding, leaks, cracks, chafing, etc.	--	✓
Visually inspect the coolant hoses and replace the hoses if they are cracked, swollen or deteriorated. Inspect all pipes, fittings and clamps; replace with GM parts as needed. To help ensure proper operation, a pressure test of the cooling system and pressure cap and cleaning the outside of the radiator and air conditioning condenser is recommended at least once a year.		✓
Inspect the wiper blades for wear or cracking.	--	✓
Inspect the restraint system components.Ensure the safety belt reminder light and all the belts, buckles, latch plates, retractors and anchorages are working properly. Look for any other loose or damaged safety belt system parts. If you see anything that might keep a safety belt system from working correctly, repair or replaced the damaged part. Replace torn or frayed safety belts, refer to Operational and Functional Checks in Seat Belts. Inspect for any opened or broken air bag coverings, and repair or replace as needed. The air bag system does require regular maintenance.	--	✓

22116_SIER_C0017

MAINTENANCE I AND II SERVICE SCHEDULES
SIERRA AND SILVERADO

When the CHANGE ENGINE OIL light appears, certain services and inspections are required.
Required services are described as Maintenance I and Maintenance II.
The first service on a vehicle should be Maintenance I, and the second service should be Maintenance II.
Alternate between the 2 thereafter. However, in some cases, Maintenance II may be required more often.
Maintenance I: Use Maintenance I if the CHANGE ENGINE OIL light comes on within 10 months
since vehicle was purchased or, if Maintenance II was performed.
Maintenance II: Use Maintenance II if the previous service performed was Maintenance I.
Always use Maintenance II whenever the CHANGE ENGINE OIL light comes on 10 months or more since the last
service, or, if the CHANGE ENGINE OIL light has not come on at all for one year.

Service	Maintenance I	Maintenance
Lubricate the body components.Lubricate all key lock cylinders, hood latch assemblies, secondary latches, pivots, spring anchor and release pawl, hood and door hinges, rear folding seats and liftgate hinges. Frequent lubrication may be required when exposed to a corrosive environment, refer to Fluid and Lubricant Recommendations . Applying dielectric silicone grease GM P/N 12345579 (Canadian P/N 1974984) or equivalent on the weatherstrips with a clean cloth.	--	✓
Inspect the transaxle fluid level and add fluid as needed.	--	✓
Inspect the suspension and steering components.Inspect the front and rear suspension and the steering system for damaged, loose or missing parts, or signs of wear. Inspect power steering lines and hoses for proper hook-up, binding, leaks, cracks, chafing, etc.	--	✓
Inspect the throttle system for interference or binding and for damaged or missing parts. Replace the parts as needed. Replace any components that have high effort or excessive wear. Do not lubricate the accelerator or the cruise control cables.	--	✓
Replace the passenger compartment air filter.	--	✓

22116_SIER_C0023

PRECAUTIONS

Before servicing any vehicle, please be sure to read all of the following precautions, which deal with personal safety, prevention of component damage, and important points to take into consideration when servicing a motor vehicle:

• Never open, service or drain the radiator or cooling system when the engine is hot; serious burns can occur from the steam and hot coolant.

• Observe all applicable safety precautions when working around fuel. Whenever servicing the fuel system, always work in a well-ventilated area. Do not allow fuel spray or vapors to come in contact with a spark, open flame, or excessive heat (a hot drop light, for example). Keep a dry chemical fire extinguisher near the work area. Always keep fuel in a container specifically designed for fuel storage; also, always properly seal fuel containers to avoid the possibility of fire or explosion. Refer to the additional fuel system precautions later in this section.

• Fuel injection systems often remain pressurized, even after the engine has been turned **OFF**. The fuel system pressure must be relieved before disconnecting any fuel lines. Failure to do so may result in fire and/or personal injury.

• Brake fluid often contains polyglycol ethers and polyglycols. Avoid contact with the eyes and wash your hands thoroughly after handling brake fluid. If you do get brake fluid in your eyes, flush your eyes with clean, running water for 15 minutes. If eye irritation persists, or if you have taken brake fluid internally, IMMEDIATELY seek medical assistance.

• The EPA warns that prolonged contact with used engine oil may cause a number of skin disorders, including cancer. You should make every effort to minimize your exposure to used engine oil. Protective gloves should be worn when changing oil. Wash your hands and any other exposed skin areas as soon as possible after exposure to used engine oil. Soap and water, or waterless hand cleaner should be used.

• All new vehicles are now equipped with an air bag system, often referred to as a Supplemental Restraint System (SRS) or Supplemental Inflatable Restraint (SIR) system. The system must be disabled before performing service on or around system components, steering column, instrument panel components, wiring and sensors. Failure to follow safety and disabling procedures could result in accidental air bag deployment, possible personal injury and unnecessary system repairs.

• Always wear safety goggles when working with, or around, the air bag system. When carrying a non-deployed air bag, be sure the bag and trim cover are pointed away from your body. When placing a non-deployed air bag on a work surface, always face the bag and trim cover upward, away from the surface. This will reduce the motion of the module if it is accidentally deployed. Refer to the additional air bag system precautions later in this section.

• Clean, high quality brake fluid from a sealed container is essential to the safe and proper operation of the brake system. You should always buy the correct type of brake fluid for your vehicle. If the brake fluid becomes contaminated, completely flush the system with new fluid. Never reuse any brake fluid. Any brake fluid that is removed from the system should be discarded. Also, do not allow any brake fluid to come in contact with a painted surface; it will damage the paint.

• Never operate the engine without the proper amount and type of engine oil; doing so WILL result in severe engine damage.

• Timing belt maintenance is extremely important. Many models utilize an interference-type, non-freewheeling engine. If the timing belt breaks, the valves in the cylinder head may strike the pistons, causing potentially serious (also time-consuming and expensive) engine damage. Refer to the maintenance interval charts for the recommended replacement interval for the timing belt, and to the timing belt section for belt replacement and inspection.

• Disconnecting the negative battery cable on some vehicles may interfere with the functions of the on-board computer system(s) and may require the computer to undergo a relearning process once the negative battery cable is reconnected.

• When servicing drum brakes, only disassemble and assemble one side at a time, leaving the remaining side intact for reference.

• Only an MVAC-trained, EPA-certified automotive technician should service the air conditioning system or its components.

BRAKES

GENERAL INFORMATION

See Figures 1 and 2.

These vehicles are equipped with either a standard antilock braking system or antilock braking system with traction control.

The following components are involved in the operation of the above systems.

Electronic brake control module (EBCM) – The EBCM controls the system functions and detects failures. The EBCM contains the following components:

• System relay – The system relay is internal to the EBCM. The system relay is energized when the ignition is ON. The system relay supplies battery positive voltage to the solenoid valves and to the pump motor. This voltage is referred to as system voltage.

• Solenoids – The solenoids are commanded ON and OFF by the EBCM to operate the appropriate valves in the brake pressure modulator valve (BPMV).

Brake pressure modulator valve (BPMV) – The BPMV uses a 3–circuit configuration to control the left front wheel, the right front wheel, and the combined rear wheels. The BPMV directs fluid to the left front and right front wheels independently. The BPMV directs fluid to the two rear wheels on a single hydraulic circuit. The BPMV contains the following components.

• Pump motor
• Three isolation valves
• Three dump valves
• A front low–pressure accumulator
• A rear low–pressure accumulator
BPMV hydraulic circuit components:

ANTI-LOCK BRAKE SYSTEM (ABS)

• (1) Master Cylinder
• (2) Master Cylinder Reservoir
• (3) Pump
• (4) Brake Pressure Modulator Valve (BPMV)
• (5) Damper
• (6) Rear Isolation Valve
• (7) Accumulator
• (8) Rear Dump Valve
• (9) Right Rear Brake
• (10) Left Rear Brake
• (11) Left Front Isolation Valve
• (12) Left Front Dump Valve
• (13) Left Front Brake
• (14) Accumulator
• (15) Right Front Brake
• (16) Right Front Dump Valve
• (17) Right Front Isolation Valve
• (18) Damper

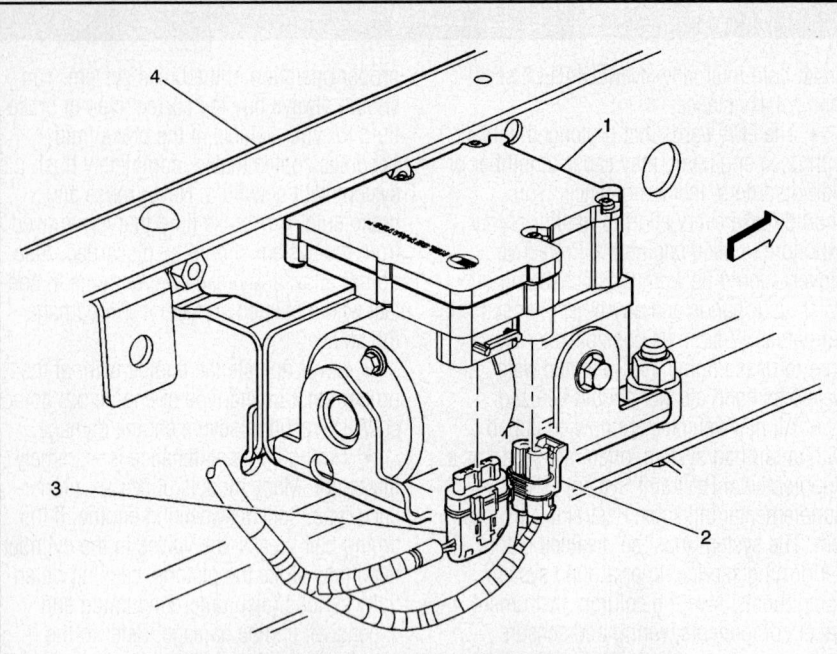

1. Electronic Brake Control Module (EBCM)
2. Electronic Brake Control Module (EBCM)
   Electrical Connector – C1
3. Electronic Brake Control Module (EBCM)
   Electrical Connector – C2
4. Left side frame rail

32085_SILV_G0079

Fig. 1 Electronic Brake Control Module (EBCM) (1), Electronic Brake Control Module (EBCM) Electrical Connector – C1 (2), Electronic Brake Control Module (EBCM) Electrical Connector – C2 (3) and left side frame rail (4)

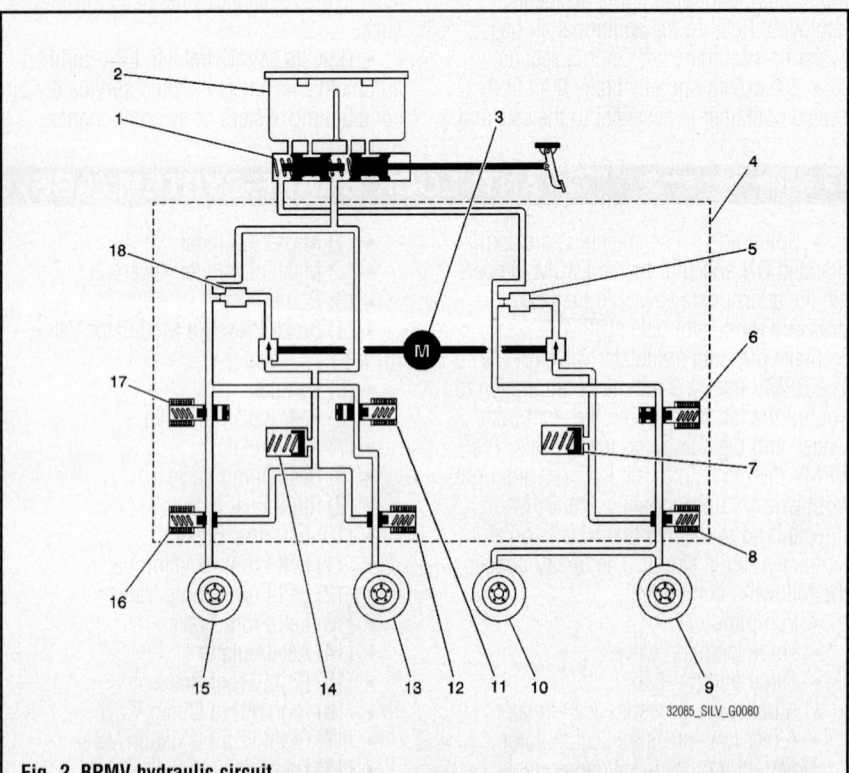

32085_SILV_G0080

Fig. 2 BPMV hydraulic circuit

Wheel Speed Sensors (WSS) – As the front wheels spin, toothed rings located at each wheel hub interrupt magnetic fields in the wheel speed sensors. This causes each wheel speed sensor to generate an AC signal. The EBCM uses these AC signals to calculate the wheel speed. The wheel speed sensors are serviceable only as part of the wheel hub and bearing assemblies. Any imperfections in the toothed ring, such as a missing or damaged tooth, can cause an inaccurate WSS signal.

Vehicle Speed Sensor (VSS) – The input signal for rear wheel speed originates at the VSS. The Powertrain Control Module (PCM) receives rear wheel speed input from the VSS and supplies this information to the EBCM.

Traction control switch (w/NW7) – The TCS is manually disabled or enabled using the traction control switch. The TCS can be programmed to be automatically enabled or disabled when the ignition is turned ON. The factory default is for the TCS to be automatically enabled. Refer to Programming the Traction Control Automatic Engagement Feature.

Initialization Sequence

The EBCM performs one initialization test each ignition cycle. The initialization of the EBCM occurs when the following conditions are met:

- The ignition is **ON**
- The bulb check has been completed
- Vehicle speed is greater than 4 mph (6 km/h)

The initialization sequence briefly cycles each solenoid and the pump motor to verify proper operation of the components. The EBCM sets one or more DTCs in accordance with any malfunction that is detected.

The EBCM defines a drive cycle as the completion of the initialization sequence.

Anti–Lock Brake System

When wheel slip is detected during a brake application, the ABS enters antilock mode. During antilock braking, hydraulic pressure in the individual wheel circuits is controlled to prevent any wheel from slipping. A separate hydraulic line and specific solenoid valves are provided for each wheel. The ABS can decrease, hold, or increase hydraulic pressure to each wheel brake. The ABS cannot, however, increase hydraulic pressure above the amount which is transmitted by the master cylinder during braking.

During antilock braking, a series of rapid pulsations is felt in the brake pedal. These pulsations are caused by the rapid changes in position of the individual solenoid valves as the EBCM responds to wheel speed sensor inputs and attempts to prevent wheel slip. These pedal pulsations are present only during antilock braking and stop when normal braking is resumed or when the vehicle comes to a stop. A ticking or popping noise may also be heard as the solenoid valves cycle rapidly. During antilock braking on dry pavement, intermittent chirping noises may be heard as the tires approach slipping. These noises and pedal pulsations are considered normal during antilock operation.

Vehicles equipped with ABS may be stopped by applying normal force to the brake pedal. Brake pedal operation during normal braking is no different than that of previous non–ABS systems. Maintaining a constant force on the brake pedal provides the shortest stopping distance while maintaining vehicle stability.

Pressure Hold

The EBCM closes the isolation valve and keeps the dump valve closed in order to isolate the slipping wheel when wheel slip occurs. This holds the pressure steady on the brake so that the hydraulic pressure does not increase or decrease.

Pressure Decrease

If a pressure hold does not correct the wheel slip condition, a pressure decrease occurs. The EBCM decreases the pressure to individual wheels during deceleration when wheel slip occurs. The isolation valve is closed and the dump valve is opened. The excess fluid is stored in the accumulator until the pump can return the fluid to the master cylinder or fluid reservoir.

Pressure Increase

After the wheel slip is corrected, a pressure increase occurs. The EBCM increases the pressure to individual wheels during deceleration in order to reduce the speed of the wheel. The isolation valve is opened and the dump valve is closed. The increased pressure is delivered from the master cylinder.

Dynamic Rear Proportioning (DRP)

The Dynamic Rear Proportioning (DRP) is a control system that replaces the hydraulic proportioning function of the mechanical proportioning valve in the base brake system. The DRP control system is part of the operation software in the EBCM. The DRP uses active control with existing ABS in order to regulate the vehicle's rear brake pressure.

The red brake warning indicator is illuminated when the dynamic rear proportioning function is disabled.

Traction Control System (TCS)

When drive wheel slip is noted while the brake is not applied, the EBCM will enter traction control mode.

The EBCM uses a 5–volt Pulse–Width Modulated (PWM) signal to request the PCM to reduce the amount of torque to the drive wheels. The PCM reduces torque to the drive wheels by retarding spark timing and by commanding the throttle actuator control. The PCM uses a 5–volt PWM signal in order to report to the EBCM the amount of torque delivered to the drive wheels.

Brake Warning Indicator

The Instrument Panel Cluster (IPC) illuminates the brake warning indicator when the following occurs:

• The Body Control Module (BCM) detects that the park brake is engaged. The IPC receives a class 2 message from the BCM requesting illumination.

• The EBCM detects a low brake fluid condition and sends a class 2 message to the IPC.

• The IPC performs the bulb check.

• An ABS–disabling malfunction also disables dynamic rear proportioning (DRP).

ABS Indicator

The IPC illuminates the ABS indicator when the following occurs:

• The electronic brake control module (EBCM) detects an ABS–disabling malfunction. The IPC receives a class 2 message from the EBCM requesting illumination.

• The IPC performs the bulb check.

• The IPC detects a loss of class 2 communications with the EBCM.

Traction Control Indicators

The TRACTION ACTIVE message is displayed on the instrument panel cluster (IPC) during a traction control event.

The EBCM illuminates the TRACTION OFF indicator if any of the following conditions are present:

• The EBCM inhibits the traction control system.

• The driver manually disables the traction control system by pressing the traction control switch.

• The automatic transmission shift lever is in the low (1) position.

The EBCM inhibits the traction control system when a TCS–disabling malfunction occurs, or when the automatic engagement feature is programmed to disable the TCS when the ignition is turned **ON**. Refer to Programming the Traction Control Automatic Engagement Feature.

Programming the Traction Control Automatic Engagement

The automatic engagement feature may be programmed so that the traction control system activates or does not activate automatically at the start of each ignition cycle. In order to change the status of the automatic engagement feature, perform the following procedure:

➡**Failure to follow the correct procedure may cause DTC C0283 to set in EBCM memory.**

1. Park the vehicle and apply the parking brake.
2. Unlock the ignition and shift the transmission into NEUTRAL (N).
3. Turn the ignition **ON**, engine **OFF**.
4. Press and hold the brake pedal and the accelerator pedal.
5. Press and hold the traction assist switch for 5 seconds.
6. Release the brake and accelerator pedals and the traction control switch.
7. Turn the ignition **OFF**.

PRECAUTIONS

• Certain components within the ABS system are not intended to be serviced or repaired individually.

• Do not use rubber hoses or other parts not specifically specified for and ABS system. When using repair kits, replace all parts included in the kit. Partial or incorrect repair may lead to functional problems and require the replacement of components.

• Lubricate rubber parts with clean, fresh brake fluid to ease assembly. Do not use shop air to clean parts; damage to rubber components may result.

• Use only DOT 3 brake fluid from an unopened container.

• If any hydraulic component or line is removed or replaced, it may be necessary to bleed the entire system.

• A clean repair area is essential. Always clean the reservoir and cap thoroughly before removing the cap. The slightest amount of dirt in the fluid may plug an orifice and impair the system function. Perform repairs after components have been thoroughly cleaned; use only denatured alcohol to clean components. Do not allow ABS components to come into contact with any substance containing mineral oil; this includes used shop rags.

• The Anti-Lock control unit is a microprocessor similar to other computer units in the vehicle. Ensure that the ignition switch is **OFF** before removing or installing controller harnesses. Avoid static electricity discharge at or near the controller.

• If any arc welding is to be done on the vehicle, the control unit should be unplugged before welding operations begin.

SPEED SENSORS

REMOVAL & INSTALLATION

Front

See Figure 3.

1. Raise and properly support the vehicle.
2. Remove the tire and wheel.
3. Remove the brake rotor .
4. Remove the WSS cable mounting clip from the knuckle.
5. Remove the WSS cable mounting clip from the upper control arm.
6. Remove the WSS cable mounting clip from the frame attachment point.
7. Remove the WSS cable electrical connector.
8. Remove the wheel speed sensor (WSS) mounting bolt.

※※ WARNING

Carefully remove the sensor by pulling it straight out of the bore. DO NOT use a screwdriver, or other device to pry the sensor out of the bore. Prying will cause the sensor body to break off in the bore.

9. Remove the wheel speed sensor from the hub/bearing assembly.

To install:

10. Plug the WSS bore to prevent debris from falling into the hub.
11. Using a wire brush or equivalent, clean the WSS mounting surface on the hub to remove any rust or corrosion.

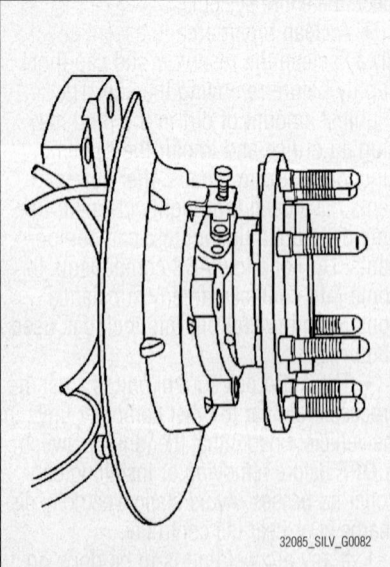

Fig. 3 Wheel speed sensor mounting bolt—2-Wheel drive

32085_SILV_G0082

12. Apply a thin layer of wheel bearing lubricant to the hub surface and the sensor O–ring prior to sensor installation.
13. Install the WSS into the hub/bearing assembly. Ensure that the sensor is seated flat against the hub.
14. Install the WSS mounting bolt.
   a. Tighten the WSS mounting bolt to 13 ft. lbs. (18 Nm).
15. Install the WSS cable mounting clip to the knuckle.
16. Install the WSS cable mounting clip to the upper control arm.
17. Install the WSS cable mounting clip to the frame attachment point.
18. Connect the WSS cable electrical connector.
19. Install the brake rotor.
20. Install the tire and wheel.
21. Using a scan tool, perform the Diagnostic System Check – ABS

Rear

Transmission Mounted

See Figure 4.

1. Disconnect the negative battery cable.
2. Raise and safely support the vehicle.
3. Unplug the sensor connector.
4. Remove the bolt and sensor by pulling the sensor from the transmission or transfer case housing.
   a. Fluid will drip out of the opening, so be ready to catch the spillage.

To install:

5. Install a new O–ring on the vehicle speed sensor and coat with transmission fluid.

6. Install the sensor, bolts and torque to:
   a. Automatic transmission: 97 inch lbs. (11 Nm).
   b. Manual transmission NV3500 and NV4500: 142 inch lbs. (16 Nm)
   c. Manual transmission ZF S6–650: 89 inch lbs. (10 Nm)
7. Engage the electrical connector.
8. Connect the negative battery cable and check transaxle or transmission fluid level.

Rear Wheel Mounted

See Figure 5.

1. Raise and properly support the vehicle.
2. Remove the tire and wheel.
3. Remove the brake rotor .
4. Remove the WSS cable mounting clip from the frame attachment point.
5. Remove the WSS cable electrical connector.
6. Remove the wheel speed sensor (WSS) mounting bolt.

※※ WARNING

Carefully remove the sensor by pulling it straight out of the bore. DO NOT use a screwdriver, or other device to pry the sensor out of the bore. Prying will cause the sensor body to break off in the bore.

7. Remove the wheel speed sensor from the hub/bearing assembly.

To install:

8. Plug the WSS bore to prevent debris from falling into the hub.
9. Using a wire brush or equivalent,

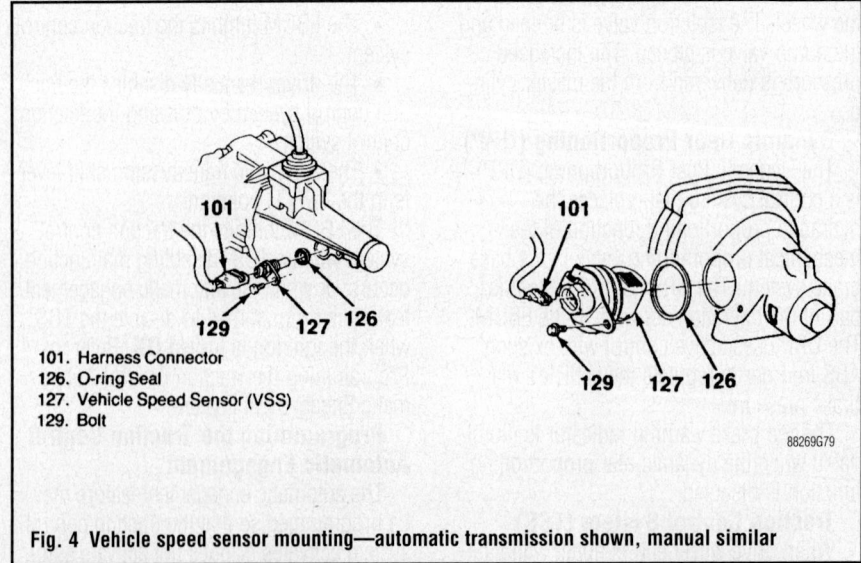

101. Harness Connector
126. O-ring Seal
127. Vehicle Speed Sensor (VSS)
129. Bolt

88269G79

Fig. 4 Vehicle speed sensor mounting—automatic transmission shown, manual similar

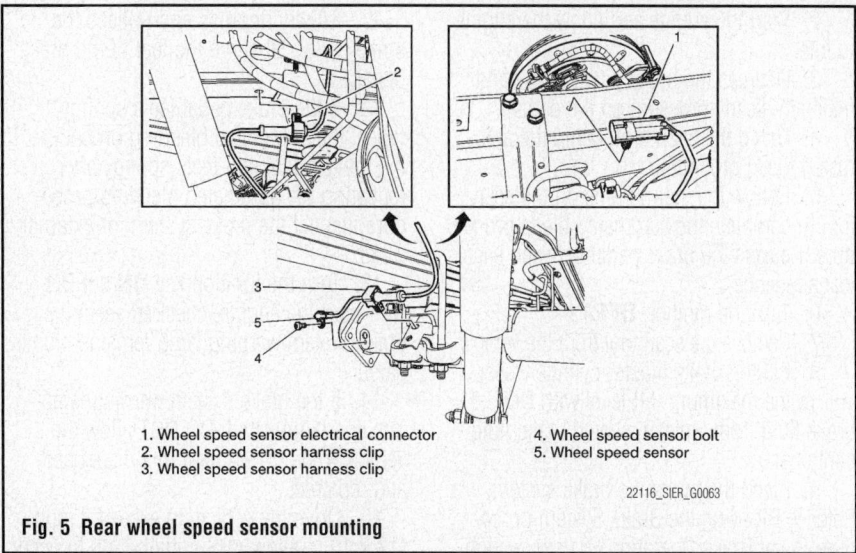

1. Wheel speed sensor electrical connector
2. Wheel speed sensor harness clip
3. Wheel speed sensor harness clip
4. Wheel speed sensor bolt
5. Wheel speed sensor

22116_SIER_G0063

Fig. 5 Rear wheel speed sensor mounting

clean the WSS mounting surface on the hub to remove any rust or corrosion.

10. Apply a thin layer of wheel bearing lubricant to the hub surface and the sensor O–ring prior to sensor installation.

11. Install the WSS. Ensure that the sensor is seated flat against the hub.

12. Install the WSS mounting bolt.

a. Tighten the WSS mounting bolt to 80 inch lbs. (9 Nm).

13. Install the WSS cable mounting clip to the frame attachment point.

14. Connect the WSS cable electrical connector.

15. Install the brake rotor.

16. Install the tire and wheel.

17. Using a scan tool, perform the Diagnostic System Check – ABS

BRAKES | BLEEDING THE BRAKE SYSTEM

BLEEDING PROCEDURE

BLEEDING PROCEDURE

Except Hydro–Boost or ABS

The brake system must be bled when any brake line is disconnected or there is air in the system.

➡**Never bleed a wheel cylinder when a drum is removed.**

1. Clean the master cylinder of excess dirt and remove the cylinder cover and the diaphragm.

2. Fill the master cylinder to the proper level. Check the fluid level periodically during the bleeding process and replenish it as necessary. Do not allow the master cylinder to run dry, or you will have to start over.

3. Before opening any of the bleeder screws, you may want to give each one a shot of penetrating solvent. This reduces the possibility of breakage when they are unscrewed.

4. Attach a length of vinyl hose to the bleeder screw of the brake to be bled. Insert the other end of the hose into a clear jar half full of clean brake fluid, so that the end of the hose is beneath the level of fluid. The correct sequence for bleeding is to work from the brake farthest from the master cylinder to the one closest; right rear, left rear, right front, left front.

5. Depress and release the brake pedal three or four times to exhaust any residual vacuum.

6. Have an assistant push down on the brake pedal and hold it down. Open the bleeder valve slightly. As the pedal reaches the end of its travel, close the bleeder screw and release the brake pedal. Repeat this process until no air bubbles are visible in the expelled fluid.

➡**Make sure your assistant presses the brake pedal to the floor slowly. Pressing too fast will cause air bubbles to form in the fluid.**

7. Repeat this procedure at each of the brakes. Remember to check the master cylinder level occasionally. Use only fresh fluid to refill the master cylinder, not the stuff bled from the system.

8. When the bleeding process is complete, refill the master cylinder, install its cover and diaphragm, and discard the fluid bled from the brake system.

Hydro–Boost

The system should be bled whenever the booster is removed and installed.

1. Fill the power steering pump until the fluid level is at the base of the pump reservoir neck. Disconnect the battery lead from the distributor.

➡**Remove the electrical lead to the fuel solenoid terminal on the injection pump before cranking the engine.**

2. Jack up the front of the car, turn the wheels all the way to the left, and crank the engine for a few seconds.

3. Check steering pump fluid level. If necessary, add fluid to the "ADD" mark on the dipstick.

4. Lower the car, connect the battery lead, and start the engine. Check fluid level and add fluid to the "ADD" mark, as necessary. With the engine running, turn the wheels from side to side to bleed air from the system. Make sure that the fluid level stays above the internal pump casting.

5. The Hydro–Boost system should now be fully bled. If the fluid is foaming after bleeding, stop the engine, let the system set for one hour, then repeat the second part of Step 4.

The preceding procedures should be effective in removing the excess air from the system, however sometimes air may still remain trapped. When this happens the booster may make a gulping noise when the brake is applied. Lightly pumping the brake pedal with the engine running should cause this noise to disappear. After the noise stops, check the pump fluid level and add as necessary.

ABS

To bleed the brakes on a vehicle equipped with ABS, please refer to the ABS bleeding procedure in this section.

BLEEDING THE ABS SYSTEM

✳✳ WARNING

When adding fluid to the brake master cylinder reservoir, use only DOT–3 brake fluid from a clean, sealed brake fluid container. The use of any type of fluid other than the recommended type of brake fluid, may cause contamination which could result in damage to the internal rubber seals and/or rubber linings of hydraulic brake system components.

✷✷ WARNING

Avoid spilling brake fluid onto painted surfaces, electrical connections, wiring, or cables. Brake fluid will damage painted surfaces and cause corrosion to electrical components. If any brake fluid comes in contact with painted surfaces, immediately flush the area with water. If any brake fluid comes in contact with electrical connections, wiring, or cables, use a clean shop cloth to wipe away the fluid.

➡The base hydraulic brake system must be bled before performing this automated bleeding procedure. Refer to Bleeding the Brake System procedure in the Brake Operating System section of this manual before proceeding.

1. Connect a scan tool to the vehicle's Data Link Connector (DLC).

2. Start the engine and allow the engine to idle.

3. Depress the brake pedal firmly and maintain steady pressure on the pedal.

4. Using the scan tool, begin the automated bleed procedure.

5. Follow the instructions on the scan tool to complete the automated bleed procedure. Release the brake pedal between each test sequence.

6. Turn the ignition OFF.

7. Remove the scan tool from the vehicle.

8. Fill the brake master cylinder reservoir to the maximum–fill level with DOT–3 brake fluid from a clean, sealed brake fluid container.

9. Bleed the hydraulic brake system. Refer to Bleeding the Brake System procedure in the Brake Operating System section of this manual.

10. With the ignition OFF, apply the brakes 3–5 times, or until the brake pedal becomes firm, in order to deplete the brake booster power reserve.

11. Slowly depress and release the brake pedal. Observe the feel of the brake pedal.

12. If the brake pedal feels spongy, repeat the automated bleeding procedure. If the brake pedal still feels spongy after repeating the automated bleeding procedure inspect the brake system for external leaks.

13. Turn the ignition key ON but DO NOT start the engine; check to see if the brake system warning lamp remains illuminated.

14. If the brake system warning lamp remains illuminated, DO NOT allow the vehicle to be driven until it is diagnosed and repaired.

15. Drive the vehicle to exceed 8 mph (13 kph) to allow ABS initialization to occur. Observe brake pedal feel.

16. If the brake pedal feels spongy, repeat the automated bleeding procedure until a firm brake pedal is obtained.

BRAKES

✷✷ CAUTION

Dust and dirt accumulating on brake parts during normal use may contain asbestos fibers from production or aftermarket brake linings. Breathing excessive concentrations of asbestos fibers can cause serious bodily harm. Exercise care when servicing brake parts. Do not sand or grind brake lining unless equipment used is designed to contain the dust residue. Do not clean brake parts with compressed air or by dry brushing. Cleaning should be done by dampening the brake components with a fine mist of water, then wiping the brake components clean with a dampened cloth. Dispose of cloth and all residue containing asbestos fibers in an impermeable container with the appropriate label. Follow practices prescribed by the Occupational Safety and Health Administration (OSHA) and the Environmental Protection Agency (EPA) for the handling, processing, and disposing of dust or debris that may contain asbestos fibers.

BRAKE CALIPER

REMOVAL & INSTALLATION

See Figures 6 through 8.

1. Remove or disconnect the following:
   • ⅔ of the brake fluid from the master cylinder
   • Tire and wheel assembly
2. Using a C–clamp or the equivalent, compress the caliper piston until the caliper piston bottoms in the bore.
   • Brake hose at caliper by removing the inlet fitting bolt. Plug the line.
   • Caliper mounting bolts
   • Caliper
3. Inspect the caliper assembly.

FRONT DISC BRAKES

To install:

4. Install or connect the following:
   • Caliper. Tighten the caliper guide pin bolts to 74 ft. lbs. (100 Nm) on 1500 series or 80 ft. lbs. (108 Nm) on 2500/3500 series.
   • Brake hose at caliper by installing the inlet fitting bolt. Tighten the inlet fitting bolt to 30 ft. lbs. (40 Nm).
5. Bleed the brakes.
   • Tire and wheel assembly

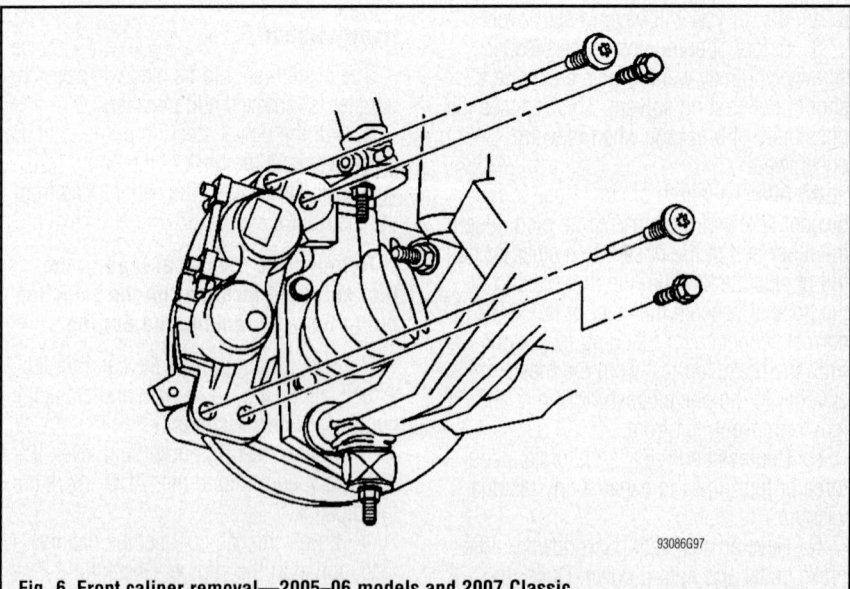

93086G97

Fig. 6 Front caliper removal—2005–06 models and 2007 Classic

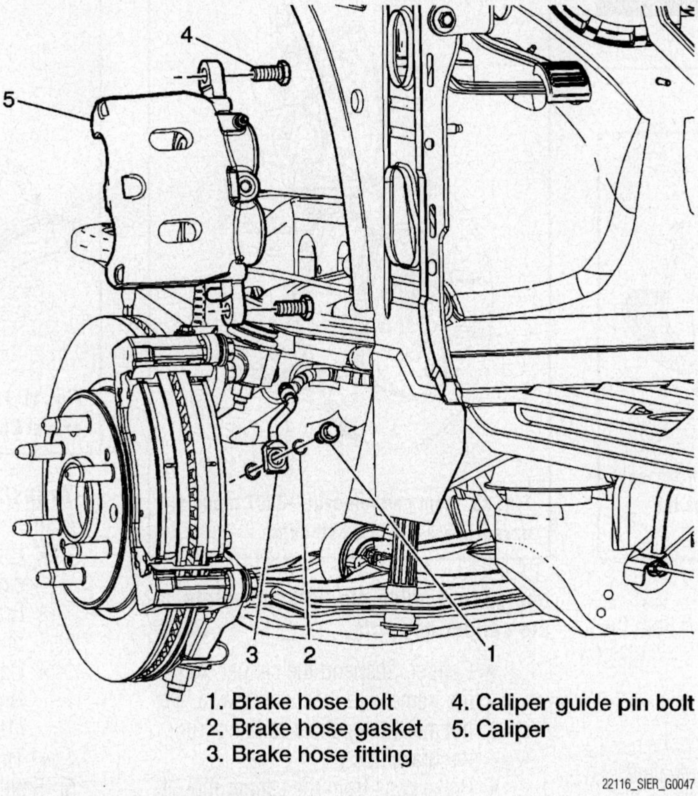

1. Brake hose bolt
2. Brake hose gasket
3. Brake hose fitting
4. Caliper guide pin bolt
5. Caliper

22116_SIER_G0047

Fig. 7 Front caliper removal—2007 models, except Classic with 6 bolt hubs

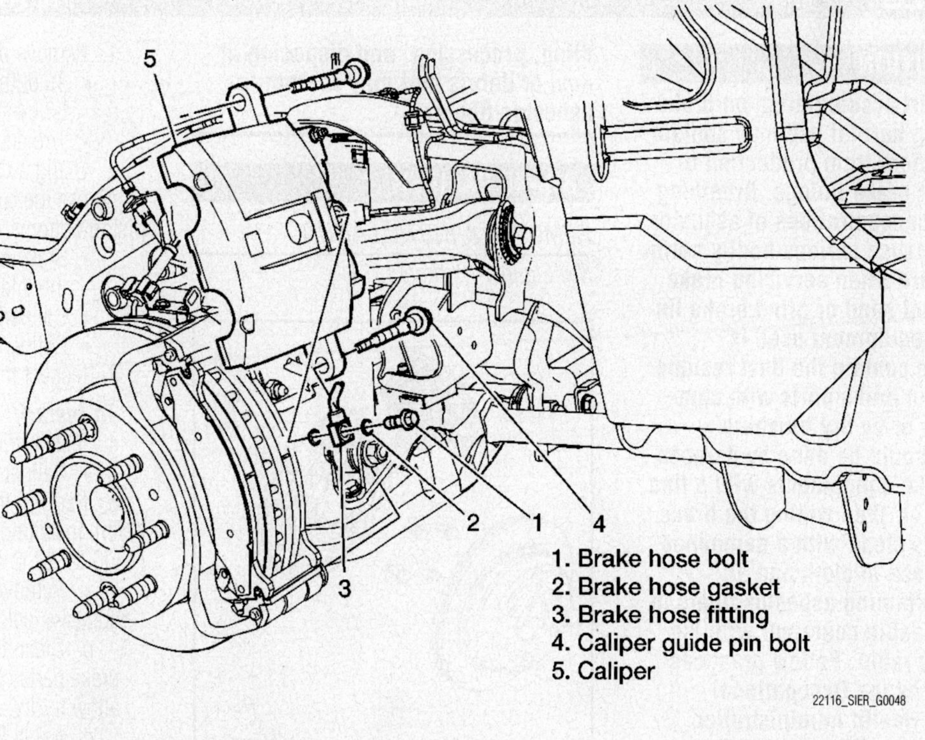

1. Brake hose bolt
2. Brake hose gasket
3. Brake hose fitting
4. Caliper guide pin bolt
5. Caliper

22116_SIER_G0048

Fig. 8 Front caliper removal—2007 models, except Classic with 8 bolt hubs

DISC BRAKE PADS

REMOVAL & INSTALLATION

See Figures 9 through 11.

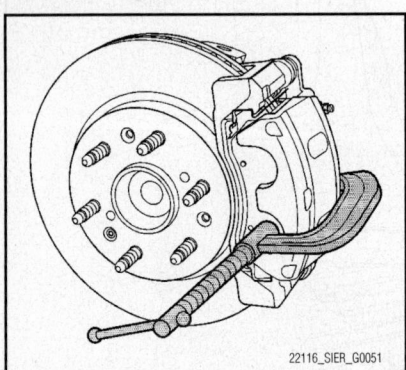

Fig. 9 Use a C–clamp to compress the piston in its bore

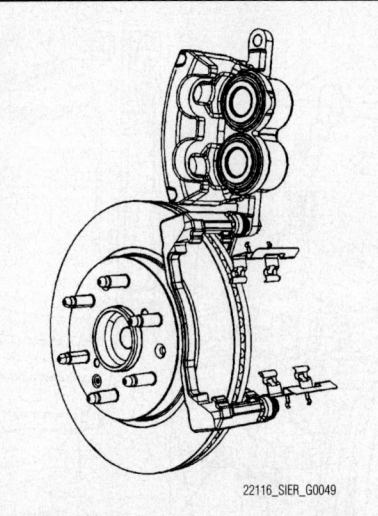

Fig. 10 Front pad removal—2007 models, except Classic with 6 bolt hubs

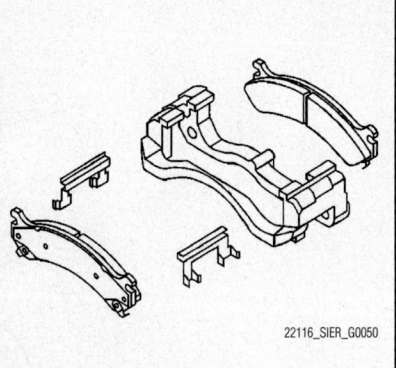

Fig. 11 Front pad removal—2007 models, except Classic with 8 bolt hubs

1. Remove ⅔ of the brake fluid from the master cylinder.
2. Remove or disconnect the following:
   • Wheel
3. Using a C–clamp or the equivalent, compress the caliper piston until the caliper piston bottoms in the bore.

➡On most models, complete removal of the caliper is not necessary. Remove one caliper guide pin bolt and rotate the caliper upwards.

   • Caliper. Suspend the caliper from the frame with mechanic's wire. Do not allow the caliper to hang from the brake hose.
   • Brake pads from the caliper mounting bracket
   • Clips from the inside ends of the caliper mounting bracket and discard

To install:

4. Install or connect the following:
   • Clips to the inside ends of the caliper mounting bracket
   • Brake pads to the caliper mounting bracket
   • Caliper. Tighten to 74 ft. lbs. (100 Nm) on 6 bolt hubs or 80 ft. lbs. (108 Nm) on 8 bolt hubs.
   • Tire and wheel assembly
5. Refill the master cylinder to the proper level with fresh brake fluid. Pump the brake pedal slowly and firmly in order to seat the brake pads. Burnish the brakes as needed.

BRAKES

✳✳ CAUTION

Dust and dirt accumulating on brake parts during normal use may contain asbestos fibers from production or aftermarket brake linings. Breathing excessive concentrations of asbestos fibers can cause serious bodily harm. Exercise care when servicing brake parts. Do not sand or grind brake lining unless equipment used is designed to contain the dust residue. Do not clean brake parts with compressed air or by dry brushing. Cleaning should be done by dampening the brake components with a fine mist of water, then wiping the brake components clean with a dampened cloth. Dispose of cloth and all residue containing asbestos fibers in an impermeable container with the appropriate label. Follow practices prescribed by the Occupational Safety and Health Administration (OSHA) and the Environmental Protection Agency (EPA) for the handling, processing, and disposing of dust or debris that may contain asbestos fibers.

BRAKE CALIPER

REMOVAL & INSTALLATION

See Figures 12 through 14.

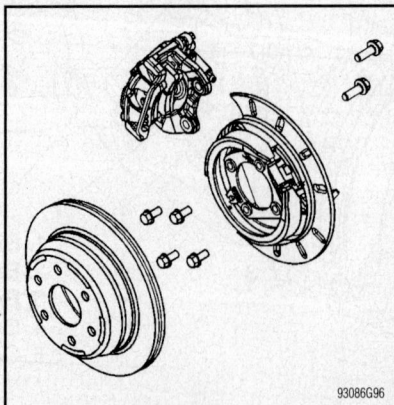

Fig. 12 Rear caliper removal—2005–06 models and 2007 Classic

REAR DISC BRAKES

1. Remove or disconnect the following:
   • ⅔ of the brake fluid from the master cylinder
   • Tire and wheel assembly
2. Using a C–clamp or the equivalent, compress the caliper piston until the caliper piston bottoms in the bore.
   • Brake hose at caliper by removing the inlet fitting bolt. Plug the line.
   • Caliper mounting bolts
   • Caliper
3. Inspect the caliper assembly.

To install:

4. Install or connect the following:
   • Caliper
5. Perform the following procedure before installing the caliper guide pin bolts (1500 series only).
   a. Remove all traces of the original adhesive patch.
   b. Clean the threads of the bolt with brake parts cleaner or the equivalent and allow to dry.
   c. Apply Red Loctite® #272 to the threads of the bolt.
6. Install or connect the following:

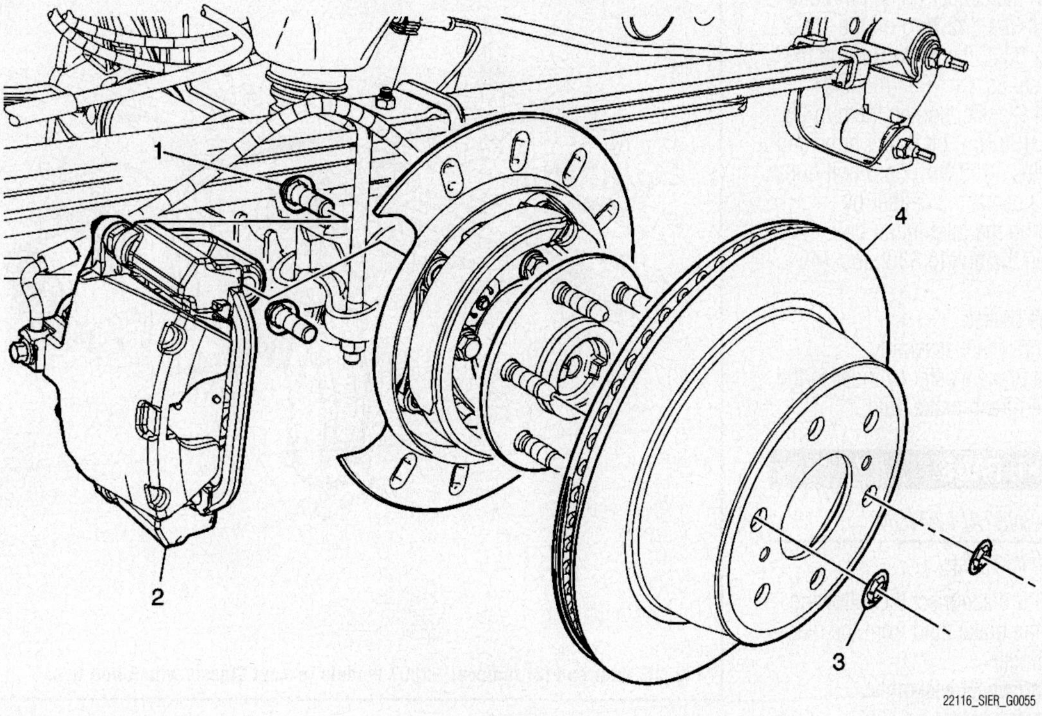
1
2
3
4
22116_SIER_G0055

Fig. 13 Rear caliper (2) removal—2007 models, except Classic with 6 bolt hubs

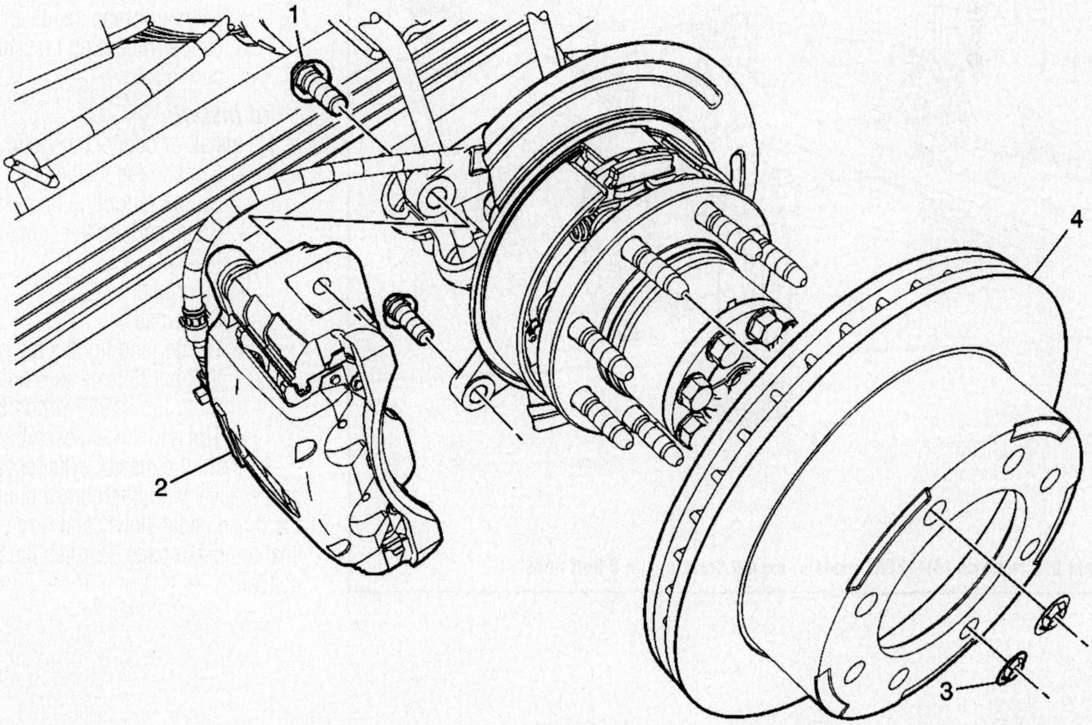
1
2
3
4
22116_SIER_G0056

Fig. 14 Rear caliper (2) removal—2007 models, except Classic with 8 bolt hubs

- Caliper mounting bolts. On 2005–06 models and 2007 Classic, tighten the caliper guide pin bolts to 31 ft. lbs. (42 Nm) on the 1500 series; 80 ft. lbs. (108 Nm) on the 2500 series. On 2007 models except Classic, tighten them to 28 ft. lbs. (38 Nm) on 6 bolt hubs and 80 ft. lbs. (108 Nm) on 8 bolt hubs.
- Brake hose at the caliper by installing the inlet fitting bolt. Tighten the bolt to 33 ft. lbs. (45 Nm).

7. Bleed the brakes.
   - Tire and wheel assembly
8. Refill the brake master cylinder to the proper level with fresh brake fluid.

DISC BRAKE PADS

REMOVAL & INSTALLATION

See Figures 15 and 16.

1. Remove or disconnect the following:
   - ⅔ of the brake fluid from the master cylinder
   - Tire and wheel assembly

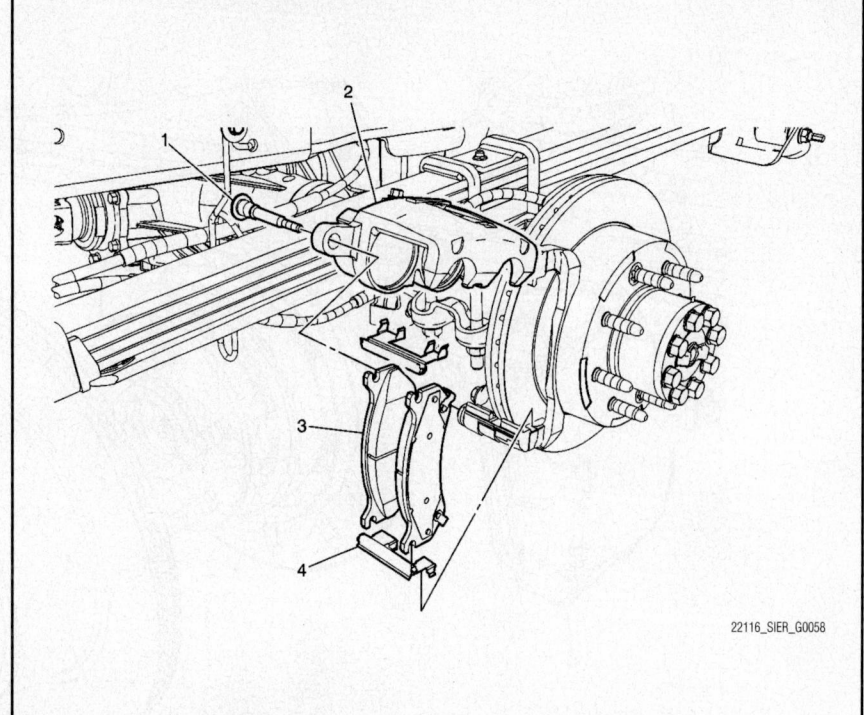

22116_SIER_G0058

Fig. 16 Rear pad (3) removal—2007 models, except Classic with 8 bolt hubs

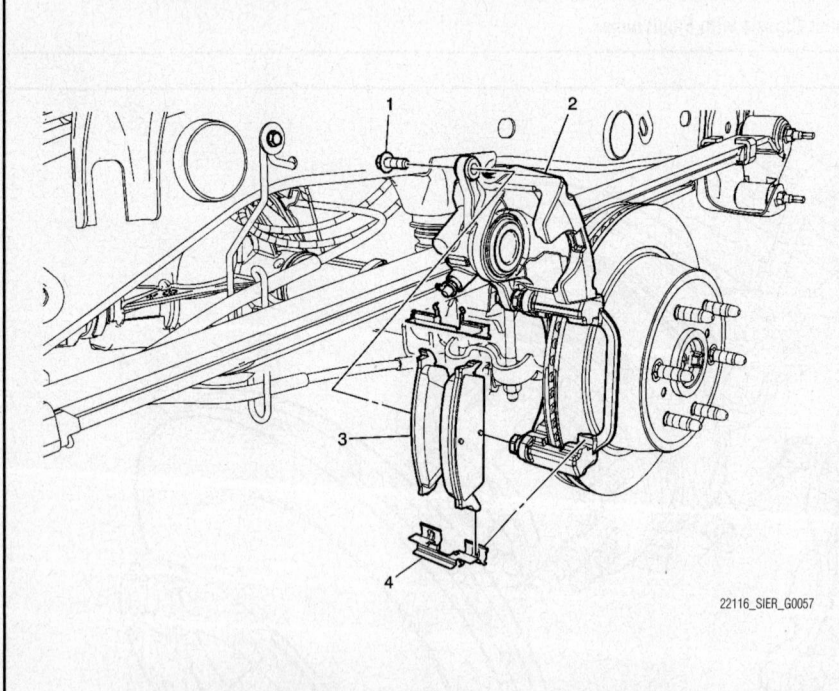

22116_SIER_G0057

Fig. 15 Rear pad removal (3)—2007 models, except Classic with 6 bolt hubs

- Caliper. Suspend the caliper from the frame with mechanic's wire. Do not allow the caliper to hang from the brake hose.
- Brake pads from the caliper mounting bracket
- Clips from the inside ends of the caliper mounting bracket and discard

To install:

2. Install or connect the following:
   - Clips to the inside ends of the caliper mounting bracket
   - Brake pads to the caliper mounting bracket
   - Inner pad
   - Outer pad
   - Caliper and tighten the bolts to 28 ft. lbs. (38 Nm) on 6 bolt hubs or 80 ft. lbs. (108 Nm) on 8 bolt hubs.
   - Tire and wheel assembly
3. Refill the master cylinder to the proper level with fresh brake fluid. Pump the brake pedal slowly and firmly in order to seat the brake pads. Burnish the brakes as needed.

BRAKES   **REAR DRUM BRAKES**

✳✳ CAUTION

Dust and dirt accumulating on brake parts during normal use may contain asbestos fibers from production or aftermarket brake linings. Breathing excessive concentrations of asbestos fibers can cause serious bodily harm. Exercise care when servicing brake parts. Do not sand or grind brake lining unless equipment used is designed to contain the dust residue. Do not clean brake parts with compressed air or by dry brushing. Cleaning should be done by dampening the brake components with a fine mist of water, then wiping the brake components clean with a dampened cloth. Dispose of cloth and all residue containing asbestos fibers in an impermeable container with the appropriate label. Follow practices prescribed by the Occupational Safety and Health Administration (OSHA) and the Environmental Protection Agency (EPA) for the handling, processing, and disposing of dust or debris that may contain asbestos fibers.

BRAKE DRUM

REMOVAL & INSTALLATION

With Semi–Floating Axles

See Figure 17.

1. Raise and support the vehicle safely.
2. Mark the relationship of the wheel to the hub and remove the wheel.
3. Mark the relationship of the drum to the hub and pull the drum from the brake assembly. If the brake drums have been scored from worn linings, the brake adjuster

must be backed off so the brake shoes will retract from the drum. The adjuster can be backed off by inserting a brake adjusting tool through the access hole provided. In some cases the access hole is provided in the brake drum. A metal cover plate is over the hole. This may be removed by using a hammer and chisel.

To install:

4. Align the mark on the drum to mark on hub and install drum
5. Align the mark on the wheel to mark on drum and install wheel
6. Adjust brake lining as needed. Pump brakes

With Full Floating Axles

To remove the drums from full floating rear axles, the axle shaft will have to be removed. Full–floating rear axles can be identified by a bearing housing that protrudes through the center of the wheel.

1. Remove or disconnect the following:
   • Wheel
   • Axle shaft
   • Retaining ring, key and adjusting nut
   • Hub and drum

To install:

2. Install or connect the following:

• Hub and drum to the tube
• Adjusting nut
• Key and retaining ring
• Axle shaft and wheel

BRAKE SHOES

REMOVAL & INSTALLATION

See Figure 18.

1. Remove or disconnect the following:
   • Tire and wheel assembly
   • Brake drums
2. Using denatured alcohol, clean the rear brake shoes.
3. Adjust the brake shoes to the lowest position. This will reduce the tension on the retractor spring.
4. Remove the adjuster spring.
5. Remove the brake adjuster lever.
6. Remove the adjuster assembly.
7. Using a pair of channel locks, remove the retractor spring from the secondary brake shoe.
8. Remove the secondary brake shoe from the backing plate.
9. Using a pair of channel locks, remove the retractor spring from the primary brake shoe.
10. Remove the primary brake shoe from the backing plate.

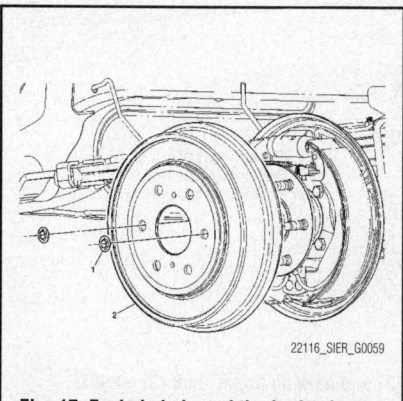

Fig. 17 Exploded view of the brake drum

22116_SIER_G0059

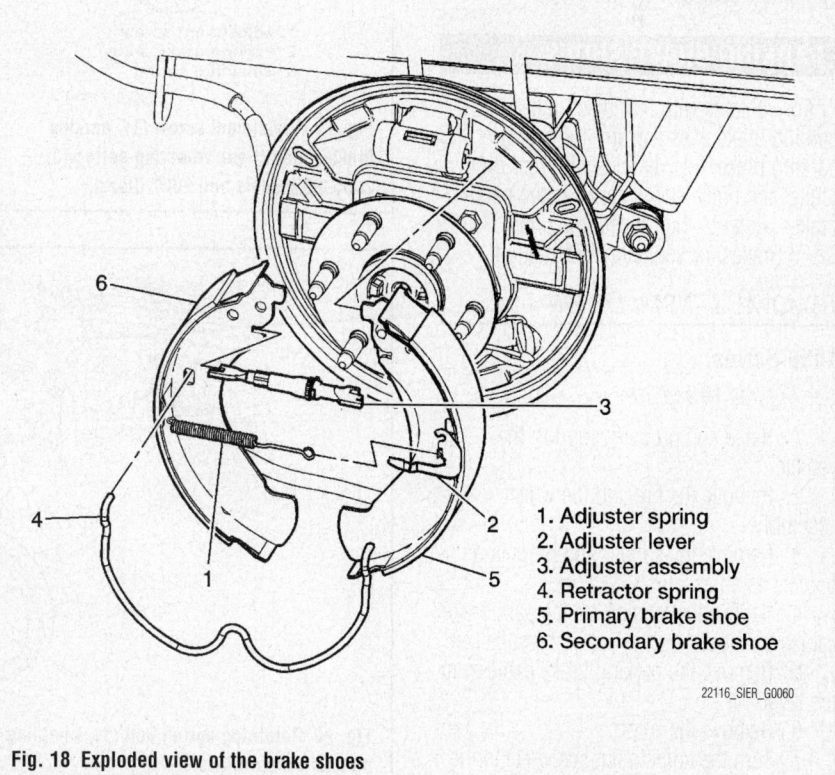

1. Adjuster spring
2. Adjuster lever
3. Adjuster assembly
4. Retractor spring
5. Primary brake shoe
6. Secondary brake shoe

22116_SIER_G0060

Fig. 18 Exploded view of the brake shoes

11. Remove the return spring.

12. Using a small flat–blade screwdriver, press the lock tab for the park brake cable.

13. Hold the lock tab in place.

14. Pushing forward on the park brake cable will unlock the cable from the retainer allowing the cable to be removed from the park brake lever.

15. Push the park brake cable forward.

16. Remove the park brake cable from the lever.

To install:

17. Apply a small amount of high temperature silicone grease or equivalent to the contact areas between the rear brake shoes and the backing plate.

18. Install the park brake cable in the lever. A snap or clip should be felt or heard. This will indicate that the park brake cable is properly in seated in the lever.

19. Install the retractor spring on the backing plate.

20. Using a pair of channel locks, install the retractor spring in the primary brake shoe.

21. Install the secondary brake shoe on the backing plate.

22. Using channel locks, install the retractor spring in the secondary brake shoe.

23. Install the adjuster spring.

24. Install the brake adjuster lever.

25. Install the adjuster assembly.

26. Adjust the rear brake shoes.

27. Install the rear brake drum.

ADJUSTMENT

1. Raise the vehicle and support it with jack stands.

2. Remove the adjusting hole cover from the rear of the backing plate.

3. Insert a brake adjustment tool into the adjusting hole and turn the starwheel on the adjusting screw while turning the wheel by hand. Keep turning the starwheel until the wheel can just be turned by hand.

4. On vehicles equipped with duo–servo drum brakes, back off the adjusting screw 33 times.

5. On vehicles equipped with leading/trailing drum brakes, back off the adjusting screw 20 times.

6. Perform this procedure at both wheels.

7. Install the adjusting hole cover and check the parking brake adjustment.

8. Lower the vehicle.

9. Make the final adjustment by driving the vehicle very slowly in reverse and pumping the brakes until the self–adjusting mechanisms adjust to the proper level and the brake pedal reaches satisfactory height.

10. Road test the vehicle.

BRAKES   PARKING BRAKE

PARKING BRAKE CABLES

ADJUSTMENT

The parking brake pedals are equipped with automatic adjusters. The Park Brake Cable Equalizer evenly distributes input force to both the left and right park brake units and the threaded park brake cable equalizers are also used to remove slack in park brake cables

PARKING BRAKE SHOES

For vehicles with rear disc brakes the parking brake uses a drum–in–hat style parking brake. For vehicles with rear drum brakes the brake shoes serve as the parking brakes. Refer to the procedures under Rear Drum Brakes for servicing information.

REMOVAL & INSTALLATION

1500 Series

See Figures 19 and 20.

1. Raise and properly support the vehicle.

2. Remove the tire and the wheel assembly.

3. Remove the caliper and mounting bracket as an assembly.

4. Relieve the tension on the park brake cables by loosening the nut at the equalizer.

5. Remove the parking brake cable from the lever.

6. Remove the rotor.

7. Turn the adjustment screw (1) to the

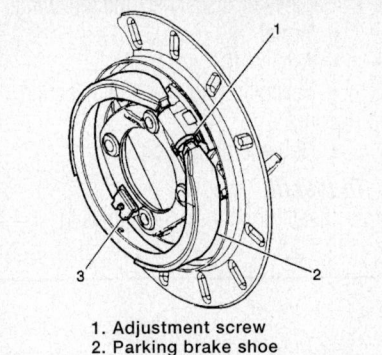

1. Adjustment screw
2. Parking brake shoe
3. Retaining spring

32085_SILV_G0067

Fig. 19 Adjustment screw (1), parking brake shoe (2) and retaining spring (3)—2005–06 models and 2007 Classic

fully home position in the notched adjustment nut.

8. Remove the park brake shoe assembly from the backing plate by removing the tips from the slots and sliding the shoe (2) towards the retaining spring (3) until the shoe is disengaged from the spring.

9. Remove the park brake shoe assembly from the vehicle by placing one of the open ends of the shoe over the axle flange and rotating the shoe until it has cleared the flange.

To install:

10. Clean the debris and the dust from the park brake components using a clean towel.

11. Align the slots in both the adjusting

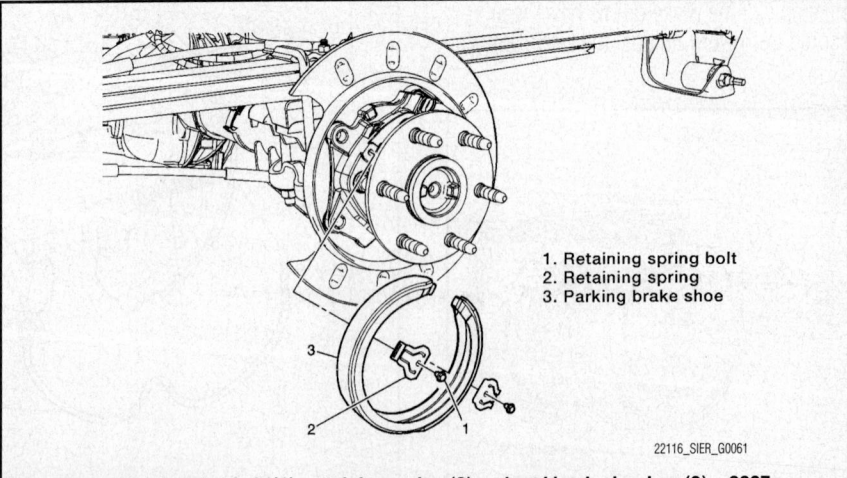

1. Retaining spring bolt
2. Retaining spring
3. Parking brake shoe

22116_SIER_G0061

Fig. 20 Retaining spring bolt (1), retaining spring (2) and parking brake shoe (3)—2007 models except Classic

screw and tappet to be parallel with the backing plate face.

12. Install the park brake shoe assembly (2) to the vehicle by placing one of the open ends of the shoe over the axle flange and rotating the shoe until it is behind the flange.

13. Position the park brake shoe on the inboard side of the actuation.

14. Slide the parking brake shoe into position and seat into the retaining spring.

15. Inspect the shoe assembly position. The shoe must be central on the backing plate with both tips located in the slots.

16. Adjust the park brake shoe.

17. Install the rotor.

18. Install the park brake cable to the park brake lever.

19. Tighten the nut to the intermediate cable at the equalizer.

   a. Tighten the nut to 31 inch lbs. (3.5 Nm).

20. Install the caliper and mounting bracket as an assembly.

21. Install the tire and wheel assembly.

22. Remove the safety stands.

23. Lower the vehicle.

24. Adjust parking brake cable

1500HD, 2500 and 3500 Series

See Figures 21 through 23.

1. For the 1500HD, relieve the tension from the park brake cable by pulling down on the park brake cable in front of the equalizer then removing the cable from the equalizer bar.

2. For the 2500/3500 series, disable the park brake cable automatic adjuster.

3. Raise and safely support the vehicle.

4. Remove the tire and the wheel.

5. Perform the following procedure to remove the cable from the backing plate:

   a. Compress the spring by pushing toward the lever.

   b. Depress the locking tabs.

   c. Pull the cable housing out of the backing plate.

   d. Remove the cable through the slot in the backing plate.

6. Remove the park brake cable from the lever.

7. Remove the rotor.

8. Remove the rear axle shaft.

9. Remove the park brake shoe return spring.

10. Remove the park brake shoe anchor springs and pins.

11. Separate the tips of the shoes from the park brake actuator and remove the park brake shoes and adjuster assembly from the vehicle.

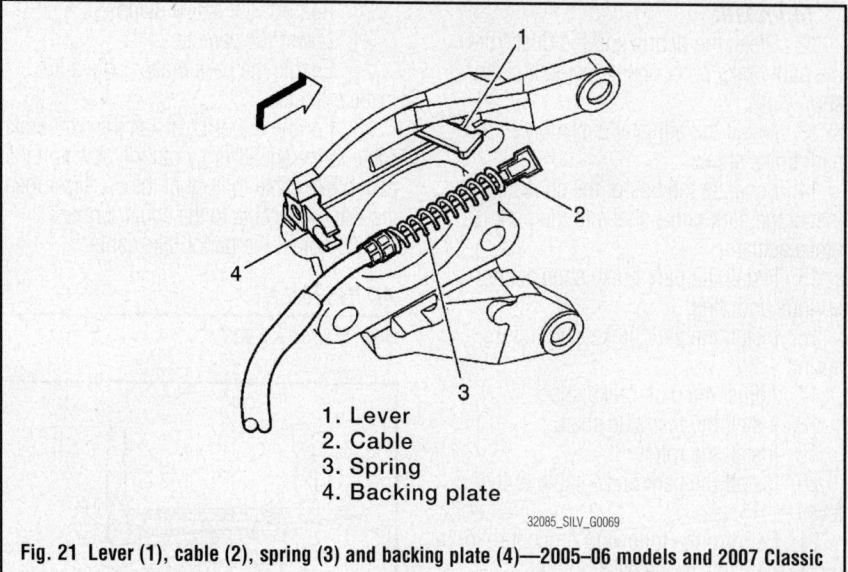

1. Lever
2. Cable
3. Spring
4. Backing plate

32085_SILV_G0069

Fig. 21 Lever (1), cable (2), spring (3) and backing plate (4)—2005–06 models and 2007 Classic

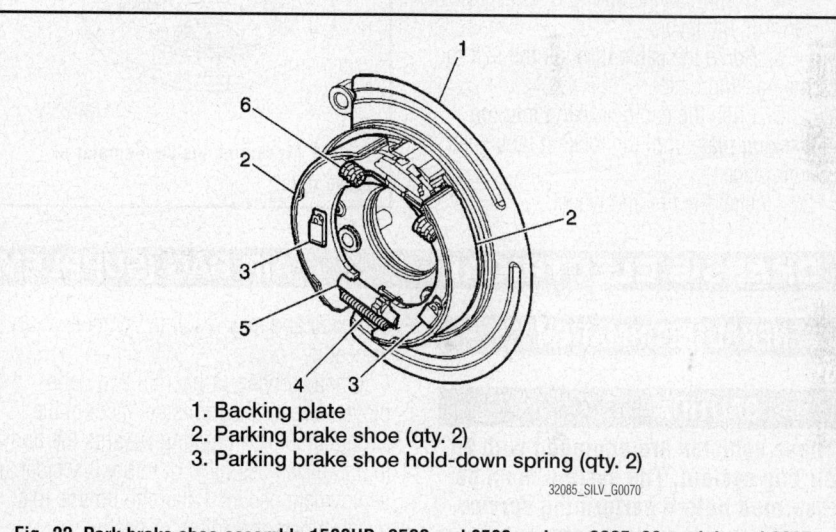

1. Backing plate
2. Parking brake shoe (qty. 2)
3. Parking brake shoe hold-down spring (qty. 2)

32085_SILV_G0070

Fig. 22 Park brake shoe assembly 1500HD, 2500 and 3500 series—2005–06 models and 2007 Classic

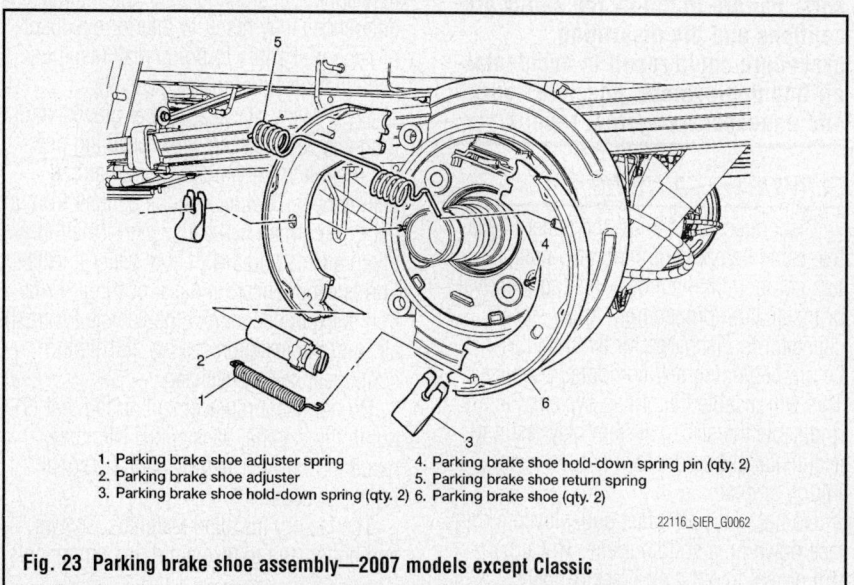

1. Parking brake shoe adjuster spring
2. Parking brake shoe adjuster
3. Parking brake shoe hold-down spring (qty. 2)
4. Parking brake shoe hold-down spring pin (qty. 2)
5. Parking brake shoe return spring
6. Parking brake shoe (qty. 2)

22116_SIER_G0062

Fig. 23 Parking brake shoe assembly—2007 models except Classic

To install:

12. Clean the debris and the dust from the park brake components using a clean shop cloth.

13. Install the adjuster assembly to the park brake shoes.

14. Separate the tips of the shoes and install the park brake shoes to the park brake actuator.

15. Install the park brake shoe anchor springs and pins.

16. Install the park brake shoe return spring.

17. Adjust the park brake shoe.

18. Install the rear axle shaft.

19. Install the rotor.

20. Install the park brake cable to the lever.

21. Perform the following procedure to install the cable to the backing plate:

   a. Compress the spring by pushing towards the lever.

   b. Route the cable through the slot in the backing plate.

   c. Push the cable housing into the backing plate until the locking tabs snap into place.

22. Install the tire and wheel.

23. Remove the safety stands.

24. Lower the vehicle.

25. Enable the park brake cable automatic adjuster.

26. For the 1500HD, install the park brake cable to the equalizer by pulling down on the park brake cable in front of the equalizer then installing the cable to the equalizer bar.

27. Adjust the park brake cable.

ADJUSTMENT

See Figures 24 and 25.

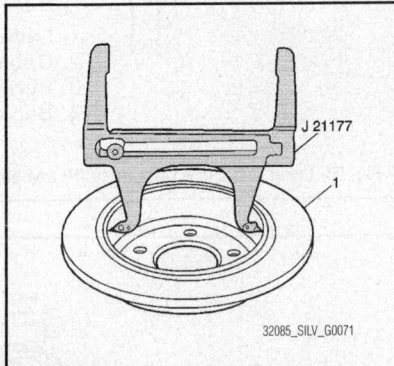

Fig. 24 Measuring inside diameter of brake rotor

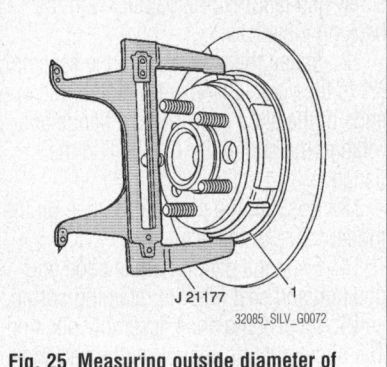

Fig. 25 Measuring outside diameter of brake rotor

1. Set the J 21177–A so that the J 21177–A contacts the inside diameter of the rotor.

2. Position the J 21177–A over the shoe and the lining at the widest point.

3. Turn the adjuster nut until the lining just contacts the J 21177–A.

4. Repeat steps 1 through 3 for the opposite side.

5. The clearance between the park brake shoe and the rotor is 0.026 inch (0.66 mm).

CHASSIS ELECTRICAL   AIR BAG (SUPPLEMENTAL RESTRAINT SYSTEM)

GENERAL INFORMATION

❋❋ CAUTION

These vehicles are equipped with an air bag system. The system must be disarmed before performing service on, or around, system components, the steering column, instrument panel components, wiring and sensors. Failure to follow the safety precautions and the disarming procedure could result in accidental air bag deployment, possible injury and unnecessary system repairs.

SERVICE PRECAUTIONS

Disconnect and isolate the battery negative cable before beginning any airbag system component diagnosis, testing, removal, or installation procedures. Allow system capacitor to discharge for two minutes before beginning any component service. This will disable the airbag system. Failure to disable the airbag system may result in accidental airbag deployment, personal injury, or death.

Do not place an intact undeployed airbag face down on a solid surface. The airbag will propel into the air if accidentally deployed and may result in personal injury or death.

When carrying or handling an undeployed airbag, the trim side (face) of the airbag should be pointing towards the body to minimize possibility of injury if accidental deployment occurs. Failure to do this may result in personal injury or death.

Replace airbag system components with OEM replacement parts. Substitute parts may appear interchangeable, but internal differences may result in inferior occupant protection. Failure to do so may result in occupant personal injury or death.

Wear safety glasses, rubber gloves, and long sleeved clothing when cleaning powder residue from vehicle after an airbag deployment. Powder residue emitted from a deployed airbag can cause skin irritation. Flush affected area with cool water if irritation is experienced. If nasal or throat irritation is experienced, exit the vehicle for fresh air until the irritation ceases. If irritation continues, see a physician.

Do not use a replacement airbag that is not in the original packaging. This may result in improper deployment, personal injury, or death.

The factory installed fasteners, screws and bolts used to fasten airbag components have a special coating and are specifically designed for the airbag system. Do not use substitute fasteners. Use only original equipment fasteners listed in the parts catalog when fastener replacement is required.

During, and following, any child restraint anchor service, due to impact event or vehicle repair, carefully inspect all mounting hardware, tether straps, and anchors for proper installation, operation, or damage. If a child restraint anchor is found damaged in any way, the anchor must be replaced. Failure to do this may result in personal injury or death.

Deployed and non-deployed airbags may or may not have live pyrotechnic material within the airbag inflator.

Do not dispose of driver/passenger/curtain airbags or seat belt tensioners unless you are sure of complete deployment. Refer to the Hazardous Substance Control System for proper disposal.

Dispose of deployed airbags and tensioners consistent with state, provincial, local, and federal regulations.

After any airbag component testing or service, do not connect the battery negative cable. Personal injury or death may result if the system test is not performed first.

If the vehicle is equipped with the Occupant Classification System (OCS), do not connect the battery negative cable before performing the OCS Verification Test using the scan tool and the appropriate diagnostic information. Personal injury or death may result if the system test is not performed properly.

Never replace both the Occupant Restraint Controller (ORC) and the Occupant Classification Module (OCM) at the same time. If both require replacement, replace one, then perform the Airbag System test before replacing the other.

Both the ORC and the OCM store Occupant Classification System (OCS) calibration data, which they transfer to one another when one of them is replaced. If both are replaced at the same time, an irreversible fault will be set in both modules and the OCS may malfunction and cause personal injury or death.

If equipped with OCS, the Seat Weight Sensor is a sensitive, calibrated unit and must be handled carefully. Do not drop or handle roughly. If dropped or damaged, replace with another sensor. Failure to do so may result in occupant injury or death.

If equipped with OCS, the front passenger seat must be handled carefully as well. When removing the seat, be careful when setting on floor not to drop. If dropped, the sensor may be inoperative, could result in occupant injury, or possibly death.

If equipped with OCS, when the passenger front seat is on the floor, no one should sit in the front passenger seat. This uneven force may damage the sensing ability of the seat weight sensors. If sat on and damaged, the sensor may be inoperative, could result in occupant injury, or possibly death.

DISARMING THE SYSTEM

1. Turn the steering wheel so that the vehicles wheels are pointing straight ahead.
2. Turn **OFF** the ignition.
3. Remove the key from the ignition.
4. With the SIR fuse removed and the ignition **ON**, the AIR BAG indicator illuminates. This is normal operation and does not indicate an SIR system malfunction.
5. Remove the SIR fuse from the fuse block.
6. Raise and support the vehicle.
7. Remove the connector position assurance (CPA) from both front end sensor connectors located on the frame crossmember.
8. Disconnect both front end sensor connectors

9. When the fuse is installed, turn **ON** the ignition, with the engine OFF.
10. The AIR BAG indicator will flash 7 times then turn off.
11. Perform the Diagnostic System Check if the AIR BAG indicator does not operate as described.

ARMING THE SYSTEM

1. Reverse the disarming procedure to arm the system.

CLOCKSPRING CENTERING

See Figures 26 and 27.

> ✳✳ **CAUTION**
>
> **The new clock spring assembly will be centered. Improper alignment of**

the clock spring assembly may damage the unit, causing an inflatable restraint malfunction.

➡ **If double wire harness strap is installed onto the wire harness assembly and column, you must reuse the holder for the wire straps during installation. Remove the wire harness strap(s) where necessary.**

1. Verify the following conditions before centering the clock spring:
   a. The wheels on the vehicle are straight ahead.
   b. The block tooth (1) of the steering shaft assembly is in the 12 o'clock position.

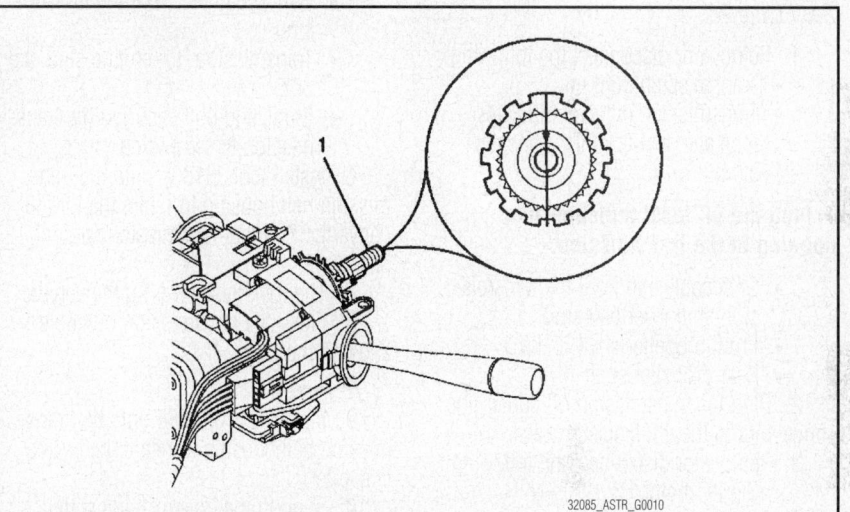

32085_ASTR_G0010

Fig. 26 Make sure the block tooth (1) of the steering shaft assembly is in the 12 o'clock position

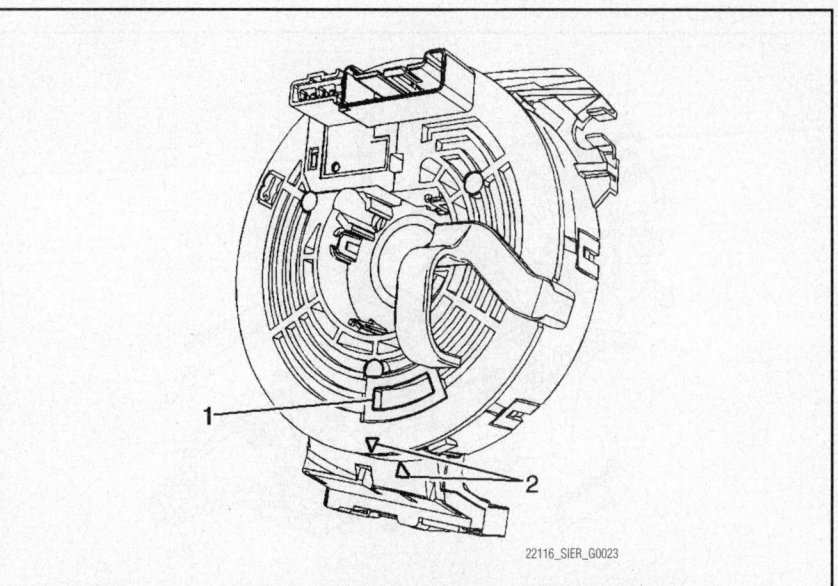

22116_SIER_G0023

Fig. 27 Clock spring assemblies with centering window (3) and without spring service lock

c. The ignition switch is in the **LOCK** position.

d. Hold the Clock spring with the face up.

e. Rotate the coil hub clockwise until the coil ribbon stops.

f. Rotate the coil hub slowly, counter-clockwise until the centering window appears yellow and both arrows (2) line up. This is the CENTER position.

g. While holding the coil hub in the CENTER position, align the clockspring with the horn tower and slide onto the steering shaft assembly.

h. If double wire harness strap is installed onto the wire harness assembly and column, you must route the wires up against the steering column. One wire harness strap will surround one lead from the coil to the steering column. The other wire harness strap will surround all leads to the steering column.

DRIVETRAIN

AUTOMATIC TRANSMISSION ASSEMBLY

REMOVAL & INSTALLATION

4L60E, 4L65E and 4L70E Transmissions

See Figure 28.

1. Remove or disconnect the following:
   - Transmission fluid
   - Transmission oil level indicator tube and seal from the transmission

➡**Plug the oil level indicator tube opening in the transmission.**

   - Shift cable end from the transmission shift lever ball stud
   - Front propeller shaft, if 4WD
   - Rear propeller shaft.

2. Plug the transmission oil cooler line connectors in the transmission case.

3. Remove or disconnect the following:
   - Starter motor

4. Support the transmission with a transmission jack.

5. Remove or disconnect the following:
   - Torque converter access plug
   - Flywheel–to–torque converter bolts
   - Transmission rear mount–to–transmission bolts and nut
   - Heat shield–to–transmission bolts
   - Transmission vent hose from the transmission
   - Fuel lines from the transmission
   - Wiring harness from the transmission
   - Transmission–to–engine stud and bolt
   - Studs and bolt securing the transmission to the engine.

6. Install tool J21366 onto the transmission bell housing to retain the torque converter. Pull the transmission straight back.

7. The transmission from the vehicle

8. Flush the transmission oil cooler and cooling lines.

To install:

9. Install Tool J21366 onto the transmission bell housing to retain the torque converter.

10. Support the transmission with a transmission jack.

11. Raise the transmission into place and remove the tool from the transmission.

12. Slide the transmission straight onto the locating pins while lining up the marks on the flywheel and the torque converter. The torque converter must be flush onto the flywheel and rotate freely by hand.

13. Install or connect the following:
   - Studs and bolt securing the transmission to the engine. Tighten to 37 ft. lbs. (50 Nm).
   - Flywheel to torque converter bolts. Tighten to 46 ft. lbs. (63 Nm) and use Loctite 242 on the threads
   - Torque converter access plug
   - Transmission vent hose to the transmission
   - Fuel lines to the transmission
   - Wiring harness to the transmission.
   - Heat shield–to–transmission bolts and tighten to 13 ft. lbs. (17 Nm)
   - Transmission rear mount–to–transmission bolt and nut and tighten to 18 ft. lbs. (25 Nm)

14. Remove the transmission jack from the transmission.

15. Unplug the transmission oil cooler line connectors in the transmission case.

16. Install or connect the following:
   - Transmission oil cooler lines
   - Front propeller shaft, if equipped
   - Rear propeller shaft
   - Shift cable end to the transmission shift lever ball stud

17. Unplug the oil level indicator tube opening in the transmission.

18. Install the transmission oil level indicator tube and seal to the transmission.

19. Tighten the oil pan bolts and fill the transmission with transmission fluid.

20. Lower the vehicle.

4L80E and 4L85E Transmissions

See Figure 29.

1. Remove or disconnect the following:
   - Transmission fluid
   - Transmission oil level indicator tube and seal from the transmission

2. Plug the oil level indicator tube opening in the transmission.

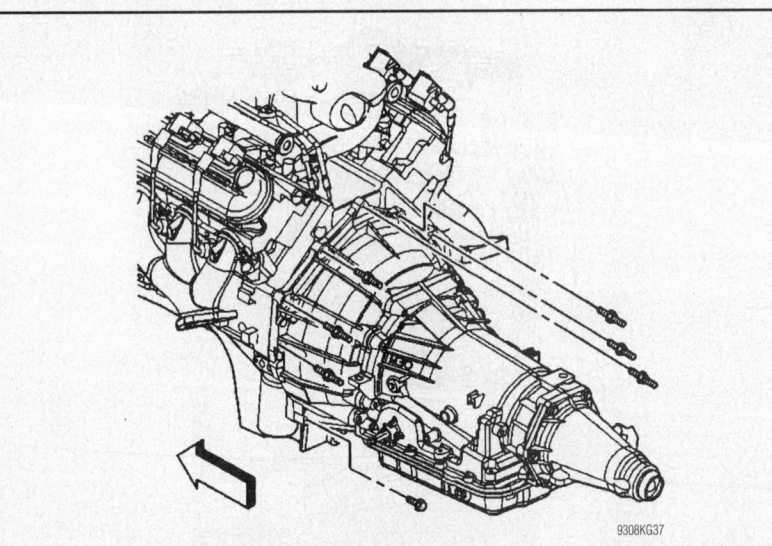

Fig. 28 4L60E removal; 4L65E and 4L70E similar

9308KG37

- Shift cable from the transmission shift lever ball stud
- Front propeller shaft, if 4WD
- Rear propeller shaft.
- Transmission oil cooler lines, then plug thee openings in the transmission case
- Starter motor

3. Support the transmission with a transmission jack.

- Heat shield
- Transmission vent hose
- Fuel lines from the transmission
- Wiring harness from the transmission
- Transmission brace–to–engine bracket and transmission nut and bolt
- Torque converter cover
- Flywheel to torque converter bolts
- Transmission rear mount
- Stud and bolt on the right side securing the transmission to the engine
- Remaining six studs and the bolt securing the transmission to the engine

4. Install Tool J21366 onto the transmission bell housing to retain the torque converter.

5. Pull the transmission straight back. Remove the transmission from the vehicle.

6. Flush the transmission oil cooler and cooling lines when you remove the transmission.

To install:

7. Install Tool J21366 onto the transmission bell housing to retain the torque converter.

8. Support the transmission with a transmission jack.

9. Raise the transmission into place and remove the tool from the transmission.

10. Slide the transmission straight onto the locating pins while lining up the marks on the flywheel and the torque converter. The torque converter must be flush onto the flywheel and rotate freely by hand.

11. Install or connect the following:

- Six studs and bolt securing the transmission to the engine. Tighten to 37 ft. lbs. (50 Nm).
- Stud and bolt on the right side securing the transmission to the engine. Tighten to 37 ft. lbs. (50 Nm).
- Flywheel–to–torque converter bolts and tighten to 44 ft. lbs. (60 Nm).
- Torque converter cover–to–engine bolts and tighten to 37 ft. lbs. (50 Nm)
- Torque converter cover–to–transmission stud and bolt and tighten to 24 ft. lbs. (33 Nm).
- Transmission vent hose
- Fuel lines
- Wiring harness
- Heat shield. Tighten the bolts to 13 ft. lbs. (17 Nm).
- Transmission rear mount–to–transmission nuts and bolt. Tighten to 18 ft. lbs. (25 Nm).
- Transmission brace. Tighten the bolts and nut to 37 ft. lbs. (50 Nm).

12. Remove the transmission jack from the transmission.

- Starter motor

13. Unplug the transmission oil cooler line connectors in the transmission case.

14. Connect the transmission oil cooler lines to the transmission.

15. Install or connect the following:

- Rear propeller shaft
- Front propeller shaft, if 4WD
- Shift cable end to the transmission shift lever ball stud

16. Unplug the oil level indicator tube opening in the transmission.

17. Install the transmission oil level indicator tube and seal to the transmission.

18. Tighten the oil pan bolts and fill the transmission with transmission fluid.

19. Lower the vehicle.

6L80E and 6L90E Transmissions

See Figure 30.

1. Remove or disconnect the following:

- Transmission fluid
- Transmission oil level indicator tube and seal from the transmission

2. Plug the oil level indicator tube opening in the transmission.

- Shift cable from the transmission shift lever ball stud
- Front propeller shaft, if 4WD
- Rear propeller shaft.
- Transmission oil cooler lines, then plug thee openings in the transmission case
- Starter motor
- Transfer case, if 4WD

3. Support the transmission with a transmission jack.

- Heat shield
- Transmission vent hose
- Fuel lines from the transmission
- Wiring harness from the transmission
- Transmission brace–to–engine bracket and transmission nut and bolt
- Torque converter cover
- Flywheel to torque converter bolts
- Transmission rear mount
- 8 bolts securing the transmission to the engine

4. Install Tool J21366 onto the transmission bell housing to retain the torque converter.

5. Pull the transmission straight back. Remove the transmission from the vehicle.

6. Flush the transmission oil cooler and cooling lines when you remove the transmission.

To install:

7. Install Tool J21366 onto the transmission bell housing to retain the torque converter.

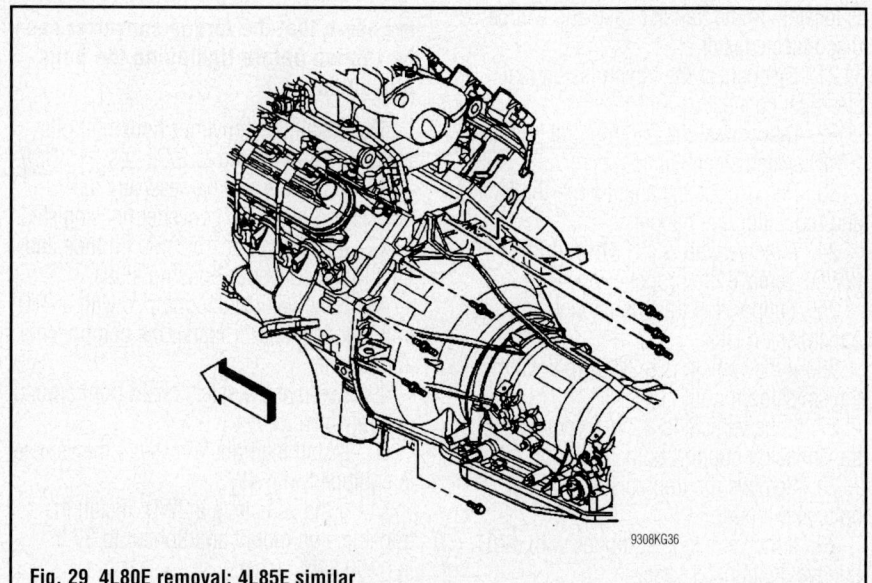

9308KG36

Fig. 29 4L80E removal; 4L85E similar

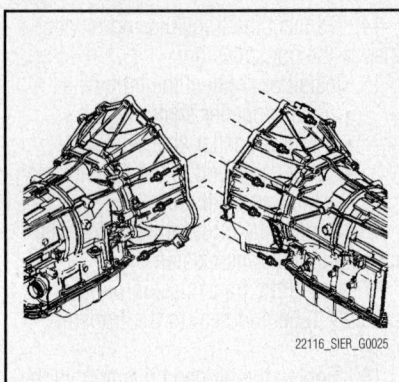

Fig. 30 6L series mounting bolt locations

22116_SIER_G0025

8. Support the transmission with a transmission jack.

9. Raise the transmission into place and remove the tool from the transmission.

10. Slide the transmission straight onto the locating pins while lining up the marks on the flywheel and the torque converter. The torque converter must be flush onto the flywheel and rotate freely by hand.

11. Install or connect the following:
- 8 bolts securing the transmission to the engine. Tighten to 37 ft. lbs. (50 Nm).
- Flywheel–to–torque converter bolts and tighten to 46 ft. lbs. (63 Nm). Use Loctite 242 on the threads
- Transmission vent hose
- Fuel lines
- Wiring harness
- Heat shield.
- Transmission rear mount–to–transmission nuts and bolt.
- Transmission brace.

12. Remove the transmission jack from the transmission.
- Starter motor
- Transfer case, if 4WD

13. Unplug the transmission oil cooler line connectors in the transmission case.

14. Connect the transmission oil cooler lines to the transmission.

15. Install or connect the following:
- Rear propeller shaft
- Front propeller shaft, if 4WD
- Shift cable end to the transmission shift lever ball stud

16. Unplug the oil level indicator tube opening in the transmission.

17. Install the transmission oil level indicator tube and seal to the transmission.

18. Tighten the oil pan bolts and fill the transmission with transmission fluid.

19. Lower the vehicle.

Allison Transmissions

1. Drain the transmission.

2. Disconnect both negative battery cables.

3. Remove the transmission fluid level indicator.

4. Remove the right front wheel and tire.

5. Remove the right front wheel house inner panel retainers.

6. Disconnect any harness retainers attached to the inner panel.

7. Remove the inner panel.

8. Remove the starter.

9. Remove the engine protection shield bolts and shield.

10. Rotate the engine clockwise, using the crankshaft bolt in order to access the torque converter bolts thru the starter opening. Have an assistant rotate the engine while aligning the bolts.

11. Remove the torque converter bolts.

12. Completely raise the vehicle.

13. Disconnect the shift cable from the selector lever ball stud and remove the cable from the bracket.

14. Remove the shift cable bracket bolts and bracket from the transmission.

15. Reposition the bracket with the cable attached off to the side.

16. Remove the fuel line retainer bolts on the left side of the transmission.

17. Remove the fuel line bracket nut from the converter housing stud.

18. Disconnect the turbine speed sensor and input speed sensor electrical connectors.

19. Disconnect the output speed sensor electrical connector.

20. If the vehicle is equipped with 4 wheel drive (4WD), the output speed sensor is located on the transfer case and will be disconnected later.

21. Disconnect the transmission main electrical connector.

22. Disconnect the park/neutral position (PNP) switch electrical connector.

23. Remove the exhaust hanger bolts and reposition the hanger.

24. If the vehicle is a 2 wheel drive (2WD), remove the propeller shaft.

25. Support the transmission with a transmission jack.

26. If the vehicle is a 2WD, remove the transmission mount nuts.

27. If the vehicle is a 2WD, remove the transmission support bolts and nuts.

28. Remove the transmission mount bolts and mount.

29. If the vehicle is equipped with 4WD, remove the transfer case.

30. Reposition any wiring harness branches out of the way.

31. Secure a safety chain around the transmission. Use care not to overlap any wiring, fuel lines, or other related components.

32. Disconnect and plug the transmission oil cooler lines from the transmission.

33. If the vehicle is equipped with a power take off (PTO) unit , disconnect and/or remove any necessary components to facilitate transmission removal.

34. Remove the transmission fill tube nuts from the converter housing studs.

35. Remove the wire harness/vent tube bracket nut from the converter housing stud and reposition the bracket.

36. Remove the remaining converter housing bolts and studs.

37. Separate the transmission from the engine.

38. Install torque converter holding tool J–21366 to the converter housing in order to keep the torque converter from sliding off of the turbine shaft.

39. Carefully lower the transmission from the vehicle while simultaneously removing the fill tube.

40. Remove the holding tool.

To install:

41. Install torque converter holding tool J–21366 to the converter housing in order to keep the torque converter from sliding off of the turbine shaft.

42. Raise the transmission into place while simultaneously installing the transmission fill tube.

43. Remove the holding tool.

44. Align the transmission with the engine using the alignment dowels located at the rear of the engine.

➡**Ensure that the torque converter can be rotated before tightening the bolts and studs.**

45. Install the converter housing bolts and studs and tighten to 37 ft. lbs. (50 Nm).

46. Install the wire harness/vent tube bracket and nut to the converter housing stud.

47. Install the transmission fill tube and nuts to the converter housing studs.

48. If the vehicle is equipped with a PTO unit, connect and/or install the components at this time.

49. Remove the safety chain from around the transmission.

50. Install the transfer case, if the vehicle is equipped with 4WD.

51. If the vehicle is a 2WD, install the transmission mount and tighten to 37 ft. lbs. (50 Nm).

52. Install the transmission support and tighten to 70 ft. lbs. (95 Nm).

53. If the vehicle is a 2WD, install the transmission mount nuts and tighten to 30 ft. lbs. (40 Nm).

54. Remove the transmission jack.

55. If the vehicle is a 2WD, install the propeller shaft.

56. Position the exhaust hanger and install the bolts.

57. Position the wiring harness branches.

58. Connect the PNP switch electrical connectors.

59. Connect the transmission main electrical connector

60. Connect the output speed sensor electrical connector. If the vehicle is equipped with 4WD, the output speed sensor is located on the transfer case and has been connected during the transfer case installation.

61. Connect the turbine speed sensor and the input speed sensor electrical connectors.

62. Install the fuel line bracket and nut to the transmission converter housing stud.

63. Install the fuel line retainer and bolts to the left side of the transmission.

64. Install the shift cable bracket and bolts to the transmission.

65. Install the shift cable to the bracket and the selector lever ball stud.

66. Remove the access hole cover on the converter housing in order to rotate the converter and align the first torque converter bolt. If reusing the torque converter bolts, clean the bolt threads and apply Loctite® or equivalent to the threads prior to installation.

67. Install the torque converter bolts and tighten to 44 ft. lbs. (760 Nm).

68. Install the converter housing access hole cover.

69. Install the engine protection shield and bolts.

70. Position and install the starter.

71. Install the inner panel.

72. Connect any harness retainers to the inner panel.

73. Install the right front wheel house inner panel retainers.

74. Install the right front wheel and tire.

75. Remove the plugs from the transmission oil cooler line fittings in the transmission case, if necessary.

76. Flush the transmission oil cooler and lines, if necessary.

77. Connect the transmission oil cooler lines to the transmission.

78. Lower the vehicle.

79. Connect both negative battery cables.

80. Fill the transmission with new transmission fluid.

81. Install the transmission fluid level indicator.

82. If a replacement transmission was installed, perform the Fast Learn procedure using a scan tool.

MANUAL TRANSMISSION ASSEMBLY

REMOVAL & INSTALLATION

NV3500 Transmissions

See Figure 31.

1. Shift the transmission into 3rd or 4th speed gear.

2. Remove or disconnect the following:
   • Shift lever
   • Shift tower
   • Transmission oil
   • If equipped with a transfer case, remove the front propeller shaft
   • Rear propeller shaft.

3. If equipped with a transfer case, remove or disconnect the following:
   • Two transfer case shields
   • Manual transfer case shift linkage
   • Bolt securing the left side support brace to the transmission
   • Bolt and stud securing the left side support brace to the transfer case
   • Bolt securing the right side support brace to the transmission
   • Bolt securing the right side support brace to the transfer case

4. Using tool J42371, push back on the white plastic sleeve on the quick connect in order to separate the hydraulic clutch line from the concentric slave cylinder quick connect.

5. Disconnect the wiring harness and connectors from the vehicle speed sensor, backup lamp switch, and transmission harness retainers.

6. If equipped with a 4.3L engine, remove the two bolts securing the clutch housing cover. Remove the transmission rear mount. Support the transmission with a transmission jack.

7. Remove or disconnect the following:
   • Bolts securing the bottom right side of the transmission to the engine
   • Stud securing the right side of the transmission to the engine
   • Bolt and six studs securing the transmission to the engine

8. Pull the transmission straight back on the clutch hub splines. Do not let the transmission hang from the clutch plate and the clutch cover.
   • Transmission from the vehicle
   • Clutch plate and the clutch cover from the engine flywheel, if required

To install:

9. Install the clutch plate and the clutch cover to the engine flywheel if removed.

10. Ensure the transmission is positioned in the 3rd or 4th speed gear. Rotate the transmission clockwise onto the clutch hub splines. Install the bolt and the studs securing the transmission to the engine. Tighten the bolts to 37 ft. lbs. (50 Nm).

11. Install or connect the following:
   • Stud securing the right side of the transmission to the engine and tighten to 37 ft. lbs. (50 Nm)
   • Bolts securing the bottom right side of the transmission to the engine and tighten to 37 ft. lbs. (50 Nm)

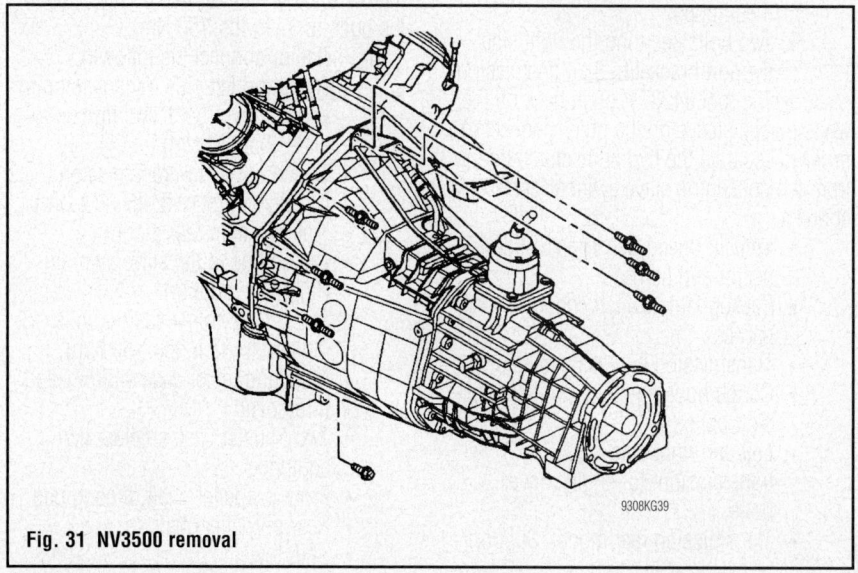

9308KG39

Fig. 31 NV3500 removal

- Clutch housing cover using the two bolts (4.3L engine). Tighten the bolts to 10 ft. lbs. (14 Nm).
- Transmission rear mount
- Clutch line to the concentric slave cylinder

12. If equipped with a transfer case, install or connect the following:
  - Right side support brace–to–transmission bolt and tighten to 37 ft. lbs. (50 Nm)
  - Right side support brace–to–transfer case bolts and tighten to 37 ft. lbs. (50 Nm)
  - Left side support brace–to–transfer case bolt(s) and stud and tighten to 37 ft. lbs. (50 Nm)
  - Left side support brace–to–transmission bolts and tighten to 37 ft. lbs. (50 Nm)
  - Manual transfer case shift linkage.
  - Two transfer case shields
  - Front propeller shaft

13. Install or connect the following:
  - The rear propeller shaft.
  - The shift tower.
  - Transmission with transmission fluid
  - Shift lever

NV4500 Transmissions

See Figure 32.

1. Shift the transmission into 3rd or 4th speed gear.
2. Remove or disconnect the following:
  - The shift lever
  - The shift tower
  - The transmission oil
  - Front propeller shaft, 4WD only
  - Rear propeller shaft
  - Two transfer case shields
  - Manual transfer case shift linkage, if equipped
  - Two bolts securing the right side support bracket to the transmission
3. Using tool J42371, push back on the white plastic sleeve on the quick connect in order to separate the hydraulic clutch line from the concentric slave cylinder quick connect.
  - Vehicle Speed Sensor (VSS) connector and harness
  - Backup lamp switch connector and harness
  - Transmission harness retainers
  - Clutch housing cover–to–transmission bolts (4)
  - Left and right side transmission–to–engine cover bolts
  - Transmission rear mount. Support

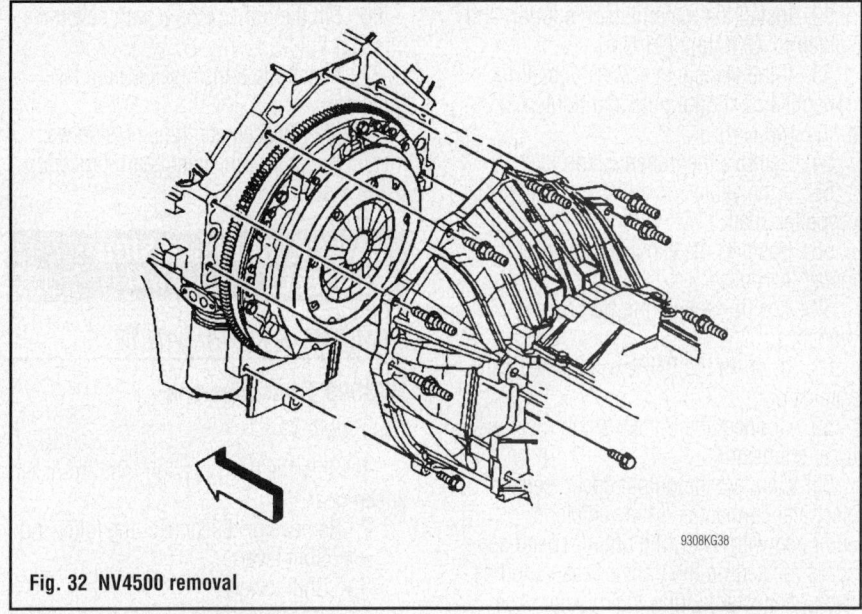

Fig. 32 NV4500 removal

the transmission with a transmission jack.
  - Bolts and studs securing the transmission to the engine.
4. Pull the transmission straight back on the clutch hub splines. Do not let the transmission hang from the clutch plate and the clutch cover. Remove the transmission from the vehicle.
5. Remove the clutch plate and the clutch cover from the engine flywheel if required.

To install:

6. Install or connect the following:
  - Clutch plate and the clutch cover to the engine flywheel, if removed
7. Ensure the transmission is positioned in the 3rd or 4th speed gear. Rotate the transmission clockwise onto the clutch hub splines. Install the bolt and the studs securing the transmission to the engine. Tighten the bolts to 37 ft. lbs. (50 Nm).
8. Install or connect the following:
  - Right and left side transmission to engine cover bolts and tighten to 10 ft. lbs. (14 Nm)
  - Clutch cover–to–transmission bolts and tighten to 10 ft. lbs. (14 Nm)
  - Transmission rear mount
  - Clutch line to the slave cylinder
  - Right side support bracket–to–transmission bolts (2). Tighten to 37 ft. lbs. (50 Nm).
  - Manual transfer case shift linkage, if removed
  - Two transfer case shields, if equipped
  - Front propeller shaft, if equipped
  - Rear propeller shaft
  - Shift tower

- Transmission with transmission fluid
- Shift lever

ZF S6–650 Transmissions

1. Shift the transmission into 3rd or 4th speed gear.
2. Remove the shift lever.
3. Raise and suitably support the vehicle.
4. If vehicle is a 2 wheel drive (2WD), remove the rear propeller shaft.
5. If equipped with 4 wheel drive (4WD), remove the transfer case.
6. Disconnect the clutch slave cylinder hydraulic hose quick connect at the master cylinder.
7. Disconnect the clutch slave cylinder line retaining clips.
8. If equipped with a 6.6L engine, disconnect the power take off, backup lamp and vehicle speed sensor connectors.
9. Remove the engine harness clips from the fuel feed/return brackets.
10. Remove the PTO connector from the fuel feed/return bracket.
11. Reposition the harness.
12. Remove the fuel lines from the fuel feed/return brackets.
13. If equipped with a 8.1L engine, disconnect the power take off, backup lamp, vehicle speed sensor and oxygen sensor connectors.
14. Remove the engine harness clips from the fuel feed/return brackets.
15. Remove the PTO connector from the fuel feed/return bracket.
16. Remove the oxygen sensors connectors from the fuel feed/return hose clip and transmission bracket.

17. Reposition the harness.

18. Remove the fuel lines from the fuel feed/return brackets.

19. If equipped with 4WD, remove the vent hose clip from the bracket.

20. Remove the vent hose clip nut and clip.

21. If equipped with 4WD, remove the vent hose clip from the fuel feed/return bracket.

22. Remove the starter.

23. Remove the exhaust pipe hanger bracket bolts and bracket.

24. Support the transmission with a suitable transmission jack.

25. Remove the transmission support

26. Remove the transmission bolts/studs.

27. Pull the transmission straight back on the clutch hub splines. Do not let the transmission hang from the clutch assembly.

28. Remove the transmission from the vehicle with the clutch hydraulic hose attached to the clutch actuator.

29. Remove the insulator from the top of the transmission.

To install:

30. Install the insulator to the top of the transmission.

➡️**Connect the clutch slave cylinder hose quick connect to the master cylinder before the transmission is fully installed. Failure to connect the hose could cause damage to the clutch pressure plate.**

31. Slowly feed the clutch hydraulic hose towards the clutch master cylinder and connect the clutch slave cylinder hydraulic hose quick connect to the master cylinder.

32. Rotate the transmission clockwise onto the clutch hub splines.

33. Position the transmission to the engine. Do not use the transmission bolts to draw up the transmission.

34. Install the transmission studs and tighten to 37 ft. lbs. (50 Nm).

35. Slowly feed the clutch hydraulic hose towards the clutch master cylinder and connect the clutch slave cylinder hydraulic hose quick connect to the master cylinder.

36. Install the transmission support.

37. Remove the transmission jack.

38. Install the exhaust pipe hanger bracket and bolts.

39. Install the starter.

40. If equipped with 4WD, install the vent hose clip to the fuel feed/return bracket.

41. Install the vent hose clip and nut.

42. Install the vent hose clip to the bracket.

43. Install the fuel lines to the fuel feed/return brackets.

44. Position the harness.

45. Install the oxygen sensors connectors to the fuel feed/return hose clip and transmission bracket.

46. Install the PTO connector to the fuel feed/return bracket.

47. Install the engine harness clips to the fuel feed/return brackets.

48. If equipped with a 8.1L engine, connect the power take off, backup lamp, vehicle speed sensor and oxygen sensor connectors.

49. Connect the clutch slave cylinder line retaining clips.

50. If equipped with 4WD, install the transfer case.

51. If equipped with a 6.6L engine, connect the power take off, backup lamp and vehicle speed sensor connectors.

52. If vehicle is a 2WD, install the rear propeller shaft.

53. Lower the vehicle.

54. Install the shift lever.

55. Fill the transmission with fluid.

56. Bleed the clutch hydraulic system, if necessary.

57. Connect the battery cables.

CLUTCH DRIVEN DISC AND PRESSURE PLATE

REMOVAL & INSTALLATION

1. Remove or disconnect the following:
   - Transmission
   - Quick disconnect from the slave cylinder

2. Install a clutch alignment tool.

3. Mark the flywheel and a clutch pressure plate lug for the installation alignment.

4. Remove the pressure plate bolts and the washers.

5. Secure the clutch pressure plate and the clutch driven plate to the flywheel.

6. Remove the clutch alignment tool.

To install:

7. Install the bolts and the washers securing the clutch pressure plate and the clutch driven plate to the flywheel.

8. Install the clutch alignment tool.

9. Align the marks made during removal or, if new align the lightest part of the clutch pressure plate identified by a yellow dot, to the heaviest part of the flywheel, identified by an "X". Tighten the clutch pressure plate to the flywheel bolts to 52 ft. lbs. (70 Nm) in a crisscross pattern.

10. Remove the clutch alignment tool.

11. Install the transmission.

12. Install the quick disconnect to the concentric slave cylinder.

ADJUSTMENTS

The hydraulic clutch system requires no adjustment.

CLUTCH MASTER CYLINDER

REMOVAL & INSTALLATION

See Figures 33 and 34.

1. Disconnect the clutch pedal position switch electrical connector.

2. Push the clutch pedal in and squeeze the pushrod bushing tabs in, in order to release the pushrod bushing from the clutch pedal.

3. If equipped with a NV 3500 or NV 4500 transmission:

   a. Disconnect the clutch slave cylinder to clutch master cylinder quick connect fitting.

   b. Remove the clutch master cylinder clip from the brake pressure module valve pipe.

4. If equipped with a ZF S6–650 transmission:

   a. Disconnect the clutch slave cylinder to clutch master cylinder quick connect fitting.

   b. Rotate the clutch master cylinder 45 degrees clockwise to the unlocked position.

5. Remove the clutch master cylinder.

To install:

6. If equipped with a ZF S6–650 transmission

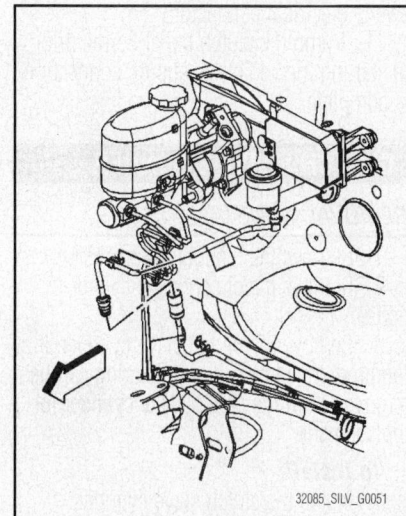

32085_SILV_G0051

Fig. 33 Clutch slave cylinder to clutch master cylinder quick connect fitting—NV 3500 or NV 4500 transmissions

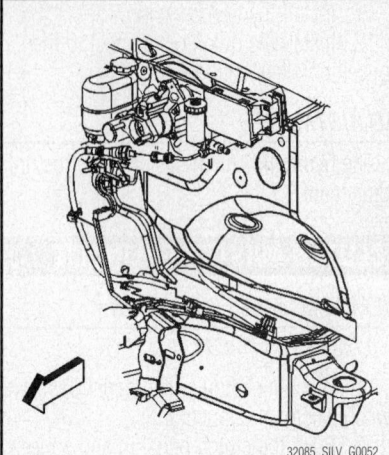

32085_SILV_G0052

Fig. 34 Clutch slave cylinder to clutch master cylinder quick connect fitting—ZF S6–650 transmission

a. Install the clutch master cylinder.

b. Push in and rotate the clutch master cylinder 45 degrees counterclockwise to the locked position.

c. Connect the clutch slave cylinder to clutch master cylinder quick connect fitting.

7. If equipped with a NV 3500 or NV 4500 transmission

a. Install the clutch master cylinder.

b. Connect the clutch slave cylinder to clutch master cylinder quick connect fitting.

8. Install the clutch master cylinder clip to the brake pressure module valve pipe.

9. Apply light pressure to the clutch pedal to couple the pushrod socket to the clutch pedal.

10. Connect the clutch pedal position switch electrical connector.

11. Pump the clutch pedal 3 time prior to starting the vehicle to ensure connection is complete.

CLUTCH SLAVE CYLINDER

REMOVAL & INSTALLATION

1. Remove the manual transmission.

2. Remove the clutch slave cylinder bolts.

3. Remove the clutch slave cylinder. If required, the clutch release bearing can be removed from the clutch slave cylinder for replacement.

To install:

4. Install the clutch slave cylinder.

5. Install the clutch slave cylinder bolts.

a. Tighten the bolts to 71 inch lbs. (8 Nm).

6. Install the manual transmission.

CLUTCH HYDRAULIC SYSTEM BLEEDING

Bleeding air from the hydraulic clutch system is necessary whenever any part of the system has been disconnected or the fluid level (in the reservoir) has been allowed to fall so low, that air has been drawn into the master cylinder.

1. Fill master cylinder reservoir with new brake fluid conforming to DOT 3 specifications.

2. Have an assistant fully depress and hold the clutch pedal, then open the bleeder screw.

3. Close the bleeder screw and have your assistant release the clutch pedal.

4. Repeat the procedure until all of the air is evacuated from the system. Check and refill master cylinder reservoir as required to prevent air from being drawn through the master cylinder.

→**Never release a depressed clutch pedal with the bleeder screw open or air will be drawn into the system.**

5. Test the clutch for proper operation.

TRANSFER CASE ASSEMBLY

REMOVAL & INSTALLATION

See Figure 35.

1. Remove or disconnect the following:
- Transfer case shields
- Front propeller shaft
- Rear propeller shaft
- Shift rod from the transfer case
- Vent hose from the transfer case
- Vehicle Speed Sensor (VSS) electrical connectors
- All necessary wiring harnesses from the transfer case

2. Support the transfer case with a transmission jack.

3. If equipped with a NV3500 manual transmission, remove or disconnect the following:
- Bolt securing the left side support brace to the transmission
- Bolt and stud securing the left side support brace to the transfer case
- Two bolts securing the right side support brace to the transmission and transfer case

4. Remove or disconnect the following:
- Six nuts securing the transfer case and bracket to the transmission or transmission adapter, as applicable
- Transfer case
- Gasket, then discard

To install:

5. Install a new gasket to the transmission. Use Teflon pipe sealant GM P/N 12346004 in order to hold the gasket in place.

6. Raise and position the transfer case to the vehicle.

7. Install or connect the following:
- Six nuts securing the transfer case and bracket to the transmission adapter or transmission. Tighten to 37 ft. lbs. (50 Nm).

8. If equipped with a manual transmission, install or connect the following:
- Bolt securing the left side support brace to the transmission and tighten to 37 ft. lbs. (50 Nm)
- Bolt and stud securing the left side support brace to the transfer case and tighten to 37 ft. lbs. (50 Nm)
- Two bolts securing the right side support brace to the transmission and transfer case and tighten to 37 ft. lbs. (50 Nm)

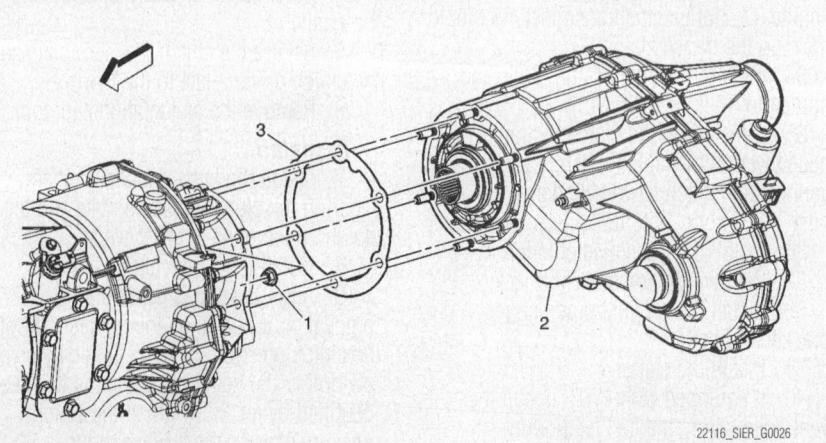

22116_SIER_G0026

Fig. 35 Transfer case mounting nuts (1), transfer case (2) and transfer case gasket (3)

9. Install or connect the following:
- Vent hose to the transfer case
10. Check the transfer case oil level.
- VSS electrical connectors
- Wiring harness to the transfer case
- Shift rod to the transfer case
- Front and rear propeller shafts
- Transfer case shields
11. Lower the vehicle.

TRANSFER CASE ENCODER MOTOR

REMOVAL & INSTALLATION

See Figure 36.

1. Remove the transfer case shield.
2. Remove the front propeller shaft.
3. Disconnect the transfer case switch electrical connector.
4. Disconnect the encoder motor electrical connector.
5. Remove the encoder motor bolts.
6. Remove the encoder motor.
7. Remove the actuator insulator gasket.
8. If replacing the encoder motor, remove the locating pins from the old motor.

To install:

➡ **If the encoder motor is being replaced because it is defective, ensure that the transfer case is in the neutral position. Manually shift the transfer case at the shift shaft, using a crescent wrench if necessary. When**

installing the encoder motor, ensure that the encoder motor is indexed correctly and the motor is flat against the transfer case before tightening the bolts.

9. Install the locating pins to the new encoder motor.
10. Position a new actuator insulator gasket to the transfer case.
11. Install the encoder motor.
12. Install encoder motor bolts and tighten in sequence to 15 ft. lbs. (20 Nm).
13. Connect the encoder motor electrical connector.
14. Connect the transfer case switch electrical connector.
15. Install the front propeller shaft.
16. Install the transfer case shield.

FRONT AXLE SHAFT, BEARING AND SEAL

REMOVAL & INSTALLATION

8.25 S4WD (Part–Time) and 9.25 Axles

See Figure 37.

1. Raise and support the vehicle.
2. Drain the differential carrier assembly.
3. If only replacing the right side inner shaft and/or housing, follow the steps below. If only replacing the left side inner shaft, proceed to step 19.
4. Remove the stabilizer shaft link assembly.

5. Disconnect the electrical connector from the electric motor actuator.
6. Disconnect the wire harness from the inner axle shaft housing.
7. Remove the drive shaft inboard flange bolts from the inner axle shaft.
8. Disconnect the wheel drive shaft from the inner axle shaft.
9. Remove the inner axle shaft housing nuts from the bracket.
10. For 2500/3500 series vehicles, remove the front axle mounting bracket to frame nuts.
11. Slide the front axle mounting bracket towards the engine. It may be necessary to pull down on the inner axle housing and/or push up on the mounting bracket in order to gain clearance.
12. Remove the inner axle shaft housing bolts from the differential carrier case.
13. Carefully remove the inner axle shaft housing assembly from the differential carrier assembly.
14. For the 8.25 inch axle, remove the following components from the inner axle shaft housing:
    a. The clutch fork inner spring (10).
    b. The clutch fork assembly (11).
    c. The clutch shaft shim (9).
    d. The clutch sleeve (8).
    e. The clutch gear (6) by doing the following:
    f. Clamp the inner axle shaft housing (4) in a vise. Clamp only on the mounting flange.
    g. Strike the inside surface of the shaft (1) flange with a hammer and a brass drift in order to dislodge the front drive axle clutch gear (6) from the inner axle shaft (1).
    h. The thrust washer (5).
15. For the 9.25 inch axle, remove the following components from the inner axle shaft housing:
    a. The clutch fork inner spring (10).
    b. The clutch fork assembly (11).
    c. The clutch shaft shim (9).
    d. The clutch sleeve (8).
    e. The retainer ring (7).
    f. The thrust washers (5, 6).
16. Remove the inner axle shaft (2). Tap out the inner axle shaft with a soft–faced mallet, if necessary.
17. Remove the inner axle seal and the bearing from the axle housing.
18. If only replacing the left side inner axle shaft, remove the wheel drive shaft inboard flange bolts from the inner axle shaft. Disconnect the wheel drive shaft from the inner axle shaft.
19. Remove the inner axle shaft using a hammer and a brass drift.

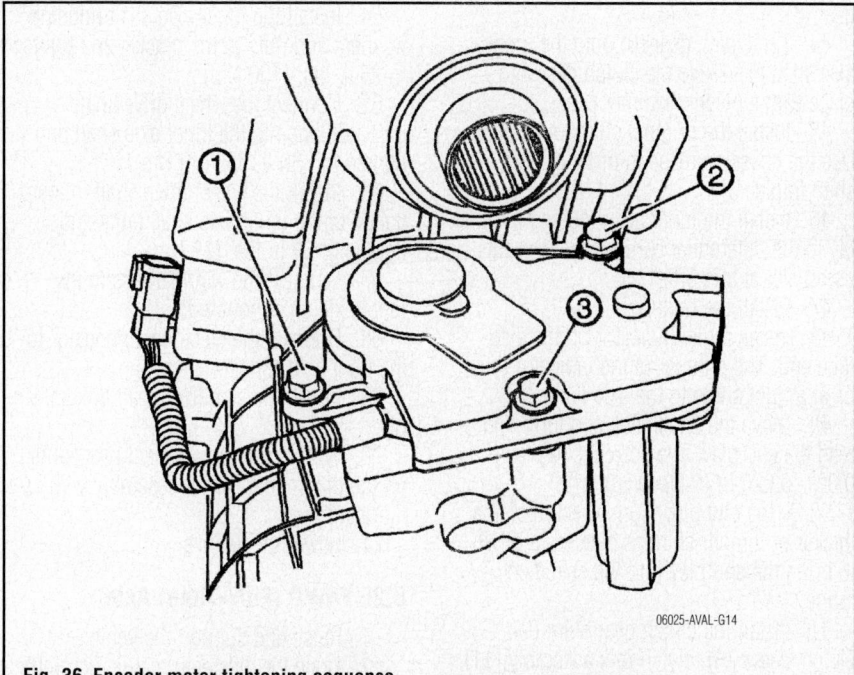

06025-AVAL-G14

Fig. 36 Encoder motor tightening sequence

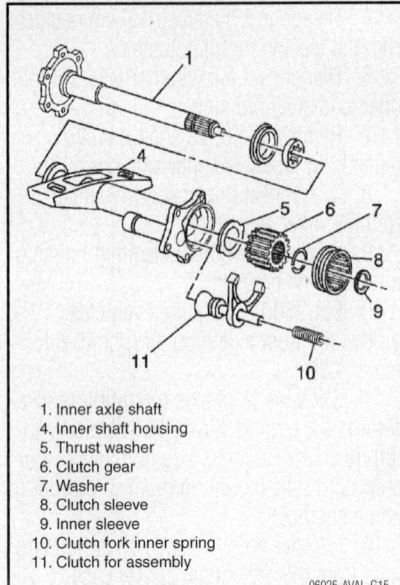

1. Inner axle shaft
4. Inner shaft housing
5. Thrust washer
6. Clutch gear
7. Washer
8. Clutch sleeve
9. Inner sleeve
10. Clutch fork inner spring
11. Clutch for assembly

06025-AVAL-G15

Fig. 37 Exploded view of the front axle assembly—8.25 S4WD and 9.25 axles

20. Install the inner axle shaft housing into a vise. Clamp only on the mounting flange of the inner axle shaft housing.

21. Install the bushing and bearing removal tool J–29369–1, 8.25 inch axle, or J–29369–2, 9.25 inch axle, behind the inner axle shaft seal or the inner axle shaft bearing as necessary.

22. Install a slide hammer to the removal tool.

23. Remove the inner axle shaft seal and/or the inner axle shaft bearing using the slide hammer.

24. If only replacing the left side seal, place an alignment mark between the inner axle shaft and the wheel drive shaft.

25. Disconnect the wheel drive shaft from the inner axle shaft.

26. Remove the inner axle shaft using a hammer and a brass drift.

27. Remove the inner axle shaft seal using a suitable seal remover tool.

To install:

28. Install the right side bearing with the square shoulder in using and axle bearing tube installer and a universal driver handle.

29. Install the new axle shaft seal using the sane tools.

30. Install the inner axle shaft into the inner axle shaft housing. Carefully tap the inner axle shaft into place with a soft–faced mallet.

31. Install the inner axle shaft and clutch fork assembly components into the inner shaft housing.

32. If only the left side inner axle shaft

was removed, install the shaft by performing the following steps:

33. Install the inner axle shaft into the differential case side gear using a soft–faced mallet until the retaining ring on the inner axle shaft is fully seated within the groove in the differential case side gear.

34. Pull back on the inner axle shaft to ensure that the inner axle shaft is properly retained in the differential case side gear.

35. Connect the halfshaft to the inner axle shaft.

36. Install the halfshaft inboard flange to inner axle shaft bolts and tighten to 58 ft. lbs. (79 Nm).

37. If the right side inner axle shaft and/or housing was removed, install the shaft and/or housing using the following steps:

38. Install the new inner axle shaft bearing and the seal to the axle housing.

39. Install the inner axle shaft (2) into the inner axle shaft housing (1). Carefully tap the inner axle shaft into place with a soft–faced mallet.

40. Place the inner axle shaft housing on end so that the splines of the inner axle shaft is facing up.

41. For the 8.25 inch axle, install the following components into the inner axle shaft housing:

➡**Use chassis grease in order to hold the thrust washer in place.**

42. The thrust washer (5) Ensure the tabs on the thrust washer are aligned with the slots in the inner axle shaft housing (4).

43. The retainer ring (7) into the clutch gear (6).

44. The clutch gear (6) onto the inner axle shaft (1). Drive the clutch gear into place with a plastic hammer.

45. Install the original shim to the shaft. Use the chassis grease in order to hold the shim in place.

46. Install the inner axle housing assembly to the differential carrier case. Do not use sealer at this time.

47. Install the bolts.

48. Install a dial indicator on the axle tube end. The plunger of the indicator must be at a right angle to the axle flange.

49. Move the shaft back and forth and read the end play. The correct end play is 0.001–0.020 in (0.03–0.51mm).

50. If the end play is incorrect, install a thicker or thinner shim as needed in order to bring the end play into the specified range.

51. Install the clutch gear shim (9). clutch sleeve (8), clutch fork assembly (11) and clutch fork inner spring (10).

52. For the 9.25 inch axle, install the following components into the inner axle shaft housing:

53. The thrust washer (5) Ensure the tabs on the thrust washer are aligned with the slots in the inner axle shaft housing (4).

54. The second thrust washer (6).

55. The retainer ring (7) onto the inner axle shaft (1).

56. Determine the clutch gear shim thickness.

57. Install the clutch gear shim (9). clutch sleeve (8), clutch fork assembly (11) and clutch fork inner spring (10).

58. Apply sealant to the inner axle housing to differential carrier sealing surface.

59. Install the inner axle shaft housing assembly to the differential carrier assembly.

60. Install the inner axle shaft housing bolts and tighten to 30 ft. lbs. (40 Nm) or 41 ft. lbs. (55 Nm) on 2007 models (except Classic) with 9.25 inch axles.

61. For 2500/3500 series vehicles, perform the following steps in order to install the front axle mounting bracket to the inner axle shaft housing:

62. Slide the front axle mounting bracket towards the frame. Install the front axle mounting bracket studs into the inner shaft housing mounting flange. It may be necessary to push up on the front axle mounting bracket and/or pull down on the inner axle housing in order to gain enough clearance to install the mounting bracket studs into the inner shaft housing.

63. Install the front axle mounting bracket to frame nuts. Tighten to 67 ft. lbs. (90 Nm).

64. Install the inner axle shaft housing washers and nuts to the bracket and tighten to 75 ft. lbs. (100 Nm).

65. Connect the wheel drive shaft inboard flange to the inner axle shaft and tighten to . 30 ft. lbs. (40 Nm).

66. Install the wheel drive shaft inboard flange to the inner axle shaft bolts and tighten to 58 ft. lbs. (79 Nm).

67. Connect the wire harness to the inner axle shaft housing.

68. Connect the electrical connector to the front axle actuator.

69. Install the stabilizer shaft link assembly.

70. With either replacement procedure, fill the differential carrier assembly with axle lubricant.

71. Lower the vehicle.

8.25 F4WD (Full–Time) Axle

1. Raise and support the vehicle.
2. Drain the differential carrier assembly.

3. If only replacing the right side inner shaft and/or housing, follow the steps below. If only replacing the left side inner shaft, proceed to step 16.

4. Remove the stabilizer shaft link assembly.

5. Remove the wheel drive shaft inboard flange bolts from the inner axle shaft.

6. Disconnect the wheel drive shaft from the inner axle shaft.

7. Disconnect the inner axle shaft from the differential case side gear using a hammer and brass drift. Remove the inner axle shaft housing nuts from the bracket.

8. Remove the inner axle shaft housing bolts from the differential carrier assembly.

9. Remove the inner axle shaft and inner axle shaft housing from the vehicle.

10. Remove the inner axle shaft from the inner axle shaft housing.

11. Remove the inner axle shaft seal and the bearing from the inner axle shaft housing.

12. Install the inner axle shaft housing into a vise. Clamp only on the mounting flange of the inner axle shaft housing.

13. Install the bushing and bearing removal tool J–29369–1 behind the inner axle shaft seal or the inner axle shaft bearing as necessary.

14. Install a slide hammer to the removal tool.

15. Remove the inner axle shaft seal and/or the inner axle shaft bearing using the slide hammer.

16. If only replacing the left side seal, place an alignment mark between the inner axle shaft and the wheel drive shaft.

17. Disconnect the wheel drive shaft from the inner axle shaft.

18. Remove the inner axle shaft using a hammer and a brass drift.

19. Remove the inner axle shaft seal using a suitable seal remover tool.

To install:

20. Install the right side bearing with the square shoulder in using and axle bearing tube installer and a universal driver handle.

21. Install the new axle shaft seal using the sane tools.

22. Install the inner axle shaft into the inner axle shaft housing. Carefully tap the inner axle shaft into place with a soft–faced mallet.

23. Install the inner axle shaft and clutch fork assembly components into the inner shaft housing.

24. If only the left side inner axle shaft was removed, install the shaft by performing the following steps:

25. Install the inner axle shaft into the differential case side gear using a soft–faced mallet until the retaining ring on the inner axle shaft is fully seated within the groove in the differential case side gear.

26. Pull back on the inner axle shaft to ensure that the inner axle shaft is properly retained in the differential case side gear.

27. Connect the halfshaft to the inner axle shaft.

28. Install the halfshaft inboard flange to inner axle shaft bolts and tighten to 58 ft. lbs. (79 Nm).

29. If the right side inner axle shaft and/or housing was removed, install the shaft and/or housing using the following steps.

30. Install the new inner axle shaft bearing and the new seal to the inner axle shaft housing.

31. Install the inner axle shaft into the inner axle shaft housing. Do not install the inner axle shaft completely into the inner axle shaft housing at this time.

32. Apply sealant to the inner axle housing to differential carrier sealing surface.

33. Install the inner axle shaft and the inner axle shaft housing to the differential carrier assembly.

34. Install the inner axle shaft housing bolts and tighten to 30 ft. lbs. (40 Nm).

35. Install the inner axle shaft housing nuts to the bracket and tighten to 75 ft. lbs. (100 Nm).

36. Install the inner axle shaft into the differential case side gear by doing the following:

37. Turn the inner axle shaft and align the splines of the inner axle shaft with the splines on the differential side gear.

38. Install the inner axle shaft into the differential case side gear using a soft–faced mallet until the retaining ring on the inner axle shaft is fully seated within the groove in the differential case side gear.

39. Pull back on the inner axle shaft to ensure that the inner axle shaft is properly retained in the differential case side gear.

40. Install the wheel drive shaft inboard flange to the inner axle shaft.

41. Install the wheel drive shaft inboard flange to inner axle shaft bolts and tighten to 58 ft. lbs. (79 Nm).

42. Install the stabilizer shaft link assembly.

43. Fill the differential carrier assembly with axle lubricant

44. Lower the vehicle.

FRONT HALFSHAFT

REMOVAL & INSTALLATION

See Figure 38.

1. Remove or disconnect the following:
   • Wheels

2. Insert a drift or a large screwdriver through the brake caliper into one of the brake rotor vanes in order to prevent the drive axle wheel drive shaft from turning.

3. Remove or disconnect the following:
   • Nut and the washer from the hub

➡ **Do not reuse the hub nut. A new nut must be used when installing the wheel drive shaft.**

   • Bolts (6) securing the wheel drive shaft inboard flange to the output shaft flange
   • Drift from the rotor
   • Stabilizer shaft link from the lower control arm

4. Wrap shop towels around both the inner and the outer wheel drive shaft boots in order to avoid damage to the boots during removal and installation.

5. Pull the wheel drive shaft through the lower control arm opening.

To install:

6. Wrap shop towels around both the inner and the outer wheel drive shaft boots in order to avoid damage to the boots during removal and installation.

➡ **Clean the steering knuckle and the wheel drive shaft splines and threads. These areas must be dry and free of grease, dirt, and contamination.**

7. Insert the wheel drive shaft splined shank into the knuckle hub.

➡ **Use only a genuine GM front wheel drive shaft nut. Installation of anything but an OEM front wheel drive shaft nut could cause damage to the vehicle.**

8. Install or connect the following:
   • Washer and the new hub nut to the wheel driveshaft. Do not tighten.
   • The wheel drive shaft inboard flange to the output shaft flange using the inboard flange bolts

9. Insert a drift or a large screwdriver through the brake caliper into 1 of the brake rotor vanes in order to prevent the wheel drive shaft from turning. Tighten the inboard flange bolts to 58 ft. lbs. (78 Nm). Tighten the hub nut to 177 ft. lbs. (240 Nm).

10. Remove the drift from the rotor.

11. Install the stabilizer shaft link.

12. Install the wheel and tire assembly.

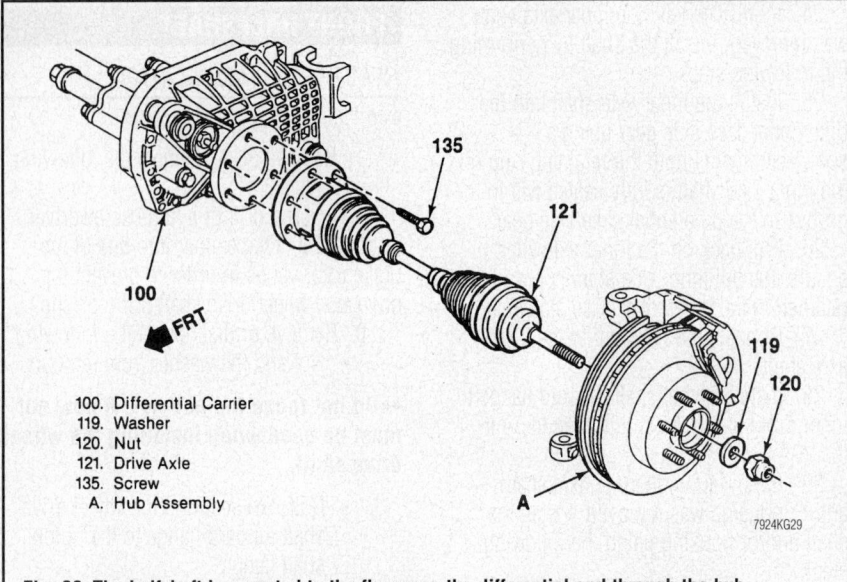

100. Differential Carrier
119. Washer
120. Nut
121. Drive Axle
135. Screw
A. Hub Assembly

Fig. 38 The halfshaft is mounted to the flange on the differential and through the hub assembly—4-Wheel drive models

CV-JOINTS OVERHAUL

Inner Joint

See Figures 39 and 40.

➡**With removal of the halfshaft for any reason, the transmission sealing surface (the tripod male/female shank of the halfshaft) should be inspected for corrosion. If corrosion is evident, the surface should be cleaned with 320 grit cloth or equivalent. Transmission fluid may be used to clean off any remaining debris. The surface should be wiped dry and the halfshaft reinstalled free of any buildup.**

1. Before servicing the vehicle, refer to the precautions in the beginning of this section.
2. Use a hand grinder in order to cut through the swage ring.
3. Remove the tripod housing from the halfshaft. Wipe the grease off of the tripod assembly roller bearings and the tripod housing. Thoroughly degrease the tripod housing. Allow the tripod housing to dry prior to assembly.

➡**Handle the tripod spider assembly with care. Tripod balls and needle rollers may separate from the spider trunnion if the tripod balls and needle rollers are not handled carefully.**

4. Use side cutters to cut away the small boot clamp.
5. Compress the tripod boot up the halfshaft away from the tripod spider assembly toward the outboard (CV joint assembly) end of the halfshaft.

6. Spread the spider spacer ring with tool J8059, or equivalent.
7. Remove the following items from the halfshaft bar:
   a. The spacer ring.
   b. The spider assembly.
   c. The tripod boot.
8. Clean the halfshaft bar. Use a wire brush in order to remove any rust in the boot mounting area (grooves).
9. Inspect the needle rollers, needle bearings, and trunnion. Check the tripod housing for unusual wear, cracks, or other damage. Replace any damaged parts.

To assemble:

10. Place the new small boot clamp onto the small end of the joint boot.
11. Compress the joint boot and small boot clamp onto the halfshaft bar.
12. Position the small end of the joint boot into the joint boot groove on the halfshaft bar.

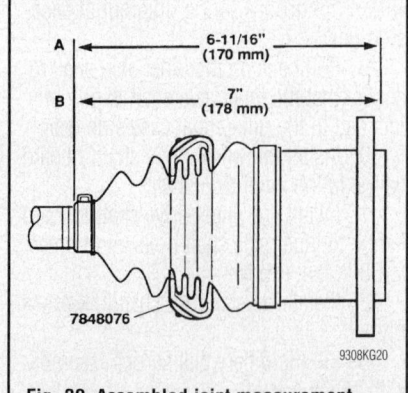

Fig. 39 Assembled joint measurement

13. Secure the small boot clamp with tool J35910, or equivalent, a breaker bar, and a torque wrench. Tighten the small boot clamp (1) to 100 ft. lbs. (136 Nm).
14. Check the gap dimension on the clamp ear. Continue tightening until the gap dimension is reached.

➡**Assemble the CV joint with the convolute retainer in the correct position, as illustrated.**

15. Install the convolute retainer over the inboard joint boot, being sure to capture three convolutions.
16. Install the tripod spider assembly onto the halfshaft bar with the counterbore towards the end of the halfshaft bar.
17. Install the spacer ring in the groove at the end of the halfshaft bar.
18. Push the spider assembly back toward the end of the halfshaft bar until the spacer ring is covered by the spider assembly counterbore.
19. Pack the tripod boot and the tripod housing with the grease supplied in the kit. The amount of grease supplied in this kit has been pre-measured for this application.
20. Reassemble the tripod housing and the tripod boot using the following procedure:
   a. Pinch the swage ring slightly by hand in order to distort it into an oval shape.
   b. Slide the distorted swage ring over the large diameter of the boot.
   c. Place the tripod housing over the spider assembly.
   d. Install the boot onto the tripod housing.
   e. Align the tripod boot with the swage ring in place, over the flat area on the tripod housing.
21. Mount tool J36652 in a vise. Install the bottom half of the split-plate swage clamp. For 1500 models, use tool J36652-98. For 2500 models, use tool J36652-1.
22. Check the inboard stroke position. Use measurement A for the 1500 models. Use measurement B for the 2500 models.
23. Position the inboard end (tripod end) of the halfshaft assembly in tool J36652. Install the top half of the proper size tool on the lower half of the tool. For 1500 models, use tool J36652-98. For 2500 models, use tool J36652-1.
24. Align the swage ring and the swage ring clamp. Insert the bolts. Hand tighten the bolts in tool J36652 until the bolts are snug.
25. Align the following during this procedure:

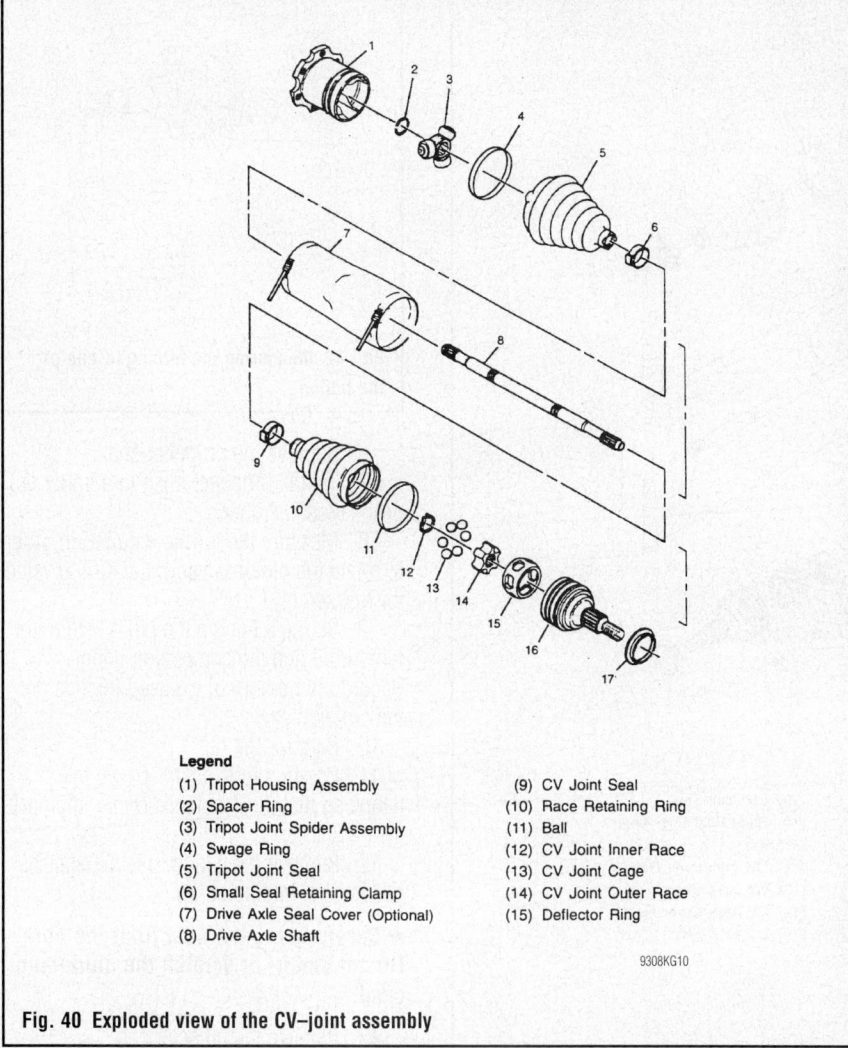

Legend
(1) Tripot Housing Assembly
(2) Spacer Ring
(3) Tripot Joint Spider Assembly
(4) Swage Ring
(5) Tripot Joint Seal
(6) Small Seal Retaining Clamp
(7) Drive Axle Seal Cover (Optional)
(8) Drive Axle Shaft

(9) CV Joint Seal
(10) Race Retaining Ring
(11) Ball
(12) CV Joint Inner Race
(13) CV Joint Cage
(14) CV Joint Outer Race
(15) Deflector Ring

9308KG10

Fig. 40 Exploded view of the CV–joint assembly

a. The tripod boot.
b. The housing.
c. The swage ring. Tighten each bolt 180 degrees at a time. Alternate between the bolts until both sides of the top half of J36652 touch the bottom half of the tool.
26. Loosen the bolts and remove the halfshaft assembly from J36652.
27. Remove the convolute retainer from the boot.

Outer Joint

See Figure 41.

1. Place protective covers over the vise jaws. Place the halfshaft in the vise.
2. Use a hand grinder to cut through the swage ring. Use side cutters to cut off the small boot clamp.
3. Slide the boot down the halfshaft bar and away from the CV–joint outer race. Wipe all grease away from the face of the CV joint.
4. Find the halfshaft bar retaining snap ring, which is located in the inner race.

5. Spread the snapring ears apart.
6. Pull the CV joint and the CV joint boot from the halfshaft bar. Discard the old CV joint boot.
7. Place a brass drift against the CV joint cage. Tap gently on the brass drift with a hammer in order to tilt the cage.
8. Remove the first chrome alloy ball when the CV joint cage tilts. Tilt the CV joint cage (1) in the opposite direction to remove the opposing chrome alloy ball. Repeat this process to remove all six of the balls.
9. Pivot the CV joint cage and the inner race 90 degrees to the center line of the outer race. At the same time, align the cage windows with the lands of the outer race. Lift out the cage and the inner race.
10. Remove the inner race from the cage by rotating the inner race upward. Clean the following items thoroughly with cleaning solvent. Remove all traces of old grease and any contaminates.
    a. Inner and outer race assemblies.
    b. CV joint cage.
    c. Chrome alloy balls.

11. Dry all the parts. Check the CV joint assembly for unusual wear, cracks, or other damage. Replace any damaged parts. Clean the halfshaft bar. Use a wire brush to remove any rust in the boot mounting area (grooves).

To assemble:

12. Inspect all of the parts for unusual wear, cracks, or other damage. Replace the CV joint assembly if necessary. Put a light coat of the recommended grease on the inner and the outer race grooves.
13. Hold the inner race at 90 degrees to the centerline of the cage. Align the lands of the inner race with the windows of the cage. Insert the inner race into the cage by rotating the inner race downward.
14. Insert the cage and inner race into the outer race.
15. Place a brass drift against the CV joint cage. Tap gently on the brass drift with a hammer in order to tilt the cage. Install the first chrome alloy ball when the CV joint cage tilts. Tilt the CV joint cage in the opposite direction to install the opposing chrome alloy ball. Repeat this process in order to install all six of the balls.
16. Pack the CV joint boot and the CV joint assembly with the grease supplied in the kit. The amount of grease supplied in this kit has been pre–measured for this application.
17. Place the new small boot clamp onto the CV joint boot.
18. Slide the CV joint boot onto the halfshaft bar.
19. Position the small end of the CV joint boot into the joint boot groove on the halfshaft bar.
20. Secure the small boot clamp, a breaker bar, and a torque wrench. Tighten the small clamp (1) to 100 ft. lbs. (136 Nm).
21. Check the gap dimension on the clamp ear. Continue tightening until the gap dimension is reached.
22. Pinch the new swage ring slightly by hand to distort it into an oval shape. Slide the distorted swage ring over the large diameter of the boot.

➡**Be sure that the retaining ring side of the CV joint inner race faces the half-shaft bar (3) before installation.**

23. Slide the CV joint onto the halfshaft bar. The retaining snap ring inside of the inner race engages in the halfshaft bar groove with a click when the CV joint is in the proper position.
24. Pull on the CV joint to verify engagement.

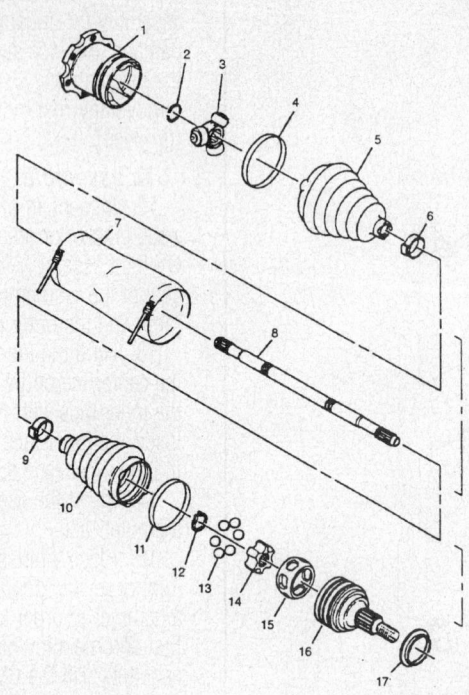

Legend

(1) Tripot Housing Assembly
(2) Spacer Ring
(3) Tripot Joint Spider Assembly
(4) Swage Ring
(5) Tripot Joint Seal
(6) Small Seal Retaining Clamp
(7) Drive Axle Seal Cover (Optional)
(8) Drive Axle Shaft
(9) CV Joint Seal
(10) Race Retaining Ring
(11) Ball
(12) CV Joint Inner Race
(13) CV Joint Cage
(14) CV Joint Outer Race
(15) Deflector Ring

9308KG10

Fig. 41 Exploded view of the CV–joint assembly

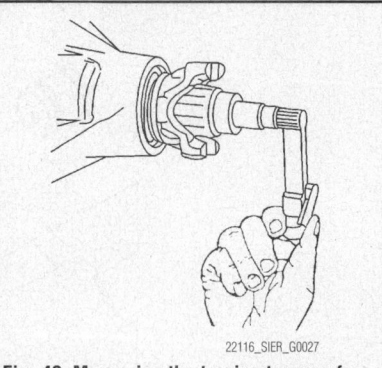

Fig. 42 Measuring the turning torque of the pinion

25. Slide the large diameter of the CV joint boot with the large swage ring in place, over the outside edge of the CV joint outer race.

26. Clamp the CV joint boot tightly to the CV joint outer race with the large swage ring, using the following procedure:

a. Mount tool J36652 in a vise.

b. Install the bottom half of the split–plate swage clamp. For 1500 models, use tool J36652–98.

c. For 2500 models, use tool J36652–1.

d. Position the CV joint end (outboard end) of the halfshaft assembly in the bottom half of tool J36652.

27. Align the following during this procedure:

a. CV joint boot.

b. CV joint assembly.

c. Swage ring.

28. Install the top half of tool J36652 onto the lower half of the tool, over the CV joint boot and the CV joint assembly.

29. Align the swage ring and the swage ring clamp.

30. Insert the bolts into J36652. Hand tighten the bolts until the bolts are snug. Tighten each bolt 180 degrees at a time. Alternate between the bolts until both sides of the top half of the tool touch the bottom half of the tool.

31. Loosen the bolts and remove the halfshaft assembly from the tool.

FRONT PINION SEAL

REMOVAL & INSTALLATION

See Figure 42.

1. Raise the vehicle on a hoist.
2. Remove the tire and wheel.
3. Remove the brake calipers.
4. Remove the differential carrier assembly shield, if equipped.
5. Reference mark the relationship of the propeller shaft to the front axle pinion yoke.

6. Remove the propeller shaft.

7. Tie the propeller shaft to a frame rail or the crossmember.

8. Measure the torque required in order to rotate the pinion. Record the torque value for reassembly.

9. Scribe a line on the pinion stem, the pinion nut and the companion flange. Record the number of exposed threads on the pinion stem.

10. Remove the nut.

11. Position tool J8614–01 on the flange so that the 4 notches on the tool face the flange.

12. Remove the flange. Use the special nut and the forcing screw.

➡**Carefully pry the seal from the bore. Do not distort or scratch the aluminum case.**

13. Remove the oil seal.

14. Inspect the pinion flange for a smooth oil seal surface. Inspect the pinion flange for worn drive splines. Replace the pinion flange if necessary.

15. Remove the dust deflector.

To install:

➡**Stake the new deflector at 3 new equally spaced positions. You must stake the new deflector in such a way that you do not damage the seal operating surface.**

16. Install and stake the dust deflector on the flange.

17. Position the oil seal in the bore. Then place a driver over the oil seal. Strike the driver with a hammer until the seal flange seats on the axle housing surface. Drive the seal in straight, not at an angle, as this will damage the aluminum housing.

➡**Do not hammer the pinion flange/yoke onto the pinion shaft. Pinion components may be damaged if the** pinion flange/yoke is hammered onto the pinion shaft.

18. Install the flange onto the pinion using tool J8614–01. Place the washer and a new nut on the pinion threads. Tighten the nut to the original scribed position using the scribe marks and the exposed threads as reference.

19. Measure the rotating torque of the pinion. Compare the measurement with the rotating torque recorded earlier. Tighten the pinion nut by small increments until the torque required in order to rotate the pinion is 3–5 inch lbs. (0.40–0.57 Nm) greater than the original torque.

20. Install the propeller shaft.

21. Install the differential carrier assembly shield, if equipped.

22. Install the brake calipers

23. Install the tire and wheel.

24. Lower the vehicle.

REAR AXLE HOUSING

REMOVAL & INSTALLATION

See Figure 43.

1. Raise and support the vehicle.

2. Place jack stands at the front end of the vehicle.

3. Support the axle with jack stands.

4. Remove the tire and wheel assemblies.

5. Disconnect the upper stabilizer shaft link from the frame.

6. Reference mark the rear propeller shaft to the rear axle pinion yoke.

7. Disconnect the propeller shaft from the axle. Support the propeller shaft as necessary.

8. Disconnect the lower mount of the shock absorbers.

9. Disconnect the vent hose.

10. Disconnect the park brake cables.

11. Disconnect the junction block and brake pipe.

12. Remove and wire the calipers out of the way.

13. Remove the nuts and the washers from the spring assembly U–bolts.

14. Remove the U–bolts, the anchor plates and the spacers from the axle.

15. Remove the axle with the aid of a hydraulic assist.

16. Remove the stabilizer shaft U–bolt nuts and the U–bolts from the axle if necessary.

17. Remove the stabilizer shaft from the axle if necessary.

To install:

18. Install the stabilizer shaft to the axle if necessary.

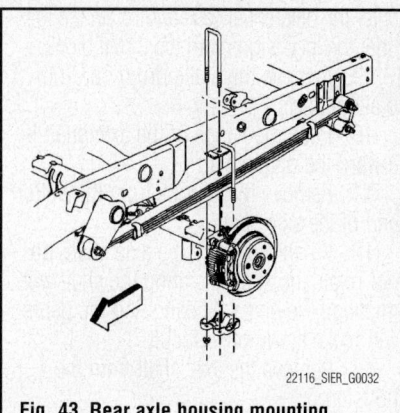

Fig. 43 Rear axle housing mounting

22116_SIER_G0032

19. Install the stabilizer shaft clamps, the U–bolts, and the nuts if necessary. Do not torque the stabilizer shaft U–bolt nuts at this time.

20. Place the axle under the vehicle.

21. Raise the axle to the springs with the aid of a hydraulic assist. Align the axle with the springs.

22. Install the spacers, the anchor plates and the U–bolts.

23. Install the washers if equipped and the nuts to the U–bolts and tighten in a crisscross pattern to:

   a. 2005–06 and 2007 Classic models
- 1500 series: 53 ft. lbs. (72 Nm)
- 1500 series w/rear steering: 110 ft. lbs. (150 Nm)
- 2500 and 3500 series: 110 ft. lbs. (150 Nm)

   b. 2007 Models (except Classic)
- 1500 series: 74 ft. lbs. (100 Nm)
- 2500 and 3500 series: 118 ft. lbs. (160 Nm)

24. Install the stabilizer shaft link to the frame if necessary.

25. Install the stabilizer shaft link bolt and the nut

26. Tighten the stabilizer shaft U–bolt nuts.

27. Install the brake calipers.

28. Install the brake pipe fitting brackets.

29. Install the brake pipe.

30. Install the brake pipe junction block.

31. Connect the park brake cables.

32. Connect the vent hose to the axle vent fitting.

33. Install the shock absorbers to the lower mount bracket.

34. Install the shock absorber bolts and the nuts.

35. Install the propeller shaft to the pinion yoke. Align the reference marks made during removal.

36. Install the propeller shaft yoke retaining clamps and the bolts.

37. Install the tire and wheel assemblies.

38. Fill the axle with lubricant.

39. Remove the jack stands.

40. Lower the vehicle.

REAR AXLE SHAFT, BEARING AND SEAL

REMOVAL & INSTALLATION

8.6 Inch With Drum Brakes

See Figure 44.

1. Raise and support the vehicle on a hoist.

2. Remove or disconnect the following:
- Tire and wheel assembly
- Rear cover and the gasket
- Pinion shaft locking screw.
- Pinion shaft, on axles without locking differential

3. On axles with a locking differential, remove the shaft part way. Rotate the case until the pinion shaft touches the housing.

4. On axles with a locking differential, use a screwdriver, or a similar tool, in order to enter the differential case and rotate the lock until the lock aligns with the thrust block.

5. Remove the brake drum.

6. Push the flange of the axle shaft toward the differential. Remove the lock from the button end of the axle shaft.

➡**When removing the axle shaft, do not rotate the shaft. Rotating the shaft will misalign the gears. Misaligning the gears will make the assembly difficult.**

7. Remove the axle shaft from the housing.

8. If replacing only the axle shaft seal, remove the seal using a suitable seal removal tool.

9. Remove the bearing using a bearing remover.

10. Inspect all the parts for damage. Replace the parts as necessary.

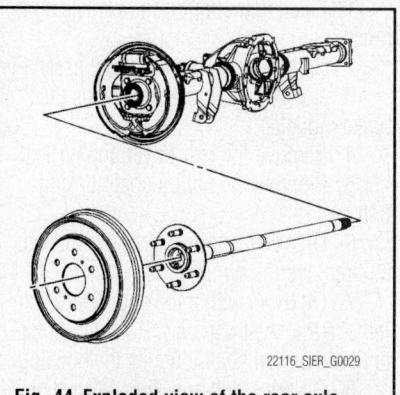

22116_SIER_G0029

Fig. 44 Exploded view of the rear axle— 8.6 inch with drum brakes

To install:

11. Install a new bearing using a bearing installer.

12. Install new seal using a seal installer. Ensure the seal is fully seated in the axle tube.

➡️**Carefully insert the axle shaft in order to not damage the seal.**

13. Install the axle shaft into the housing. Slide the axle shaft into place allowing the splines to engage the differential side gear.

14. On axles without a locking differential, place the lock on the button end of the axle shaft.

15. On axles with a locking differential, keep the pinion shaft partially withdrawn.

16. Install the brake drum.

17. On axles with a locking differential, place the lock on the axle shaft so that the ends are flush with the thrust block. Pull the shaft flange outward in order to seat the lock in the differential gear.

➡️**Anytime you remove a differential pinion shaft locking screw, coat the screw threads with Loctite® 242 before reinstalling the screws. The screw has an adhesive coating in order to prevent the screw from loosening in the case. Removing the screw removes the adhesive on the screw.**

18. Align the hole in the pinion shaft with the screw hole in the differential case.

19. Install or connect the following:
- Pinion flange locking bolt and tighten to 25 ft. lbs. (34 Nm).
- Rear cover and the gasket
- Tire and wheel assembly

20. Fill the rear axle.

21. Remove the supports and lower the vehicle.

8.6 and 9.5 Inch Rear Axles

See Figure 45.

1. Raise and support the vehicle on a hoist.

2. Remove the tire and wheel assembly.

3. Remove the brake caliper on disc brake models.

4. Remove the rear cover and gasket.

5. Remove the pinion shaft locking bolt.

6. On axles without a locking differential, remove the pinion shaft.

7. On axles with a locking differential, remove the shaft part way. Rotate the case until the pinion shaft touches the housing.

8. On axles with a locking differential, use a screwdriver, or a similar tool, in order to enter the differential case and rotate the lock until the lock aligns with the thrust block.

9. Remove the brake drum on drum brake models.

10. Push the flange of the axle shaft in toward the differential.

11. Remove the C–lock from the button end of the axle shaft.

12. When removing the axle shaft, do not rotate the shaft. Rotating the shaft will misalign the gears. Misaligning the gears will make assembly difficult.

13. Remove the axle shaft from the housing.

To install:

14. Install the axle shaft into the rear axle housing.

15. Slide the axle shaft into place allowing the splines to engage the differential side gear.

16. On axles without a locking differential, place the C–lock on the button end of the axle shaft.

17. On axles with a locking differential, keep the pinion shaft partially withdrawn.

18. Install the brake drum on drum brake models.

19. On axles with a locking differential, place the C–lock on the axle shaft so that the ends are flush with the thrust block.

20. Pull the shaft flange outward in order to seat the lock in the differential gear.

21. Align the hole in the pinion shaft with the bolt hole in the differential case.

22. Install the new pinion shaft locking bolt and tighten to 27 ft. lbs. (36 Nm) on 8.5 inch axles or 37 ft. lbs. (50 Nm) on 9.5 inch axles.

23. Install the rear cover and the gasket.

24. Install the caliper on disc brake models.

25. Install the tire and wheel assembly.

26. Fill the rear axle, using the proper fluid.

27. Lower the vehicle.

9.75 Inch Rear Axles

See Figure 46.

1. Release the parking brake.

2. Raise and support the vehicle.

3. Remove the tire and wheel assembly.

4. Remove the rear steering gear assembly.

5. Remove the steering knuckle assembly.

6. Remove the lock clip from the axle shaft end. The lock clip is spring loaded and fits securely in the axle shaft slot and may need to be push off the shaft end with a screw driver or related tool. Pushing the axle shaft inwards towards the gears my help in removal of the lock clip.

7. When removing the axle shaft do not rotate the shaft. Rotating the shaft will cause the gears to move. Misalignment of the gears will make the assembly difficult.

8. Remove the axle shaft.

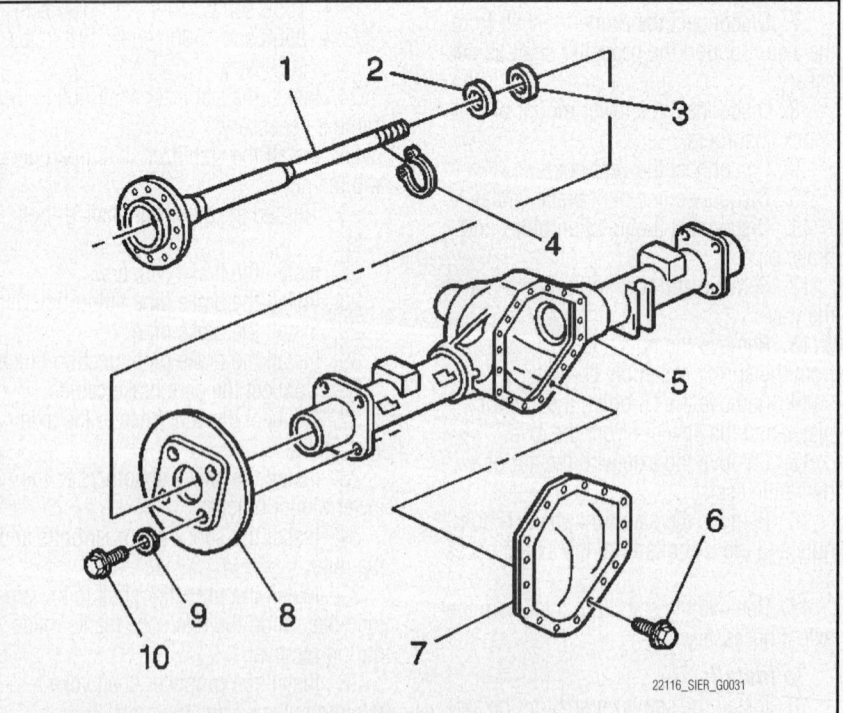

22116_SIER_G0031

Fig. 45 Exploded view of the rear axle assembly—8.6 and 9.5 inch axles

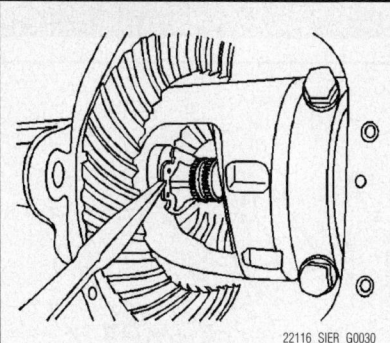

Fig. 46 Removing the lock clip—9.75 inch axles

To install:

9. Install the axle shaft.

10. Install the spring loaded lock clip to the axle shaft end.

11. Install the steering knuckle assembly.

12. Install the rear steering gear assembly.

13. Install the tire and wheel assembly.

14. Lower the vehicle.

10.5 and 11.5 Inch Rear Axles

See Figure 47.

1. Remove or disconnect the following:
   - Tire and wheel
   - Brake caliper
   - Brake rotor
   - Flange bolts

2. Lightly rap the axle shaft with a soft–faced hammer in order to loosen the shaft. Grip the rib on the axle shaft flange with a locking pliers. Twist the axle shaft flange in order to start the axle shaft

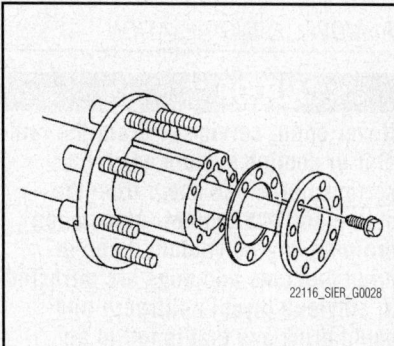

Fig. 47 Rear axle shaft removal—10.5 and 11.5 inch axles

removal. Remove the axle shaft from the tube.

3. Remove the gasket.

4. Clean the axle shaft flange and the outside face of the hub assembly. Inspect all the parts. Replace the parts as necessary.

To install:

5. Install or connect the following:
   - Gasket onto the axle shaft
   - Gasket and axle shaft into the tube. Ensure the shaft splines mesh into the differential side gear. Align the holes in the axle flange and the gasket with the holes in the hub.
   - Axle flange bolts and tighten to 110 ft. lbs. (150 Nm).
   - Rotor
   - Caliper
   - Wheel and tire

REAR PINION SEAL

REMOVAL & INSTALLATION

See Figure 48.

1. Raise the vehicle.

2. Remove the tire and wheel assemblies.

3. Remove the rear brake calipers and rotors or drums.

4. Remove the axle shafts on 10.5 inch and 11.5 inch axles.

5. Reference mark the rear propeller shaft to the rear axle pinion yoke.

6. Disconnect the propeller shaft from the axle.

7. Measure the torque required to turn the pinion. Record the torque number measurement which gives the combined pinion bearing, seal, carrier bearing, axle bearing and seal preload.

8. Make and accurate alignment mark on the pinion flange. Record the number of exposed threads on the pinion stem.

9. Remove the pinion flange nut and the washer. Use a container in order to catch any lubricant.

➡**Use care not to damage any of the machined surfaces.**

10. Remove the pinion flange.

➡**The pinion flange has an oil seal that is part of the pinion flange assembly.**

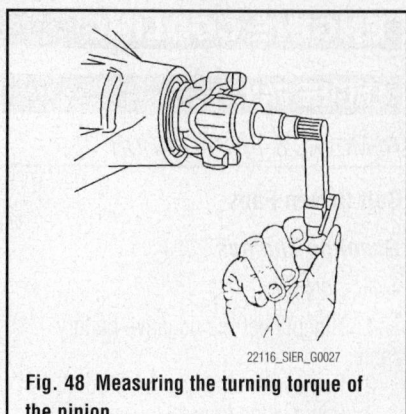

Fig. 48 Measuring the turning torque of the pinion

The pinion flange must be inspected to ensure that the seal is not damaged.

11. Pry the oil seal from the bore.

12. Thoroughly clean any foreign material from the contact area. Replace any parts as necessary.

To install:

13. Lubricate the cavity between the lips of the oil seal with wheel bearing lubricant.

14. Install the oil seal into the bore using a driver.

➡**Do not hammer the pinion flange onto the pinion stem.**

15. Install the pinion flange. Use the alignment marks in the installation of the pinion flange.

16. Install the washer and a new nut. Tighten the nut on the pinion stem as close as possible to the alignment marks without going past the marks. Use the alignment marks and the thread count as a reference. Tighten the nut a little at a time. Turn the pinion flange several times after each tightening in order to seat the rollers.

17. Measure the torque required to rotate the pinion flange. Compare this to the original torque. Tighten the pinion nut, in small increments, until the rotating torque is 3 inch lbs. (0.35 Nm) GREATER than the original torque.

18. Align the propeller shaft with the alignment marks. Connect the propeller shaft.

19. Install the axle shafts on 10.5 inch and 11.5 inch axle.

20. Install the rear brake calipers and rotors or drums.

21. Install the tire and wheel assemblies.

ENGINE COOLING

ENGINE FAN

REMOVAL & INSTALLATION

Belt Driven Fans

Gasoline Engines

See Figure 49.

1. Disconnect the negative battery cable.
2. Remove the radiator fan shroud.
3. Remove the drive belt, if necessary.
4. Remove the four fan clutch–to–water pump pulley nuts and lift out the fan/clutch assembly.
5. Remove the fan clutch bolts and separate the fan from the clutch.

To install:

6. Install the fan on the fan clutch and tighten the bolts to 17 ft. lbs. (23 Nm).
7. Position the fan/clutch assembly on the water pump pulley. Tighten the nuts to 18 ft. lbs. (24 Nm).
8. Install the fan shroud.
9. Connect the battery cable.

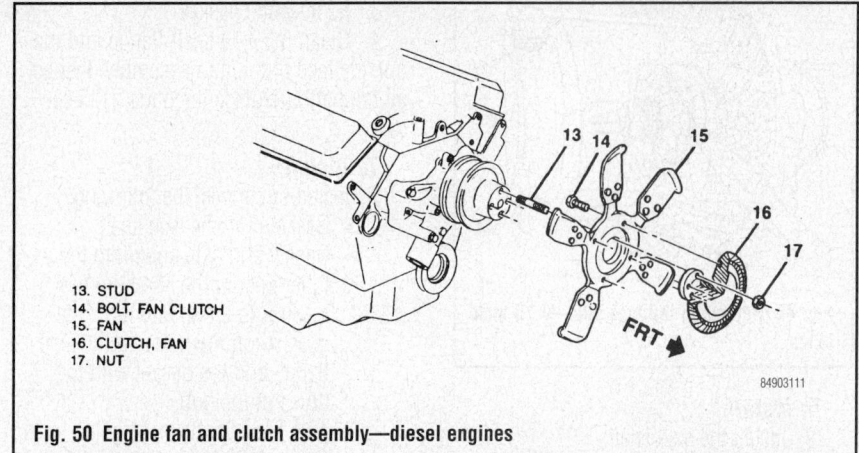

13. STUD
14. BOLT, FAN CLUTCH
15. FAN
16. CLUTCH, FAN
17. NUT

84903111

Fig. 50 Engine fan and clutch assembly—diesel engines

To install:

7. Install the fan on the fan clutch and tighten the bolts to 18 ft. lbs. (24 Nm).
8. Position the fan/clutch assembly on the water pump pulley so that the reference marks on each hub align. Tighten the nuts to 18 ft. lbs. (24 Nm).
9. Install the fan shroud.
10. Connect the battery cable.

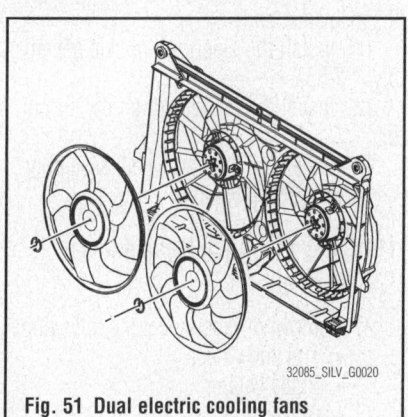

32085_SILV_G0020

Fig. 51 Dual electric cooling fans

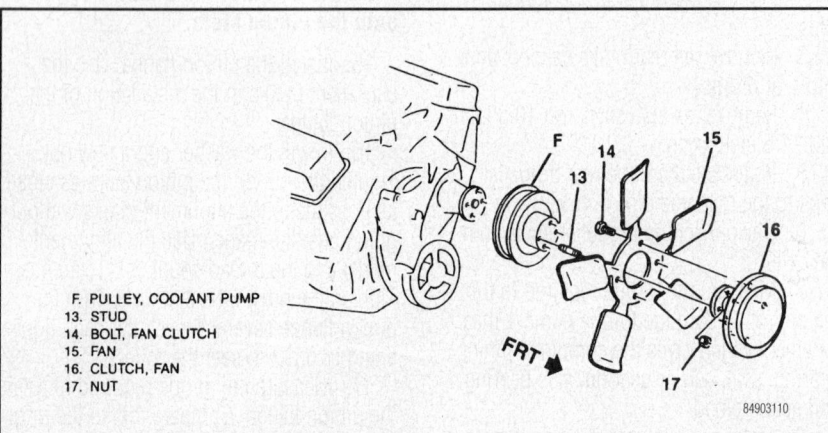

F. PULLEY, COOLANT PUMP
13. STUD
14. BOLT, FAN CLUTCH
15. FAN
16. CLUTCH, FAN
17. NUT

84903110

Fig. 49 Engine fan and clutch assembly—gasoline engines

Diesel Engines

See Figure 50.

1. Disconnect the negative battery cable.
2. Remove the radiator shroud.
3. Locate the yellow dot on the fan clutch hub and matchmark the water pump pulley.
4. Remove the drive belt, if necessary.
5. Remove the fan clutch–to–water pump pulley nuts and lift out the fan/clutch assembly.
6. Remove the fan clutch bolts and separate the fan from the clutch.

Dual Electric Fans

See Figure 51.

1. Remove the cooling fan and shroud.
2. Remove the cooling fan blade retainers.
3. Remove the cooling fan blades.

To install:

➡ The electric cooling fan assembly uses a 5–blade fan and a 7–blade fan, it does not matter which side the fan blades are installed on. DO NOT install two 5–blade assemblies or two 7–blade assemblies, as this would cause a noise issue.

4. Install the cooling fan blades.
5. Install the cooling fan blade retainers.
6. Install the cooling fan and shroud.

RADIATOR

REMOVAL & INSTALLATION

✳✳ CAUTION

Never open, service or drain the radiator or cooling system when hot; serious burns can occur from the steam and hot coolant. Also, when draining engine coolant, keep in mind that cats and dogs are attracted to ethylene glycol antifreeze and could drink any that is left in an uncovered container or in puddles on the ground. This will prove fatal in sufficient quantities. Always drain coolant into a sealable container. Coolant should be reused unless it is contaminated or is several years old.

Gasoline Engines

See Figure 52.

1. Remove the upper intake manifold sight shield using the following procedure:

    a. Remove the retaining bolt in the front of the shield.

    b. Lift–up on the front of the shield.

    c. Lift the shield off the rear bracket.

2. Drain the engine coolant.

3. Remove the radiator inlet hose from the water outlet tube.

4. Remove the bolt and wiring harness bracket at the thermostat housing.

5. Disconnect the turbocharger coolant hose from the turbocharger bypass valve.

6. Remove the turbocharger bypass valve and sealing washer from the water outlet tube.

7. Remove the 2 bolts retaining the water outlet tube to the left valve rocker arm cover.

8. Remove the bolt retaining the water outlet tube to the thermostat housing.

9. Remove the water outlet tube.

10. Remove and discard the O–ring seal.

To install:

11. Install a new O–ring seal on the water outlet tube.

12. Lightly lubricate the O–ring seal with coolant.

13. Install the water outlet tube.

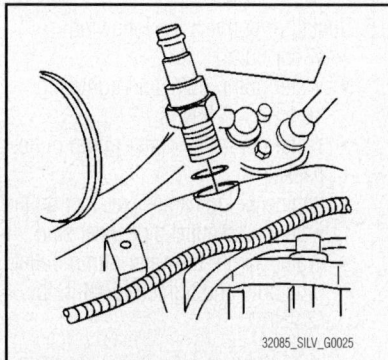

Fig. 58 Turbocharger bypass valve and sealing washer—6.6L engines

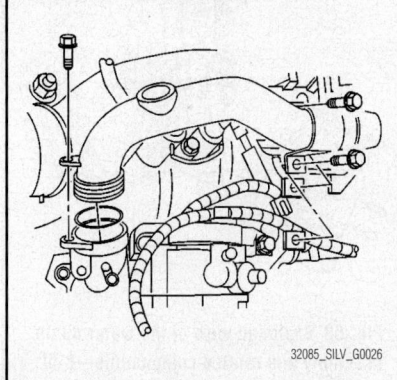

Fig. 59 Water outlet tube—6.6L engines

14. Install the bolt retaining the water outlet tube to the thermostat housing.

    a. Tighten the water outlet tube to thermostat housing bolt to 15 ft. lbs. (21 Nm).

15. Install the 2 bolts retaining the water outlet tube to the valve rocker arm cover.

    a. Tighten the water outlet tube to valve rocker arm cover bolts to 15 ft. lbs. (21 Nm).

16. Install the turbocharger bypass valve and sealing washer to the water outlet tube.

    a. Tighten the turbocharger bypass valve to 44 ft. lbs. (60 Nm).

17. Connect the turbocharger coolant hose to the turbocharger bypass valve.

18. Install the bolt and wiring harness bracket to the thermostat housing.

    a. Tighten the wiring harness bracket bolt to 71 inch lbs. (8 Nm).

19. Install the radiator inlet hose to the water outlet tube.

20. Fill the engine coolant.

21. Install the upper intake manifold sight shield.

    a. Tighten the upper intake manifold shield bolt to 80 inch lbs. (9 Nm).

22. With the engine idling, add coolant to the radiator until the coolant level reaches the bottom of the filler neck.

23. Install the radiator cap to the radiator.

24. Inspect the coolant system for leaks.

8.1L Engine

See Figure 60.

1. Drain the cooling system.

2. Reposition the inlet hose clamp at the water outlet.

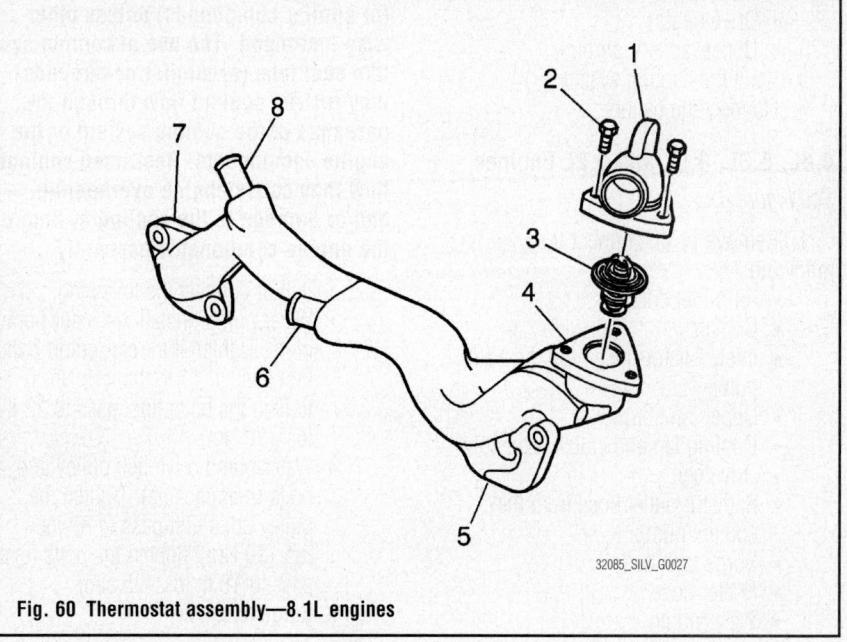

Fig. 60 Thermostat assembly—8.1L engines

3. Remove the inlet hose from the water outlet.

4. Remove the water outlet bolts (2).

5. Remove the water outlet (1).

6. Remove the thermostat (3).

To install:

7. Install the thermostat (3).

8. Install the water outlet (1).

9. Install the water outlet bolts (2).

    a. Tighten the bolts to 22 ft. lbs. (30 Nm).

10. Install the inlet hose to the water outlet.

11. Position the inlet hose clamp at the water outlet.

12. Fill the cooling system.

13. With the engine idling, add coolant to the radiator until the coolant level reaches the bottom of the filler neck.

14. Install the radiator cap to the radiator.

15. Inspect the coolant system for leaks.

WATER PUMP

REMOVAL & INSTALLATION

4.3L Engine

See Figure 61.

1. Drain the radiator.

2. Remove or disconnect the following:

- Fan shroud
- Negative battery cable
- Drive belt(s)
- Alternator and other accessories, if necessary
- Fan, fan clutch and pulley
- Accessory brackets that might interfere with water pump removal

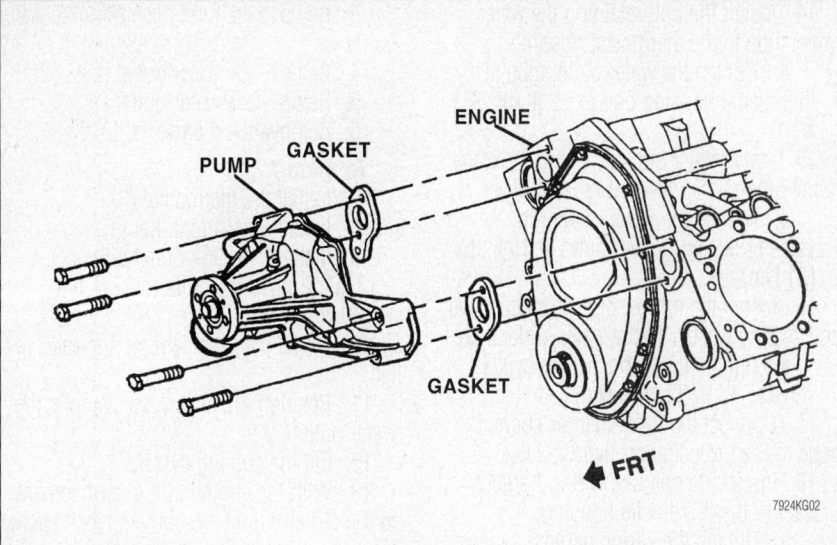

Fig. 61 Exploded view of the water pump mounting—4.3L engines

- Lower radiator hose from the water pump inlet
- Heater hose from the nipple on the pump
- Water pump assembly away from the timing cover

To install:

3. Clean all old gasket material from the timing chain cover.
4. Install or connect the following:
   - Pump assembly with a new gasket. Torque the bolts to 33 ft. lbs. (45 Nm).
   - Hose between the water pump inlet and the pump
   - Fan, fan clutch and pulley
   - Alternator and other accessories, if necessary
   - Drive belt(s)
   - Upper radiator shroud
5. Refill the cooling system.
6. Connect the battery.

4.8L, 5.3L, 6.0L and 6.2L Engines

See Figure 62.

1. Remove or disconnect the following:
   - Air outlet duct
   - Coolant
   - Inlet radiator hose from the water pump
   - Upper fan shroud
   - Cooling fan and clutch assembly
   - Drive belt
   - Radiator outlet hose from the coolant pump
   - Surge tank hose
   - Heater hose
   - Water pump

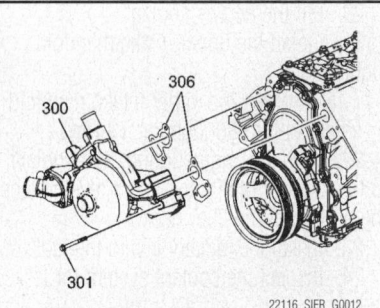

Fig. 62 Exploded view of the water pump assembly—4.8L, 5.3L, 6.0L and 6.2L engines

To install:

➡**DO NOT use cooling system seal tabs (or similar compounds) unless otherwise instructed. The use of cooling system seal tabs (or similar compounds) may restrict coolant flow through the passages of the cooling system or the engine components. Restricted coolant flow may cause engine overheating and/or damage to the cooling system or the engine components/assembly.**

2. Install or connect the following:
   - Water pump. Install the water pump bolts. Tighten the water pump bolts first pass to 11 ft. lbs. (15 Nm); tighten the bolts final pass to 22 ft. lbs. (30 Nm).
   - Water pump drive belt pulley and bolts (if applicable). Tighten the pulley bolts first pass to 89 inch lbs. (10 Nm); tighten the bolts final pass to 18 ft. lbs. (25 Nm).
   - Surge tank hose

- Heater hose
- Outlet radiator hose to the coolant pump
- Drive belt
- Cooling fan and clutch assembly
- Upper fan shroud
- Inlet radiator hose to the water pump
- Air inlet duct
- Coolant

6.6L Engine

See Figure 63.

1. Remove the left front fender wheelhouse inner panel.
2. Drain the coolant.
3. Remove or disconnect the following:
   - Thermostat housing crossover
   - Fan clutch
   - Crankshaft balancer
   - Water pump outlet pipe–to–water pump nuts
   - Engine wiring harness retainer front the inner stud
   - Water pump bolts, noting their locations as they are different lengths
   - Water pump and gasket

To install:

4. Lubricate the water pump O–ring with engine oil.
5. Install or connect the following:
   - Water pump
   - Water pump bolts and tighten to 18 ft. lbs. (25 Nm)
   - Water pump–to–water pump outlet gasket
   - Engine wiring harness retainer on the water pump outlet pipe inner stud
   - Water pump–to–water pump outlet pipe nuts and tighten to 18 ft. lbs. (25 Nm)

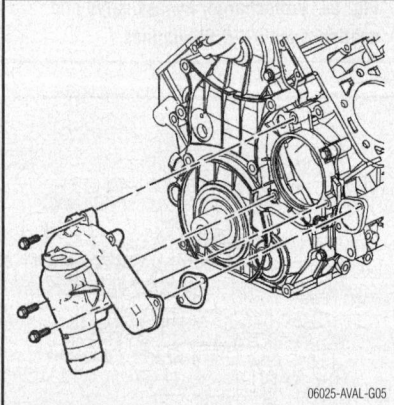

Fig. 63 Exploded view of the water pump assembly and related components—6.6L diesel engines

- Thermostat housing crossover
- Crankshaft balancer
- Fan clutch

6. Fill the cooling system and install the left front fender wheelhouse inner panel.

8.1L Engine

See Figure 64.

1. Remove or disconnect the following:
   - Coolant
   - Drive belt
   - Fan clutch
   - Outlet hose clamp and hose
2. Reposition the bypass hose clamps at the water pump and water crossover
   - Bypass hose
   - Water pump bolt and pump. Discard the water pump gaskets.

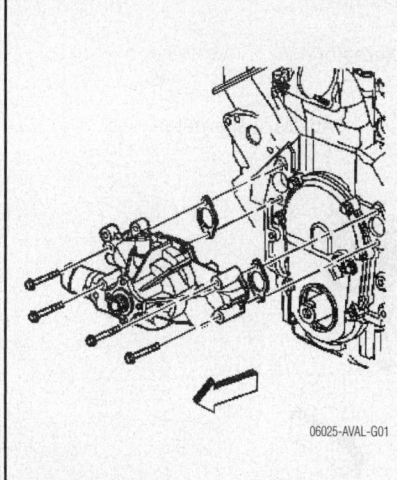

Fig. 64 Exploded view of the water pump assembly—8.1L engines

To install:

3. Install or connect the following:
   - New water pump gaskets.
   - Water pump and bolts. Tighten the water pump bolts 37 ft. lbs. (50 Nm).
   - Bypass hose and clamps
   - Outlet hose and clamp
   - Fan clutch
   - Drive belt
   - Surge tank hose
   - Heater hose
   - Outlet radiator hose to the coolant pump
   - Drive belt
   - Cooling fan and clutch assembly
   - Upper fan shroud
   - Inlet radiator hose to the water pump
   - Air inlet duct
   - Coolant

ENGINE ELECTRICAL

CHARGING SYSTEM

ALTERNATOR

REMOVAL & INSTALLATION

4.3L Engine

See Figure 65.

1. Remove or disconnect the following:
   - Negative battery cable
   - Wires
   - Accessory belt(s)
   - Mounting bracket, if necessary
   - Alternator

To install:

2. Install or connect the following:
   - Alternator
   - Mounting bracket. Torque the bolts to 18 ft lbs. (25 Nm).

- Mounting bolts. Torque the right bolt to 18 ft lbs. (25 Nm) and left bolt to 37 ft. lbs. (50 Nm).
- Accessory belt(s)
- Wires. Torque the battery feed wire to 71 inch lbs. (8 Nm).
- Negative battery cable

4.8L, 5.3L, 6.0L and 6.2L Engines

See Figure 66.

1. Disconnect the negative battery cable.
2. Remove or disconnect the following:
   - Accessory drive belt
   - Engine sight shield, if necessary
   - Electrical connections from the alternator

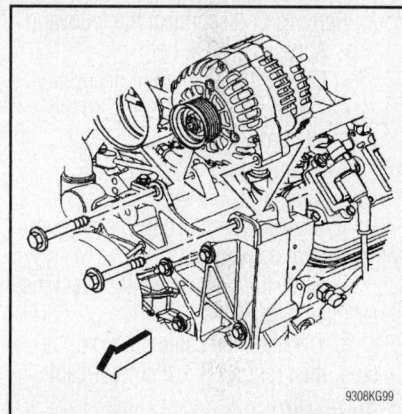

Fig. 66 Alternator mounting—4.8L, 5.3L, 6.0L and 6.2L engines; 8.1L similar

- Mounting bolts
- Alternator

To install:

3. Install the alternator.
4. Install or connect the following:
   - Alternator mounting bolts. Tighten the bolts to 37 ft. lbs. (50 Nm) on 2005–06 models and 2007 Classic. On other 2007 models, tighten to 41 ft. lbs. (55 Nm).
   - Electrical connections to the alternator. Tighten the B+ nut to 80 inch. lbs. (9 Nm).
   - Engine sight shield, if removed
   - Accessory drive belt
5. Connect the negative battery cable.

6.6L Engine

See Figure 67.

➡This procedure applies to both the main and auxiliary alternators.

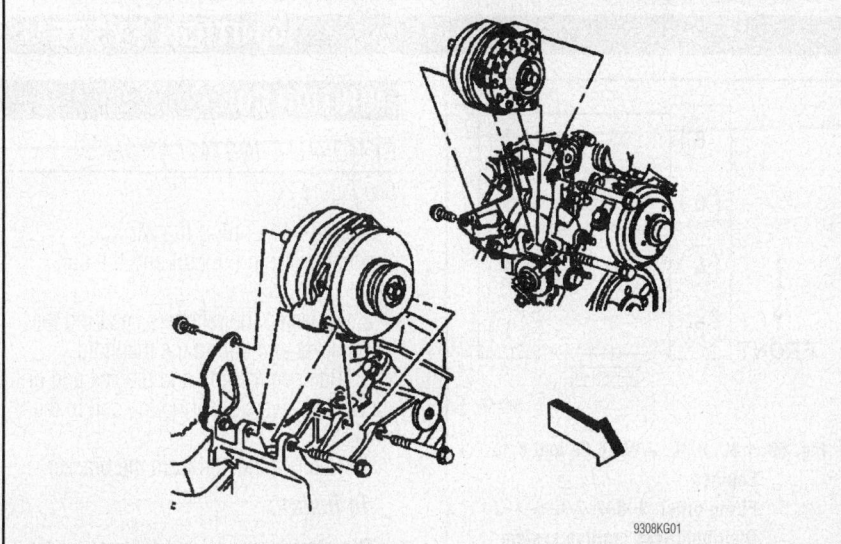

Fig. 65 Exploded view of the alternator mounting—4.3L engines

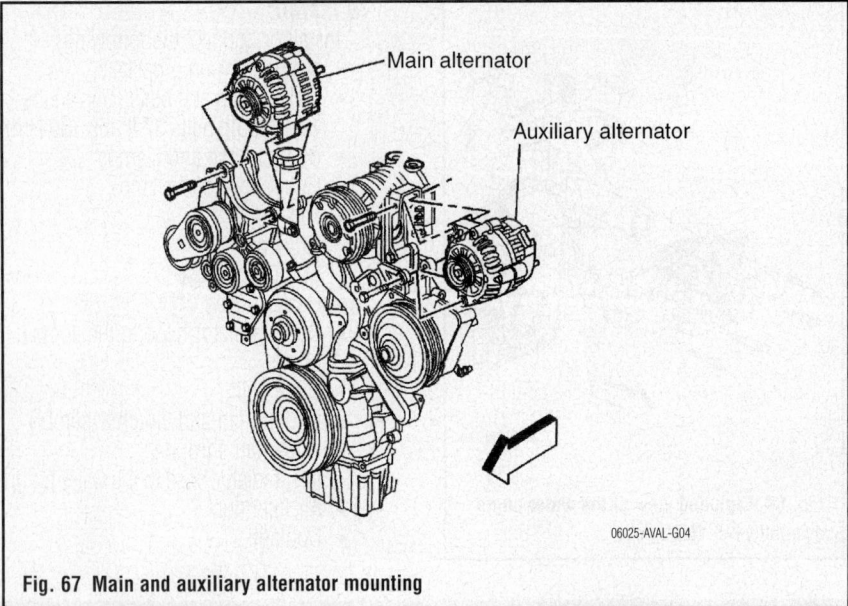

Fig. 67 Main and auxiliary alternator mounting

1. Disconnect the negative battery cable.
2. Remove or disconnect the following:
   - Accessory drive belt
   - Engine sight shield, if necessary
   - Electrical connections from the alternator
   - Mounting bolts
   - Alternator
3. If necessary, remove the cable from the alternator as follows:
   a. Slide the boot down, to reveal the terminal stud.
   b. Unfasten the cable nut from the stud, then remove the alternator cable.

To install:

4. Connect the alternator cable, secure with the nut and tighten to 80 inch lbs. (9 Nm). Slide the boot back over the terminal stud.

5. Install the alternator.

➡Use the correct fastener in the correct location. Replacement fasteners must be the correct part number for that application. Fasteners requiring replacement or fasteners requiring the use of thread locking compound or sealant are identified in the service procedure. Do not use paints, lubricants, or corrosion inhibitors on fasteners or fastener joint surfaces unless specified. These coatings affect fastener torque and joint clamping force and may damage the fastener. Use the correct tightening sequence and specifications when installing fasteners in order to avoid damage to parts and systems.

6. Install or connect the following:
   - Alternator mounting bolts and tighten to 37 ft. lbs. (50 Nm)
   - Electrical connections to the alternator. Tighten the B+ nut to 13 ft. lbs. (18 Nm).
   - Engine sight shield, if removed
   - Accessory drive belt
7. Connect the negative battery cable.

8.1L Engine

1. Disconnect the negative battery cable.
2. Remove or disconnect the following:
   - Electrical connections from the alternator
3. Remove the cable from the alternator as follows:
   a. Slide the boot down, to reveal the terminal stud.
   b. Unfasten the cable nut from the stud, then remove the alternator cable.
   - Accessory drive belt
   - Mounting bolts
   - Alternator
   - Mounting bolts securing the alternator to the brace and bracket
   - Alternator

To install:

4. Install or connect the following:
   - Alternator
   - Alternator mounting bolts. Tighten the bolts to 37 ft. lbs. (50 Nm).
   - Accessory drive belt
5. Connect the alternator cable, secure with the nut and tighten to 80 inch lbs. (9 Nm). Slide the boot back over the terminal stud.
   - Electrical connections to the alternator
6. Connect the negative battery cable.

ENGINE ELECTRICAL

FIRING ORDER

See Figures 68 and 69.

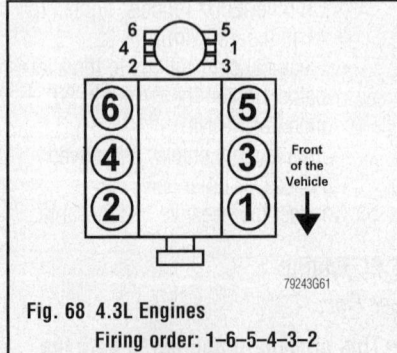

Fig. 68 4.3L Engines
Firing order: 1–6–5–4–3–2
Distributor rotation: Clockwise

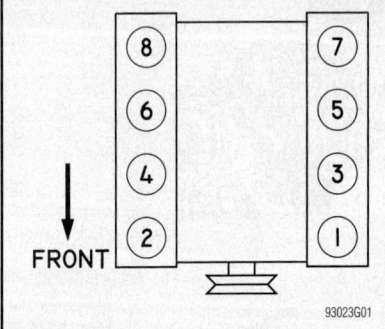

Fig. 69 4.8L, 5.3L, 6.0L, 6.2L and 8.1L Engines
Firing order: 1–8–7–2–6–5–4–3
Distributorless ignition system (one coil for each cylinder)

IGNITION SYSTEM

IGNITION COIL

REMOVAL & INSTALLATION
See Figure 70.

1. Tag and unplug the wiring connectors from the coil and the coil wire.
2. Unfasten the retainers securing the coil bracket and coil to the manifold.
3. Remove the coil and bracket and drill out the two rivets securing the coil to the bracket.
4. Remove the coil from the bracket.

To install:

➡The replacement coil kit may come with the two screws to attach the coil to

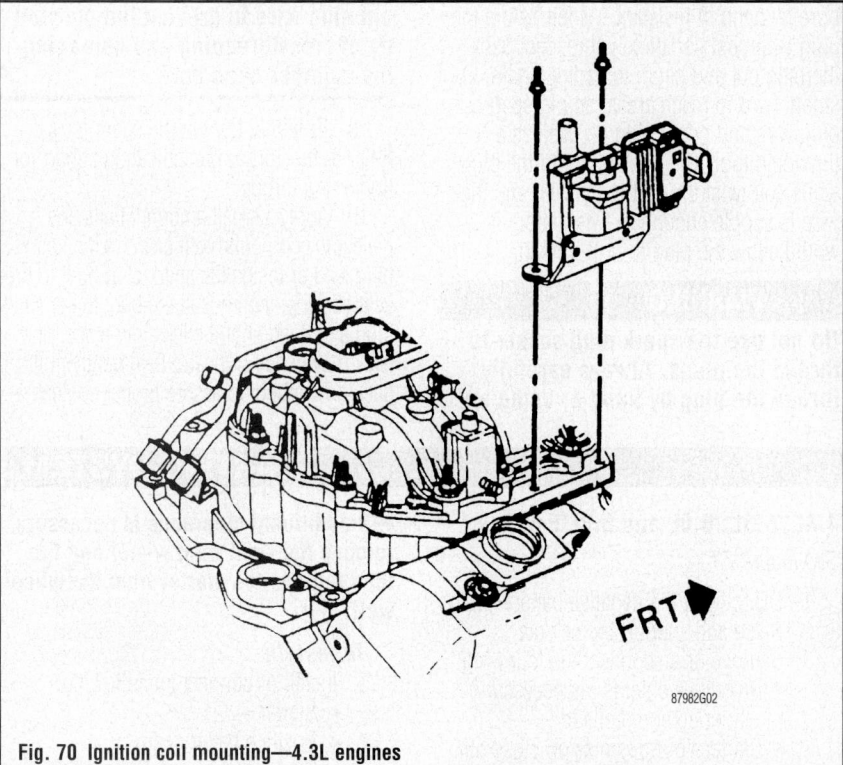

Fig. 70 Ignition coil mounting—4.3L engines

the bracket. If not, you must supply your own screws.

5. Fasten the coil to the bracket using two screws.
6. Fasten the coil and bracket to the manifold. Tighten the retainers until they are snug.
7. Engage the coil wire and the wiring connectors to the coil.

IGNITION TIMING

ADJUSTMENT

The ignition timing is controlled by the Powertrain Control Module (PCM). No adjustment is necessary or possible.

SPARK PLUGS

REMOVAL & INSTALLATION

See Figure 71.

➡ **All models were originally equipped with platinum–tip spark plugs which can be used for as–long–as 100,000 miles (161,000 km). This holds true unless internal engine wear or damage and/or improperly operating emissions controls cause plug fouling. If you suspect this, you may wish to remove and inspect the platinum plugs before the recommended mileage. Most platinum plugs should not be cleaned or re-gapped. If you find their condition unsuitable, they should be replaced.**

When removing the spark plugs, work on 1 at a time. Don't start by removing the plug wires all at once because unless you number them, they're going to get mixed up. On some models though, it will be more convenient for you to remove all of the wires before you start to work on the plugs. If this is necessary, take a minute before you begin and number the wires with tape before you take them off. The time you spend here will pay off later.

1. Disconnect the negative battery cable, and if the vehicle has been run recently, allow the engine to thoroughly cool. Attempting to remove plugs from a hot cylinder head could cause the plugs to seize and damage the threads in the cylinder head.

2. Check for access to the plugs on your vehicle. The wheel wells of some vehicles covered by this manual are designed to allow access to the sides of the engine. A rubber cover may be draped over the opening, and it may require removal of 1 or more plastic body snap–fasteners (which are carefully pried loose using a special C–shaped tool) before you can move it aside for clearance. If this is your best access point, raise and support the vehicle safely then remove the front tire and wheel assemblies.

➡ **On some models, the engine cover may be removed to provide additional**

access to the spark plugs. This will be necessary if you also plan to check the spark plug wires at this time anyway.

3. Carefully twist the spark plug wire boot to loosen it, then pull upward and remove the boot from the plug. Be sure to pull on the boot and not on the wire, otherwise the connector located inside the boot may become separated.

➡ **A spark plug wire removal tool is recommended as it will make removal easier and help prevent damage to the boot and wire assembly.**

4. Using compressed air (and SAFETY GLASSES), blow any water or debris from the spark plug well to assure that no harmful contaminants are allowed to enter the combustion chamber when the spark plug is removed. If compressed air is not available, use a rag or a brush to clean the area.

➡ **Remove the spark plugs when the engine is cold, if possible, to prevent damage to the threads. If plug removal is difficult, apply a few drops of penetrating oil or silicone spray to the area around the base of the plug, and allow it a few minutes to work.**

5. Using a spark plug socket (usually a ⅝ in. socket on these engines) that is equipped with a rubber insert to properly hold the plug, turn the spark plug counterclockwise to loosen and remove the spark plug from the bore.

✳✳ WARNING

AVOID the use of a flexible extension on the socket. Use of a flexible extension may allow a shear force to be applied to the plug. A shear force could break the plug off in the cylinder head, leading to costly and frustrating repairs.

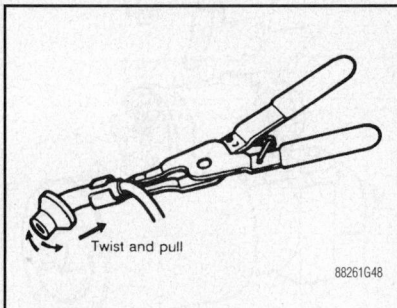

Fig. 71 A spark plug wire removal tool is recommended to prevent wire damage (and to make it easier)

To install:

6. Inspect the spark plug boot for tears or damage. If a damaged boot is found, the spark plug wire must be replaced. As mentioned earlier, this is an excellent time to check each of the spark plug wires for proper resistance and/or for damage.

7. Using a wire feeler gauge, check and adjust the spark plug gap. When using a gauge, the proper size should pass between the electrodes with a slight drag. The next larger size should not be able to pass while the next smaller size should pass freely.

8. Carefully thread the plug into the bore by hand. If resistance is felt before the plug is almost completely threaded, back the plug out and begin threading again. In small, hard to reach areas, an old spark plug wire and boot could be used as a threading tool. The boot will hold the plug while you twist the end of the wire and the wire is supple enough to twist before it would allow the plug to crossthread.

✳ WARNING

Do not use the spark plug socket to thread the plugs. Always carefully thread the plug by hand or using an old plug wire to prevent the possibility of crossthreading and damaging the cylinder head bore.

9. Carefully tighten the spark plug. Refer to the Torque Specifications chart for tightening torque.

10. Apply a small amount of silicone dielectric compound to the end of the spark plug lead or inside the spark plug boot to prevent sticking, then install the boot to the spark plug and push until it clicks into place. The click may be felt or heard, then gently pull back on the boot to assure proper contact.

ENGINE ELECTRICAL

STARTER

REMOVAL & INSTALLATION

4.3L Engine

See Figure 72.

1. Remove or disconnect the following:
   • Negative battery cable
   • Bracket and shield
   • Wires
   • Mounting bolts and shims
   • Starter

To install:

2. Install or connect the following:
   • Starter
   • Mounting bolts and shim. Torque the bolts to 33 ft lbs. (45 Nm).
   • Wires. Torque battery wire nut to 89 inch lbs. (10 Nm) and ignition nut to 18 inch lbs. (2 Nm).
   • Bracket and shield. Torque the nuts to 53 inch lbs. (6 Nm).
   • Negative battery cable

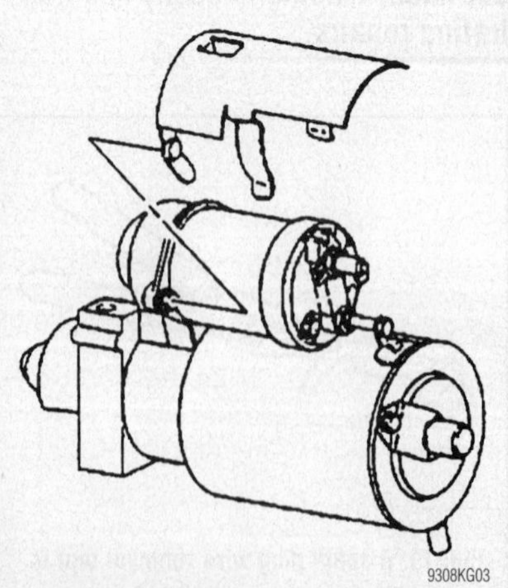

Fig. 72 Exploded view of the starter motor–4.3L engines

4.8L, 5.3L, 6.0L and 6.2L Engines

See Figure 73.

1. Disconnect the negative battery cable.
2. Raise and support the vehicle.
3. Remove or disconnect the following:
   • Protective shields (as necessary)
   • Starter solenoid shield
   • Starter–to–transmission close out cover bolt
   • Engine oil level sensor connection
4. Slide the starter forward until the starter clears the transmission.
   • Starter transmission close out cover
   • Positive battery cable and wiring harness from the starter
   • Starter

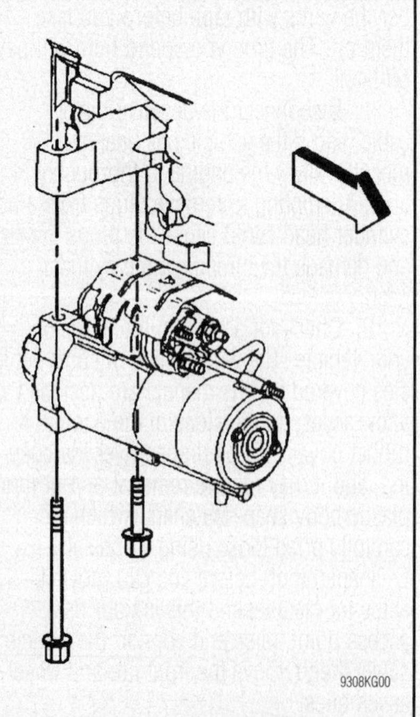

Fig. 73 Starter removal—4.8L, 5.3L, 6.0L and 6.2L engines

STARTING SYSTEM

➡If additional clearance is necessary, remove the right front wheel and tire, then remove the starter from the wheel well.

To install:

5. Install or connect the following:
   • Starter
   • Positive battery cable.
   • Starter transmission close out cover
   • Mounting bolts to the engine block and tighten to 37 ft. lbs. (50 Nm)
   • Oil level sensor connection
   • Starter–to–transmission close out cover bolt
   • Starter solenoid shield
   • Protective shields (as necessary)
6. Remove the safety stands.
7. Lower the vehicle.
8. Connect the negative battery cable.

6.6L Engine

See Figure 74.

1. Remove or disconnect the following:
   • Negative battery cables
   • Right front wheel and fender splash shield
   • Turbocharger exhaust pipe
   • Mounting bolts/nuts and shim, if used
   • Starter
   • Wires
   • Heat shield and bracket

To install:

2. Install or connect the following:
   • Heat shield and bracket.
   • Wires. Tighten the solenoid nut to 30 inch lbs. (3.4 Nm) and the positive battery cable nut to 80 inch lbs. (9 Nm).
   • Starter
   • Mounting bolts/nuts and shim,

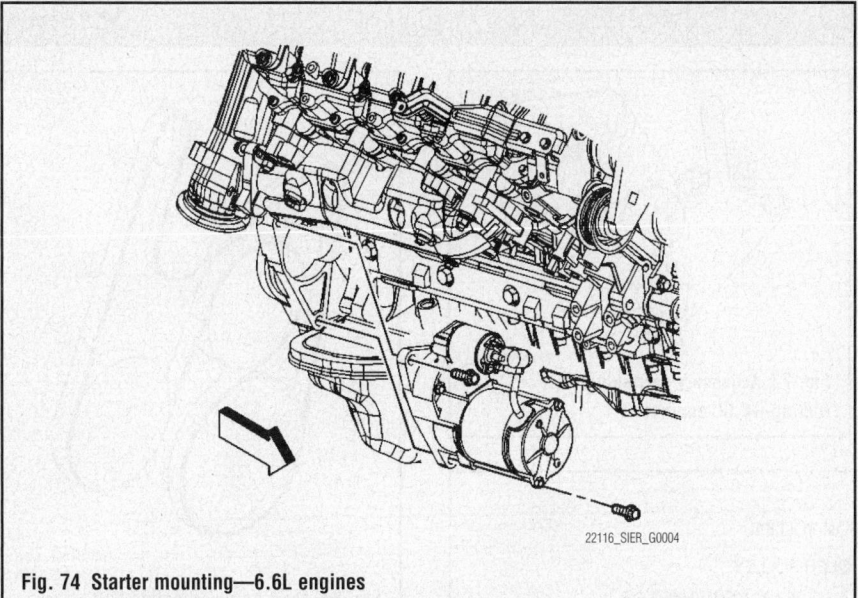

Fig. 74 Starter mounting—6.6L engines

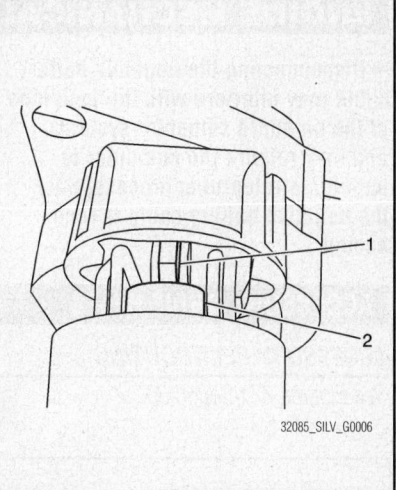

Fig. 76 Make sure that the drive gear lever (1) is properly installed into the solenoid plunger (2) loop

if used. Tighten the starter bolts to 63 ft. lbs. (85 Nm).
- Turbocharger exhaust pipe
- Right front fender splash shield and wheel
- Negative battery cables

8.1L Engine

1. Remove or disconnect the following:
   - Negative battery cable
   - Positive battery cable nut
   - Positive cable from the solenoid
   - Engine harness ground nut and ground from the solenoid
   - Mounting bolts and starter
   - Heat shield bolts, nut and shield, if necessary

To install:

2. Install or connect the following:
   - Heat shield, bolts and nut if removed. Tighten the bolts to 35 inch lbs. (3 Nm) and the nut to 44 inch lbs. (5 Nm).
   - Starter and bolts. Tighten to 37 ft. lbs. (50 Nm).
   - Ground wire and nut. Tighten to 30 inch lbs. (3.4 Nm).
   - Positive cable and nut. Tighten to 80 inch lbs. (9 Nm).
   - Negative battery cable.

SOLENOID REPLACEMENT

See Figures 75 and 76.

1. Remove the starter motor.
2. Reposition the M–terminal stud weather cover.
3. Clean the epoxy coating from the M–terminal stud.
4. Loosen the M–terminal stud nut.

5. Remove the cable from the M–terminal stud.
6. Remove the solenoid bolts.
7. Separate the solenoid from the housing and unhook the solenoid plunger from the drive gear lever.
8. Note that the spring (3) is positioned against the drive gear lever (1) and the drive gear lever is placed inside the solenoid plunger loop (2).
9. Remove the solenoid housing.
10. If necessary, remove the solenoid plunger and spring.

To install:

11. If necessary, install the solenoid plunger and spring.
12. Using Three Bond silicone 1207B, GM P/N 97720043, seal the starter solenoid attachment area.

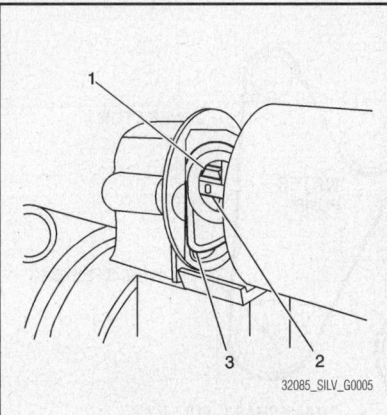

Fig. 75 Spring (3) is positioned against the drive gear lever (1) and the drive gear lever is placed inside the solenoid plunger loop (2)

❊❊ WARNING

Make sure that the drive gear lever (1) is properly installed into the solenoid plunger (2) loop. Improper installation of the drive gear lever will cause an abnormal or no operation condition of the starter.

13. Install the solenoid, making sure to insert the drive gear lever (1) into the solenoid plunger (2) loop, perform the following:
   a. Pull the gear lever (1) out away from the starter housing and pull the plunger (2) out away from the solenoid.
   b. Tip the solenoid and insert the lever into the loop, push the solenoid against the housing.
14. Install the solenoid bolts and tighten the bolts to 89 inch lbs. (10 Nm).
15. Wipe the excess silicone pressed out during the solenoid installation from around the base of the solenoid to make a weather proof seal.
16. Install the cable to the M–terminal stud between the washers and terminal nut.
17. Tighten the M–terminal stud nut and tighten the nut to 71 inch lbs. (8 Nm).
18. Using Three Bond silicone 1207B, GM P/N 97720043, seal the M–terminal stud connection.
19. Reposition the M–terminal stud weather cover.
20. Bench test the starter in a free–run condition prior to installation.
21. Install the starter motor.

ENGINE MECHANICAL

➡️Disconnecting the negative battery cable may interfere with the functions of the on board computer systems and may require the computer to undergo a relearning process, once the negative battery cable is reconnected.

ACCESSORY DRIVE BELTS

ACCESSORY BELT ROUTING

See Figures 77 through 80.

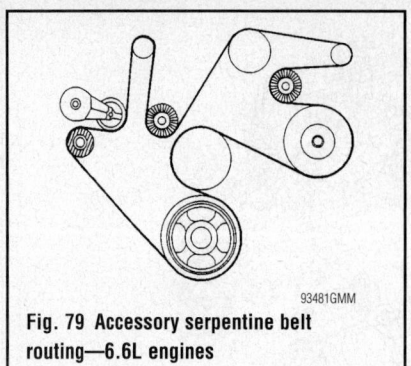

Fig. 79 Accessory serpentine belt routing—6.6L engines

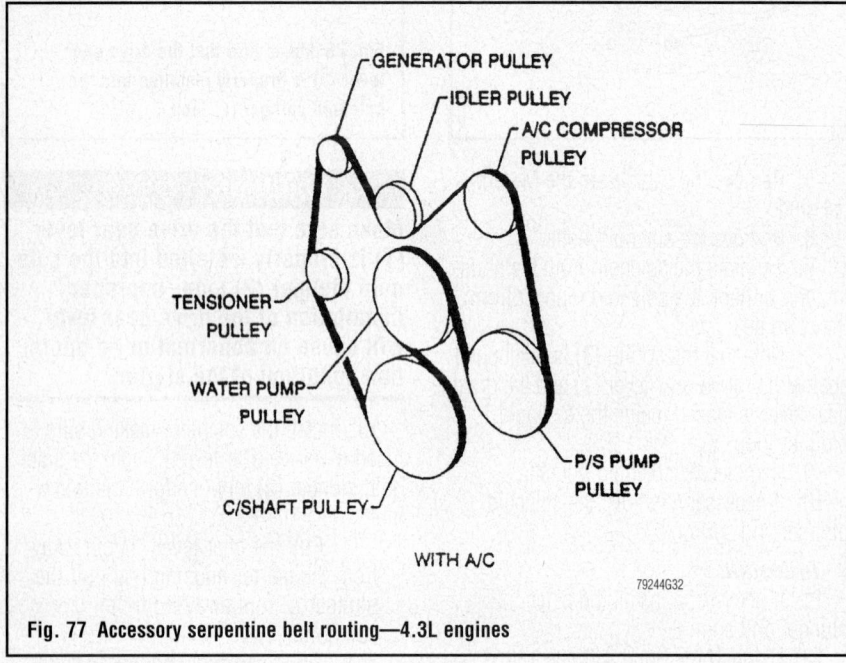

Fig. 77 Accessory serpentine belt routing—4.3L engines

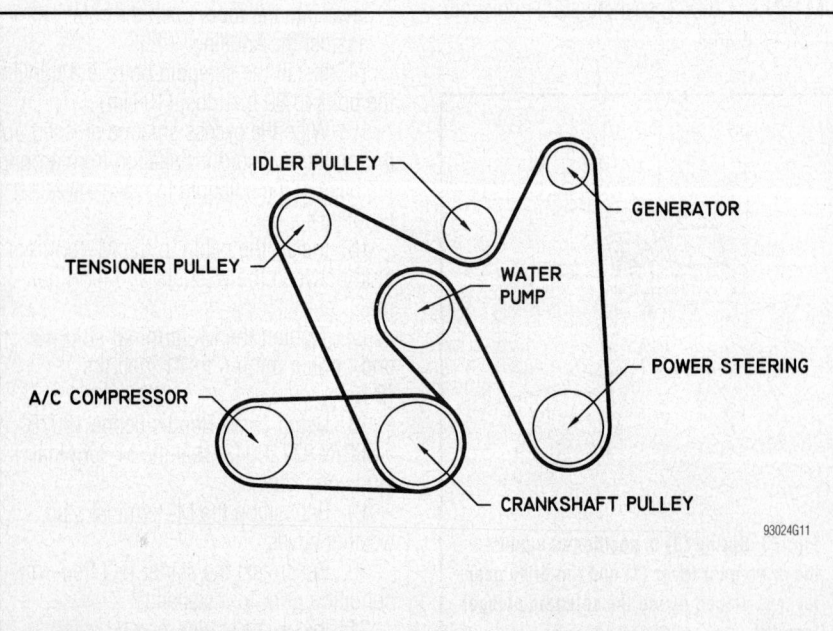

Fig. 78 Accessory serpentine belt routing—4.8L, 5.3L, 6.0L and 6.2L engines

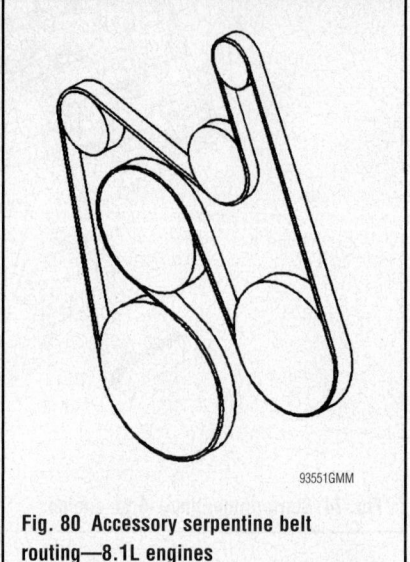

Fig. 80 Accessory serpentine belt routing—8.1L engines

INSPECTION

Inspect the drive belt for signs of glazing or cracking. A glazed belt will be perfectly smooth from slippage, while a good belt will have a slight texture of fabric visible. Cracks will usually start at the inner edge of the belt and run outward. All worn or damaged drive belts should be replaced immediately.

ADJUSTMENT

These vehicles are equipped with a single serpentine belt and spring loaded tensioner. The proper belt adjustment is automatically maintained by the tensioner, therefore, no periodic adjustment is needed. If the pointer is past the scale on the tensioner replace the belt. If correct belt tension cannot be achieved make sure the correct belt is installed. If the correct tension is still not achieved and check for proper mounting off all accessory drives.

REMOVAL & INSTALLATION

Belt replacement is a relatively simple matter rotating the tensioner off the belt (to relieve tension) and holding the tensioner in this position as the belt is slipped from its pulley. The tensioner arm contains a machined receiver for a ⅜ in. driver from a ratchet or breaker bar.

1. Before you begin, visually confirm the belt routing to the engine compartment label (if present) or to the appropriate diagram in this section (if the label is not present). If you cannot make a match (perhaps it is not the original motor for this vehicle), scribble your own diagram before proceeding.

2. Disconnect the negative battery cable for safety.

3. Install the appropriate sized breaker bar, wrench, or socket to the tensioner arm or pulley, as applicable.

4. Rotate the tensioner to the left (counterclockwise) and slip the belt from the tensioner pulley.

5. Once the belt is free from the tensioner, CAREFULLY rotate the tensioner back into position. DO NOT allow the tensioner to suddenly snap into place or damage could occur to the assembly.

6. Slip the belt from the remaining pulleys (this can get difficult is there is little room between the radiator/fan assembly and the accessory pulleys. Work slowly and be patient.

7. Once the belt is free, remove it from the engine compartment.

To install:

8. Route the belt over all the pulleys except the water pump and/or the tensioner. Refer to the routing illustration that you identified as a match before beginning.

9. Rotate the tensioner pulley to the left (counterclockwise) and hold it while you finish slipping the belt into position. Slowly allow the tensioner into contact with the belt.

10. Check to see if the correct V–groove tracking is around each pulley.

✳✳ WARNING

Improper V–groove tracking will cause the belt to fail in a short period of time.

11. Connect the negative battery cable.

BALANCE SHAFT

REMOVAL & INSTALLATION

4.3L Engine

See Figure 81.

✳✳ CAUTION

Before beginning this procedure, refer to the precautions at the beginning of the Heating & Air Conditioning Section. Only a MVAC–trained, EPA–certified, automotive technician should service the A/C system or its components.

1. Discharge and recover the air conditioning system using a proper refrigerant recovery/recycling station.

2. Properly relieve the fuel system pressure, as outlined in the Fuel System Section, then disconnect the negative battery cable.

3. Remove the air cleaner intake duct.

4. Drain the engine cooling system.

5. Remove the A/C compressor and its brackets.

6. Remove the radiator and air conditioning condenser from the vehicle.

7. Remove the fan assembly.

8. Carefully release the belt tension, then remove the serpentine drive belt.

9. Remove the water pump.

10. Remove the crankshaft pulley and damper.

11. Drain the oil and remove the oil pan.

12. Remove the front cover.

13. Remove the timing chain and sprockets.

14. Unfasten the balance shaft gear bolt, then remove the gear.

15. Remove the balance shaft retainer.

16. Remove the intake manifold assembly.

17. Remove the hydraulic lifter retainer.

18. Remove the balance shaft and front bearing by gently driving them out using a soft faced mallet.

19. Using tool J–38834 or its equivalent, remove the balance shaft rear bearing.

➡ **The balance shaft and drive and driven gears are serviced only as a set, including the gear bolt. The balance shaft and front bearing are serviced as a package.**

✳✳ WARNING

The front bearing must not be removed from the balance shaft

To install:

20. Inspect the balance shaft gears for damage, such as nicks and burrs.

21. Using a suitable gasket scraper, clean the gasket mounting surfaces. Using solvent, clean the oil and grease from the gasket mounting surfaces.

22. Lubricate the balance shaft rear bearing with clean engine oil, then install the bearing using tool J–38834 or its equivalent.

23. Lubricate the balance shaft with clean engine oil, then install the balance shaft into the block.

24. Install the balance shaft bearing retainer and bolts. Tighten the bolts to 106 inch. lbs. (12 Nm).

25. Install the balance shaft driven gear and bolt. Tighten the bolt to 15 ft. lbs. (20 Nm) plus an additional 35° using a torque/angle meter.

26. Install the hydraulic lifter retainer, then rotate the balance shaft by hand and check that there is clearance between the balance shaft and the lifter retainer.

27. Temporarily install the balance shaft drive gear so that the timing mark on the gear points straight up, then remove the drive gear, turn the balance shaft so the timing mark on the driven gear is facing straight down.

28. Install the drive gear and make sure the timing marks on both gears line up (dot–to–dot).

29. Install the drive gear retaining bolt and tighten to 12 ft. lbs. (16 Nm).

30. Install the intake manifold assembly.

31. Install the timing chain and sprocket assemblies.

32. Install the front cover, seal, bolts and the oil pan assembly.

33. Using tool J–39046 or its equivalent engage the crankshaft pulley and damper.

34. Install the water pump.

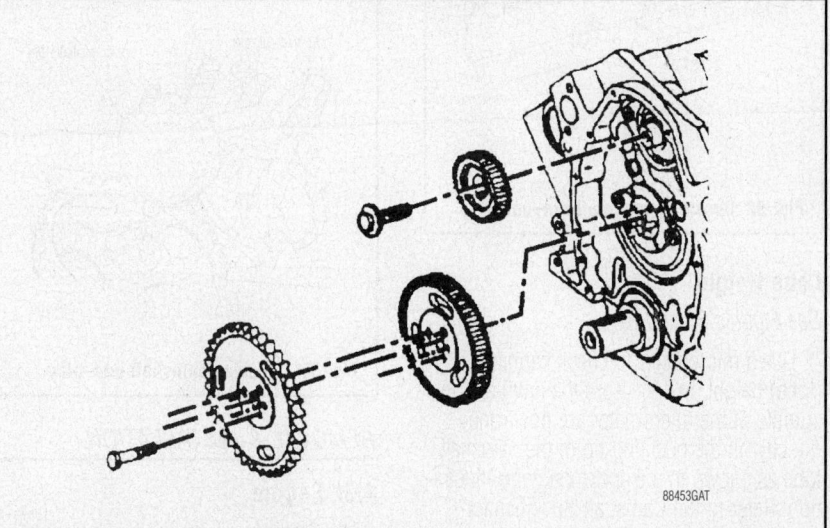

88453GAT

Fig. 81 View of the balance shaft drive and driven gears—4.3L engines

35. Install the serpentine drive belt.
36. Install the fan assembly.
37. Install the air conditioning condenser and the radiator assemblies. Engage all hoses removed from the radiator.
38. Install the A/c compressor.
39. Engage the oil and transmission cooler lines at the radiator, then install the radiator shroud.
40. Install the air cleaner assembly and connect the negative battery cable.
41. Fill the crankcase with the correct grade and amount of oil.
42. Fill the cooling system with coolant.
43. Start the vehicle and check for leaks.
44. Charge the air conditioning system using a proper refrigerant recovery/recycling station.

CAMSHAFT AND VALVE LIFTERS

INSPECTION

Run–Out

See Figure 82.

Camshaft run–out should be checked when the camshaft has been removed from the engine. An accurate dial indicator is needed for this procedure. If the run–out exceeds the limit replace the camshaft. Refer to the Camshaft Specifications chart.

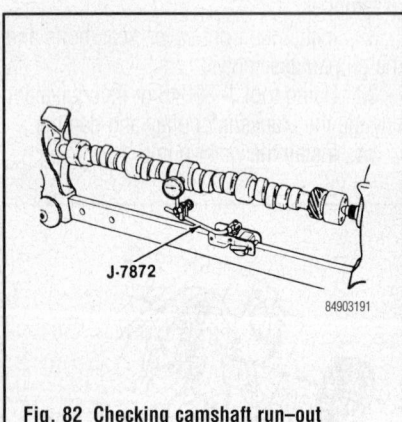

Fig. 82 Checking camshaft run–out

Lobe Height

See Figures 83 and 84.

Use a micrometer to check camshaft (lobe) height, making sure the anvil and the spindle of the micrometer are positioned directly on the heel and tip of the camshaft lobe as shown in the accompanying illustration. Refer to the Camshaft Specifications chart.

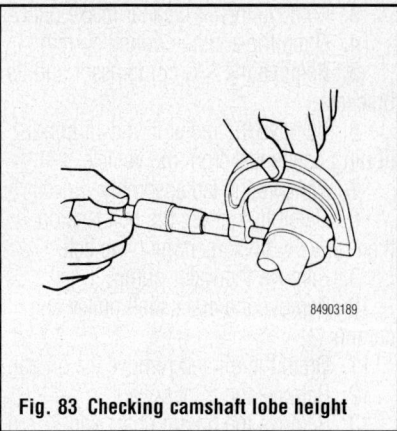

Fig. 83 Checking camshaft lobe height

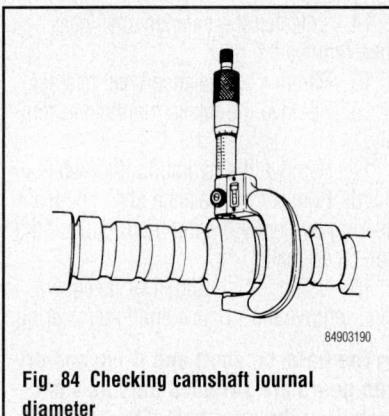

Fig. 84 Checking camshaft journal diameter

End–Play

See Figure 85.

After the camshaft has been installed, end–play should be checked. The camshaft sprocket should be installed on the cam. Use a dial gauge to check the end–play, by moving the camshaft forward and backward. Refer to the Camshaft Specifications chart.

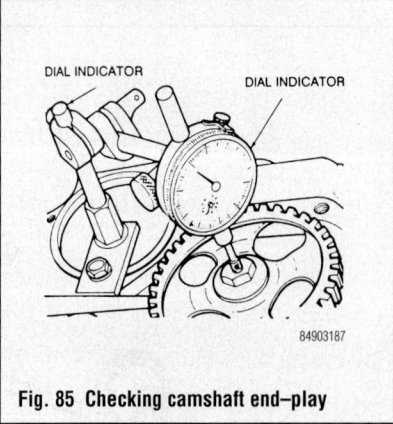

Fig. 85 Checking camshaft end–play

REMOVAL & INSTALLATION

4.3L Engine

1. Properly relieve the fuel system pressure.

2. Drain the engine cooling system.
3. Remove or disconnect the following:
   • Negative battery cable
   • Radiator
   • Cooling fan
   • Water pump
   • Rocker arm covers from the engine
   • Intake manifold assembly
   • Rocker arms, pushrods and lifters
   • Crankshaft pulley and hub
   • Engine front cover
4. Align the timing marks on the crankshaft and camshaft sprockets.
   • Camshaft sprocket and timing chain
   • Balance shaft drive gear, if equipped
   • Camshaft thrust plate

➡**Install the sprocket bolts or longer bolts of the same thread into the end of the camshaft as a handle.**

   • Camshaft

To install:

5. Lubricate the camshaft journals with clean engine oil or a suitable pre–lube.
6. Install or connect the following:
   • Camshaft
   • Camshaft thrust plate
   • Balance shaft drive gear, if equipped
   • Timing chain and camshaft sprocket
   • Engine front cover
   • Crankshaft pulley and hub
   • Valve lifters
   • Pushrods and rocker arms, properly adjust the valve clearance
   • Intake manifold assembly
   • Rocker arm covers to the engine
   • Radiator to the vehicle
   • Negative battery cable
7. Refill the engine cooling system.

4.8L, 5.3L, 6.0L and 6.2L Engines

See Figures 86 and 87.

1. Raise the hood to the servicing position and secure it. Move the hood hinge bolt to hold the hood in the servicing position.
2. Remove or disconnect the following:
   • Battery negative cable
   • Coolant
   • Upper and lower radiator hoses from the engine
   • Air cleaner duct from the engine
   • A/C condenser mounting bolts, if equipped
   • Radiator support and radiator
   • Engine cooling fan
   • Drive belt

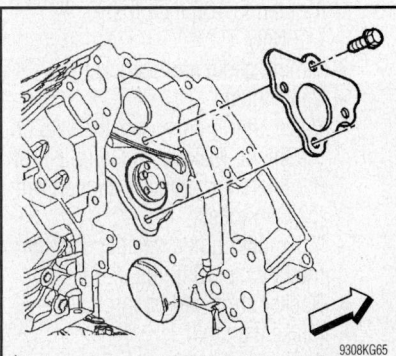

Fig. 86 Camshaft sensor removal—4.8L, 5.3L, 6.0L and 6.2L engines

- A/C drive belt, if equipped
- Engine sight shield
- Electrical wiring harness from the thermostat housing
- Water pump
3. Raise the vehicle.
- Starter motor
- Right side closeout cover and bolt
- Crankshaft balancer
- Engine oil pan
- Engine front cover
- Cylinder heads from the engine
- Valve lifters from the engine
4. Align the timing marks on the camshaft and crankshaft sprockets. Make sure that the number 1 piston is in the firing position.
- Camshaft sprocket
- Camshaft sensor bolt and sensor
- Camshaft retainer bolts and retainer

➡️**All camshaft journals are the same diameter, so care must be used in removing or installing the camshaft to avoid damage to the camshaft bearings.**

Fig. 87 Camshaft retainer removal—4.8L, 5.3L, 6.0L and 6.2L engines

5. Install the three M8–1.25 x 100 mm bolts in the camshaft front bolt holes. Using the bolts as a handle, carefully rotate and pull the camshaft out of the engine block. Remove the bolts from the front of the camshaft.
6. Clean and inspect all sealing surfaces.

To install:

➡️**If camshaft replacement is required, the valve lifters must also be replaced.**

7. Lubricate the camshaft journals and the bearings with clean engine oil. Install three M8–1.25 x 100 mm (M8–1.25 x 4.0 in) bolts into the camshaft front bolt holes.

➡️**All camshaft journals are the same diameter, so care must be used in removing or installing the camshaft to avoid damage to the camshaft bearings.**

8. Using the bolts as a handle, carefully install the camshaft into the engine block. Remove the three bolts from the front of the camshaft.

➡️**Install the retainer plate with the sealing gasket facing the engine block. The gasket surface on the engine block should be clean and free of dirt or debris.**

9. Install or connect the following:
- Camshaft retainer and the bolts. Tighten the camshaft retainer bolts to 18 ft. lbs. (25 Nm).
10. Inspect the camshaft sensor O–ring seal. If the O–ring seal is not cut or damaged, it may be reused. Lubricate the O–ring seal with clean engine oil.
- Camshaft sensor and bolt. Tighten the bolt to 18 ft. lbs. (25 Nm).
- Camshaft sprocket and timing chain
- Valve lifters
- Cylinder heads
- Engine front cover to the engine
- Oil pan
- Right side closeout cover
- Starter motor
- Crankshaft balancer to the crankshaft
- Water pump
- Electrical wiring harness to the thermostat housing
- A/C drive belt, if equipped
- Drive belt
- Engine sight shield
- Radiator support and radiator
- A/C condenser mounting bolts
- Engine cooling fan
- Air cleaner duct
- Negative battery cable

6.6L Engine

See Figures 88 through 90.

➡️**This procedure requires the use of the following special tools: Flywheel Holding Tool No. J 44643, Magnetic Base J 26900–13 and Dial Indicator J 26900–12.**

1. Properly discharge the A/C system.
2. Remove or disconnect the following:
- Both cylinder heads
- Valve lifter guide hold–down bracket bolts
- Valve lifter guide hold–down brackets
- Valve lifter guides
- Valve lifters
- Charged air cooler
- A/C condenser
- Starter
3. Install the Flywheel Holding Tool No. J 44643 in the starter opening. Make sure the tool is flush to the flywheel opening. The holding tool will be used to remove the crankshaft balancer bolt and camshaft drive gear bolt.
- Engine front cover
- Oil pump driven gear nut and gear

➡️**The crankshaft reluctor and oil pump drive gear are timed together at the factory. Do NOT remove the reluctor from the oil pump drive gear.**

- Oil pump drive gear and crankshaft reluctor assembly. Do not remove the reluctor bolts or damage the reluctor teeth

4. Using the Magnetic Base J 26900–13 and Dial Indicator J 26900–12, measure the camshaft end–play. The production value is 0.002–0.0045 in. (0.050–0.114mm) and the service limit is 0.008 in. (0.20mm). Replace

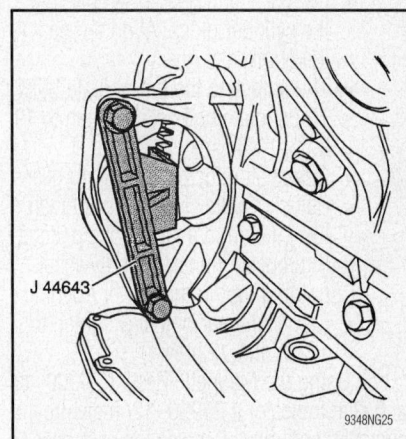

Fig. 88 Proper installation of the flywheel holding tool in the starter opening—6.6L engines

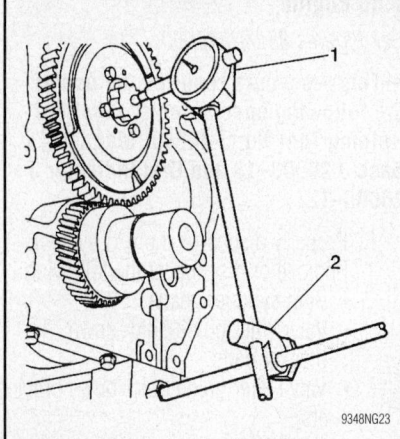

Fig. 89 Use the dial indicator (1) and magnetic base (2) to measure the camshaft end–play—6.6L engines

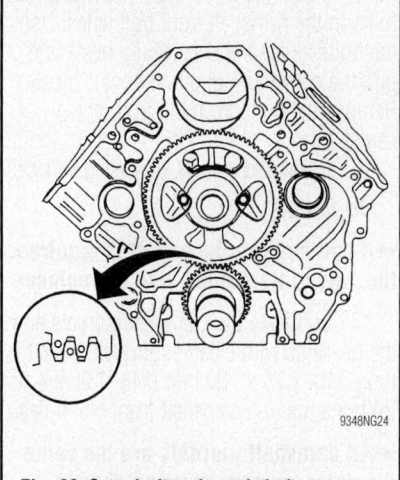

Fig. 90 Camshaft and crankshaft gear alignment—6.6L engines

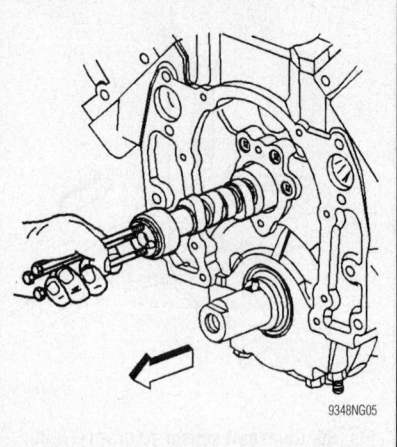

Fig. 91 Use the 3 bolts as a handle to carefully remove and install the camshaft—8.1L engines

the cam gear or thrust plate if the measured value exceeds the service limit.
- Camshaft reluctor screws and reluctor

➡**Use the flywheel holding tool to hold the engine from turning while loosening the camshaft gear bolt.**

- Loosen the camshaft gear bolt and leave the bolt finger–tight
- Camshaft thrust plate bolts through the holes in the camshaft gear
- Camshaft with the gear attached
- Cam gear bolt and gear
- Thrust plate

5. Clean and inspect the camshaft and bearings.

To install:

6. Install or connect the following:
- Camshaft thrust plate
- Camshaft driven gear
- New driven gear bolt (finger–tight)
- Camshaft and gear assembly into the cylinder block. Align the gear to the crankshaft gear
- Threadlock to the thrust plate bolts
- Thrust plate bolts and tighten to 19 ft. lbs. (26 Nm)
- Camshaft reluctor to the cam gear
- Reluctor bolts. Tighten to 80 inch lbs. (9 Nm) in a crisscross pattern.
- If removed, reinstall the flywheel holding tool in the starter opening
- Camshaft gear bolt and tighten to 173 ft. lbs. (234 Nm)

7. Using the Magnetic Base J 26900–13 and Dial Indicator J 26900–12, measure the camshaft end–play. Replace the cam gear or thrust plate if the measured value exceeds the service limit; refer to the Camshaft Specifications chart.

- Oil pump drive gear and reluctor to the crankshaft. Do not damage the teeth of the reluctor.
- Oil pump driven gear and nut. Tighten to 74 ft. lbs. (100 Nm).
- Engine front cover
- A/C condenser
- Charged air cooler

8. Apply clean engine oil to the roller and outside of the lifters.
- Valve lifters
- Valve lifter guides
- Valve lifter guide hold–down brackets. Make sure that both tabs of the bracket are in the holes of the valve lifter guides.
- Valve lifter guide hold–down bracket bolts. Tighten to 97 inch lbs. (11 Nm).

8.1L Engine
See Figure 91.

1. Properly discharge the air conditioning system.
2. Remove or disconnect the following:
- Grille
- A/C condenser
- Intake manifold
- Rocker arms and pushrods
- Valve lifter guide retainer bolts and retainer
- Valve lifter guides, keeping them in proper order for reassembly
- Valve lifters
- Timing chain and sprocket
- Camshaft retaining bolts
- Camshaft retainer

➡**If any lifters are stuck in their bores, use a suitable valve lifter to remove them.**

All of the cam journals are the same size so be very careful when removing and installing the camshaft that you do not damage the bearings.

3. Install three 8–1.25 x 100mm bolts in the holes in the front of the camshaft and carefully pull the camshaft from the block.
4. Remove the bolts from the front of the camshaft.
5. Clean and inspect the camshaft for damage.

To install:

6. Liberally coat camshaft and bearings with heavy engine oil or engine assembly lubricant.
7. Install the camshaft, using the 3 bolts threaded into the camshaft bolt holes as a handle, then remove the bolts.

➡**If a new camshaft is installed, you MUST install new valve lifters.**

8. Install or connect the following:
- Camshaft retainer and bolts. Tighten to 106 inch lbs. (12 Nm).
- Timing chain and sprocket
- Valve lifters
- Valve lifter guides over the flats on the lifters. Make sure the rollers of the lifters are properly aligned with the cam lobes.
- Valve lifter guide retainer. Tighten the bolts to 18 ft. lbs. (25 Nm).
- Rocker arms and pushrods
- Intake manifold
- A/C condenser
- Grille

9. Recharge the A/C system.

CAMSHAFT BEARING REPLACEMENT

See Figures 92 through 96.

If excessive camshaft wear is found, or if the engine is completely rebuilt, the camshaft bearings should be replaced.

➡**The front and rear bearings should be removed last, and installed first. Those bearings act as guides for the other bearings and pilot.**

1. Remove the engine.
2. Drive the camshaft rear plug from the block.
3. Assemble the removal puller with its shoulder on the bearing to be removed. Gradually tighten the puller nut until the bearing is removed.
4. Remove the remaining bearings, leaving the front and rear for last. To remove these, reverse the position of the puller, so

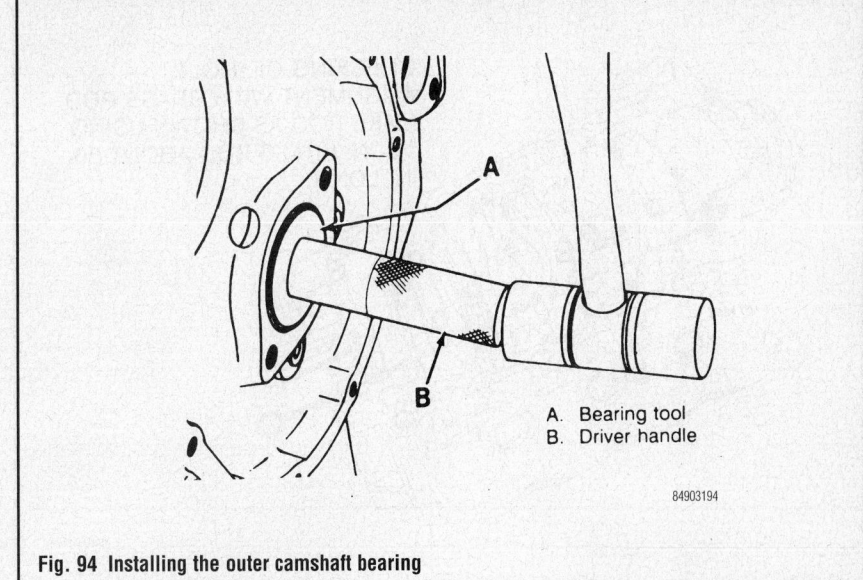

A. Bearing tool
B. Driver handle

Fig. 94 Installing the outer camshaft bearing

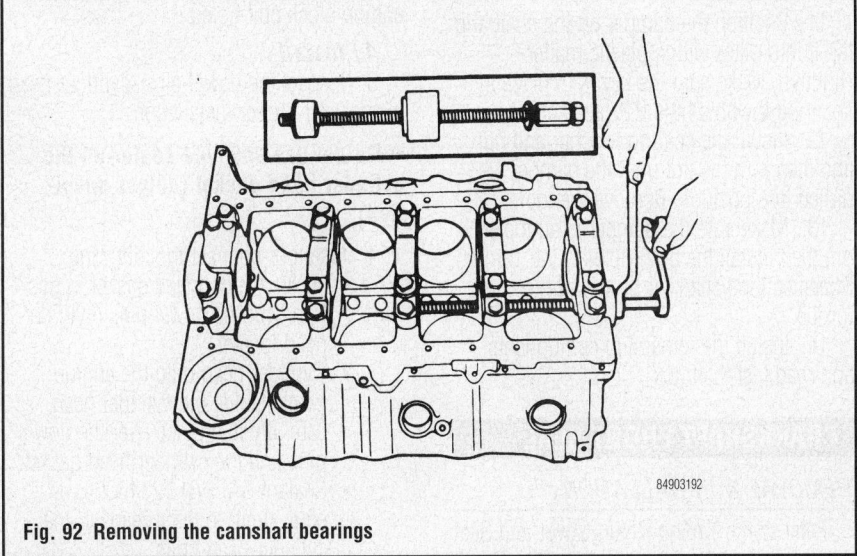

Fig. 92 Removing the camshaft bearings

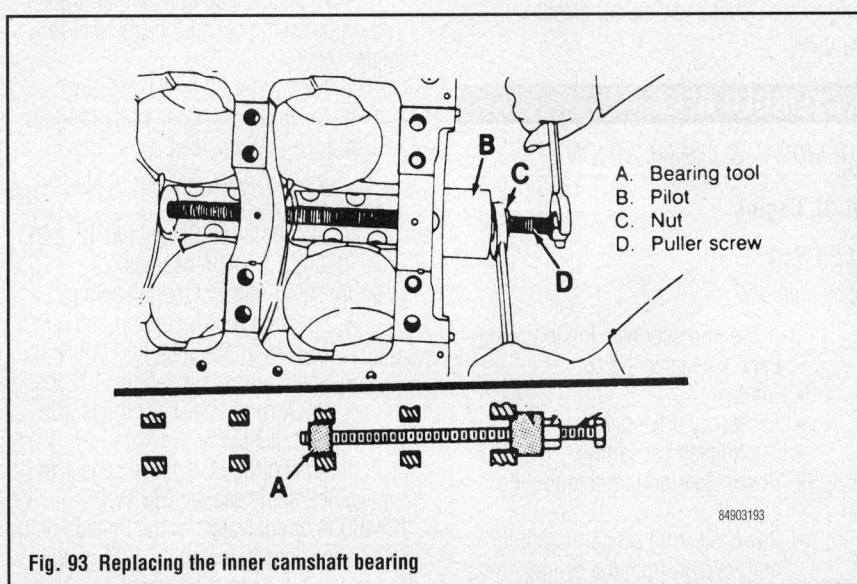

A. Bearing tool
B. Pilot
C. Nut
D. Puller screw

Fig. 93 Replacing the inner camshaft bearing

as to pull the bearings towards the center of the block. Leave the tool in this position, pilot the new front and rear bearings on the installer, and pull them into position.

5. Return the puller to its original position and pull the remaining bearings into position.

➡**You must make sure that the oil holes of the bearings and block align when installing the bearings. If they don't align, the camshaft will not get proper lubrication and may seize or at least be seriously damaged. To check for correct oil hole alignment, use a piece of brass rod with a 90° bend in the end as shown in the illustration. Check all oil hole openings. The wire must enter each hole, or the hole is not properly aligned.**

6. Replace the camshaft rear plug, and stake it into position. On diesel engines,

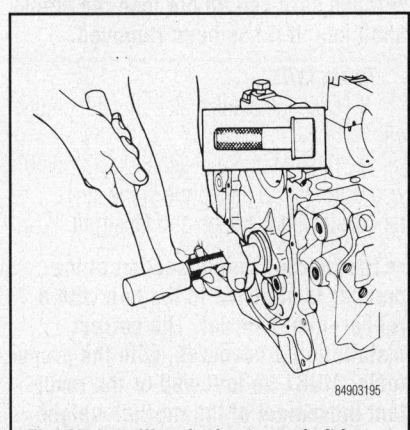

Fig. 95 Installing the front camshaft bearing on diesel engines. The bearing tool is shown in the inset

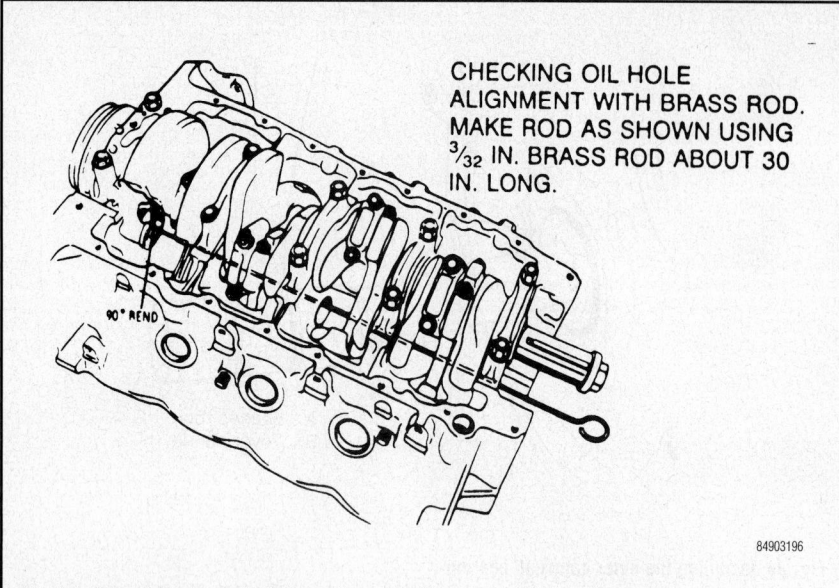

CHECKING OIL HOLE ALIGNMENT WITH BRASS ROD. MAKE ROD AS SHOWN USING 3/32 IN. BRASS ROD ABOUT 30 IN. LONG.

84903196

Fig. 96 Make this simple tool to check camshaft bearing oil hole alignment

coat the outer diameter of the new plug with GM sealant #1052080 or equivalent, and install it flush to 1/32 in. (0.794mm) deep.

CRANKSHAFT DAMPER

REMOVAL & INSTALLATION

➡A torsional damper puller tool is required to perform this procedure.

1. Disconnect the negative battery cable.
2. Remove the fan shroud assembly.
3. Remove the fan belts, fan and pulley.
4. If necessary, remove the radiator.
5. Remove the accessory drive pulley (crankshaft pulley on diesel engines).
6. Remove the torsional damper bolt.
7. Remove the torsional damper using tool J–39046 or its equivalent puller.

➡Make sure you do not lose the crankshaft key, if it has been removed.

To install:

8. Coat the crankshaft stub with engine oil.
9. Position the crankshaft key if one was used. If you pulled the crank seal, replace it with the open end facing in.

➡The inertial weight section of the damper is attached to the hub with a rubber–like material. The correct installation procedures, with the proper tools, MUST be followed or the resultant movement of the inertial weight will destroy the tuning of the damper!

10. Thread the stud on the tool into the end of the crankshaft.

11. Position the damper on the shaft and tap it into place with a plastic mallet (lightly!). Make sure the key is in place by securing it with a little RTV sealant.
12. Install the bearing, washer and nut and then turn the nut until the damper is pulled into position. Remove the tool.
13. Make sure the damper is all the way on, then install the bolt. Refer to the Torque Specifications chart for proper tightening torque.
14. Install the remaining components and road test the truck.

CRANKSHAFT FRONT SEAL

REMOVAL & INSTALLATION

Refer to the Timing Chain Cover and Seal procedure for gasoline engines or the Timing Gears Cover and Seal for diesel engines.

CYLINDER HEAD

REMOVAL & INSTALLATION

4.3L Engine

Left Side

See Figure 97.

1. Remove or disconnect the following:
   - Battery negative cable
   - Coolant
   - Accessory drive belt
   - Cooling fan assembly
   - Power steering pump mounting bracket
   - Power steering pump mounting bracket stud from the cylinder head

   - Lower intake manifold
   - Exhaust manifold
   - Spark plug wire harness and the spark plug wire support
   - Valve pushrods
   - Ground strap and ground wire bolt from the rear of the cylinder head
   - Engine Coolant Temperature (ECT) sensor (if applicable)
   - ECT gauge sensor (if applicable)
   - Spark plugs
   - Spark plug wire support
   - Cylinder head bolts
   - Cylinder head and the gasket

➡Clean all dirt, debris, and coolant from the engine block cylinder head bolt holes. Failure to remove all foreign material may result in damaged threads, improperly tightened fasteners or damage to components.

2. Clean the cylinder head bolts and the engine block bolt holes.

To install:

3. Inspect the dowel pins (cylinder head locator) for proper installation.

➡Do not use any type sealer on the cylinder head gasket (unless specified).

4. Install or connect the following:
   - NEW cylinder head gasket in position over the dowel pins (cylinder head locator)
   - Cylinder head onto the engine block. Guide the cylinder head carefully into place over the dowel pins and the cylinder head gasket.
   - Sealant GM P/N 12346004, or equivalent, to the threads of the cylinder head bolts
   - Cylinder head bolts finger–tight

5. Tighten the cylinder head bolts in sequence:
   a. First pass: 22 ft. lbs. (30 Nm).
   b. Second pass: Long bolts (1, 4, 5, 8, and 9)–+ 75 degrees.
   c. Second pass: Medium bolts (12 and 13)–+ 65 degrees.
   d. Second pass: Short bolts (2, 3, 6, 7, 10, and 11)–+ 55 degrees.

6. Install or connect the following:
   - Spark plug wire support and bolts. Tighten to 106 inch lbs. (12 Nm).
   - Spark plugs. Tighten to 11 ft. lbs. (15 Nm), if USED; 22 ft. lbs. (30 Nm), if NEW.

7. If reusing the ECT gauge sensor (if applicable), apply sealant GM P/N 12346004 or equivalent to the threads of the ECT gauge sensor. Install the ECT gauge

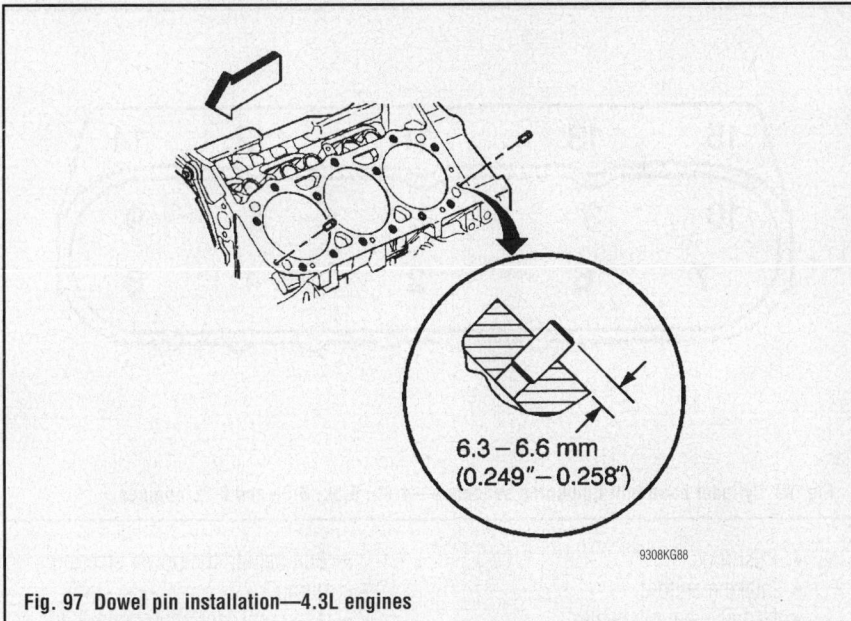

Fig. 97 Dowel pin installation—4.3L engines

6.3 – 6.6 mm
(0.249" – 0.258")

9308KG88

sensor (if applicable). Tighten the sensor to 15 ft. lbs. (20 Nm).

8. Install or connect the following:
- Ground strap and the ground wire bolt. Tighten the bolt to 12 ft. lbs. (16 Nm).
- Valve pushrods
- Lower intake manifold
- Exhaust manifold
- Stud for the power steering pump mounting bracket to the cylinder head. Tighten the power steering pump mounting bracket stud to 15 ft. lbs. (20 Nm).
- Power steering pump mounting bracket
- Engine cooling fan assembly
- Coolant
- Battery negative cable

Right Side

1. Remove or disconnect the following:
- Battery negative cable
- Coolant
- Engine cooling fan assembly
- Alternator mounting bracket
- Alternator mounting bracket stud from the cylinder head
- Lower intake manifold
- Exhaust manifold
- Spark plug wire harness and spark plug wire support
- Valve pushrods
- Cylinder head and the gasket

2. Clean the engine block and the cylinder head sealing surfaces.

To install:

3. Inspect the dowel pins (cylinder head locator) for proper installation.

➡️Do not use any type sealer on the cylinder head gasket (unless specified).

4. Install or connect the following:
- NEW cylinder head gasket in position over the dowel pins (cylinder head locator)
- Cylinder head onto the engine block. Guide the cylinder head carefully into place over the dowel pins and the cylinder head gasket.
- Sealant GM P/N 12346004 or equivalent to the threads of the cylinder head bolts
- Cylinder head bolts finger–tight

5. Tighten the cylinder head bolts in sequence:
  a. First pass: 22 ft. lbs. (30 Nm).
  b. Second pass: Long bolts (1, 4, 5, 8, and 9)–+ 75 degrees.
  c. Second pass: Medium bolts (12 and 13)–+ 65 degrees.
  d. Second pass: Short bolts (2, 3, 6, 7, 10, and 11)–+ 55 degrees.

6. Install or connect the following:
- Spark plug wire support and bolts. Tighten only the rear support bolt to 106 inch lbs. (12 Nm).

➡️ The front spark plug wire support bolt is used to fasten the oil level indicator tube, and will be installed within the oil level indicator tube installation procedure.

- Front spark plug wire support bolt
- Spark plugs. Tighten to 11 ft. lbs. (15 Nm), if USED; 22 ft. lbs. (30 Nm), if NEW.
- Valve pushrods

- Lower intake manifold
- Spark plug wire harness and wire support. Tighten to 106 inch lbs. (12 Nm).
- Exhaust manifold
- Stud for the alternator mounting bracket. Tighten the alternator mounting bracket stud to 15 ft. lbs. (20 Nm).
- Alternator mounting bracket
- Engine cooling fan assembly
- Coolant
- Battery negative cable

4.8L, 5.3L, 6.0L and 6.2L Engines

Right Side

See Figures 98 and 99.

✳✳ CAUTION

Before servicing any electrical component, the ignition key must be in the OFF or LOCK position and all electrical loads must be OFF, unless instructed otherwise in these procedures.

1. Remove or disconnect the following:
- Negative battery cable
- Coolant air bleed pipe
- Intake manifold
- Push rods
- Exhaust manifold(s)
- Alternator
- Alternator mounting bracket–to–cylinder head bolts
- Bolt behind the power steering pump
- Alternator mounting bracket and set it aside
- Bolt holding the oil level indicator tube to the right side cylinder head
- Oil level indicator tube
- Cylinder head(s) from the engine
- Spark plugs

➡️The M11 cylinder head bolts are NOT reusable. Install NEW M11 cylinder head bolts during reassembly.

- Cylinder head bolts

➡️After removal, place the cylinder head on two wood blocks to prevent damage.

2. Remove the gasket. Discard the gasket. Discard the M11 cylinder head bolts.

To install:

➡️Do not use any type sealant on the cylinder head gasket (unless specified). The cylinder head gaskets must be installed in the proper direction and position.

3. Clean the engine block cylinder head bolt holes (if required). Thread repair tool J 42385–107 may be used to clean the threads of old thread locking material.

4. Spray cleaner GM P/N 12346139, P/N 12377981, or equivalent into the hole.

5. Clean the cylinder head bolt holes with compressed air.

6. Check the cylinder head locating pins for proper installation.

➡When properly installed, the tab on the right cylinder head gasket will be located right of center or closer to the front of the engine.

7. Install or connect the following:
- NEW right cylinder head gasket onto the locating pins
- Cylinder head onto the locating pins and the gasket
- NEW M11 cylinder head bolts. Apply a 0.20 in. (5mm) band of threadlock GM P/N 12345382 or equivalent to the threads of the M8 cylinder head bolts.
- M8 cylinder head bolts.

8. Tighten the cylinder head bolts as follows:

a. M11 bolts (1–10) 1st pass: in sequence to 22 ft. lbs. (30 Nm).

b. M11 bolts (1–10) 2nd pass: in sequence + 90 degrees.

c. M11 bolts (1–10): + 70 degrees.

d. M8 cylinder head bolts (11,12,13,14,15) to 22 ft. lbs. (30 Nm). Begin with the center bolt (11) and alternating side–to–side, work outward tightening all of the bolts.

9. Install or connect the following:
- Alternator
- Exhaust manifold(s)

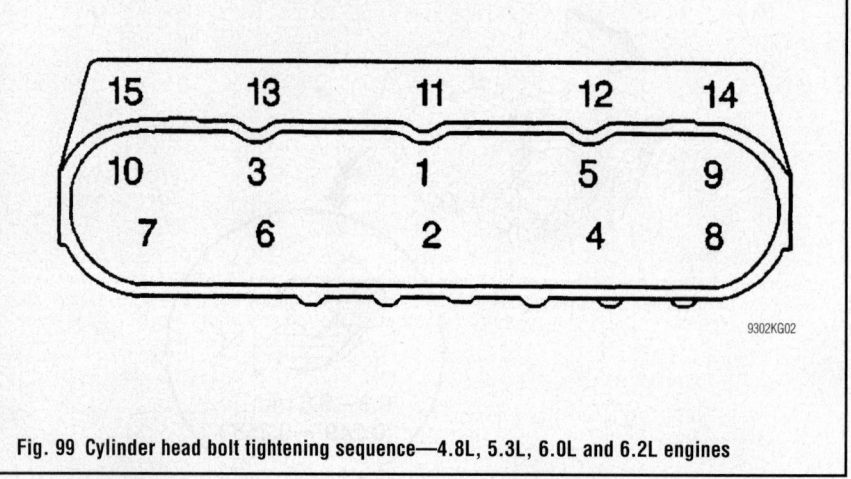

Fig. 99 Cylinder head bolt tightening sequence—4.8L, 5.3L, 6.0L and 6.2L engines

- Pushrods
- Intake manifold
- Negative battery cable

Left Side

See Figures 98 and 99.

> **✷✷ CAUTION**
>
> Before servicing any electrical component, the ignition key must be in the OFF or LOCK position and all electrical loads must be OFF, unless instructed otherwise in these procedures.

1. Remove or disconnect the following:
- Negative battery cable
- Intake manifold
- Push rods
- Exhaust manifold(s)
- Alternator
- Alternator mounting bracket–to–cylinder head bolts

- Bolt behind the power steering pump
- Alternator mounting bracket and set it aside
- Oil level indicator tube–to–cylinder head bolt
- Oil level indicator tube
- Cylinder head from the engine
- Spark plugs

➡The M11 cylinder head bolts are NOT reusable. Install NEW M11 cylinder head bolts during assembly.

2. Remove the cylinder head bolts.

➡After removal, place the cylinder head on two wood blocks to prevent damage.

3. Remove the gasket. Discard the gasket. Discard the M11 cylinder head bolts.

To install:

➡Do not use any type sealant on the cylinder head gasket (unless specified). The cylinder head gaskets must be installed in the proper direction and position.

4. Clean the engine block cylinder head bolt holes (if required). Thread repair tool J 42385–107 may be used to clean the threads of old thread locking material.

5. Spray cleaner GM P/N 12346139, P/N 12377981, or equivalent into the hole.

6. Clean the cylinder head bolt holes with compressed air.

7. Check the cylinder head locating pins for proper installation.

➡When properly installed, the tab on the left cylinder head gasket will be located left of center or closer to the front of the engine.

8. Install or connect the following:

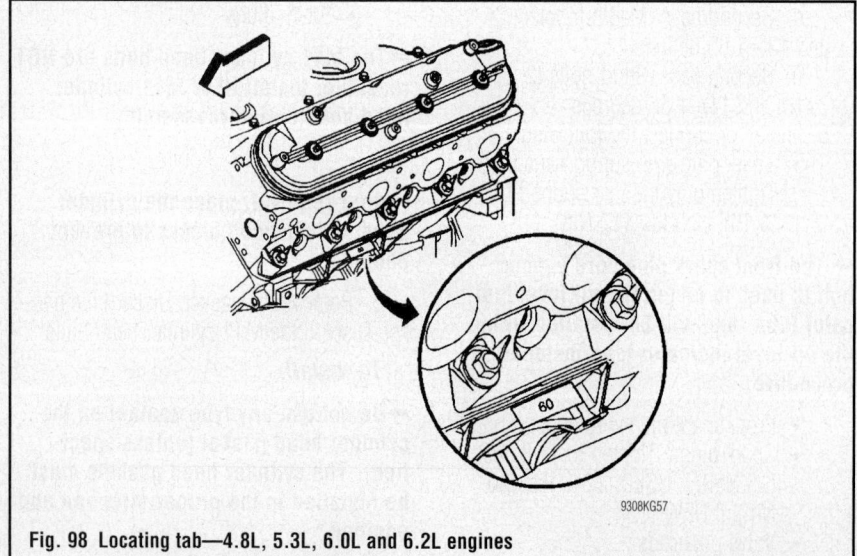

Fig. 98 Locating tab—4.8L, 5.3L, 6.0L and 6.2L engines

- NEW left cylinder head gasket onto the locating pins
- Cylinder head onto the locating pins and the gasket
- NEW M11 cylinder head bolts.

9. Apply a 0.20 in. (5mm) band of threadlock GM P/N 12345382 or equivalent to the threads of the M8 cylinder head bolts.

- M8 cylinder head bolts
- M8 cylinder head bolts.

10. Tighten the cylinder head bolts as follows:

a. M11 bolts (1–10) 1st pass: in sequence to 22 ft. lbs. (30 Nm).

b. M11 bolts (1–10) 2nd pass: in sequence + 90 degrees.

c. M11 bolts (1–10): + 70 degrees.

d. M8 cylinder head bolts (11,12,13,14,15) to 22 ft. lbs. (30 Nm). Begin with the center bolt (11) and alternating side–to–side, work outward tightening all of the bolts.

11. Install or connect the following:

- Alternator mounting bracket. Tighten the four bolts to 37 ft. lbs. (50 Nm).
- Bolt at the rear of the power steering pump and tighten to 37 ft. lbs. (50 Nm).
- Exhaust manifold(s)
- Pushrods
- Intake manifold
- Negative battery cable

6.6L Engine

See Figures 100 and 101.

1. Relieve the fuel system pressure.
2. Drain the coolant system.
3. Remove or disconnect the following:
- Negative battery cables
- Left or right front splash shield from the fender well, as applicable
- Turbocharger
- Turbocharger charged air cooler inlet duct
- Thermostat housing crossover
- Left or right intake manifold, as necessary
- Upper left or right valve cover
- Fuel rail assembly
- Left or right exhaust manifold
- Bolt and ground straps from the rear of the cylinder head
- Lower left or right valve cover
- Rocker arm shaft assembly
- Glow plugs
- Fuel injector return pipe eye bolts and washers
- Fuel injector return pipe assembly
- Fuel injector bracket bolts

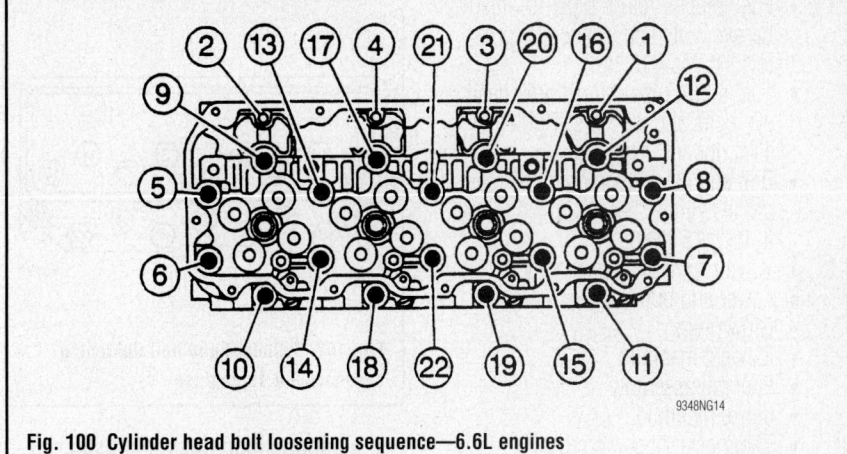

Fig. 100 Cylinder head bolt loosening sequence—6.6L engines

9348NG14

- Fuel injectors with the brackets, using a suitable removal tool
- Injector bracket pins
- Cylinder head bolts, in the proper sequence
- Cylinder head and gasket. Discard the gasket

To install:

4. Clean the mating surfaces of the heads and block thoroughly.

5. Position a new left or right side head gasket on the block. Note that the left and right side gaskets are NOT interchangeable.

➡**The cylinder head bolts on these vehicles are pre–coated with an application of a molybdenum disulfide for thread lubrication. Do not remove the coating or add any additional lubrication.**

6. Install the cylinder head and bolts.

7. Tighten the cylinder head bolts, in sequence, as follows:

a. Step 1: M12 bolts to 37 ft. lbs. (50 Nm).

b. Step 2: M12 bolts to 59 ft. lbs. (80 Nm).

c. Step 3: Using a torque angle meter, tighten the M12 bolts an additional 90 degrees on 2005 models or 60 degrees on 2006–07 models.

d. Step 4: Using a torque angle meter, tighten the M12 bolts an additional 75 degrees on 2005 models or 60 degrees on 2006–07 models.

e. Step 5: M8 bolts to 18 ft. lbs. (25 Nm).

8. Install or connect the following:

- New O–ring onto the fuel injectors after coating with clean engine oil
- New copper washer into the fuel injector bore in the cylinder head
- Fuel injector bracket pin

➡**If you are reusing the old injectors, clean the carbon from the tips, but do not use a wire brush.**

- Fuel injector bracket bolt and tighten to 37 ft. lbs. (50 Nm)
- Fuel injector return pipe assembly

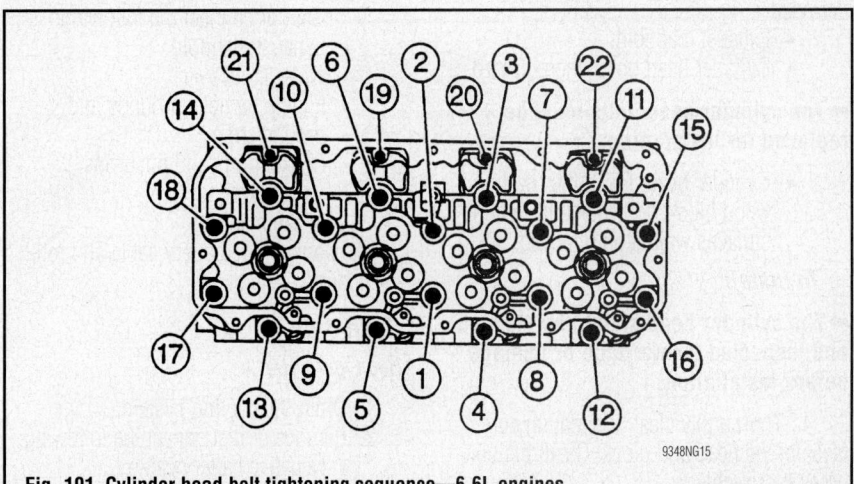

Fig. 101 Cylinder head bolt tightening sequence—6.6L engines

9348NG15

- Fuel injector return pipe–to–injector eye bolts and washers. Tighten to 11 ft. lbs. (15 Nm).
- Fuel return pipe–to–cylinder head eye bolts and washers. Tighten to 11 ft. lbs. (15 Nm).
- Bolt and ground straps to the rear of the cylinder head. Tighten to 18 ft. lbs. (25 Nm).
- Valve rocker shaft assembly
- Lower and upper valve covers
- Glow plugs
- Exhaust manifold
- Fuel rail assembly
- Intake manifold
- Thermostat housing crossover
- Turbocharger charged air cooler duct
- Clamp and hose to the charged air cooler. Tighten to 53 inch lbs. (6 Nm).
- Turbocharger
- Fender splash shield
- Negative battery cables

9. Refill the cooling system with the proper type and quantity of antifreeze.

10. Recharge the air conditioning system.

8.1L Engine

Left Side

See Figure 102.

1. Drain the cooling system.
2. Remove or disconnect the following:
   - Negative battery cable
   - Water crossover
   - Intake manifold
   - Valve cover
   - Rocker arms and pushrods, keeping them in order for installation
   - Engine harness ground bolts
3. Reposition the engine harness grounds and ground straps from the cylinder head.
   - Exhaust manifold
   - Cylinder head bolts, then discard

➡ **The cylinder head bolts must be replaced for installation.**

- Cylinder head. Place the head on 2 wood blocks to protect the sealing surfaces while it is removed.

To install:

➡ **The cylinder head should be cleaned and inspected for warpage or damage before installation.**

4. Thoroughly clean the mating surfaces of the head and block. Clean the bolt holes thoroughly.

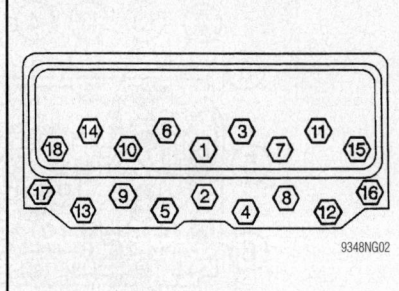

Fig. 102 Cylinder head bolt tightening sequence—8.1L engines

9348NG02

➡ **If a composition gasket is used, do not use sealer.**

5. Align the cylinder head gasket locating marks to face up. Make sure that the gasket tabs are located of the No. 1 and 2 cylinder for proper installation.

6. Install or connect the following:
   - New cylinder head gasket
   - Cylinder head
   - Sealer to the threads of new cylinder head bolts, if not pre–applied

➡ **The long bolts are used in locations 1, 2, 3, 6, 7, 8, 9, 10, 11, 14, 16, and 17. The medium length bolts are used in locations 15 and 18. The short bolts are used in locations 4, 5, 12, and 13.**

7. Tighten the head bolts, in sequence, in 4 stages, as follows:
   a. Step 1: 22 ft. lbs. (30 Nm).
8. Step 2: 22 ft. lbs. (30 Nm)
   a. Step 3: Additional 120 degrees using a torque angle meter.
   b. Step 4: Torque bolt numbers. 1, 2, 3, 6, 7, 8, 9, 10, 11, 14, 16 and 17 an additional 60 degrees.
   c. Tighten bolts 15 and 18 an additional 45 degrees, and bolt numbers 4, 5, 12 and 13 an additional 30 degrees.
9. Install or connect the following:
   - Exhaust manifold
   - Water crossover
   - Engine harness grounds and ground strap
   - Rocker arms and pushrods
   - Valve cover
   - Intake manifold
10. Connect the battery cable and refill the cooling system.

Right Side

See Figure 102.

1. Drain the cooling system.
2. Remove or disconnect the following:
   - Negative battery cable
   - Intake manifold

- Valve cover
- Rocker arms and pushrods, keeping them in order for installation
- Engine Coolant Temperature (ECT) sensor clip from the bracket
- ECT sensor
- ECT sensor bracket bolt and bracket
- Heater inlet and outlet hoses from the hose bracket
- Water crossover
- Exhaust manifold
- Cylinder head bolts, then discard

➡ **The cylinder head bolts must be replaced for installation.**

- Cylinder head. Place the head on 2 wood blocks to protect the sealing surfaces while it is removed.

To install:

➡ **The cylinder head should be cleaned and inspected for warpage or damage before installation.**

3. Thoroughly clean the mating surfaces of the head and block. Clean the bolt holes thoroughly.

➡ **If a composition gasket is used, do not use sealer.**

4. Align the cylinder head gasket locating marks to face up. Make sure that the gasket tabs are located of the no. 1 and 2 cylinder for proper installation.

5. Install or connect the following:
   - New cylinder head gasket
   - Cylinder head
   - Sealer to the threads of new cylinder head bolts, if not pre–applied

➡ **The long bolts are used in locations 1, 2, 3, 6, 7, 8, 9, 10, 11, 14, 16, and 17. The medium length bolts are used in locations 15 and 18. The short bolts are used in locations 4, 5, 12, and 13.**

6. Tighten the head bolts, in sequence, in 4 stages, as follows:
   a. Step 1: 22 ft. lbs. (30 Nm).
7. Step 2: 22 ft. lbs. (30 Nm)
   a. Step 3: Additional 120 degrees using a torque angle meter.
   b. Step 4: Torque bolt numbers. 1, 2, 3, 6, 7, 8, 9, 10, 11, 14, 16 and 17 an additional 60 degrees.
   c. Tighten bolts 15 and 18 an additional 45 degrees, and bolt numbers 4, 5, 12 and 13 an additional 30 degrees.
8. Install or connect the following:
   - Exhaust manifold
   - Water crossover
   - Heater hose bracket and bolts. Tighten the bolts to 37 ft. lbs. (50 Nm).

- ECT sensor bracket and bolt. Tighten to 37 ft. lbs. (50 Nm).
- ECT sensor
- ECT sensor clip
- Rocker arms and pushrods
- Valve cover
- Intake manifold

9. Connect the battery cable and refill the cooling system.

ENGINE ASSEMBLY

REMOVAL & INSTALLATION

4.3L Engine

See Figures 103 and 104.

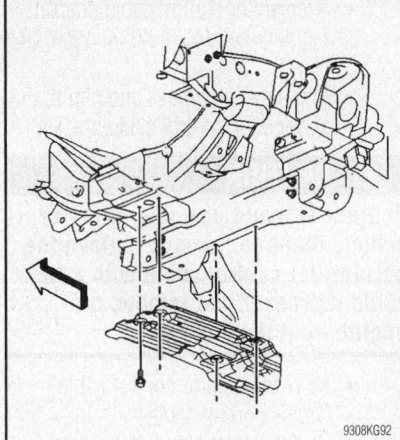

Fig. 103 Engine shield removal—4.3L engines

1. Remove or disconnect the following:
   - Battery negative cable
   - Coolant
   - A/C refrigerant, if equipped
   - Oil pan skid plate
   - Engine shield
   - Starter.
   - Transmission cover
   - Bolt holding the bracket for the starter cables and transmission cooler lines, if equipped
   - Nuts at the catalytic converter pipe
   - Exhaust pipes from the exhaust manifolds
   - Bolts holding the brackets to the oil pan for both battery cables
   - Crankshaft Position (CKP) sensor electrical connector and remove the harness from the retainer
   - Low oil level sensor electrical connector and remove the wire harness from the retainer
   - Bolt holding the battery negative cable and ground cable to the engine

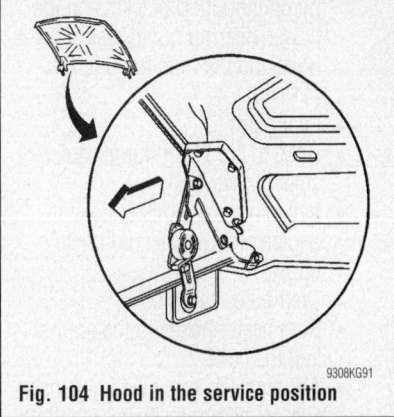

Fig. 104 Hood in the service position

- Torque converter–to–flywheel bolts, if equipped, through the starter opening
- Engine to transmission bolts

2. Move the hood hinge bolts to hold the hood in the service position.

3. Remove or disconnect the following:
   - Positive Crankcase Ventilation (PCV) hose from the air cleaner outlet duct
   - Air cleaner outlet duct from the throttle body and the air cleaner assembly
   - Fan shroud
   - Drive belt
   - Engine cooling fan
   - Radiator inlet and outlet hoses from the engine

✱✱ CAUTION

In order to avoid possible injury or vehicle damage, always replace the accelerator control cable with a NEW cable whenever you remove the engine from the vehicle.

✱✱ WARNING

In order to avoid cruise control cable damage, position the cable out of the way while you remove or install the engine.

- Accelerator control cable
- Cruise control cable from the throttle body and the bracket on the throttle body and intake manifold, if equipped
- Engine wiring harness and clip from the accelerator control cable bracket
- Accelerator control cable bracket from the throttle body
- A/C hoses from the compressor and the accumulator, if equipped
- Secondary Air Injection (AIR) crossover pipe from the AIR pipe assemblies

➡**Remove the AIR pipes before engine removal. The AIR pipes can break or damage easily causing erratic engine operation.**

- AIR pipe assemblies from the left exhaust manifold, if equipped
- AIR pipe assembly from the AIR pump
- AIR pipe assembly from the right exhaust manifold, if equipped.
- A/C pressure switch, if equipped
- A/C compressor clutch, if equipped
- Exhaust Gas Recirculation (EGR) valve
- Battery positive cable
- Fuel meter body
- Idle Air Control (IAC) motor
- Throttle Position (TP) sensor
- Engine Coolant Temperature (ECT) sensor
- EVAP canister purge solenoid valve
- Manifold Absolute Pressure (MAP) sensor
- Ignition Control Module (ICM)
- Ignition coil
- Engine oil pressure gauge sensor
- Distributor
- Knock Sensor (KS)
- Nuts holding the bracket for the engine wiring harness to the intake manifold studs
- Bolt holding the engine wiring harness clip to the battery positive cable junction block bracket
- Bracket for the battery positive cable junction block from the power steering pump mounting bracket
- Battery positive and negative cables, if not done already
- Nut holding the ground wire to the stud at the rear of the right cylinder head
- Stud holding the engine wiring harness bracket to the rear of the right cylinder head
- Nut holding the engine wiring harness bracket to the stud for the EVAP canister purge solenoid valve
- Bolt holding the ground strap and the ground wire to the rear of the left cylinder head. Move the engine wiring harness aside.
- Both heater hoses from the engine and the cowl
- Distributor cap
- Fuel pipes at the rear of the engine
- Hose from the EVAP purge canister solenoid valve

- Power brake booster vacuum hose
- Nuts holding the power steering pump rear bracket to the side and front of the engine
- Three bolts and the nut holding the power steering pump mounting bracket to the engine

4. With the power steering pump and the A/C compressor still attached, slide the power steering pump mount bracket off the stud and set aside.

- Water outlet
- EGR valve inlet pipe from the intake and exhaust manifold

5. Attach the engine crane to the left front and right rear intake manifold mounting bolts.

6. Remove the engine motor mount to frame bracket bolts.

7. Support the transmission with a suitable jack.

8. Remove the engine.

To install:

9. Install or connect the following:

- Engine in the vehicle
- Engine mount to frame bracket bolts. Tighten the bolts to 48 ft. lbs. (65 Nm).

10. Remove the lifting device.

11. Apply thread lock GM P/N 12345382 or equivalent to the threads of the lower intake manifold bolts. Install the bolts and tighten as follows:

    a. First pass: 27 inch lbs. (3 Nm)

    b. Second pass: 106 inch lbs. (12 Nm)

    c. Final pass: 11 ft. lbs. (15 Nm)

12. Loosely install one transmission to engine bolt. Remove the support jack from under the transmission.

13. Install the EGR valve inlet pipe to the intake and the exhaust manifold and tighten as follows:

    a. Tighten the EGR valve inlet pipe intake nut to 18 ft. lbs. (25 Nm).

    b. Tighten the EGR valve inlet pipe exhaust nut to 22 ft. lbs. (30 Nm).

    c. Tighten the EGR valve inlet pipe clamp bolt to 18 ft. lbs. (25 Nm).

14. Install the water outlet.

15. Slide the power steering pump mounting bracket with the power steering pump and the A/C compressor on the stud.

16. Position the power steering pump rear bracket on the studs.

17. Install or connect the following:

- Power steering pump mounting bracket bolts and the nut
- Nut for the power steering pump rear bracket to the front of the engine. Tighten the power steering

pump mounting bracket and the power steering pump rear bracket bolts and the nuts to 30 ft. lbs. (41 Nm).

- Fuel pipes
- Hose to the EVAP purge canister solenoid valve
- Vacuum brake booster hose to engine and the vacuum brake booster
- Distributor cap
- Both heater hoses to the engine and the cowl
- AIR pipe assembly with new gaskets to the right exhaust manifold, if equipped
- AIR pipe nuts and bracket bolt. Tighten the nuts to 18 ft. lbs. (25 Nm) and the bolt to 89 inch lbs. (10 Nm).
- AIR pipe assembly to the AIR pump
- AIR pipe assembly with new gaskets to the left exhaust manifold, if equipped. Install the AIR pipe nuts and bracket bolt. Tighten the nuts to 18 ft. lbs. (25 Nm) and the bolt to 89 inch lbs. (10 Nm).
- AIR crossover pipe to the AIR pipe assemblies
- Engine wiring harness
- A/C pressure switch
- A/C compressor clutch
- EGR valve
- Alternator battery positive cable
- Fuel meter body assembly
- IAC motor
- TP sensor
- ECT sensor
- EVAP canister purge solenoid valve
- MAP sensor
- ICM
- Ignition coil
- Engine oil pressure gauge sensor
- Distributor
- Knock sensor

18. Install the bolt holding the ground strap and the ground wire to the rear of the left cylinder head. Tighten the ground strap and ground wire bolt to 12 ft. lbs. (16 Nm).

19. Position the engine wiring harness bracket on the EVAP purge canister solenoid valve stud and install the nut.

20. Install the stud holding the wire harness bracket to the rear of the right cylinder head. Tighten the nut on the EVAP solenoid to 80 inch lbs. (9 Nm). Tighten the stud at rear of the cylinder head to 18 ft. lbs. (25 Nm).

21. Install the nut holding the ground wire on the stud at the rear of the right cylinder head. Tighten the ground wire nut to 12 ft. lbs. (16 Nm).

22. Position the battery positive and negative cables. Do not connect the negative battery cable to the battery.

23. Install or connect the following:

- Battery positive cable junction block bracket and bolt to the power steering pump mounting bracket. Tighten the bolt to 18 ft. lbs. (25 Nm).
- Bolt holding the engine wiring harness bracket to battery positive cable junction block bracket
- Engine wiring harness bracket on the intake manifold studs. Tighten the nuts to 106 inch lbs. (12 Nm) and the bolt to 80 inch lbs. (9 Nm).
- A/C hoses
- Accelerator control cable bracket. Tighten the nuts to 80 inch lbs. (9 Nm).
- Engine wire harness and clip to the accelerator control cable bracket

❊❊ CAUTION

In order to avoid possible injury or vehicle damage, always replace the accelerator control cable with a NEW cable whenever you remove the engine from the vehicle.

- NEW accelerator control cable
- Cruise control cable
- Radiator inlet and outlet hoses
- Engine cooling fan
- Drive belt
- Upper and lower radiator shroud
- Air cleaner outlet duct to the throttle body and the air cleaner assembly
- PCV hose to the air inlet duct

24. Move the hood hinge bolts from the service position to the normal operating position.

25. Raise the vehicle.

26. Install or connect the following:

- Remaining transmission to engine bolts except for the one where the transmission cover mounts
- Torque converter to flywheel
- Transmission cover and bolts. Tighten the transmission cover to oil pan bolt to 106 inch lbs. (12 Nm). Tighten the transmission cover to transmission bolt to 34 ft. lbs. (47 Nm).
- Bolt holding the bracket for the starter cables and the transmission cooler pipe and tighten to 80 inch lbs. (9 Nm)
- Positive and negative battery cable brackets–to–oil pan bolts and tighten to 106 inch lbs. (12 Nm).

- Bolt for the battery negative cable and ground wire to the front of the engine. Tighten the battery negative cable and ground wire bolt to 18 ft. lbs. (25 Nm).
- CKP sensor and install the harness in the retainer
- Low oil level sensor and install the wire harness in the retainer
- Exhaust pipe to the exhaust manifolds and tighten the nuts at the catalytic converter flange
- Starter motor
- Oil pan skid plate and tighten bolt to 15 ft. lbs. (20 Nm)
- Engine shield

27. Lower the vehicle.
- Battery negative cable
- Engine oil
- Coolant

28. Recharge the A/C system.

4.8L, 5.3L, 6.0L and 6.2L Engines

2005–06 Models And 2007 Classic

See Figures 105 through 109.

> ❈❈ **CAUTION**
>
> **Before servicing any electrical component, the ignition key must be in the OFF or LOCK position and all electrical loads must be OFF, unless instructed otherwise in these procedures.**

1. Remove or disconnect the following:
- Negative battery cable
- Coolant
- A/C refrigerant

2. Raise the hood to the servicing position. Move the hood hinge bolt to hold the hood in the servicing position.
- Upper and the lower radiator hoses from the engine
- Air cleaner duct from the engine
- A/C condenser mounting bolts
- Radiator support from the vehicle
- A/C compressor
- Coolant hose from the throttle body
- Heater hoses from the engine and the cowl
- Engine sight shield from the intake manifold
- Accelerator control cable mounting bracket from the intake manifold

> ❈❈ **CAUTION**
>
> **In order to avoid possible injury or vehicle damage, always replace the accelerator control cable with a NEW cable whenever you remove the engine from the vehicle. In order to avoid cruise control cable damage, position the cable out of the way while you remove or install the engine.**

- Accelerator control cable and the cruise control cable, if equipped, from the throttle shaft

3. Open the large electrical harness retainer. Remove one 10 mm nut in order to release the engine harness from the intake manifold.

4. Disconnect the electrical connectors from the following:
- Eight injectors
- Idle Air Control (IAC) motor
- Throttle Position (TP) sensor
- Evaporative Emissions (EVAP) canister purge solenoid
- Manifold Absolute Pressure (MAP) sensor
- Camshaft Position (CMP) sensor
- Ground splice at the rear of the right side of the block
- Ground splice and the ground strap at the rear of the left side of the block
- Coolant Temperature (CTS) sensor
- Oil pressure sensor/switch
- Electrical connector from intake and disconnect from harness
- Junction block bracket from alternator bracket

5. Set the electrical harness aside.

6. Remove or disconnect the following:
- EVAP canister purge solenoid vent tube from the solenoid by squeez-

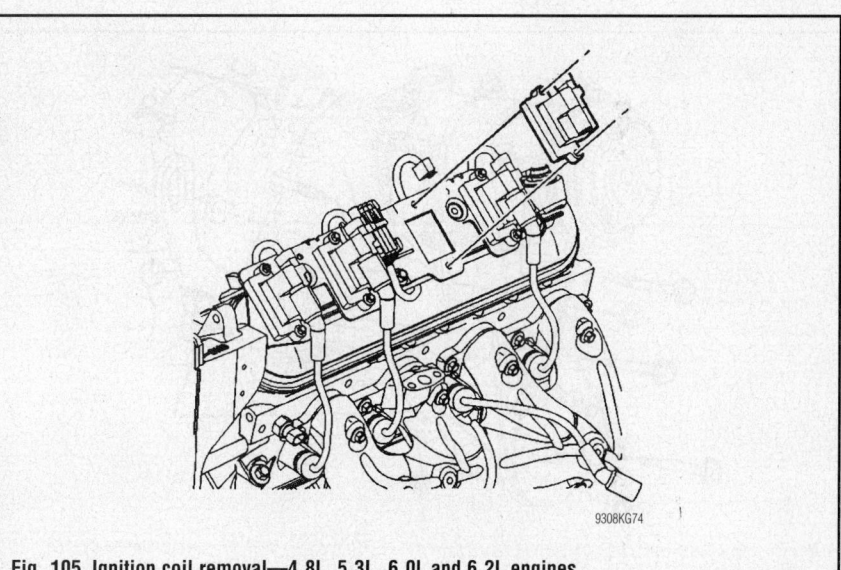

Fig. 105 Ignition coil removal—4.8L, 5.3L, 6.0L and 6.2L engines

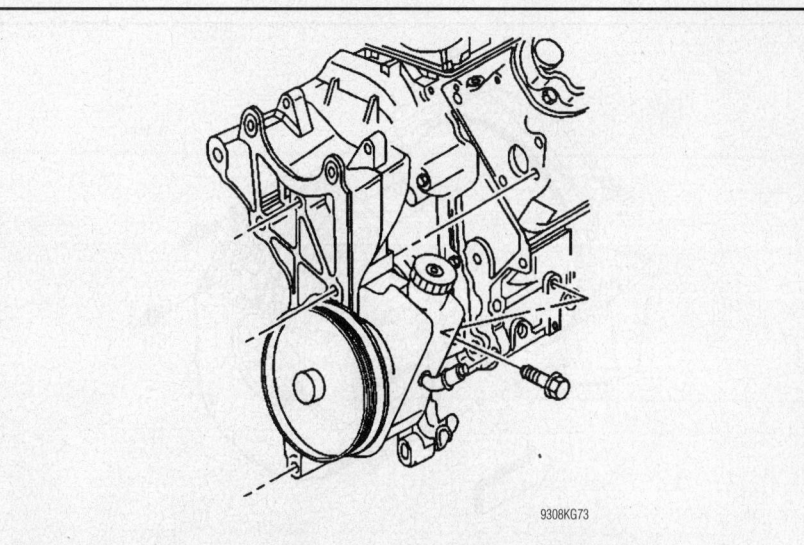

Fig. 106 Power steering pump removal—4.8L, 5.3L, 6.0L and 6.2L engines

ing the retainer, then release the tube from the solenoid
- Battery negative cable from the engine block
- Drive belt
- Bolts holding the alternator mounting bracket to the cylinder head and block
- Bolt behind the power steering pump to engine block
- Alternator mounting bracket. Position the bracket aside.
- Fuel pipes from the engine

7. Raise the vehicle.
- Steering linkage under body shield, if equipped
- Engine oil pan under body shield, if equipped
- Engine oil
- Starter motor

8. Disconnect the engine wiring harness from the following components:
- Crankshaft Position (CKP) sensor
- Engine oil level sensor
- Block heater, if equipped
- Oil pan wiring harness

9. Reposition wiring from the lower engine area.
- Exhaust pipes from the exhaust manifolds
- Transmission cooler pipe retainer from the right side of the engine block, if equipped
- Torque converter shield from the engine
- Torque converter bolts
- Nut and the transmission oil level indicator tube from the bell housing stud

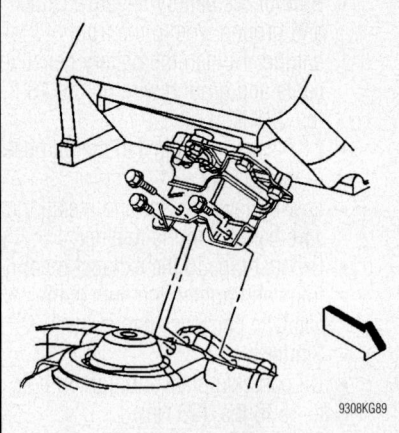

Fig. 109 Engine mount disconnect—4.8L, 5.3L, 6.0L and 6.2L engines

- Lower bell housing studs from the engine

10. Lower the vehicle.
- Remaining bell housing bolts
- Engine electrical harness aside
- Ignition coil(s)

11. Install an engine crane.

12. Install a floor jack or stands to transmission for support.

13. Remove the engine mount bolts.

➡ **Use care while moving the engine assembly in order to avoid breaking the MAP sensor locating tabs. Broken MAP sensor tabs may result in decreased engine performance.**

14. Remove the engine from the vehicle.

To install:

15. Install or connect the following:
- Engine to the vehicle
- Engine mount bolts
- Upper bell housing bolts

16. Remove transmission support apparatus.

17. Remove the lifting device.

18. Remove the lift brackets from both cylinder heads.

19. Install the ignition coil(s) and the spark plug wire(s).

20. Route the engine wiring harness to the lower right hand side of the engine.

21. Raise the vehicle.

22. Install or connect the following:
- Remaining bell housing bolts
- Torque converter bolts
- Torque converter shield
- Transmission oil level indicator tube and nut to bell housing stud
- A/C compressor
- Transmission cooler pipe retainer to right side of engine block
- Engine exhaust pipes to the exhaust manifolds

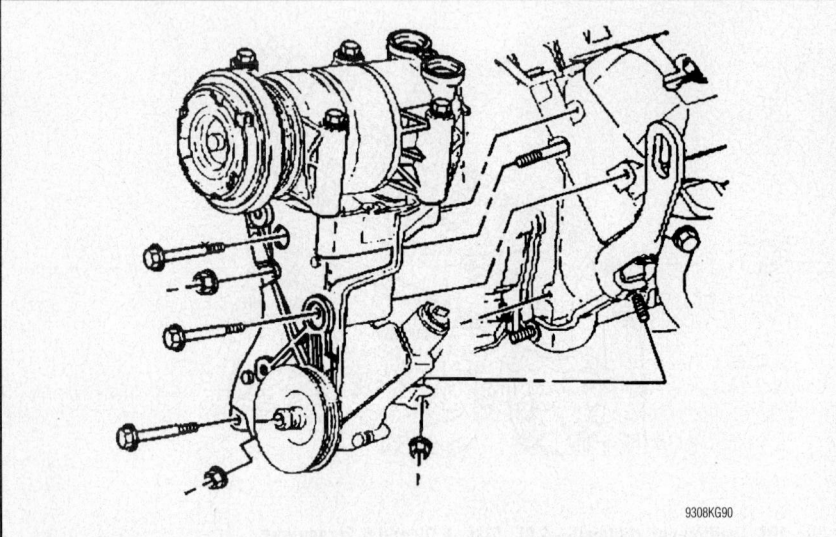

Fig. 107 Power steering mount bracket removal—4.8L, 5.3L, 6.0L and 6.2L engines

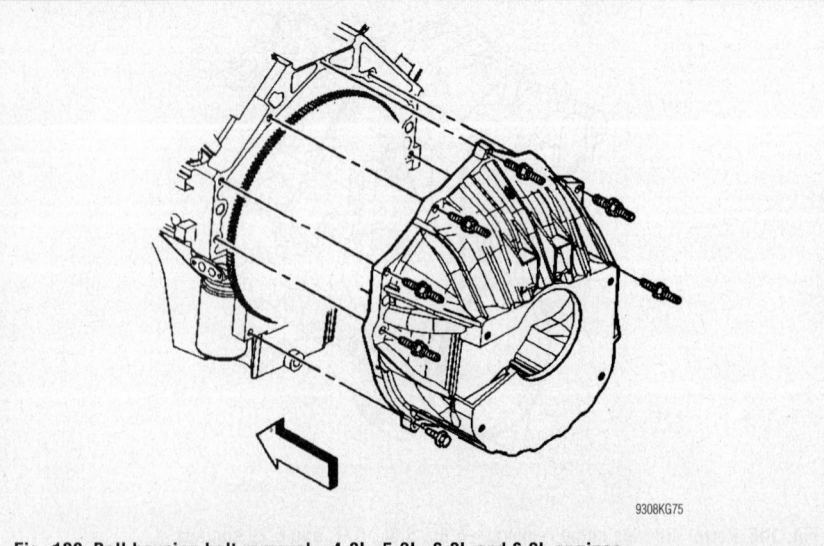

Fig. 108 Bell housing bolt removal—4.8L, 5.3L, 6.0L and 6.2L engines

23. Reroute wiring to lower engine area and install bolt to oil pan.

24. Connect electrical connectors to the CKP sensor, the engine oil level sensor and the block heater, if equipped.

25. Install or connect the following:
- Starter motor
- Engine oil pan under body shield, if equipped
- Steering linkage under body shield

26. Lower the vehicle.
- Fuel pipes to the engine
- Alternator mounting bracket to the cylinder head using the nuts and the bolts. Tighten the bolts to 37 ft. lbs. (50 Nm).
- Bolt at the rear of the power steering pump to the engine block and tighten to 37 ft. lbs. (50 Nm)
- Alternator
- Drive belt
- Battery negative cable to the engine block
- EVAP canister purge solenoid to the intake manifold

27. Route the engine harness over the top of the engine. Attach the connectors for following components:
- Eight injectors
- IAC motor
- TP sensor
- EVAP canister purge solenoid.
- MAP sensor
- CMP sensor
- Ground splice at the rear of the right side of engine block
- Ground splice and the ground strap at the rear of the left side of engine block
- CTS sensor

28. Install or connect the following:
- Nut to the engine wiring harness bracket and tighten to 89 inch lbs. (10 Nm)

❋❋ CAUTION

In order to avoid possible injury or vehicle damage, always replace the accelerator control cable with a NEW cable whenever you remove the engine from the vehicle. In order to avoid cruise control cable damage, position the cable out of the way while you remove or install the engine.

- NEW accelerator control cable
- Cruise control cable, if equipped, to the throttle shaft
- Bolts for the accelerator control cable mounting bracket and tighten to 89 inch lbs. (10 Nm)

- Engine sight shield to the intake manifold
- Heater hoses to the cowl and the engine
- Coolant hose to the throttle body
- Radiator support in the vehicle
- A/C condenser mounting bolts
- Air cleaner duct
- Lower radiator hoses to the engine

29. Lower the hood.
30. Fill the engine with oil.
31. Fill the engine with coolant.
32. Connect the negative battery cable.

2007 Models, Except Classic

❋❋ CAUTION

Before servicing any electrical component, the ignition key must be in the OFF or LOCK position and all electrical loads must be OFF, unless instructed otherwise in these procedures.

1. Remove or disconnect the following:
- Negative battery cable
- Coolant
- Engine oil
- A/C refrigerant

2. Raise the hood to the servicing position. Move the hood hinge bolt to hold the hood in the servicing position.
- Hood latch and radiator support
- Intake manifold
- Upper and the lower radiator hoses from the engine
- Heater hoses from the engine and the cowl
- Harness connectors from the oil pressure sensor and lifter oil manifold
- Ground strap from the left cylinder head
- Negative battery cable and harness ground from the right cylinder head

3. Raise and safely support the vehicle.
- Harness grounds and clips from the engine block
- Transmission oil cooler line clip bolt from the oil pan
- Starter
- Harness connectors for the knock sensors, CMP sensor, A/C pressure sensor, CKP sensor and oil level sensor
- Block heater connector, if equipped

4. Lower the vehicle.
- Power steering pump engine block bolt
- Alternator bracket assembly and set aside with the power steering pump

- Ignition coils to allow attachment of the engine lift brackets
- Transmission dipstick tube nut and tube

5. Install engine lift brackets J41798 or equivalent. Tighten the M8 bolts to 18 ft. lbs. (25 Nm) and the M10 bolts to 37 ft. lbs. (50 Nm).
- Engine mount bolts

6. Raise and safely support the vehicle.
- Engine shield or skid plate
- Exhaust pipes from the exhaust manifolds and catalytic converters
- Torque converter bolts
- Transmission mounting bolts

7. Lower the vehicle.
8. Install an engine crane.
9. Install a floor jack or stands to transmission for support.
10. Remove the engine from the vehicle.

To install:

11. Position the engine in the vehicle. Make sure the engine is properly aligned and mated with the transmission, then remove the crane.
12. Install the engine mount bolts; start with the middle bolt then the outer bolts. Tighten to 48 ft. lbs. (65 Nm).
13. Install the transmission bolts. Tighten to 37 ft. lbs. (50 Nm).
14. Align the torque converter bolt holes and install the bolts. Tighten to 47 ft. lbs. (63 Nm) except on 4L80E transmissions. On the 4L80E, tighten the bolts to 44 ft. lbs. (60 Nm).
15. The remaining installation is the reverse of removal.

6.6L Engine

See Figures 110 and 111.

➡**In order to remove the engine, the vehicle must be on a lift. the front tires also need to be removed. You will have to support the vehicle by its frame for tire removal.**

1. Drain the cooling system.
2. Discharge and recover the air conditioning system.
3. Drain the engine oil.
4. Raise the hood to the servicing position. Move the hood hinge bolt to hold the hood in the servicing position.
5. Disconnect the battery cables.
6. Remove the upper intake manifold sight shield as follows:
   a. Remove the retaining bolt in the front of the shield.
   b. Lift up on the front of the shield, then left the shield off the rear bracket.

7. Remove or disconnect the following:

➡**After you remove the duct, cover the turbocharger openings and ducts with tape to prevent foreign objects from entering.**

- Air cleaner outlet duct from the air cleaner and turbocharger.
- Mass Air Flow (MAF) switch connector
- A/C pressure cycling switch connector
- Surge tank switch
- Engine wire harness clip from the accumulator
- Engine wire harness clips from the wheelhouse inner panel and engine bracket
- Air cleaner assembly and bracket
- Surge tank

8. Raise the vehicle.
- Front tires and wheels
- Both front fender wheelhouse inner panels

9. Lower the vehicle.
- Charged air cooler pipes and hoses from the engine and charged air cooler
- Radiator inlet hose form the radiator and engine
- Upper and lower fan shrouds
- Radiator outlet hose from the radiator
- Outlet heater hose from the outlet radiator hose
- Hose clips from the frame
- Radiator outlet hose from the engine
- Bolt securing the outlet heater hose pipe to the alternator mounting bracket
- Nut securing the outlet heater hose pipe to the fuel filter mounting bracket
- Secure the heater hose aside
- Upper radiator support
- Radiator
- Charged air cooler
- A/C condenser
- Alternator harness connector
- A/C refrigerant switch connector
- Dual alternator harness connector, if equipped
- A/C compressor clutch connector
- Harness clip from the A/C compressor bracket
- Battery cable from the alternator and auxiliary alternator, if equipped
- Battery cable harness clips from the bracket
- Bolt securing the battery cable junction block from the power steering pump

- Move and secure the battery cables aside
- Both fuel injection control module harness connectors, by flipping the latch up
- Engine wire harness from the retainer
- Fuel lines at the engine
- Remove the nut and the fuel line bracket from the upper valve rocker arm cover stud
- Fuel lines aside
- Power supply cable from the glow plug relay
- Drive belt
- Suction hose from the accumulator. You can leave the compressor end on the compressor.
- A/C compressor bolts, then move the compressor, with the hoses attached, to the right side of the engine compartment
- Wiring harness to the left side of the engine and tie aside
- Bolts holding the power steering pump front bracket to the pump and A/C compressor mounting bracket
- A/C compressor and power steering pump bracket. Once the battery cables are removed from the engine, the power steering pump can be removed further out of the way
- Positive Crankcase Ventilation (PCV) oil separator from the bracket
- Bolts securing the PCV separator bracket and fuel bleed valve
- Right idler pulley (ribbed)
- Alternator mounting bracket and secure aside. You do not have to remove the alternator or the belt tensioner
- Inlet heater hose from the heater core inlet, using Quick Connect–Disconnect tool No. J 43181
- Bolt and ground wires from the rear of the left cylinder head

10. Raise the vehicle
- Oil pan skid plate
- Engine protection shield, if equipped
- Bolt for the negative battery cable and engine wiring harness ground wire from the left side of the engine
- Bolts holding the battery cable channel retainer to the lower crankcase
- Engine coolant heater cord
- Starter motor

- Nut securing the battery cable bracket to the right side of the lower crankcase
- Bolt holding the auxiliary negative battery cable and the engine wiring harness ground wires to the right side of the engine
- Position the battery cables aside
- Exhaust pipe–to–exhaust outlet clamp
- Lower oil pan, if 4WD

11. If equipped with an automatic transmission, matchmark the installed position of the flywheel and torque converter.
- Torque converter bolts through the starter opening
- Transmission oil line clip nut if equipped with A/T
- Nuts securing the transmission fluid fill tube bracket, if equipped with A/T
- Transmission–to–engine stud and bolts. Note the location of the studs and any brackets attached to the studs

12. Lower the vehicle to work through the wheel opening
- Engine mount–to–frame bracket bolts

13. Lower the vehicle.

14. Install Engine Lifting Bracket tool No. J 36857 to the rear of the left cylinder head with a suitable bolt.

15. Install Engine Lifting Bracket tool No. J 36857 to the front of the right cylinder head with a suitable bolt.

16. Install a suitable lifting device. The engine will have to be angled to remove it. Use a load positioning sling to help in angling the engine.

17. Raise the vehicle off the engine mounts.

18. Remove the left and right engine mount frame brackets.

19. Remove the engine assembly from the vehicle.

20. Secure the engine on an engine stand by removing the following components:
- Flywheel/flexplate
- Rear main seal
- Exhaust outlet
- Oil pan
- Flywheel housing

To install:

21. Install Engine Lifting Bracket tool No. J 36857 to the rear of the left cylinder head with a suitable bolt.

22. Install Engine Lifting Bracket tool No. J 36857 to the front of the right cylinder head with a suitable bolt.

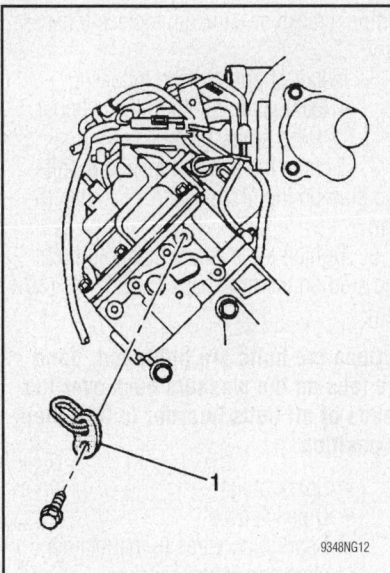

Fig. 110 Install the engine lifting bracket to the rear of the left cylinder head—6.6L engines

23. Install a suitable lifting device. The engine will have to be angled to install it. Use a load positioning sling to help in angling the engine.

24. Install or connect the following:
- Engine in the vehicle
- 2 transmission–to–engine bolts, loosely
- Left and right side engine mount frame brackets and tighten to 55 ft. lbs. (75 Nm)
- Engine mount–to–frame bracket bolts and tighten to 50 ft. lbs. (65 Nm)

25. Remove the lifting brackets from the cylinder heads.

- Transmission–to–engine bolts/studs and tighten to 37 ft. lbs. (50 Nm)
- Torque converter bolts and tighten to 44 ft. lbs. (60 Nm)

26. Install the remaining components in the reverse of the removal procedure, noting the following important specifications and steps:
- Transmission fluid tube bracket nuts: 13 ft. lbs. (18 Nm)
- Transmission oil cooler line clip bolt: 80 inch lbs. (9 Nm)
- Exhaust pipe clamp: 30 ft. lbs. (40 Nm)
- Ground wire bolt: 25 ft. lbs. (34 Nm)
- Battery cable bracket bolts: 106 inch lbs. (12 Nm)
- Cable and ground wire bolts: 25 ft. lbs. (34 Nm)
- Oil pan skid plate bolts: 15 ft. lbs. (20 Nm)
- Engine protection shield bolts: 15 ft. lbs. (20 Nm)
- Alternator bracket bolt: 37 ft. lbs. (50 Nm)
- Idler pulley bolt: 32 ft. lbs. (43 Nm)
- A/C compressor bolts: 37 ft. lbs. (50 Nm)

27. Refill the crankcase and the cooling system.

28. Recharge the air conditioning system.

8.1L Engine

See Figure 112.

1. Raise the hood to the servicing position. Move the hood hinge bolt to hold the hood in the servicing position.

2. Release the fuel system pressure.

3. Remove or disconnect the following:
- Negative, then positive battery cables
- Coolant
- A/C refrigerant
- Engine oil cooler lines from the engine block
- Transmission–to–engine bolts
- Clutch pressure plate bolts, if equipped
- Torque converter bolts, if equipped
- Catalytic converter
- Exhaust manifold pipe
- Hoses from power steering pump, then plug the lines and ports
- Starter motor

4. Raise the vehicle.
- Engine electrical harness and tie aside
- Alternator
- Ground cable bolt from engine block
- Exhaust Gas Recirculation (EGR) valve adapter
- Vacuum lines (tag before removal)
- Throttle Actuator Control (TAC) module electrical connector

5. Install Engine Lift Brackets part No. J 36857, or equivalent, to the rear of the right cylinder head and the front of the left cylinder head.

6. Install the attaching bolt and washer. Use part No. 9428217 with 1560963. Tighten the bolts to 30 ft. lbs. (40 Nm).

7. Remove or disconnect the following:
- Engine mount heat shield bolt and shields
- Engine mount–to–engine mount bracket bolts

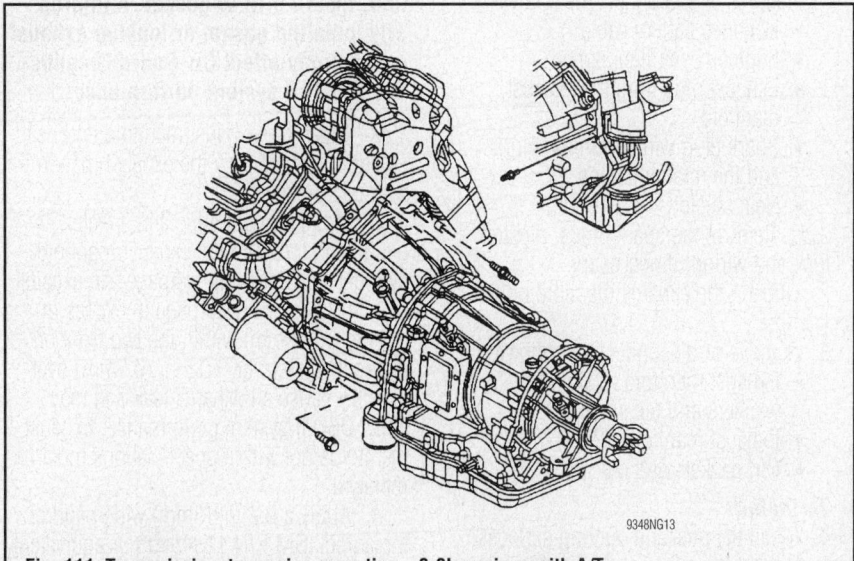

Fig. 111 Transmission–to–engine mounting—6.6L engines with A/T

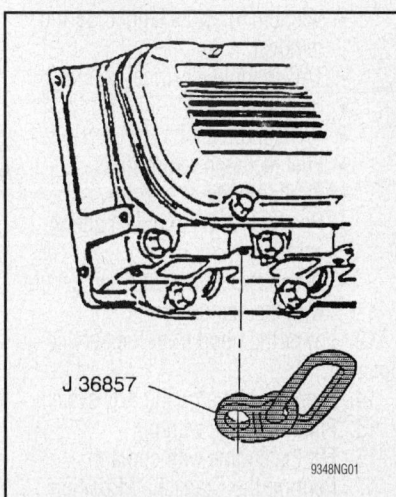

J 36857

Fig. 112 Install suitable lift brackets to the rear of the right head and the front of the left head

- Engine from the vehicle, using a suitable lifting device. Place on a suitable stand.
- A/C compressor/power steering pump bracket from the cylinder head
- Lift brackets from the cylinder head

To install:

8. Install Engine Lift Brackets part No. J 36857, or equivalent, to the rear of the right cylinder head and the front of the left cylinder head.

9. Install the attaching bolt and washer. Use part No. 9428217 with 1560963. Tighten the bolts to 30 ft. lbs. (40 Nm).

10. Install or connect the following:
- A/C compressor/power steering mounting bracket. Tighten the bolts and nut to 37 ft. lbs. (50 Nm).
- Alternator bracket
- Engine into the vehicle
- Engine mount–to–engine mount bracket bolts
- Engine mount heat shield and bolts

11. Remove the lift hooks from the cylinder heads, then raise the vehicle.
- Engine oil cooler lines
- Transmission–to–engine bolts
- Clutch pressure plate bolts, if equipped
- Torque converter bolts, if equipped
- Catalytic converter
- Exhaust manifold pipe
- Hoses to the power steering pump
- Starter motor

12. Lower the vehicle.
- Engine electrical harness. Make sure the harness is properly routed.
- Alternator
- Ground cable bolt to engine block and tighten to 12 ft. lbs. (16 Nm)
- EGR valve adapter
- Vacuum lines, as tagged during removal
- TAC module electrical connector
- Radiator
- A/C compressor
- Fuel feed and return lines
- Ignition coils
- Positive, then negative battery cables
- Air cleaner outlet duct and secure with the clamp

13. Lower the hood from the service position.

14. Properly recharge the A/C system.

15. Fill the engine with oil.

16. Fill the engine with coolant.

17. Perform the Crankshaft Position (CKP) sensor variation learn procedure:
  a. Install a suitable scan tool and check for Diagnostic Trouble Codes

(DTCs). If any DTCs, other than P1336 are set, resolve those codes first, before proceeding with this procedure.
  b. With the scan tool, select the crankshaft position variation learn procedure.
  c. Observe the fuel cut–off for the 8.1L engine.
  d. The scan tool will instruct you to perform certain steps, make sure you follow all directions given by the scan tool exactly.
  e. Enable the crankshaft position system variation learn procedure.

➡While the learn procedure is in progress, release the throttle immediately when the engine started to decelerate. The engine control is returned to the operator and the engine responds to throttle position after the learn procedure is complete.

  f. Slowly increase the engine speed to the RPM that you observed.
  g. Immediately release the throttle when fuel cut–out is reached.
  h. The scan tool displays: Learn Status: Learned this ignition. If the scan tool does NOT display this message and not other DTCs set, you must perform further troubleshooting.
  i. Turn the ignition **OFF** for 30 seconds after the learn procedure has been completed successfully.

18. Start and run the engine, then check for leaks.

EXHAUST MANIFOLD

REMOVAL & INSTALLATION

4.3L Engine

1. Remove or disconnect the following:
- Negative battery cable
- Engine cover, if equipped
- Exhaust pipe from the exhaust manifold
- Spark plug wires from the plugs and the retaining clips
- Heat shields
  j. Remove the spark plugs, dipstick tube and wiring, if necessary.

2. Unbend the exhaust manifold bolt lock tangs.

3. Remove or disconnect the following:
- Exhaust manifold retaining bolts, washers and tab washers
- Exhaust manifold
- Old gaskets and discard

To install:

4. Clean the gasket mounting surfaces.

5. Inspect the exhaust manifold for distortion, cracks or damage; replace if necessary.

6. Install or connect the following:
- Exhaust manifold to the cylinder using a new gasket.

7. Tighten the exhaust manifold bolts and stud on the first pass to 11 ft. lbs. (5 Nm).

8. Tighten the exhaust manifold bolts and stud on the final pass to 22 ft. lbs.(30 Nm).

➡Once the bolts are tightened, bend the tabs on the washers back over the heads of all bolts in order to lock them in position.

- Spark plugs
- Dipstick tube
- Spark plug wires to the retainer clips and plugs
- Exhaust pipe to the manifold
- Engine cover (if equipped)
- Negative battery cable

4.8L, 5.3L, 6.0L and 6.2L Engines

See Figure 113.

1. Remove or disconnect the following:
- Spark plug wires from the spark plugs

➡Do not remove the spark plug wires from the ignition coils unless required.

- Exhaust manifold, bolts, and gasket. Discard the gasket.
- Heat shield and bolts from the manifold, if required

To install:

➡Do not reuse the exhaust manifold–to–cylinder head gaskets. Upon installation of the exhaust manifold, install a NEW gasket. A improperly installed gasket or leaking exhaust system may effect On–Board Diagnostics (OBD) II system performance.

2. Clean the exhaust manifold and heat shield in solvent. Dry the exhaust manifold with compressed air.

3. Use a straight edge and a feeler gauge and measure the exhaust manifold cylinder head deck for warpage. An exhaust manifold deck with warpage in excess of 0.01 in. (0.25mm) within the two front or two rear runners or 0.02 in. (0.5mm) overall, may cause an exhaust leak and may affect OBD II system performance. Exhaust manifolds not within specifications must be replaced.

4. Apply a 0.2 in. (5mm) wide band of threadlock GM P/N 12345493 or equivalent to the threads of the exhaust manifold bolts.

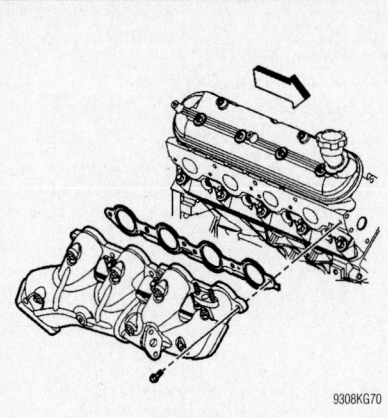

Fig. 113 Right exhaust manifold removal—4.8L, 5.3L, 6.0L and 6.2L; left side similar

5. Install the exhaust manifold gasket and exhaust manifold

6. Install the exhaust manifold bolts and tighten, beginning with the center two bolts. Alternate from side–to–side, and work toward the outside bolts.

   a. Tighten the exhaust manifold bolts first pass to 11 ft. lbs. (15 Nm). Begin with the center 2 bolts, then alternate from side to side working outwards.

   b. Tighten the exhaust manifold bolts final pass to 18 ft. lbs. (25 Nm). Begin with the center 2 bolts, then alternate from side to side working outwards. Using a flat punch, bend over the exposed edge of the exhaust manifold gasket at the front of the right cylinder head.

7. Install or connect the following:
- Heat shield and bolts and tighten to 80 inch lbs. (9 Nm)
- Spark plug wires

6.6L Engine

Left Side

See Figure 114.

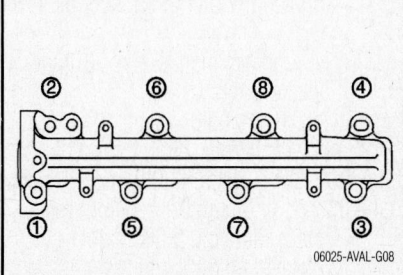

Fig. 114 Left and right side exhaust manifold bolt removal and installation sequence—6.6L engines

1. Raise the vehicle.
2. Remove or disconnect the following:
- Bolts securing the left exhaust pipe heat shield and move the heat shield aside
- Left exhaust pipe–to–manifold bolts
- Left front wheel
- Left front fender splash shield
- Charge air cooler duct
- Exhaust manifold heat shield bolts and shield
- 2 nuts and 6 bolts with the plain washer and bell view washer from the left manifold
- Exhaust manifold by removing it from the rear, then the front studs and sliding it out the bottom, past the oil filter
- Exhaust manifold gasket and discard

To install:

3. Installation is the reverse of the removal procedure. Tighten the retainers as follows:

   a. Exhaust manifold nuts and bolts, in sequence, in 2 passes to 25 ft. lbs. (34 Nm).

   b. Heat shield bolts: 71 inch lbs. (8 Nm).

   c. Exhaust pipe–to–manifold bolts: 39 ft. lbs. (59 Nm).

Right Side

See Figure 114.

1. Raise the vehicle.
2. Remove or disconnect the following:
- Right front wheel
- Right front fender splash shield
- Exhaust manifold heat shield bolts and shield
- Right exhaust pipe–to–manifold bolts
- 2 nuts and 6 bolts with the plain washer and bell view washer from the left manifold
- Exhaust manifold by removing it from the rear, then the front studs and sliding it out the bottom, past the oil filter
- Bolt for the oil level dipstick tube, to remove the gasket
- Exhaust manifold gasket and discard

To install:

3. Installation is the reverse of the removal procedure. Tighten the retainers as follows:

   a. Oil level dipstick tube: 15 ft. lbs. (20 Nm).

   b. Exhaust manifold nuts and bolts, in sequence, in 2 passes: 25 ft. lbs. (34 Nm).

   c. Heat shield bolts: 71 inch lbs. (8 Nm).

   d. Exhaust pipe–to–manifold bolts: 39 ft. lbs. (59 Nm).

8.1L Engine

1. Remove or disconnect the following:
- Spark plug wires
- Spark plugs
- Exhaust manifold heat shield bolts and shield
- Exhaust manifold bolt and nuts
- Exhaust manifold
- Exhaust manifold gasket and discard

To install:

2. Clean the mating surfaces and the retainer threads.

3. Install or connect the following:
- New exhaust manifold gasket
- Exhaust manifold
- Exhaust manifold bolt and nuts. Tighten the bolt to 26 ft. lbs. (35 Nm) and the nuts to 12 ft. lbs. (16 Nm).
- If removed, tighten the studs to 15 ft. lbs. (20 Nm).
- Heat shield. Tighten the retaining bolts and nuts to 18 ft. lbs. (25 Nm).
- Spark plugs and plug wires

INTAKE MANIFOLD

REMOVAL & INSTALLATION

4.3L Engine

See Figure 115.

1. Before servicing the vehicle, refer to the precautions in the beginning of this section.

2. Relieve the fuel system pressure
3. Remove or disconnect the following:
- Negative battery cable
- Air intake duct
- Wiring harness connectors and brackets from the manifold
- Throttle linkage and bracket from the upper manifold
- Cruise control cable, if equipped
- Fuel lines at the rear of the lower intake manifold
- Brake booster vacuum hose from the upper intake manifold
- Ignition coil and bracket
- Purge solenoid and bracket
- Studs and intake manifold attaching bolts, mark for reassembly

- Upper intake manifold
- Distributor housing and rotor, mark for reassembly
- Upper radiator hose from the thermostat housing
- Heater hoses and the bypass hose from the lower intake manifold
- Exhaust Gas Recirculation (EGR) valve
- Transmission dipstick tube, if equipped
- Positive Crankcase Ventilation (PCV) valve and hoses
- Air conditioning compressor and bracket. Without disconnecting, position aside
- Alternator bracket and bolt next to the thermostat housing, if needed
- Lower intake manifold mounting bolts and the lower manifold

To install:

4. Clean all gasket mating surfaces thoroughly.

5. Position the new gaskets on the cylinder heads with the port blocking plates at the rear and the words **THIS SIDE UP** facing up.

6. Apply a ³⁄₁₆ inch (5mm) bead of RTV to the front and rear sealing surfaces on the engine block. Extend the bead ½ inch (13mm) up each cylinder head to retain the gasket.

7. Carefully position the lower intake manifold onto the engine.

8. Apply GM 1052080 or equivalent sealer to the lower intake manifold bolts

9. Torque the bolts using 3 steps in the sequence shown:

   a. Step 1: 27 inch lbs. (3 Nm).
   b. Step 2: 106 inch lbs. (12 Nm).
   c. Step 3: 11 ft. lbs. (15 Nm).

10. Install or connect the following:

- Alternator bracket and bolts near the thermostat housing, if removed
- Air conditioning compressor

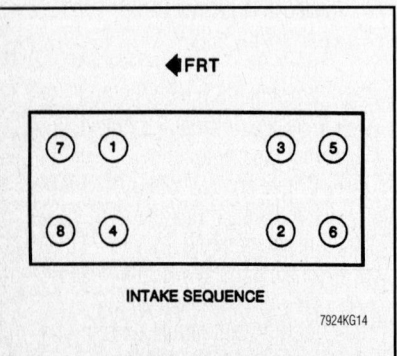

Fig. 115 Lower intake manifold bolt tightening sequence—4.3L engines

- PCV valve and hose
- Transmission dipstick tube, if equipped
- EGR valve
- Upper radiator and bypass hose to the thermostat housing
- Distributor.

11. Position the upper intake manifold gasket on the lower manifold.

☀ WARNING

Be careful not to pinch the injector tubes between the upper and lower manifolds.

- Upper intake manifold. Torque the bolts and studs to 88 inch lbs. (10 Nm).
- Purge control bracket and valve
- Ignition coil
- Brake booster vacuum
- Fuel lines
- Accelerator cable
- Cruise control cable, if equipped
- Wiring harness brackets and connections
- Air intake duct
- Negative battery cable

12. Refill and bleed the cooling system.

13. Pressurize the fuel system and check for leaks.

4.8L, 5.3L, 6.0L and 6.2L Engines

See Figures 116 and 117.

➡ **The intake manifold, throttle body, fuel injection rail, and fuel injectors may be removed as an assembly. If not servicing the individual components, remove the manifold as a complete assembly.**

1. Remove or disconnect the following:

- Alternator
- Positive Crankcase Ventilation (PCV) hose and valve
- Manifold Absolute Pressure (MAP) sensor, if required
- Engine coolant air bleed clamp and hose from the throttle body
- Knock sensor connector, if required.
- Accelerator control cable bracket and bolts, if required
- Fuel rail with injectors, if required
- EVAP solenoid, bolt, and isolator
- Any additional engine harness attachment points and set aside
- Intake manifold bolts
- Intake manifold with gaskets
- Intake manifold–to–cylinder head gaskets from the manifold. Discard the intake manifold gaskets.

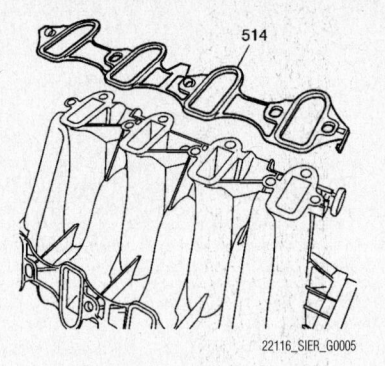

Fig. 116 Always use new gaskets—4.8L, 5.3L, 6.0L and 6.2L engines

2. Clean the intake manifold in solvent.

3. Dry the intake manifold with compressed air.

4. Inspect the intake manifold vacuum passages for debris or restrictions.

5. Inspect for damaged or broken vacuum fittings, damaged MAP sensor mounting bore, or broken MAP sensor retaining tabs.

6. Inspect the composite intake manifold assembly for cracks or other damage.

7. Inspect the areas between the intake runners. Inspect all the gasket sealing surfaces for damage.

8. Inspect the fuel injector bores for excessive scoring or damage. Inspect the intake manifold cylinder head deck for warpage.

9. Locate a straight edge across the intake manifold cylinder head deck surface. Position the straight edge across a minimum of two runner port openings.

10. Insert a feeler gauge between the intake manifold and the straight edge. A intake manifold with warpage in excess of 0.118 in. (3mm) over a 7.87 in. (200mm) area is warped and should be replaced.

To install:

11. Install or connect the following:

- MAP sensor
- EVAP solenoid, bolt, and isolator. Tighten the bolt to 89 inch lbs. (10 Nm).
- NEW intake manifold–to–cylinder head gaskets
- Intake manifold

12. Apply a 0.20 in. (5mm) band of threadlock GM P/N 12345382 or equivalent to the threads of the intake manifold bolts.

- Intake manifold bolts. Tighten intake manifold bolts first pass in sequence to 44 inch lbs. (5 Nm). Tighten intake manifold bolts final pass in sequence to 89 inch lbs. (10 Nm).

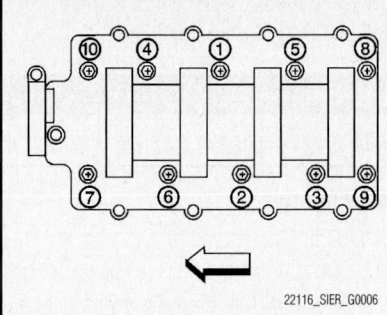

Fig. 117 Lower intake manifold bolt tightening sequence—4.8L, 5.3L, 6.0L and 6.2L engines

- PCV valve and hose
- Coolant air bleed hose and clamp onto the throttle body
- Accelerator control cable bracket and bolts. Tighten the bolts to 89 inch lbs. (10 Nm).
- Alternator

6.6L Engine

Center Manifold

See Figure 118.

1. Remove the Exhaust Gas Recirculation (EGR) valve cooler tube.
2. Remove the intake manifold tube.
3. Remove and discard the 2 intake manifold tube gaskets.
4. Remove the turbocharger.
5. Remove the center intake manifold bolts/nuts.
6. Pull–up the center intake manifold in order to remove.
7. Remove and discard the gaskets.
8. Clean the center intake manifold in cleaning solvent and air dry.

To install:

9. Install new center intake manifold gaskets.
10. Install the center intake manifold.
11. Install the center intake manifold

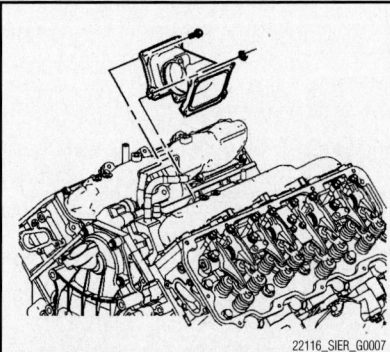

Fig. 118 Center intake manifold—6.6L engines

bolts/nuts and tighten to 89 inch lbs. (10 Nm).

12. Install the turbocharger.
13. Install 2 new O–rings onto the intake manifold tube.
14. Lubricate the O–rings with clean engine oil to aid in the installation.
15. Install the intake manifold tube.
16. Install the EGR valve cooler tube.

Left and Right Manifolds

See Figures 119 and 120.

1. Drain the cooling system.
2. Remove or disconnect the following:
   - Batteries cables
   - Center intake manifold
   - Fuel junction block
   - Left or right fuel rail
   - Intake manifold tube
   - 9 bolts and 2 nuts from the intake manifold. A bolt is located in the manifold opening.

➡The intake manifold uses sealer. If necessary, pry at the area by the common rail bolt holes and be careful to avoid damaging the sealing surfaces.

   - Intake manifold from the head. Cover the head openings to prevent debris from entering.

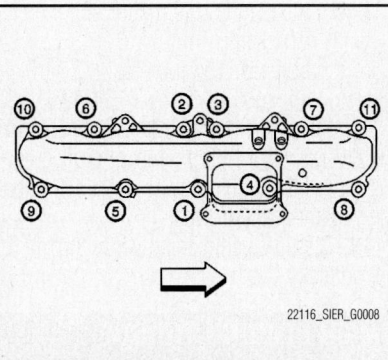

Fig. 119 Left side intake manifold bolt tightening sequence—6.6L engines

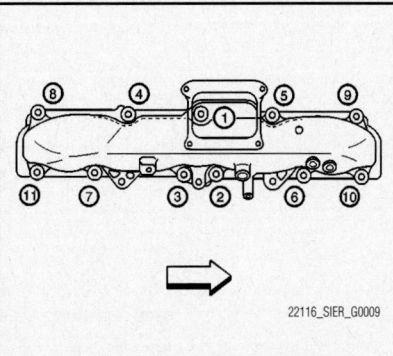

Fig. 120 Right side intake manifold bolt tightening sequence—6.6L engines

3. Clean all gaskets surface.

To install:

4. Install or connect the following:
   - A ⅛ in. (2–3mm) wide to ¹⁄₁₆ in (0.5–1.5mm) high bead of sealant to the sealing surface of the intake manifold

➡The left and right side manifolds are NOT interchangeable.

   - Intake manifold
   - Bolts and nuts. Tighten to 15 ft. lbs. (20 Nm), in sequence.
   - Intake manifold tube
   - Fuel rail
   - Fuel junction block
   - Turbocharger
   - Negative battery cables
5. Fill cooling system.

8.1L Engine

See Figures 121 and 122.

➡The intake manifold, throttle body, fuel rail and injectors can be removed as an assembly. If you do not need to service these components individually, remove the manifold as a complete assembly.

1. Relieve the fuel system pressure and drain the cooling system.
2. Remove or disconnect the following:
   - Air cleaner outlet duct
   - Intake manifold sight shield
   - Fuel feed and return pipes
   - Engine harness clips from the studs on the front of the dash
   - Engine harness clip from the wheelhouse splash shield
   - Pressure cycling switch, surge tank switch and Mass Air Flow (MAF) electrical connectors
3. Reposition the engine harness to the top of the engine
   - Connector Position Assurance (CPA) retainer from the ignition coil harness
   - Manifold Absolute Pressure (MAP) sensor connector
   - Ignition coil connector(s)
   - Engine Coolant Temperature (ECT) sensor electrical connector
   - Engine harness bolt and studs
   - CPA retainer from the ignition coil harness
   - Alternator connector
   - Injector harness connector
   - Ignition coil harness connector
   - Throttle Position (TP) sensor connector

- Electronic Throttle Control (ETC) connector
- Purge valve solenoid connector

4. Reposition the engine harness to the driver's side of the engine compartment.

- Bypass valve vacuum hose from the intake manifold
- EVAP tubes
- Exhaust Gas Recirculation (EGR) valve electrical connector
- EGR pipe bolts from the EGR adapter. Reposition the EGR pipe
- EGR valve pipe gasket and discard
- Secondary Air Injection (AIR) pipe nut from the fuel rail stud, if equipped
- Fuel pressure regulator vacuum hose
- Fuel rail studs and fuel rail, ONLY if replacing the manifold
- Intake manifold bolts

✳✳ WARNING

Do NOT try to remove the intake manifold by prying under the sealing surfaces.

- Intake manifold
- Intake manifold side gaskets and end seals and discard

➡**The splash shield is reusable and secured using a snap–in fit. Do not distort the shield during removal.**

- Splash shield

To install:

5. Clean all gasket surfaces completely.
6. Install or connect the following:
- Splash shield. Make sure the shield

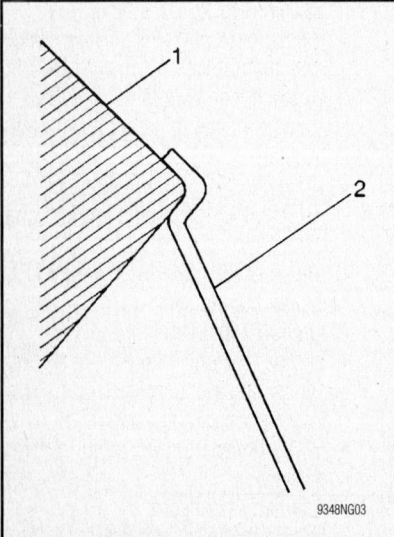

Fig. 121 Make sure that the splash shield snap fits between the cylinder heads— 8.1L engines

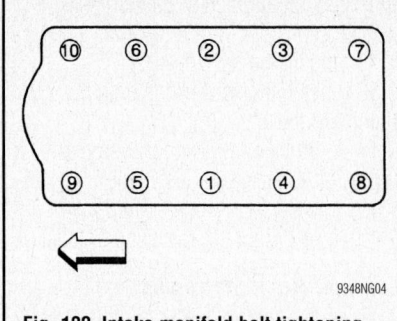

Fig. 122 Intake manifold bolt tightening sequence—8.1L engines

fits properly between the cylinder head.

➡**Make sure the manifold gasket tabs align with the hole in the head gasket.**

- New intake manifold end seals
- New intake manifold side gaskets onto the heads. Make sure the stamped **This Side Up** is showing.
- Intake manifold to the block
- Apply a suitable thread locking material to at least 8 threads of the intake manifold bolts

7. Install the intake manifold bolts and tighten, in the sequence shown, in 4 passes:
   a. 1st pass: 44 inch lbs. (5 Nm).
   b. 2nd pass: 71 inch lbs. (8 Nm).
   Check the manifold joints for shifting and fix as necessary.
   c. 3rd pass: 106 inch lbs. (12 Nm).
   d. 4th pass: 11 ft. lbs. (15 Nm).

8. Install the remaining components in the reverse order of the removal procedure.
9. Fill the cooling system, then connect the negative battery cable
10. Start the vehicle and verify that there are no leaks.

MAIN BEARING TORQUE SEQUENCE

See Figure 123.

Refer to the accompanying illustration for main bearing torque sequence.

OIL PAN

REMOVAL & INSTALLATION

4.3L Engine

1. Drain the engine oil.
2. Disconnect the negative battery cable.
3. Raise and support the vehicle.
4. Remove or disconnect the following:
- Oil pan skid plate bolts and plate, if equipped
- Engine oil and filter
- Crossmember bolts and bar
- On 4WD, the front differential carrier
- Battery cable bracket bolts.
- Starter
- Transmission cover
- Positive battery cable clip bolt
- Oil level sensor electrical connector
- Transmission
- Oil level sensor and discard
- Oil pan bolts and oil pan
- Oil pan gasket

To install:

5. Thoroughly clean all gasket surfaces,
6. Apply a 5 mm wide and 25 mm long bead of sealant to both the right and left sides of the engine front cover to engine block junction at the oil pan sealing surfaces.
7. Apply a 5 mm wide and 25 mm long bead of sealant to both the right and left sides of the crankshaft rear oil seal housing to engine block junction at the oil pan sealing surfaces.
8. Install or connect the following:
- Transmission
- New gasket
- Oil pan and new gasket
- Install the oil pan bolts and nuts, but do not tighten

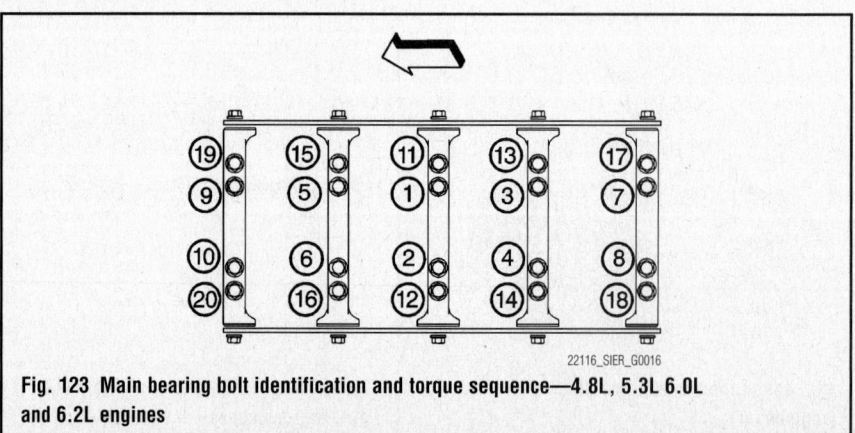

Fig. 123 Main bearing bolt identification and torque sequence—4.8L, 5.3L 6.0L and 6.2L engines

9. Measure the pan–to–transmission housing clearance using a feeler gage and a straight edge. Use a feeler gage to check the clearance between the oil pan–to–transmission housing measurement points. If the clearance exceeds 0.011 in. (0.3 mm) at any of the 3 oil pan–to–transmission housing measurement points (1), then repeat the step until the oil pan–to–transmission housing clearance is within the specification. The oil pan must always be forward of the rear face of the engine block.

10. Install the oil pan bolts, nuts and reinforcements. Torque bolts in sequence to 18 ft. lbs. (25 Nm).
- Oil level sensor electrical connector
- Positive battery cable clip bolt
- Transmission cover
- Starter
- Battery cable bracket bolts.
- On 4WD, the front differential carrier
- Crossmember bolts and bar
- Engine oil and filter
- Oil pan skid plate bolts and plate, if equipped
- Negative battery cable
11. Refill the engine with oil.

4.8L, 5.3L, 6.0L and 6.2L Engines

See Figures 124 through 127.

➡The original oil pan gasket is retained and aligned to the oil pan by rivets. When installing a new gasket, it is not necessary to install new rivets. DO NOT reuse the oil pan gasket. When installing the oil pan, install a NEW oil pan gasket.

1. Remove or disconnect the following:
- Negative battery cable

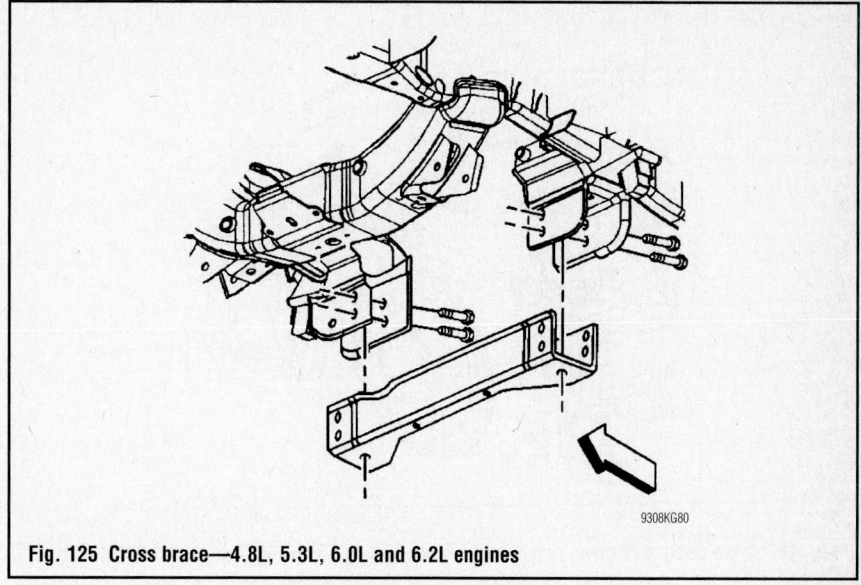

Fig. 125 Cross brace—4.8L, 5.3L, 6.0L and 6.2L engines

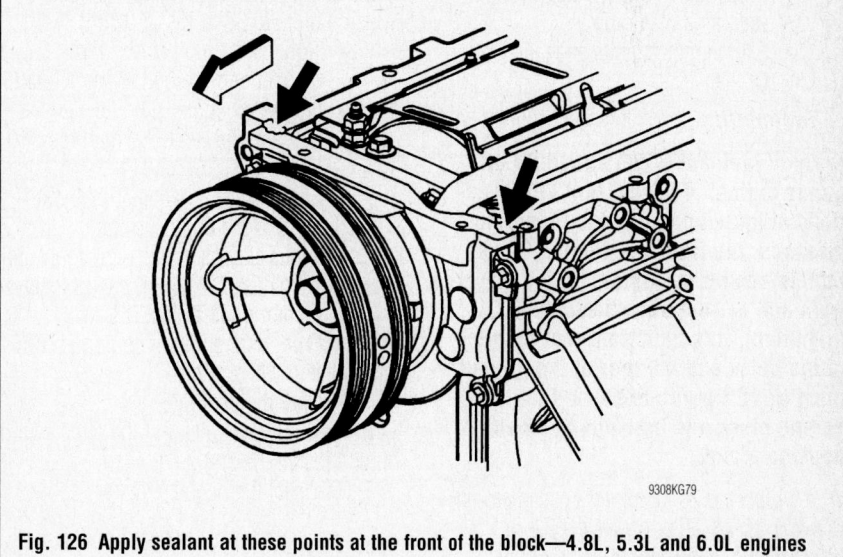

Fig. 126 Apply sealant at these points at the front of the block—4.8L, 5.3L and 6.0L engines

- Front differential if equipped with four wheel drive
- Under body shield from the vehicle
- Oil pan shield
- On 2007 models (except Classic), unbolt steering rack and hang downwards
- Cross brace if equipped
- Engine oil and filter
- Transmission–to–oil pan bolts
- Oil level sensor electrical connector
- Two front wiring harness retainer bolts
- Engine wiring harness retainer bolts from the engine oil pan
- Engine oil cooler pipe–to–oil pan bolt
- Transmission oil cooler pipe retainer and the bolt from the oil pan

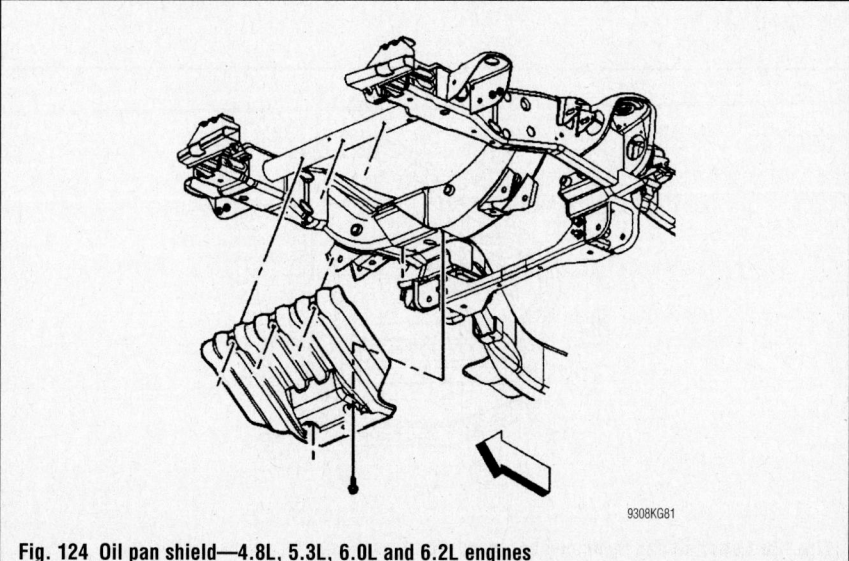

Fig. 124 Oil pan shield—4.8L, 5.3L, 6.0L and 6.2L engines

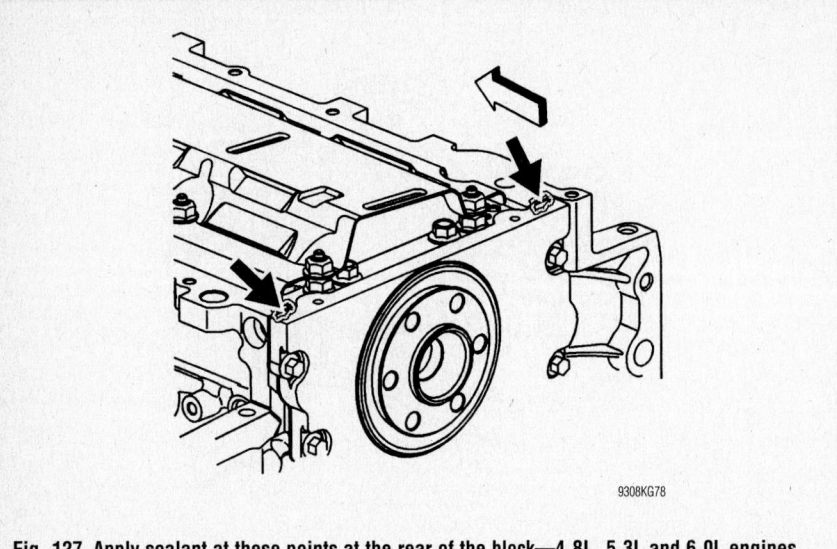

Fig. 127 Apply sealant at these points at the rear of the block—4.8L, 5.3L and 6.0L engines

- Closeout covers and bolts (one each side of engine)
- Engine mount bolts each side
- Oil pan

To install:

➡**The alignment of the structural oil pan is critical. The rear bolt hole locations of the oil pan provide mounting points for the transmission bell housing. To ensure the rigidity of the powertrain and correct transmission alignment, it is important that the rear of the block and the rear of the oil pan must NEVER protrude beyond the engine block and transmission bell housing plane.**

2. Apply a 0.20 in. (5mm) bead of sealant GM P/N 12378190 or equivalent 0.8 in. (20mm) long to the engine block. Apply the sealant directly onto the tabs of the front cover gasket that protrudes into the oil pan surface.

➡**Be sure to align the oil gallery passages in the oil pan and engine block properly with the oil pan gasket.**

3. Pre–assemble the oil pan gasket to the pan. Install the oil pan bolts to the pan through the gasket.
4. Install or connect the following:
   - Oil pan gasket
   - Oil pan
   - Oil pan bolts, finger–tight. Do not over tighten.
   - Two lower bell housing bolts to position the oil pan correctly

5. Snug the lower bell housing bolt finger–tight. Do not over tighten. Tighten the oil pan–to–block and oil pan–to–oil pan front cover bolts to 18 ft. lbs. (25 Nm). Tighten the oil pan–to–rear cover bolts to

106 inch lbs. (12 Nm). Tighten the bell housing bolts to 37 ft. lbs. (50 Nm).
   - Transmission oil cooler pipe retainer and the bolt to the oil pan
   - Engine oil cooler pipe–to–oil pan bolt and tighten to 89 inch lbs. (10 Nm)
   - Engine wiring harness retainer bolts to the engine oil pan
   - Oil level sensor electrical connector
   - Transmission–to–oil pan bolts and tighten to 41 ft. lbs. (55 Nm)
   - Front differential, if equipped with four wheel drive
   - Underbody shield

6. Lower the vehicle. Fill the engine with oil and install the engine oil filter.
7. Connect the negative battery cable.

6.6L Engine

Lower Oil Pan

See Figure 128.

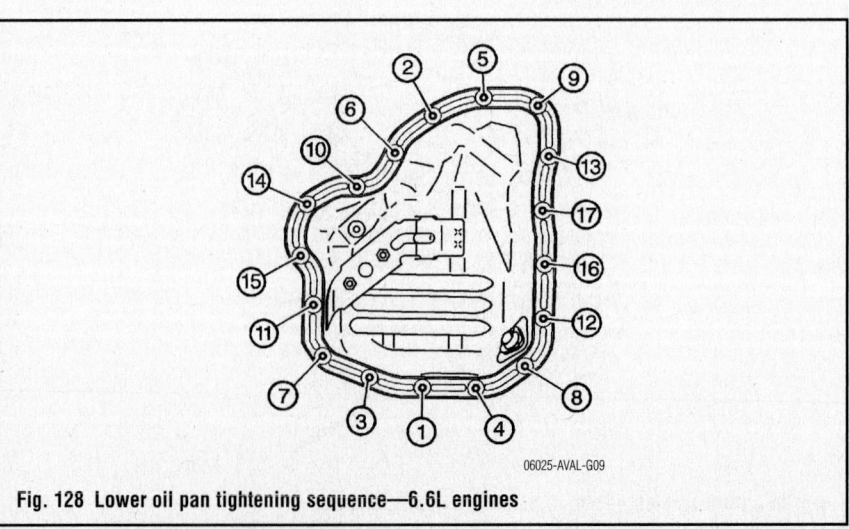

Fig. 128 Lower oil pan tightening sequence—6.6L engines

1. Drain the engine oil.
2. Remove or disconnect the following:
   - Oil pan skid plate (2WD vehicles)
   - Crossbar
   - Oil level sensor connector
   - Lower oil pan bolts and nuts
   - Lower oil pan from the lower crankcase
   - Lower oil pan

To install:

3. Clean all sealing surfaces
4. Apply a ⅛ in. (2mm) bead of sealant to the oil pan sealing surface.
5. Install the oil pan. Tighten the bolts and nuts in sequence to 89 inch lbs. (10 Nm)
6. The remainder of installation is the reverse of the removal procedure.
7. Refill engine with oil.

Upper Oil Pan

See Figures 129 and 130.

1. Drain the engine oil.
2. Remove or disconnect the following:
   - Front differential carrier (4WD vehicles)
   - Relay rod from the pitman arm and idler arm (2WD vehicles)
   - Transmission
   - Lower oil pan
   - Flywheel/flexplate
   - Positive and negative battery cable bracket bolts and bracket from the front of the upper oil pan
   - Positive and negative battery cable bracket nut and bracket from the right side of the upper oil pan
   - 2 engine flywheel housing to upper oil pan bolts (refer to denoted black triangles on accompanying figure)

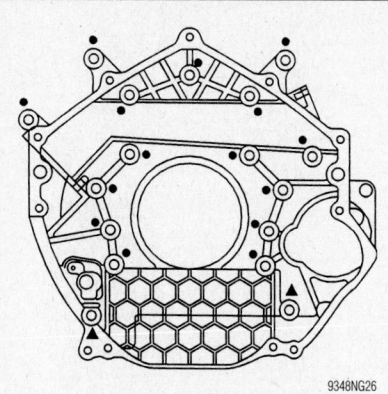

Fig. 129 Remove only the flywheel housing–to–upper oil pan bolts designated with a black triangle—6.6L engines

- Upper oil pan bolts and any brackets
- Upper oil pan from the engine block
- Upper oil pan. The oil dipstick tube needs to be removed while lowering the upper oil pan.

To install:

3. Clean all sealing surfaces.

4. Apply a ⅛ in. (2mm) bead of sealant to the oil pan and flywheel sealing surfaces.

5. Install or connect the following:
- Upper oil pan; make sure the dipstick is installed into the upper pan
- Upper pan bolts and brackets. Tighten, in sequence, to 15 ft. lbs. (20 Nm).
- 2 engine flywheel housing to upper oil pan bolts (refer to denoted black triangles on accompanying figure). Torque to 37 ft. lbs. (50 Nm).

6. The remainder of installation is the reverse of the removal procedure.

7. Refill engine with oil.

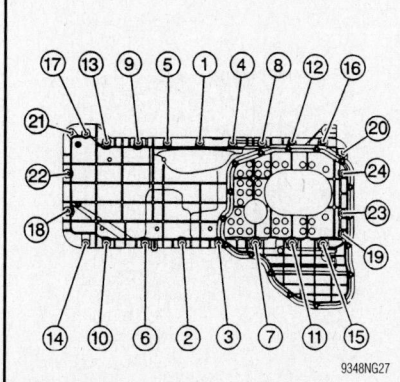

Fig. 130 Upper oil pan bolt tightening sequence—6.6L engines

8.1L Engine

See Figure 131.

1. Disconnect the negative battery cable and drain the engine oil.

2. Remove or disconnect the following:
- Front differential, if equipped with 4WD
- Starter motor
- Oil pan skid plate bolts and plate
- Crossbar bolt(s) and crossbar
- Oil level dipstick
- Oil level sensor electrical connector
- Engine harness clip from the oil pan
- Battery cable channel bolt
- Battery cable channel and reposition
- Oil pan bolts, oil pan and gasket

➡ **You can reuse the oil pan gasket, if it is not damaged**

To install:

➡ **You must install the oil pan within 5 minutes of applying the sealer.**

3. Before servicing the vehicle, refer to the precautions in the beginning of this section.

4. Apply sealant to the sides of the front and rear crankshaft bearing caps on the left and right sides.

5. Install or connect the following:
- Oil pan gasket into the oil pan groove
- Oil pan and bolts

6. Tighten the oil pan bolts, in sequence, as follows:
   a. 1st pass: 89 inch lbs. (10 Nm).
   b. 2nd pass: 18 ft. lbs. (25 Nm).

7. Install or connect the following:
- Battery cable channel and bolt. Tighten to 80 inch lbs. (9 Nm).
- Oil level sensor and tighten to 15 ft. lbs. (20 Nm)
- Engine harness clip

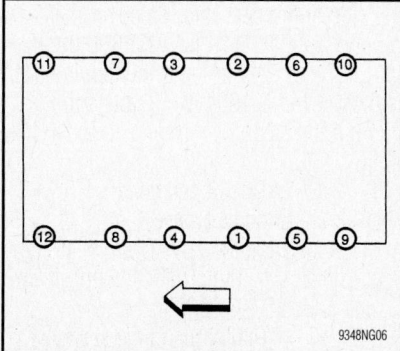

Fig. 131 Oil pan bolt tightening sequence—8.1L engines

- Oil level sensor connector
- Oil level dipstick
- Crossbar and bolt(s). Tighten to 74 ft. lbs. (100 Nm).
- Skid plate. Tighten the bolts to 15 ft. lbs. (20 Nm).
- Starter motor
- Front differential
- Negative battery cable

8. Fill the crankcase with oil.

OIL PUMP

REMOVAL & INSTALLATION

4.3L Engine

1. Remove or disconnect the following:
- Oil pan
- Oil pump mounting bolt
- Oil pump

To install:

2. Inspect the oil pump locator pins for damage, and replace if required.

3. Clean and inspect the oil pump.

4. Position the oil pump onto the locator pins.

5. Install the oil pump bolt and tighten the bolt to 66 ft. lbs. (90 Nm).

6. Install the oil pan.

4.8L, 5.3L, 6.0L and 6.2L Engines

See Figures 132 and 133.

1. Remove or disconnect the following:
- Engine front cover
- Oil pan
- Oil pump screen bolt and nuts
- Oil pump screen with O–ring seal.
- O–ring seal from the pump screen. Discard the O–ring seal.
- Remaining crankshaft oil deflector nuts.
- Crankshaft oil deflector
- Oil pump bolts

➡ **Do not allow dirt or debris to enter the oil pump assembly, cap ends as necessary.**

- Oil pump

➡ **The internal parts of the oil pump assembly are not serviced separately (excluding the spring). If the oil pump components are worn or damaged, replace the oil pump as an assembly. Do not attempt to repair the wire mesh portion of the pump and screen assembly.**

To install:

➡ **Inspect the oil pump and engine block oil gallery passages. These**

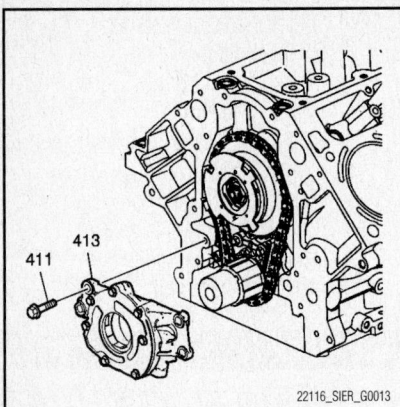

Fig. 132 Exploded view of the oil pump mounting—4.8L, 5.3L, 6.0L and 6.2L engines

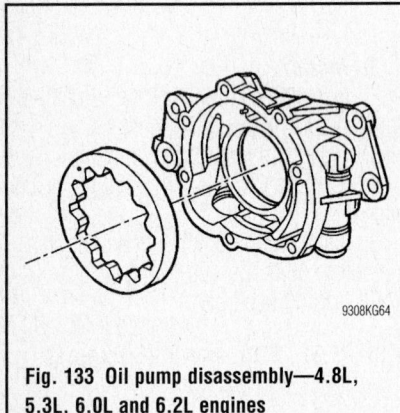

Fig. 133 Oil pump disassembly—4.8L, 5.3L, 6.0L and 6.2L engines

surfaces must be clear and free of debris or restrictions.

2. Align the splined surfaces of the crankshaft sprocket and the oil pump drive gear and install the oil pump. Install the oil pump onto the crankshaft sprocket until the pump housing contacts the face of the engine block.

3. Install or connect the following:
- Oil pump bolts. Tighten the oil pump bolts to 18 ft. lbs. (25 Nm).
- Crankshaft oil deflector

➡**Lubricate a NEW oil pump screen O-ring seal with clean engine oil.**

- NEW O-ring seal onto the oil pump screen

➡**Push the oil pump screen tube completely into the oil pump prior to tightening the bolt. Do not allow the bolt to pull the tube into the pump.**

4. Align the oil pump screen mounting brackets with the correct crankshaft bearing cap studs.

5. Install or connect the following:
- Oil pump screen

- Oil pump screen bolt and the deflector nuts. Tighten the bolt to 106 inch lbs. (12 Nm) and the nuts to 18 ft. lbs. (25 Nm).
- Oil pan
- Engine front cover

6.6L Engine

See Figures 134 and 135.

1. Drain the engine oil
2. Remove or disconnect the following:
- Engine flywheel housing (2WD vehicles)
- Engine front cover
- Lower and upper oil pans
- Oil pump pipe and screen and gasket

3. Block the crankshaft from turning with a wooden dowel.
- Oil pump driven gear nut
- Oil pump driven gear

➡**The crankshaft reluctor and oil pump drive gear are timed together at the factory. Do NOT remove the reluctor from the oil pump drive gear or damage the reluctor teeth.**

- Oil pump drive gear and crankshaft reluctor assembly using a brass drift and tapping as close to the center of the reluctor assembly
- 3 hex head and 1 Allen head bolt
- Oil pump
- Oil pump O-ring seal
- Oil pump gear cover bolts and cover

4. Measure the clearance between the gear teeth and oil pump housing using a feeler gauge. The production clearance is 0.0049–0.0087 in. (0.125–0.221mm) and the service limit is 0.0087 in. (0.221mm). Replace the pump if the clearance exceeds the service limit.

5. Use a feeler gauge and a straightedge to measure the clearance between the side of the gear and the cover. The production clearance is 0.0025–0.0043 in. (0.064–0.109mm) and the service limit is 0.0043 in. (0.109mm). Replace the pump if the clearance exceeds the service limit.

6. Calculate the driven gear shaft-to-bushing clearance:

a. Measure the driven gear shaft outside diameter. The production specification is 0.7853–0.7858 in. (19.947–19.960mm) and the service limit is 0.7819 in. (19.86mm).

b. Measure the driven gear bushing

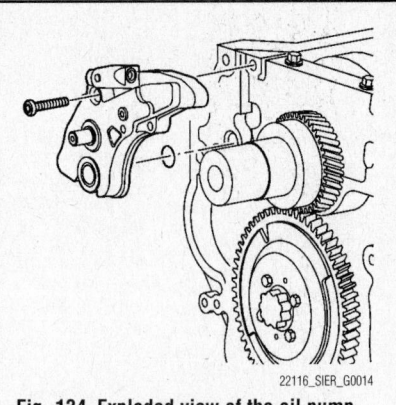

Fig. 134 Exploded view of the oil pump mounting—6.6L engines

inside diameter. The production value is 0.7874 in. (20mm).

c. Calculate the driven gear shaft-to-bushing clearance. The service limit is 0.0055 in. (0.14mm).

d. Replace the pump if the clearance exceeds the service limit.

To install:

7. Install or connect the following:
- Oil pump gear cover and bolts. Tighten to 15 ft. lbs. (20 Nm).
- New O-ring seal for the oil pump
- Oil pump and bolts. Tighten to 15 ft. lbs. (20 Nm).

8. Check the oil pump drive gear for wear and replace the gear pin if necessary.
- Oil pump drive gear and reluctor
- Oil pump driven gear and nut. Block the crankshaft from moving, then tighten to 74 ft. lbs. (100 Nm)
- Oil pump pipe and screen gasket to the oil pump (4WD vehicle)
- Oil pump pipe and screen (4WD vehicle)
- Oil pump pipe and screen bolts and nuts (4WD vehicle). Tighten to 18 ft. lbs. (25 Nm).

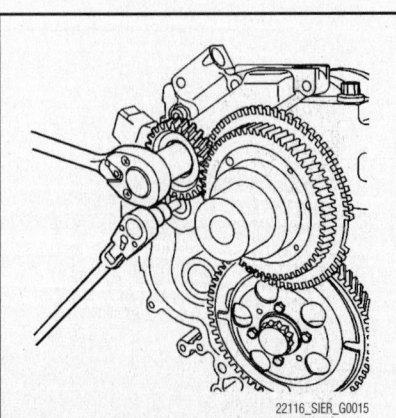

Fig. 135 Installing the oil pump drive gear—6.6L engines

- Engine front cover
- Engine flywheel housing (2WD vehicle)
- Upper and lower oil pans
9. Refill the crankcase with oil.

8.1L Engine

See Figure 136.

1. Remove or disconnect the following:
   - Oil pan
   - Oil pump screen bolt
   - Oil pump, retainer and driveshaft. Discard the driveshaft retainer
   - Crankshaft oil deflector nuts
   - Crankshaft oil deflector
   - Oil pump bolts
   - Oil pump
2. Clean and inspect the oil pump

To install:

3. Install the crankshaft oil deflector. Tighten the nuts to 37 ft. lbs. (50 Nm).

➡ **Always replace the retainer between the oil pump and the shaft, when installing the oil pump. During assembly, install a new oil pump driveshaft retainer. To ease installation, slightly heat the retainer to above room temperature.**

4. Assemble the oil pump, driveshaft and a new retainer.
5. Install or connect the following:
   - Oil pump, positioning it on the locating pins
   - Oil pump bolt and tighten to 56 ft. lbs. (75 Nm)
   - Oil pan
6. Refill the engine crankcase
7. Disable the ignition system; crank engine for approximately 10 seconds to aid in priming the oil pump and reducing the risk of engine damage.

➡**If the oil pump does not build up oil pressure almost immediately, remove the pan and check for a loose oil pump–to–pick–up tube attachment. If necessary dismantle the pump and pack the pump cavity with petroleum jelly. Running the engine without measurable oil pressure will cause extensive damage.**

INSPECTION

4.3L Engine

See Figure 137.

✳✳ CAUTION

Wear safety glasses in order to avoid eye damage.

1. Clean the oil pump components in cleaning solvent.
2. Dry the components with compressed air.
3. Inspect the oil pump for the following conditions:
   - Scoring on the top of the gears (1)
   - Damaged gears (2) for the following:
   - Chipping
   - Galling
   - Wear
   - Scoring, damage or casting imperfections to the body (3)
   - Damaged or scored gear shaft (4)
   - Damaged or scored gear shaft (5)
   - Damaged bolt hole threads
   - Worn oil pump driveshaft bore
   - Damaged or sticking oil pump pressure relief valve Minor imper-

fections may be removed with a fine oil stone.
   - Collapsed or broken oil pump pressure relief valve spring
   - If the oil pump is to be reused, install a NEW oil pump pressure relief valve spring.
   - During oil pump installation, install a NEW oil pump driveshaft retainer.

4.8L, 5.3L, 6.0L and 6.2L Engines

See Figure 138.

✳✳ CAUTION

Wear safety glasses in order to avoid eye damage.

➡**The internal parts of the oil pump assembly are not serviced separately, excluding the spring. If the oil pump components are worn or damaged, replace the oil pump as an assembly.**

➡**The oil pump pipe and screen are to be serviced as an assembly. Do not attempt to repair the wire mesh portion of the pump and screen assembly.**

1. Clean the parts in solvent.
2. Dry the parts with compressed air.
   - Inspect the oil pump housing (413) and the cover (409) for cracks, excessive wear, scoring, or casting imperfections.
   - Inspect the oil pump housing–to–engine block oil gallery surface for scratches or gouging.
   - Inspect the oil pump housing for damaged bolt hole threads.
   - Inspect the relief valve plug (416) and plug bore for damaged threads.
   - Inspect the oil pump internal oil passages for restrictions.
   - Inspect the drive gear (410) and driven gear (412) for chipping, galling or wear. Minor burrs or imperfections on the gears may be removed with a fine oil stone.

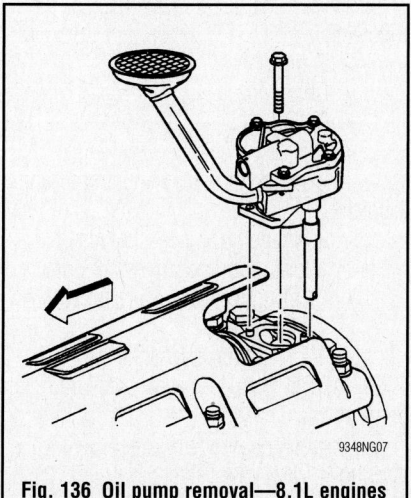

9348NG07

Fig. 136 Oil pump removal—8.1L engines

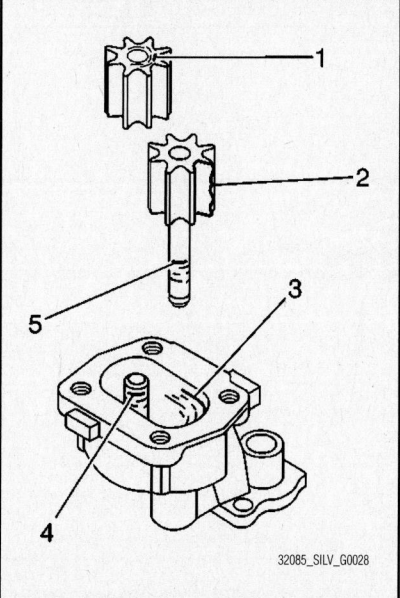

32085_SILV_G0028

Fig. 137 Exploded view of the oil pump—4.3L engines

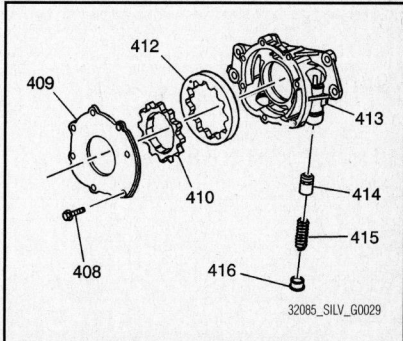

32085_SILV_G0029

Fig. 138 Exploded view of oil pump—4.8L, 5.3L, 6.0L and 6.2L engines

- Inspect the drive gear splines for excessive wear.
- Inspect the pressure relief valve (414) and bore for scoring or wear. The valve must move freely in the bore with no restrictions.
- Inspect the oil pump screen for debris or restrictions.
- Inspect the oil pump screen for broken or loose wire mesh.

6.6L Engine

See Figures 139 through 141.

✳✳ CAUTION

Wear safety glasses in order to avoid eye damage.

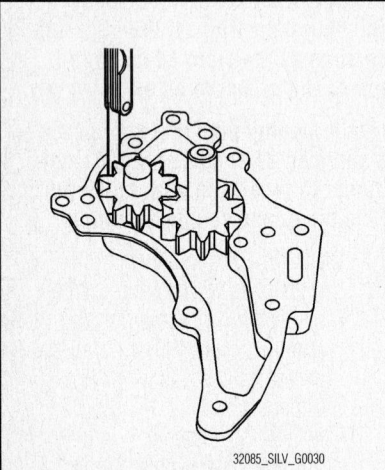

Fig. 139 Use a feeler gauge to measure the clearance between the gear teeth and the oil pump housing—6.6L engines

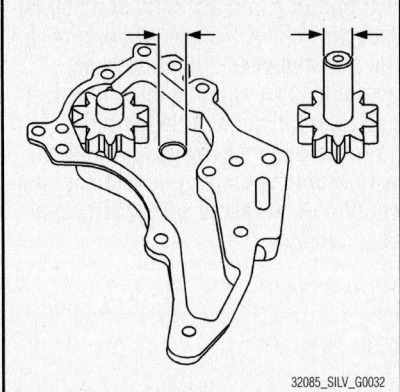

32085_SILV_G0032

Fig. 141 Measuring driven gear shaft and bushing—6.6L engines

1. Remove the oil pump gear cover bolts and oil pump gear cover.

2. Use a feeler gauge to measure the clearance between the gear teeth and the oil pump housing. The production clearance is 0.005–0.009 inch (0.125–0.221 mm) and the service limit is 0.009 inch (0.221 mm).

3. Replace the oil pump assembly if the clearance exceeds the service limit.

4. Use a feeler gauge and a straightedge to measure the clearance between the side of the gear and the cover. The production clearance is 0.003–0.004 inch (0.064–0.109 mm) and the service limit is 0.004 inch (0.109 mm).

5. Replace the oil pump assembly if the clearance exceeds the service limit.

6. Calculate the driven gear shaft to bushing clearance.

   a. Measure the driven gear shaft outside diameter. The production specification is (0.785–0.786 inch

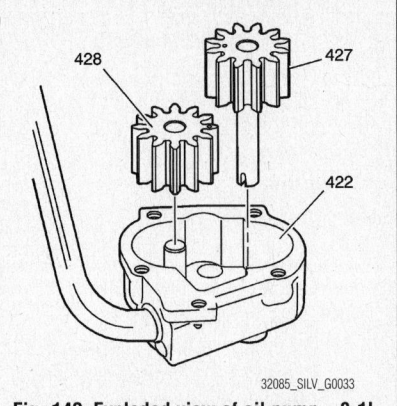

32085_SILV_G0033

Fig. 142 Exploded view of oil pump—8.1L engines

(19.947–19.960 mm) and the service limit is 0.782 inch (19.86 mm).

   b. Measure the driven gear bushing inside diameter. The production value is 0.787 inch (20 mm).

   c. Calculate the driven gear shaft to bushing clearance. The service limit is 0.006 inch (0.14 mm)

7. Replace the oil pump assembly if the clearance exceeds the service limit.

8. Install the oil pump gear cover to the oil pump assembly.

9. Install the oil pump gear cover bolts.

   a. Tighten the oil pump gear cover bolts to 15 ft. lbs. (21 Nm).

8.1L Engine

See Figure 142.

✳✳ CAUTION

Wear safety glasses in order to avoid eye damage.

1. Clean the oil pump components in cleaning solvent.

2. Dry the components with compressed air.

3. Inspect the gears (427, 428) for the following:
   - Scoring
   - Chipping
   - Galling
   - Excessive wear

4. Inspect the oil pump housing for the following:
   - Damaged bolt hole threads
   - Worn oil pump driveshaft bore
   - Scoring or excessive wear within the housing
   - Worn driven gear shaft

5. Inspect for a collapsed pressure relief valve spring.

6. Inspect the pressure relief valve for scoring or wear. The valve should move freely within the bore of the housing.

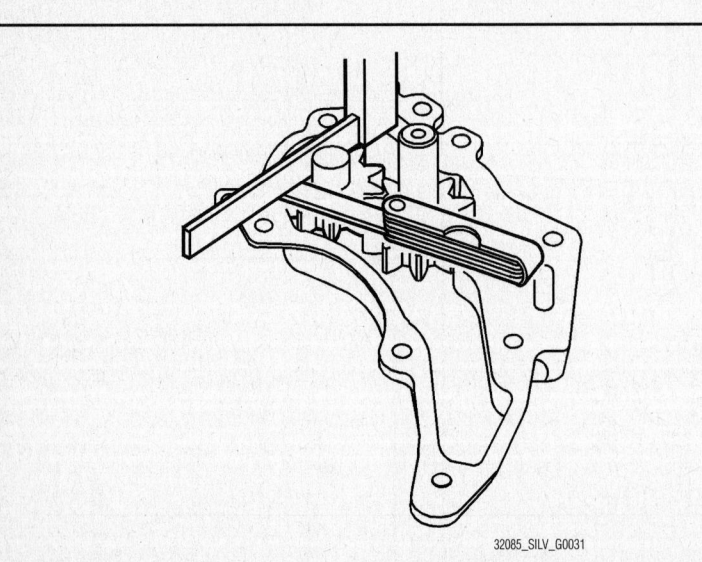

32085_SILV_G0031

Fig. 140 Use a feeler gauge and a straightedge to measure the clearance between the side of the gear and the cover—6.6L engines

PISTON AND RING

POSITIONING

See Figures 143 through 146.

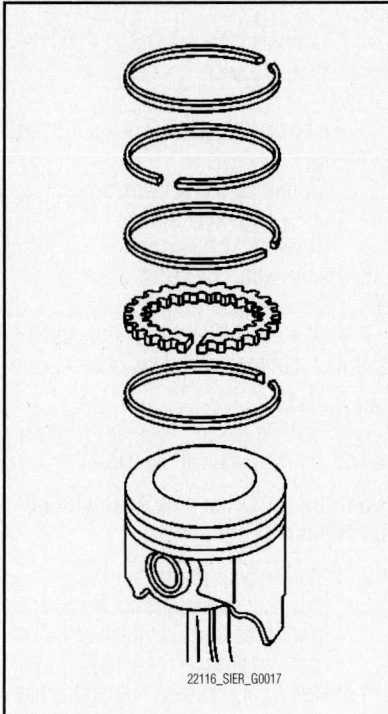

Fig. 143 Piston and connecting rod assembly positioning; place the ring gaps 120 degrees apart—4.3L engines

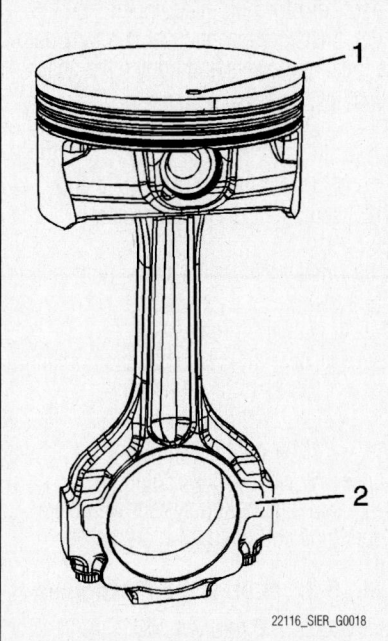

Fig. 144 Piston and connecting rod assembly; place the ring gaps 180 degrees apart—4.8L, 5.3L, 6.0L and 6.2L engines

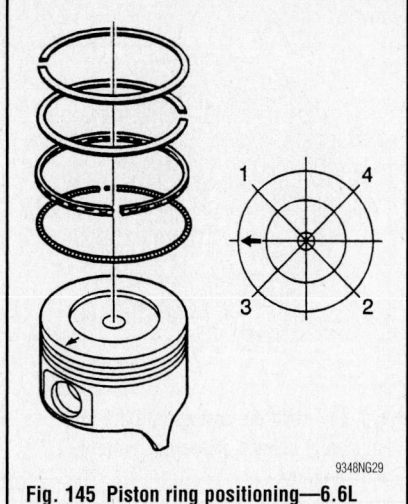

Fig. 145 Piston ring positioning—6.6L engines

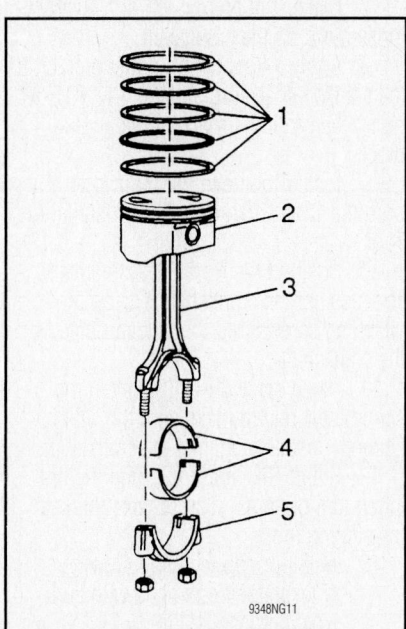

Fig. 146 Piston rings (1), piston (2), connecting rod (3) and related components—8.1L engines

REAR MAIN SEAL

REMOVAL & INSTALLATION

Except 6.6L and 8.1L Engines

Please note that the entire transmission assembly and flywheel/flexplate must be removed to perform this procedure.

1. Remove or disconnect the following:
   • Negative battery cable
   • Transfer case, if equipped
   • Transmission assembly
   • Clutch assembly and flywheel, if equipped with manual transmission

• Flexplate, if equipped with automatic transmission
• Crankshaft rear main oil seal by inserting a suitable prying tool and prying the seal out. Take care not to damage the crankshaft sealing surface.

To install:

2. Clean the oil seal bore in the block thoroughly before installation of the new seal.

3. Inspect the crankshaft for grit, rust or burrs and correct as necessary. Also inspect the portion of the crankshaft where the oil seal makes contact, for wear due to the rubbing action of the oil seal.

4. Clean the seal running surface of the crankshaft with a non–abrasive cleaner.

5. Lubricate the inner diameter of the new seal and the outer diameter of the crankshaft with engine oil.

6. Install or connect the following:
   • Rear main oil seal, using installation tool J 38841, J–35621–B or J–41479, until the tool bottoms against the block and crankshaft rear main bearing cap.
   • Flywheel and clutch
   • Flexplate, as required
   • Transmission assembly
   • Transfer case, if equipped
   • Negative battery cable

7. Start the engine and verify no oil leaks.

6.6L Engine

Please note that the entire transmission assembly must be removed before performing this procedure. Before a new seal is installed, the Crankcase Depression Regulator (CDR) and crankcase ventilation system should be cleaned and inspected. In addition, use care removing the flywheel. Some models use a heavy, dual mass flywheel that must be handled with care.

1. Before servicing the vehicle, refer to the precautions in the beginning of this section.

2. Remove or disconnect the following:
   • Negative battery cables
   • Transfer case, if equipped
   • Transmission assembly
   • Clutch assembly and flywheel, if equipped with manual transmission
   • Flexplate, if equipped with automatic transmission
   • Crankshaft rear main oil seal by inserting a suitable crankshaft seal removal tool and prying the seal out

To install:

3. Clean the oil seal bore in the block thoroughly before installation of the new seal.

4. Inspect the crankshaft for grit, rust or burrs and correct as necessary. Also inspect the portion of the crankshaft where the oil seal makes contact, for wear due to the rubbing action of the oil seal.

➡ **Because of rear crankshaft wear or grooving, the new oil seal should be seated in a new location. The J 39084 installation tool will control the seal positioning. This will provide a new surface on the crankshaft for the seal to ride on.**

5. Clean the running surface of the crankshaft with a non–abrasive cleaner.

6. Lubricate the inner diameter of the new seal and the outer diameter of the crankshaft with engine oil.

7. Install or connect the following:
- Rear main oil seal using a crankshaft rear oil seal installation tool
- Flywheel.
- Transmission assembly
- Transfer case, if equipped
- Negative battery cables

8. Start the engine and verify no oil leaks.

8.1L Engine

See Figure 147.

Please note that the entire transmission assembly and flywheel/flexplate must be removed to perform this procedure. This procedure requires the use of the following tools: Crankshaft Rear Seal Puller tool No. J 43320 and Crankshaft Rear Seal Installer tool No. J 42849.

1. Remove or disconnect the following:
- Negative battery cable
- Transfer case, if equipped
- Transmission assembly
- Clutch assembly and flywheel, if equipped with manual transmission
- Flexplate, if equipped with automatic transmission

2. Install the guide pins from the Crankshaft Rear Sear Puller into the crankshaft.

3. Install the Rear Seal Puller over the guide pins.

4. Using a drill, insert 8 of the self–drilling sheet metal screws into the rear crankshaft seal, using a crisscross pattern as shown. The self tapping screws are included with the Crankshaft Rear Seal Puller.

5. Thread the center bolt of the Crankshaft Rear Seal Puller into the crankshaft to remove the seal.

6. Remove the guide pins from the crankshaft.

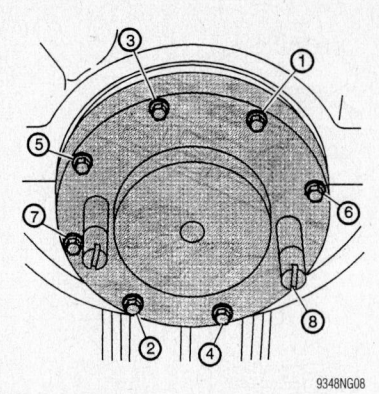

Fig. 147 Drill the screws into the rear main seal using a crisscross pattern— 8.1L engines

9348NG08

To install:

7. Make sure there is no dirt, rust or loose burrs on the crankshaft.

8. Apply a light coating of engine oil to the crankshaft sealing surface. Do NOT get oil on the sealing surface of the engine block.

9. Install the new rear main seal onto the Crankshaft Rear Seal Installation Tool.

10. Position the Rear Seal Installation Tool against the crankshaft. Thread the attaching screws into the tapped holes in the crankshaft.

11. Use a screwdriver to tighten the screws securely to make sure the seal is squarely installed against the crankshaft.

12. Rotate the center nut until the installation tool bottoms, then remove the seal installation tool.

13. Install or connect the following:
- Flexplate, if equipped with automatic transmission
- Clutch assembly and flywheel, if equipped with manual transmission
- Transmission assembly
- Transfer case, if equipped
- Negative battery cable

TIMING CHAIN COVER AND SEAL

REMOVAL & INSTALLATION

4.3L Engine

1. Drain the cooling system.
2. Remove or disconnect the following:
- Negative battery cable
- Fan shroud assembly
- Belts, pulleys and water pump assembly
- Crankshaft pulley and damper
- Oil pan–to–front cover bolts

➡ **If equipped with a composite front cover, it must be replaced with a new one. Reusing the front cover may result in oil leaks.**

3. Remove the engine shield bolts and shield.

4. Disconnect the Crankshaft Position (CKP) sensor electrical connector, if equipped.

5. Remove the CKP sensor and discard the o–ring.
- Screws holding the timing chain cover to the block
- Cover and gaskets.

6. Remove the crankshaft position (CKP) sensor reluctor ring, if equipped.

7. Use a suitable tool to pry the old seal out of the front face of the cover.

To install:

8. Clean the gasket mounting surfaces of all remaining traces of old gasket.

➡ **Coat the lip of the new seal with oil prior to installation.**

9. Install or connect the following:
- New seal so that the open end is toward the inside of the cover, using seal driver J–22102
- New front pan seal, cutting the tabs off.

10. Coat a new cover gasket with adhesive sealer and position it on the block.

11. Apply a ⅛ in. (3mm) bead of RTV gasket material to the front cover.

12. Install the crankshaft position (CKP) sensor reluctor ring, if equipped.

13. Install the front cover carefully onto the locating dowels and tighten the attaching screws

14. Install the CKP sensor and new o–ring.

15. Connect the Crankshaft Position (CKP) sensor electrical connector, if equipped.

16. Install the engine shield bolts and shield.
- Oil pan, if removed
- Cover–to–pan bolts and tighten to 106 inch lbs. (12 Nm)
- Torsional damper
- Water pump assembly
- Negative battery cable

17. Fill the cooling system with the proper type and quantity of antifreeze.

4.8L, 5.3L, 6.0L and 6.2L Engines

See Figures 148 through 150.

1. Drain the cooling system.
2. Remove or disconnect the following:
- Negative battery cable

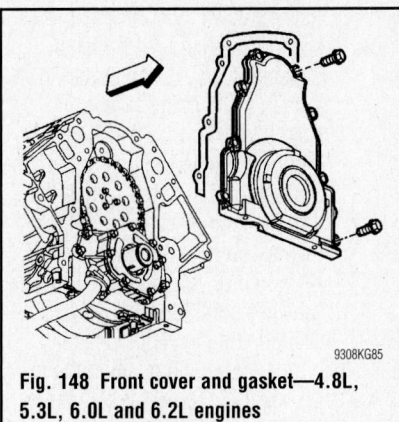

Fig. 148 Front cover and gasket—4.8L, 5.3L, 6.0L and 6.2L engines

- Water pump
- Crankshaft balancer from the crank-shaft
- Front cover bolts
- Front cover and gasket. Discard the front cover gasket.
- Crankshaft front oil seal from the cover

To install:

➡**Do not lubricate the oil seal sealing surface.**

3. Lubricate the outer edge of the oil seal with clean engine oil. Lubricate the front cover oil seal bore with clean engine oil.

4. Install the crankshaft front oil seal with an installer.

➡**Do not apply any type of sealant to the front cover gasket (unless specified). Special tools are used to properly align the engine front cover at the oil pan surface and to center the crankshaft front oil seal.**

5. Install the front cover gasket, cover, and bolts onto the engine. Tighten the cover bolts finger—tight. Do not over tighten.

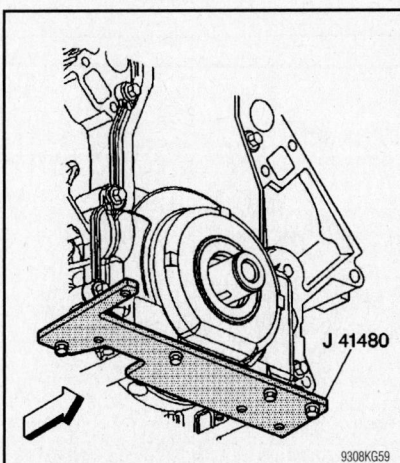

Fig. 149 J41480 installation—4.8L, 5.3L, 6.0L and 6.2L engines

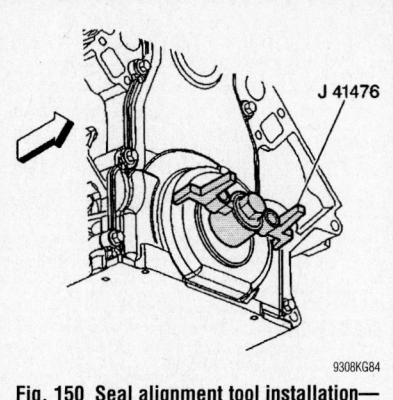

Fig. 150 Seal alignment tool installation— 4.8L, 5.3L, 6.0L and 6.2L engines

6. Start the J41480 tool–to–front cover bolts. Don't tighten the bolts yet.

➡**Align the tapered legs of the tool with the machined alignment surfaces on the front cover.**

7. Install tool J41476 . Install the crankshaft balancer bolt. Tighten the crank-shaft balancer bolt by hand until snug. Do not over tighten. Tighten the J41480 bolts and front cover bolts to 18 ft. lbs. (25 Nm).

8. Remove the tools.

9. Install the used crankshaft balancer bolt and tighten to 240 ft. lbs. (330 Nm).

10. Remove the used bolt.

➡ **The nose of the crankshaft should be recessed 0.094–0.176 in (2.4–4.48 mm) into the balancer bore.**

11. Install a NEW crankshaft balancer bolt and tighten to 37 ft. lbs. (50 Nm), then tighten an additional 140 degrees.

12. Place a straight edge across the engine block and front cover oil pan sealing surfaces. Avoid contact with the portion of the gasket that protrudes into the oil pan surface. Insert a feeler gauge between the front cover and the straight edge tool. The cover must be flush with the oil pan surface or no more than 0.02 in. (0.5mm) below flush. If the front cover–to–engine block oil pan surface align-ment is not within specifications, repeat the cover alignment procedure. If the correct front cover–to–engine block alignment cannot be obtained, replace the front cover.

13. Snug the oil pan–to–cover bolts in order to position the cover at the pan rail.

14. Tighten the oil pan–to–front cover bolts to 18 ft. lbs. (25 Nm).

15. Tighten the front cover bolts to 18 ft. lbs. (25 Nm).

16. Install the water pump.

8.1L Engine

See Figures 151 and 152.

1. Drain the cooling system.
2. Remove or disconnect the following:
   - Negative battery cable
   - Water pump
   - Crankshaft balancer from the crank-shaft
   - Camshaft Position (CMP) sensor connector
   - Engine harness clips from the bat-tery cable channel
   - CMP sensor bolt and sensor
   - Battery cable channel bolt
   - Battery cable channel and reposition
   - Front cover bolts, front cover and gasket

➡**The front cover gasket can be reused if it is not damaged.**

To install:

3. Use clean engine oil to lubricate the sealing surfaces of the front oil seal.

4. Install or connect the following:
   - New seal into the front cover, using a suitable seal installation tool

➡**The front cover must be installed while the sealant is still wet to the touch.**

- Sealant to the 2 places on the engine block where the front cover meets the oil pan
- Front cover gasket into the cover

5. Install the front cover, referring to the accompanying figure and using the follow-ing steps only:

a. Hold the front cover (1) up to the crankshaft (2).

b. Lift the cover (1) while sliding the cover over the crankshaft (2).

c. Slide the front cover toward the engine block (5) while keeping the cover raised.

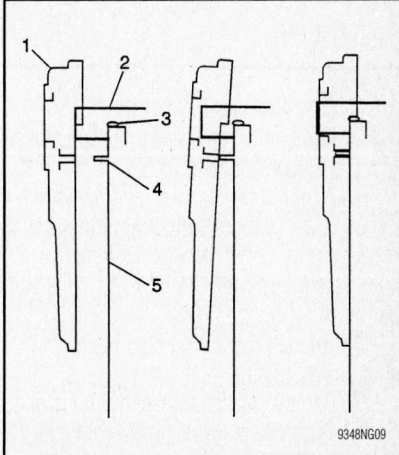

Fig. 151 Proper front cover installation sequence—8.1L engines

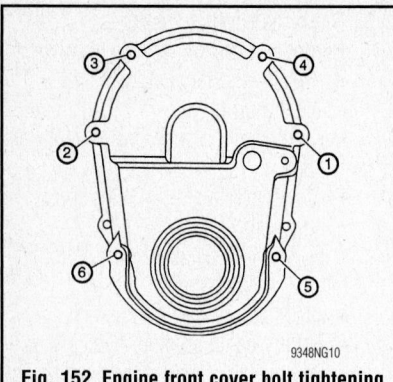

Fig. 152 Engine front cover bolt tightening sequence—8.1L engines

d. Lower the cover down over the dowel pin (4), allowing the front cover to rest on the sealant (3).

6. Install the front cover bolts and tighten, in sequence, as follows:

    a. 1st pass: 53 inch lbs. (6 Nm)

    b. 2nd pass: 106 inch lbs. (12 Nm)

7. Install or connect the following:
- Battery cable channel and bolt. Tighten to 80 inch lbs. (9 Nm).
- CMP sensor. Inspect the O–ring first, replace if necessary and coat with oil before installation
- CMP sensor bolt to 106 inch lbs. (12 Nm)
- Engine harness clips to the battery cable channel
- CMP sensor electrical connector
- Crankshaft balancer
- Water pump
- Negative battery cable.

8. Fill the cooling system with the proper type and quantity of antifreeze.

TIMING CHAIN AND SPROCKETS

REMOVAL & INSTALLATION

4.3L Engine

See Figure 153.

1. Drain the cooling system.
2. Remove or disconnect the following:
- Negative battery cable
- Timing chain cover and gaskets

3. Rotate the crankshaft until the timing marks on the camshaft and crankshaft sprockets are in proper alignment. This will put no. 4 cylinder at TDC.

4. Unsnap the timing chain tensioner shoe from the pin.

5. Remove or disconnect the following:
- Camshaft sprocket–to–camshaft nut and/or bolts
- Camshaft sprocket (along with the timing chain), if the sprocket is dif-

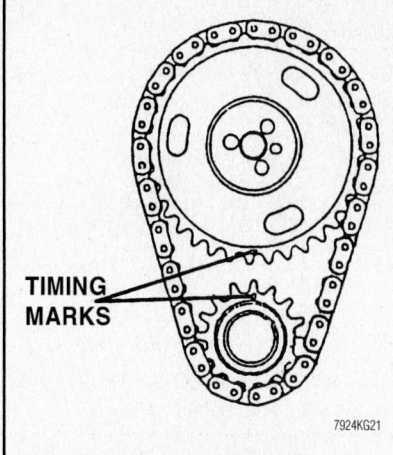

Fig. 153 Timing mark alignment for timing chain removal and installation—4.3L engines

ficult to remove, use a plastic mallet to bump the sprocket from the camshaft.

➡**The camshaft sprocket (located by a dowel) is lightly pressed onto the camshaft and should come off easily. The chain comes off with the camshaft sprocket.**

6. If necessary use J–5825–A, or equivalent, crankshaft sprocket removal tool to free the timing sprocket from the crankshaft.

7. Remove the crankshaft balancer key.

8. If necessary, remove the timing chain tensioner bracket bolt and bracket.

To install:

9. Inspect the timing chain and the timing sprockets for wear or damage, replace the damaged parts as necessary.

10. Clean the gasket mounting surfaces of all remaining traces of old gasket.

➡**During installation, coat the thrust surfaces lightly with Molykote® or equivalent pre–lube.**

11. If necessary, install the timing chain tensioner bracket and bolt and tighten to 106 inch lbs. (12 Nm).

12. Install the key into the crankshaft keyway. The crankshaft balancer key should be parallel to the crankshaft or with a slight incline.

13. Install or connect the following:
- Crankshaft sprocket onto the crankshaft, use tool J–5590, crankshaft sprocket installation tool, and a hammer, without disturbing the position of the engine.
- Timing chain, arrange the camshaft sprocket in such a way that the tim-

ing marks will align between the shaft centers and the camshaft locating dowel will enter the dowel hole in the cam sprocket.
- Cam sprocket, with the chain mounted under it in position on the front of the camshaft. Torque the camshaft sprocket–to–camshaft retainer bolts to 106 inch lbs. (12 Nm) on 5.0L and 5.7L, or 18 ft. lbs. (25 Nm) on 4.3L.

14. Install the timing chain tensioner shoe onto the bracket and position the top of the shoe under the tab at the top of the bracket.

15. With the timing chain installed, turn the crankshaft 2 complete revolutions, then check to make certain that the timing marks are in correct alignment between the shaft centers.
- Timing chain cover with a new seal
- Negative battery cable

16. Fill the cooling system with the proper type and quantity of antifreeze.

4.8L, 5.3L, 6.0L and 6.2L Engines

See Figures 154 through 156.

1. Drain the cooling system.
2. Remove or disconnect the following:
- Negative battery cable
- Front cover and gasket. Discard the front cover gasket.
- Oil pump

3. Rotate the crankshaft until the timing marks on the crankshaft and the camshaft sprockets are aligned.

➡**Do not turn the crankshaft assembly after the timing chain has been removed in order to prevent damage to the piston assemblies or the valves.**

4. Remove or disconnect the following:
- Camshaft sprocket bolts

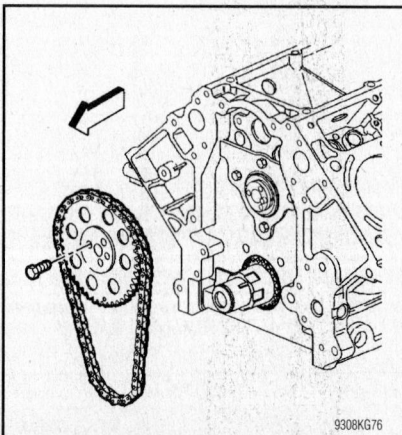

Fig. 154 Sprocket and chain removal—4.8L, 5.3L, 6.0L and 6.2L engines

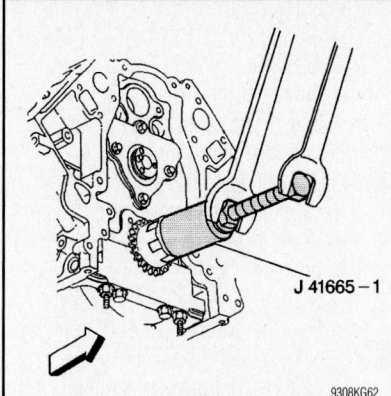

Fig. 155 Crankshaft sprocket installation—4.8L, 5.3L, 6.0L and 6.2L engines

- Camshaft sprocket and timing chain
- Crankshaft sprocket
- Crankshaft sprocket key

To install:

5. Install or connect the following:
- Key into the crankshaft keyway
- Crankshaft sprocket onto the front of the crankshaft. Align the crankshaft key with the crankshaft sprocket keyway. Rotate the crankshaft sprocket until the alignment mark is in the 12 o'clock position.
- Camshaft sprocket and timing chain. Locate the camshaft sprocket alignment mark in the 6 o'clock position.
- Camshaft sprocket bolts and tighten to 26 ft. lbs. (35 Nm)

6. Install the oil pump and the front cover. Be sure to use a new gasket and oil seal.

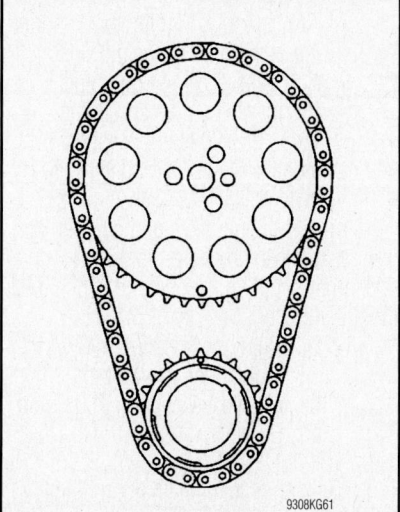

Fig. 156 Timing mark alignment—4.8L, 5.3L, 6.0L and 6.2L engines

8.1L Engine

➡This procedure requires the use of Crankshaft Sprocket Installer tool No. J 22102 and Crankshaft Protector Button tool No. J 42846.

1. Drain the cooling system.
2. Remove or disconnect the following:
- Negative battery cable
- Front cover bolts, front cover and gasket
3. Align the timing marks on the camshaft and crankshaft sprockets.
- Camshaft sprocket bolts
- Camshaft sprocket and timing chain
4. Install Crankshaft Protector Button tool No. J 42846 into the end of the crankshaft and remove the crankshaft sprocket using a 3-jawed puller.
5. Clean and inspect the timing chain and sprockets.

To install:

6. Use the Crankshaft Sprocket Installer tool No. J 22102 to install the crankshaft sprocket. Align the keyway of the sprocket with the crankshaft pin.
7. Remove the installation tool.
8. Rotate the crankshaft until the crankshaft sprocket alignment mark is in the 12 o'clock position.
9. Install the camshaft sprocket and timing chain, noting the following important points:
   a. The cam sprocket must be installed with the alignment mark at the 6 o'clock position.
   b. The sprocket teeth must mesh with the timing chain to avoid damaging the camshaft retainer.
   c. Never use a hammer to install the sprocket onto the camshaft.
10. Make sure the crankshaft sprocket is alignment at the 12 o'clock position and the cam sprocket is at the 6 o'clock position.
11. Install the camshaft sprocket bolts and tighten, in two passes, to 22 ft. lbs. (30 Nm).
12. Install the front cover.
13. Fill the cooling system with the proper type and quantity of antifreeze.

TIMING GEARS COVER AND SEAL

REMOVAL & INSTALLATION

6.6L Engine

See Figure 157.

➡The 6.6L engine uses gears in place of a timing chain. For removal and installation of the gears, please see the Camshaft and Lifters procedure. This procedure covers the removal of the front cover and seal.

1. Remove the upper intake manifold sight shield as follows:
   a. Remove the retaining bolt in the front of the shield.
   b. Lift up on the front of the shield, then lift the shield off the rear bracket.
2. Drain the cooling system.
3. Remove or disconnect the following:
- Negative battery cables
- Right front wheel
- Right front fender splash shield
- Upper fan shroud
- Fan clutch
- Drive belt
- Oil dipstick tube
- Thermostat housing crossover
- Crankshaft balancer
- Crankshaft front oil seal
- Water pump
- Camshaft sensor electrical connector
- Camshaft sensor bolt and sensor
- Crankshaft Position (CKP) sensor connector, bolt and sensor
- CKP sensor spacer bolts and spacer
- 5 bolts securing the upper oil pan to the front cover
- Bracket bolts and the bracket for the turbocharger outlet coolant pipe
- Engine front cover bolts
- Use a suitable seal cutter to separate the front cover from the cylinder block and upper oil pan
- O-ring from the front cover
- Oil pressure relief valve from the front cover

➡Do not bend the turbocharger outlet pipe.

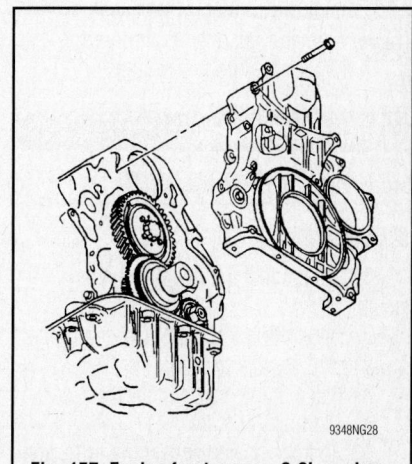

Fig. 157 Engine front cover—6.6L engines

To install:

4. Clean and inspect all sealing surfaces.

5. Install or connect the following:
- Oil pressure relief valve with a new O–ring. Tighten to 30 ft. lbs. (41 Nm).
- Apply a 1/8 in. (2–3mm) wide to 1/16 in. (0.5–1.5mm) high bead of sealant to the front cover sealing surfaces to the engine block and oil pan.
- New front cover O–ring after lubricating it with engine oil
- Front cover and bolts. Tighten to 18 ft. lbs. (25 Nm).
- Upper oil pan–to–front cover bolts. Tighten to 15 ft. lbs. (20 Nm).
- Turbocharger coolant outlet pipe bracket and bolts. Tighten to 15 ft. lbs. (20 Nm).
- Camshaft sensor and bolt. Tighten to 80 inch lbs. (9 Nm).
- Camshaft sensor connector

➡ **The CKP sensor spacers are machined with different timing positions. If you have to replace a spacer, make sure it has the same part number.**

- CKP sensor spacer and spacer bolts. Tighten to 89 inch lbs. (10 Nm).
- CKP sensor and bolt. Tighten to 89 inch lbs. (10 Nm).
- Water pump
- Crankshaft front oil seal
- Crankshaft balancer
- Thermostat housing crossover
- Oil fill tube
- Drive belt
- Upper fan shroud
- Right front fender splash shield and wheel
- Negative battery cables

6. Refill the cooling system with the proper type and quantity of antifreeze.

7. Inspect the engine for leaks.

TURBOCHARGER

REMOVAL & INSTALLATION

6.6L Engine

1. Disconnect the negative battery cables.

2. Open the hood and move the hinge bolts to the service position.

3. Raise the vehicle.

4. Drain the coolant.

5. Remove or disconnect the following:
- Left and right wheelhouse liners
- Exhaust pipe–to–exhaust outlet clamp. Move the clamp onto the exhaust pipe
- Transmission fluid fill tube–to–bell housing nuts if equipped with an A/T. Position the tube to the right side of the vehicle; it does not need to be removed from the transmission.

➡ **If necessary, the entire transmission can be removed to gain additional clearance**

- 3 nuts and left exhaust heat shield from the front of the lower dash panel
- Left exhaust pipe heat shield bolts

6. Position the left exhaust pipe heat shield to access the left exhaust pipe–to–manifold bolts. Do not remove the heat shield from the vehicle at this time.

➡ **Do not bend the exhaust pipe at the expansion area.**

- Left, then the right exhaust pipe–to–exhaust manifold bolts
- Gaskets and discard
- Lower bolt for the exhaust outlet shield

7. Lower the vehicle.
- Upper intake manifold sight shield front retaining bolt
- Sight shield
- Air cleaner outlet duct from the air cleaner and turbocharger. Cover the openings to prevent debris from entering
- Charged air cooler outlet duct–to–intake hose clamps (loosen only)
- Hose from the charged air cooler duct–to–intake manifold tube
- A/C compressor clutch electrical connector
- A/C cut–out switch connector
- Drive belt
- A/C compressor mounting bolts; position the compressor aside with the lines attached
- Turbocharger inlet coolant hose from the bypass valve
- Turbocharger outlet coolant hose from the turbocharger
- Crankcase hose from the left valve cover and position aside
- Wire connector from the intake heater
- Intake air heater relay, if equipped
- Heat shield–to–turbocharger bolts and heat shield
- Remaining 2 bolts from the exhaust outlet heat shield
- Exhaust outlet heat shield
- 4 bolts and 2 nuts from the exhaust outlet. You do not have to remove the outlet for turbocharger removal

8. Move the exhaust outlet to one side in order to access the right exhaust pipe–to–turbocharger bolts.
- Exhaust outlet gasket and discard
- Right exhaust pipe–to–turbocharger bolts
- Right exhaust pipe and gasket

9. Move the exhaust outlet to one side for access to the left pipe.
- Left exhaust pipe heat shield
- Left exhaust pipe–to–turbocharger bolts
- Left exhaust pipe and gasket
- Turbocharger oil supply hose eye bolt and washers. Move the hose aside
- Turbocharger oil drain pipe nuts from the flywheel housing
- Turbocharger mounting bolts
- Turbocharger with the oil drain pipe

10. If replacing the turbocharger, remove the oil drain pipe and coolant hose.

To install:

11. Thoroughly clean the gasket surfaces.

12. Install or connect the following:
- Turbocharger oil drain pipe and new gasket. Tighten the bolts to 15 ft. lbs. (21 Nm).
- Turbocharger inlet coolant hose
- Turbocharger oil supply hose to the engine block
- Turbocharger oil supply hose eye bolt and washers and tighten to 31 ft. lbs. (42 Nm) except on 2007 models. On 2007 models, tighten to 25 ft. lbs. (34 Nm)
- Turbocharger lower heat shield
- Turbocharger. Tighten the 3 mounting bolts to 80 ft. lbs. (108 Nm).
- New gasket for oil drain pipe
- Oil drain pipe nuts and tighten to 15 ft. lbs. (20 Nm) except on 2007 models. On 2007 models, tighten to 18 ft. lbs. (25 Nm)

13. If installing a new turbocharger, pour 4–5 oz. of clean engine oil into the turbocharger supply hose opening, while rotating the impeller.
- Oil supply hose, using new washers. Tighten the eye bolt to 31 ft. lbs. (42 Nm) except on 2007 models. On 2007 models, tighten to 25 ft. lbs. (34 Nm)

14. Install the remaining components in the reverse order of removal, noting the following important points:

- When installing the exhaust pipe, use new gaskets and align the tabs and make sure the proper pipe flange is towards the turbocharger, as they are different. Tighten the exhaust pipe–to–turbocharger bolts to 39 ft. lbs. (53 Nm).
- Tighten the turbocharger heat shield bolts to 80 inch lbs. (9 Nm)
- Tighten the A/C compressor bolts to 37 ft. lbs. (50 Nm)
- Tighten the exhaust pipe clamp to 30 ft. lbs. (40 Nm)

15. Fill the cooling system and connect the negative battery cables.

➡**Operate the engine at idle for at least 3 minutes after installing the turbocharger**

VALVE LASH

ADJUSTMENT

Except 6.6L Engine

All gasoline engines use hydraulic lifters, which require no periodic adjustment.

6.6L Engine

See Figures 158 and 159.

1. Remove the fan clutch.
2. Remove both upper valve covers.
3. Rotate the engine in the normal direction and place the No. 1 piston at Top Dead Center (TDC) of the compression stroke. The No. 1 cylinder is at the right side front. While turning the engine, watch the intake valve to open and close. Align the mark on the crankshaft balancer with the pointer on the engine.
4. Loosen the valve clearance adjusting screws for the valve being adjusted.
5. Insert the feeler gauge between the tip of the rocker arm and the valve bridge.

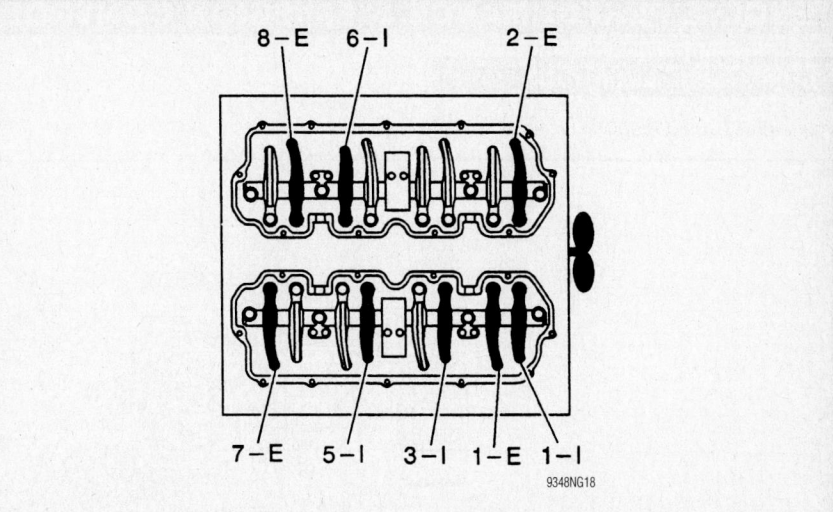

Fig. 158 Location of the valves that are adjusted at TDC of the compression stroke—6.6L engines

6. Adjust the intake and the exhaust valve clearance to 0.012 in. (0.3mm) with the engine cold. Refer to the figure for the valves that can be adjusted TDC of the compression stroke.
7. Tighten the valve adjusting screw lock nut to 16 ft. lbs. (22 Nm).
8. Turn the engine one rotation in the normal direction and put the No. 1 piston at TDC of the exhaust stroke to adjust the remaining valve clearance. While turning the engine, watch the exhaust valve to open and close. Align the mark on the crankshaft balancer with the pointer on the engine.
9. Loosen the valve clearance adjusting screws for the valves being adjusted.
10. Insert the feeler gauge between the tip of the rocker arm and the valve bridge.
11. Adjust the intake and the exhaust valve clearance to 0.012 in. (0.3mm) with the engine cold. Refer to the figure for the valves that can be adjusted TDC of the exhaust stroke.

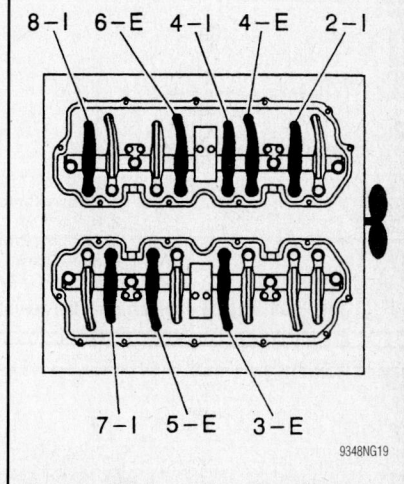

Fig. 159 Location of the valves that are adjusted at TDC of the exhaust stroke— 6.6L engines

12. Tighten the valve adjusting screw lock nut to 16 ft. lbs. (22 Nm).
13. Install the upper and lower valve cover and fan clutch, as necessary.

ENGINE PERFORMANCE & EMISSION CONTROL

COMPONENT LOCATIONS

See Figures 160 through 176.

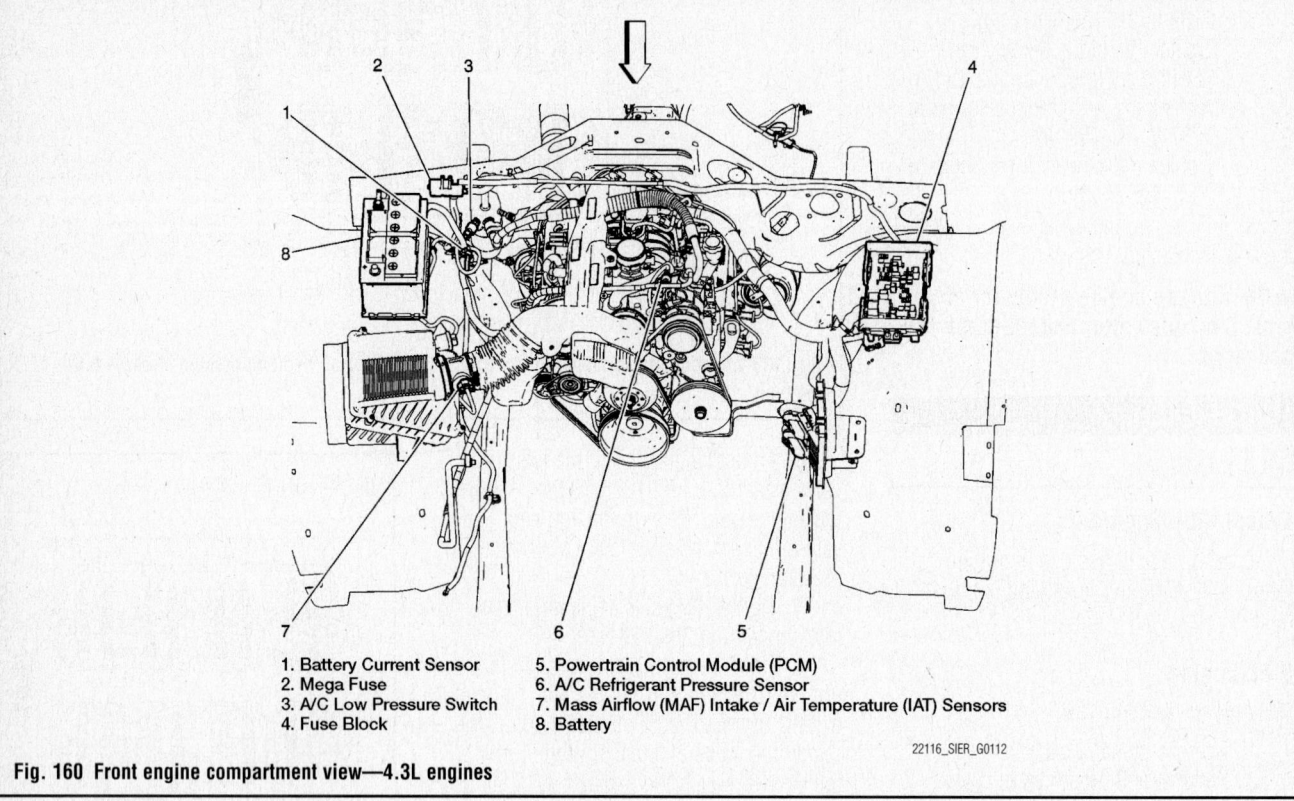

1. Battery Current Sensor
2. Mega Fuse
3. A/C Low Pressure Switch
4. Fuse Block
5. Powertrain Control Module (PCM)
6. A/C Refrigerant Pressure Sensor
7. Mass Airflow (MAF) Intake / Air Temperature (IAT) Sensors
8. Battery

22116_SIER_G0112

Fig. 160 Front engine compartment view—4.3L engines

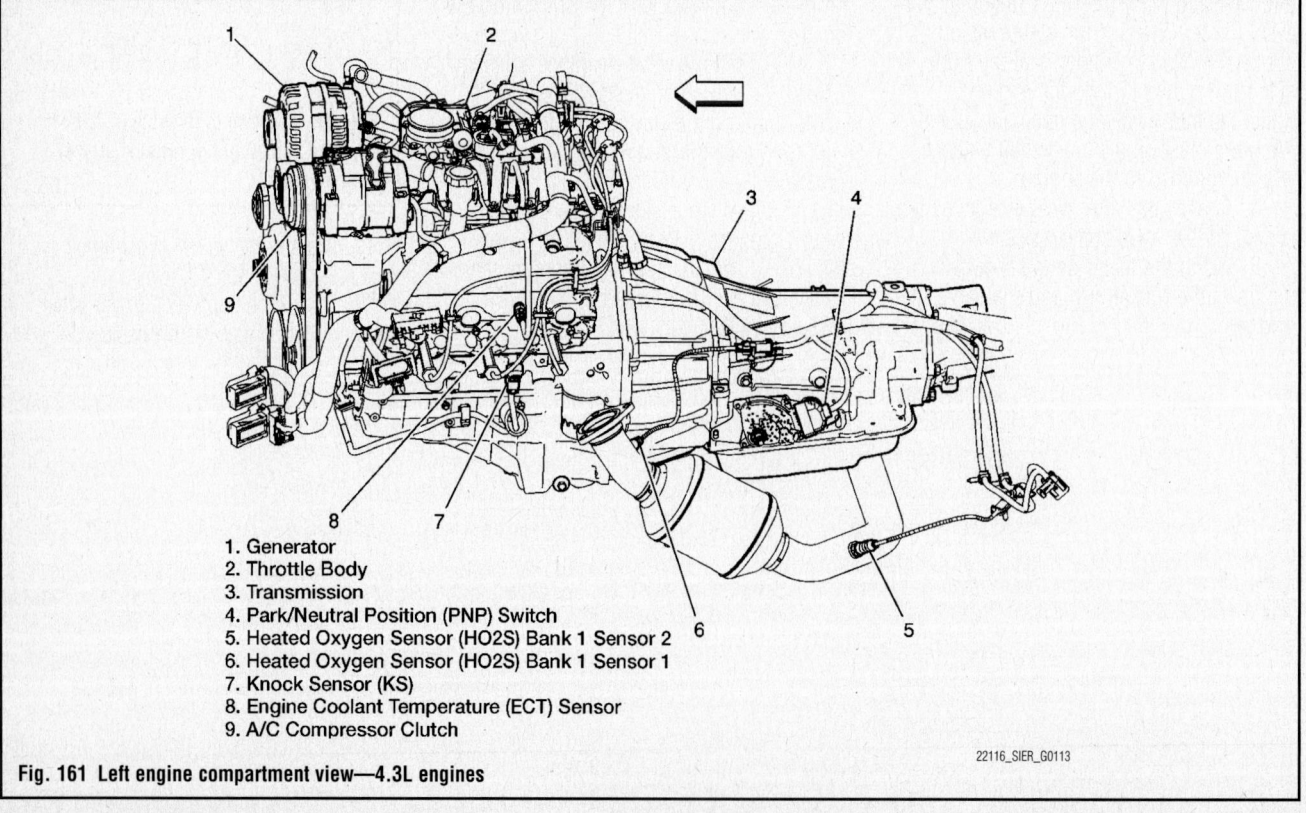

1. Generator
2. Throttle Body
3. Transmission
4. Park/Neutral Position (PNP) Switch
5. Heated Oxygen Sensor (HO2S) Bank 1 Sensor 2
6. Heated Oxygen Sensor (HO2S) Bank 1 Sensor 1
7. Knock Sensor (KS)
8. Engine Coolant Temperature (ECT) Sensor
9. A/C Compressor Clutch

22116_SIER_G0113

Fig. 161 Left engine compartment view—4.3L engines

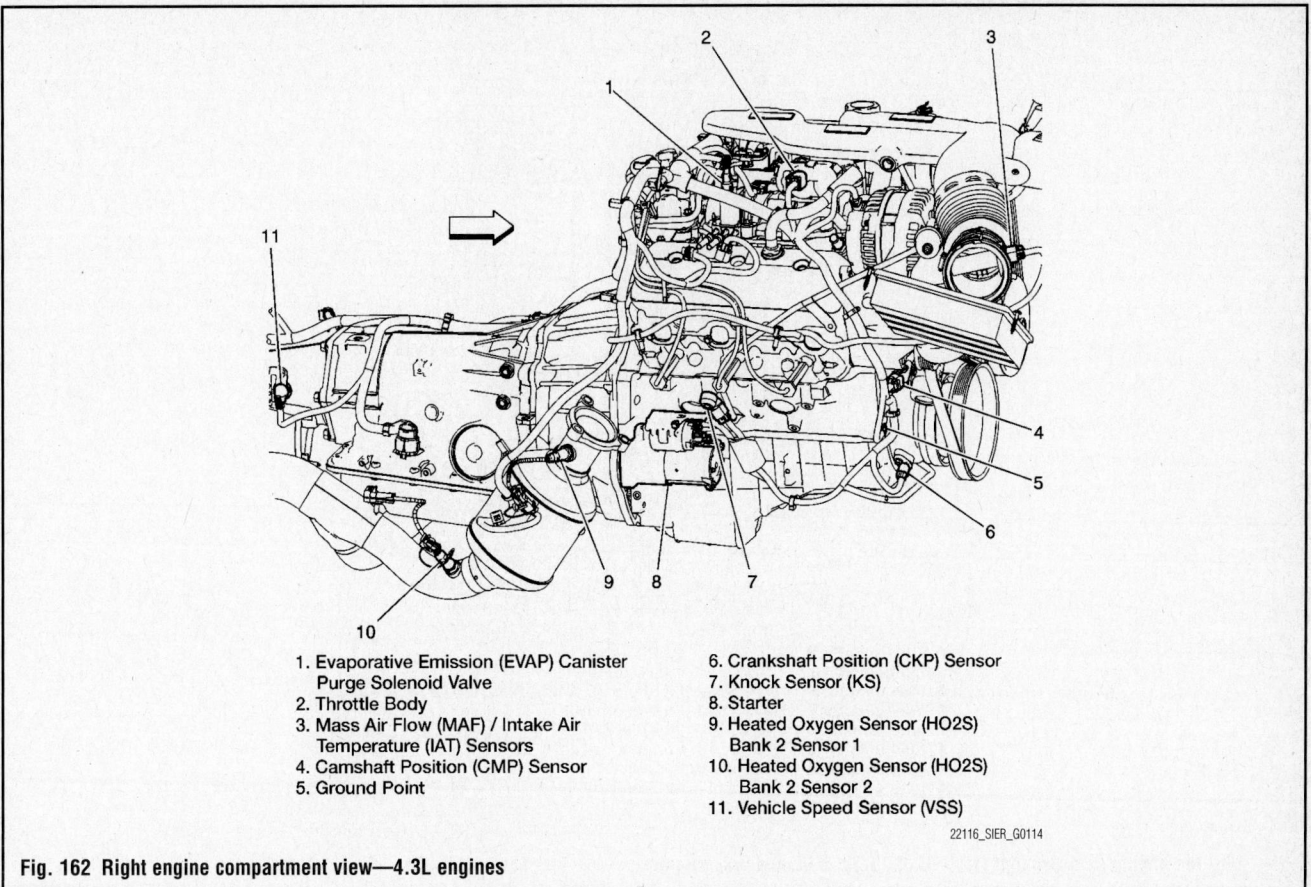

1. Evaporative Emission (EVAP) Canister Purge Solenoid Valve
2. Throttle Body
3. Mass Air Flow (MAF) / Intake Air Temperature (IAT) Sensors
4. Camshaft Position (CMP) Sensor
5. Ground Point
6. Crankshaft Position (CKP) Sensor
7. Knock Sensor (KS)
8. Starter
9. Heated Oxygen Sensor (HO2S) Bank 2 Sensor 1
10. Heated Oxygen Sensor (HO2S) Bank 2 Sensor 2
11. Vehicle Speed Sensor (VSS)

22116_SIER_G0114

Fig. 162 Right engine compartment view—4.3L engines

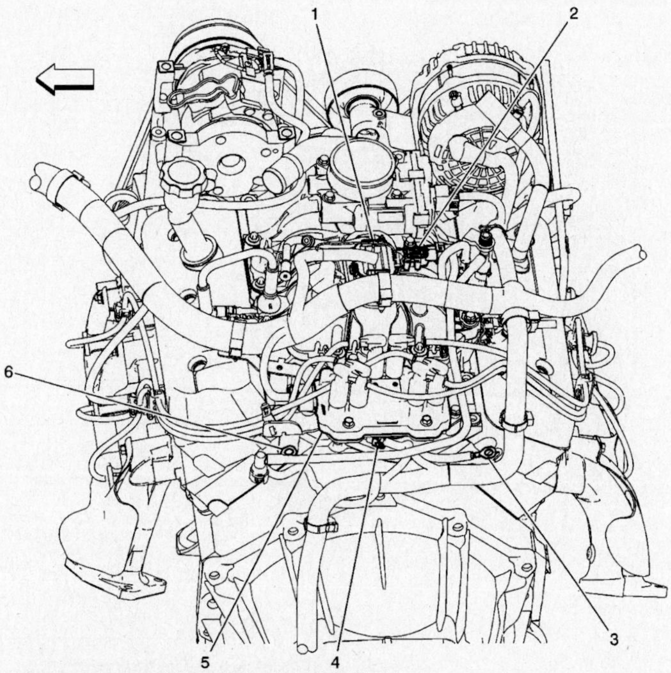

1. Central Sequential Fuel Injection (SFI) Module
2. Manifold Absolute Pressure (MAP) Sensor
3. Ground Point
4. Engine Oil Pressure (EOP) Sensor
5. Ignition Control Module (ICM)
6. Ground Point

22116_SIER_G0115

Fig. 163 Rear engine compartment view—4.3L engines

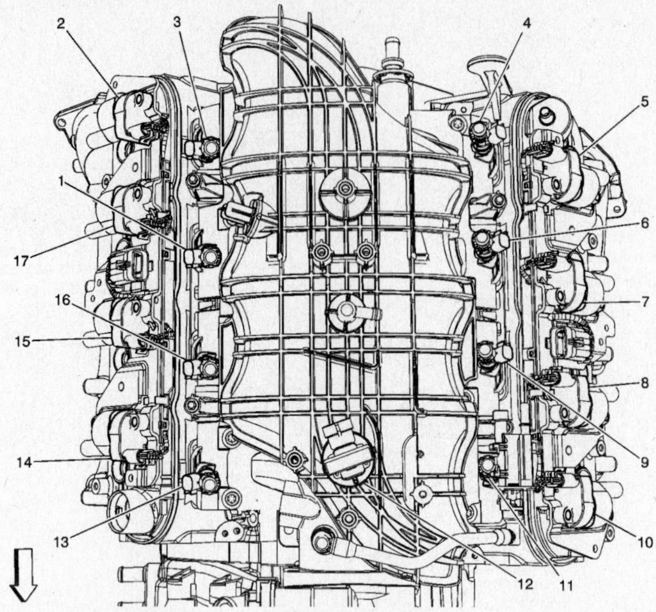

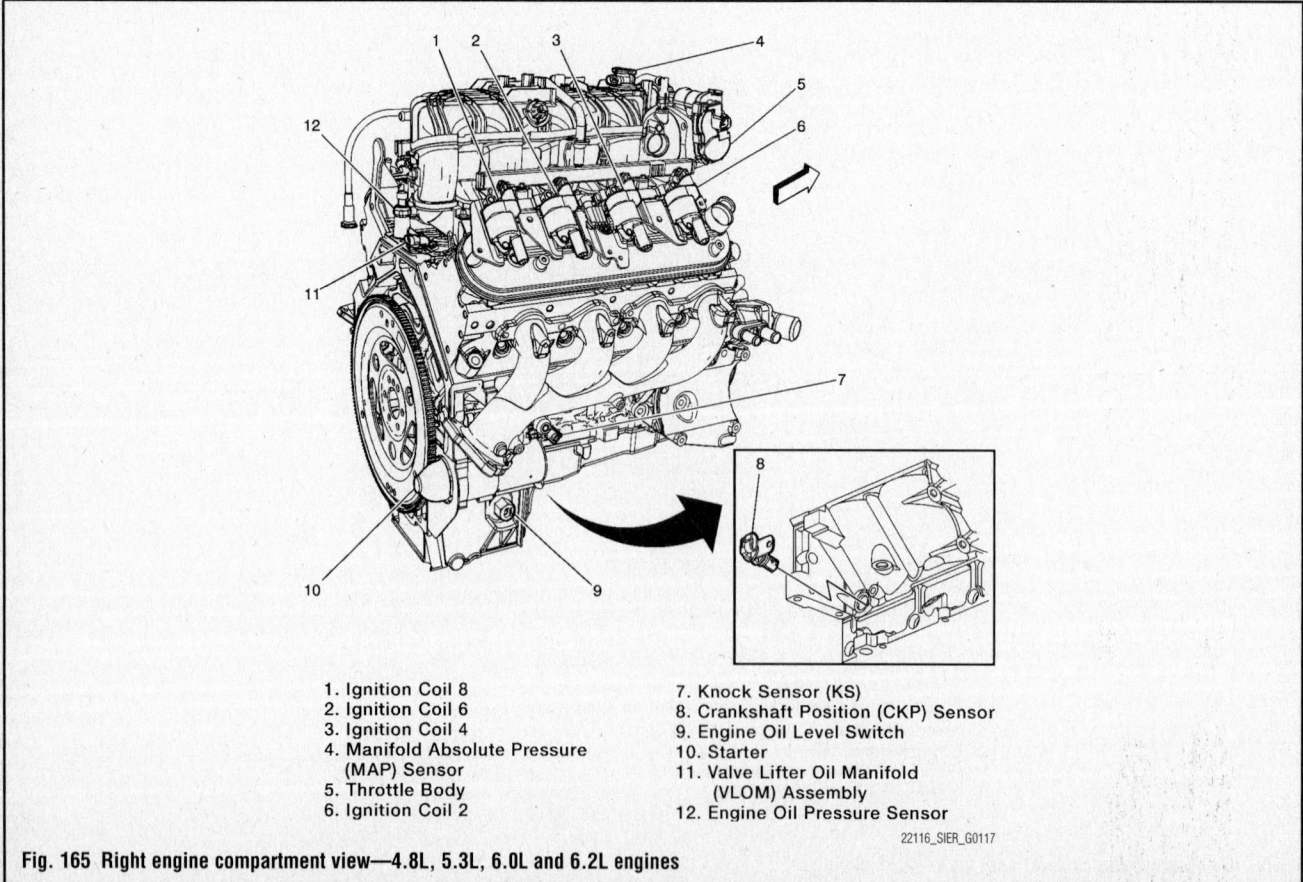

1. Fuel Injector 6
2. Ignition Coil 8
3. Fuel Injector 8
4. Fuel Injector 7
5. Ignition Coil 7
6. Fuel Injector 5
7. Ignition Coil 5
8. Ignition Coil 3
9. Fuel Injector 3
10. Ignition Coil 1
11. Fuel Injector 1
12. Manifold Absolute Pressure (MAP) Sensor
13. Fuel Injector 2
14. Ignition Coil 2
15. Ignition Coil 4
16. Fuel Injector 4
17. Ignition Coil 6

22116_SIER_G0116

Fig. 164 Top engine compartment view—4.8L, 5.3L, 6.0L and 6.2L engines

1. Ignition Coil 8
2. Ignition Coil 6
3. Ignition Coil 4
4. Manifold Absolute Pressure (MAP) Sensor
5. Throttle Body
6. Ignition Coil 2
7. Knock Sensor (KS)
8. Crankshaft Position (CKP) Sensor
9. Engine Oil Level Switch
10. Starter
11. Valve Lifter Oil Manifold (VLOM) Assembly
12. Engine Oil Pressure Sensor

22116_SIER_G0117

Fig. 165 Right engine compartment view—4.8L, 5.3L, 6.0L and 6.2L engines

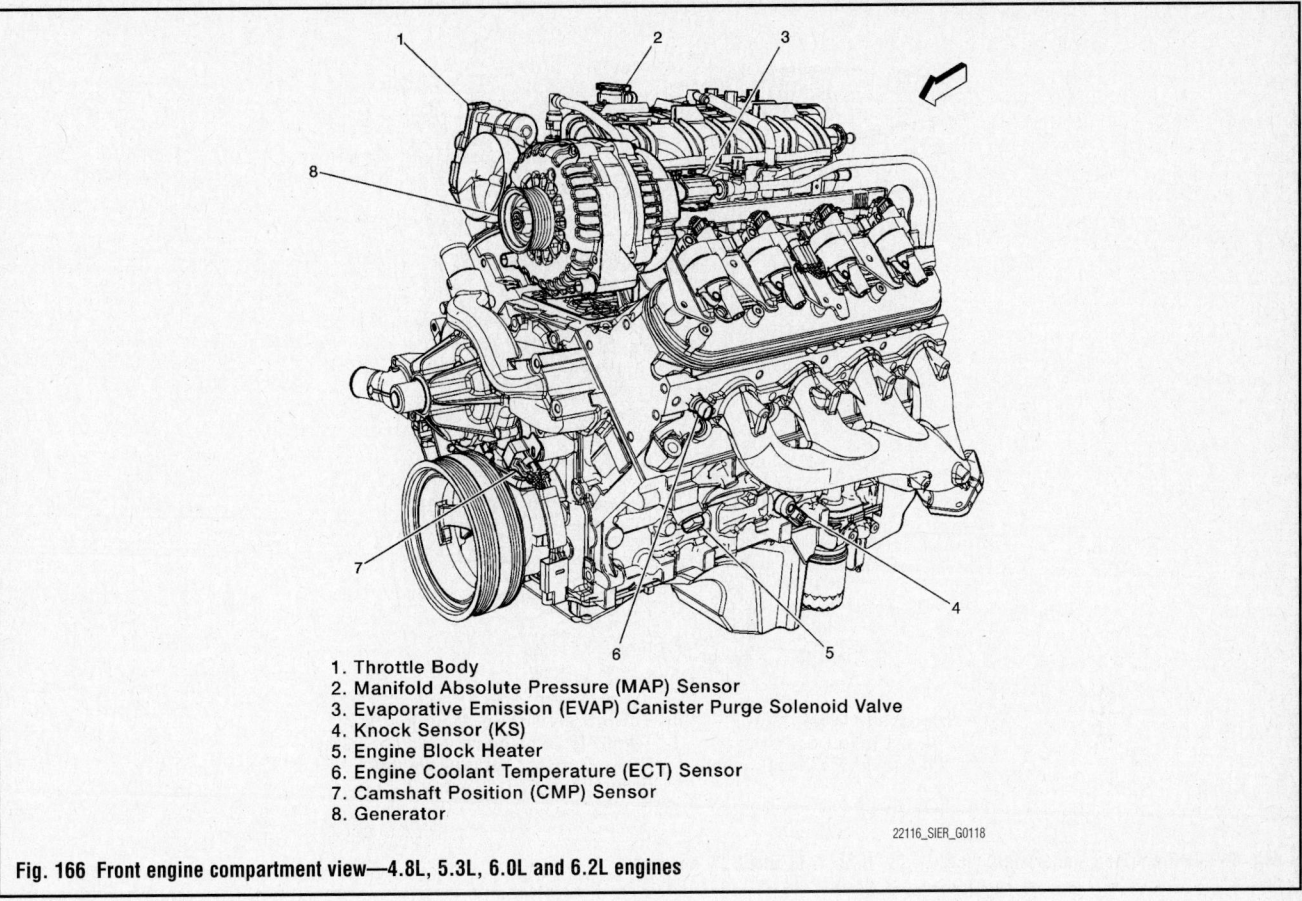

1. Throttle Body
2. Manifold Absolute Pressure (MAP) Sensor
3. Evaporative Emission (EVAP) Canister Purge Solenoid Valve
4. Knock Sensor (KS)
5. Engine Block Heater
6. Engine Coolant Temperature (ECT) Sensor
7. Camshaft Position (CMP) Sensor
8. Generator

22116_SIER_G0118

Fig. 166 Front engine compartment view—4.8L, 5.3L, 6.0L and 6.2L engines

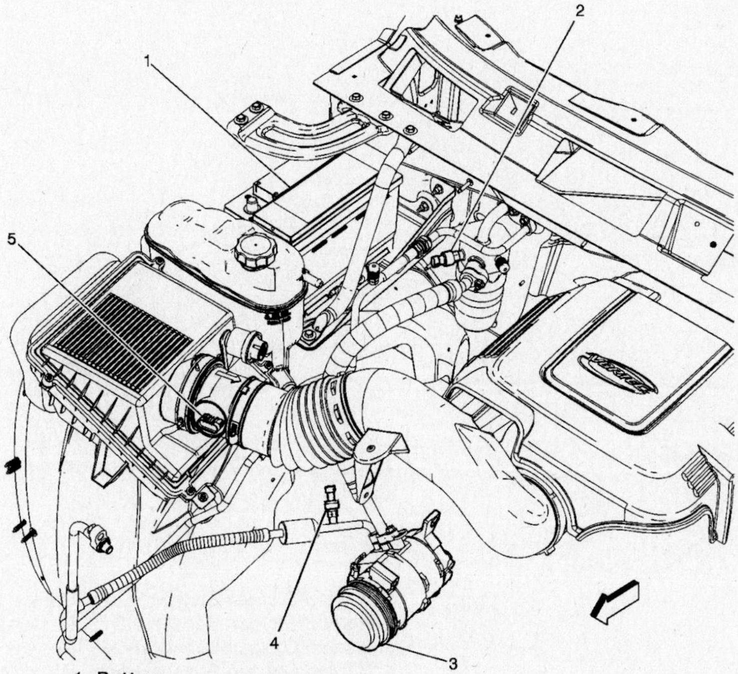

1. Battery
2. A/C Low Pressure Switch
3. A/C Compressor Clutch
4. A/C Refrigerant Pressure Switch
5. Mass Air Flow (MAF)/Intake Air Temperature (IAT) Sensor

22116_SIER_G0119

Fig. 167 Right rear engine compartment view—4.8L, 5.3L, 6.0L and 6.2L engines

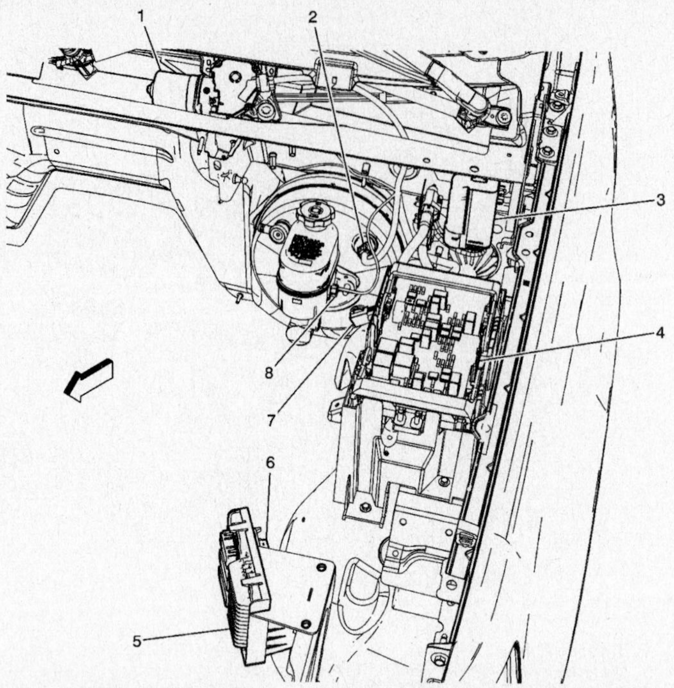

1. Windshield Wiper Motor
2. Power Brake Booster
3. Windshield Washer Solvent Heater
4. Fuse Block
5. Powertrain Control Module (PCM)
6. Transmission Control Module (TCM)
7. Brake Booster Vacuum Sensor
8. Brake Fluid Level Switch

22116_SIER_G0120

Fig. 168 Left engine compartment view—4.8L, 5.3L, 6.0L and 6.2L engines

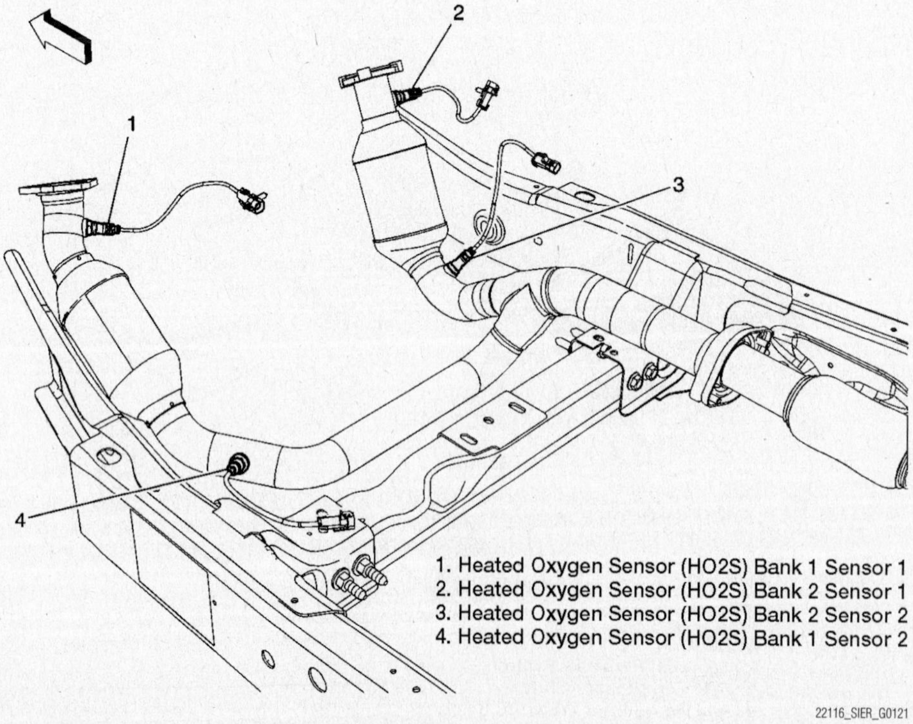

1. Heated Oxygen Sensor (HO2S) Bank 1 Sensor 1
2. Heated Oxygen Sensor (HO2S) Bank 2 Sensor 1
3. Heated Oxygen Sensor (HO2S) Bank 2 Sensor 2
4. Heated Oxygen Sensor (HO2S) Bank 1 Sensor 2

22116_SIER_G0121

Fig. 169 Oxygen sensor locations—4.8L, 5.3L, 6.0L and 6.2L engines

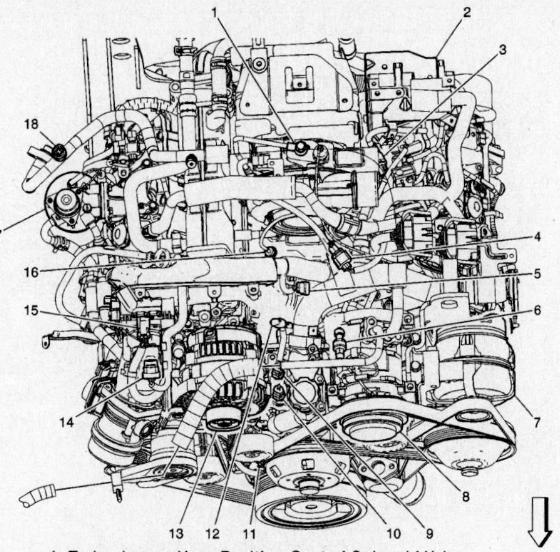

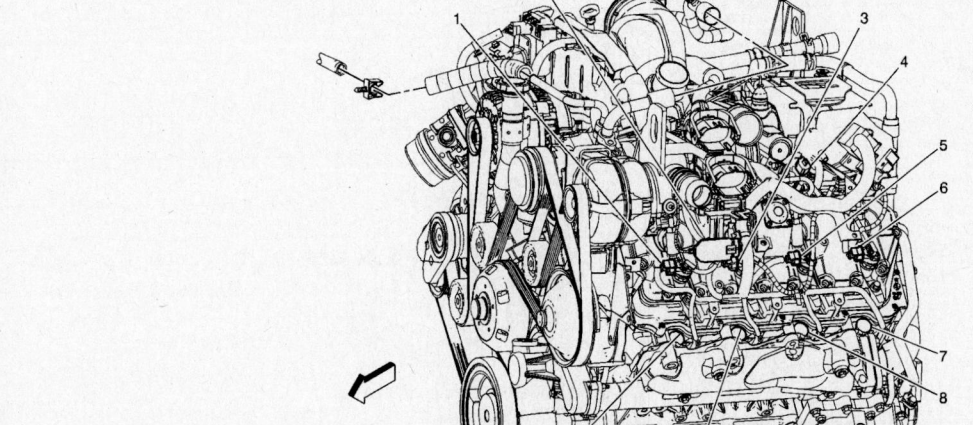

1. Turbocharger Vane Position Control Solenoid Valve
2. Glow Plug Control Module (GPCM)
3. Fuel Rail Temperature (FRT) Sensor
4. Intake Air Temperature (IAT) Sensor 2 Connector
5. Fuel Pressure Regulator Connector
6. A/C Refrigerant Pressure Sensor
7. Generator
8. A/C Compressor Clutch
9. Engine Coolant Temperature (ECT) Sensor 1
10. Engine Coolant Temperature (ECT) Sensor 2
11. Camshaft Position (CMP) Sensor
12. Connector X127
13. Generator – Right
14. Manifold Absolute Pressure (MAP) Sensor
15. Intake Air Heater (IAH) Module
16. Intake Air Temperature (IAT) Sensor 2
17. Fuel Heater
18. A/C Low Pressure Switch

22116_SIER_G0122

Fig. 170 Top engine compartment view—6.6L engines

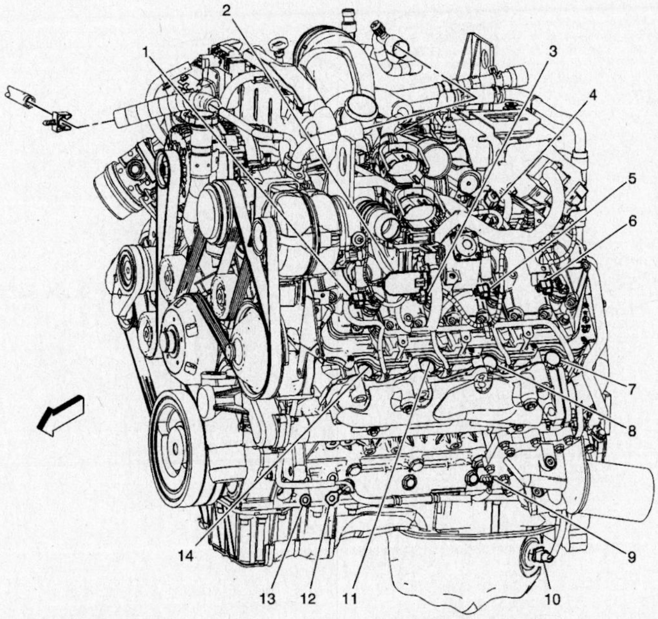

1. Fuel Injector 2
2. Turbocharger Vane Position Sensor
3. Fuel Injector 4
4. Fuel Rail Pressure Sensor
5. Fuel Injector 6
6. Fuel Injector 8
7. Glow Plug 8
8. Glow Plug 6
9. Engine Oil Pressure (EOP) Sensor
10. Engine Oil Level Switch
11. Glow Plug 4
12. Ground Point
13. Ground Point
14. Glow Plug 2

22116_SIER_G0123

Fig. 171 Left engine compartment view—6.6L engines

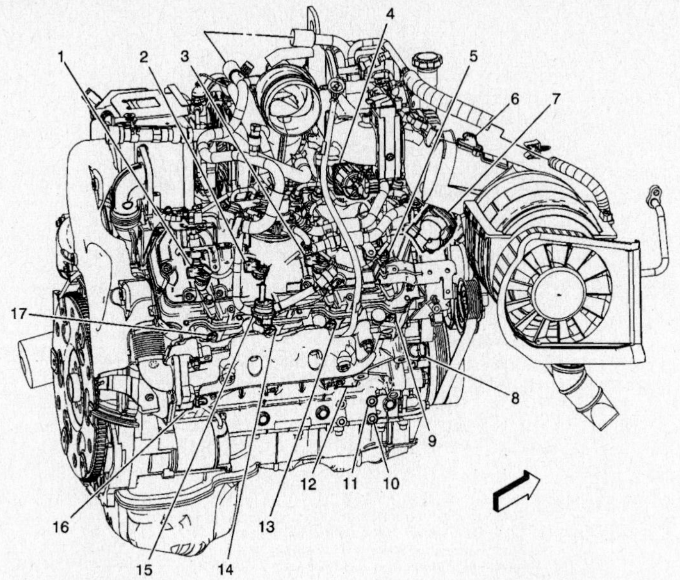

1. Fuel Injector 7
2. Fuel Injector 5
3. Fuel Injector 3
4. Exhaust Gas Recirculation (EGR) Valve
5. Fuel Injector 1
6. Mass Air Flow (MAF)/Intake Air Temperature (IAT) Sensor
7. Intake Air Valve
8. Crankshaft Position (CKP) Sensor
9. Glow Plug 1
10. Ground Point
11. Ground Point
12. Block Heater
13. Glow Plug 3
14. Glow Plug 5
15. Water In Fuel Sensor
16. Starter
17. Glow Plug 7

22116_SIER_G0124

Fig. 172 Right engine compartment view—6.6L engines

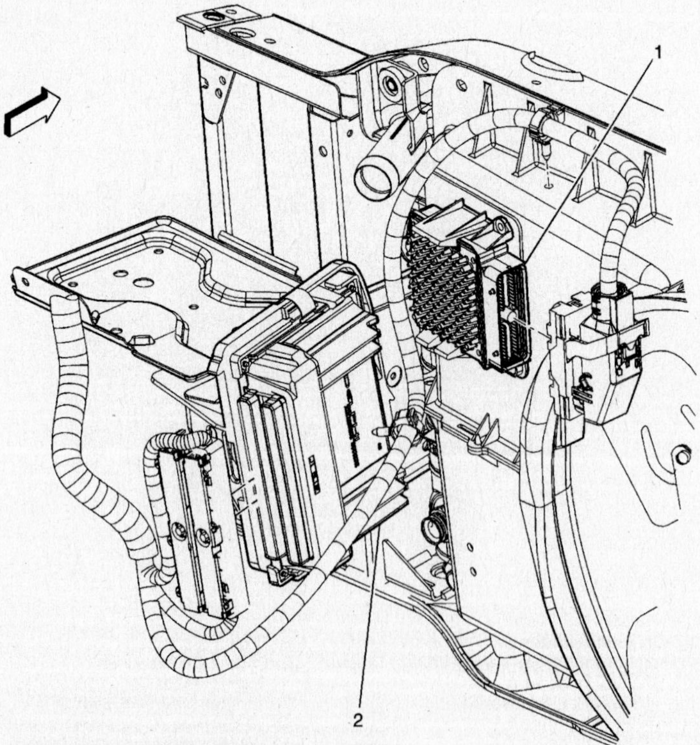

1. Transmission Control Module (TCM)
2. Powertrain Control Module (PCM)

22116_SIER_G0146

Fig. 173 Left front engine compartment view—8.1L engines

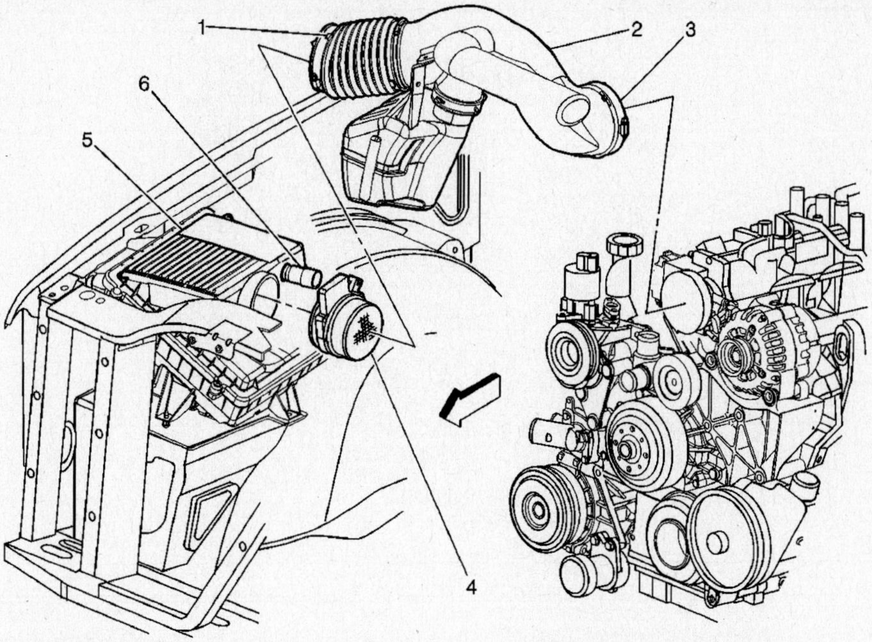

1. Clamp
2. Air Duct
3. Clamp
4. Mass Air Flow (MAF)/Intake
   Air Temperature (IAT) Sensor
5. Air Cleaner Assembly
6. Air Restriction Indicator

22116_SIER_G0147

Fig. 174 Right front engine compartment view—8.1L engines

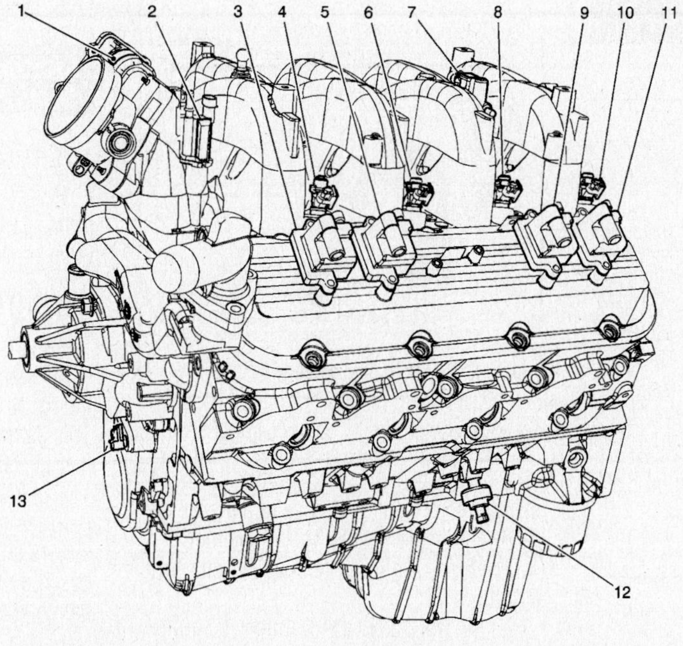

1. Throttle Body
2. Evaporative Emission (EVAP)
   Canister Purge Solenoid Valve
3. Ignition Coil 1
4. Fuel Injector 1
5. Ignition Coil 3
6. Fuel Injector 3
7. Manifold Absolute Pressure (MAP) Sensor
8. Fuel Injector 5
9. Ignition Coil 5
10. Fuel Injector 7
11. Ignition Coil 7
12. Knock Sensor (KS)
13. Camshaft Position (CMP) Sensor

22116_SIER_G0148

Fig. 175 Left side engine compartment view—8.1L engines

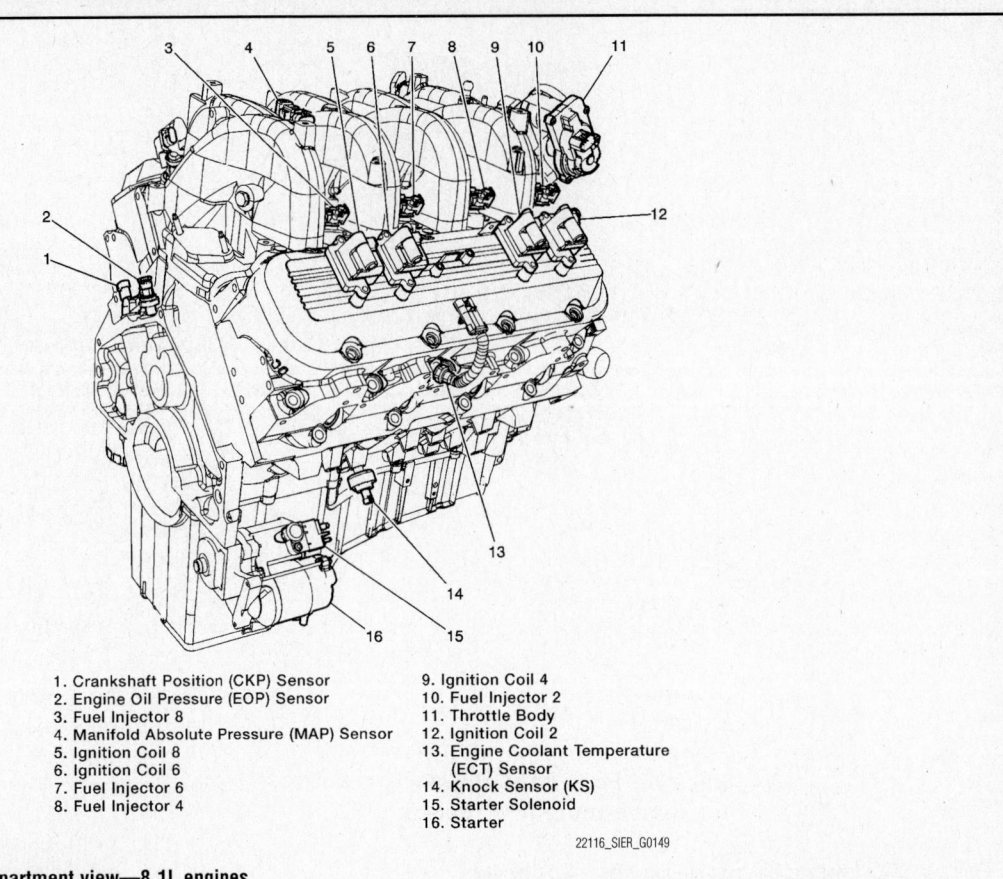

1. Crankshaft Position (CKP) Sensor
2. Engine Oil Pressure (EOP) Sensor
3. Fuel Injector 8
4. Manifold Absolute Pressure (MAP) Sensor
5. Ignition Coil 8
6. Ignition Coil 6
7. Fuel Injector 6
8. Fuel Injector 4
9. Ignition Coil 4
10. Fuel Injector 2
11. Throttle Body
12. Ignition Coil 2
13. Engine Coolant Temperature (ECT) Sensor
14. Knock Sensor (KS)
15. Starter Solenoid
16. Starter

22116_SIER_G0149

Fig. 176 Right side engine compartment view—8.1L engines

ACCELERATOR PEDAL POSITION (APP) SENSOR

LOCATION

The Accelerator Pedal Position (APP) sensor is mounted inside the accelerator pedal control assembly.

OPERATION

The sensor is made up of the two individual sensors within a single housing. Each sensor has a unique functionality to determine pedal position. The APP system along with the Powertrain Control Module (PCM) is used to calculate and control the amount of acceleration and deceleration through fuel injector control.

REMOVAL & INSTALLATION

See Figure 177.

1. Remove the driver's side knee bolster.
2. Push down on the small tab and disengage the electrical connector.
3. Remove the pedal bolts and remove the pedal and sensor assembly.
4. Installation is the reverse of removal. Tighten the bolts to 80 inch lbs. (9 Nm).

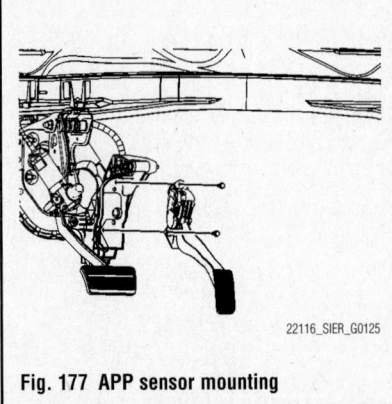

22116_SIER_G0125

Fig. 177 APP sensor mounting

TESTING

1. Install a 3 amp fused jumper wire between the 5–volt reference terminal of the APP sensor and 5 volts. Install a jumper wire between the low reference terminal and a ground.
2. Sweep the sensor through the entire range while monitoring the voltage between the signal terminal and the low reference terminal with a digital multimeter. The voltage should vary between 0.30–4.98 volts without any spikes or dropouts.
3. If the voltage is not within the specified range or is erratic, replace the accelerator pedal assembly.

CAMSHAFT POSITION (CMP) SENSOR

LOCATION

Refer to the component locator illustrations. The CMP sensor is located above the crankshaft pulley.

OPERATION

The PCM uses the Camshaft Position (CMP) sensor to determine the position of the No. 1 piston during its power stroke. This signal is used by the PCM to calculate fuel injection mode of operation.

If the cam signal is lost while the engine is running, the fuel injection system will shift to a calculated fuel injected mode based on the last fuel injection pulse, and the engine will continue to run.

REMOVAL & INSTALLATION

4.3L Engines

See Figure 178.

1. Unplug the harness connector from the CMP sensor.

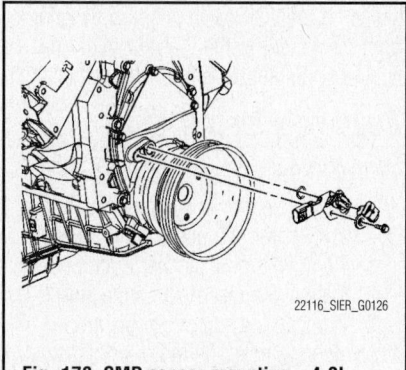

Fig. 178 CMP sensor mounting—4.3L engines

2. Remove the water pump.
3. Remove the CMP sensor bolt, then remove the sensor from the engine.
4. Installation is the reverse of removal. Lubricate a new O–ring with clean engine oil. Tighten the bolt to 89 inch lbs. (10 Nm).

4.8L, 5.3L, 6.0L and 6.2L Engines

See Figure 179.

1. Unplug the harness connector from the CMP sensor.
2. Remove the CMP sensor harness bolts, then remove the sensor from the engine.
3. Installation is the reverse of removal. Lubricate a new O–ring with clean engine oil. Tighten the bolt to 106 inch lbs. (12 Nm).

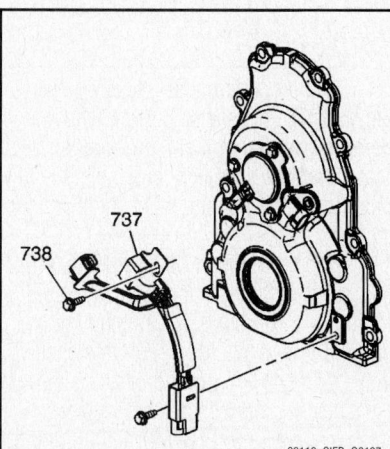

Fig. 179 CMP sensor harness mounting— 4.8L, 5.3L, 6.0L and 6.2L engines

6.6L Engines

See Figure 180.

1. Remove the cooling fan pulley.
2. Unplug the harness connector from the CMP sensor.
3. Remove the CMP sensor bolt, then remove the sensor from the engine.

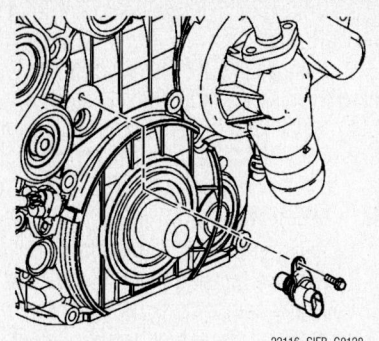

Fig. 180 CMP sensor mounting—6.6L engines

4. Installation is the reverse of removal. Tighten the bolt to 89 inch lbs. (10 Nm).

8.1L Engines

See Figure 181.

1. Unplug the harness connector from the CMP sensor.
2. Remove the water pump.
3. Remove the CMP sensor bolt, then remove the sensor from the engine.
4. Installation is the reverse of removal. Lubricate a new O–ring with clean engine oil. Tighten the bolt to 106 inch lbs. (12 Nm).

Fig. 181 CMP sensor mounting—8.1L engines

TESTING

1. Inspect the CMP sensor for correct installation. Remove the CMP sensor from the engine and inspect the sensor O–ring for damage. If the sensor is loose, incorrectly installed, or damaged, replace the CMP sensor.
2. Engage the CMP sensor harness connector to the CMP sensor.
3. Connect the scan tool to the diagnostic connector.

4. With the ignition ON, engine OFF observe the CMP Active counter parameter on the scan tool.
5. Pass a flat steel object across the tip of the sensor repeatedly. The CMP Active counter parameter should increment with each pass of the steel object.
6. If the parameter does not increment, replace the CMP sensor.

CRANKSHAFT POSITION (CKP) SENSOR

LOCATION

Refer to the component locator illustrations. The CKP sensor is located next to the crankshaft pulley except on 4.8L, 5.3L, 6.0L and 6.2L engines. On these engines, it is located on the side of the engine block.

OPERATION

The Crankshaft Position (CKP) sensor senses the crank angle (piston position) of each cylinder and converts it into a pulse signal. The PCM receives this signal and then computes the engine speed and controls the fuel injector timing and ignition timing based on this input.

REMOVAL & INSTALLATION

➡**Use of a scan tool is required to complete this procedure. Anytime the CKP sensor is replaced, the variation learn procedure must be performed.**

4.3L Engines

See Figure 182.

1. Raise and safely support the vehicle.
2. Remove the skid plate, if equipped.
3. Unplug the harness connector from the sensor.
4. Remove the bolt securing the sensor, then remove it from the engine.
5. Installation is the reverse of removal. Lubricate a new O–ring with clean engine

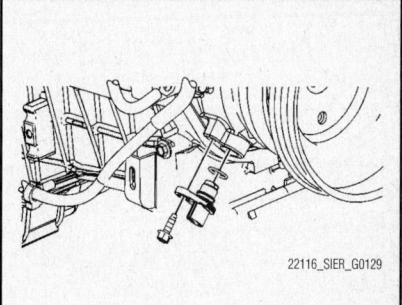

Fig. 182 CKP sensor mounting—4.3L engines

oil. Tighten the bolt to 89 inch lbs. (10 Nm). Connect the scan tool to the vehicle and perform the CKP sensor variation learn procedure.

4.8L, 5.3L, 6.0L and 6.2L Engines

See Figure 183.

1. Raise and safely support the vehicle.
2. Remove the starter.
3. Working through the wheel well opening, unplug the harness connector from the sensor.
4. Clean the area around the sensor to prevent debris from entering the engine.
5. Remove the bolt securing the sensor, then remove it from the engine.
6. Installation is the reverse of removal. Lubricate a new O–ring with clean engine oil. Tighten the bolt to 18 ft. lbs. (25 Nm). Connect the scan tool to the vehicle and perform the CKP sensor variation learn procedure.

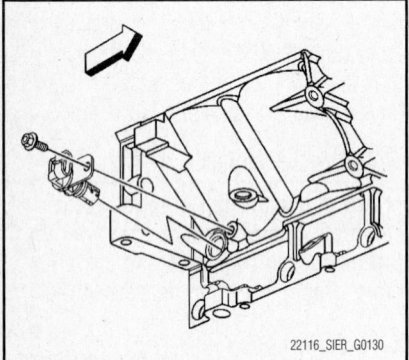

Fig. 183 CKP sensor mounting—4.8L, 5.3L, 6.0L and 6.2L engines

6.6L Engines

See Figure 184.

1. Disconnect the negative battery cable.
2. Remove the right wheelhouse liner to gain access to the CKP sensor.

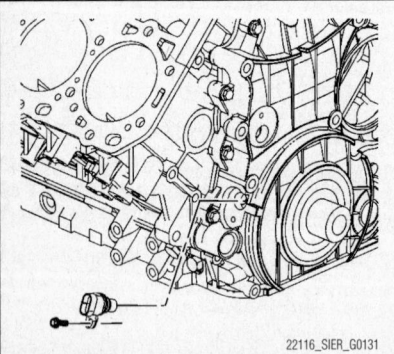

Fig. 184 CKP sensor mounting—6.6L engines

3. Unplug the harness connector from the CKP sensor.
4. Remove the CKP sensor bolt, then remove the sensor from the engine.
5. Installation is the reverse of removal. Tighten the bolt to 89 inch lbs. (10 Nm).

8.1L Engines

1. Raise and safely support the vehicle.
2. Remove the skid plate, if equipped. Remove any components necessary to ease access to the sensor (ignition coils, etc).
3. Unplug the harness connector from the sensor.
4. Remove the bolt securing the sensor, then remove it from the engine.
5. Installation is the reverse of removal. Lubricate a new O–ring with clean engine oil. Tighten the bolt to 106 inch lbs. (12 Nm). Connect the scan tool to the vehicle and perform the CKP sensor variation learn procedure.

TESTING

1. Inspect the CKP sensor for correct installation. Remove the CKP sensor from the engine and inspect the sensor O–ring for damage. If the sensor is loose, incorrectly installed, or damaged, replace the CKP sensor.
2. Engage the CKP sensor harness connector to the CKP sensor.
3. Connect the scan tool to the diagnostic connector.
4. With the ignition ON, engine OFF observe the CKP Active counter parameter on the scan tool.
5. Pass a flat steel object across the tip of the sensor repeatedly. The CKP Active counter parameter should increment with each pass of the steel object.
6. If the parameter does not increment, replace the CKP sensor.

EGR VALVE POSITION (EVP) SENSOR

LOCATION

The EGR Valve Position (EVP) sensor is located on the end of the EGR valve. It is used on 6.6L diesel engines.

OPERATION

The PCM uses the EGR position sensor to determine the position of the EGR valve. The PCM sends a reference voltage through the 5–volt reference circuit to the EGR position sensor. The PCM provides a voltage return path for the sensor through the low reference circuit. A variable voltage signal, based on the EGR valve position, is sent from the sensor to the PCM through the EGR position sensor signal circuit.

REMOVAL & INSTALLATION

See Figure 185.

If the EVP sensor is defective the entire EGR valve motor will need to be replaced.

1. Remove the air cleaner duct.
2. Detach the electrical connector.
3. Remove the screws securing the motor, then remove the motor and spacer (if equipped) from the valve.
4. Installation is the reverse of removal. Tighten the screws to 18 inch lbs. (2 Nm).

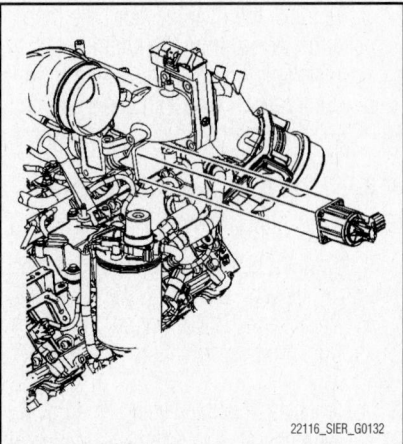

Fig. 185 EVP sensor mounting—6.6L engines

TESTING

1. With the ignition OFF, test for less than 1 ohm of resistance between the low reference circuit terminal B and ground. If greater than the specified range, test the low reference circuit for an open or high resistance.
2. With the ignition ON, test for 4.8–5.2 volts between the 5–volt reference circuit terminal A and ground. If less than the specified range, test the 5–volt reference circuit for a short to ground or an open/high resistance. If greater than the specified range, test the 5–volt reference circuit for a short to voltage. If a short is not found, the PCM is faulty.
3. With the ignition ON, and the EGR valve disconnected, observe that the EGR Position parameter on the scan tool is 0 volt. If the EGR Position parameter is more than 0 volt, test the signal circuit for a short to voltage. If a short is not found, the PCM is faulty.
4. With the ignition ON and the EGR valve disconnected, connect a jumper wire between the 5–volt reference circuit terminal

A of the EGR valve and the signal circuit terminal C of the EGR valve and observe with a scan tool that the EGR sensor parameter displays 4.98–5.02 volts. If the EGR Sensor parameter is less than 4.98 volts, test the signal circuit for an open, short to ground, or high resistance.

5. If all tests are normal, but the sensor is throwing a DTC code, then the sensor is faulty.

ENGINE COOLANT TEMPERATURE (ECT) SENSOR

LOCATION

Refer to the component locations. The ECT sensor is threaded into the cylinder head. The 6.6L diesel engines use 2 ECT sensors; they are located side by side.

OPERATION

The Engine Coolant Temperature (ECT) sensor resistance changes in response to engine coolant temperature. The sensor resistance decreases as the coolant temperature increases, and increases as the coolant temperature decreases. This provides a reference signal to the PCM, which indicates engine coolant temperature. The signal sent to the PCM by the ECT sensor helps the PCM to determine spark advance, EGR flow rate, air/fuel ratio, and engine temperature. The ECT is a two wire sensor, a 5–volt reference signal is sent to the sensor and the signal return is based upon the change in the measured resistance due to temperature.

REMOVAL & INSTALLATION

See Figures 186 through 188.

1. Drain the cooling system to a level below the ECT sensor.

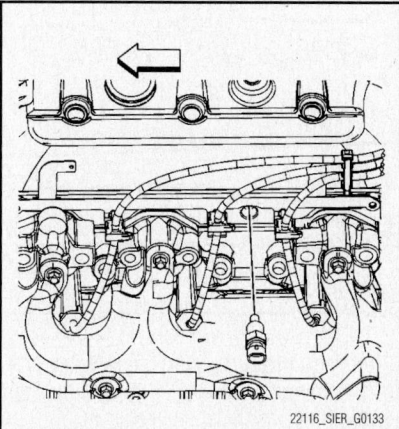

Fig. 186 ECT sensor mounting—4.3L engines

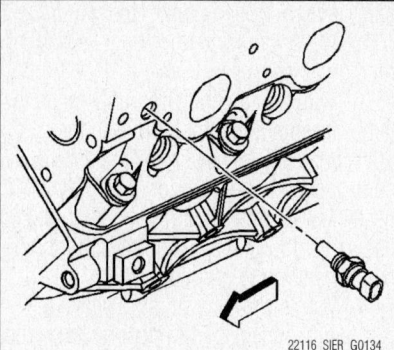

22116_SIER_G0134

Fig. 187 ECT sensor mounting—4.8L, 5.3L, 6.0L and 6.2L engines

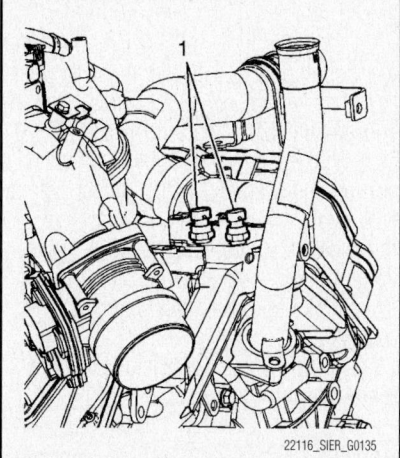

22116_SIER_G0135

Fig. 188 ECT sensor mounting—6.6L engines

2. On 6.6L diesel engines, remove the alternator.

3. Unplug the harness connector from the ECT sensor.

4. Remove the ECT sensor from the engine.

5. Installation is the reverse of removal. If reusing the old sensor, coat the threads with GM sealant 12346004 or equivalent. New sensors are already coated; additional sealant is not needed. Tighten the sensor to 15 ft. lbs. (20 Nm).

TESTING

1. Remove the ECT sensor.
2. Measure and record the resistance of the ECT sensor at various temperatures, then compare those measurements to the following. The change in resistance should occur smoothly. If there are any sudden changes, the sensor is faulty.
   - -4°F: 28680 ohms
   - 14°F: 16180 ohms
   - 32°F: 9420 ohms
   - 50°F: 5670 ohms
   - 68°F: 3520 ohms
   - 86°F: 2238 ohms
   - 104°F: 1459 ohms
   - 122°F: 973 ohms
   - 158°F: 467 ohms
   - 194°F: 241 ohms
   - 230°F: 132 ohms
   - 266°F: 77 ohms

3. If the sensor tests outside of these ranges, replace the sensor.

HEATED OXYGEN (HO2S) SENSOR

LOCATION

Refer to the component locations. The Heated Oxygen Sensors (HO2S) are threaded into the exhaust pipes.

OPERATION

The Heated Oxygen Sensor (HO2S) is a device which produces an electrical voltage when exposed to the oxygen present in the exhaust gases. The oxygen sensors are electrically heated internally for faster switching when the engine is started cold. The oxygen sensor produces a voltage within 0 and 1 volt. When there is a large amount of oxygen present (lean mixture), the sensor produces a low voltage (less than 0.4v). When there is a lesser amount present (rich mixture) it produces a higher voltage (0.6–1.0v). The stoichiometric or correct fuel to air ratio will read between 0.4 and 0.6v. By monitoring the oxygen content and converting it to electrical voltage, the sensor acts as a rich–lean switch. The voltage is transmitted to the PCM.

Two sensors per bank are used, one before the catalyst and one after. This is done for a catalyst efficiency monitor that is a part of the diagnostic system of the engine controls. The one before the catalyst measures the exhaust emissions right out of the engine, and sends the signal to the PCM about the state of the mixture as previously talked about. The second sensor reports the difference in the emissions after the exhaust gases have gone through the catalyst. This sensor reports to the PCM the amount of emissions reduction the catalyst is performing.

The oxygen sensor will not work until a predetermined temperature is reached, until this time the PCM is running in what is known as open loop operation. Open loop means that the PCM has not yet begun to correct the air–to–fuel ratio by reading the oxygen sensor. After the engine comes to operating temperature, the PCM will monitor the oxygen sensor and correct the air/fuel ratio from the sensor's readings. This is what is known as closed loop operation.

REMOVAL & INSTALLATION

See Figure 189.

➡**Replace the sensor if the pigtail wiring, connector, or terminal is damaged. The external clean air reference is obtained by way of the sensor signal and heater wires. Any attempt to repair the wires or connectors could result in obstruction of the air reference. Make sure the lead wires are not sharply bent or kinked as the air reference could become blocked.**

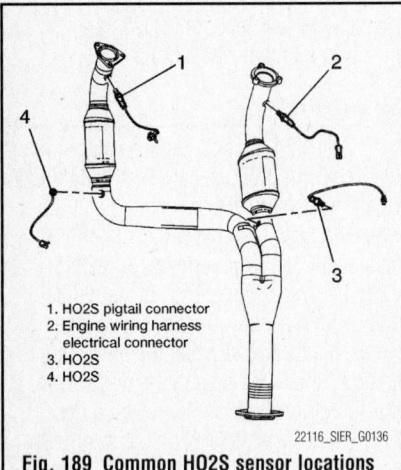

1. HO2S pigtail connector
2. Engine wiring harness electrical connector
3. HO2S
4. HO2S

22116_SIER_G0136

Fig. 189 Common HO2S sensor locations on the exhaust pipes

1. Remove the wheelhouse liner for access to the sensor.
2. Remove the connector position assurance retainer.
3. Unplug the sensor connector. Remove the clip from the engine harness.
4. Remove the sensor from the exhaust pipe.
5. Installation is the reverse of removal. If reusing the old sensor, coat the threads with GM anti-seize compound 12377953 or equivalent. New sensors are already coated; additional compound is not needed. Tighten the sensor to 31 ft. lbs. (42 Nm).

TESTING

Heater

1. With the ignition OFF, disconnect the harness connector at the appropriate HO2S.
2. With the ignition ON, verify that a test lamp illuminates between the appropriate HO2S heater voltage supply circuit and ground. If the test lamp does not illuminate, test the HO2S heater voltage supply circuit for a short to ground or an open/high resistance. If the circuit tests normal and the HO2S heater voltage

supply circuit fuse is open, test all components connected to the fuse and replace as necessary.

3. With the ignition ON, verify that a test lamp does not illuminate between the appropriate HO2S heater voltage supply control circuit and the appropriate HO2S heater low control circuit. If the lamp illuminates, test the HO2S heater low control circuit for a short to ground.

4. With the engine running, leave the test lamp connected from the previous step. The lamp should flash or be ON steady. If the test lamp is not ON steady or flashing, test the HO2S heater low control circuit for a short to voltage or an open/high resistance.

5. With the ignition OFF, install a 30A fused jumper wire between the appropriate HO2S heater voltage supply circuit and the appropriate HO2S heater low control circuit. With the engine running, verify the appropriate scan tool HO2S Heater parameter is less than 0.1 amp. If more than the specified range, test the HO2S heater voltage supply and HO2S heater low control circuits for more than 1 ohm of resistance.

6. If the PCM and all circuits test normal, replace the appropriate HO2S.

Sensor

➡**If any HO2S heater circuit DTC's are set, test the heater circuit first.**

1. Allow the engine to reach operating temperature.
2. With the engine running, observe the affected HO2S parameter with a scan tool.:
   a. The pre-catalyst oxygen sensors value should vary from below 200 mV to above 800 mV and respond to fueling changes.
   b. The post-catalyst oxygen sensors value should change more than 200 mV when the throttle is quickly cycled 3 times from closed to wide open and back to closed after running the engine at 1,500 RPM for 30 seconds.
3. If the sensor did not perform as indicated, replace the sensor.

INTAKE AIR TEMPERATURE (IAT) SENSOR

LOCATION

Refer to the component locations. The IAT sensor is integrated with the MAF sensor. The 6.6L diesel engines utilize an additional IAT sensor located on the intake manifold.

OPERATION

The Intake Air Temperature (IAT) sensor determines the air temperature entering the intake manifold. Resistance changes in response to the ambient air temperature. The sensor has a negative temperature coefficient. As the temperature of the sensor rises the resistance across the sensor decreases. This provides a signal to the PCM indicating the temperature of the incoming air charge. This sensor helps the PCM to determine spark timing and air/fuel ratio. Information from this sensor is added to the pressure sensor information to calculate the air mass being sent to the cylinders. The IAT receives a 5-volt reference signal and the signal return is based upon the change in the measured resistance due to temperature.

REMOVAL & INSTALLATION

See Figure 190.

This procedure is for the intake manifold mounted IAT sensor on 6.6L engines. Refer to the MAF sensor removal and installation procedure for other IAT sensors.

1. Remove the air intake pipe.
2. Unplug the harness connector from the IAT sensor.
3. Remove the sensor from the intake manifold.
4. Installation is the reverse of removal. Tighten the sensor to 18 ft. lbs. (25 Nm).

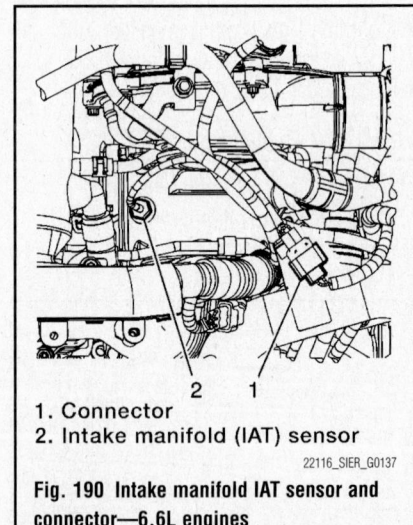

1. Connector
2. Intake manifold (IAT) sensor

22116_SIER_G0137

Fig. 190 Intake manifold IAT sensor and connector—6.6L engines

TESTING

1. Remove the IAT sensor.
2. Measure and record the resistance of the IAT sensor at various temperatures, then compare those measurements to the following. The change in resistance should occur smoothly. If there are any sudden changes, the sensor is faulty.

Gasoline engines:
- -4°F: 28680 ohms
- 14°F: 16180 ohms
- 32°F: 9420 ohms
- 50°F: 5670 ohms
- 68°F: 3520 ohms
- 86°F: 2238 ohms
- 104°F: 1459 ohms
- 122°F: 973 ohms
- 158°F: 467 ohms
- 194°F: 241 ohms
- 230°F: 132 ohms
- 266°F: 77 ohms

Diesel engines; MAF mounted:
- -4°F: 14700 ohms
- 14°F: 8970 ohms
- 32°F: 5650 ohms
- 50°F: 3660 ohms
- 68°F: 2440 ohms
- 86°F: 1650 ohms
- 104°F: 1150 ohms
- 122°F: 810 ohms
- 158°F: 430 ohms
- 194°F: 240 ohms
- 212°F: 190 ohms

Diesel engines; manifold mounted:
- -4°F: 38480 ohms
- 14°F: 23670 ohms
- 32°F: 15000 ohms
- 50°F: 9765 ohms
- 68°F: 6517 ohms
- 86°F: 4448 ohms
- 104°F: 3100 ohms
- 122°F: 2203 ohms
- 158°F: 1171 ohms
- 194°F: 662 ohms
- 212°F: 508 ohms
- 248°F: 310 ohms
- 284°F: 198 ohms

3. If the sensor tests outside of these ranges, replace the sensor.

KNOCK SENSOR (KS)

LOCATION

Refer to the component locations. The Knock Sensor (KS) sensor is located on the sides of the engine block. It is used on gasoline engines only.

OPERATION

The knock sensor system enables the PCM to control ignition timing for best performance while protecting the engine from detonation.

The KS system uses one or 2 flat response 2–wire sensors. The sensor uses piezo–electric crystal technology that produces an AC voltage signal of varying amplitude and frequency based on the engine vibration or noise level. The control

module receives the KS signal through a signal circuit. The KS ground is supplied by the control module through a low reference circuit. The control module learns a minimum noise level, or background noise, at idle from the KS and uses calibrated values for the rest of the RPM range.

In order to determine which cylinders are knocking, the control module only uses KS signal information when each cylinder is near Top Dead Center (TDC) of the firing stroke. If knock is present, the signal will range outside of the noise channel. If the control module has determined that knock is present, it will retard the ignition timing to attempt to eliminate the knock. The control module will always try to work back to a zero compensation level, or no spark retard.

REMOVAL & INSTALLATION

See Figures 191 through 193.

1. Raise and safely support the vehicle.
2. On 4.3L engines, remove the skid plates if equipped.
3. Remove the tire to ease access to the knock sensor.

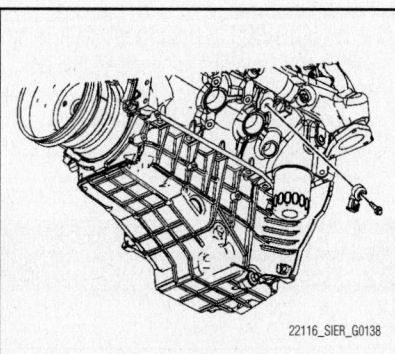
Fig. 191 Knock sensor mounting—4.3L engines

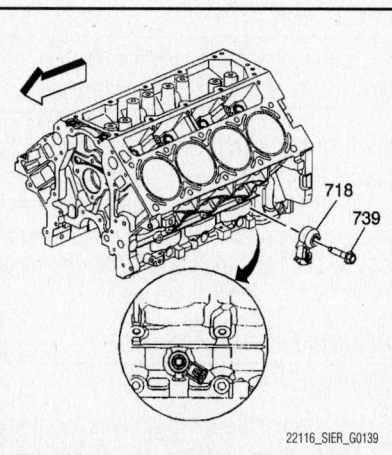
Fig. 192 Knock sensor mounting—4.8L, 5.3L, 6.0L and 6.2L engines

Fig. 193 Knock sensor mounting—8.1L engines

4. If equipped, remove the knock sensor shield.
5. Unplug the harness connection from the knock sensor.
6. Remove the bolt securing the sensor, then remove it from the engine.
7. Installation is the reverse of removal. Tighten the bolt to 18 ft. lbs. (25 Nm).

TESTING

1. Connect a digital multimeter to the KS signal circuit and to the KS low reference circuit at the KS.
2. Set the multimeter to the 400 mv AC hertz scale and wait for the display to stabilize at 0 Hz.
3. Tap on the engine block with a non–metallic object near the KS while observing the signal indicated on the multimeter.

➡**Do not tap on plastic engine components.**

4. The multimeter should display a fluctuating frequency while tapping on the engine block. If not, replace the sensor.

MASS AIR FLOW (MAF) SENSOR

LOCATION

Refer to the component locations. The Manifold Airflow (MAF) sensor is located on the air cleaner assembly or air intake tube. The IAT sensor is integrated with the MAF sensor.

OPERATION

The Mass Air Flow (MAF) sensor directly measures the mass of air being drawn into the engine. The sensor output is used to calculate injector pulse width. The MAF sensor is what is referred to as a "hot–wire sensor". The sensor uses a thin platinum wire filament, wound on a ceramic bobbin and coated with glass, that is heated to 417°F (200°C) above the ambient air temperature and subjected to the intake airflow stream. A "cold–wire" is used inside the MAF sensor to determine the ambient air temperature.

Battery voltage, a reference signal, and a ground signal from the PCM are supplied to the MAF sensor. The sensor returns a signal proportionate to the current flow required to keep the "hot–wire" at the required temperature. The increased airflow across the "hot–wire" acts as a cooling fan, lowering the resistance and requiring more current to maintain the temperature of the wire. The increased current is measured by the voltage in the circuit, as current increases, voltage increases. As the airflow increases the signal return voltage of a normally operating MAF sensor will increase.

REMOVAL & INSTALLATION

Gasoline Engines

See Figure 194.

1. Remove the air intake tube from the air cleaner assembly.
2. Detach the electrical connector from the MAF sensor.
3. Loosen the clamp securing the MAF sensor to the air cleaner.
4. Pull the MAF sensor out of the air cleaner assembly.
5. Installation is the reverse of removal.

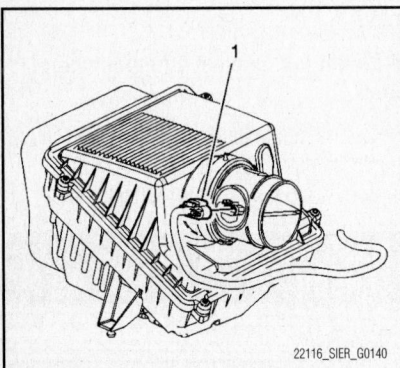

Fig. 194 MAF sensor mounting—gasoline engines

Diesel Engines

See Figure 195.

1. Detach the electrical connector from the MAF sensor.
2. Remove the screws securing the MAF sensor.
3. Pull the MAF sensor out of the air cleaner assembly.
4. Installation is the reverse of removal. Tighten the screws to 70 inch lbs. (8 Nm).

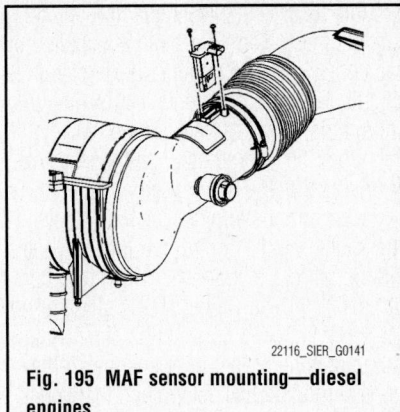

Fig. 195 MAF sensor mounting—diesel engines

TESTING

1. Turn OFF the ignition.
2. Connect tool J 38522 to the vehicle. Connect the battery voltage supply, and ground the black lead.
3. Connect the red lead to the signal circuit of the MAF sensor.
4. Set the Duty Cycle switch to Normal.
5. Set the Frequency switch to 5 K.
6. Set the Signal switch to 5 V.
7. Start the engine. Observe the MAF Sensor parameter for the correct range of 4,950–5,025 Hz.
   a. If the MAF Sensor parameter is not within the specified range, replace the ECM.
   b. If the MAF Sensor parameter is within the specified range, replace the MAF sensor.

MANIFOLD ABSOLUTE PRESSURE (MAP) SENSOR

LOCATION

Refer to the component locations. The Manifold Absolute Pressure (MAP) sensor is located on the intake manifold.

OPERATION

Using the pressure and temperature data, the PCM calculates the intake air mass. It is connected to the engine intake manifold and takes readings of the absolute pressure.

Atmospheric pressure is measured both when the engine is started and when driving fully loaded, then the pressure sensor information is adjusted accordingly.

REMOVAL & INSTALLATION

See Figure 196.

1. Detach the electrical connection from the MAP sensor.
2. Remove the screws securing the sensor, then remove it from the intake manifold.

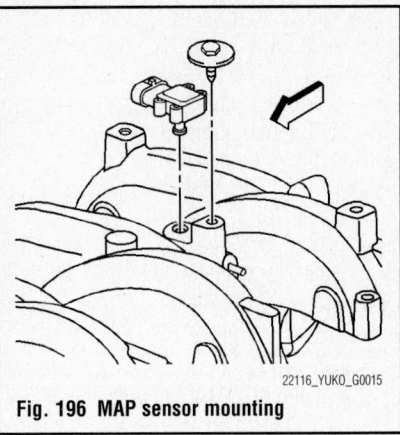

Fig. 196 MAP sensor mounting

3. Installation is the reverse of removal. If reusing the sensor, replace the seal.

TESTING

1. Turn ON the ignition, with the engine OFF, and remove the MAP sensor.
2. Install a 3 amp fused jumper wire between the 5–volt reference circuit and the corresponding terminal of the MAP sensor.
3. Install a jumper wire between the low reference circuit of the MAP sensor and ground.
4. Install a jumper wire at the MAP sensor signal circuit.
5. Connect a digital multimeter between the jumper wire from the MAP sensor signal circuit and ground.
6. Install hand vacuum pump to the MAP sensor vacuum port. Slowly apply vacuum to the sensor while observing the voltage on the multimeter. The voltage should vary between 0–5.2 volts without any spikes or dropouts.
7. If the voltage is not within the specified range or is erratic, replace the MAP sensor.

POWERTRAIN CONTROL MODULE (PCM)

LOCATION

Refer to the component locations. The PCM is located on a bracket on the side of the engine compartment.

OPERATION

The Powertrain Control Module (PCM) performs many functions on your vehicle. The module accepts information from various sensors and computes the required fuel flow rate necessary to maintain the correct amount of air/fuel ratio throughout the entire engine operational range and controls the shifting of the transmission.

Based on the information that is received and programmed into the PCM's memory, the PCM generates output signals to control relays, actuators and solenoids. The module automatically senses and compensates for any changes in altitude when driving your vehicle.

REMOVAL & INSTALLATION

See Figures 197 and 198.

➡️**It is necessary to record the remaining engine oil life. If the replacement module is not programmed with the remaining engine oil life, the engine oil life will default to 100 percent. If**

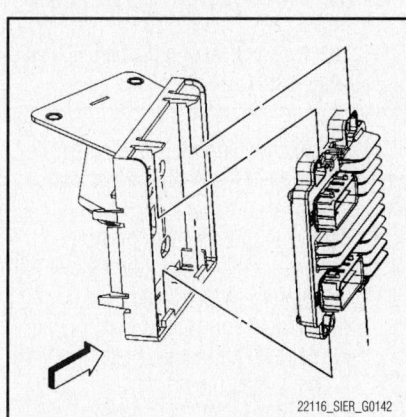

Fig. 197 PCM mounting—gasoline engines

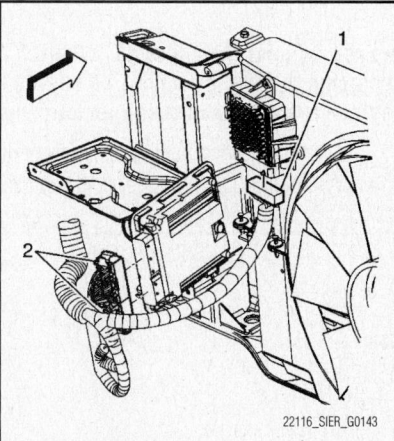

Fig. 198 PCM mounting—diesel engines

the replacement module is not programmed with the remaining engine oil life, the engine oil must be changed at 3,000 miles (5,000km) from the last oil change. A scan tool must be used to retrieve the PCM data. This information must be transferred to the new PCM.

1. Disconnect the negative battery cable.
2. Disengage the harness connections from the PCM.
3. Disengage the retainer tabs securing the PCM to the bracket. Remove the PCM from the engine compartment.
4. Installation is the reverse of removal. Program the PCM.

TESTING

Service of the Powertrain Control Module (PCM) should consist of either replacement of the PCM or programming of the Electrically Erasable Programmable Read Only Memory (EEPROM). If the diagnostic procedures call for the PCM to be replaced, the replacement PCM should be checked to ensure that the correct part is being used. If the correct part is being used, remove the faulty PCM and install the new service PCM

VEHICLE SPEED SENSOR (VSS)

LOCATION

The Vehicle Speed Sensor (VSS) is located on the tail section of the transmission on 2WD models. On 4WD models, it is located on the transfer case.

OPERATION

The VSS supplies vehicle speed information to the PCM.

REMOVAL & INSTALLATION

See Figures 199 and 200.

1. Raise and safely support the vehicle.
2. Detach the electrical connector from the VSS sensor.
3. Remove the sensor from the transmission or transfer case.

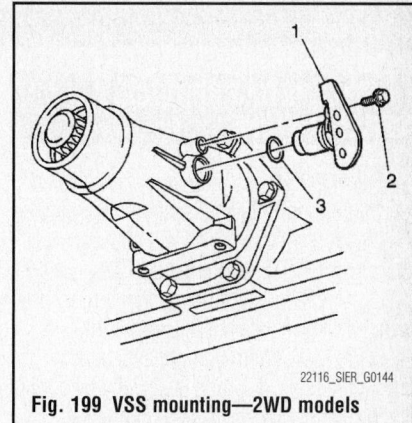

Fig. 199 VSS mounting—2WD models

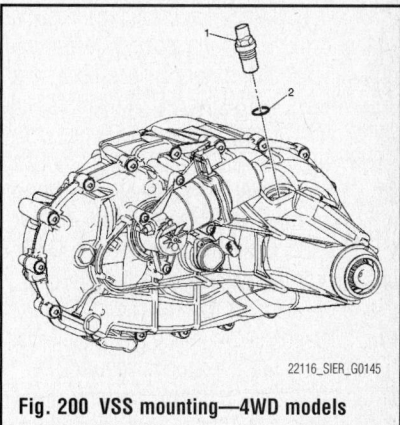

Fig. 200 VSS mounting—4WD models

4. Remove the O–ring seal.
5. Installation is the reverse of removal. Coat a new O–ring with transmission fluid. Tighten the bolt to 97 inch lbs. (11 Nm) on 2WD models or the sensor to 13 ft. lbs. (17 Nm) on 4WD models.

TESTING

1. Remove the VSS.
2. Connect a digital multimeter set to the 0 to 1 AC volt scale to the terminals.
3. Pass a flat steel object across the tip of the sensor repeatedly.
4. The digital multimeter should indicate voltage each time the steel object passes the tip of the sensor. If not, replace the sensor.

FUEL GASOLINE FUEL INJECTION SYSTEM

FUEL SYSTEM SERVICE PRECAUTIONS

Safety is the most important factor when performing not only fuel system maintenance but any type of maintenance. Failure to conduct maintenance and repairs in a safe manner may result in serious personal injury or death. Maintenance and testing of the vehicle's fuel system components can be accomplished safely and effectively by adhering to the following rules and guidelines.

• To avoid the possibility of fire and personal injury, always disconnect the negative battery cable unless the repair or test procedure requires that battery voltage be applied.

• Always relieve the fuel system pressure prior to disconnecting any fuel system component (injector, fuel rail, pressure regulator, etc.), fitting or fuel line connection. Exercise extreme caution whenever relieving fuel system pressure to avoid exposing skin, face and eyes to fuel spray. Please be advised that fuel under pressure may penetrate the skin or any part of the body that it contacts.

• Always place a shop towel or cloth around the fitting or connection prior to loosening to absorb any excess fuel due to spillage. Ensure that all fuel spillage (should it occur) is quickly removed from engine surfaces. Ensure that all fuel soaked cloths or towels are deposited into a suitable waste container.

• Always keep a dry chemical (Class B) fire extinguisher near the work area.

• Do not allow fuel spray or fuel vapors to come into contact with a spark or open flame.

• Always use a back-up wrench when loosening and tightening fuel line connection fittings. This will prevent unnecessary stress and torsion to fuel line piping.

• Always replace worn fuel fitting O-rings with new Do not substitute fuel hose or equivalent where fuel pipe is installed.

Before servicing the vehicle, make sure to also refer to the precautions in the beginning of this section as well.

RELIEVING FUEL SYSTEM PRESSURE

A Schrader valve is provided on these fuel systems, in order to conveniently test or release the system pressure. A fuel pressure gauge and adapter will be necessary to connect the gauge to the fitting. Most of the MFI systems utilize a service valve on one end of the fuel rail assembly. The CMFI system covered here uses a valve located on

the inlet pipe fitting, immediately before it enters the CMFI assembly (towards the rear of the engine)

1. Before servicing the vehicle, refer to the precautions in the beginning of this section.
2. Turn the ignition **OFF**.
3. Disconnect the negative battery cable.
4. Loosen the fuel filler cap in order to relieve the fuel tank vapor pressure.
5. Connect a fuel pressure gauge to the fuel pressure valve/fitting.
6. Wrap a shop towel around the fitting while connecting the gauge in order to avoid spillage.
7. Install the bleed hose of the gauge into an approved container.
8. Open the valve on the gauge to bleed the system pressure.

The fuel connections are now safe for servicing. Drain any fuel remaining in the gauge into an approved container.

FUEL FILTER

REMOVAL & INSTALLATION

On gasoline engines, the fuel filter is integral with the fuel pump/sender assembly in the fuel tank. Refer to the Fuel Pump removal procedure.

FUEL INJECTORS

REMOVAL & INSTALLATION

4.3L Engine

See Figures 201 and 202.

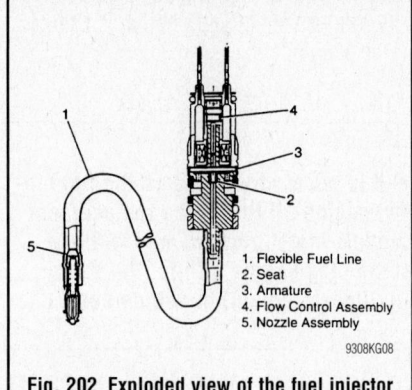

1. Flexible Fuel Line
2. Seat
3. Armature
4. Flow Control Assembly
5. Nozzle Assembly

9308KG08

Fig. 202 Exploded view of the fuel injector assembly–CSFI systems

1. Before servicing the vehicle, refer to the precautions in the beginning of this section.
2. Relieve the fuel system pressure.
3. Remove or disconnect the following:
   • Negative battery cable
   • Electrical connection
   • Fuel feed and return hoses from the engine fuel pipes
   • Upper manifold assembly
   • Poppet nozzle out of the casting socket
   • Fuel meter body by releasing the locktabs

➡**Each injector is calibrated. When replacing the fuel injectors, be sure to replace it with the correct injector.**

   • Lower hold–down plate and nuts
4. While pulling the poppet nozzle tube

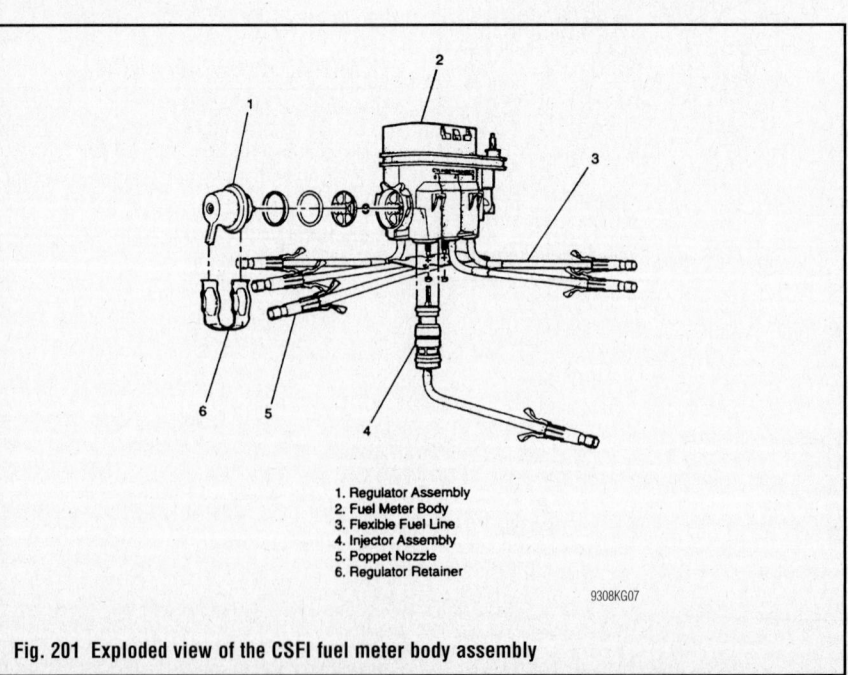

1. Regulator Assembly
2. Fuel Meter Body
3. Flexible Fuel Line
4. Injector Assembly
5. Poppet Nozzle
6. Regulator Retainer

9308KG07

Fig. 201 Exploded view of the CSFI fuel meter body assembly

downward, push with a small prytool down between the injector terminals and remove the injectors.

To install:

5. Lubricate the new injector O–ring seats with engine oil.

6. Install or connect the following:
- O–rings on the injector
- Fuel injector into the fuel meter body injector socket
- Lower hold–down plate and nuts. Torque the nuts to 27 inch lbs. (3 Nm).
- Fuel meter body assembly into the intake manifold. Torque the fuel meter bracket retainer bolts to 88 inch. lbs. (10 Nm).

✳✳ CAUTION

To reduce the risk of fire or injury ensure that the poppet nozzles are properly seated and locked in their casting sockets

- Fuel meter body into the bracket and lock all the tabs in place
- Poppet nozzles into the casting sockets
- Electrical connections
- New O–ring seals on the fuel return and feed hoses
- Fuel feed and return hoses. Torque the fuel pipe nuts to 22 ft. lbs. (30 Nm).
- Negative battery cable

7. Turn the ignition **ON** for 2 seconds and then turn it **OFF** for 10 seconds. Again turn the ignition **ON** and check for leaks.
- Manifold plenum

4.8L, 5.3L, 6.0L and 6.2L Engines

See Figures 203 and 204.

1. Relieve the fuel system pressure.
2. Remove or disconnect the following:
- Negative battery cable
- Engine sight shield bolts and bracket
- Accelerator control and cruise control cables from the cable bracket and throttle body
- Upper engine wire harness retainer nut
- Evaporative Emission (EVAP) purge valve harness connector

3. Position the upper engine wire harness aside

4. Tag the injector connectors for identification, then pull the top part of the injector connector up. Do not pull the top part of the connector past the top of the white portion.

5. Push the tab on the lower side of the injector connector to release the connect from the injection. Perform these steps on each injector connector.

6. Remove or disconnect the following:
- Fuel feed and return pipes from the fuel rail
- Fuel pressure regulator vacuum line
- Crossover tube–to–right fuel rail retainer screw
- Fuel rail attaching bolts and fuel rail

➡**Use care in removing the fuel injectors in order to prevent damage to the electrical connector pins on the injector and to prevent damage to the nozzle. Service the fuel injector as a complete assembly only. The fuel injector is an electrical component. DO NOT immerse the fuel injector in any type of cleaner.**

- Injector retainer clip. Insert the fork of a fuel injector assembly removal tool behind the injector connector between the fuel rail pod and the 3 protruding retaining clip ledges. Use a prying motion while inserting the tool in order to force the injector out of the fuel rail pod.
- Injector retainer clip
- Injector O–ring seals from both ends of the injector. Discard the O–ring seals.

To install:

➡**When ordering new fuel injectors, be sure to order the correct injector for the**

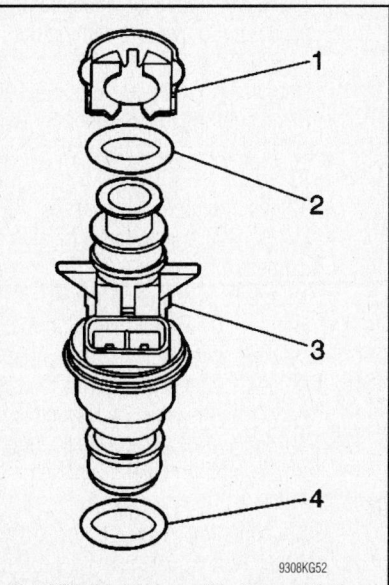

Fig. 203 Fuel injector (3), O-rings (2,4) and retaining clip (1)—4.8L, 5.3L, 6.0L and 6.2L engines

9308KG52

application being serviced. The fuel injector assembly is stamped with a part number identification.

7. Lubricate the new injector O–ring seals with clean engine oil.

8. Install or connect the following:
- New injector O–ring seals on the injector
- New retainer clip on the injector

9. Push the fuel injector into the fuel rail injector socket with the electrical connector facing outward. The retainer clip locks on to a flange on the fuel rail injector socket.

10. Remove the crossover tube–to–right fuel rail retainer, then remove the crossover tube.

11. Replace the crossover tube O–ring with a new, lubricated one.

12. Install or connect the following:
- Crossover tube and loosely install the retainer
- Fuel rail to the intake manifold
- Apply a 0.020 in. (5mm) band of threadlock to the fuel rail retaining bolts
- Fuel rail bolts and tighten to 89 inch lbs. (10 Nm)
- Crossover pipe retainer and tighten to 34 inch lbs. (3.8 Nm)
- Fuel pressure regulator vacuum line
- Fuel feed and return pipes
- Fuel injector electrical connectors, as tagged. Rotate the injectors as necessary to avoid stretching the wire harness.
- Upper engine wire harness
- EVAP purge solenoid electrical connector
- Upper engine wire harness retainer nut and tighten to 49 inch lbs. (5.5 Nm)

Fig. 204 Fuel rail assembly—4.8L, 5.3L, 6.0L and 6.2L engines

9308KG51

- Accelerator control and cruise control cables
- Engine sight shield mounting bracket and bolts

13. Tighten the fuel cap.
14. Connect the negative battery cable.
15. Turn the ignition **ON** for 2 seconds.
16. Turn the ignition **OFF** for 10 seconds.
17. Turn the ignition **ON**.
18. Inspect for fuel leaks.
19. Install the engine sight shield. Tighten the engine sight shield bolts to 89 inch lbs. (10 Nm).

8.1L Engine

1. Relieve the fuel system pressure.
2. Remove or disconnect the following:
- Negative battery cable
- Engine sight shield nuts and bracket
- Alternator harness connector
- Evaporative Emission (EVAP) purge valve harness connector
- Throttle Position (TP) sensor electrical connector
- Electronic Throttle Control (ETC) electrical connector
- Upper engine wire harness bracket studs, and position the harness aside

3. Tag the injector connectors for identification, then pull the top part of the injector connector up. Do not pull the top part of the connector past the top of the white portion.
4. Push the tab on the lower side of the injector connector to release the connect from the injector. Perform these steps on each injector connector.
5. Remove or disconnect the following:
- Fuel feed and return pipes from the fuel rail
- Fuel pressure regulator vacuum line
- Fuel rail attaching bolts and fuel rail

➡Use care in removing the fuel injectors in order to prevent damage to the electrical connector pins on the injector and to prevent damage to the nozzle. Service the fuel injector as a complete assembly only. The fuel injector is an electrical component. DO NOT immerse the fuel injector in any type of cleaner.

- Injector retainer clip. Insert the fork of a fuel injector assembly removal tool behind the injector connector between the fuel rail pod and the 3

protruding retaining clip ledges. Use a prying motion while inserting the tool in order to force the injector out of the fuel rail pod.
- Injector retainer clip
- Injector from the fuel rail pod
- Injector O–ring seals from both ends of the injector. Discard the O–ring seals.

To install:

➡When ordering new fuel injectors, be sure to order the correct injector for the application being serviced. The fuel injector assembly is stamped with a part number identification.

6. Lubricate the new injector O–ring seals with clean engine oil.
7. Install or connect the following:
- New injector O–ring seals on the injector
- New retainer clip on the injector

8. Push the fuel injector into the fuel rail injector socket with the electrical connector facing outward. The retainer clip locks on to a flange on the fuel rail injector socket.
9. Install or connect the following:
- Fuel rail to the intake manifold
- Apply a 0.020 (5mm) band of threadlock to the fuel rail retaining bolts
- Fuel rail bolts and tighten to 106 inch lbs. (12 Nm)
- Fuel pressure regulator vacuum line
- Fuel feed and return pipes
- Fuel injector electrical connectors, as tagged. Rotate the injectors as necessary to avoid stretching the wire harness
- Upper engine wire harness bracket
- Retainer studs to the upper engine wire harness and tighten the nut to 89 inch lbs. (10 Nm)
- Alternator electrical connector
- EVAP purge solenoid electrical connector
- TP and ETC sensor connectors
- Engine sight shield mounting bracket and bolts

10. Tighten the fuel cap.
11. Connect the negative battery cable.
12. Turn the ignition **ON** for 2 seconds.
13. Turn the ignition **OFF** for 10 seconds.
14. Turn the ignition **ON**.
15. Inspect for fuel leaks.
16. Install the engine sight shield. Tighten the engine sight shield bolts to 89 inch lbs. (10 Nm).

FUEL PUMP

REMOVAL & INSTALLATION

See Figure 205.

1. Before servicing the vehicle, refer to the precautions in the beginning of this section.
2. Remove or disconnect the following:
- Negative battery cable
3. Relieve the fuel system pressure.
4. Drain the fuel tank.
5. Remove or disconnect the following:
- Fuel tank

✳✳ WARNING

Do not handle the fuel sender assembly by the fuel pipes. The amount of leverage generated by handling the fuel pipes could damage the joints.

- Fuel sender assembly retaining ring using a fuel tank sending unit wrench. Remove the fuel sender assembly and the seal. Discard the seal.

6. Note the position of the fuel strainer on the fuel sender. Support the fuel sender assembly with one hand and grasp the strainer with the other hand. Pull the strainer off the fuel sender. Discard the strainer after inspection. Inspect the strainer. Replace a contaminated strainer and clean the fuel tank.
- Fuel pump electrical connector
- Electrical connector retaining clip from the fuel level sensor
- Sensor electrical connector from under the fuel sender cover
- Fuel level sensor retaining clip

7. Squeeze the locking tangs and remove the fuel level sensor.
8. Remove the fuel pressure sensor.

To install:

9. Install or connect the following:

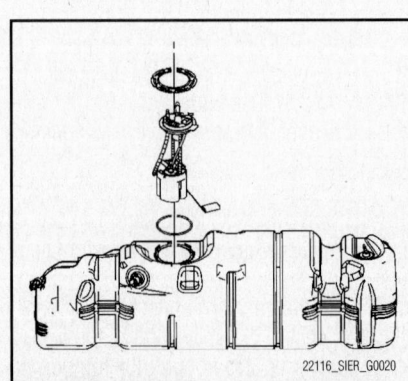

22116_SIER_G0020

Fig. 205 Exploded view of the fuel pump assembly mounting

- Fuel pressure sensor
- Fuel level sensor
- Sensor retaining clip
- Electrical connector to the fuel level sensor
- Electrical connector retaining clip to the fuel level sensor
- Fuel pump electrical connector

➡**Always install a new fuel strainer when replacing the fuel tank fuel pump module.**

- New fuel strainer in the same position as noted during disassembly. Push the strainer on the bottom of the fuel sender until the strainer is fully seated.
- New seal on the fuel tank

➡**The fuel pump strainer must be in a horizontal position when the fuel sender is installed in the tank. When installing the fuel sender assembly, assure that the fuel pump strainer does not block full travel of the float arm.**

- Fuel sender assembly into the fuel tank
- Fuel sender assembly retaining ring
- Fuel tank. Install the fuel tank strap attaching bolts. Tighten the bolts to 30 ft. lbs. (40 Nm).

10. Refill the fuel tank. Install the fuel filler cap. Connect the negative battery cable.
11. Turn the ignition **ON** for 2 seconds.
12. Turn the ignition **OFF** for 10 seconds.
13. Turn the ignition **ON**.
14. Inspect for fuel leaks.

FUEL TANK

REMOVAL & INSTALLATION

See Figure 206.

✷✷ CAUTION

Before servicing any electrical component, the ignition key must be in the OFF or LOCK position and all electrical loads must be OFF, unless instructed otherwise in these procedures. If a tool or equipment could easily come in contact with a live exposed electrical terminal, also disconnect the negative battery cable. Failure to follow these precautions may cause personal injury and/or damage to the vehicle or its components.

1. Disconnect the negative battery cable.

➡**Clean the fuel and EVAP connections before disconnecting them to prevent fuel system contamination. Cap the lines to prevent leakage and contamination.**

2. Relieve the fuel system pressure.
3. Drain the fuel tank.
4. Remove the fuel filler pipe and remove the tank shield, if equipped.
5. Label and disconnect the EVAP lines and electrical connection from the fuel tank assembly.
6. Disconnect the fuel line from the tank.
7. Support the fuel tank using a suitable jack. Remove the strap bolts and the straps.
8. Lower the tank halfway. Be sure the fill neck does not get hung up on the chassis harness. Detach the harness clip from the crossmember.
9. Lower the tank enough so that the electrical connections are accessible. Detach the connections then fully lower the tank and remove it from under the vehicle.

To install:

10. Installation is the reverse of removal. When installing the tank, be sure to inspect all lines, hoses and electrical connections first. Repair or replace as necessary. Tighten the strap bolts to 30 ft. lbs. (40 Nm).
11. To check for leaks, refill the tank then turn the ignition ON (engine OFF) for 2 seconds. Turn the ignition OFF for 10 seconds. Turn the ignition ON again (engine OFF) and inspect the tank and lines for leaks.

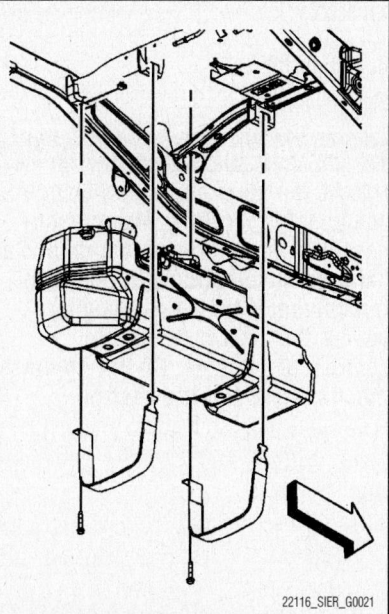

22116_SIER_G0021

Fig. 206 Exploded view of the fuel tank assembly mounting

IDLE SPEED

ADJUSTMENT

Idle speed is maintained by the Powertrain Control Module (PCM). No adjustment is necessary or possible.

THROTTLE BODY

REMOVAL & INSTALLATION

4.3L Engine

See Figure 207.

1. Disconnect the negative battery cable.
2. Remove the engine cover.
3. Remove the air cleaner outlet resonator.
4. Remove the air cleaner outlet resonator adapter stud.
5. Remove the cruise control cable.
6. Remove the stud and nuts retaining the accelerator control cable bracket and position bracket aside.
7. Disconnect the Idle air Control (IAC) valve harness connector.
8. Disconnect the Throttle Position (TP) sensor harness connector.
9. Remove the throttle body retaining studs.
10. Remove the throttle body assembly.
11. Discard the throttle body seal.

To install:

✷✷ CAUTION

Wear safety glasses in order to avoid eye damage.

12. Clean the gasket surface on the intake manifold.
13. Install the throttle body assembly with a new seal.

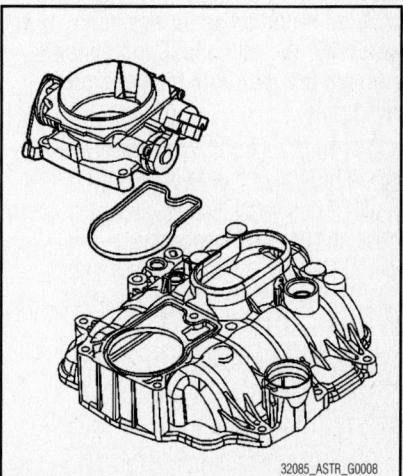

32085_ASTR_G0008

Fig. 207 Exploded view of throttle body, gasket and intake manifold—4.3L engines

14. Install the throttle body assembly retaining studs.

   a. Tighten the studs to 80 inch lbs. (9 Nm).

15. Install the air cleaner outlet resonator adapter stud.

   a. Tighten the studs to 71 inch lbs. (8 Nm).

16. Connect the TP sensor harness connector.

17. Connect the IAC valve harness connector.

18. Install the accelerator control cable bracket using the fasteners.

   a. Tighten the fasteners to 106 inch lbs. (12 Nm).

❈❈ WARNING

Ensure the accelerator and the cruise control cables do not hold the throttle open.

19. Install the accelerator cable.
20. Install the cruise control cable.
21. Install the air cleaner outlet resonator.
22. Install the engine cover.
23. Connect the negative battery cable.

❈❈ WARNING

The accelerator pedal should operate freely without binding between full and closed throttle.

24. Use the following procedure in order to check the accelerator pedal operation.

   a. Depress the pedal to the floor.

   b. Release the accelerator pedal.

4.8L, 5.3L, 6.0L and 6.2L Engines
See Figure 208.

➡ **The intake manifold, throttle body, fuel injection rail, and fuel injectors may be removed as an assembly. If not servicing the individual components, remove the manifold as a complete assembly.**

1. Remove the electrical wire harness connectors from the throttle body.

2. Remove the engine coolant air bleed hose and clamp, if applicable.

3. Remove the throttle body nuts.

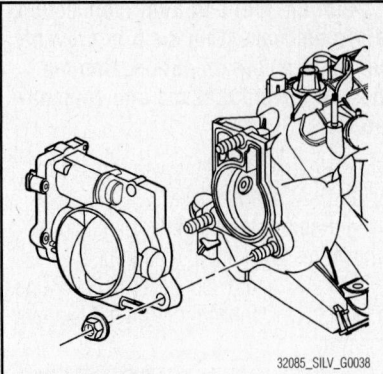
Fig. 208 Throttle body—4.8L, 5.3L, 6.0L and 6.2L engines

32085_SILV_G0038

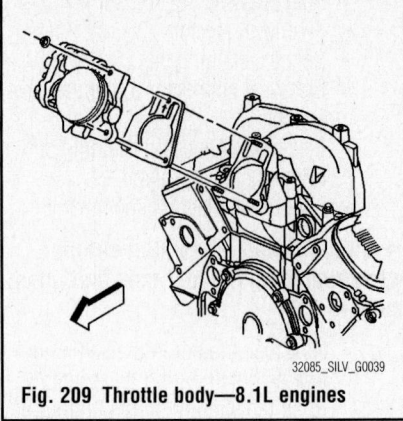
Fig. 209 Throttle body—8.1L engines

32085_SILV_G0039

4. Remove the throttle body.
5. Remove the throttle body gasket.
6. Discard the gasket.
7. Remove the throttle body studs, if required.

To install:

8. Install the throttle body studs, if required.

   a. Tighten the throttle body studs to 53 inch lbs. (6 Nm).

➡ **DO NOT use the throttle body gasket again. Install a NEW gasket during assembly.**

9. Install the new throttle body gasket to the intake manifold.

10. Install the throttle body and nuts.

   a. Tighten the throttle body nuts to 89 inch lbs. (10 Nm).

11. Install the engine coolant air bleed hose and clamp to the throttle body, if applicable.

8.1L Engine
See Figure 209.

❈❈ WARNING

Handle the electronic throttle control components carefully. Use cleanliness in order to prevent damage. Do not drop the electronic throttle control components. Do not roughly handle the electronic throttle control components. Do not immerse the electronic throttle control

components in cleaning solvents of any type.

➡ **An 8 digit part identification number is stamped on the throttle body casting. Refer to this number if servicing, or part replacement is required.**

1. Remove the intake air resonator.

2. Disconnect the throttle actuator motor electrical connector.

➡ **Cover or plug any openings when servicing the throttle body in order to prevent possible contamination.**

3. Remove the throttle body nuts.
4. Remove the throttle body.
5. Remove and discard the throttle body gasket.

To install:

6. Install a NEW throttle body gasket.

7. Install the throttle body.

8. Install the throttle body nuts.

   a. Tighten the nuts to 89 inch lbs. (10 Nm).

9. Connect the throttle actuator motor electrical connector.

10. Install the intake air resonator.

11. Connect a scan tool in order to test for proper throttle—opening and throttle—closing range.

12. Operate the accelerator pedal and monitor the throttle angles. The accelerator pedal should operate freely, without binding, between a closed throttle, and a wide open throttle (WOT).

FUEL | **DIESEL FUEL INJECTION SYSTEM**

FUEL SYSTEM SERVICE PRECAUTIONS

Safety is the most important factor when performing not only fuel system maintenance but any type of maintenance. Failure to conduct maintenance and repairs in a safe manner may result in serious personal injury or death. Maintenance and testing of the vehicle's fuel system components can be accomplished safely and effectively by adhering to the following rules and guidelines.

• To avoid the possibility of fire and personal injury, always disconnect the negative battery cable unless the repair or test procedure requires that battery voltage be applied.

• Always relieve the fuel system pressure prior to disconnecting any fuel system component (injector, fuel rail, pressure regulator, etc.), fitting or fuel line connection. Exercise extreme caution whenever relieving fuel system pressure to avoid exposing skin, face and eyes to fuel spray. Please be advised that fuel under pressure may penetrate the skin or any part of the body that it contacts.

• Always place a shop towel or cloth around the fitting or connection prior to loosening to absorb any excess fuel due to spillage. Ensure that all fuel spillage (should it occur) is quickly removed from engine surfaces. Ensure that all fuel soaked cloths or towels are deposited into a suitable waste container.

• Always keep a dry chemical (Class B) fire extinguisher near the work area.

• Do not allow fuel spray or fuel vapors to come into contact with a spark or open flame.

• Always use a back-up wrench when loosening and tightening fuel line connection fittings. This will prevent unnecessary stress and torsion to fuel line piping.

• Always replace worn fuel fitting O-rings with new. Do not substitute fuel hose or equivalent where fuel pipe is installed.

Before servicing the vehicle, make sure to also refer to the precautions in the beginning of this section as well.

RELIEVING FUEL SYSTEM PRESSURE

Fuel system pressure can be released by wrapping a fuel fitting in a heavy shop towel and slightly loosening the fitting. NEVER perform this with any source of ignition nearby!

FUEL FILTER

REMOVAL & INSTALLATION
See Figure 210.

1. Disconnect the negative battery cables.
2. If necessary, remove the wheelhouse liner for additional access.
3. Drain the fuel from the fuel filter as follows:
   a. Install a hose on the water drain on the water–in–fuel sensor.
   b. Place the other end of the hose into an approved container.
   c. Drain as much fuel as possible from the fuel filter housing.
   d. Tighten the water drain on the water–in–fuel sensor.
4. Remove or disconnect the following:
   • Water–in–fuel sensor harness connector
   • Fuel filter from the fuel filter/heater element housing
   • Water–in–fuel sensor from the fuel filter

To install:
5. Install or connect the following:
   • Water–in–fuel sensor in the fuel filter

➡**Check the fuel filter/heater element housing and the filter for a dislocated** filter seal or foreign debris. Contamination on the filter/heater housing may cause leakage at the fuel filter. Coat the seal with clean engine oil.

   • Fuel filter on the fuel filter/heater element housing
   • Water–in–fuel harness connector
   • Negative battery cables
6. Prime the fuel system:
   a. Pump the primer located on top of the fuel filter 30 times or until stiff.
   b. Try to start and run the engine. If the engine does not start, repeat the previous step.
   c. Allow the engine to run for 5 minutes at idle.
   d. Check for fuel leaks and clear all Diagnostic Trouble Codes (DTCs).

DRAINING WATER FROM THE SYSTEM
See Figures 211 through 213.

1. Attach a small piece of hose to the drain cock onto the water–in–fuel sensor.
2. Place an approved fuel–resistant container under the fuel filter.
3. Open the drain cock 3 or 4 turns or until the water contaminated fuel seeps from the drain cock.
4. Operate the priming pump until only diesel fuel is visible. Allow the pump to return upward between pushes.
5. Tighten the drain cock.
6. Remove the container and hose.

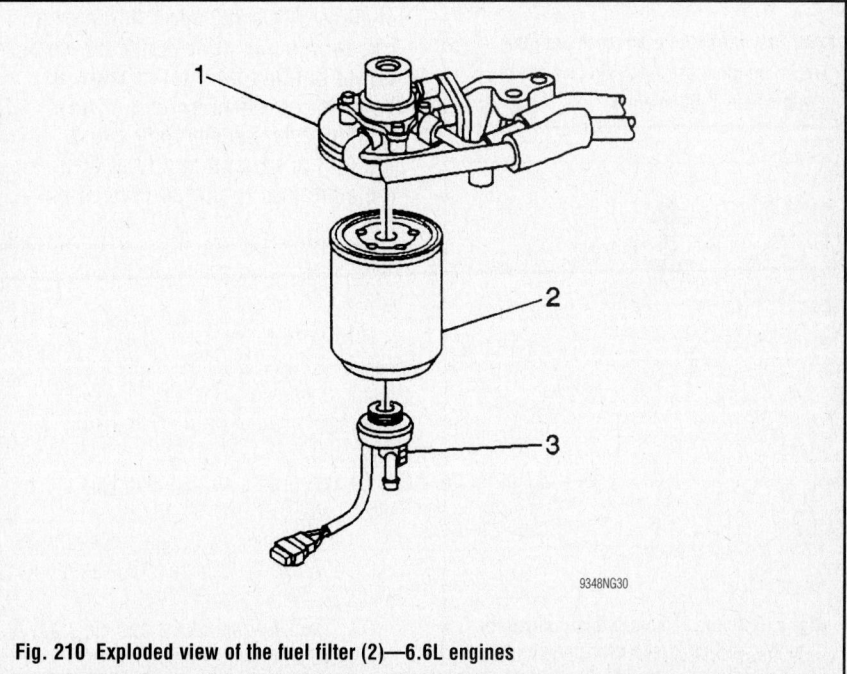

9348NG30

Fig. 210 Exploded view of the fuel filter (2)—6.6L engines

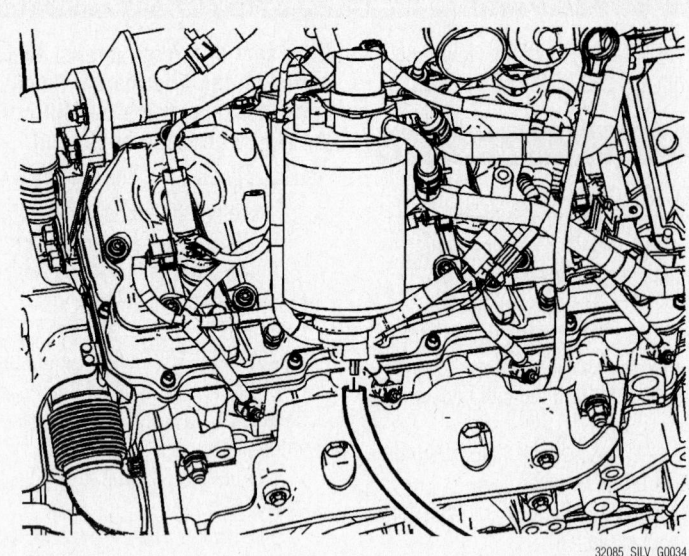

32085_SILV_G0034

Fig. 211 Attach a hose to the drain cock onto the water–in–fuel sensor—6.6L engines

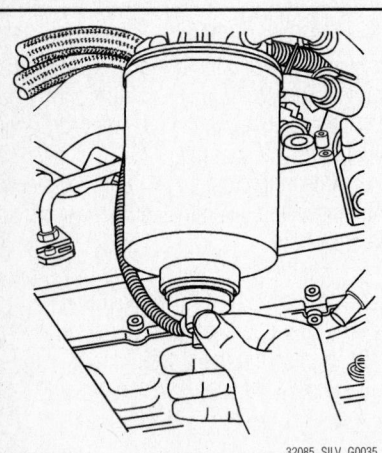

32085_SILV_G0035

Fig. 212 Open the drain cock until the water contaminated fuel seeps from the drain cock—6.6L engines

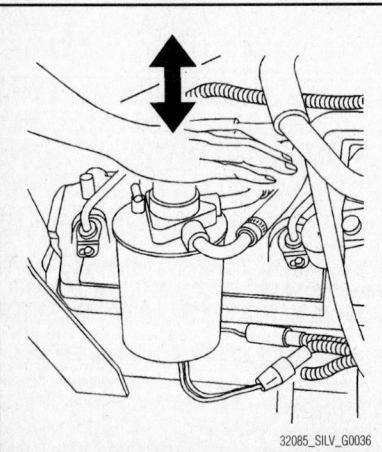

32085_SILV_G0036

Fig. 213 Operate the priming pump until only diesel fuel is visible—6.6L engines

FUEL SYSTEM PURGING

BLEEDING

1. Open the air bleed valve on the fuel manager/filter.
2. Connect a hose to the air bleed valve and place the other of the hose in a suitable container.

✳✳ CAUTION

The Diesel/water mixture is flammable and may be hot. To avoid personal injury or property damage, do not allow the Diesel/water mixture to come in contact with skin, open flame or a hot engine. Do not overfill the container holding the fuel mixture as heat from a warm engine or any another heat source may cause the fuel to expand and leak from the container that may lead to a fire.

3. Remove the F/SOL fuse from the fuse panel.
4. Crank the engine in short intervals of 10–to–15 seconds until clear fuel is observed at the air bleed hose (wait for 1 minute between cranking intervals).
5. Remove the hose and close the air bleed valve.
6. Install the F/SOL fuse and start the vehicle. Allow the vehicle to run at idle for 5 minutes.
7. Check for fuel leaks, and clear any Diagnostic Trouble Codes (DTCs).

INJECTION TIMING

ADJUSTMENT

On diesel engines the idle speed and injection timing is controlled by the Powertrain Control Module (PCM). There is no provision for adjustment.

INJECTION LINES

REMOVAL & INSTALLATION

See Figures 214 through 220.

1. Remove the fuel feed pipe attaching nuts and bolts.
2. Remove the fuel feed pipe.
3. Disconnect the fuel rail balance pipe from fuel rails.
4. Remove the fuel rail balance pipe bolts.
5. Remove the fuel rail balance pipe.
6. Remove the left fuel return hose.
7. Remove the right fuel return hose.
8. Disconnect the fuel hoses from the fuel injector pump.
9. Remove the distribution block and fuel line assembly bolts.
10. Remove the distribution block and fuel line assembly.
11. Remove the fuel pipe assembly bracket bolts.
12. Remove the fuel pipe assembly bracket.
13. Remove the coolant pipe bolt and nut.
14. Remove the coolant pipe.
15. Remove the left fuel rail to pump pipe.
16. Remove the EGR mounting bracket bolts.
17. Remove the EGR mounting brackets.
18. Using compressed air to blow away any debris between the fuel injector line and the fittings. Wipe clean the fittings of debris.

✳✳ WARNING

DO NOT use compressed air to clean debris from the fuel injector inlet after the fuel line is removed. Using compressed air can allow debris to enter the fuel injector inlet and damage the fuel injector.

19. Spray lithium grease, GM P/N 12346293 or equivalent, between the fuel injector line and fitting to contain any debris during removal.
20. Remove the left fuel injector pipes.
21. Remove the right fuel injector pipes.
22. Remove the left fuel rail and bracket bolts.
23. Remove the left fuel rail and bracket.

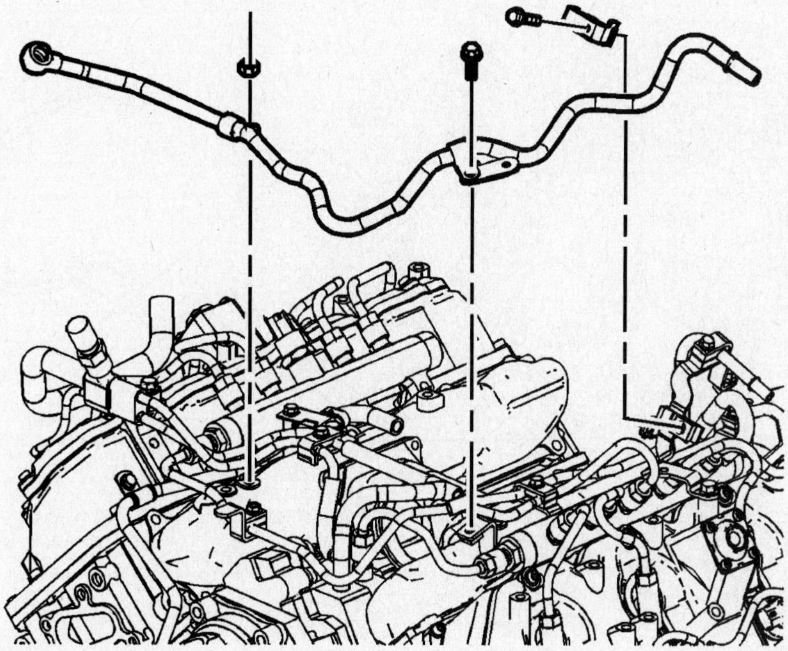

32085_SILV_G0042

Fig. 214 Remove the fuel feed pipe

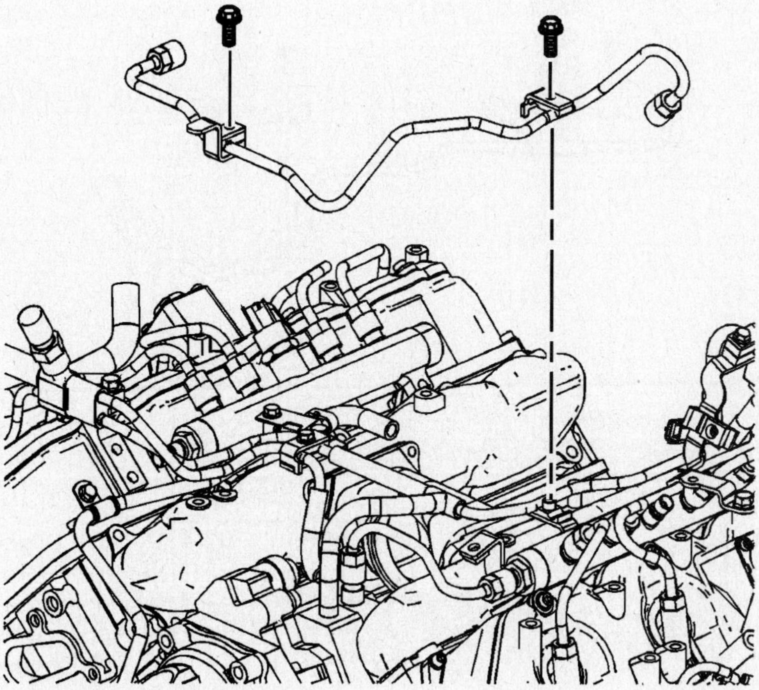

32085_SILV_G0043

Fig. 215 Remove the fuel rail balance pipe

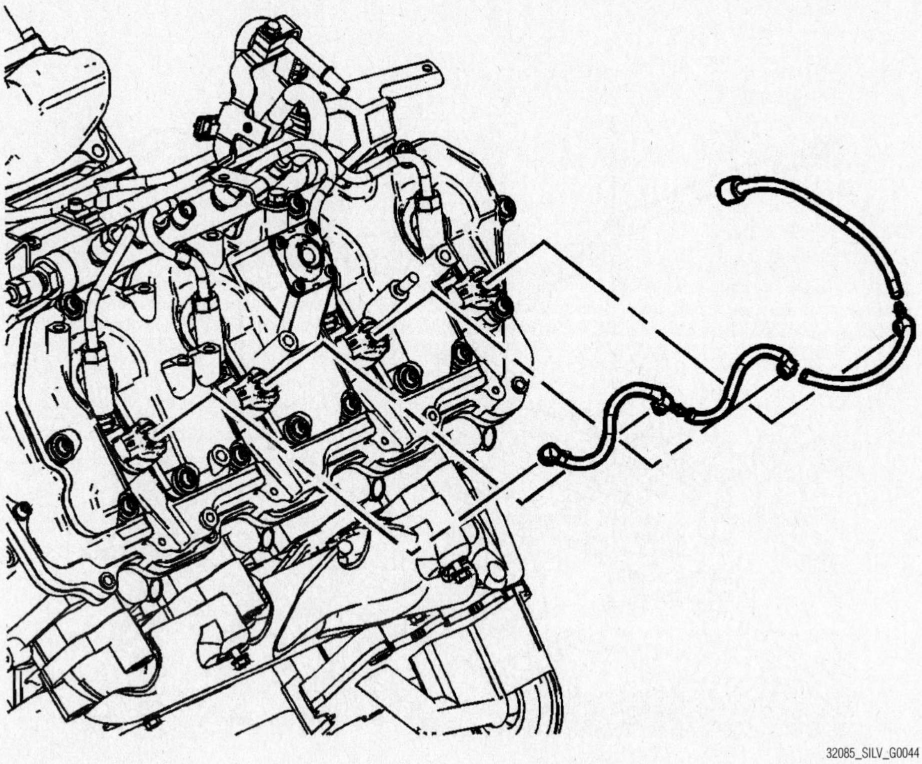

32085_SILV_G0044

Fig. 216 Fuel return hose—left side shown

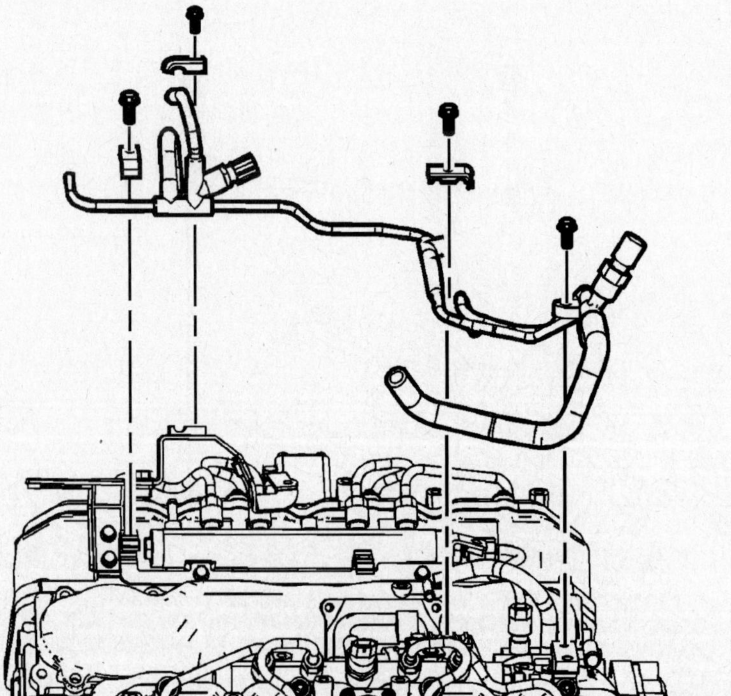

32085_SILV_G0045

Fig. 217 Remove the distribution block and fuel line assembly

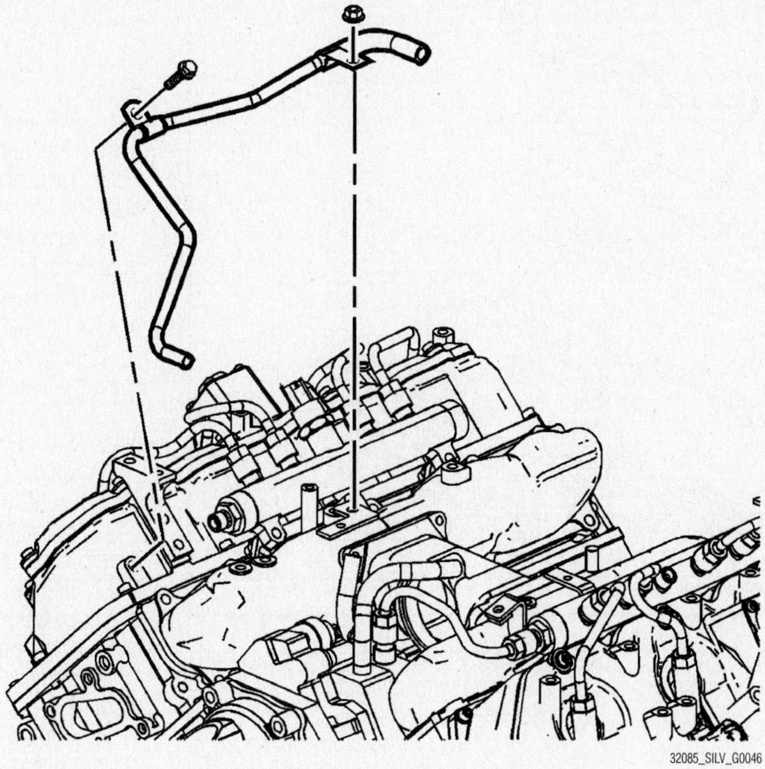

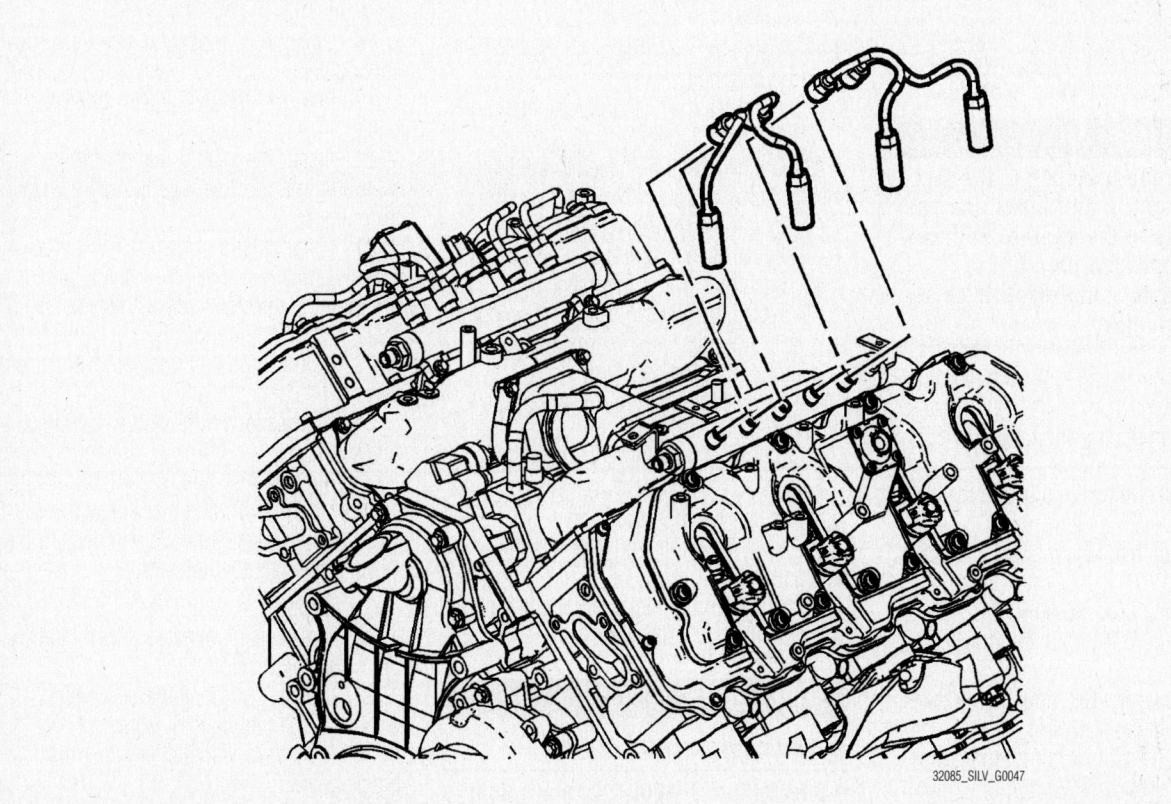

32085_SILV_G0046

Fig. 218 Remove the coolant pipe

32085_SILV_G0047

Fig. 219 Fuel injector pipes—left side shown

Fig. 220 Fuel rail and bracket—left side shown

24. Remove the right fuel rail bolts.
25. Remove the right fuel rail.

To install:

26. Install the right fuel rail.
27. Install the right fuel rail mounting bolts.
28. Tighten the right fuel rail mounting bolts to 18 ft. lbs. (25 Nm).
29. Install the left fuel rail.
30. Install the left fuel rail mounting bolts.
31. Tighten the left fuel rail mounting bolts to 18 ft. lbs. (25 Nm).

✳✳ CAUTION

Improper torque methods of the fuel lines will result in fuel leaks and possible damage to the engine. Failure to follow proper fuel line fitting torque methods could result in serious personal injury.

32. Install the injection pipes to the right bank.
    a. Tighten the injection pipes to 30 ft. lbs. (41 Nm)
33. Install the injection pipes to the left bank.
    a. Tighten the injection pipes to 30 ft. lbs. (41 Nm)
34. Install the EGR mounting brackets.
35. Install the EGR mounting bracket bolts.
    a. Tighten the EGR mounting bracket bolts to 15 ft. lbs. (20 Nm).
36. Install the left fuel rail to pump pipe.
    a. Tighten the fuel rail to pump pipe nut to 30 ft. lbs. (41 Nm).
37. Install the coolant pipe.

38. Install the coolant pipe bolt and nut.
    a. Tighten the coolant pipe bolt and nut to 18 ft. lbs. (25 Nm).
39. Install the fuel pipe assembly bracket.
40. Install the fuel pipe assembly bracket bolts.
    a. Tighten the fuel pipe assembly bracket bolts to 18 ft. lbs. (25 Nm).
41. Install the distribution block and fuel line assembly.
42. Install the distribution block and fuel line assembly bolts.
    a. Tighten the fuel line assembly bolts to 18 ft. lbs. (25 Nm).
43. Connect the fuel hoses to the fuel injector pump.
44. Install the right fuel return hose.
45. Install the left fuel return hose.
46. Install the fuel rail balance pipe.
47. Install the fuel rail balance pipe bolts.
    a. Tighten the fuel rail balance pipe bolts to 15 ft. lbs. (21 Nm).
48. Connect the fuel rail balance pipe to the fuel rails.
    a. Tighten the fuel rail balance pipe nuts to 30 ft. lbs. (41 Nm).
49. Install the fuel feed pipe.
50. Install the fuel feed pipe attaching nuts and bolts.
    a. Tighten the fuel feed pipe bolts and nut to 18 ft. lbs. (25 Nm).

INJECTORS

REMOVAL & INSTALLATION

➡**Special tool J–46594, or equivalent, an injector removal tool, will be necessary for this procedure.**

1. Drain the cooling system.
2. Disconnect the negative battery cable.
3. On the left side, remove the charged air cooler inlet duct connector from the turbocharger.
4. Remove the main engine electrical harness connectors.
5. Disconnect the barometric sensor electrical connector.
6. Remove the engine wire harness from the clip.
7. Remove the main electrical harness bracket bolts and bracket.
8. Disconnect the glow plug controller electrical connector.
9. Remove the positive crankcase ventilation (PCV) hose/pipe.
10. On the right side, remove the air cleaner outlet duct.
11. Loosen the charged air cooler outlet duct to intake hose clamp.
12. Remove the charged air cooler outlet duct from the intake.
13. Remove the fuel filter and bracket.
14. Remove the fuel injection control module.
15. Prior to removing the fuel injector pipes, use compressed air to blow any debris from between the injector line and fittings. Wipe the fittings clean of debris.
16. Remove the fuel injector pipes.
17. Remove the fuel return hose from the injectors.
18. Disconnect the fuel injector electrical connectors.
19. Remove the fuel injector bracket bolts.
20. Install the injector removal tool J–46594 into the bolt hole in the fuel injector bracket.
21. Install a flare nut wrench onto the tool and pull back away from the fuel injector, until the injector releases from its seat.
22. Remove the tool.
23. Remove the fuel injectors with brackets.
24. If necessary, remove the fuel injector bracket pins.
25. If necessary, remove and discard the copper washer from the fuel injector bore.
26. If necessary, remove and discard the O–ring from the fuel injector.

To install:

27. If necessary, install a new O–ring onto the fuel injector.
28. If necessary, install a new copper washer to the fuel injector bore.
29. If necessary, install the fuel injector bracket pins.
30. Install the fuel injectors with brackets.

31. Install the fuel injector bracket bolts and tighten to 22 ft. lbs. (30 Nm).

32. Connect the fuel injector electrical connectors.

33. Install the fuel return hose to the injectors.

34. Install the fuel return hose clips.

35. Install the fuel injector pipes and tighten to 30 ft. lbs. (40 Nm).

36. On the left side, install the positive crankcase ventilation (PCV) hose/pipe.

37. Connect the glow plug controller electrical connector.

38. Install the main electrical harness bracket bolts and bracket.

39. Install the engine wire harness to the clip.

40. Connect the barometric sensor electrical connector.

41. Install the main engine electrical harness connectors.

42. Install the charged air cooler inlet duct connector to the turbocharger.

43. On the right side, install the fuel injection control module.

44. Install the fuel filter and bracket.

45. Install the charged air cooler outlet duct to the intake.

46. Tighten the charged air cooler outlet duct to intake hose clamp.

47. Install the air cleaner outlet duct.

48. Connect the negative battery cable.

49. Refill the cooling system.

FUEL SUPPLY PUMP

REMOVAL & INSTALLATION

See Figure 221.

1. Disconnect the negative battery cable.

➡ **Clean the fuel connections before disconnecting them to prevent fuel system contamination. Cap the lines to prevent leakage and contamination.**

2. Relieve the fuel system pressure and open the fuel filler cap.

3. Raise and safely support the vehicle.

4. Detach the electrical connector from the pump.

5. Disconnect the fuel lines from the pump, then slide the pump out of its bracket.

To install:

6. Install the pump using new O-rings. Tighten the fittings to 22 ft. lbs. (30 Nm).

7. Engage the electrical connection and install the fuel filler cap.

8. Purge the fuel system of air. Start the vehicle and check for leaks.

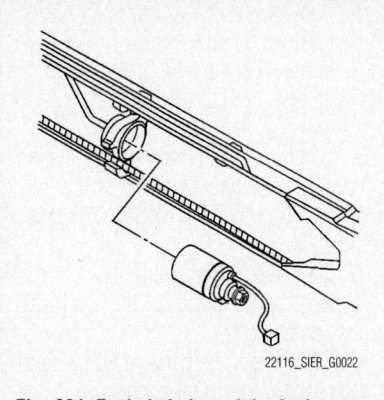

Fig. 221 Exploded view of the fuel pump assembly mounting—6.6L engines

INJECTION PUMP

REMOVAL & INSTALLATION

See Figure 222.

1. Drain the cooling system

2. Remove or disconnect the following:
   - Negative battery cables
   - Air intake duct. Cover the end to prevent dirt from entering
   - Intake manifold cover
   - Fuel fill cap in order to relieve the fuel pressure
   - Fuel Injection Control Module (FICM) electrical connectors
   - Fuel injection control module
   - Upper fan shroud
   - Fan blade assembly
   - Drive belt
   - Bolt holding the positive battery cable junction box and bracket and position aside
   - A/C compressor and power steering pump and position aside with the lines attached
   - Oil dipstick tube
   - A/C and power steering pump bracket
   - Drive belt tensioner and bolt.
   - Alternator
   - Thermostat housing bracket, wiring and fuel test port and 2 nuts
   - Positive Crankcase Ventilation (PCV) catch tank from the PCV bracket and the bolt below holding the lower line, then position aside
   - Alternator bracket
   - Turbo cooling hose return line clamp and hose
   - Upper radiator hose at the outlet pipe. Remove the bracket and support the bracket at the valve cover and swing out of the way
   - Bolt holding the wiring support bracket at the thermostat housing

3. Move the main wiring harness by disconnecting the following:
   a. The fuel pressure regulator connector on the fuel injection pump
   b. Fuel injection control module connectors

4. Flip the wire harness and harness tray towards the back and position aside.

5. Remove or disconnect the following:
   - Heater pipe bolt and temperature sensor wire from the thermostat housing
   - Air intake pipe
   - Water crossover assembly
   - Hose from the turbo water feed line

➡ **Cap all open fuel connections to prevent contaminants from entering.**

   - High pressure fuel lines and support pipe and hose at the fuel injection pump and junction block
   - Fuel return hose from the fuel injection pump
   - Y–junction banjo fitting from the junction block
   - Bolts securing the fuel injection pump at the front cover and block

➡ **When removing the pump, be careful not to damage any of the mating surfaces.**

   - Fuel injection pump from the block using 2 pry tools to work the pump from the block toward the rear of the engine, keeping the pump straight.

6. Prepare the fuel pump as follows:
   a. Hold the fuel pump by the drive gear in a vise with copper jaw liners.
   b. Loosen the gear nut until the nut is even with the end of the gear shaft.
   c. Separate the pump and adapter by removing the 3 bolts and spacers.
   d. Inspect the O–ring for damage on the pump adapter and replace if

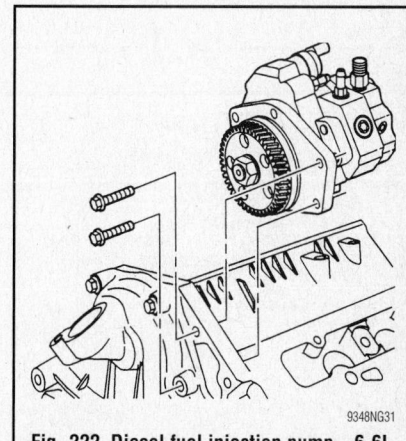

Fig. 222 Diesel fuel injection pump—6.6L engines

necessary. Lubricate the O–ring with clean engine oil.

  e. Clean all mating surfaces.

  f. Install the adapter on the pump

  g. Using the bolts and spacers, reassemble the pump. Tighten the bolts to 15 ft. lbs. (20 Nm).

  h. Install the gear and nut and tighten to 52 ft. lbs. (70 Nm).

To install:

7. Installation is the reverse of removal, noting the following tightening specifications:

- Fuel injection pump mounting bolts: 15 ft. lbs. (20 Nm)
- Y–junction banjo fitting: 11 ft. lbs. (15 Nm)
- High pressure fuel lines: 40 ft. lbs. (54 Nm)
- Heater pipe bracket and water crossover bolts: 15 ft. lbs. (20 Nm)
- Upper radiator hose mounting bolts: 89 inch lbs. (10 Nm)
- A/C and power steering pump bracket bolts: 34 ft. lbs. (46 Nm)

8. Refill the cooling system, then start the engine and check for leaks.

INJECTION TIMING

On the 6.6L engine, the Powertrain Control Module (PCM) controls the fuel injection timing, no further adjustment is possible.

FUEL PRESSURE REGULATOR

REMOVAL & INSTALLATION

See Figures 223 and 224.

1. Remove the air intake pipe.

2. Disconnect the air conditioning (A/C) compressor clutch electrical connector.

3. Disconnect the A/C cut out switch electrical connector.

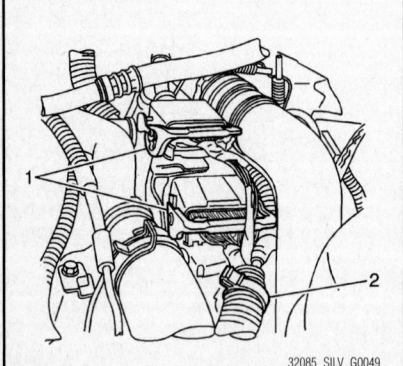

32085_SILV_G0049

Fig. 223 Main engine electrical harness connector

4. Remove the A/C compressor bolts.

5. Remove the alternator.

6. Reposition the A/C compressor (with the hoses attached) to the right side of the engine compartment.

7. Disconnect the main engine electrical harness connectors. Lift up on the latches (1) in order to disconnect the connectors.

8. Open the harness clip (2).

9. Remove the main engine electrical harness connectors.

10. Disconnect the barometric pressure (BARO) sensor electrical connector.

11. Remove the main engine harness electrical connector bolts.

12. Remove the main connectors from the bracket.

13. Disconnect the engine coolant temperature (ECT) sensor electrical connector.

14. Remove the water outlet tube.

15. Disconnect the fuel temperature sensor electrical connector.

16. Disconnect the fuel pressure regulator electrical connector.

17. Disconnect the oil level sensor harness electrical connector.

18. Reposition the distribution block hose clamps.

19. Remove the distribution block hoses from the distribution block.

20. Remove the Exhaust Gas Recirculation (EGR) coolant pipe bolts.

21. Loosen the EGR coolant pipe clamp and position the hose aside.

22. Clean the fuel pressure regulator and high pressure injection pump thoroughly with solvent, such as GM P/N 12377981 (Canadian P/N 10953463) or equivalent.

23. Using compressed air, thoroughly blow dry the regulator and pump.

24. Remove the 3 fuel pressure regulator screws using a T25 TORX®.

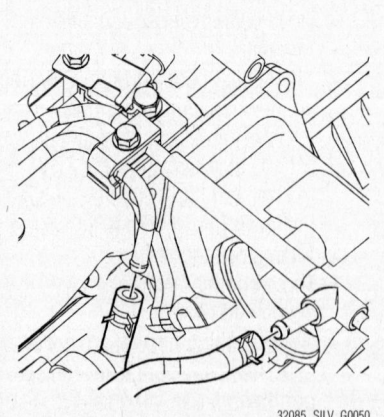

32085_SILV_G0050

Fig. 224 Remove the distribution block hoses from the distribution block

25. Remove the fuel pressure regulator.

26. If dirt or debris is found in the bore or seating surfaces of the fuel injection pump, perform the following:

  a. Place a clean rag over the bore on order to collect the excess fuel

  b. Bump the engine over in order to flush any debris out of the regulator bore

To install:

➡ If the pressure regulator is being re–used, check the O–rings for damage. If the O–rings are damaged, install NEW O–rings.

27. Lubricate and install NEW O–rings onto the regulator. Lubricate the O–rings with clean, NEW engine oil.

❋❋ WARNING

If the regulator is installed at an angle the O–rings may be damaged, resulting in possible fuel leakage.

28. Install the fuel pressure regulator.

29. Install the 3 fuel pressure regulator screws using a T25 TORX®, as follows:

  a. Tighten the screws a first pass to 35 inch lbs. (4 Nm).

  b. Tighten the screws a final pass to 62 inch lbs. (7 Nm).

30. Position the EGR coolant pipe clamp and install the coolant pipe to the thermostat housing.

31. Install the EGR coolant pipe retaining bolts and tighten to 15 ft. lbs. (21 Nm).

32. Install the distribution block hoses to the distribution block.

33. Position the distribution block hose clamps.

34. Connect the oil level sensor harness electrical connector.

35. Connect the fuel pressure regulator electrical connector.

36. Connect the fuel temperature sensor electrical connector.

37. Install the water outlet tube.

38. Connect the ECT sensor electrical connector.

39. Install the main connectors to the bracket.

40. Install the main engine harness electrical connector bolts:

  a. Tighten the bolts to 15 ft. lbs. (21 Nm).

41. Connect the BARO sensor electrical connector.

42. Connect the main engine electrical harness connectors.

43. Push down on the latches (1) in order to connect the connectors.

44. Close the harness clip (2).

45. Position the A/C compressor.

46. Install the A/C compressor bolts. Tighten the bolts to 37 ft. lbs. (50 Nm).

47. Connect the A/C cut out switch electrical connector.

48. Connect the A/C compressor clutch electrical connector.

49. Install the alternator.

50. Install the air intake pipe.

51. Prime the fuel system.

52. Start the engine. If the engine stalls, repeat the above step.

53. Once the engine starts, inspect for fuel leaks.

GLOW PLUGS

REMOVAL & INSTALLATION

1. Remove or disconnect the following:
   - Negative battery cables
   - Front tire
   - Inner splash shield from the fender well
   - Air cleaner outlet duct
   - Electrical nuts from the glow plug(s)
   - Harness from the glow plug(s)

➡ **On vehicles with Federal emissions systems, there is a buss bar connecting the glow plugs on each bank of the engine.**

   - Glow plug(s)

To install:

2. Install or connect the following:
   - Glow plug and tighten to 13 ft. lbs. (18 Nm)
   - Buss bar and wiring
   - Glow plug electrical nut and tighten to 13 inch lbs. (1.5 Nm)
   - Air cleaner outlet duct
   - Splash shield to the fender well
   - Negative battery cables

HEATING & AIR CONDITIONING SYSTEM

BLOWER MOTOR

REMOVAL & INSTALLATION

Delphi Blower Motor

See Figure 225.

1. If equipped, remove the sound insulator panel.

2. Remove the blower motor insulating cover screws.

3. Disconnect the electrical connector from the blower motor.

4. Remove the blower motor insulating cover.

5. Pull the retaining tab down while turning the blower motor counterclockwise in order to disengage the blower motor from the heater/ventilation module.

6. Remove the blower motor.

To install:

7. Install the blower motor.

8. Install the blower motor to the heater/ventilation module. Turn the blower assembly clockwise until the retaining tab locks into place.

9. Install the blower motor insulating cover.

10. Connect the electrical connector to the blower motor.

11. Install the blower motor insulating cover screws.

   a. Tighten the screws to 14 inch lbs. (1.6 Nm).

12. If equipped, install the sound insulator panel.

Visteon Blower Motor

See Figure 226.

1. Remove the sound insulator panel.

2. Disconnect the electrical connector (2) from the blower motor (1).

3. Remove the screws from the blower motor (1).

4. Remove the blower motor (1) from the HVAC module (3).

5. Remove the retainer from the blower motor wheel. Discard the retainer.

6. Remove the blower motor wheel from the blower motor (1).

To install:

7. Install the blower motor wheel to the blower motor (1).

8. Install the New retainer to the blower motor wheel.

9. Install the blower motor (1) to the HVAC module (3).

10. Install the screws to the blower motor (1).

   a. Tighten the screws to 18 inch lbs. (2 Nm).

11. Connect the electrical connector (2) to the blower motor (1).

12. Install the sound insulator panel.

HEATER CORE

REMOVAL & INSTALLATION

See Figures 227 and 228.

32085_SILV_G0086

Fig. 225 Pull the retaining tab down while turning the blower motor counterclockwise in order to disengage the blower motor

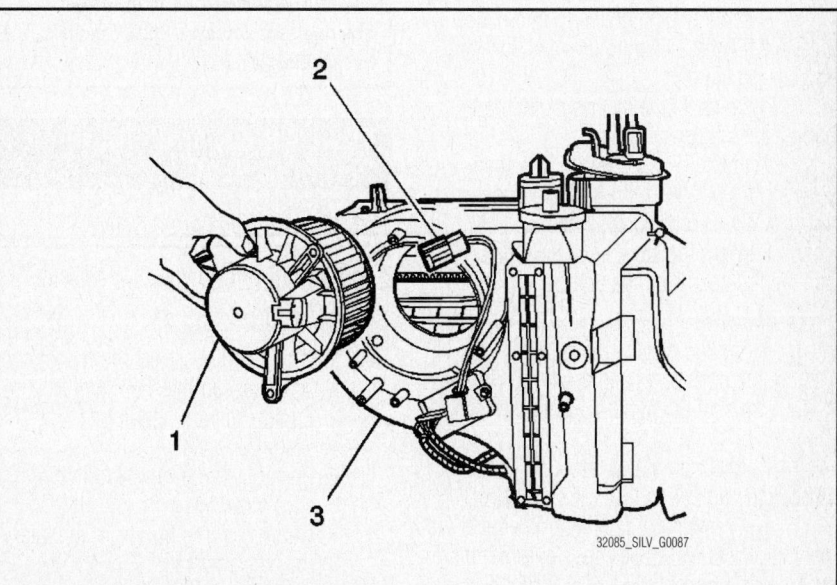

32085_SILV_G0087

Fig. 226 Replacing blower motor—Visteon

1. Drain the engine cooling system into a clean container for reuse.
2. Remove or disconnect the following:
   - Negative battery cable
   - Heater hoses from the heater core
   - Temperature control cable from the heater case assembly
   - Disconnect the mode control cable from the heater case assembly
   - Instrument panel carrier to provide access to the heater case assembly
   - Electrical connectors that may interfere with the heater case assembly removal
   - Heater case assembly–to–chassis screws/nuts and the assembly. Place the heater case assembly on a bench.
   - Heater core cover screws
   - Heater core from the heater case

To install:

3. Install or connect the following:
   - Heater core to the heater case

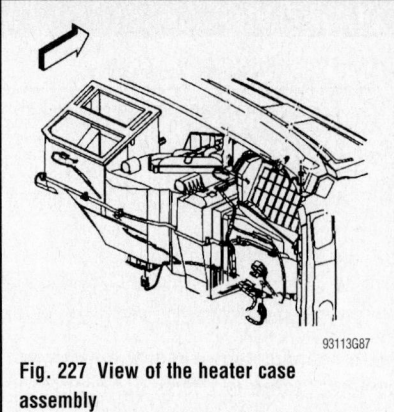

Fig. 227 View of the heater case assembly

- Heater core cover screws and tighten to 14 inch lbs. (1.5 Nm)
- Heater case assembly and the assembly–to–chassis screws, then, tighten the screws to 35 inch lbs. (4 Nm) and the nuts to 80 inch lbs. (9 Nm)
- Electrical connectors, as necessary
- Instrument panel carrier

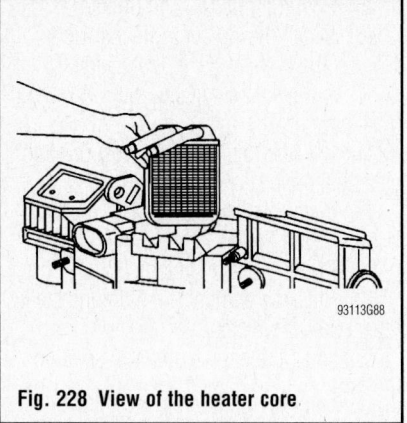

Fig. 228 View of the heater core

- Mode control cable to the heater case assembly
- Temperature control cable to the heater case assembly
- Heater hoses to the heater core
- Negative battery cable.
4. Refill the engine cooling system.
5. Run the engine to normal operating temperatures; then, check the climate control operation and check for leaks.

STEERING

POWER STEERING GEAR

REMOVAL & INSTALLATION

See Figure 229.

1. Raise and support the front end on jack stands.
2. Remove as much power steering fluid from the reservoir as possible.
3. Remove the engine under cover.
4. On diesel models, remove the wheelhouse liner.
5. Disconnect the hoses from the steering gear. Plug the lines to prevent leakage and contamination.
6. Disconnect the steering shaft coupling from the gear.
7. Remove the pitman arm nut, then separate the arm from the relay rod using puller J24319–B or equivalent.
8. Remove the steering gear bolts and remove the gear from the vehicle.

To install:

9. Install the gear in the vehicle. Tighten the bolts to 110 ft. lbs. (150 Nm).
10. Connect the pitman arm to the relay rod.
11. Connect the power steering hoses. Tighten the fittings to 24 ft. lbs. (32 Nm).
12. The remaining installation is the reverse of removal. Bleed the power steering system.

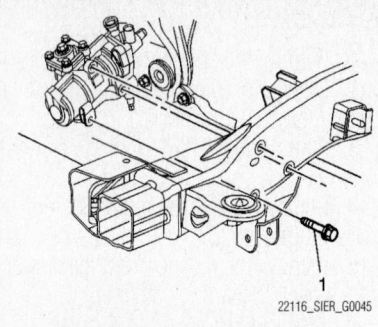

Fig. 229 Exploded view of the power steering gear assembly—2007 models, except Classic

POWER RACK AND PINION STEERING GEAR

REMOVAL & INSTALLATION

2005–06 and 2007 Classic Models

See Figure 230.

1. Remove or disconnect the following:
   - Wheel assemblies
   - Engine shield, if equipped
   - Stabilizer shaft
   - Power steering high and low pressure lines
   - Coupler clamp bolt from the intermediate shaft

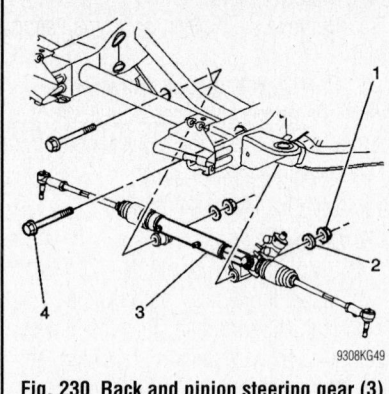

Fig. 230 Rack and pinion steering gear (3)

- Outer tie rod ends from steering knuckle
- Intermediate shaft from the rack and pinion assembly
- Rack and pinion assembly mounting nuts, washers and bolts
- Rack and pinion assembly from the vehicle

To install:

2. Install or connect the following:
   - Rack and pinion assembly into the vehicle
   - Rack and pinion assembly mounting bolts, washers and nuts. Tighten the nuts to 136 ft. lbs. (185 Nm).

- Intermediate shaft to the rack and pinion assembly
- Coupler clamp bolt to the intermediate shaft. Tighten the bolt to 33 ft. lbs. (45 Nm).
- Low pressure hose
- High pressure hose. Tighten the hoses to 20 ft. lbs. (27 Nm).
- Outer tie rod ends
- Engine protection shield, if equipped
- Stabilizer shaft
- Wheels

3. Lower the vehicle.

4. Fill and bleed the power steering system.

2007 Models, Except Classic

See Figure 231.

1. Remove as much power steering fluid from the reservoir as possible.

2. Remove or disconnect the following:
- Wheel assemblies
- Engine shield, if equipped
- Coupler clamp bolt from the intermediate shaft
- Outer tie rod ends from steering knuckle
- Power steering high and low pressure line retaining plate
- Power steering high and low pressure lines, then plug them to prevent leakage and contamination
- Rack and pinion assembly mounting nuts, washers and bolts
- Rack and pinion assembly from the vehicle

To install:

3. Install or connect the following:
- Rack and pinion assembly into the vehicle

- Rack and pinion assembly mounting bolts, washers and nuts. Tighten the left side bolts to 148 ft. lbs. (200 Nm) and the right side bolts to 74 ft. lbs. (100 Nm).
- Intermediate shaft to the rack and pinion assembly
- Coupler clamp bolt to the intermediate shaft. Tighten the bolt to 33 ft. lbs. (45 Nm).
- Low pressure line and high pressure line. Tighten the retaining plate to 106 inch lbs. (12 Nm)
- Outer tie rod ends
- Engine protection shield, if equipped
- Wheels

4. Lower the vehicle.

5. Fill and bleed the power steering system.

POWER STEERING PUMP

REMOVAL & INSTALLATION

4.3L Engine

1. Before servicing the vehicle, refer to the precautions in the beginning of this section.

2. Disconnect the hoses at the pump. When the hoses are disconnected, secure the ends in a raised position to prevent leakage. Cap the ends of the hoses to prevent the entrance of dirt.

3. Cap the pump fittings.

4. Loosen the belt tensioner.

5. Remove the pump drive belt.

6. Remove the pulley with a pulley puller such as J–29785–A.

7. Remove the following fasteners front mounting bolts

8. Lift out the pump.

To install:

9. Observe the following torque:
- Front mounting bolts: 37 ft. lbs. (50 Nm)

10. Install the pulley with J–25033–B.

11. Install the drive belt.

12. Install the hoses.

13. Fill and bleed the system.

Except 4.3L Engine

See Figure 232.

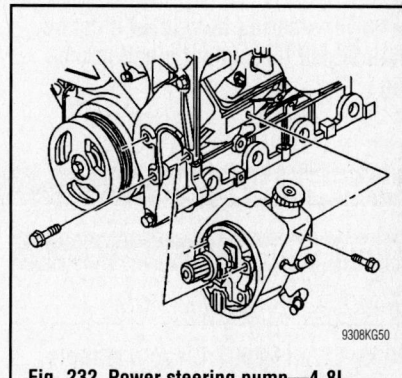

Fig. 232 Power steering pump—4.8L, 5.3L and 6.0L engines shown

1. Before servicing the vehicle, refer to the precautions in the beginning of this section.

2. Remove or disconnect the following:
- Upper radiator fan shroud, if necessary
- Drive belt
- Pulley.
- Nut and clamp retaining the filler neck to the power steering pump, if equipped

3. Place a drain pan under the pump. Remove the hoses from the pump.
- Bolts from the rear of the pump
- Bolts from the front of the pump
- Pump from the vehicle

To install:

4. Install or connect the following:
- Power steering pump
- Bolts to the front and the rear of the pump. Tighten the bolts to 37 ft. lbs. (50 Nm)
- Hoses to the pump. Tighten the nut to 20 ft. lbs. (28 Nm)
- Nut and clamp retaining the filler neck to the power steering pump, if equipped
- Pulley. Install the pulley with 0.020 in (0.5 mm) play
- Drive belt
- Upper radiator shroud.

5. Fill and bleed the power steering system.

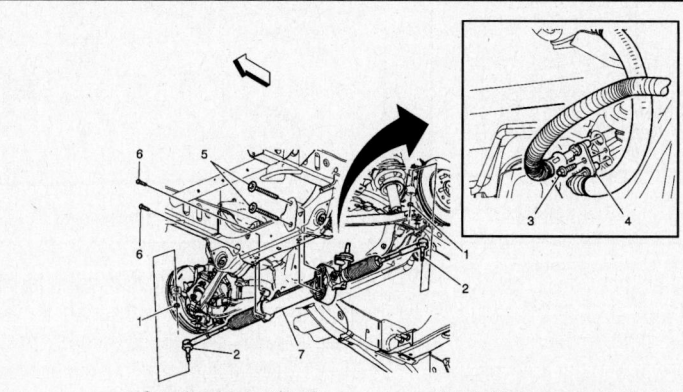

1. Outer tie rod end nut (qty. 2)
2. Outer tie rod (qty. 2)
3. Power steering gear inlet hose retaining plate bolt
4. Power steering gear inlet/outlet hose (qty. 2)
5. Left side steering gear bolt (qty. 2)
6. Right side steering gear bolts (qty. 2)
7. Steering gear

22116_SIER_G0046

Fig. 231 Exploded view of the rack and pinion steering gear assembly—2007 models, except Classic

BLEEDING

Observe the following:
- Use clean, new power steering fluid type only
- Hoses touching the frame, body or engine may cause system noise. Verify that the hoses do not touch any other part of the vehicle.
- Loose connections may not leak, but could allow air into the steering system. Verify that all hose connections are tight.

➡️**Power steering fluid level must be maintained throughout bleed procedure.**

1. Fill pump reservoir with fluid to minimum system level, FULL COLD level, or middle of hash mark on cap stick fluid level indicator.

➡️**With hydro–boost only, the oil level will appear falsely high if the hydro–boost accumulator is not fully charged. Do not apply the brake pedal with the engine OFF. This will discharge the hydro–boost accumulator.**

2. If equipped with hydro–boost, fully charge the hydro–boost accumulator using the following procedure:
   a. Start the engine.
   b. Firmly apply the brake pedal 10–15 times.
   c. Turn the engine **OFF**

3. Raise the vehicle until the front wheels are off the ground.

4. With key in the **ON** position and the engine **OFF**, turn the steering wheel from stop to stop 12 times. Vehicles equipped with hydro–boost systems or longer length power steering hoses may require turns up to 15 to 20 stop to stops.

5. Verify power steering fluid level per operating specification.

6. Start the engine. Rotate steering wheel from left to right. Check for sign of cavitation or fluid aeration (pump noise/whining).

7. Verify the fluid level. Repeat the bleed procedure if necessary.

SUSPENSION   FRONT SUSPENSION

COIL SPRING

REMOVAL & INSTALLATION

2005–06 and 2007 Classic Models

See Figures 233 through 237.

1. Raise and support the vehicle.
2. Remove or disconnect the following:
   - Engine protection shield
   - Frame cross bar (2500 series only)
   - Tire and wheel assembly
   - Shock absorber
   - Front stabilizer shaft link
3. Install tool J23028–15 using the outboard locating tab (1500 series), or, the inboard locating tab (2500 series).
4. Attach the retaining hook to the control arm. Tighten the wing nut until free–play is eliminated.
5. Securely attach tool J23028–01 to a

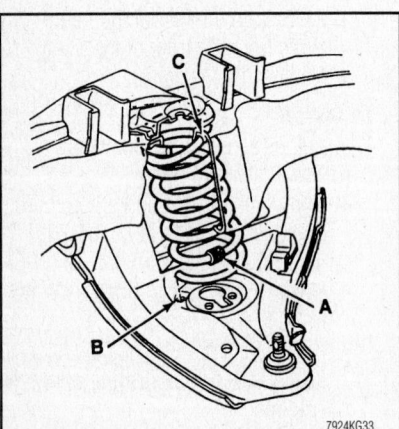

Fig. 233 Position the coil spring so the bottom end of the spring covers only one drain hole—the other hole must remain open

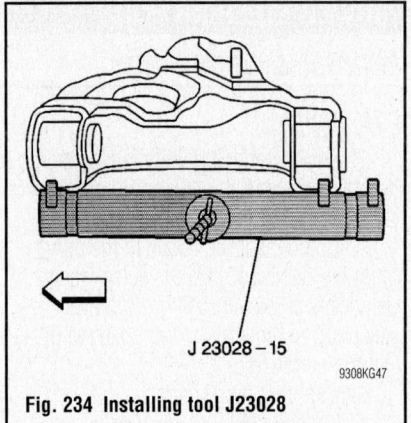

Fig. 234 Installing tool J23028

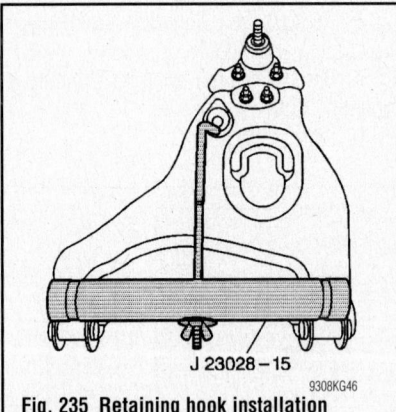

Fig. 235 Retaining hook installation

suitable transmission jack. Raise the jack until the yokes of tool J23028–01 line up with the notches in J23028–15.

6. Using the tools and the transmission jack, relieve the spring tension from the lower control arm pivot bolts.

7. Remove or disconnect the following:
   - Lower control arm pivot bolt nuts
   - Rear pivot bolt
   - Front pivot bolt

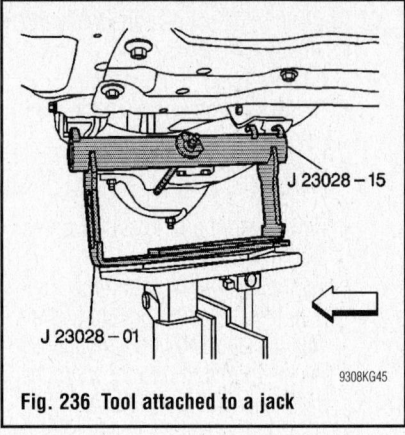

Fig. 236 Tool attached to a jack

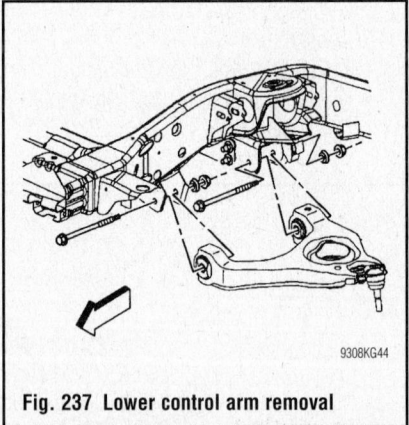

Fig. 237 Lower control arm removal

8. Slowly lower the transmission jack in order to unload the front coil spring. It may be necessary to use a pry bar in order to guide the lower control arm out of position.

9. Remove the coil spring and the insulator.

To install:

10. Install the coil spring and the insulator to the lower control arm.

11. Raise the transmission jack in order to compress the front coil spring. It may be necessary to use a pry bar in order to guide the lower control arm into position.

12. Install or connect the following:
- Front pivot bolt
- Rear pivot bolt
- Lower control arm pivot nuts. Tighten the pivot bolt nuts to 107 ft. lbs. (145 Nm).

13. Lower the jack. Remove the tool from the control arm.
- Front stabilizer shaft link
- Shock absorber
- Tire and wheel assembly
- Frame cross bar (2500 series only). Tighten the nuts to 74 ft. lbs. (100 Nm).

14. Install the engine protection shield.

15. Remove the safety stands. Lower the vehicle.

2007 Models, Except Classic

2-Wheel Drive And 4-Wheel Drive 1500 Series

Refer to the Shock Absorber removal procedure to replace the coil spring.

CONTROL LINKS

REMOVAL & INSTALLATION

See Figures 238 and 239.

1. Raise and properly support the vehicle.

2. Remove the tire and wheel assembly.

3. Remove cotter pin (if equipped) and the nut from outer tie rod stud.

4. Loosen the jam nut (2) on the inner tie rod assembly (1).

5. Disconnect the outer tie rod assembly (2) from the steering knuckle using J 24319 or equivalent.

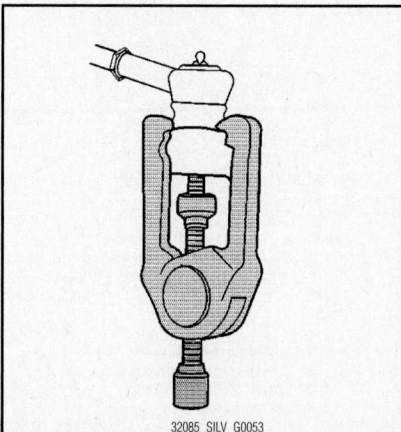

32085_SILV_G0053

Fig. 238 Disconnecting the outer tie rod from the steering knuckle

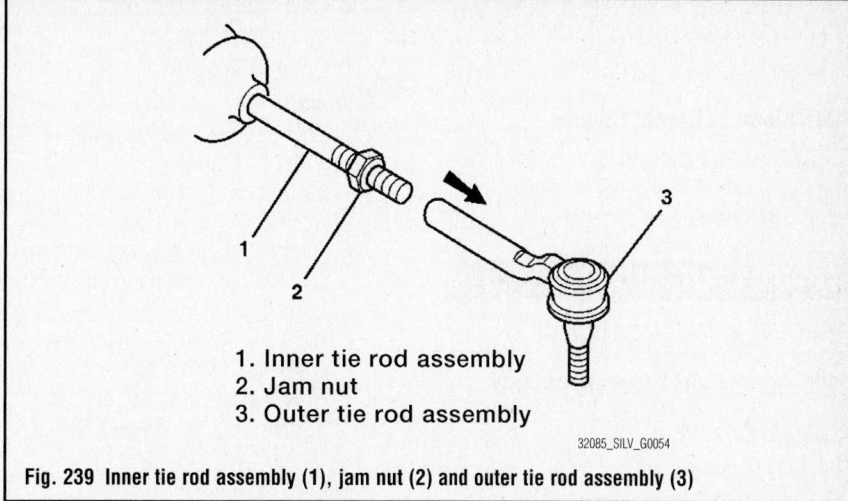

1. Inner tie rod assembly
2. Jam nut
3. Outer tie rod assembly

32085_SILV_G0054

Fig. 239 Inner tie rod assembly (1), jam nut (2) and outer tie rod assembly (3)

6. Remove the outer tie rod assembly (3) from the inner tie rod assembly (1).

To install:

7. Connect the outer tie rod assembly (3) to the inner tie rod (1). Do not tighten the jam nut (2).

8. Connect the outer tie rod assembly (3) to the steering knuckle.

9. Install outer tie rod nut to the outer tie rod stud (1).

   a. Tighten the outer tie rod nut to 33–37 ft. lbs. (45–50 Nm) on 2005–06 and 2007 Classic models or 44 ft. lbs. (60 Nm) on 2007 models, except Classic.

   b. If equipped with cotter pin install new cotter pin. If necessary further tighten nut until holes align and install cotter pin.

➡ **If equipped with rack and pinion steering, make sure the rack and pinion boot is not twisted after the toe adjustment.**

10. Check and adjust the wheel alignment as necessary.

11. Tighten jam nut (2).

LOWER BALL JOINT

REMOVAL & INSTALLATION

2005–06 and 2007 Classic Models

2-Wheel Drive Models

1. Raise and support the vehicle.

2. Remove or disconnect the following:
- Tire and wheel assembly
- Front coil spring
- Lower control arm

3. Secure the lower control arm in a bench vise or equivalent.

4. Center punch the rivet heads.

5. Drill out the rivets.

To install:

6. Install or connect the following:
- Ball joint to the lower control arm
- Replacement bolts to the lower control arm
- Nuts to the bolts. Tighten the nuts to 52 ft. lbs. (70 Nm).

7. Remove the lower control arm from the bench vise.
- Lower control arm
- Coil spring
- Tire and wheel tire assembly

8. Remove the safety stands.

9. Lower the vehicle.

10. Verify the wheel alignment.

4-Wheel Drive Models

1. Raise and support the vehicle.

2. Remove or disconnect the following:
- Tire and wheel assembly
- Lower control arm

3. Place the lower control arm in a bench vise.

4. Using a chisel, remove the 4 securing crimps from the ball joint body (1500 series only).

5. Using a press, remove the ball joint from the lower control arm.

To install:

➡ **Use the outer flange of the ball joint in order to press the ball joint into place.**

6. Install the new ball joint using a press.

7. Place the lower control arm in a bench vise.

8. Using a punch, install 4 crimps to the ball joint. Use the replaced ball joint as a reference (1500 series only).

9. Install or connect the following:
- Lower control arm
- Tire and wheel assembly

10. Remove the safety stands.
11. Lower the vehicle.
12. Verify the wheel alignment.

2007 Models, Except Classic

The lower ball joint is integrated with the lower control arm. If worn or damaged, the entire control arm must be replaced.

LOWER CONTROL ARM

REMOVAL & INSTALLATION

2005–06 and 2007 Classic Models

2-Wheel Drive Models

See Figures 240 and 241.

1. Raise and support the vehicle.
2. Remove or disconnect the following:
   - Tire and wheel assembly
   - Coil spring on vehicles with rack and pinion steering
   - Torsion bar on vehicles with recirculating ball steering
   - Shock absorber
   - Front stabilizer shaft link
   - Lower control arm nuts and the washers
   - Lower control arm bolts
   - Lower ball joint stud nut

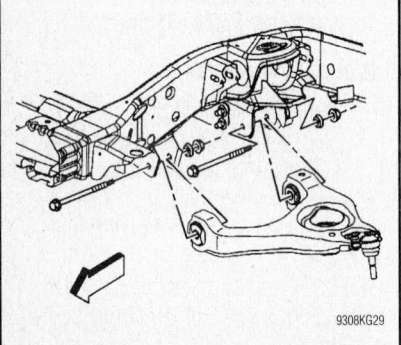

Fig. 240 2WD lower control arm—1500 series, 2005–06 models and 2007 Classic

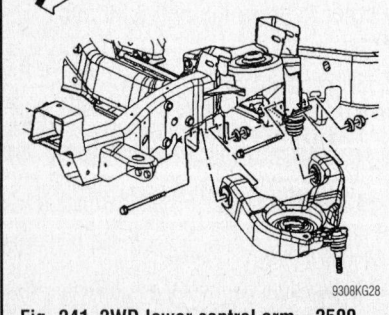

Fig. 241 2WD lower control arm—2500 series, 2005–06 models and 2007 Classic

- Lower ball joint stud from the steering knuckle
- Lower control arm

To install:

3. Install or connect the following:
   - Lower control arm
   - Ball joint stud to the steering knuckle
   - Lower ball joint stud nut. Tighten the lower ball joint stud nut to 74 ft. lbs. (100 Nm)
   - Front coil spring or torsion bar
   - Lower control arm bolt
   - Lower control arm nuts and the washers. Tighten the nuts to 129 ft. lbs. (175 Nm)
   - Front stabilizer shaft link.
   - Shock absorber
   - Tire and wheel assembly
4. Remove the safety stands. Lower the vehicle. Verify the wheel alignment.

4-Wheel Drive Models

See Figure 242.

1. Raise and support the vehicle.
2. Remove or disconnect the following:
   - Tire and wheel assembly
   - Stabilizer shaft links from the lower control arm
   - Shock absorber nut and the bolt
   - Torsion bars
   - Halfshaft
   - Lower ball joint stud nut
   - Lower ball joint stud from the steering knuckle
   - Lower control arm nuts and the washers
   - Lower control arm bolts
   - Lower control arm

To install:
   - Lower control arm
   - Lower control arm bolts
   - Washers with the shoulder facing the arm

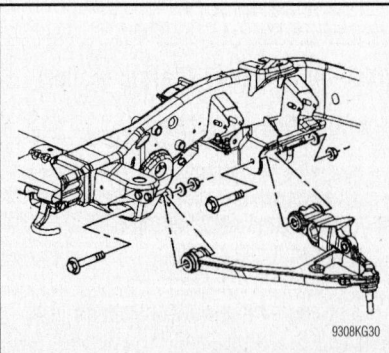

Fig. 242 4WD lower control arm—1500 series, 2005–06 models and 2007 Classic

- Nuts and tighten to 129 ft. lbs. (175 Nm)
- Halfshaft
- Lower ball joint stud to the steering knuckle. Install the nut to the ball joint stud. Tighten the nut to 74 ft. lbs. (100 Nm).
- Torsion bars
- Shock absorber through nut and bolt
- Stabilizer shaft links to the lower control arm
- RTD link rod to the sensor (if equipped)
- Tire and wheel assembly

3. Remove the safety stands. Lower the vehicle. Verify the wheel alignment.

2007 Models, Except Classic

See Figure 243.

1. Raise and support the vehicle.
2. Remove or disconnect the following:
   - Tire and wheel assembly
   - Stabilizer shaft links from the lower control arm
   - Electronic suspension control electrical connector
   - Torsion bars, if equipped
   - Halfshaft, on four wheel drive
   - Lower ball joint stud nut
   - Lower shock absorber bolts. Support the knuckle and upper control arm assembly with wire
   - Lower ball joint stud from the steering knuckle
   - Lower control arm nuts and the washers
   - Lower control arm bolts
   - Lower control arm

To install:
   - Lower control arm
   - Lower control arm bolts

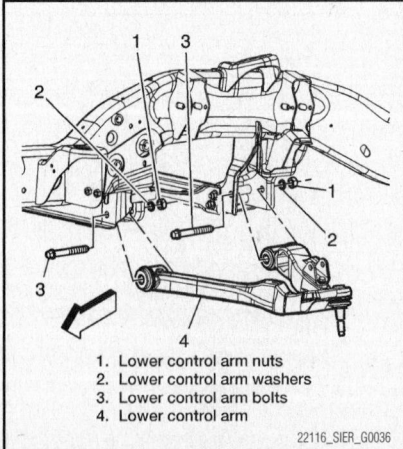

1. Lower control arm nuts
2. Lower control arm washers
3. Lower control arm bolts
4. Lower control arm

Fig. 243 Lower control arm assembly—2007 models, except Classic

- Washers
- Nuts and tighten to 129 ft. lbs. (175 Nm)
- Torsion bars, if equipped
- Halfshaft, on four wheel drive
- Lower ball joint stud to the steering knuckle. Install the nut to the ball joint stud. Tighten the nut to 74 ft. lbs. (100 Nm)
- Shock absorber bolts
- Stabilizer shaft links to the lower control arm
- Electronic suspension control electrical connector
- Tire and wheel assembly

3. Remove the safety stands. Lower the vehicle. Verify the wheel alignment.

SHOCK ABSORBERS

REMOVAL & INSTALLATION

2005–06 and 2007 Classic Models

2-Wheel Drive Models

See Figures 244 through 247.

1. Raise and support the vehicle.
2. If equipped with selectable ride, disconnect the Real Time Damping (RTD) link rod from the sensor. Grasp the connector lock tabs. Rotate the connector lock tabs (1) and (2) counter–clockwise until the connector is unlocked. Disengage the connector from the tennon by firmly pulling the connector up. Hold the tennon end with a wrench while removing the nut. Remove the nut.
3. Remove the upper insulator. Do not discard the plastic pilot ring.
4. Remove the shock absorber mounting bolts at the lower control arm. Remove the shock absorber through the lower control arm from below.

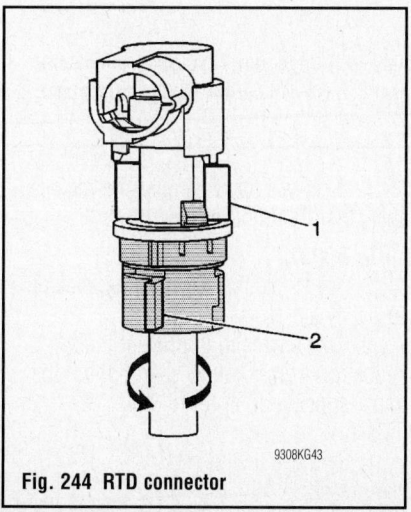

Fig. 244 RTD connector

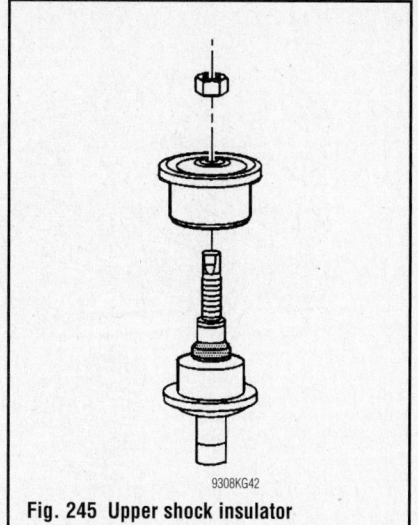

Fig. 245 Upper shock insulator

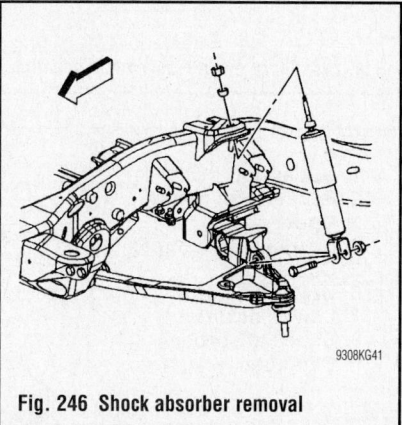

Fig. 246 Shock absorber removal

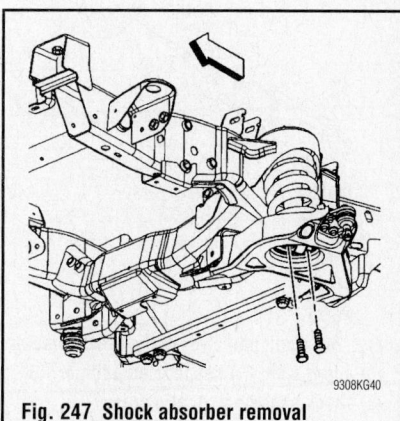

Fig. 247 Shock absorber removal

To install:

5. Support the lower control arm with a suitable jack in order to align the tennon with the mounting hole if equipped with selectable ride.
6. Install or connect the following:
   - Shock absorber through the lower control arm from below
   - Tennon through the mounting hole in the upper spring pocket
7. Align the shock absorber with the mounting holes in the lower control arm.
   - Shock absorber mounting bolts to the lower control arm. Tighten to 18 ft. lbs. (25 Nm).

➡The upper insulators are substantially larger that the lower insulators. The upper insulator must be installed above the shock mounting bracket on the frame. The plastic pilot ring will assist the alignment of the isolators.

- Upper insulator to the shock absorber
- Nut to the tennon end. Do not tighten the nut.
- RTD link rod to the sensor (if equipped).

8. Remove the safety stands.
9. Lower the vehicle. Hold the tennon end with a wrench while torquing the nut. Tighten the nut to 15 ft. lbs. (20 Nm).
10. Connect the electrical connector using the following procedure:
   a. Verify that the connector is unlocked.
   b. Align the connector so that the tabs are perpendicular to the wrench flats on the tennon end.
   c. Engage the connector to the tennon by firmly pushing the connector down.
   d. Grasp the connector lock tabs. Rotate the connector counter clockwise.
11. The connector is locked into place when you hear an audible snap and the tabs are aligned.

4-Wheel Drive Models

1. Raise and support the vehicle.
2. Remove or disconnect the following:
   - Real Time Damping (RTD) link rod from the sensor, if equipped
   - Electrical connector, if equipped with selectable ride. Grasp the connector lock tabs. Rotate the connector tabs counter clockwise until the connector is unlocked. Disengage the connector from the tennon by firmly pulling the connector up. Hold the tennon end with a wrench while removing the nut. Remove the nut.
   - Upper insulator. Do not discard the plastic pilot ring.
   - Shock absorber mounting bolt at the lower control arm

➡The lower shock mounting bushing is serviceable by driving the bushing out with the appropriate tool.

- Shock absorber

To install:

3. Install the shock absorber. Insert the stem through the hole in the shock bracket on the frame. Align the shock absorber with the mounting holes in the lower control arm.

4. Install or connect the following:
- Shock absorber through bolt to the lower control arm
- Shock absorber through bolt nut and tighten to 59 ft. lbs. (80 Nm)

➡**The upper insulators are substantially larger that the lower insulators. The upper insulator must be installed above the shock mounting bracket on the frame. The plastic pilot ring will assist the alignment of the isolators.**

- Upper insulator to the shock absorber
- Nut to the tennon end. Do not tighten the nut
- RTD link rod to the sensor, if equipped

5. Remove the safety stands. Lower the vehicle. Hold the tennon end with a wrench while torquing the nut. Tighten the nut to 15 ft. lbs. (20 Nm).

6. Connect the electrical connector using the following procedure if equipped with selectable ride.

a. Verify that the connector is unlocked.

b. Align the connector so that the tabs (1) are perpendicular to the wrench flats on the tennon end.

c. Engage the connector to the tennon by firmly pushing the connector down.

d. Grasp the connector lock tabs (1, 2). Rotate the connector counter clockwise. The connector is locked into place when you hear an audible snap and the tabs are aligned.

2007 Models, Except Classic

2-Wheel Drive And 4-Wheel Drive 1500 Series

See Figures 248 and 249.

1. Raise and support the vehicle.
2. Remove or disconnect the following:
- Front wheels
- Outer tie rod from the steering knuckle
- Lower shock mounting bolts
- Electronic suspension control electrical connector

3. Support the lower arm, then remove the 3 upper shock mounting nuts and remove the assembly from the vehicle.

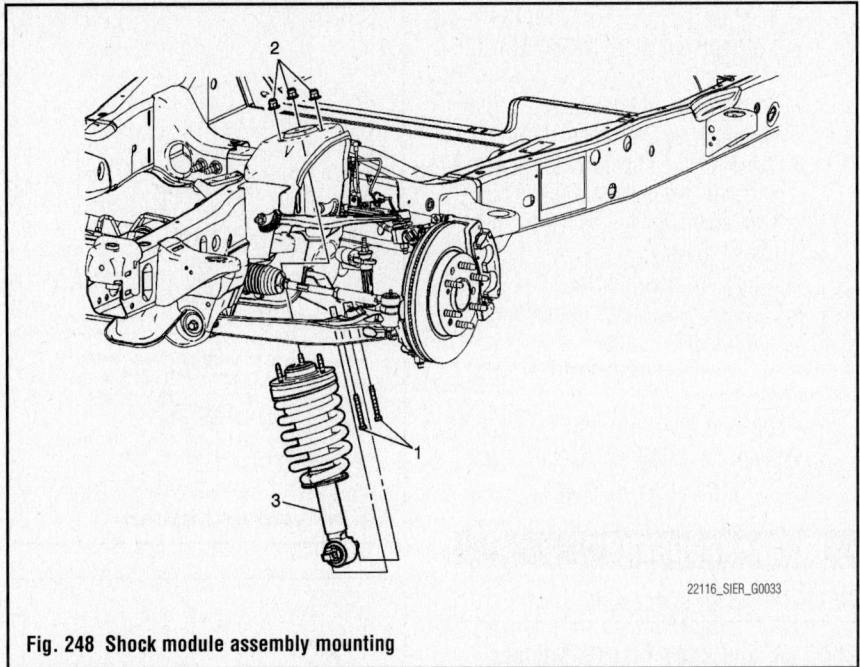

Fig. 248 Shock module assembly mounting

22116_SIER_G0033

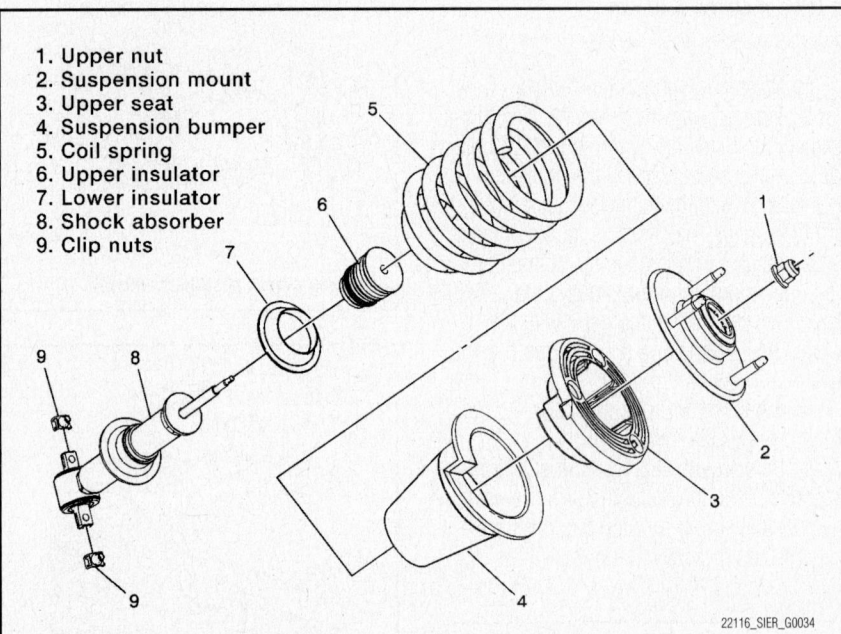

1. Upper nut
2. Suspension mount
3. Upper seat
4. Suspension bumper
5. Coil spring
6. Upper insulator
7. Lower insulator
8. Shock absorber
9. Clip nuts

Fig. 249 Exploded view of the shock module assembly—(1) Upper nut, (2) suspension mount, (3) upper seat, (4) suspension bumper, (5) upper insulator, (6) coil spring, (7) lower insulator, (8) shock absorber, (9) clip nuts

22116_SIER_G0034

4. Compress the coil spring using tool J45400 or equivalent.

5. Make sure one of the mount studs is aligned with the centerline of the shock absorber dog bone.

6. Use a wrench to prevent the shock rod from rotating, then remove the upper shock mount nut.

➡**When disassembling the shock absorber assembly, do not let the shock rod rotate. It may damage the shock.**

7. Separate the assembly and replace any components necessary.

To install:

8. Assemble the components, making sure they are properly aligned.

9. Use a wrench to prevent the shock rod from rotating, then tighten the upper shock mount nut to 37 ft. lbs. (50 Nm).

10. Remove the coil spring compressor.

11. Install the shock absorber assembly on the vehicle. Tighten the upper mounting nuts and lower bolts to 37 ft. lbs. (50 Nm).

12. The remaining installation is the reverse of removal.

4-Wheel Drive 2500 And 3500 Series

See Figure 250.

1. Raise and support the vehicle.
2. Remove or disconnect the following:
   - Front wheels
   - Support the lower control arm, then remove the upper shock mounting nut.
   - Lower mounting bolt
   - Shock absorber

To install:

3. Install the shock absorber on the vehicle. Tighten the lower mounting bolt to 59 ft. lbs. (80 Nm) and the upper nut to 17 ft. lbs. (24 Nm).

4. The installation is the reverse of removal.

STABILIZER BAR

REMOVAL & INSTALLATION

1. Raise and support the vehicle.
2. Remove the tire and wheel.

3. Remove the stabilizer shaft nut from the link bolt.

4. Remove the stabilizer shaft link bolt.

5. Remove the stabilizer shaft link insulators and spacers.

6. Remove the oil pan skid plate, if equipped.

7. Remove the stabilizer shaft insulator bracket bolts.

8. Remove the stabilizer shaft bracket.

9. Remove the stabilizer shaft.

10. Remove the stabilizer shaft insulators.

11. Inspect all of the parts for wear and damage.

To install:

12. Install the insulators to the stabilizer shaft.

13. Install the stabilizer shaft.

14. Install the brackets over the insulators and the stabilizer shaft.

15. Install insulator bracket bolts and tighten to 37 ft. lbs. (50 Nm).

16. Install the stabilizer shaft link insulators and spacers.

17. Apply Loctite® on the threads of the stabilizer link bolts then install the bolts.

18. On 2005–06 and 2007 Classic models, install the stabilizer shaft nut to the link bolt and tighten to 89 inch lbs. (10 Nm),

and continue to tighten the nut until 2–4 threads protrude above the nut. On 2007 models except Classic, tighten the nuts to 17 ft. lbs. (23 Nm).

19. Install the oil pan skid plate, if equipped.

20. Install the tire and wheel assembly.

21. Remove the safety stands

22. Lower the vehicle.

STEERING KNUCKLE

REMOVAL & INSTALLATION

See Figure 251.

1. Raise and support the vehicle.
2. Remove the tire and wheel.
3. Remove the wheel hub and bearing.
4. Support the lower control arm with a suitable jack.
5. Disconnect the outer tie rod from the knuckle.
6. Remove the brake hose bracket retaining bolt from the knuckle.
7. Remove the retaining nut and separate the upper and lower ball joints from the steering knuckle using a ball joint remover and adapters.
8. Remove the steering knuckle.

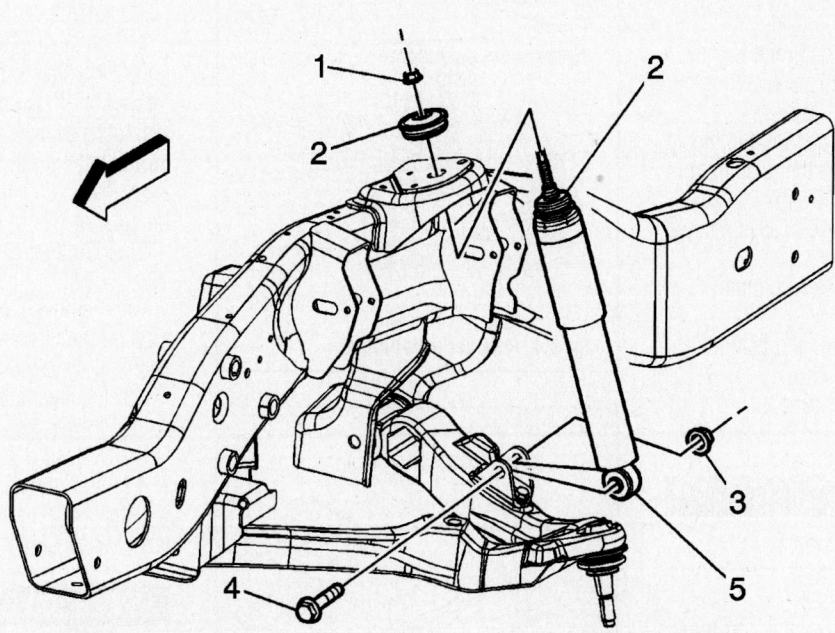

1. Shock absorber retaining nut
2. Insulator (qty. 2)
3. Retaining nut
4. Mounting bolt
5. Shock Absorber

22116_SIER_G0035

Fig. 250 Exploded view of the shock absorber mounting—4WD 2500 series and 3500 series

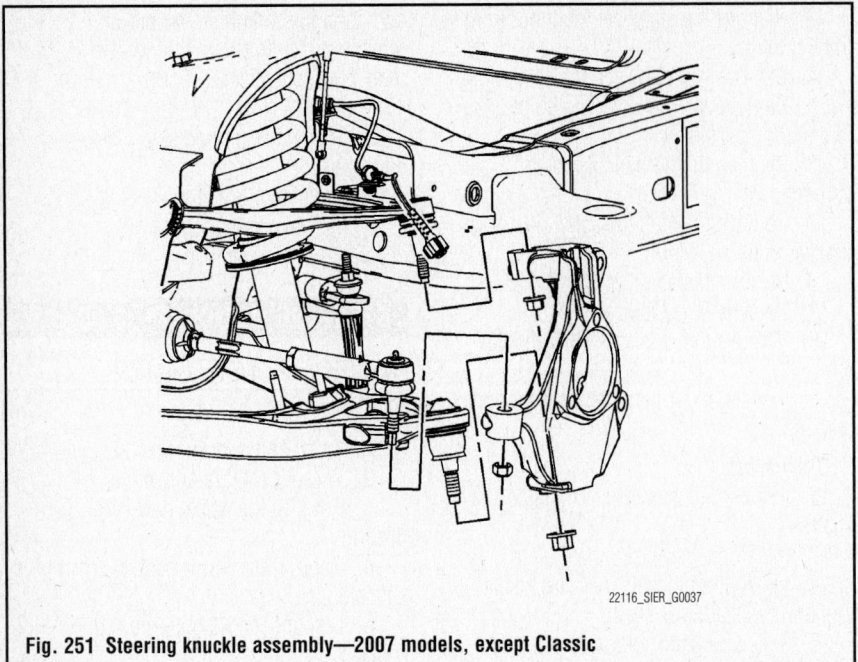

Fig. 251 Steering knuckle assembly—2007 models, except Classic

To install:

9. Clean all grease and contaminants from the tapered section and the threads of the upper ball joint, the lower ball joint, and the tie rod end.

10. Clean and inspect the taper holes and the mounting surfaces of the steering knuckle. If any of the tapered holes are elongated, out of round, or damaged, the replace the steering knuckle.

11. Install the steering knuckle.

12. Connect the lower ball joint to the steering knuckle and install the retaining nut and tighten to 74 ft. lbs. (100 Nm).

13. Connect the upper ball joint to the steering knuckle and install the retaining nut and tighten to 37 ft. lbs. (50 Nm).

14. Install the brake hose bracket retaining bolt to the knuckle.

15. Connect the outer tie rod to the steering knuckle.

16. Install the wheel hub and bearing.

17. Install the tire and wheel.

18. Remove the safety stands.

19. Lower the vehicle.

TORSION BAR

REMOVAL & INSTALLATION

See Figures 252 through 254.

➡**This procedure requires the removal of both torsion bars.**

1. Raise and support the vehicle.

2. Mark the adjustment bolt setting. Install tool J36202 to the adjustment arm and the crossmember.

3. Increase the tension on the adjust-ment arm until the load is removed from the adjustment bolt and the adjuster nut.

4. Remove or disconnect the following:
- Adjustment bolt and the adjuster nut
- Tool, allowing the torsion bar to unload.

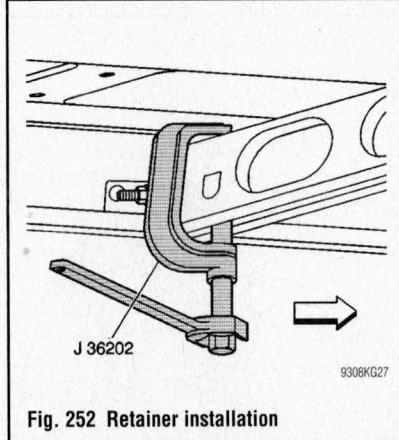

Fig. 252 Retainer installation

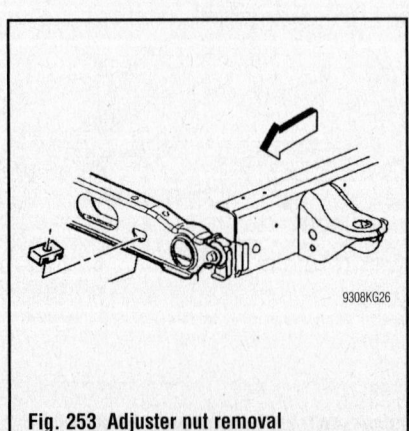

Fig. 253 Adjuster nut removal

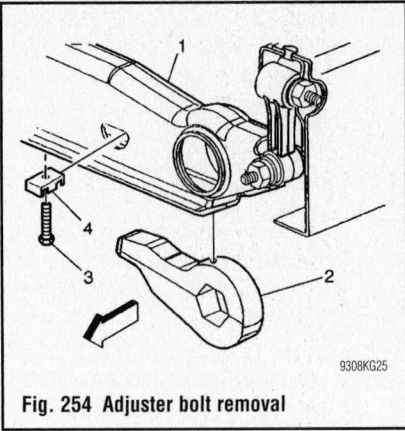

Fig. 254 Adjuster bolt removal

- Adjustment arm by sliding the tor-sion bar forward until the torsion bar clears the adjustment arm. Use your hand to support the adjust-ment arm as the adjustment arm releases from the torsion bar.
- Torsion bar crossmember bolts
- Torsion bar crossmember
- Torsion bars

➡**Note the position of the torsion bars as the left and right bars are different.**

To install:

5. Install or connect the following:
- Torsion bars
- Torsion bar crossmember
- Torsion bar crossmember bolts. Tighten the bolt to 70 ft. lbs. (95 Nm)

6. While supporting the adjustment arm, slide the torsion bar rearward until the torsion bar fully engages the adjustment arm. Install tool J36202 to the adjustment arm and the crossmember. Increase the ten-sion on the adjustment arm in order to load the torsion bar.
- Adjustment bolt and the adjuster nut

7. Remove the tool, releasing the ten-sion on the torsion bar until the load is taken up by the adjustment bolt.

8. Remove the safety stands.

9. Lower the vehicle.

10. Measure the ride height.

11. Turn the adjustment bolt clockwise to increase the ride height and counterclock-wise to decrease it.

UPPER BALL JOINT

REMOVAL & INSTALLATION

2005–06 and 2007 Classic Models

1. Raise and support the vehicle.

2. Remove or disconnect the following:
- Tire and wheel assembly

- Upper control arm
- Upper ball joint, using a press

To install:

➡ **The ball joint must be installed with the flat edges or notches in the same position as the replaced ball joint. The ball joint is directional and damage will occur if this procedure is not followed.**

3. Install or connect the following:
   - Upper ball joint, using a press
   - Upper control arm
   - Tire and wheel assembly
4. Remove the safety stands.
5. Lower the vehicle.
6. Verify the wheel alignment.

2007 Models, Except Classic

The upper ball joint is integrated with the upper control arm. If worn or damaged, the entire control arm must be replaced.

UPPER CONTROL ARM

REMOVAL & INSTALLATION

See Figure 255.

1. Raise and support the vehicle.
2. Remove or disconnect the following:
   - Tire and wheel assembly
   - Real Time Damping (RTD) link rod from the sensor, if equipped
   - Retaining bolt for the brake hose and the wheel speed sensor brackets
   - Halfshaft
   - Nut at the upper ball joint. Discard the nut
   - Upper control arm from the steering knuckle
   - Upper control arm nuts and the adjustment cams
   - Upper control arm bolts
   - Upper control arm

To install:

3. Install or connect the following:
   - Upper control arm
   - Upper control arm bolts
   - Upper control arm nuts and the adjustment cams. Tighten the nuts to 140 ft. lbs. (190 Nm)
   - Upper control arm to the steering knuckle
   - Halfshaft
   - New nut to the upper ball joint stud. Tighten the nut to 37 ft. lbs. (50 Nm).
   - Retaining bolts for the brake hose and wheel speed sensor brackets.

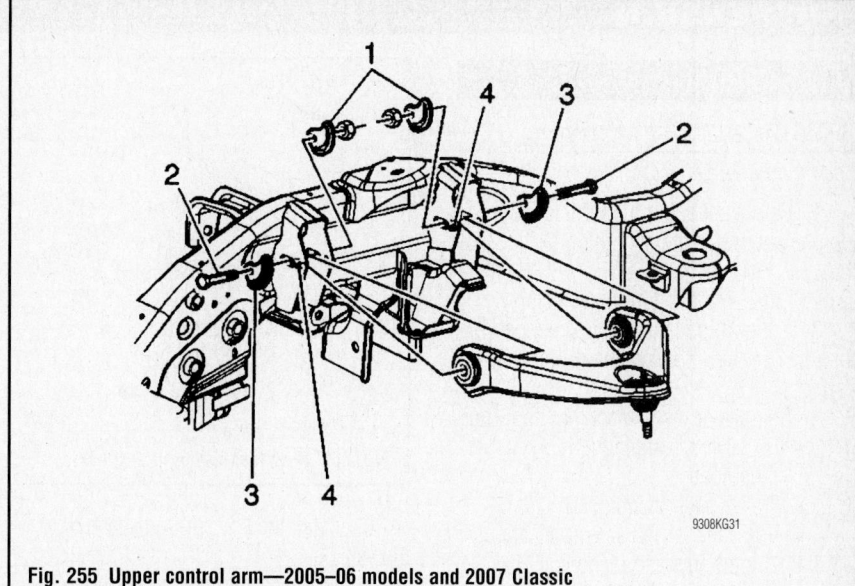

Fig. 255 Upper control arm—2005–06 models and 2007 Classic

Tighten the bolts to 80 inch lbs. (9 Nm).
   - RTD link rod to the sensor, if equipped
   - Tire and wheel assembly
4. Remove the safety stands.
5. Lower the vehicle. Verify the wheel alignment.

WHEEL HUB AND BEARINGS

REMOVAL & INSTALLATION

See Figure 256.

1. Raise and support the vehicle.
2. Remove or disconnect the following:
   - Tire and wheel assembly
   - Caliper and rotor
   - Wheel speed sensor and brake hose mounting bracket bolt from the steering knuckle
   - Electrical connection for the wheel speed sensor
   - Front drive halfshaft assembly on four wheel drive models
   - Hub and bearing assembly mounting bolts
   - Hub and bearing assembly
   - O–ring seal from the steering knuckle bore (2500 series)
3. Clean and inspect the O–ring seal (2500 series).

To install:

4. Clean all corrosion or contaminates from the steering knuckle bore and the hub and bearing assembly.

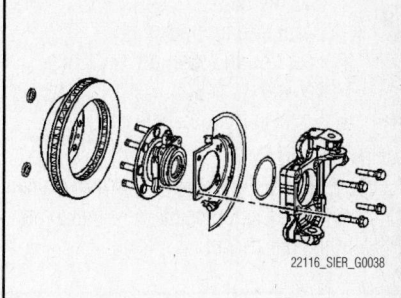

Fig. 256 Exploded view of the front hub assembly—2500 shown, 1500 similar

5. Install the O–ring to the steering knuckle (2500 series).
6. Lubricate the steering knuckle bore with wheel bearing grease or the equivalent.
7. Install or connect the following:
   - Hub and bearing assembly
   - Hub and bearing assembly mounting bolts. Tighten the bolts to 133 ft. lbs. (180 Nm).
   - Front drive halfshaft assembly on four wheel drive models
   - Electrical connection for the wheel speed sensor
   - Wheel speed sensor and brake hose mounting bracket bolt to the steering knuckle. Tighten to 106 inch lbs. (12 Nm).
   - Rotor
   - Tire and wheel assembly.

SUSPENSION

REAR SUSPENSION

LEAF SPRING

REMOVAL & INSTALLATION

See Figures 257 and 258.

1. Before servicing the vehicle, refer to the precautions in the beginning of this section.
2. Raise and support the vehicle.
3. Support the rear axle independently in order to relieve the tension on the leaf springs.
4. Remove or disconnect the following:
   - Real Time Damping (RTD) sensors, if equipped
   - Trailer hitch if equipped
   - Fuel tank for left side applications
   - U–bolt nuts and U–bolts
   - Spring spacer and anchor plate
   - Shackle to the frame bracket nut and the bolt
   - Front spring bracket bolt
   - Leaf spring assembly from the vehicle
   - Shackle from the spring

To install:

5. Loosely assemble the spring shackle bracket to the frame. Install the shackle bolt. Install the shackle nut.

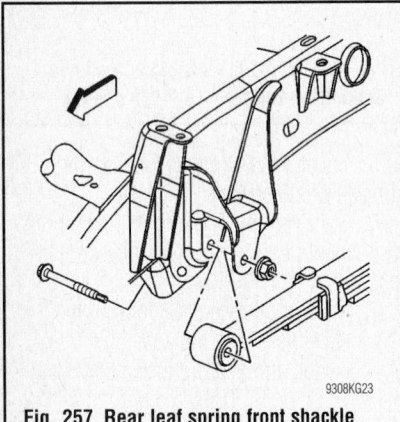

Fig. 257 Rear leaf spring front shackle

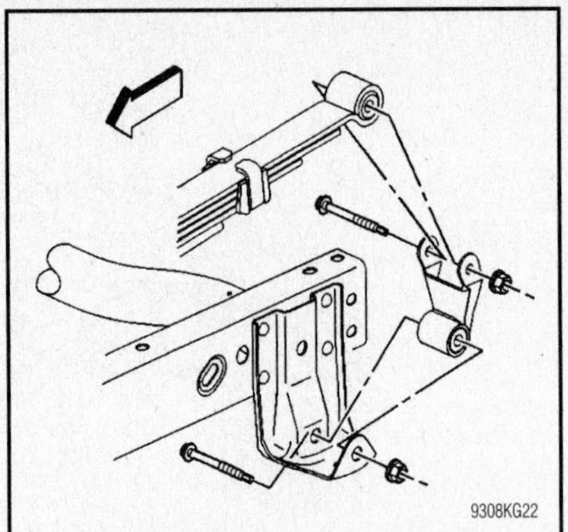

9308KG23

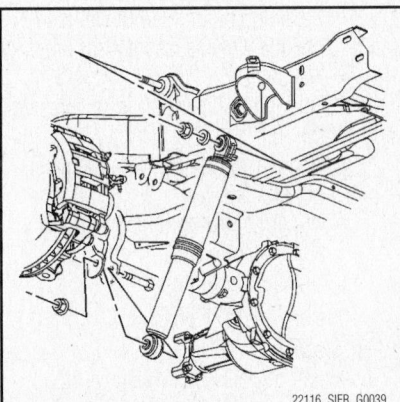

Fig. 258 Rear leaf spring rear shackle

9308KG22

6. Install the leaf spring assembly to the vehicle.
7. Loosely assemble the spring to the front hanger bracket.
8. Install or connect the following:
   - Front spring hanger bracket bolt
   - Front spring hanger bracket nut
   - Shackle to the spring bolt
   - Shackle to the spring nut

➡**Do not reuse the U–bolts.**

   - Spring spacer
   - U–bolts
   - Anchor plate
   - U–bolt nuts

9. Tighten in a crisscross pattern to:
   a. 2005–06 and 2007 Classic models
   - 1500 series: 53 ft. lbs. (72 Nm)
   - 1500 series w/rear steering: 110 ft. lbs. (150 Nm)
   - 2500 and 3500 series: 110 ft. lbs. (150 Nm)
   b. 2007 Models, except Classic
   - 1500 series: 74 ft. lbs. (100 Nm)
   - 2500 and 3500 series: 118 ft. lbs. (160 Nm)

10. Tighten the front hanger bracket nut to 110 ft. lbs. (150 Nm) on 2005–06 and 2007 Classic models or 70 ft. lbs. (95 Nm) on 2007 models, except Classic.

11. Tighten the rear hanger bracket nut to 70 ft. lbs. (95 Nm).
12. Install the fuel tank for left side applications.
13. Install the trailer hitch if equipped.
14. Connect the RTD sensors, if equipped
15. Remove the rear axle support.
16. Remove the safety stands. Lower the vehicle.

SHOCK ABSORBER

REMOVAL & INSTALLATION

See Figure 259.

1. Raise and support the vehicle.
2. Remove or disconnect the following:
   - Electrical connector, if equipped with selectable ride
   - Upper shock absorber nut and bolt
   - Lower shock absorber nut and bolt
   - Shock absorber

To install:

3. Installation is the reverse of removal. Tighten the nuts to 70 ft. lbs. (95 Nm).
4. Connect the electrical connector if equipped with Selectable Ride. Remove the safety stands. Lower the vehicle.

Fig. 259 Exploded view of the rear shock absorber mounting

22116_SIER_G0039

PONTIAC AND SATURN

Sky • Solstice

21

SPECIFICATIONS AND MAINTENANCE CHARTS

ENGINE AND VEHICLE IDENTIFICATION

Engine							Model Year	
Code ①	Liters	Cu. In.	Cyl.	Fuel Sys.	Engine Type	Eng. Mfg.	Code ②	Year
B	2.4	146	4	MFI	DOHC	GM	6	2006
M	2.0	122	4	MFI	DOHC	GM	7	2007
							8	2008

MFI: Multi-port Fuel Injection

DOHC: Double Overhead Camshafts

NA: Information not available

① 8th digit of VIN

② 10th digit of VIN

22116_SOLS_C0001

GENERAL ENGINE SPECIFICATIONS

Year	Model	Engine Displacement Liters	Engine VIN	Net Horsepower @ rpm	Net Torque @ rpm (ft. lbs.)	Bore x Stroke (in.)	Com-pression Ratio	Oil Pressure @ rpm
2006	Solstice	2.4	B	177@6600	166@4800	3.467x3.861	10:01	50-80@1000
2007	Sky	2.4	B	177@6600	166@4800	3.467x3.861	10:01	50-80@1000
	Sky	2.0	M	260@5300	260@5250	3.388x3.338	9.2:1	50-80@1000
	Solstice	2.4	B	177@6600	166@4800	3.467x3.861	10:01	50-80@1000
	Solstice	2.0	M	260@5300	260@5250	3.388x3.338	9.2:1	50-80@1000
2008	Sky	2.4	B	177@6600	166@4800	3.467x3.861	10:01	50-80@1000
	Sky	2.0	M	260@5300	260@5250	3.388x3.338	9.2:1	50-80@1000
	Solstice	2.4	B	177@6600	166@4800	3.467x3.861	10:01	50-80@1000
	Solstice	2.0	M	260@5300	260@5250	3.388x3.338	9.2:1	50-80@1000

22116_SOLS_C0002

GASOLINE ENGINE TUNE-UP SPECIFICATIONS

Year	Engine Displacement Liters	Engine VIN	Spark Plug Gap (in.)	Ignition Timing (deg.) MT	AT	Fuel Pump (psi)	Idle Speed (rpm) MT	AT	Valve Clearance In.	Ex.
2006	2.4	B	0.037-0.043	①	①	50-60	①	①	HYD	HYD
2007	2.4	B	0.037-0.043	①	①	50-60	①	①	HYD	HYD
	2.0	M	0.030-0.035	①	①	50-60	①	①	HYD	HYD
2008	2.4	B	0.037-0.043	①	①	50-60	①	①	HYD	HYD
	2.0	M	0.030-0.035	①	①	50-60	①	①	HYD	HYD

NOTE: The Vehicle Emission Control Information label often reflects specification changes changes made during production.

The label figures must be used if they differ from those in this chart.

HYD: Hydraulic

① Electronically controlled and cannot be adjusted

22116_SOLS_C0003

CAPACITIES

Year	Model	Engine VIN	Engine Displacement Liters	Engine Oil with Filter (qts.)	Transmission (pts.)		Rear Axle (pts.)	Fuel Tank (gal.)	Cooling System (qts.)
					Manual	Auto. *			
2006	Solstice	B	2.4	5.0	5.5	18	2.74 ②	13.8	8.9
2007	Sky	B	2.4	5.0	5.5	18	2.74 ②	13.8	8.9
	Sky	M	2.0	5.0	5.5	18	2.74 ②	13.8	8.7 ①
	Solstice	B	2.4	5.0	5.5	18	2.74 ②	13.8	8.9
	Solstice	M	2.0	5.0	5.5	18	2.74 ②	13.8	8.7 ①
2008	Sky	B	2.4	5.0	5.5	18	2.74 ②	13.8	8.9
	Sky	M	2.0	5.0	5.5	18	2.74 ②	13.8	8.7 ①
	Solstice	B	2.4	5.0	5.5	18	2.74 ②	13.8	8.9
	Solstice	M	2.0	5.0	5.5	18	2.74 ②	13.8	8.7 ①

* Dry fill

① Manual transmission 9.5qts

② Use limited slip additive 3.38oz dry or 2.37oz drain and fill

22116_SOLS_C0004

FLUID SPECIFICATIONS

Year	Model	Engine Displacement Liters	Engine ID/VIN	Engine Oil	Auto. Trans.	Drive Axle	Power Steering Fluid	Brake Master Cylinder	Engine Coolant
2006	Solstice	2.4	B	5W-30	Dexron® VI ②	75W-90 ③	GM PS Fluid	DOT 3	Dex-Cool
2007	Sky	2.4	B	5W-30	Dexron® VI ②	75W-90 ③	GM PS Fluid	DOT 3	Dex-Cool
	Sky	2.0	M	5W-30 ①	Dexron® VI ②	75W-90 ③	GM PS Fluid	DOT 3	Dex-Cool
	Solstice	2.4	B	5W-30	Dexron® VI ②	75W-90 ③	GM PS Fluid	DOT 3	Dex-Cool
	Solstice	2.0	M	5W-30 ①	Dexron® VI ②	75W-90 ③	GM PS Fluid	DOT 3	Dex-Cool
2008	Sky	2.4	B	5W-30	Dexron® VI ②	75W-90 ③	GM PS Fluid	DOT 3	Dex-Cool
	Sky	2.0	M	5W-30 ①	Dexron® VI ②	75W-90 ③	GM PS Fluid	DOT 3	Dex-Cool
	Solstice	2.4	B	5W-30	Dexron® VI ②	75W-90 ③	GM PS Fluid	DOT 3	Dex-Cool
	Solstice	2.0	M	5W-30 ①	Dexron® VI ②	75W-90 ③	GM PS Fluid	DOT 3	Dex-Cool

DOT: Department Of Transpotation

① Synthetic motor oil is recommended

② Manual transmission (GM part number 89021806)

③ Sythetic axle lubricant and limited-slip addative
   for limited-slip differentials

22116_SOLS_C0011

VALVE SPECIFICATIONS

Year	Engine Displacement Liters	Engine VIN	Seat Angle (deg.)	Face Angle (deg.)	Spring Test Pressure (lbs. @ in.)	Spring Installed Height (in.)	Stem-to-Guide Clearance (in.)		Stem Diameter (in.)	
							Intake	Exhaust	Intake	Exhaust
2006	2.4	B	NA	NA	NA	1.28	0.0012-0.0022	0.0020-0.0026	0.2344-0.2355	0.2337-0.2343
2007	2.4	B	NA	NA	NA	1.28	0.0012-0.0022	0.0020-0.0026	0.2344-0.2355	0.2337-0.2343
	2.0	M	NA	NA	NA	1.28	0.0012-0.0022	0.0020-0.0026	0.2344-0.2355	0.2337-0.2343
2008	2.4	B	NA	NA	NA	1.28	0.0012-0.0022	0.0020-0.0026	0.2344-0.2355	0.2337-0.2343
	2.0	M	NA	NA	NA	1.28	0.0012-0.0022	0.0020-0.0026	0.2344-0.2355	0.2337-0.2343

22116_SOLS_C0005

CAMSHAFT AND BEARING SPECIFICATIONS CHART
All measurements are given in inches.

Year	Engine Displ. Liters	Engine VIN	Journal Dia.	Brg. Oil Clearance	Shaft End-play	Runout	Journal Bore	Lobe Height	
								Intake	Exhaust
2006	2.4	B	1.0604-1.0614	NA	0.0016-0.0057	NA	NA	NA	NA
2007	2.4	B	1.0604-1.0614	NA	0.0016-0.0057	NA	NA	NA	NA
	2.0	M	1.0604-1.0614	NA	0.0016-0.0121	NA	NA	NA	NA
2008	2.4	B	1.0604-1.0614	NA	0.0016-0.0057	NA	NA	NA	NA
	2.0	M	1.0604-1.0614	NA	0.0016-0.0121	NA	NA	NA	NA

NA: Not Available

22116_SOLS_C0006

CRANKSHAFT AND CONNECTING ROD SPECIFICATIONS
All measurements are given in inches.

Year	Engine Displacement Liters	Engine VIN	Crankshaft				Connecting Rod		
			Main Brg. Journal Dia.	Main Brg. Oil Clearance	Shaft End-play	Thrust on No.	Journal Diameter	Oil Clearance	Side Clearance
2006	2.4	B	2.2045-2.2050	0.0012-0.0026	0.0012-0.0150	2	1.19291-1.9297	0.0011-0.0027	0.0028-0.0146
2007	2.4	B	2.2045-2.2050	0.0012-0.0026	0.0012-0.0150	2	1.19291-1.9297	0.0011-0.0027	0.0028-0.0146
	2.0	M	2.2045-2.2050	0.0012-0.0026	0.0012-0.0150	2	1.19291-1.9297	0.0011-0.0027	0.0028-0.0146
2008	2.4	B	2.2045-2.2050	0.0012-0.0026	0.0012-0.0150	2	1.19291-1.9297	0.0011-0.0027	0.0028-0.0146
	2.0	M	2.2045-2.2050	0.0012-0.0026	0.0012-0.0150	2	1.19291-1.9297	0.0011-0.0027	0.0028-0.0146

22116_SOLS_C0007

PISTON AND RING SPECIFICATIONS

All measurements are given in inches.

Year	Engine Displacement Liters	Engine VIN	Piston Clearance	Ring Gap Top Compression	Bottom Compression	Oil Control	Ring Side Clearance Top Compression	Bottom Compression	Oil Control
2006	2.4	B	0.0004-0.0016	0.006-0.012	0.008-0.018	0.006-0.020	0.0015-0.0031	0.0012-0.0030	0.0011-0.0069
2007	2.4	B	0.0004-0.0016	0.006-0.012	0.008-0.018	0.006-0.020	0.0015-0.0031	0.0012-0.0030	0.0011-0.0069
	2.0	M	0.0004-0.0016	0.0078-0.0138	0.014-0.0220	0.010-0.0300	0.0016-0.0031	0.0001-0.0027	0.0009-0.0069
2008	2.4	B	0.0004-0.0016	0.006-0.012	0.008-0.018	0.006-0.020	0.0015-0.0031	0.0012-0.0030	0.0011-0.0069
	2.0	M	0.0004-0.0016	0.0039-0.0098	0.014-0.0220	0.010-0.0300	0.0016-0.0031	0.0001-0.0027	0.0009-0.0069

22116_SOLS_C0008

TORQUE SPECIFICATIONS

All readings in ft. lbs.

Year	Engine Displacement Liters	Engine VIN	Cylinder Head Bolts	Main Bearing Bolts	Rod Bearing Bolts	Crankshaft Damper Bolts	Flywheel Bolts	Manifold Intake	Exhaust	Spark Plugs	Oil Pan Drain Plug
2006	2.4	B	①	②	③	④	⑤	⑥	10	15	18
2007	2.4	B	①	②	③	④	⑤	⑥	10	15	18
	2.0	M	①	②	③	④	⑤	⑥	10	15	18
2008	2.4	B	①	②	③	④	⑤	⑥	10	15	18
	2.0	M	①	②	③	④	⑤	⑥	10	15	18

① Step 1: 22 ft. lbs. (30 Nm).
Step 2: plus 155 degress
For 2.4L front chaincase bolts: 26 ft. lbs.

② Bedplate-to-block
Cap bolts
Step 1: 15 ft. lbs. (20 Nm).
Step 2: plus 79 degrees
Perimeter bolts: 18 ft. lbs.

③ Step 1: 18 ft. lbs. (25 Nm).
Step 2: plus 100 degrees

④ Step 1: 74 ft. lbs. (100 Nm).
Step 2: plus 125 degrees

⑤ Step 1: 39 ft. lbs. (53 Nm).
Step 2: plus 25 degrees

⑥ Bolts and nuts: 89 inch. lbs. (10 Nm);
studs: 53 inch. lbs. (6 Nm).

22116_SOLS_C0009

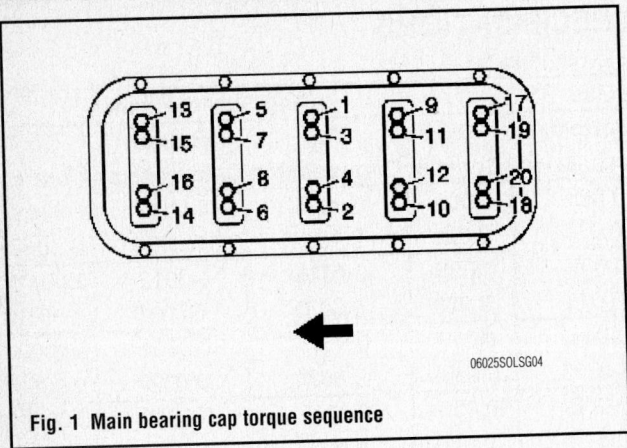

Fig. 1 Main bearing cap torque sequence

WHEEL ALIGNMENT

Year	Model		Caster Range (+/-Deg.)	Caster Preferred Setting (Deg.)	Camber Range (+/-Deg.)	Camber Preferred Setting (Deg.)	Toe-in (in.)
2006	Solstice	F	0.60	+8.00	0.60	-0.50	0.10+/-0.20
		R	0.75	-4.00	0.50	-0.50	0.10+/-0.20
2007	Sky	F	0.60	+8.00	0.60	-0.50	0.10+/-0.20
		R	0.75	-4.00	0.50	-0.50	0.10+/-0.20
	Solstice	F	0.60	+8.00	0.60	-0.50	0.10+/-0.20
		R	0.75	-4.00	0.50	-0.50	0.10+/-0.20
2008	Sky	F	0.60	+8.00	0.60	-0.50	0.10+/-0.20
		R	0.75	-4.00	0.50	-0.50	0.10+/-0.20
	Solstice	F	0.60	+8.00	0.60	-0.50	0.10+/-0.20
		R	0.75	-4.00	0.50	-0.50	0.10+/-0.20

22116_SOLS_C0010

TIRE, WHEEL AND BALL JOINT SPECIFICATIONS

Year	Model	OEM Tires Standard	OEM Tires Optional	Tire Pressures (psi) Front	Tire Pressures (psi) Rear	Wheel Size	Ball Joint Inspection	Lug Nuts (ft. lbs.)
2006	Solstice	P245/45R18	none	①	①	8J	②	100
2007	Sky	P245/45R18	none	①	①	8J	②	100
	Solstice	P245/45R18	none	①	①	8J	②	100
2007	Sky	P245/45R18	none	①	①	8J	②	100
	Solstice	P245/45R18	none	①	①	8J	②	100

OEM: Original Equipment Manufacturer

PSI: Pounds Per Square Inch

① See placard on vehicle

② Replace if any movement is noted

22116_SOLS_C0012

BRAKE SPECIFICATIONS
All measurements in inches unless noted

| Year | Model | | Brake Disc | | | Minimum Lining Thickness | Brake Caliper | |
			Original Thickness	Minimum Thickness	Maximum Run-out		Bracket Bolts (ft. lbs.)	Mounting Bolts (ft. lbs.)
2006	Solstice	F	1.023	0.906	0.002	NA	85	25
		R	0.465	0.394	0.002	NA	85	20
2007	Sky	F	1.023	0.906	0.002	NA	85	25
		R	0.465	0.394	0.002	NA	85	20
	Solstice	F	1.023	0.906	0.002	NA	85	25
		R	0.465	0.394	0.002	NA	85	20
2008	Sky	F	1.023	0.906	0.002	NA	85	25
		R	0.465	0.394	0.002	NA	85	20
	Solstice	F	1.023	0.906	0.002	NA	85	25
		R	0.465	0.394	0.002	NA	85	20

NA: Information not available

22116_SOLS_C0013

SCHEDULED MAINTENANCE INTERVALS
2006-08 PONTIAC Solstice/SATURN Sky

TO BE SERVICED	TYPE OF SERVICE	VEHICLE MILEAGE INTERVAL (x1000)															
		5	10	15	20	25	30	35	40	45	50	55	60	65	70	75	80
Accessory drive belt	S/I	Every 150,000 miles															
Air cleaner filter ①	S/I			✓			✓			✓			✓			✓	
Automatic transmission fluid and filter ②	R										✓						
Brake fluid level	I	Every 6 months															
Clutch fluid level	I	Every 6 months															
Engine coolant system ③	S/I	Every 150,000 miles or 60 months															
Engine oil & filter ④	R	✓	✓	✓	✓	✓	✓	✓	✓	✓	✓	✓	✓	✓	✓	✓	✓
Hinges and latches	L	Once a year															
Restraint system	I	Every 6 months															
Tires ⑤	Rotate		✓		✓		✓		✓		✓		✓		✓		✓
Spark plugs	R	Every 100,000 miles															
Wiper blades	S/I	Every 6 months															

R: Replace   S/I: Inspect and service, if necessary   L: Lubricate

① Replace as necessary, but, replace every 45,000 miles if not previously done.

② Replace at this interval if driven under any of these conditons:

　Heavy city traffic where the outside temperature regularly reaches 32°C (90°F) or higher

　Hilly or mountainous terrain

　Frequent trailer towing

　Taxi, police or delivery service

　Otherwise, change every 100,000 miles

③ Drain an flush

④ For vehicle with a Driver Information Center, change the oil and filter when specified by the DIC.

⑤ Check wear and inflation every month

After each oil change, reset the Engine Oil Life System as follows:

1. Turn the ignition switch to RUN with the engine OFF.

2. Press the Information and Reset buttons on the DIC at the same time to enter the personalization menu.

3. Press the Information button to scroll through the menu to Oil Life Reset.

4. Press and hold the Reset button until the display shows Acknowledged.

5. Turn the key to OFF.

22116_SOLS_C0014

PRECAUTIONS

Before servicing any vehicle, please be sure to read all of the following precautions, which deal with personal safety, prevention of component damage, and important points to take into consideration when servicing a motor vehicle:

• Never open, service or drain the radiator or cooling system when the engine is hot; serious burns can occur from the steam and hot coolant.

• Observe all applicable safety precautions when working around fuel. Whenever servicing the fuel system, always work in a well-ventilated area. Do not allow fuel spray or vapors to come in contact with a spark, open flame, or excessive heat (a hot drop light, for example). Keep a dry chemical fire extinguisher near the work area. Always keep fuel in a container specifically designed for fuel storage; also, always properly seal fuel containers to avoid the possibility of fire or explosion. Refer to the additional fuel system precautions later in this section.

• Fuel injection systems often remain pressurized, even after the engine has been turned **OFF**. The fuel system pressure must be relieved before disconnecting any fuel lines. Failure to do so may result in fire and/or personal injury.

• Brake fluid often contains polyglycol ethers and polyglycols. Avoid contact with the eyes and wash your hands thoroughly after handling brake fluid. If you do get brake fluid in your eyes, flush your eyes with clean, running water for 15 minutes. If eye irritation persists, or if you have taken brake fluid internally, IMMEDIATELY seek medical assistance.

• The EPA warns that prolonged contact with used engine oil may cause a number of skin disorders, including cancer. You should make every effort to minimize your exposure to used engine oil. Protective gloves should be worn when changing oil. Wash your hands and any other exposed skin areas as soon as possible after exposure to used engine oil. Soap and water, or waterless hand cleaner should be used.

• All new vehicles are now equipped with an air bag system, often referred to as a Supplemental Restraint System (SRS) or Supplemental Inflatable Restraint (SIR) system. The system must be disabled before performing service on or around system components, steering column, instrument panel components, wiring and sensors. Failure to follow safety and disabling procedures could result in accidental air bag deployment, possible personal injury and unnecessary system repairs.

• Always wear safety goggles when working with, or around, the air bag system. When carrying a non-deployed air bag, be sure the bag and trim cover are pointed away from your body. When placing a non-deployed air bag on a work surface, always face the bag and trim cover upward, away from the surface. This will reduce the motion of the module if it is accidentally deployed. Refer to the additional air bag system precautions later in this section.

• Clean, high quality brake fluid from a sealed container is essential to the safe and proper operation of the brake system. You should always buy the correct type of brake fluid for your vehicle. If the brake fluid becomes contaminated, completely flush the system with new fluid. Never reuse any brake fluid. Any brake fluid that is removed from the system should be discarded. Also, do not allow any brake fluid to come in contact with a painted surface; it will damage the paint.

• Never operate the engine without the proper amount and type of engine oil; doing so WILL result in severe engine damage.

• Timing belt maintenance is extremely important. Many models utilize an interference-type, non-freewheeling engine. If the timing belt breaks, the valves in the cylinder head may strike the pistons, causing potentially serious (also time-consuming and expensive) engine damage. Refer to the maintenance interval charts for the recommended replacement interval for the timing belt, and to the timing belt section for belt replacement and inspection.

• Disconnecting the negative battery cable on some vehicles may interfere with the functions of the on-board computer system(s) and may require the computer to undergo a relearning process once the negative battery cable is reconnected.

• When servicing drum brakes, only disassemble and assemble one side at a time, leaving the remaining side intact for reference.

• Only an MVAC-trained, EPA-certified automotive technician should service the air conditioning system or its components.

BRAKES

ANTI-LOCK BRAKE SYSTEM (ABS)

GENERAL INFORMATION

This vehicle is equipped with the MK 25 E Continental Teves antilock braking system.

The vehicle is equipped with the following braking systems:

• Antilock Brake System (ABS)
• Engine Drag Control (EDC)
• Electronic Brake Distribution (EBC)
• Hydraulic Brake Booster
• Traction Control System (TCS)
• Vehicle Stability Enhancement System (VSES) (w/JL4)

When wheel slip is detected during a brake application, the ABS enters antilock mode. During antilock braking, hydraulic pressure in the individual wheel circuits is controlled to prevent any wheel from slipping. A separate hydraulic line and specific solenoid valves are provided for each wheel. The ABS can decrease, hold, or increase hydraulic pressure to each wheel brake. The ABS cannot, however, increase hydraulic pressure above the amount which is transmitted by the master cylinder during braking.

During antilock braking, a series of rapid pulsations is felt in the brake pedal. These pulsations are caused by the rapid changes in position of the individual solenoid valves as the EBCM responds to wheel speed sensor inputs and attempts to prevent wheel slip. These pedal pulsations are present only during antilock braking and stop when normal braking is resumed or when the vehicle comes to a stop. A ticking or popping noise may also be heard as the solenoid valves cycle rapidly. During antilock braking on dry pavement, intermittent chirping noises may be heard as the tires approach slipping. These noises and pedal pulsations are considered normal during antilock operation

Vehicles equipped with ABS may be stopped by applying normal force to the brake pedal. Brake pedal operation during normal braking is no different than that of previous non-ABS systems. Maintaining a constant force on the brake pedal provides the shortest stopping distance while maintaining vehicle stability.

PRECAUTIONS

• Certain components within the ABS system are not intended to be serviced or repaired individually.

- Do not use rubber hoses or other parts not specifically specified for and ABS system. When using repair kits, replace all parts included in the kit. Partial or incorrect repair may lead to functional problems and require the replacement of components.

- Lubricate rubber parts with clean, fresh brake fluid to ease assembly. Do not use shop air to clean parts; damage to rubber components may result.

- Use only DOT 3 brake fluid from an unopened container.

- If any hydraulic component or line is removed or replaced, it may be necessary to bleed the entire system.

- A clean repair area is essential. Always clean the reservoir and cap thoroughly before removing the cap. The slightest amount of dirt in the fluid may plug an orifice and impair the system function. Perform repairs after components have been thoroughly cleaned; use only denatured alcohol to clean components. Do not allow ABS components to come into contact with any substance containing mineral oil; this includes used shop rags.

- The Anti-Lock control unit is a microprocessor similar to other computer units in the vehicle. Ensure that the ignition switch is **OFF** before removing or installing controller harnesses. Avoid static electricity discharge at or near the controller.

- If any arc welding is to be done on the vehicle, the control unit should be unplugged before welding operations begin.

WHEEL SPEED SENSORS

REMOVAL & INSTALLATION

The wheel speed sensors are part of the wheel hub and bearing assembly. Refer to wheel hub and bearing section.

BRAKES

BLEEDING THE BRAKE SYSTEM

BLEEDING PROCEDURE

BLEEDING PROCEDURE

1. Before servicing the vehicle, refer to the Precautions Section.

✳✳ CAUTION

When adding fluid to the brake master cylinder reservoir, use only Delco Supreme 11®, GM P/N 12377967 (Canadian P/N 992667), or equivalent DOT-3 brake fluid from a clean, sealed brake fluid container. The use of any type of fluid other than the recommended type of brake fluid, may cause contamination which could result in damage to the internal rubber seals and/or rubber linings of hydraulic brake system components.

2. Place a clean shop cloth beneath the brake master cylinder to prevent brake fluid spills.

3. With the ignition OFF and the brakes cool, apply the brakes 3-5 times, or until the brake pedal effort increases significantly, in order to deplete the brake booster power reserve.

4. If you have performed a brake master cylinder bench bleeding on this vehicle, or if you disconnected the brake pipes from the master cylinder, or disconnected the brake pipes from the proportioning valve assembly or the brake modulator assembly, you must perform the following steps to bleed air at the ports of the hydraulic component:

a. Ensure that the brake master cylinder reservoir is full to the maximum-fill level. If necessary, add GM approved, or equivalent DOT-3 brake fluid from a clean, sealed brake fluid container. If removal of the reservoir cap and diaphragm is necessary, clean the outside of the reservoir on and around the cap prior to removal.

b. With the brake pipes installed securely to the master cylinder, proportioning valve assembly, or brake modulator assembly, loosen and separate one of the brake pipes from the port of the component. For the proportioning valve assembly or the brake modulator assembly perform these steps in the sequence of system flow; begin with the fluid feed pipes from the master cylinder.

c. Allow a small amount of brake fluid to gravity bleed from the open port of the component.

d. Reconnect the brake pipe to the component port and tighten securely.

e. Have an assistant slowly depress the brake pedal fully and maintain steady pressure on the pedal.

f. Loosen the same brake pipe to purge air from the open port of the component.

g. Tighten the brake pipe, then have the assistant slowly release the brake pedal.

h. Wait 15 seconds, then repeat steps 3-7 until all air is purged from the same port of the component.

i. With the brake pipe installed securely to the master cylinder, proportioning valve assembly, or brake modulator assembly-after all air has been purged from the first port of the component that was bled-loosen and separate the next brake pipe from the component, then repeat steps 3-8 until each of the ports on the component have been bled.

j. After completing the final component port bleeding procedure, ensure that each of the brake pipe-to-component fittings are properly tightened.

5. Fill the brake master cylinder reservoir with GM approved, or equivalent DOT-3 brake fluid from a clean, sealed brake fluid container. Ensure that the brake master cylinder reservoir remains at least half-full during this bleeding procedure. Add fluid as needed to maintain the proper level. Clean the outside of the reservoir on and around the reservoir cap prior to removing the cap and diaphragm.

6. Install a proper box-end wrench onto the RIGHT REAR wheel hydraulic circuit bleeder valve.

7. Install a transparent hose over the end of the bleeder valve.

8. Submerge the open end of the transparent hose into a transparent container partially filled with GM approved, or equivalent DOT-3 brake fluid from a clean, sealed brake fluid container.

9. Have an assistant slowly depress the brake pedal fully and maintain steady pressure on the pedal.

10. Loosen the bleeder valve to purge air from the wheel hydraulic circuit.

11. Tighten the bleeder valve, then have the assistant slowly release the brake pedal.

12. Wait 15 seconds, then repeat steps 8-10 until all air is purged from the same wheel hydraulic circuit.

13. With the right rear wheel hydraulic circuit bleeder valve tightened securely, after all air has been purged from the right rear hydraulic circuit, install a proper box-end wrench onto the LEFT FRONT wheel hydraulic circuit bleeder valve.

14. Install a transparent hose over the end of the bleeder valve, then repeat steps 7-11.

15. With the left front wheel hydraulic circuit bleeder valve tightened securely, after all air has been purged from the left front hydraulic circuit, install a proper box-end

wrench onto the LEFT REAR wheel hydraulic circuit bleeder valve.

16. Install a transparent hose over the end of the bleeder valve, then repeat steps 7-11.

17. With the left rear wheel hydraulic circuit bleeder valve tightened securely, after all air has been purged from the left rear hydraulic circuit, install a proper box-end wrench onto the RIGHT FRONT wheel hydraulic circuit bleeder valve.

18. Install a transparent hose over the end of the bleeder valve, then repeat steps 7-11.

19. After completing the final wheel hydraulic circuit bleeding procedure, ensure that each of the 4 wheel hydraulic circuit bleeder valves are properly tightened.

20. Fill the brake master cylinder reservoir to the maximum-fill level with GM approved, or equivalent DOT-3 brake fluid from a clean, sealed brake fluid container.

21. Slowly depress and release the brake pedal. Observe the feel of the brake pedal.

➡**If it is determined that air was inducted into the system upstream of the ABS modulator prior to servicing, the ABS Automated Bleed Procedure must be performed.**

22. If the brake pedal feels spongy, repeat the bleeding procedure again. If the brake pedal still feels spongy after repeating the bleeding procedure, perform the following steps:

a. Inspect the brake system for external leaks.

b. Pressure bleed the hydraulic brake system in order to purge any air that may still be trapped in the system.

23. Turn the ignition key ON, with the engine OFF. Check to see if the brake system warning lamp remains illuminated.

BLEEDING THE ABS SYSTEM

The automated bleed procedure is recommended when one of the following conditions exist:

• Base brake system bleeding does not achieve the desired pedal height or feel

• Extreme loss of brake fluid has occurred

• Air ingestion is suspected in the secondary circuits of the brake modulator assembly

The ABS Automated Bleed Procedure uses a scan tool to cycle the system solenoid valves and run the pump in order to purge any air from the secondary circuits. These circuits are normally closed off, and are only opened during system initialization at vehicle start up and during ABS operation. The automated bleed procedure opens these secondary circuits and allows any air trapped in these circuits to flow out toward the brake corners.

➡**The Auto Bleed Procedure may be terminated at any time during the process by pressing the EXIT button. No further Scan Tool prompts pertaining to the Auto Bleed procedure will be given. After exiting the bleed procedure, relieve bleed pressure and disconnect bleed equipment per manufacturer's instructions. Failure to properly relieve pressure may result in spilled brake fluid causing damage to components and painted surfaces.**

1. Perform the automated bleed procedure as follows.

2. Raise and support the vehicle.

3. Inspect the brake system for leaks and visual damage.

4. Lower the vehicle.

5. Inspect the battery state of charge.

6. Install a scan tool.

7. Turn the ignition ON, with the engine OFF.

8. With the scan tool, establish communications with the ABS system. Select Special Functions. Select Automated Bleed from the Special Functions menu.

9. Raise and support the vehicle.

10. Following the directions given on the scan tool, pressure bleed the base brake system.

11. Follow the scan tool directions until the desired brake pedal height is achieved.

12. If the bleed procedure is aborted, a malfunction exists. Perform the following steps before resuming the bleed procedure:

a. If a DTC is detected, diagnose the appropriate DTC.

b. If the brake pedal feels spongy, perform the conventional brake bleed procedure again.

13. When the desired pedal height is achieved, press the brake pedal to inspect for firmness.

14. Lower the vehicle.

15. Remove the scan tool.

16. Install the tire and wheel assemblies.

17. Inspect the brake fluid level.

18. Road test the vehicle while inspecting that the pedal remains high and firm.

BRAKES

FRONT DISC BRAKES

BRAKE CALIPER

REMOVAL & INSTALLATION

See Figure 2.

1. Before servicing the vehicle, refer to the Precautions Section.

2. Raise and support the vehicle.

3. Remove the tire and wheel.

4. Remove the brake hose bolt.

5. Remove the brake hose bolt washers.

6. Remove the front brake hose.

7. Cap or plug the brake hose to prevent fluid loss and contamination

8. Remove the brake caliper bolt.

9. Remove the brake caliper.

To install:

10. Installation is the reverse of removal procedure.

11. Please take note of the following tightening specifications:

• Tighten the caliper mounting bolts to 25 ft. lbs. (34 Nm).

• Tighten the brake hose bolt to 30 ft. lbs. (40 Nm).

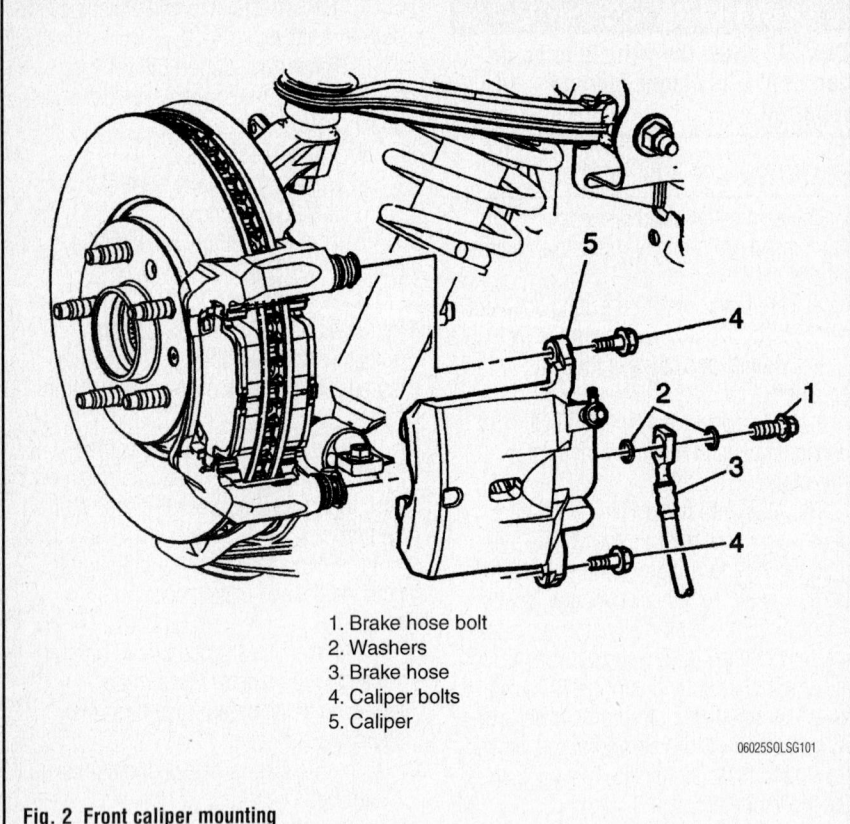

1. Brake hose bolt
2. Washers
3. Brake hose
4. Caliper bolts
5. Caliper

06025SOLSG101

Fig. 2 Front caliper mounting

To install:

10. Installation is the reverse of removal procedure.

11. Please take note of the following tightening specifications:
   - Tighten the caliper bolt to 25 ft. lbs. (34 Nm).

12. Apply brake lubricant to the front caliper guide pins ensuring adequate lubrication to both pin areas of the front brake caliper bracket with GM P/N 22688644 or equivalent.

➡ **DO NOT reuse the old brake pad springs if replacing the brake pads, use new springs.**

13. Gradually apply pressure to the brake pedal until a firm pedal is felt. If a firm pedal is not achieved, wait 15 seconds and repeat until a firm pedal is obtained.

14. Fill the master cylinder reservoir to the proper level.

15. Burnish the brake pads and rotors.

BRAKE PAD & ROTOR BURNISHING

✳✳ CAUTION

Road test a vehicle under safe conditions and while obeying all traffic laws. Do not attempt any maneuvers that could jeopardize vehicle

12. Bleed the brakes.

13. Gradually apply pressure to the brake pedal until a firm pedal is felt. If a firm pedal is not achieved, wait 15 seconds and repeat until a firm pedal is obtained.

14. Fill the master cylinder to the proper level.

✳✳ WARNING

Do not reuse the brake hose bolt washers.

DISC BRAKE PADS

REMOVAL & INSTALLATION

See Figure 3.

1. Before servicing the vehicle, refer to the Precautions Section.

2. Raise and support the vehicle.

3. Remove the tire and wheel.

4. Lower brake caliper guide pin bolt.

5. Rotate the brake caliper up and forward until it rests on the brake caliper mounting bracket. The brake hose does not have to be removed from the brake caliper.

6. Remove the brake pads.

7. Remove the brake pad springs.

8. Remove about half of the fluid from the master cylinder.

9. Using an appropriate tool, force the caliper piston back into the caliper.

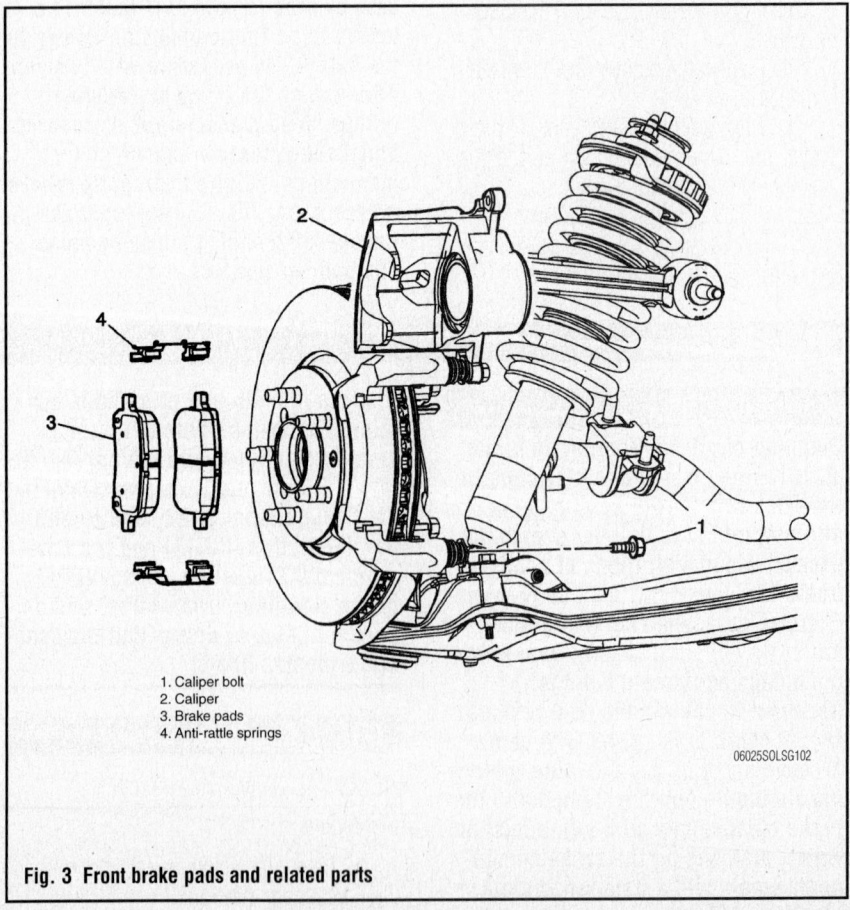

1. Caliper bolt
2. Caliper
3. Brake pads
4. Anti-rattle springs

06025SOLSG102

Fig. 3 Front brake pads and related parts

control. Failure to adhere to these precautions could lead to serious personal injury and vehicle damage.

Burnishing the brake pads and brake rotors is necessary in order to ensure that the braking surfaces are properly prepared after service has been performed on the disc brake system.

This procedure should be performed whenever the disc brake rotors have been refinished or replaced, and/or whenever the disc brake pads have been replaced.

1. Select a smooth road with little or no traffic.
2. Accelerate the vehicle to 48 km/h (30 mph).
3. Using moderate to firm pressure, apply the brakes to bring the vehicle to a stop. Do not allow the brakes to lock.

➡ Use care to avoid overheating the brakes while performing this step.

4. Using moderate to firm pressure, apply the brakes to bring the vehicle to a stop. Do not allow the brakes to lock.
5. Repeat steps 2 and 3 until approximately 20 stops have been completed. Allow sufficient cooling periods between stops in order to properly burnish the brake pads and rotors

BRAKES

✳ CAUTION

Dust and dirt accumulating on brake parts during normal use may contain asbestos fibers from production or aftermarket brake linings. Breathing excessive concentrations of asbestos fibers can cause serious bodily harm Exercise care when servicing brake parts. Do not sand or grind brake lining unless equipment used is designed to contain the dust residue. Do not clean brake parts with compressed air or by dry brushing. Cleaning should be done by dampening the brake components with a fine mist of water, then wiping the brake components clean with a dampened cloth. Dispose of cloth and all residue containing asbestos fibers in an impermeable container with the appropriate label. Follow practices prescribed by the Occupational Safety and Health Administration (OSHA) and the Environmental Protection Agency (EPA) for the handling, processing, and disposing of dust or debris that may contain asbestos fibers.

BRAKE CALIPER

REMOVAL & INSTALLATION
See Figure 4.

1. Before servicing the vehicle, refer to the Precautions Section.
2. Raise and support the vehicle.
3. Remove the tire and wheel.
4. Release the tension from the park brake cables.
5. Disconnect the park brake cable from the actuator lever on the brake caliper.
6. Remove the brake hose bolt.
7. Remove the brake hose bolt washers.
8. Remove the brake hose.

9. Cap or plug the brake hose to prevent fluid loss and contamination
10. Remove the brake caliper bolt.
11. Remove the brake caliper.

To install:
12. Installation is the reverse of removal procedure.
13. Please take note of the following tightening specifications:
- Tighten the caliper mounting bolts to 20 ft. lbs. (27 Nm).
- Tighten the brake hose bolt to 30 ft. lbs. (40 Nm).

REAR DISC BRAKES

✳ WARNING

Do not reuse the brake hose bolt washers.

14. Bleed the hydraulic brake system.
15. Gradually apply pressure to the brake pedal until a firm pedal is felt. If a firm pedal is not achieved, wait 15 seconds and repeat until a firm pedal is obtained.
16. Fill the master cylinder reservoir to the proper level.
17. Connect the park brake cable to the actuator lever on the caliper.

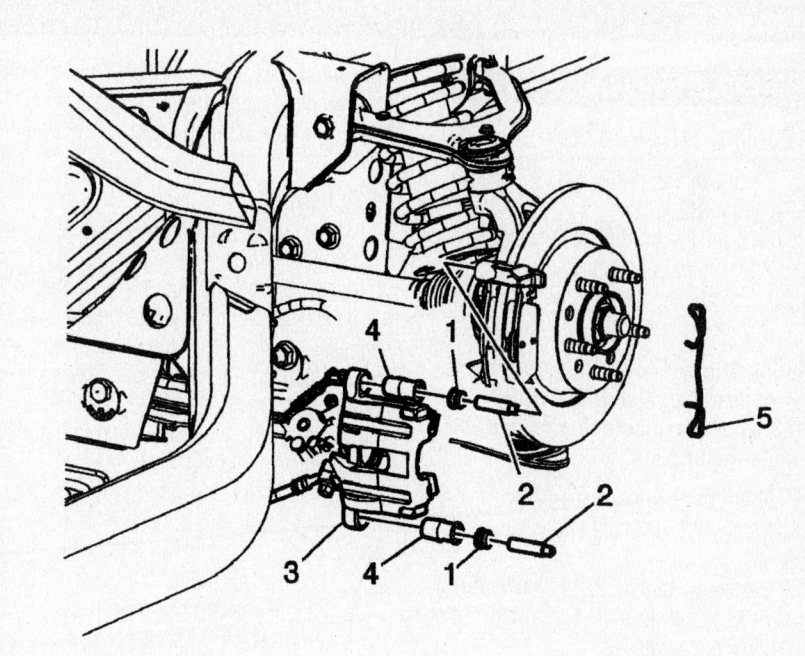

1. Guide pin seal
2. guide pin
3. Caliper
4. Bushing
5. Anti-rattle spring

06025SOLSG104

Fig. 4 Rear brake caliper and related parts

18. Adjust the tension of the park brake cables.

19. Burnish the brake pads and rotors.

DISC BRAKE PADS

REMOVAL & INSTALLATION

1. Before servicing the vehicle, refer to the Precautions Section.

2. Raise and support the vehicle.

3. Remove the tire and wheel.

4. Lower brake caliper guide pin bolt.

5. Rotate the brake caliper up and forward until it rests on the brake caliper mounting bracket. The brake hose does not have to be removed from the brake caliper.

6. Remove the brake pads.

7. Remove the brake pad springs.

8. Remove about half of the fluid from the master cylinder.

9. Using an appropriate tool, force the caliper piston back into the caliper.

To install:

10. Installation is the reverse of removal procedure.

11. Please take note of the following tightening specifications:

• Tighten the caliper bolt to 20 ft. lbs. (27 Nm).

12. Apply brake lubricant to the front caliper guide pins ensuring adequate lubrication to both pin areas of the front brake caliper bracket with GM P/N 22688644 or equivalent.

➡ **DO NOT reuse the old brake pad springs if replacing the brake pads, use new springs.**

13. Gradually apply pressure to the brake pedal until a firm pedal is felt. If a firm pedal is not achieved, wait 15 seconds and repeat until a firm pedal is obtained.

14. Fill the master cylinder reservoir to the proper level.

15. Burnish the brake pads and rotors.

BRAKE PAD & ROTOR BURNISHING

※ CAUTION

Road test a vehicle under safe conditions and while obeying all traffic laws. Do not attempt any maneuvers that could jeopardize vehicle control. Failure to adhere to these precautions could lead to serious personal injury and vehicle damage.

Burnishing the brake pads and brake rotors is necessary in order to ensure that the braking surfaces are properly prepared after service has been performed on the disc brake system.

This procedure should be performed whenever the disc brake rotors have been refinished or replaced, and/or whenever the disc brake pads have been replaced.

1. Select a smooth road with little or no traffic.

2. Accelerate the vehicle to 48 km/h (30 mph).

3. Using moderate to firm pressure, apply the brakes to bring the vehicle to a stop. Do not allow the brakes to lock.

➡ **Use care to avoid overheating the brakes while performing this step.**

4. Using moderate to firm pressure, apply the brakes to bring the vehicle to a stop. Do not allow the brakes to lock.

5. Repeat steps 2 and 3 until approximately 20 stops have been completed. Allow sufficient cooling periods between stops in order to properly burnish the brake pads and rotors

BRAKES

PARKING BRAKE CABLE

REMOVAL & INSTALLATION

1. Before servicing the vehicle, refer to the Precautions Section.

2. Remove the front floor console.

3. With the park brake lever fully released, completely back off the adjustment nut.

➡ **The park brake cable adjusting nut is a nylon lock type. Use ONLY HAND TOOLS whenever tightening or loosening the adjusting nut.**

4. Raise and support the vehicle.

5. Remove the rear tire and wheel assemblies.

6. Carefully position the driveline tunnel insulator downward just enough to access the cable equalizer.

7. Rotate the front cable end to release the cable from the equalizer.

8. Release the wheel speed sensor harness clips from the park brake cable.

9. Disconnect the park brake cables from the park brake actuator levers on the brake calipers.

10. Remove parking brake retainer clips.

11. Move the cable conduit rearward to

clear the tunnel bracket, then lift the cables to release the cables from the bracket

12. Remove parking brake cable assembly.

To install:

13. Install the parking brake cable assembly.

14. Reconnect the park brake cables to the park brake actuator levers on the brake calipers.

15. Reattach the wheel speed sensor harness clips to the park brake cable.

16. Rotate the front cable end to install the cable to the equalizer.

17. Reconnect driveline tunnel insulator.

18. Install the rear tire and wheel assemblies.

19. Lower the vehicle.

20. Adjust parking brake cable.

21. Install the front floor console.

ADJUSTMENT

1. Remove the front floor console.

2. Cycle the park lever several times. Verify the lever releases fully.

3. Turn the ignition ON. Verify the red BRAKE warning lamp is not illuminated. If the warning lamp is illuminated, verify the following:

PARKING BRAKE

• The lever is fully released and against the stop.

• There is not excessive slack in the cables.

• If the warning lamp remained illuminated and there were no visible causes, check hydraulic system.

• Turn the ignition OFF.

• Raise and support the vehicle enough to raise the rear tire and wheel assemblies off the ground.

4. Ensure the park brake lever is fully released.

5. Loosen the cable tension adjusting nut just enough to back the nut away from the lever cam.

6. Tighten the adjusting nut just until slack in the front cable is removed and the nut rests against the lever cam.

➡ **The park brake cable adjusting nut is a nylon lock type. Use ONLY HAND TOOLS whenever tightening or loosening the adjusting nut.**

7. Cycle the park brake lever several times.

8. With the lever fully released, tighten the adjusting nut just enough to remove slack in the front cable.

9. Raise the lever 1 detent position, then attempt to rotate the rear wheels. Both sides should require high effort to rotate.

10. Raise the lever 1 more detent, to the second position, then attempt to rotate the rear wheels. One side should be locked,

the other side should require high effort to rotate.

11. Raise the lever 1 more detent, to the third detent position, then attempt to rotate the rear wheels. Both sides should be locked.

12. Release the park brake lever, then

rotate the rear wheels to inspect for drag.

13. There should not be any drag from the park brake system.

14. Inspect the brake caliper park brake levers to ensure that they are resting against the stops.

CHASSIS ELECTRICAL

AIR BAG (SUPPLEMENTAL RESTRAINT SYSTEM)

GENERAL INFORMATION

✳✳ CAUTION

These vehicles are equipped with an air bag system. The system must be disarmed before performing service on, or around, system components, the steering column, instrument panel components, wiring and sensors. Failure to follow the safety precautions and the disarming procedure could result in accidental air bag deployment, possible injury and unnecessary system repairs.

SERVICE PRECAUTIONS

Disconnect and isolate the battery negative cable before beginning any airbag system component diagnosis, testing, removal, or installation procedures. Allow system capacitor to discharge for two minutes before beginning any component service. This will disable the airbag system. Failure to disable the airbag system may result in accidental airbag deployment, personal injury, or death.

Do not place an intact undeployed airbag face down on a solid surface. The airbag will propel into the air if accidentally deployed and may result in personal injury or death.

When carrying or handling an undeployed airbag, the trim side (face) of the airbag should be pointing towards the body to minimize possibility of injury if accidental deployment occurs. Failure to do this may result in personal injury or death.

Replace airbag system components with OEM replacement parts. Substitute parts may appear interchangeable, but internal differences may result in inferior occupant protection. Failure to do so may result in occupant personal injury or death.

Wear safety glasses, rubber gloves, and long sleeved clothing when cleaning powder residue from vehicle after an airbag deployment. Powder residue emitted from

a deployed airbag can cause skin irritation. Flush affected area with cool water if irritation is experienced. If nasal or throat irritation is experienced, exit the vehicle for fresh air until the irritation ceases. If irritation continues, see a physician.

Do not use a replacement airbag that is not in the original packaging. This may result in improper deployment, personal injury, or death.

The factory installed fasteners, screws and bolts used to fasten airbag components have a special coating and are specifically designed for the airbag system. Do not use substitute fasteners. Use only original equipment fasteners listed in the parts catalog when fastener replacement is required.

During, and following, any child restraint anchor service, due to impact event or vehicle repair, carefully inspect all mounting hardware, tether straps, and anchors for proper installation, operation, or damage. If a child restraint anchor is found damaged in any way, the anchor must be replaced. Failure to do this may result in personal injury or death.

Deployed and non-deployed airbags may or may not have live pyrotechnic material within the airbag inflator.

Do not dispose of driver/passenger/curtain airbags or seat belt tensioners unless you are sure of complete deployment. Refer to the Hazardous Substance Control System for proper disposal.

Dispose of deployed airbags and tensioners consistent with state, provincial, local, and federal regulations.

After any airbag component testing or service, do not connect the battery negative cable. Personal injury or death may result if the system test is not performed first.

If the vehicle is equipped with the Occupant Classification System (OCS), do not connect the battery negative cable before performing the OCS Verification Test using the scan tool and the appropriate diagnostic information. Personal injury or death may result if the system test is not performed properly.

Never replace both the Occupant Restraint Controller (ORC) and the Occupant Classification Module (OCM) at the same time. If both require replacement, replace one, then perform the Airbag System test before replacing the other.

Both the ORC and the OCM store Occupant Classification System (OCS) calibration data, which they transfer to one another when one of them is replaced. If both are replaced at the same time, an irreversible fault will be set in both modules and the OCS may malfunction and cause personal injury or death.

If equipped with OCS, the Seat Weight Sensor is a sensitive, calibrated unit and must be handled carefully. Do not drop or handle roughly. If dropped or damaged, replace with another sensor. Failure to do so may result in occupant injury or death.

If equipped with OCS, the front passenger seat must be handled carefully as well. When removing the seat, be careful when setting on floor not to drop. If dropped, the sensor may be inoperative, could result in occupant injury, or possibly death.

If equipped with OCS, when the passenger front seat is on the floor, no one should sit in the front passenger seat. This uneven force may damage the sensing ability of the seat weight sensors. If sat on and damaged, the sensor may be inoperative, could result in occupant injury, or possibly death.

DISARMING THE SYSTEM

Zone 1

See Figures 5 and 6.

1. Before servicing the vehicle, refer to the Precautions Section.

2. Turn the steering wheel so that the vehicles wheels are pointing straight ahead.

3. Place the ignition switch to the OFF position.

4. Remove the passenger floor mat and remove the kick up panel covering the body control module (BCM) fuse center.

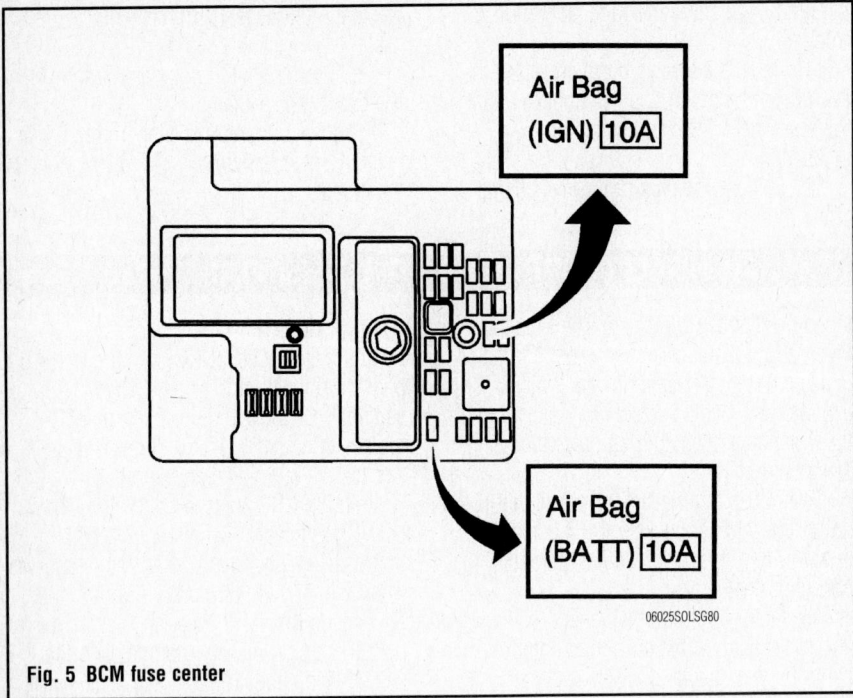

Fig. 5 BCM fuse center

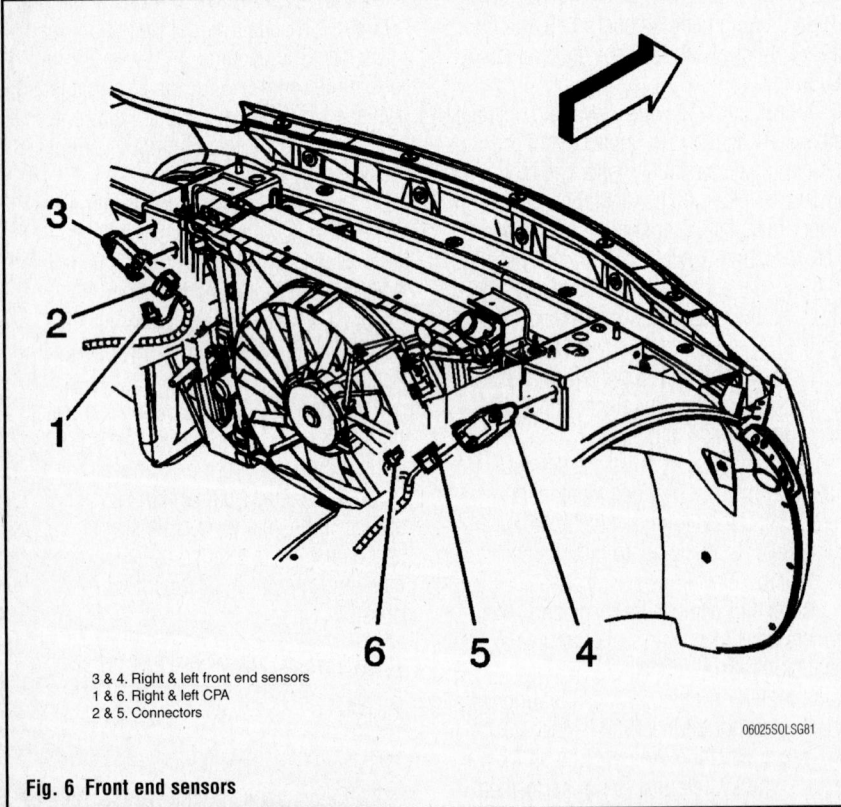

3 & 4. Right & left front end sensors
1 & 6. Right & left CPA
2 & 5. Connectors

Fig. 6 Front end sensors

> ❈❈ **WARNING**
>
> This sensing and diagnostic module (SDM) has two fused power inputs. To ensure there is no unwanted SIR deployment, personal injury, or unnecessary SIR system repairs, remove both AIR BAG (IGN) and AIR BAG (BATT) fuses from the BCM fuse center. With the AIR BAG fuses removed and the ignition switch in the ON position, the AIR BAG warning indicator illuminates. This is normal operation, and does not indicate an SIR system malfunction.

5. Locate and remove the AIR BAG (IGN) and AIR BAG (BATT) fuses from the BCM fuse center.

6. Open front hood and locate both the right and left front end sensors.

7. Remove both the right and left connector position assurance (CPA) from the right and left front end sensor connector.

8. Remove both connectors from left and right front end sensors.

Zone 3
See Figure 7.

1. Before servicing the vehicle, refer to the Precautions Section.

2. Turn the steering wheel so that the vehicles wheels are pointing straight ahead.

3. Place the ignition switch to the OFF position.

4. Remove the passenger floor mat and remove the kick up panel covering the body control module (BCM) fuse center.

> ❈❈ **WARNING**
>
> This sensing and diagnostic module (SDM) has two fused power inputs. To ensure there is no unwanted SIR deployment, personal injury, or unnecessary SIR system repairs, remove both AIR BAG (IGN) and AIR BAG (BATT) fuses from the BCM fuse center. With the AIR BAG fuses removed and the ignition switch in the ON position, the AIR BAG warning indicator illuminates. This is normal operation, and does not indicate an SIR system malfunction.

5. Locate and remove the AIR BAG (IGN) and AIR BAG (BATT) fuses from the BCM fuse center.

6. On the back side of the steering wheel there are 2 openings to access the fasteners securing the steering wheel module.

7. Insert a 3.175 mm (⅛ inch) diameter blunt ended punch or equivalent tool into each of the holes in order to release the fastener securing the module to the steering wheel.

8. Pull the steering wheel module gently away from the steering wheel.

9. Remove both connector position assurance (CPA) from the steering wheel module connectors.

10. Remove both connectors from the steering wheel module.

11. Remove the steering wheel module.

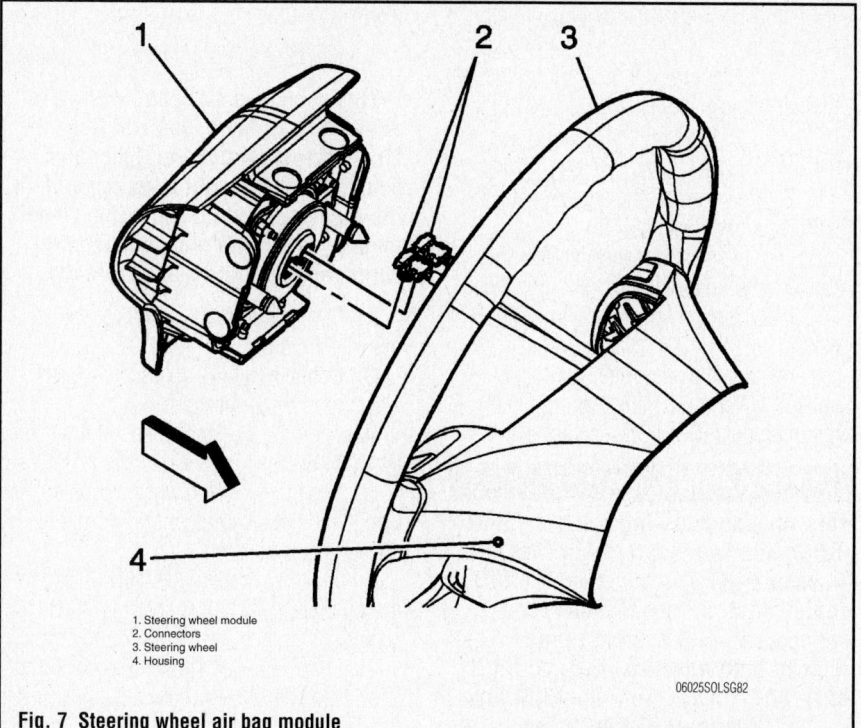

1. Steering wheel module
2. Connectors
3. Steering wheel
4. Housing

06025SOLSG82

Fig. 7 Steering wheel air bag module

Zone 4

See Figure 8.

1. Before servicing the vehicle, refer to the Precautions Section.

2. Turn the steering wheel so that the vehicles wheels are pointing straight ahead.

3. Place the ignition switch to the OFF position.

4. Remove the passenger floor mat and remove the kick up panel covering the body control module (BCM) fuse center.

✳✳ WARNING

This sensing and diagnostic module (SDM) has two fused power inputs. To ensure there is no unwanted SIR deployment, personal injury, or unnecessary SIR system repairs, remove both AIR BAG (IGN) and AIR BAG (BATT) fuses from the BCM fuse center. With the AIR BAG fuses removed and the ignition switch in the ON position, the AIR BAG warning indicator illuminates. This is normal operation, and does not indicate an SIR system malfunction.

5. Locate and remove the AIR BAG (IGN) and AIR BAG (BATT) fuses from the BCM fuse center.

6. Open and lower glove box door fully.

7. Locate the I/P module yellow connector and remove the connector position assurance (CPA) from the vehicle harness yellow connector.

8. Disconnect the I/P module yellow connector from the vehicle harness yellow connector.

9. Remove passenger and driver sill plates and front seat back body panel.

10. Locate the right seat belt retractor pretensioner.

11. Remove the right CPA connector from the seat belt retractor pretensioner.

12. Disconnect the connector from the right seat belt retractor pretensioner.

13. Locate the left seat belt retractor pretensioner.

14. Remove the left CPA connector from the seat belt retractor pretensioner.

15. Disconnect the connector from the left seat belt retractor pretensioner.

16. On the back side of the steering wheel there are 2 openings to access the fasteners securing the steering wheel module.

17. Insert a 3.175 mm (⅛ inch) diameter blunt ended punch or equivalent tool into each of the holes in order to release the fastener securing the module to the steering wheel.

18. Pull the steering wheel module gently away from the steering wheel.

19. Remove both CPAs from the steering wheel module connectors.

20. Remove both connectors from the steering wheel module.

21. Remove the steering wheel module.

Zone 5

1. Before servicing the vehicle, refer to the Precautions Section.

2. Turn the steering wheel so that the vehicles wheels are pointing straight ahead.

3. Place the ignition switch to the OFF position.

4. Remove the passenger floor mat and remove the kick up panel covering the body control module (BCM) fuse center.

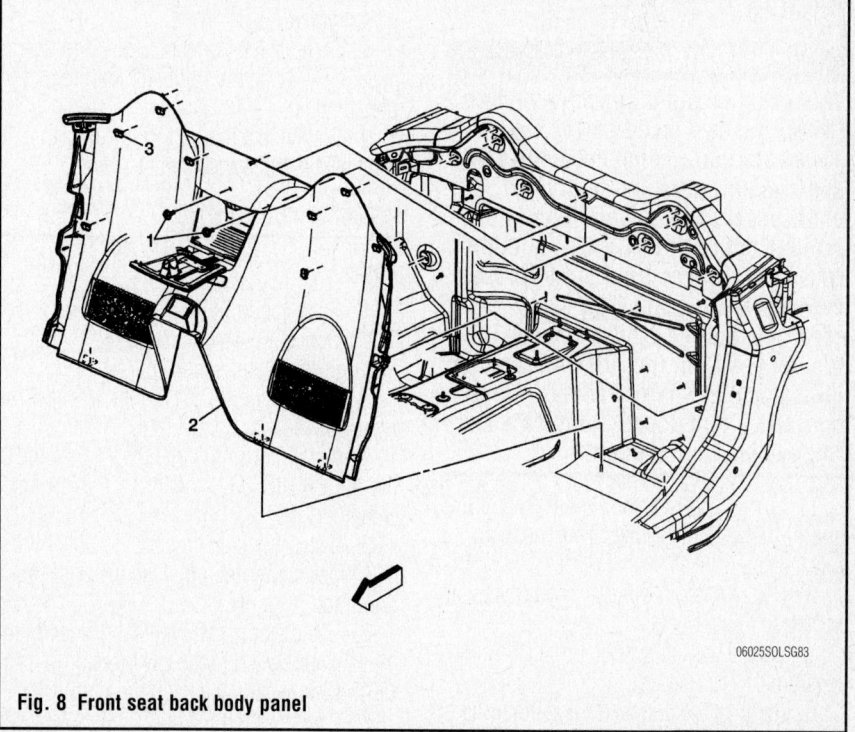

06025SOLSG83

Fig. 8 Front seat back body panel

✳✳ WARNING

This sensing and diagnostic module (SDM) has two fused power inputs. To ensure there is no unwanted SIR deployment, personal injury, or unnecessary SIR system repairs, remove both AIR BAG (IGN) and AIR BAG (BATT) fuses from the BCM fuse center. With the AIR BAG fuses removed and the ignition switch in the ON position, the AIR BAG warning indicator illuminates. This is normal operation, and does not indicate an SIR system malfunction.

5. Locate and remove the AIR BAG (IGN) and AIR BAG (BATT) fuses from the BCM fuse center.
6. Open and lower glove box door fully.
7. Locate the I/P module yellow connector and remove the connector position assurance (CPA) from the vehicle harness yellow connector.
8. Disconnect the I/P module yellow connector from the vehicle harness yellow connector.

Zone 7

1. Before servicing the vehicle, refer to the Precautions Section.
2. Turn the steering wheel so that the vehicles wheels are pointing straight ahead.
3. Place the ignition switch to the OFF position.
4. Remove the passenger floor mat and remove the kick up panel covering the body control module (BCM) fuse center.

✳✳ WARNING

This sensing and diagnostic module (SDM) has two fused power inputs. To ensure there is no unwanted SIR deployment, personal injury, or unnecessary SIR system repairs, remove both AIR BAG (IGN) and AIR BAG (BATT) fuses from the BCM fuse center. With the AIR BAG fuses removed and the ignition switch in the ON position, the AIR BAG warning indicator illuminates. This is normal operation, and does not indicate an SIR system malfunction.

5. Locate and remove the AIR BAG (IGN) and AIR BAG (BATT) fuses from the BCM fuse center.
6. Remove driver sill plate and front seat back body panel.
7. Locate the left seat belt retractor pretensioner.
8. Remove the connector position assurance (CPA) from the left seat belt retractor pretensioner.
9. Disconnect the connector from the left seat belt retractor pretensioner.

Zone 9

1. Before servicing the vehicle, refer to the Precautions Section.
2. Turn the steering wheel so that the vehicles wheels are pointing straight ahead.
3. Place the ignition switch to the OFF position.
4. Remove the passenger floor mat and remove the kick up panel covering the body control module (BCM) fuse center.

✳✳ WARNING

This sensing and diagnostic module (SDM) has two fused power inputs. To ensure there is no unwanted SIR deployment, personal injury, or unnecessary SIR system repairs, remove both AIR BAG (IGN) and AIR BAG (BATT) fuses from the BCM fuse center. With the AIR BAG fuses removed and the ignition switch in the ON position, the AIR BAG warning indicator illuminates. This is normal operation, and does not indicate an SIR system malfunction.

5. Locate and remove the AIR BAG (IGN) and AIR BAG (BATT) fuses from the BCM fuse center.
6. Remove passenger sill plate and front seat back body panel.
7. Locate the right seat belt retractor pretensioner.
8. Remove the connector position assurance (CPA) from the right seat belt retractor pretensioner.
9. Disconnect the connector from the right seat belt retractor pretensioner.

ARMING THE SYSTEM

Zone 1

1. Place the ignition in the OFF position.
2. Connect both connectors to the left and right front end sensors.
3. Connect both CPAs to the left and right front sensor connectors.
4. Install both AIR BAG (IGN) fuse and the AIR BAG (BATT) fuse into the BCM fuse center.
5. Install the kick up panel to cover the BCM fuse center then replace the passenger floor mat.
6. Use caution while reaching in and turn the ignition switch to the ON position. The AIR BAG indicator will flash then turn OFF.

Zone 3

1. Place the ignition in the OFF position.

➡This vehicle is equipped with dual stage air bags, you will find 2 connectors. Match the right color connector to the right color opening in the module. Route the steering wheel module wires, the redundant control wires, and the horn wires correctly.

2. Connect both connectors to the steering wheel module.
3. Connect both CPA's to the steering wheel module connectors.
4. Align the steering wheel module fasteners to the steering wheel fastener holes.
5. Push the steering wheel module firmly into the steering wheel in order to engage the fasteners.
6. Install both AIR BAG (IGN) fuse and the AIR BAG (BATT) fuse into the BCM fuse center.
7. Install the kick up panel to cover the BCM fuse center then replace the passenger floor mat.
8. Use caution while reaching in and turn the ignition switch to the ON position. The AIR BAG indicator will flash then turn OFF.

Zone 4

1. Place the ignition in the OFF position.

➡This vehicle is equipped with dual stage air bags. You will find 2 connectors. Match the right color connector to the right color opening in the module. Route the steering wheel module wires, the redundant control wires, and the horn wires correctly.

2. Connect both connectors to the steering wheel module.
3. Connect both CPAs to the steering wheel module connectors.
4. Align the steering wheel module fasteners to the steering wheel fastener holes.
5. Push the steering wheel module firmly into the steering wheel in order to engage the fasteners.
6. Connect the connector to the left seat belt retractor pretensioner.
7. Connect the left CPA connector to the seat belt retractor pretensioner.
8. Connect the connector to the right seat belt retractor pretensioner.
9. Connect the CPA to the right seat belt retractor pretensioner.
10. Install passenger and driver sill plates and front seat back body panel.
11. Connect the I/P module yellow connector to the vehicle harness yellow connector.

12. Connect the CPA to the vehicle harness yellow connector.

13. Close the glove box.

14. Install both AIR BAG (IGN) fuse and the AIR BAG (BATT) fuse into the BCM fuse center.

15. Install the kick up panel to cover the BCM fuse center then replace the passenger floor mat.

16. Use caution while reaching in and turn the ignition switch to the ON position. The AIR BAG indicator will flash then turn OFF.

Zone 5

1. Place the ignition in the OFF position.

2. Connect the I/P module yellow connector to the vehicle harness yellow connector.

3. Connect the CPA to the vehicle harness yellow connector.

4. Close the glove box.

5. Install both AIR BAG (IGN) fuse and the AIR BAG (BATT) fuse into the BCM fuse center.

6. Install the kick up panel to cover the BCM fuse center then replace the passenger floor mat.

7. Use caution while reaching in and turn the ignition switch to the ON position. The AIR BAG indicator will flash then turn OFF.

Zone 7

1. Place the ignition in the OFF position.

2. Connect the connector to the left seat belt retractor pretensioner.

3. Connect the CPA to the left seat belt retractor pretensioner.

4. Install driver sill plate and front seat back body panel.

5. Install both AIR BAG (IGN) fuse and

the AIR BAG (BATT) fuse into the BCM fuse center.

6. Install the kick up panel to cover the BCM fuse center then replace the passenger floor mat.

7. Use caution while reaching in and turn the ignition switch to the ON position. The AIR BAG indicator will flash then turn OFF.

Zone 9

1. Place the ignition in the OFF position.

2. Connect the connector to the right seat belt retractor pretensioner.

3. Connect the CPA to the right seat belt retractor pretensioner.

4. Install passenger sill plate and front seat back body panel.

5. Install both AIR BAG (IGN) fuse and the AIR BAG (BATT) fuse into the BCM fuse center.

6. Install the kick up panel to cover the BCM fuse center then replace the passenger floor mat.

7. Use caution while reaching in and turn the ignition switch to the ON position. The AIR BAG indicator will flash then turn OFF.

CLOCKSPRING CENTERING

See Figure 9.

1. Verify the following conditions before centering the supplemental inflatable restraint (SIR) steering wheel module coil:

a. The wheels on the vehicle are straight ahead.

b. The block tooth and the centering mark (1) of the steering shaft is in the 12 o'clock position. If available, remove the yellow retaining tab (1) from the SIR

steering wheel module coil and save the tab for reassembly.

2. Hold the SIR steering wheel module coil face up by the casing (2).

a. Slowly turn the SIR steering wheel module coil hub (3) clockwise until the coil ribbon stops.

b. Slowly rotate the SIR steering wheel module coil hub (3) counterclockwise 2.5 revolutions until the centering window (4) turns yellow. This indicates the CENTER position.

➡If the retaining tab is not available, the use of tape to secure the SIR steering wheel module coil is recommended for installation to the steering column.

3. Install the yellow retaining tab (1) to the SIR steering wheel module coil.

4. Slide the centered SIR steering wheel module coil onto the steering shaft.

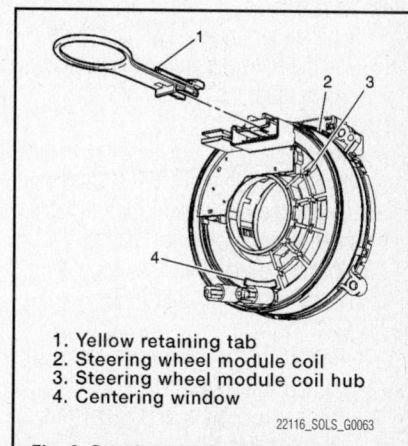

1. Yellow retaining tab
2. Steering wheel module coil
3. Steering wheel module coil hub
4. Centering window

22116_SOLS_G0063

Fig. 9 Steering wheel module coil

DRIVETRAIN

AUTOMATIC TRANSMISSION ASSEMBLY

REMOVAL & INSTALLATION

1. Before servicing the vehicle, refer to the Precautions Section.

2. Disconnect the negative battery cable.

3. Remove the starter motor to gain access to the torque converter bolts.

4. Remove the left side transmission to engine mounting bolt.

5. Remove the two upper transmission mounting bolts.

6. Remove the turbocharger, If equipped. Refer to Turbocharger Replacement.

7. Remove the right side transmission to engine mounting bolts.

8. Raise and support the vehicle.

9. Remove the exhaust system pipe.

10. Remove the front closeout panel.

11. Drain the transmission fluid if disassembly of the transmission is necessary.

12. Remove the transmission manual shift shaft nut.

13. Disconnect the shift linkage from the transmission.

14. Place the transmission in Neutral by rotating the transmission shift shaft clockwise 2 clicks.

15. Remove the propeller shaft.

16. Disconnect the transmission wiring harness connector from the transmission by rotating the locking latch counterclockwise.

17. Disconnect the wiring harness clips from the transmission, and position the wiring harness aside.

18. Remove the flywheel inspection cover bolt and cover.

19. Mark the torque converter to flexplate/flywheel orientation to ensure proper realignment.

20. Repeat the following steps for all 3 torque converter bolts:

a. Rotate the harmonic balancer center bolt clockwise only, in order to align the torque converter bolt with the starter motor opening in the engine block.

b. Remove and discard the torque converter bolt. The bolt is self locking and is not reusable.

21. Place an oil drain pan under the transmission fluid cooler pipes.

22. Remove the bolt securing the transmission fluid cooler pipes retainer to the transmission.

23. Remove the transmission fluid cooler pipes from the transmission, and position aside.

24. Remove the O-rings. Do not reuse the O-rings.

25. Plug the open outlet ports to prevent fluid loss and contamination.

26. Position a suitable transmission jack under the transmission.

27. Remove the transmission mount.

28. Remove the left side transmission to engine mounting bolts.

29. Remove the right side transmission to engine mounting bolts.

30. Pull the transmission free from the engine dowels.

31. Carefully lower the transmission from the vehicle.

32. Flush the transmission oil cooler.

33. If the transmission is being replaced, remove the drive flange and install it on the replacement unit.

To install:

34. Using the transmission jack, carefully raise the transmission to the vehicle.

35. Align the transmission with the engine dowels.

36. Install the right transmission mounting bolts and tighten to 37 ft. lbs. (50 Nm).

37. Install the left transmission mounting bolts and tighten to 37 ft. lbs. (50 Nm).

38. Install the transmission mount and tighten mounting bolts to 41 ft. lbs. (55 Nm).

39. Remove transmission jack from under the transmission.

40. Place new seals over the transmission fluid cooler pipes.

41. Insert the transmission fluid cooler pipes into the transmission.

42. Install the bolt securing the transmission fluid cooler pipe retainer to the transmission. Tighten the bolt to 18 ft. lbs. (25 Nm).

43. Align the torque converter to flexplate/flywheel orientation marks made during the removal procedure.

✳✳ WARNING

Torque converter bolts are self locking and must be replaced with new torque converter bolts every time the bolts are removed.

44. Repeat the following steps for all 3 torque converter bolts:

   a. Rotate the harmonic balancer center bolt clockwise ONLY, in order to align the torque converter bolt holes in the flexplate/flywheel with the starter motor opening in the engine block.

   b. To aid in alignment of the torque converter to the flexplate/flywheel. Install all 3 NEW torque converter bolts before fully tightening.

45. Tighten torque converter bolts to 46 ft. lbs. (63 Nm).

46. Install the flywheel inspection cover and bolt.

47. Connect the wiring harness clips to the transmission.

48. Connect the transmission wiring harness connector to the transmission by rotating the locking latch clockwise.

49. Install the propeller shaft.

50. Place the transmission in the park position by rotating the shift shaft fully counterclockwise.

51. Connect the shift linkage to the transmission.

52. Install the transmission manual shift shaft nut and tighten to 80 inch. lbs. (9 Nm).

53. Check the transmission fluid level (fill as needed).

54. Adjust the shift control linkage.

55. Install the exhaust system pipe and tighten the nuts to 13 ft. lbs. (17 Nm).

56. Install the front closeout panel, tighten mounting bolts to 80 inch. lbs. (9 Nm).

57. Lower the vehicle.

58. Install the right transmission mounting bolts and tighten to 37 ft. lbs. (50 Nm).

59. Install the turbocharger, If equipped. Refer to Turbocharger Replacement.

60. Install the two upper transmission mounting bolts and tighten to 37 ft. lbs. (50 Nm).

61. Install the left transmission mounting bolt and tighten to 37 ft. lbs. (50 Nm).

62. Install the starter motor and tighten mounting bolts to 30 ft. lbs. (40 Nm).

63. Tighten starter solenoid terminal no. nut to 89 inch. lbs. (10 Nm).

64. Tighten starter solenoid "S" terminal no. nut to 27 inch. lbs. (3 Nm).

65. Connect the negative battery cable.

66. The transmission control module must be programmed with the proper software/calibrations.

67. Complete the following procedure after the transmission is installed in the vehicle:

   • With the ignition OFF or disconnected, crank the engine several times. Listen for any unusual noises or evidence that any parts are binding.

   • Start the engine and listen for abnormal conditions.

   • While the engine continues to idle raise and support the vehicle.

   • Inspect for fluid leaks while the engine is idling.

   • Lower the vehicle.

   • Perform a final inspection for the proper fluid level.

   • Reset the Transmission Adaptive Functions (TAP) values.

   • Road test the vehicle.

MANUAL TRANSMISSION ASSEMBLY

REMOVAL & INSTALLATION

See Figures 10 and 11.

1. Before servicing the vehicle, refer to the Precautions Section.

2. Remove the control lever knob and boot assembly.

3. Remove the turbocharger, if equipped. Refer to Turbocharger Replacement.

4. Remove the clutch hose/pipe assembly retainer clip from the clutch master cylinder.

5. Disconnect the clutch hose/pipe assembly from the clutch master cylinder.

6. Cap the clutch hose/pipe assembly in order to prevent fluid loss and contamination. It is not necessary to plug the lower hose end or slave cylinder fitting as they are equipped with check valves, only minimal fluid loss may be experienced.

7. Remove the transmission support.

8. Drain the transmission fluid if necessary.

9. Disconnect the electrical connector from the backup lamp switch.

10. Disconnect the electrical connector from the Vehicle Speed Sensor (VSS).

11. Disconnect the wiring harness from the clip bracket.

12. Disconnect the wiring harness clips from the clip brackets, and position the harness aside.

13. Support the transmission using a transmission jack.

14. Remove the propeller shaft and driveline support.

15. Remove the 5 transmission to engine mounting bolts.

16. Remove the 2 engine to transmission mounting bolts.

17. Remove the 2 remaining transmission mounting bolts.

✳✳ WARNING

Do not allow the transmission to hang from the clutch assembly.

18. Pull the transmission straight back off the clutch hub splines.

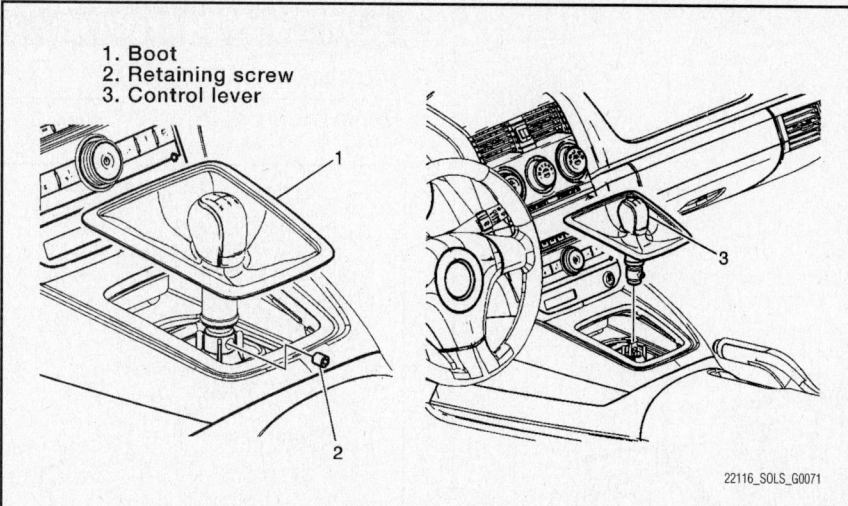

1. Boot
2. Retaining screw
3. Control lever

22116_SOLS_G0071

Fig. 10 Control lever knob and boot assembly Saturn Sky shown, Pontiac Solstice similar

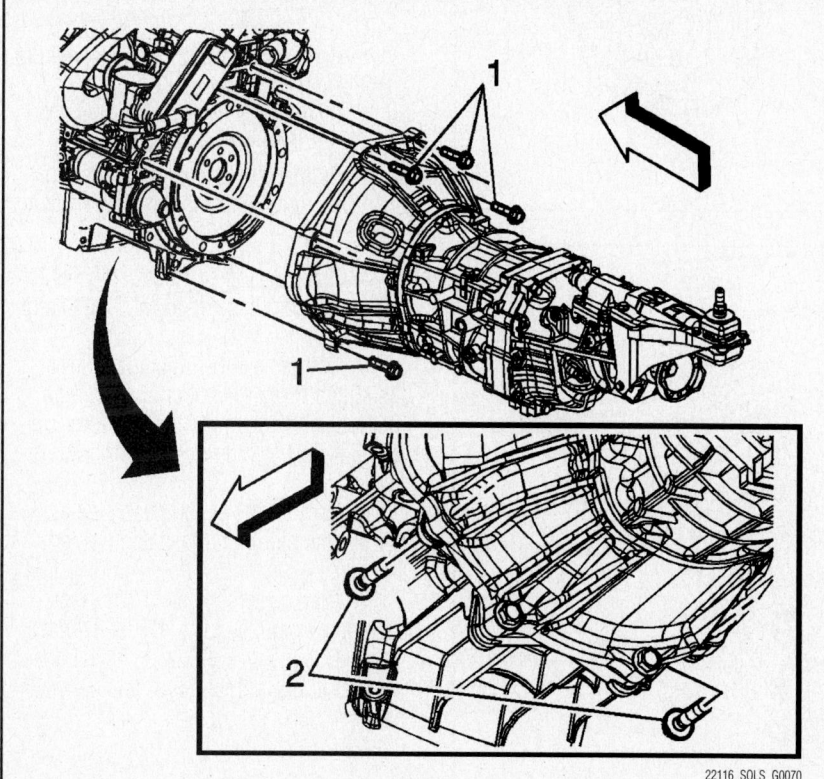

22116_SOLS_G0070

Fig. 11 Manual transmission and mounting bolts

19. Using the transmission jack, carefully lower the transmission from the vehicle.

To install:

20. Ensure clearance is maintained between the transmission and the following:
   • The catalytic converter
   • The clutch assembly
   • The engine wiring harness
21. Using the transmission jack, carefully raise the transmission to the engine.

22. Align the transmission with the engine dowels
23. Install the 2 transmission mounting bolts and tighten to 37 ft. lbs. (50 Nm).
24. Install the 2 engine to transmission mounting bolts and tighten to 37 ft. lbs. (50 Nm).
25. Install the 5 transmission to engine mounting bolts and tighten to 37 ft. lbs. (50 Nm).

26. Install the driveline support and propeller shaft.
27. Remove the transmission jack.
28. Lay the engine wiring harness over the transmission.
29. Connect the wiring harness clips to the clip brackets.
30. Connect the wiring harness to the clip bracket.
31. Connect the electrical connector to the VSS.
32. Connect the electrical connector to the backup lamp switch.
33. Fill the transmission fluid if removed.
34. Install the transmission support and closeout panels.

� WARNING

Ensure the clutch hydraulic hose does not come in contact with any sharp or potentially hot surfaces.

35. Install the clutch hose/pipe assembly retainer clip to the clutch master cylinder.
36. Connect the clutch hose/pipe assembly to the clutch master cylinder.
37. Tug gently on the clutch hose/pipe assembly to ensure proper retention into the clutch master cylinder.
38. Install the turbocharger, if equipped. Refer to Turbocharger Replacement.
39. Install the control lever knob and boot assembly.

CLUTCH DRIVEN DISC & PRESSURE PLATE

REMOVAL & INSTALLATION

See Figures 12 and 13.

1. Before servicing the vehicle, refer to the Precautions Section.
2. Remove the transmission.
3. Remove the clutch cover bolts one turn at a time, until spring pressure is relieved.
4. Remove the clutch cover and the clutch disc.

To install:

5. Install the clutch disc and the clutch cover.
6. Hand-start the clutch cover to flywheel bolts, leaving the clutch cover loose enough to reposition for alignment.
7. Install a clutch alignment tool to center the disc.
8. Tighten the clutch cover to flywheel bolts in the sequence shown. Tighten the bolts to 30 Nm (22 ft. lbs.).
9. Recheck each bolt torque using the tightening sequence.

Fig. 12 Clutch components

06025SOLSG68

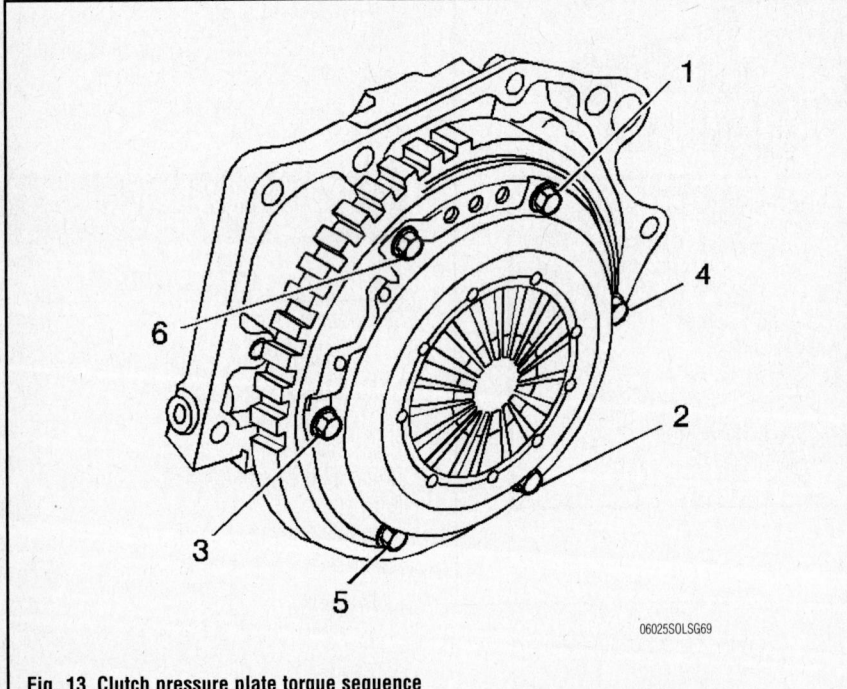

Fig. 13 Clutch pressure plate torque sequence

06025SOLSG69

➡**Excessive amounts of lubricant on the input shaft splines may contaminate the clutch disc and cause clutch shudder.**

10. Lubricate the inside diameter of the bearing with Saturn P/N 21005995, or equivalent.

11. Install the transmission.
12. Bleed the hydraulic system.
13. Connect the negative battery cable.

ADJUSTMENTS

This vehicle has a self-adjusting clutch that is constantly adjusting.

CLUTCH MASTER CYLINDER

REMOVAL & INSTALLATION

See Figures 14 and 15.

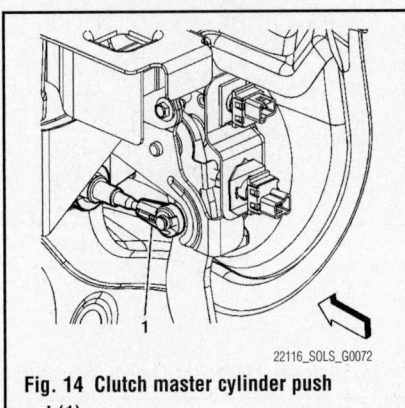

22116_SOLS_G0072

Fig. 14 Clutch master cylinder push rod (1)

1. Before servicing the vehicle, refer to the Precautions Section.
2. Remove the instrument panel left closeout/insulator panel.
3. Remove the clutch master cylinder push rod from the clutch pedal arm integral stud.
4. Place a shop towel under the clutch master cylinder in order to catch any fluid loss.
5. Disconnect the clutch hose from the clutch master cylinder and position the hose end above the brake master cylinder reservoir in order to prevent fluid loss.
6. Remove the clutch hose/pipe assembly retainer clip from the clutch master cylinder.
7. Disconnect the clutch hose/pipe assembly from the clutch master cylinder.
8. Cap the reservoir and clutch hoses in order to prevent fluid loss and contamination.

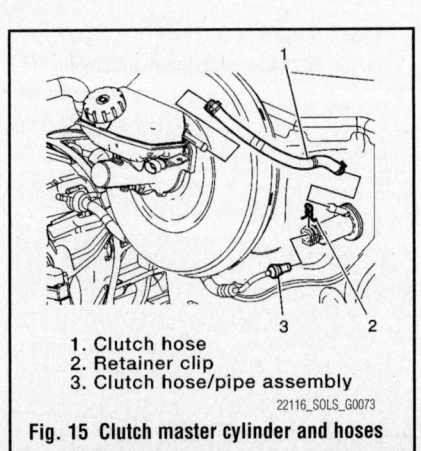

1. Clutch hose
2. Retainer clip
3. Clutch hose/pipe assembly

22116_SOLS_G0073

Fig. 15 Clutch master cylinder and hoses

9. Rotate the clutch master cylinder one ¼ turn clockwise and remove the cylinder from the cowl.

To install:

➡**While installing, ensure that the clutch master cylinder pushrod is aligned with the clutch pedal.**

10. Align the keys of the clutch master cylinder with the tabs on the cowl.

11. Install the clutch master cylinder to the cowl and rotate ¼ turn counterclockwise. The clutch fluid reservoir hose connection will be at the 12:00 position when the clutch master cylinder is properly installed.

12. Uncap the reservoir and hydraulic lines.

13. Install the clutch hose/pipe assembly retainer clip to the clutch master cylinder.

14. Connect the clutch hose/pipe assembly (3) to the clutch master cylinder.

15. Tug gently on the clutch hose/pipe assembly (3) to ensure proper retention into the clutch master cylinder.

16. Connect the clutch hose to the clutch master cylinder.

17. Install the clutch master cylinder push rod to the clutch pedal arm integral stud.

18. Install the instrument panel left closeout/insulator panel.

19. Bleed the clutch hydraulic system.

CLUTCH PEDAL POSITION SWITCH ADJUSTMENT

See Figure 16.

1. Before servicing the vehicle, refer to the Precautions Section.

2. Remove the instrument panel left closeout/insulator panel.

3. Push the clutch pedal bottom of travel switch (4) in fully until bottomed against the switch retainer clip.

4. Using a continuous steady force, push the clutch pedal all the way forward until it stops to set the switch. While pushing the pedal forward, a clicking should be heard as the switch threads pass through the locking barbs within the retainer clip. Note if no clicking sound is heard, the switch may not have been fully bottomed against the switch retainer and may be out of adjustment.

5. Release the clutch top of travel switch (3) from the retainer by rotating the switch counterclockwise approximately 60 degrees.

6. Slide the switch into the retainer until the switch plunger is fully depressed into the barrel against the clutch pedal. Do not move or push the clutch pedal.

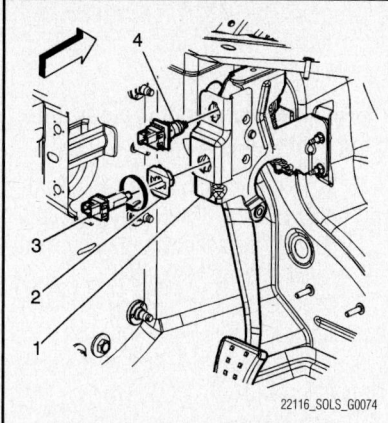

Fig. 16 Clutch pedal position switch, upper and lower

7. Rotate the switch clockwise approximately 60 degrees to engage the switch with the retainer. A detent should be felt or possibly a click type noise should be heard as the switch is engaged with the retainer.

8. Perform verification test for the switch by checking to see if the vehicle will not start without depressing the clutch pedal. then depress the clutch pedal until the vehicle starts.

9. Install the instrument panel left closeout/insulator panel.

CLUTCH SLAVE CYLINDER

REMOVAL & INSTALLATION

See Figure 17.

1. Before servicing the vehicle, refer to the Precautions Section.

2. Disconnect the negative battery cable.

3. Raise the vehicle.

4. Remove the clutch hose/pipe assembly retainer clip from the clutch actuator cylinder, (slave cylinder).

5. Disconnect the clutch hose/pipe assembly from the clutch actuator cylinder.

6. Drain the fluid from the hose/pipe assembly into a suitable container.

7. Remove the transmission.

8. Remove the clutch actuator cylinder bolts.

9. Remove the clutch actuator cylinder.

10. Install the clutch actuator cylinder.

11. Install the clutch actuator cylinder bolts and tighten to 89 inch. lbs. (10 Nm).

12. Install the transmission.

13. Reconnect the clutch hose/pipe assembly from the clutch actuator cylinder and install retainer clip.

14. Check transmission fluid level and add as needed.

15. Lower the vehicle

16. Connect the negative battery cable.

17. Fill the brake/clutch reservoir with DOT 3 hydraulic fluid to the proper fluid level.

18. Bleed the clutch hydraulic system.

CLUTCH HYDRAULIC SYSTEM BLEEDING

MANUAL BLEEDING

➡**Maintain the fluid in the brake reservoir at the MAX level with DOT 3 hydraulic brake fluid. The MAX level marker can be found on the side of the brake reservoir that faces the engine, If the fluid in the brake reservoir is not at the MAX level, the portion of the brake reservoir that is connected to the clutch hydraulic system may not contain fluid. The portion of the brake reservoir that is connected to the clutch hydraulic system is located in the left, rear corner of the brake reservoir.**

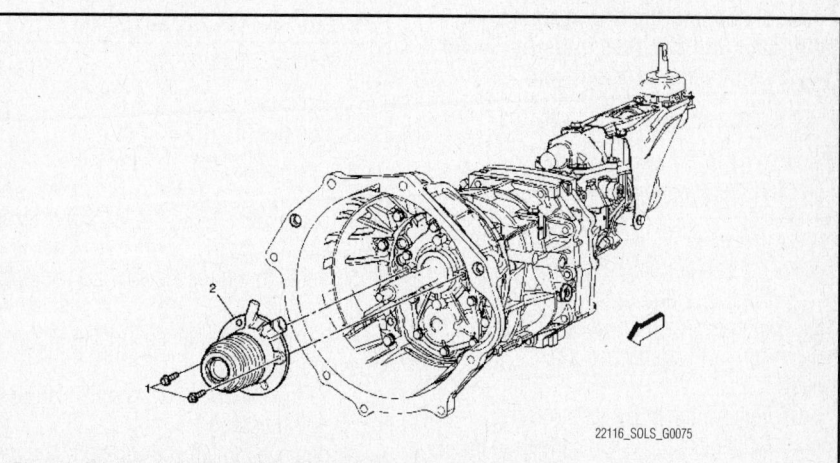

Fig. 17 Clutch actuator cylinder, (slave cylinder) and transmission

1. Verify all clutch hydraulic lines and connectors are dry, secure and properly routed.

2. Clean dirt and grease from the cap in order to ensure that no foreign substances enter the system.

3. Remove the brake reservoir cap and fill the entire brake reservoir to the MAX level.

4. Depress the clutch pedal slowly to the full depressed position.

5. Let the clutch pedal return to the up stop position and hold for 5 seconds.

6. Check the brake reservoir to see if the portion of the brake reservoir that is connected to the clutch hydraulic system has the same fluid level as the rest of the brake reservoir. If the fluids are not the same, add DOT 3 hydraulic brake fluid until the entire brake reservoir is at the MAX level.

7. Repeat steps 3—5 until air is purged from the clutch system and the clutch pedal feels firm.

8. Replace the cap on the brake reservoir.

✳✳ CAUTION

Do not start the engine while the transmission is in gear, only while in the neutral position. This vehicle is equipped with a concentric actuator cylinder and may move if started in gear.

9. Fully apply the PARK brake.

10. Place the transmission into the neutral position, depress the clutch pedal, and start the engine.

11. Pump the clutch pedal until firm.

12. Pump the brake pedal until firm.

13. If needed, add additional DOT 3 hydraulic brake fluid to fill the brake reservoir to the MAX level.

➡**The clutch and braking systems are integrated into one reservoir. The brake may be soft when first applying.**

14. Road test the vehicle to ensure proper operation.

VACUUM BLEEDING

1. Verify that all the hydraulic lines are dry, secure and correctly routed.

2. Clean dirt and grease from the brake reservoir cap in order to ensure that no foreign substances enter the system.

3. Remove the brake reservoir cap.

4. Fill the entire brake reservoir to the MAX level using DOT 3 hydraulic brake fluid.

5. Install the J 43485 power steering bleeder adapter and the J 35555 metal mighty vac to the reservoir.

➡**Make sure equipment is clean and free of contaminants.**

6. Hold the J 43485 into position while applying 51-68 kPa (15-20 hg) of vacuum.

7. Remove the adapter and refill the brake reservoir to the MAX level.

8. Depress the clutch pedal slowly to the full depressed position.

9. Let the clutch pedal return to the up stop position and hold for 5 seconds.

10. Repeat steps 4—9 until all air is removed from the clutch system.

11. Replace the cap on the brake reservoir.

✳✳ CAUTION

Do not start the engine while the transmission is in gear, only while in the neutral position. This vehicle is equipped with a concentric actuator cylinder and may move if started in gear.

12. Fully apply the PARK brake.

13. Place the transmission into the neutral position, depress the clutch pedal, and start the engine.

14. Pump the clutch pedal until firm.

➡**The clutch and braking systems are integrated into one reservoir. The brake may be soft when first applying.**

15. Pump the brake pedal until firm.

16. If needed, add additional DOT 3 hydraulic brake fluid to fill the brake reservoir to the MAX level.

17. Road test the vehicle to ensure proper operation.

REAR AXLE HOUSING

REMOVAL & INSTALLATION

See Figures 18 through 20.

1. Raise and support the vehicle.

2. Remove propeller shaft.

3. Remove the rear tire and wheel assemblies.

4. Remove the right and left wheel drive axle shafts.

5. Position a transmission jack beneath the differential.

6. Firmly secure the differential to the transmission jack.

7. Remove the front differential carrier bracket to frame bolt.

8. Remove the left and right differential rear mounting bolts.

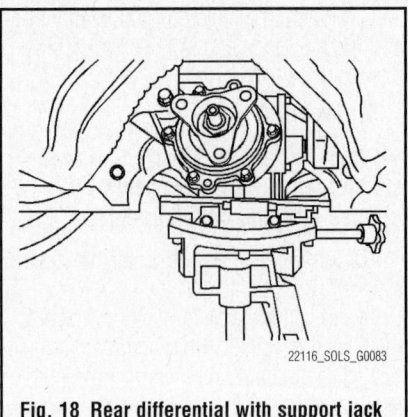
Fig. 18 Rear differential with support jack

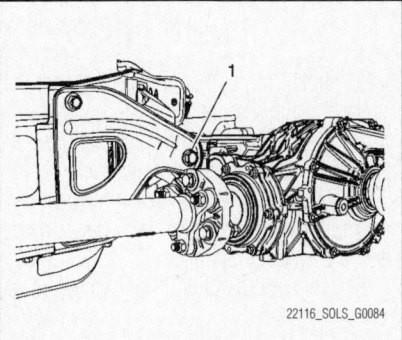
Fig. 19 Front differential carrier bracket to frame bolt (1)

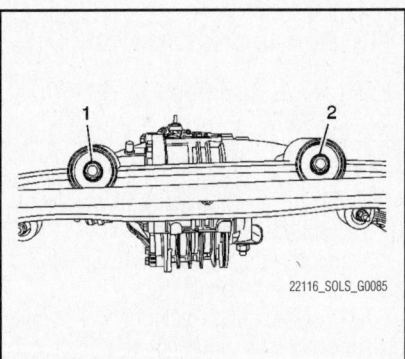
Fig. 20 Left (1) and right (2) differential rear mounting bolts

9. Lower the jack slightly until the mounting ear at the front of the differential clears the support attachment point.

10. Remove the differential from the vehicle.

To install:

➡**The differential is shipped with a plastic vent plug. Remove the plastic vent plug prior to differential vent installation.**

11. When replacing the differential. remove the plastic vent plug and install

a new differential vent. The vent flange must be fully seated.

12. With the differential firmly attached to the jack, raise the differential to the vehicle.

13. Hand install the differential carrier bracket-to-frame bolt (1) in order to locate the differential to the rear support.

14. With the differential firmly attached to the jack, raise the differential to the rear support.

15. Position the differential to the support.

16. Install the left and right differential rear mounting bolts. Tighten the differential mounting bolts to 129 ft. lbs. (175 Nm).

17. Tighten the differential carrier bracket to frame bolt to 129 ft. lbs. (175 Nm).

18. Remove the transmission jack.

19. Install propeller shaft.

20. Install the wheel drive shafts.

21. Install the rear tire and wheel assemblies.

22. Inspect the differential lubricant level.

23. Lower the vehicle.

REAR AXLE SHAFT SEAL

REMOVAL & INSTALLATION

1. Before servicing the vehicle, refer to the Precautions Section.

2. Raise and suitably support the vehicle.

3. Remove the appropriate rear tire and wheel assembly.

4. Remove the appropriate wheel drive shaft.

5. Using a flat bladed tool remove the differential output shaft seal.

➡**Take care not to damage any sealing surfaces.**

To install:

6. Lubricate the wheel drive shaft sealing surface of the oil seal with (75W90) synthetic axle lubricant.

7. Carefully install the differential output shaft seal with a seal driver.

8. Install the wheel drive shaft.

9. Inspect the fluid level.

10. Install the rear tire and wheel assembly.

11. Lower the vehicle.

REAR HALFSHAFT

REMOVAL & INSTALLATION

See Figures 21 through 23.

1. Before servicing the vehicle, refer to the Precautions Section.

2. Raise and support the vehicle.

3. Remove the tire and wheel assembly.

4. Remove the rear brake rotor.

❊❊ WARNING

The wheel drive shaft spindle nut must not be reused. Replace the wheel drive shaft spindle nut with a new nut whenever it is removed.

5. Remove and discard the wheel drive shaft spindle nut.

6. Using a Universal Hub Puller, disengage the wheel drive shaft from the wheel bearing/hub.

7. Remove the adjustment link.

8. Separate the upper ball joint from the rear knuckle.

9. Using a suitable tool, carefully release the wheel drive shaft from the rear differential enough to install the J 44394 seal protector.

❊❊ WARNING

J-44394 must be installed into the differential output shaft seal prior to removing and installing the wheel drive shaft. Failure to install J-44394 as indicated may cause the splines of the wheel drive shaft to cut the differential output seal.

10. Carefully install the J 44394 over the wheel drive shaft

11. Carefully slide the J 44394 into the differential output shaft seal.

12. Remove the wheel drive shaft from the vehicle.

13. If reusing the wheel drive shaft, remove and discard the wheel drive shaft retaining ring. The wheel drive shaft retaining ring is on the splined shaft of the cross groove joint.

To install:

14. Install the new wheel drive shaft retaining ring. The wheel drive shaft retaining ring is on the splined shaft of the cross groove joint.

15. If previously removed, carefully install J 44394 into the differential output shaft seal.

➡**In order to prevent lubricant leaks, use care when installing the wheel drive shaft to the differential. Do not damage the oil seal. Replace the oil seal if it becomes nicked, distorted, or is otherwise damaged.**

16. Carefully install the wheel drive shaft into the differential until the splines are past the J 44394. Ensure that the retaining ring is installed in the upright position.

17. Carefully remove the J 44394 from the differential output shaft seal.

18. Carefully remove J 44394 from the wheel drive shaft.

19. Carefully install the wheel drive shaft into the differential until the retaining ring is engaged.

20. Ensure the wheel drive shaft retaining ring is fully engaged to the differential by grasping the inner housing and pulling outward. The wheel drive shaft will stay positively engaged if properly installed to the differential.

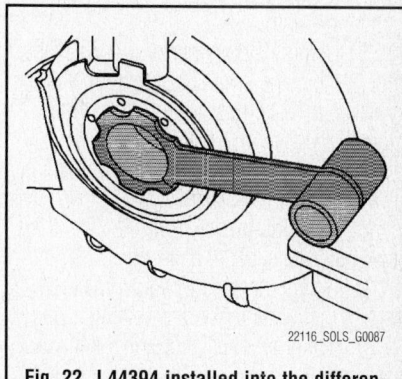

Fig. 22 J 44394 installed into the differential output shaft seal

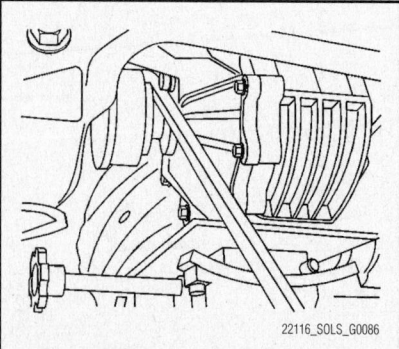

Fig. 21 Releasing the wheel drive shaft from the rear differential

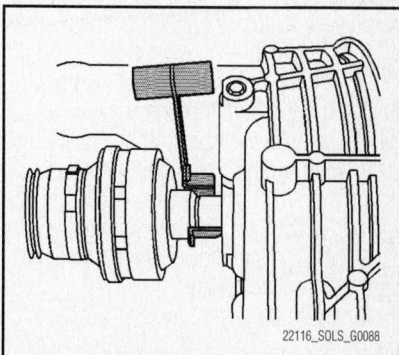

Fig. 23 J 44394 removal from the differential output shaft seal

21. Install the upper ball joint to the rear knuckle.

22. Loosely install the new wheel drive shaft spindle nut.

23. Install the adjustment link.

24. Use the new wheel drive shaft spindle nut to slowly pull the spindle to the wheel hub and bearing assembly.

25. Tighten the wheel drive shaft spindle nut to 159 ft. lbs. (215 Nm).

26. Install the rear brake rotor.

27. Install the tire and wheel assembly.

28. Inspect the differential lubricant level.

29. Lower the vehicle.

CV-JOINTS OVERHAUL

Inner Joint

See Figures 24 through 27.

1. Before servicing the vehicle, refer to the Precautions Section.

2. Remove the halfshaft assembly from the vehicle.

3. Wrap a shop towel around the halfshaft bar.

4. Place the halfshaft horizontally in a bench vise.

5. Using a side cutter or other suitable tool, remove the large boot retaining clamp from the inner joint boot and discard the retaining clamp.

6. Using a side cutter or other suitable tool, remove the small boot retaining clamp from the inner joint boot and discard the clamp.

7. Slide the boot along the halfshaft bar away from the joint face.

8. Wipe the grease from the face of the joint inner race, cage, balls, etc.

9. Using snapring pliers, spread the ears of the joints inner race retaining ring.

10. Hold the inner joint horizontally to the shaft.

11. Position a brass drift on the inner race.

12. Carefully strike the brass drift with a hammer to remove the inner joint assembly from the halfshaft.

13. Remove and discard both halfshaft retaining rings from the axle shaft.

14. Remove the boot from the halfshaft.

15. Remove the small boot retaining clamp from the halfshaft.

16. Remove the halfshaft from the vise.

17. Wrap a shop towel around the joint outer race splined shaft.

18. Place the outer race vertically in a bench vise.

➥**All traces of old grease and any contaminates must be removed.**

19. Clean all parts thoroughly with a safe solvent.

20. Thoroughly air dry all of the parts.

21. Inspect all parts for damage and/or wear.

To install:

22. Insert approximately 60 percent of the grease from the service kit into the inner joint. Spread the most of that 60 percent onto the ball tracks, the balls, the cage and the inner race. Spread the remainder of the grease into the bottom of the outer race.

23. Remove the inner joint from the bench vise.

24. Wrap a shop towel around the halfshaft.

25. Place the halfshaft horizontally in a bench vise.

26. Install a new small boot retaining clamp onto the halfshaft.

27. Slide the boot onto the halfshaft.

28. Place the new large retaining clamp over the large end of the boot.

29. Install the new halfshaft large retaining ring onto drive shaft.

30. Seat the new halfshaft large retaining ring into the large ring groove.

31. Install the new halfshaft small retaining ring onto drive shaft.

32. Seat the new halfshaft small retaining ring into the small ring groove.

33. Push the inner joint assembly onto the halfshaft until the small retaining ring seats itself in the retaining groove on the halfshaft.

34. Insert the remaining grease from the service kit into the boot.

35. Position the small boot retaining clamp onto the neck of the boot.

36. Position the boot and small retaining clamp to the axle shaft as shown.

➥**The boot retaining clamp must not be over-tightened or under-tightened.**

37. Using the crimping pliers, crimp the small boot retaining clamp. Tighten the small boot clamp until the base of the omega shape has a gap of 1 mm (0.039 in.)

38. The clamping hold time must be no less than 2 seconds.

➥**The inner boot must not be dimpled, stretched, or out of shape in any way. If necessary, equalize the air pressure in the inner boot and shape properly by hand.**

39. Position the large boot retaining clamp onto the boot.

40. Position the boot and large retaining clamp to the joint's boot groove as shown.

41. Measure the distance (1) between the boot edges. The gap should be 88.6 mm (3.50 in.)

➥**The boot must not be dimpled, stretched or otherwise deformed.**

42. Inspect the boot for proper shape. If the boot is not shaped correctly, equalize the pressure in the boot by lifting the boot edge slightly and shape the boot properly by hand.

43. Inspect the boot for damage. If the boot has been cut or punctured during assembly, you must discard and replace the boot.

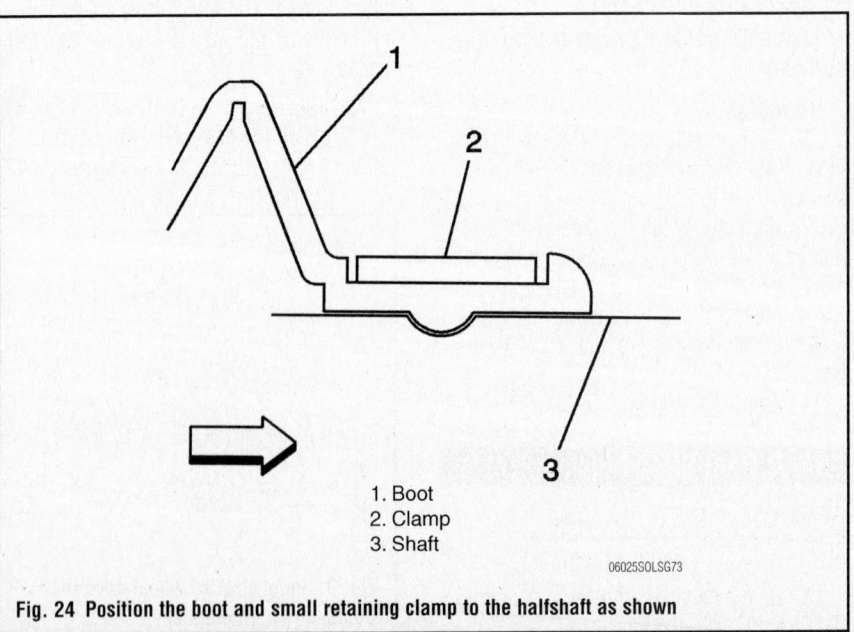

06025SOLSG73

Fig. 24 Position the boot and small retaining clamp to the halfshaft as shown

1. Boot
2. Clamp
3. Shaft

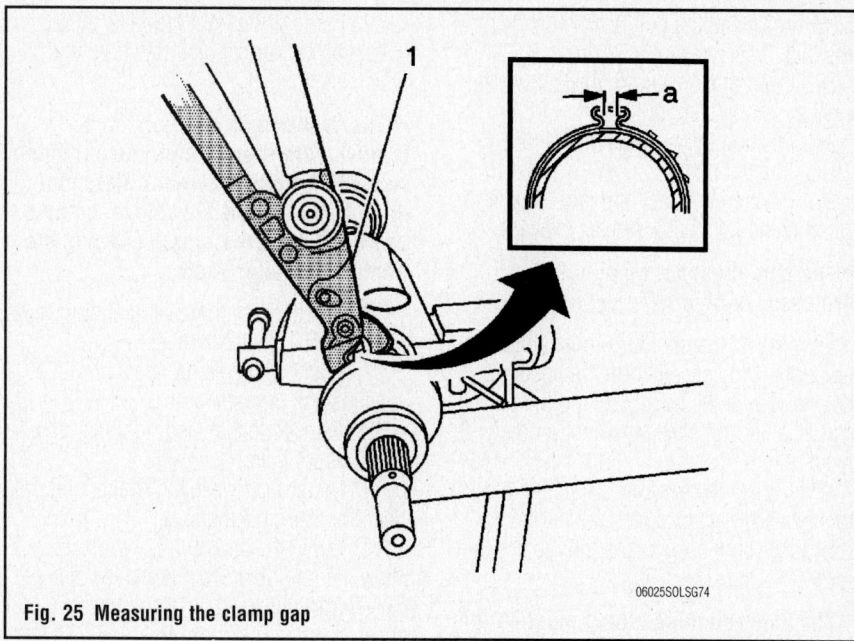

Fig. 25 Measuring the clamp gap

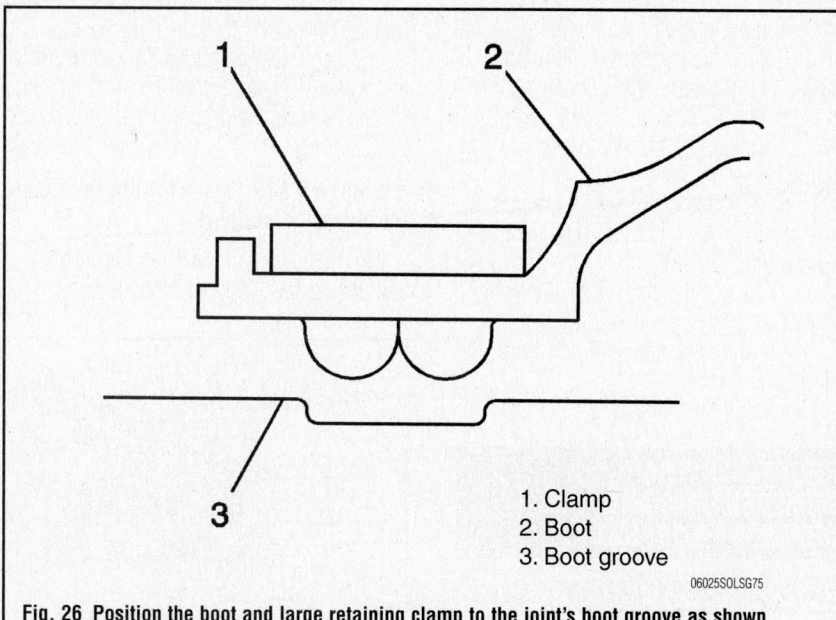

1. Clamp
2. Boot
3. Boot groove

Fig. 26 Position the boot and large retaining clamp to the joint's boot groove as shown

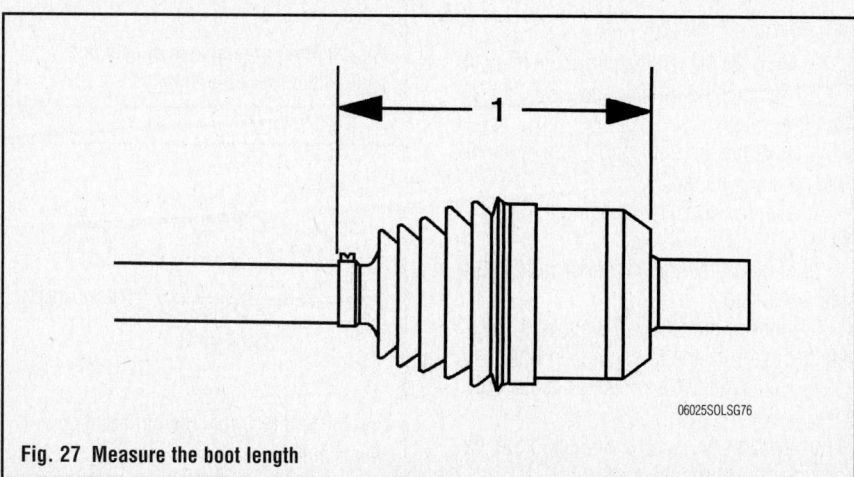

Fig. 27 Measure the boot length

➡ **The boot retaining clamp must not be over-tightened or under-tightened.**

44. Crimp the large boot retaining clamp. Tighten the large boot clamp until the base of the omega shape has a gap of 1 mm (0.039 in.).

45. Inspect the inner joint for smooth operation. This will also distribute the grease within the joint.
  a. Hold the halfshaft vertically, with the inner joint at the bottom.
  b. Rotate the halfshaft 4 or 5 times in a circular motion.
  c. Install the halfshaft.

Outer Joint

1. Before servicing the vehicle, refer to the Precautions Section.
2. Remove the halfshaft from the vehicle.
3. Wrap a shop towel around the shaft.
4. Place the halfshaft horizontally in a bench vise.
5. Using a side cutter or other suitable tool, remove the large boot retaining clamp from the outer joint boot and discard the clamp.
6. Using a side cutter or other suitable tool, remove the small boot retaining clamp from the outer joint boot and discard the clamp.
7. Separate the boot from the joint outer race at the large diameter end.
8. Slide the boot away from the joint face.
9. Wipe the grease from the face of the joint inner race, cage, balls, etc.
10. Remove the outer joint from the axle shaft using the following steps:
  a. Hold the outer joint housing horizontally to the shaft.
  b. Position a brass drift on the inner race.
  c. Strike the brass drift with a hammer to compress the axle shaft retaining clip.
  d. Continue to strike the brass drift in order to remove the outer joint from the axle shaft.
11. Remove and discard the narrow retaining ring from the outer narrow ring groove at the end of the halfshaft.
12. Remove and discard the wide spacer ring from the wide ring groove of the halfshaft.
13. Remove the boot from the axle shaft.
14. Remove the halfshaft from the vise.
15. Wrap a shop towel around the joint outer race splined shaft.
16. Place the outer race vertically in a bench vise.

➡**All traces of old grease and any contaminates must be removed.**

17. Clean all parts thoroughly with safe solvent.

18. Thoroughly air dry all of the parts.

19. Inspect all parts for damage and/or wear.

To install:

20. Insert approximately 60 percent of the grease from the service kit into the outer joint. Spread most of the grease onto the ball tracks, the balls, the cage, and the inner race. Spread the remainder of the grease into the bottom of the outer race.

21. Remove the inner joint from the bench vise.

22. Wrap a shop towel around the axle shaft.

23. Place the halfshaft horizontally in a bench vise.

24. Install a new small boot retaining clamp onto the axle shaft.

25. Install the boot onto the axle shaft.

26. Install the New narrow retaining ring to the outer narrow ring groove at the end of the halfshaft.

27. Install the New wide spacer ring to the wide ring groove of the halfshaft.

28. Position the outer joint horizontally.

29. Engage the inner race splines onto the axle shaft splines.

30. Compress the axle shaft ring spacer.

    a. Press the end of the retaining ring, using a flat-bladed tool, into the axle shaft groove while firmly pressing the inner joint onto the axle shaft.

    b. Continue to work around the retaining ring, until it is compressed.

➡**The axle shaft and inner race must be fully seated to each other.**

31. Install the outer joint to the axle shaft.

    a. Position a wood block over the end of the outer joint threaded shaft.

    b. Use a hammer to drive the outer joint onto the shaft.

    c. Continue to drive the outer joint until the inner joint seats fully onto the axle shaft.

32. Position the small boot retaining clamp into the boot groove.

33. Position the boot and small retaining clamp to the shaft boot groove as shown.

➡**The boot retaining clamp must not be over-tightened or under-tightened.**

34. Crimp the small boot retaining clamp. Tighten the small boot clamp until the base of the omega ohms shape has a gap of 1 mm (0.039 in).

35. The clamping hold time must be no less than 2 seconds.

36. Insert the remaining grease from the service kit into the boot.

37. Position the large boot retaining clamp onto the boot.

38. Position the boot and large retaining clamp to the joint outer race as shown.

➡**The boot must not be dimpled, stretched, or otherwise deformed.**

39. Inspect the boot for proper shape. If the boot is not shaped correctly, equalize the pressure in the boot by lifting the boot edge slightly and shape the boot properly by hand.

40. Inspect the boot for damage. If the boot has been cut or punctured during assembly, you must discard and replace the boot.

➡**The boot retaining clamp must not be over-tightened or under-tightened.**

41. Crimp the large boot retaining clamp. Tighten the large boot clamp until the base of the omega ohms shape has a gap of 1 mm (0.039 in).

42. The clamping hold time must be no less than 2 seconds.

43. Inspect the outer joint for smooth operation. This will also distribute the grease within the joint.

    a. Hold the halfshaft vertically, with the outer joint at the bottom.

    b. Rotate the halfshaft 4 or 5 times in a circular motion.

    c. Install the halfshaft.

PROPELLER SHAFT, DIFFERENTIAL, AND DRIVELINE SUPPORT

REMOVAL & INSTALLATION

With Manual Transmission

See Figures 28 through 33.

1. Remove the left rear wheel drive shaft.

2. Remove the muffler and exhaust pipe from the vehicle.

3. Remove the floor panel tunnel panel front closeout panel.

4. Remove the floor panel tunnel rear panel

5. Support the transmission with a suitable jack stand.

6. Loosen but DO NOT remove the driveline support to the transmission bolts.

7. Remove the transmission close out panel.

8. Loosen, but DO NOT remove the left and right motor mount bolts.

9. Remove the front propeller shaft bolts and washer support tabs from the transmission.

➡**The proper nuts and bolts to be removed are those where the nut is the closest or facing the rear differential drive flange. DO NOT remove the nuts and bolt where the nuts are facing the front or propeller shaft.**

10. Remove the propeller shaft nuts and bolts from the rear differential.

11. Support the rear differential with a transmission jack stand.

12. Remove the left and right rear differential mount bolts.

13. Lower the rear differential enough to clear the rear crossmember.

14. Using the J 44394 seal protector , move the rear differential to the left side of the vehicle, remove the right rear wheel drive shaft.

15. Remove the four differential carrier bracket bolts.

16. Separate the differential carrier from the driveline support bracket

17. Remove the propeller shaft from the vehicle.

➡**Steps 18 and 19 are for the replacing the driveline support.**

18. Remove the driveline support bolts and the washers from the transmission.

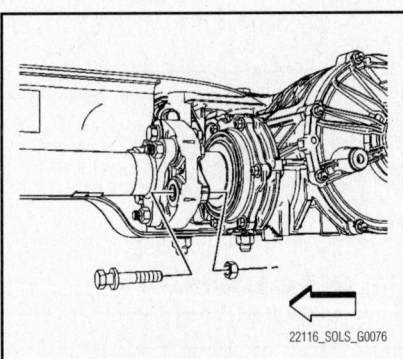

Fig. 28 Rear propeller shaft nuts and bolts at the rear differential

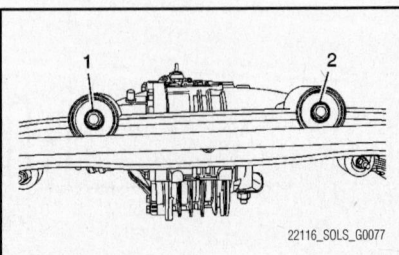

Fig. 29 Left and right rear differential mount bolts

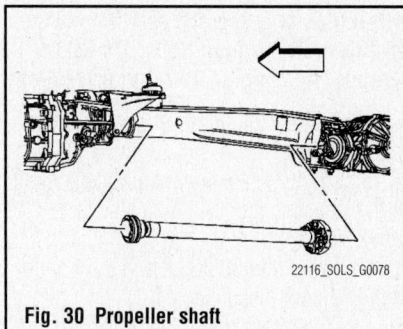

Fig. 30 Propeller shaft

19. Remove the driveline support from the transmission and the rear differential assembly.

➡️**Support the right rear wheel drive shaft with mechanics wire or equivalent.**

To install:

20. Clean the bolt holes in the differential carrier with brake cleaner or other suitable solvents to remove any adhesive.

21. If servicing the driveline support, position the driveline support (4) on the differential housing.

22. Install the bolt plate, bolts, nuts for the driveline support on the differential housing. Tighten the nuts to 177 ft. lbs. (240 Nm).

23. Position the driveline support on the transmission.

24. Install the driveline support bolts and washers. Leave the bolts loose.

25. Raise the differential to just below the rear crossmember.

26. Clean the pilot shaft and the pilot hole of any dirt or debris

27. Apply a small amount of chassis lube on the pilot shaft.

28. Align the pilot shaft and the pilot hole.

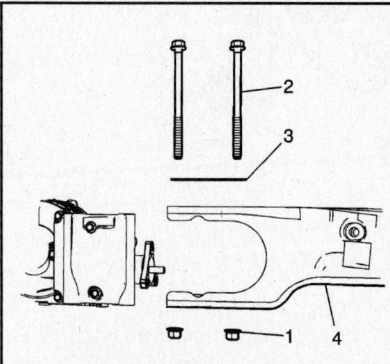

1. Driveline support mounting nut
2. Driveline support mounting bolt
3. Washer block
4. Driveline support

Fig. 31 Driveline support

29. Install the propeller shaft to the transmission and differential.

➡️**In steps 11 and 12, finger tighten the front and rear propeller shaft nuts and bolts only. DO NOT torque the propeller shaft nuts and bolts until the differential and driveline support have been aligned and torqued to specifications.**

30. Install the propeller shaft bolts and washer support tabs in the transmission drive flange.

31. Install the propeller shaft nuts and bolts to the differential drive flange.

32. Remove the wheel drive shaft from the mechanics wire.

33. Position the J 44394 on the right wheel drive shaft.

34. Moving the differential to the right, install the wheel drive shaft.

35. Remove the J 44394 from the wheel drive shaft.

36. Align the differential carrier and the torque beam bracket.

37. Install the four new driveline support bracket bolts.

➡️**Use only hands tools to tighten the bolts.**

38. Tighten the four new driveline support bracket bolts to 66 ft. lbs. (90 Nm).

39. Raise and position the differential in the rear support.

40. Hand install the left and right rear differential mounting bolts tighten to 129 ft. lbs. (175 Nm).

41. Tighten the rear propeller shaft bolts to 63 ft. lbs. (85 Nm).

42. Tighten the front propeller shaft bolts in sequence to 30 ft. lbs. (40 Nm).

43. Install the left rear wheel drive shaft.

❋❋ WARNING

Failing to perform the following service procedure will create the wrong driveline angle for the propeller shaft and alignment of the transmission and the rear differential.

44. Position a scale or known straight edge across the floor pan where the driveline tunnel closeout mounts to the body.

45. Position another scale at the transmission output shaft oil seal slinger.

46. Using the jack stand, raise or lower the transmission until a measurement of 3.150 inch. (80 mm) is obtained.

47. Tighten the driveline support bolts at the transmission to 177 ft. lbs. (240 Nm).

48. Remove the jack stand from the rear differential.

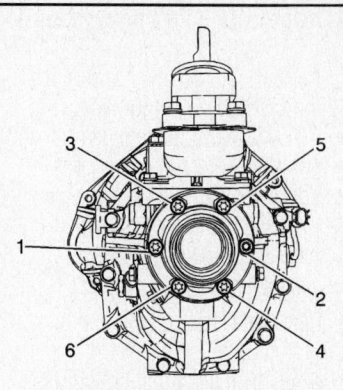

Tighten the front propeller shaft bolts in sequence (1-6).

Fig. 32 Front propeller shaft bolts tightening sequence

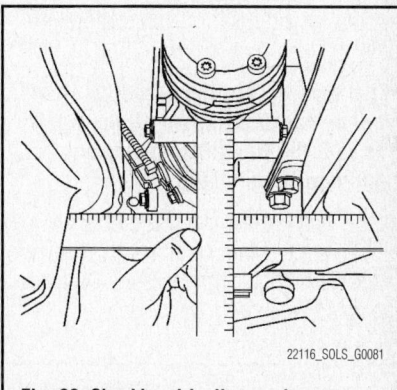

Fig. 33 Checking driveline angle measurement for 3.150 inch. (80 mm)

49. Tighten the left and right motor mount bolts.

50. Remove the transmission jack stand.

51. Install the transmission close out panel.

52. Install the floor panel tunnel panel front closeout panel.

53. Install the floor panel tunnel rear panel.

54. Install the muffler and exhaust pipe from the vehicle.

PROPELLER SHAFT

REMOVAL & INSTALLATION

With Automatic Transmission

See Figures 34 and 35.

1. Raise and support the vehicle.

2. Remove the exhaust pipe and muffler.

3. Remove the floor panel rear panel.

4. Support the rear differential assembly with a suitable jack stand.

5. Remove the left and right rear differential support bolts.

6. Remove the front differential support bolt.

7. Remove the propeller shaft bolts from the transmission output flange.

8. Remove the propeller shaft nut and bolts from the differential drive flange.

9. Lower the rear differential assembly enough to remove the propeller shaft from the vehicle.

To install:

10. Remove all debris from the pilot shaft.

11. Apply a small amount of chassis lube on the pilot shaft and pilot shaft hole in the propeller shaft.

12. Position the propeller shaft on the transmission output flange.

13. Raise the rear differential at the same time as aligning the propeller shaft pilot shaft and the propeller shaft pilot hole.

➡ **DO NOT tighten the propeller shaft front or rear fasteners until the front and rear differential support bolts are tighten to specifications.**

14. Hand tighten the propeller shaft bolts to the transmission output shaft flange.

15. Hand tighten the nuts and bolts to the rear differential drive flange.

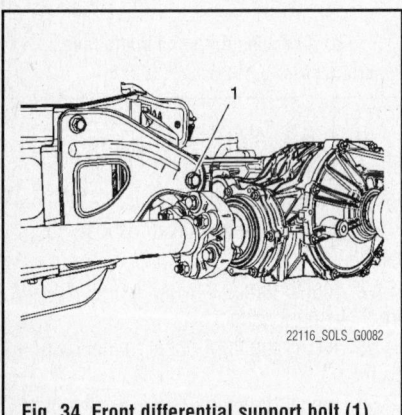

22116_SOLS_G0082

Fig. 34 Front differential support bolt (1)

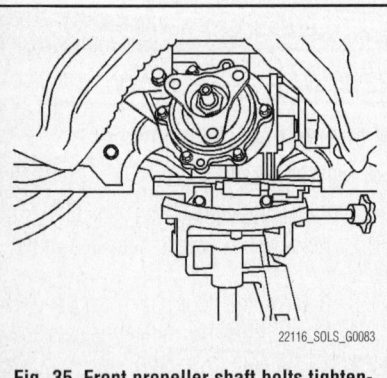

22116_SOLS_G0083

Fig. 35 Front propeller shaft bolts tightening sequence

16. Position the rear differential assembly in the support.

17. Install the left and right rear differential support bolts and tighten to 129 ft. lbs. (175 Nm).

18. Install the front differential support bolt and tighten to 129 ft. lbs. (175 Nm).

19. Remove the jack stand from the rear differential assembly.

20. Tighten the front propeller shaft bolts in sequence to 30 ft. lbs. (40 Nm).

21. Tighten the rear propeller shaft bolts to 63 ft. lbs. (85 Nm).

22. Install the floor panel rear panel.

23. Install the exhaust pipe and muffler.

24. Remove the support and lower the vehicle.

REAR PINION SEAL

REMOVAL & INSTALLATION

See Figures 36 and 37.

1. Raise and support vehicle.

2. Remove the floor panel tunnel rear panel.

➡ **The following service procedure is for those vehicles equipped with a manual transmission and drive line support. For vehicles equipped with a automatic transmission, proceed to Step 4.**

3. Remove the propeller shaft, differential and driveline support.

➡ **Remove only the driveshaft coupler-to-differential flange bolts. Do NOT remove the coupler from the driveshaft.**

4. Remove the propeller shaft from the rear differential.

5. Carefully position the propeller shaft to the side and support using a suitable jack stand..

6. Lower the driveshaft and the front of the RDM until disconnected.

7. Carefully position the driveshaft out of the way and support the driveshaft using a suitable jack.

8. Install a holding tool on the flange.

9. Remove the drive pinion nut.

10. Using a puller, remove the flange.

11. Using a flat-bladed tool, remove the drive pinion seal. Take care not to damage any sealing surfaces.

To install:

12. Lubricate the drive pinion flange sealing surface of the drive pinion seal with synthetic gear oil.

13. Using a seal driver, install the pinion seal to the differential.

14. Install the pinion flange on the drive pinion shaft.

➡ **The pinion shaft threads and the pinion flange nut must be free of residue and debris prior to application of threadlocker in order to ensure proper adhesion and fastener retention.**

15. Prepare the pinion shaft threads and the pinion flange nut for assembly:

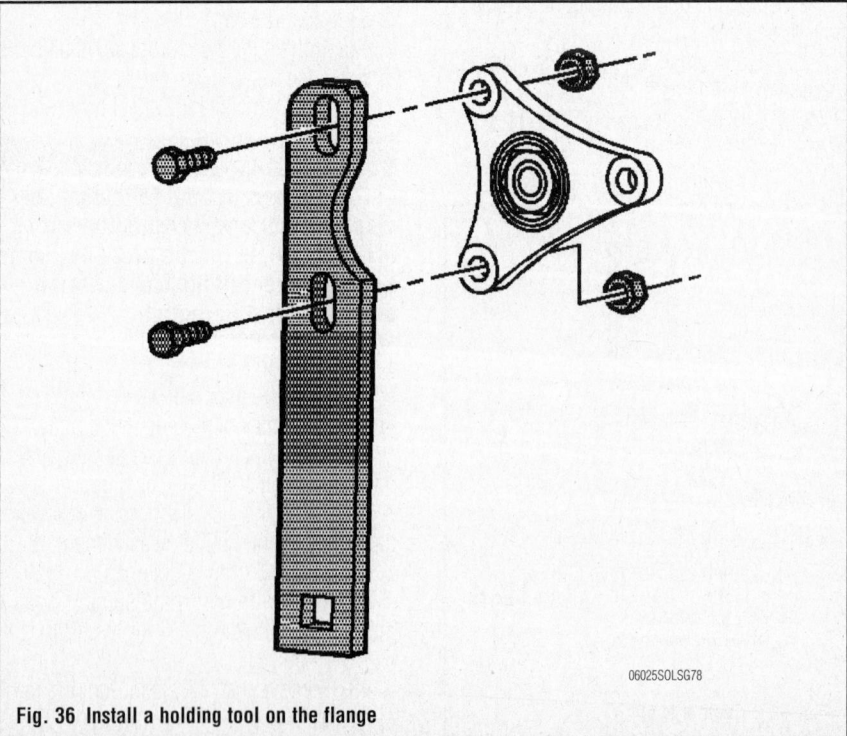

06025SOLSG78

Fig. 36 Install a holding tool on the flange

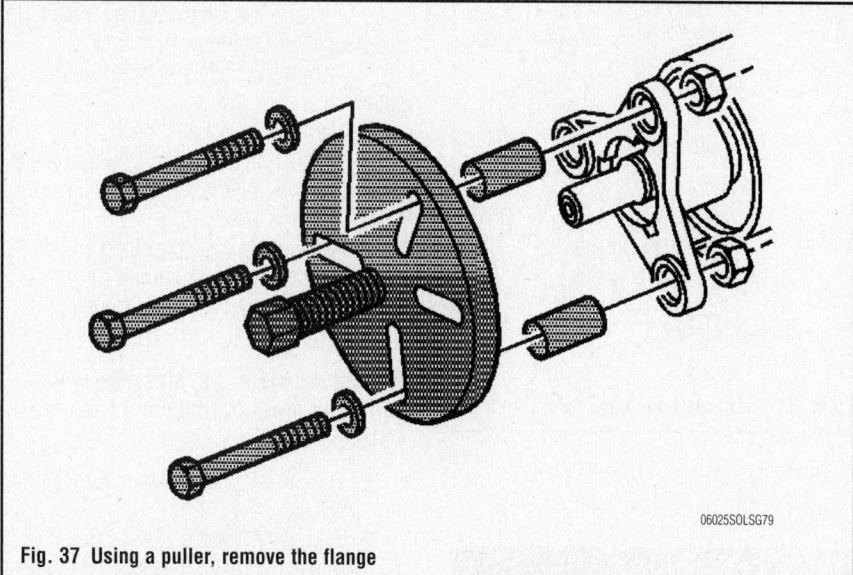

Fig. 37 Using a puller, remove the flange

a. Thoroughly clean the residue from the pinion shaft threads by using denatured alcohol or equivalent and allow to dry.

b. Thoroughly clean the residue from the pinion flange nut by using denatured alcohol or equivalent and allow to dry.

16. Apply threadlocker GM P/N 12345382 (Canadian P/N 10953489), or equivalent to ⅔ of the threaded length of the pinion shaft threads. Ensure that there are no gaps in the threadlocker along the length of the filled area of the pinion shaft threads.

17. Allow the threadlocker to cure approximately 10 minutes before installation.

18. Install the drive pinion flange nut to the pinion shaft. Hold the pinion flange with the holding tool.

19. Tighten the drive pinion flange nut to 181 ft. lbs. (245 Nm).

➡ **The following service procedure is for those vehicles equipped with a manual transmission and drive line support. For vehicles equipped with a automatic transmission, proceed to Step 15.**

20. Install the propeller shaft, differential and driveline support.

21. Install the propeller shaft to the differential.

22. Install the floor panel tunnel rear panel.

23. Inspect the fluid level.

24. Remove the support and lower the vehicle.

ENGINE COOLING

ENGINE FAN

REMOVAL & INSTALLATION

2.4L (LE5) & 2.0L (LNF) Engines
See Figure 38.

1. Remove the air cleaner assembly.
2. Remove the air cleaner duct.
3. Disconnect the cooling fan motor electrical connector.
4. Remove fan assembly mounting bolts.
5. Remove fan assembly.

To install:
6. Install fan assembly.
7. Install fan assembly mounting bolts and tighten to 18 ft. lbs. (25 Nm).

8. Reconnect the cooling fan motor electrical connector.
9. Install the air cleaner duct.
10. Install the air cleaner assembly.

RADIATOR

REMOVAL & INSTALLATION

2.4L (LE5) & 2.0L (LNF) Engines
See Figure 39.

1. Drain the cooling system.
2. Remove the upper radiator air baffle.
3. Remove the fan shroud assembly.

4. Remove the radiator inlet hose from the radiator.
5. Remove the radiator outlet hose from the radiator.
6. Remove the surge tank inlet hose from radiator.
7. Remove the radiator support brackets.
8. Remove the A/C condenser bolt and bracket.
9. Remove radiator assembly.

To install:
10. Install radiator assembly.
11. Install the A/C condenser bolt and bracket.

Fig. 38 Electric fan assembly

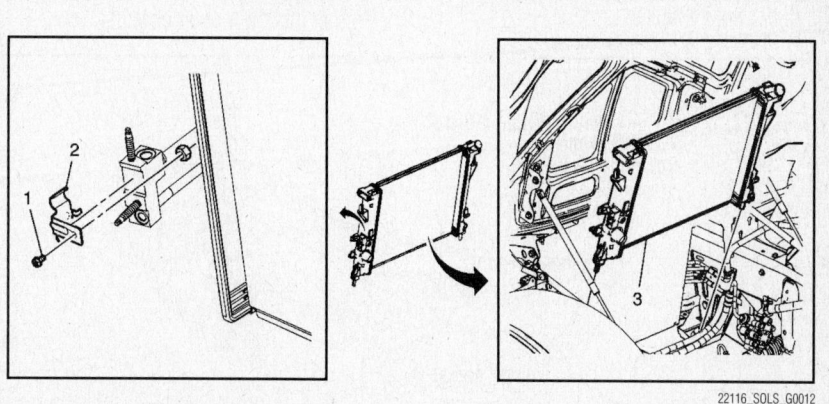

Fig. 39 Radiator assembly, (3) condenser bracket, (2) bolt, (1)

12. Tighten the condenser bracket bolt to 80 inch. lbs. (9 Nm).

13. Install the radiator support brackets and tighten to 80 inch. lbs. (9 Nm).

14. Install the surge tank inlet hose to the radiator.

15. Install the radiator outlet and inlet hoses to the radiator.

16. Install the fan shroud assembly.

17. Install the upper radiator air baffle.

18. Refill and bleed cooling system.

19. Check for leaks.

THERMOSTAT

REMOVAL & INSTALLATION

2.4L (LE5) & 2.0L (LNF) Engines

See Figures 40 and 41.

1. Drain the cooling system.

2. Remove the air inlet grille panel.

3. Reposition the radiator outlet hose clamp at the thermostat housing.

4. Remove the radiator outlet hose from the thermostat housing.

5. Remove the radiator outlet hose clip from the outlet hose bracket for 2.4L engines.

6. Remove the thermostat housing cover bolts and cover.

7. Remove the thermostat.

8. Remove and discard the thermostat housing O-ring seal.

To install:

9. Install a new thermostat housing cover O-ring seal onto the housing.

10. Install the thermostat housing cover and bolts.

11. Tighten mounting bolts to 89 inch. lbs. (10 Nm).

12. Install the radiator outlet hose to the thermostat housing.

13. Reposition the radiator outlet hose clamp at the thermostat housing.

14. Install the radiator outlet hose clip to the outlet hose bracket.

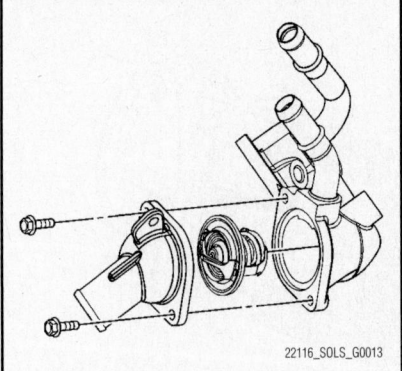

Fig. 41 Thermostat and housing assembly

15. Install the air inlet grille panel.

16. Fill and bleed the cooling system.

WATER PUMP

REMOVAL & INSTALLATION

2.4L (LE5) & 2.0L (LNF) Engines

See Figures 42 through 47.

1. Before servicing the vehicle, refer to the Precautions Section.

2. Drain the cooling system.

➡**A drain has been provided at the bottom of the water pump for engine block coolant drainage.**

3. Drain the coolant from the engine block at the water pump drain. After the coolant has drained, tighten the drain bolt.

4. Lower the vehicle.

5. Disconnect the engine coolant temperature (ECT) sensor electrical connector.

6. Remove the ECT sensor, if necessary.

7. Reposition the surge tank outlet hose clamp at the thermostat housing.

8. Remove the surge tank outlet hose from the thermostat housing.

9. Reposition the radiator outlet hose clamp at the thermostat housing.

10. Remove the radiator outlet hose from the thermostat housing.

11. Remove the exhaust heat shield bolts.

12. Remove the exhaust heat shield.

13. Reposition the heater inlet and outlet hose clamps at the thermostat housing pipes.

14. Disconnect the heater inlet and outlet hoses from the thermostat housing pipes.

15. Remove the thermostat housing bolts.

➡**Twist the water transfer pipe while pulling in order to remove it from the water pump.**

16. Remove the thermostat housing from the vehicle.

17. Remove the water transfer pipe from the thermostat housing, if necessary.

18. Remove and discard the water transfer pipe O-ring seals, if necessary.

19. Remove the thermostat housing cover bolts and cover, if necessary.

20. Remove the thermostat, if necessary.

21. Remove and discard the thermostat housing O-ring seal, if necessary.

22. Remove all debris and thread sealant from the engine coolant temperature sensor and bolt holes if the housing is being re-used.

23. Remove the water pump access plate from the front cover.

24. Remove the right hand fender liner.

➡**A drain plug has been provided at the bottom of the water pump assembly for additional coolant drainage from the engine block and water pump.**

25. Drain the coolant from the water pump using the plug at the bottom of the pump.

➡**The water pump holding tool supports the sprocket and chain during water pump service. The tool must be used or the balance shaft must be re-timed.**

26. Install water pump holding tool J 43651 into position.

27. Tighten the bolts on the water pump holding tool into the threads on the water pump sprocket.

28. Install the access cover bolts that were removed earlier to secure the water pump holding tool to the front cover assembly.

29. Remove the 3 inner water pump sprocket to water pump bolts.

➡**Be sure to remove both water pump bolts from the front of the engine block.**

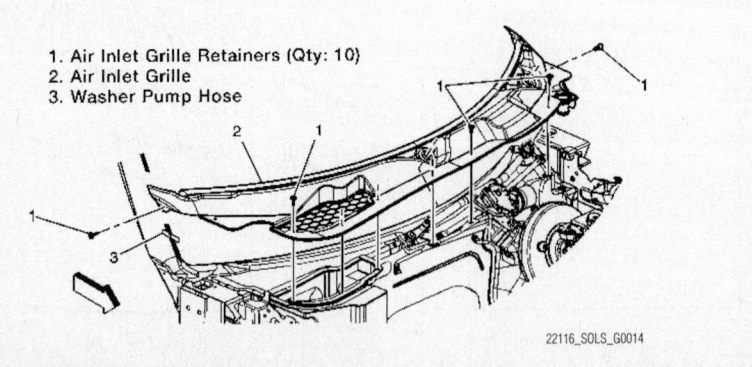

1. Air Inlet Grille Retainers (Qty: 10)
2. Air Inlet Grille
3. Washer Pump Hose

Fig. 40 Air inlet grille panel removal

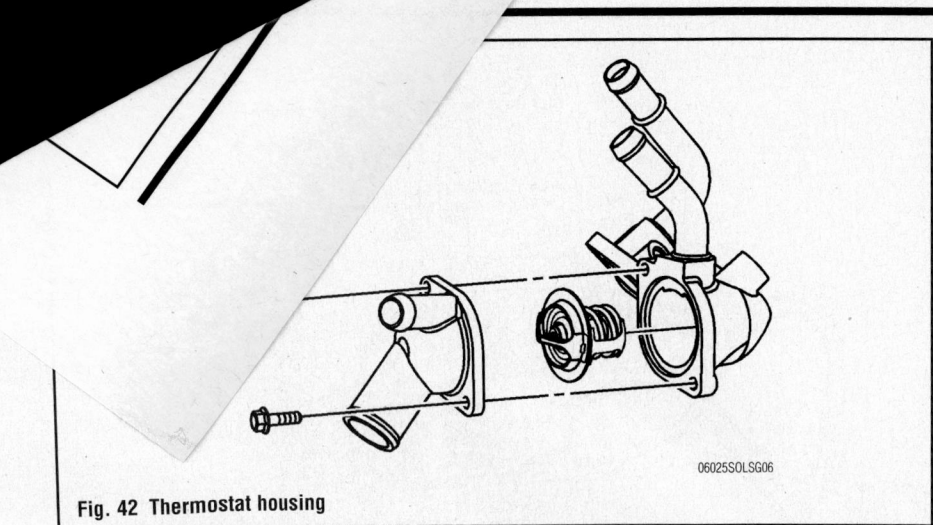

Fig. 42 Thermostat housing

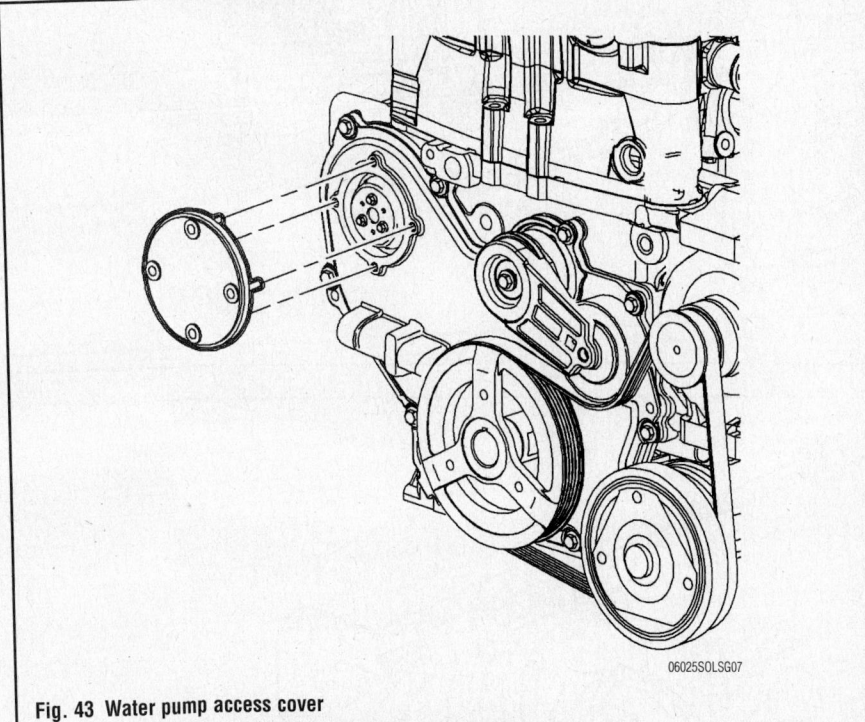

Fig. 43 Water pump access cover

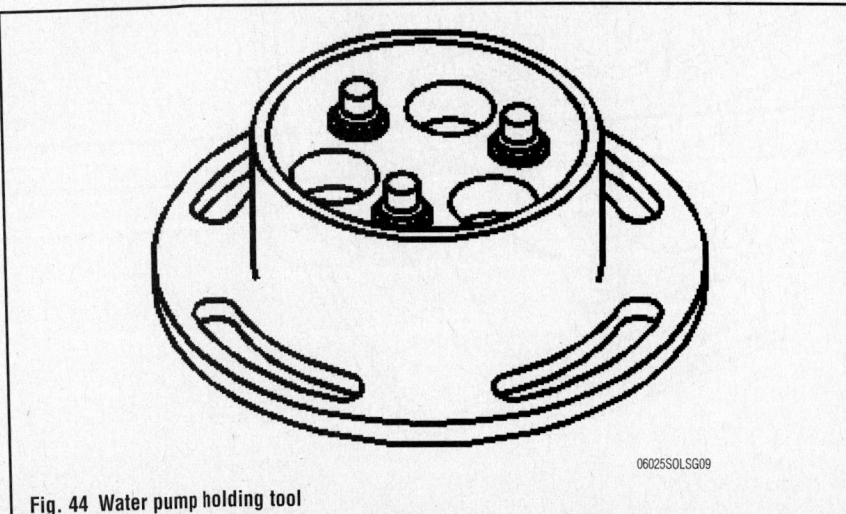

Fig. 44 Water pump holding tool

30. Remove the 2 water pump bolts.
31. Remove the rear 2 water pump bolts.
32. Remove the water pump.
33. Remove and discard the water pump O-ring seal.

To install:

➡ **Prior to installing the water pump, read the entire procedure. This will help avoid balance shaft chain re-timing and ensure proper sealing.**

34. Install a NEW water pump O-ring seal.

➡ **A guide pin can be created to aid in water pump alignment. Use an M 6 m x 6 mm stud. Thread the pin into the water pump sprocket.**

35. Using the guide pin, align the pin with the water pump holding tool.
36. Position the water pump against the engine block and hand tighten the water pump bolts.
37. Install the inner water pump sprocket bolts. After 2 are snug, remove the guide pin and install the 3rd bolt. Tighten the bolts to 25 Nm (18 ft. lbs.).
38. Tighten the water pump sprocket bolts last. Tighten the bolts to 89 inch. lbs. (10 Nm).
39. Remove the tool.
40. Install the water pump access plate and bolts. Tighten the bolts to 89 inch. lbs. (10 Nm).
41. Install the right hand fender liner.
42. Install a NEW thermostat housing cover O-ring seal into the recess groove.
43. Install the thermostat, if necessary.
44. Install the thermostat housing cover bolts, if necessary. Tighten the bolts to 89 inch. lbs. (10 Nm).
45. Install a NEW thermostat housing to engine gasket onto the thermostat housing.
46. Load the thermostat housing assembly into position while the vehicle is lowered.
47. Raise and support the vehicle.

➡ **The water feed pipe seals can be lightly lubricated with coolant to aid during installation.**

48. Install NEW O-ring seals onto the water feed pipe.

➡ **Lubricate the O-rings with coolant ONLY.**

49. Install the water feed pipe into the thermostat housing aligning locator tab.
50. Align the water pipe to water pump.
51. Seat the water feed O-ring seal by pushing inward toward the water pump. Take care not to tear or damage the O-ring.

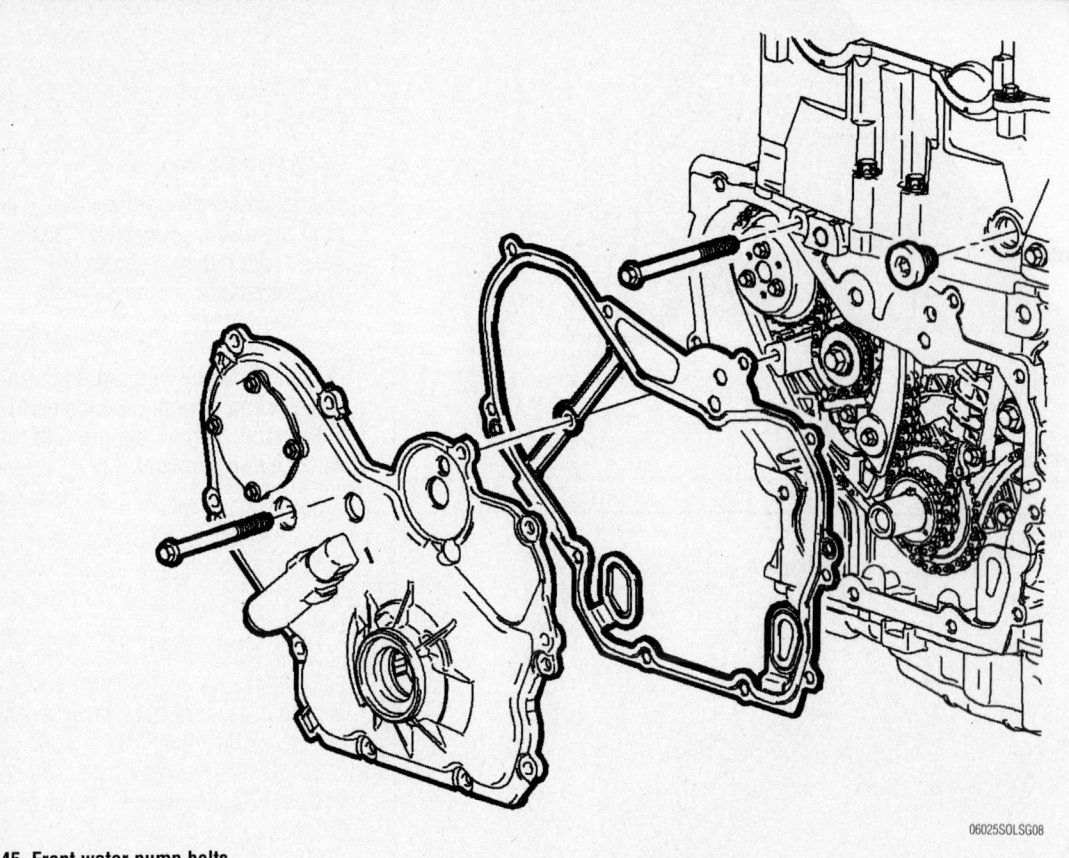

06025SOLSG08

Fig. 45 Front water pump bolts

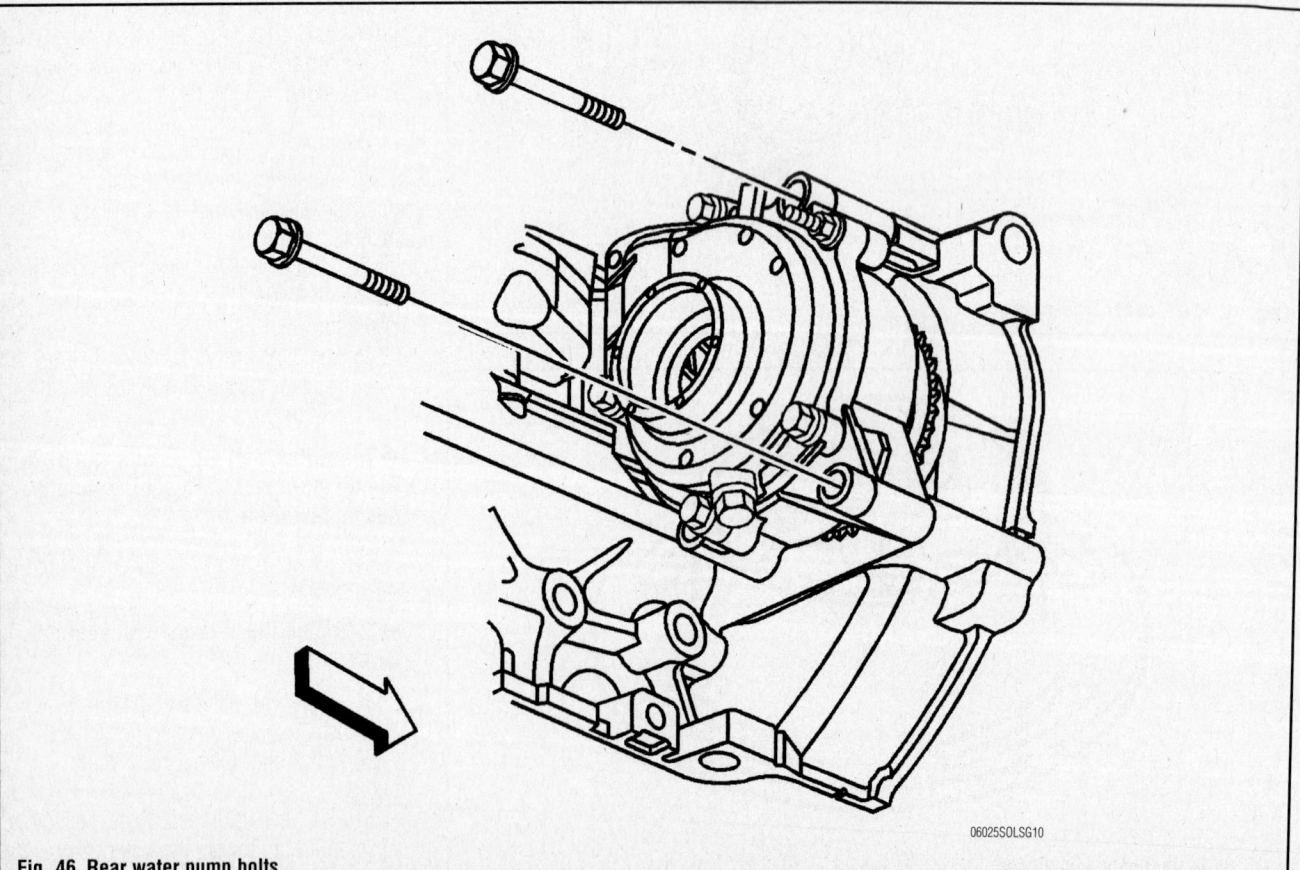

06025SOLSG10

Fig. 46 Rear water pump bolts

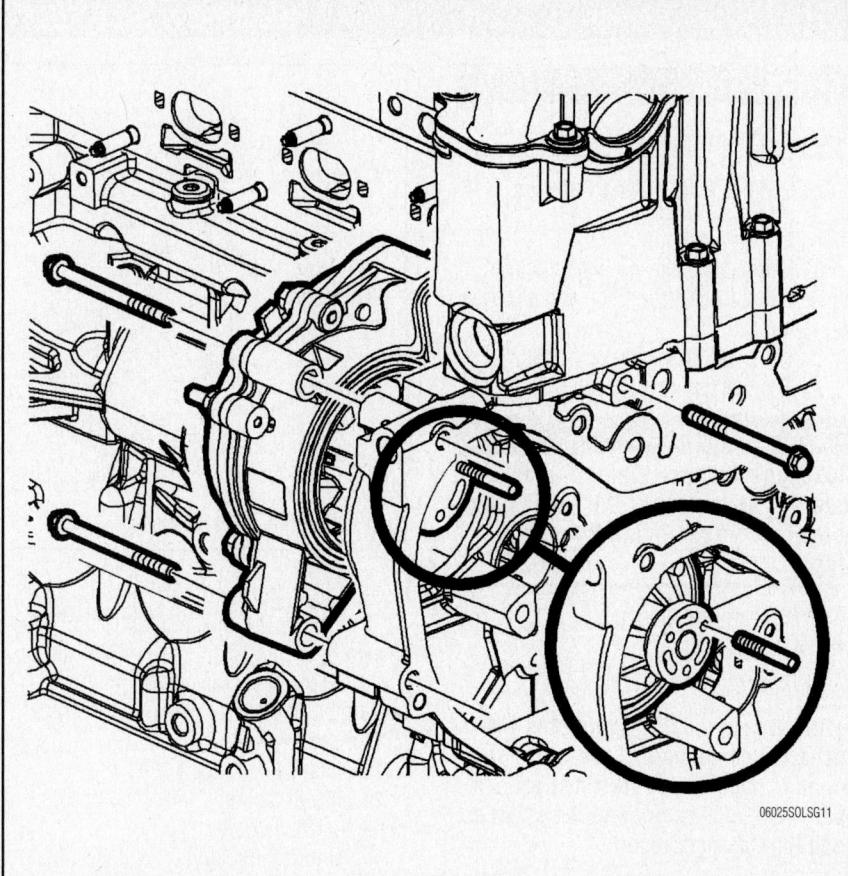

Fig. 47 Guide pin installation

52. Lower the vehicle.
53. Position the thermostat housing against the engine.
54. Install the thermostat housing bolts. Tighten the bolts to 89 inch. lbs. (10 Nm).
55. Connect the heater inlet and outlet hoses to the thermostat housing pipes.
56. Position the heater inlet and outlet hose clamps at the thermostat housing pipes.
57. Install the exhaust heat shield.
58. Install the exhaust heat shield bolts. Tighten the bolts to 17 ft. lbs. (23 Nm).
59. Install the radiator outlet hose to the thermostat housing.
60. Position the radiator outlet hose clamp at the thermostat housing.
61. Install the surge tank outlet hose to the thermostat housing.
62. Position the surge tank outlet hose clamp at the thermostat housing.
63. Install the ECT sensor, if necessary.
64. Connect the ECT sensor electrical connector.

➡ **The vehicle must be level when filling the cooling system.**

65. Verify the drain valves at the radiator and water pump are closed.
66. Fill the cooling system.
67. Lower the vehicle.
68. Check for any leaks.

ENGINE ELECTRICAL

CHARGING SYSTEM

ALTERNATOR

REMOVAL & INSTALLATION

See Figure 48.

1. Before servicing the vehicle, refer to the Precautions Section.
2. Disconnect the negative battery cable.
3. Remove the drive belt.
4. Disconnect the alternator wiring.
5. Remove the bolts.
6. Installation is the reverse of removal. Torque the mounting bolts to 16 ft. lbs. (22 Nm).

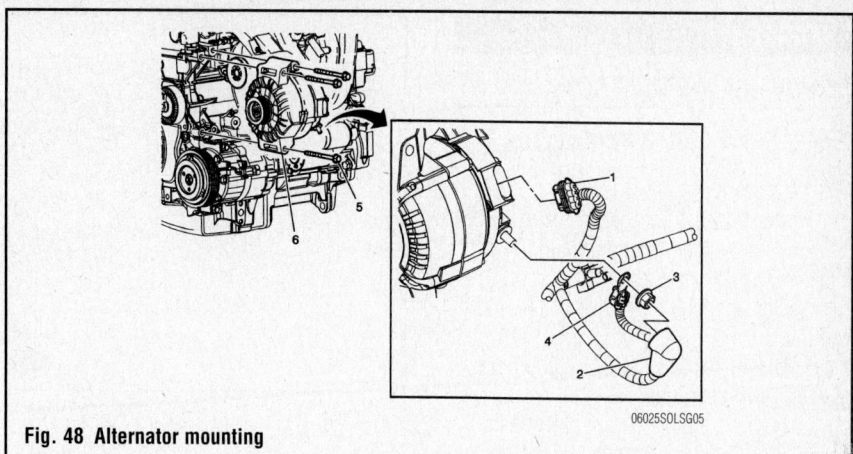

Fig. 48 Alternator mounting

ENGINE ELECTRICAL   **IGNITION SYSTEM**

IGNITION COIL

REMOVAL & INSTALLATION

2.4L (LE5) & 2.0L (LNF) Engines

1. Remove the intake manifold cover.
2. Disconnect the ignition coil electrical connectors.
3. Remove the ignition coil bolts.
4. Remove the ignition coils.

To install:

5. Apply dielectric compound to the spark plug boots and make sure no corrosion is present.
6. Install the ignition coils.
7. Install the ignition coil bolts and tighten to 89 inch. lbs. (10 Nm).
8. Connect the ignition coil electrical connectors.
9. Install the intake manifold cover.

IGNITION TIMING

ADJUSTMENT

The ignition timing is controlled by the Powertrain Control Module (PCM). No adjustment is necessary or possible.

SPARK PLUGS

REMOVAL & INSTALLATION

2.4L (LE5) & 2.0L (LNF) Engines

See Figure 49.

1. Remove the intake manifold cover.
2. Disconnect the ignition coil electrical connectors.
3. Remove the ignition coil bolts.
4. Remove the ignition coils.

※※ WARNING

Make sure that any water and/or debris is blown out of the spark plug holes prior to removing the spark plugs.

5. Remove the spark plugs using a ⅝ inch spark plug socket.

To install:

→**Do not coat spark plug threads with anti-seize compound. If anti-seize compound is used and spark plugs are over—torqued, damage to the cylinder head threads may result.**

6. Check that the spark plug gap is 0.042 inch. (1.06 mm).

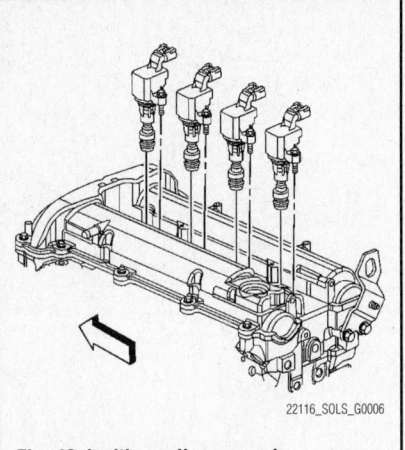

Fig. 49 Ignition coils removed

7. Install the spark plugs.
8. Tighten the plugs to 15 ft. lbs. (20 Nm).
9. Apply dielectric compound to the spark plug boots and make sure no corrosion is present.
10. Install the ignition coils.
11. Install the ignition coil bolts and tighten to 89 inch. lbs. (10 Nm).
12. Connect the ignition coil electrical connectors.
13. Install the intake manifold cover.

ENGINE ELECTRICAL   **STARTING SYSTEM**

STARTER

REMOVAL & INSTALLATION

2.4L (LE5) & 2.0L (LNF) Engines

See Figure 50.

1. Disconnect the negative battery cable.
2. Remove the intake manifold. Refer to intake manifold removal.
3. Disconnect the positive battery cable and nut.
4. Disconnect the starter solenoid terminal no. wire and nut.
5. Remove engine harness terminals
6. Remove starter motor.

To install:

7. Install starter motor and tighten mounting bolts to 30 ft. lbs. (40 Nm).
8. Install the engine harness terminals
9. Reconnect the starter solenoid terminal no. wire and nut. Tighten to 27 inch. lbs. (3 Nm).
10. Reconnect the positive battery cable and nut. Tighten to 89 inch. lbs. (10 Nm).
11. Install the intake manifold.
12. Connect the negative battery cable.

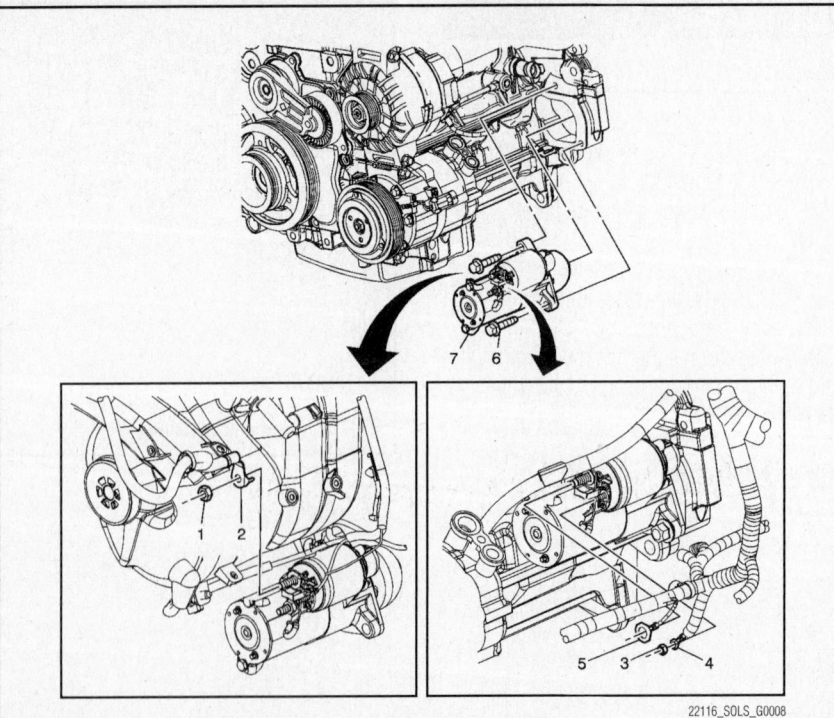

Fig. 50 Starter motor, mounting bolts and electrical connectors

ENGINE MECHANICAL

➡**Disconnecting the negative battery cable may interfere with the functions of the on board computer systems and may require the computer to undergo a relearning process, once the negative battery cable is reconnected.**

ACCESSORY DRIVE BELTS

ACCESSORY BELT ROUTING

See Figures 51 and 52.

INSPECTION

Inspect the drive belt for signs of glazing or cracking. A glazed belt will be perfectly smooth from slippage, while a good belt will have a slight texture of fabric visible. Cracks will usually start at the inner edge of the belt and run outward. All worn or damaged drive belts should be replaced immediately.

ADJUSTMENT

The drive belts for this model are equipped with automatic belt tensioners.

REMOVAL & INSTALLATION

Primary Drive Belt

See Figure 53.

1. Remove the intake manifold cover.
2. Raise the vehicle.
3. Rotate the power steering belt tensioner pulley clockwise to release the tension on the power steering pump drive belt.
4. Remove power steering drive belt.
5. Lower vehicle.
6. Remove the air cleaner.
7. Rotate the primary drive belt tensioner pulley counter clockwise to release the tension on the primary drive belt.
8. Remove primary drive belt.

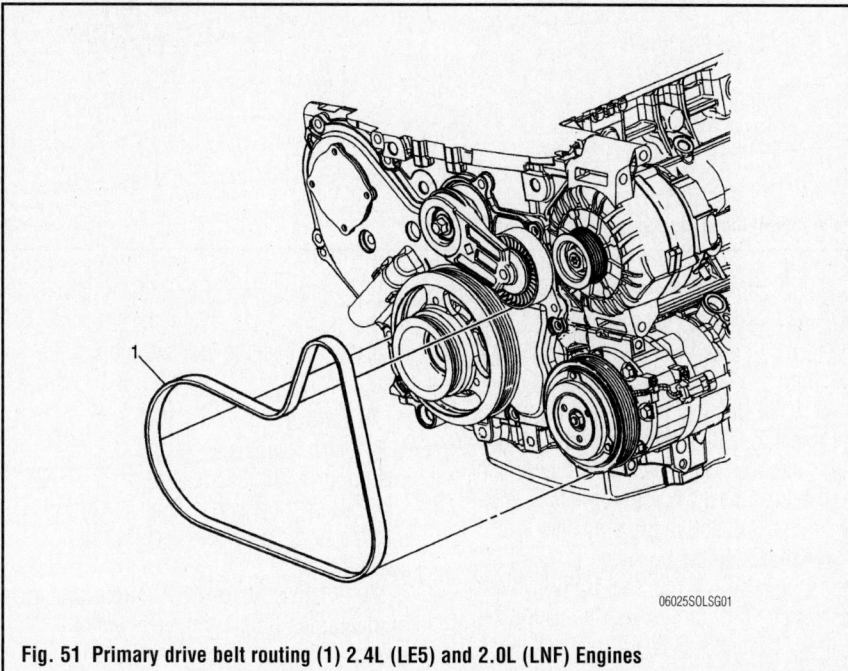

Fig. 51 Primary drive belt routing (1) 2.4L (LE5) and 2.0L (LNF) Engines

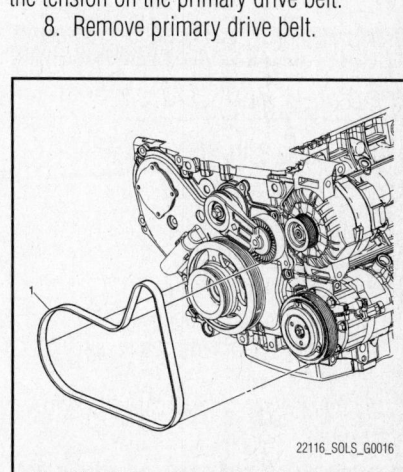

Fig. 53 Primary drive belt (1) with a/c shown

To install:

9. Rotate the primary drive belt tensioner pulley counter clockwise and install primary drive belt.
10. Install air cleaner.
11. Raise vehicle.
12. Rotate the power steering belt tensioner pulley clockwise and install power steering belt.
13. Lower vehicle.

Power Steering Belt

See Figure 54.

1. Raise the vehicle.
2. Rotate the power steering belt tensioner pulley clockwise to release the tension on the power steering pump drive belt.
3. Remove power steering drive belt.

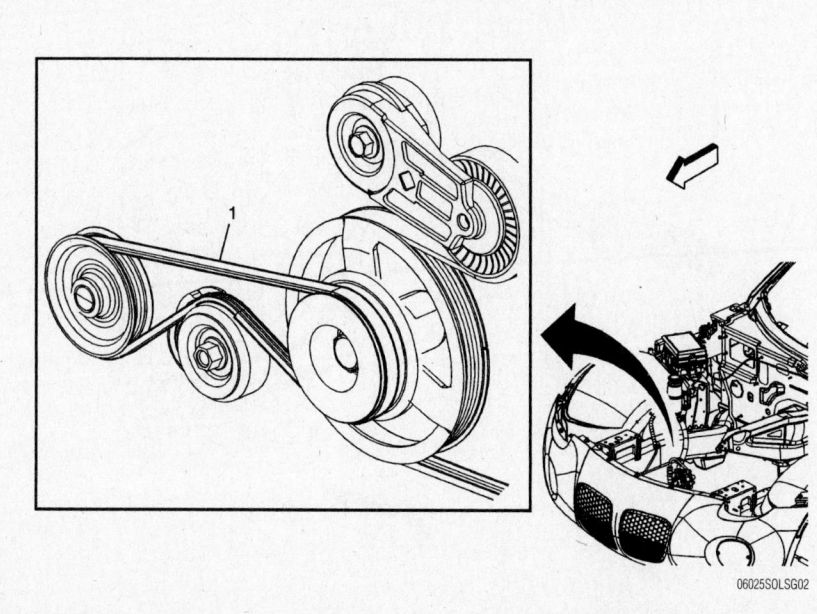

Fig. 52 Power steering belt (1) routing 2.4L (LE5) and 2.0L (LNF) Engines

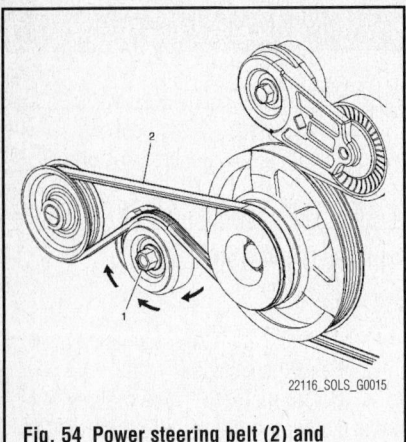

Fig. 54 Power steering belt (2) and tensioner rotation (1) shown

To install:

4. Rotate the power steering belt tensioner pulley clockwise and install power steering belt.

5. Lower vehicle.

BALANCE SHAFTS

REMOVAL & INSTALLATION

2.4L (LE5) & 2.0L (LNF) Engines

See Figures 55 through 57.

1. Before servicing the vehicle, refer to the Precautions Section.

2. Remove the radiator.

3. Remove A/C condenser

4. Remove the timing chain, sprocket and tensioner.

5. Remove the balance shaft bearing carrier bolts.

❊❊ WARNING

It is possible to install the intake side balance shaft into the exhaust side and vice versa. Please use care not to install the balance shafts into the wrong bores. Engine vibration will result. Do not remove the bolt holding the sprocket.

6. Remove the balance shaft assemblies.

❊❊ WARNING

Proper centering of the tool is required on the balance shaft bushing. If the tool is not properly centered then damage to the bearing bore and block will occur.

7. Install tool J 43650 into the balance shaft hole. Insert the tool with the foot parallel to the shaft.

8. When the tool is inserted in the

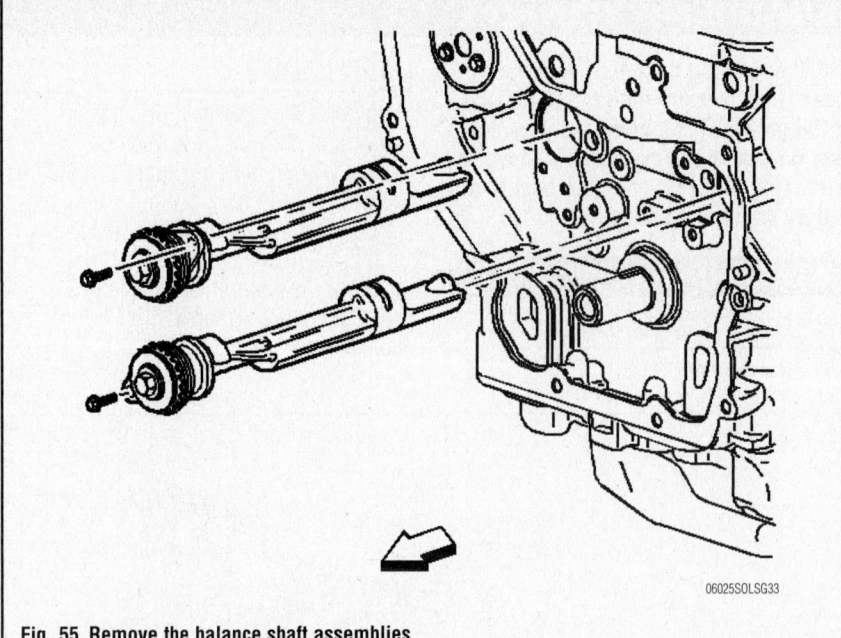

Fig. 55 Remove the balance shaft assemblies

block turn the tool so that the foot becomes perpendicular to the shaft. Center the foot of the tool on the balance shaft bushing.

9. Once the tool is centered on the balance shaft bushing, then insert the centering guide into the front balance shaft bore and tighten the nut with an appropriate wrench. When tool J 43650 is properly installed, before removing the bushing, the end of the tool should be 116 mm (4.6 in) (a) from the block face. If the tool is less than approximately 114 mm (4.5 in) (a), recheck the tool alignment.

10. Tighten the nut on tool J 43650 until the tension releases. When the tension releases, remove the tool and the balance shaft bushing.

To install:

11. Install the balance shaft bushing using tool J 43650.

12. Seat the balance shaft bushing into the bore using tool J 43650 and a wrench.

13. When tool J 43650 is fully seated in the engine block remove it with a wrench.

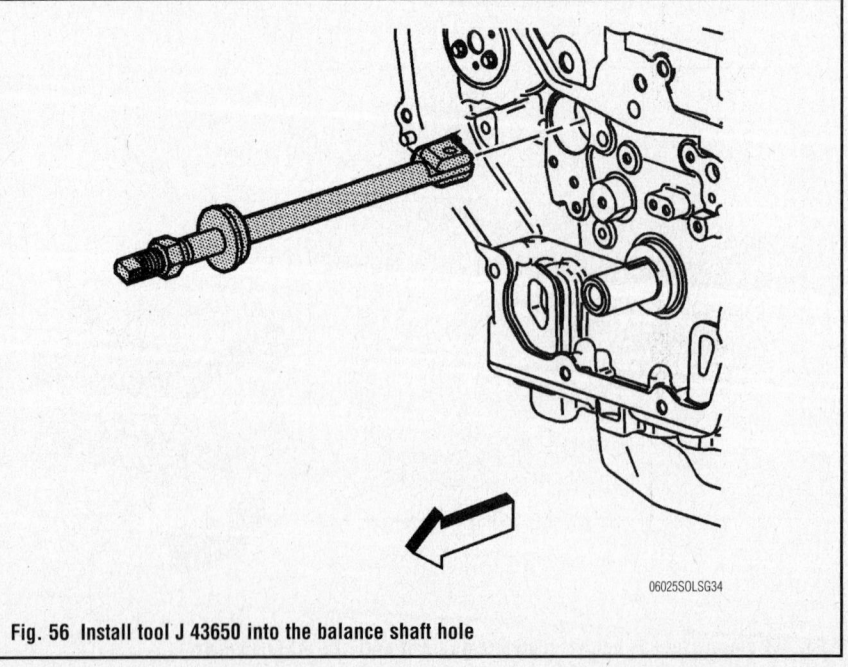

Fig. 56 Install tool J 43650 into the balance shaft hole

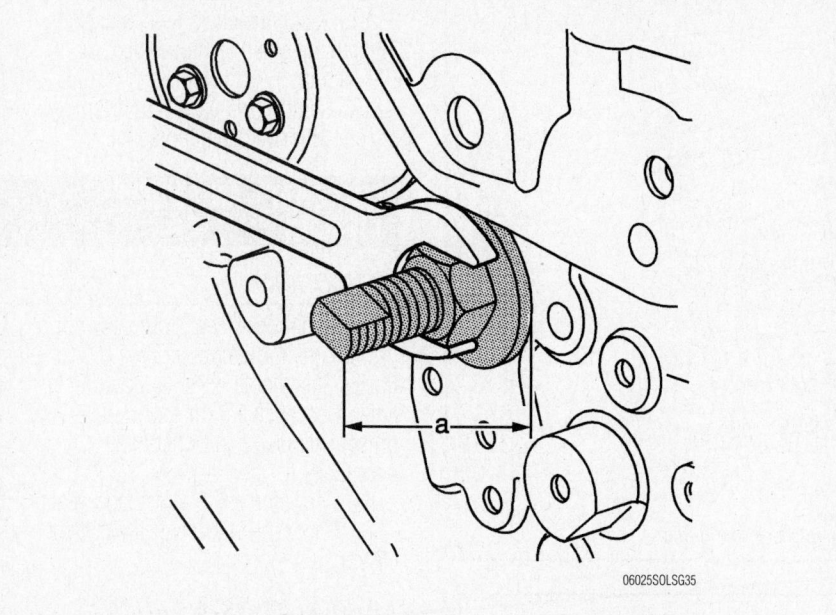

Fig. 57 When tool J 43650 is properly installed, before removing the bushing, the end of the tool should be 116 mm (4.6 in) (a) from the block face

➡**If the balance shafts are not properly timed to the engine, the engine may vibrate or make noise.**

14. Place the number one piston at top dead center (TDC).

15. Lubricate the balance shaft lobes with engine oil.

16. Install the balance shafts into their bores.

17. Install the balance shaft retaining bolts. Tighten the balance shaft retaining bolts to 10 Nm (89 inch lbs.).

18. Install the timing chain, sprocket and tensioner.

19. Install the A/C condenser.

20. Install the radiator.

BALANCE SHAFT CHAIN

REMOVAL & INSTALLATION

2.4L (LE5) & 2.0L (LNF) Engines
See Figures 58 through 61.

1. Before servicing the vehicle, refer to the Precautions Section.

2. Remove the balance shaft drive chain tensioner bolts and tensioner.

3. Remove the adjustable balance shaft chain guide bolt and guide.

4. Remove the small balance shaft drive chain guide bolts and guide.

5. Remove the upper balance shaft drive chain guide bolts and guide.

➡**The balance shaft drive chain will be easier to remove if you gather all of the**

slack in the chain between the crankshaft and water pump sprockets.

6. Remove the balance shaft drive chain.

To install:

➡**If the balance shafts are not properly timed to the engine, the engine may vibrate and make noise.**

7. Install the upper balance shaft chain guide and bolts. Tighten the upper balance shaft chain guide bolts to 15 Nm (11 ft. lbs.).

8. Install the small balance shaft chain guide.

9. Install the balance shaft chain guide bolts. Tighten the chain guide bolts to 15 Nm (11 ft. lbs.).

10. Install the adjustable balance shaft drive chain guide.

11. Install the adjustable balance shaft drive chain guide bolts. Tighten the chain guide bolts to 10 Nm (89 inch lbs.).

12. Reset the timing chain tensioner by performing the following steps:

a. Turn the tensioner plunger 90 degrees in its bore and compress the plunger.

b. Turn the tensioner back to the original 12 o'clock position and insert a paper clip through the hole in the plunger body and into the hole in the tensioner plunger.

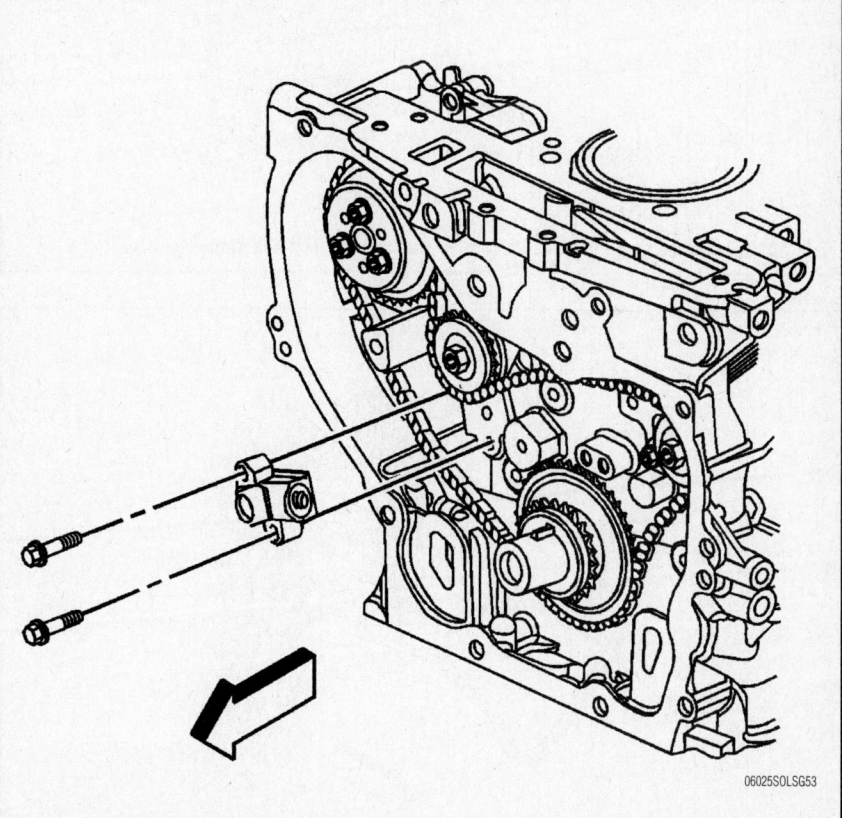

Fig. 58 Remove the balance shaft drive chain tensioner bolts and tensioner

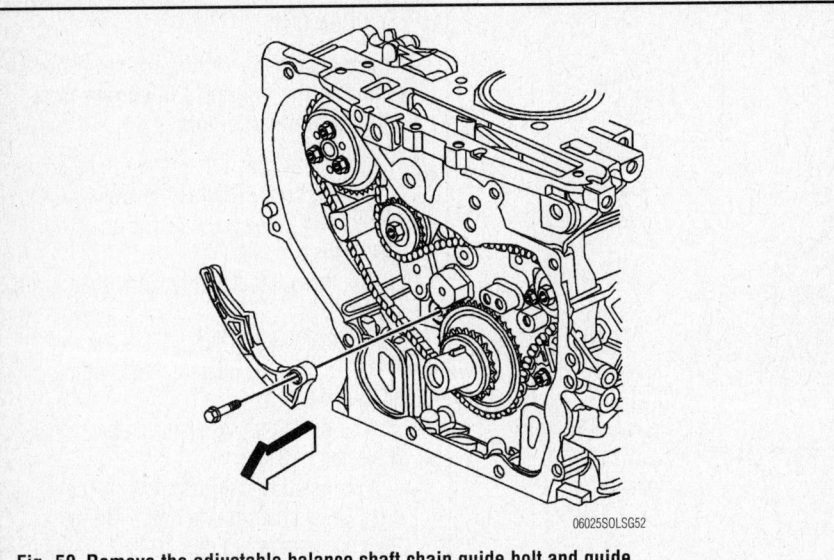

Fig. 59 Remove the adjustable balance shaft chain guide bolt and guide

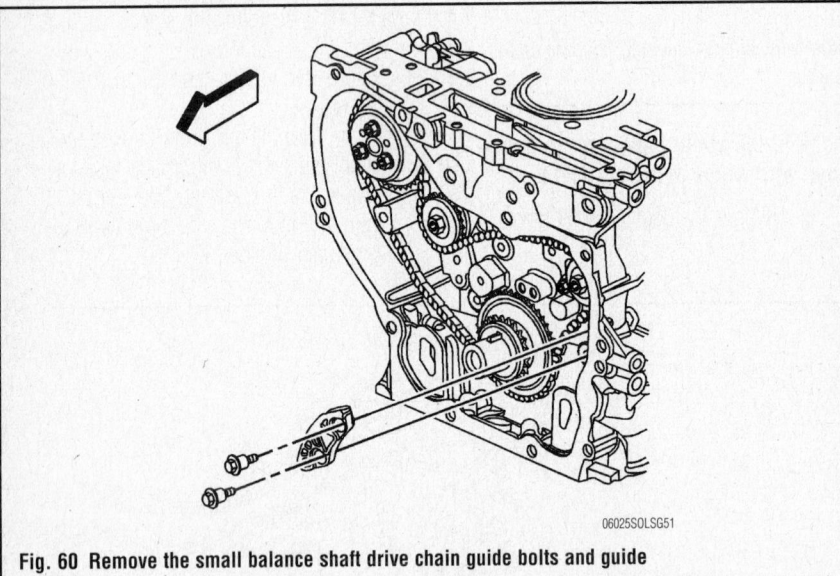

Fig. 60 Remove the small balance shaft drive chain guide bolts and guide

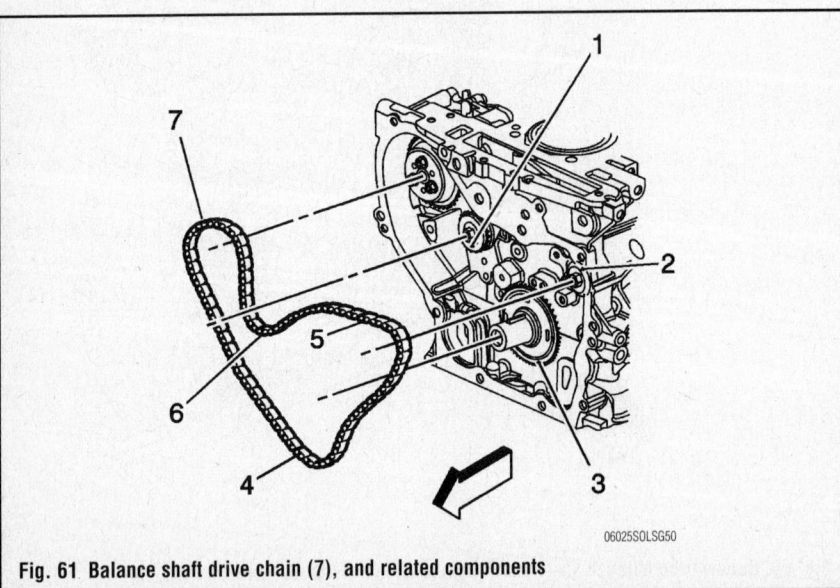

Fig. 61 Balance shaft drive chain (7), and related components

13. Install the timing chain tensioner.

14. Install the chain tensioner bolts. Tighten the chain tensioner bolts to 10 Nm (89 inch lbs.).

15. Remove the paper clip from the balance shaft drive chain tensioner.

CAMSHAFT AND VALVE LIFTERS

INSPECTION

1. Inspect camshaft lobes for pitting or damage in the contact area. Minor pitting is acceptable outside the contact area. If excessive pitting or damage is present replace components as necessary.

2. Check for valve tappet face wear.

3. Check for excessive valve tappet clearance.

REMOVAL & INSTALLATION

2.4L (LE5) Engine

INTAKE

See Figures 62 through 66.

1. Before servicing the vehicle, refer to the Precautions Section.

2. Remove the camshaft cover.

3. Remove the upper timing chain guide bolts and guide.

4. Install tool J 43655, or equivalent.

5. Remove and discard both the intake and exhaust camshaft sprocket bolts.

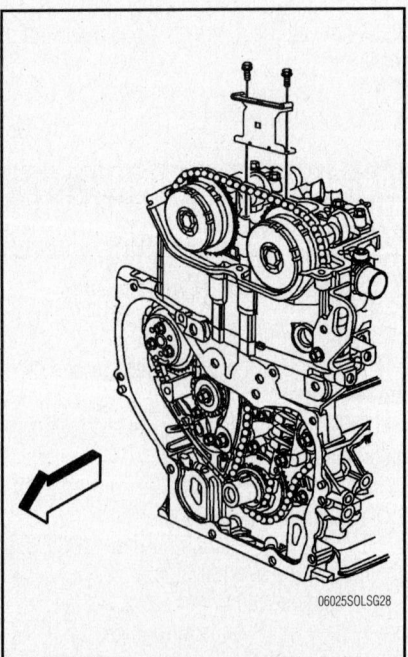

Fig. 62 Remove the upper timing chain guide bolts and guide

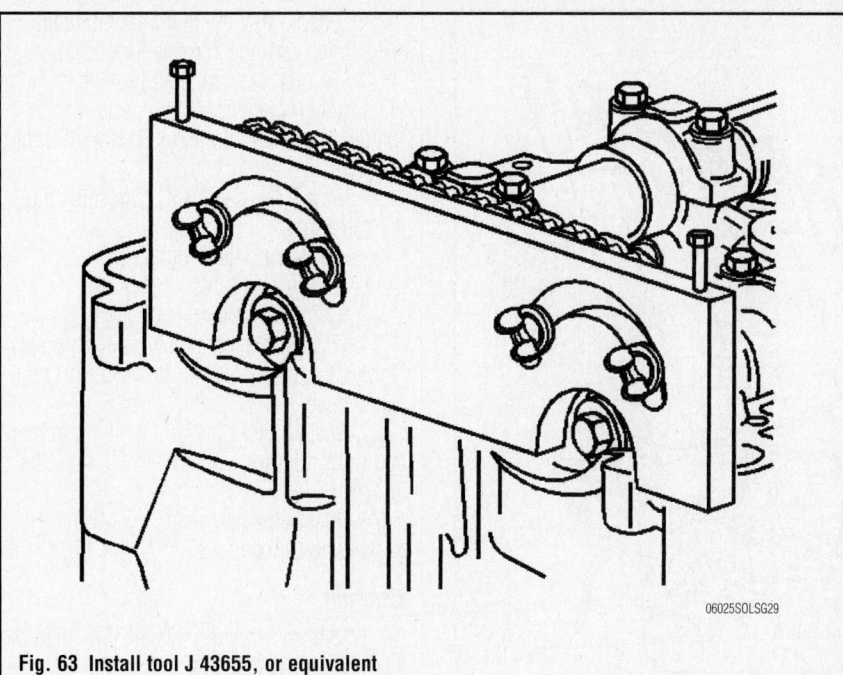

Fig. 63 Install tool J 43655, or equivalent

6. Slide the camshaft sprockets forward.

➡ **Remove each bolt on each cap one turn at a time until there is no spring tension pushing on the camshaft.**

7. Mark the bearing caps to ensure they are installed in the original position.
8. Remove the bearing cap bolts.
9. Remove the bearing caps.
10. Remove the intake camshaft.

➡ **Keep all of the roller followers and hydraulic adjusters in order so that they can be reinstalled in their respective locations.**

11. Remove the camshaft roller followers.
12. Remove the hydraulic adjusters.

To install:

13. Install the hydraulic element lash adjusters into their bores in the cylinder head.

Fig. 64 Remove the camshaft roller followers

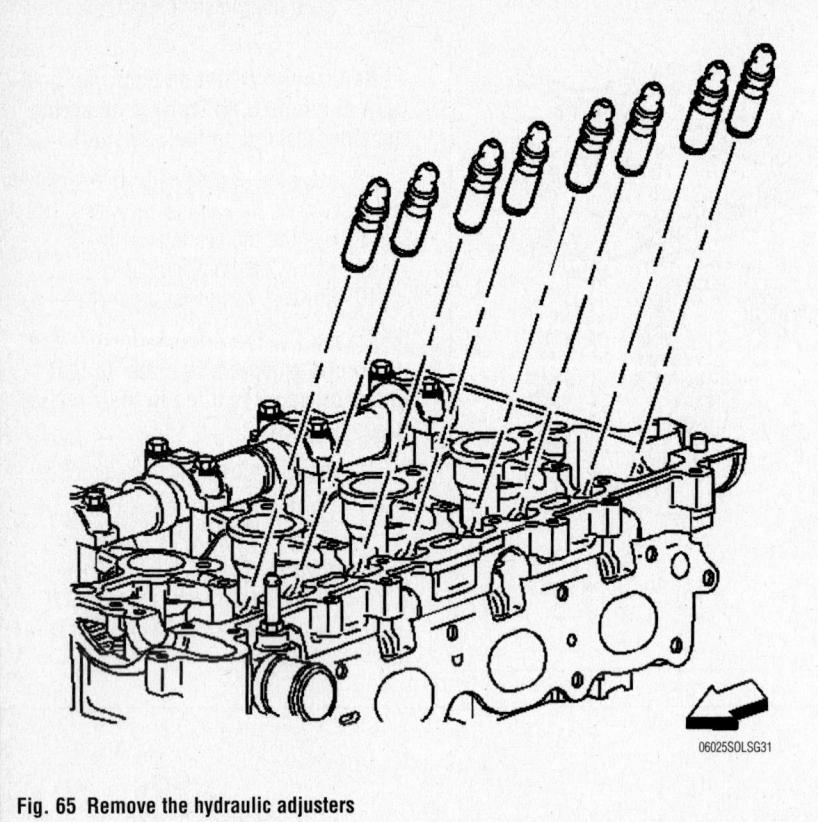

Fig. 65 Remove the hydraulic adjusters

14. Lubricate the hydraulic lash adjusters with GM PN 12345501 (Canadian PN 992704) or equivalent.

15. Lubricate the valve tips.

➥Used roller followers MUST be returned to their original position on the camshaft. If the camshaft is being replaced, the roller followers actuated by the camshaft must also be replaced.

16. Position the camshaft roller followers on the tip of the valve stem and on the lash adjuster. Lubricate the roller followers with GM PN 12345501 (Canadian PN 992704) or equivalent.

17. Install the intake camshaft. Lubricate with GM PN 12345501 (Canadian PN 992704) or equivalent.

18. Install the camshaft bearing caps. Hand-tighten the cap bolts.

19. Ensure that the alignment notches are aligned with the camshaft sprocket.

20. Tighten the camshaft bearing cap bolts in increments of 3 turns until they are seated. Tighten the bolts to 10 Nm (89 inch lbs.).

21. Install the camshaft sprockets onto the camshafts.

22. Install and hand tighten new camshaft sprocket bolts.

23. Remove the tool.

24. Tighten the camshaft sprocket bolts. Tighten the bolts to 63 ft. lbs. (85 Nm) plus 30 degrees.

25. Install the upper timing chain guide and bolts. Tighten the bolts to 89 inch. lbs. (10 Nm).

26. Install the camshaft cover with new gasket and tighten to 89 inch. lbs. (10 Nm).

Exhaust

1. Before servicing the vehicle, refer to the Precautions Section.

2. Remove the camshaft cover.

3. Remove the upper timing chain guide bolts and guide.

4. Install tool J 43655, or equivalent.

5. Remove and discard both the intake and exhaust camshaft sprocket bolts.

6. Slide the camshaft sprockets forward.

❋❋ WARNING

Remove each bolt on each cap one turn at a time until there is no spring tension pushing on the camshaft.

7. Mark the bearing caps to ensure they are installed in the original position.

8. Remove the bearing cap bolts.

9. Remove the bearing caps.

10. Remove the exhaust camshaft.

❋❋ WARNING

Keep all of the roller followers and hydraulic adjusters in order so that they can be reinstalled in their respective locations.

11. Remove the camshaft roller followers.

12. Remove the hydraulic element adjusters.

To install:

13. Install the hydraulic element adjusters into their bores in the cylinder head. Lubricate the hydraulic lash adjusters with GM PN 12345501 (Canadian PN 992704) or equivalent.

14. Lubricate the valve tips with GM PN 12345501 (Canadian PN 992704) or equivalent.

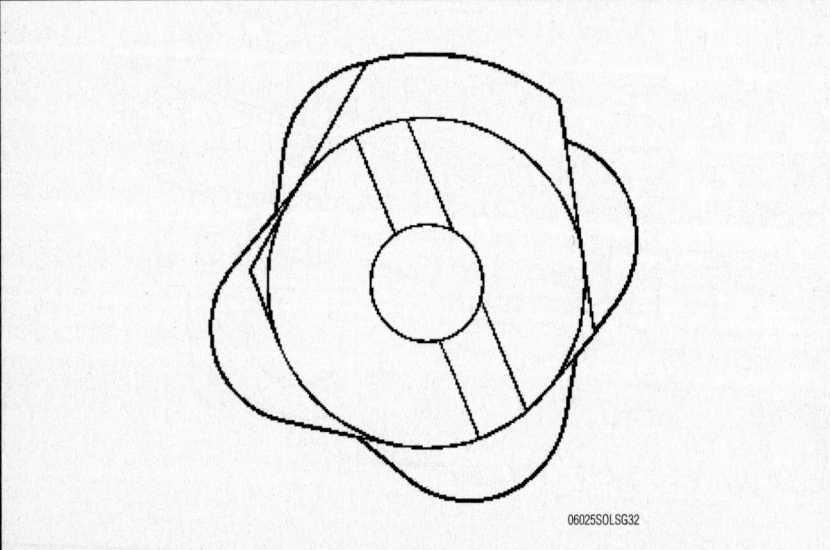

Fig. 66 Ensure that the alignment notches are aligned with the camshaft sprocket

❋❋ WARNING

Used roller followers MUST be returned to the original position on the camshaft. If the camshaft is being replaced, the roller followers actuated by the camshaft must also be replaced.

15. Position the roller followers on the tip of the valve stem and on the lash adjuster. Apply lubricate GM PN 12345501 (Canadian PN 992704) or equivalent.

16. Install the exhaust camshaft. Lubricate with GM PN 12345501 (Canadian PN 992704) or equivalent.

17. Install the camshaft bearing caps.

18. Install and hand tighten the camshaft bearing cap bolts.

19. Ensure that the alignment notches are aligned with the camshaft sprocket.

20. Install and hand tighten the camshaft bearing cap bolts in increments of 3 turns until they are seated.

21. Tighten the camshaft bearing cap bolts to 89 inch. lbs. (10 Nm).

22. Install camshaft sprockets onto the camshafts.

23. Hand tighten the NEW camshaft sprocket bolts.

24. Remove the tool.

25. Tighten the camshaft sprocket bolts. Tighten the bolts to 63 ft. lbs. (85 Nm) plus 30 degrees.

26. Install the upper timing chain guide and bolts. Tighten the bolts to 89 inch. lbs. (10 Nm).

27. Install the camshaft cover with new gasket and tighten to 89 inch. lbs. (10 Nm).

2.0L (LNF) Engine

Intake

See Figures 67 through 72.

1. Before servicing the vehicle, refer to the Precautions Section.

2. Remove the camshaft cover.

3. Remove the camshaft position intake actuator. Refer to timing chain and gears.

4. Remove the high pressure fuel pump.

5. Mark the camshaft bearing caps to ensure they are installed in the same position.

6. Remove the camshaft bearing cap bolts and caps. Remove each bolt on each cap one turn at a time until there is no spring tension pushing on the camshaft.

7. Remove the high pressure fuel pump roller lifter.

8. Remove the cylinder head opening plate bolts and plate.

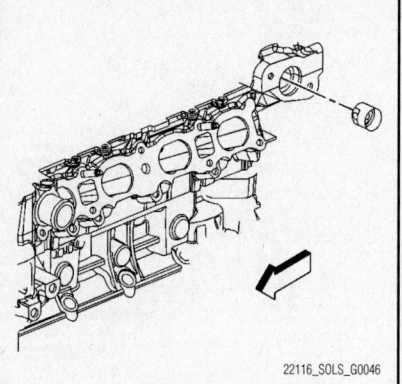

Fig. 67 High pressure fuel pump roller lifter shown

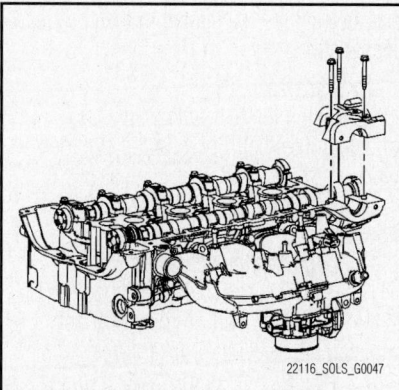

Fig. 68 Cylinder head opening plate bolts and plate

9. Remove the rear bearing cap bolts and cap.

10. Remove the intake camshaft.

11. Remove the valve rocker arms. Keep all of the roller followers and hydraulic valve lash adjusters in order so that they can be reinstalled in their respective locations.

12. Remove the valve rocker arms.

13. Remove the hydraulic valve lash adjusters. Keep all of the rocker arms and hydraulic valve lash adjusters in order so that they can be reinstalled in their respective locations.

To install:

14. Install the hydraulic valve lash adjusters into their bores in the cylinder head.

15. Lubricate the hydraulic lash adjusters.

16. Lubricate the valve tips.

➡**Used valve rocker arms MUST be returned to their original position on the camshaft. If the camshaft is being replaced, the rocker arms MUST also be replaced.**

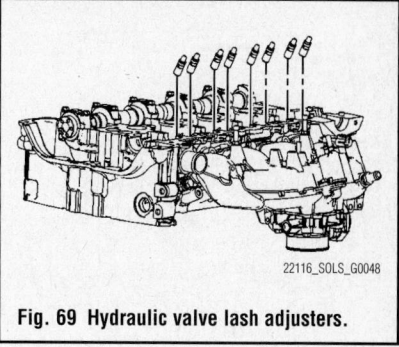

Fig. 69 Hydraulic valve lash adjusters.

17. Position the valve rocker arms on the tip of the valve stem and on the valve lash adjuster. Lubricate the rocker arms.

18. Install the intake camshaft. Lubricate the camshaft.

19. Apply a 3.5 mm (0.138 in) bead of sealer (1) to the cylinder head.

20. In areas were the rear bearing cap ends on the perimeter rail, extend the bead of sealer 4.0 mm (0.1575 in) beyond the edge of the cap (a).

21. Run the bead of sealer to within 4.0 mm (0.1575 in) of end points (b).

22. Install the rear bearing cap and bolts, tighten to 89 inch. lbs. (10 Nm).

23. Install the cylinder head opening plate and bolts, tighten to 89 inch. lbs. (10 Nm).

24. Install the high pressure fuel pump roller lifter.

25. Position the camshaft bearing caps. Install the bearing cap bolts hand tight.

❋❋ WARNING

The caps should be installed on the cylinder head in sequence as shown on top of the bearing caps.

26. Tighten the bearing cap bolts in increments of 3 turns until they are seated.

27. Tighten bearing cap bolts to 89 inch. lbs. (10 Nm).

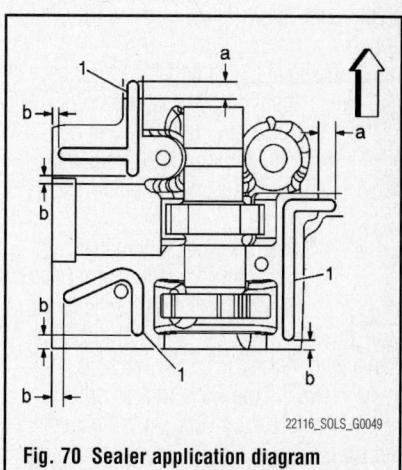

Fig. 70 Sealer application diagram

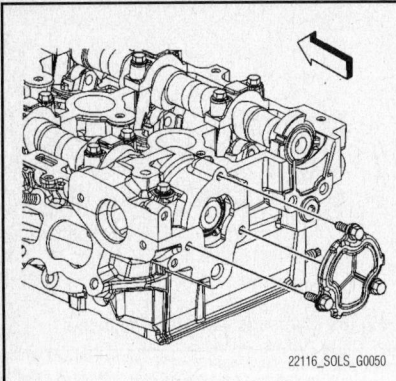

Fig. 71 Cylinder head opening plate and bolts

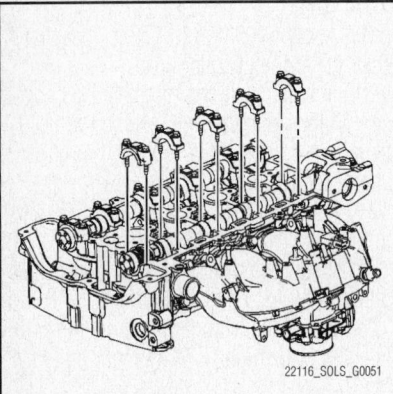

Fig. 72 Bearing caps and bolts shown

28. Install the high pressure fuel pump.

29. Install the camshaft position intake actuator.

30. Install the camshaft cover with new gasket and tighten to 89 inch. lbs. (10 Nm).

Exhaust

See Figure 73.

1. Remove the camshaft position intake actuator. Refer to timing chain and gears.

2. Mark the camshaft bearing caps to ensure they are installed in the same position.

3. Remove the camshaft bearing cap bolts and caps. Remove each bolt on each cap one turn at a time until there is no spring tension pushing on the camshaft.

4. Remove the camshaft bearing cap bolts and cap.

5. Remove the exhaust camshaft.

6. Remove the valve rocker arms. Keep all of the rocker arms and hydraulic valve lash adjusters in order so that they can be reinstalled in their respective locations.

7. Remove the valve rocker arms.

8. Remove the hydraulic valve lash adjusters. Keep all of the rocker arms and

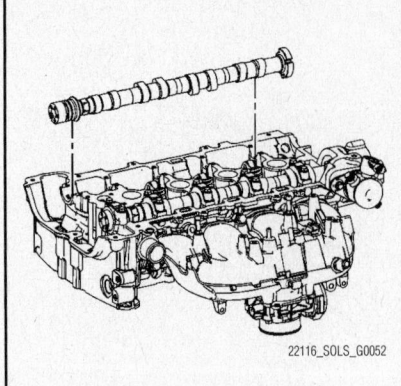

Fig. 73 Exhaust camshaft removal

hydraulic valve lash adjusters in order so that they can be reinstalled in their respective locations.

To install:

9. Install the hydraulic valve lash adjusters into their bores in the cylinder head.

10. Lubricate the hydraulic valve lash adjusters.

11. Lubricate the valve tips.

12. Position the rocker arms on the tip of the valve stem and on the valve lash adjuster. Lubricate the rocker arms.

➡**Used rocker arms MUST be returned to the original position on the camshaft. If the camshaft is being**

replaced, the rocker arms MUST also be replaced.

13. Position the rocker arms on the tip of the valve stem and on the valve lash adjuster. Lubricate the rocker arms.

14. Install the exhaust camshaft. Lubricate the camshaft.

15. Position the camshaft bearing caps. Install the bearing cap bolts hand tight.

16. Tighten the bearing cap bolts in increments of 3 turns until they are seated.

17. Tighten the bolts to 89 inch lbs. (10 Nm).

18. Install the camshaft position exhaust actuator.

19. Install the camshaft cover with new gasket and tighten to 89 inch. lbs. (10 Nm).

CRANKSHAFT DAMPER

REMOVAL & INSTALLATION

2.4L (LE5) & 2.0L (LNF) Engines

See Figure 74.

1. Before servicing the vehicle, refer to the Precautions Section.

2. Remove the engine drive belt.

3. Use the crankshaft holding tool J 38122-A, or equivalent, in order to prevent the crankshaft from rotating while loosening the crankshaft balancer bolt.

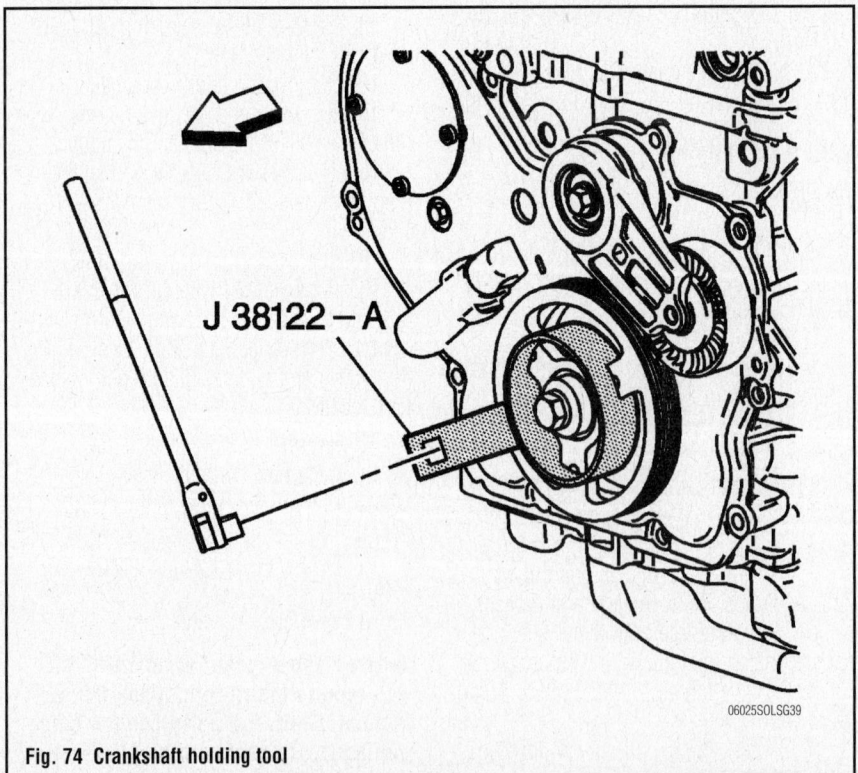

Fig. 74 Crankshaft holding tool

4. Remove and discard the crankshaft balancer bolt.

5. Remove the balancer using a universal removal tool.

To install:

⁂ WARNING

Ensure both components are aligned correctly or serious engine damage will occur.

6. Install the crankshaft balancer onto the crankshaft indexing keyway. Use care to properly align the keyway and the flats on the balancer with the oil pump drive.

7. Install the crankshaft balancer using a universal balancer installer.

8. Install a new crankshaft balancer bolt and washer. Prevent the crankshaft from rotating when tightening the bolt.

9. Tighten the bolt to 100 Nm (74 ft. lbs.) plus an additional 125 degrees.

10. Install the engine drive belt.

CRANKSHAFT FRONT SEAL

REMOVAL & INSTALLATION

2.4L (LE5) & 2.0L (LNF) Engines

1. Before servicing the vehicle, refer to the Precautions Section.

2. Remove the crankshaft balancer/damper.

3. Using a flat-bladed tool, remove the oil seal from the front cover.

To install:

4. Use a seal driver to install the oil seal in the front cover.

5. Install the crankshaft balancer.

CYLINDER HEAD

REMOVAL & INSTALLATION

2.4L (LE5) Engine

See Figures 75 through 77.

1. Before servicing the vehicle, refer to the Precautions Section.

2. Remove the intake manifold.

3. Remove the exhaust manifold.

4. Remove the timing chain.

5. Drain the cooling system.

6. Remove the negative battery cable ground terminal no. bolt.

7. Disconnect the intake Camshaft Position (CMP) sensor electrical connector.

8. Remove the Evaporative Emission (EVAP) canister purge solenoid valve.

9. Disconnect the exhaust CMP sensor electrical connector.

10. Remove the engine harness ground terminal no. bolt and terminal.

11. Disconnect the Engine Coolant Temperature (ECT) sensor electrical connector.

12. Remove the cylinder head bolts in the sequence shown. Discard the bolts.

13. Remove the cylinder head.

14. Remove the cylinder head gasket.

15. Clean all of the gasket surfaces.

16. Use the following steps when cleaning the cylinder head and cylinder block surfaces:

- Use a razor blade gasket scraper to clean the cylinder head and cylinder block gasket surfaces. Do not scratch or gouge either surface

➡DO NOT use any other method or technique to clean these gasket surfaces.

- Use a NEW razor blade on the cylinder head and a NEW blade on the cylinder block.

➡Be careful not to gouge or scratch the gasket surfaces. DO NOT gouge or scrape the combustion chamber surfaces. The feel of the gasket surface is important, not the appearance. There will be indentations from the gasket left in the cylinder head after all of the gasket material is removed. These small indentations will be filled in by the NEW gasket.

- Hold the razor blade as parallel to the gasket surface as possible
- Clean the old sealer/lube and any dirt from around the bolt holes.

➡DO NOT use a tap to clean the cylinder head bolt holes.

- Clean the bolts holes with a nylon bristle brush.
- When cleaning the cylinder head bolt holes use suitable commercial spray liquid solvent and compressed air from an extended-tip blow gun in order to reach the bottom of the holes.

To install:

➡DO NOT use any sealing material.

17. Install the cylinder head gasket.

18. Install the cylinder head.

19. Lightly apply clean engine oil to the threads and the bottom side flange of the head bolts and allow the oil to drain before installing.

20. Install NEW cylinder head bolts.

21. Install and tighten the cylinder head bolts in the sequence shown. Tighten the bolts to 22 ft. lbs. (30 Nm) plus an additional 155 degrees.

22. Install the NEW front cylinder head bolts. Tighten the bolts to 26 ft. lbs (35 Nm).

23. Connect the ECT sensor electrical connector.

24. Install the engine harness ground terminal no. and bolt. Tighten the bolt to 89 inch. lbs. (10 Nm).

25. Connect the exhaust CMP sensor electrical connector.

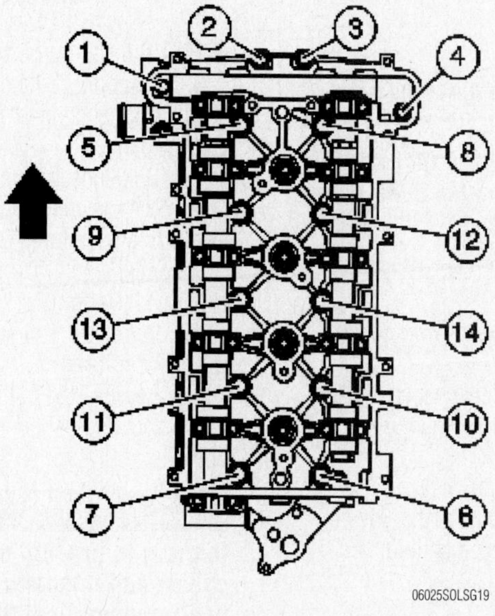

Fig. 75 Head bolt removal sequence

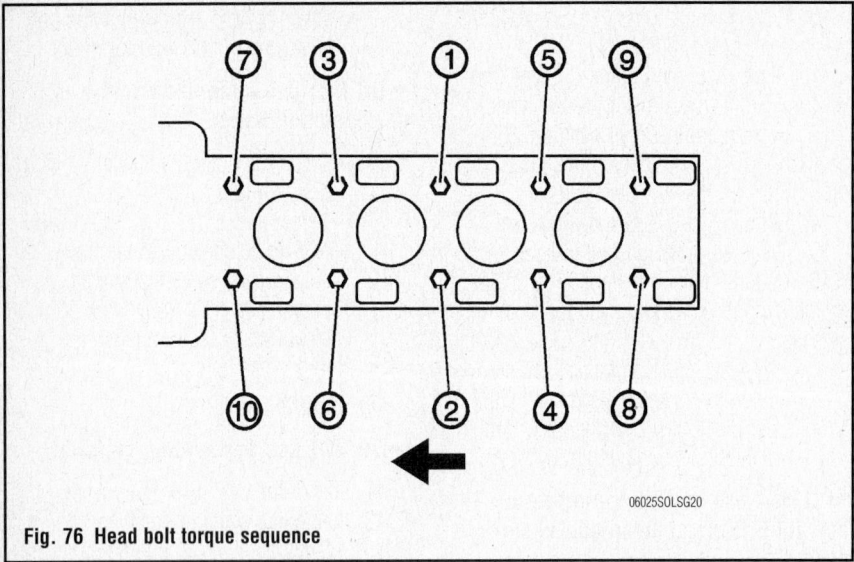

Fig. 76 Head bolt torque sequence

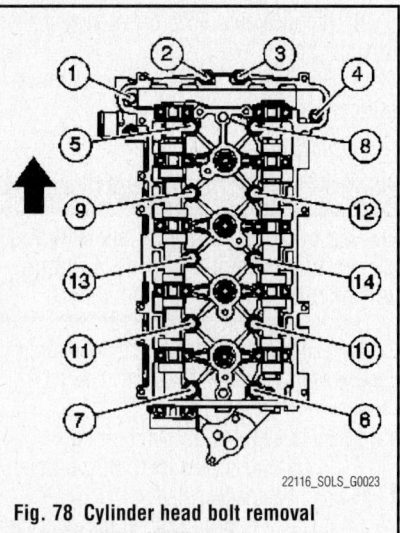

Fig. 78 Cylinder head bolt removal sequence 2.0L (LNF) engine

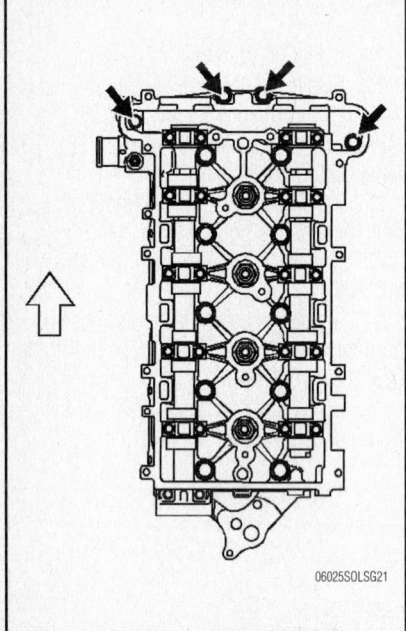

Fig. 77 Tighten these front bolts last

➡️**Ensure that the intake CMP sensor wire is routed behind the EVAP purge solenoid valve bracket.**

26. Install the EVAP canister purge solenoid valve.
27. Connect the intake CMP sensor electrical connector.
28. Install the negative battery cable ground terminal no. bolt. Tighten the bolt to 89 inch. lbs. (10 Nm).
29. Install the timing chain.
30. Install the exhaust manifold.
31. Install the intake manifold.
32. Fill the cooling system.

2.0L (LNF) Engine

See Figures 78 through 80.

1. Before servicing the vehicle, refer to the Precautions Section.
2. Remove the hood.
3. Remove the fuel rail.
4. Remove the exhaust manifold.
5. Remove the turbocharger coolant feed pipe.
6. Remove the timing chain.
7. Drain the cooling system.
8. Remove the fuel pump acoustic cover.
9. Remove the negative battery cable ground terminal no. bolt.
10. Remove the negative battery cable ground terminal no. from the engine lift bracket.
11. Disconnect the engine wiring harness electrical connector from the intake Camshaft Position (CMP) sensor.
12. Remove the Evaporative Emission (EVAP) canister purge solenoid valve.
13. Disconnect the engine wiring harness electrical connector from the exhaust CMP sensor.
14. Disconnect the engine wiring harness electrical connector from the Engine Coolant Temperature (ECT) sensor.
15. Reposition the radiator inlet hose clamp at the engine.
16. Remove the radiator inlet hose from the cylinder head.
17. Remove the cylinder head bolts in the sequence shown. Discard the bolts.

☀☀ WARNING

In order to prevent damage to the valves and injectors during cylinder head removal, set the cylinder head on blocks

18. Remove the cylinder head and place on clean work blocks.
19. Remove the cylinder head gasket.
20. Clean all of the gasket surfaces
21. Use the following steps when cleaning the cylinder head and cylinder block surfaces:
    a. Use a razor blade gasket scraper to clean the cylinder head and cylinder block gasket surfaces. Do not scratch or gouge either surface.
    b. Use a new razor blade on the cylinder head and a new blade on the cylinder block.
    c. Hold the razor blade as parallel to the gasket surface as possible.

☀☀ WARNING

Be careful not to gouge or scratch the gasket surfaces. DO NOT gouge or scrape the combustion chamber surfaces. The feel of the gasket surface is important, not the appearance. There will be indentations from the gasket left in the cylinder head after all of the gasket material is removed. These small indentations will be filled in by the new gasket.

☀☀ WARNING

DO NOT use any other method or technique to clean these gasket surfaces. DO NOT use a tap to clean the cylinder head bolt holes.

22. Clean the bolts holes with a nylon bristle brush.
23. When cleaning the cylinder head bolt holes use suitable commercial spray liquid solvent and compressed air from an

extended-tip blow gun in order to reach the bottom of the holes.

To install:

❄❄ WARNING
DO NOT use any sealing material.

24. Install the cylinder head gasket.
25. Install the cylinder head.
26. Lightly apply clean engine oil to the threads and the bottom side flange of the head bolts and allow the oil to drain before installing.
27. Install new cylinder head bolts.
28. Install and tighten the cylinder head bolts in the sequence shown.
29. Tighten the bolts to 22 ft. lbs. (30 Nm) plus an additional 155 degrees using a angle meter.
30. Install the new front cylinder head bolts. Tighten the bolts to 26 ft. lbs. (35 Nm).
31. Install the radiator inlet hose to the cylinder head.
32. Position the radiator inlet hose clamp at the engine.
33. Connect the engine wiring harness electrical connector to the exhaust CMP sensor.
34. Connect the engine wiring harness electrical connector to the ECT sensor.
35. Install the EVAP canister purge solenoid valve.
36. Connect the engine wiring harness electrical connector to the intake CMP sensor.
37. Position the negative battery cable ground terminal no. to the engine lift bracket.
38. Install the negative battery cable ground terminal no. bolt and tighten to 89 inch. lbs. (10 Nm).
39. Install the fuel pump acoustic cover.
40. Fill the cooling system.
41. Install the timing chain.

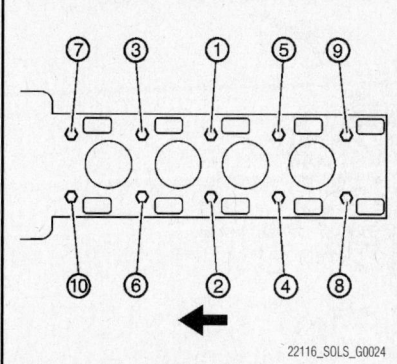

22116_SOLS_G0024

Fig. 79 Cylinder head bolt tightening sequence 2.0L (LNF) engine

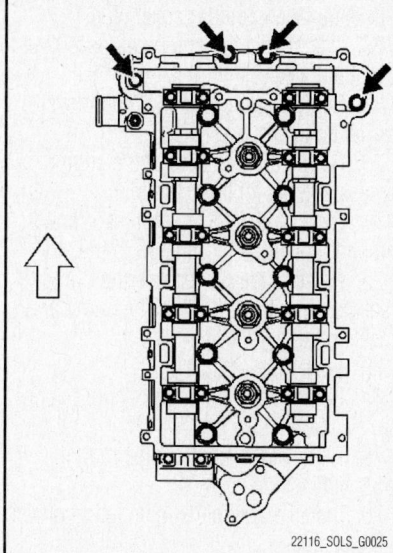

22116_SOLS_G0025

Fig. 80 Front cylinder head bolts shown 2.0L (LNF) engine

42. Install the turbocharger coolant feed pipe.
43. Install the exhaust manifold.
44. Install the fuel rail.
45. Install the hood.

ENGINE ASSEMBLY

REMOVAL & INSTALLATION

2.4L (LE5) Engine

See Figure 81.

1. Remove the hood.
2. Recover the Air Conditioning (A/C) system.
3. Remove the drive belt.
4. Drain the cooling system.
5. Remove the radiator.
6. Relieve the fuel system pressure.
7. Disconnect the Evaporative Emission (EVAP) canister purge solenoid tube from the valve.
8. Disconnect the fuel feed pipe from the fuel rail.
9. Remove the transmission.
10. For manual transmission. After the transmission is removed, reinstall the bolt from the differential case bracket assembly to body, in order to remove the support from under the rear drive module.
11. Remove the starter.
12. Reposition the radiator inlet hose clamp at the engine.
13. Remove the radiator inlet hose.
14. If the vehicle is equipped with a engine oil cooler perform the following steps, otherwise proceed to step (23).

15. Reposition the radiator outlet hose clamps at the thermostat housing and oil cooler
16. Remove the radiator outlet hose from the thermostat housing and oil cooler.
17. Reposition the outlet hose out of the way.
18. Reposition the surge tank outlet hose clamps at the thermostat housing and oil cooler.
19. Remove the surge tank outlet hose from the thermostat housing and oil cooler.
20. Reposition the surge tank outlet hose clamp at the surge tank
21. Remove the surge tank clip from the oil level indicator tube bracket.
22. Remove the surge tank outlet hose. Proceed to step (26).
23. If the vehicle is not equipped with a engine oil cooler, reposition the radiator outlet hose clamp at the thermostat housing.
24. Remove the radiator outlet hose from the thermostat housing.
25. Remove the radiator outlet hose clip from the outlet hose bracket.
26. Reposition the surge tank air bleed hose clamp at the engine.
27. Remove the surge tank air bleed hose from the engine.
28. Reposition the air bleed hose out of the way.
29. Reposition the heater inlet and outlet hose clamps at the thermostat housing.
30. Remove the heater inlet and outlet hoses from the thermostat housing.
31. Raise and suitably support the vehicle.
32. Drain the engine oil.
33. Disconnect the engine wiring harness electrical connector from the Crankshaft Position (CKP) sensor.
34. Disconnect the engine wiring harness electrical connector from the oil pressure sensor.
35. Lower the vehicle.
36. Remove the positive battery cable clip from the bracket.
37. Cut the engine harness tie straps.
38. Remove the negative battery cable ground bolt.
39. Remove the negative battery cable ground terminal no. and engine harness ground terminal no. from the cylinder head.
40. Disconnect the engine wiring harness electrical connector from the generator.
41. Reposition the positive battery cable terminal no. boot.
42. Remove the generator terminal no. nut.
43. Remove the positive battery cable terminal no. from the generator.

44. Disconnect the engine wiring harness electrical connector from the A/C compressor.

45. Reposition the negative/positive battery cable.

46. Disconnect the engine wiring harness electrical connector from the A/C refrigerant pressure sensor.

47. Disconnect the engine wiring harness electrical connector from the windshield wiper motor.

48. Remove the engine harness clip from the wiper motor hole.

49. Remove the engine harness clip from the surge tank air bleed hose.

50. Disconnect the engine wiring harness electrical connector from the intake Camshaft Position (CMP) actuator.

51. Disconnect the engine wiring harness electrical connector from the exhaust CMP actuator.

52. Remove the engine harness clip from the camshaft cover.

53. Disconnect the engine wiring harness electrical connectors from the ignition coils.

54. Remove the Connector Position Assurance (CPA) retainers from the heated oxygen sensor (HO2S) electrical connectors.

55. Disconnect the engine wiring harness electrical connector from the front HO2S.

56. Disconnect the engine wiring harness electrical connector from the rear HO2S.

57. Disconnect the engine harness clips from the junction block bracket.

58. Disconnect the HO2S electrical connector clip from the strut.

59. Disconnect the engine wiring harness electrical connector from the intake CMP sensor.

60. Disconnect the engine wiring harness electrical connector from the exhaust CMP sensor.

61. Remove the engine harness ground terminal no. bolt and reposition the engine harness ground terminal.

62. Disconnect the engine wiring harness electrical connector from the engine coolant temperature (ECT) sensor.

63. Disconnect the engine wiring harness electrical connector from the EVAP canister purge solenoid.

64. Disconnect the engine harness clip from the EVAP canister purge solenoid valve bracket.

65. Disconnect the engine harness clips from the camshaft cover.

66. Remove the EVAP canister purge solenoid valve.

67. Remove the engine harness bracket from the intake manifold cover stud.

68. Disconnect the engine harness clip from the bracket

69. Remove the intake manifold cover bracket bolts and bracket.

70. Gather all branches of the engine harness and lay off to the side.

71. Remove the A/C compressor line bolt and reposition the line off to the side.

72. Remove the power steering pump bracket bolts and reposition the pump and bracket off to the side.

73. Lower the vehicle.

74. Remove the left engine mount upper nut.

75. Remove the right engine mount upper nut.

76. Install a suitable engine lifting devise to the engine.

77. Remove the engine from the vehicle.

✳✳ WARNING

It may be necessary to remove the chamfer (bevel) from the edge of an 18 mm socket in order to get full engagement on the thin headed flywheel bolts.

78. For manual transmission remove the clutch pressure plate and disc.

79. Remove the flywheel bolts and flywheel.

80. Install the engine to an engine stand.

81. Remove the A/C compressor bolt and compressor.

82. Remove the catalytic converter to bracket bolt.

83. Remove the catalytic converter nuts.

84. Remove the catalytic converter gasket and converter from the engine.

To install:

85. Install the catalytic converter gasket and converter to the engine.

86. Install the catalytic converter nuts and tighten to 18 ft. lbs. (25 Nm).

87. Install the catalytic converter to bracket bolt and tighten to 18 ft. lbs. (25 Nm).

88. Install the A/C compressor and bolts.

89. Tighten the bolts in sequence to 16 ft. lbs. (22 Nm).

90. Install a suitable engine lifting devise to the engine.

91. Remove the engine from the stand.

92. Using a nylon bristle brush clean the thread adhesive from the flywheel bolt holes, if necessary.

93. Install the flywheel and bolts and tighten to 39 ft. lbs. (53 Nm), plus an additional 25 degrees.

94. For manual transmission, install the clutch pressure plate and disc. Tighten mounting bolts in a star sequence to 22 ft. lbs. (30 Nm).

95. Install the engine to the vehicle.

96. Install the right and left engine mount upper nuts and tighten to 37 ft. lbs. (50 Nm).

97. Remove engine lifting devise from the engine.

98. Raise and support the vehicle.

99. Position the power steering pump and bracket to the engine and install the bracket bolts.

100. Tighten the power steering pump bracket bolts to 43 ft. lbs. (58 Nm).

101. Lower the vehicle.

102. Position the A/C compressor line and install the bolt .

103. Tighten A/C compressor line mounting bolt to 16 ft. lbs. (22 Nm).

104. Install the transmission and tighten mounting bolts to 37 ft. lbs. (50 Nm).

105. Lower the vehicle.

106. Install the intake manifold cover bracket and tighten mounting bolts to 18 ft. lbs. (20 Nm).

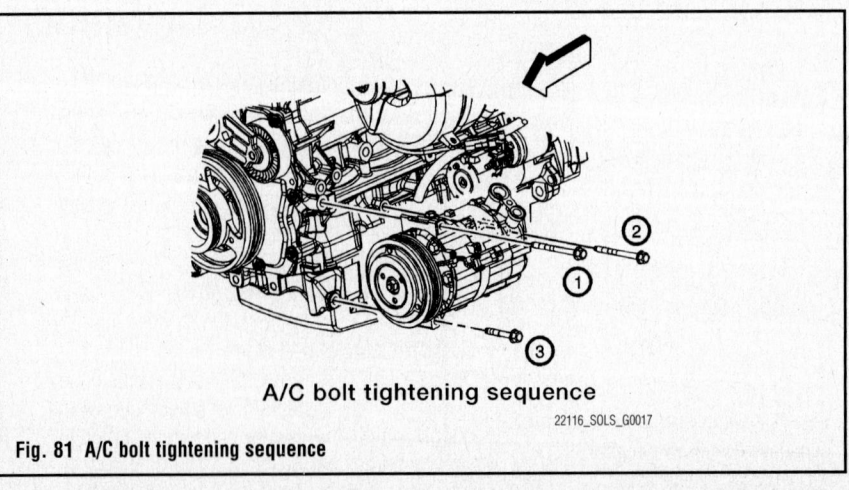

A/C bolt tightening sequence

22116_SOLS_G0017

Fig. 81 A/C bolt tightening sequence

107. Position the branches of the engine harness to the engine.

108. Connect the engine harness clip to the bracket.

109. Install the engine harness bracket to the intake manifold cover stud.

110. Install the EVAP canister purge solenoid valve.

111. Connect the engine harness clips to the camshaft cover.

112. Connect the engine harness clip to the EVAP canister purge solenoid valve bracket.

113. Connect the engine wiring harness electrical connector to the EVAP canister purge solenoid.

114. Connect the engine wiring harness electrical connector to the ECT sensor.

115. Position the engine wiring harness ground terminal no. and install the bolt. Tighten to 89 inch. lbs. (10 Nm).

116. Connect the engine wiring harness electrical connector to the exhaust CMP sensor.

117. Connect the engine wiring harness electrical connector to the intake CMP sensor.

118. Connect the HO2S electrical connector clip to the strut.

119. Connect the engine harness clips to the junction block bracket.

120. Connect the engine wiring harness electrical connector to the rear HO2S.

121. Connect the engine wiring harness electrical connector to the front HO2S.

122. Install the CPA retainers to the HO2S electrical connectors

123. Connect the engine wiring harness electrical connectors to the ignition coils.

124. Install the engine harness clip to the camshaft cover.

125. Connect the engine wiring harness electrical connector to the exhaust CMP actuator.

126. Connect the engine wiring harness electrical connector to the intake CMP actuator

127. Install the engine harness clip to the surge tank air bleed hose.

128. Connect the engine wiring harness electrical connector to the windshield wiper motor.

129. Install the engine harness clip to the wiper motor hole.

130. Connect the engine wiring harness electrical connector to the A/C refrigerant pressure sensor.

131. Position the negative/positive battery cable.

132. Connect the engine wiring harness electrical connector to the A/C compressor.

133. Install the positive battery cable terminal no. to the generator.

134. Install the generator terminal no. nut and tighten to 15 ft. lbs. (20 Nm).

135. Position the positive battery cable terminal no. boot (4).

136. Connect the engine wiring harness electrical connector (1) to the generator.

137. Position the engine harness ground terminal no. behind the negative battery cable terminal no. and position against the cylinder head.

138. Install the negative battery cable ground terminal no. bolt and tighten to 89 inch. lbs. (10 Nm).

139. Install new tie straps to the engine harness.

140. Install the positive battery cable clip to the bracket.

141. Raise and support the vehicle.

142. Connect the engine wiring harness electrical connector to the oil pressure sensor.

143. Connect the engine wiring harness electrical connector to the CKP sensor.

144. Install the heater inlet and outlet hoses to the thermostat housing.

145. Position the heater inlet and outlet hose clamps at the thermostat housing.

146. Position the air bleed hose.

147. Install the surge tank air bleed hose to the engine.

148. Position the surge tank air bleed hose clamp at the engine.

149. If the vehicle is not equipped with a engine oil cooler perform the following steps, otherwise proceed to step 66.

150. Install the radiator outlet hose to the thermostat housing.

151. Reposition the radiator outlet hose clamp at the thermostat housing.

152. Install the radiator outlet hose clip to the outlet hose bracket. Proceed to step 71.

153. If the vehicle is equipped with a engine oil cooler, install the surge tank outlet hose.

154. Install the surge tank clip to the oil level indicator tube bracket.

155. Position the surge tank outlet hose clamp at the surge tank.

156. Install the surge tank outlet hose to the thermostat housing and oil cooler.

157. Position the surge tank outlet hose clamps at the thermostat housing and oil cooler.

158. Position the outlet hose.

159. Install the radiator outlet hose to the thermostat housing and oil cooler.

160. Position the radiator outlet hose clamps at the thermostat housing and oil cooler.

161. Install the radiator inlet hose.

162. Position the radiator inlet hose clamp at the engine.

163. Install the starter.

164. Install the air inlet grille panel.

165. Connect the fuel feed pipe to the fuel rail.

166. Connect the EVAP canister purge solenoid tube to the valve.

167. Install the radiator.

168. Install the drive belt.

169. Vacuum and recharge the A/C system.

170. Install the hood.

171. Fill the engine oil.

172. Fill and bleed cooling system.

2.0L (LNF) Engine

See Figure 82.

1. Remove the hood.

2. Recover the Air Conditioning (A/C) system.

3. Remove the drive belt.

4. Drain the cooling system.

5. Remove the radiator.

6. Relieve the fuel system pressure.

7. Disconnect the Evaporative Emission (EVAP) canister purge solenoid tube from the valve.

8. Disconnect the fuel feed pipe from the fuel rail.

9. Remove the transmission.

10. For Manual transmission. After the transmission is removed, reinstall the bolt from the differential case bracket assembly to body, in order to remove the support from under the rear drive module.

11. Remove the turbocharger heat shield bolts and shield.

12. Remove the charge air cooler pipe to turbocharger bolts.

13. Remove the charge air cooler pipe and gasket from the turbocharger.

14. Cap or plug the turbocharger opening.

15. Reposition the radiator inlet hose clamp at the engine.

16. Remove the radiator inlet hose from the engine.

17. Reposition the radiator inlet hose out of the way.

18. Reposition the radiator outlet hose clamp at the thermostat housing.

19. Reposition the radiator outlet hose clamp at the oil cooler.

20. Remove the radiator outlet hose from the thermostat housing and oil cooler.

21. Remove the radiator outlet hose clip from the bracket.

22. Reposition the radiator outlet hose out of the way.

23. Reposition the surge tank outlet hose clamp at the thermostat housing.

24. Reposition the surge tank outlet hose clamp at the oil cooler.

25. Remove the surge tank outlet hose from the thermostat housing and oil cooler.

26. Reposition the surge tank outlet hose clamp at the surge tank.

27. Remove the surge tank outlet hose from the surge tank.

28. Remove the surge tank clip from the oil level indicator tube bracket.

29. Remove the surge tank outlet hose from the vehicle.

30. Reposition the surge tank air bleed hose clamp at the engine.

31. Remove the surge tank air bleed hose clip from the surge tank bracket.

32. Remove the surge tank air bleed hose from the engine.

33. Reposition the air bleed hose out of the way.

34. Reposition the heater inlet and outlet hose clamps at the thermostat housing.

35. Remove the heater inlet and outlet hoses from the thermostat housing.

36. Raise and suitably support the vehicle.

37. Drain the engine oil.

38. Disconnect the engine wiring harness electrical connector from the Crankshaft Position (CKP) sensor.

39. Disconnect the engine wiring harness electrical connector from the oil pressure sensor.

40. Disconnect the engine wiring harness electrical connector from the brake booster vacuum pump.

41. Remove the positive battery cable lead nut at the starter.

42. Remove the positive battery cable lead from the starter.

43. Remove the engine wiring harness clip from the oil level indicator tube bracket.

44. Remove the engine wiring harness terminal no. from the starter.

45. Remove the engine wiring harness terminal no. nut from the starter.

46. Remove the engine wiring harness terminal no. from the starter.

47. Remove the engine wiring harness clip from the oil level indicator tube.

48. Lower the vehicle.

49. Disconnect the engine wiring harness electrical connector from the Mass Air Flow (MAF) sensor.

50. Cut the engine harness tie straps.

51. Remove the negative battery cable ground bolt from the front engine lift bracket.

52. Remove the negative battery cable ground terminal no. from the engine lift bracket.

53. Reposition the negative/positive battery cable out of the way.

54. Disconnect the engine wiring harness electrical connector from the transmission oil cooler pump.

55. Disconnect the engine wiring harness electrical connector from the knock sensor.

56. Remove the engine wiring harness clip from the oil level indicator tube bracket.

57. Disconnect the engine wiring harness electrical connector from the generator.

58. Reposition the positive battery cable terminal no. boot.

59. Remove the generator terminal no. nut.

60. Remove the positive battery cable terminal no. from the generator.

61. Disconnect the engine wiring harness electrical connector from the A/C compressor.

62. Disconnect the engine wiring harness electrical connector from the fuel injector jumper electrical connector.

63. Disconnect the engine wiring harness electrical connector from the throttle actuator.

64. Disconnect the engine wiring harness electrical connector from the knock sensor.

65. Remove the engine wiring harness clip from the intake manifold brace.

66. Disconnect the engine wiring harness electrical connector from the EVAP canister purge solenoid valve.

67. Disconnect the engine wiring harness electrical connector from the Manifold Absolute Pressure (MAP) sensor.

68. Disconnect the engine wiring harness electrical connector from the A/C refrigerant pressure sensor.

69. Disconnect the engine wiring harness electrical connector from the brake booster vacuum sensor.

70. Disconnect the engine wiring harness electrical connector from the windshield wiper motor.

71. Remove the engine harness clip from the wiper motor hole.

72. Disconnect the engine wiring harness electrical connector from the intake Camshaft Position (CMP) sensor.

73. Disconnect the engine wiring harness electrical connector from the high pressure fuel pump.

74. Remove the engine wiring harness clip from the high pressure fuel pump bracket.

75. Disconnect the engine wiring harness electrical connector from the intake CMP actuator.

76. Disconnect the engine wiring harness electrical connector from the exhaust CMP actuator.

77. Remove the engine harness clip from the camshaft cover.

78. Disconnect the engine wiring harness electrical connectors from the ignition coils.

79. Disconnect the engine wiring harness electrical connector from the Heated Oxygen Sensor (HO2S) (3).

80. Disconnect the engine wiring harness electrical connector from the exhaust CMP sensor.

81. Remove the engine harness ground terminal no. bolt and reposition the engine harness ground terminal.

82. Disconnect the engine wiring harness electrical connector from the Engine Coolant Temperature (ECT) sensor.

83. Disconnect the engine harness clips from the camshaft cover.

84. Disconnect the engine harness clip from the camshaft cover.

85. Remove the engine wiring harness clip from the turbocharger coolant feed pipe stud.

86. Remove the engine wiring harness clip from the turbocharger coolant feed pipe tab.

87. Disconnect the engine wiring harness electrical connector from the boost sensor.

88. Remove the engine wiring harness ground bolt from the cylinder head.

89. Remove the engine wiring harness ground terminal no. from the cylinder head.

90. Remove the engine harness clips from the front studs.

91. Gather all branches of the engine harness and lay off to the side.

92. Reposition the vacuum hose clamp at the turbocharger.

93. Remove the vacuum hose from the turbocharger.

94. Remove the vacuum hose from the turbocharger coolant feed pipe clips.

95. Reposition the vacuum hose out of the way.

96. Remove the turbocharger coolant feed pipe bolt at the turbocharger.

97. Remove the turbocharger coolant feed pipe fitting from the cylinder head.

98. Remove the turbocharger coolant feed pipe bracket bolt from the cylinder head.

99. Remove the turbocharger coolant feed pipe bracket from the vehicle.

100. Remove the A/C compressor line bolt and reposition the line off to the side.

101. Remove the power steering pump bracket bolts and reposition the pump and bracket off to the side.

102. Lower the vehicle.

103. Remove the left engine mount upper nut.

104. Remove the right engine mount upper nut.

105. Install engine support adapter to the engine, if necessary

106. Install a suitable engine lifting devise to the engine.

107. Remove the engine from the vehicle.

✳✳ WARNING

It may be necessary to remove the chamfer (bevel) from the edge of an 18 mm socket in order to get full engagement on the thin headed flywheel bolts.

108. For manual transmission remove the clutch pressure plate and disc.

109. Remove the flywheel bolts and flywheel.

110. Install the engine to an engine stand.

111. Remove the A/C compressor bolts and compressor.

112. Remove the catalytic converter to bracket bolts.

113. Remove the catalytic converter nuts.

114. Remove the catalytic converter and gasket from the turbocharger and bracket.

To install:

115. Install the catalytic converter and gasket to the turbocharger and bracket.

116. Install the catalytic converter nuts and tighten to 43 ft. lbs. (59 Nm).

117. Install the catalytic converter to bracket bolts and tighten to 16 ft. lbs. (22 Nm).

118. Install the A/C compressor and bolts and tighten in sequence to 16 ft. lbs. (22 Nm).

119. Install a suitable engine lifting devise to the engine.

120. Remove the engine from the stand.

121. Using a nylon bristle brush clean the thread adhesive from the flywheel bolt holes, if necessary.

122. Install the flywheel and bolts and tighten to 39 ft. lbs. (53 Nm), plus an additional 25 degrees.

123. For manual transmission, install the clutch pressure plate and disc. Tighten mounting bolts in a star sequence to 22 ft. lbs. (30 Nm).

124. Install the engine to the vehicle.

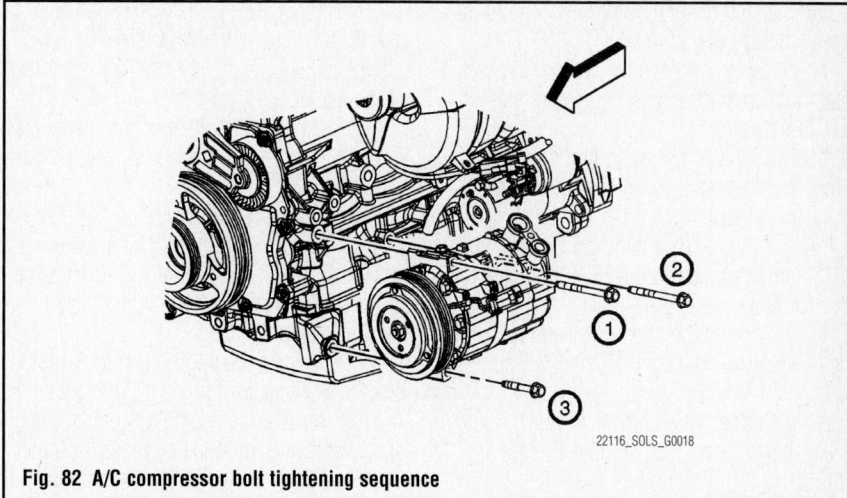

22116_SOLS_G0018

Fig. 82 A/C compressor bolt tightening sequence

125. Install the right and left engine mount upper nuts and tighten to 37 ft. lbs. (50 Nm).

126. Remove engine lifting devise from the engine.

127. Raise and support the vehicle.

128. Position the power steering pump and bracket to the engine and install the bracket bolts.

129. Tighten the power steering pump bracket bolts to 43 ft. lbs. (58 Nm).

130. Lower the vehicle.

131. Position the A/C compressor line and install the bolt and tighten to 16 ft. lbs. (22 Nm).

132. Position the turbocharger coolant feed pipe to the vehicle.

133. Install the turbocharger coolant feed pipe bracket bolt to the cylinder head. Tighten the bolt to 89 inch. lbs. (10 Nm).

134. Install the turbocharger coolant feed pipe fitting to the cylinder head. Tighten the fittings to 26 ft. lbs. (35 Nm).

135. Install the turbocharger coolant feed pipe bolt at the turbocharger. Tighten the bolt to 26 ft. lbs. (35 Nm).

136. Position the vacuum hose to the turbocharger.

137. Install the vacuum hose to the turbocharger.

138. Position the vacuum hose clamp at the turbocharger.

139. Install the vacuum hose to the turbocharger coolant feed pipe clips.

140. Position the branches of the engine harness to the engine.

141. Install the engine harness clips to the front studs.

142. Install the engine wiring harness ground terminal no. to the cylinder head.

143. Install the engine wiring harness ground bolt to the cylinder head and tighten to 18 ft. lbs. (25 Nm).

144. Connect the engine wiring harness electrical connector to the boost sensor.

145. Install the engine wiring harness clip to the turbocharger coolant feed pipe tab.

146. Install the engine wiring harness clip to the turbocharger coolant feed pipe stud.

147. Connect the engine harness clips to the camshaft cover.

148. Connect the engine harness clip to the camshaft cover.

149. Connect the engine wiring harness electrical connector to the exhaust CMP sensor.

150. Connect the engine wiring harness electrical connector to the ECT sensor.

151. Position the engine harness ground terminal, install the engine harness ground terminal no. bolt. Tighten the bolt to 18 ft. lbs. (25 Nm).

152. Connect the engine wiring harness electrical connector to the HO2S.

153. Connect the engine wiring harness electrical connectors to the ignition coils.

154. Install the engine harness clip to the camshaft cover.

155. Connect the engine wiring harness electrical connector to the intake CMP actuator.

156. Connect the engine wiring harness electrical connector to the exhaust CMP actuator.

157. Connect the engine wiring harness electrical connector to the intake CMP sensor.

158. Connect the engine wiring harness electrical connector to the high pressure fuel pump.

159. Install the engine wiring harness clip to the high pressure fuel pump bracket.

160. Connect the engine wiring harness electrical connector to the windshield wiper motor.

161. Install the engine harness clip to the wiper motor hole.

162. Connect the engine wiring harness electrical connector to the brake booster vacuum sensor.

163. Connect the engine wiring harness electrical connector to the A/C refrigerant pressure sensor

164. Connect the engine wiring harness electrical connector to the EVAP canister purge solenoid valve.

165. Connect the engine wiring harness electrical connector to the MAP sensor.

166. Connect the engine wiring harness electrical connector to the throttle actuator.

167. Connect the engine wiring harness electrical connector to the knock sensor.

168. Install the engine wiring harness clip to the intake manifold brace.

169. Connect the engine wiring harness electrical connector to the fuel injector jumper electrical connector.

170. Install the positive battery cable terminal no. to the generator.

171. Install the generator terminal no. nut and tighten to 15 ft. lbs. (20 Nm).

172. Position the positive battery cable terminal no. boot.

173. Connect the engine wiring harness electrical connector (4) to the A/C compressor

174. Connect the engine wiring harness electrical connector to the generator.

175. Connect the engine wiring harness electrical connector to the knock sensor.

176. Install the engine wiring harness clip to the oil level indicator tube bracket.

177. Connect the engine wiring harness electrical connector to the transmission oil cooler pump.

178. Position the negative/positive battery cable to the engine.

179. Install the negative battery cable ground terminal no. to the engine lift bracket.

180. Install the negative battery cable ground bolt to the front engine lift bracket and tighten to 18 ft. lbs. (25 Nm).

181. Install NEW tie straps to the engine wiring harness.

182. Connect the engine wiring harness electrical connector to the MAF sensor.

183. Raise the vehicle.

184. Install the engine wiring harness terminal no. to the starter.

185. Install the engine wiring harness terminal no. to the starter.

186. Install the engine wiring harness terminal no. nut to the starter and tighten to 27 inch. lbs. (3 Nm).

187. Install the engine wiring harness clip to the oil level indicator tube.

188. Install the positive battery cable lead to the starter.

189. Install the positive battery cable lead nut at the starter and tighten to 89 inch. lbs (10 Nm).

190. Install the engine wiring harness clip to the oil level indicator tube bracket.

191. Connect the engine wiring harness electrical connector to the brake booster vacuum pump.

192. Connect the engine wiring harness electrical connector to the CKP sensor.

193. Connect the engine wiring harness electrical connector to the oil pressure sensor.

194. Install the heater inlet and outlet hoses to the thermostat housing.

195. Position the heater inlet and outlet hose clamps at the thermostat housing.

196. Position the air bleed hose to the engine.

197. Install the surge tank air bleed hose to the engine.

198. Install the surge tank air bleed hose clip to the surge tank bracket.

199. Position the surge tank air bleed hose clamp at the engine.

200. Install the surge tank clip to the oil level indicator tube bracket.

201. Position the surge tank outlet hose clamp at the surge tank.

202. Install the surge tank outlet hose to the thermostat housing and oil cooler.

203. Position the surge tank outlet hose clamp at the oil cooler.

204. Position the surge tank outlet hose clamp at the thermostat housing.

205. Position the outlet hose to the engine.

206. Install the radiator outlet hose clip to the bracket.

207. Install the radiator outlet hose to the thermostat housing and oil cooler.

208. Position the radiator outlet hose clamp at the oil cooler.

209. Position the radiator outlet hose clamp at the thermostat housing.

210. Position the inlet hose to the engine.

211. Install the radiator inlet hose to the engine.

212. Position the radiator inlet hose clamp at the engine.

213. Remove the cap or plug from the turbocharger opening.

214. Install the charge air cooler pipe to the turbocharger.

215. Install the charge air cooler pipe to turbocharger bolts and tighten to 16 ft. lbs. (22 Nm).

216. Install the turbocharger heat shield

and bolts. Tighten bolts to 89 inch. lbs. (10 Nm).

217. Install the transmission.

218. Install the air inlet grille panel.

219. Install the charge air cooler inlet and outlet pipes.

220. Connect the fuel feed pipe to the fuel line.

221. Connect the EVAP canister purge solenoid tube to the valve .

222. Install the radiator.

223. Install the drive belt.

224. Vacuum and recharge the A/C system.

225. Install the hood.

226. Connect the negative battery cable.

227. Fill the engine with oil.

228. Fill and bleed cooling system.

EXHAUST MANIFOLD

REMOVAL & INSTALLATION

2.4L (LE5) Engine

See Figures 83 and 84.

1. Before servicing the vehicle, refer to the Precautions Section.

2. Remove the exhaust manifold heat shield bolts.

3. Remove the exhaust manifold heat shield.

4. Remove the block heater if equipped.

5. Remove the oxygen sensor.

6. Remove and discard the exhaust manifold to cylinder head retaining nuts.

7. Remove the exhaust manifold.

8. If the exhaust manifold is being replaced, transfer the following parts:
   - The exhaust manifold heat shield
   - The oxygen sensor

To install:

→**Do not reuse the exhaust manifold-to-cylinder head gaskets. Upon installation of the exhaust manifold, install a NEW gasket. An improperly installed gasket or leaking exhaust system may effect On-Board Diagnostics (OBD) II system performance. Remove the oxygen sensor prior to cleaning the manifold, do not submerge the oxygen sensor in cleaning solvent.**

9. Remove the oxygen sensor from the manifold.

10. Clean the exhaust manifold in solvent.

✳✳ CAUTION

Wear safety glasses in order to avoid eye damage.

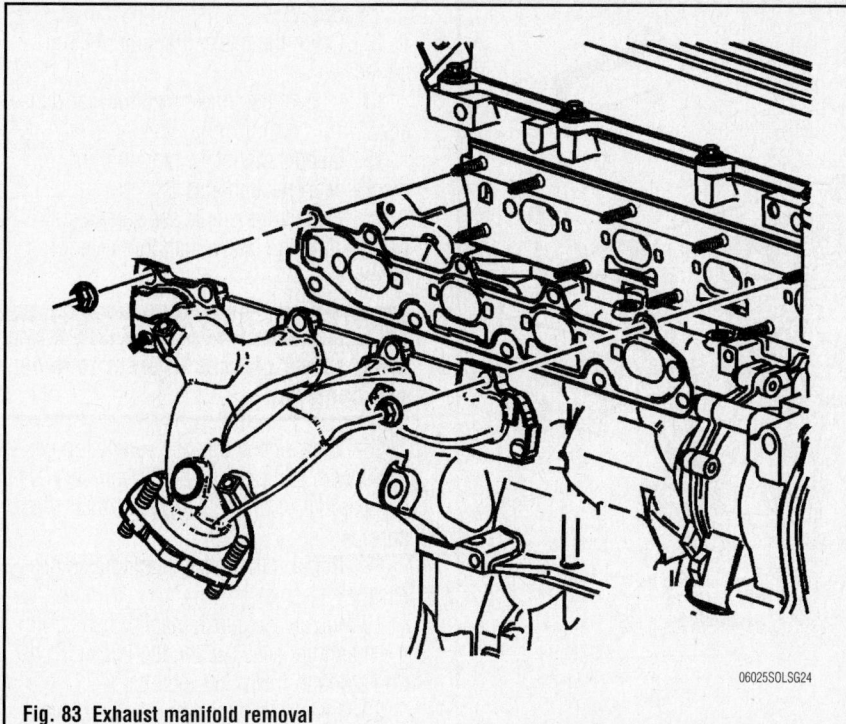

Fig. 83 Exhaust manifold removal

11. Dry the exhaust manifold with compressed air.

12. Inspect the heat shield for damage.

13. Use a straightedge and a feeler gage and measure the exhaust manifold mounting face for warpage. An exhaust manifold face with warpage in excess of 0.010 inch. (0.25 mm) may cause an exhaust leak and may affect OBD II system performance. Exhaust manifolds not within specifications must be replaced.

14. Install new exhaust manifold studs. Tighten the studs to 89 inch. lbs. (10 Nm).

15. Install the exhaust manifold gasket.

16. Install the exhaust manifold to the cylinder head.

17. Install NEW exhaust manifold to cylinder head retaining nuts finger tight.

18. Tighten the NEW exhaust manifold to cylinder head retaining nuts in sequence. Tighten the nuts to 10 ft. lbs. (14 Nm).

19. Coat the threads of the oxygen sensor with anti-seize P/N 12397953, or equivalent.

20. Install the oxygen sensor. Tighten the oxygen sensor to 31 ft. lbs. (42 Nm).

21. Install the exhaust manifold heat shield.

22. Install the exhaust manifold heat shield bolts. Tighten the bolts to 16 ft. lbs. (22 Nm).

2.0L (LNF) Engine

See Figure 85.

1. Before servicing the vehicle, refer to the Precautions Section.

2. Remove the turbocharger. Refer to turbocharger removal.

3. Remove the exhaust manifold heat shield bolts.

4. Remove the heat shield.

5. Remove and discard the exhaust manifold nuts.

6. Remove the exhaust manifold.

7. Remove and discard the exhaust manifold gasket.

To install:

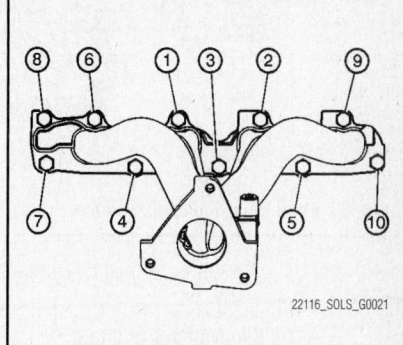

Fig. 85 Exhaust manifold tightening sequence 2.0L (LNF) engine

8. Install a new exhaust manifold gasket onto the studs.

9. Install the exhaust manifold.

10. Install the new exhaust manifold nuts.

11. Tighten the exhaust manifold nuts in the sequence shown to 10 ft. lbs. (14 Nm).

12. Install the heat shield.

13. Install the exhaust manifold heat shield bolts and tighten to 18 ft. lbs. (25 Nm).

14. Install the turbocharger.

INTAKE MANIFOLD

REMOVAL & INSTALLATION

2.4L (LE5) Engine

See Figures 86 and 87.

❄ WARNING

Never attempt to remove the intake manifold from a hot engine, allow the engine to cool to ambient temperature. The intake manifold is made of a composite plastic and can be damaged if it is removed when the engine is hot.

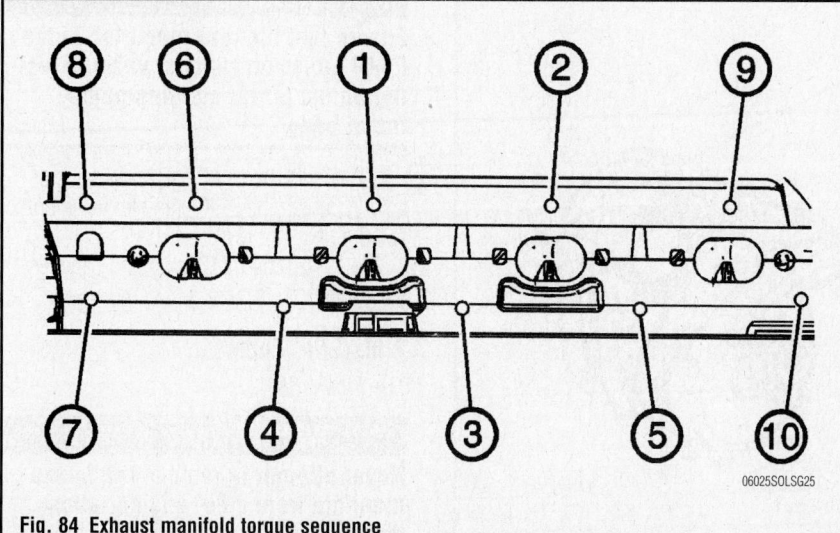

Fig. 84 Exhaust manifold torque sequence

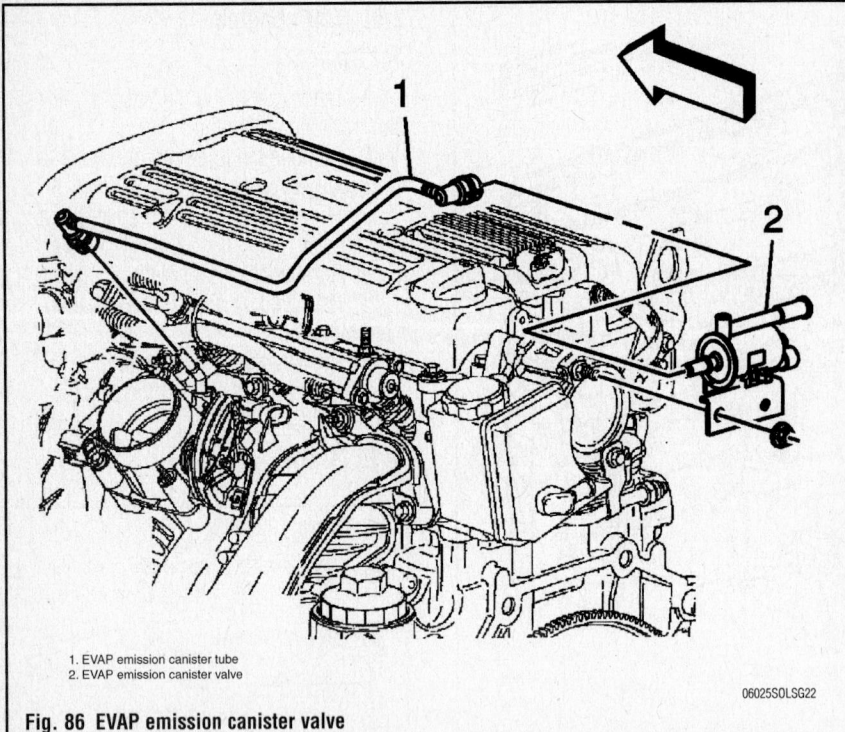

1. EVAP emission canister tube
2. EVAP emission canister valve

06025SOLSG22

Fig. 86 EVAP emission canister valve

1. Before servicing the vehicle, refer to the Precautions Section.
2. Remove the evaporative emission (EVAP) canister valve tube.
3. Remove the EVAP canister valve.
4. Remove the throttle body bolts.
5. Remove the throttle body.
6. Remove fuel pipes and clips.
7. Remove the fuel rail bolts.

8. Remove the fuel rail.
9. Remove the fuel injector tip insulators and discard.
10. Remove the intake manifold retaining nuts and bolts.
11. Remove the intake manifold.
12. Remove the intake manifold gasket, if necessary. The gasket can be used again if it is not damaged.

06025SOLSG23

Fig. 87 Intake manifold

To install:

13. Clean the intake manifold mating surfaces.
14. Inspect the intake manifold for damage.
15. Inspect the intake manifold for cracks near metallic inserts.
16. Inspect the crankcase ventilation passages in the intake manifold face for blockage.

※※ CAUTION

Wear safety glasses in order to avoid eye damage.

17. Clean the crankcase ventilation passages with compressed air if necessary. Use a maximum of 172 kPa (25 psi) of air pressure.
18. Replace the intake manifold as necessary.
19. Install the intake manifold studs in the manifold face. Tighten the intake manifold studs to 6 Nm (53 inch lbs.).
20. Install a new intake manifold gasket on the intake manifold.
21. Install the intake manifold.
22. Install the intake manifold bolts and nuts. Tighten the bolts and nuts to 89 inch. lbs. (10 Nm).
23. Lubricate the fuel injector tip insulators with engine oil.
24. Install new fuel injector tip insulators.
25. Lubricate the fuel injector oil rings with engine oil.
26. Install the fuel rail assembly.
27. Install the fuel rail bolts. Tighten the bolts to 89 inch. lbs. (10 Nm).
28. Install a new throttle body gasket.
29. Install the throttle body. Tighten the bolts and nuts to 89 inch. lbs. (10 Nm).

※※ WARNING

Ensure that the rear metal tab of the EVAP emission canister valve is resting on the power steering pump metal body.

30. Install the EVAP emission canister valve. Tighten the EVAP canister valve bolt to 16 ft. lbs. (22 Nm).
31. Install the EVAP emission canister valve tube.

2.0L (LNF) Engine

See Figure 88.

※※ WARNING

Never attempt to remove the intake manifold from a hot engine, allow the engine to cool to ambient tem-

perature. **The intake manifold is
made of a composite plastic and can
be damaged if it is removed when
the engine is hot.**

1. Before servicing the vehicle, refer to the Precautions Section.
2. Remove the intake manifold cover
3. Remove the oil level indicator tube.
4. Disconnect the fuel feed line quick connect fitting from the fuel rail.
5. Disconnect the Evaporative Emission (EVAP) line quick connect fitting from the EVAP purge solenoid.
6. Reposition the brake booster vacuum hose clamp at the intake manifold.
7. Remove the brake booster hose from the intake manifold.
8. Remove the knock sensor electrical connector (1) clip from the intake manifold brace.
9. Remove the knock sensor electrical connector clip from the oil level indicator tube bracket.
10. Disconnect the engine wiring harness electrical connector from the EVAP canister purge solenoid
11. Disconnect the engine wiring harness electrical connector from the manifold absolute pressure (MAP) sensor.
12. Disconnect the engine wiring harness electrical connector from the charge air bypass vale solenoid.
13. Disconnect the engine wiring harness electrical connector from the Throttle Actuator Control (TAC) module.
14. Remove the engine wiring harness clip from the intake manifold brace
15. Reposition the surge tank air bleed hose clamp at the engine.
16. Remove the surge tank air bleed hose from the engine.
17. Remove the surge tank air bleed hose clip from the surge tank bracket.
18. Reposition the surge tank air bleed hose out of the way.
19. Reposition the charge air bypass valve vacuum hose clamp at the intake manifold.
20. Remove the charge air bypass valve vacuum hose from the intake manifold.
21. Remove the charge air bypass valve solenoid bolts.
22. Reposition the charge air bypass valve solenoid assembly out of the way.
23. Remove the surge tank bracket bolt and stud.
24. Remove the surge tank bracket.
25. Remove the surge tank hose retainer and hose from the surge tank bracket.
26. Disconnect the metal quick connect fitting from the fuel feed pipe.

27. Disconnect the fuel feed pipe fitting from the fuel pump.
28. Remove the fuel feed pipe bolts.
29. Remove the fuel feed pipe.
30. Inspect the fuel feed pipe nut for damaged threads.
31. Inspect the fuel feed pipe sealing bail for damage or debris.
32. Replace the fuel feed pipe if any damage is found.
33. Unbolt and reposition the power brake booster pump
34. Remove the intake manifold brace bolt.
35. Remove the intake manifold brace.
36. Remove the intake manifold bolts and nuts.
37. Remove the intake manifold and place on a clean work surface.

➡**The intake manifold gasket is
reusable. Only replace the gasket if
damage has occurred.**

38. Remove the intake manifold gasket, if necessary

To install:
39. Install new intake manifold gasket, if necessary.
40. Install the intake manifold to the studs.
41. Install the intake manifold bolts and nuts, tighten to 16 ft. lbs.(22 Nm).
42. Install the intake manifold brace.
43. Loosely install the intake manifold brace bolt.
44. Position and install the power brake booster pump.
45. Tighten the intake manifold brace bolt to 16 ft. lbs.(22 Nm).
46. Lubricate the high pressure fuel pump fuel feed pipe connection threads with silicon free engine oil.
47. Place the fuel feed pipe on top of the intake manifold.
48. Connect the fuel feed pipe fitting to the high pressure fuel pump.
49. Install the fuel feed pipe bolts.

a. Tighten the bolts to 89 inch. lbs. (10 Nm).
b. Tighten the fittings to 22 ft. lbs. (30 Nm).
50. Connect the metal quick connect fitting to the fuel feed pipe.
51. Position the surge tank bracket to the intake manifold.
52. Install the surge tank bracket bolt and stud. Tighten the bolt and stud to 80 inch. lbs. (9 Nm).
53. Install the surge tank hose retainer and hose to the surge tank bracket.
54. Position the charge air bypass valve solenoid assembly to the intake manifold.
55. Install the charge air bypass valve solenoid bolts and tighten to 89 inch. lbs. (10 Nm).
56. Install the charge air bypass valve vacuum hose to the intake manifold.
57. Position the charge air bypass valve vacuum hose clamp at the intake manifold.
58. Position the surge tank air bleed hose to the engine.
59. Install the surge tank air bleed hose to the engine.
60. Position the surge tank air bleed hose clamp at the engine.
61. Install the surge tank air bleed hose clip to the surge tank bracket.
62. Connect the engine wiring harness electrical connector to the TAC module.
63. Install the engine wiring harness clip to the intake manifold brace.
64. Connect the engine wiring harness electrical connector to the charge air bypass vale solenoid
65. Connect the engine wiring harness electrical connector to the MAP sensor.
66. Connect the engine wiring harness electrical connector to the EVAP canister purge solenoid.
67. Install the knock sensor electrical connector clip to the intake manifold brace.
68. Install the knock sensor electrical connector clip to the oil level indicator tube bracket.

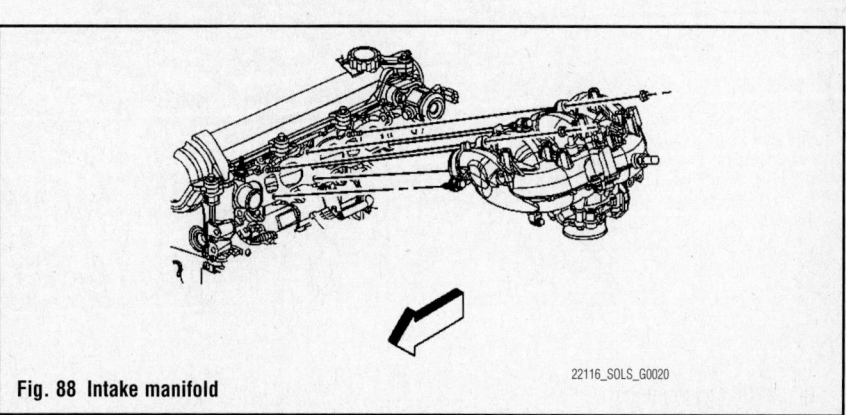

Fig. 88 Intake manifold

22116_SOLS_G0020

69. Install the brake booster hose to the intake manifold.

70. Position the brake booster vacuum hose clamp at the intake manifold.

71. Connect the EVAP line quick connect fitting to the EVAP purge solenoid.

72. Connect the fuel feed line quick connect fitting from the fuel rail.

73. Install the oil level indicator tube.

74. Install the intake manifold cover.

OIL PAN

REMOVAL & INSTALLATION

2.4L (LE5) & 2.0L (LNF) Engines

See Figures 89 and 90.

1. Before servicing the vehicle, refer to the Precautions Section.

2. Remove the engine from vehicle.

3. Remove the oil pan bolts.

4. Remove the oil pan at pry points.

5. Clean the oil pan mating surface.

6. Clean the oil pan. Remove all the sludge and the oil deposits.

7. Inspect the threads for the engine oil drain plug.

8. Inspect the oil pan for cracking near the pan rail and the transmission mounting points.

9. Inspect the oil pan for cracking resulting from impact or flying road debris.

➡ **The oil pan baffle and pickup screen are not removable from the oil pan.**

10. Inspect the oil pan baffle and pickup screen.

11. Repair or replace the oil pan as necessary.

12. Make sure that the oil pan and mounting surface on the lower crankcase are free of all oil and debris.

13. Apply a 3.5 mm bead of GM P/N

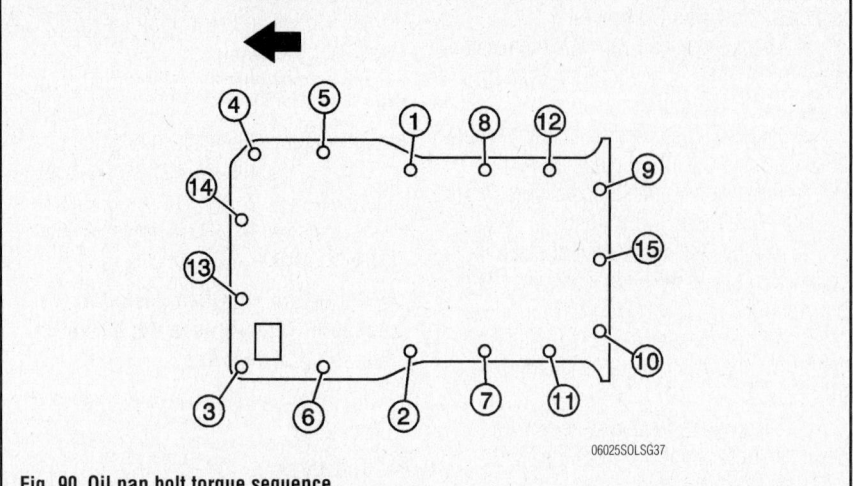

06025SOLSG37

Fig. 90 Oil pan bolt torque sequence

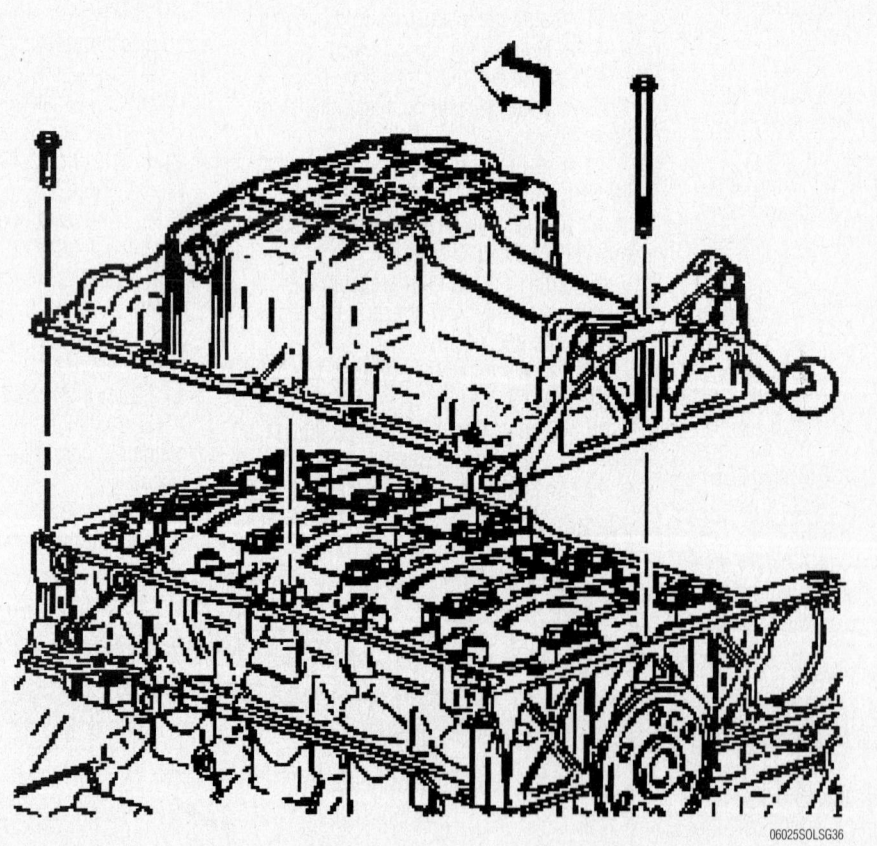

06025SOLSG36

Fig. 89 Oil pan pry points

12378521 (Canadian P/N 88901148) or equivalent around the perimeter of the oil pan and the oil suction port opening.

14. Install the oil pan.

15. Install the oil pan bolts. Tighten the oil pan bolts to 25 Nm (18 ft. lbs.) in sequence.

16. Install engine in vehicle.

17. Refill crankcase, check and refill fluids as needed.

OIL PUMP

REMOVAL & INSTALLATION

2.4L (LE5) & 2.0L (LNF) Engines

See Figures 91 through 93.

1. Remove the hood.

2. Remove the drive belt and tensioner.

3. Remove the crankshaft balancer.

4. Remove the engine front cover bolts.

5. Remove the engine front cover to water pump bolt.

6. Remove and discard the engine front cover gasket.

7. Remove the crankshaft front cover oil seal with an appropriate tool.

8. Remove and discard the friction washer.

9. Disassemble the pressure relief valve.

10. Remove the oil pump gerotor cover and bolts.

11. Clean all of the parts in cleaning solvent. Remove varnish, sludge, and dirt.

To install:

12. Lubricate all oil pump parts with engine oil.

13. Install the inner gear into the outer gear.

➡️ **If gears are improperly installed in the front cover, the gerotor cover will not bolt on.**

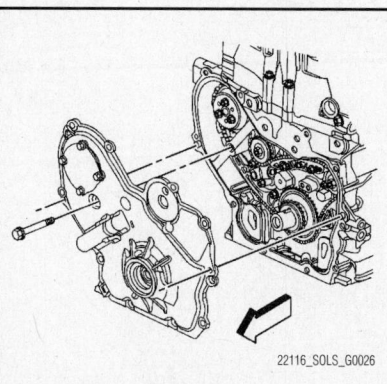

Fig. 91 Engine front cover

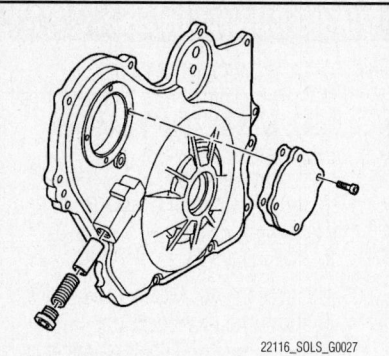

Fig. 92 Oil pressure relief valve removal shown

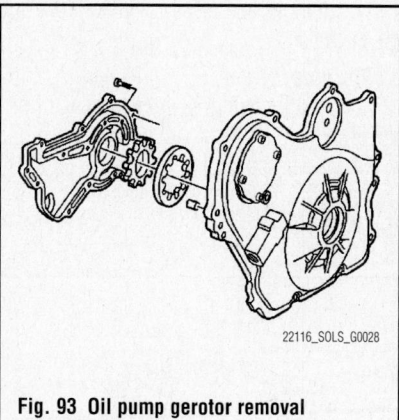

Fig. 93 Oil pump gerotor removal

14. Install the gears together into the front cover with the hub of the center gear facing the front cover.

15. Install the oil pump gerotor cover and bolts.

16. Tighten the oil pump gerotor cover bolts to 53 inch. lbs. (6 Nm).

17. Install the pressure relief valve piston.

18. Install the pressure relief valve spring.

19. Tighten the pressure relief valve plug to 30 ft. lbs. (40 Nm).

20. Install a new crankshaft front oil seal.

21. Install a new friction washer.

22. Position and install a new engine front cover gasket to the dowel pins.

23. Position and install the engine front cover.

24. Install the engine front cover to water pump bolt and tighten to 18 ft. lbs. (25 Nm).

25. Install the engine front cover bolts and tighten to 18 ft. lbs. (25 Nm).

26. Install the crankshaft balancer.

27. Install the drive belt and tensioner.

28. Install the hood.

INSPECTION

1. Clean all of the parts in cleaning solvent. Remove varnish, sludge and dirt.

2. Inspect the oil pump for wear and scoring. Insure that all components are within specifications. Refer to engine mechanical specifications.

3. Replace the front cover and oil pump assembly if it is out of specification or damaged.

PISTON AND RING

POSITIONING

See Figure 94.

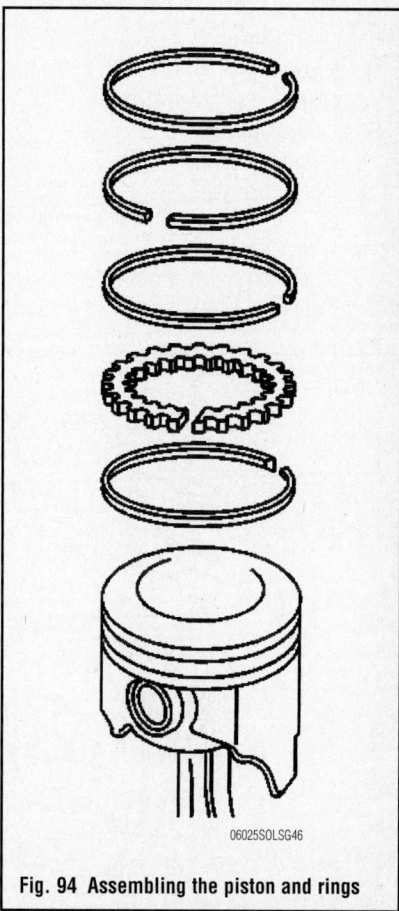

Fig. 94 Assembling the piston and rings

REAR MAIN SEAL

REMOVAL & INSTALLATION

2.4L (LE5) & 2.0L (LNF) Engines

See Figure 95.

1. Before servicing the vehicle, refer to the Precautions Section.

2. Remove the transmission and, if equipped, the clutch.

➡️ **It may be necessary to remove the chamfer (bevel) from the edge of an 18 mm socket in order to get full engagement on the thin-headed flywheel bolts.**

3. Remove the flywheel bolts.

➡ **Do not orientate the flywheel to the crankshaft. It is balanced separately from the engine.**

4. Remove the flywheel.

5. Clean the thread adhesive from the flywheel bolt holes. Use a nylon bristle brush to clean the holes in the crankshaft.

➡ **Do not damage the outside diameter of the crankshaft or chamber with any tool.**

6. Pry out the crankshaft rear oil seal using a flat-bladed tool.

To install:

7. Using a seal driver, install a NEW crankshaft real oil seal.

8. Install the flywheel.

9. Install the flywheel bolts. Tighten the bolts to 53 Nm (39 ft. lbs.) plus an additional 25 degrees.

10. Install the clutch, if equipped.

11. Install the transmission.

TIMING CHAIN COVER

REMOVAL & INSTALLATION

2.4L (LE5) & 2.0L (LNF) Engines

See Figure 96.

1. Before servicing the vehicle, refer to the Precautions Section.

2. Remove the hood.

3. Remove the accessory drive belts.

4. Remove the drive belt tensioner.

5. Remove the crankshaft balancer.

6. Remove the engine front cover bolts.

7. Remove the engine front cover-to-water pump bolt.

8. Remove and discard the engine front cover gasket.

To install:

9. Position and install the engine front cover.

10. Install the engine front cover to water pump bolt. Tighten the bolt to 25 Nm (18 ft. lbs.).

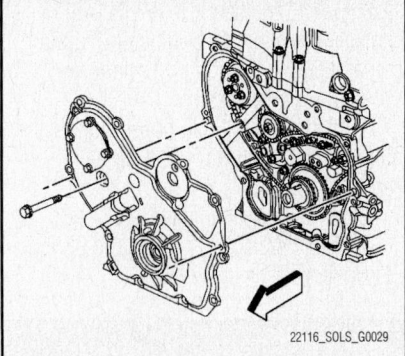

22116_SOLS_G0029

Fig. 96 Engine front cover 2.4L & 2.0L engines

11. Install the engine front cover bolts. Tighten the bolts to 25 Nm (18 ft. lbs.).

12. Install the crankshaft balancer.

13. Install the drive belt tensioner. Torque to 33 ft. lbs. (45 Nm).

14. Install drive belt.

15. Install hood.

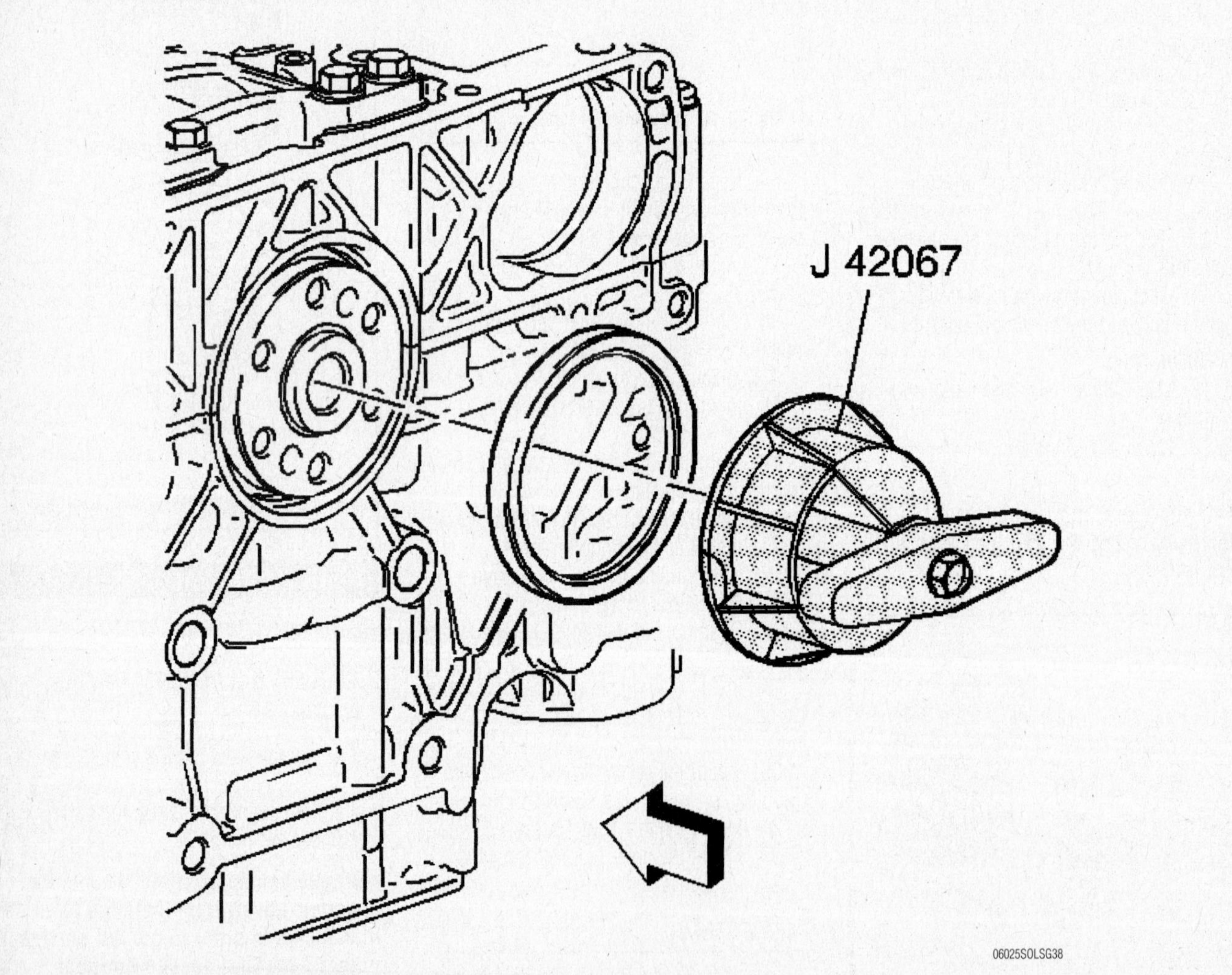

J 42067

06025SOLSG38

Fig. 95 Rear main seal installation

TIMING CHAIN AND SPROCKETS

REMOVAL & INSTALLATION

2.4L (LE5) & 2.0L (LNF) Engines

See Figures 97 through 110.

1. Remove the hood.
2. Remove the #1 cylinder spark plug.
3. Rotate the crankshaft in the engine rotational direction clockwise, until the #1 piston is at top dead center (TDC) on the compression stroke.
4. Remove the camshaft cover.
5. Remove the engine front cover.
6. Remove the upper timing chain guide bolts and guide.

✳✳ WARNING

The timing chain tensioner must be removed to unload chain tension before the timing chain is removed. If it is not, the timing chain will become cocked and it will be difficult to remove.

7. Remove the timing chain tensioner.
8. Install a 24 mm wrench on the hex on the exhaust camshaft in order to hold the camshaft.
9. Remove and discard the exhaust camshaft actuator bolt.
10. Remove the exhaust camshaft actuator from the camshaft and timing chain.
11. Remove the timing chain tensioner guide bolt and guide.

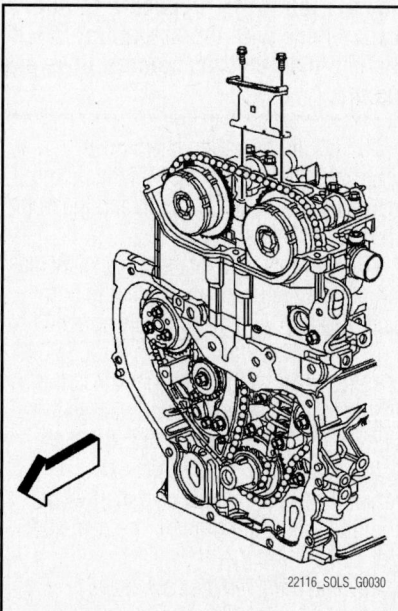

Fig. 97 Timing chain guide bolts and guide removal

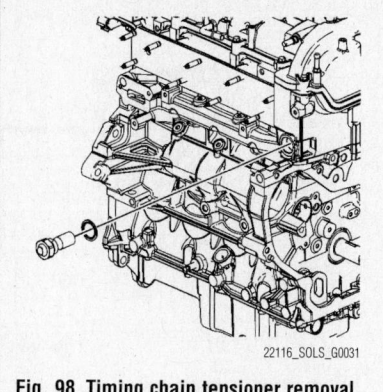

Fig. 98 Timing chain tensioner removal

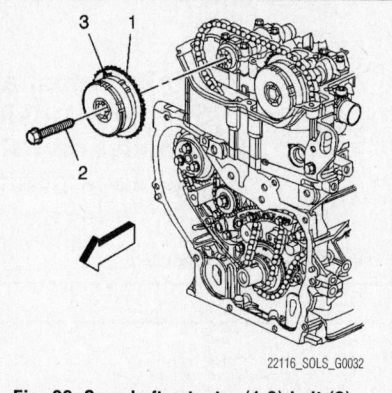

Fig. 99 Camshaft actuator (1,3) bolt (2)

12. Remove the fixed timing chain guide access plug.
13. Remove the fixed timing chain guide bolts and guide.
14. Install a 24 mm wrench on the hex on the intake camshaft in order to hold the camshaft.
15. Remove and discard the intake camshaft actuator bolt.
16. Remove the intake camshaft actuator, and the timing chain through the top of the cylinder head.
17. Remove the timing chain crankshaft sprocket.

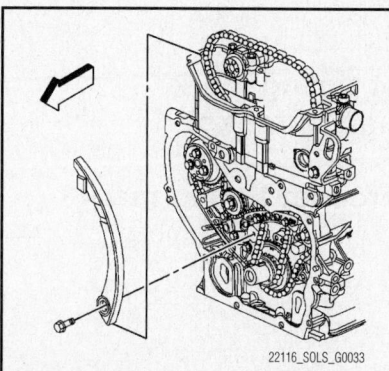

Fig. 100 Timing chain tensioner guide bolt and guide

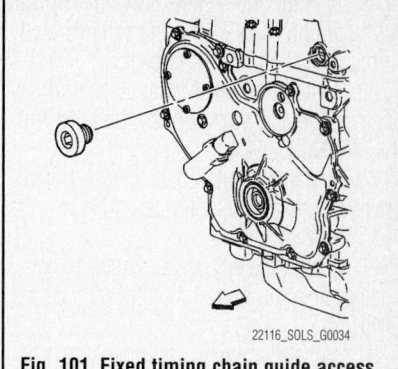

Fig. 101 Fixed timing chain guide access plug

18. If replacing the balance shaft timing chain and sprocket, perform the following steps, if not proceed to step 10 in the installation procedure.
19. Remove the balance shaft drive chain tensioner bolts and tensioner.
20. Remove the adjustable balance shaft chain guide bolt and guide.
21. Remove the small balance shaft drive chain guide bolts and guide.
22. Remove the upper balance shaft drive chain guide bolts and guide.

➡ **It may ease removal of the balance shaft drive chain to get all the slack in the chain between the crankshaft and water pump sprockets.**

23. Remove the balance shaft drive chain.

To install:

24. If replacing the balance shaft timing chain, perform the following steps, if not proceed to step 10.
25. Install the balance shaft drive sprocket.

✳✳ WARNING

If the balance shafts are not properly timed to the engine, the engine may vibrate or make noise.

26. Install the balance shaft drive chain (1) with the colored link lined up with the marks on the balance shaft sprockets and the balance shaft drive sprocket.
27. There are three colored links on the chain. Two are chrome and one is copper. Use the following steps in order to line up the links with the sprockets:
   a. Working clockwise around the chain, place the chrome link (4) in line with the timing mark (3) on the balance shaft drive sprocket. (Approximately 6 o'clock position on the sprocket.)
   b. Place the chain (7) on the water pump drive sprocket. The alignment is not critical.

c. Align the last chrome link (6) with the timing mark (1) on the exhaust side balance shaft drive sprocket.

28. Install the upper balance shaft drive chain guide and bolts, tighten bolts to 11ft. lbs. (15 Nm).

29. Install the small balance shaft drive chain guide and bolts, tighten bolts to 11ft. lbs. (15 Nm).

30. Install the adjustable balance shaft chain guide and bolt, tighten to 89 inch lbs. (10 Nm).

31. Reset the timing chain tensioner by performing the following steps:

   a. Rotate the tensioner plunger 90 degrees in its bore and compress the plunger.

   b. Rotate the tensioner back to the original 12 o'clock position and insert a paper clip through the hole in the plunger body and into the hose in the tensioner plunger.

32. Install the balance shaft drive chain tensioner and bolts.

33. Remove the paper clip from the balance shaft drive chain tensioner.

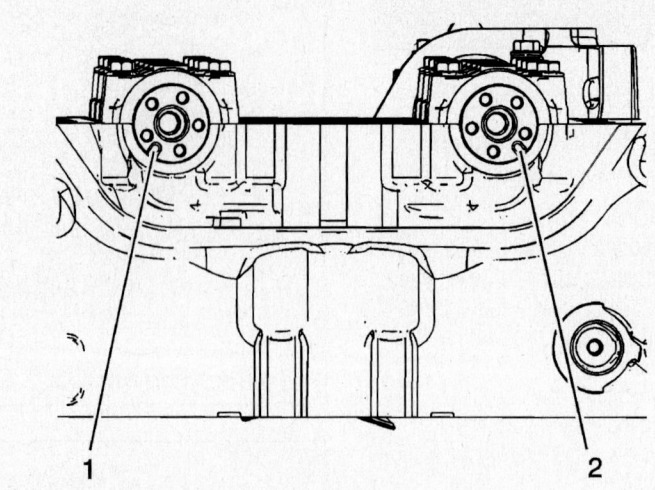

1. **Intake camshaft notch is in the 5 o'clock position**
2. **Exhaust camshaft notch is in the 7 o'clock position**

22116_SOLS_G0037

Fig. 103 Camshaft alignment

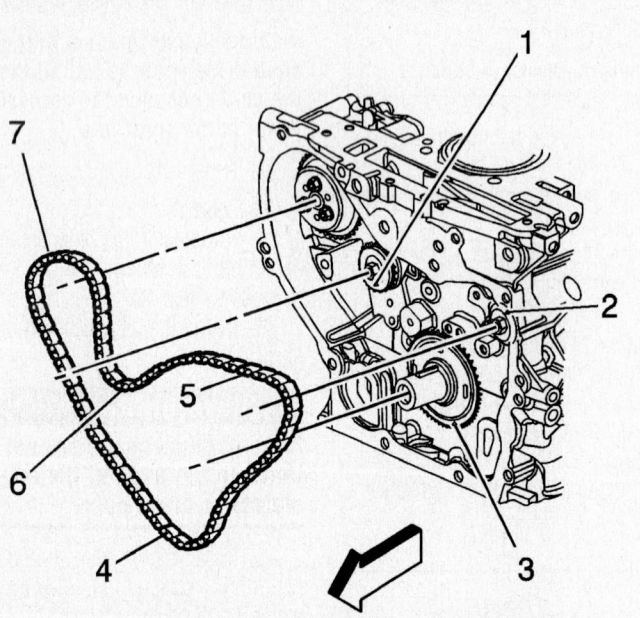

1. **Balance shaft sprocket timing mark**
2. **Intake side balance shaft sprocket timing mark**
3. **Balance shaft drive sprocket timing mark**
4. **Chrome link**
5. **Copper link**
6. **Chrome link**
7. **Timing chain**

22116_SOLS_G0036

Fig. 102 Timing chain alignment

34. Ensure the intake camshaft notch is in the 5 o'clock position (2) and the exhaust camshaft notch is in the 7 o'clock position (1). The number 1 piston should be at top dead center (TDC), crankshaft key at 12 o'clock.

⁂ WARNING

There are 3 colored links on the timing chain. 2 links are of matching color, and 1 link is of a unique color. Use the following procedure to line up the links with the actuators. Orient the chain so that the colored links are visible.

35. Install the timing chain drive sprocket to the crankshaft with the timing mark in the 5 o'clock position and the front of the sprocket facing out.

36. Assemble the intake camshaft actuator into the timing chain with the timing mark lined up with the uniquely colored link

37. Lower the timing chain through the opening in the cylinder head. Use care to ensure that the chain goes around both sides of the cylinder block bosses.

38. Install the intake camshaft actuator onto the intake camshaft while aligning the dowel pin into the camshaft slot.

39. Hand tighten the new intake camshaft actuator bolt.

40. Route the timing chain around the crankshaft sprocket and line up the first

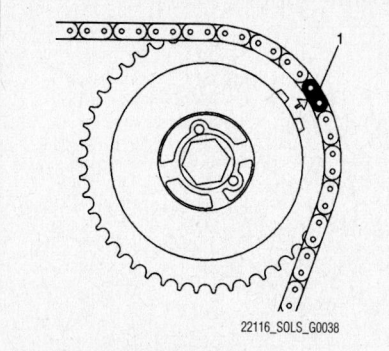

Fig. 104 Camshaft actuator and timing chain mark alignment

matching colored link with the timing mark on the crankshaft sprocket, in approximately the 5 o'clock position.

41. Rotate the crankshaft clockwise to remove all chain slack. Do not rotate the intake camshaft.

42. Install the adjustable timing chain guide down through the opening in the cylinder head and install the adjustable timing chain bolt.

43. Tighten the adjustable timing chain guide bolt to 89 inch. lbs. (10 Nm).

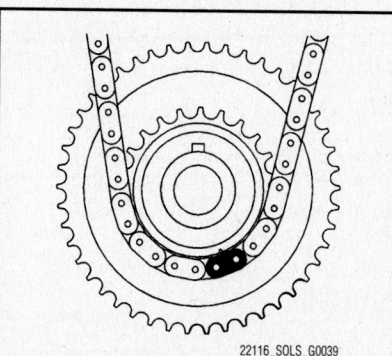

Fig. 105 Crankshaft sprocket and timing chain mark alignment

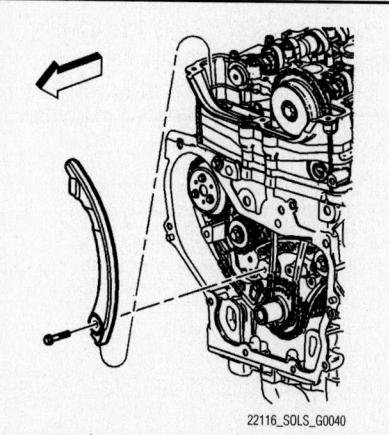

Fig. 106 Installation of the adjustable timing chain guide

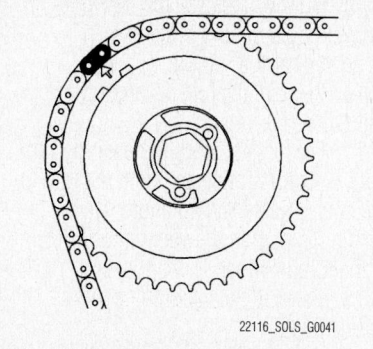

Fig. 107 Camshaft actuator and timing chain mark alignment

➡**Always install new actuator bolts.**

44. Install the exhaust camshaft actuator into the timing chain with the timing mark lined up with the second matching colored link.

45. Install the exhaust camshaft actuator onto the exhaust camshaft, aligning the dowel pin into the camshaft slot.

46. Using a 23 mm open end wrench, rotate the exhaust camshaft approximately 45 degrees until the dowel pin in the camshaft actuator goes into the camshaft slot.

47. When the actuator seats on the cam, tighten the new exhaust camshaft actuator bolt hand tight.

48. Verify that all of the colored links and the appropriate timing marks are still aligned. If they are not aligned, repeat the portion of the procedure necessary to align the timing marks.

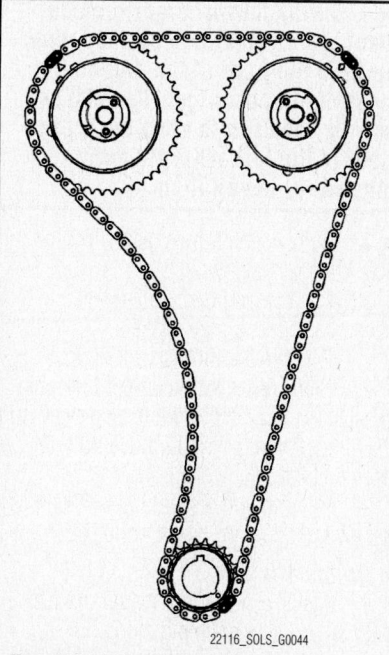

Fig. 108 Timing chain, colored links, and marks

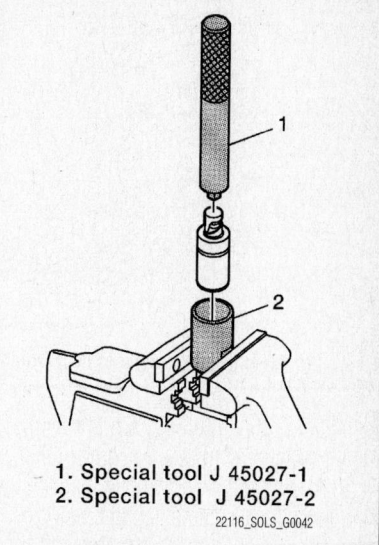

1. Special tool J 45027-1
2. Special tool J 45027-2

Fig. 109 Timing chain tensioner and tools shown for resetting

49. Install the fixed timing chain guide and bolts. Tighten the fixed timing chain guide bolts to 106 inch. lbs. 12 Nm).

50. Install the upper timing chain guide and bolts, tighten to 89 inch. lbs. (10 Nm).

51. Reset the timing chain tensioner by performing the following steps:

   a. Remove the snap ring.

   b. Remove the piston assembly from the body of the timing chain tensioner.

   c. Install the J 45027-2 (2) into a vise.

   d. Install the notch end of the piston assembly into the J 45027-2 (2).

   e. Using the J 45027-1 (1), turn the ratchet cylinder into the piston

   f. Reinstall the piston assembly into the body of the tensioner.

   g. Install the snap ring.

52. Inspect the timing chain tensioner seal for damage. If damaged, replace the seal.

53. Inspect to ensure all dirt and debris is removed from the timing chain tensioner threaded hole in the cylinder head.

✳✳ WARNING

Ensure the timing chain tensioner seal is centered throughout the torque procedure to eliminate the possibility of an oil leak.

54. Install the timing chain tensioner assembly and tighten to 55 ft. lbs. (75 Nm).

55. The timing chain tensioner is released by compressing it 0.079 inch (2 mm), which will release the locking mechanism in the ratchet. To release the timing chain tensioner, use a suitable tool with a rubber tip on the end. Feed the tool down through the cam drive chest to rest on the

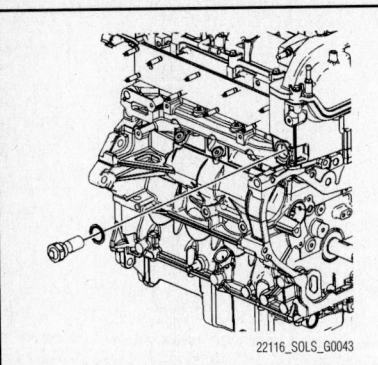

Fig. 110 Timing chain tensioner installation

cam chain. Then give a sharp jolt diagonally downwards to release the tensioner.

56. Using a 23 mm wrench, engage the hex on the intake camshaft, and using a torque wrench, tighten the camshaft actuator bolt.

57. Tighten the intake camshaft position actuator bolt to 22 ft. lbs. (30 Nm). plus an additional 100 degrees using a angle meter.

58. Using a 23 mm wrench, engage the hex on the exhaust camshaft, and using a torque wrench, tighten the camshaft actuator bolt.

59. Tighten the intake camshaft position actuator bolt to 22 ft. lbs. (30 Nm). plus an additional 100 degrees using a angle meter.

60. Install the timing chain oiling nozzle, and tighten to 89 inch. lbs. (10 Nm).

61. Apply sealant compound to the thread of the timing chain guide bolt access hole plug.

62. Install the timing chain guide bolt access hole plug and tighten to 66ft. lbs. 90 Nm).

63. Install the engine front cover.

64. Install the camshaft cover.

65. Install the #1 cylinder spark plug.

66. Install the hood.

TURBOCHARGER

REMOVAL & INSTALLATION

2.0L (LNF) Engine

See Figure 111.

1. Before servicing the vehicle, refer to the Precautions Section.

2. Drain the cooling system.

3. Remove the charge air cooler inlet pipe.

4. Remove the charge air cooler pipe bolts at the turbocharger.

5. Remove the charge air cooler pipe from the turbocharger.

6. Remove the turbocharger heat shield bolts and shield.

7. Remove the catalytic converter

8. Remove the catalytic converter bracket bolt, nut, and bracket.

9. Lower the vehicle

10. Remove the turbocharger brace nut and brace.

11. Disconnect the engine wiring harness electrical connector from the turbocharger wastegate solenoid valve.

12. Reposition the vacuum hose clamp at the turbocharger.

13. Remove the vacuum hose from the turbocharger.

14. Remove the engine wiring harness clip from the turbocharger coolant feed pipe.

15. Remove the turbocharger coolant feed pipe bolt at the turbocharger.

16. Remove and discard the turbocharger coolant feed pipe gasket.

17. Remove the turbocharger coolant feed pipe bolt from the cylinder head.

18. Reposition the turbocharger coolant feed pipe out of the way.

19. Remove the Positive Crankcase Ventilation (PCV) fitting bolt from the turbocharger. Reposition the PCV pipe (with fitting) out of the way.

20. Remove the turbocharger coolant return pipe bolts and pipe.

21. Remove and discard the turbocharger coolant return pipe gaskets.

> **❋❋ WARNING**
>
> **Do not twist the turbocharger oil feed pipe. Twisting of the feed pipe will result in the collapse and deformation of the plastic pipe, restricting oil flow and causing turbocharger damage. During turbocharger replacement, gently push the oil feed pipe towards the front of the engine to clear the turbocharger. Assistance may be required to keep the pipes clear of the turbocharger during removal or installation.**

22. Remove the turbocharger oil feed pipe bolts and pipe.

23. Remove and discard the turbocharger oil feed pipe gaskets.

24. Remove the turbocharger nuts.

25. Remove the turbocharger from the exhaust manifold studs while also removing the turbocharger oil return hose from the engine block.

26. Remove and discard the turbocharger gasket and oil return hose O-ring seal.

To install:

27. Install a new turbocharger gasket onto the exhaust manifold studs.

28. Lubricate and install a new turbocharger oil return hose O-ring seal.

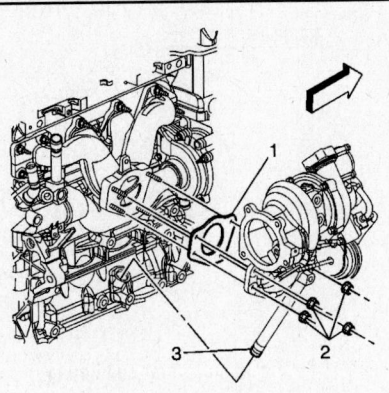

1. Turbocharger gasket
2. Turbocharger mounting nuts
3. Oil return hose O-ring seal

Fig. 111 Turbocharger—2.0L (LNF) engine

29. Install the turbocharger oil return hose to the engine block while also installing the turbocharger to the exhaust manifold studs.

30. Install the turbocharger nuts and tighten to 26 ft. lbs. (35 Nm).

31. Install new gaskets onto the turbocharger oil feed pipe fittings.

32. Install the turbocharger oil feed pipe and bolts. Tighten the bolts to 24 ft. lbs. (32 Nm).

33. Install new gaskets onto the turbocharger coolant return pipe fittings.

34. Install the turbocharger coolant return pipe and bolts. Tighten the bolts to 26ft. lbs. (35 Nm).

35. Install a new o—ring seal to the PCV fitting.

36. Position the PCV pipe (with fitting) and install the PCV fitting bolt to the turbocharger. Tighten the bolt to 89 inch. lbs. (10 Nm).

37. Position the turbocharger coolant feed pipe to the turbocharger.

38. Install NEW gaskets onto the turbocharger coolant feed pipe fitting.

39. Install the turbocharger coolant feed pipe bolt at the turbocharger. Tighten the bolt to 26 ft. lbs. (35 Nm).

40. Install the turbocharger coolant feed pipe bolt to the cylinder head. Tighten the bolt to 89 inch. lbs. (10 Nm).

41. Install the engine wiring harness clip to the turbocharger coolant feed pipe.

42. Install the vacuum hose to the turbocharger.

43. Position the vacuum hose clamp at the turbocharger.

44. Connect the engine wiring harness electrical connector to the turbocharger wastegate solenoid valve.

45. Install the turbocharger brace bolt and nut. Tighten the nut to 43 ft. lbs. (58 Nm).

46. Raise and suitably support the vehicle.

47. Position the catalytic converter bracket to the engine.

48. Install the catalytic converter bracket bolt, and nut until snug.

49. Install the catalytic converter

50. Tighten the catalytic converter bracket bolt and nut.

51. Tighten the bolt and nut to 43 ft. lbs. (58 Nm).

52. Lower the vehicle.

53. Install the turbocharger heat shield and bolts. Tighten the bolts to 89 inch. lbs. (10 Nm).

54. Install the charge air cooler pipe and gasket to the turbocharger.

55. Install the charge air cooler pipe bolts at the turbocharger. Tighten the bolts to 16 ft. lbs. (22 Nm).

56. Install the charge air cooler inlet pipe.

57. Fill and bleed the cooling system.

VALVE LASH

ADJUSTMENT

Hydraulic lash adjusters are used on all engines and no adjustment is necessary.

ENGINE PERFORMANCE & EMISSION CONTROL

COMPONENT LOCATIONS

See Figures 112 through 122.

ACCELERATOR PEDAL POSITION (APP) SENSOR

LOCATION

The Accelerator Pedal Position (APP) Sensor is located inside the vehicle. It is mounted at the top of the accelerator pedal and is part of the assembly.

OPERATION

The accelerator pedal contains 2 individual Accelerator Pedal Position (APP) sensors within the assembly. The APP sensors 1 and 2 are potentiometer type sensors each with 3 circuits:

- A 5-volt reference circuit
- A low reference circuit
- A signal circuit

The APP sensors are used to determine the pedal angle. The Engine Control Module (ECM) provides each APP sensor a 5-volt reference circuit and a low reference circuit. The APP sensors provide the ECM with signal voltage proportional to the pedal movement. The APP sensor 1 signal voltage at rest position is near the low reference and increases as the pedal is actuated. The APP sensor 2 signal voltage at rest position is also near the low reference and increases as the pedal is actuated.

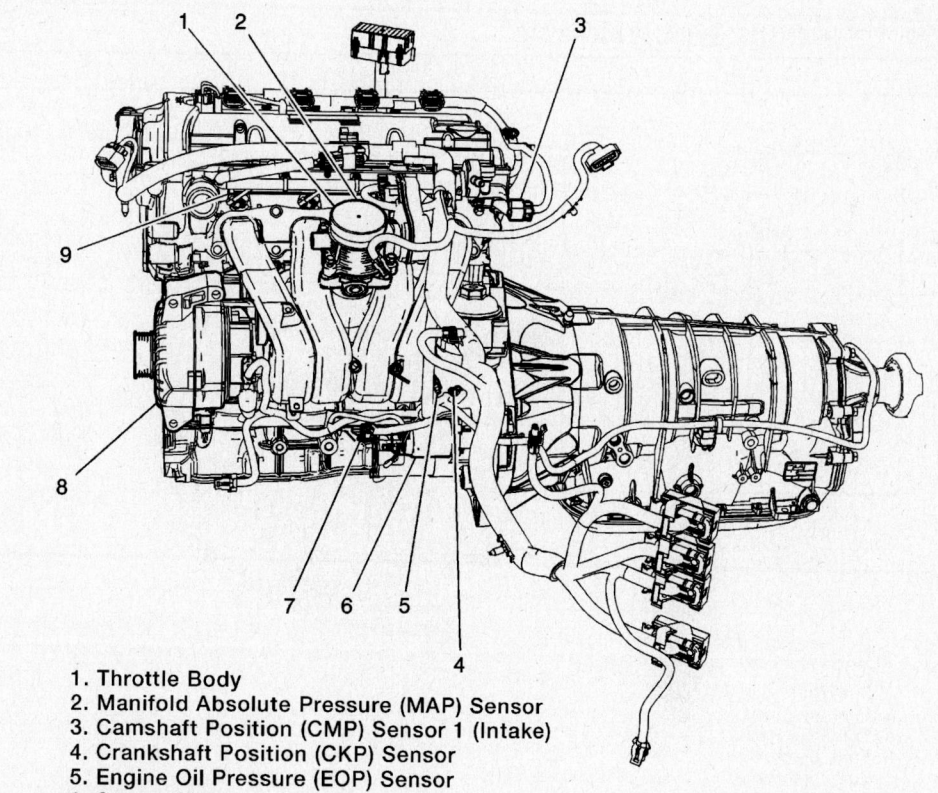

1. Throttle Body
2. Manifold Absolute Pressure (MAP) Sensor
3. Camshaft Position (CMP) Sensor 1 (Intake)
4. Crankshaft Position (CKP) Sensor
5. Engine Oil Pressure (EOP) Sensor
6. Starter Motor
7. Knock Sensor Pigtail Connector
8. Generator
9. Fuel Injector Rail

22116_SOLS_G0139

Fig. 112 2.4L (LE5) Engine components left side automatic transmission

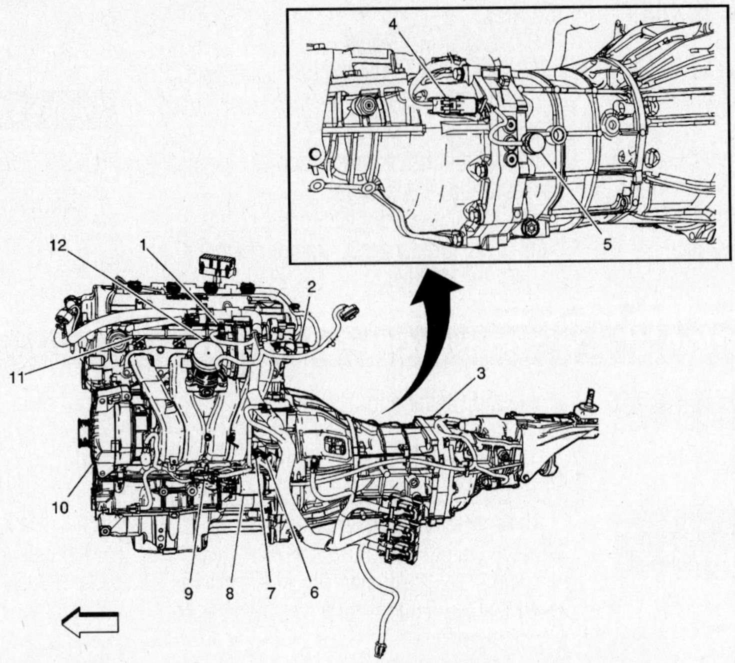

1. Throttle Body
2. Camshaft Position (CMP) Sensor 1 (Intake)
3. Manual Transmission
4. Vehicle Speed Sensor (VSS)
5. Backup Lamp Switch
6. Crankshaft Position (CKP) Sensor
7. Engine Oil Pressure (EOP) Sensor
8. Starter Motor
9. Knock Sensor Pigtail Connector
10. Generator
11. Fuel Injector Rail
12. Manifold Absolute Pressure (MAP) Sensor

22116_SOLS_G0140

Fig. 113 2.4L (LE5) Engine components left side manual transmission

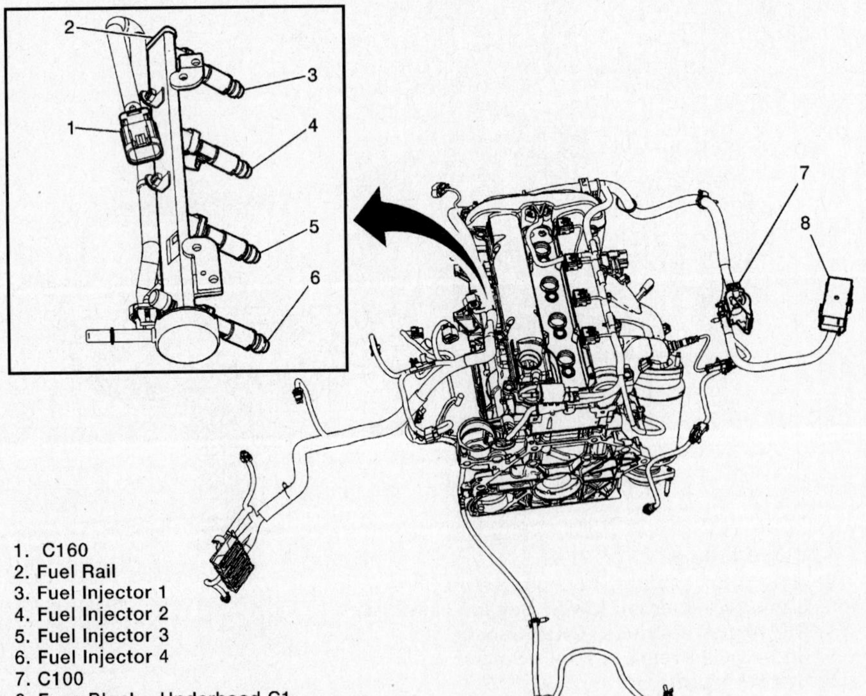

1. C160
2. Fuel Rail
3. Fuel Injector 1
4. Fuel Injector 2
5. Fuel Injector 3
6. Fuel Injector 4
7. C100
8. Fuse Block - Underhood C1

22116_SOLS_G0141

Fig. 114 2.4L (LE5) Engine components top view

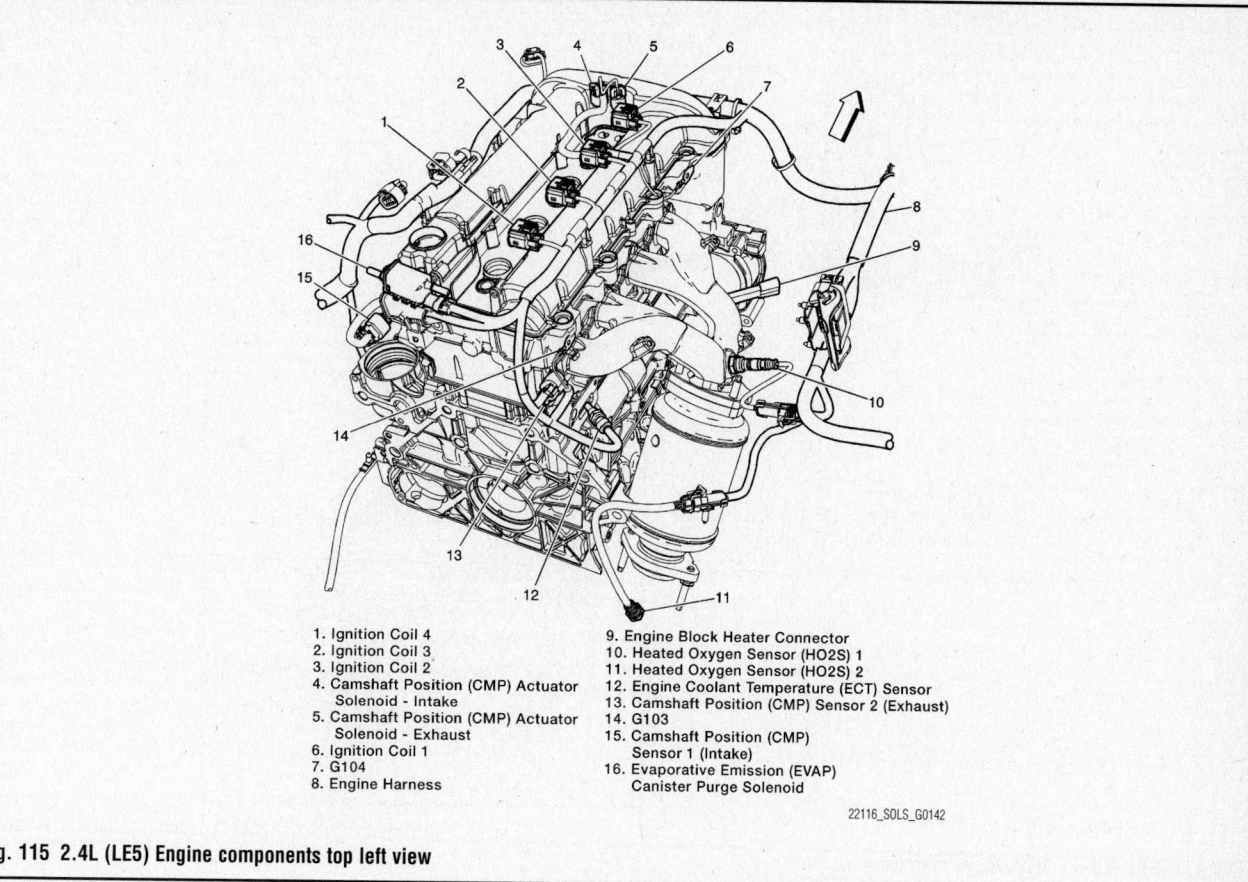

1. Ignition Coil 4
2. Ignition Coil 3
3. Ignition Coil 2
4. Camshaft Position (CMP) Actuator
   Solenoid - Intake
5. Camshaft Position (CMP) Actuator
   Solenoid - Exhaust
6. Ignition Coil 1
7. G104
8. Engine Harness
9. Engine Block Heater Connector
10. Heated Oxygen Sensor (HO2S) 1
11. Heated Oxygen Sensor (HO2S) 2
12. Engine Coolant Temperature (ECT) Sensor
13. Camshaft Position (CMP) Sensor 2 (Exhaust)
14. G103
15. Camshaft Position (CMP)
    Sensor 1 (Intake)
16. Evaporative Emission (EVAP)
    Canister Purge Solenoid

22116_SOLS_G0142

Fig. 115 2.4L (LE5) Engine components top left view

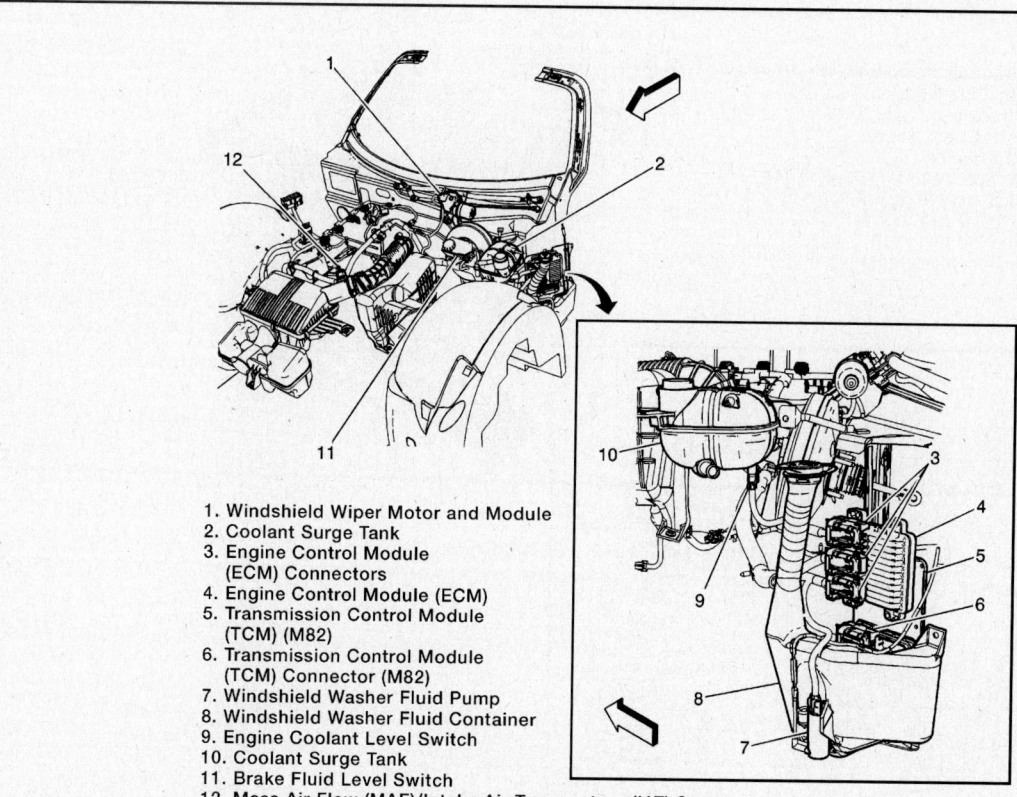

1. Windshield Wiper Motor and Module
2. Coolant Surge Tank
3. Engine Control Module
   (ECM) Connectors
4. Engine Control Module (ECM)
5. Transmission Control Module
   (TCM) (M82)
6. Transmission Control Module
   (TCM) Connector (M82)
7. Windshield Washer Fluid Pump
8. Windshield Washer Fluid Container
9. Engine Coolant Level Switch
10. Coolant Surge Tank
11. Brake Fluid Level Switch
12. Mass Air Flow (MAF)/Intake Air Temperature (IAT) Sensor

22116_SOLS_G0143

Fig. 116 2.4L (LE5) Engine front compartment view

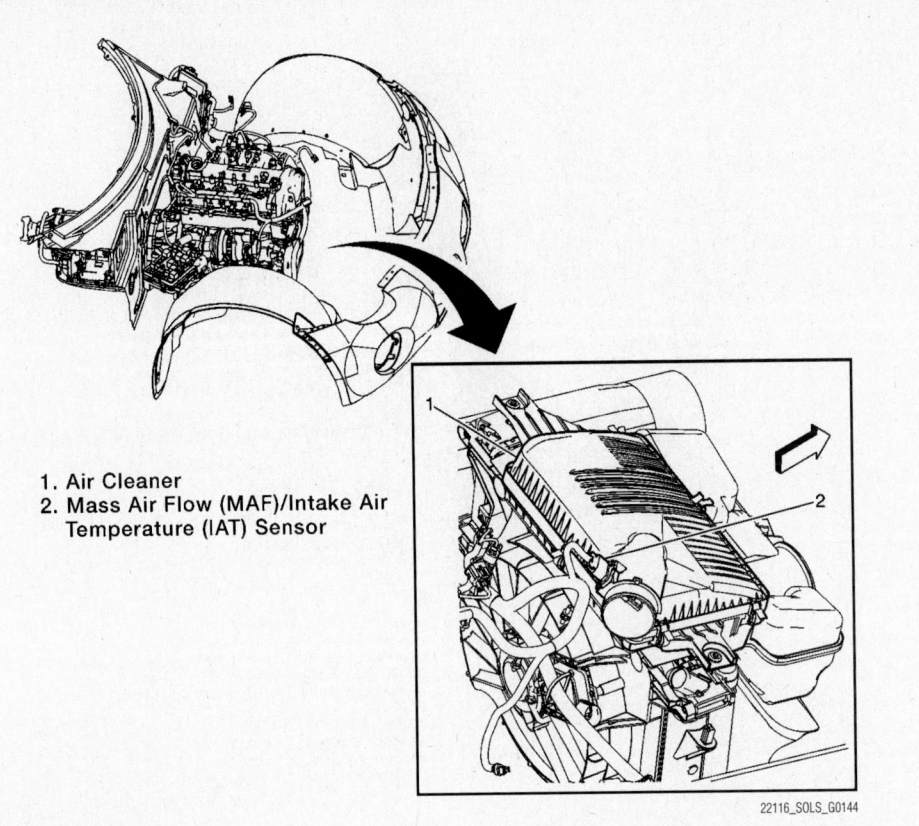

1. Air Cleaner
2. Mass Air Flow (MAF)/Intake Air Temperature (IAT) Sensor

22116_SOLS_G0144

Fig. 117 2.0L (LNF) Engine above radiator view

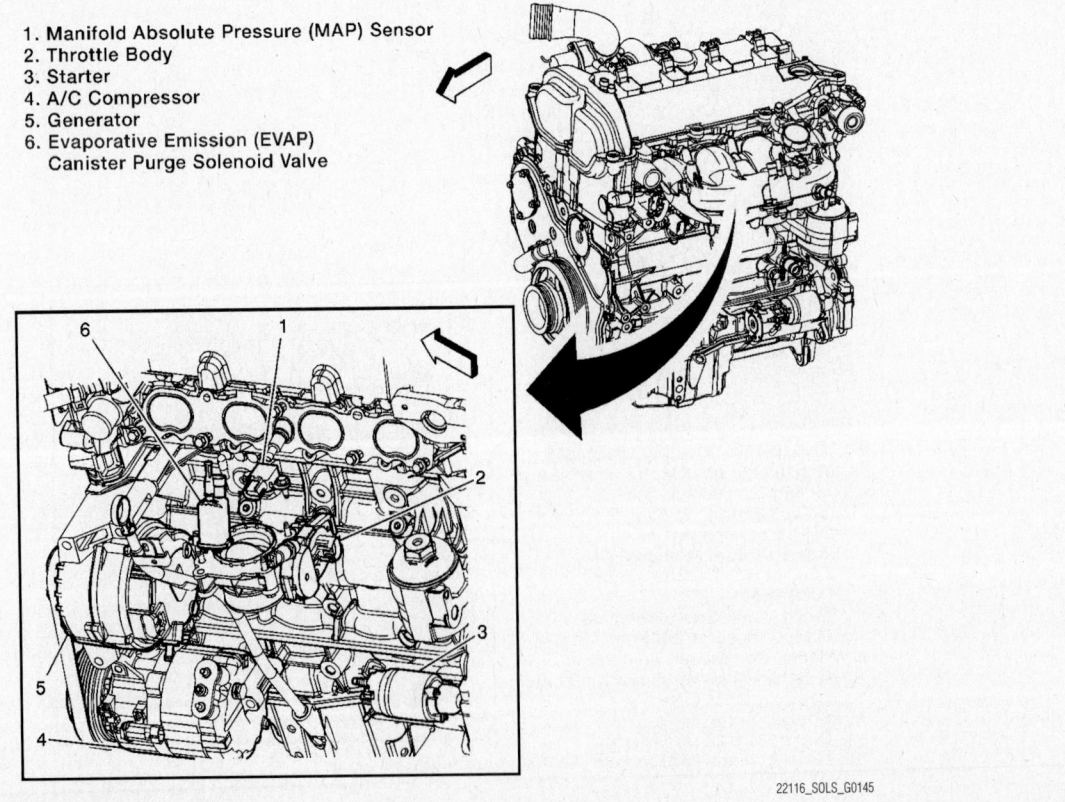

1. Manifold Absolute Pressure (MAP) Sensor
2. Throttle Body
3. Starter
4. A/C Compressor
5. Generator
6. Evaporative Emission (EVAP) Canister Purge Solenoid Valve

22116_SOLS_G0145

Fig. 118 2.0L (LNF) Engine components left side view

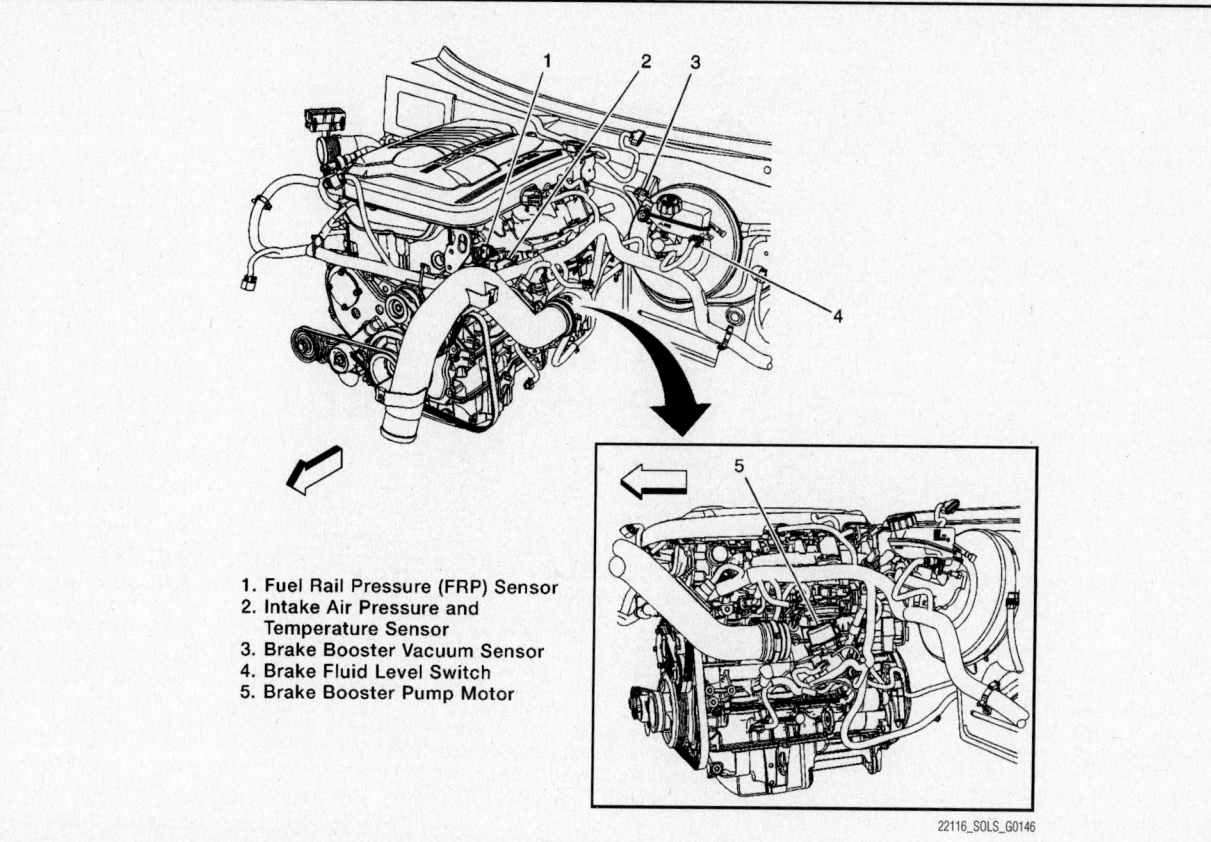

1. Fuel Rail Pressure (FRP) Sensor
2. Intake Air Pressure and
   Temperature Sensor
3. Brake Booster Vacuum Sensor
4. Brake Fluid Level Switch
5. Brake Booster Pump Motor

22116_SOLS_G0146

Fig. 119 2.0L (LNF) Engine compartment left side view

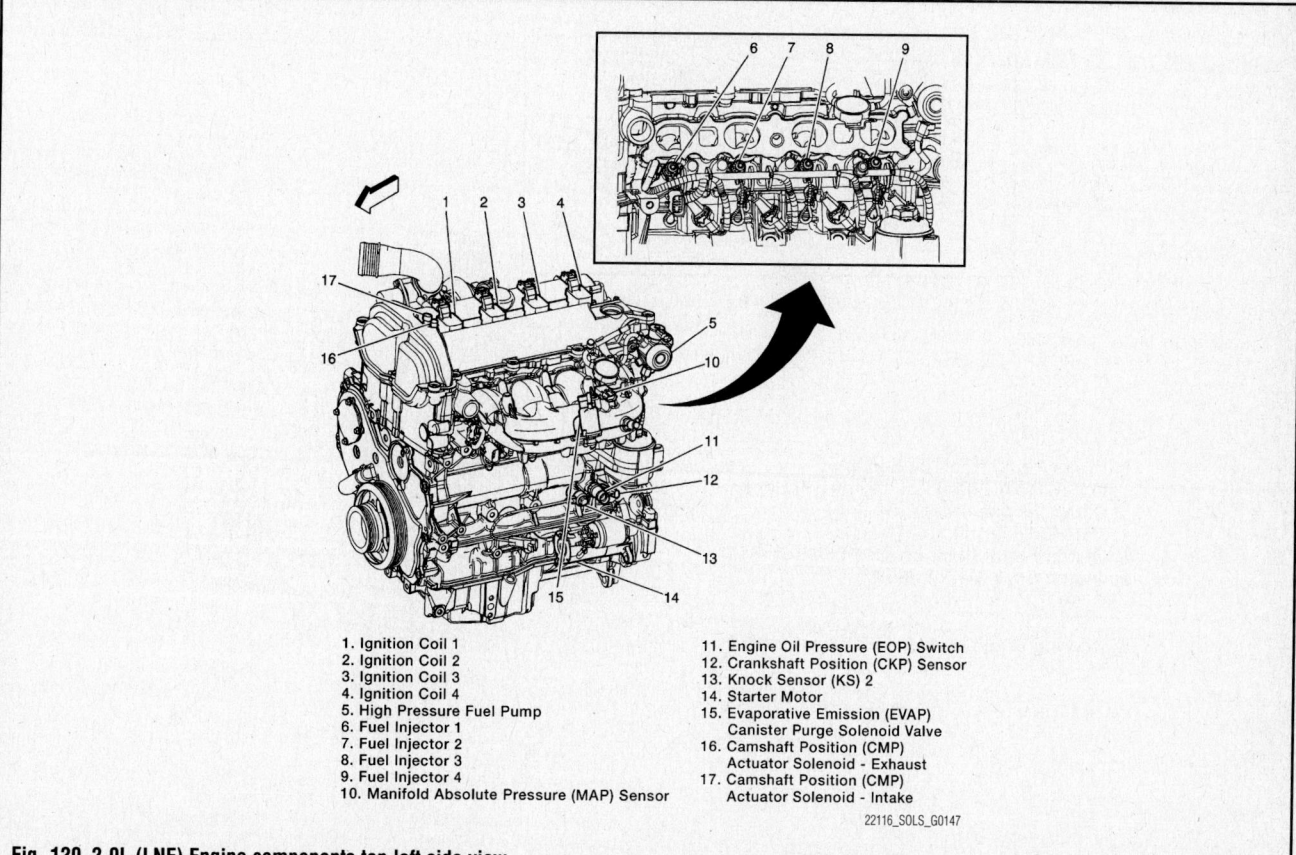

1. Ignition Coil 1
2. Ignition Coil 2
3. Ignition Coil 3
4. Ignition Coil 4
5. High Pressure Fuel Pump
6. Fuel Injector 1
7. Fuel Injector 2
8. Fuel Injector 3
9. Fuel Injector 4
10. Manifold Absolute Pressure (MAP) Sensor

11. Engine Oil Pressure (EOP) Switch
12. Crankshaft Position (CKP) Sensor
13. Knock Sensor (KS) 2
14. Starter Motor
15. Evaporative Emission (EVAP)
    Canister Purge Solenoid Valve
16. Camshaft Position (CMP)
    Actuator Solenoid - Exhaust
17. Camshaft Position (CMP)
    Actuator Solenoid - Intake

22116_SOLS_G0147

Fig. 120 2.0L (LNF) Engine components top left side view

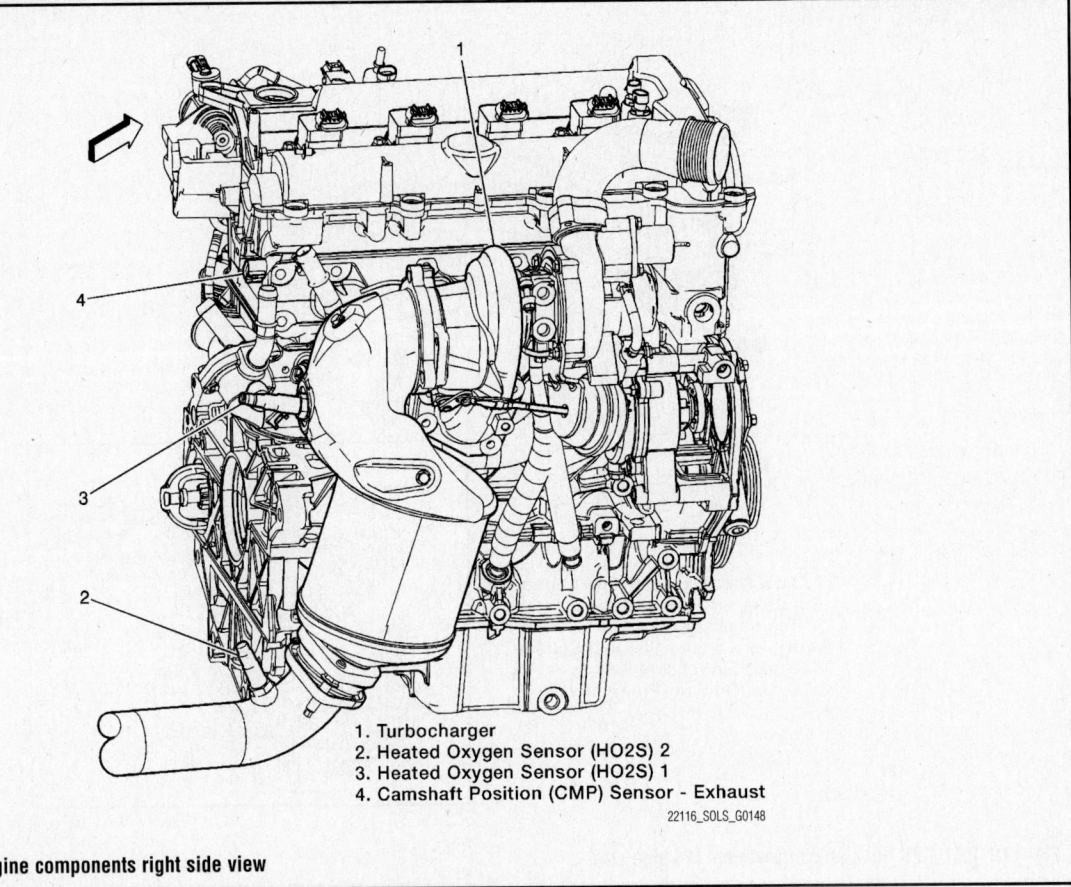

1. Turbocharger
2. Heated Oxygen Sensor (HO2S) 2
3. Heated Oxygen Sensor (HO2S) 1
4. Camshaft Position (CMP) Sensor - Exhaust

22116_SOLS_G0148

Fig. 121 2.0L (LNF) Engine components right side view

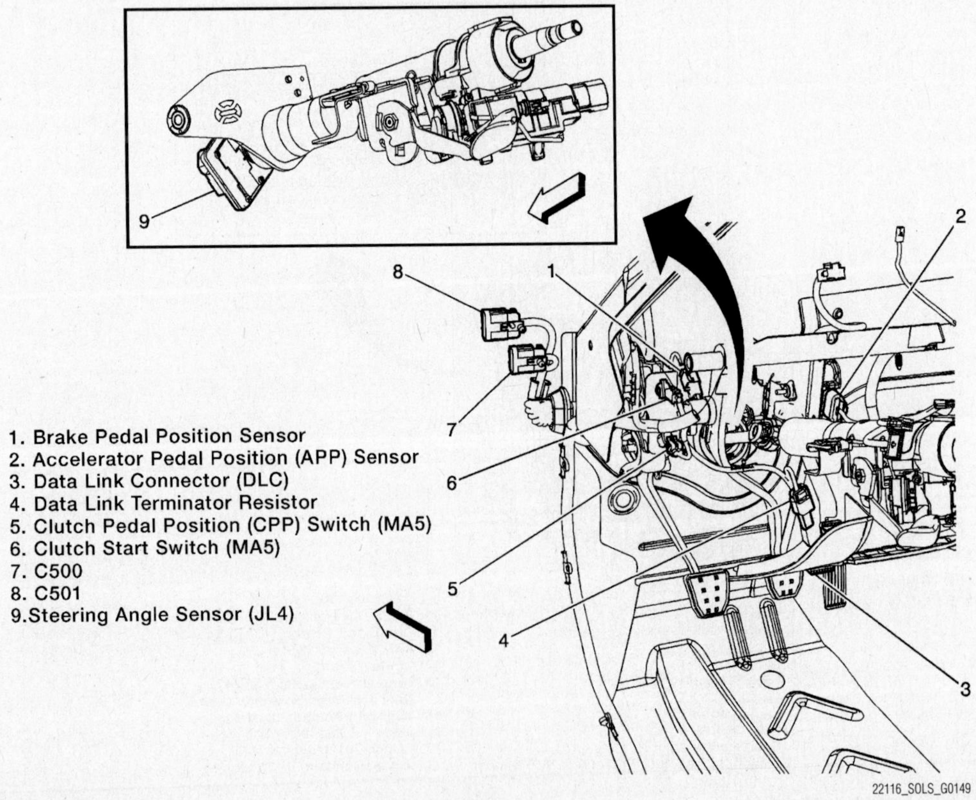

1. Brake Pedal Position Sensor
2. Accelerator Pedal Position (APP) Sensor
3. Data Link Connector (DLC)
4. Data Link Terminator Resistor
5. Clutch Pedal Position (CPP) Switch (MA5)
6. Clutch Start Switch (MA5)
7. C500
8. C501
9. Steering Angle Sensor (JL4)

22116_SOLS_G0149

Fig. 122 Lower left side of instrument panel

REMOVAL & INSTALLATION

See Figure 123.

1. Remove the knee bolster.
2. Disconnect the Accelerator Pedal Position (APP) sensor electrical connector.
3. Remove the APP sensor nuts.
4. Remove the APP sensor from the vehicle.

To install:

5. Install the APP sensor to the vehicle.
6. Install the APP sensor nuts and tighten to 89 inch lbs. (10 Nm).
7. Connect the APP sensor electrical connector.
8. Confirm that the APP sensor connector locking clip is fully secured.
9. Verify the operation of the accelerator pedal.
10. Install the knee bolster.

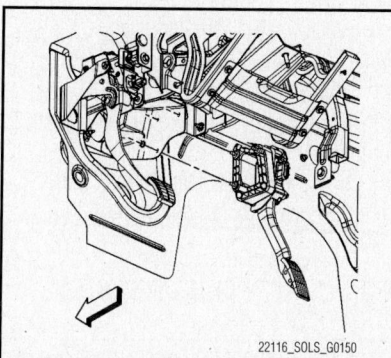

Fig. 123 Accelerator Pedal Position (APP) sensor

TESTING

See Figure 124.

1. Disconnect the Accelerator Pedal Position (APP) electrical connector.
2. With digital multimeter check pin C for 5 volt reference signal.
3. With digital multimeter check pin F for 5 volt reference signal.

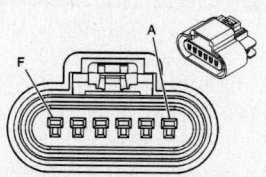

(A) Low Reference
(B) APP Sensor 2 Signal
(C) 5-Volt Reference 1
(D) Low Reference
(E) APP Sensor 1 Signal
(F) 5-Volt Reference 2

22116_SOLS_G0151

Fig. 124 Accelerator Pedal Position (APP) Sensor electrical connector

4. If 5 volt reference signal is not present, repair circuit in question.

CAMSHAFT POSITION (CMP) SENSOR

LOCATION

There are two Camshaft Position Sensors (CMP). They are located to the rear of the engine cylinder head. The exhaust (CMP) sensor is located just below the canister purge valve and the intake sensor is on opposite side of cylinder head.

OPERATION

The Camshaft Position Sensors (CMP) sensors are triggered by a notched reluctor wheels built onto the intake and the exhaust camshaft sprockets. Both of the CMP sensors provide four signal pulses every camshaft revolution. Each notch, or feature of the reluctor wheel is of a different size which is used to identify the compression stroke of each cylinder and to enable sequential fuel injection. Both of the CMP sensors are connected to the ECM by the following circuits:

- A 5-volt reference circuit
- A low reference circuit
- A signal circuit

REMOVAL & INSTALLATION

2.4L (LE5) & 2.0L (LNF) Engine Intake Sensor

1. Disconnect the intake Camshaft Position (CMP) sensor electrical connector.
2. Remove the CMP sensor bolt.
3. Remove the CMP sensor.

To install:

➡**Inspect the CMP sensor for damage, replace as necessary.**

4. Lubricate the CMP sensor O-ring seal with clean engine oil.
5. Install the CMP sensor.
6. Install the CMP sensor bolt and tighten to 89 inch. lbs. (10 Nm).

2.4L (LE5) & 2.0L (LNF) Engine Exhaust Sensor

1. Disconnect the exhaust Camshaft Position (CMP) sensor electrical connector.
2. Remove the CMP sensor bolt.
3. Remove the CMP sensor.

To install:

➡**Inspect the CMP sensor for damage, replace as necessary.**

4. Lubricate the CMP sensor O-ring seal with clean engine oil.

5. Install the CMP sensor.
6. Install the CMP sensor bolt and tighten to 89 inch. lbs. (10 Nm).

TESTING

See Figures 125 and 126.

1. Ignition OFF, disconnect the affected Camshaft Position (CMP) sensor connector.
2. Test for less than 1 ohm of resistance between Electronic Control Module (ECM) side of the low reference circuit and ground.
   a. If greater than the specified value, test the low reference circuit for an open/high resistance. If the circuit tests normal, replace the ECM.
3. Ignition ON, test for 4.8–5.2 volts between the ECM side of the 5 volt reference circuit and ground.
   a. If less than the specified range, test the 5 volt reference circuit for an open/high resistance or short to ground. If the circuit tests normal, replace the ECM.
   b. If greater than the specified range, test the 5 volt reference circuit for a short to voltage. If the circuit tests normal, replace the ECM.
4. Ignition ON, test for 4.8–5.2 volts between the signal circuit and ground.
   a. If less than the specified range, test the affected signal circuit for an open/high resistance or short to ground. If the circuit tests normal, replace the ECM.
   b. If greater than the specified range, test the affected signal circuit for a short to voltage. If the circuit tests normal, replace the ECM.
5. Ignition ON, using a jumper wire connected to ground, momentarily touch the CMP sensor signal circuit repeatedly. The applicable CMP active counter parameter should increment.
   a. If the CMP active counter does not increment, replace the ECM.

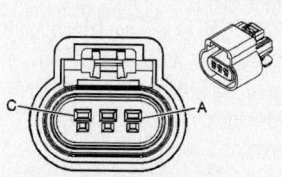

(A) 5-Volt Reference 1
(B) Low Reference
(C) Camshaft Position Exhaust Sensor Signal

22116_SOLS_G0152

Fig. 125 Camshaft exhaust position sensor electrical connector 2.4L (LE5) & 2.0L (LNF) Engines

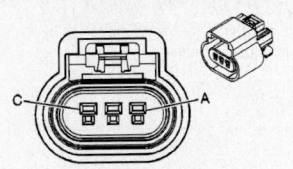

(A) 5-Volt Reference 1
(B) Low Reference
(C) Camshaft Position
Intake Sensor Signal

22116_SOLS_G0153

Fig. 126 Camshaft intake position sensor electrical connector 2.4L (LE5) & 2.0L (LNF) Engines

6. If the circuits test normal, replace the CMP sensor.

CRANKSHAFT POSITION (CKP) SENSOR

LOCATION

The 2.4L (LE5) and 2.0L (LNF) engine Crankshaft Position (CKP) sensor is mounted to the rear of the engine block, and above the starter motor.

OPERATION

The Crankshaft Position (CKP) sensor is connected to the Electronic Control Module (ECM) by the following circuits:

- A 5-volt reference circuit
- A low reference circuit
- A signal circuit

The CKP sensor is an internally magnetic biased digital output integrated circuit sensing device. The sensor detects magnetic flux changes of the teeth and slots of a 58-tooth reluctor wheel on the crankshaft. Each tooth on the reluctor wheel is spaced at 60-tooth spacing, with 2 missing teeth for the reference gap. The CKP sensor produces an ON/OFF DC voltage of varying frequency, with 58 output pulses per crankshaft revolution. The frequency of the CKP sensor output depends on the rotational velocity of the crankshaft. The CKP sensor sends a digital signal, which represents an image of the crankshaft reluctor wheel, to the ECM as each tooth on the wheel rotates past the CKP sensor. The ECM uses each CKP signal pulse to determine crankshaft speed and decodes the crankshaft reluctor wheel reference gap to identify crankshaft position. This information, along with information from the CMP sensors is then used to determine the optimum ignition and fuel injection points of the engine. The ECM also uses CKP sensor output information to determine the camshaft relative position to the crankshaft, to control camshaft phasing, and to detect cylinder misfire.

REMOVAL & INSTALLATION

1. Disconnect the negative battery cable.
2. Disconnect the Crankshaft Position (CKP) sensor electrical connector.
3. Remove the oil level indicator tube.
4. Remove the positive battery cable nut from the starter solenoid.
5. Remove the positive battery cable from the starter solenoid.
6. Remove Starter motor.
7. Remove the CKP sensor bolt
8. Remove the CKP sensor.

To install:

9. Lubricate the CKP sensor O-ring seal with clean engine oil.
10. Install the CKP sensor.
11. Install the CKP sensor bolt and tighten to 89 inch. lbs. (10 Nm).
12. Ensure that the engine harness terminal no. is still installed on the starter solenoid.
13. Install starter motor.
14. Install the positive battery cable to the starter solenoid.
15. Install the positive battery cable nut to the starter solenoid and tighten to 89 inch. lbs. (10 Nm).
16. Connect the CKP sensor electrical connector (3).
17. Install the oil level indicator tube.
18. Connect the negative battery cable.

TESTING

See Figure 127.

1. Disconnect the Crankshaft Position (CKP) sensor connector.
2. Test for less than 1 ohm of resistance between low reference circuit and ground.
   a. If greater than the specified value, test the low reference circuit for an open/high resistance. If the circuit tests normal, replace the Electronic Control Module (ECM).
3. Ignition ON, test for 4.8–5.2 volts between the 5 volt reference circuit and ground.
   a. If less than the specified range, test the 5 volt reference circuit for an open/high resistance or short to ground. If the circuit tests normal, replace the ECM.
   b. If greater than the specified range, test the 5volt reference circuit for a short to voltage. If the circuit tests normal, replace the ECM.
4. Ignition ON, test for 4.8–5.2 volts between the signal circuit and ground.
   a. If less than the specified range, test the signal circuit for an open/high resis-

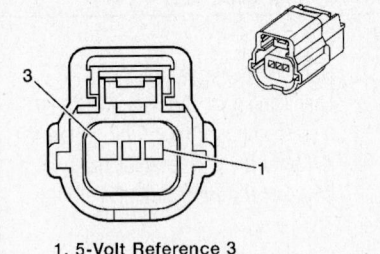

1. 5-Volt Reference 3
2. Low Reference
3. Crankshaft Position Sensor Signal

22116_SOLS_G0154

Fig. 127 Crankshaft sensor electrical connector 2.4L (LE5) & 2.0L (LNF) Engines

tance or short to ground. If the circuit tests normal, replace the ECM.
   b. If greater than the specified range, test the signal circuit for a short to voltage. If the circuit tests normal, replace the ECM.
5. Ignition ON, using a jumper wire connected to ground, momentarily touch the CKP sensor signal circuit repeatedly. The CKP Active Counter parameter should increment
   a. If the CKP Active Counter parameter does not increment, replace the ECM.

CRANKSHAFT POSITION SYSTEM VARIATION LEARN

The Crankshaft Position (CKP) system variation learn procedure is required when the following service procedures have been performed, regardless of whether DTC P0315 is set:

- Engine replacement
- Engine Control Module (ECM) replacement
- Crankshaft damper replacement
- Crankshaft replacement
- CKP sensor replacement
- Any engine repairs which disturb the crankshaft to CKP sensor relationship

The scan tool monitors certain component signals to determine if all the conditions are met to continue with the CKP system variation learn procedure. The scan tool only displays the condition that inhibits the procedure. The scan tool monitors the following components:

- CKP sensor activity—If there is a CKP sensor condition, refer to the applicable DTC that set.
- Camshaft Position (CMP) signal activity—If there is a CMP signal condition, refer to the applicable DTC that set.
- Engine Coolant Temperature (ECT)—If the engine coolant temperature is not warm enough, idle the engine until the engine

coolant temperature reaches the correct temperature.

1. Install a scan tool.

2. Monitor the ECM for DTCs with a scan tool. If other DTCs are set, except DTC P0315, refer to Diagnostic Trouble Code (DTC) List.

3. With a scan tool, select the CKP system variation learn procedure and perform the following:

a. Observe the fuel cut-off for the applicable engine.

b. Block the drive wheels.

c. Set the parking brake.

d. Place the vehicle's transmission in Park or Neutral.

e. Turn the Air Conditioning (A/C) OFF.

f. Cycle the ignition from OFF to ON.

g. Apply and hold the brake pedal for the duration of the procedure.

h. Start and idle the engine.

i. Accelerate to Wide Open Throttle (WOT). The engine should not accelerate beyond the calibrated fuel cut-off RPM value noted in step (A). Release the throttle immediately if the value is exceeded.

➡ **While the learn procedure is in progress, release the throttle immediately when the engine starts to decelerate. The engine control is returned to the operator and the engine responds to throttle position after the learn procedure is complete.**

j. Release the throttle when fuel cut-off occurs.

4. The scan tool displays Learn Status: Learned this Ignition. If the scan tool indicates that DTC P0315 ran and passed, the CKP variation learn procedure is complete. If the scan tool indicates DTC P0315 failed or did not run, refer to DTC P0315. If any other DTCs set, refer to Diagnostic Trouble Code (DTC).

5. Turn OFF the ignition for 30 seconds after the learn procedure is completed successfully.

ELECTRONIC CONTROL MODULE (ECM)

LOCATION

The Electronic Control Module (ECM) is located in the left front fender above windshield washer container.

OPERATION

The Electronic Control Module (ECM) is in the engine compartment. The ECM is the control center of the engine controls system. The ECM controls the following components:

- The fuel injection system
- The ignition system
- The emission control systems
- The on-board diagnostics
- The A/C and fan systems
- The Throttle Actuation Control (TAC) system

The ECM constantly monitors the information from various sensors and other inputs, and controls the systems that affect the vehicle performance and the emissions. The ECM also performs diagnostic tests on various parts of the system. The ECM can recognize operational problems and alert the driver via the MIL. When the ECM detects a malfunction, the ECM stores a DTC. The condition area is identified by the particular DTC that is set. This aids the technician in making repairs.

The engine control module (ECM) can supply 5 volts or 12 volts to the various sensors or switches. This is done through pull-up resistors to the regulated power supplies within the ECM. In some cases, even an ordinary shop voltmeter will not give an accurate reading because the resistance is too low. Therefore, a DMM with at least 10 megaohms input impedance is required in order to ensure accurate voltage readings.

The ECM controls the output circuits by controlling the ground or the power feed circuit through the transistors or a device called an output driver module.

REMOVAL & INSTALLATION

❋❋ **WARNING**

Turn the ignition OFF when installing or removing the control module connectors and disconnecting or reconnecting the power to the control module (battery cable, Powertrain Control Module (PCM) Electronic Control Module (ECM) Transaxle Control Module (TCM) pigtail, control module fuse, jumper cables, etc.) in order to prevent internal control module damage. Control module damage may result when the metal case contacts battery voltage. DO NOT contact the control module metal case with battery voltage when servicing a control module, using battery booster cables, or when charging the vehicle battery.

❋❋ **WARNING**

In order to prevent any possible electrostatic discharge damage to the control module, do not touch the connector pins or the soldered components on the circuit board. Remove any debris from around the control module connector surfaces before servicing the control module. Inspect the control module connector gaskets when diagnosing or replacing the control module. Ensure that the gaskets are installed correctly. The gaskets prevent contaminant intrusion into the control module

➡ **The replacement control module must be programmed.**

1. Using a scan tool, retrieve the percentage of remaining engine oil. Record the remaining engine oil life.

2. Record the preset radio stations.

3. Turn the ignition OFF.

4. Disconnect the negative battery cable.

5. Remove the left front fender.

6. Remove the windshield washer solvent container.

7. Release the Engine Control Module (ECM) bracket upper and lower retaining tabs using a small screwdriver or other suitable tool.

8. Remove the ECM from the bracket by lifting upward after releasing the tabs.

9. Disconnect the engine wiring harness electrical connectors from the ECM.

To install:

10. Connect the engine wiring harness electrical connectors to the ECM.

11. Slide the ECM into the bracket.

12. Push down on the ECM until the upper and lower retaining tabs snap into place.

13. Connect the negative battery cable.

14. Install the windshield washer solvent container.

15. Install the left front fender.

16. Reset the clock and preset radio stations.

17. If a new ECM was installed, the ECM must be programmed.

TESTING

See Figures 128 through 132.

1. Test the voltage and ground circuits to the control module for the following:

- A short
- High resistance
- An open

2. If all circuits test normal, suspect the ECM.

➡ **The replacement control module must be programmed.**

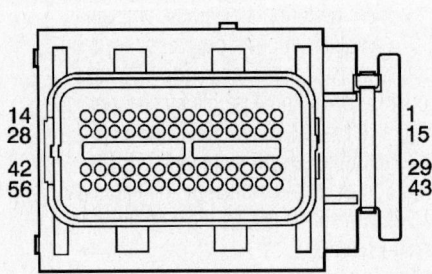

1-5	**13**	**34**	**44**	**53**
--	D-GN/WH	GY	PU	D-GN/WH
--	465	2709	1589	459
Not Used	Fuel Pump Relay Control	5-Volt Reference 1	Fuel Level Sensor Signal	A/C Compressor Clutch Relay Control (C60)
6	**14-17**	**35**	**45-46**	**54**
BN/WH	--	TN	--	D-BU
379	--	1274	--	473
CPP Switch Signal (MA5)	Not Used	5-Volt Reference 1	Not Used	High Speed Cooling Fan Relay Control
7	**18**	**36**	**47**	
L-BU	BN	BN	D-BU	**55**
20	4	1271	1161	WH
Stop Lamp Supply Voltage	Accessory Voltage	Low Reference	APP Sensor 1 Signal	1310
8	**19**	**37**	**48**	EVAP Canister Vent Solenoid Control
--	PK	PU	D-GN	
--	1039	1272	890	**56**
Not Used	Ignition 1 Voltage	Low Reference	Fuel Tank Pressure Sensor Signal	YE
9	**20**	**38-39**		447
TN	RD/WH	--	**49**	Starter Relay Coil Control
2759	840	--	L-BU	
Low Reference	Battery Positive Voltage	Not Used	1162	
10-11	**21-32**	**40**	APP Sensor 2 Signal	
--	--	BN		
--	--	5069	**50-52**	
Not Used	Not Used	Main Relay Control	--	
12	**33**	**41-43**	--	
BN/WH	WH/BK	--	Not Used	
419	1164	--		
MIL Control	5-Volt Reference 2	Not Used		

22116_SOLS_G0155

Fig. 128 2.4L (LE5) Engine Control Module (ECM) C1

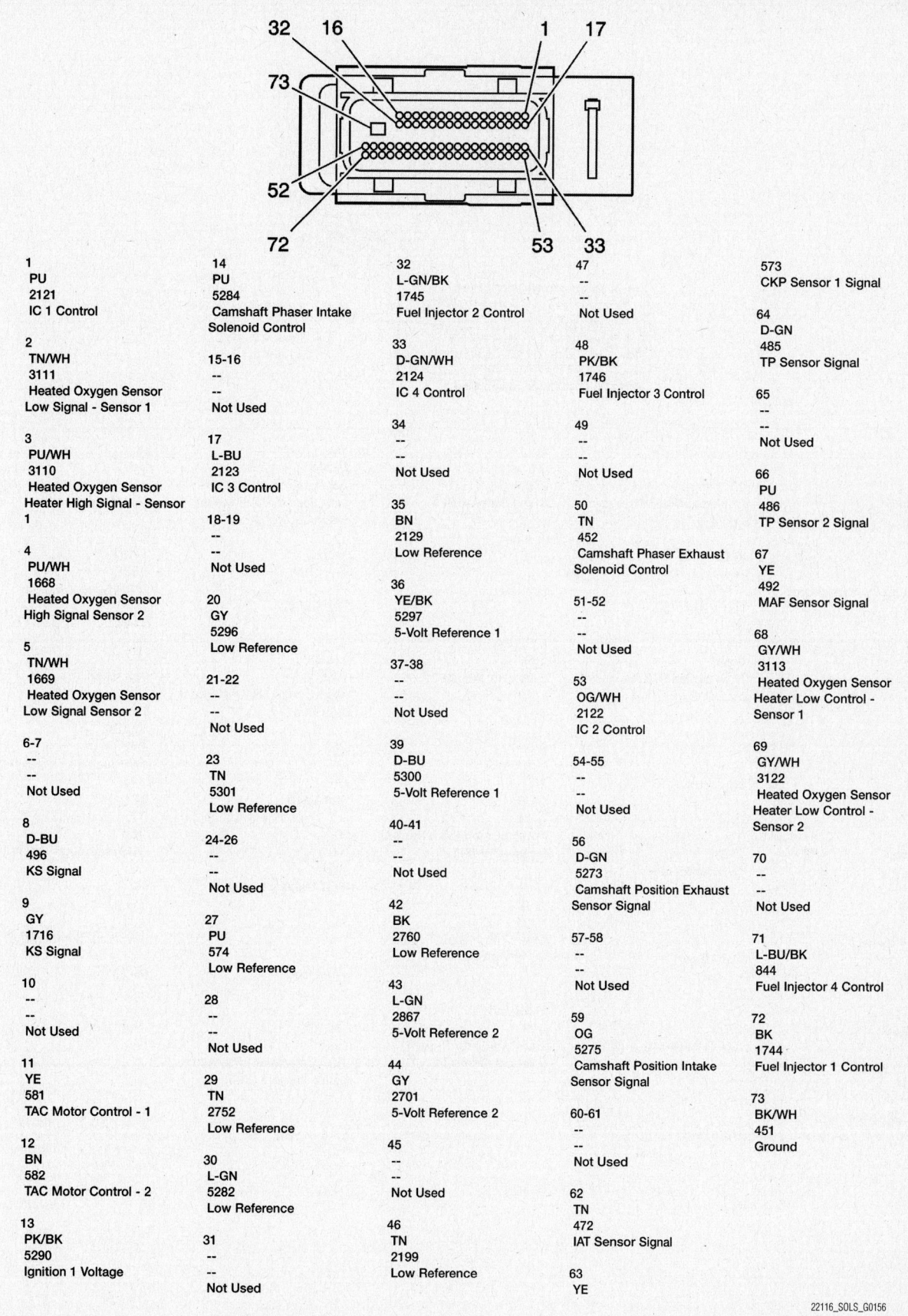

1
PU
2121
IC 1 Control

2
TN/WH
3111
Heated Oxygen Sensor
Low Signal - Sensor 1

3
PU/WH
3110
Heated Oxygen Sensor
Heater High Signal - Sensor
1

4
PU/WH
1668
Heated Oxygen Sensor
High Signal Sensor 2

5
TN/WH
1669
Heated Oxygen Sensor
Low Signal Sensor 2

6-7
--
--
Not Used

8
D-BU
496
KS Signal

9
GY
1716
KS Signal

10
--
--
Not Used

11
YE
581
TAC Motor Control - 1

12
BN
582
TAC Motor Control - 2

13
PK/BK
5290
Ignition 1 Voltage

14
PU
5284
Camshaft Phaser Intake
Solenoid Control

15-16
--
--
Not Used

17
L-BU
2123
IC 3 Control

18-19
--
--
Not Used

20
GY
5296
Low Reference

21-22
--
--
Not Used

23
TN
5301
Low Reference

24-26
--
--
Not Used

27
PU
574
Low Reference

28
--
--
Not Used

29
TN
2752
Low Reference

30
L-GN
5282
Low Reference

31
--
--
Not Used

32
L-GN/BK
1745
Fuel Injector 2 Control

33
D-GN/WH
2124
IC 4 Control

34
--
--
Not Used

35
BN
2129
Low Reference

36
YE/BK
5297
5-Volt Reference 1

37-38
--
--
Not Used

39
D-BU
5300
5-Volt Reference 1

40-41
--
--
Not Used

42
BK
2760
Low Reference

43
L-GN
2867
5-Volt Reference 2

44
GY
2701
5-Volt Reference 2

45
--
--
Not Used

46
TN
2199
Low Reference

47
--
--
Not Used

48
PK/BK
1746
Fuel Injector 3 Control

49
--
--
Not Used

50
TN
452
Camshaft Phaser Exhaust
Solenoid Control

51-52
--
--
Not Used

53
OG/WH
2122
IC 2 Control

54-55
--
--
Not Used

56
D-GN
5273
Camshaft Position Exhaust
Sensor Signal

57-58
--
--
Not Used

59
OG
5275
Camshaft Position Intake
Sensor Signal

60-61
--
--
Not Used

62
TN
472
IAT Sensor Signal

63
YE

573
CKP Sensor 1 Signal

64
D-GN
485
TP Sensor Signal

65
--
--
Not Used

66
PU
486
TP Sensor 2 Signal

67
YE
492
MAF Sensor Signal

68
GY/WH
3113
Heated Oxygen Sensor
Heater Low Control -
Sensor 1

69
GY/WH
3122
Heated Oxygen Sensor
Heater Low Control -
Sensor 2

70
--
--
Not Used

71
L-BU/BK
844
Fuel Injector 4 Control

72
BK
1744
Fuel Injector 1 Control

73
BK/WH
451
Ground

22116_SOLS_G0156

Fig. 129 2.4L (LE5) Engine Control Module (ECM) C2

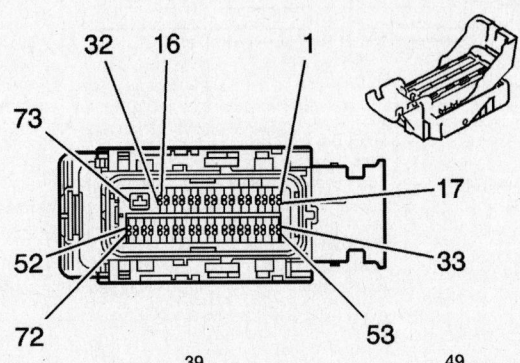

1-6
--
--
Not Used

7
OG
225
Generator Turn On Signal

8-20
--
--
Not Used

21
BK/WH
2751
Low Reference (C60)

22
--
--
Not Used

23
OG/BK
469
Low Reference

24-27
--
--
Not Used

28
TN/WH
1704
Low Reference

29
GY
23
Generator Field Duty Cycle
Signal

30-32
--
--
Not Used

33
TN
2501
High Speed GMLAN Serial
Data Bus (-)

34
--
--
Not Used

35
TN
2761
Low Reference

36
--
--
Not Used

37
GY
2700
5-Volt Reference 1 (C60)

38
--
--
Not Used

39
GY
2704
5-Volt Reference 1

40-43
--
--
Not Used

44
L-BU/BK
1688
5-Volt Reference 2

45
--
--
Not Used

46
OG/BK
1786
Transmission Park/Neutral
Signal (1) (M82)

47
D-GN
1433
PNP/Clutch Start Switch
Signal (MA5)

48
D-GN/WH
428
EVAP Canister Purge
Solenoid Control

49
D-GN
335
Low Speed Cooling Fan
Relay Control

50-52
--
--
Not Used

53
TN/BK
2500
High Speed GMLAN Serial
Data Bus (+)

54
--
--
Not Used

55
YE
410
ECT Sensor Signal

56
--
--
Not Used

57
OG/BK
380
A/C Refrigerant Pressure
Sensor Signal (C60)

58
--
--
Not Used

59
L-GN
432
MAP Sensor Signal

60-64
--
--
Not Used

65
TN/BK
231
Oil Pressure Switch Signal

66
YE
400
VSS High Signal (MA5)

67
PU
401
VSS Low Signal (MA5)

68-73
--
--
Not Used

22116_SOLS_G0157

Fig. 130 2.4L (LE5) Engine Control Module (ECM) C3

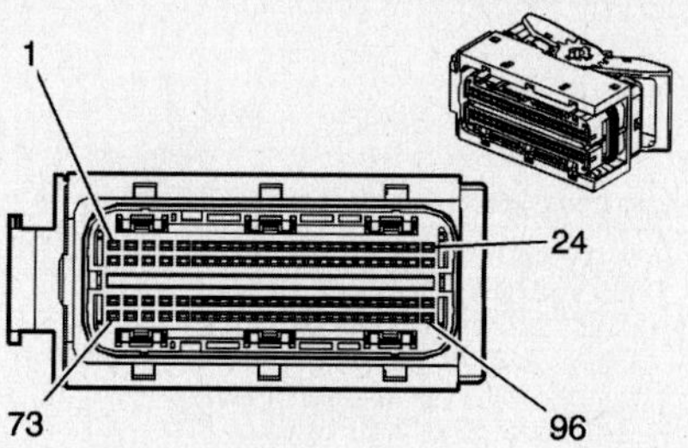

1	24	41	59	81
L-GN	YE	TN	D-BU	--
5282	581	552	496	--
Camshaft Phaser Exhaust Solenoid Control	TAC Motor Control - 1	Low Reference	KS 1 Signal	Not Used
	25	42	60	82
2	--	TN	GY	YE
PU	--	808	2303	410
5284	Not Used	Low Reference	KS 2 Signal	ECT Sensor Signal
Camshaft Phaser Intake Soleniod Control	26	43	61-63	
	L-BU	--	--	83
3-4	4804	--	--	GY
--	Direct Fuel Injector (DFI) High Voltage Control Cylinder 4	Not Used	Not Used	1716
--				KS 1 Signal
Not Used		44	64	
	27	TN	TN	84
5	L-BU/WH	2761	407	L-BU
YE	4904	Low Reference	Low Reference	1876
7301	Direct Fuel Injector (DFI) High Voltage Supply Cylinder 4			KS 2 Signal
High Pressure Fuel Pump Actuator High Control		45	65	
		GY	--	85
6	28	605	--	--
D-GN/WH	D-BU	5-Volt Reference 3	Not Used	--
428	4802			Not Used
EVAP Canister Purge Solenoid Control	Direct Fuel Injector (DFI) High Voltage Control Cylinder 2	46	66	86
		TN	PU	L-BU
7		452	7330	7329
OG	29	Low Reference	Pre-Throttle Air Temp and Press (TMAP) Air Pressure Signal	Pre-Throttle Air Temp and Press (TMAP) Temperature Signal
5275	D-BU/WH			
Camshaft Position Intake Sensor Signal	4902	47		
	Direct Fuel Injector (DFI) High Voltage Supply Cylinder 2	--	67	87
8-9		--	TN/WH	--
--		Not Used	3111	--
--	30		Heated Oxygen Sensor Low Signal Sensor 1	Not Used
Not Used	GY	48		
	23	BN	68	88
10	Generator Field Duty Cycle Signal	582	WH	TN
OG		TAC Motor Control - 2	5279	2752
225			Heated Oxygen Sensor Pump Current Sensor 1	Low Reference
Generator Turn On Signal	31-33	49-50		
	--	--		89
11-12	--	--	69-72	PU
--	Not Used	Not Used	--	486
--			--	TP Sensor 2 Signal
Not Used	34	51	Not Used	
	D-GN	BN		90
13	5273	4801	73	D-GN
BN/WH	Camshaft Position Exhaust Sensor Signal	Direct Fuel Injector (DFI) High Voltage Control Cylinder 1	PU	485
2130			7300	TP Sensor 1 Signal
Low Reference			High Pressure Fuel Pump Actuator Low Control	
	35	52		91
14	YE	D-GN		L-GN
--	573	4803	74	5278
--	CKP Sensor Signal	Direct Fuel Injector (DFI) High Voltage Control Cylinder 3	--	Heated Oxygen Sensor Input Pump Current Sensor 1
Not Used			--	
	36	53	Not Used	
15	YE	D-GN/WH		92
GY	2918	4903	75	PU/WH
705	FRP Sensor Signal	Direct Fuel Injector (DFI) High Voltage Supply Cylinder 3	BN/WH	3110
5-Volt Reference 2			4901	Heated Oxygen Sensor High Signal Sensor 1
	37		Direct Fuel Injector (DFI) High Voltage Supply Cyl 1	
16	L-GN	54		93-94
D-GN	432	BN/WH	76-77	--
6391	MAP Sensor Signal	419	--	--
Turbo Bypass Valve Control		MIL Control	--	Not Used
	38		Not Used	
17	GY	55		95
TN/BK	598	PU	78	GY
231	5-Volt Reference 1	2121	BN	597
Oil Pressure Switch Signal		IC 1 Control	2129	5-Volt Reference 1
	39		Low Reference	
18	GY	56		96
YE	2701	D-GN/WH	79	GY/WH
258	5-Volt Reference 3	2124	L-BU	3113
Wastegate Solenoid Control		IC 4 Control	2123	Heated Oxygen Sensor Heater Low Control Sensor 1
	40		IC 3 Control	
19-23	--	57-58		
--	--	--	80	
--	Not Used	--	OG/WH	
Not Used		Not Used	2122	
			IC 2 Control	

22116_SOLS_G0158

Fig. 131 2.0L (LNF) Engine Control Module (ECM) C1

1
BK/WH
451
Ground

2
BK/WH
451
Ground

3
PK/BK
5290
Ignition 1 Voltage

4
BK/WH
451
Ground

5
PK/BK
5290
Ignition 1 Voltage

6
PK/BK
5290
Ignition 1 Voltage

7
GY/WH
3122
Heated Oxygen Sensor
Heater Low Control Sensor
2

8
--
--
Not Used

9
TN
2759
Low Reference

10
D-GN/WH
465
Fuel Pump Relay Control

11
TN
5514
A/C Refrigerant Pressure
Sensor Low Reference (C60)

12
YE
447
Starter Relay Coil Control

13
YE
492
MAF Sensor Signal

14
GY
2709
5-Volt Reference 1

15
D-BU
1161
APP Sensor 1 Signal

16
BN/WH
379
CPP Switch Signal (MA5)

17
OG/BK
1786
Transmission Park/Neutral
Signal (M82)

18
L-GN
24
Backup Lamp Supply
Voltage (M82)

19
WH
1310
EVAP Canister Vent
Solenoid Control

20
BN
7448
Vacuum Assist Pump Relay
Coil Control

21
--
--
Not Used

22
TN
2760
Low Reference

23
TN/WH
3121
Heated Oxygen Sensor
Low Signal Sensor 2

24
--
--
Not Used

25
L-BU
1162
APP Sensor 2 Signal

26
--
--
Not Used

27
D-GN
890
Fuel Tank Pressure Sensor
Signal

28
--
--
Not Used

29
D-BU
1809
Brake Booster Vacuum
Sensor Signal

30
--
--
Not Used

31
D-BU
6306
Clutch Start Neutral Start
Signal (MA5)

32-33
--
--
Not Used

34
BN
1271
Low Reference

35
GY
2700
5-Volt Reference 3 (C60)

36
PU
1589
Fuel Level Sensor Signal

37
--
--
Not Used

38
PU
3120
Heated Oxygen Sensor
High Signal Sensor 2

39
OG/BK
380
A/C Refrigerant Pressure
Sensor Signal (C60)

40
PU
401
OSS Low Signal (MA5)

41
BN
4
Accessory Voltage

42
TN/BK
2500
High Speed GMLAN Serial
Data Bus (+)

43
--
--
Not Used

44
D-GN/WH
459
A/C Compressor Clutch
Relay Control (C60)

45
--
--
Not Used

46
WH
2368
Cooling Fan Speed Control

47
PU
1272
Low Reference

48
TN
1274
5-Volt Reference 3

49
WH/BK
1164
5-Volt Reference 2

50
L-BU
6289
Induction Air Temperature
Sensor Signal

51
--
--
Not Used

52
L-BU
20
Stop Lamp Supply Voltage
(M82)

53
YE
400
OSS High Signal (MA5)

54
PK
1039
Ignition 1 Voltage

55
TN
2501
High Speed GMLAN Serial
Data BUS (-)

56
RD/WH
840
Battery Positive Voltage

57
--
--
Not Used

58
YE
5991
Powertrain Relay Coil
Control

22116_SOLS_G0159

Fig. 132 2.0L (LNF) Engine Control Module (ECM) C2

ENGINE COOLANT TEMPERATURE (ECT) SENSOR

LOCATION

2.4L (LE5) Engine

The Engine Coolant Temperature (ECT) sensor is located to the rear of engine just below the Camshaft Position (CMP) sensor.

2.0L (LNF) Engine

The Engine Coolant Temperature (ECT) sensor is located to the rear of engine and behind the turbocharger. It is mounted between two coolant pipes next to the thermostat housing.

OPERATION

The Engine Control Module (ECM) supplies a 5 volt signal to the engine coolant temperature sensor through a resistor in the ECM and measures the voltage. The voltage will be high when the engine is cold, and low when the engine is hot. By measuring the voltage, the ECM calculates the engine coolant temperature. Engine coolant temperature affects most systems the ECM controls.

REMOVAL & INSTALLATION

2.4L (LE5) & 2.0L (LNF) Engines

1. Partially drain the cooling system.
2. Disconnect the engine wiring harness electrical connector from the Engine Coolant Temperature (ECT) sensor.
3. Remove the ECT.

To install:

4. Install the ECT.
5. Tighten the ECT sensor to (15 ft. lbs. (20 Nm).
6. Connect the engine wiring harness electrical connector to the ECT sensor.
7. Fill and bleed the cooling system as needed.

TESTING

See Figures 133 and 134.

1. Ignition OFF, disconnect the harness connector at the ECT sensor.
2. Ignition OFF for 90 seconds, test for less than 5 ohms of resistance between the low reference circuit terminal no. A and ground.

  a. If greater than the specified range, test the low reference circuit for an open/high resistance. If the circuit tests normal, replace the Electronic Control Module (ECM).

3. Ignition ON, verify the scan tool ECT parameter is less than -39°C (-38°F).

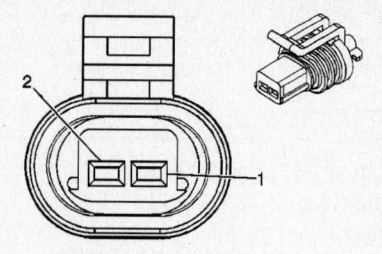

1. TN
2761
Low Reference

2. YE
410
ECT Sensor Signal

22116_SOLS_G0160

Fig. 133 2.4L (LE5) & 2.0L (LNF) Engine Coolant Temperature (ECT) sensor

  a. If greater than the specified range, test the signal circuit terminal no. B or 2 for a short to ground. If the circuit tests normal, replace the ECM.

4. Install a 3-amp fused jumper wire between the signal circuit terminal no. B or 2 and the low reference circuit terminal no. A or 1. Verify the scan tool ECT parameter is greater than 149°C (300°F).

5. If less than the specified range, test the signal circuit for a short to voltage or an open/high resistance. If the circuit tests normal, replace the ECM.

6. If all circuits test normal, test or replace the ECT sensor.

7. Measure and record the resistance of the ECT sensor at various ambient temperatures, then compare those measurements to the temperature versus resistance table.

HEATED OXYGEN (HO2S) SENSOR

LOCATION

2.4L (LE5) Engine

The front (1) Heated Oxygen Sensors (HO2S) is mounted in the exhaust manifold and before the catalytic converter.

The rear (2) Heated Oxygen Sensors (HO2S) in mounted in the front exhaust pipe and after the catalytic converter.

2.0L (LNF) Engine

The front (1) Heated Oxygen Sensors (HO2S) is mounted in the exhaust manifold

Temperature Versus Resistance

°C	°F	OHMS
		Temperature vs Resistance Values (Approximate)
150	302	47
140	284	60
130	266	77
120	248	100
110	230	132
100	212	177
90	194	241
80	176	332
70	158	467
60	140	667
50	122	973
45	113	1188
40	104	1459
35	95	1802
30	86	2238
25	77	2796
20	68	3520
15	59	4450
10	50	5670
5	41	7280
0	32	9420
-5	23	12300
-10	14	16180
-15	5	21450
-20	-4	28680
-30	-22	52700
-40	-40	100700

22116_SOLS_G0161

Fig. 134 Temperature versus resistance table

after the turbocharger and before the catalytic converter.

The rear (2) Heated Oxygen Sensors (HO2S) in mounted in the front exhaust pipe and after the catalytic converter

OPERATION

Heated Oxygen Sensors (HO2S) are used for fuel control and post catalyst monitoring. Each HO2S compares the oxygen content of the surrounding air with the oxygen content in the exhaust stream. The HO2S must reach operating temperature to provide an accurate voltage signal. Heating elements inside the HO2S minimize the time required for the sensors to reach operating temperature. The Engine Control Module (ECM) supplies the HO2S with a reference, or bias, voltage of about 450 mV. When the engine is first started, the ECM operates in Open Loop, ignoring the HO2S voltage signal. Once the HO2S reaches operating temperature and Closed Loop is achieved, the HO2S generates a voltage within a range of 0–1,000 mV that fluctuates above and below bias voltage. High HO2S voltage indicates a rich exhaust stream. Low HO2S voltage indicates a lean exhaust stream.

The wide band heated oxygen sensor (HO2S) measures the amount of oxygen in the exhaust stream more quickly and accurately than the switching style HO2S. The wide band sensor consists of an oxygen sensing cell, an oxygen pumping cell, and a heater. The exhaust gas sample passes through a diffusion gap between the sensing cell and the pumping cell. The engine control module (ECM) supplies a signal voltage to the HO2S and uses this voltage as a reference to the amount of oxygen in the exhaust system. An electronic circuit within the ECM controls the pump current through the oxygen pumping cell in order to maintain a constant signal voltage. The ECM monitors the voltage variation on the signal circuit and attempts to keep the voltage constant by increasing or decreasing the amount of current flow or reversing the direction of the current flow to the pumping cell. By measuring the direction and amount of current required to maintain the signal voltage, the ECM can determine the concentration of oxygen in the exhaust. The signal voltage is displayed as a lambda value. A lambda value of 1 is equal to a stoichiometric air fuel ratio of 14.7:1. Under normal operating conditions, the lambda value will remain around 1. When the system is lean, the oxygen level will be high and the lambda value will be high, or more than 1. When the system is rich, the oxygen level is low and the lambda value will be low, or less than 1. The ECM uses this information to maintain the proper air/fuel ratio.

REMOVAL & INSTALLATION

2.4L (LE5) Engine Front (1) and Rear (2)

See Figure 135.

> **❈❈ WARNING**
>
> **The oxygen sensor uses a permanently attached pigtail and connector. Do not remove the pigtail from the oxygen sensor. Damage to or removal of the pigtail connector could affect proper operation of the oxygen sensor. The use of excessive force may damage the threads in the exhaust manifold/pipe.**

➡ The Heated Oxygen Sensors (HO2S) may be difficult to remove when the engine temperature is less than 48°C (120°F).

1. Open the hood.
2. Remove the Connector Position Assurance (CPA) retainer.
3. Disconnect the HO2S electrical connector.
4. Remove the HO2S electrical connector clip from the junction block bracket.
5. Raise and support the vehicle for removal of the rear HO2S only.
6. Using an approved oxygen sensor wrench remove the HO2S.

To install:

➡ A special anti-seize compound is used on the HO2S threads. The compound consists of a liquid graphite and glass beads. The graphite will burn away, but the glass beads will remain, making the sensor easier to remove. New or service sensors will have the

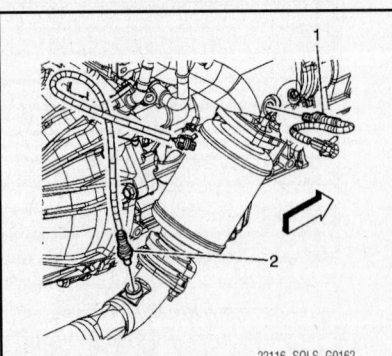

Fig. 135 Front (1) and Rear (2) Heated Oxygen Sensors

22116_SOLS_G0162

compound applied to the threads. If a sensor is removed and is to be reinstalled, the threads must have an anti-seize compound applied before installation.

7. If reinstalling the old HO2S, coat the threads with anti-seize compound.
8. Using an approved oxygen sensor wrench install the HO2S.
9. Tighten the HO2S to 30 ft. lbs. (41 Nm).
10. Lower vehicle if rear HO2S was installed.
11. Connect the HO2S electrical connector.
12. Install the CPA retainer.
13. Close the hood.

2.0L (LNF) Engine Front (1) and Rear (2)

See Figures 136 and 137.

> **❈❈ WARNING**
>
> **The oxygen sensor uses a permanently attached pigtail and connector. Do not remove the pigtail from the oxygen sensor. Damage to or removal of the pigtail connector could affect proper operation of the oxygen sensor. The use of excessive force may damage the threads in the exhaust manifold/pipe.**

➡ The Heated Oxygen Sensors (HO2S) may be difficult to remove when the engine temperature is less than 48°C (120°F).

1. Open the hood.
2. Remove the Connector Position Assurance (CPA) retainer.
3. Disconnect the HO2S electrical connector from the engine wiring harness electrical connector.
4. Raise and support the vehicle for removal of the rear HO2S only.
5. Using an approved oxygen sensor wrench remove the HO2S.

To install:

➡ A special anti-seize compound is used on the HO2S threads. The compound consists of a liquid graphite and glass beads. The graphite will burn away, but the glass beads will remain, making the sensor easier to remove. New or service sensors will have the compound applied to the threads. If a sensor is removed and is to be reinstalled, the threads must have an anti-seize compound applied before installation.

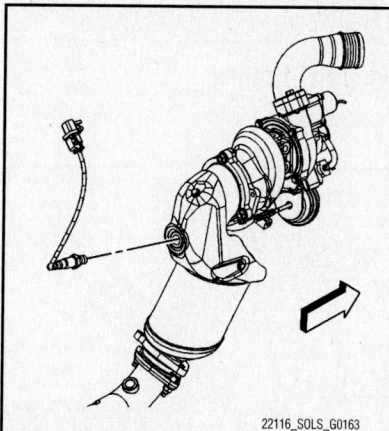

Fig. 136 Front (1) Heated Oxygen Sensors 2.0L (LNF) Engine

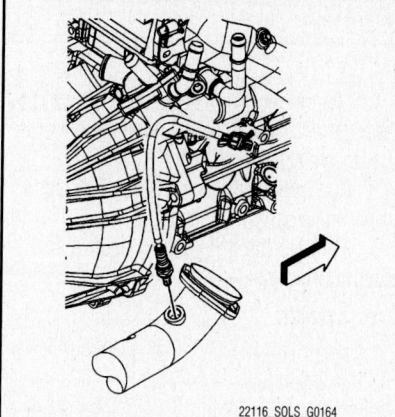

Fig. 137 Rear (2) Heated Oxygen Sensors 2.0L (LNF) Engine

6. If reinstalling the old HO2S, coat the threads with anti-seize compound.

7. Using an approved oxygen sensor wrench install the HO2S.

8. Tighten the HO2S to 31 ft. lbs. (42 Nm).

9. Lower vehicle if rear HO2S was installed.

10. Connect the HO2S electrical connector.

11. Install the CPA retainer.

12. Close the hood.

TESTING

Front (1) HO2S

See Figure 138.

1. Ignition OFF, disconnect the HO2S 1.

2. Ignition ON, test for 2.9 volts between the HO2S 1 High Signal circuit terminal no. 6 and ground.

   a. If more than the specified value, test the circuit for a short to voltage. If the circuit tests normal, replace the Electronic Control Module (ECM).

b. If less than the specified value, test the circuit for an open/high resistance or a short to ground. If the circuit tests normal, replace the ECM.

3. Ignition ON, test for 2.5 volts between the HO2S 1 low signal circuit terminal no. 2 and ground

   a. If more than the specified value, test the circuit for a short to voltage. If the circuit tests normal, replace the ECM.

   b. If less than the specified value, test the circuit for an open/high resistance or a short to ground. If the circuit tests normal, replace the ECM.

4. Ignition ON, test for 2.8 volts between the HO2S 1 Output Pump Current circuit terminal no. 1 and ground.

   a. If more than the specified value, test the circuit for a short to voltage. If the circuit tests normal, replace the ECM.

   b. If less than the specified value, test the circuit for an open/high resistance or a short to ground. If the circuit tests normal, replace the ECM.

5. Ignition ON, test for 2.8 volts between the HO2S 1 Input Pump Current circuit terminal no. 5 and ground.

   a. If more than the specified value, test the circuit for a short to voltage. If the circuit tests normal, replace the ECM.

   b. If less than the specified value, test the circuit for an open/high resistance or a short to ground. If the circuit tests normal, replace the ECM.

6. Ignition OFF, disconnect the ECM connector C1.

7. Ignition OFF, test for infinite ohms between each HO2S 1 circuit terminal no. and all other HO2S 1 circuit terminals.

   a. If less than the specified value, repair as necessary.

8. If the ECM and all circuits test normal, replace the HO2S 1.

Rear (2) HO2S

See Figure 139.

1. If present clear the DTCs with a scan tool.

2. Operate the vehicle within the conditions for running and setting the DTC. The DTC should not set.

➡**All modules must be powered down or misdiagnosis may result.**

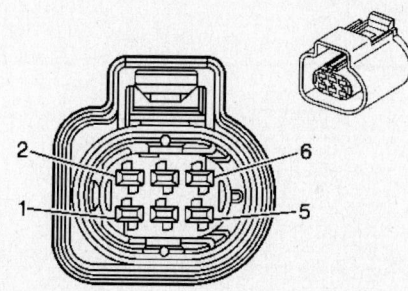

1. WH
5279
Heated Oxygen Sensor Pump Current - Sensor 1

2. TN/WH
3111
Heated Oxygen Sensor Low Signal - Sensor 1

3. GY/WH
3113
Heated Oxygen Sensor Heater Low Control - Sensor 1

4. PK/BK
5291
Ignition 1 Voltage

5. L-GN
5278
Heated Oxygen Sensor Input Pump Current - Sensor 1

6. PU/WH
3110
Heated Oxygen Sensor High Signal - Sensor 1

Fig. 138 Front HO2S (1) Electrical connector

3. Ignition OFF, disconnect the scan tool and wait 60 seconds to ensure all modules are powered down.

4. Ignition OFF, disconnect the harness connector at the HO2S 2.

5. Ignition OFF, measure for less than 5 ohms resistance between the HO2S 2 low signal circuit terminal no. A and ground.

   a. If more than the specified range, test the HO2S 2 low signal circuit for an open/high resistance. If the circuit tests normal, replace the Electronic Control Module (ECM).

6. Ignition ON, verify the scan tool HO2S 2 parameter is approximately 450 mV.

   a. If more than the specified value, test the HO2S 2 high signal circuit for a short to voltage. If the circuit tests normal, replace the ECM.

   b. If less than the specified value, test the HO2S 2 high signal circuit for a short to ground. If the circuit tests normal, replace the ECM.

7. Ignition ON, install a 3A fused jumper wire at the HO2S 2 high signal circuit terminal no. B. Toggle the jumper wire between the HO2S 2 low signal circuit terminal no. A and battery voltage. Verify the scan tool HO2S 2 parameter toggles between 0 mV and approximately 1,000 mV.

8. If the scan tool HO2S 2 parameter does not toggle correctly, test the HO2S 2 high signal circuit for an open/high resistance. If the circuits test normal, replace the ECM.

9. If all circuits test normal, replace the HO2S 2.

INTAKE AIR TEMPERATURE (IAT) SENSOR

LOCATION

2.0L (LNF) Engine

The intake air temperature and pressure sensor is mounted to the fresh air tube before the throttle body.

OPERATION

2.0L (LNF) Engine

The Intake Air Temperature (IAT) sensor 2 is integrated with the boost pressure sensor. The IAT sensor 2 is a variable resistor that measures the temperature of the air after the turbocharger and the charge air cooler, and before it enters the engine intake manifold. The Engine Control Module (ECM) supplies 5 volts to the IAT sensor 2 signal circuit and supplies a ground to the low reference circuit.

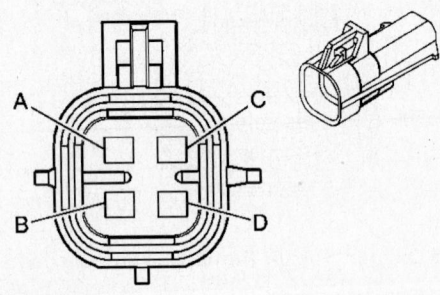

A. TN/WH
3121
Heated Oxygen Sensor Low Signal - Sensor 2

B. PU
3120
Heated Oxygen Sensor High Signal - Sensor 2

C. GY/WH
3122
Heated Oxygen Sensor Heater Low Control - Sensor 2

D. PK/BK
5291
Ignition 1 Voltage

22116_SOLS_G0165

Fig. 139 Rear HO2S (2) Electrical connector

REMOVAL & INSTALLATION

2.0L (LNF) Engine

See Figure 140.

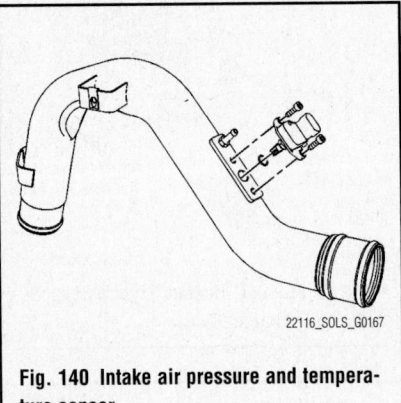

22116_SOLS_G0167

Fig. 140 Intake air pressure and temperature sensor

1. Disconnect the engine wiring harness electrical connector from the intake air pressure and temperature sensor.

2. Remove the intake air pressure and temperature sensor bolts.

3. Remove the intake air pressure and temperature sensor.

To install:

4. Lubricate the intake air pressure and temperature sensor O-ring with clean engine oil.

5. Install the intake air pressure and temperature sensor.

6. Install the intake air pressure and temperature sensor bolts.

7. Tighten the bolts to 80 inch. lbs. (9 Nm).

8. Connect the engine wiring harness electrical connector to the intake air pressure and temperature sensor.

TESTING

2.0L (LNF) Engine

See Figures 141 and 142.

If the ignition has been OFF for 8 hours or greater, the Intake Air Temperature (IAT), the IAT 2 and the Engine Coolant Temperature (ECT) should be within 9°C (16°F) of each other and also the ambient temperature. Ignition ON, observe the scan tool IAT Sensor, IAT 2 Sensor and the ECT Sensor parameters. Compare those sensor parameters to each other and also to the ambient temperature to determine if the condition is current.

Engine running, observe the scan tool IAT Sensor 2 parameter. The reading should be between -39 and +140°C (-38 and +284°F) depending on the current ambient temperature, the vehicle operating conditions, and the engine load.

1. Test the circuit, with ignition OFF, disconnect the IAT sensor 2 harness connector at the boost pressure sensor.

2. Ignition OFF for 90 seconds, test for less than 5 ohms of resistance between the low reference circuit terminal no. A and ground.

   a. If greater than the specified range, test the low reference circuit for an open/high resistance. If the circuit tests normal, Engine Control Module (ECM)

3. Ignition ON, verify the scan tool IAT Sensor 2 parameter is less than -39°C (-38°F).

   a. If greater than the specified range, test the signal circuit for a short to ground. If the circuit tests normal, replace the ECM.

4. Install a 3A fused jumper wire between the signal circuit terminal no. B and ground. Verify the scan tool IAT Sensor 2 parameter is greater than 140°C (284°F).

   a. If less than the specified range, test the signal circuit for a short to voltage or an open/high resistance. If the circuit tests normal replace the ECM.

5. If the circuits test normal, test the IAT sensor 2 by Measuring and recording the resistance of the IAT sensor 2 at various ambient temperatures, then compare those measurements to the Temperature vs. Resistance table.

Temperature Versus Resistance

°C	°F	OHMS
Temperature vs Resistance Values (Approximate)		
150	302	47
140	284	60
130	266	77
120	248	100
110	230	132
100	212	177
90	194	241
80	176	332
70	158	467
60	140	667
50	122	973
45	113	1188
40	104	1459
35	95	1802
30	86	2238
25	77	2796
20	68	3520
15	59	4450
10	50	5670
5	41	7280
0	32	9420
-5	23	12300
-10	14	16180
-15	5	21450
-20	-4	28680
-30	-22	52700
-40	-40	100700

22116_SOLS_G0169

Fig. 142 Temperature versus resistance table

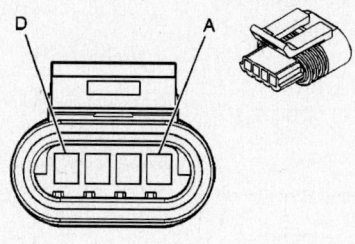

A. TN
407
Low Reference

B. L-BU
7329
Pre-Throttle Air Temp and Press (TMAP) Temperature Signal

C. GY
597
5-Volt Reference 1

D. PU
7330
Pre-Throttle Air Temp and Press (TMAP) Air Pressure Signal

22116_SOLS_G0168

Fig. 141 2.0L (LNF) Engine intake air and pressure sensor electrical connector

KNOCK SENSOR (KS)

LOCATION

2.4L (LE5) Engine

The Knock Sensor (KS) is located at the left rear of the engine block and just before the oil filter housing.

2.0L (LNF) Engine

The 2.0L (LNF) engine uses two Knock Sensors (KS) that are mounted on the left side of the engine block. The sensors are mounted parallel to each other.

OPERATION

The Knock Sensor (KS) system enables the control module to control the ignition timing for the best possible performance while protecting the engine from potentially damaging levels of detonation. The control module uses the KS system to test for abnormal engine noise that may indicate detonation, also known as spark knock.

This KS system uses one or two flat response two-wire sensors. The sensor uses piezo-electric crystal technology that produces an AC voltage signal of varying amplitude and frequency based on the engine vibration or noise level. The amplitude and frequency are dependent upon the level of knock that the KS detects. The control module receives the KS signal through 2 isolated signal circuits.

The control module learns a minimum noise level, or background noise, at idle from the KS and uses calibrated values for the rest of the RPM range. The control module uses the minimum noise level to calculate a noise channel. A normal KS signal will ride within the noise channel. As engine speed and load change, the noise channel upper and lower parameters will change to accommodate the KS signal, keeping the signal within the channel. In order to determine which cylinders are knocking, the control module only uses KS signal information when each cylinder is near Top Dead Center (TDC) of the firing stroke. If knock is present, the signal will range outside of the noise channel.

If the control module has determined that knock is present, it will retard the ignition timing to attempt to eliminate the knock. The control module will always try to work back to a zero compensation level, or no spark retard. An abnormal KS signal will stay outside of the noise channel or will not be present. KS diagnostics are calibrated to detect faults with the KS circuitry inside the control module, the KS wiring, the KS voltage output, or constant noise from an outside influence such as a loose/damaged component or excessive engine mechanical noise.

REMOVAL & INSTALLATION

2.4L (LE5) Engine

1. Disconnect the Knock Sensor (KS) electrical connector.
2. Remove the KS electrical connector clip from the oil level indicator tube bracket.
3. Remove the KS bolt.
4. Remove the KS.

To install:

➡ Rotate the pigtail 90 degrees from vertical before securing the fastener.

5. Install the KS.
6. Install the KS bolt and tighten to 18 ft. lbs. (25 Nm).
7. Disconnect the KS electrical connector.
8. Install the KS electrical connector clip to the oil level indicator tube bracket.

2.0L (LNF) Engine

1. Disconnect the engine wiring harness electrical connector from the front knock sensor, if required.
2. Disconnect the engine wiring harness electrical connector from the rear knock sensor, if required.
3. Remove the front knock sensor clip from the oil level indicator tube, if required.
4. Remove the rear knock sensor clip from the intake manifold brace, if required.
5. Loosen the appropriate knock bolt.
6. Remove the appropriate knock sensor.

To install:

➡ Rotate the pigtail 90 degrees from vertical before securing the fastener.

7. Position the appropriate knock sensor to the engine block.
8. Tighten the appropriate knock sensor mounting bolt to 18 ft. lbs. (25 Nm).
9. Install the front knock sensor clip to the oil level indicator tube, if required.
10. Install the rear knock sensor clip to the intake manifold brace, if required.
11. Connect the engine wiring harness electrical connector to the rear knock sensor.
12. Connect the engine wiring harness electrical connector to the front knock sensor.

TESTING

See Figures 143 and 144.

1. Connect the Digital Multi-Meter (DMM) across both Knock Sensor (KS) signal circuits on the sensor side of the KS harness connector.
2. Set the DMM to the 400 mV AC hertz scale and wait for the DMM to stabilize at 0 Hz.

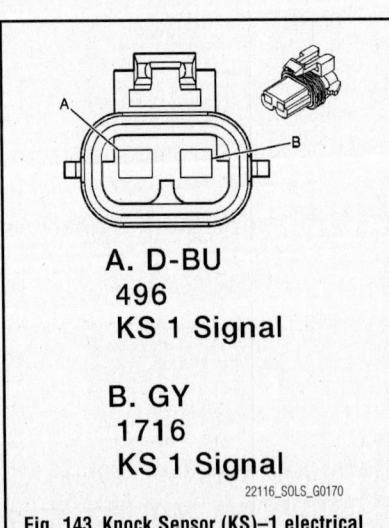

A. D-BU
496
KS 1 Signal

B. GY
1716
KS 1 Signal

Fig. 143 Knock Sensor (KS)–1 electrical connector

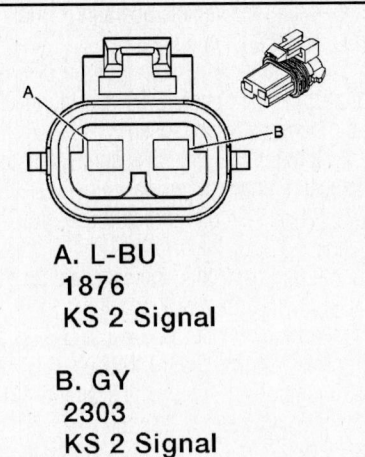

A. L-BU
1876
KS 2 Signal

B. GY
2303
KS 2 Signal

22116_SOLS_G0171

Fig. 144 Knock Sensor (KS)–2 electrical connector

3. Tap on the engine block with a non-metallic object near the KS while observing the signal indicated on the DMM.

➡ DO NOT tap on any plastic engine components.

4. The DMM should display a fluctuating frequency while tapping on the engine block.

MASS AIR FLOW (MAF) SENSOR

LOCATION

The Mass Air Flow (MAF) sensor is mounted on the top of the air filter housing.

OPERATION

On 2.4L (LE5) engines the Mass Air Flow (MAF) sensor is integrated with the Intake Air Temperature (IAT) sensor. The MAF sensor is an air flow meter that measures the amount of air entering the engine. The Engine Control Module (ECM) uses the MAF sensor signal to provide the correct fuel delivery for all engine speeds and loads. A small quantity of air entering the engine indicates a deceleration or idle condition. A large quantity of air entering the engine indicates an acceleration or high load condition. The MAF/IAT sensor has an ignition 1 voltage circuit, a ground circuit, a MAF sensor signal circuit, and IAT sensor signal circuit, and a low reference circuit.

The ECM applies 5 volts to the MAF sensor on the MAF sensor signal circuit. The sensor uses the voltage to produce a frequency based on the inlet air flow through the sensor bore. The frequency varies in a range of near 2,000 Hertz at idle to near 10,000 Hertz at maximum engine load.

REMOVAL & INSTALLATION

1. Disconnect the Mass Air Flow (MAF)/Intake Air Temperature (IAT) sensor electrical connector.

➡ **For 2.0L (LNF) engines the (IAT) is not part of the MAF.**

2. Remove the MAF/IAT sensor screws.
3. Remove the MAF/IAT sensor.

To install:

4. Install the MAF/IAT sensor.
5. Install the MAF/IAT sensor screws and tighten to 5 inch. lbs. (0.6 Nm).
6. Connect the MAF/IAT sensor electrical connector.

TESTING

See Figure 145.

1. Verify the integrity of the entire air induction system by inspecting for the following conditions:
   - Any damaged components
   - Loose or improper installation
   - An air flow restriction
   - Any vacuum leaks
   - Water intrusion
   - In cold climates, inspect for any snow or ice buildup
2. Ignition OFF, disconnect the Mass Air Flow (MAF)/Intake Air Temperature (IAT) harness connector at the MAF/IAT sensor.
3. Ignition OFF for 90 seconds, test for less than 5.0 ohms of resistance between the ground circuit terminal no. C and ground.
   a. If greater than the specified range, test the ground circuit for an open/high resistance.
4. Ignition ON, verify that a test lamp illuminates between the ignition circuit terminal no. B and ground.
   a. If the test lamp does not illuminate, test the ignition circuit for a short to ground or an open/high resistance.
5. Ignition ON, test for 4.8-5.2 volts between the signal circuit terminal no. A and ground.
   a. If less than the specified range, test the signal circuit for a short to ground or an open/high resistance. If the circuit tests normal, replace the Engine Control Module (ECM).
   b. If greater than the specified range, test the signal circuit for a short to voltage. If the circuit tests normal, replace the ECM.

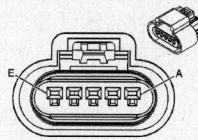

A. YE
492
MAF Sensor Signal

B. BK/WH
451
Ground

C. PK/BK
5291
Ignition 1 Voltage

D. BK
2760
Low Reference

E. L-BU
6289
Induction Air Temperature Sensor Signal

22116_SOLS_G0172

Fig. 145 Mass Air Flow (MAF) sensor electrical connector

MANIFOLD ABSOLUTE PRESSURE (MAP) SENSOR

LOCATION

2.4L (LE5) Engine

The Manifold Absolute Pressure (MAP) sensor is mounted in the intake manifold and sits under the throttle body.

2.0L (LNF) Engine

The Manifold Absolute Pressure (MAP) sensor is mounted on top of the intake manifold.

OPERATION

The Manifold Absolute Pressure (MAP) sensor has a 5-volt reference circuit, a low reference circuit, and a signal circuit. The control module supplies 5 volts to the MAP sensor on a 5-volt reference circuit, and provides a ground on a low reference circuit. The MAP sensor provides a voltage signal to the control module on a signal circuit relative to the intake manifold pressure changes.

REMOVAL & INSTALLATION

2.4L (LE5) Engine

1. Remove the throttle body.
2. Disconnect the Manifold Absolute Pressure (MAP) sensor electrical connector.
3. Remove the MAP sensor and the MAP sensor port seal if it is still retained in the intake manifold

To install:

4. Install the MAP sensor with the port seal into the intake manifold
5. Connect the MAP sensor electrical connector.
6. Install the throttle body.

2.0L (LNF) Engine

1. Disconnect the engine wiring harness electrical connector from the Manifold Absolute Pressure (MAP) sensor.
2. Remove the MAP sensor bolts.
3. Remove the MAP sensor and O-ring seal from the intake manifold.

To install:

4. Lubricate the O-ring seal with clean engine oil.
5. Install the MAP sensor to the intake manifold.
6. Install the MAP sensor bolts.
7. Tighten the bolts to 89 inch. lbs. (10 Nm).
8. Connect the engine wiring harness electrical connector to the MAP sensor.

TESTING

See Figure 146.

1. Ignition OFF, disconnect the harness connector at the Manifold Absolute Pressure (MAP) sensor.
2. Ignition OFF for 90 seconds, test for less than 5 ohms of resistance between the low reference circuit terminal no. 2 and ground.
   a. If greater than the specified range, test the low reference circuit for an open/high resistance. If the circuit tests normal, replace the Engine Control Module (ECM).
3. Ignition ON, test for 4.8-5.2 volts between the 5-volt reference circuit terminal no. 1 and ground.
   a. If less than the specified range, test the 5-volt reference circuit for a short to ground or an open/high resistance. If the circuit tests normal, replace the ECM.
   b. If greater than the specified range, test the 5-volt reference circuit for a short to voltage. If the circuit tests normal, replace the ECM.
4. Verify the scan tool MAP Sensor parameter is less than 2 kPa.
   a. If greater than the specified range, test the signal circuit terminal no. 3 for a short to voltage. If the circuit tests normal, replace the ECM.
5. Install a 3A fused jumper wire between the signal circuit terminal no. 3 and the 5-volt reference circuit terminal no. 1. Verify the scan tool MAP parameter is greater than 126 kPa.

a. If less than the specified range, test the signal circuit for short to ground or an open/high resistance. If the circuit tests normal, replace the ECM.

6. If all circuits test normal, test or replace the MAP sensor.

To test (MAP) sensor observe the following procedure:

• Ignition OFF, remove the MAP sensor.

• Install a 3A fused jumper wire between the 5-volt reference circuit terminal no. 1 and the corresponding terminal no. of the MAP sensor.

• Install a jumper wire between the low reference circuit terminal no. no. 2 of the MAP sensor and ground.

• Install a jumper wire at terminal no. 3 of the MAP sensor.

• Connect a DMM between the jumper wire from terminal no. 3 of the MAP sensor and ground.

• Ignition ON, with a vacuum pump slowly apply vacuum to the sensor while observing the voltage on the DMM. The voltage should vary between 0-5.2 volts, without any spikes or dropouts.

• If the voltage reading is erratic, replace the MAP sensor.

7. Ignition OFF, disconnect the harness connector at the MAP sensor.

8. Ignition OFF for 90 seconds, test for less than 5 ohms of resistance between the low reference circuit terminal no. 2 and ground.

a. If greater than the specified range, test the low reference circuit for an open/high resistance. If the circuit tests normal, replace the ECM.

9. Ignition ON, test for 4.8-5.2 volts between the 5-volt reference circuit terminal no. 1 and ground.

a. If less than the specified range, test the 5-volt reference circuit for a short to ground or an open/high resistance. If the circuit tests normal, replace the ECM.

b. If greater than the specified range, test the 5-volt reference circuit for a short to voltage. If the circuit tests normal, replace the ECM.

10. Verify the scan tool MAP Sensor parameter is less than 2 kPa.

a. If greater than the specified range, test the signal circuit terminal no. 3 for a short to voltage. If the circuit tests normal, replace the ECM.

11. Install a 3A fused jumper wire between the signal circuit terminal no. 3 and the 5-volt reference circuit terminal no. 1. Verify the scan tool MAP parameter is greater than 126 kPa.

a. If less than the specified range, test the signal circuit for short to ground or

an open/high resistance. If the circuit tests normal, replace the ECM.

12. If all circuits test normal, test or replace the MAP sensor.

To test (MAP) sensor observe the following procedure:

• Ignition OFF, remove the MAP sensor.

• Install a 3A fused jumper wire between the 5-volt reference circuit terminal no. 1 and the corresponding terminal no. of the MAP sensor.

• Install a jumper wire between the low reference circuit terminal no. 2 of the MAP sensor and ground.

• Install a jumper wire at terminal no. 3 of the MAP sensor.

• Connect a DMM between the jumper wire from terminal no. 3 of the MAP sensor and ground.

• Ignition ON, with a vacuum pump slowly apply vacuum to the sensor while observing the voltage on the DMM. The voltage should vary between 0-5.2 volts, without any spikes or dropouts.

• If the voltage reading is erratic, replace the MAP sensor.

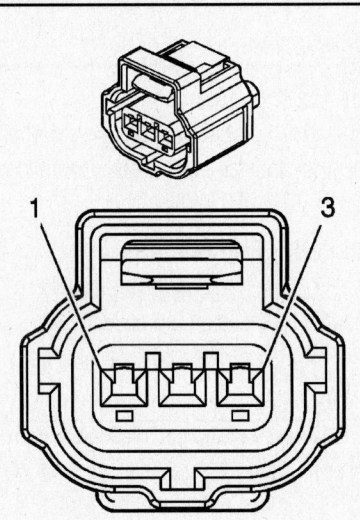

1. GY
597
5-Volt Reference 1

2. TN
407
Low Reference

3. L-GN
432
MAP Sensor Signal

22116_SOLS_G0173

Fig. 146 Manifold Absolute Pressure (MAP) sensor electrical connector

THROTTLE POSITION SENSOR (TPS)

LOCATION

The Throttle Position (TP) sensors 1 and 2 are located within the throttle body assembly.

OPERATION

There are 2 individual Throttle Position (TP) sensors within the throttle body assembly. The TP sensors are used to determine the throttle plate angle. The TP sensors provide the engine control module (ECM) with a signal voltage proportional to throttle plate movement. The TP sensor 1 signal voltage at closed throttle is near the 5-volt reference and decreases as the throttle plate is opened. The TP sensor 2 signal voltage at closed throttle is near the low reference and increases as the throttle plate is opened.

REMOVAL & INSTALLATION

2.4L (LE5) Engine

✳✳ WARNING

Do not use solvent of any type when cleaning the gasket surfaces on the intake manifold and the throttle body assembly, as damage to the gasket surfaces and throttle body assembly may result. Use care in cleaning the gasket surfaces on the intake manifold and the throttle body assembly, as sharp tools may damage the gasket surfaces. Do not use any solvent that contains Methyl Ethyl Ketone Peroxide (MEKP). This solvent may damage fuel system components.

1. Remove the intake manifold cover.
2. Remove the air cleaner outlet.
3. Disconnect the Electronic Throttle Control (ETC) electrical connector.
4. Remove the throttle body bolts.
5. Remove the throttle body from the intake manifold.

To install:

6. Inspect the throttle body gasket and replace if necessary.
7. Position the throttle body to the intake manifold.
8. Install the throttle body bolts and tighten to 89 inch. lbs. (10 Nm).
9. Connect the ETC electrical connector.
10. Install the air cleaner outlet.
11. Install the intake manifold cover.

2.0L (LNF) Engine

✵✵ WARNING

Do not use solvent of any type when cleaning the gasket surfaces on the intake manifold and the throttle body assembly, as damage to the gasket surfaces and throttle body assembly may result. Use care in cleaning the gasket surfaces on the intake manifold and the throttle body assembly, as sharp tools may damage the gasket surfaces. Do not use any solvent that contains Methyl Ethyl Ketone Peroxide (MEKP). This solvent may damage fuel system components.

1. Remove the charge air cooler outlet pipe.

2. Disconnect the engine wiring harness electrical connector from the Electronic Throttle Control (ETC).

3. Disconnect the engine wiring harness electrical connector from the brake booster auxiliary pump.

4. Remove the brake booster auxiliary pump electrical connector clip from the bracket.

5. Remove the throttle body bolts.

6. Remove the throttle body and seal from the intake manifold.

To install:

7. Inspect the throttle body seal, and replace if necessary.

8. Position the throttle body to the intake manifold.

9. Install the throttle body bolts and tighten to 89 inch. lbs. (10 Nm).

10. Connect the engine wiring harness electrical connector to the brake booster auxiliary pump.

11. Install the brake booster auxiliary pump electrical connector clip to the bracket.

12. Connect the engine wiring harness electrical connector (1) to the ETC.

13. Install the charge air cooler outlet pipe.

TESTING

See Figure 147.

1. Ignition OFF, disconnect the harness connector at the throttle body.

2. Ignition OFF for 90 seconds, test for less than 5 ohms of resistance between the low reference circuit terminal no. C and ground.

  a. If greater than 5 ohms, test the low reference circuit for an open/high resistance. If the circuit tests normal, replace the Engine Control Module (ECM).

3. Ignition ON, test for 4.8–5.2 volts between 5-volt reference circuit terminal no. E and ground.

  a. If less than 4.8 volts, test 5-volt reference circuit for a short to ground or an open/high resistance. If the circuit tests normal, replace the ECM.

  b. If greater than 5.2 volts, test the 5-volt reference circuit for a short to voltage. If the circuit tests normal, replace the ECM.

4. Verify the scan tool Throttle position (TP) sensor 1 voltage is less than 0.1 volt.

  a. If greater than 0.1 volt, test the signal circuit terminal no. D for a short to voltage. If the circuit tests normal, replace the ECM.

5. Verify the scan tool TP sensor 2 voltage is greater than 4.8 volts.

  a. If less than 4.8 volts, test the signal circuit for a short to ground. If the circuit tests normal, replace the ECM.

6. Install a 3A fused jumper wire between the signal circuit terminal no. D and the 5-volt reference circuit terminal no. E of the TP sensor 1. Verify the TP sensor 1 voltage is greater than 4.8 volts.

  a. If less than 4.8 volts, test the TP sensor 1 signal circuit for a short to ground or an open/high resistance. If the circuit tests normal, replace the ECM.

7. Install a 3A fused jumper wire between the signal circuit terminal no. F and the low reference circuit terminal no. C of the TP sensor 2. Verify that the TP sensor 2 voltage is less than 0.1 volt

  a. If greater than 1.0 volt, test the TP sensor 2 signal circuit for a short to voltage or an open/high resistance. If the circuit tests normal, replace the ECM.

8. Ignition OFF for 90 seconds, disconnect the harness connector at the ECM.

9. Test for less than 5 ohms of resistance on all TP sensor circuits between the following terminals:

  a. ECM C2 signal circuit terminal no. 65 to TP terminal no. D

  b. ECM C2 signal circuit terminal no. 63 to TP terminal no. F

  c. ECM C2 5-volt reference circuit terminal no. 3 to terminal no. E

10. If greater than 5 ohms, repair the affected circuit for open/high resistance.

11. Test for infinite resistance between TP sensor 1 signal circuit terminal no. D and TP sensor signal circuit terminal no. F.

  a. If less than infinite resistance, repair the short between TP sensor 1 signal circuit and TP sensor 2 signal circuit.

12. If all circuits test normal, replace the throttle body.

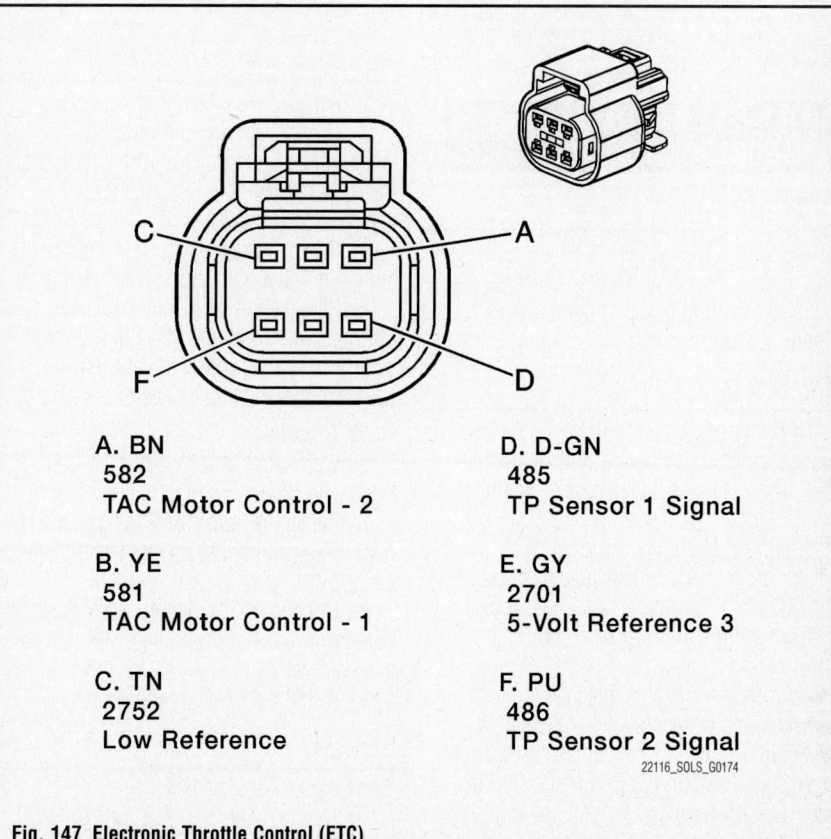

A. BN	**D. D-GN**
582	485
TAC Motor Control - 2	TP Sensor 1 Signal
B. YE	**E. GY**
581	2701
TAC Motor Control - 1	5-Volt Reference 3
C. TN	**F. PU**
2752	486
Low Reference	TP Sensor 2 Signal

22116_SOLS_G0174

Fig. 147 Electronic Throttle Control (ETC)

THROTTLE RELEARN PROCEDURE

➡ **Do NOT perform this procedure if DTCs are set.**

1. Start and idle the engine in PARK for 3 minutes.
2. With a scan tool, monitor desired and actual RPM.
3. The Engine Control Module (ECM) will start to learn the new idle cells and Desired RPM should start to decrease.
4. Ignition OFF for 60 seconds.
5. Start and idle the engine in PARK for 3 minutes.
6. After the 3 minute run time the engine should be idling normal.

➡ **During the drive cycle the check engine light may come on with idle speed DTCs. If idle speed codes are set, clear codes so the ECM can continue to learn.**

- If the engine idle speed has not been learned the vehicle will need to be driven at speeds above 70 km/h (44 mph) with several decelerations and extended idles.

7. After the drive cycle, the engine should be idling normally.

- If the engine idle speed has not been learned, turn OFF the ignition for 60 seconds and repeat step 6.

8. Once the engine speed has returned to normal, clear DTCs.

VARIABLE CAMSHAFT TIMING OIL CONTROL SOLENOID

LOCATION

The Camshaft Position (CMP) actuator sensors are located under the intake manifold cover in front of the ignition coil module for cylinder no. 1.

OPERATION

The Camshaft Position (CMP) actuator system is controlled by the control module. The control module sends a pulse width modulated 12-volt signal to each CMP actuator solenoid to control the amount of engine oil flow to a camshaft actuator passage. There are 2 different passages for oil to flow through, a passage for camshaft advance and a passage for camshaft retard. The camshaft actuator is attached to each camshaft and is hydraulically operated to change the angle of each camshaft relative to Crankshaft Position (CKP). Engine Oil Pressure (EOP), viscosity, temperature, and engine oil level can affect camshaft actuator

performance. The control module calculates the optimum camshaft position through the following inputs:

- Engine speed
- Manifold Absolute Pressure (MAP)
- Throttle position indicated angle
- CKP
- CMP
- Engine load
- Barometric Pressure (BARO)

A locking pin keeps the CMP actuators in the parked position to avoid valve train noise upon engine start-up. The parked position is 0 degrees of camshaft actuation. The locking pin will release the actuator after the EOP is sufficient to overcome the locking pin spring pressure. The exhaust CMP actuators also have return springs. The return springs are necessary to assist the CMP actuators to return to the parked position due to the rotational inertia of the valve train components upon engine shutdown. The control module uses the following inputs before assuming control of the CMP actuator:

- Engine Coolant Temperature (ECT)
- Closed loop fuel control
- Engine oil temperature (EOT
- EOP
- Engine oil level
- CMP actuator solenoid circuit state
- Ignition 1 signal voltage
- BARO

REMOVAL & INSTALLATION

1. Remove the intake manifold cover.
2. Disconnect the engine harness electrical connectors from the Camshaft Position (CMP) actuator solenoid valves.
3. Remove the exhaust CMP actuator solenoid valve bolt and valve, if required.
4. Remove the intake CMP actuator solenoid valve bolt and valve, if required.
5. Inspect the solenoid valve O-ring seals for damage, replace as necessary.

To install:

6. Lubricate the solenoid valve O-ring seals with clean engine oil.
7. Install the intake CMP actuator solenoid valves and bolts, tighten to 89 inch. lbs. (10 Nm).
8. Connect the engine harness electrical connector to the appropriate CMP actuator solenoid valves.
9. Install the intake manifold cover.

TESTING

See Figures 148 and 149.

1. Ignition OFF, disconnect the Camshaft Position (CMP) actuator sole-

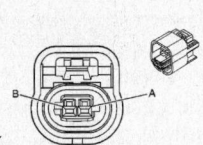

A. PK/BK
5293
Powertrain Main Relay Fused Supply (4)

B. PU
5284
Camshaft Phaser Intake Solenoid Control

22116_SOLS_G0175

Fig. 148 Camshaft Position (CMP) actuator solenoid—intake Electrical connector

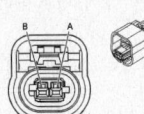

A. PK/BK
5293
Powertrain Main Relay Fused Supply (4)

B. L-GN
5282
Camshaft Phaser Exhaust Solenoid Control

22116_SOLS_G0176

Fig. 149 Camshaft Position (CMP) actuator solenoid—exhaust Electrical connector

noid harness connector at the CMP actuator solenoid.

➡ **Ensure component is tested at 20°C (68°F).**

2. Test for 4.6–7.5 ohms of resistance between the high control terminal no. A and the low reference terminal no. B of the CMP actuator solenoid.
3. If the resistance is not within the specified range, replace the CMP actuator solenoid.

VEHICLE SPEED SENSOR (VSS)

➡ **The Vehicle Speed Sensor (VSS) is also known as the Output Shaft Speed (OSS) sensor.**

LOCATION

Automatic Transmission 5L40—E/5L50—E Output Shaft Speed Sensor (OSS)

See Figure 150.

The Output Shaft Speed Sensor (OSS) is located inside the transmission. The pan must be removed to access the sensor that is mounted near the right rear corner.

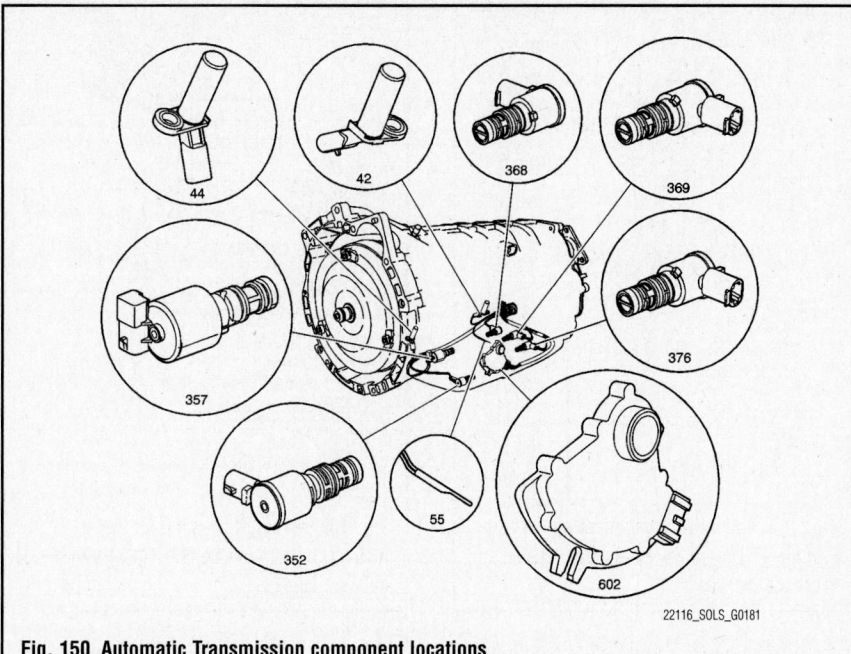

Fig. 150 Automatic Transmission component locations

Manual Transmission Aisin—AR5 Vehicle Speed Sensor (VSS) electrical connector

See Figure 151.

The Vehicle Speed Sensor (VSS) is externally mounted and located on the left rear of the transmission.

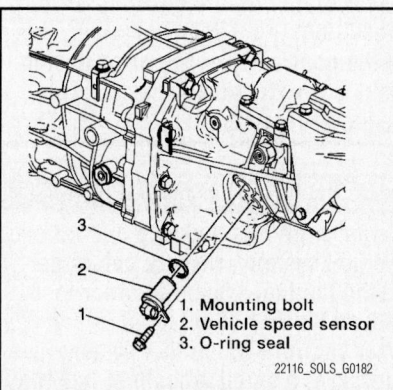

1. Mounting bolt
2. Vehicle speed sensor
3. O-ring seal

22116_SOLS_G0182

Fig. 151 Vehicle Speed Sensor (VSS)

OPERATION

The Vehicle Speed Sensor or Output Shaft Speed Sensor (VSS)/(OSS) is a magnetic inductive pickup that relays vehicle speed information to the Transmission Control Module (TCM). The TCM uses this information in order to control shift timing, line pressure, and TCC apply and release.

The VSS mounts in the case extension at the vehicle speed sensor reluctor wheel, which is pressed onto the final drive carrier assembly. An air gap of 0.011–0.062 inch. (0.27–1.57 mm) occurs between the sensor

and the teeth on the vehicle speed sensor reluctor wheel as the final drive carrier assembly rotates.

The sensor consists of a permanent magnet surrounded by a coil of wire. As the vehicle speed sensor reluctor wheel on the final drive carrier assembly rotates, an AC signal is produced by the VSS. This AC signal consists of a voltage and frequency that changes based on vehicle speed. The TCM uses the frequency portion of this signal to determine vehicle speed. Higher vehicle speeds induce a higher frequency and a higher voltage measurement at the sensor. The voltage portion of the signal is used in diagnostic procedures.

REMOVAL & INSTALLATION

Automatic Transmission 5L40—E/5L50—E Output Speed Sensor (OSS)

See Figures 152 and 153.

1. Raise and support the vehicle.
2. Remove the floor panel tunnel.
3. Drain the transmission fluid.
4. Remove the transmission fluid pan and filter.
5. Disconnect the electrical wiring harness connector from the output speed sensor.
6. Remove the output speed sensor bolt.
7. Remove the output speed sensor.
8. Remove the output speed sensor spacer.
9. Inspect the output speed sensor for the following conditions:

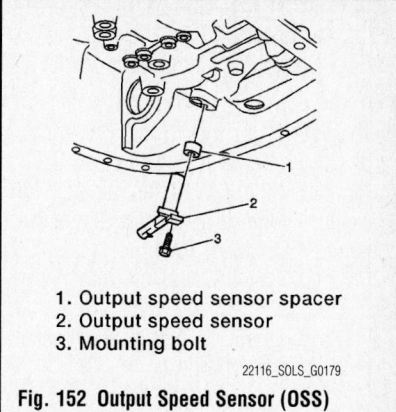

1. Output speed sensor spacer
2. Output speed sensor
3. Mounting bolt

22116_SOLS_G0179

Fig. 152 Output Speed Sensor (OSS)

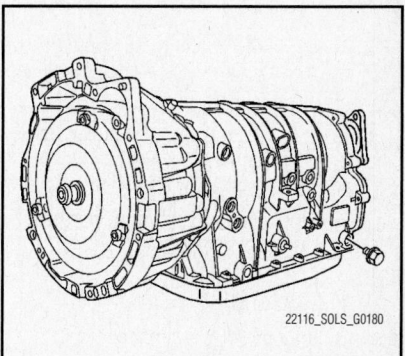

22116_SOLS_G0180

Fig. 153 Transmission fluid check plug location

a. Damaged or missing magnet
b. Damaged housing
c. Bent or missing electrical terminals

To install:

10. Install the output speed sensor spacer.
11. Install the output speed sensor.
12. Install the output speed sensor mounting bolt and tighten to 97 inch. lbs. (11 Nm).
13. Connect the electrical wiring harness connector to the output speed sensor.
14. Install the transmission fluid pan and filter.
15. Tighten the transmission pan bolts to 97 inch. lbs. (11 Nm).
16. Add DEXRON®VI automatic transmission fluid in increments of 0.5 L (0.5 qt) until the fluid drains from the hole plug.
17. Install the floor panel tunnel.
18. Lower vehicle.
19. Recheck fluid level if needed.

Manual Transmission Aisin—AR5 Vehicle Speed Sensor (VSS) Electrical Connector

1. Raise and support the vehicle.
2. Remove the front floor closeout panel.
3. Disconnect the Vehicle Speed Sensor (VSS) electrical connector.

4. Remove the VSS bolt.

5. Remove the VSS.

6. Remove the O-ring seal from the VSS.

To install:

7. Install the O-ring seal to the VSS.

8. Install the VSS to the transmission.

9. Install the VSS mounting bolt and tighten to 13 ft. lbs. (17 Nm).

10. Connect the VSS electrical connector.

11. Install the front floor closeout panel.

12. Lower the vehicle.

TESTING

See Figures 154 and 155.

1. Disconnect Vehicle Speed Sensor or Output Speed Sensor (VSS)/(OSS) electrical connector from sensor.

2. With a digital multimeter check resistance between pin A VSS/OSS low signal and pin B VSS/OSS high signal.

3. Sensor resistance should measure between 1,650–2,200 ohms at 20°C 68°F.

4. If resistance reading is not as stated suspect faulty VSS/OSS sensor.

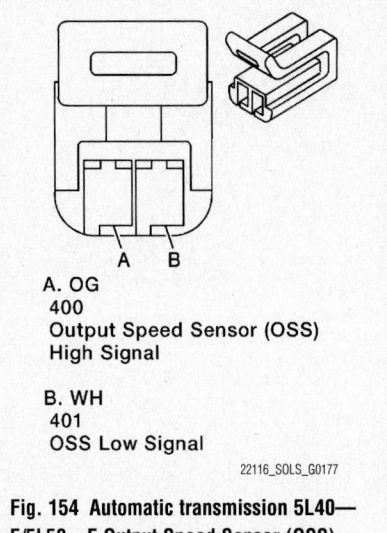

A. OG
400
Output Speed Sensor (OSS) High Signal

B. WH
401
OSS Low Signal

22116_SOLS_G0177

Fig. 154 Automatic transmission 5L40—E/5L50—E Output Speed Sensor (OSS) electrical connector

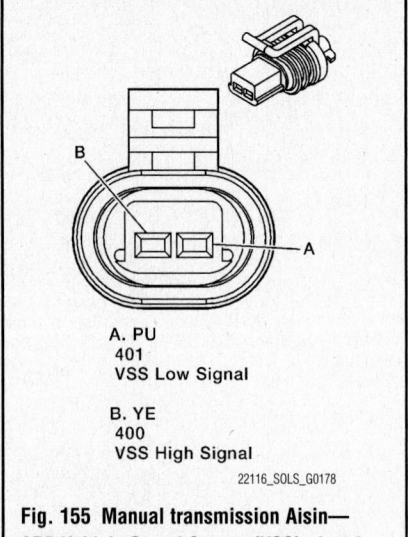

A. PU
401
VSS Low Signal

B. YE
400
VSS High Signal

22116_SOLS_G0178

Fig. 155 Manual transmission Aisin—AR5 Vehicle Speed Sensor (VSS) electrical connector

5. With a digital multimeter check voltage between pin A VSS low signal and pin B VSS/OSS high signal.

6. Safely lift wheels off of the ground and run in gear to check voltage readings.

7. Check for output voltage this will vary with vehicle speed from a minimum of 0.5 volts AC at 100 RPM to 200 volts at 6,000 RPM.

8. If no voltage reading is present suspect internal transmission problem or faulty VSS/OSS sensor.

FUEL

GASOLINE FUEL INJECTION SYSTEM

FUEL SYSTEM SERVICE PRECAUTIONS

Safety is the most important factor when performing not only fuel system maintenance but any type of maintenance. Failure to conduct maintenance and repairs in a safe manner may result in serious personal injury or death. Maintenance and testing of the vehicle's fuel system components can be accomplished safely and effectively by adhering to the following rules and guidelines.

• To avoid the possibility of fire and personal injury, always disconnect the negative battery cable unless the repair or test procedure requires that battery voltage be applied.

• Always relieve the fuel system pressure prior to disconnecting any fuel system component (injector, fuel rail, pressure regulator, etc.), fitting or fuel line connection. Exercise extreme caution whenever relieving fuel system pressure to avoid exposing skin, face and eyes to fuel spray. Please be advised that fuel under pressure may penetrate the skin or any part of the body that it contacts.

• Always place a shop towel or cloth around the fitting or connection prior to loosening to absorb any excess fuel due to spillage. Ensure that all fuel spillage (should it occur) is quickly removed from engine surfaces. Ensure that all fuel soaked cloths or towels are deposited into a suitable waste container.

• Always keep a dry chemical (Class B) fire extinguisher near the work area.

• Do not allow fuel spray or fuel vapors to come into contact with a spark or open flame.

• Always use a back-up wrench when loosening and tightening fuel line connection fittings. This will prevent unnecessary stress and torsion to fuel line piping.

• Always replace worn fuel fitting O-rings with new Do not substitute fuel hose or equivalent where fuel pipe is installed.

Before servicing the vehicle, make sure to also refer to the precautions in the beginning of this section as well.

RELIEVING FUEL SYSTEM PRESSURE

LOW PRESSURE SIDE WITH FUEL GAUGE

❊❊ CAUTION

Gasoline or gasoline vapors are highly flammable. A fire could occur if an ignition source is present. Never drain or store gasoline or diesel fuel in an open container, due to the possibility of fire or explosion. Have a dry chemical (Class B) fire extinguisher nearby.

❊❊ CAUTION

Remove the fuel tank cap and relieve the fuel system pressure before servicing the fuel system in order to reduce the risk of personal injury. After you relieve the fuel system pressure, a small amount of fuel may be released when servicing the fuel lines, the fuel injection pump, or the connections. In order to reduce the risk of personal injury, cover the fuel system components with a shop towel before disconnection. This will catch any fuel that may leak out. Place the towel in an approved container when the disconnection is complete.

1. Remove the engine cover, if required.

2. Loosen the fuel fill cap in order to relieve the fuel tank vapor pressure.

3. Remove the fuel rail service port cap.

4. Wrap a shop towel around the fuel rail service port.

5. Connect the adapter to the fuel rail service port.

6. Connect service port adapter to pressure tester.

7. Place the relief hose on the tester into an approved gasoline container.

8. Open the valve on the tester in order to bleed any fuel from the fuel rail.

9. Close the valve on the tester.

10. Remove the relief hose on the tester from the approved gasoline container.

11. Disconnect service port adapter and tester.

12. Install the fuel rail service port cap.

13. Install fuel cap.

LOW PRESSURE SIDE W/O FUEL GAUGE

✳✳ CAUTION

Gasoline or gasoline vapors are highly flammable. A fire could occur if an ignition source is present. Never drain or store gasoline or diesel fuel in an open container, due to the possibility of fire or explosion. Have a dry chemical (Class B) fire extinguisher nearby.

✳✳ CAUTION

Remove the fuel tank cap and relieve the fuel system pressure before servicing the fuel system in order to reduce the risk of personal injury. After you relieve the fuel system pressure, a small amount of fuel may be released when servicing the fuel lines, the fuel injection pump, or the connections. In order to reduce the risk of personal injury, cover the fuel system components with a shop towel before disconnection. This will catch any fuel that may leak out. Place the towel in an approved container when the disconnection is complete.

1. Loosen the fuel fill cap in order to relieve the fuel tank vapor pressure.

2. Remove the engine cover, if required.

3. Remove the fuel rail service port cap.

4. Wrap a shop towel around the fuel rail service port and using a small flat bladed tool, depress (open) the fuel rail test port valve.

5. Remove the shop towel from around the fuel rail service port, and place in an approved gasoline container.

6. Install the fuel rail service port cap.

7. Install fuel cap.

HIGH PRESSURE SIDE

✳✳ CAUTION

Fuel that flows out at high pressure can cause serious injury to the skin and eyes. ALWAYS depressurize the fuel system before removing components that are under high fuel pressure.

✳✳ CAUTION

Gasoline or gasoline vapors are highly flammable. A fire could occur if an ignition source is present. Never drain or store gasoline or diesel fuel in an open container, due to the possibility of fire or explosion. Have a dry chemical (Class B) fire extinguisher nearby.

✳✳ CAUTION

Remove the fuel tank cap and relieve the fuel system pressure before servicing the fuel system in order to reduce the risk of personal injury. After you relieve the fuel system pressure, a small amount of fuel may be released when servicing the fuel lines, the fuel injection pump, or the connections. In order to reduce the risk of personal injury, cover the fuel system components with a shop towel before disconnection. This will catch any fuel that may leak out. Place the towel in an approved container when the disconnection is complete.

1. Install a scan tool to the vehicle and command the fuel pump relay OFF, allowing the low pressure fuel pump to shut off.

2. Start the vehicle and allow the engine to idle until the engine stops. The engine will stop in approximately 20-30 seconds.

3. Turn the ignition OFF.

4. Using the scan tool, verify that there is little to no fuel pressure, if there still is fuel pressure repeat step 2.

✳✳ WARNING

If a scan tool is not available, WAIT at LEAST 2 hours after the engine has been run, before removing the high pressure fuel line.

5. Remove the high pressure fuel line.

FUEL FILTER

REMOVAL & INSTALLATION

There is no routinely replaced fuel filter. A plastic mesh strainer is part of the fuel pump module located in the fuel tank.

FUEL INJECTORS

REMOVAL & INSTALLATION

2.4L (LE5) Engine

See Figures 156 and 157.

✳✳ CAUTION

Gasoline or gasoline vapors are highly flammable. A fire could occur if an ignition source is present. Never drain or store gasoline or diesel fuel in an open container, due to the possibility of fire or explosion. Have a dry chemical (Class B) fire extinguisher nearby.

✳✳ CAUTION

Remove the fuel tank cap and relieve the fuel system pressure before servicing the fuel system in order to reduce the risk of personal injury. After you relieve the fuel system pressure, a small amount of fuel may be released when servicing the fuel lines, the fuel injection pump, or the connections. In order to reduce the risk of personal injury, cover the fuel system components with a shop towel before disconnection. This will catch any fuel that may leak out. Place the towel in an approved container when the disconnection is complete.

1. Before servicing the vehicle, refer to the Precautions Section.

2. Relieve the fuel system pressure.

3. Remove the air cleaner outlet duct.

4. Disconnect the fuel injector inline electrical connector.

5. Disconnect the electronic throttle control (ETC) electrical connector.

6. Remove the 2 engine harness clips from the fuel rail tabs.

7. Remove the fuel rail bolts.

➥Use care when removing the fuel rail assembly in order to prevent damage to the fuel injectors electrical connector terminals and spray tips.

8. Pull the fuel rail back and upward in

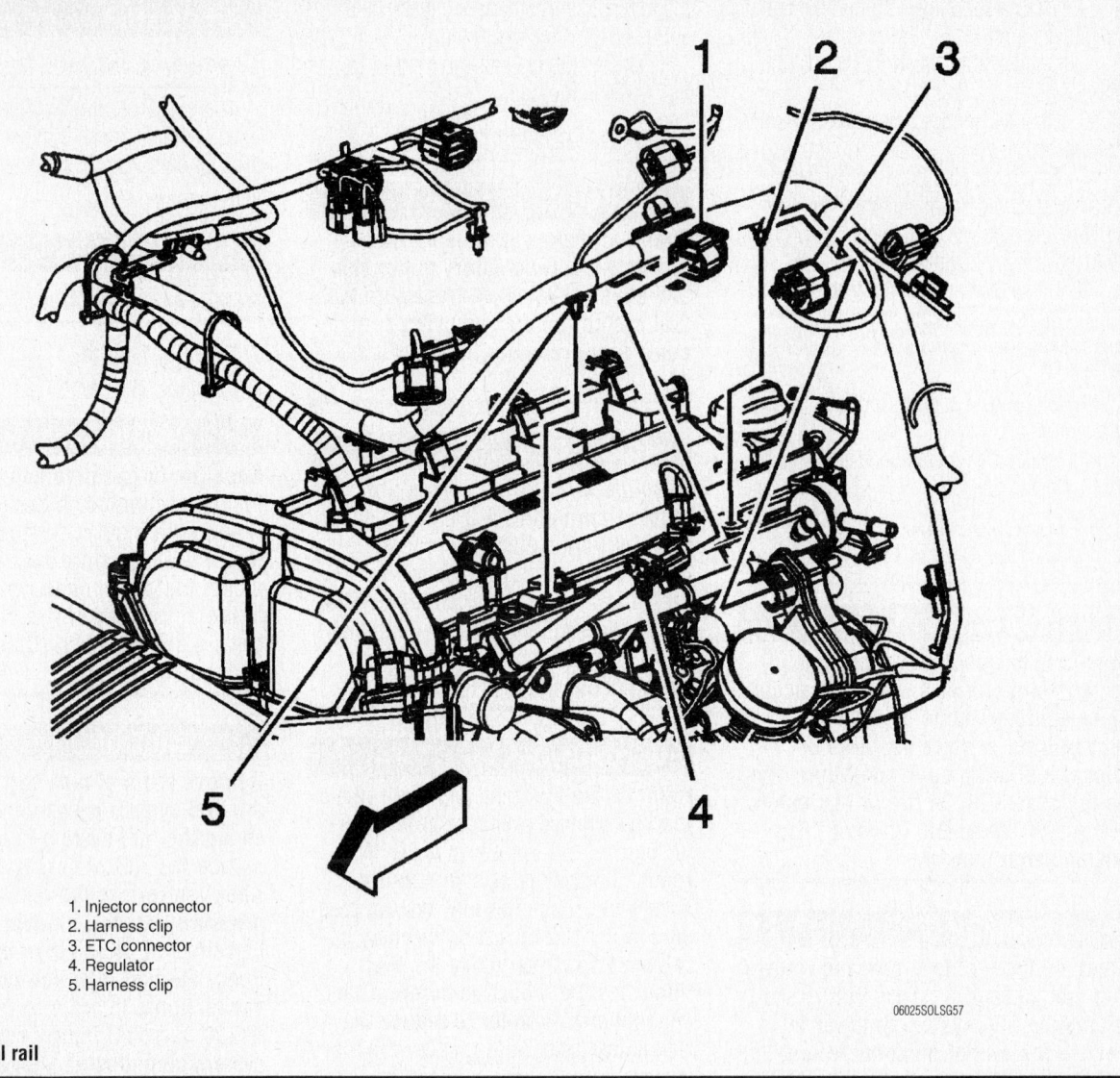

1. Injector connector
2. Harness clip
3. ETC connector
4. Regulator
5. Harness clip

06025SOLSG57

Fig. 156 Fuel rail

order to release the fuel injectors from the cylinder head ports.

9. Remove the fuel rail.

※※ WARNING

Use care in removing the fuel injectors in order to prevent damage to the fuel injector electrical connector pins or the fuel injector nozzles. Do not immerse the fuel injector in any type of cleaner. The fuel injector is an electrical component and may be damaged by this cleaning method.

➡ **If the fuel injectors are found to be leaking, the engine oil may be contaminated with fuel.**

10. Remove the fuel injector retaining clip.

11. Remove the fuel injector from the fuel rail.

12. Remove the fuel injector upper O-ring.

13. Remove the fuel injector lower O-ring.

To install:

➡ **Be sure to use the correct part number when ordering replacement fuel injectors.**

14. The fuel injector assembly is stamped with a part number identification.

15. Lubricate the new injector O-rings with clean engine oil.

16. Install the fuel injector upper O-ring.

17. Install the fuel injector lower O-ring.

18. Install the fuel injector to the fuel rail.

19. Install the fuel injector retaining clip.

➡ **Install NEW lower O-rings when reusing fuel injectors. Lubricate the lower O-rings prior to installing the injectors into the intake manifold.**

20. With the fuel injectors positioned downward, lower the fuel injectors into the cylinder head ports.

21. Carefully push the fuel injectors into the cylinder head ports.

22. Install the fuel rail bolts. Tighten the bolts to 10 Nm (89 inch lbs.).

23. Install the 2 engine harness clips to the fuel rail tabs.

24. Connect the ETC electrical connector.

25. Connect the fuel injector inline electrical connector.

26. Install the air cleaner outlet duct.

27. Connect the negative battery cable.

28. Inspect for fuel leaks using the following procedure:

- Turn ON the ignition, with the engine OFF for 2 seconds.
- Turn OFF the ignition for 10 seconds.
- Turn ON the ignition.
- Inspect for fuel leaks.

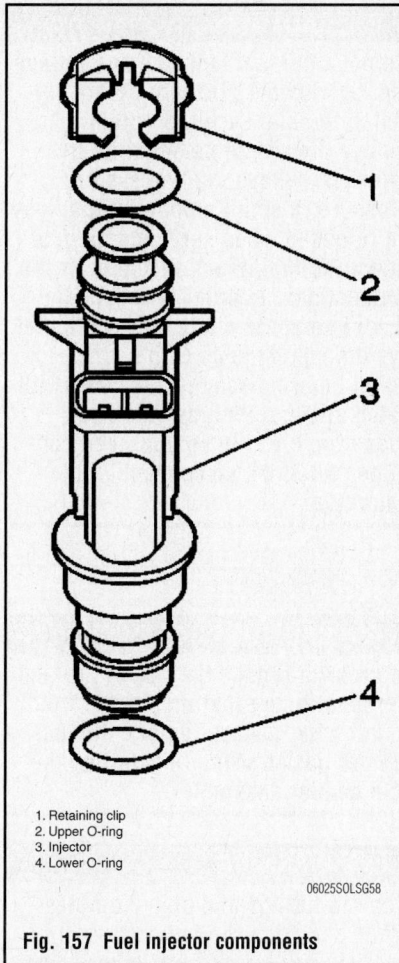

1. Retaining clip
2. Upper O-ring
3. Injector
4. Lower O-ring

06025SOLSG58

Fig. 157 Fuel injector components

2.0L (LNF) Engine

See Figures 158 through 162.

⚠️ **CAUTION**

Gasoline or gasoline vapors are highly flammable. A fire could occur if an ignition source is present. Never drain or store gasoline or diesel fuel in an open container, due to the possibility of fire or explosion. Have a dry chemical (Class B) fire extinguisher nearby.

⚠️ **CAUTION**

Remove the fuel tank cap and relieve the fuel system pressure before servicing the fuel system in order to reduce the risk of personal injury. After you relieve the fuel system pressure, a small amount of fuel may be released when servicing the fuel lines, the fuel injection pump, or the connections. In order to reduce the risk of personal injury, cover the fuel system components with a shop towel before disconnection. This will catch any fuel that may leak out.

Place the towel in an approved container when the disconnection is complete.

1. Before servicing the vehicle, refer to the Precautions Section.
2. Disconnect the engine wiring harness electrical connector from the fuel injector wiring harness electrical connector.
3. Remove the intake manifold.
4. Remove the fuel injector insulator.
5. Relieve the high side fuel system pressure.
6. Disconnect the engine wiring harness electrical connector from the high pressure fuel pump.
7. Remove the high pressure fuel pump cover bolts.
8. Remove the high pressure fuel pump cover.
9. Remove the engine wiring harness clip from the high pressure fuel pump cover.
10. Remove the high pressure fuel pump insulator.
11. Loosen the high pressure fuel pipe fitting at the fuel pump.
12. Loosen the high pressure fuel pipe fitting at the fuel rail.
13. Remove and discard the high pressure fuel pipe.
14. Disconnect the fuel injector wiring harness electrical connectors from the fuel injectors.
15. Remove the fuel rail bolts.
16. Carefully remove the fuel rail.

➡️**The fuel injectors may come out of the cylinder head with the fuel rail.**

17. Remove and discard the direct fuel injector hold down clamps.
18. Remove the direct fuel injectors.
19. If necessary, use a slide hammer and the J-37281-A injector removal adapter in order to remove the direct fuel injectors.

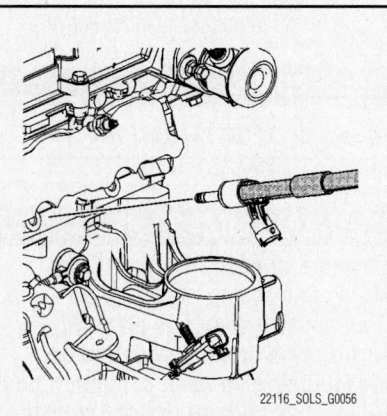

22116_SOLS_G0056

Fig. 158 Direct fuel injector removal 2.0L (LNF) engine

20. Remove and discard the upper O-ring seal and plastic spacer from the injector.
21. Carefully remove and discard the lower nylon seal from the injector.

To install:

22. Install a new plastic spacer onto the fuel injector.
23. Lubricate a new O-ring seal with silicon free engine oil
24. Carefully install the new O-ring seal onto the fuel injector.
25. From the EN-48266 , position the EN 48266-1 to the injector tip.
26. Install a new seal onto the EN 48266-1.

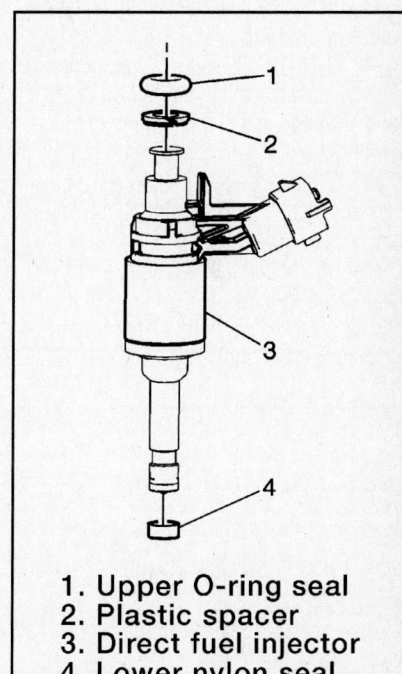

1. **Upper O-ring seal**
2. **Plastic spacer**
3. **Direct fuel injector**
4. **Lower nylon seal**

22116_SOLS_G0057

Fig. 159 Direct fuel injector view

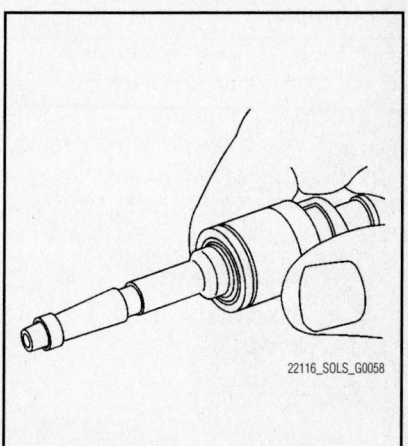

22116_SOLS_G0058

Fig. 160 Fuel injector with EN 48266-1 tool and O-ring

27. Pull the new seal by hand over the EN 48266-1 and into the groove in the injector.

28. Remove the EN 48266-1 from the injector tip.

29. From the EN-48266, install the EN 48266-2 to the injector tip.

30. Using the EN 48266-2, resize the seal. Install the EN 48266-2, until it bottoms out against the injector body, and rotate the EN 48266-2 while applying only moderate force 180 degrees in one direction and then 180 degrees back in the other direction.

31. Remove the EN 48266-2.

32. Install the direct fuel injectors to the cylinder head.

33. Install the new direct fuel injector hold down clamps.

34. Place the fuel rail into position.

35. Install the outer fuel rail bolts first, hand tight and install the remaining bolts, hand tight.

36. Connect the fuel injector wiring harness electrical connectors to the fuel injectors.

37. Tighten the fuel rail bolts in the sequence shown to:

   a. Tighten the bolts a first pass to 16 ft. lbs. (22 Nm).

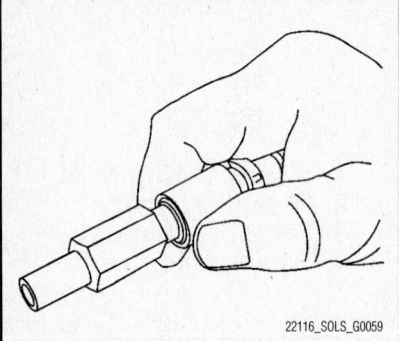

Fig. 161 Fuel injector with EN 48266-2 tool installed

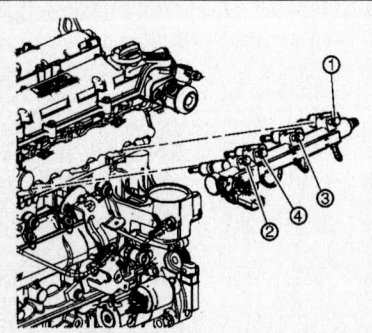

Fig. 162 Fuel rail tightening sequence 2.0L (LNF) engine

   b. Tighten the bolts a final pass to 16 ft. lbs. (22 Nm).

38. Ensure that the high pressure fuel pump, and fuel rail fittings are clean prior to assembly.

39. Lubricate the high pressure fuel pump, and the fuel rail fittings with silicon free engine oil

40. Install the new high pressure fuel pipe.

41. Tighten the new high pressure fuel pipe fitting to the fuel rail hand tight.

42. Tighten the new high pressure fuel pipe fitting to the fuel pump hand tight.

43. Tighten the fittings to 24 ft. lbs. (32 Nm).

44. Install the high pressure fuel pump insulator.

45. Install the high pressure fuel pump cover.

46. Install the high pressure fuel pump cover bolts and tighten to 89 inch lbs. (10 Nm).

47. Connect the engine wiring harness electrical connector to the high pressure fuel pump

48. Install the engine wiring harness clip (3) to the high pressure fuel pump cover.

49. Install the fuel injector insulator.

50. Install the intake manifold.

51. Connect the engine wiring harness electrical connector (1) to the fuel injector wiring harness electrical connector.

52. Inspect for leaks using the following procedure:

- Turn ON the ignition, with the engine OFF for 2 seconds.
- Turn OFF the ignition, for 10 seconds.
- Turn ON the ignition, with the engine OFF.
- Inspect for fuel leaks.

53. Install the low side fuel pressure service port cap.

54. Tighten the fuel fill cap.

55. Install the intake manifold cover.

FUEL PUMP

REMOVAL & INSTALLATION

See Figures 163 through 165.

> ❊❊ **CAUTION**
>
> **Gasoline or gasoline vapors are highly flammable. A fire could occur if an ignition source is present. Never drain or store gasoline or diesel fuel in an open container, due to the possibility of fire or explosion. Have a dry chemical (Class B) fire extinguisher nearby.**

> ❊❊ **CAUTION**
>
> **Remove the fuel tank cap and relieve the fuel system pressure before servicing the fuel system in order to reduce the risk of personal injury. After you relieve the fuel system pressure, a small amount of fuel may be released when servicing the fuel lines, the fuel injection pump, or the connections. In order to reduce the risk of personal injury, cover the fuel system components with a shop towel before disconnection. This will catch any fuel that may leak out. Place the towel in an approved container when the disconnection is complete.**

1. Before servicing the vehicle, refer to the Precautions Section.

> ❊❊ **CAUTION**
>
> **In order to reduce the risk of fire and personal injury that may result from a fuel leak, always replace the fuel sender gasket when reinstalling the fuel sender assembly.**

> ❊❊ **WARNING**
>
> **Cap the fittings and plug the holes when servicing the fuel system in order to prevent dirt and other contaminants from entering the open pipes and passages.**

2. Relieve the fuel system pressure.

3. Remove the rear compartment trim panel.

4. Remove the fuel sending unit access cover bolts.

5. Remove the access cover.

6. Disconnect the fuel sender electrical connector.

7. Disconnect the fuel pressure sensor electrical connector.

8. Disconnect the fuel fill pipe evaporative emission (EVAP) pipe quick connect fitting.

9. Disconnect the fuel feed pipe quick connect fitting.

> ❊❊ **WARNING**
>
> **Avoid damaging the lockring. Use only tool J-45722 to prevent damage to the lockring.**

> ❊❊ **WARNING**
>
> **Do Not handle the fuel sender assembly by the fuel pipes. The**

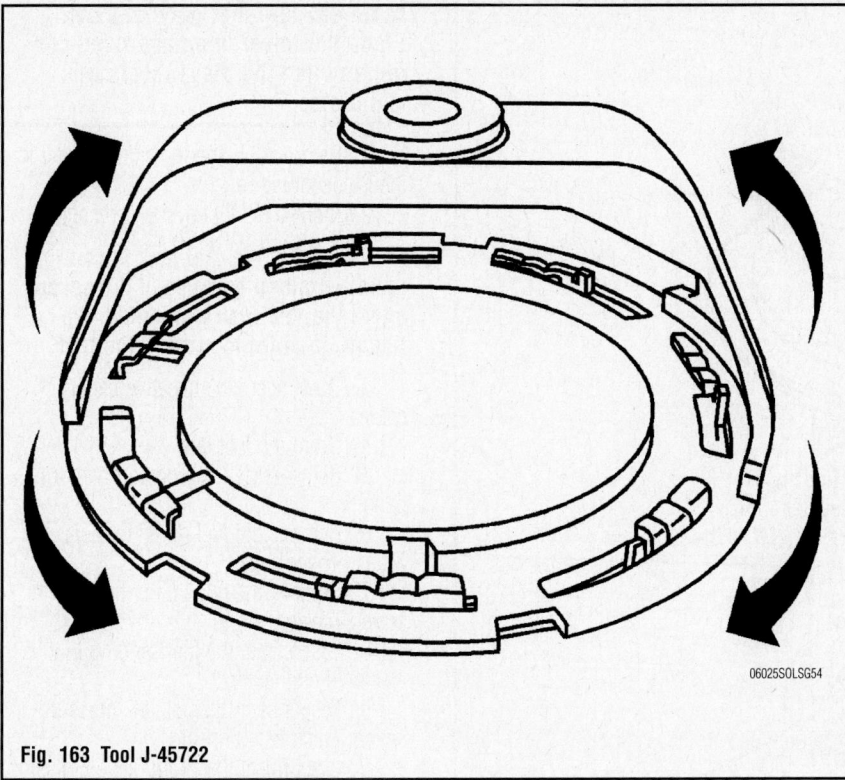

Fig. 163 Tool J-45722

amount of leverage generated by handling the fuel pipes could damage the joints.

➡ The fuel sender assembly may spring up from its position. When removing the fuel sender assembly from the fuel tank, be aware that the reservoir bucket is full of fuel. It must be tipped slightly during removal to avoid damage to the float. Discard the fuel sender assembly O-ring and replace it with a new one. Carefully discard the fuel in the reservoir bucket into an approved container.

➡Do NOT use impact tools. Significant force will be required to release the lockring. The use of a hammer and screwdriver is not recommended. Secure the fuel tank in order to prevent fuel tank rotation.

10. Use tool J 45722 and a long breaker-bar in order to unlock the fuel sender lockring. Turn the fuel sender lockring in a counterclockwise direction.
11. Raise the fuel sender up slightly.
12. Connect the large EVAP canister quick connect fitting.
13. Remove the fuel sender assembly.
14. Remove and discard the fuel sender O-ring.

➡Some lockrings were manufactured with DO NOT REUSE stamped into

them. These lockrings may be reused if they are not damaged or warped.

➡Inspect the lockring for damage due to improper removal or installation procedures. If damage is found, install a NEW lockring.

➡Check the lockring for flatness.

15. Place the lockring on a flat surface. Measure the clearance between to lockring and the flat surface using a feeler gage at 7 points.
16. If the warpage is less than 0.41 mm (0.016 in.), the lockring does not require replacement.

17. If the warpage is greater than 0.41 mm (0.016 in.), the lockring must be replaced.

To install:
18. Install a NEW fuel sender O-ring.
19. Install the fuel sender assembly.

➡Always replace the fuel sender seal when installing the fuel sender assembly. Replace the lockring if necessary. Do not apply any type of lubrication in the seal groove. Ensure the lockring is installed with the correct side facing upward. A correctly installed lockring will only turn in a clockwise direction.

20. Using the tool, rotate the fuel sender assembly lockring clockwise until the ring is locked into place on the fuel tank.
21. Connect the large EVAP canister quick connect fitting.
22. Connect the fuel feed pipe quick connect fitting.
23. Connect the fuel fill pipe EVAP pipe quick connect fitting.
24. Connect the fuel pressure sensor electrical connector.
25. Connect the fuel sender electrical connector.
26. Install the access cover.
27. Install the fuel sending unit access cover bolts.
28. Install the rear compartment trim panel.
29. Refill the tank.
30. Connect the negative battery cable.
31. Inspect for fuel leaks through the following steps:
- Turn the ignition to the ON position for 2 seconds.
- Turn the ignition to the OFF position for 10 seconds.
- Turn the ignition to the ON position
- Check for fuel leaks.

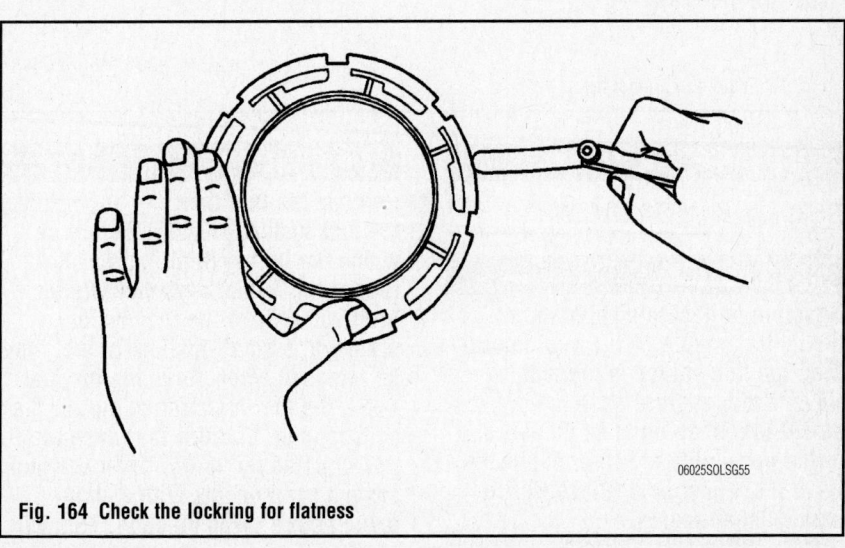

Fig. 164 Check the lockring for flatness

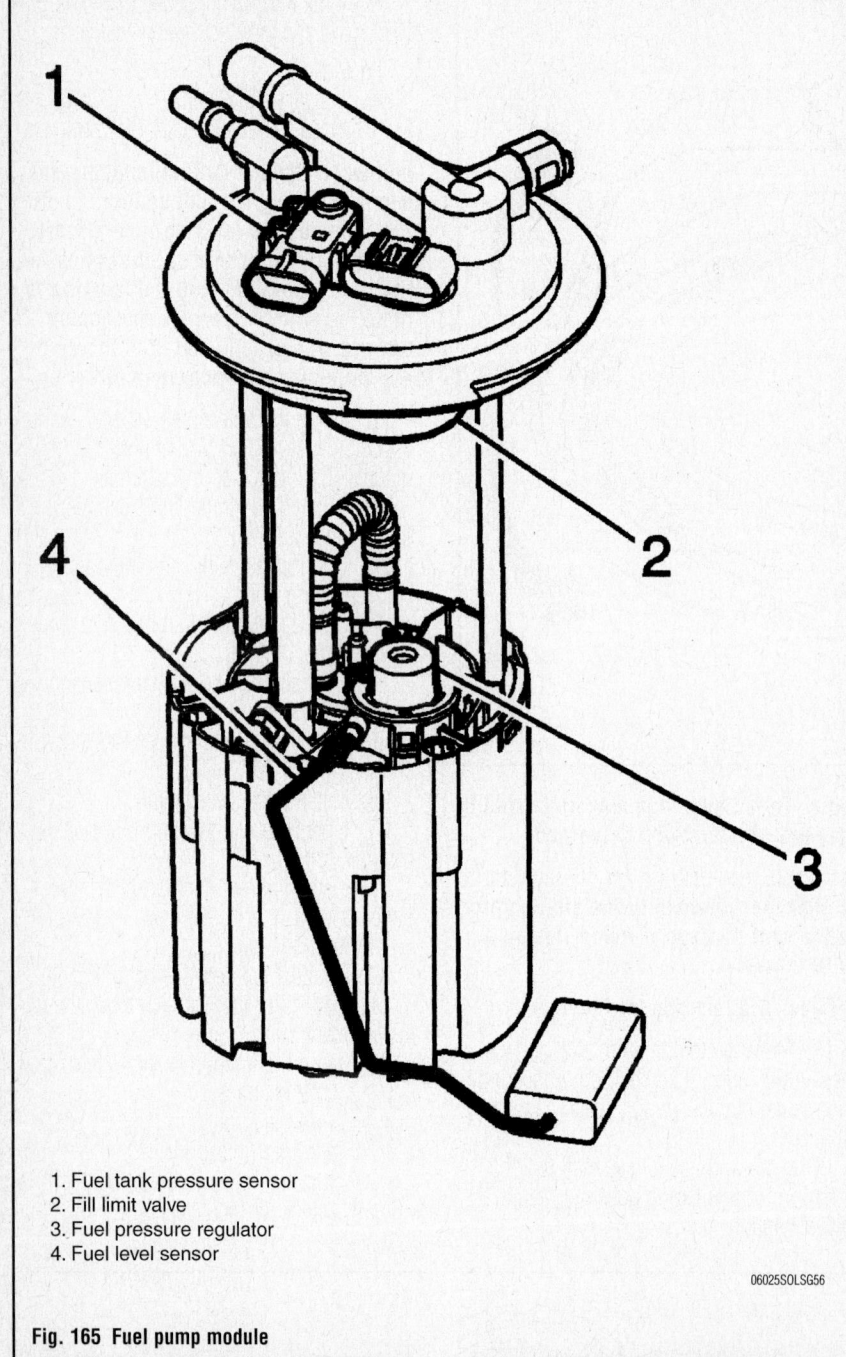

1. Fuel tank pressure sensor
2. Fill limit valve
3. Fuel pressure regulator
4. Fuel level sensor

06025SOLSG56

Fig. 165 Fuel pump module

FUEL TANK

REMOVAL & INSTALLATION

❋❋ CAUTION

Gasoline or gasoline vapors are highly flammable. A fire could occur if an ignition source is present. Never drain or store gasoline or diesel fuel in an open container, due to the possibility of fire or explosion. Have a dry chemical (Class B) fire extinguisher nearby.

❋❋ CAUTION

Remove the fuel tank cap and relieve the fuel system pressure before servicing the fuel system in order to reduce the risk of personal injury. After you relieve the fuel system pressure, a small amount of fuel may be released when servicing the fuel lines, the fuel injection pump, or the connections. In order to reduce the risk of personal injury, cover the fuel system components with a shop towel before disconnection. This will catch any fuel that may leak out. Place the towel in an approved container when the disconnection is complete.

1. Before servicing the vehicle, refer to the Precautions Section.
2. Relieve the fuel system pressure.

➡Ensure that the fuel tank is completely drained because of the severe angle that the tank will need to be tipped, in order to remove the tank.

3. Disconnect the negative battery cable.
4. Drain the fuel tank.
5. Remove the rear compartment trim panel.
6. Remove the fuel pump module access cover bolts.
7. Remove the fuel pump module access cover.
8. Disconnect the fuel sending unit electrical connector.
9. Disconnect the fuel tank pressure sensor electrical connector.
10. Disconnect the Evaporative Emission (EVAP) canister vent solenoid electrical connector.
11. Disconnect the fuel pump fuel feed line quick connect fitting .
12. Disconnect the EVAP canister purge line quick connect fitting from the module.
13. Secure the fuel feed and EVAP purge lines up out of the way.
14. Remove the fuel fill pipe.
15. Disconnect the fuel tank fill pipe EVAP line quick connect fitting (1) from the module.
16. Remove the fuel tank fill EVAP line out through the access hole in order to prevent damage to the pipe when removing the tank.
17. Remove the rear suspension cross-member.
18. Remove the stabilizer shaft.
19. Position an adjustable jack under the fuel tank.
20. Remove the fuel tank strap/support bolts.
21. Remove the fuel tank support bolts.
22. Remove the fuel tank supports.
23. Remove the adjustable jack from under the fuel tank and with the aid of an assistant, tilt the tank down towards the left side of the vehicle and carefully remove the tank.
24. Place the fuel tank onto a suitable work surface.
25. Cap or plug the fuel feed and EVAP lines in order to prevent fuel loss and/or system contamination.

To install:

26. Remove the caps or plugs from the fuel feed and EVAP lines.

27. With the aid of an assistant tilt the tank up and carefully install the tank in from the left side of the vehicle.

28. Position an adjustable jack under the fuel tank.

29. Position the fuel tank supports.

30. Install the fuel tank strap/support bolts and tighten to 16 ft. lbs. (22 Nm).

31. Install the fuel tank support bolts and tighten to 16 ft. lbs. (22 Nm).

32. Remove adjustable jack from under the fuel tank.

33. Install the stabilizer shaft.

34. Install the rear suspension crossmember.

35. Install the fuel tank fill EVAP line in through the access hole.

36. Connect the fuel tank fill pipe EVAP line quick connect fitting to the module.

37. Install the fuel fill pipe.

38. Unsecure the fuel feed and EVAP purge lines and position to the module.

39. Connect the EVAP canister purge line quick connect fitting to the module.

40. Connect the fuel pump fuel feed line quick connect fitting to the module.

41. Connect the EVAP canister vent solenoid electrical connector.

42. Connect the fuel tank pressure sensor electrical connector.

43. Connect the fuel sending unit electrical connector.

44. Install the pump module access cover.

45. Install the fuel pump module access cover bolts and tighten to 89 inch. lbs. (10 Nm).

46. Install the rear compartment trim panel.

47. Connect the negative battery cable.

48. Inspect for leaks using the following procedures:

- Turn ON the ignition, with the engine OFF for 2 seconds.
- Turn OFF the ignition for 10 seconds.
- Turn ON the ignition, with the engine OFF.
- Inspect for fuel leaks.

HIGH PRESSURE FUEL PUMP

REMOVAL & INSTALLATION

2.0L (LNF) Engine

See Figures 166 and 167.

✳✳ CAUTION

Gasoline or gasoline vapors are highly flammable. A fire could occur if an ignition source is present. Never drain or store gasoline or diesel fuel in an open container, due to the possibility of fire or explosion. Have a dry chemical (Class B) fire extinguisher nearby.

✳✳ CAUTION

Remove the fuel tank cap and relieve the fuel system pressure before servicing the fuel system in order to reduce the risk of personal injury. After you relieve the fuel system pressure, a small amount of fuel may be released when servicing the fuel lines, the fuel injection pump, or the connections. In order to reduce the risk of personal injury, cover the fuel system components with a shop towel before disconnection. This will catch any fuel that may leak out. Place the towel in an approved container when the disconnection is complete.

1. Before servicing the vehicle, refer to the Precautions Section.

2. Relieve the low and high side fuel system pressure.

3. Disconnect the engine wiring harness electrical connector from the high pressure fuel pump.

4. Remove the engine wiring harness clip from the high pressure fuel pump cover.

5. Remove the high pressure fuel pump cover bolts.

6. Remove the high pressure fuel pump cover.

7. Remove the high pressure fuel pump insulator.

8. Loosen the fuel feed pipe to fuel pump fitting.

9. Remove the fuel feed pipe bolts.

10. Remove the fuel feed pipe from the intake manifold.

11. Loosen the high pressure fuel pipe fitting at the fuel pump.

12. Loosen the high pressure fuel pipe fitting at the fuel rail.

13. Remove and discard the high pressure fuel pipe.

14. Remove and discard the high pressure fuel pump bolts.

15. Remove the high pressure fuel pump.

16. Remove and discard the high pressure fuel pump gasket.

17. Remove and discard the high pressure fuel pump O-ring.

18. Remove the high pressure fuel pump roller lifter, if necessary.

22116_SOLS_G0061

Fig. 166 High pressure fuel pump removal 2.0L (LNF) engine

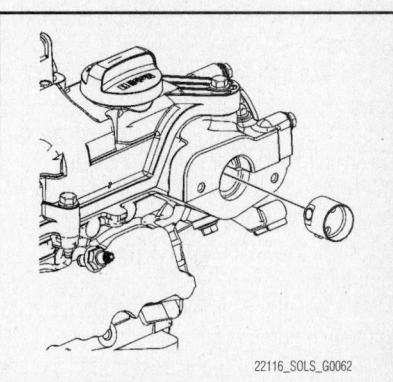

22116_SOLS_G0062

Fig. 167 High pressure fuel pump roller lifter 2.0L (LNF) engine

To install:

19. Lubricate the high pressure fuel pump cylinder head bore and roller lifter with silicon free engine oil.

20. Install the high pressure fuel pump roller lifter, if necessary.

21. Install a new high pressure fuel pump O-ring.

22. Position the new high pressure fuel pump gasket to the cylinder head.

➡**Ensure the plastic bolt retainers are installed in the high pressure fuel pump mounting holes prior to installing.**

23. Install the high pressure fuel pump. Push the pump into the cylinder head bore by hand, applying force to the top of the pump.

24. Install the new high pressure fuel pump bolts hand tight.

25. Ensure that the high pressure fuel pump, and fuel rail fittings are clean prior to assembly.

26. Lubricate the high pressure fuel pump, and the fuel rail fittings with silicon free engine oil.

27. Install the new high pressure fuel pipe.

28. Tighten the high pressure fuel pipe fitting to the fuel rail hand tight.

29. Tighten the high pressure fuel pipe fitting to the fuel pump hand tight.

30. Place the fuel feed pipe onto the intake manifold.

31. Install the fuel feed pipe bolts hand tight.

32. Tighten the fuel feed pipe to fuel pump fitting hand tight.

33. Tighten the fuel feed pipe bolts to 89 inch. lbs. (10 Nm).

34. Tighten the fuel feed pipe to fuel pump fitting to 22 ft. lbs. (30 Nm).

35. Tighten the high pressure fuel pipe fittings to 24 ft. lbs. (32 Nm).

36. Tighten the high pressure fuel pump bolts evenly to 11 ft. lbs. (15 Nm).

37. Install the high pressure fuel pump insulator.

38. Position the high pressure fuel pump cover.

39. Install the high pressure fuel pump cover bolts and tighten to 89 inch. lbs. (10 Nm).

40. Connect the engine wiring harness electrical connector to the high pressure fuel pump.

41. Install the engine wiring harness clip to the fuel pump cover.

42. Inspect for fuel leaks through the following steps:

- Turn ON the ignition, with the engine OFF for 2 seconds.
- Turn the ignition to the OFF position for 10 seconds.
- Turn ON the ignition, with the engine OFF.
- Check for fuel leaks.

43. Install the low side fuel pressure service port cap.

44. Tighten the fuel fill cap.

45. Install the intake manifold cover.

IDLE SPEED

ADJUSTMENT

Idle speed is maintained by the Powertrain Control Module (PCM). No adjustment is necessary or possible.

THROTTLE BODY

REMOVAL & INSTALLATION

2.4L (LE5) Engine

See Figure 168.

✳✳ WARNING

Do not use solvent of any type when cleaning the gasket surfaces on the intake manifold and the throttle body

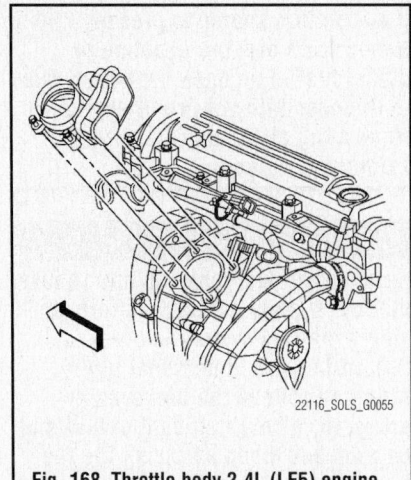

Fig. 168 Throttle body 2.4L (LE5) engine

assembly, as damage to the gasket surfaces and throttle body assembly may result. Use care in cleaning the gasket surfaces on the intake manifold and the throttle body assembly, as sharp tools may damage the gasket surfaces. Do not use any solvent that contains Methyl Ethyl Ketone (MEK). This solvent may damage fuel system components.

1. Before servicing the vehicle, refer to the Precautions Section.

2. Remove the intake manifold cover.

3. Remove the air cleaner outlet.

4. Disconnect the Electronic Throttle Control (ETC) electrical connector.

5. Remove the throttle body bolts.

6. Remove the throttle body from the intake manifold.

To install:

7. Inspect the throttle body gasket and replace if necessary.

8. Position the throttle body to the intake manifold.

9. Install the throttle body bolts and tighten to 89 inch. lbs. (10 Nm).

10. Connect the ETC electrical connector.

11. Install the air cleaner outlet.

12. Install the intake manifold cover.

2.0L (LNF) Engine

See Figure 169.

✳✳ WARNING

Do not use solvent of any type when cleaning the gasket surfaces on the intake manifold and the throttle body assembly, as damage to the gasket surfaces and throttle body assembly

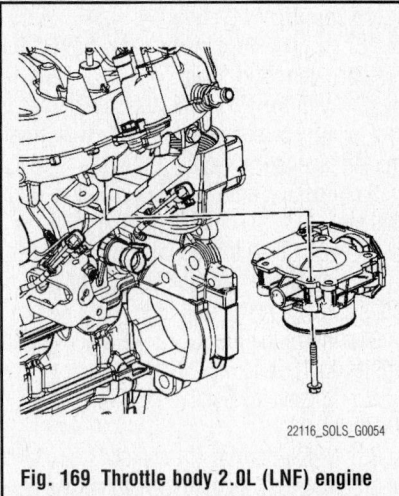

Fig. 169 Throttle body 2.0L (LNF) engine

may result. Use care in cleaning the gasket surfaces on the intake manifold and the throttle body assembly, as sharp tools may damage the gasket surfaces. Do not use any solvent that contains Methyl Ethyl Ketone (MEK). This solvent may damage fuel system components.

1. Before servicing the vehicle, refer to the Precautions Section.

2. Remove the charge air cooler outlet pipe.

3. Disconnect the engine wiring harness electrical connector from the Electronic Throttle Control (ETC).

4. Disconnect the engine wiring harness electrical connector from the brake booster auxiliary pump.

5. Remove the brake booster auxiliary pump electrical connector clip from the bracket.

6. Remove the throttle body bolts.

7. Remove the throttle body and seal from the intake manifold.

To install:

8. Inspect the throttle body seal, and replace if necessary.

9. Position the throttle body to the intake manifold.

10. Install the throttle body bolts and tighten to 89 inch lbs. (10 Nm).

11. Connect the engine wiring harness electrical connector to the brake booster auxiliary pump.

12. Install the brake booster auxiliary pump electrical connector clip to the bracket.

13. Connect the engine wiring harness electrical connector to the ETC.

14. Install the charge air cooler outlet pipe.

HEATING & AIR CONDITIONING SYSTEM

BLOWER MOTOR

REMOVAL & INSTALLATION

See Figure 170.

1. Before servicing the vehicle, refer to the Precautions Section.
2. Remove the instrument panel (I/P) compartment.
3. Disconnect the blower motor resistor electrical connector.
4. Remove blower motor resistor screws.
5. Remove blower motor resistor.
6. Remove blower motor screws.
7. Remove blower motor assembly.

To install:

8. Install blower motor assembly.
9. Install blower motor screws and tighten to 13 inch. lbs. (1.5 Nm).
10. Install blower motor resistor.
11. Install blower motor resistor screws and tighten to 13 inch. lbs. (1.5 Nm).
12. Reconnect the blower motor resistor electrical connector.
13. Install the instrument panel (I/P) compartment.

HEATER CORE

REMOVAL & INSTALLATION

2006–08 Pontiac Solstice

See Figures 171 through 177.

1. Before servicing the vehicle, refer to the Precautions Section.
2. Disable the SIR system.
3. Disconnect the negative battery cable.
4. Drain the cooling system.
5. Recover the refrigerant.
6. Remove the A/C compressor tube assembly nut.
7. Remove the sealing washer.
8. Remove the thermal expansion valve bolt.
9. Remove the sealing washer.
10. Remove the evaporator tube from the thermal expansion valve.
11. Remove the air inlet grille panel.
12. Remove the heater inlet hose from the heater core.
13. Remove the heater outlet hose from the heater core.
14. Remove the shift knob, if equipped with a manual transmission.

15. Remove the console shift lever bezel, if equipped with an automatic transmission.
16. Remove the instrument panel assist handle.
17. Remove the instrument panel cluster (IPC) trim plate.
18. Remove the driver knee bolster trim panel.
19. Remove the instrument panel (I/P) compartment.
20. Disable the supplemental inflatable restraint (SIR) system Zone 5.
21. Remove the I/P inflatable restraint.
22. Remove the right and left I/P outer trim covers.
23. Remove the right and left windshield pillar garnish moldings.
24. Remove the I/P extension trim plate.
25. Remove the knee bolster panel.
26. Remove the knee bolster bracket.
27. Remove the steering column trim panels.
28. Disable the supplemental inflatable restraint (SIR) system Zone 3.
29. Insert a small flat bladed tool through the access openings, on the left and right of the steering wheel.

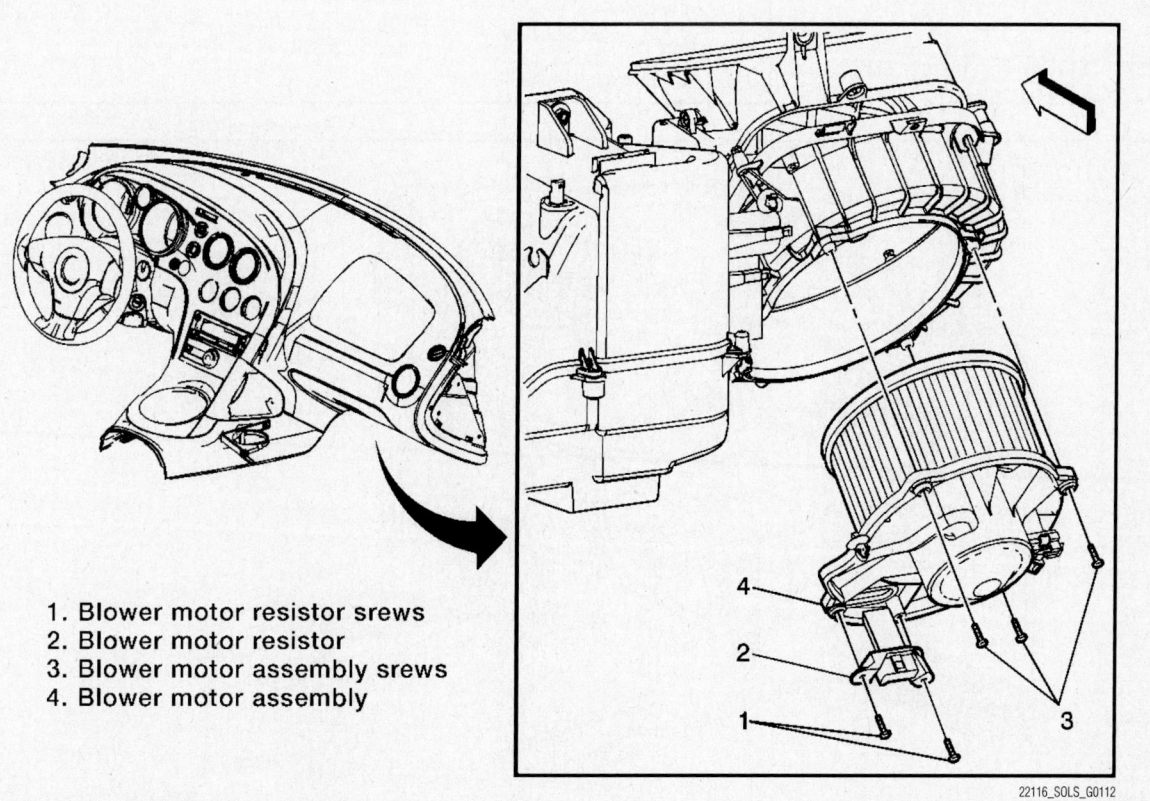

1. Blower motor resistor srews
2. Blower motor resistor
3. Blower motor assembly srews
4. Blower motor assembly

22116_SOLS_G0112

Fig. 170 Blower motor assembly and resistor

30. Push on the flat bladed tool to release the steering wheel inflator from the steering wheel.

31. Remove the steering wheel.

32. Lower and position the steering column out of the way.

33. Remove the instrument panel carrier bolt.

34. Remove the instrument panel carrier screw.

35. Remove the instrument panel carrier nut.

36. Remove the instrument panel carrier assembly.

➡ **Note the routing of the I/P wiring harness around the I/P tie bar to aid in the reinstallation procedure**

37. Remove the nuts securing the air distribution duct to the I/P tie bar.

38. Remove the bolts securing the I/P tie bar to the brake pedal bracket.

39. Disconnect the HVAC module assembly electrical connectors.

40. Disconnect the actuator electrical connectors from the recirculation case.

41. Remove the air outlet duct screw.

42. Remove the air outlet duct.

43. Remove the heater core cover screw.

44. Remove the heater core cover.

45. Remove the heater core pass-through seal.

46. Remove the air distribution case screw.

47. Remove the air distribution case.

48. Remove the heater core.

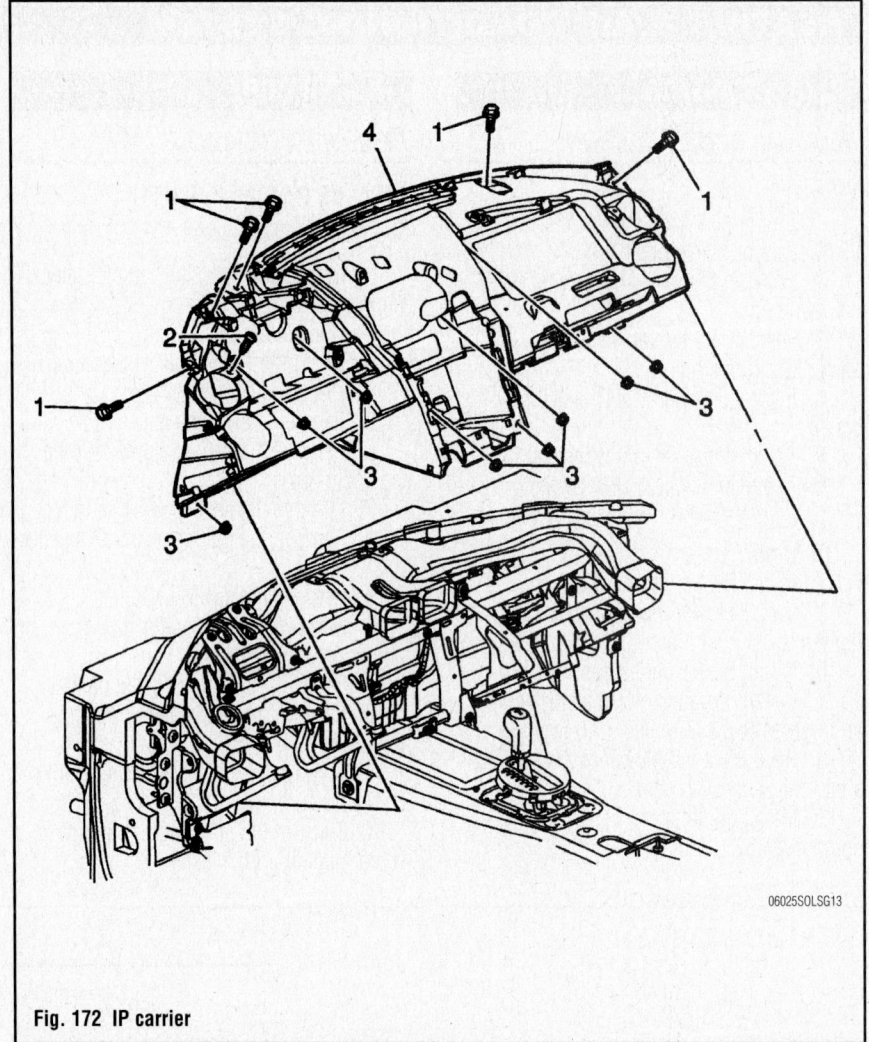

Fig. 172 IP carrier

06025SOLSG13

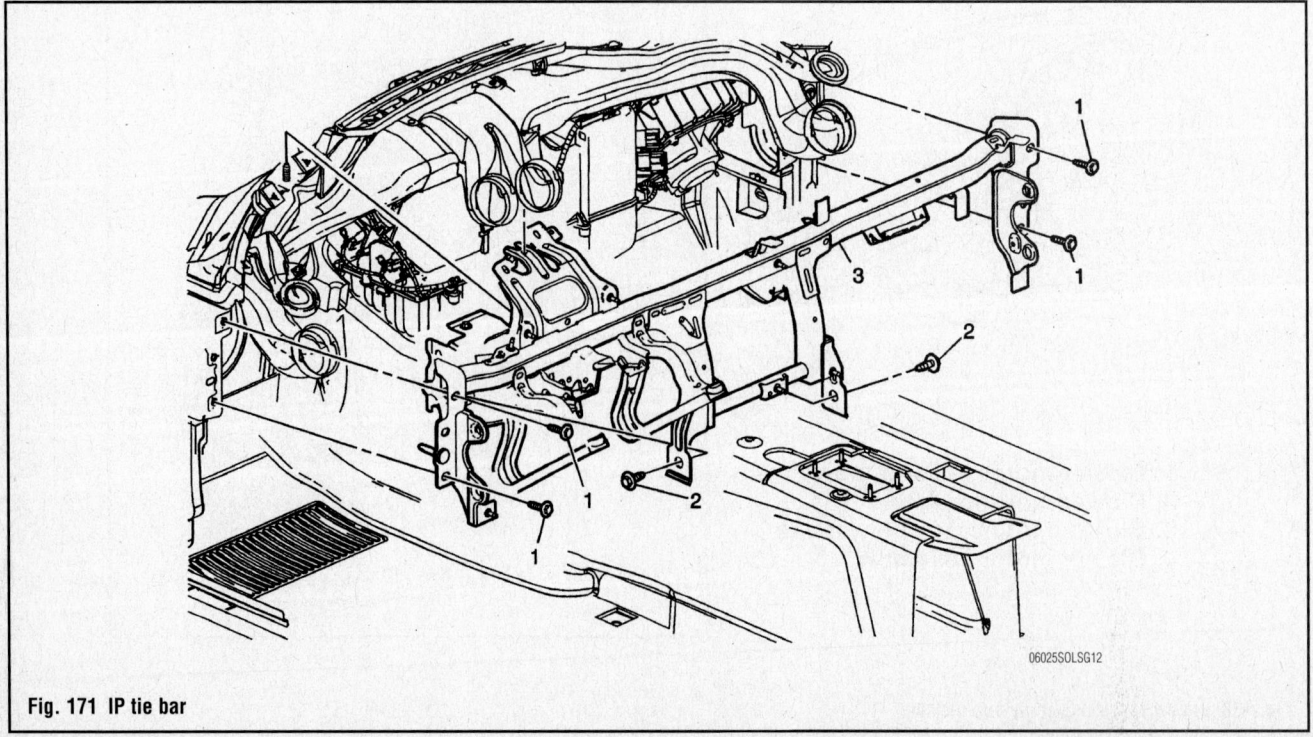

Fig. 171 IP tie bar

06025SOLSG12

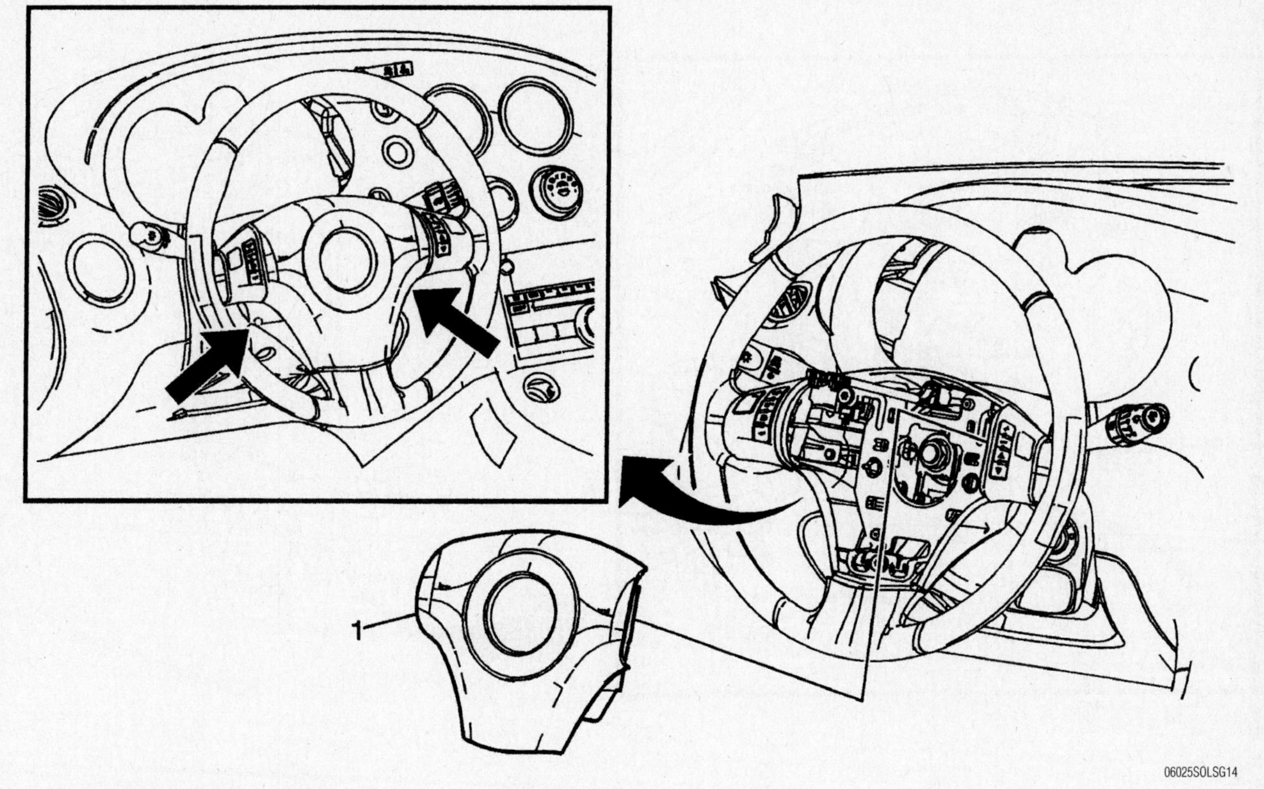

Fig. 173 Steering wheel inflator module

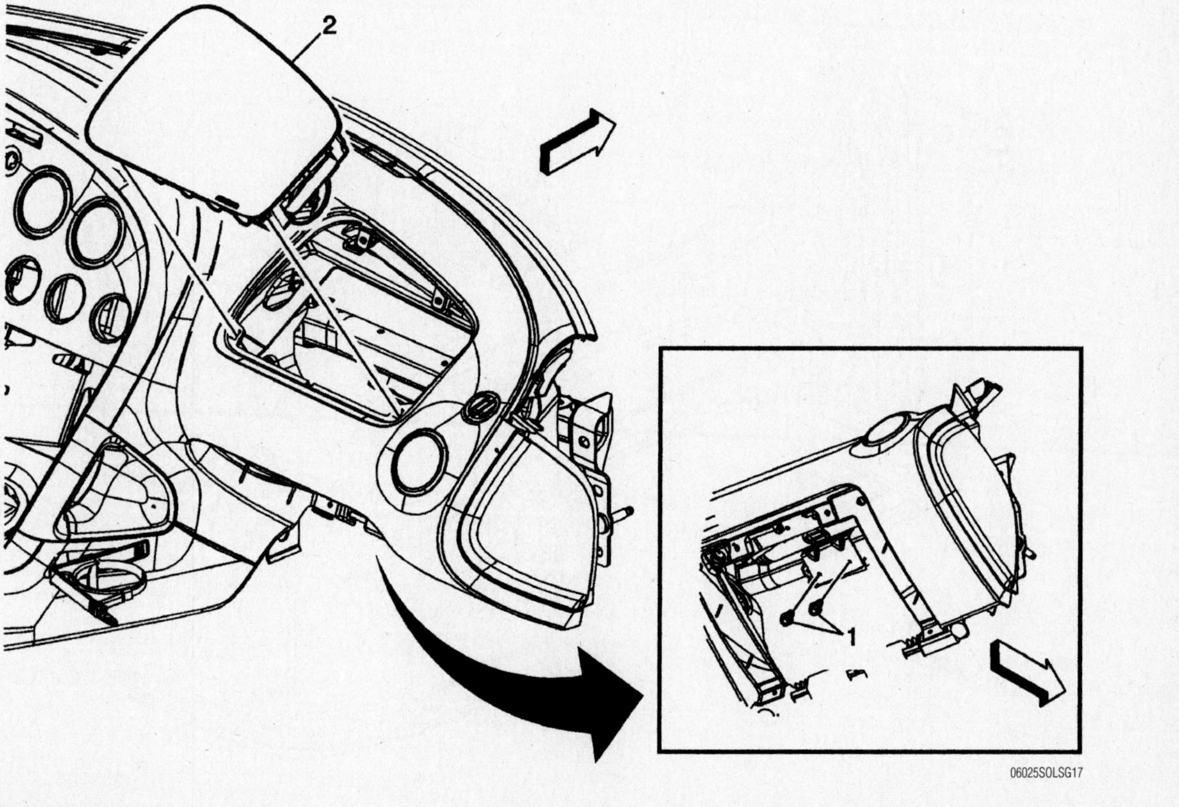

06025SOLSG14

Fig. 174 IP inflator module

06025SOLSG17

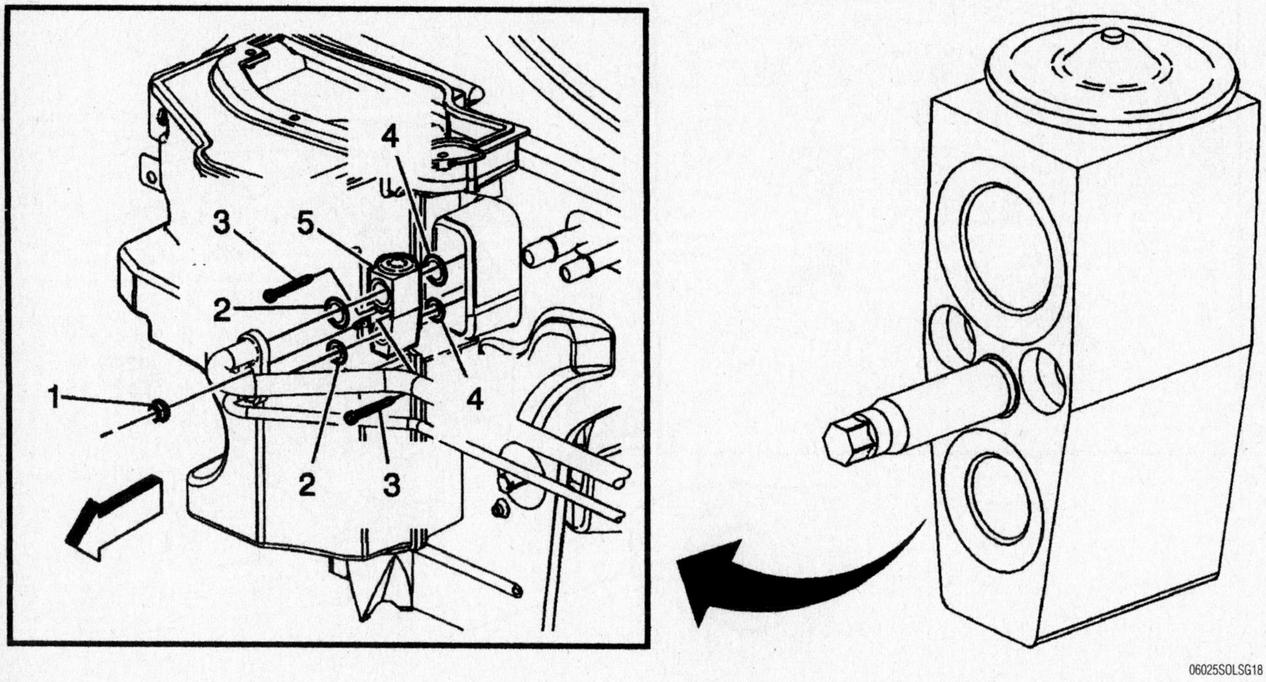

Fig. 175 Thermal expansion valve

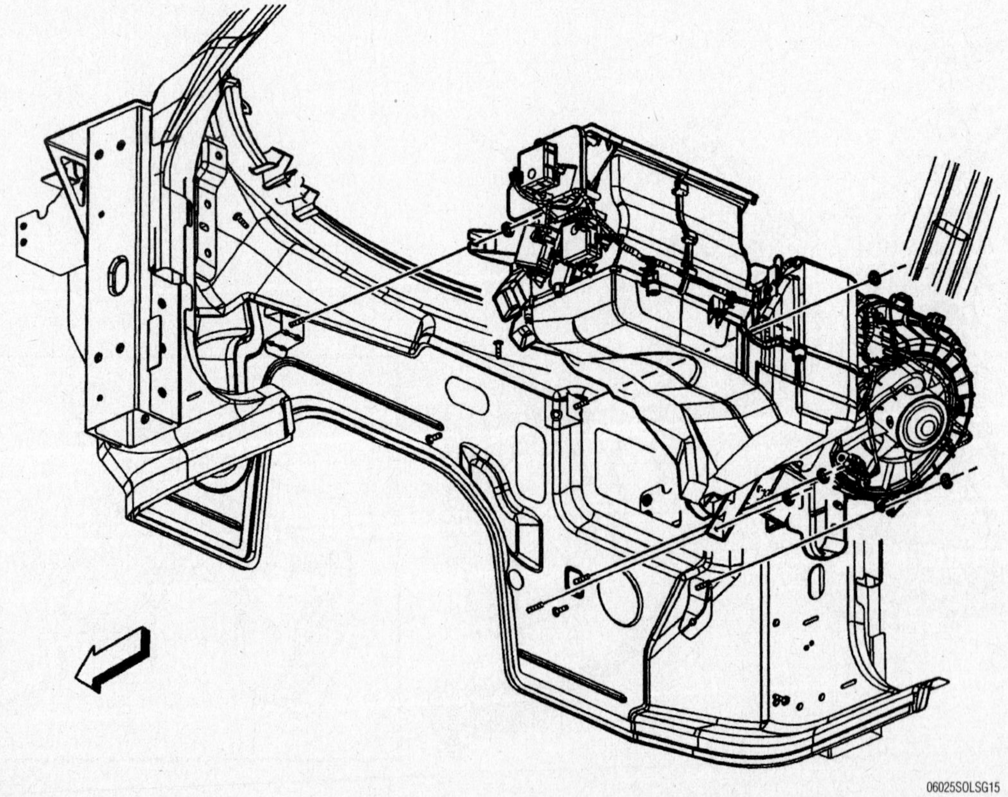

06025SOLSG18

Fig. 176 HVAC unit

06025SOLSG15

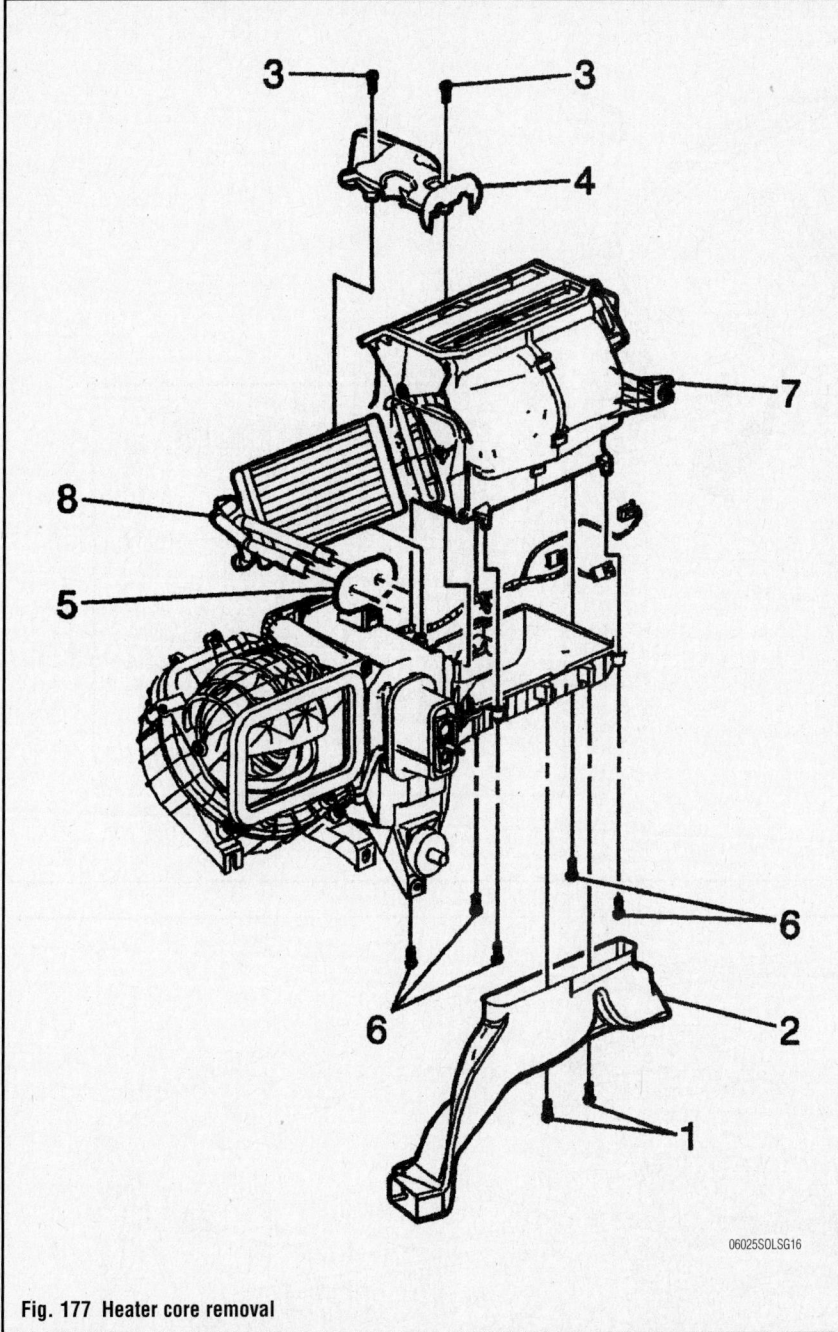

Fig. 177 Heater core removal

06025SOLSG16

4. Drain the cooling system.

5. Recover the refrigerant.

6. Remove the thermal expansion valve nut.

7. Remove the evaporator tube from the thermal expansion valve. Remove and discard the sealing washer.

8. Remove the air inlet grille panel.

9. Remove the heater inlet hose from the heater core.

10. Remove the heater outlet hose from the heater core.

11. Remove the windshield garnish molding.

12. Remove the instrument panel outer trim covers.

13. Remove the instrument panel cluster housing.

14. Remove the knee bolster.

15. Remove the instrument panel accessory trim plate.

16. Remove the instrument panel compartment door frame.

17. Remove the instrument panel lower trim panel.

18. Remove the instrument panel inflatable restraint module.

19. Remove the instrument panel (I/P) upper trim panel.

20. Remove the I/P cluster.

21. Remove the radio.

22. Remove the HVAC control module.

23. Remove the bolts and nuts securing the column to the instrument panel, lower and position the steering column out of the way. Refer to steering column replacement.

24. Remove the instrument panel (I/P) carrier assembly.

25. Note the routing of the I/P wiring harness around the I/P tie bar to ensure the proper reinstallation.

26. Remove the nuts securing the air distribution duct to the I/P tie bar.

27. Remove the bolts securing the I/P tie bar to the brake pedal bracket.

28. Disconnect the HVAC module assembly electrical connectors.

29. Remove the air outlet duct screw.

30. Remove the air outlet duct.

31. Remove the heater core cover screw.

32. Remove the heater core cover.

33. Remove the heater core pass-through seal.

34. Remove the air distribution case screw.

35. Remove the air distribution case.

36. Remove the heater core.

To install:

37. Installation is the reverse of removal procedure.

To install:

49. Installation is the reverse of removal procedure.

50. Please take note of the following tightening specifications:

- HVAC module nuts: 89 inch. lbs. (10 Nm)
- A/C compressor tube nut: 12 ft. lbs. (16 Nm)
- Thermal expansion valve bolt: 12 ft. lbs. (16 Nm)
- IP tie bar bolts: (1) 18 ft. lbs. (25 Nm)
- IP tie bar bolts: (2) 106 inch. lbs. (12 Nm)

- IP carrier fasteners: 80 inch. lbs. (9 Nm)

51. Replace all seals.

52. Evacuate and recharge A/C system.

53. Refill and bleed the cooling system.

54. Enable the SIR system.

55. Connect the negative battery cable.

2007–08 Saturn Sky

See Figures 178 through 185.

1. Before servicing the vehicle, refer to the Precautions Section.

2. Disable the SIR system.

3. Disconnect the negative battery cable.

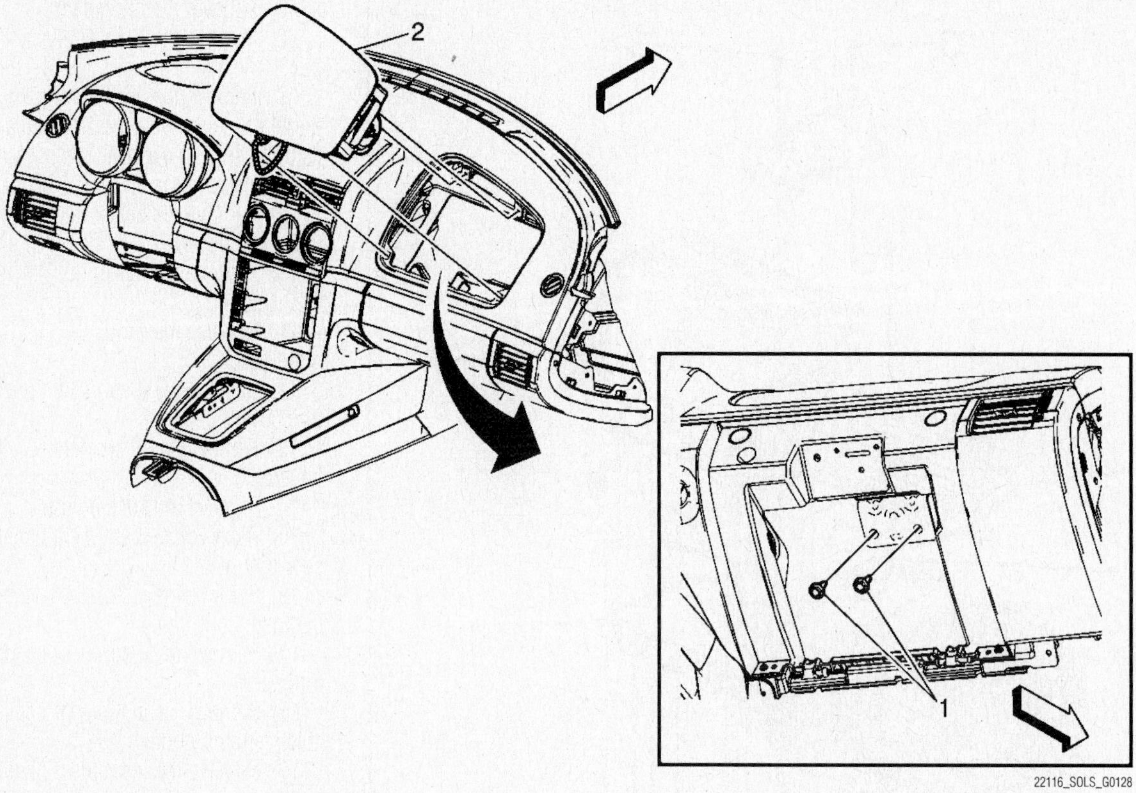

Fig. 178 Inflatable restraint instrument panel module

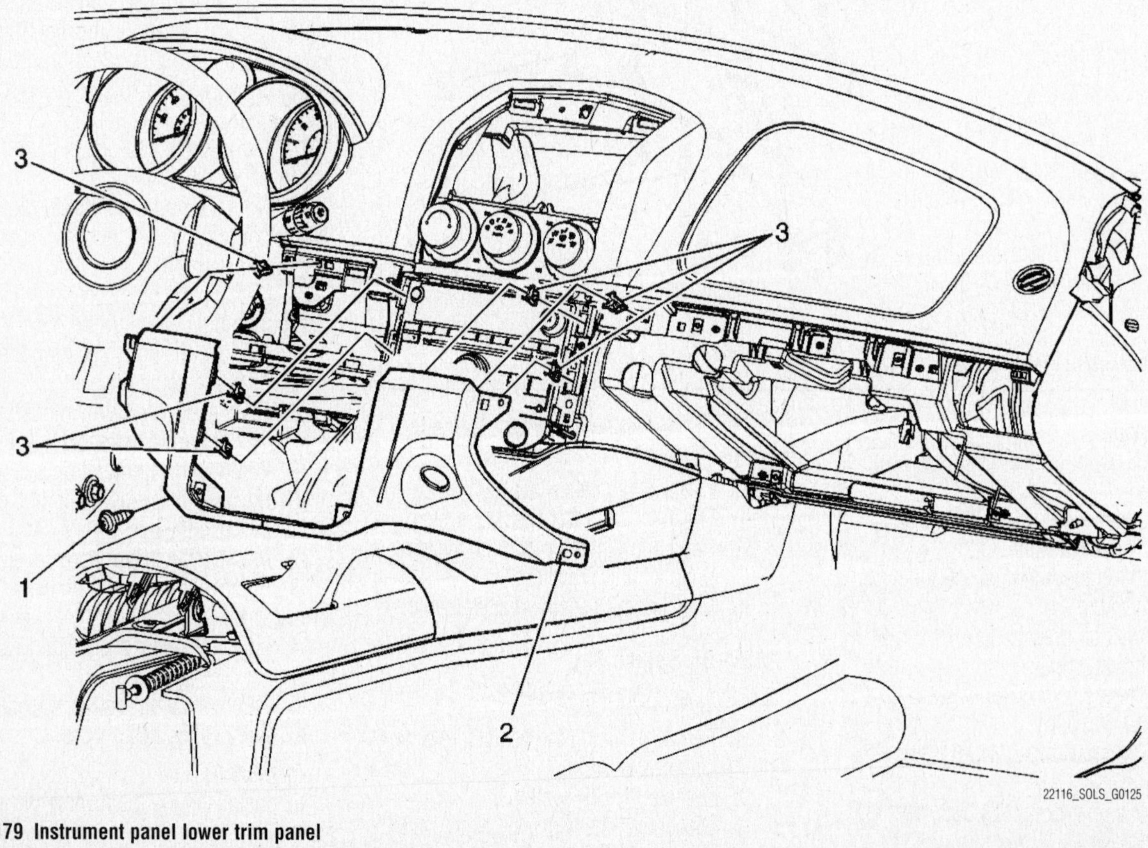

Fig. 179 Instrument panel lower trim panel

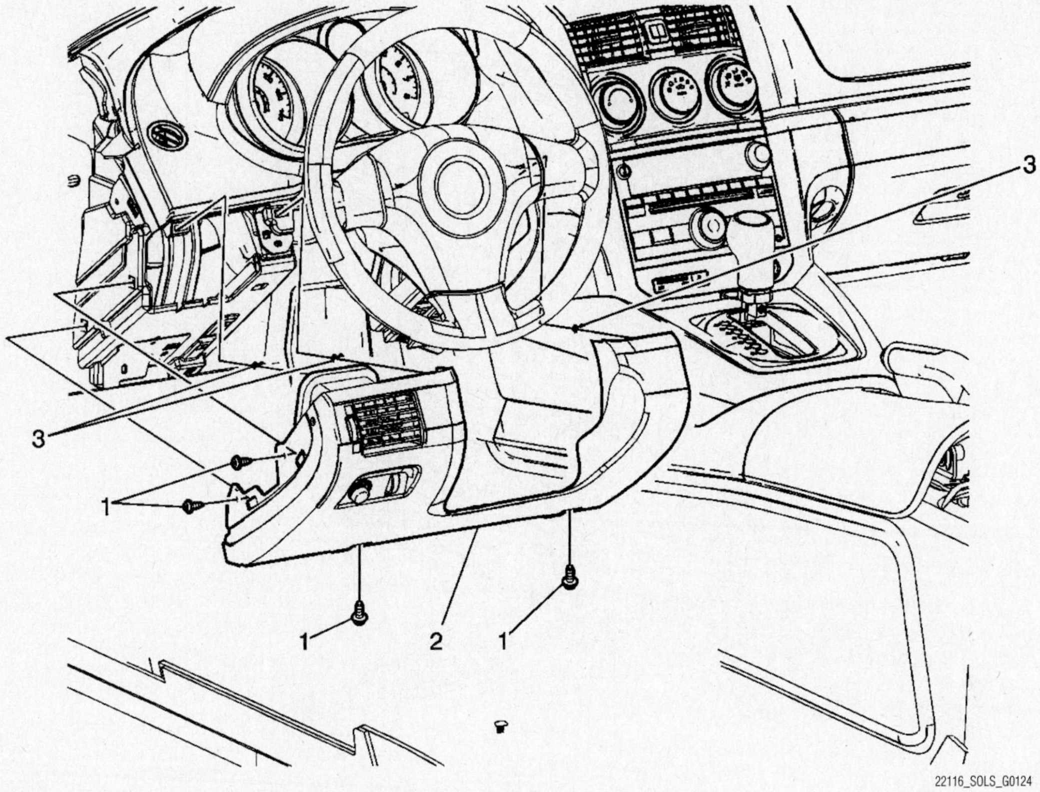

Fig. 180 Knee bolster

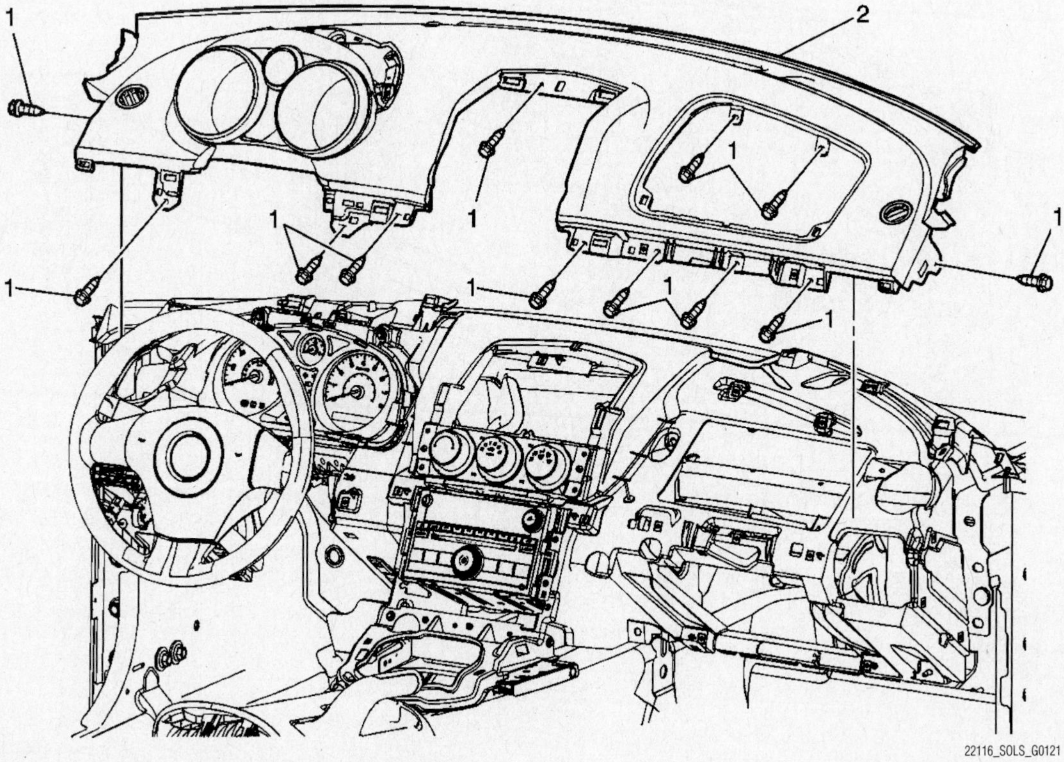

Fig. 181 Saturn Sky instrument upper trim panel

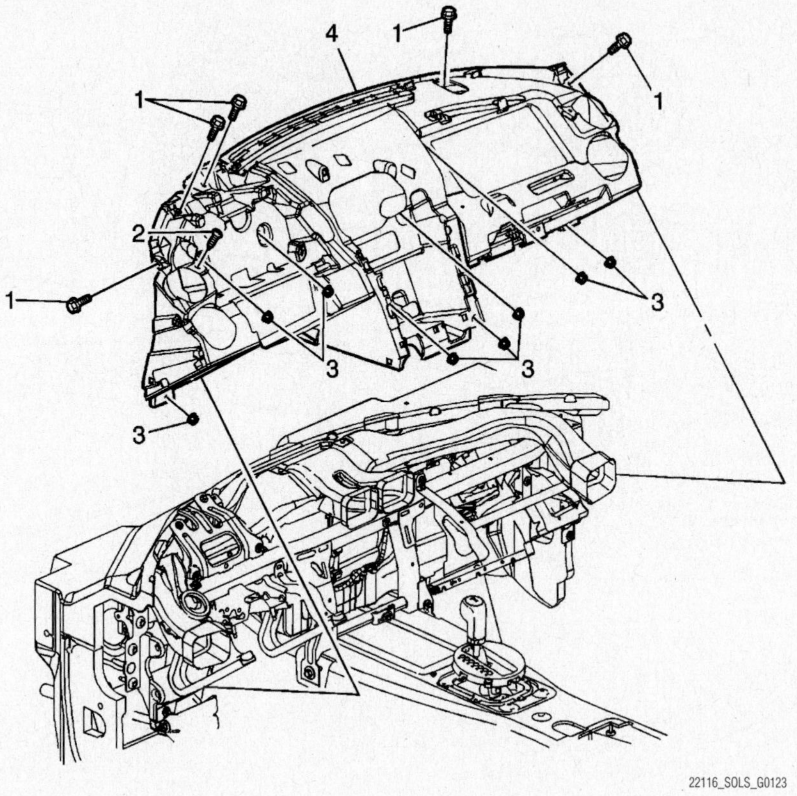

Fig. 182 Instrument panel carrier

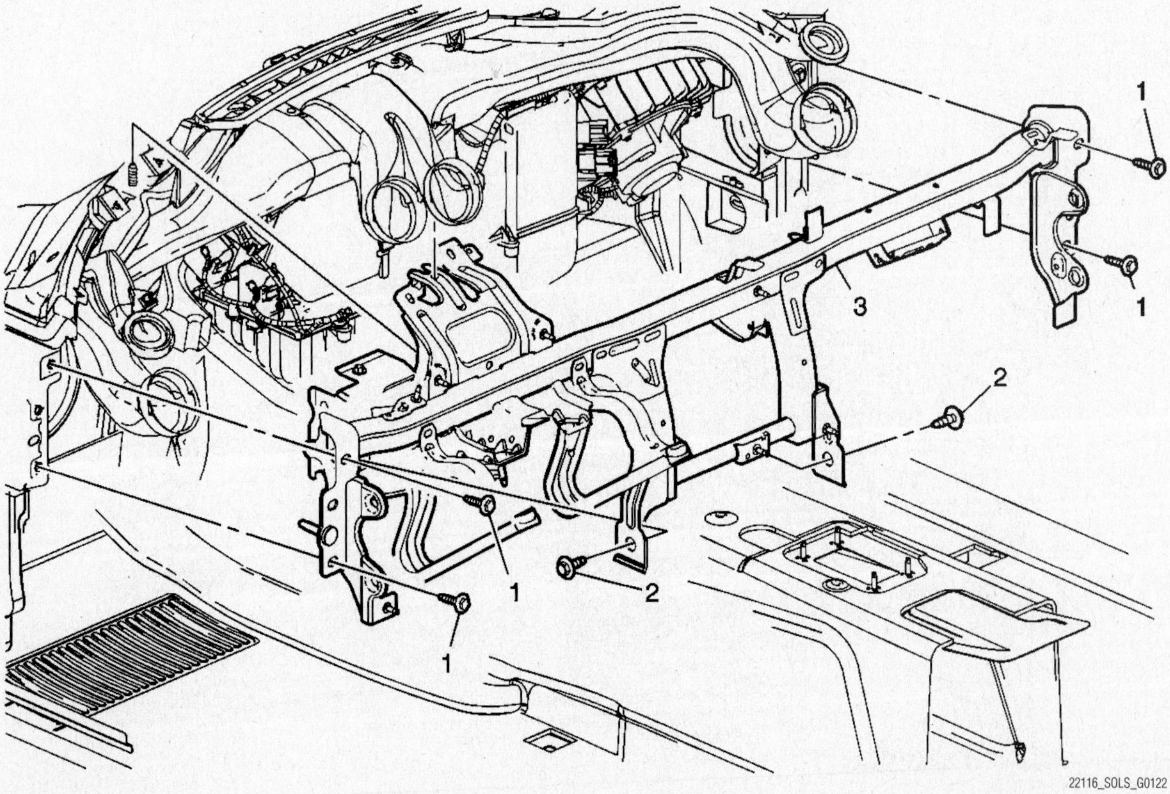

Fig. 183 Instrument panel tie bar

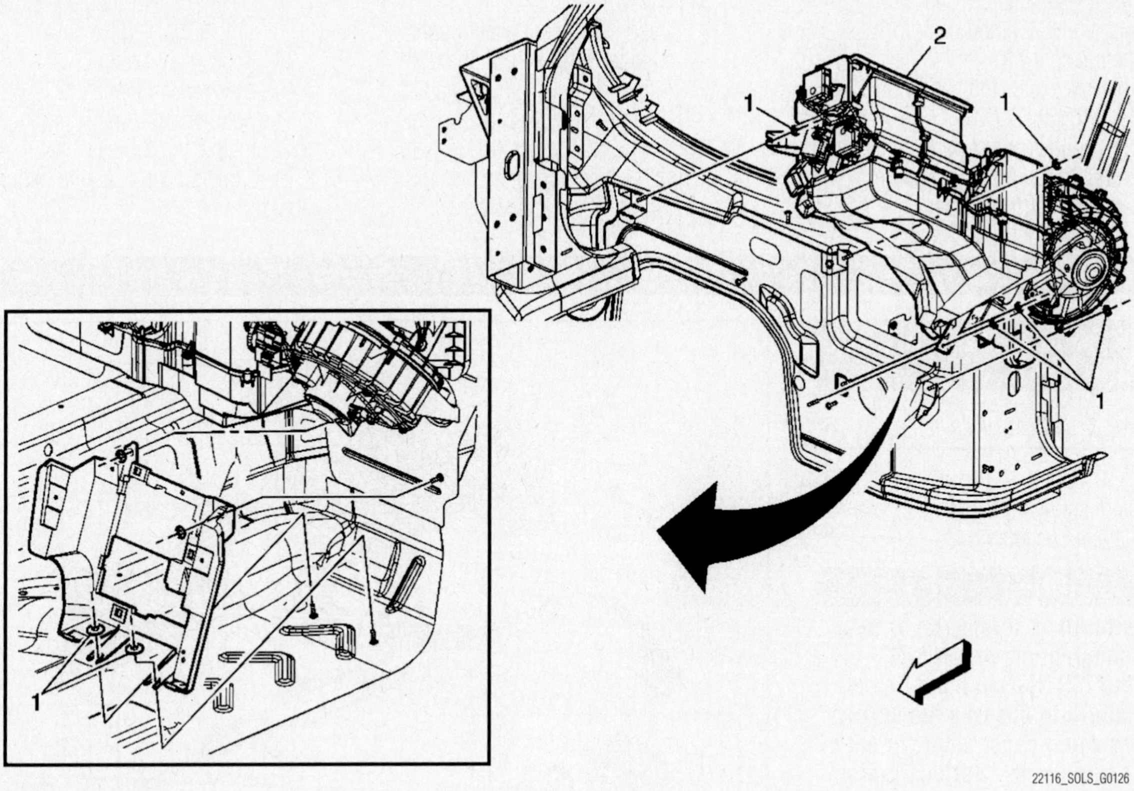
2
1
1
1
1
22116_SOLS_G0126

Fig. 184 HVAC module assembly

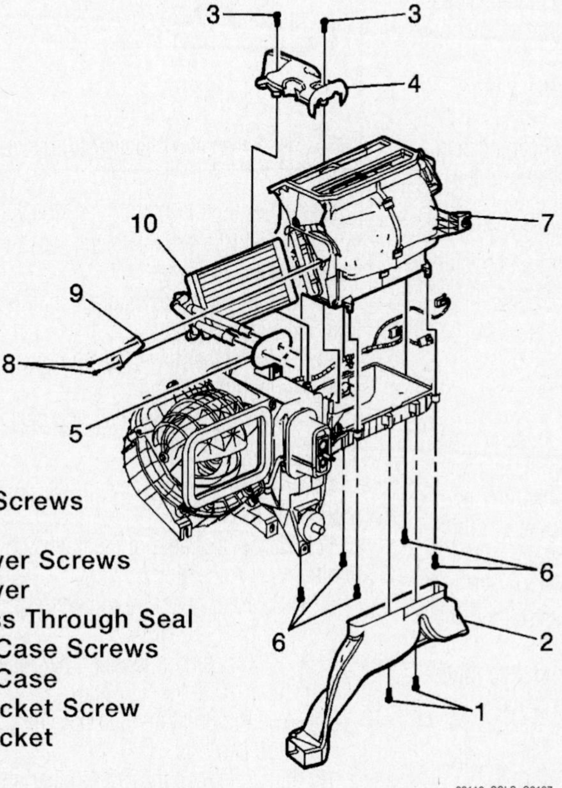
3
3
4
7
10
9
8
5
6
6
2
1
22116_SOLS_G0127

1. Air Outlet Duct Screws
2. Air Outlet Duct
3. Heater Core Cover Screws
4. Heater Core Cover
5. Heater Core Pass Through Seal
6. Air Distribution Case Screws
7. Air Distribution Case
8. Heater Core Bracket Screw
9. Heater Core Bracket
10. Heater Core

Fig. 185 Heater core and related parts

38. Please take note of the following tightening specifications:
- Tighten HVAC module nuts to 89 inch. lbs. (10 Nm)
- Thermal expansion valve nut: 12 ft. lbs. (16 Nm)
- Tighten instrument panel tie bar bolts, (1) to 18 ft. lbs. (25 Nm)
- Tighten instrument panel tie bar

bolts, (2) to 106 inch. lbs. (12 Nm)
- Tighten instrument panel upper trim panel screws 12 ft. lbs. (16 Nm)
- Tighten instrument panel carrier fasteners to 80 inch. lbs. (9 Nm)
- Tighten knee bolster screws to 22 inch. lbs. (2.5 Nm).

- Tighten inflatable restraint instrument panel Module Bolts to 89 inch. lbs. (10 Nm).

39. Replace all seals.
40. Evacuate and recharge A/C system.
41. Refill and bleed the cooling system.
42. Enable the SIR system.
43. Connect the negative battery cable.

STEERING

POWER RACK & PINION STEERING GEAR

REMOVAL & INSTALLATION

See Figure 186.

1. Before servicing the vehicle, refer to the Precautions Section.

❈❈ CAUTION

When performing service on or near the SIR components or the SIR wiring, the SIR system must be disabled. Failure to observe the correct procedure could cause deployment of the SIR components. Serious injury can occur. Failure to observe the correct procedure could also result in unnecessary SIR system repairs.

2. Disable the Supplemental Inflatable Restraint (SIR) system and wait at least one minute.
3. Disconnect the negative battery cable.
4. Secure the steering wheel utilizing a strap to prevent rotation. Locking of the steering column will prevent damage and a possible malfunction of the SIR system. The steering wheel must be secured in position before disconnecting the following components:
- The steering column
- The intermediate shaft
- The steering gear

5. After disconnecting these components, do not move the front tires and wheels. Failure to follow these procedures may cause improper alignment of some components during installation and result in possible damage to the SIR coil.
6. Raise and safely support the vehicle.
7. Remove the wheels.
8. Remove the tie rod end outer nut.
9. Using a 2-jawed tool, remove the outer tie rod end.
10. Drain the power steering system.
11. Disconnect the power steering outlet pipe/hose fitting.

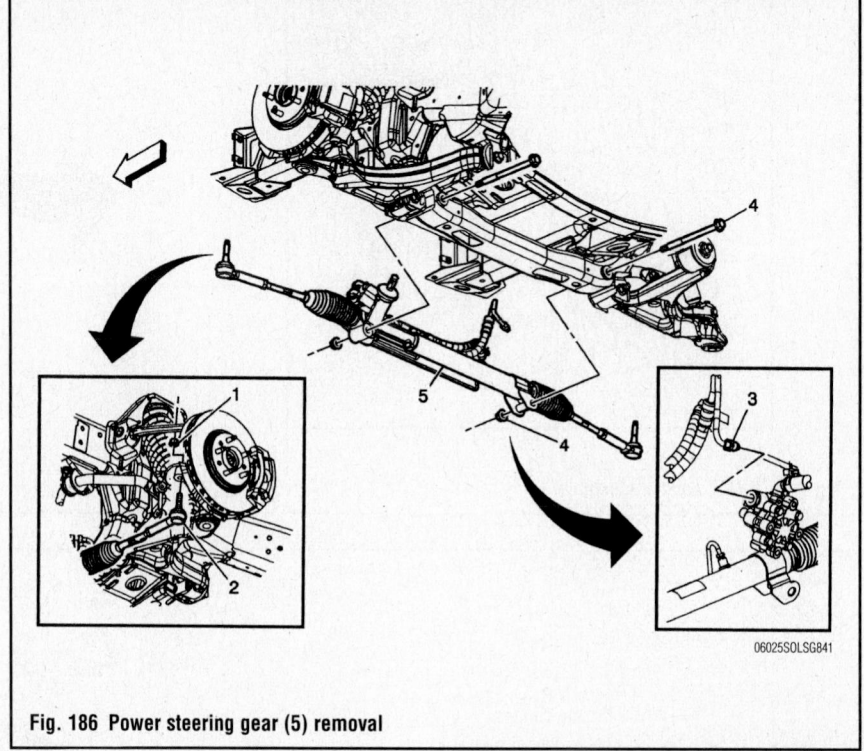

Fig. 186 Power steering gear (5) removal

12. Using tool J 42640 Steering Column Anti-Rotation Pin, or equivalent, lock the steering wheel in place.
13. Remove the intermediate shaft bolt from the steering gear.
14. Remove the power steering gear mounting nuts/bolts.
15. Remove the power steering gear.

To install:
16. Installation is the reverse of removal procedure.
17. Please take note of the following tightening specifications:
- Steering gear mount bolts/nuts: 81 ft. lbs. (110 Nm).
- Power steering outlet pipe/hose fitting: 20 ft. lbs. (27 Nm).
- Tie rod end ball stud nut: 44 ft. lbs. (60 Nm)
18. Fill and bleed the power steering system.
19. Adjust the front toe.

POWER STEERING PUMP

REMOVAL & INSTALLATION

See Figure 187.

1. Before servicing the vehicle, refer to the Precautions Section.
2. Remove the intake manifold cover.
3. Remove the air cleaner assembly.
4. Use the remover J 25034-C to remove the power steering pump pulley.
5. Remove the power steering outlet hose clamp.
6. Remove the outlet hose.
7. Remove the power steering pressure hose fitting.
8. Remove the power steering mounting bolts.
9. Remove the steering pump.

To install:
10. Install the steering pump.
11. Install the power steering

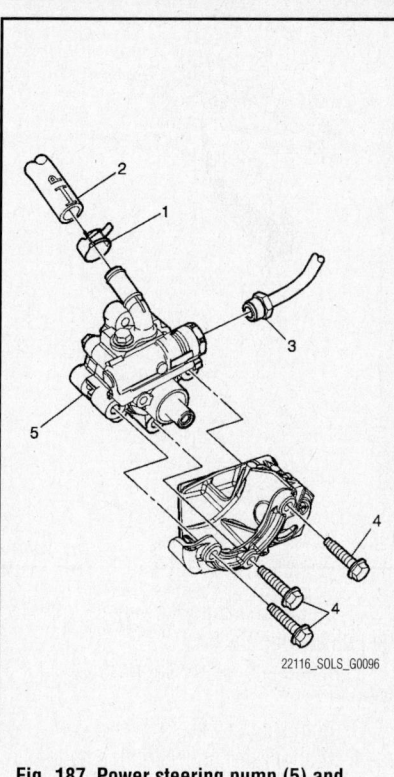

Fig. 187 Power steering pump (5) and related parts

mounting bolts and tighten to 16 ft. lbs. (22 Nm).

12. Install the power steering pressure hose and tighten fitting to 20 ft. lbs. (27 Nm).

13. Install the power steering outlet hose and tighten clamp.

14. Use installer J 25033-C to install the power steering pump pulley.

15. Fill and bleed the power steering system.

BLEEDING

> ❊❊ **WARNING**
>
> **Use clean, new power steering fluid type only. See the Maintenance and Lubrication subsection for fluid specifications. Hoses touching the frame, body or engine may cause system noise. Verify that the hoses do not touch any other part of the vehicle. Loose connections may not leak, but could allow air into the steering system. Verify that all hose connections are tight.**

1. Fill pump reservoir with fluid to minimum system level, FULL COLD level, or middle of hash mark on cap stick fluid level indicator.

2. If equipped with hydro-boost, fully charge the hydro-boost accumulator using the following procedure:

   a. Start the engine.

   b. Firmly apply the brake pedal 10–15 times.

   c. Turn the engine OFF.

3. Raise the vehicle until the front wheels are off the ground.

4. Key on engine OFF, turn the steering wheel from stop to stop 12 times.

5. Vehicles equipped with hydro-boost systems or longer length power steering hoses may require turns up to 15 to 20 steering stop to steering stop.

➡**Power steering fluid level must be maintained throughout bleed procedure.**

6. Verify power steering fluid level per operating specification.

7. Start the engine. Rotate steering wheel from left to right. Check for signs of cavitation or fluid aeration (pump noise/whining).

8. Verify the fluid level. Repeat the bleed procedure, if necessary.

SUSPENSION

COIL SPRING

REMOVAL & INSTALLATION

See Figures 188 and 189.

1. Before servicing the vehicle, refer to the Precautions Section.

2. Raise and support the vehicle.

3. Remove the tire and wheel.

4. Remove the shock module from the vehicle.

5. Install the shock module into the spring compressor.

6. Mark the upper control arm assembly and insulator for proper installation.

7. Turn the spring compressor forcing screw until the coil spring is compressed.

8. Remove the shock absorber upper retaining nut.

9. Remove the shock absorber from the shock module.

10. Loosen the compressor forcing screw until the upper mounting plate and the coil spring may be removed.

11. Remove the upper control arm bracket assembly, the insulator, and the coil spring from the spring compressor.

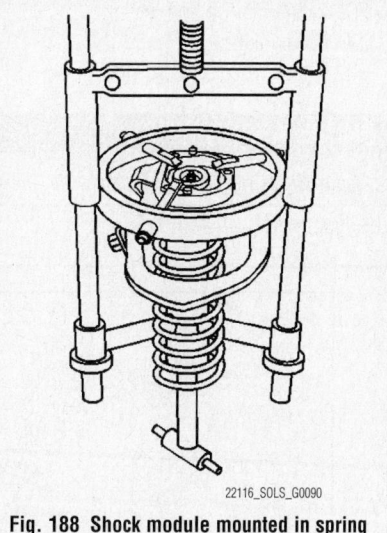

Fig. 188 Shock module mounted in spring compressor

To install:

➡**Ensure the alignment pins in the upper control arm bracket are orientated 90 degrees with the shock absorber lower mounting holes.**

12. Install the coil spring, the insulator, the upper control arm bracket assembly, and the shock absorber to the spring compres-

FRONT SUSPENSION

sor, aligning all marks made in disassembly procedure.

13. Turn the spring compressor forcing screw until the coil spring is compressed.

14. Install the shock absorber retaining nut and tighten to 31 ft. lbs. (42 Nm).

15. Remove the shock module from the spring compressor.

16. Install the shock module to the vehicle.

17. Install the tire and wheel.

18. Lower the vehicle.

19. Check wheel alignment.

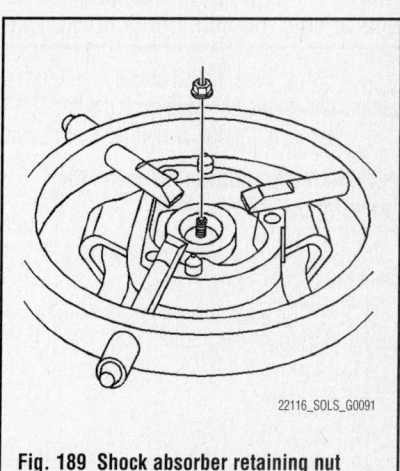

Fig. 189 Shock absorber retaining nut

CONTROL LINKS

REMOVAL & INSTALLATION

1. Before servicing the vehicle, refer to the Precautions Section.
2. Raise and support the vehicle.
3. Remove the tire and wheel.
4. Remove upper and lower control link retaining nuts.
5. Remove control link.

To install:

6. Install control link.
7. Tighten upper and lower control link retaining nuts to 53 ft. lbs. (72 Nm).
8. Install the tire and wheel.
9. Lower vehicle.

LOWER CONTROL ARM

REMOVAL & INSTALLATION

See Figure 190.

1. Before servicing the vehicle, refer to the Precautions Section.
2. Raise and support the vehicle.
3. Remove the tire and wheel.
4. Disconnect the stabilizer link from the lower control arm.
5. Disconnect the shock module from the lower control arm.
6. Separate the outer tie rod end from the steering knuckle. DO NOT loosen the adjustment jamb nut.

➡**Loosen but DO NOT remove the nut until the ball stud has been separated from the knuckle.**

❊❊ WARNING

The ball stud must not rotate during disassembly or reassembly. Hand tools must be used to keep the ball stud from rotating. If air tools are used and the stud is allowed to rotate, damage to the ball stud and/or stud mounting hole may occur.

7. Using the J-42188-B Ball Joint Separator, separate the ball stud from the knuckle.
8. Remove the lower ball joint stud nut.

➡**Mark frame alignment cams for installation.**

9. Remove the lower control arm to frame nuts and cam.
10. Remove the lower control arm to frame alignment cam bolts.
11. Remove the lower control arm.

To install:

12. Install the lower control arm.
13. Install the lower control arm to frame alignment cam bolts.

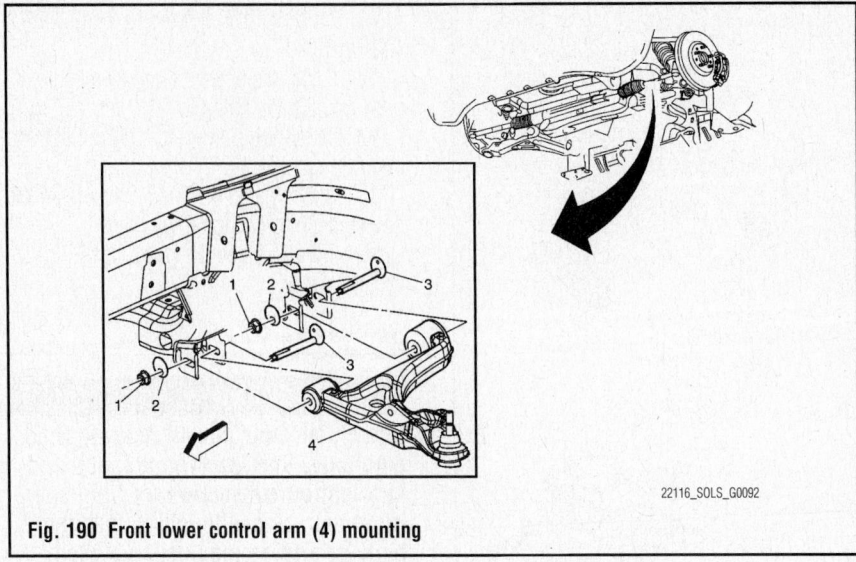

Fig. 190 Front lower control arm (4) mounting

22116_SOLS_G0092

14. Install the lower control arm to frame nuts and cams.
15. Position the cams to previous marks.
16. Tighten lower control arm nuts to 122 ft. lbs. (165 Nm).
17. Install the lower ball joint stud nut and tighten to 30 ft. lbs. (40 Nm), plus an additional 135°
18. Reconnect the shock module to the lower control arm.
19. Reconnect the stabilizer link to the lower control arm.
20. Install the tire and wheel.
21. Lower vehicle.
22. Check wheel alignment.

SHOCK ABSORBERS

REMOVAL & INSTALLATION

See Figure 191.

1. Before servicing the vehicle, refer to the Precautions Section.
2. Raise and safely support the vehicle.
3. Remove the wheels.
4. Without disconnecting the hydraulic brake hose from the caliper, remove and support the brake caliper with bracket as an assembly.
5. Separate the lower control arm ball stud from the steering knuckle.
6. Remove the lower shock mounting bolts.
7. Remove the upper shock mounting nuts.

➡**Raise the steering knuckle and upper control arm while removing the shock module toward the rear of the vehicle.**

8. Remove the shock module.

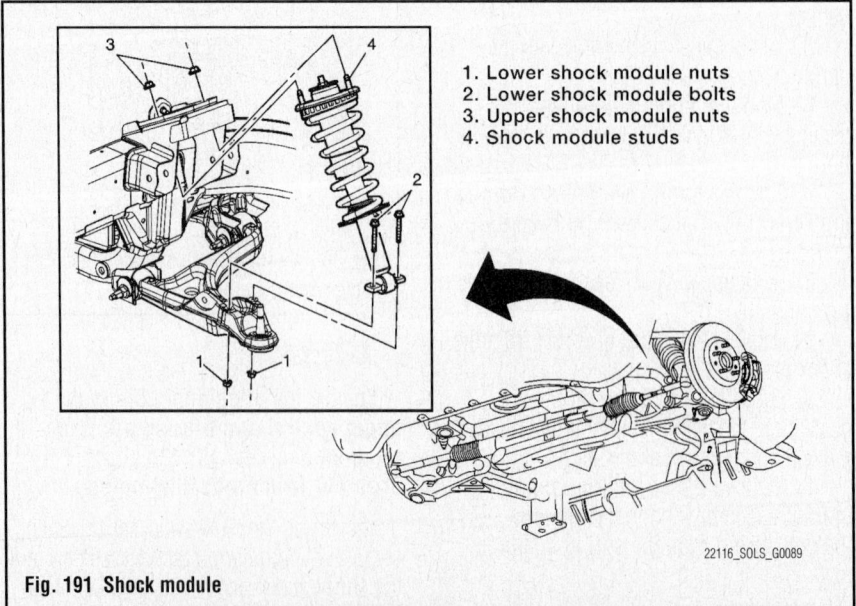

1. Lower shock module nuts
2. Lower shock module bolts
3. Upper shock module nuts
4. Shock module studs

Fig. 191 Shock module

22116_SOLS_G0089

To install:

9. Install the shock module.

10. Install the upper strut nuts and tighten to 35 ft. lbs. (47 Nm)

11. Install the lower strut bolts, nuts and tighten to 21 ft. lbs. (28 Nm)

12. Reconnect the lower control arm ball stud to the steering knuckle and tighten to 30 ft. lbs. (40 Nm) plus an additional 135°

13. Install brake caliper assembly and tighten caliper bracket bolts to 85ft. lbs. (115 Nm).

14. Install the wheels.

15. Lower vehicle.

16. Check wheel alignment.

TESTING

1. Test drive vehicle.

2. Inspect each shock absorber for external fluid leakage.

3. Use your hands in order to lift up and push down each corner of the vehicle 3 times.

4. Remove your hands from the vehicle.

5. Replace any shock that exceeds more than two bounces.

STABILIZER BAR

REMOVAL & INSTALLATION

1. Before servicing the vehicle, refer to the Precautions Section.

2. Raise and support the vehicle.

3. Remove the tire and wheel.

4. Remove the stabilizer shaft bar from the stabilizer shaft links.

5. Remove stabilizer shaft bar bolts.

6. Remove stabilizer shaft bar and brackets.

7. If replacing bar remove insulators and replace if necessary.

To install:

8. Install insulators if previously replaced.

9. Lift stabilizer shaft bar into place with brackets.

10. Install bracket mounting bolts and tighten to 41 ft. lbs. (55 Nm).

11. Reattach the stabilizer shaft bar to the stabilizer shaft links.

12. Tighten stabilizer link retaining nuts to 53 ft. lbs. (72 Nm).

13. Install the tires and wheels.

14. Lower vehicle.

STEERING KNUCKLE

REMOVAL & INSTALLATION

See Figure 192.

1. Before servicing the vehicle, refer to the Precautions Section.

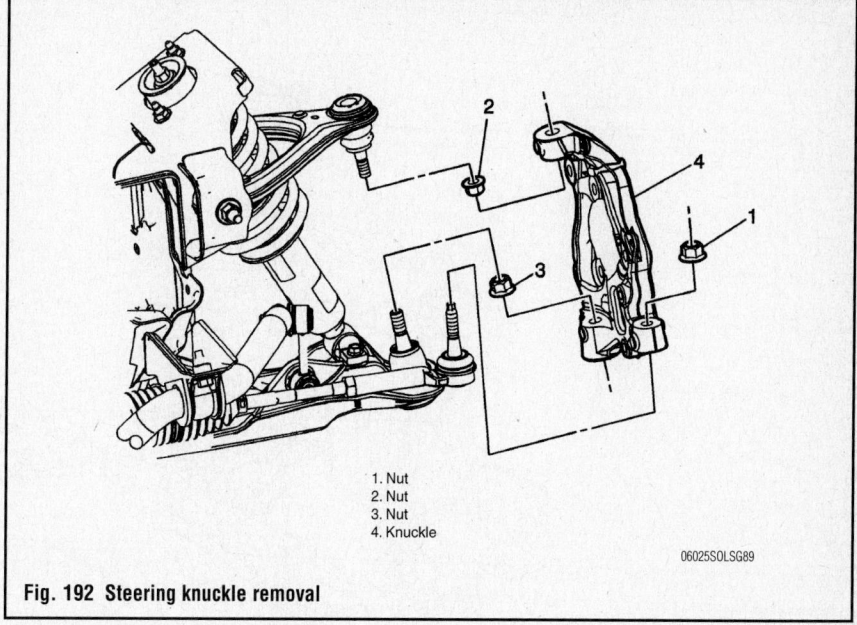

1. Nut
2. Nut
3. Nut
4. Knuckle

06025SOLSG89

Fig. 192 Steering knuckle removal

2. Raise and support the vehicle.

3. Remove the tire and wheel.

4. Remove the tie rod end nut.

5. Using the appropriate tool, remove the tie rod end from the steering knuckle.

➥**Loosen but DO NOT remove the nuts until the ball studs have been separated from the knuckle.**

6. Use the appropriate tool to remove the upper and lower ball joint from the steering knuckle.

7. Remove the upper and lower ball joint nuts.

8. Remove the steering knuckle.

To install:

9. Install the steering knuckle.

10. Install the upper and lower ball joint nuts.

11. Tighten the upper ball joint retaining nut to 22 ft. lbs. (30 Nm). plus an additional 150°

12. Tighten the lower ball joint retaining nut to 30 ft. lbs. (40 Nm). plus an additional 135°

13. Install tie rod end and retaining nut and tighten to 22 ft. lbs. (30 Nm). plus an additional 115°

14. Install the tire and wheel.

15. Lower vehicle.

16. Check wheel alignment.

UPPER CONTROL ARM

REMOVAL & INSTALLATION

See Figure 193.

1. Before servicing the vehicle, refer to the Precautions Section.

2. Raise and support the vehicle.

3. Remove the tire and wheel.

4. Remove the shock module.

➥**Loosen but DO NOT remove the nut until the ball stud has been separated from the knuckle.**

✷✷ WARNING

The ball stud must not rotate during disassembly or reassembly. Hand tools must be used to keep the ball stud from rotating. If air tools are used and the stud is allowed to rotate, damage to the ball stud and/or stud mounting hole may occur.

5. Using the J-42188-B Ball Joint Separator, separate the ball stud from the knuckle.

6. Remove the upper ball joint stud nut.

7. Disconnect the wiring harness from the upper control arm.

8. Remove the upper control arm mounting bolts.

9. Remove the upper control arm.

To install:

10. Install the upper control arm.

11. Install the upper control arm mounting bolts and tighten to 81 ft. lbs. (110 Nm).

12. Reconnect the wiring harness to the upper control arm.

13. Install the upper ball joint stud nut. Tighten to 22 ft. lbs. (30 Nm), plus an additional 150°

14. Install the shock module.

15. Install the tire and wheel.

16. Lower vehicle.

17. Check wheel alignment.

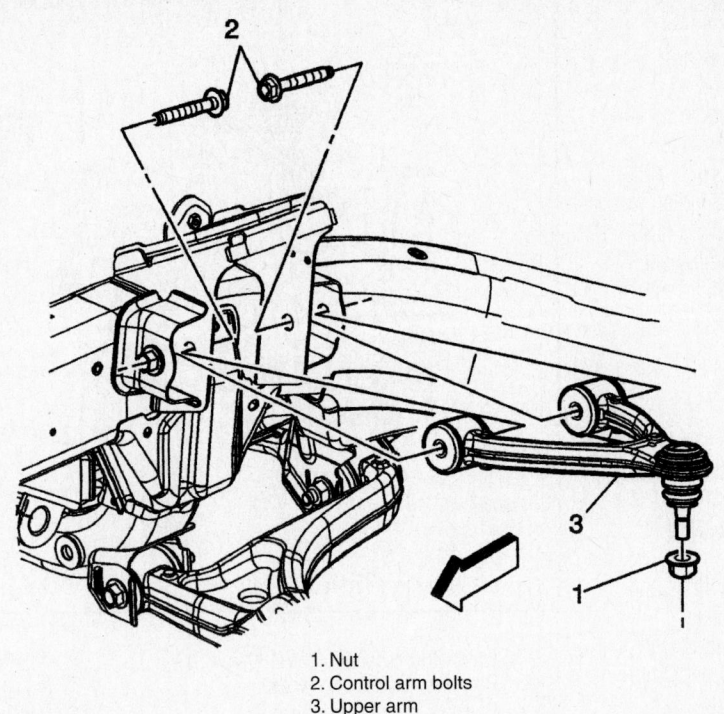

1. Nut
2. Control arm bolts
3. Upper arm

06025SOLSG87

Fig. 193 Front upper control arm mounting

WHEEL HUB AND BEARING

REMOVAL & INSTALLATION

See Figure 194.

1. Before servicing the vehicle, refer to the Precautions Section.

2. Raise and support the vehicle.
3. Remove the tire and wheel.
4. Remove the brake caliper with mounting bracket.
5. Remove the brake rotor.
6. Disconnect the speed sensor electrical connector and the wiring harness from the retainers on the steering knuckle.
7. Remove the wheel hub mounting bolts.
8. Remove the wheel hub/bearing/speed sensor assembly.

To install:

9. Install the wheel hub and bearing/speed sensor assembly.
10. Tighten the wheel hub and bearing assembly mounting bolts to 85 ft. lbs. (115 Nm).
11. Reconnect the speed sensor electrical connector and the wiring harness to the retainers on the steering knuckle.
12. Install the brake rotor.
13. Install brake caliper assembly and tighten bracket mounting bolts to 85 ft. lbs. (115 Nm).
14. Install the tire and wheel.
15. Lower vehicle.

ADJUSTMENT

The front wheel hub and bearing assembly is a sealed unit and does not require adjustments or repacking.

REPACKING

The front wheel hub and bearing assembly is a sealed unit and does not require adjustments or repacking.

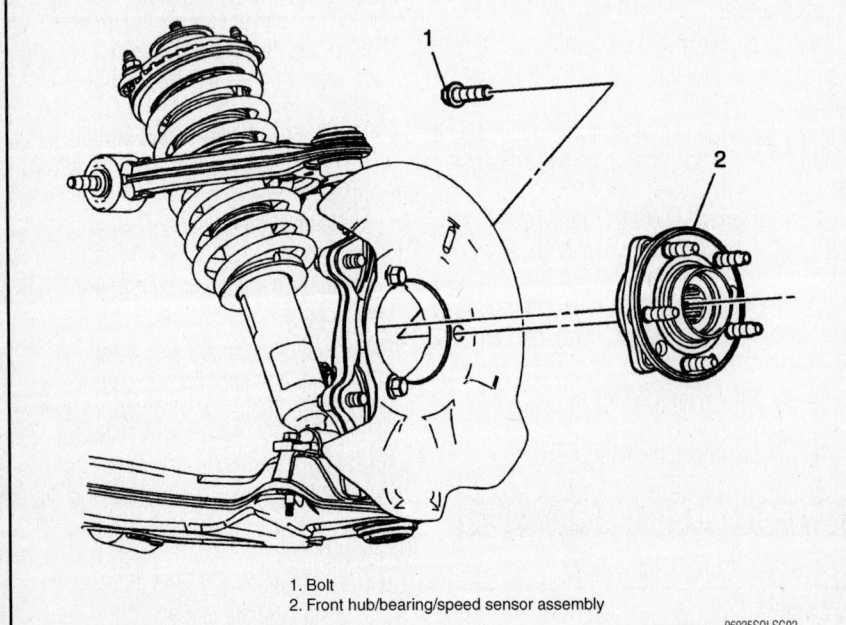

1. Bolt
2. Front hub/bearing/speed sensor assembly

06025SOLSG92

Fig. 194 Front hub/bearing/speed sensor

SUSPENSION

REAR SUSPENSION

COIL SPRING

REMOVAL & INSTALLATION

See Figures 195 and 196.

1. Before servicing the vehicle, refer to the Precautions Section.
2. Raise and support the vehicle.
3. Remove the tire and wheel.
4. Remove the shock module from the vehicle.
5. Install the shock module into the spring compressor.
6. Mark the upper control arm assembly and insulator for proper installation.
7. Turn the spring compressor forcing screw until the coil spring is compressed.
8. Remove the shock absorber upper retaining nut.
9. Remove the shock absorber from the shock module.
10. Loosen the compressor forcing screw until the upper mounting plate and the coil spring may be removed.
11. Remove the upper control arm bracket assembly, the insulator, and the coil spring from the spring compressor.

To install:

➡**Ensure the alignment pins in the upper control arm bracket are orientated 90 degrees with the shock absorber lower mounting holes.**

12. Install the coil spring, the insulator, the upper control arm bracket assembly, and the shock absorber to the spring compres-

sor, aligning all marks made in disassembly procedure.
13. Turn the spring compressor forcing screw until the coil spring is compressed.
14. Install the shock absorber retaining nut and tighten to 31 ft. lbs. (42 Nm).
15. Remove the shock module from the spring compressor.

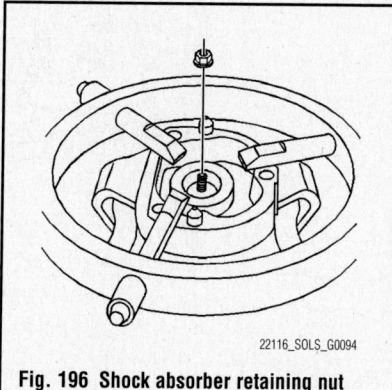

Fig. 196 Shock absorber retaining nut

16. Install the shock module to the vehicle.
17. Install the tire and wheel.
18. Lower the vehicle.
19. Check wheel alignment.

KNUCKLE

REMOVAL & INSTALLATION

See Figure 197.

1. Before servicing the vehicle, refer to the Precautions Section.
2. Raise and support the vehicle.
3. Remove the tire and wheel.
4. Remove the wheel bearing hub assembly.
5. Remove the outer tie rod end retaining nut.
6. Use the appropriate tool to remove the tie rod end from the steering knuckle.
7. Remove the upper ball joint retaining nut.
8. Use the appropriate tool to remove the upper ball joint from the knuckle.
9. Remove the lower ball joint retaining nut.
10. Use the appropriate tool to remove the lower ball joint ball joint from the knuckle.
11. Remove the steering knuckle.

To install:

12. Installation is the reverse of removal procedure.
13. Please take note of the following tightening specifications:

- Tie rod end stud nut: 22 ft. lbs. (30 Nm) plus an additional 150°
- Upper ball stud nut: 22 ft. lbs. (30 Nm) plus an additional 150°
- Lower ball stud nut: 30 ft. lbs. (40 Nm) plus an additional 135°

14. Check the alignment.

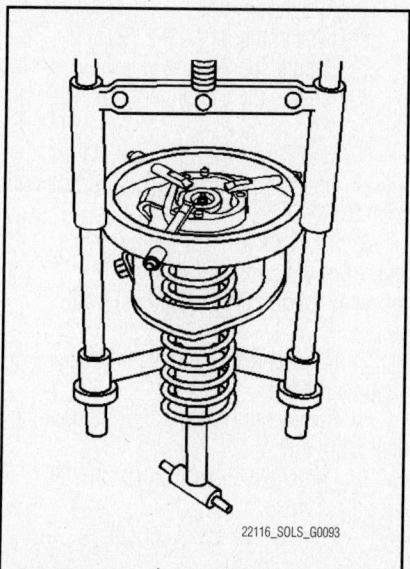

Fig. 195 Shock module mounted in spring compressor

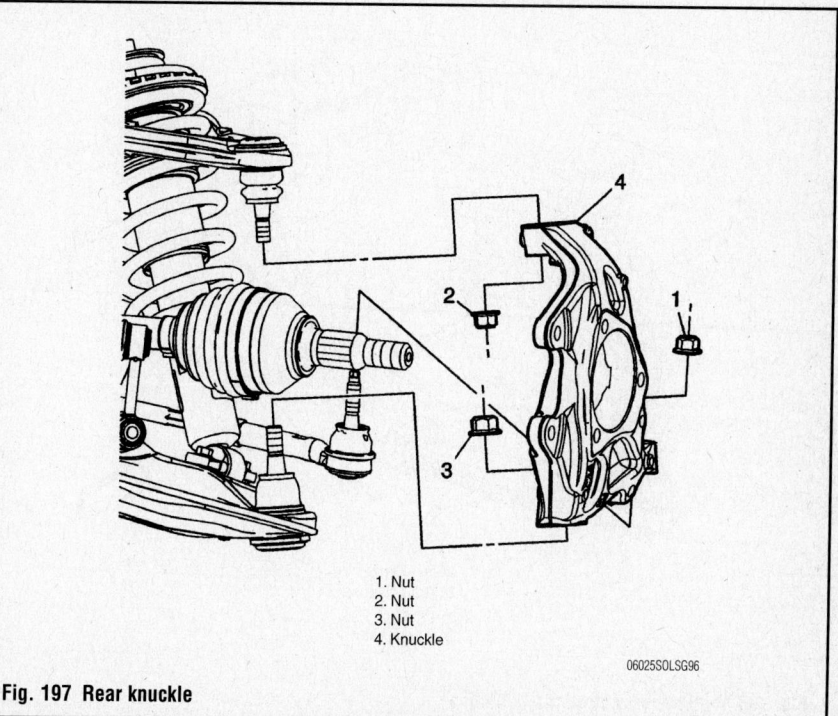

1. Nut
2. Nut
3. Nut
4. Knuckle

Fig. 197 Rear knuckle

LOWER CONTROL ARM

REMOVAL & INSTALLATION

See Figure 198.

1. Before servicing the vehicle, refer to the Precautions Section.
2. Raise and support the vehicle.
3. Remove the tire and wheel.
4. Disconnect the stabilizer link from the lower control arm.
5. Disconnect the shock module from the lower control arm.
6. Separate the rear adjustment link from the suspension knuckle. DO NOT loosen the adjustment jamb nut.
7. Remove the lower control arm ball joint nut.
8. Using the appropriate tool, separate the lower control arm ball joint from the knuckle.

➡ **Mark alignment adjusting cams for installation.**

9. Remove the lower control arm nuts.
10. Remove the adjusting cams.
11. Remove the lower control arm to frame bolts.
12. Remove the lower control arm.

To install:

13. Install the lower control arm.
14. Install the lower control arm to frame bolts.
15. Install adjusting cams and control arm nuts.

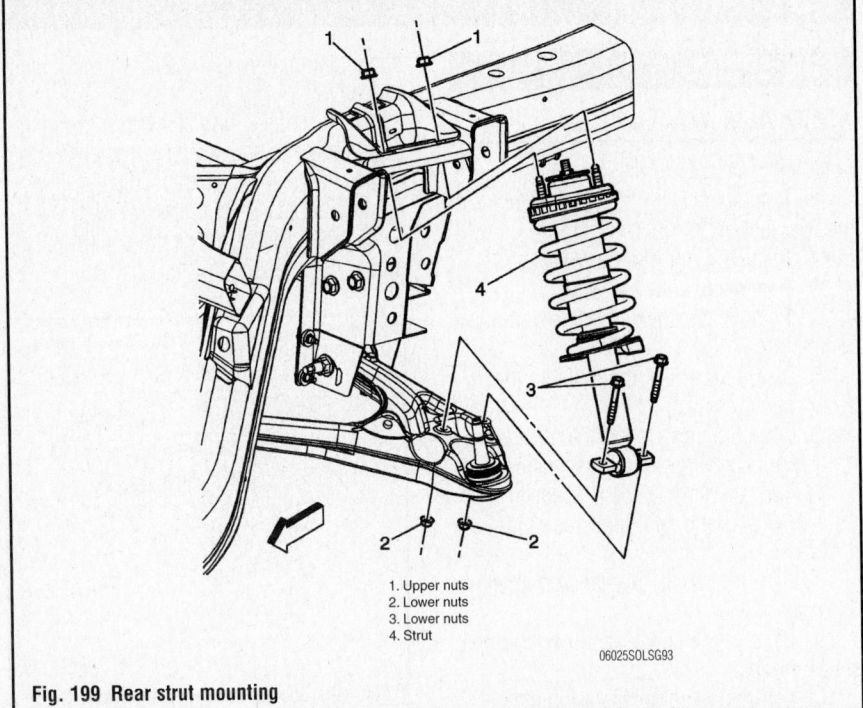

1. Upper nuts
2. Lower nuts
3. Lower nuts
4. Strut

06025SOLSG93

Fig. 199 Rear strut mounting

➡ **Install cams in original location previously marked.**

16. Tighten the lower control arm nuts to 122 ft. lbs. (165 Nm).
17. Install the lower control arm ball joint stud in the knuckle.
18. Install the lower control arm ball joint retaining nut to 30 ft. lbs. (40 Nm). plus an additional 135°

19. Reconnect the shock module to the lower control arm.
20. Reconnect the stabilizer link to the lower control arm.
21. Install the tire and wheel.
22. Lower vehicle.
23. Check wheel alignment.

SHOCK ABSORBER

REMOVAL & INSTALLATION

See Figure 199.

1. Before servicing the vehicle, refer to the Precautions Section.
2. Raise and support the vehicle.
3. Remove the tire and wheel.
4. Remove the adjustment link retaining nut.
5. Using the J-42188-B Ball Joint Separator, separate the adjustment link ball stud from the knuckle.
6. Separate the rear adjustment link from the suspension knuckle. DO NOT loosen the adjustment jamb nut.
7. Remove the upper shock module mounting nuts.
8. Remove the lower shock module mounting nuts.
9. Remove the lower shock module mounting bolts.
10. Remove the shock module.

➡ **Remove the strut toward the rear of the vehicle.**

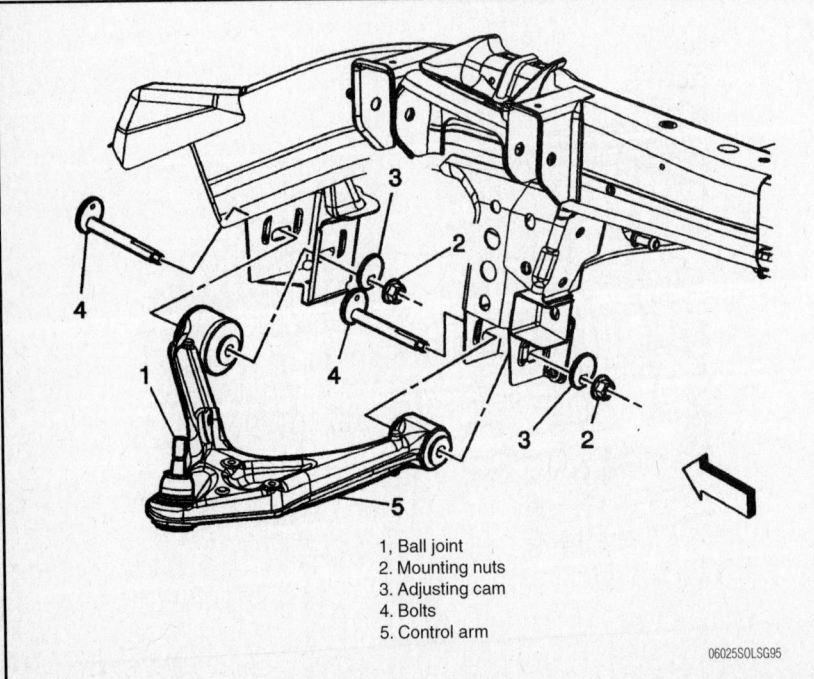

1. Ball joint
2. Mounting nuts
3. Adjusting cam
4. Bolts
5. Control arm

06025SOLSG95

Fig. 198 Rear lower control arm mounting

To install:

11. Install the shock module.

12. Install the lower shock module mounting bolt sand nuts. Tighten the nuts to 21 ft. lbs. (28 Nm).

13. Install the upper shock module mounting nuts and tighten to 35 ft. lbs. (47 Nm).

14. Reconnect the rear adjustment link and tighten the retaining nut to 22 ft. lbs. (30 Nm). plus an additional 150°

15. Install tire and wheel.

16. Lower vehicle.

TESTING

1. Test drive vehicle.

2. Inspect each shock absorber for external fluid leakage.

3. Use your hands in order to lift up and push down each corner of the vehicle 3 times.

4. Remove your hands from the vehicle.

5. Replace any shock that exceeds more than two bounces.

STABILIZER BAR & END LINKS

REMOVAL & INSTALLATION

See Figures 200 and 201.

1. Before servicing the vehicle, refer to the Precautions Section.

2. Raise and support the vehicle.

3. Remove the tires and wheels.

4. Disconnect the heated oxygen sensor (HO₂S) electrical connector.

➡**The HO₂S uses a permanently attached pigtail and connector. This pigtail should not be removed from the sensor. Damage or removal of the pigtail or connector will affect proper operation of the sensor.**

5. Remove the HO₂S.

6. Remove the catalytic converter to muffler nuts.

7. Have an assistant support the muffler assembly.

8. Separate the muffler insulators from the hangers.

9. With the aid of an assistant, remove the muffler assembly.

10. Remove the stabilizer shaft link mounting nuts.

11. Remove the stabilizer shaft links.

12. Remove the stabilizer shaft mounting bracket bolts.

13. Remove the stabilizer shaft mounting brackets.

14. Remove the stabilizer shaft.

To install:

15. Installation is the reverse of removal procedure.

16. Please take note of the following tightening specifications:

- Mounting bracket bolts: 41 ft. lbs. (55 Nm).
- End link nuts: 53 ft. lbs. (72 Nm).
- Catalytic converter to muffler nuts: 13 ft. lbs. (17 Nm).
- HO₂S: 30 ft. lbs. (41 Nm).

✱✱ WARNING

The oxygen sensor uses a permanently attached pigtail and connector. Do not remove the pigtail from the oxygen sensor. Damage to or removal of the pigtail connector could affect proper operation of the oxygen sensor.

✱✱ WARNING

The use of excessive force may damage the threads in the exhaust manifold/pipe.

➡**The in-line connector and louvered end must be kept clear of grease, dirt or other contaminants. Avoid using cleaning solvents of any type. DO NOT drop or roughly handle the heated oxygen sensor (HO₂S).**

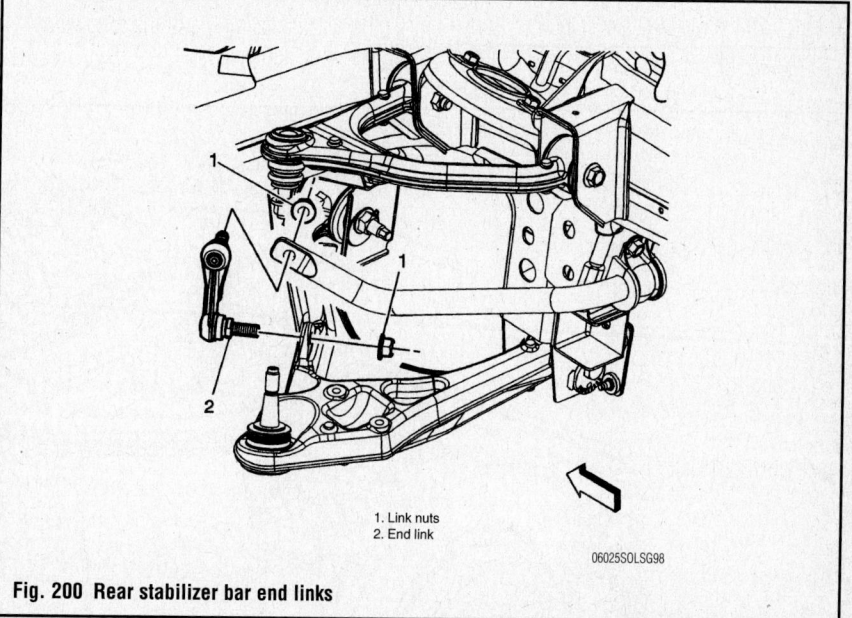

1. Link nuts
2. End link

06025SOLSG98

Fig. 200 Rear stabilizer bar end links

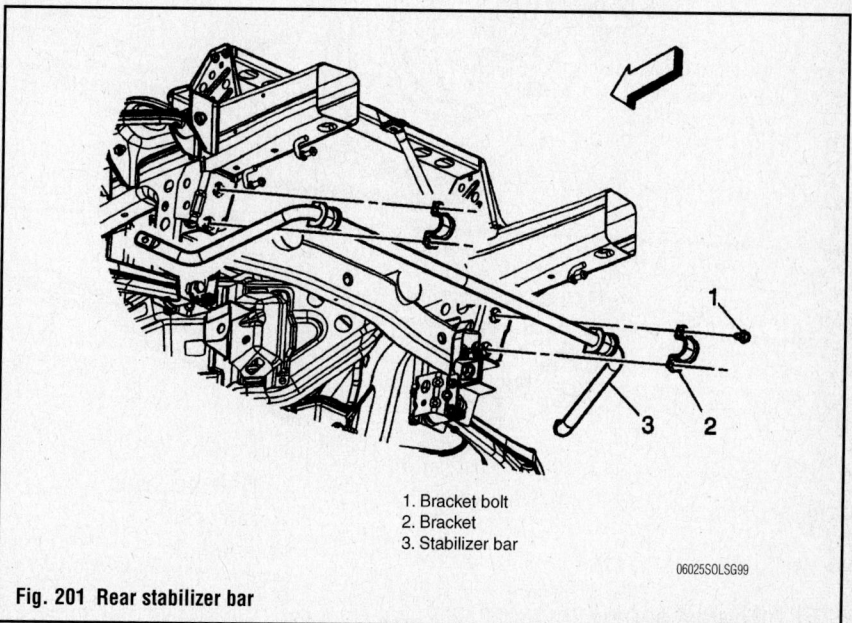

1. Bracket bolt
2. Bracket
3. Stabilizer bar

06025SOLSG99

Fig. 201 Rear stabilizer bar

➡The HO2S may be difficult to remove when the engine temperature is less than 48°C (120°F).

➡A special anti-seize compound is used on the HO2S threads. The compound consists of a liquid graphite and glass beads. The graphite will burn away, but the glass beads will remain, making the sensor easier to remove. New or service sensors will have the compound applied to the threads. If a sensor is removed and is to be reinstalled, the threads must have an anti-seize compound applied before installation.

TOE LINKS

REMOVAL & INSTALLATION

See Figure 202.

1. Before servicing the vehicle, refer to the Precautions Section.
2. Raise and support the vehicle.
3. Remove the tire and wheel.
4. Remove the toe link retaining nut.
5. Use the appropriate tool to remove the toe link ball joint from the rear knuckle.
6. Clean off threads and apply a small amount of penetrating oil to the thread of the link and allow to sit for a very minutes. This will aid in the removal of the nut and not damage the threads.
7. Remove the toe link-to-frame nut.
8. Remove the toe link.

To install:

9. Installation is the reverse of removal procedure.
10. Please take note of the following tightening specifications:

- Toe link retaining nut: 74 ft. lbs. (100 Nm).
- Toe link to frame nut: 44 ft. lbs. (60 Nm).

11. Adjust the rear toe.

UPPER CONTROL ARM

REMOVAL & INSTALLATION

See Figure 203.

1. Before servicing the vehicle, refer to the Precautions Section.
2. Raise and support the vehicle.
3. Remove the tire and wheel.
4. Remove the upper ball joint nut.
5. Using the appropriate tool, separate the upper control arm ball joint from the knuckle.
6. Remove the rear shock module.

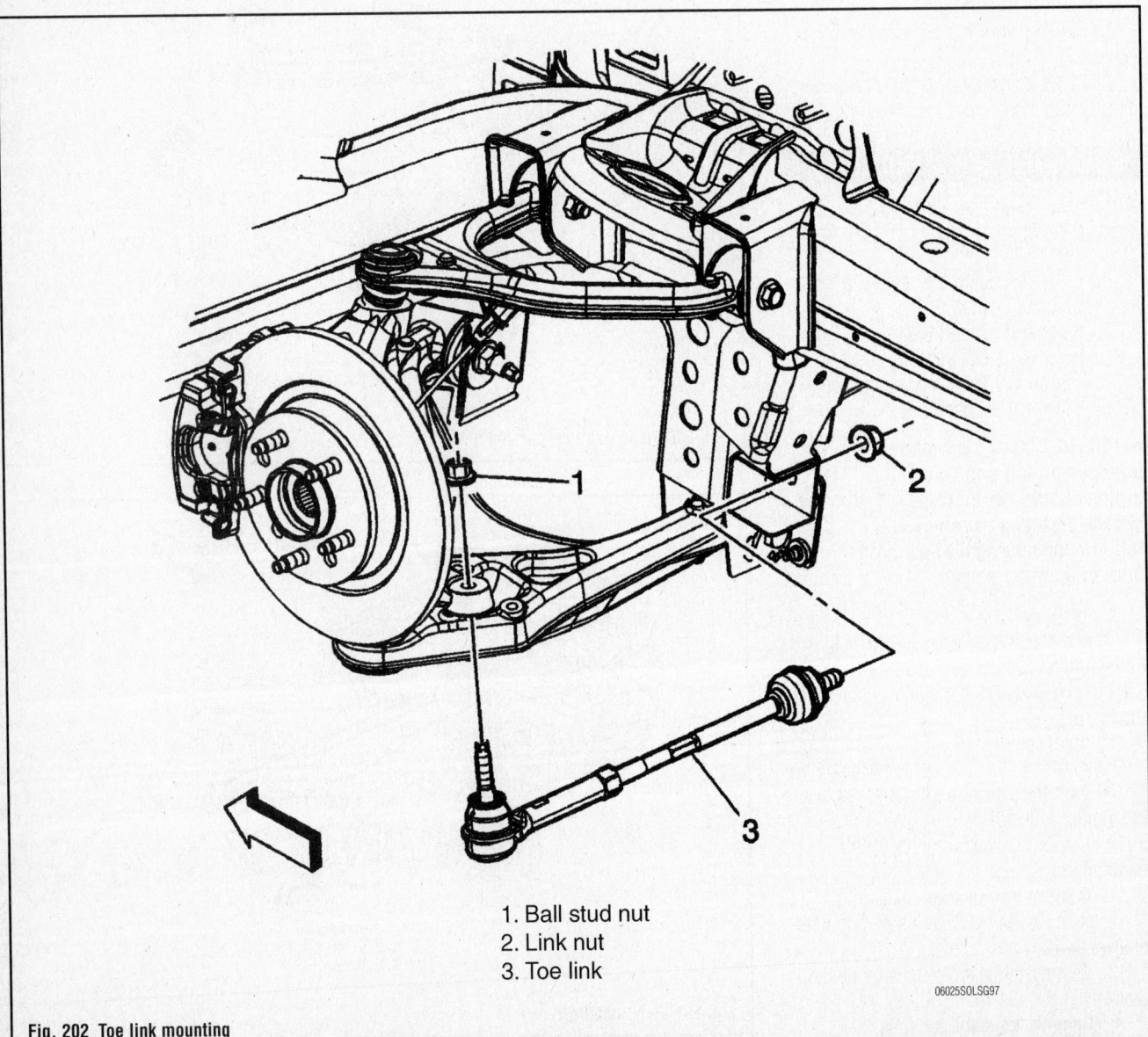

1. Ball stud nut
2. Link nut
3. Toe link

06025SOLSG97

Fig. 202 Toe link mounting

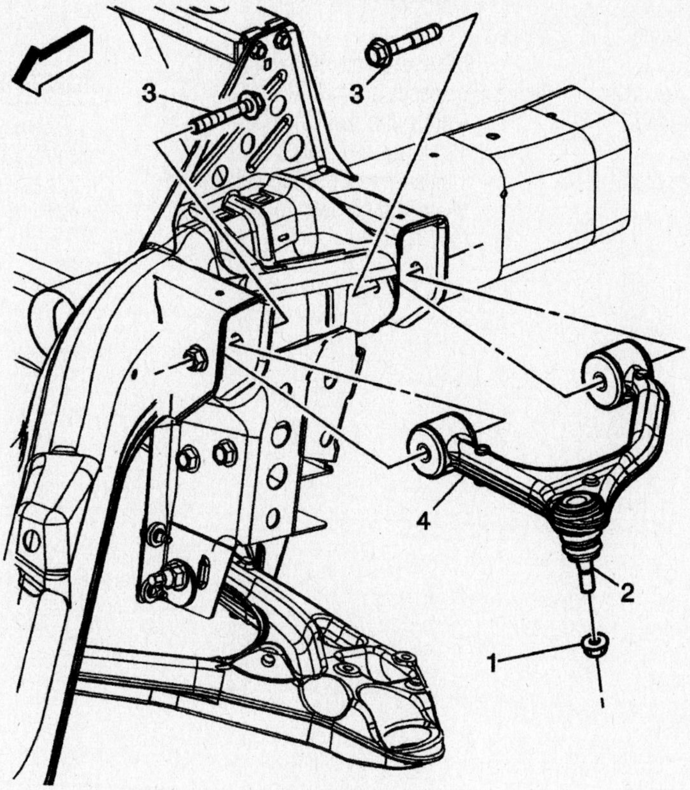

1. Ball stud nut
2. Ball joint
3. Mounting bolts
4. Control arm

06025SOLSG94

Fig. 203 Rear upper control arm removal

7. Remove the upper control arm mounting bolts.

8. Remove the upper control arm.

To install:

9. Install the upper control arm.

10. Install the upper control arm mounting bolts and tighten to 81 ft. lbs. (110 Nm).

11. Install the rear shock module.

12. Install ball stud into knuckle and start ball joint retaining nut.

13. Tighten ball joint retaining nut to 22 ft. lbs. (30 Nm). plus an additional 150°

14. Install the tire and wheel.

15. Lower vehicle.

WHEEL HUB AND BEARING

REMOVAL & INSTALLATION

See Figure 204.

1. Before servicing the vehicle, refer to the Precautions Section.

2. Raise and support the vehicle.

3. Remove the tire and wheel.

4. Remove the brake caliper mounting bracket.

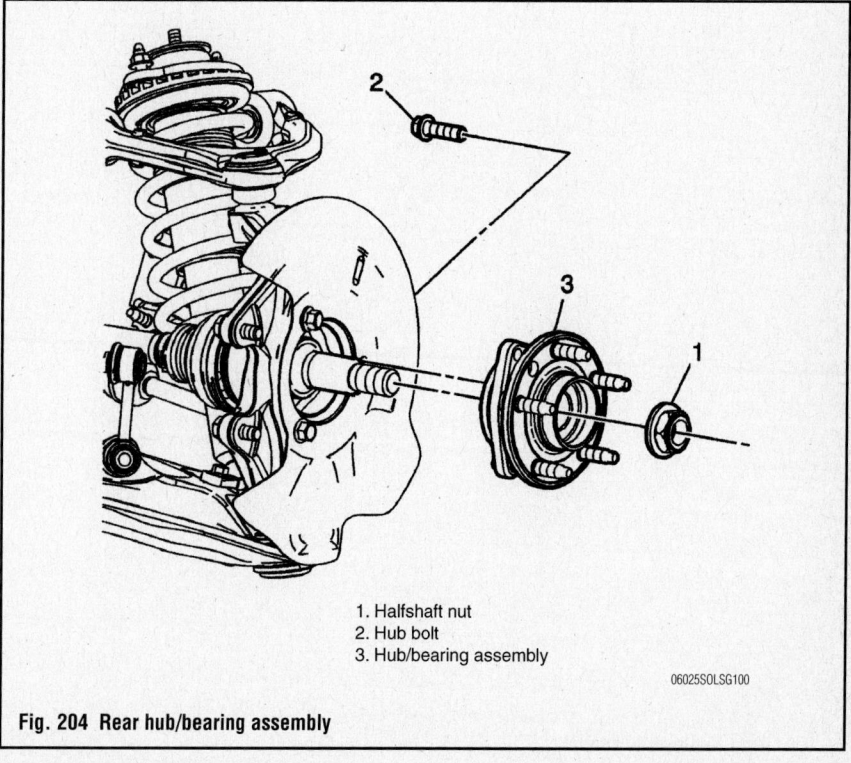

1. Halfshaft nut
2. Hub bolt
3. Hub/bearing assembly

06025SOLSG100

Fig. 204 Rear hub/bearing assembly

5. Remove the drive axle retaining nut.

6. Remove the wheel/hub mounting bolt.

7. Using a small flat-blade screw driver, remove the speed sensor wiring harness from the upper control arm.

8. Disconnect the speed sensor electrical connector.

9. Remove the wheel hub.

To install:

10. Installation is the reverse of removal procedure.

11. Please take note of the following tightening specifications:
- Tighten the new halfshaft nut to 118 ft. lbs. (160 Nm).
- Tighten wheel bearing hub assembly mounting bolts to 85 ft. lbs. (115 Nm).
- Tighten caliper mounting bracket bolts to 85 ft. lbs. (115 Nm).

ADJUSTMENT

The rear wheel hub and bearing assembly is a sealed unit and does not require adjustments or repacking.

CADILLAC

SRX

22

SPECIFICATIONS AND MAINTENANCE CHARTS

VEHICLE AND ENGINE IDENTIFICATION CHART

Engine							Model Year		
Code	Liters	Cu. In.	Cyl.	Fuel Sys.	Engine Type	Eng. Mfg.		Code	Year
7	3.6	217	6	SEFI	DOHC	GM		5	2005
A	4.6	279	8	SEFI	DOHC	GM		6	2006
								7	2007

SEFI: Sequential Electronic Fuel Injection

22116_SSRX_C0001

GENERAL ENGINE SPECIFICATIONS

Year	Engine Displacement Liters	Engine VIN	Net Horsepower @ rpm	Net Torque @ rpm (ft. lbs.)	Bore x Stroke (in.)	Compression Ratio	Oil Pressure @ rpm
2005	3.6	7	260@6500	252@2800	3.70x3.37	10.2:1	20@2000
	4.6	A	320@6400	315@4400	3.66x3.30	10.5:1	35@2000
2006	3.6	7	255@6500	252@2800	3.70x3.37	10.2:1	20@2000
	4.6	A	320@6400	315@4400	3.66x3.30	10.5:1	35@2000
2007	3.6	7	255@6500	252@2800	3.70x3.37	10.2:1	20@2000
	4.6	A	320@6400	315@4400	3.66x3.30	10.5:1	35@2000

22116_SSRX_C0002

GASOLINE ENGINE TUNE-UP SPECIFICATIONS

Year	Engine Displacement Liters	Engine VIN	Spark Plugs Gap (in.)	Ignition Timing (deg.) MT	AT	Fuel Pump (psi)	Idle Speed (rpm) MT	AT	Valve Clearance In.	Ex.
2005	3.6	7	0.044	—	①	55-60	—	②	HYD	HYD
	4.6	A	0.051	—	①	55-60	—	②	HYD	HYD
2006	3.6	7	0.044	—	①	55-60	—	②	HYD	HYD
	4.6	A	0.040	—	①	55-60	—	②	HYD	HYD
2007	3.6	7	0.044	—	①	55-60	—	②	HYD	HYD
	4.6	A	0.040	—	①	55-60	—	②	HYD	HYD

NOTE: The Vehicle Emission Control Information label often reflects specification changes changes made during production.

The label figures must be used if they differ from those in this chart.

HYD: Hydraulic

① Controlled by the Powertrain Control Module (PCM) and cannot be manually adjusted.

② 600 with A/C off, 700 with A/C on.

22116_SSRX_C0003

CAPACITIES

Year	Model	Engine Displacement Liters	Engine VIN	Engine Oil with Filter (qts.)	Transmission (pts.) 4-Spd	5-Spd	Auto.	Drive Axle Front (pts.)	Rear (pts.)	Fuel Tank (gal.)	Cooling System (qts.)
2005	SRX	3.6	7	6.0	—	—	18	①	①	20	9.7
		4.6	A	8.0	—	—	18	①	①	20	10.4
2006	SRX	3.6	7	6.0	—	—	18	①	①	20	9.7
		4.6	A	8.0	—	—	18	①	①	20	10.4
2007	SRX	3.6	7	6.0	—	—	18	①	①	20	9.7
		4.6	A	8.0	—	—	18	①	①	20	10.4

NOTE: All capacities are approximate. Add fluid gradually and check to be sure a proper fluid level is obtained.

① Front and rear is 1.37 qts. Transfer case capacity is 0.53 qts.

22116_SSRX_C0004

FLUID SPECIFICATIONS

Year	Model	Engine Displacement Liters	Engine ID/VIN	Engine Oil	Auto. Trans.	Drive Axle	Power Steering Fluid	Brake Master Cylinder
2005	SRX	3.6	7	5W-30	Dexron VI	①	GM PS Fluid	DOT-3
		4.6	A	5W-30	Dexron VI	①	GM PS Fluid	DOT-3
2006	SRX	3.6	7	5W-30	Dexron VI	①	GM PS Fluid	DOT-3
		4.6	A	5W-30	Dexron VI	①	GM PS Fluid	DOT-3
2007	SRX	3.6	7	5W-30	Dexron VI	①	GM PS Fluid	DOT-3
		4.6	A	5W-30	Dexron VI	①	GM PS Fluid	DOT-3

DOT: Department Of Transpotation

① Front and rear axles: 75W90 Synthetic

22116_SSRX_C0010

VALVE SPECIFICATIONS

Year	Engine VIN	Engine Displacement Liters	Seat Angle (deg.)	Face Angle (deg.)	Spring Test Pressure (lbs. @ in.)	Spring Installed Height (in.)	Stem-to-Guide Clearance (in.) Intake	Exhaust	Stem Diameter (in.) Intake	Exhaust
2005	7	3.6	45	44.25	224@1.16	1.377	0.0010-0.0026	0.0014-0.0030	0.2344-0.2352	0.2341-0.2348
	A	4.6	45.75	45	224@1.16	1.378	0.0011-0.0027	0.0020-0.0039	0.2331-0.2339	0.2331-0.2339
2006	7	3.6	45	44.25	134-139 @0.9449	1.378	0.0010-0.0026	0.0014-0.0030	0.2344-0.2352	0.2341-0.2348
	A	4.6	45.75	45	130-142 @0.965	1.378	0.0011-0.0027	0.0020-0.0039	0.2331-0.2339	0.2331-0.2339
2007	7	3.6	45	44.25	134-139 @0.9449	1.378	0.0010-0.0026	0.0014-0.0030	0.2344-0.2352	0.2341-0.2348
	A	4.6	45.75	45	130-142 @0.965	1.378	0.0011-0.0027	0.0020-0.0039	0.2331-0.2339	0.2331-0.2339

22116_SSRX_C0005

CAMSHAFT AND BEARING SPECIFICATIONS CHART

All measurements are given in inches.

Year	Engine Displ. Liters	Engine ID/VIN	Journal Dia.	Brg. Oil Clearance	Shaft End-play	Runout	Journal Bore	Lobe Height Intake	Exhaust
2005	3.6	7	①	NA	0.0018-0.0085	0.002	②	0.4252	0.4252
	4.6	A	1.0610-1.0619	0.0016-0.0035	0.0050-0.0087	0.002	NA	0.2421	0.2339
2006	3.6	7	①	NA	0.0018-0.0085	0.002	②	0.4252	0.4252
	4.6	A	1.0610-1.0619	0.0016-0.0035	0.0050-0.0087	0.002	NA	0.2421	0.2339
2007	3.6	7	①	NA	0.0018-0.0085	0.002	②	0.4252	0.4252
	4.6	A	1.0610-1.0619	0.0016-0.0035	0.0050-0.0087	0.002	NA	0.2421	0.2339

NA: Not Available

① Bore 1: 1.3779-1.3787

  Bore 2-4: 1.0630-1.0638

② Bore 1: 1.3754-1.3764

  Bore 2-4: 1.605-1.0614

22116_SSRX_C0006

CRANKSHAFT AND CONNECTING ROD SPECIFICATIONS

All measurements are given in inches.

Year	Engine Displ. Liters	Engine VIN	Crankshaft Main Brg. Journal Dia.	Main Brg. Oil Clearance	Shaft End-play	Thrust on No.	Connecting Rod Journal Diameter	Oil Clearance	Side Clearance
2005	3.6	7	2.6768-2.6775	0.0004-0.0024	0.0039-0.0130	NA	2.2044-2.2050	0.0004-0.0028	0.0374-0.0140
	4.6	A	2.5335-2.5341	0.0006-0.0022	0.0020-0.0197	NA	2.1239-2.1245	0.0010-0.0014	0.0079-0.0197
2006	3.6	7	2.6768-2.6775	0.0004-0.0024	0.0039-0.0130	NA	2.2044-2.2050	0.0004-0.0028	0.0374-0.0140
	4.6	A	2.5335-2.5341	0.0006-0.0022	0.0020-0.0197	NA	2.1239-2.1245	0.0010-0.0014	0.0079-0.0197
2007	3.6	7	2.6768-2.6775	0.0004-0.0024	0.0039-0.0130	NA	2.2044-2.2050	0.0004-0.0028	0.0374-0.0140
	4.6	A	2.5335-2.5341	0.0006-0.0022	0.0020-0.0197	NA	2.1239-2.1245	0.0010-0.0014	0.0079-0.0197

NA: Not available

22116_SSRX_C0007

PISTON AND RING SPECIFICATIONS

All measurements are given in inches.

Year	Engine Displ. Liters	Engine VIN	Piston Clearance	Ring Gap			Ring Side Clearance		
				Top Comp.	Bottom Comp.	Oil Control	Top Comp.	Bottom Comp.	Oil Control
2005	3.6	7	0.0008-0.0013	0.0059-0.0118	0.0110-0.0189	0.00989-0.0295	0.0012-0.0026	0.0002-0.0013	0.0083-0.0155
	4.6	A	0.0008-0.0020	0.0098-0.0157	0.0138-0.0200	0.0098-0.0299	0.0016-0.0037	0.0016-0.0037	Snug
2006	3.6	7	0.0010-0.0021	0.0059-0.0118	0.0110-0.0189	0.0059-0.0236	0.0012-0.0026	0.0006-0.0024	0.0012-0.0067
	4.6	A	0.0008-0.0020	0.0098-0.0157	0.0138-0.0200	0.0098-0.0299	0.0016-0.0037	0.0016-0.0037	Snug
2007	3.6	7	0.0010-0.0021	0.0059-0.0118	0.0110-0.0189	0.0059-0.0236	0.0012-0.0026	0.0006-0.0024	0.0012-0.0067
	4.6	A	0.0008-0.0020	0.0098-0.0157	0.0138-0.0200	0.0098-0.0299	0.0016-0.0037	0.0016-0.0037	Snug

22116_SSRX_C0008

TORQUE SPECIFICATIONS

All readings in ft. lbs.

Year	Engine VIN	Engine Displacement Liters	Cylinder Head Bolts	Main Bearing Bolts	Rod Bearing Bolts	Crankshaft Damper Bolts	Flywheel Bolts	Manifold		Spark Plugs	Oil Pan Drain Plug
								Intake	Exhaust		
2005	7	3.6	①	②	③	④	⑤	17	15	13	18
	A	4.6	⑥	⑦	⑧	⑨	⑩	⑪	15	11	18
2006	7	3.6	①	②	③	④	⑤	17	15	13	18
	A	4.6	⑥	⑦	⑧	⑨	⑩	⑪	15	11	18
2007	7	3.6	①	②	③	④	⑤	17	15	13	18
	A	4.6	⑥	⑦	⑧	⑨	⑩	⑪	15	11	18

① M8 bolt step 1: 10 ft. lbs.
   Step 2: plus 60 degrees
   M11 bolt step 1: 33 ft. lbs.
   Step 2: plus 120 degrees

② Inner bolt step 1: 15 ft. lbs.
   Step 2: plus 80 degrees
   Outer bolt step1: 10 ft. lbs.
   Step 2: plus 110 degrees

③ Step 1: 22 ft. lbs.
   Step 2: loosen to zero degrees
   Step 3: 18 ft. lbs.
   Step 4: plus 110 degrees

④ Step 1: 74 ft. lbs.
   Step 2: plus 150 degrees

⑤ Step 1: 22 ft. lbs.
   Step 2: plus 150 degrees

⑥ M6 bolt: 106 inch lbs.
   M11 bolt step 1: 22 ft. lbs.
   Step 2: plus 60 degrees
   Step 3: plus 60 degrees
   Step 4: plus 60 degrees

⑦ M8 bolt: 22 ft. lbs.
   M10 bolt step 1: 15 ft. lbs.
   Step 2: plus 65 degrees

⑧ Step 1: 22 ft. lbs.
   Step 2: loosen to zero degrees
   Step 3: 18 ft. lbs.
   Step 4: plus 100 degrees

⑨ Step 1: 37 ft. lbs.
   Step 2: plus 150 degrees

⑩ Step 1: 11 ft. lbs.
   Step 2: plus 50 degrees

⑪ 89 inch lbs.

22116_SSRX_C0009

WHEEL ALIGNMENT

Year	Model		Caster Range (+/-Deg.)	Caster Preferred Setting (Deg.)	Camber Range (+/-Deg.)	Camber Preferred Setting (Deg.)	Toe-in (Deg.)
2005	SRX	Front	0.50	+4.10	0.50	-0.50	0.20+/-0.20
		Rear	—	—	0.75	-1.00	-0.40+/-0.10
2006	SRX	Front	0.60	+4.10	0.60	-0.50	0.20+/-0.20
		Rear	—	—	0.50	-1.00	-0.20+/-0.20
2007	SRX	Front	0.60	+4.10	0.60	-0.50	0.20+/-0.20
		Rear	—	—	0.50	-1.00	-0.20+/-0.20

22116_SSRX_C0011

TIRE AND WHEEL SPECIFICATIONS

Year	Model	OEM Tires Front	OEM Tires Rear	Tire Pressures (psi) Front	Tire Pressures (psi) Rear	Wheel Size	Lug Nut (ft. lbs.)
2005	SRX-V6	P235/65R17	P255/60R17	①	①	②	100
	SRX-V8	P235/60R18	P255/55R18	①	①	②	100
2006	SRX-V6	P235/65R17	P255/60R17	①	①	②	100
	SRX-V8	P235/60R18	P255/55R18	①	①	②	100
2007	SRX-V6	P235/65R17	P255/60R17	①	①	②	100
	SRX-V8	P235/60R18	P255/55R18	①	①	②	100

OEM: Original Equipment Manufacturer

PSI: Pounds Per Square Inch

① See vehicle tire placard.

22116_SSRX_C0012

BRAKE SPECIFICATIONS

All measurements in inches unless noted

Year	Model		Brake Disc Original Thickness	Brake Disc Minimum Thickness	Brake Disc Maximum Runout	Minimum Lining Thickness Front	Minimum Lining Thickness Rear	Brake Caliper Bracket Bolts (ft. lbs.)	Brake Caliper Mounting Bolts (ft. lbs.)
2005	SRX	F	1.270	1.210	0.002	①	—	96	25
		R	1.020	0.944	0.002	—	①	88	44
2006	SRX	F	1.267	1.209	0.002	①	—	96	25
		R	1.020	0.944	0.002	—	①	88	44
2007	SRX	F	1.267	1.209	0.002	①	—	96	25
		R	1.020	0.944	0.002	—	①	88	44

① Not available

22116_SSRX_C0013

MAINTENANCE I AND II SERVICE SCHEDULES
SRX

When the CHANGE ENGINE OIL light appears, certain services and inspections are required.

Required services are described as Maintenance I and Maintenance II.

The first service on a vehicle should be Maintenance I, and the second service should be Maintenance II.

Alternate between the 2 thereafter. However, in some cases, Maintenance II may be required more often.

Maintenance I: Use Maintenance I if the CHANGE ENGINE OIL light comes on within 10 months since vehicle was purchased or, if Maintenance II was performed.

Maintenance II: Use Maintenance II if the previous service performed was Maintenance I. Always use Maintenance I whenever the CHANGE ENGINE OIL light comes on 10 months or more since the last service, or, if the CHANGE ENGINE OIL light has not come on at all for one year.

Service	Maintenance I	Maintenance II
Change the engine oil and filter. Reset the oil life system.	✓	✓
Visually inspect the vehicle for leaks or damage. A fluid loss in the vehicle system could indicate a problem. Inspected, repair and add fluid to the system if necessary.	✓	✓
Inspect the engine air cleaner filter. If necessary, replace the filter.	✓	✓
Rotate the tires. Inspect the tire inflation pressures and the tire wear.	✓	✓
Visually inspect the brake lines and hoses for proper hook-up, binding, leaks, cracks, chafing, etc. Inspect the disc brake pads for wear and the rotors for surface condition. Inspect the drum brake linings for wear or cracks. Inspect other brake parts, including drums, wheel cylinders, calipers, parking brake, etc. Inspect the parking brake adjustment.	✓	✓
Inspect the engine coolant and the windshield washer fluid levels. Add fluid as needed.	✓	✓
Inspect the suspension and steering components. Inspect the front and rear suspension and the steering system for damaged, loose or missing parts, or signs of wear. Inspect the power steering lines and the hoses for proper hook-up, binding, leaks, cracks,	--	✓
Visually inspect the coolant hoses and replace the hoses if they are cracked, swollen or deteriorated. Inspect all pipes, fittings and clamps; replace with GM parts as needed. To help ensure proper operation, a pressure test of the cooling system and pressure cap and cleaning the outside of the radiator and air conditioning condenser is recommended at least once a year.	--	✓
Inspect the front and rear suspension and the steering system for damaged, loose or missing parts, or signs of wear. Inspect power steering lines and hoses for proper hook-up, binding, leaks, cracks, chafing, etc.	--	✓
Inspect the throttle system for interference or binding and for damaged or missing parts. Replace the parts as needed. Replace any components that have high effort or excessive wear. Do not lubricate the accelerator or the cruise control cables.	--	✓
Replace the passenger compartment air filter.	--	✓

Press the CLR button located to the right of the DIC display to acknowledge the Change Engine Oil message. This will clear the message from the display and reset it.

To reset the oil life indicator, use the following steps:

1. Press the up or down arrow on the INFO button located to the right of the DIC display to access the DIC menu.

2. Once XXX% ENGINE OIL LIFE menu item is highlighted, press and hold the CLR button.

The percentage will return to 100, and the oil life indicator will be reset.

3. Turn the key to OFF.

22116_SSRX_C0014

ADDITIONAL MAINTENANCE SERVICES
SRX

TO BE SERVICED	TYPE OF SERVICE	VEHICLE MILEAGE INTERVAL (x1000)					
		25	50	75	100	125	150
Air cleaner filter	R		✓		✓		✓
Accessory drive belt	I						✓
Auto. Trans. Fluid and Filter①	R		✓		✓		✓
Cooling system hoses and clamps	S/I						✓
Engine coolant	R						✓
Fuel system	I	✓	✓	✓	✓	✓	✓
Exhaust system & heat shields	S/I	✓	✓	✓	✓	✓	✓
Supercharger oil level	S/I	✓	✓	✓	✓	✓	✓
Spark plugs and wires	R				✓		

R: Replace   S/I: Inspect and service, if necessary

① Replace if any of the following conditions are met:

   Heavy city traffic where the outside temperature regularly reaches 32°C (90°F) or higher

   Hilly or mountainous terrain

   Frequent trailer towing

   Taxi, police or delivery service

   Otherwise, change every 100,000 miles

22116_SSRX_C0015

PRECAUTIONS

Before servicing any vehicle, please be sure to read all of the following precautions, which deal with personal safety, prevention of component damage, and important points to take into consideration when servicing a motor vehicle:

• Never open, service or drain the radiator or cooling system when the engine is hot; serious burns can occur from the steam and hot coolant.

• Observe all applicable safety precautions when working around fuel. Whenever servicing the fuel system, always work in a well-ventilated area. Do not allow fuel spray or vapors to come in contact with a spark, open flame, or excessive heat (a hot drop light, for example). Keep a dry chemical fire extinguisher near the work area. Always keep fuel in a container specifically designed for fuel storage; also, always properly seal fuel containers to avoid the possibility of fire or explosion. Refer to the additional fuel system precautions later in this section.

• Fuel injection systems often remain pressurized, even after the engine has been turned **OFF**. The fuel system pressure must be relieved before disconnecting any fuel lines. Failure to do so may result in fire and/or personal injury.

• Brake fluid often contains polyglycol ethers and polyglycols. Avoid contact with the eyes and wash your hands thoroughly after handling brake fluid. If you do get brake fluid in your eyes, flush your eyes with clean, running water for 15 minutes. If eye irritation persists, or if you have taken

brake fluid internally, IMMEDIATELY seek medical assistance.

• The EPA warns that prolonged contact with used engine oil may cause a number of skin disorders, including cancer. You should make every effort to minimize your exposure to used engine oil. Protective gloves should be worn when changing oil. Wash your hands and any other exposed skin areas as soon as possible after exposure to used engine oil. Soap and water, or waterless hand cleaner should be used.

• All new vehicles are now equipped with an air bag system, often referred to as a Supplemental Restraint System (SRS) or Supplemental Inflatable Restraint (SIR) system. The system must be disabled before performing service on or around system components, steering column, instrument panel components, wiring and sensors. Failure to follow safety and disabling procedures could result in accidental air bag deployment, possible personal injury and unnecessary system repairs.

• Always wear safety goggles when working with, or around, the air bag system. When carrying a non-deployed air bag, be sure the bag and trim cover are pointed away from your body. When placing a non-deployed air bag on a work surface, always face the bag and trim cover upward, away from the surface. This will reduce the motion of the module if it is accidentally deployed. Refer to the additional air bag system precautions later in this section.

• Clean, high quality brake fluid from a sealed container is essential to the safe and

proper operation of the brake system. You should always buy the correct type of brake fluid for your vehicle. If the brake fluid becomes contaminated, completely flush the system with new fluid. Never reuse any brake fluid. Any brake fluid that is removed from the system should be discarded. Also, do not allow any brake fluid to come in contact with a painted surface; it will damage the paint.

• Never operate the engine without the proper amount and type of engine oil; doing so WILL result in severe engine damage.

• Timing belt maintenance is extremely important. Many models utilize an interference-type, non-freewheeling engine. If the timing belt breaks, the valves in the cylinder head may strike the pistons, causing potentially serious (also time-consuming and expensive) engine damage. Refer to the maintenance interval charts for the recommended replacement interval for the timing belt, and to the timing belt section for belt replacement and inspection.

• Disconnecting the negative battery cable on some vehicles may interfere with the functions of the on-board computer system(s) and may require the computer to undergo a relearning process once the negative battery cable is reconnected.

• When servicing drum brakes, only disassemble and assemble one side at a time, leaving the remaining side intact for reference.

• Only an MVAC-trained, EPA-certified automotive technician should service the air conditioning system or its components.

BRAKES

GENERAL INFORMATION

When wheel slip is detected during a brake application, the ABS enters antilock mode. During antilock braking, hydraulic pressure in the individual wheel circuits is controlled to prevent any wheel from slipping. A separate hydraulic line and specific solenoid valves are provided for each wheel. The ABS can decrease, hold, or increase hydraulic pressure to each wheel brake. The ABS cannot, however, increase hydraulic pressure above the amount which is transmitted by the master cylinder during braking.

During antilock braking, a series of rapid pulsations is felt in the brake pedal. These pulsations are caused by the rapid changes in position of the individual solenoid valves

as the EBCM responds to wheel speed sensor inputs and attempts to prevent wheel slip. These pedal pulsations are present only during antilock braking and stop when normal braking is resumed or when the vehicle comes to a stop. A ticking or popping noise may also be heard as the solenoid valves cycle rapidly. During antilock braking on dry pavement, intermittent chirping noises may be heard as the tires approach slipping. These noises and pedal pulsations are considered normal during antilock operation.

Vehicles equipped with ABS may be stopped by applying normal force to the brake pedal. Brake pedal operation during normal braking is no different than that of previous non-ABS systems. Maintaining a constant force on the brake pedal provides

ANTI-LOCK BRAKE SYSTEM (ABS)

the shortest stopping distance while maintaining vehicle stability.

PRECAUTIONS

• Certain components within the ABS system are not intended to be serviced or repaired individually.

• Do not use rubber hoses or other parts not specifically specified for and ABS system. When using repair kits, replace all parts included in the kit. Partial or incorrect repair may lead to functional problems and require the replacement of components.

• Lubricate rubber parts with clean, fresh brake fluid to ease assembly. Do not use shop air to clean parts; damage to rubber components may result.

• Use only DOT 3 brake fluid from an unopened container.

• If any hydraulic component or line is removed or replaced, it may be necessary to bleed the entire system.

• A clean repair area is essential. Always clean the reservoir and cap thoroughly before removing the cap. The slightest amount of dirt in the fluid may plug an orifice and impair the system function. Perform repairs after components have been thoroughly cleaned; use only denatured alcohol to clean components. Do not allow ABS components to come into contact with any substance containing mineral oil; this includes used shop rags.

• The Anti-Lock control unit is a microprocessor similar to other computer units in the vehicle. Ensure that the ignition switch is **OFF** before removing or installing controller harnesses. Avoid static electricity discharge at or near the controller.

• If any arc welding is to be done on the vehicle, the control unit should be unplugged before welding operations begin.

BRAKES | **BLEEDING THE BRAKE SYSTEM**

BLEEDING PROCEDURE

BLEEDING PROCEDURE

❋❋ WARNING

Clean, high quality brake fluid is essential to the safe and proper operation of the brake system. You should always buy the highest quality brake fluid that is available. If the brake fluid becomes contaminated, drain and flush the system, then refill the master cylinder with new fluid. Never reuse any brake fluid. Any brake fluid that is removed from the system should be discarded. Also, do not allow any brake fluid to come in contact with a painted surface; it will damage the paint.

❋❋ CAUTION

Brake fluid contains polyglycol ethers and polyglycols. Avoid contact with the eyes and wash your hands thoroughly after handling brake fluid. If you do get brake fluid in your eyes, flush your eyes with clean, running water for 15 minutes. If eye irritation persists, or if you have taken brake fluid internally, IMMEDIATELY seek medical assistance.

1. Place a clean shop cloth beneath the brake master cylinder to prevent brake fluid spills.

2. With the ignition OFF and the brakes cool, apply the brakes 3-5 times, or until the brake pedal effort increases significantly, in order to deplete the brake booster power reserve.

Fill the brake master cylinder reservoir with DOT-3 brake fluid from a clean, sealed brake fluid container. Ensure that the brake master cylinder reservoir remains at least half-full during this bleeding procedure. Add fluid as needed to maintain the proper level. Clean the outside of the reservoir on and around the reservoir cap prior to removing the cap and diaphragm.

3. Install a proper box-end wrench onto the RIGHT REAR wheel hydraulic circuit bleeder valve.

4. Install a transparent hose over the end of the bleeder valve.

5. Submerge the open end of the transparent hose into a transparent container partially filled DOT-3 brake fluid from a clean, sealed brake fluid container.

6. Have an assistant slowly depress the brake pedal fully and maintain steady pressure on the pedal.

7. Loosen the bleeder valve to purge air from the wheel hydraulic circuit.

8. Tighten the bleeder valve, then have the assistant slowly release the brake pedal.

9. Wait 15 seconds, then repeat these steps until all air is purged from the same wheel hydraulic circuit.

10. Repeat this procedure with the LEFT FRONT, then LEFT REAR and finally the RIGHT FRONT.

11. Fill the brake master cylinder reservoir to the maximum-fill level with DOT-3 brake fluid from a clean, sealed brake fluid container.

12. Slowly depress and release the brake pedal. Observe the feel of the brake pedal.

➡**If it is determined that air was induced into the system upstream of the ABS modulator prior to servicing, the ABS Automated Bleed Procedure must be performed.**

If the brake pedal feels spongy, repeat the bleeding procedure again. Turn the ignition key ON, with the engine OFF. Check to see if the brake system warning lamp remains illuminated.

BLEEDING THE ABS SYSTEM

❋❋ WARNING

Clean, high quality brake fluid is essential to the safe and proper operation of the brake system. You should always buy the highest quality brake fluid that is available. If the brake fluid becomes contaminated, drain and flush the system, then refill the master cylinder with new fluid. Never reuse any brake fluid. Any brake fluid that is removed from the system should be discarded. Also, do not allow any brake fluid to come in contact with a painted surface; it will damage the paint.

❋❋ WARNING

Before performing the ABS Automated Bleed Procedure, first perform a pressure bleed of the base brake system.

The ABS Automated Bleed Procedure uses a scan tool to cycle the system solenoid valves and run the pump in order to purge any air from the secondary circuits. These circuits are normally closed off, and are only opened during system initialization at vehicle start up and during ABS operation. The automated bleed procedure opens these secondary circuits and allows any air trapped in these circuits to flow out toward the brake corners.

➡**The Auto Bleed Procedure may be terminated at any time during the process by pressing the EXIT button. No further Scan Tool prompts pertaining to the Auto Bleed procedure will be given. After exiting the bleed procedure, relieve bleed pressure and disconnect bleed equipment per manufacturer's instructions. Failure to properly relieve pressure may result in spilled brake fluid causing damage to components and painted surfaces.**

1. Before servicing the vehicle, refer to the Precautions Section.

2. Raise and support the vehicle.

3. Remove all four tire and wheel assemblies.

4. Inspect the brake system for leaks and visual damage.

5. Inspect the battery state of charge.

6. Install a scan tool.

7. Turn the ignition ON, with the engine OFF.

8. With the scan tool, establish

communications with the ABS system. Select Special Functions. Select Automated Bleed from the Special Functions menu.

9. Following the directions given on the scan tool, pressure bleed the base brake system.

10. Follow the scan tool directions until the desired brake pedal height is achieved.

11. If the bleed procedure is aborted, a malfunction exists. Perform the following steps before resuming the bleed procedure:
- If a DTC is detected, diagnose the appropriate DTC.
- If the brake pedal feels spongy, perform the conventional brake bleed procedure again.

12. When the desired pedal height is achieved, press the brake pedal to inspect for firmness.

13. Remove the scan tool.

14. Install the tire and wheel assemblies.

15. Inspect the brake fluid level.

16. Lower the vehicle.

17. Road test the vehicle while inspecting that the pedal remains high and firm.

BRAKES

✴✴ CAUTION

Dust and dirt accumulating on brake parts during normal use may contain asbestos fibers from production or aftermarket brake linings. Breathing excessive concentrations of asbestos fibers can cause serious bodily harm. Exercise care when servicing brake parts. Do not sand or grind brake lining unless equipment used is designed to contain the dust residue. Do not clean brake parts with compressed air or by dry brushing. Cleaning should be done by dampening the brake components with a fine mist of water, then wiping the brake components clean with a dampened cloth. Dispose of cloth and all residue containing asbestos fibers in an impermeable container with the appropriate label. Follow practices prescribed by the Occupational Safety and Health Administration (OSHA) and the Environmental Protection Agency (EPA) for the handling, processing, and disposing of dust or debris that may contain asbestos fibers.

BRAKE CALIPER

REMOVAL & INSTALLATION

See Figure 1.

1. Before servicing the vehicle, refer to the Precautions Section.

➡**If brake fluid level is midway between the maximum-full point and the minimum allowable level, no fluid needs to be removed from the reservoir.**

2. Remove ½ of the brake fluid from the brake master cylinder reservoir. Properly dispose of the brake fluid.

3. Raise and safely support the vehicle.

4. Remove the wheel and tire assembly.

5. Install a large C-clamp over the rear

of the caliper and against the outer brake pad.

6. Tighten the clamp until the caliper piston is compressed into the caliper bore enough to clear the rotor.

7. Remove the C-clamp.

8. Remove the brake line, discard the 2 copper washers and plug the line openings.

9. Remove the 2 brake pin retainer bolts.

10. Remove the disc brake caliper from the vehicle.

To install:

11. Inspect the guide pin boots for tears or cuts and replace as needed.

12. Seat the guide pin boots into the guide pin retaining seat.

13. Clean the guide pin bolt threads, then apply Threadlock to two-thirds of the lower guide pin bolt threads and allow it 10 minutes to dry.

14. Apply a thin coat of high temperature brake lubricant to the guide bolts.

15. Ensure that the disc brake pads are properly positioned and that the lining material is facing the rotor.

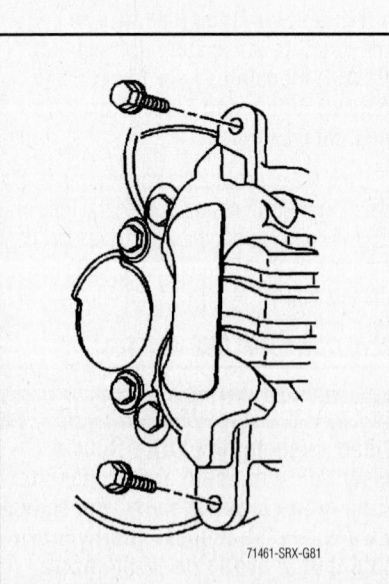

71461-SRX-G81

Fig. 1 Front brake caliper mounting

FRONT DISC BRAKES

16. Place the disc brake caliper over the rotor and tighten the brake pin retainer bolts-to-guide pin bolts to 25 ft. lbs. (34 Nm) for front brakes, or 44 ft. lbs. (60 Nm) for rear brakes.

17. Unplug and install the brake hose and retaining bolt to the disc brake caliper using new copper sealing washers on each side of the hose fitting. Tighten the brake hose bolts to 37 ft. lbs. (50 Nm).

18. Bleed the brake system, then apply the brake pedal two-thirds down and slowly release the pedal. Wait 15 seconds and repeat until a firm pedal is obtained.

19. Install the wheel and tire assembly. Torque the lug nuts to 100 ft. lbs. (136 Nm).

20. Lower the vehicle.

21. Check and fill the brake master cylinder as required.

22. Road-test the vehicle and check for proper brake operation.

DISC BRAKE PADS

REMOVAL & INSTALLATION

1. Before servicing the vehicle, refer to the Precautions Section.

2. Remove ½ of the brake fluid from the brake master cylinder reservoir. Properly dispose of the brake fluid.

3. Raise and safely support the vehicle.

4. Remove the wheel and tire assembly.

5. Install a large C-clamp over the rear of the caliper and against the outer brake pad.

6. Tighten the clamp until the caliper piston is compressed into the caliper bore enough to clear the rotor.

7. Remove the C-clamp.

8. Remove the lower brake pin retainer bolt.

9. Pivot the caliper upward away from the rotor.

10. Hang the disc brake caliper with a length of wire or equivalent to prevent damage to the brake hose.

11. Remove the inner and outer disc brake pads and the retainers.

12. Inspect the disc brake rotor surfaces for grooves, cracks or glazing. Resurface or replace as required. If resurfacing, observe the minimum thickness specification.

To install:

13. Inspect the guide pin boots for tears or cuts and replace as needed.

14. Seat the guide pin boot into the guide pin retaining seat.

15. Clean the guide pin bolt threads, then apply Threadlock to two-thirds of the lower guide pin bolt threads and allow it 10 minutes to dry.

16. Apply a thin coat of high temperature brake lubricant to the guide bolt.

17. Retract the caliper piston fully into the caliper bore using a C-clamp and wood block or equivalent. This will allow room for the new disc brake pads.

18. Install new inner and outer disc brake pads and the retainers. Ensure that the disc brake pads are properly positioned and that the lining material is facing the rotor.

19. Ensure that the disc brake pads are properly positioned and that the lining material is facing the rotor.

20. Place the disc brake caliper over the rotor and tighten the brake pin retainer bolts-to-guide pin bolts to 25 ft. lbs. (34 Nm) for front brakes, or 44 ft. lbs. (60 Nm) for rear brakes.

21. Install the wheel and tire assembly. Torque the lug nuts to 100 ft. lbs. (136 Nm).

22. Lower the vehicle.

23. Pump the brake pedal to position the brake pads before attempting to move the vehicle.

24. Check and fill the brake master cylinder reservoir, as required.

25. Road-test the vehicle and check for proper brake system operation.

BRAKES

✳✳ CAUTION

Dust and dirt accumulating on brake parts during normal use may contain asbestos fibers from production or aftermarket brake linings. Breathing excessive concentrations of asbestos fibers can cause serious bodily harm. Exercise care when servicing brake parts. Do not sand or grind brake lining unless equipment used is designed to contain the dust residue. Do not clean brake parts with compressed air or by dry brushing. Cleaning should be done by dampening the brake components with a fine mist of water, then wiping the brake components clean with a dampened cloth. Dispose of cloth and all residue containing asbestos fibers in an impermeable container with the appropriate label. Follow practices prescribed by the Occupational Safety and Health Administration (OSHA) and the Environmental Protection Agency (EPA) for the handling, processing, and disposing of dust or debris that may contain asbestos fibers.

BRAKE CALIPER

REMOVAL & INSTALLATION
See Figure 2.

1. Before servicing the vehicle, refer to the Precautions Section.

➡**If brake fluid level is midway between the maximum-full point and the minimum allowable level, no fluid needs to be removed from the reservoir.**

2. Remove ½ of the brake fluid from the brake master cylinder reservoir. Properly dispose of the brake fluid.

3. Raise and safely support the vehicle.

4. Remove the wheel and tire assembly.

5. Install a large C-clamp over the rear of the caliper and against the outer brake pad.

6. Tighten the clamp until the caliper piston is compressed into the caliper bore enough to clear the rotor.

7. Remove the C-clamp.

8. Remove the brake line, discard the 2 copper washers and plug the line openings.

9. Remove the 2 brake pin retainer bolts.

10. Remove the disc brake caliper from the vehicle.

To install:

11. Inspect the guide pin boots for tears or cuts and replace as needed.

12. Seat the guide pin boots into the guide pin retaining seat.

13. Clean the guide pin bolt threads, then apply Threadlock to two-thirds of the lower guide pin bolt threads and allow it 10 minutes to dry.

14. Apply a thin coat of high temperature brake lubricant to the guide bolts.

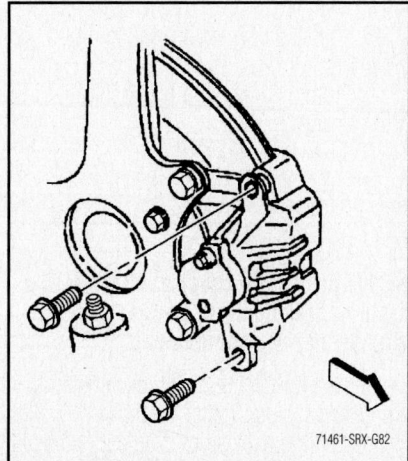

71461-SRX-G82

Fig. 2 Rear brake caliper mounting

REAR DISC BRAKES

15. Ensure that the disc brake pads are properly positioned and that the lining material is facing the rotor.

16. Place the disc brake caliper over the rotor and tighten the brake pin retainer bolts-to-guide pin bolts to 25 ft. lbs. (34 Nm) for front brakes, or 44 ft. lbs. (60 Nm) for rear brakes.

17. Unplug and install the brake hose and retaining bolt to the disc brake caliper using new copper sealing washers on each side of the hose fitting. Tighten the brake hose bolts to 37 ft. lbs. (50 Nm).

18. Bleed the brake system, then apply the brake pedal two-thirds down and slowly release the pedal. Wait 15 seconds and repeat until a firm pedal is obtained.

19. Install the wheel and tire assembly. Torque the lug nuts to 100 ft. lbs. (136 Nm).

20. Lower the vehicle.

21. Check and fill the brake master cylinder as required.

22. Road-test the vehicle and check for proper brake operation.

DISC BRAKE PADS

REMOVAL & INSTALLATION

1. Before servicing the vehicle, refer to the Precautions Section.

2. Remove ½ of the brake fluid from the brake master cylinder reservoir. Properly dispose of the brake fluid.

3. Raise and safely support the vehicle.

4. Remove the wheel and tire assembly.

5. Install a large C-clamp over the rear of the caliper and against the outer brake pad.

6. Tighten the clamp until the caliper piston is compressed into the caliper bore enough to clear the rotor.

7. Remove the C-clamp.

8. Remove the lower brake pin retainer bolt.

9. Pivot the caliper upward away from the rotor.

10. Hang the disc brake caliper with a length of wire or equivalent to prevent damage to the brake hose.

11. Remove the inner and outer disc brake pads and the retainers.

12. Inspect the disc brake rotor surfaces for grooves, cracks or glazing. Resurface or replace as required. If resurfacing, observe the minimum thickness specification.

To install:

13. Inspect the guide pin boots for tears or cuts and replace as needed.

14. Seat the guide pin boot into the guide pin retaining seat.

15. Clean the guide pin bolt threads, then apply Threadlock to two-thirds of the lower guide pin bolt threads and allow it 10 minutes to dry.

16. Apply a thin coat of high temperature brake lubricant to the guide bolt.

17. Retract the caliper piston fully into the caliper bore using a C-clamp and wood block or equivalent. This will allow room for the new disc brake pads.

18. Install new inner and outer disc brake pads and the retainers. Ensure that the disc brake pads are properly positioned and that the lining material is facing the rotor.

19. Ensure that the disc brake pads are properly positioned and that the lining material is facing the rotor.

20. Place the disc brake caliper over the rotor and tighten the brake pin retainer bolts-to-guide pin bolts to 25 ft. lbs. (34 Nm) for front brakes, or 44 ft. lbs. (60 Nm) for rear brakes.

21. Install the wheel and tire assembly. Torque the lug nuts to 100 ft. lbs. (136 Nm).

22. Lower the vehicle.

23. Pump the brake pedal to position the brake pads before attempting to move the vehicle.

24. Check and fill the brake master cylinder reservoir, as required.

25. Road-test the vehicle and check for proper brake system operation.

BRAKES

PARKING BRAKE

PARKING BRAKE CABLES

ADJUSTMENT

The cable is self adjusting. Refer to parking brake shoe adjustment procedure.

PARKING BRAKE SHOES

REMOVAL & INSTALLATION

See Figures 3 and 4.

1. Before servicing the vehicle, refer to the Precautions Section.

2. Remove the wheel bearing and hub assembly.

3. Rotate the parking brake adjusting nut (2) until all park brake shoe adjustment has been removed.

4. Remove the parking brake shoe retaining spring (1).

5. Remove the park brake shoe assembly (1) by grasping the shoe and spreading slightly while pulling the shoe from the actuator assembly.

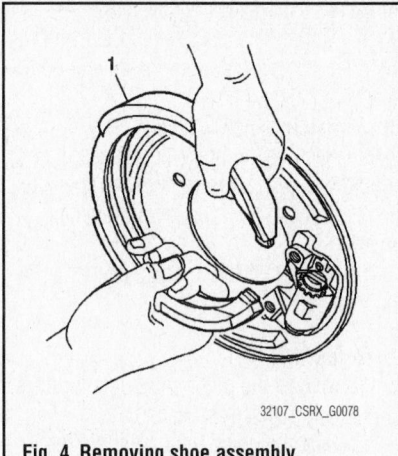

Fig. 4 Removing shoe assembly

To install:

6. Install the park brake shoe assembly (1) by grasping the shoe and spreading slightly while pulling the shoe over the actuator assembly.

7. Install the parking brake shoe retaining spring (1).

8. Install the wheel bearing and hub assembly.

9. Adjust the parking brake shoe-to-drum clearance.

10. Lower the vehicle.

ADJUSTMENT

See Figures 5 and 6.

➡This procedure requires the use of a drum to brake caliper gauge, special tool J21177-A or equivalent.

Adjustments to the park brake shoe are not necessary after replacing the park brake lever or park brake cables. The park brake is adjusted automatically by cycling the park brake lever three times.

➡DO not operate the park brake lever with the rear disc brake rotor(s) removed.

1. Before servicing the vehicle, refer to the Precautions Section.

2. Apply and fully release the parking brake three times.

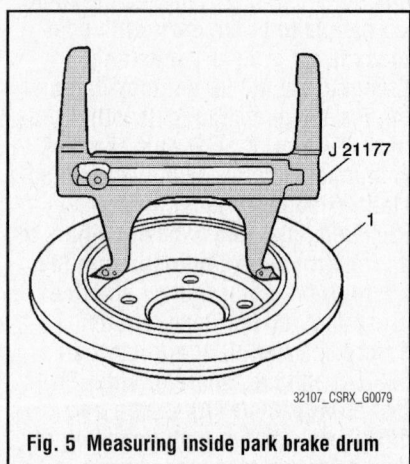

Fig. 5 Measuring inside park brake drum

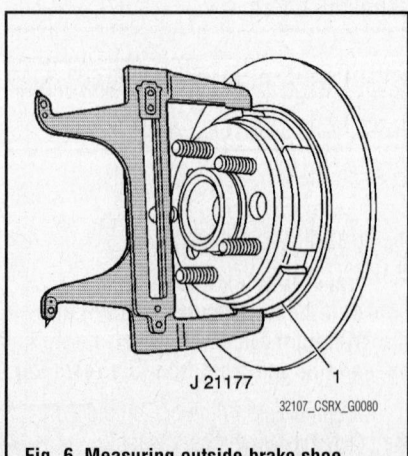

Fig. 6 Measuring outside brake shoe

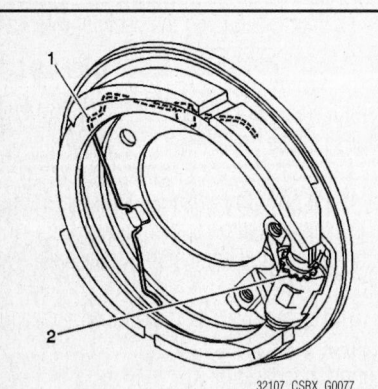

Fig. 3 Park brake adjustment nut (2) and retaining spring (1)

3. Verify that the parking brake pedal releases completely.

4. Raise and suitably support the vehicle.

5. Remove the rear tire and wheel assembly.

6. Remove the rear brake caliper brackets.

7. Remove the rear brake rotors (1).

8. Set the J21177-A inside of the park brake drum at the widest point and tighten the set screw on the tool.

9. Position the J21177-A over the park brake shoe (1) at the widest point.

10. Turn the adjuster on the actuator until the park brake shoe just contacts the J21177-A.

11. Install the rear brake rotors.

12. Install the rear caliper brackets.

13. Install the rear tire and wheel.

14. Set and release the park brake lever 3 times.

➡**If the rear wheels rotate during the following test, readjust the parking brake shoes.**

15. Release the parking brake. Verify that the wheels rotate freely.

16. Lower the vehicle.

CHASSIS ELECTRICAL

AIR BAG (SUPPLEMENTAL RESTRAINT SYSTEM)

GENERAL INFORMATION

❊❊ CAUTION

These vehicles are equipped with an air bag system. The system must be disarmed before performing service on, or around, system components, the steering column, instrument panel components, wiring and sensors. Failure to follow the safety precautions and the disarming procedure could result in accidental air bag deployment, possible injury and unnecessary system repairs.

SERVICE PRECAUTIONS

Disconnect and isolate the battery negative cable before beginning any airbag system component diagnosis, testing, removal, or installation procedures. Allow system capacitor to discharge for two minutes before beginning any component service. This will disable the airbag system. Failure to disable the airbag system may result in accidental airbag deployment, personal injury, or death.

Do not place an intact undeployed airbag face down on a solid surface. The airbag will propel into the air if accidentally deployed and may result in personal injury or death.

When carrying or handling an undeployed airbag, the trim side (face) of the airbag should be pointing towards the body to minimize possibility of injury if accidental deployment occurs. Failure to do this may result in personal injury or death.

Replace airbag system components with OEM replacement parts. Substitute parts may appear interchangeable, but internal differences may result in inferior occupant protection. Failure to do so may result in occupant personal injury or death.

Wear safety glasses, rubber gloves, and long sleeved clothing when cleaning powder residue from vehicle after an airbag deployment. Powder residue emitted from a deployed airbag can cause skin irritation. Flush affected area with cool water if irritation is experienced. If nasal or throat irritation is experienced, exit the vehicle for fresh air until the irritation ceases. If irritation continues, see a physician.

Do not use a replacement airbag that is not in the original packaging. This may result in improper deployment, personal injury, or death.

The factory installed fasteners, screws and bolts used to fasten airbag components have a special coating and are specifically designed for the airbag system. Do not use substitute fasteners. Use only original equipment fasteners listed in the parts catalog when fastener replacement is required.

During, and following, any child restraint anchor service, due to impact event or vehicle repair, carefully inspect all mounting hardware, tether straps, and anchors for proper installation, operation, or damage. If a child restraint anchor is found damaged in any way, the anchor must be replaced. Failure to do this may result in personal injury or death.

Deployed and non-deployed airbags may or may not have live pyrotechnic material within the airbag inflator.

Do not dispose of driver/passenger/curtain airbags or seat belt tensioners unless you are sure of complete deployment. Refer to the Hazardous Substance Control System for proper disposal.

Dispose of deployed airbags and tensioners consistent with state, provincial, local, and federal regulations.

After any airbag component testing or service, do not connect the battery negative cable. Personal injury or death may result if the system test is not performed first.

If the vehicle is equipped with the Occupant Classification System (OCS), do not connect the battery negative cable before performing the OCS Verification Test using the scan tool and the appropriate diagnostic information. Personal injury or death may result if the system test is not performed properly.

Never replace both the Occupant Restraint Controller (ORC) and the Occupant Classification Module (OCM) at the same time. If both require replacement, replace one, then perform the Airbag System test before replacing the other.

Both the ORC and the OCM store Occupant Classification System (OCS) calibration data, which they transfer to one another when one of them is replaced. If both are replaced at the same time, an irreversible fault will be set in both modules and the OCS may malfunction and cause personal injury or death.

If equipped with OCS, the Seat Weight Sensor is a sensitive, calibrated unit and must be handled carefully. Do not drop or handle roughly. If dropped or damaged, replace with another sensor. Failure to do so may result in occupant injury or death.

If equipped with OCS, the front passenger seat must be handled carefully as well. When removing the seat, be careful when setting on floor not to drop. If dropped, the sensor may be inoperative, could result in occupant injury, or possibly death.

If equipped with OCS, when the passenger front seat is on the floor, no one should sit in the front passenger seat. This uneven force may damage the sensing ability of the seat weight sensors. If sat on and damaged, the sensor may be inoperative, could result in occupant injury, or possibly death.

DISABLING AND ENABLING THE SYSTEM

The Supplemental Restraint System (SRS) is designed to work in conjunction with the standard 3-point safety belts to reduce injury in a head-on collision.

❊❊ CAUTION

The SRS can actually cause physical injury or death if the safety belts are not used, or if the manufacturer's warnings are not followed. The manufacturer's warnings can be found in your owner's manual, or, in some cases, on your sun visor.

The SRS is comprised of the following components:

- Driver's side air bag module
- Passenger's side air bag module
- Right-hand and left-hand primary crash front air bag sensors
- Air bag diagnostic monitor computer
- Electrical wiring

The SRS primary crash front air bag sensors are hard-wired to the air bag modules and determine when the air bags are deployed. During a frontal collision, the sensors quickly inflate the 2 air bags to reduce injury by cushioning the driver and front passenger from striking the dashboard, windshield, steering wheel and any other hard surfaces. The air bag inflates so quickly (in a fraction of a second) that in most cases it is fully inflated before you actually start to move during a collision.

Since the SRS is a complicated and essentially important system, its components are constantly being tested by a diagnostic computer. The computer illuminates the air bag indicator light on the instrument cluster for approximately 6 seconds when the ignition switch is turned to the **RUN** position when the SRS is functioning properly. After being illuminated for the 6 seconds, the indicator light should then turn off.

If the air bag light does not illuminate at all, stays on continuously, or flashes at any time, a problem has been detected by the diagnostic computer.

✳✳ CAUTION

If at any time the air bag light indicates that the computer has noted a problem, immediately diagnose the problem. A faulty SRS can cause severe physical injury or death.

Zone 1

See Figure 7.

1. Turn the steering wheel so that the vehicles wheels are pointing straight ahead.
2. Turn the ignition switch to the OFF position.
3. Remove the key from the ignition switch.
4. Adjust the right rear seat to the rear of vehicle.
5. Pull the carpet away from under the right side of rear seat.
6. When the carpet is pulled away from the right rear seat the right rear fuse center will be exposed, then remove the fuse center top cover.

➡**With the SIR fuse removed and the ignition switch in the ON position, the**

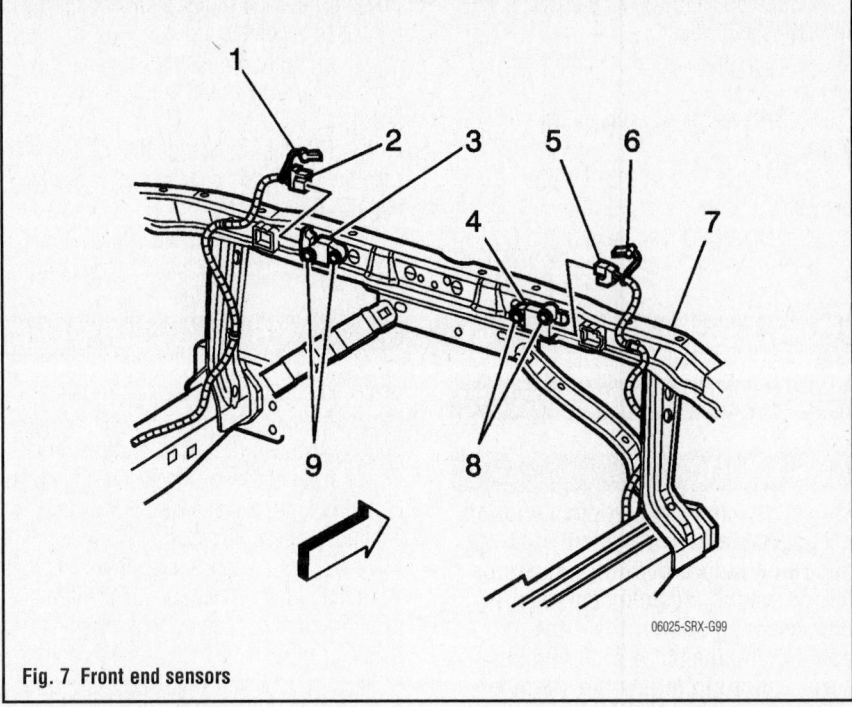

Fig. 7 Front end sensors

AIR BAG warning indicator illuminates. This is normal operation, and does not indicate an SIR system malfunction.

7. Locate and remove the SIR fuse from the right rear fuse center.
8. Open front hood, and locate both front end sensors (3, 4).
9. Remove both connector position assurance (CPA) (1, 6) from left and right front end sensor connectors (2, 5).
10. Remove both connectors (2, 5) from left and right front end sensors (3, 4).

Enabling Procedure:

11. Remove the key from the ignition switch.
12. Connect both connectors (2, 5) to the left and right front end sensors (3, 4).
13. Install both CPAs (1, 6) to the left and right front end sensor connectors (2, 5).
14. Close front hood.
15. Install the SIR fuse into the right rear fuse center.
16. Install the right rear fuse center cover.
17. Position the carpet back under the right rear seat.
18. Use caution while reaching in and turn the ignition switch to the ON position. The AIR BAG indicator will flash then turn OFF.

Zone 2

See Figure 8.

1. Turn the steering wheel so that the vehicle's wheels are pointing straight ahead.
2. Turn the ignition switch to the OFF position.

3. Remove the key from the ignition switch.
4. Adjust the right rear seat to the rear of vehicle.
5. Pull the carpet away from under the right side of rear seat.
6. When the carpet is pulled away from the rear seat the right rear fuse center (1) will be exposed, then remove the fuse center top cover.

➡**With the SIR fuse removed and the ignition switch in the ON position, the AIR BAG warning indicator illuminates. This is normal operation, and does not indicate an SIR system malfunction.**

7. Locate and remove the SIR fuse from the right rear fuse center.
8. When disabling the roof rail module, go to step 9. If the side impact sensor (SIS) needs disabling, go to step 12.
9. Remove the left carpet retainer trim.
10. Remove the connector position assurance (CPA) from the left/driver roof rail module yellow connector.
11. Disconnect the left roof rail module connector from the left roof rail module.
12. Remove the left center pillar trim panel.
13. Remove the SIS CPA (1) from the left SIS connector (2).
14. Remove the SIS connector (2) from the SIS (3).

Enabling Procedure:

15. Remove the key from the ignition switch.
16. When enabling the SIS, proceed to

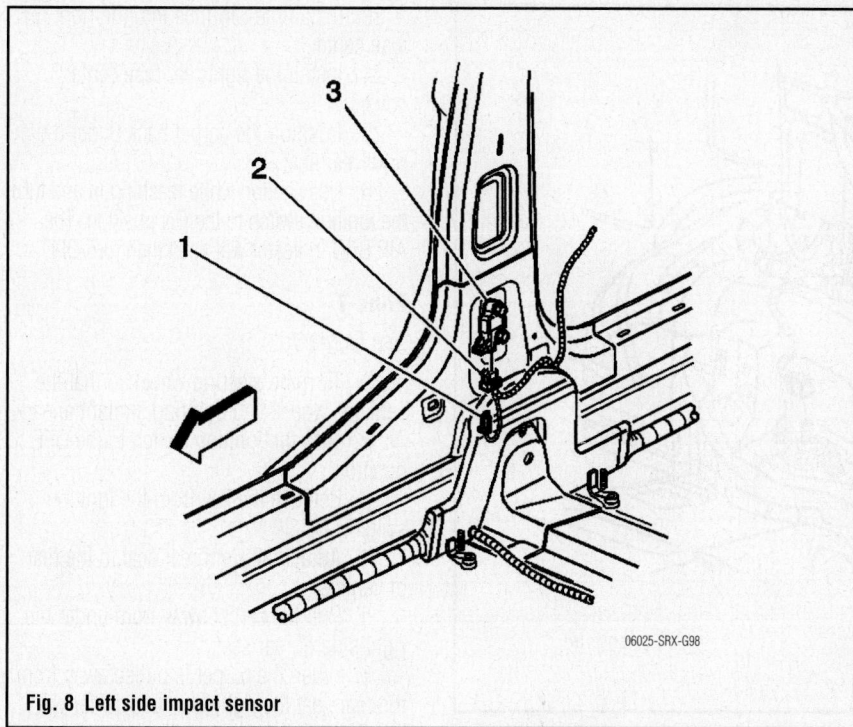

06025-SRX-G98

Fig. 8 Left side impact sensor

step 3. If the roof rail module needs enabling, go to step 6.

17. Connect the SIS connector to the SIS.

18. Connect the CPA to the SIS connector.

19. Install the left center pillar trim panel.

20. Connect the roof rail module yellow connector to the left roof rail module.

21. Install the CPA to the left roof rail module connector.

22. Install the left carpet retainer trim.

23. Install the SIR fuse into the right rear fuse center.

24. Install the right rear fuse center cover.

25. Position the carpet back under the right rear seat.

26. Use caution while reaching in and turn the ignition switch to the ON position. The AIR BAG indicator will flash then turn OFF.

Zone 3

1. Turn the steering wheel so that the vehicle's wheels are pointing straight ahead.

2. Turn the ignition switch to the OFF position.

3. Remove the key from the ignition switch.

4. Adjust the right rear seat to the rear of vehicle.

5. Pull the carpet away from under the right side of rear seat.

6. When the carpet is pulled away from

the rear seat the right rear fuse center will be exposed, then remove the fuse center top cover.

➡**With the SIR fuse removed and the ignition switch in the ON position, the AIR BAG warning indicator illuminates. This is normal operation, and does not indicate an SIR system malfunction.**

7. Locate and remove the SIR fuse from the right rear fuse center.

8. Remove the left/driver sound insulator from the instrument panel (I/P).

9. Remove the connector position assurance (CPA) from the steering wheel module coil yellow connector.

10. Disconnect the steering wheel module coil yellow connector from the vehicle harness yellow connector.

Enabling Procedure:

11. Remove the key from the ignition switch.

12. Connect the steering wheel module coil yellow connector to the vehicle harness yellow connector.

13. Install the CPA to the steering wheel module coil yellow connector.

14. Install the left sound insulator to the I/P.

15. Install the SIR fuse into the right rear fuse center.

16. Install the right rear fuse center cover.

17. Position the carpet back under the right rear seat.

18. Use caution while reaching in and

turn the ignition switch to the ON position. The AIR BAG indicator will flash then turn OFF.

Zone 5

1. Turn the steering wheel so that the vehicle's wheels are pointing straight ahead.

2. Turn the ignition switch to the OFF position.

3. Remove the key from the ignition switch.

4. Adjust the right rear seat to the rear of vehicle.

5. Pull the carpet away from under the right side of rear seat.

6. When the carpet is pulled away from the rear seat the right rear fuse center will be exposed, then remove the fuse center top cover.

➡**With the SIR fuse removed and the ignition switch in the ON position, the AIR BAG warning indicator illuminates. This is normal operation, and does not indicate an SIR system malfunction.**

7. Locate and remove the SIR fuse from the right rear fuse center.

8. Remove the right/passenger sound insulator from the instrument panel (I/P).

9. Remove the connector position assurance (CPA) from the I/P module yellow connector.

10. Disconnect the I/P module yellow connector from the vehicle harness yellow connector.

Enabling procedure:

11. Remove the key from the ignition switch.

12. Connect the I/P module yellow connector to the vehicle harness yellow connector.

13. Install the CPA to the I/P module yellow connector.

14. Install the right sound insulator to the I/P.

15. Install the SIR fuse into the right rear fuse center.

16. Install the right rear fuse center cover.

17. Position the carpet back under the right rear seat.

18. Use caution while reaching in and turn the ignition switch to the ON position. The AIR BAG indicator will flash then turn OFF.

Zone 6

See Figure 9.

1. Turn the steering wheel so that the vehicle's wheels are pointing straight ahead.

2. Turn the ignition switch to the OFF position.

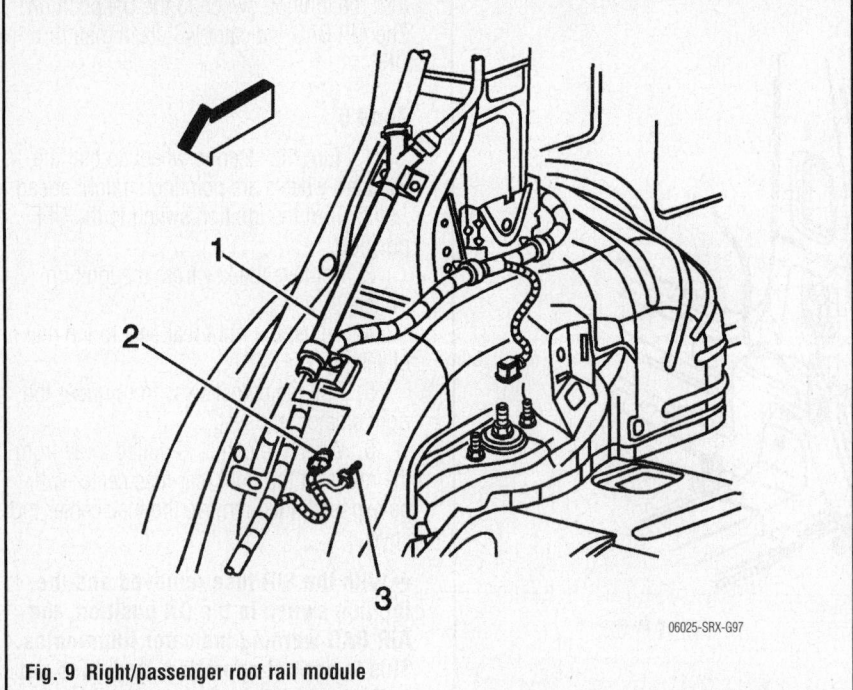

Fig. 9 Right/passenger roof rail module

06025-SRX-G97

3. Remove the key from the ignition switch.

4. Adjust the right rear seat to the rear of vehicle.

5. Pull the carpet away from under the right side of rear seat.

6. When the carpet is pulled away from the rear seat the right rear fuse center will be exposed, then remove the fuse center top cover.

➡**With the SIR fuse removed and the ignition switch in the ON position, the AIR BAG warning indicator illuminates. This is normal operation, and does not indicate an SIR system malfunction.**

7. Locate and remove the SIR fuse from the right rear fuse center.

8. When disabling the roof rail module, go to step 9. If the side impact sensor (SIS) needs disabling, go to step 12.

9. Remove the right carpet retainer trim.

10. Remove the connector position assurance (CPA) (2) from the right/passenger roof rail module yellow connector (3).

11. Disconnect the right roof rail module connector from the right roof rail module (1).

12. Remove the right center pillar trim panel.

13. Remove the SIS CPA from the left SIS connector.

14. Remove the SIS connector from the SIS.

Enabling Procedure:

15. Remove the key from the ignition switch.

16. When enabling the SIS, proceed to step 3. If the roof rail module needs enabling, go to step 6.

17. Connect the SIS connector to the SIS.

18. Connect the CPA to the SIS connector.

19. Install the right center pillar trim panel.

20. Connect the roof rail module yellow connector to the right roof rail module.

21. Install the CPA to the right roof rail module connector.

22. Install the right carpet retainer trim.

23. Install the SIR fuse into the right rear fuse center.

24. Install the right rear fuse center cover.

25. Position the carpet back under the right rear seat.

26. Use caution while reaching in and turn the ignition switch to the ON position. The AIR BAG indicator will flash then turn OFF.

Zone 7

See Figure 10.

1. Turn the steering wheel so that the vehicles wheels are pointing straight ahead.

2. Turn the ignition switch to the OFF position.

3. Remove the key from the ignition switch.

4. Adjust the right rear seat to the rear of vehicle.

5. Pull the carpet away from under the right side of rear seat.

6. When the carpet is pulled away from the rear seat the right rear fuse center will be exposed, then remove the fuse center top cover.

➡**With the SIR fuse removed and the ignition switch in the ON position, the AIR BAG warning indicator illuminates. This is normal operation, and does not indicate an SIR system malfunction.**

7. Locate and remove the SIR fuse from the right rear fuse center.

8. Remove both connector position assurance (CPA) from the LF/driver's side impact module and seat belt pretensioner yellow connector (1) which is located under the front of driver's seat.

06025-SRX-G96

Fig. 10 LF/driver's side impact module

9. Disconnect the LF side impact module and pretensioner yellow connector from the vehicle harness yellow connector.

Enabling Procedure:

10. Remove the key from the ignition switch.

11. Connect the LF side impact module and pretensioner yellow connector (1) to the vehicle harness yellow connector.

12. Install both CPA locks to the LF side impact module and pretensioner yellow connector.

13. Install the SIR fuse into the right rear fuse center.

14. Install the right rear fuse center cover.

15. Position the carpet back under the right rear seat.

16. Use caution while reaching in and turn the ignition switch to the ON position. The AIR BAG indicator will flash then turn OFF.

Zone 8

1. Turn the steering wheel so that the vehicle's wheels are pointing straight ahead.

2. Turn the ignition switch to the OFF position.

3. Remove the key from the ignition switch.

4. Adjust the right rear seat to the rear of vehicle.

5. Pull the carpet away from under the right side of rear seat.

6. When the carpet is pulled away from the rear seat the right rear fuse center will be exposed, then remove the fuse center top cover.

➡ **With the SIR fuse removed and the ignition switch in the ON position, the AIR BAG warning indicator illuminates. This is normal operation, and does not indicate an SIR system malfunction.**

7. Locate and remove the SIR fuse from the right rear fuse center.

8. Remove the right carpet retainer trim.

9. Remove the connector position assurance (CPA) from the right/passenger roof rail module yellow connector.

10. Disconnect the right roof rail module connector from the right roof rail module.

11. Remove the right/passenger sound insulator from the instrument panel (I/P).

12. Remove the CPA from the I/P module yellow connector.

13. Disconnect the I/P module yellow connector from the vehicle harness yellow connector.

14. Remove both CPA locks from the passenger/RF side impact module and seat

belt pretensioner yellow connector located under the front of passenger seat.

15. Disconnect the RF side impact module and pretensioner yellow connector from the vehicle harness yellow connector.

16. Remove the driver/left sound insulator from the I/P.

17. Remove the CPA from the steering wheel module coil yellow connector.

18. Disconnect the steering wheel module coil yellow connector from the vehicle harness yellow connector.

19. Remove both CPA locks from the driver/LF side impact module and seat belt pretensioner yellow connector located under the front of driver seat.

20. Disconnect the LF side impact module and pretensioner yellow connector from the vehicle harness yellow connector.

21. Remove the left carpet retainer trim.

22. Remove the CPA from the left/driver roof rail module yellow connector.

23. Disconnect the left roof rail module connector from the left roof rail module.

Enabling Procedure:

24. Remove the key from the ignition switch.

25. Connect the roof rail module yellow connector to the left roof rail module.

26. Install the CPA to the left roof rail module connector.

27. Install the left carpet retainer trim.

28. Connect the driver/LF side impact module and seat belt pretensioner yellow connector to the vehicle harness yellow connector located under the front of driver seat.

29. Install both CPA locks to the LF side impact module and pretensioner yellow connector.

30. Connect the steering wheel module coil yellow connector to the vehicle harness yellow connector.

31. Install the CPA to the steering wheel module coil yellow connector.

32. Install the driver/left sound insulator to the I/P.

33. Connect the passenger/I/P module yellow connector to the vehicle harness yellow connector.

34. Install the CPA to the I/P module yellow connector.

35. Install the passenger/right sound insulator to the I/P.

36. Connect the passenger/RF side impact module and seat belt pretensioner yellow connector to the vehicle harness yellow connector located under the front of passenger seat.

37. Install both CPA locks to the RF side impact module and pretensioner yellow connector.

38. Connect the roof rail module yellow connector to the right roof rail module.

39. Install the CPA to the right roof rail module connector.

40. Install the right carpet retainer trim.

41. Install the SIR fuse into the right rear fuse center.

42. Install the right rear fuse center cover.

43. Position the carpet back under the right rear seat.

44. Use caution while reaching in and turn the ignition switch to the ON position. The AIR BAG indicator will flash then turn OFF.

Zone 9

1. Turn the steering wheel so that the vehicles wheels are pointing straight ahead.

2. Turn the ignition switch to the OFF position.

3. Remove the key from the ignition switch.

4. Adjust the right rear seat to the rear of vehicle.

5. Pull the carpet away from under the right side of rear seat.

6. When the carpet is pulled away from the rear seat the right rear fuse center will be exposed, then remove the fuse center top cover.

➡ **With the SIR fuse removed and the ignition switch in the ON position, the AIR BAG warning indicator illuminates. This is normal operation, and does not indicate an SIR system malfunction.**

7. Locate and remove the SIR fuse from the right rear fuse center.

8. Remove both connector position assurance (CPA) from the RF/passenger side impact module and seat belt pretensioner yellow connector which is located under the front of passenger seat.

9. Disconnect the RF side impact module and pretensioner yellow connector from the vehicle harness yellow connector.

Enabling Procedure:

10. Remove the key from the ignition switch.

11. Connect the RF side impact module and pretensioner yellow connector to the vehicle harness yellow connector.

12. Install both CPA locks to the RF side impact module and pretensioner yellow connector.

13. Install the SIR fuse into the right rear fuse center.

14. Install the right rear fuse center cover.

15. Position the carpet back under the right rear seat.

16. Use caution while reaching in and turn the ignition switch to the ON position. The AIR BAG indicator will flash then turn OFF.

CLOCKSPRING CENTERING

Verify the following before centering the inflatable restraint steering wheel module coil:

• The wheels on the vehicle are straight ahead.

• The block tooth of the upper steering shaft is in the 12 o'clock position.

• The ignition and start switch is in the **LOCK** position.

With Centering Window

With Spring Lock

If the front of the inflatable restraint steering wheel module coil has a centering window, and on the back side a spring service lock, perform the following steps.

1. Hold the coil with the face up.

2. While depressing the spring service lock, rotate the coil hub clockwise until the coil ribbon stops.

3. Rotate the coil hub slowly, counterclockwise, until the centering window appears yellow and both arrows line up.

4. Release the spring service lock between the locking tab. The coil is now centered.

5. Align the centered coil with the turn signal switch cancel cam and it slide onto the upper steering shaft.

Without Spring Lock

If the front of the inflatable restraint steering wheel module coil has a centering window and no spring service lock on the back side, perform the following steps.

1. Hold the coil with the face up.

2. Rotate the coil hub clockwise until the coil ribbon stops.

3. Rotate the coil hub slowly, counterclockwise until the centering window appears yellow and both arrows line up. This is the CENTER position.

4. While holding the coil hub in the CENTER position, align the coil with the turn signal switch cancel cam and slide it onto the upper steering shaft.

Without Centering Window

With Spring Lock

If no centering window is present on the front side of the inflatable restraint steering wheel module coil, but a spring service lock

is on the back side, perform the following steps.

1. Hold the coil with the back side up.

2. While depressing the spring service lock, rotate the coil hub in the direction of the arrow until the coil ribbon stops.

3. Still pressing the spring service lock, rotate the coil hub in the opposite direction 2.5 revolutions.

4. Release the spring service lock between locking tabs. The coil is now centered.

5. Align the centered coil with the turn signal switch cancel cam and slide it onto the upper steering shaft.

Without Spring Lock

If there is no centering window on the front side of the inflatable restraint steering wheel module coil and no spring service lock on the back side, perform the following steps.

1. Hold the coil with the face up.

2. Rotate the coil hub in the direction of the arrow until the coil ribbon stops.

3. Rotate the coil hub, slowly, counterclockwise, for 2.5 revolutions. This is the CENTER position.

4. While maintaining the coil hub in the CENTER position, align it with the turn signal switch cancel cam and slide it onto the upper steering shaft.

DRIVETRAIN

AUTOMATIC TRANSMISSION ASSEMBLY

REMOVAL & INSTALLATION

1. Before servicing the vehicle, refer to the Precautions Section.

2. Drain the transmission fluid

3. Remove or disconnect the following:

• Negative battery cable
• Thermostat housing
• Exhaust system
• Propeller shaft
• On 4WD models, the transfer case
• Shift linkage
• Transmission wiring harness connector
• Wiring harness retainers
• Transmission fluid cooler lines and plug the openings
• Starter on 3.6L engines
• Mark the torque converter to flywheel orientation
• Front air deflector

4. Rotate the harmonic balancer center bolt clockwise ONLY to align the torque converter bolts with the access hole.

5. Remove and discard the torque converter bolts.

6. Remove the front differential heat shield and bracket, if equipped.

7. Place a transmission jack under the transmission and lower the transmission enough to access the upper 2 transmission mounting bolts.

8. Remove the 2 upper transmission mounting bolts.

9. Raise the transmission so the engine and transmission are in the normal position, then place a jack under the engine to keep it level.

10. Remove the lower transmission mounting bolts.

11. Carefully pull the transmission back off the engine dowels, then lower the transmission away from the vehicle.

To install:

➡**Torque converter bolts are self-locking and must be replaced with new bolts.**

12. Place the transaxle on a suitable jack and carefully raise it into position.

13. Install the lower transmission mounting bolts. Tighten the M10 bolts to 37 ft. lbs. (50 Nm). Tighten the M12 bolts to 55 ft. lbs. (75 Nm).

• Lower the transmission and install the upper bolts. Tighten the M10 bolts to 37 ft. lbs. (50 Nm). Tighten the M12 bolts to 55 ft. lbs. (75 Nm).

14. Install or connect the following:

• Torque converter bolts and tighten to 46 ft. lbs. (63 Nm).
• Differential heat shield and bracket.
• Front air deflector
• Starter on 3.6L engines
• Transmission fluid cooler lines
• Wiring harness retainers
• Transmission wiring harness connector
• Shift linkage
• On 4WD models, the transfer case
• Propeller shaft
• Exhaust system
• Thermostat housing
• Negative battery cable

15. Fill the transmission with fluid to the correct level.

16. Adjust the shift control linkage.

17. Start the vehicle and check for leaks and check the fluid level.

TRANSFER CASE ASSEMBLY

REMOVAL & INSTALLATION

4.6L AWD Models

See Figures 11 and 12.

1. Before servicing the vehicle, refer to the Precautions Section.
2. Drain the transfer case fluid.
3. Remove or disconnect the following:
   - Negative battery cable
   - Exhaust system
   - Rear propeller shaft
4. Support the transmission with a jack
5. Remove the rear transmission mount-to-body bolts.
6. Remove the transmission mount-to-transmission bolts.
7. Insert a flat bladed tool into the notch on the transfer case flange and carefully move the front propeller shaft forward and remove the transfer case flange.
8. Wire the propeller shaft up and out of the way.
9. Support the transfer case with a jack and remove the mounting bolts.
10. Remove the transfer case.

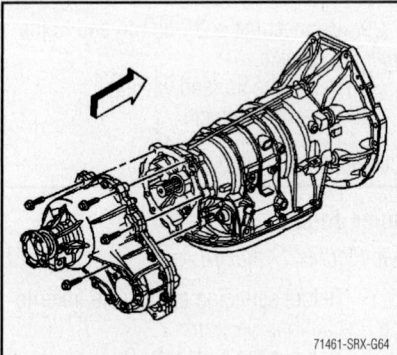

Fig. 11 Transfer case mounting—4.6L engine AWD models

71461-SRX-G64

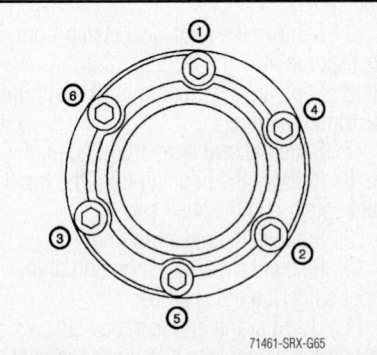

Fig. 12 Transfer case flange bolt tightening sequence—4.6L engine AWD models

71461-SRX-G65

To install:

11. Install the transfer case and tighten the bolts to 44 ft. lbs. (60 Nm).
12. Remove the jack.
13. Untie the front propeller shaft and position it to the transfer case so the coned end CV joint is installed into the transfer case flange.
14. Clean the transfer case flange bolts and apply threadlock to the threads and allow it to dry for 10 minutes.
15. Install the transfer case flange bolts with the crescent washers and tighten the bolts in sequence to 22 ft. lbs. (30 Nm).
16. Install or connect the following:
   - Transmission mount-to-transmission bolts. Tighten to 81 ft. lbs. (110 Nm).
   - Rear transmission mount-to-body bolts. Tighten the bolts to 44 ft. lbs. (60 Nm).
17. Remove the jack.
18. Install or connect the following:
   - Rear propeller shaft
   - Exhaust system
   - Negative battery cable
19. Fill the transfer case with fluid to the correct level.

FRONT AXLE HOUSING

REMOVAL & INSTALLATION

See Figure 13.

1. Before servicing the vehicle, refer to the Precautions Section.
2. Remove the front wheels.
3. Remove the front frame assembly. See the procedure in suspension.
4. Remove or disconnect the following:
   - Front propeller shaft
   - Front axle shafts
   - Intermediate drive shaft support bearing
5. Secure the differential to a transmission jack.

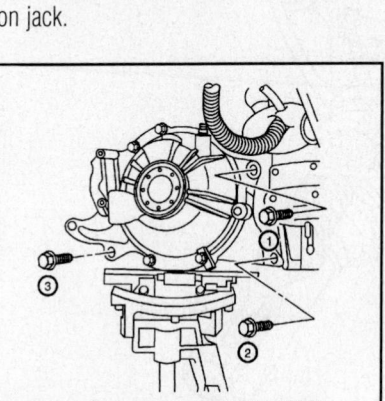

Fig. 13 Front differential bolt tightening sequence—AWD models

71461-SRX-G71

6. Remove the differential-to-oil pan bolts.
7. Remove the differential and the intermediate drive shaft as an assembly.

To install:

8. Installation is the reverse of the removal procedure. Tighten the differential bolts in the sequence shown to 81 ft. lbs. (110 Nm).
9. Check the differential fluid level and fill as needed.

FRONT HALFSHAFT

REMOVAL & INSTALLATION

See Figures 14 through 16.

➡**Do not begin this removal procedure unless a new wheel hub retainer nut and a new retainer circlip are available. Once removed, these parts must not be reused during assembly. Their torque holding ability, or retention capability, is diminished during removal.**

➡**This procedure requires the use of Slide Hammer and Adapter J-2619-01, or equivalent, Extension J-29794, Axle Shaft Puller J-35341, Seal Protector J-44394 and Wheel Hub Remover J-45859.**

1. Before servicing the vehicle, refer to the Precautions Section.
2. Raise and support the vehicle.
3. Remove or disconnect the following:
   - Front wheels
   - Outer tie rod end, but DO NOT loosen the jam nut
   - Axle hub nut and washer. Discard the nut.
   - Anti-lock Brake System (ABS) sensor connector
   - Upper ball joint
4. Install tool J-45859 onto the wheel hub and secure with 2 lug nuts.
5. Use the tool to disengage the halfshaft from the wheel hub and bearing. Support the halfshaft.
6. Remove the tool from the wheel hub.
7. Assemble tools J-2619-01, J-29794 and J-45341 and install it to the halfshaft inner joint pull groove.
8. On the left side, use the tool to separate the wheel halfshaft from the intermediate wheel driveshaft.
9. Remove the halfshaft from the left side.
10. On the right side, use the tool to disengage the halfshaft away from the differential enough to install tool J-44394.

11. Install tool J-44394 over the half-shaft and into the differential output seal to protect the seal.

12. Remove the halfshaft from the right side.

13. If reusing the halfshaft, remove and discard the retaining ring from the intermediate shaft ring groove.

To install:

14. On the left side install a new O-ring to the intermediate shaft O-ring groove.

15. On both sides, install a new retainer circlip on the splined end of the shaft.

16. On the left side, apply a small amount of grease to the intermediate drive-shaft splines.

17. Install the left halfshaft into the intermediate driveshaft.

18. Verify that the shaft is engaged by pulling outward on the inner joint housing. The shaft should remain firmly engaged.

19. On the right side, install tool J-44394 into the differential output shaft seal.

20. Install the right halfshaft into the differential until the splines are past the tool opening.

21. Remove the tool from the differential seal.

22. Continue to install the halfshaft until the retaining ring is fully seated.

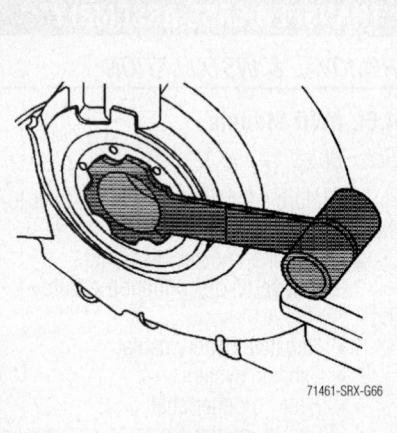

Fig. 16 Using tool J-44394 to protect the right side differential output seal

23. Verify that the shaft is engaged by pulling outward on the inner joint housing. The shaft should remain firmly engaged.

24. On both sides, install the halfshaft into the wheel hub and bearing.

25. Connect the upper ball joint to the steering knuckle.

26. Connect the ABS sensor connector.

27. Loosely install the NEW wheel axle nut.

28. Hold the brake rotor from turning and tighten the axle nut to 118 ft. lbs. (160 Nm).

29. Connect the outer tie rod end to the steering knuckle.

30. Install the tire and wheel.

31. Lower the vehicle.

CV-JOINTS OVERHAUL

Inner Joint

See Figures 17 and 18.

1. Before servicing the vehicle, refer to the Precautions Section.

2. Remove the halfshaft.

3. Wrap a towel around the halfshaft and place it horizontally in a vise.

4. Remove the small seal clamp using side cutters.

5. Remove the large seal clamp from the tripot joint.

6. Separate the inboard joint seal from the tripot bushing.

7. Slide the seal away from the joint.

8. Remove the housing from the tripot joint spider and the shaft bar.

9. Remove the retaining ring.

10. Reference mark the position of the tripot spider on the shaft bar.

11. Using a drift and hammer, tap around the spider face to remove the joint from the bar.

12. Remove the joint seal from the bar.

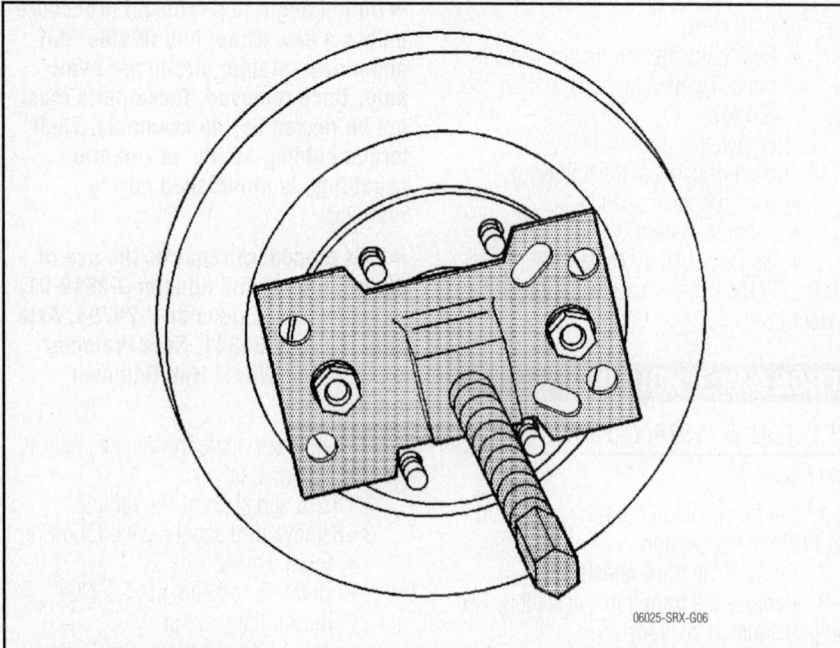

Fig. 14 Install Special Tool J-45859 to disengage the halfshaft from the wheel hub assembly.

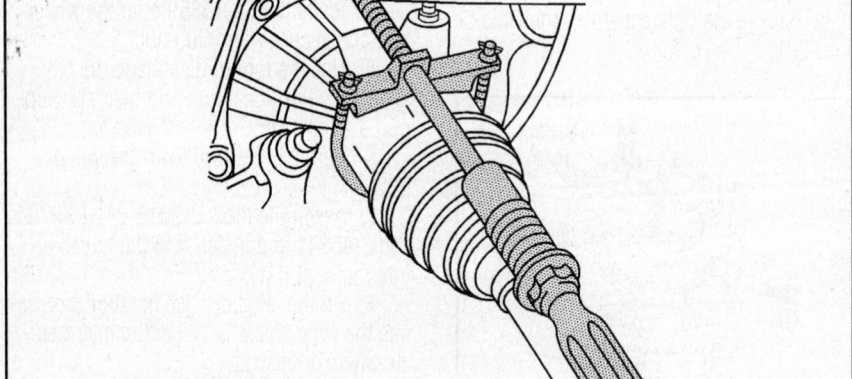

Fig. 15 Special tools J-2619-01, J-29794 and J-45341 assembled on the inner joint.

13. Inspect the parts for wear or damage and replace as necessary.

To assemble:

14. Place a new small seal clamp on the small end of the inner joint seal.

15. Slide the inner joint seal and the small seal clamp into the boot groove on the shaft bar.

16. Position the small end of the inner joint seal into the inner joint seal groove.

17. Crimp the small seal clamp until the crimping joint gap is 0.039 inch (1mm).

➡ **The clamping hold time must be no less than 2 seconds.**

18. Align the reference marks and install the tripot spider to the shaft bar.

19. Install a new retaining ring.

20. Pull out on the spider to verify that the spider is fully engaged.

21. Place half of the grease from the service kit in the shaft inboard seal. Use the remainder of the grease to repack the housing.

22. Install the tripot bushing to the housing.

23. Position the large seal clamp on the inboard seal.

24. Slide the housing over the joint spider.

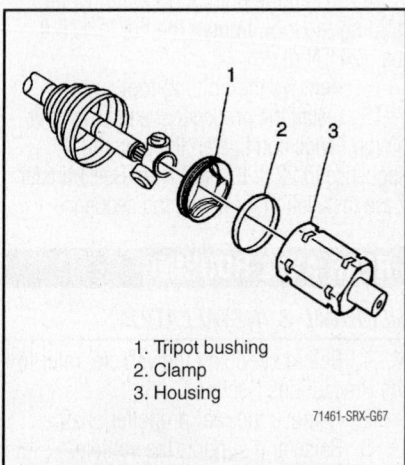

1. Tripot bushing
2. Clamp
3. Housing

71461-SRX-G67

Fig. 17 Exploded view of front inner CV joint assembly

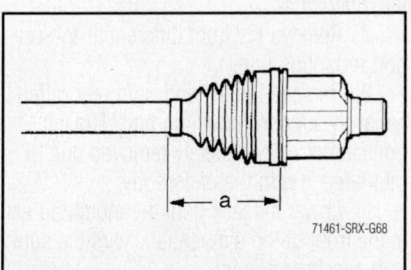

71461-SRX-G68

Fig. 18 Measuring installed boot seal distance—front inner joint

25. Slide the large inboard seal with the large clamp in place, over the bushing and locate the lip of the seal in the groove.

26. Ensure the seal is properly shaped around the circumference of the joint.

27. Measure the distance (a) between the seal edges. The correct distance is 4.12 inches (104.7mm).

28. Remove the air from the inner joint seal.

29. Using crimping pliers, crimp the large clamp around the boot, ensuring the tangs are fully engaged.

30. Rotate the inner tripot housing a few times to fully distribute the gear into the bearings.

Outer Joint

See Figure 19.

1. Before servicing the vehicle, refer to the Precautions Section.

2. Remove the halfshaft.

3. Wrap a towel around the halfshaft and place it horizontally in a vise.

4. Remove the small and large seal clamps using side cutters.

5. Separate the seal from the joint outer race at the large end.

6. Wipe the grease away from the joint face.

7. Hold the outer joint housing horizontally and position a wood block between the seal and the joint on the joint face.

8. Hammer around the wood block to remove the outer joint from the axle shaft.

9. Remove and discard the shaft retaining ring.

10. Remove the seal from the shaft.

11. Remove the axle shaft from the vise.

12. Wrap a towel around the joint outer face and place the joint in a vise vertically.

13. Using a drift and hammer, tap gently on the inner cage until it tilts up enough to remove the first ball.

14. Repeat this procedure using the proper sequence until all the balls are removed.

15. Position the cage and inner race 90° to the centerline of the outer race.

16. Remove the cage and inner race from the outer race.

17. Position the cage and inner race so the larger radius corners of the race windows are up. Rotate the inner race 90° to the centerline of the cage.

18. Align the lands of the inner race with the windows of the cage.

19. Insert an inner race land into a cage window.

20. Pivot the inner down and remove it from the cage.

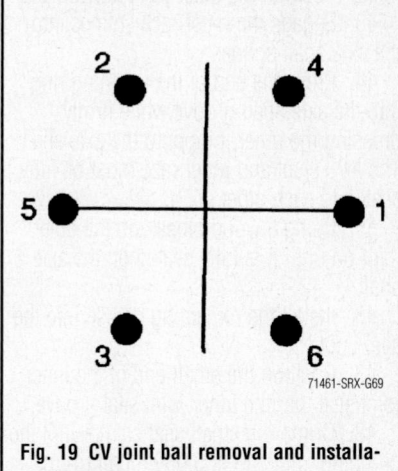

71461-SRX-G69

Fig. 19 CV joint ball removal and installation sequence

21. Clean all parts thoroughly with solvent and allow to air dry.

22. Inspect all parts for wear or damage and replace as necessary.

To assemble:

23. Position the cage so the large radius corners of the cage windows are up.

24. Position the inner race 90° to the centerline of the cage.

25. Insert the inner race up through the bottom of the cage.

26. Align a land of the inner race to a window of the cage.

27. Insert the inner race land into cage window.

28. Rotate the remainder of the inner race into the cage.

29. Align the inner race ball tracks with the cage windows.

30. Wrap a towel around the splined shaft and place the shaft vertically in a vise with the joint opening up.

31. Position the cage and inner race 90° to the centerline of the outer race.

32. Align 2 cage windows 180° apart.

33. Place a cage window and inner race ball track in position to insert the ball.

34. Insert a ball through the cage window and into the ball track. Tap the ball with a plastic hammer until it is fully engaged.

35. Repeat the procedure using the same sequence as the removal.

36. Insert about 60 percent of the grease from the service kit into the outer joint.

37. Remove the outer joint from the vise.

38. Wrap a towel around the axle shaft and place it horizontally in a vise.

39. Install a new small seal retaining clamp on the axle shaft.

40. Install the seal on the axle shaft.

41. Install a new retaining ring on the axle shaft.

42. Position the outer joint horizontally.

43. Engage the inner race splines into the axle shaft splines.

44. Press the end of the retaining ring into the axle shaft groove while firmly pressing the outer joint onto the axle shaft. The axle shaft and inner race must be fully seated to each other.

45. Using a wood block, tap the outer joint on until it is fully seated on the axle shaft.

46. Install the remaining grease into the seal boot.

47. Position the small end of the inner joint seal into the inner joint seal groove.

48. Crimp the small seal clamp until the crimping joint gap is 0.039 inch (1mm).

49. Position the large clamp onto the boot seal

50. Slide the large inboard seal with the large clamp in place, over the bushing and locate the lip of the seal in the groove.

51. Ensure the seal is properly shaped around the circumference of the joint.

52. Remove the air from the inner joint seal.

53. Using crimping pliers, crimp the large clamp around the boot, until the crimping joint gap is 0.039 inch (1mm).

54. Rotate the outer joint a few times to fully distribute the gear into the bearings.

FRONT OUTPUT SHAFT SEAL

REMOVAL & INSTALLATION

See Figure 20.

1. Before servicing the vehicle, refer to the Precautions Section.

2. Raise and support the vehicle.

3. Remove the right front wheel.

4. Remove the right halfshaft.

5. Pry the output shaft seal from the seal opening.

To install:

6. Lubricate the seal surface with synthetic gear oil.

7. Using a seal installer, install the new seal.

8. Install the right halfshaft.

9. Install the right wheel.

10. Lower the vehicle.

FRONT PINION SEAL

REMOVAL & INSTALLATION

See Figures 21 and 22.

1. Before servicing the vehicle, refer to the Precautions Section.

2. Remove the front propeller shaft-to-drive pinion flange bolts and carefully slide the shaft away from the flange.

3. Wire the propeller shaft up with mechanics wire.

4. Install holding tool J-45012 to the pinion flange.

5. While holding the tool rigid, remove the pinion flange nut.

6. Remove the holding tool and install

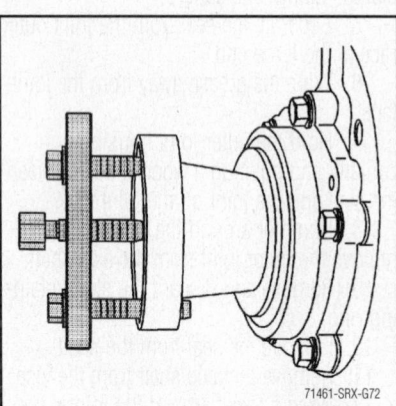

Fig. 21 Remove the front drive pinion flange using tool J-45019—AWD models

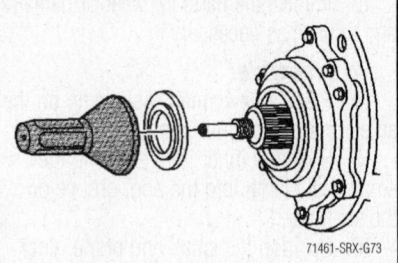

Fig. 22 Installing the front pinion seal using tool J-46262—AWD models

J-45019 to the pinion flange and tighten the tool to remove the pinion flange.

7. Pry the pinion seal from the seal opening.

To install:

8. Lubricate the pinion flange sealing surface with synthetic gear oil.

9. Using installer tool J-46262, install the new pinion seal.

10. Install the drive pinion flange.

11. Clean the pinion shaft threads and pinion nut.

12. Apply Threadlock to two-thirds of the pinion shaft threads and allow it 10 minutes to dry.

13. Install the pinion nut to the pinion flange.

14. Install the holding tool and while holding the tool, tighten the nut to 178 ft. lbs. (241 Nm).

15. Remove the holding tool.

16. Install the propeller shaft to the drive pinion flange and tighten the bolts in sequence to 22 ft. lbs. (30 Nm). See Transfer Case installation for tightening sequence.

REAR AXLE HOUSING

REMOVAL & INSTALLATION

1. Before servicing the vehicle, refer to the Precautions Section.

2. Remove the rear propeller shaft.

3. Raise and support the vehicle.

4. Remove the rear wheels.

5. Remove the right halfshaft.

6. Position a transmission jack under the differential.

7. Remove the front differential-to-support mounting bolt.

8. Remove the left and right rear differential-to-support mounting bolt. The left bolt cannot be completely removed due to interference with the underbody.

9. Lower the jack until the mounting ear at the front of the differential clears the support attachment point.

10. Pry the left halfshaft away from the differential enough to install tool J-44394.

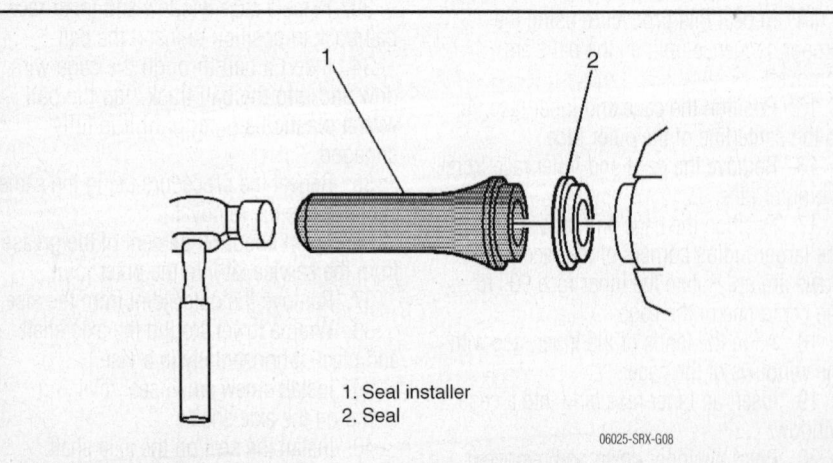

1. Seal installer
2. Seal

06025-SRX-G08

Fig. 20 Using the seal installer tool (1) to install the output shaft seal (2).

11. Install seal protector J-44394 over the halfshaft and into the differential output seal to protect the seal.

12. Continue lowering the jack while disengaging the halfshaft.

13. Remove the differential.

To install:

14. Installation is the reverse of the removal procedure. Tighten the differential mounting bolts to 129 ft. lbs. (175 Nm).

15. Check the differential fluid level and fill as needed.

REAR HALFSHAFT

REMOVAL & INSTALLATION

➡**Do not begin this removal procedure unless a new wheel hub retainer nut and a new retainer circlip are available. Once removed, these parts must not be reused during assembly. Their torque holding ability, or retention capability, is diminished during removal.**

1. Before servicing the vehicle, refer to the Precautions Section.

2. Raise and support the vehicle.

3. Remove or disconnect the following:
   • Rear wheels
   • Axle hub nut and washer. Discard the nut.
   • Rear knuckle assembly

4. Pry the halfshaft away from the differential enough to install tool J-44394.

5. Install tool J-44394 over the halfshaft and into the differential output seal to protect the seal.

6. Remove the halfshaft from the vehicle.

7. If reusing the halfshaft, remove and discard the retaining ring from the intermediate shaft ring groove.

To install:

8. Install a new retainer circlip on the splined end of the shaft.

9. Install tool J-44394 into the differential output shaft seal.

10. Install the halfshaft into the differential until the splines are past the tool opening.

11. Remove the tool from the differential seal.

12. Continue to install the halfshaft until the retaining ring is fully seated.

13. Verify that the shaft is engaged by pulling outward on the inner joint housing. The shaft should remain firmly engaged.

14. Install the rear knuckle.

15. Loosely install the NEW wheel axle nut.

16. Hold the brake rotor from turning and tighten the axle nut to 118 ft. lbs. (160 Nm).

17. Install the tire and wheel.

18. Lower the vehicle.

CV-JOINTS OVERHAUL

Outer Joint

See Figure 23.

1. Before servicing the vehicle, refer to the Precautions Section.

2. Remove the halfshaft.

3. Wrap a towel around the halfshaft and place it horizontally in a vise.

4. Remove the small and large seal clamps using side cutters.

5. Separate the seal from the joint outer race at the large end.

6. Wipe the grease away from the joint face.

7. Hold the outer joint housing horizontally and position a wood block between the seal and the joint on the joint face.

8. Hammer around the wood block to remove the outer joint from the axle shaft.

9. Remove and discard the shaft retaining ring.

10. Remove the seal from the shaft.

11. Remove the axle shaft from the vise.

12. Wrap a towel around the joint outer face and place the joint in a vise vertically.

13. Using a drift and hammer, tap gently on the inner cage until it tilts up enough to remove the first ball.

14. Repeat this procedure using the proper sequence until all the balls are removed.

15. Position the cage and inner race 90° to the centerline of the outer race.

16. Remove the cage and inner race from the outer race.

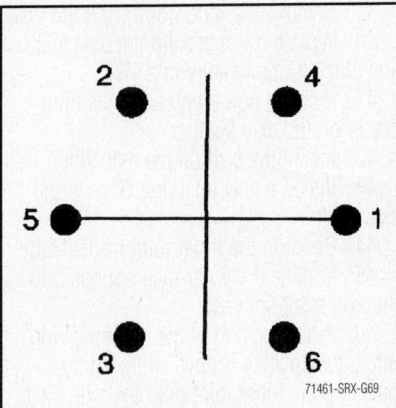

2   4

5   1

3   6

71461-SRX-G69

Fig. 23 CV joint ball removal and installation sequence

17. Position the cage and inner race so the larger radius corners of the race windows are up. Rotate the inner race 90° to the centerline of the cage.

18. Align the lands of the inner race with the windows of the cage.

19. Insert an inner race land into a cage window.

20. Pivot the inner down and remove it from the cage.

21. Clean all parts thoroughly with solvent and allow to air dry.

22. Inspect all parts for wear or damage and replace as necessary.

To assemble:

23. Position the cage so the large radius corners of the cage windows are up.

24. Position the inner race 90° to the centerline of the cage.

25. Insert the inner race up through the bottom of the cage.

26. Align a land of the inner race to a window of the cage.

27. Insert the inner race land into the cage window.

28. Rotate the remainder of the inner race into the cage.

29. Align the inner race ball tracks with the cage windows.

30. Wrap a towel around the splined shaft and place the shaft vertically in a vise with the joint opening up.

31. Position the cage and inner race 90° to the centerline of the outer race.

32. Align 2 cage windows 180° apart.

33. Place a cage window and inner race ball track in position to insert the ball.

34. Insert a ball through the cage window and into the ball track. Tap the ball with a plastic hammer until it is fully engaged.

35. Repeat the procedure using the same sequence as the removal.

36. Insert about 60 percent of the grease from the service kit into the outer joint.

37. Remove the outer joint from the vise.

38. Wrap a towel around the axle shaft and place it horizontally in a vise.

39. Install a new small seal retaining clamp on the axle shaft.

40. Install the seal on the axle shaft.

41. Install a new retaining ring on the axle shaft.

42. Position the outer joint horizontally.

43. Engage the inner race splines into the axle shaft splines.

44. Press the end of the retaining ring into the axle shaft groove while firmly pressing the outer joint onto the axle shaft. The axle shaft and inner race must be fully seated to each other.

45. Using a wood block, tap the outer joint on until it is fully seated on the axle shaft.

46. Install the remaining grease into the seal boot.

47. Position the small end of the inner joint seal into the inner joint seal groove.

48. Crimp the small seal clamp until the crimping joint gap is 0.039 inch (1mm).

49. Position the large clamp onto the boot seal

50. Slide the large inboard seal with the large clamp in place, over the bushing and locate the lip of the seal in the groove.

51. Ensure the seal is properly shaped around the circumference of the joint.

52. Remove the air from the inner joint seal.

53. Using crimping pliers, crimp the large clamp around the boot, until the crimping joint gap is 0.039 inch (1mm).

54. Rotate the outer joint a few times to fully distribute the gear into the bearings.

Inner Joint

See Figure 24.

1. Before servicing the vehicle, refer to the Precautions Section.

2. Remove the halfshaft:

3. Wrap a towel around the halfshaft and place it horizontally in a vise.

4. Remove the small and large seal clamps using side cutters.

5. Separate the seal from the joint outer race at the large end.

6. Slide the seal away from the joint face.

7. Wipe the grease away from the joint face.

8. Hold the inner joint housing horizontally and position a drift on the inner face.

9. Tap the drift to compress the axle shaft retaining ring.

10. Remove and discard the shaft retaining ring.

11. Use the hammer and drift again to remove the inner joint.

12. Remove the seal from the shaft.

13. Remove the axle shaft from the vise.

14. Wrap a towel around the joint outer face and place the joint in a vise vertically.

15. Using a drift and hammer, tap gently on the inner cage until it tilts up enough to remove the first ball.

16. Repeat this procedure using the proper sequence until all the balls are removed.

17. Position the cage and inner race 90° to the centerline of the outer race.

18. Remove the cage and inner race from the outer race.

19. Position the cage and inner race so the larger radius corners of the race windows are up. Rotate the inner race 90° to the centerline of the cage.

20. Align the lands of the inner race with the windows of the cage.

21. Insert an inner race land into a cage window.

22. Pivot the inner down and remove it from the cage.

23. Clean all parts thoroughly with solvent and allow to air dry.

24. Inspect all parts for wear or damage and replace as necessary.

To assemble:

25. Position the cage so the large radius corners of the cage windows are up.

26. Position the inner race 90° to the centerline of the cage.

27. Insert the inner race up through the bottom of the cage.

28. Align a land of the inner race to a window of the cage.

29. Insert the inner race land into the cage window.

30. Rotate the remainder of the inner race into the cage.

31. Align the inner race ball tracks with the cage windows.

32. Wrap a towel around the splined shaft and place the shaft vertically in a vise with the joint opening up.

33. Position the cage and inner race 90° to the centerline of the outer race.

34. Align 2 cage windows 180° apart.

35. Place a cage window and inner race ball track in position to insert the ball.

36. Insert a ball through the cage window and into the ball track. Tap the ball with a plastic hammer until it is fully engaged.

37. Repeat the procedure using the same sequence as in removal.

38. Insert about 60 percent of the grease from the service kit into the inner joint.

39. Remove the inner joint from the vise.

40. Wrap a towel around the axle shaft and place it horizontally in a vise.

41. Install a new small seal retaining clamp on the axle shaft.

42. Install the seal on the axle shaft.

43. Install a new retaining ring on the axle shaft.

44. Position the inner joint horizontally.

45. Engage the inner race splines into the axle shaft splines.

46. Press the end of the retaining ring into the axle shaft groove while firmly pressing the inner joint onto the axle shaft. The axle shaft and inner race must be fully seated to each other.

47. Using a wood block, tap the inner joint on until it is fully seated on the axle shaft.

48. Install the remaining grease into the seal boot.

49. Position the small end of the inner joint seal into the inner joint seal groove.

50. Crimp the small seal clamp until the crimping joint gap is 0.039 inch (1mm).

51. Position the large clamp onto the boot seal

52. Slide the large inboard seal with the large clamp in place, over the bushing and locate the lip of the seal in the groove.

53. Ensure the seal is properly shaped around the circumference of the joint.

54. Measure the distance (a) between the seal edges. The correct distance is 3.42 inches (86.85mm) for AWD, or 3.50 inches (88.6mm).

55. Using crimping pliers, crimp the large clamp around the boot, until the crimping joint gap is 0.039 inch (1mm).

56. Rotate the inner joint a few times to fully distribute the gear into the bearings.

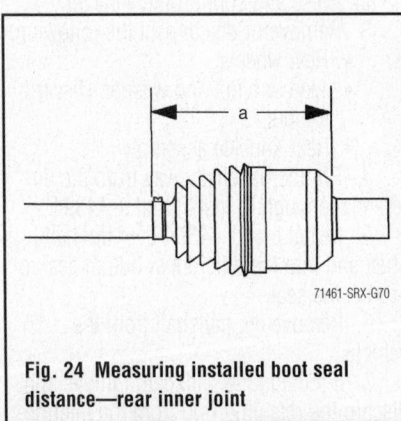

71461-SRX-G70

Fig. 24 Measuring installed boot seal distance—rear inner joint

REAR PINION SEAL

REMOVAL & INSTALLATION

See Figures 25 and 26.

1. Before servicing the vehicle, refer to the Precautions Section.

2. Raise and support the vehicle.

3. Remove the rear propeller shaft coupler-to-drive pinion flange bolts and carefully slide the shaft away from the flange.

4. Wire the propeller shaft up with mechanics wire.

5. Install holding tool J-45012 to the pinion flange.

6. While holding the tool rigid, remove the pinion flange nut.

7. Remove the holding tool and install

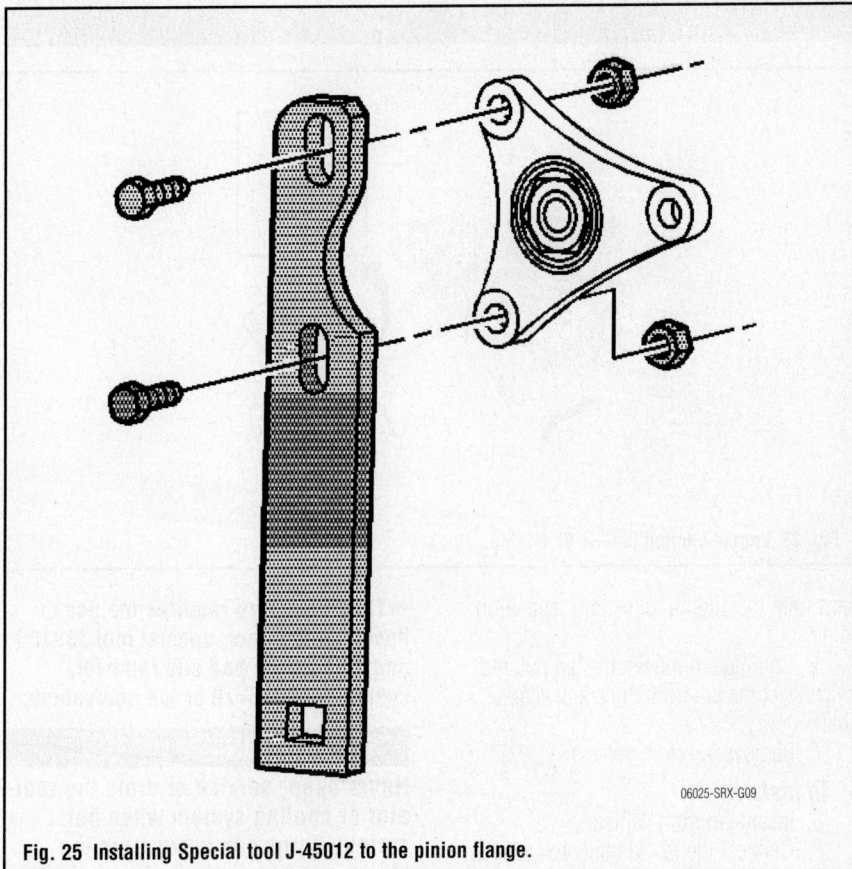

06025-SRX-G09

Fig. 25 Installing Special tool J-45012 to the pinion flange.

J-45019 to the pinion flange and tighten the tool to remove the pinion flange.

8. Pry the pinion seal from the seal opening.

9. Lubricate the pinion flange sealing surface with synthetic gear oil.

10. Using a seal installer, install the new pinion seal.

11. Install the drive pinion flange.

12. Clean the pinion shaft threads and pinion nut.

13. Apply Threadlock to two-thirds of the pinion shaft threads and allow it 10 minutes to dry.

14. Install the pinion nut to the pinion flange.

15. Install the holding tool and while holding the tool, tighten the nut to 210 ft. lbs. (285 Nm).

16. Remove the holding tool.

17. Clean the propeller shaft coupler bolts.

18. Apply threadlock to two-thirds of the coupler bolt threads and allow it 10 minutes to dry.

19. Install the propeller shaft and coupler to the drive pinion flange.

20. Install the bolts and washers and tighten the bolts 63 ft. lbs. (85 Nm).

21. Lower the vehicle.

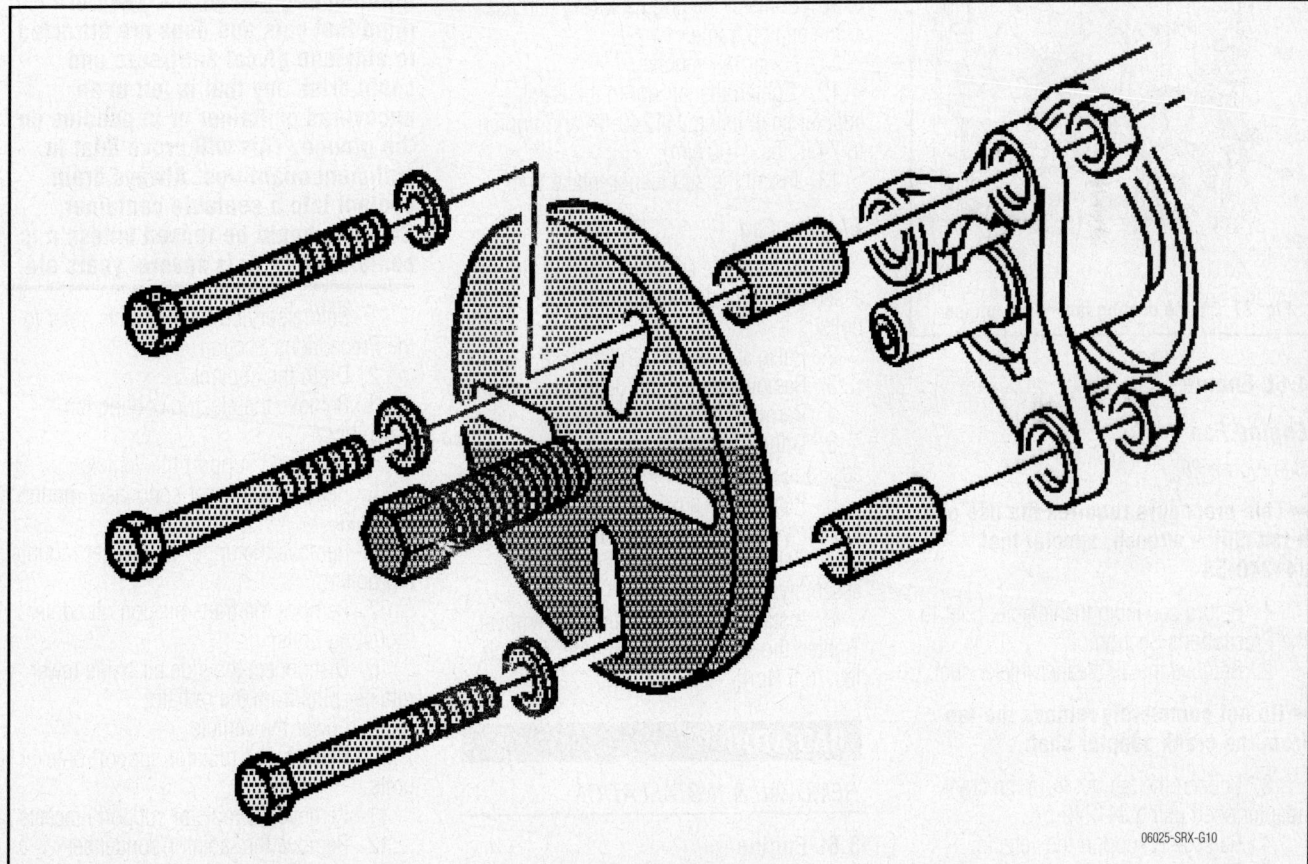

06025-SRX-G10

Fig. 26 Install Special tool J-45019 to the pinion flange and tighten to remove the flange.

ENGINE COOLING

ENGINE FAN

REMOVAL & INSTALLATION

3.6L Engine

See Figure 27.

1. Before servicing the vehicle, refer to the Precautions Section.
2. Remove the air cleaner outlet duct.
3. Unplug the cooling fan electrical connectors.
4. Disconnect the condenser tube from the cooling fan shroud retainer clip.
5. Disengage the surge tank inlet hose from the retaining features on the cooling fan shroud and reposition aside.
6. Remove the cooling fan shroud to radiator retaining bolts.
7. Remove the cooling fan assembly.
8. Installation is the reverse of removal. Tighten the shroud retaining bolts 58 inch lbs. (6.5 Nm).

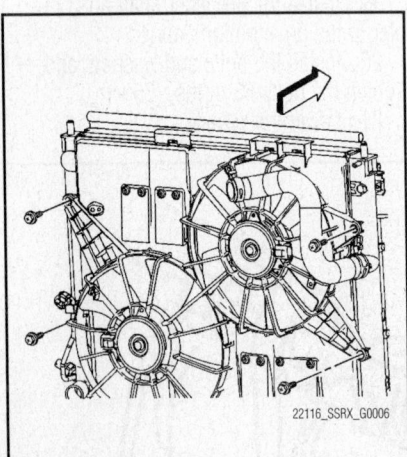

Fig. 27 Engine cooling fan—3.6L engine

4.6L Engine

Engine Fan

See Figure 28.

➥This procedure requires the use of a fan clutch wrench, special tool J41240-5A

1. Before servicing the vehicle, refer to the Precautions Section.
2. Remove the air cleaner intake duct.

➥Do not completely remove the fan from the crank adapter shaft.

3. Loosen the fan nut from the crank adapter shaft using J41240-5A .
4. Raise and support the vehicle.
5. Disconnect the engine wiring har-

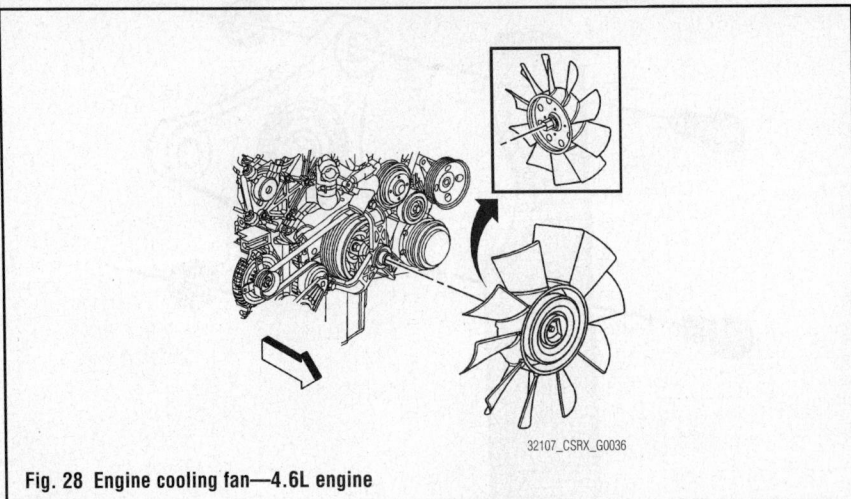

Fig. 28 Engine cooling fan—4.6L engine

ness from the engine frame and reposition aside.

6. Continue to loosen the fan nut and disconnect the fan from the crank adapter shaft.
7. Remove fan from vehicle.

To install:

8. Install fan from vehicle.
9. Connect the fan to the crank adapter shaft.
10. Connect the engine wiring harness to the engine frame.
11. Lower the vehicle.
12. Tighten the fan nut to the crank adapter shaft using J41240-5A and tighten to 74 ft. lbs. (100 Nm).
13. Install the air cleaner intake duct.

Electric Fan

1. Remove the auxiliary cooling fan assembly to condenser upper mounting bolts.
2. Raise and support the vehicle.
3. Remove the front air deflector retainers.
4. Remove the front air deflector.
5. Unplug the auxiliary cooling fan assembly electrical connectors.
6. Remove the auxiliary cooling fan assembly to condenser lower mounting bolts.
7. Remove the auxiliary cooling fan assembly.
8. Installation is the reverse of removal. Tighten the shroud retaining bolts 58 inch lbs. (6.5 Nm).

RADIATOR

REMOVAL & INSTALLATION

3.6L Engine

See Figures 29 through 31.

➥This procedure requires the use of hose clamp pliers, special tool J38185 and a door trim pad clip remover, special tool J38778 or the equivalents.

❊❊ CAUTION

Never open, service or drain the radiator or cooling system when hot; serious burns can occur from the steam and hot coolant. Also, when draining engine coolant, keep in mind that cats and dogs are attracted to ethylene glycol antifreeze and could drink any that is left in an uncovered container or in puddles on the ground. This will prove fatal in sufficient quantities. Always drain coolant into a sealable container. Coolant should be reused unless it is contaminated or is several years old.

1. Before servicing the vehicle, refer to the Precautions Section.
2. Drain the coolant.
3. Remove the electric cooling fan assembly.
4. Raise and support the vehicle.
5. Remove the lower condenser mounting bolts.
6. Remove the upper condenser mounting bolts.
7. Remove the transmission oil cooler mounting bolts.
8. Disconnect the side air baffle lower retainer pins from the radiator.
9. Lower the vehicle.
10. Remove the radiator support bracket bolts.
11. Remove the radiator support brackets.
12. Remove the radiator/condenser upper support using J38778 .

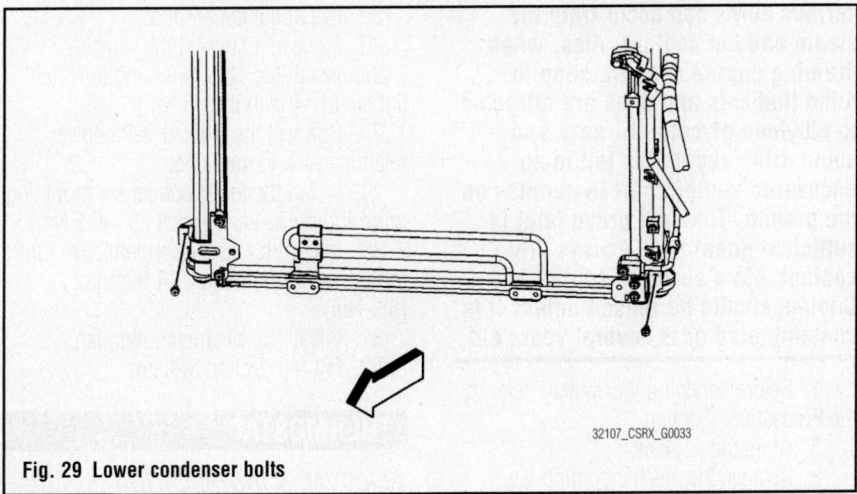

Fig. 29 Lower condenser bolts

32107_CSRX_G0033

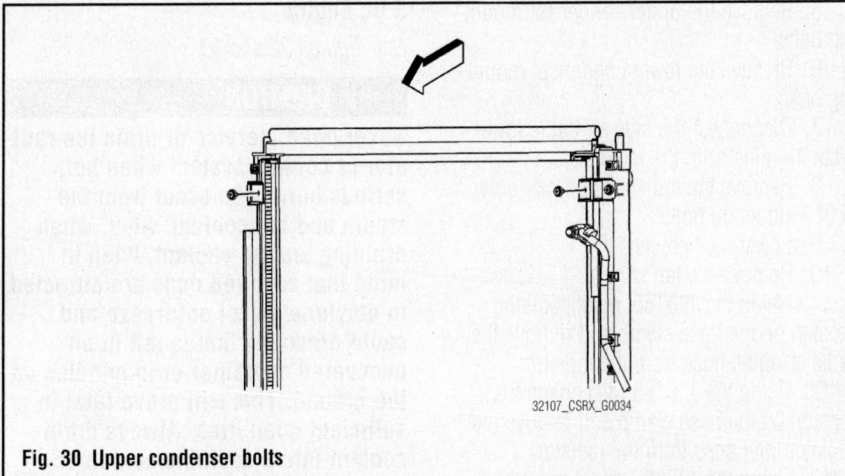

Fig. 30 Upper condenser bolts

32107_CSRX_G0034

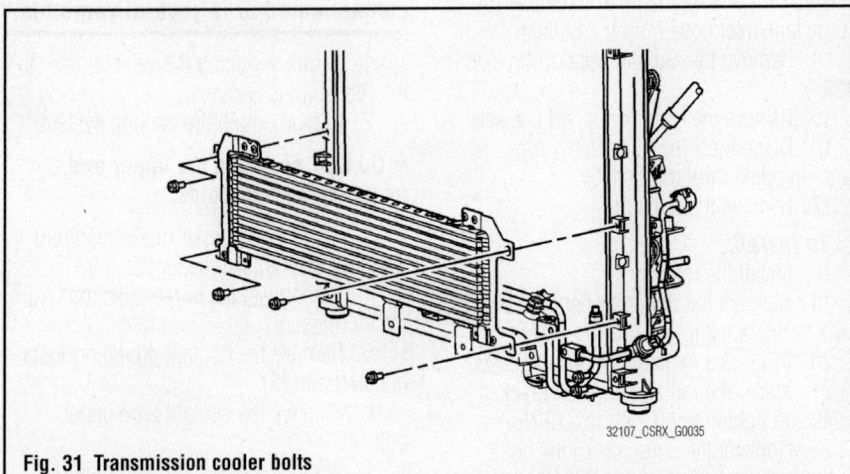

Fig. 31 Transmission cooler bolts

32107_CSRX_G0035

13. Disconnect the surge tank inlet hose from the radiator using the J38185 and reposition aside.

14. Using the J38185 tool, disengage tension on the radiator inlet hose clamp and disconnect from the radiator.

15. Using the J38185 tool, disengage tension on the radiator outlet hose clamp and disconnect from the radiator.

16. Disconnect the side air baffle upper retainer pins from the radiator.

17. Remove the radiator.

To install:

18. Install the radiator.

19. Connect the side air baffle upper retainer pins to the radiator.

20. Connect the radiator outlet hose to the radiator and using the J38185, position

the radiator outlet hose clamp to secure the hose.

21. Connect the radiator inlet hose to the radiator and using the J38185, position the radiator inlet hose clamp to secure the hose.

22. Connect the surge tank inlet hose to the radiator and using the J38185, position the hose clamp to secure the hose.

23. Install the radiator/condenser upper support.

24. Install the radiator support brackets.

25. Install the radiator support bracket bolts and tighten to 80 inch lbs. (9 Nm).

26. Raise and support the vehicle.

27. Connect the side air baffle lower retainer pins to the radiator.

28. Install the transmission oil cooler mounting bolts and tighten to 44 inch lbs. (5 Nm).

29. Install the upper condenser mounting bolts and tighten to 58 inch lbs. (6.5 Nm).

30. Install the lower condenser mounting bolts and tighten to 58 inch lbs. (6.5 Nm).

31. Lower the vehicle.

32. Install the electric cooling fan assembly.

33. Fill the cooling system.

4.6L Engine

Standard Cooling

See Figures 29 through 31.

➡ **This procedure requires the use of hose clamp pliers, special tool J38185 or equivalent.**

❋❋ CAUTION

Never open, service or drain the radiator or cooling system when hot; serious burns can occur from the steam and hot coolant. Also, when draining engine coolant, keep in mind that cats and dogs are attracted to ethylene glycol antifreeze and could drink any that is left in an uncovered container or in puddles on the ground. This will prove fatal in sufficient quantities. Always drain coolant into a sealable container. Coolant should be reused unless it is contaminated or is several years old.

1. Before servicing the vehicle, refer to the Precautions Section.

2. Drain the coolant.

3. Remove the electric cooling fan.

4. Raise and support the vehicle.

5. Remove the upper condenser mounting bolts.

6. Remove the lower condenser mounting bolts.

7. Disconnect the side air baffle lower retaining pins from the radiator.

8. Remove the transmission oil cooler (TOC) mounting bolts.

9. Lower the vehicle.

10. Using the J38185, disengage the tension on the hose clamp and remove the radiator outlet hose from the radiator.

11. Using the J38185, disengage the tension on the hose clamp and remove the radiator inlet hose from the radiator.

12. Using the J38185, disengage the tension on the hose clamp and remove the surge tank inlet hose from the radiator.

13. Remove the radiator support bracket bolts.

14. Remove the radiator support brackets.

15. Disconnect the upper air baffle retaining pins from the radiator.

16. Remove the radiator.

To install:
17. Install the radiator.

18. Connect the upper air baffle retaining pins to the radiator.

19. Install the radiator support brackets.

20. Install the radiator support bracket bolts and tighten to 80 inch lbs. (9 Nm).

21. Connect the surge tank inlet hose to the radiator and using the J38185, position the surge tank inlet hose clamp to secure the hose.

22. Connect the radiator inlet hose to the radiator and using the J38185, position the radiator inlet hose clamp to secure the hose.

23. Connect the radiator outlet hose to the radiator and using the J38185, position the radiator outlet hose clamp to secure the hose.

24. Raise and support the vehicle.

25. Install the TOC mounting bolts and tighten to 44 inch lbs. (5 Nm).

26. Connect the side air baffle lower retaining pins to the radiator.

27. Install the lower condenser mounting bolts and tighten to 58 inch lbs. (6.5 Nm).

28. Install the upper condenser mounting bolts and tighten to 58 inch lbs. (6.5 Nm).

29. Install the electric cooling fan.

30. Fill the cooling system.

Heavy Duty Cooling
See Figures 29 through 31.

➡This procedure requires the use of hose clamp pliers, special tool J38185 or equivalent.

✻✻ CAUTION
Never open, service or drain the radiator or cooling system when hot;

serious burns can occur from the steam and hot coolant. Also, when draining engine coolant, keep in mind that cats and dogs are attracted to ethylene glycol antifreeze and could drink any that is left in an uncovered container or in puddles on the ground. This will prove fatal in sufficient quantities. Always drain coolant into a sealable container. Coolant should be reused unless it is contaminated or is several years old.

1. Before servicing the vehicle, refer to the Precautions Section.

2. Drain the coolant.

3. Remove the electric cooling fan.

4. Raise and support the vehicle.

5. Remove the upper condenser mounting bolts.

6. Remove the lower condenser mounting bolts.

7. Disconnect the side air baffle lower retaining pins from the radiator.

8. Remove the transmission oil cooler (TOC) mounting bolts.

9. Lower the vehicle.

10. Remove the fan shroud.

11. Using the J38185, disengage the tension on the hose clamp and remove the radiator outlet hose from the radiator.

12. Using the J38185, disengage the tension on the hose clamp and remove the radiator inlet hose from the radiator.

13. Using the J38185, disengage the tension on the hose clamp and remove the surge tank inlet hose from the radiator.

14. Remove the radiator support bracket bolts.

15. Remove the radiator support brackets.

16. Disconnect the upper air baffle retaining pins from the radiator.

17. Remove the radiator.

To install:
18. Install the radiator.

19. Connect the upper air baffle retaining pins to the radiator.

20. Install the radiator support brackets.

21. Install the radiator support bracket bolts and tighten to 80 inch lbs. (9 Nm).

22. Connect the surge tank inlet hose to the radiator and using the J38185, position the surge tank inlet hose clamp to secure the hose.

23. Connect the radiator inlet hose to the radiator and using the J38185 , position the radiator inlet hose clamp to secure the hose.

24. Connect the radiator outlet hose to the radiator and using the J38185 , position the radiator outlet hose clamp to secure the hose.

25. Install the fan shroud.

26. Raise and support the vehicle.

27. Install the TOC mounting bolts and tighten to 44 inch lbs. (5 Nm).

28. Connect the side air baffle lower retaining pins to the radiator.

29. Install the lower condenser mounting bolts and tighten to 58 inch lbs. (6.5 Nm).

30. Install the upper condenser mounting bolts and tighten to 58 inch lbs. (6.5 Nm).

31. Install the electric cooling fan.

32. Fill the cooling system.

THERMOSTAT

REMOVAL & INSTALLATION

3.6L Engine
See Figures 32 and 33.

✻✻ CAUTION
Never open, service or drain the radiator or cooling system when hot; serious burns can occur from the steam and hot coolant. Also, when draining engine coolant, keep in mind that cats and dogs are attracted to ethylene glycol antifreeze and could drink any that is left in an uncovered container or in puddles on the ground. This will prove fatal in sufficient quantities. Always drain coolant into a sealable container. Coolant should be reused unless it is contaminated or is several years old.

1. Before servicing the vehicle, refer to the Precautions Section.

2. Partially drain the cooling system.

➡Do NOT separate the upper and lower intake manifolds.

3. Remove the upper intake manifold with the lower intake manifold.

4. Disconnect the surge tank hose from the thermostat.

5. Remove the coolant pipe/thermostat housing bolt (2).

6. Remove the coolant pipe upper bolt (7).

7. Remove the coolant inlet pipe (4) from the thermostat.

8. Remove the thermostat bolts.

9. Remove the thermostat and discard the thermostat seal.

To install:
10. Install the thermostat with a NEW thermostat seal.

11. Install the thermostat bolts and tighten to 89 inch lbs. (10 Nm).

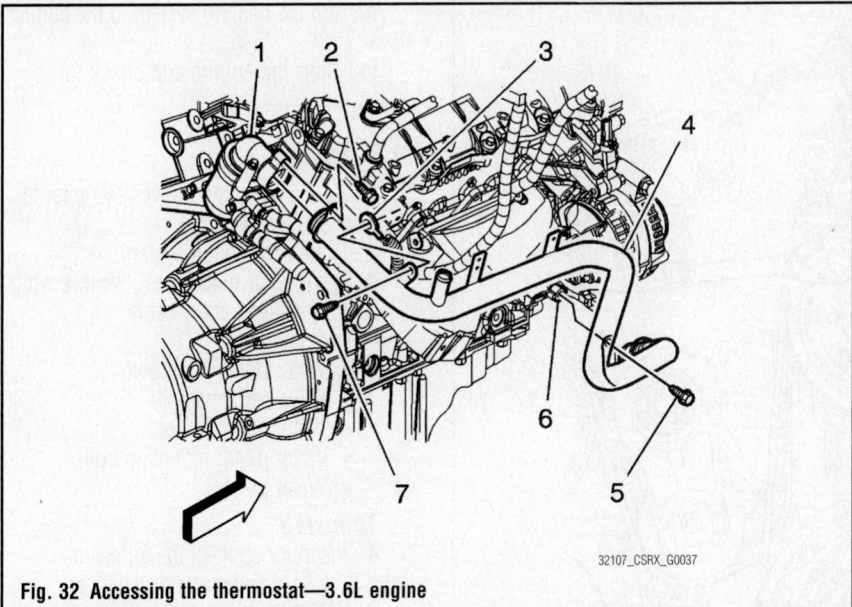

Fig. 32 Accessing the thermostat—3.6L engine

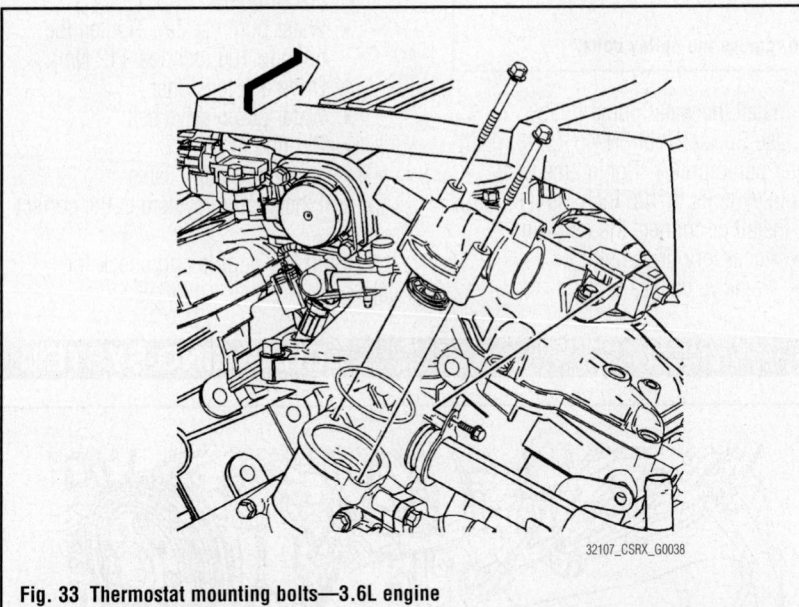

Fig. 33 Thermostat mounting bolts—3.6L engine

12. Install the coolant pipe (4), NEW seal, and fasteners (2 and 7).

13. Install the surge tank hose to the thermostat.

14. Install the upper intake manifold with the lower intake manifold.

15. Fill the cooling system.

4.6L Engine

See Figure 34.

❊❊ CAUTION

Never open, service or drain the radiator or cooling system when hot; serious burns can occur from the steam and hot coolant. Also, when draining engine coolant, keep in mind that cats and dogs are attracted

to ethylene glycol antifreeze and could drink any that is left in an uncovered container or in puddles on the ground. This will prove fatal in sufficient quantities. Always drain coolant into a sealable container. Coolant should be reused unless it is contaminated or is several years old.

1. Before servicing the vehicle, refer to the Precautions Section.

2. Drain the cooling system.

3. Remove the air cleaner outlet duct.

4. Remove the radiator hose from the thermostat housing.

5. Remove the heater hose from the thermostat housing.

6. Remove the thermostat housing bolts.

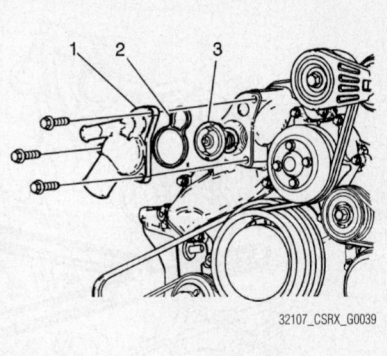

Fig. 34 Accessing the thermostat—4.6L engine

7. Remove the thermostat housing (1) with thermostat (3), from the water housing.

8. Remove and discard the seal ring (2).

9. Remove the thermostat from the thermostat housing.

To install:

10. Clean the thermostat housing and water housing sealing surfaces.

11. Install the new thermostat to the thermostat housing.

12. Install the NEW seal (2) to the thermostat housing.

13. Install the thermostat housing (1) with the thermostat (3) and the seal (2) to the water housing.

14. Install the thermostat housing bolts and tighten to 89 inch lbs. (10 Nm).

15. Install the heater hose to the thermostat housing.

16. Install the radiator hose to the thermostat housing.

17. Install the air cleaner outlet duct.

18. Fill the cooling system.

WATER PUMP

REMOVAL & INSTALLATION

3.6L Engine

See Figure 35.

1. Before servicing the vehicle, refer to the Precautions Section.

2. Drain the cooling system.

3. Remove or disconnect the following:

- Negative battery cable
- Accessory drive belt

4. Use Special Tool EN-46104 to retain the water pump pulley.

5. Remove or disconnect the following:
- Water pump pulley
- Water pump

06025-SRX-G01

Fig. 35 Using water pump pulley holding tool EN-46104 to remove the pulley bolts.

To install:

➡ **Clean the water pump sealing surfaces**

6. Install the water pump and new gasket. Tighten the bolts to 89 inch lbs. (10 Nm).

7. Install the water pump pulley.
8. Use Special Tool EN-46104 to retain the water pump pulley. Tighten the water pump pulley bolts to 106 inch lbs. (12 Nm).
9. Install or connect the following:
   • Accessory drive belt
   • Negative battery cable

10. Fill the cooling system to the correct level.
11. Start the engine and check for leaks.

4.6L Engine

1. Before servicing the vehicle, refer to the Precautions Section.
2. Drain the cooling system.
3. Remove or disconnect the following:
   • Negative battery cable
   • Cooling fan
   • Water pump drive belt
   • Drive belt tensioner
   • Water pump pulley
   • Water pump mounting bolts
   • Water pump

To install:

4. Install or connect the following:
   • Water pump and new gasket. Tighten the bolts to 89 inch lbs. (10 Nm).
   • Water pump pulley. Tighten the bolts to 106 inch lbs. (12 Nm).
   • Drive belt tensioner
   • Water pump drive belt
   • Cooling fan
   • Negative battery cable
5. Fill the cooling system to the correct level.
6. Start the engine and check for leaks.

ENGINE ELECTRICAL   CHARGING SYSTEM

ALTERNATOR

REMOVAL & INSTALLATION

3.6L Engine

See Figure 36.

1. Before servicing the vehicle, refer to the Precautions Section.
2. Disconnect the negative battery cable.
3. Remove the accessory drive belt.
4. Raise and support the vehicle.
5. Disconnect the alternator wiring connector.
6. Remove the positive cable nut.
7. Remove the alternator.

To install:

8. Position the alternator on the engine.
9. Install the alternator mounting bolts. Tighten the bolts to 37 ft. lbs. (50 Nm).
10. Tighten the positive cable nut to 89 inch lbs. (10 Nm).
11. Connect the wiring connector.
12. Install and tension the accessory drive belt.
13. Connect the negative battery cable.

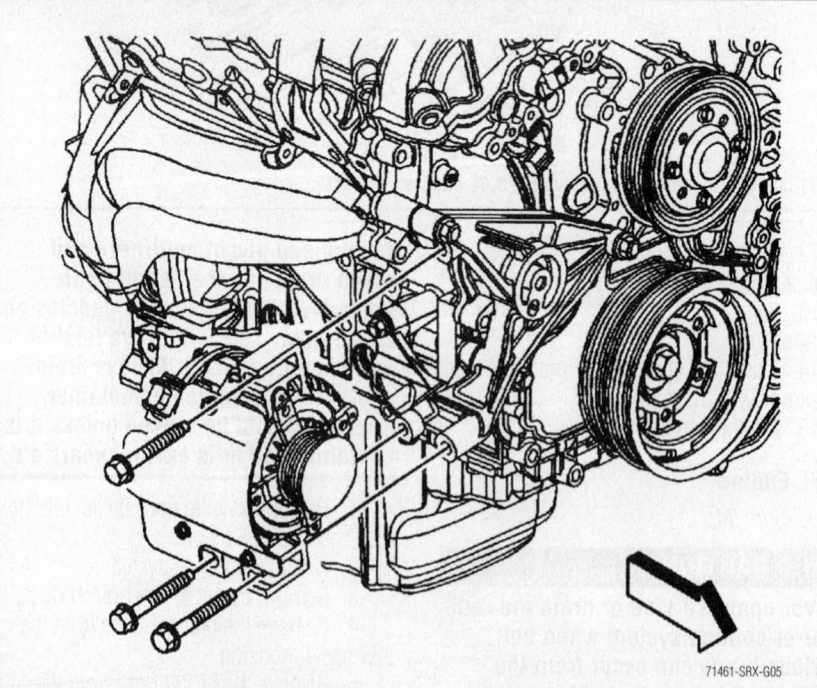

71461-SRX-G05

Fig. 36 Alternator mounting—3.6L engine

4.6L Engine

2WD Models

See Figure 37.

1. Before servicing the vehicle, refer to the Precautions Section.
2. Disconnect the negative battery cable.
3. Remove the accessory drive belt.
4. Remove the alternator upper mounting bolts.
5. Raise and support the vehicle.
6. Remove the front air deflector.
7. Remove the lower alternator mounting bolt.
8. Disconnect the alternator wiring connector.
9. Remove the positive cable nut.
10. Remove the alternator.

To install:

11. Install alternator positive lead and tighten to 111 inch lbs. (13 Nm).
12. Connect the wiring connector.
13. Install the lower alternator mounting bolt but do not tighten.
14. Lower the vehicle.
15. Install the upper mounting bolts. Tighten all bolts to 37 ft. lbs. (50 Nm).
16. Install the front air deflector.
17. Install and tension the accessory drive belt.
18. Connect the negative battery cable.

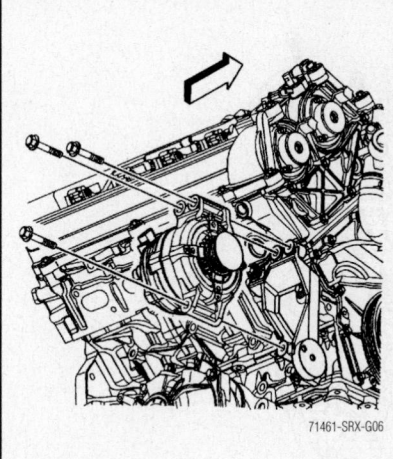

Fig. 37 Alternator mounting—4.6L engine

AWD Models

See Figure 37.

1. Before servicing the vehicle, refer to the Precautions Section.
2. Disconnect the negative battery cable.
3. Remove the accessory drive belt.
4. Remove the alternator upper mounting bolts.
5. Raise and support the vehicle.
6. Remove the front air deflector.
7. Remove the right front wheel.
8. Remove the right wheel splash shield.

9. Remove the right and left front stabilizer bar links at the lower control arms.
10. Rotate the stabilizer bar down enough to access the alternator.
11. Remove the lower alternator mounting bolt.
12. Disconnect the alternator wiring connector.
13. Remove the positive cable nut.
14. Remove the alternator through the wheelhouse opening.

To install:

15. Install alternator positive lead and tighten to 111 inch lbs. (13 Nm).
16. Connect the wiring connector.
17. Install the lower alternator mounting bolt but do not tighten.
18. Lower the vehicle.
19. Install the upper mounting bolts. Tighten all bolts to 37 ft. lbs. (50 Nm).
20. Raise the vehicle.
21. Install the right and left front stabilizer bar links at the lower control arms.
22. Install the right wheel splash shield.
23. Install the right front wheel.
24. Install the front air deflector.
25. Install and tension the accessory drive belt.
26. Connect the negative battery cable.

ENGINE ELECTRICAL

IGNITION SYSTEM

IGNITION COIL

REMOVAL & INSTALLATION

3.6L Engine

Bank 1

See Figures 38 and 39.

1. Before servicing the vehicle, refer to the Precautions Section.
2. Turn the ignition **OFF**.
3. Remove the engine cover.

➡**Do NOT disconnect the fuel pipes and/or hoses.**

4. If you are replacing the ignition coil for cylinder 1 or 3, remove and reposition the intake manifold. Perform the following steps:
5. Remove or disconnect the following:

- Disconnect the air cleaner duct from the throttle body.
- Disconnect the positive crankcase ventilation (PCV) hose from the right bank camshaft cover.

➡**Do NOT separate the upper intake manifold from the lower intake manifold.**

- Remove the intake manifold bolts.
- Remove the intake manifold brace bolts (1 and 2) and the brace.
6. Remove and reposition the upper

intake manifold with the lower intake manifold in order to gain sufficient clearance for ignition coil removal.

7. Remove the ignition coil electrical connector(s).
8. Remove the ignition coil bolt(s).
9. Remove the ignition coil(s).

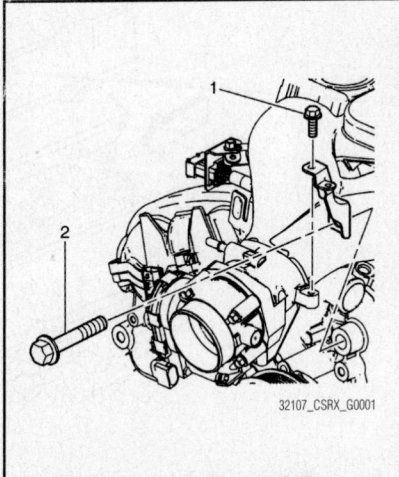

Fig. 38 Intake manifold brace bolts

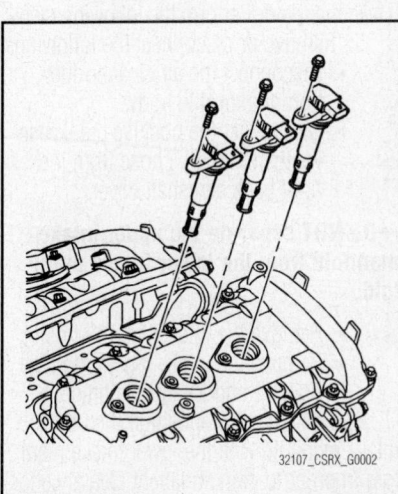

Fig. 39 Bank 1 ignition coils—3.6L engine

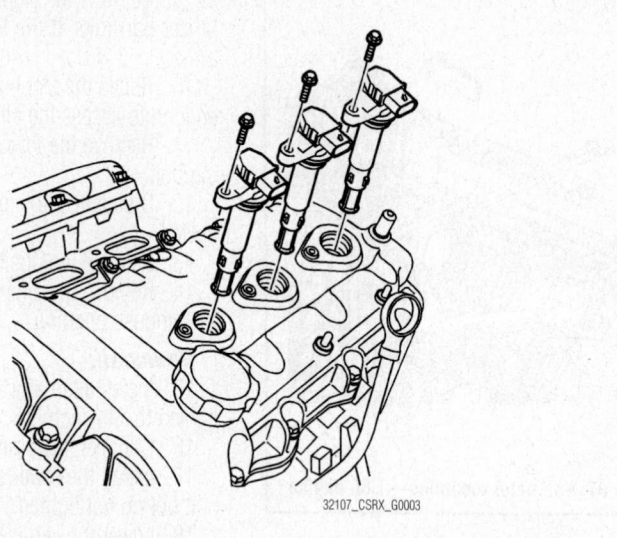

Fig. 40 Bank 2 ignition coils—3.6L engine

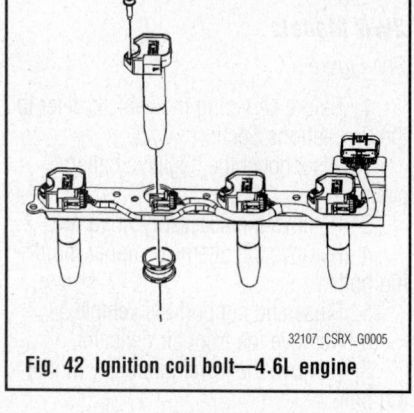

Fig. 42 Ignition coil bolt—4.6L engine

To install:

10. Install or connect the following:
   - Install the ignition coil(s).
   - Install the ignition coil bolt(s) and tighten to 89 inch lbs. (10 Nm).
   - Install the ignition coil electrical connector(s).
11. If removed, install the intake manifold.
12. Install the engine cover.

Bank 2

See Figures 38 and 40.

1. Before servicing the vehicle, refer to the Precautions Section.
2. Turn the ignition **OFF**.
3. Remove the engine cover.

➡**Do NOT disconnect the fuel pipes and/or hoses.**

4. If you are replacing the ignition coil for cylinder 2, remove and reposition the intake manifold. Perform the following steps:
5. Remove or disconnect the following:
   - Disconnect the air cleaner duct from the throttle body.
   - Disconnect the positive crankcase ventilation (PCV) hose from the right bank camshaft cover.

➡**Do NOT separate the upper intake manifold from the lower intake manifold.**

   - Remove the intake manifold bolts.
   - Remove the intake manifold brace bolts (1 and 2) and the brace.
6. Remove and reposition the upper intake manifold with the lower intake manifold in order to gain sufficient clearance for ignition coil removal.

7. Remove the ignition coil electrical connector(s).
8. Remove the ignition coil bolt(s).
9. Remove the ignition coil(s).

To install:

10. Install or connect the following:
11. Install the ignition coil(s).
12. Install the ignition coil bolt(s) and tighten to 89 inch lbs. (10 Nm).
13. Install the ignition coil electrical connector(s).
14. If removed, install the upper intake manifold.

4.6L Engine

Bank 1

See Figures 41 and 42.

1. Before servicing the vehicle, refer to the Precautions Section.
2. Remove the fuel injector sight shield.
3. Remove the ignition coil cover from the cam cover by lifting straight up.
4. Disconnect the ignition coil wiring harness electrical connector from the coil that needs to be replaced.
5. Remove the ignition coil retaining bolt.
6. Carefully remove the ignition coil.

To install:

➡**Ensure that the spark plug seals are in place when installing the ignition coil.**

7. Install or connect the following:
8. Install the ignition coil.
9. Install the ignition coil retaining bolt and tighten to 89 inch lbs. (10 Nm).
10. Reconnect the ignition coil electrical connector.
11. Install the ignition coil cover to the cam cover.
12. Install the fuel injector sight shield.

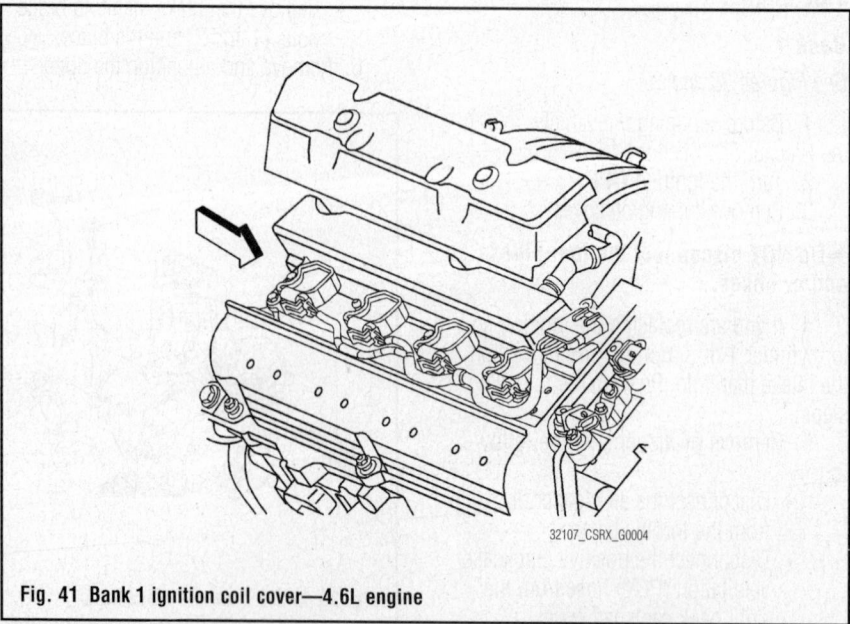

Fig. 41 Bank 1 ignition coil cover—4.6L engine

Bank 2

See Figures 42 and 43.

1. Before servicing the vehicle, refer to the Precautions Section.
2. Remove the fuel injector sight shield.
3. Remove the ignition coil cover from the cam cover by lifting straight up.

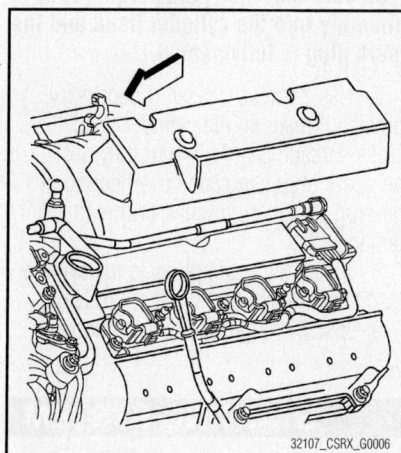

32107_CSRX_G0006

Fig. 43 Bank 2 ignition coil cover—4.6L engine

4. Disconnect the ignition coil wiring harness electrical connector from the coil that needs to be replaced.
5. Remove the ignition coil retaining bolt.
6. Carefully remove the ignition coil.

To install:

➡**Ensure that the spark plug seals are in place when installing the ignition coil.**

7. Install or connect the following:
8. Install the ignition coil.
9. Install the ignition coil retaining bolt and tighten to 89 inch lbs. (10 Nm).
10. Reconnect the ignition coil electrical connector.
11. Install the ignition coil cover to the cam cover.
12. Install the fuel injector sight shield.

IGNITION TIMING

ADJUSTMENT

The ignition timing is controlled by the Powertrain Control Module (PCM). No adjustment is necessary or possible.

SPARK PLUGS

REMOVAL & INSTALLATION

3.6L Engine

See Figure 44.

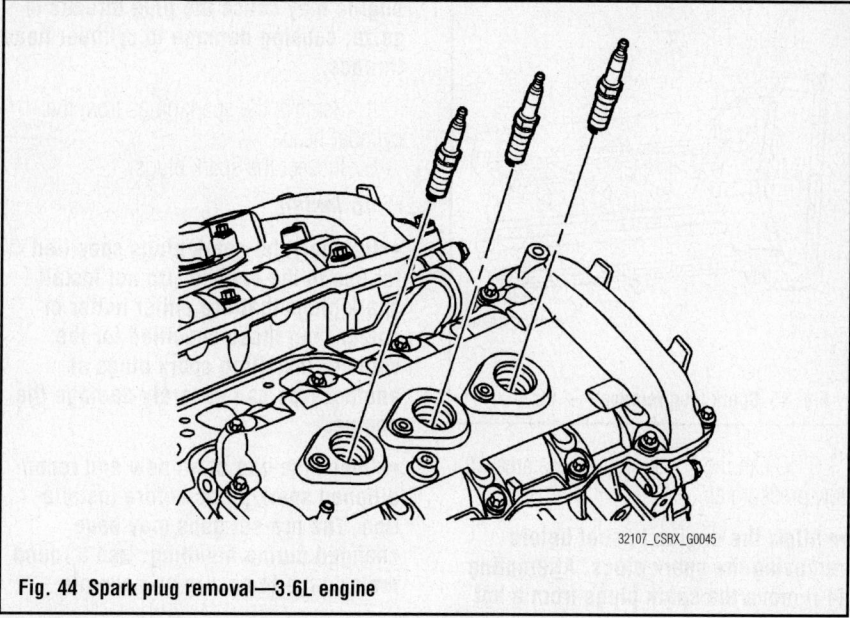

32107_CSRX_G0045

Fig. 44 Spark plug removal—3.6L engine

1. Before servicing the vehicle, refer to the Precautions Section.
2. Turn the ignition **OFF**.
3. Remove the ignition coil.

➡**Clean the spark plug recess area before removing the spark plug. Failure to do so could result in engine damage because of dirt or foreign material entering the cylinder head, or by the contamination of the cylinder head threads. The contaminated threads may prevent the proper seating of the new plug. Use a thread chaser to clean the threads of any contamination.**

4. Use compressed air in order to remove debris from the spark plug cavity.

➡**Allow the engine to cool before removing the spark plugs. Attempting to remove the spark plugs from a hot engine may cause the plug threads to seize, causing damage to cylinder head threads.**

5. Remove the spark plug.

To install:

➡**Use only the spark plugs specified for use in the vehicle. Do not install spark plugs that are either hotter or colder than those specified for the vehicle. Installing spark plugs of another type can severely damage the engine.**

➡**Check the gap of all new and reconditioned spark plugs before installation. The pre-set gaps may have changed during handling. Use a round feeler gage to ensure an accurate check. Installing the spark plugs with the wrong gap can cause poor engine**

performance and may even damage the engine. Ensure that the spark plug gap is equivalent to the spark plug gap specification.

➡**Be sure that the spark plug threads smoothly into the cylinder head and the spark plug is fully seated. Use a thread chaser, if necessary, to clean threads in the cylinder head. Cross-threading or failing to fully seat the spark plug can cause overheating of the plug, exhaust blow-by, or thread damage.**

6. Install the spark plug and tighten to 15 ft. lbs. (20 Nm).
7. Install the ignition coil.

4.6L Engine

See Figure 45.

1. Before servicing the vehicle, refer to the Precautions Section.
2. Remove the ignition control modules.

❋❋ CAUTION

Wear safety glasses when using compressed air, as flying dirt particles may cause eye injury.

➡**Clean the spark plug recess area before removing the spark plug. Failure to do so could result in engine damage because of dirt or foreign material entering the cylinder head, or by the contamination of the cylinder head threads. The contaminated threads may prevent the proper seating of the new plug. Use a thread chaser to clean the threads of any contamination.**

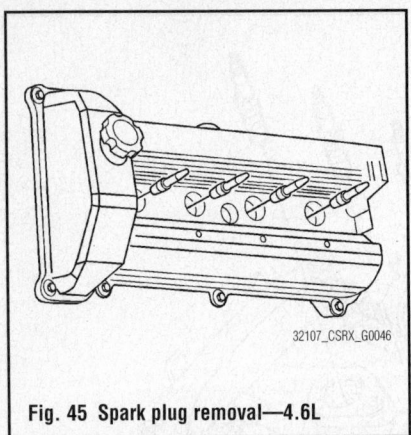

Fig. 45 Spark plug removal—4.6L

3. Clean the spark plug recess area with low pressure air.

➡**Allow the engine to cool before removing the spark plugs. Attempting to remove the spark plugs from a hot** engine may cause the plug threads to seize, causing damage to cylinder head threads.

4. Remove the spark plugs from the cylinder heads.
5. Inspect the spark plugs.

To install:

➡**Use only the spark plugs specified for use in the vehicle. Do not install spark plugs that are either hotter or colder than those specified for the vehicle. Installing spark plugs of another type can severely damage the engine.**

➡**Check the gap of all new and reconditioned spark plugs before installation. The pre-set gaps may have changed during handling. Use a round feeler gage to ensure an accurate** check. Installing the spark plugs with the wrong gap can cause poor engine performance and may even damage the engine.

6. Measure the spark plug gap on the spark plugs to be installed, correct as necessary.

➡**Be sure that the spark plug threads smoothly into the cylinder head and the spark plug is fully seated.**

7. Use a thread chaser, if necessary, to clean threads in the cylinder head. Cross-threading or failing to fully seat the spark plug can cause overheating of the plug, exhaust blow-by, or thread damage.
8. Install the spark plugs to the cylinder heads and tighten to 15 ft. lbs. (20 Nm).
9. Install the ignition control modules.

ENGINE ELECTRICAL

STARTER

REMOVAL & INSTALLATION

3.6L Engine

See Figure 46.

1. Before servicing the vehicle, refer to the Precautions Section.
2. Disconnect the negative battery cable.
3. Raise and support the vehicle safely.
4. Disconnect the starter electrical harness.
5. Remove the upper starter bolt.
6. Support the starter and remove the lower bolt.
7. Remove the starter from the vehicle.

To install:

8. Position the starter in the vehicle.
9. Install the upper and lower bolts. Tighten to 37 ft. lbs. (50 Nm).
10. Connect the starter electrical harness.
11. Lower the vehicle.
12. Connect the negative battery cable.

STARTING SYSTEM

4.6L Engine

See Figure 47.

1. Before servicing the vehicle, refer to the Precautions Section.
2. Disconnect the negative battery cable.
3. Remove the intake manifold.
4. Disconnect the starter electrical harness.
5. Remove the starter mounting bolts.
6. Remove the starter from the engine.

To install:

7. Position the starter on the engine.
8. Install or connect the following:
   - Starter mounting bolts. Tighten to 22 ft. lbs. (30 Nm).
   - Starter electrical harness. Tighten the motor stud nut to 84 inch lbs. (9.5Nm) and tighten the solenoid stud nut to 30 inch lbs. (3.4Nm).
   - Intake manifold
   - Negative battery cable

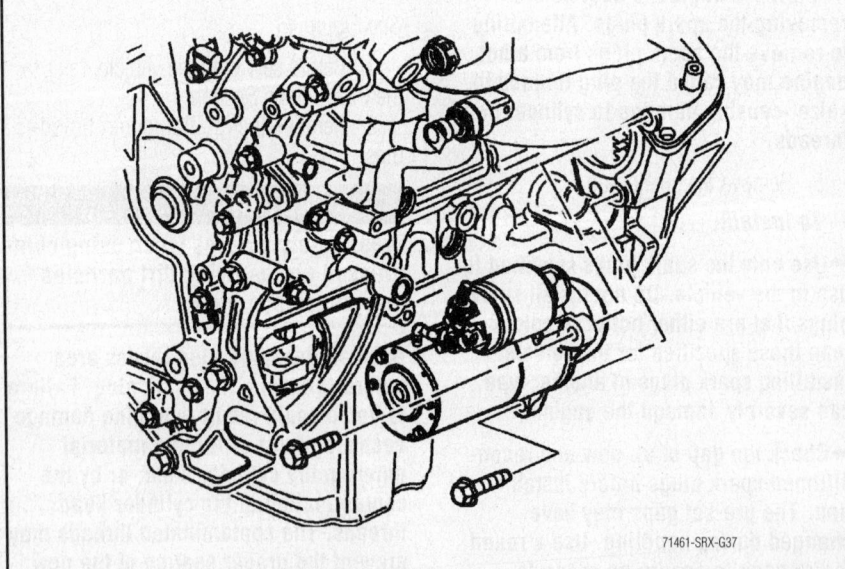

Fig. 46 Starter motor mounting—3.6L engine

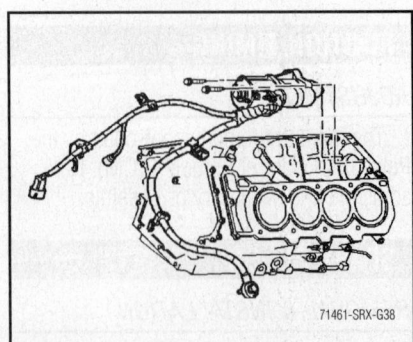

Fig. 47 Starter motor mounting—4.6L engine

ENGINE MECHANICAL

➡Disconnecting the negative battery cable may interfere with the functions of the on board computer systems and may require the computer to undergo a relearning process, once the negative battery cable is reconnected.

ACCESSORY DRIVE BELTS

ACCESSORY BELT ROUTING

See Figures 48 through 51.

INSPECTION

Inspect the drive belt for signs of glazing or cracking. A glazed belt will be perfectly smooth from slippage, while a good belt will have a slight texture of fabric visible. Cracks will usually start at the inner edge of the belt and run outward. All worn or damaged drive belts should be replaced immediately.

71461-SRX-G02

Fig. 49 Engine accessory drive belt routing—3.6L engine crankshaft, A/C compressor, tensioner and power steering pump belt

71461-SRX-G01

Fig. 48 Engine accessory drive belt routing—3.6L engine crankshaft, alternator and water pump belt

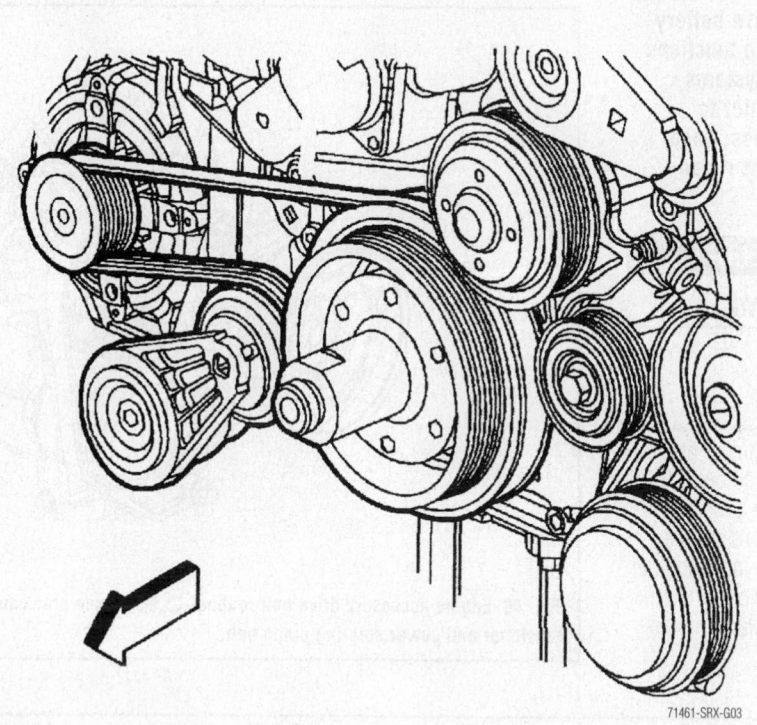

Fig. 50 Engine accessory drive belt routing—4.6L engine crankshaft, alternator and tensioner belt

Fig. 51 Engine accessory drive belt routing—4.6L engine crankshaft, A/C compressor, tensioner, idler and power steering pump belt

ADJUSTMENT

➡ **Belt tension is maintained by an automatic tensioner. No adjustment is necessary.**

REMOVAL & INSTALLATION

3.6L Engine

Generator and Water Pump

See Figure 52.

1. Before servicing the vehicle, refer to the Precautions Section.
2. Rotate the drive belt tensioner clockwise to release the drive belt tension.
3. Slide the drive belt off of the water pump pulley.
4. Slowly release the drive belt tensioner.
5. Remove the drive belt from the accessory drive pulleys.

To install:

6. Install the drive belt to the crankshaft pulley, the tensioner and the generator.
7. Rotate the drive belt tensioner clockwise.
8. Install the drive belt to the water pump.
9. Ensure the drive belt is properly aligned and seated into the grooves of the accessory drive pulleys.
10. Slowly release the drive belt tensioner.

Power Steering and A/C Compressor

See Figure 53.

1. Before servicing the vehicle, refer to the Precautions Section.
2. Remove the generator and water pump drive belt.
3. Rotate the drive belt tensioner clockwise in order to release the drive belt tension.
4. Remove the drive belt from the power steering pulley.
5. Slowly release the drive belt tensioner.
6. Remove the drive belt from the accessory drive pulleys.

To install:

7. Install the drive belt to the crankshaft pulley, the idler pulley and the A/C compressor.
8. Rotate the drive belt tensioner clockwise.
9. Install the drive belt to the power steering pulley.

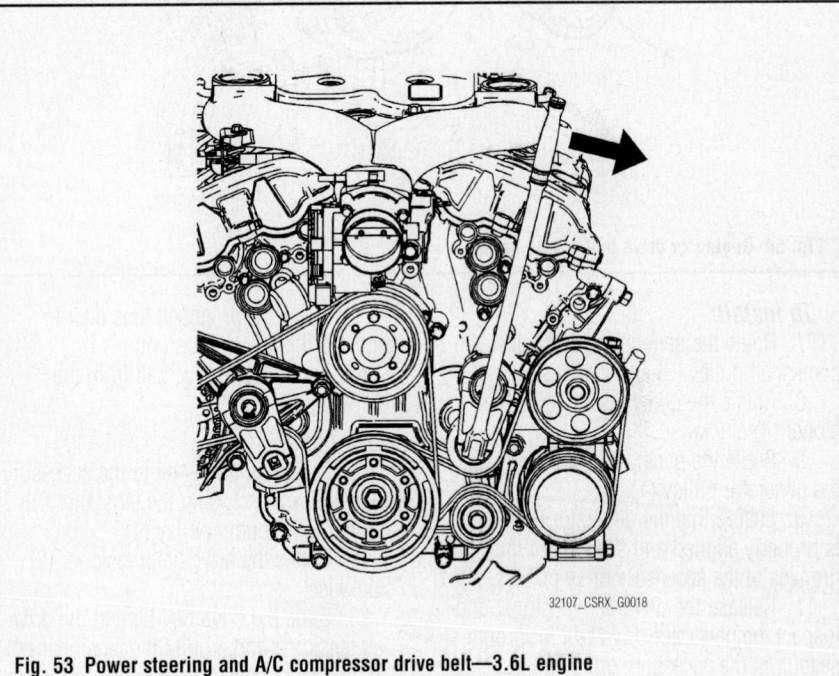

Fig. 53 Power steering and A/C compressor drive belt—3.6L engine

10. Slowly release the drive belt tensioner.
11. Ensure the drive belt is properly aligned and seated into the grooves of the accessory drive pulleys.
12. Install the generator and water pump drive belt.

4.6L Engine

Generator

See Figure 54.

1. Before servicing the vehicle, refer to the Precautions Section.
2. Remove the air conditioning, power steering, and water pump belt.
3. Rotate the generator drive belt tensioner (4) clockwise to release drive belt tension.
4. Slide the generator drive belt from the generator pulley (1).
5. Allow the drive belt tensioner to return to the relaxed position.
6. Remove the generator drive belt from the pulleys.

Fig. 52 Generator and water pump drive belt—3.6L engine

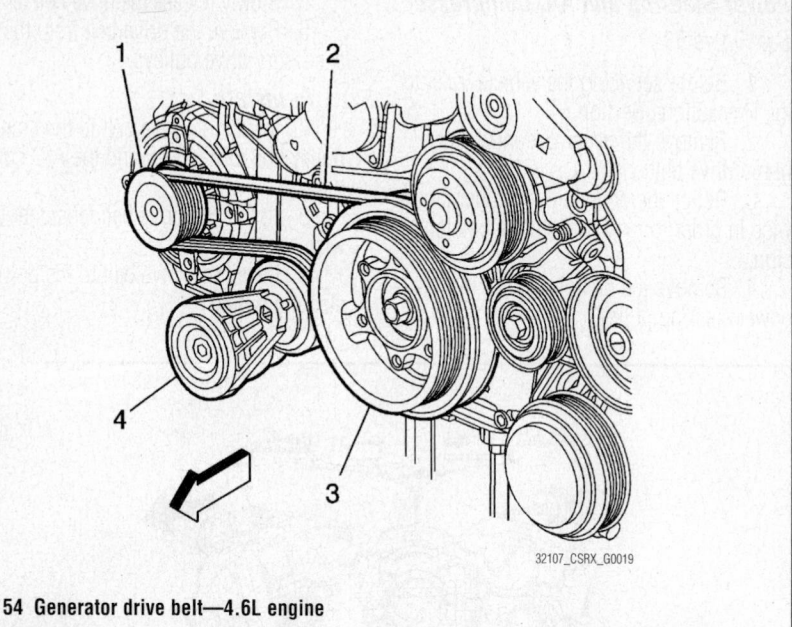

Fig. 54 Generator drive belt—4.6L engine

To install:

7. Route the generator drive belt to the crankshaft pulley (3) and the tensioner (4).

8. Rotate the generator drive belt tensioner (4) clockwise.

9. Route the generator drive belt over the generator pulley (1).

10. Ensure that the generator drive belt is properly aligned and seated into the grooves of the accessory drive pulleys.

11. Release the drive belt tensioner and inspect the generator drive belt for proper seating in the accessory drive pulleys.

12. Install the air conditioning, power steering, and water pump belt.

A/C Compressor, Power Steering and Water Pump

See Figure 55.

1. Before servicing the vehicle, refer to the Precautions Section.

2. Remove the fuel injector sight shield.

3. Remove the air cleaner outlet duct.

4. Remove the power steering fluid reservoir mounting nuts and position the reservoir aside. It is not necessary to remove the fluid lines.

5. If equipped with a crankshaft driven cooling fan, remove the cooling fan bracket.

6. Rotate the drive belt tensioner (2) clockwise to release drive belt tension.

7. Slide the drive belt from the water pump pulley (1).

8. Slide the drive belt out from behind the drive belt tensioner. Access the belt from the side of the tensioner pulley in the location of the lower reservoir mounting nut.

9. Allow the drive belt tensioner to return to the relaxed position.

10. Remove the drive belt from the remaining pulleys.

To install:

11. Route the drive belt to the accessory drive pulleys, excluding the tensioner (2) and the water pump pulley (1).

12. Rotate the drive belt tensioner (2) clockwise.

13. Slide the drive belt behind the drive belt tensioner and around the tensioner pulley. Access the belt from the side of the tensioner pulley in the location of the lower reservoir mounting nut.

14. Route the drive belt under the water pump pulley (1).

15. Ensure the drive belt is properly aligned and seated into the grooves of the accessory drive pulleys.

16. Release the drive belt tensioner and inspect the drive belt for proper seating in the accessory drive pulleys.

17. If equipped with a crankshaft driven cooling fan, install the cooling fan bracket.

18. Install the power steering fluid reservoir to the engine.

19. Install the air cleaner outlet duct.

20. Install the fuel injector sight shield.

CAMSHAFT AND VALVE LIFTERS

INSPECTION

Run-Out

See Figure 56.

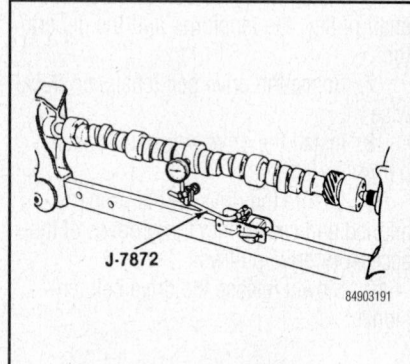

Fig. 56 Checking camshaft run-out

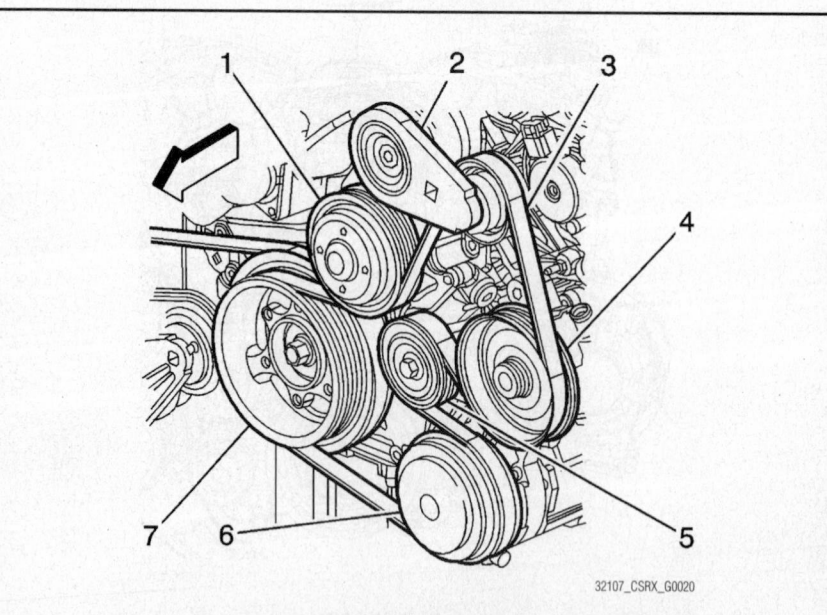

Fig. 55 A/C compressor, power steering and water pump drive belt—4.6L engine

Camshaft run-out should be checked when the camshaft has been removed from the engine. An accurate dial indicator is needed for this procedure. If the run-out exceeds the limit replace the camshaft. Refer to the Camshaft Specifications chart.

Lobe Height

See Figures 57 and 58.

Use a micrometer to check camshaft (lobe) height, making sure the anvil and the spindle of the micrometer are positioned directly on the heel and tip of the camshaft lobe as shown in the accompanying illustration. Refer to the Camshaft Specifications chart.

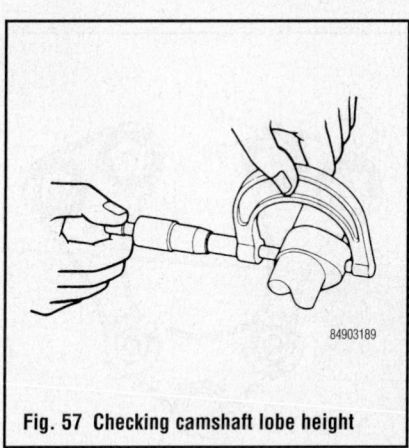

Fig. 57 Checking camshaft lobe height

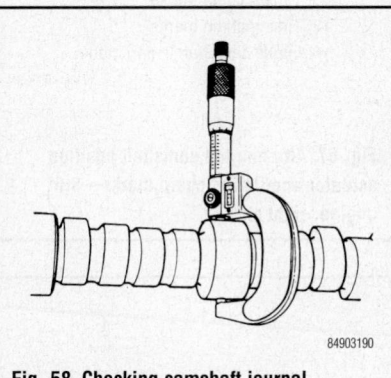

Fig. 58 Checking camshaft journal diameter

End-Play

See Figure 59.

After the camshaft has been installed, end-play should be checked. The camshaft sprocket should be installed on the cam. Use a dial gauge to check the end-play, by moving the camshaft forward and backward. Refer to the Camshaft Specifications chart.

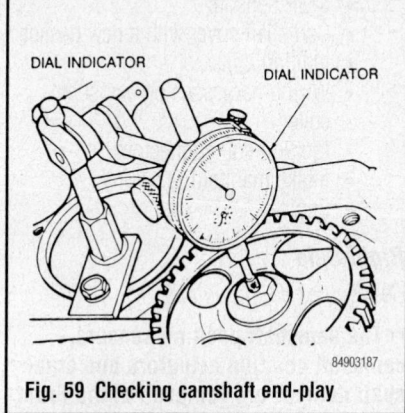

DIAL INDICATOR   DIAL INDICATOR

84903187

Fig. 59 Checking camshaft end-play

REMOVAL & INSTALLATION

3.6L Engine

Left Side

See Figures 60 through 64.

➡The camshaft position sensors, camshaft position actuators and crankshaft damper are removed in the

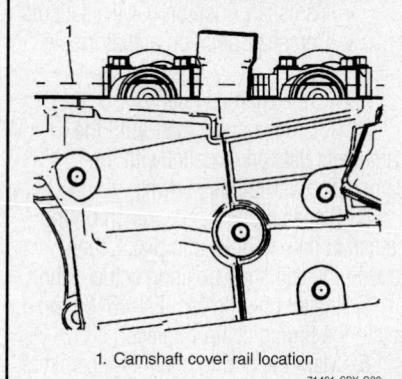

1. Camshaft cover rail location

71461-SRX-G20

Fig. 60 Aligning the camshaft flats with the camshaft cover rail—3.6L engine left side

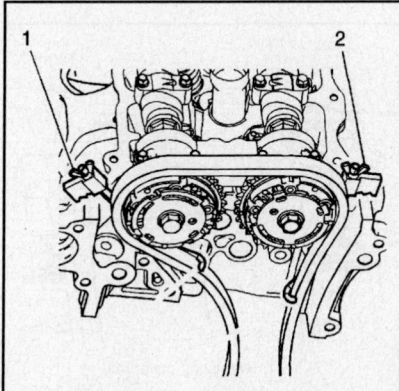

1-2. Timing chain retaining tool EN-46108

71461-SRX-G21

Fig. 61 Installing tool EN-46108 to lock the timing chain—3.6L engine left side

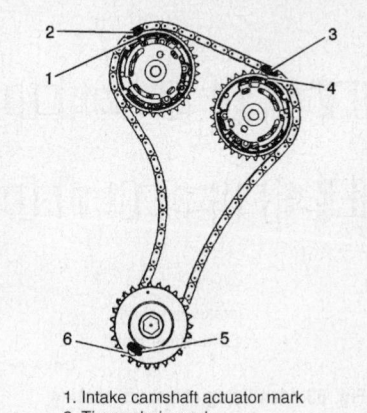

1. Intake camshaft actuator mark
2. Timng chain mark
3. Exhaust camshaft actuator mark
4. Timing chain mark

71461-SRX-G22

Fig. 62 Aligning the camshaft position actuators and timing chain marks—3.6L engine

Front Cover and Timing Chain procedure.

1. Before servicing the vehicle, refer to the Precautions Section.
2. Remove or disconnect the following:
   - Engine
   - Intake manifold assembly
   - Ignition coil connectors
   - Wiring harnesses on camshaft cover
   - Ignition coils
   - Camshaft cover
   - Camshaft Position (CMP) sensors
   - Camshaft position actuator solenoid
   - Crankshaft damper
3. Rotate the crankshaft until the camshafts flats are parallel with the camshaft cover rail as shown.
4. Place an open end wrench on the camshaft flats to hold it in place, then loosen the camshaft position actuator bolt.
5. Install holding tool EN-46108 to retain the timing chain in place.
6. Mark the timing chain and camshaft position actuators for reassembly reference.
7. Remove the camshaft position actuator bolt.
8. Note the locations of the camshaft bearing caps for reassembly reference.
9. Remove the camshaft bearing caps.
10. Remove the camshafts.

To install:

11. Install the camshaft sealing rings in the camshaft grooves.
12. Ensure the camshafts are placed in the correct position by locating the

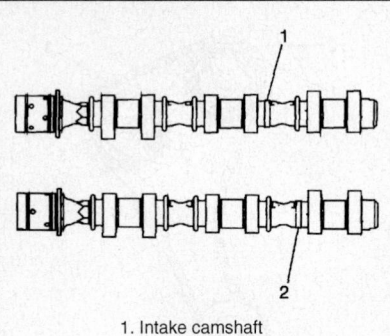

1. Intake camshaft
2. Exhaust camshaft

71461-SRX-G23

Fig. 63 Identifying camshaft locating numbers—3.6L engine left side

identification numbers on the appropriate camshaft.

13. Apply engine lubricant to the camshaft journals and carriers and the camshaft bearing caps.

14. Install the camshafts.

15. Ensure the camshafts flats are parallel with the camshaft cover rail as shown.

16. Install thrust cap in the first camshaft journal.

17. Install the camshaft bearing caps in the correct locations so the raised boss is toward the center of the engine.

18. Hand tighten the bearing cap bolts.

19. Tighten the bearing caps bolt in the sequence shown to 89 inch lbs. (10 Nm).

20. Loosen the bolts number 1, 2, 3 and 4, then retighten the bolts to 89 inch lbs. (10 Nm).

21. Place an open end wrench on the camshaft flats to hold it in place, then tighten the camshaft position actuator bolt to 48 ft. lbs. (58 Nm).

22. Install or connect the following:
- Crankshaft damper
- Camshaft position actuator solenoids

- CMP sensors
- Camshaft cover with a new gasket
- Ignition coils
- Wiring harnesses on camshaft cover
- Ignition coil connectors
- Intake manifold
- Engine

Right Side

See Figures 65 through 69.

➡The camshaft position sensors, camshaft position actuators and crankshaft damper are removed in the Front Cover and Timing Chain procedure.

1. Before servicing the vehicle, refer to the Precautions Section.

2. Remove or disconnect the following:
- Engine
- Intake manifold
- Ignition coil connectors
- Wiring harnesses on camshaft cover
- Ignition coils
- Camshaft cover
- Camshaft Position (CMP) sensors
- Camshaft position actuator solenoid
- Crankshaft damper

3. Rotate the crankshaft until the camshafts flats are parallel with the camshaft cover rail as shown.

4. Place an open end wrench on the camshaft flats to hold it in place, then loosen the camshaft position actuator bolt.

5. Install holding tool EN-46108 to retain the timing chain in place.

6. Mark the timing chain and camshaft position actuators for reassembly reference.

7. Remove the camshaft position actuator bolt.

8. Note the locations of the camshaft bearing caps for reassembly reference.

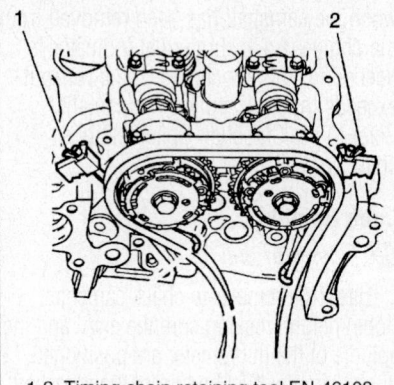

1-2. Timing chain retaining tool EN-46108

71461-SRX-G26

Fig. 66 Installing tool EN-46108 to lock the timing chain—3.6L engine, right side

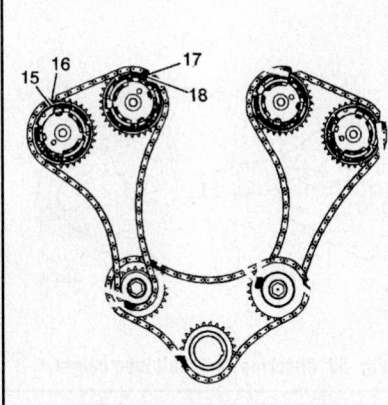

15. Exhaust camshaft timing marks
16. Timing chain marks
17. Timing chain marks
18. Intake camshaft timing marks

71461-SRX-G27

Fig. 67 Aligning the camshaft position actuator and timing chain marks—3.6L engine, right side

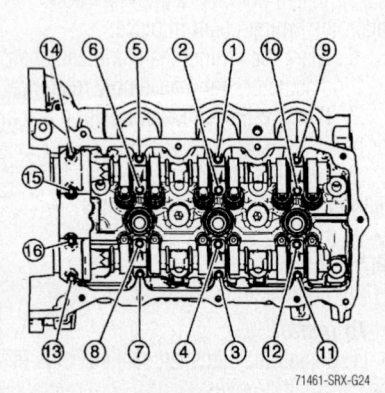

71461-SRX-G24

Fig. 64 Camshaft bearing cap tightening sequence—3.6L engine, left side

1. Camshaft cover rail

71461-SRX-G25

Fig. 65 Aligning the camshaft flats with the camshaft cover rail—3.6L engine, right side

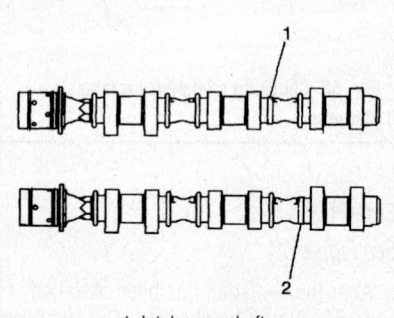

1. Intake camshaft
2. Exhaust camshaft

71461-SRX-G28

Fig. 68 Identifying camshaft locating numbers—3.6L engine right side

9. Remove the camshaft bearing caps.

10. Remove the camshafts.

To install:

11. Install the camshaft sealing rings in the camshaft grooves.

12. Ensure the camshafts are placed in the correct position by locating the identification numbers on the appropriate camshaft.

13. Apply engine lubricant to the camshaft journals and carriers and the camshaft bearing caps.

14. Install the camshafts.

15. Ensure the camshafts flats are parallel with the camshaft cover rail as shown.

16. Install thrust cap in the first camshaft journal.

17. Install the camshaft bearing caps in the correct locations so the raised boss is toward the center of the engine.

18. Hand tighten the bearing cap bolts.

19. Tighten the bearing caps bolt in the sequence shown to 89 inch lbs. (10 Nm).

20. Loosen the bolts number 1, 2, 3 and 4, then retighten the bolts to 89 inch lbs. (10 Nm).

21. Place an open end wrench on the camshaft flats to hold it in place, then tighten the camshaft position actuator bolt to 48 ft. lbs. (58 Nm).

22. Install or connect the following:
- Crankshaft damper
- Camshaft position actuator solenoids
- CMP sensors
- Camshaft cover with a new gasket
- Ignition coils
- Wiring harnesses on camshaft cover
- Ignition coil connectors
- Intake manifold
- Engine

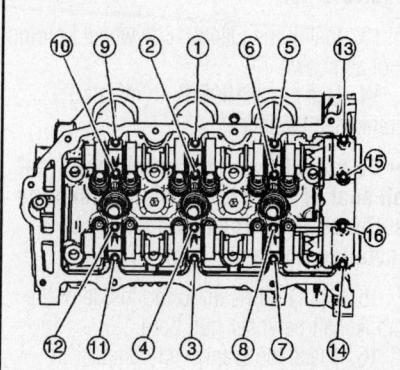

Fig. 69 Camshaft bearing cap tightening sequence—3.6L engine right side

4.6L Engine

Left Side

See Figures 70 through 72.

➡**The camshaft position actuators and timing chains are removed in the Front Cover and Timing Chain procedure.**

1. Before servicing the vehicle, refer to the Precautions Section.

2. Remove or disconnect the following:
- Engine
- Intake manifold
- Camshaft cover
- Front cover
- Timing chains
- Camshaft position actuators
- Camshaft bearing caps

➡**Observe the positions of the camshaft bearing caps. The arrow on the cap points toward the front of the engine, the I or E indicates intake or exhaust and the number indicates the journal position from the front of the engine.**

3. Remove the camshafts.

To install:

4. Apply engine lubricant to the camshaft journals and carriers and the camshaft bearing caps.

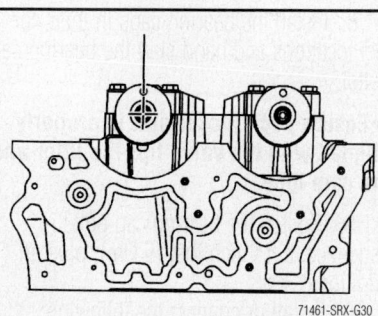

Fig. 70 Installing camshafts with locating pins at top of the rotation—4.6L engine, left side

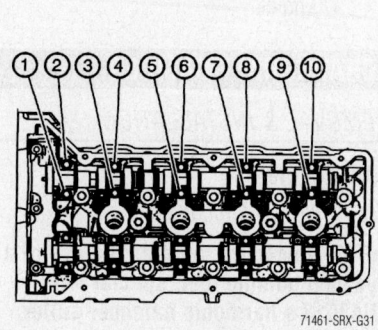

Fig. 71 Camshaft bearing cap tightening sequence—4.6L engine, left side intake

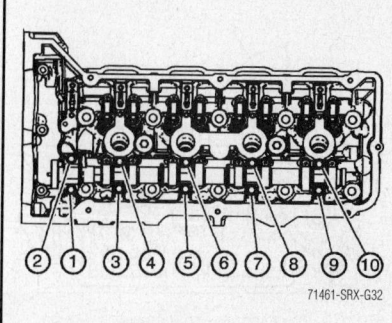

Fig. 72 Camshaft bearing cap tightening sequence—4.6L engine, left side exhaust

5. Ensure the camshafts are placed in the correct position by locating the identification letters stamped near the rear journal. For example: L-INT indicates left intake camshaft.

6. Install the camshafts with the camshaft sprocket drive pins at the top of their rotation and the lobes in the neutral position.

7. Install the bearing caps in their correct locations and hand start the bearing cap bolts.

➡**Ensure each rocker arm is properly aligned with the valve tip, the lifter and the cam lobe.**

8. Tighten the bearing cap bolts in sequence to 44 inch lbs. (5 Nm), plus an additional 30°.

9. Install or connect the following:
- Camshaft position actuators
- Timing chains
- Front cover
- Camshaft cover
- Ignition coils
- Wiring harnesses on camshaft cover
- Ignition coil connectors
- Intake manifold
- Engine

Right Side

See Figures 73 through 76.

➡**The camshaft position actuators and timing chains are removed in the Front Cover and Timing Chain procedure.**

1. Before servicing the vehicle, refer to the Precautions Section.

2. Remove or disconnect the following:
- Engine
- Intake manifold
- Camshaft cover
- Front cover
- Timing chains
- Camshaft position actuators
- Camshaft bearing caps

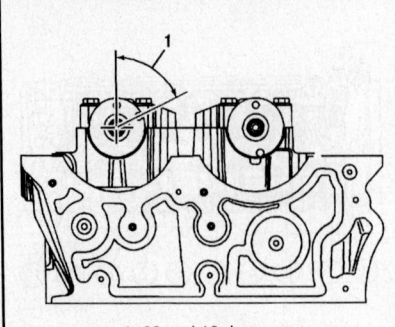

1. 60 and 10 degrees

71461-SRX-G33

Fig. 73 Installing the right exhaust camshaft with locating pins at 10 and 60 degree locations—4.6L engine, right side

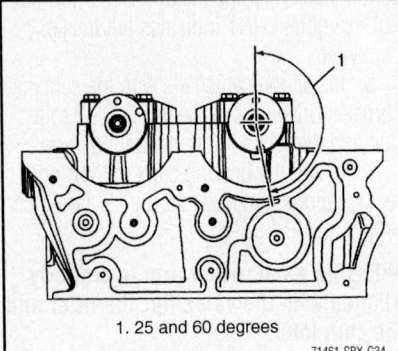

1. 25 and 60 degrees

71461-SRX-G34

Fig. 74 Installing the right intake camshaft with locating pins at 25 and 60 degree locations—4.6L engine, right side

➡Observe the positions of the camshaft bearing caps. The arrow on the cap points toward the front of the engine, the I or E indicates intake or exhaust and the number indicates the journal position from the front of the engine.

3. Remove the camshafts.

To install:

4. Apply engine lubricant to the camshaft journals and carriers and the camshaft bearing caps.

5. Ensure the camshafts are placed in the correct position by locating the identification letters stamped near the rear journal. For example: R-INT indicates right intake camshaft.

6. Install the right exhaust camshaft with the camshaft sprocket drive pins at the 10 and 60 degree locations and the lobes in the neutral position.

7. Install the right intake camshaft with the camshaft sprocket drive pins at the 25 and 60 degree locations and the lobes in the neutral position.

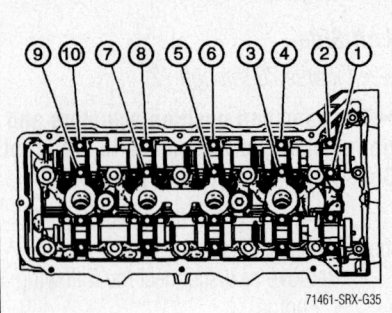

71461-SRX-G35

Fig. 75 Camshaft bearing cap tightening sequence—4.6L engine, right side intake

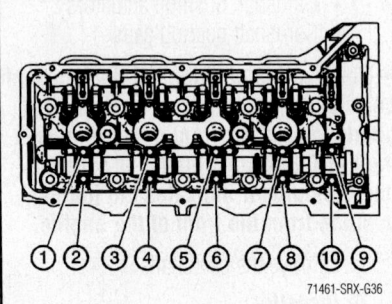

71461-SRX-G36

Fig. 76 Camshaft bearing cap tightening sequence—4.6L engine, right side exhaust

8. Install the bearing caps in their correct locations and hand start the bearing cap bolts.

➡Ensure each rocker arm is properly aligned with the valve tip, the lifter and the cam lobe.

9. Tighten the bearing cap bolts in sequence to 44 inch lbs. (5 Nm), plus an additional 30°.

10. Install or connect the following:
• Camshaft position actuators
• Timing chains
• Front cover
• Camshaft cover
• Intake manifold
• Engine

CRANKSHAFT DAMPER

REMOVAL & INSTALLATION

3.6L Engine

See Figures 77 through 80.

➡This procedure requires the use of a flywheel holding tool, special tool EN48018 a harmonic balancer puller, special tool J24420-C and a crankshaft button, special tool J38416-2 or the equivalents.

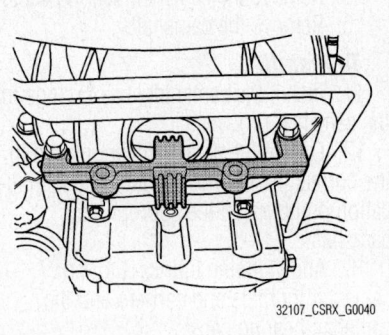

32107_CSRX_G0040

Fig. 77 Flywheel holding tool EN48018—3.6L engine

1. Before servicing the vehicle, refer to the Precautions Section.

2. Remove the A/C compressor and power steering pump drive belt.

3. Remove the generator and water pump drive belt.

4. Raise and support the vehicle.

5. Remove the transmission bell housing inspection hole cover.

6. Install the EN48018 flywheel holding tool as shown.

7. Remove the front air deflector.

8. Remove the crankshaft balancer bolt.

9. Install the J38416-2 in the nose of the crankshaft.

10. Install the J24420-C in order to remove the crankshaft balancer.

11. Pull the crankshaft balancer off by tightening the center bolt on the J24420-C until the crankshaft balancer pulls off of the crankshaft end.

12. Remove the J24420-C from the crankshaft balancer.

To install:

➡This procedure requires the use of a flywheel holding tool, special tool EN48018 a harmonic balancer installer, special tool J41998-B and a angle meter, special tool J45059 or the equivalents.

13. Install the EN48018 flywheel holding tool as shown.

14. Use the J41998-B, to install the crankshaft balancer.

➡Do not lubricate the crankshaft front oil seal or crankshaft balancer sealing surfaces. The crankshaft balancer is installed into a dry seal.

15. Apply lubricant to the inside of the crankshaft balancer hub bore.

16. Place the crankshaft balancer in position on the crankshaft.

17. Thread the J41998-B in the crankshaft by at least 10 threads.

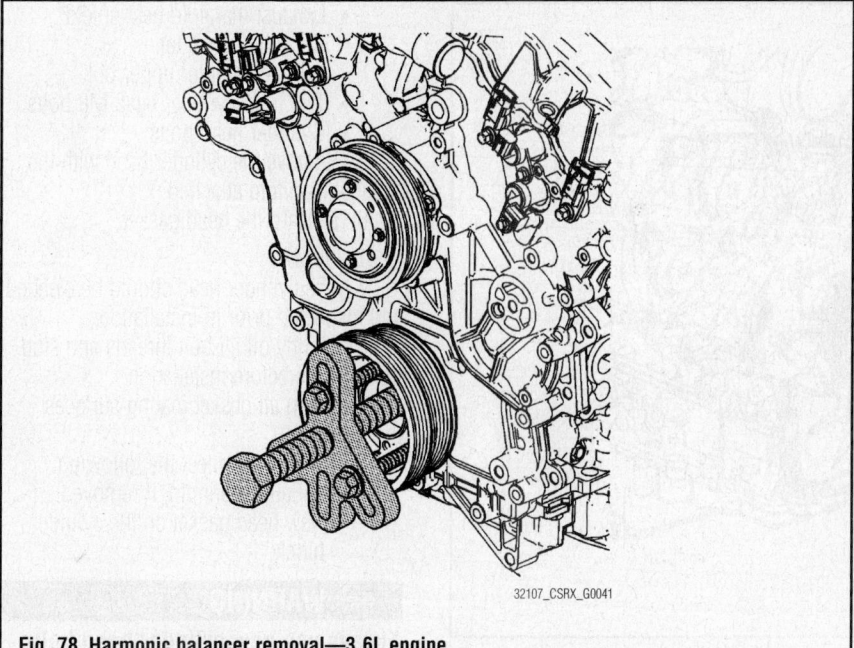

Fig. 78 Harmonic balancer removal—3.6L engine

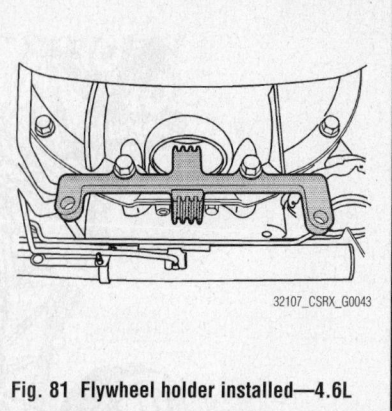

Fig. 81 Flywheel holder installed—4.6L

Fig. 79 Lubricate the inside of the balancer bore

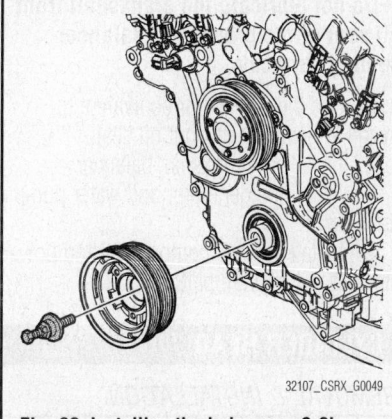

Fig. 80 Installing the balancer—3.6L engine

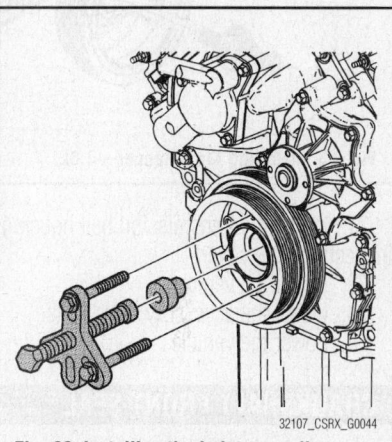

Fig. 82 Installing the balancer puller—4.6L

18. Push the crankshaft balancer into position by tightening the nut on the J41998-B until the large washer bottoms out on the crankshaft end.

19. Remove the J41998-B .

20. Install the crankshaft balancer bolt.

21. Tighten the crankshaft balancer bolt to 74 ft. lbs. (100 Nm).

22. Tighten the crankshaft balancer bolt an additional 150 degrees using the J45059.

23. Install the front air deflector.

24. Remove the EN48018 flywheel holding tool.

25. Install the transmission bell housing inspection hole cover.

26. Install the generator and water pump drive belt.

27. Install the A/C compressor and power steering pump drive belt.

4.6L Engine

See Figures 81 through 83.

This procedure requires the use of the following special tools or the equivalents:

• Crankshaft balancer remover J24420-C

• Crankshaft button J38416-2

• Crankshaft balancer installer J41998-B

• Angle meter J45059

• Flywheel holding tool EN48018

1. Before servicing the vehicle, refer to the Precautions Section.

2. Remove the accessory drive belts.

3. Raise and support the vehicle.

4. Remove the transmission bell housing inspection hole cover.

5. Install the EN48018 flywheel holding tool as shown.

6. Remove the front air deflector.

7. Remove the crankshaft balancer bolt.

8. Place the J38416-2 crankshaft button into the end of the crankshaft.

9. Install the J24420-C on the crankshaft balancer.

10. Remove the crankshaft balancer using the J24420-C .

11. Clean and inspect the crankshaft balancer.

To install:

12. Position the crankshaft balancer on the nose of the crankshaft.

13. Press the crankshaft balancer in place using the J41998-B.

14. Clean the crankshaft balancer bolt threads.

15. Apply engine oil to the crankshaft balancer bolt threads.

16. Install the crankshaft balancer bolt.

17. First Pass, tighten the crankshaft balancer bolt to 37 ft. lbs. (50 Nm).

18. Final Pass, tighten the crankshaft balancer bolt an additional 120 degrees using the J45059 .

19. Install the front air deflector.

20. Remove the EN48018 flywheel holding tool.

Fig. 83 Installing the balancer—4.6L

21. Install the transmission bell housing inspection hole cover.
22. Lower the vehicle.
23. Install the accessory drive belts.
24. Lower the vehicle.

CRANKSHAFT FRONT SEAL

REMOVAL & INSTALLATION

See Figure 84.

➡️**This procedure requires the use of an oil seal installer, special tool J29184 or equivalent.**

1. Remove the A/C compressor and power steering pump drive belt.
2. Remove the generator and water pump drive belt.
3. Remove the crankshaft balancer.
4. Use a flat-bladed tool in order to remove the crankshaft oil seal.

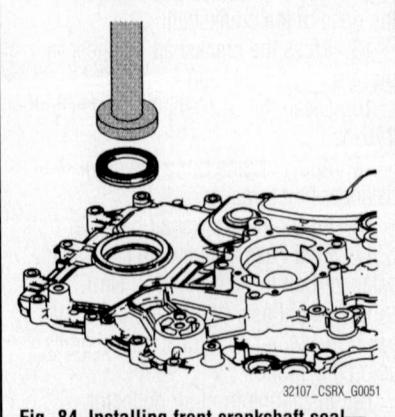

Fig. 84 Installing front crankshaft seal—3.6L engine

To install:

➡️**Do not lubricate the crankshaft front oil seal or the crankshaft balancer sealing surfaces.**

5. Use the J29184 or equivalent to install the crankshaft front oil seal.
6. Install the crankshaft balancer.
7. Install the generator and water pump drive belt.
8. Install the A/C compressor and power steering pump drive belt.

CYLINDER HEAD

REMOVAL & INSTALLATION

3.6L Engine

Left Side

See Figure 85.

1. Before servicing the vehicle, refer to the Precautions Section.
2. Relieve the fuel system pressure.
3. Drain the cooling system.
4. Remove or disconnect the following:
- Negative battery cable
- Left side secondary timing chain
- Oil level indicator
- Coolant temperature sensor heat shield
- Coolant temperature sensor electrical connector
- Wiring harness ground, connector and connector bracket
- Power steering pump pulley
- Power steering pump, but leave the fluid lines attached
- Surge tank hose

- Exhaust manifold heat shield
- Catalytic converter
- Oil filter adapter upper bolt
- Two front cylinder head M8 bolts
- Cylinder head bolts
5. Remove the cylinder head with the exhaust manifold attached.
6. Discard the head gasket.

To install:

7. The cylinder head should be cleaned and inspected prior to installation.
8. Lightly oil all bolt threads and stud bolt threads before installation.
9. Clean all gasket mating surfaces thoroughly.
10. Install or connect the following:
- Exhaust manifold, if removed.
- New head gasket on the cylinder block.

❋❋ WARNING

Always use new cylinder head bolts when installing the cylinder head or damage to the engine may occur.

- Cylinder head on the cylinder block.
- Tighten the M11 cylinder head bolts in steps following the proper torque sequence. The first step is 33 ft. lbs. (45 Nm), the second step is an additional 120°.
- Tighten the front M8 cylinder head bolts in steps following the proper torque sequence. The first step is 11 ft. lbs. (15 Nm), the second step is an additional 60°.
- Oil filter adapter upper bolt
- Catalytic converter
- Exhaust manifold heat shield
- Surge tank hose
- Power steering pump, but leave the fluid lines attached
- Power steering pump pulley
- Wiring harness ground, connector and connector bracket

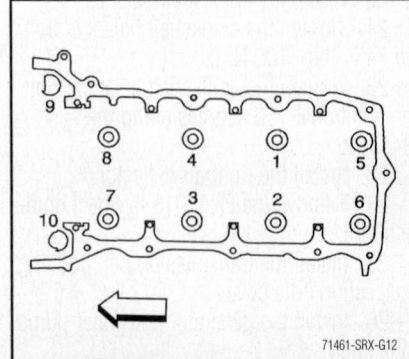

Fig. 85 Left side cylinder head bolt torque sequence—3.6L engine

- Coolant temperature sensor electrical connector
- Coolant temperature sensor heat shield
- Oil level indicator
- Left side secondary timing chain
- Negative battery cable
11. Fill and bleed the cooling system.

➡ **Engine coolant is corrosive to engine bearing material. Replace the engine oil after removal of any coolant-carrying component to help prevent potential bearing damage.**

12. Change the engine oil and filter
13. Connect the negative battery cable.
14. Start the engine and check for leaks.

Right Side
See Figure 86.

1. Before servicing the vehicle, refer to the Precautions Section.
2. Relieve the fuel system pressure.
3. Drain the cooling system.
4. Remove or disconnect the following:
- Negative battery cable
- Right side secondary timing chain
- Coolant inlet pipe
- Wiring harness ground and harness bracket
- Negative battery cable bolt on head
- Exhaust manifold heat shield
- Catalytic converter
- Cylinder head bolts
5. Remove the cylinder head with the exhaust manifold attached.
6. Discard the head gasket.

To install:

7. The cylinder head should be cleaned and inspected prior to installation.
8. Lightly oil all bolt threads and stud bolt threads before installation.
9. Clean all gasket mating surfaces thoroughly.
10. Install or connect the following:

- Exhaust manifold, if removed.
- New head gasket on the cylinder block.

✳✳ WARNING

Always use new cylinder head bolts when installing the cylinder head or damage to the engine may occur.

- Cylinder head on the cylinder block.
- Tighten the M11 cylinder head bolts in steps following the proper torque sequence. The first step is 33 ft. lbs. (45 Nm), the second step is an additional 120°.
- Catalytic converter
- Exhaust manifold heat shield
- Negative battery cable bolt on head
- Wiring harness ground and harness bracket. Tighten bolt to 89 inch lbs. (10 Nm).
- Coolant inlet pipe
- Right side secondary timing chain
- Negative battery cable
11. Fill and bleed the cooling system.
12. Start the engine and check for leaks.

4.6L Engine

Left Side
See Figure 87.

1. Before servicing the vehicle, refer to the Precautions Section.
2. Relieve the fuel system pressure.
3. Drain the cooling system.
4. Remove or disconnect the following:
- Negative battery cable
- Exhaust manifold
- Throttle body
- Intake manifold
- Manifold Absolute Pressure (MAP) sensor
- EVAP canister purge valve hose
- Thermostat housing hoses
- Thermostat housing

- Left side secondary timing chain
- Left camshafts
- Power steering reservoir return hose bracket
- Cylinder head bolts
5. Remove the cylinder head and discard the head gasket.

To install:

6. The cylinder head should be cleaned and inspected prior to installation.
7. Lightly oil all bolt threads and stud bolt threads before installation.
8. Clean all gasket mating surfaces thoroughly.

➡ **Ensure the M11 cylinder head bolts have the proper pitch or engine damage will occur. The bolts have been revised. Identify the bolts before installation. Bolts with a pitch of 1.5mm have a thread length of about 1.89 inches (48mm). Bolts with a pitch of 2mm have a thread length of about 2.64 inches (67mm).**

9. Install or connect the following:
- New head gasket on the cylinder block.

✳✳ WARNING

Always use new cylinder head bolts when installing the cylinder head or damage to the engine may occur.

- Cylinder head on the cylinder block.
- Tighten the M11 cylinder head bolts in steps following the proper torque sequence. The first step is 22 ft. lbs. (30 Nm), the second step is an additional 60°, the third step is an additional 60° and the fourth step is a final 60°.
- Tighten the M6 bolts at the front of the head to 106 inch lbs. (12 Nm).
- Power steering reservoir return hose bracket
- Left camshafts
- Left side secondary timing chain
- Thermostat housing and tighten the bolts to 18 ft. lbs. (25 Nm).
- Thermostat housing hoses
- EVAP canister purge valve hose
- MAP sensor
- Throttle body
- Intake manifold
- Exhaust manifold
- Coolant
- Negative battery cable
10. Fill and bleed the cooling system.
11. Start the engine and check for leaks.

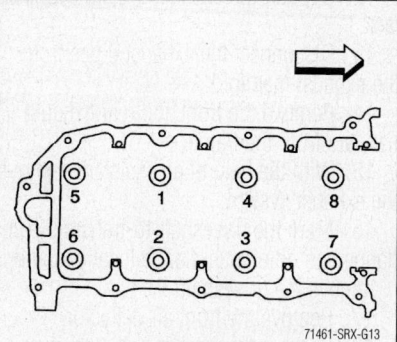

Fig. 86 Right side cylinder head bolt torque sequence—3.6L engine

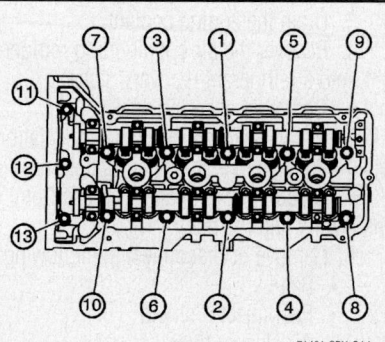

Fig. 87 Left side cylinder head bolt torque sequence—4.6L engine

Right Side

See Figure 88.

1. Before servicing the vehicle, refer to the Precautions Section.
2. Relieve the fuel system pressure.
3. Remove or disconnect the following:
   - Negative battery cable
   - Coolant
   - Exhaust manifold
   - Throttle body
   - Intake manifold
   - Manifold Absolute Pressure (MAP) sensor
   - EVAP canister purge valve hose
   - Thermostat housing hoses
   - Thermostat housing
   - Right side secondary timing chain
   - Right camshafts
   - Cylinder head bolts
4. Remove the cylinder head and discard the head gasket.

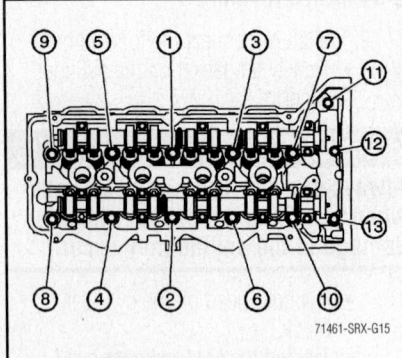

Fig. 88 Right side cylinder head bolt torque sequence—4.6L engine

To install:

5. The cylinder head should be cleaned and inspected prior to installation.
6. The cylinder head should be cleaned and inspected prior to installation.
7. Lightly oil all bolt threads and stud bolt threads before installation.
8. Clean all gasket mating surfaces thoroughly.

➡**Ensure the M11 cylinder head bolts have the proper pitch or engine damage will occur. The bolts have been revised. Identify the bolts before installation. Bolts with a pitch of 1.5mm have a thread length of about 1.89 inches (48mm). Bolts with a pitch of 2mm have a thread length of about 2.64 inches (67mm).**

9. Install or connect the following:
   - New head gasket on the cylinder block.

✷✷ WARNING

Always use new cylinder head bolts when installing the cylinder head or damage to the engine may occur.

- Cylinder head on the cylinder block.
- Tighten the M11 cylinder head bolts in steps following the proper torque sequence. The first step is 22 ft. lbs. (30 Nm), the second step is an additional 60°, the third step is an additional 60 ° and the fourth step is a final 60°.
- Tighten the M6 bolts at the front of the head to 106 inch lbs. (12 Nm).
- Right camshafts
- Right side secondary timing chain
- Thermostat housing and tighten the bolts to 18 ft. lbs. (25 Nm).
- Thermostat housing hoses
- EVAP canister purge valve hose
- MAP sensor
- Throttle body
- Intake manifold
- Exhaust manifold
- Coolant
- Negative battery cable
10. Fill and bleed the cooling system.
11. Start the engine and check for leaks.

ENGINE ASSEMBLY

REMOVAL & INSTALLATION

3.6L Engine

See Figures 89 and 90.

➡**The front wheels must be in the straight ahead position and the steering column locked before disconnecting the intermediate shaft. Failure to do so may result in damage to the Supplemental Restraint System (SRS) coil.**

1. Before servicing the vehicle, refer to the Precautions Section.
2. Relieve the fuel system pressure.
3. Drain the engine coolant.
4. Recover the air conditioning refrigerant, into a refrigerant recovery station.
5. Center the steering wheel.
6. Install Steering Column Anti-rotation pin J-42640 to lock the steering column.
7. Disconnect the battery cables from the battery and the body.
8. Remove or disconnect the following:
   - Battery
   - Fuel injector shield
   - Air cleaner duct
   - Cooling fan connectors
   - Surge tank hoses

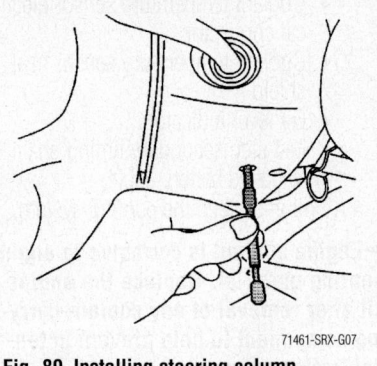

Fig. 89 Installing steering column anti-rotation pin

- Heater hoses
- Purge solenoid line
- Fuel line from fuel rail
- Wiper module
- A/C suction hose from evaporator
- Suction hose bracket
- A/C pressure switch connector
- Radiator support brackets
- Brake booster check valve and vacuum hose
- Brake fluid level switch connector
- Mass Air Flow (MAF) sensor connector
- Instrument panel connector at rear of left cylinder head
- Engine module connectors from underhood electrical center
- Transmission Control Module (TCM) wiring harness
- Ground bolt and cable from frame rail
- Engine harness connector from frame rail
- Without removing the brake lines, unbolt the master cylinder and secure it to the engine
9. Raise and support the vehicle.
10. Remove the oxygen sensors from the exhaust pipes.
11. Remove the floor panel tunnel brace from under the vehicle.
12. Support the exhaust system with a jack.
13. Disconnect the exhaust pipes from the exhaust manifold.
14. Remove the front and rear exhaust hangers from the frame.
15. With the help of an assistant, remove the exhaust system.
16. Mark the driveshaft-to-transmission flange and differential flange locations and remove the driveshaft.
17. Remove the front air deflector.
18. Remove the washer bottle bracket, but not the washer bottle.
19. Remove the radiator side air baffles.

20. Disconnect the front brake pipe retainers.

21. Disconnect the 2 center pipes from the brake proportion modulator valve and cap the openings.

22. Remove the front wheels.

23. Remove the upper to center intermediate steering shaft bolt.

24. Remove the lower intermediate steering shaft-to-steering gear bolt.

25. Remove the center intermediate steering shaft with the lower shaft attached.

26. Remove the lower engine mount nuts.

27. Disconnect the transmission shift linkage.

28. Disconnect the oil level sensor connector.

29. Remove the headlight leveling sensors.

30. Secure the shock modules to the lower control arms with a suitable strap to avoid damage to the brake lines.

31. Remove the shock yoke.

32. Remove the left and right shock module upper mounting nuts.

33. Raise the vehicle enough to place a suitable engine lift table under the engine, transmission, front frame and front suspension assembly.

34. Lower the vehicle or raise the lift until the engine assembly is supported by the lift.

35. Remove the transmission brace-to-underbody bolts.

36. Remove the 4 front frame bolts.

37. With the aid of an assistant, remove the engine, transmission, front frame and front suspension assembly from the vehicle.

38. If the engine itself is to be serviced, the engine will have to be separated from the transmission and the front frame and suspension assembly.

To install:

39. With the aid of an assistant, raise the table and/or lift the vehicle to install the engine, transmission, front frame and front suspension assembly to the vehicle.

40. Install the front frame bolts. Tighten the bolts to 141 ft. lbs. (191 Nm).

41. Install the transmission support to underbody bolts. Tighten the bolt 44 ft. lbs. (60 Nm).

42. Remove the powertrain lift/support table.

43. Install the right and left shock module upper mounting bolts. Tighten the bolts to 83 ft. lbs. (112 Nm).

44. Install the headlamp leveling sensors.

45. Connect the transmission shift linkage to the transmission.

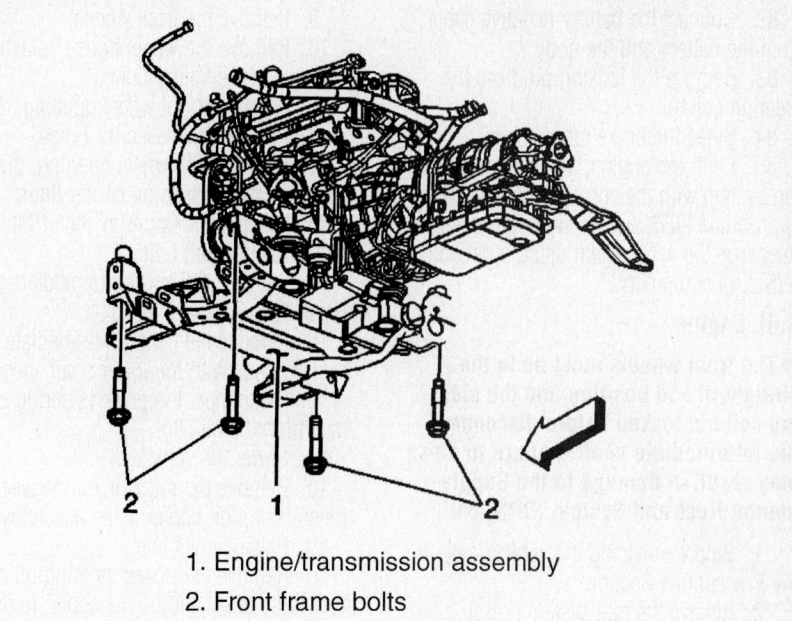

1. Engine/transmission assembly
2. Front frame bolts

71461-SRX-G08

Fig. 90 Removing the front frame mounting bolts—3.6L engine

46. Connect the low oil level sensor electrical connector.

47. Install the lower engine mount nuts. Tighten the nut to 59 ft. lbs. (80 Nm).

48. Install the lower and intermediate steering shafts. Tighten the bolts to 23 ft. lbs. (80 Nm).

49. Install the front tire and wheel assemblies.

50. Install the front brake pipes and retainers to the underbody.

51. Connect the rear brake pipes (two center pipes) to the brake pressure modulator valve (BPVM).

52. Connect the radiator side air baffles to the radiator.

53. Install the washer bottle bracket.

54. Install the air deflector.

55. Install the propeller shaft using the reference marks previously made. Tighten the bolts to 63 ft. lbs. (85 Nm).

56. Install the exhaust system. Tighten the exhaust pipe-to-manifold nuts to 22 ft. lbs. (30 Nm).

57. Install the floor tunnel brace. Tighten the bolts to 18 ft. lbs. (25 Nm).

58. Install the master cylinder.

59. Connect the engine harness electrical connector to the frame rail.

60. Install the ground wire and bolt to the longitudinal rail. Tighten the bolt to 89 inch lbs. (10 Nm).

61. Connect the wiring harness to the TCM.

62. Connect the engine module wiring

harness connectors to the underhood electrical center.

63. Connect and lock the instrument panel electrical connector to the engine at the rear of the left cylinder head.

64. Connect the mass air flow sensor electrical connector.

65. Connect the brake fluid level switch electrical connector from the master cylinder.

66. Connect the brake booster vacuum hose.

67. Install the radiator support brackets.

68. Connect the purge line to the purge solenoid.

69. Connect the fuel pipe to the fuel rail.

70. Connect the heater hoses to the heater core.

71. Install the air inlet duct.

72. Position the surge tank inlet hose to the vehicle.

73. Connect the surge tank inlet hose to the water outlet housing and the radiator.

74. Connect the surge tank outlet hose to the surge tank.

75. Connect the A/C pressure switch electrical connector and the liquid line to the evaporator.

76. Connect the air conditioning suction hose to the evaporator and install the suction hose bracket to the shock tower.

77. Install the cooling fan wiring harnesses to the fan shroud.

78. Install the cooling fan electrical connectors.

79. Install the wiper module.

80. Install the fuel injector sight shield.

81. Connect the battery cables.

82. Connect the battery negative cable from the battery and the body.

83. Remove the locking pin from the steering column.

84. Bleed the brake rear circuits

85. Refill the engine, transaxle and cooling system with the correct amount of the appropriate fluids before starting the engine. Recharge the A/C system using approved recycling equipment.

4.6L Engine

➡ **The front wheels must be in the straight ahead position and the steering column locked before disconnect the intermediate shaft. Failure to do so may result in damage to the Supplemental Restraint System (SRS) coil.**

1. Before servicing the vehicle, refer to the Precautions Section.

2. Relieve the fuel system pressure.

3. Drain the engine coolant.

4. Recover the air conditioning refrigerant, into a refrigerant recovery station.

5. Center the steering wheel.

6. Install Steering Column Anti-rotation pin J-42640 to lock the steering column.

7. Disconnect the battery cables from the battery and wire them to the engine. Remove or disconnect the following:
- Cross vehicle brace
- Fuel injector shield
- Air cleaner assembly
- Surge tank hoses
- A/C suction hose fitting on shock tower
- A/C liquid hose from condenser
- Brake booster vacuum hose
- Brake fluid level switch connector
- Without removing the brake lines, unbolt the master cylinder and secure it to the engine
- Fuel line retainer
- Engine harness connector at firewall
- Underhood fuse block connector near right shock tower
- Underhood electrical center cover
- Ground bolt from right shock tower
- Positive battery cable from inside electrical center
- Chassis electrical connector from right shock tower
- Transmission Control Module (TCM) wiring harness
- Engine wiring harness connector inside electrical center
- Electrical connector at right frame rail
- Cooling fans

8. Raise and support the vehicle.

9. Remove the front wheels.

10. Remove the wheel house splash shields and the fender liners.

11. From the right wheel opening, disconnect the washer reservoir brace.

12. From the left wheel opening, disconnect the transmission oil cooler lines.

13. Remove the upper to center intermediate steering shaft bolt.

14. Remove the lower intermediate steering shaft-to-steering gear bolt.

15. Remove the center intermediate steering shaft with the lower shaft attached.

16. Disconnect the power steering cooler lines from the radiator.

17. Lower the vehicle.

18. Remove the radiator, condenser and transmission oil cooler as an assembly.

19. Raise the vehicle.

20. Remove the power steering oil cooler from the bracket and tie the cooler to the engine.

21. On 4WD models, remove the transfer case.

22. Remove the transmission.

23. Remove the brake bundle clips from both frame rails.

24. Disconnect the fuel line from the filter.

25. Disconnect the EVAP hose from the rear of the fuel filter.

26. Disconnect the rear brake lines from the bracket above the rear axle assembly.

27. Remove the fuel and brake line bundle retainers from the frame rail the length of the vehicle. Do not remove the retainers from the lines.

28. Remove the fuel filter bracket to provide a removal path for the fuel and brake line bundle assembly.

29. Remove the fuel and brake line bundle bracket from the right side wheelhouse.

30. Lower the vehicle.

31. Disconnect the heater outlet hose from the heater outlet pipe at the right frame rail. Position the hose to the engine.

32. Disconnect the heater inlet hose from the water housing and position the hose to the vehicle.

33. If the vehicle is equipped with Magnaride®, disconnect the electrical connectors from the top of the right and left shock modules.

34. Secure the shock modules to the lower control arms with a suitable strap to avoid damage to the brake lines.

35. Remove the shock yoke.

36. Remove the left and right shock module upper mounting nuts.

37. Raise the vehicle enough to place a suitable engine lift table under the engine,

transmission, front frame and front suspension assembly.

38. Support the rear of the vehicle with jack stands.

39. Raise the lift table and/or lower the vehicle to preload the weight of the engine, front frame, and front suspension assembly.

40. Remove the 4 front frame bolts.

41. With the aid of an assistant, lower the table and/or raise the vehicle to remove the engine, front frame, fuel/brake bundle and front suspension assembly from the vehicle.

42. Ensure that all the hoses, wires, pipes and shock modules clear the vehicle during the removal process.

43. If the engine itself is to be serviced, the engine will have to be separated from the transmission and the front frame and suspension assembly.

To install:

44. With the aid of an assistant, raise the table and/or lift the vehicle to install the engine, fuel/brake bundle, front frame and front suspension assembly to the vehicle.

45. Install the front frame bolts. Tighten the bolts to 141 ft. lbs. (191 Nm).

46. Install the right and left shock module upper mounting bolts. Tighten the bolts to 83 ft. lbs. (112 Nm).

47. Connect the shock module connectors, if equipped with Magnaride®.

48. Connect the heater inlet hose to the water housing.

49. Connect the heater outlet hose to the outlet pipe.

50. Raise and support the vehicle.

51. Install the fuel and brake line bundle to the right side wheelhouse. Tighten bundle bracket to 80 inch lbs. (9 Nm).

52. Install the fuel filter bracket. Tighten the bracket bolt to 80 inch lbs. (9 Nm).

53. Install the fuel/brake line bundle to the bundle brackets the length of the vehicle.

54. Install the rear brake line to the rear axle assembly. Tighten the bracket bolt to 80 inch lbs. (9 Nm).

55. Connect the EVAP hose to the fuel filter.

56. Connect the fuel line to the fuel filter.

57. Install the brake lines to the bundle clips on the left and right frame rails.

58. Install the transmission.

59. On 4WD models, install the transfer case.

60. Install the power steering oil cooler to the mounting bracket.

61. Lower the vehicle.

62. Install the radiator, condenser and transmission oil cooler as an assembly.

63. Raise and support the vehicle.
64. Connect the power steering cooler lines to the radiator.
65. Install the lower and intermediate steering shafts. Tighten the bolts to 23 ft. lbs. (30 Nm).
66. From the left wheel opening, connect the transmission oil cooler lines.
67. From the right wheel opening, connect the washer reservoir brace.
68. Install the wheel house splash shields and the fender liners.
69. Install the front wheels. Install or connect the following:
- Cooling fans
- Electrical connector at right frame rail
- Engine wiring harness connector inside electrical center
- Transmission Control Module (TCM) wiring harness
- Chassis electrical connector to right shock tower
- Positive battery cable inside electrical center
- Ground bolt to right shock tower
- Underhood electrical center cover
- Underhood fuse block connector near right shock tower
- Engine harness connector at firewall
- Fuel line retainer
- Master cylinder. Tighten the retaining nuts to 18 ft. lbs. (25 Nm).
- Brake fluid level switch connector
- Brake booster vacuum hose
- A/C liquid hose to condenser
- A/C suction hose fitting on shock tower
- Surge tank hoses
- Air cleaner assembly
- Fuel injector shield
- Cross vehicle brace
70. Connect the battery cables.
71. Remove the locking pin from the steering column.
72. Bleed the brake circuits.
73. Refill the engine, transaxle and cooling system with the correct amount of the appropriate fluids before starting the engine. Recharge the A/C system using approved recycling equipment.

EXHAUST MANIFOLD

REMOVAL & INSTALLATION

3.6L Engine

➡Spray the exhaust system fasteners with penetrating lubricant before removing them to help prevent broken studs and bolts. The use of a 6-point socket is highly recommended when removing exhaust system fasteners.

❋ CAUTION

To prevent serious burns, allow the exhaust manifold to cool down before attempting to remove it.

1. Before servicing the vehicle, refer to the Precautions Section.
2. Disconnect the negative battery cable.
3. Raise and support the vehicle safely on jackstands.
4. Disconnect the catalytic converter from the exhaust manifold.
5. Remove the heat shield.
6. On the left side, remove the upper insulator from the oil dipstick tube.
7. Remove the exhaust manifold.

To install:

8. Clean all gasket mating surfaces thoroughly.
9. Install a new exhaust manifold gasket and the exhaust manifold on the cylinder head. Start 2 bolts to hold the manifold in position.
10. Install the remaining bolts. Tighten the bolts to 18 ft. lbs. (25 Nm).
11. Raise and support the vehicle safely.
12. Connect the dual converter Y-pipe.
13. Install the heat shield.
14. Install the upper insulator on the left side.
15. Connect the negative battery cable.
16. Start the engine and check for exhaust leaks.

4.6L Engine

See Figure 91.

➡Spray the exhaust system fasteners with penetrating lubricant before removing them to help prevent broken studs and bolts. The use of a 6-point socket is highly recommended when removing exhaust system fasteners.

❋ CAUTION

To prevent serious burns, allow the exhaust manifold to cool down before attempting to remove it.

1. Before servicing the vehicle, refer to the Precautions Section.
2. Disconnect the negative battery cable.
3. Raise and support the vehicle safely on jackstands.
4. Disconnect the catalytic converter from the exhaust manifold.

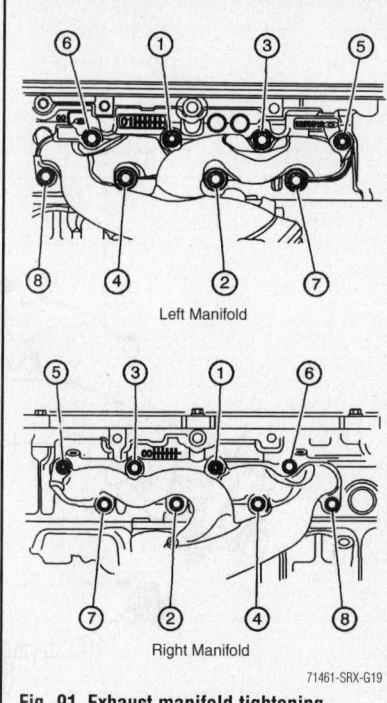

Fig. 91 Exhaust manifold tightening sequence—4.6L engine

5. Remove the heat shield.
6. Remove the exhaust manifold.

To install:

7. Clean all gasket mating surfaces thoroughly.
8. Install a new gasket and the exhaust manifold on the cylinder head.
9. Install the bolts. Tighten the bolts in the sequence shown to 18 ft. lbs. (25 Nm).
10. Install the heat shield.
11. Raise and support the vehicle safely on jackstands.
12. Connect the catalytic converter.
13. Lower the vehicle.
14. Connect the negative battery cable.
15. Start the engine and check for exhaust leaks.

INTAKE MANIFOLD

REMOVAL & INSTALLATION

3.6L Engine

See Figures 92 and 93.

1. Before servicing the vehicle, refer to the Precautions Section.
2. Relieve the fuel system pressure.
3. Drain the cooling system.
4. Remove or disconnect the following:
- Negative battery cable
- Engine cover
- Air intake assembly
- Brake booster hose
- Intake manifold brace

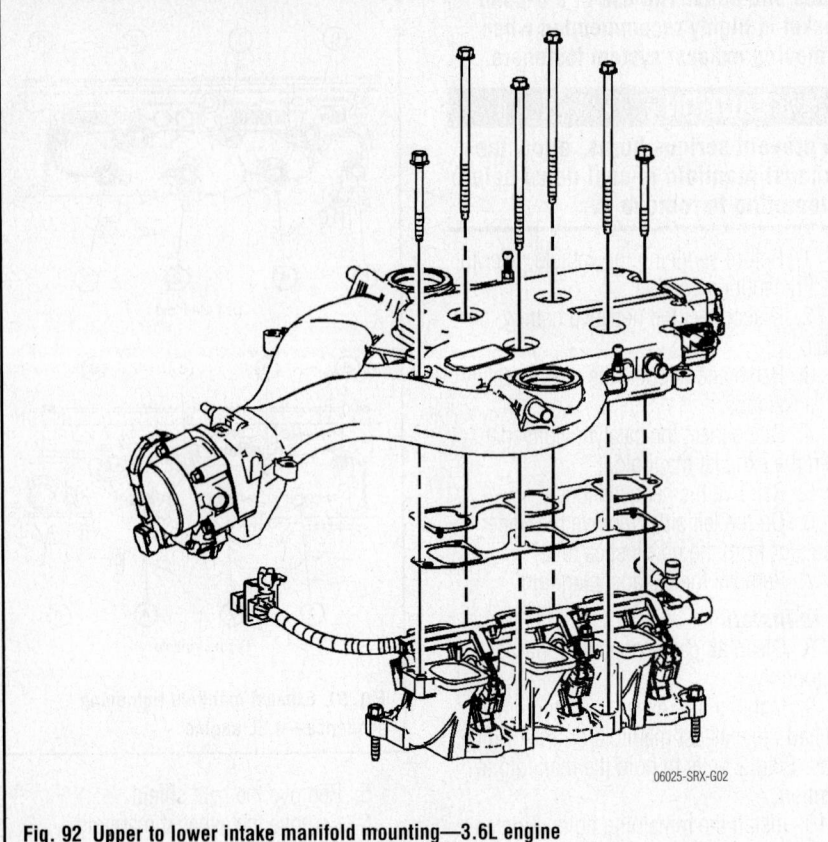

Fig. 92 Upper to lower intake manifold mounting—3.6L engine

06025-SRX-G02

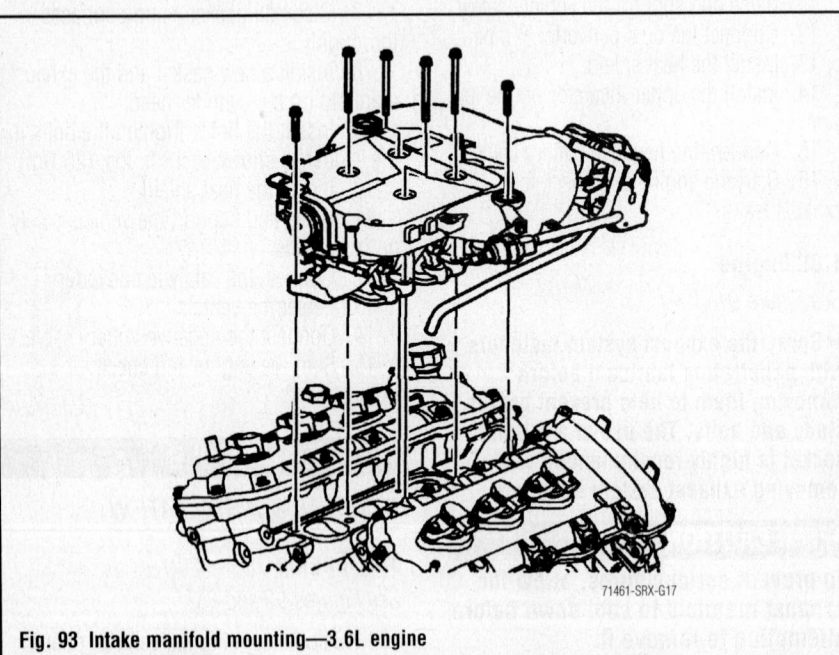

Fig. 93 Intake manifold mounting—3.6L engine

71461-SRX-G17

- PCV tube assembly
- EVAP hose
- EVAP solenoid
- All necessary electrical connectors
- Intake manifold mounting bolts
- Intake manifold

To install:

5. Installation is the reverse of the removal procedure, using the following torque specifications.
- New intake manifold gasket
- Upper-to-lower intake manifold bolts, if removed, to 17 ft. lbs. (23 Nm).

- Intake manifold bolts and tighten all bolts in a circular manner from the center outward to 17 ft. lbs. (23 Nm).
- Intake manifold brace–Bolt 1 to 89 inch lbs. (10 Nm). Bolt 2 to 48 ft. lbs. (65 Nm).

6. Fill and bleed the engine cooling system.

7. Connect the negative battery cable.

8. Start the engine and check for leaks.

4.6L Engine

See Figure 94.

1. Before servicing the vehicle, refer to the Precautions Section.

2. Drain the cooling system.

3. Relieve the fuel system pressure.

4. Remove or disconnect the following:
- Cross brace
- Engine cover/sight shield
- PCV air tubes
- Sight shield bracket
- Fuel rail and injector assembly
- Intake manifold retaining bolts
- Intake manifold

To install:

5. Lightly grease the inside edge of the rubber plenum duct.

6. Install new intake manifold gaskets and position the front of the manifold into the plenum duct.

7. Seat the manifold on the cylinder heads and install the manifold bolts.

8. Tighten the bolts in sequence to 89 inch lbs. (10 Nm).

9. Ensure the plenum duct is fully attached to the manifold, then install the plenum duct clamp.

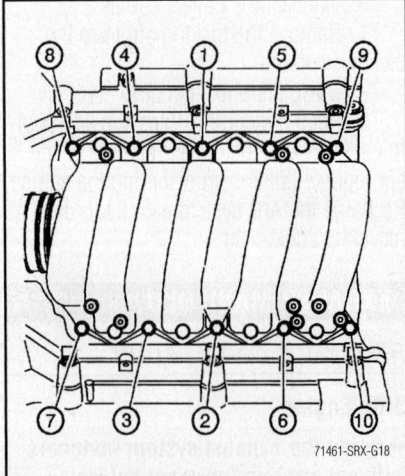

71461-SRX-G18

Fig. 94 Intake manifold tightening sequence—4.6L engine

10. Lightly lubricate the fuel injector bores with clean engine oil.

11. Install the fuel rail and injectors and tighten to 89 inch lbs. (10 Nm).

12. Install or connect the following.
- Sight shield bracket
- PCV air tubes

13. Fill and bleed the cooling system.

14. Start the engine and check for leaks.

MAIN BEARING BOLT TORQUE SEQUENCE

See Figures 95 through 99.

Refer to the accompanying illustrations for main bearing bolt tightening sequence.

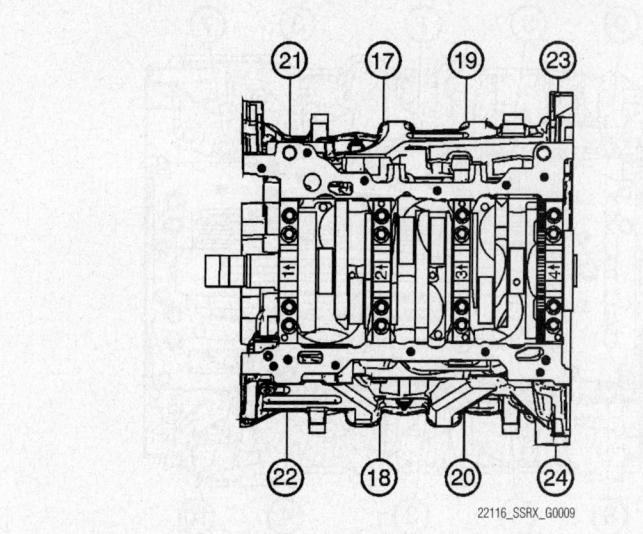

Fig. 97 Side main bearing bolt torque sequence—3.6L engine

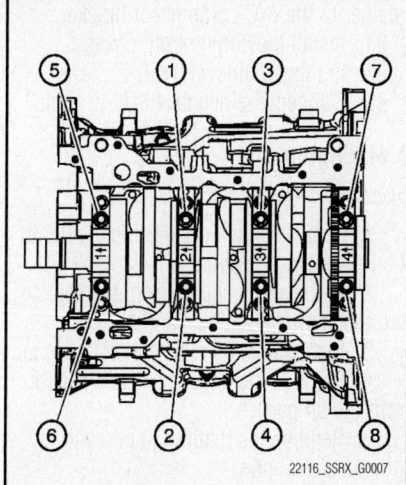

Fig. 95 Inner main bearing bolt torque sequence—3.6L engine

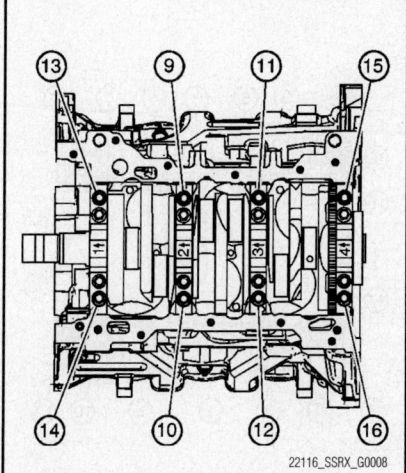

Fig. 96 Outer main bearing bolt torque sequence—3.6L engine

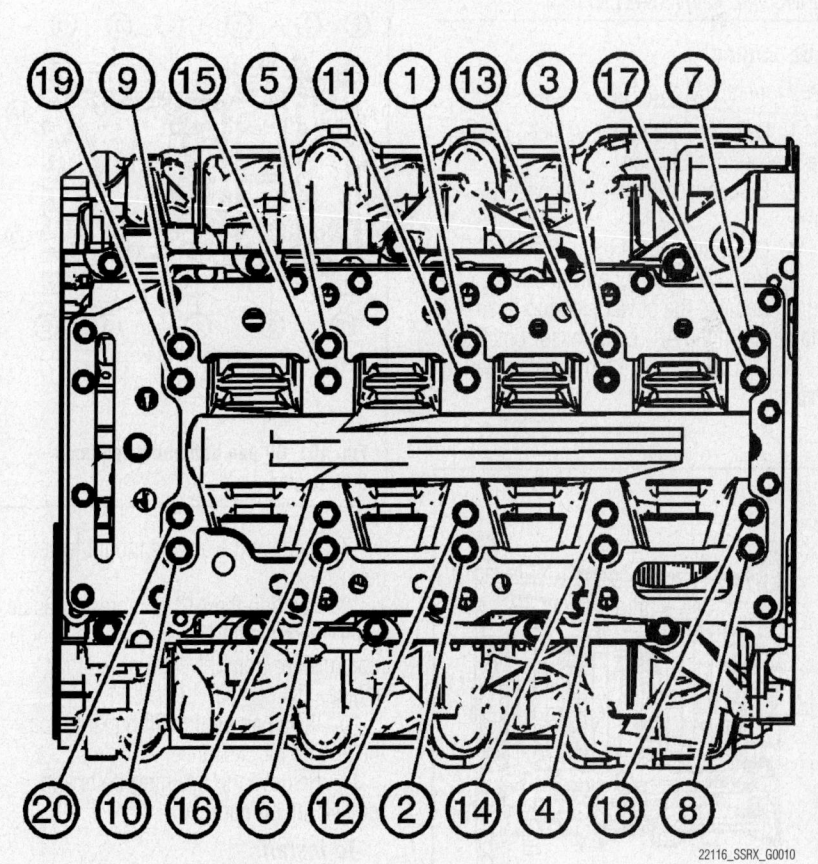

Fig. 98 Inner main bearing bolt torque sequence—4.6L engine

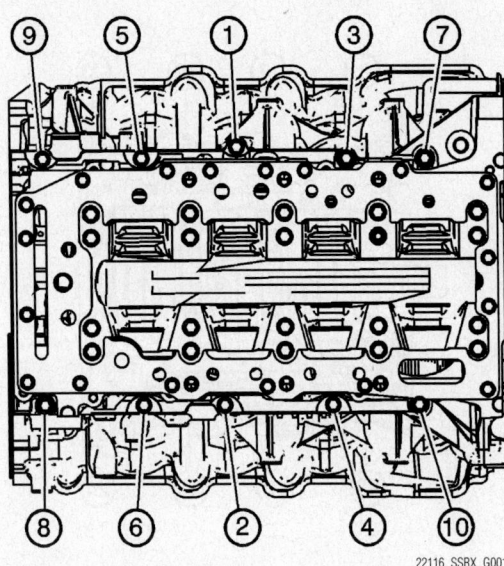

Fig. 99 Outer main bearing bolt torque sequence—4.6L engine

OIL PAN

REMOVAL & INSTALLATION

3.6L Engine

See Figures 100 and 101.

1. Before servicing the vehicle, refer to the Precautions Section.
2. Disconnect the negative battery cable.
3. Drain the engine oil.
4. Remove the engine front cover.
5. Remove the power steering hose retainer from the A/C compressor bracket.
6. Disconnect the intermediate steering shaft.

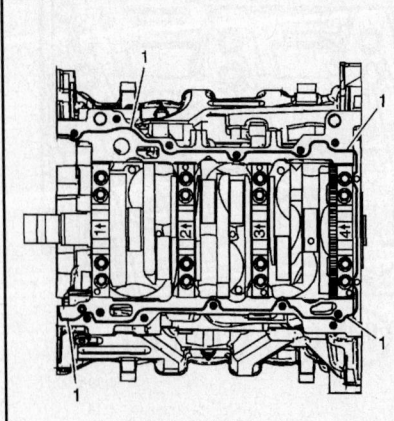

1. Sealant application areas

Fig. 100 Oil pan sealant application locations—3.6L engine

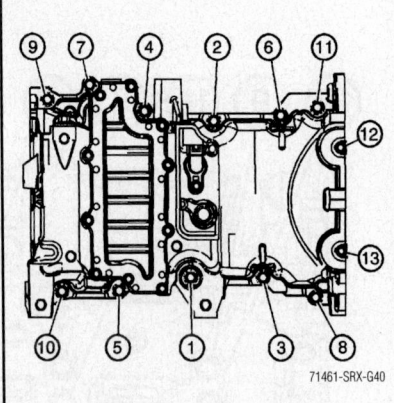

Fig. 101 Oil pan tightening sequence—3.6L engine

7. Remove the engine mount lower nuts.
8. Position the A/C compressor aside.
9. Remove the transmission oil cooler pipe retainer from the right side of the engine.
10. Install an engine lifting kit to raise the engine for clearance.
11. Remove the retaining bolts and remove the oil pan.

To install:

12. Clean the gasket mating surfaces thoroughly.
13. Trial fit the oil pan to the cylinder block. Ensure that enough clearance has been provided to allow the oil pan to be installed without sealant being scraped

off when pan is positioned under the engine.

14. Apply a bead of silicone sealer to the oil pan flange as shown.
15. Install the oil pan and loosely install the attaching bolts.
16. Tighten the bolts in sequence. Tighten bolts 1–11 to 17 ft. lbs. (23 Nm). Tighten bolts 11–12 to 89 inch lbs. (10 Nm).
17. Lower the engine to engage the engine mounts.
18. Remove the engine lift.
19. Install the transmission oil cooler pipe retainer to the right side of the engine.
20. Reposition the A/C compressor.
21. Install the engine mount lower nuts. Tighten the nuts to 59 ft. lbs. (80 Nm).
22. Connect the intermediate steering shaft.
23. Install the power steering hose retainer to the A/C compressor bracket.
24. Install the engine front cover.
25. Fill the engine with oil.
26. Connect the negative battery cable.

4.6L Engine

See Figure 102.

1. Before servicing the vehicle, refer to the Precautions Section.
2. Remove the engine from the vehicle and place on an engine stand.
3. Rotate the engine so the oil pan is up.
4. Remove the engine oil level sensor from the oil pan.
5. Remove the retaining bolts and remove the oil pan.

To install:

6. Clean the gasket mating surfaces thoroughly.

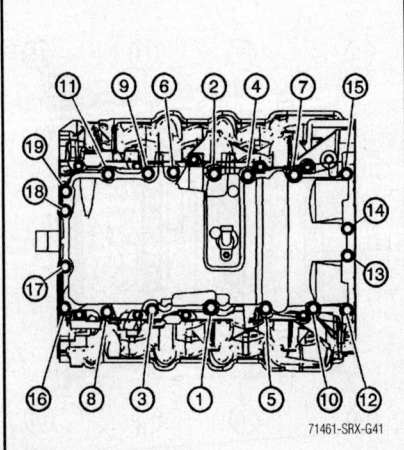

Fig. 102 Oil pan tightening sequence—4.6L engine

7. Install a new oil pan gasket.

8. Install the oil pan so it is flush within 0.020 inch (0.50mm) forward of the rear face of the block.

9. Install the oil pan and loosely install the attaching bolts.

10. Tighten the bolts in sequence as shown to 89 inch lbs. (10 Nm).

11. Install the oil level sensor.

OIL PUMP

REMOVAL & INSTALLATION

3.6L Engine

See Figure 103.

1. Before servicing the vehicle, refer to the Precautions Section.

2. Disconnect the negative battery cable.

3. Drain the engine oil.

4. Remove the primary timing chain.

5. Remove the crankshaft sprocket.

6. Remove the oil pump attaching bolts. Slide the oil pump from the crankshaft.

To install:

7. Install the oil pump so the rotor aligns with the crankshaft flats.

8. Tighten the oil pump retaining bolts to 17 ft. lbs. (23 Nm).

9. Install the crankshaft sprocket.

10. Install the primary timing chain.

11. Fill the engine with clean oil.

12. Connect the negative battery cable.

➡**Check for proper engine oil pressure immediately after starting the engine. If engine oil pressure is not within specification a few seconds after**

starting the engine, stop the engine and determine the reason for the low oil pressure condition. Running an engine with low oil pressure may result in serious engine damage.

13. Start the engine and check for leaks.

4.6L Engine

See Figure 104.

1. Before servicing the vehicle, refer to the Precautions Section.

2. Disconnect the negative battery cable.

3. Drain the engine oil.

4. Remove the engine front cover.

5. Remove the oil pump attaching bolts. Slide the oil pump from the crankshaft.

To install:

6. Install the oil pump drive spacer so the drive flat engages the pump rotor.

7. Tighten the oil pump retaining bolts and tighten in sequence to 89 inch lbs. (10 Nm), plus an additional 35°.

8. Install the engine front cover.

9. Fill the engine with clean oil.

10. Connect the negative battery cable.

➡**Check for proper engine oil pressure immediately after starting the engine. If engine oil pressure is not within specification a few seconds after**

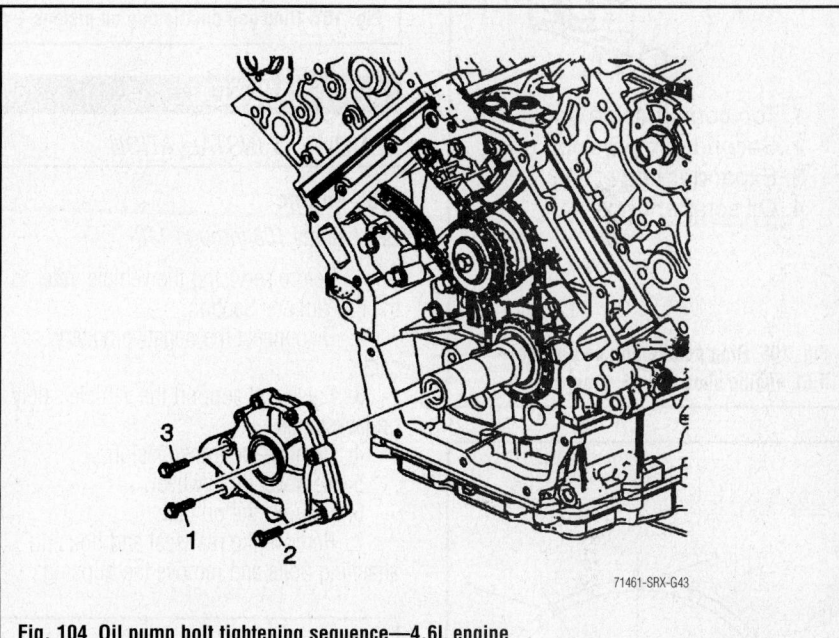

Fig. 104 Oil pump bolt tightening sequence—4.6L engine

starting the engine, stop the engine and determine the reason for the low oil pressure condition. Running an engine with low oil pressure may result in serious engine damage.

11. Start the engine and check for leaks.

INSPECTION

There are no serviceable components within the oil pump. Disassemble the pump only to diagnose an oiling concern. A disassembled oil pump must not be reused. A disassembled oil pump must be replaced.

PISTON AND RING

POSITIONING

See Figures 105 through 107.

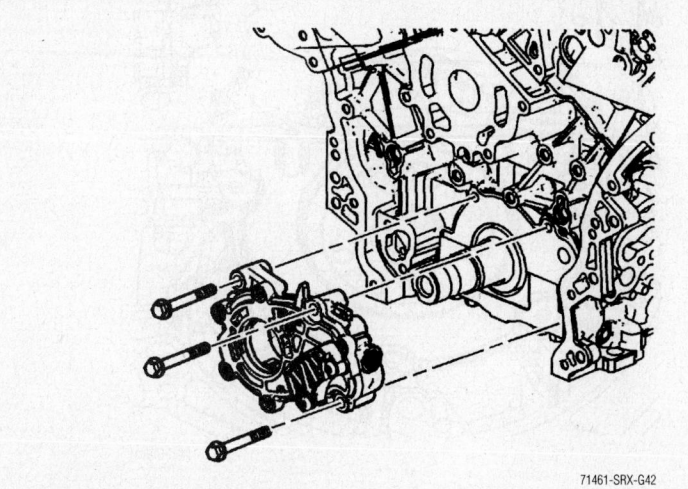

Fig. 103 Oil pump mounting—3.6L engine

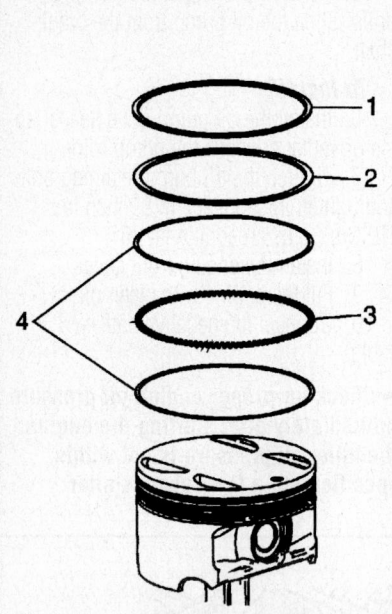

1. Top compression ring
2. Second compression ring
3. Expander ring
4. Oil scraper rings

71461-SRX-G59

Fig. 105 Ring positioning on pistons—3.6L engine shown; 4.6L similar

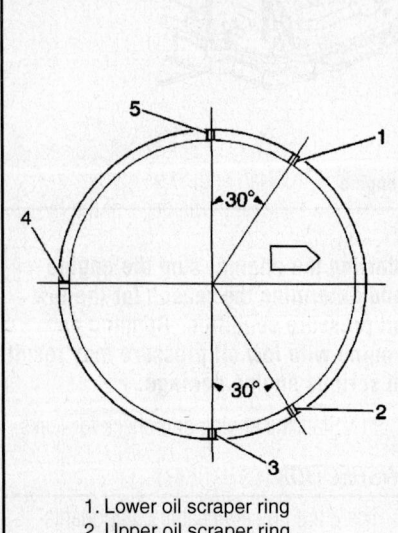

1. Lower oil scraper ring
2. Upper oil scraper ring
3. Top compression ring
4. Expander ring
5. Second compression ring

71461-SRX-G60

Fig. 106 Ring gap positioning on pistons—3.6L engine

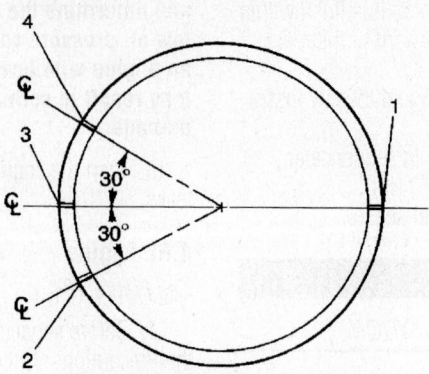

1. Expander and second compression ring
2. Upper oil scraper ring
3. Top compression ring
4. Lower oil scraper ring

71461-SRX-G61

Fig. 107 Ring gap positioning on pistons—4.6L engine

REAR MAIN SEAL

REMOVAL & INSTALLATION

3.6L Engine

See Figures 108 through 110.

1. Before servicing the vehicle, refer to the Precautions Section.
2. Disconnect the negative battery cable.
3. Raise and support the vehicle safely on jackstands.
4. Remove the transmission.
5. Remove the flywheel.
6. Remove the oil pan.
7. Remove the real seal and housing attaching bolts and remove the housing.

To install:

8. Install Crankshaft Rear Oil Seal Installation Tool EN-47839 onto the rear of the crankshaft flange.
9. Place a bead of RTV sealant around the seal housing mounting surface.
10. Install the seal housing and tighten the bolts to 89 inch lbs. (10 Nm).
11. Remove Installation Tool EN-47839.
12. Install the oil pan.
13. Install the flywheel. Tighten the NEW bolts to 22 ft. lbs. (30 Nm), plus an additional 45°.
14. Install the transmission.
15. Lower the vehicle and connect the battery.

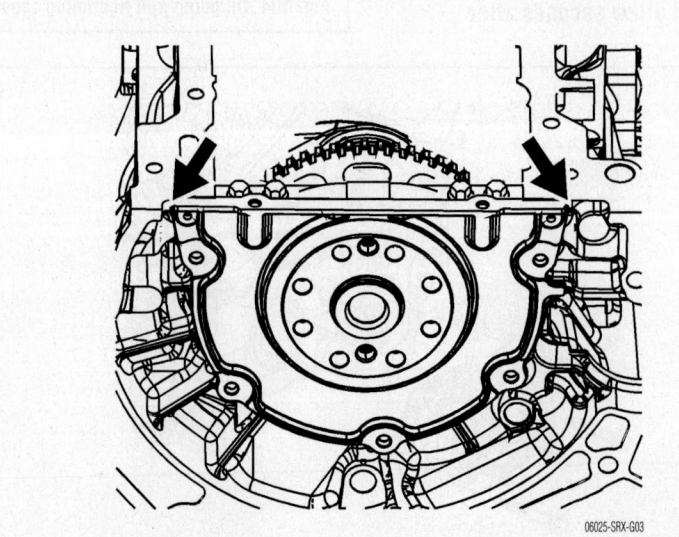

06025-SRX-G03

Fig. 108 Location of the pry points to remove the rear main seal—3.6L engine

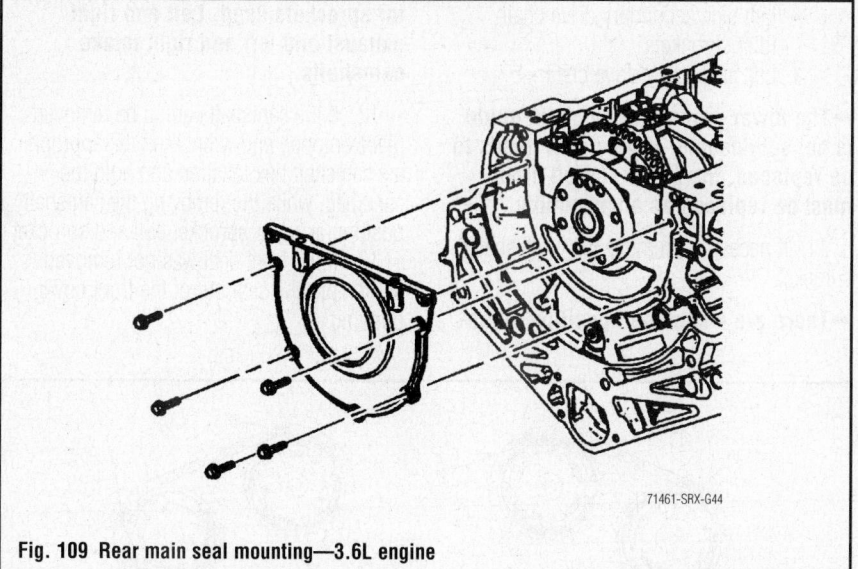

Fig. 109 Rear main seal mounting—3.6L engine

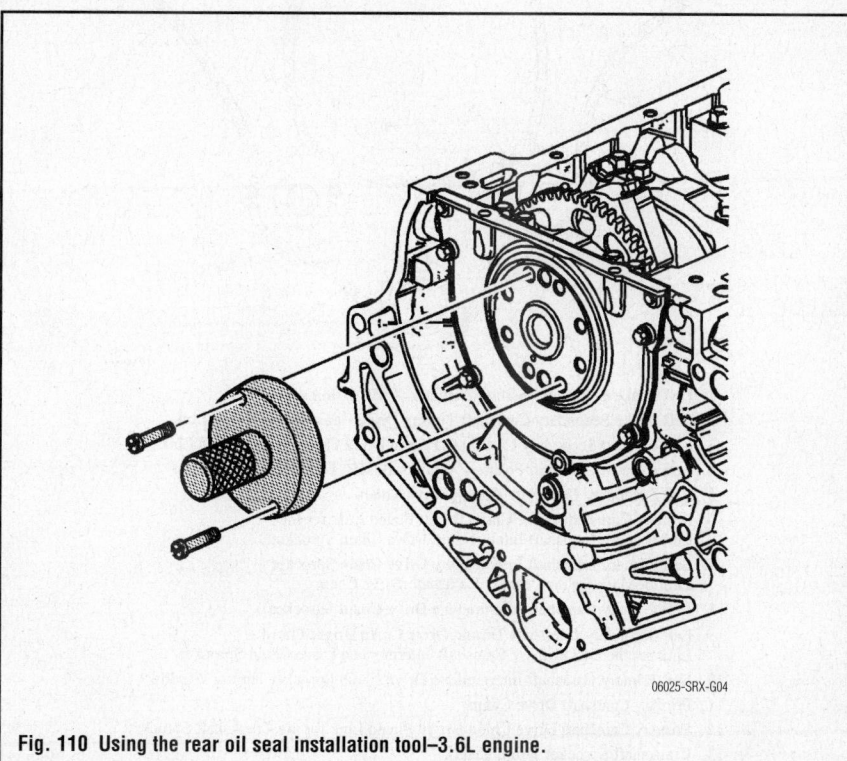

Fig. 110 Using the rear oil seal installation tool–3.6L engine.

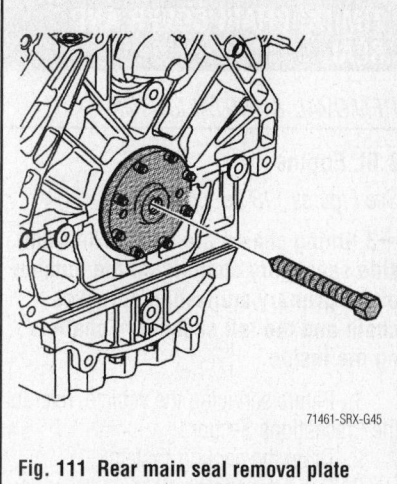

Fig. 111 Rear main seal removal plate and forcing screw—4.6L engine

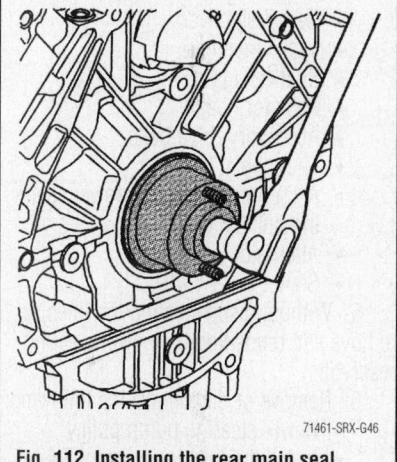

Fig. 112 Installing the rear main seal using tool J-45930—4.6L engine

4.6L Engine

See Figures 111 and 112.

1. Before servicing the vehicle, refer to the Precautions Section.
2. Disconnect the negative battery cable.
3. Remove the transmission.
4. Remove the flywheel.
5. Install seal remover J-42841 onto the seal using 2 retaining bolts.
6. Using a variable speed drill, screw in eight 1 inch (25mm) self-tapping screws into the holes in the seal remover. Reduce drill speed when screws start threading into the seal.
7. Remove seal remover retaining bolts.
8. Install a center forcing screw into the remover.
9. Using a socket wrench, tighten the center screw until the seal is pulled off the crankshaft.

To install:

10. Using a stiff piece of wire, clean the seal mounting area of any grease.
11. Place a small amount of gasket maker at the crankshaft split line across the end of the upper/lower crankcase seal.
12. Coat the outer diameter of the seal opening with clean engine oil.
13. Wipe the outer diameter of the flywheel flange clean.
14. Lubricate the outer rubber surface of the new seal with clean engine oil. Do not get any oil on the Green coating applied to the inner diameter of the seal.
15. Install the new seal onto mounting tool J-45930, and install the tool to the crankshaft.
16. Tighten 3 mounting bolts into the tool until the tool is firmly mounted.
17. Tighten the tool center bolt until the tool bottoms against the crankcase.
18. Remove the tool and inspect the seal mounting. The seal depth must be equal around the circumference. If the depth is not equal, reinstall the tool and repeat the procedure.
19. Install the flywheel and tighten the bolts to 11 ft. lbs. (15 Nm), plus an additional 50°.

TIMING CHAIN COVER AND SEAL

REMOVAL & INSTALLATION

3.6L Engine

See Figures 113 through 121.

➡**3 timing chains are used. The right side secondary chain is on the outside of the primary crankshaft sprocket chain and the left secondary chain is on the inside.**

1. Before servicing the vehicle, refer to the Precautions Section.
2. Drain the cooling system.
3. Drain the engine oil.
4. Remove or disconnect the following:
   - Negative battery cable
   - Engine appearance cover
   - Camshaft covers
   - Intake manifold
   - Spark plugs
   - Radiator hoses
   - Accessory drive belts
   - Thermostat housing
   - A/C compressor and power steering belt tensioners
   - Alternator
   - Starter
5. Without disconnecting the lines, remove and reposition the power steering reservoir.
6. Remove or disconnect the following:
   - Power steering pump pulley
   - Install flywheel locking tool EN-46106 in the starter mounting holes
   - Crankshaft damper bolt
   - Using a gear puller, remove the crankshaft damper
7. To remove the front seal only, pry the seal out of the front cover opening.
8. Remove or disconnect the following:
   - 4 Camshaft Position (CMP) sensors
   - 4 CMP actuator solenoids
   - Water pump pulley
   - Front cover bolts, cover and gasket
9. Ensure the engine is placed in the Stage 2 timing drive chain alignment position as shown.
10. Remove or disconnect the following:
    - Right side secondary drive chain tensioners, guides and shoes
    - Right secondary drive chain
    - Primary drive chain tensioner and upper guide
    - Primary drive chain
    - Right side secondary drive chain idler sprockets
    - Left side secondary drive chain tensioners, guides and shoes
    - Left side secondary drive chain idler sprockets
    - Left secondary drive chain

➡**The lower primary drive chain guide is not serviceable. If the guide needs to be replaced, the guide and oil pump must be replaced as an assembly.**

11. If necessary, remove the crankshaft sprocket.

➡**There are 4 camshaft position actuator sprockets used. Left and right exhaust and left and right intake camshafts.**

12. If the camshafts are to be removed, place an open end wrench on the appropriate camshaft hex location and hold the camshaft, while the removing the camshaft position actuator sprocket bolt and sprocket.

13. If the front seal was not removed earlier, pry the seal out of the front cover opening.

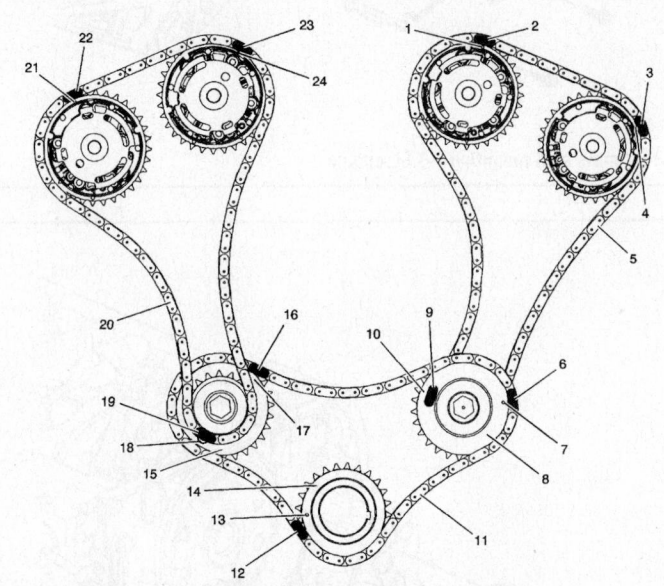

1. Left Intake Camshaft Position Actuator (CMP) Timing Mark
2. Left Intake Secondary Camshaft Timing Drive Chain Bright Plated Link
3. Left Exhaust Secondary Camshaft Timing Drive Chain Bright Plated Link
4. Left Exhaust Camshaft Position Actuator (CMP) Timing Mark
5. Left Secondary Camshaft Timing Drive Chain
6. Primary Camshaft Drive Chain Bright Plated Link for the Left Primary Camshaft Intermediate Drive Chain Sprocket
7. Left Primary Camshaft Intermediate Drive Chain Sprocket Timing Mark for the Primary Camshaft Drive Chain
8. Left Primary Camshaft Intermediate Drive Chain Sprocket
9. Left Secondary Camshaft Timing Drive Chain Bright Plated Link for the Left Primary Camshaft Intermediate Drive Chain Sprocket
10. Left Primary Camshaft Intermediate Drive Chain Sprocket Timing Window
11. Primary Camshaft Drive Chain
12. Primary Camshaft Drive Chain Bright Plated Link for the Crankshaft Sprocket
13. Crankshaft Sprocket Timing Mark
14. Crankshaft Sprocket
15. Right Primary Camshaft Intermediate Drive Chain Sprocket
16. Primary Camshaft Drive Chain Bright Plated Link for the Right Primary Camshaft Intermediate Drive Chain Sprocket
17. Right Primary Camshaft Intermediate Drive Chain Sprocket Timing Mark for the Primary Camshaft Drive Chain
18. Right Primary Camshaft Intermediate Drive Chain Sprocket Timing Mark/Window for the Right Secondary Camshaft Timing Drive Chain
19. Right Secondary Camshaft Timing Drive Chain Bright Plated Link for the Right Primary Camshaft Intermediate Drive Chain Sprocket
20. Right Secondary Camshaft Timing Drive Chain
21. Right Exhaust Camshaft Position Actuator (CMP) Timing Mark
22. Right Exhaust Secondary Camshaft Timing Drive Chain Bright Plated Link
23. Right Intake Camshaft Position Actuator (CMP) Timing Mark
24. Right Intake Camshaft Position Actuator (CMP) Timing Mark

71461-SRX-G47

Fig. 113 Stage 2 timing drive chain alignment position—3.6L engine

To install:

14. Clean all the gasket mating surfaces.

15. If the camshafts were removed, install the camshafts using the procedure described under Camshafts.

16. Install the camshaft position actuator sprockets and tighten the bolts to 43 ft. lbs. (58 Nm).

17. If the front cover was removed, use a seal installer and install a new front seal into the front cover opening.

18. If removed, install the crankshaft sprocket with the timing mark out and placed in the Stage 1 timing drive position.

19. Install camshaft holding tools EN-46105 on the camshaft rear flats to hold them in position.

20. Install the left side secondary drive chain idler sprockets with the part number outs and the larger sprocket on the outside. Tighten the bolt to 48 ft. lbs. (65 Nm).

21. Install the left secondary timing chain on the inner idler sprocket with the bright plate chain drive link aligned with the hole in the outer sprocket as shown.

22. Place the timing chain around the camshaft sprockets and ensure there are 7 links between the bright links as shown.

23. There will be 18 darkened links between the left camshaft intermediate drive chain idler bright plated secondary camshaft drive chain link and each left camshaft position actuator sprocket bright plated secondary camshaft drive chain link.

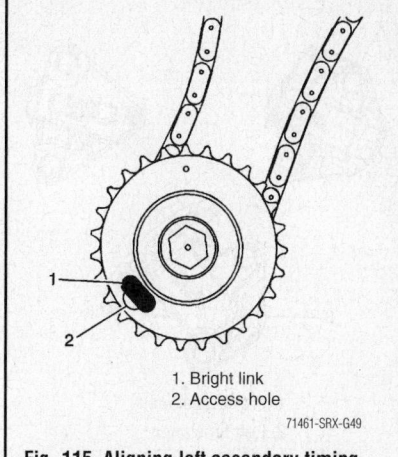

1. Bright link
2. Access hole

71461-SRX-G49

Fig. 115 Aligning left secondary timing chain to lower idler sprocket—3.6L engine

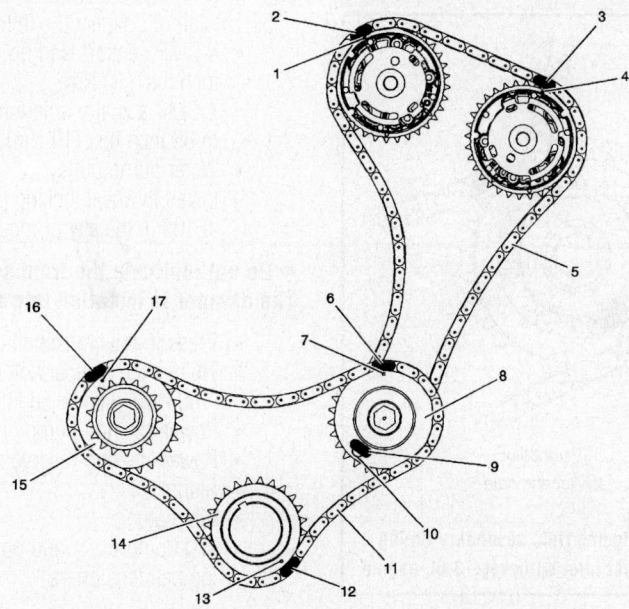

1. Left Intake Camshaft Position Actuator (CMP) Timing Mark
2. Left Intake Secondary Camshaft Timing Drive Chain Bright Plated Link
3. Left Exhaust Secondary Camshaft Timing Drive Chain Bright Plated Link
4. Left Exhaust Camshaft Position Actuator (CMP) Timing Mark
5. Left Secondary Camshaft Timing Drive Chain
6. Primary Camshaft Drive Chain Bright Plated Link for the Left Primary Camshaft Intermediate Drive Chain Sprocket
7. Left Primary Camshaft Intermediate Drive Chain Sprocket Timing Mark for the Primary Camshaft Drive Chain
8. Left Primary Camshaft Intermediate Drive Chain Sprocket
9. Left Secondary Camshaft Timing Drive Chain Bright Plated Link for the Left Primary Camshaft Intermediate Drive Chain Sprocket
10. Left Primary Camshaft Intermediate Drive Chain Sprocket Timing Window for the Left Secondary Camshaft Timing Drive Chain Bright Plated Link
11. Primary Camshaft Drive Chain
12. Primary Camshaft Drive Chain Bright Plated Link for the Crankshaft Sprocket
13. Crankshaft Sprocket Timing Mark
14. Crankshaft Sprocket
15. Right Primary Camshaft Intermediate Drive Chain Sprocket
16. Primary Camshaft Drive Chain Bright Plated Link for the Right Primary Camshaft Intermediate Drive Chain Sprocket
17. Right Primary Camshaft Intermediate Drive Chain Sprocket Timing Mark

71461-SRX-G48

Fig. 114 Stage 1 timing drive chain alignment position—3.6L engine

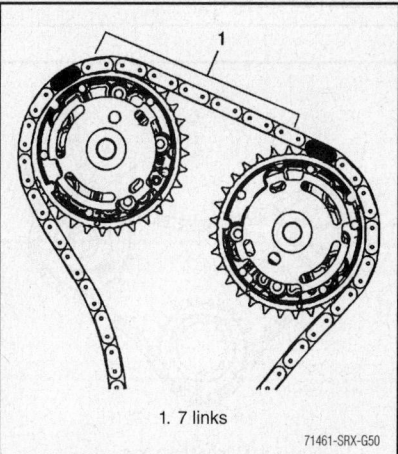

1. 7 links

71461-SRX-G50

Fig. 116 Aligning left secondary timing chain to camshaft sprockets—3.6L engine

24. Ensure that the correct tensioner is installed in the correct positions as shown.

25. Using tensioner tool J-45027 reset the left tensioner plunger.

26. Install the plunger in the tensioner body and lock it in place with a paper clip.

27. Release the pressure on the tensioner and ensure it remains compressed.

28. Install a new gasket on the tensioner, install the tensioner and tighten the bolts to 17 ft. lbs. (23 Nm).

29. Install the left side chain guide and chain shoe and tighten the bolts to 17 ft. lbs. (23 Nm).

30. Install the right side secondary drive chain idler sprockets with the part number outs and the larger sprocket on the outside. Tighten the bolt to 48 ft. lbs. (65 Nm).

31. Place the primary timing chain around the camshaft idler sprockets and crankshaft sprocket with the links and timing marks aligned as shown.

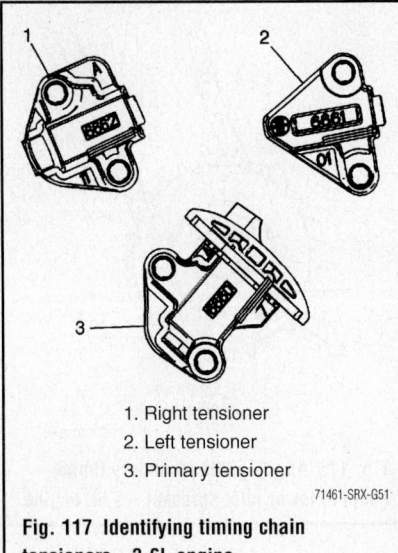

1. Right tensioner
2. Left tensioner
3. Primary tensioner

71461-SRX-G51

Fig. 117 Identifying timing chain tensioners—3.6L engine

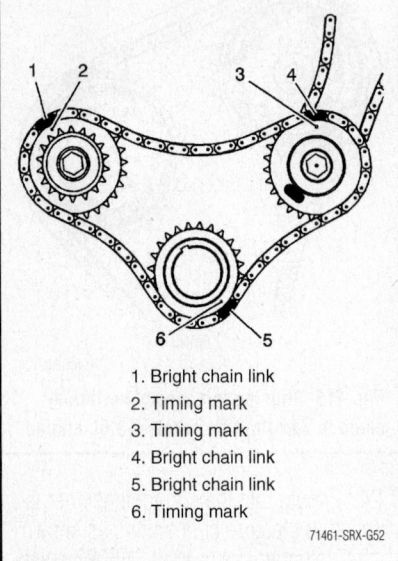

1. Bright chain link
2. Timing mark
3. Timing mark
4. Bright chain link
5. Bright chain link
6. Timing mark

71461-SRX-G52

Fig. 118 Aligning primary timing chain to camshaft idler and crankshaft sprockets—3.6L engine

32. Using tensioner tool J-45027 reset the primary tensioner plunger.

33. Install the plunger in the tensioner body and lock it in place with a paper clip.

34. Release the pressure on the tensioner and ensure it remains compressed.

35. Install a new gasket on the tensioner, install the tensioner and tighten the bolts to 44 inch lbs. (5 Nm) and then a final pass of 17 ft. lbs. (23 Nm).

36. Release the tension on the primary tensioner, and ensure the primary and left side timing chains are in the Stage 1 position.

37. Remove the camshaft holding tool from the left camshafts.

38. Rotate the crankshaft sprocket clockwise from the Stage 1 to the Stage 2 posi-

tion. The rotation is approximately 15 degrees.

39. Install the right secondary timing chain on the outer idler sprocket with the bright plate chain drive link aligned with the hole in the inner sprocket as shown.

40. Place the timing chain around the camshaft sprockets and ensure there are 7 links between the bright links as shown.

41. There will be 18 darkened links between the right camshaft intermediate drive chain idler bright plated secondary camshaft drive chain link and each right camshaft position actuator sprocket bright plated secondary camshaft drive chain link.

42. Using tensioner tool J-45027 reset the right tensioner plunger.

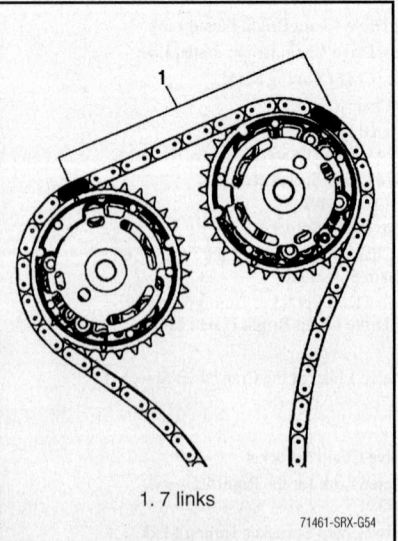

1. Bright link
2. Access hole

71461-SRX-G53

Fig. 119 Aligning right secondary timing chain to lower idler sprocket—3.6L engine

1. 7 links

71461-SRX-G54

Fig. 120 Aligning right secondary timing chain to camshaft sprockets—3.6L engine

43. Install the plunger in the tensioner body and lock it in place with a paper clip.

44. Release the pressure on the tensioner and ensure it remains compressed.

45. Install a new gasket on the tensioner, install the tensioner and tighten the bolts to 17 ft. lbs. (23 Nm).

46. Install the right side chain guide and chain shoe and tighten the bolts to 17 ft. lbs. (23 Nm).

47. Verify the timing chains are aligned in the Stage 2 timing drive chain alignment position as shown.

48. Install a new front cover-to-cylinder block seal.

49. Place a bead of RTV sealant onto the front cover as shown.

50. Install the front cover and tighten the bolts to 17 ft. lbs. (23 Nm).

51. Install or connect the following:
- 4 CMP sensors and tighten to 89 inch lbs. (10 Nm).
- 4 CMP actuator solenoids tighten to 89 inch lbs. (10 Nm).
- Water pump pulley
- Install flywheel locking tool EN-46106 in the starter mounting holes

➡ **Do not lubricate the front seal bore. The damper is installed into a dry bore.**

- Press in the crankshaft damper
- Tighten the damper bolt to 74 ft. lbs. (100 Nm), plus an additional 150°.
- Power steering pump pulley
- Power steering reservoir
- Starter
- Alternator
- A/C compressor and power steering belt tensioners

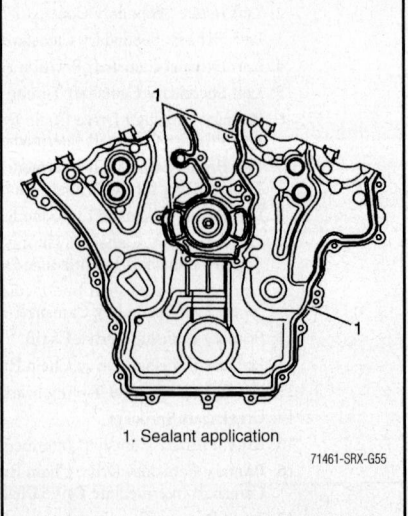

1. Sealant application

71461-SRX-G55

Fig. 121 Front cover sealant application areas—3.6L engine

- Thermostat housing
- Accessory drive belts
- Radiator hoses
- Spark plugs
- Intake manifold
- Camshaft covers
- Engine appearance cover
- Negative battery cable

52. Fill the cooling system to the correct level.

53. Fill the engine with oil to the correct level.

54. Start the engine and verify proper operation.

4.6L Engine

See Figures 122 through 124.

➡**3 timing chains are used. The right side secondary chain is on the outside, the left secondary chain is in the middle and the primary chain is on the inside of the camshaft intermediate sprocket.**

1. Before servicing the vehicle, refer to the Precautions Section.
2. Drain the cooling system.
3. Drain the engine oil.
4. Remove or disconnect the following:
   - Negative battery cable
   - Radiator hoses
   - Camshaft covers
   - Accessory drive belts
   - Drive belt tensioners
   - Drive belt idler pulley
   - Water pump pulley
   - Fan adapter, if equipped
   - Starter
   - Water pump pulley
5. Install a flywheel holding tool in the starter mounting holes.
6. Remove or disconnect the following:
   - Crankshaft damper bolt
   - Using a puller, remove the crankshaft damper
   - Engine front cover and gasket
   - Oil pump
7. Rotate the crankshaft until the primary timing marks are aligned as shown.
8. Remove or disconnect the following:
   - Right side Camshaft Position (CMP) sensors
   - Right side CMP solenoids.
   - Right side CMP actuator housings
   - Install camshaft holding tool EN-46328 on the right side camshafts
   - Right side timing chain tensioner
9. Place an open end wrench on the exhaust camshaft hex to hold the camshaft and remove the oil control valve.

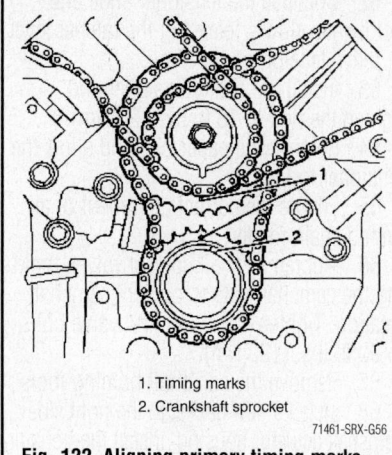

1. Timing marks
2. Crankshaft sprocket

71461-SRX-G56

Fig. 122 Aligning primary timing marks— 4.6L engine

10. Slide the right exhaust camshaft position actuator off of the camshaft and remove the secondary timing chain from the actuator.

11. Place an open end wrench on the intake camshaft hex to hold the camshaft and remove the oil control valve.

12. Slide the right intake camshaft position actuator off of the camshaft and remove the secondary timing chain from the actuator.

13. Remove the timing chain.

14. Remove the timing chain guide and shoe.

15. Remove or disconnect the following:
   - Left side Camshaft Position (CMP) sensors
   - Left side CMP actuator solenoids
   - Left side CMP actuator housings
   - Install camshaft holding tool EN-46328 on the left side camshafts
   - Left side timing chain tensioner

16. Place an open end wrench on the exhaust camshaft hex to hold the camshaft and remove the oil control valve.

17. Slide the left exhaust camshaft position actuator off of the camshaft and remove the secondary timing chain from the actuator.

18. Place an open end wrench on the intake camshaft hex to hold the camshaft and remove the oil control valve.

19. Slide the left intake camshaft position actuator off of the camshaft and remove the secondary timing chain from the actuator.

20. Remove the timing chain.

21. Remove the timing chain guide and shoe.

22. Remove the primary timing chain tensioner.

23. Remove the oil outlet tube.

24. Remove the camshaft intermediate sprocket bolt.

25. Remove the primary timing drive chain guide.

26. Remove the intermediate sprocket, primary drive chain and crankshaft sprocket as an assembly.

27. Pry the front seal from the timing cover.

To install:

28. Clean all the gasket mating surfaces.

29. Using a seal installer, press in a new front crankshaft seal into the front cover.

30. Align the intermediate and crankshaft sprocket timing marks so they are vertical as shown.

31. Install the primary timing chain around the intermediate and crankshaft sprockets,

32. Verify that the no. 1 piston is at TDC and the crankshaft keyway is at about the 5° ATDC position.

33. Install the intermediate/crankshaft sprocket/timing chain assembly onto the crankshaft and camshaft driveshafts.

34. Install the intermediate sprocket bolt and tighten to 44 ft. lbs. (60 Nm).

35. Install the primary drive chain guide and tighten the bolts to 18 ft. lbs. (25 Nm).

36. Holding the primary drive chain tensioner in one hand, rotate the ratchet release lever counterclockwise with the other hand and place a paper clip to hold it.

37. Collapse the tensioner shoe and hold while slowly releasing the ratchet lever to relive tension on the shoe.

38. Install the chain tensioner and tighten the bolt to 18 ft. lbs. (25 Nm).

39. Remove the paper clip and allow the tensioner to load.

40. Install the oil outlet tube and tighten the bolts to 89 inch lbs. (10 Nm).

41. Install the left side drive chain guide and shoe and tighten the bolts to 18 ft. lbs. (25 Nm).

42. Guide the left timing chain through the cylinder head and onto the inner row of the intermediate drive chain sprocket teeth.

43. Install the left camshaft position actuators into the drive chain.

44. Install the camshaft sprockets on the camshafts.

➡**Ensure the camshaft sprockets notches marked LI or LE engage the proper camshaft pins.**

45. Loosely install the actuator oil control valves.

46. Verify that the camshaft sprocket notches and the camshaft pins are 90° perpendicular to each other.

47. Install camshaft locking tool J-46328 to the left camshafts.

48. Install the upper drive chain shoe guide bolt and then tighten the upper and lower bolts to 18 ft. lbs. (25 Nm).

49. Holding the left drive chain tensioner in one hand, rotate the ratchet release lever counterclockwise with the other hand and place a paper clip to hold it.

50. Collapse the tensioner shoe and hold while slowly releasing the ratchet lever to relive tension on the shoe.

51. Install the chain tensioner and tighten the bolt to 18 ft. lbs. (25 Nm).

52. Remove the paper clip and allow the tensioner to load.

53. Install the right side drive chain guide and shoe and tighten the bolts to 18 ft. lbs. (25 Nm).

54. Guide the right timing chain through the cylinder head and onto the outer row of the intermediate drive chain sprocket teeth.

55. Install the right camshaft position actuators into the drive chain.

56. Install the camshaft sprockets on the camshafts.

➡**Ensure the camshaft sprockets notches marked RI or RE engage the proper camshaft pins.**

57. Loosely install the actuator oil control valves.

58. Verify that the camshaft sprocket notches and the camshaft pins are 90° perpendicular to each other.

59. Install camshaft locking tool J-46328 to the right camshafts.

60. Install the upper drive chain shoe guide bolt and then tighten the upper and lower bolts to 18 ft. lbs. (25 Nm).

61. Holding the right drive chain tensioner in one hand, rotate the ratchet release lever counterclockwise with the other hand and place a paper clip to hold it.

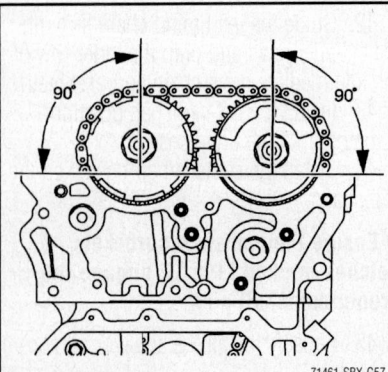

Fig. 123 Aligning left camshaft sprocket marks and camshaft pin marks—4.6L engine; right side similar

62. Collapse the tensioner shoe and hold while slowly releasing the ratchet lever to relive tension on the shoe.

63. Install the chain tensioner and tighten the bolt to 18 ft. lbs. (25 Nm).

64. Remove the paper clip and allow the tensioner to load.

65. Ensure the correct alignment of all timing chain marks.

66. Tighten all 4 oil control valves, holding the camshaft flats to prevent camshaft rotation. Tighten the oil control valve bolts to 90 ft. lbs. (120 Nm).

67. Remove the camshaft holding tools.

68. Install a new gasket to the right side camshaft actuator housing, install the housing and tighten the bolts to 89 inch lbs. (10 Nm).

➡**The camshaft position actuators solenoids must be precisely aligned to the camshaft position actuator oil control valves on the ends of the camshafts. This is done with an alignment pin. Failure to align the solenoids correctly can lead to poor engine performance and component damage.**

69. Fabricate an alignment pin using a 15/64 inch drill bit at least 2 inches long.

70. Verify the alignment pin will pass through intake actuator solenoid alignment hole and the control valve alignment hole.

71. Apply a bead of RTV sealant around the actuator solenoid flange.

72. Install the actuator over the oil control valve and insert the alignment pin to align the valve to the solenoid.

73. Tighten the actuator solenoid bolts to 71 inch lbs. (8 Nm).

74. Install a new actuator solenoid plug.

75. Repeat this procedure on the right exhaust actuator solenoid, and both left side actuator solenoids.

76. Install the oil pump.

77. Clean the front cover gasket surface.

78. Place a small amount of sealant to the split line of the upper and lower crankcases and the top edge of the block face.

79. Install a new front cover gasket over the crankcase dowel pins.

80. Install the front cover and hand tighten the bolts.

81. Tighten the front cover bolts in the sequence shown to 106 inch lbs. (12 Nm).

82. Install the 4 CMP sensors and tighten to 89 inch lbs. (10 Nm).

83. Install the camshaft covers.

84. Press the crankshaft damper on.

85. Coat the damper bolt with clean engine oil, install the bolt and tighten to 37 ft. lbs. (50 Nm), plus an additional 120°.

86. Remove the crankshaft holding tool from the starter opening and install the starter.

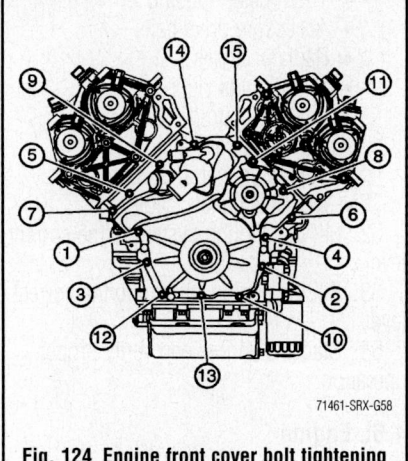

Fig. 124 Engine front cover bolt tightening sequence—4.6L engine

87. Install the water pump pulley and tighten the bolts to 89 inch lbs. (10 Nm).

88. Install the drive belt idler pulley and tighten to 37 ft. lbs. (50 Nm).

89. Install or connect the following:
- Fan adapter, if equipped
- Drive belt tensioners
- Accessory drive belts
- Radiator hoses
- Engine appearance cover
- Air outlet duct
- Negative battery cable

90. Fill the cooling system to the correct level.

91. Fill the engine with oil to the correct level.

92. Start the engine and verify proper operation.

TIMING CHAIN AND SPROCKETS

REMOVAL & INSTALLATION

3.6L Engine

Primary

See Figure 125.

1. Before servicing the vehicle, refer to the Precautions Section.

2. Remove the spark plugs in order to ease crankshaft/engine rotation.

3. Remove the engine front cover.

4. Remove the right bank secondary camshaft drive chain tensioner.

5. Remove the right bank secondary camshaft drive chain shoe.

6. Remove the right bank secondary camshaft drive chain guide.

7. Remove the right bank secondary camshaft drive chain.

8. Remove the primary camshaft drive chain tensioner.

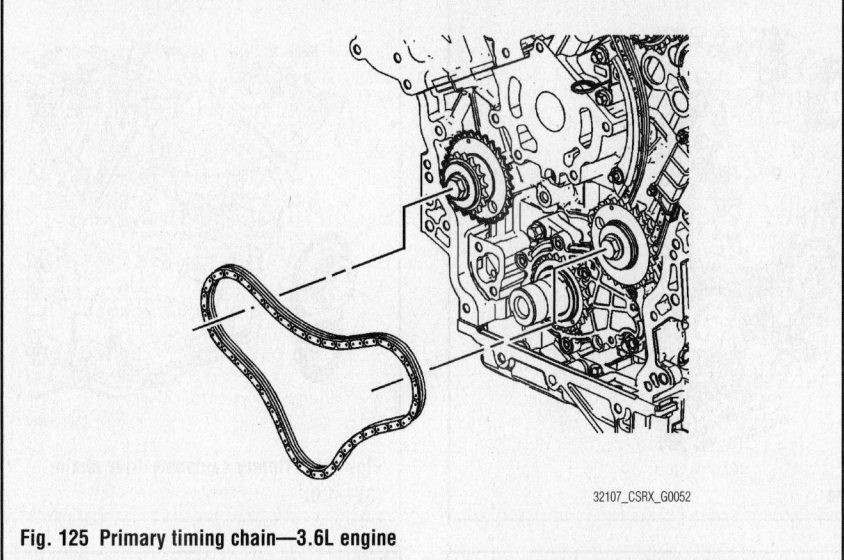

Fig. 125 Primary timing chain—3.6L engine

32107_CSRX_G0052

9. Remove the primary camshaft drive chain upper guide.

10. Remove the primary camshaft timing chain.

To install:

11. Install the primary camshaft timing chain.

12. Install the primary upper camshaft drive chain guide.

13. Install the primary camshaft drive chain tensioner.

14. Install the right bank secondary camshaft drive chain.

15. Install the right bank secondary camshaft drive chain guide.

16. Install the right bank secondary camshaft drive chain shoe.

17. Install the right bank secondary camshaft drive chain tensioner.

18. Install the spark plugs.

19. Install the engine front cover.

Left Secondary

See Figure 126.

1. Before servicing the vehicle, refer to the Precautions Section.

2. Remove the spark plugs in order to ease crankshaft/engine rotation.

3. Remove the engine front cover.

4. Remove the right bank secondary camshaft drive chain tensioner.

5. Remove the right bank secondary camshaft drive chain shoe.

6. Remove the right bank secondary camshaft drive chain guide.

7. Remove the right bank secondary camshaft drive chain.

8. Remove the primary camshaft drive chain tensioner.

9. Remove the primary upper camshaft drive chain guide.

10. Remove the primary camshaft drive chain.

11. Remove the right bank camshaft intermediate drive chain idler.

12. Remove the left bank secondary camshaft drive chain tensioner.

13. Remove the left bank secondary camshaft drive chain shoe.

14. Remove the left bank secondary camshaft drive chain guide.

15. Remove the left bank camshaft intermediate drive chain idler.

16. Remove the left bank secondary camshaft drive chain.

17. Clean and inspect all of the camshaft timing drive components. Replace components as necessary.

To install:

18. Install the left bank secondary camshaft drive chain.

19. Install the left bank camshaft intermediate drive chain idler.

20. Install the left bank secondary camshaft drive chain guide.

21. Install the left bank secondary camshaft drive chain shoe.

22. Install the left bank secondary camshaft drive chain tensioner.

23. Install the right bank camshaft intermediate drive chain idler.

24. Install the primary camshaft drive chain.

25. Install the primary upper camshaft drive chain guide.

26. Install the primary camshaft drive chain tensioner.

27. Install the right bank secondary camshaft drive chain.

28. Install the right bank secondary camshaft drive chain guide.

29. Install the right bank secondary camshaft drive chain shoe.

30. Install the right bank secondary camshaft drive chain tensioner.

31. Install the spark plugs.

32. Install the engine front cover.

Right Secondary

See Figure 127.

1. Before servicing the vehicle, refer to the Precautions Section.

2. Remove the spark plugs in order to ease crankshaft/engine rotation.

3. Remove the engine front cover.

4. Remove the right bank secondary camshaft drive chain tensioner.

5. Remove the right bank secondary camshaft drive chain shoe.

6. Remove the right bank secondary camshaft drive chain guide.

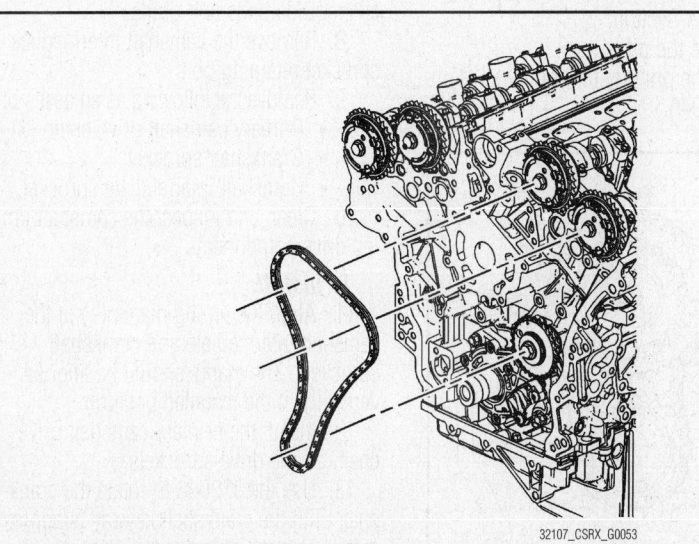

Fig. 126 Left secondary timing chain—3.6L engine

32107_CSRX_G0053

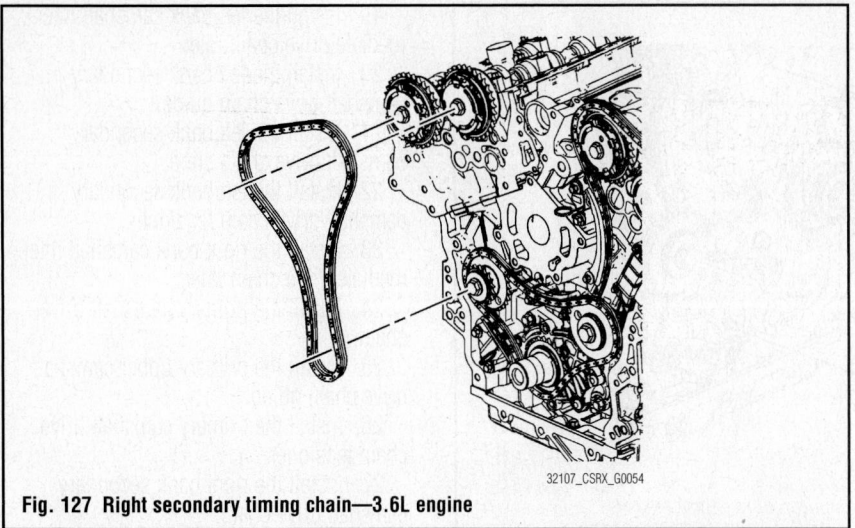

Fig. 127 Right secondary timing chain—3.6L engine

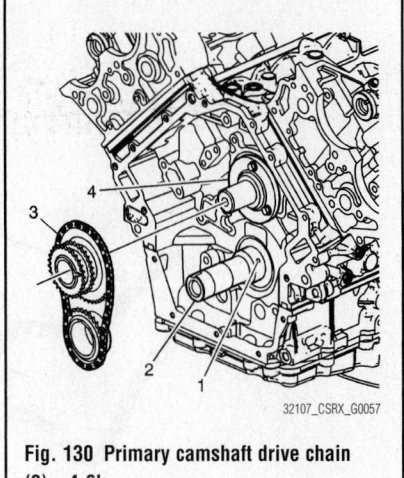

Fig. 130 Primary camshaft drive chain (3)—4.6L

7. Remove the right bank secondary camshaft drive chain. .

To install:

8. Install the right bank secondary camshaft drive chain.

9. Install the right bank secondary camshaft drive chain guide.

10. Install the right bank secondary camshaft drive chain shoe.

11. Install the right bank secondary camshaft drive chain tensioner.

12. Install the spark plugs.

13. Install the engine front cover.

4.6L Engine

Primary

See Figures 128 through 132.

➡**This procedure requires the use of a crankshaft socket, special tool J39946 or equivalent.**

1. Before servicing the vehicle, refer to the Precautions Section.

2. Remove the oil pump.

3. Align the primary timing marks (1) using the J39946.

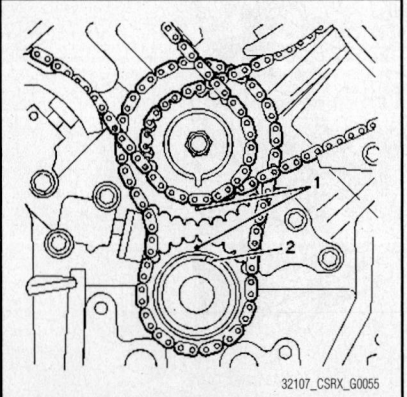

Fig. 128 Aligning timing marks (1)—4.6L

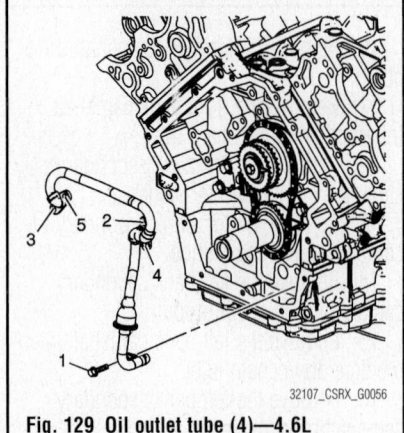

Fig. 129 Oil outlet tube (4)—4.6L

4. Remove the secondary camshaft drive chains.

5. Remove the primary drive chain tensioner.

6. Remove the oil outlet tube (4).

7. Remove the primary camshaft drive chain guide bolts and guide.

8. Remove the camshaft intermediate sprocket retaining bolt.

9. Remove the following as an assembly:
   - Primary camshaft drive chain (3).
   - Crankshaft sprocket.
   - Camshaft intermediate sprocket.

10. Clean and inspect the camshaft timing drive components.

To install:

11. Align the timing marks (1) of the camshaft intermediate and crankshaft sprockets. The marks should be aligned vertically in the installed position.

12. Install the primary camshaft drive chain on the drive sprockets.

13. Use the J39946 to rotate the crankshaft until the crankshaft keyway is approximately at the 1 o'clock position.

14. Install the following as an assembly:

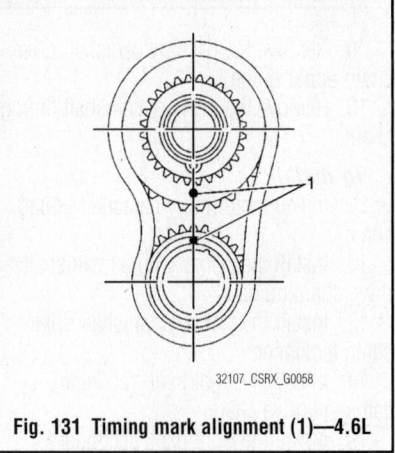

Fig. 131 Timing mark alignment (1)—4.6L

   - Primary camshaft drive chain (3).
   - Crankshaft sprocket.
   - Camshaft intermediate sprocket.

15. Install the camshaft intermediate sprocket retaining bolt and tighten to 44 ft. lbs. (60 Nm).

16. Install the primary drive chain guide.

17. Install the primary drive chain guide bolts tighten to 18 ft. lbs. (25 Nm).

Fig. 132 Primary drive chain guide—4.6L

18. Install the primary drive chain tensioner.

19. Install the oil outlet tube (4) and bolts and tighten to 89 inch lbs. (10 Nm).

20. Install the secondary camshaft drive chains.

21. Remove the pin from the primary timing chain tensioner release lever.

22. Ensure the primary timing marks (1) are aligned vertically.

23. Install the oil pump.

Left Secondary

See Figures 128 and 133 through 137.

➡**This procedure requires the use of a crankshaft socket, special tool J39946 and a camshaft holding tool, special tool EN46328.**

1. Before servicing the vehicle, refer to the Precautions Section.

2. Remove the right secondary timing chain.

3. Using the J39946 , rotate the crankshaft until the primary timing gear alignment marks (1) are adjacent to each other as shown.

4. Remove the left camshaft position actuator housing. DO NOT remove the actuator solenoids from the housing.

✳ CAUTION

The camshaft holding tools must be installed on the camshafts to prevent camshaft rotation. When performing service to the valve train and/or timing components, valve spring pressure can cause the camshafts to rotate unexpectedly and can cause personal injury

5. Install the EN46328 (1) on the bank 2 (left) camshafts (2).

6. Loosen and remove the left secondary timing chain tensioner bolts and tensioner.

✳ WARNING

A wrench must be used on the hex of the camshaft when loosening or tightening in order to prevent component damage. Failure to prevent the torque reaction against the timing drive chain can lead to timing drive chain failure.

7. Use an open-end wrench on the hex cast into the camshaft in order to prevent the camshaft from rotating when removing the camshaft oil control valve.

8. Loosen and remove the bank 2 (left) exhaust camshaft position oil control valve.

9. Slide the left exhaust camshaft position actuator off of the camshaft and remove the secondary timing chain from the camshaft actuator teeth.

10. Use an open-end wrench on the hex cast into the camshaft in order to prevent the camshaft from rotating when removing the camshaft oil control valve.

11. Loosen and remove the bank 2 (left) intake camshaft position oil control valve.

12. Slide the left intake camshaft position actuator off of the camshaft and remove the secondary timing chain from the camshaft actuator teeth.

13. Remove the left secondary timing chain from the engine.

14. Clean and inspect the camshaft timing drive components.

To install:

The secondary timing chain (2) has 3 black links that aid in timing the camshaft position actuators to the intermediate sprocket. The black link (4) is aligned with the bank 2 exhaust actuator timing mark. The black link (3) is aligned with the bank 2 intake actuator timing mark. The black link (1) is aligned with the intermediate sprocket.

➡**The intermediate sprocket left bank timing mark is labeled left bank (LB) as shown.**

15. Assemble the secondary timing chain to the intermediate sprocket aligning the sprocket LB timing mark to the timing chain black link.

16. Align the timing mark (5) of the LB intake camshaft position actuator with the timing chain black link (3) and install the actuator on the camshaft with the actuator timing mark perpendicular (90 degrees) to the cylinder head deck surface at the top of its rotation.

17. Loosely install the oil control valve (10) to secure the intake actuator.

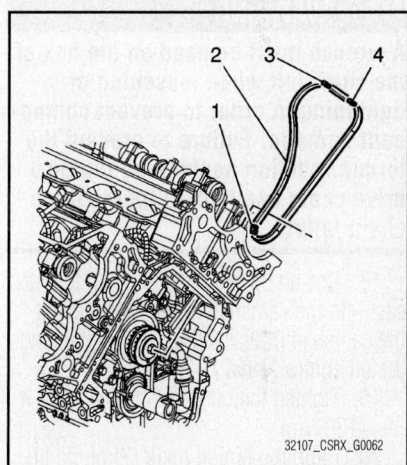

32107_CSRX_G0062

Fig. 135 Location of black timing links—4.6L

32107_CSRX_G0060

Fig. 133 Installing the EN46328 (1)—4.6L

32107_CSRX_G0061

Fig. 134 Holding camshaft with wrench—4.6L

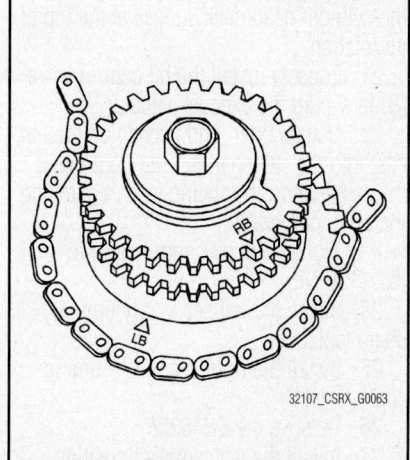

32107_CSRX_G0063

Fig. 136 Intermediate sprocket—4.6L

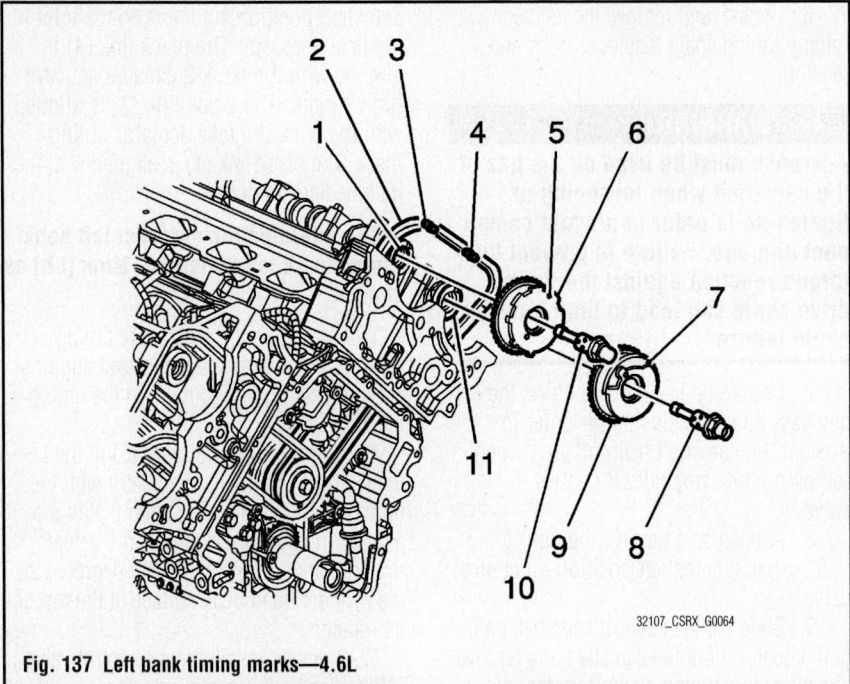

Fig. 137 Left bank timing marks—4.6L

32107_CSRX_G0064

※ WARNING

A wrench must be used on the hex of the camshaft when loosening or tightening in order to prevent component damage. Failure to prevent the torque reaction against the timing drive chain can lead to timing drive chain failure.

18. Use an open-end wrench on the hex cast into the camshaft in order to prevent the camshaft from rotating when tightening the oil control valve.

19. Tighten the oil control valve to 89 ft. lbs. (120 Nm).

20. Align the timing mark (7) of the LB exhaust camshaft position actuator with the timing chain black link (4) and install the actuator on the camshaft with the actuator timing mark perpendicular (90 degrees) to the cylinder head deck surface at the top of its rotation.

21. Loosely install the oil control valve (8) to secure the exhaust actuator.

22. Use an open-end wrench on the hex cast into the camshaft in order to prevent the camshaft from rotating when tightening the oil control valve.

23. Tighten the oil control valve to 89 ft. lbs. (120 Nm).

24. Install the left secondary timing chain tensioner.

25. Install the right secondary timing chain.

26. Remove the EN46328 .

27. Install the left camshaft position actuator housing.

Right Secondary

See Figures 128 and 138 through 142.

➡This procedure requires the use of a crankshaft socket, special tool J39946 and a camshaft holding tool, special tool EN46328.

1. Remove the oil pump.

2. Using the J39946, rotate the crankshaft until the primary timing gear marks (1) are adjacent to each other as shown.

3. Remove the right camshaft position

actuator housing. DO NOT remove the actuator solenoids from the housing.

※ CAUTION

The camshaft holding tools must be installed on the camshafts to prevent camshaft rotation. When performing service to the valve train and/or timing components, valve spring pressure can cause the camshafts to rotate unexpectedly and can cause personal injury

4. Install the EN46328 (1) on the bank 1 (right) camshafts (2).

5. Loosen and remove the right secondary timing chain tensioner bolts and tensioner.

※ WARNING

A wrench must be used on the hex of the camshaft when loosening or tightening in order to prevent component damage. Failure to prevent the torque reaction against the timing drive chain can lead to timing drive chain failure.

6. Use an open-end wrench on the hex cast into the camshaft in order to prevent the camshaft from rotating when removing the camshaft oil control valve.

7. Loosen and remove the bank 1 (right) exhaust camshaft position oil control valve.

8. Slide the right exhaust camshaft position actuator off of the camshaft and

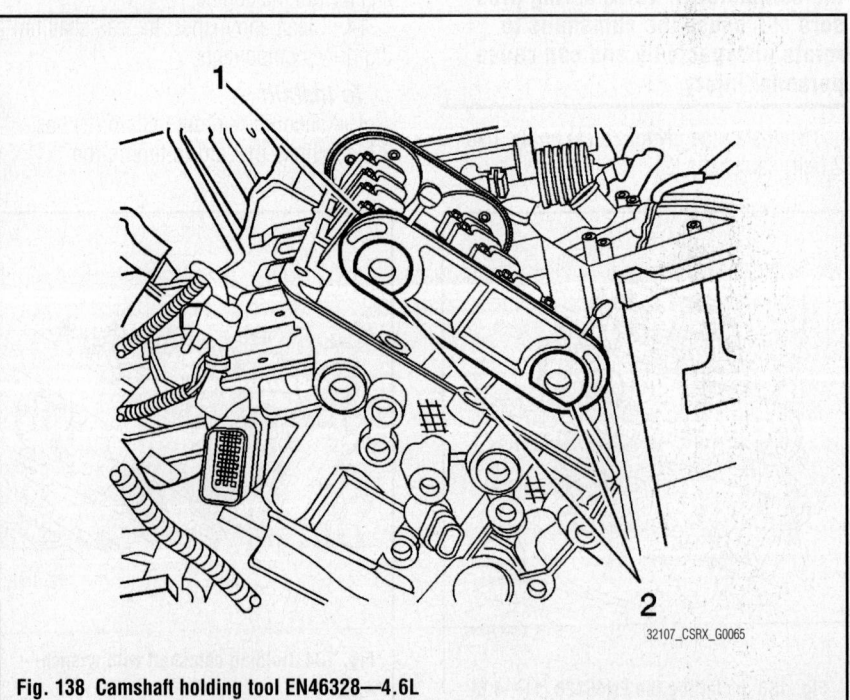

Fig. 138 Camshaft holding tool EN46328—4.6L

32107_CSRX_G0065

remove the secondary timing chain from the camshaft actuator teeth.

9. Use an open-end wrench on the hex cast into the camshaft in order to prevent the camshaft from rotating when removing the camshaft oil control valve.

10. Loosen and remove the bank 1 (right) intake camshaft position oil control valve.

11. Slide the right intake camshaft position actuator off of the camshaft and remove the secondary timing chain from the camshaft actuator teeth.

12. Remove the right secondary timing chain from the engine.

13. Clean and inspect the camshaft timing drive components.

To install:

The secondary timing chain has 3 black links that aid in timing the camshaft position actuators to the intermediate

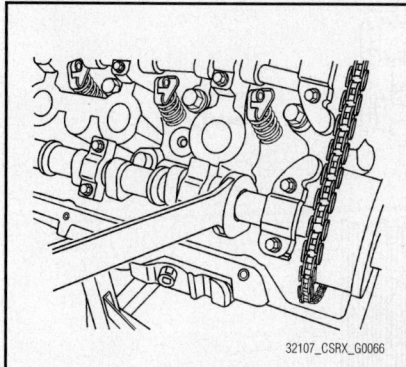

Fig. 139 Holding hex on camshaft—4.6L

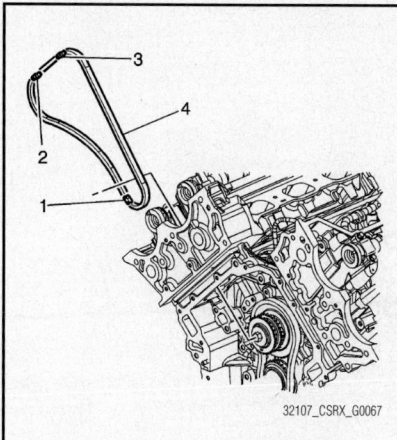

Fig. 140 Location of black timing links— 4.6L

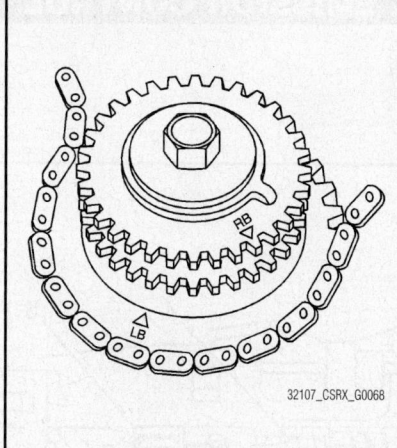

Fig. 141 Right bank timing marks—4.6L

sprocket. The black link (2) is aligned with the bank 1 exhaust actuator timing mark. The black link (3) is aligned with the bank 1 intake actuator timing mark. The black link (1) is aligned with the intermediate sprocket.

➡**The intermediate sprocket right bank timing mark is labeled right bank (RB) as shown.**

14. Assemble the secondary timing chain to the intermediate sprocket aligning the sprocket RB timing mark to the timing chain black link.

15. Align the timing mark (5) of the RB intake camshaft position actuator with the timing chain black link (8) and install the actuator on the camshaft with the actuator timing mark perpendicular (90 degrees) to

the cylinder head deck surface near the top of its rotation.

16. Loosely install the oil control valve (2) to secure the intake actuator.

17. Use an open-end wrench on the hex cast into the camshaft in order to prevent the camshaft from rotating when tightening the oil control valve.

18. Tighten the oil control valve to 89 ft. lbs. (120 Nm).

19. Align the timing mark (3) of the RB exhaust camshaft position actuator with the timing chain black link and install the actuator on the camshaft with the actuator timing mark perpendicular (90 degrees) to the cylinder head deck surface near the top of its rotation.

20. Loosely install the oil control valve (1) to secure the exhaust actuator.

21. Use an open-end wrench on the hex cast into the camshaft in order to prevent the camshaft from rotating when tightening the oil control valve.

22. Tighten the oil control valve to 89 ft. lbs. (120 Nm).

23. Install the right secondary timing chain tensioner.

24. Remove the EN46328 .

25. Install the right camshaft position actuator housing.

26. Install the oil pump.

VALVE LASH

ADJUSTMENT

These engines use hydraulic lifters, which require no periodic adjustment.

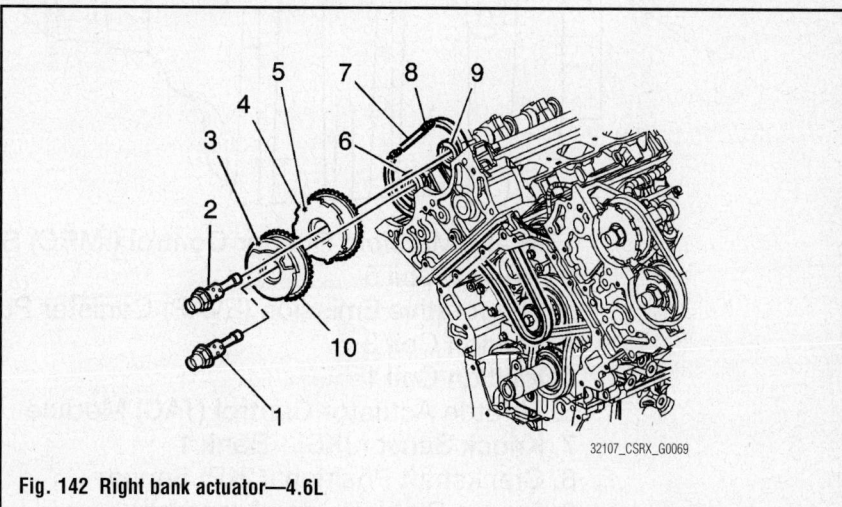

Fig. 142 Right bank actuator—4.6L

ENGINE PERFORMANCE & EMISSION CONTROL

COMPONENT LOCATIONS

See Figures 143 through 148.

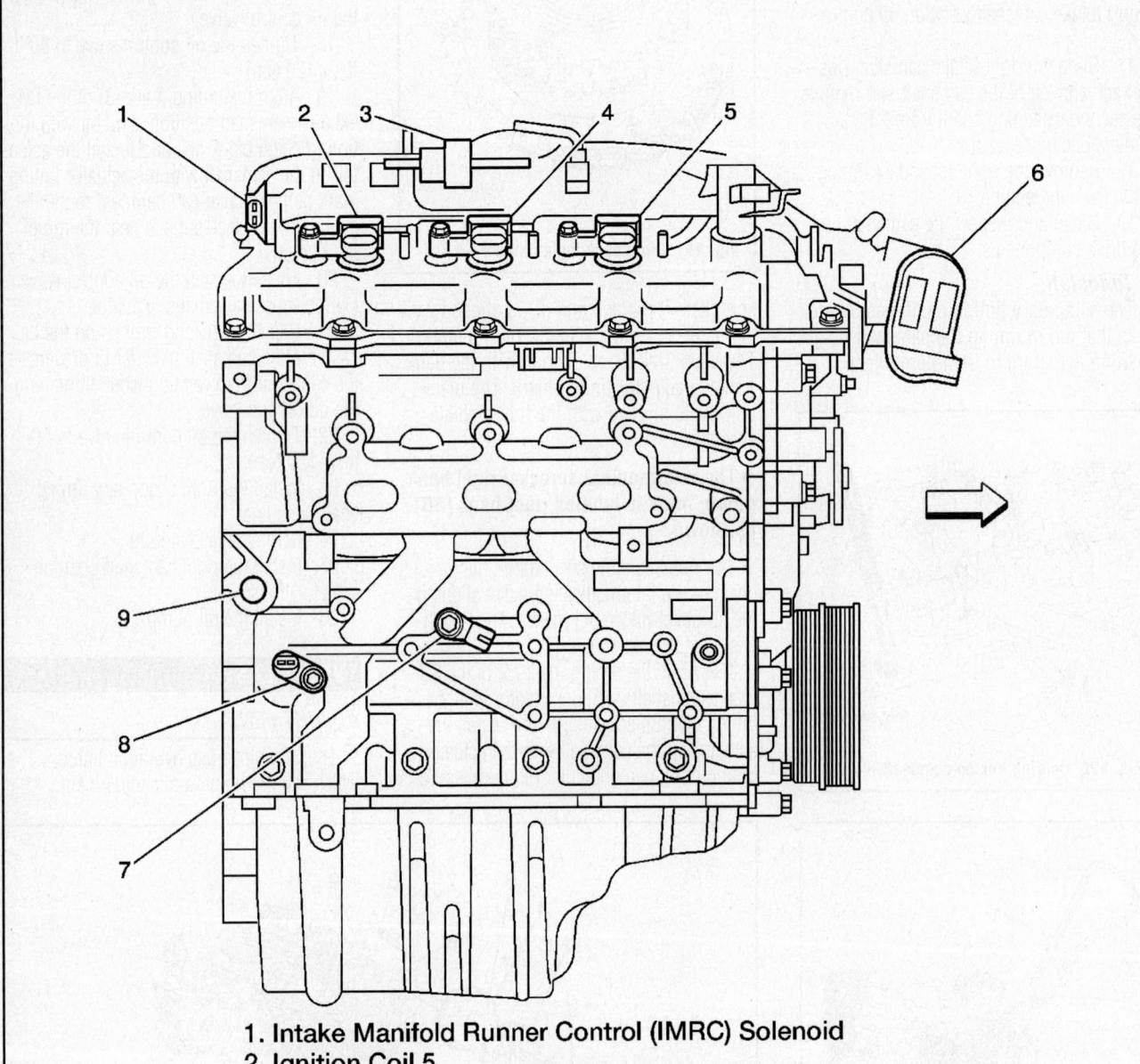

1. Intake Manifold Runner Control (IMRC) Solenoid
2. Ignition Coil 5
3. Evaporative Emission (EVAP) Canister Purge Solenoid Valve
4. Ignition Coil 3
5. Ignition Coil 1
6. Throttle Actuator Control (TAC) Module
7. Knock Sensor (KS) - Bank 1
8. Crankshaft Position (CKP) Sensor
9. Engine Block Heater Assembly

22116_SSRX_G0039

Fig. 143 Engine control components—3.6L engine

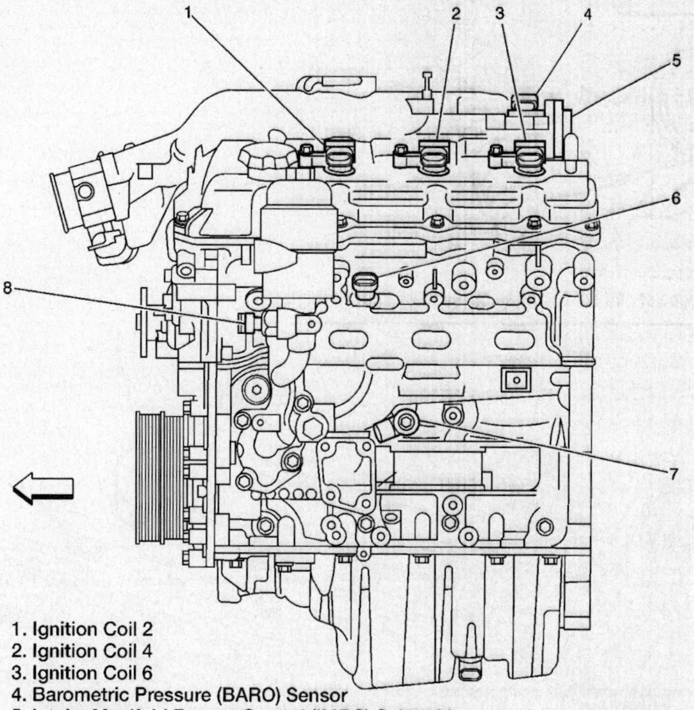

1. Ignition Coil 2
2. Ignition Coil 4
3. Ignition Coil 6
4. Barometric Pressure (BARO) Sensor
5. Intake Manifold Runner Control (IMRC) Solenoid
6. Engine Coolant Temperature (ECT) Sensor
7. Knock Sensor (KS) - Bank 2
8. Engine Oil Pressure (EOP) Sensor

22116_SSRX_G0040

Fig. 144 Engine control components—3.6L engine

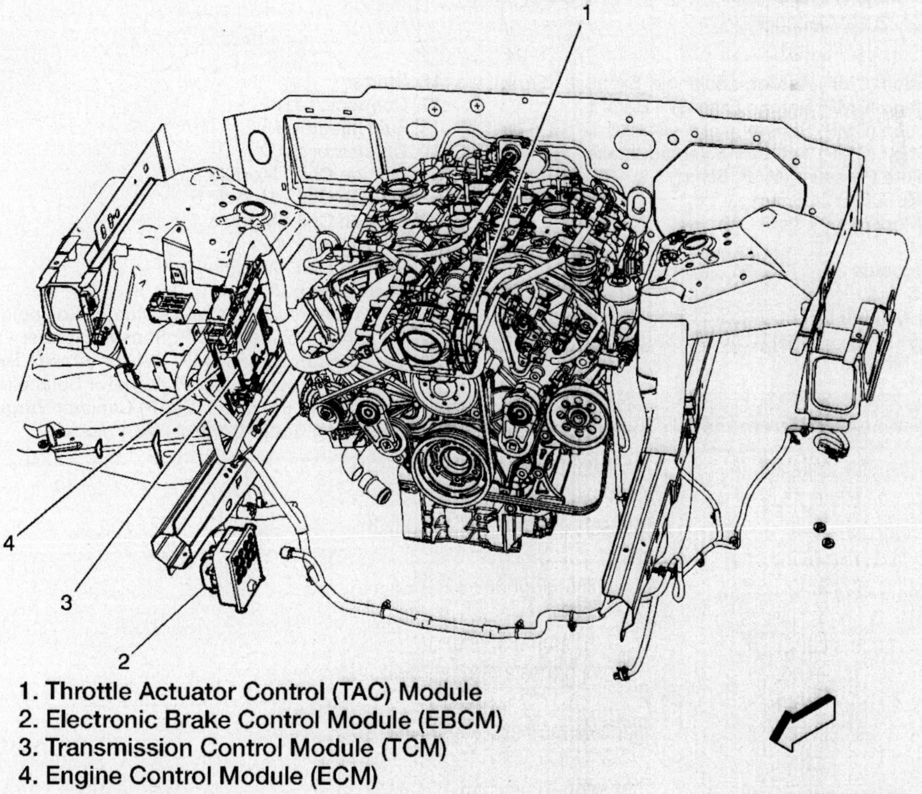

1. Throttle Actuator Control (TAC) Module
2. Electronic Brake Control Module (EBCM)
3. Transmission Control Module (TCM)
4. Engine Control Module (ECM)

22116_SSRX_G0041

Fig. 145 Engine control modules—3.6L engine

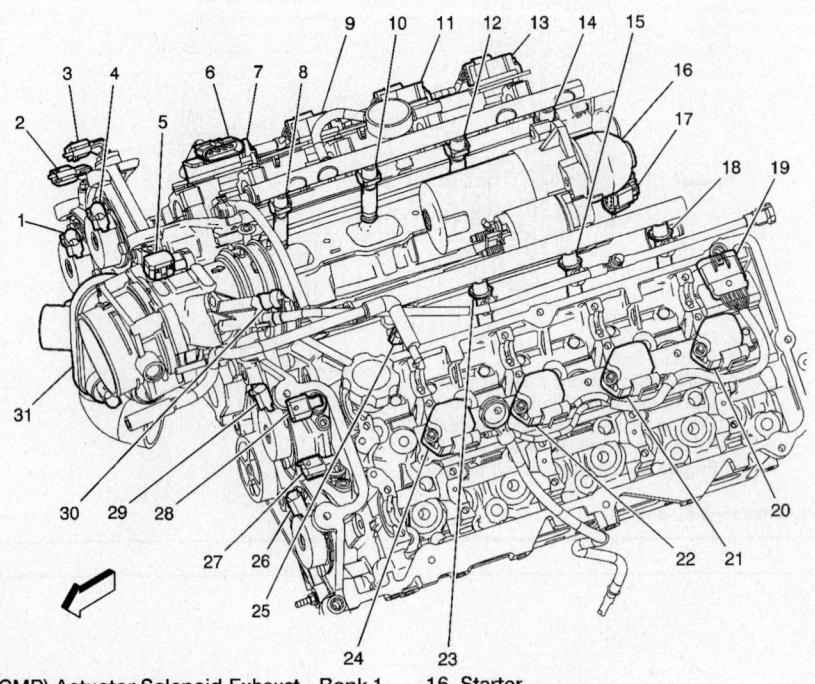

1. Camshaft Position (CMP) Actuator Solenoid Exhaust - Bank 1
2. Camshaft Position (CMP) Sensor Exhaust - Bank 1
3. Camshaft Position (CMP) Sensor Intake - Bank 1
4. Camshaft Position (CMP) Actuator Solenoid Intake - Bank 1
5. Manifold Absolute Pressure (MAP) Sensor
6. Connector #140
7. Ignition Coil - Module 1
8. Fuel Injector 1
9. Ignition Coil - Module 3
10. Fuel Injector 3
11. Ignition Coil - Module 5
12. Fuel Injector 5
13. Ignition Coil - Module 7
14. Fuel Injector 7
15. Fuel Injector 6

16. Starter
17. Connector #102
18. Fuel Injector 8
19. Connector #139
20. Ignition Coil - Module 8
21. Ignition Coil - Module 6
22. Ignition Coil - Module 4
23. Fuel Injector 4
24. Ignition Coil - Module 2
25. Fuel Injector 2
26. Camshaft Position (CMP) Actuator Solenoid Exhaust - Bank 2
27. Camshaft Position (CMP) Sensor Exhaust - Bank 2
28. Camshaft Position (CMP) Sensor Intake - Bank 2
29. Camshaft Position (CMP) Actuator Solenoid Intake - Bank 2
30. Evaporative Emission (EVAP) Canister Purge Valve
31. Throttle Actuator Control (TAC) Module

22116_SSRX_G0042

Fig. 146 Engine control components—4.6L engine

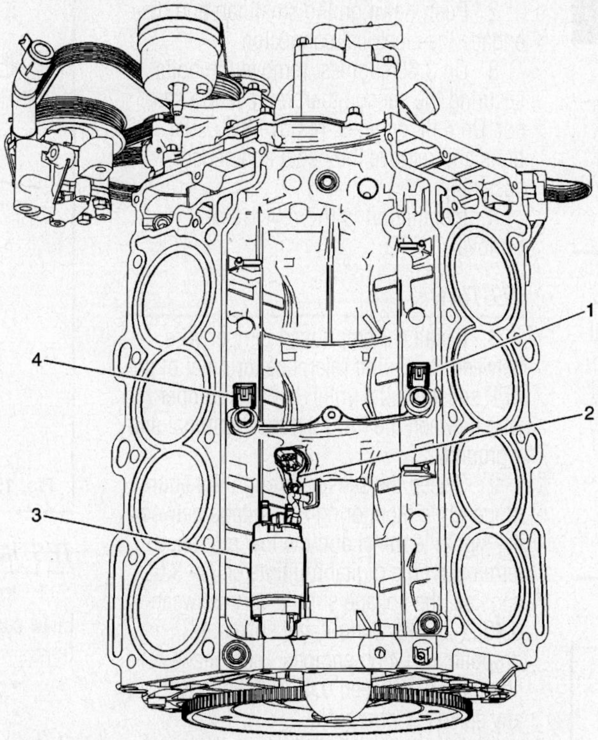

1. Knock Sensor (KS) 1
2. Crankshaft Position (CKP) Sensor
3. Starter Motor
4. Knock Sensor (KS) 2

22116_SSRX_G0043

Fig. 147 Engine control components—4.6L engine

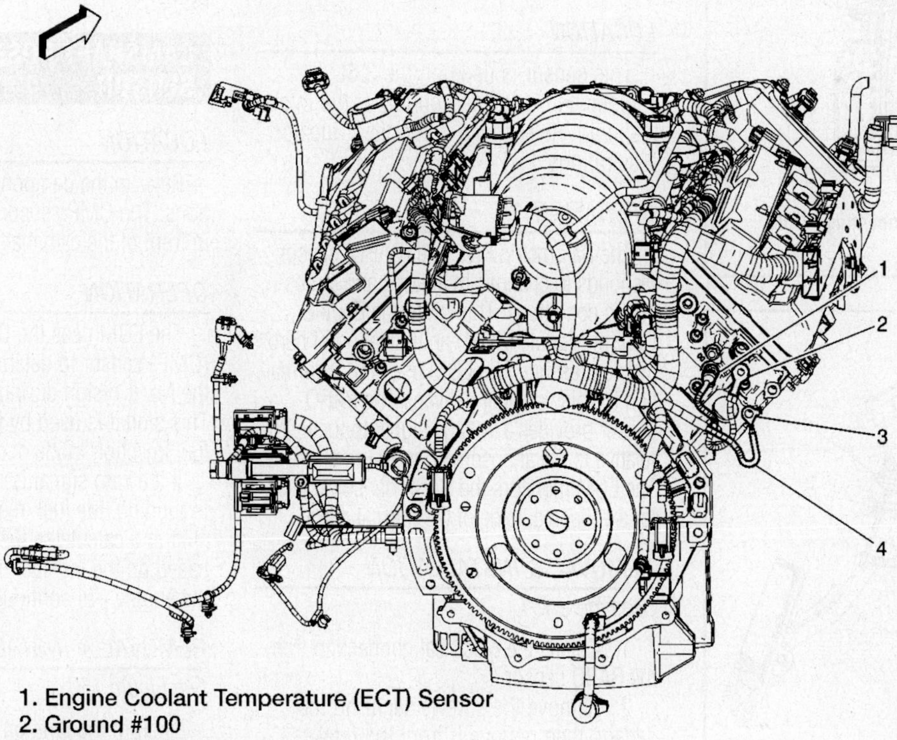

1. Engine Coolant Temperature (ECT) Sensor
2. Ground #100
3. Ground #107
4. Engine Harness

22116_SSRX_G0044

Fig. 148 Engine control components—4.6L engine

ACCELERATOR PEDAL POSITION (APP) SENSOR

LOCATION

The Accelerator Pedal Position (APP) sensor is mounted inside the accelerator pedal control assembly.

OPERATION

The sensor is made up of the two individual sensors within a single housing. Each sensor has a unique functionality to determine pedal position. The APP system along with the Electronic Control Module (ECM) is used to calculate and control the amount of acceleration and deceleration through fuel injector control.

REMOVAL & INSTALLATION

See Figures 149 and 150.

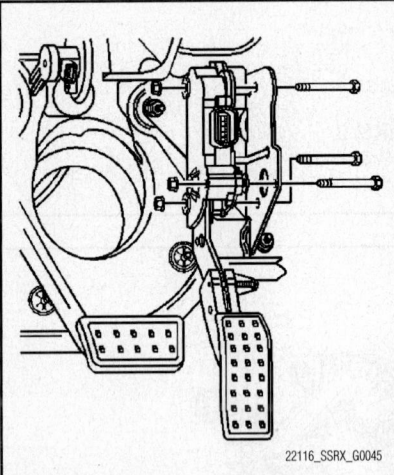

Fig. 149 APP sensor mounting—3.6L engine

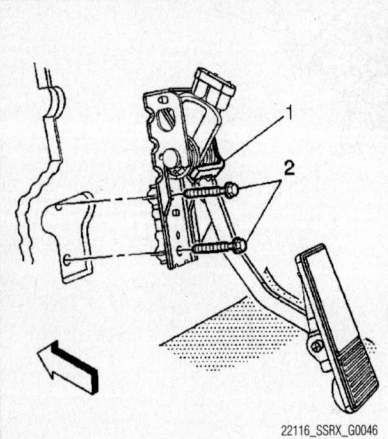

Fig. 150 On 4.6L engines, the sensor is integrated with the pedal assembly

1. Remove the driver's side knee bolster.
2. Push down on the small tab and disengage the electrical connector.
3. On 3.6L engines, remove the bolts securing the sensor, then remove the sensor. On 4.6L engines, remove the pedal bolts and remove the pedal and sensor assembly.
4. Installation is the reverse of removal.

TESTING

1. Install a 3 amp fused jumper wire between the 5–volt reference terminal of the APP sensor and 5 volts. Install a jumper wire between the low reference terminal and a ground.
2. Sweep the sensor through the entire range while monitoring the voltage between the signal terminal and the low reference terminal with a digital multimeter. On 3.6L engines, the voltage should vary between 0.40–2.2 volts without any spikes or dropouts. On 4.6L engines, the voltage should vary between 0.40–4.5 volts without any spikes or dropouts.
3. If the voltage is not within the specified range or is erratic, replace the accelerator pedal/sensor assembly.

BAROMETRIC PRESSURE (BARO) SENSOR

LOCATION

This sensor is used on the 3.6L engines and is located on top of the intake manifold. Refer to the component locator illustrations.

OPERATION

The Barometric Pressure (BARO) sensor responds to changes in altitude and atmospheric conditions. This gives the Engine Control Module (ECM) an indication of barometric pressure. The ECM uses this information to calculate fuel delivery. The BARO sensor provides a voltage signal to the ECM relative to the atmospheric pressure changes. The ECM monitors the BARO sensor signal for a voltage outside of the normal range.

REMOVAL & INSTALLATION

See Figure 151.

1. Detach the electrical connection from the BARO sensor.
2. Remove the screws securing the sensor, then remove it from the intake manifold.
3. Installation is the reverse of removal. If reusing the sensor, replace the seal.

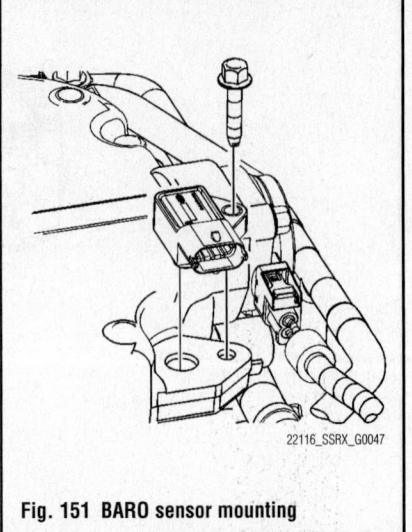

Fig. 151 BARO sensor mounting

TESTING

1. Inspect the atmospheric vent on the ECM case for one of the following conditions:
   - Moisture in the vent inlet
   - Debris in the vent inlet
2. If a condition exists, attempt to clean or dry the atmospheric inlet.
3. Start the engine. Observe the DTC information with a scan tool. DTC P2227, P2228, or P2229 should not set. If DTC P2227, P2228, or P2229 sets, replace the ECM.

CAMSHAFT POSITION (CMP) SENSOR

LOCATION

Refer to the component locator illustrations. The CMP sensor is located above or in front of the camshaft covers.

OPERATION

The ECM uses the Camshaft Position (CMP) sensor to determine the position of the No. 1 piston during its power stroke. This signal is used by the ECM to calculate fuel injection mode of operation.

If the cam signal is lost while the engine is running, the fuel injection system will shift to a calculated fuel injected mode based on the last fuel injection pulse, and the engine will continue to run.

REMOVAL & INSTALLATION

See Figure 152.

1. Turn the ignition **OFF**.
2. On 3.6L engines, if replacing one of the left side sensors, remove the power steering fluid reservoir bolts and reposition the power steering fluid reservoir aside.

➡️**Do not disconnect the power steering fluid lines/hoses from the reservoir.**

3. Unplug the CMP sensor electrical connector.

4. Remove the CMP sensor bolt.

5. Remove the CMP sensor.

6. Installation is the reverse of removal. Tighten the bolt to 89 inch lbs. (10 Nm).

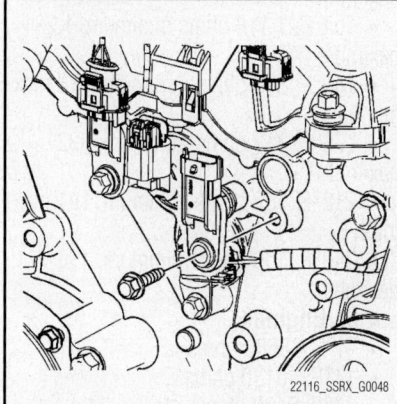

Fig. 152 Unplug the electrical connector, then remove the bolt securing the CMP sensor

TESTING

1. Inspect the CMP sensor for correct installation. Remove the CMP sensor from the engine and inspect the sensor O–ring for damage. If the sensor is loose, incorrectly installed, or damaged, replace the CMP sensor.

2. Engage the CMP sensor harness connector to the CMP sensor.

3. Connect the scan tool to the diagnostic connector.

4. With the ignition **ON**, engine off observe the CMP Active counter parameter on the scan tool.

5. Pass a flat steel object across the tip of the sensor repeatedly. The CMP Active counter parameter should increment with each pass of the steel object.

6. If the parameter does not increment, replace the CMP sensor.

CRANKSHAFT POSITION (CKP) SENSOR

LOCATION

Refer to the component locator illustrations. The CKP sensor is located near the bellhousing on the side of the engine block on 3.6L engines. On 4.6L engines, it is located under the intake manifold.

OPERATION

The Crankshaft Position (CKP) sensor senses the crank angle (piston position) of each cylinder and converts it into a pulse signal. The ECM receives this signal and then computes the engine speed and controls the fuel injector timing and ignition timing based on this input.

REMOVAL & INSTALLATION

See Figure 153.

➡️**Use of a scan tool is required to complete this procedure. Anytime the CKP sensor is replaced, the variation learn procedure must be performed.**

1. On 3.6L engines, raise and safely support the vehicle.

2. On 4.6L engines, remove the intake manifold.

3. Unplug the harness connector from the sensor.

4. Clean the area around the sensor to prevent debris from entering the engine.

5. Remove the bolt securing the sensor, then remove it from the engine.

6. Installation is the reverse of removal. Lubricate a new O–ring with clean engine oil. Tighten the bolt to 89 inch lbs. (10 Nm). Connect the scan tool to the vehicle and perform the CKP sensor variation learn procedure.

Fig. 153 Remove the bolt securing the CKP sensor, then remove it

TESTING

1. Inspect the CKP sensor for correct installation. Remove the CKP sensor from the engine and inspect the sensor O–ring for damage. If the sensor is loose, incorrectly installed, or damaged, replace the CKP sensor.

2. Engage the CKP sensor harness connector to the CKP sensor.

3. Connect the scan tool to the diagnostic connector.

4. With the ignition **ON**, engine off observe the CKP Active counter parameter on the scan tool.

5. Pass a flat steel object across the tip of the sensor repeatedly. The CKP Active counter parameter should increment with each pass of the steel object.

6. If the parameter does not increment, replace the CKP sensor.

ELECTRONIC CONTROL MODULE (ECM)

LOCATION

Refer to the component location illustrations. The ECM is located on a bracket on the side of the engine compartment.

OPERATION

The Electronic Control Module (ECM) performs many functions on your vehicle. The module accepts information from various sensors and computes the required fuel flow rate necessary to maintain the correct amount of air/fuel ratio throughout the entire engine operational range and controls the shifting of the transmission.

Based on the information that is received and programmed into the ECM's memory, the ECM generates output signals to control relays, actuators and solenoids. The module automatically senses and compensates for any changes in altitude when driving your vehicle.

REMOVAL & INSTALLATION

See Figure 154.

➡️**It is necessary to record the remaining engine oil and transmission fluid life. If the replacement module is not programmed with the remaining engine oil life, the engine oil life will default to 100 percent. If the replacement module is not programmed with the remaining engine oil life, the engine oil must be changed at 3,000 miles (5,000km) from the last oil change. The transmission fluid life will default to 100 percent as well. If the replacement module is not programmed with the remaining transmission fluid life, the fluid must be changed at 50,000 miles (83,000km) from the last change. A scan tool must be used to retrieve the ECM data. This information must be transferred to the new ECM.**

1. Disconnect the negative battery cable.

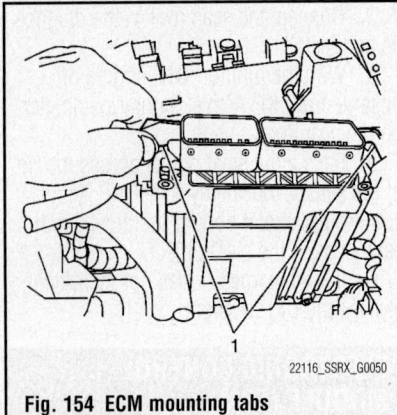

Fig. 154 ECM mounting tabs

2. Disengage the harness connections from the ECM.

3. Disengage the retainer tabs securing the ECM to the bracket. Remove the ECM from the engine compartment.

4. Installation is the reverse of removal. Program the ECM.

TESTING

Service of the ECM should consist of either replacement of the ECM or programming of the Electrically Erasable Programmable Read Only Memory (EEPROM). If the diagnostic procedures call for the ECM to be replaced, the replacement ECM should be checked to ensure that the correct part is being used. If the correct part is being used, remove the faulty ECM and install the new service ECM

ENGINE COOLANT TEMPERATURE (ECT) SENSOR

LOCATION

Refer to the component location illustrations. The Engine Coolant Temperature (ECT) sensor is threaded into the cylinder head.

OPERATION

The ECT sensor resistance changes in response to engine coolant temperature. The sensor resistance decreases as the coolant temperature increases, and increases as the coolant temperature decreases. This provides a reference signal to the ECM, which indicates engine coolant temperature. The signal sent to the ECM by the ECT sensor helps the ECM to determine spark advance, EGR flow rate, air/fuel ratio, and engine temperature. The ECT is a two wire sensor, a 5–volt reference signal is sent to the sensor and the signal return is based upon the change in the measured resistance due to temperature.

REMOVAL & INSTALLATION

See Figures 155 and 156.

1. Drain the cooling system to a level below the ECT sensor.
2. Unplug the harness connector from the ECT sensor.
3. Remove the ECT sensor from the engine.
4. Installation is the reverse of removal. If reusing the old sensor, coat the threads with GM sealant 12346004 or equivalent. New sensors are already coated; additional sealant is not needed. Tighten the sensor to 16 ft. lbs. (22 Nm) on 3.6L engines or 15 ft. lbs. (20 Nm) on 4.6L engines.

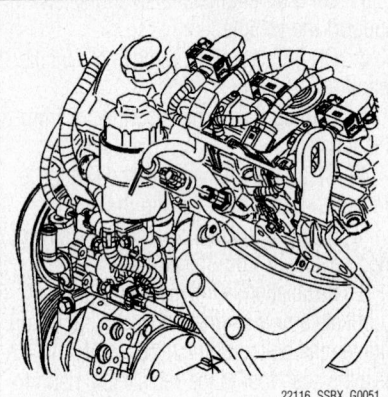

Fig. 155 ECT sensor mounting—3.6L engine

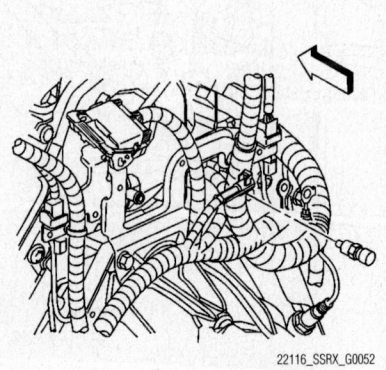

Fig. 156 ECT sensor mounting—4.6L engine

TESTING

1. Remove the ECT sensor.
2. Measure and record the resistance of the ECT sensor at various temperatures, then compare those measurements to the following. The change in resistance should occur smoothly. If there are any sudden changes, the sensor is faulty.

3.6L Engines

- -4°F: 14,096 ohms minimum, 16,827 maximum
- 14°F: 8,642 ohms minimum, 10,152 maximum
- 32°F: 5,466 ohms minimum, 6,326 maximum
- 68°F: 2,351 ohms minimum, 2,649 maximum
- 77°F: 1,941 ohms minimum, 2,173 maximum
- 104°F: 1,118 ohms minimum, 1,231 maximum
- 140°F: 573 ohms minimum, 618 maximum
- 176°F: 313 ohms minimum, 332 maximum
- 212°F: 182 ohms minimum, 191 maximum
- 248°F: 109 ohms minimum, 116 maximum

4.6L Engines

- -4°F: 28680 ohms
- 14°F: 16180 ohms
- 32°F: 9420 ohms
- 50°F: 5670 ohms
- 68°F: 3520 ohms
- 86°F: 2238 ohms
- 104°F: 1459 ohms
- 122°F: 973 ohms
- 158°F: 467 ohms
- 194°F: 241 ohms
- 230°F: 132 ohms
- 266°F: 77 ohms

3. If the sensor tests outside of these ranges, replace the sensor.

HEATED OXYGEN (HO2S) SENSOR

LOCATION

Refer to the component location illustrations. The Heated Oxygen Sensors (HO2S) are threaded into the exhaust pipes.

OPERATION

The Heated Oxygen Sensor (HO2S) is a device that produces an electrical voltage when exposed to the oxygen present in the exhaust gases. The oxygen sensors are electrically heated internally for faster switching when the engine is started cold. The oxygen sensor produces a voltage within 0 and 1 volt. When there is a large amount of oxygen present (lean mixture), the sensor produces a low voltage (less than 0.4v). When there is a lesser amount present (rich mixture) it produces a higher voltage (0.6–1.0v). The stoichiometric or correct fuel to air ratio will read between 0.4 and 0.6v. By monitoring the oxygen content and converting it to electrical voltage, the sensor acts as a rich–lean switch. The voltage is transmitted to the ECM.

Two sensors per bank are used, one before the catalyst and one after. This is done for a catalyst efficiency monitor that is a part of the diagnostic system of the engine controls. The one before the catalyst measures the exhaust emissions right out of the engine, and sends the signal to the ECM about the state of the mixture as previously talked about. The second sensor reports the difference in the emissions after the exhaust gases have gone through the catalyst. This sensor reports to the ECM the amount of emissions reduction the catalyst is performing.

The oxygen sensor will not work until a predetermined temperature is reached, until this time the ECM is running in what is known as open loop operation. Open loop means that the ECM has not yet begun to correct the air–to–fuel ratio by reading the oxygen sensor. After the engine comes to operating temperature, the ECM will monitor the oxygen sensor and correct the air/fuel ratio from the sensor's readings. This is what is known as closed loop operation.

REMOVAL & INSTALLATION

See Figure 157.

➡**Replace the sensor if the pigtail wiring, connector, or terminal is damaged. The external clean air reference is obtained by way of the sensor signal and heater wires. Any attempt to repair the wires or connectors could result in obstruction of the air reference. Make sure the lead wires are not sharply bent or kinked as the air reference could become blocked.**

1. Raise and safely support the vehicle.
2. Unplug the sensor connector. Remove the clip from the harness.

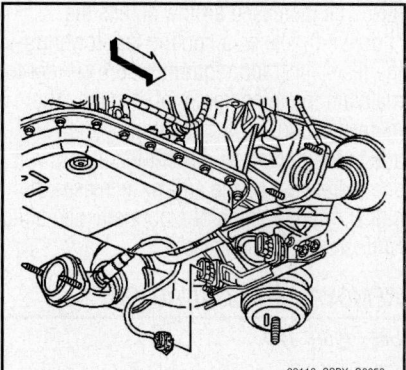

22116_SSRX_G0053

Fig. 157 Common HO2S sensor mounting

3. Remove the sensor from the exhaust pipe or catalytic converter.
4. Installation is the reverse of removal. If reusing the old sensor, coat the threads with GM anti-seize compound 12377953 or equivalent. New sensors are already coated; additional compound is not needed. Tighten the sensor to 30 ft. lbs. (40 Nm).

TESTING

Heater

1. With the ignition **OFF**, disconnect the harness connector at the appropriate HO2S.
2. With the ignition **ON**, verify that a test lamp illuminates between the appropriate HO2S heater voltage supply circuit and ground. If the test lamp does not illuminate, test the HO2S heater voltage supply circuit for a short to ground or an open/high resistance. If the circuit tests normal and the HO2S heater voltage supply circuit fuse is open, test all components connected to the fuse and replace as necessary.
3. With the ignition **ON**, verify that a test lamp does not illuminate between the appropriate HO2S heater voltage supply control circuit and the appropriate HO2S heater low control circuit. If the lamp illuminates, test the HO2S heater low control circuit for a short to ground.
4. With the engine running, leave the test lamp connected from the previous step. The lamp should flash or be on steady. If the test lamp is not on steady or flashing, test the HO2S heater low control circuit for a short to voltage or an open/high resistance.
5. With the ignition **OFF**, install a 30A fused jumper wire between the appropriate HO2S heater voltage supply circuit and the appropriate HO2S heater low control circuit. With the engine running, verify the appropriate scan tool HO2S Heater parameter is less than 0.1 amp. If more than the specified range, test the HO2S heater voltage supply and HO2S heater low control circuits for more than 1 ohm of resistance.
6. If the ECM and all circuits test normal, replace the appropriate HO2S.

Sensor

➡**If any HO2S heater circuit DTC's are set, test the heater circuit first.**

1. Allow the engine to reach operating temperature.
2. With the engine running, observe the affected HO2S parameter with a scan tool.:

   a. The pre–catalyst oxygen sensors value should vary from below 200 mV to above 800 mV and respond to fueling changes.

   b. The post–catalyst oxygen sensors value should change more than 200 mV when the throttle is quickly cycled 3 times from closed to wide open and back to closed after running the engine at 1,500 RPM for 30 seconds.

3. If the sensor did not perform as indicated, replace the sensor.

INTAKE AIR TEMPERATURE (IAT) SENSOR

LOCATION

Refer to the component location illustrations. The IAT sensor is integrated with the MAF sensor.

OPERATION

The Intake Air Temperature (IAT) sensor determines the air temperature entering the intake manifold. Resistance changes in response to the ambient air temperature. The sensor has a negative temperature coefficient. As the temperature of the sensor rises the resistance across the sensor decreases. This provides a signal to the ECM indicating the temperature of the incoming air charge. This sensor helps the ECM to determine spark timing and air/fuel ratio. Information from this sensor is added to the pressure sensor information to calculate the air mass being sent to the cylinders. The IAT receives a 5–volt reference signal and the signal return is based upon the change in the measured resistance due to temperature.

REMOVAL & INSTALLATION

Refer to the MAF sensor removal and installation procedure for the IAT sensors.

TESTING

See Figure 158.

1. Unplug the IAT/MAF sensor connector.
2. Measure and record the resistance of the IAT sensor at terminals C and D on 3.6L

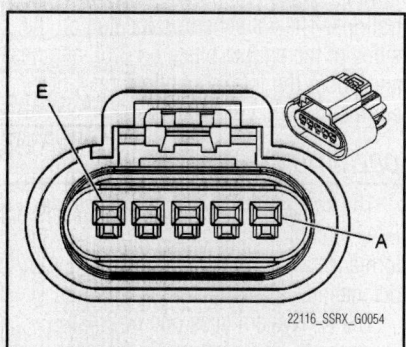

22116_SSRX_G0054

Fig. 158 IAT/MAF connector terminal identification

engines or B and E on 4.6L engines at various temperatures, then compare those measurements to the following. The change in resistance should occur smoothly. If there are any sudden changes, the sensor is faulty.

3.6L Engines:
- -4°F: 14,096 ohms minimum, 16,827 maximum
- 14°F: 8,642 ohms minimum, 10,152 maximum
- 32°F: 5,466 ohms minimum, 6,326 maximum
- 68°F: 2,351 ohms minimum, 2,649 maximum
- 77°F: 1,941 ohms minimum, 2,173 maximum
- 104°F: 1,118 ohms minimum, 1,231 maximum
- 140°F: 573 ohms minimum, 618 maximum
- 176°F: 313 ohms minimum, 332 maximum
- 212°F: 182 ohms minimum, 191 maximum
- 248°F: 109 ohms minimum, 116 maximum

4.6L Engines
- -4°F: 28680 ohms
- 14°F: 16180 ohms
- 32°F: 9420 ohms
- 50°F: 5670 ohms
- 68°F: 3520 ohms
- 86°F: 2238 ohms
- 104°F: 1459 ohms
- 122°F: 973 ohms
- 158°F: 467 ohms
- 194°F: 241 ohms
- 230°F: 132 ohms
- 266°F: 77 ohms

3. If the sensor tests outside of these ranges, replace the sensor.

KNOCK SENSOR (KS)

LOCATION

Refer to the component location illustrations. The KS sensor is located on the sides of the engine block on 3.6L engines and under the intake manifold on 4.6L engines.

OPERATION

The knock sensor system enables the ECM to control ignition timing for best performance while protecting the engine from detonation.

The KS system uses one or 2 flat response 2–wire sensors. The sensor uses piezo–electric crystal technology that produces an AC voltage signal of varying

amplitude and frequency based on the engine vibration or noise level. The control module receives the KS signal through a signal circuit. The KS ground is supplied by the control module through a low reference circuit. The control module learns a minimum noise level, or background noise, at idle from the KS and uses calibrated values for the rest of the RPM range.

In order to determine which cylinders are knocking, the control module only uses KS signal information when each cylinder is near Top Dead Center (TDC) of the firing stroke. If knock is present, the signal will range outside of the noise channel. If the control module has determined that knock is present, it will retard the ignition timing to attempt to eliminate the knock. The control module will always try to work back to a zero compensation level, or no spark retard.

REMOVAL & INSTALLATION

See Figure 159.

1. On 3.6L engines, raise and safely support the vehicle.
2. On 4.6L engines, remove the intake manifold.
3. If equipped, remove the knock sensor shield.
4. Unplug the harness connection from the knock sensor.
5. Remove the bolt securing the sensor, then remove it from the engine.
6. Installation is the reverse of removal. Tighten the bolt to 17 ft. lbs. (23 Nm) on 3.6L engines or 15 ft. lbs. (20 Nm) on 4.6L engines.

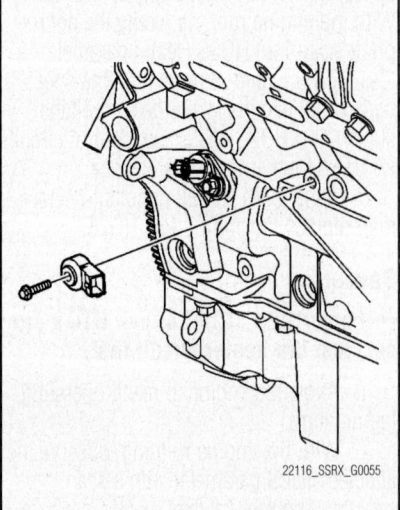

22116_SSRX_G0055

Fig. 159 Knock sensor mounting—3.6L engines

TESTING

1. Connect a digital multimeter to the KS signal circuit and to the KS low reference circuit at the KS.
2. Set the multimeter to the 400 mv AC hertz scale and wait for the display to stabilize at 0 Hz.
3. Tap on the engine block with a non–metallic object near the KS while observing the signal indicated on the multimeter.

➡**Do not tap on plastic engine components.**

4. The multimeter should display a fluctuating frequency while tapping on the engine block. If not, replace the sensor.

MASS AIR FLOW (MAF) SENSOR

LOCATION

Refer to the component location illustrations. The MAF sensor is located on the air cleaner assembly. The IAT sensor is integrated with the MAF sensor.

OPERATION

The Mass Air Flow (MAF) sensor directly measures the mass of air being drawn into the engine. The sensor output is used to calculate injector pulse width. The MAF sensor is what is referred to as a "hot–wire sensor". The sensor uses a thin platinum wire filament, wound on a ceramic bobbin and coated with glass, that is heated to 417°F (200°C) above the ambient air temperature and subjected to the intake airflow stream. A "cold–wire" is used inside the MAF sensor to determine the ambient air temperature.

Battery voltage, a reference signal, and a ground signal from the ECM are supplied to the MAF sensor. The sensor returns a signal proportionate to the current flow required to keep the "hot–wire" at the required temperature. The increased airflow across the "hot–wire" acts as a cooling fan, lowering the resistance and requiring more current to maintain the temperature of the wire. The increased current is measured by the voltage in the circuit, as current increases, voltage increases. As the airflow increases the signal return voltage of a normally operating MAF sensor will increase.

REMOVAL & INSTALLATION

See Figure 160.

1. Remove the air intake tube from the air cleaner assembly.

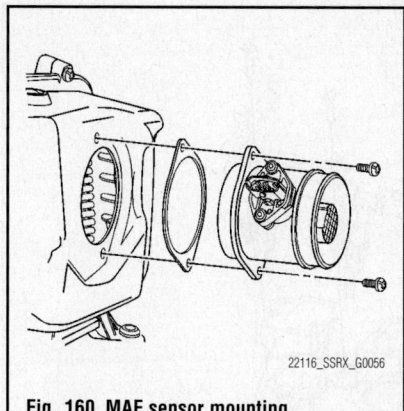

Fig. 160 MAF sensor mounting

2. Detach the electrical connector from the MAF sensor.

3. Remove the screws securing the MAF sensor to the air cleaner.

4. Pull the MAF sensor out of the air cleaner assembly.

5. Installation is the reverse of removal. Use a new seal.

TESTING

1. Turn **OFF** the ignition.

2. Connect tool J 38522 to the vehicle. Connect the battery voltage supply, and ground the black lead.

3. Connect the red lead to the signal circuit of the MAF sensor.

4. Set the Duty Cycle switch to Normal.

5. Set the Frequency switch to 5 K.

6. Set the Signal switch to 5 V.

7. Start the engine. Observe the MAF Sensor parameter for the correct range of 4,950–5,025 Hz.

   a. If the MAF Sensor parameter is not

within the specified range, replace the ECM.

   b. If the MAF Sensor parameter is within the specified range, replace the MAF sensor

MANIFOLD ABSOLUTE PRESSURE (MAP) SENSOR

LOCATION

Refer to the component location illustrations. It is located on the intake manifold and is used on the 4.6L engines.

OPERATION

Using the pressure and temperature data, the ECM calculates the intake air mass. It is connected to the engine intake manifold and takes readings of the absolute pressure.

Atmospheric pressure is measured both when the engine is started and when driving fully loaded, then the pressure sensor information is adjusted accordingly.

REMOVAL & INSTALLATION

See Figure 161.

1. Detach the electrical connection from the MAP sensor.

2. Remove the screws securing the sensor, then remove it from the intake manifold.

3. Installation is the reverse of removal. If reusing the sensor, replace the seal.

TESTING

1. Turn **ON** the ignition, with the engine off, and remove the MAP sensor.

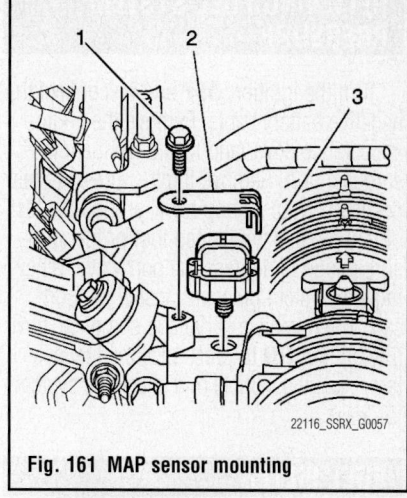

Fig. 161 MAP sensor mounting

2. Install a 3 amp fused jumper wire between the 5–volt reference circuit and the corresponding terminal of the MAP sensor.

3. Install a jumper wire between the low reference circuit of the MAP sensor and ground.

4. Install a jumper wire at the MAP sensor signal circuit.

5. Connect a digital multimeter between the jumper wire from the MAP sensor signal circuit and ground.

6. Install hand vacuum pump to the MAP sensor vacuum port. Slowly apply vacuum to the sensor while observing the voltage on the multimeter. The voltage should vary between 0–5.2 volts without any spikes or dropouts.

7. If the voltage is not within the specified range or is erratic, replace the MAP sensor.

FUEL · · · · · · · · · · · · · · · · · · GASOLINE FUEL INJECTION SYSTEM

FUEL SYSTEM SERVICE PRECAUTIONS

Safety is the most important factor when performing not only fuel system maintenance but any type of maintenance. Failure to conduct maintenance and repairs in a safe manner may result in serious personal injury or death. Maintenance and testing of the vehicle's fuel system components can be accomplished safely and effectively by adhering to the following rules and guidelines.

• To avoid the possibility of fire and personal injury, always disconnect the negative battery cable unless the repair or test procedure requires that battery voltage be applied.

• Always relieve the fuel system pressure prior to disconnecting any fuel system component (injector, fuel rail, pressure regulator, etc.), fitting or fuel line connection. Exercise extreme caution whenever relieving fuel system pressure to avoid exposing skin, face and eyes to fuel spray. Please be advised that fuel under pressure may penetrate the skin or any part of the body that it contacts.

• Always place a shop towel or cloth around the fitting or connection prior to loosening to absorb any excess fuel due to spillage. Ensure that all fuel spillage (should it occur) is quickly removed from engine surfaces. Ensure that all fuel soaked cloths or towels are deposited into a suitable waste container.

• Always keep a dry chemical (Class B) fire extinguisher near the work area.

• Do not allow fuel spray or fuel vapors to come into contact with a spark or open flame.

• Always use a back-up wrench when loosening and tightening fuel line connection fittings. This will prevent unnecessary stress and torsion to fuel line piping.

• Always replace worn fuel fitting O-rings with new Do not substitute fuel hose or equivalent where fuel pipe is installed.

Before servicing the vehicle, make sure to also refer to the precautions in the beginning of this section as well.

RELIEVING FUEL SYSTEM PRESSURE

Turn the ignition **OFF** and disconnect the negative battery cable. Remove the engine appearance cover and locate the fuel pressure test port. Remove the fuel pressure test port cap. Wrap a shop towel around the test port and use a flat bladed tool or fuel pressure gauge to depress the port valve, relieving any system pressure. Install the port cap. When vehicle service is complete, turn the ignition **ON** to pressurize the fuel system. Start the vehicle and check the system for leaks.

FUEL FILTER

REMOVAL & INSTALLATION

1. Before servicing the vehicle, refer to the Precautions Section.
2. Relieve the fuel system pressure.
3. Raise and support the vehicle safely on jackstands.
4. Place a rag under the fuel filter to catch any residual fuel that may leak out when the filter is removed.
5. Remove the quick-connect fitting at the fuel filter inlet.
6. Remove the threaded fitting at the fuel outlet line.
7. Remove the discard the O-ring.
8. Remove the fuel filter.

To install:

9. Lubricate a new O-ring with clean engine oil and install it.
10. Install the fuel filter in its bracket, ensuring proper direction of flow.
11. Connect the fuel inlet and outlet lines. Tighten the outlet fitting to 22 ft. lbs. (30 Nm).
12. Start the engine and check the filter connections for leaks by running the tip of your finger around each connection.
13. Turn the engine off and lower the vehicle.

FUEL INJECTORS

REMOVAL & INSTALLATION

3.6L Engine

See Figures 162 and 163.

1. Before servicing the vehicle, refer to the Precautions Section.
2. Disconnect the negative battery cable.
3. Relieve the fuel system pressure.
4. Remove the intake manifold.
5. Remove the fuel line retaining clip.

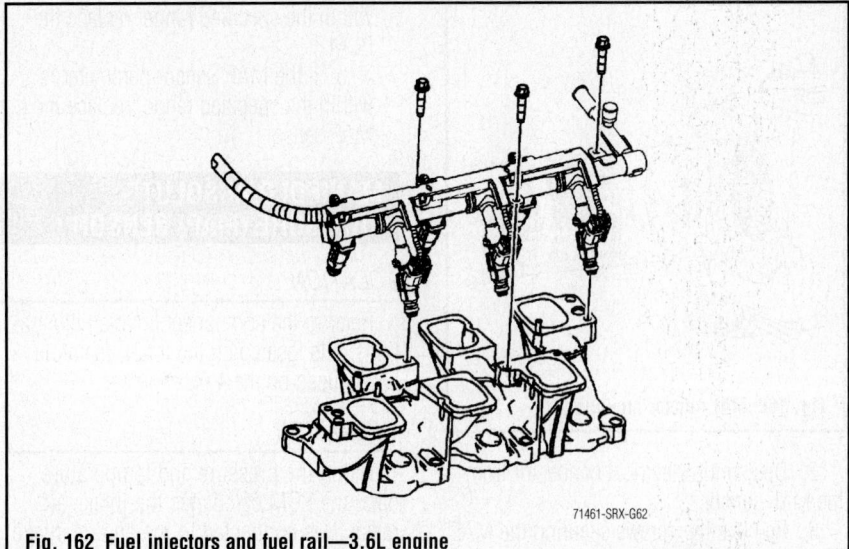

Fig. 162 Fuel injectors and fuel rail—3.6L engine

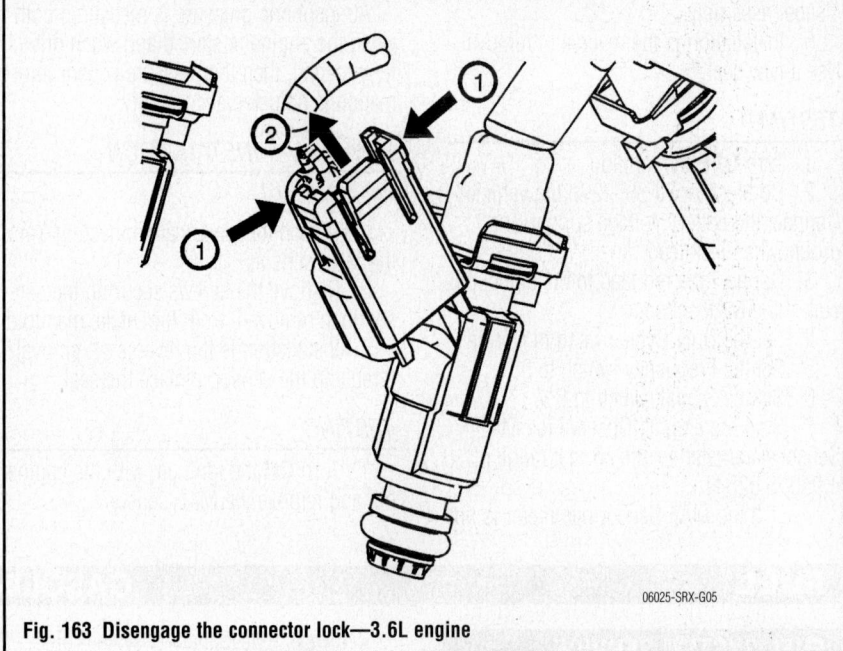

Fig. 163 Disengage the connector lock—3.6L engine

6. Disconnect the feed line from the fuel rail.
7. Remove the fuel rail attaching bolts and remove the fuel rail with the injectors.
8. Disengage the fuel injector electrical connector lock.
9. Disconnect the injector electrical connectors.
10. Remove the retaining clips and remove the fuel injectors. Discard the seals.

To install:

11. Install new fuel injector seals.
12. Reverse the removal procedure to install the fuel rail and injectors. Tighten the fuel rail bolts to 89 inch lbs. (10 Nm).
13. Start the engine and check for fuel leaks.

4.6L Engine

See Figure 164.

1. Before servicing the vehicle, refer to the Precautions Section.
2. Disconnect the negative battery cable.
3. Relieve the fuel system pressure.
4. Remove the front end cross vehicle brace.
5. Disconnect the feed line from the fuel rail.
6. Remove the PCV air hose.
7. Disconnect the EVAP quick connect fitting.
8. Open the fuel line retainers at the rear of the engine.
9. Disconnect the fuel injector electrical connectors.

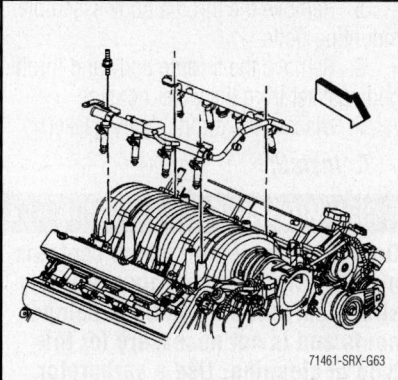

Fig. 164 Fuel injectors and fuel rail—4.6L engine

10. Remove the injector shield bracket.

11. Remove the fuel rail attaching bolts and remove the fuel rail with the injectors.

12. Remove the retaining clips and remove the fuel injectors. Discard the O-ring seals.

To install:

13. Install new fuel injector seals after coating them with clean engine oil.

14. Reverse the removal procedure to install the fuel rail and injectors. Tighten the fuel rail bolts to 89 inch lbs. (10 Nm).

15. Turn the ignition on for 2 seconds. Turn the ignition off for 10 seconds. Turn the ignition on and check for fuel leaks.

FUEL PUMP

REMOVAL & INSTALLATION

➥The following procedure applies to both the primary and secondary fuel pump modules. To gain access to the fuel pump, it is necessary to remove the fuel tank.

1. Before servicing the vehicle, refer to the Precautions Section.

2. Disconnect the negative battery cable.

3. Depressurize the fuel system and drain the fuel into a suitable container.

4. Remove the fuel tank.

5. Disconnect the electrical connectors and fuel line fittings.

6. Remove any dirt that has accumulated around the fuel pump module attaching flange to prevent it from entering the tank during service.

7. Turn the fuel pump module locking ring counterclockwise using a locking ring removal tool, and remove the locking ring.

8. Raise the fuel pump and disconnect the fuel transfer tube.

9. Remove the fuel pump module.

10. Remove the seal gasket and discard it.

To install:

11. Ensure the new seal bead is facing the fuel tank.

12. Reverse the removal procedure to install the fuel pump(s).

13. Install the tank in the vehicle.

14. Install a minimum of 10 gallons (38L) of fuel and check for leaks.

15. Check for fuel leaks at the fittings.

16. Turn the ignition **ON** for 2 seconds. Turn the ignition **OFF** for 10 seconds. Turn the ignition **ON** and check for fuel leaks.

FUEL TANK

REMOVAL & INSTALLATION

See Figures 165 and 166.

1. Before servicing the vehicle, refer to the Precautions Section.

2. Drain the fuel tank.

3. Relieve the fuel system pressure.

4. Remove the exhaust system.

5. Remove the propeller shaft.

6. Disconnect the filler hose from the fuel tank.

7. Disconnect the filler vent tube from the evaporative emission hose.

8. Disconnect the fuel feed hose, the fuel return hose and the fuel EVAP hose from the chassis bundle.

9. Unplug the fuel tank electrical connector.

10. Disconnect the EVAP hoses from the EVAP canister.

11. Pull outward on the retainer tab in order to disengage the retainer from the chassis.

12. Unplug the electrical connector from the EVAP canister.

13. Raise the lower control arms using a suitable screw jack in order to remove the load from the lower shock bolts. Remove the lower shock bolts, then remove the screw jack.

14. Position the screw jack under the rear frame near the adjuster tie bar, in order to support the front of the rear frame. Remove the 2 front bolts from the rear frame. Use care not to over extend the rear brake hoses.

15. Lower the screw jack until there is approximately 2 inches (50 mm) between the front mounting surface of the rear frame and the chassis. This will allow clearance to access the fuel tank strap bolts.

16. Remove the fuel tank strap bolts. Position the fuel tank straps downward

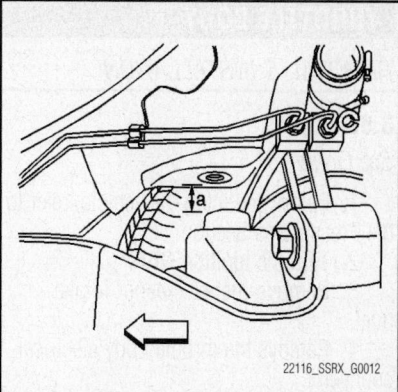

Fig. 165 Lower the rear frame so there is a gap of about 2 inches (a)

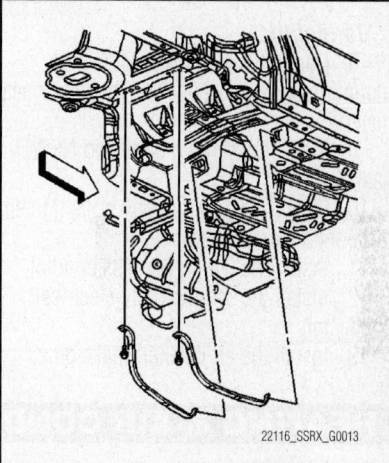

Fig. 166 Fuel tank strap mounting locations

around the rear frame. Carefully bend the fuel tank straps ONLY enough to allow the fuel tank to be removed.

17. Ensure the following are free from the surrounding components while lowering the fuel tank:

a. The fuel tank wiring harness

b. The EVAP wiring harness

c. The EVAP hoses at the EVAP canister

d. The fuel and EVAP hoses at the chassis pipes

18. With the aid of an assistant, carefully lower the fuel tank from the vehicle.

19. Installation is the reverse of removal. Tighten the tank strap bolts to 37 ft. lbs. (50 Nm).

IDLE SPEED

ADJUSTMENT

Idle speed is maintained by the Powertrain Control Module (PCM). No adjustment is necessary or possible.

THROTTLE BODY

REMOVAL & INSTALLATION

3.6L Engine

See Figure 167.

1. Before servicing the vehicle, refer to the Precautions Section.
2. Turn the ignition **OFF**.
3. Remove the air cleaner intake duct.
4. Remove the throttle body electrical connector.
5. Unlock and reposition the wiring harness conduit.
6. Remove the throttle body bolts.
7. Remove the throttle body and gasket.

To install:

8. Carefully clean the throttle body mounting surfaces of any gasket and/or seal material.
9. Install the throttle body and NEW gasket.
10. Install the throttle body bolts tighten to 89 inch lbs. (10 Nm).
11. Install the wiring harness conduit.
12. Install the throttle body electrical connector.
13. Install the air cleaner intake duct.

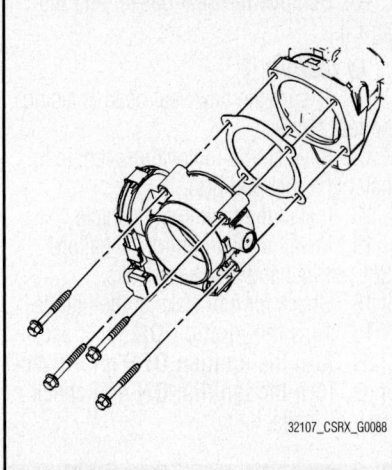

Fig. 167 Throttle body mounting bolts— 3.6L engine

14. Use a scan tool to perform the idle learn procedure and clear all DTCs.

4.6L Engine

1. Before servicing the vehicle, refer to the Precautions Section.
2. Remove the fuel injector sight shield.
3. Remove the air cleaner outlet duct.
4. Disconnect the electrical connector from the throttle body assembly.

5. Remove the throttle body assemble mounting bolts.
6. Remove the throttle body and throttle body gasket from the water housing.
7. Discard the throttle body gasket.

To install:

> **☀☀ WARNING**
>
> Do not use a cleaner which contains methyl ethyl ketone. This extremely strong solvent may damage components and is not necessary for this type of cleaning. Use a carburetor cleaner in order to remove deposits. Refer to the instructions provided with the cleaner. Do not reuse the old throttle body gasket.

8. Install the NEW gasket to the throttle body assembly.
9. Install the throttle body assembly to the water housing.
10. Install the throttle body assembly mounting bolts tighten to 89 inch lbs. (10 Nm).
11. Connect the electrical connector to the throttle body assembly.
12. Install the air cleaner outlet duct.
13. Install the fuel injector sight shield.

HEATING & AIR CONDITIONING SYSTEM

BLOWER MOTOR

REMOVAL & INSTALLATION

See Figure 168.

1. Before servicing the vehicle, refer to the Precautions Section.
2. Remove the right closeout insulator panel.
3. Remove the instrument panel (I/P) compartment.
4. Disconnect the blower motor electrical connector.
5. Disconnect the blower motor processor electrical connector.
6. Remove the screws (1) that retain the blower motor.
7. Remove the blower motor.

To install:

8. Install the blower motor.
9. Install the blower motor screws (1) and tighten to 13 inch lbs. (1.5 Nm).
10. Connect the blower motor processor electrical connector.
11. Connect the blower motor electrical connector.
12. Install the I/P compartment.
13. Install the right closeout insulator panel.

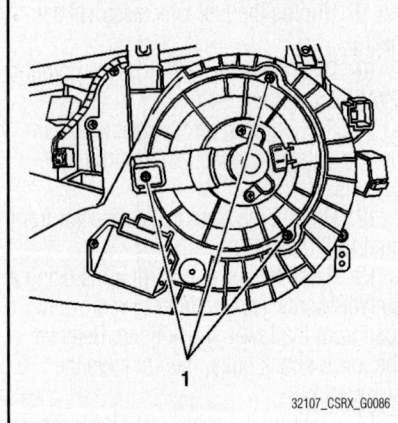

Fig. 168 Blower motor mounting screws (1)

HEATER CORE

REMOVAL & INSTALLATION

See Figure 169.

1. Before servicing the vehicle, refer to the Precautions Section.
2. Disconnect the negative battery cable.

3. Drain the cooling system into a clean container for reuse.
4. Recover the air conditioning refrigerant, into a refrigerant recovery station.
5. Disable the air bag system.
6. Disconnect the heater hoses from the heater core inlet and outlet tubes in the engine compartment.
7. Disconnect both A/C line fittings at the cowl. Remove the quick connect fittings, then remove and discard the O-rings.
8. Remove the instrument panel.
9. Remove the air inlet assembly.
10. Disconnect the HVAC module connector.
11. Press the tabs and release the left and right rear heater ducts from the HVAC module.
12. Remove the drain tube.
13. Remove the upper and lower HVAC mounting screws and remove the HVAC module.
14. Remove the heater core pipe bracket screw and bracket.
15. Remove the heater core.

To install:

16. Install the heater core to the HVAC module.

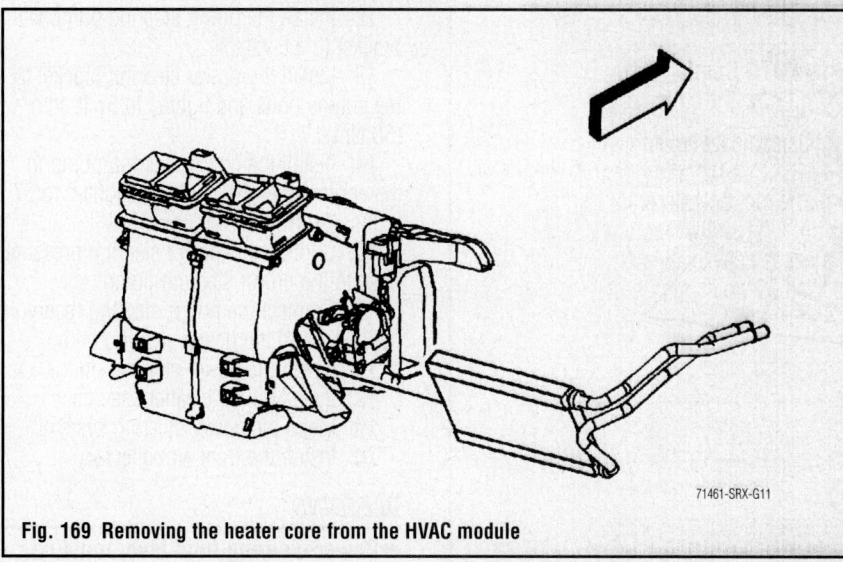

Fig. 169 Removing the heater core from the HVAC module

17. Install the heater core pipe bracket and screw.

18. Install the HAVC module. Tighten the mounting nuts to 89 inch lbs. (10 Nm).

19. Connect left and right rear heater ducts to the HVAC module

20. Install the drain tube.

21. Connect the HVAC module connector.

22. Install the air inlet assembly.

23. Install new O-rings to the A/C suction and liquid lines and connect them to the HVAC module.

24. Connect the heater hoses.

25. Install the instrument panel.

26. Recharge the air conditioning refrigerant.

27. Fill the cooling system.

28. Connect the negative battery cable.

29. Start the vehicle and check for leaks.

STEERING

POWER RACK & PINION STEERING GEAR

REMOVAL & INSTALLATION

See Figure 170.

➡**The front wheels must be in the straight ahead position and the steering column locked before disconnect the intermediate shaft. Failure to do so may result in damage to the SRS coil.**

1. Before servicing the vehicle, refer to the Precautions Section.

2. Center the steering wheel.

3. Install Steering Column Anti-rotation pin J-42640 to lock the steering column.

4. Remove or disconnect the following:

- Front wheels
- Front air deflector

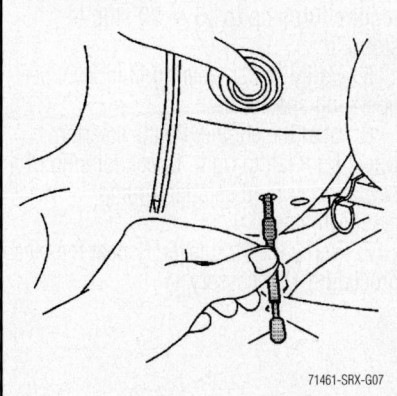

Fig. 170 Installing steering column anti-rotation pin

- Intermediate steering shaft lower pinch bolt
- Intermediate shaft from the steering gear
- Variable effort steering harness connector
- Outer tie rod retaining nuts
- Outer tie rods from steering knuckles
- Power steering hoses from steering gear
- Left brake line from brake hose and plug opening
- On AWD models, place a jack under the front differential
- On AWD models, remove the right engine mount-to-frame nut
- Raise the differential enough to clear the steering rack bolt

5. On all models, remove the steering gear mounting bolts.

6. Remove the left rear lower control arm-to-frame mounting bolt and nut.

7. Remove the steering gear through the left wheel opening.

To install:

8. Install the steering gear through the left wheel opening.

9. Install the left rear lower control arm-to-frame mounting bolt and nut.

10. Install the steering gear mounting bolts. Tighten the bolts to 134 ft. lbs. (180 Nm).

11. On AWD models, lower the differential.

12. On AWD models, install the right engine mount-to-frame nut and tighten to 59 ft. lbs. (80 Nm).

13. On AWD models, remove the differential jack.

14. Install or connect the following:

- Left brake line to brake hose
- Power steering hoses
- Outer tie rod to steering knuckles. Tighten the nuts to 52 ft. lbs. (70 Nm).
- Variable effort steering harness connector
- Intermediate shaft-to-steering gear
- Intermediate shaft pinch bolt and tighten to 37 ft. lbs. (50 Nm).
- Front air deflector
- Front wheels

15. Lower the vehicle.

16. Remove the steering wheel anti-rotation pin.

17. Fill the power steering oil reservoir.

18. Bleed the steering system.

19. Check and adjust the front wheel toe.

20. Start the vehicle and check for leaks.

POWER STEERING PUMP

REMOVAL & INSTALLATION

3.6L Engine

See Figure 171.

1. Before servicing the vehicle, refer to the Precautions Section.

2. Remove the front air deflector.

3. Remove the power steering pulley.

4. Remove the air cleaner assembly.

5. Disconnect the power steering reservoir outlet hose from the power steering pump.

6. Disconnect the power steering pressure hose from the power steering pump.

7. Remove the power steering bracket to the engine mounting bolts (1, 2, and 3).

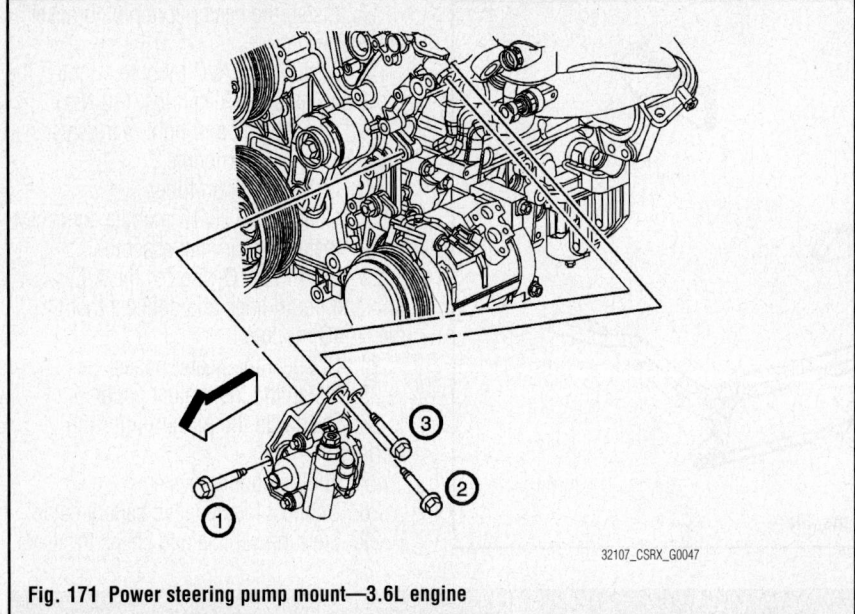

Fig. 171 Power steering pump mount—3.6L engine

8. Remove the power steering pump with bracket from the vehicle.

9. Remove the power steering pump bracket from the power steering pump.

To install:

10. Install the power steering pump to the power steering pump bracket and tighten to 18 ft. lbs. (25 Nm)

11. Install the power steering pump with bracket to the vehicle.

12. Install the power steering pump bracket to the engine mounting bolts (1, 2 and 3) and tighten in sequence to 37 ft. lbs. (50 Nm).

13. Connect the power steering pressure hose to the power steering pump.

14. Connect the power steering reservoir outlet hose to the power steering pump.

15. Install the power steering pulley.

16. Install the air cleaner assembly.

17. Bleed the power steering system.

18. Install the front air deflector.

4.6L Engine

See Figure 171.

1. Before servicing the vehicle, refer to the Precautions Section.

2. Remove the front air deflector.

3. Remove the power steering pulley.

4. Remove the air cleaner assembly.

5. Disconnect the power steering reservoir outlet hose from the power steering pump.

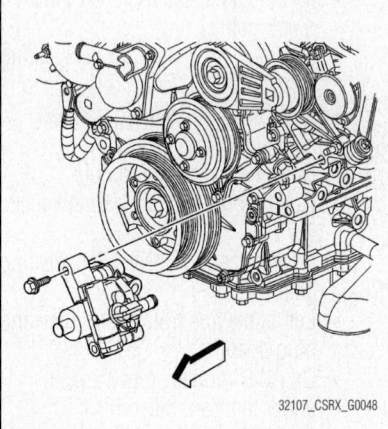

Fig. 172 Power steering pump mount—4.6L engine

6. Disconnect the power steering pressure hose from the power steering pump.

7. Remove the power steering pump to engine mounting bolt.

8. Remove the power steering bracket to the engine bolts.

9. Remove the power steering pump with bracket from the vehicle.

10. Remove the power steering pump to power steering bracket.

To install:

11. Install the power steering pump to power steering bracket and tighten the bolts to 18 ft. lbs. (25 Nm).

12. Install the power steering pump with bracket to the vehicle.

13. Install the power steering bracket to the engine bolts and tighten to 37 ft. lbs. (50 Nm).

14. Install the power steering pump to the engine mounting bolt and tighten to 37 ft. lbs. (50 Nm).

15. Connect the power steering pressure hose to the power steering pump.

16. Connect the power steering reservoir outlet hose to the power steering pump.

17. Install the power steering pulley.

18. Install the air cleaner assembly.

19. Bleed the power steering system.

20. Install the front air deflector.

BLEEDING

➡**Power steering fluid level must be maintained throughout bleed procedure.**

1. Fill pump reservoir with fluid to minimum system level; FULL COLD level, or middle of hash mark on cap stick fluid level indicator.

➡**With hydro-boost only, the oil level will appear falsely high if the hydro-boost accumulator is not fully charged. Do not apply the brake pedal with the engine OFF. This will discharge the hydro-boost accumulator.**

2. If equipped with hydro-boost, fully charge the hydro-boost accumulator using the following procedure:
   - Start the engine.
   - Firmly apply the brake pedal 10-15 times.
   - Turn the engine OFF.

3. Raise the vehicle until the front wheels are off the ground.

4. Key on engine OFF, turn the steering wheel from stop to stop 12 times. Vehicles equipped with hydro-boost systems or longer length power steering hoses may require turns up to 15 to 20 stop to stops.

5. Verify power steering fluid level per operating specification.

6. Start the engine. Rotate steering wheel from left to right. Check for sign of cavitation or fluid aeration (pump noise/whining).

7. Verify the fluid level. Repeat the bleed procedure, if necessary.

SUSPENSION

FRONT SUSPENSION

COIL SPRING

REMOVAL & INSTALLATION

See Figures 173 and 174.

※※ WARNING

Use care when handling the coil springs in order to avoid chipping or scratching the coating. Damage to the coating will result in premature failure of the coil springs.

➡ **This procedure requires the use of a universal spring compressor.**

1. Raise and support the vehicle.
2. Remove the tire and wheel.
3. Remove the shock module from the vehicle.
4. Install the shock module into the spring compressor.
5. Mark the upper control arm assembly and insulator for proper installation.

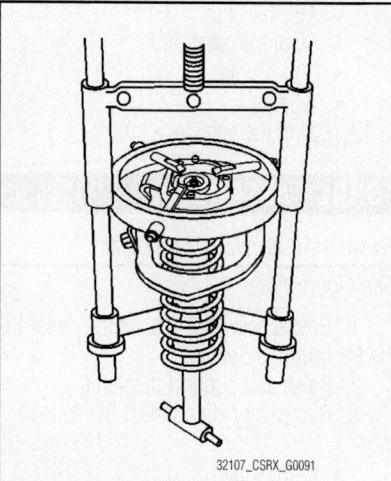

32107_CSRX_G0091

Fig. 173 Installing shock module into spring compressor

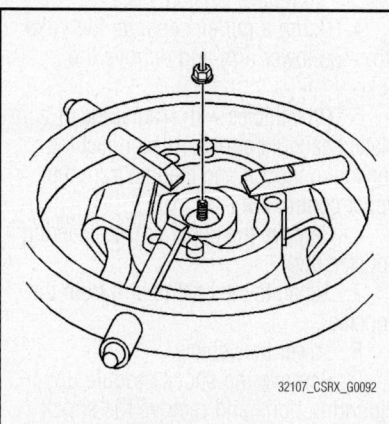

32107_CSRX_G0092

Fig. 174 Magnaride sensor nut

6. Turn the spring compressor forcing screw until the coil spring is compressed.
7. Remove the Magnaride sensor nut.
8. Remove the shock absorber upper retaining nut.
9. Remove the shock absorber from the shock module.
10. Loosen the compressor forcing screw until the upper mounting plate and coil spring may be removed.
11. Remove the upper control arm bracket assembly, insulator and coil spring from the spring compressor.

To install:

➡ **Ensure the alignment pins in the upper control arm bracket is orientated 90 degrees with the shock absorber lower mounting holes.**

12. Install the coil spring, insulator, upper control arm bracket assembly, and shock absorber to the spring compressor aligning all marks.
13. Turn the spring compressor forcing screw until the coil spring is compressed.
14. Install the shock absorber retaining nut and tighten to 18 ft. lbs. (25 Nm).
15. Install the Magnaride sensor nut.
16. Remove the shock module from the spring compressor.
17. Install the shock module to the vehicle.
18. Install the tire and wheel.
19. Lower the vehicle.

FRONT SUSPENSION FRAME

REMOVAL & INSTALLATION

See Figure 175.

1. Before servicing the vehicle, refer to the Precautions Section.
2. Install an engine support fixture to the top of the engine.
3. Raise and support the vehicle.
4. Remove the front wheels.
5. Remove the front air deflector.
6. Remove or disconnect the following:
   - Wheel speed sensor
   - Outer tie rod nuts
   - Separate the outer tie rods
   - Power steering return and pressure hose clamp bolts
   - Engine Control Module (ECM) and retaining bracket
   - Power steering cooler from the A/C condenser
   - Variable effort steering harness connector
   - Power steering lines from steering gear
   - Intermediate steering shaft lower pinch bolt
   - Intermediate shaft from steering gear
   - Brake lines from brake hoses
   - ABS module nuts and harness connector
   - Upper ball joint nuts
   - Separate the ball joint from steering knuckle
   - Shock yoke-to-shock nuts and bolts
   - Washer bottle-to-knuckle bolts
   - Engine mount lower retaining nuts

7. Install frame support table J-39580 under the vehicle and lower the vehicle to the frame support.
8. Remove the 6 frame mounting bolts.
9. With an assistant, slowly raise the body up away from the frame.
10. Remove the lower control arms and the stabilizer bar.
11. Remove the frame from the support fixture.

To install:

12. Install the frame to the support fixture.
13. Install the stabilizer bar.
14. Install the lower control arms.

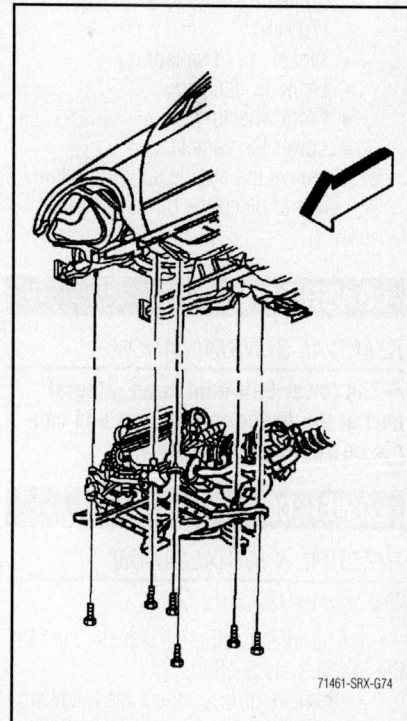

71461-SRX-G74

Fig. 175 Removing front suspension frame mounting bolts

15. Place the frame assembly under the vehicle.

16. Carefully lower the vehicle to the frame.

17. Install the frame mounting bolts and tighten to 141 ft. lbs. (191 Nm).

18. Raise the vehicle from the support fixture.

19. Install the engine mount lower nuts and tighten to 59 ft. lbs. (80 Nm).

20. Install or connect the following:

- Washer bottle
- Shock yoke-to-shock retainers and tighten to 133 ft. lbs. (180 Nm).
- Ball joint to steering knuckle
- Upper ball joint nuts and tighten 15 ft. lbs., plus an additional 210°
- ABS module nuts and harness connector
- Brake lines to brake hoses
- Intermediate shaft to steering gear
- Intermediate steering shaft lower pinch bolt and tighten to 37 ft. lbs. (50 Nm)
- Power steering lines to steering gear
- Variable effort steering harness connector
- Power steering cooler to the A/C condenser
- ECM and retaining bracket
- Power steering return and pressure hose clamp bolts
- Connect the outer tie rods and tighten the nuts to 52 ft. lbs. (70 Nm)
- Wheel speed sensor
- Front air deflector
- Front wheels
- Lower the vehicle

21. Remove the engine support fixture.

22. Fill and bleed the power steering system

LOWER BALL JOINT

REMOVAL & INSTALLATION

➡The lower ball joint is an integral part of the lower control arm and cannot be serviced separately.

LOWER CONTROL ARM

REMOVAL & INSTALLATION

See Figures 176 and 177.

1. Before servicing the vehicle, refer to the Precautions Section.

2. Remove or disconnect the following:

- Wheel
- Shock yoke
- Stabilizer shaft link

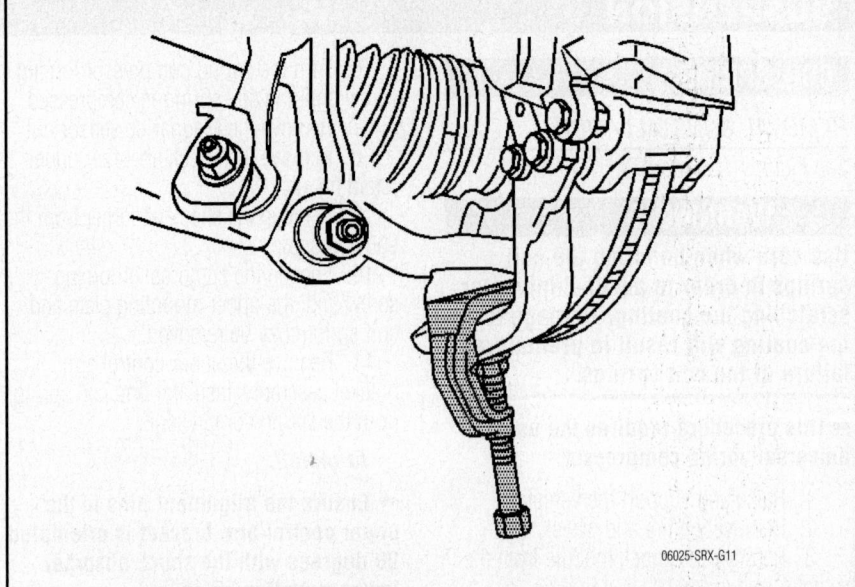

Fig. 176 Using the ball joint remover tool to separate the lower control arm from the knuckle.

06025-SRX-G11

- ABS harness
- Lower control arm-to-steering knuckle nut

3. Separate the lower control arm from knuckle using Ball Joint Remover J-43631.

4. Loosen the steering gear mounting nuts and raise the steering gear.

5. Remove the control arm to cradle nuts and bolts.

6. Lower the control arm at the frame and move the ball joint upward.

7. Remove the lower control arm.

To install:

8. Install the lower arm on the ball joint and move the arm up to meet the cradle.

9. Install the lower arm-to-cradle nuts and bolts. Tighten the nuts to 96 ft. lbs. (135 Nm).

10. Lower the steering gear and install the bolts. Tighten the bolts to 89 ft. lbs. (120 Nm).

11. Install or connect the following:

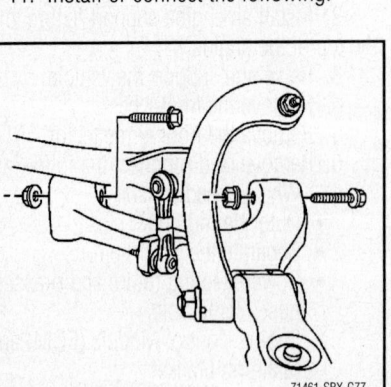

Fig. 177 Front lower control arm-to-cradle mounting bolts

71461-SRX-G77

- Lower control arm-to-steering knuckle nut. Tighten to 15 ft. lbs. (20 Nm) plus 210°
- ABS harness
- Stabilizer shaft link
- Shock yoke
- Wheels

12. Lower the vehicle.

SHOCK ABSORBERS

REMOVAL & INSTALLATION

See Figure 178.

1. Before servicing the vehicle, refer to the Precautions Section.

2. Raise and support the vehicle.

3. Remove or disconnect the following:

- Front wheel
- Shock-to yoke retaining nut
- Shock-to-yoke retaining bolt by pulling up on the lower control arm to relieve tension

4. Using a puller, separate the yoke from the lower arm and remove the yoke.

5. On vehicles with Magnaride or automatic headlight aiming, disconnect the sensor connector and the link from the upper control arm.

6. Remove the upper arm-to-steering knuckle nut.

7. Separate the control arm from the knuckle.

8. Lower the vehicle.

9. Remove the shock module upper mounting bolts and remove the shock module.

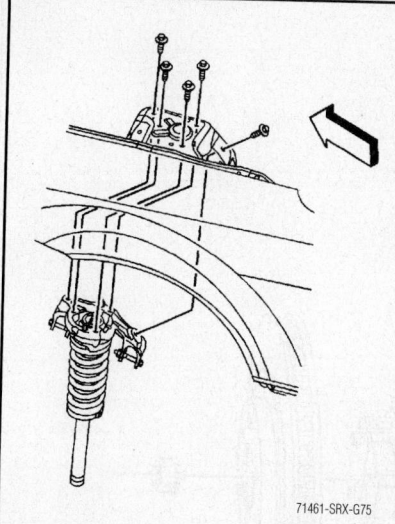

Fig. 178 Front shock module assembly mounting

To install:

10. Install the shock module and tighten the upper mounting nuts to 83 ft. lbs. (112 Nm).

11. Install the upper control arm to the knuckle and tighten the nut to 18 ft. lbs. (20 Nm), plus an additional 210°.

12. On vehicles with Magnaride or automatic headlight aiming, connect the sensor connector and the link to the upper control arm.

13. Connect the yoke to the lower arm and install the nut.

14. Install the yoke to the shock.

15. Tighten the shock-to-yoke nut to 81 ft. lbs. (110 Nm), and the yoke to lower control arm nut to 133 ft. lbs. (180 Nm).

16. Install the front wheel.

17. Lower the vehicle.

STABILIZER BAR

REMOVAL & INSTALLATION

1. Raise and safely support the vehicle.
2. Remove the wheels.
3. Remove the stabilizer bar link nuts.
4. Disconnect the stabilizer shaft links from the stabilizer bar.
5. Remove the bar mounting bolts and bracket.
6. Remove the insulators from the stabilizer shaft.
7. Remove the stabilizer bar.

To install:

8. Install the stabilizer bar.
9. Install the bar insulators to the shaft with the slits facing rearward.
10. Install the stabilizer shaft bracket and bolts but do not tighten.

11. Connect the shaft links to the bar and tighten the nuts to 95 ft. lbs. (115 Nm), and the bolts to 81 ft. lbs. (110 Nm).

12. Install the wheels and lower the vehicle.

STEERING KNUCKLE

REMOVAL & INSTALLATION

See Figure 179.

1. Before servicing the vehicle, refer to the Precautions Section.
2. Raise and safely support the vehicle.
3. Remove the wheel and tire assembly.
4. Remove the wheel hub/bearing assembly.
5. Remove the outer tie rod-to-steering knuckle nut.
6. Disconnect the tie rod from the steering knuckle.
7. Remove the brake hose bracket bolts.
8. Remove the upper and lower control arm ball joint-to-knuckle nuts.
9. Separate the lower ball joint from the knuckle.
10. Remove the steering knuckle.
11. If the ball joints are to be removed, press the appropriate ball joint out the mounting.

To install:

12. If a ball joint was removed, install the appropriate ball joint.
13. Install the steering knuckle to the upper and lower ball joints.
14. Install new ball joint nuts and tighten the nuts to 15 ft. lbs. (20 Nm), plus an additional 210°.
15. Install the brake hose bracket bolts.

16. Connect the outer tie rod to the steering knuckle and tighten the retaining nut to 52 ft. lbs. (70 Nm).

17. Install the wheel hub/ bearing assembly.

18. Install the wheel and tire assembly.

UPPER BALL JOINT

REMOVAL & INSTALLATION

➡**The upper ball joint is an integral part of the upper control arm/shock absorber assembly and cannot be serviced separately.**

UPPER CONTROL ARM

REMOVAL & INSTALLATION

Refer to the shock absorber removal procedure.

WHEEL HUB AND BEARINGS

REMOVAL & INSTALLATION

See Figure 180.

The wheel bearing is integral with the wheel hub and cannot be replaced separately. If the wheel bearing is found to be defective, the wheel hub must be replaced as an assembly.

1. Before servicing the vehicle, refer to the Precautions Section.
2. Raise and safely support the vehicle.
3. Remove the wheel and tire assembly.
4. On AWD models, remove axle hub nut and discard.
5. On all models, remove the brake caliper and wire it out of the way.

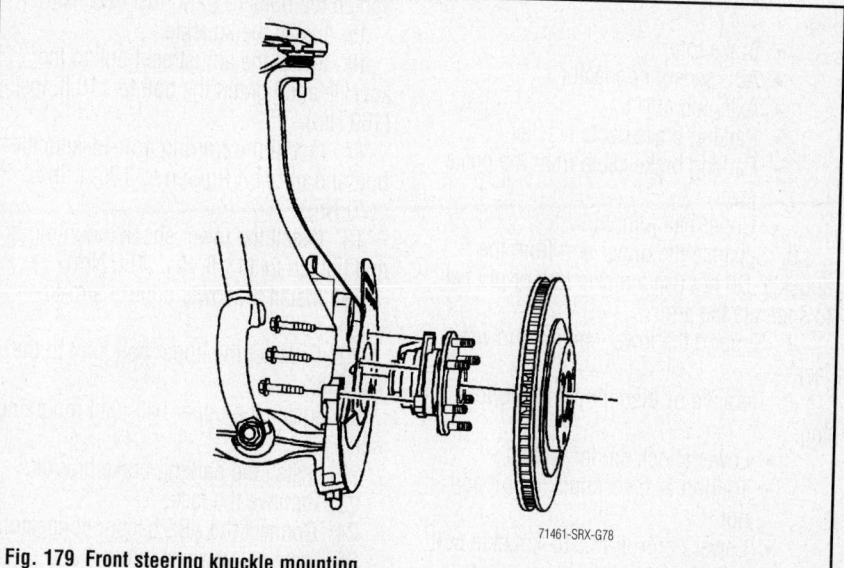

Fig. 179 Front steering knuckle mounting

6. Remove the brake rotor.

7. Disconnect the ABS sensor connector.

8. On AWD models, install tool J-45859 onto the wheel hub and secure with 2 lug nuts.

9. Use the tool to disengage the half-shaft from the wheel hub and bearing. Support the halfshaft.

10. On all models from the backside, remove the wheel hub/bearing retaining bolts.

11. Remove the wheel hub/bearing assembly.

To install:

12. Install the wheel hub/bearing and tighten the bolts to 100 ft. lbs. (135 Nm).

13. Install a new axle shaft nut and tighten the nut to 118 ft. lbs. (160 Nm).

14. Install or connect the following:
- ABS sensor connector
- Brake rotor
- Brake caliper
- Wheel and tire assembly

ADJUSTMENT

No adjustment is necessary

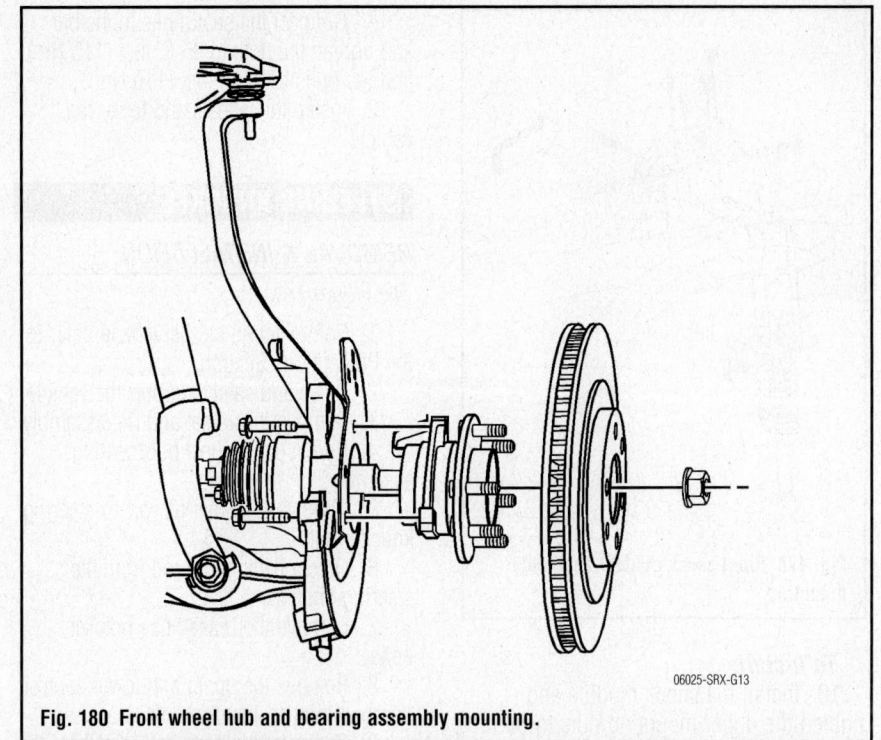

Fig. 180 Front wheel hub and bearing assembly mounting.

06025-SRX-G13

SUSPENSION

BALL JOINTS AND KNUCKLE

REMOVAL & INSTALLATION

1. Before servicing the vehicle, refer to the Precautions Section.

2. Raise and safely support the vehicle.

3. Remove the wheel and tire assembly.

4. Remove the brake caliper and wire it out of the way.

5. Remove or disconnect the following:
- Brake rotor
- ABS sensor connector
- Axle hub nut
- Parking brake cable bracket
- Parking brake cable from the brake lever
- Upper ball joint nut

6. Separate the upper arm from the knuckle. Do not use a pickle fork or pry bar to separate the arm.

7. Support the lower control arm with a jack.

8. Remove or disconnect the following:
- Lower shock mounting bolt
- Trailing arm-to-knuckle bolt and nut
- Lower control arm-to-knuckle bolt
- Adjustment link-to-knuckle nut

9. Install tool J-45859 onto the wheel hub and secure with 2 lug nuts.

10. Use the tool to disengage the half-shaft from the wheel hub and bearing. Support the halfshaft.

11. Remove the knuckle.

12. Separate the wheel hub/bearing from the knuckle and backing plate.

To install:

13. Install the wheel hub/bearing to the knuckle and backing plate.

14. Install the wheel hub/bearing and tighten the bolts to 92 ft. lbs. (125 Nm).

15. Install the knuckle.

16. Install the adjustment link to the knuckle and tighten the bolt to 118 ft. lbs. (160 Nm).

17. Install the trailing arm-to-knuckle bolt and nut and tighten to 125 ft. lbs. (170 Nm).

18. Install the lower shock mounting bolt and tighten to 111 ft. lbs. (150 Nm).

19. Install the lower control arm-to-knuckle bolt.

20. Connect the upper ball joint to the knuckle.

21. Install the upper ball joint mounting nut.

22. Install the parking brake bracket.

23. Remove the jack.

24. Connect the ABS sensor connector.

25. Install a new axle hub nut and tighten to 118 ft. lbs. (160 Nm).

REAR SUSPENSION

26. Install the brake rotor.

27. Install the brake caliper.

28. Install the wheel and tire assembly.

COIL SPRING

REMOVAL & INSTALLATION

See Figure 181.

1. Before servicing the vehicle, refer to the Precautions Section.

2. Raise and safely support the vehicle.

3. Remove the rear wheels.

4. Disconnect the Magnaride and headlight adjustment sensor link from the upper control arm.

5. Raise and support the lower control arm with a jack.

6. Remove the shock absorber lower mounting bolt.

7. Lower the control arm and remove the jack.

8. Support the rear frame with a jack.

9. Remove the 4 rear frame to body bolts and lower the frame far enough to remove the coil spring without going past the guide pins.

10. Remove the coil spring.

To install:

11. Install the coil spring.

12. Raise the frame and install the mounting bolts. Tighten the front bolts to

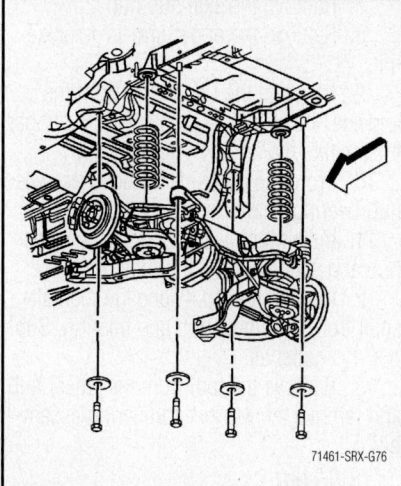
Fig. 181 Removing the rear coil spring

195 ft. lbs. (265 Nm), and the rear bolts to 140 ft. lbs. (191 Nm).

13. Remove the frame jack.

14. Place a jack under the lower control arm.

15. Raise the jack until the shock absorber aligns with the lower control arm.

16. Install the lower shock bolt and tighten the bolt to 111 ft. lbs. (150 Nm).

17. Remove the jack.

18. Connect the Magnaride and headlight adjustment link to the upper control arm.

19. Install the rear wheels.

20. Lower the vehicle.

LOWER CONTROL ARM

REMOVAL & INSTALLATION

1. Before servicing the vehicle, refer to the Precautions Section.

2. Remove or disconnect the following:
- Wheel
- Stabilizer shaft link
- Coil spring
- Lower arm-to-knuckle bolt
- Lower arm-to-frame bolt
- Lower control arm

To install:

3. Install the lower arm and the retaining bolts and nuts.

4. Install the coil spring.

5. Tighten the lower arm-to-frame bolt and nut to 100 ft. lbs. (135 Nm).

6. Tighten the lower arm-to-knuckle bolt to 118 ft. lbs. (160 Nm).

7. Install or connect the following:
- Coil spring
- Stabilizer shaft link
- Wheel

SHOCK ABSORBER

REMOVAL & INSTALLATION

1. Before servicing the vehicle, refer to the Precautions Section.

2. Remove the rear interior trim panel to access the upper shock mounting.

3. Move the sound insulator away from the shock tower.

4. On vehicles with Magnaride®, disconnect the electrical connector.

5. Remove the upper shock mounting nuts.

6. Raise and support the vehicle.

7. Disconnect the Magnaride connector from the shock.

8. Remove the lower shock mounting bolt.

9. Remove the shock absorber.

To install:

10. Install the shock to the vehicle.

11. Tighten the lower mounting bolt to 111 ft. lbs. (150 Nm).

12. Connect the connector to the shock.

13. Install the shock into the shock tower and tighten the upper nuts to 18 ft. lbs. (25 Nm).

14. Connect the Magnaride connector.

15. Reposition the sound insulator.

16. Install the trim panel.

UPPER CONTROL ARM

REMOVAL & INSTALLATION

See Figure 182.

1. Before servicing the vehicle, refer to the Precautions Section.

2. Remove or disconnect the following:
- Wheel
- Upper arm-to-knuckle nut

3. Separate the upper arm from the knuckle using Ball Joint Remover J-43631. Do not use a pickle fork or pry bar to separate the arm.

4. Remove the upper arm-to-frame mounting bolts and nuts and remove the upper control arm.

To install:

5. Install the upper control arm and loosely install the mounting nuts and bolts.

6. Connect the arm to the knuckle.

7. Tighten the arm-to-knuckle nut to 15 ft. lbs. (20 Nm), plus an additional 210°. Tighten the arm-to-frame nuts and bolts to 111 ft. lbs. (150 Nm).

8. Install the wheel.

WHEEL HUB AND BEARING

REMOVAL & INSTALLATION

See Figure 183.

1. Before servicing the vehicle, refer to the Precautions Section.

2. Raise and safely support the vehicle.

3. Remove the wheel and tire assembly.

4. Remove the brake caliper and wire it out of the way.

5. Remove the brake rotor.

6. Disconnect the ABS sensor connector.

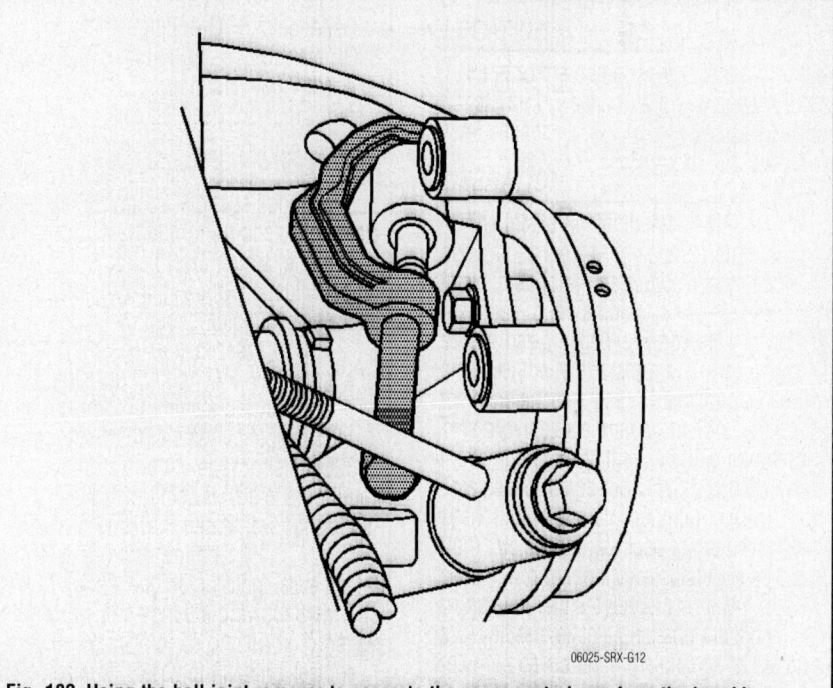
Fig. 182 Using the ball joint remover to separate the upper control arm from the knuckle.

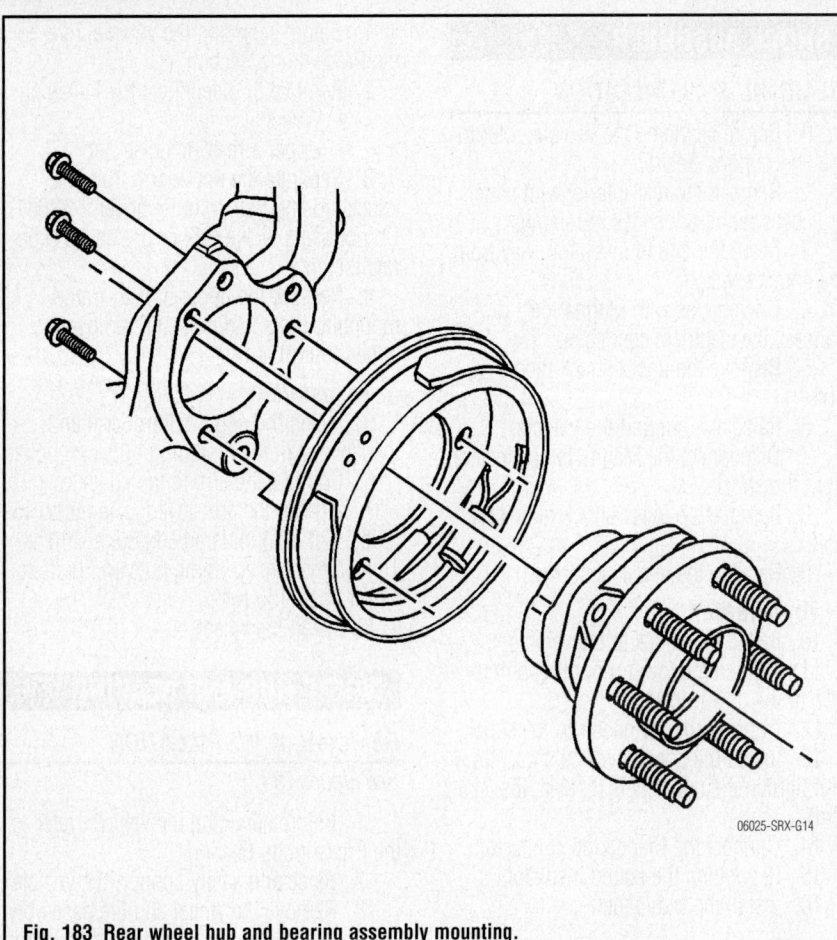

Fig. 183 Rear wheel hub and bearing assembly mounting.

7. Remove the axle hub nut.

8. Remove the upper arm-to-knuckle nut

9. Separate the upper arm from the knuckle. Do not use a pickle fork or pry bar to separate the arm.

10. From the backside, remove the wheel hub/bearing retaining bolts.

11. Install tool J-45859 onto the wheel hub and secure with 2 lug nuts.

12. Use the tool to disengage the halfshaft from the wheel hub and bearing. Support the halfshaft.

13. Remove the tool from the wheel hub and remove the wheel hub/bearing assembly.

To install:

14. Install the wheel hub/bearing and tighten the bolts to 92 ft. lbs. (125 Nm).

15. Connect the arm to the knuckle and tighten the nut to 15 ft. lbs. (20 Nm), plus an additional 210°.

16. Install a new axle shaft nut and tighten the nut to 118 ft. lbs. (160 Nm).

17. Install or connect the following:
- ABS sensor connector
- Brake rotor
- Brake caliper
- Wheel and tire assembly

ADJUSTMENT

➡**No adjustment is necessary.**

SPECIFICATIONS AND MAINTENANCE CHARTS

ENGINE AND VEHICLE IDENTIFICATION

Engine								Model Year	
Code	Liters (cc)	Cu. In.	Cyl.	Fuel Sys.	Engine Type	Eng. Mfg.		Code ①	Year
1ZZ-FE	1.8 (1794)	109	4	EFI	DOHC	Toyota		5	2005
2ZZ-GE	1.8 (1796)	109.5	4	EFI	DOHC	Toyota		6	2006
								7	2007

EFI: Electronic Fuel Injection

DOHC: Double Overhead Camshaft

① 10th digit of VIN

22116_VIBE_C0001

GENERAL ENGINE SPECIFICATIONS

Year	Model	Engine Displacement Liters (VIN)	Net Horsepower @ rpm	Net Torque @ rpm (ft. lbs.)	Bore x Stroke (in.)	Com- pression Ratio	Oil Pressure @ idle
2005	Vibe	1.8 (1ZZ-FE)	①	②	3.11x3.60	10.0:1	4.2
	Vibe	1.8 (2ZZ-GE)	180@7600	130@6800	3.23x3.35	11.5:1	2.8
2006	Vibe	1.8 (1ZZ-FE)	①	②	3.11x3.60	10.0:1	4.2
	Vibe	1.8 (2ZZ-GE)	180@7600	130@6800	3.23x3.35	11.5:1	2.8
2007	Vibe	1.8 (1ZZ-FE)	①	②	3.11x3.60	10.0:1	4.2
	Vibe	1.8 (2ZZ-GE)	170@7600	130@6800	3.23x3.35	11.5:1	2.8

EFI: Electronic Fuel Injection

① 2WD models: 130@6000

  4WD models: 123@6000

② 2WD models: 125@4400

  4WD models: 118@4400

22116_VIBE_C0002

ENGINE TUNE-UP SPECIFICATIONS

Year	Engine Displacement Liters (VIN)	Spark Plug Gap (in.)	Ignition Timing (deg.)	Fuel Pump (psi)	Idle Speed (rpm)		Valve Clearance	
					MT	AT	Intake	Exhaust
2005	1.8 (1ZZ-FE)	0.043	①	44-50	650-750	650-750	0.0059-0.0098	0.0098-0.0138
	1.8 (2ZZ-GE)	0.043	②	44-50	750-850	700-800	0.0031-0.0071	0.0087-0.0126
2006	1.8 (1ZZ-FE)	0.043	①	44-50	650-750	650-750	0.0059-0.0098	0.0098-0.0138
	1.8 (2ZZ-GE)	0.043	②	44-50	750-850	700-800	0.0031-0.0071	0.0087-0.0126
2007	1.8 (1ZZ-FE)	0.040-0.048	①	44-50	650-750	650-750	0.0059-0.0098	0.0098-0.0138
	1.8 (2ZZ-GE)	0.040-0.051	②	44-50	750-850	700-800	0.0031-0.0071	0.0087-0.0126

NOTE: The Vehicle Emission Control Information label often reflects specification changes made during production. The label figures must be used if they differ from those in this chart.

① With terminal TC and CG of DLC3 connected: 8-12 degrees BTDC
  With terminal TC and CG of DLC3 disconnected: 10-18 degrees BTDC

② With terminal TC and CG of DLC3 connected: 8-12 degrees BTDC
  A59 With terminal TC and CG of DLC3 disconnected:
  A/T: 10-18 degrees BTDC
  M/T: 4-12 degrees BTDC

22116_VIBE_C0004

CAPACITIES

Year	Model	Engine Displacement Liters (VIN)	Engine Oil with Filter	Transmission (pts.)			Drive Axle		Fuel Tank (gal.)	Cooling System (qts.)
				5-Spd	6-Spd	Auto.	Front (pts.)	Rear (pts.)		
2005	Vibe	1.8 (1ZZ-FE)	3.9	4.0	4.0	6.0	3.0	—	12.0	6.9
	Vibe	1.8 (2ZZ-GE)	4.8	4.8	4.8	6.6	①	—	13.0	7.1
2006	Vibe	1.8 (1ZZ-FE)	3.9	4.0	4.0	6.0	3.0	—	12.0	6.9
	Vibe	1.8 (2ZZ-GE)	4.8	4.8	4.8	6.6	①	—	13.0	7.1
2007	Vibe	1.8 (1ZZ-FE)	3.9	4.0	4.0	6.0	3.0	—	12.0	6.9
	Vibe	1.8 (2ZZ-GE)	4.8	4.8	4.8	6.6	①	—	13.0	7.1

Note: All capacities are approximate. Add fluid gradually and check to be sure a proper fluid level is obtained.

① Included in transaxle capacity

22116_VIBE_C0003

FLUID SPECIFICATIONS

Year	Model	Engine Displacement Liters (VIN)	Engine Oil	Auto. Trans.	Drive Axle	Power Steering Fluid	Brake Master Cylinder
2005	Vibe	1.8 (1ZZ-FE)	①	②	—	③	DOT 3
2006	Vibe	1.8 (1ZZ-FE)	①	②	—	③	DOT 3
2007	Vibe	1.8 (1ZZ-FE)	①	②	—	③	DOT 3

DOT: Department Of Transpotation

① 5W-30 oil meeting GM Standard GM6094M

② T-IV Automatic Transmission Fluid (GM Part No. U.S. 88900925, in Canada 22689186).

③ DEXRON®-VI Automatic Transmission Fluid

22116_VIBE_C0010

VALVE SPECIFICATIONS

Year	Engine Displacement Liters (VIN)	Seat Angle (deg.)	Face Angle (deg.)	Spring Test Pressure (lbs. @ in.)	Spring Installed Height (in.)	Stem-to-Guide Clearance (in.)		Stem Diameter (in.)	
						Intake	Exhaust	Intake	Exhaust
2005	1.8 (1ZZ-FE)	45	44.5	31.3-34.8@ 1.252	1.323	0.0010- 0.0024	0.0012- 0.0026	0.2154- 0.2159	0.2152- 0.2158
	1.8 (2ZZ-GE)	45	44.5	①	1.516	0.0010- 0.0023	0.0012- 0.0025	0.2145- 0.2156	0.2144- 0.2154
2006	1.8 (1ZZ-FE)	45	44.5	31.3-34.8@ 1.252	1.323	0.0010- 0.0024	0.0012- 0.0026	0.2154- 0.2159	0.2152- 0.2158
	1.8 (2ZZ-GE)	45	44.5	①	1.516	0.0010- 0.0023	0.0012- 0.0025	0.2145- 0.2156	0.2144- 0.2154
2007	1.8 (1ZZ-FE)	45	45	31.3-34.8@ 1.252	②	0.0010- 0.0023	0.0011- 0.0028	0.2150- 0.2155	0.2143- 0.2153
	1.8 (2ZZ-GE)	45	45	①	②	0.0010- 0.0023	0.0011- 0.0028	0.2150- 0.2155	0.2143- 0.2153

① Intake: 49.6-55.5@1.516

Exhaust: 47.6-52.6@1.516

② Intake: 1.831

Exhaust: 1.830

22116_VIBE_C0005

CRANKSHAFT AND CONNECTING ROD SPECIFICATIONS

All measurements are given in inches.

Year	Engine Displacement Liters (VIN)	Crankshaft				Connecting Rod		
		Main Brg. Journal Dia.	Main Brg. Oil Clearance	Shaft End-play	Thrust on No.	Journal Diameter	Oil Clearance	Side Clearance
2005	1.8 (1ZZ-FE)	1.8893-1.8898	0.0006-0.0013	0.0008-0.0087	3	1.7320-1.7323	0.0011-0.0024	0.0063-0.0135
	1.8 (2ZZ-GE)	1.8893-1.8898	0.0006-0.0013	0.0016-0.0094	3	1.7713-1.7717	0.0011-0.0020	0.0063-0.0135
2006	1.8 (1ZZ-FE)	1.8893-1.8898	0.0006-0.0013	0.0008-0.0087	3	1.7320-1.7323	0.0011-0.0024	0.0063-0.0135
	1.8 (2ZZ-GE)	1.8893-1.8898	0.0006-0.0013	0.0016-0.0094	3	1.7713-1.7717	0.0011-0.0020	0.0063-0.0135
2007	1.8 (1ZZ-FE)	1.8893-1.8898	0.0006-0.0013	0.0016-0.0094	3	1.7320-1.7323	0.0011-0.0024	0.0063-0.0135
	1.8 (2ZZ-GE)	1.8893-1.8898	0.0006-0.0013	0.0016-0.0094	3	1.7713-1.7717	0.0011-0.0020	0.0063-0.0135

22116_VIBE_C0006

PISTON AND RING SPECIFICATIONS

All measurements are given in inches.

Year	Engine Displacement Liters (VIN)	Piston Clearance	Ring Gap			Ring Side Clearance		
			Top Compression	Bottom Compression	Oil Control	Top Compression	Bottom Compression	Oil Control
2005	1.8 (1ZZ-FE)	0.0026-0.0035	0.0098-0.0138	0.0138-0.0197	0.0059-0.0197	0.0009-0.0028	0.0012-0.0028	0.0012-0.0043
	1.8 (2ZZ-GE)	0.0003-0.0015	0.0098-0.0138	0.0138-0.0197	NA	0.0009-0.0028	0.0012-0.0028	NA
2006	1.8 (1ZZ-FE)	0.0026-0.0035	0.0098-0.0138	0.0138-0.0197	0.0059-0.0197	0.0009-0.0028	0.0012-0.0028	0.0012-0.0043
	1.8 (2ZZ-GE)	0.0003-0.0015	0.0098-0.0138	0.0138-0.0197	NA	0.0009-0.0028	0.0012-0.0028	NA
2007	1.8 (1ZZ-FE)	0.0039	0.0098-0.0138	0.0138-0.0197	0.0059-0.0197	0.0009-0.0028	0.0012-0.0028	0.0012-0.0043
	1.8 (2ZZ-GE)	0.0039	0.0098-0.0138	0.0138-0.0197	0.0059-0.0197	0.0009-0.0028	0.0012-0.0028	NA

NA - Not available

22116_VIBE_C0007

TORQUE SPECIFICATIONS

All readings in ft. lbs.

Year	Engine Displacement Liters (VIN)	Cylinder Head Bolts	Main Bearing Bolts	Rod Bearing Bolts	Crankshaft Damper Bolts	Flywheel Bolts	Manifold		Spark Plugs	Oil Pan Drain Plug
							Intake	Exhaust		
2005	1.8 (1ZZ-FE)	①	②	③	102	①	22	27	18	26
	1.8 (2ZZ-GE)	④	⑤	⑥	87	①	⑦	37	13	26
2006	1.8 (1ZZ-FE)	①	②	③	102	①	22	27	18	26
	1.8 (2ZZ-GE)	④	⑤	⑥	87	①	⑦	37	13	26
2007	1.8 (1ZZ-FE)	⑧	⑨	③	105	⑩	13	37	21	26
	1.8 (2ZZ-GE)	④	⑤	⑥	87	⑪	⑦	37	21	26

① Step 1: 36 ft. lbs.
Step 2: 90 degree turn

② 12 pointed bolts:
Step 1: 33 ft. lbs.
Step 2: 90 degree turn
Hex head bolts: 14 ft. lbs.

③ Step 1: 15 ft. lbs.
Step 2: 90 degree turn

④ Step 1: 26 ft. lbs.
Step 2: 180 degree turn

⑤ 12 pointed bolts:
Step 1: 16 ft. lbs.
Step 2: 32 ft. lbs.
Step 3: 45 degree turn
Step 4: 45 degree turn
Hex head bolts: 13 ft. lbs

⑥ Step 1: 22 ft. lbs.
Step 2: 90 degree turn

⑦ Bolt A: 25 ft. lbs.
Bolt B: 34 ft. lbs.

⑧ Step 1: 18 ft. lbs.
Step 2: 36 ft. lbs.
Step 3: 36 ft. lbs. Plus a 90 degree turn

⑨ Step 1: 16 ft. lbs.
Step 2: 32 ft. lbs.
Step 2: 32 ft. lbs. Plus a 90 degree turn

⑩ Automatic transmission: 61 ft. lbs.
Manual transmission: 36 ft. lbs. plus a 90 degree turn

⑪ Automatic transmission: 65 ft. lbs.
Manual transmission: 36 ft. lbs. plus a 90 degree turn

22116_VIBE_C0008

WHEEL ALIGNMENT

Year	Model		Caster Range (+/-Deg.)	Caster Preferred Setting (Deg.)	Camber Range (+/-Deg.)	Camber Preferred Setting (Deg.)	Toe-in (in.)
2005	Vibe - 2WD	F	0.75	+2.78	0.75	-0.77	0+/-0.08
		R	—	—	0.50	-1.45	0.11+/-0.11
	Vibe - 4WD	F	0.75	+2.77	0.75	-0.48	0+/-0.08
		R	—	—	0.75	-0.73	0.08+/-0.08
2006	Vibe - 2WD	F	0.75	+2.78	0.75	-0.77	0+/-0.08
		R	—	—	0.50	-1.45	0.11+/-0.11
	Vibe - 4WD	F	0.75	+2.77	0.75	-0.48	0+/-0.08
		R	—	—	0.75	-0.73	0.08+/-0.08
2007	Vibe - 2WD	F	0.75	+2.78	0.75	-0.77	0+/-0.08
		R	—	—	0.50	-1.45	0.11+/-0.11
	Vibe - 4WD	F	0.75	+2.77	0.75	-0.48	0+/-0.08
		R	—	—	0.75	-0.73	0.08+/-0.08

22116_VIBE_C0011

TIRE, WHEEL AND BALL JOINT SPECIFICATIONS

Year	Model	OEM Tires Standard	OEM Tires Optional	Tire Pressures (psi) Front	Tire Pressures (psi) Rear	Wheel Size	Ball Joint Inspection	Lug Nuts (ft. lbs.)
2005	Vibe	205/55R16	—	33	33	6.5-JJ	9-26 in. ①	76
2006	Vibe	205/55R16	—	33	33	6.5-JJ	9-26 in. ①	76
2007	Vibe	205/55R16	—	33	33	6.5-JJ	9-26 in. ①	76

OEM: Original Equipment Manufacturer

PSI: Pounds Per Square Inch

STD: Standard

OPT: Optional

① Torque required in inch lbs. to rotate ball joint when removed from the knuckle

22116_VIBE_C0012

BRAKE SPECIFICATIONS
All measurements in inches unless noted

Year	Model		Brake Disc			Brake Drum Diameter			Minimum Lining Thickness	Brake Caliper	
			Original Thickness	Minimum Thickness	Maximum Runout	Original Inside Diameter	Max. Wear Limit	Maximum Machine Diameter		Bracket Bolts (ft. lbs.)	Mounting Bolts (ft. lbs.)
2005	Vibe	F	0.984	0.906	0.0020	—	—	—	0.039	79	25
		R	0.354	0.295	0.0059	9.00	—	9.04	0.039	34	—
2006	Vibe	F	0.984	0.906	0.0020	—	—	—	0.039	79	25
		R	0.354	0.295	0.0059	9.00	—	9.04	0.039	34	—
2007	Vibe	F	0.984	0.906	0.0020	—	—	—	0.039	79	25
		R	0.354	0.295	0.0059	9.00	—	9.04	0.039	34	—

F: Front

R: Rear

22116_VIBE_C0013

SCHEDULED MAINTENANCE INTERVALS
PONTIAC—VIBE

TO BE SERVICED	TYPE OF SERVICE	VEHICLE MILEAGE INTERVAL (x1000)												
		7.5	15	22.5	30	37.5	45	52.5	60	67.5	75	82.5	90	97.5
Engine oil & filter	R	✔	✔	✔	✔	✔	✔	✔	✔	✔	✔	✔	✔	✔
Drive belts	S/I								✔	✔	✔	✔	✔	✔
Automatic transaxle fluid & filter	S/I		✔		✔		✔		✔		✔		✔	
Ball joints & dust covers	S/I		✔		✔		✔		✔		✔		✔	
Bolts & nuts on body & chassis	S/I		✔		✔		✔		✔		✔		✔	
Brake line pipes & hoses	S/I		✔		✔		✔		✔		✔		✔	
Brake linings & drums	S/I		✔		✔		✔		✔		✔		✔	
Brake pads & discs (front & rear if equipped)	S/I		✔		✔		✔		✔		✔		✔	
Differential oil	S/I		✔		✔		✔		✔		✔		✔	
Drive shaft boots (except Supra)	S/I		✔		✔		✔		✔		✔		✔	
Manual transaxle oil	S/I		✔		✔		✔		✔		✔		✔	
Steering gear housing oil	S/I		✔		✔		✔		✔		✔		✔	
Steering linkage	S/I		✔		✔		✔		✔		✔		✔	
Air filter	R				✔				✔				✔	
Spark plugs	R				✔				✔				✔	
Spark plugs (platinum tip)	R								✔					
Exhaust system	S/I				✔				✔				✔	
Fuel lines & connections	S/I				✔				✔				✔	
Valve clearance	S/I				✔				✔				✔	
Engine coolant	R						✔				✔			
Fuel tank cap gasket	R								✔					
Charcoal canister	S/I								✔					

R: Replace   S/I: Service or Inspect

FREQUENT OPERATION MAINTENANCE (SEVERE SERVICE)

If a vehicle is operated under any of the following conditions it is considered severe service:

- Extremely dusty areas.

- 50% or more of the vehicle operation is in 32°C (90°F) or higher temperatures, or constant operation in temperatures below 0°C (32°F).

- Prolonged idling (vehicle operation in stop and go traffic).

- Frequent short running periods (engine does not warm to normal operating temperatures).

- Police, taxi, delivery usage or trailer towing usage.

Oil & oil filter: change every 6000 miles.

Bolts & nuts on chassis & body: tighten every 7500 miles.

Ball joints & dust covers: service or inspect every 12,000 miles.

Brake linings & drums: service or inspect ever 12,000 miles.

Brake pads & discs (front & rear if equipped): service or inspect every 12,000 miles.

Drive shaft boots & except Supra): service or inspect every 12,000 miles.

Steering linkage: service or inspect every 12,000 miles.

Air filter: service or inspect every 15,000 miles.

Exhaust system: service or inspect every 15,000 miles.

Timing belt: replace every 60,000 miles.

22116_VIBE_C0009

PRECAUTIONS

Before servicing any vehicle, please be sure to read all of the following precautions, which deal with personal safety, prevention of component damage, and important points to take into consideration when servicing a motor vehicle:

• Never open, service or drain the radiator or cooling system when the engine is hot; serious burns can occur from the steam and hot coolant.

• Observe all applicable safety precautions when working around fuel. Whenever servicing the fuel system, always work in a well-ventilated area. Do not allow fuel spray or vapors to come in contact with a spark, open flame, or excessive heat (a hot drop light, for example). Keep a dry chemical fire extinguisher near the work area. Always keep fuel in a container specifically designed for fuel storage; also, always properly seal fuel containers to avoid the possibility of fire or explosion. Refer to the additional fuel system precautions later in this section.

• Fuel injection systems often remain pressurized, even after the engine has been turned **OFF**. The fuel system pressure must be relieved before disconnecting any fuel lines. Failure to do so may result in fire and/or personal injury.

• Brake fluid often contains polyglycol ethers and polyglycols. Avoid contact with the eyes and wash your hands thoroughly after handling brake fluid. If you do get brake fluid in your eyes, flush your eyes with clean, running water for 15 minutes. If eye irritation persists, or if you have taken

brake fluid internally, IMMEDIATELY seek medical assistance.

• The EPA warns that prolonged contact with used engine oil may cause a number of skin disorders, including cancer. You should make every effort to minimize your exposure to used engine oil. Protective gloves should be worn when changing oil. Wash your hands and any other exposed skin areas as soon as possible after exposure to used engine oil. Soap and water, or waterless hand cleaner should be used.

• All new vehicles are now equipped with an air bag system, often referred to as a Supplemental Restraint System (SRS) or Supplemental Inflatable Restraint (SIR) system. The system must be disabled before performing service on or around system components, steering column, instrument panel components, wiring and sensors. Failure to follow safety and disabling procedures could result in accidental air bag deployment, possible personal injury and unnecessary system repairs.

• Always wear safety goggles when working with, or around, the air bag system. When carrying a non-deployed air bag, be sure the bag and trim cover are pointed away from your body. When placing a non-deployed air bag on a work surface, always face the bag and trim cover upward, away from the surface. This will reduce the motion of the module if it is accidentally deployed. Refer to the additional air bag system precautions later in this section.

• Clean, high quality brake fluid from a sealed container is essential to the safe and

proper operation of the brake system. You should always buy the correct type of brake fluid for your vehicle. If the brake fluid becomes contaminated, completely flush the system with new fluid. Never reuse any brake fluid. Any brake fluid that is removed from the system should be discarded. Also, do not allow any brake fluid to come in contact with a painted surface; it will damage the paint.

• Never operate the engine without the proper amount and type of engine oil; doing so WILL result in severe engine damage.

• Timing belt maintenance is extremely important. Many models utilize an interference-type, non-freewheeling engine. If the timing belt breaks, the valves in the cylinder head may strike the pistons, causing potentially serious (also time-consuming and expensive) engine damage. Refer to the maintenance interval charts for the recommended replacement interval for the timing belt, and to the timing belt section for belt replacement and inspection.

• Disconnecting the negative battery cable on some vehicles may interfere with the functions of the on-board computer system(s) and may require the computer to undergo a relearning process once the negative battery cable is reconnected.

• When servicing drum brakes, only disassemble and assemble one side at a time, leaving the remaining side intact for reference.

• Only an MVAC-trained, EPA-certified automotive technician should service the air conditioning system or its components.

BRAKES

GENERAL INFORMATION

When wheel slip is detected during a brake application, the ABS enters antilock mode. During antilock braking, hydraulic pressure in the individual wheel circuits is controlled to prevent any wheel from slipping. A separate hydraulic line and specific solenoid valves are provided for each wheel. The ABS can decrease, hold, or increase hydraulic pressure to each wheel brake. The ABS cannot, however, increase hydraulic pressure above the amount which is transmitted by the master cylinder during braking.

During antilock braking, a series of rapid pulsations is felt in the brake pedal. These pulsations are caused by the rapid changes in position of the individual sole-

noid valves as the electronic brake control module responds to wheel speed sensor inputs and attempts to prevent wheel slip. These pedal pulsations are present only during antilock braking and stop when normal braking is resumed or when the vehicle comes to a stop. A ticking or popping noise may also be heard as the solenoid valves cycle rapidly. During antilock braking on dry pavement, intermittent chirping noises may be heard as the tires approach slipping. These noises and pedal pulsations are considered normal during antilock operation.

PRECAUTIONS

• Certain components within the ABS system are not intended to be serviced or repaired individually.

ANTI-LOCK BRAKE SYSTEM (ABS)

• Do not use rubber hoses or other parts not specifically specified for and ABS system. When using repair kits, replace all parts included in the kit. Partial or incorrect repair may lead to functional problems and require the replacement of components.

• Lubricate rubber parts with clean, fresh brake fluid to ease assembly. Do not use shop air to clean parts; damage to rubber components may result.

• Use only DOT 3 brake fluid from an unopened container.

• If any hydraulic component or line is removed or replaced, it may be necessary to bleed the entire system.

• A clean repair area is essential. Always clean the reservoir and cap thoroughly before removing the cap. The slightest amount of dirt in the fluid may plug an orifice and impair the system function. Perform repairs after components have been thoroughly cleaned; use only denatured alcohol to clean components. Do not allow ABS components to come into contact with any substance containing mineral oil; this includes used shop rags.

• The Anti-Lock control unit is a microprocessor similar to other computer units in the vehicle. Ensure that the ignition switch is **OFF** before removing or installing controller harnesses. Avoid static electricity discharge at or near the controller.

• If any arc welding is to be done on the vehicle, the control unit should be unplugged before welding operations begin.

SPEED SENSORS

REMOVAL & INSTALLATION

Front

See Figures 2 through 4.

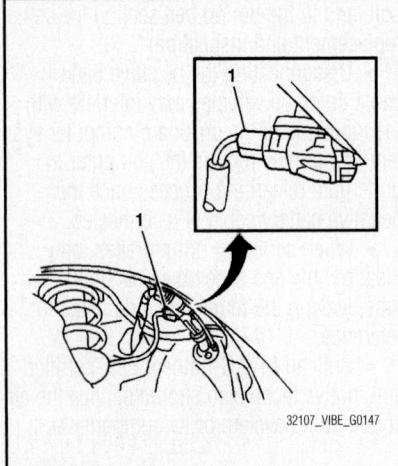

Fig. 2 Disconnect the wheel speed sensor electrical connector (1)

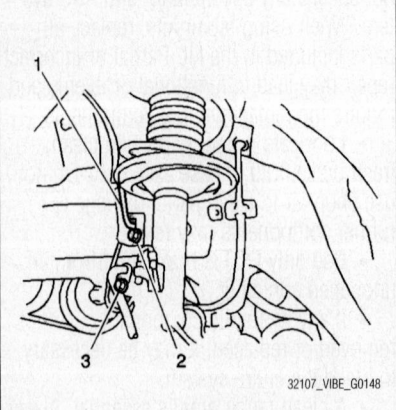

Fig. 3 Remove the 2 bolts retaining the wheel speed sensor pigtail harness

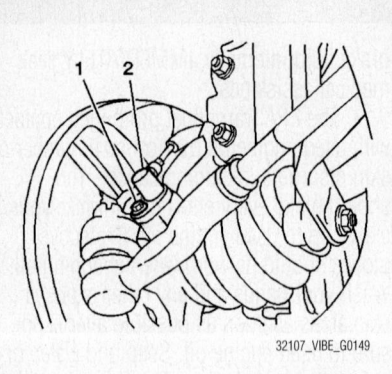

Fig. 4 Remove the wheel speed sensor retaining bolt (1) and remove the wheel speed sensor (2) from the steering knuckle

1. Remove the wheel housing.

➡ **The wheel speed sensor is serviceable only as an assembly. Do NOT attempt to service the sensor harness pigtail.**

2. Disconnect the wheel speed sensor electrical connector (1).

3. Remove the 2 bolts retaining the wheel speed sensor pigtail harness.

4. Remove the wheel speed sensor retaining bolt (1) and remove the wheel speed sensor (2) from the steering knuckle.

To install:

5. Install the wheel speed sensor (2) to the steering knuckle. Secure with 1 bolt. Tighten the front wheel speed sensor bolt to 71 inch lbs (8 Nm).

6. Connect the wheel speed wiring harness (1) to the vehicle. Secure with 2 bolts. Tighten the pigtail harness nut (2) to 71 inch lbs (8 Nm) and pigtail harness nut (3) to 21 ft. lbs. (29 Nm).

7. Connect the wheel speed sensor electrical connector (1).

8. Install the wheelhousing.

Rear

FWD Vehicles

See Figures 5 through 7.

✲ WARNING

The wheel speed sensor is serviceable only as an assembly. Do NOT attempt to service the sensor harness pigtail.

1. Disconnect the electrical connector (6) from the wheel speed sensor.

2. Remove the rear axle hub and bearing assembly.

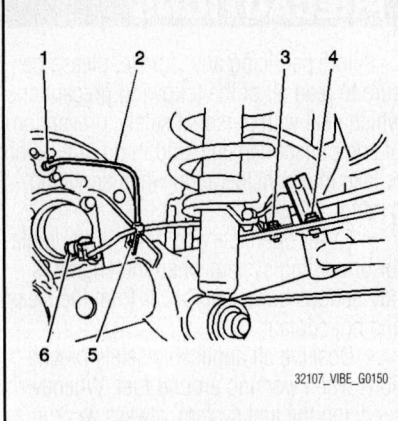

Fig. 5 Disconnect the electrical connector (6) from the wheel speed sensor.

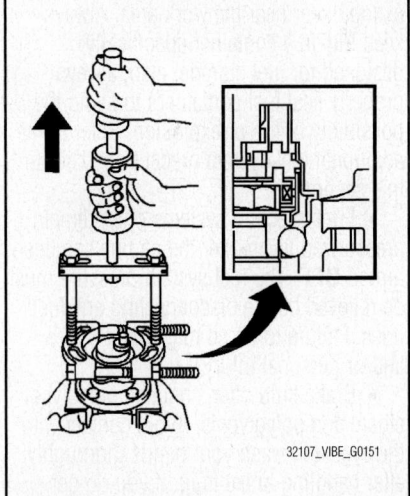

Fig. 6 Remove the wheel speed sensor from the rear axle hub.

3. Remove the wheel speed sensor from the rear axle hub.

To install:

✲ WARNING

Use the correct fastener in the correct location. Replacement fasteners must be the correct part number for that application. Fasteners requiring replacement or fasteners requiring the use of thread locking compound or sealant are identified in the service procedure. Do not use paints, lubricants, or corrosion inhibitors on fasteners or fastener joint surfaces unless specified. These coatings affect fastener torque and joint clamping force and may damage the fastener. Use the correct tightening sequence and specifications when installing fasteners in order to avoid damage to parts and systems. Install

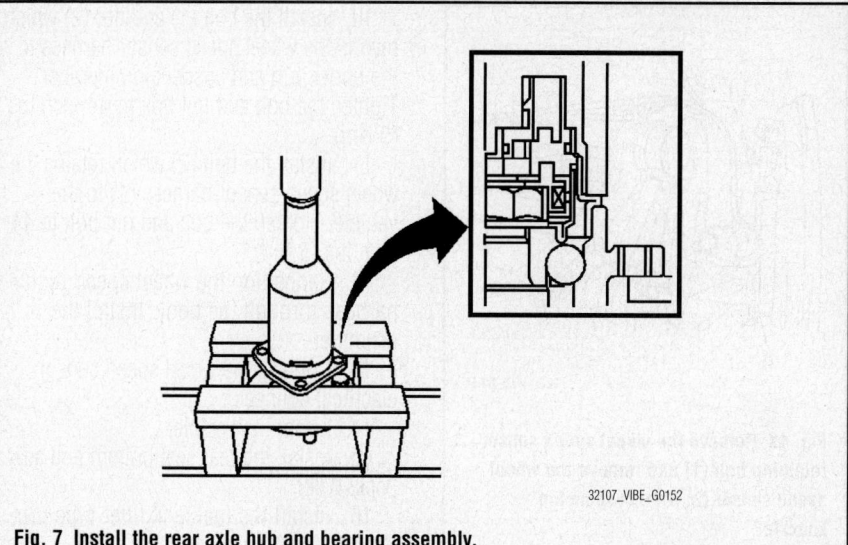

Fig. 7 Install the rear axle hub and bearing assembly.

the wheel speed sensor to rear wheel hub.

4. Install the rear axle hub and bearing assembly.
5. Connect the wheel speed sensor electrical connector (6).

AWD Vehicles

See Figures 8 through 12.

1. Remove the fuel tank filler pipe protector bolts (2) and remove the fuel tank filler pipe protector (1).
2. Remove the rear seat bottom and seat back.

❄❄ **WARNING**

The wheel speed sensor is serviceable only as an assembly. Do NOT attempt to service the sensor harness pigtail.

Fig. 9 Disconnect the electrical connector (1) from the wheel speed sensor

3. Disconnect the electrical connector (1) from the wheel speed sensor.

4. Raise and suitably support the vehicle.
5. Pull the sensor harness and grommet out through the body.
6. Remove the bolt (2) which retains the wheel speed sensor harness (1) to the vehicle.
7. Remove the bolt (1) and nut (2) which retains the wheel speed sensor harness to the upper arm and suspension member.
8. Remove the wheel speed sensor retaining bolt (1) and remove the wheel speed sensor (2) from suspension knuckle.

To install:

❄❄ **WARNING**

Use the correct fastener in the correct location. Replacement fasteners must be the correct part number for that application. Fasteners requiring replacement or fasteners requiring the use of thread locking compound or sealant are identified in the service procedure. Do not use paints, lubricants, or corrosion inhibitors on fasteners or fastener joint surfaces unless specified. These coatings affect fastener torque and joint clamping force and may damage the fastener. Use the correct tightening sequence and specifications when installing fasteners in order to avoid damage to parts and systems.

9. Install the wheel speed sensor (2) to the steering knuckle. Tighten the rear wheel speed sensor bolt (1) to 71 inch lbs (8 Nm).

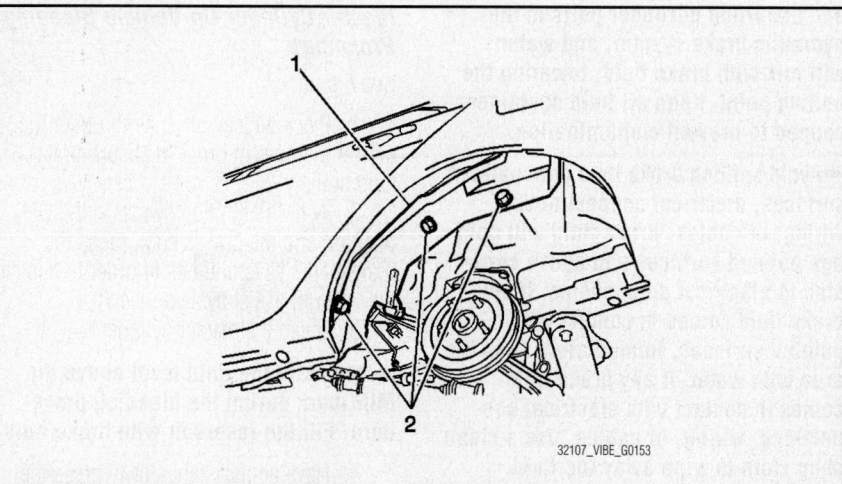

Fig. 8 Remove the fuel tank filler pipe protector bolts (2) and remove the fuel tank filler pipe protector (1)

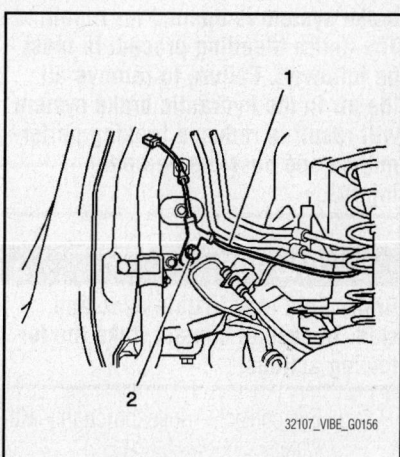

Fig. 10 Remove the bolt (2) which retains the wheel speed sensor harness (1) to the vehicle.

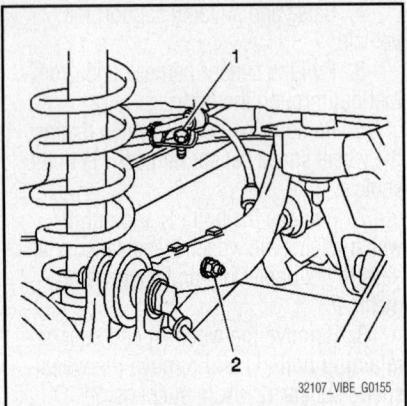

Fig. 11 Remove the bolt (1) and nut (2) which retains the wheel speed sensor harness to the upper arm and suspension member

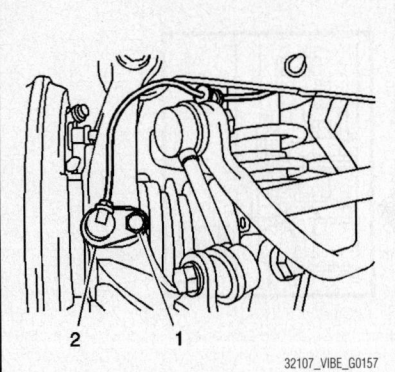

Fig. 12 Remove the wheel speed sensor retaining bolt (1) and remove the wheel speed sensor (2) from suspension knuckle.

10. Install the bolt (1) and nut (2) which retains the wheel speed sensor harness to the upper arm and suspension member. Tighten the bolt and nut bolt to 44 inch lbs (5 Nm).

11. Install the bolt (2) which retains the wheel speed sensor harness (1) to the vehicle. Tighten the bolt and nut bolt to 44 inch lbs (5 Nm).

12. Reposition the wheel speed pigtail harness through the body. Install the grommet.

13. Connect the wheel speed sensor electrical connector (1).

14. Lower the vehicle.

15. Install the rear seat bottom and seat back. Refer

16. Install the fuel tank filler pipe protector (1). Secure with 3 bolts (2).

BRAKES
BLEEDING THE BRAKE SYSTEM

BLEEDING PROCEDURE

BLEEDING PROCEDURE

Hydraulic Brake System Bleeding

Tools Required:
- J 29532 Diaphragm Pressure Bleeder
- J 39801-VIBE Pressure Bleeder Adapter

✳ CAUTION

Do not move the vehicle until a firm brake pedal is obtained. Air in the brake system can cause the loss of brakes with possible personal injury.

✳ CAUTION

Remove all the air from the hydraulic brake system anytime the hydraulic brake system is opened for repair. The entire bleeding procedure must be followed. Failure to remove all the air in the hydraulic brake system will result in reduced braking performance and possible personal injury.

✳ CAUTION

Brake fluid may irritate eyes and skin. In case of contact, take the following actions:

- Eye contact—rinse thoroughly with water.
- Skin contact—wash with soap and water.
- If ingested—consult a physician immediately.

✳ CAUTION

Caution: Use only Delco Supreme 11, GM P/N 12377967 (Canadian P/N 992667), or equivalent DOT 3 brake fluid from a clean, sealed container. Do not use fluid from an open container that may be contaminated with water. Improper or contaminated fluid could result in damage to components, or loss of braking, with possible injury.

➡ When filling the master cylinder, use only Delco Supreme 11, GM P/N 12377967 (Canadian P/N 992667), or equivalent DOT 3 brake fluid. Do not use a container which has been used for petroleum based fluids, or a container which is wet with water. Petroleum based fluids will cause swelling and distortion of rubber parts in the hydraulic brake system, and water will mix with brake fluid, lowering the boiling point. Keep all fluid containers capped to prevent contamination.

➡Avoid spilling brake fluid onto painted surfaces, electrical connections, wiring, or cables. Brake fluid will damage painted surfaces and cause corrosion to electrical components. If any brake fluid comes in contact with painted surfaces, immediately flush the area with water. If any brake fluid comes in contact with electrical connections, wiring, or cables, use a clean shop cloth to wipe away the fluid.

1. Bleed the hydraulic brake system in the following sequence:

a. The master cylinder
b. Right rear bleeder valve
c. Left rear bleeder valve
d. Right front bleeder valve
e. Left front bleeder valve

If air enters the hydraulic brake system due to low brake fluid level, bleed the system at the master cylinder and at the 4 bleeder valves.

If you disconnect a brake pipe from the master cylinder, bleed the system at the master cylinder and at the 4 bleeder valves.

If you disconnect a brake pipe or a fitting between the master cylinder and the wheels, bleed the system at the bleeder valve served by the brake pipe or fitting.

If you disconnect a brake pipe or brake hose at only 1 wheel, bleed the system at the bleeder valve for that wheel.

Master Cylinder On-Vehicle Bleeding Procedure

See Figure 13.

1. Place a clean shop cloth under the master cylinder in order to absorb brake fluid spills.

2. With the ignition switch in the OFF position and the brakes cool, press the brake pedal several times in order to deplete the vacuum assist system reserve.

3. Clean the master cylinder.

➡ **Maintain the fluid level above the MIN mark during the bleeding procedure. Fill the reservoir with brake fluid.**

4. Have an assistant slowly press the brake pedal and maintain pressure on the brake pedal.

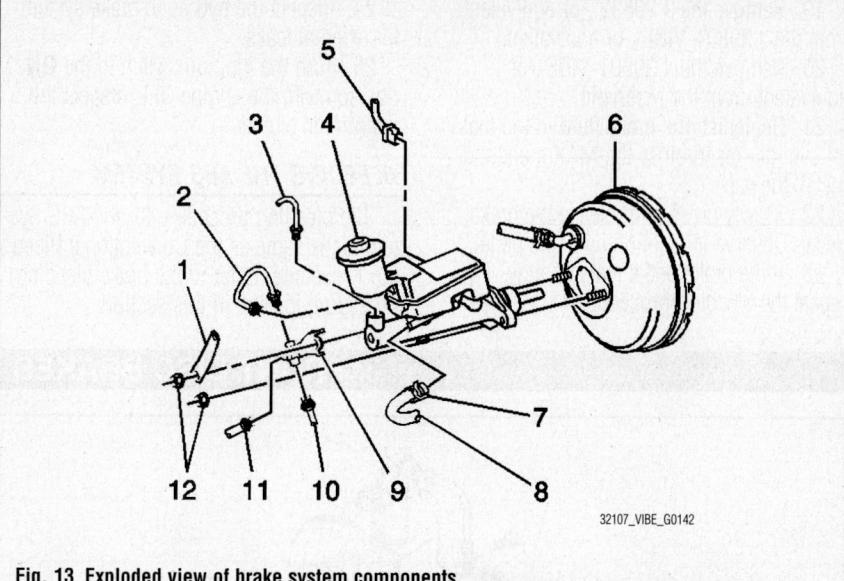

Fig. 13 Exploded view of brake system components

5. Loosen the flare nut for the front brake pipe (3) in order to purge air from the front of the master cylinder.

6. Tighten the flare nut. Tighten the flare nut to 11.2 ft. lbs. (15.2 Nm).

7. Have the assistant slowly release the brake pedal.

8. Wait 15 seconds.

9. Repeat this procedure until air is purged from the front of the master cylinder.

10. Remove the rear brake pipe (2) from the master cylinder.

11. Allow a small amount of brake fluid to drip from the open port of the master cylinder.

12. Install the brake pipe to the master cylinder. Tighten the flare nut to 11.2 ft. lbs. (15.2 Nm).

13. Have the assistant slowly press the brake pedal and maintain pressure on the brake pedal.

14. Loosen the flare nut for the rear brake pipe in order to purge air from the rear of the master cylinder.

15. Tighten the flare nut. Tighten the flare nut to 11.2 ft. lbs. (15.2 Nm).

16. Have the assistant slowly release the brake pedal.

17. Wait 15 seconds.

18. Repeat this procedure until air is purged from the rear of the master cylinder.

Manual Bleeding Procedure

See Figure 14.

1. With the ignition switch in the OFF position and the brakes cool, press the brake pedal several times in order to deplete the vacuum assist system reserve.

➡ **Maintain the fluid level above the MIN mark during the bleeding procedure.**

2. Fill the reservoir with brake fluid.

3. Remove the bleeder valve cap.

4. Install a transparent hose (1) over the end of the bleeder valve (2). Submerge the other end of the hose in a transparent container (5) partially filled with brake fluid.

5. Have the assistant slowly press the brake pedal and maintain pressure on the brake pedal.

6. Loosen the bleeder valve in order to purge air from the wheel hydraulic circuit.

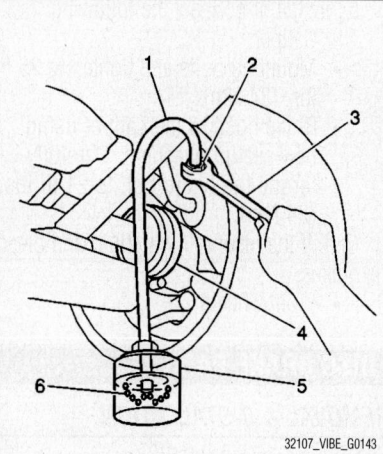

Fig. 14 Install a transparent hose (1) over the end of the bleeder valve (2). Submerge the other end of the hose in a transparent container (5) partially filled with brake fluid.

7. Close the bleeder valve. Tighten the bleeder valve to 73.5 inch lbs (8.3 Nm).

8. Have the second technician slowly release the pedal.

9. Wait 15 seconds.

10. Repeat this procedure until air (6) is purged from the wheel hydraulic circuit.

11. Install the bleeder valve cap.

12. Repeat this procedure at all bleeder valves that require bleeding.

13. Replenish the brake fluid in the master cylinder reservoir to the MAX mark and install the cap.

14. Slowly press and release the brake pedal. Observe the feel of the brake pedal.

15. If the brake pedal feels spongy, repeat the bleeding procedure.

16. Inspect the hydraulic brake system for external leaks.

17. Turn the ignition switch to the **ON** position with the engine OFF. Inspect the instrument cluster.

Pressure Bleeding Procedure

See Figure 14.

✳✳ WARNING

Pressure bleeding equipment must be the diaphragm type and must have a rubber diaphragm between the air supply and the brake fluid. Air, moisture, oil and other contaminants can damage the hydraulic system.

1. Clean the outside of the brake fluid reservoir and the cap.

2. Remove the reservoir cap.

3. Remove the reservoir diaphragm.

4. Install the J 39801-VIBE , or equivalent, to the reservoir.

5. Add brake fluid to the J 29532 , or equivalent, in order to raise the fluid level above the half mark.

6. Connect the J 29532 , or equivalent, to the J 39801-VIBE , or equivalent.

7. Charge the J 29532 , or equivalent, to 25 - 30 phi (175 - 205 kappa).

8. Open the fluid tank valve for the J 29532 , or equivalent, in order to allow pressurized brake fluid to enter the hydraulic brake system.

9. Wait 30 seconds.

10. Inspect the hydraulic brake system for external leaks.

11. Remove the bleeder valve cap.

12. Install a transparent hose (1) over the end of the bleeder valve (2). Submerge the other end of the hose in a transparent container (5) partially filled with brake fluid.

13. Loosen the bleeder valve in order to purge air from the wheel hydraulic circuit.

14. Close the bleeder valve. Tighten the bleeder valve to 73.5 inch lbs (8.3 Nm).

15. Repeat this procedure until air (6) is purged from the wheel hydraulic circuit.

16. Install the bleeder valve cap.

17. Repeat this procedure at all bleeder valves that require bleeding.

18. Close the fluid tank valve for the J 29532 , or equivalent.

19. Remove the J 29532 , or equivalent, from the J 39801-VIBE , or equivalent.

20. Remove the J 39801-VIBE , or equivalent, from the reservoir.

21. Replenish the brake fluid in the master cylinder reservoir to the MAX mark and install the cap.

22. Slowly press and release the brake pedal. Observe the feel of the brake pedal.

23. If the brake pedal feels spongy, repeat the bleeding procedure.

24. Inspect the hydraulic brake system for external leaks.

25. Turn the ignition switch to the **ON** position with the engine OFF. Inspect the instrument cluster.

BLEEDING THE ABS SYSTEM

The bleeding procedure for the ABS System is the same as the Conventional Bleeding Procedure. Refer to the brake bleeding procedure located in this section.

BRAKES   FRONT DISC BRAKES

✳✳ CAUTION

Dust and dirt accumulating on brake parts during normal use may contain asbestos fibers from production or aftermarket brake linings. Breathing excessive concentrations of asbestos fibers can cause serious bodily harm. Exercise care when servicing brake parts. Do not sand or grind brake lining unless equipment used is designed to contain the dust residue. Do not clean brake parts with compressed air or by dry brushing. Cleaning should be done by dampening the brake components with a fine mist of water, then wiping the brake components clean with a dampened cloth. Dispose of cloth and all residue containing asbestos fibers in an impermeable container with the appropriate label. Follow practices prescribed by the Occupational Safety and Health Administration (OSHA) and the Environmental Protection Agency (EPA) for the handling, processing, and disposing of dust or debris that may contain asbestos fibers.

BRAKE CALIPER

REMOVAL & INSTALLATION

See Figure 15.

1. Before servicing the vehicle, refer to the precautions section.

2. Remove some fluid from the reservoir with a suction pump.

3. Remove or disconnect the following:
   • Front wheels
   • Banjo bolt and disconnect the brake hose from the caliper. Plug the hose to prevent fluid loss and contamination.
   • Mounting bolts while holding the slide pin
   • Caliper

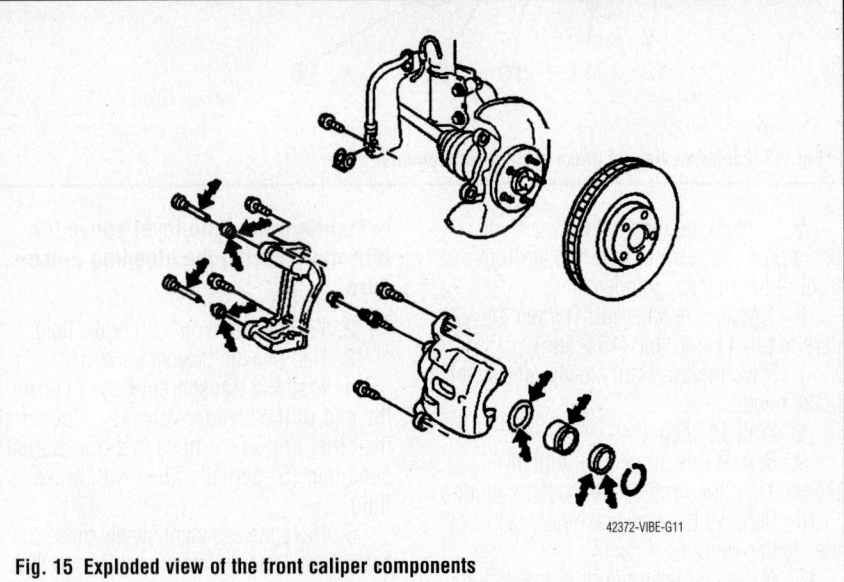

Fig. 15 **Exploded view of the front caliper components**

To Install:

4. Compress the caliper piston using a C–clamp or other suitable tool.

5. Install or connect the following:
   • Caliper
   • Mounting bolts and tighten to 25 ft. lbs. (34 Nm)
   • Brake hose to the caliper using new sealing washers. Carefully torque the banjo bolt to 21 ft. lbs. (29 Nm).

6. Fill the reservoir with fluid and bleed the brakes.
   • Front wheels

DISC BRAKE PADS

REMOVAL & INSTALLATION

See Figures 16 through 20.

1. Before servicing the vehicle, refer to the precautions section.

2. Use a siphon in order to remove half of the brake fluid from the master cylinder reservoir.

3. Raise and support the vehicle.

4. Remove the tire and wheel assembly from the vehicle.

5. Install a large C–clamp over the brake caliper. Position the ends of the C–clamp against the rear of the caliper body and against the outer brake pad.

6. Tighten the C–clamp in order to compress the caliper piston into the caliper bore.

7. Remove the C–clamp from the caliper.

8. Remove the 2 caliper bolts.

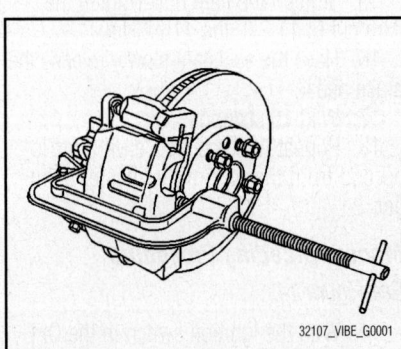

Fig. 16 **Install large C–clamp over brake caliper**

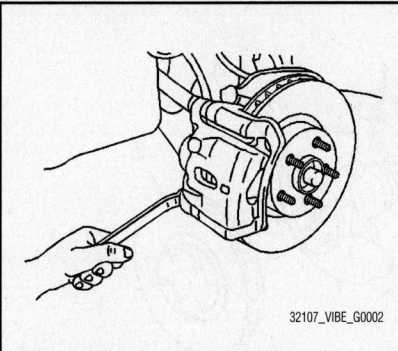

Fig. 17 Remove 2 Caliper Bolts

➡**Support the brake caliper with heavy mechanic's wire, or equivalent, whenever it is separated from its mount and the hydraulic flexible brake hose is still connected. Failure to support the caliper in this manner will cause the flexible brake hose to bear the weight of the caliper, which may cause damage to the brake hose and in turn may cause a brake fluid leak.**

9. Remove the caliper housing (2) from the caliper bracket. Support the caliper with a wire (1) in order to prevent damage to the brake hose.

10. Remove the 2 brake pads (6,10).

11. Remove the inner pad wear indicator (3) from the inner pad.

12. Remove the outer pad wear indicator (5), if equipped, from the outer pad.

13. Remove the 2 insulators (1,7).

14. Remove the 2 pad insulators (2,8).

➡**Note the location of the upper retainer and the lower retainer. The upper retainer is not interchangeable with the lower retainer.**

15. Remove the 2 brake pad retainers (4,9).

16. Inspect the brake pads for wear. If the pad thickness is less than specification, replace the disc brake pads in axle sets. The minimum brake pad lining thickness is 1 mm (0.039 in).

17. Clean the 2 brake pad retainers (4,9). Inspect the retainers for the following conditions:

- Sufficient rebound
- No deformation
- No cracks
- No wear
- No rust
- No dirt

f. If the retainers meet the above conditions, re-use the retainers.

18. Clean and inspect the disc brake hardware. Replace components if necessary.

19. Clean and inspect the caliper. Repair or replace components as necessary.

❋❋ **WARNING**

Refinish or replace the rotor ONLY if the condition of the rotor requires service. DO NOT refinish the rotor if the brake pads are the only components requiring service.

20. Measure the brake rotor thickness. Refinish or replace the rotor as necessary.

21. Measure the brake rotor thickness variation. Refinish or replace the rotor as necessary.

22. Inspect the surface of the brake rotor. Refinish or replace the rotor as necessary.

23. Measure the brake rotor assembled lateral runout. Refinish or replace the rotor as necessary.

To install:

24. If the caliper piston is not compressed into the caliper bore, complete the following steps:

a. Place an old brake pad (2) or a block of wood against the caliper piston.

b. Install a large C-clamp over the body of the brake caliper.

c. Position the ends of the C-clamp against the rear of the caliper body and against the pad or the wood.

d. Tighten the C-clamp in order to compress the caliper piston into the caliper bore.

e. Remove the C-clamp.

25. Install the upper brake pad retainer (4) to the caliper bracket.

26. Install the lower brake pad retainer (9) to the caliper bracket.

27. Install the inner wear indicator (3) to the inner pad (10).

28. Install the outer wear indicator (5), if equipped, to the outer pad (6).

29. Apply disc brake grease to both sides of the inner pad insulator (2).

30. Install the inner pad insulator to the inner pad.

31. Install the inner insulator (1) to the inner pad insulator.

32. Install the inner brake pad to the caliper bracket with the wear indicator facing upward.

33. Apply disc brake grease to both sides of the outer pad insulator (8).

34. Install the outer pad insulator to the outer pad (6).

35. Install the outer insulator (7) to the outer pad insulator.

36. Install the outer brake pad to the caliper bracket.

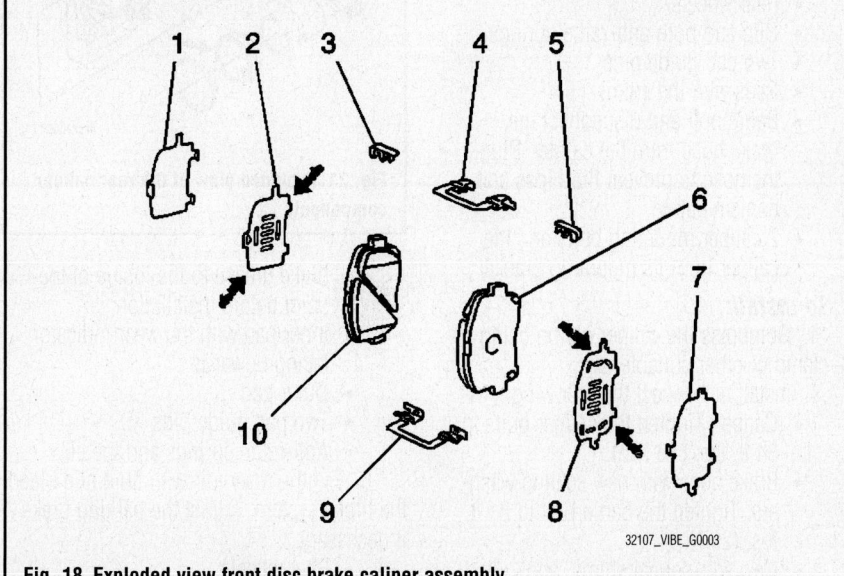

Fig. 18 Exploded view front disc brake caliper assembly

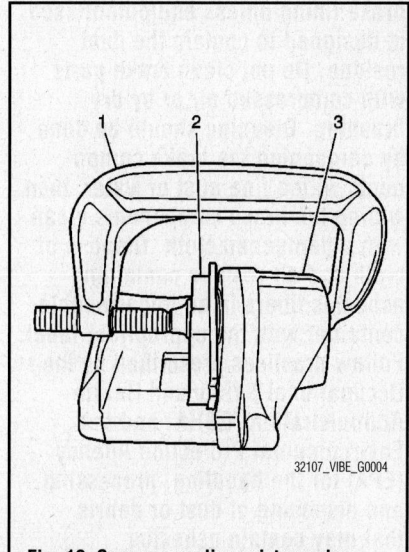

Fig. 19 Compress caliper piston using C-clamp

37. Install the caliper housing (10) to the caliper bracket (14).

✳✳ CAUTION

Use the correct fastener in the correct location. Replacement fasteners must be the correct part number for that application. Fasteners requiring replacement or fasteners requiring the use of thread locking compound or sealant are identified in the service procedure. Do not use paints, lubricants, or corrosion inhibitors on fasteners or fastener joint surfaces unless specified. These coatings affect fastener torque and joint clamping force and may damage the fastener. Use the correct tightening sequence and specifications when installing fasteners in order to avoid damage to parts and systems.

38. Install the caliper bolts (11,18). Tighten the bolts to 25.30 ft. lbs. (34.3 Nm).
39. Install the tire and wheel assembly to the vehicle.
40. Lower the vehicle.
41. With the engine OFF, gradually apply

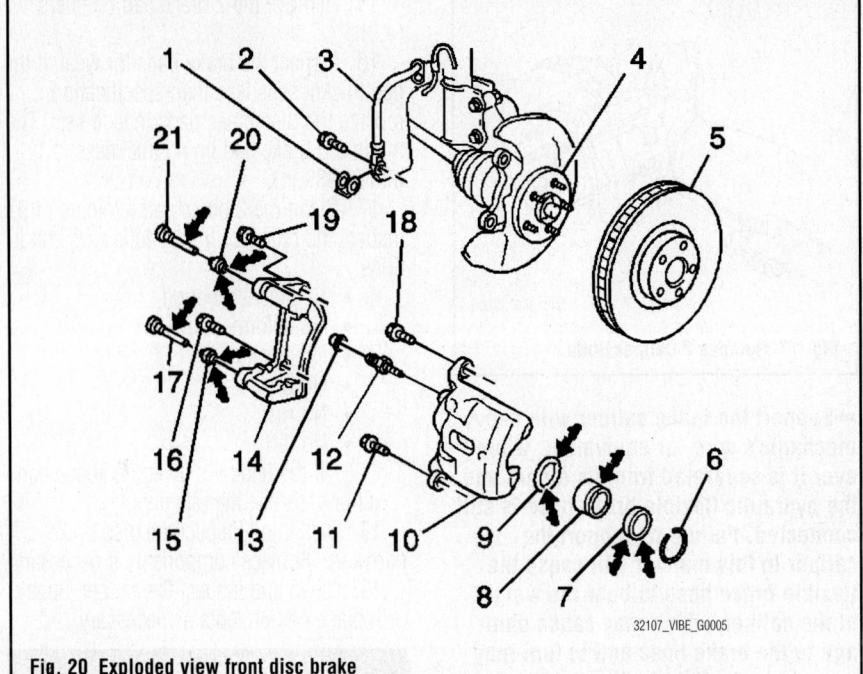

Fig. 20 Exploded view front disc brake

and release the brake pedal several times in order to position the caliper pistons and the brake pads.

42. Fill the master cylinder fluid reservoir.
43. Burnish the pads and the rotors.

BRAKES   REAR DISC BRAKES

✳✳ CAUTION

Dust and dirt accumulating on brake parts during normal use may contain asbestos fibers from production or aftermarket brake linings. Breathing excessive concentrations of asbestos fibers can cause serious bodily harm. Exercise care when servicing brake parts. Do not sand or grind brake lining unless equipment used is designed to contain the dust residue. Do not clean brake parts with compressed air or by dry brushing. Cleaning should be done by dampening the brake components with a fine mist of water, then wiping the brake components clean with a dampened cloth. Dispose of cloth and all residue containing asbestos fibers in an impermeable container with the appropriate label. Follow practices prescribed by the Occupational Safety and Health Administration (OSHA) and the Environmental Protection Agency (EPA) for the handling, processing, and disposing of dust or debris that may contain asbestos fibers.

BRAKE CALIPER

REMOVAL & INSTALLATION

See Figure 21.

1. Before servicing the vehicle, refer to the precautions section.
2. Remove some fluid from the reservoir with a suction pump.
3. Remove or disconnect the following:
   - Rear wheels
   - Clip and both anti-rattle springs
   - Two pad guide pins
   - Pads with the shims
   - Banjo bolt and disconnect the brake hose from the caliper. Plug the hose to prevent fluid loss and contamination.
   - 2 caliper mounting bolts and the caliper from its mounting bracket

To Install:

4. Compress the caliper piston using a C–clamp or other suitable tool.
5. Install or connect the following:
   - Caliper. Tighten the caliper bolts to 34 ft. lbs. (46 Nm).
   - Brake hose with new sealing washers. Tighten the banjo bolt to 21 ft. lbs. (29 Nm).
   - New anti-squeal shims, apply disc

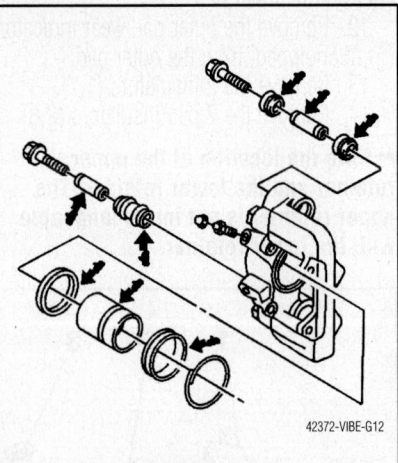

Fig. 21 Exploded view of the rear caliper components

brake grease to the inside of the shim before installation
   - Inner pad with the wear indicator facing upwards
   - Outer pad
   - Two pad guide pins
   - Anti-rattle springs and the clip
6. Fill the reservoir with fluid and bleed the brake system. Adjust the parking brake if necessary.
   - Rear wheels

DISC BRAKE PADS

REMOVAL & INSTALLATION

See Figure 22.

1. Before servicing the vehicle, refer to the precautions section.
2. Remove some fluid from the reservoir with a suction pump.
3. Remove or disconnect the following:
   - Rear wheels
   - Clip and both anti-rattle springs
   - Two pad guide pins
   - Pads with the shims

To Install:

4. Compress the caliper piston using a C–clamp or other suitable tool.
5. Install or connect the following:
   - New anti-squeal shims, apply disc brake grease to the inside of the shim before installation

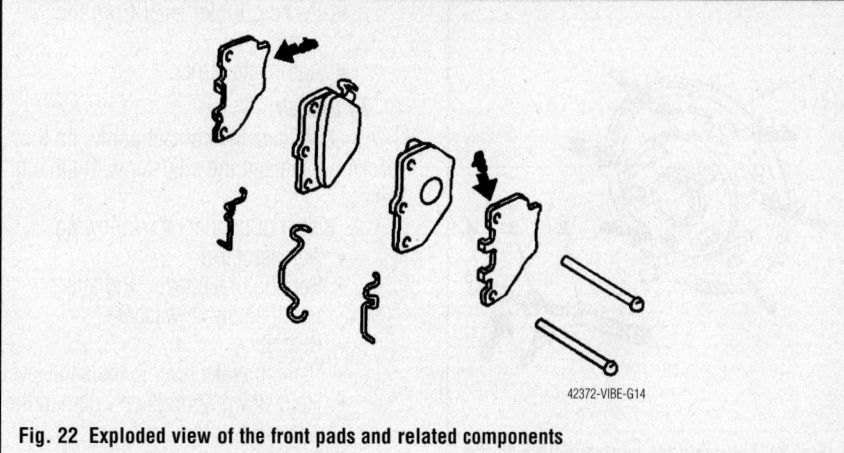

Fig. 22 Exploded view of the front pads and related components

   - Inner pad with the wear indicator facing upwards
   - Outer pad
   - Two pad guide pins
   - Anti-rattle springs and the clip

6. Fill the reservoir with fluid and bleed the brake system. Adjust the parking brake if necessary.
   - Rear wheels

BRAKES

✳✳ CAUTION

Dust and dirt accumulating on brake parts during normal use may contain asbestos fibers from production or aftermarket brake linings. Breathing excessive concentrations of asbestos fibers can cause serious bodily harm. Exercise care when servicing brake parts. Do not sand or grind brake lining unless equipment used is designed to contain the dust residue. Do not clean brake parts with compressed air or by dry brushing. Cleaning should be done by dampening the brake components with a fine mist of water, then wiping the brake components clean with a dampened cloth. Dispose of cloth and all residue containing asbestos fibers in an impermeable container with the appropriate label. Follow practices prescribed by the Occupational Safety and Health Administration (OSHA) and the Environmental Protection Agency (EPA) for the handling, processing, and disposing of dust or debris that may contain asbestos fibers.

BRAKE DRUM

REMOVAL & INSTALLATION

1. Before servicing the vehicle, refer to the precautions section.
2. Remove or disconnect the following:
   - Wheel

   - Brake drum. If the drum will not pull of the axle, back off the automatic adjuster by turning the adjusting wheel.

To install:

3. Install or connect the following:
   - Drum on the axle
   - Wheel
4. Refill the master cylinder and pump pedal to attain full brake pedal before road-testing the vehicle.

BRAKE SHOES

REMOVAL & INSTALLATION

See Figures 23 and 24.

1. Before servicing the vehicle, refer to the precautions section.

REAR DRUM BRAKES

2. Remove or disconnect the following:
   - Wheel
   - Brake drum. If the drum will not pull of the axle, back off the automatic adjuster by turning the adjusting wheel.
   - Upper return spring
   - Lower return spring
   - Hold-down springs and pins from the front shoe
   - Anchor side spring using needle nosed pliers
   - Front shoe with the adjuster lever
   - Adjuster lever and spring from the front shoe
   - Hold-down springs and pins from the rear shoe
   - Parking brake cable from the rear shoe using needle nosed pliers

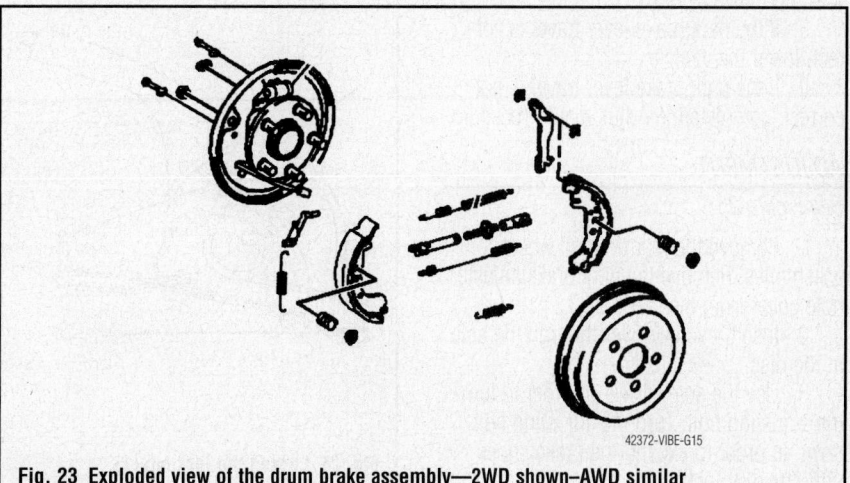

Fig. 23 Exploded view of the drum brake assembly—2WD shown–AWD similar

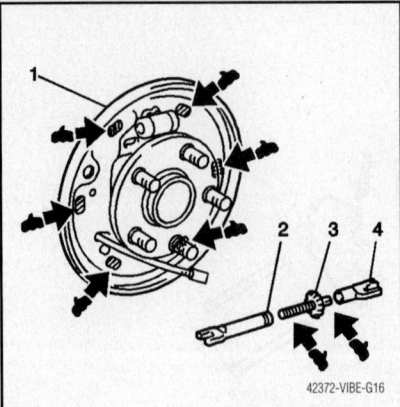

Fig. 24 Lubricate the contact points on the backing plate and the adjuster with lithium grease

- Rear brake shoe
- C-washer using a suitable pry tool from the shoe

- Parking brake lever from the shoe
- Automatic strut

To install:

3. Lubricate the contact points on the backing plate and the adjuster with lithium grease.

4. Install or connect the following:
- Adjuster strut
- Parking brake lever, and attach using a new C-washer
- Rear shoe
- Parking brake lever to the shoe lever
- Hold-down springs and pins to the rear shoe
- Automatic adjuster lever and spring to the front shoe
- Front shoe
- Anchor spring
- Hold-down springs and pins to the front shoe
- Lower return spring

- Upper return spring
- Drum

ADJUSTMENT

1. Adjust the rear brakes as follows:
a. Temporarily install the drum and hub nuts.
b. Remove the hole plug from the backing plate.
c. Turn the adjuster to expand the shoe until the drum locks.
d. Back off the adjuster eight notches using a suitable adjustment tool.
e. Install the hole plug into the backing plate to prevent dirt and moisture from entering.
f. Readjust the parking brake cable as necessary.
2. Install the wheels.
3. Refill the master cylinder and pump pedal to attain full brake pedal before Road-testing the vehicle.

BRAKES

PARKING BRAKE CABLES

INSPECTION

1. Raise and support the vehicle.
2. Pull the park brake lever with approximately 20 kg (44.1 lb) of force.
3. Count the number of clicks or ratchet notches considering the following specifications:
- The minimum number of clicks is 5.
- The maximum number of clicks is 7.
4. Attempt to rotate the rear wheels. Verify the rear wheels do not rotate.
5. Release the park brake.
6. Attempt to rotate the rear wheels. Verify the rear wheels rotate freely.
7. Turn the ignition switch to the **ON** position. Verify the red **BRAKE** BRAKE warning indicator is **OFF**.
8. If the park brake lever travel is correct, lower the vehicle.
9. If the park brake lever travel is not correct, complete the Adjustment Procedure.

ADJUSTMENT

See Figure 25.

1. Remove the rear tire and wheel assemblies. Remove the park brake adjuster hole cover from the rear disc.
2. Insert a screwdriver through the hole in the disc.
3. Use the screwdriver in order to turn the adjusting bolt. Turn the adjusting bolt down in order to expand the brake shoes until the disc locks.

4. Turn the adjusting bolt up 8 notches in order to adjust the shoes to the proper distance away from the drum portion of the rear disc.
5. Install the adjuster hole cover.
6. Install the rear tire and wheel assemblies.
7. Remove the rear center console.
8. Loosen the lock nut.
9. Turn the adjusting nut (2) in order to adjust the park brake lever travel. Refer to the Inspection Procedure above.
10. Tighten the lock nut. Tighten the nut to 44.25 inch lbs (5.0 Nm)
11. Install the rear center console.

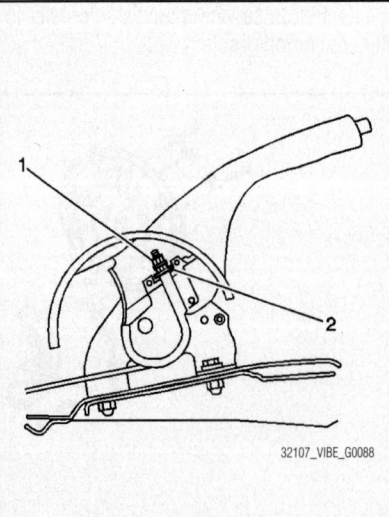

Fig. 25 Loosen the lock nut (1)

PARKING BRAKE

PARKING BRAKE SHOES

REMOVAL & INSTALLATION

With Rear Drum Brakes

The rear drum brake shoes serve as the parking brakes. Refer to the procedures under Rear Drum Brakes.

With Rear Disc Brakes

See Figures 26 through 30.

1. Remove the rear disc (rotor).
2. Remove the return springs (1, 2)
3. Remove the tension spring (1).
4. Separate the adjuster (15) from the front brake shoe (17).
5. Remove the hold-down spring (16) and the pin (1) from the front shoe.

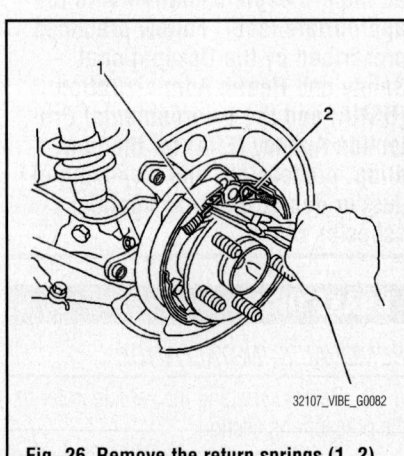

Fig. 26 Remove the return springs (1, 2)

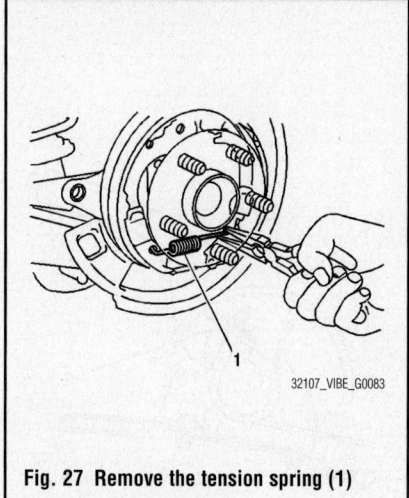

Fig. 27 Remove the tension spring (1)

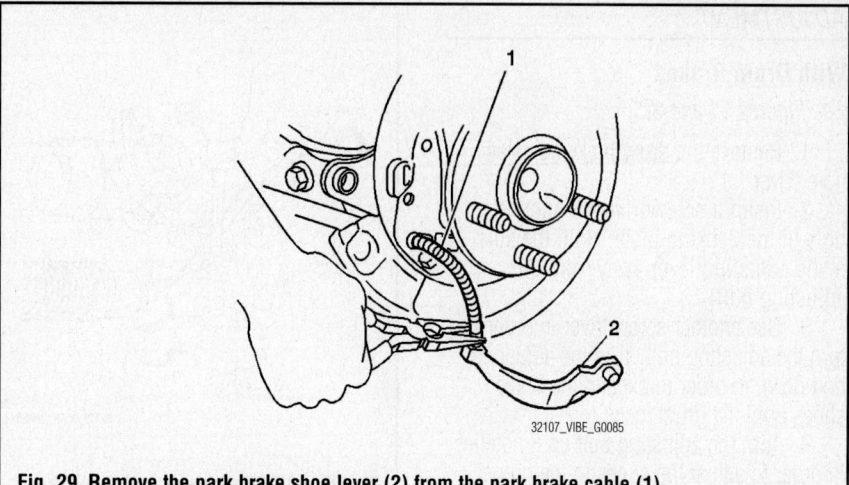

Fig. 29 Remove the park brake shoe lever (2) from the park brake cable (1).

6. Remove the front shoe.

7. Separate the adjuster from the rear brake shoe (8).

8. Remove the adjuster and the adjuster strut (7).

9. Disassemble the adjuster (10,11,15)

10. Remove the hold-down spring (9) and the pin (2) from the rear shoe.

11. Separate the rear shoe from the park brake shoe lever (6).

12. Remove the rear shoe.

13. Remove the park brake shoe lever (2) from the park brake cable (1).

14. Inspect the park brake hardware.

To install:

15. Apply Jubilate® Lubricant, GM P/N 1050109 (Canadian P/N 5264008), or the equivalent, to the metal contact points on the following components:

- The backing plate (1)

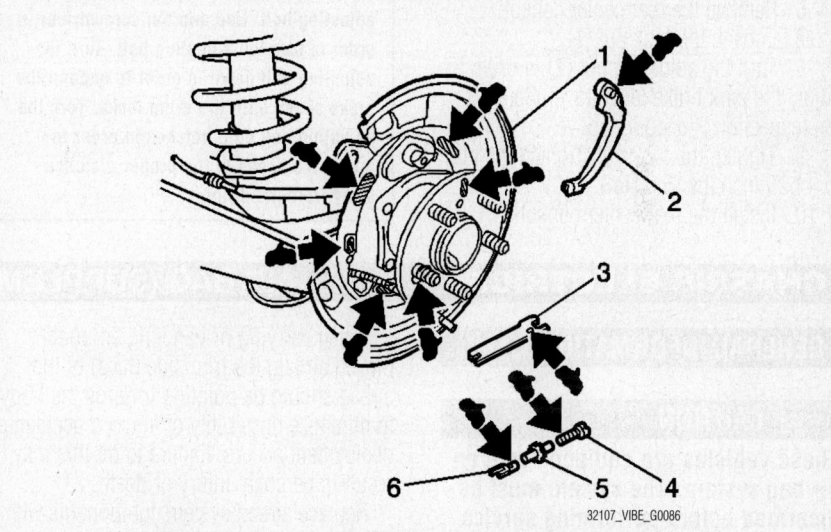

Fig. 30 Exploded view of components: the backing plate (1), the park brake shoe lever (2), the adjuster strut (3), the adjuster (4, 5, 6)

- The park brake shoe lever (2)
- The adjuster strut (3)
- The adjuster (4, 5, 6)

16. Assemble the adjuster.

17. Install the park brake shoe lever (2) to the park brake cable (1).

18. Install the park brake shoe lever (6) and the rear shoe (8).

19. Install the pin (2) and the hold-down spring (9) to the rear shoe.

20. Install the adjuster (10,11,15) and the adjuster strut (7) to the rear shoe.

21. Install the front shoe (17).

22. Install the pin (1) and the hold-down spring (16) to the front shoe.

23. Connect the adjuster to the front shoe.

24. Install the tension spring (1).

25. Install the return springs (1, 2).

26. Install the rear disc.

27. Adjust the park brake.

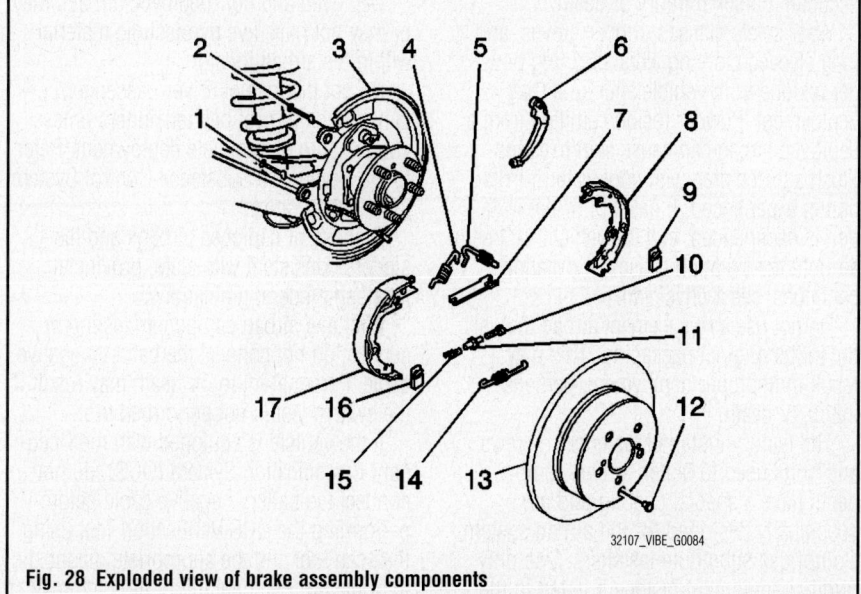

Fig. 28 Exploded view of brake assembly components

ADJUSTMENT

With Drum Brakes

See Figures 31 and 32.

1. Remove the drum brake adjuster hole cover.
2. Insert a screwdriver through the hole in the backing plate. Hold the automatic adjusting lever away from the adjusting bolt.
3. Use another screwdriver in order to turn the adjusting bolt. Turn the adjusting bolt down in order to expand the brake shoes until the drum locks.
4. Turn the adjusting bolt up 8 notches in order to adjust the shoes to the proper distance away from the drum.
5. Install the adjuster hole cover.
6. Remove the rear center console.
7. Loosen the lock nut (1).
8. Turn the adjusting nut (2) in order to adjust the park brake lever travel. Refer to the Inspection Procedure above.
9. Tighten the lock nut. Tighten the nut to 44.25 inch lbs (5.0 Nm).
10. Install the rear center console.

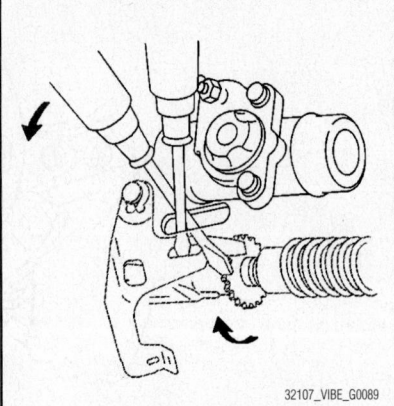

32107_VIBE_G0089

Fig. 31 Insert a screwdriver through the hole in the backing plate. Hold the automatic adjusting lever away from the adjusting bolt. Use another screwdriver in order to turn the adjusting bolt. Turn the adjusting bolt down in order to expand the brake shoes until the drum locks. Turn the adjusting bolt up 8 notches in order to adjust the shoes to the proper distance away from the drum.

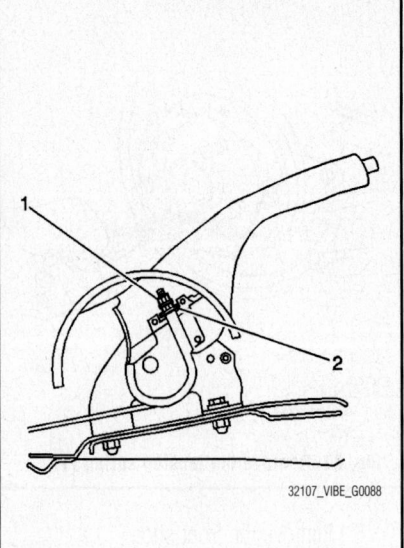

32107_VIBE_G0088

Fig. 32 Loosen the lock nut (1). Turn the adjusting nut (2) in order to adjust the park brake lever travel. Refer to the Inspection Procedure above.

CHASSIS ELECTRICAL

AIR BAG (SUPPLEMENTAL RESTRAINT SYSTEM)

GENERAL INFORMATION

✴✴ CAUTION

These vehicles are equipped with an air bag system. The system must be disarmed before performing service on, or around, system components, the steering column, instrument panel components, wiring and sensors. Failure to follow the safety precautions and the disarming procedure could result in accidental air bag deployment, possible injury and unnecessary system repairs.

SERVICE PRECAUTIONS

Disconnect and isolate the battery negative cable before beginning any airbag system component diagnosis, testing, removal, or installation procedures. Allow system capacitor to discharge for two minutes before beginning any component service. This will disable the airbag system. Failure to disable the airbag system may result in accidental airbag deployment, personal injury, or death.

Do not place an intact undeployed airbag face down on a solid surface. The airbag will propel into the air if accidentally deployed and may result in personal injury or death.

When carrying or handling an undeployed airbag, the trim side (face) of the airbag should be pointing towards the body to minimize possibility of injury if accidental deployment occurs. Failure to do this may result in personal injury or death.

Replace airbag system components with OEM replacement parts. Substitute parts may appear interchangeable, but internal differences may result in inferior occupant protection. Failure to do so may result in occupant personal injury or death.

Wear safety glasses, rubber gloves, and long sleeved clothing when cleaning powder residue from vehicle after an airbag deployment. Powder residue emitted from a deployed airbag can cause skin irritation. Flush affected area with cool water if irritation is experienced. If nasal or throat irritation is experienced, exit the vehicle for fresh air until the irritation ceases. If irritation continues, see a physician.

Do not use a replacement airbag that is not in the original packaging. This may result in improper deployment, personal injury, or death.

The factory installed fasteners, screws and bolts used to fasten airbag components have a special coating and are specifically designed for the airbag system. Do not use substitute fasteners. Use only original equipment fasteners listed in the parts catalog when fastener replacement is required.

During, and following, any child restraint anchor service, due to impact event or vehicle repair, carefully inspect all mounting hardware, tether straps, and anchors for proper installation, operation, or damage. If a child restraint anchor is found damaged in any way, the anchor must be replaced. Failure to do this may result in personal injury or death.

Deployed and non-deployed airbags may or may not have live pyrotechnic material within the airbag inflator.

Do not dispose of driver/passenger/curtain airbags or seat belt tensioners unless you are sure of complete deployment. Refer to the Hazardous Substance Control System for proper disposal.

Dispose of deployed airbags and tensioners consistent with state, provincial, local, and federal regulations.

After any airbag component testing or service, do not connect the battery negative cable. Personal injury or death may result if the system test is not performed first.

If the vehicle is equipped with the Occupant Classification System (OCS), do not connect the battery negative cable before performing the OCS Verification Test using the scan tool and the appropriate diagnostic information. Personal injury or death may result if the system test is not performed properly.

Never replace both the Occupant Restraint Controller (ORC) and the Occupant Classification Module (OCM) at the same time. If both require replacement, replace one, then perform the Airbag System test before replacing the other.

Both the ORC and the OCM store Occupant Classification System (OCS) calibration data, which they transfer to one another when one of them is replaced. If both are replaced at the same time, an irreversible fault will be set in both modules and the OCS may malfunction and cause personal injury or death.

If equipped with OCS, the Seat Weight Sensor is a sensitive, calibrated unit and must be handled carefully. Do not drop or handle roughly. If dropped or damaged, replace with another sensor. Failure to do so may result in occupant injury or death.

If equipped with OCS, the front passenger seat must be handled carefully as well. When removing the seat, be careful when setting on floor not to drop. If dropped, the sensor may be inoperative, could result in occupant injury, or possibly death.

If equipped with OCS, when the passenger front seat is on the floor, no one should sit in the front passenger seat. This uneven force may damage the sensing ability of the seat weight sensors. If sat on and damaged, the sensor may be inoperative, could result in occupant injury, or possibly death.

DISARMING THE SYSTEM

Zone 1

1. Turn the steering wheel so that the vehicle's wheels are pointing straight ahead.
2. Turn the ignition switch to the **OFF** position.

➡**With the SIR fuse removed and the ignition switch in the ON position, the AIR BAG warning indicator illuminates. This is normal operation, and does not indicate a SIR system malfunction.**

3. Locate and remove the AM2 Fuse from the junction block, which is located near the base of the steering column.
4. Disconnect the battery negative cable.
5. Locate the front end sensor - right electrical connector.
6. Remove the Connector Position Assurance (CPA) from the front end sensor - right connector.
7. Remove the front end sensor - right electrical connector from the front end sensor - right.

8. Open the hood, and locate the front end discriminating sensor - left electrical connector.
9. Remove the CPA from the front end sensor - left connector.
10. Remove the front end sensor - left electrical connector from the front end sensor - left.

Zone 2

1. Turn the steering wheel so that the vehicle wheels are pointing straight ahead.
2. Turn the ignition switch to the **OFF** position.
3. With the SIR fuse removed and the ignition switch in the ON position, the AIR BAG warning indicator illuminates. This is normal operation, and does not indicate an SIR system malfunction.
4. Locate and remove the AM2 Fuse from the junction block, which is located near the base of the steering column.
5. Disconnect the battery negative cable.
6. Remove the front door sill plate.
7. Remove the rear door sill plate.
8. Remove the center pillar lower trim panel.
9. Remove the front seat belt retractor.
10. Disconnect the SIS electrical connector.
11. Remove the quarter upper trim panel.
12. Remove the center pillar upper trim panel.
13. Disconnect the left roof rail module wiring harness yellow connector from the left roof rail module.

Zone 4

1. Turn the steering wheel so that the vehicle wheels are pointing straight ahead.
2. Turn the ignition switch to the **OFF** position.

➡**With the SIR fuse removed and the ignition switch in the ON position, the AIR BAG warning indicator illuminates. This is normal operation, and does not indicate an SIR system malfunction.**

3. Locate and remove the AM2 fuse from the junction block, which is located near the base of the steering column.
4. Disconnect the battery negative cable.
5. Release the inflatable restraint steering wheel module coil connector locking mechanism.
6. Disconnect the inflatable restraint steering wheel module coil connector C3.
7. Remove the Instrument Panel (I/P) glove compartment.

8. Release then unlock the I/P module connector.
9. Disconnect the I/P module pigtail.
10. Release and unlock the driver and passenger seat module connectors.
11. Disconnect the driver and passenger seat modules.
12. Remove the quarter upper trim panel.
13. Remove the center pillar upper trim panel.
14. Disconnect the left and right roof rail module wiring harness yellow connectors from the roof rail modules.

Zone 5

1. Turn the steering wheel so that the vehicle wheels are pointing straight ahead.
2. Turn the ignition switch to the **OFF** position.

➡**With the SIR fuse removed and the ignition switch in the ON position, the AIR BAG warning indicator illuminates. This is normal operation, and does not indicate an SIR system malfunction.**

3. Locate and remove the AM2 fuse from the junction block, which is located near the base of the steering column.
4. Disconnect the negative battery cable.
5. Remove the glove compartment.
6. Release then unlock the Instrument Panel (I/P) module connector.
7. Disconnect the I/P module pigtail.

Zone 6

1. Turn the steering wheel so that the vehicle wheels are pointing straight ahead.
2. Turn the ignition switch to the **OFF** position.

➡**With the SIR fuse removed and the ignition switch in the ON position, the AIR BAG warning indicator illuminates. This is normal operation, and does not indicate an SIR system malfunction.**

3. Locate and remove the AM2 fuse from the junction block, which is located near the base of the steering column.
4. Disconnect the negative battery cable.
5. Remove the front door sill plate.
6. Remove the rear door sill plate.
7. Remove the center pillar lower trim panel.
8. Remove the front seat belt retractor.
9. Disconnect the SIS electrical connector.
10. Remove the quarter upper trim panel.
11. Remove the center pillar upper trim panel.

12. Disconnect the right roof rail module wiring harness yellow connector from the right roof rail module.

Zone 7

1. Turn the steering wheel so that the vehicle wheels are pointing straight ahead.
2. Turn the ignition switch to the **OFF** position.

➡**With the SIR fuse removed and the ignition switch in the ON position, the AIR BAG warning indicator illuminates. This is normal operation, and does not indicate an SIR system malfunction.**

3. Locate and remove the AM2 fuse from the junction block, which is located near the base of the steering column.
4. Disconnect the negative battery cable.
5. Release and unlock the Driver Seat Module (DSM) connector.
6. Disconnect the DSM connector.

Zone 9

1. Turn the steering wheel so that the vehicle wheels are pointing straight ahead.
2. Turn the ignition switch to the **OFF** position.

➡**With the SIR fuse removed and the ignition switch in the ON position, the AIR BAG warning indicator illuminates. This is normal operation, and does not indicate an SIR system malfunction.**

3. Locate and remove the AM2 fuse from the junction block, which is located near the base of the steering column.
4. Disconnect the negative battery cable.
5. Release and unlock the Passenger Seat Module (PSM) connector.
6. Disconnect the PSM connector.

Zone 10

1. Turn the steering wheel so that the vehicle wheels are pointing straight ahead.
2. Turn the ignition switch to the **OFF** position.

➡**With the SIR fuse removed and the ignition switch in the ON position, the AIR BAG warning indicator illuminates. This is normal operation, and does not indicate an SIR system malfunction.**

3. Locate and remove the AM2 fuse from the junction block, which is located near the base of the steering column.
4. Disconnect the negative battery cable.
5. Remove the rear door sill plate.

6. Remove the rear seat garnish molding.
7. Disconnect the Side Impact Sensor (SIS) electrical connector.

Zone 12

1. Turn the steering wheel so that the vehicle wheels are pointing straight ahead.
2. Turn the ignition switch to the **OFF** position.

➡**With the SIR fuse removed and the ignition switch in the ON position, the AIR BAG warning indicator illuminates. This is normal operation, and does not indicate an SIR system malfunction.**

3. Locate and remove the AM2 fuse from the junction block, which is located near the base of the steering column.
4. Disconnect the negative battery cable.
5. Remove the rear door sill plate.
6. Remove the rear seat garnish molding.
7. Disconnect the Side Impact Sensor (SIS) electrical connector.

ARMING THE SYSTEM

Zone 1

1. Connect the front end sensor - left electrical connector from the front end sensor - left.
2. Connect the CPA from the front end sensor - left connector.
3. Connect the front end sensor - right electrical connector from the front end sensor - right.
4. Connect the CPA from the front end sensor - right connector.
5. Connect the battery negative cable.
6. Install the AM2 Fuse into the junction block.

❉❉ CAUTION

Use caution while reaching in and turn the ignition switch to the ON position.

7. The AIR BAG indicator will flash then turn OFF.
8. Perform the Diagnostic System Check - Vehicle if the AIR BAG warning indicator does not operate as described.

Zone 2

1. Connect the SIS electrical connector.
2. Install the front seat belt retractor.
3. Install the center pillar lower trim panel.
4. Interior Trim.
5. Install the rear door sill plate.

6. Install the front door sill plate.
7. Connect the left roof rail module wiring harness yellow connector to the left roof rail module.
8. Install the center pillar upper trim panel.
9. Install the quarter upper trim panel.
10. Connect the battery negative cable.
11. Install the AM2 Fuse into the junction block.

❉❉ CAUTION

Use caution while reaching in and turn the ignition switch to the ON position.

12. The AIR BAG indicator will flash then turn OFF.
13. Perform the Diagnostic System Check - Vehicle if the AIR BAG warning indicator does not operate as described.

Zone 4

1. Remove the key from the ignition switch.
2. Connect the left and right roof rail module wiring harness yellow connectors to the roof rail modules.
3. Install the center pillar upper trim panel.
4. Install the quarter upper trim panel.
5. Install the yellow 2-way connectors to the driver and passenger seat modules.
6. Connect the connectors and lock the connectors with the connector lock levers.
7. Install the yellow 2-way connector to the inflatable restraint I/P module pigtail. Connect the connector and lock the connector with the connector lock lever.
8. Install the I/P glove compartment.
9. Install the yellow 2-way connector for the inflatable restraint steering wheel module coil. Connect the connector and lock the connector with the connector lock lever.
10. Install the lower steering column trim cover.
11. Connect the battery negative cable.
12. Install the AM2 fuse into the junction block.

❉❉ CAUTION

Use caution while reaching in and turn the ignition switch to the ON position.

13. The AIR BAG indicator will flash then turn OFF. Perform the Diagnostic System Check - Vehicle if the AIR BAG

warning indicator does not operate as described.

Zone 5

1. Install the yellow 2-way connector to the inflatable restraint I/P module pigtail. Connect the connector and lock the connector with the connector lock lever.
2. Install the glove compartment.
3. Connect the battery negative cable.
4. Install the AM2 fuse into the junction block.

✳✳ CAUTION

Use caution while reaching in and turn the ignition switch to the ON position.

5. The AIR BAG indicator will flash then turn OFF.
6. Perform the Diagnostic System Check - Vehicle if the AIR BAG warning indicator does not operate as described.

Zone 6

1. Connect the SIS electrical connector.
2. Install the front seat belt retractor.
3. Install the center pillar lower trim panel.
4. Install the rear door sill plate.
5. Install the front door sill plate.
6. Connect the right roof rail module wiring harness yellow connector to the right roof rail module.
7. Install the center pillar upper trim panel.
8. Install the quarter upper trim panel.
9. Connect the negative battery cable.
10. Install the AM2 fuse into the junction block.

✳✳ CAUTION

Use caution while reaching in and turn the ignition switch to the ON position.

11. The AIR BAG indicator will flash then turn OFF.
12. Perform the Diagnostic System Check - Vehicle if the AIR BAG warning indicator does not operate as described.

Zone 7

1. Install the yellow 2-way connector to the DSM.
2. Connect the connector and lock the connector with the connector lock lever.
3. Connect the negative battery cable.
4. Install the AM2 fuse into the junction block.

✳✳ CAUTION

Use caution while reaching in and turn the ignition switch to the ON position.

5. The AIR BAG indicator will flash then turn OFF.
6. Perform the Diagnostic System Check - Vehicle if the AIR BAG warning indicator does not operate as described.

Zone 9

1. Install the yellow 2-way connector to the PSM.
2. Connect the connector and lock the connector with the connector lock lever.
3. Connect the negative battery cable.
4. Install the AM2 fuse into the junction block.

✳✳ CAUTION

Use caution while reaching in and turn the ignition switch to the ON position.

5. The AIR BAG indicator will flash then turn OFF.

6. Perform the Diagnostic System Check - Vehicle if the AIR BAG warning indicator does not operate as described.

Zone 10

1. Connect the SIS electrical connector.
2. Install the rear seat garnish molding.
3. Connect the negative battery cable.
4. Install the AM2 fuse into the junction block.

✳✳ CAUTION

Use caution while reaching in and turn the ignition switch to the ON position.

5. The AIR BAG indicator will flash then turn OFF.
6. Perform the Diagnostic System Check - Vehicle if the AIR BAG warning indicator does not operate as described.

Zone 12

1. Connect the SIS electrical connector.
2. Install the rear seat garnish molding.
3. Install the rear door sill plate.
4. Connect the negative battery cable.
5. Install the AM2 fuse into the junction block.

✳✳ CAUTION

Use caution while reaching in and turn the ignition switch to the ON position.

6. The AIR BAG indicator will flash then turn OFF.
7. Perform the Diagnostic System Check - Vehicle if the AIR BAG warning indicator does not operate as described.

DRIVETRAIN

AUTOMATIC TRANSAXLE ASSEMBLY

REMOVAL & INSTALLATION

FWD—A246E & U240E Transaxles

See Figures 33 through 35.

1. Before servicing the vehicle, refer to the precautions section.
2. Drain the transaxle fluid.
3. Remove or disconnect the following:
   - Negative battery cable
   - Hood
   - No. 2 cylinder head cover

- Battery and battery carrier
- Air cleaner assembly with hose
- Floor shift cable transmission control shift
- Transmission control cable support
- No. 1 transmission control cable bracket

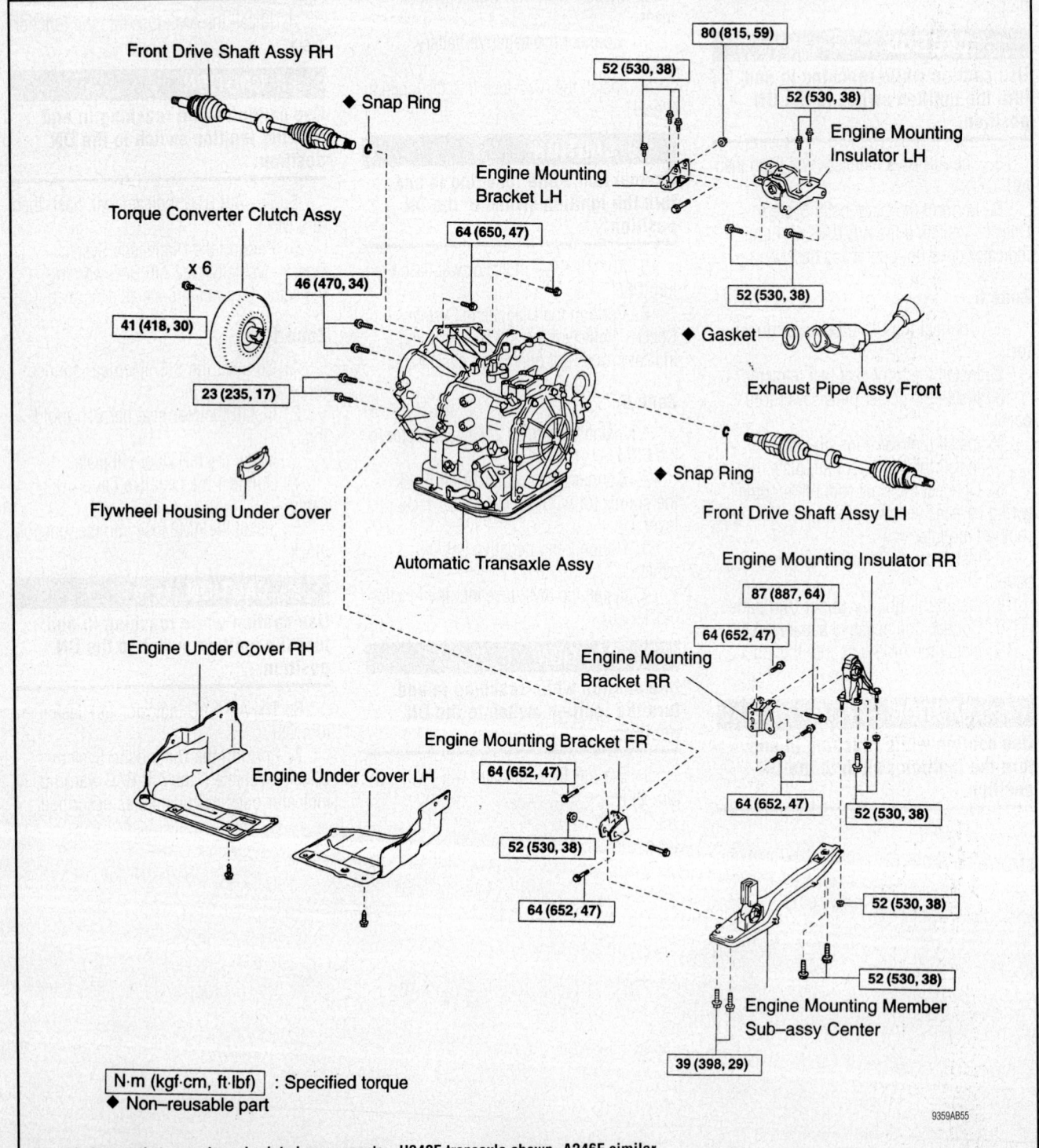

Fig. 33 Automatic transaxle and related components—U240E transaxle shown, A246E similar

9359AB55

- Wiring harness and brackets
- Transmission wire connector
- Park/neutral position switch connector, with Anti-lock Brake System (ABS)
- Speedometer sensor connector, without ABS
- Transmission revolution sensor connectors, if equipped
- Transmission fluid filler tube
- No. 1 oil cooler inlet and outlet tubes
- Foot rest
- Floor carpet
- Oxygen (O_2) sensor connector

4. Suspend the engine as follows:

   a. Disconnect the 2 Positive Crankcase Ventilation (PCV) hoses.

   b. Install the No. 1 and No. 2 engine hangers in the correct direction.

   c. No. 1 engine hanger: P/N 12281-22021 (A246E) or 12281-88600 (U240E).

   d. No. 2 engine hanger: P/N 12281-15040 (A246E) or 12281-88600 (U240E).

   e. Bolt: P/N 91512-B1016.

   f. Torque the bolt to 28 ft. lbs. (38 Nm).

   g. Attach an engine chain hoist to the engine hangers.

- Front wheels
- Right and left engine undercovers
- Front floor panel brace, U240E transaxle
- Front exhaust pipe
- Front halfshafts
- Automatic transmission case protector
- Starter

5. Support the transaxle with a floor jack

- Left side transverse engine mounting insulator and bracket
- Right side front and rear engine mount insulators
- 4 bolts, dynamic damper and member sub-assembly
- Front and rear right side transverse engine mounting brackets
- Flywheel housing undercover
- Automatic transaxle. Turn the crankshaft for access to the 6 bolts while holding the crankshaft pulley bolt with a wrench.
- Torque converter clutch

6. Installation is the reverse of the removal procedure, noting the following specifications:

   a. Automatic transaxle: Bolt "A" to 47 ft. lbs. (64 Nm), bolt "B" to 34 ft. lbs. (47 Nm) and bolt "C" to 17 ft. lbs. (23 Nm).

   b. Torque converter bolts: 20 ft. lbs. (28 Nm).

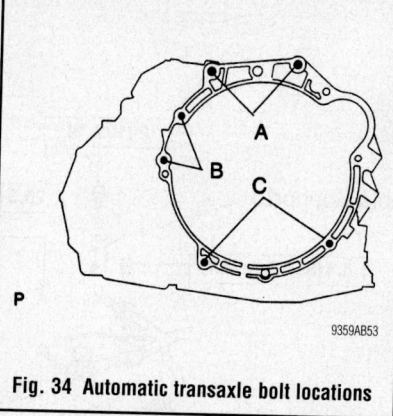

Fig. 34 Automatic transaxle bolt locations

   c. Front and rear right transverse engine mounting bracket bolts: 47 ft. lbs. (64 Nm).

   d. Member sub-assembly center bolts: "A" bolts to 29 ft. lbs. (39 Nm) and "B" bolts to 38 ft. lbs. (52 Nm).

   e. Right rear engine mounting insulator-to-engine mounting bracket bolt: 64 ft. lbs. (87 Nm).

   f. Right rear engine mount insulator nuts and bolt: 38 ft. lbs. (52 Nm).

   g. Left side engine mounting bracket-to-transaxle bolts: 38 ft. lbs. (52 Nm).

   h. Left side engine mounting insulator bolts and nut: Bolt "A" to 38 ft. lbs. (52 Nm), Bolt "B" and Nut "B" to 59 ft. lbs. (80 Nm).

   i. Front right engine mount insulator-to-mounting bracket bolt and nut: 38 ft. lbs. (52 Nm).

   j. Starter bolts: 29 ft. lbs. (39 Nm).

   k. Automatic transmission case protector bolts: 14 ft. lbs. (18 Nm).

   l. Wheel lug nuts: 76 ft. lbs. (103 Nm).

   m. Oil cooler clamp bolts: 49 inch lbs. (5.5 Nm).

   n. Oil cooler inlet and outlet tubes: 25 ft. lbs. (34 Nm).

   o. Wire harness bracket bolt: 9 ft. lbs. (13 Nm).

   p. Transmission control cable bracket bolts: 9 ft. lbs. (12 Nm).

   q. Transmission control cable support: 9 ft. lbs. (12 Nm).

   r. Battery carrier: 10 ft. lbs. (13 Nm).

   s. Air cleaner assembly: 62 inch lbs. (7 Nm).

   t. Cylinder head cover bolts: 62 inch lbs. (7 Nm).

   u. Hood bolts: 10 ft. lbs. (13 Nm).

7. Fill the transaxle fluid to the proper level.

8. Start the vehicle, check for leaks and repair if necessary.

AWD—U341F Transaxle

See Figure 36.

1. Before servicing the vehicle, refer to the precautions section.

2. Drain the transaxle fluid.

3. Remove or disconnect the following:

- Negative battery cable
- Engine and transaxle assembly
- Transfer case
- Automatic transmission case protector
- Front left side halfshaft
- Transmission control cable support and bracket
- Wire harness clamp bracket, bolts and 2 wire harnesses
- Transmission wire connector
- Park/neutral position switch connector
- Transmission revolution sensor connectors, if equipped
- Transmission fluid filler tube
- Oil cooler inlet and outlet tubes

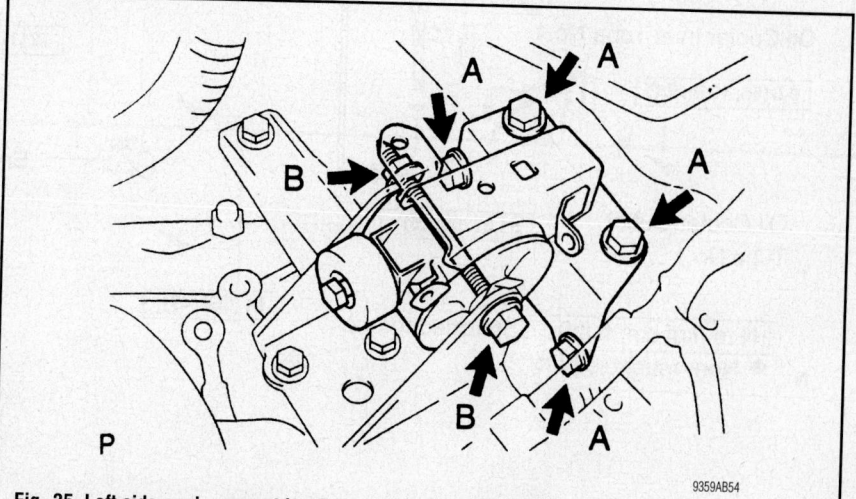

Fig. 35 Left side engine mount insulator bolt and nut locations

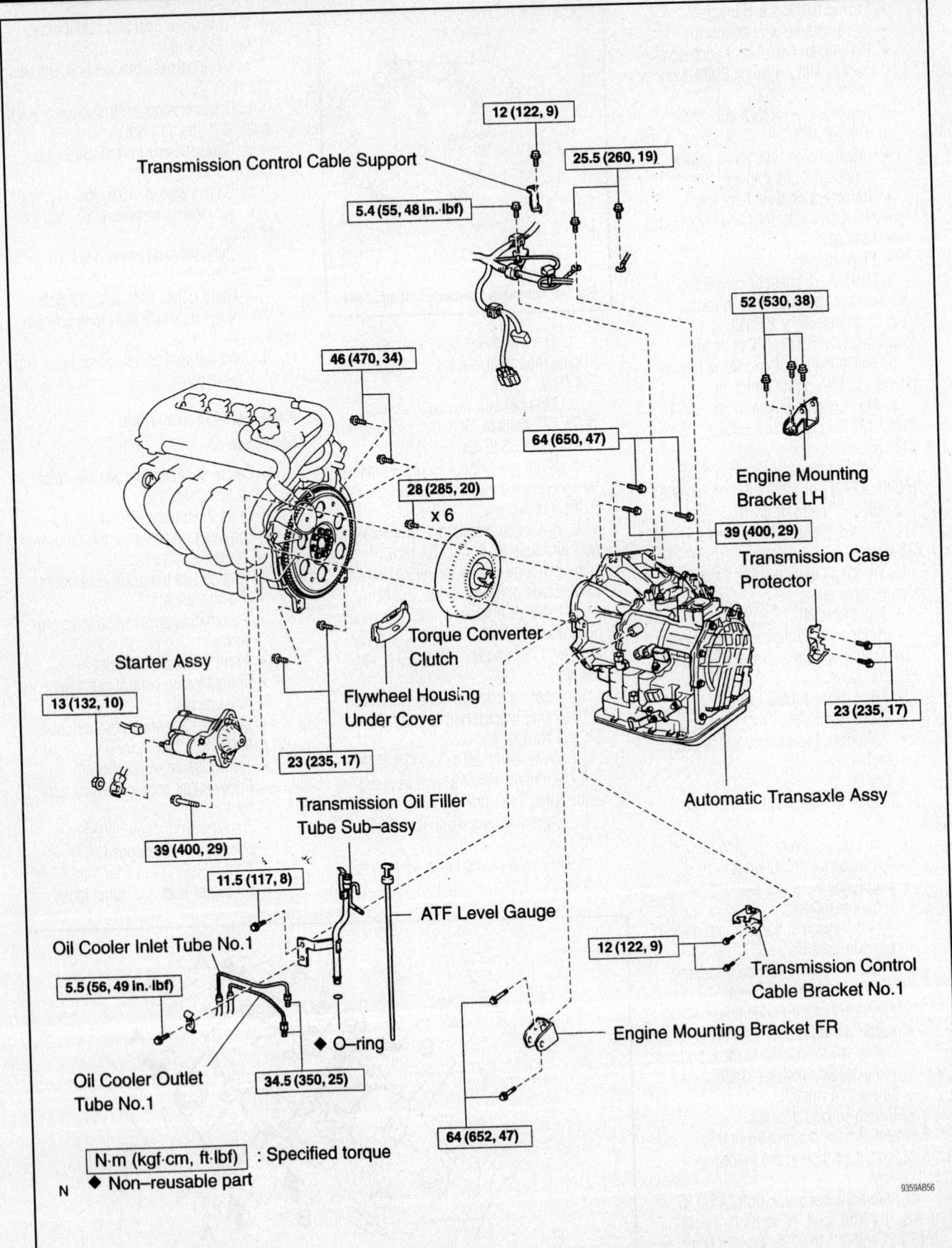

12 (122, 9)

Transmission Control Cable Support

25.5 (260, 19)

5.4 (55, 48 in. lbf)

52 (530, 38)

46 (470, 34)

64 (650, 47)

Engine Mounting
Bracket LH

28 (285, 20)

x 6

39 (400, 29)

Transmission Case
Protector

Torque Converter
Clutch

Starter Assy

Flywheel Housing
Under Cover

13 (132, 10)

23 (235, 17)

23 (235, 17)

Automatic Transaxle Assy

Transmission Oil Filler
Tube Sub–assy

39 (400, 29)

11.5 (117, 8)

ATF Level Gauge

Oil Cooler Inlet Tube No.1

12 (122, 9)

Transmission Control
Cable Bracket No.1

5.5 (56, 49 in. lbf)

◆ O–ring

Oil Cooler Outlet
Tube No.1

34.5 (350, 25)

Engine Mounting Bracket FR

64 (652, 47)

N·m (kgf·cm, ft·lbf) : Specified torque

N ◆ Non–reusable part

9359AB56

Fig. 36 Automatic transaxle and related components—U341F transaxle

- Transverse engine mounting brackets
- Flywheel housing undercover
- Automatic transaxle. Turn the crankshaft for access to the 6 bolts while holding the crankshaft pulley bolt with a wrench.
- Torque converter clutch

4. Installation is the reverse of the removal procedure, noting the following specifications:

   a. Automatic transaxle: Bolt "A" to 47 ft. lbs. (64 Nm), bolt "B" to 34 ft. lbs. (47 Nm) and bolt "C" to 17 ft. lbs. (23 Nm).

   b. Oil cooler clamp bolts: 8 ft. lbs. (11 Nm) for the top bolt and 49 inch lbs. (5.5 Nm) for the bottom bolt

   c. Oil cooler inlet and outlet tube bolts: 25 ft. lbs. (34 Nm).

   d. Wire harness clamp bracket bolt: 48 inch lbs. (5 Nm).

   e. Transmission control cable bracket and support bolts: 9 ft. lbs. (12 Nm).

   f. Automatic transmission case protector bolts: 17 ft. lbs. (23 Nm).

5. Fill the transaxle fluid to the proper level.

6. Start the vehicle, check for leaks and repair if necessary.

MANUAL TRANSAXLE ASSEMBLY

REMOVAL & INSTALLATION

1. Before servicing the vehicle, refer to the precautions section.

✳✳ CAUTION

Before servicing any electrical component, the ignition key must be in the OFF or LOCK position and all electrical loads must be OFF, unless instructed otherwise in these procedures. If a tool or equipment could easily come in contact with a live exposed electrical terminal, also disconnect the negative battery cable. Failure to follow these precautions may cause personal injury and/or damage to the vehicle or its components.

2. Remove the battery and tray.
3. Remove the air cleaner case assembly.
4. Remove the cruise control servo from the vehicle.
5. Remove the cylinder head cover from the engine.
6. Disconnect the wire harness from the transaxle.

7. Remove the 2 bolts, then disconnect the 2 wire harness brackets.
8. Remove the 2 bolts and the ground cables from the transaxle.
9. Disconnect the backup lamp connector.
10. Disconnect the vehicle speed sensor connector.
11. Remove the clutch actuator cylinder and the piping from the transaxle assembly.
12. Remove the clip and the washer, then disconnect the shift cable from the transaxle.
13. Remove the clip, then disconnect the shift cable from the bracket.
14. Remove the clip and washer, then disconnect the shift cable from the transaxle.
15. Remove the clip, then disconnect the shift cable from the bracket. Remove the starter assembly from the vehicle.
16. Install the engine support fixture.
17. Remove the front wheels.
18. Remove the left and right lower splash shields.
19. Remove the exhaust pipe from the vehicle.
20. Remove the transaxle drain plug and the oil.
21. Remove the left and right drive shafts.
22. Remove the front suspension crossmember.
23. Support the transaxle with a suitable jack.
24. Remove the 5 bolts from the left engine mount, then remove the mount from the vehicle.
25. Remove the 3 bolts from the left engine mount bracket, then remove the bracket from the vehicle.
26. Remove the 6 bolts that secure the transaxle to the engine.
27. Slightly lower the transaxle.
28. Remove the transaxle from the engine.

To install:

29. Align the input shaft with the clutch disc and install the transaxle to the engine.
30. Install the 6 bolts that secure the transaxle to the engine. Torque the "A" bolts to 47 ft. lbs. (64 Nm), the "B" bolts to 35 ft. lbs. (47 Nm) and the "C" bolts to 17 ft. lbs. (23 Nm).
31. Install the left engine mounting bracket to the transaxle with the 3 bolts. Tighten to 38 ft. lbs. (52 Nm).
32. Install the left engine mount with the 5 bolts and nuts. Tighten the "A" bolts to 38 ft. lbs. (52 Nm) and the "B" bolts to 59 ft. lbs. (80 Nm).

33. Lower the jack from the transaxle.
34. Install the front suspension crossmember.
35. Install the left and right drive shafts.
36. Install the left and right lower splash shields.
37. Install the exhaust pipe in the vehicle.
38. Install the front wheels.
39. Install the drain plug with a new gasket. Tighten to 29 ft. lbs. (39 Nm).
40. Fill the transaxle with 2.0 qts. (1.9L) of API GL-4 or GL-5 SAE 75W-90 or equivalent.
41. Install the fill plug with a new gasket. Tighten to 29 ft. lbs. (39 Nm).
42. Remove the engine support fixture.
43. Install the starter assembly from the vehicle.
44. Connect the shift cable to the transaxle, then install the clip and the washer.
45. Connect the shift cable to the bracket, then install the clip.
46. Connect the shift cable to the transaxle, then install the clip and the washer.
47. Connect the shift cable to the bracket, then install the clip.
48. Install the clutch actuator cylinder and the piping.
49. Connect the backup lamp connector.
50. Connect the vehicle speed sensor connector.
51. Connect the wire harness to the transaxle.
52. Connect the 2 wire harness brackets, then install the 2 bolts.
53. Install the 2 bolts and the ground cables to the transaxle.
54. Install the cruise control servo in the vehicle.
55. Install the battery tray and the 4 bolts.

✳✳ CAUTION

Before servicing any electrical component, the ignition key must be in the OFF or LOCK position and all electrical loads must be OFF, unless instructed otherwise in these procedures. If a tool or equipment could easily come in contact with a live exposed electrical terminal, also disconnect the negative battery cable. Failure to follow these precautions may cause personal injury and/or damage to the vehicle or its components.

56. Install the battery.
57. Install the air cleaner case assembly.

58. Install the cylinder head cover in the engine.

CLUTCH DRIVEN DISC & PRESSURE PLATE

REMOVAL & INSTALLATION

See Figure 37.

1. Before servicing the vehicle, refer to the precautions section.

➡**Do not allow grease or oil to get on any part of the disc, pressure plate, or flywheel surfaces.**

2. Remove or disconnect the following:
   • Negative battery cable. On vehicles equipped with an air bag, wait at least 90 seconds before proceeding
   • Transaxle assembly

3. Make matchmarks on the clutch cover (pressure plate) and flywheel so that the pressure plate can be returned to its original position during installation.

4. Remove or disconnect the following:
   • Release fork bearing clips
   • Release bearing hub, complete with the release bearing
   • Release fork and support

❊❊ CAUTION

Slowly unfasten the bolts which attach the pressure plate. Loosen each bolt 1 turn at a time until the spring tension is released. If the bolts are released improperly the clutch assembly could fly apart, causing possible injury.

   • Pressure plate from the clutch cover/spring assembly

5. Inspect the disc, pressure plate and flywheel for damage and wear using a caliper to measure depth and width and a dial indicator to measure runout.

   a. The minimum clutch disc rivet head depth is 0.012 in. (0.3mm).
   b. The maximum clutch disc runout is 0.031 in. (0.8mm).
   c. The maximum pressure plate spring depth is 0.024 in. (0.6mm).
   d. The maximum pressure plate spring width is 0.197 in. (5.0mm).
   e. The maximum flywheel runout is 0.004 in. (0.1mm).

6. Replace or machine parts as necessary.

To install:

7. When reassembling, apply a thin coating of multipurpose grease to the release bearing hub and release fork contact points. Also, pack the groove inside the

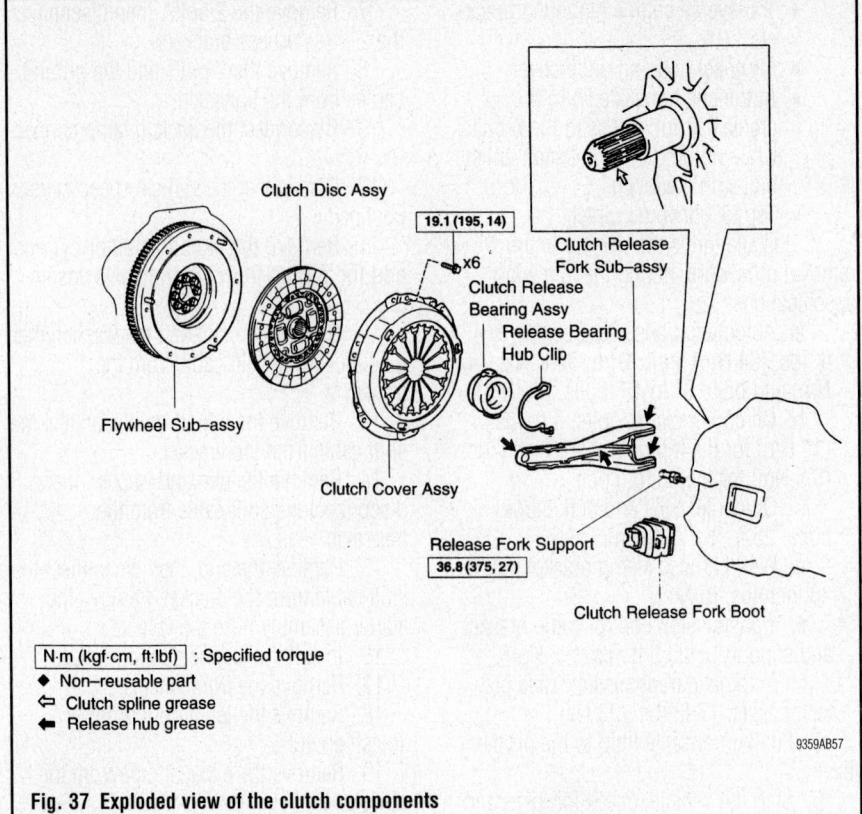

Fig. 37 Exploded view of the clutch components

clutch hub with multipurpose grease and lubricate the pivot points of the release fork.

8. Install or connect the following:
   • Clutch disc and pressure plate. The bolts should be tightened in 2 or 3 steps, gradually and evenly. Final bolt torque is 14 ft. lbs. (19 Nm).
   • Release bearing, fork and boot
   • Transaxle assembly
   • Negative battery cable

ADJUSTMENTS

Hydraulic clutch actuating systems used in these vehicles do not require adjustment.

CLUTCH MASTER CYLINDER

REMOVAL & INSTALLATION

1. Remove the brake booster assembly from the vehicle.
2. Disconnect the clutch reservoir tube from the clutch master cylinder assembly.
3. Disconnect the pipe from the clutch master cylinder.
4. Remove the clutch master cylinder push rod clevis pin and clip.
5. Remove the 2 clutch master cylinder retaining nuts.
6. Remove the clutch master cylinder from the vehicle.

To install:

7. Install the clutch master cylinder in the vehicle.
8. Install the clutch master cylinder retaining nuts and tighten to 9 ft. lbs. (12 Nm).
9. Install the clevis pin and clip.
10. Install the hydraulic pipe to the clutch master cylinder.
11. Install the brake booster assembly in the vehicle.
12. Connect the reservoir tube to the clutch master cylinder.
13. Bleed the clutch.

CLUTCH SLAVE CYLINDER

REMOVAL & INSTALLATION

1. Remove the clutch actuator cylinder fluid line from the clutch actuator cylinder.
2. Remove the clutch actuator cylinder bolts.
3. Remove the clutch actuator cylinder from the transaxle.

To install:

4. Install the clutch actuator cylinder to the transaxle.

➡**Use the correct fastener in the correct location. Replacement fasteners must be the correct part number for** that application. Fasteners requiring replacement or fasteners requiring the use of thread locking compound or sealant are identified in the service procedure. Do not use paints, lubricants, or corrosion inhibitors on fasteners or fastener joint surfaces unless specified. These coatings affect fastener torque and joint clamping force and may damage the fastener. Use the correct tightening sequence and specifications when installing fasteners in order to avoid damage to parts and systems.

5. Install the clutch actuator cylinder bolts and tighten to 9 ft. lbs. (12 Nm).

6. Install the clutch actuator cylinder fluid line to the clutch actuator cylinder.

7. Bleed the hydraulic clutch system.

CLUTCH HYDRAULIC SYSTEM BLEEDING

➡If any maintenance on the clutch system was performed or the system is suspected of containing air, bleed the system. Use care; brake fluid will remove the paint from any surface. If the brake fluid spills onto any painted surface, wash it off immediately with soap and water.

1. Before servicing the vehicle, refer to the precautions section.

2. Fill the clutch reservoir with brake fluid. Check the reservoir level frequently and add fluid as needed.

3. Connect one end of a vinyl tube to the bleeder plug on the slave cylinder and submerge the other end into a clear container half-filled with brake fluid.

4. Slowly pump the clutch pedal several times.

5. Have an assistant hold the clutch pedal down and loosen the bleeder plug until fluid and/or air starts to run out of the bleeder plug. Close the bleeder plug while the pedal is held to the floor.

➡Do not allow the pedal to rise back-up while the bleeder is still open. If this happens, it will allow air to re-enter the slave cylinder and cause the clutch system not to work properly.

6. Repeat Steps 2 and 3 until all the air bubbles are removed from the system.

7. Tighten the bleeder plug when all the air is gone.

8. Refill the master cylinder to the proper level as required.

9. Check the system for leaks.

TRANSFER CASE ASSEMBLY

REMOVAL & INSTALLATION

See Figure 38.

1. Before servicing the vehicle, refer to the precautions section.

2. Drain the transfer case fluid.

3. Remove or disconnect the following:
   - Negative battery cable. Due to the air bag system, wait at least 90 seconds before proceeding
   - Engine and transaxle assembly
   - Separate vane pump
   - Steering gear
   - Crossmember
   - Manifold stay
   - Oxygen (O_2) sensor
   - Exhaust manifold heat shield
   - Exhaust manifold
   - Starter
   - Right side halfshaft
   - Transverse engine mounting bracket
   - Center and right side transfer stiffener plates

❊❊ WARNING

When removing the transfer case, DO NOT touch the oil seal.

   - Transfer case bolts, and transfer assembly, using a mallet to dislodge it from the transaxle

4. Installation is the reverse of the removal procedure, noting the following specifications:

   a. Transfer case stiffener case bolts: 25 ft. lbs. (34 Nm).

   b. Engine mounting bracket bolts: 47 ft. lbs. (64 Nm).

5. Add fluid to the transfer case, and check for leaks.

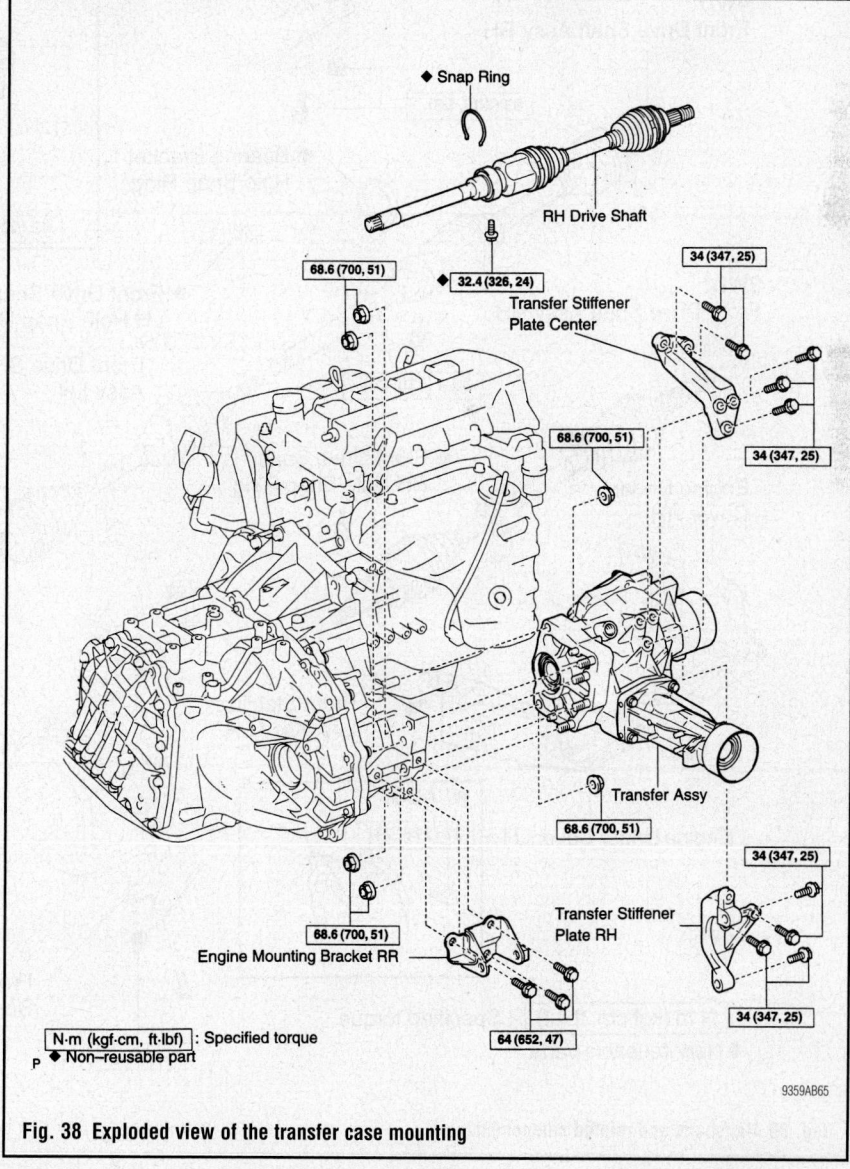

◆ Snap Ring

RH Drive Shaft

68.6 (700, 51)

◆ 32.4 (326, 24)

Transfer Stiffener Plate Center

34 (347, 25)

68.6 (700, 51)

34 (347, 25)

Transfer Assy

68.6 (700, 51)

34 (347, 25)

Transfer Stiffener Plate RH

68.6 (700, 51)

Engine Mounting Bracket RR

64 (652, 47)

34 (347, 25)

N·m (kgf·cm, ft·lbf) : Specified torque
◆ Non–reusable part

9359AB65

Fig. 38 Exploded view of the transfer case mounting

FRONT HALFSHAFTS

REMOVAL & INSTALLATION

See Figure 39.

➡The hub bearing could be damaged if subjected to the full weight of the vehicle, such as if the vehicle is moved without the halfshafts. If it is absolutely necessary to place the full vehicle weight on the hub bearing, first support the bearing with SST No. 09608–16041.

1. Before servicing the vehicle, refer to the precautions section.

2. Drain the transaxle fluid.
3. Remove or disconnect the following:

- Negative battery cable. Due to the air bag system, wait at least 90 seconds before proceeding.
- Both front wheels

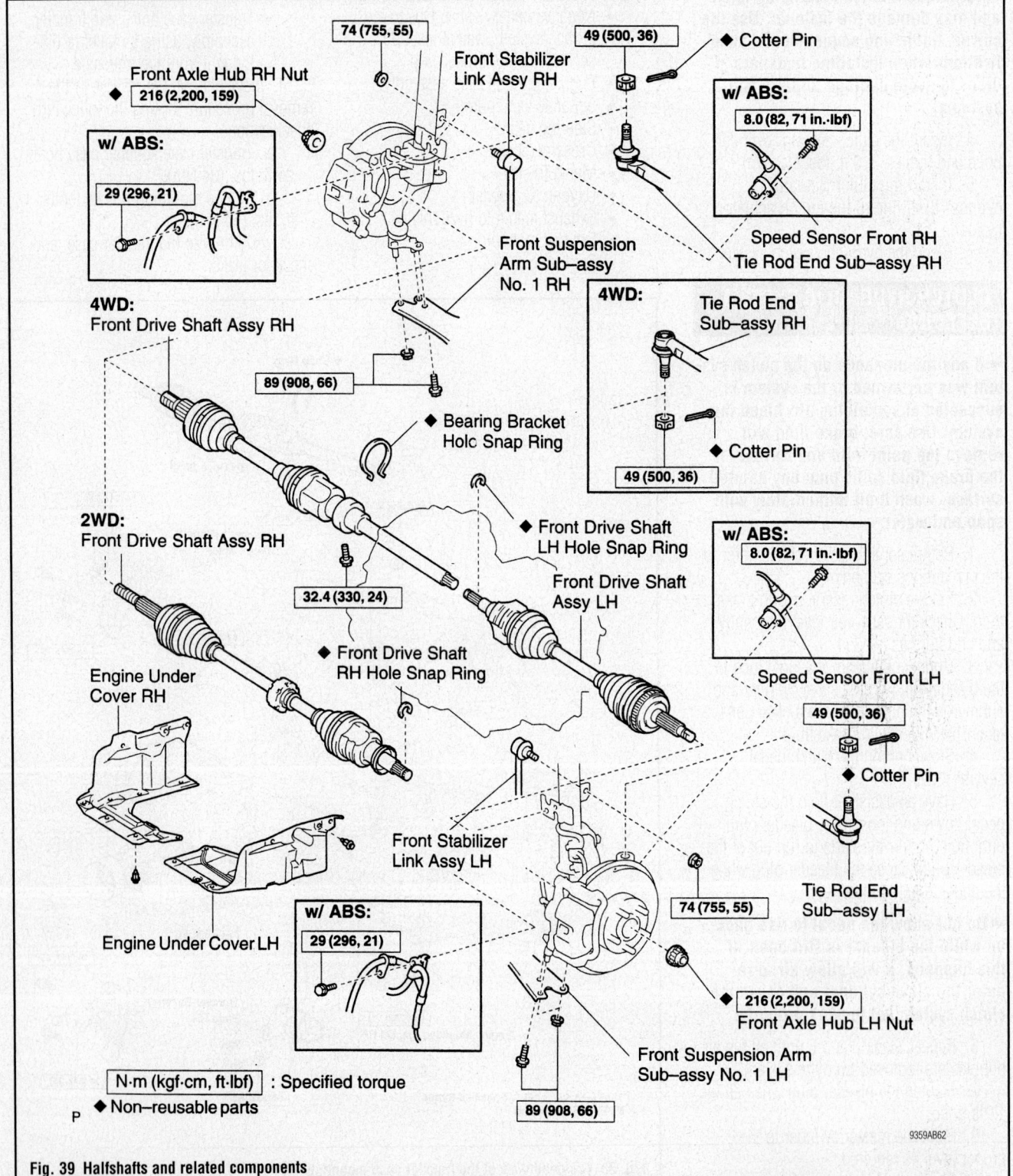

Fig. 39 Halfshafts and related components

- Cotter pin, locknut cap, and the hub nut
- Undercovers
- Speed sensors
- Tie rod ball joint from the steering knuckle
- Stabilizer bar link from the lower suspension arm
- Lower ball joint from the lower suspension arm
- Halfshaft from the knuckle

➡ **Be careful not to damage the inner oil seal or the ABS sensor rotor on the halfshaft.**

4. To remove the left side halfshaft, separate the halfshaft from the transaxle.

5. To remove the right side halfshaft perform the following steps:

- Remove the 2 bolts of the center bearing bracket
- Pull the halfshaft out together with the center bearing case and the center halfshaft.
- Remove the center shaft with the right-hand halfshaft from the transaxle through the bearing bracket.

➡ **Do not damage the oil seal lip.**

To install:

6. Install or connect the following:

- Snapring opening side facing downward, on the oiled inboard joint tulip
- Left side halfshaft into the transaxle
- Right side halfshaft, with the bearing case and center shaft, into the transaxle
- Center bearing case (right side).

7. After installing either halfshaft, check that there is 0.08–0.12 in. (2–3mm) of axial play. Check that the halfshaft is making contact with the pinion shaft and that the halfshaft cannot be pulled out.

8. Install or connect the following:

- Halfshaft into the knuckle
- Lower suspension arm to the lower ball joint. Torque the bolt and nuts to 66 ft. lbs. (89 Nm).
- Tie rod end to the steering knuckle. Tighten the nut to 36 ft. lbs. (49 Nm).
- Stabilizer bar link to the lower suspension arm. Torque the nuts to 55 ft. lbs. (74 Nm).
- Front wheels
- Hub nut and washer and tighten to 159 ft. lbs. (216 Nm)
- Negative battery cable
- Locknut cap and a new cotter pin.
- Speed sensors
- Undercover

9. Fill the transaxle fluid to the proper level

10. Start the vehicle, check for leaks and repair if necessary.

CV-JOINTS OVERHAUL

See Figures 40 and 41.

1. Before servicing the vehicle, refer to the precautions section.

2. Remove or disconnect the following:

- Inboard joint boot clips
- Inboard joint tulip from the driveshaft
- Snapring

- Using a brass rod and hammer, the tri-pot joint off the driveshaft without hitting the joint roller
- Inboard joint boot
- Clamp and driveshaft damper
- Clamps and the outboard drive boot. DO NOT disassemble the outboard joint.

To assemble:

3. Install or connect the following:

➡ **Before installing the boot, wrap the spline end of the shaft with masking tape to prevent damage to the boot.**

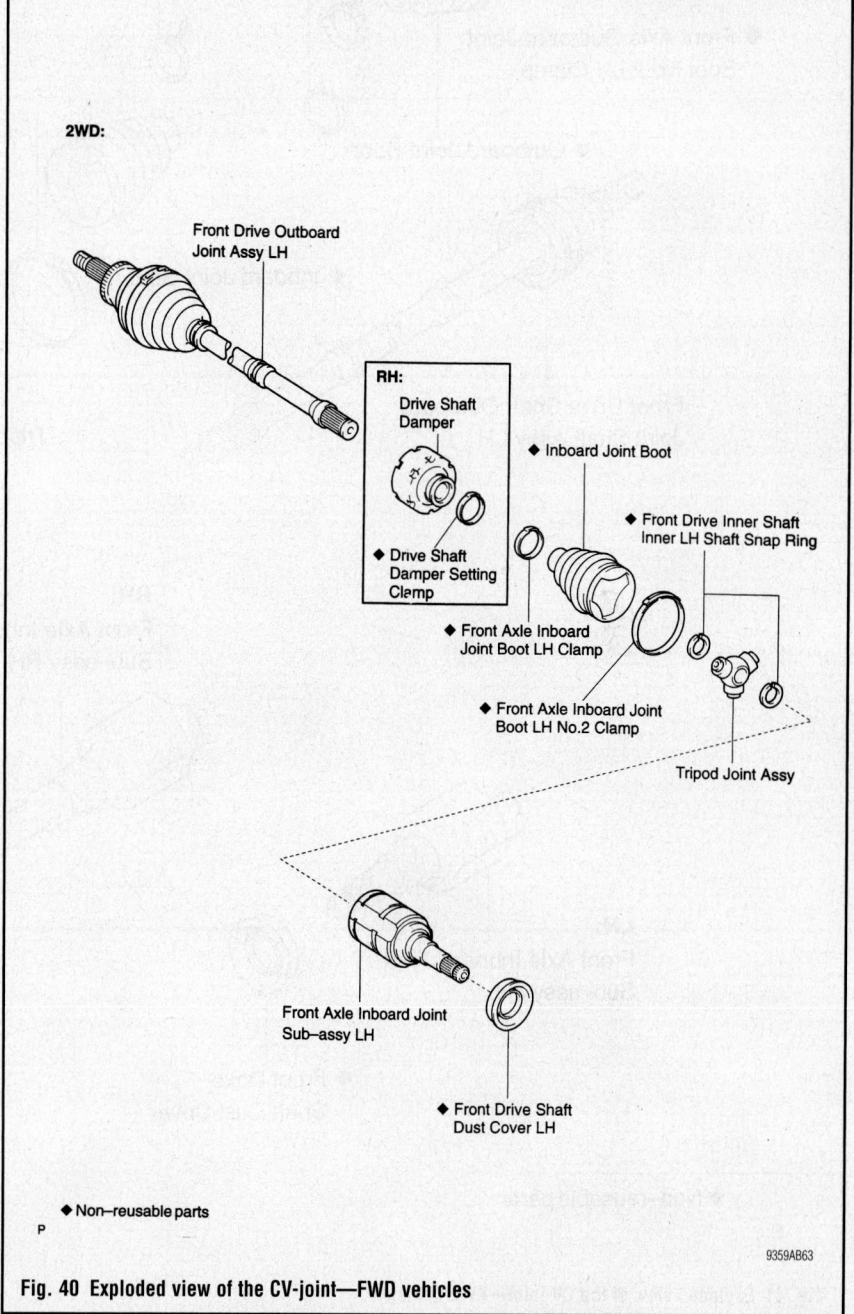

Fig. 40 Exploded view of the CV-joint—FWD vehicles

9359AB63

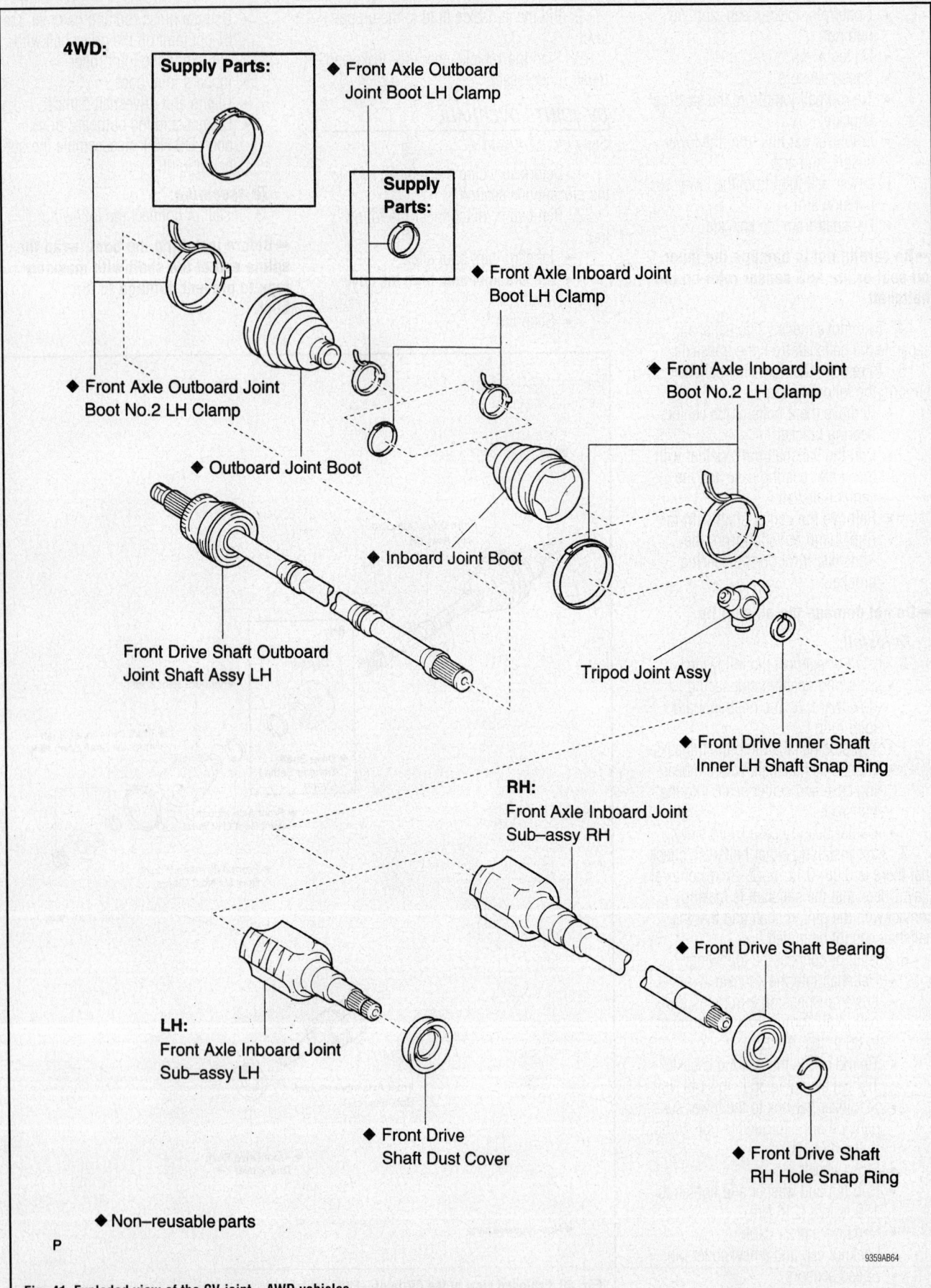

4WD:

Supply Parts:

◆ Front Axle Outboard Joint Boot LH Clamp

Supply Parts:

◆ Front Axle Inboard Joint Boot LH Clamp

◆ Front Axle Outboard Joint Boot No.2 LH Clamp

◆ Front Axle Inboard Joint Boot No.2 LH Clamp

◆ Outboard Joint Boot

◆ Inboard Joint Boot

Front Drive Shaft Outboard Joint Shaft Assy LH

Tripod Joint Assy

◆ Front Drive Inner Shaft Inner LH Shaft Snap Ring

RH:
Front Axle Inboard Joint Sub–assy RH

◆ Front Drive Shaft Bearing

LH:
Front Axle Inboard Joint Sub–assy LH

◆ Front Drive Shaft Dust Cover

◆ Front Drive Shaft RH Hole Snap Ring

◆ Non–reusable parts

P

9359AB64

Fig. 41 Exploded view of the CV-joint—AWD vehicles

- Driveshaft damper with a new clamp
- Temporarily, the inboard boot with new clamp to the drive joint

➡**The inboard boot and clamp are larger than those of the outboard boot.**

- The tri-pot onto the driveshaft with a brass rod and hammer without hitting the joint roller
- The snapring

4. Pack the outboard tulip joint and the outboard boot with about 0.26–0.33 lbs. ounces of grease that was supplied with the boot kit.
5. Install or connect the following:
- Boot onto the outboard joint

6. Pack the inboard tulip joint and boot with ½ lb. of grease that was supplied with the boot kit.
- Inboard tulip joint onto the driveshaft
- Boot onto the driveshaft

7. Before checking the standard length, bend the band and lock it. Make sure that the boot is not stretched or squashed when the driveshaft is at standard length. Standard driveshaft length:

LH: 540.2 mm (21.268 in.); RH: 857.4 mm (33.756 in.)

REAR AXLE SHAFT, BEARING & SEAL

REMOVAL & INSTALLATION

1. Raise and support the vehicle.
2. Remove the 4 bolts and the 2 clips that attach the brake pipes, brake hoses, parking brake cables and wheel speed sensor wires to the rear axle.
3. Remove the 2 backing plates.
4. Remove the stabilizer shaft.
5. Support the rear axle with a block of wood and a jack.
6. Remove the shock absorbers to rear axle bolts, nuts and retainers.
7. Remove the 2 bolts and the 2 nuts and the rear axle.
8. If necessary, use a press in order to remove the rear axle bushings.

To install:

9. If you removed the bushings, use a press in order to install the bushings.
10. Use a jack and a block of wood in order to raise and support the rear axle.

➡**Do not tighten the nuts or the bolts. The weight of the vehicle must be on the tire and wheel assemblies before tightening the nuts and the bolts.**

11. Install the 2 bolts and nuts that attach he rear axle to the body.
12. Install the shock absorbers to the rear axle retainers.
13. Install the stabilizer shaft.
14. Install the 2 backing plates.
15. Install the bolts and clips that attach the brakes hoses, clips and other components to the rear axle.
16. Remove the jack and lower the vehicle.
17. Bleed the brake system.
18. Bounce the rear of the vehicle in order to stabilize the suspension.

➡**The weight of the vehicle must be on the tire and wheel assemblies.**

19. Tighten the 2 nuts and the 2 bolts that retain the axle to the body to 62 ft. lbs. (85 Nm).
20. Tighten the 2 nuts and the 2 bolts that retain the shock absorbers to the axle to 59 ft. lbs. (80 Nm).
21. Measure and adjust the rear wheel alignment if needed.

ENGINE COOLING

ENGINE FAN

REMOVAL & INSTALLATION
See Figure 42.

1. Disconnect the reservoir hose from the radiator.
2. Disconnect the fan motor electrical connector.
3. On vehicles equipped with an air pump:
a. Disconnect the 2 hoses from the air pump outlet pipe.
b. Remove the 2 bolts from the air pump outlet pipe.
4. Disconnect the 2 fan motor electrical harness clamps from the fan shroud.
5. Remove the 2 fan shroud bolts.
6. Remove the fan shroud and motor assembly.
7. Remove the fan retaining nut.
8. Remove the 2 radiator fan mount bolts.
9. Remove the radiator fan motor.

To install:
10. Position the radiator fan and the radiator fan motor to the shroud.
11. Install one radiator fan nut. Tighten the radiator fan nut to 55 inch lbs. (6.2 Nm).

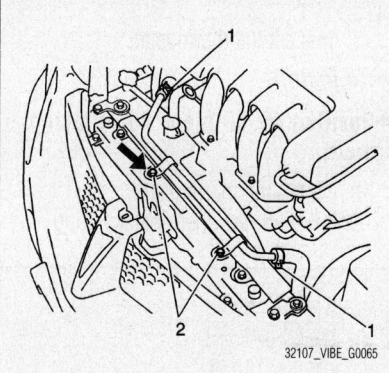
Fig. 42 Air pump outlet pipe hoses (1) and bolts (2).

32107_VIBE_G0065

12. Install the 2 radiator fan mount bolts. Tighten the radiator fan bolts to 34 inch lbs. (3.8 Nm).
13. Position the radiator fan and shroud assembly into the vehicle; then install the 2 fan shroud bolts. Tighten the radiator fan shroud bolts to 53 inch lbs (6 Nm).
14. Connect the 2 fan motor electrical harness clamps to the fan shroud.
15. Connect the fan motor electrical connector.

16. If equipped with an air pump:
a. Install the 2 bolts to the air pump outlet pipe (2). Tighten the air pump outlet pipe bolts to 62 inch lbs (7 Nm).
b. Connect the 2 hoses to the air pump outlet pipe (1).
17. Connect the reservoir hose to the radiator.

RADIATOR

REMOVAL & INSTALLATION
See Figures 42 and 43.

1. Disconnect the negative battery cable.
2. Drain the cooling system.
3. Remove the radiator inlet hose.
4. Remove the radiator outlet hose.
5. Disconnect transmission oil cooler lines.
6. If equipped with an air pump:
a. Disconnect the 2 hoses from the air pump outlet pipe.
b. Remove the 2 bolts from the air pump outlet pipe.
7. Disconnect the fan motor electrical connector.
8. Disconnect two fan motor electrical harness clamps from the fan shroud.

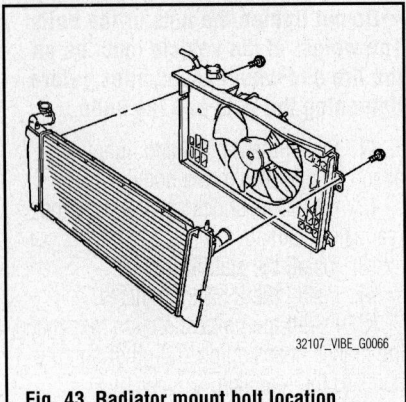

Fig. 43 Radiator mount bolt location

9. Remove two radiator mount bolts.

10. Remove the radiator fan with the motor

11. Transfer all necessary components onto the replacement radiator.

To install:

➡ Use the correct fastener in the correct location. Replacement fasteners must be the correct part number for that application. Fasteners requiring replacement or fasteners requiring the use of thread locking compound or sealant are identified in the service procedure. Do not use paints, lubricants, or corrosion inhibitors on fasteners or fastener joint surfaces unless specified. These coatings affect fastener torque and joint clamping force and may damage the fastener. Use the correct tightening sequence and specifications when installing fasteners in order to avoid damage to parts and systems.

12. Position the radiator and fan shroud assembly. Tighten the radiator bolts to 14 ft. lbs. (19 Nm).

13. Connect the 2 fan motor electrical harness clamps to the fan shroud.

14. Connect the fan motor electrical connector.

15. If equipped with an air pump:
   a. Install the 2 bolts from the air pump outlet pipe. Tighten the air pump outlet pipe bolts to 62 inch lbs. (7 Nm).
   b. Connect the 2 hoses from the air pump outlet pipe.

16. Connect the transmission oil cooler lines.

17. Install the radiator outlet hose.

18. Install the radiator inlet hose.

19. Refill the cooling system.

20. Connect the negative battery cable.

✳✳ WARNING

Watch for a potential overheating condition while the engine is operating with the radiator cap off.

21. Start and run the engine until the coolant is at operating temperature.

22. Inspect the transmission fluid level, on vehicles with automatic transmission.

23. Tighten any loose connections as necessary.

THERMOSTAT

REMOVAL & INSTALLATION

See Figures 44 and 45.

1. Drain the cooling system.
2. Remove the generator.
3. Remove the following components from the cylinder block:
   a. The 2 nuts securing the thermostat cup
   b. The thermostat housing
4. Remove the following components from the thermostat housing:
   a. The thermostat
   b. The O-ring
5. Clean the following materials from the thermostat cap:
   a. Corrosion
   b. Debris
6. Clean the cylinder block mating surfaces.
7. Inspect the thermostat.

To install:

➡ Position the air bleed valve facing upward.

8. Install the thermostat.
9. Install a new thermostat O-ring.

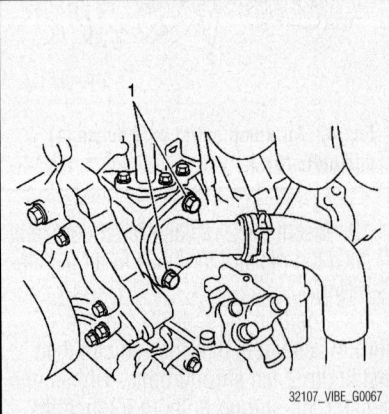

Fig. 44 Remove the 2 nuts (1) from the cylinder block.

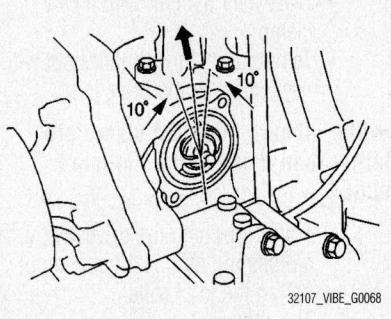

Fig. 45 Position the air bleed valve facing upward.

10. Install the thermostat housing to the cylinder block.

✳✳ WARNING

Use the correct fastener in the correct location. Replacement fasteners must be the correct part number for that application. Fasteners requiring replacement or fasteners requiring the use of thread locking compound or sealant are identified in the service procedure. Do not use paints, lubricants, or corrosion inhibitors on fasteners or fastener joint surfaces unless specified. These coatings affect fastener torque and joint clamping force and may damage the fastener. Use the correct tightening sequence and specifications when installing fasteners in order to avoid damage to parts and systems.

11. Use the 2 nuts (1) in order to secure the thermostat cap.
   - On low output engine, tighten the thermostat cap nuts to 8 ft. lbs. (11 Nm).
   - On high output engine, tighten the thermostat cap nuts to 7 ft. lbs. (10 Nm).

12. Install the generator.

13. Fill the radiator using approved coolant.

14. Start the engine.

15. Run the engine until the coolant is at operating temperature. The coolant is at operating temperature when the following conditions exist:
   - The hoses feel warm.
   - The coolant is flowing through the radiator.

16. Inspect for leaks in the cooling system.

17. Turn off the engine.

18. Install the radiator cap.

WATER PUMP

REMOVAL & INSTALLATION

1ZZ-FE Engine

See Figure 46.

1. Before servicing the vehicle, refer to the precautions section.
2. Drain the cooling system.
3. Remove or disconnect the following:

- Negative battery cable
- Right-hand engine under cover
- Drive belt
- Alternator
- Water pump

To install:

4. Install or connect the following:
- Water pump. Torque bolts marked **A** (short) to 80 inch lbs. (9 Nm) and bolts marked **B** (long) to 96 inch lbs. (11 Nm).

- Alternator
- Drive belt
- Right engine under cover
- Negative battery cable

5. Fill the cooling system to the proper level.

6. Start the vehicle, check for leaks and repair if necessary.

2ZZ-GE Engine

See Figures 47 and 48.

1. Before servicing the vehicle, refer to the precautions section.
2. Drain the cooling system.
3. Remove or disconnect the following:
- Negative battery cable
- Right-hand engine under cover
- Drive belt
- Alternator
- Water pump pulley, using SST 09960-10010
- Water pump and O-ring

To install:

4. Install or connect the following:
- Water pump with new O-ring. Torque the bolts to 80 inch lbs. (9 Nm).
- Water pump pulley, using SST 09960-10010. Torque the bolts to 11 ft. lbs. (15 Nm).
- Alternator
- Drive belt
- Right engine under cover
- Negative battery cable

5. Fill the cooling system to the proper level.

6. Start the vehicle, check for leaks and repair if necessary.

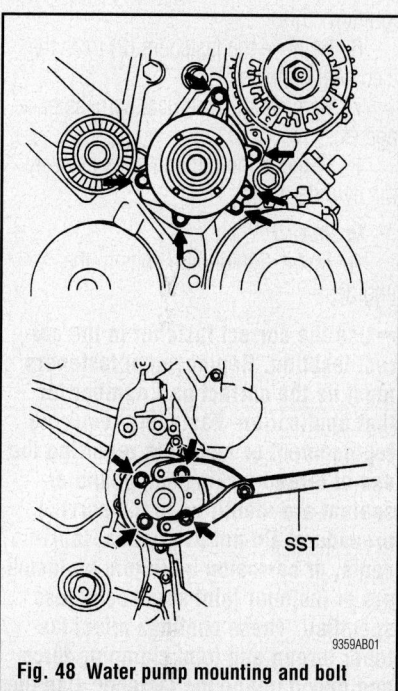

Fig. 48 Water pump mounting and bolt locations—2ZZ-GE engine

Fig. 46 Water pump bolt identification— 1.8L (1ZZ-FE) engine

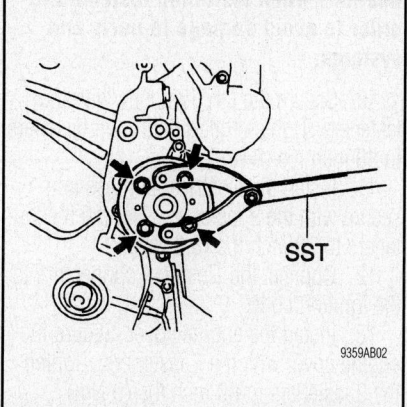

Fig. 47 View of the special tool needed to remove and install the water pump pulley

ENGINE ELECTRICAL

ALTERNATOR

REMOVAL & INSTALLATION

1. Before servicing the vehicle, refer to the precautions section.
2. Remove or disconnect the following:
- Negative battery cable
- Drive belt

- Wire clamp from the clip on the end frame
- Rubber clamp and nut
- Alternator wiring and connector
- Alternator

To install:

3. Install or connect the following:
- Alternator. Torque the 12mm bolt

CHARGING SYSTEM

to 18 ft. lbs. (25 Nm) and the 14mm bolt to 39 ft. lbs. (54 Nm).
- Alternator connector and wiring
- Rubber clamp and nut
- Wire clamp
- Drive belt
- Negative battery cable

IGNITION COIL

REMOVAL & INSTALLATION

1ZZ-FE Engine

See Figures 49 and 50.

1. Remove the 2 fasteners.
2. Remove the 2 plastic retainers.
3. Remove the engine cover from the engine.
4. Disconnect the 4 electrical connectors from the ignition coils (3).
5. Remove the fasteners (4) from the ignition coils.
6. Remove the fasteners (2) from the electrical harness (1).
7. Remove the electrical harness package (1).
8. Remove the ignition coils (3) from the cylinder head.

To install:

9. Install the ignition coils to the engine.

➥Use the correct fastener in the correct location. Replacement fasteners must be the correct part number for that application. Fasteners requiring replacement or fasteners requiring the use of thread locking compound or sealant are identified in the service procedure. Do not use paints, lubricants, or corrosion inhibitors on fasteners or fastener joint surfaces unless specified. These coatings affect fastener torque and joint clamping force and may damage the fastener. Use the correct tightening sequence and speci-

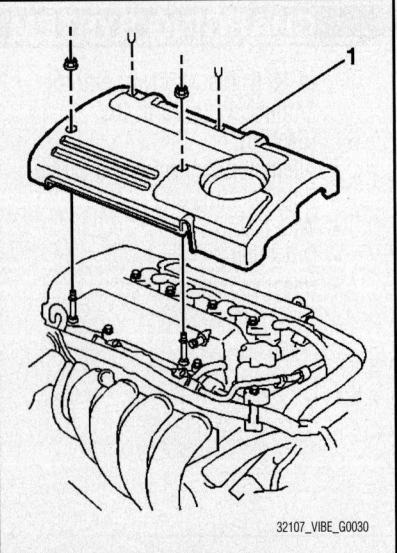

Fig. 49 Remove engine cover from engine

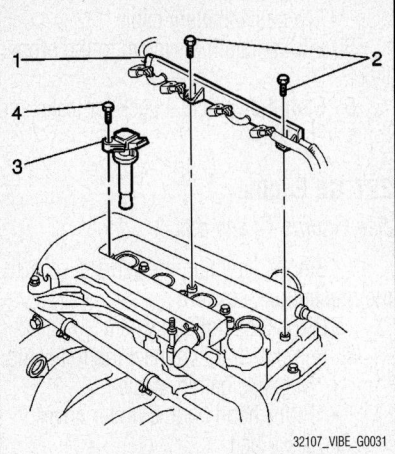

Fig. 50 (1) Electrical harness, (2) Electrical harness fasteners, (3) Ignition coils, (4) Ignition coil fasteners

fications when installing fasteners in order to avoid damage to parts and systems.

10. Secure the ignition coils with the fasteners. Tighten the ignition coil fasteners to 80 inch lbs (9 Nm).
11. Install the electrical harness and secure with the 2 fasteners. Tighten the fasteners to 78 inch lbs (8.8 Nm).
12. Connect the electrical connectors to the ignition coils.
13. Install the engine cover. Secure the engine cover with the 2 fasteners. Tighten the 2 fasteners to 80 inch lbs (9 Nm).
14. Install the 2 plastic retainers.

2ZZ-GE Engine

See Figures 50 and 51.

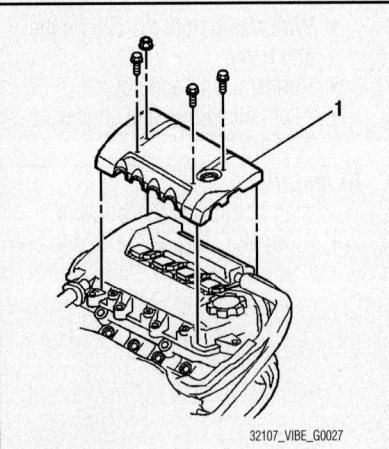

Fig. 51 Remove the four fasteners from the engine cover (1).

1. Remove the four fasteners from the engine cover.
2. Remove the engine cover from the engine.
3. Disconnect the 4 electrical connectors from the ignition coils.
4. Remove the fasteners from the ignition coils.
5. Remove the fasteners from the electrical harness.
6. Remove the electrical harness package.
7. Remove the ignition coils from the cylinder head.

To install:

8. Install the ignition coils to the engine.

➥Use the correct fastener in the correct location. Replacement fasteners must be the correct part number for that application. Fasteners requiring replacement or fasteners requiring the use of thread locking compound or sealant are identified in the service procedure. Do not use paints, lubricants, or corrosion inhibitors on fasteners or fastener joint surfaces unless specified. These coatings affect fastener torque and joint clamping force and may damage the fastener. Use the correct tightening sequence and specifications when installing fasteners in order to avoid damage to parts and systems.

9. Secure the ignition coils with the fasteners. Tighten the ignition coil fasteners to 80 inch lbs (9 Nm).
10. Install the electrical harness and secure with the 2 fasteners. Tighten the fasteners to 78 inch lbs (8.8 Nm).
11. Connect the electrical connectors to the ignition coils.
12. Install the engine cover to the engine.
13. Secure the engine cover with the four fasteners. Tighten the fasteners to 62 inch lbs (7 Nm).

IGNITION TIMING

ADJUSTMENT

The ignition timing is controlled by the Powertrain Control Module (PCM). No adjustment is necessary or possible.

SPARK PLUGS

REMOVAL & INSTALLATION

2ZZ-GE Engine

See Figures 50 through 53.

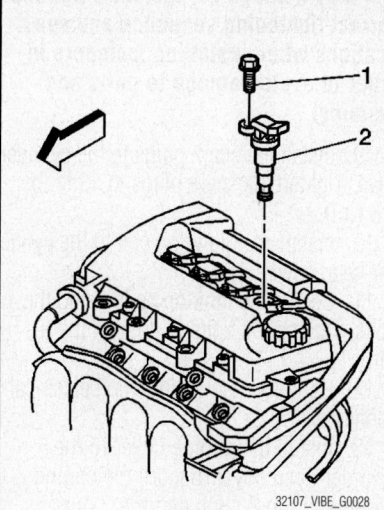

32107_VIBE_G0028

Fig. 52 Remove the bolt (1) securing each ignition coil from the cylinder head cover. Then remove each ignition coil (2) from the cylinder head cover.

1. Remove the four fasteners from the engine cover.

2. Remove the engine cover from the engine.

3. Disconnect the electrical connector from each ignition coil.

4. Remove the bolt securing each ignition coil from the cylinder head cover.

5. Remove each ignition coil from the cylinder head cover.

➡ This engine is equipped with an aluminum cylinder head. Allow the engine to cool before removing spark plugs. Removing the spark plugs from an engine at operating temperature may damage the spark plug threads in the cylinder head. Also be sure to clean any dirt or debris from around spark plug holes prior to removing spark plugs.

6. Remove the spark plugs from the cylinder head.

7. Inspect the spark plugs for electrode wear, carbon deposits and insulator damage.

To install:

Important: Use one of the following types of iridium tipped spark plugs.

• Denso Type SK20R11

• NGK Type IFR6A11

8. Replace the spark plugs every 90,000 mi (144,000 km).

Important:

• Do not touch the tip of the spark plug.

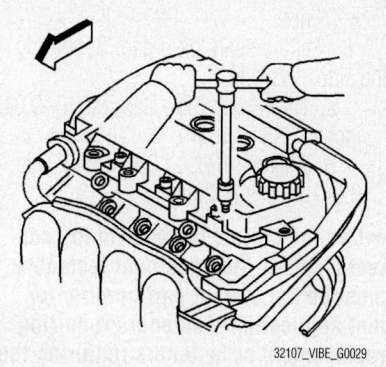

32107_VIBE_G0029

Fig. 53 Remove the spark plugs from the cylinder head.

• Do not damage the iridium surface of the electrode when gapping the plug.

• Do not adjust the gap on used spark plugs. Replace the spark plug if the gap is greater than specification.

9. Set the spark plug gap to 0.051 in.

➡ Use the correct fastener in the correct location. Replacement fasteners must be the correct part number for that application. Fasteners requiring replacement or fasteners requiring the use of thread locking compound or sealant are identified in the service procedure. Do not use paints, lubricants, or corrosion inhibitors on fasteners or fastener joint surfaces unless specified. These coatings affect fastener torque and joint clamping force and may damage the fastener. Use the correct tightening sequence and specifications when installing fasteners in order to avoid damage to parts and systems.

10. Install the spark plugs to the cylinder head. Tighten the spark plugs to 13 ft. lbs. (18 Nm).

11. Install the spark plugs to the cylinder head. Tighten the spark plugs to 13 ft. lbs. (18 Nm).

12. Install each ignition coil to the cylinder head cover.

13. Secure the ignition coils using the bolts. Tighten the bolts to 80 inch lbs (9 Nm).

14. Connect each ignition coil electrical connector.

15. Install the engine cover on the engine.

16. Secure the engine cover with the four fasteners. Tighten the fasteners to 62 inch lbs (7 Nm).

1ZZ-FE Engine

See Figures 50, 54 and 55.

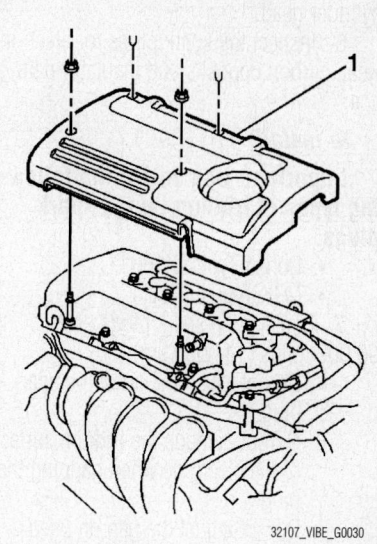

32107_VIBE_G0030

Fig. 54 Remove the 2 clips and the 2 nuts that secure the engine cover (1) to the cylinder head cover

1. Remove the 2 clips and the 2 nuts that secure the engine cover to the cylinder head cover.

2. Remove the engine cover from the cylinder head cover.

3. Disconnect the electrical connector from each ignition coil.

4. Remove the bolt securing each ignition coil from the cylinder head cover and remove each ignition coil from the cylinder head cover.

➡ This engine is equipped with an aluminum cylinder head. Allow the engine to cool before removing spark plugs. Removing the spark plugs from an engine at operating temperature may damage the spark plug threads in the cylinder head. Also be sure to clean any dirt or debris from around spark plug holes prior to removing spark plugs.

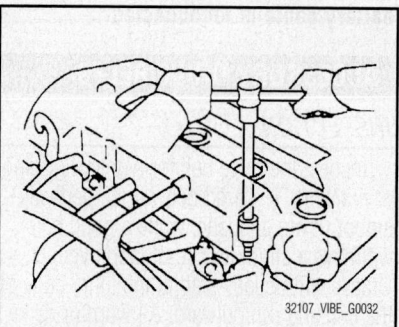

32107_VIBE_G0032

Fig. 55 Remove the spark plugs from the cylinder head

5. Remove the spark plugs from the cylinder head.

6. Inspect the spark plugs for electrode wear, carbon deposits and insulator damage.

To install:

Important: Use one of the following types of iridium tipped spark plugs.

- Denso Type SK16R11
- NGK Type IFR5A11

7. Replace the spark plugs every 90,000 miles (144,000 km).

- Do not touch the tip of the spark plug.
- Do not damage the iridium surface of the electrode when gapping the plug.
- Do not adjust the gap on used spark plugs. Replace the spark plug

if the gap is greater than specification.

8. Set the spark plug gap. Bend only the side electrode.

a. New Spark Plug Gap: 0.040–0.043 inches (1.0–1.1mm)

b. Maximum Used Spark Plug Gap: 0.047 inches (1.2mm)

➡**Use the correct fastener in the correct location. Replacement fasteners must be the correct part number for that application. Fasteners requiring replacement or fasteners requiring the use of thread locking compound or sealant are identified in the service procedure. Do not use paints, lubricants, or corrosion inhibitors on fasteners or fastener joint surfaces unless specified. These coatings affect fastener torque and joint clamping force**

and may damage the fastener. Use the correct tightening sequence and specifications when installing fasteners in order to avoid damage to parts and systems.

9. Install the spark plugs to the cylinder head. Tighten the spark plugs to 13 ft. lbs. (18 Nm).

10. Install each ignition coil to the cylinder head cover.

11. Secure the ignition coils using the bolts. Tighten the bolts to 80 inch lbs (9 Nm).

12. Connect each ignition coil electrical connector.

13. Install the engine cover to the cylinder head cover. Secure the engine cover with the 2 clips and the 2 nuts. Tighten the nuts to 80 inch lbs (9 Nm).

ENGINE ELECTRICAL   STARTING SYSTEM

STARTER

REMOVAL & INSTALLATION

See Figure 56.

1. Before servicing the vehicle, refer to the precautions section.

2. Remove or disconnect the following:

- Negative battery cable
- Right side engine undercover
- Starter wiring
- Starter

3. Installation is the reverse of removal. Torque the bolts to 27 ft. lbs. (37 Nm) and the nut to 7 ft. lbs. (10 Nm).

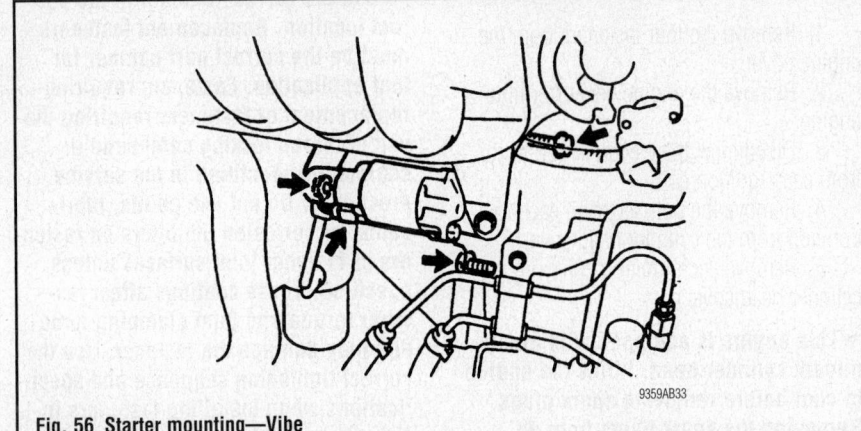

Fig. 56 Starter mounting—Vibe

ENGINE MECHANICAL

➡**Disconnecting the negative battery cable may interfere with the functions of the on board computer systems and may require the computer to undergo a relearning process, once the negative battery cable is reconnected.**

ACCESSORY DRIVE BELTS

INSPECTION

Inspect the drive belt for signs of glazing or cracking. A glazed belt will be perfectly smooth from slippage, while a good belt will have a slight texture of fabric visible. Cracks will usually start at the inner edge of the belt and run outward. All worn or damaged drive belts should be replaced immediately.

ADJUSTMENT

The belt tension is maintained by an automatic tensioner. No adjustment is necessary or possible.

REMOVAL & INSTALLATION

1ZZ-FE Engine

See Figure 57.

1. Disconnect the negative battery cable.

2. Use a wrench and rotate the belt tensioner clockwise.

3. With pressure applied to the wrench, and tension relieved from the drive belt, remove the accessory drive belt.

To install:

4. Raise and safely support the vehicle.

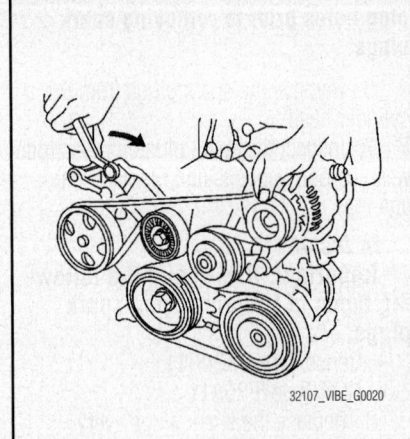

Fig. 57 Use a wrench and rotate the belt tensioner clockwise.

5. Remove the right side lower engine splash shield.

6. Properly route and install the accessory drive belt onto the drive pulleys.

7. Use a wrench and rotate the belt tensioner clockwise.

8. With pressure applied to the wrench, install the accessory drive belt.

9. With the accessory drive belt installed properly, release the belt tensioner.

10. Install the right side lower engine splash shield.

11. Connect the negative battery cable. Tighten the battery cable bolt to 11 ft. lbs. (15 Nm).

2ZZ-GE Engine

See Figures 58 through 60.

1. Disconnect the negative battery cable.

2. Remove the bolt, then reposition the wiring harness clamp bracket.

3. Remove the 2 nuts, then reposition the A/C hose aside.

4. Use a wrench and rotate the belt tensioner clockwise.

5. With pressure applied to the wrench, and tension relieved from the drive belt, remove the accessory drive belt.

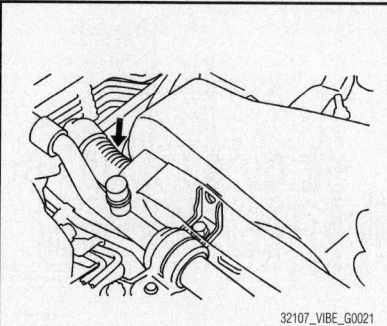

Fig. 58 Remove the bolt, then reposition the wiring harness clamp bracket

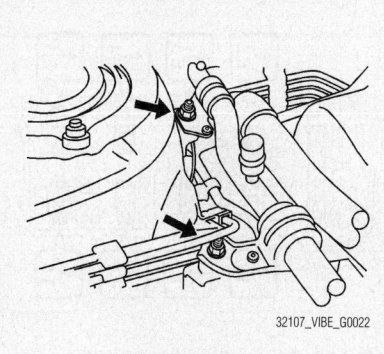

Fig. 59 A/C hose indicated by arrow

Fig. 60 Use a wrench and rotate the belt tensioner clockwise.

To install:

6. Raise and safely support the vehicle.

7. Remove the right side lower engine splash shield.

8. Properly route and install the accessory drive belt onto the drive pulleys.

9. Use a wrench and rotate the belt tensioner clockwise.

10. With pressure applied to the wrench, install the accessory drive belt.

11. With the accessory drive belt installed properly, release the belt tensioner.

12. Install the right side lower engine splash shield.

13. Position the A/C hose and install the 2 retaining nuts. Tighten the A/C hose nuts to 7 ft. lbs. (10 Nm).

14. Position the wiring harness clamp bracket and install the bolt. Tighten the wire harness clamp bracket bolt to 7 ft. lbs. (10 Nm).

15. Connect the negative battery cable. Tighten the battery cable bolt to 11 ft. lbs. (15 Nm).

CAMSHAFT AND VALVE LIFTERS

INSPECTION

See Figures 61 and 62.

1. Inspect the camshaft journals and lobes for wear or scoring (1, 2).

2. Wash the cylinder head in solvent.

3. Inspect the cylinder head for cracks or other signs of damage.

4. Inspect the camshaft bearing caps for wear, cracks and scoring.

5. Inspect the camshaft bearing journals in the cylinder head for wear, cracks and scoring.

6. If excessive wear or scoring is present, or if the cylinder head is cracked, replace the cylinder head with bearing caps.

7. Measure the camshaft lobe height using a micrometer. The minimum measure-

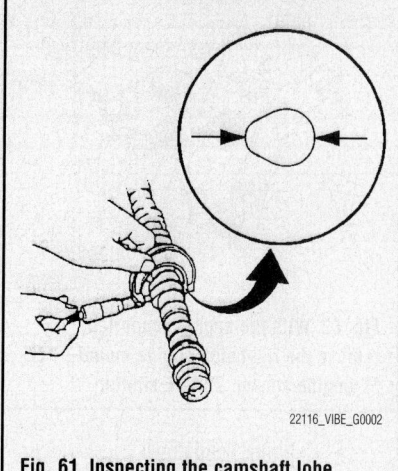

Fig. 61 Inspecting the camshaft lobe height using a micrometer

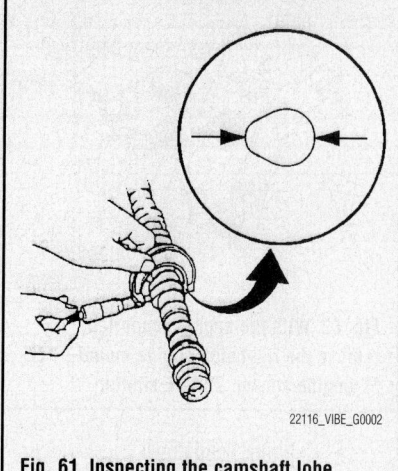

Fig. 62 Inspecting the camshaft lobe runout using a dial indicator

ment for the exhaust lobe height is 1.5693 inch on the No: 1 lobe and 1.5240 inch on the No: 2 lobe. The minimum measurement for the intake lobe height is 1.5925 inch on the No: 1 lobe and 1.5201 inch on the No: 2 lobe.

8. Replace the camshaft if any lobe is below the minimum.

9. Place the camshaft (1) onto V-blocks. Measure the camshaft runout using a dial indicator. The maximum runout is 0.0012 inch. If the runout exceeds specifications, replace the camshaft.

REMOVAL & INSTALLATION

See Figures 63 through 80.

1. Before servicing the vehicle, refer to the precautions section.

2. Remove or disconnect the following:
- Negative battery cable
- Right side engine under cover

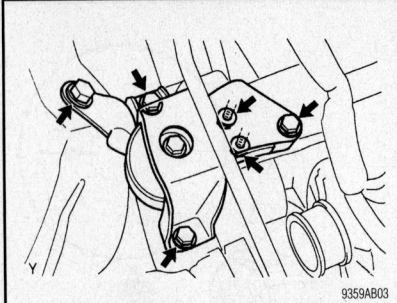

Fig. 63 With the engine supported, remove the right side engine mount—1ZZ-FE engine shown, 2ZZ-GE similar

- Cylinder head cover
- Suction hose sub-assembly, 2ZZ-GE engine
- Drive belt
- Power steering pump reservoir and position it aside, 1ZZ-FE engine

3. Place a jack with a wooden block under the vehicle for support, then remove the 4 bolts and 2 nuts and remove the right side engine mount.

4. Remove the engine wire, on 1ZZ-FE engines:

   a. Remove the 5 clamps from the brackets.

   b. Detach the connectors.

   c. Remove the ignition coil connectors.

   d. Bolt and nut holding the engine wire.

5. Remove or disconnect the following:
- Ignition coil assembly

- Positive Crankcase Ventilation (PCV) hoses from the valve cover
- Valve (cylinder head) cover sub-assembly

6. Set the No. 1 cylinder to Top Dead Center (TDC) of the compressor stroke as follows:

   a. Turn the crankshaft pulley, and align its groove with the "0" timing mark of the timing chain cover.

   b. Make sure the point marks of the camshaft timing sprockets and VVT timing sprockets are in a straight line as shown. If not, turn the crankshaft 1 complete revolution (360°) and align the marks.

7. Remove the drive belt tensioner.

✳✳ WARNING

Do not turn the crankshaft without the tensioner installed.

8. Make sure the No. 1 cylinder is at TDC of the compression stroke.

9. Matchmark the timing chain and camshaft sprockets

10. Remove the 2 nuts and chain tensioner.

11. Hold the camshafts with a wrench and loosen the camshaft set bolt.

12. Using several passes, gradually remove the bearing cap bolts from the No. 2 camshaft, in the proper sequence.

13. Remove the camshaft and timing gear as shown.

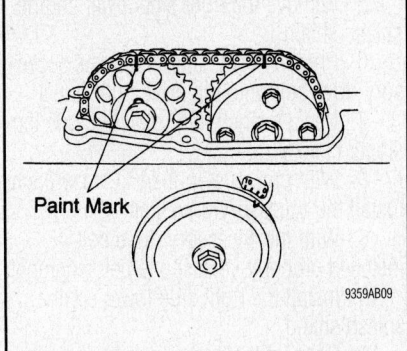

Fig. 65 Matchmark the timing chain and cam sprockets

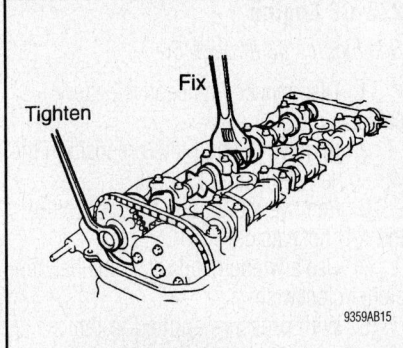

Fig. 66 Hold the camshaft with a wrench while removing the set bolt

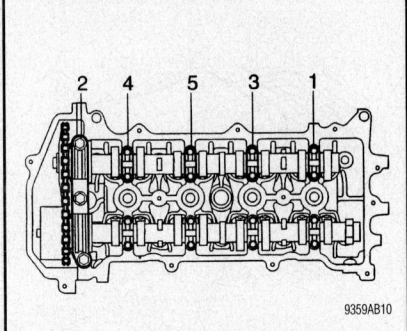

Fig. 67 Camshaft bearing cap bolt removal sequence—1ZZ-FE engine

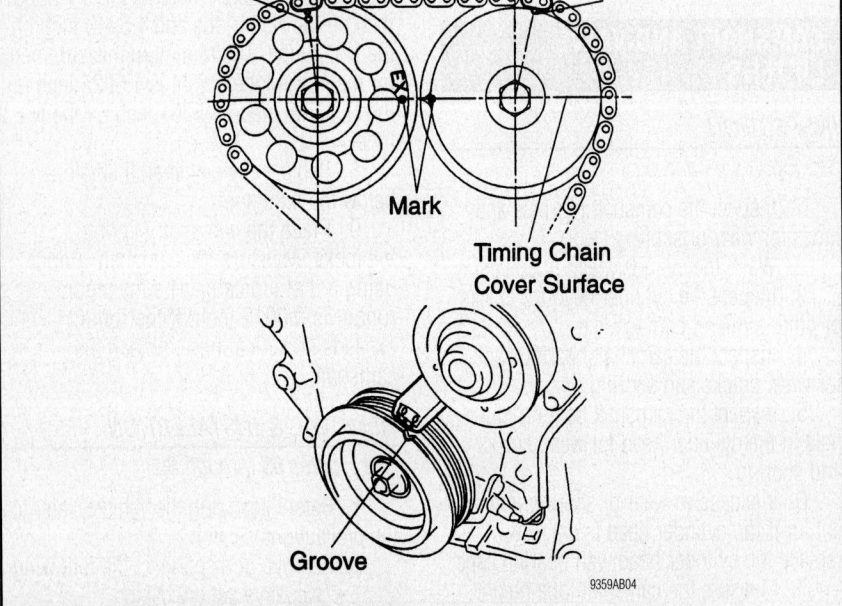

Fig. 64 Proper timing mark alignment for TDC

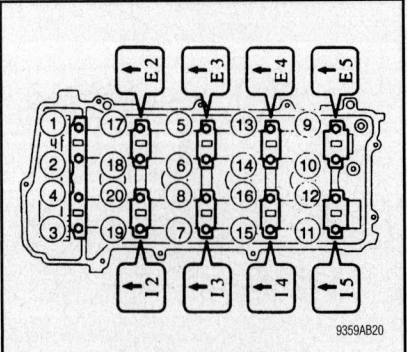

Fig. 68 Camshaft bearing cap bolt removal sequence—2ZZ-GE engine

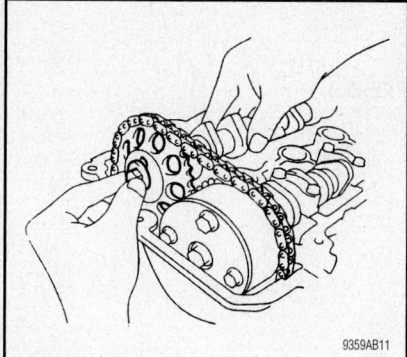

Fig. 69 Carefully remove the cam and timing gear

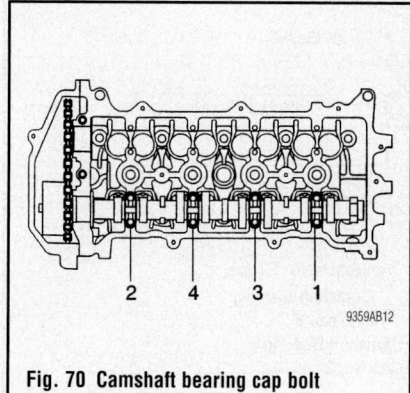

Fig. 70 Camshaft bearing cap bolt removal sequence—1ZZ-FE engine

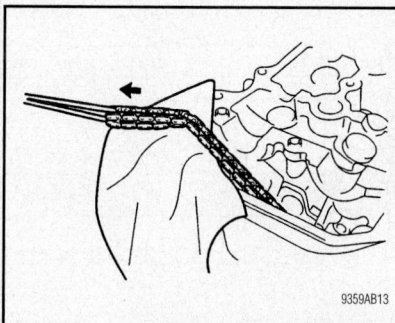

Fig. 71 Secure the timing chain with string to prevent it from slipping down into the timing chain cover

14. Using several passes, gradually remove the bearing cap bolts from the other camshaft, in the proper sequence.

15. Remove the camshaft while holding the timing chain.

✳✳ WARNING

Do not let anything drop down into the timing chain cover while the camshafts are removed.

16. Tie the timing chain with a string as shown, to prevent it from dropping down into the timing chain cover.

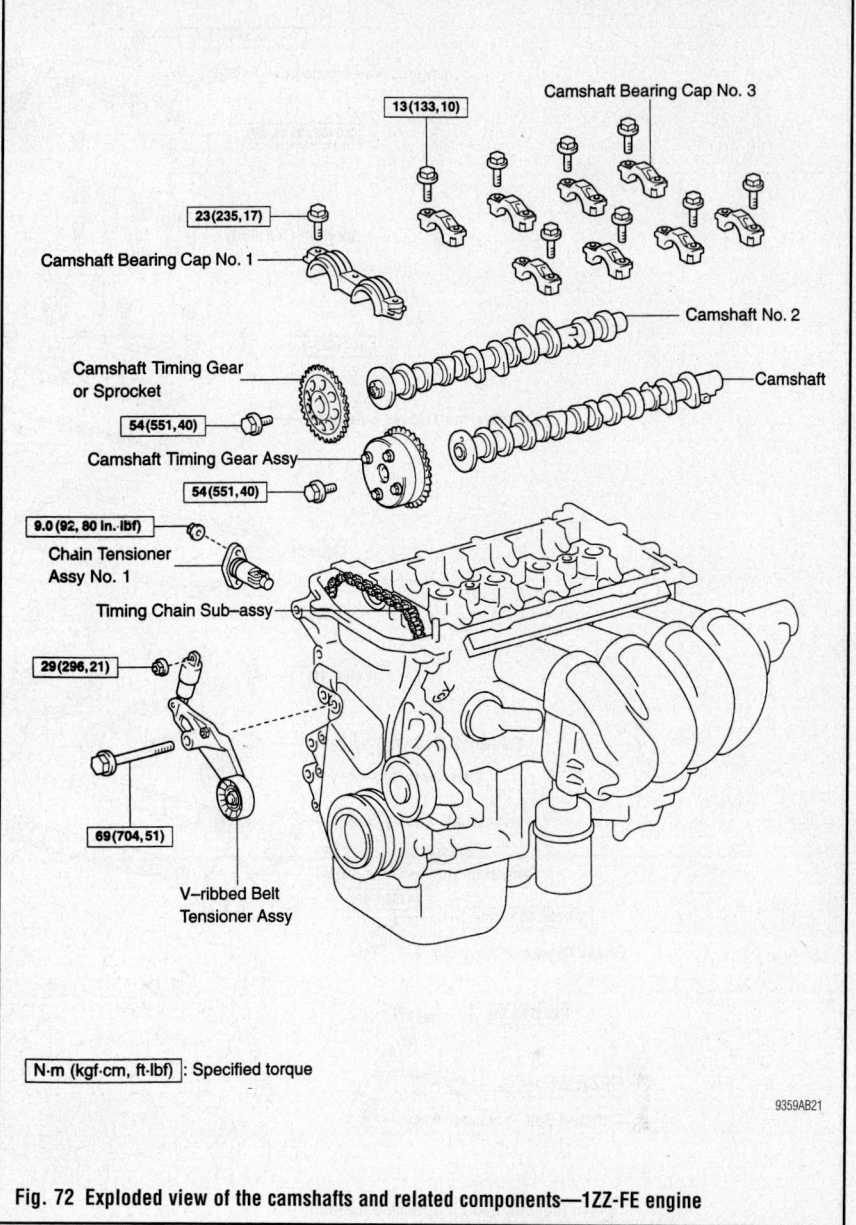

Fig. 72 Exploded view of the camshafts and related components—1ZZ-FE engine

Camshaft Bearing Cap No. 3
13(133, 10)
23(235, 17)
Camshaft Bearing Cap No. 1
Camshaft No. 2
Camshaft Timing Gear or Sprocket
54(551, 40)
Camshaft
Camshaft Timing Gear Assy
54(551, 40)
9.0 (92, 80 in.·lbf)
Chain Tensioner Assy No. 1
Timing Chain Sub–assy
29(296, 21)
V–ribbed Belt Tensioner Assy
69(704, 51)

N·m (kgf·cm, ft·lbf) : Specified torque

To install:

17. Position the camshaft on the cylinder head, then install the timing chain on the cam timing gear, with the painted links aligned with the marks on the timing gear.

18. Check the front marks and numbers and torque the camshaft cap bolts, in sequence, to 10 ft. lbs. (13 Nm) for 1ZZ-FE engine, or to 14 ft. lbs. (19 Nm) for 2ZZ-GE engines.

19. Put camshaft No. 2 on the cylinder head, with the painted links of the chain aligned with the mark on the timing gear.

20. Tighten the camshaft gear set bolt temporarily.

21. Check the front marks and numbers and torque the camshaft cap bolts, in sequence, to 10 ft. lbs. (13 Nm). Install the

No. 1 bearing cap and tighten to 17 ft. lbs. (23 Nm).

22. Hold the camshaft secure with a wrench and tighten the set bolt to 40 ft. lbs. (54 Nm). Be careful not the damage the lifters.

23. Check to be sure the matchmarks on the timing chain and cam sprockets, and the alignment of the pulley groove with the timing mark on the cover are still aligned.

24. Install the chain tensioner:

a. Make sure the O-ring is clean, then set the hook as shown.

b. Oil the tensioner, then install and tighten to 80 inch lbs. (9 Nm).

➡**When installing the tensioner, set the hook again if the hook releases the plunger.**

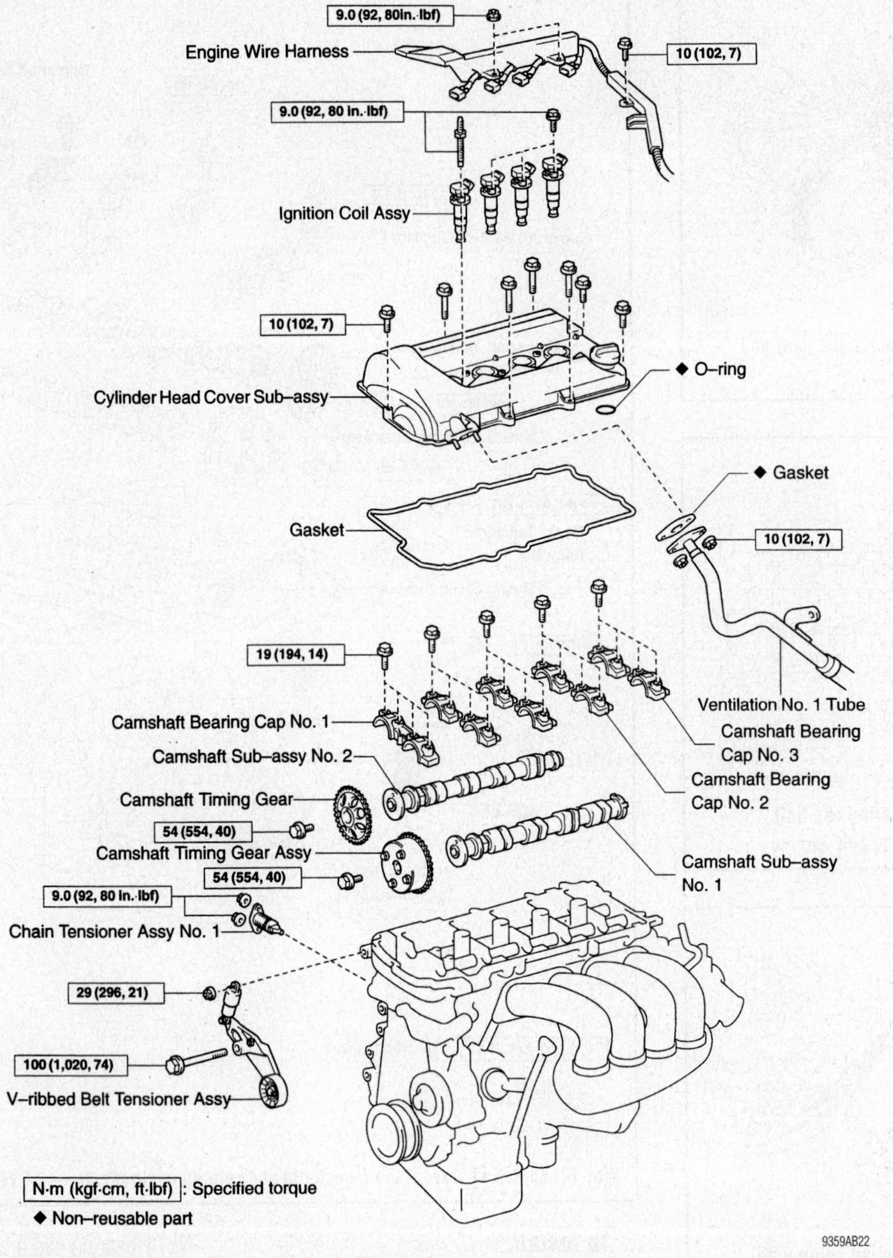

9.0 (92, 80in.·lbf)
Engine Wire Harness
10 (102, 7)
9.0 (92, 80 in.·lbf)
Ignition Coil Assy
10 (102, 7)
◆ O–ring
Cylinder Head Cover Sub–assy
◆ Gasket
Gasket
10 (102, 7)
19 (194, 14)
Ventilation No. 1 Tube
Camshaft Bearing Cap No. 1
Camshaft Bearing Cap No. 3
Camshaft Sub–assy No. 2
Camshaft Bearing Cap No. 2
Camshaft Timing Gear
54 (554, 40)
Camshaft Timing Gear Assy
54 (554, 40)
Camshaft Sub–assy No. 1
9.0 (92, 80 in.·lbf)
Chain Tensioner Assy No. 1
29 (296, 21)
100 (1,020, 74)
V–ribbed Belt Tensioner Assy
N·m (kgf·cm, ft·lbf) : Specified torque
◆ Non–reusable part
9359AB22

Fig. 73 Exploded view of the camshafts and related components—2ZZ-GE engine

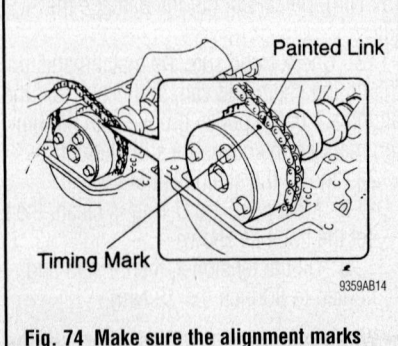

Painted Link
Timing Mark
9359AB14

Fig. 74 Make sure the alignment marks on the timing chain and camshaft gear match up

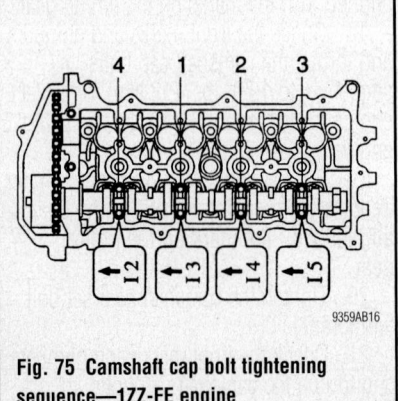

4
1
2
3
I2
I3
I4
I5
9359AB16

Fig. 75 Camshaft cap bolt tightening sequence—1ZZ-FE engine

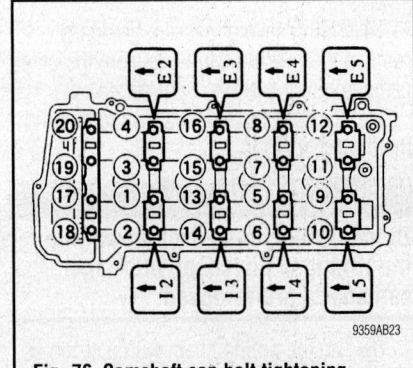

E2
E3
E4
E5
20
4
16
8
12
19
3
15
7
11
17
1
13
5
9
18
2
14
6
10
I2
I3
I4
I5
9359AB23

Fig. 76 Camshaft cap bolt tightening sequence—2ZZ-GE engine

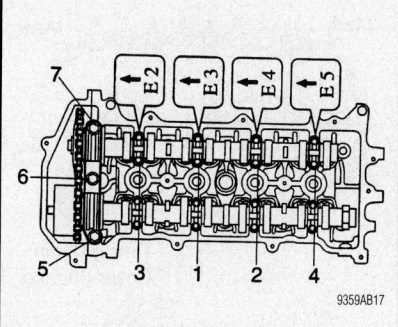

Fig. 77 Camshaft cap bolt tightening sequence—1ZZ-FE

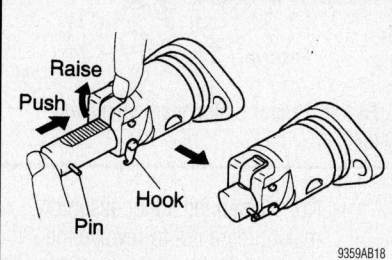

Fig. 78 Set the timing chain tensioner hook properly

c. Turn the crankshaft counterclockwise, and disconnect the plunger knock pin from the hook.

d. Turn the crankshaft clockwise and check that the slipper is pushed by the plunger. If the plunger does not spring out, press the slipper into the chain tensioner with a screwdriver so that the hook is released from the knock pin and the plunger springs out.

25. Check the valve clearance and make adjustments as needed.

26. Install or connect the following:
• Belt tensioner. Tighten the nut to 21 ft. lbs. (29 Nm) and the bolt to 51 ft. lbs. (69 Nm).
• Cylinder head sub-assembly cover. Install seal packing into the locations shown and install within 3 minutes. Tighten the "A" bolts to

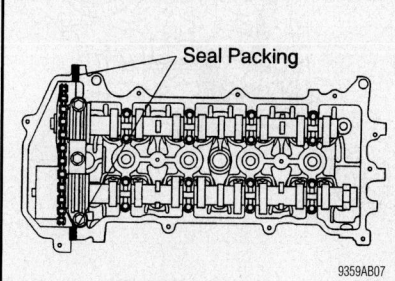

Fig. 79 Seal packing installation locations

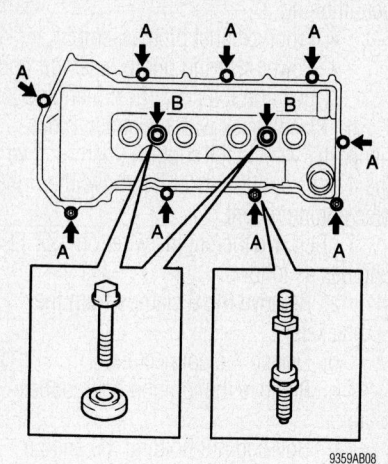

Fig. 80 Cylinder head (valve) cover bolt locations—1ZZ-FE engine

8 ft. lbs. (11 Nm) and the "B" bolts to 80 inch lbs. (9 Nm) for 1ZZ-FE engine and to 7 ft. lbs. (10 Nm) for 2ZZ-GE engines.
• Ignition coil assembly. Torque the bolts to 80 inch lbs. (9 Nm).
• Engine wire and tighten to 80 inch lbs. (9 Nm)
• Right side engine mount. Tighten to 38 ft. lbs. (52 Nm).
• Cylinder head (valve) cover
• Negative battery cable

CRANKSHAFT DAMPER

REMOVAL & INSTALLATION
See Figure 81.

➡This procedure requires the use of Pinion Flange Holder J 8614, or equivalent special tool.

1. Disconnect the negative battery cable.
2. Remove the accessory drive belt.
3. Raise and suitably support the vehicle.
4. Remove the right splash shield.
5. Remove the crankshaft pulley retaining bolt using J 8614-01 to prevent crankshaft rotation when loosening the bolt.

To install:
6. Lubricate the front seal and the sealing surface of the crankshaft pulley with Chassis Grease GM P/N 1051344 (Canadian P/N 993037) or equivalent.
7. Install the crankshaft pulley onto the crankshaft indexing keyway.
8. Install the crankshaft pulley retaining bolt using J 8614-01 to prevent crankshaft rotation when tightening the bolt. Tighten the bolt to 105 ft. lbs. (142 Nm).

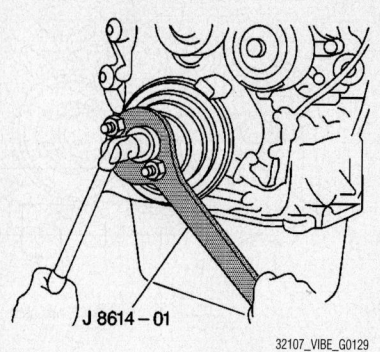

Fig. 81 Remove the crankshaft pulley retaining bolt using J 8614-01 to prevent crankshaft rotation when loosening the bolt.

9. Install the right splash shield.
10. Lower the vehicle.
11. Install the accessory drive belt.
12. Connect the negative battery cable. Tighten the battery cable bolt to 11 ft. lbs. (15 Nm).

CRANKSHAFT FRONT SEAL

REMOVAL & INSTALLATION
See Figures 82 and 83.

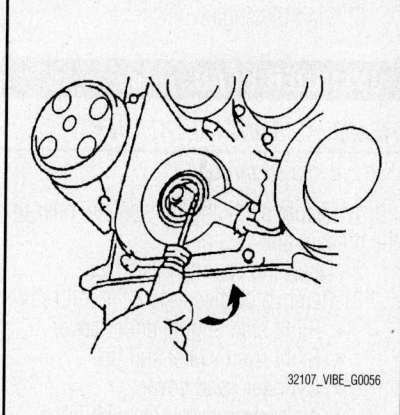

Fig. 82 Use the tip of a screwdriver wrapped in tape to pry out the crankshaft front oil seal.

1. Disconnect the negative battery cable.
2. Remove the crankshaft pulley.

❋❋ WARNING
To protect the crankshaft from damage, wrap the tip of the screwdriver with tape.

3. Use a screwdriver and pry out the crankshaft front oil seal.

Fig. 83 Using a hammer and an appropriate driver, lightly tap the crankshaft front oil seal into place.

To install:

4. Lubricate the new crankshaft front oil seal with Chassis Grease GM P/N 1051344 (Canadian P/N 993037) or equivalent.

5. Using a hammer and an appropriate driver, lightly tap the crankshaft front oil seal into place.

✲✲ WARNING

Tap the oil seal in until its surface is flush with the crankshaft front oil seal retainer edge.

6. Install the crankshaft pulley.
7. Connect the negative battery cable.
8. Start the engine.

CYLINDER HEAD

REMOVAL & INSTALLATION

See Figures 84 through 90.

1. Before servicing the vehicle, refer to the precautions section.
2. Drain the cooling system.
3. Remove or disconnect the following:
- Right side engine under cover
- Right front wheel and tire
- Cylinder head cover
- Air cleaner assembly with hose
- Accelerator control cable
- Wire harness clamp and suction hose assembly, 2ZZ-GE engine only
- Water bypass hoses
- Fuel pipe clamp
- Fuel tube sub-assembly
- Union-to-connector tube hose
- Radiator and heater inlet hoses
- Drive belt

4. Separate the vane pipe assembly, but do not disconnect the hose, 1ZZ-FE engine.
- Alternator bracket, 2ZZ-GE
- Alternator

5. Separate the compressor and mag-

netic clutch, on 2ZZ-GE engines with air conditioning.
- Front exhaust pipe assembly
- Power steering pump reservoir and position it aside, 1ZZ-FE engine

6. Place a jack with a wooden block under the vehicle for support, then remove the 4 bolts and 2 nuts and remove the right side engine mount.

7. Remove the engine wire, on 1ZZ-FE engines as follows:
   a. Remove the 5 clamps from the brackets.
   b. Detach the connectors.
   c. Remove the ignition coil connectors.
   d. Bolt and nut holding the engine wire.

8. Remove or disconnect the following:
- Ignition coil assembly
- Positive Crankcase Ventilation (PCV) hoses
- Valve (cylinder head) cover sub-assembly

9. Set the No. 1 cylinder to Top Dead Center (TDC) of the compressor stroke as follows:
   a. Turn the crankshaft pulley, and align its groove with the "0" timing mark of the timing chain cover.
   b. Make sure the point marks of the camshaft timing sprockets and Variable Valve Timing (VVT) timing sprockets are in a straight line as shown. If not, turn the crankshaft 1 complete revolution (360°) and align the marks.

10. Remove or disconnect the following:
- Crankshaft pulley, using SST 09960-10010
- Belt tensioner
- Exhaust manifold stay and head insulator, 2ZZ-GE engine
- Water pump pulley and pump
- Transverse engine mounting bracket
- Crankshaft Position (CKP) sensor

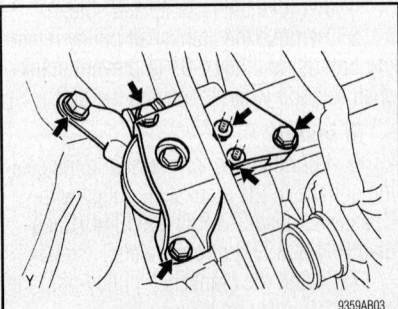

Fig. 84 With the engine supported, remove the right side engine mount—1ZZ-FE engine shown, 2ZZ-GE similar

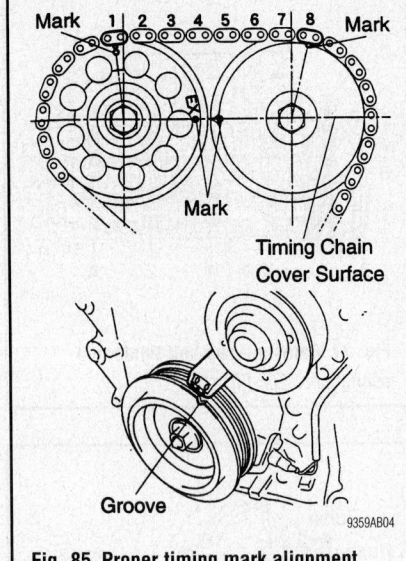

Fig. 85 Proper timing mark alignment for TDC

- No. 1 chain tensioner assembly, making sure not to revolve the crankshaft without the tensioner
- Timing chain or belt cover
- Timing gear cover oil seal
- CKP sensor plate No. 1
- Timing chain tensioner slipper
- Timing chain vibration damper No. 1

➡**In case you turn the camshafts with the timing chain removed, turn the crankshaft ¼ turn for the valve to avoid contact with the pistons.**

- Timing chain sub-assembly. Remove the chain with the crankshaft gear, using screwdrivers as shown.
- Surge tank stay, 2ZZ-GE engine
- Intake manifold
- Oil level gauge
- Water bypass pipe bolts and pipe, 1ZZ-FE engine
- Camshafts

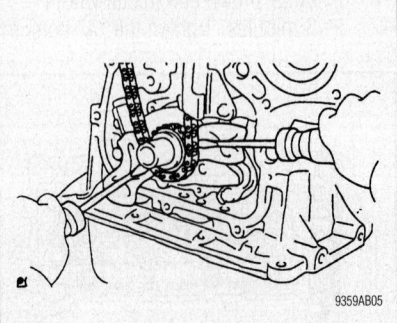

Fig. 86 Remove the timing chain with the crankshaft gear

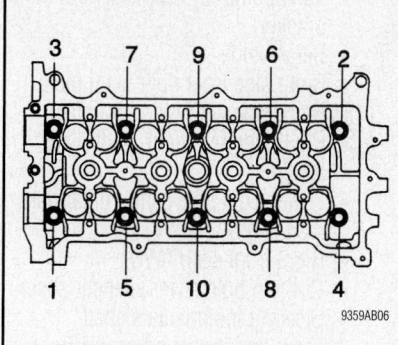

Fig. 87 Cylinder head bolt loosening sequence

- Camshaft timing oil control valve, 1ZZ-FE engine
- Manifold stay, 1ZZ-FE engine
- Cylinder head bolts in sequence. To prevent damage to the cylinder head, loosen each bolt about ¼ of a turn during each pass until the bolts are loose.
- Cylinder head

To install:

11. Clean and degrease the surface of the cylinder head and engine block.

12. Check the length of the cylinder head bolts. They should be 5.780–5.835 in. (146.8–148.2mm) long. If they are longer than 5.846 in. (148.5mm), they must be replaced.

13. Install or connect the following:
- New gasket on the engine block with the Lot No. stamp facing up.
- Cylinder head
- Apply a light coat of oil to cylinder head bolt threads;

14. On 1ZZ-FE engines tighten the bolts as follows:

    a. Step 1: 36 ft. lbs. (49 Nm)

    b. Step 2: Tighten an additional 90 degrees.

15. On 2ZZ-GE engines tighten the bolts as follows:

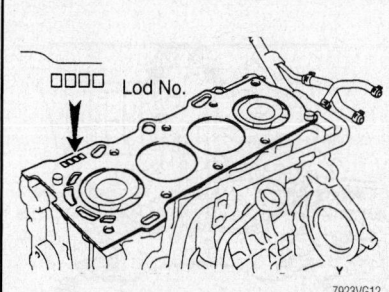

Fig. 88 Position the head gasket correctly on the cylinder head—1.8L (1ZZ-FE) engine

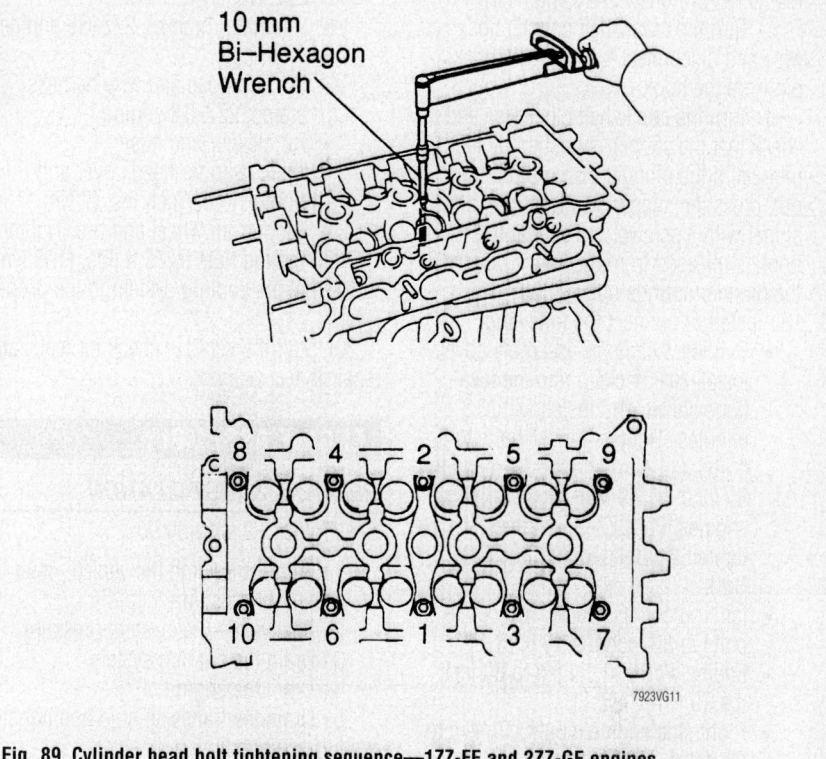

Fig. 89 Cylinder head bolt tightening sequence—1ZZ-FE and 2ZZ-GE engines

    a. Step 1: 16 ft. lbs. (25 Nm)

    b. Step 2: 36 ft. lbs. (49 Nm)

    c. Step 3: 36 ft. lbs. (49 Nm), plus an additional 90 degrees.

16. Install or connect the following:
- Manifold stay, 1ZZ-FE engine. Tighten the bolts to 36 ft. lbs. (49 Nm).
- Camshaft timing oil control valve, on 1ZZ-FE engines, and tighten to 80 inch lbs. (9 Nm)
- Camshaft
- Water by-pass pipe, on 1ZZ-FE engines, and tighten to 80 inch lbs. (9 Nm)
- Oil level gauge
- Intake manifold
- Surge tank stay, 2ZZ-GE engine. Tighten to 18 ft. lbs. (24 Nm).
- Timing chain
- Timing chain vibration damper. Tighten the bolts to 80 inch lbs. (9 m).
- Timing chain tensioner slipper and tighten the bolt to 14 ft. lbs. (19 Nm).
- Crankshaft position sensor plate, with the "F" mark facing forward.
- Timing gear cover oil seal
- Timing cover. For 1ZZ-FE engine, tighten the "A" bolts to 10 ft. lbs. (13 Nm), the "B" bolts to 14 ft. lbs.

(19 Nm) and the stud bolt to 84 inch lbs. (9.5 Nm), using a Torx® wrench. For 2ZZ-GE engines, tighten the M8 bolts to 15 ft. lbs. (21 m), the M6 bolts to 8 ft. lbs. (11 Nm) and the stud bolt to 84 inch lbs. (9.5 Nm).

➡**When installing the tensioner, make sure to set the hook again if the hook releases the plunger.**

- Timing chain tensioner. Torque the nuts to 80 inch lbs. (9 Nm).
- CKP sensor and tighten the bolts to 80 inch lbs. (9 Nm)
- Transverse engine mounting bracket. Tighten the bolts to 35 ft. lbs. (47 Nm).
- Water pump and pulley
- Exhaust manifold stay and heat insulator, 2ZZ-GE engine
- Belt tensioner. Tighten the nut to 21 ft. lbs. (29 Nm) and the bolt to 51 ft. lbs. (69 Nm) on 1ZZ-FE engines or to 74 ft. lbs. (100 Nm) on 2ZZ-GE engines.

17. Install the crankshaft pulley, as follows:

    a. Align the pulley set key with the key groove of the pulley and slide on the pulley.

    b. Use SST 09960-11010 to install the bolt and tighten to 102 ft. lbs.

(138 Nm) for 1ZZ-FE engine or to 87 ft. lbs. (118 Nm) on 2ZZ-GE engines.

c. Turn the crankshaft counterclockwise and disconnect the plunger knock pin from the hook.

d. Turn the crankshaft clockwise and check that the slipper is pushed by the plunger. If the plunger does not spring out, press the slipper into the chain tensioner with a screwdriver so that the hook is released from the knock pin and the plunder springs out.

18. Install or connect the following:

- Cylinder head sub-assembly cover. Install seal packing into the locations shown and install within 3 minutes. Tighten the "A" bolts to 8 ft. lbs. (11 Nm) and the "B" bolts to 80 inch lbs. (9 Nm) for 1ZZ-FE engines. For 2ZZ-GE engines, tighten the bolts to 7 ft. lbs. (10 Nm).
- Ignition coil assembly. Torque the bolts to 80 inch lbs. (9 Nm).
- Engine wire and tighten to 80 inch lbs. (9 Nm), 1ZZ-FE
- Right side engine mount. Tighten to 38 ft. lbs. (52 Nm).
- Front exhaust pipe
- Vane pump, 1ZZ-FE

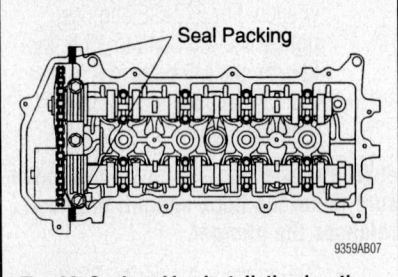

Fig. 90 Seal packing installation locations

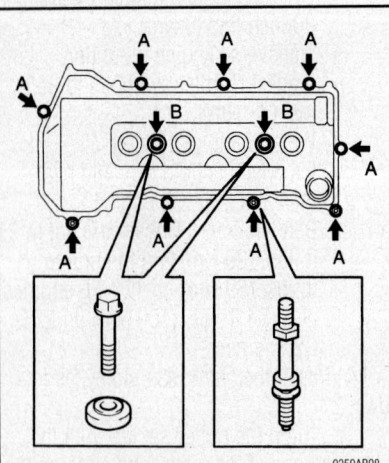

Fig. 91 Cylinder head (valve) cover bolt locations—1ZZ-FE engine

- Compressor and magnetic clutch, 2ZZ-GE
- Alternator bracket, 2ZZ-GE engine
- Alternator
- Suction hose and wire harness clamp, 2ZZ-GE engine
- Air cleaner and hose
- Main cylinder head cover and tighten to 62 inch lbs. (7 Nm)
- Right front wheel and tire. Tighten the lug nuts to 76 ft. lbs. (103 Nm).

19. Fill the cooling system to the proper level.

20. Start the vehicle, check for leaks and repair if necessary.

ENGINE ASSEMBLY

REMOVAL & INSTALLATION

See Figures 92 through 96.

1. Before servicing the vehicle, refer to the precautions section.
2. Relieve the fuel system pressure.
3. Drain the cooling system.
4. Drain the engine oil.
5. Drain the transaxle fluid and transfer fluid, if equipped.
6. Remove or disconnect the following:

- Negative battery cable. Wait at least 90 seconds before proceeding.
- Battery
- Hood
- Undercovers
- Radiator inlet and outlet hoses
- Radiator hose outlet
- Oil cooler inlet and outlet tubes
- Upper radiator support and radiator, if equipped with A/C
- Battery
- Air cleaner assembly
- Fuel pipe clamp
- Fuel tube sub-assembly
- Accelerator control cable
- Cruise control actuator, if equipped
- Union-to-connector tube hose
- Heater inlet and outlet hoses
- Transmission shift cable(s)
- Clutch release cylinder, on manual transaxle
- Glove compartment door
- Engine relay block cover
- 3 connectors from the relay block
- 2 ground cables
- Engine wire from the Engine Control Module (ECM) and junction block
- Engine wire from the cabin
- Drive belt
- Compressor and magnetic clutch, if equipped with A/C. Unbolt and position aside, DO NOT disconnect the lines.

- Vane pump oil reservoir from the bracket
- Return tube
- Right side front door scuff plate
- Right side cowl side trim plate
- Right side rear door scuff plate, AWD
- Lower right side center pillar garnish, AWD
- Right front seat, AWD
- Column hole cover silencer sheet
- Steering intermediate shaft
- Front floor panel brace, FWD
- Center exhaust pipe, AWD
- Propeller shaft with center bearing shaft, AWD
- Front exhaust pipe
- Front hub nuts
- Tie rod ends from the steering knuckles

7. Separate the front stabilizer links and lower control arm ball joints

- Front halfshafts

8. Remove the engine from the vehicle, as follows:

a. Set the engine lifter.

b. Remove the bolts and nuts, then remove the engine mounting insulator.

c. Remove the through bolt and nut, then detach the engine mounting insulator from the vehicle.

d. Remove the 6 bolts as shown.

e. Use a suitable tool to suspend the engine assembly, as shown in the figure.

f. No. 1 engine hanger: P/N 12281-15040 (1ZZ-FE), 12281-88600 (2ZZ-GE).

g. No. 2 engine hanger: P/N 12281-22021 (1ZZ-FE), 12281-88600 (2ZZ-GE).

h. Bolt: P/N 91512-B1016.

i. Torque the bolts to 28 ft. lbs. (38 Nm).

✳✳ CAUTION

Do not try to suspend the engine by hooking the chain to any other part.

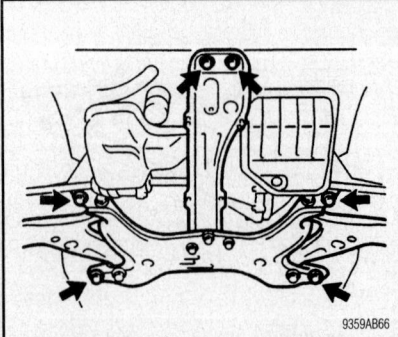

Fig. 92 Remove the 6 bolts, as indicated by arrows

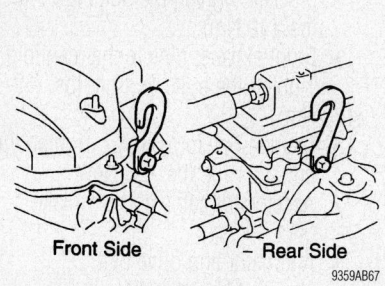

Fig. 93 Install the engine hangers—1ZZ-FE shown, 2ZZ-GE similar

j.   Attach an engine chain hoist to the hangers.

k.   Using the chain block and sling device, suspend the engine.

l.   Remove the engine and transaxle assembly from the vehicle.

9.   Remove or disconnect the following components, as necessary:

- Vane pump
- Steering gear
- Crossmember
- Manifold stay
- Oxygen (O₂) sensor
- Exhaust manifold
- Starter
- Transaxle
- Transfer case
- Clutch
- Flywheel
- Alternator
- Ignition coil
- Fuel delivery pipe
- Intake manifold
- Oil level gauge
- Water inlet and bypass pipes
- Thermostat
- Oil pressure switch
- Crankshaft Position (CKP) sensor
- Knock Sensor (KS)
- Drive belt tensioner
- Engine mounts and brackets
- Coolant Temperature Sensor (CTS)

To install:

10.   Install any removed components to the engine and transaxle assembly.

11.   To install the engine:

a.   Place the engine and transaxle on an engine lifter.

b.   Install the engine with the transaxle to the vehicle.

c.   Temporarily install the crossmember and 6 bolts.

d.   Install the left engine mounting insulator. Tighten the bolts to 59 ft. lbs. (80 Nm).

e.   Install the right engine mounting

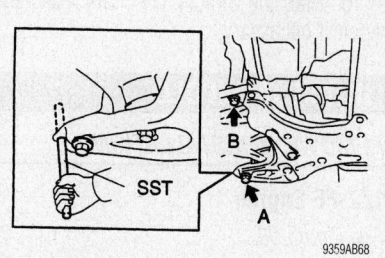

Fig. 94 Insert the SST to the positioning holes of the right handle crossmember and on the right handle of the vehicle. Temporarily tighten bolt A, then bolt B

insulator. Tighten the bolts to 38 ft. lbs. (52 Nm).

f.   Insert SST 09670-00010 to the positioning holes of the right handle crossmember and on the right handle of the vehicle. Temporarily tighten bolt A, then bolt B.

g.   Insert SST 09670-00010 to the positioning holes of the left handle crossmember and on the left handle of the vehicle. Temporarily tighten bolt A, then bolt B.

h.   Insert the SST to the positioning holes on the right-handle crossmember and right handle. Tighten bolt A to 116 ft. lbs. (157 Nm) and bolt B to 83 ft. lbs. (113 Nm).

i.   Insert the SST to the positioning holes on the left-handle crossmember and left handle. Tighten bolt A to 116 ft. lbs. (157 Nm) and bolt B to 83 ft. lbs. (113 Nm).

j.   Tighten the 2 crossmember bolts, shown in the figure, to 29 ft. lbs. (39 Nm).

12.   Installation of the remaining components is the reverse of the removal procedure.

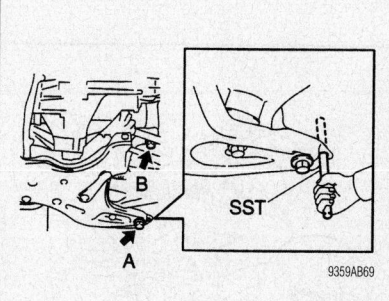

Fig. 95 Insert the SST to the positioning holes of the left handle crossmember and on the left handle of the vehicle. Temporarily tighten bolt A, then bolt B

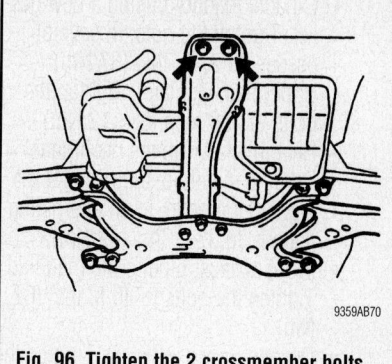

Fig. 96 Tighten the 2 crossmember bolts, indicated by arrows

13.   Make sure all fluid levels are accurate, then start the engine check for leaks.

EXHAUST MANIFOLD

REMOVAL & INSTALLATION

1ZZ-FE Engine

See Figure 97.

1.   Before servicing the vehicle, refer to the precautions section.

2.   Drain the cooling system.

3.   Remove or disconnect the following:

- Negative battery cable
- Drive belt and alternator
- Air intake duct
- Accelerator cable
- Exhaust pipe from the manifold
- Exhaust manifold support bracket
- Heat insulator from the dash panel
- Upper heat insulator
- Exhaust manifold and gasket
- If necessary, the lower heat insulator from the exhaust manifold.

To install:

4.   Install or connect the following:

- Lower heat insulator on the exhaust manifold. Tighten the bolts to 108 inch lbs. (12 Nm).

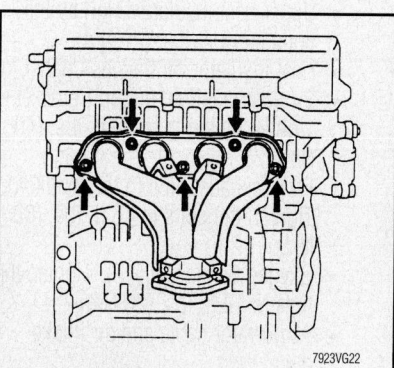

Fig. 97 Exhaust manifold mounting nut locations—1.8L (1ZZ-FE) engine

- Exhaust manifold using a new gasket. Tighten the nuts, in several passes, to 27 ft. lbs. (37 Nm).
- Upper heat insulator. Tighten the bolts to 108 inch lbs. (12 Nm).
- Heat insulator on the dash panel
- Exhaust manifold support bracket. Tighten the bolts, in an alternating pattern, to 37 ft. lbs. (49 Nm).
- Front exhaust pipe to the manifold. Tighten the bolts to 46 ft. lbs. (62 Nm).
- Oxygen Sensor (O$_2$S). Tighten the nuts to 14 ft. lbs. (20 Nm).
- Accelerator cable and air intake duct
- Alternator and drive belt
- Negative battery cable

5. Fill the cooling system.
6. Start the vehicle, check for leaks and repair if necessary.

2ZZ-GE Engine

1. Before servicing the vehicle, refer to the precautions section.
2. Drain the cooling system.
3. Remove or disconnect the following:
- Negative battery cable
- Drive belt and alternator
- Air intake duct
- Accelerator cable
- Exhaust pipe from the manifold
- Exhaust manifold support bracket
- Heat insulator from the dash panel
- Upper heat insulator
- Exhaust manifold and gasket
- If necessary, the lower heat insulator from the exhaust manifold.

To install:

4. Install or connect the following:
- Lower heat insulator on the exhaust manifold. Tighten the bolts to 15 ft. lbs. (20 Nm).
- Exhaust manifold using a new gasket. Tighten the nuts, in several passes to 37 ft. lbs. (50 Nm).
- Upper heat insulator. Tighten the bolts to 15 ft. lbs. (20 Nm).
- Heat insulator on the dash panel.
- Exhaust manifold support bracket. Tighten the bolts to 37 ft. lbs. (49 Nm).
- Front exhaust pipe to the manifold. Tighten the bolts to 46 ft. lbs. (62 Nm).
- Oxygen Sensor (O$_2$S). Tighten the nuts to 14 ft. lbs. (20 Nm).
- Accelerator cable and air intake duct.
- Alternator and drive belt.
- Negative battery cable

5. Fill the cooling system.
6. Start the vehicle, check for leaks and repair if necessary.

INTAKE MANIFOLD

REMOVAL & INSTALLATION

1ZZ-FE Engine

See Figure 98.

1. Before servicing the vehicle, refer to the precautions section.
2. Drain the cooling system.
3. Remove or disconnect the following:
- Negative battery cable
- Drive belt and alternator
- Air intake duct
- Accelerator cable
- Exhaust pipe from the manifold.
- Exhaust manifold support bracket
- Spark plug wires, then ignition coils
- Spark plugs
- Positive Crankcase Ventilation (PCV) hoses
- Throttle body assembly
- 2 bolts securing the wiring harness protector
- Wiring connectors and ground wires
- Intake manifold support bracket
- Intake manifold and gasket

To install:

4. Install or connect the following:
- Intake manifold with a new gasket. Torque the bolts to 22 ft. lbs. (30 Nm).
- Harness wiring to the cylinder head and harness protector
- Fuel injectors, throttle body and the PCV hoses
- Spark plugs and ignition coils. Tighten the bolts and nuts to 80 inch lbs. (9 Nm).
- Exhaust manifold and support

bracket. Tighten the bolts to 37 ft. lbs. (49 Nm).
- Front exhaust pipe to the manifold. Tighten the bolts to 46 ft. lbs. (62 Nm).
- Oxygen Sensor (O$_2$S). Tighten the nuts to 14 ft. lbs. (20 Nm).
- Accelerator cable and air intake duct
- Alternator and drive belt
- Negative battery cable

5. Fill the cooling system.
6. Start the vehicle, check for leaks and repair if necessary.

2ZZ-GE Engine

See Figure 99.

1. Before servicing the vehicle, refer to the precautions section.
2. Drain the cooling system.
3. Remove or disconnect the following:
- Negative battery cable
- Drive belt and alternator
- Air intake duct
- Accelerator cable
- Spark plug wires, then ignition coils
- Spark plugs
- Positive Crankcase Ventilation (PCV) hoses
- Throttle body assembly
- Wiring harness
- Hoses and tubes connected to the head
- Intake manifold support bracket
- Intake manifold and gasket

To install:

4. Install or connect the following:
- Intake manifold with a new gasket. Tighten bolts A to 25 ft. lbs. (34 Nm) and bolt B to 34 ft. lbs. (46 Nm).
- Harness wiring to the cylinder head and harness protector

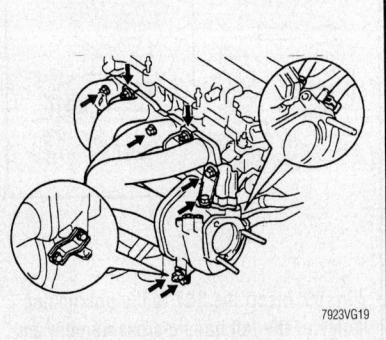

Fig. 98 Intake manifold mounting fastener locations—1.8L (1ZZ-FE) engine

7923VG19

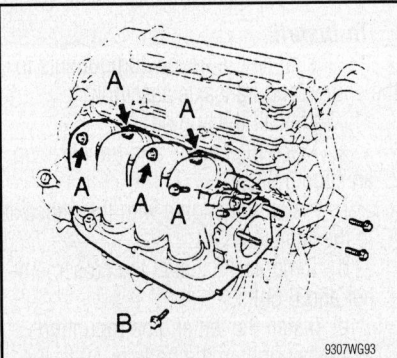

Fig. 99 Intake manifold bolt installation—2ZZ-GE engine

9307WG93

- Fuel injectors, throttle body and the PCV hoses
- Spark plugs and ignition coils. Tighten the bolts and nuts to 80 inch lbs. (9 Nm).
- Oxygen Sensor (O_2S). Tighten the nuts to 14 ft. lbs. (20 Nm).
- Accelerator cable and air intake duct
- Alternator and drive belt
- Negative battery cable

5. Fill the cooling system.
6. Start the vehicle, check for leaks and repair if necessary.

OIL PAN

REMOVAL & INSTALLATION

1ZZ-FE Engine

See Figure 100.

1. Before servicing the vehicle, refer to the precautions section.
2. Drain the engine oil.
3. Remove or disconnect the following:
   - Negative battery cable
   - Undercovers
   - Front exhaust pipe
   - Oil pan mounting bolts and nuts
   - Oil pan, cutting off the applied sealer.

To install:

4. Remove any old sealant from the oil pan flange and thoroughly clean the sealing surface.

5. Install or connect the following:
   - Oil pan. Tighten the bolts and nuts in several passes to 80 inch lbs. (9 Nm).
   - Front exhaust pipe
   - Negative battery cable
   - Undercovers
6. Fill the engine with clean oil.
7. Start the vehicle, check for leaks and repair if necessary.

2ZZ-GE Engine

1. Before servicing the vehicle, refer to the precautions section.
2. Drain the engine oil.
3. Remove or disconnect the following:
   - Negative battery cable. On vehicles equipped with an air bag, wait at least 90 seconds before proceeding.
   - Undercovers
   - Front exhaust pipe
   - Oil pan mounting bolts and nuts
   - Oil pan, cutting off the applied sealer

To install:

4. Remove any old sealant from the oil pan flange and thoroughly clean the sealing surface.
5. Install or connect the following:
   - Oil pan. Tighten the bolts and nuts in several passes to 80 inch lbs. (9 Nm).
   - Front exhaust pipe
   - Negative battery cable
   - Undercovers

6. Fill the engine with clean oil.
7. Start the vehicle, check for leaks and repair if necessary.

OIL PUMP

REMOVAL & INSTALLATION

1ZZ-FE Engine

See Figure 101.

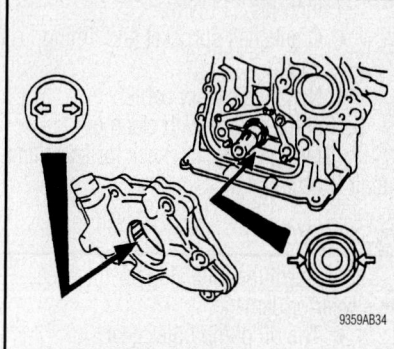

Fig. 101 Oil pump mounting—1ZZ-FE and 2ZZ-GE engines

1. Before servicing the vehicle, refer to the precautions section.
2. Drain the engine oil.
3. Remove or disconnect the following:
   - Negative battery cable
   - Timing chain and crankshaft sprocket
   - Timing chain vibration damper
   - Oil pump bolts, pump and gasket

To install:

4. Clean the mounting surface.
5. Install or connect the following:
   - Oil pump, with new gasket. Engage the spline teeth of the oil pump drive rotor with the larger teeth of the crankshaft, and slide the pump on.
   - Oil pump bolts and tighten to 97 inch lbs. (11 Nm)
   - Crankshaft vibration damper and tighten to 80 inch lbs. (9 Nm)
   - Crankshaft sprocket and timing chain
   - Negative battery cable
6. Fill the engine with clean oil.
7. Start the vehicle, check for leaks and repair if necessary.

2ZZ-GE Engine

1. Before servicing the vehicle, refer to the precautions section.
2. Drain the engine oil.
3. Remove or disconnect the following:
   - Negative battery cable

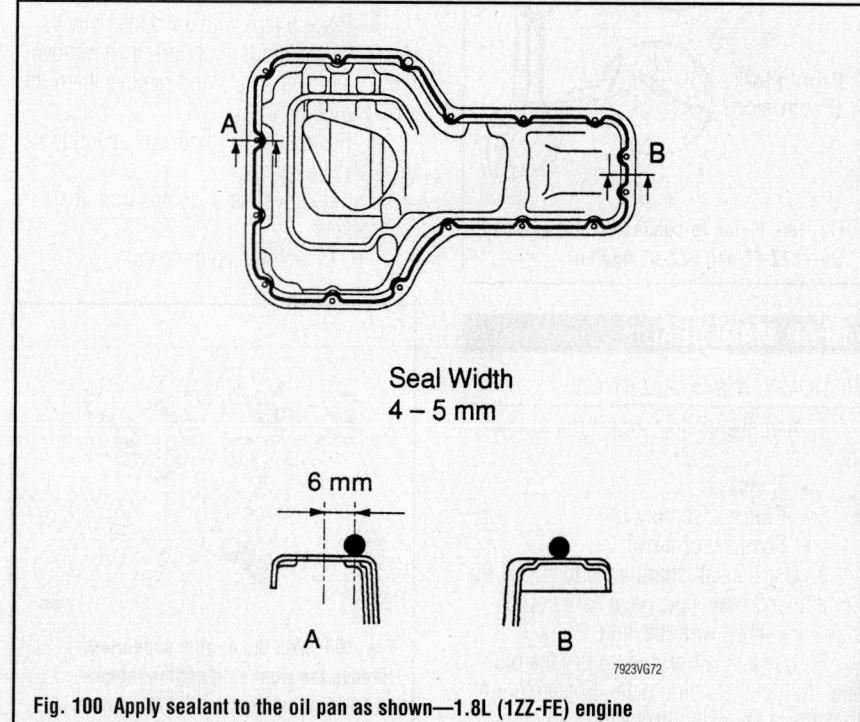

Seal Width
4 – 5 mm

6 mm

A   B

Fig. 100 Apply sealant to the oil pan as shown—1.8L (1ZZ-FE) engine

- Timing chain and crankshaft sprocket
- Oil pump and gasket

To install:

4. Clean the mounting surface.

5. Install or connect the following:
- Oil pump, with new gasket. Engage the spline teeth of the oil pump drive rotor with the larger teeth of the crankshaft, and slide the pump on.
- Oil pump bolts and tighten to 97 inch lbs. (11 Nm)
- Crankshaft sprocket and timing chain
- Negative battery cable

6. Fill the engine with clean oil.

7. Start the vehicle, check for leaks and repair if necessary.

INSPECTION

1. Inspect the following for the excessive wear or damage:
- The oil pump outer gear
- The oil pump inner gear
- The oil pump cover
- The oil pump body

2. Measure the radial clearance between the oil pump outer gear and the oil pump body using a feeler gage. Replace the oil pump outer gear and/or oil pump if the clearance exceeds 0.01280 inches (0.325mm).

3. Measure the side clearance between the oil pump gears and a straightedge using a feeler gage. Replace the gears if the clearance exceeds 0.0062 inches (0.16mm).

4. Measure the tip clearance between the oil pump gear tips using a feeler gage. Replace the gears if the clearance exceeds 0.35 mm (0.0138 in).

PISTON AND RING

POSITIONING

See Figures 102 through 105.

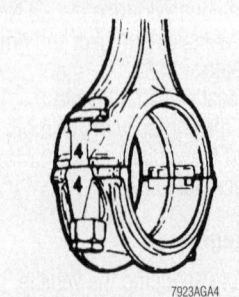

Fig. 102 Before removing the caps from the connecting rods, be sure to matchmark them as shown

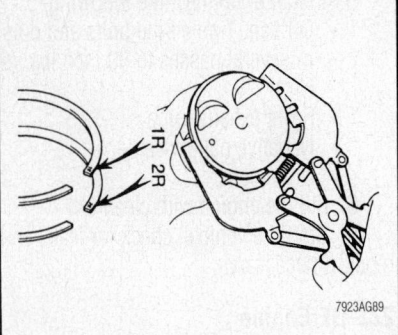

Fig. 103 Piston ring identification mark locations—1ZZ-FE and 2ZZ-GE engines

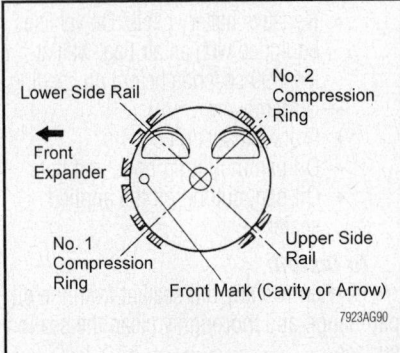

Fig. 104 Piston ring end-gap spacing— 1ZZ-FE and 2ZZ-GE engines

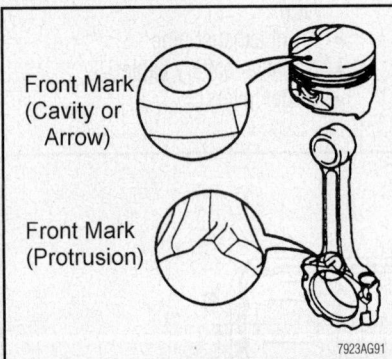

Fig. 105 Piston-to-connecting rod assembly—1ZZ-FE and 2ZZ-GE engines

REAR MAIN SEAL

REMOVAL & INSTALLATION

1. Remove or disconnect the following:
- Transaxle
- Clutch assembly
- Flywheel or flexplate

2. Use a small sharp knife to cut off the lip of the oil seal. Take great care not to score any metal with the knife.

3. Use a small prytool to pry the old seal from the retaining plate. Be careful not to damage the plate. Protect the tip of the

tool with tape and pad the fulcrum point with cloth.

4. Inspect the crankshaft and seal lip contact surfaces for any sign of damage.

To install:

5. Apply a light coat of multi-purpose grease to the lip of a new oil seal. Loosely fit the seal into place by hand, making sure it is not crooked.

6. Use a seal driver of the correct size to install the seal. Tap it into place until the surface of the seal is flush with the edge of the housing.

TIMING CHAIN, SPROCKETS, FRONT COVER AND SEAL

REMOVAL & INSTALLATION

See Figures 106 through 116.

1. Before servicing the vehicle, refer to the precautions section.

2. Drain the cooling system.

3. Remove or disconnect the following:
- Right side engine under cover
- Right front wheel and tire
- Cylinder head cover
- Wire harness clamp and suction hose assembly, 2ZZ-GE engine
- Drive belt

4. Separate the vane pipe assembly, but do not disconnect the hose, 1ZZ-FE engine.
- Alternator bracket, 2ZZ-GE
- Alternator
- Power steering pump reservoir and position it aside, 1ZZ-FE engine

5. Place a jack with a wooden block under the vehicle for support, then remove the 4 bolts and 2 nuts and remove the right side engine mount.

6. Remove the engine wire as follows, on 1ZZ-FE engines:
   a. Remove the 5 clamps from the brackets.
   b. Detach the connectors.

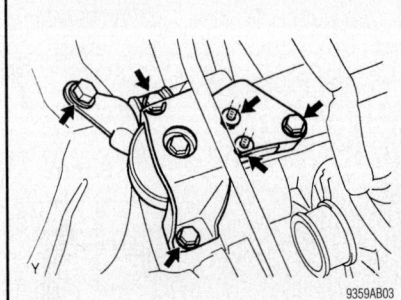

Fig. 106 With the engine supported, remove the right side engine mount— 1ZZ-FE engine shown, 2ZZ-GE similar

c. Remove the ignition coil connectors.

d. Bolt and nut holding the engine wire.

7. Remove the engine wire as follows, on 2ZZ-GE engines:

a. Detach the ignition coil, oil control valve and Crankshaft Position (CKP) sensor electrical connectors.

b. Bolt and nut for the engine ground, then position the engine wire aside

8. Remove or disconnect the following:

- Ignition coil assembly
- Positive Crankcase Ventilation (PCV) hoses from the cylinder head cover, if necessary
- Cylinder head (valve) cover sub-assembly

9. Set the No. 1 cylinder to Top Dead Center (TDC) of the compressor stroke as follows:

a. Turn the crankshaft pulley, and align its groove with the "0" timing mark of the timing chain cover.

b. Make sure the point marks of the camshaft timing sprockets and VVT timing sprockets are in a straight line as shown. If not, turn the crankshaft 1 complete revolution (360°) and align the marks.

- Crankshaft pulley, using SST 09960-10010
- Belt tensioner
- Water pump pulley, if equipped, and pump

- Transverse engine mounting bracket
- Crankshaft Position (CKP) sensor
- No. 1 chain tensioner assembly, making sure not to revolve the crankshaft without the tensioner
- Timing chain cover. The cover is retained with 11 bolts and nuts and a Torx® stud bolt. Pry the cover between the cylinder head and block to remove it.
- Timing gear cover oil seal
- CKP sensor plate No. 1
- Timing chain tensioner slipper

➡In case you turn the camshafts with the timing chain removed, turn the crankshaft ¼ turn for the valve to avoid contact with the pistons.

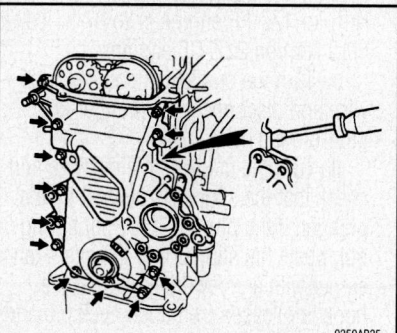

Fig. 108 Timing chain cover mounting— 1ZZ-FE engine shown, 2ZZ-GE similar

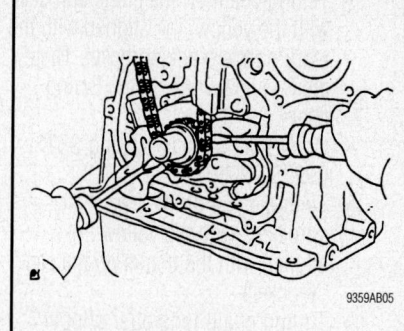

Fig. 109 Remove the timing chain with the crankshaft gear

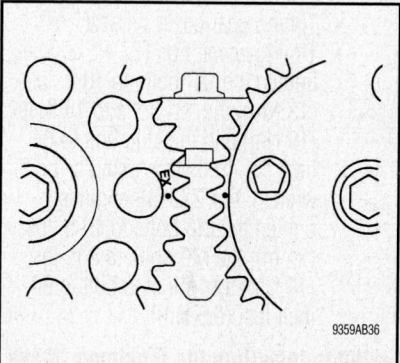

Fig. 110 Proper alignment of the camshaft sprockets—1ZZ-FE engine

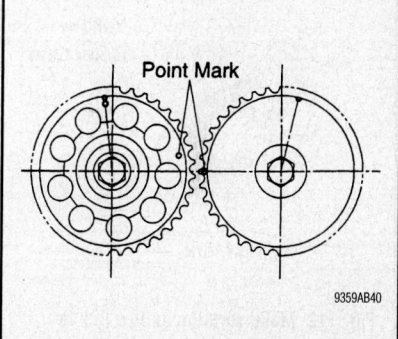

Fig. 111 Proper alignment of the camshaft sprockets—2ZZ-GE engine

- Timing chain sub-assembly. Remove the chain with the crankshaft gear, using screwdrivers as shown.

To install:

10. Set the No. 1 cylinder to TDC of the compression stroke:

a. Turn the hexagonal wrench head part of the camshafts, and align the point marks of the cam sprockets.

b. Using the crankshaft pulley bolt, turn the crankshaft and position the crankshaft set key upward.

11. Install or connect the following:

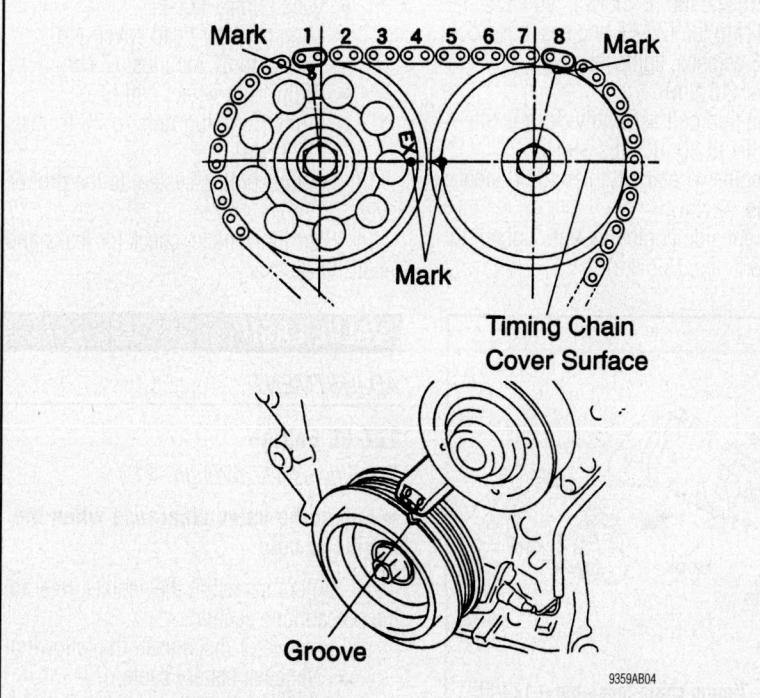

Fig. 107 Proper timing mark alignment for TDC

- Timing chain on the crank sprocket with the yellow link aligned with the mark on the crank sprocket. There are 3 yellow links on the timing chain.
- Crankshaft sprocket, using SST 09223-22010
- Timing chain on the camshaft sprockets with the yellow links aligned with the marks on the cam sprockets
- Timing chain tensioner slipper and tighten the bolt to 14 ft. lbs. (19 Nm)
- Crankshaft position sensor plate, with the "F" mark facing forward
- Timing gear cover oil seal
- Timing cover. For 1ZZ-FE engine, tighten the "A" bolts to 10 ft. lbs. (13 Nm), the "B" bolts to 14 ft. lbs. (19 Nm) and the stud bolt to 84 inch lbs. (9.5 Nm), using a Torx® wrench. For 2ZZ-GE engines, tighten the M8 bolts to 15 ft. lbs. (21 m), the M6 bolts to 8 ft. lbs. (11 Nm) and the stud bolt to 84 inch lbs. (9.5 Nm).

➡**When installing the tensioner, make sure to set the hook again if the hook releases the plunger.**

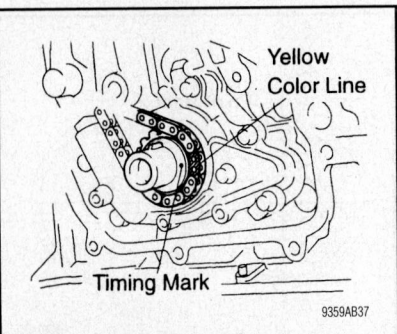

Fig. 112 Make sure the yellow link is aligned with the crankshaft sprocket timing mark—1ZZ-FE and 2ZZ-GE engines

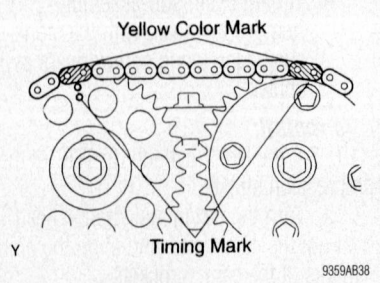

Fig. 113 The yellow links of the timing chain must align with the camshaft sprocket timing marks—1ZZ-FE and 2ZZ-GE engines

- Timing chain tensioner. Torque the nuts to 80 inch lbs. (9 Nm).
- CKP sensor and tighten the bolts to 80 inch lbs. (9 Nm)
- Transverse engine mounting bracket. Tighten the bolts to 35 ft. lbs. (47 Nm).
- Water pump and pulley
- Drive belt tensioner. Tighten the nut to 21 ft. lbs. (29 Nm) and the bolt to 51 ft. lbs. (69 Nm) on 1ZZ-FE engines or to 74 ft. lbs. (100 Nm) on 2ZZ-GE engines.

12. Install the crankshaft pulley, as follows:

　a. Align the pulley set key with the key groove of the pulley and slide on the pulley.

　b. Use SST 09960-11010 to install the bolt and tighten to 102 ft. lbs. (138 Nm) for 1ZZ-FE engine or to 87 ft. lbs. (118 Nm) on 2ZZ-GE engines.

　c. Turn the crankshaft counterclockwise and disconnect the plunger knock pin from the hook.

　d. Turn the crankshaft clockwise and check that the slipper is pushed by the plunger. If the plunger does not spring out, press the slipper into the chain tensioner with a screwdriver so that the hook is released from the knock pin and the plunder springs out.

- Cylinder head sub-assembly cover. Install seal packing into the locations shown and install within 3 minutes. Tighten the "A" bolts to 8 ft. lbs. (11 Nm) and the "B" bolts to 80 inch lbs. (9 Nm) for 1ZZ-FE engines. For 2ZZ-GE engines, tighten the bolts to 7 ft. lbs. (10 Nm).
- Ignition coil assembly. Torque the bolts to 80 inch lbs. (9 Nm).
- Engine wire and tighten to 80 inch lbs. (9 Nm)
- Right side engine mount. Tighten to 38 ft. lbs. (52 Nm).

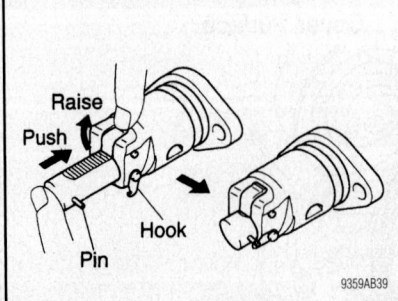

Fig. 114 Timing chain tensioner—1ZZ-FE engine

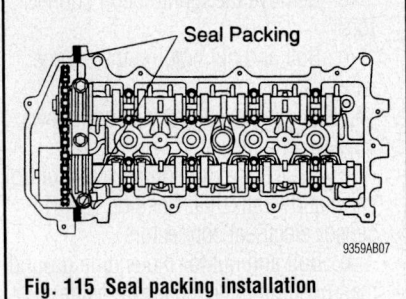

Fig. 115 Seal packing installation locations

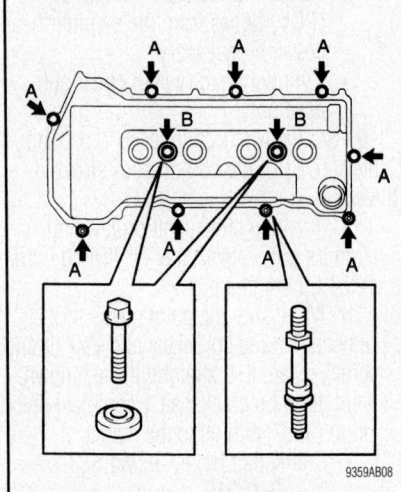

Fig. 116 Cylinder head (valve) cover bolt locations—1ZZ-FE engine

- Alternator bracket, 2ZZ-GE engine
- Alternator
- Vane pump, 1ZZ-FE
- Main cylinder head cover and tighten to 62 inch lbs. (7 Nm)
- Right front wheel and tire. Tighten the lug nuts to 76 ft. lbs. (103 Nm).

13. Fill the cooling system to the proper level.

14. Start the vehicle, check for leaks and repair if necessary.

VALVE LASH

ADJUSTMENT

1ZZ-FE Engine

See Figures 117 through 121.

➡**Adjust the valve clearance when the engine is cold.**

1. Before servicing the vehicle, refer to the precautions section.

2. Remove or disconnect the following:
- Negative battery cable.
- Cylinder head covers
- Engine wire

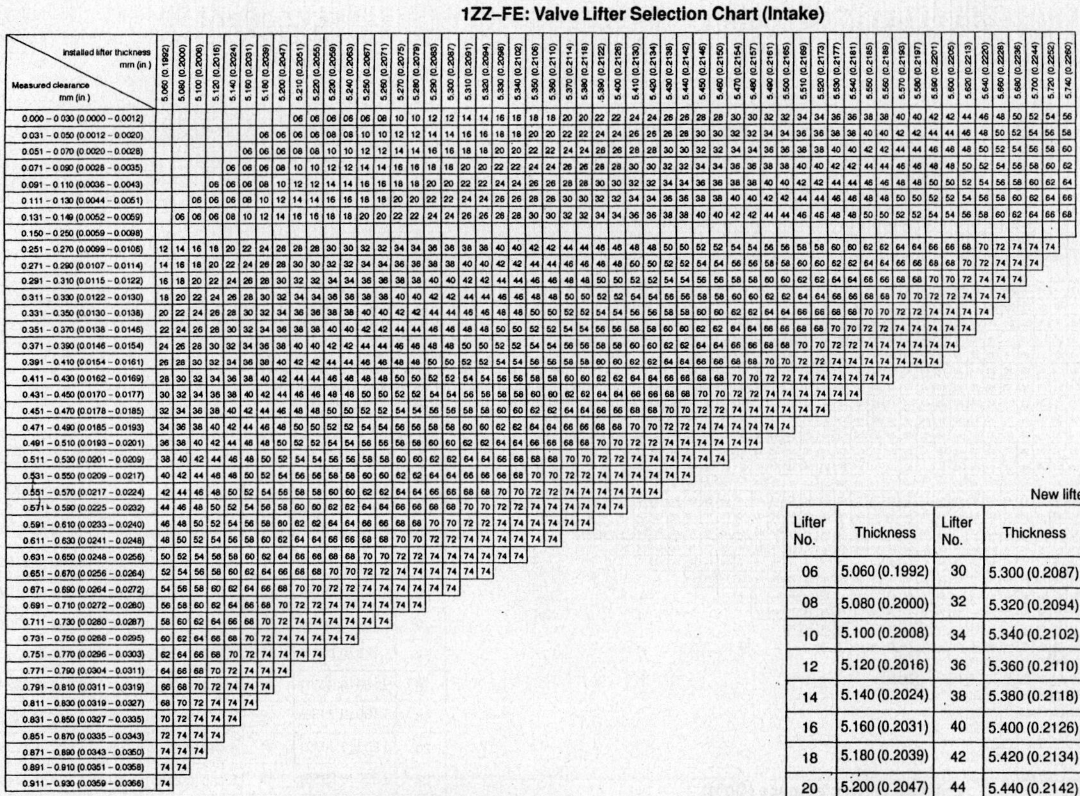

1ZZ–FE: Valve Lifter Selection Chart (Intake)

Installed lifter thickness column headers (mm (in)): 5.060 (0.1992), 5.080 (0.2000), 5.100 (0.2008), 5.120 (0.2016), 5.140 (0.2024), 5.160 (0.2031), 5.180 (0.2039), 5.200 (0.2047), 5.210 (0.2051), 5.220 (0.2055), 5.230 (0.2059), 5.240 (0.2063), 5.260 (0.2071), 5.270 (0.2075), 5.280 (0.2079), 5.290 (0.2083), 5.300 (0.2087), 5.310 (0.2091), 5.320 (0.2094), 5.340 (0.2102), 5.360 (0.2106), 5.370 (0.2110), 5.380 (0.2114), 5.390 (0.2118), 5.400 (0.2122), 5.410 (0.2126), 5.420 (0.2130), 5.430 (0.2134), 5.440 (0.2138), 5.460 (0.2142), 5.470 (0.2146), 5.480 (0.2150), 5.490 (0.2154), 5.500 (0.2157), 5.510 (0.2161), 5.520 (0.2169), 5.540 (0.2173), 5.550 (0.2177), 5.560 (0.2181), 5.570 (0.2189), 5.580 (0.2193), 5.600 (0.2197), 5.620 (0.2201), 5.640 (0.2205), 5.660 (0.2213), 5.680 (0.2220), 5.700 (0.2228), 5.720 (0.2236), 5.740 (0.2252), 5.740 (0.2260)

Measured clearance rows (mm (in)): 0.000 – 0.030 (0.0000 – 0.0012), 0.031 – 0.050 (0.0012 – 0.0020), 0.051 – 0.070 (0.0020 – 0.0028), 0.071 – 0.090 (0.0028 – 0.0035), 0.091 – 0.110 (0.0036 – 0.0043), 0.111 – 0.130 (0.0044 – 0.0051), 0.131 – 0.149 (0.0052 – 0.0059), 0.150 – 0.250 (0.0059 – 0.0098), 0.251 – 0.270 (0.0099 – 0.0106), 0.271 – 0.290 (0.0107 – 0.0114), 0.291 – 0.310 (0.0115 – 0.0122), 0.311 – 0.330 (0.0122 – 0.0130), 0.331 – 0.350 (0.0130 – 0.0138), 0.351 – 0.370 (0.0138 – 0.0146), 0.371 – 0.390 (0.0146 – 0.0154), 0.391 – 0.410 (0.0154 – 0.0161), 0.411 – 0.430 (0.0162 – 0.0169), 0.431 – 0.450 (0.0170 – 0.0177), 0.451 – 0.470 (0.0178 – 0.0185), 0.471 – 0.490 (0.0185 – 0.0193), 0.491 – 0.510 (0.0193 – 0.0201), 0.511 – 0.530 (0.0201 – 0.0209), 0.531 – 0.550 (0.0209 – 0.0217), 0.551 – 0.570 (0.0217 – 0.0224), 0.571 – 0.590 (0.0225 – 0.0232), 0.591 – 0.610 (0.0233 – 0.0240), 0.611 – 0.630 (0.0241 – 0.0248), 0.631 – 0.650 (0.0248 – 0.0256), 0.651 – 0.670 (0.0256 – 0.0264), 0.671 – 0.690 (0.0264 – 0.0272), 0.691 – 0.710 (0.0272 – 0.0280), 0.711 – 0.730 (0.0280 – 0.0287), 0.731 – 0.750 (0.0288 – 0.0295), 0.751 – 0.770 (0.0296 – 0.0303), 0.771 – 0.790 (0.0304 – 0.0311), 0.791 – 0.810 (0.0311 – 0.0319), 0.811 – 0.830 (0.0319 – 0.0327), 0.831 – 0.850 (0.0327 – 0.0335), 0.851 – 0.870 (0.0335 – 0.0343), 0.871 – 0.890 (0.0343 – 0.0350), 0.891 – 0.910 (0.0351 – 0.0358), 0.911 – 0.930 (0.0359 – 0.0366)

New lifter thickness   mm (in.)

Lifter No.	Thickness	Lifter No.	Thickness	Lifter No.	Thickness
06	5.060 (0.1992)	30	5.300 (0.2087)	54	5.540 (0.2181)
08	5.080 (0.2000)	32	5.320 (0.2094)	56	5.560 (0.2189)
10	5.100 (0.2008)	34	5.340 (0.2102)	58	5.580 (0.2197)
12	5.120 (0.2016)	36	5.360 (0.2110)	60	5.600 (0.2205)
14	5.140 (0.2024)	38	5.380 (0.2118)	62	5.620 (0.2213)
16	5.160 (0.2031)	40	5.400 (0.2126)	64	5.640 (0.2220)
18	5.180 (0.2039)	42	5.420 (0.2134)	66	5.660 (0.2228)
20	5.200 (0.2047)	44	5.440 (0.2142)	68	5.680 (0.2236)
22	5.220 (0.2055)	46	5.460 (0.2150)	70	5.700 (0.2244)
24	5.240 (0.2063)	48	5.480 (0.2157)	72	5.720 (0.2252)
26	5.260 (0.2071)	50	5.500 (0.2165)	74	5.740 (0.2260)
28	5.280 (0.2079)	52	5.520 (0.2173)		

Intake valve clearance (Cold):
0.15 – 0.25 mm (0.006 – 0.010 in.)
EXAMPLE: The 5.250 mm (0.2067 in.) lifter is installed, and the measured clearance is 0.400 mm (0.0157 in.).
Replace the 5.250 mm (0.2067 in.) lifter with a new No. 48 lifter.

9307WG70

Fig. 117 Adjusting shim chart (intake)—1ZZ-FE engine

- Ignition coil
- Positive Crankcase Ventilation (PCV) hoses
- Cylinder head cover sub-assembly

3. Set the No. 1 cylinder to Top Dead Center (TDC) of the compressor stroke as follows:

a. Turn the crankshaft pulley, and align its groove with the "0" timing mark of the timing chain cover.

b. Make sure the point marks of the camshaft timing sprockets and VVT timing sprockets are in a straight line as shown. If not, turn the crankshaft 1 complete revolution (360°) and align the marks.

4. Check the valve clearance of the first set of the valves shown:

c. Use a feeler gauge to measure the clearance between the valve lifter and camshaft. The clearance of the intake valves should be 0.0059–0.0098 in. (0.15–0.25mm). The clearance of the exhaust valves should be 0.0098–0.0138 in. (0.25–0.35mm).

d. Note the out-of-specification valve clearance measurements. You will need them later to determine the required replacement valve lifter.

e. Turn the crankshaft 1 revolution (360°) to set the No. 4 cylinder to TDC.

5. Check the valve clearance of the second set of the valves shown:

f. Use a feeler gauge to measure the clearance between the valve lifter and camshaft. The clearance of the intake valves should be 0.0059–0.0098 in. (0.15–0.25mm). The clearance of the exhaust valves should be 0.0098–0.0138 in. (0.25–0.35mm).

g. Note the out-of-specification valve clearance measurements. You will need them later to determine the required replacement valve lifter.

6. Remove or disconnect the following:
- Drive belt
- Right side engine mount
- Drive belt tensioner

✽✽ WARNING

DO NOT turn the crankshaft while the tensioner is removed!

7. Set the No. 1 cylinder to TDC of the compression stroke.
- Camshafts
- Valve lifters.

8. Use a micrometer to measure the thickness of the used lifter. Calculate the thickness of a new lifter. so the valve clearance comes within the specified value:

a. A: Thickness of new lifter.

b. B: Thickness of used lifter.

c. C: Measured valve clearance.

d. Intake valve clearance: $A = B + (C - 0.0079\ \text{in. (0.20mm)})$.

1ZZ–FE: Valve Lifter Selection Chart (Exhaust)

Installed lifter thickness mm (in.)

Measured clearance mm (in.):

Measured clearance mm (in.)
0.000 – 0.030 (0.0000 – 0.0012)
0.031 – 0.050 (0.0012 – 0.0020)
0.051 – 0.070 (0.0020 – 0.0026)
0.071 – 0.090 (0.0028 – 0.0035)
0.091 – 0.110 (0.0036 – 0.0043)
0.111 – 0.130 (0.0044 – 0.0051)
0.131 – 0.150 (0.0052 – 0.0059)
0.151 – 0.170 (0.0059 – 0.0067)
0.171 – 0.190 (0.0067 – 0.0075)
0.191 – 0.210 (0.0075 – 0.0083)
0.211 – 0.230 (0.0083 – 0.0091)
0.231 – 0.249 (0.0091 – 0.0098)
0.250 – 0.350 (0.0098 – 0.0138)
0.351 – 0.370 (0.0138 – 0.0146)
0.371 – 0.390 (0.0146 – 0.0154)
0.391 – 0.410 (0.0154 – 0.0161)
0.411 – 0.430 (0.0162 – 0.0169)
0.431 – 0.450 (0.0170 – 0.0177)
0.451 – 0.470 (0.0178 – 0.0185)
0.471 – 0.490 (0.0185 – 0.0193)
0.491 – 0.510 (0.0193 – 0.0201)
0.511 – 0.530 (0.0201 – 0.0209)
0.531 – 0.550 (0.0209 – 0.0217)
0.551 – 0.570 (0.0217 – 0.0224)
0.571 – 0.590 (0.0225 – 0.0232)
0.591 – 0.610 (0.0233 – 0.0240)
0.611 – 0.630 (0.0241 – 0.0248)
0.631 – 0.650 (0.0248 – 0.0256)
0.651 – 0.670 (0.0256 – 0.0264)
0.671 – 0.690 (0.0264 – 0.0272)
0.691 – 0.710 (0.0272 – 0.0280)
0.711 – 0.730 (0.0280 – 0.0287)
0.731 – 0.750 (0.0288 – 0.0295)
0.751 – 0.770 (0.0296 – 0.0303)
0.771 – 0.790 (0.0304 – 0.0311)
0.791 – 0.810 (0.0311 – 0.0319)
0.811 – 0.830 (0.0319 – 0.0327)
0.831 – 0.850 (0.0327 – 0.0335)
0.851 – 0.870 (0.0335 – 0.0343)
0.871 – 0.890 (0.0343 – 0.0350)
0.891 – 0.910 (0.0351 – 0.0358)
0.911 – 0.930 (0.0359 – 0.0366)
0.931 – 0.950 (0.0367 – 0.0374)
0.951 – 0.970 (0.0374 – 0.0382)
0.971 – 0.990 (0.0382 – 0.0390)
0.991 – 1.010 (0.0390 – 0.0398)
1.011 – 1.030 (0.0398 – 0.0406)

New lifter thickness mm (in.)

Lifter No.	Thickness	Lifter No.	Thickness	Lifter No.	Thickness
06	5.060 (0.1992)	30	5.300 (0.2087)	54	5.540 (0.2181)
08	5.080 (0.2000)	32	5.320 (0.2094)	56	5.560 (0.2189)
10	5.100 (0.2008)	34	5.340 (0.2102)	58	5.580 (0.2197)
12	5.120 (0.2016)	36	5.360 (0.2110)	60	5.600 (0.2205)
14	5.140 (0.2024)	38	5.380 (0.2118)	62	5.620 (0.2213)
16	5.160 (0.2031)	40	5.400 (0.2126)	64	5.640 (0.2220)
18	5.180 (0.2039)	42	5.420 (0.2134)	66	5.660 (0.2228)
20	5.200 (0.2047)	44	5.440 (0.2142)	68	5.680 (0.2236)
22	5.220 (0.2055)	46	5.460 (0.2150)	70	5.700 (0.2244)
24	5.240 (0.2063)	48	5.480 (0.2157)	72	5.720 (0.2252)
26	5.260 (0.2071)	50	5.500 (0.2165)	74	5.740 (0.2260)
28	5.280 (0.2079)	52	5.520 (0.2173)		

Exhaust valve clearance (Cold):
0.25 – 0.35 mm (0.010 – 0.014 in.)
EXAMPLE: The 5.340 mm (0.2102 in.) lifter is installed, and the measured clearance is 0.440 mm (0.0173 in.).
Replace the 5.340 mm (0.2102 in.) lifter with a new No. 48 lifter.

9307WG71

Fig. 118 Adjusting shim chart (exhaust)—1ZZ-FE engine

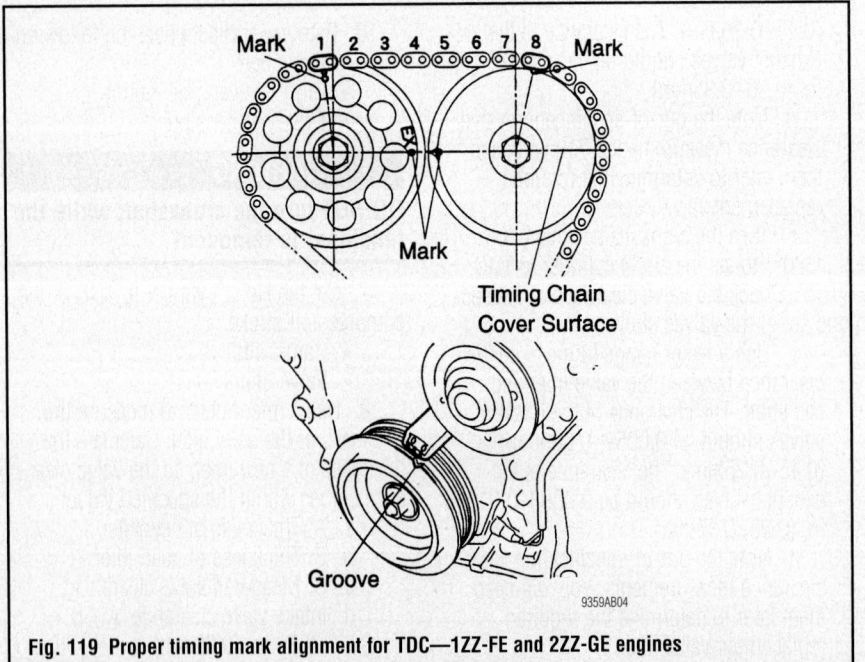

Mark 1 2 3 4 5 6 7 8 Mark

Mark

Timing Chain Cover Surface

Groove

9359AB04

Fig. 119 Proper timing mark alignment for TDC—1ZZ-FE and 2ZZ-GE engines

e. Exhaust valve clearance: $A = B + (C - 0.0118$ in. (0.30mm).

f. Select a new lifter with a thickness as close as possible to the calculated values. Lifters come in 35 sizes in increments of 0.0008 in. (0.020mm) from 0.1992–0.2260 in (5.060–5.740mm).

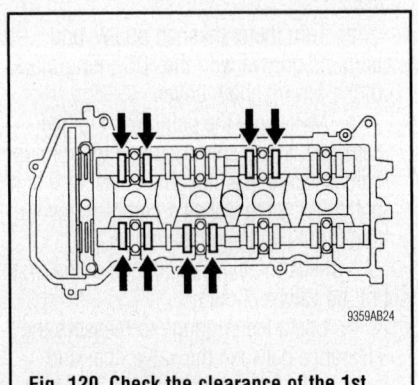

9359AB24

Fig. 120 Check the clearance of the 1st set of valves–1ZZ-FE engine

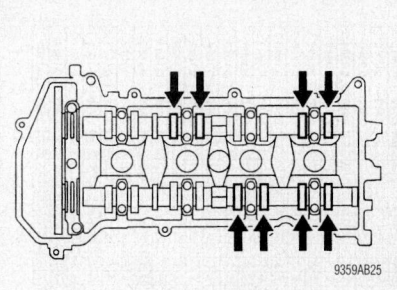

Fig. 121 Check the clearance of the 2nd set of valves–1ZZ-FE engine

9. Install or connect the following:
- Camshafts
- Drive belt tensioner
- Right hand engine mount
- Cylinder head (valve) cover sub-assembly
- Ignition coil
- Engine wire
- Cylinder head (valve) cover
- Negative battery cable

2ZZ-GE Engine

See Figures 122 through 128.

→**Adjust the valve clearance when the engine is cold.**

1. Before servicing the vehicle, refer to the precautions section.
2. Remove or disconnect the following:
- Negative battery cable.
- Right side engine under cover
- Cylinder head cover
- Ignition coil assembly
- Wire harness clamp
- Suction hose sub-assembly
- Cylinder head cover sub-assembly
- Drive belt
- Right side engine mount

3. Set the No. 1 cylinder to Top Dead Center (TDC) of the compressor stroke as follows:

a. Turn the crankshaft pulley, and align its groove with the "0" timing mark of the timing chain cover.

b. Make sure the point marks of the camshaft timing sprockets and VVT timing sprockets are in a straight line as shown. If not, turn the crankshaft 1 complete revolution (360°) and align the marks.

4. Check the valve clearance of the first set of the valves shown:

c. Use a feeler gauge to measure the clearance between the valve lifter and camshaft. The clearance of the intake valves should be 0.0031–0.0071 in. (0.08–0.18mm). The clearance of the exhaust valves should be 0.0087–0.0126 in. (0.22–0.32mm).

d. Note the out-of-specification valve clearance measurements. You will need them later to determine the required replacement valve lifter.

e. Turn the crankshaft 1 revolution (360°) to set the No. 4 cylinder to TDC.

5. Check the valve clearance of the second set of the valves shown:

f. Use a feeler gauge to measure the clearance between the valve lifter and camshaft. The clearance of the intake valves should be 0.0031–0.0071 in. (0.08–0.18mm). The clearance of the exhaust valves should be 0.0087–0.0126 in. (0.22–0.32mm).

g. Note the out-of-specification valve clearance measurements. You will need them later to determine the required replacement valve lifter.

6. To adjust the intake valve clearance:

a. Set the SST. Turn the crankshaft so the related rocker arm, where the valve clearance is adjusted, is fully pushed down.

→**Remove the spark plug and take off the compression.**

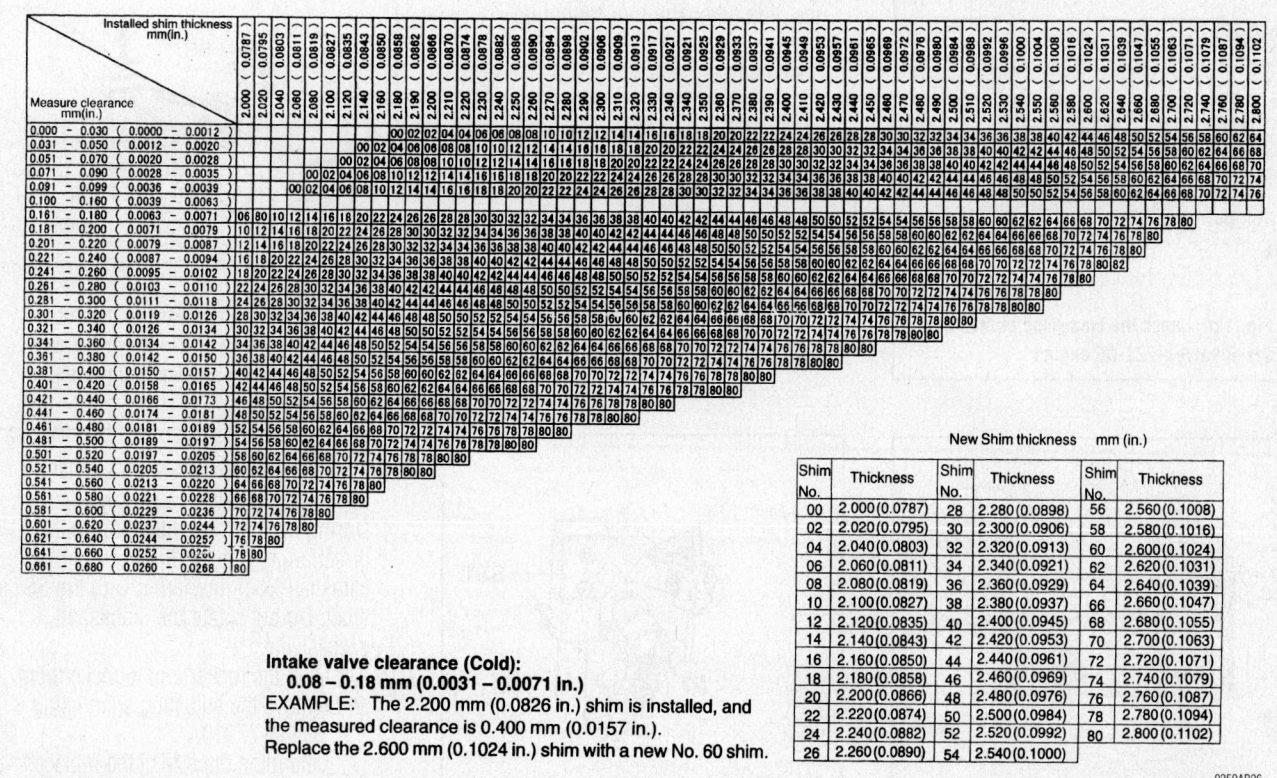

Intake valve clearance (Cold):
0.08 – 0.18 mm (0.0031 – 0.0071 in.)
EXAMPLE: The 2.200 mm (0.0826 in.) shim is installed, and the measured clearance is 0.400 mm (0.0157 in.).
Replace the 2.600 mm (0.1024 in.) shim with a new No. 60 shim.

New Shim thickness   mm (in.)

Shim No.	Thickness	Shim No.	Thickness	Shim No.	Thickness
00	2.000 (0.0787)	28	2.280 (0.0898)	56	2.560 (0.1008)
02	2.020 (0.0795)	30	2.300 (0.0906)	58	2.580 (0.1016)
04	2.040 (0.0803)	32	2.320 (0.0913)	60	2.600 (0.1024)
06	2.060 (0.0811)	34	2.340 (0.0921)	62	2.620 (0.1031)
08	2.080 (0.0819)	36	2.360 (0.0929)	64	2.640 (0.1039)
10	2.100 (0.0827)	38	2.380 (0.0937)	66	2.660 (0.1047)
12	2.120 (0.0835)	40	2.400 (0.0945)	68	2.680 (0.1055)
14	2.140 (0.0843)	42	2.420 (0.0953)	70	2.700 (0.1063)
16	2.160 (0.0850)	44	2.440 (0.0961)	72	2.720 (0.1071)
18	2.180 (0.0858)	46	2.460 (0.0969)	74	2.740 (0.1079)
20	2.200 (0.0866)	48	2.480 (0.0976)	76	2.760 (0.1087)
22	2.220 (0.0874)	50	2.500 (0.0984)	78	2.780 (0.1094)
24	2.240 (0.0882)	52	2.520 (0.0992)	80	2.800 (0.1102)
26	2.260 (0.0890)	54	2.540 (0.1000)		

Fig. 122 Adjusting shim chart (intake)—2ZZ-GE engine

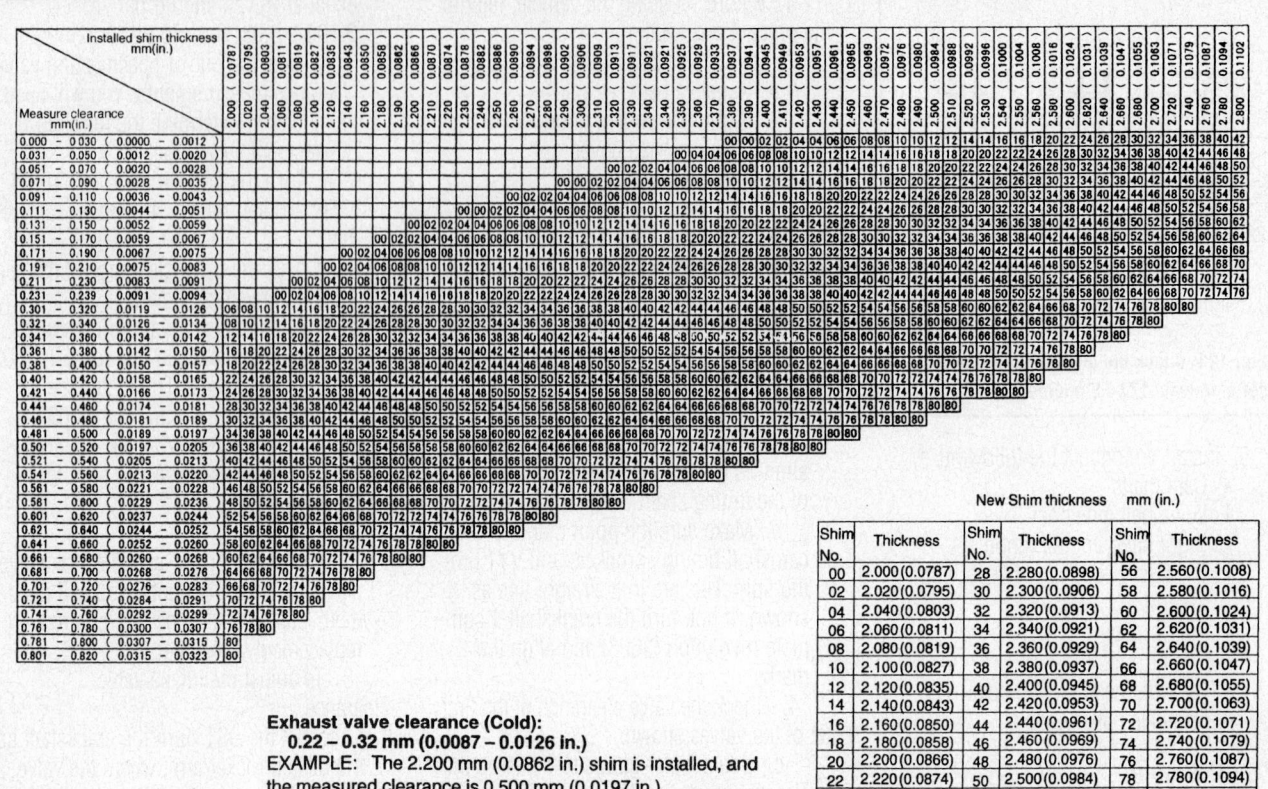

Exhaust valve clearance (Cold):
0.22 – 0.32 mm (0.0087 – 0.0126 in.)
EXAMPLE: The 2.200 mm (0.0862 in.) shim is installed, and the measured clearance is 0.500 mm (0.0197 in.). Replace the 2.540 mm (0.1000 in.) shim with a new No. 54 shim.

New Shim thickness   mm (in.)

Shim No.	Thickness	Shim No.	Thickness	Shim No.	Thickness
00	2.000(0.0787)	28	2.280(0.0898)	56	2.560(0.1008)
02	2.020(0.0795)	30	2.300(0.0906)	58	2.580(0.1016)
04	2.040(0.0803)	32	2.320(0.0913)	60	2.600(0.1024)
06	2.060(0.0811)	34	2.340(0.0921)	62	2.620(0.1031)
08	2.080(0.0819)	36	2.360(0.0929)	64	2.640(0.1039)
10	2.100(0.0827)	38	2.380(0.0937)	66	2.660(0.1047)
12	2.120(0.0835)	40	2.400(0.0945)	68	2.680(0.1055)
14	2.140(0.0843)	42	2.420(0.0953)	70	2.700(0.1063)
16	2.160(0.0850)	44	2.440(0.0961)	72	2.720(0.1071)
18	2.180(0.0858)	46	2.460(0.0969)	74	2.740(0.1079)
20	2.200(0.0866)	48	2.480(0.0976)	76	2.760(0.1087)
22	2.220(0.0874)	50	2.500(0.0984)	78	2.780(0.1094)
24	2.240(0.0882)	52	2.520(0.0992)	80	2.800(0.1102)
26	2.260(0.0890)	54	2.540(0.1000)		

Fig. 123 Adjusting shim chart (exhaust)—2ZZ-GE engine

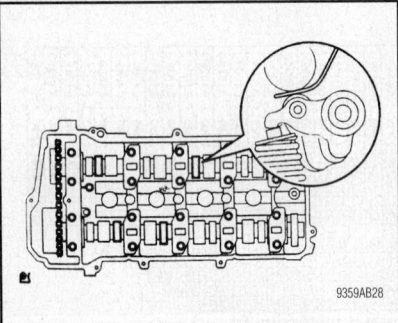

Fig. 124 Check the clearance of the 1st set of valves–2ZZ-GE engine

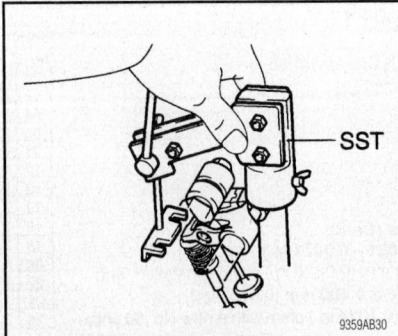

Fig. 126 Insert the special tool into the plug tube—2ZZ-GE

Fig. 125 Check the clearance of the 2nd set of valves–2ZZ-GE engine

b. Insert SST 09248-77010 into the plug tube. The tool cannot be inserted unless the set screw is loosened.

c. Operate the lever so that the SST's seat surface comes to contact with the valve retainer and lock them with the set screw. Clearance between the valve retainer and SST's set surface is not allowed. Be careful not to make clearance when inserting the SST, since clearance may unlock the keeper.

d. Lock the set screw on the tube side of the SST.

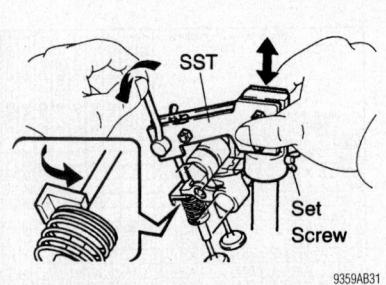

Fig. 127 Operate the lever so that the SST's seat surface comes to contact with the valve retainer and lock them with the set screw

e. Rotate the crankshaft so that the camshaft is position as shown. During rotation, pay attention to the direction, to prevent the nose of the camshaft from interfering with the SST's shaft. Do not rotate the crankshaft excessively.

f. Lift the rocker arm to make room and remove the adjusting shim using SST 09248-77010.

7. Determine the size of the replaced shim according to the chart or the following formula:

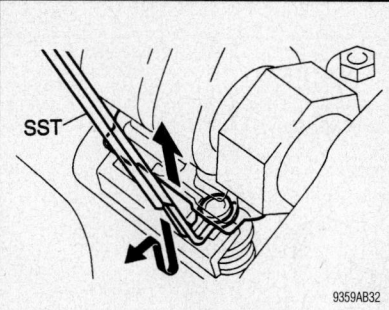

Fig. 128 Setting the tool from the right side, makes shim removal easier—2ZZ-GE

a. Use a dial indicator to measure the thickness of the removed shim.

b. Calculate the thickness of a new shim so that the valve clearance comes within the specified value.

c. A: Thickness of new shim.

d. B: Thickness of used shim.

e. C: Measured valve clearance.

f. Intake: A = B + (C - 0.005 in. [0.13mm])

g. Exhaust: A = B + (C - 0.011 in. [0.27mm])

h. Select a new shim with a thickness as close as possible to the calculated values. Shims come in 41 sizes in incre-ments of 0.0008 in. (0.020mm) from 0.0787–0.1102 in (2.0–2.8mm).

8. Lift the rocker arm to make room, then install the adjusting shim using the SST. To remove the tool from the shim, push down on the rocker arm.

9. Turn the crankshaft so the related rocker arm, where the valve clearance is adjusted, is fully pushed down.

10. Loosen the 2 set-screws, then remove the SST.

11. Install all components in the reverse of the removal procedure.

ENGINE PERFORMANCE & EMISSION CONTROL

COMPONENT LOCATIONS

See Figures 129 through 131.

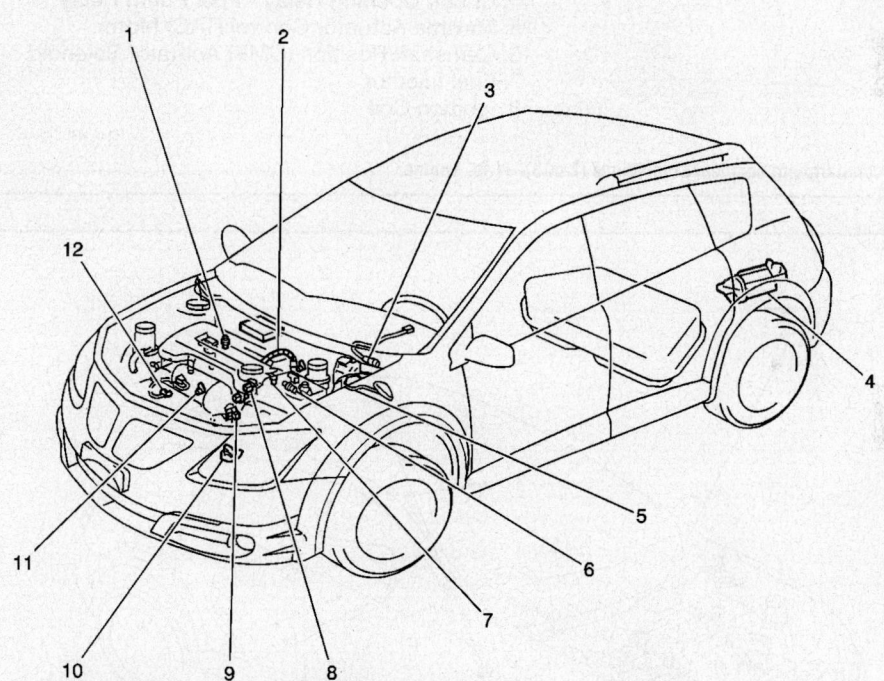

1. Power Steering Pressure Switch
2. Heated Oxygen Sensor 1 - HO2S 1
3. Heated Oxygen Sensor 2- HO2S 2
4. EVAP Vacuum Leak Pump Assembly, includes Fuel Tank Pressure (FTP) Sensor
5. Accelerator Pedal Position (APP) Sensor
6. Engine Coolant Temperature (ECT) Sensor
7. Mass Air Flow (MAF) Sensor
8. Camshaft Position (CMP) Sensor
9. Throttle Actuator Control (TAC) Module, includes TP Sensor 1 and TP Sensor 2
10. PNP Switch, Automatic Transmission only
11. Knock (KS) Sensor
12. Crankshaft Position (CKP) Sensor

22116_VIBE_G0013

Fig. 129 Vibe engine compartment component locations (1 of 3)—1.8L engine

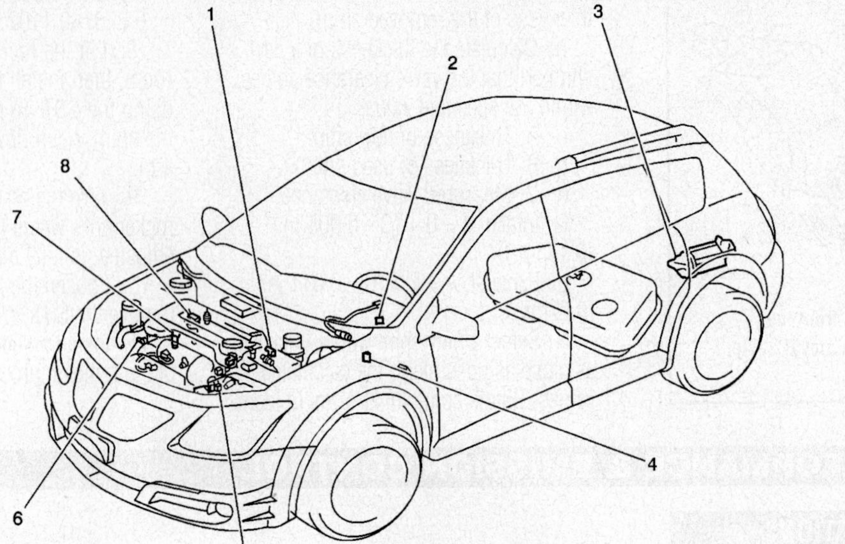

1. EVAP Purge Solenoid
2. Malfunction Indicator Lamp (MIL)
3. EVAP Vacuum Leak Pump Assembly,
   includes EVAP Vent Solenoid
4. Circuit Opening Relay - Fuel Pump Relay
5. Throttle Actuator Control (TAC) Motor
6. Camshaft Position (CMP) Actuator Solenoid
7. Fuel Injector
8. Ignition Coil

22116_VIBE_G0014

Fig. 130 Vibe engine compartment component locations (2 of 3)—1.8L engine

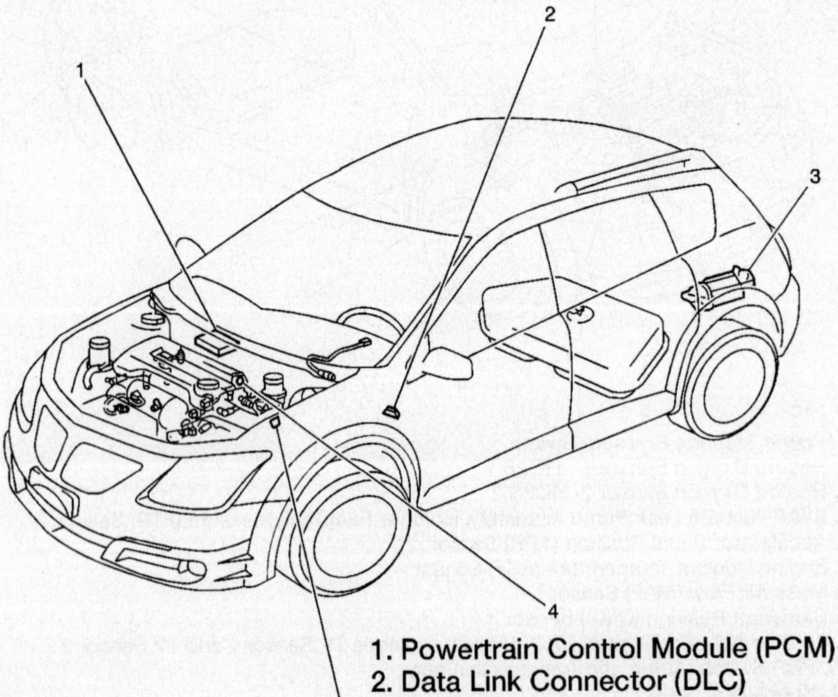

1. **Powertrain Control Module (PCM)**
2. **Data Link Connector (DLC)**
3. **EVAP Canister and Canister Air Filter**
4. **Noise Filter, for Ignition System**
5. **EFI Relay**

22116_VIBE_G0015

Fig. 131 Vibe engine compartment component locations (3 of 3)—1.8L engine

ACCELERATOR PEDAL POSITION (APP) SENSOR

LOCATION

The Accelerator Pedal Position (APP) sensor is attached to the pedal.

OPERATION

The sensor is made up of the two individual sensors within a single housing. Each sensor has a unique functionality to determine pedal position. The APP system along with the Powertrain Control Module (PCM) is used to calculate and control the amount of acceleration and deceleration through fuel injector control.

REMOVAL & INSTALLATION

1. Disconnect the Connector Position Assurance (CPA) from the Accelerator Pedal Position (APP) sensor connector.
2. Disconnect the APP sensor harness connector.
3. Remove the APP assembly attachment bolts from the pedal assembly.
4. Remove the APP assembly from the vehicle

To install:

5. Installation is the reverse of removal.

TESTING

See Figure 132.

1. Check the condition of the connector. Make sure the connector is firmly attached. Check for broken or bent connector pins. Repair any connector damage before continuing with troubleshooting the issue.
2. Check the condition of the wiring to the connector. If the wiring is damaged, repair the wiring before continuing with any further tests.
3. Turn OFF the ignition.
4. Disconnect the accelerator pedal connector.
5. Turn ON the ignition, with the engine OFF.
6. Measure the voltage of the APP sensor 5-volt reference voltage circuit to a good ground. The reading should be 5 volts. If not check the wiring for an open, short or high resistance.
7. Turn ON the ignition, with the engine OFF.
8. Measure the voltage between the APP sensor 5-volt reference voltage circuit and signal circuit. If the reading is 5 volts replace the sensor.

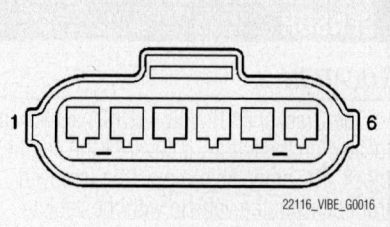

22116_VIBE_G0016

Fig. 132 Accelerator Pedal Position (APP) sensor terminals; (1) Low reference, (6) 5 volt reference

CAMSHAFT POSITION (CMP) ACTUATOR SOLENOID

LOCATION

The actuator is located underneath the engine cover below the fuel rail.

OPERATION

The Camshaft Position (CMP) actuator system enables the Powertrain Control Module (PCM) to change the intake camshaft timing while the engine is running. The CMP actuator solenoid controls the advance or retard of the camshaft. The CMP actuator solenoid is controlled by a pulse width modulated (PWM) signal from the PCM. The CMP sensor monitors the camshaft position or the camshaft angle, and compares that position or phase to the Crankshaft Position (CKP) sensor signal. The PCM determines whether the camshaft angle is correct by comparing the actual camshaft position to the target camshaft position. By continuously analyzing the input of the CMP sensor and the CKP sensor the PCM can detect a failure in the CMP actuator system.

REMOVAL & INSTALLATION

1. Remove the engine cover.
2. Disconnect the electrical connector from the CMP actuator solenoid valve.
3. Remove the fastener retaining the CMP actuator solenoid valve from the cylinder head.
4. Remove the CMP actuator solenoid valve and the O-ring from the cylinder head.

To install:

5. Installation is the reverse of removal. Make sure to use a new O-ring.

TESTING

See Figure 133.

1. Check the condition of the connector. Make sure the connector is firmly attached.

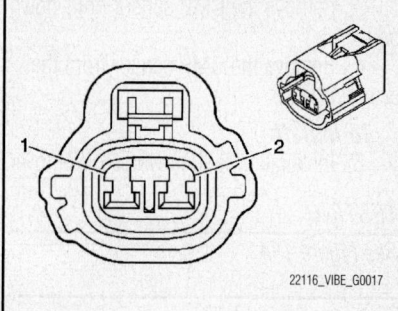

22116_VIBE_G0017

Fig. 133 Camshaft Position (CMP) actuator solenoid terminals; (1) CMP Actuator High Control, (2) CMP Actuator Low Control

Check for broken or bent connector pins. Repair any connector damage before continuing with troubleshooting the issue.

2. Check the condition of the wiring to the connector. If the wiring is damaged, repair the wiring before continuing with any further tests.
3. Turn OFF the ignition.
4. Remove the CMP actuator solenoid.
5. Connect the CMP actuator solenoid to B+ and to ground with a pair of fused jumper wires.
6. Observe the movement of the solenoid plunger when electrical power is applied and released.
7. The solenoid plunger must extend to at least 0.125 inches when voltage is applied and then retract when voltage is removed. If not, replace the actuator.

CAMSHAFT POSITION (CMP) SENSOR

LOCATION

The Camshaft Position (CMP) sensor is located on the front left of the engine. Refer to the illustration for further clarification.

OPERATION

The PCM uses the Camshaft Position (CMP) sensor to determine the position of the No. 1 piston during its power stroke. This signal is used by the PCM to calculate fuel injection mode of operation.

If the cam signal is lost while the engine is running, the fuel injection system will shift to a calculated fuel injected mode based on the last fuel injection pulse, and the engine will continue to run.

REMOVAL & INSTALLATION

1. Remove the engine cover from the engine.
2. Disconnect the CMP electrical connector.

3. Remove the CMP sensor hold-down bolt.

4. Remove the CMP sensor from the cylinder head.

To install:

5. Installation is the reverse of removal.

TESTING

See Figure 134.

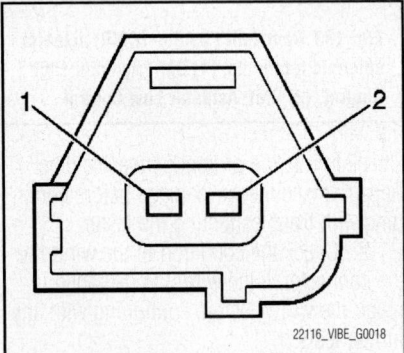

22116_VIBE_G0018

Fig. 134 Camshaft Position (CMP) sensor terminals; (1) Camshaft position input, (2) Sensor ground

1. Check the condition of the connector. Make sure the connector is firmly attached. Check for broken or bent connector pins. Repair any connector damage before continuing with troubleshooting the issue.

2. Check the condition of the wiring to the connector. If the wiring is damaged, repair the wiring before continuing with any further tests.

3. Visually inspect the CMP sensor reluctor ring for damage, repair as needed.

4. Measure the voltage from the 5-volt reference circuit of the CMP sensor to a good ground. The voltage should be 5 volts. If not check the wiring for an open or short.

5. Measure the resistance of the low reference circuit of the CMP sensor. The resistance should be 5 Ohms. If the resistance is not as specified, check the low reference circuit of the CMP sensor for an open or high resistance.

6. Measure the resistance of the 5-volt reference circuit of the CMP sensor The resistance should be 5 Ohms. If the resistance is not as specified, check the 5-volt reference circuit of the CMP sensor for an open or high resistance.

7. If there are no issues with the wiring and connectors, replace the sensor.

CRANKSHAFT POSITION (CKP) SENSOR

LOCATION

The Crankshaft Position (CKP) sensor is located on the left front cover of the engine block. The stone shield must be removed from beneath the vehicle with the vehicle raised to access the sensor.

OPERATION

The Crankshaft Position (CKP) sensor senses the crank angle (piston position) of each cylinder and converts it into a pulse signal. The PCM receives this signal and then computes the engine speed and controls the fuel injector timing and ignition timing based on this input.

REMOVAL & INSTALLATION

1. Raise the vehicle and remove the stone shield.

2. Disconnect the crankshaft position (CKP) sensor electrical connector.

3. Remove the CKP sensor bolt.

4. Remove the CKP sensor

To install:

5. Installation is the reverse of removal.

TESTING

See Figure 135.

1. Check the condition of the connector. Make sure the connector is firmly attached. Check for broken or bent connector pins. Repair any connector damage before continuing with troubleshooting the issue.

2. Check the condition of the wiring to the connector. If the wiring is damaged, repair the wiring before continuing with any further tests.

3. Remove the CKP sensor.

4. Inspect the CKP sensor for the following:

- Physical damage
- Excessive play or looseness
- Improper installation
- Foreign material passing between the CKP sensor and the reluctor wheel
- Electromagnetic interference in the CKP sensor circuits

5. Inspect the CKP reluctor wheel for the following:

- Physical damage
- Excessive play or looseness
- Improper installation

6. Turn OFF the ignition.

7. Disconnect the crankshaft position (CKP) sensor electrical connector.

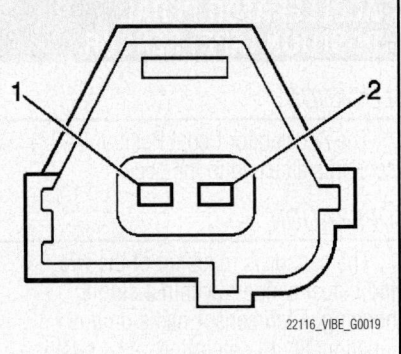

22116_VIBE_G0019

Fig. 135 Crankshaft Position (CKP) sensor terminals; (1) Crankshaft position input, (2) Sensor ground

8. Measure the resistance of the CKP sensor. The resistance should be 1,630-2,740 Ohms at -10 to +50°C (+14 to +122°F) or 2,065-3,225 ohms at 50-100°C (122-212°F). If not, replace the crankshaft position sensor.

9. Connect the CKP sensor electrical connector.

10. Disconnect the powertrain control module (PCM) electrical connector C1.

11. Connect the multimeter across the PCM harness connector C1 terminal 27 and terminal 34.

12. Observe the AC voltage while cranking the engine. The voltage should be 1.4–1.6 volts.

13. Connect the multimeter to terminal 27 of the PCM harness connector C1 and ground.

14. Observe the AC voltage while cranking the engine. If the voltage reads 1.4–1.6 volts, repair the open in the CKP ground circuit. If not, repair the open or short on the CKP input circuit.

15. If there are no issues with the wiring and connectors, replace the sensor.

ENGINE COOLANT TEMPERATURE (ECT) SENSOR

LOCATION

The Engine Coolant Temperature (ECT) sensor is located on the right side of the engine. Refer to the illustration for further clarification.

OPERATION

The Engine Coolant Temperature (ECT) sensor resistance changes in response to engine coolant temperature. The sensor resistance decreases as the coolant temperature increases, and increases as the coolant temperature decreases. This provides a reference signal to the PCM, which indicates engine coolant temperature. The signal sent to the PCM by the ECT sensor helps the PCM to determine spark advance, EGR flow rate, air/fuel ratio, and engine temperature. The ECT is a two wire sensor, a 5–volt reference signal is sent to the sensor and the signal return is based upon the change in the measured resistance due to temperature.

REMOVAL & INSTALLATION

See Figure 136.

> **❊❊ WARNING**
>
> **Use care when handling the engine coolant temperature (ECT) sensor. Damage to the ECT sensor will affect proper operation of the fuel injection system.**

1. Drain the engine coolant.
2. Disconnect the ECT sensor electrical connector from the ECT sensor located next to the upper radiator hose on the cylinder head.
3. Remove the ECT sensor from the cylinder head.

To install:

> **❊❊ WARNING**
>
> **Replacement components must be the correct part number for the application. Components requiring the use of the thread locking compound, lubricants, corrosion inhibitors, or sealants are identified in the service procedure. Some replacement components may come with these coatings already applied. Do not use these coatings on components unless**

specified. These coatings can affect the final torque, which may affect the operation of the component. Use the correct torque specification when installing components in order to avoid damage.

4. Install the ECT sensor into cylinder head. Tighten the ECT sensor to 14 ft. lbs. (20 Nm).
5. Connect the ECT sensor electrical connector.
6. Refill the engine coolant.

TESTING

See Figure 137.

1. Before servicing the vehicle, refer to the precautions section.
2. Drain and recycle the engine coolant.
3. Remove the coolant temperature sensor.
4. Place the sensor in a container of water with a temperature approximately 20 degrees C (68 F).
5. Using an ohmmeter, check resistance between the terminals. The resistance should be 2.32–2.59 Kohms.
6. Raise the temperature of the container of water to approximately 80 degrees C (176F).
7. Using an ohmmeter, check resistance between the terminals. The resistance should be 0.310–0.326 Kohms.

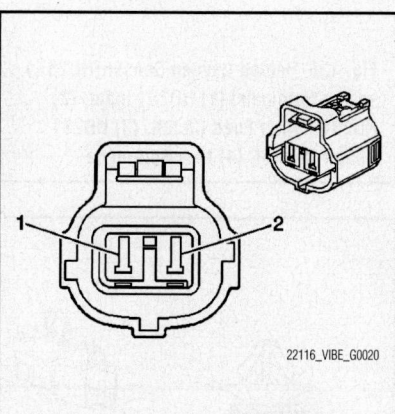

Fig. 137 Engine Coolant Temperature (ECT) sensor terminals; (1) Sensor ground, (2) ECT input

HEATED OXYGEN (HO2S) SENSOR

LOCATION

The two Heated Oxygen Sensors (HO2S) are located on different parts of the vehicle.

Refer to the illustration for further clarification.

OPERATION

The Heated Oxygen Sensor (HO2S) is a device which produces an electrical voltage when exposed to the oxygen present in the exhaust gases. The oxygen sensors are electrically heated internally for faster switching when the engine is started cold. The oxygen sensor produces a voltage within 0 and 1 volt. When there is a large amount of oxygen present (lean mixture), the sensor produces a low voltage (less than 0.4v). When there is a lesser amount present (rich mixture) it produces a higher voltage (0.6–1.0v). The stoichiometric or correct fuel to air ratio will read between 0.4 and 0.6v. By monitoring the oxygen content and converting it to electrical voltage, the sensor acts as a rich–lean switch. The voltage is transmitted to the PCM.

Two sensors per bank are used, one before the catalyst and one after. This is done for a catalyst efficiency monitor that is a part of the diagnostic system of the engine controls. The one before the catalyst measures the exhaust emissions right out of the engine, and sends the signal to the PCM about the state of the mixture as previously talked about. The second sensor reports the difference in the emissions after the exhaust gases have gone through the catalyst. This sensor reports to the PCM the amount of emissions reduction the catalyst is performing.

The oxygen sensor will not work until a predetermined temperature is reached, until this time the PCM is running in what is known as open loop operation. Open loop means that the PCM has not yet begun to correct the air–to–fuel ratio by reading the oxygen sensor. After the engine comes to operating temperature, the PCM will monitor the oxygen sensor and correct the air/fuel ratio from the sensor's readings. This is what is known as closed loop operation.

REMOVAL & INSTALLATION

Front

1. Remove the engine cover.
2. Note the routing of the Heated Oxygen Sensor (HO2S) electrical harness.
3. Disconnect the HO2S electrical connector.
4. Using a suitable Oxygen sensor socket remove the sensor.

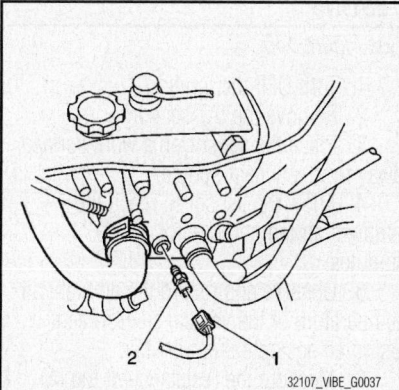

Fig. 136 Disconnect the ECT sensor electrical connector (1) from the ECT sensor (2) located next to the upper radiator hose on the cylinder head. Remove the ECT sensor from the cylinder head.

To install:

➡ **A special anti-seize compound is used on the HO2S threads. The compound consists of a liquid graphite and glass beads. The graphite will burn away but the glass beads will remain, making the sensor easier to remove. New or service sensors already have the compound applied to the threads. If the sensor is removed and is to be reinstalled, the threads must be coated with an anti-seize compound before reinstallation.**

5. If reinstalling the old HO2S, coat the threads with anti-seize compound.

6. Carefully install the HO2S to the pipe. Tighten the sensor to 32 ft. lbs. (44 Nm).

7. Attach the sensor electrical connections.

Rear

1. Remove the carpet retaining pin from the front floor console.

2. Pull back the carpet from the area near the front floor console.

3. Note the routing of the Heated Oxygen Sensor (HO2S) electrical harness.

4. Disconnect the HO2S electrical connector.

5. Using a suitable Oxygen sensor socket remove the sensor from below the vehicle.

To install:

➡ **A special anti-seize compound is used on the HO2S threads. The compound consists of a liquid graphite and glass beads. The graphite will burn away but the glass beads will remain, making the sensor easier to remove. New or service sensors already have the compound applied to the threads. If the sensor is removed and is to be reinstalled, the threads must be coated with an anti-seize compound before reinstallation.**

6. If reinstalling the old HO2S, coat the threads with anti-seize compound.

7. Carefully install the HO2S to the pipe. Tighten the sensor to 32 ft. lbs. (44 Nm).

8. Attach the sensor electrical connections.

TESTING

See Figures 138 and 139.

1. Turn OFF the ignition.

2. Disconnect the HO2S connector.

3. Measure the resistance of the HO2S, between the heater control and the

ignition voltage circuits. If the resistance is not 1.8-3.4 ohms at 20°C (68°F), replace the sensor.

4. Turn ON the ignition, with the engine OFF.

5. Probe the ignition voltage circuit of the HO2S with a test lamp connected to a good ground. If the lamp does not illuminate, check the wiring circuit, for an open, short or high resistance.

6. Connect the HO2S.

7. Using a test lamp connected to a good ground, backprobe the HO2S heater control circuit at the powertrain control module (PCM) connector.

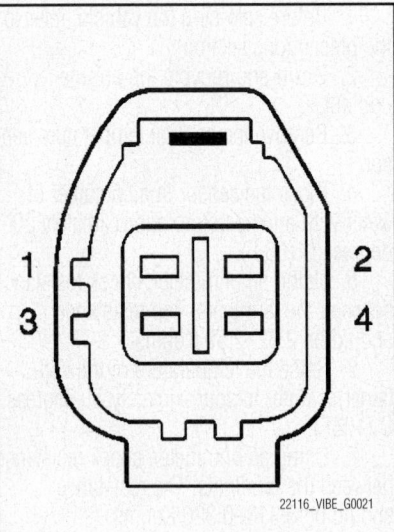

Fig. 138 Heated Oxygen Sensor (HO2S) 1 sensor terminals; (1) HO2S1 Input, (2) HO2S1 Heater Feed Circuit, (3) HO2S1 Heater Control, (4) Low Reference

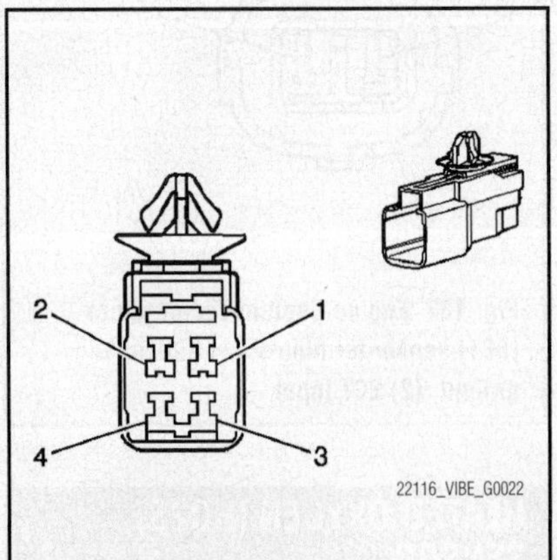

Fig. 139 Heated Oxygen Sensor (HO2S) 2 sensor terminals; (1) HO2S2 Feed Circuit, (2) HO2S2 Heater Control, (3) Ground, (4) HO2S2 Heater Control

8. Turn ON the ignition, with the engine OFF. If the test lamp does not illuminate, check the heater control circuit of the HO2S for an open or a high resistance.

9. If there are no issues with the wiring and connectors, replace the sensor.

INTAKE AIR TEMPERATURE (IAT) SENSOR

LOCATION

The Intake Air temperature (IAT) sensor is an integral part of The Mass air Flow (MAF) sensor located on the air cleaner housing. Refer to the component location illustration for further clarification.

OPERATION

IAT sensor is a thermistor that is an integral part of the mass air flow (MAF) sensor. The electrical resistance of the IAT sensor is high when the air temperature is cold, and the resistance is low when the air temperature is warm. The IAT sensor is wired in series with a fixed resistor located in the powertrain control module (PCM). The PCM applies 5 volts to the IAT sensor. The PCM monitors the voltage across the IAT sensor and converts the voltage into a temperature reading. The voltage measured by the PCM will be high when the air temperature is cold, and low when the air temperature is warm.

REMOVAL & INSTALLATION

1. Refer to the Mass Air Flow (MAF) sensor replacement.

TESTING

See Figure 140.

1. Turn OFF the ignition.

2. Remove the IAT sensor.

3. Place the sensor on a work surface away from any heat source.

4. Allow the sensor to reach the ambient air temperature for 30-60 minutes.

5. Observe and record the ambient air temperature of the vehicle environment using an accurate thermometer.

6. Measure the resistance of the IAT sensor 2 and record the value.

7. Compare the resistance measurement of the IAT sensor to the ambient air temperature on the Temperature vs. Resistance chart illustration. If not within specification, replace the sensor.

Temperature Versus Resistance

°C	°F	OHMS
Temperature vs Resistance Values (Approximate)		
150	302	47
140	284	60
130	266	77
120	248	100
110	230	132
100	212	177
90	194	241
80	176	332
70	158	467
60	140	667
50	122	973
45	113	1188
40	104	1459
35	95	1802
30	86	2238
25	77	2796
20	68	3520
15	59	4450
10	50	5670
5	41	7280
0	32	9420
-5	23	12300
-10	14	16180
-15	5	21450
-20	-4	28680
-30	-22	52700
-40	-40	100700

22116_IION_G0041

Fig. 140 Temperature versus resistance chart

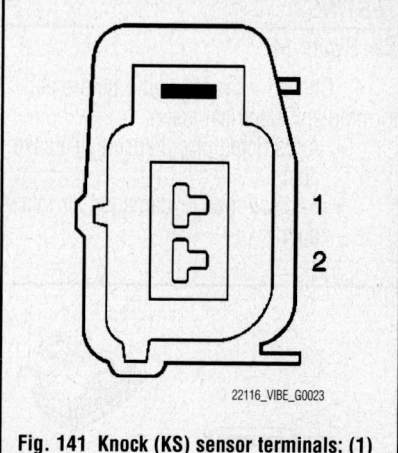

22116_VIBE_G0023

Fig. 141 Knock (KS) sensor terminals; (1) Knock sensor signal low, (2) Knock sensor signal high

9. Measure the resistance between the KS Signal High circuit and the KS Signal Low circuit. The resistance should be 200 KOhms at 68 degrees F (20 degrees C). if not, check the sensor connections.

10. If there are no issues with the wiring and connectors, replace the sensor.

MASS AIR FLOW (MAF) SENSOR

LOCATION

The Mass Air Flow (MAF) sensor located on the air cleaner housing. Refer to the illustration for further clarification.

OPERATION

The MAF sensor is a hot wire design. A platinum hot wire and a thermistor are located in the intake air bypass passage of the MAF sensor housing. The temperature of the platinum hot wire is affected by exposure to air flow and by exposure to air temperature. The platinum hot wire is maintained at a set temperature by controlling the current flow through the wire. The MAF sensor converts the changes in current flow to a voltage signal. The voltage signal from the MAF sensor enables the PCM to detect changes in air density and changes in air volume.

REMOVAL & INSTALLATION

1. Disconnect the electrical connector from the mass air flow (MAF) sensor.
2. Remove the two fasteners.
3. Remove the MAF sensor and O-ring from the air cleaner housing.

To install:
4. Installation is the reverse of removal. Use a new o-ring.

KNOCK SENSOR (KS)

LOCATION

The Knock Sensor (KS) is located on the engine block behind the starter.

OPERATION

The KS is non-resonant design that is constructed of a piezoelectric element which generates an AC signal when vibrated. Normal engine operation will cause the KS to generate signals of known frequencies. When engine knock is present, the KS frequency changes. This signals the powertrain control module (PCM) to retard ignition timing. The PCM sends a bias voltage of 5 volts to the KS on the KS Signal High circuit. The PCM expects approximately 2.5 volts back on the KS Signal Low circuit. The KS generated AC signal rides on top of the bias voltage provided by the PCM.

REMOVAL & INSTALLATION

1. Remove the starter.
2. Disconnect the Knock Sensor (KS) harness connector.
3. Remove the KS retaining bolt.
4. Remove the KS.

To install:
5. Installation is the reverse of removal.

TESTING

See Figure 141.

1. Turn OFF the ignition.
2. Disconnect the Knock Sensor (KS) electrical connector.
3. Turn ON the ignition, with the engine OFF.
4. Measure the voltage across the KS connector, harness side. The voltage should be 5 volts.
5. Measure the voltage from the KS Signal High circuit to a good ground. . The voltage should be 5 volts. If the voltage is less, check for an open in the signal low circuit. If the voltage is greater than 5 volts, check for an open or short in the signal high circuit.
6. Turn OFF the ignition.
7. Connect the KS electrical connector.
8. Disconnect the powertrain control module (PCM) electrical connector C2.

TESTING

See Figure 142.

1. Check for the following before performing any electrical tests:
- A restricted or collapsed air intake duct
- A misaligned or damaged air intake duct

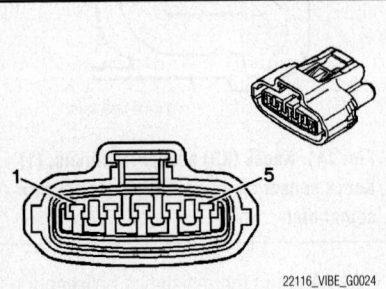

22116_VIBE_G0024

Fig. 142 Mass Air Flow (MAF) sensor terminals; (1) MAF Feed Circuit, (2) MAF Signal Low, (3) MAF Signal High, (4) IAT Sensor Input, (5) Sensor Ground

- Loose clamps on the air intake duct
- A dirty or deteriorating air filter element
- Water in the induction system
- Any objects blocking or restricting the air inlet probe of the MAF sensor
- Any contamination or debris on the sensing elements in the probe of the MAF sensor

2. Turn OFF the ignition.

3. Disconnect the mass air flow (MAF) sensor electrical connector.

4. Turn ON the ignition, with the engine OFF.

5. Probe the ignition positive voltage circuit with a test lamp connected to ground. If the test lamp does not illuminate, check the ignition positive voltage wiring for an open circuit.

6. Turn OFF the ignition.

7. Connect the MAF sensor electrical connector.

8. Turn ON the ignition, with the engine OFF.

9. Backprobe the MAF signal high circuit at the powertrain control module (PCM) with a meter connected to ground. The voltage should be 0.5–3 volts. If not check the circuit for an open or short to ground on the signal wire.

10. Remove the MAF sensor from the air cleaner housing. Continue to backprobe the MAF signal high circuit at the PCM.

11. Observe the voltage on the MAF signal high circuit while blowing gently into the MAF sensor orifice. The signal high circuit voltage increase when blowing air into the sensor orifice. If not check the wiring for open, short or high resistance.

12. If there are no issues with the wiring and connectors, replace the sensor.

POWERTRAIN CONTROL MODULE (PCM)

LOCATION

The PCM is located behind a close out panel below the instrument panel (I/P) glove box.

OPERATION

The Powertrain Control Module (PCM) performs many functions on your vehicle. The module accepts information from various sensors and computes the required fuel flow rate necessary to maintain the correct amount of air/fuel ratio throughout the entire engine operational range and controls the shifting of the transmission.

Based on the information that is received and programmed into the PCM's memory, the PCM generates output signals to control relays, actuators and solenoids. The module automatically senses and compensates for any changes in altitude when driving your vehicle.

REMOVAL & INSTALLATION

1. Disconnect the negative battery cable.

2. Remove the 2 retainers from the PCM close out panel below the instrument panel (I/P) glove box.

3. Swing the PCM close out panel down.

4. Open the I/P compartment.

5. Push in on both sides of the I/P compartment in order to release the safety catches.

6. Remove the I/P compartment door assembly from the I/P.

7. Remove the 2 PCM bracket fasteners.

8. Pull the PCM with brackets toward you and swing both down away from under the I/P.

9. Disconnect the four PCM electrical connectors.

10. Remove the four fasteners and the two brackets from the PCM.

➡ **Do not touch the connector pins or soldered components on the circuit board in order to prevent possible electrostatic discharge (ESD) damage to the PCM.**

➡ **Turn the ignition OFF when installing or removing the PCM connectors and disconnecting or reconnecting the power to the PCM (battery cable, PCM pigtail, PCM fuse, jumper cables, etc.) in order to prevent internal PCM damage.**

To install:

11. Installation is the reverse of removal.

12. Program the vehicle identification number (VIN) to the replacement PCM.

TESTING

1. Install a scan tool.

2. Clear the scan tool information.

3. Turn OFF the ignition, in order to initialize the powertrain control module (PCM).

4. Turn ON the ignition.

5. Wait 10 seconds and check for DTCs.

6. If DTC P0606 sets, check for a short to ground at the 5 volt reference circuit.

7. If DTC's P0601, P0604, P0607 or P2610 set, replace the PCM.

THROTTLE POSITION SENSOR (TPS)

LOCATION

1. The throttle position (TP) sensors are located within the throttle body assembly and if defective the throttle body assembly must be replaced. Refer to the illustration for further clarification.

OPERATION

The TP sensor used with the throttle actuator control (TAC) system is actually a Hall Effect switch. The Hall Effect switch is surrounded by a magnetic yoke that induces a flux in the magnetic field when the throttle shaft is rotated. The PCM provides a 5-volt reference voltage to the sensor circuits in the TAC module. An integrated circuit (IC) receives and converts the magnetic pulses into two separate TP signal, each with their own characteristics. Both TP sensor signal voltages are low at closed throttle and increase as the throttle opens. TP sensor 1 determines the actual throttle valve position. TP sensor 2 has a voltage that is more than twice that of TP sensor 1 at idle. TP sensor 2 provides a backup value for TP sensor 1.

REMOVAL & INSTALLATION

1ZZ-FE Engine

See Figures 143 through 146.

1. Remove the 2 nuts and the 2 retainers from the engine cover.

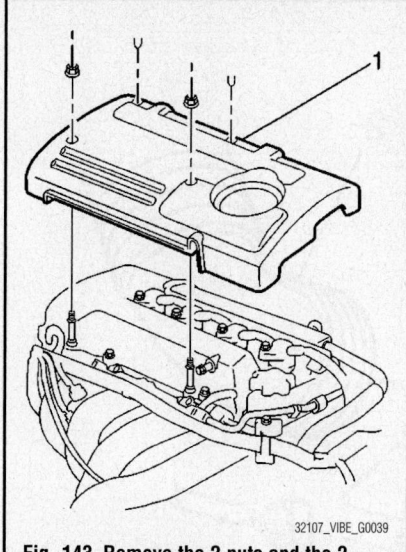

**Fig. 143 Remove the 2 nuts and the 2
retainers from the engine cover (1).**

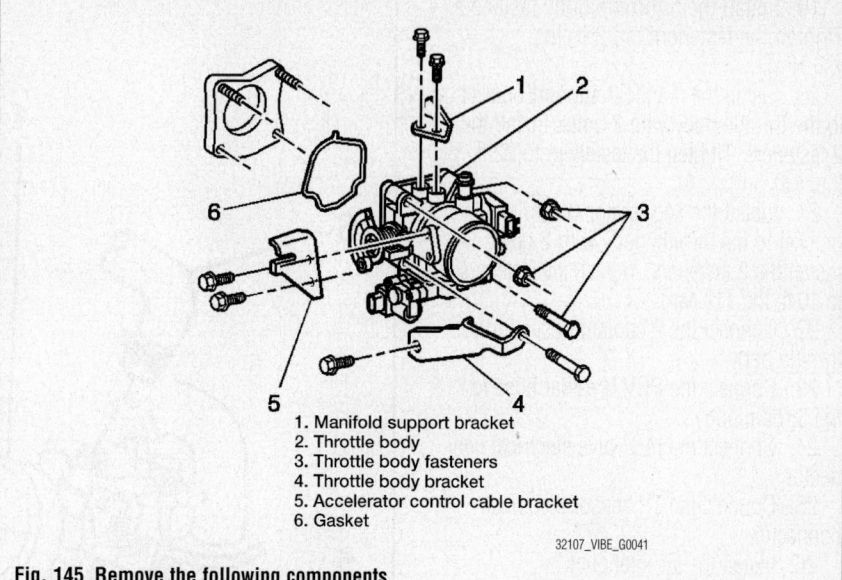

1. Manifold support bracket
2. Throttle body
3. Throttle body fasteners
4. Throttle body bracket
5. Accelerator control cable bracket
6. Gasket

32107_VIBE_G0041

Fig. 145 Remove the following components

2. Remove the engine cover from the engine.

3. Remove the air inlet duct from the throttle body assembly.

4. Remove the positive crankcase ventilation (PCV) breather hose.

5. Remove the throttle position (TP) sensor connector.

6. Rotate the throttle lever and disconnect the accelerator cable and the throttle valve cable, if equipped.

7. Disconnect the electrical connector of the idle air control (IAC) valve.

8. Drain the cooling system.

9. Remove the 2 coolant hoses from the throttle body.

10. Remove the 2 bolts and the accelerator control cable bracket.

11. Remove the 2 fasteners and the throttle body bracket.

12. Remove the 3 throttle body fasteners.

13. Remove the 2 fasteners and the manifold support bracket.

14. Remove the throttle body and the gasket from the intake manifold.

15. Clean any remaining throttle body gasket from the intake manifold.

To install:

16. Install a new throttle body gasket onto the intake manifold.

17. Install the throttle body onto the intake manifold with the 3 fasteners.

18. Install the throttle body bracket and the 2 bolts to the throttle body.

➡**Use the correct fastener in the correct location. Replacement fasteners must be the correct part number for that application. Fasteners requiring replacement or fasteners requiring the use of thread locking compound or sealant are identified in the service procedure. Do not use paints, lubricants, or corrosion inhibitors on fasteners or fastener joint surfaces unless specified. These coatings affect fastener torque and joint clamping force and may damage the fastener. Use the correct tightening sequence and specifications when installing fasteners in order to avoid damage to parts and systems.**

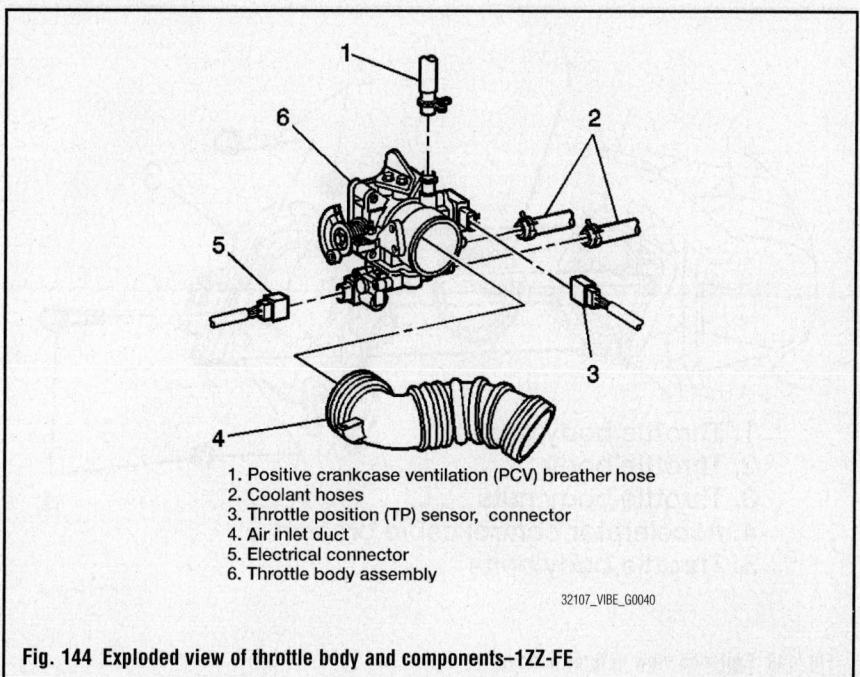

1. Positive crankcase ventilation (PCV) breather hose
2. Coolant hoses
3. Throttle position (TP) sensor, connector
4. Air inlet duct
5. Electrical connector
6. Throttle body assembly

32107_VIBE_G0040

Fig. 144 Exploded view of throttle body and components–1ZZ-FE

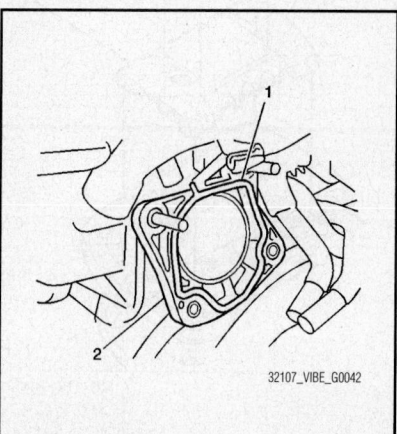

32107_VIBE_G0042

Fig. 146 Install a new throttle body gasket (1) onto the intake manifold (2).

19. Install the 5 throttle body fasteners. Tighten the fasteners to 22 ft. lbs. (30 Nm).

20. Install the manifold support bracket to the throttle body with 2 bolts. Install the 2 fasteners. Tighten the fasteners to 22 ft. lbs. (30 Nm).

21. Install the accelerator control cable bracket to the throttle body with 2 bolts. Install the 2 fasteners. Tighten the fasteners to 10 ft. lbs. (13 Nm).

22. Connect the 2 coolant hoses to the throttle body.

23. Connect the PCV breather hose to the throttle body.

24. Connect the IAC valve electrical connector.

25. Connect the TP sensor electrical connector.

26. Install the air inlet duct.

27. Refill the cooling system.

28. Install the engine cover to the engine and secure engine cover with the 2 nuts. Secure the engine cover with the 2 nuts. Tighten the fasteners to 62 inch lbs (7 Nm).

29. Install the 2 retainers to the engine cover.

2ZZ-GE Engine

See Figures 147 through 150.

1. Remove the 4 fasteners from the engine cover.

2. Remove the engine cover from the engine.

3. Remove the air inlet duct from the throttle body assembly.

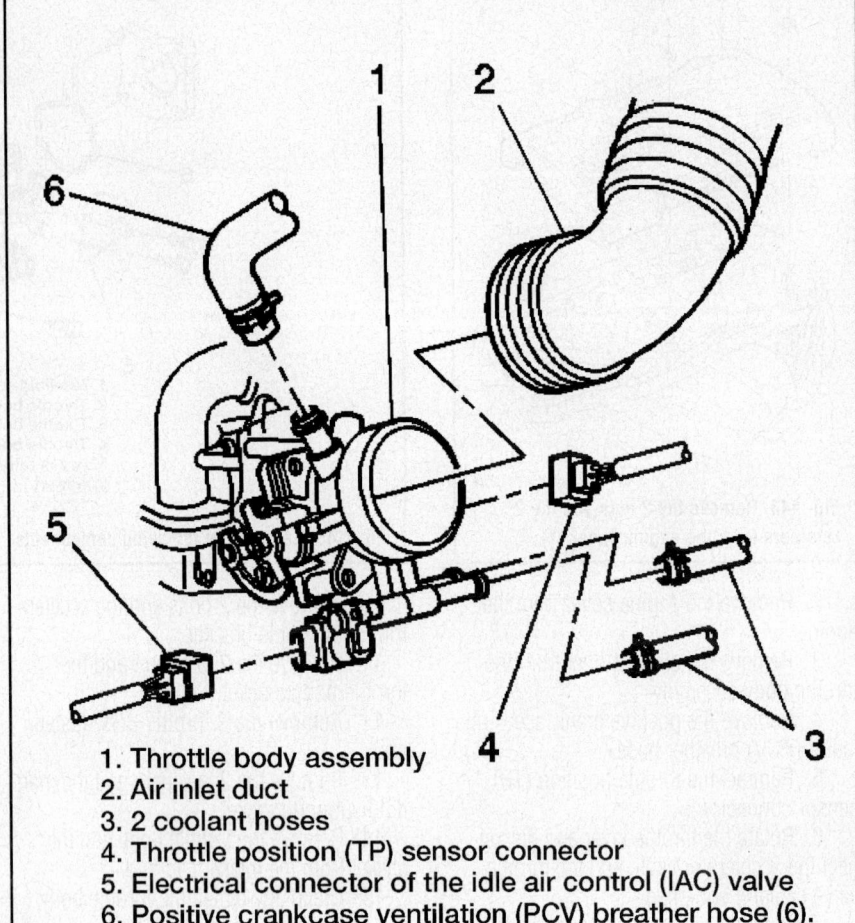

1. **Throttle body assembly**
2. **Air inlet duct**
3. **2 coolant hoses**
4. **Throttle position (TP) sensor connector**
5. **Electrical connector of the idle air control (IAC) valve**
6. **Positive crankcase ventilation (PCV) breather hose (6).**

32107_VIBE_G0047

Fig. 148 Exploded view of throttle body and components

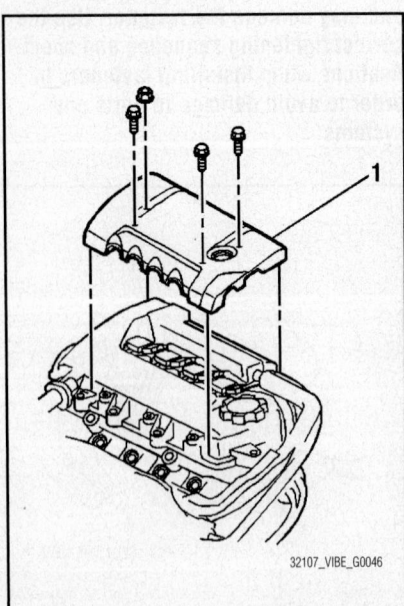

Fig. 147 Remove the 4 fasteners from the engine cover (1).

32107_VIBE_G0046

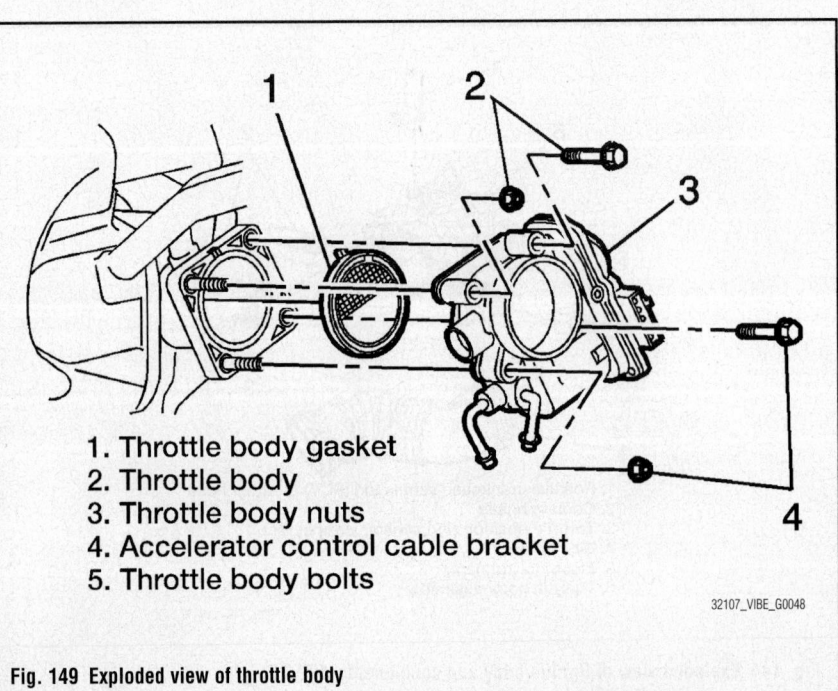

1. **Throttle body gasket**
2. **Throttle body**
3. **Throttle body nuts**
4. **Accelerator control cable bracket**
5. **Throttle body bolts**

32107_VIBE_G0048

Fig. 149 Exploded view of throttle body

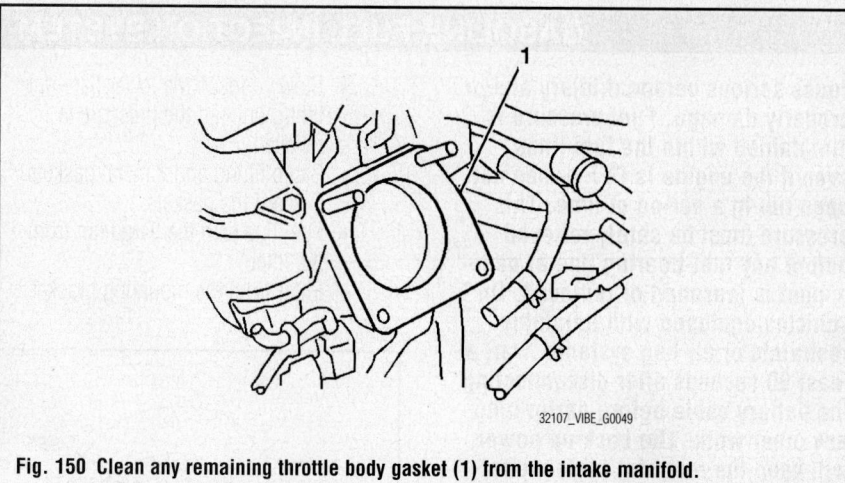

Fig. 150 Clean any remaining throttle body gasket (1) from the intake manifold.

4. Remove the positive crankcase ventilation (PCV) breather hose.

5. Remove the throttle position (TP) sensor connector.

6. Rotate the throttle lever and disconnect the accelerator cable and the throttle valve cable, if equipped.

7. Disconnect the electrical connector of the idle air control (IAC) valve.

8. Drain the cooling system.

9. Remove the 2 coolant hoses from the throttle body.

10. Remove the 2 throttle body nuts and the accelerator control cable bracket.

11. Remove the 2 throttle body bolts.

12. Remove the throttle body and the gasket from the intake manifold.

13. Clean any remaining throttle body gasket from the intake manifold.

To install:

14. Install a new throttle body gasket.

15. Install the throttle body onto the intake manifold with the 2 bolts.

16. Install the accelerator cable bracket and the 2 nuts to the throttle body.

➡ **Use the correct fastener in the correct location. Replacement fasteners must be the correct part number for that application. Fasteners requiring replacement or fasteners requiring the use of thread locking compound or sealant are identified in the service**
procedure. Do not use paints, lubricants, or corrosion inhibitors on fasteners or fastener joint surfaces unless specified. These coatings affect fastener torque and joint clamping force and may damage the fastener. Use the correct tightening sequence and specifications when installing fasteners in order to avoid damage to parts and systems.

17. Tighten the 4 throttle body fasteners. Tighten the fasteners to 16 ft. lbs. (22 Nm).

18. Connect the 2 coolant hoses to the throttle body.

19. Connect the PCV breather hose to the throttle body.

20. Connect the IAC valve electrical connector.

21. Connect the TP sensor electrical connector.

22. Install the air inlet duct.

23. Refill the cooling system.

24. Install the engine cover to the engine.

25. Secure the engine cover with the 4 fasteners. Tighten the fasteners to 62 inch lbs. (7 Nm).

TESTING

See Figure 151.

1. Turn OFF the ignition.

2. Disconnect the throttle body harness connector.

3. Turn ON the ignition, with the engine OFF.

4. Measure the voltage from the 5 volt reference circuit of the TP sensor to a good ground. The voltage should be 4.9–5.1 volts. If not check sensor 5-volt reference circuit for an open, short to ground of high resistance and repair as needed.

5. Connect a fused jumper wire between the 5 volt reference circuit and the signal circuit of TP sensor. The voltage should be 4.8–5 volts. If not check sensor 5 volt signal circuit for an open, short to ground of high resistance and repair as needed.

6. If the wiring circuits are not defective, replace the throttle body assembly.

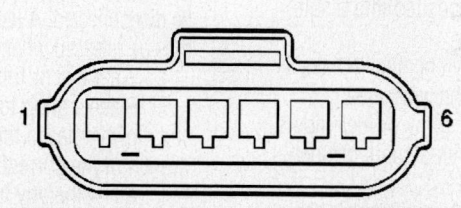

1. Motor Control Low
2. Motor Control High
3. Sensor Ground
4. TP Signal Sensor 2
5. 5-Volt Reference
6. TP Signal Sensor 1

Fig. 151 Throttle Position Sensor (TPS) sensor terminals

FUEL SYSTEM SERVICE PRECAUTIONS

Safety is the most important factor when performing not only fuel system maintenance but any type of maintenance. Failure to conduct maintenance and repairs in a safe manner may result in serious personal injury or death. Maintenance and testing of the vehicle's fuel system components can be accomplished safely and effectively by adhering to the following rules and guidelines.

• To avoid the possibility of fire and personal injury, always disconnect the negative battery cable unless the repair or test procedure requires that battery voltage be applied.

• Always relieve the fuel system pressure prior to disconnecting any fuel system component (injector, fuel rail, pressure regulator, etc.), fitting or fuel line connection. Exercise extreme caution whenever relieving fuel system pressure to avoid exposing skin, face and eyes to fuel spray. Please be advised that fuel under pressure may penetrate the skin or any part of the body that it contacts.

• Always place a shop towel or cloth around the fitting or connection prior to loosening to absorb any excess fuel due to spillage. Ensure that all fuel spillage (should it occur) is quickly removed from engine surfaces. Ensure that all fuel soaked cloths or towels are deposited into a suitable waste container.

• Always keep a dry chemical (Class B) fire extinguisher near the work area.

• Do not allow fuel spray or fuel vapors to come into contact with a spark or open flame.

• Always use a back-up wrench when loosening and tightening fuel line connection fittings. This will prevent unnecessary stress and torsion to fuel line piping.

• Always replace worn fuel fitting O-rings with new Do not substitute fuel hose or equivalent where fuel pipe is installed.

Before servicing the vehicle, make sure to also refer to the precautions in the beginning of this section as well.

RELIEVING FUEL SYSTEM PRESSURE

✳✳ CAUTION

Failure to relieve fuel pressure before repairs or disassembly can cause serious personal injury and/or property damage. Fuel pressure is maintained within the fuel lines, even if the engine is OFF or has not been run in a period of time. This pressure must be safely relieved before any fuel-bearing line or component is loosened or removed. On vehicles equipped with inflatable restraints or air bag systems, wait at least 90 seconds after disconnecting the battery cable before performing any other work. The back-up power will keep the restraint system energized for a period of time after the battery is disconnected.

1. Before servicing the vehicle, refer to the precautions section.
2. Perform the following:
   a. Remove the rear seat cushion.
   b. Remove the rear floor service hole cover.
   c. Disconnect the fuel pump connector.
   d. Start and run the engine, until it stalls.
   e. Turn the ignition key to the **LOCK** position.
   f. Disconnect the negative battery cable.
   g. Connect the fuel pump connector.
   h. Install the service hole cover and rear seat cushion.
   i. Place a catch-pan under the joint to be disconnected. A large quantity of fuel may be released when the joint is opened.
   j. Wear eye or full face protection.
   k. Place a shop towel over the area and slowly release the joint using a wrench of the correct size.
   l. Allow the any fuel left in the line to bleed off slowly before fully disconnecting the joint.
   m. Plug the opened lines.

FUEL FILTER

REMOVAL & INSTALLATION
See Figure 152.

1. Before servicing the vehicle, refer to the precautions section.
2. Relieve the fuel system pressure.
3. Remove or disconnect the following:
   • Negative battery cable
   • Protective shield for the fuel filter
   • Air cleaner hose and cap, if necessary
   • Charcoal canister, if necessary

• Slowly loosen the lower flare nut fitting until all the pressure is relieved
• Banjo fitting and 2 metal gaskets. Discard the gaskets.
• Fuel line with the flared nut from the filter
• Filter from the mounting bracket

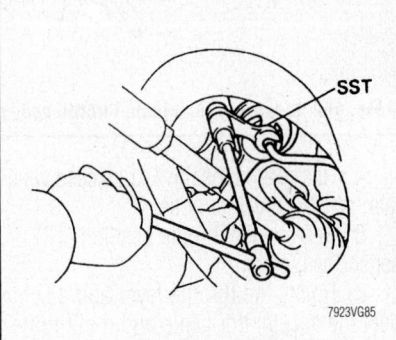

Fig. 152 A line wrench with an extension may be needed to loosen the inlet line at the filter

To install:
4. Install or connect the following:
   • New fuel filter
   • Banjo fitting with a new metal gasket on each side and install the union bolt. Bolt: 22 ft. lbs. (30 Nm).
   • Flare nut to the lower connection. Nut: 22 ft. lbs. (30 Nm).
   • Charcoal canister
   • Air cleaner hose and cap
   • Protective shield
   • Negative battery cable

FUEL INJECTORS

REMOVAL & INSTALLATION

1ZZ-FE Engine
See Figure 153.

1. Before servicing the vehicle, refer to the precautions section.
2. Properly relieve the fuel system pressure.
3. Remove or disconnect the following:
   • Negative battery cable.
   • No. 2 cylinder head cover
   • Positive Crankcase Ventilation (PCV) hose
   • Engine wire, unplugging the injector connectors and clamps
   • Fuel pipe clamp
   • Fuel line/tube sub-assembly

✳✳ WARNING

Be careful not to drop the fuel injectors when removing the delivery pipe.

- Fuel delivery pipe sub-assembly with the injectors attached
- Delivery pipe and injectors
- Spacers from the head
- Injectors from the delivery pipe
- O-ring and grommet from each injector

To install:

4. Install or connect the following:
   - New grommets
   - New O-rings coated with light machine oil
   - Injectors on the delivery pipe

➡**Coat the contact point on the pipe with light machine oil and twist the injectors into place. The connector should face outward.**

   - Spacers

➡**Coat the seats in the head where the injectors contact, with light machine oil.**

- Delivery pipe and injectors

5. Loosely install the hold-down bolts and check that the injectors rotate smoothly. If they don't, the probable cause is incorrect O-ring installation. Torque the delivery pipe hold-down bolts to 14 ft. lbs. (19 Nm) and the fuel pipe bolt to 80 inch lbs. (9 Nm).

- Engine wire, attaching the injector connectors and clamps
- Fuel line/tube sub-assembly
- PCV hose
- No. 2 cylinder head (valve) cover

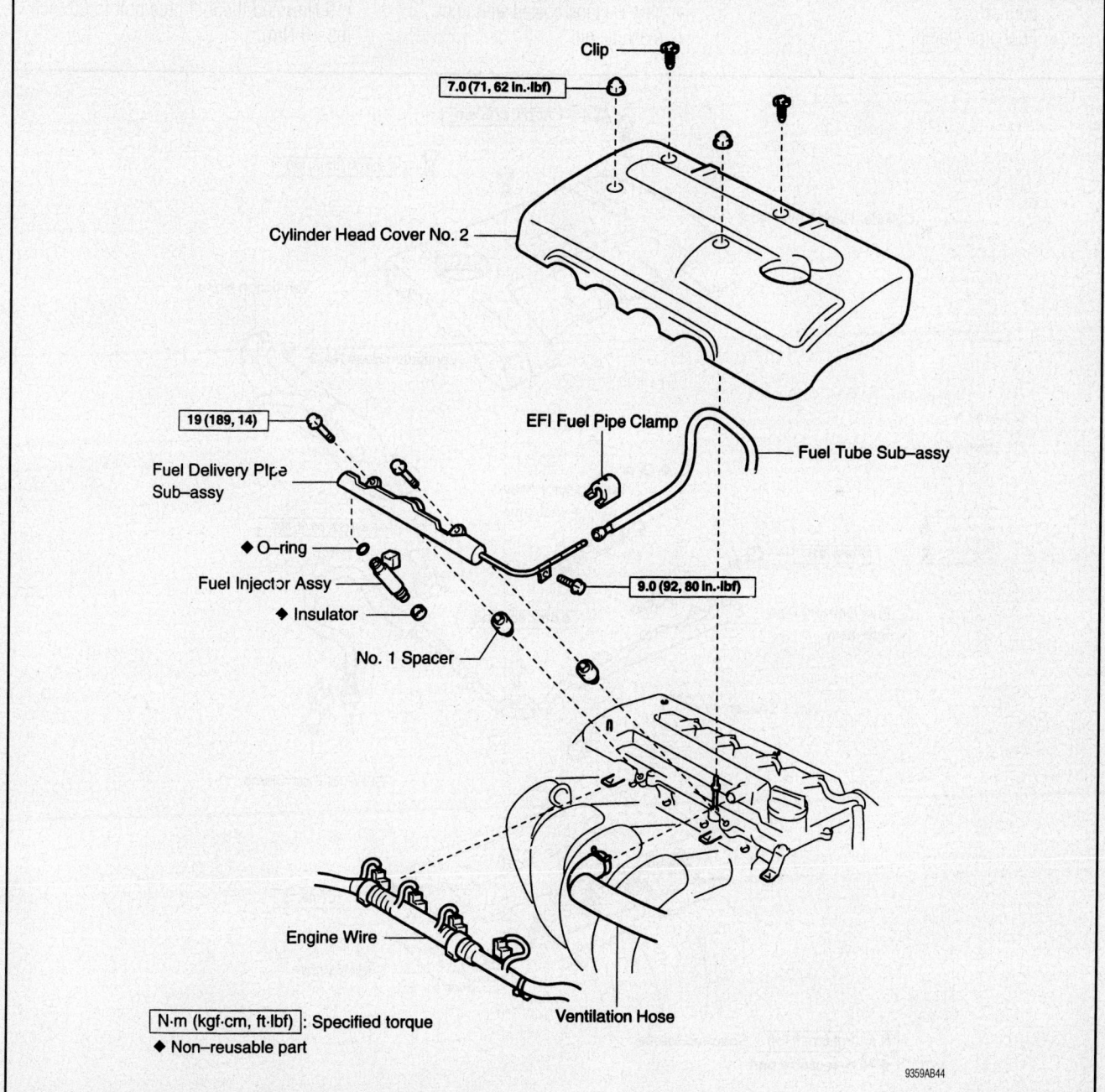

Fig. 153 Fuel injector removal and installation—1ZZ-FE engine

2ZZ-GE Engine

See Figure 154.

1. Before servicing the vehicle, refer to the precautions section.

2. Properly relieve the fuel system pressure.

3. Remove or disconnect the following:

- Negative battery cable.
- No. 2 cylinder head cover
- Positive Crankcase Ventilation (PCV) hose
- Engine wire, by removing the bolt, then unplugging the injector and Camshaft Position (CMP) sensor connectors
- Fuel pipe clamp

✳✳ WARNING

Be careful not to drop the fuel injectors when removing the delivery pipe.

- Fuel delivery pipe sub-assembly with the injectors attached
- Delivery pipe and injectors
- Spacers from the head
- Injectors from the delivery pipe
- O-ring and grommet from each injector

To install:

4. Install or connect the following:
- New grommets
- New O-rings coated with light machine oil

- Injectors on the delivery pipe

➡Coat the contact point on the pipe with light machine oil and twist the injectors into place. The connector should face outward.

- Spacers

➡Coat the seats in the head where the injectors contact, with light machine oil.

- Delivery pipe and injectors

5. Loosely install the hold-down bolts and check that the injectors rotate smoothly. If they don't, the probable cause is incorrect O-ring installation. Torque the delivery pipe hold-down bolts to 14 ft. lbs. (19 Nm) and the fuel pipe bolt to 80 inch lbs. (9 Nm).

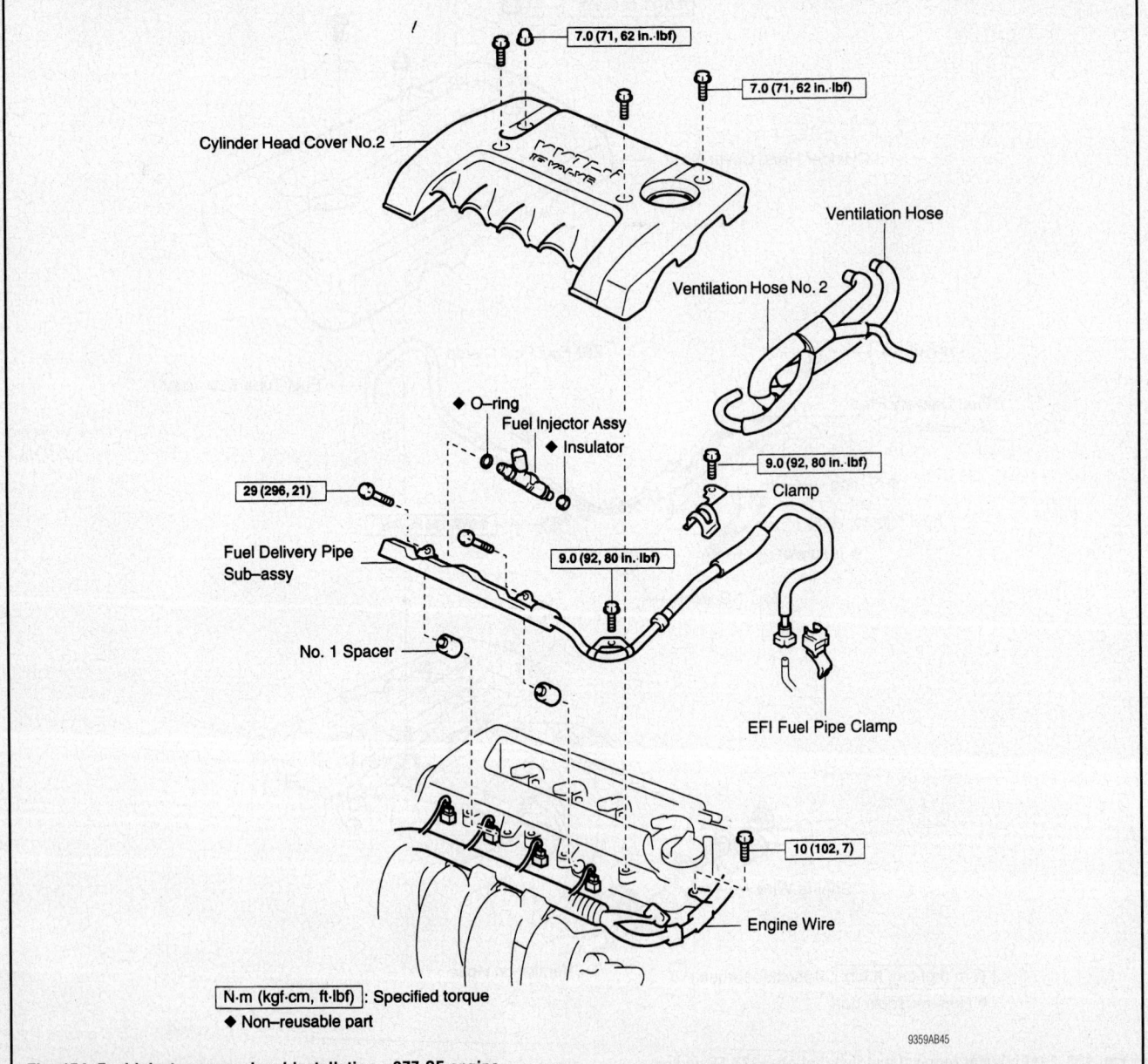

Fig. 154 Fuel injector removal and installation—2ZZ-GE engine

- Fuel line/tube sub-assembly
- PCV hose
- Engine wire, by connecting the CMP sensor and injector connectors and installing the bolt. Tighten the bolt to 7 ft. lbs. (10 Nm).
- No. 2 cylinder head (valve) cover

FUEL PUMP

REMOVAL & INSTALLATION

See Figures 155 through 157.

1. Before servicing the vehicle, refer to the precautions section.

2. Remove or disconnect the following:
   - Negative battery cable
   - Rear seat cushion and floor service hole cover
   - Fuel pump and vapor pressure sensor connectors
   - Start and run the engine, until it stalls

3. Turn the ignition key to the **LOCK** position.
   - Negative battery cable

4. Connect the fuel pump connector.
   - Fuel tank protector, AWD vehicles
   - Fuel tank main tube sub-assembly

- Fuel emission tube sub-assembly No. 1, FWD vehicles
- Fuel tank vent tube set plate. The plate is secured with 8 bolts on FWD vehicles, or 5 bolts on AWD vehicles.
- Fuel pump assembly, being careful not to damage the filter or bend the arm of the fuel sender gauge
- Fuel suction tube set gasket
- Fuel suction support No. 2
- Fuel pump rubber cushion
- Fuel sender gauge assembly. Unplug the connector, then use

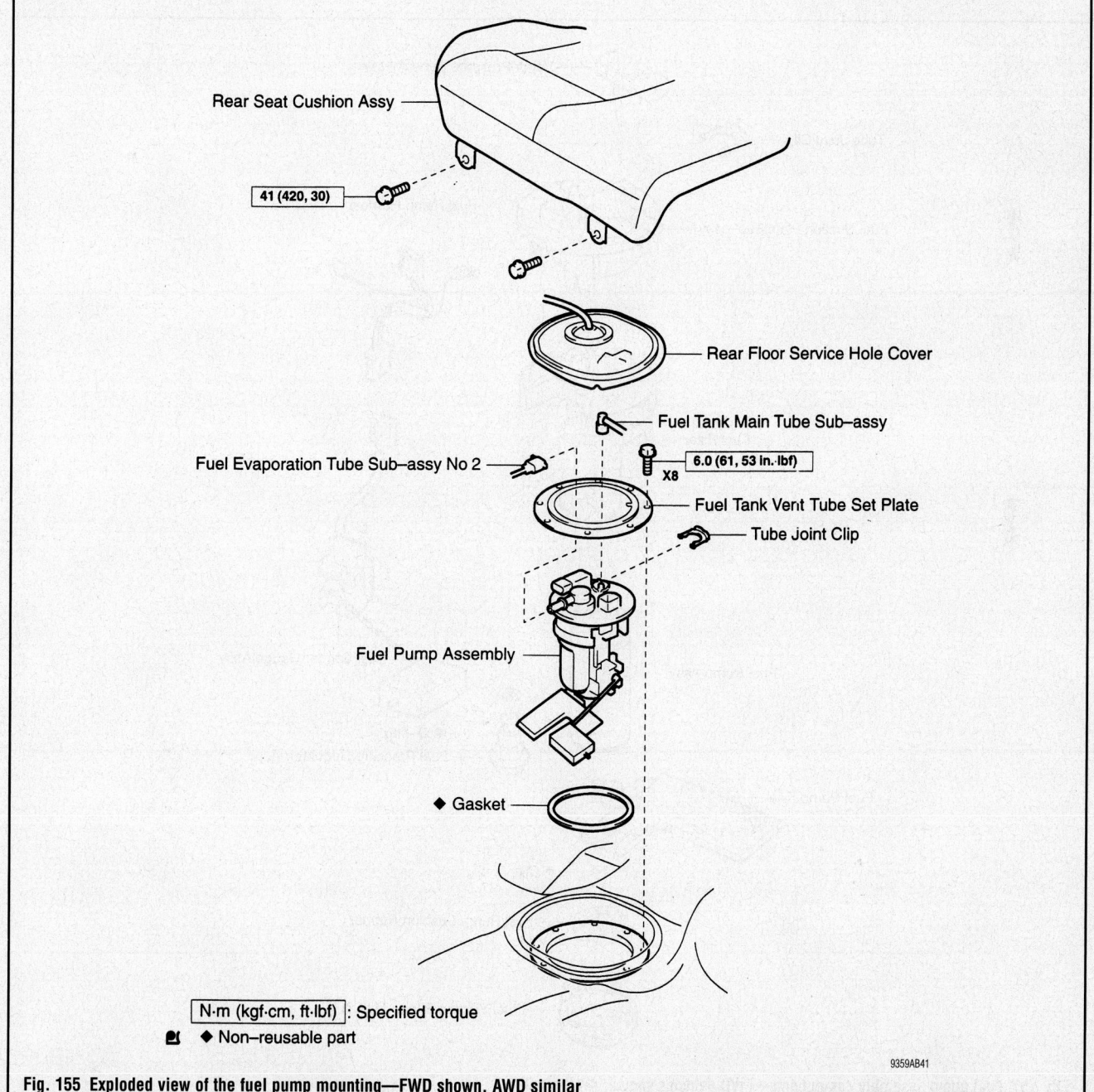

Rear Seat Cushion Assy

41 (420, 30)

Rear Floor Service Hole Cover

Fuel Tank Main Tube Sub-assy

Fuel Evaporation Tube Sub-assy No 2

6.0 (61, 53 in.·lbf)
X8

Fuel Tank Vent Tube Set Plate

Tube Joint Clip

Fuel Pump Assembly

◆ Gasket

N·m (kgf·cm, ft·lbf) : Specified torque

◆ Non-reusable part

9359AB41

Fig. 155 Exploded view of the fuel pump mounting—FWD shown, AWD similar

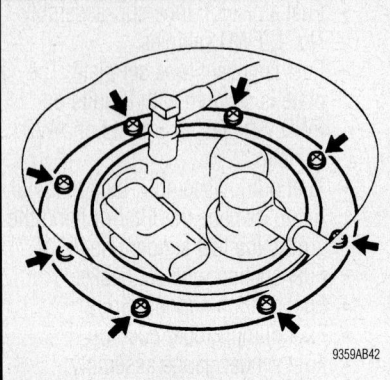

Fig. 156 The fuel tank vent tube set plate is secured with 8 bolts on FWD vehicles

a screwdriver to unlock the gauge and slide it to remove.
- Fuel section plate sub-assembly
- Vapor pressure sensor
- Fuel pump harness
- Fuel pump
- Fuel pump filter
- Fuel pressure regulator and O-ring

To install:

5. Install or connect the following:
- New regulator O-ring and regulator
- Fuel pump filter
- Fuel pump
- Vapor pressure sensor
- Fuel suction tube set gasket
- Fuel pump assembly
- Fuel tank vent tube set plate. Tighten the bolts to 53 inch lbs. (6 Nm).
- Connect the fuel emission tube sub-assembly
- Fuel tank main tube sub-assembly
- Fuel tank protector No. 2, AWD vehicles
- Negative battery cable. Check for fuel leaks.
- Floor service hole cover. Use butyl tape to seal the cover.
- Rear seat cushion

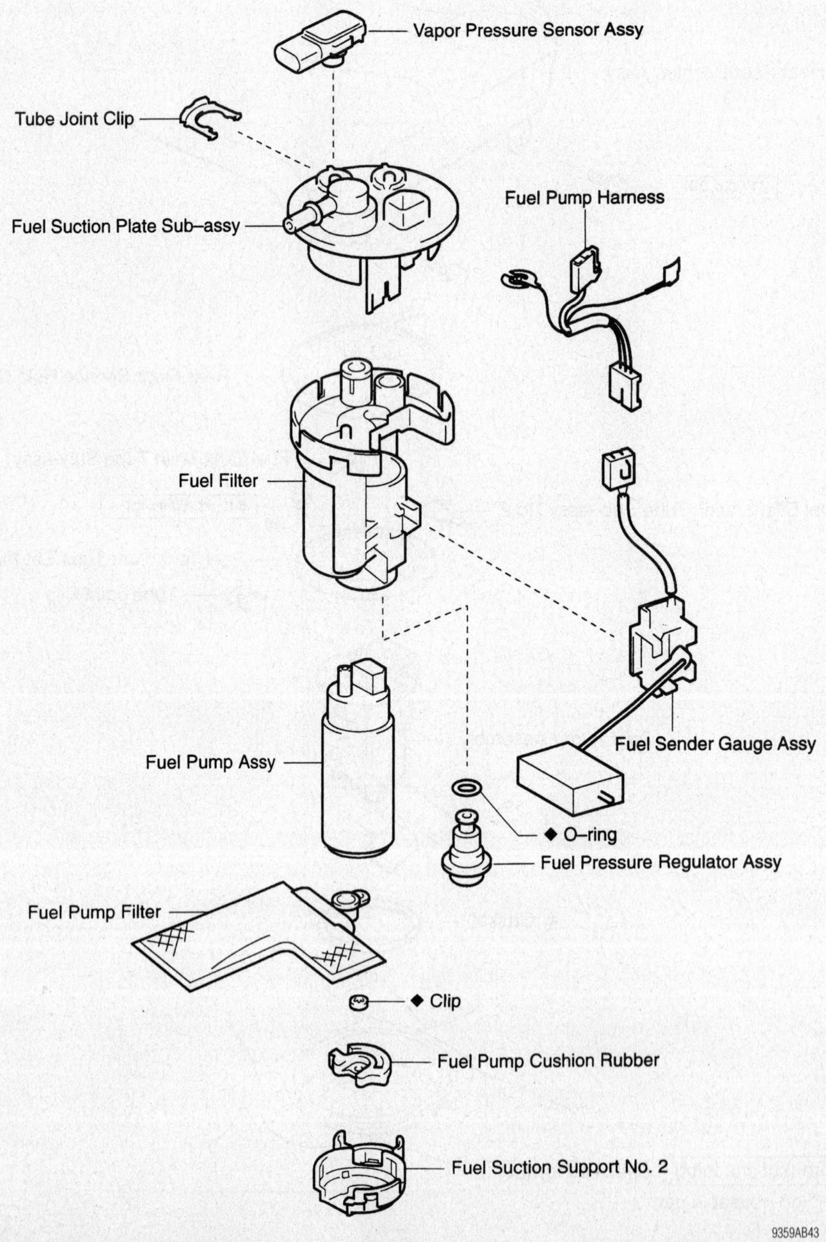

Vapor Pressure Sensor Assy

Tube Joint Clip

Fuel Suction Plate Sub-assy

Fuel Pump Harness

Fuel Filter

Fuel Pump Assy

Fuel Sender Gauge Assy

◆ O-ring

Fuel Pressure Regulator Assy

Fuel Pump Filter

◆ Clip

Fuel Pump Cushion Rubber

Fuel Suction Support No. 2

Fig. 157 Fuel pump assembly components—FWD vehicles shown, AWD similar

FUEL TANK

REMOVAL & INSTALLATION

➡The fuel tank equipped with ORVR components require special handling. Follow all instructions for servicing the fuel tank as specified in the service procedures. Damage to the fuel system components and the failure to meet the Federal Regulations may result from incorrect servicing of the fuel tank.

1. Drain the fuel tank.
2. Raise and suitably support the vehicle.
3. Remove the catalytic converter and intermediate pipe assembly from the vehicle.
4. Remove the 2 left side bolts and the 3 right side bolts from the rear exhaust heat shield.
5. Remove the rear exhaust heat shield from the underbody.
6. Remove the 2 bolts securing the parking brake cable on the right side of the vehicle.
7. Disconnect the fuel supply line.
8. Disconnect the fuel tank vapor line with the quick release fitting from the fuel vapor pipe. Loosen the fuel filler hose clamp.
9. Disconnect the fuel filler hose (2) from the fuel tank.
10. Disconnect the ORVR vent line from the Fill Limiter Vent Valve (FLVV) of the evap canister.
11. Remove the 4 bolts and the fuel tank straps from the vehicle.
12. Remove the fuel tank from the vehicle.
13. If replacing the fuel tank, remove all lines and hoses, and install on the replacement fuel tank.

To install:
14. Installation is the reverse of removal. Tighten the strap bolts to 29 ft. lbs. (39 Nm). Make sure all fuel lines and hoses are properly connected.
15. Start the vehicle and check for leaks.

IDLE SPEED

ADJUSTMENT

Idle speed is maintained by the Powertrain Control Module (PCM). No adjustment is necessary or possible.

THROTTLE BODY

REMOVAL & INSTALLATION

1ZZ-FE Engine

See Figures 158 through 161.

1. Remove the 2 nuts and the 2 retainers from the engine cover.
2. Remove the engine cover from the engine.
3. Remove the air inlet duct from the throttle body assembly.
4. Remove the positive crankcase ventilation (PCV) breather hose.

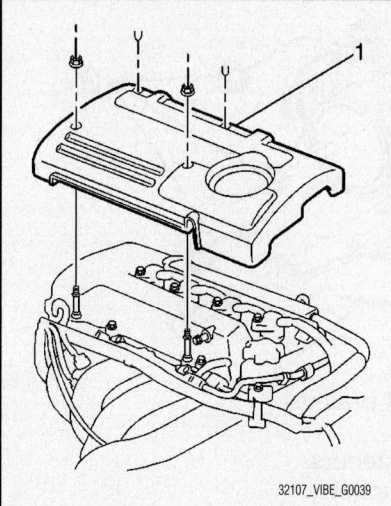

Fig. 158 Remove the 2 nuts and the 2 retainers from the engine cover (1).

5. Remove the throttle position (TP) sensor connector.
6. Rotate the throttle lever and disconnect the accelerator cable and the throttle valve cable, if equipped.
7. Disconnect the electrical connector of the idle air control (IAC) valve.
8. Drain the cooling system.
9. Remove the 2 coolant hoses from the throttle body.
10. Remove the 2 bolts and the accelerator control cable bracket.
11. Remove the 2 fasteners and the throttle body bracket.
12. Remove the 3 throttle body fasteners.
13. Remove the 2 fasteners and the manifold support bracket.
14. Remove the throttle body and the gasket from the intake manifold.
15. Clean any remaining throttle body gasket from the intake manifold.

To install:
16. Install a new throttle body gasket onto the intake manifold.
17. Install the throttle body onto the intake manifold with the 3 fasteners.
18. Install the throttle body bracket and the 2 bolts to the throttle body.

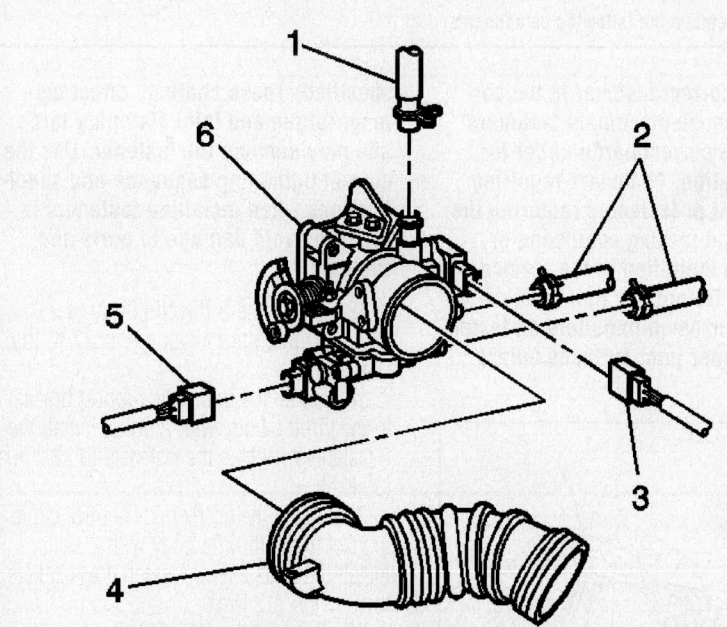

1. Positive crankcase ventilation (PCV) breather hose
2. Coolant hoses
3. Throttle position (TP) sensor, connector
4. Air inlet duct
5. Electrical connector
6. Throttle body assembly

Fig. 159 Exploded view of throttle body and components–1ZZ-FE

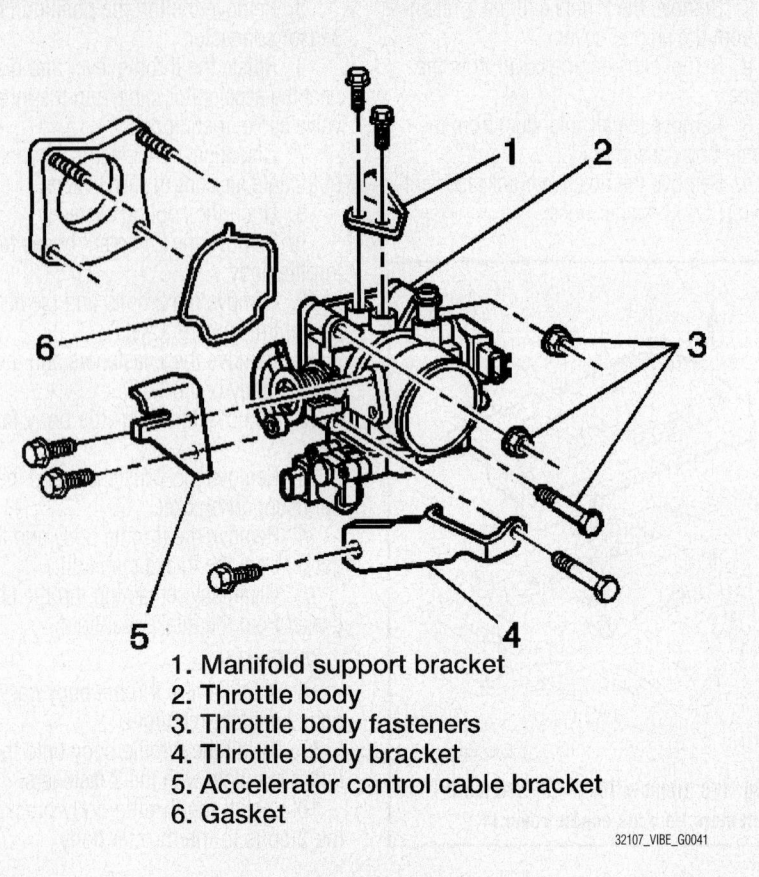

1. Manifold support bracket
2. Throttle body
3. Throttle body fasteners
4. Throttle body bracket
5. Accelerator control cable bracket
6. Gasket

32107_VIBE_G0041

Fig. 160 Remove the following components:

➡️Use the correct fastener in the correct location. Replacement fasteners must be the correct part number for that application. Fasteners requiring replacement or fasteners requiring the use of thread locking compound or sealant are identified in the service procedure. Do not use paints, lubricants, or corrosion inhibitors on fasteners or fastener joint surfaces unless specified. These coatings affect fastener torque and joint clamping force and may damage the fastener. Use the correct tightening sequence and specifications when installing fasteners in order to avoid damage to parts and systems.

19. Install the 5 throttle body fasteners. Tighten the fasteners to 22 ft. lbs. (30 Nm).

20. Install the manifold support bracket to the throttle body with 2 bolts. Install the 2 fasteners. Tighten the fasteners to 22 ft. lbs. (30 Nm).

21. Install the accelerator control cable bracket to the throttle body with 2 bolts. Install the 2 fasteners. Tighten the fasteners to 10 ft. lbs. (13 Nm).

22. Connect the 2 coolant hoses to the throttle body.

23. Connect the PCV breather hose to the throttle body.

24. Connect the IAC valve electrical connector.

25. Connect the TP sensor electrical connector.

26. Install the air inlet duct.

27. Refill the cooling system.

28. Install the engine cover to the engine and secure engine cover with the 2 nuts. Secure the engine cover with the 2 nuts. Tighten the fasteners to 62 inch lbs (7 Nm).

29. Install the 2 retainers to the engine cover.

2ZZ-GE Engine

See Figures 162 through 164.

1. Remove the 4 fasteners from the engine cover.

2. Remove the engine cover from the engine.

3. Remove the air inlet duct from the throttle body assembly.

4. Remove the positive crankcase ventilation (PCV) breather hose.

5. Remove the throttle position (TP) sensor connector.

6. Rotate the throttle lever and disconnect the accelerator cable and the throttle valve cable, if equipped.

7. Disconnect the electrical connector of the idle air control (IAC) valve.

8. Drain the cooling system.

9. Remove the 2 coolant hoses from the throttle body.

10. Remove the 2 throttle body nuts and the accelerator control cable bracket.

11. Remove the 2 throttle body bolts.

12. Remove the throttle body and the gasket from the intake manifold.

13. Clean any remaining throttle body gasket from the intake manifold.

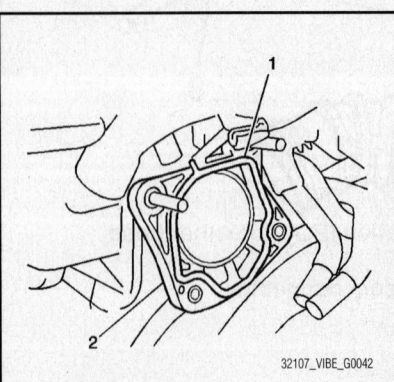

32107_VIBE_G0042

Fig. 161 Install a new throttle body gasket (1) onto the intake manifold (2).

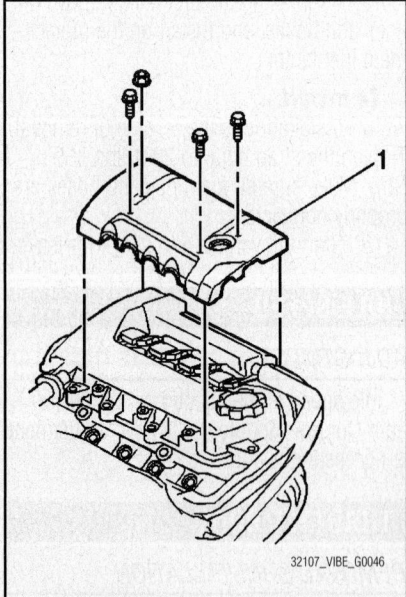

32107_VIBE_G0046

Fig. 162 Remove the 4 fasteners from the engine cover (1).

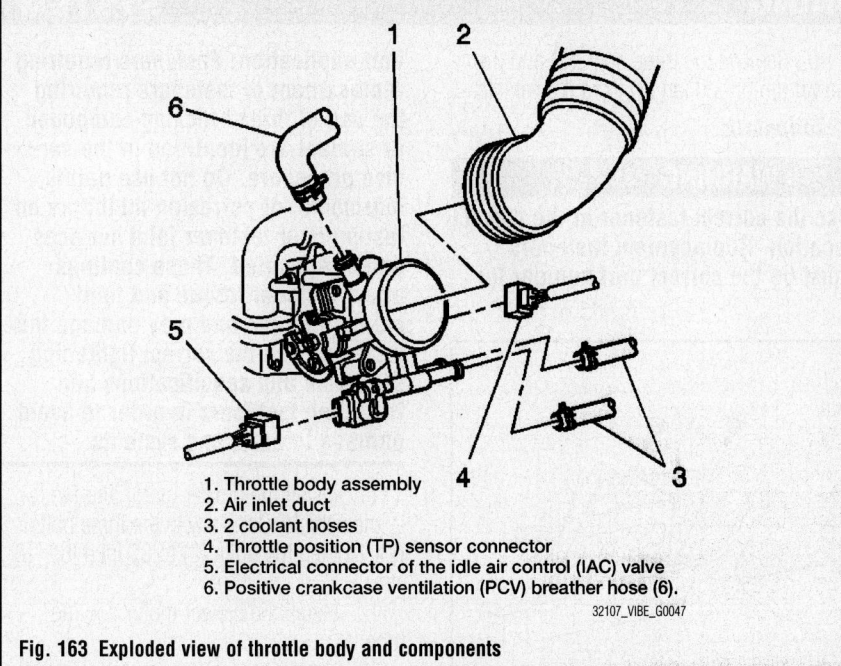

1. Throttle body assembly
2. Air inlet duct
3. 2 coolant hoses
4. Throttle position (TP) sensor connector
5. Electrical connector of the idle air control (IAC) valve
6. Positive crankcase ventilation (PCV) breather hose (6).

32107_VIBE_G0047

Fig. 163 Exploded view of throttle body and components

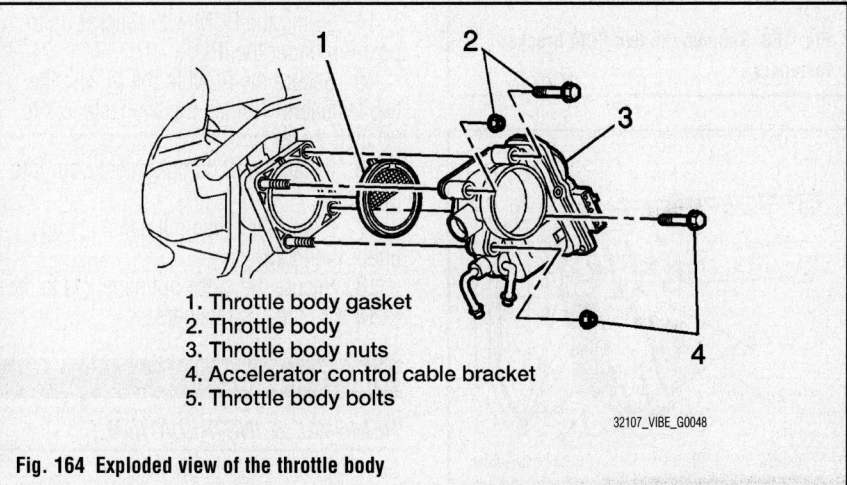

1. Throttle body gasket
2. Throttle body
3. Throttle body nuts
4. Accelerator control cable bracket
5. Throttle body bolts

32107_VIBE_G0048

Fig. 164 Exploded view of the throttle body

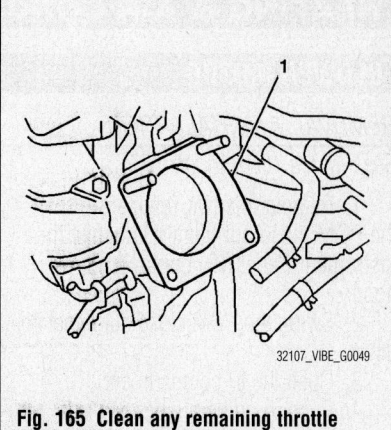

32107_VIBE_G0049

Fig. 165 Clean any remaining throttle body gasket (1) from the intake manifold.

that application. Fasteners requiring replacement or fasteners requiring the use of thread locking compound or sealant are identified in the service procedure. Do not use paints, lubricants, or corrosion inhibitors on fasteners or fastener joint surfaces unless specified. These coatings affect fastener torque and joint clamping force and may damage the fastener. Use the correct tightening sequence and specifications when installing fasteners in order to avoid damage to parts and systems.

17. Tighten the 4 throttle body fasteners. Tighten the fasteners to 16 ft. lbs. (22 Nm).
18. Connect the 2 coolant hoses to the throttle body.
19. Connect the PCV breather hose to the throttle body.
20. Connect the IAC valve electrical connector.
21. Connect the TP sensor electrical connector.
22. Install the air inlet duct.
23. Refill the cooling system.
24. Install the engine cover to the engine.
25. Secure the engine cover with the 4 fasteners. Tighten the fasteners to 62 inch lbs. (7 Nm).

To install:
14. Install a new throttle body gasket.
15. Install the throttle body onto the intake manifold with the 2 bolts.
16. Install the accelerator cable bracket and the 2 nuts to the throttle body.

➡ Use the correct fastener in the correct location. Replacement fasteners must be the correct part number for

BLOWER MOTOR

REMOVAL & INSTALLATION

See Figures 166 through 170.

1. Remove the two retainers from the PCM close out panel (1) below the Instrument Panel (IP) compartment door.

2. Swing the PCM close out panel (1) down.

3. Open the IP compartment.

4. Push in on both sides of the IP compartment in order to release the safety catches.

5. Remove the IP compartment door assembly from the IP.

6. Remove the two PCM bracket fasteners.

7. Pull the PCM (2) with brackets (3) toward you and swing both down away from under the IP.

8. Disconnect the blower motor electrical connector.

9. Remove the blower motor cooling tube.

10. Remove the three bolts (2) and the blower motor and fan (1) from the vehicle.

To install:

⁂ WARNING

Use the correct fastener in the correct location. Replacement fasteners must be the correct part number for

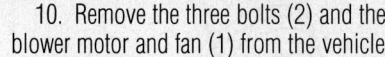

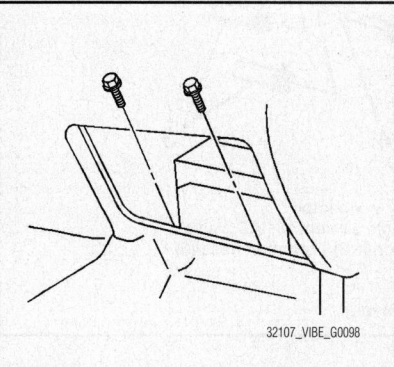

Fig. 168 Remove the two PCM bracket fasteners

that application. Fasteners requiring replacement or fasteners requiring the use of thread locking compound or sealant are identified in the service procedure. Do not use paints, lubricants, or corrosion inhibitors on fasteners or fastener joint surfaces unless specified. These coatings affect fastener torque and joint clamping force and may damage the fastener. Use the correct tightening sequence and specifications hen installing fasteners in order to avoid damage to parts and systems.

11. Install the blower motor and fan (1) to the vehicle. Secure with the three bolts (2). Tighten the bolts (2) to 89 inch lbs (10 Nm).

12. Install the blower motor cooling tube.

13. Connect the blower motor electrical connector.

14. Swing the PCM with bracket up in position under the IP.

15. Secure the PCM to the IP with the two fasteners. Tighten the two fasteners to 80 inch lbs (9 Nm).

16. Install the IP compartment door into the IP.

17. Swing the close out panel (1) up under the PCM.

18. Secure the close out panel (1) to the PCM with the two retainers.

HEATER CORE

REMOVAL & INSTALLATION

See Figures 171 through 180.

1. Before servicing the vehicle, refer to the precautions section.

2. Drain the cooling system.

3. Discharge and recover the A/C system refrigerant using approved equipment.

4. Remove or disconnect the following:

- Negative battery cable
- Heater hoses from the core
- Evaporator inlet and outlet tubes from the evaporator and cap the lines to avoid system contamination

➡**This procedure requires the removal of the instrument panel, as outlined below.**

5. Disable the air bag system.

6. Using a taped flat–bladed tool, care-

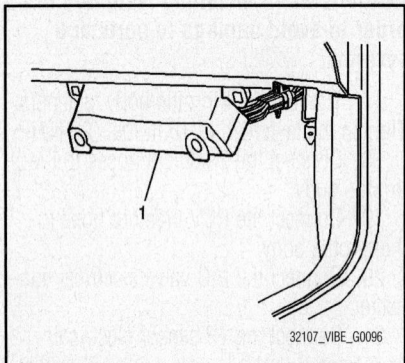

Fig. 166 Remove the two retainers from the PCM close out panel (1) below the Instrument Panel (IP) compartment door

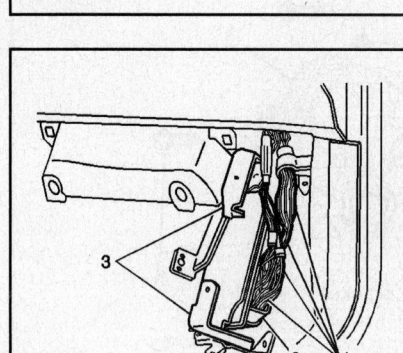

Fig. 169 Pull the PCM (2) with brackets (3) toward you and swing both down away from under the IP.

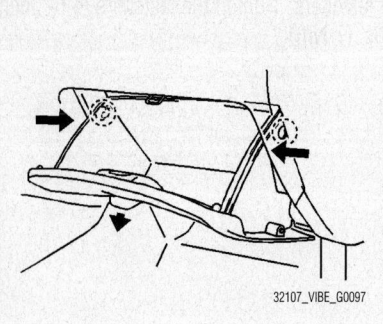

Fig. 167 Push in on both sides of the IP compartment in order to release the safety catches.

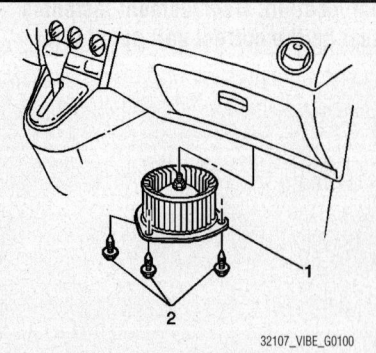

Fig. 170 Remove the three bolts (2) and the blower motor and fan (1) from the vehicle.

fully pry the retaining clips attaching the center trim plate to the instrument panel.

7. Disconnect the A/C switch, hazard switch; rear defogger switch and passenger seat belt indicator switch electrical connections.

8. Remove the radio retaining screws, clamp from the radio bracket, slide the radio forward to disconnect the power and antenna connections. Remove the radio.

9. Remove the A/C switch and screw.

10. Remove the hazard switch.

11. Remove the rear defogger switch.

12. Remove the manual transmission shift knob.

13. Using a taped flat–bladed tool, carefully pry the retaining clips attaching the front floor console trim plate to the floor console assembly.

14. Disconnect the 2 cigar lighter connectors.

15. Disconnect the accessory power receptacle connectors.

16. Remove the cigar lighters and power receptacle.

17. Place both wheels in the straight ahead position.

18. Remove the bolts from the steering wheel module.

19. Release the Connector Position Assurance (CPA) from the inflator module.

20. Disconnect the steering wheel module connectors.

21. Remove the steering wheel module.

22. Matchmark the steering wheel nut–to–shaft position, then remove the steering wheel nut and the wheel.

23. Remove the upper and lower steering column cover screws and the covers.

24. Disconnect the turn signal/headlamp assembly connectors.

25. Remove the turn signal/headlamp switch assembly

26. Remove the wiper switch by depressing the tab.

27. Remove the glove box.

28. Disconnect the instrument panel connector.

29. Remove the instrument panel module connectors and the passenger air bag assembly.

30. Remove the cluster trim plate by disengaging the clips.

31. Remove the cluster screw and disengage the 2 lower clips.

32. Disconnect the cluster electrical connectors and remove the cluster.

33. Remove the windshield garnish moldings.

34. Using a taped flat–bladed tool, carefully pry the retaining clips attaching the instrument panel left trim plate to the instrument panel.

35. Disconnect the power mirror and dimmer switch connectors.

36. Remove the power mirror and dimmer switches.

37. Disconnect any remaining electrical connections.

38. Remove the upper instrument panel screws and the panel by pulling towards the rear to disengage the tabs.

39. Disconnect the steering wheel coil connector.

40. Release the 3 claws and remove the coil assembly.

41. If the vehicle is equipped with an automatic transmission, insert the key into the cylinder, turn to the ACC position, push in the release butt, disconnect the park lock cable, remove the key from the cylinder and lock the steering wheel.

42. Move the silencer pad from the column.

43. Matchmark the steering shaft coupling to the shaft.

44. Loosen the upper bolt on the coupling.

45. Remove the lower bolt from the coupling.

46. Move the coupling onto the column shaft.

47. Disconnect the wiring harness clamps from the column.

48. Remove the 3 bolts and the column.

49. Remove the body hinge trim panels.

50. Remove the sill plates.

51. Remove the front floor console storage door.

52. Remove the screws attaching the console to the instrument panel, pull the console rewards and up and remove the front floor console.

53. Remove the HVAC retaining screw; disconnect the electrical connectors and module control, temperature control and A/C cables. Remove the unit.

54. Push in the clip and disconnect the cable from the manual selector shifter assembly.

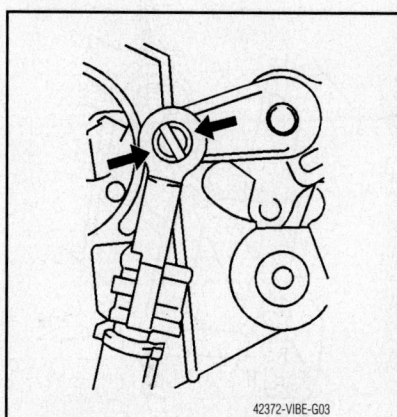

Fig. 173 Push in the clip and disconnect the cable from the manual selector shifter assembly

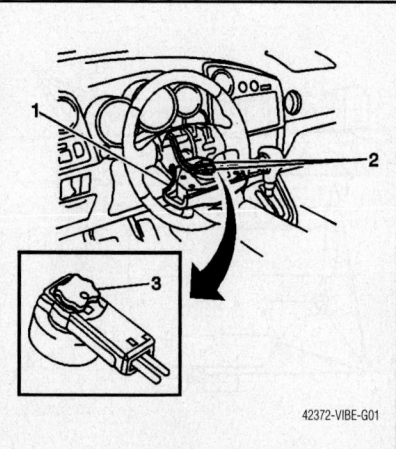

Fig. 171 Exploded view of the CPA assembly

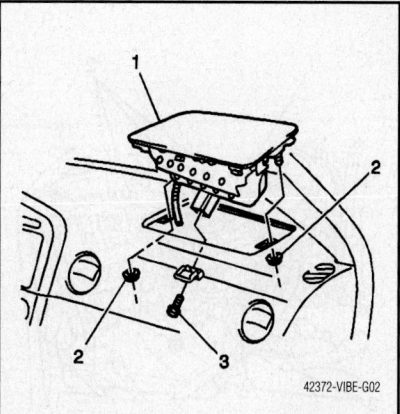

Fig. 172 Remove the instrument panel module connectors and the passenger air bag assembly

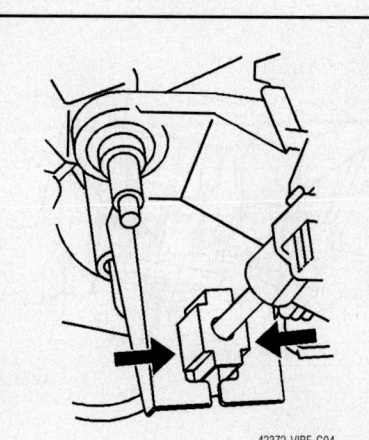

Fig. 174 Using a suitable prytool, disconnect the park lock cable from the bracket

55. Using a suitable prytool, disconnect the park lock cable from the bracket.

56. Disconnect the shift select cable from the manual selector lever.

57. Using a suitable prytool, disconnect the shift select cable from the shift lever plate.

58. Disconnect the electrical connectors and the wire harness clip.

59. Remove the nuts from the selector and remove the selector.

60. Disconnect the hood release cable from the release handle.

61. Remove the 8 bolts, 4 push retainers and the wire harness clamps from the lower instrument panel and remove the panel.

62. Disengage the wiring harness clips, remove the bolts retaining the lower instrument panel pad and the pad.

63. Remove the ground cable.

64. Remove the connector housing bracket from the right instrument panel center support brace.

65. Remove the left brace nut, right brace nut, left brace bolt, right brace bolt, left center support brace and right center support brace.

66. Remove the windshield defroster nozzle duct from the heater case.

67. Remove the 5 bolts and the nuts from the instrument panel reinforcement at the hinge pillars.

68. Remove the instrument panel reinforcement.

69. Disconnect the blower motor connector.

70. Disconnect the rear ducts from the HVAC module.

71. Remove the HVAC module.

72. Remove the 12 bolts from the core case.

73. Remove the heater core.

To install:

74. Install the heater core.

75. Install the 12 bolts from the core case and tighten to 89 inch lbs. (10 Nm).

76. Install the HVAC module.

77. Connect the rear ducts to the HVAC module.

78. Connect the blower motor connector.

79. Install the instrument panel reinforcement.

80. Install the 5 bolts and the nuts to the instrument panel reinforcement at the hinge pillars. Tighten to 21 ft. lbs. (28 Nm).

81. Install the windshield defroster nozzle duct to the heater case.

82. Install left center support brace and right center support brace. Tighten the nuts and bolt to 15 ft. lbs. (20 Nm).

83. Install the connector housing bracket.

84. Connect the ground cable.

85. Install the lower instrument panel pad and the bolts and attach the wiring harness clips.

86. Connect the hood release cable to the release handle.

87. Install the lever and tighten the nuts to 12 ft. lbs. (18 Nm).

88. Connect the manual selector electrical connections.

89. Attach the shift cable to the shift lever plate.

90. Connect the shift select cable to the selector lever.

91. Install the park lock cable to the shift lever plate.

92. Connect the park lock cable to the manual selector lever.

93. Connect the electrical connectors and module control, temperature control and A/C cables. Install the HVAC unit.

94. Adjust the temperature control cable by setting the temperature control dial to coldest. Hold the door lever fully rearwards, clockwise. Attach the cable to the control clip.

95. Adjust the Mode linkage by setting

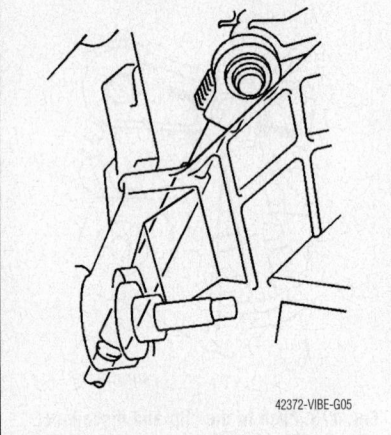

Fig. 175 Disconnect the shift select cable from the manual selector lever

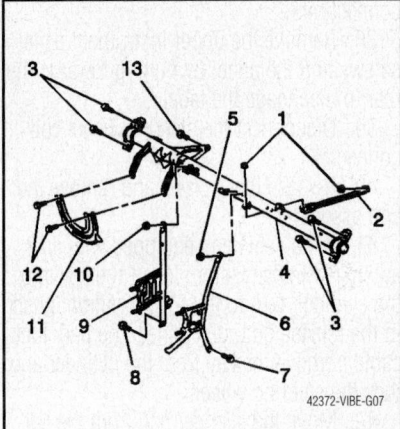

Fig. 177 Exploded view of the instrument panel reinforcement

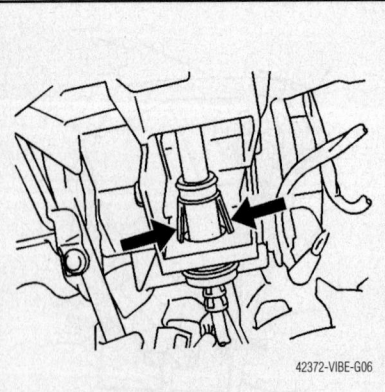

Fig. 176 Using a suitable prytool, disconnect the shift select cable from the shift lever plate

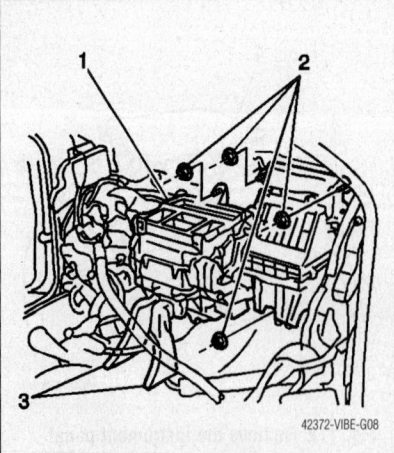

Fig. 178 Remove the HVAC module

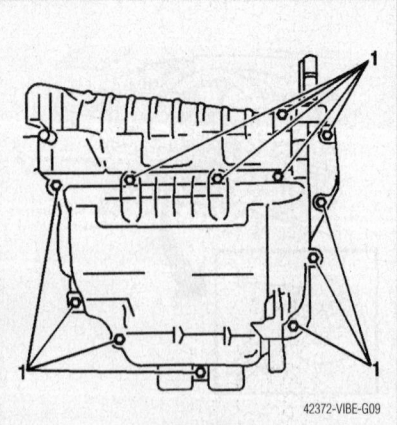

Fig. 179 Remove the 12 bolts from the core case to access the heater core

the dial to defrost. Hold the door lever fully rearward, clockwise. Attach the cable to the control clip.

96. Install the front floor console and tighten the screws.

97. Install the front floor console storage door.

98. Install the sill plates.

99. Install the column.

100. Install the 3 bolts and tighten the lower bolt to 16 ft. lbs. (21 Nm) and the 2 upper bolts to 16 ft. lbs. (21 Nm).

101. Align the matchmarks made prior to removal.

102. Lower the coupling onto the shaft. Install the bolts and tighten to 26 ft. lbs. (35 Nm).

103. Connect the wiring harness clamps to the column.

104. Move the silencer pad to the column.

105. If the vehicle is equipped with an automatic transmission, insert the key into the cylinder, turn to the ACC position, insert the park lock cable making sure the release button engages. Make sure the key will not rotate to the lock position unless the shifter is in the park position, remove the key from the cylinder and lock the steering wheel.

106. Install the body hinge trim panels.

107. Make sure the turn signal switch is in the neutral position.

108. If installing a new coil, remove the lock pin.

109. Install the coil making sure the 3 claws engage.

110. While holding the coil casing, turn the coil center casing counterclockwise until the coil reaches its stop.

111. Turn the coil center casing clockwise 2 ½ turns.

112. Align the center casing with the arrow on the outer casing.

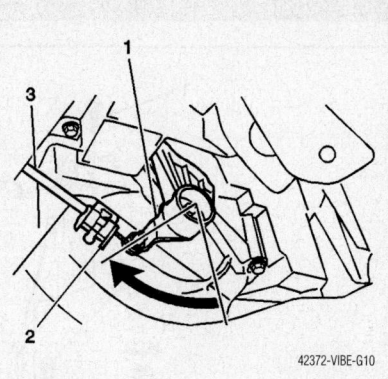

Fig. 180 Location of the components used to adjust the temperature control cable (3) clip (2), door lever (1).

113. Connect the coil electrical connector.

114. Install the upper instrument panel and screws.

115. Connect the electrical connections.

116. Install the power mirror and dimmer switches.

117. Connect the power mirror and dimmer switch connectors.

118. Install the instrument panel left trim plate to the instrument panel.

119. Install the windshield garnish moldings.

120. Connect the cluster electrical connectors and install the cluster.

121. Engage the cluster lower clips and install the screw.

122. Install the cluster trim plate.

123. Install the passenger air bag assembly and the instrument panel module connectors.

124. Connect the instrument panel connector.

125. Install the glove box.

126. Install the wiper switch.

127. Install the turn signal/headlamp switch assembly

128. Connect the turn signal/headlamp assembly connectors.

129. Install the upper and lower steering column covers and screws.

130. Install the steering wheel and nut aligning the matchmarks made prior to removal and tighten the nut to 37 ft. lbs. (50 Nm).

131. Connect the steering wheel module connectors.

132. Install the CPA to the inflator module.

133. Install the steering wheel module and tighten the retainers 78 inch lbs. (9 Nm)

134. Install cigar lighters and power receptacle.

135. Connect the accessory power receptacle connectors.

136. Connect the 2 cigar lighter connectors.

137. Install the front floor console trim plate to the floor console assembly.

138. Install the manual transmission shift knob.

139. Install the rear defogger switch.

140. Install the hazard switch.

141. Install the A/C switch and screw.

142. Install the radio.

143. Connect the A/C switch, hazard switch, rear defogger switch and passenger seat belt indicator switch electrical connections.

144. Install the center trim plate to the instrument panel.

145. Connect the evaporator inlet and outlet tubes.

146. Connect the heater hoses to the core.

147. Connect the negative battery cable.

148. Recharge the A/C system and fill the cooling system.

STEERING

POWER STEERING GEAR

REMOVAL & INSTALLATION

FWD Vehicles

See Figures 181 through 183.

➡ The steering column must be in the LOCK position before disconnecting the following components:

- The steering column
- The steering shaft coupling
- The intermediate shaft
- The lower steering shaft

✷✷ WARNING

After disconnecting these components, do not move the front tires and wheels. Failure to follow these procedures may cause improper alignment of some components during installation and result in possible damage to the SIR coil.

1. LOCK the steering column and verify the front wheels are in the straight ahead position.

2. Move the silencer pad away from the steering column.

3. Use paint in order to place match marks on the steering shaft coupling (3) and on the intermediate shaft (4).

4. Loosen the upper coupling bolt (7).

5. Remove the lower coupling bolt (6).

6. Remove the steering column hole cover (4) from the bulkhead.

7. Install the Engine Support Fixture.

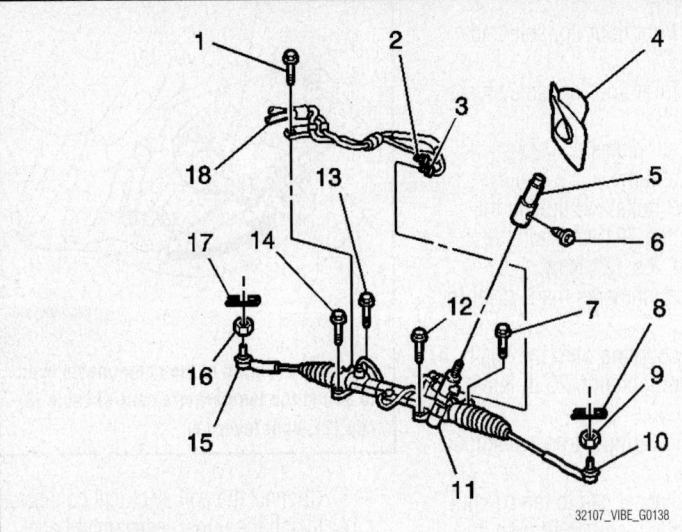

Fig. 182 Exploded view of components

8. Raise and support the vehicle.

9. Remove the front tire and wheel assemblies.

10. Remove the left engine splash shield.

11. Remove the right engine splash shield.

12. Remove the 2 outer tie rod ends (10,15).

13. Place a drain pan under the vehicle in order to collect the fluid from the power steering system.

14. Remove the pressure and return pipes (2,3) from the steering gear.

15. Remove the bolt and the pipe bracket from the steering gear.

16. Remove the following components together as a unit.

- The steering gear
- The intermediate steering shaft
- The front suspension crossmember
- The trans support
- The 2 control arms
- The front stabilizer shaft

17. Remove the bolt and the rear engine mount insulator from the crossmember.

18. Remove the 3 bolts and the rear engine mount bracket from the crossmember.

19. Use paint in order to place match marks on the intermediate shaft (3) and on the steering gear (2).

20. Remove the bolt (5).

21. Remove the intermediate shaft (4).

22. Remove the 4 bolts and the steering gear from the crossmember.

To install:

23. Install the rear engine mount bracket to the crossmember.

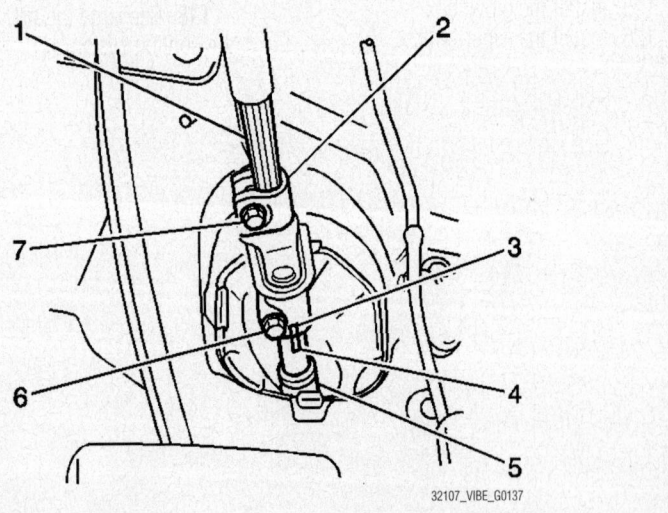

Fig. 181 Use paint in order to place match marks on the steering shaft coupling (3) and on the intermediate shaft (4). Loosen the upper coupling bolt (7). Remove the lower coupling bolt (6).

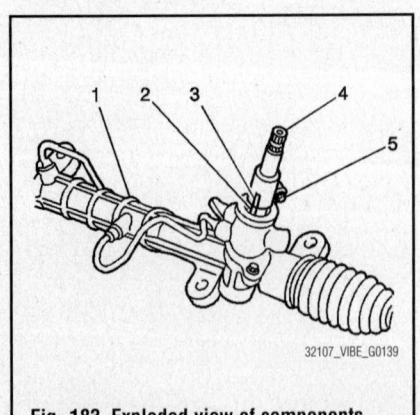

Fig. 183 Exploded view of components

24. Install the 3 bolts to the rear engine mount bracket. Tighten the bolts to 47 ft. lbs. (64 Nm).

25. Install the rear engine mount insulator to the crossmember.

26. Install the bolt to the rear engine mount insulator. Tighten the bolt to 64 ft. lbs. (87 Nm).

27. If you are replacing the steering gear or the intermediate shaft, copy the match marks from the old parts to the same locations on the new parts.

28. Install the steering gear (11) and the 4 bolts (7,12,13,14) to the crossmember. Tighten the bolts to 58 Nm (42.8 lb ft).

29. Install the intermediate shaft (5) to the steering gear. Align the match marks.

30. Install the bolt (6) to the intermediate shaft. Tighten the bolt to 26 ft. lbs. (35 Nm).

31. Install the steering column hole cover (4) to the bulkhead.

32. Install the following components as a unit.

- The steering gear
- The intermediate steering shaft
- The front suspension crossmember
- The trans support
- The 2 control arms
- The front stabilizer shaft

33. Install the 2 outer tie rod ends (10,15).

34. Install the pressure and return pipes (18) to the steering gear. Tighten the pipe nuts to 17 ft. lbs. (23 Nm).

35. Install the pipe bracket bolt (1). Tighten the bolt to 69.04 inch lbs (7.8 Nm).

36. Install the left engine splash shield.

37. Install the right engine splash shield.

38. Install the front tire and wheel assemblies.

39. Lower the vehicle.

40. Remove the Engine Support Fixture.

41. Align the match marks on the intermediate shaft (4) and on the steering shaft coupling (3).

42. Install the lower coupling bolt (6). Tighten the bolt to 26 ft. lbs. (35 Nm).

43. Tighten the upper coupling bolt (7). Tighten the bolt to 26 ft. lbs. (35 Nm).

44. Place the silencer pad into the correct position.

45. Fill the power steering fluid reservoir.

46. Bleed the power steering system.

47. Inspect the power steering system for leaks. Repair as necessary.

48. Measure the wheel alignment. Adjust as necessary.

AWD Vehicles

See Figures 184 through 186.

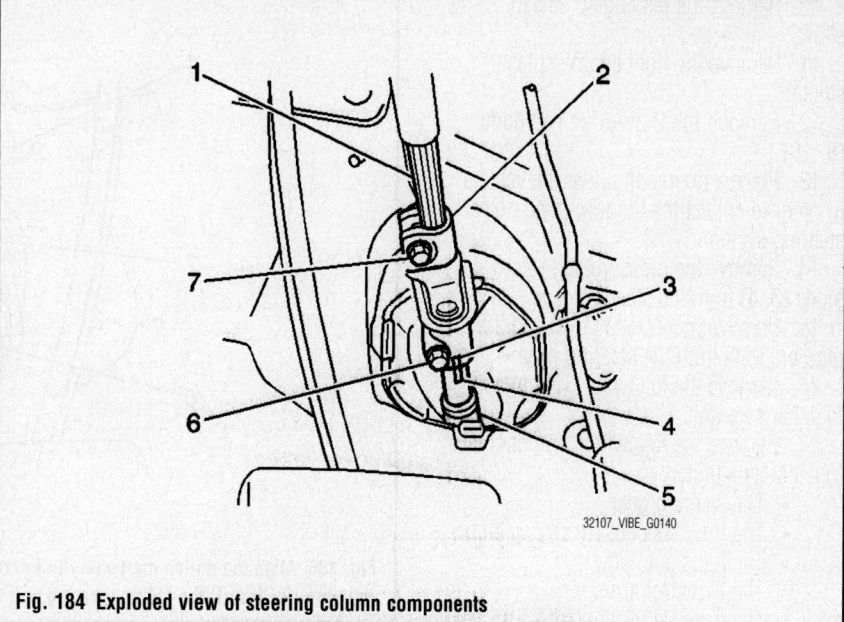

Fig. 184 Exploded view of steering column components

➡The steering column must be in the LOCK position before disconnecting the following components:

- The steering column
- The steering shaft coupling
- The intermediate shaft
- The lower steering shaft

※ WARNING

After disconnecting these components, do not move the front tires and wheels. Failure to follow these procedures may cause improper alignment of some components during installation and result in possible damage to the SIR coil.

1. LOCK the steering column and verify the front wheels are in the straight ahead position.

2. Move the silencer pad away from the steering column.

3. Use paint in order to place match marks on the steering shaft coupling (3) and on the steering gear pinion shaft (4).

4. Loosen the upper coupling bolt (7).

5. Remove the lower coupling bolt (6).

6. Remove the steering column hole cover (5) from the bulkhead.

7. Install the Engine Support Fixture.

8. Raise and support the vehicle.

9. Remove the front tire and wheel assemblies.

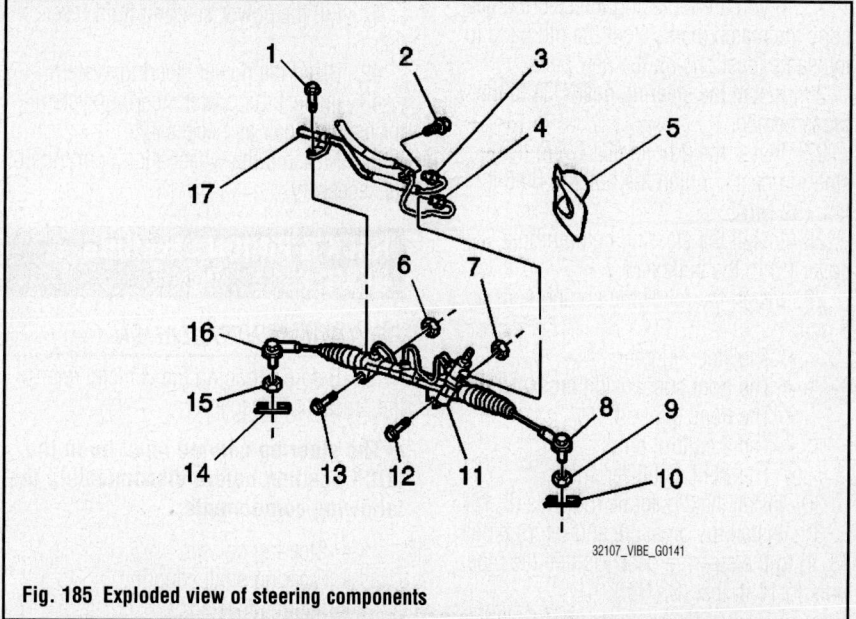

Fig. 185 Exploded view of steering components

10. Remove the left engine splash shield.

11. Remove the right engine splash shield.

12. Remove the 2 outer tie rod ends (8, 16).

13. Place a drain pan under the vehicle in order to collect the fluid from the power steering system.

14. Remove the pressure and return pipes (3, 4) from the steering gear.

15. Remove the 2 bolts (1, 2) and the pipe brackets from the steering gear.

16. Remove the following components together as a unit.

17. Remove the following components together as a unit.

- The steering gear
- The front suspension crossmember
- The trans support
- The 2 control arms
- The front stabilizer shaft

18. Remove the bolt and the rear engine mount insulator from the crossmember.

19. Remove the 3 bolts and the rear engine mount bracket from the crossmember.

20. Remove the 2 bolts (12,13) and the steering gear from the crossmember.

To install:

21. Install the rear engine mount bracket to the crossmember.

22. Install the 3 bolts to the rear engine mount bracket. Tighten the bolts to 47 ft. lbs. (64 Nm).

23. Install the rear engine mount insulator to the crossmember.

24. Install the bolt to the rear engine mount insulator. Tighten the bolt to 64 ft. lbs. (87 Nm).

25. If you are replacing the steering gear, copy the match marks from the old parts to the same locations on the new parts.

26. Install the steering gear (11) to the crossmember.

27. Install the 2 bolts (12,13) to the steering gear. Tighten the bolts to 60.5 ft. lbs. (82 Nm).

28. Install the steering column hole cover (5) to the bulkhead.

29. Install the following components as a unit.

- The steering gear
- The front suspension crossmember
- The trans support
- The 2 control arms
- The front stabilizer shaft

30. Install the 2 outer tie rod ends (8, 16).

31. Install the pressure and return pipes (3, 4) to the steering gear. Tighten the pipe nuts to 17 ft. lbs. (23 Nm).

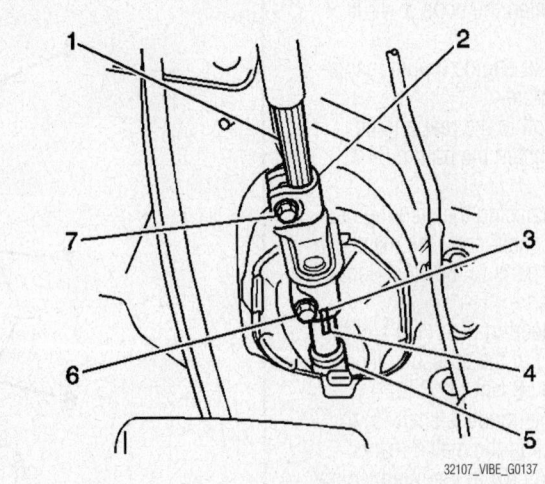

Fig. 186 Align the match marks on the intermediate shaft (4) and on the steering shaft coupling (3). Install the lower coupling bolt (6).

32107_VIBE_G0137

32. Install the 2 pipe bracket bolts (1, 2). Tighten the bolts to 69 inch lbs (7.8 Nm).

33. Install the left engine splash shield. Install the right engine splash shield.

34. Install the front tire and wheel assemblies.

35. Lower the vehicle.

36. Remove the Engine Support Fixture.

37. Align the match marks on the steering gear pinion shaft (4) and on the steering shaft coupling (3).

38. Install the lower coupling bolt (6). Tighten the bolt to 26 ft. lbs. (35 Nm).

39. Tighten the upper coupling bolt (7). Tighten the bolt to 26 ft. lbs. (35 Nm).

40. Place the silencer pad into the correct position.

41. Fill the power steering fluid reservoir.

42. Bleed the power steering system.

43. Inspect the power steering system for leaks. Repair as necessary.

44. Measure the wheel alignment. Adjust as necessary.

RACK & PINION STEERING GEAR

REMOVAL & INSTALLATION

1. Before servicing the vehicle, refer to the precautions section.

➡**The steering column must be in the LOCK position before disconnecting the following components:**

- Steering column
- Steering shaft coupling
- Intermediate shaft
- Lower steering shaft

➡**After disconnecting these components, do not move the front tires and wheels. Failure to follow these procedures may cause improper alignment of some components during installation and result in possible damage to the SIR coil.**

2. LOCK the steering column and verify the front wheels are in the straight ahead position.

3. Move the silencer pad away from the steering column.

4. Use paint in order to place match marks on the steering shaft coupling and on the intermediate shaft.

5. Loosen the upper coupling bolt.

6. Remove the lower coupling bolt.

7. Remove the steering column hole cover from the bulkhead.

8. Install the Engine Support Fixture.

9. Remove the front tire and wheel assemblies.

10. Remove the engine splash shields.

11. Remove the 2 outer tie rod ends.

12. Place a drain pan under the vehicle in order to collect the fluid from the power steering system.

13. Remove the pressure and return pipes from the steering gear.

14. Remove the bolt and the pipe bracket from the steering gear.

15. Remove the following components together as a unit:

- Steering gear
- Intermediate steering shaft
- Front suspension crossmember
- Trans support

- Control arms
- Front stabilizer shaft

16. Remove the bolt and the rear engine mount insulator from the crossmember.

17. Remove the 3 bolts and the rear engine mount bracket from the crossmember.

18. Use paint in order to place match marks on the intermediate shaft and on the steering gear.

19. Remove the bolt and the intermediate shaft (4).

20. Remove the 4 bolts and the steering gear from the crossmember.

To install:

21. Install the rear engine mount bracket to the crossmember.

22. Install the 3 bolts to the rear engine mount bracket. Tighten to 47 ft. lbs. (64 Nm).

23. Install the rear engine mount insulator to the crossmember.

24. Install the bolt to the rear engine mount insulator. Tighten to 64 ft. lbs. (87 Nm).

25. If you are replacing the steering gear or the intermediate shaft, copy the match marks from the old parts to the same locations on the new parts.

26. Install the steering gear and the 4 bolts to the crossmember. Tighten to 42 ft. lbs. (58 Nm).

27. Install the intermediate shaft to the steering gear. Align the match marks.

28. Install the bolt to the intermediate shaft. Tighten to 26 ft. lbs. (35 Nm).

29. Install the steering column hole cover to the bulkhead.

30. Install the following components as a unit:

- Steering gear
- Intermediate steering shaft
- Front suspension crossmember
- Trans support
- Control arms
- Front stabilizer shaft

31. Install the 2 outer tie rod ends.

32. Install the pressure and return pipes to the steering gear. Tighten the fittings to 17 ft. lbs. (23 Nm).

33. Install the pipe bracket bolt. Tighten to 69 inch lbs. (8 Nm).

34. Install the splash shields.

35. Install the front tire and wheel assemblies.

36. Remove the Engine Support Fixture.

37. Align the match marks on the intermediate shaft and on the steering shaft coupling.

38. Install the lower coupling bolt. Tighten to 26 ft. lbs. (35 Nm).

39. Tighten the upper coupling bolt. Tighten to 26 ft. lbs. (35 Nm).

40. Place the silencer pad into the correct position.

41. Fill the power steering fluid reservoir.

42. Bleed the power steering system.

43. Inspect the power steering system for leaks. Repair as necessary.

44. Measure the wheel alignment. Adjust as necessary

POWER STEERING PUMP

REMOVAL & INSTALLATION

See Figures 187 and 188.

1. Disconnect the negative battery cable.

2. Remove the right side front wheel.

3. Drain power steering fluid

4. Remove the right hand engine under cover.

5. Remove the drive belt.

6. Remove the clip and disconnect the oil reservoir to pump hose No.1.

7. Disconnect the pressure feed tube assembly .

8. Remove the bolt and disconnect the pressure feed tube clamp.

9. Disconnect the oil pressure switch connector.

10. Remove the 2 bolts, nuts and pump assembly .

To install:

11. Install the pump assembly with the 2 bolts and nuts. Tighten to 27 ft. lbs. (37 Nm).

12. Connect the oil pressure switch connector.

➡**Be careful that the oil does not adhere to the connector.**

13. Using SST 09023-38401, connect the pressure feed tube assembly . Tighten to 30 ft. lbs. (41 Nm) using a torque wrench with a fulcrum length of 13.58 in. (345 mm).

14. Connect the pressure feed tube clamp with the bolt. Tighten to 69 in. lbs. (8 Nm).

15. Connect the oil reservoir to pump hose No.1 with the clip.

16. Install the drive belt.

17. Install the wheel.

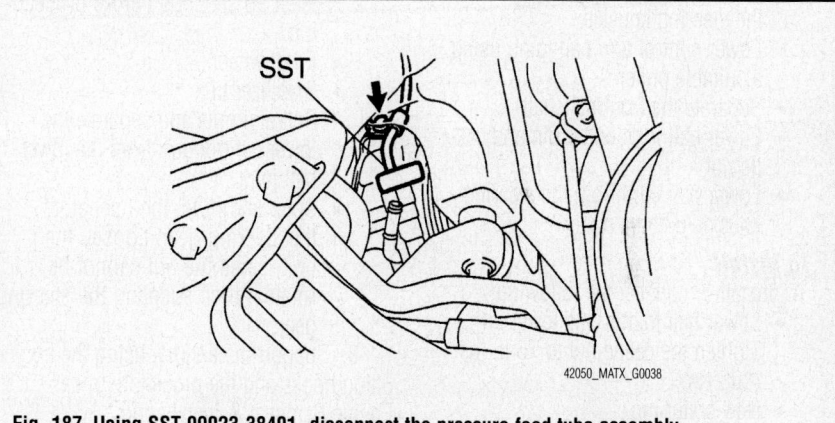

42050_MATX_G0038

Fig. 187 Using SST 09023-38401, disconnect the pressure feed tube assembly

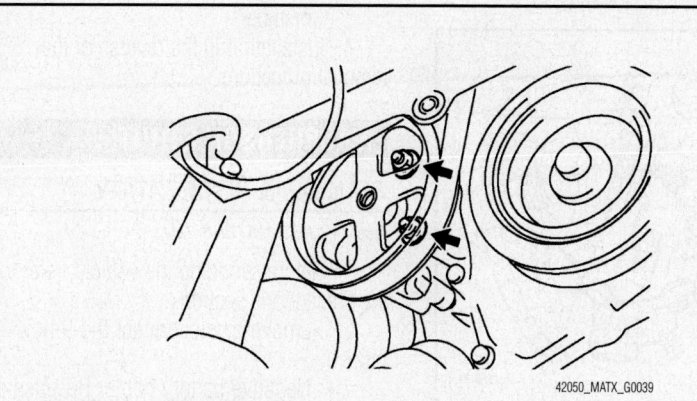

42050_MATX_G0039

Fig. 188 Location of the power steering pump assembly

18. Fill and bleed the power steering system.

19. Install the engine under cover.

BLEEDING

1. Check the fluid level and top off as needed.

2. Jack up the front of the vehicle and support it with safety stands.

3. With the engine OFF, turn the wheel from lock to lock slowly several times.

4. Lower the vehicle and start the engine and allow to idle for a few minutes.

5. With the engine warm and at idle, turn the steering wheel to the left or right lock position and hold it there for 2 to 3 seconds , then turn the wheel to the opposite side lock and hold for 2 to 3 seconds.

6. Repeat these last two steps several times.

7. Turn the vehicle off and check the fluid level.

8. if there is a lot of foam in the reservoir, check the system for leaks and repair, then bleed the system again.

SUSPENSION

LOWER BALL JOINT

REMOVAL & INSTALLATION

See Figure 189.

1. Before servicing the vehicle, refer to the precautions section.

2. Remove or disconnect the following:
- Negative battery cable. Wait at least 90 seconds before proceeding.
- Front wheel

3. Depress the brake pedal and loosen the hub nut
- ABS speed sensor, if equipped
- Cotter pin and nut from the tie rod end. Using a tie rod end removal tool, separate the tie rod end from the steering knuckle.
- Lower control arm ball joint, using a suitable puller
- Separate the front halfshaft
- Lower ball joint cotter pin and castle nut
- Lower ball joint from the steering knuckle using a puller

To install:

4. Install or connect the following:
- Lower ball joint to the lower arm. Tighten the castle nut to 76 ft. lbs. (103 Nm).
- New cotter pin
- Front halfshaft
- Lower control arm

- Tie rod end to the knuckle
- ABS speed sensor
- Hub nut
- Wheel
- Negative battery cable

5. Check and adjust the alignment, if needed.

LOWER CONTROL ARM

REMOVAL & INSTALLATION

1. Before servicing the vehicle, refer to the precautions section.

2. Remove or disconnect the following:

- Negative battery cable. Wait at least 90 seconds before proceeding.
- Front wheel
- Stabilizer link
- Bolt and nuts and separate the lower control arm from the lower ball joint
- Bolts and nuts, then separate the steering gear. Loosen the bolt, since the nut cannot be rotated, then suspend the steering gear.

3. Support the engine, using the engine lifting hooks and the procedure under Engine Removal & Installation.
- Crossmember
- Lower control arm from the crossmember

4. Installation is the reverse of the removal procedure.

MACPHERSON STRUT

REMOVAL & INSTALLATION

See Figures 190 and 191.

1. Before servicing the vehicle, refer to the precautions section.

2. Remove or disconnect the following:

- Negative battery cable. Because of the air bag system, wait at least 90 seconds before proceeding

FRONT SUSPENSION

✶✶ WARNING

Do not support the weight of the vehicle on the suspension arm; the arm will deform under its weight.

- Wheel
- Stabilizer link from the strut
- Bolt, and disconnect the brake hose from the strut
- With ABS brakes, speed sensor wiring harness from the strut
- Lower strut bolts and nuts
- Upper strut nuts
- Strut from the steering knuckle
- Strut

3. To disassemble the strut:
- Install a bolt and 2 nuts to the bracket at the lower portion of the strut shell and secure it in a vise
- Compress the coil spring
- Dust cover and hold the spring seat so that it will not turn
- Nut on the top of the strut
- Suspension support, bearing, dust seal, spring seat, spring, insulators and bumper

To install:

4. To assemble the strut:
- Install the spring bumper to piston

5. Using a spring compressor, compress the spring.
- Coil spring to the strut. Fit the lower end of the coil spring into the gap of the lower seat.
- Spring seat with the insulator
- Dust seal on the spring seat
- Suspension support and tighten 35 ft. lbs. (47 Nm). After the nut has been tighten, release the compressor tool tension.

6. Pack multipurpose grease into the suspension support.
- Dust cover.

➥**Do not use an impact wrench to tighten the nut. Also, check that the bearing fits into the recess in the suspension support.**

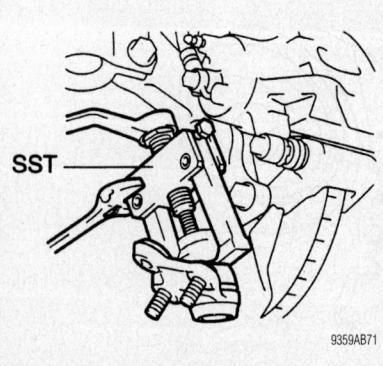

Fig. 189 Removing the ball joint from the knuckle

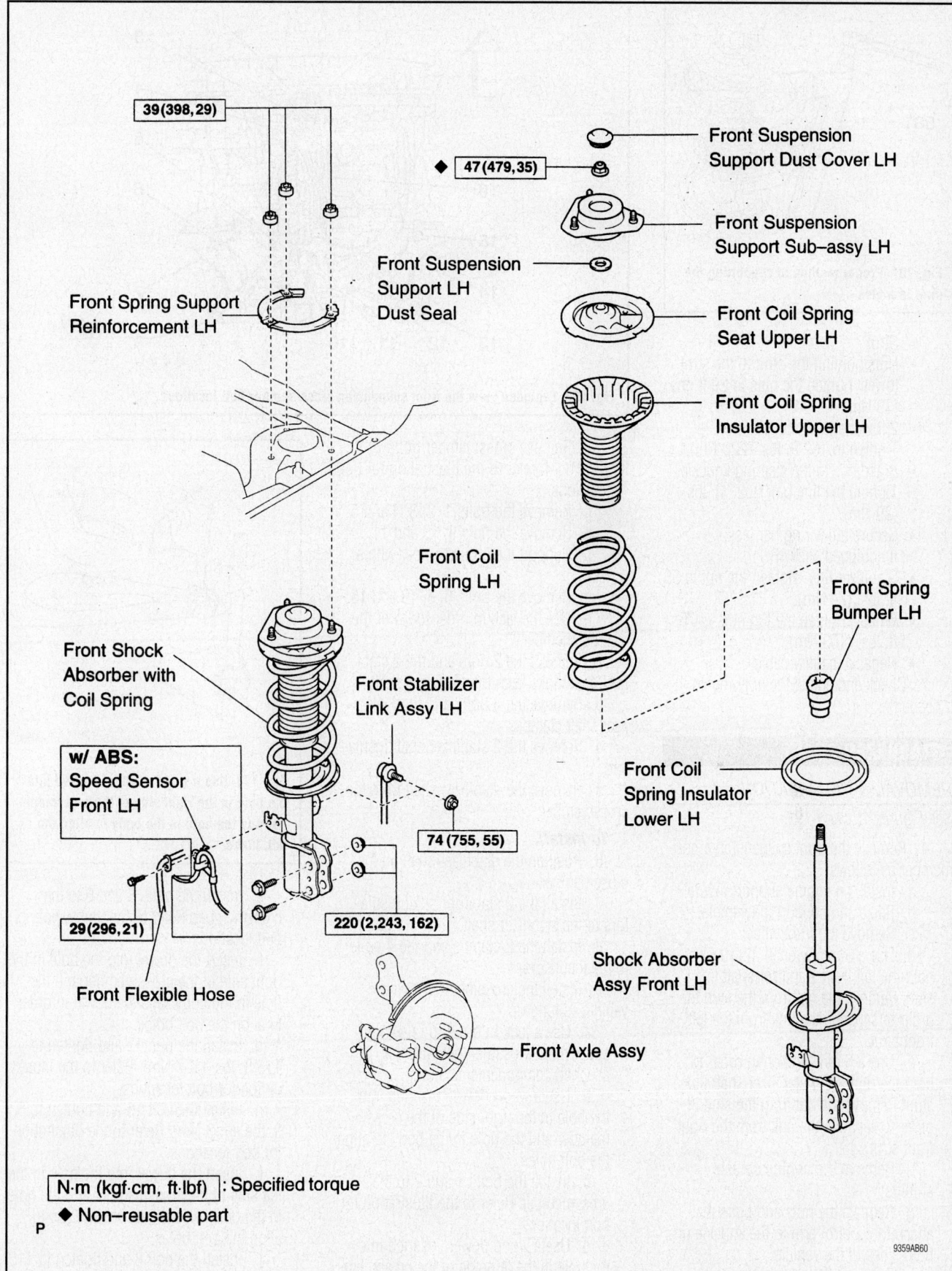

39(398, 29)

47(479, 35)

Front Suspension
Support Dust Cover LH

Front Suspension
Support Sub–assy LH

Front Spring Support
Reinforcement LH

Front Suspension
Support LH
Dust Seal

Front Coil Spring
Seat Upper LH

Front Coil Spring
Insulator Upper LH

Front Coil
Spring LH

Front Spring
Bumper LH

Front Shock
Absorber with
Coil Spring

Front Stabilizer
Link Assy LH

Front Coil
Spring Insulator
Lower LH

w/ ABS:
Speed Sensor
Front LH

74 (755, 55)

29(296, 21)

220 (2,243, 162)

Front Flexible Hose

Shock Absorber
Assy Front LH

Front Axle Assy

N·m (kgf·cm, ft·lbf) : Specified torque

P ◆ Non–reusable part

9359AB60

Fig. 190 Common coil spring and strut component assembly

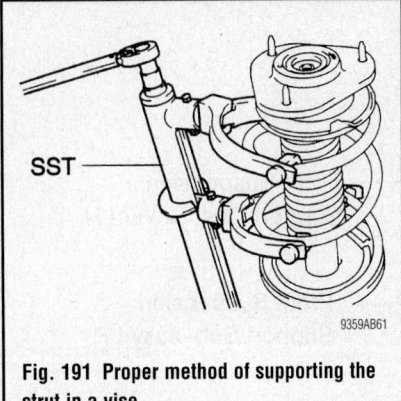

Fig. 191 Proper method of supporting the strut in a vise

- Strut
- Nuts holding the strut to the strut tower. Tighten the nuts to 29 ft. lbs. (39 Nm).
- 2 lower strut bolts and nuts. Tighten to 162 ft. lbs. (220 Nm).
- Brake line to the steering knuckle. Tighten the line bolt to 21 ft. lbs. (29 Nm).
- Secure the wiring harness, if equipped with ABS
- Stabilizer link. Tighten the nut to 55 ft. lbs. (74 Nm).
- Wheel. Tighten the lug nuts to 76 ft. lbs. (103 Nm).
- Negative battery cable

7. Check and adjust the alignment, if needed

STABILIZER SHAFT

REMOVAL & INSTALLATION

See Figures 192 and 193.

1. Remove the front suspension crossmember as follows:

    a. Install an engine support fixture.

    b. Raise and support the vehicle.

    c. Remove the front wheel.

    d. Use a 6 mm wrench in order to hold the left front stabilizer shaft link stud. Remove the nut from the stud in order to separate the link from the left front strut.

    e. Use a 6 mm wrench in order to hold the right front stabilizer shaft link stud. Remove the nut from the stud in order to separate the link from the right front strut.

    f. Remove the engine splash shields.

    g. Remove the nuts and bolts that attach the control arm to the knuckle on both sides of the vehicle.

    h. Suspend the steering gear using wire.

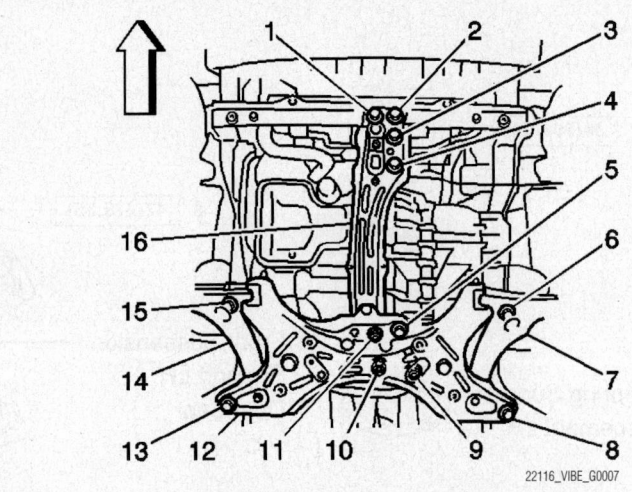

Fig. 192 Exploded view the front suspension crossmember bolt locations

    i. Remove crossmember bolts 7, 12, 13 and 14. refer to the illustration for bolt locations.

    j. Remove the bolts 1, 2, 3, 4 and 5.

    k. Remove the nuts 9, 10 and 11.

    l. Support the crossmember with a jack.

    m. Remove the bolts 6, 8, 13 and 15.

    n. Use the jack in order to lower the crossmember.

2. Remove the 2 nuts and the 2 stabilizer shaft links from the stabilizer shaft.

3. Remove the 4 bolts and the 2 stabilizer shaft clamps.

4. Remove the 2 stabilizer shaft insulators.

5. Remove the stabilizer shaft from the crossmember.

To install:

6. Position the stabilizer shaft on the crossmember.

7. Install the 2 stabilizer shaft insulators to the stabilizer shaft.

8. Install the 2 clamps and the 4 bolts to the insulators.

9. Install the crossmember to the vehicle as follows:

    a. Use a jack in order to raise and support the crossmember with the attached components as a unit.

    b. Use a wood dowel, inserted into the hole in the right side of the crossmember and the hole in the body to align the bolt holes.

    c. Install the bolts 1 and 2 to the crossmember. Refer to the illustration for bolt locations.

    d. Use a wood dowel, inserted into the hole in the left side of the crossmember and the hole in the body to align the bolt holes

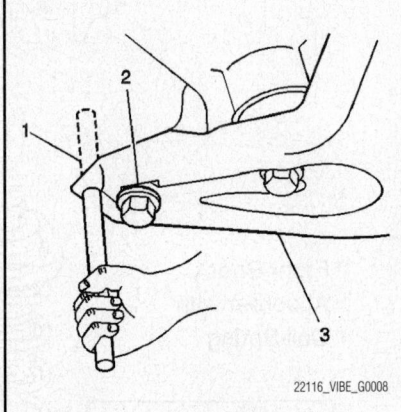

Fig. 193 Use a wood dowel, inserted into the hole in the right side of the crossmember and the hole in the body to align the bolt holes

    e. Install the bolts 8 and 6 to the crossmember. Refer to the illustration for bolt locations.

    f. Insert the dowel into the hole in the right side of the crossmember and the hole in the body. Use the dowel in order to align the bolt holes.

    g. Install the bolt 13 and tighten to 115 ft. lbs. (157 Nm). Refer to the illustration for bolt locations.

    h. Install the bolt 15 and tighten to 83 ft. lbs. (113 Nm). Refer to the illustration for bolt locations.

    i. Insert the dowel into the hole in the left side of the crossmember and the hole in the body. Use the dowel in order to align the bolt holes.

    j. Install the bolt 8 and tighten to 115 ft. lbs. (157 Nm). Refer to the illustration for bolt locations.

k. Install the bolt 6 and tighten to 83 ft. lbs. (113 Nm). Refer to the illustration for bolt locations.

l. Remove the jack from the cross-member.

m. Install the nuts 9, 10 and 11. Tighten to 38 ft. lbs. (52 Nm). Refer to the illustration for bolt locations.

n. Install the bolts 1, 2, 3, 4 and 5. Tighten to 38 ft. lbs. (52 Nm). Refer to the illustration for bolt locations.

o. Install the bolts 7, 12, 13 and 14. Tighten to 42 ft. lbs. (58 Nm). Refer to the illustration for bolt locations.

p. Remove the wire from the steering gear.

q. Install the control arm to knuckle nuts and bolts. Tighten to 65 ft. lbs. (89 Nm).

r. Install the splash shields.

s. Use a 6 mm wrench in order to hold the left front stabilizer shaft link stud to the stabilizer link. Install the nut and the stud to the strut bracket. Tighten the nut to 54 ft. lbs. (74 Nm).

t. Use a 6 mm wrench in order to hold the right front stabilizer shaft link stud to the stabilizer link. Install the nut and the stud to the strut bracket. Tighten the nut to 54 ft. lbs. (74 Nm).

u. Install the front tire and lower the vehicle.

v. Remove the engine support fixture.

STEERING KNUCKLE

REMOVAL & INSTALLATION

See Figures 194 through 196.

Tools Required
• J 6627-A Tie Rod Puller
• J 24319-B Steering Linkage and Tie Rod Puller

You may remove the following components as an assembly:
• The steering knuckle
• The lower ball joint
• The front hub
• The wheel studs
• The front wheel bearing
• The disc brake shield

1. Raise and support the vehicle.

2. Remove the front tire and wheel assembly.

3. If the vehicle has ABS, remove the ABS wheel speed sensor from the steering knuckle. Position the sensor to the side.

4. Unstake the front wheel drive shaft nut.

5. Remove the drive shaft nut from the drive axle while an assistant presses the brake pedal.

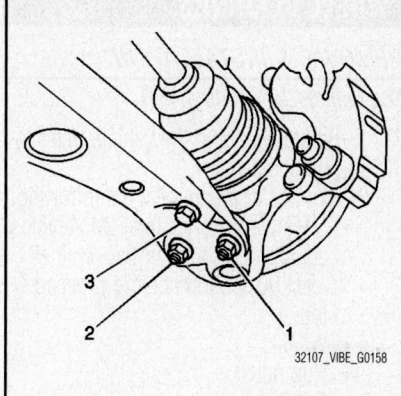

Fig. 194 Remove the 2 nuts (1, 2) and the bolt (3) from the lower control arm

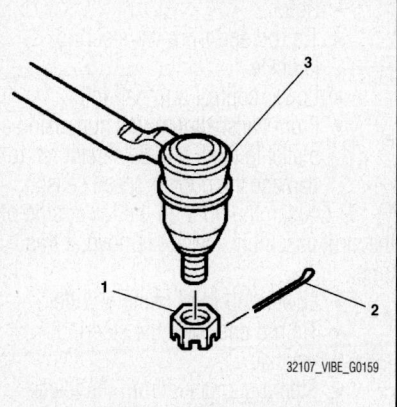

Fig. 195 Outer tie rod nut (1) and cotter pin (2)

6. Remove the 2 nuts (1, 2) and the bolt (3) from the lower control arm.

7. Remove the brake rotor.

8. Loosen the nuts on the lower side of the strut assembly. Do not remove the bolts.

9. Remove the outer tie rod cotter pin (2).

10. Remove the outer tie rod nut (1).

11. Use the J 6627-A , or equivalent, in order to disconnect the outer tie rod from the knuckle.

12. Remove the 2 nuts and the 2 bolts from lower side of the strut assembly.

13. Remove the steering knuckle from the strut.

➡>**If you are replacing the steering knuckle, continue with this procedure.**

14. Remove the front wheel bearing and the disc brake shield.

15. Remove the steering knuckle cotter pin (5) and the ball stud nut (4).

16. Use the J 24319-B , or equivalent, in order to remove the ball joint (3) from the steering knuckle.

To install:

➡**Do not loosen the nut in order to insert the cotter pin.**

17. Install the ball joint (3) and the nut (4) to the steering knuckle (2). Tighten the nut to 103 Nm (76.0 lb ft). Tighten the nut up to ⅙ additional turn in order to insert the cotter pin.

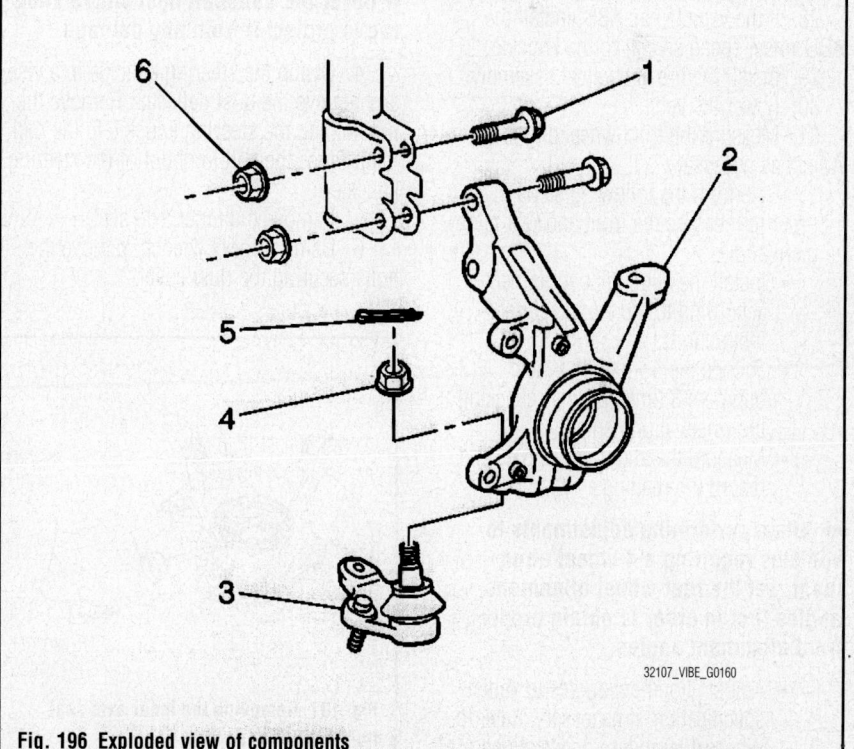

Fig. 196 Exploded view of components

18. Install a NEW cotter pin (5) to the ball joint stud. Bend the cotter pin ends in order to retain the nut.

19. Install the front wheel bearing and the disc brake shield to the steering knuckle.

➡**Do not tighten the nuts or the bolts.**

20. Install the following components to the lower side of the strut assembly:
- The steering knuckle
- The 2 bolts
- The 2 nuts

➡**Do not loosen the nut in order to insert the cotter pin.**

21. Install the outer tie rod and the nut to the steering knuckle. Tighten the outer tie rod nut to 49 Nm (36 lb ft). Tighten the nut up to ⅙ additional turn in order to insert the cotter pin.

22. Install a NEW cotter pin to the tie rod ball joint stud. Bend the cotter pin ends in order to retain the nut.

23. Install the front brake rotor.

24. Install a NEW drive shaft nut while an assistant applies the brakes. Tighten the nut to 159 ft. lbs. (216 Nm).

25. Stake the drive shaft nut into the slot on the wheel drive shaft.

26. Install the bolt (3) and the 2 nuts (1, 2) to the control arm. Tighten the bolt and the 2 nuts to 89 Nm (65.6 lb ft).

27. Tighten the nuts and the bolts on the lower side of the strut assembly. Tighten the nuts and bolts to 220 Nm (162.3 lb ft).

28. If the vehicle has ABS, install the ABS wheel speed sensor to the knuckle.

29. Install the tire and wheel assembly.

30. Lower the vehicle.

31. Measure the front wheel alignment. Adjust as necessary.

  a. Perform the following steps in order to measure the front and rear alignment angles:
- Install the alignment equipment according to the manufacturer's instructions.
- Jounce the front and the rear bumpers 3 times prior to checking the wheel alignment.
- Measure the alignment angles and record the readings.

➡ **When performing adjustments to vehicles requiring a 4-wheel alignment, set the rear wheel alignment angles first in order to obtain proper front alignment angles.**

- Adjust alignment angles to vehicle specification, if necessary. Refer to Wheel Alignment Specifications.

WHEEL BEARINGS

REMOVAL & INSTALLATION

See Figures 197 through 201.

1. Before servicing the vehicle, refer to the precautions section.

2. Remove or disconnect the following:
- Negative battery cable. On vehicles equipped with an air bag, wait at least 90 seconds before proceeding.
- Wheels
- Hub nut
- Front stabilizer link
- Anti-lock Brake System (ABS) speed sensor
- Brake caliper
- Rotor
- Tie rod end from the steering knuckle
- Lower control arm ball joint
- Front halfshaft from the hub, using a mallet to tap it out. Be careful not to damage the boot or speed sensor.

3. Loosen the nuts on the lower side of the strut assembly. Do not remove at this time.
- Lower ball joint using a puller
- Tie rod end from the steering knuckle
- Steering knuckle from the lower control arm
- Knuckle from the strut assembly
- Hub

➡**Cover the halfshaft boot with a shop rag to protect it from any damage.**

4. Clamp the steering knuckle in a vise and remove the dust deflector. Remove the nut holding the steering knuckle to the ball joint. Press the ball joint out of the steering knuckle.

5. Remove the inner axle seal.

6. Using a Torx® wrench, remove the bolts securing the dust cover.

7. Using hub puller, remove the hub and backing plate from the steering knuckle.

8. Using a proper sized driver and a press, remove the inner hub race from the axle hub.

9. Using seal removal tool, remove the outer axle seal.

10. Using snapring pliers, remove the snapring from the inner side of the steering knuckle.

11. Using a proper sized driver and a press, remove the bearing from the steering knuckle. The bearing is pressed from the front of the steering knuckle and is removed through the back of the steering knuckle.

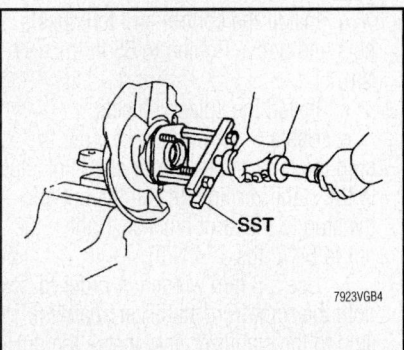

Fig. 198 Removing the axle hub from the knuckle

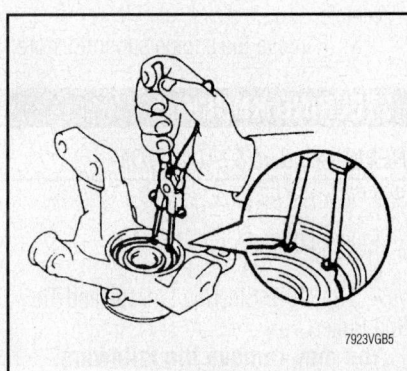

Fig. 199 Removing the snapring from the knuckle before pressing out the bearing

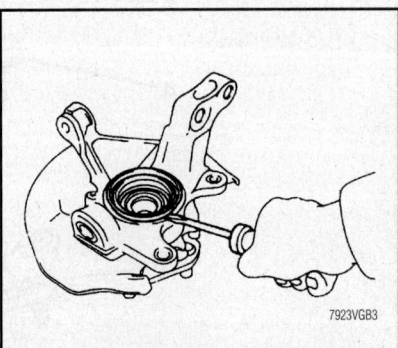

Fig. 197 Removing the inner axle seal from the hub assembly

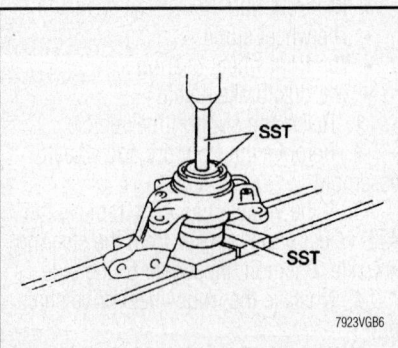

Fig. 200 Removing the bearing from the steering knuckle using a press

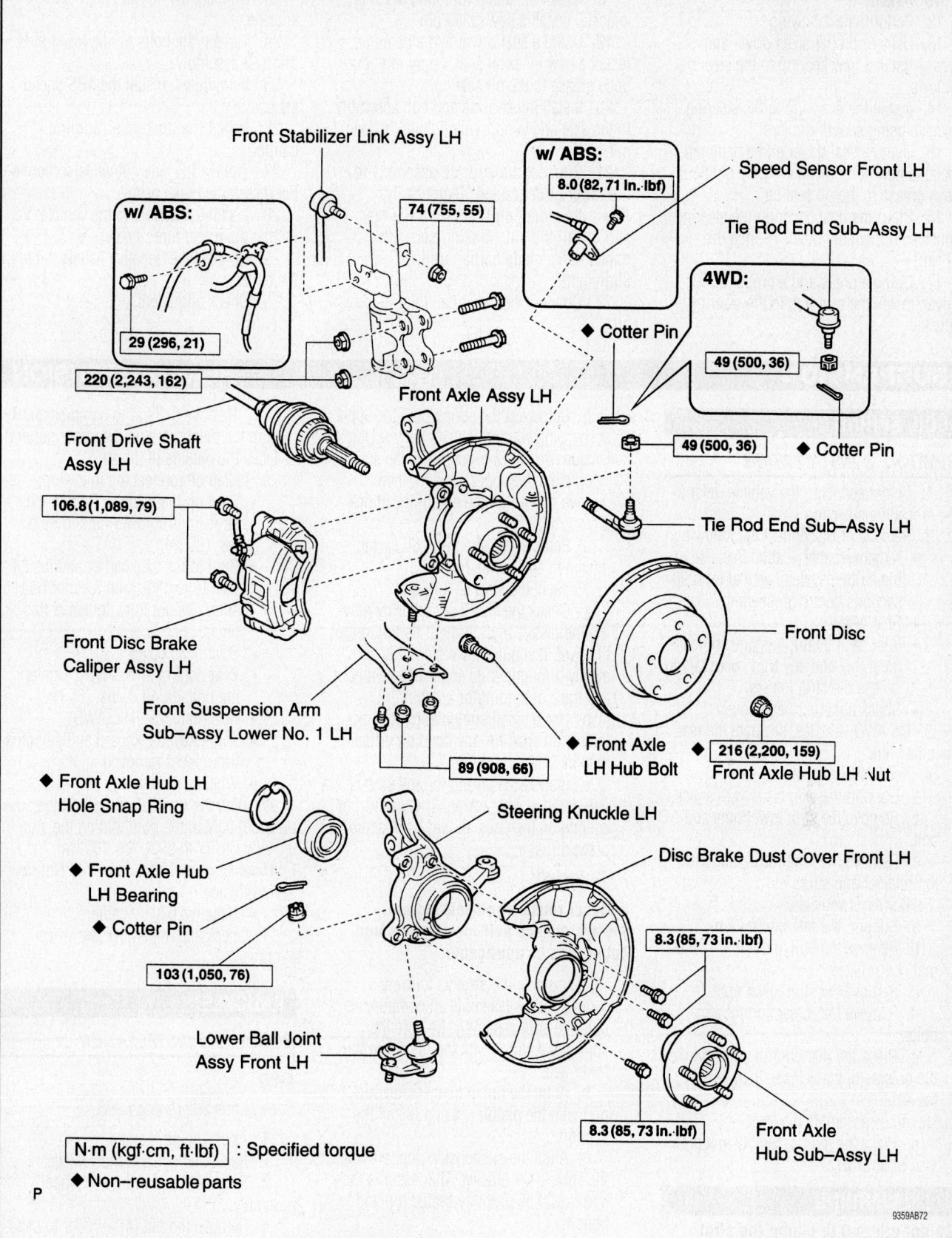

Front Stabilizer Link Assy LH

w/ ABS:

8.0 (82, 71 in.·lbf)

Speed Sensor Front LH

Tie Rod End Sub–Assy LH

w/ ABS:

29 (296, 21)

220 (2,243, 162)

74 (755, 55)

4WD:

49 (500, 36)

◆ Cotter Pin

Front Axle Assy LH

49 (500, 36)

◆ Cotter Pin

Front Drive Shaft
Assy LH

Tie Rod End Sub–Assy LH

106.8 (1,089, 79)

Front Disc

Front Disc Brake
Caliper Assy LH

Front Suspension Arm
Sub–Assy Lower No. 1 LH

◆ Front Axle
LH Hub Bolt

216 (2,200, 159)
Front Axle Hub LH Nut

89 (908, 66)

◆ Front Axle Hub LH
Hole Snap Ring

Steering Knuckle LH

Disc Brake Dust Cover Front LH

◆ Front Axle Hub
LH Bearing

8.3 (85, 73 in.·lbf)

◆ Cotter Pin

103 (1,050, 76)

Lower Ball Joint
Assy Front LH

8.3 (85, 73 in.·lbf)

Front Axle
Hub Sub–Assy LH

N·m (kgf·cm, ft·lbf) : Specified torque

◆ Non–reusable parts

P

9359AB72

Fig. 201 Exploded view of the front hub and bearing, and related components

To install:

12. Perform the following:

13. Using a proper sized driver and a press, install a new bearing to the steering knuckle.

14. Install the snapring to the steering knuckle using snapring pliers.

15. Using a seal driver and a hammer, install a new outer oil seal. Apply multipurpose grease to the oil seal lip.

16. Place the dust cover on the steering knuckle. Tighten the bolts: 78 inch lbs. (9 Nm).

17. Using a press and a proper sized driver, install the axle hub to the steering knuckle.

18. Attach the ball joint to the steering knuckle. Install a new cotter pin.

19. Using a seal driver and a hammer, install a new inner oil seal. Apply multipurpose grease to the oil seal lip.

20. Install the knuckle and hub assembly to the axle and temporarily tighten the axle nut.

21. Connect the knuckle assembly to the lower strut bracket. Temporarily insert the mounting bolts from the rear and install the nuts making sure the matchmarks made earlier are in alignment.

22. Connect the lower ball joint to lower arm.

23. Connect the tie rod end to the knuckle.

24. Tighten the bolts on the lower side of the strut assembly.

25. If equipped, install the ABS speed sensor.

26. Install the brake disc and the caliper.

27. Tighten the axle nut while someone depresses the brake pedal.

28. Install the wheels to the vehicle. Verify that the wheel turns freely.

29. Connect the negative battery cable to the battery.

30. Check alignment.

SUSPENSION

REAR SUSPENSION

COIL SPRING

REMOVAL & INSTALLATION

1. Before servicing the vehicle, refer to the precautions section.

2. Remove or disconnect the following:
   - Negative battery cable. Because of the air bag system, wait at least 90 seconds before proceeding.
   - Rear wheel
   - Rear deck board, luggage compartment tray and any trim necessary to access the strut towers
   - Shock absorber head cover

3. On AWD vehicles, separate the rear stabilizer link.

4. For FWD vehicles:
   a. Support the axle beam with a jack.
   b. Remove the strut tower nuts and bolt.
   c. Remove the lower strut nut, cushion retainer and strut .

5. For AWD vehicles:
   a. Support the rear control arm.
   b. Remove the bolt and nut from the rear control arm.
   c. Remove the strut tower nuts.
   d. Remove the 3 rear control arm bolts.
   e. Press the rear control arm down to the outside of the vehicle, then remove the strut.

6. To disassemble the strut:
   a. Place the strut assembly in a pipe vise or strut vise.

❊❊ WARNING

Do not attempt to clamp the strut assembly in a flat jaw vise as this will result in damage to the strut tube.

   b. Compress the spring until the upper suspension support is free of any spring tension. Do not over-compress the spring.
   c. Hold the upper support, then remove the nut on the end of the shock piston rod.
   d. Remove the support, coil spring, insulator, and bumper.

7. Inspect the strut as follows:
   a. Check the shock absorber by moving the piston shaft through its full range of travel. It should move smoothly and evenly throughout its entire travel without any trace of binding or notching.
   b. Use a small straightedge to check the piston shaft for any bending or deformation.
   c. Inspect the spring for any sign of deterioration or cracking. The waterproof coating on the coils should be intact to prevent rusting.

To install:

➡**Never reuse a self-locking nut. Always replace self-locking nuts and cotter pins as applicable.**

8. Assemble the strut as follows:
   a. Loosely assemble all components onto the strut assembly. Be sure the spring end aligns with the hollow in the lower seat.
   b. Align the upper suspension support with the piston rod and install the support.
   c. Align the suspension support with the strut lower bracket. This assures the spring will be properly seated top and bottom.
   d. Compress the spring to expose the strut piston rod threads.
   e. Install a new strut piston nut and tighten to 41 ft. lbs. (56 Nm).

   f. Remove the spring compressor. Be sure the paint mark on the upper support faces the outside of the strut.

9. Install or connect the following:
   - Strut on the vehicle. Tighten the strut-to-strut tower nuts to 59 ft. lbs. (80 Nm).
   - Strut to the axle carrier and install the nut and cushion retainer/bolt snug. Do not fully tighten at this time.
   - Strut head cover
   - Rear control arm (AWD). Tighten the bolts to 48 ft. lbs. (65 Nm).
   - Rear stabilizer link (AWD)
   - Trunk tray, deckboard and any other trim pieces removed
   - Wheel

10. With the vehicle's weight on the suspension, tighten the bolt holding the strut to the axle carrier to 59 ft. lbs. (80 Nm) for FWD vehicles, or 103 ft. lbs. (140 Nm) for AWD vehicles.
    - Negative battery cable

11. Check and adjust the rear wheel alignment.

KNUCKLE

REMOVAL & INSTALLATION

AWD

See Figures 202 through 206.

1. Apply the park brake.

2. Raise and support the vehicle.

3. Remove the rear tire and wheel assembly.

4. Remove the nut (4) in order to separate the stabilizer shaft link stud from the knuckle.

5. Remove and discard the cotter pin from the wheel drive shaft nut.

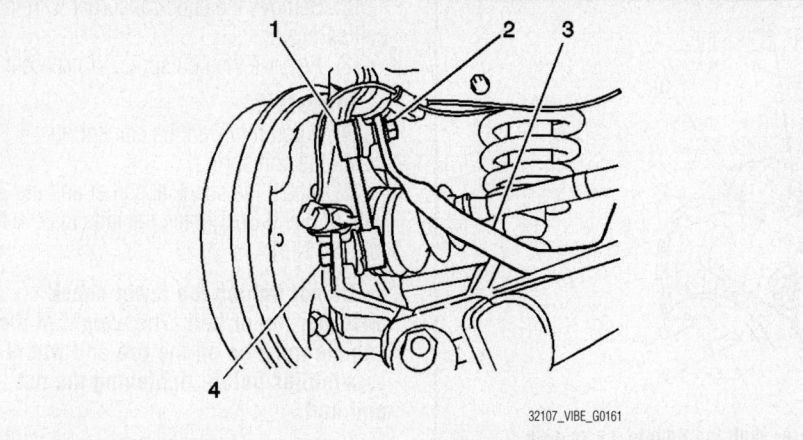

Fig. 202 Remove the nut (4) in order to separate the stabilizer shaft link stud from the knuckle.

6. Remove the lock cap from the wheel drive shaft nut.

7. Remove and discard the wheel drive shaft nut.

8. Release the park brake.

9. If the vehicle has ABS, remove the rear wheel speed sensor and pigtail.

10. Remove the brake drum

11. Remove the brake shoes and the brake hardware.

12. Use containers in order to catch the brake fluid.

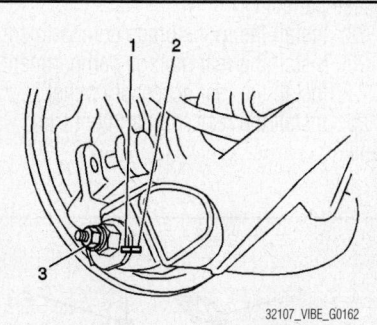

Fig. 203 Use paint in order to place match marks (1, 2) on the camber adjust cams. Remove the nut (3) and the cam.

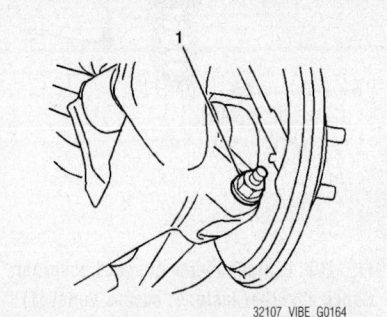

Fig. 204 Remove the nut (1) and the bolt in order to separate the lower control arm from the knuckle.

13. Remove the wheel cylinder.

14. Use paint in order to place match marks (1, 2) on the camber adjust cams.

15. Remove the nut (3) and the cam.

16. Remove the cam bolt.

17. Remove the nut (1) and the bolt in order to separate the lower control arm from the knuckle.

18. Remove the nut (2) and the bolt (3) in order to separate the upper control arm (1) from the knuckle.

➡ Support the wheel drive shaft.

19. Remove the knuckle from the wheel drive shaft.

20. Remove the wheel bearing and hub assembly.

21. Remove the drum brake backing plate.

To install:

22. Install the drum brake backing plate and the wheel bearing and hub assembly to the knuckle.

23. Install the knuckle to the wheel drive shaft.

➡ Do not tighten the nuts or the bolts on the control arms. The weight of the vehicle must be on the tire and wheel assemblies before tightening the nuts and the bolts.

24. Install the bolt (3) and the nut (2) in order to retain the knuckle to the upper control arm (1).

25. Install the bolt and the nut (1) to the front of the rear lower control arm.

26. Align the match marks (1, 2) and install the cam bolt to the rear of the rear lower control arm.

27. Align the match marks and install the cam to the cam bolt.

28. Install the nut (3) to the cam bolt.

29. Install the wheel cylinder.

30. Install the brake shoes and the brake hardware.

31. Install the brake drum.

32. Apply the park brake.

33. Install a NEW wheel drive shaft spindle nut.

34. Slowly tighten the nut in order to draw the wheel drive shaft spindle into the wheel bearing and hub. Tighten the nut to 159.3 ft. lbs. (216 Nm).

35. Install the lock cap.

36. Install a NEW cotter pin.

37. If the vehicle has ABS, install the rear wheel speed sensor and pigtail.

38. Install the nut (4) in order to retain the stabilizer shaft link stud to the knuckle. Tighten the nut to 32.5 ft. lbs. (44 Nm).

39. Install the rear tire and wheel assembly.

40. Lower the vehicle.

41. Bounce the rear of the vehicle in order to stabilize the suspension.

➡ The weight of the vehicle must be on the tire and wheel assemblies.

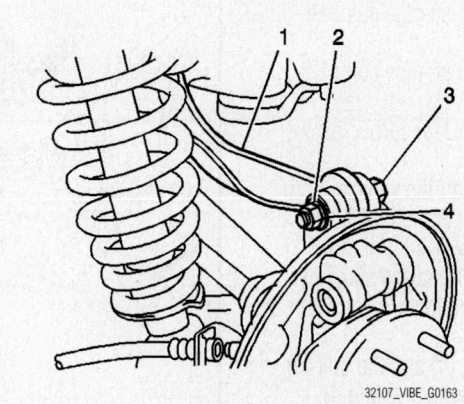

Fig. 205 Remove the nut (2) and the bolt (3) in order to separate the upper control arm (1) from the knuckle.

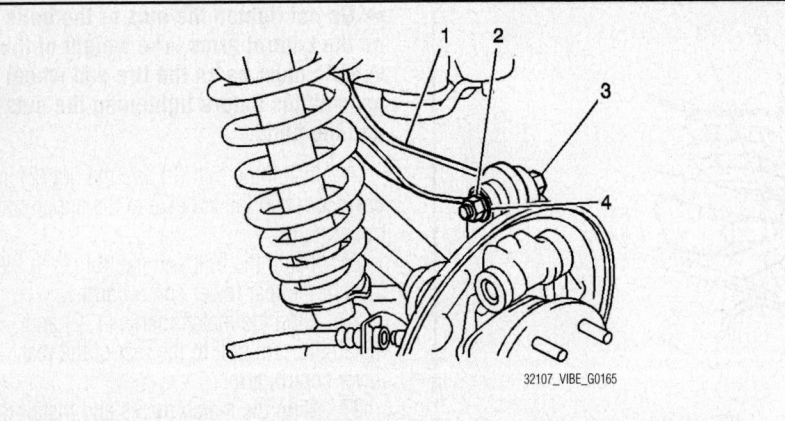

Fig. 206 Install the nut (4) in order to retain the stabilizer shaft link stud to the knuckle.

42. Tighten the nut and the bolt that retains the upper control arm to the knuckle. Tighten the nut and the bolt to 54.6 ft. lbs. (74 Nm).

43. Align the match marks and tighten the nut and the cam bolt that retains the rear of the lower control arm to the knuckle. Tighten the nut and the bolt to 54.6 ft. lbs. (74 Nm).

44. Tighten the nut and the bolt that retains the front of the lower control arm to the knuckle. Tighten the nut and the bolt to 54.6 ft. lbs. (74 Nm).

45. Release the park brake.

46. Bleed the brake system.

47. Measure the wheel alignment. Adjust if necessary.

SHOCK ABSORBER

REMOVAL & INSTALLATION

AWD Vehicles

See Figures 207 through 209.

1. Remove the rear compartment trim panel.

2. Remove the rear accessory panel.

3. Remove the rear storage compartment.

4. Remove the tool storage compartment.

5. Remove the shock absorber fastener access panel (1).

6. Raise and support the vehicle.

7. Use a block of wood and a jack in order to support the lower control arm.

8. Remove the nut and the stabilizer shaft link stud from the lower control arm.

9. Remove the nut (4) and the bolt (5).

10. Remove the 3 bolts (1,3,and 4).

11. Move the front of the lower control arm (2) down and toward the outside of the vehicle.

12. Remove the shock absorber with the coil spring.

13. Remove the coil spring, if necessary.

To install:

14. If you removed the coil spring, install the coil spring.

15. Install the shock absorber and the 3 nuts (2,3,and 6). Tighten the nuts to 59.0 ft. lbs. (80 Nm).

➡ **Do not tighten the lower shock absorber nut or bolt. The weight of the vehicle must be on the tire and wheel assemblies before tightening the nut and bolt.**

16. Install the bolt (5) and the nut (4).

17. Install the 3 bolts in order to retain the lower control arm to the body. Tighten the bolts to 47.9 ft. lbs. (65 Nm).

➡ **Do not tighten the stabilizer shaft link nut. The weight of the vehicle must be on the tire and wheel assemblies before tightening the nut.**

18. Install the nut and the stabilizer shaft link stud to the lower control arm.

19. Remove the jack and the block of wood.

20. Lower the vehicle.

21. Install the shock absorber fastener access panel (1).

22. Install the tool storage compartment.

23. Install the rear storage compartment.

24. Install the rear accessory panel.

25. Install the rear compartment trim panel.

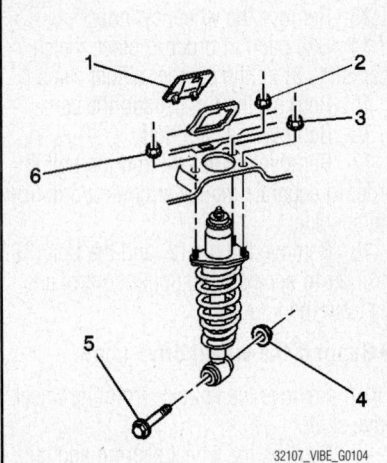

Fig. 207 Exploded view of shock absorber components. Shock absorber fastener access panel (1) and 3 nuts (2,3,6) Stabilizer shaft link stud from the lower control arm the nut (4) and the bolt (5).

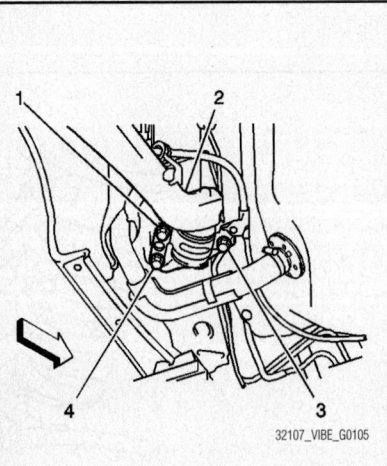

Fig. 208 Remove the shock absorber with the coil spring.

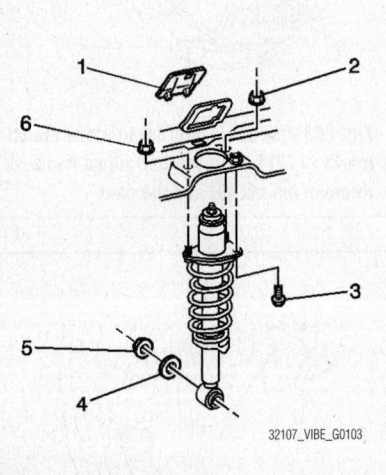

Fig. 209 Exploded view of shock absorber: Shock absorber fastener access panel (1) and 3 nuts (2,3,6) Stabilizer shaft link stud from the lower control arm, the nut (4) and the bolt (5).

26. Bounce the rear of the vehicle in order to stabilize the suspension.

27. Tighten the lower shock absorber nut (4) and the bolt (5). Tighten the nut and the bolt to 103.3 ft. lbs. (140 Nm).

28. Tighten the nut to the stabilizer shaft link stud. Tighten the nut to 32.5 ft. lbs. (44 Nm).

29. Measure the wheel alignment. Adjust if necessary.

FWD Vehicles

See Figure 207.

1. Remove the rear compartment trim panel.

2. Remove the rear accessory panel.

3. Remove the rear storage compartment.

4. Remove the tool storage compartment.

5. Remove the shock absorber fastener access panel (1).

6. Remove the 2 nuts (2,6).

7. Raise and support the vehicle.

8. Use a block of wood and a jack in order to support the rear axle.

9. Remove the bolt (3).

10. Remove the nut (5) and the washer (4).

11. Remove the shock absorber with the coil spring.

12. Remove the coil spring, if necessary.

To install:

13. If you removed the coil spring, install the coil spring.

14. Install the shock absorber and the bolt (3). Tighten the bolt to 59.0 ft. lbs. (80 Nm).

➡ **Do not tighten the lower shock absorber nut. The weight of the vehicle must be on the tire and wheel assemblies before tightening the nut.**

15. Install the washer (4) and the nut (5).

16. Remove the jack and the block of wood.

17. Lower the vehicle.

18. Bounce the rear of the vehicle in order to stabilize the suspension.

19. Install the 2 nuts (2,6). Tighten the nuts to 59.0 ft. lbs. (80 Nm).

20. Install the shock absorber fastener access panel (1).

21. Install the tool storage compartment.

22. Install the rear storage compartment.

23. Install the rear accessory panel.

24. Install the rear compartment trim panel.

25. Tighten the lower shock absorber nut (5). Tighten the nut to 59.0 ft. lbs. (80 Nm).

26. Measure the wheel alignment. Adjust if necessary.

UPPER CONTROL ARM

REMOVAL & INSTALLATION

AWD Only

1. Before servicing the vehicle, refer to the precautions section.

2. Remove or disconnect the following:
- Negative battery cable. Wait at least 90 seconds before proceeding
- Rear wheel
- Exhaust pipe
- Propeller shaft with center bearing shaft
- Rear stabilizer links
- Rear hub nuts
- Rear brake drum
- Speed sensor
- Front brake shoe
- Parking brake shoe strut set
- Rear brake shoe
- Parking brake cables
- Rear brake hoses
- Separate the rear suspension arms
- Separate the upper control arm
- Rear drive axle assembly
- Rear strut nut and bolt
- Rear strut
- Rear suspension arm
- Rear suspension member
- Upper control arm assembly. Matchmark the camber adjust cams and rear suspension member prior to removal.

3. Installation is the reverse of the removal procedure.

WHEEL BEARINGS

REMOVAL & INSTALLATION

See Figure 210.

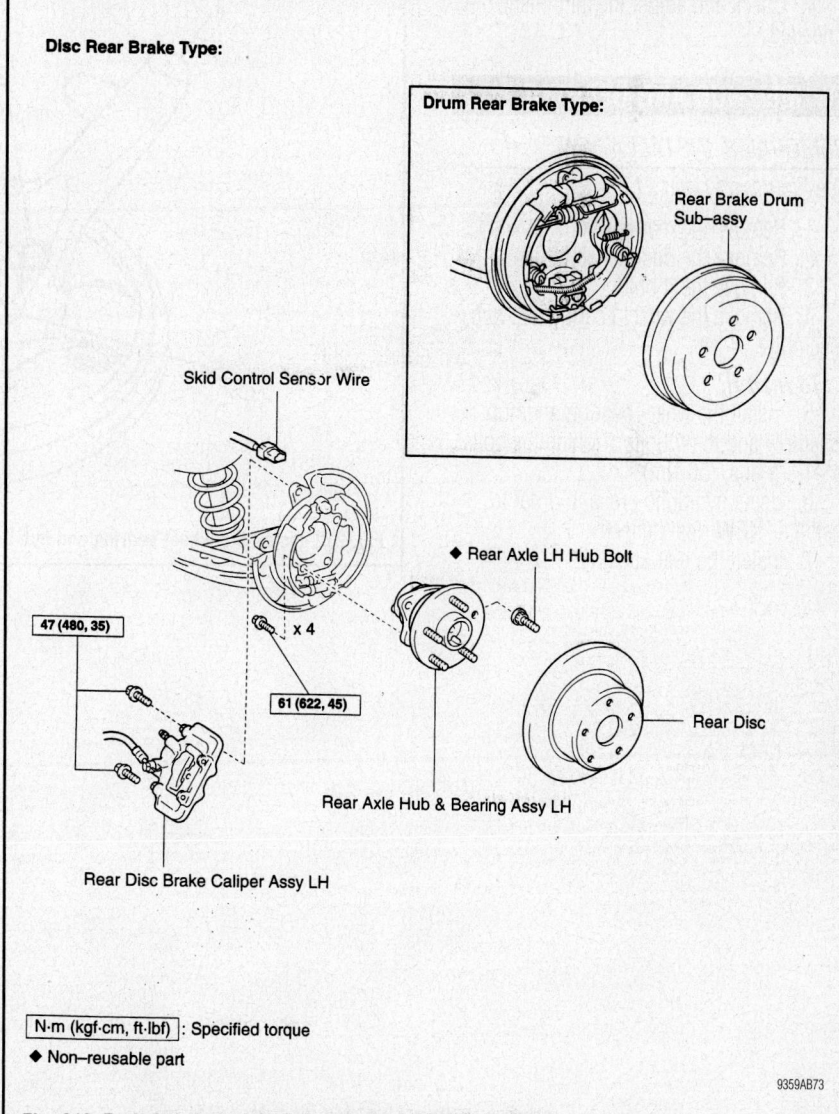

Disc Rear Brake Type:

Drum Rear Brake Type:

Rear Brake Drum Sub–assy

Skid Control Sensor Wire

47 (480, 35)

◆ Rear Axle LH Hub Bolt

x 4

61 (622, 45)

Rear Disc

Rear Axle Hub & Bearing Assy LH

Rear Disc Brake Caliper Assy LH

N·m (kgf·cm, ft·lbf) : Specified torque

◆ Non–reusable part

9359AB73

Fig. 210 Exploded view of the hub and wheel bearing assembly

1. Before servicing the vehicle, refer to the precautions section.
2. Remove or disconnect the following:
   - Negative battery cable. On vehicles equipped with an air bag, wait at least 90 seconds before proceeding.
   - Wheel
   - Brake drum or rotor
   - With ABS brakes, ABS wheel speed sensor or skid control sensor, as applicable
   - 4 hub retaining bolts
   - Hub

To install:
3. Install or connect the following:
   - Hub to the knuckle. Tighten the bolts to 45 ft. lbs. (61 Nm).
   - ABS wheel speed or skid control sensor, if equipped
   - Brake drum or rotor
   - Wheel
   - Negative battery cable
4. Check and adjust the alignment, if needed.

WHEEL HUB AND BEARING

REMOVAL & INSTALLATION

See Figures 211 and 212.

1. Remove the rear knuckle.
2. Remove the dust deflector (2).
3. Remove the 4 bolts.
4. Remove the wheel bearing and hub assembly.

To install:
5. Install the wheel bearing and hub assembly and the 4 bolts. Tighten the bolts to 41.3 ft. lbs. (56 Nm).
6. Use a hydraulic press in order to install a **NEW** dust deflector.
7. Install the rear knuckle.

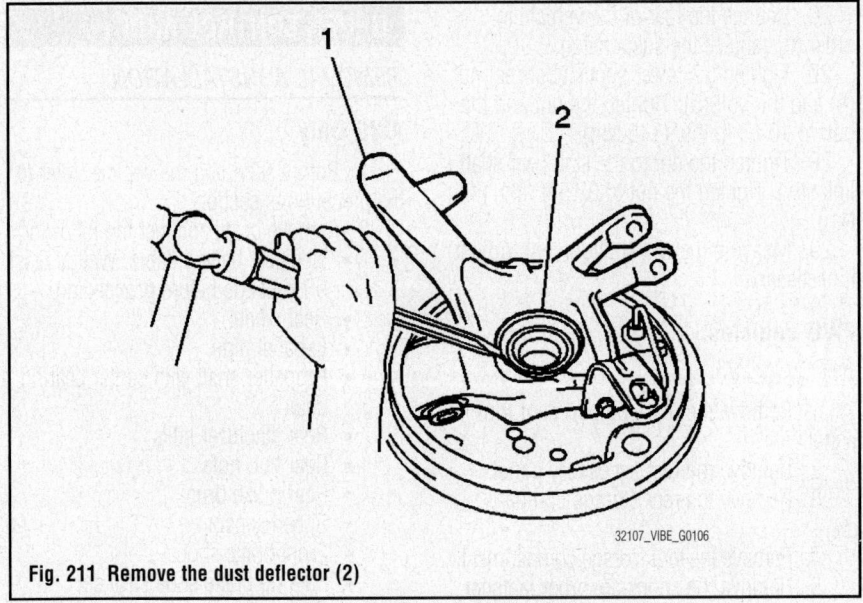

Fig. 211 Remove the dust deflector (2)

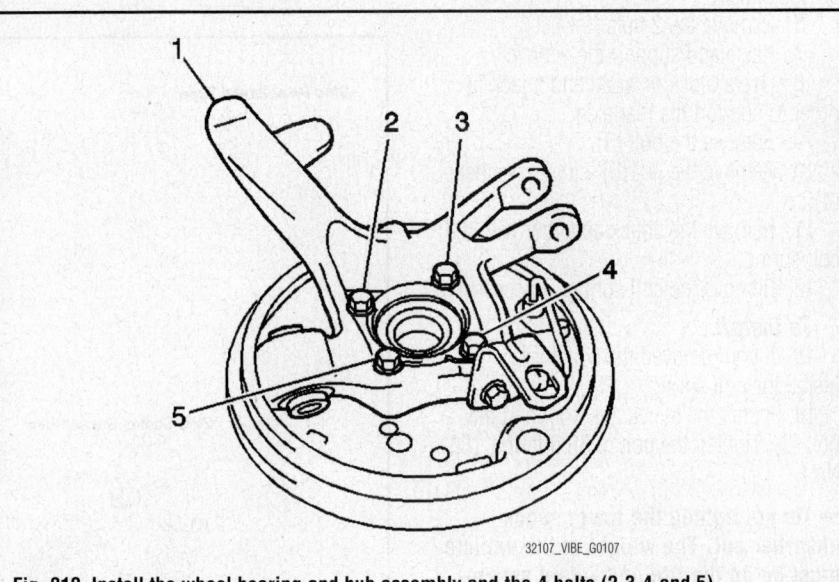

Fig. 212 Install the wheel bearing and hub assembly and the 4 bolts (2,3,4,and 5).

SATURN

Vue

SPECIFICATIONS AND MAINTENANCE CHARTS

ENGINE AND VEHICLE IDENTIFICATION

		Engine						Model Year	
Code ①	Liters (cc)	Cu. In.	Cyl.	Fuel Sys.	Engine Type	Eng. Mfg.		Code ②	Year
D	2.2 (2199)	134	4	SFI	DOHC	Saturn		5	2005
5	2.4 (2398)	146	4	MFI	DOHC	Saturn		6	2006
4	3.5 (3471)	212	6	SFI	DOHC	Honda		7	2007

MFI: Multi-point Fuel Injection

SFI: Sequential Fuel Injection

DOHC: Double Overhead Camshafts

① 8th digit of VIN

② 10th digit of VIN

22116_SVUE_C0001

GENERAL ENGINE SPECIFICATIONS

Year	Model	Engine Displacement Liters (VIN)	Net Horsepower @ rpm	Net Torque @ rpm (ft. lbs.)	Bore x Stroke (in.)	Compression Ratio	Oil Pressure @ rpm
2005	VUE	2.2 (D)	143@5400	152@4000	3.38x3.72	10.0:1	50-80@1000
		3.5 (4)	250@5800	242@4500	3.50x3.66	10.0:1	71@3000
2006	VUE	2.2 (D)	143@5400	152@4000	3.38x3.72	10.0:1	50-80@1000
		3.5 (4)	250@5800	242@4500	3.50x3.66	10.0:1	71@3000
2007	VUE	2.2 (D)	143@5400	152@4000	3.38x3.72	10.0:1	50-80@1000
		2.4 (5)	164@6400	159@5000	3.47x3.86	10.1:1	50-80@1000
		3.5 (4)	250@5800	242@4500	3.50x3.66	10.0:1	71@3000

22116_SVUE_C0002

ENGINE TUNE-UP SPECIFICATIONS

Year	Engine Displacement Liters (VIN)	Spark Plug Gap (in.)	Ignition Timing (deg.) MT	AT	Fuel Pump (psi) ①	Idle Speed (rpm) MT ②	AT ②	Valve Clearance In.	Ex.
2005	2.2 (D)	0.045	③	③	50-60	④	④	HYD	HYD
	3.5 (4)	0.051	③	③	48-56	④	④	HYD	HYD
2006	2.2 (D)	0.045	③	③	50-60	④	④	HYD	HYD
	3.5 (4)	0.051	③	③	48-56	④	④	HYD	HYD
2007	2.2 (D)	0.045	③	③	50-60	④	④	HYD	HYD
	2.4 (5)	0.040	③	③	50-60	④	④	HYD	HYD
	3.5 (4)	0.051	③	③	48-56	④	④	HYD	HYD

NOTE: The Vehicle Emission Control Information label often reflects specification changes made during production. The label figures must be used if they differ from those in this chart.

HYD: Hydraulic

① Pressure measured at idle

② Idle speed measured with manual transmission in Neutral; automatic transmission in D (Drive)

③ Engines equipped with Distributorless Ignition System (DIS). Ignition timing is not adjustable

④ Refer to the Vehicle Emission Control Information label

22116_SVUE_C0003

CAPACITIES

Year	Model	Engine Displacement Liters (VIN)	Engine Oil with Filter (qts.)	Transaxle (qts.)		Fuel Tank (gal.)	Cooling System (qts.)
				Manual	**Auto.**		
2005	VUE	2.2 (D)	5.0	1.7	①	15.7	②
		3.5 (4)	4.5	—	①	16.5	10.3
2006	VUE	2.2 (D)	5.0	1.7	①	16.6	②
		3.5 (4)	4.5	—	①	16.6	10.3
2007	VUE	2.2 (D)	5.0	1.7	①	16.6	②
		2.4 (5)	5.0	—	7.0	16.6	9.3
		3.5 (4)	4.5	—	①	16.6	10.3

NOTE: All capacities are approximate. Add fluid gradually and ensure a proper fluid level is obtained.

① 5-Speed Automatic - 4.5 qts.

　5-Speed Automatic AWD - 4.1 qts.

　4-Speed Automatic - 7.0 qts.

② 2.2L with Manual Transaxle - 9.1 qts.

　2.2L with Automatic Transaxle - 8.8 qts.

22116_SVUE_C0004

FLUID SPECIFICATIONS

Year	Model	Engine Displacement Liters	Engine ID/VIN	Engine Oil	Auto. Trans.	Manual Trans.	Power Steering Fluid	Brake Master Cylinder
2005	VUE	2.2	D	5W-30	Dexron VI	①	GM Part No. 89021184	②
		3.5	4	5W-30	③	—	GM Part No. 89021184	②
2006	VUE	2.2	D	5W-30	Dexron VI	①	GM Part No. 89021184	②
		3.5	4	5W-30	③	—	GM Part No. 89021184	②
2007	VUE	2.2	D	5W-30	Dexron VI	①	GM Part No. 89021184	②
		2.4	5	5W-30	Dexron VI	—	GM Part No. 89021184	②
		3.5	4	5W-30	③	—	GM Part No. 89021184	②

DOT: Department Of Transportation

① Manual Transmission Fluid (GM Part No. U.S. 88861800, in Canada 88861801).

② Delco® Supreme 11 brake fluid or equivalent DOT-3 brake fluid.

③ ATF Z1 Automatic Transmission Fluid (Saturn Part No. 22717466).

22116_SVUE_C0005

VALVE SPECIFICATIONS

Year	Engine Displacement Liters (VIN)	Seat Angle (deg.)	Face Angle (deg.)	Spring Test Pressure (lbs. @ in.)	Spring Free-Length (in.)	Stem-to-Guide Clearance (in.)		Stem Diameter (in.)	
						Intake	Exhaust	Intake	Exhaust
2005	2.2 (D)	44.5-45.4	45-45.5	①	1.6100	0.0012	0.0020	0.2344	0.2337
				②		0.0022	0.0026	0.2355	0.2343
	3.5 (4)	45-60	③	NA	④	0.0008	0.0022	0.2159	0.2146
						0.0018	0.0031	0.2163	0.2150
2006	2.2 (D)	44.5-45.4	45-45.5	①	1.6100	0.0012	0.0020	0.2344	0.2337
				②		0.0022	0.0026	0.2355	0.2343
	3.5 (4)	45-60	③	NA	④	0.0008	0.0022	0.2159	0.2146
						0.0018	0.0031	0.2163	0.2150
2007	2.2 (D)	44.5-45.4	45-45.5	①	1.6100	0.0012	0.0020	0.2344	0.2337
				②		0.0022	0.0026	0.2355	0.2343
	2.4 (5)	44.5-45.4	45-45.5	⑤	NA	0.0012	0.0020	0.2344	0.2337
				⑥		0.0022	0.0026	0.2355	0.2343
	3.5 (4)	45-60	③	NA	④	0.0008	0.0022	0.2159	0.2146
						0.0018	0.0031	0.2163	0.2150

NA: Not available

① Valve spring load closed: 245-271 N
② Valve spring load open: 525-575 N
③ Intake: 45-60-70
   Exhaust: 40-60
④ Intake: 2.029
   Exhaust: 2.01
⑤ Valve spring load closed: 252-575 N at 22.5mm
⑥ Valve spring load open: 245-271 N at 32mm

CAMSHAFT AND BEARING SPECIFICATIONS CHART

All measurements are given in inches.

Year	Engine Displ. Liters	Engine ID/VIN	Journal Dia.	Brg. Oil Clearance	Shaft End-play	Runout	Journal Bore	Lobe Height	
								Intake	Exhaust
2005	2.2	D	1.0604-1.0614	NA	0.0016-0.0057	NA	NA	NA	NA
	3.5	4	1.6900-1.6910	①	②	③	NA	④	1.4302
2006	2.2	D	1.0604-1.0614	NA	0.0016-0.0057	NA	NA	NA	NA
	3.5	4	1.6900-1.6910	①	②	③	NA	④	1.4302
2007	2.2	D	1.0604-1.0614	NA	0.0016-0.0057	NA	NA	NA	NA
	2.4	5	1.0604-1.0614	NA	0.0016-0.0057	NA	NA	NA	NA
	3.5	4	1.6900-1.6910	①	②	③	NA	④	1.4302

NA: Not Available

① Production: 0.002 - 0.0035 in.
   Service: 0.006 in.
② Production: 0.002 - 0.008 in.
   Service: 0.008 in.
③ Production: 0.001 in.
   Service: 0.002 in.
④ Intake Primary: 1.3796 in.
   Intake Mid: 1.4348 in.
   Intake Secondary: 1.3891 in.

CRANKSHAFT AND CONNECTING ROD SPECIFICATIONS

All measurements are given in inches.

Year	Engine Displacement Liters (VIN)	Crankshaft				Connecting Rod		
		Main Brg. Journal Dia.	Main Brg. Oil Clearance	Shaft End-play	Thrust on No.	Journal Diameter	Oil Clearance	Side Clearance
2005	2.2 (D)	2.2045-2.2050	0.0012 0.0026	0.0012-0.0150	3	1.9291-1.9297	0.0001-0.0021	0.0028-0.0146
	3.5 (4)	2.8337-2.8346	0.0008 0.0017	0.0004-0.0140	3	2.1644-2.1654	0.0008-0.0017	NA
2006	2.2 (D)	2.2045-2.2050	0.0012 0.0026	0.0012-0.0150	3	1.9291-1.9297	0.0001-0.0021	0.0028-0.0146
	3.5 (4)	2.8337-2.8346	0.0008 0.0017	0.0004-0.0140	3	2.1644-2.1654	0.0008-0.0017	NA
2007	2.2 (D)	2.2045-2.2050	0.0012 0.0026	0.0012-0.0150	3	1.9291-1.9297	0.0001-0.0021	0.0028-0.0146
	2.4 (5)	2.2045-2.2050	0.0012 0.0026	0.0012-0.0150	3	2.0519-2.0525	0.0001-0.0029	0.0028-0.0146
	3.5 (4)	2.8337-2.8346	0.0008 0.0017	0.0004-0.0140	3	2.1644-2.1654	0.0008-0.0017	NA

NA: Not available

22116_SVUE_C0008

PISTON AND RING SPECIFICATIONS

All measurements are given in inches.

Year	Engine Displacement Liters (VIN)	Piston Clearance	Ring Gap			Ring Side Clearance		
			Top Compression	Bottom Compression	Oil Control	Top Compression	Bottom Compression	Oil Control
2005	2.2 (D)	0.0004-0.0016	0.008-0.016	0.0014 0.0022	0.0010 0.0030	0.0028-0.0146	0.0005-0.0024	SNUG
	3.5 (4)	0.0006-0.0016	0.0008-0.0014	0.0160 0.0220	0.008-0.0280	0.0022-0.0031	0.0012-0.0022	SNUG
2006	2.2 (D)	0.0004-0.0016	0.008-0.016	0.0014 0.0022	0.0010 0.0030	0.0028-0.0146	0.0005-0.0024	SNUG
	3.5 (4)	0.0006-0.0016	0.0008-0.0014	0.0160 0.0220	0.008-0.0280	0.0022-0.0031	0.0012-0.0022	SNUG
2007	2.2 (D)	0.0004-0.0016	0.008-0.016	0.0014 0.0022	0.0010 0.0030	0.0028-0.0146	0.0005-0.0024	SNUG
	2.4 (5)	0.0004-0.0016	0.006-0.012	0.0080 0.0180	0.0060 0.0020	0.0015-0.0031	0.0012-0.0030	SNUG
	3.5 (4)	0.0006-0.0016	0.0008-0.0014	0.0160 0.0220	0.008-0.0280	0.0022-0.0031	0.0012-0.0022	SNUG

22116_SVUE_C0009

TORQUE SPECIFICATIONS
All readings in ft. lbs.

Year	Engine Displacement Liters (VIN)	Cylinder Head Bolts	Main Bearing Bolts	Rod Bearing Bolts	Crankshaft Damper Bolts	Flywheel Bolts	Manifold Intake	Manifold Exhaust	Spark Plugs	Oil Pan Drain Plug
2005	2.2 (D)	①	②	③	④	⑤	⑥	13	15	18
	3.5 (4)	⑦	⑧	⑨	181	54	⑩	31	13	29
2006	2.2 (D)	①	②	③	④	⑤	⑥	13	15	18
	3.5 (4)	⑦	⑧	⑨	181	54	⑩	31	13	29
2007	2.2 (D)	①	②	③	④	⑤	⑥	13	15	18
	2.4 (5)	①	⑪	③	④	⑤	⑫	⑥	15	18
	3.5 (4)	⑦	⑧	⑨	181	54	⑩	31	13	29

① Step 1: 22 ft. lbs.
  Step 2: 155 degrees

② Step 1: 15 ft. lbs.
  Step 2: plus 70 degrees

③ 18 ft. lbs. Plus 100 degrees

④ 74 ft. lbs. Plus 125 degrees

⑤ 39 ft. lbs. Plus 25 degrees

⑥ Nut: 124 inch lbs.
  Stud: 89 inch lbs.

⑦ Step 1: 29 ft. lbs.
  Step 2: 51 ft. lbs.
  Step 3: 72.3 ft. lbs.

⑧ Bottom M11 bolts: 54 ft. lbs.
  Side M10 bolts: 36 ft. lbs.

⑨ 14 ft. lbs. Plus 90 degrees

⑩ Intake manifold nuts and bolts:
  Step 1: 97 inch lbs.
  Step 2: 16 ft. lbs.
  Intake manifold top cover gasket:
  Step 1: 53 inch lbs.
  Step 2: 106 inch lbs.

⑪ 15 ft. lbs. Plus 70 degrees

⑫ Nut and bolt: 89 inch lbs.
  Stud: 53 inch lbs.

22116_SVUE_C0010

WHEEL ALIGNMENT

Year	Model		Caster Range (+/-Deg.)	Caster Preferred Setting (Deg.)	Camber Range (+/-Deg.)	Camber Preferred Setting (Deg.)	Toe-in (in.)
2005	VUE	F	0.75	①	0.75	②	+0.20 +/- 0.20
		R	—	—	0.75	-0.45	+0.20 +/- 0.20
2006	VUE	F	0.75	①	0.75	②	+0.20 +/- 0.20
		R	—	—	0.75	-0.45	+0.20 +/- 0.20
2007	VUE	F	0.75	①	0.75	②	+0.20 +/- 0.20
		R	—	—	0.75	-0.45	+0.20 +/- 0.20

① Except Red Line and Green Line: 3.00 degrees +/- 0.75 degrees
  Red Line and Green Line: 3.15 degrees +/- 0.75 degrees

② Except Red Line and Green Line: -0.60 degrees +/- 0.75 degrees
  Red Line and Green Line: -0.75 degrees +/- 0.75 degrees

22116_SVUE_C0011

PRECAUTIONS

Before servicing any vehicle, please be sure to read all of the following precautions, which deal with personal safety, prevention of component damage, and important points to take into consideration when servicing a motor vehicle:

• Never open, service or drain the radiator or cooling system when the engine is hot; serious burns can occur from the steam and hot coolant.

• Observe all applicable safety precautions when working around fuel. Whenever servicing the fuel system, always work in a well-ventilated area. Do not allow fuel spray or vapors to come in contact with a spark, open flame, or excessive heat (a hot drop light, for example). Keep a dry chemical fire extinguisher near the work area. Always keep fuel in a container specifically designed for fuel storage; also, always properly seal fuel containers to avoid the possibility of fire or explosion. Refer to the additional fuel system precautions later in this section.

• Fuel injection systems often remain pressurized, even after the engine has been turned **OFF**. The fuel system pressure must be relieved before disconnecting any fuel lines. Failure to do so may result in fire and/or personal injury.

• Brake fluid often contains polyglycol ethers and polyglycols. Avoid contact with the eyes and wash your hands thoroughly after handling brake fluid. If you do get brake fluid in your eyes, flush your eyes with clean, running water for 15 minutes. If eye irritation persists, or if you have taken

brake fluid internally, IMMEDIATELY seek medical assistance.

• The EPA warns that prolonged contact with used engine oil may cause a number of skin disorders, including cancer. You should make every effort to minimize your exposure to used engine oil. Protective gloves should be worn when changing oil. Wash your hands and any other exposed skin areas as soon as possible after exposure to used engine oil. Soap and water, or waterless hand cleaner should be used.

• All new vehicles are now equipped with an air bag system, often referred to as a Supplemental Restraint System (SRS) or Supplemental Inflatable Restraint (SIR) system. The system must be disabled before performing service on or around system components, steering column, instrument panel components, wiring and sensors. Failure to follow safety and disabling procedures could result in accidental air bag deployment, possible personal injury and unnecessary system repairs.

• Always wear safety goggles when working with, or around, the air bag system. When carrying a non-deployed air bag, be sure the bag and trim cover are pointed away from your body. When placing a non-deployed air bag on a work surface, always face the bag and trim cover upward, away from the surface. This will reduce the motion of the module if it is accidentally deployed. Refer to the additional air bag system precautions later in this section.

• Clean, high quality brake fluid from a sealed container is essential to the safe and

proper operation of the brake system. You should always buy the correct type of brake fluid for your vehicle. If the brake fluid becomes contaminated, completely flush the system with new fluid. Never reuse any brake fluid. Any brake fluid that is removed from the system should be discarded. Also, do not allow any brake fluid to come in contact with a painted surface; it will damage the paint.

• Never operate the engine without the proper amount and type of engine oil; doing so WILL result in severe engine damage.

• Timing belt maintenance is extremely important. Many models utilize an interference-type, non-freewheeling engine. If the timing belt breaks, the valves in the cylinder head may strike the pistons, causing potentially serious (also time-consuming and expensive) engine damage. Refer to the maintenance interval charts for the recommended replacement interval for the timing belt, and to the timing belt section for belt replacement and inspection.

• Disconnecting the negative battery cable on some vehicles may interfere with the functions of the on-board computer system(s) and may require the computer to undergo a relearning process once the negative battery cable is reconnected.

• When servicing drum brakes, only disassemble and assemble one side at a time, leaving the remaining side intact for reference.

• Only an MVAC-trained, EPA-certified automotive technician should service the air conditioning system or its components.

BRAKES

GENERAL INFORMATION

The purpose of the Antilock Brake System (ABS) is to minimize wheel slip during heavy braking. The ABS performs this function by monitoring the speed of each wheel and controlling the brake fluid pressure to each wheel independently during an braking event. This allows the driver to maintain directional stability while minimizing stopping distance.

During normal braking, the ABS system is transparent to the operator. Internally, each control piston is in the uppermost or home position allowing brake fluid pressure to pass to the wheels unrestricted. A small internal Expansion Spring Brake (ESB) device is applied to each piston, preventing it from being forced downward by the pressurized fluid passing above it.

When impending wheel lock is noted at one or more wheels, the Electronic Brake Control Module (EBCM) commands the system into ABS mode. Solenoids in each front wheel circuit close. The brakes on the pistons are released and the pistons are driven downward by the electric motors through a system of driven gears and against the spring pressure. The amount of current applied to the motors controls the speed and distance traveled. As the motors move backwards, the piston moves downward, allowing a check valve to seat. The brake pressure to the wheel is now a function of the controlled volume within the piston chamber.

To reduce pressure, the motor continues to drive the piston downward. If an increase in pressure is necessary, the piston is driven

ANTI-LOCK BRAKE SYSTEM (ABS)

upward. Total pressure available is limited to the amount present when ABS was entered.

The rear brakes are controlled in similar fashion. Wheel speed signals are received from each rear wheel. The EBCM uses a Select Low strategy, controlling a single motor to control output to the rear brakes based on the wheel with the greatest tendency to lock.

Many of the service procedures, including troubleshooting and control assembly overhaul require the use the Saturn Portable Diagnostic Tool (PDT) or an equivalent scan tool.

PRECAUTIONS

• Certain components within the ABS system are not intended to be serviced or repaired individually.

• Do not use rubber hoses or other parts not specifically specified for and ABS system. When using repair kits, replace all parts included in the kit. Partial or incorrect repair may lead to functional problems and require the replacement of components.

• Lubricate rubber parts with clean, fresh brake fluid to ease assembly. Do not use shop air to clean parts; damage to rubber components may result.

• Use only DOT 3 brake fluid from an unopened container.

• If any hydraulic component or line is removed or replaced, it may be necessary to bleed the entire system.

• A clean repair area is essential. Always clean the reservoir and cap thoroughly before removing the cap. The slightest amount of dirt in the fluid may plug an orifice and impair the system function. Perform repairs after components have been thoroughly cleaned; use only denatured alcohol to clean components. Do not allow ABS components to come into contact with any substance containing mineral oil; this includes used shop rags.

• The Anti-Lock control unit is a microprocessor similar to other computer units in the vehicle. Ensure that the ignition switch is **OFF** before removing or installing controller harnesses. Avoid static electricity discharge at or near the controller.

• If any arc welding is to be done on the vehicle, the control unit should be unplugged before welding operations begin.

SPEED SENSORS

REMOVAL & INSTALLATION

Front

See Figure 1.

1. Before servicing the vehicle, refer to the Precautions Section.
2. Raise and safely support the vehicle.
3. Remove the tire and wheel assembly.
4. Remove the brake rotor.
5. Disconnect the wheel speed sensor electrical connector.
6. Remove the wheel speed sensor bolt.
7. Remove the wheel speed sensor.

To install:

8. Install the wheel speed sensor to the wheel bearing/hub assembly.
9. Install the wheel speed sensor mounting bolt.
10. Tighten the bolt to 71 inch lbs. (8 Nm).

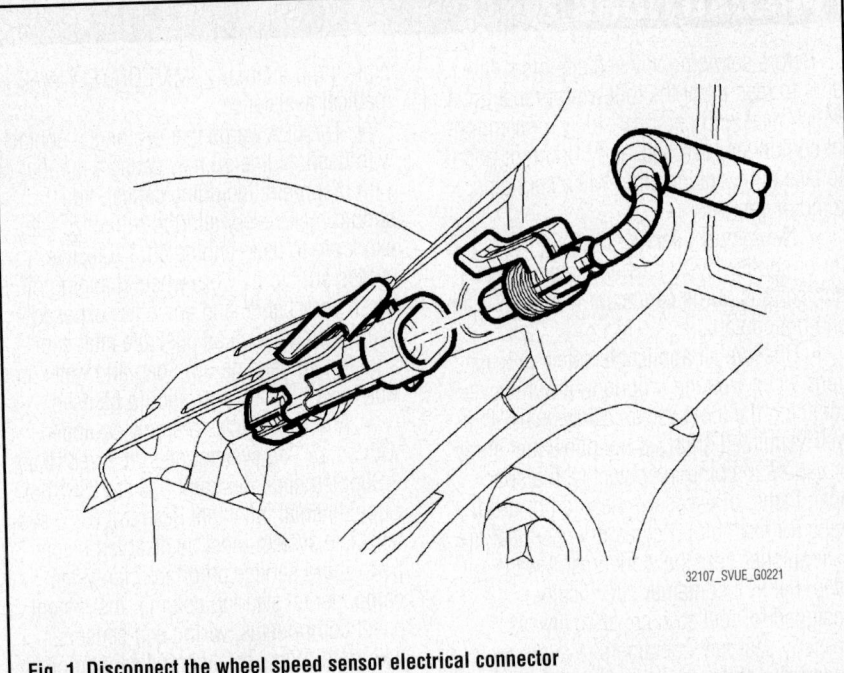

Fig. 1 Disconnect the wheel speed sensor electrical connector

11. Connect the wheel speed sensor electrical connector.
12. Install the brake rotor.
13. Install the tire and wheel assembly. Tighten the wheel lug nuts to 100 ft. lbs. (136 Nm).
14. Lower the vehicle.

Rear

See Figure 2.

1. Before servicing the vehicle, refer to the Precautions Section.
2. Raise and safely support the vehicle.
3. Remove the tire and wheel assembly.
4. Remove the brake shoes.
5. Disconnect the wheel speed sensor electrical connector.
6. Remove the wheel speed sensor bolt.

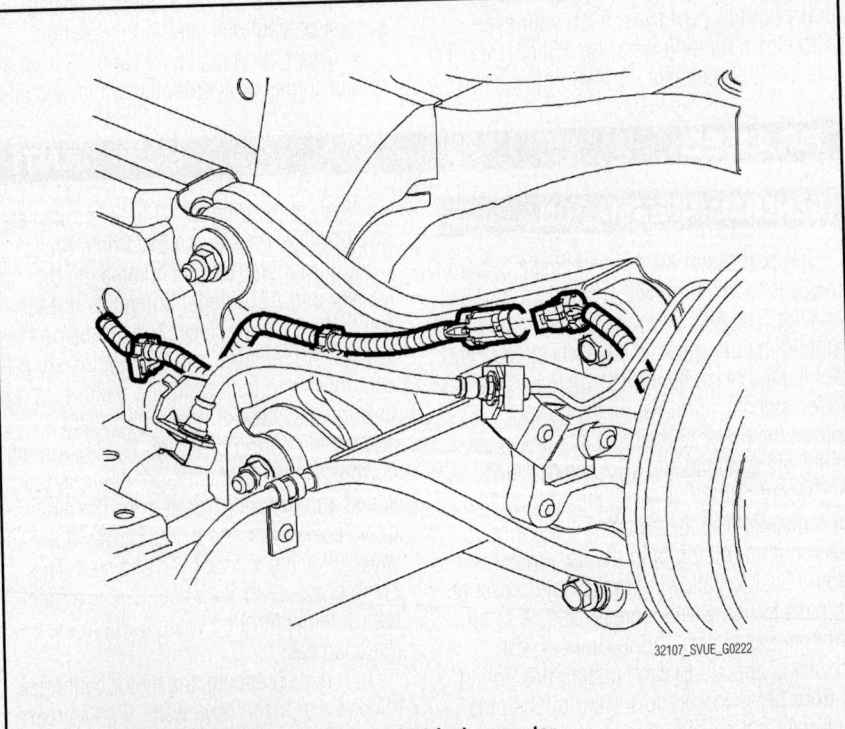

Fig. 2 Disconnect the wheel speed sensor electrical connector.

7. Remove the wheel speed sensor through the drum brake backing plate.

To install:

8. Install the wheel speed sensor through the drum brake backing plate to the wheel bearing/hub assembly.

9. Seat the wheel speed sensor harness grommet into the backing plate.

10. Install the wheel speed sensor mounting bolt. Tighten the bolt to 71 inch lbs. (8 Nm).

11. Connect the wheel speed sensor electrical connector.

12. Install the brake shoes.

13. Install the tire and wheel assembly. Tighten the wheel lug nuts to 100 ft. lbs. (136 Nm).

14. Lower the vehicle.

BRAKES   BLEEDING THE BRAKE SYSTEM

BLEEDING PROCEDURE

BLEEDING PROCEDURE

Manual Brake Bleeding

❊❊ WARNING

When adding fluid to the brake master cylinder reservoir, use only GM approved or equivalent DOT-3 brake fluid from a clean, sealed brake fluid container. The use of any type of fluid other than the recommended type of brake fluid may cause contamination which could result in damage to the internal rubber seals and/or rubber linings of hydraulic brake system components.

❊❊ WARNING

Avoid spilling brake fluid onto painted surfaces, electrical connections, wiring, or cables. Brake fluid will damage painted surfaces and cause corrosion to electrical components. If any brake fluid comes in contact with painted surfaces, immediately flush the area with water. If any brake fluid comes in contact with electrical connections, wiring, or cables, use a clean shop cloth to wipe away the fluid.

1. Place a clean shop cloth beneath the brake master cylinder to catch brake fluid spills.

2. With the ignition **OFF** and the brakes cool, apply the brakes 3–5 times, or until the brake pedal effort increases significantly, in order to deplete the brake booster power reserve.

3. If you have performed a brake master cylinder bench bleeding on this vehicle, or if you disconnected the brake pipes from the master cylinder, or if you have disconnected the brake pipes from the proportioning valve assembly or the brake modulator assembly, you must perform the following steps to bleed air at the ports of the hydraulic component:

a. If removal of the reservoir cap and diaphragm is necessary, clean the outside of the reservoir on and around the cap prior to removal.

b. With the brake pipes installed securely to the master cylinder, proportioning valve assembly, or brake modulator assembly, loosen and separate one of the brake pipes from the port of the component. For the proportioning valve assembly or the brake modulator assembly, perform these steps in the sequence of system flow; begin with the fluid feed pipes from the master cylinder.

c. Allow a small amount of brake fluid to gravity bleed from the open port of the component.

d. Reconnect the brake pipe to the component and tighten securely.

e. Have an assistant slowly depress the brake pedal fully and maintain steady pressure on the pedal.

f. Loosen the same brake pipe to purge air from the open port of the component.

g. Tighten the brake pipe, then have the assistant slowly release the brake pedal.

h. Wait 15 seconds, then repeat the steps until all air is purged from the same port of the component.

i. With the brake pipe installed securely to the master cylinder, proportioning valve assembly, or brake modulator assembly, and after all air has been purged from the first port of the component that was bled, loosen and separate the next brake pipe from the component, then repeat the steps until each of the ports on the component has been bled.

j. After completing the final component port bleeding procedure, ensure that each of the brake pipe-to-component fittings is properly tightened.

4. Ensure the brake master cylinder reservoir remains at least half-full during this bleeding procedure. Add fluid as needed to maintain the proper level. Clean the outside of the reservoir on and around the reservoir cap prior to removing the cap and diaphragm.

5. Install a proper box-end wrench onto the RIGHT REAR wheel hydraulic circuit bleeder valve.

6. Install a transparent hose over the end of the bleeder valve.

7. Have an assistant slowly depress the brake pedal fully and maintain steady pressure on the pedal.

8. Loosen the bleeder valve to purge air from the wheel hydraulic circuit.

9. Tighten the bleeder valve, then have the assistant slowly release the brake pedal.

10. Wait 15 seconds, then repeat steps 8–10 until all air is purged from the same wheel hydraulic circuit.

11. With the right rear wheel hydraulic circuit bleeder valve tightened securely, and after all air has been purged from the right rear hydraulic circuit, install a proper box-end wrench onto the LEFT FRONT wheel hydraulic circuit bleeder valve.

12. Install a transparent hose over the end of the bleeder valve, then repeat steps 7–11.

13. With the left front wheel hydraulic circuit bleeder valve tightened securely, and after all air has been purged from the left front hydraulic circuit, install a proper box-end wrench onto the LEFT REAR wheel hydraulic circuit bleeder valve.

14. Install a transparent hose over the end of the bleeder valve, then repeat steps 7–11.

15. With the left rear wheel hydraulic circuit bleeder valve tightened securely, and after all air has been purged from the left rear hydraulic circuit, install a proper box-end wrench onto the RIGHT FRONT wheel hydraulic circuit bleeder valve.

16. Install a transparent hose over the end of the bleeder valve, then repeat steps 7–11.

17. After completing the final wheel hydraulic circuit bleeding procedure, ensure that each of the 4 wheel hydraulic circuit bleeder valves is properly tightened.

18. Slowly depress and release the brake pedal. Observe the feel of the brake pedal.

19. If the brake pedal feels spongy, repeat the bleeding procedure again. If the brake pedal still feels spongy after repeating

the bleeding procedure, perform the following steps:

   a. Inspect the brake system for external leaks.

   b. Pressure bleed the hydraulic brake system in order to purge any air that may still be trapped in the system.

20. Turn the ignition key **ON**, with the engine **OFF**. Check to see if the brake system warning lamp remains illuminated.

Pressure Brake Bleeding

❄❄ WARNING

When adding fluid to the brake master cylinder reservoir, use only GM approved or equivalent DOT-3 brake fluid from a clean, sealed brake fluid container. The use of any type of fluid other than the recommended type of brake fluid may cause contamination which could result in damage to the internal rubber seals and/or rubber linings of hydraulic brake system components.

❄❄ WARNING

Avoid spilling brake fluid onto painted surfaces, electrical connections, wiring, or cables. Brake fluid will damage painted surfaces and cause corrosion to electrical components. If any brake fluid comes in contact with painted surfaces, immediately flush the area with water. If any brake fluid comes in contact with electrical connections, wiring, or cables, use a clean shop cloth to wipe away the fluid.

1. Place a clean shop cloth beneath the brake master cylinder to catch brake fluid spills.

2. With the ignition **OFF** and the brakes cool, apply the brakes 3–5 times, or until the brake pedal becomes firm, in order to deplete the brake booster power reserve.

3. If you have performed a brake master cylinder bench bleeding on this vehicle, or if you disconnected the brake pipes from the master cylinder, or if you have disconnected the brake pipes from the proportioning valve assembly or the brake modulator assembly, you must perform the following steps to bleed air at the ports of the hydraulic component:

   a. If removal of the reservoir cap and diaphragm is necessary, clean the outside of the reservoir on and around the cap prior to removal.

   b. With the brake pipes installed securely to the master cylinder, proportioning valve assembly, or brake modulator assembly, loosen and separate one of the brake pipes from the port of the component. For the proportioning valve assembly or the brake modulator assembly, perform these steps in the sequence of system flow; begin with the fluid feed pipes from the master cylinder.

   c. Allow a small amount of brake fluid to gravity bleed from the open port of the component.

   d. Reconnect the brake pipe to the component and tighten securely.

   e. Have an assistant slowly depress the brake pedal fully and maintain steady pressure on the pedal.

   f. Loosen the same brake pipe to purge air from the open port of the component.

   g. Tighten the brake pipe, then have the assistant slowly release the brake pedal.

   h. Wait 15 seconds, then repeat steps 3c–3g until all air is purged from the same port of the component.

   i. With the brake pipe installed securely to the master cylinder, proportioning valve assembly, or brake modulator assembly, and after all air has been purged from the first port of the component that was bled, loosen and separate the next brake pipe from the component, then repeat steps 3c–3h until each of the ports on the component has been bled.

   j. After completing the final component port bleeding procedure, ensure that each of the brake pipe-to-component fittings is properly tightened.

4. Clean the outside of the reservoir on and around the reservoir cap prior to removing the cap and diaphragm.

5. Install the J 44894-A, Brake Pressure Bleeder Adapter, to the brake master cylinder reservoir.

6. Connect the J 29532, Diaphragm Type Brake Pressure Bleeder, or equivalent, to the J 44894-A .

7. Charge the J 29532, or equivalent, air tank to 25–30 psi (175-205 kPa).

8. Open the J 29532, or equivalent, fluid tank valve to allow pressurized brake fluid to enter the brake system.

9. Wait approximately 30 seconds, then inspect the entire hydraulic brake system in order to ensure that there are no existing external brake fluid leaks. Any brake fluid leaks identified require repair prior to completing this procedure.

10. Install a proper box-end wrench onto the RIGHT REAR wheel hydraulic circuit bleeder valve.

11. Install a transparent hose over the end of the bleeder valve.

12. Loosen the bleeder valve to purge air from the wheel hydraulic circuit. Allow fluid to flow until air bubbles stop flowing from the bleeder, then tighten the bleeder valve.

13. With the right rear wheel hydraulic circuit bleeder valve tightened securely, and after all air has been purged from the right rear hydraulic circuit, install a proper box-end wrench onto the LEFT FRONT wheel hydraulic circuit bleeder valve.

14. Install a transparent hose over the end of the bleeder valve, then repeat steps 13–14.

15. With the left front wheel hydraulic circuit bleeder valve tightened securely, and after all air has been purged from the left front hydraulic circuit, install a proper box-end wrench onto the LEFT REAR wheel hydraulic circuit bleeder valve.

16. Install a transparent hose over the end of the bleeder valve, then repeat steps 13–14.

17. With the left rear wheel hydraulic circuit bleeder valve tightened securely, and after all air has been purged from the left rear hydraulic circuit, install a proper box-end wrench onto the RIGHT FRONT wheel hydraulic circuit bleeder valve.

18. Install a transparent hose over the end of the bleeder valve, then repeat steps 13–14.

19. After completing the final wheel hydraulic circuit bleeding procedure, ensure that each of the 4 wheel hydraulic circuit bleeder valves is properly tightened.

20. Close the J 29532, or equivalent, fluid tank valve, then disconnect the J 29532, or equivalent, from the J 44894-A.

21. Remove the J 44894-A from the brake master cylinder reservoir.

22. Slowly depress and release the brake pedal. Observe the feel of the brake pedal.

23. If the brake pedal feels spongy perform the following steps:

   a. Inspect the brake system for external leaks.

   b. If equipped with antilock brakes, using a scan tool, perform the antilock brake system automated bleeding procedure to remove any air that may have been trapped in the Brake Pressure Modulator Valve (BPMV). Refer to ABS Automated Bleed Procedure in Antilock Brake System.

AUTOMATED BLEED PROCEDURE

➡**Before performing the Antilock Brake System (ABS) Automated Bleed Procedure, first perform a manual or pressure bleed of the base brake system.**

The automated bleed procedure is recommended when Base brake system bleeding does not achieve the desired pedal height or feel, extreme loss of brake fluid has occurred or air ingestion is suspected in the secondary circuits of the brake modulator assembly.

The ABS Automated Bleed Procedure uses a scan tool to cycle the system solenoid valves and run the pump in order to purge any air from the secondary circuits. These circuits are normally closed off, and are only opened during system initialization at vehicle start up and during ABS operation. The automated bleed procedure opens these secondary circuits and allows any air trapped in these circuits to flow out toward the brake corners.

❊❊ WARNING

The Auto Bleed Procedure may be terminated at any time during the process by pressing the EXIT button. No further Scan Tool prompts pertaining to the Auto Bleed procedure will be given. After exiting the bleed procedure, relieve bleed pressure and disconnect bleed equipment per manufacturer's instructions. Failure to properly relieve pressure may result in spilled brake fluid causing damage to components and painted surfaces.

1. Raise and safely support the vehicle.
2. Remove all 4 tire and wheel assemblies.
3. Inspect the brake system for leaks and visual damage and repair or replace components as needed.
4. Lower the vehicle.
5. Inspect the battery state of charge.
6. Install a scan tool.
7. Turn the ignition **ON**, with the engine **OFF**.
8. With the scan tool, establish communications with the ABS system. Select Special Functions then Automated Bleed from the Special Functions menu.
9. Raise and support the vehicle.

10. Following the directions given on the scan tool, pressure bleed the base brake system.
11. Follow the scan tool directions until the desired brake pedal height is achieved.
12. If the bleed procedure is aborted, a malfunction exists. Perform the following steps before resuming the bleed procedure:
   a. If a DTC is detected, refer to the Diagnostic Trouble Codes listed in this section.
   b. If the brake pedal feels spongy, perform the conventional brake bleed procedure again.
13. When the desired pedal height is achieved, press the brake pedal to inspect for firmness.
14. Lower the vehicle.
15. Remove the scan tool.
16. Install the tire and wheel assemblies. Tighten the wheel lug nuts to 100 ft. lbs. (136 Nm).
17. Inspect the brake fluid level.
18. Road test the vehicle while inspecting that the pedal remains high and firm.

BRAKES   FRONT DISC BRAKES

❊❊ CAUTION

Dust and dirt accumulating on brake parts during normal use may contain asbestos fibers from production or aftermarket brake linings. Breathing excessive concentrations of asbestos fibers can cause serious bodily harm. Exercise care when servicing brake parts. Do not sand or grind brake lining unless equipment used is designed to contain the dust residue. Do not clean brake parts with compressed air or by dry brushing. Cleaning should be done by dampening the brake components with a fine mist of water, then wiping the brake components clean with a dampened cloth. Dispose of cloth and all residue containing asbestos fibers in an impermeable container with the appropriate label. Follow practices prescribed by the Occupational Safety and Health Administration (OSHA) and the Environmental Protection Agency (EPA) for the handling, processing, and disposing of dust or debris that may contain asbestos fibers.

BRAKE CALIPER

REMOVAL & INSTALLATION

See Figure 3.

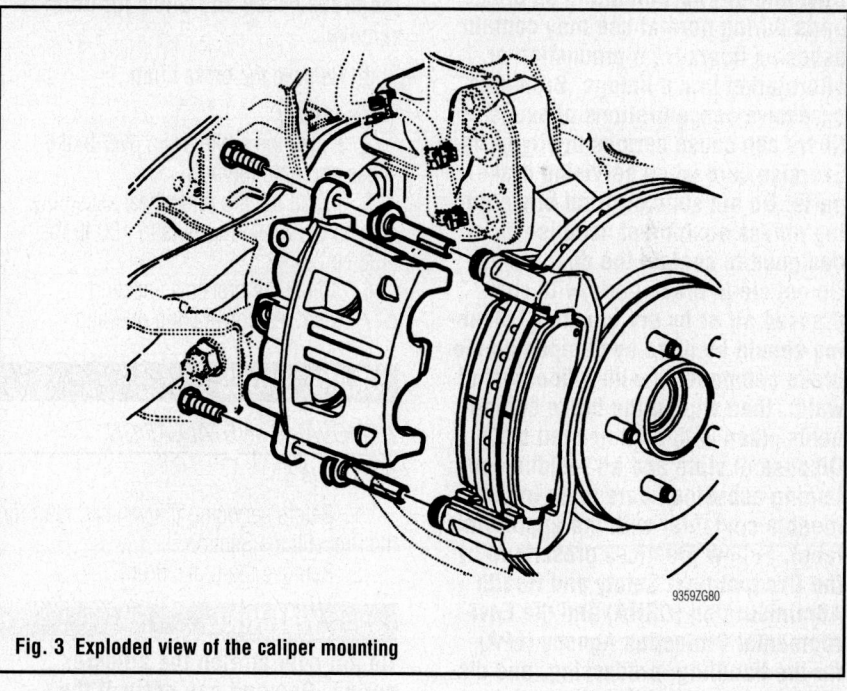

Fig. 3 Exploded view of the caliper mounting

1. Before servicing the vehicle, refer to the Precautions Section.
2. Remove or disconnect the following:
   • The front wheel and tire assembly
   • The brake hose from the caliper and discard the 2 copper washers. Plug the openings to prevent system contamination or excessive fluid loss
   • The lock pin and guide pin from the caliper

   • The caliper from the support, being careful not to damage the pin boots
   • The pin boots from the caliper support and inspect for damage

To install:
3. If necessary, bottom the caliper piston by using a C-clamp.
4. If removed, install the brake pads and clips to the caliper support.

5. Lubricate the pin boots and guide pins with silicone grease.

6. Install the pin boots into the caliper support, using the pin to assure that the boot passes all the way through the support.

7. Install the caliper onto the support and over the brake pads.

8. Lubricate the non-threaded portion of the guide and lock pins with silicone grease.

9. Install the pins through the caliper and torque to 32 ft. lbs. (44 Nm).

➡ **Make sure the brake line is properly routed with loop to the rear and that the hose is not twisted.**

10. Install the bake hose using 2 new copper washers. Torque the fitting bolt to 32 ft. lbs. (44 Nm).

11. Properly bleed the hydraulic brake system.

12. Install the wheel. Tighten the wheel lug nuts to 100 ft. lbs. (136 Nm).

DISC BRAKE PADS

REMOVAL & INSTALLATION

1. Before servicing the vehicle, refer to the Precautions Section.

2. Remove the front wheels.

3. Remove the caliper lower lock pin.

4. Either pivot the caliper up on the guide pin or remove the upper guide pin and support the caliper from the strut using a mechanics wire or suitable wire.

5. Remove the 2 brake pads and the pad clips from the caliper support. Discard the old pad clips.

6. Check the caliper pins, pin boots, and the piston boot for deterioration or damage. Replace as necessary.

To install:

7. Using a C-clamp, bottom the piston all the way into the caliper bore.

8. Carefully lift the inner edge of the piston boot by hand to release any trapped air.

9. Install the new pad clips into the caliper support.

10. Install the inner and outer brake pads into the support. When installed, remove the temporary support wire from the caliper.

11. Install the caliper body on the support and upper guide pin into position. Compress the boots by hand as the caliper is positioned onto the support.

12. Lubricate the smooth ends of the removed pin(s) with silicone grease.

13. Install the pin(s) and torque to 32 ft. lbs. (44 Nm). Do not get grease on the pin threads.

14. Install the wheels. Tighten the wheel lug nuts to 100 ft. lbs. (136 Nm).

15. Prior to operating the vehicle, depress the brake pedal a few times until the brake pads are seated against the rotor.

BRAKES

REAR DRUM BRAKES

✳✳ CAUTION

Dust and dirt accumulating on brake parts during normal use may contain asbestos fibers from production or aftermarket brake linings. Breathing excessive concentrations of asbestos fibers can cause serious bodily harm. Exercise care when servicing brake parts. Do not sand or grind brake lining unless equipment used is designed to contain the dust residue. Do not clean brake parts with compressed air or by dry brushing. Cleaning should be done by dampening the brake components with a fine mist of water, then wiping the brake components clean with a dampened cloth. Dispose of cloth and all residue containing asbestos fibers in an impermeable container with the appropriate label. Follow practices prescribed by the Occupational Safety and Health Administration (OSHA) and the Environmental Protection Agency (EPA) for the handling, processing, and disposing of dust or debris that may contain asbestos fibers.

BRAKE DRUM

REMOVAL & INSTALLATION

1. Before servicing the vehicle, refer to the Precautions Section.

2. Remove the rear wheel and tire assembly.

➡ **If necessary, turn the starwheel of the brake adjuster assembly to loosen the brake shoes and allow for drum removal.**

3. Remove the brake drum.

To install:

4. Install the brake drum over brake shoes and onto the hub.

5. Install the tire and wheel assembly. Tighten the wheel lug nuts to 100 ft. lbs. (136 Nm).

6. Adjust the brakes as needed.

7. Road test for braking operation.

BRAKE SHOES

REMOVAL & INSTALLATION

See Figure 4.

1. Before servicing the vehicle, refer to the Precautions Section.

2. Remove the brake drum.

✳✳ WARNING

Do not over stretch the adjuster spring. Damage can occur if the spring is over stretched.

3. Disengage the adjuster spring hook end from the tab on the adjuster actuator.

4. Remove or disconnect the following:
- The straight end of the adjuster spring from the brake shoe
- The adjuster actuator from the brake shoe

- The return spring from the brake shoes
- The park brake cable from the parking brake actuator lever
- The brake shoe hold-down springs and retainers from the brake shoes
- The adjuster from the brake shoes and the parking brake actuator lever
- The horseshoe clip retaining the parking brake actuator lever to the brake shoe
- The parking brake actuator lever and wave washer from the brake shoe

5. Clean all of the drum brake system components with denatured alcohol.

6. Inspect all of the drum brake system components.

7. Inspect the wheel cylinder for the following conditions:
   a. Brake fluid leakage.
   b. Worn or damaged dust boots.

8. Replace damaged or leaking wheel cylinders as necessary.

To install:

9. Lubricate the adjuster assembly, the 6 backing plate raised shoe contact pads, the brake lever pin, and surfaces which contact brake shoe webs with brake lubricant.

10. Install or connect the following:
- The parking brake actuator lever to the lever pivot pin
- The horseshoe clip to the parking brake actuator lever pivot pin
- The brake shoes to the brake backing plate

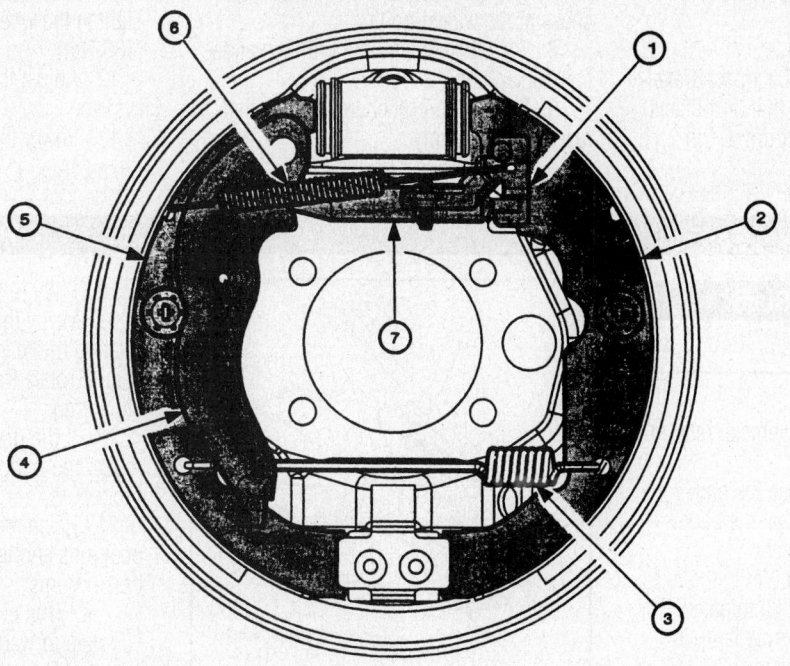

1. Adjuster lever
2. Leading (front) brake shoe
3. Lower return spring
4. Park brake lever
5. Trailing (rear) brake shoe
6. Upper return spring
7. Adjuster assembly

9359ZG81

Fig. 4 View of the installed drum brake assembly components

- The brake shoe hold-down pins, springs and retainers to the brake shoes
- The parking brake cable to the park brake actuator lever

➡**Make sure that the adjuster engages the brake shoe and the parking brake actuator properly.**

11. Install the adjuster screw to the brake shoe and the parking brake actuator.

12. Apply a thin, light coat of high temperature, silicone brake lubricant to the adjuster actuator/brake shoe interface.

13. Install the adjuster actuator to the brake shoe.

➡**Do not over stretch the adjuster spring. Damage can occur if the spring is over stretched.**

14. Install the straight end of the adjuster spring to the brake shoe.

15. Install the adjuster spring hook end to the tab on the adjuster actuator.

16. Install the return spring to the brake shoes.

17. Make sure that the adjuster operates properly.

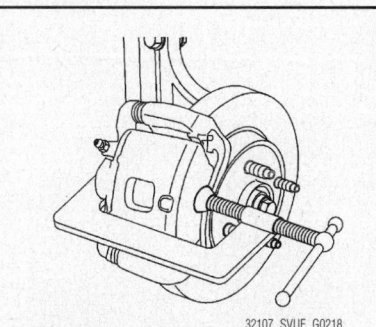

32107_SVUE_G0218

Fig. 5 Set the Drum-to-Brake Shoe Clearance Gauge, so that it contacts the inside diameter of the drum at the widest point

18. Move the parking brake actuator lever in order to spread the brake shoes apart. The adjuster actuator lever should move downward, then upward as the park brake actuator lever is released, forcing the adjuster wheel to rotate. If the adjuster does not operate properly, remove, then reinstall the adjuster.

19. Adjust the brake shoes.
20. Adjust the parking brake cable.
21. Install the brake drum.

ADJUSTMENT

See Figure 5.

1. Before servicing the vehicle, refer to the Precautions Section.

2. Raise and safely support the vehicle.

3. Remove the rear wheels and tires.

4. Relieve cable tension from the park brake system at the equalizer. There should be no tension on the park brake cables,

so that the brake shoes are positioned only by the adjuster strut.

5. Remove the rear drums.

6. Set the J 21177-A, Drum-to-Brake Shoe Clearance Gauge, so that it contacts the inside diameter of the drum at the widest point.

7. Position the J 21177-A over the shoes at the widest point.

8. Turn the adjuster nut until the shoes just contact the J 21177-A.

9. Repeat the procedure for the other rear brake assembly.

10. Install the rear drums.

11. Install the rear wheels and tires. Tighten the wheel lug nuts to 100 ft. lbs. (136 Nm).

12. Adjust the park brake cable system.

13. Lower the vehicle.

PARKING BRAKE CABLES

ADJUSTMENT

See Figure 6.

1. Before servicing the vehicle, refer to the Precautions Section.

2. Apply and fully release the park brake several times. Verify that the park brake lever releases completely.

3. Turn **ON** the ignition. Verify the red BRAKE warning lamp is not illuminated.

4. If the red BRAKE warning lamp is illuminated, verify the following:

a. The park brake lever is in the fully released position and against the stop.

b. There is no slack in the park brake cable.

5. Turn **OFF** the ignition.

6. Disable the SIR system. Refer to Air Bag (Supplemental Restraint System), disarming the system.

7. Remove the front floor console.

8. With the park brake lever in the released position, using ONLY hand tools, loosen the adjusting nut completely to the end of the front cable threaded rod.

9. Raise and safely support the vehicle.

10. Remove the rear tire and wheel assemblies.

11. Adjust the rear drum brakes.

12. Ensure there is no brake shoe drag after adjustment by rotating the brake drums. If drag exists, re-center the brake

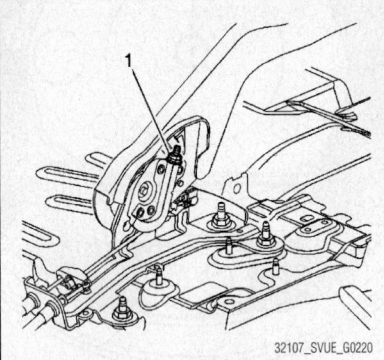

32107_SVUE_G0220

Fig. 6 Tighten the park brake cable adjusting nut (1) until light to moderate drag is exhibited while rotating the rear brake drums

shoes and perform the brake shoe adjustment again.

13. Install 2 wheel nuts to the wheel studs and firmly hand tighten in order to retain the brake drums.

14. Lower the vehicle to permit access to the park brake lever.

15. Raise the park brake lever 1 detent position.

16. Using ONLY hand tools, tighten the park brake cable adjusting nut (1) until light to moderate drag is exhibited while rotating the rear brake drums

17. Attempt to rotate the rear brake drums. There should be no rotation forward or rearward.

18. Fully release the park brake lever.

19. Verify the park brake is released by rotating the rear brake drums. The drums should rotate freely and exhibit no brake shoe drag.

20. If the drums do not rotate freely, repeat the park brake cable adjustment procedure.

21. Raise the park brake lever 3 detent positions and attempt to rotate the rear brake drums:

a. One of the brake drums should not rotate forward or rearward.

b. The other brake drum should not rotate forward or rearward, or should require substantial effort to rotate

22. Raise the vehicle.

23. Remove the wheel nuts retaining the brake drums.

24. Install the rear tire and wheel assemblies.

25. Lower the vehicle.

26. Install the front floor console.

27. Release the park brake lever.

28. Enable the SIR system. Refer to Air Bag (Supplemental Restraint System), arming the system.

PARKING BRAKE SHOES

REMOVAL & INSTALLATION

The rear drum brake shoes serve as the parking brakes. Refer to the procedures under Rear Drum Brakes.

CHASSIS ELECTRICAL   AIR BAG (SUPPLEMENTAL RESTRAINT SYSTEM)

GENERAL INFORMATION

✱✱ CAUTION

These vehicles are equipped with an air bag system. The system must be disarmed before performing service on, or around, system components, the steering column, instrument panel components, wiring and sensors. Failure to follow the safety precautions and the disarming procedure could result in accidental air bag deployment, possible injury and unnecessary system repairs.

SERVICE PRECAUTIONS

Disconnect and isolate the battery negative cable before beginning any airbag system component diagnosis, testing, removal, or installation procedures. Allow system capacitor to discharge for two minutes before beginning any component service. This will disable the airbag system. Failure to disable the airbag system may result in accidental airbag deployment, personal injury, or death.

Do not place an intact undeployed airbag face down on a solid surface. The airbag will propel into the air if accidentally deployed and may result in personal injury or death.

When carrying or handling an undeployed airbag, the trim side (face) of the airbag should be pointing towards the body to minimize possibility of injury if accidental deployment occurs. Failure to do this may result in personal injury or death.

Replace airbag system components with OEM replacement parts. Substitute parts may appear interchangeable, but internal differences may result in inferior occupant protection. Failure to do so may result in occupant personal injury or death.

Wear safety glasses, rubber gloves, and long sleeved clothing when cleaning powder residue from vehicle after an airbag deployment. Powder residue emitted from a deployed airbag can cause skin irritation. Flush affected area with cool water if irritation is experienced. If nasal or throat irritation is experienced, exit the vehicle for fresh air until the irritation ceases. If irritation continues, see a physician.

Do not use a replacement airbag that is not in the original packaging. This may result in improper deployment, personal injury, or death.

The factory installed fasteners, screws and bolts used to fasten airbag components have a special coating and are specifically designed for the airbag system. Do not use substitute fasteners. Use only original equipment fasteners listed in the parts catalog when fastener replacement is required.

During, and following, any child restraint anchor service, due to impact event or vehicle repair, carefully inspect all mounting hardware, tether straps, and anchors for proper installation, operation, or damage. If a child restraint anchor is found damaged in any way, the anchor must be replaced. Failure to do this may result in personal injury or death.

Deployed and non-deployed airbags may or may not have live pyrotechnic material within the airbag inflator.

Do not dispose of driver/passenger/curtain airbags or seat belt tensioners unless you are sure of complete deployment. Refer to the Hazardous Substance Control System for proper disposal.

Dispose of deployed airbags and tensioners consistent with state, provincial, local, and federal regulations.

After any airbag component testing or service, do not connect the battery negative cable. Personal injury or death may result if the system test is not performed first.

If the vehicle is equipped with the Occupant Classification System (OCS), do not connect the battery negative cable before performing the OCS Verification Test using the scan tool and the appropriate diagnostic information. Personal injury or death may result if the system test is not performed properly.

Never replace both the Occupant Restraint Controller (ORC) and the Occupant Classification Module (OCM) at the same time. If both require replacement, replace one, then perform the Airbag System test before replacing the other.

Both the ORC and the OCM store Occupant Classification System (OCS) calibration data, which they transfer to one another when one of them is replaced. If both are replaced at the same time, an irreversible fault will be set in both modules and the OCS may malfunction and cause personal injury or death.

If equipped with OCS, the Seat Weight Sensor is a sensitive, calibrated unit and must be handled carefully. Do not drop or handle roughly. If dropped or damaged, replace with another sensor. Failure to do so may result in occupant injury or death.

If equipped with OCS, the front passenger seat must be handled carefully as well. When removing the seat, be careful when setting on floor not to drop. If dropped, the sensor may be inoperative, could result in occupant injury, or possibly death.

If equipped with OCS, when the passenger front seat is on the floor, no one should sit in the front passenger seat. This uneven force may damage the sensing ability of the seat weight sensors. If sat on and damaged, the sensor may be inoperative, could result in occupant injury, or possibly death.

DISARMING THE SYSTEM

1. Before servicing the vehicle, refer to the Precautions Section.
2. Align the steering wheel so the vehicle wheels are pointing in the straight-ahead position.
3. Turn the ignition switch to the **LOCK** position.
4. Remove the SIR or AIR BAG fuse from the fuse block.
5. Disable the passenger side air bag as follows:
   a. Locate the SIR connector attached to the HVAC blower motor and disconnect the clip.

➥**Do not remove the upper trim panel as you are able to disable the passenger side air bag from the underside of the instrument panel.**

   b. Remove the Connector Position Assurance (CPA) device, then disengage the yellow 2-way SIR wiring harness connector.
6. Disable the driver's side air bag as follows:
7. Remove the Connector Position Assurance (CPA) device, then disengage the yellow 2-way SIR wiring harness connector at the base of the steering column.
8. Disable the curtain air bag as follows:
   a. Remove the center push pins located in the upper headliner trim panel.
   b. Remove the left D-pillar upper trim panel.
   c. Using a flat bladed tool, partially remove the right and left coat hook center retainers, then remove the coat hooks.
   d. Pull back the headliner gently to access the yellow 2-way connectors.
   e. Remove the Connector Position Assurance (CPA) device, then disengage the yellow 2-way SIR wiring harness connector.

ARMING THE SYSTEM

1. Before servicing the vehicle, refer to the Precautions Section.

2. Turn the ignition switch to the **LOCK** position.

3. Engage the yellow 2-way connectors for the airbags, then install the Connector Position Assurance (CPA) device.

4. Install any removed trim pieces.

5. Reinstall the Supplemental Inflatable Restraint (SIR) or AIR BAG fuse.

6. Turn the ignition switch to the **RUN** position.

7. Verify the SIR indicator light flashes 7–9 times, if not, inspect the system for malfunction.

CLOCKSPRING CENTERING

See Figure 7.

1. Before servicing the vehicle, refer to the Precautions Section.

> ✳✳ **CAUTION**

The new Supplemental Inflatable Restraint (SIR) coil assembly will be

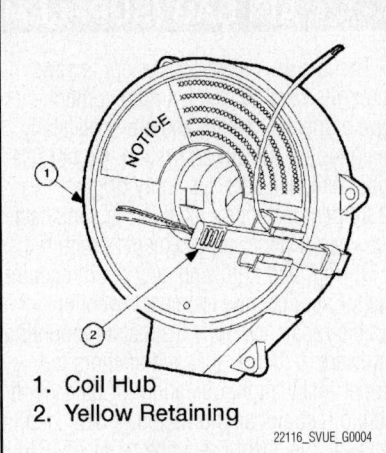

1. Coil Hub
2. Yellow Retaining

22116_SVUE_G0004

Fig. 7 SIR steering wheel module coil centering showing location of the coil hub & yellow retaining tab

centered. Improper alignment of the SIR coil assembly may damage the unit, causing an inflatable restraint malfunction.

2. If available, remove the yellow tab (2) and save for reassembly.

3. Gently rotate the coil hub (1) clockwise until a slight tension is present.

4. Count the number of revolutions, while gently rotating the coil hub (1) counter clockwise until a slight tension is present.

5. Gently rotate the coil hub (1) clockwise one half of the previously counted revolutions.

6. Rotate the coil hub as required to align the yellow tab (2).

➡ **If the yellow retaining tab is not available, the use of tape to secure the SIR steering wheel module coil is recommended for installation to the steering column.**

7. Install the yellow tab (2) into the coil hub.

8. Slide the centered SIR steering wheel module coil onto the steering shaft.

DRIVETRAIN

AUTOMATIC TRANSAXLE ASSEMBLY

REMOVAL & INSTALLATION

4T40–E & 4T45–E

See Figures 8 through 14.

Before servicing any vehicle, please be sure to read the precautions section, which deals with personal safety, prevention of component damage, and important points to take into consideration when servicing a motor vehicle.

1. Remove the battery tray.

2. Disconnect the air duct hose from the intake plenum.

3. Disconnect the shift control cable (3) from the range select lever (4).

4. Release the shift control cable retaining clip (2) and remove the cable from the shift control cable bracket (1).

5. Disconnect the transaxle wiring harness from the main transaxle electrical connector, and the Park Neutral Position (PNP) switch.

6. Install the engine support fixture.

7. Tie the radiator, air conditioning condenser, and fan module assembly to the upper radiator support to keep the assembly with the vehicle when the frame is lowered.

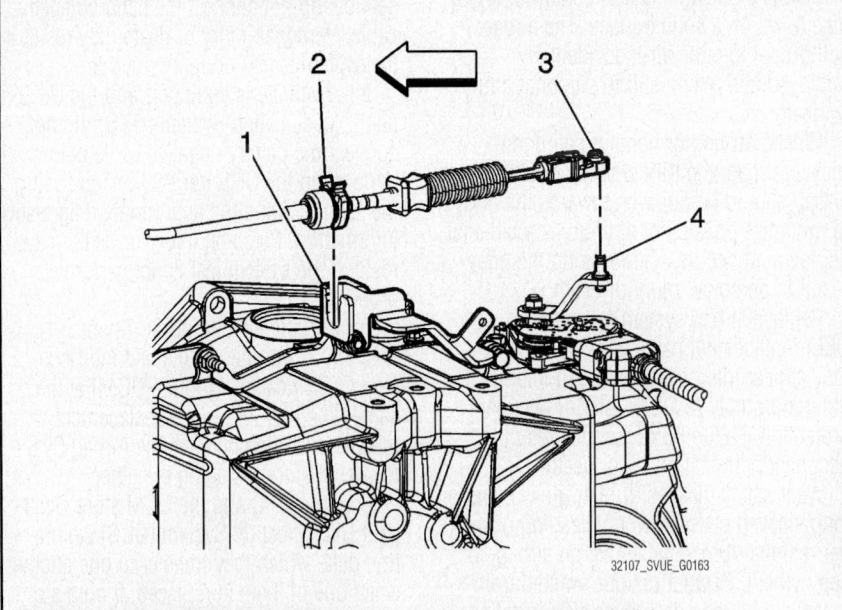

32107_SVUE_G0163

Fig. 8 Disconnect the shift control cable (3) from the range select lever (4)

8. Remove the upper transaxle to engine bolts (1, 3, 5, 6) and stud (2).

9. Safely support the engine.

10. Remove the transaxle mount to transaxle bolts.

11. Remove the transaxle mount to frame rail bolts.

12. Remove the mount from the engine.

13. Remove the left transaxle mount

14. Raise and safely support the vehicle.

15. Remove the front wheel and tire assemblies.

16. Remove the splash shield.

17. Remove the bolts (2, 3) from the transaxle brace.

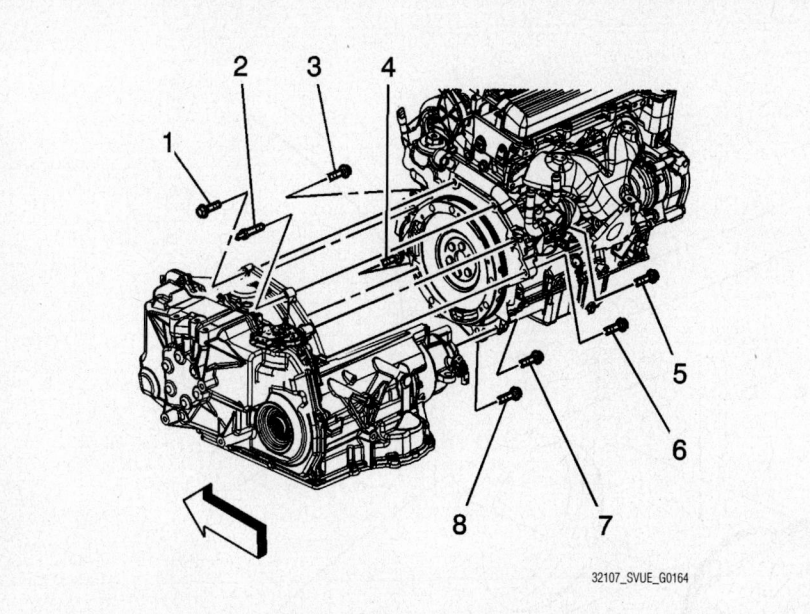

Fig. 9 Remove the upper transaxle to engine bolts (1, 3, 5, 6) and stud (2)

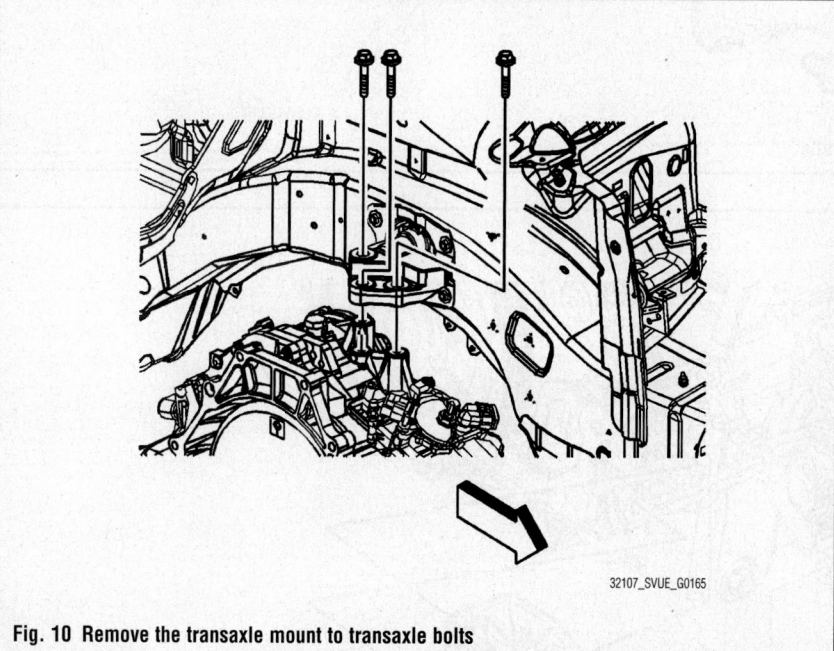

Fig. 10 Remove the transaxle mount to transaxle bolts

18. Remove the transaxle brace (1).
19. Remove the starter.
20. Mark the relationship of the flywhee l to the torque converter for reassembly.
21. Use the J 43653, Flywheel Holding Tool, to prevent the crankshaft from rotating.
22. Remove the torque converter to flywheel bolts.
23. Remove the nut holding the transaxle cooler line retainer to the transaxle.
24. Disconnect the transaxle cooler lines from the transaxle.

25. Disconnect the Vehicle Speed Sensor (VSS) wiring harness from the sensor.
26. Remove the steering gear intermediate shaft pinch bolt.
27. Disconnect the tie rods from the steering knuckle.
28. Disconnect the stabilizer shaft links from the stabilizer shaft.
29. Disconnect the ball joints from the steering knuckles.
30. Remove the frame.
31. Disconnect the wheel drive shafts from the transaxle.

32. Support the transaxle with a suitable jack.
33. Remove the lower transaxle to engine bolts (5, 6, 7, 8).
34. Separate the engine and the transaxle.
35. Remove the transaxle from the vehicle.
36. Flush the transaxle cooler and the lines with J 35944-A, Transaxle Oil Cooler Flusher.
37. Remove the following only if replacing the transaxle.
    a. Remove the shift cable bracket bolt (3), nut (1), and bracket (2).
    b. Remove the PNP switch.
    c. Remove the transaxle mounts.

To install:
38. Install the following if previously removed
    a. Install the shift cable bracket (2), bolt (3), and nut (1).
    b. Tighten the bolt (3) and nut (1) to 16 ft. lbs. (22 Nm).
39. Install the PNP switch.
40. Install the transaxle mounts.
41. Position the transaxle in the vehicle.
42. Install the lower transaxle to engine bolts. Tighten the bolts to 55 ft. lbs. (75 Nm).
43. Install the wheel drive shafts to the transaxle.
44. Install the frame.
45. Lubricate the transaxle cooler pipes before inserting into seals.
46. Connect the transaxle cooler pipes to the transaxle.
47. Install the transaxle cooler pipes retainer nut. Tighten the nut to 62 inch lbs. (7 Nm).
48. Use the J 43653, Flywheel Holding Tool, to prevent the crankshaft from rotating.
49. Install the torque converter to flywheel bolts. Tighten the torque converter bolts to 44 ft. lbs. (60 Nm).
50. Install the starter.
51. Install the frame.
52. Install the steering gear intermediate shaft pinch bolt.
53. Connect the ball joints to the steering knuckles.
54. Connect the stabilizer shaft links to the stabilizer shaft.
55. Connect the tie rods to the steering knuckle.
56. Connect the wiring harness to the VSS.
57. Install the transaxle brace.
58. Install the transaxle brace bolts. Tighten the bolts to 39 ft. lbs. (53 Nm).
59. Install the front splash shields.
60. Install the front wheel and tire assemblies.

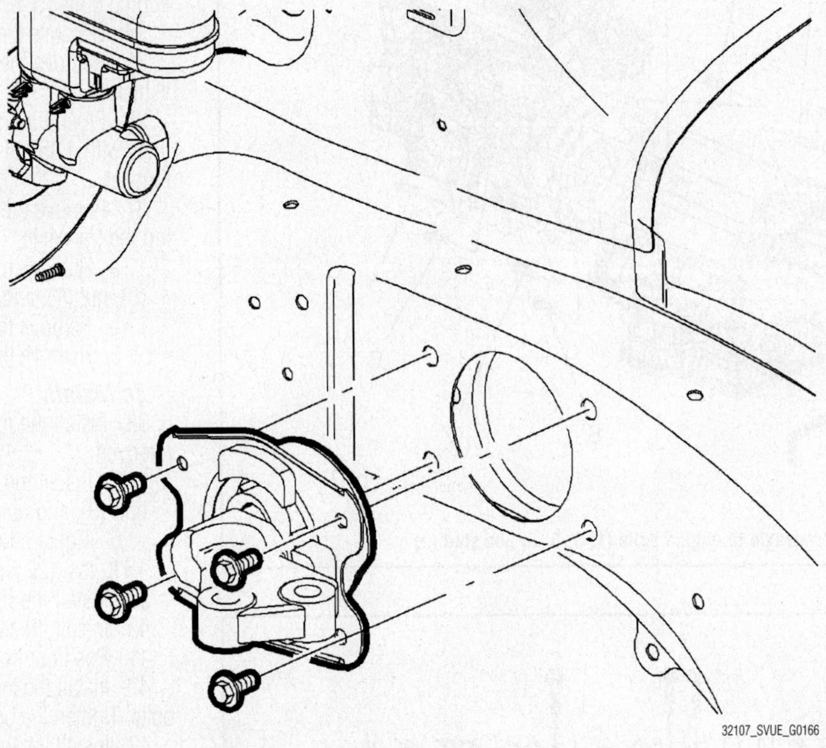

32107_SVUE_G0166

Fig. 11 Remove the transaxle mount to frame rail bolts

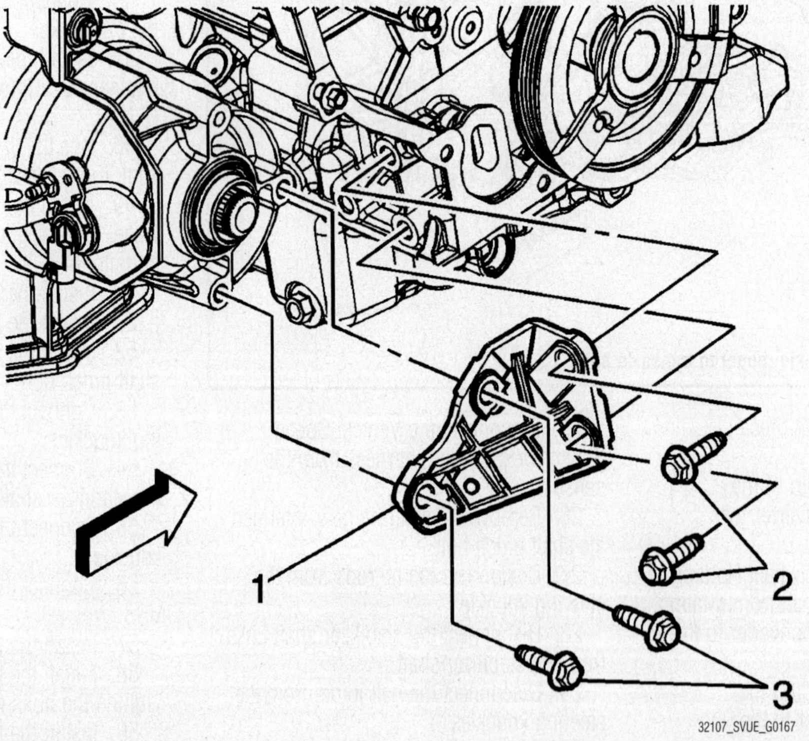

32107_SVUE_G0167

Fig. 12 Remove the bolts (2, 3) from the transaxle brace

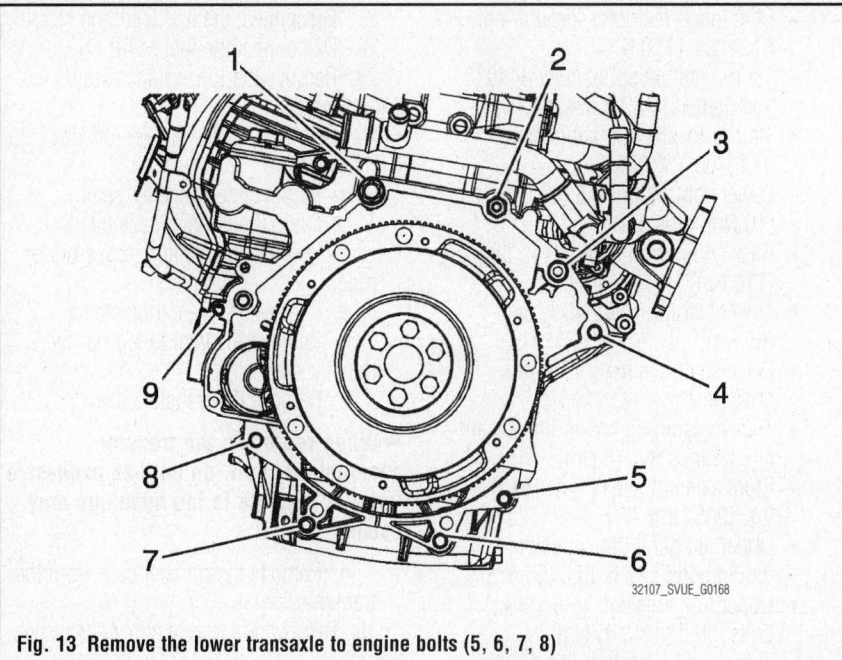

Fig. 13 Remove the lower transaxle to engine bolts (5, 6, 7, 8)

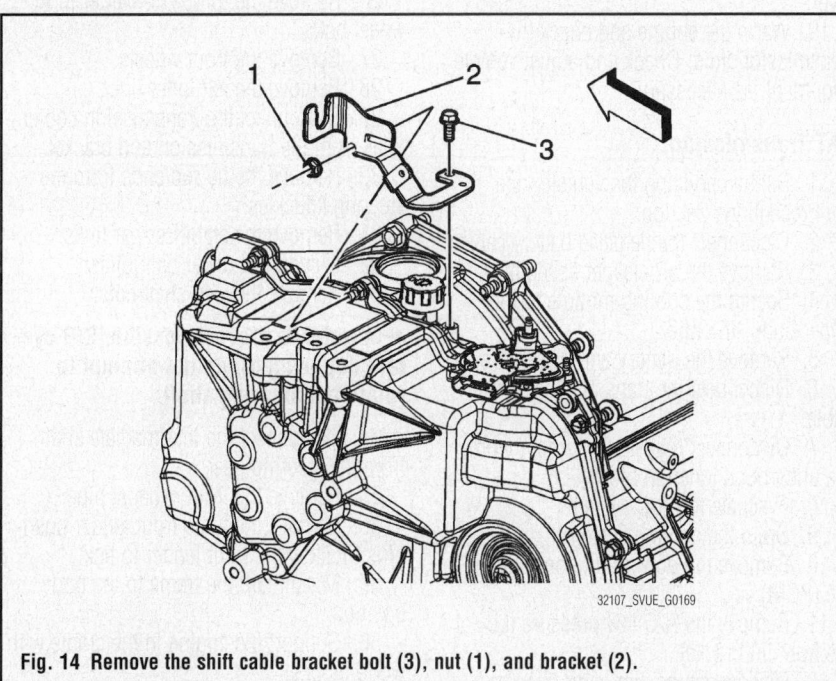

Fig. 14 Remove the shift cable bracket bolt (3), nut (1), and bracket (2).

61. Lower the vehicle.

62. Install the left transaxle mount.

63. Install the upper transaxle to engine bolts and stud. Tighten all of the bolts and stud to 55 ft. lbs. (75 Nm).

64. Untie the radiator, air conditioning condenser, and fan module assembly.

65. Remove the engine support fixture.

66. Connect the transaxle wiring harness to the main transaxle electrical connector, and the PNP switch.

67. Install the shift control cable to the shift control cable bracket. Ensure the cable retaining clip is fully seated.

68. Connect the shift control cable to the range select lever.

69. Connect the air duct hose to the intake plenum.

70. Install the battery tray.

71. Inspect the transaxle fluid level.

➡**It is recommended that Transmission Adaptive Pressure (TAP) information be reset. Resetting the TAP values using a scan tool will erase all learned values in all cells. As a result, the ECM, PCM or TCM will need to relearn TAP values. Transaxle performance may be affected as new TAP values are learned.**

72. Reset the TAP values.

The 4T45 automatic transaxle uses a line pressure control system, which has the ability to continuously adapt the system line pressure. This compensates for normal wear of clutch fiber plates, seals, and springs.

The Transmission Control Module (TCM) maintains the Upshift Adapt parameters for the transaxle. The TCM monitors the Input Speed Sensor (ISS) and the Output Speed Sensor (OSS) during commanded shifts in order to determine if a shift is occurring too fast or too slow. The TCM adjusts the signal from the transaxle Pressure Control (PC) solenoid in order to maintain a set shift feel. Transaxle adapts must be set again when the transaxle is overhauled or replaced. In order to set the transaxle adapts again, select the following:

- Scan Tool
- Transmission/Transaxle
- Special Functions
- Reset Transmission Adapts

AUTOMATIC TRANSMISSION ASSEMBLY

REMOVAL & INSTALLATION

Except 5AT Transmission

1. Before servicing the vehicle, refer to the Precautions Section.

2. Drain the transmission fluid.

3. Remove or disconnect the following:
- Both battery cables
- The battery and battery tray bracket
- The control cable from the Transmission Range Switch using pry-tool J36346
- The control cable from the bracket
- The TRS electrical connection
- The input and output speed sensor connections
- The positive battery cable from the transmission stud
- The headlamp fasteners and wire radiator to the core support

4. Install an engine support fixture.

5. Remove or disconnect the following:
- The transmission fluid dipstick tube
- The upper left hand transmission mount
- The wheels
- The splash shields
- The front air deflector
- The transmission cooler line nut
- The transmission cooler lines from the transmission

➡**Mark the position of the Power take Off (PTO) prior to removal.**

- The drive shaft from the PTO marking alignment locations prior to removal
- The lower stabilizer nut from the cradle on both sides
- The lower control arm from the knuckle
- The ball joints and tie rods from the knuckle
- The front pitch restrictor bolts, through bolts and restrictor
- The rear restrictor through bolt from the cradle

6. Position a support table under the cradle.

7. Remove the cradle bolts and lower the cradle onto the table.

8. Remove the left side drive axle drive shaft using removal tool J45341 and slide hammer SA9173G and secure the axle aside.

➡**The stub shaft may disengage from the PTO. If this occurs, plug the PTO to avoid fluid loss.**

9. Remove or disconnect the following:
- The right side drive axle from the PTO using removal tool J45341 and slide hammer SA9173G
- The PTO-to-engine bracket
- The starter
- The torque converter-to-flywheel bolts through the starter hole
- The 3 lower transmission-to-engine bolts
- The 1 engine-to-transmission bolt located above the PTO

10. Attach the transmission to a suitable transmission jack.

11. Separate the engine from the transmission, lower the assembly and disconnect the PTO hose.

12. Remove the PTO, if necessary.

To install:

13. Installation is the reverse of removal, please note the following torque specifications:
- Transmission-to-engine bolts: 55 ft. lbs. (75 Nm)
- PTO bracket bolts: 44 ft. lbs. (60 Nm)
- Torque converter-to-flexplate bolts: 44 ft. lbs. (60 Nm)
- Bracket-to-engine bolts: 26 ft. lbs. (35 Nm)
- Cradle bolts: 114 ft. lbs. (155 Nm)
- Rear pitch restrictor through bolt: 81 ft. lbs. (110 Nm)
- Front pitch restrictor bolts: 37 ft. lbs. (50 Nm)

- Front pitch restrictor through bolt: 81 ft. lbs. (110 Nm)
- Tie rod end using installer J44015 and tighten to 30 ft. lbs. (40 Nm)
- Tie rod-to-steering knuckle nut: 37 ft. lbs. (50 Nm)
- Lower control arm nut: 89 inch lbs. (10 Nm) plus 150°
- Rack and pinion bolts: 81 ft. lbs. (110 Nm)
- Lower stabilizer nut: 48 ft. lbs. (65 Nm)
- Drive shaft retainers: 74 ft. lbs. (100 Nm)
- Transmission oil cooler line assembly: 71 inch lbs. (8 Nm)
- Front axle stub shaft nut: 151 ft. lbs. (205 Nm)
- Upper left hand transmission mount bolts : 37 ft. lbs. (50 Nm)
- Upper transmission-to-engine bolts: 55 ft. lbs. (75 Nm)

14. Fill the transmission to the proper level.

15. Warm the engine and check the transmission fluid. Check and adjust vehicle alignment, as necessary.

5AT Transmission

1. Before servicing the vehicle, refer to the Precautions Section.

2. Disconnect the negative battery cable.

3. Remove the air cleaner assembly.

4. Secure the cooling module to the upper body structure.

5. Remove the battery and battery tray.

6. Disconnect the transmission shiftier cable.

7. Disconnect the wiring harness from the underhood junction block.

8. Evacuate the A/C system.

9. Drain the cooling system.

10. Remove the powertrain control module (PCM).

11. Remove the A/C low pressure tube at the front lift bracket.

12. Disconnect the alternator positive cable.

13. Disconnect the A/C high pressure switch harness.

14. Remove the A/C tube from the A/C compressor.

15. Disconnect the A/C line from the condenser to the compressor.

16. Disconnect the coolant reservoir hose from the engine.

17. Disconnect the radiator hoses from the engine.

18. Remove the heater hoses.

19. Remove the starter positive cable.

20. Relieve the fuel pressure.

21. Disconnect the fuel feed line.

22. Disconnect the fuel EVAP line.

23. Remove the lower transmission-to-engine bolts.

24. Remove the Power Take-off Unit (PTU) as follows:
   a. Remove the propeller shaft.
   b. Drain the transfer case oil.
   c. Remove the exhaust cross-under pipe.
   d. Remove the vent tube clamp.
   e. Remove the vent tube from the transfer case.
   f. Remove the transfer case.

➡**When removing the transfer case/output shaft, do not use excessive force or damage to the bushings may occur.**

   g. Remove the transfer case from the transmission.

25. Remove the torque converter inspection cover.

26. Remove the torque converter to flywheel bolts.

27. Remove the front wheels.

28. Remove the left inner liner.

29. Disconnect the transmission cooler lines from the transmission and bracket.

30. Remove the tie rod ends from the steering knuckles.

31. Remove the stabilizer bar links.

32. Disconnect lower ball joints.

33. Remove the axle shaft nuts.

➡**In order to prevent possible SIR system deployment, do not attempt to rotate the steering shaft.**

34. Disconnect the intermediate shaft from the steering gear.

35. Remove the front exhaust pipe.

36. Remove the three front fender push-pins to allow the front fender to flex.

37. Matchmark the frame to the body position.

38. Support the engine in the cradle with wood blocks.

39. Disconnect the front engine mount from the body.

40. Lower the vehicle to 3 feet off the ground in order to position the Engine Support Table J 39580 under the frame.

41. Remove the cradle bolts.

42. Slowly lower the table to the floor.

43. Remove the starter.

44. Remove the following components:
   a. The transmission shift cable bracket.
   b. The Park/Neutral position switch.
   c. The transmission vent hose.
   d. The transmission mount from the transmission.

e. The rear transmission mount bracket.

45. Separate the transmission from the engine.

46. Remove the transfer case, if equipped.

To install:

47. Attach the engine to the transmission.

48. Install the rear mount.

49. Install the front engine mount to the engine

50. Install the following components:
   a. The transmission vent hose.
   b. The Park/Neutral position switch.
   c. The transmission shift cable bracket and bolts. Tighten the bolts to 89 inch lbs. (10 Nm).
   d. The starter.

51. Install the engine and transmission assembly in the vehicle.

52. Install the cradle bolts. Tighten the bolts to 114 ft. lbs. (155 Nm).

53. Remove the lift table.

54. Install the front engine mount bolts to the body. Tighten the transmission mount-to-frame bolts to 37 ft. lbs. (50 Nm) and the transmission mount-to-bracket through bolt, while aligning the transmission mount to the bracket to 81 ft. lbs. (110 Nm).

55. Remove the wood blocks from the cradle.

56. Install the lower transmission-to-engine bolts and tighten to 47 ft. lbs. (64 Nm).

57. Install the PTU as follows:
   a. Install the transfer case to the transmission and tighten the bolts to 38 ft. lbs. (51 Nm).
   b. Install the vent hose and the clamp to the transfer case.
   c. Install the exhaust cross-under pipe.

58. Remove the transfer case check plug and fill the transfer case with synthetic gear oil.

59. Install the check plug and gasket to the case and tighten to 33 ft. lbs. (44 Nm).

60. Install the torque converter-to-flywheel bolts and tighten to 80 inch lbs. (12 Nm).

61. Install the torque converter inspection cover and tighten to 80 inch lbs. (12 Nm).

62. Install the 3 front fender push-pins.

63. Install the front exhaust pipe.

64. Connect the intermediate shaft from the steering gear.

65. Install the propeller shaft.

66. Install the axle shaft nuts.

67. Connect the lower ball joints.

68. Install the stabilizer bar links.

69. Install tie rod ends to the steering knuckles.

70. Connect the transmission cooler lines to the transmission and bracket.

71. Install the left inner liner.

72. Install the front wheels. Tighten the wheel lug nuts to 100 ft. lbs. (136 Nm).

73. Install the fuel EVAP line.

74. Connect the fuel feed line.

75. Connect the starter positive cable.

76. Install the heater hoses.

77. Connect the radiator hoses to the engine.

78. Attach the A/C tube to the A/C compressor.

79. Connect the coolant reservoir hose.

80. Connect the A/C line from the condenser to compressor.

81. Connect the A/C high pressure switch harness.

82. Connect the alternator wiring.

83. Install the A/C lower pressure tube at the front lift bracket.

84. Install the PCM.

85. Connect the radiator hoses to the engine.

86. Fill the cooling system to the proper level.

87. Connect the wiring harness to the underhood junction block.

88. Connect the transmission shifter cable.

89. Remove the cooling module support.

90. Install the battery tray and battery.

91. Install the air cleaner assembly and ducts.

92. Connect the negative battery cable

MANUAL TRANSAXLE ASSEMBLY

REMOVAL & INSTALLATION

See Figures 15 and 16.

1. Before servicing the vehicle, refer to the Precautions Section.

2. Drain the transaxle fluid.

3. Remove both battery cables

4. Install an engine support fixture.

5. Fasten the radiator to the upper radiator support.

6. Remove or disconnect the following:
   • The front wheels
   • The splash shields
   • The ball joints and tie rods from the knuckle
   • The lower control arm from the knuckle
   • The lower stabilizer bar links
   • The steering gear from the steering gear assembly

   • The rear transaxle mount-to-cradle bolts
   • The rear transaxle mount bracket-to-transaxle bolts
   • The front lower mount through bolt from the cradle
   • The front air deflector from the body, but leave it attached to the cradle

7. Support the cradle with a jack.

8. Remove or disconnect the following:
   • The cradle bolts and the cradle
   • The shift lever cable from the shift control housing using tool J36346
   • The shift lever cable from the bracket
   • The pressure line from the clutch actuator by removing the C-clip and pulling it away from the actuator
   • The back-up lamp switch connector
   • The front transaxle mount from the transaxle
   • The right side drive axle from the intermediate drive shaft using removal tool J45341 and slide hammer SA9173G

9. Secure the drive axle from the intermediate drive shaft.

➡**Remove the retainer ring from the stub shaft before removing the tool and discard the ring.**

10. Remove the intermediate drive shaft using removal tool J440177 and axle seal puller SA9133T.

11. Remove the left side drive axle drive shaft using removal tool J45341 and slide hammer SA9173G and secure the axle aside.

12. Remove the top transaxle mount bolts.

13. Use the engine support fixture to lower the transaxle enough so that the assembly can be removed.

14. Attach the transaxle to a suitable transaxle jack.

15. Remove the transaxle bolts on the engine side and the transaxle bolt on the transaxle side.

To install:

16. Installation is the reverse of removal, please note the following torque specifications:
   • The transaxle-to-engine and engine-to-transaxle bolts: 55 ft. lbs. (75 Nm)
   • The top mount-to-transaxle bolts: 37 ft. lbs. (50 Nm)
   • The front transaxle mount bolts: 37 ft. lbs. (50 Nm)

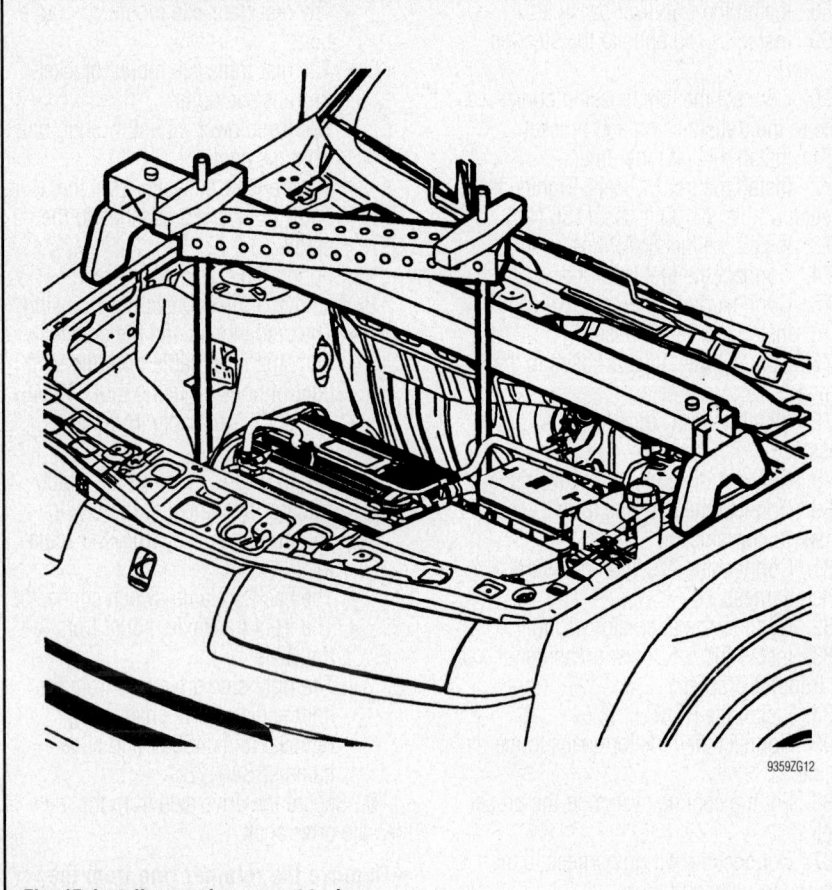

Fig. 15 Install an engine support tool

9359ZG12

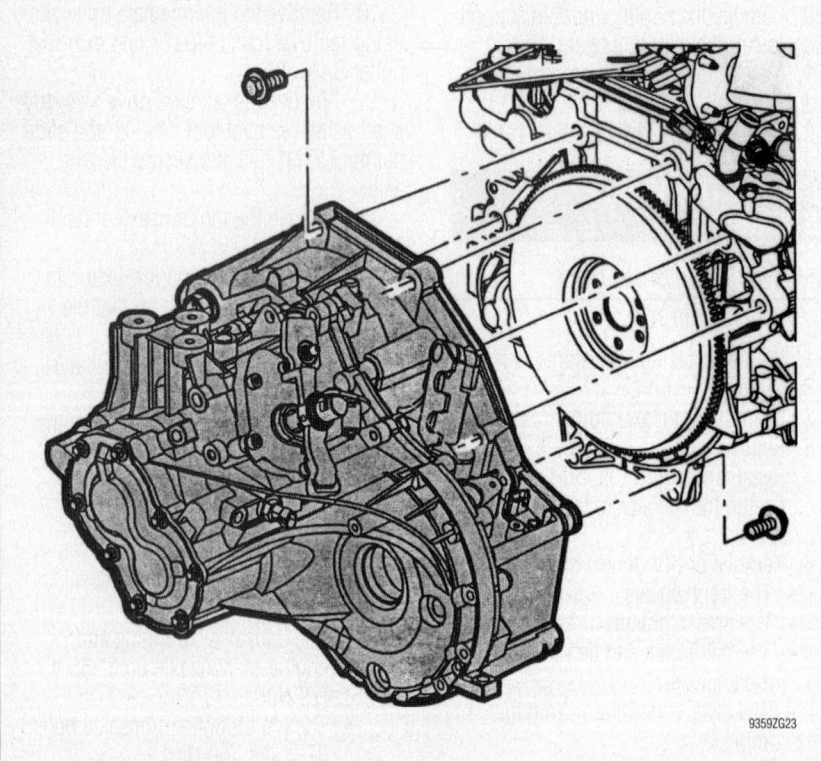

Fig. 16 Remove the engine to manual transaxle bolts

9359ZG23

- The rear transaxle mount-to-transaxle bolts: 37 ft. lbs. (50 Nm)
- The cradle-to-body bolts: 114 ft. lbs. (155 Nm)
- The front transaxle mount through bolt: 81 ft. lbs. (110 Nm)
- The rear transaxle mount through bolt: 81 ft. lbs. (110 Nm)
- The steering gear-to-column bolt: 25 ft. lbs. (34 Nm)
- The lower control arm nut: 89 inch lbs. (10 Nm) plus 150°
- The stabilizer bar link: 48 ft. lbs. (65 Nm)
- The tie rod end using installer J44015 and tighten to 30 ft. lbs. (40 Nm)
- The tie rod-to-steering knuckle nut: 37 ft. lbs. (50 Nm)

17. Fill the transaxle to the proper level.

18. Warm the engine and check the transaxle fluid. Check and adjust vehicle alignment, as necessary.

CLUTCH DRIVEN DISC & PRESSURE PLATE

REMOVAL & INSTALLATION

1. Before servicing the vehicle, refer to the Precautions Section.

2. Remove the transaxle from the vehicle.

3. Remove the pressure plate and clutch disc.

4. Inspect the pressure plate, as follows:

   a. Check for excessive wear, chatter marks, cracks or overheating (indicated by a blue discoloration). Black random spots on the friction surface of the pressure plate is normal.

   b. Check the plate for warpage using a straightedge and a feeler gauge; the maximum allowable warpage is 0.006 in. (0.15mm).

   c. Replace the plate, if necessary.

5. Inspect the clutch disc, as follows:

   a. Check the disc face for oil or burned spots.

   b. Check the disc for loose damper springs, hub or rivets.

   c. Replace the disc, if necessary.

6. Check the flywheel, as follows:

   a. Check the ring gear for wear or damage.

   b. Check the friction surface for excessive wear, chatter marks, cracks or overheating.

   c. Check flywheel thickness; the minimum allowable is 1.102 in. (28mm).

d. Measure flywheel run-out using a dial indicator, positioned for at least 2 flywheel revolutions. Push the crankshaft forward to take up thrust bearing clearance. Maximum flywheel run-out is 0.006 in. (0.15mm).

e. Check the flywheel for warpage using a straight-edge and a feeler gauge; the maximum allowable warpage is 0.006 in. (0.15mm).

f. Replace the flywheel, if necessary.

7. If necessary, remove the flywheel retaining bolts and remove the flywheel from the crankshaft.

To install:

8. Install or connect the following:
- The flywheel (if removed) and torque the bolts in a crisscross pattern to 39 ft. lbs. (53 Nm) plus 25°
- The clutch disc and pressure plate and loosely install the pressure plate bolts
- The clutch alignment tool in the clutch disc, and push in until it bottoms out in the crankshaft

9. Tighten the pressure plate bolts using multiple passes of a crisscross sequence to 17 ft. lbs. (24 Nm) and remove the alignment tool.

10. Lubricate the splines of the input shaft lightly with a high temperature grease.

11. Install the transaxle assembly.

ADJUSTMENTS

The hydraulic clutch system is self-adjusting.

CLUTCH MASTER CYLINDER

REMOVAL & INSTALLATION

See Figures 17 through 19.

Before servicing any vehicle, please be sure to read the precautions section, which deals with personal safety, prevention of component damage, and important points to take into consideration when servicing a motor vehicle.

1. Clean the clutch fluid reservoir cap and area around the cap.

2. Remove the clutch fluid reservoir cap and remove enough brake fluid to clear a passage to the clutch master cylinder.

3. Remove the clutch pedal retainer.

4. Remove the clutch master cylinder pushrod from the clutch pedal assembly, 1st design.

5. Remove the clutch master cylinder pushrod from the clutch pedal assembly, 2nd design.

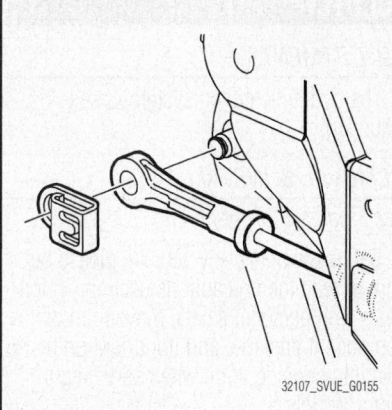

Fig. 17 Remove the clutch master cylinder pushrod from the clutch pedal assembly, 1st design

32107_SVUE_G0155

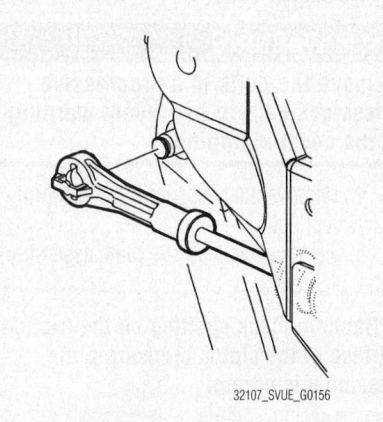

Fig. 18 Remove the clutch master cylinder pushrod from the clutch pedal assembly, 2nd design

32107_SVUE_G0156

✳✳ WARNING

Avoid spilling brake fluid onto painted surfaces, electrical connections, wiring, or cables. Brake fluid will damage painted surfaces and cause corrosion to electrical components. If any brake fluid comes in contact with painted surfaces, immediately flush the area with water. If any brake fluid comes in contact with electrical connections, wiring, or cables, use a clean shop cloth to wipe away the fluid.

6. Place a shop towel under the clutch master cylinder in order to catch any fluid loss.

7. Using a pick tool on the strut tower side, disconnect the clutch line from clutch master cylinder.

8. Cap the reservoir and hydraulic lines in order to prevent fluid loss and contamination.

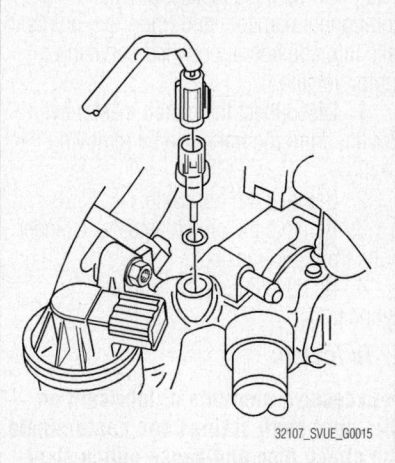

32107_SVUE_G0015

Fig. 19 Remove the clutch master cylinder mounting nuts and slide the clutch fluid reservoir up and out

✳✳ WARNING

Do not damage the pushrod boot when sliding it through the front of the dash.

9. Remove the clutch master cylinder mounting nuts and slide the clutch fluid reservoir up and out.

➡**Do not damage the pushrod boot when sliding it through the front of the dash.**

10. Uncap the fluid reservoir and hydraulic lines.

11. Slide the clutch fluid reservoir into the mounting slot and install the clutch master cylinder mounting nuts. Tighten the nuts to 17 ft. lb (23 Nm).

12. Install the clutch master cylinder pushrod to the clutch pedal assembly, 1st design.

13. Install the clutch pedal retainer.

14. Install the clutch master cylinder pushrod to the clutch pedal assembly, 2nd design.

15. Remove the shop towel and discard into a suitable container.

16. Connect the clutch line to the clutch master cylinder.

17. Connect the clutch master cylinder pushrod to the clutch pedal.

18. Install the clutch pedal retainer, nuts and bolts.

19. Bleed the clutch hydraulic system

CLUTCH SLAVE CYLINDER

REMOVAL & INSTALLATION

See Figure 20.

Before servicing any vehicle, please be sure to read the precautions section, which deals with personal safety, prevention of component damage, and important points to take into consideration when servicing a motor vehicle.

1. Disconnect the clutch master cylinder line from the transaxle by removing the C-clip.

2. Remove the transaxle.

3. Remove the clutch actuator cylinder bolts from the transaxle.

4. Remove the clutch actuator cylinder.

To install:

➡**Excessive amounts of lubricant on the input shaft splines can contaminate the clutch disc and cause clutch shudder.**

5. Lightly lubricate the inside diameter of the bearing with input shaft lubricant P/N 21005995 or equivalent.

6. Install the clutch actuator cylinder (1) to the transaxle.

7. Install the clutch actuator cylinder bolts.

8. Tighten the bolts to 89 inch lbs. (10 Nm).

9. Install the transaxle.

10. Connect the clutch master cylinder line to the transaxle by pushing it in until it seats.

11. Bleed the clutch hydraulic system.

CLUTCH

ADJUSTMENTS

The hydraulic clutch system is self-adjusting.

REMOVAL & INSTALLATION

See Figures 21 through 25.

Before servicing any vehicle, please be sure to read the precautions section, which deals with personal safety, prevention of component damage, and important points to take into consideration when servicing a motor vehicle.

1. Remove the transaxle.

2. Inspect the actuator release bearing minimal bearing drag.

3. Replace the actuator assembly if no or little drag is found.

❊❊ WARNING

Remove the bolts in a progressive crisscross pattern to prevent warping of the cover stamping.

4. Remove the pressure plate assembly to flywheel bolts.

5. Remove the pressure plate assembly and clutch disc.

➡**Random black spotting on the friction surface of the clutch pressure plate assembly is normal.**

6. Inspect the clutch pressure plate assembly surface for the following conditions:

   a. Excessive wear.

   b. Chatter marks.

   c. Cracks.

   d. Overheating—indicated by blue discoloration.

7. Replace the clutch pressure plate assembly if damaged.

8. Using a straight edge and a feeler gage, inspect the clutch pressure plate assembly for warpage. Maximum warpage: 0.006 in. (0.15mm).

9. Inspect the clutch disc facings for oil or burned spots.

10. Replace the clutch disc if necessary.

11. Inspect the clutch disc for the following conditions: Loose damper springs, hub, or rivets.

12. Replace the clutch disc if any components are broken or excessively loose.

13. Inspect the flywheel ring gear for wear or damage.

14. Replace the flywheel if damaged.

➡**Random black spotting on the friction surface of the flywheel is normal.**

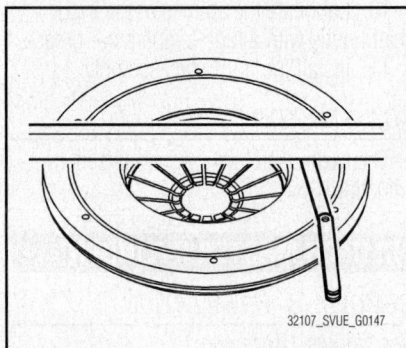

Fig. 21 Using a straight edge and a feeler gage, inspect the clutch pressure plate assembly for warpage

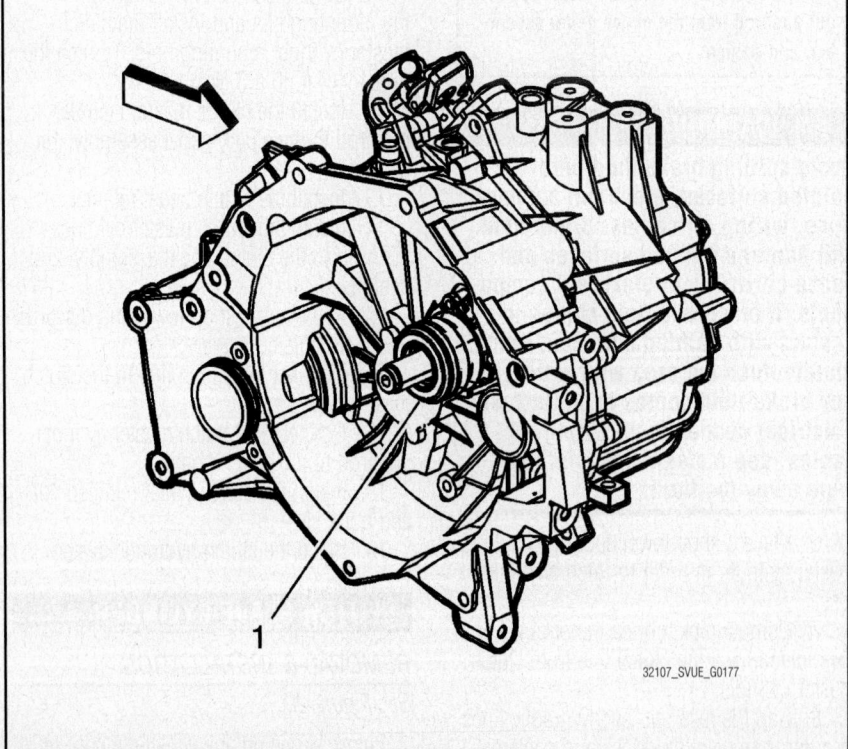

Fig. 20 Install the clutch actuator cylinder (1) to the transaxle

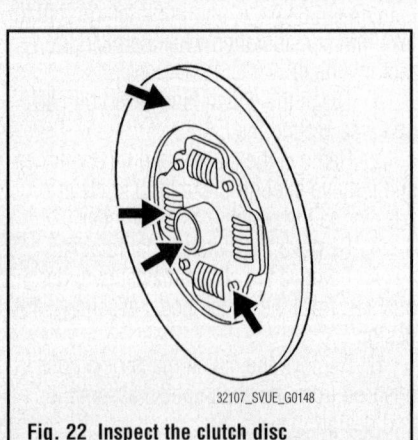

Fig. 22 Inspect the clutch disc

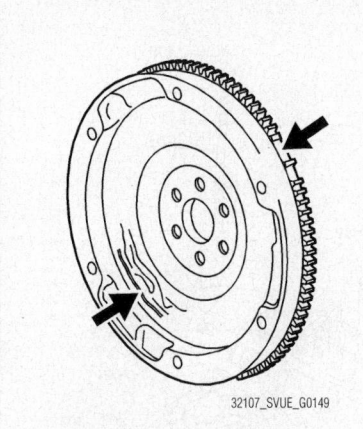

Fig. 23 Inspect the flywheel to clutch disc contact surface

15. Inspect the flywheel to clutch disc contact surface for the following conditions:
   a. Wear.
   b. Cracks.
   c. Chatter marks.
   d. Overheating—indicated by blue discoloration.
16. Repair or replace the flywheel if necessary.
17. Using a dial indicator, for at least two revolutions, measure flywheel runout. Maximum runout: 0.006 in. (0.15mm).
18. Repair or replace the flywheel if not within specification.
19. Using a straight edge and a feeler gage, inspect the flywheel for warpage. Maximum warpage: 0.006 in. (0.15mm).
20. If the flywheel is being replaced, remove and discard the flywheel-to-crankshaft bolts and remove the flywheel.

To install:

21. Install the flywheel and the new flywheel-to-crankshaft bolts. Hand start the bolts.

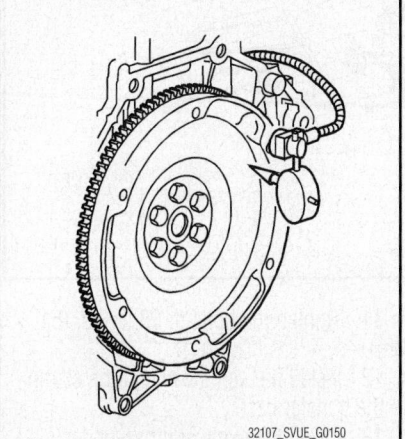

Fig. 24 Using a dial indicator, for at least two revolutions, measure flywheel runout

22. Install the flywheel-to-crankshaft bolts in a crisscross pattern. Tighten the bolts to 39 ft. lbs. (53 Nm) plus 25°.

✳✳ WARNING
Ensure that the straps on the clutch pressure plate fit into the slots on the flywheel.

23. Install the clutch disc and the clutch pressure plate assembly to the flywheel.
24. Loosely install the clutch pressure plate bolts.
25. Install the J 43482, Clutch Alignment Arbor, in the clutch disc and push in until it bottoms out in the crankshaft.

✳✳ WARNING
Do not tighten the pressure plate assembly bolts more than half a turn at a time or the pressure plate assembly may warp.

26. Install the pressure plate assembly bolts using a progressive crisscross pattern to prevent warping of the pressure plate assembly. Tighten the bolts to 17 ft. lbs. (24 Nm).

✳✳ WARNING
Excessive amounts of lubricant on the input shaft splines can contaminate the clutch disc and cause clutch shudder.

27. Lightly lubricate the input shaft splines with clutch spline lubricant P/N 21005995 or equivalent.
28. Install the transaxle.
29. Bleed the clutch hydraulic system.

CLUTCH HYDRAULIC SYSTEM BLEEDING

BLEEDING PROCEDURE

Before servicing any vehicle, please be sure to read the precautions section, which deals with personal safety, prevention of component damage, and important points to take into consideration when servicing a motor vehicle.

Vacuum Bleeding

This procedure outlines how to bleed the hydraulic clutch with the transaxle in the vehicle. Only **DOT 3** brake fluid should be added to the system.

1. Before servicing the vehicle, refer to the Precautions Section.
2. Remove the reservoir cap and fill the reservoir with new brake fluid.
3. Install a Bleeder Adapter Tool J23738A, to the reservoir and connect a pressure bleeder to the adapter.
4. Charge the pressure bleeder to 15–20 psi (103–138 kPa).
5. Attach a transparent hose over the clutch bleeder screw nipple and submerge

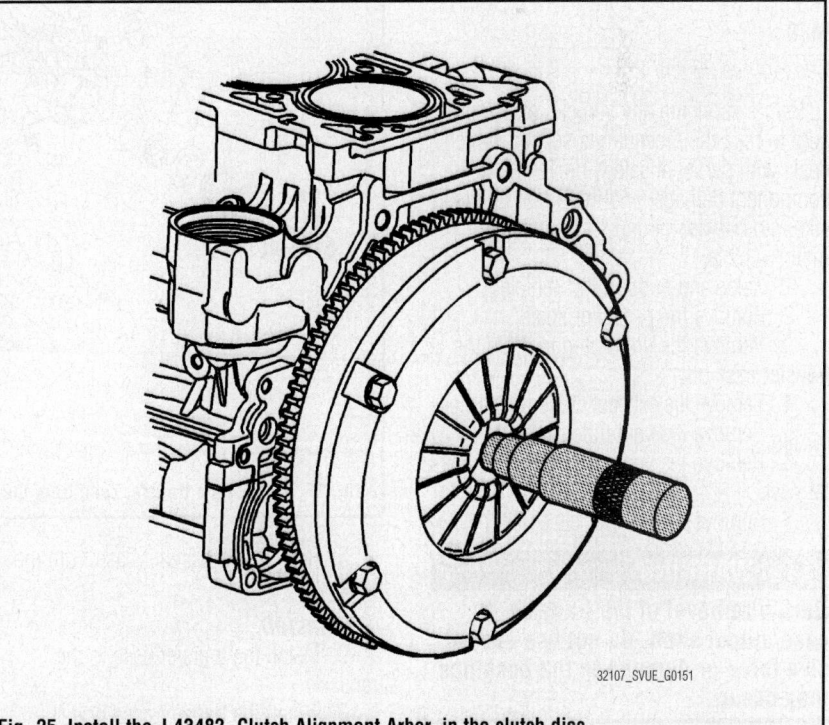

Fig. 25 Install the J 43482, Clutch Alignment Arbor, in the clutch disc

the opposite end of the hose in a container of brake fluid.

6. Loosen the bleeder screw on the transaxle hydraulic fitting.

7. Bleed the system until no air bubbles are seen in the hose.

8. Tighten the bleeder screw.

9. Check the clutch pedal for a spongy feel. If the pedal feels soft, repeat the bleeding procedure.

10. Remove the bleeder tools and top off the fluid level if necessary.

Manual Bleeding

1. Before servicing the vehicle, refer to the Precautions Section.

2. Fill the clutch reservoir with brake fluid. Check the reservoir level frequently and add fluid as needed.

3. Connect one end of a vinyl tube to the bleeder plug on the slave cylinder and submerge the other end into a clear container half-filled with clean brake fluid.

4. Slowly pump the clutch pedal 10–15 times without bring the pedal the full way up.

5. Repeat Steps 2 and 3 until all of the air bubbles are removed from the system.

6. Tighten the bleeder screw to 62 inch lbs. (7 Nm).

7. Refill the master cylinder to the proper level.

8. Check the system for leaks.

TRANSFER CASE ASSEMBLY

REMOVAL & INSTALLATION

MJ8

See Figures 26 and 27.

Before servicing any vehicle, please be sure to read the precautions section, which deals with personal safety, prevention of component damage, and important points to take into consideration when servicing a motor vehicle.

1. Raise and support the vehicle.

2. Remove the propeller shaft.

3. Remove the drain plug to drain the transfer case oil.

4. Remove the exhaust cross-under pipe.

5. Remove the vent tube clamp .

6. Remove the vent tube from the transfer case.

7. Remove the transfer case.

✳✳ WARNING

During removal of the transfer case/output shaft, do not use excessive force or damage to the bushings may occur.

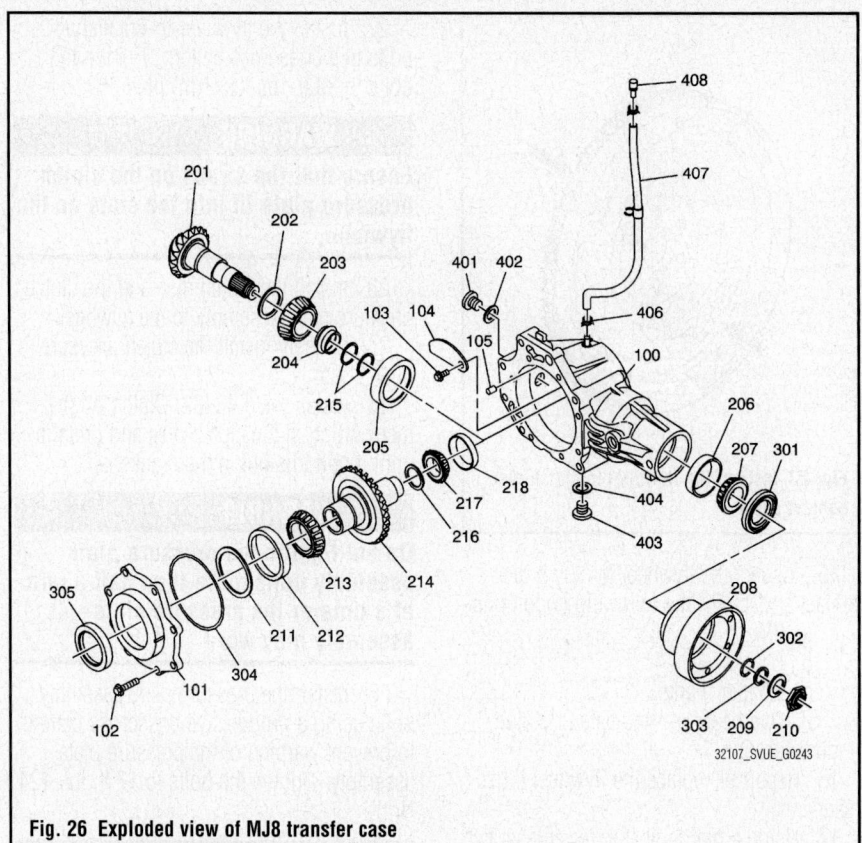

Fig. 26 Exploded view of MJ8 transfer case

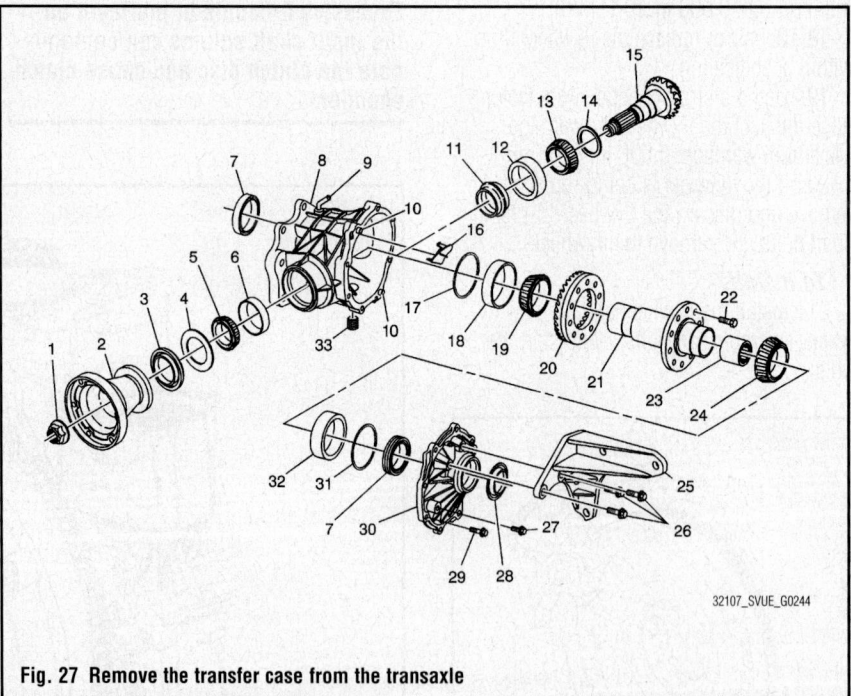

Fig. 27 Remove the transfer case from the transaxle

8. Remove the transfer case from the transaxle .

To install:

9. Install the transfer case to the transaxle.

10. Install the transfer case bolts.

11. Tighten the bolts to 38 ft. lbs. (51 Nm).

12. Install the vent hose and the clamp to the transfer case.

13. Install the exhaust cross-under pipe.

14. Install the propeller shaft.

15. Remove the transfer case check plug and fill the transfer case with the specified synthetic gear oil.

16. Install the check plug and gasket to the case.

17. Tighten the check plug to 33 ft. lbs. (44 Nm).

18. Lower the vehicle.

NVG 900

See Figures 28 through 30.

Before servicing any vehicle, please be sure to read the precautions section, which deals with personal safety, prevention of component damage, and important points to take into consideration when servicing a motor vehicle.

1. Raise and safely support the vehicle.

2. Remove the intermediate drive shaft.

➡**Remove the retainer ring from the stub shaft for tool installation. Discard the used retainer ring.**

➡**Use the proper container for fluid loss when the stub shaft is removed. Plug the Power Take-off Unit (PTU) to minimize fluid loss.**

3. Disengage the PTU stub shaft from the PTU using the J 44017, Shaft Remover, and SA9133T, Slide Hammer.

4. Remove the propshaft center bearing to underbody bolts.

➡**Index mark the propshaft to PTU for re-installation.**

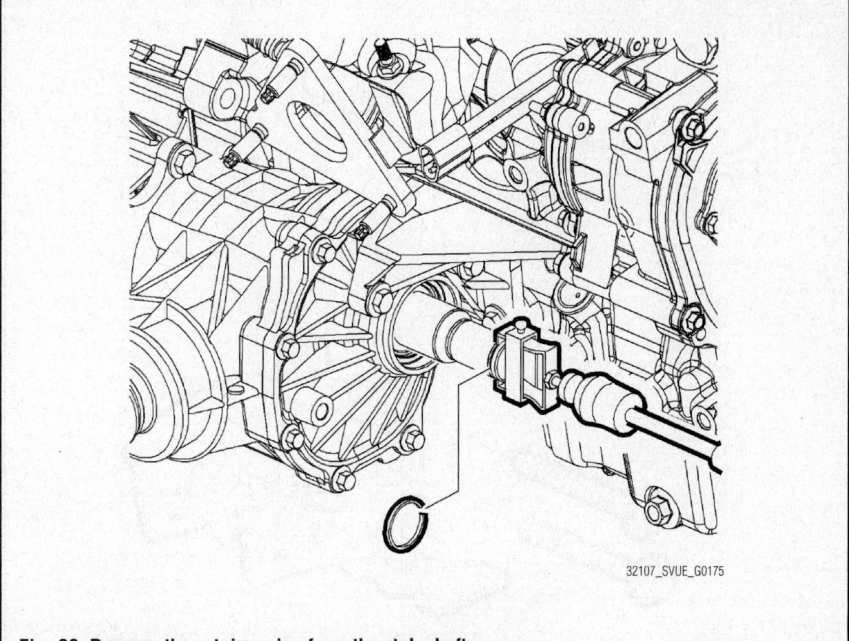

32107_SVUE_G0175

Fig. 29 Remove the retainer ring from the stub shaft

5. Remove the front propshaft attachment bolts.

6. Compress the CV joint and disengage the propshaft from the PTU and secure with wire.

7. Separate the steering gear from the cradle for clearance.

8. Remove the rear powertrain mount bracket bolts from the PTU.

9. Remove the PTU brace bolts and remove the brace.

10. Remove the PTU to transaxle bolts.

11. Remove the PTU vent hose.

To install:

➡**Lubricate the seal with transaxle fluid prior to PTU installation.**

12. Inspect the transaxle output shaft seal, replace if damaged.

13. Install the PTU to transaxle. Ensure the PTU is fully engaged. Hand start the PTU to transaxle bolts. DO NOT tighten.

14. Install the PTU brace. Hand start all 6 bolts.

15. Tighten the PTU to transaxle bolts.

16. Tighten the bolts to 44 ft. lbs. (60 Nm).

17. Tighten the PTU brace bolts.

18. Tighten the bolts to 44 ft. lbs. (60 Nm).

19. Hand start all the powertrain mount to PTU bolts and tighten.

➡**Use the index mark for reassembly.**

20. Hand start the propshaft center bearing bolts.

21. Ensure all the PTU flange and propshaft coupling area is clean. Insert coupling into the PTU flange.

➡**Apply Permatex Threadlocker® Blue to bolt threads.**

22. Hand start all propshaft coupling bolts. Tighten the bolts to 19 ft. lbs. (25 Nm).

23. Install the center bearing bolts. Tighten the bolts to 19 ft. lbs. (25 Nm).

24. Install the intermediate drive shaft.

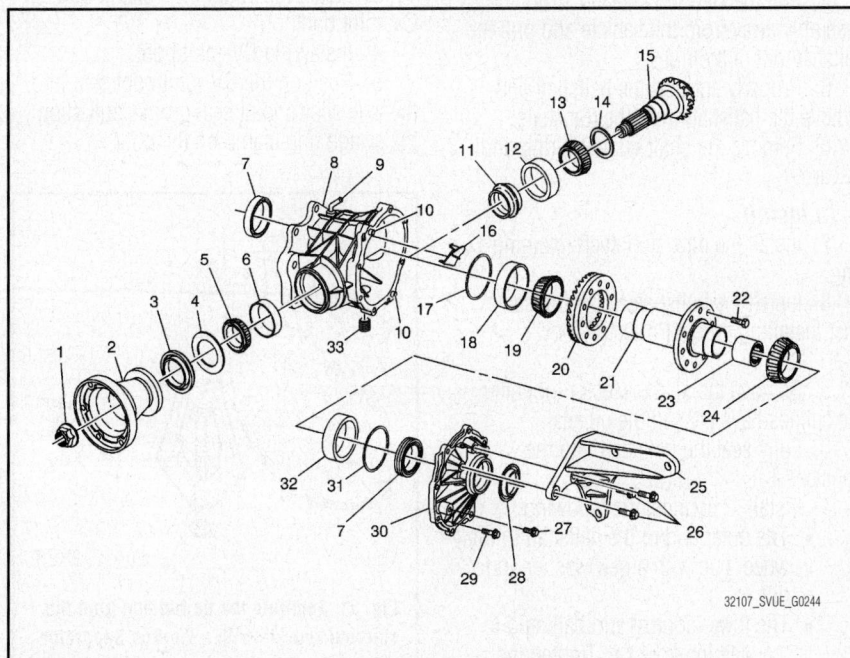

32107_SVUE_G0244

Fig. 28 Exploded view of NVG900 transfer case.

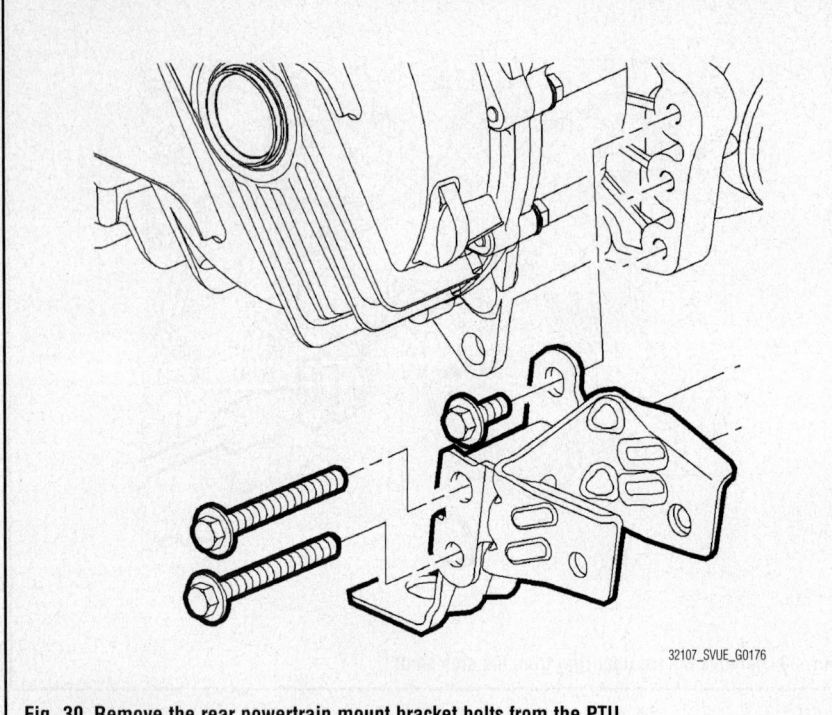

Fig. 30 Remove the rear powertrain mount bracket bolts from the PTU

25. Position the steering gear mounts to the cradle.

26. Install the PTU vent hose.

➡**Use sealant GM P/N 12345493 or equivalent on the fill plug.**

27. Check the PTU fluid fill. Remove the fluid fill plug. Fill until fluid is just below the bottom of the fill hole. Specification: Add 17 oz. (500 ml) PTU fluid.

28. Tighten the fill plug to 11 ft. lbs. (15 Nm).

29. Lower the vehicle.

30. Start the engine and observe the idle. Compare to pre-removal condition. If necessary, perform the powertrain balance procedure.

31. Check the transaxle oil level and fill as required.

FRONT HALFSHAFTS

REMOVAL & INSTALLATION

See Figures 31 through 33.

1. Before servicing the vehicle, refer to the Precautions Section.

2. Remove the wheel cover or the center cap for access to the halfshaft nut. Have an assistant depress the brake pedal and loosen the front halfshaft nut.

3. Remove or disconnect the following:
- The wheel
- The tie rod end torque prevailing nut and discard it
- The tie rod end from the steering knuckle, using a Tie Rod Separator Tool SA91100C
- The lower control arm to steering knuckle
- The stabilizer bar link nut

➡**Do not allow the steering knuckle to contact the ball stud seal. Contact may cause the seal to rip and the ball stud will need replacement.**

4. Pull the steering knuckle/strut assembly away from the vehicle and pull the halfshaft out of the hub.

5. Properly support the halfshaft and remove the halfshaft from the transaxle.

6. Remove the shaft retaining ring and discard it.

To install:

7. Install the new stub shaft retaining ring.

8. Install the halfshaft to the transaxle after installing a Seal Protector Tool SA91112T.

9. Remove the seal protector tool after the splines have passed the oil seal.

10. Fully seat the halfshaft into the transaxle.

11. Install or connect the following:
- The outer end of the halfshaft to the wheel hub with a new washer and nut
- The lower control arm ball stud to the steering knuckle. Tighten the fastener to 30 ft. lbs. (40 Nm)
- The stabilizer bar link nut to 48 ft. lbs. (65 Nm)
- The tie rod end to the steering knuckle using tool J44015. When seated properly, torque the fastener to 30 ft. lbs. (40 Nm)
- The wheel. Tighten the wheel lug nuts to 100 ft. lbs. (136 Nm)
- The Halfshaft to wheel nut. Torque the nut to 151 ft. lbs. (205 Nm)
- The cotter pin

12. Fill the transaxle to the proper level.

13. Check and adjust the front end alignment as necessary.

CV-JOINTS OVERHAUL

Constant Velocity (Outer) Joint

1. Before servicing the vehicle, refer to the Precautions Section.

2. Remove or disconnect the following:
- The front wheel
- The halfshaft
- The swage ring using a hand grinder
- The large CV-joint boot clamp
- The CV-joint boot by sliding it away from the tri-pod joint
- The tri-pod housing from the tri-pod spider
- The inboard spacer ring slide it rearward on the shaft
- The outboard retaining ring
- The tri-pod joint spider assembly
- The inboard spacer ring and CV-joint boot

To install:

3. Install the swage ring clamp on the CV-joint boot.

4. Install the CV-joint boot.

5. Position the CV-joint boot seal into the axle shaft's joint seal groove and align the swage ring clamp on the boot.

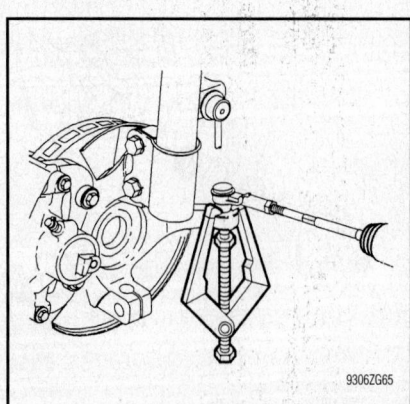

Fig. 31 Separate the tie rod end from the steering knuckle with a Tie Rod Separator tool

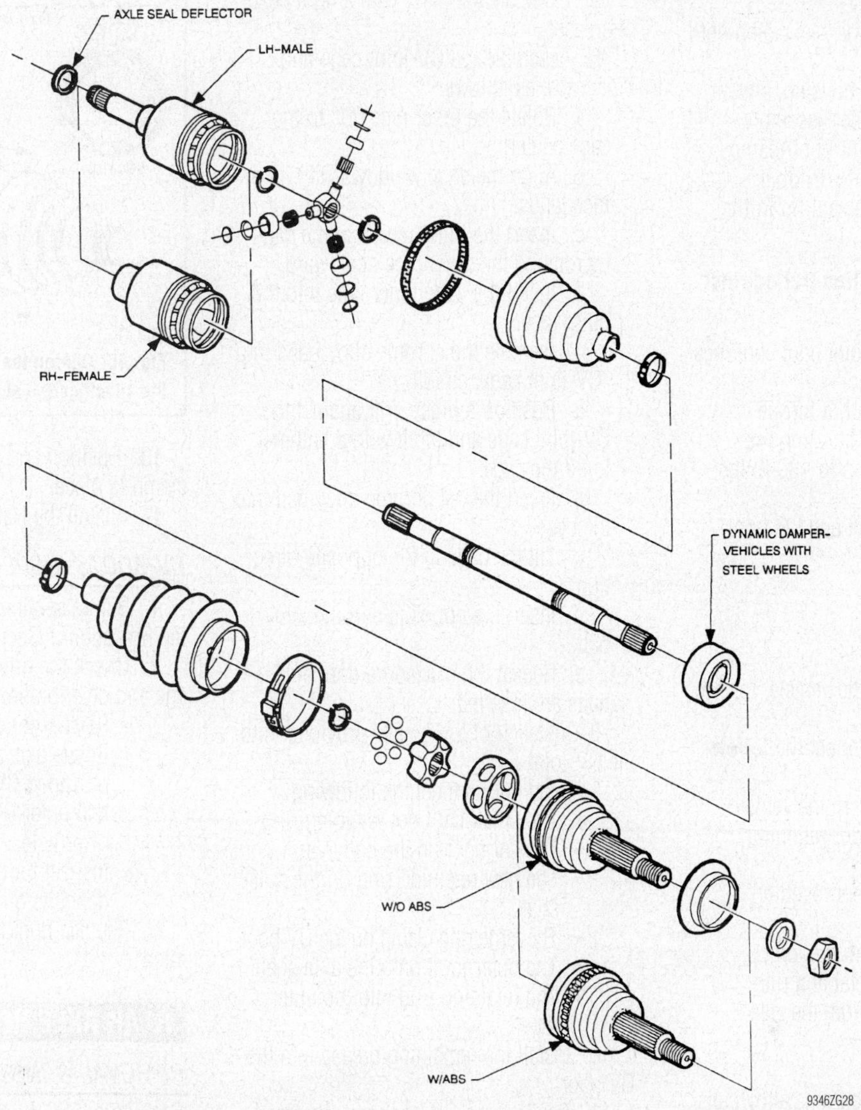

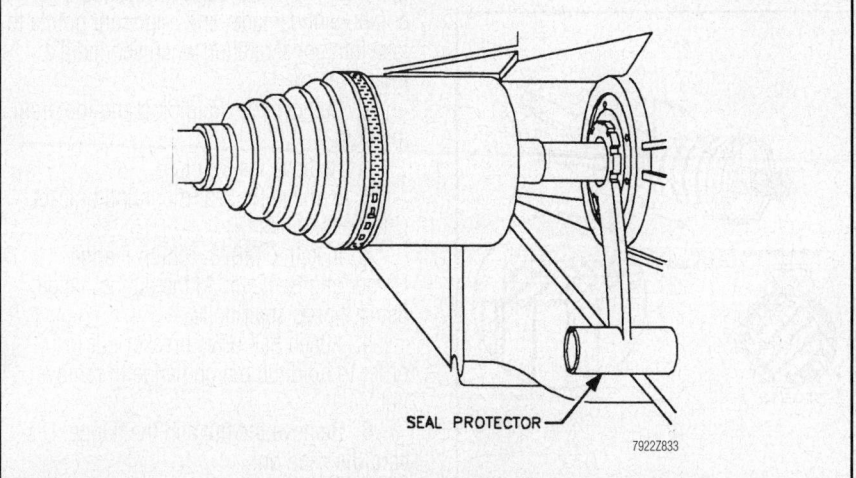

AXLE SEAL DEFLECTOR

LH-MALE

RH-FEMALE

DYNAMIC DAMPER-
VEHICLES WITH
STEEL WHEELS

W/O ABS

W/ABS

9346ZG28

Fig. 32 Exploded view of a typical axle shaft assembly

SEAL PROTECTOR

7922Z833

Fig. 33 Failure to use a seal protector may allow the halfshaft splines to damage the transaxle seal

✳✳ WARNING
Make sure that there are no pinch points on the inboard seal.

6. Crimp the swage ring.
7. Install or connect the following:
   - The inboard spacer ring, slide it rearward on the shaft
   - The tri-pod joint spider assembly onto the shaft
   - The outboard retaining ring into the axle shaft groove
   - The tri-pod joint spider assembly, slide it against the outboard retaining ring
   - The inboard spacer ring, seat it in the groove
8. Pack ½ of the grease kit into the boot.

9. Pack ½ of the grease kit into the tri-pod housing.

10. Install the new large seal clamp onto the CV-joint boot.

11. Install the tri-pod housing, slide it over the tri-pod joint spider assembly.

12. Install the CV-joint boot/clamp, slide it into place, over the trilobal tri-pod bushing with the seal lip in the groove.

→**Make sure the boot lies flat against the trilobal bushing.**

13. Position the CV-joint boot so it measures 4.9 in. (125mm).

14. Using a crimp tool, a torque wrench, and a breaker bar, crimp the large CV-joint boot clamp to 130 ft. lbs. (176 Nm).

15. Install the halfshaft and the front wheel.

Tri-Pot (Inner) Joint

See Figures 34 and 35.

1. Before servicing the vehicle, refer to the Precautions Section.

2. Remove or disconnect the following:

- The axle shaft from the vehicle
- The large CV boot retaining clamp
- The small CV boot retaining clamp
- The CV boot from the joint
- The axle shaft retaining ring
- The outer joint from the axle shaft
- The CV boot

3. Disassemble the chrome alloy balls from the CV-joint cage as follows:

a. Position a brass drift against the CV-joint cage and tap it with a hammer to tilt the cage.

b. Remove the 1st chrome alloy ball from the cage.

c. Tilt the cage in the opposite direction.

d. Remove the opposite chrome alloy ball.

e. Repeat the procedure until all 6 balls are removed.

4. Disassemble the CV-joint cage and inner race as follows:

a. Pivot the cage and race 90° to the center line of the outer race.

b. Align the cage windows with outer race lands.

c. Remove the cage from the outer race.

d. Rotate the inner race upward and remove it from the cage.

To install:

5. Lubricate the parts with a light coat of grease.

6. Assemble the CV-joint cage and inner race, as follows:

a. Rotate the inner race 90° to the cage centerline.

b. Align the cage windows with inner race lands.

c. Insert the inner race into the cage by rotating the inner race downward.

d. Insert the cage/inner race into the outer race.

7. Assemble the chrome alloy balls into the CV-joint cage, as follows:

a. Position a brass drift against the CV-joint cage and tap it with a hammer to tilt the cage.

b. Insert the 1st chrome alloy ball into the cage.

c. Tilt the cage in the opposite direction.

d. Insert the opposite chrome alloy ball.

e. Repeat the procedure until all 6 balls are inserted.

8. Install ½ of the grease provided, into the CV-joint.

9. Install or connect the following:

- The small CV boot retaining ring
- The CV boot on the halfshaft
- The new retaining ring on the halfshaft
- The large ring clamp on the CV boot
- The outer joint onto the axle shaft
- The retaining ring into the outer race

10. Install the remaining grease into the CV boot.

11. Position the CV boot and the small boot clamp.

12. Crimp the small boot clamp.

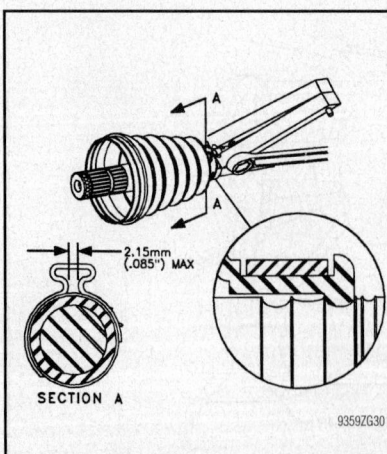

Fig. 34 Tighten the small boot clamp to the specification shown

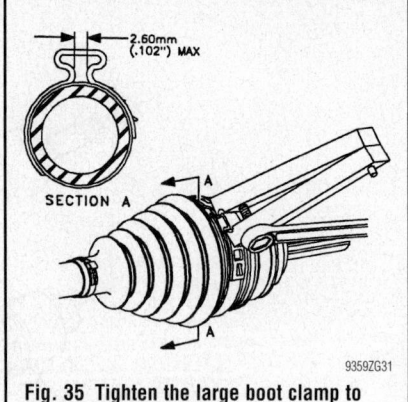

Fig. 35 Tighten the large boot clamp to the specification shown

13. Position and crimp the large boot clamp in place.

14. Install the Halfshaft in the vehicle.

CV-BOOTS INSPECTION

1. Before servicing the vehicle, refer to the Precautions Section.

2. Check the driveshaft boots for damage and deterioration.

- Raise front of vehicle
- Rotate axle and inspect for cracked or ripped CV boot material on inner and outer CV joints on both sides of vehicle
- Inspect for excessive grease deposits on or around the CV boot

3. Replace boot if damaged or deteriorated.

REAR AXLE HOUSING

REMOVAL & INSTALLATION

See Figures 36 through 52.

Before servicing any vehicle, please be sure to read the precautions section, which deals with personal safety, prevention of component damage, and important points to take into consideration when servicing a motor vehicle.

1. Remove the drain plug and the drain the fluid.

2. Remove the fill plug.

3. Remove the rear mounting bracket (2) and the bolts (3).

4. Install J 44873, Pinion Flange Holder and Remover, to the pinion flange using 2 prop shaft bolts.

5. Attach half drive breaker bar in order to hold the pinion flange to remove nut.

6. Remove the nut and the flange. Discard the used nut.

7. Remove the dust deflector from the flange, if required.

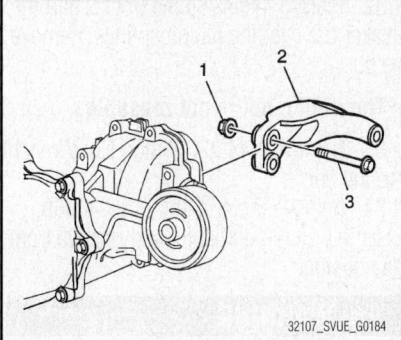

Fig. 36 Remove the rear mounting bracket (2) and the bolts (3)

8. Remove the input flange oil seal from the clutch cover.

9. Remove the bolts and the clutch cover from the differential housing.

10. Remove the filter assembly.

11. Remove the dowel pins.

✳✳ WARNING

Do not submerge the clutch drum in solvent. This will damage the friction material and gerotor pump.

➡The clutch drum is not serviceable. If inoperative conditions are found, replace the unit.

12. Remove the clutch drum from the clutch cover.

13. Remove the snapring (1) from the clutch cover.

14. Remove the bearing. Only remove the bearing if it is going to be replaced. It must be pressed out by the inner race.

15. Remove the clutch drum rear oil seal from the housing.

16. Attach the assembly holding fixture J 44869 to the housing, using 4 clutch cover bolts.

17. Install the housing (1) and the fixture into J 43964, Engine Stand Fixture Adapter (2) adapter.

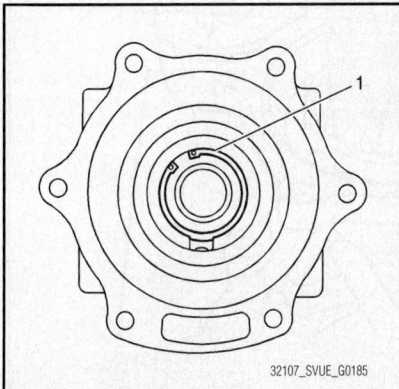

Fig. 37 Remove the snapring (1)

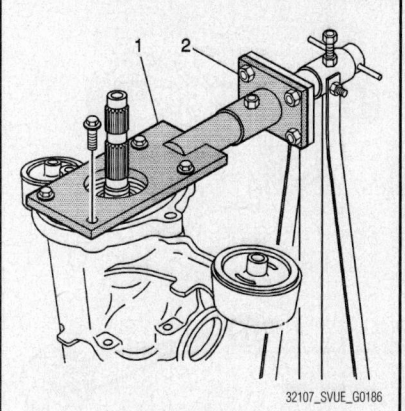

Fig. 38 Install the housing (1) and the fixture into J 43964, Engine Stand Fixture Adapter (2) adapter

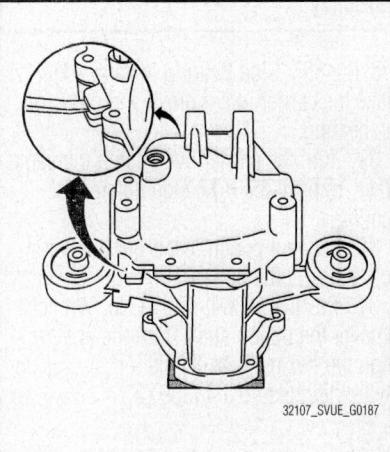

Fig. 39 Remove the rear cover by prying it off at the pry point locations

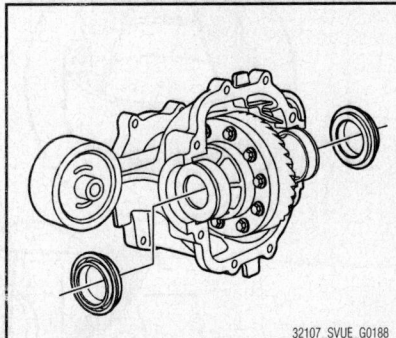

Fig. 40 Remove the right and the left axle shaft oil seals.

18. Remove the rear cover bolts: 4 M8 and 4 M10.

✳✳ WARNING

Use the pry point only. Do not pry on the sealing surface.

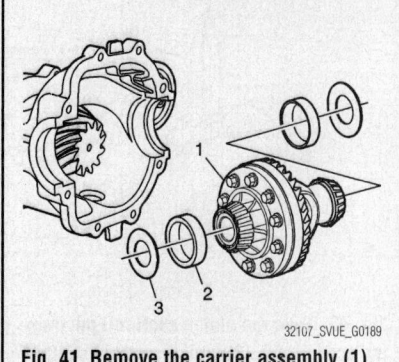

Fig. 41 Remove the carrier assembly (1), bearing races (2), and shims (3)

➡The rear differential carrier may come out with the cover.

19. Remove the rear cover by prying it off at the pry point locations.

20. Remove the right and the left axle shaft oil seals.

21. Remove the differential carrier. Place a screw driver in the axle differential bore and pry up.

22. Mark or tag the bearing races and the shims for assembly.

23. Remove the carrier assembly (1), bearing races (2), and shims (3).

➡The ring gear bolts are not to be reused. Use new bolts during assembly.

24. Remove the bolts and the ring gear from the carrier.

25. Identify the lock pin location (1) within the differential case.

26. Drive the pinion shaft roll pin from the access hole (3) until the pinion shaft (2) can be removed from the differential case (1).

27. Remove the washers (1), pinion gears (2) and side gears (3) from the differential case.

28. Using J 44854, Side Bearing Remover (3), J 22912-01 Bearing Puller (2),

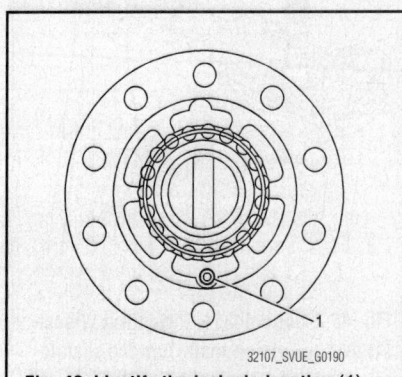

Fig. 42 Identify the lock pin location (1) within the differential case

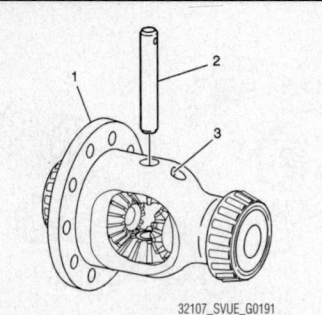

Fig. 43 Drive the pinion shaft roll pin from the access hole (3) until the pinion shaft (2) can be removed from the differential case (1)

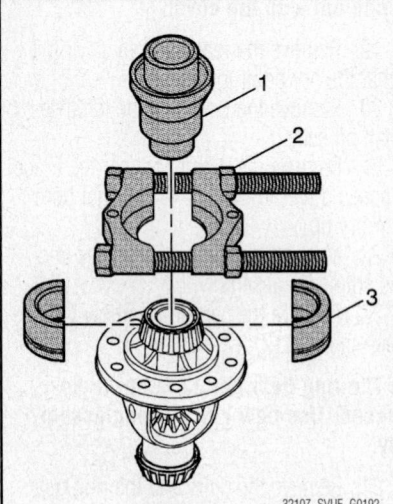

Fig. 44 Using J 44854, Side Bearing Remover (3), J 22912-01 Bearing Puller (2), and J 44855, Side Bearing Installer (1), place the carrier into a press and press off the bearing

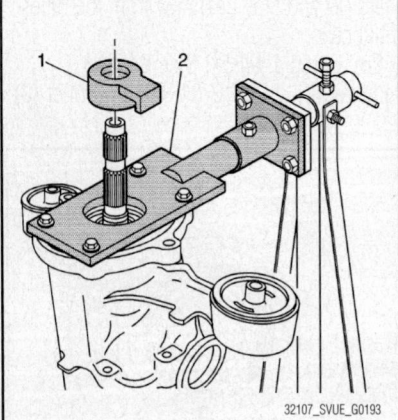

Fig. 45 Place J 44864, Pinion Nut Wrench (1) over the pinion shaft. Turn the shaft to align the hex nut with the flat on the assembly holding fixture J 44869 (2)

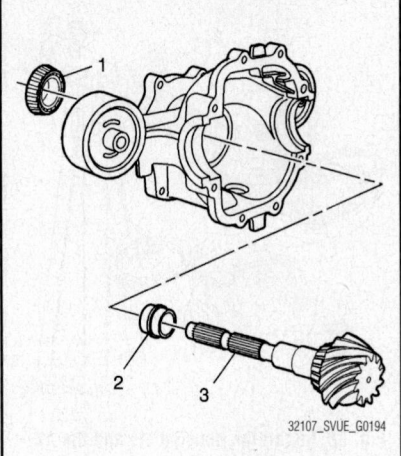

Fig. 46 Remove the front bearing (1), the collapsible spacer (2) and the pinion shaft (3).

and J 44855, Side Bearing Installer (1), place the carrier into a press and press off the bearing.

29. Turn the carrier over, using the same press, remove the right side differential bearing.

30. Using a punch, bend out the flat on both sides of the pinion nut.

31. Place J 44864, Pinion Nut Wrench (1) over the pinion shaft. Turn the shaft to align the hex nut with the flat on the assembly holding fixture J 44869 (2).

32. Place J 44865 Spline Socket and the breaker bar over the pinion splines. Remove the nut.

➡ **The pinion nut is not reusable.**

33. Remove J 44864, Pinion Nut Wrench and the nut.

34. Remove the 4 bolts from J 44869, Assembly Holding Fixture, and remove from the housing.

✳✳ WARNING

Inspect the press bar surface. Do not press the housing against a rough surface. Sealing surfaces could be damaged.

35. Position the differential housing into a press in order to remove the pinion shaft.

➡ **The collapsible spacer is not reusable.**

36. Remove the front bearing (1), the collapsible spacer (2) and the pinion shaft (3).

✳✳ WARNING

If dowel pins are still in the housing, remove them before pressing. Pressing on dowels will damage the housing.

➡ **The bolt is left-hand threaded on J 3940, Bearing Race Remover.**

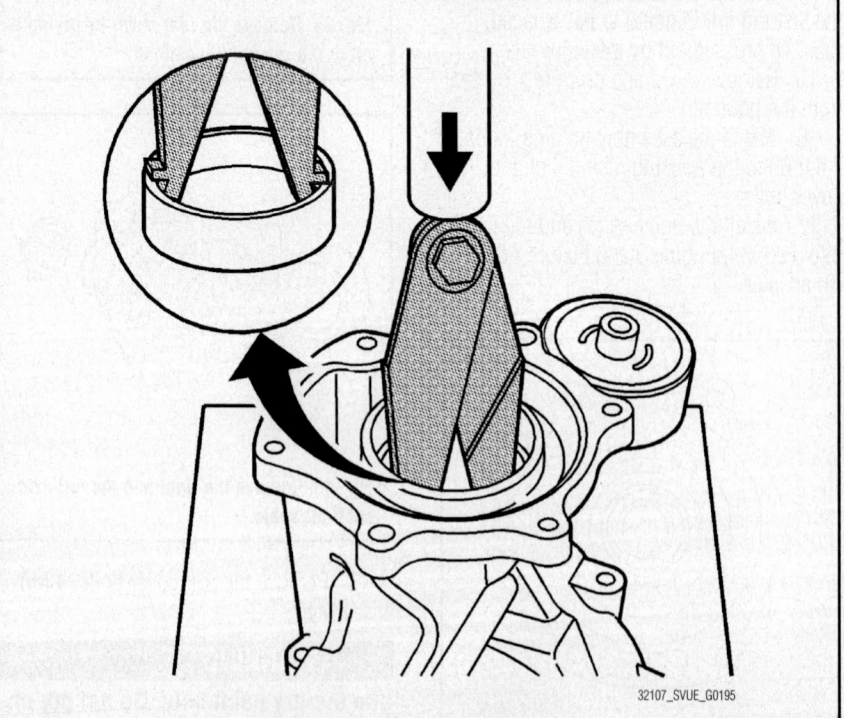

Fig. 47 Place J 3940, Bearing Race Remover, behind the front bearing race in the grooves

37. Place J 3940, Bearing Race Remover, behind the front bearing race in the grooves. Spread the arms and tighten the lock bolt.

38. Place the housing in a press and remove the race.

➡**The bolt is left-hand threaded on J 3940, Bearing Race Remover.**

39. Place J 3940, Bearing Race Remover, behind the rear pinion bearing race in the grooves. Spread the arms and tighten the lock bolt.

40. Place the housing in a press and remove the race.

41. Using J 44858 Pinion Bearing Remover (2), and J 22912-01 Bearing Puller (1), place the V of the split plate in the groove of J 44858 Pinion Bearing Remover (2). Tighten the nuts.

➡**The pinion shim is located under the bearing. Measure and mark or tag when removed.**

42. Place the pinion shaft and the tools in a press; then remove the bearing and the shim.

To install:

✳✳ WARNING

Do not use excessive amounts of sealer. Excess sealer could plug the vent passage, the oil pump, and/or the oil pump screen causing internal damage.

➡**Ensure sealing surface is still clean and oil free.**

43. Apply sealer Saturn P/N 21019581 to the rear housing sealing surface (1). Do not apply sealer to vent walls (2). Apply a constant bead of sealer 0.098 in. (2.5mm) wide and thick.

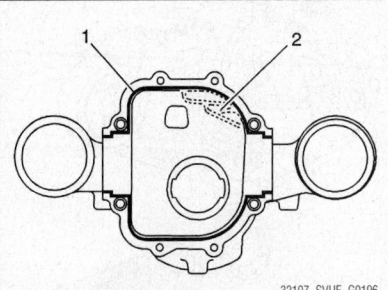

Fig. 48 Apply sealer Saturn P/N 21019581 to the rear housing sealing surface (1). Do not apply sealer to vent walls (2). Apply a constant bead of sealer 0.098 in. (2.5mm) wide and thick

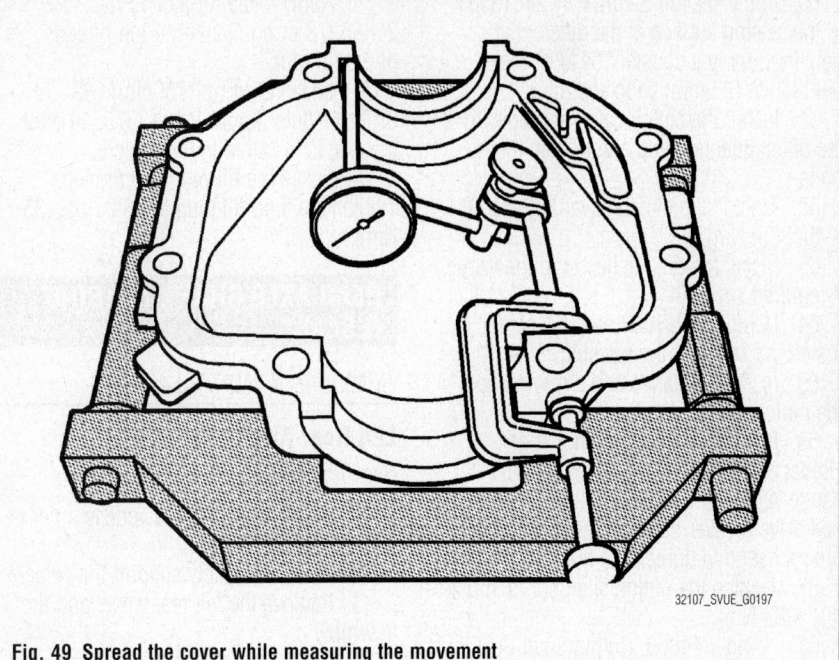

Fig. 49 Spread the cover while measuring the movement

44. Install the dial indicator on the cover at the top of the bearing bore. Preload the indicator and zero it out.

45. Install J 44868, Housing Spreader, on the cover.

46. Spread the cover while measuring the movement. Do not spread the cover more than 0.012–0.016 in. (0.30–0.40mm).

47. After the spread is reached, remove the dial indicator.

48. Install the cover.

49. Install the 4 (M8) cover bolts and tighten in a criss-cross pattern. Tighten the cover bolts (M8) to 18 ft. lbs. (24 Nm).

50. Remove the housing spreader J 44868 .

51. Install 4 (M10) cover bolts and tighten in a criss-cross pattern. Tighten the cover bolts (M10) to 38 ft. lbs. (52 Nm).

52. Using J 44853, Rear Clutch Drum Seal Installer, install the clutch drum rear oil seal to the differential housing.

53. Install the bearing and the snapring to the clutch cover. If removed, the bearing will have to be pressed in. Press the bearing from the outer race. Use SA9114T, Converter Bearing Installer, from SA1991T2 automatic transaxle tool kit or equivalent.

54. Using J 44852 install the front clutch drum oil seal.

55. Install the filter assembly.

56. Install the dowel pins.

57. Align the clutch with the pump and the pump bushing. Place J 46607, Alignment Tool, in the splines of the clutch. Twist J 46607 back and forth to align the pump and the bushing. With a properly aligned

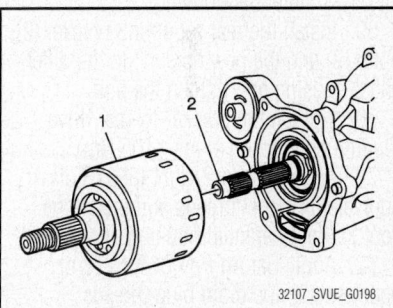

Fig. 50 Install the clutch drum (1) on the pinion shaft (2) carefully.

clutch, the groove on J 46607 will be flush with the drum. Remove J 46607 by pulling straight out.

58. Install the clutch drum (1) on the pinion shaft (2) carefully.

59. A properly installed clutch drum will be fully engaged into the seal.

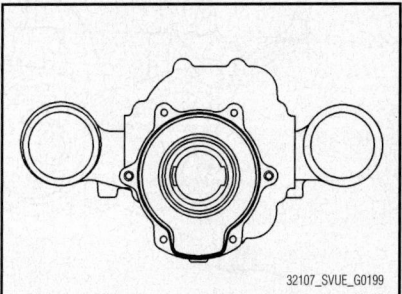

Fig. 51 Apply sealant Saturn P/N 21019581 to the sealing surface of the differential housing

60. Apply sealant Saturn P/N 21019581 to the sealing surface of the differential housing. Apply a constant bead of sealer 0.098 inch (2.5mm) wide and thick.

61. Install the clutch cover and bolts to the differential housing and tighten the bolts.

62. Tighten the clutch cover bolts to 18 ft. lbs. (24 Nm).

63. Install the dust deflector to the flange if required.

64. Using J 44851, Pinion Seal Installer, install the seal into the housing.

65. Install the flange and a new nut to the pinion shaft.

66. Install J 44873, Pinion Flange Holder and Remover (1), to the pinion flange (2) using 2 shoulder bolts. Attach half drive breaker bar in order to hold the pinion flange to tighten the nut.

67. Tighten the pinion shaft nut to 150 ft. lbs. (203 Nm).

68. Using J 44809, Output Shaft Seal Installer, install the right axle shaft oil seal into the differential housing.

69. Install the rear mounting bracket (2), bolts (3) and the new nuts (1) to the differential housing and tighten the bolt.

70. Tighten the bracket-to-rear drive module bolts to 77 ft. lbs. (105 Nm).

71. Apply Saturn P/N 21485278 or equivalent on the threads and install the vent to the differential housing, if removed.

72. Apply Saturn P/N 21485278 or equivalent to the drain plug threads.

73. Install the drain plug to the differential housing and tighten. Tighten the drain plug to 22 ft. lbs. (30 Nm).

74. Apply sealant Saturn P/N 21485278 or equivalent to the threads of the fill plug.

75. Install 25.4 oz. (750mm) GM VERSATRAK®fluid Saturn P/N 12378514 after the axle is installed in the vehicle.

76. Install the fill plug and tighten. Tighten the fluid fill plug to 26 ft. lbs. (35 Nm).

REAR AXLE SHAFT, BEARING & SEAL

REMOVAL & INSTALLATION

Left Rear Axle

See Figure 53.

1. Before servicing the vehicle, refer to the Precautions Section.
2. Raise and safely support the vehicle.
3. Remove the left rear wheel and tire assembly.
4. Remove the left rear wheel half shaft.
5. Carefully pry out the output shaft seal and discard.

To install:

6. Install the new output shaft seal using the J 44809, Output Shaft Seal Installer.
7. Install the left rear wheel drive shaft.
8. Inspect the rear drive module fluid level.
9. Install the left rear wheel and tire assembly.
10. Lower the vehicle.

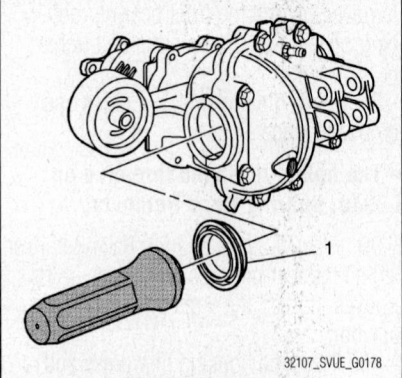

Fig. 53 Carefully pry out the output shaft seal. Use the special tool to install the output shaft seal (1)—left rear axle.

Right Rear Axle

See Figure 54.

1. Before servicing the vehicle, refer to the Precautions Section.
2. Raise and safely support the vehicle.
3. Remove the right rear wheel and tire assembly.
4. Remove the right rear wheel drive shaft.
5. Carefully pry out the output shaft seal and discard.

To install:

6. Install the new output shaft seal using the J 44809, Output Shaft Seal Installer.
7. Install the right rear wheel drive shaft.
8. Inspect the rear drive module fluid level.
9. Install the right rear wheel and tire assembly.
10. Lower the vehicle.

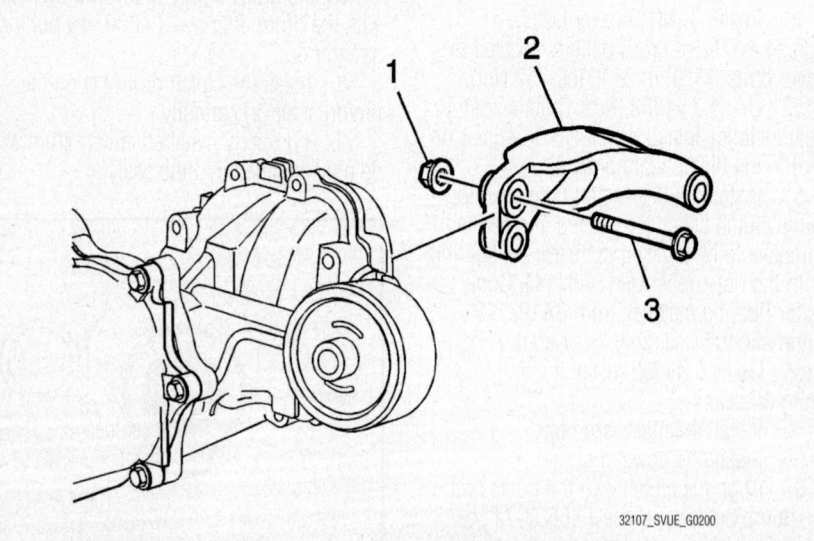

Fig. 52 Install the rear mounting bracket (2), bolts (3) and the new nuts (1) to the differential housing

Fig. 54 Carefully pry out the output shaft seal. Remove the output shaft seal (1) using the special tool—right rear axle.

REAR HALFSHAFT

REMOVAL & INSTALLATION

Tools Required:
- J 45341 Rear Wheel Drive Shaft Removal Tool
- J 44394 Seal Protector
- J-2619-A Slide Hammer w/Adapter
- J 45059 Angle Meter

1. Before servicing the vehicle, refer to the Precautions Section.

2. Raise and support the vehicle.

3. Remove the tire and wheel assembly.

4. Remove and discard the wheel drive shaft spindle nut.

5. While holding the stabilizer link with a wrench, remove the stabilizer link-to-lower control arm nut.

6. Disconnect the link from the control arm.

7. Place a stand under the lower control arm and support the control arm.

8. Remove the lower shock absorber mounting bolt and nut.

9. Remove the toe link nut, bolt, and washer.

10. Loosen, but do not remove, the lower suspension jounce bumper nut.

11. Remove the lower control arm-to-suspension knuckle bolt and nut.

✳✳ CAUTION

Relieve spring tension slowly in order to avoid sudden release of the coil spring.

12. Slowly lower support stand until coil spring tension is relieved and remove coil spring.

13. Loosen, but do not remove, the upper control arm-to-suspension knuckle nut.

✳✳ WARNING

Support the wheel drive shaft while it is disengaged from the wheel hub and bearing assembly in order to avoid damaging the wheel drive shaft seals.

14. Place a block of wood against the wheel drive shaft spindle and tap with a hammer to release the spindle from the wheel hub and bearing assembly.

15. Rotate the suspension knuckle upward and secure with heavy mechanics wire, or equivalent.

16. Assemble the J 45341 and the J-2619-A to the wheel drive shaft inner tripot joint.

17. Disengage the tripot joint from the Rear Drive Module (RDM).

18. Remove the rear wheel drive half-shaft from the vehicle.

19. Remove and discard the wheel drive shaft retaining ring.

To install:

20. Install a new wheel drive shaft retaining ring to the inner tripot joint.

21. Install the J 44394 to the wheel drive shaft oil seal.

22. Align the splines of the inner tripot joint to the output shaft of the RDM.

23. Install the wheel drive shaft to the output shaft:

a. Guide the wheel drive shaft tripot joint squarely onto the output shaft.

b. After the splined end of the wheel drive shaft passes the oil seal, remove the J 44394 from the oil seal.

c. Firmly engage the wheel drive shaft to the output shaft.

d. Ensure that the tripot joint is fully seated on the output shaft by grasping the tripot joint and attempting to pull free of the output shaft.

e. Ensure that the tripot slinger does not become damaged.

24. Rotate the suspension knuckle downward while simultaneously guiding the Constant Velocity (CV) joint spindle to the wheel hub and bearing assembly of the suspension knuckle.

25. Hand install a new wheel drive shaft spindle nut.

26. Position the insulators to the coil spring and align the ends of the coil spring with the abutments of the insulators.

27. Secure each of the insulators to the coil spring using 2 plastic tie straps positioned 180° apart and through the relieves molded into the insulators.

28. Cut off any excess length of the tie straps.

29. Position the coil spring assembly to the lower control arm.

30. Position a support stand under the lower control arm.

31. Carefully raise the lower control arm while simultaneously guiding the coil spring assembly into the rear suspension cradle.

32. Position the suspension knuckle to the lower control arm.

➡**Ensure that the hex head of the suspension knuckle bolt faces the rear of the vehicle.**

33. Install the lower control arm-to-suspension knuckle bolt and nut. Tighten the bolt and nut to 118 ft. lbs. (160 Nm). Tighten the upper control arm-to-suspension knuckle bolt and nut. Tighten the bolt and nut to 100 ft. lbs. (135 Nm).

34. Install the lower shock absorber mounting bolt and nut. Tighten the bolt and nut to 77 ft. lbs. (105 Nm).

35. Slowly lower and remove the support stand.

36. Tighten the lower jounce bumper nut. Tighten the nut to 47 ft. lbs. (63 Nm).

37. Position the rear toe link to the suspension knuckle.

38. Install the washer, bolt, and nut to the suspension knuckle and the toe link assembly. Tighten the bolt and nut to 81 ft. lbs. (110 Nm).

39. Position the stabilizer bar link to the lower control arm.

40. Install the nut to the stabilizer bar link.

41. While holding the stabilizer bar link stationary with a wrench, tighten the nut. Tighten the nut to 11 ft. lbs. (15 Nm).

42. Tighten the wheel drive shaft spindle nut. Using the J 45059, tighten the nut to 63 ft. lbs. (86 Nm) plus 36°.

43. Install the tire and wheel assembly. Tighten the wheel lug nuts to 100 ft. lbs. (136 Nm).

44. Lower the vehicle.

CV-JOINTS OVERHAUL

Constant Velocity (Outer) Joint

1. Before servicing the vehicle, refer to the Precautions Section.

2. Remove or disconnect the following:
- The wheel
- The halfshaft
- The swage ring using a hand grinder
- The large CV-joint boot clamp
- The CV-joint boot by sliding it away from the tri-pod joint
- The tri-pod housing from the tri-pod spider
- The inboard spacer ring slide it rearward on the shaft
- The outboard retaining ring
- The tri-pod joint spider assembly
- The inboard spacer ring and CV-joint boot

To install:

3. Install the swage ring clamp on the CV-joint boot.

4. Install the CV-joint boot.

5. Position the CV-joint boot seal into the axle shaft's joint seal groove and align the swage ring clamp on the boot.

✳✳ WARNING

Make sure that there are no pinch points on the inboard seal.

6. Crimp the swage ring.

7. Install or connect the following:
- The inboard spacer ring, slide it rearward on the shaft
- The tri-pod joint spider assembly onto the shaft
- The outboard retaining ring into the axle shaft groove
- The tri-pod joint spider assembly, slide it against the outboard retaining ring
- The inboard spacer ring, seat it in the groove

8. Pack ½ of the grease kit into the boot.

9. Pack ½ of the grease kit into the tri-pod housing.

10. Install the new large seal clamp onto the CV-joint boot.

11. Install the tri-pod housing, slide it over the tri-pod joint spider assembly.

12. Install the CV-joint boot/clamp, slide it into place, over the trilobal tri-pod bushing with the seal lip in the groove.

➡**Make sure the boot lies flat against the trilobal bushing.**

13. Position the CV-joint boot so it measures 4.9 in. (125mm).

14. Using a crimp tool, a torque wrench, and a breaker bar, crimp the large CV-joint boot clamp to 130 ft. lbs. (176 Nm).

15. Install the halfshaft and the wheel.

Tri-Pot (Inner) Joint

See Figures 55 and 56.

1. Before servicing the vehicle, refer to the Precautions Section.

2. Remove or disconnect the following:
- The axle shaft from the vehicle
- The large CV boot retaining clamp
- The small CV boot retaining clamp
- The CV boot from the joint
- The axle shaft retaining ring

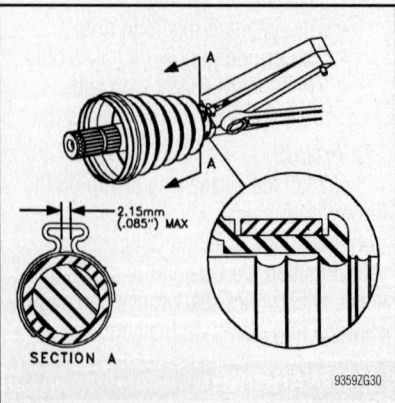

Fig. 55 Tighten the small boot clamp to the specification shown

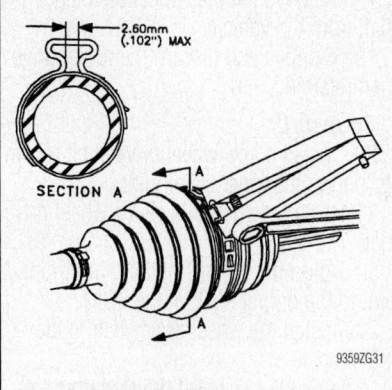

Fig. 56 Tighten the large boot clamp to the specification shown

- The outer joint from the axle shaft
- The CV boot

3. Disassemble the chrome alloy balls from the CV-joint cage as follows:

a. Position a brass drift against the CV-joint cage and tap it with a hammer to tilt the cage.

b. Remove the 1st chrome alloy ball from the cage.

c. Tilt the cage in the opposite direction.

d. Remove the opposite chrome alloy ball.

e. Repeat the procedure until all 6 balls are removed.

4. Disassemble the CV-joint cage and inner race as follows:

a. Pivot the cage and race 90° to the center line of the outer race.

b. Align the cage windows with outer race lands.

c. Remove the cage from the outer race.

d. Rotate the inner race upward and remove it from the cage.

To install:

5. Lubricate the parts with a light coat of grease.

6. Assemble the CV-joint cage and inner race, as follows:

a. Rotate the inner race 90° to the cage centerline.

b. Align the cage windows with inner race lands.

c. Insert the inner race into the cage by rotating the inner race downward.

d. Insert the cage/inner race into the outer race.

7. Assemble the chrome alloy balls into the CV-joint cage, as follows:

a. Position a brass drift against the CV-joint cage and tap it with a hammer to tilt the cage.

b. Insert the 1st chrome alloy ball into the cage.

c. Tilt the cage in the opposite direction.

d. Insert the opposite chrome alloy ball.

e. Repeat the procedure until all 6 balls are inserted.

8. Install ½ of the grease provided, into the CV-joint.

9. Install or connect the following:
- The small CV boot retaining ring
- The CV boot on the halfshaft
- The new retaining ring on the halfshaft
- The large ring clamp on the CV boot
- The outer joint onto the axle shaft
- The retaining ring into the outer race

10. Install the remaining grease into the CV boot.

11. Position the CV boot and the small boot clamp.

12. Crimp the small boot clamp.

13. Position and crimp the large boot clamp in place.

14. Install the Halfshaft in the vehicle.

REAR PINION SEAL

REMOVAL & INSTALLATION

See Figures 57 through 60.

Before servicing any vehicle, please be sure to read the precautions section, which deals with personal safety, prevention of component damage, and important points to take into consideration when servicing a motor vehicle.

1. Raise and safely support the vehicle.

2. Remove the propeller shaft underbody guard loop bolts.

3. Remove the guard loop.

4. Reference mark the propeller shaft flange-to-input flange relationship at the Rear Drive Module (RDM).

5. Remove the propeller shaft flange mounting bolts at the RDM input flange.

6. Position the end of the propeller shaft away from the RDM and secure with heavy mechanics wire, or equivalent.

7. Remove the propeller shaft shield mounting bolts (1) and the propeller shaft shield (2).

8. Place a container under the RDM housing.

9. Remove the RDM drain plug.

10. Drain the RDM fluid.

11. Install the J 44873, Pinion Flange Holder and Remover, (1) to the pinion flange (2).

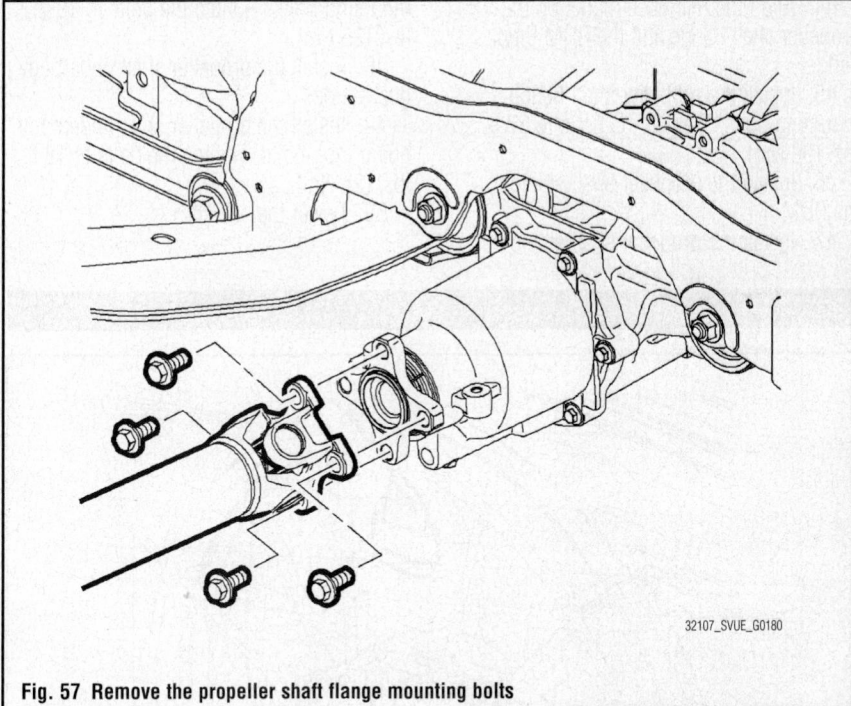

Fig. 57 Remove the propeller shaft flange mounting bolts

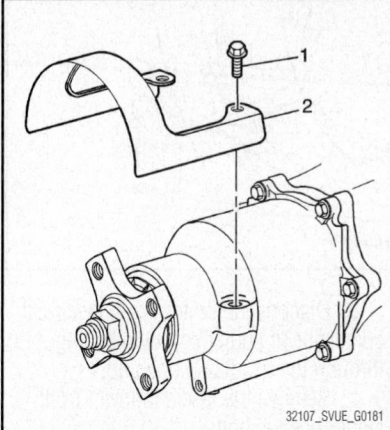

Fig. 58 Remove the propeller shaft shield mounting bolts (1) and the propeller shaft shield (2)

12. Use a breaker bar to hold the J 44873, Pinion Flange Holder and Remover, stationary and loosen the pinion flange nut.

13. Remove and discard the input flange nut.

14. Remove the input flange.

15. Remove the RDM housing cover bolts.

16. Carefully remove the housing cover from the RDM.

✳✳ WARNING

Do not gouge the housing cover and RDM sealing surfaces.

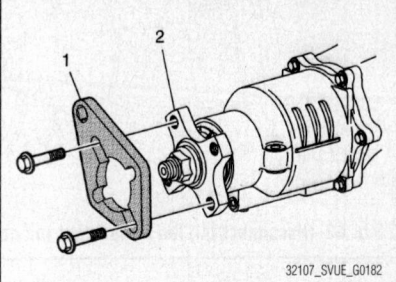

Fig. 59 Install the J 44873, Pinion Flange Holder and Remover, (1) to the pinion flange (2).

17. Remove all traces of sealer from the housing cover and RDM sealing surfaces.

18. Clean the housing cover and RDM sealing surfaces with denatured alcohol or equivalent, and dry with a clean, lint free cloth.

19. Remove the clutch drum from the housing cover.

20. Remove the input flange oil seal from the housing cover.

21. Remove and discard the filter assembly.

22. Install a new filter assembly.

23. Install the locating pins, if removed.

24. Install the clutch drum to the pinion shaft by shaking the drum while rotating the drum back and forth to engage the splines of the pump rotor and bushing.

25. When properly engaged, the clutch drum will be fully seated against the clutch drum oil seal.

26. Apply a continuous bead of sealer Saturn P/N 12346240 of equal height and width to the RDM housing sealing surface. Apply sealer to a height and width of 0.098 inch (2.5mm).

➡ **Do not disturb the sealer bead applied to the RDM sealing surface.**

27. Install the clutch housing cover to the RDM.

28. Hand install the clutch housing cover bolts.

29. Install the housing cover mounting bolts. Tighten the bolts to 19 ft. lbs. (26 Nm).

➡ **Strict adherence to the sealer cure time must be observed.**

30. Allow the sealer to cure a minimum of 8 hours.

31. Using the J 44851 Pinion Seal Installer (1) install the input shaft seal (2) to the housing cover (3).

32. Install the dust deflector to the input flange if removed.

33. Install the input flange to the clutch shaft.

34. Hand install a new input flange nut to the clutch shaft.

35. Install the J 44873, Pinion Flange Holder and Remover, to the pinion flange.

36. Using a breaker bar to hold the J 44873, Pinion Flange Holder and Remover stationary, tighten the pinion nut. Tighten the nut to 150 ft. lbs. (203 Nm).

37. Thoroughly clean the drain plug threads and apply thread sealer Saturn P/N 21485278 to the plug threads.

38. Install the RDM drain plug. Tighten the plug to 22 ft. lbs. (30 Nm).

39. Remove the RDM fill plug.

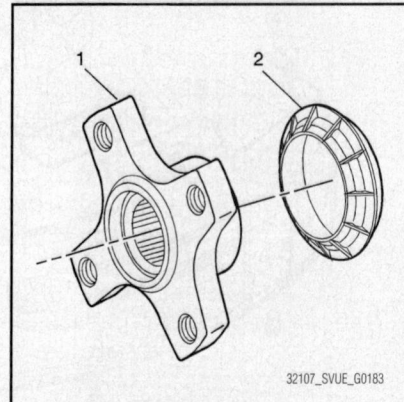

Fig. 60 Using the J 44851 Pinion Seal Installer (1) install the input shaft seal (2) to the housing cover (3)

40. Thoroughly clean the fill plug threads and apply thread sealer Saturn P/N 21485278 to the plug threads.

41. Fill the RDM with lubricant.

42. Install the fill plug. Tighten the plug to 26 ft. lbs. (35 Nm).

43. Thoroughly clean and apply a thread-locker, Saturn P/N 21005994, to the propeller shaft flange mounting bolt threads.

44. Align the reference marks on the propeller shaft flange and the RDM input flange.

45. Install the propeller shaft flange mounting bolts. Tighten the bolts to 37 ft. lbs. (50 Nm).

46. Install the propeller shaft shield to the RDM.

47. Install the propeller shaft shield

mounting bolts. Tighten the bolts to 18 ft. lbs. (25 Nm).

48. Install the propeller shaft underbody guard loop.

49. Install the propeller shaft underbody guard loop bolts. Tighten the bolts to 18 ft. lbs. (24 Nm).

50. Lower the vehicle.

ENGINE COOLING

ENGINE FAN

REMOVAL & INSTALLATION

2.2L Engine

See Figures 61 through 65.

Before servicing any vehicle, please be sure to read the precautions section, which deals with personal safety, prevention of component damage, and important points to take into consideration when servicing a motor vehicle.

1. Disconnect the negative battery cable.

2. Remove the front fascia:

    a. Remove the front side marker lamps.

    b. Remove the headlamps.

    c. Remove the front air deflector.

    d. Remove the front wheelhouse push-pins and move the wheelhouse liner rearward.

Fig. 62 Disconnect the fan motor from the engine harness.

    e. Disconnect the fog lamp electrical connector (if equipped), by reaching through the headlamp opening.

    f. Remove the fascia to lower front fender bracket bolts.

    g. Remove the fascia to body push-in retainers.

    h. Separate the fascia from the front fenders.

    i. Remove the fascia to fascia support push-in retainers.

    j. Remove the fascia from the vehicle.

3. Drain the coolant.

4. Disconnect the fan motor from the engine harness.

5. Unclip the wire harness from the fan assembly.

6. Unclip the transaxle cooler lines from the fan assembly.

7. Remove the battery box inlet air duct.

8. Remove the condenser splash shield.

9. Remove the radiator inlet hose.

10. Remove the radiator outlet hose.

11. Remove the upper Condenser Radiator Fan Module (CRFM) bracket assemblies.

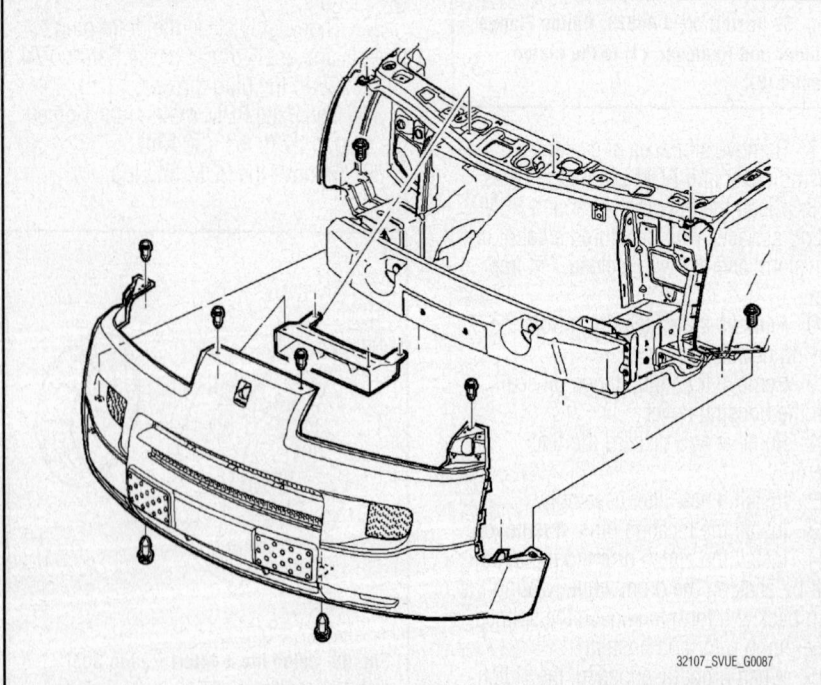

Fig. 61 Separate the fascia from the front fenders.

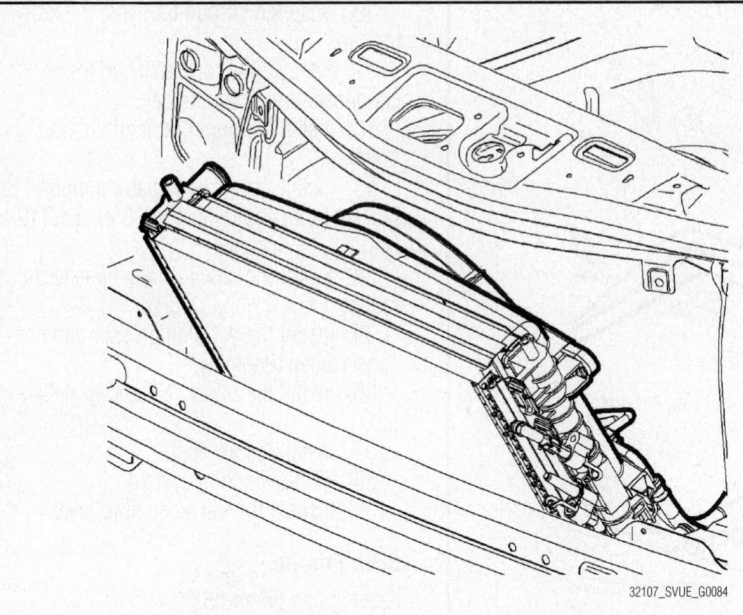

Fig. 63 Lift the CRFM assembly from the lower brackets and carefully move the bottom of the assembly rearward while tilting the top forward.

12. Lift the CRFM assembly from the lower brackets and carefully move the bottom of the assembly rearward while tilting the top forward.

13. Remove the fan assembly to radiator bolt.

14. Remove the fan assembly.

To install:

15. Install the fan assembly by guiding the lower tabs of the fan assembly into the corresponding radiator hooks.

16. Install the fan assembly to radiator bolts.

17. Install the lower radiator pins into the cradle brackets.

18. Install the upper CRFM bracket assemblies.

19. Install the radiator outlet hose.

20. Position the clamp at 5 o'clock.

21. Install the radiator inlet hose.

22. Position the clamp at 6 o'clock.

23. Install the condenser splash shield.

24. Install the battery box inlet air duct.

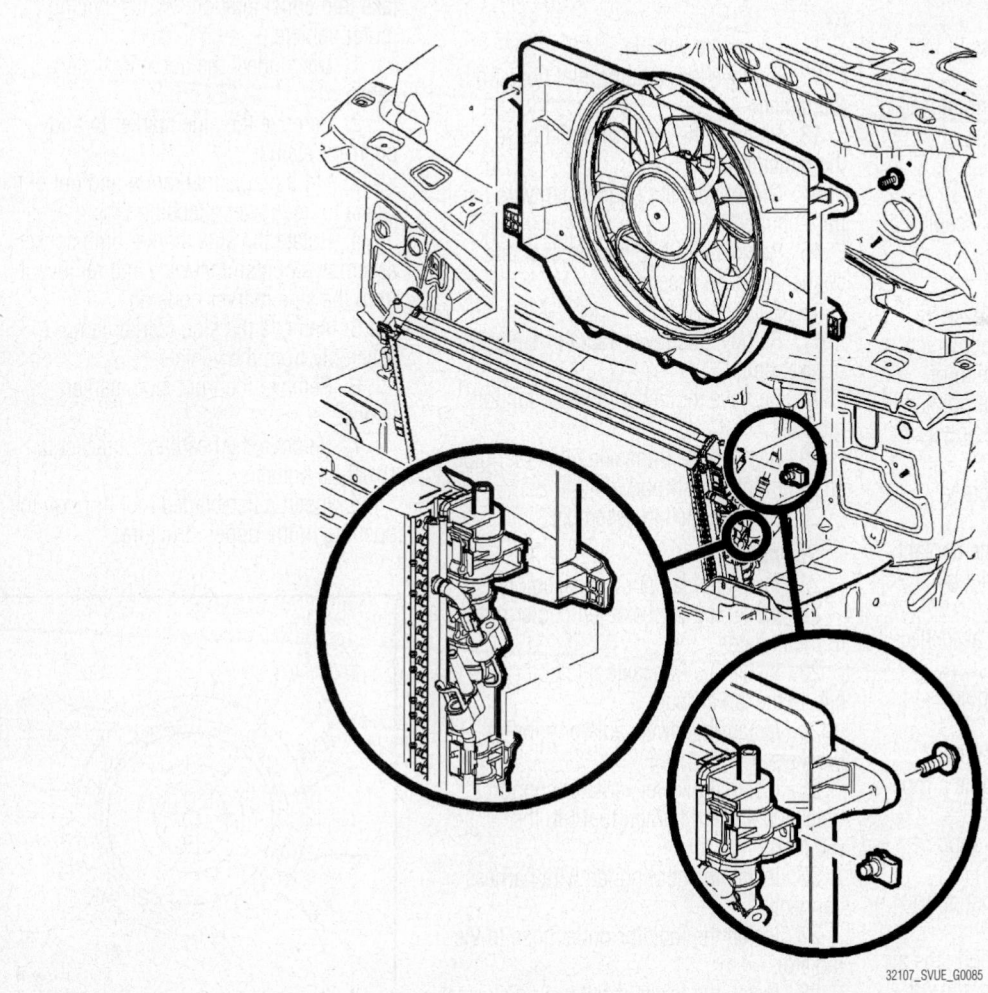

Fig. 64 Install the fan assembly by guiding the lower tabs of the fan assembly into the corresponding radiator hooks

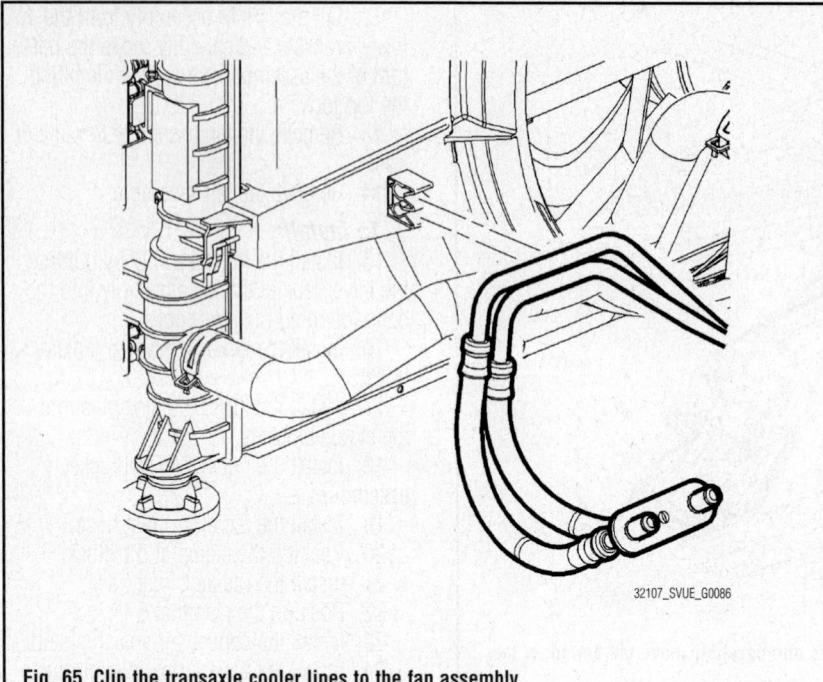

Fig. 65 Clip the transaxle cooler lines to the fan assembly.

25. Clip the transaxle cooler lines to fan assembly.

26. Clip the engine wire harness to fan assembly.

27. Connect the fan motor to engine harness.

28. Install the front fascia.

29. Fill the cooling system.

30. Connect the negative battery cable.

2.4L Engine

Before servicing any vehicle, please be sure to read the precautions section, which deals with personal safety, prevention of component damage, and important points to take into consideration when servicing a motor vehicle.

1. Disconnect the negative battery cable.

2. Drain and recycle the engine coolant.

3. Remove the air cleaner outlet air duct.

4. Remove the upper radiator air deflector.

5. Remove the transaxle oil cooler pipes from the radiator.

6. Loop a rope around each of the upper 2 tabs of the condenser and tie a rope around the upper tie bar.

7. Remove the upper radiator support bracket bolts.

8. Remove the upper radiator support brackets.

9. Pry upward on the fan shroud tabs at the radiator clips to release the fan shroud from the radiator.

10. Remove the lower radiator air deflector.

11. Lower the vehicle.

12. Remove the radiator inlet hose from the radiator.

13. Remove the radiator outlet hose from the radiator.

14. Disconnect the cooling fan wire harness connectors.

15. Remove the A/C compressor and condenser hose assembly.

16. Raise the vehicle.

17. Remove the lower radiator support bracket bolts.

18. Remove the lower radiator support brackets.

19. Remove the transaxle oil cooler pipe clip from the fan shroud.

20. Remove the fan assembly.

To install:

21. Install the fan shroud assembly.

22. Install the transaxle oil cooler pipes to the radiator.

23. Install the transaxle oil cooler pipe clip to the fan shroud.

24. Install the lower radiator support brackets.

25. Install the lower radiator support bracket bolts and tighten to 44 ft. lbs. (60 Nm).

26. Install the cooling fan wire harness connectors.

27. Install the radiator outlet hose to the radiator.

28. Install the lower radiator air deflector.

29. Lower the vehicle.

30. Snap fan shroud tabs into the radiator clips.

31. Remove the rope attached to the condenser and upper tie bar.

32. Install the upper radiator support brackets.

33. Install the upper radiator support bracket bolts and tighten to 89 in. lbs. (10 Nm).

34. Install the radiator inlet hose to the radiator.

35. Install the A/C compressor and condenser hose assembly.

36. Install the upper radiator air deflector.

37. Install the air duct.

38. Fill the cooling system.

39. Inspect the transaxle fluid level.

3.5L Engine

See Figures 66 and 67.

Before servicing any vehicle, please be sure to read the precautions section, which deals with personal safety, prevention of component damage, and important points to take into consideration when servicing a motor vehicle.

1. Disconnect the negative battery cable.

2. Remove the side marker to body push-in retainer.

3. Lift the side marker up and out of the fascia to free lower attaching tabs.

4. Rotate the side marker bulb socket assembly counterclockwise and remove it from the side marker housing.

5. Remove the side marker lamp assembly from the vehicle.

6. Remove the front side marker lamps.

7. Remove the headlamp bracket to structure bolts.

8. Insert a flat-bladed tool through the opening in the upper structure.

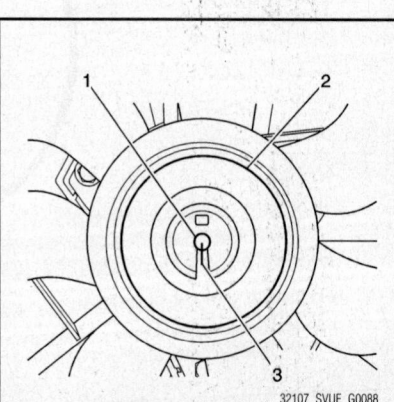

Fig. 66 Place a scribe mark (3) on the fan (2) hub and the motor shaft (1).

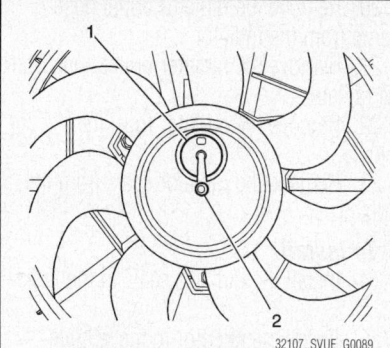

Fig. 67 Remove the fan retaining clip (1) from the motor shaft (2).

9. Gently push the locking tab toward the rear of the vehicle with flat-bladed tool to detach the headlamp bracket lower arm.

10. Lift headlamp assembly upward.

11. Disconnect the electrical connector from the headlamp assembly.

12. Remove the headlamp assembly away from the vehicle, if necessary.

13. Rotate the headlamp bulb assembly counterclockwise to remove it from the headlamp housing.

14. Remove the park/turn bulb socket from the housing by rotating the socket counterclockwise, if necessary.

15. Gently pull the park/turn bulb from the socket , if necessary.

16. Remove the front air deflector to fascia screws.

17. Remove the front air deflector to engine cradle push-in retainers.

18. Remove the front air deflector by lowering from the vehicle.

19. Remove the front wheelhouse push-pins and move the wheelhouse liner rearward.

20. Disconnect the fog lamp electrical connector (if equipped), by reaching through the headlamp opening.

21. Remove the fascia to lower front fender bracket bolts.

22. Remove the fascia to body push-in retainers.

23. Separate the fascia from the front fenders.

24. Remove the fascia to fascia support push-in retainers.

25. Remove the fascia from the vehicle.

26. Drain the coolant.

27. Disconnect the electrical connectors from the fan motors.

28. Unclip the wire harness from the fan assembly.

29. Unclip the transaxle cooler lines from the fan assembly.

30. Remove the Condenser Radiator Fan Module (CRFM) closeout panel retainers from the condenser.

31. Remove the CRFM closeout panel from the condenser.

32. Remove the radiator inlet hose clamp from the radiator.

33. Remove the radiator inlet hose from the radiator.

34. Remove the radiator inlet hose retaining straps from the radiator support.

35. Remove the radiator outlet hose clamp from the radiator.

36. Remove the radiator outlet hose from the radiator.

37. Remove the CRFM mounting bracket bolts from the radiator support.

38. Remove the CRFM mounting brackets from the radiator support.

39. Lift the CRFM assembly from the lower mounts and carefully move the bottom of the assembly rearward while tilting the top forward.

40. Remove the fan assembly bolts from the radiator.

41. Remove the fan assembly from the radiator.

➡**The fan and motor assembly is a balanced assembly. Be sure to mark the relationship of the fan to the motor shaft to ensure the balance is maintained.**

42. Place a scribe mark (3) on the fan (2) hub and the motor shaft (1).

43. Remove the fan retaining clip (1) from the motor shaft (2).

44. Discard fan retaining clip (1).

45. Remove the fan (1) from the motor (2).

To install:

46. Install the fan (1) to the motor (2).

47. Align the scribe marks (3) previously made on the fan (2) hub and the motor shaft (1).

➡**Ensure that the scribe marks remain aligned during fan retaining clip (1) installation.**

48. Install a new fan retaining clip (1) to the motor shaft (2). Ensure the retaining clip (1) is fully seated.

49. Install the cooling fan and shroud to the vehicle.

50. Install the fan assembly to the radiator by guiding the lower tabs into the corresponding hooks on the radiator.

❊❊ WARNING

Use the correct fastener in the correct location. Replacement fasteners must be the correct part number for that application. Fasteners requiring replacement or fasteners requiring the use of thread locking compound or sealant are identified in the service procedure. Do not use paints, lubricants, or corrosion inhibitors on fasteners or fastener joint surfaces unless specified. These coatings affect fastener torque and joint clamping force and may damage the fastener. Use the correct tightening sequence and specifications when installing fasteners in order to avoid damage to parts and systems.

51. Install the fan assembly bolts to the radiator.

52. Tighten the bolts to 71 inch lbs. (8 Nm).

53. Position the CRFM assembly onto the lower mounts.

54. Install the CRFM mounting brackets to the radiator support.

55. Install the CRFM mounting bracket bolts to the radiator support.

56. Tighten the bolts to 71 inch lbs (8 Nm).

57. Install the radiator outlet hose to the radiator.

58. Install the radiator outlet hose clamp to the radiator.

59. Install the radiator inlet hose to the radiator.

60. Install the radiator inlet hose clamp to the radiator.

61. Install the CRFM closeout panel to the condenser.

62. Install the CRFM closeout panel retainers to the condenser.

63. Clip the transaxle cooler lines to the fan assembly.

64. Clip the engine wire harness to fan assembly.

65. Install the electrical connectors to the fan motors.

66. Install the front fascia.

67. Fill the cooling system.

RADIATOR

REMOVAL & INSTALLATION

2.2L Engine
See Figures 68 through 72.

Before servicing any vehicle, please be sure to read the precautions section, which deals with personal safety, prevention of component damage, and important points to take into consideration when servicing a motor vehicle.

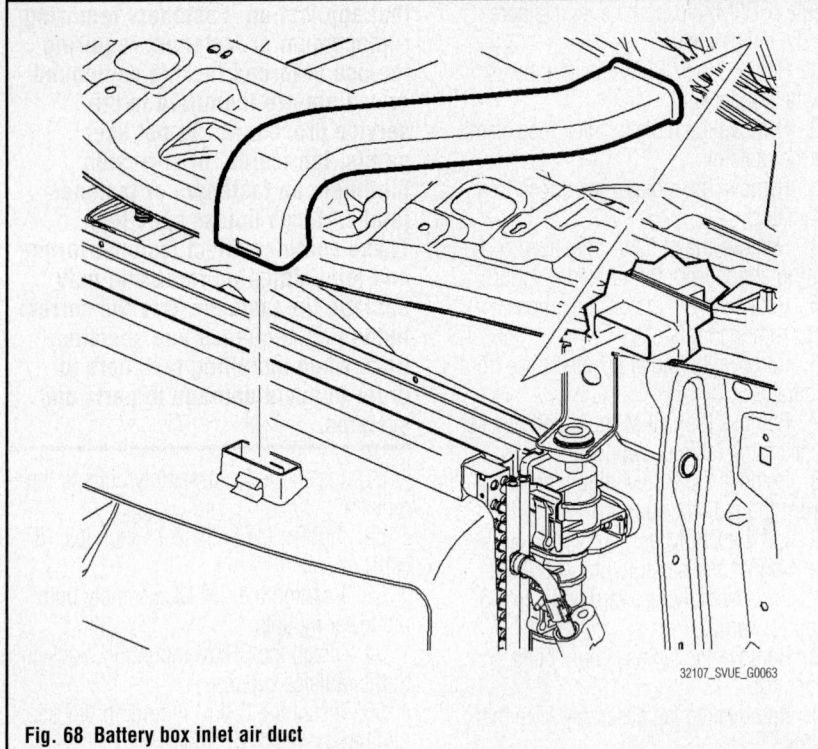

Fig. 68 Battery box inlet air duct

1. Disconnect the negative battery cable.

2. Drain the cooling system.

3. Remove the front fascia.

   a. Remove headlight assemblies, front bumper fascia support and lower fascia for standard front bumper.

   b. Remove headlamp assemblies, front bumper fascia support, and front bumper fascia upper grille for Redline.

4. Remove the battery box inlet air duct.

5. Remove the Condenser Radiator Fan Module (CRFM) closeout panel retainers from the condenser.

6. Remove the CRFM closeout panel from the condenser.

7. Remove the fan assembly bolts from the radiator.

8. Lift the fan assembly to disengage the lower retention tabs.

9. Position the fan assembly away from the radiator.

10. Lift the condenser while holding the upper retention tabs forward.

11. Position the condenser away from the radiator.

12. Disconnect the transaxle cooler liners from the transaxle cooler, if equipped.

13. Remove the transaxle cooler bolt from the radiator, if equipped.

14. Lift the transaxle cooler while holding the upper retention tabs forward, if equipped.

15. Remove the transaxle cooler from the vehicle

16. Remove the CRFM bracket bolts from the radiator support.

17. Remove the CRFM brackets from the radiator.

18. Remove the radiator inlet hose clamp from the radiator.

19. Remove the radiator inlet hose from the radiator.

20. Remove the radiator outlet hose clamp from the radiator.

21. Remove the radiator outlet hose from the radiator.

22. Remove the radiator from the vehicle.

23. Remove the radiator seals from the radiator.

To install:

24. Install the radiator seals to the radiator.

25. Install the radiator to the vehicle.

26. Install the radiator outlet hose to the radiator.

27. Install the radiator outlet hose clamp to the radiator.

28. Install the radiator inlet hose to the radiator.

29. Install the radiator inlet hose clamp to the radiator.

30. Install the CRFM bracket to the radiator support.

➡ **Use the correct fastener in the correct location. Replacement fasteners must be the correct part number for that application. Fasteners requiring replacement or fasteners requiring the use of thread locking compound or sealant are identified in the service procedure. Do not use paints, lubricants, or corrosion inhibitors on fasteners or fastener joint surfaces unless specified. These coatings affect fastener torque and joint clamping force**

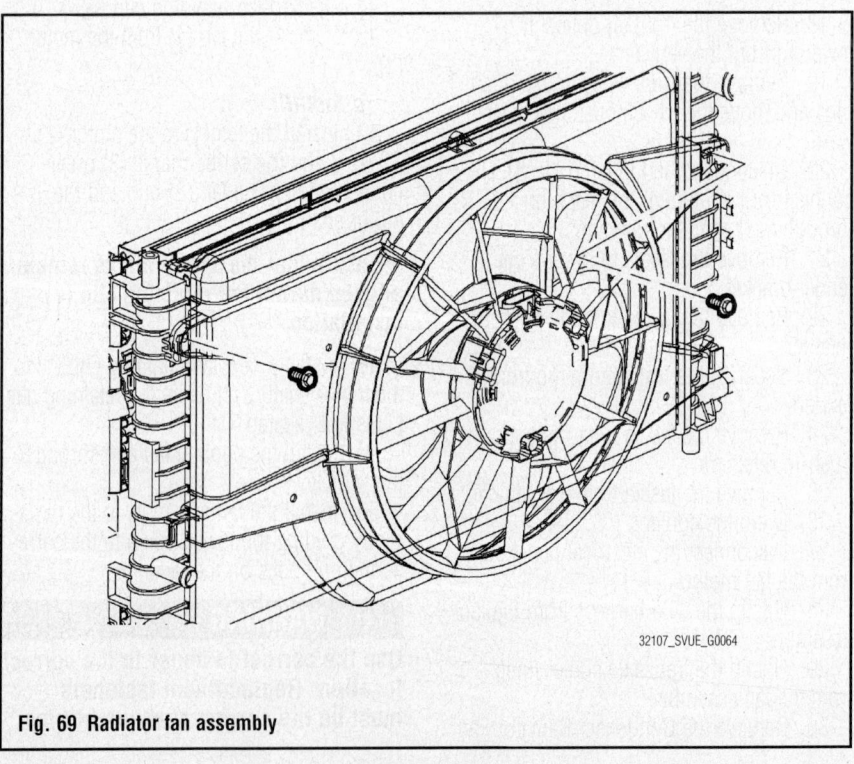

Fig. 69 Radiator fan assembly

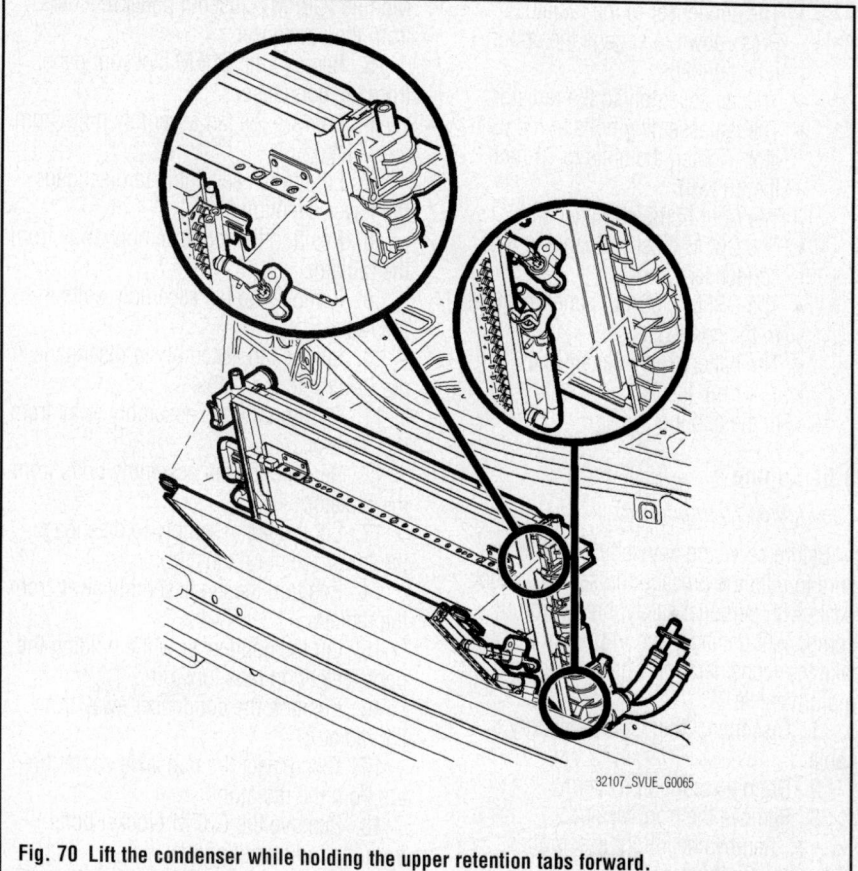

Fig. 70 Lift the condenser while holding the upper retention tabs forward.

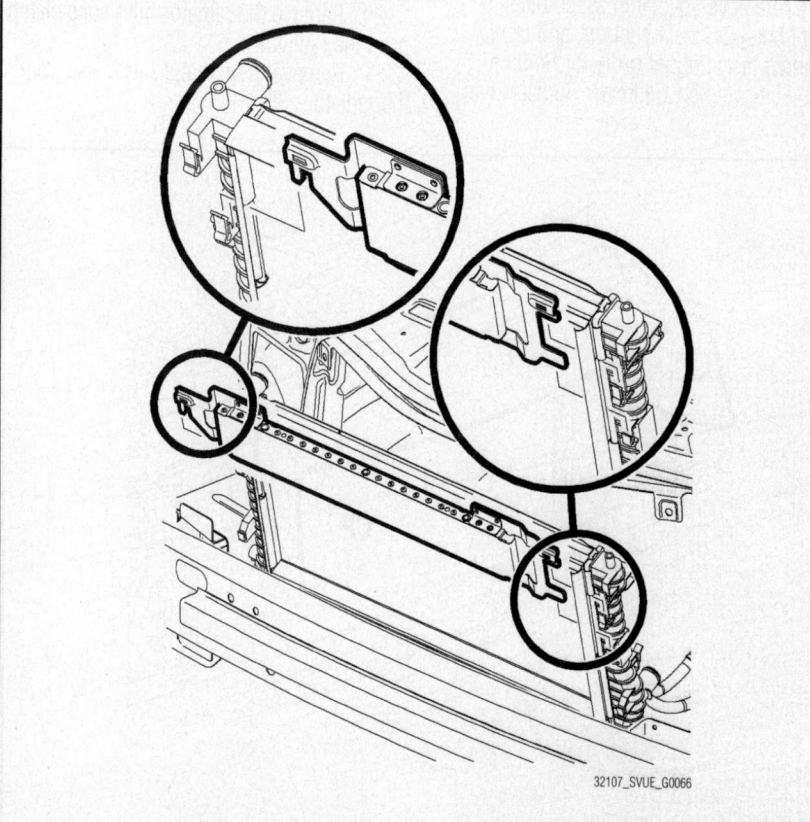

Fig. 71 Lift the transaxle cooler while holding the upper retention tabs forward, if equipped

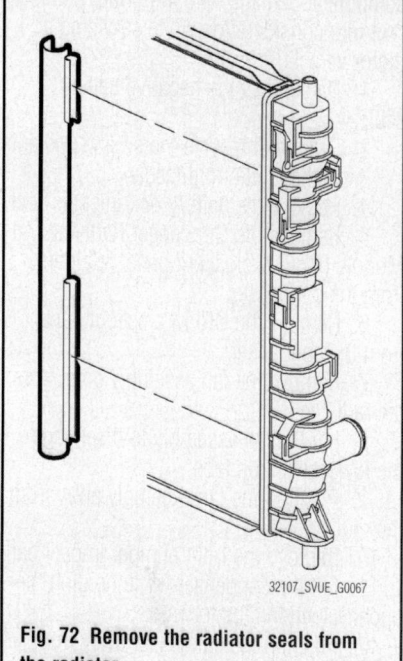

Fig. 72 Remove the radiator seals from the radiator

and may damage the fastener. Use the correct tightening sequence and specifications when installing fasteners in order to avoid damage to parts and systems.

31. Install the CRFM brackets bolts to the radiator. Tighten the bolts to 71 inch lbs. (8 Nm).

32. Install the transaxle cooler to the vehicle, if equipped. Press down to engage the upper retention tabs.

33. Install the transaxle cooler bolt to the radiator, if equipped. Tighten the bolt to 71 inch lbs. (8 Nm).

34. Connect the transaxle cooler liners to the transaxle cooler, if equipped.

35. Install the condenser to the radiator. Press down to engage the upper retention tabs.

36. Install the fan assembly to the radiator.

37. Install the fan assembly bolts to the radiator. Tighten the bolts to 71 inch lbs. (8 Nm).

38. Install the CRFM closeout panel to the condenser.

39. Install the CRFM closeout panel retainers to the condenser.

40. Install the battery box inlet air duct.

41. Install the front fascia.

42. Fill the cooling system.

2.4L Engine

Before servicing any vehicle, please be sure to read the precautions section, which deals with personal safety, prevention of component damage, and important points to take into consideration when servicing a motor vehicle.

1. Disconnect the negative battery cable.
2. Drain and recycle the engine coolant.
3. Remove the front fascia.
4. Remove the battery box inlet air duct.
5. Remove the Condenser Radiator Fan Module (CRFM) closeout panel retainers from the condenser.
6. Remove the CRFM closeout panel from the condenser.
7. Remove the fan assembly bolts from the radiator.
8. Lift the fan assembly to disengage the lower retention tabs.
9. Position the fan assembly away from the radiator.
10. Remove the front bumper impact bar.
11. Lift the condenser while holding the upper retention tabs forward.
12. Position the condenser away from the radiator.
13. Remove or disconnect the following:
- The transaxle cooler lines from the radiator, if equipped
- The CRFM bracket bolts from the radiator support
- The CRFM brackets from the radiator
- The radiator inlet hose clamp from the radiator
- The radiator inlet hose from the radiator
- The radiator outlet hose clamp from the radiator
- The radiator outlet hose from the radiator
- The radiator from the vehicle
- The radiator seals from the radiator

To install:
14. Install or connect the following:
- The radiator seals to the radiator
- The radiator to the vehicle
- The radiator outlet hose to the radiator
- The radiator outlet hose clamp to the radiator
- The radiator inlet hose to the radiator
- The radiator inlet hose clamp to the radiator
- The CRFM bracket to the radiator support
- The CRFM brackets bolts to the radiator. Tighten the bolt to 71 inch lbs. (8 Nm)
- The transaxle cooler lines to the radiator, if equipped. Tighten the fittings to 12 ft. lbs. (16 Nm)

- The condenser to the radiator. Press down to engage the upper retention tabs
- The fan assembly to the radiator
- The fan assembly bolts to the radiator. Tighten the bolts to 71 inch lbs. (8 Nm)
- The front bumper impact bar
- The CRFM closeout panel to the condenser
- The CRFM closeout panel retainers to the condenser
- The battery box inlet air duct
- The front fascia
15. Fill the cooling system.

3.5L Engine

See Figures 73 through 75.

Before servicing any vehicle, please be sure to read the precautions section, which deals with personal safety, prevention of component damage, and important points to take into consideration when servicing a motor vehicle.

1. Disconnect the negative battery cable.
2. Drain the cooling system.
3. Remove the front fascia:
   a. Remove headlight assemblies, front bumper fascia support and lower fascia for standard front bumper.
   b. Remove headlamp assemblies, front bumper fascia support, and front bumper fascia upper grille for Redline.
4. Remove the Condenser Radiator Fan Module (CRFM) closeout panel retainers from the condenser.
5. Remove the CRFM closeout panel from the condenser.
6. Remove the fan assembly bolts from the radiator.
7. Lift the fan assembly to disengage the lower retention tabs.
8. Position the fan assembly away from the radiator.
9. Remove the fan assembly bolts from the radiator.
10. Lift the fan assembly to disengage the lower retention tabs.
11. Position the fan assembly away from the radiator.
12. Remove the fan assembly bolts from the radiator.
13. Lift the fan assembly to disengage the lower retention tabs.
14. Position the fan assembly away from the radiator.
15. Lift the condenser while holding the upper retention tabs forward.
16. Position the condenser away from the radiator.
17. Disconnect the transaxle cooler liners from the radiator.
18. Remove the CRFM bracket bolts from the radiator support.
19. Remove the CRFM brackets from the radiator.
20. Remove the radiator inlet hose clamp from the radiator.
21. Remove the radiator inlet hose from the radiator.

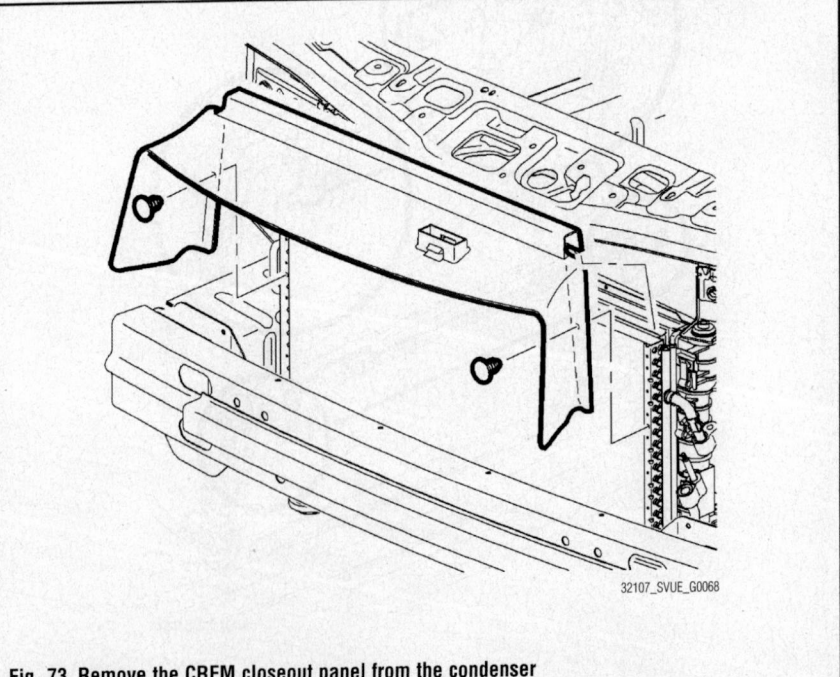

32107_SVUE_G0068

Fig. 73 Remove the CRFM closeout panel from the condenser

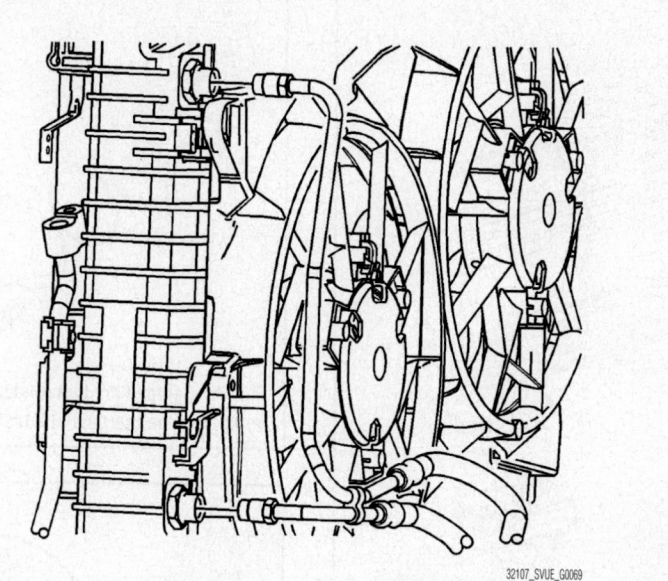

Fig. 74 Disconnect the transaxle cooler liners from the radiator.

22. Remove the radiator outlet hose clamp from the radiator.

23. Remove the radiator outlet hose from the radiator.

24. Remove the radiator from the vehicle.

25. Remove the radiator seals from the radiator.

To install:

26. Install or connect the following:
- The radiator seals to the radiator
- The radiator to the vehicle
- The radiator outlet hose to the radiator
- The radiator outlet hose clamp to the radiator

• The CRFM bracket to the radiator support

➡ **Use the correct fastener in the correct location. Replacement fasteners must be the correct part number for that application. Fasteners requiring replacement or fasteners requiring the use of thread locking compound or sealant are identified in the service procedure. Do not use paints, lubricants, or corrosion inhibitors on fasteners or fastener joint surfaces unless specified. These coatings affect fastener torque and joint clamping force and may damage the fastener. Use the correct tightening sequence and specifications when installing fasteners in order to avoid damage to parts and systems.**

- The CRFM brackets bolts to the radiator. Tighten the bolt to 71 inch lbs. (8 Nm)

27. Connect the transaxle cooler liners to the radiator
- The condenser to the radiator. Press down to engage the upper retention tabs
- The fan assembly to the radiator
- The fan assembly bolts to the radiator. Tighten the bolts to 71 inch lbs. (8 Nm)
- The CRFM closeout panel to the condenser
- The CRFM closeout panel retainers to the condenser
- The front fascia

28. Fill the cooling system.

THERMOSTAT

REMOVAL & INSTALLATION

2.2L Engine

See Figures 76 through 80.

Before servicing any vehicle, please be sure to read the precautions section, which deals with personal safety, prevention of component damage, and important points to take into consideration when servicing a motor vehicle.

❋ WARNING

The thermostat will not function correctly once it is contacted by oil. If oil is found in the cooling system, it must be flushed and the thermostat cartridge replaced.

1. Drain the coolant.
2. Remove the exhaust heat shield bolts.

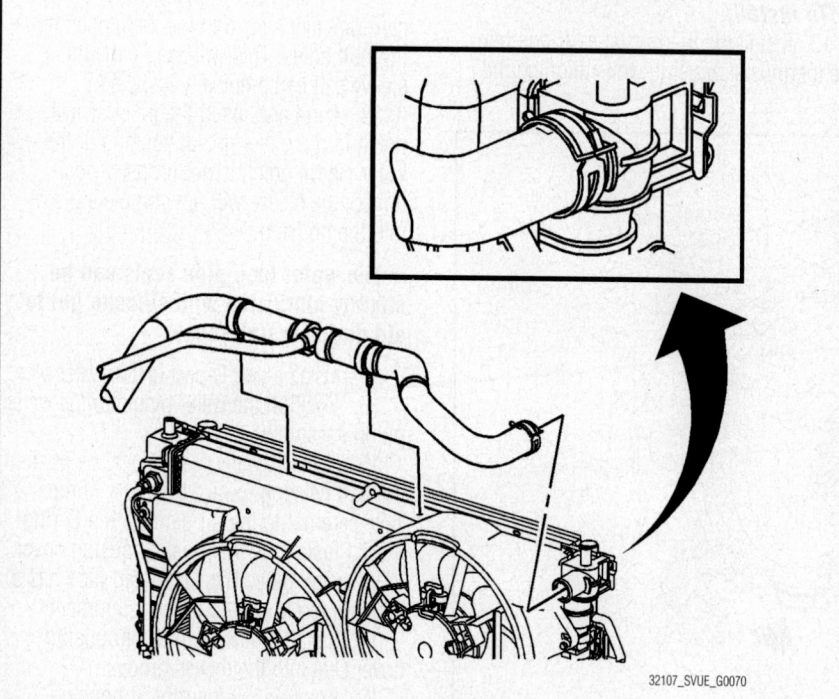

Fig. 75 Remove the radiator inlet hose clamp from the radiator.

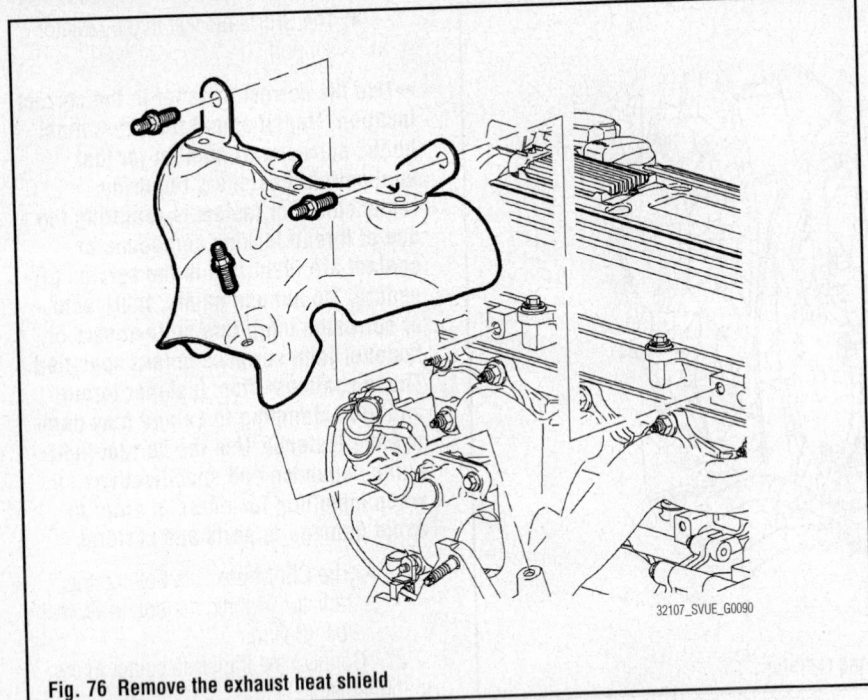

Fig. 76 Remove the exhaust heat shield

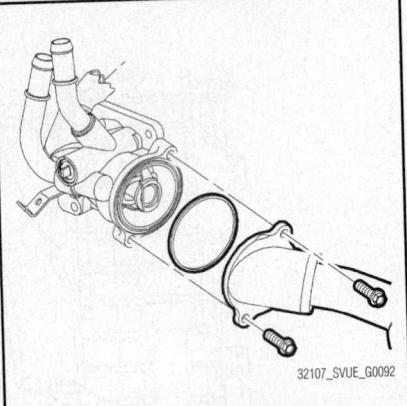

Fig. 78 Remove the thermostat cover bolts from the thermostat housing.

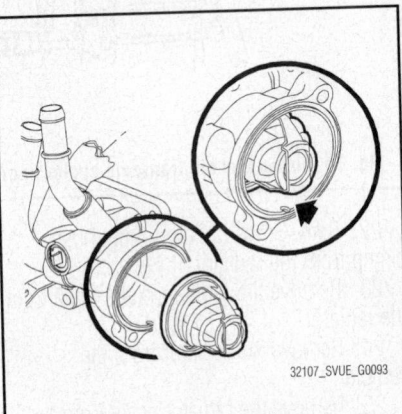

Fig. 79 Install the thermostat cartridge into the thermostat housing

3. Remove the exhaust heat shield.
4. Raise the vehicle.

➡**A drain plug has been provided at the bottom of the water pump assembly for additional coolant drainage from the engine block and water pump.**

5. Drain the coolant from the water pump drain plug.
6. Remove the thermostat cover bolts from the thermostat housing.
7. Remove and discard the thermostat housing O-seal.

➡**Twist the water feed pipe while pulling to remove it from the water pump.**

8. Remove the water pipe from the water pump assembly.
9. Remove and discard the seals from the water pipe.
10. Remove the inner thermostat sleeve.
11. Remove the thermostat assembly.

To install:

12. Install the thermostat cartridge into the thermostat housing while aligning the cartridge tangs up with the thermostat housing bolt holes. This will assure the inner sleeve can be completely installed.

13. Align and insert the inner sleeve notch into the thermostat housing. If the inner sleeve notch is not properly positioned, the sleeve will not completely seat into the housing.

➡**The water feed pipe seals can be slightly lubricated with silicone gel to aid during installation.**

14. Install a new O-seal on the water pipe.
15. Position the water pipe into the water pump assembly.
16. Seat the water feed O-seal by pushing and twisting toward the water pump. Take care not to tear or damage the O-ring.
17. Install the thermostat housing cover to the water pipe. The water feed pipe has a locating tab to assure proper alignment.
18. Install a new thermostat housing cover seal into the recess groove.
19. Position the thermostat housing cover into position.
20. Install the thermostat housing cover bolts.

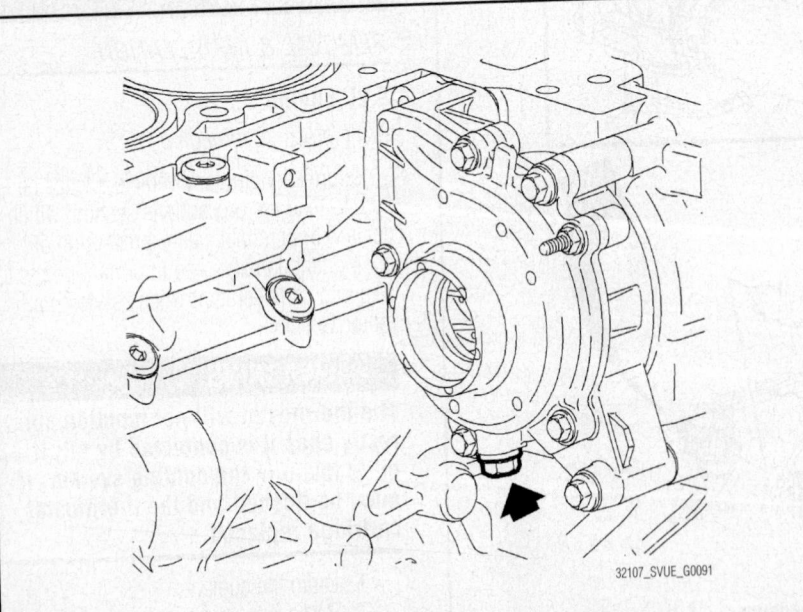

Fig. 77 Drain the coolant from the water pump drain plug

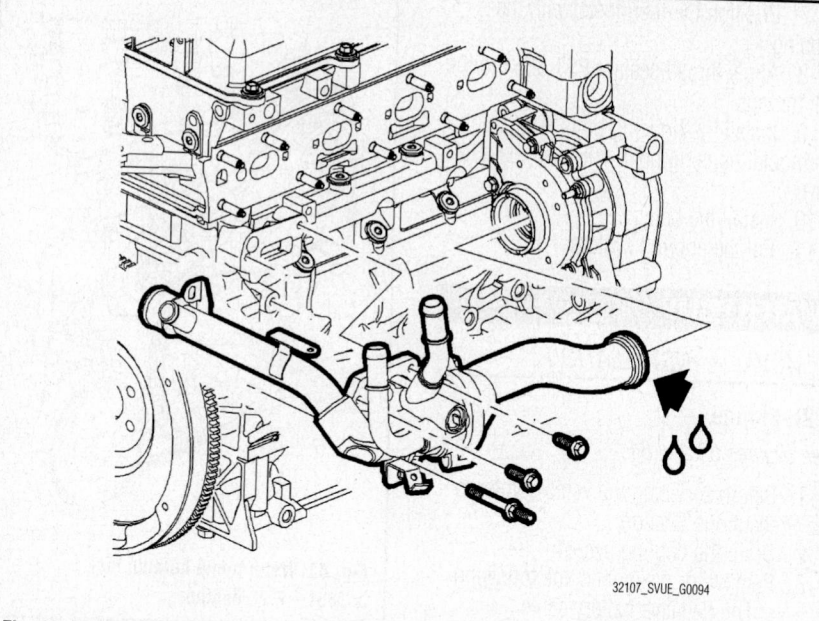

32107_SVUE_G0094

Fig. 80 Position the water pipe into the water pump assembly

21. Tighten the thermostat housing cover-to-thermostat housing bolts to 89 inch lbs. (10 Nm).

22. Lower the vehicle.

23. Install the exhaust manifold heat shield.

24. Install the exhaust manifold heat shield bolts. Tighten the exhaust manifold heat shield bolts to 17 ft. lbs. (23 Nm).

➡**The vehicle must be level when filling the cooling system.**

25. Verify the drain valve at the radiator and the water pump are closed.

26. Fill the engine coolant .

27. Verify the repair and inspect for any leaks.

2.4L Engine

See Figure 81.

Before servicing any vehicle, please be sure to read the precautions section, which deals with personal safety, prevention of component damage, and important points to take into consideration when servicing a motor vehicle.

1. Drain and recycle the engine coolant.

➡**A drain has been provided at the bottom of the water pump for engine block coolant drainage.**

2. Drain the coolant from the engine block at the water pump drain. After the coolant has drained, tighten the drain bolt.

3. Lower the vehicle.

4. Remove or disconnect the following:
  * The battery tray

* The engine wiring harness electrical connector from the Engine Coolant Temperature (ECT) sensor
* The Heated Oxygen Sensor (HO2S) electrical connector rosebud clip from the thermostat housing

5. Reposition the radiator outlet hose clamp at the thermostat cover.

6. Remove or disconnect the following:
  * The radiator outlet hose from the thermostat cover
  * The exhaust heat shield bolts
  * The exhaust heat shield
  * The auxiliary heater water pump hose clip from the heater outlet hose

7. Reposition the auxiliary heater water pump hose clamp at the thermostat housing.

8. Remove the auxiliary heater water pump hose from the thermostat housing.

9. Reposition the heater inlet hose clamp at the thermostat housing.

10. Remove the heater inlet hose from the thermostat housing.

11. Raise and support the vehicle.

12. Remove or disconnect the following:

  * The ECT sensor, if necessary
  * The thermostat housing bolts

➡**Twist the water transfer pipe while pulling in order to remove it from the water pump.**

  * The water transfer pipe from the thermostat housing, if necessary
  * The water transfer pipe O-ring seals and discard

* The thermostat cover bolts and cover, if necessary
* The thermostat

13. Remove and discard the thermostat cover O-ring seal.

14. Remove all debris and thread sealant from the Engine Coolant Temperature (ECT) sensor and bolt holes if the housing is being re-used.

To install:

15. Install a NEW thermostat cover O-ring seal into the recess groove.

16. Install the thermostat.

17. Install the thermostat cover bolts.

18. Install a NEW thermostat housing to engine gasket onto the thermostat housing.

19. Load the thermostat housing assembly into position.

➡**The water feed pipe seals can be lightly lubricated with coolant to aid during installation.**

20. Install NEW O-ring seals onto the water feed pipe.

➡**Lubricate the O-rings with coolant ONLY.**

21. Install the water feed pipe into the thermostat housing aligning locator tab.

22. Align the water pipe to water pump.

23. Seat the water feed O-ring seal by pushing inward toward the water pump. Take care not to tear or damage the O-ring.

24. Position the thermostat housing against the engine.

25. Install the thermostat housing bolts. Tighten the bolts to 89 in. lbs. (10 Nm).

26. If reinstalling the old sensor, coat the threads with sealant.

27. Install the ECT sensor, if necessary. Tighten the sensor to 15 ft. lbs. (20 Nm).

28. Lower the vehicle.

29. Install the heater inlet hose to the thermostat housing.

30. Position the heater inlet hose clamp at the thermostat housing.

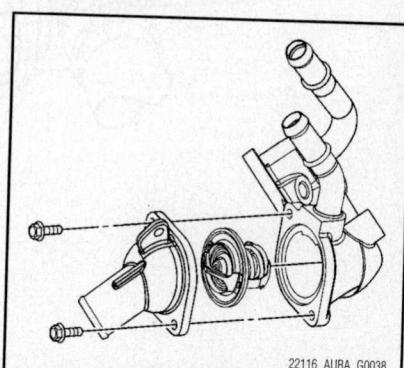

22116_AURA_G0038

Fig. 81 Exploded view of the thermostat housing assembly—2.4L engine

31. Install the auxiliary heater water pump hose to the thermostat housing.

32. Position the auxiliary heater water pump hose clamp at the thermostat housing.

33. Install the auxiliary heater water pump hose clip to the heater outlet hose.

34. Install the exhaust heat shield.

35. Install the exhaust heat shield bolts. Tighten the bolts to 16 ft. lbs. (22 Nm).

36. Install the radiator outlet hose to the thermostat cover.

37. Position the radiator outlet hose clamp at the thermostat cover.

38. Connect the engine wiring harness electrical connector to the ECT sensor.

39. Install the HO2S electrical connector rosebud clip to the thermostat housing.

40. Install the battery tray.

41. Verify the drain valves at the radiator and water pump are closed.

42. Lower the vehicle.

43. Fill the cooling system

3.5L Engine

See Figure 82.

Before servicing any vehicle, please be sure to read the precautions section, which deals with personal safety, prevention of component damage, and important points to take into consideration when servicing a motor vehicle.

1. Drain the coolant.

2. Remove the battery.

3. Remove the thermostat housing.

4. Remove the thermostat.

To install:

5. Install the thermostat with housing.

6. Install a new gasket.

7. Position the thermostat with the housing.

8. Apply thread sealant PST 565® to the bolt threads.

9. Install the housing bolts. Tighten the thermostat housing bolts 106 inch lbs. (12 Nm).

10. Install the battery.

11. Fill the cooling system.

WATER PUMP

REMOVAL & INSTALLATION

2.2L Engine

See Figures 83 and 84.

1. Before servicing the vehicle, refer to the Precautions Section.

2. Drain the cooling system.

3. Remove or disconnect the following:
   - The negative battery cable
   - The air cleaner assembly
   - The thermostat housing pipe-to-cylinder head bolt (near the front of the engine)
   - The exhaust manifold heat shield
   - The water pump access plate
   - The right hand wheel and splash shield
   - The drain plug from the bottom of the pump and drain the remaining coolant
   - The engine Coolant Temperature (ECT) sensor connection
   - The thermostat housing bolts, then move the housing towards the left hand side of the vehicle while twisting the feed pipe from the rear

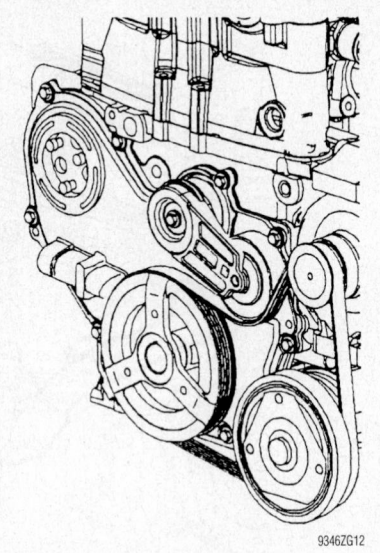

Fig. 83 Water pump holding tool J43651—2.2L engine

of the pump. Leave the coolant hoses and the housing connected
   - The water feed pipe and discard the seals

4. Install a Water Pump Holding Tool J43651. Tighten the bolts on the tool into threads on the pump sprocket, then install some of the access plate bolts to attach the tool to the front cover.

5. Remove the water pump retaining bolts.

6. Remove the water pump.

To install:

7. Install or connect the following:
   - The water pump with a new seal and torque the bolts to 18 ft. lbs. (25 Nm)

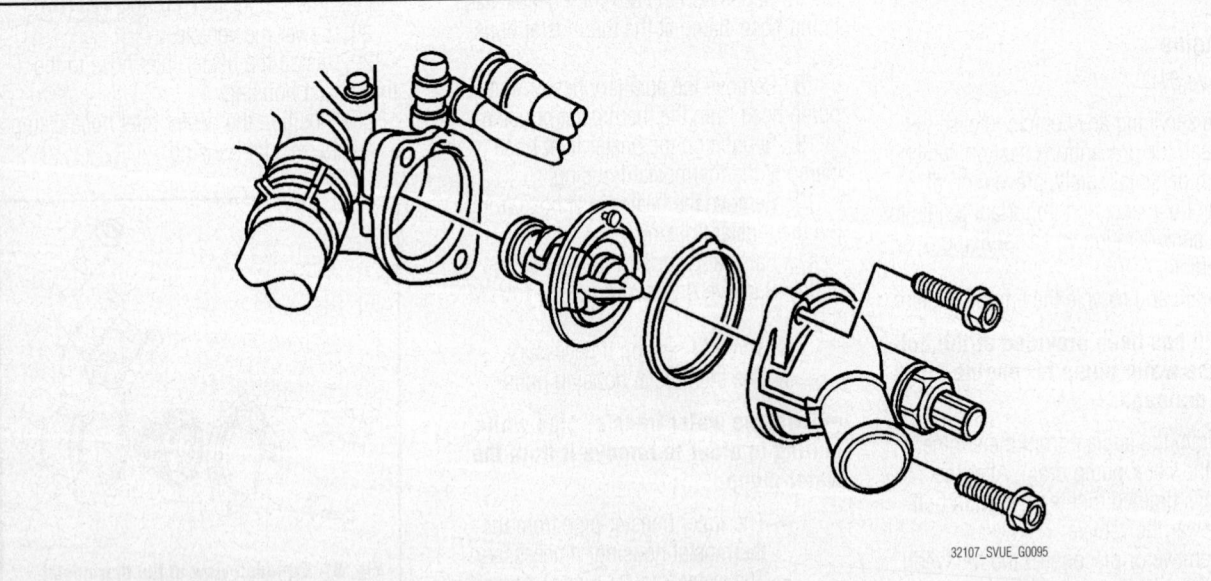

Fig. 82 Remove the thermostat housing.

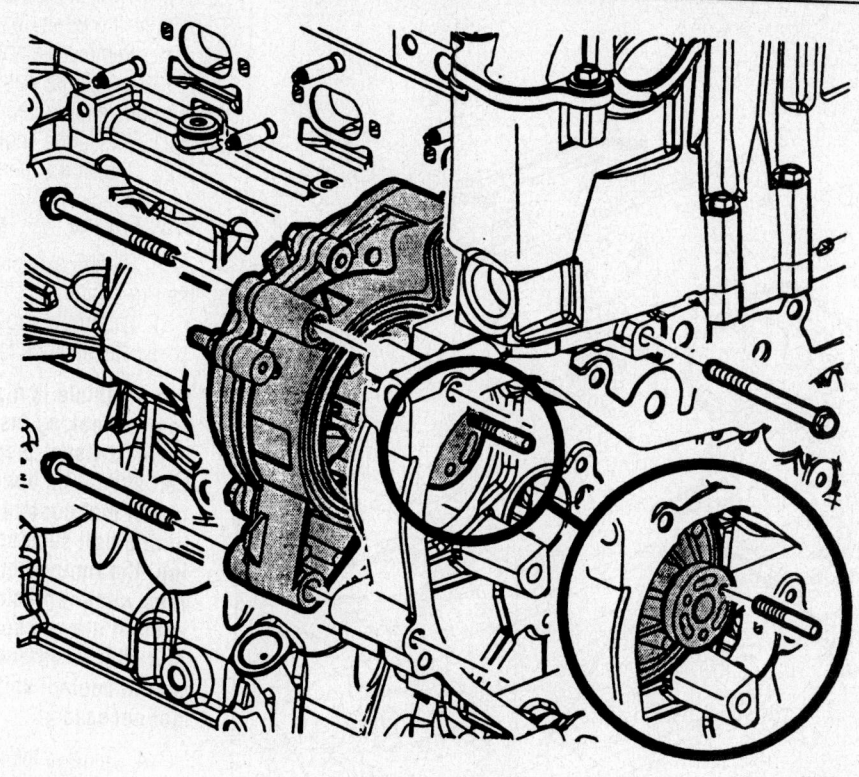

Fig. 84 Exploded view of the water pump mounting—2.2L engine

- The water pump sprocket and torque the bolts to 89 inch lbs. (10 Nm)
- The water pump sprocket access plate and torque the bolts to 89 inch lbs. (10 Nm)
- The water feed tube after lubricating the O-ring with coolant
- The thermostat housing and torque the bolts to 89 inch lbs. (10 Nm)
- The exhaust manifold heat shield
- The air cleaner assembly
- The negative battery cable

8. Fill the cooling system.
9. Start the vehicle and check for leaks, repair if necessary.

2.4L Engine

See Figures 85 and 86.

1. Before servicing the vehicle, refer to the Precautions Section.
2. Drain and recycle the engine coolant.
3. Remove the thermostat housing.
4. Remove the engine splash shield.
5. Remove the water pump access plate from the front cover.

➡**A drain plug has been provided at the bottom of the water pump assembly** for additional coolant drainage from the engine block and water pump.

6. Drain the coolant from the water pump using the plug at the bottom of the pump.

❊❊ WARNING

The water pump holding tool supports the sprocket and chain during water pump service. The tool must be used or the balance shaft must be re-timed.

7. Install a water pump holding tool such as J 43651 into position.
8. Tighten the bolts on the water pump holding tool into the threads on the water pump sprocket. Install the access cover bolts that were removed earlier to secure the water pump holding tool to the front cover assembly.
9. Remove the 3 inner water pump sprocket to water pump bolts.

➡**Be sure to remove both water pump bolts from the front of the engine block.**

10. Remove the front 2 water pump bolts.
11. Remove the rear 2 water pump bolts.
12. Remove the water pump.

13. Remove and discard the water pump O-ring seal.

To install:

❊❊ WARNING

Prior to installing the water pump, read the entire procedure. This will help avoid balance shaft chain re-timing and ensure proper sealing.

14. Install a NEW water pump O-ring seal.

➡**A guide pin can be created to aid in water pump alignment. Use an M6 6mm stud. Thread the pin into the water pump sprocket.**

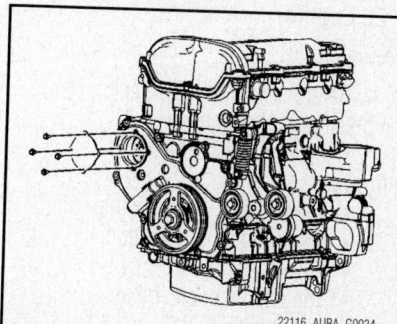

Fig. 85 Removing the thermostat housing—2.4L engine

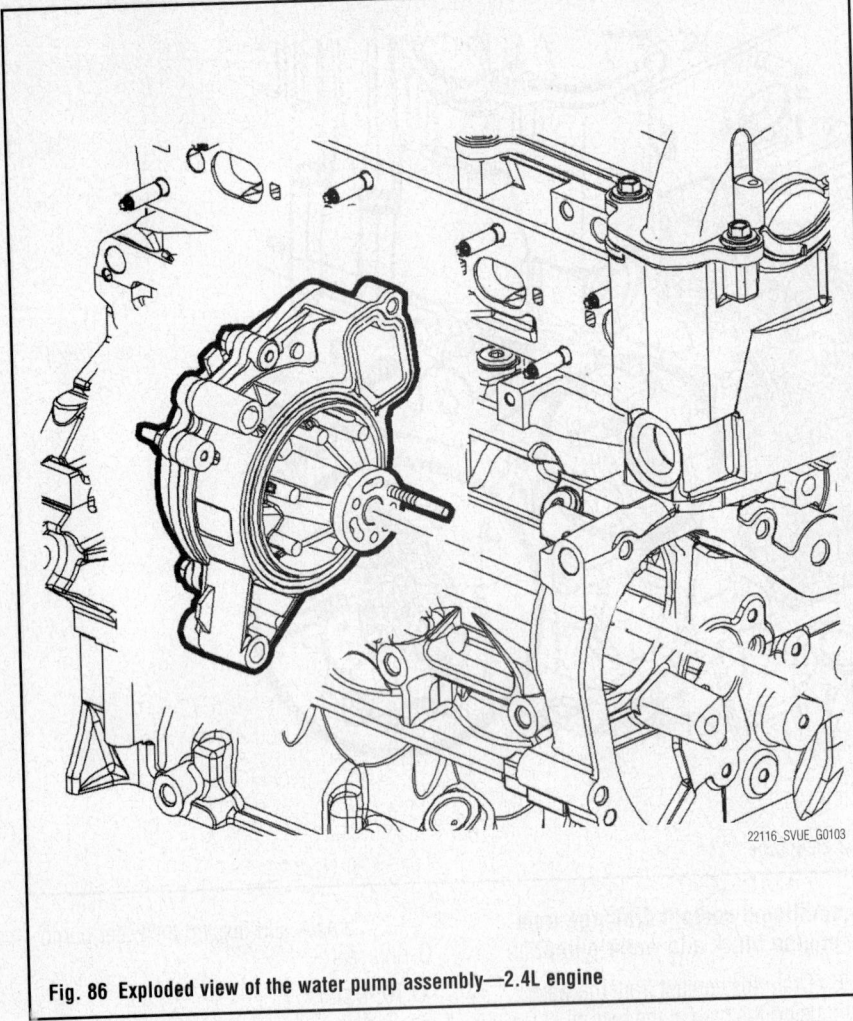

Fig. 86 Exploded view of the water pump assembly—2.4L engine

15. Using the guide pin, align the pin with the water pump holding tool.

16. Position the water pump against the engine block and hand tighten the water pump bolts.

17. Install the inner water pump sprocket bolts. After 2 are snug, remove the guide pin and install the 3rd bolt. Tighten the water pump bolts to 18 ft. lbs. (25 Nm).

18. Tighten the water pump sprocket bolts last to 89 in. lbs. (10 Nm).

19. Remove the water pump holding tool.

20. Install the water pump access plate and bolts and tighten to 89 in. lbs. (10 Nm).

21. Install the engine splash shield.

22. Install the thermostat housing.

3.5L Engine

1. Before servicing the vehicle, refer to the Precautions Section.

2. Drain the coolant.

3. Remove the timing belt cover.

➡If a vehicle is diagnosed to have coolant leaking inside the timing belt cover, a visual inspection of the timing belt should be done. If there is an indication that coolant has leaked onto the timing belt such as wetness or staining, the timing belt should be replaced. Also when replacing the water pump, coolant may be spilled onto the timing belt. Replacement of the timing belt due to coolant spillage on the belt is not necessary.

4. Remove the water pump assembly bolts.

5. Remove the water pump and O-ring.

To install:

6. Clean the water pump mating surfaces.

7. Install a new water pump O-ring seal to the water pump.

8. Install the water pump assembly and tighten the bolts to 106 inch lbs. (12 Nm).

9. Install the timing belt cover.

10. Fill the cooling system.

ENGINE ELECTRICAL

ALTERNATOR

REMOVAL & INSTALLATION

2.2L Engine

See Figure 87.

1. Before servicing the vehicle, refer to the precautions section.

2. Remove or disconnect the following:

- The negative battery cable
- The throttle body air duct
- The accessory drive belt
- The alternator electrical connectors
- The alternator bolts
- The alternator

CHARGING SYSTEM

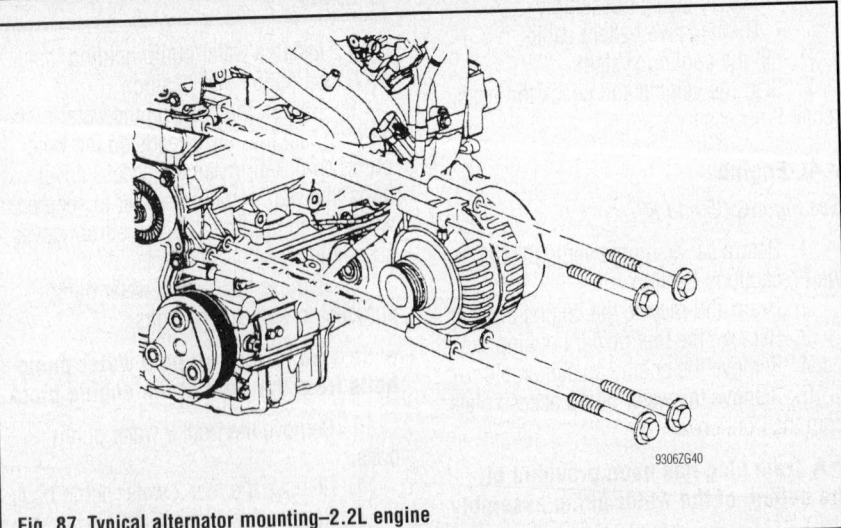

Fig. 87 Typical alternator mounting–2.2L engine

To install:

3. Install or connect the following:
- The alternator and torque the bolts to 26 ft. lbs. (35 Nm)
- The alternator electrical connectors
- The accessory drive belt
- The throttle body air duct
- The negative battery cable

2.4L Engine

1. Before servicing the vehicle, refer to the precautions section.
2. Disconnect the negative battery cable.
3. Remove the accessory drive belt.
4. Remove the alternator electrical connections.

5. Remove the alternator mounting nuts and bolts.
6. Remove the alternator.
7. Installation is the reverse of removal, tighten the bolts to 37 ft. lbs. (50 Nm) and the nuts to 22 ft. lbs. (30 Nm).

3.5L Engine

1. Before servicing the vehicle, refer to the precautions section.
2. Disconnect the negative battery cable.
3. Remove the air cleaner.
4. Remove the accessory drive belt tensioner.
5. Install an engine support fixture.
6. Remove the front of the engine

mount through bolt and raise the engine for clearance.
7. Remove the alternator.

To install:

8. Install or connect the following:
- Alternator and hand-tighten the top bolts.
- Bottom bolts and tighten all the bolts to 33 ft. lbs. (44 Nm).
- Lower the engine and tighten the engine mount through bolt to 81 ft. lbs. (110 Nm).
- Remove the engine support fixture.
9. Install or connect the following:
- The accessory drive belt tensioner
- The air cleaner assembly
- The negative battery cable

ENGINE ELECTRICAL

FIRING ORDER

See Figure 88.

Firing order—3.5L Engine:
1–4–2–5–3–6.

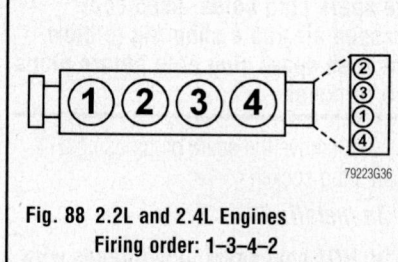

79223G36

Fig. 88 2.2L and 2.4L Engines
Firing order: 1–3–4–2
Distributorless ignition system

IGNITION COIL

REMOVAL & INSTALLATION

2.2L Engine

Before servicing any vehicle, please be sure to read the precautions section, which deals with personal safety, prevention of component damage, and important points to take into consideration when servicing a motor vehicle.

1. Remove the intake manifold cover.
2. Disconnect the ignition coil connectors from the ignition coils.
3. Remove the retaining bolts from the ignition coils.
4. Remove the ignition coils from the engine.

To install:

➡**Make sure that the ignition coil seals are properly seated to the valve cover.**

5. Install the ignition coil.
6. Install the ignition coil retaining bolts, and tighten the ignition coil retaining bolts to 89 inch lbs. (10 Nm).
7. Replace the ignition coil connectors.
8. Install the intake manifold cover.

2.4L Engine

See Figure 89.

1. Remove the intake manifold cover.
2. Disconnect the ignition coil connectors from the ignition coils.
3. Remove the retaining bolts from the ignition coils.
4. Remove the ignition coils from the engine.

To install:

➡**Make sure that the ignition coil seals are properly seated to the valve cover.**

5. Install the ignition coil.
6. Install the ignition coil retaining bolts,

IGNITION SYSTEM

and tighten the ignition coil retaining bolts to 89 inch lbs. (10 Nm).
7. Replace the ignition coil connectors.
8. Install the intake manifold cover.

3.5L Engine

Bank 1

See Figures 90 and 91.

Before servicing any vehicle, please be sure to read the precautions section, which deals with personal safety, prevention of component damage, and important points to take into consideration when servicing a motor vehicle.

1. Remove the air cleaner outlet duct assembly as follows:
   a. Loosen clamp at the air cleaner assembly and the front outlet duct seal assembly.
   b. Remove the attachment bolt from the support bracket.
   c. Remove the outlet resonator/duct assembly.

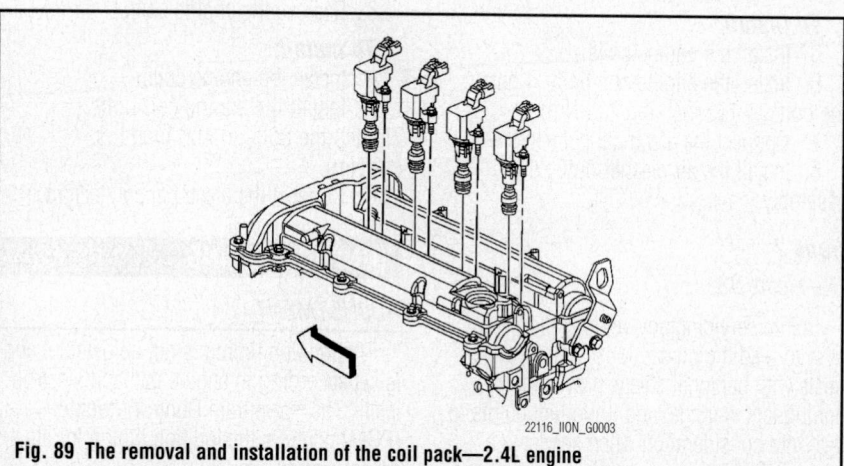

22116_IION_G0003

Fig. 89 The removal and installation of the coil pack—2.4L engine

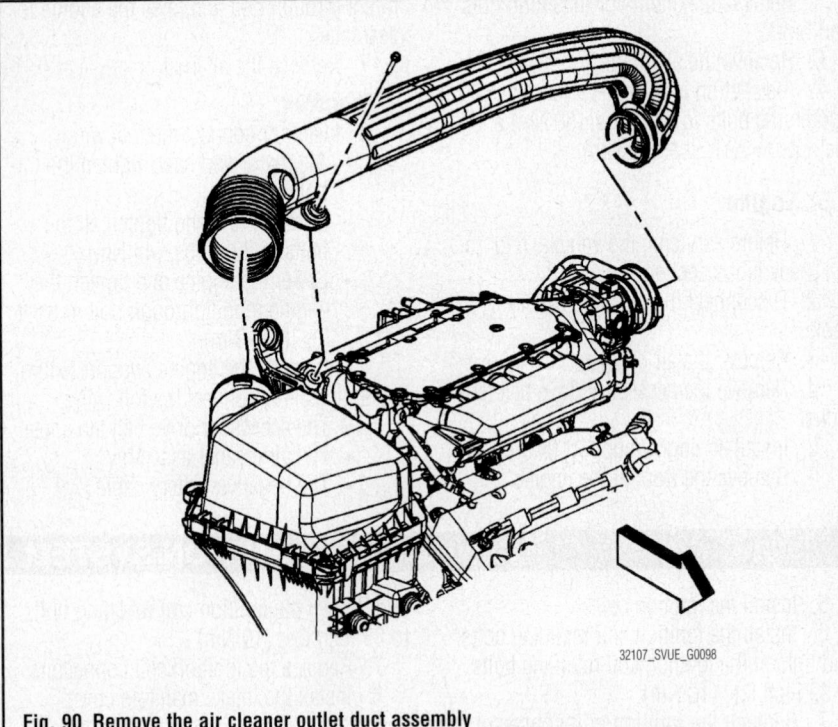

Fig. 90 Remove the air cleaner outlet duct assembly

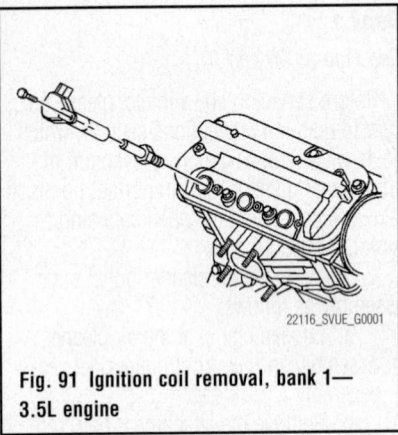

Fig. 91 Ignition coil removal, bank 1—3.5L engine

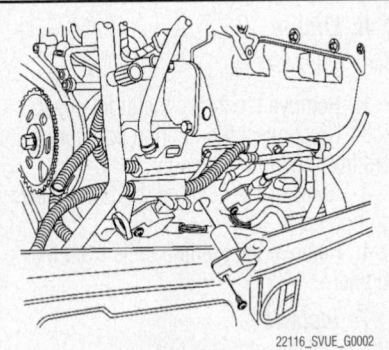

Fig. 92 Ignition coil removal, bank 2—3.5L engine

2. Disconnect the electrical connectors.
3. Remove the engine coil bolts.
4. Remove the engine coils.

To install:

5. Install the engine coils.
6. Install the engine coil bolts. Tighten the bolts to 106 inch lbs. (12 Nm).
7. Connect the electrical connectors.
8. Install the air cleaner outlet duct assembly.

Bank 2

See Figure 92.

Before servicing any vehicle, please be sure to read the precautions section, which deals with personal safety, prevention of component damage, and important points to take into consideration when servicing a motor vehicle.

1. Disconnect the electrical connectors.
2. Remove the engine coil bolts.
3. Remove the engine coils.

To install:

4. Install the engine coils.
5. Install the engine coil bolts. Tighten the bolts to 106 inch lbs. (12 Nm).
6. Connect the electrical connectors.

IGNITION TIMING

ADJUSTMENT

The ignition timing is not adjustable, and is set according to engine demand electronically. The Powertrain Control Module (PCM) controls the ignition timing for all driving conditions.

SPARK PLUGS

REMOVAL & INSTALLATION

2.2L Engine

See Figures 93 through 96.

1. Disconnect the Intake Air Temperature (IAT) sensor connector.
2. Loosen the clamp at the air cleaner assembly.
3. Remove the push-pin attachment from the outlet resonator/duct assembly to support bracket.
4. Loosen the clamp at the throttle body assembly.
5. Remove the outlet resonator/duct assembly.
6. Disconnect the EI module electrical connector.
7. Remove the ignition module attachment bolts.
8. Remove the ignition module housing assembly with the spark plug boots from the spark plugs.

✳✳ WARNING

To avoid getting water and debris into the spark plug holes, used compressed air and a shop rag to blow out each spark plug hole before plugs are removed.

9. Remove the spark plugs using a spark plug socket.

To install:

➡**Do NOT coat spark plug threads with anti-seize compound. If anti-seize compound is used and spark plugs are over-torqued, damage to the cylinder head threads may result.**

10. Gap the spark plugs to 0.045 inch (1.1mm).
11. Install spark plugs and tighten to 15 ft. lbs. (20 Nm).
12. Apply dielectric compound to the spark plug boots and ensure no corrosion is present.
13. Install the ignition module housing assembly with spark plug boots into position and tighten the ignition module-to-camshaft cover bolts to 89 inch lbs. (10 Nm).
14. Connect the EI module harness connector. Push in until a click is heard and pull back to confirm a positive engagement.
15. Position the outlet resonator/duct assembly into position.
16. Connect the PCV fresh air vent hose assembly.
17. Tighten the clamp at the throttle body assembly.

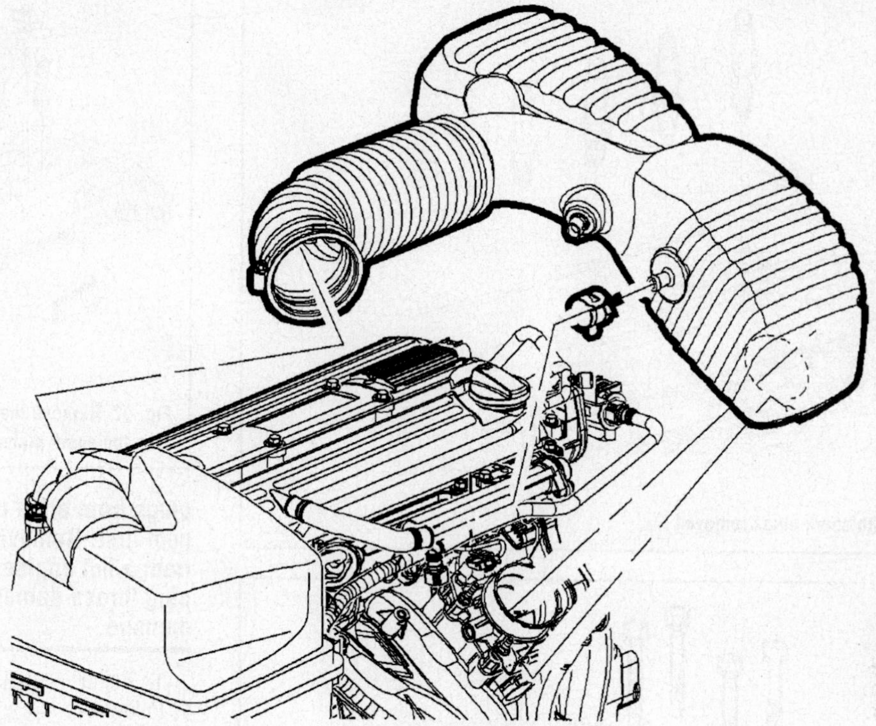

32107_SVUE_G0010

Fig. 93 Resonator/duct assembly removed

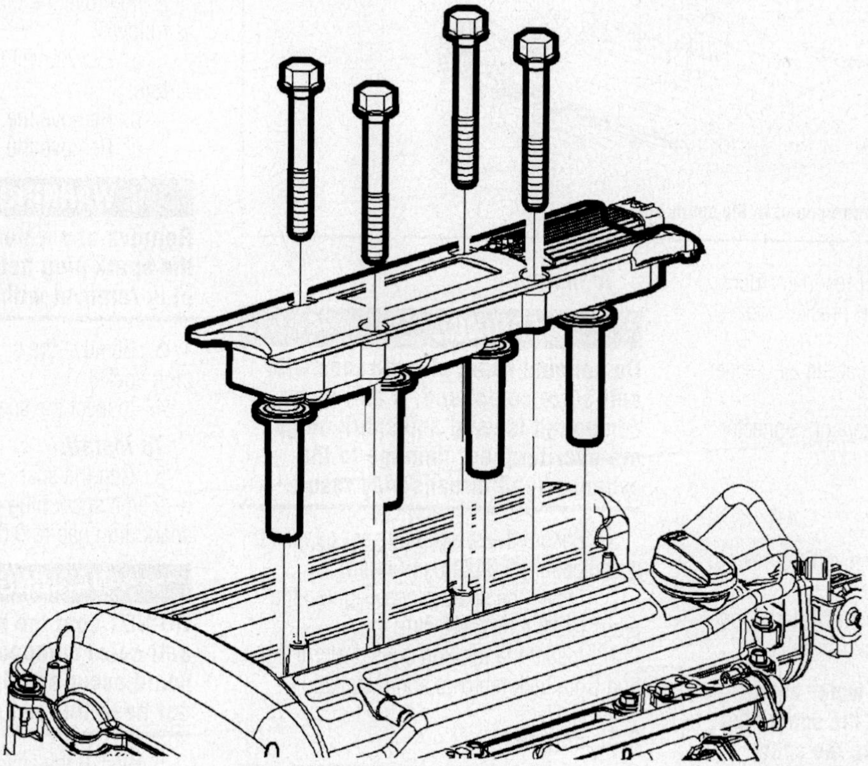

32107_SVUE_G0011

Fig. 94 Ignition Module attachment bolts

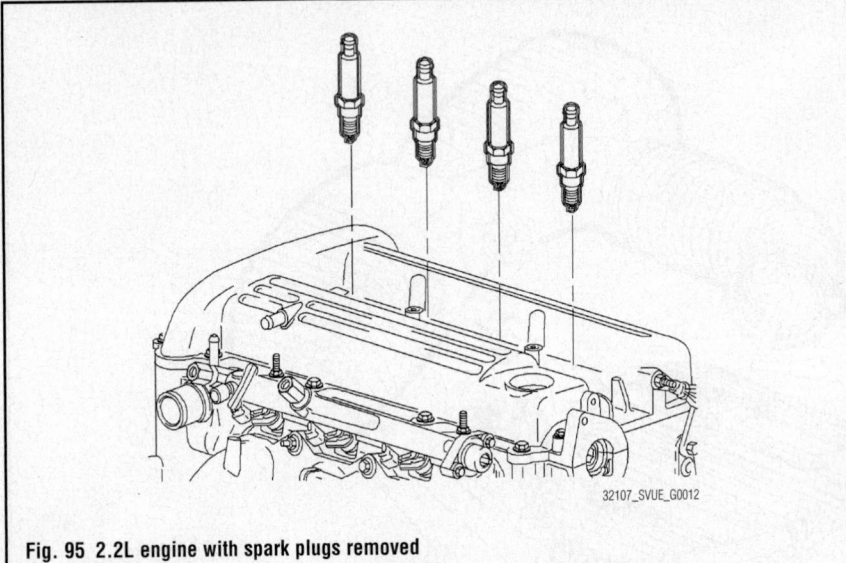

Fig. 95 2.2L engine with spark plugs removed

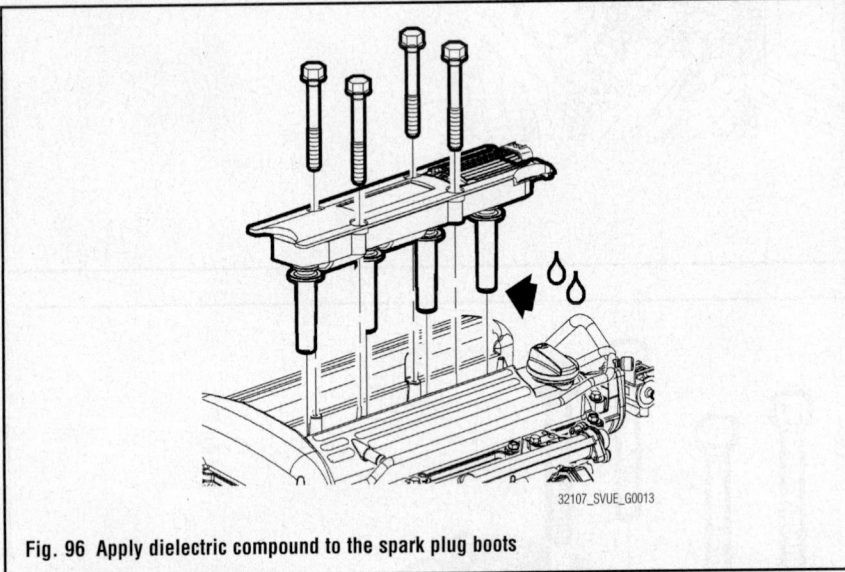

Fig. 96 Apply dielectric compound to the spark plug boots

18. Position the outlet resonator/duct assembly up with support bracket and install the push-pin.

19. Tighten the clamp at the air cleaner assembly.

20. Connect the IAT sensor connector.

2.4L Engine

See Figure 97.

1. Before servicing the vehicle, refer to the Precautions Section.

2. Remove ignition coils. Refer to Ignition Coil Pack removal and installation.

➡ Make sure that any water and/or debris is blown out of the spark plug holes prior to removing the spark plugs.

3. Remove the spark plugs using a ⅝ inch spark plug socket.

To install:

✲✲ WARNING

Do not coat spark plug threads with anti-seize compound. If anti-seize compound is used and spark plugs are over-torqued, damage to the cylinder head threads may result.

4. Ensure the spark plugs are gapped to specification: 0.042 in. (1.06mm).

5. Install the spark plugs. Tighten the plugs to 15 ft. lbs. (20 Nm).

6. Install the ignition coils. Refer to Ignition Coil Pack removal and installation.

3.5L Engine

✲✲ WARNING

This engine has aluminum cylinder heads. Do not remove the spark

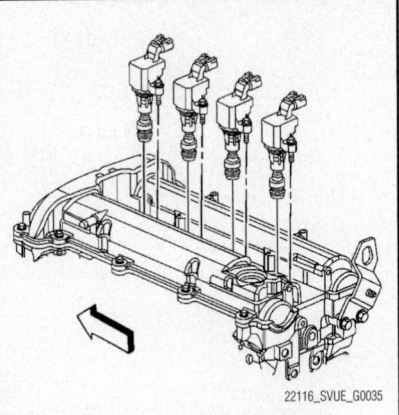

Fig. 97 Remove the ignition coils and then the spark plugs—2.4L engine

plugs from a hot engine, allow it to cool first. Removing the spark plugs from a hot engine may cause spark plug thread damage or cylinder head damage.

1. Remove the ignition coils on Bank 1 as follows:

    a. Remove the air cleaner outlet duct assembly.

    b. Disconnect the electrical connectors.

    c. Remove the engine coil bolts.

    d. Remove the engine coils.

2. Remove the ignition coils on Bank 2 as follows:

    a. Disconnect the electrical connectors.

    b. Remove the engine coil bolt.

    c. Remove the engine coils.

✲✲ WARNING

Remove any water and debris from the spark plug holes before spark plug removal with compressed air.

3. Remove the spark plugs with a spark plug socket.

4. Inspect the spark plugs.

To install:

5. Gap the spark plug, using a round wire type spark plug gap gauge. Adjust spark plug gap to 0.043 inch (1.1mm).

✲✲ WARNING

DO NOT coat the spark plugs with anti-seize compound. Over-tightening could occur and damage to the cylinder head threads may result.

6. Install the spark plugs with a spark plug socket. Tighten the spark plugs to 13 ft. lbs. (18 Nm).

7. Install the ignition coils.

ENGINE ELECTRICAL

STARTER

REMOVAL & INSTALLATION

2.2L Engine

See Figure 98.

1. Before servicing the vehicle, refer to the precautions section.
2. Remove or disconnect the following:
   • The negative battery cable
   • The starter electrical connections
   • The starter bolts
   • The starter assembly by pulling it toward the left side of the vehicle

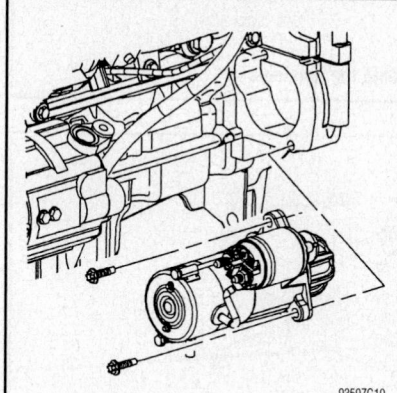

Fig. 98 Starter assembly removal–2.2L engine

To install:

3. Install or connect the following:
   • The starter to the flywheel housing and torque the bolts to 30 ft. lbs. (40 Nm)

• The starter electrical connectors and torque the solenoid ignition wire to 44 inch lbs. (5 Nm) and the positive battery cable to 89 inch lbs. (10 Nm)
• The negative battery cable

2.4L Engine

1. Before servicing the vehicle, refer to the precautions section.
2. Disconnect the negative battery cable.
3. Raise and support the vehicle.
4. Disconnect the engine wiring harness electrical connector from the alternator control module coolant pump.
5. Remove the alternator control module coolant pump bolt.
6. Remove the alternator control module coolant pump with the hoses attached from the oil pan.
7. Reposition and secure the alternator control module coolant pump with the hoses attached out of the way.
8. Disconnect the engine wiring harness electrical connector from the starter.
9. Remove the positive battery cable to starter motor nut.
10. Remove the positive battery cable lead from the starter motor.
11. Remove the starter motor bolts and starter.

To install:

12. Install the starter motor and bolts. Tighten to 39 ft. lbs. (53 Nm).
13. Install the positive battery cable lead to the starter motor.
14. Install the positive battery cable to starter motor nut.

15. Connect the engine wiring harness electrical connector to the starter.
16. Unfasten the alternator control module coolant pump.
17. Position the alternator control module coolant pump with the hoses attached to the oil pan. Ensure that the anti-rotation tab is inserted into the hole in the oil pan.
18. Install the alternator control module coolant pump bolt. Tighten to 16 ft. lbs. (22 Nm).
19. Connect the engine wiring harness electrical connector to the alternator control module coolant pump.
20. Lower the vehicle.
21. Connect the negative battery cable.

3.5L Engine

1. Before servicing the vehicle, refer to the precautions section.

➡**Record all pre-set radio stations.**

2. Disconnect the negative battery cable.
3. Remove starter electrical connections.
4. Remove the lower starter–to–transaxle bolt and Oxygen (O$_2$) sensor connector bracket.
5. Remove the upper starter–to–transaxle bolt.
6. Remove the starter.

To install:

7. Install the starter. Tighten the starter bolts to 33 ft. lbs. (44 Nm).
8. Install the starter electrical connections.
9. Connect the negative battery cable and reprogram the radio stations

ENGINE MECHANICAL

➡**Disconnecting the negative battery cable may interfere with the functions of the on board computer systems and may require the computer to undergo a relearning process, once the negative battery cable is reconnected.**

ACCESSORY DRIVE BELTS

ACCESSORY BELT ROUTING

See Figures 99 through 101.

INSPECTION

Inspect the drive belt for signs of glazing or cracking. A glazed belt will be perfectly

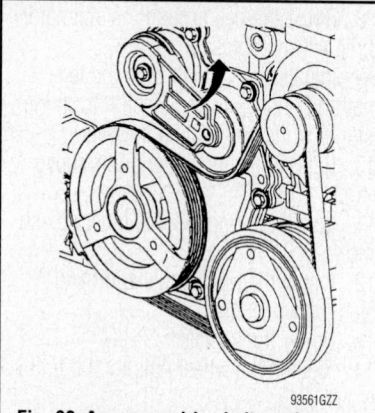

Fig. 99 Accessory drive belt routing—2.2L engine

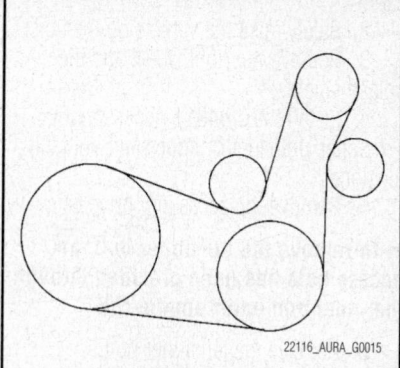

Fig. 100 Accessory drive routing—2.4L engine

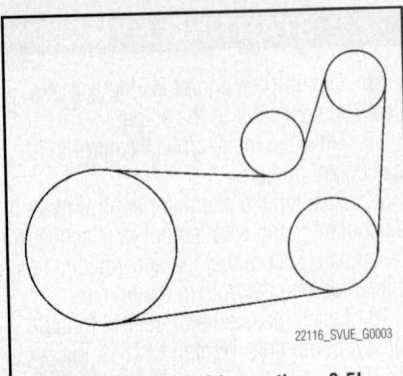

Fig. 101 Accessory drive routing—3.5L engine

smooth from slippage, while a good belt will have a slight texture of fabric visible. Cracks will usually start at the inner edge of the belt and run outward. All worn or damaged drive belts should be replaced immediately.

ADJUSTMENT

The accessory drive belt adjustment is maintained by an automatic tensioner.

REMOVAL & INSTALLATION

2.2L Engine

See Figures 102 and 103.

Before servicing any vehicle, please be sure to read the precautions section, which deals with personal safety, prevention of component damage, and important points to take into consideration when servicing a motor vehicle.

✳✳ CAUTION

The internal parts of the tensioner assembly are not serviceable. To avoid injury, do not disassemble the tensioner.

1. Disconnect the negative battery cable.
2. Safely raise the vehicle on the hoist.
3. Remove the right wheel and the splash shield.
4. Install the J 44811 Accessory Belt Tensioner Unloader or equivalent onto the tensioner.
5. Remove the accessory drive belt.

➡ **To remove the tensioner bolt, an access hole has been provided through the inner and outer engine rail.**

6. Remove the tensioner bolt.

To install:

7. Install the tensioner assembly and bolt (if removed). Tighten the drive belt tensioner bolt to 33 ft. lbs. (45 Nm).

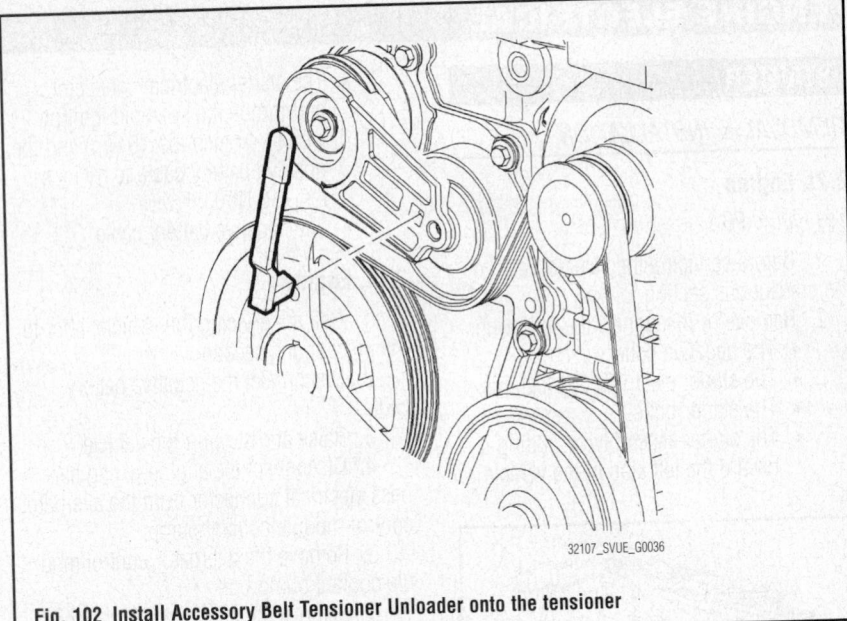

Fig. 102 Install Accessory Belt Tensioner Unloader onto the tensioner

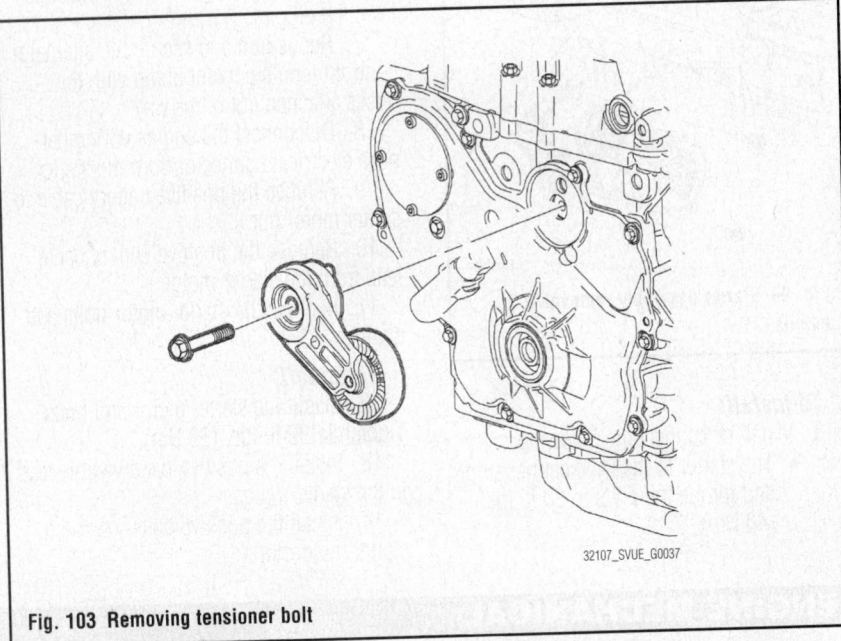

Fig. 103 Removing tensioner bolt

8. Route the belt around the alternator and the A/C compressor.
9. Install the J 44811 onto the tensioner and unload spring tension from the tensioner while positioning the belt.
10. Release the tensioner and remove the tool.
11. Install the right engine inner splash shield.
12. Install the right wheel and hand tighten the wheel nuts.
13. Lower the vehicle.
14. Tighten the wheel nuts to 100 ft. lbs. (136 Nm).
15. Connect the negative battery cable
16. Tighten the battery terminal bolt to 13 ft. lbs. (17 Nm).

2.4L Engine

Before servicing any vehicle, please be sure to read the precautions section, which deals with personal safety, prevention of component damage, and important points to take into consideration when servicing a motor vehicle.

1. Remove the air cleaner assembly.
2. Install a hydraulic belt tensioner compressor such as EN-48079 to the drive belt tensioner spring.
3. Compress the drive belt tensioner spring fully using the hydraulic belt tensioner compressor.
4. Install a box wrench to the drive belt tensioner) and rotate the tensioner clock-

wise in order to release the tension from the drive belt.

5. With the tensioner released, remove the drive belt from under the middle idler pulley.

6. Slowly rotate the tensioner clockwise in order to allow the tensioner to rest.

7. Remove the drive belt from the vehicle.

To install:

8. Install and position the drive belt around all of the pulleys except for the middle idler pulley.

9. Install a box wrench to the drive belt tensioner and rotate the tensioner counterclockwise in order to release the tensioner.

10. Install the drive belt under the middle idler pulley.

11. Slowly rotate the tensioner counterclockwise in order to allow the tensioner to rest against the drive belt.

12. Loosen the forcing bolt on the hydraulic belt tensioner compressor and remove from the drive belt tensioner spring.

13. Ensure that the drive belt tensioner idler is fully seated against the drive belt.

14. Install the air cleaner assembly.

3.5L Engine

See Figure 104.

Before servicing any vehicle, please be sure to read the precautions section, which deals with personal safety, prevention of component damage, and important points to take into consideration when servicing a motor vehicle.

1. Remove the air cleaner assembly:

    a. Loosen the clamp at the air cleaner assembly.

    b. Disconnect the Intake Air Temperature (IAT) 1 sensor connector

    c. Remove the air cleaner assembly top cover and filter element

    d. Remove the air cleaner assembly bolt.

    e. Remove the air cleaner assembly.

2. Loosen the drive belt tensioner by rotating the tensioner pulley clockwise while sliding the accessory drive belt off the tensioner.

3. Remove the accessory drive belt.

4. Clean and inspect the accessory drive belt surfaces.

To install:

5. Route the belt around all pulleys, except the tensioner.

➡**Ensure that the drive belt is aligned into the proper grooves on the drive pulley.**

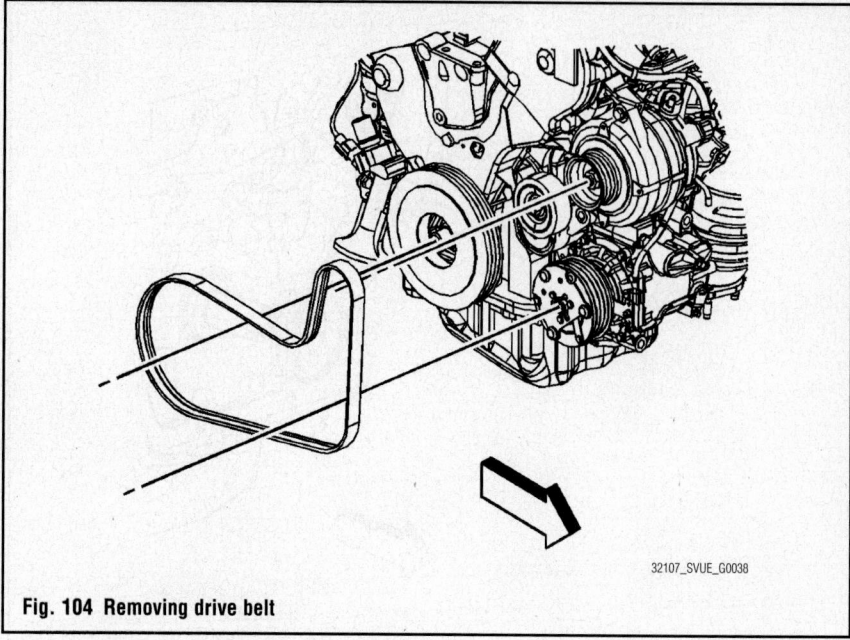

Fig. 104 Removing drive belt

6. Rotate the tensioner pulley clockwise and install the drive belt .

7. Install the air cleaner assembly:

    a. Install the air cleaner assembly into position, aligning locking pins into the front panel.

    b. Install the air cleaner attachment bolt and tighten to 89 inch lbs.(10 Nm).

    c. Install the filter element and air cleaner assembly top cover.

    d. Tighten the clamp at the air cleaner assembly to 35 inch lbs. (4 Nm).

    e. Connect the IAT 1 sensor connector.

BALANCE SHAFT

REMOVAL & INSTALLATION

2.2L Engine

See Figures 105 through 107.

Before servicing any vehicle, please be sure to read the precautions section, which deals with personal safety, prevention of component damage, and important points to take into consideration when servicing a motor vehicle.

1. Remove the balance shaft bearing carrier bolts.

❋❋ WARNING

It is possible to install the intake side balance shaft into the exhaust side and vice versa. Please use care not to install the balance shafts into the wrong bores. Engine vibration will result.

➡**Do not remove the bolt holding the sprocket.**

2. Remove the balance shaft assemblies.

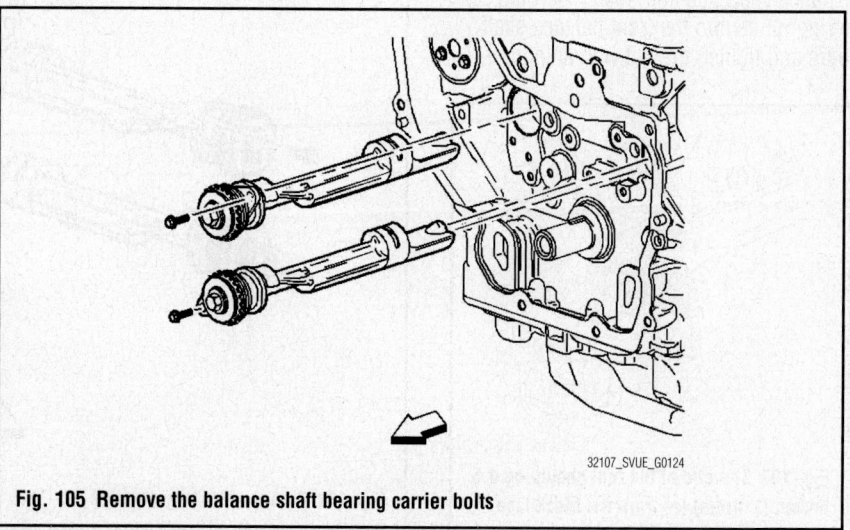

Fig. 105 Remove the balance shaft bearing carrier bolts

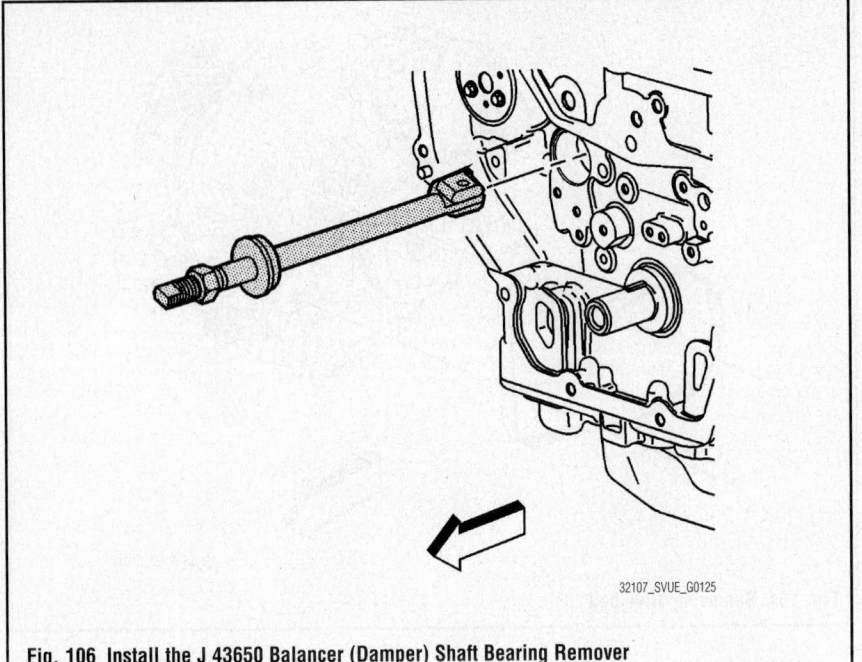

Fig. 106 Install the J 43650 Balancer (Damper) Shaft Bearing Remover

To install:

> ⁂ **WARNING**
>
> **Proper centering of the tool is required on the balance shaft bushing. If the tool is not properly centered then damage to the bearing bore and block will occur.**

3. Install the J 43650 Balancer (Damper) Shaft Bearing Remover or equivalent into the balance shaft hole. Insert the tool with the foot parallel to the shaft.

4. When the J 43650 is inserted in the block turn the J 43650 so that the foot becomes perpendicular to the shaft.

5. Center the foot of the J 43650 on the balance shaft bushing.

6. Once the J 43650 is centered on the balance shaft bushing, then insert the centering guide into the front balance shaft bore and tighten the nut with an appropri-ate wrench. When the J 43650 is properly installed, before removing the bushing, the end of the tool should be 4.6 inch (116mm) (a) from the block face. If the J 43650 is less than approximately 4.5 inches (114mm) (a), recheck the tool alignment.

7. Tighten the nut on the J 43650 until the tension releases. When the tension releases, remove the J 43650 and the balance shaft bushing.

2.4L Engine

See Figures 108 through 110.

1. Before servicing the vehicle, refer to the Precautions Section.

2. Remove the balance shaft bearing carrier bolts.

> ⁂ **WARNING**
>
> **It is possible to install the intake side balance shaft into the exhaust side and vice versa. Please use care not to install the balance shafts into the wrong bores. Engine vibration will result. Do not remove the bolt holding the sprocket.**

3. Remove the balance shaft assemblies.

> ⁂ **WARNING**
>
> **Proper centering of the tool is required on the balance shaft bushing. If the tool is not properly centered, then damage to the bearing bore and block will occur.**

4. Install tool J 43650 into the balance shaft hole. Insert the tool with the foot parallel to the shaft.

5. When the J 43650 is inserted in the block turn the tool so that the foot becomes perpendicular to the shaft.

6. Center the foot of the tool on the balance shaft bushing.

7. Once the tool is centered on the balance shaft bushing, then insert the centering guide into the front balance shaft bore and tighten the nut with an appropriate wrench. When the tool is properly installed, before removing the bushing, the end of the tool should be 4.6 inches (116mm) (a) from the

Fig. 107 The end of the tool should be 4.5 inches (114mm) (a) from the block face

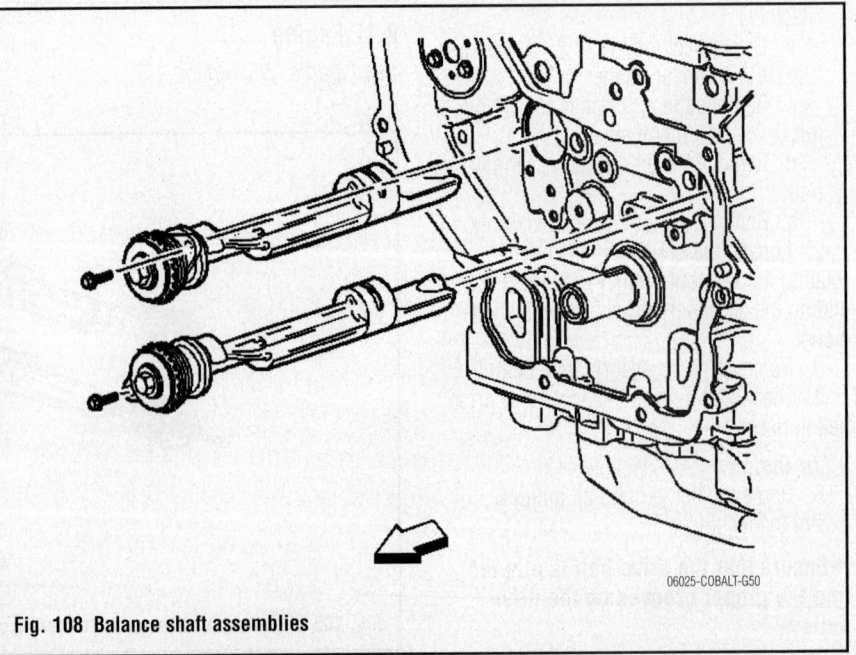

Fig. 108 Balance shaft assemblies

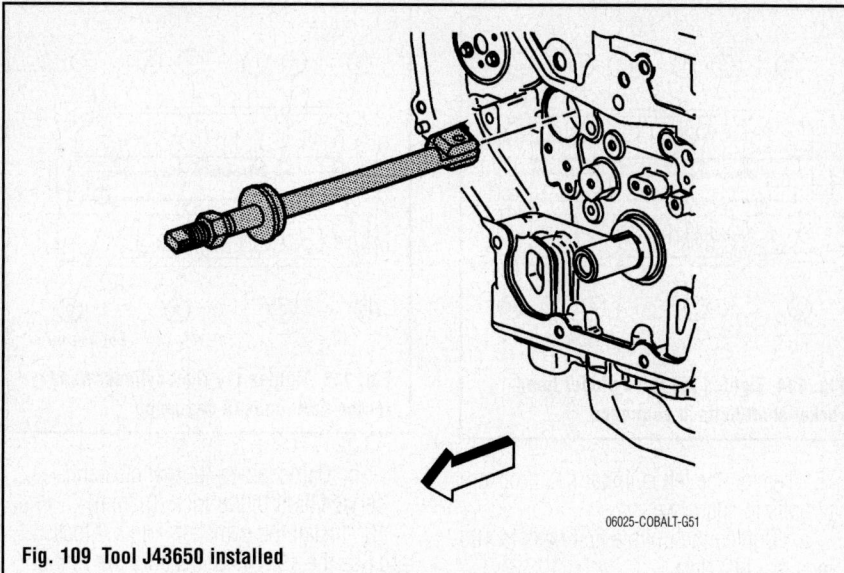

Fig. 109 Tool J43650 installed

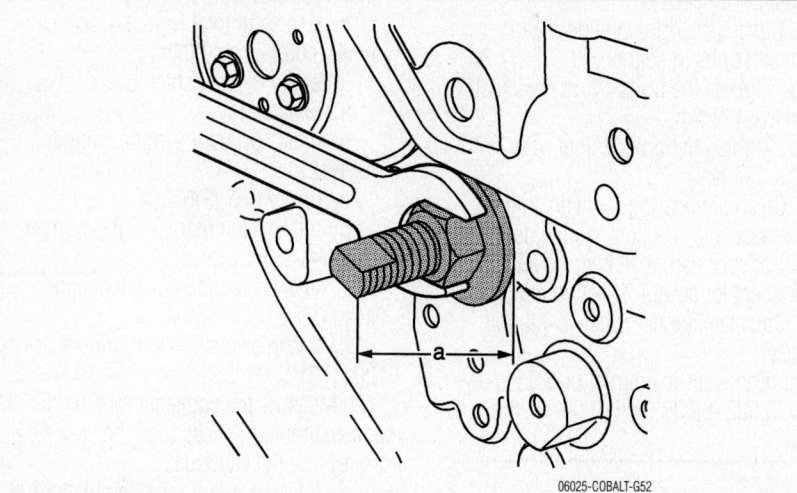

Fig. 110 When the J 43650 is inserted in the block turn the tool so that the foot becomes perpendicular to the shaft

block face. If the tool is less than approximately 4.5 inches (114mm) (a), recheck the tool alignment.

8. Tighten the nut on the tool until the tension releases. When the tension releases, remove the tool and the balance shaft bushing.

To install:

9. Install the balance shaft bushing using the J 43650.

10. Seat the balance shaft bushing into the bore using the J 43650 and a wrench.

11. When the J 43650 is fully seated in the engine block, remove it with a wrench.

✳✳ WARNING

If the balance shafts are not properly timed to the engine, the engine may vibrate or make noise.

12. Install the balance shaft assemblies to the engine using the following steps:

a. Place the number one piston at Top Dead Center (TDC).

b. Lubricate the balance shaft lobes with engine oil.

c. Install the balance shafts into their bores.

d. Install the balance shaft retaining bolts. Tighten the balance shaft retaining bolts to 89 inch lbs. (10 Nm).

CAMSHAFT AND VALVE LIFTERS

INSPECTION

2.2L Engine

1. Inspect the camshaft journals and lobes for wear or scoring.

2. Inspect the camshaft sprocket alignment notch for damage.

3. Inspect the camshaft cover for damage or loose oil control baffles.

4. Clean the camshaft cover.

5. Wash the camshaft in solvent.

6. Oil the camshaft.

7. Inspect the camshaft cover for cracks or other signs of damage.

2.4L Engine

See Figure 111.

1. Clean the camshaft in solvent.

2. Dry the camshaft with compressed air.

3. Inspect the camshaft for the following conditions:

a. Worn, scored, or damaged bearing journals

b. Worn camshaft lobes

c. Damaged sprocket pin

4. Measure the camshaft journals with a micrometer to be sure they are within specification.

5. Measure for a bent camshaft or excessive camshaft runout using J 7872, Magnetic Base Dial Indicator.

6. Mount the camshaft in V-blocks between centers.

7. Use the J 7872 in order to measure for a bent camshaft.

8. Replace the camshaft if runout exceeds specifications.

9. Inspect the camshaft bearings and bearing cap surfaces for the following:

a. Wear

b. Scoring

c. Overheating from lack of lubrication

10. Inspect the bearing clearances with gauging plastic.

11. Inspect the camshaft for excessive end play.

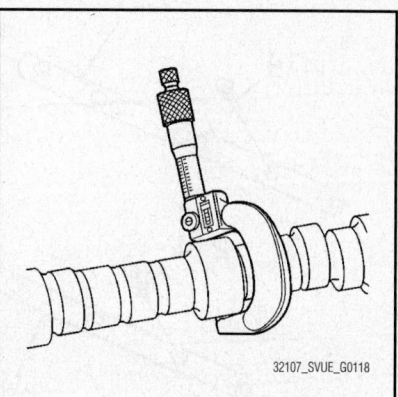

Fig. 111 Measure the camshaft journals with a micrometer

3.5L Engine

See Figures 112 through 121.

1. Clean the camshaft and inspect for pitted, scored or excessively worn lobes.

2. Measure the diameter of each bearing journal.

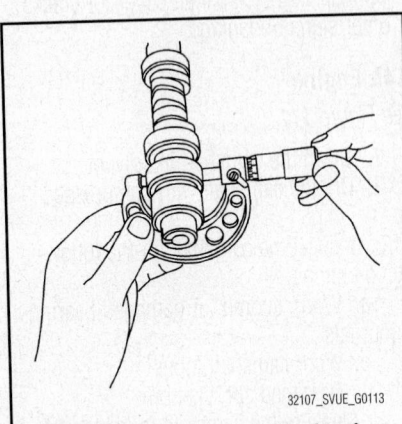

Fig. 112 Measure the diameter of each bearing journal

➡ **In order to properly measure the camshaft journal bores, the rocker arm shafts must be bolted to the cylinder heads.**

3. Remove the rocker arms (215, 218) and springs (219) from the shafts (220, 221).

4. Lubricate the bolt threads and flanges with clean engine oil.

5. Install the rocker arm shafts and bolts to the cylinder heads.

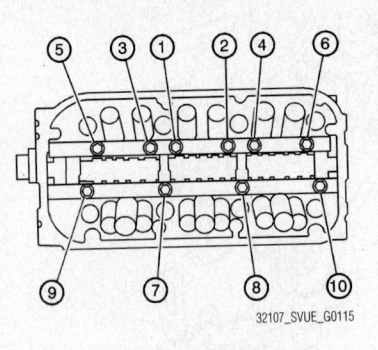

Fig. 114 Tighten the left cylinder head rocker shaft bolts in sequence

6. Tighten the left cylinder head rocker shaft bolts in sequence:

   a. Tighten the bolts a first pass to 106 inch lbs. (12 Nm).

   b. Tighten the bolts a final pass to 17 ft. lbs. (24 Nm).

7. Tighten the right cylinder head rocker shaft bolts in sequence:

   a. Tighten the bolts a first pass to 106 inch lbs. (12 Nm).

   b. Tighten the bolts a final pass to 17 ft. lbs. (24 Nm).

8. Clean the bearing surfaces in the cylinder head and measure the inside diameter (ID) of each camshaft bearing surface. Also, inspect for an out-of-round condition.

9. Calculate the camshaft-to-journal clearance:

   a. Camshaft-to-journal clearance—new: 0.002–0.008 inch (0.05–0.2mm)

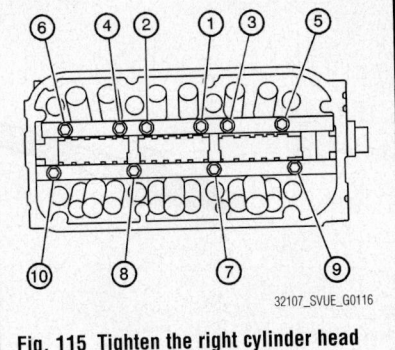

Fig. 115 Tighten the right cylinder head rocker shaft bolts in sequence

   b. Camshaft-to-journal clearance—service limit 0.008 inch (0.2mm)

10. Install the camshaft into V-blocks and use the J 7872 to measure the runout:

   a. Camshaft total runout—new: 0.001 inch (0.03mm)

   b. Camshaft total runout—service limit: 0.002 inch (0.04mm)

11. Identify the camshaft lobes:

   a. Exhaust (1)

   b. Intake primary—right cylinder head (2)

   c. Intake mid (3)

   d. Intake secondary—right cylinder head (4)

   e. Intake secondary—left cylinder head (5)

   f. Intake primary—left cylinder head (6)

12. Measure the camshaft lobe height. If the measurement is less than the specification, replace the camshaft.

   a. Intake primary lobe height: 1.3796 inch (35.041mm)

   b. Intake mid lobe height: 1.4348 inch (36.445mm)

   c. Intake secondary lobe height: 1.3891 inch (35.284mm)

   d. Exhaust lobe height: 1.4302 inch (36.326mm)

13. To check camshaft endplay:

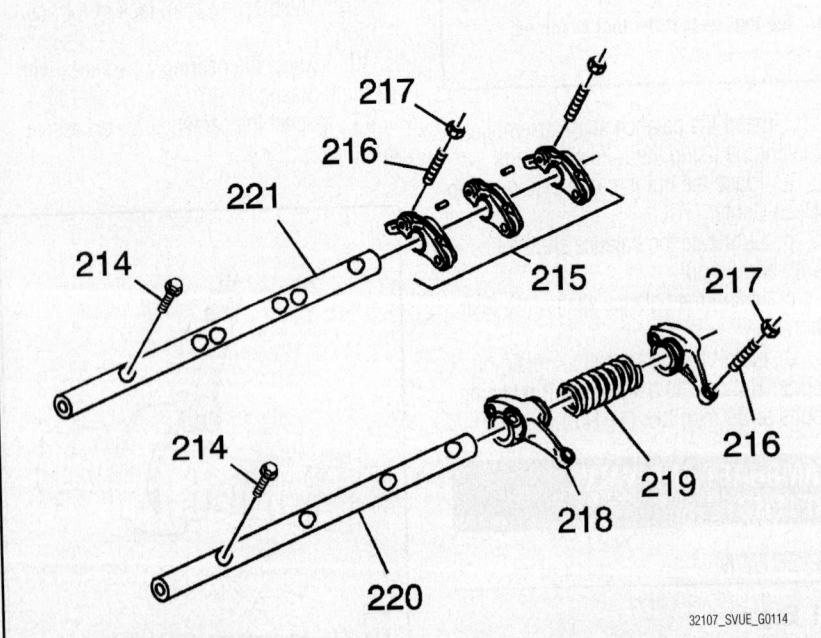

Fig. 113 Remove the rocker arms (215, 218) and springs (219) from the shafts (220, 221)

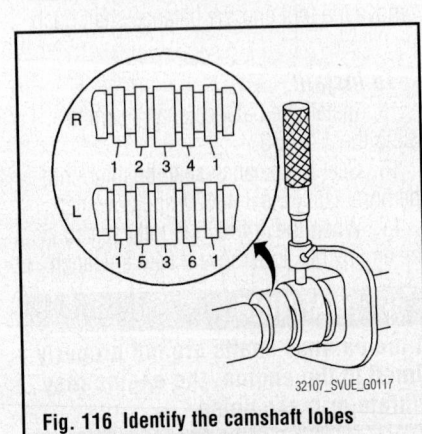

Fig. 116 Identify the camshaft lobes

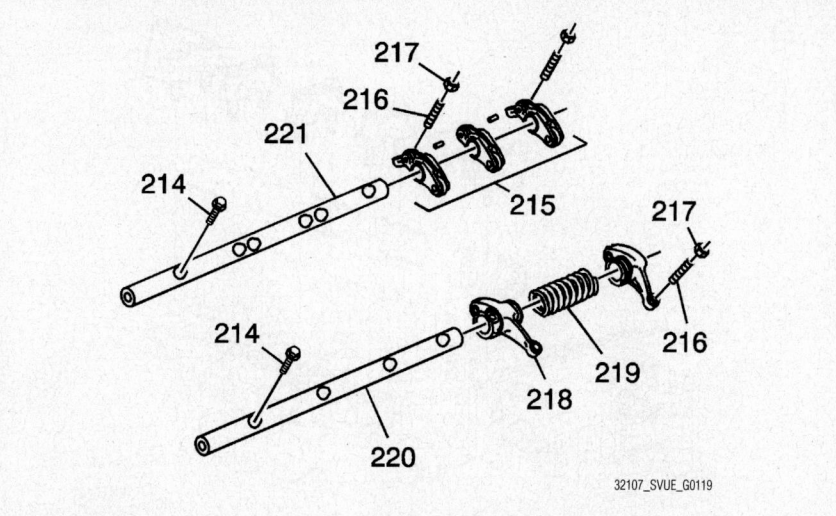

Fig. 117 Remove the rocker arms (215 and 218) and springs (219) from the shafts (220 and 221)

➡**In order to properly measure camshaft end play, the rocker arm shafts must be bolted to the cylinder heads.**

e. Remove the rocker arms (215 and 218) and springs (219) from the shafts (220 and 221).

f. Lubricate the bolt (214) threads and flanges with clean engine oil.

g. Install the rocker arm shafts (220, 221) and bolts (214) to the cylinder heads.

h. Tighten the left cylinder head rocker shaft bolts in sequence:

- Tighten the bolts a first pass to 106 inch lbs. (12 Nm)
- Tighten the bolts a final pass to 17 ft. lbs (24 Nm)

i. Tighten the right cylinder head rocker shaft bolts in sequence:

- Tighten the bolts a first pass to 106 inch lbs (12 Nm)
- Tighten the bolts a final pass to 17 ft. lbs. (24 Nm)

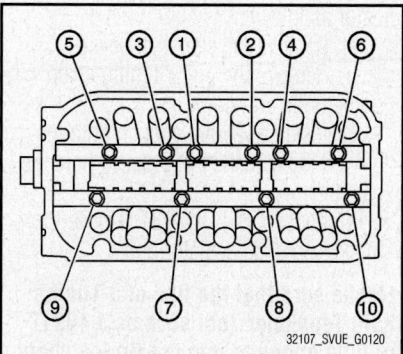

Fig. 118 Tighten the left cylinder head rocker shaft bolts in sequence

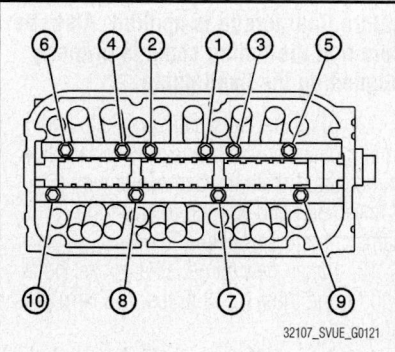

Fig. 119 Tighten the right cylinder head rocker shaft bolts in sequence

j. Install the camshafts (209), caps (211), and bolts (212).

k. Tighten the bolts to 16 ft. lbs. (22 Nm).

l. Seat the camshaft by pushing it toward the rear of the cylinder head.

m. Use the SA9179NE Dial Indicator in order to measure the end play. Zero the dial indicator against the end of the camshaft. Push the camshaft forward and rearward and measure the end play:

- Camshaft end play—new: 0.05–0.2 mm (0.002–0.008 in)
- Camshaft end play—service limit: 0.2 mm (0.008 in)

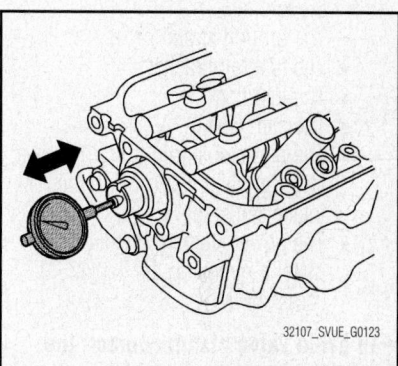

Fig. 121 Use the SA9179NE Dial Indicator in order to measure the end play

REMOVAL & INSTALLATION

2.2L Engine

See Figures 122 and 123.

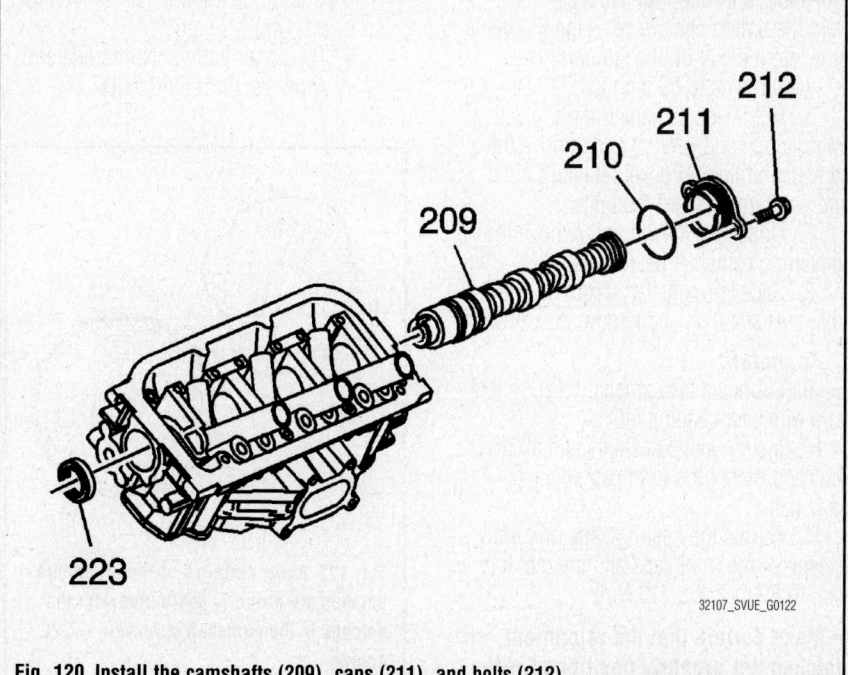

Fig. 120 Install the camshafts (209), caps (211), and bolts (212)

➡Be very careful when working around the camshaft sprockets and timing chain cover during this procedure. If a bolt or washer is accidentally dropped between the front cover and engine assembly, the cover will have to be removed for retrieval.

1. Before servicing the vehicle, refer to the Precautions Section.
2. Relieve the fuel system pressure.
3. Remove or disconnect the following:
   - The negative battery cable
   - The air cleaner assembly
   - The ignition coil
   - The coolant degas hose clips from the fuel rail
   - The ground strap
   - The fuel rail bracket
   - The fuel line
   - The cam cover
   - The purge solenoid from the power steering plate, if removing the intake camshaft
   - The power steering block off the plate, if removing the intake camshaft

➡To avoid valve piston contact, the No. 1 cylinder piston must be positioned at 60 degrees Before Top Dead Center (BTDC). The pistons are properly aligned when the diamond shaped hole on the intake camshaft sprocket is located at 12 o'clock.

4. Remove the upper timing chain guide and front camshaft caps.
5. Install a camshaft sprocket holding tool J43655 through the sprocket holes from the timing chain side. Align the guide pins into the slot on the support head. Torque the pins to 89 inch lbs. (10 Nm).
6. Hold each camshaft in place with a 24mm open end wrench and remove the camshaft timing sprocket retaining bolts and washers. Discard the bolts.
7. Uniformly loosen and remove the remaining camshaft bearing caps.
8. Slide the camshaft sprockets away from the camshafts and remove the camshaft.

To install:

9. Lubricate the camshaft bearing journals with clean engine oil.
10. Install both camshafts and all bearing caps except the front cap on each camshaft.
11. Torque the bearing caps uniformly, except for the front caps and the rear intake cap, to 89 inch lbs. (10 Nm).

➡Make certain that the alignment notches are properly positioned with

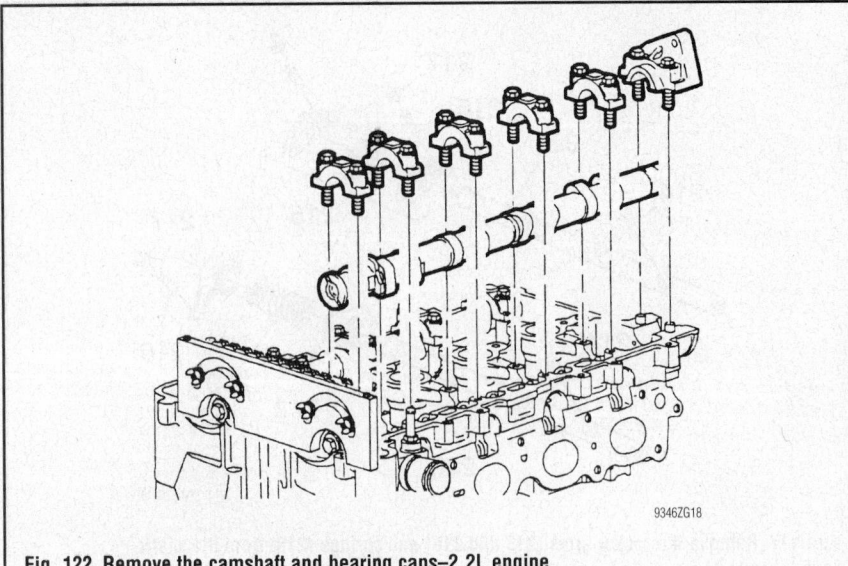

Fig. 122 Remove the camshaft and bearing caps–2.2L engine

the notches in the camshaft sprockets before final torque is applied. Also, be sure that the timing chain is properly aligned on the fixed guide.

12. Slide the camshaft sprockets and timing chain on the guide pins toward the camshafts. Rotate the camshafts with a 24mm open end wrench to align the camshaft and sprocket.
13. Install new camshaft sprocket bolts and torque them to 63 ft. lbs. (85 Nm) plus 30°.
14. Remove the camshaft sprocket holding tool.
15. Install or connect the following:
   - The front camshaft bearing caps and torque the bolts to 89 inch lbs. (10 Nm)
   - The upper timing chain guide and apply Loctite® to the bolts

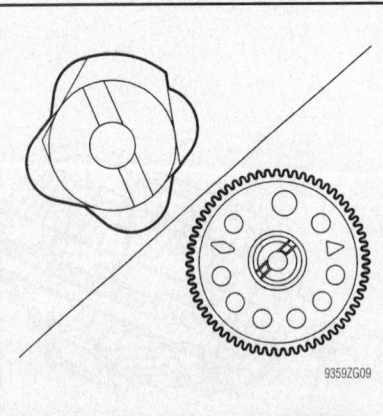

Fig. 123 Make certain that the alignment notches are properly positioned with the notches in the camshaft sprockets—2.2L engine

- The rear intake camshaft bearing cap and torque the bolts 19 ft. lbs. (25 Nm)
- The power steering block off plate and torque the bolts to 19 ft. lbs. (25 Nm)
- The cam cover
- The fuel line and tighten the fitting to 89 inch lbs. (10 Nm)
- The fuel line bracket and tighten to 89 inch lbs. (10 Nm)
- The ground strap
- The coolant degas hose
- The ignition coil
- The air cleaner assembly
- The negative battery cable

16. Start the vehicle and check for leaks, repair if necessary.

2.4L Engine

Intake

See Figures 124 through 126.

1. Before servicing the vehicle, refer to the Precautions Section.
2. Remove the intake camshaft position actuator as follows:
   a. Remove the camshaft cover.
   b. Remove the upper timing chain guide bolts and guide.
   c. Install a 24 mm wrench onto the hex on the camshaft in order to hold the camshaft.
   d. Loosen, but DO NOT remove the intake camshaft actuator bolt.

➡Make sure that the tips of a Timing Chain Tensioner Tool such as J 44217 are fully engaged into the timing chain.

   e. Install one of the tools from a Timing Chain Tensioner Tool such as

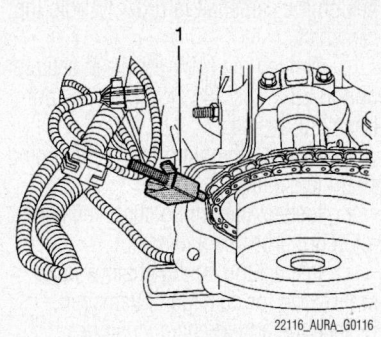

Fig. 124 Make sure that the tips of a Timing Chain Tensioner Tool such as J 44217 are fully engaged into the timing chain—2.4L engine

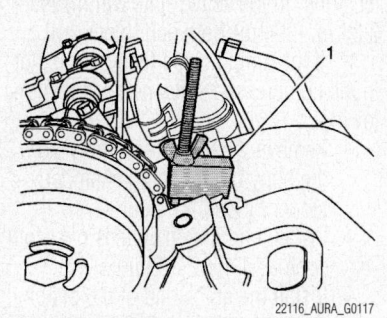

Fig. 125 Install the tools (1) from a Timing Chain Tensioner Tool such as J 44217 to the exhaust camshaft side of the timing chain assembly in order to retain the timing chain—2.4L engine

J 44217 to the exhaust camshaft side of the timing chain assembly in order to retain the timing chain. Firmly tighten the nuts.

→**Ensure that the tips from a Timing Chain Tensioner Tool such as J 44217 are fully engaged into the timing chain.**

f. Install one of the tools from a Timing Chain Tensioner Tool such as J 44217 to the intake camshaft side of the timing chain assembly in order to retain the timing chain. Firmly tighten the nuts.

g. Ensure that the timing chain and the camshaft position actuators are marked for proper assembly.

h. Mark the intake and exhaust camshaft actuators and the respective locations on the timing chain.

i. Install a 24 mm wrench onto the hex on the camshaft in order to hold the camshaft.

j. Remove and discard the intake camshaft actuator bolt.

k. Remove the intake camshaft actuator from the camshaft while also removing the actuator from the timing chain.

→**Remove each bolt on each cap one turn at a time until there is no spring tension pushing on the camshaft.**

3. Mark the bearing caps to ensure they are installed in the original position.
4. Remove the bearing cap bolts.
5. Remove the bearing caps.
6. Remove the intake camshaft.

→**Keep all of the roller followers and hydraulic adjusters in order so that they can be reinstalled in their respective locations.**

7. Remove the camshaft roller followers.
8. Remove the hydraulic element lash adjusters.

To install:

9. Install the hydraulic element lash adjusters into their bores in the cylinder head.
10. Lubricate the hydraulic lash adjusters with GM Molylube®.
11. Lubricate the valve tips with GM Molylube®.

→**Used roller followers MUST be returned to their original position on the camshaft. If the camshaft is being replaced, the roller followers actuated by the camshaft must also be replaced.**

12. Position the camshaft roller followers on the tip of the valve stem and on the lash adjuster. Lubricate the roller followers with GM Molylube®.
13. Install the intake camshaft and lubricate with GM Molylube®.
14. Install the camshaft bearing caps. Hand tighten the cap bolts.
15. Tighten the bearing cap bolts in increments of 3 turns until they are seated to 89 in. lbs. (10 Nm).
16. Install the intake camshaft position actuator as follows:

→**Ensure that the alignment mark made previously on the exhaust camshaft actuator is still aligned properly with the mark on the timing chain.**

a. Install the timing chain onto the intake camshaft actuator.
b. Align the intake camshaft actuator alignment mark made previously with the timing chain mark and install the actuator onto the camshaft.
c. Install a NEW intake camshaft actuator bolt until snug.

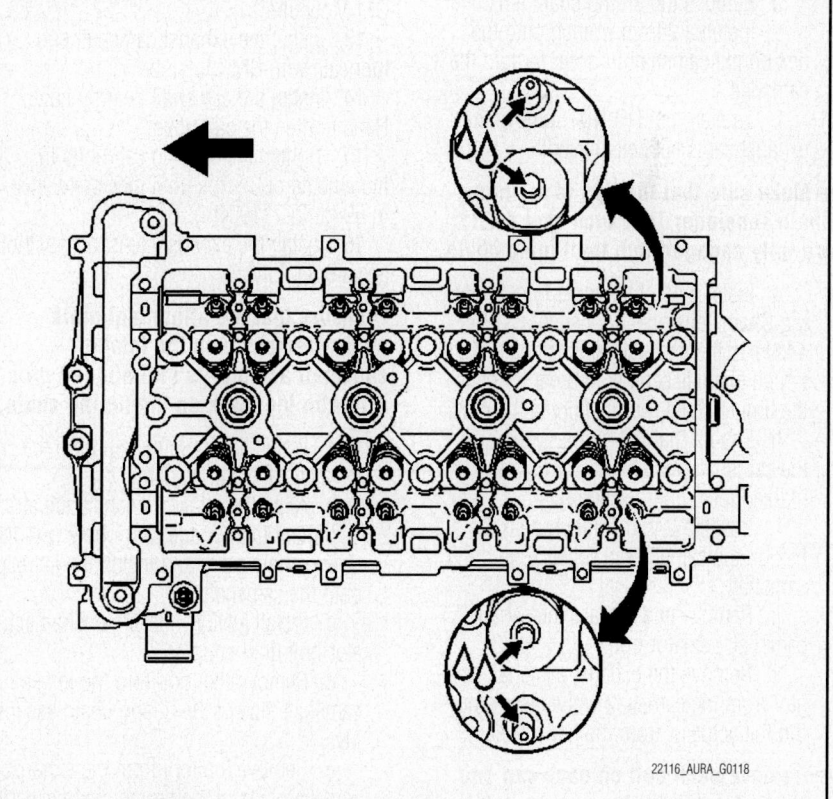

Fig. 126 Lubricate the hydraulic lash adjusters—2.4L engine

d. Remove the tool from the intake camshaft side of the timing chain assembly.

e. Remove the tool from the exhaust camshaft side of the timing chain assembly.

f. Install a 24 mm wrench onto the hex on the camshaft in order to hold the camshaft.

g. Tighten the NEW camshaft actuator bolt to 63 ft. lbs. (85 Nm) plus 30°.

h. Install the upper timing chain guide and bolts. Tighten the bolts to 89 in. lbs. (10 Nm).

i. Install the camshaft cover.

Exhaust

See Figures 124 through 127.

1. Before servicing the vehicle, refer to the Precautions Section.

2. Remove the exhaust camshaft position actuator as follows:

a. Remove the camshaft cover.

➡**Ensure that the timing chain and the camshaft position actuators are marked for proper assembly.**

b. Mark the intake and exhaust camshaft actuators and the respective locations on the timing chain.

c. Remove the upper timing chain guide bolts and guide.

d. Remove the timing chain tensioner.

e. Install a 24mm wrench onto the hex on the camshaft in order to hold the camshaft.

f. Loosen, but DO NOT remove the exhaust camshaft actuator bolt.

➡**Make sure that the tips of a Timing Chain Tensioner Tool such as J 44217 are fully engaged into the timing chain.**

g. Install one of the tools from a Timing Chain Tensioner Tool such as J 44217 to the exhaust camshaft side of the timing chain assembly in order to retain the timing chain. Firmly tighten the nuts.

h. Ensure that the timing chain and the camshaft position actuators are marked for proper assembly.

i. Install a 24mm wrench onto the hex on the camshaft in order to hold the camshaft.

j. Remove and discard the exhaust camshaft actuator bolt.

k. Remove the exhaust camshaft actuator from the camshaft while also removing the actuator from the timing chain.

➡**Remove each bolt on each cap one turn at a time until there is no spring tension pushing on the camshaft.**

3. Mark the bearing caps to ensure they are installed in the original position.

4. Remove the bearing cap bolts.

5. Remove the bearing caps.

6. Remove the exhaust camshaft.

➡**Keep all of the roller followers and hydraulic adjusters in order so that they can be reinstalled in their respective locations.**

7. Remove the camshaft roller followers.

8. Remove the hydraulic element lash adjusters.

To install:

9. Install the hydraulic element lash adjusters into their bores in the cylinder head.

10. Lubricate the hydraulic lash adjusters with GM Molylube®.

11. Lubricate the valve tips with GM Molylube®.

➡**Used roller followers MUST be returned to their original position on the camshaft. If the camshaft is being replaced, the roller followers actuated by the camshaft must also be replaced.**

12. Position the camshaft roller followers on the tip of the valve stem and on the lash adjuster. Lubricate the roller followers with GM Molylube®.

13. Install the exhaust camshaft and lubricate with GM Molylube®.

14. Install the camshaft bearing caps. Hand tighten the cap bolts.

15. Tighten the bearing cap bolts in increments of 3 turns until they are seated to 89 in. lbs. (10 Nm).

16. Install the exhaust camshaft position actuator as follows:

➡**Ensure that the alignment mark made previously on the intake camshaft actuator is still aligned properly with the mark on the timing chain.**

a. Install the timing chain onto the exhaust camshaft actuator.

b. Align the intake camshaft actuator alignment mark made previously with the timing chain mark and install the actuator onto the camshaft.

c. Install a NEW intake camshaft actuator bolt until snug.

d. Remove the tool from the intake camshaft side of the timing chain assembly.

e. Remove the tool from the exhaust camshaft side of the timing chain assembly.

f. Install a 24 mm wrench onto the hex on the camshaft in order to hold the camshaft.

g. Tighten the NEW camshaft actuator bolt to 63 ft. lbs. (85 Nm) plus an additional 30 degrees.

h. Remove the old oil from the timing chain tensioner.

i. Inspect the timing chain tensioner for scoring or free movement.

j. Inspect the timing chain washer and O-ring for damage. If damaged, replace the timing chain tensioner.

k. Measure the timing chain tensioner assembly from end to end. A NEW tensioner should be supplied in the fully compressed non-active state. A tensioner in the compressed state will measure 2.83 in. (72mm) from end to end (a). A tensioner in the active state will measure 3.35 in. (85mm) from end to end (a).

l. If the timing chain tensioner is not in the compressed state, perform the following:

- Remove the piston assembly from the body of the timing chain tensioner by pulling it out
- Install a timing chain tensioner tool such as J 45027-2 into a vise
- Install the notch end of the piston assembly into the tool
- Using the tool, turn the ratchet cylinder into the piston

m. Inspect the bore of the tensioner body for dirt, debris, and damage. If any damage appears, replace the tensioner. Clean dirt or debris with a lint free cloth.

n. Install the compressed piston assembly back into the timing chain tensioner body until the assembly stops at the bottom of the bore. Do not compress the piston assembly against the bottom of the bore. If the piston assembly is compressed against the bottom of the bore, the assembly will activate the tensioner, which will then need to be reset again.

o. At the point the tension should measure approximately 2.83 in. (72mm) from end to end. If the tensioner does not measure 2.83 in. (72mm) repeat the steps using the timing chain tensioner tool.

p. Ensure that all dirt and debris is removed from the timing chain tensioner threaded hole in the cylinder head.

Install the timing chain tensioner and tighten to 66 ft. lbs. (75 Nm).

q. The timing chain tensioner is released by compressing the tensioner 0.079 in. (2mm) which will release the locking mechanism in the ratchet. To release the timing chain tensioner, use a

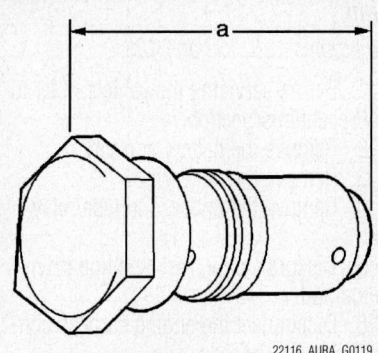

Fig. 127 Measure the timing chain tensioner assembly from end to end. A NEW tensioner should be supplied in the fully compressed non-active state. A tensioner in the compressed state will measure 2.83 in. (72mm) from end to end (a). A tensioner in the active state will measure 3.35 in. (85mm) from end to end (a)—2.4L engine

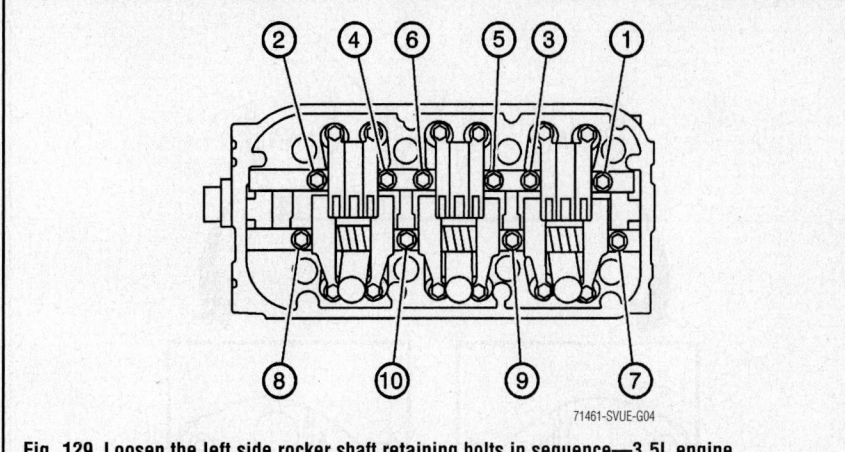

Fig. 129 Loosen the left side rocker shaft retaining bolts in sequence—3.5L engine

suitable tool with a rubber tip on the end. Feed the tool down through the cam chest to rest on the timing chain, then give a sharp jolt diagonally downwards to release the tensioner.

   r. Install the upper timing chain guide and bolts. Tighten to 89 in. lbs. (10 Nm).

   s. Install the camshaft cover.

3.5L Engine

Left

See Figures 128 through 131.

   1. Before servicing the vehicle, refer to the Precautions Section.

   2. Remove the battery and tray.

   3. Drain the cooling system.

   4. Remove the upper radiator hose.

   5. Remove the Exhaust Gas Recirculation (EGR) valve.

   6. Remove the oil dipstick tube.

   7. Remove the oil fill cap.

   8. Remove the Positive Crankcase Ventilation (PCV) valve and bolt.

   9. Disconnect the ignition wiring harness from the ignition coils and retaining bracket.

   10. Remove the wiring harness bracket bolt from the cylinder head.

   11. Remove the bolts the ignition coils.

   12. Remove the bolts, grommets, valve cover and gasket.

   13. Remove the seals, if required.

   14. Remove the left camshaft drive sprocket as follows:

     a. Remove the timing belt.

     b. Use timing belt alignment kit EN 46337 to retain the camshaft sprocket.

   15. Remove the camshaft bolt and sprocket.

   16. Loosen the adjusting nuts and bolts.

   17. Loosen the left side rocker shaft retaining bolts in the sequence illustrated .

   18. Loosen the valve rocker shaft mounting bolts two turns at a time in sequence, to prevent damaging the valves or rocker arms.

➡**Make sure to not each components location as it is being removed so that it may be installed in its correction location upon assembly. When removing or installing the rocker arm shaft assembly, do not remove the rocker arm shaft mounting bolts. The bolts will retain the springs and rocker arms on the shaft.**

   19. Remove the bolts, valve rocker arm and shaft assemblies.

   20. Remove the lash adjusters.

   21. Remove the intake valve rocker arms as an assembly from the shaft.

   22. Remove the exhaust valve rocker arms and springs from the shaft.

   23. Remove the nuts and bolts.

   24. Note the installed location of the exhaust valve rocker arms.

   25. Remove the rear camshaft cap, bolts, and O-ring.

   26. Remove the camshaft from the cylinder head.

   27. Remove the camshaft seal.

   28. Clean all of the bearing surfaces and sealing surfaces.

To install:

   29. Lubricate the camshaft journals and bores with clean engine oil.

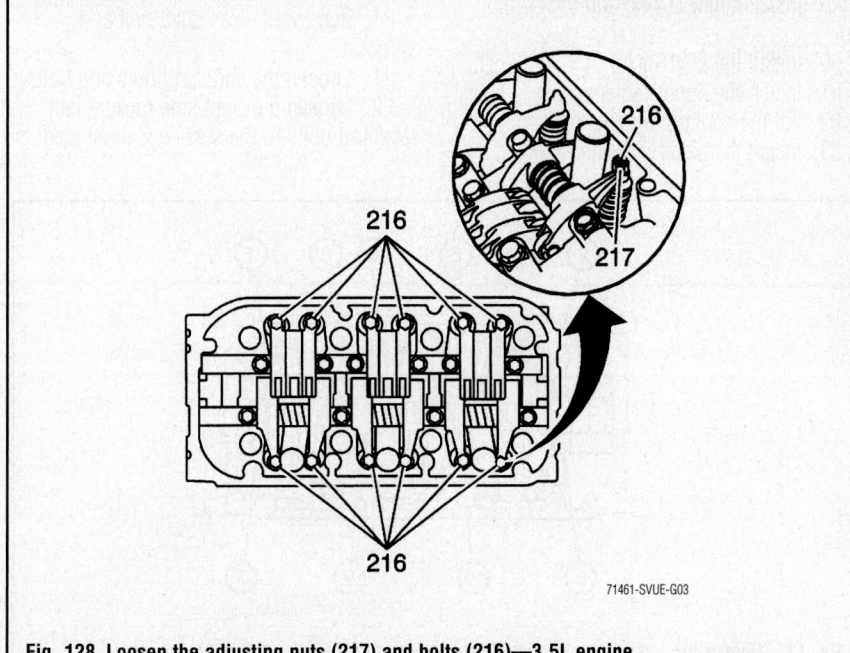

Fig. 128 Loosen the adjusting nuts (217) and bolts (216)—3.5L engine

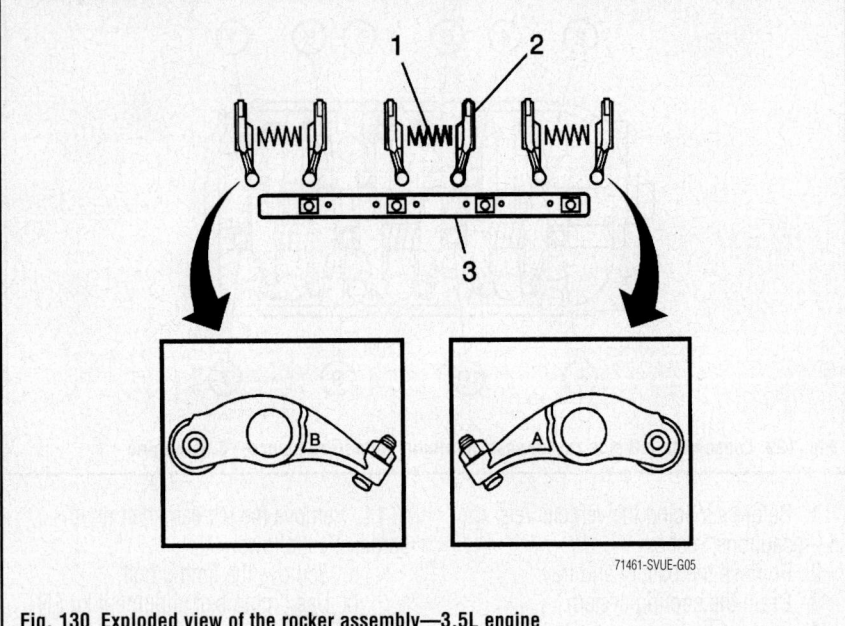

Fig. 130 Exploded view of the rocker assembly—3.5L engine

30. Install the camshaft, with new O-ring, cap, and bolts. Tighten the bolts to 16 ft. lbs. (22 Nm).

31. Install a new camshaft seal.

32. Install the bolts and nuts. Do not tighten the nuts at this time.

33. Install the intake valve rocker arm assemblies onto the shaft.

34. Install the bolts to the shaft.

35. Install the exhaust valve rocker arms and springs onto the shaft.

36. Note the installed position of the exhaust valve rocker arms.

37. Install the bolts onto the shaft.

38. Install the lash adjusters.

➡**The intake rocker arm shaft front locating pin serves as an oil passage for VTEC system operation. During assembly, use care to locate the shaft onto the pin. Replace pins that are bent or damaged.**

39. Install the rocker arm and shaft assemblies and bolts.

40. Tighten the left side rocker shaft retaining bolts in the sequence illustrated. Tighten the bolts 2 turns at a time in, to ensure that the rocker arms do not bind on the valves as follows:

    a. First pass: 106 inch lbs. (12 Nm).

    b. Final pass: 27 ft. lbs. (24 Nm).

41. Install the left camshaft drive sprocket.

42. Install new seals, new gasket and the cover

43. Install new grommets and the bolts, tighten the bolts in sequence as follows:

    a. First pass: 53 inch lbs. (6 Nm).

    b. Final pass: 106 inch lbs. (12 Nm).

44. Install the ignition coils and tighten the bolts to 106 inch lbs. (12 Nm).

45. Install the wiring harness bracket bolt to the cylinder head and tighten to 89 inch lbs. (10 Nm).

46. Connect the ignition wiring harness to the retaining bracket and ignition coils.

47. Install the oil dipstick tube and new O-rings.

48. Install a new O-rings, the PCV valve and bolt. Tighten the bolt to 106 inch lbs. (12 Nm.

49. Install a new O-ring and the oil fill cap.

50. Install the EGR valve.

51. Install the upper radiator hose.

52. Fill the cooling system.

53. Install the battery tray and tray.

Right

See Figures 128, 132 and 133.

1. Before servicing the vehicle, refer to the Precautions Section.

2. Remove the battery and tray.

3. Remove the battery tray.

4. Remove the underhood fuse/relay box.

5. Disconnect the fuel feed line from the fuel rail.

6. Disconnect the engine harness connectors to gain access.

7. Remove the Powertrain Control Module (PCM).

8. Disconnect the vacuum brake booster hose.

9. Disconnect the Manifold Absolute Pressure (MAP) sensor connector.

10. Disconnect the Intake Air Temperature (IAT) sensor connector.

11. Disconnect the Engine Coolant Temperature (ECT) sensor connector.

12. Disconnect the EVAP purge hose from the purge valve.

13. Remove the intake manifold.

14. Disconnect the fuel injector connectors.

15. Remove the wiring harness bracket bolt from the valve rocker arm cover.

16. Remove the ignition coils.

17. Remove the bolts, grommets, valve cover and gasket.

18. Remove the seals, if required.

19. Remove the right camshaft drive sprocket as follows:

    a. Remove the timing belt.

    b. Use timing belt alignment kit EN 46337 to retain the camshaft sprocket.

20. Remove the camshaft bolt and sprocket.

21. Loosen the adjusting nuts and bolts.

22. Loosen the right side rocker shaft retaining bolts in the sequence illustrated.

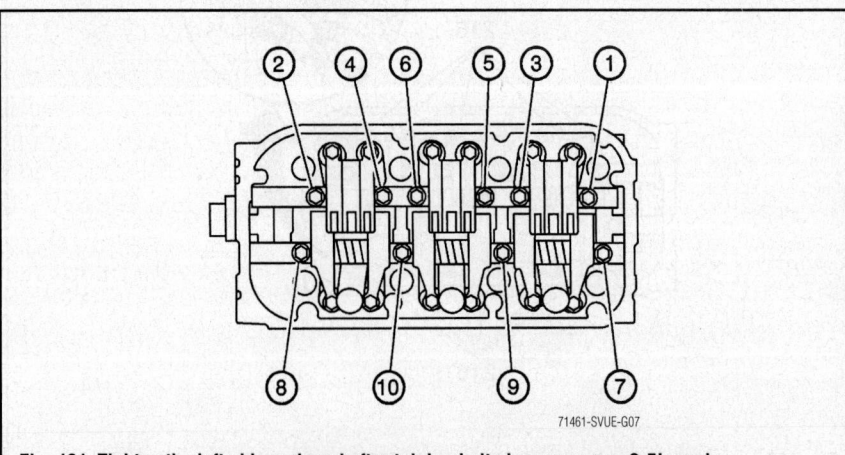

Fig. 131 Tighten the left side rocker shaft retaining bolts in sequence—3.5L engine

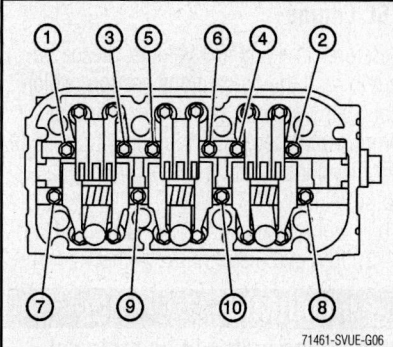

Fig. 132 Loosen the right side rocker shaft retaining bolts in sequence—3.5L engine

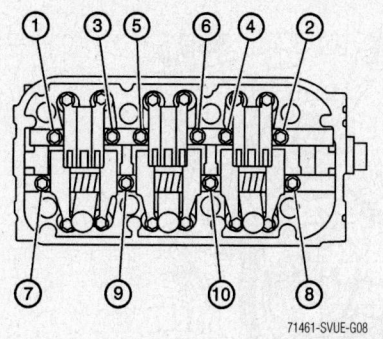

Fig. 133 Tighten the right side rocker shaft retaining bolts in sequence—3.5L engine

23. Loosen the valve rocker shaft mounting bolts two turns at a time in sequence, to prevent damaging the valves or rocker arms.

➡ **Make sure to not each components location as it is being removed so that it may be installed in its correction location upon assembly. When removing or installing the rocker arm shaft assembly, do not remove the rocker arm shaft mounting bolts. The bolts will retain the springs and rocker arms on the shaft.**

24. Remove the lash adjusters.

25. Remove the intake valve rocker arms as an assembly from the shaft.

26. Remove the exhaust valve rocker arms and springs from the shaft.

27. Remove the nuts and bolts.

28. Note the installed location of the exhaust valve rocker arms.

29. Remove the rear camshaft cap, bolts, and O-ring.

30. Remove the camshaft from the cylinder head.

31. Remove the camshaft seal.

32. Clean all of the bearing surfaces and sealing surfaces.

To install:

33. Lubricate the camshaft journals and bores with clean engine oil.

34. Install the camshaft, with new O-ring, cap, and bolts. Tighten the bolts to 16 ft. lbs. (22 Nm).

35. Install a new camshaft seal.

36. Install the bolts and nuts. Do not tighten the nuts at this time.

37. Install the intake valve rocker arm assemblies onto the shaft.

38. Install the bolts to the shaft.

39. Install the exhaust valve rocker arms and springs onto the shaft.

40. Note the installed position of the exhaust valve rocker arms.

41. Install the bolts onto the shaft.

42. Install the lash adjusters.

➡ **The intake rocker arm shaft front locating pin serves as an oil passage for VTEC system operation. During assembly, use care to locate the shaft onto the pin. Replace pins that are bent or damaged.**

43. Install the rocker arm and shaft assemblies and bolts.

44. Tighten the right side rocker shaft retaining bolts in the sequence illustrated. Tighten the bolts 2 turns at a time in, to ensure that the rocker arms do not bind on the valves as follows:
   a. First pass: 106 inch lbs. (12 Nm).
   b. Final pass: 27 ft. lbs. (24 Nm).

45. Install the left camshaft drive sprocket.

46. Install new seals, new gasket and the cover

47. Install new grommets and the bolts, tighten the bolts in sequence as follows:
   a. First pass: 53 inch lbs. (6 Nm).
   b. Final pass: 106 inch lbs. (12 Nm).

48. Install the ignition coils and tighten the bolts to 106 inch lbs. (12 Nm).

49. Install the wiring harness bracket bolt to the cylinder head and tighten to 89 inch lbs. (10 Nm).

50. Connect the fuel injector connectors.

51. Install the intake manifold.

52. Connect the EVAP purge hose.

53. Connect the IAT sensor connector.

54. Connect the MAP sensor connector.

55. Connect the vacuum brake booster hose.

56. Connect the ECT sensor connector.

57. Install the PCM.

58. Connect the engine harness connectors .

59. Connect the fuel feed line to the fuel rail.

60. Install the underhood fuse/relay box.

61. Install the battery tray and tray.

CAMSHAFT BEARING REPLACEMENT

Check each bearing for damage. If the bearing surface is excessively damaged, replace the cylinder head assembly or camshaft bearing cap, as necessary.

CRANKSHAFT DAMPER

REMOVAL & INSTALLATION

2.2L Engine

See Figures 134 and 135.

Before servicing any vehicle, please be sure to read the precautions section, which deals with personal safety, prevention of component damage, and important points to take into consideration when servicing a motor vehicle.

1. Install the J 38122-A, Harmonic Balancer Holder (also known as a crankshaft damper holder).

2. Remove the damper retaining bolt and washer. Use the J 38122-A and a breaker bar in order to prevent the crankshaft from rotating when loosening the bolt. Discard the bolt.

3. Remove the damper assembly.

To install:

> ✳✳ **WARNING**
>
> **Ensure both components are aligned correctly or serious engine damage will occur.**

4. Install the damper onto the crankshaft indexing keyway. Use care to properly align the keyway and flats on the damper with the oil pump drive.

5. Install the J 38122-A, Harmonic Balancer Holder (Crankshaft Damper Holder).

> ✳✳ **WARNING**
>
> **Use the correct fastener in the correct location. Replacement fasteners must be the correct part number for that application. Fasteners requiring replacement or fasteners requiring the use of thread locking compound or sealant are identified in the service procedure. Do not use paints, lubricants, or corrosion inhibitors on fasteners or fastener joint surfaces unless specified. These coatings affect fastener torque and joint clamping force and may damage the fastener. Use the correct tightening sequence and specifications when installing fasteners in order to avoid damage to parts and systems.**

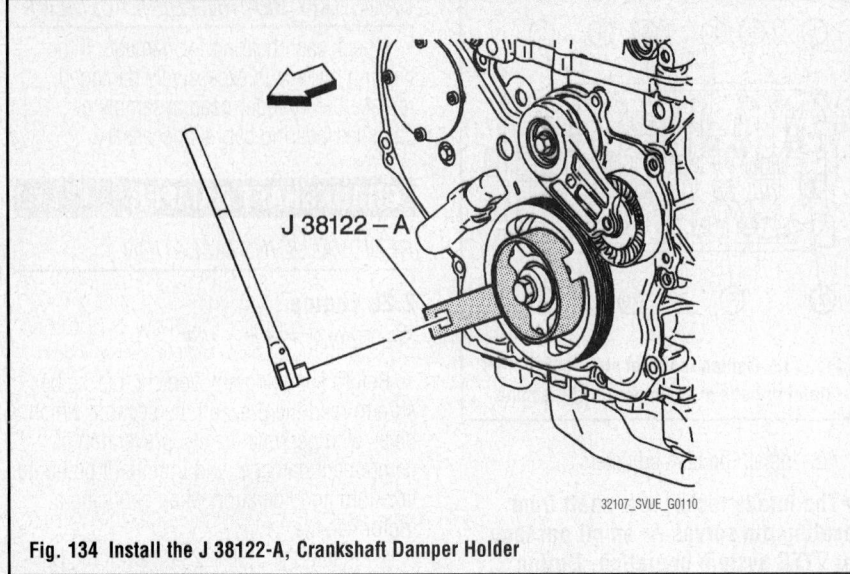

Fig. 134 Install the J 38122-A, Crankshaft Damper Holder

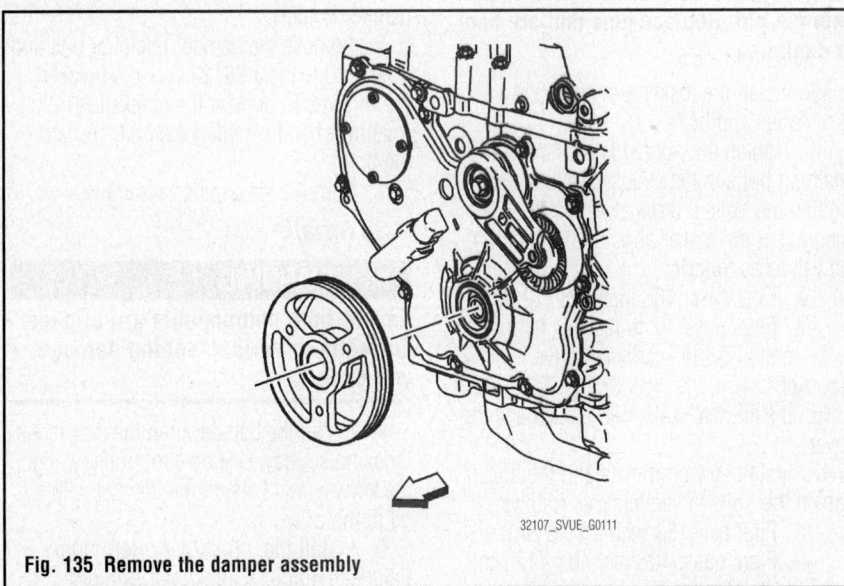

Fig. 135 Remove the damper assembly

➡**Always install a new crankshaft damper retaining bolt and washer.**

6. Install a new retaining bolt and washer. Use the J 38122-A and a breaker bar in order to prevent the crankshaft from rotating when tightening the bolt.

7. Tighten the bolt to 74 ft. lbs. (100 Nm) plus 125° using the J 45059, Angle Meter or equivalent.

2.4L Engine

See Figures 136 through 138.

Before servicing any vehicle, please be sure to read the precautions section, which deals with personal safety, prevention of component damage, and important points to take into consideration when servicing a motor vehicle.

1. Remove the accessory drive belt.

2. Remove the engine splash shield.

3. Install a crankshaft holding tool and a breaker bar to the damper in order to prevent the damper from rotating when loosening the damper bolt.

4. Remove and discard the crankshaft damper bolt.

5. Remove the crankshaft damper.

To install:

6. Position the crankshaft damper.

7. Install a NEW crankshaft damper bolt.

8. Install the holding tool and a breaker bar to the damper in order to prevent the damper from rotating while tightening the bolt.

9. Tighten the crankshaft damper bolt to 74 ft. lbs. (100 Nm) plus an additional 125°.

10. Install the engine splash shield.

11. Install the accessory drive belt.

3.5L Engine

Before servicing any vehicle, please be sure to read the precautions section, which deals with personal safety, prevention of component damage, and important points to take into consideration when servicing a motor vehicle.

1. Remove the accessory drive belt.

2. Remove the right front wheel.

✱✱ WARNING

If the timing belt is to be removed, the crankshaft damper must be rotated to position number 1 piston at Top Dead Center (TDC) of compression stroke to avoid valve-to-piston contact.

3. Turn the crankshaft so its white mark (1) lines up with the pointer (2).

4. Inspect for cylinder number 1 piston at TDC. The pointer on the upper cover (2) will be aligned with the number 1 cylinder TDC mark (1) on the camshaft pulley.

5. Use the EN 46337, Camshaft Sprocket/Crankshaft Balancer Holder (Crankshaft Damper Holder) or equivalent, and a breaker bar in order to retain the damper.

6. Remove the bolt (227), balancer/damper (228) and guide (236).

To install:

7. Clean all oil from the balancer/damper (228), guide (236), bolt (227) and crankshaft.

8. Lubricate the threads of the bolt (227) with clean engine oil.

9. Install the guide (236), balancer/damper (228) and bolt (227). Install the guide with the concave surface facing the damper.

10. Use the EN 46337 and a breaker bar in order to retain the crankshaft damper.

11. Tighten the damper bolt to 181 ft. lbs. (245 Nm).

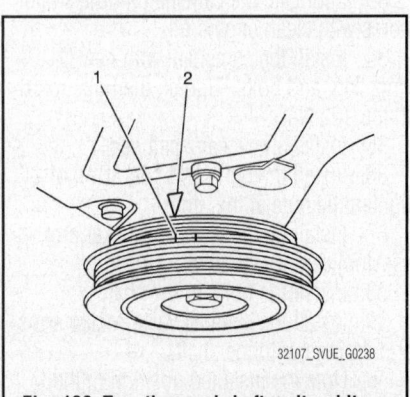

Fig. 136 Turn the crankshaft so its white mark (1) lines up with the pointer (2).

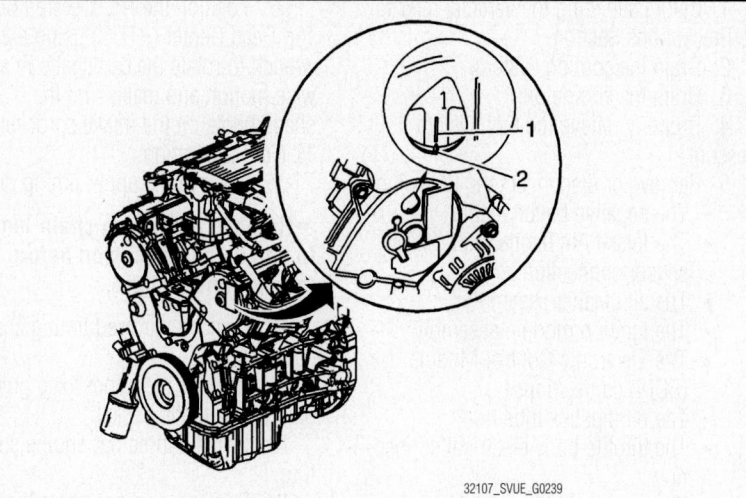

Fig. 137 The pointer on the upper cover (2) will be aligned with the number 1 cylinder TDC mark (1) on the camshaft pulley

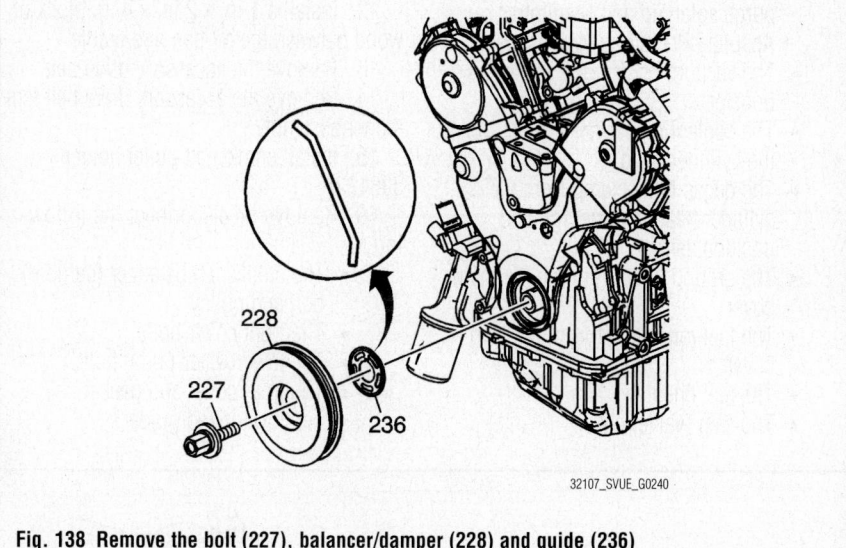

Fig. 138 Remove the bolt (227), balancer/damper (228) and guide (236)

12. Install the right front wheel. Tighten the wheel lug nuts to 100 ft. lbs. (136 Nm).

13. Install the accessory drive belt.

CRANKSHAFT FRONT SEAL

REMOVAL & INSTALLATION

2.2L Engine

See Figure 139.

1. Before servicing the vehicle, refer to the Precautions Section.

2. Remove the crankshaft damper.

3. Remove the drive belt tensioner.

4. Remove the engine front cover to water pump bolt.

5. Remove the remaining engine front cover bolts.

6. Remove the engine front cover.

To install:

7. If removed install a new engine front cover gasket.

8. Install the engine front cover.

9. Install the engine front cover bolts. Tighten the engine front cover bolts to 18 ft. lbs. (25 Nm).

10. Install the water pump bolt. Tighten the water pump bolt to 18 ft. lbs. (25 Nm).

11. Install the drive belt tensioner.

12. Install the drive belt tensioner bolt. Tighten the drive belt tensioner bolt to 33 ft. lbs. (45 Nm).

13. Install the crankshaft damper.

2.4L Engine

See Figures 140 and 141.

1. Before servicing the vehicle, refer to the Precautions Section.

2. Remove the crankshaft damper. Refer to Crankshaft Damper removal and installation.

3. Use a flat-bladed tool to remove the seal from the front cover.

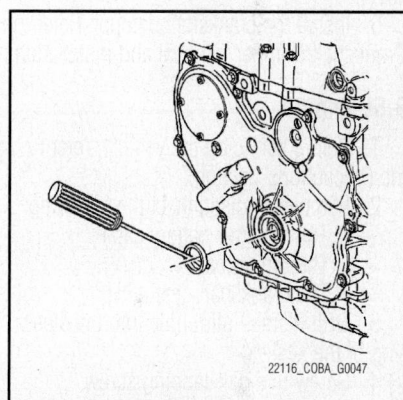

Fig. 140 Using a flat-bladed tool to remove the front seal—2.4L engine

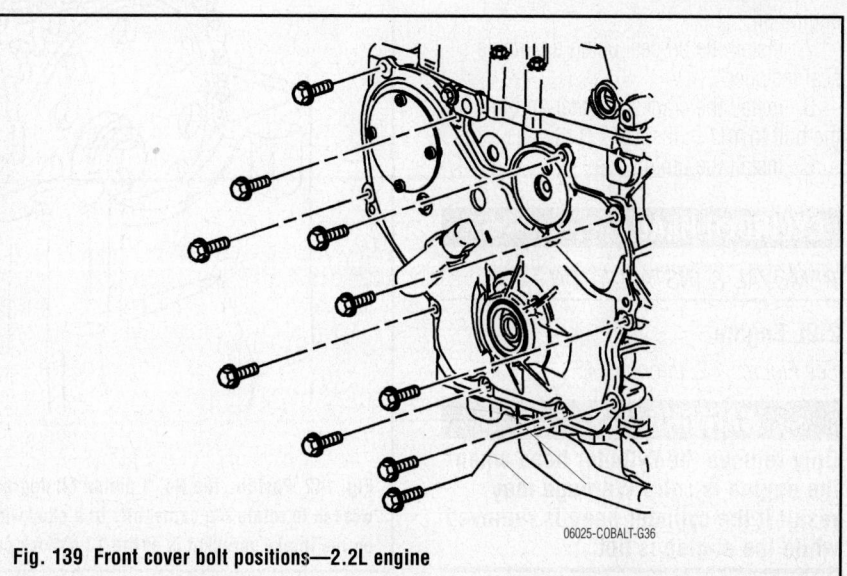

Fig. 139 Front cover bolt positions—2.2L engine

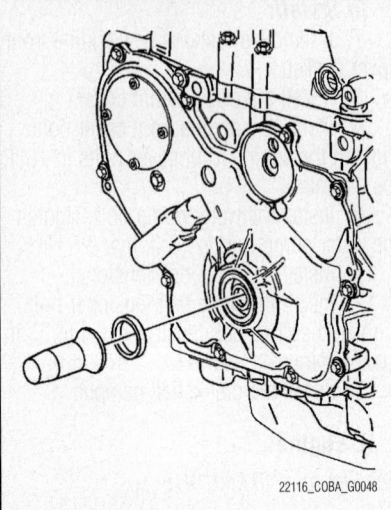

Fig. 141 Using the J 35268-A to install the crankshaft front oil seal—2.4L engine

To install:

4. Use the J 35268-A to install the crankshaft front oil seal to the engine front cover.

5. Install the crankshaft damper. Refer to Crankshaft Damper removal and installation.

3.5L Engine

1. Before servicing the vehicle, refer to the Precautions Section.

2. Remove or disconnect the following:
   - The negative battery cable
   - The timing belt
   - The crankshaft gear

3. Drill a small pilot hole into the steel ring of the seal.

4. Screw in a self-tapping screw.

5. Use a pliers to pull out the oil seal.

To install:

6. Coat the lip of the new oil seal with engine oil.

7. Install the oil seal using a suitable seal installer.

8. Install the crankshaft gear and torque the bolt to 181 ft. lbs. (245 Nm).

9. Install the timing belt.

CYLINDER HEAD

REMOVAL & INSTALLATION

2.2L Engine

See Figures 142 through 145.

❊❊ WARNING

Only remove the cylinder head when the engine is cold. Warpage may result if the cylinder head is removed while the engine is hot.

1. Before servicing the vehicle, refer to the Precautions Section.

2. Drain the cooling system.

3. Drain the engine oil.

4. Properly relieve the fuel system pressure.

5. Remove or disconnect the following:
   - The negative battery cable
   - The Intake Air Temperature (IAT) sensor connection
   - The air cleaner assembly
   - The ignition module assembly
   - The Electronic Control Module (ECM) connections
   - The oil dipstick tube bolt
   - The throttle body electrical connection
   - The electrical connector from the fuel injector harness and attachment at the bottom of the intake manifold
   - The electrical connector at the purge solenoid and Manifold Absolute Pressure (MAP) sensor
   - The vacuum hose at the brake booster
   - The coolant pipe bracket bolts from the cylinder head
   - The degas hose clamp from the cylinder head and fuel rail and position aside
   - The ground strap from the rear cam cover
   - The fuel rail bracket from the cam cover
   - The fuel lines
   - The cam (valve) cover

6. Position the No. 1 piston 60° Before Top Dead Center (BTDC) using a 24mm wrench to rotate the camshafts in a clockwise motion and make sure the diamond shaped hole on the intake sprocket is at the 12 o'clock position.

7. Remove the upper timing guide.

➡ **Remove the timing chain tensioner to unload chain tension before removing the timing chain.**

8. Remove the fixed timing chain guide access plug.

9. Remove the upper fixed guide bolt using a magnetic socket.

10. Install a three bar engine support fixture.

11. Remove or disconnect the following:
    - The right hand engine mount
    - The right hand mount bracket
    - The right wheel splash shield

12. Install a 1 in. x 2 in. x 4 in. block of wood between the oil pan and cradle.

13. Remove the accessory drive belt.

14. Remove the accessory drive belt tensioner assembly.

15. Install crankshaft pullet holder J38122A.

16. Remove or disconnect the following:
    - The crankshaft balancer (damper) bolt and pulley
    - The front cover bolts
    - The lower water pump bolt
    - The front cover and gasket
    - The lower fixed guide

Fig. 142 Position the No. 1 piston 60 degrees Before Top Dead Center (BTDC) using a 24mm wrench to rotate the camshafts in a clockwise motion and make sure the diamond shaped hole on the intake sprocket is at the 12 o'clock position—2.2L engine

- The upper radiator hose from the cylinder head
- The exhaust manifold pipe nuts
- The front and rear Oxygen (O$_2$S) sensor electrical connector
- The down pipe-to-intermediate pipe nuts
- The down pipe
- The exhaust camshaft sprocket bolts while holding the camshaft with a 24mm wrench and discard the camshaft sprocket bolts
- The exhaust sprocket
- The adjustable guide through the top of the cylinder head
- The intake camshaft sprocket bolts while holding the camshaft with a 24mm wrench and discard the camshaft sprocket bolts
- The intake sprocket
- The timing chain assembly
- The timing drive sprocket from the crankshaft

17. Install a floor jack to support the engine and remove the engine support fixture.

18. Remove the cylinder head bolts using the proper sequence.

19. Remove the cylinder head.

To install:

➡**Set the crankshaft to 60° Before Top Dead Center (BTDC) to prevent contact between the pistons and valves.**

20. Install or connect the following:
- The new cylinder head gasket with the side imprinted **OPEN** facing up
- The cylinder head and align it on the dowels

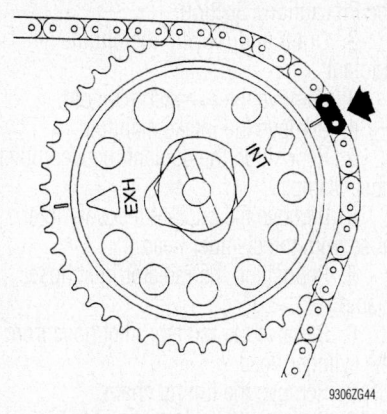

Fig. 144 Align the copper link on the timing chain with the INT diamond timing mark

- The new cylinder head bolts and torque them in sequence to 22 ft. lbs. (30 Nm) plus 155°
- The front 4 cylinder head bolts coated with Loctite® and torque them to 26 ft. lbs. (35 Nm)

21. Position the exhaust camshaft with the offset slot in the 2 o'clock position and the intake camshaft with the offset slot in the 11 o'clock position.

22. Install or connect the following:
- The timing chain around the intake camshaft sprocket with the copper link aligned with the **INT** diamond timing mark
- The sprocket to the camshaft and align it with the offset slot
- The new camshaft sprocket bolt, but do not tighten yet

- The timing chain around the crankshaft sprocket and align the silver link to the timing mark
- The adjustable timing chain guide through the opening on top of the cylinder head and torque the bolt to 89 inch lbs. (10 Nm)
- The timing chain around the exhaust camshaft sprocket with the silver link aligned with the offset slot. Install but do not tighten a new sprocket bolt

❋❋ WARNING

Make certain that all timing marks and colored links are aligned properly before proceeding to the next step. If the timing chain is not aligned properly, severe engine damage may occur.

23. Torque the intake and exhaust camshaft bolts to 63 ft. lbs. (85 Nm) plus 30°.

24. Install or connect the following:
- The fixed timing guide and torque the bolt to 89 inch lbs. (10 Nm)
- The fixed timing guide bolt access plug after applying Loctite® to the threads and torque it to 30 ft. lbs. (40 Nm)
- The timing chain tensioner and torque the bolts 55 ft. lbs. (75 Nm)

25. Tap the top of the timing chain between the camshaft sprockets to engage the tensioner.

26. Install or connect the following:
- The upper timing chain guide and torque the bolts to 89 inch lbs. (10 Nm)

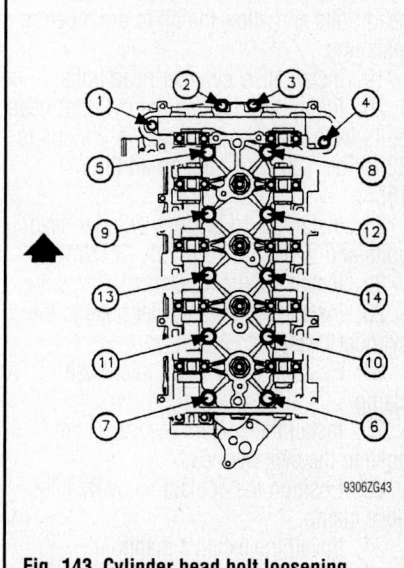

Fig. 143 Cylinder head bolt loosening sequence—2.2L engine

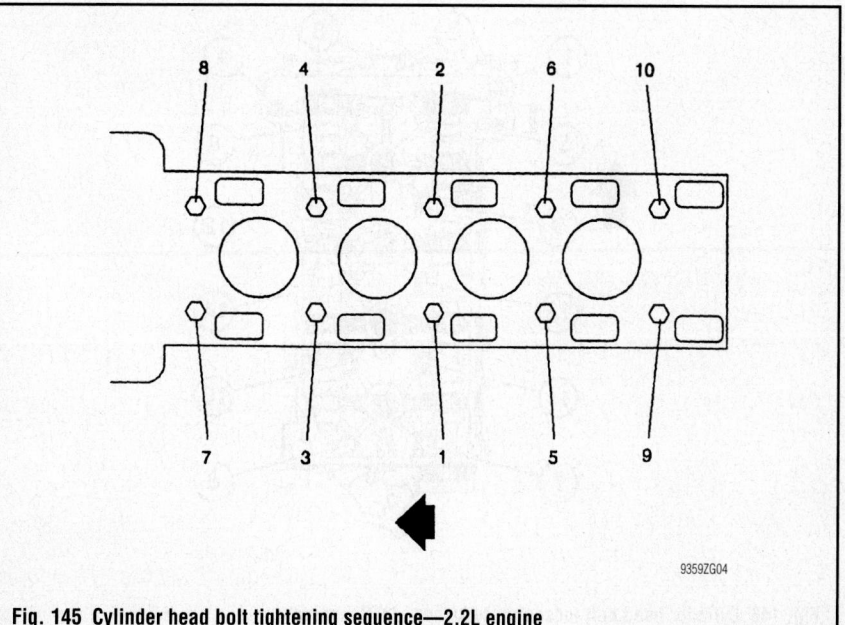

Fig. 145 Cylinder head bolt tightening sequence—2.2L engine

- The front cover with a new gasket and torque the bolts to 18 ft. lbs. (25 Nm)
- The water pump bolt and torque it to 18 ft. lbs. (25 Nm)
- The crankshaft damper and torque the bolt to 74 ft. lbs. (100 Nm) plus 75°
- The accessory drive belt tensioner and torque the bolts to 30 ft. lbs. (40 Nm)
- The exhaust manifold pipe to the manifold and tighten the nuts to 22 ft. lbs. (30 Nm)
- The oil dipstick tube bolt to 89 inch lbs. (10 Nm)
- The engine mount bracket and torque the bolts to 66 ft. lbs. (90 Nm)
- The engine mount to body nuts to 81 ft. lbs. (110 Nm)
- The engine mount to the bracket and torque the bolts to 41 ft. lbs. (55 Nm)

27. Install the remaining components in the reverse order of removal.

28. Fill the engine with the proper amount of clean oil.

29. Fill the cooling system.

30. Prime the fuel system by cycling the ignition **ON** for 5 seconds and **OFF** for 10 seconds a few times without cranking the engine.

31. Start the engine, check for leaks, and repair if necessary.

2.4L Engine

See Figures 146 through 148.

1. Before servicing the vehicle, refer to the Precautions Section.

2. Drain and recycle the engine coolant.

3. Remove the exhaust manifold.

4. Remove the intake manifold.

5. Reposition the coolant recovery inlet hose clamp.

6. Remove the coolant recovery inlet hose from the cylinder head.

7. Reposition the radiator inlet hose clamp.

8. Remove the radiator inlet hose from the cylinder head.

9. Remove the timing chain.

10. Remove the cylinder head bolts in the sequence shown. Discard the bolts.

11. Remove the cylinder head.

12. Remove the cylinder head gasket.

13. Clean the old sealer/lube and any dirt from around the bolt holes.

➡ **DO NOT use a tap to clean the cylinder head bolt holes.**

14. Clean the bolts holes with a nylon bristle brush.

15. When cleaning the cylinder head bolt holes use suitable commercial spray liquid solvent and compressed air from an extended-tip blow gun in order to reach the bottom of the holes.

To install:

➡ **DO NOT use any sealing material.**

16. Install the cylinder head gasket.

17. Install the cylinder head.

18. Lightly apply clean engine oil to the threads and the bottom side flange of the

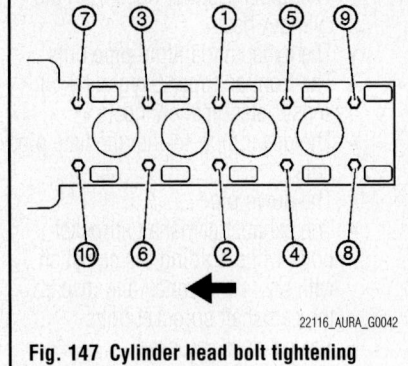

Fig. 147 Cylinder head bolt tightening sequence—2.4L engine

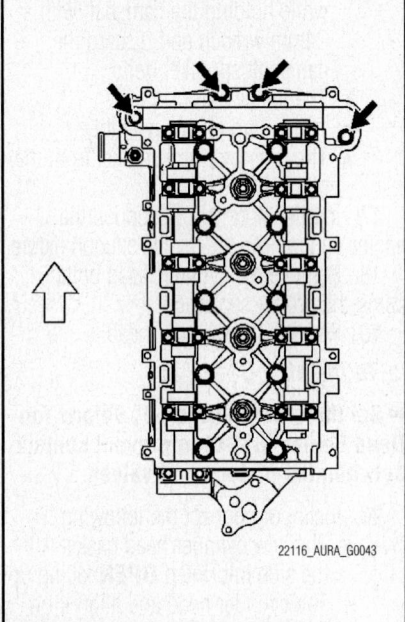

Fig. 148 Location of the front cylinder head bolts—2.4L engine

head bolts and allow the oil to drain before installing.

19. Install NEW cylinder head bolts.

20. Install and tighten the cylinder head bolts in the sequence shown in 2 steps to 22 ft. lbs. (30 Nm) plus an additional 155°.

21. Install the NEW front cylinder head bolts and tighten to 26 ft. lbs. (35 Nm).

22. Install the timing chain.

23. Install the radiator inlet hose to the cylinder head.

24. Position the radiator inlet hose clamp.

25. Install the coolant recovery inlet hose to the cylinder head.

26. Position the coolant recovery inlet hose clamp.

27. Install the exhaust manifold.

28. Install the intake manifold.

29. Fill the cooling system.

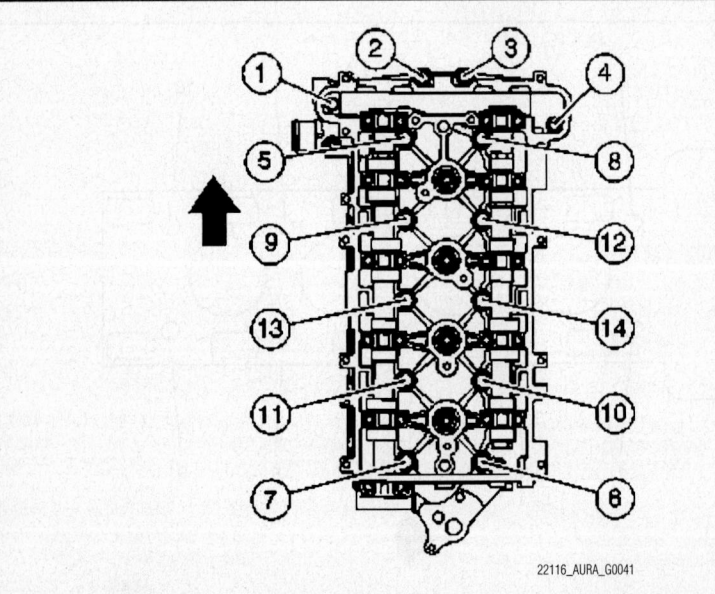

Fig. 146 Cylinder head bolt loosening sequence—2.4L engine

3.5L Engine

Left

See Figures 149 and 150.

1. Before servicing the vehicle, refer to the Precautions Section.
2. Remove the oil dipstick tube.
3. Remove the oil fill cap.
4. Remove the Positive Crankcase Ventilation (PCV) valve and bolt.
5. Disconnect the ignition wiring harness from the ignition coils and retaining bracket.
6. Remove the wiring harness bracket bolt from the cylinder head.
7. Remove the bolts the ignition coils.
8. Remove the bolts, grommets, valve cover and gasket.
9. Remove the seals, if required.
10. Remove the timing belt.
11. Remove the coolant bridge.
12. Disconnect the left bank Oxygen (O2S) sensors.
13. Remove the cylinder head bolts.
14. Remove the cylinder head and gasket.

To install:

15. Install a new gasket and the cylinder head.
16. Install the cylinder head bolts and tighten in the following sequence:
    a. First pass: 29 ft. lbs. (39 Nm).
    b. Second pass: 51 ft. lbs. (69 Nm).
    c. Final pass: 72 ft. lbs. (98 Nm).
17. Connect the left bank O2S sensors.
18. Install the coolant bridge.
19. Install the timing belt.
20. Install new seals, new gasket and the cover.

21. Install new grommets and the bolts, tighten the bolts in sequence as follows:
    a. First pass: 53 inch lbs. (6 Nm).
    b. Final pass: 106 inch lbs. (12 Nm).
22. Install the ignition coils and tighten the bolts to 106 inch lbs. (12 Nm).
23. Install the wiring harness bracket bolt to the cylinder head and tighten to 89 inch lbs. (10 Nm).
24. Connect the ignition wiring harness to the retaining bracket and ignition coils.
25. Install the oil dipstick tube and new O-rings.
26. Install a new O-rings, the PCV valve and bolt. Tighten the bolt to 106 inch lbs. (12 Nm).
27. Install a new O-ring and the oil fill cap.

Right

1. Before servicing the vehicle, refer to the Precautions Section.
2. Disconnect the vacuum brake booster hose.
3. Disconnect the Manifold Absolute Pressure (MAP) sensor connector.
4. Disconnect the Intake Air Temperature (IAT) sensor connector.
5. Disconnect the Engine Coolant Temperature (ECT) sensor connector.
6. Disconnect the EVAP purge hose from the purge valve.
7. Remove the intake manifold.
8. Disconnect the fuel injector connectors.
9. Remove the wiring harness bracket bolt from the valve rocker arm cover.
10. Remove the ignition coils.
11. Remove the bolts, grommets, valve cover and gasket.
12. Remove the seals, if required.
13. Remove the timing belt.
14. Remove the coolant bridge.
15. Disconnect the right bank Oxygen (O2S) sensors.
16. Remove the cylinder head bolts.
17. Remove the cylinder head and gasket.

To install:

18. Install a new gasket and the cylinder head.
19. Install the cylinder head bolts and tighten in the following sequence:
    a. First pass: 29 ft. lbs. (39 Nm).
    b. Second pass: 51 ft. lbs. (69 Nm).
    c. Final pass: 72 ft. lbs. (98 Nm).
20. Connect the right bank O2S sensors.
21. Install the coolant bridge.
22. Install the timing belt.
23. Install new seals, new gasket and the cover.

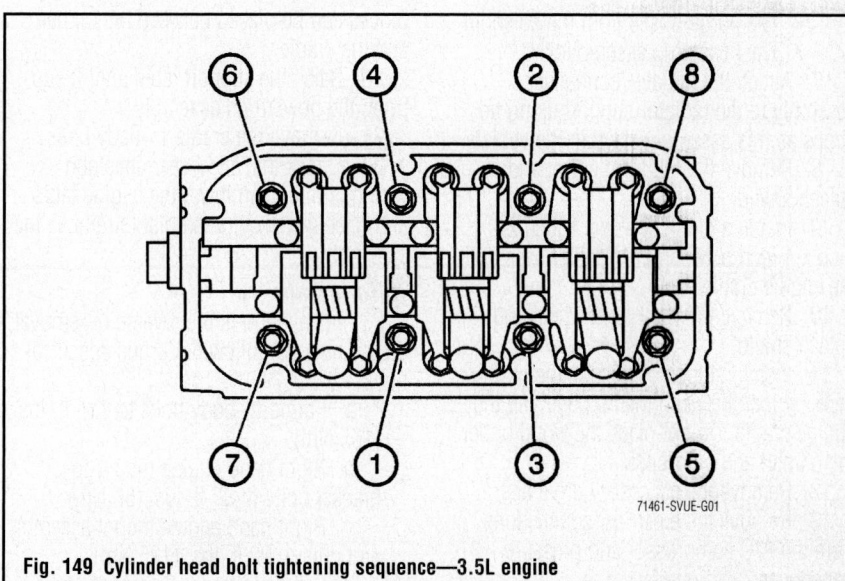

Fig. 149 Cylinder head bolt tightening sequence—3.5L engine

71461-SVUE-G01

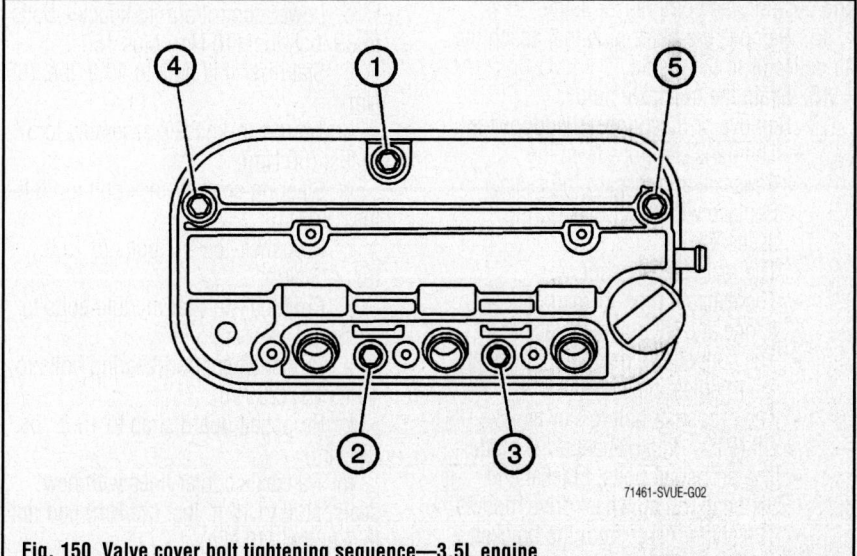

Fig. 150 Valve cover bolt tightening sequence—3.5L engine

71461-SVUE-G02

24. Install new grommets and the bolts, tighten the bolts in sequence as follows:
   a. First pass: 53 inch lbs. (6 Nm).
   b. Final pass: 106 inch lbs. (12 Nm).
25. Install the ignition coils and tighten the bolts to 106 inch lbs. (12 Nm).
26. Install the wiring harness bracket bolt to the cylinder head and tighten to 89 inch lbs. (10 Nm).
27. Connect the fuel injector connectors.
28. Install the intake manifold.
29. Connect the EVAP purge hose.
30. Connect the IAT sensor connector.
31. Connect the MAP sensor connector.
32. Connect the vacuum brake booster hose.
33. Connect the ECT sensor connector.

ENGINE ASSEMBLY

REMOVAL & INSTALLATION

2.2L Engine

See Figure 150.

1. Before servicing the vehicle, refer to the Precautions Section.
2. Properly relieve the fuel system pressure.
3. Drain the engine coolant.
4. Drain the engine oil.
5. Drain the power steering fluid.
6. Remove or disconnect the following:

   - Both battery cables
   - The battery
   - The air cleaner and intake duct assembly
   - The Intake Air Temperature (IAT) sensor electrical connector
   - The underhood fuse panel cover
   - The 3 connector through bolts from the fuse block
   - The battery and electronic power steering feed wire nut and the wires from the stud
   - The fuse block connectors from the fuse block
   - The fuse block and battery tray bolts, then the fuse block and the battery tray
   - The electrical connectors from the Transmission Control Module (TCM), if equipped
   - The rear Heated Oxygen (HO2) sensor electrical connector
   - The 8-way electrical connection
   - The main harness connector

➡ **Do not remove the shifter cable from the bracket before removing the cable from the switch.**

- The shift cable from the transaxle range switch by slightly prying between the cable plastic retainer and the switch, if equipped
- The shift lever cables from the shift control housing using tool J36346, manual transaxle only
- The shift lever cable from the bracket, manual transaxle only
- The pressure line from the clutch actuator
- The back-up lamp switch
- The upper radiator hose from the cylinder head
- The lower radiator hose at the coolant pipe
- The degas hose at the surge tank
- The surge hose at the surge tank
- The heater hoses from the core at the firewall
- The fuel lines
- The purge hoses from the solenoid
- The headlamp assemblies

7. Attach the radiator/condenser assembly to the radiator support using tie straps as this assembly stays in the vehicle.
8. Remove the left front wheel and splash shield.
9. Install a block of wood 1 inch x 2 inch x 4 inch between the transfer case and the engine cradle.
10. Remove the right front wheel and splash shield.
11. Install a block of wood 1 inch x 2 inch x 4 inch between the oil pane and the engine cradle. Do not place the wood under the oil pan and plug boss.
12. Remove the accessory drive belt.
13. Remove the electrical connections from the A/C compressor and pressure transducer.
14. Remove the A/C compressor bolts and position the compressor aside.
15. Remove the push-pins that attach the air deflector to the cradle.
16. Drain the transaxle fluid.
17. Remove or disconnect the following:

   - The transaxle lines from the transaxle and discard the seals. Replace with new seals during assembly
   - The rear HO2S sensor
   - The exhaust pipe-to-manifold flange and intermediate fasteners
   - The converter pipe and support the intermediate pipe
   - The propshaft bolt to Power Take Off (PTO) on all wheel drive models
   - The propshaft bolts, bracket and the shaft, on all wheel drive models
   - The shifter cable from the bracket, on automatic transaxle models

- The power steering gear-to-intermediate shaft bolt
- The tie rod from the knuckles
- The lower control arms from the knuckles
- The stabilizer link nuts
- The left hand axle shaft from the transaxle
- The right hand shaft from the intermediate shaft using tool J45341
- The right hand engine mount and the left hand transaxle mount and let the engine rest on the wood blocks

➡ **Support the rear of the vehicle with a jackstand prior to engine removal.**

18. Place an engine support table under the engine.
19. Place blocks of wood to level the powertrain assembly, if necessary. The blocks can be placed between the oil pan and the cradle.
20. Raise the support table until it supports the powertrain assembly.
21. Remove the cradle-to-body bolts.
22. Check that all hoses, lines and wiring is free, then lower the engine table and raise the body on a hoist to remove the assembly.

To install:

23. Installation is the reverse of removal, please note the following torque specifications:
   a. Frame-to-body bolts to 114 ft. lbs. (155 Nm).
   b. Right hand engine mount-to-bracket bolts to 37 ft. lbs. (50 Nm).
   c. Right hand engine mount assembly and nuts to 92 ft. lbs. (125 Nm).
   d. Left hand transaxle mount-to-bracket bolts to 37 ft. lbs. (50 Nm).
   e. Lower control arm to knuckle bolts to 89 inch lbs. (10 Nm) plus 150°.
   f. Stabilizer link nuts to 48 ft. lbs. (65 Nm).
   g. Tie rod-to-knuckle assembly to 37 ft. lbs. (50 Nm).
   h. Steering shaft-to-rack bolt to 25 ft. lbs. (34 Nm).
   i. Propshaft-to-PTU bolts to 19 ft. lbs. (25 Nm).
   j. Propshaft-to-rear module bolts to 37 ft. lbs. (50 Nm).
   k. Propshaft support bearing bolts to 19 ft. lbs. (25 Nm).
   l. Propshaft guard strap to 19 ft. lbs. (25 Nm).
   m. Transaxle cooler lines with new seals, stud to 15 ft. lbs. (20 Nm) and nut to 7 ft. lbs. (10 Nm).

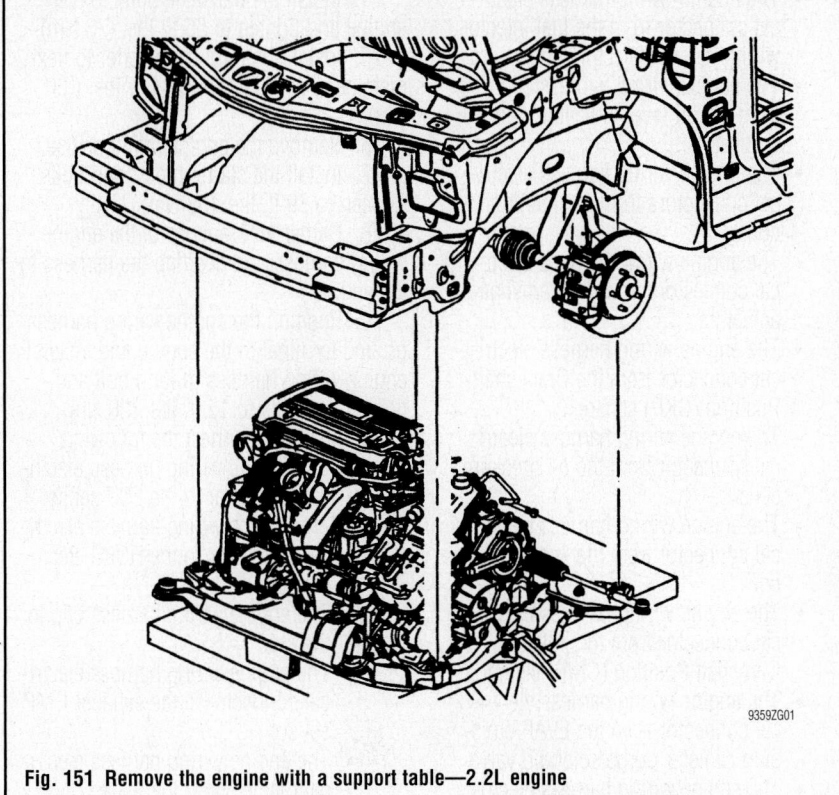

Fig. 151 Remove the engine with a support table—2.2L engine

n. Down pipe-to-manifold nuts to 22 ft. lbs. (30 Nm).

o. Down pipe-to-intermediate pipe nuts to 37 ft. lbs. (50 Nm).

p. A/C compressor bolts to 18 ft. lbs. (25 Nm).

q. Engine ground-to-body bolt to 15 ft. lbs. (20 Nm).

24. Fill the engine with the proper amount of coolant.

25. Fill the engine with the proper amount of new oil.

26. Prime the fuel system by cycling the ignition **ON** for 5 seconds and **OFF** for 10 seconds a few times without cranking the engine.

27. Start the engine, check for leaks, and repair as necessary.

2.4L Engine

1. Before servicing the vehicle, refer to the Precautions Section.

2. Relieve the fuel system pressure.

3. Remove the air cleaner assembly.

4. Disconnect the fuel feed pipe quick connect fitting at the fuel rail.

5. Disconnect the Evaporative Emission (EVAP) line quick connect fitting from the EVAP purge solenoid.

6. Remove the fuel feed pipe clip from the fuel line bracket.

7. Remove the transaxle shift cable clip from the fuel line bracket.

8. Remove the battery tray.

9. Remove the alternator starter.

10. Reposition the vacuum brake booster hose clamp at the intake manifold.

11. Remove the vacuum brake booster hose from the intake manifold. Reposition the brake booster hose out of the way.

12. Remove the coolant recovery inlet hose clamp at the cylinder head.

13. Remove the coolant recovery inlet pipe clip from the fuel rail.

14. Remove the coolant recovery inlet hose from the cylinder head. Reposition the hose/pipe out of the way.

15. Reposition the radiator inlet hose clamp.

16. Remove the radiator inlet hose from the cylinder head.

17. Remove the radiator outlet hose.

18. Reposition the alternator control module coolant hose clamp at the alternator control module.

19. Remove the alternator control module coolant hose from the alternator control module.

20. Disconnect the engine wiring harness electrical connector from the transaxle auxiliary pump module.

21. Reposition the heater inlet hose clamp at the thermostat housing.

22. Remove the heater inlet hose from the thermostat housing.

23. Reposition the coolant recovery reservoir/heater inlet hose clamp at the thermostat housing.

24. Remove the coolant recovery reservoir/heater inlet hose from the thermostat housing.

25. Raise and support the vehicle.

26. Drain the engine oil.

27. Disconnect the engine wiring harness electrical connector from the alternator control module coolant pump.

28. Disconnect the engine wiring harness electrical connector from the Air Conditioning (A/C) compressor.

29. Remove the alternator control module coolant pump bolt and pump.

30. Unbolt the A/C compressor and reposition out of the way.

31. Remove the positive battery cable to starter motor nut.

32. Remove the positive battery cable lead from the starter motor.

33. Remove the positive battery cable from in between the starter and the engine. Reposition the positive battery cable out of the way.

34. Disconnect the engine wiring harness electrical connector from the auxiliary heater water pump.

35. Remove the auxiliary heater water pump bolt and pump.

36. Lower the vehicle.

37. Remove the transaxle shift cable from the range select lever.

38. Release the shift control cable retaining clip and remove the cable from the shift control cable bracket.

➡**The radiator/condenser/fan assembly will stay in the vehicle during engine removal.**

39. Using long tie straps, secure the radiator/condenser/fan assembly to the radiator support.

40. Raise the vehicle.

41. Remove the front wheels and tires.

42. Remove the front fender liners.

➡**A piece of hardwood should be used between the transaxle and the engine cradle. This wood will support the engine when the left side engine mount bolts are removed.**

43. Install a piece of hardwood 1 in. x 2 in. x 4 in. between the transaxle and the engine cradle.

44. Drain the transaxle fluid.

45. Remove the transaxle oil cooler line to transaxle nut.

46. Remove the transaxle oil cooler lines from the transaxle.

47. Remove the catalytic converter.

➡ **Secure the steering wheel in the straight forward position before separating the intermediate shaft from the steering gear, or damage to the SIR coil will occur.**

48. Remove the intermediate to steering gear pinch bolt and disconnect the intermediate shaft from the steering gear. Discard the pinch bolt.

49. Remove and discard both outer tie rod to steering knuckle nuts.

➡ **Hold the ball stud to prevent turning during removal of the nut.**

50. Separate the tie rods from the steering knuckles.

51. Remove the stabilizer link to stabilizer shaft nuts and disconnect the stabilizer links from the stabilizer shaft.

52. Remove and discard both of the lower control arm ball stud cotter pins.

53. Loosen the ball stud nuts until the nuts are level with the top of the ball stud.

54. Separate the lower control arms from the steering knuckles.

55. Remove the ball stud nuts.

56. Remove the wheel drive shafts.

57. Lower the vehicle.

58. Remove the engine mount to bracket bolts.

59. Remove the transaxle mount to transaxle bolts.

60. Raise the vehicle.

➡ **During the powertrain removal support the vehicle body by placing a jack at the rear of the vehicle. Position a engine support table under the powertrain assembly.**

➡ **Blocks of wood can be used between the front of the cradle and the oil pan to table in order to level the powertrain during the removal.**

61. With the table positioned, fully raise the table to contact with the powertrain assembly.

62. Remove the cradle to body bolts. Discard the bolts.

➡ **When lowering the engine/transaxle assembly, verify all brake lines, shifter cables and other components are free during removal.**

63. Lower the engine table and raise the body on the hoist until the engine/transaxle and cradle are free from the vehicle.

64. Remove or disconnect the following:

- The engine wiring harness electrical connector from the throttle actuator

- The engine wiring harness electrical connector from the fuel injector wiring harness electrical connector
- The engine wiring harness clip from the oil level indicator tube bracket
- The engine wiring harness electrical connectors from the ignition coils
- The engine wiring harness electrical connectors from the camshaft actuators
- The engine wiring harness electrical connector from the Crankshaft Position (CKP) sensor
- The engine wiring harness electrical connector from the oil pressure sensor
- The engine wiring harness electrical connector from the knock sensor
- The engine wiring harness electrical connector from the intake Camshaft Position (CMP) sensor
- The engine wiring harness electrical connector from the EVAP emission canister purge solenoid valve
- The engine wiring harness electrical connector from the exhaust CMP sensor
- The engine wiring harness electrical connector from the Engine Coolant Temperature (ECT) sensor
- The engine wiring harness electrical connector from the Heated Oxygen Sensor (HO2S) electrical connector
- The engine wiring harness clip from the stud
- The engine wiring harness ground bolt and reposition the ground terminal from the engine

65. Gather all branches of the engine wiring harness and reposition the harness out of the way.

66. Remove the starter motor bolts and starter.

67. Remove the torque converter to flexplate bolts.

68. Install a suitable lifting devise to the engine.

69. Remove the transaxle bolts from the engine.

70. Separate the engine from the transaxle.

71. Install the engine to a suitable engine stand.

To install:

72. Install a suitable lifting devise to the engine.

73. Using the lifting devise, position and install the engine to the transaxle.

74. Install the transaxle bolts to the engine and tighten to 55 ft. lbs. (75 Nm).

75. Install the torque converter to flexplate bolts and tighten to 44 ft. lbs. (60 Nm).

76. Remove the engine lifting devise.

77. Install the starter motor and bolts. Tighten to 39 ft. lbs. (53 Nm).

78. Gather all branches of the engine wiring harness and position the harness to the engine.

79. Position the engine wiring harness ground terminal to the engine and install the engine wiring harness ground bolt and tighten the bolts to 15 ft. lbs. (20 Nm).

80. Install or connect the following:

- The engine wiring harness electrical connector to the ECT sensor
- The engine wiring harness electrical connector to the HO2S electrical connector
- The engine wiring harness clip to the stud
- The engine wiring harness electrical connector to the exhaust CMP sensor
- The engine wiring harness electrical connector to the intake CMP sensor
- The engine wiring harness electrical connector to the EVAP emission canister purge solenoid valve
- The engine wiring harness electrical connector to the CKP sensor
- The engine wiring harness electrical connector to the oil pressure sensor
- The engine wiring harness electrical connector to the knock sensor
- The engine wiring harness electrical connectors to the ignition coils
- The engine wiring harness electrical connectors to the camshaft actuators
- The engine wiring harness electrical connector to the throttle actuator
- The engine wiring harness electrical connector to the fuel injector wiring harness electrical connector
- The engine wiring harness clip to the oil level indicator tube bracket

81. Position the powertrain and support table under the vehicle.

82. Raise the powertrain into position under the vehicle.

83. With the table positioned, if required, lower the vehicle over the powertrain.

84. Align the lower radiator pins with the cradle. Ensure all hoses and electrical harnesses are correctly routed and free from the loading path of the powertrain.

85. Install the NEW cradle to body bolts and tighten to 114 ft. lbs. (155 Nm).

86. Lower the vehicle.

87. Install the transaxle mount to transaxle bolts. Tighten to 41 ft. lbs. (55 Nm).

➡**The engine mount to bracket bolts must be hand started. Do not pry the engine mount to align the holes.**

88. Install the engine mount to bracket bolts and tighten to 37 ft. lbs. (50 Nm).

89. Install the wheel drive shafts.

90. Install the control arm ball studs into the steering knuckles.

91. Install the ball stud nuts and tighten to 30 ft. lbs. (40 Nm).

92. Continue to tighten the nuts only enough to align the castle nut slots with the ball stud, install NEW cotter pins.

93. Connect the stabilizer links to the stabilizer shaft and install the stabilizer link to stabilizer shaft nuts. Tighten to 48 ft. lbs. (65 Nm).

94. Connect the outer tie rods to the steering knuckles. Tighten to 30 ft. lbs. (40 Nm).

95. Install NEW outer tie rod to steering knuckle nuts. Tighten to 48 ft. lbs. (65 Nm) plus an additional 90°.

96. Position the intermediate shaft to the steering gear and install a NEW pinch bolt. Tighten to 25 ft. lbs. (34 Nm).

97. Install the catalytic converter.

98. Install the transaxle oil cooler lines to the transaxle.

99. Install the transaxle oil cooler line to transaxle nut. Tighten to 27 in. lbs. (4 Nm).

100. Remove the wood from between the oil pan and the engine cradle.

101. Remove the wood from between the transaxle and the engine cradle.

102. Install the front fender liners.

103. Install the front wheels and tires. Tighten the wheel lug nuts to 100 ft. lbs. (136 Nm).

104. Lower the vehicle.

105. Unsecure and position the radiator/condenser/fan assembly.

106. Install the shift control cable to the shift control cable bracket and engage the shift control cable retaining clip.

107. Install the transaxle shift cable to the range select lever.

108. Raise and support the vehicle.

109. Install the auxiliary heater water pump and bolt. Tighten the bolt to 80 in. lbs. (9 Nm).

110. Connect the engine wiring harness electrical connector to the auxiliary heater water pump.

111. Position and install the positive battery cable between the starter and the engine.

112. Install the positive battery cable lead to the starter motor.

113. Install the positive battery cable to starter motor nut.

114. Position the A/C compressor and install the bolts. Tighten to 37 ft. lbs. (50 Nm).

115. Install the alternator control module coolant pump and bolt. Tighten to 18 ft. lbs. (25 Nm).

116. Connect the engine wiring harness electrical connector to the alternator control module coolant pump.

117. Connect the engine wiring harness electrical connector to the A/C compressor.

118. Lower the vehicle.

119. Install the coolant recovery reservoir/heater inlet hose to the thermostat housing.

120. Position the coolant recovery reservoir/heater inlet hose clamp at the thermostat housing.

121. Install the heater inlet hose to the thermostat housing.

122. Position the heater inlet hose clamp at the thermostat housing.

123. Connect the engine wiring harness electrical connector to the transaxle auxiliary pump module.

124. Install the alternator control module coolant hose to the alternator control module.

125. Position the alternator control module coolant hose clamp at the alternator control module.

126. Reposition the radiator inlet hose clamp.

127. Remove the radiator inlet hose from the cylinder head.

128. Remove the radiator outlet hose.

129. Position and install the coolant recovery inlet hose to the cylinder head.

130. Install the coolant recovery inlet pipe clip to the fuel rail.

131. Install the coolant recovery inlet hose clamp at the cylinder head.

132. Position and install the vacuum brake booster hose to the intake manifold.

133. Position the vacuum brake booster hose clamp at the intake manifold.

134. Install the alternator starter.

135. Install the battery tray.

136. Install the transaxle shift cable clip to the fuel line bracket.

137. Install the fuel feed pipe clip to the fuel line bracket.

138. Connect the EVAP line quick connect fitting to the EVAP purge solenoid.

139. Connect the fuel feed pipe quick connect fitting at the fuel rail.

140. Install the air cleaner assembly.

141. Fill the transaxle with the proper amount of fluid.

142. Refill the engine with the proper amount of new oil.

143. Start the engine and allow the engine to run, inspect for leaks. Repair as necessary.

3.5L Engine

1. Before servicing the vehicle, refer to the Precautions Section.

2. Place the wheels in the straight forward position, remove the key from the ignition.

3. Disconnect the battery cables.

4. Remove the air cleaner assembly.

5. Secure the cooling module to the upper body structure.

6. Remove the battery and battery tray.

7. Disconnect the transaxle shifter cable.

8. Disconnect the wiring harness from the underhood junction block.

9. Evacuate the A/C system.

10. Drain the cooling system.

11. Remove the Powertrain Control Module (PCM).

12. Remove the A/C low pressure tube at the front lift bracket.

13. Disconnect the alternator positive cable and the A/C high pressure switch harness.

14. Remove the A/C tube from the compressor.

15. Disconnect the A/C line from the condenser to the compressor.

16. Disconnect the coolant reservoir hose from the engine.

17. Disconnect the radiator inlet and outlet hoses at the engine.

18. Disconnect the heater hoses.

19. Remove the starter positive cable.

20. Relieve the fuel pressure.

21. Disconnect the fuel feed line.

22. Disconnect the fuel Evaporative Emission (EVAP) line.

23. Remove the lower transaxle-to-engine bolts.

24. Remove the PTU as follows:

   a. Remove the propeller shaft.

   b. Drain the transfer case oil.

   c. Remove the exhaust cross-under pipe.

   d. Remove the vent tube clamp.

   e. Remove the vent tube from the transfer case.

   f. Remove the transfer case.

➡**When removing the transfer case/output shaft, do not use excessive force or damage to the bushings may occur.**

g. Remove the transfer case from the transaxle .

25. Remove the torque converter inspection cover.

26. Remove the torque converter to flywheel bolts.

27. Remove the front wheels.

28. Remove the left inner liner.

29. Disconnect the transaxle cooler lines from the transaxle and bracket.

30. Remove the tie rod ends from the steering knuckles.

31. Remove the stabilizer bar links.

32. Disconnect the lower ball joints.

33. Remove the axle shaft nuts.

34. Disconnect the intermediate shaft from the steering gear.

35. Remove the front exhaust pipe.

36. Remove the 3 front fender pushpins to allow the front fender to flex.

37. Matchmark the frame to the body position for installation purposes.

38. Support the engine in the cradle with wood blocks.

39. Disconnect the front engine mount from the body.

40. Lower the vehicle to 3 feet off the ground in order to position an engine support table such as J 39580 under the frame.

41. Remove the cradle bolts.

42. Lower the table to the floor slowly.

43. Remove the starter.

44. Remove the A/C compressor.

45. Remove the alternator.

46. Remove the front covers.

47. Remove the rocker covers.

48. Remove the catalytic converters.

49. Remove the timing belt.

50. Remove the cylinder heads.

51. Remove the front engine mount from the engine.

52. Remove the right engine mount.

53. Separate the engine from the transaxle.

To install:

54. Attach the engine to the transaxle.

55. Install or connect the following:
- The right engine mount
- The front engine mount to the engine
- The cylinder heads
- The timing belt
- The catalytic converters
- The rocker covers
- The front covers
- The alternator
- The A/C compressor
- The starter
- The engine and transaxle assembly in the vehicle

- The cradle bolts. Tighten the bolts to 114 ft. lbs. (155 Nm)

56. Remove the lift table.

57. Install the front engine mount bolts to the body. Tighten the transaxle mount-to-frame bolts to 37 ft. lbs. (50 Nm) and the transaxle mount-to-bracket through bolt, while aligning the transaxle mount to the bracket to 81 ft. lbs. (110 Nm).

58. Remove the wood blocks from the cradle.

59. Install the lower transaxle-to-engine bolts and tighten to 47 ft. lbs. (64 Nm).

60. Install the PTU as follows:

a. Install the transfer case to the transaxle and tighten the bolts to 38 ft. lbs. (51 Nm).

61. Install the vent hose and the clamp to the transfer case.

62. Install the exhaust cross-under pipe.

63. Remove the transfer case check plug and fill the transfer case with synthetic gear oil.

64. Install the check plug and gasket to the case and tighten to 33 ft. lbs. (44 Nm).

65. Install the torque converter–to–flywheel bolts and tighten to 9 ft. lbs. (12 Nm).

66. Install the torque converter inspection cover and tighten to 9 ft. lbs. (12 Nm).

67. Install the 3 front fender push-pins

68. Install the front exhaust pipe.

69. Connect the intermediate shaft from the steering gear.

70. Install the propeller shaft.

71. Install the axle shaft nuts.

72. Connect the lower ball joints.

73. Install the stabilizer bar links.

74. Install tie rod ends to the steering knuckles.

75. Connect the transaxle cooler lines to the transaxle and bracket.

76. Install the left inner liner.

77. Install the front tires.

78. Install the fuel EVAP line.

79. Connect the fuel feed line.

80. Connect the starter positive cable.

81. Install the heater hoses.

82. Connect the radiator hoses to the engine.

83. Attach the A/C tube to the A/C compressor.

84. Connect the coolant reservoir hose.

85. Connect the A/C line from the condenser to compressor.

86. Connect the A/C high pressure switch harness.

87. Connect the alternator wiring.

88. Install the A/C lower pressure tube at the front lift bracket.

89. Install the PCM.

90. Connect the radiator hoses to the engine.

91. Fill the cooling system.

92. Connect the wiring harness to the underhood junction block.

93. Connect the transaxle shifter cable.

94. Remove the cooling module support.

95. Install the battery tray and battery.

96. Install the air cleaner assembly and ducts.

97. Connect the positive and negative battery cables.

EXHAUST MANIFOLD

REMOVAL & INSTALLATION

2.2L Engine

See Figure 152.

1. Before servicing the vehicle, refer to the Precautions Section.

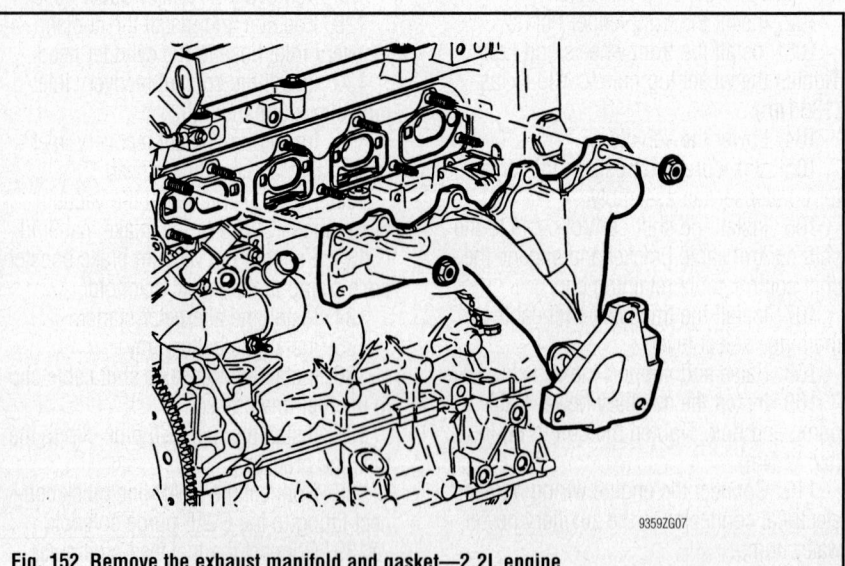

Fig. 152 Remove the exhaust manifold and gasket—2.2L engine

9359ZG07

2. Remove or disconnect the following:
- The negative battery cable
- The air cleaner assembly
- The exhaust manifold heat shield
- The Oxygen (O$_2$S) sensor from the manifold
- The exhaust pipe from the manifold
- The exhaust pipe-to-resonator pipe nuts from behind the converter
- The exhaust manifold pipe and resonator pipe
- The exhaust manifold

To install:

3. Install or connect the following:
- The exhaust manifold with a new gasket and torque the bolts, starting from the center and working outward, to 13 ft. lbs. (18 Nm)
- The O$_2$S sensor and torque it to 33 ft. lbs. (45 Nm)
- The exhaust pipe to the manifold with a new gasket and torque the nuts to 22 ft. lbs. (30 Nm)
- The exhaust pipe-to-resonator pipe nuts and tighten to 31 ft. lbs. (42 Nm)
- The exhaust manifold heat shield and torque the bolts to 18 ft. lbs. (25 Nm)
- The air cleaner assembly
- The negative battery cable

4. Start the vehicle and check for leaks, repair if necessary.

2.4L Engine

See Figure 153.

1. Before servicing the vehicle, refer to the Precautions Section.
2. Remove the exhaust manifold heat shield.
3. Remove the Heated Oxygen Sensor (HO2S).
4. Remove the exhaust manifold pipe.

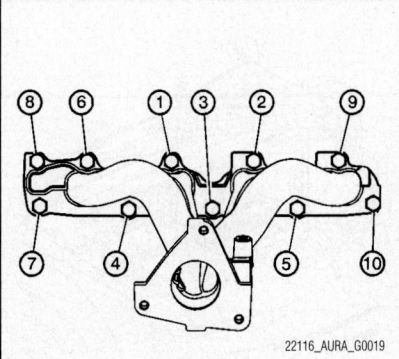

Fig. 153 Exhaust manifold torque sequence—2.4L engine

5. Lower the vehicle.
6. Remove the upper exhaust manifold brace bolt.
7. Remove and discard the exhaust manifold nuts.
8. Remove the exhaust manifold/catalytic converter assembly.
9. Remove and discard the exhaust manifold gasket.

To install:

10. Install a NEW exhaust manifold gasket onto the manifold studs.
11. Install the exhaust manifold/catalytic converter assembly.
12. Install the NEW exhaust manifold nuts finger tight.
13. Install the upper exhaust manifold brace bolt to 43 ft. lbs. (58 Nm).
14. Tighten the manifold bolts in the sequence shown to 10 ft. lbs. (14 Nm).
15. Raise and suitably support the vehicle.
16. Install the exhaust manifold pipe.
17. Install the HO2S.
18. Install the exhaust manifold heat shield.

3.5L Engine

1. Before servicing the vehicle, refer to the Precautions Section.
2. Disconnect the Intake Air Temperature (IAT) sensor connector.
3. Loosen the clasp at the air cleaner assembly.
4. Remove the push-pin attachment from the outlet resonator/duct assembly to support the bracket.
5. Loosen the clamp at the throttle body assembly.
6. Disconnect the Positive Crankcase Ventilation (PCV) hose at the cam cover.
7. Remove the outlet resonator/duct assembly.
8. Remove the exhaust manifold heat shield bolts.
9. Remove the exhaust manifold heat shield.
10. Disconnect the front and rear Oxygen (O$_2$S) sensor connectors.
11. Remove the O$_2$S sensor if the exhaust manifold is being replaced.
12. Remove the exhaust manifold pipe-to-manifold nuts.
13. Remove the exhaust manifold pipe-to-resonator pipe nuts behind the converter.
14. Disconnect the rear O$_2$S sensor wire from the heat shield.
15. Separate the exhaust manifold pipe and resonator pipe and discard the gaskets.

16. Remove the exhaust manifold nuts.
17. Remove the exhaust manifold assembly and discard the gasket.

To install:

18. Install a new manifold gasket on the cylinder head.
19. Install the exhaust manifold and torque the nuts to 13 ft. lbs. (18 Nm).
20. If necessary, transfer the O$_2$S sensor from the old manifold.

➡**Whenever the oxygen sensor is removed, coat the threads with a nickel-based anti-seize.**

21. Install the O2 O$_2$S sensor into the exhaust manifold and tighten to 33 ft. lbs. (45 Nm).
22. Install the gasket and exhaust pipe to the intermediate pipe and tighten the nuts to 22 ft. lbs. (30 Nm).
23. Attach the rear O$_2$S sensor wire to the heat shield.
24. Install a new exhaust manifold gasket onto the exhaust manifold flange studs.
25. Attach the exhaust manifold pipe to the exhaust manifold studs and install the exhaust manifold nuts. Tighten the nuts to 31 ft. lbs. (42 Nm).
26. Install the exhaust manifold heat shield and tighten the bolts to 17 ft. lbs. (23 Nm).
27. Install the outlet resonator/duct assembly.
28. Connect the PVC fresh air vent hose.
29. Tighten the clamp at the throttle body assembly.
30. Position the outlet resonator/duct. assembly up with the support bracket and install the push-pin.
31. Tighten the air cleaner assembly.
32. Connect the IAT sensor connector.

INTAKE MANIFOLD

REMOVAL & INSTALLATION

2.2L Engine

See Figure 154.

1. Before servicing the vehicle, refer to the Precautions Section.
2. Remove or disconnect the following:
- The negative battery cable
- The Intake Air Temperature (IAT) sensor electrical connector
- The air cleaner assembly
- The throttle body electrical connection
- The throttle cable and automatic transaxle downshift cable from the throttle body

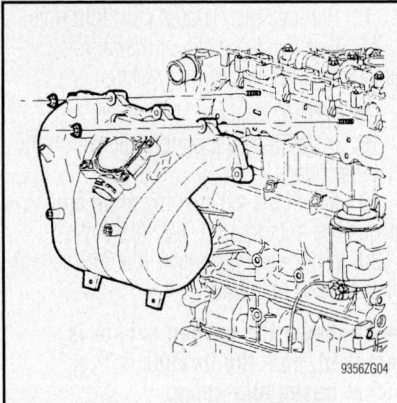

Fig. 154 Intake manifold mounting—2.2L engine

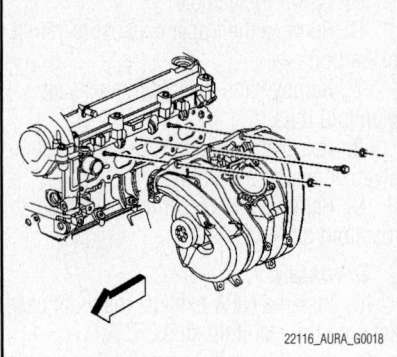

Fig. 155 Intake manifold mounting—2.4L engine

- The throttle body
- The intake manifold

To install:

3. Install or connect the following:
- The intake manifold with a new gasket and torque the nuts to 89 inch lbs. (10 Nm) starting from the center and working outward
- The throttle body to the intake manifold and torque the bolts to 89 inch lbs. (10 Nm)
- The throttle cable and automatic transaxle downshift cable from the throttle body
- The throttle body electrical connection
- The air cleaner assembly
- The IAT sensor electrical connector
- The negative battery cable

4. Start the engine, check for leaks, and repair if necessary.

2.4L Engine

See Figure 155.

1. Before servicing the vehicle, refer to the Precautions Section.
2. Remove the air cleaner outlet duct.
3. Remove the battery box cover.
4. Disconnect the engine wiring harness electrical connectors from the intake and exhaust camshaft position actuator solenoid valves.
5. Remove the ignition coils.
6. Remove the engine harness clips from the cover.
7. Reposition the engine wiring harness out of the way.
8. Remove the fuel feed line retainers from the engine brackets.
9. Remove the camshaft cover bolts.
10. Remove the camshaft cover.
11. Installation is the reverse of removal, tighten the cover bolts to 89 in. lbs. (10 Nm).

3.5L Engine

1. Before servicing the vehicle, refer to the Precautions Section.
2. Remove the outlet resonator/duct assembly.
3. Remove the throttle body.
4. Disconnect the Positive Crankcase Ventilation (PCV) hoses from the intake manifold.
5. Disconnect the brake booster hose from the intake manifold.
6. Remove the intake manifold top cover nuts and bolts.
7. Remove and discard the intake manifold top cover gasket.
8. Remove the Intake Air Temperature (IAT) sensor .
9. Remove the air outlet duct bracket.
10. Remove the intake manifold nuts and bolts.
11. Remove the intake manifold and gasket and discard the gasket.
12. Remove and discard the intake manifold gasket.

To install:

13. Install the intake manifold with a new gasket.
14. Install the intake manifold nuts and bolts in using two passes. On the first pass, tighten to 97 inch lbs. (11 Nm) and the second pass to 16 ft. lbs. (22 Nm) starting in the center and working outwards in a circular pattern.
15. Install the outlet duct bracket and nuts and tighten the nuts to 89 inch lbs. (10 Nm).
16. Install the IAT sensor and tighten to 13 ft. lbs. (18 Nm).
17. Install the intake manifold top cover gasket.
18. Install the intake manifold top cover, nuts, and bolts using two passes. On the first pass, tighten to 53 inch lbs. (6 Nm) and the second pass to 106 inch lbs.

(12 Nm) starting in the center and working outwards in a circular pattern.
19. Install the throttle body.
20. Connect the PCV hoses.
21. Connect the brake booster hose.
22. Install the outlet resonator/duct assembly.

OIL PAN

REMOVAL & INSTALLATION

2.2L Engine

See Figures 156 and 157.

1. Before servicing the vehicle, refer to the Precautions Section.
2. Drain the engine oil.
3. Remove the negative battery cable.
4. Remove the oil dipstick tube.
5. Install an engine support fixture.
6. Remove the Right hand engine mount and raise the engine 3 inches using the support tool.
7. Remove the lower A/C compressor bolt.
8. Remove the oil pan bolts.
9. Using a flat blade tool, pry the oil pan from the engine block.

To install:

10. Apply a 0.08 in. (2mm) bead of RTV sealer to the pan flange. Be sure the RTV is applied to the inner side of the flange.
11. Install the oil pan and torque the bolts in the proper sequence to 11 ft. lbs. (15 Nm).
12. Install the lower A/C compressor bolt and tighten to 15 ft. lbs. (20 Nm).
13. Install the right hand engine mount.
14. Remove the engine support fixture.
15. Install the oil dipstick tube.
16. Connect the negative battery cable.
17. Fill the engine with the proper amount of clean oil.
18. Start the vehicle and check for leaks, repair if necessary.

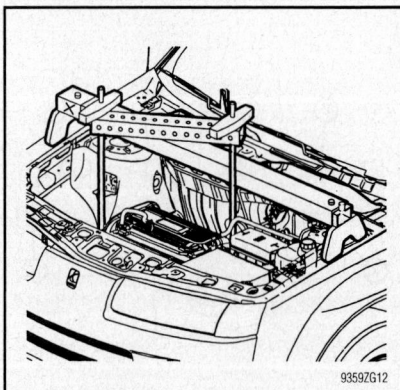

Fig. 156 Use the engine support tool to raise the engine—2.2L engines

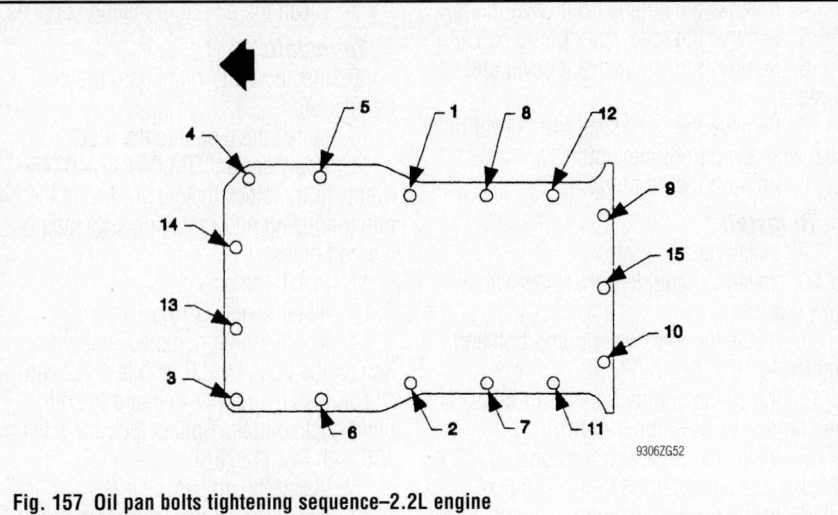

Fig. 157 Oil pan bolts tightening sequence–2.2L engine

2.4L Engine

See Figure 158.

1. Before servicing the vehicle, refer to the Precautions Section.
2. Remove the accessory drive belt.
3. Remove the oil level indicator tube.

➡**The support fixture bar must be installed to provide enough access to remove and properly tighten the oil pan bolts.**

4. Install the engine support fixture.
5. Remove engine mount.
6. Using the engine support fixture, raise the engine approximately 3 inches.
7. Raise and support the vehicle.
8. Loosen the upper Air Conditioning (A/C) compressor bolts.
9. Remove the lower A/C compressor bolt.
10. Place a suitable drain pan under the oil pan drain plug.
11. Remove the oil pan drain plug.
12. Drain the engine oil.
13. Reinstall the oil pan drain plug until snug.
14. Disconnect the engine wiring harness electrical connector from the alternator control module coolant pump.
15. Remove the alternator control module coolant pump bolt.
16. Remove the alternator control module coolant pump from the oil pan.
17. Remove the 4 oil pan to transaxle bolts.
18. Remove the oil pan bolts.
19. Remove the oil pan
20. Remove any old oil pan sealant.

To install:

21. Ensure that the oil pan and the sealing surface on the lower crankcase are free of all oil and debris. Apply a 2mm bead of sealant around the perimeter of the oil pan and the oil suction port opening. DO NOT over apply the sealant. More than a 2mm bead is not required.
22. Install the oil pan.
23. Install the oil pan bolts and hand tighten.
24. Install the 4 oil pan to transaxle bolts. Tighten the bolts to 55 ft. lbs. (75 Nm).
25. Tighten the oil pan bolts in the sequence shown to 18 ft. lbs. (25 Nm).
26. Install the alternator control module coolant pump to the oil pan. Ensure that the anti-rotation tab is inserted into the hole in the oil pan.
27. Install the alternator control module coolant pump bolt and tighten to 18 ft. lbs. (25 Nm).
28. Connect the engine wiring harness electrical connector to the alternator control module coolant pump.
29. Lower the vehicle.
30. Using the engine support fixture, lower the engine.

31. Install the engine mount.
32. Remove the engine support fixture.
33. Install the oil level indicator tube.
34. Install the accessory drive belt.
35. Fill the engine oil to the proper level.

3.5L Engine

1. Before servicing the vehicle, refer to the Precautions Section.
2. Drain the engine oil.
3. Remove the rear engine cover.
4. Remove the cross-under exhaust pipe brace and pipe.
5. Remove the oil pan bolts and pan.
6. Clean the pan mating surfaces.

To install:

7. Apply sealant GM P/N 12346240 evenly to the oil pan mating surface of the engine block.
8. Install the oil pan to the engine. Tighten the bolts in two passes:
    a. First pass to 53 inch lbs. (6 Nm).
    b. Second pass to 106 inch lbs. (12 Nm).
9. Install the rear engine cover.
10. Install the cross-under exhaust pipe brace and pipe.
11. Refill the engine with the proper type and amount of engine oil.

OIL PUMP

REMOVAL & INSTALLATION

2.2L Engine

See Figure 159.

1. Before servicing the vehicle, refer to the Precautions Section.
2. Drain the engine oil.
3. Remove or disconnect the following:
   - The negative battery cable
   - The air cleaner assembly
   - The right front wheel and splash shield

Fig. 158 Oil pan bolt tightening sequence—2.4L engine

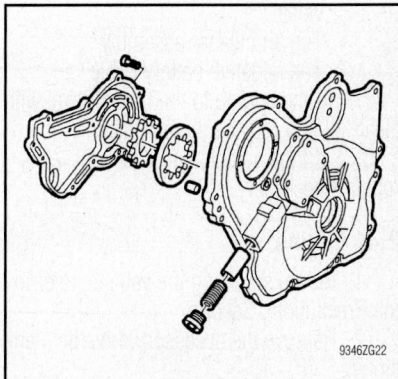

Fig. 159 Front cover and oil pump assembly—2.2L engine

- The accessory drive belt
- The crankshaft damper pulley
- The belt tensioner

4. Install an engine support fixture.
5. Remove or disconnect the following:
- The right front engine mount
- The front cover bolts and the 13mm bolt under the water pump
- The front cover
- The oil pump cover plate
- The drive rotor and driven rotor
- The pressure relief valve

To install:

➡**Whenever the oil pump is installed, the assembly must be packed with petroleum jelly in order to prime the pump.**

6. Install or connect the following:
- The new relief valve into the cover bore, if removed. Coat the valve with clean engine oil and tap it into the bore. Torque the plug to 30 ft. lbs. (40 Nm)
- The drive and driven rotors into the pump with the chamfer toward the front oil seal
- The oil pump body cover using new bolts and torque the bolts to 53 inch lbs. (6 Nm)
- The front cover with a new oil seal and torque the perimeter and center bolts to 19 ft. lbs. (25 Nm) and the lower center bolt to 89 inch lbs. (10 Nm)
- The right side engine mount and torque the bolts to 41 ft. lbs. (55 Nm)
- The engine support fixture
- The drive belt tensioner and torque the bolts 37 ft. lbs. (50 Nm)
- The crankshaft damper pulley and torque the bolt to 74 ft. lbs. (100 Nm) plus 75°
- The accessory drive belt
- The right front splash shield and wheel
- The air cleaner assembly
- The negative battery cable

7. Fill the engine to the proper level with clean oil and replace the oil filter.
8. Start the vehicle and check for leaks, repair if necessary.

2.4L Engine

1. Before servicing the vehicle, refer to the Precautions Section.
2. Remove the accessory drive belt tensioner.
3. Remove the drive belt tensioner bracket.

4. Remove the engine front cover bolts.
5. Remove the long water pump bolt.
6. Remove the engine front cover and gaskets.
7. Remove the crankshaft front cover oil seal with an appropriate tool.
8. Remove the oil pump.

To install:

9. Install the oil pump.
10. Install the engine front cover with a new gasket.
11. Install the long water pump bolt and tighten to 18 ft. lbs. (25 Nm).
12. Install the engine front cover bolts and tighten to 18 ft. lbs. (25 Nm).
13. Install the drive belt tensioner bracket and tighten to 33 ft. lbs. (45 Nm).
14. Install the accessory drive belt tensioner and tighten to 33 ft. lbs. (45 Nm).

3.5L Engine

See Figure 160.

1. Before servicing the vehicle, refer to the Precautions Section.
2. Remove the timing belt.
3. Remove the timing belt idler pulley.
4. Remove the oil flow control module.
5. Remove the oil pan.
6. Remove the oil pump pickup tube.
7. Remove the oil pump bolts and pump.

8. Clean the oil pump mating surfaces.

To install:

9. Install new O-rings onto the oil transfer pipe.
10. Install the pipe into the block.
11. Apply sealant GM P/N 12346240 evenly to the block mating surface of the oil pump housing and to the inner threads of the bolt holes.
12. Install the pins.
13. Install a new O-ring.
14. Install the oil pump assembly and tighten the bolts to 106 inch lbs. (12 Nm).
15. Install a new O-ring and the oil pump pickup tube. Tighten the tube bolts to 106 inch lbs. (12 Nm).
16. Install the oil pan.
17. Install the oil flow control module.
18. Install the timing belt idler pulley.
19. Install the timing belt.

INSPECTION

See Figures 161 through 163.

1. With the timing chain front cover and the oil pump body cover removed, use a feeler gauge to measure the clearance between the driven rotor and pump body. Clearance should not exceed 0.011 in. (0.277mm).
2. Use a feeler gauge to measure the clearance between the both rotor tips.

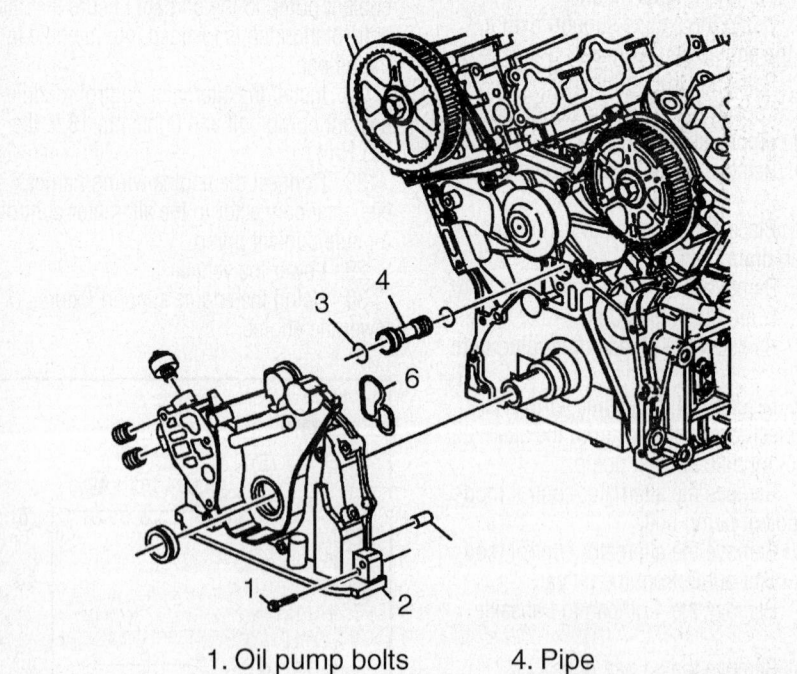

1. Oil pump bolts	4. Pipe
2. Oil pump	5. Pins
3. O-ring	6. O-ring

71461-SVUE-G09

Fig. 160 Exploded view of the oil pump assembly—3.5L engine

Clearance should not exceed 0.006 in. (0.150mm).

3. Using Plastigage®or a feeler gauge, temporarily install the pump cover and measure the rotor-to-cover clearance. Clearance should not exceed 0.005 in. (0.128mm).

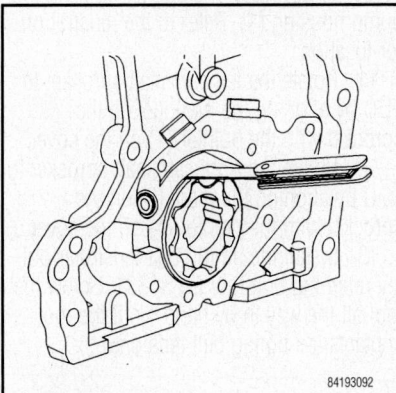

Fig. 161 Use a feeler gauge to measure the clearance between the driven rotor and pump body

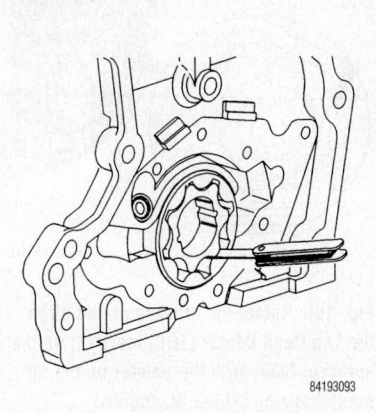

Fig. 162 Use a feeler gauge to measure the clearance between both rotor tips

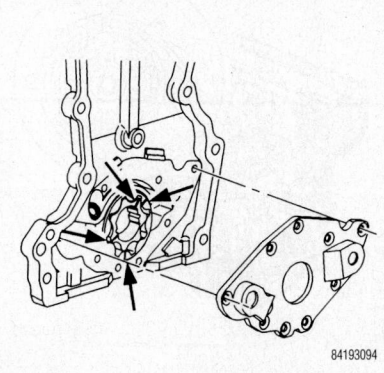

Fig. 163 Temporarily install the pump cover and measure the rotor-to-cover clearance

4. If necessary, replace the pump components and/or the front cover assembly.

PISTON AND RING

POSITIONING

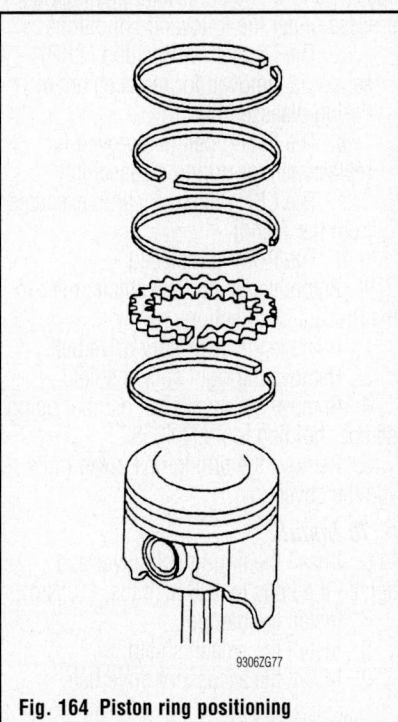

Fig. 164 Piston ring positioning

REAR MAIN SEAL

REMOVAL & INSTALLATION

2.2L Engine

See Figure 165.

1. Before servicing the vehicle, refer to the Precautions Section.

2. Remove or disconnect the following:
   • The negative battery cable
   • The transaxle
   • The clutch/pressure plate assembly, if equipped with a manual transaxle
   • The flywheel

3. Center punch the steel ring of the oil seal.

4. Drill a small hole into the steel ring.

5. Install a self-tapping screw and using a pliers, pull out the rear main oil seal.

✷✷ WARNING

Be careful not to damage or scratch the seal mounting surfaces.

To install:

6. Lubricate the new rear main bearing seal with engine oil.

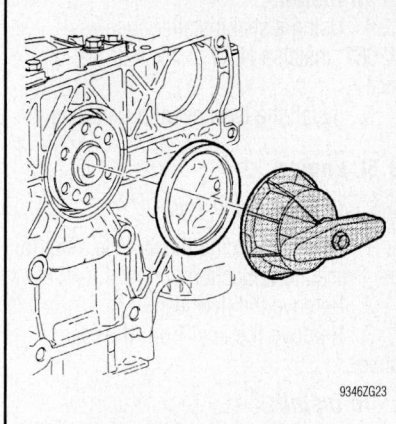

Fig. 165 Rear oil seal and installation tool J42067—2.2L engine

7. Install or connect the following:
   • A NEW rear main seal using a Rear Main Bearing Oil Seal Installer Tool J42067 until it is flush with the block
   • The flywheel
   • The clutch/pressure plate assembly, if equipped with a manual transaxle
   • The transaxle
   • The negative battery cable

8. Start the engine and check for leaks, repair if necessary.

2.4L Engine

See Figure 166.

1. Before servicing the vehicle, refer to the Precautions Section.

2. Remove the transaxle and flywheel.

➡Do not damage the outside diameter of the crankshaft or chamber with any tool.

3. Pry out the crankshaft rear oil seal using a flat-bladed tool.

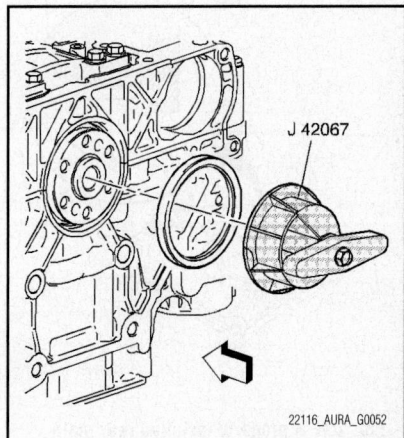

Fig. 166 Installing the rear seal—2.4L engine

To install:

4. Using a seal installer such as J 42067, install a NEW crankshaft real oil seal.

5. Install the flywheel and transaxle

3.5L Engine

See Figures 167 and 168.

1. Before servicing the vehicle, refer to the Precautions Section.

2. Remove the flywheel.

3. Remove the seal from the rear cover.

To install:

4. Lubricate the lip of the oil seal with a light coat of grease.

5. Use the driver handle tool EN 46342 and driver tool EN 46351 to install the seal squarely into the housing.

6. Drive the new crankshaft oil seal until the tool bottoms onto the housing. A properly installed seal will be flush with the face of the housing.

7. Install the engine flywheel.

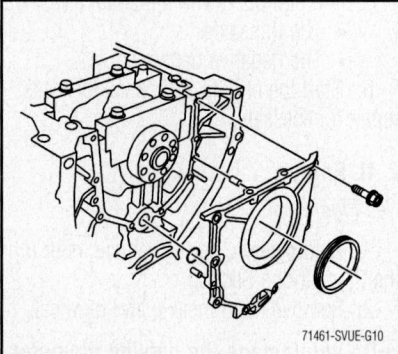

Fig. 167 Exploded view of the rear main seal—3.5L engine

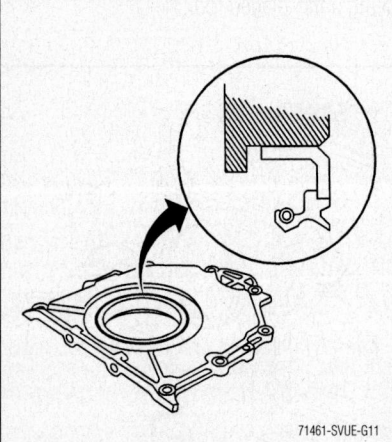

Fig. 168 A properly installed rear main seal will be flush with the face of the housing—3.5L engine

TIMING BELT FRONT COVER

REMOVAL & INSTALLATION

3.5L Engine

The Powertrain Control Module (PCM) has to perform the crankshaft position learn process under the following conditions:

a. The Crankshaft Position (CKP) sensor is removed for replacement or during disassembly.

b. The timing belt is removed for replacement or during disassembly.

c. The CKP Pattern Clear is executed from the Tech II.

d. The PCM is replaced

1. Before servicing the vehicle, refer to the Precautions Section.

2. Remove the accessory drive belt.

3. Remove the right splash shield.

4. Remove the crankshaft damper using damper holding tool EN 46337.

5. Remove the timing belt cover bolts and the cover.

To install:

6. Install the timing belt cover and tighten the bolts to 106 inch lbs. (12 Nm).

7. Install the damper.

8. Install the splash shield.

9. Install the accessory drive belt.

TIMING BELT AND SPROCKETS

REMOVAL & INSTALLATION

3.5L Engine

See Figures 169 through 175.

The Powertrain Control Module (PCM) has to perform the crankshaft position learn process under the following conditions:

a. The Crankshaft Position (CKP) sensor is removed for replacement or during disassembly.

b. The timing belt is removed for replacement or during disassembly.

c. The CKP Pattern Clear is executed from the Tech II.

d. The PCM is replaced

1. Before servicing the vehicle, refer to the Precautions Section.

2. Remove the accessory drive belt.

3. Remove the right splash shield.

4. Remove the crankshaft damper using damper holding tool EN 46337.

5. Remove the timing belt cover bolts and the cover.

6. Use timing belt tensioner pulley retaining bolt tool EN 36331 to retain the tensioner pulley.

7. Loosen the idler pulley bolt about 5 or 6 turns.

8. Remove the timing belt from the pulleys.

To install:

9. Clean the belt pulleys and covers.

10. Rotate the crankshaft and align the Top Dead Center (TDC) mark (2) on the sprocket (237) with the pointer on the oil pump housing (1). Refer to the illustration for location.

11. Rotate the left camshaft sprocket to TDC by aligning the mark (2) on the sprocket with the pointer (1) on the cover.

12. Rotate the right camshaft sprocket to TDC by aligning the mark (2) on the sprocket with the pointer (1) on the cover.

13. Install the timing belt tensioner pulley retaining bolt tool EN 36331. Screw the tool all the way in by hand, until the tool contacts the timing belt tensioner.

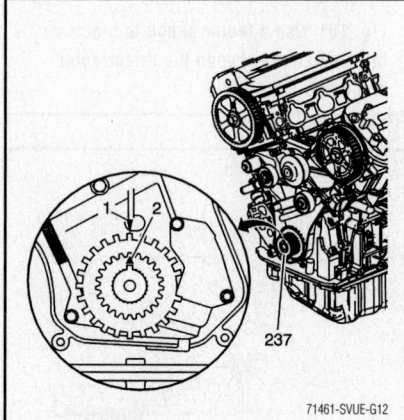

Fig. 169 Rotate the crankshaft and align the Top Dead Center (TDC) mark (2) on the sprocket (237) with the pointer on the oil pump housing (1)—3.5L engine

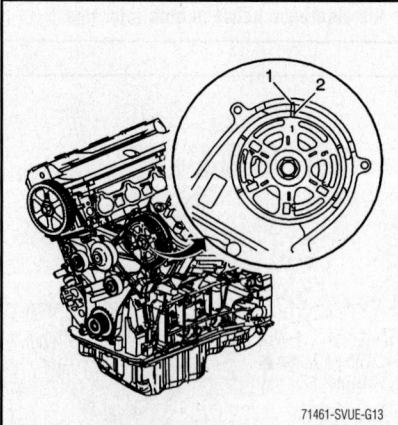

Fig. 170 Rotate the left camshaft sprocket to TDC by aligning the mark (2) on the sprocket with the pointer (1) on the cover—3.5L engine

Fig. 171 Rotate the right camshaft sprocket to TDC by aligning the mark (2) on the sprocket with the pointer (1) on the cover—3.5L engine

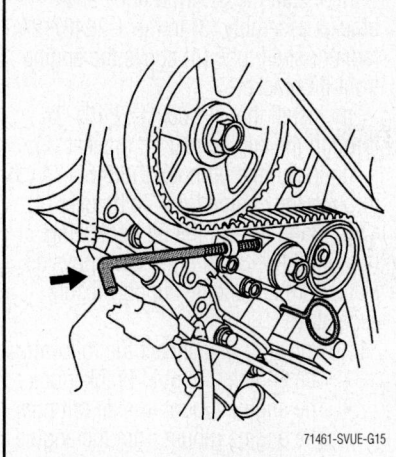

Fig. 172 Install timing belt tensioner pulley retaining bolt tool EN 36331—3.5L engine

Fig. 173 Install timing belt onto the sprockets—3.5L engine

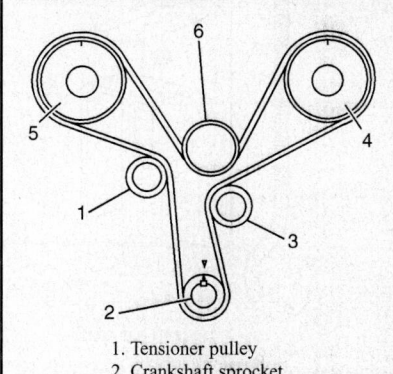

1. Tensioner pulley
2. Crankshaft sprocket
3. Idler pulley
4. Camshaft sprocket - left
5. Camshaft sprocket - right
6. Water pump

Fig. 174 Install timing belt on the pulleys in the sequence shown—3.5L engine

14. Install the belt onto the sprockets. Install the timing belt in a clockwise sequence starting with the tensioner pulley in the sequence illustrated.

15. Tighten the idler pulley bolt to 33 ft. lbs. (44 Nm).

16. Remove the tools.

17. Install the guide (236), balancer/damper (228), and bolt (227) and tighten the bolt until snug.

18. Using the damper holding tool EN 46337 rotate the crankshaft clockwise about 5 or 6 complete revolutions to position the timing belt on the sprockets.

19. Align the mark (2) on the sprocket with the pointer (1) on the oil pump housing.

20. Inspect the left camshaft sprocket for proper alignment. The TDC mark (2) on the sprocket should align with the pointer (1) on the cover.

21. Inspect the right camshaft sprocket for proper alignment. The TDC mark (2) on the sprocket should align with the pointer (1) on the cover.

22. Remove the damper.

23. Install the timing belt cover and tighten the bolts to 106 inch lbs. (12 Nm).

24. Install the damper.

25. Install the splash shield.

26. Install the accessory drive belt.

TIMING CHAIN COVER AND SEAL

REMOVAL & INSTALLATION

2.2L Engine

See Figure 176.

1. Before servicing the vehicle, refer to the Precautions Section.

2. Remove or disconnect the following:
- The crankshaft damper. Refer to Crankshaft Damper removal and installation
- The drive belt tensioner
- The idler pulley
- The timing chain cover to water pump bolt
- The remaining cover bolts
- The engine timing chain front cover

3. If the seal is damaged, remove the front engine mount and seal.

To install:

4. If removed, install a new seal.

5. Install the front engine mount.

6. Install or connect the following:
- The timing chain front cover
- The cover bolts. Tighten the cover bolts to 18 ft. lbs. (25 Nm)

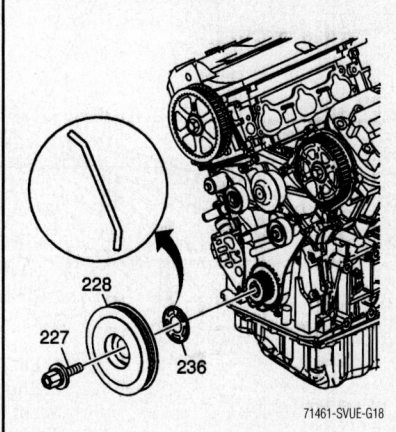

Fig. 175 Install the guide (236), balancer/damper (228), and bolt (227)—3.5L engine

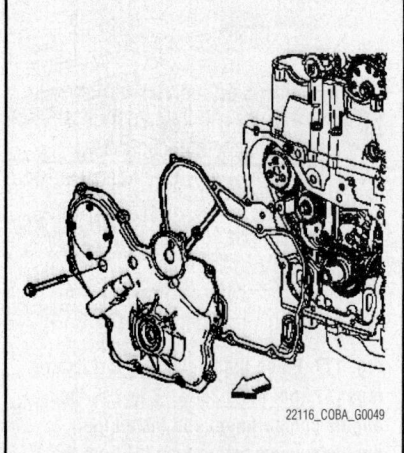

Fig. 176 Removing long water pump bolt and remaining cover bolts

- The water pump bolt. Tighten the water pump bolt to 18 ft. lbs. (25 Nm)
- The idler pulley. Tighten the bolts to 18 ft. lbs. (25 Nm)
- The drive belt tensioner
- The drive belt tensioner bolts. Tighten the drive belt tensioner bolts to 33 ft. lbs. (45 Nm)
- The crankshaft damper. Refer to Crankshaft Damper removal and installation.

2.4L Engine

See Figures 177 through 184.

1. Before servicing the vehicle, refer to the Precautions Section.
2. Remove or disconnect the following:
- The drive belt tensioner
- The crankshaft damper
- The air cleaner assembly.
- The windshield washer solvent reservoir
3. Install the engine support fixture:
   a. Place the engine support fixture legs (1) from the J 28467-B across the engine compartment.
   b. Install the engine support fixture legs (1) from the J 28467-500 on the engine support fixture long bar (2).
   c. Install the radiator shelf tube J-28467-2A (1) on top of the strut tower tube J-28467-3 (2) above the engine front (right back) lift hook bracket.
   d. Install the round tube of the front support assembly J-28467-4A (3) through the large hole in the radiator shelf tube J-28467-2A.

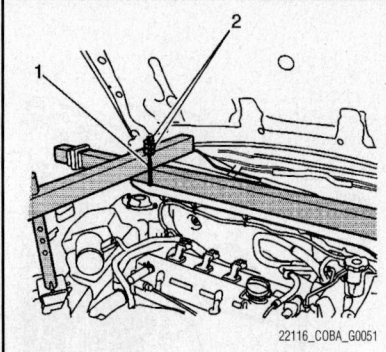

Fig. 178 Install the J-28467-1A cross bracket assembly (1) and hand tighten the J-28467-1A cross bracket wing nuts (2)—2.4L engine

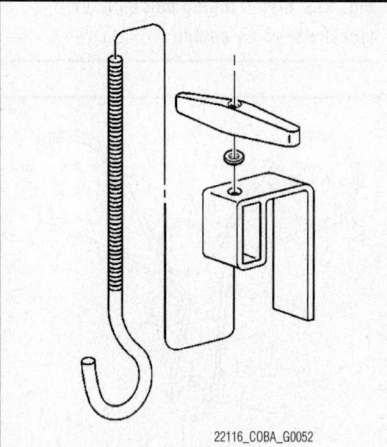

Fig. 179 View of the J-28467-7A bolt hook and the J-28467-34 lift hook wing nut and washer for installing the engine support fixture—2.4L engine

e. Position the J-28467-4A front support assembly on to the upper tie bar.

f. Install the J-28467-9 7/16 inch x 2.0 inch quick-release pin (4) through the top hole in the J-28467-4A front support assembly.

g. Install the J-28467-1A cross bracket assembly (1).

h. Hand tighten the J-28467-1A cross bracket wing nuts (2).

i. Install the J-28467-7A bolt hook through the J-28467-6A bracket.

j. Install the J-28467-34 lift hook wing nut and washer to the J-28467-7A lift hook.

k. Repeat the previous 2 steps in order to assemble 2 lift hooks and brackets.

l. Install one of the lift hook and bracket assemblies (1) to the engine support fixture long bar (2).

m. Install the other lift hook and bracket assembly (3) to the J-28467-2A radiator shelf tube (4) above the engine front lift bracket.

n. Install the lift hook J-28467-7A through the engine rear lift bracket (2).

o. Install the lift hook J-28467-7A (3) through the engine front lift bracket (4).

p. Hand tighten the lift hook wing nuts J-28467-34 in order to remove all slack from the engine support fixture assembly.

4. Remove or disconnect the following:
- The engine mount to bracket bolts
- The engine mount to side rail nuts
- The engine mount from the engine compartment

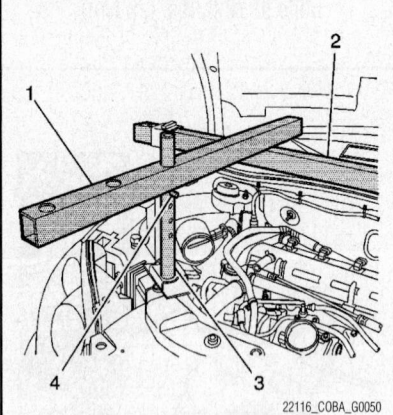

Fig. 177 Place the engine support fixture legs (1) from the J 28467-B across the engine compartment and install the engine support fixture legs (1) from the J 28467-500 on the engine support fixture long bar (2)—2.4L engine

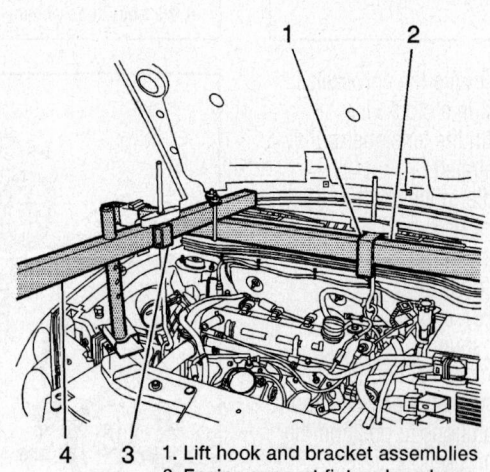

1. Lift hook and bracket assemblies
2. Engine support fixture long bar
3. Lift hook and bracket assembly
4. J-28467-2A radiator shelf tube

Fig. 180 Installing lift hook and bracket assemblies to the engine support fixture long bar, lift hook, and bracket assembly to the J-28467-2A radiator shelf tube—2.4L engine

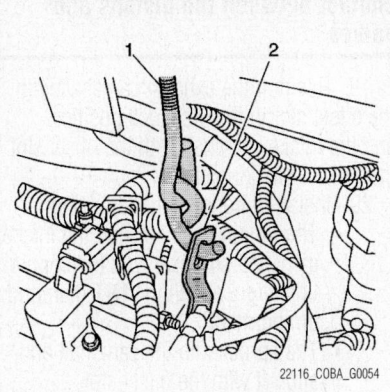

Fig. 181 Install the lift hook J-28467-7A through the engine rear lift bracket (2)—2.4L engine

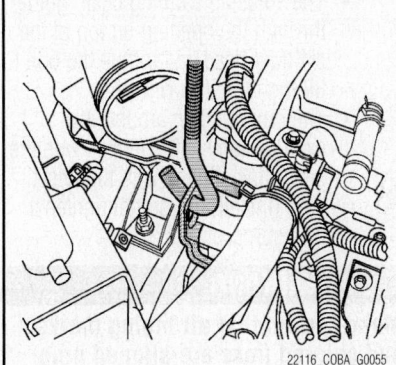

Fig. 182 Install the lift hook J-28467-7A (3) through the engine front lift bracket (4)—2.4L engine

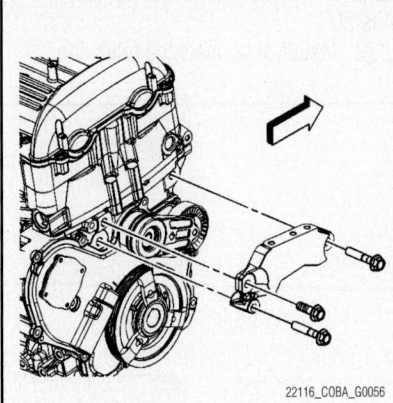

Fig. 183 Removing the engine mount bracket to engine bolts—2.4L engine

- The engine mount bracket to engine bolts
- The engine mount bracket
- The engine front cover to water pump bolt

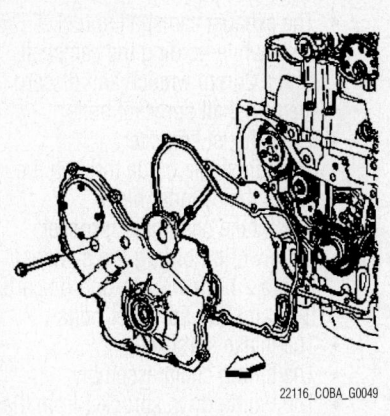

Fig. 184 Removing long water pump bolt and remaining cover bolts

5. Raise and suitably support the vehicle.

6. Remove the timing chain cover bolts.

7. Remove the timing chain cover.

8. Remove and discard the timing chain cover seal.

To install:

9. Install a NEW timing chain cover seal.

10. Install the timing chain cover.

11. Install the timing chain cover bolts. Tighten the bolts to 18 ft. lbs. (25 Nm).

12. Lower the vehicle.

13. Install the timing chain cover to water pump bolt. Tighten the bolt to 18 ft. lbs. (25 Nm).

14. Position the engine mount bracket to the engine.

15. Install the engine mount bracket bolts in the following locations:

    a. The long bolts in the forward and lower rear holes.

    b. The short bolt in the upper rear hole.

16. Tighten the engine mount bracket bolts in the following sequence:

    a. Upper rear.

    b. Lower rear.

    c. Forward..

    d. Tighten the bolts to 37 ft. lbs. (50 Nm).

17. Install the engine mount to the engine compartment.

18. Install the engine mount to side rail nuts. Tighten the nuts to 74 ft. lbs. (100 Nm).

19. Install the engine mount to bracket bolts.

20. Tighten the engine mount to bracket bolts in the following sequence:

    a. Middle

    b. Rear

    c. Front

    d. Tighten the bolts to 37 ft. lbs. (50 Nm).

21. Remove the engine support fixture. Removal is reverse of the installation.

22. Install or connect the following:

- The windshield washer solvent reservoir
- The air cleaner assembly
- The crankshaft damper. Refer to Crankshaft Damper removal and installation
- The accessory drive belt tensioner

TIMING CHAIN AND SPROCKETS

REMOVAL & INSTALLATION

2.2L Engine

See Figures 185 through 188.

1. Before servicing the vehicle, refer to the Precautions Section.

2. Drain the cooling system.

3. Drain the engine oil.

4. Properly relieve the fuel system pressure.

5. Remove or disconnect the following:

- The negative battery cable
- The Intake Air Temperature (IAT) sensor connection
- The air cleaner assembly
- The ignition module assembly
- The Electronic Control Module (ECM) connections
- The oil dipstick tube bolt
- The throttle body electrical connection
- The electrical connector from the fuel injector harness and attachment at the bottom of the intake manifold
- The electrical connector at the purge solenoid and Manifold Absolute Pressure (MAP) sensor
- The vacuum hose at the brake booster
- The coolant pipe bracket bolts from the cylinder head
- The degas hose clamp from the cylinder head and fuel rail and position aside
- The ground strap from the rear cam cover
- The fuel rail bracket from the cam cover
- The fuel lines
- The cam cover

6. Position the No. 1 piston 60° Before Top dead center (BTDC) using a 24mm wrench to rotate the camshafts in a clockwise motion and make sure the diamond

shaped hole on the intake sprocket is at the 12 o'clock position.

7. Remove the upper timing guide.

➡**Remove the timing chain tensioner to unload chain tension before removing the timing chain.**

9359ZG03

Fig. 185 Position the No. 1 piston 60 degrees Before Top dead center (BTDC) using a 24mm wrench to rotate the camshafts in a clockwise motion and make sure the diamond shaped hole on the intake sprocket is at the 12 o'clock position—2.2L engine

8. Remove the fixed timing chain guide access plug.

9. Remove the upper fixed guide bolt using a magnetic socket

10. Install a three bar engine support fixture.

11. Remove the right hand engine mount.

12. Remove the right hand mount bracket.

13. Remove the right wheel splash shield.

14. Install a 1 in. x 2 in. x 4 in. block of wood between the oil pan and cradle.

15. Remove the accessory drive belt.

16. Remove the accessory drive belt tensioner assembly.

17. Install crankshaft pullet holder J38122A.

18. Remove or disconnect the following:
- The crankshaft damper bolt and pulley
- The front cover bolts
- The lower water pump bolt
- The front cover and gasket
- The lower fixed guide
- The upper radiator hose from the cylinder head
- The exhaust manifold pipe nuts
- The front and rear Oxygen (O2S) sensor electrical connector
- The down pipe-to-intermediate pipe nuts

- The down pipe
- The exhaust camshaft sprocket bolts while holding the camshaft with a 24mm wrench and discard the camshaft sprocket bolts
- The exhaust sprocket
- The adjustable guide through the top of the cylinder head
- The intake camshaft sprocket bolts while holding the camshaft with a 24mm wrench and discard the camshaft sprocket bolts
- The intake sprocket
- The timing chain assembly
- The timing drive sprocket from the crankshaft

To install:

✳✳ WARNING

Set the crankshaft to 60° Before Top Dead Center (BTDC) to prevent

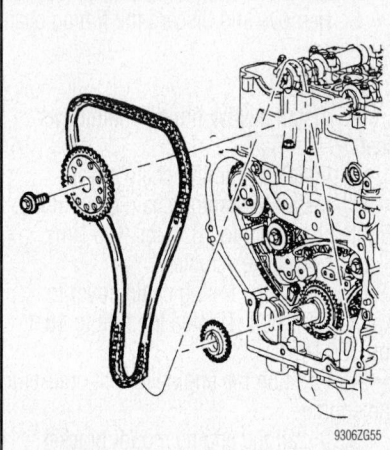

9306ZG55

Fig. 186 Remove the timing chain through the top of the cylinder head—2.2L engine

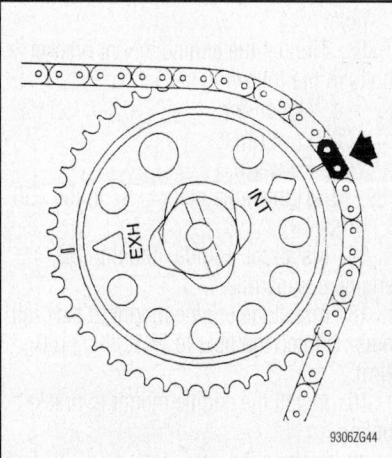

9306ZG44

Fig. 187 Align the copper link on the timing chain with the INT diamond timing mark

contact between the pistons and valves.

19. Position the exhaust camshaft with the offset slot in the 2 o'clock position and the intake camshaft with the offset slot in the 11 o'clock position.

20. Install or connect the following:
- The timing chain around the intake camshaft sprocket with the copper link aligned with the **INT** diamond timing mark
- The sprocket to the camshaft and align it with the offset slot
- The new camshaft sprocket bolt but do not tighten
- The timing chain around the crankshaft sprocket and align the silver link to the timing mark
- The adjustable timing chain guide through the opening on top of the cylinder head and torque the bolt to 89 inch lbs. (10 Nm)
- The timing chain around the exhaust camshaft sprocket with the silver link aligned with the offset slot. (Install, but do not tighten a new sprocket bolt)

✳✳ WARNING

Make certain that all timing marks and colored links are aligned properly before proceeding to the next step. If the timing chain is not aligned properly, severe engine damage may occur.

21. Torque the intake and exhaust camshaft bolts to 63 ft. lbs. (85 Nm) plus 30°.

22. Install or connect the following:

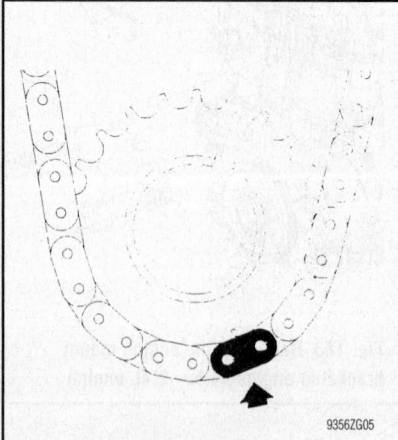

9356ZG05

Fig. 188 Route the timing chain around the crankshaft sprocket and align the silver link to the timing mark (5 o'clock position)—2.2L engines

- The fixed timing guide and torque the bolt to 89 inch lbs. (10 Nm)
- The fixed timing guide bolt access plug after applying Loctite®to the threads and torque it to 30 ft. lbs. (40 Nm)
- The timing chain tensioner and torque the bolts 55 ft. lbs. (75 Nm)

23. Tap the top of the timing chain between the camshaft sprockets to engage the tensioner.

24. Install or connect the following:
- The upper timing chain guide and torque the bolts to 89 inch lbs. (10 Nm)
- The front cover with a new gasket and torque the bolts to 18 ft. lbs. (25 Nm)
- The water pump bolt and torque it to 18 ft. lbs. (25 Nm)
- The crankshaft damper and torque the bolt to 74 ft. lbs. (100 Nm) plus 75 degrees
- The drive belt tensioner and torque the bolts to 30 ft. lbs. (40 Nm)
- The exhaust manifold pipe to the manifold and tighten the nuts to 22 ft. lbs. (30 Nm).
- The oil dipstick tube bolt to 89 inch lbs. (10 Nm).
- The engine mount bracket and torque the bolts to 66 ft. lbs. (90 Nm)
- The engine mount to body nuts to 81 ft. lbs. (110 Nm)
- The engine mount to the bracket and torque the bolts to 41 ft. lbs. (55 Nm)

25. Install the remaining components in the reverse order of removal.

26. Fill the engine to the proper level with clean oil.

27. Fill the cooling system.

28. Prime the fuel system by cycling the ignition **ON** for 5 seconds and **OFF** for 10 seconds a few times without cranking the engine.

29. Start the engine, check for leaks, and repair if necessary

2.4L Engine

See Figures 189 through 199.

1. Remove the No. 1 cylinder spark plug.

2. Rotate the crankshaft in the engine rotational direction clockwise, until the No. 1 piston is at Top Dead Center (TDC) on the compression stroke.

3. Remove the camshaft cover.

4. Remove the engine front cover as follows:

a. Remove the accessory drive belt tensioner.

b. Remove the crankshaft damper.

c. Install the engine support fixture.

d. Remove the engine mount to bracket bolts.

e. Remove the engine mount to side rail nuts.

f. Remove the engine mount from the engine compartment.

g. Remove the engine mount bracket to engine bolts.

h. Remove the engine mount bracket.

i. Remove the engine front cover to water pump bolt.

j. Raise and suitably support the vehicle.

k. Remove the engine front cover bolts.

l. Remove the engine front cover.

m. Remove and discard the engine front cover gasket.

5. Remove the upper timing chain guide bolts and guide.

➡**The timing chain tensioner must be removed to unload chain tension before the timing chain is removed. If it is not, the timing chain will become cocked and it will be difficult to remove.**

6. Remove the timing chain tensioner.

7. Install a 24mm wrench on the hex on the exhaust camshaft in order to hold the camshaft.

8. Remove and discard the exhaust camshaft actuator bolt.

9. Remove the exhaust camshaft actuator from the camshaft and timing chain.

10. Remove the timing chain tensioner guide bolt and guide.

11. Remove the fixed timing chain guide access plug.

12. Remove the fixed timing chain guide bolts and guide.

13. Install a 24mm wrench on the hex on the intake camshaft in order to hold the camshaft.

14. Remove and discard the intake camshaft actuator bolt.

15. Remove the intake camshaft actuator, and the timing chain through the top of the cylinder head.

16. Remove the timing chain crankshaft sprocket.

17. If replacing the balance shaft timing chain and sprocket, perform the following:

a. Remove the balance shaft drive chain tensioner bolts and tensioner.

b. Remove the adjustable balance shaft chain guide bolt and guide.

c. Remove the small balance shaft drive chain guide bolts and guide.

d. Remove the upper balance shaft drive chain guide bolts and guide.

➡**It may ease removal of the balance shaft drive chain to get all the slack in the chain between the crankshaft and water pump sprockets.**

18. Remove the balance shaft drive chain.

19. Remove the balance shaft drive sprocket .

To install:

20. If replacing the balance shaft timing chain, perform the following:

a. Install the balance shaft drive sprocket.

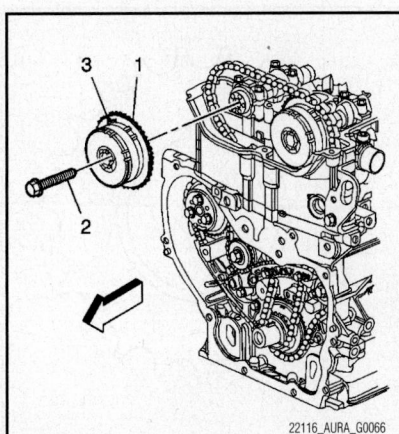

Fig. 189 Remove and discard the exhaust camshaft actuator bolt (2). Remove the exhaust camshaft actuator (1, 3) from the camshaft and timing chain—2.4L engine

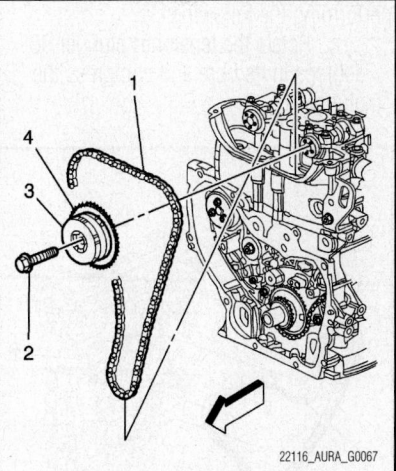

Fig. 190 Remove and discard the intake camshaft actuator bolt (2). Remove the intake camshaft actuator (3), and the timing chain through the top of the cylinder head—2.4L engine

➡ **If the balance shafts are not properly timed to the engine, the engine may vibrate or make noise.**

b. Install the balance shaft drive chain with the colored link lined up with the marks on the balance shaft sprockets and the balance shaft drive sprocket. There are 3 colored links on the chain. Two are chrome and 1 is copper.

c. Use the following steps in order to line up the links with the sprockets:

- Place the copper link (5) so that it lines up with the timing mark (2) on the intake side balance shaft sprocket
- Working clockwise around the chain, place the chrome link (4) in line with the timing mark (3) on the balance shaft drive sprocket. (approximately 6 o'clock position on the sprocket)
- Place the chain (7) on the water pump drive sprocket. The alignment is not critical Align the last chrome link (6) with the timing mark (1) on the exhaust side balance shaft drive sprocket.

d. Install the upper balance shaft drive chain guide and bolts and tighten to 11 ft. lbs. (15 Nm).

e. Install the small balance shaft drive chain guide and bolts and tighten to 11 ft. lbs. (15 Nm).

21. Install the adjustable balance shaft chain guide and bolt and tighten to 89 in. lbs. (10 Nm).

22. Reset the timing chain tensioner by performing the following:

a. Rotate the tensioner plunger 90 degrees in its bore and compress the plunger.

b. Rotate the tensioner back to the original 12 o'clock position and insert a paper clip through the hole in the plunger body and into the hose in the tensioner plunger.

c. Install the balance shaft drive chain tensioner and bolt and tighten to 89 in. lbs. (10 Nm).

d. Remove the paper clip from the balance shaft drive chain tensioner.

23. Ensure the intake camshaft notch is in the 5 o'clock position (2) and the exhaust camshaft notch is in the 7 o'clock position (1). The number 1 piston should be at top dead center (TDC), crankshaft key at 12 o'clock.

24. Install the timing chain drive sprocket to the crankshaft with the timing mark in the 5 o'clock position and the front of the sprocket facing out.

➡ **There are 3 colored links on the timing chain. Two links are of matching color, and 1 link is of a unique color. Use the following procedure to line up the links with the actuators. Orient the chain so that the colored links are visible. Always use new actuator bolts.**

25. Assemble the intake camshaft actuator into the timing chain with the timing mark lined up with the uniquely colored link.

26. Lower the timing chain through the opening in the cylinder head. Use care to ensure that the chain goes around both sides of the cylinder block bosses (1, 2).

27. Install the intake camshaft actuator onto the intake camshaft while aligning the dowel pin into the camshaft slot.

28. Hand tighten the new intake camshaft actuator bolt.

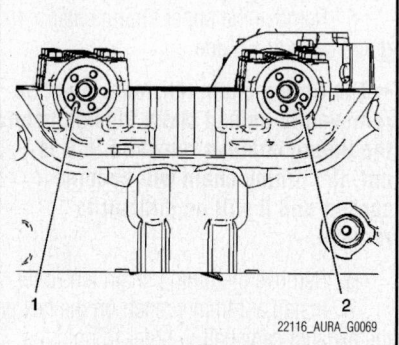

Fig. 192 Ensure the intake camshaft notch is in the 5 o'clock position (2) and the exhaust camshaft notch is in the 7 o'clock position (1). The number 1 piston should be at top dead center (TDC), crankshaft key at 12 o'clock—2.4L engine

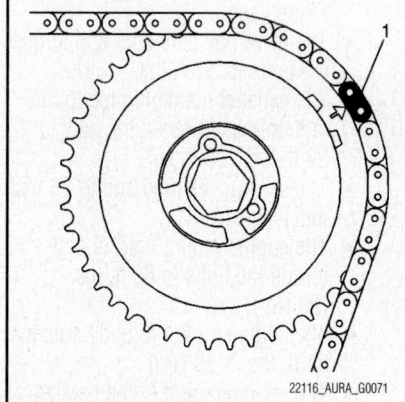

Fig. 194 Assemble the intake camshaft actuator into the timing chain with the timing mark lined up with the uniquely colored link (1)—2.4L engine

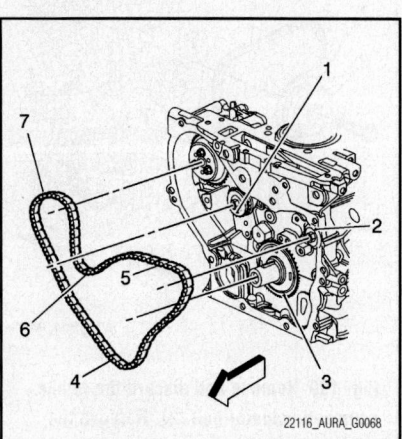

Fig. 191 Balance shaft drive chain components—2.4L engine

Fig. 193 Install the timing chain drive sprocket to the crankshaft with the timing mark in the 5 o'clock position and the front of the sprocket facing out—2.4L engine

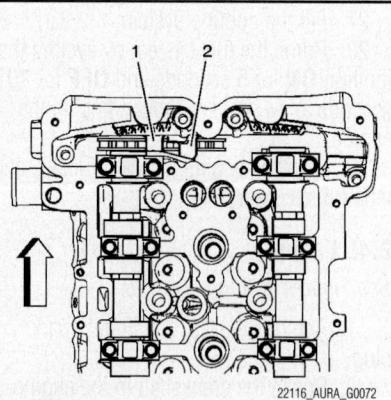

Fig. 195 Lower the timing chain through the opening in the cylinder head. Use care to ensure that the chain goes around both sides of the cylinder block bosses (1, 2)—2.4L engine

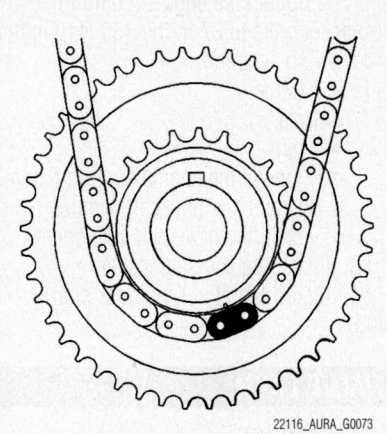

Fig. 196 Route the timing chain around the crankshaft sprocket and line up the first matching colored link (2) with the timing mark on the crankshaft sprocket, in approximately the 5 o'clock position—2.4L engine

29. Route the timing chain around the crankshaft sprocket and line up the first matching colored link (2) with the timing mark on the crankshaft sprocket, in approximately the 5 o'clock position.

30. Rotate the crankshaft clockwise to remove all chain slack. Do not rotate the intake camshaft.

31. Install the adjustable timing chain guide down through the opening in the cylinder head and install the adjustable timing chain bolt and tighten to 89 in. lbs. (10 Nm).

➡ **Always install NEW actuator bolts.**

32. Install the exhaust camshaft actuator into the timing chain with the timing mark lined up with the second matching colored link.

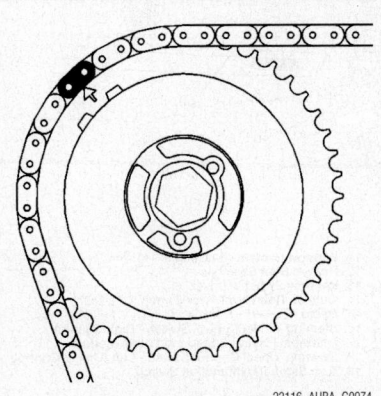

Fig. 197 Install the exhaust camshaft actuator into the timing chain with the timing mark lined up with the second matching colored link—2.4L engine

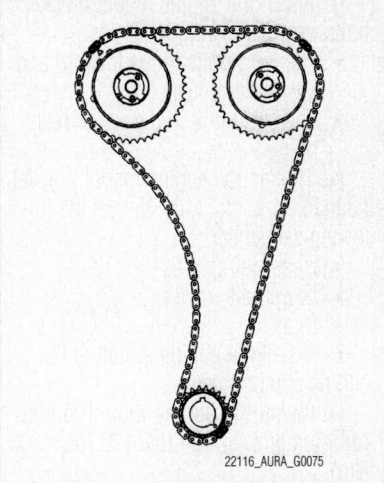

Fig. 198 Verify that all of the colored links and the appropriate timing marks are still aligned. If they are not aligned, repeat the portion of the procedure necessary to align the timing marks—2.4L engine

33. Install the exhaust camshaft actuator onto the exhaust camshaft, aligning the dowel pin into the camshaft slot.

34. Using a 23 mm open end wrench, rotate the exhaust camshaft approximately 45° until the dowel pin in the camshaft actuator goes into the camshaft slot.

35. When the actuator seats on the cam, tighten the new exhaust camshaft actuator bolt hand tight.

36. Verify that all of the colored links and the appropriate timing marks are still aligned. If they are not aligned, repeat the portion of the procedure necessary to align the timing marks.

37. Install the fixed timing chain guide and bolts and tighten to 106 in. lbs. (12 Nm).

38. Install the upper timing chain guide and bolts and tighten to 89 in. lbs. (10 Nm).

39. Reset the timing chain tensioner by performing the following:

    a. Remove the snap ring.

    b. Remove the piston assembly from the body of the timing chain tensioner.

    c. Install tensioner tool J 45027-2 (2) into a vise.

    d. Install the notch end of the piston assembly into the tool.

    e. Using the J 45027-1 handle (1), turn the ratchet cylinder into the piston.

    f. Reinstall the piston assembly into the body of the tensioner.

    g. Install the snap ring.

40. Inspect the timing chain tensioner seal for damage. If damaged, replace the seal.

41. Inspect to ensure all dirt and debris

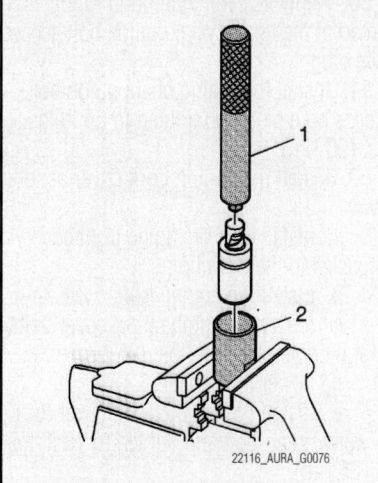

Fig. 199 Install tensioner tool J 45027-2 (2) into a vise, Install the notch end of the piston assembly into the tool and using the J 45027-1 handle (1), turn the ratchet cylinder into the piston—2.4L engine

is removed from the timing chain tensioner threaded hole in the cylinder head.

➡ **Ensure the timing chain tensioner seal is centered throughout the torque procedure to eliminate the possibility of an oil leak.**

42. Install the timing chain tensioner assembly.

43. Tighten the timing chain tensioner to 55 ft. lbs. (75 Nm).

➡ **The timing chain tensioner is released by compressing it 0.079 inch (2mm), which will release the locking mechanism in the ratchet.**

44. To release the timing chain tensioner, use a suitable tool with a rubber tip on the end. Feed the tool down through the cam drive chest to rest on the cam chain. Then give a sharp jolt diagonally downwards to release the tensioner.

45. Using a 23mm wrench, engage the hex on the intake camshaft, and using a torque wrench, tighten the camshaft actuator bolt.

46. Tighten the intake camshaft position actuator bolt to 22 ft. lbs. (30 Nm), plus an additional 100 degrees.

47. Using a 23mm wrench, engage the hex on the exhaust camshaft, and using a torque wrench, tighten the camshaft actuator bolt.

48. Tighten the exhaust camshaft position actuator bolt to 22 ft. lbs. (30 Nm), plus an additional 100 degrees.

49. Install the timing chain oiling nozzle and bolt and tighten to 89 in. lbs. (10 Nm).

50. Apply sealant compound to the thread of the timing chain guide bolt access hole plug.

51. Install the timing chain guide bolt access hole plug and tighten to 66 ft. lbs. lbs. (90 Nm).

52. Install the engine front cover as follows:

   a. Install a NEW engine front cover gasket to the dowel pins.

   b. Install the engine front cover.

   c. Install the engine front cover bolts and tighten to 18 ft. lbs. (25 Nm).

   d. Lower the vehicle.

   e. Install the engine front cover to water pump bolt and tighten to 18 ft. lbs. (25 Nm).

   f. Position the engine mount bracket to the engine.

   g. Install the engine mount bracket bolts in the following locations:
- The long bolts in the forward and lower rear holes
- The short bolt in the upper rear hole

   h. Tighten the engine mount bracket bolts to 74 ft. lbs. (100 Nm) in the following sequence:
- Upper left
- Lower left
- Right

   i. Install the engine mount to the engine compartment.

   j. Install the engine mount to side rail nuts and tighten to 74 ft. lbs. (100 Nm).

   k. Install the engine mount to bracket bolts.

   l. Tighten the engine mount to bracket bolts to 37 ft. lbs. (50 Nm) in the following sequence:
- Middle
- Rear
- Front

   m. Remove the engine support fixture.

   n. Install the crankshaft damper.

   o. Install the drive belt tensioner.

53. Install the camshaft cover.

54. Install the No. 1 cylinder spark plug.

VALVE LASH

ADJUSTMENT

All engines utilize hydraulic lash adjusters; no adjustment is necessary.

ENGINE PERFORMANCE & EMISSION CONTROL

MALFUNCTION INDICATOR LIGHT (MIL) RESET PROCEDURES

1. Proper operation of the Malfunction Indicator Lamp (MIL):
- The MIL will illuminate with the ignition switch ON and the engine OFF
- The MIL will turn OFF when the engine is started
- The MIL will remain ON if the self-diagnostic system has detected a malfunction
- The MIL may turn OFF if the malfunction is no longer present
- If the MIL is illuminated and then the engine stalls, the MIL will remain illuminated as long as the ignition switch is ON
- If the MIL is not illuminated and the engine stalls, the MIL will not illuminate until the ignition switch is cycled OFF, then ON

2. Resetting the MIL:
- The control module turns OFF the Malfunction Indicator Lamp (MIL) after 3 consecutive ignition cycles that the diagnostic system runs and does not fail
- A current Diagnostic Trouble Code (DTC) clears when the diagnostic cycle runs and passes
- There may still be a history of DTC's stored in the system. These will clear after 40 consecutive warm-up cycles, if no failures are reported by any other related diagnostic system
- Manual resetting of the MIL and

any DTC stored in the system, requires the use of an OBD2 scan tool connected to the data link connector for communication with the vehicle. Follow the instructions of the scan tool for both retrieval and resetting of DTC's.

➡ **If the error symptoms causing the MIL to illuminate have been corrected, the MIL will return to normal operation.**

COMPONENT LOCATIONS

See Figures 200 through 210.

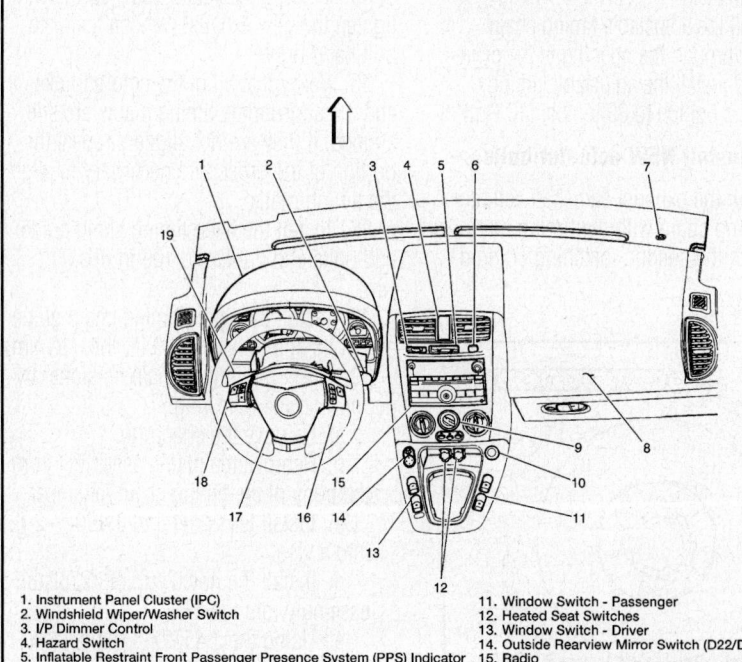

1. Instrument Panel Cluster (IPC)
2. Windshield Wiper/Washer Switch
3. I/P Dimmer Control
4. Hazard Switch
5. Inflatable Restraint Front Passenger Presence System (PPS) Indicator
6. Fog Lamp (T96) or Traction Control Switch (NW9)
7. Ambient Light Sensor
8. Inflatable Restraint I/P Module
9. HVAC Control Module
10. Cigar Lighter (DT4)
11. Window Switch - Passenger
12. Heated Seat Switches
13. Window Switch - Driver
14. Outside Rearview Mirror Switch (D22/DG7)
15. Radio
16. Steering Wheel Control Switch - Right (Radio)
17. Inflatable Restraint Steering Wheel Module
18. Steering Wheel Control Switch - Left (Cruise Control)
19. Turn Signal/Multifunction Switch

22116_SVUE_G0036

Fig. 200 Instrument Panel (I/P) component view

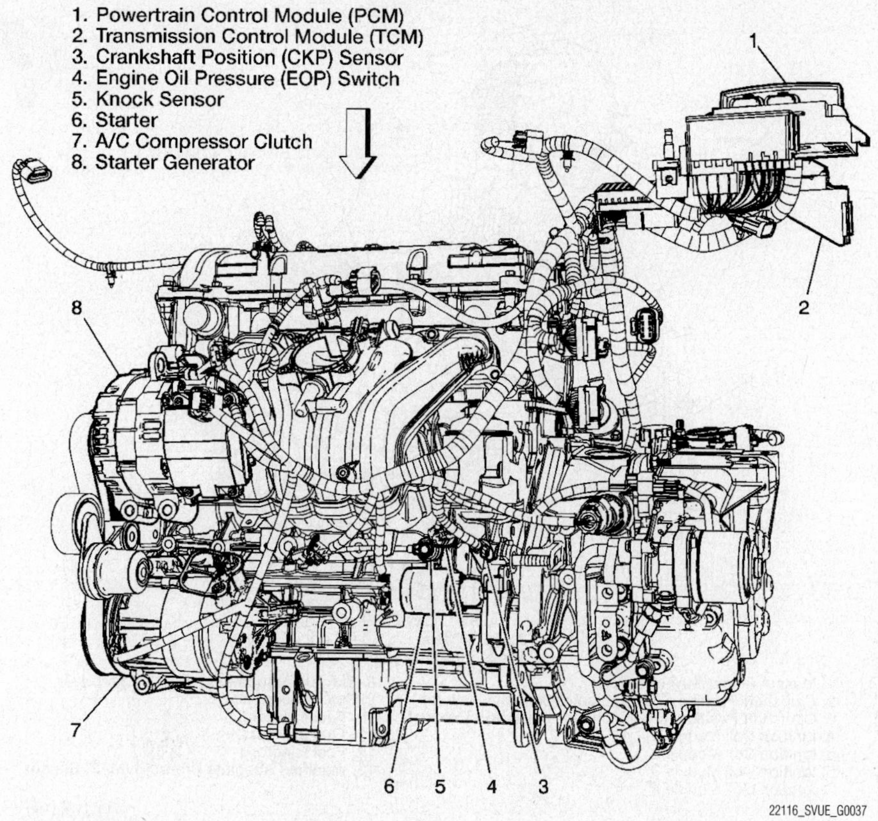

1. Powertrain Control Module (PCM)
2. Transmission Control Module (TCM)
3. Crankshaft Position (CKP) Sensor
4. Engine Oil Pressure (EOP) Switch
5. Knock Sensor
6. Starter
7. A/C Compressor Clutch
8. Starter Generator

22116_SVUE_G0037

Fig. 201 Engine component view (front)—2.2L & 2.4L engines

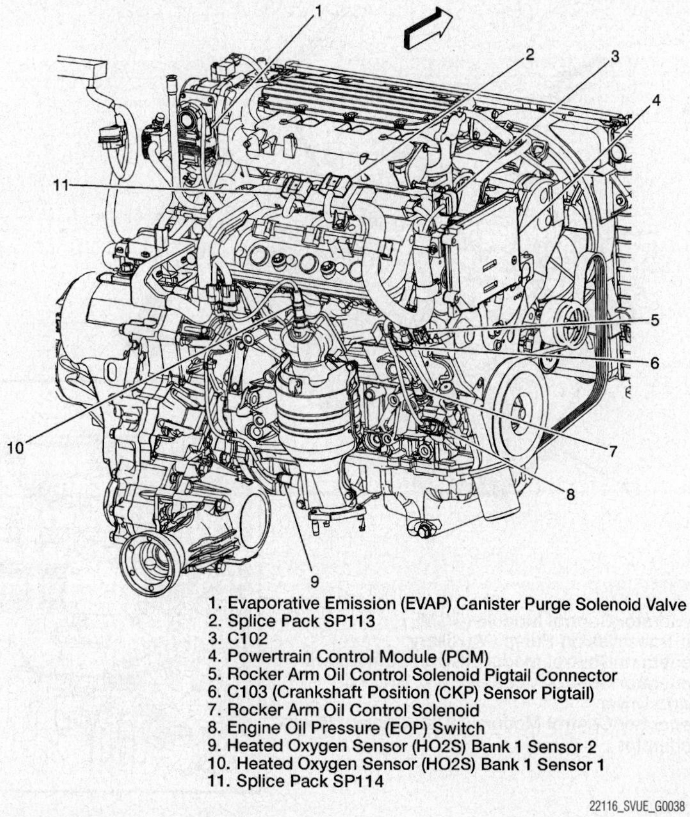

1. Evaporative Emission (EVAP) Canister Purge Solenoid Valve
2. Splice Pack SP113
3. C102
4. Powertrain Control Module (PCM)
5. Rocker Arm Oil Control Solenoid Pigtail Connector
6. C103 (Crankshaft Position (CKP) Sensor Pigtail)
7. Rocker Arm Oil Control Solenoid
8. Engine Oil Pressure (EOP) Switch
9. Heated Oxygen Sensor (HO2S) Bank 1 Sensor 2
10. Heated Oxygen Sensor (HO2S) Bank 1 Sensor 1
11. Splice Pack SP114

22116_SVUE_G0038

Fig. 202 Engine component view (rear)—2.2L & 2.4L engines

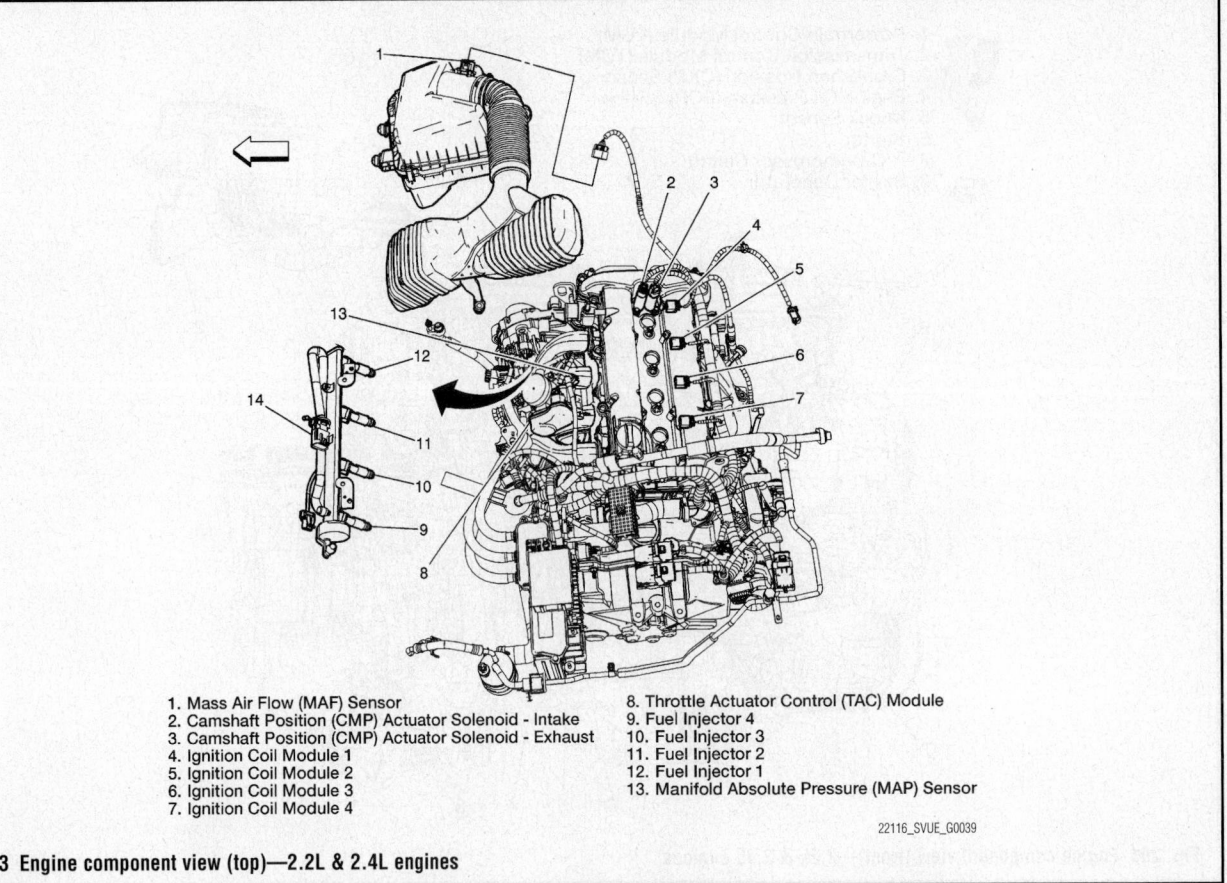

1. Mass Air Flow (MAF) Sensor
2. Camshaft Position (CMP) Actuator Solenoid - Intake
3. Camshaft Position (CMP) Actuator Solenoid - Exhaust
4. Ignition Coil Module 1
5. Ignition Coil Module 2
6. Ignition Coil Module 3
7. Ignition Coil Module 4
8. Throttle Actuator Control (TAC) Module
9. Fuel Injector 4
10. Fuel Injector 3
11. Fuel Injector 2
12. Fuel Injector 1
13. Manifold Absolute Pressure (MAP) Sensor

22116_SVUE_G0039

Fig. 203 Engine component view (top)—2.2L & 2.4L engines

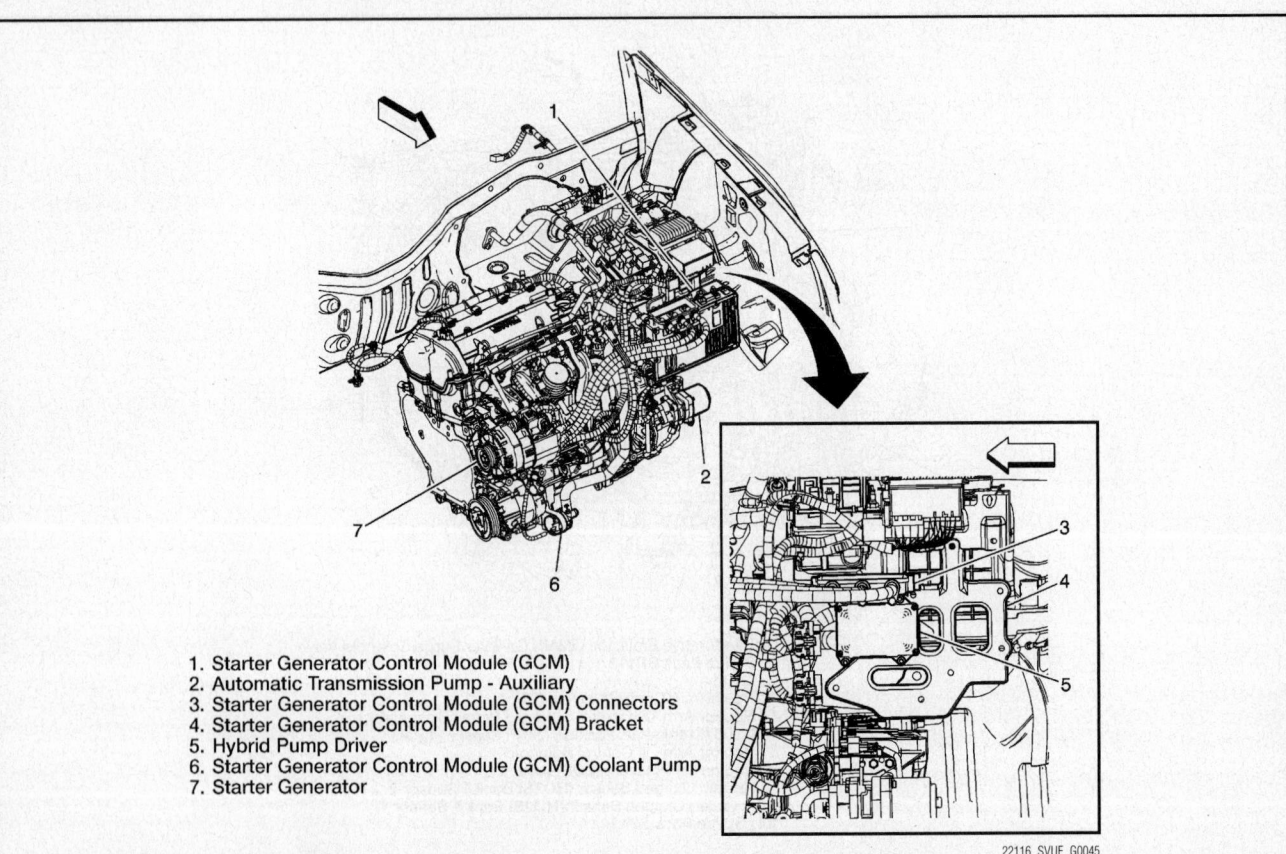

1. Starter Generator Control Module (GCM)
2. Automatic Transmission Pump - Auxiliary
3. Starter Generator Control Module (GCM) Connectors
4. Starter Generator Control Module (GCM) Bracket
5. Hybrid Pump Driver
6. Starter Generator Control Module (GCM) Coolant Pump
7. Starter Generator

22116_SVUE_G0045

Fig. 204 Engine component view (front)—2.4L hybrid engine

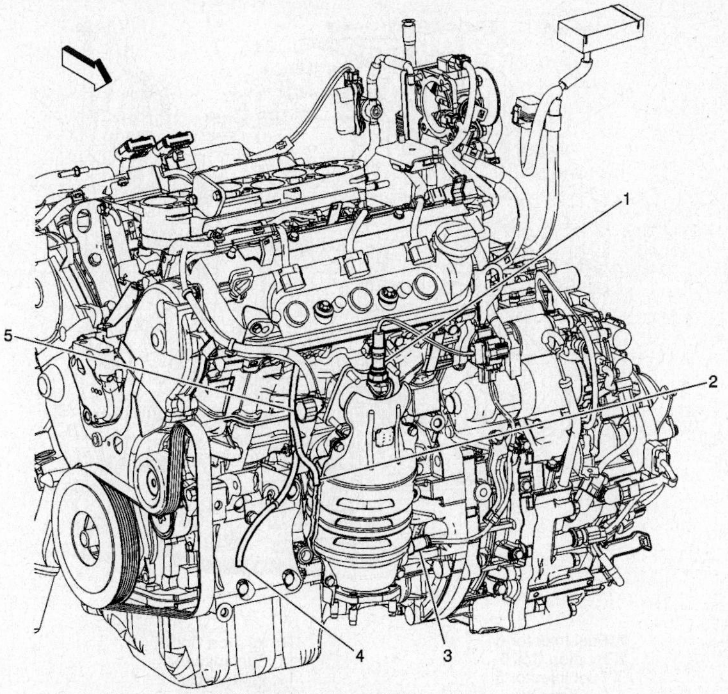

1. Heated Oxygen Sensor (HO2S) Bank 2 Sensor 1
2. A/C High Pressure Switch (Incomplete)
3. Heated Oxygen Sensor (HO2S) Bank 2 Sensor 2
4. A/C Compressor Clutch (Incomplete)
5. Generator Connector

22116_SVUE_G0040

Fig. 205 Engine component view (front)—3.5L engine

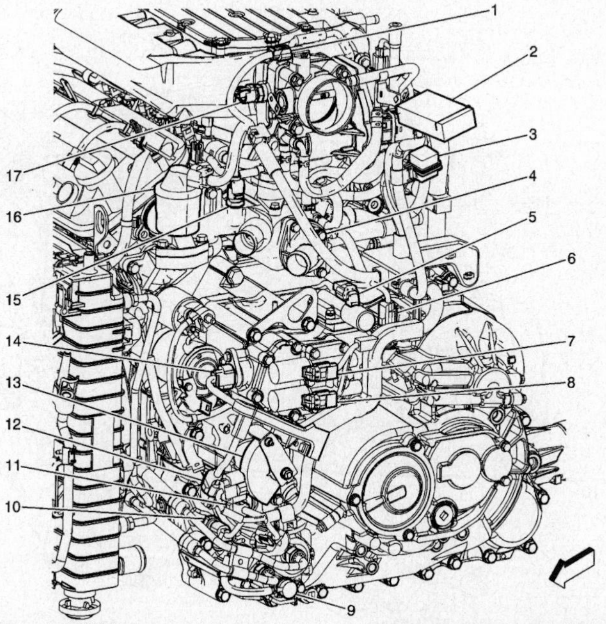

1. Manifold Absolute Pressure (MAP) Sensor
2. Fuse Block-Underhood C2
3. Starter Relay
4. G107
5. (5)Torque Converter Clutch (TCC) Pressure Control Solenoid Valve
6. 4th Clutch Pressure Switch
7. Clutch Pressure Control Solenoid Valve 1
8. Clutch Pressure Control Solenoid Valve 2
9. Transmission Fluid Temperature (TFT) Sensor
10. 3rd Clutch Pressure Switch
11. Transmission Output Shaft Speed Sensor
12. Transmission Input Shaft Speed Sensor
13. Park / Neutral Position (PNP) Switch
14. C100 Engine Harness to Transmission Harness
15. Engine Coolant Temperature (ECT) Sensor
16. Exhaust Gas Recirculation (EGR) Valve
17. Intake Air Temperature (IAT) Sensor 2

22116_SVUE_G0041

Fig. 206 Engine component view (left side)—3.5L engine

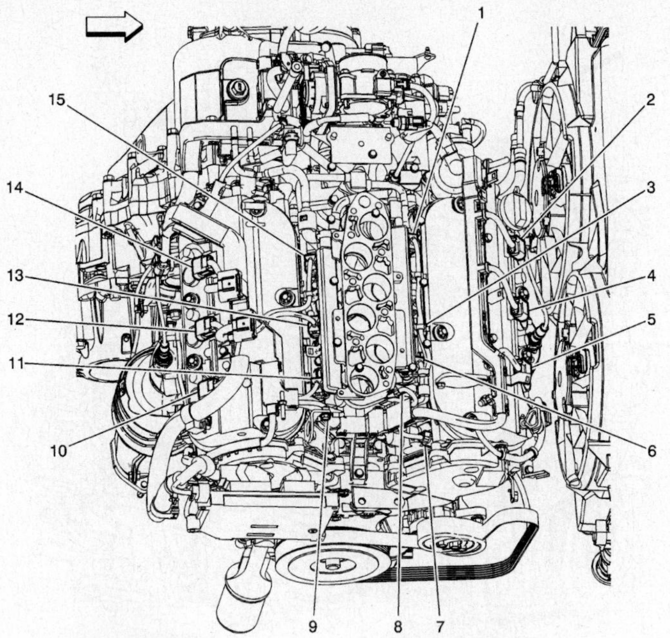

1. Fuel Injector 6
2. Ignition Coil 6
3. Fuel Injector 5
4. Ignition Coil 5
5. Ignition Coil 4
6. Fuel Injector 4
7. Camshaft Position (CMP) Sensor
8. Knock Sensor (KS)
9. G109
10. Ignition Coil 1
11. Fuel Injector 1
12. Ignition Coil 2
13. Fuel Injector 2
14. Ignition Coil 3
15. Fuel Injector 3

22116_SVUE_G0042

Fig. 207 Engine component view (top)—3.5L engine

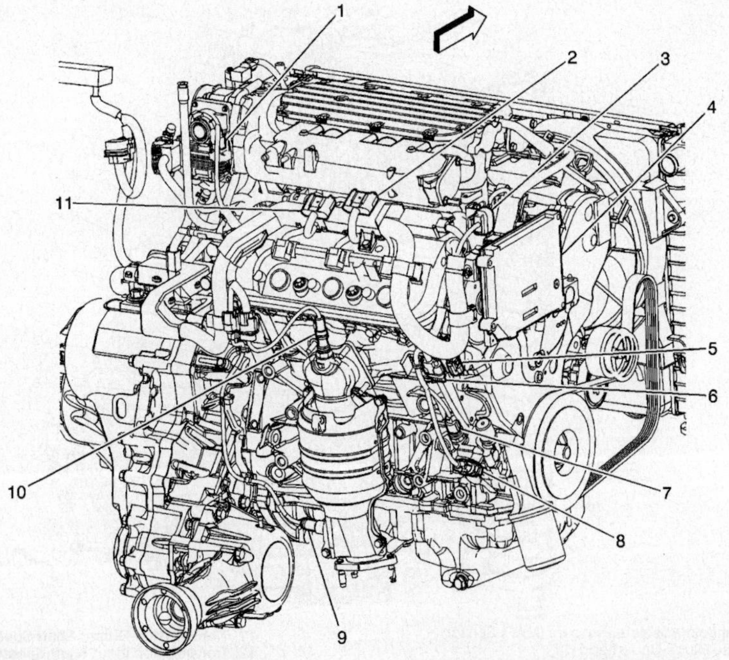

1. Evaporative Emission (EVAP) Canister Purge Solenoid Valve
2. Splice Pack SP113
3. C102
4. Powertrain Control Module (PCM)
5. Rocker Arm Oil Control Solenoid Pigtail Connector
6. C103 (Crankshaft Position (CKP) Sensor Pigtail)
7. Rocker Arm Oil Control Solenoid
8. Engine Oil Pressure (EOP) Switch
9. Heated Oxygen Sensor (HO2S) Bank 1 Sensor 2
10. Heated Oxygen Sensor (HO2S) Bank 1 Sensor 1
11. Splice Pack SP114

22116_SVUE_G0043

Fig. 208 Engine component view (rear)—3.5L engine

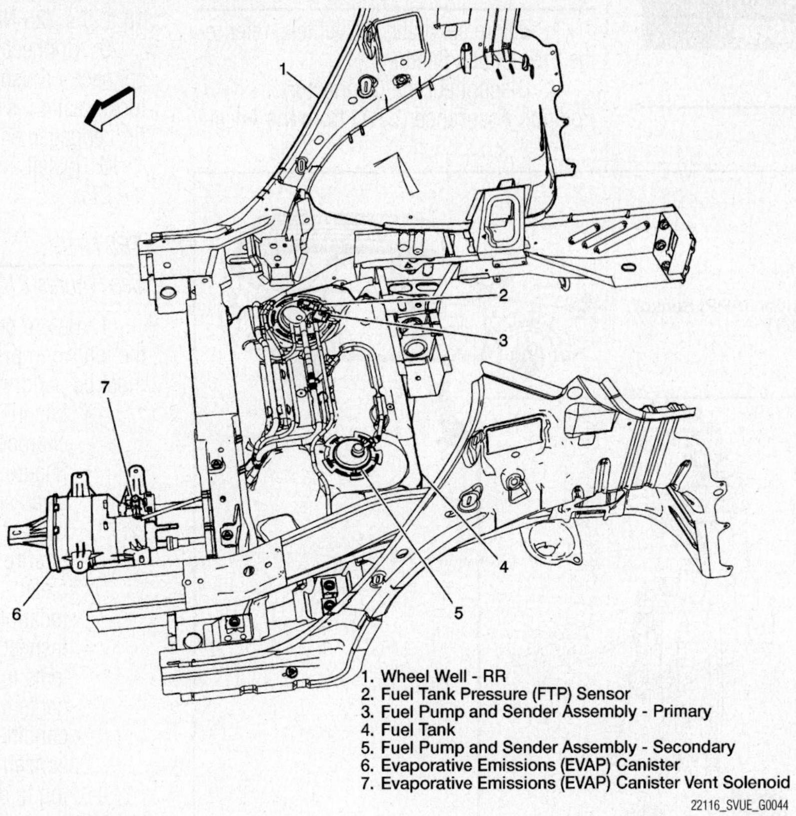

1. Wheel Well - RR
2. Fuel Tank Pressure (FTP) Sensor
3. Fuel Pump and Sender Assembly - Primary
4. Fuel Tank
5. Fuel Pump and Sender Assembly - Secondary
6. Evaporative Emissions (EVAP) Canister
7. Evaporative Emissions (EVAP) Canister Vent Solenoid

22116_SVUE_G0044

Fig. 209 Fuel Tank and related components view

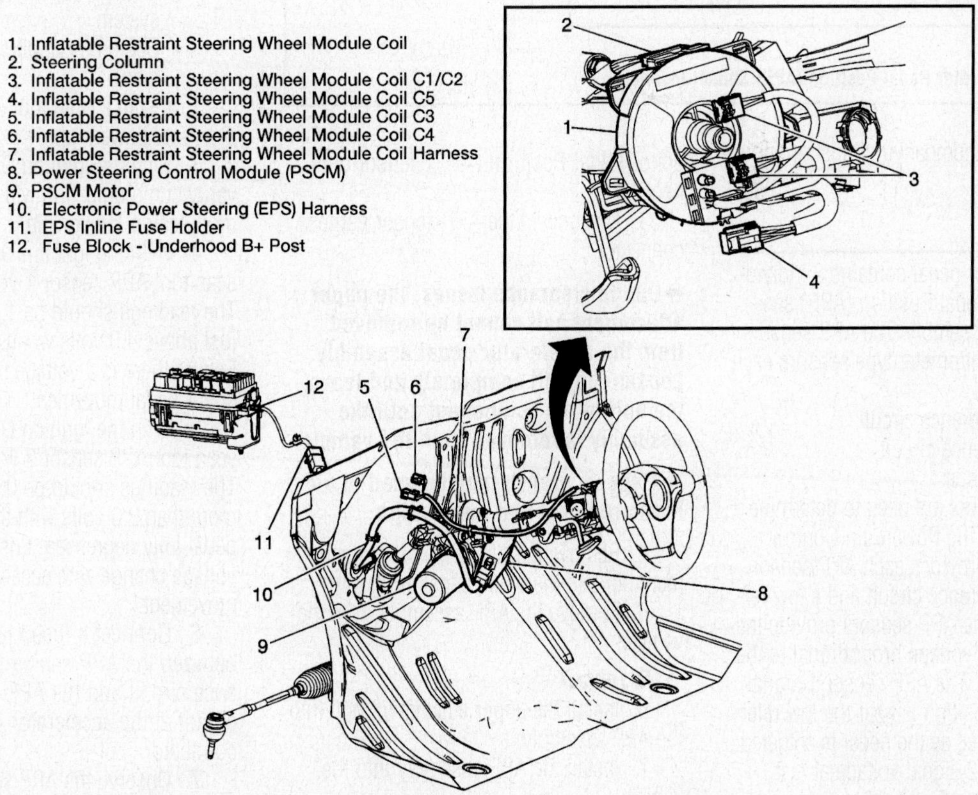

1. Inflatable Restraint Steering Wheel Module Coil
2. Steering Column
3. Inflatable Restraint Steering Wheel Module Coil C1/C2
4. Inflatable Restraint Steering Wheel Module Coil C5
5. Inflatable Restraint Steering Wheel Module Coil C3
6. Inflatable Restraint Steering Wheel Module Coil C4
7. Inflatable Restraint Steering Wheel Module Coil Harness
8. Power Steering Control Module (PSCM)
9. PSCM Motor
10. Electronic Power Steering (EPS) Harness
11. EPS Inline Fuse Holder
12. Fuse Block - Underhood B+ Post

22116_SVUE_G0006

Fig. 210 Expanded view of the electronic power steering and related components

ACCELERATOR PEDAL POSITION (APP) SENSOR

LOCATION

See Figure 211.

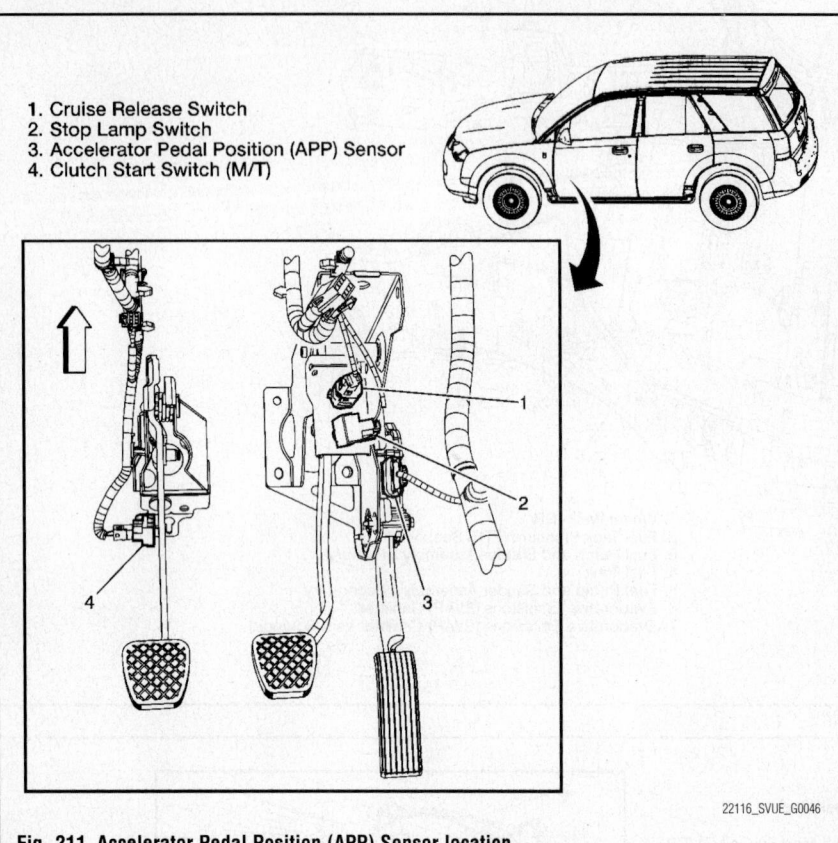

1. Cruise Release Switch
2. Stop Lamp Switch
3. Accelerator Pedal Position (APP) Sensor
4. Clutch Start Switch (M/T)

22116_SVUE_G0046

Fig. 211 Accelerator Pedal Position (APP) Sensor location

Refer to the accompanying illustration for sensor location.

OPERATION

The accelerator pedal contains 2 individual Accelerator Pedal Position (APP) sensors within the assembly. The APP sensors 1 and 2 are potentiometer type sensors each with 3 circuits:

- A 5-volt reference circuit
- A low reference circuit
- A signal circuit

The APP sensors are used to determine the pedal angle. The Powertrain Control Module (PCM) provides each APP sensor with a 5-volt reference circuit and a low reference circuit. The APP sensors provide the PCM with signal voltage proportional to the pedal movement. The APP sensor 1 signal voltage at rest position is near the low reference and increases as the pedal is actuated. The APP sensor 2 signal voltage at rest position is near the 5-volt reference and decreases as the pedal is actuated.

REMOVAL & INSTALLATION

1. Before servicing the vehicle, refer to the Precautions Section.
2. Disconnect the Connector Position Assurance (CPA) from the Accelerator Pedal Position (APP) sensor connector.
3. Disconnect the APP sensor harness connector.

➡**Due to clearance issues, the upper attachment bolt cannot be removed from the accelerator pedal assembly. Loosen the bolt completely and leave the bolt in the component until the assembly is removed from the vehicle.**

➡**A speed wrench may be used to aid in the removal and installation.**

4. Remove the APP assembly attachment bolts to the brake pedal assembly.
5. Remove the APP assembly from the vehicle.

To install:

6. Install the upper attachment bolt into the APP assembly.
7. Install the APP assembly into the vehicle.
8. Install the attachment bolts into the APP assembly. Tighten the accelerator pedal position assembly-to-brake bracket bolt to 18 ft. lbs. (25 Nm).
9. Connect the APP sensor harness connector. Push the connector in until the lock position is felt, then pull back to confirm engagement.
10. Install the APP sensor and connect the CPA.

TESTING

See Figures 212 through 214.

1. Before beginning vehicle diagnosis, the following preliminary inspections/tests must be performed:

- Ensure that the battery is fully charged
- Ensure that the battery cables are clean and tight
- Inspect for any open fuses
- Ensure that the grounds are clean, tight, and in the correct location
- Inspect the easily accessible systems or the visible system components for obvious damage or conditions that could cause the concern. This would include checking to ensure that all connections/connectors are fully seated and secured
- Inspect for aftermarket devices that could affect the operation of the system
- Search for applicable service bulletins

2. Install a scan tool. Verify that the scan tool powers up.
3. With the ignition ON, engine OFF, verify communication with all of the control modules on the vehicle.
4. With the ignition ON, observe the scan tool APP sensor 1 voltage parameter. The readings should be 1.0 volt at rest to just above 4.0 volts when fully depressed. Ensure there is a voltage change with accelerator pedal movement.
5. With the ignition ON, observe the scan tool APP sensor 2 voltage parameter. The readings should be 0.5 volts at rest to more than 2.0 volts with the accelerator pedal fully depressed. Ensure there is a voltage change with accelerator pedal movement.
6. Connect a fused jumper wire between the APP sensor 2 5-volt reference circuit and the APP sensor 2 signal circuit at the accelerator pedal harness connector.
7. Observe the APP sensor 2 voltage parameter with a scan tool. It should read 4.6–5.2 volts.

8. Turn OFF the ignition. Remove the fused jumper.

9. Turn ON the ignition, with the engine OFF.

10. Measure the voltage of the APP sensor 5-volt reference circuit with a DMM. It should read 4.6–5.2 volts.

11. If the reference voltage is below the acceptable range, check the low reference circuit for an open or high resistance interruption.

12. If all circuits are functioning properly and there is no voltage change when the accelerator pedal is moved, replace the APP.

LOCATION

See Figures 215 and 216.

Refer to the accompanying illustrations for sensor locations.

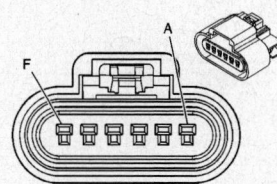

Pin	Wire Color	Circuit No.	Function
A	PU	1272	5-Volt Reference - A
B	L-BU	1162	APP Sensor 2 Signal
C	TN	1274	Low Reference
D	BN	1271	Low Reference
E	D-BU	1161	APP Sensor 1 Signal
F	WH/BK	1164	5-Volt Reference - B

22116_SVUE_G0047

Fig. 212 Accelerator Pedal Position (APP) connector end view—2.2L engine

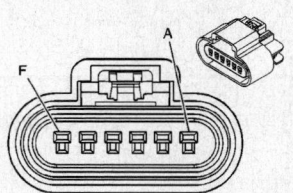

Pin	Wire Color	Circuit No.	Function
A	TN	1274	Low Reference
B	L-BU	1162	APP Sensor 2 Signal
C	PU	1272	5-Volt Reference - 1
D	BN	1271	Low Reference
E	D-BU	1161	APP Sensor 1 Signal
F	WH/BK	1164	5-Volt Reference - 2

22116_SVUE_G0048

Fig. 213 Accelerator Pedal Position (APP) connector end view—2.4L engine

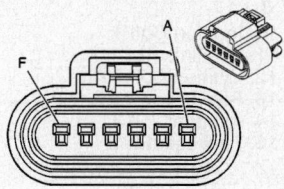

Pin	Wire Color	Circuit No.	Function
A	PU	1272	Low Reference
B	L-BU	1162	APP Sensor 2 Signal
C	TN	1274	5-Volt Reference - B
D	BN	1271	Low Reference
E	D-BU	1161	APP Sensor 1 Signal
F	WH/BK	1164	5-Volt Reference - A

22116_SVUE_G0049

Fig. 214 Accelerator Pedal Position (APP) connector end view—3.5L engine

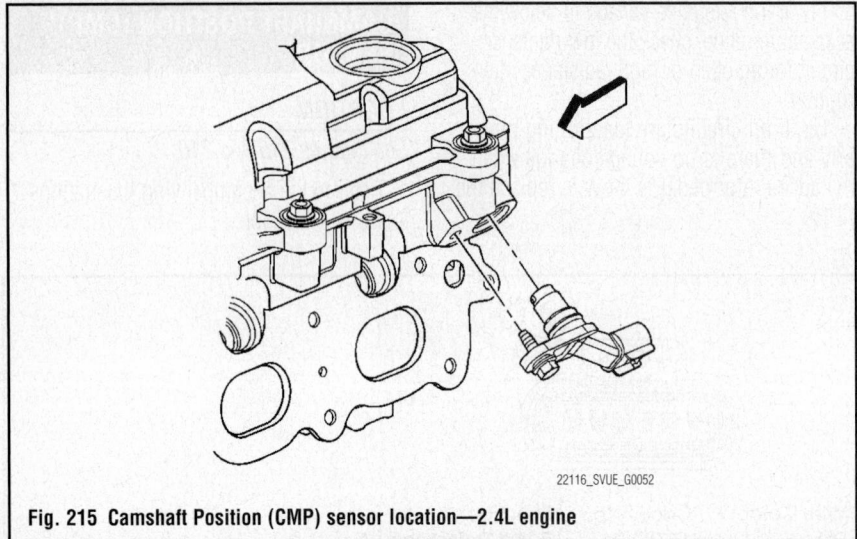

Fig. 215 Camshaft Position (CMP) sensor location—2.4L engine

22116_SVUE_G0052

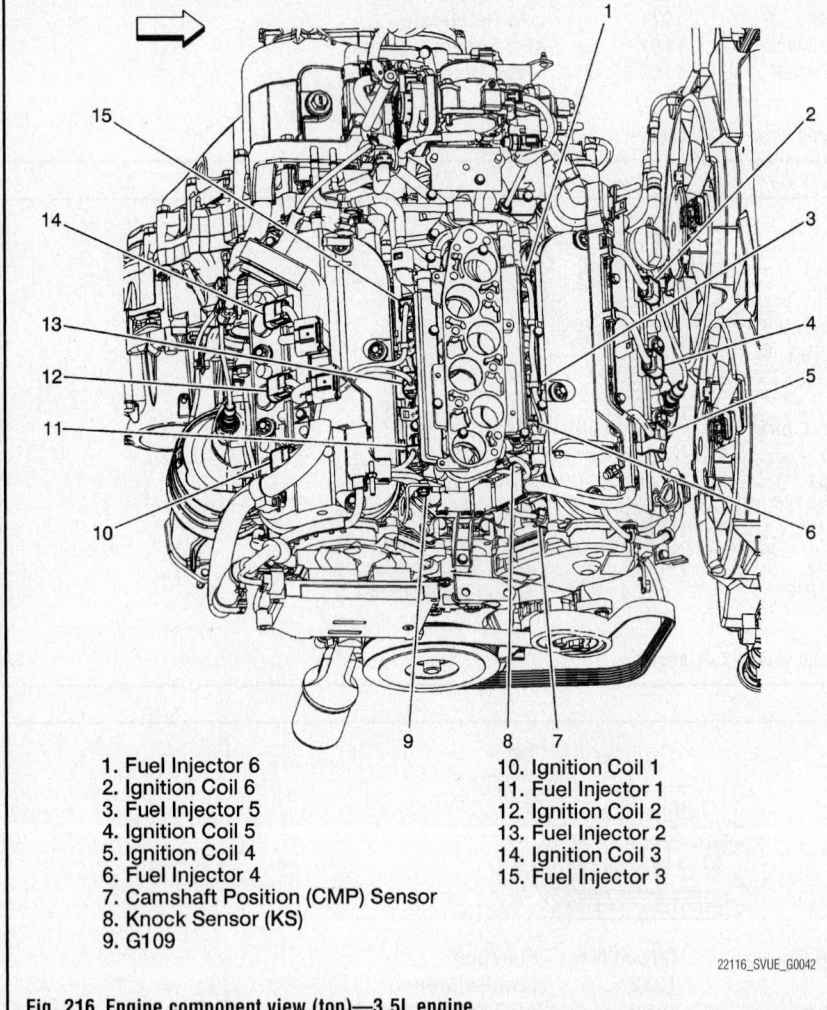

1. Fuel Injector 6
2. Ignition Coil 6
3. Fuel Injector 5
4. Ignition Coil 5
5. Ignition Coil 4
6. Fuel Injector 4
7. Camshaft Position (CMP) Sensor
8. Knock Sensor (KS)
9. G109
10. Ignition Coil 1
11. Fuel Injector 1
12. Ignition Coil 2
13. Fuel Injector 2
14. Ignition Coil 3
15. Fuel Injector 3

22116_SVUE_G0042

Fig. 216 Engine component view (top)—3.5L engine

OPERATION

The Camshaft Position (CMP) sensor is triggered by a notched reluctor wheel built onto the camshaft sprocket. The CMP sensor provides four signal pulses every camshaft revolution. Each notch, or feature of the reluctor wheel, is of a different size which is used to identify the compression stroke of each cylinder and to enable sequential fuel injection. The CMP sensor is connected to the PCM by the following circuits:

- A 5-volt circuit
- A low reference circuit
- A signal circuit

REMOVAL & INSTALLATION

2.4L Engine

Intake

1. Before servicing the vehicle, refer to the Precautions Section.
2. Remove the generator battery control module cover.
3. Disconnect the engine wiring harness electrical connector from the intake Camshaft Position (CMP) sensor.
4. Remove the CMP sensor bolt.
5. Remove the CMP sensor.

To install:

➡ **Inspect the CMP sensor for damage, replace as necessary.**

6. Lubricate the CMP sensor O-ring seal with clean engine oil.
7. Install the CMP sensor.
8. Install the CMP sensor bolt. Tighten the bolt to 89 inch lbs. (10 Nm).
9. Connect the engine wiring harness electrical connector to the intake CMP sensor.
10. Install the generator battery control module.

Exhaust

1. Before servicing the vehicle, refer to the Precautions Section.
2. Disconnect the engine wiring harness electrical connector from the exhaust Camshaft Position (CMP) sensor.
3. Remove the CMP sensor bolt.
4. Remove the CMP sensor.

To install:

➡ **Inspect the CMP sensor for damage, replace as necessary.**

5. Lubricate the CMP sensor O-ring seal with clean engine oil.
6. Install the CMP sensor.
7. Install the CMP sensor bolt. Tighten the bolt to 89 inch lbs. (10 Nm).
8. Connect engine wiring harness electrical connector to the exhaust CMP sensor.

3.5L Engine

See Figures 217 and 218.

1. Before servicing the vehicle, refer to the Precautions Section.
2. Remove the left camshaft sprocket.
3. Remove the bolt (240), sprocket

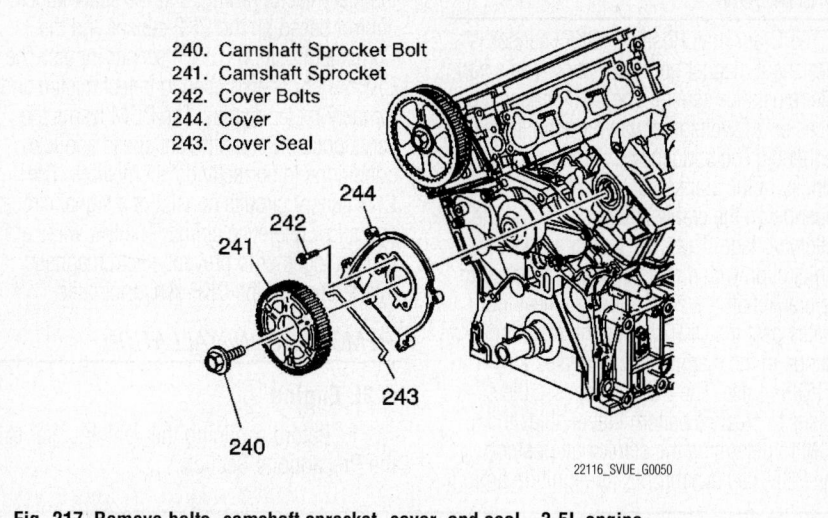

240. Camshaft Sprocket Bolt
241. Camshaft Sprocket
242. Cover Bolts
244. Cover
243. Cover Seal

22116_SVUE_G0050

Fig. 217 Remove bolts, camshaft sprocket, cover, and seal—3.5L engine

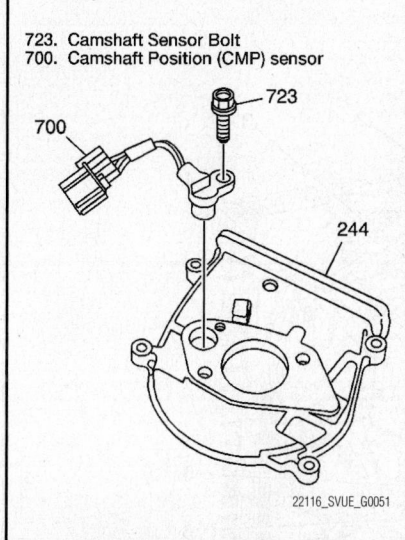

723. Camshaft Sensor Bolt
700. Camshaft Position (CMP) sensor

22116_SVUE_G0051

Fig. 218 Remove the Camshaft Position (CMP) sensor—3.5L engine

(241), bolts (242), cover (244), and seal (243).

4. Remove the bolt (723) and camshaft position (CMP) sensor (700).

To install:

5. Install the CMP sensor (700) and bolt (723). Tighten the bolt to 35 inch lbs. (4 Nm).

6. Install the cover (244), NEW seal (243) and bolts (242). Tighten the bolts to 16 ft. lbs. (22 Nm).

7. Install the left camshaft sprocket.

TESTING

See Figures 219 through 221.

During normal operation the PCM controls all ignition functions. If either the Crankshaft Position (CKP) or Camshaft

Position (CMP) sensor signal is lost, the engine will continue to run because the PCM will default to a limp home mode using the remaining sensor input. Diagnostic trouble codes are available to accurately diagnose the ignition system with an OBD2 scan tool.

1. Inspect the CMP sensor for correct installation. Remove the CMP sensor from the engine and inspect the sensor O-ring for

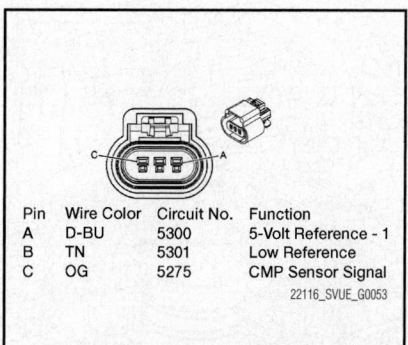

Pin	Wire Color	Circuit No.	Function
A	D-BU	5300	5-Volt Reference - 1
B	TN	5301	Low Reference
C	OG	5275	CMP Sensor Signal

22116_SVUE_G0053

Fig. 219 Camshaft Position (CMP) sensor connector end view (intake)—2.4L engine

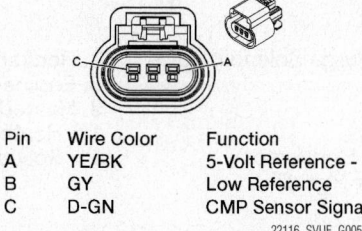

Pin	Wire Color	Function
A	YE/BK	5-Volt Reference - 1
B	GY	Low Reference
C	D-GN	CMP Sensor Signal

22116_SVUE_G0054

Fig. 220 Camshaft Position (CMP) sensor connector end view (exhaust)—2.4L engine

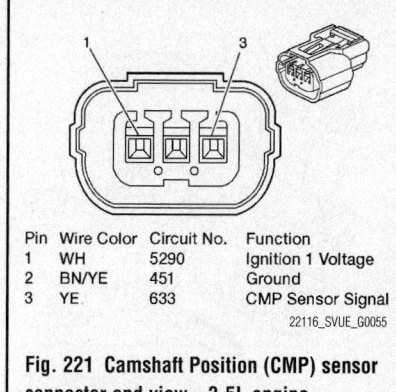

Pin	Wire Color	Circuit No.	Function
1	WH	5290	Ignition 1 Voltage
2	BN/YE	451	Ground
3	YE	633	CMP Sensor Signal

22116_SVUE_G0055

Fig. 221 Camshaft Position (CMP) sensor connector end view—3.5L engine

damage. If the sensor is loose, incorrectly installed, or damaged, replace the CMP sensor.

2. Engage the CMP sensor harness connector to the CMP sensor.

3. Connect the scan tool to the diagnostic connector.

4. With the ignition ON, engine OFF observe the CMP active counter parameter on the scan tool.

5. Pass a flat steel object across the tip of the sensor repeatedly. The CMP active counter parameter should increment with each pass of the steel object.

6. If the parameter does not increment, replace the CMP sensor.

CRANKSHAFT POSITION (CKP) SENSOR

LOCATION

See Figures 222 through 224.

Refer to the accompanying illustrations for sensor locations.

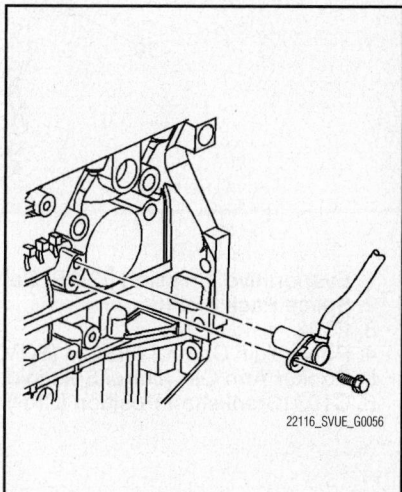

22116_SVUE_G0056

Fig. 222 Crankshaft Position (CKP) sensor location—2.2L engine

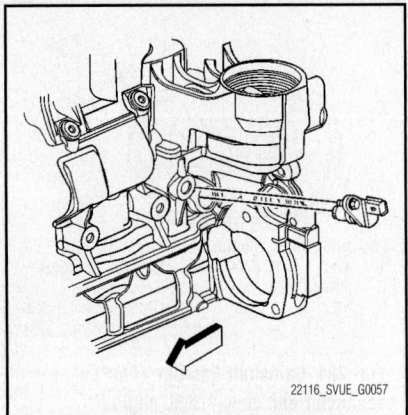

Fig. 223 Crankshaft Position (CKP) sensor location—2.4L engine

22116_SVUE_G0057

OPERATION

The Crankshaft Position (CKP) sensor is a permanent magnet generator known as a variable reluctance sensor. The CKP sensor produces an AC voltage of varying amplitude and frequency. The frequency depends on the velocity of the crankshaft. The AC output depends on the crankshaft position and the battery voltage. The CKP sensor works in conjunction with a reluctor wheel attached to the crankshaft. As each reluctor wheel tooth rotates past the CKP sensor, the resulting change in the magnetic field creates an ON/OFF pulse. The PCM processes the pulses to create a pattern that enables the PCM to determine the crankshaft position. The PCM can synchronize the ignition timing, the fuel injector timing, and the spark knock control based on the CKP sensor and the Camshaft Position (CMP) sensor inputs. The CKP sensor is also used to detect misfire and for tachometer display. The PCM learns the variations between different speed and load conditions to correctly detect misfires. The CKP sensor circuits consist of a signal circuit and a low reference circuit. The two wires are twisted together to prevent electromagnetic interference on the CKP sensor circuits.

REMOVAL & INSTALLATION

2.2L Engine

1. Before servicing the vehicle, refer to the Precautions Section.

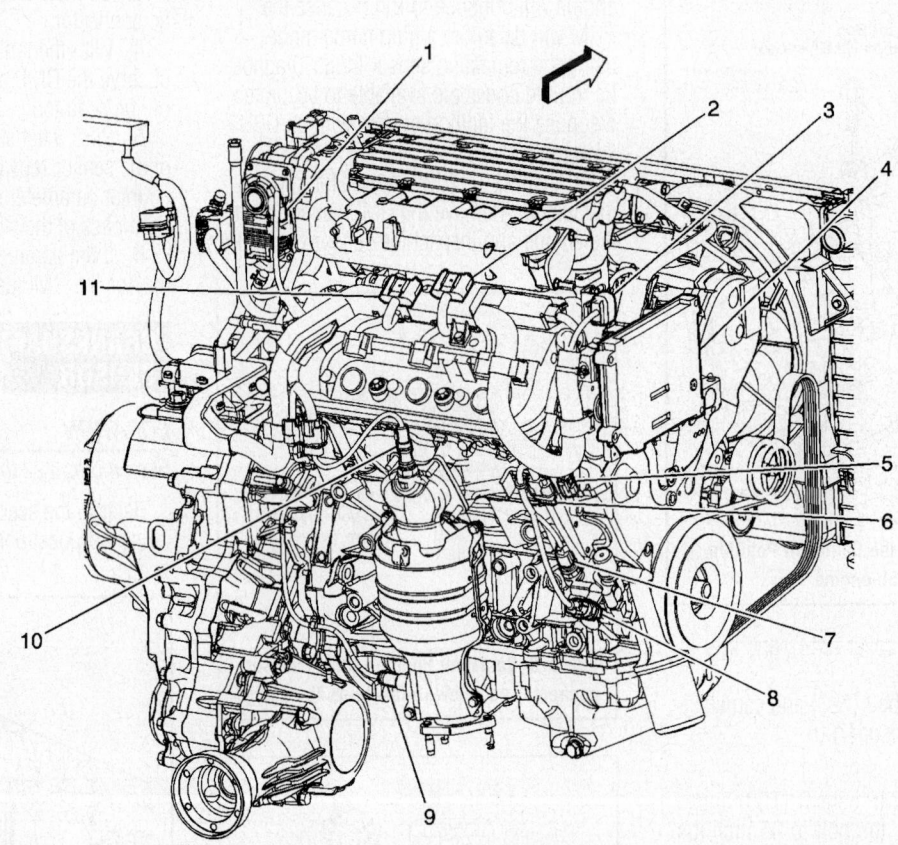

1. Evaporative Emission (EVAP) Canister Purge Solenoid Valve
2. Splice Pack SP113
3. C102
4. Powertrain Control Module (PCM)
5. Rocker Arm Oil Control Solenoid Pigtail Connector
6. C103 (Crankshaft Position (CKP) Sensor Pigtail)
7. Rocker Arm Oil Control Solenoid
8. Engine Oil Pressure (EOP) Switch
9. Heated Oxygen Sensor (HO2S) Bank 1 Sensor 2
10. Heated Oxygen Sensor (HO2S) Bank 1 Sensor 1
11. Splice Pack SP114

22116_SVUE_G0043

Fig. 224 Engine component view (rear)—3.5L engine

2. Remove the starter. Refer to Starter, removal & installation.

3. Disconnect the Crankshaft Position (CKP) sensor electrical connector.

4. Remove the CKP sensor bolt.

5. Remove the CKP sensor.

To install:

6. Gently insert the CKP sensor into the block.

☀☀ WARNING

Use the correct fastener in the correct location. Replacement fasteners must be the correct part number for that application. Fasteners requiring replacement or fasteners requiring the use of thread locking compound or sealant are identified in the service procedure. Do not use paints, lubricants, or corrosion inhibitors on fasteners or fastener joint surfaces unless specified. These coatings affect fastener torque and joint clamping force and may damage the fastener. Use the correct tightening sequence and specifications when installing fasteners in order to avoid damage to parts and systems.

7. Install the CKP sensor bolt. Tighten the CKP sensor bolt to 71 inch lbs. (8 Nm).

8. Reconnect the CKP sensor electrical connector.

9. Install the starter. Refer to Starter, removal & installation.

➡**The CKP system Variation Learn Procedure must be followed after replacing the CKP sensor.**

The Crankshaft Position (CKP) system variation learn procedure is required when the following service procedures have been performed, regardless of whether a Diagnostic Trouble Code (DTC) is set:

• Engine replacement
• Engine Control Module (ECM) replacement
• Crankshaft damper replacement
• Crankshaft replacement
• CKP sensor replacement
• Any engine repairs which disturb the crankshaft to CKP sensor relationship

The scan tool monitors certain component signals to determine if all the conditions are met to continue with the CKP system variation learn procedure. The scan tool only displays the condition that inhibits the procedure. The scan tool monitors the following components:

• CKP sensor activity. If there is a CKP sensor condition, refer to the applicable DTC that was set.

• Camshaft Position (CMP) signal activity. If there is a CMP signal condition, refer to the applicable DTC that was set.

• Engine Coolant Temperature (ECT). If the ECT is not warm enough, idle the engine until the ECT reaches the correct temperature.

10. Install a scan tool.

11. Monitor the ECM for DTC's with a scan tool. If other DTC's are set, make repairs as necessary before continuing.

12. With a scan tool, select the CKP system variation learn procedure and perform the following:

a. Observe the fuel cut-off for the applicable engine.

b. Block the drive wheels.

c. Set the parking brake.

d. Place the vehicle's transmission in Park or Neutral.

e. Turn the Air Conditioning (A/C) **OFF**.

f. Cycle the ignition from **OFF** to **ON**.

g. Apply and hold the brake pedal for the duration of the procedure.

h. Start and idle the engine.

i. Accelerate to Wide Open Throttle (WOT). The engine should not accelerate beyond the calibrated fuel cut-off RPM value noted above. Release the throttle immediately if the value is exceeded.

➡**While the learn procedure is in progress, release the throttle immediately when the engine starts to decelerate. The engine control is returned to the operator and the engine responds to throttle position after the learn procedure is complete.**

j. Release the throttle when fuel cut-off occurs.

13. The scan tool displays Learn Status: Learned this Ignition.

14. Turn **OFF** the ignition for 30 seconds after the learn procedure is completed successfully in order to store the CKP system variation values in the PCM memory.

2.4L Engine

1. Before servicing the vehicle, refer to the Precautions Section.

2. Remove the starter. Refer to Starter, removal & installation.

3. Disconnect the engine wiring harness electrical connector from the Crankshaft Position (CKP) sensor.

4. Remove the CKP sensor bolt.

5. Remove the CKP sensor.

To install:

6. Lubricate the CKP sensor O-ring seal with clean engine oil.

7. Install the CKP sensor.

8. Install the CKP sensor bolt. Tighten the sensor bolt to 89 inch lbs. (10 Nm).

9. Connect the engine wiring harness electrical connector to the CKP sensor.

10. Install the starter. Refer to Starter, removal & installation.

3.5L Engine

1. Before servicing the vehicle, refer to the Precautions Section.

2. Remove the engine front cover. Refer to Front Cover, removal & installation.

3. Remove the timing belt guide (703).

4. Remove the crank sensor and harness.

To install:

5. Install the crank sensor and harness.

6. Install the timing belt guide (703). Tighten the timing belt fasteners to 88 inch lbs. (10 Nm).

7. Install the front cover. Refer to Front Cover, removal & installation.

➡**The idle learn procedure must be followed after replacing the Crankshaft Position Sensor (CKP).**

8. Install a scan tool.

9. Diagnose and repair any DTC's before proceeding with this procedure.

10. Ensure that all electrical loads and accessories are OFF.

11. Turn OFF the air conditioning.

12. Ensure that the vehicle is in PARK or NEUTRAL.

13. Turn ON the ignition.

14. Clear the DTC information with the scan tool.

15. Wait 5 seconds and start the engine.

16. Operate the engine with no load at 3,000 RPM until the ECT reaches 194°F (90°C).

➡**If the engine cooling fan turns ON during the idle portion of this procedure, do not include the fan run time in the total idle time.**

17. Let the engine idle with the THROTTLE CLOSED and the engine cooling fan OFF, for a total of 5 minutes.

18. The PCM has a new learned idle position.

19. The idle learn procedure is required when the following service procedures have been performed:

• The throttle body assembly is replaced
• The throttle valve is cleaned— deposits can build up in the throttle body requiring periodic cleaning of the throttle valve and throttle bore area

- The Clear DTC's function has been performed
- The PCM has been programmed.
- The PCM is replaced

TESTING

During normal operation, the PCM controls all ignition functions. If either the Crankshaft Position (CKP) or Camshaft Position (CMP) sensor signal is lost, the engine will continue to run because the PCM will default to a limp home mode using the remaining sensor input. Diagnostic trouble codes are available to accurately diagnose the ignition system with an OBD2 scan tool.

1. Inspect the CKP sensor for correct installation. Remove the CKP sensor from the engine and inspect the sensor O—ring for damage. If the sensor is loose, incorrectly installed, or damaged, replace the CKP sensor.

2. Engage the CKP sensor harness connector to the CKP sensor.

3. Connect the scan tool to the diagnostic connector.

4. With the ignition ON, engine OFF observe the CKP active counter parameter on the scan tool.

5. Pass a flat steel object across the tip of the sensor repeatedly. The CKP active counter parameter should increment with each pass of the steel object.

6. If the parameter does not increment, replace the CKP sensor.

EGR VALVE POSITION (EVP) SENSOR

LOCATION

See Figure 225.

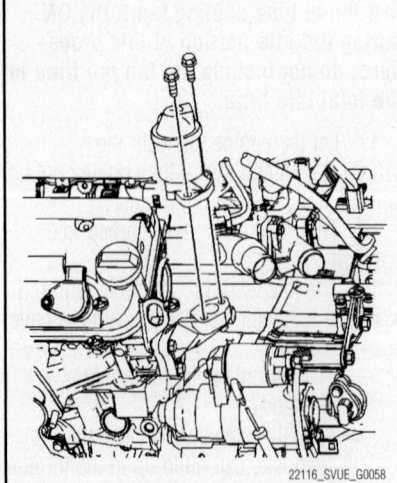

22116_SVUE_G0058

Fig. 225 Exhaust Gas Recirculation (EGR) valve location—3.5L engine

Refer to the accompanying illustration for sensor location.

OPERATION

The Exhaust Gas Recirculation (EGR) system is used to reduce the amount of nitrogen oxide (NOx) emission levels caused by combustion temperatures exceeding 1,500°F (816°C). It does this by introducing small amounts of exhaust gas back into the combustion chamber. The exhaust gas absorbs a portion of the thermal energy produced by the combustion process and thus decreases combustion temperature. The EGR system will only operate under specific temperature, Barometric Pressure (BARO) and engine load conditions in order to prevent drivability concerns and to increase engine performance.

The PCM calculates the amount of EGR needed based on the following inputs:
- The Engine Coolant Temperature (ECT) sensor
- The Intake Air Temperature (IAT) sensor
- The Barometric Pressure (BARO)
- The Manifold Absolute Pressure (MAP) sensor
- The Throttle Position (TP) sensor
- The Mass Air Flow (MAF) sensor

The control module tests the EGR system during deceleration. The control module does this by momentarily commanding the EGR valve to open while monitoring the signal circuit of the Manifold Absolute Pressure (MAP) sensor. When the EGR valve is opened, the control module will expect to see a predetermined increase in MAP. If the expected increase in MAP is not detected, the control module records the amount of MAP difference that was detected and adjusts a calibrated fail counter towards a calibrated fail threshold level. The number of EGR flow test counts required to exceed the fail threshold may vary according to the amount of detected EGR flow error.

The EGR Valve Position (EVP) sensor is monitored by the control module. The 5-volt reference circuit, the low reference circuit, and the EVP signal circuit are used by the control module to determine the EGR valve position. The control module compares the EVP sensor parameter with the desired EGR position parameter when the valve is commanded open or closed.

The control module controls the EGR valve with a solid state device called a driver. The driver supplies the EGR solenoid with 12 volts that is Pulse Width Modulated (PWM) through the EGR solenoid high control circuit. A ground path is provided by the control module through the EGR sole-

noid low control circuit. The driver has the ability to detect an electrical malfunction on the EGR solenoid control circuits.

When the ignition switch is turned ON, the control module records the EGR learned minimum position. The control module compares the EGR learned minimum position parameter to the EVP parameter.

The control module will only allow one EGR flow test during an ignition cycle. To aid in verifying a repair, the control module will allow 9–16 EGR flow test counts during the first ignition cycle following a code clear event or a battery disconnect.

REMOVAL & INSTALLATION

3.5L Engine

1. Before servicing the vehicle, refer to the Precautions Section.
2. Turn the ignition OFF.
3. Disconnect the Exhaust Gas Recirculation (EGR) valve electrical connector.
4. Remove the EGR valve retaining nuts.
5. Remove the EGR valve assembly.
6. Remove the gasket.
7. Clean the EGR valve mating surface.

To install:

8. Install the EGR valve with a new gasket to the engine.
9. Install the EGR valve nuts. Tighten the nuts to 16 ft. lbs. (22 Nm).
10. Connect the EGR valve electrical connector.

TESTING

See Figures 226 and 227.

1. With the ignition ON and the engine OFF, command the EGR from 0–90 percent. The Exhaust Gas Recirculation (EGR) position sensor parameter should remain within 3 percent of the desired EGR position parameter through the entire range.

2. With the ignition OFF, disconnect the EGR valve harness connector.

3. Turn the ignition ON, connect a test lamp between B and A. The test lamp should illuminate.

   a. If the test lamp does not illuminate, test the EGR low control circuit for an open/high resistance.

   b. If the circuit tests normal, replace the ECM.

4. Connect a test lamp between the EGR control circuit and a ground. Command the EGR valve from 0–90 percent and exit the EGR solenoid output control. The test lamp should turn ON when commanded between 10–90 percent and turn OFF when commanded to 0 percent.

   a. If the test lamp is ON when

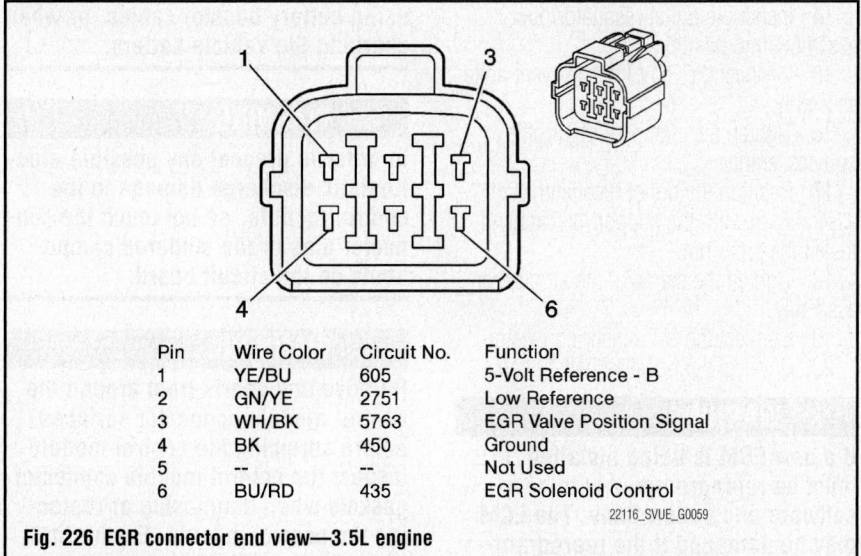

Fig. 226 EGR connector end view—3.5L engine

Pin	Wire Color	Circuit No.	Function
1	YE/BU	605	5-Volt Reference - B
2	GN/YE	2751	Low Reference
3	WH/BK	5763	EGR Valve Position Signal
4	BK	450	Ground
5	--	--	Not Used
6	BU/RD	435	EGR Solenoid Control

22116_SVUE_G0059

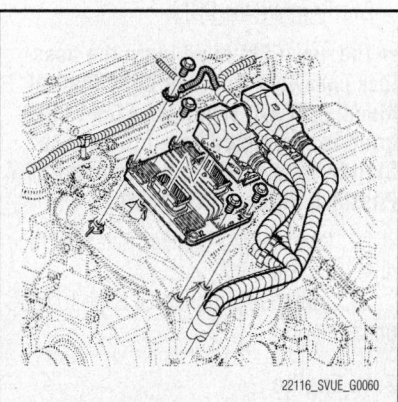

1. Cap-Sensor
2. Sensor-EGR Pintle Position
3. Pole Piece-Primary
4. Bobbin and Coil Assembly
5. Sleeve-Armature
6. Valve-Pintle
7. Armature and Base Assembly

22116_LUCE_G0040

Fig. 227 EGR linear valve cut-away view

commanded to 0 percent, test the EGR high control circuit for a short to voltage.

b. If the circuit tests normal, replace the ECM.

c. If the test lamp is always OFF while commanding the EGR valve from 0–90 percent, test the EGR high control circuit for an open, high resistance, or a short to ground.

d. If the circuit tests normal, replace the ECM.

5. If all circuits test normal, replace the EGR valve.

ELECTRONIC CONTROL MODULE (ECM)

LOCATION

See Figures 228 and 229.

Refer to the accompanying illustrations for ECM locations.

OPERATION

The Electronic (or Engine) Control Module (ECM), interacts with many emis-

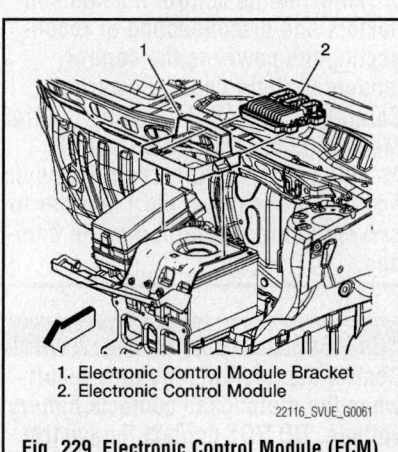

22116_SVUE_G0060

Fig. 228 Electronic Control Module (ECM) location—2.2L engine

1. Electronic Control Module Bracket
2. Electronic Control Module

22116_SVUE_G0061

Fig. 229 Electronic Control Module (ECM) location—2.4L engine

sion related components and systems, and monitors the emission related components and systems for deterioration. OBD2 diagnostics monitor the system performance and a Diagnostic Trouble Code (DTC) sets if the system performance degrades. The Malfunction Indicator Lamp (MIL) operation and the DTC storage are dictated by the DTC type. A DTC is ranked as a Type A or Type B if the DTC is emissions related. Type C is a non-emissions related DTC.

The ECM is in the engine compartment and is the control center of the engine controls system. The ECM controls the following components:

• The fuel injection system
• The ignition system
• The emission control systems
• The on-board diagnostics
• The A/C and fan systems
• The Throttle Actuation Control (TAC) system

The ECM constantly monitors the information from various sensors and other inputs, and controls the systems that affect the vehicle performance and the emissions. The ECM also performs diagnostic tests on various parts of the system. The ECM can recognize operational problems and alert the driver via the MIL. When the ECM detects a malfunction, the ECM stores a DTC. The condition area is identified by the particular DTC that is set.

REMOVAL & INSTALLATION

2.2L Engine

✳✳ WARNING

Turn the ignition OFF when installing or removing the control module connectors and disconnecting or reconnecting the power to the control module (battery cable, Powertrain Control Module (PCM)/Engine Control Module (ECM)/Transaxle Control Module (TCM) pigtail, control module fuse, jumper cables, etc.) in order to prevent internal control module damage.

✳✳ WARNING

Control module damage may result when the metal case contacts battery voltage. DO NOT contact the control module metal case with battery voltage when servicing a control module, using battery booster cables, or when charging the vehicle battery.

⁂ WARNING

In order to prevent any possible electrostatic discharge damage to the control module, do not touch the connector pins or the soldered components on the circuit board.

⁂ WARNING

Remove any debris from around the control module connector surfaces before servicing the control module. Inspect the control module connector gaskets when diagnosing or replacing the control module. Ensure that the gaskets are installed correctly. The gaskets prevent contaminant intrusion into the control module.

➡The replacement control module must be programmed.

➡It is necessary to record the remaining engine oil life. If the replacement module is not programmed with the remaining engine oil life, the engine oil life will default to 100 percent. If the replacement module is not programmed with the remaining engine oil life, the engine oil will need to be changed at 3,000 miles (5,000 km) from the last engine oil change.

1. Using a scan tool, retrieve the percentage of remaining engine oil. Record the remaining engine oil life.
2. Disconnect the negative battery cable.
3. Disconnect the Intake Air Temperature (IAT) sensor.
4. Loosen the clamp at the air cleaner assembly.
5. Remove the push pin attachment from the outlet resonator/duct assembly to support bracket.
6. Loosen the clamp at the throttle body assembly.
7. Disconnect the Positive Crankcase Ventilation (PCV) fresh air hose at the cam cover.
8. Remove the outlet resonator/duct assembly.
9. Remove the J 1 and J 2 connectors at the ECM.
10. Remove the 4 ECM attachment bolts.

To install:
11. Install the ECM.
12. Install the ECM bolts. Tighten the engine control module bolts to 71 inch lbs. (8 Nm).
13. Connect the J 1 and J 2 ECM electrical connectors.

14. Install the outlet resonator/duct assembly into position.
15. Connect the PCV fresh air vent hose assembly.
16. Tighten the clamp at the throttle body assembly.
17. Position the outlet resonator/duct assembly up with the support bracket and install the push-pin.
18. Tighten the clamp at the air cleaner assembly.
19. Connect the IAT sensor connector.
20. Connect the negative battery cable.

⁂ WARNING

If a new ECM is being installed, it must be reprogrammed with new software and calibrations. The ECM may be damaged if the reprogramming process is interrupted. Make sure the scan tool is connected securely to the Data Link Connector (DLC) and the vehicle battery has sufficient charge.

➡Ensure the original ECM has the correct VIN and vehicle options.

21. Program the ECM.

➡The new ECM must learn the passlock password from the Body Control Module (BCM). When the ECM reprogram is completed, use the Service Stall System (SSS) to perform the ECM Passlock Relearn Procedure.

22. Perform the Passlock Relearn Procedure using the SSS.
23. Turn the ignition to OFF for 10 seconds.

2.4L Engine

⁂ WARNING

Turn the ignition OFF when installing or removing the control module connectors and disconnecting or reconnecting the power to the control module (battery cable, Powertrain Control Module (PCM)/Engine Control Module (ECM)/Transaxle Control Module (TCM) pigtail, control module fuse, jumper cables, etc.) in order to prevent internal control module damage.

⁂ WARNING

Control module damage may result when the metal case contacts battery voltage. DO NOT contact the control module metal case with battery voltage when servicing a control module, using battery booster cables, or when charging the vehicle battery.

⁂ WARNING

In order to prevent any possible electrostatic discharge damage to the control module, do not touch the connector pins or the soldered components on the circuit board.

⁂ WARNING

Remove any debris from around the control module connector surfaces before servicing the control module. Inspect the control module connector gaskets when diagnosing or replacing the control module. Ensure that the gaskets are installed correctly. The gaskets prevent contaminant intrusion into the control module.

➡The replacement control module must be programmed.

➡It is necessary to record the remaining engine oil life. If the replacement module is not programmed with the remaining engine oil life, the engine oil life will default to 100 percent. If the replacement module is not programmed with the remaining engine oil life, the engine oil will need to be changed at 3,000 miles (5,000 km) from the last engine oil change.

1. Using a scan tool, retrieve the percentage of remaining engine oil. Record the remaining engine oil life.
2. Remove the generator battery control module cover.
3. Disconnect the negative battery cable.
4. Disconnect the body wiring harness electrical connector from the Engine Control Module (ECM).
5. Disconnect the engine wiring harness electrical connectors from the ECM.
6. Remove the 36 volt positive battery cable retainer from the ECM bracket.

⁂ WARNING

Control module damage may result when the metal case contacts battery voltage. DO NOT contact the control module metal case with battery voltage when servicing a control module, using battery booster cables or when charging the vehicles battery.

7. Remove the ECM bracket from the battery hold-down bracket.

8. Remove the ECM from the ECM bracket.

To install:

9. Install the ECM to the ECM bracket.

10. Install the ECM bracket to the battery hold down bracket.

11. Install the 36 volt positive battery cable retainer to the ECM bracket.

12. Connect the engine wiring harness electrical connectors to the ECM.

13. Connect the body wiring harness electrical connector 1) to the ECM.

14. Connect the negative battery cable.

15. Install the generator battery control module cover.

16. Program the ECM.

3.5L Engine

For the 3.5L engine, refer to Powertrain Control Module (PCM) for the removal & installation.

TESTING

1. Perform a careful underhood inspection when performing any diagnostic procedure or diagnosing the cause of an emission test failure. This can often lead to repairing a condition without further steps. Use the following guidelines when performing an inspection:

a. Inspect all of the vacuum hoses for correct routing, pinches, cuts, or disconnects

b. Inspect any hoses that are difficult to see

c. Inspect all of the wires in the engine compartment for the following conditions:

- Burned or chafed spots
- Pinched wires
- Contact with sharp edges
- Contact with hot exhaust manifolds

The Electronic Control Module (ECM), also called the Engine Control Module (ECM), is programmed with test routines that test the operation of the various systems the ECM controls. Some tests monitor internal ECM functions. Many tests are run continuously. Other tests run only under specific conditions, referred to as conditions for running the Diagnostic Trouble Code (DTC). When the vehicle is operating within the conditions for running a particular test, the ECM monitors certain parameters and determines if the values are within an expected range. The parameters and values considered outside the range of normal operation are listed as conditions for setting the DTC. When the conditions for setting the DTC occur, the ECM executes the action taken when the DTC sets. Some DTC's alert

the driver via the Malfunction Indicator Lamp (MIL) or a message. Other DTC's do not trigger a driver warning, but are stored in memory. The ECM also saves data and input parameters when most DTC's are set.

The DTC's are categorized by type. The DTC type is determined by the MIL operation and the manner in which the fault data is stored when a particular DTC fails. In some cases, there may be exceptions to this structure. Therefore, when diagnosing the system it is important to read the action taken when the DTC sets and the conditions for clearing the DTC.

Many intermittent open or shorted circuits come and go with harness and connector movement caused by vibration, engine torque, bumps, and rough pavement.

2. Test the wiring harness and connectors by performing the following:

- Move the related ECM connectors and wiring while monitoring the appropriate scan tool data
- With the engine running, move the related connectors and wiring while monitoring engine operation
- If harness or connector movement affects the data displayed, the component and system operation, or the engine operation, inspect and repair the harness or connections as necessary

3. Test the electrical connections and/or wiring by performing the following:

- Inspect for incorrect mating of the connector halves or terminals not fully seated in the connector body
- Inspect for improperly formed or damaged terminals. Test for incorrect terminal tension
- Inspect for poor terminal to wire connections including terminals crimped over insulation. This requires removing the terminal from the connector body
- Inspect for corrosion or water intrusion. Pierced or damaged insulation can allow moisture to enter the wiring. The conductor can corrode inside the insulation with little visible evidence. Look for swollen and stiff sections of wire in the suspect circuits
- Inspect for wires that are broken inside the insulation

ENGINE COOLANT TEMPERATURE (ECT) SENSOR

LOCATION

See Figures 230 through 233.

Refer to the accompanying illustrations for sensor locations.

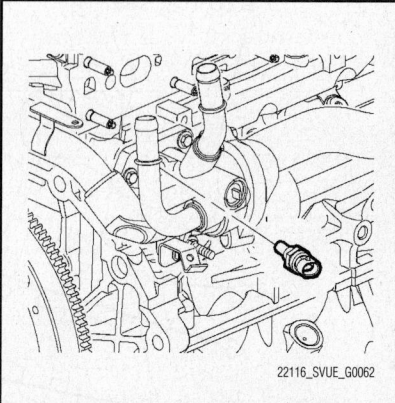

22116_SVUE_G0062

Fig. 230 Engine Coolant Temperature (ECT) sensor location—2.2L engine

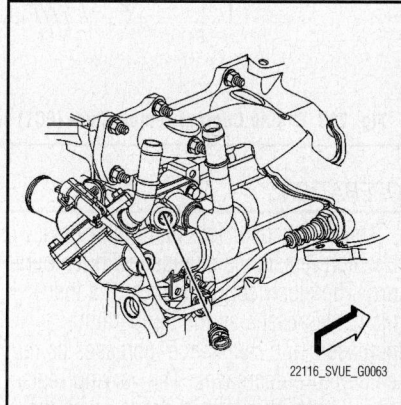

22116_SVUE_G0063

Fig. 231 Engine Coolant Temperature (ECT) sensor location—2.4L engine

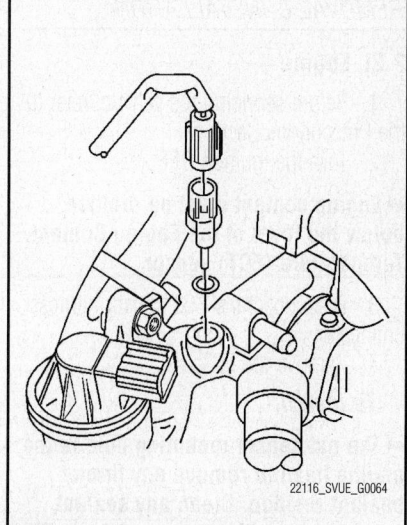

22116_SVUE_G0064

Fig. 232 Engine Coolant Temperature (ECT) sensor location (sensor 1)—3.5L engine

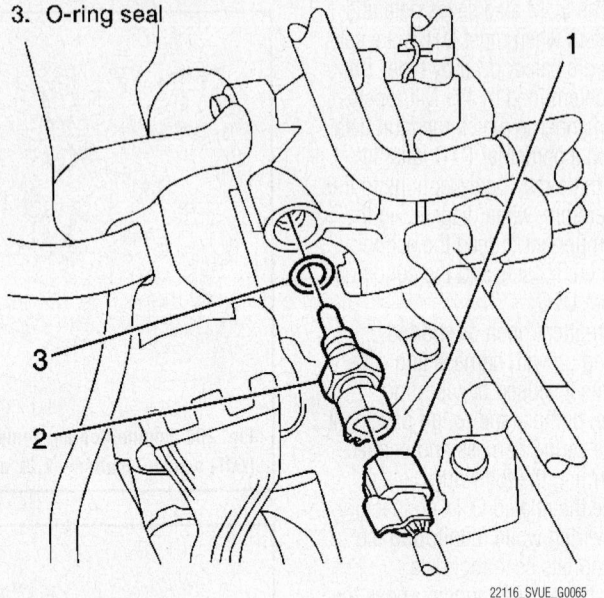

1. Wiring Harness Electrical Connector
2. Engine Coolant Temperature (ECT) sensor
3. O-ring seal

22116_SVUE_G0065

Fig. 233 Engine Coolant Temperature (ECT) sensor location (sensor 2)—3.5L engine

OPERATION

The ECT sensor is a thermistor device in which resistance changes with temperature. The electrical resistance of a thermistor decreases as the temperature increases, and resistance increases as the temperature decreases. The varying resistance affects the voltage drop across the sensor terminals and provides electrical signals to the PCM corresponding to temperature.

REMOVAL & INSTALLATION

2.2L Engine

1. Before servicing the vehicle, refer to the Precautions Section.
2. Turn the ignition OFF.

➡Engine coolant must be drained below the level of the Engine Coolant Temperature (ECT) sensor.

3. Disconnect the ECT sensor harness connector.
4. Remove the ECT.

To install:

➡Tap out sensor mounting hole in the engine head to remove any thread sealant residue. Clean any sealant residue from old sensor and apply RTV sealant to threads if the old sensor is going to be reused.

5. Apply thread sealant Saturn P/N

21485277 Loctite 242® Threadlocker, or equivalent, to sensor threads.

6. Install the ECT sensor. Tighten the engine coolant temperature sensor to 89 inch lbs. (10 Nm).

7. Connect the ECT sensor harness connector. Push in the connector until a click is heard, then pull back to confirm a positive engagement.

8. Fill engine coolant to proper level.

2.4L Engine

1. Before servicing the vehicle, refer to the Precautions Section.

✳✳ WARNING

Use care when handling the coolant sensor. Damage to the coolant sensor will affect the operation of the fuel control system.

2. Drain the cooling system.
3. Disconnect the engine wiring harness electrical connector from the Engine Coolant Temperature (ECT) sensor.
4. Remove the ECT sensor.

To install:

✳✳ WARNING

Replacement components must be the correct part number for the application. Components requiring the use of the thread locking compound, lubricants, corrosion inhibitors, or

sealants are identified in the service procedure. Some replacement components may come with these coatings already applied. Do not use these coatings on components unless specified. These coatings can affect the final torque, which may affect the operation of the component. Use the correct torque specification when installing components in order to avoid damage.

5. If reinstalling the original sensor, or if installing a NEW sensor without a sealer, coat the threads with sealant.

6. Install the ECT sensor. Tighten the sensor to 15 ft. lbs. (20 Nm).

7. Connect the engine wiring harness electrical connector to the ECT sensor.

8. Fill the cooling system to the proper level.

3.5L Engine

Sensor 1

1. Before servicing the vehicle, refer to the Precautions Section.

2. Drain the coolant to a level below the Engine Coolant Temperature (ECT) sensor.

3. Disconnect the engine wiring harness electrical connector from the ECT sensor.

4. Remove the ECT sensor and O-ring seal.

To install:

➡Clean out the sensor hole with a tap in order to remove any thread sealant residue. Clean any sealant residue from the old sensor and apply sealant to the threads if the old sensor is being reused.

5. Apply thread sealant SA P/N 21485277, Loctite 242® Threadlocker, or equivalent to the sensor threads.

6. Install the NEW ECT sensor with a new O-ring. Tighten the sensor to 13 ft. lbs. (18 Nm).

7. Connect the engine wiring harness electrical connector to the ECT sensor.

8. Fill the cooling system to the proper level.

Sensor 2

See Figure 233.

1. Before servicing the vehicle, refer to the Precautions Section.

2. Drain the coolant to a level below the Engine Coolant Temperature (ECT) sensor.

3. Disconnect the engine wiring harness electrical connector (1) from the ECT sensor.

4. Remove the ECT sensor (2) and O-ring seal (3).

To install:

➡ Clean out the sensor hole with a tap in order to remove any thread sealant residue. Clean any sealant residue from the old sensor and apply sealant to the threads if the old sensor is being reused.

5. Apply thread sealant SA P/N 21485277, Loctite 242® Threadlocker, or equivalent to the sensor threads.

6. Install the NEW ECT sensor (2) with a new O-ring (3). Tighten the sensor to 13 ft. lbs. (18 Nm).

7. Connect the engine wiring harness electrical connector (1) to the ECT sensor.

8. Fill the cooling system to the proper level.

TESTING

See Figures 234 through 236.

➡ If the PCM receives a high engine temperature signal from the Engine Coolant Temperature (ECT), it adjusts fueling rates to protect the engine from damage due to overheating.

1. Turn OFF the ignition.

2. Inspect the cooling system surge tank for the proper coolant level.

3. If the ignition has been OFF for 8 hours or more, the ECT and the Intake Air Temperature (IAT) should be within 27°F (15°C) of each other and also the ambient temperature.

4. Turn ON the ignition, with the engine OFF, and use a scan tool to observe the IAT and the ECT sensor parameters.

5. Use the scan tool to verify the proper operation of the engine cooling system fans.

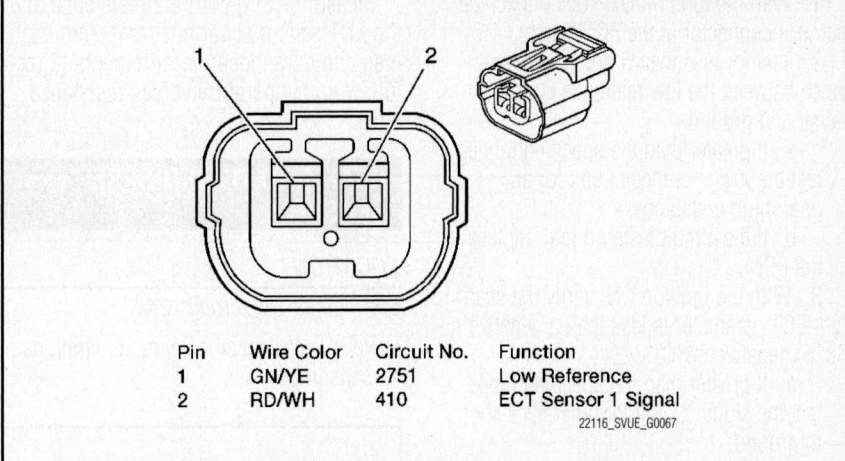

Pin	Wire Color	Circuit No.	Function
1	GN/YE	2751	Low Reference
2	RD/WH	410	ECT Sensor 1 Signal

22116_SVUE_G0067

Fig. 235 Engine Coolant Temperature (ECT) sensor connector end view (sensor 1)—3.5L engine

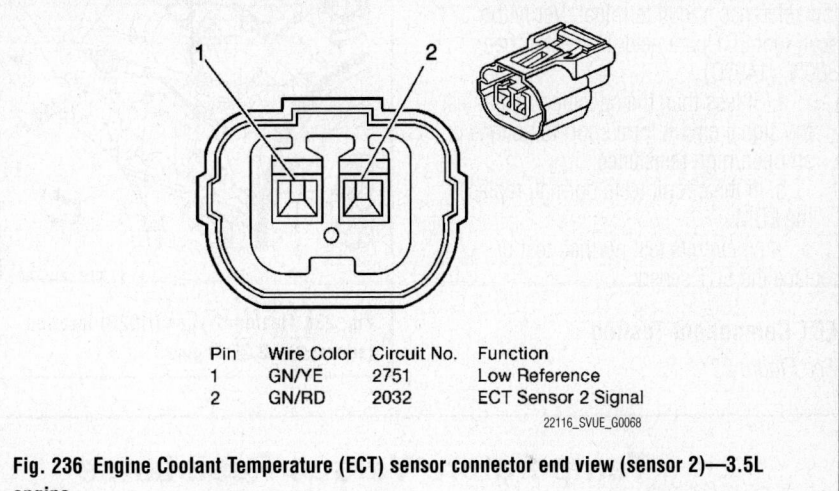

Pin	Wire Color	Circuit No.	Function
1	GN/YE	2751	Low Reference
2	GN/RD	2032	ECT Sensor 2 Signal

22116_SVUE_G0068

Fig. 236 Engine Coolant Temperature (ECT) sensor connector end view (sensor 2)—3.5L engine

➡ A critical analysis of the operation of the thermostat is important to the proper diagnosis of the ECT.

6. Verify the proper heat range and the operation of the thermostat.

Circuit/System Testing

➡ All electrical components and accessories must be turned OFF and allowed to power down.

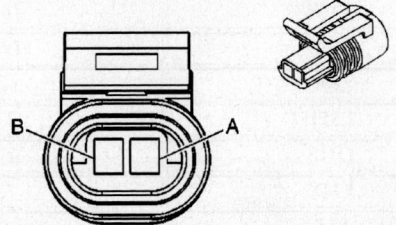

Pin	Wire Color	Circuit No.	Function
A	BK	2761	Low Reference
B	YE	410	ECT Sensor Signal

22116_SVUE_G0066

Fig. 234 Engine Coolant Temperature (ECT) sensor connector end view—2.2L & 2.4L engines

1. With the ignition OFF, disconnect the harness connector at the ECT sensor.

2. Test for less than 5 ohms of resistance between the low reference circuit terminal and ground.

   a. If greater than the specified range, test the low reference circuit for an open/high resistance.

   b. If the circuit tests normal, replace the ECM.

3. With the ignition ON, verify the scan tool ECT parameter is less than a negative 38°F (negative 39°C).

   a. If greater than the specified range, test the signal circuit terminal for a short to ground.

   b. If the circuit tests normal, replace the ECM.

4. Install a 3-amp fused jumper wire between the signal circuit terminal and the low reference circuit terminal. Verify the scan tool ECT parameter is greater than 300°F (149°C).

   a. If less than the specified range, test the signal circuit for a short to voltage or an open/high resistance.

   b. If the circuit tests normal, replace the ECM.

5. If all circuits test normal, test or replace the ECT sensor.

ECT Component Testing

See Figure 237.

Measure and record the resistance of the ECT sensor at various temperatures, then compare those measurements to the following temperature verses resistance table.

HEATED OXYGEN (HO2S) SENSOR

LOCATION

See Figures 238 through 243.

Refer to the accompanying illustrations for sensor locations.

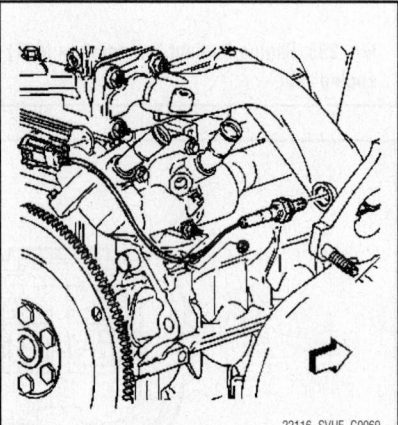

Fig. 238 Heated Oxygen (HO2S) location (sensor 1)—2.2L engine

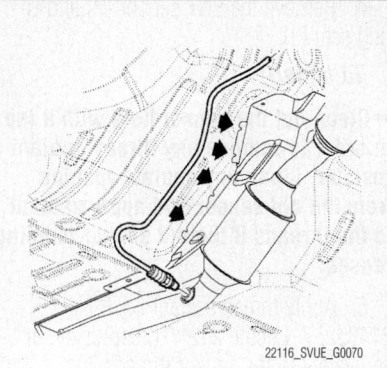

Fig. 239 Heated Oxygen (HO2S) location (sensor 2)—2.2L engine

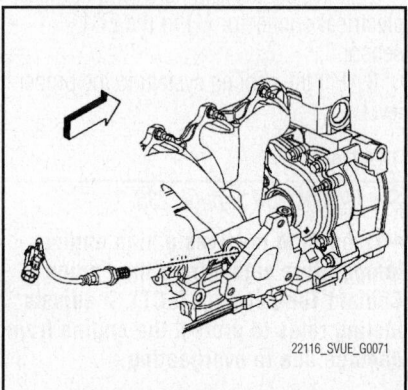

Fig. 240 Heated Oxygen (HO2S) location (sensor 1)—2.4L engine

Temperature Versus Resistance

Temperature	Resistance Minimum	Resistance Maximum
C°/F°	Ohms	Ohms
Engine Coolant Temperature (ECT)		
-40/-40	40,490	50,136
-20/-4	14,096	16,827
-10/14	8,642	10,152
0/32	5,466	6,326
20/68	2,351	2,649
25/77	1,941	2,173
40/104	1,118	1,231
60/140	573	618
80/176	313	332
100/212	182	191
120/248	109	116
140/284	068	074

Fig. 237 Temperature verses resistance table for ECT sensor

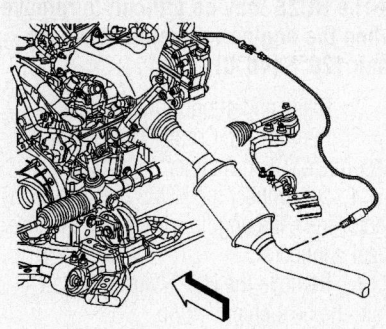

Fig. 241 Heated Oxygen (HO2S) location (sensor 2)—2.4L engine

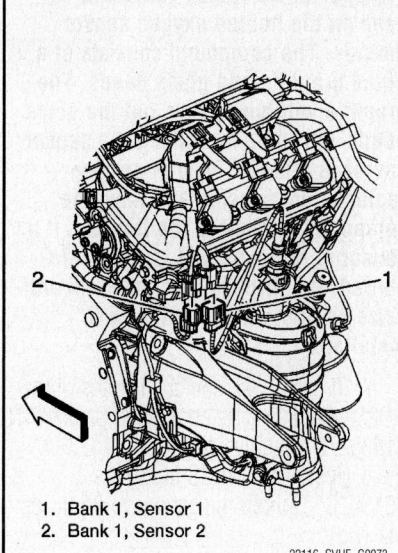

1. Bank 1, Sensor 1
2. Bank 1, Sensor 2

Fig. 242 Heated Oxygen (HO2S) location (bank 1, sensors 1 & 2)—3.5L engine

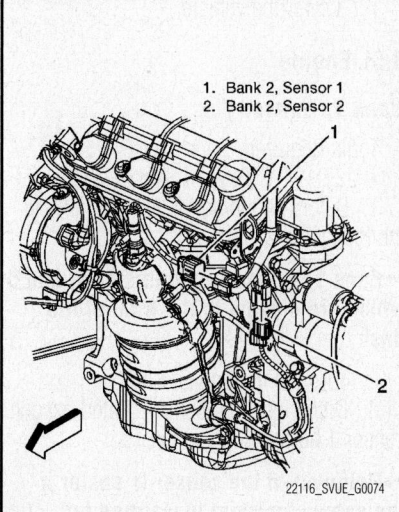

1. Bank 2, Sensor 1
2. Bank 2, Sensor 2

Fig. 243 Heated Oxygen (HO2S) location (bank 2, sensors 1 & 2)—3.5L engine

OPERATION

Heated Oxygen Sensors (HO2S) are used for fuel control and post catalyst monitoring. Each HO2S compares the oxygen content of the surrounding air with the oxygen content in the exhaust stream. The HO2S must reach operating temperature to provide an accurate voltage signal. A heating element inside the HO2S minimizes the time required for the sensor to reach operating temperature. Voltage is provided to the heater by the ignition 1 voltage circuit through a fuse. With the engine running, a ground is provided to the heater by the HO2S heater low control circuit through a low side driver within the Powertrain Control Module (PCM). The PCM commands the heater ON or OFF to maintain a specific HO2S operating temperature range. The PCM monitors the voltage on the HO2S heater low control circuit for heater fault diagnosis. If the PCM detects that the HO2S heater low control circuit voltage is not within a specified range, a DTC is set.

REMOVAL & INSTALLATION

2.2L Engine

Sensor 1

Tool Required:
• J 39194-C O2 Sensor Wrench
1. Before servicing the vehicle, refer to the Precautions Section.

❋❋ WARNING

The HO2S uses a permanently attached pigtail and connector. This pigtail should not be removed from the HO2S. Damage to, or removal of, the pigtail or connector could affect proper operation of the sensor.

2. Turn the ignition OFF.
3. Disconnect the HO2S-1 harness connector.
4. Remove the sensor harness and connector from the attachment clip.
5. Use a liquid penetrate before removing the sensor.

➡**Removal of the sensor is easier if the exhaust system is slightly warmed up. Be careful that the exhaust is not too hot to work on safely. Moving the sensor back and forth while applying penetrating oil to the threads will aid in removal and will decrease the chance of exhaust pipe thread damage.**

6. Remove the HO2S-1 using the J 39194-C, or equivalent.

To install:

❋❋ WARNING

Silicone based products will contaminate the HO2S. Use only a nickel based anti-seize compound that does not contain silicone.

7. Apply a small amount of anti-seize compound Saturn P/N 21485279, or equivalent, to the threads of the HO2S-1.
8. Install the HO2S-1 using the J 39194-C, or equivalent. Tighten the oxygen sensor-to-exhaust manifold pipe to 33 ft. lbs. (45 Nm).
9. Install the sensor harness and connector to the attachment clip.
10. Connect the HO2S-1 harness connector. Push in the connector until a click is heard and pull back to confirm a positive engagement.

Sensor 2

Tool Required:
• J 39194-C O2 Sensor Wrench
1. Before servicing the vehicle, refer to the Precautions Section.

❋❋ WARNING

The HO2S uses a permanently attached pigtail and connector. This pigtail should not be removed from the HO2S. Damage to, or removal of, the pigtail or connector could affect proper operation of the sensor.

2. Turn the ignition OFF.

❋❋ CAUTION

Ensure that the vehicle is properly supported and squarely positioned. To help avoid personal injury when a vehicle is on a hoist, provide additional support for the vehicle on the opposite end from which the components are being removed.

3. Raise the vehicle.
4. Disconnect the HO2S-2 harness connector.
5. Remove the HO2S-2 harness clip from the heat shield attachment.
6. Use a liquid penetrate before removing the sensor.
7. Remove the HO2S-2 using the J 39194-C, or equivalent.

To install:

✹✹ WARNING

Silicone based products will contaminate the HO2S. Use only a nickel based anti-seize compound that does not contain silicone.

8. Apply a small amount of anti-seize compound Saturn P/N 21485279, or equivalent, to the threads of the HO2S-2.

9. Install the HO2S-2 using the J 39194-C, or equivalent. Tighten the HO2S-2 sensor-to-exhaust pipe to 33 ft. lbs. (45 Nm).

➡ **Do Not apply any material in the HO2S-2 harness connector such as grease or dielectric compound. The wires carry air reference to the sensor in order for the sensor to operate properly.**

10. Install the HO2S-2 harness clip to the heat shield attachment bolt. Tighten the bolt to 35 inch lbs. (4 Nm).

11. Connect the HO2S-2 harness connector. Push in the connector until a click is heard, then pull back to confirm a positive engagement.

12. Ensure the HO2S-2 harness pigtail connector is secure to the chassis.

2.4L Engine

Sensor 1

Tool Required:
- J 39194-C Oxygen Sensor Wrench
1. Before servicing the vehicle, refer to the Precautions Section.

✹✹ WARNING

The HO2S uses a permanently attached pigtail and connector. This pigtail should not be removed from the HO2S. Damage to, or removal of, the pigtail or connector could affect proper operation of the sensor.

✹✹ WARNING

The use of excessive force may damage the threads in the exhaust manifold/pipe.

➡ **The in-line connector and louvered end must be kept clear of grease, dirt, or other contaminants. Avoid using cleaning solvents of any type. DO NOT drop or roughly handle the Heated Oxygen Sensor (HO2S).**

➡ **The HO2S may be difficult to remove when the engine temperature is less than 120°F (48°C).**

2. Raise and support the vehicle.

3. Remove the Connector Position Assurance (CPA) retainer.

4. Disconnect the engine wiring harness electrical connector from the HO2S.

5. Remove the HO2S connector clip from the thermostat housing.

6. Remove the HO2S using the J 39194-C.

To install:

➡ **A special anti-seize compound is used on the heated oxygen sensor threads. The compound consists of a liquid graphite and glass beads. The graphite will burn away, but the glass beads will remain, making the sensor easier to remove. New or service replacement sensors will have the compound applied to the threads. If a sensor is removed and is to be reinstalled, the threads must have an anti-seize compound applied prior to installation.**

7. If necessary, coat the threads of the HO2S with anti-seize compound Saturn P/N 21485279 or equivalent.

8. Install the HO2S using the J 39194-C. Tighten the sensor to 31 ft. lbs. (42 Nm).

9. Install the HO2S connector clip to the thermostat housing.

10. Connect the engine wiring harness electrical connector to the HO2S.

11. Install the CPA retainer.

Sensor 2

Tool Required:
- J 39194-C Oxygen Sensor Wrench
1. Before servicing the vehicle, refer to the Precautions Section.

✹✹ WARNING

The HO2S uses a permanently attached pigtail and connector. This pigtail should not be removed from the HO2S. Damage to, or removal of, the pigtail or connector could affect proper operation of the sensor.

✹✹ WARNING

The use of excessive force may damage the threads in the exhaust manifold/pipe.

➡ **The in-line connector and louvered end must be kept clear of grease, dirt, or other contaminants. Avoid using cleaning solvents of any type. DO NOT drop or roughly handle the Heated Oxygen Sensor (HO2S).**

➡ **The HO2S may be difficult to remove when the engine temperature is less than 120°F (48°C).**

2. Raise and support the vehicle.

3. Remove the Connector Position Assurance (CPA) retainer.

4. Disconnect the HO2S electrical connector from the engine wiring harness electrical connector.

5. Remove the HO2S wiring pigtail from the heat shield crimp.

6. Remove the HO2S using the J 39194.

To install:

➡ **A special anti-seize compound is used on the heated oxygen sensor threads. The compound consists of a liquid graphite and glass beads. The graphite will burn away, but the glass beads will remain, making the sensor easier to remove. New or service replacement sensors will have the compound applied to the threads. If a sensor is removed and is to be reinstalled, the threads must have an anti-seize compound applied prior to installation.**

7. If necessary, coat the threads of the HO2S with anti-seize compound Saturn P/N 21485279 or equivalent.

8. Install the HO2S using the J 39194-C. Tighten the sensor to 31 ft. lbs. (42 Nm).

9. Install the HO2S wiring pigtail to the heat shield crimp.

10. Connect the HO2S electrical connector to the engine wiring harness electrical connector.

11. Install the CPA retainer.

12. Lower the vehicle.

3.5L Engine

Bank 1, Sensor 1

Tools Required:
- J 39194-C Oxygen Sensor Wrench
1. Before servicing the vehicle, refer to the Precautions Section.

➡ **Bank 1 includes cylinders 1, 3, and 5 which are closest to the front of the dash.**

2. Turn the ignition OFF.

3. Disconnect the bank 1 heated oxygen sensor 1 harness connector.

➡ **Removal of the sensor is easier if the exhaust system is warmed up slightly. Be careful that it is not too hot to work on safely. Applying penetrating oil to the threads while moving the** sensor back and forth will also aid in removal and will decrease the chance of exhaust pipe thread damage.

4. Remove the oxygen sensor using the J 39194-C.

To install:

5. Apply a small amount of the anti-seize compound SA P/N 21485279, or equivalent, to the threads of the heated oxygen sensor 1.

6. Install the heated oxygen sensor 1 using the J 39194-C. Tighten the oxygen sensor to 33 ft. lbs. (44 Nm).

7. Attach the bank 1 heated oxygen sensor 1 harness connector. Make sure the locking tab is in the full closed position.

8. Start the engine and make sure no exhaust leaks exist.

Bank 1, Sensor 2

Tools Required:
- J 39194-C Oxygen Sensor Wrench

1. Before servicing the vehicle, refer to the Precautions Section.

➡**Bank 1 includes cylinders 1, 3, and 5 which are the closest to the front of the dash.**

2. Turn the ignition OFF.

3. Disconnect the bank 1 heated oxygen sensor 2 harness connector.

4. Disconnect the connectors from the retaining bracket.

5. Remove the heated oxygen sensor connector retaining bracket and bolt.

6. Raise and support the vehicle.

7. Remove the heated oxygen sensor wiring harness bracket and bolt.

➡**Removal of the sensor is easier if the exhaust system is warmed up slightly. Be careful that it is not too hot to work on safely. Applying penetrating oil to the threads while moving the sensor back and forth will also aid in removal and will decrease the chance of exhaust pipe thread damage.**

8. Remove the bank 1 heated oxygen sensor 2 using the J 39194-C.

To install:

9. Apply a small amount of anti-seize compound SA P/N 21485279, or equivalent, to the threads of the heated sensor 2.

10. Install the bank 1 heated oxygen sensor 2 using the J 39194-C. Tighten the oxygen sensor to 33 ft. lbs. (44 Nm).

11. Install the heated oxygen sensor wiring harness bracket and bolt. Tighten the bolt to 89 inch lbs. (10 Nm).

12. Lower the vehicle.

13. Install the heated oxygen sensor connector retaining bracket and bolt. Tighten the bolt to 89 inch lbs. (10 Nm).

14. Connect the bank 1 heated oxygen sensor 2 harness connector. Make sure the locking tab is in the full closed position.

15. Connect the connectors to the retaining bracket.

16. Start the engine and make sure no exhaust leaks exist.

Bank 2, Sensor 1

Tools Required:
- J 39194-C Oxygen Sensor Wrench

1. Before servicing the vehicle, refer to the Precautions Section.

➡**Bank 2 includes cylinders 2, 4, and 6 which are closest to the front of the vehicle.**

2. Turn the ignition OFF.

3. Disconnect the bank 2 heated oxygen sensor 1 harness connector.

➡**Removal of the sensor is easier if the exhaust system is warmed up slightly. Be careful that it is not too hot to work on safely. Applying penetrating oil to the threads while moving the sensor back and forth will also aid in removal and will decrease the chance of exhaust pipe thread damage.**

4. Remove the bank 2 heated oxygen sensor 1 using the J 39194-C.

To install:

5. Apply a small amount of the anti-seize compound SA P/N 21485279, or equivalent, to the threads of the heated oxygen sensor.

6. Install the bank 2 heated oxygen sensor 1 using the J 39194-C. Tighten the oxygen sensors (exhaust manifold) to 33 ft. lbs. (44 Nm).

7. Connect the heated oxygen sensor harness connector. Make sure the locking tab is in the full closed position.

8. Start the engine and make sure no exhaust leaks exist.

Bank 2, Sensor 2

Tools Required:
- J 39194-C Oxygen Sensor Wrench

1. Before servicing the vehicle, refer to the Precautions Section.

➡**Bank 2 includes cylinders 2, 4, and 6 which are closest to the front of the vehicle.**

2. Turn the ignition OFF.

3. Disconnect the bank 2 heated oxygen sensor 2 harness connector and disconnect from the retaining bracket.

4. Raise and support the vehicle.

5. Remove the left transaxle mount just enough to gain access to the heated oxygen sensor.

6. Remove the heated oxygen sensor wiring harness bracket and bolt.

➡**Removal of the sensor is easier if the exhaust system is warmed up slightly. Be careful that it is not too hot to work on safely. Applying penetrating oil to the threads while moving the sensor back and forth will also aid in removal and will decrease the chance of exhaust pipe thread damage.**

7. Remove the bank 2 heated oxygen sensor 2 using the J 39194-C.

To install:

8. Apply a small amount of the anti-seize compound SA P/N 21485279, or equivalent, to the threads of the heated oxygen sensor.

9. Install the bank 2 heated oxygen sensor 2 using the J 39194-C. Tighten the oxygen sensors (exhaust manifold) to 33 ft. lbs. (44 Nm).

10. Install the heated oxygen sensor wiring harness bracket and bolt. Tighten the bolt to 30 ft. lbs. (40 Nm).

11. Install the left transaxle mount.

12. Lower the vehicle.

13. Connect the heated oxygen sensor harness connector. Make sure the locking tab is in the full closed position.

14. Start the engine and make sure no exhaust leaks exist.

TESTING

See Figures 244 through 251.

1. With an OBD2 scan tool connected to the datalink port:

   a. Start the engine and allow it to reach normal operating temperature.

   b. If the engine is at operating temperature when started, wait 15 seconds to allow the Heated Oxygen Sensor (HO2S) heater current to stabilize.

   c. Observe the affected HO2S heater parameter with a scan tool.

   d. The HO2S heater parameter should be within the specified range: 0.5–2.0 Amps.

2. Replace the affected HO2S as necessary.

3. Probe for circuit voltage:

   a. Turn engine OFF.

   b. Disconnect the affected HO2S.

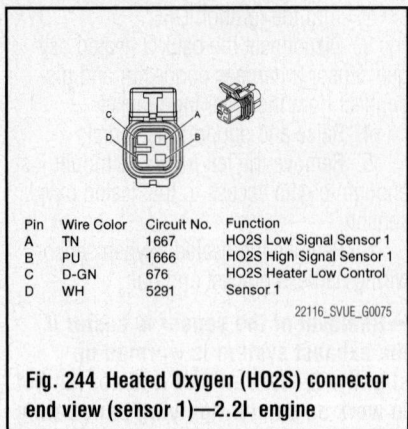

Pin	Wire Color	Circuit No.	Function
A	TN	1667	HO2S Low Signal Sensor 1
B	PU	1666	HO2S High Signal Sensor 1
C	D-GN	676	HO2S Heater Low Control
D	WH	5291	Sensor 1

22116_SVUE_G0075

Fig. 244 Heated Oxygen (HO2S) connector end view (sensor 1)—2.2L engine

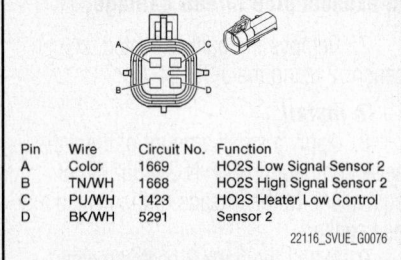

Pin	Wire Color	Circuit No.	Function
A	1669		HO2S Low Signal Sensor 2
B	TN/WH	1668	HO2S High Signal Sensor 2
C	PU/WH	1423	HO2S Heater Low Control
D	BK/WH	5291	Sensor 2

22116_SVUE_G0076

Fig. 245 Heated Oxygen (HO2S) connector end view (sensor 2)—2.2L engine

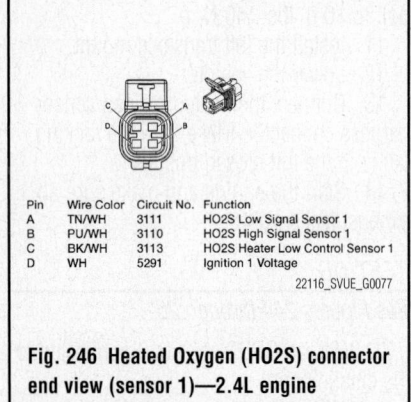

Pin	Wire Color	Circuit No.	Function
A	TN/WH	3111	HO2S Low Signal Sensor 1
B	PU/WH	3110	HO2S High Signal Sensor 1
C	BK/WH	3113	HO2S Heater Low Control Sensor 1
D	WH	5291	Ignition 1 Voltage

22116_SVUE_G0077

Fig. 246 Heated Oxygen (HO2S) connector end view (sensor 1)—2.4L engine

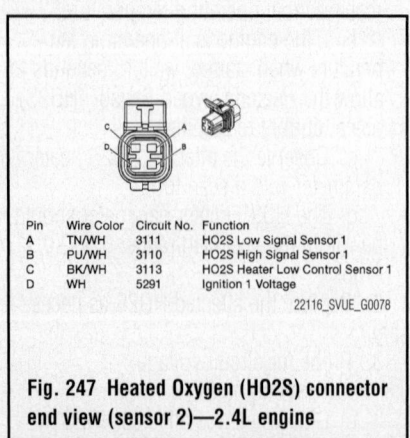

Pin	Wire Color	Circuit No.	Function
A	TN/WH	3111	HO2S Low Signal Sensor 1
B	PU/WH	3110	HO2S High Signal Sensor 1
C	BK/WH	3113	HO2S Heater Low Control Sensor 1
D	WH	5291	Ignition 1 Voltage

22116_SVUE_G0078

Fig. 247 Heated Oxygen (HO2S) connector end view (sensor 2)—2.4L engine

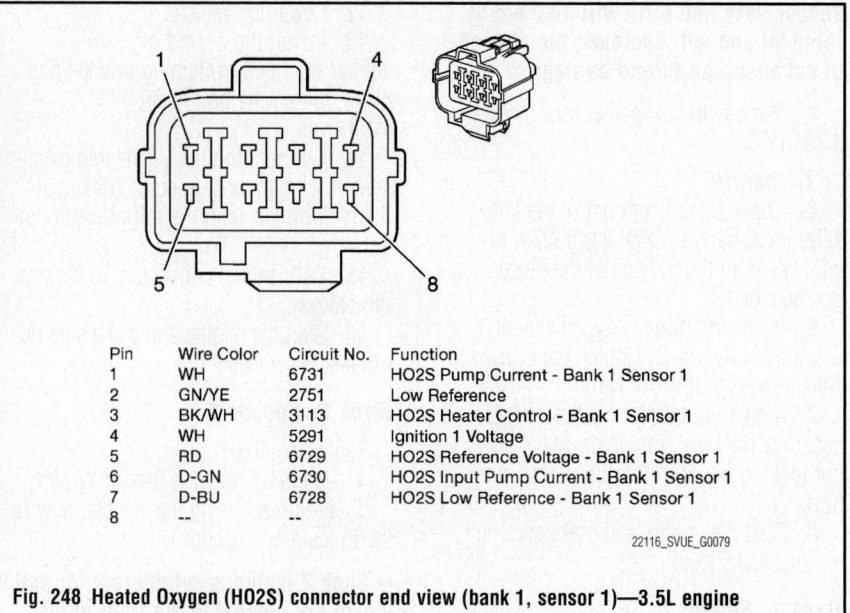

Pin	Wire Color	Circuit No.	Function
1	WH	6731	HO2S Pump Current - Bank 1 Sensor 1
2	GN/YE	2751	Low Reference
3	BK/WH	3113	HO2S Heater Control - Bank 1 Sensor 1
4	WH	5291	Ignition 1 Voltage
5	RD	6729	HO2S Reference Voltage - Bank 1 Sensor 1
6	D-GN	6730	HO2S Input Pump Current - Bank 1 Sensor 1
7	D-BU	6728	HO2S Low Reference - Bank 1 Sensor 1
8	--	--	

22116_SVUE_G0079

Fig. 248 Heated Oxygen (HO2S) connector end view (bank 1, sensor 1)—3.5L engine

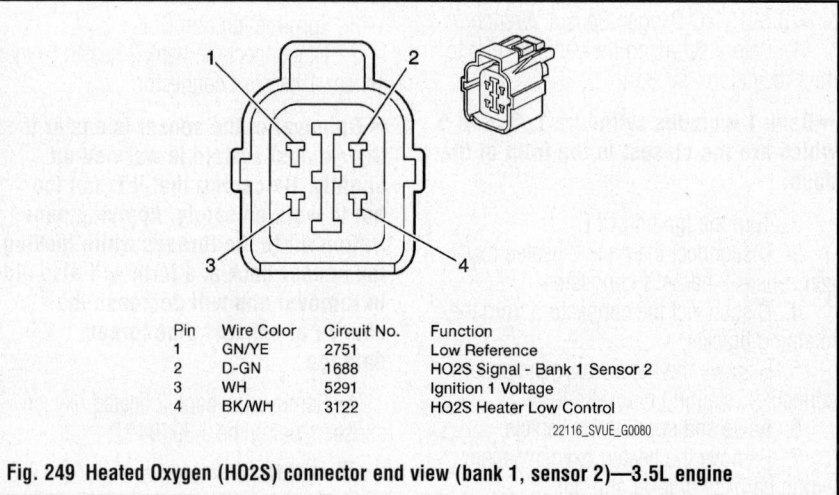

Pin	Wire Color	Circuit No.	Function
1	GN/YE	2751	Low Reference
2	D-GN	1688	HO2S Signal - Bank 1 Sensor 2
3	WH	5291	Ignition 1 Voltage
4	BK/WH	3122	HO2S Heater Low Control

22116_SVUE_G0080

Fig. 249 Heated Oxygen (HO2S) connector end view (bank 1, sensor 2)—3.5L engine

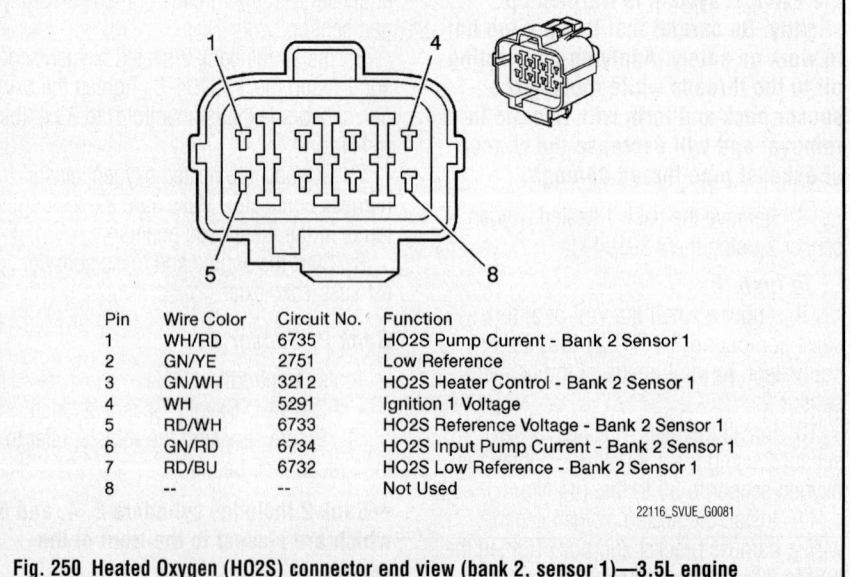

Pin	Wire Color	Circuit No.	Function
1	WH/RD	6735	HO2S Pump Current - Bank 2 Sensor 1
2	GN/YE	2751	Low Reference
3	GN/WH	3212	HO2S Heater Control - Bank 2 Sensor 1
4	WH	5291	Ignition 1 Voltage
5	RD/WH	6733	HO2S Reference Voltage - Bank 2 Sensor 1
6	GN/RD	6734	HO2S Input Pump Current - Bank 2 Sensor 1
7	RD/BU	6732	HO2S Low Reference - Bank 2 Sensor 1
8	--	--	Not Used

22116_SVUE_G0081

Fig. 250 Heated Oxygen (HO2S) connector end view (bank 2, sensor 1)—3.5L engine

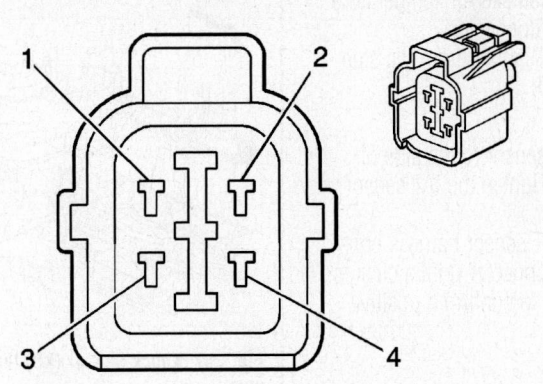

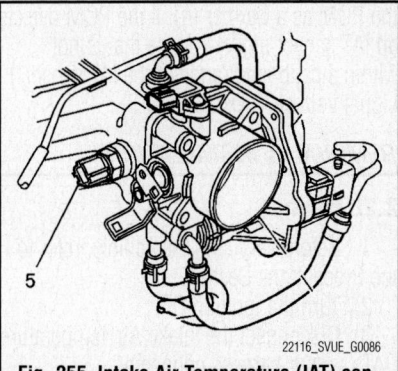

Fig. 255 Intake Air Temperature (IAT) sensor location (sensor 2)—3.5L engine

Pin	Wire Color	Circuit No.	Function
1	GN/YE	2751	Low Reference
2	WH	1670	HO2S Signal - Bank 2 Sensor 2
3	WH	5291	Ignition 1 Voltage
4	GN/RD	3223	HO2S Heater Low Control

22116_SVUE_G0082

Fig. 251 Heated Oxygen (HO2S) connector end view (bank 2, sensor 2)—3.5L engine

INTAKE AIR TEMPERATURE (IAT) SENSOR

LOCATION

See Figures 252 through 255.

Refer to the accompanying illustrations for sensor locations.

c. Turn ON the ignition, with the engine OFF.

d. Probe the ignition 1 voltage circuit of the HO2S harness connector on the engine harness side with a test lamp that is connected to a good ground.

e. The test lamp should illuminate.

4. Test the ground circuit:

a. Turn OFF the ignition.

b. Probe the HO2S heater low control circuit of the HO2S harness connector on the engine harness side with a test lamp connected to battery voltage.

c. With the ignition still OFF, observe the test lamp.

d. The test lamp should illuminate.

5. If the ECM and all circuits test normal, replace the appropriate HO2S.

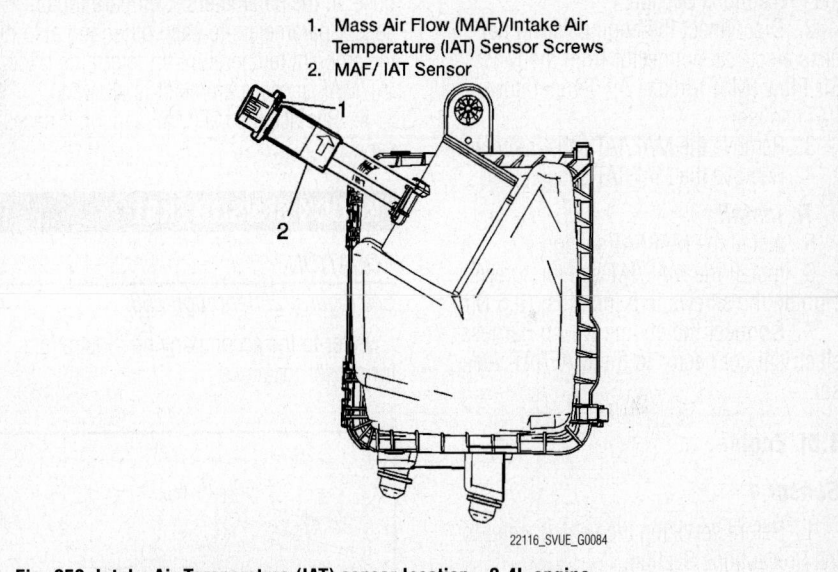

1. Mass Air Flow (MAF)/Intake Air Temperature (IAT) Sensor Screws
2. MAF/ IAT Sensor

22116_SVUE_G0084

Fig. 253 Intake Air Temperature (IAT) sensor location—2.4L engine

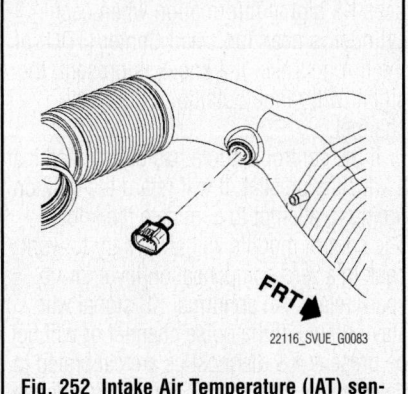

22116_SVUE_G0083

Fig. 252 Intake Air Temperature (IAT) sensor location—2.2L engine

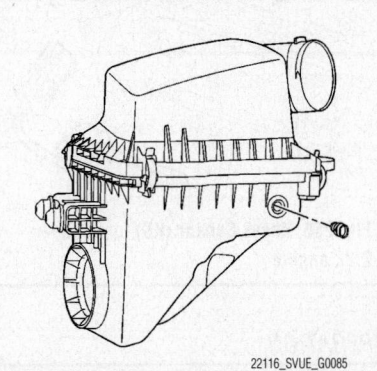

22116_SVUE_G0085

Fig. 254 Intake Air Temperature (IAT) sensor location (sensor 1)—3.5L engine

OPERATION

The Intake Air Temperature (IAT) sensor is a variable resistor that measures the temperature of the air entering the engine intake manifold. The Powertrain Control Module (PCM) supplies 5 volts to the IAT signal circuit and a ground for the IAT low reference circuit. When the sensor is cold, the resistance is greater. This results in a greater voltage on the signal circuit that is interpreted by the PCM as a colder IAT. As the sensor becomes warmer, the resistance decreases. This results in a lesser voltage on the IAT signal circuit that is interpreted by the PCM as a warmer IAT. If the PCM detects an IAT sensor signal voltage that is not within a calibrated range of the IAT sensor 1 signal voltage, a DTC is set.

REMOVAL & INSTALLATION

2.2L Engine

1. Before servicing the vehicle, refer to the Precautions Section.
2. Turn the ignition OFF.
3. Disconnect the Intake Air Temperature (IAT) sensor harness connector.
4. Remove the IAT sensor by pulling it out of the air induction tube.

To install:

5. Install the IAT sensor.
6. Connect the IAT sensor harness connector. Push in the connector until a click is heard, then pull back to confirm a positive engagement.

2.4L Engine

1. Before servicing the vehicle, refer to the Precautions Section.
2. Disconnect the engine wiring harness electrical connector from the Mass Sir Flow (MAF)/Intake Air Temperature (IAT) sensor.
3. Remove the MAF/IAT sensor screws.
4. Remove the MAF/IAT sensor.

To install:

5. Install the MAF/IAT sensor.
6. Install the MAF/IAT sensor screws. Tighten the screws to 5 inch lbs. (0.6 Nm).
7. Connect the engine wiring harness electrical connector to the MAF/IAT sensor.

3.5L Engine

Sensor 1

1. Before servicing the vehicle, refer to the Precautions Section.
2. Turn the ignition OFF.
3. Disconnect the Intake Air Temperature (IAT) sensor harness connector.
4. Remove the IAT sensor by pulling it out of the air cleaner housing.

To install:

5. Install the IAT sensor with a new O-ring.
6. Connect the IAT sensor harness connector. Push in the connector until a click is heard, then pull back to confirm a positive engagement.

Sensor 2

1. Before servicing the vehicle, refer to the Precautions Section.
2. Turn the ignition OFF.

3. Disconnect the Intake Air Temperature (IAT) sensor harness connector.
4. Remove the IAT sensor from the side of the intake manifold.

To install:

5. Install the IAT sensor to the side of the intake manifold. Tighten the IAT sensor to 13 ft. lbs. (18 Nm).
6. Connect the IAT sensor harness connector. Push in the connector until a click is heard, then pull back to confirm a positive engagement.

TESTING

1. Determine the ambient temperature by using an accurate thermometer.
2. If the ignition has been OFF for 8 hours or more, the Intake Air Temperature (IAT)/Mass Air Flow (MAF) sensor parameter and the Engine Coolant Temperature (ECT) sensor parameter should be within 27°F (15°C) of each other and also the ambient temperature.
3. Turn ON the ignition, and immediately observe the parameters. Compare those sensor parameters to each other and also to the ambient temperature to determine if the IAT/MAF sensor parameter is skewed.
4. Replace the IAT/MAF sensor, if necessary.

KNOCK SENSOR (KS)

LOCATION

See Figures 256 through 258.

Refer to the accompanying illustrations for sensor locations.

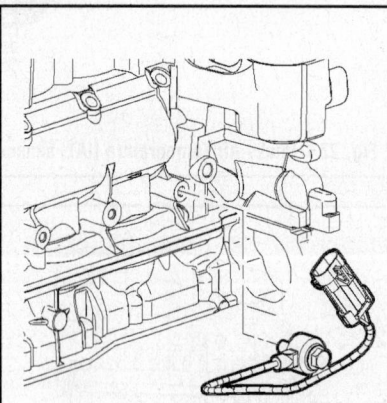

Fig. 256 Knock Sensor (KS) location—2.2L engine

OPERATION

The Knock Sensor (KS) system enables the control module to control the ignition

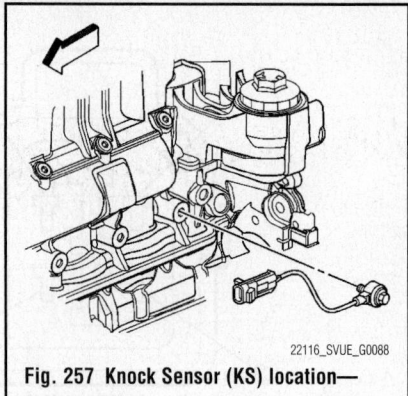

Fig. 257 Knock Sensor (KS) location—2.4L engine

timing for the best possible performance while protecting the engine from potentially damaging levels of detonation. The control module uses the KS system to test for abnormal engine noise that may indicate detonation, also known as spark knock.

This KS system uses one or two flat response two-wire sensors. The sensor uses piezo-electric crystal technology that produces an AC voltage signal of varying amplitude and frequency based on the engine vibration or noise level. The amplitude and frequency are dependent upon the level of knock that the KS detects. The control module receives the KS signal through a signal circuit. The KS ground is supplied by the control module through a low reference circuit.

The control module learns a minimum noise level, or background noise, at idle from the KS and uses calibrated values for the rest of the RPM range. The control module uses the minimum noise level to calculate a noise channel. A normal KS signal will ride within the noise channel. As engine speed and load change, the noise channel upper and lower parameters will change to accommodate the normal KS signal, keeping the signal within the channel. In order to determine which cylinders are knocking, the control module only uses KS signal information when each cylinder is near Top Dead Center (TDC) of the firing stroke. If a knock is present, the signal will range outside of the noise channel.

If the control module has determined that a knock is present, it will retard the ignition timing to attempt to eliminate the knock. The control module will always try to work back to a zero compensation level, or no spark retard. An abnormal KS signal will stay outside of the noise channel or will not be present. KS diagnostics are calibrated to detect faults with the KS circuitry inside the control module, the KS wiring, and the KS

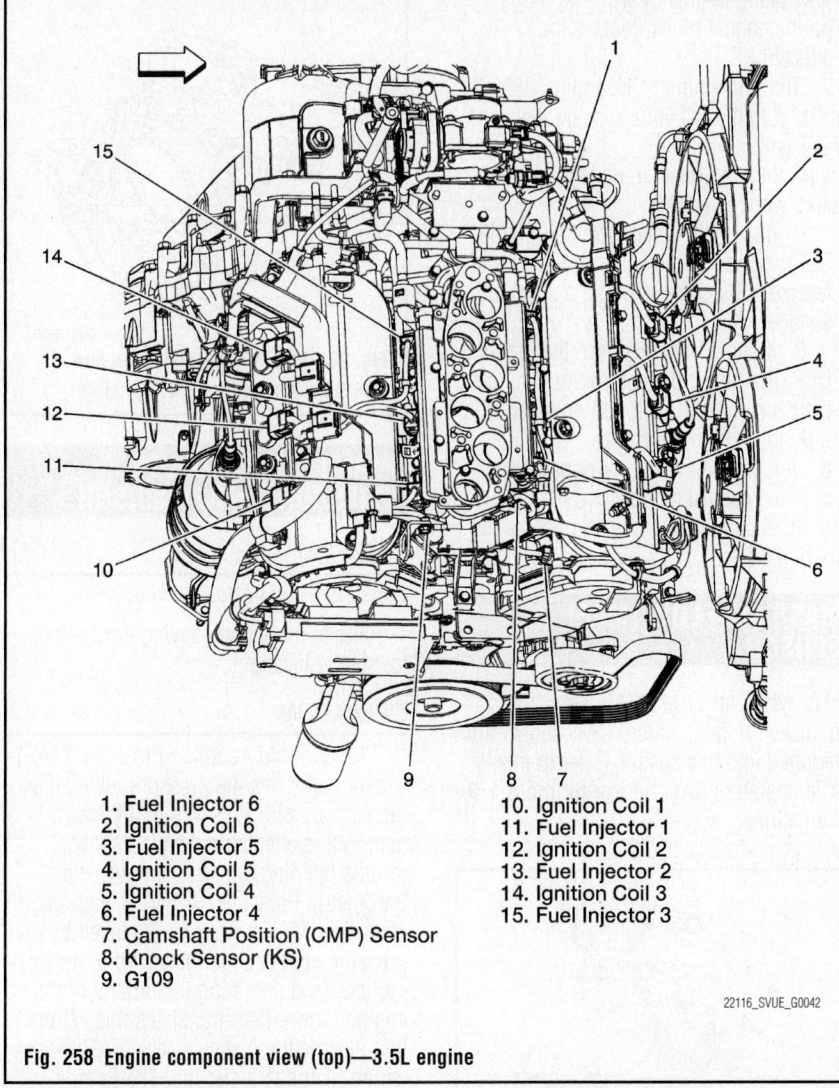

1. Fuel Injector 6
2. Ignition Coil 6
3. Fuel Injector 5
4. Ignition Coil 5
5. Ignition Coil 4
6. Fuel Injector 4
7. Camshaft Position (CMP) Sensor
8. Knock Sensor (KS)
9. G109
10. Ignition Coil 1
11. Fuel Injector 1
12. Ignition Coil 2
13. Fuel Injector 2
14. Ignition Coil 3
15. Fuel Injector 3

22116_SVUE_G0042

Fig. 258 Engine component view (top)—3.5L engine

voltage output. Some diagnostics are also calibrated to detect constant noise from an outside influence such as a loose/damaged component or excessive engine mechanical noise.

REMOVAL & INSTALLATION

2.2L Engine

1. Before servicing the vehicle, refer to the Precautions Section.
2. Disconnect the negative battery cable.
3. Remove the knock sensor harness connector.
4. Remove the knock sensor connector from the retaining clip by inserting a flat-bladed screwdriver between the connector and clip while sliding the connector upward.
5. Remove the knock sensor.

To install:

➡If a new knock sensor pigtail connector retaining clip is going to be used, the old one must be removed from the intake manifold. Use a push pin removal tool to remove the clip from the intake manifold.

6. Insert the knock sensor pigtail connector with retaining clip into the intake manifold hole or slide the knock sensor pigtail connector over the retaining clip from the top.
7. Connect the knock sensor harness connector. Push in the connector until a click is heard, then pull back to confirm a positive engagement.

➡The larger metal contact area of the knock sensor MUST be toward the engine block. The DTC P0327 may result if the sensor is installed backwards.

8. Install the knock sensor at the 9 o'clock position and attachment bolt. Tighten the knock-sensor-engine block bolt to 18 ft. lbs. (25 Nm).
9. Connect the negative battery cable.

2.4L Engine

1. Before servicing the vehicle, refer to the Precautions Section.
2. Raise and support the vehicle.
3. Disconnect the engine wiring harness electrical connector from the knock sensor pigtail electrical connector.
4. Remove the knock sensor electrical connector pigtail clip from the oil level indicator tube bracket.
5. Remove the knock sensor bolt.
6. Remove the knock sensor.

To install:

➡Rotate the pigtail 90° from vertical before securing the fastener.

7. Install the knock sensor.
8. Install the knock sensor bolt. Tighten the bolt to 18 ft. lbs. (25 Nm).
9. Connect the engine wiring harness electrical connector to the knock sensor pigtail electrical connector.
10. Install the knock sensor electrical connector pigtail clip to the oil level indicator tube bracket.
11. Lower the vehicle.

3.5L Engine

1. Before servicing the vehicle, refer to the Precautions Section.
2. Remove the lower left intake manifold.
3. Disconnect the wiring harness connector from the Knock Sensor (KS).
4. Remove the KS from the engine block.

To install:

> ❈❈ **WARNING**
>
> **DO NOT apply thread sealant to the sensor threads. The sensor threads are coated at the factory and applying additional sealant affects the sensors ability to detect detonation.**

5. Install the KS into engine block. Tighten the KS to 23 ft. lbs. (31 Nm).
6. Connect the KS wiring harness connector to the knock sensor.
7. Install the lower left intake manifold.

TESTING

See Figures 258 and 260.

1. Inspect the Knock Sensor (KS) for physical damage. A KS that is dropped or damaged may cause a DTC to set.
2. Inspect the KS for proper installation. A KS that is loose or over-tightened may

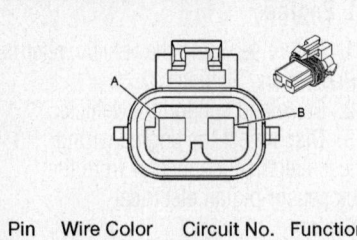

Pin	Wire Color	Circuit No.	Function
A	D-BU	496	KS Signal
B	GY	1716	KS Signal

22116_SVUE_G0089

Fig. 259 Knock Sensor (KS) connector end view—2.2L & 2.4L engines

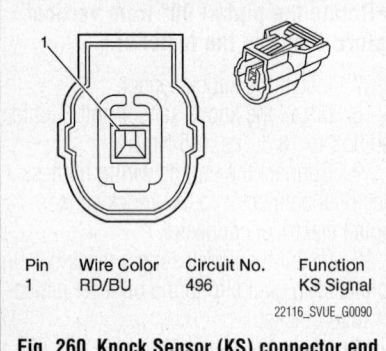

Pin	Wire Color	Circuit No.	Function
1	RD/BU	496	KS Signal

22116_SVUE_G0090

Fig. 260 Knock Sensor (KS) connector end view—3.5L engine

cause a DTC to set. The KS should be free of thread sealant other than the factory coating.

3. The KS mounting surface should be free of burrs, casting flash, and foreign material.

➡**If an engine mechanical noise can be heard, repair the condition before proceeding to test the KS.**

4. Test for an intermittent or poor connection at the affected KS.

5. With the ignition OFF, disconnect the affected KS.

   a. Measure the resistance for infinite ohms from the sensor signal terminal on the KS to a good ground with a Digital Multi-Meter (DMM).

   b. If resistance does not measure infinite ohms, replace the affected KS.

✳✳ WARNING

DO NOT tap on plastic engine components.

6. Connect the DMM to the terminal of the affected KS. Set the DMM to the 400 Hz scale, let it stabilize at 0 Hz.

   a. Tap on engine block with a non-metallic object near the affected KS while observing the signal indicated on the DMM.

   b. If the DMM does not display a

fluctuating frequency while tapping on the engine block, replace the affected KS.

7. Turn the ignition ON, engine OFF. Set the DMM to the DC voltage scale. Measure for 4.2 volts from the KS signal circuit to a good ground with the DMM.

   c. If over 4.2 volts, turn the ignition OFF, disconnect the control module and test the KS signal circuit for a short to voltage.

   d. If under 4.2 volts, turn the ignition OFF, disconnect the control module test the KS signal circuit for an open, short to ground, or high resistance.

8. Test for intermittent or poor connections at the control module.

9. If all circuits test normal, replace the control module.

MASS AIR FLOW (MAF) SENSOR

The Mass Air Flow (MAF) sensor and the Intake Air Temperature (IAT) sensor are integrated into one sensor. Refer to Intake Air Temperature (IAT) Sensor for more information.

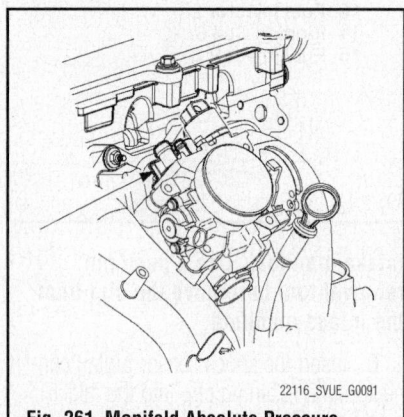

22116_SVUE_G0091

Fig. 261 Manifold Absolute Pressure (MAP) sensor location—2.2L engine

22116_SVUE_G0092

Fig. 262 Manifold Absolute Pressure (MAP) sensor location—2.4L engine

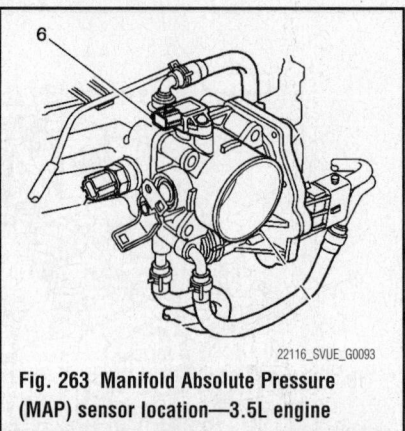

22116_SVUE_G0093

Fig. 263 Manifold Absolute Pressure (MAP) sensor location—3.5L engine

MANIFOLD ABSOLUTE PRESSURE (MAP) SENSOR

LOCATION

See Figures 261 through 263.

Refer to the accompanying illustrations for sensor locations.

OPERATION

The Manifold Absolute Pressure (MAP) sensor measures the pressure inside the intake manifold. Pressure in the intake manifold is affected by engine speed, throttle opening, air temperature, and Barometric Pressure (BARO). A diaphragm within the MAP sensor is displaced by the pressure changes that occur from the varying load and operating conditions of the engine. The sensor translates this action into electrical resistance. The MAP sensor wiring includes 3 circuits. The Engine Control Module (ECM) supplies a regulated 5 volts to the sensor on a 5 volt reference circuit. The ECM supplies a ground on a low reference circuit. The MAP sensor provides a signal voltage to the ECM, relative to the pressure changes, on the MAP sensor signal circuit. The ECM converts the signal voltage input to a pressure value.

Under normal operation the greatest pressure that can exist in the intake manifold is equal to BARO. This occurs when the vehicle is operated at Wide Open Throttle (WOT) or when the ignition is ON while the engine is OFF. Under these conditions, the ECM uses the MAP sensor to determine the current BARO. The least manifold pressure occurs when the vehicle is idling or decelerating. MAP can range from 10 kPa, when pressures are less, to as great as 104 kPa, depending on the current BARO. The ECM monitors the MAP sensor signal for pressure outside of the normal range.

REMOVAL & INSTALLATION

2.2L Engine

1. Before servicing the vehicle, refer to the Precautions Section.

2. Disconnect the Intake Air Temperature (IAT) sensor connector.

3. Loosen the clamp at the air cleaner assembly.

4. Remove the push-pin attachment from the outlet resonator/duct assembly to support bracket.

5. Loosen the clamp at the throttle body assembly.

6. Disconnect the Positive Crankcase Ventilation (PCV) fresh air vent hose at the cam cover.

7. Remove the outlet resonator/duct assembly.

8. Disconnect the Manifold Absolute Pressure (MAP) sensor electrical connector.

9. Remove the MAP sensor and the MAP sensor port seal if it is still retained in the intake manifold.

To install:

10. Install the MAP sensor with port seal into the intake manifold.

11. Connect the MAP sensor electrical connector. Push in the connector until a click is heard and pull back to confirm a positive engagement.

12. Install the outlet resonator/duct assembly into position.

13. Connect the PCV fresh air vent hose assembly.

14. Tighten the clamp at the throttle body assembly. Tighten the clamp to 35 inch lbs. (4 Nm).

15. Position the outlet resonator/duct assembly up with the support bracket and install the push-pin.

16. Tighten the clamp at the air cleaner assembly. Tighten the clamp to 35 inch lbs. (4 Nm).

17. Connect the IAT sensor connector.

2.4L Engine

1. Before servicing the vehicle, refer to the Precautions Section.

2. Disconnect the Evaporative Emission (EVAP) canister purge tube from the intake manifold.

3. Reposition the EVAP canister purge tube out of the way.

4. Disconnect the fuel injector wiring harness electrical connector from the engine wiring harness electrical connector.

5. Remove the fuel injector wiring harness clips from the fuel rail and reposition the wiring harness out of the way.

6. Disconnect the engine harness electrical connector from the Manifold Absolute Pressure (MAP) sensor.

7. Remove the MAP sensor and seal.

To install:

8. Lubricate the NEW MAP sensor seal with clean engine oil.

9. Install the MAP sensor into the intake manifold.

10. Position the fuel injector wiring harness and install the fuel injector wiring harness clips to the fuel rail.

11. Connect the fuel injector wiring harness electrical connector to the engine wiring harness electrical connector.

12. Position the EVAP canister purge tube to the intake manifold.

13. Connect the EVAP canister purge tube to the intake manifold.

3.5L Engine

1. Before servicing the vehicle, refer to the Precautions Section.

2. Turn the ignition OFF.

3. Disconnect the Manifold Absolute Pressure (MAP) sensor harness connector.

4. Remove the MAP sensor attachment screw and remove the MAP sensor and O-ring.

To install:

5. Make sure the MAP sensor mounting surface is clean. Install the MAP sensor with the new O-ring and attachment bolt. Tighten the manifold absolute pressure sensor screw to 35 inch lbs. (4 Nm).

6. Connect the MAP sensor harness connector. Push the connector in until the lock position is felt, then pull back to confirm engagement.

TESTING

See Figures 264 through 266.

Poor idle characteristics may be due to uncontrolled fueling caused by an open or high resistance in the Heated Oxygen Sensor (HO2S) 1 low signal circuit. Before replacing any component, ensure that this condition does not exist.

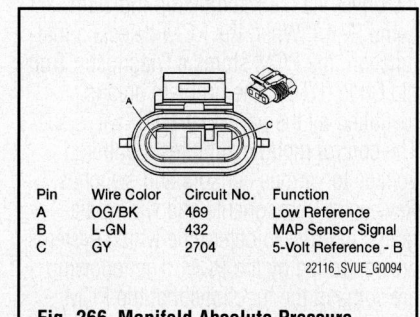

Pin	Wire Color	Circuit No.	Function
A	OG/BK	469	Low Reference
B	L-GN	432	MAP Sensor Signal
C	GY	2704	5-Volt Reference - B

22116_SVUE_G0094

Fig. 266 Manifold Absolute Pressure (MAP) connector end view—2.2L engine

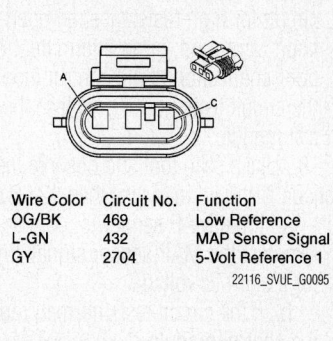

Pin	Wire Color	Circuit No.	Function
A	OG/BK	469	Low Reference
B	L-GN	432	MAP Sensor Signal
C	GY	2704	5-Volt Reference 1

22116_SVUE_G0095

Fig. 265 Manifold Absolute Pressure (MAP) connector end view—2.4L engine

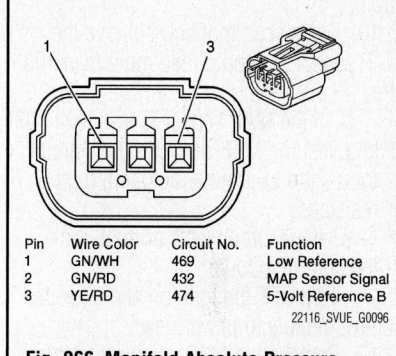

Pin	Wire Color	Circuit No.	Function
1	GN/WH	469	Low Reference
2	GN/RD	432	MAP Sensor Signal
3	YE/RD	474	5-Volt Reference B

22116_SVUE_G0096

Fig. 266 Manifold Absolute Pressure (MAP) connector end view—3.5L engine

1. Start the engine.

2. Monitor the DTC information with the scan tool.

3. Turn the engine OFF.

4. If other DTC codes are set, correct these codes first, if possible.

5. Verify the integrity of the entire air induction system by inspecting for the following conditions:

- Any damage to, or hairline fractures of, the Manifold Absolute Pressure (MAP) sensor housing
- Disconnected, damaged, or incorrectly routed vacuum hoses
- MAP sensor disconnected from the vacuum source
- Restrictions in the MAP sensor vacuum source
- Intake manifold vacuum leaks
- Inspect for a properly functioning oxygen sensor

6. With the ignition ON, and the engine OFF, disconnect the MAP sensor.

7. Using a Digital Multi-Meter (DMM), measure the 5-volt reference circuit of the MAP sensor to a good ground. The reading should be 4.8–5.2 volts.

a. If more than 5.2 volts, then test the circuit for a short to voltage. If the circuit tests normal, replace the control module.

b. If less than 4.8 volts, then test the circuit for high resistance, an open, a short to ground, or an intermittent or poor connection at the control module. If the circuit tests normal, replace the control module.

8. Use a scan tool and observe the MAP sensor. It should read less than 12 kPa.

a. If the MAP sensor is more than 12 kPa, test the MAP sensor signal circuit for a short to voltage.

b. If the circuit tests normal, replace the control module.

9. Use a 3-Amp fused jumper wire and connect it between the MAP sensor 5-volt reference circuit and the MAP sensor signal circuit.

10. Use a scan tool and observe the MAP sensor. It should read more than 103 kPa.

a. If the MAP sensor is less than 103 kPa, test the MAP sensor signal circuit for a short to ground, an open, high resistance.

b. If the circuit tests normal, replace the control module.

11. Turn OFF the ignition and allow the control module to power down.

12. Remove the MAP sensor from the engine vacuum source, but leave the MAP sensor connected to the engine harness.

13. Connect the J 23738-A, or a similar vacuum pump, to the MAP sensor.

14. Turn ON the ignition, with the engine OFF.

15. Observe the MAP sensor pressure with the scan tool.

16. Apply vacuum to the MAP sensor with the J 23738-A in 1 inch Hg increments until 15 inches Hg is reached. Each 1 inch Hg should decrease MAP sensor pressure by 3–4 kPa. Monitor the MAP sensor pressure to see if the decrease in pressure is consistent.

a. If decrease in pressure is not consistent then, test for intermittent and poor connections at the MAP sensor.

b. If connections test OK, replace the MAP sensor.

17. Apply vacuum with the J 23738-A until 20 inches Hg is reached. Observe the MAP sensor pressure. It should read less than 34 kPa.

a. If the pressure is more than 34 kPa, test for an intermittent or poor connection at the MAP sensor.

b. If connections test OK, replace the MAP sensor.

18. With a DMM, measure the resistance between the low reference circuit of the MAP sensor and battery negative post. It should read less than 5 ohms.

a. If the resistance is more than 5 ohms, test the low reference circuit for a high resistance.

b. If the circuit tests normal, replace the control module.

POWERTRAIN CONTROL MODULE (PCM)

LOCATION

See Figure 267.

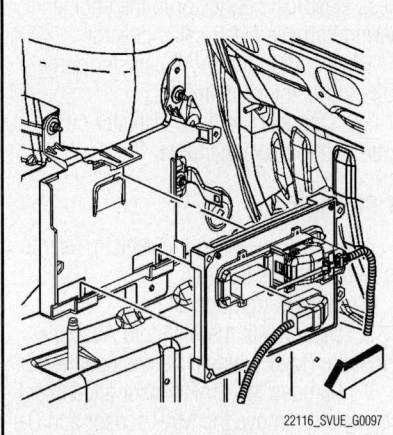

22116_SVUE_G0097

Fig. 267 Powertrain Control Module (PCM) location—3.5L engine

Refer to the accompanying illustration for PCM location.

OPERATION

The powertrain has electronic controls to reduce exhaust emissions while maintaining excellent drivability and fuel economy. The Powertrain Control Module (PCM) is the control center of this system. The PCM monitors numerous engine and vehicle functions. The PCM constantly looks at the information from various sensors and other inputs, and controls the systems that affect vehicle performance and emissions. The PCM also performs the diagnostic tests on various parts of the system. The PCM can recognize operational problems and alert the driver via the Malfunction Indicator Lamp (MIL). When the PCM detects a malfunction, the PCM stores a Diagnostic Trouble Code (DTC). The problem area is identified by the particular DTC that is set. The control module supplies a buffered voltage to various sensors and switches. Review the components and wiring diagrams in order to determine which systems are controlled by the PCM. The following are some of the functions that the PCM controls:

- The engine fueling

- The Ignition Control (IC)
- The Knock Sensor (KS) system
- The Evaporative Emissions (EVAP) system
- The Secondary Air Injection (AIR) system (if equipped)
- The Exhaust Gas Recirculation (EGR) system
- The automatic transmission functions
- The alternator
- The A/C clutch control
- The cooling fan control

REMOVAL & INSTALLATION

2.2L & 2.4L Engines

For the 2.2L & 2.4L engines, refer to Electronic Control Module (ECM) for the removal & installation.

3.5L Engine

1. Before servicing the vehicle, refer to the Precautions Section.

✳✳ WARNING

Turn the ignition OFF when installing or removing the control module connectors and disconnecting or reconnecting the power to the control module (battery cable, Powertrain Control Module (PCM)/Engine Control Module (ECM)/Transaxle Control Module (TCM) pigtail, control module fuse, jumper cables, etc.) in order to prevent internal control module damage.

✳✳ WARNING

Control module damage may result when the metal case contacts battery voltage. DO NOT contact the control module metal case with battery voltage when servicing a control module, using battery booster cables, or when charging the vehicle battery.

✳✳ WARNING

In order to prevent any possible electrostatic discharge damage to the control module, do not touch the connector pins or the soldered components on the circuit board.

✳✳ WARNING

Remove any debris from around the control module connector surfaces before servicing the control module. Inspect the control module

connector gaskets when diagnosing or replacing the control module. Ensure that the gaskets are installed correctly. The gaskets prevent contaminant intrusion into the control module.

➡**The replacement control module must be programmed.**

➡**It is necessary to record the remaining engine oil life. If the replacement module is not programmed with the remaining engine oil life, the engine oil life will default to 100 percent. If the replacement module is not programmed with the remaining engine oil life, the engine oil will need to be changed at 3,000 miles (5,000 km) from the last engine oil change.**

2. Using a scan tool, retrieve the percentage of remaining engine oil. Record the remaining engine oil life.

3. Disconnect the battery negative cable.

4. Disconnect the wiring harness.

5. Depress the retaining tab and remove the Powertrain Control Module (PCM).

6. Remove the PCM from the housing.

To install:

7. Install the PCM into the housing bracket.

8. Connect the wiring harness.

9. Connect the battery negative cable.

10. Program the PCM.

TESTING

The Powertrain Control Module (PCM) is programmed with test routines that test the operation of the various systems the PCM controls. Some tests monitor internal PCM functions. Many tests are run continuously. Other tests run only under specific conditions, referred to as conditions for running a Diagnostic Trouble Code (DTC). When the vehicle is operating within the conditions for running a particular test, the PCM monitors certain parameters and determines if the values are within an expected range. The parameters and values considered outside the range of normal operation are listed as conditions for setting the DTC. When the conditions for setting the DTC occur, the PCM executes the action taken when the DTC Sets. Some DTC's alert the driver via the Mal-

function Indicator Lamp (MIL) or a message. Other DTC's do not trigger a driver warning, but are stored in memory. The PCM also saves data and input parameters when most DTC's are set. This data is stored in the freeze frame and/or failure records.

The DTC's are categorized by type. The DTC type is determined by the MIL operation and the manner in which the fault data is stored when a particular DTC fails. In some cases there may be exceptions to this structure. Therefore, when diagnosing the system it is important to read the action taken when the DTC sets and the conditions for clearing the DTC.

Many intermittent open or shorted circuits come and go with harness and connector movement caused by vibration, engine torque, bumps, and rough pavement.

1. Test the wiring harness and connectors by performing the following:
- Move the related PCM connectors and wiring while monitoring the appropriate scan tool data
- With the engine running, move the related connectors and wiring while monitoring engine operation
- If harness or connector movement affects the data displayed, the component and system operation, or the engine operation, inspect and repair the harness or connections as necessary

2. Test the electrical connections and/or wiring by performing the following:
- Inspect for incorrect mating of the connector halves, or terminals not fully seated in the connector body, backed-out
- Inspect for improperly formed or damaged terminals. Test for incorrect terminal tension
- Inspect for poor terminal to wire connections including terminals crimped over insulation. This requires removing the terminal from the connector body
- Inspect for corrosion or water intrusion. Pierced or damaged insulation can allow moisture to enter the wiring. The conductor can corrode inside the insulation with little visible evidence. Look for swollen and stiff sections of wire in the suspect circuits
- Inspect for wires that are broken inside the insulation

VARIABLE CAMSHAFT TIMING OIL CONTROL SOLENOID

LOCATION

See Figure 268.

Refer to the accompanying illustration for solenoid location.

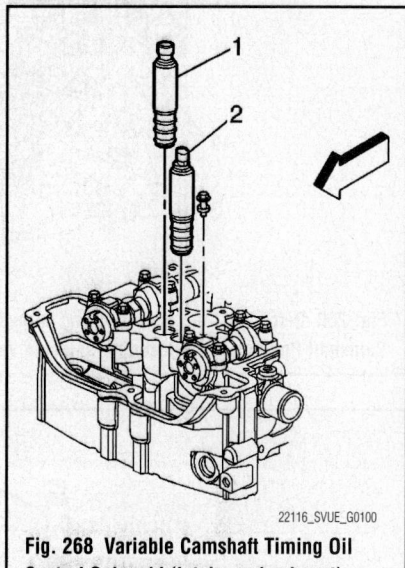

22116_SVUE_G0100

Fig. 268 Variable Camshaft Timing Oil Control Solenoid (intake and exhaust) location—3.5L engine

OPERATION

The variable camshaft timing oil control solenoid (also called the Camshaft Position (CMP) actuator) is attached to each camshaft and is hydraulically operated in order to change the angle of the camshaft relative to Crankshaft Position (CKP). The variable camshaft timing oil control solenoid is controlled by the control module. The control module sends a pulse width modulated 12 volt signal to a variable camshaft timing oil control solenoid. The solenoid controls the amount of engine oil flow. The variable camshaft timing oil control solenoid can change the camshaft angle. The control module increases the pulse width to accomplish the desired camshaft operation.

REMOVAL & INSTALLATION

2.4L Engine

See Figures 269 and 270.

1. Before servicing the vehicle, refer to the Precautions Section.

2. Remove the air cleaner outlet duct.

3. Disconnect the engine wiring harness electrical connectors (2, 3) from the appropriate Camshaft Position (CMP) actuator solenoid valve, also known as the

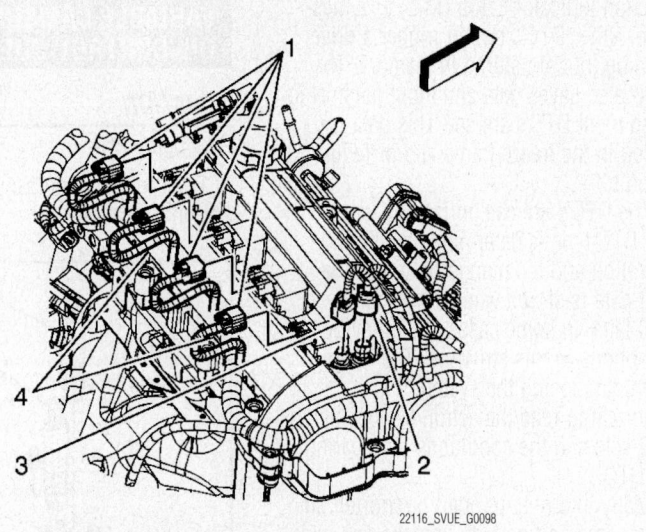

Fig. 269 Disconnect the engine wiring harness electrical connectors from the appropriate Camshaft Position (CMP) actuator solenoid valve—3.5L engine

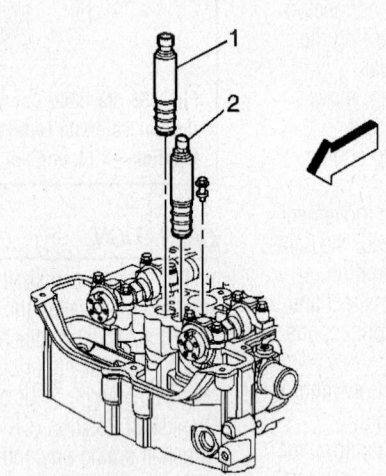

1. Variable Camshaft Timing Oil Control Solenoid (exhaust)
2. Variable Camshaft Timing Oil Control Solenoid (intake)

22116_SVUE_G0099

Fig. 270 Remove the intake and exhaust CMP actuator solenoid valve bolts and valves—3.5L engine

Variable Camshaft Timing Oil Control Solenoid.

4. Remove the exhaust CMP actuator solenoid valve bolt and valve (1), if required.

5. Remove the intake CMP actuator solenoid valve bolt and valve (2), if required.

6. Inspect the solenoid valve O-ring seals for damage, replace as necessary.

To install:

7. Lubricate the solenoid valve O-ring seals with clean engine oil.

8. Install the intake (2) CMP actuator

solenoid valve and bolt, if required. Tighten the bolt to 89 inch lbs. (10 Nm).

9. Install the exhaust (1) CMP actuator solenoid valve and bolt, if required. Tighten the bolt to 89 inch lbs. (10 Nm).

10. Connect the engine wiring harness electrical connector (2, 3) to the appropriate CMP actuator solenoid valve.

11. Install the air cleaner outlet duct.

TESTING

1. Before servicing the vehicle, refer to the Precautions Section.

2. Ensure the vehicle has the proper oil viscosity.

3. Observe the engine oil level. The engine oil level should be within the operating range.

4. Allow the engine to reach operating temperature.

5. Increase the engine speed to 1,500 RPM.

6. Command each solenoid to 25 percent. The angle desired parameter should match the solenoid actual parameter.

Component Testing

1. Measure the resistance of each variable camshaft timing oil control solenoid valve assembly. Resistance should be between 8–12 ohms.

2. Connect a jumper wire between the variable camshaft timing oil control solenoid low reference circuit at the solenoid and a good ground.

3. Connect a fused jumper wire to the high control circuit at the solenoid.

   a. Momentarily touch the fused jumper to B+.

   b. Observe the spool valve inside the variable camshaft timing oil control solenoid. The spool valve should move from fully closed to fully opened position.

   c. If the spool valve does not move, replace the variable camshaft timing oil control solenoid.

VEHICLE SPEED SENSOR (VSS)

LOCATION

See Figures 271 and 272.

Refer to the accompanying illustrations for sensor locations.

22116_SVUE_G0101

Fig. 271 Vehicle Speed Sensor (VSS) location (automatic transaxle)—4T45–E

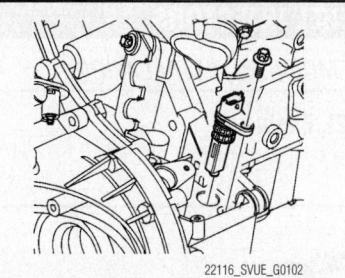

22116_SVUE_G0102

Fig. 272 Vehicle Speed Sensor (VSS) location (manual transaxle)—Getrag 5 speed

OPERATION

The Vehicle Speed Sensor (VSS) system is a pulse generator consisting of a speed sensor assembly, located in the case extension, and a toothed vehicle speed sensor reluctor wheel, which is pressed onto the final drive carrier assembly. As the vehicle drives forward, the vehicle speed sensor reluctor wheel rotates. This rotation produces a variable AC signal in the pickup coil that is proportional to vehicle speed. The Powertrain Control Module (PCM) uses this signal in order to calculate vehicle speed, shift timing, and gear ratios. If the PCM detects a low vehicle speed with a high engine speed while in a drive range, then a DTC is set.

REMOVAL & INSTALLATION

Automatic Transaxle—4T45–E

1. Before servicing the vehicle, refer to the Precautions Section.

2. Disconnect the negative battery cable.
3. Raise and support the vehicle.
4. Remove the electrical connector from the Vehicle Speed Sensor (VSS).
5. Remove the retaining stud and the VSS. Pull straight out in order to avoid damage to the case.

To install:

6. Clean and dry the VSS.
7. Install the VSS and the retaining stud. Tighten the stud to 106 inch lbs. (12 Nm).
8. Install the electrical connector to the VSS.
9. Lower the vehicle.
10. Connect the negative battery cable.

Manual Transaxle—Getrag 5 speed

1. Before servicing the vehicle, refer to the Precautions Section.
2. Raise and support the vehicle.
3. Disconnect the Vehicle Speed Sensor (VSS) electrical connector.
4. Remove the VSS retaining bolt.
5. Remove the VSS.

To install:

6. Install the VSS.
7. Install the VSS retaining bolt. Tighten the bolt to 106 inch lbs. (12 Nm).
8. Connect the VSS electrical connector.
9. Lower the vehicle.

TESTING

1. Ensure the Vehicle Speed Sensor (VSS) is correctly tightened to the transmission housing.
2. Install a scan tool.
3. Turn ON the ignition, with the engine OFF.

➡**Before clearing any DTC's, use the scan tool in order to record the Freeze Frame and Failure Records. Using the Clear Info function erases the Freeze Frame and Failure Records from the PCM. Record the DTC Freeze Frame and Failure Records, then clear any DTC's.**

✳✳ WARNING

Support the lower control arms in the normal horizontal position in order to avoid damage to the drive axles. Do not operate the vehicle in gear with the wheels hanging down at full travel.

4. Raise and support the drive wheels.
5. Start and idle the engine.
6. Place the transmission in DRIVE.
7. Monitor Transmission OSS on the scan tool.
8. With the drive wheels rotating, increase and decrease the throttle position.
9. The Transmission OSS RPM should increase when the wheel speed increases.

FUEL   **GASOLINE FUEL INJECTION SYSTEM**

FUEL SYSTEM SERVICE PRECAUTIONS

Safety is the most important factor when performing not only fuel system maintenance but any type of maintenance. Failure to conduct maintenance and repairs in a safe manner may result in serious personal injury or death. Maintenance and testing of the vehicle's fuel system components can be accomplished safely and effectively by adhering to the following rules and guidelines.

• To avoid the possibility of fire and personal injury, always disconnect the negative battery cable unless the repair or test procedure requires that battery voltage be applied.

• Always relieve the fuel system pressure prior to disconnecting any fuel system component (injector, fuel rail, pressure regulator, etc.), fitting or fuel line connection. Exercise extreme caution whenever relieving fuel system pressure to avoid exposing skin, face

and eyes to fuel spray. Please be advised that fuel under pressure may penetrate the skin or any part of the body that it contacts.

• Always place a shop towel or cloth around the fitting or connection prior to loosening to absorb any excess fuel due to spillage. Ensure that all fuel spillage (should it occur) is quickly removed from engine surfaces. Ensure that all fuel soaked cloths or towels are deposited into a suitable waste container.

• Always keep a dry chemical (Class B) fire extinguisher near the work area.

• Do not allow fuel spray or fuel vapors to come into contact with a spark or open flame.

• Always use a back-up wrench when loosening and tightening fuel line connection fittings. This will prevent unnecessary stress and torsion to fuel line piping.

• Always replace worn fuel fitting O-rings with new Do not substitute fuel hose or equivalent where fuel pipe is installed.

Before servicing the vehicle, make sure to also refer to the precautions in the beginning of this section as well.

RELIEVING FUEL SYSTEM PRESSURE

See Figure 273.

1. Before servicing the vehicle, refer to the Precautions Section.

2. Unless battery voltage is necessary for testing, disconnect the negative battery cable. This will prevent the fuel pump from running and causing a fuel spill through the disconnected components if the ignition key is accidentally turned **ON**.

3. Remove the air cleaner assembly, for access.

4. Connect gauge bar 53476 to fuel gauge pressure adapter 309725 using a flexible hose from gauge bar set SA9127E. Make sure the needle valve on the pressure adapter is off.

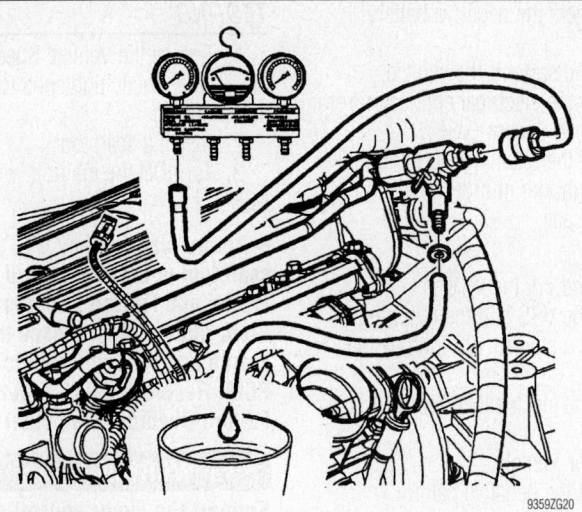

Fig. 273 Connect gauge bar 53476 to fuel gauge pressure adapter 309725 using a flexible hose from gauge bar set SA9127E

➡**Do not use tools to tighten the adapter to the pressure port. If the adapter will not hand-tighten the seals are defective and needs to be replaced.**

5. Wrap a shop rag around the fuel test port fitting, located at the lower rear of the engine, then remove the cap and connect fuel pressure gauge.

6. Install the bleed hose from the pressure gauge into an approved container and open the valve to bleed the system pressure.

7. After the pressure is bled, remove the gauge from the test port and recap it.

8. Install the air cleaner assembly.

9. After servicing the vehicle, connect the negative battery cable and prime the fuel system as follows:

   a. Turn the ignition **ON** for 5 seconds, then **OFF** for 10 seconds.

   b. Repeat the **ON/OFF** cycle 2 more times.

   c. Crank the engine until it starts.

   d. If the engine does not readily start, repeat sub-steps A–C.

10. Run the engine and check for leaks.

FUEL FILTER

REMOVAL & INSTALLATION

See Figure 274.

1. Before servicing the vehicle, refer to the Precautions Section.

2. Properly relieve the fuel system pressure.

3. Remove or disconnect the following:
   • The negative battery cable
   • The fuel filter bracket screw

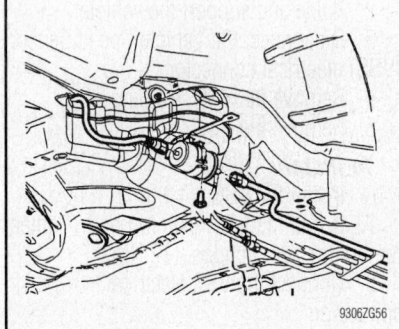

Fig. 274 Remove the fuel filter bracket attaching screw

   • The fuel feed and return lines from the filter
   • The fuel filter from the bracket

To install:

4. Install or connect the following:
   • The new fuel filter into the bracket
   • The new fuel line retainers to the female portion of the quick connect fittings
   • The fuel feed and return lines
   • The fuel filter bracket attaching screw and torque it to 18 inch lbs. (2 Nm)
   • The negative battery cable

5. Prime the fuel system as follows:

   a. Turn the ignition **ON** for 5 seconds, then **OFF** for 10 seconds.

   b. Repeat the **ON/OFF** cycle 2 more times.

   c. Crank the engine until it starts.

   d. If it does not start, repeat the sub-steps A–C.

6. Start the engine and check for leaks, repair if necessary.

FUEL INJECTORS

REMOVAL & INSTALLATION

2.2L Engine
See Figure 275.

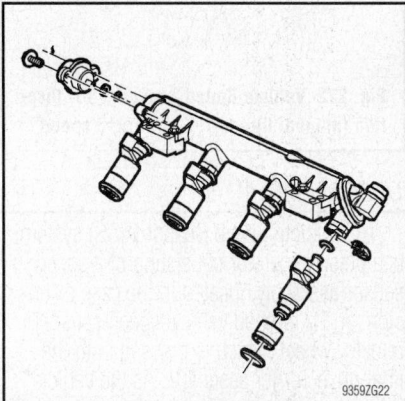

Fig. 275 Remove the retainer clip from the fuel injector—2.2L engine

1. Before servicing the vehicle, refer to the Precautions Section.

2. Properly relieve the fuel system pressure.

3. Remove or disconnect the following:
   • The negative battery cable
   • The air cleaner assembly
   • The engine harness and position aside
   • The fuel rail bracket from the rear of the can cover
   • The fuel feed line
   • The fuel injector electrical connectors
   • The fuel rail bolts
   • The fuel rail with the injectors as an assembly
   • The fuel injector retaining clip off the injector
   • The fuel injector
   • The fuel injector O-rings

To install:

4. Lubricate the new fuel injector O-ring with clean engine oil.

5. Install or connect the following:
   • The new O-ring seals on the fuel injector
   • The fuel injector to the fuel rail
   • The retaining clip to the fuel injector
   • The fuel rail and torque the bolts to 89 inch lbs. (10 Nm)
   • The fuel injector electrical connectors
   • The fuel feed line and tighten the fitting to 89 inch lbs. (10 Nm)
   • The fuel line bracket and tighten the retainer to 89 inch lbs. (10 Nm)

- The air cleaner assembly
- The negative battery cable

6. Start the vehicle and check for leaks, repair if necessary.

2.4L Engine

1. Before servicing the vehicle, refer to the Precautions Section.
2. Properly relieve the fuel system pressure.
3. Remove the air cleaner outlet duct.
4. Disconnect the fuel feed line quick connect fitting from the fuel rail
5. Disconnect the engine wiring harness electrical connector from the fuel injector wiring harness electrical connector.
6. Disconnect the fuel injector wiring harness electrical from the Manifold Absolute Pressure (MAP) sensor.
7. Remove the engine wiring harness clips from the fuel rail tabs.
8. Remove the fuel rail bolts.

✖✖ WARNING

Use care when removing the fuel rail assembly in order to prevent damage to the fuel injector spray tips.

9. Pull the fuel rail back and upward in order to release the fuel injectors from the cylinder head ports.
10. Remove the fuel rail.

➡**The fuel injector tip insulators may be located on the injector or may still be located in the cylinder head. Either way, ensure that all 4 injector tip insulators are removed and discarded.**

11. Remove and discard the fuel injector tip insulators.
12. Disconnect the fuel injector wiring harness electrical connectors from the fuel injectors.
13. Remove the fuel injector wiring harness clips from the fuel rail.
14. Remove the fuel injector wiring harness from the fuel rail.
15. Remove the fuel injector retainer.
16. Remove the fuel injector from the fuel rail.
17. Remove the fuel injector upper O-ring.
18. Remove the fuel injector lower O-ring.

To install:

➡**The fuel injector assembly is stamped with a part number identification. Be sure to use the correct part number when ordering replacement fuel injectors.**

19. Lubricate the NEW fuel injector O-rings with clean engine oil.
20. Install the NEW fuel injector O-rings.
21. Install the fuel injector to the fuel rail.
22. Install the fuel injector retainer.
23. Install the fuel injector wiring harness clips to the fuel rail.
24. Connect the fuel injector wiring harness electrical connectors to the fuel injectors.
25. Lubricate the NEW fuel injector tip insulators with clean engine oil.
26. Install the NEW fuel injector tip insulators to the cylinder head.
27. With the fuel injectors positioned downward, lower the fuel injectors into the cylinder head ports.
28. Carefully push down on the fuel rail in order to insert the injectors into the cylinder head ports.
29. Install the fuel rail bolts. Tighten the bolts to 89 in. lbs. (10 Nm).
30. Install the engine wiring harness clips to the fuel rail tabs).
31. Connect the fuel injector wiring harness electrical to the MAP sensor.
32. Connect the engine wiring harness electrical connector to the fuel injector wiring harness electrical connector.
33. Connect the fuel feed line quick connect fitting to the fuel rail.
34. Install the air cleaner outlet duct.
35. Connect the negative battery cable.
36. Inspect for fuel leaks using the following procedure:
    a. Turn ON the ignition, with the engine OFF for 2 seconds.
    b. Turn OFF the ignition for 10 seconds
    c. Turn ON the ignition
    d. Inspect for fuel leaks.

3.5L Engine

See Figure 278.

1. Before servicing the vehicle, refer to the Precautions Section.
2. Relieve the fuel system pressure.
3. Remove the intake manifold.
4. Disconnect the fuel injector electrical connectors.
5. Remove the fuel rail bolts.
6. Remove the fuel rail and injectors from the manifold as an assembly.
7. Remove the fuel injector retaining clip off the injector.
8. Remove the fuel injector.
9. Fuel injector O-rings and discard.

To install:

10. Lubricate the new fuel injector O-ring with clean engine oil.

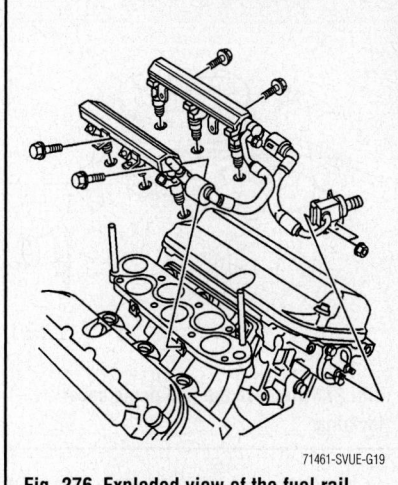

Fig. 276 Exploded view of the fuel rail assembly—3.5L engine

71461-SVUE-G19

11. Install new O-ring seals on the fuel injector.
12. Install the fuel injector to the fuel rail.
13. Install the retaining clip to the fuel injector.
14. Install new O-rings to the injectors.
15. Install the fuel rail and injectors as an assembly to the manifold. Torque the bolts to 87 inch lbs. (10 Nm).
16. Connect the fuel injector electrical connectors.
17. Install the intake manifold.
18. Inspect for fuel leaks using the following procedure:
    a. With the engine OFF, turn ON the ignition for 2 seconds and inspect for fuel leaks.
    b. Turn the ignition OFF for at least 10 seconds.
    c. With the engine OFF, turn ON the ignition for 2 seconds and inspect for fuel leaks.
19. Turn the ignition OFF.

FUEL PUMP

REMOVAL & INSTALLATION

See Figure 277.

1. Before servicing the vehicle, refer to the Precautions Section.
2. Properly relieve the fuel system pressure.
3. Remove or disconnect the following:
    - The negative battery cable
    - The fuel tank
    - The fuel pump electrical connector
    - The fuel lines and hoses from the fuel pump module cover
    - The fuel pump module retaining ring with Wrench SA9156E

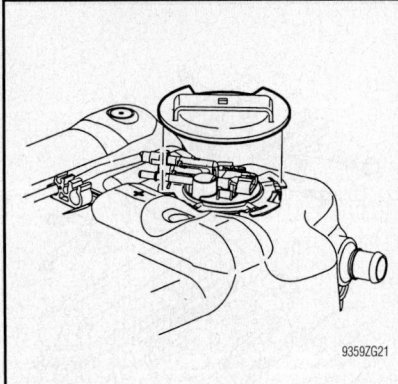

Fig. 277 Remove the fuel pump cover lockring

4. Pull the retaining clip toward the float arm and lift up.

5. Remove the fuel pump straight up from the fuel tank.

6. Remove the fuel pump tank seal and discard the seal.

To install:

7. Install or connect the following:
- The fuel pump with new seal
- The duel pump cover lock ring with Tool SA9156E
- The duel lines, hoses and wiring harness
- The duel tank
- The negative battery cable

8. Start the vehicle and check for leaks, repair if necessary

FUEL TANK

REMOVAL & INSTALLATION

2.2L & 3.5L Engines

1. Before servicing the vehicle, refer to the Precautions Section.

> ※※ CAUTION
>
> **Do not allow smoking or the use of open flames in the area where work on the fuel or EVAP system is taking place. Anytime work is being done on the fuel system, disconnect the negative battery cable, except for those tests where battery voltage is required.**

2. Ensure that the fuel level in the tank is less than ¼ full. If necessary, drain the fuel tank to at least this level.

> ※※ CAUTION
>
> **Fuel supply lines will remain pressurized for long periods of time after the engine is shutdown. This**

pressure must be relieved before servicing the fuel system.

3. Relieve the fuel system pressure.

4. Disconnect the negative battery cable.

5. Raise and support the vehicle .

6. Remove the rubber exhaust hangers on order to allow the exhaust system to drop slightly.

7. Remove the propeller shaft, if equipped.

➡**Clean all fuel pipe connections and surrounding areas before disconnecting the fuel pipes to avoid contamination of the fuel system.**

8. Disconnect the Evaporative Emission (EVAP) canister vent and fresh air hoses:

a. Grasping both sides of the quick-connect fitting, twist the female connector ¼ turn in each direction in order to loosen dirt within the quick-connect fitting.

b. Blow any dirt out of the quick-connect fitting using compressed air.

c. Squeeze the plastic retainer release tabs.

d. Pull the connection apart.

e. Inspect both ends of the quick-connect fitting for dirt and burrs.

9. Remove the fuel filler pipe, EVAP vent hose, and fresh air hose from the fuel tank.

> ※※ CAUTION
>
> **Whenever fuel lines are removed, catch fuel in an approved container. Container opening must be a minimum of 12 inches (300mm) diameter to adequately catch the fluid.**

10. Disconnect the chassis fuel supply line from the tank.

11. Disconnect the electrical connectors:

a. The fuel tank electrical connectors.

b. The EVAP solenoid electrical connector.

> ※※ WARNING
>
> **Do not bend the fuel tank straps. Bending the fuel tank straps may cause damage to the straps.**

➡**Do not disassemble the Rear Drive Module (RDM). It is not necessary to touch the RDM for fuel tank removal.**

12. Support the fuel tank.

13. Remove the fuel tank strap bolts and fuel tank straps.

14. Lower the fuel tank from the underbody of the vehicle.

15. Remove the fuel tank module assemblies.

To install:

16. Install the fuel tank module assemblies.

17. Install the fuel tank heat shield and fuel tank assembly into the vehicle.

18. Install the fuel tank straps and tighten the bolts. Tighten the fuel tank strap-to-body bolts to 18 ft. lbs. (25 Nm).

19. Install the fuel filler pipe, EVAP vent, and fresh air hoses to the fuel tank.

20. Connect the electrical connectors:

a. The fuel tank electrical connector.

b. The EVAP solenoid electrical connectors.

21. Tighten the hose clamp on the filler pipe-to-fuel tank connecting hose. Tighten the fuel fill neck-to-fuel tank clamp to 44 inch lbs. (5 Nm).

22. Connect the EVAP canister vent and fresh air hoses to the fuel tank hoses.

23. If equipped, install the propeller shaft.

24. Install the rubber exhaust hangers.

25. Lower the vehicle .

26. Fill the fuel tank with gasoline.

27. Connect the negative battery cable.

28. Prime the fuel system:

a. Cycle the ignition ON for 5 seconds and then OFF for 10 seconds.

b. Repeat the previous step twice.

c. Crank the engine until it starts. The maximum starter motor cranking time is 20 seconds.

d. If the engine does not start, repeat steps A–C.

2.4L Engine

1. Before servicing the vehicle, refer to the Precautions Section.

> ※※ CAUTION
>
> **Do not allow smoking or the use of open flames in the area where work on the fuel or EVAP system is taking place. Anytime work is being done on the fuel system, disconnect the negative battery cable, except for those tests where battery voltage is required.**

2. Ensure that the fuel level in the tank is less than ¼ full. If necessary, drain the fuel tank to at least this level.

> ※※ CAUTION
>
> **Fuel supply lines will remain pressurized for long periods of time after the engine is shutdown. This**

pressure must be relieved before servicing the fuel system.

3. Relieve the fuel system pressure.
4. Disconnect the negative battery cable.
5. Raise and support the vehicle .
6. Remove the muffler.
7. Remove the propeller shaft, if equipped.

➡**Clean all fuel pipe connections and surrounding areas before disconnecting the fuel pipes to avoid contamination of the fuel system.**

8. Disconnect the evaporative emission (EVAP) canister vent and fresh air hoses:
   a. Grasping both sides of the quick-connect fitting, twist the female connector ¼ turn in each direction in order to loosen dirt within the quick-connect fitting.
   b. Blow any dirt out of the quick-connect fitting using compressed air.
   c. Squeeze the plastic retainer release tabs.
   d. Pull the connection apart.
   e. Inspect both ends of the quick-connect fitting for dirt and burrs.
9. Remove the fuel filler pipe, EVAP vent hose, and fresh air hose from the fuel tank.

✳✳ CAUTION

Whenever fuel lines are removed, catch fuel in an approved container. Container opening must be a minimum of 12 inches (300mm) diameter to adequately catch the fluid.

10. Disconnect the chassis fuel supply line from the tank.
11. Disconnect the electrical connectors:
   a. The fuel tank electrical connectors.
   b. The EVAP solenoid electrical connector.
12. Remove the 36-volt battery positive cable, if equipped.

✳✳ WARNING

Do not bend the fuel tank straps. Bending the fuel tank straps may cause damage to the straps.

➡**Do not disassemble the Rear Drive Module (RDM). It is not necessary to touch the RDM for fuel tank removal.**

13. Support the fuel tank.
14. Remove the fuel tank strap bolts and fuel tank straps.
15. Lower the fuel tank from the underbody of the vehicle.

16. Remove the fuel tank module assemblies.

To install:
17. Install the fuel tank module assemblies.
18. Install the fuel tank heat shield and fuel tank assembly into the vehicle.
19. Install the fuel tank straps and tighten the bolts. Tighten the bolts to 18 ft. lbs. (25 Nm).
20. Install the 36-volt battery positive cable, if equipped.
21. Install the fuel filler pipe, EVAP vent, and fresh air hoses to the fuel tank.
22. Connect the electrical connectors:
   a. The fuel tank electrical connector.
   b. The EVAP solenoid electrical connectors.
23. Tighten the hose clamp on the filler pipe-to-fuel tank connecting hose. Tighten the clamp to 44 inch lbs. (5 Nm).
24. Connect the EVAP canister vent and fresh air hoses to the fuel tank hoses.
25. Install the muffler.
26. If equipped, install the propeller shaft.
27. Lower the vehicle .
28. Fill the fuel tank with gasoline.
29. Connect the negative battery cable.
30. Prime the fuel system:
   a. Cycle the ignition ON for 5 seconds and then OFF for 10 seconds.
   b. Repeat the previous step twice.
   c. Crank the engine until it starts. The maximum starter motor cranking time is 20 seconds.
   d. If the engine does not start, repeat steps A–C.

IDLE SPEED

ADJUSTMENT

The idle speed is maintained by the Powertrain Control Module (PCM). No adjustment is necessary or possible.

THROTTLE BODY

REMOVAL & INSTALLATION

2.2L Engine
See Figures 278 through 281.

1. Before servicing the vehicle, refer to the Precautions Section.
2. Disconnect the negative battery cable.
3. Disconnect the Intake Air Temperature (IAT) sensor connector.
4. Loosen the clamp at the air cleaner assembly.
5. Remove the push pin attachment

from the outlet resonator/duct assembly to support bracket.
6. Loosen the clamp at the throttle body assembly.
7. Disconnect the Positive Crankcase Ventilation (PCV) fresh air vent hose at the cam cover.
8. Remove the outlet resonator/duct assembly.

➡**Cover the throttle body with a shop towel. Using air, clean the base of the throttle body to prevent debris from entering the manifold when the throttle body is removed.**

➡**Cover the throttle body opening with a shop towel and use the shop air to remove any dirt at the base of the throttle body.**

9. Disconnect the electrical connector at throttle body.

10. Remove the throttle body bolts.
11. Remove the throttle body.

➡**The throttle body-to-manifold gasket is not reusable.**

12. Remove the gasket and discard.

➡**Cover the intake manifold opening with a shop towel whenever the throttle body is removed to prevent foreign material entry.**

13. Block the intake manifold opening with a clean shop towel to prevent dirt from entering.

To install:
14. Remove the shop towel from the throttle body opening.
15. Install the throttle body gasket.
16. Install the throttle body assembly and bolts.
17. Tighten the throttle body-to-intake manifold bolts to 89 inch lbs (10 Nm).
18. Connect the throttle body electrical connector.
19. Position the outlet resonator/duct assembly into position.
20. Connect PCV fresh air vent hose assembly.
21. Tighten the clamp at throttle body assembly.
22. Position the outlet resonator/duct assembly up with support bracket and install the push-pin.
23. Tighten the clamp at the air cleaner assembly.
24. Connect the IAT sensor connector.
25. Connect the negative battery cable.
26. Turn the ignition **ON** for one minute

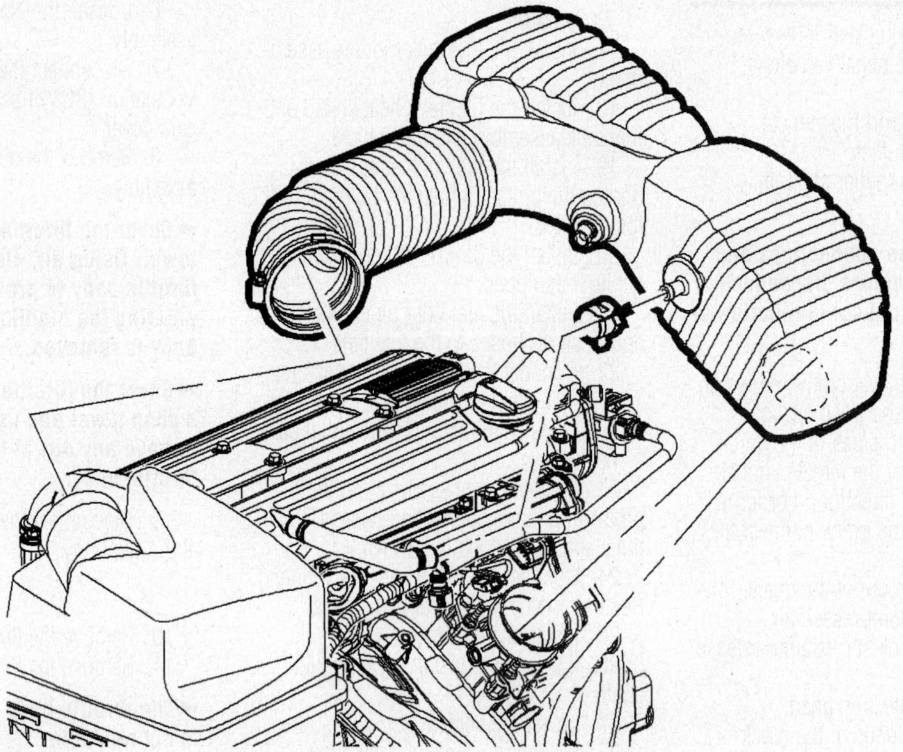

Fig. 278 Remove the outlet resonator/duct assembly

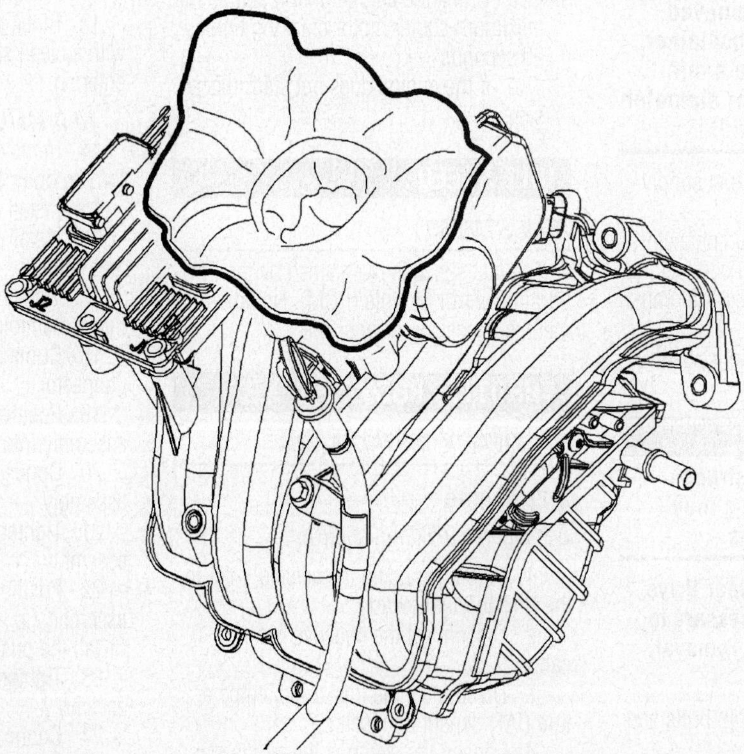

32107_SVUE_G0130

Fig. 279 Cover the throttle body opening with a shop towel

32107_SVUE_G0131

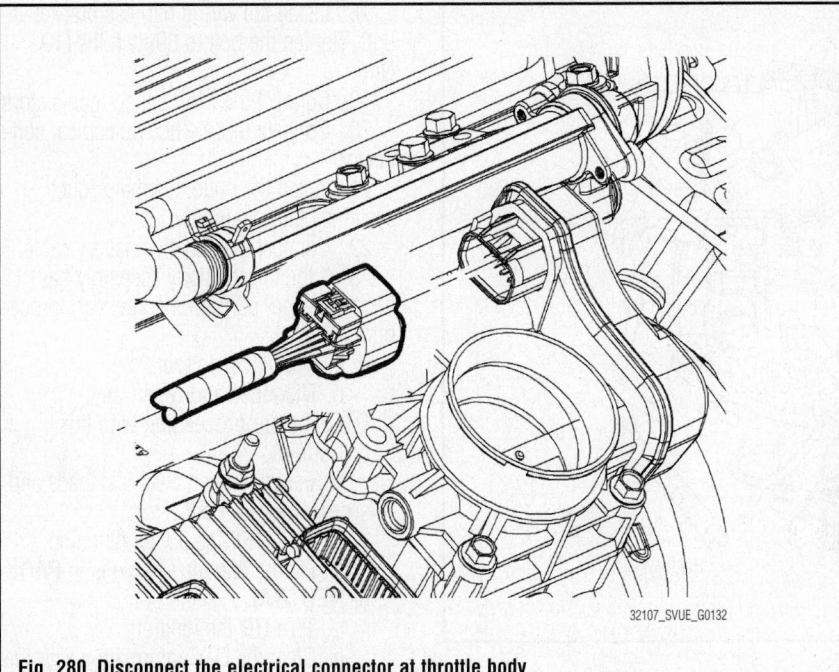

32107_SVUE_G0132

Fig. 280 Disconnect the electrical connector at throttle body

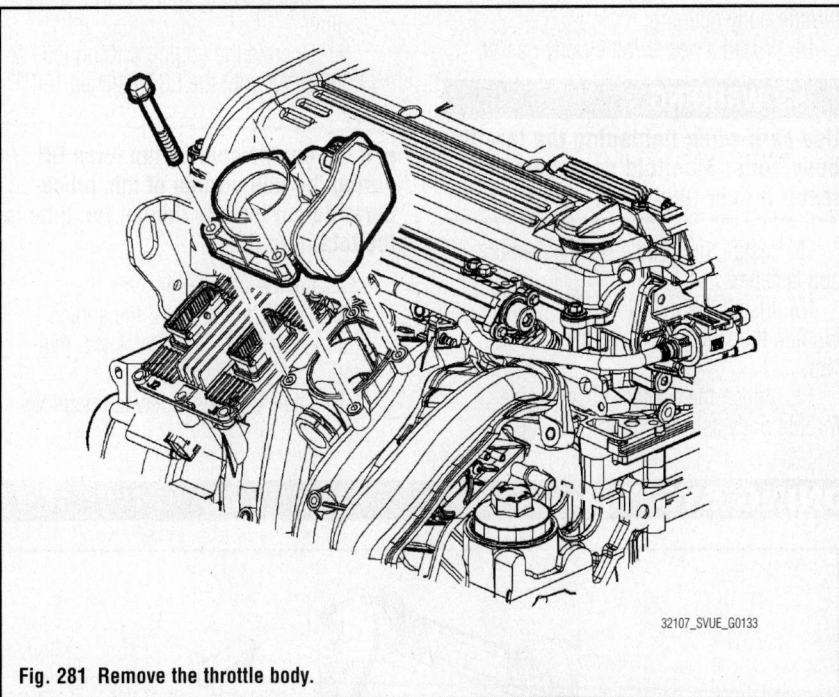

32107_SVUE_G0133

Fig. 281 Remove the throttle body.

while the Engine Control Module (ECM) automatically relearns throttle position.

2.4L Engine

> ※※ **WARNING**
>
> **Do not use solvent of any type when cleaning the gasket surfaces on the intake manifold and the throttle body assembly, as damage to the gasket surfaces and throttle body assembly may result. Use care in cleaning the gasket surfaces on**

the intake manifold and the throttle body assembly, as sharp tools may damage the gasket surfaces.

> ※※ **WARNING**
>
> **Do not use any solvent that contains Methyl Ethyl Ketone (MEK). This solvent may damage fuel system components.**

➡**DO NOT prop open the throttle blade with the ignition key in the ON position**

as it may set a Diagnostic Trouble Code (DTC).

1. Before servicing the vehicle, refer to the Precautions Section.
2. Remove the air cleaner outlet duct.
3. Disconnect the engine wiring harness electrical connector from the Electronic Throttle Control (ETC).
4. Remove the throttle body bolts.
5. Remove the throttle body .
6. Inspect the throttle body gasket, and replace if necessary.

To install:

7. Install the throttle body. Tighten the bolts to 89 in. lbs. (10 Nm).
8. Connect the engine wiring harness electrical connector to the ETC.
9. Install the air cleaner outlet duct

3.5L Engine

See Figures 282 and 283.

1. Before servicing the vehicle, refer to the Precautions Section.
2. Disconnect the negative battery cable.
3. Remove the outlet resonator/duct assembly, as follows:
   a. Loosen clamp at the air cleaner assembly and the front outlet duct seal assembly.
   b. Remove the attachment bolt from the support bracket.
   c. Remove the outlet resonator/duct assembly.
4. Cover the throttle body opening with a shop towel and use shop air to remove any dirt at the base of the throttle body.
5. Disconnect the MAP sensor connector.
6. Disconnect the throttle control connector at throttle body.
7. Clamp off the hoses to avoid leaking coolant on engine.
8. Remove the wiring harness bracket bolt from the throttle body.
9. Remove the coolant hoses at throttle body (4).
10. Remove the throttle body fasteners.
11. Remove the throttle body.

> ※※ **WARNING**
>
> **Cover the intake manifold opening with a shop towel whenever the throttle body is removed to prevent foreign material entry.**

12. Block the intake manifold opening with a clean shop towel to prevent dirt from entering.

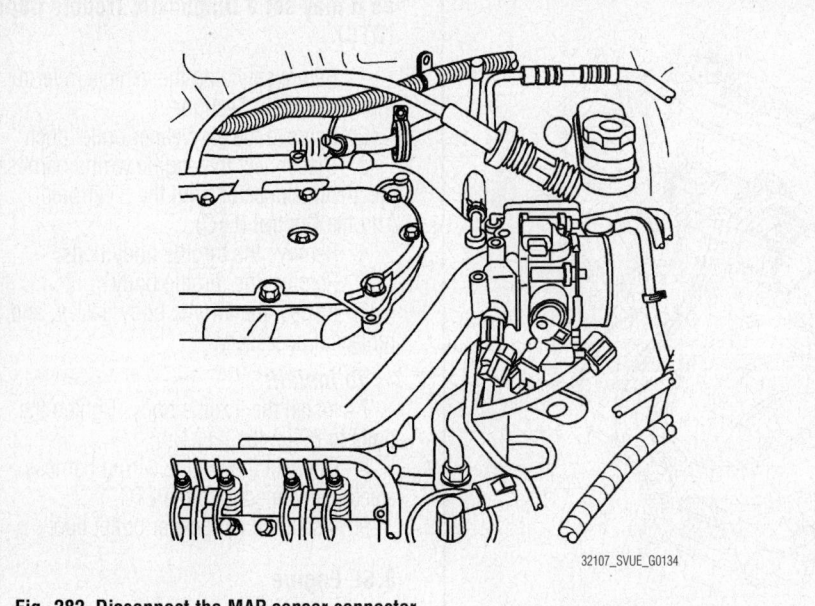

Fig. 282 Disconnect the MAP sensor connector.

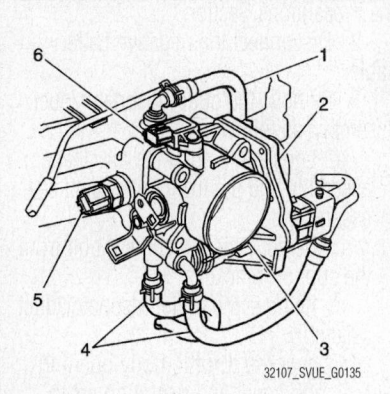

Fig. 283 Remove the coolant hoses at throttle body

To install:

13. Remove the shop towel from the throttle body opening.

14. Install a new throttle body gasket.

✳✳ WARNING

Use care when tightening the throttle body bolts. Manifold damage will result if over-tightened.

15. Install the throttle body assembly and fasteners.

16. Install the throttle body fasteners. Tighten the fasteners to 16 inch lbs (22 Nm).

17. Attach the coolant hoses to the throttle body assembly and unclamp.

18. Install the wiring harness bracket bolt. Tighten the bolt to 89 inch lbs (10 Nm).

19. Connect the MAP sensor connectors.

20. Connect throttle body electrical connector.

21. Install the outlet resonator/duct assembly into position. .

22. Connect the negative battery cable.

23. If the throttle body assembly has been replaced, perform the idle learn procedure as follows:

a. Install a scan tool.

b. Diagnose and repair any DTC's before proceeding with this procedure.

c. Ensure that all electrical loads and accessories are **OFF** .

d. Turn **OFF** the air conditioning.

e. Ensure that the vehicle is in **PARK** or **NEUTRAL** .

f. Turn **ON** the ignition.

g. Clear the DTC information with the scan tool.

h. Wait 5 seconds and start the engine.

i. Operate the engine with no load at 3,000 RPM until the ECT reaches 194°F (190°C).

➡**If the engine cooling fan turns ON during the idle portion of this procedure, do not include the fan run time in the total idle time.**

j. Let the engine idle with the THROTTLE CLOSED and the engine cooling fan **OFF** , for a total of 5 minutes.

k. The PCM has a new learned idle position.

HEATING & AIR CONDITIONING SYSTEM

BLOWER MOTOR

REMOVAL & INSTALLATION

See Figures 284 and 285.

1. Before servicing the vehicle, refer to the Precautions Section.

2. Remove the passenger side insulator/closeout panel.

3. Disconnect the electrical connector from the blower motor.

4. Remove the blower motor screws from the HVAC module.

5. Remove the blower motor from the HVAC module.

To install:

6. Install the blower motor to the HVAC module.

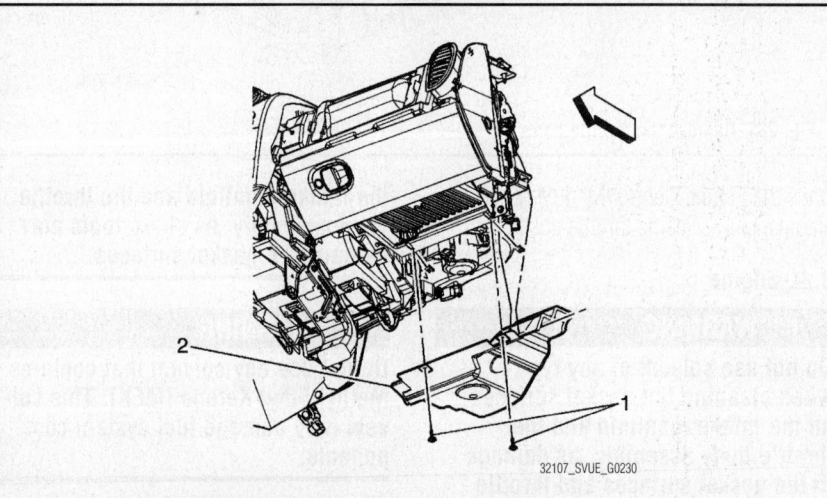

Fig. 284 Remove the passenger side insulator/closeout panel retainers (1) and panel (2)

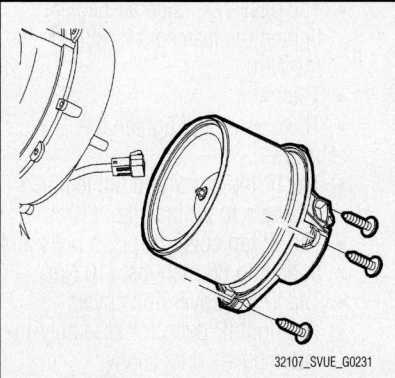

Fig. 285 Remove the blower motor screws from the HVAC module

7. Install the blower motor screws to the HVAC module.

8. Tighten the screws to 9 inch lbs. (1 Nm).

9. Connect the electrical connector to the blower motor.

10. Install the passenger side insulator/closeout panel.

HEATER CORE

REMOVAL & INSTALLATION

See Figures 286 through 289.

1. Before servicing the vehicle, refer to the Precautions Section.

2. Disable the SIR system. Refer to Air Bag (Supplemental Restraint System), disarming the system.

3. Record all preset radio stations.

4. Disconnect the negative battery cable.

5. Drain and recycle the engine coolant.

6. Recover the A/C system refrigerant using approved equipment.

7. Remove or disconnect the following:
- The suction line from the Thermal Expansion Valve (TXV) and cap the TXV and the line
- The TXV thermistor connection
- The heater core outlet and inlet hoses from the core and plug the lines
- The Instrument Panel (IP) right end panel by gently tugging to disengage the clip
- The IP knee bolster panel
- The IP left end panel by gently tugging to disengage the clip
- The door jamb switch electrical connections on both sides

8. Place the shifter in neutral.

9. Remove or disconnect the following:
- The horse shoe bezel at the shifter by first pulling up at the rear to disengage the clips and slide it up and over the shifter to access the electrical connections. Disengage all electrical connections
- The glove box-to-IP screws and upper glove box-to-radio bezel screws
- The glove box
- The radio bezel by pulling the lower edge forward first and then the top to disengage the clips
- The temperature cable, blower switch, and IP 20-way connections from the controller
- The air bag telltale, foglamp switch, dimmer switch, and hazard switch connections
- The upper and lower steering column shrouds
- The cluster bezel screws and the bezel
- The A-pillar garnish moldings
- The right IP deflector assembly-to-intermediate duct screw

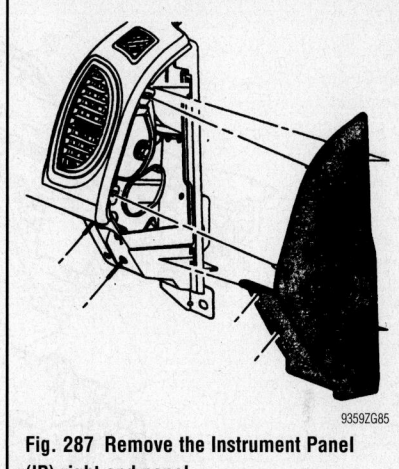

Fig. 287 Remove the Instrument Panel (IP) right end panel

- The IP cover-to-cross car beam bolt covers and the cover-to-beam bolts
- The IP cover-to-IP retaining screws at the lower edge of the cover and the radio opening
- The IP cover by lifting it then moving it rearwards passenger side first and walk the cluster opening around the steering wheel and out the driver's side door
- The cluster-to-IP screws and the cluster
- The radio
- The passenger side air bag
- The center, right, and left shifter closeout panels
- The right and left intermediate ducts
- The cluster connector from the retainer
- The IP fuse block from the bracket
- The IP ground wire from the H brace
- The Brake Control Module (BCM) from the retainer
- The Data Link Controller (DLC) from the retainer
- The right door sill plate trim
- The IP retainer fasteners and retainer
- The heater duct
- The heater core cover
- The heater core pipe cover and pipe foam seal

10. Grab the heater core at the end tanks and remove the core. If the core sticks, spray the perimeter of the core seal and the pipes at the front of the dash with soapy water to aid in removal.

To install:

11. Spray the dash seal at the core pipe openings with soapy water to aid in installation.

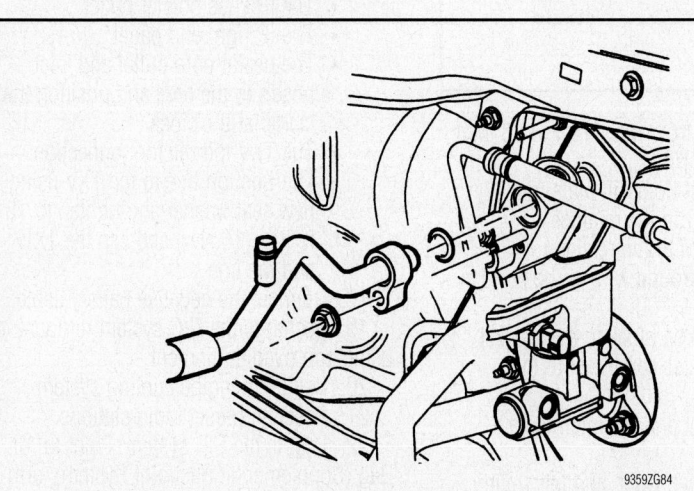

Fig. 286 Disconnect the suction line from the Thermal Expansion Valve (TXV)

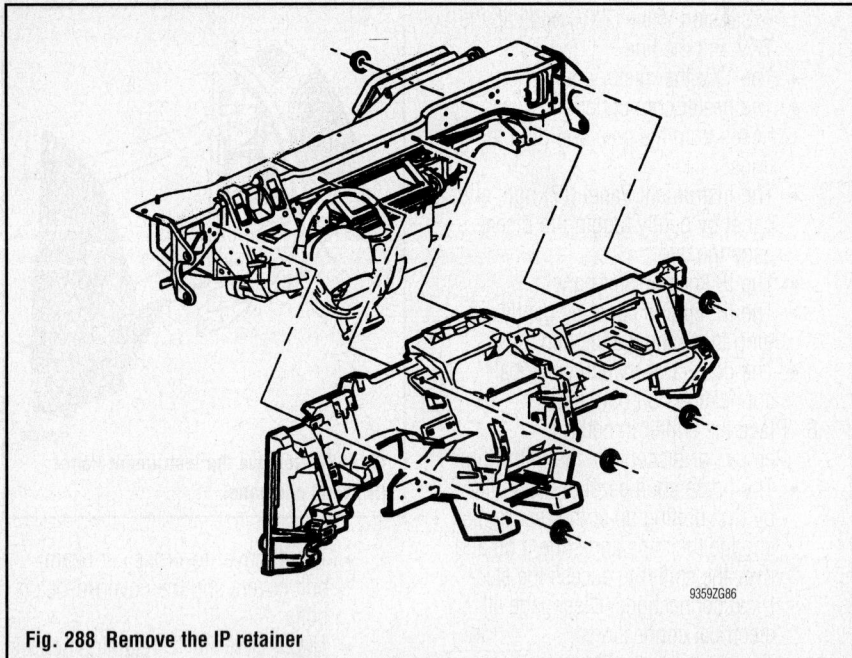

9359ZG86

Fig. 288 Remove the IP retainer

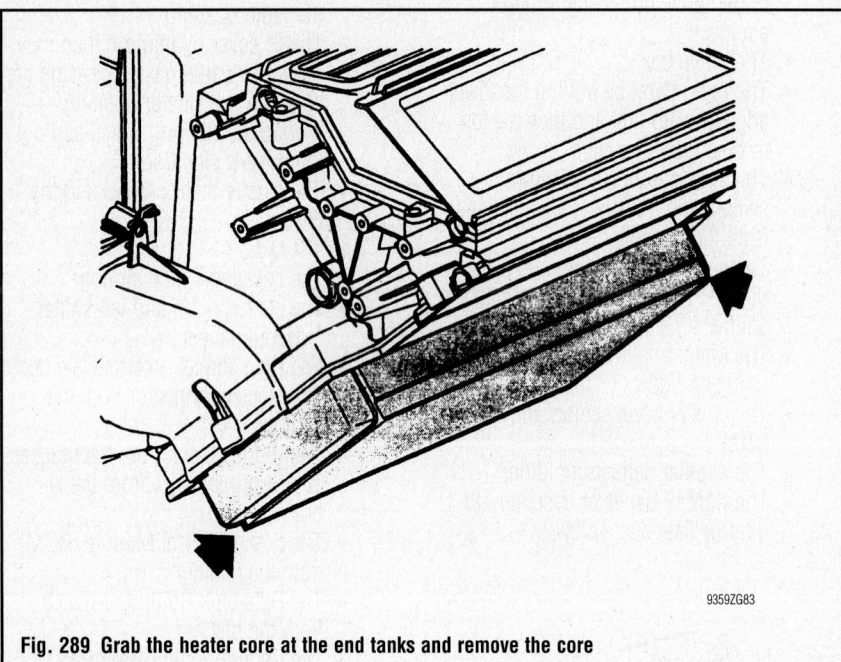

9359ZG83

Fig. 289 Grab the heater core at the end tanks and remove the core

- The passenger side air bag and tighten the fasteners to 88 inch lbs. (10 Nm)
- The radio
- The cluster and tighten the screws
- The IP top cover and tighten the retainers to 22 inch lbs. (3 Nm)
- The IP top cover-to-beam bolts and tighten to 88 inch lbs. (10 Nm)
- The IP top cover bolt covers
- The right IP deflector assembly-to-intermediate duct screw
- The A-pillar garnish moldings
- The cluster bezel and screws
- The upper and lower steering column shrouds

13. Center the temperature knob by aligning the controller housing alignment tab with the slot in the shaft.

14. Align the air temperature cable lug with the detent spring point.

15. Install or connect the following:
- The temperature cable to the control head by aligning the retention tabs and the knob shaft and snap into place
- The IP harness to the blower switch and controller
- The air bag telltale, foglamp switch, dimmer switch, and hazard switch connections
- The radio bezel
- The glove box

16. Place the shifter in neutral.

17. Install or connect the following:
- The horse shoe bezel electrical connections
- The horse shoe bezel and place the shifter in park
- The door jamb switch electrical connections on both sides
- The IP left end panel
- The IP knee bolster panel
- The IP right end panel
- The heater core outlet and inlet hose's to the core and position the clamp at 9 o'clock
- The TXV thermistor connection
- The Suction line to the TXV using new seal washer and tighten to 12 ft. lbs. (16 Nm) and cap the TXV and the line

18. Connect the negative battery cable.

19. Recharge the A/C system refrigerant using approved equipment.

20. Refill the engine cooling system.

21. Reset all preset radio stations.

22. Enable the SIR system. Refer to Air Bag (Supplemental Restraint System), arming the system.

12. Install or connect the following:
- The heater core
- The pipe seal and cover. Tighten the cover retainers to 9 inch lbs. (1 Nm)
- The heater core cover and tighten the cover retainers to 9 inch lbs. (1 Nm)
- The heater duct
- The IP retainer by aligning the 4-way locator (tapered boss) and outboard locators with the corresponding holes or slots in the beam, then tighten the fasteners

starting from the center to 88 inch lbs. (10 Nm)
- The right door sill plate trim
- The DLC to the retainer
- The BCM to the retainer
- The IP ground wire to the H brace
- The IP fuse block to the bracket
- The cluster connector to the retainer
- The right and left intermediate ducts
- The center, right, and left shifter closeout panels

STEERING

POWER RACK & PINION STEERING GEAR

REMOVAL & INSTALLATION

See Figures 290 and 291.

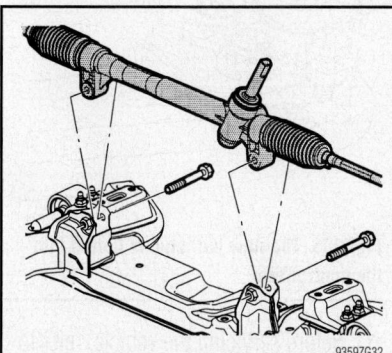

Fig. 290 Steering gear-to-frame assembly bolts

1. Before servicing the vehicle, refer to the Precautions Section.
2. Remove or disconnect the following:
   - The negative battery cable
   - The front wheels
   - The tie rods from the steering knuckles
   - The intermediate shaft from the

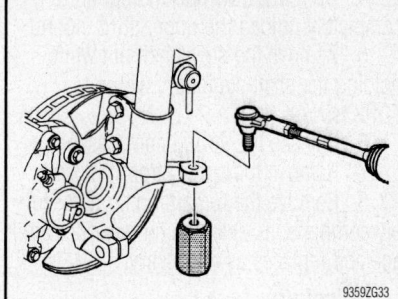

Fig. 291 Use installer tool J44015 to attach the tie rods to the steering knuckle

steering gear pinch bolt and discard the bolt
   - The shaft from the gear
   - The stabilizer bar link nuts, links and swing the bar upwards
   - The shift cable clip from the gear housing, if equipped
   - The steering gear-to-cradle bolts
   - The steering gear by sliding it out the right side of the vehicle

To install:

3. Install the steering gear through the right wheel opening.
4. Center the gear mounting bushings into the cradle supports.

5. Install or connect the following:
   - The steering gear-to-mounting bolts and tighten to 81 ft. lbs. (110 Nm)
   - The shift cable clip to the gear housing, if equipped
   - The intermediate shaft to the steering gear and torque the new pinch bolt to 25 ft. lbs. (34 Nm)
   - The stabilizer bar into position
   - The stabilizer bar links and nuts, then tighten the nuts to 48 ft. lbs. (65 Nm)
   - The tie rods to the steering knuckles using installer tool JJ44015 and tighten to 30 ft. lbs. (40 Nm)
6. Install a new tie rod nut and tighten to 44 ft. lbs. (60 Nm).
7. Install the wheels. Tighten the wheel lug nuts to 100 ft. lbs. (136 Nm).
8. Install the negative battery cable.
9. Check the alignment and adjust if necessary.

POWER STEERING PUMP

REMOVAL & INSTALLATION

See Figure 292.

This vehicle uses electronic power steering.

1. Inflatable Restraint Steering Wheel Module Coil
2. Steering Column
3. Inflatable Restraint Steering Wheel Module Coil C1/C2
4. Inflatable Restraint Steering Wheel Module Coil C5
5. Inflatable Restraint Steering Wheel Module Coil C3
6. Inflatable Restraint Steering Wheel Module Coil C4
7. Inflatable Restraint Steering Wheel Module Coil Harness
8. Power Steering Control Module (PSCM)
9. PSCM Motor
10. Electronic Power Steering (EPS) Harness
11. EPS Inline Fuse Holder
12. Fuse Block - Underhood B+ Post

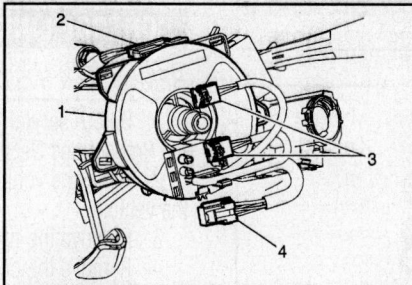

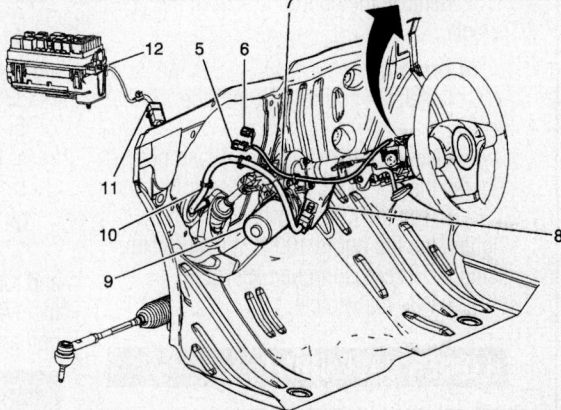

Fig. 292 Expanded view of the electronic power steering and related components

SUSPENSION

COIL SPRING

REMOVAL & INSTALLATION

See Figures 293 and 294.

1. Before servicing the vehicle, refer to the Precautions Section.
2. Remove the strut from the vehicle.
3. Place the strut into spring compressor J45400 or a similar compressor.

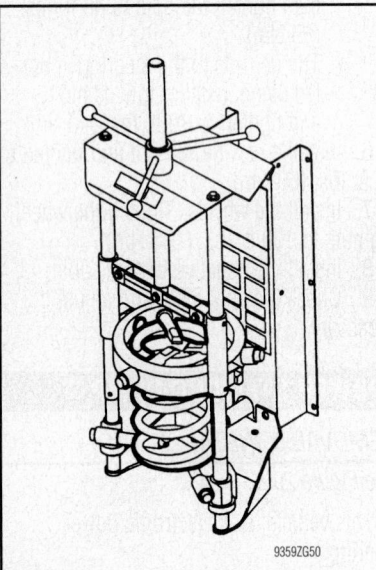

Fig. 293 Place the strut into spring compressor J45400

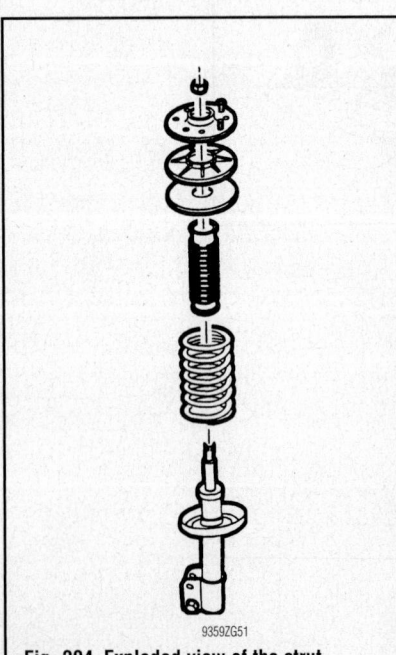

Fig. 294 Exploded view of the strut assembly

4. Compress the spring enough to completely unload the upper strut mount.
5. Remove the strut shaft nut while holding the shaft stationary with a TORX®socket.
6. Release the spring compressor.
7. Remove the spring from the strut
8. Remove the remaining strut assembly components, examine for wear or damage and replaces as necessary.

To install:

9. Install or connect the following:
   - The strut into spring compressor
   - Extend the strut shaft to its full travel
   - The strut to the spring
   - The upper spring seat onto the strut shaft and align the flat with the strut-to-knuckle bracket
   - The top mount onto the strut shaft and align the flat 180° from the flat on the upper spring seat
   - The strut top nut and tighten with a wrench while holding the strut shaft with a socket
10. Make sure the flats are aligned on the upper spring seat and top mount before tightening the nut. Then tighten the nut to 55 ft. lbs. (75 Nm).
11. Release the spring compressor tool.
12. Install the strut to the vehicle.

CONTROL LINKS

REMOVAL & INSTALLATION

1. Before servicing the vehicle, refer to the Precautions Section.
2. Raise the vehicle and safely support the vehicle.
3. Remove the tire and wheel assembly.
4. Remove the control link bolt and nut.
5. Remove the control link from the vehicle.

To install:

6. Install the control link into the vehicle.
7. Install the control link bolt and nut. Tighten the nut to 17 ft. lbs. (23 Nm).
8. Install the tire and wheel assembly. Tighten the lug nut to 100 ft. lbs. (136 Nm) using a crisscross torque pattern.
9. Lower the vehicle.

LOWER BALL JOINT

REMOVAL & INSTALLATION

See Figure 295.

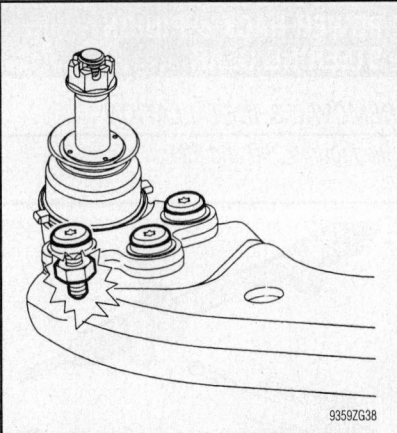

Fig. 295 The new ball stud is bolted into the control arm

1. Before servicing the vehicle, refer to the Precautions Section.
2. Remove the lower control arm from the vehicle.
3. Remove the rivets retaining the ball joint to the control arm using a 5⁄16 in. (8mm) drill bit.
4. Remove the ball joint from the control arm

To install:

5. Install the ball joint into the control arm.
6. Install the nuts and bolts (included with new ball joint kit) as shown and torque them to 50 ft. lbs. (68 Nm).
7. Install the control arm to the vehicle.

LOWER CONTROL ARM

REMOVAL & INSTALLATION

See Figure 296.

1. Before servicing the vehicle, refer to the Precautions Section.
2. Remove the wheel.
3. Remove the ball stud bolt.
4. Separate the ball stud from the steering knuckle by using ball joint removal tool J43828.
5. Remove the lower control arm-to-frame retainers.
6. Remove the lower control arm.

To install:

7. Install the control arm to the frame and torque the rear bolts and nuts to 52 ft. lbs. (70 Nm) and the front arm-to-frame bolt and nut to 148 ft. lbs. (200 Nm).

✳✳ WARNING

There are 2 different ball studs used on this vehicle. The ball stud type

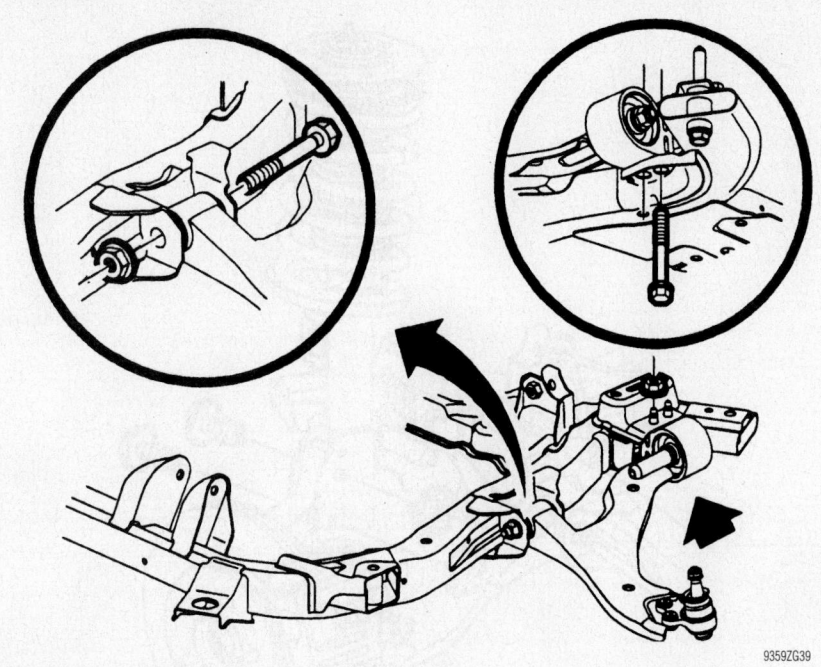

Fig. 296 Remove the lower control arm to frame bolts

must be identified in order to use the correct torque value when tightening the ball stud nut. If the wrong torque is used, damage could occur to the ball stud.

8. If the bottom of the ball stud has a cup and is silver, tighten the nut to 44 ft. lbs. (60 Nm).

9. If the bottom of the ball stud is flat and black, tighten the nut to 30 ft. lbs. (40 Nm).

10. Install the wheels. Tighten the wheel lug nuts to 100 ft. lbs. (136 Nm).

11. Check and adjust the alignment, if necessary.

MACPHERSON STRUT

REMOVAL & INSTALLATION

See Figures 297 through 299.

1. Before servicing the vehicle, refer to the Precautions Section.

2. Remove or disconnect the following:
   - The strut to body attaching nuts
   - The front wheel
   - The brake hose bracket from the strut assembly
   - Loosen the steering knuckle-to-strut fasteners, but do not remove them
   - The stabilizer bar link to the strut assembly attaching nut and move it toward the rear of the vehicle
   - Place a rag over the CV-joint seal

to protect it from damage, then remove the 2 steering knuckle-to-strut housing bolts
   - The steering knuckle-to-strut fasteners
   - The strut assembly from the vehicle

To install:

3. Install or connect the following:
   - The strut to the body and torque the new attaching nuts and bolt to 18 ft. lbs. (25 Nm)
   - The strut to the steering knuckle and torque the new fasteners to 133 ft. lbs. (180 Nm)
   - The stabilizer bar link to the strut and torque the fastener to 48 ft. lbs. (65 Nm)
   - The brake hose bracket to the strut
   - The front wheel
   - The negative battery cable

4. Check and adjust the alignment as necessary.

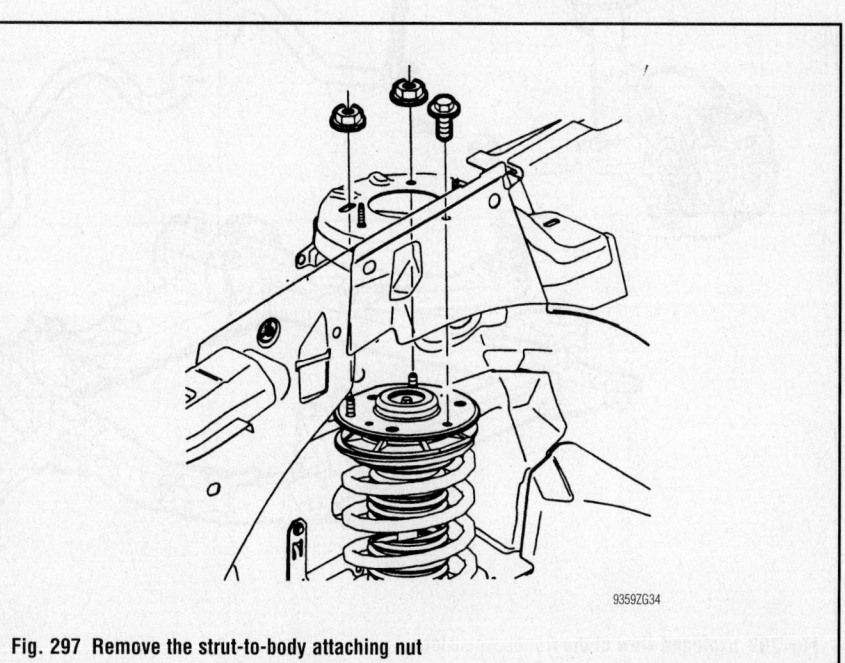

Fig. 297 Remove the strut-to-body attaching nut

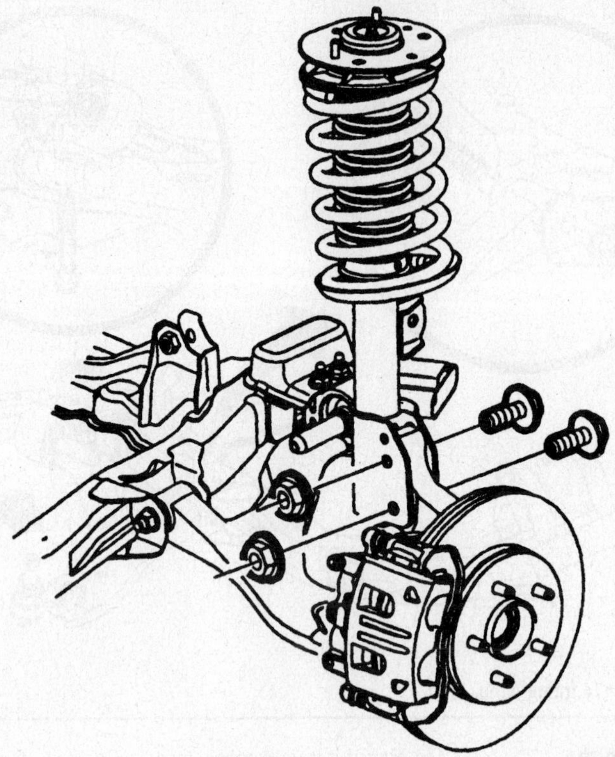

9359ZG35

Fig. 298 Remove the steering knuckle-to-strut fasteners

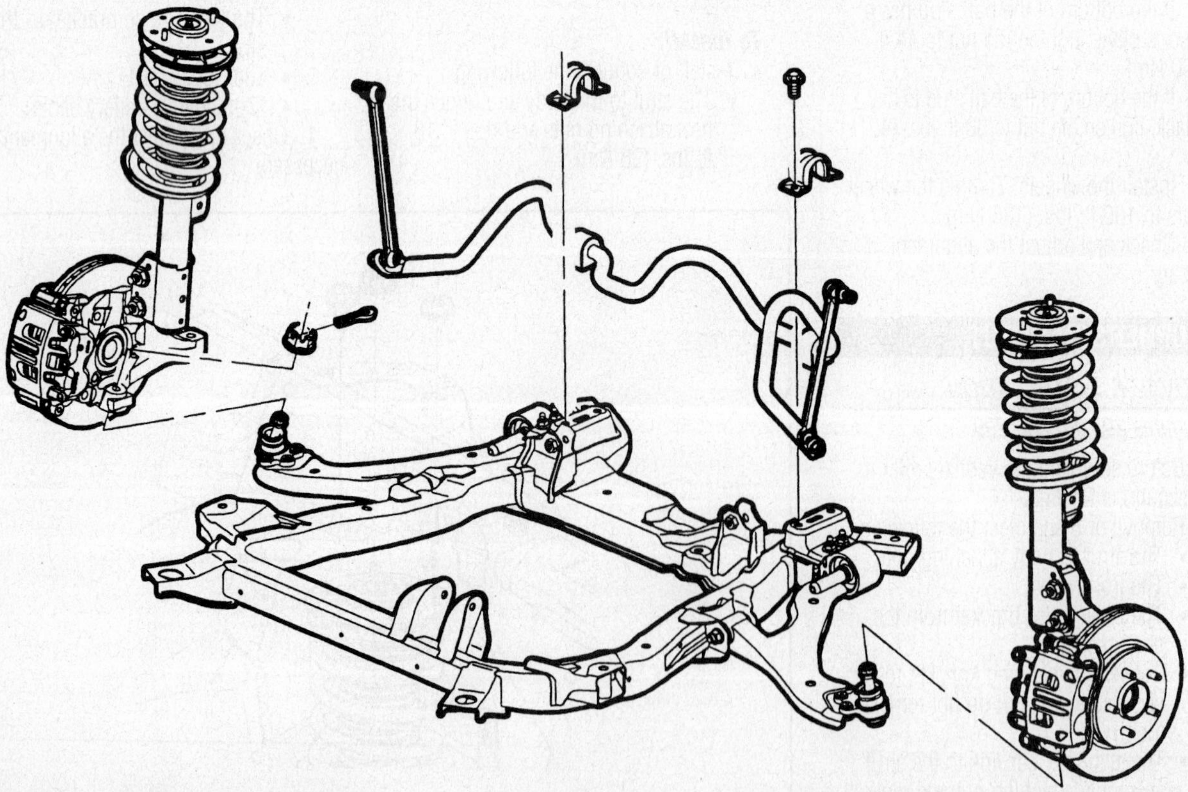

9359ZG36

Fig. 299 Exploded view of the front suspension

OVERHAUL

See Figures 300 and 301.

1. Before servicing the vehicle, refer to the Precautions Section.

2. Remove the strut from the vehicle.

3. Install the strut in a strut compressor tool, such as J 45400.

➡**The spring is compressed when the strut moves freely.**

4. Turn the spring compressor forcing screw until the coil spring is compressed.

5. Use a 45 TORX® socket in order to hold the strut shaft. Remove the upper strut mount nut.

6. Remove the strut from the compressor.

7. Loosen the compressor forcing screw until the upper strut mount and coil spring may be removed.

8. Remove the upper strut mount and the coil spring from the compressor.

To assemble:

9. Install the coil spring and upper strut mount in the compressor.

10. Turn the spring compressor forcing screw until the coil spring is compressed.

11. Install the strut to the coil spring and upper strut mount.

12. Install the strut retaining nut. Install the strut mount nut. Tighten the strut mount nut to 55 ft. lbs. (75 Nm).

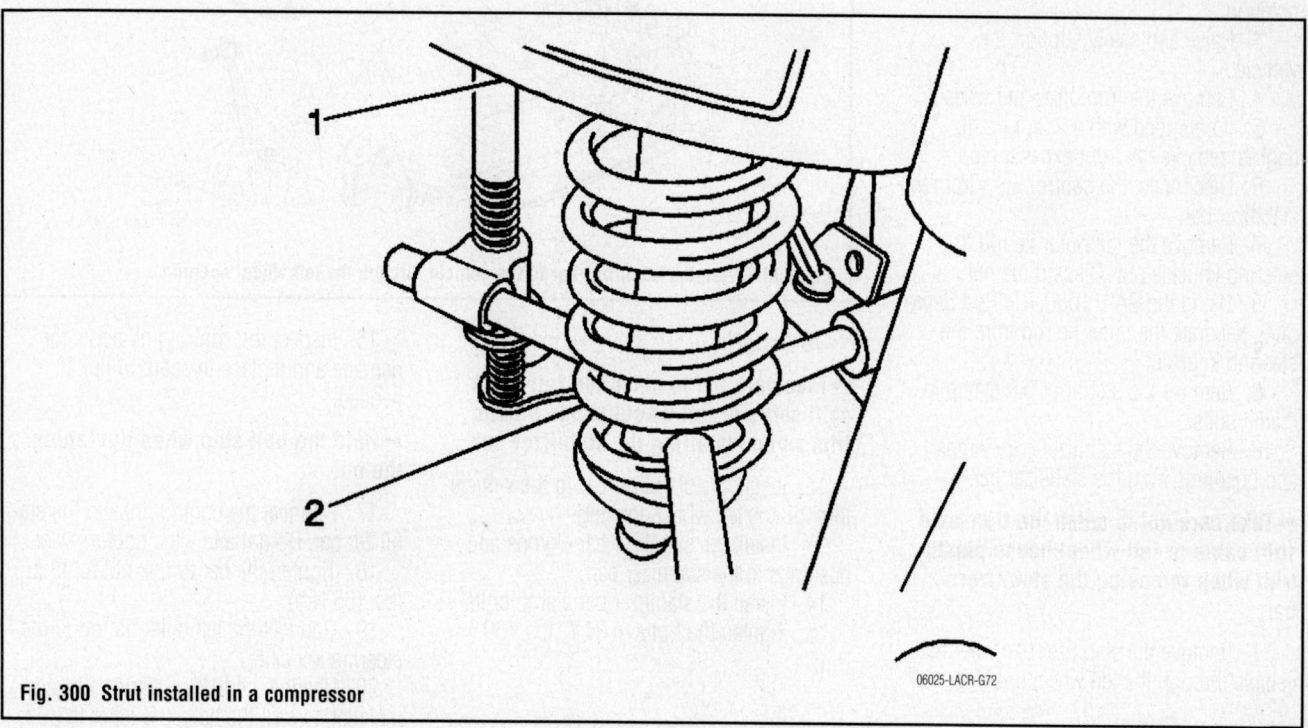

Fig. 300 Strut installed in a compressor

06025-LACR-G72

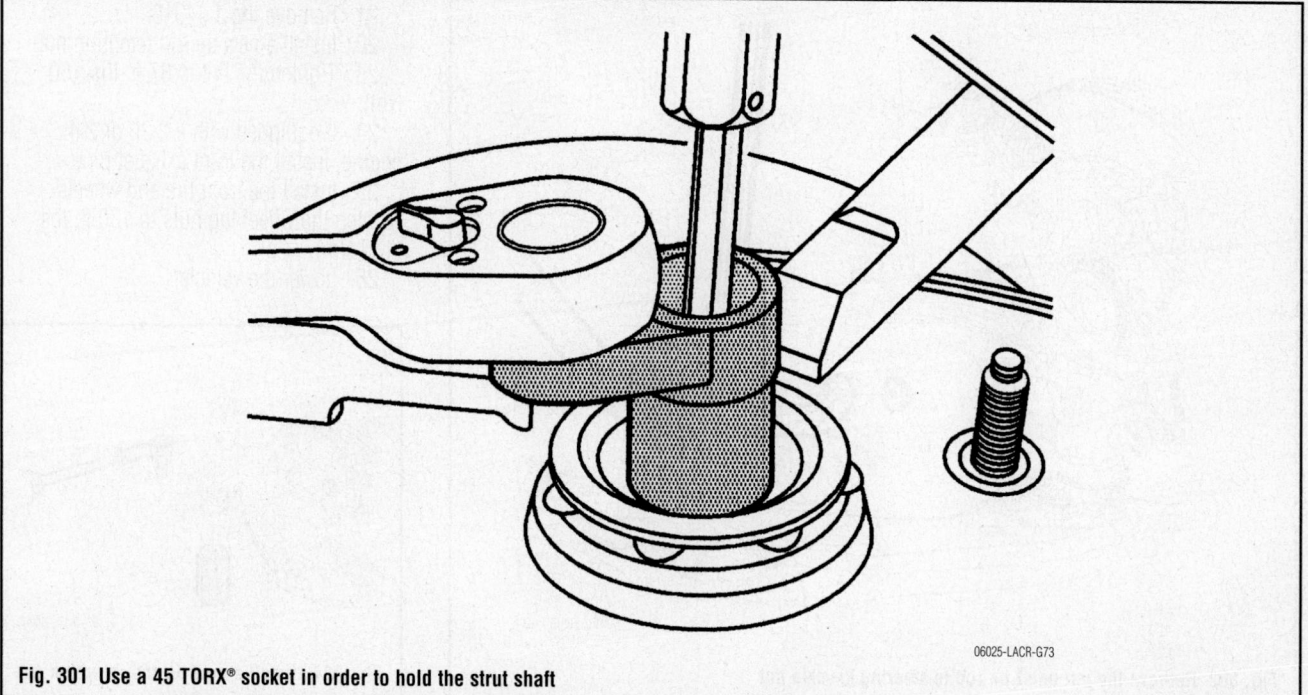

Fig. 301 Use a 45 TORX® socket in order to hold the strut shaft

06025-LACR-G73

13. Remove the strut from the compressor.

14. Install the strut.

STABILIZER BAR

REMOVAL & INSTALLATION

See Figures 302 through 304.

1. Before servicing the vehicle, refer to the Precautions Section.

2. Turn the front wheels to the full right position.

3. Raise and safely support the vehicle.

4. Remove the front tires and wheels.

5. If equipped with a 2.2L or 2.4L engine, remove the front exhaust pipe.

6. Disconnect the control links from the stabilizer bar.

7. Remove the left outer tie rod to steering knuckle nut. Discard the nut.

8. Using the SA91100C, Tie Rod Separator, separate the outer tie rod from the steering knuckle.

9. Remove the stabilizer bar clamp to cradle bolts.

10. Remove the stabilizer bar clamps and bushings from the stabilizer bar.

➡**Take care not to catch the transaxle shift cable or left wheel house plastic trim when removing the stabilizer bar.**

11. Remove the stabilizer bar from the vehicle through the left wheel opening.

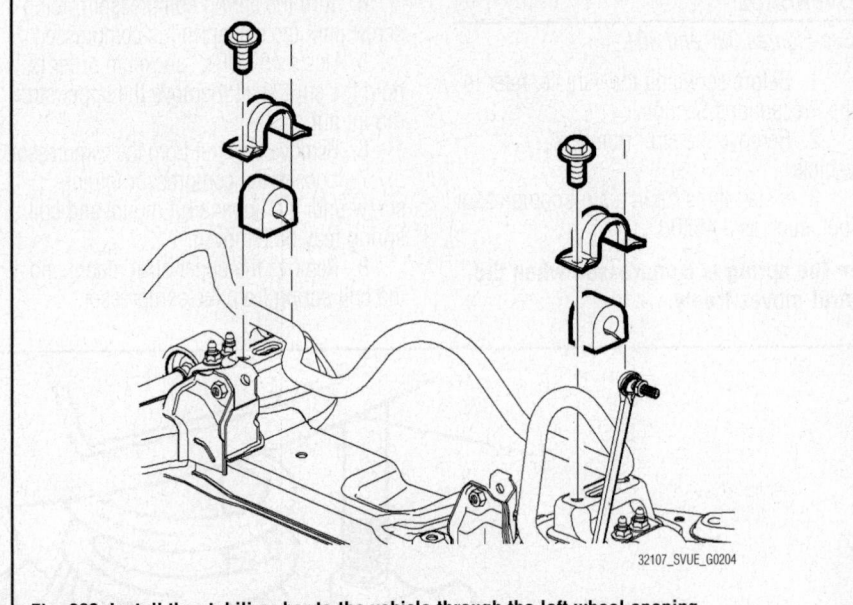

Fig. 303 Install the stabilizer bar to the vehicle through the left wheel opening

To install:

➡**Take care not to catch the transaxle shift cable or left wheel house plastic trim when installing the stabilizer bar.**

12. Install the stabilizer bar to the vehicle through the left wheel opening.

13. Install the stabilizer bar clamps and bushings to the stabilizer bar.

14. Install the stabilizer bar clamp bolts.

15. Tighten the bolts to 37 ft. lbs. (50 Nm).

16. Inspect the control link boots for damage and replace the control link if needed.

➡**Hold the ball stud when tightening the nut.**

17. Connect the control links to the stabilizer bar. Do not allow the boot to twist.

18. Tighten the bar to link nut to 48 ft. lbs. (65 Nm).

19. Connect the left outer tie rod to the steering knuckle.

20. Use the J 44015, Steering Linkage Installer, to seat the ball stud taper to 30 ft. lbs. (40 Nm).

21. Remove the J 44015.

22. Install a new tie rod retention nut.

23. Tighten the nut to 37 ft. lbs. (50 Nm).

24. If equipped with a 2.2L or 2.4L engine, install the front exhaust pipe.

25. Install the front tire and wheels. Tighten the wheel lug nuts to 100 ft. lbs. (136 Nm).

26. Lower the vehicle.

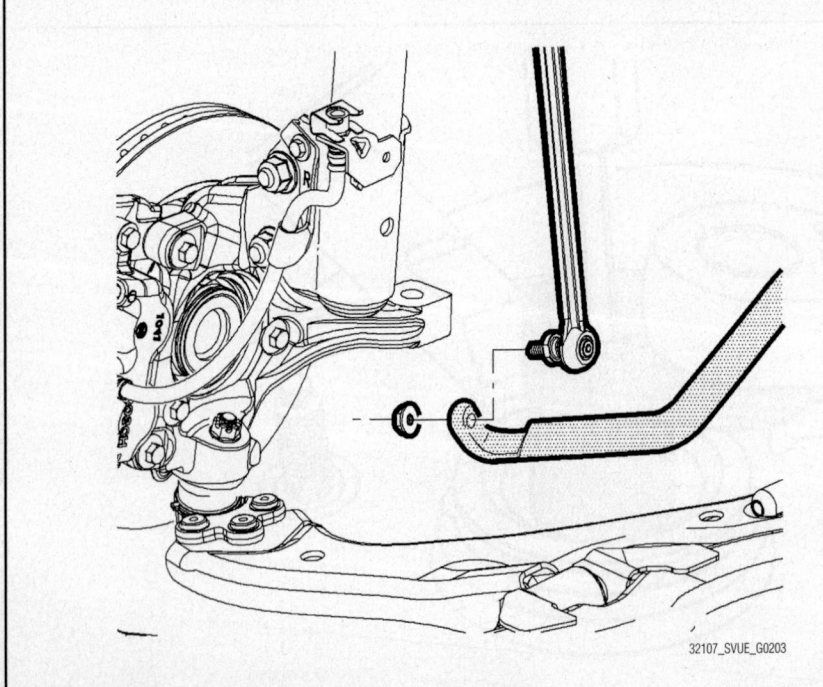

Fig. 302 Remove the left outer tie rod to steering knuckle nut

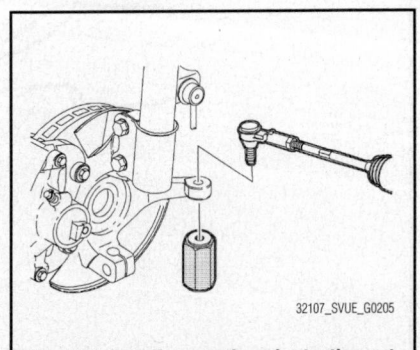

Fig. 304 Install a new tie rod retention nut

STEERING KNUCKLE

REMOVAL & INSTALLATION

See Figures 305 and 306.

1. Before servicing the vehicle, refer to the Precautions Section.
2. Raise and safely support the vehicle.
3. Remove the tire and wheel.

➡**Do not allow the stabilizer link ball stud to rotate while removing the link nut.**

4. Disconnect the stabilizer link from the strut assembly.
5. Loosen the steering knuckle to strut bolts and nuts.
6. Remove the wheel bearing/hub assembly.
7. Remove and discard the lower ball joint cotter pin.
8. Loosen the ball stud nut, until level with the top of the ball stud.
9. Using the J 43828, Ball Joint

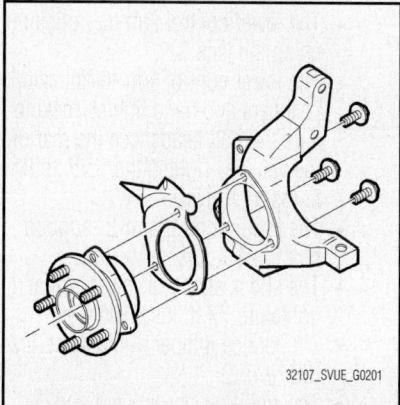

Fig. 305 Remove the wheel bearing/hub assembly

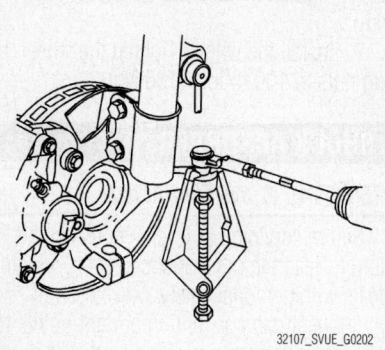

Fig. 306 Using the SA91100C, Tie Rod Separator, separate the outer tie rod from the steering knuckle

Remover, separate the lower control arm from the steering knuckle.
10. Remove the lower control arm and nut from the steering knuckle.
11. Remove the outer tie rod end to knuckle nut.
12. Using the SA91100C, Tie Rod Separator, separate the outer tie rod from the steering knuckle.
13. Remove the steering knuckle to strut bolts and nuts. Discard the bolts and nuts.
14. Remove the steering knuckle from the vehicle.

To install:

15. Install the steering knuckle to strut assembly.
16. Loosely install the strut to steering knuckle bolts and nuts.
17. Install the control arm ball stud into the steering knuckle.

⁂ **WARNING**

There are 2 different ball studs used on this vehicle. The ball stud type must be identified in order to use the correct torque value when tightening the ball stud nut. If the wrong torque is used, damage could occur to the ball stud.

18. Using the SA9140E, Torque Angle Gauge, install the ball stud nut.
19. If the bottom of the ball stud has a cup and is silver, tighten the nut to 44 ft. lbs. (60 Nm).
20. If the bottom of the ball stud is flat and black, tighten the nut to 30 ft. lbs. (40 Nm).
21. Tighten the strut to steering knuckle bolts and nuts. Tighten the bolts and nuts to 133 ft. lbs. (180 Nm).

➡**Do not loosen the castle nut for cotter pin installation.**

22. Tighten the castle nut enough to allow for cotter pin installation.

⁂ **WARNING**

The cotter pin must not contact the wheel speed sensor or drive axle.

23. Install the cotter pin.
24. Install the wheel bearing/hub assembly.
25. Connect the outer tie rod end to the steering knuckle.
26. Use the J 44015, Steering Linkage Installer, to seat the ball stud taper to 30 ft. lbs. (40 Nm).

27. Remove the J 44015, Steering Linkage Installer.
28. Install a new tie rod retention nut. Tighten the nut to 18 ft. lbs. (25 Nm) plus 90°.

⁂ **WARNING**

Do not allow the stabilizer link ball stud to rotate while installing the link nut.

29. Connect the stabilizer link to the strut assembly.
30. Tighten the nut to 48 ft. lbs. (65 Nm).
31. Install the tire and wheel.
32. Lower the vehicle.
33. Perform a wheel alignment.

WHEEL HUB AND BEARINGS

REMOVAL & INSTALLATION

See Figures 307 and 308.

1. Before servicing the vehicle, refer to the Precautions Section.
2. Remove or disconnect the following:
   - The wheel
   - The brake caliper mounting bracket bolts and suspend the assembly from the strut spring with wire
   - The brake rotor
   - The ABS sensor electrical connection, if equipped
   - The ABS sensor electrical connection from the bracket, if equipped
   - The drive shaft axle nut
3. Support the axle with wire.
4. Remove the halfshaft from the knuckle.
5. Remove the bearing bolts, the bearing assembly, and shield.

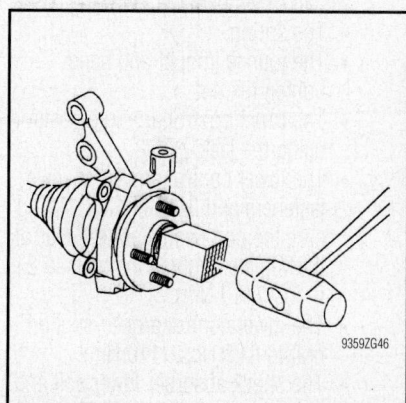

Fig. 307 Separate the axle from the wheel hub

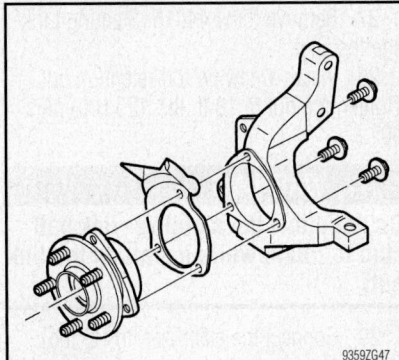

Fig. 308 Exploded view of the front bearing/hub assembly

To install:

➡**Make sure the drive shaft splines are aligned with the wheel bearing assembly splines. If you do not align the splines you could damage the bearing or drive shaft assemblies.**

6. Install or connect the following:
   • The bearing assembly with the shield. Tighten the bearing assembly bolts to 96 ft. lbs. (130 Nm)
   • The drive shaft axle nut and torque to 151 ft. lbs. (205 Nm)

• The ABS sensor electrical connection to the bracket, if equipped
• The ABS sensor electrical connection, if equipped
• The brake rotor
• The brake caliper
• The wheel. Tighten the wheel lug nuts to 100 ft. lbs. (136 Nm).

ADJUSTMENT

The wheel bearings are sealed at the factory and do not require any adjustment or maintenance.

SUSPENSION

COIL SPRING

REMOVAL & INSTALLATION

1. Before servicing the vehicle, refer to the Precautions Section.
2. Remove the wheel.
3. Remove the control link-to-lower control arm nut.
4. Remove the trailing arm bracket-to-underbody bolts.
5. Support the lower control arm with a suitable jack.
6. Remove or disconnect the following:
   • The lower shock bolt
   • The jounce jumper nut from the lower control arm
   • The lower control arm-to-support frame bolt
   • The lower control arm-to-knuckle retainers
   • The lower the jack supporting the control arm slowly to unload the spring
   • The spring

To install:

7. Install or connect the following:
   • The spring
   • The jounce jumper and hand tighten the nut
   • The lower control arm into position using the jack
   • The lower control arm-to-knuckle fasteners and hand tighten making sure the bolt heads face the rear of the vehicle. Tighten the bolts to 81 ft. lbs. (110 Nm).
   • The lower control arm-to-support bolt to 81 ft. lbs. (110 Nm)
   • The shock absorber lower bolt and tighten to 81 ft. lbs. (110 Nm)
   • The jounce jumper nut to 46 ft. lbs. (63 Nm)

   • The stabilizer bar link nut and tighten to 11 ft. lbs. (15 Nm)
8. When installing the trailing arm, push upward and install the front bolt, then use a drift to align the rear holes and install the bolts. Tighten the bolts to 81 ft. lbs. (110 Nm).
9. Install the wheel. Tighten the wheel lug nuts to 100 ft. lbs. (136 Nm).

LOWER CONTROL ARM

REMOVAL & INSTALLATION

1. Before servicing the vehicle, refer to the Precautions Section.
2. Remove or disconnect the following:
   • The wheel
   • The stabilizer link-to-lower control arm nut
   • The trailing arm bracket-to-underbody bolts
3. Support the lower control arm with a suitable jack.
4. Remove or disconnect the following:
   • The lower shock bolt
   • The jounce jumper nut from the lower control arm
   • The lower control arm-to-support frame bolt
   • The lower control arm-to-knuckle retainers
   • The lower jack supporting the control arm slowly to unload the spring
   • The lower control arm-to-knuckle retainers
   • The spring
   • The lower control arm-to-support nut and bolt
   • The lower control arm

REAR SUSPENSION

To install:

5. Install or connect the following:
   • The lower control arm
   • The lower control arm-to-support and hand tighten the nut
   • The spring
   • The jounce jumper and hand tighten the nut
   • The lower control arm into position using the jack
   • The lower control arm-to-knuckle fasteners and hand tighten making sure the bolt heads face the rear of the vehicle. Tighten the bolts to 81 ft. lbs. (110 Nm).
   • The lower control arm-to-support bolt to 81 ft. lbs. (110 Nm)
   • The shock absorber lower bolt and tighten to 77 ft. lbs. (105 Nm)
   • The jounce jumper nut to 46 ft. lbs. (63 Nm)
   • The stabilizer bar link nut and tighten to 11 ft. lbs. (15 Nm)
6. When installing the trailing arm, push upward and install the front bolt, then use a drift to align the rear holes and install the bolts. Tighten the bolts to 81 ft. lbs. (110 Nm).
7. Install the wheel. Tighten the wheel lug nuts to 100 ft. lbs. (136 Nm).

SHOCK ABSORBER

REMOVAL & INSTALLATION

Before servicing any vehicle, please be sure to read the precautions section, which deals with personal safety, prevention of component damage, and important points to take into consideration when servicing a motor vehicle.

1. Raise and safely support the vehicle.

2. Remove the lower shock bolt.

3. Remove the rear wheelhouse liner push-in retainers.

4. Remove the rear wheelhouse liner from the vehicle

5. Remove the upper shock bolt.

6. Remove the shock from the vehicle.

To install:

7. Install the shock to the vehicle.

8. Install the upper shock bolt. Tighten the bolt to 77 ft. lbs. (105 Nm).

9. Install the wheelhouse liner.

10. Install the lower shock bolt. Tighten the bolt to 77 ft. lbs. (105 Nm).

11. Lower the vehicle.

TESTING

1. Check the rubber parts for damage or deterioration.

2. Check for correct height and proper return of shock absorber to original height.

3. Check the shock absorber for abnormal resistance or unusual sounds.

4. Check for oil leakage around seals.

5. Replace if necessary.

UPPER CONTROL ARM

REMOVAL & INSTALLATION

See Figure 309.

1. Before servicing the vehicle, refer to the Precautions Section.

2. Remove or disconnect the following:

- The trailing arm bracket-to-under-body bolts
- The Anti-lock Brake System (ABS) harness from the upper control arm, if equipped
- The upper control arm-to-knuckle fasteners
- The upper control arm-to-support frame retainers
- The upper control arm

To install:

3. Install or connect the following:

- The upper control arm

➡**Make sure the bolt heads face the front of the vehicle.**

- The upper control arm-to-knuckle fasteners and hand tighten
- The upper control arm-to-support frame nut

4. Tighten the control arm-to-knuckle bolts to 118 ft. lbs. (160 Nm)

5. Tighten the upper control arm-to-support bolt to 118 ft. lbs. (160 Nm)

6. Connect the ABS harness to the upper control arm, if equipped

7. When installing the trailing arm, push upward and install the front bolt, then use a drift to align the rear holes and install the bolts. Tighten the bolts to 81 ft. lbs. (110 Nm).

8. Align the vehicle.

WHEEL HUB AND BEARING

REMOVAL & INSTALLATION

See Figure 310.

1. Before servicing the vehicle, refer to the Precautions Section.

2. Remove or disconnect the following:

- The negative battery cable
- The rear wheel
- The brake drum
- The drive axle nut, if equipped with All Wheel Drive (AWD)
- The ABS electrical connector, if equipped

3. Support the axle shaft with wire.

4. Remove the axle shaft from the hub.

5. Remove the hub-to-knuckle bolts.

6. Remove the hub.

To install:

7. Install or connect the following:

- The hub to the knuckle and torque the new bolts to 62 ft. lbs. (84 Nm)
- The ABS electrical connector through the hole and seat the rubber grommet, if equipped

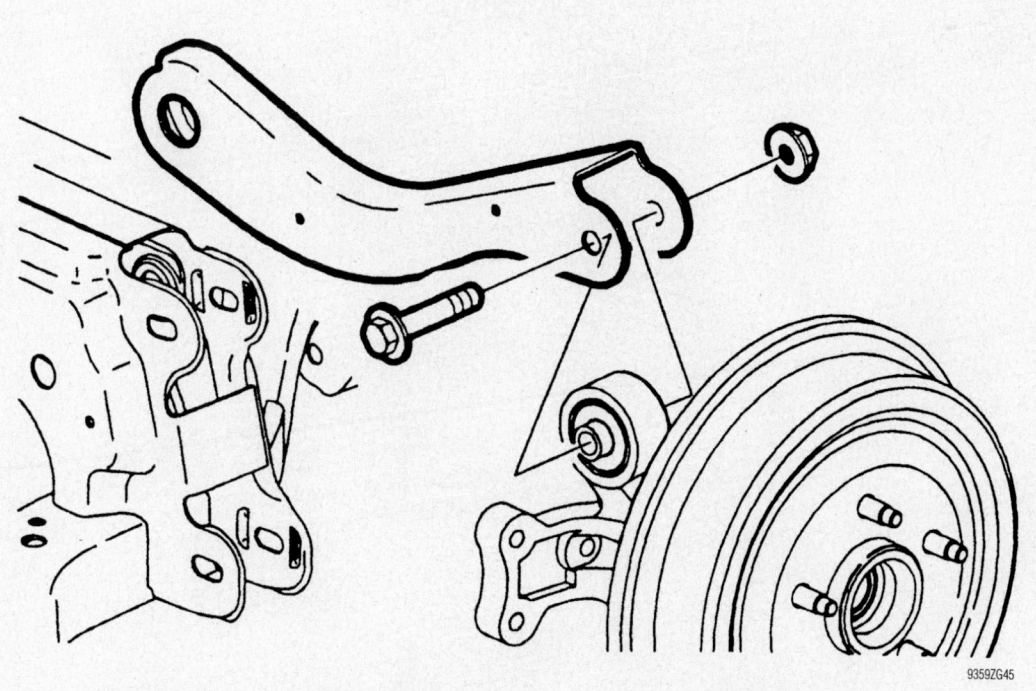

Fig. 309 Remove the lower control arm

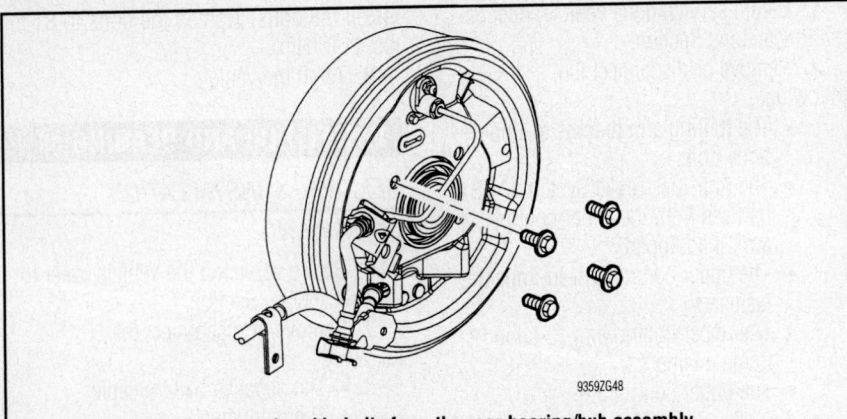

9359ZG48

Fig. 310 Remove the hub-to-knuckle bolts from the rear bearing/hub assembly

- The ABS electrical connector, if equipped
- The drive axle nut and torque to 92 ft. lbs. (125 Nm), if equipped with All Wheel Drive (AWD)
- The brake drum
- The rear wheel. Tighten the wheel lug nuts to 100 ft. lbs. (136 Nm)

ADJUSTMENT

All models use sealed wheel bearings that are pre-adjusted. If the bearing needs replacing, replace the rear wheel hub/bearing assembly.

GENERAL MOTORS

Diagnostic Trouble Codes

DIAGNOSTIC TROUBLE CODES

OBD II VEHICLE APPLICATIONS

GENERAL MOTORS

G6
2005–2007
2.4L ....VIN B
3.5L ....VIN 8
3.5L ....VIN N
3.6L ....VIN 7
3.9L ....VIN 1

GTO
2005–2006
6.0L ....VIN U

LaCrosse
2006–2007
3.6L ....VIN 7
3.8L ....VIN 1
3.5L ....VIN 6
3.7L ....VIN E

Lucerne
2006–2007
3.8L ....VIN K
4.6L ....VIN Y
2.4L ....VIN B

Malibu/Mailbu MAXX
2005–2007
2.2L ....VIN F
3.5L ....VIN 8
3.9L ....VIN 1

Montana SV6
2005–2006
3.5L ....VIN L
3.9L ....VIN 1

Relay
2005–2007
3.5L ....VIN L
3.9L ....VIN 1

Rendezvous
2005–2007
3.4L ....VIN E
3.5L ....VIN L
3.6L ....VIN 7

Sierra Gas Engine
2005–2007
4.3L ....VIN X
4.8L ....VIN C

4.8L ....VIN V
5.3L ....VIN 3
5.3L ....VIN B
5.3L ....VIN J
5.3L ....VIN M
5.3L ....VIN O
5.3L ....VIN T
5.3L ....VIN Z
6.0L ....VIN K
6.0L ....VIN N
6.0L ....VIN U
6.0L ....VIN Y
6.2L ....VIN 8
8.1L ....VIN G

Sierra Diesel Engine
2005–2007
6.6L ....VIN 2
6.6L ....VIN 6
6.6L ....VIN D

Silverado Gas Engine
2005–2007
4.3L ....VIN X
4.8L ....VIN C
4.8L ....VIN V
5.3L ....VIN 3
5.3L ....VIN B
5.3L ....VIN J
5.3L ....VIN M
5.3L ....VIN O
5.3L ....VIN T
5.3L ....VIN Z
6.0L ....VIN K
6.0L ....VIN N
6.0L ....VIN U
6.0L ....VIN Y
6.2L ....VIN 8
8.1L ....VIN G

Silverado Diesel Engine
2005–2007
6.6L ....VIN 2
6.6L ....VIN 6
6.6L ....VIN D

Sky
2007
2.0L ....VIN M
2.4L ....VIN B

Solstice
2006–2007
2.0L ....VIN M
2.4L ....VIN B

SRX
2005–2007
3.6L ....VIN 7
4.6L ....VIN A

Terraza
2005–2007
3.5L ....VIN L
3.9L ....VIN 1

Uplander
2005–2007
3.5L ....VIN L
3.9L ....VIN 1

Vibe
2005–2007
1.8L 1-ZZ-FE
1.8L 1-ZZ-GE

GM REFERENCE INFORMATION

OBD II TROUBLE CODE LIST

To use this information, first read and record All codes in memory along with Freeze Frame data. *If a PCM Reset function is done prior to recording this data,* All *codes and freeze frame data are lost!*

Look up the appropriate trouble code in the list on the following pages. The left hand column includes the code number, the number of trips to set the code (e.g., **1T or 2T**), the year, model description and type of OBD II Monitor that failed (e.g., **CCM or O2S**). This data can be used to determine how to drive a vehicle after a repair in order to validate the repair has been completed.

The **(N/MIL)** designator in the left hand column indicates the trouble code does not turn on the Malfunction Indicator Lamp or MIL. The **(STS Lamp)** indicator in the left column indicates a code that turns on the Service Transmission Soon lamp. This code may or may not turn "on" the MIL.

OBD II Trouble Code List (P0xxx Codes)

DTC	Trouble Code Title, Conditions & Possible Causes
DTC: P0005 **1T CCM, MIL: Yes** **Years:** 2005, 2006, 2007 **Models:** Sierra, Silverado **Engines:** 6.0L CNG **Transmissions:** All	**Camshaft Phasing System Malfunction** Engine started; system voltage from 6-18v, and the PCM detected the Actual and Commanded state of the High Pressure Lock-Off (HPL) solenoid did not match for more than one second. **Possible Causes:** • AF lock-off relay circuit to the HPL solenoid is open • HPL solenoid control circuit is open, shorted or grounded • HPL solenoid is damaged or it has failed • PCM has failed
DTC: P0008 **1T CCM, MIL: Yes** **Years:** 2005, 2006, 2007 **Models:** LaCrosse, Rendezvous, SRX **Engines:** 3.5L, 3.6L, 3.9L **Transmissions:** All	**Camshaft Phasing System Malfunction** DTCs P0010, P0011, P0013, P0014, P0020, P0021, P0023, P0024, P0341, P0342, P0343, P0346, P0347, P0348, P0366, P0367, P0368, P0391, P0392, P0393, P2088, P2089, P2090, P2091, P2092, P2093, P2094, and P2095 are not set. The engine is operating. ECM has learned the camshaft positions. ECM detects that both camshafts on bank 1 of the engine are mis-aligned with the crankshaft for more than 4 seconds. The presence of DTCs P0008 and P0009 along with P0016, P0017, P0018, and P0019 indicates a possible condition with the primary timing chain and the alignment between both intermediate sprockets and the crankshaft. Or, the crankshaft reluctor wheel has moved and is no longer referenced to top dead center (TDC). **Possible Causes:** • Timing chain or tensioner wear or misalignment • Crankshaft reluctor wheel for being mispositioned on the crankshaft • Another related DTC is setting
DTC: P0009 **1T CCM, MIL: Yes** **Years:** 2005, 2006, 2007 **Models:** LaCrosse, Rendezvous, SRX **Engines:** 3.5L, 3.6L, 3.9L **Transmissions:** All	**Engine Position System Performance Bank** DTCs P0010, P0011, P0013, P0014, P0020, P0021, P0023, P0024, P0341, P0342, P0343, P0346, P0347, P0348, P0366, P0367, P0368, P0391, P0392, P0393, P2088, P2089, P2090, P2091, P2092, P2093, P2094, and P2095 are not set. The engine is operating. ECM detects that both camshafts on bank 2 of the engine are mis-aligned with the crankshaft for more than 4 seconds. The presence of DTCs P0008 and P0009 along with P0016, P0017, P0018, and P0019 indicates a possible condition with the primary timing chain and the alignment between both intermediate sprockets and the crankshaft. Or, the crankshaft reluctor wheel has moved and is no longer referenced to top dead center (TDC). **Possible Causes:** • Timing chain or tensioner wear or misalignment • Crankshaft reluctor wheel for being mispositioned on the crankshaft • Another related DTC is setting
DTC: P0010 **2T CCM, MIL: Yes** **Years:** 2006, 2007 **Models:** G6, GTO, LaCrosse, Malibu, Montana, Montana SV6, Relay, Rendezvous, Sky, Solstice, SRX, Terraza, Uplander, Vibe **Engines:** 1.8L, 2.0L, 2.2L, 2.4L, 3.4L, 3.6L, 3.9L, 4.6L, 6.0L **Transmissions:** All	**Intake Camshaft Position (CMP) Actuator Solenoid Control Circuit** The engine is running. The ECM detects an open, short to ground, or a short to voltage on the high control circuit or an open on the low reference circuit for more than 0.25 second. **Possible Causes:** • CMP actuator control circuit is open or shorted to ground • CMP actuator control circuit is shorted to voltage • CMP actuator control circuit has high resistance • Engine oil pressure is low • CMP actuator control or solenoid has failed
DTC: P0011 **2T CCM, MIL: Yes** **Years:** 2006, 2007 **Models:** G6, GTO, LaCrosse, Malibu, Montana, Montana SV6, Relay, Rendezvous, Sky, Solstice, SRX, Terraza, Uplander, Vibe **Engines:** 1.8L, 2.0L, 2.2L, 2.4L, 3.4L, 3.6L, 3.9L, 4.6L, 6.0L **Transmissions:** All	**Intake Camshaft Position (CMP) System Performance** The engine is running at more than 1300 RPM. The difference between the desired CMP actuator angle and the actual CMP actuator angle is more than 6 degrees. CMP actuator is steady for 3 seconds. The condition is present for 13.5 seconds. **Possible Causes:** • CMP actuator control circuit is open or shorted to ground • CMP actuator control circuit is shorted to voltage • CMP actuator control circuit has high resistance • Engine oil pressure is low • CMP actuator control or solenoid has failed
DTC: P0013 **2T CCM, MIL: Yes** **Years:** 2006, 2007 **Models:** G6, GTO, LaCrosse, Malibu, Montana, Montana SV6, Relay, Rendezvous, Sky, Solstice, SRX, Uplander **Engines:** 2.0L, 2.2L, 2.4L, 3.6L, 3.9L, 4.6L, 6.0L **Transmissions:** All	**Exhaust Camshaft Position (CMP) Actuator Solenoid Control Circuit** The engine is running. The ECM detects an open, short to ground, or a short to voltage on the high control circuit or an open on the low reference circuit for more than 0.25 second. **Possible Causes:** • CMP actuator control circuit is open or shorted to ground • CMP actuator control circuit is shorted to voltage • CMP actuator control circuit has high resistance • Engine oil pressure is low • CMP actuator control or solenoid has failed

DTC	Trouble Code Title, Conditions & Possible Causes
DTC: P0014 **2T CCM, MIL: Yes** **Models:** G6, GTO, LaCrosse, Malibu, Montana SV6, Relay, Rendezvous, Sky, Solstice, SRX, Terraza, Uplander **Engines:** 2.0L, 2.2L, 2.4L, 3.5L, 3.6L, 3.9L, 4.6L, 6.0L **Transmissions:** All	**Exhaust Camshaft Position (CMP) System Performance** The engine is running at more than 1300 RPM. The difference between the desired CMP actuator angle and the actual CMP actuator angle is more than 6 degrees. CMP actuator is steady for 3 seconds. The condition is present for 13.5 seconds. **Possible Causes:** • CMP actuator control circuit is open or shorted to ground • CMP actuator control circuit is shorted to voltage • CMP actuator control circuit has high resistance • Engine oil pressure is low • CMP actuator control or solenoid has failed
DTC: P0016 **2T CCM, MIL: Yes** **Years:** 2006, 2007 **Models:** G6, GTO, LaCrosse, Malibu, Montana, Montana SV6, Relay, Rendezvous, Sky, Solstice, SRX, Terraza, Uplander, Vibe **Engines:** 1.8L, 2.0L, 2.2L, 2.4L, 3.4L, 3.6L, 3.9L, 4.6L, 6.0L **Transmissions:** All	**Crankshaft Position (CKP) - Intake Camshaft Position (CMP) Correlation** DTCs P0335, P0336, P0340, P0341, P0365 and P0366 are not set. Engine is running for more than 5 seconds. ECM detects 8 of the last 10 cam pulses occur during incorrect crankshaft position. **Possible Causes:** • Improper crankshaft balancer torque • Failed CKP solenoid • Incorrect valve timing
DTC: P0016 **2T CCM, MIL: Yes** **Years:** 2005, 2006, 2007 **Models:** Sierra, Silverado **Engines:** 6.6L Diesel **Transmissions:** All	**Camshaft Position Sensor - Intake Camshaft Position Correlation** Engine cranking or running, and the PCM detected the CMP sensor pulses received by the ECM did not equal 3 or 0 for two crankshaft revolutions. The ECM monitors the CKP and CMP sensor signals to determine if they are synchronized. An error is detected if both of these signals are not observed within a narrow window of time. **Possible Causes:** • CMP sensor is damaged causing a variance in sensor signal • Distributor installed one tooth off in advance or retard position • Distributor hold-down bolt loose or the rotor is loose on shaft • Excessive free play in the timing chain and gear assembly
DTC: P0017 **2T CCM, MIL: Yes** **Years:** 2006, 2007 **Models:** G6, GTO, LaCrosse, Sky, Solstice, SRX **Engines:** 2.0L, 2.2L, 2.4L, 3.6L, 3.9L, 4.6L, 6.0L **Transmissions:** All	**Crankshaft Position (CKP) - Exhaust Camshaft Position (CMP) Correlation Bank 2** DTCs P0335, P0336, P0340, P0341, P0365 and P0366 are not set. Engine is running for more than 5 seconds. CPM actuator is commanded to zero. ECM detects 25 out of the last 35 cam revolutions occur with 2 cam sensor pulses outside the CKP window. **Possible Causes:** • Improper crankshaft balancer torque • Failed CKP solenoid • Incorrect valve timing
DTC: P0018 **2T CCM, MIL: Yes** **Years:** 2006, 2007 **Models:** G6, GTO, LaCrosse, Sky, Solstice, SRX **Engines:** 2.0L, 2.2L, 2.4L, 3.6L, 3.9L, 4.6L, 6.0L **Transmissions:** All	**Crankshaft Position (CKP) - Exhaust Camshaft Position (CMP) Correlation Bank 2** DTCs P0335, P0336, P0340, P0341, P0365 and P0366 are not set. Engine is running for more than 5 seconds. CPM actuator is commanded to zero. ECM detects 25 out of the last 35 cam revolutions occur with 2 cam sensor pulses outside the CKP window. **Possible Causes:** • Improper crankshaft balancer torque • Failed CKP solenoid • Incorrect valve timing
DTC: P0019 **2T CCM, MIL: Yes** **Years:** 2006, 2007 **Models:** G6, GTO, LaCrosse, Sky, Solstice, SRX **Engines:** 2.0L, 2.2L, 2.4L, 3.6L, 3.9L, 4.6L, 6.0L **Transmissions:** All	**Crankshaft Position (CKP) - Intake Camshaft Position (CMP) Correlation Bank 2** DTCs P0335, P0336, P0340, P0341, P0365 and P0366 are not set. Engine is running for more than 5 seconds. CPM actuator is commanded to zero. ECM detects 25 out of the last 35 cam revolutions occur with 2 cam sensor pulses outside the CKP window. **Possible Causes:** • Improper crankshaft balancer torque • Failed CKP solenoid • Incorrect valve timing

DTC	Trouble Code Title, Conditions & Possible Causes
DTC: P0030 **2T CCM, MIL: Yes** **Years:** 2005, 2006, 2007 **Models:** G6, GTO, LaCrosse, Malibu, Montana, Montana SV6, Relay, Rendezvous, Sky, Solstice, SRX, Terraza, Uplander **Engines:** 2.0L, 2.2L, 2.4L, 3.4L, 3.5L, 3.6L, 3.8L, 3.9L, 4.6L, 6.0L, 6.0L **Transmissions:** All	**HO2S-11 (Bank 1 Sensor 1) Heater Circuit Malfunction** Engine started; system voltage from 9-18v, and the PCM detected the HO2S-11 heater current was more than 1.25 amps for 20 seconds. The PCM controls the HO2S-11 heater low control circuit with a low side driver, and tests the current draw through the driver. **Possible Causes:** • HO2S low side control circuit is shorted to system power (B+) • HO2S low side control circuit driver is shorted inside the PCM • HO2S heater has failed (it may be shorted internally) • PCM has failed
DTC: P0036 **2T CCM, MIL: Yes** **Years:** 2006, 2007 **Models:** G6, GTO, LaCrosse, Malibu, Montana, Montana SV6, Relay, Rendezvous, Sky, Solstice, SRX, Terraza, Uplander **Engines:** 2.0L, 2.2L, 2.4L, 3.4L, 3.5L, 3.6L, 3.8L, 3.9L, 4.6L, 6.0L, 6.0L **Transmissions:** All	**HO2S-21 (Bank 1 Sensor 1) Heater Circuit Malfunction** Engine started. Ignition 1 Signal parameter is between 10-18 volts. The engine speed is more than 400 RPM. The ECM detects that the affected HO2S heater low control circuit is not within a specified range. **Possible Causes:** • HO2S heater voltage supply circuit has a short to ground or an open/high resistance • HO2S heater voltage supply circuit fuse is open • HO2S heater low control circuit has a short to ground • HO2S heater low control circuit has a short to voltage or an open/high resistance • ECM has failed
DTC: P0053 **2T CCM, MIL: Yes** **Years:** 2006, 2007 **Models:** G6, GTO, LaCrosse, Malibu, Montana SV6, Relay, Rendezvous, Sky, Solstice, SRX, Terraza, Uplander **Engines:** 2.0L, 2.2L, 2.4L, 3.5L, 3.6L, 3.8L, 3.9L, 4.6L, 6.0L **Transmissions:** All	**HO2S Heater Resistance Sensor 1** DTCs P0112, P0113, P0117, P0118 are not set. The engine is started. The ignition is OFF for more than 10 hours. ECT Sensor parameter is between 0-40°C (32-104°F) at engine start-up. ECT Sensor parameter minus the IAT Sensor parameter is less than 8°C (14°F) at engine start-up. The ECM detects that the affected HO2S heater low control circuit is not within a specified range at engine start-up. **Possible Causes:** • HO2S heater voltage supply circuit has a short to ground or an open/high resistance • HO2S heater voltage supply circuit fuse is open • HO2S heater low control circuit has a short to ground • HO2S heater low control circuit has a short to voltage or an open/high resistance • ECM has failed
DTC: P0054 **2T CCM, MIL: Yes** **Years:** 2006, 2007 **Models:** G6, GTO, LaCrosse, Malibu, Montana SV6, Relay, Rendezvous, Sky, Solstice, SRX, Terraza, Uplander **Engines:** 2.0L, 2.2L, 2.4L, 3.5L, 3.6L, 3.8L, 3.9L, 4.6L, 6.0L **Transmissions:** All	**HO2S Heater Resistance Sensor 2** DTCs P0112, P0113, P0117, P0118 are not set. The engine is started. The ignition is OFF for more than 10 hours. ECT Sensor parameter is between 0-40°C (32-104°F) at engine start-up. ECT Sensor parameter minus the IAT Sensor parameter is less than 8°C (14°F) at engine start-up. The ECM detects that the affected HO2S heater low control circuit is not within a specified range at engine start-up. **Possible Causes:** • HO2S heater voltage supply circuit has a short to ground or an open/high resistance • HO2S heater voltage supply circuit fuse is open • HO2S heater low control circuit has a short to ground • HO2S heater low control circuit has a short to voltage or an open/high resistance • ECM has failed
DTC: P0068 **2T CCM, MIL: Yes** **Years:** 2005, 2006, 2007 **Models:** All **Engines:** All **Transmissions:** All	**TP Sensor Signal Range/Performance** DTC P0101, P0102, P0103, P0106, P0107, P0108, P0122, P0123, P0506 and P0507 not set, engine runtime 2 minutes, ECT sensor over 158°F, MAP sensor under 43 kPa for the TP sensor "skewed" high test, or the MAP sensor above 67 kPa for TP sensor "skewed" low test, MAP sensor steady and TP sensor steady (1.5%) for 2 seconds, and the PCM detected the TP sensor was more than the predicted value with the MAP under 43 kPa, or it was below a predicted value with MAP sensor more than 67 kPa for 1 second. **Possible Causes:** • TP sensor signal circuit open or shorted to ground (intermittent) • TP sensor VREF circuit is open or shorted (intermittent fault) • TP sensor is damaged or it failed (may be cracked or sticking) • TSB 76-65-04 contains a repair procedure for this code

DTC	Trouble Code Title, Conditions & Possible Causes
DTC: P0087 **1T CCM, MIL: Yes** **Years:** 2005, 2006, 2007 **Models:** Sierra, Silverado **Engines:** 6.6L Diesel **Transmissions:** A/T	**Fuel Rail Pressure Sensor Circuit Low Input** DTC P0192, P0193 or P0641 not set, Key on or engine running; and the PCM detected the actual FRP sensor signal was less than 0.0 MPa at 0-400 RPM, or the actual FRP was less than 22.5 MPa at more than 600 RPM. The ECM monitors the fuel rail pressure (FRP) using the FRP sensor. If the sensor indicates a pressure less than the commanded rail pressure plus a possible transitional overshoot, the ECM will set DTC P0087 for fuel rail pressure too low **Possible Causes:** • Check the engine oil for fuel contamination • Fuel filter is clogged or restricted • Fuel supply lines between fuel tank and injector pump clogged • Fuel rail pressure sensor signal circuit is shorted to ground • Fuel rail pressure sensor is out-of-calibration or it has failed • ECM has failed
DTC: P0088 **1T CCM, MIL: Yes** **Years:** 2005, 2006, 2007 **Models:** Sierra, Silverado **Engines:** 6.6L Diesel **Transmissions:** A/T	**Fuel Rail Pressure Sensor Circuit High Input** DTC P0192, P0193 or P0641 not set, Key on or engine running; and the PCM detected the actual FRP sensor signal was more than 167 MPa. The ECM monitors the fuel rail pressure (FRP) using the FRP sensor. If the sensor indicates a pressure less than the commanded rail pressure plus a possible transitional overshoot, the ECM will set DTC P0088 for fuel rail pressure too high. **Possible Causes:** • FRP pressure sensor signal circuit is open • FRP sensor signal circuit has a high resistance condition • FRP sensor is damaged or it has failed • FRP regulator is damaged or it has failed • ECM has failed
DTC: P0089 **1T CCM, MIL: Yes** **Years:** 2005, 2006, 2007 **Models:** Sierra, Silverado **Engines:** 6.6L Diesel **Transmissions:** A/T	**Fuel Rail Pressure Sensor Signal Range/Performance** DTC P0192, P0193 or P0641 not set, key on, and the PCM detected the difference between the Actual and Desired FRP sensor was over 20 MPa with Commanded fuel pump flow was 100 mm^3/second or less. The ECM uses the commanded fuel pump flow to determine a desired fuel rail pressure. The actual fuel pressure is monitored using the FRP sensor. If the PCM detects the FRP sensor pressure is 20 MPa more than desired value, it will set DTC P0089. **Possible Causes:** • FRP pressure sensor signal circuit is shorted to ground • FRP sensor is damaged or it has failed • FRP regulator is damaged or it has failed • ECM has failed
DTC: P0090 **1T CCM, MIL: Yes** **Years:** 2005, 2006, 2007 **Models:** Sierra, Silverado **Engines:** 6.6L Diesel **Transmissions:** A/T	**Fuel Rail Pressure Regulator Circuit Malfunction** DTC P0192, P0193 or P0641 not set, key on, and the PCM detected the difference between the Actual and Desired FRP sensor was over 20 MPa with Commanded fuel pump flow was 100 mm³/second or less. The ECM supplies power and ground to the fuel rail pressure (FRP) regulator. The PCM monitors the circuit current to detect when it is out of its normal range. **Possible Causes:** • Fuel rail pressure regulator control circuit is open or grounded • Fuel rail pressure regulator supply circuit is open or grounded • Fuel rail pressure regulator is damaged or it has failed • ECM has failed
DTC: P0101 **2T CCM, MIL: Yes** **Years:** 2005, 2006, 2007 **Models:** G6, GTO, LaCrosse, Malibu, Montana, Montana SV6, Relay, Rendezvous, Sky, Solstice, SRX, Terraza, Uplander, Vibe **Engines:** 1.8L, 2.0L, 2.2L, 2.4L, 3.4L, 3.5L, 3.6L, 3.9L, 4.6L, 6.0L **Transmissions:** All	**MAF Sensor Signal Range/Performance** DTC P0102, P0103, P0107, P0108, P0121, P0122, P0123, P0401, P0403, P0404, P0405, P0440, P0442, P0443, P0446, P0449, P1404 and P1441 not set, engine started, MAP sensor less than 63 kPa (3 kPa), TP angle less than 25% (1.5%), and the PCM detected the Actual MAF frequency value was not within a predetermined range of the calculated MAF value for 10 seconds. **Possible Causes:** • Base engine vacuum leak, PCV valve leaking or stuck open • Engine oil dipstick missing or not fully seated • MAF sensor element (wire) is contaminated or dirty • MAF sensor signal or ground circuit has a high resistance • MAF sensor is damaged or it has failed • PCM has failed

DTC	Trouble Code Title, Conditions & Possible Causes
DTC: P0101 **2T CCM, MIL: Yes** **Years:** 2005, 2006, 2007 **Models:** Sierra, Silverado **Engines:** 4.3L, 4.8L, 5.3L, 6.0L, 6.2L, 6.6L Diesel, 8.1L **Transmissions:** All	**MAF Sensor Signal Range/Performance** DTC P0102, P0103, P0106, P0107, P0108, P0120, P0121, P0122, P0123, P0220, P0442, P0443, P0446, P0449, P0455, P0496, P1404 and P2135 not set, engine cranking or running, system voltage from 11-18v, TP angle under 95% (5%), MAP sensor over 17 kPa (3 kPa), All conditions met for 1.5 seconds, and the PCM detected the Actual MAF sensor frequency was not within a predetermined range of the Calculated MAF value for 4 seconds. **Possible Causes:** • Base engine vacuum leak, PCV valve leaking or stuck open • Engine oil dipstick missing or not fully seated • MAF sensor element (wire) is contaminated or it has failed • MAF sensor signal circuit or ground circuit has high resistance • PCM has failed
DTC: P0102 **2T CCM, MIL: Yes** **Years:** 2005, 2006, 2007 **Models:** G6, GTO, LaCrosse, Malibu, Montana, Montana SV6, Relay, Rendezvous, Sky, Solstice, SRX, Terraza, Uplander, Vibe **Engines:** 1.8L, 2.0L, 2.2L, 2.4L, 3.4L, 3.5L, 3.6L, 3.9L, 4.6L, 6.0L **Transmissions:** All	**MAF Sensor Circuit Low Frequency** Engine started, system voltage from 10-18v, IAC motor more than 2 counts, and the PCM detected the MAF sensor frequency was less than 1,200 Hz, condition met for 1 second. **Possible Causes:** • MAF sensor element hot wire contaminated or the sensor failed • MAF sensor signal shorted to ground or ground circuit problem • MAF sensor wiring routed close to the ignition wires, generator, solenoids or electric motors • PCM has failed
DTC: P0102 **2T CCM, MIL: Yes** **Years:** 2005, 2006, 2007 **Models:** Sierra, Silverado **Engines:** 4.3L, 4.8L, 5.3L, 6.0L, 6.2L, 6.6L Diesel, 8.1L **Transmissions:** All	**MAF Sensor Circuit Low Frequency** Engine started; engine runtime over 3 seconds, system voltage over 8v, and the PCM detected the MAF sensor frequency was less than 1,200 Hz or less for 1.2 seconds. The MAF sensor is an airflow meter that measures how much air enters the engine. The PCM uses the MAF sensor signal to provide the correct fuel delivery for All engine speeds and loads. A small quantity of air entering the engine indicates a deceleration or idle condition. A large quantity of air entering the engine indicates acceleration or high load condition. **Possible Causes:** • MAF sensor element hot wire contaminated or the sensor failed • MAF sensor signal shorted to ground or ground circuit problem • MAF sensor wiring routed close to the ignition wires, generator, solenoids or electric motors (this causes it to pick up EMI/RFI) • PCM has failed • TSB 76-65-04 contains a repair procedure for this code
DTC: P0103 **2T CCM, MIL: Yes** **Years:** 2005, 2006, 2007 **Models:** G6, GTO, LaCrosse, Malibu, Montana, Montana SV6, Relay, Rendezvous, Sky, Solstice, SRX, Terraza, Uplander, Vibe **Engines:** 1.8L, 2.0L, 2.2L, 2.4L, 3.4L, 3.5L, 3.6L, 3.9L, 4.6L, 6.0L **Transmissions:** All	**MAF Sensor Circuit High Frequency** The engine speed is more than 300 RPM.. The ignition 1 signal is more than 8 volts. The ECM detects that the MAF Sensor parameter is more than 14,500 Hz for more than 5 seconds. A wide open throttle (WOT) acceleration from a stop should cause the MAF sensor parameter on the scan tool to increase rapidly. This increase should be from 6-10 g/s at idle to 380 g/s or more at the time of the 1-2 shift. **Possible Causes:** • Any electrical aftermarket devices not properly connected and grounded • Low reference circuit for an open/high resistance • Signal circuit for a short to ground or an open/high resistance • Signal circuit for a short to voltage • Ignition circuit for a short to ground or an open/high resistance • ECM has failed
DTC: P0103 **2T CCM, MIL: Yes** **Years:** 2005, 2006, 2007 **Models:** Sierra, Silverado **Engines:** 4.3L, 4.8L, 5.3L 6.0L, 6.2L, 6.6L Diesel, 8.1L **Transmissions:** All	**MAF Sensor Circuit High Frequency** Engine started; engine runtime over 3 seconds and the PCM detected the MAF sensor frequency was more than 13,500 Hz for over 1.2 seconds. The MAF sensor is an airflow meter that measures how much air enters the engine. The PCM uses the MAF sensor to provide the correct fuel delivery for All engine speeds and loads. A small quantity of air entering the engine indicates a deceleration or idle condition. A large quantity of air entering the engine indicates an acceleration or high load condition. **Possible Causes:** • MAF sensor power circuit has a high resistance condition • MAF sensor is contaminated, dirty or it has failed • MAF sensor wiring routed close to Generator or ignition wires • Water enters the air intake system reaches the MAF sensor, cools it, and causes it to indicate excessive airflow (check AIR system) • PCM has failed

DTC	Trouble Code Title, Conditions & Possible Causes
DTC: P0106 **2T CCM, MIL: Yes** **Years:** 2005, 2006, 2007 **Models:** G6, GTO, LaCrosse, Malibu, Montana, Montana SV6, Relay, Rendezvous, SV6, Sky, Solstice, SRX, Terraza, Uplander **Engines:** 2.0L, 2.2L, 2.4L, 3.4L, 3.5L, 3.6L, 3.9L, 4.6L, 6.0L **Transmissions:** All	**MAP Sensor Performance** DTCs P0016, P0102, P0103, P0107, P0108, P0112, P0113, P0116, P0117, P0118, P0128, P0335, or P0336 are not set. The engine is running. The intake air temperature is between −7 and +125°C (+19.4 and +257°F). ECM detects that the actual measured airflow from MAF, MAP, and TP is not within range of the calculated airflow that is derived from the system of models for more than 2 seconds. **Possible Causes:** • MAP sensor seal is missing or damage, intake manifold leaks • MAP sensor is contaminated, dirty, skewed or has failed • MAP sensor vacuum line is loose, restricted or contains "ice" • PCM has failed
DTC: P0106 **2T CCM, MIL: Yes** **Years:** 2005, 2006, 2007 **Models:** Sierra, Silverado **Engines:** 4.3L, 4.8L, 5.3L 6.0L, 6.2L, 6.6L Diesel, 8.1L **Transmissions:** All	**MAP Sensor Signal Range/Performance** DTC P0101, P0102, P0103, P0107, P0108, P0121, P0122, P0123, P0401, P0404, P0405, P0410, P0440, P0442, P0443 and P0446 not set, engine started, engine running at 400-5000 RPM with any change less than 125 RPM, PTO and Traction Control inactive, any change in IAC position less than 10 g/sec, any change in EGR position less than 20%, A/C clutch, power steering, Clutch and Brake switch signals All constant, and the PCM detected the MAP sensor signal was not within a predicted range for 2 seconds. The MAP sensor responds to pressure changes in the intake manifold that occur based on the amount of engine load. **Possible Causes:** • MAP sensor seal is missing or damage, intake manifold leaks • MAP sensor is contaminated, dirty, skewed or has failed • MAP sensor vacuum line is loose, restricted or contains "ice" • PCM has failed
DTC: P0107 **2T CCM, MIL: Yes** **Years:** 2005, 2006, 2007 **Models:** G6, GTO, LaCrosse, Malibu, Montana, Montana SV6, Relay, Rendezvous, SV6, Sky, Solstice, SRX, Terraza, Uplander **Engines:** 2.0L, 2.2L, 2.4L, 3.4L, 3.5L, 3.6L, 3.8L, 3.9L, 4.6L, 6.0L **Transmissions:** All	**MAP Sensor Circuit Low Input** DTC P0121, P0122 and P0123 not set, system voltage at 8-18v, TP angle over 0% with engine speed under 1000 RPM or more than 10% with engine speed above 1000 RPM, and the PCM detected the MAP sensor was less than 0.10v (Scan Tool reads 12 kPa) for 3 seconds. The PCM supplies the MAP sensor with a 5v reference and a ground circuit. **Possible Causes:** • MAP sensor signal circuit shorted to sensor ground • MAP sensor power circuit open between the sensor and PCM • MAP sensor is damaged or has failed • PCM has failed
DTC: P0107 **2T CCM, MIL: Yes** **Years:** 2005, 2006, 2007 **Models:** Sierra, Silverado **Engines:** 4.3L, 4.8L, 5.3L 6.0L, 6.2L, 6.6L Diesel, 8.1L **Transmissions:** All	**MAP Sensor Circuit Low Input** DTC P0120, P0121, P0122, P0123, P0220, P1125, P1514, P1515, P1516, P1518, P2108, P2120, P2121, P2125, P2126, P2130, P2131 and P2135 not set, TP angle at 0% with engine speed under 800 RPM, or TP angle over 12.5% with engine speed over 800 RPM, and PCM detected the MAP sensor was under 0.10v for 4 seconds. **Possible Causes:** • MAP sensor signal circuit shorted to sensor or chassis ground • MAP sensor power circuit open between the sensor and PCM • MAP sensor is damaged or has failed • PCM has failed
DTC: P0108 **2T CCM, MIL: Yes** **Years:** 2005, 2006, 2007 **Models:** G6, GTO, LaCrosse, Malibu, Montana, Montana SV6, Relay, Rendezvous, SV6, Sky, Solstice, SRX, Terraza, Uplander **Engines:** 2.0L, 2.2L, 2.4L, 3.4L, 3.5L, 3.6L, 3.8L, 3.9L, 4.6L, 6.0L **Transmissions:** All	**MAP Sensor Circuit High Input** DTC P0121-P0123 not set, engine runtime 1-2 minutes (depends on the ECT sensor at startup), TP angle below 2% with engine speed under 3000 RPM or TP angle over 30% with engine speed over 3000 RPM, and the PCM detected the MAP sensor was over 4.30v for 3 seconds. The MAP sensor signal is relative to the pressure changes in the manifold. The MAP signal voltage is with low MAP (idle speed or deceleration), and a high voltage with high MAP (KOEO, WOT). **Possible Causes:** • MAP sensor signal circuit is open or it is shorted to VREF • MAP sensor ground circuit open between sensor and the PCM • MAP sensor is damaged or has failed • PCM has failed • This code can set due to a backfire or engine cranking too long
DTC: P0108 **2T CCM, MIL: Yes** **Years:** 2005, 2006, 2007 **Models:** Sierra, Silverado **Engines:** 4.3L, 4.8L, 5.3L 6.0L, 6.2L, 6.6L Diesel, 8.1L **Transmissions:** All	**MAP Sensor Circuit High Input** DTC P012, P0122 and P0123 not set, engine started, system voltage 10-18v, TP angle over 0% with the engine speed under 1200 RPM (under 600 RPM on 7.4L), or TP angle less than 20% with engine speed over 1200 RPM (over 600 RPM on 7.4L), and the PCM detected the MAP sensor was more than 4.40v for 2 seconds. **Possible Causes:** • MAP sensor signal circuit is open or it is shorted to VREF • MAP sensor ground circuit open between sensor and the PCM • MAP sensor is damaged or has failed • This code can set due to a backfire or engine cranking too long • PCM has failed

DTC	Trouble Code Title, Conditions & Possible Causes
DTC: P0112 **2T CCM, MIL: Yes** **Years:** 2005, 2006, 2007 **Models:** G6, GTO, LaCrosse, Malibu, Montana, Montana SV6, Relay, Rendezvous, Sky, Solstice, SRX, Terraza, Uplander, Vibe **Engines:** 1.8L, 2.0L, 2.2L, 2.4L, 3.4L, 3.5L, 3.6L, 3.9L, 4.6L, 6.0L **Transmissions:** All	**IAT Sensor Circuit Low Input** DTC P0101, P0102, P0103, P0116, P0117, P0118, P0125, P0128, P0502 and P0503 not set, engine started, engine runtime over 10 seconds, VSS more than 25 MPH, and the PCM detected the IAT sensor was more than 253-275°F for 20 seconds in the CCM test. **Possible Causes:** • IAT sensor signal circuit is shorted to sensor or chassis ground • IAT sensor is damaged or has failed (it may be shorted) • PCM has failed • TSB 02-06-03-005 contains a repair procedure for this code
DTC: P0112 **2T CCM, MIL: Yes** **Years:** 2005, 2006, 2007 **Models:** Sierra, Silverado **Engines:** 4.3L, 4.8L, 5.3L 6.0L, 6.2L, 8.1L **Transmissions:** All	**IAT Sensor Circuit Low Input** DTC P0522 and P0523 not set, engine started, engine runtime over 45 seconds, VSS more than 2-40 MPH, and the PCM detected the IAT sensor was more than 262-282°F for 1 second. The IAT sensor is a variable resistor that includes a signal circuit and low reference circuit to measure the temperature of the air entering the engine. **Possible Causes:** • IAT sensor signal circuit is shorted to sensor or chassis ground • IAT sensor is damaged or has failed (it may be shorted) • PCM has failed
DTC: P0112 **2T CCM, MIL: Yes** **Years:** 2005, 2006, 2007 **Models:** Sierra, Silverado **Engines:** 6.6L Diesel **Transmissions:** All	**IAT Sensor Circuit Low Input** Key on or engine running, ECT sensor less than 109°F, and the PCM detected the IAT sensor was more than 304°F for 2 seconds. The IAT sensor is a variable resistor that has both an IAT signal and a low reference circuit to measure the temperature of incoming air. **Possible Causes:** • IAT sensor signal circuit is shorted to sensor or chassis ground • IAT sensor is damaged or has failed (it may be shorted) • PCM has failed
DTC: P0113 **2T CCM, MIL: Yes** **Years:** 2005, 2006, 2007 **Models:** G6, GTO, LaCrosse, Malibu, Montana, Montana SV6, Relay, Rendezvous, Sky, Solstice, SRX, Terraza, Uplander, Vibe **Engines:** 1.8L, 2.0L, 2.2L, 2.4L, 3.4L, 3.5L, 3.6L, 3.9L, 4.6L, 6.0L **Transmissions:** All	**IAT Sensor Circuit High Input** DTC P0116-P0118, P0125, P0128, P0502 and P0503 not set, engine started, engine runtime over 180 seconds, ECT sensor more than 140°F, MAF sensor less than 12 g/sec, VSS less than 35 MPH, and the PCM detected the IAT sensor indicated less than −38°F for a period of 3-20 seconds. The IAT sensor is a variable resistor that includes an IAT signal circuit and a low reference circuit to measure the temperature of the air entering the engine. When the IAT sensor is cold, its resistance is high. When the air temperature increases, its resistance decreases. With high sensor resistance, the IAT sensor signal voltage is high. With lower sensor resistance, the IAT sensor signal voltage should be a lower voltage. **Possible Causes:** • IAT sensor signal circuit is open between the sensor and PCM • IAT sensor signal circuit is shorted to VREF or system power • IAT sensor is damaged or has failed (it may be open) • PCM has failed • TSB 02-06-03-005 contains a repair procedure for this code
DTC: P0113 **2T CCM, MIL: Yes** **Years:** 2005, 2006, 2007 **Models:** Sierra, Silverado **Engines:** 4.3L, 4.8L, 5.3L 6.0L, 6.2L, 8.1L **Transmissions:** All	**IAT Sensor Circuit High Input** DTC P0101, P0102, P0103, P0116, P0117, P0118, P0125, P0128, P0502 and P0503 not set, engine runtime over 120 seconds, ECT sensor more than 140°F (more than 32°F on 7.4L), MAF sensor less than 15 g/sec, VSS less than 7 MPH, and the PCM detected the IAT sensor was less than −36°F for 1 second. **Possible Causes:** • IAT sensor signal circuit is open between the sensor and PCM • IAT sensor signal circuit is shorted to VREF or system power • IAT sensor is damaged or has failed (it may be open) • PCM has failed
DTC: P0113 **2T CCM, MIL: Yes** **Years:** 2005, 2006, 2007 **Models:** Sierra, Silverado **Engines:** 6.6L Diesel **Transmissions:** All	**IAT Sensor Circuit High Input** Engine started; engine runtime over 8 minutes and the PCM detected the IAT sensor indicated less than or equal to −40°F for 2 seconds during the CCM test. **Possible Causes:** • IAT sensor signal circuit is open between the sensor and PCM • IAT sensor signal circuit is shorted to VREF or system power • IAT sensor is damaged or has failed (it may be open) • PCM has failed

DTC	Trouble Code Title, Conditions & Possible Causes
DTC: P0116 **2T CCM, MIL: Yes** **Years:** 2005, 2006, 2007 **Models:** G6, GTO, LaCrosse, Malibu, Montana, Montana SV6, Relay, Rendezvous, Sky, Solstice, SRX, Terraza, Uplander, Vibe **Engines:** 1.8L, 2.0L, 2.2L, 2.4L, 3.4L, 3.5L, 3.6L, 3.9L, 4.6L, 6.0L **Transmissions:** All	**ECT Sensor Signal Range/Performance** DTC P0112, P0113, P0117, P0118, P0125, P0128, P0601, P0602, P0604, P0606, P1621 and P1683 not set, minimum soak time over 8 hours, key on, IAT sensor more than 59°F, and the PCM detected the difference between the ECT sensor and IAT sensor values was more than 59°F. If the vehicle soak time is from 8-10 hours, the ECT and IAT sensors should be with 10°F of each other at initial key on. **Possible Causes:** • ECT sensor circuit has an intermittent high resistance condition • ECT sensor circuit has an intermittent grounded condition • ECT sensor is out of calibration or "skewed" high • IAT sensor is out of calibration or it is "skewed" high or low • TSB 01-06-04-052 contains a repair procedure for this code
DTC: P0116 **2T CCM, MIL: Yes** **Years:** 2005, 2006, 2007 **Models:** Sierra, Silverado **Engines:** 4.3L, 4.8L, 5.3L 6.0L, 6.2L, 6.6L Diesel, 8.1L **Transmissions:** All	**ECT Sensor Signal Range/Performance** DTC P0112, P0113, P0117, P0118, P0125, P0128, P0601, P0602, P1621 or P1683 not set, minimum soak time of 8 hours, key on, the difference between the ECT and IAT sensors over 27-36°F, engine started, VSS over 15 MPH for 5 minutes. If the IAT sensor decreases more than 12.6°F, a block heater is indicated and the test is aborted. If the IAT sensor does not decrease and the PCM detects difference between the ECT and IAT sensor signals at startup is more than 252°F, and the engine is cranked for 10 seconds, this code will set. **Possible Causes:** • ECT sensor circuit has an intermittent high resistance condition • ECT sensor circuit has an intermittent grounded condition • ECT sensor is out of calibration or "skewed"
DTC: P0117 **2T CCM, MIL: Yes** **Years:** 2005, 2006, 2007 **Models:** G6, GTO, LaCrosse, Malibu, Montana, Montana SV6, Relay, Rendezvous, Sky, Solstice, SRX, Terraza, Uplander, Vibe **Engines:** 1.8L, 2.0L, 2.2L, 2.4L, 3.4L, 3.5L, 3.6L, 3.9L, 4.6L, 6.0L **Transmissions:** All	**ECT Sensor Circuit Low Input** Engine started; engine runtime over 3 seconds and the PCM detected the ECT sensor was less than 0.10v (Scan Tool reads over 283°F) for 15-25 seconds. The PCM supplies the ECT sensor with a 5v signal and a low reference ground circuit. When the ECT sensor is cold, its resistance is high. As the engine coolant temperature increases, its resistance decreases. With high sensor resistance, the ECT sensor signal voltage is high. With lower sensor resistance, the ECT sensor signal voltage should be a lower voltage. **Possible Causes:** • ECT sensor signal circuit shorted to sensor or chassis ground • ECT sensor is damaged or has failed (it may be shorted) • PCM has failed
DTC: P0117 **2T CCM, MIL: Yes** **Years:** 2005, 2006, 2007 **Models:** Sierra, Silverado **Engines:** 4.3L, 4.8L, 5.3L 6.0L, 6.2L, 6.6L Diesel, 8.1L **Transmissions:** All	**ECT Sensor Circuit Low Input** Engine started; engine runtime over 10 seconds or with the engine runtime under 10 seconds and the IAT sensor signal less than 122°F, the PCM detected the ECT sensor was more than 282°F for 20 seconds. When the coolant is cold, sensor resistance is high, and as it warms, the sensor resistance decreases. With high sensor resistance, the signal voltage is high. **Possible Causes:** • ECT sensor signal circuit shorted to sensor or chassis ground • ECT sensor is damaged or has failed (it may be shorted) • PCM has failed
DTC: P0118 **2T CCM, MIL: Yes** **Years:** 2005, 2006, 2007 **Models:** G6, GTO, LaCrosse, Malibu, Montana, Montana SV6, Relay, Rendezvous, Sky, Solstice, SRX, Terraza, Uplander, Vibe **Engines:** 1.8L, 2.0L, 2.2L, 2.4L, 3.4L, 3.5L, 3.6L, 3.9L, 4.6L, 6.0L **Transmissions:** All	**ECT Sensor Circuit High Input** Engine started and the PCM detected the ECT sensor indicated less than −36°F for a period of 15-25 seconds during the CCM test period. **Possible Causes:** • ECT sensor signal circuit is open between the sensor and PCM • ECT sensor signal circuit is shorted to VREF or system power • ECT sensor is damaged or has failed (it may be open) • PCM has failed
DTC: P0118 **2T CCM, MIL: Yes** **Years:** 2005, 2006, 2007 **Models:** Sierra, Silverado **Engines:** 4.3L, 4.8L, 5.3L 6.0L, 6.2L, 6.6L Diesel, 8.1L **Transmissions:** All	**ECT Sensor Circuit High Input** Engine started; engine runtime over 10 seconds, or engine runtime under 10 seconds with the IAT sensor more than 32°F, and the PCM detected the ECT sensor was over 4.90v (Scan Tool reads less than −36°F) for 20 seconds during the CCM test period. **Possible Causes:** • ECT sensor connector is damaged, loose or open • ECT sensor signal circuit is open between the sensor and PCM • ECT sensor signal circuit is shorted to VREF • ECT sensor is damaged or has failed (it may be open) • PCM has failed

DTC	Trouble Code Title, Conditions & Possible Causes
DTC: P0120 **1T CCM, MIL: Yes** **Years:** 2006, 2007 **Models:** G6, GTO, LaCrosse, Malibu, Montana, Montana SV6, Relay, Rendezvous, Sky, Solstice, SRX, Terraza, Uplander, Vibe **Engines:** 1.8L, 2.0L, 2.2L, 2.4L, 3.4L, 3.5L, 3.6L, 3.9L, 4.6L, 6.0L **Transmissions:** All	**TP Sensor 1 Signal Range/Performance** DTC P0641 is not set. The system voltage is more than 5.23 volts. The ignition is in the Unlock/Accessory or Run position. TP sensor 1 voltage is less than 0.27 volt or more than 4.67 volts for more than 0.5 second. The control module commands the TAC system to operate in the Reduced Engine Power mode. A message center or an indicator displays Reduced Engine Power. Under certain conditions, the control module commands the engine OFF. **Possible Causes:** • Low reference circuit has an open/high resistance • 5-volt reference circuit has a short to ground or an open/high resistance • Signal circuit terminal A has a short to voltage • signal circuit terminal D for a short to ground • TP sensor 1 signal circuit has a short to ground or an open/high resistance • TP sensor 2 signal circuit has a short to voltage or an open/high resistance • Short between TP sensor 1 signal circuit and TP sensor 2 signal circuit • Circuits have less than 5 ohms resistance • Failed TP sensor • Failed throttle body • Failed ECM
DTC: P0120 **1T CCM, MIL: Yes** **Years:** 2005, 2006, 2007 **Models:** Sierra, Silverado **Engines:** 4.3L, 4.8L, 5.3L 6.0L, 6.2L, 8.1L **Transmissions:** All	**TP Sensor 1 Signal Range/Performance** DTC P1510 and P2108 not set, engine cranking or running, system voltage over 5.23v, and the PCM detected the TP sensor 1 signal was less than 0.37v or more than 4.51v for 1 second. If the TAC module detects an internal condition, several TAC system codes can be set due to the many redundant tests run continuously on this system. Locating and repairing one individual condition may correct more than one code. **Possible Causes:** • TAC connector contaminated with water (causes other codes) • TP Sensor 1 low reference circuit is shorted to ground • TP Sensor 1 signal circuit is open or shorted to ground • APP Sensor signal or VREF circuit is open or shorted to power • APP Sensor ground circuit is open or shorted to system power • APP Sensor is damaged or it has failed (it may be cracked) • APP Sensor assembly is damaged or it has failed • TAC assembly is damaged or it has failed • TSB 03-04-06-034 contains a repair procedure for this code
DTC: P0121 **2T CCM, MIL: Yes** **Years:** 2005, 2006, 2007 **Models:** G6, GTO, LaCrosse, Malibu, Montana, Montana SV6, Relay, Rendezvous, Sky, Solstice, SRX, Terraza, Uplander, Vibe **Engines:** 1.8L, 2.0L, 2.2L, 2.4L, 3.4L, 3.5L, 3.6L, 3.9L, 4.6L, 6.0L **Transmissions:** All	**TP Sensor Signal Range/Performance** Ignition is ON or engine running. The difference between the TP sensor 1 signal and the TP sensor 2 signal is less than 0.8 volt for at least 2 seconds, or, difference between the TP sensor 1 signal and the TP sensor 2 signal is more than 1.6 volts for at least 2 seconds. **Possible Causes:** • TP sensor signal circuit open or shorted to ground (intermittent) • TP sensor VREF circuit is open or shorted (intermittent fault) • TP sensor is damaged or it failed (may be cracked or sticking) • TSB 76-65-04 contains a repair procedure for this code
DTC: P0121 **2T CCM, MIL: Yes** **Years:** 2005, 2006, 2007 **Models:** Sierra, Silverado **Engines:** 4.3L **Transmissions:** All	**TP Sensor Signal Range/Performance** DTC P0101, P0102, P0103, P0106, P0107, P0108, P0122, P0123, P0506 and P0507 not set, engine runtime 2 minutes, ECT sensor over 158°F, MAP sensor under 43 kPa for the TP sensor "skewed" high test, or the MAP sensor above 67 kPa for TP sensor "skewed" low test, MAP sensor steady and TP sensor steady (1.5%) for 2 seconds, and the PCM detected the TP sensor was more than the predicted value with the MAP under 43 kPa, or it was below a predicted value with MAP sensor more than 67 kPa for 1 second. **Possible Causes:** • TP sensor signal circuit open or shorted to ground (intermittent) • TP sensor VREF circuit is open or shorted (intermittent fault) • TP sensor is damaged or it failed (may be cracked or sticking) • TSB 76-65-04 contains a repair procedure for this code
DTC: P0121 **2T CCM, MIL: Yes** **Years:** 2005, 2006, 2007 **Models:** Sierra, Silverado **Engines:** 6.6L Diesel **Transmissions:** All	**Accelerator Pedal Position Sensor 1 Performance** Engine speed over 300 RPM, system voltage over 8.0v, and the PCM detected a difference of over 230 mv between the APP 1 and APP 2 signals, a difference between the APP 1 and APP 3 signals of over 500 mv for 2 seconds. STS lamp is "on" with multiple APP faults. **Possible Causes:** • APP sensor circuit open or shorted to ground (intermittent) • APP sensor VREF circuit is open or shorted (intermittent fault) • APP sensor is damaged or it failed (may be cracked or sticking)

DTC	Trouble Code Title, Conditions & Possible Causes
DTC: P0122 **1T CCM, MIL: Yes** **Years:** 2005, 2006, 2007 **Models:** G6, GTO, LaCrosse, Malibu, Montana, Montana SV6, Relay, Rendezvous, Sky, Solstice, SRX, Terraza, Uplander, Vibe **Engines:** 1.8L, 2.0L, 2.2L, 2.4L, 3.4L, 3.5L, 3.6L, 3.9L, 4.6L, 6.0L **Transmissions:** All	**TP Sensor Circuit Low Input** Key on or engine running; and the PCM detected the TP sensor signal was less than 0.1v for over 1 second. The PCM uses the TP sensor signal to determine the throttle plate angle for various engine controls. The TP sensor output is an analog signal that varies from 0-5v. **Possible Causes:** • TP sensor signal circuit is shorted to sensor ground • TP sensor signal circuit is open • TP sensor VREF circuit is open between sensor and PCM • TP sensor is damaged or it failed (it may be shorted) • PCM is damaged or has failed
DTC: P0122 **1T CCM, MIL: Yes** **Years:** 2005, 2006, 2007 **Models:** Sierra, Silverado **Engines:** 4.3L **Transmissions:** All	**TP Sensor Circuit Low Input** Key on or engine running; and the PCM detected the TP sensor indicated less than 0.10v for 1 second. The PCM uses the TP sensor signal to determine the throttle plate angle for various engine controls. The TP sensor output is an analog signal that varies from 0-5v. **Possible Causes:** • TP sensor signal circuit is shorted to sensor ground • TP sensor VREF circuit is open between sensor and PCM • TP sensor is damaged or it failed (it may be shorted) • PCM is damaged or has failed
DTC: P0123 **2T CCM, MIL: Yes** **Years:** 2005, 2006, 2007 **Models:** G6, GTO, LaCrosse, Malibu, Montana, Montana SV6, Relay, Rendezvous, Sky, Solstice, SRX, Terraza, Uplander, Vibe **Engines:** 1.8L, 2.0L, 2.2L, 2.4L, 3.4L, 3.5L, 3.6L, 3.9L, 4.6L, 6.0L **Transmissions:** All	**TP Sensor Circuit High Input** Key on or engine running; and the PCM detected the TP sensor signal was more than 4.90v for 1 second. Rotation of the TP sensor rotor from closed throttle position to the wide open throttle (WOT) position provides the PCM with a signal voltage from below 1.0v to over 4.0v. **Possible Causes:** • TP sensor signal circuit is shorted to VREF or system power • TP sensor ground circuit is open between the sensor and PCM • TP sensor is damaged or it failed (it may be open) • PCM is damaged or has failed
DTC: P0123 **2T CCM, MIL: Yes** **Years:** 2005, 2006, 2007 **Models:** Sierra, Silverado **Engines:** 4.3L **Transmissions:** All	**TP Sensor Circuit High Input** DTC P1635 and P1639 not set, Key on or engine running; and the PCM detected the TP sensor signal was more than 4.70-4.90v for over 1 second during the CCM test. **Possible Causes:** • TP sensor signal circuit is shorted to VREF or system power • TP sensor ground circuit is open between the sensor and PCM • TP sensor is damaged or it failed (it may be open) • PCM is damaged or has failed
DTC: P0125 **2T CCM, MIL: Yes** **Years:** 2005, 2006, 2007 **Models:** G6, GTO, LaCrosse, Malibu, Montana, Montana SV6, Relay, Rendezvous, Sky, Solstice, SRX, Terraza, Uplander, Vibe **Engines:** 1.8L, 2.0L, 2.2L, 2.4L, 3.4L, 3.5L, 3.6L, 3.9L, 4.6L, 6.0L **Transmissions:** All	**ECT Excessive Time To Enter Closed Loop** DTC P0112, P0113, P0117 and P0118 not set, startup ECT sensor more than 19°F, minimum IAT sensor more than 19°F, then while in: **Region 1** Startup ECT sensor more than 50°F and IAT sensor more than 50°F, then with engine runtime over 127 seconds, the engine did not reach a closed loop temperature of 64°F after a calibrated amount of total airflow and maximum idle time of more than 95 seconds. **Region 2** Startup ECT sensor between 20-50°F and IAT sensor more than 20°F, then with engine runtime over 20 seconds, the engine did not reach closed loop temperature of 64°F after a calibrated amount of total airflow and maximum idle time of more than 210 seconds. **Region 3** Startup ECT from −20°F to 40°F and IAT sensor more than 20°F, then with engine runtime over 439 seconds, the engine did not reach closed loop temperature of 64°F after a calibrated amount of total airflow and maximum idle time of more than 329 seconds. **Possible Causes:** • Check the operation of the thermostat (it may be stuck open) • Coolant level is too low, or the coolant mixture is incorrect • ECT sensor signal circuit has a high resistance condition • ECT sensor is damaged or it has failed

DTC	Trouble Code Title, Conditions & Possible Causes
DTC: P0125 **2T CCM, MIL: Yes** **Years:** 2005, 2006, 2007 **Models:** Sierra, Silverado **Engines:** 4.3L, 4.8L, 5.3L 6.0L, 6.2L, 8.1L **Transmissions:** All	**ECT Excessive Time To Enter Closed Loop** DTC P0101, P0102, P0103, P0112, P0113, P0116, P0117, P0118, P0500, P0502, P0503, P1111, P1112, P1114 and P1115 not set, and with the engine started with the ECT sensor from −31°F to 104°F, IAT sensor more than −40°F, accumulated airflow since startup more than 9000 grams and idle time under 360 seconds, and the PCM detected the ECT sensor was less than 68°F after 8 minutes (Test 1), or with the engine was started with the ECT sensor more than 20°F, accumulated airflow since startup more than 5500 grams with idle time less than 225 seconds, and the PCM detected the ECT sensor was less than 68°F after 2 minutes (Test 2), or the engine was started with the ECT sensor more than 50°F, accumulated airflow since startup more than 2000 grams and idle time less than 90 seconds, and the PCM detected the ECT sensor was less than 68°F after 2 minutes (Test 3). **Possible Causes:** • Check the operation of the thermostat (it may be stuck open) • Coolant level is too low, or the coolant mixture is incorrect • ECT sensor signal circuit has a high resistance condition • ECT sensor is damaged or it has failed
DTC: P0128 **2T CCM, MIL: Yes** **Years:** 2005, 2006, 2007 **Models:** G6, GTO, LaCrosse, Malibu, Montana, Montana SV6, Relay, Rendezvous, Sky, Solstice, SRX, Terraza, Uplander, Vibe **Engines:** 1.8L, 2.0L, 2.2L, 2.4L, 3.4L, 3.5L, 3.6L, 3.9L, 4.6L, 6.0L **Transmissions:** All	**ECT Sensor Below Thermostat Regulating Temperature** DTC P0112, P0113, P0116, P0117, P0118, P1111, P1112, P1114 or P1115 not set, ECT sensor from −40°F to 172°F and IAT sensor more than 19°F at started, engine started, engine runtime from 2 to 30 minutes, vehicle driven to over 15 MPH for 1 mile, average MAF reading more than 15 g/sec, and the PCM detected the time it took tool long for the ECT sensor to reach 170°F (one test per key cycle). **Possible Causes:** • Check the operation of the thermostat (it may be stuck open) • Coolant level is too low, or the coolant mixture is incorrect • ECT sensor signal circuit has a high resistance condition • ECT sensor is damaged or it has failed
DTC: P0128 **2T CCM, MIL: Yes** **Years:** 2005, 2006, 2007 **Models:** Sierra, Silverado **Engines:** 4.3L, 4.8L, 5.3L 6.0L, 6.2L, 8.1L **Transmissions:** All	**ECT Sensor Below Thermostat Regulating Temperature** DTC P0101, P0102, P0103, P0112, P0113, P0116, P0117, P0118, P0125, P0500, P0502, P0503, P1111, P1112, P1114 and P1115 not set, ECT sensor from −40°F to 158°F, IAT sensor 19°F or more, engine runtime from 2-22 minutes, VSS over 5 MPH for 1.5 miles, MAF average reading over 23 g/sec, and the PCM detected the time to reach closed loop temperature had been exceeded. **Possible Causes:** • Check the operation of the thermostat (it may be stuck open) • Coolant level is too low, or the coolant mixture is incorrect • ECT sensor signal circuit has a high resistance condition • ECT sensor is damaged or it has failed
DTC: P0130 **2T O2S, MIL: Yes** **Years:** 2005, 2006, 2007 **Models:** G6, GTO, LaCrosse, Malibu, Montana, Montana SV6, Relay, Rendezvous, Sky, Solstice, SRX, Terraza, Uplander, Vibe **Engines:** 1.8L, 2.0L, 2.2L, 2.4L, 3.4L, 3.5L, 3.6L, 3.9L, 4.6L, 6.0L **Transmissions:** All	**HO2S-11 (Bank 1 Sensor 1) Closed Loop Performance** DTC P0101-P0103, P0107, P0108, P0112, P0113, P0116-P0118, P0121-P0123, P0125, P0128, P0201-P0206, P0410, P0440, P0442, P0443, P0446, P0449 and P1441 not set, engine started, engine speed 550-3000 RPM for 4 minutes, MAF sensor from 8-35 g/sec, TP angle from 3-35%, ECT sensor more than 158°F, and the PCM detected the HO2S signal had an improper voltage amplitude. The HO2S is used for fuel control and post-catalyst monitoring. This sensor compares the oxygen content of the surrounding air with the oxygen content of the exhaust stream. At initial startup, the PCM operates in open loop mode, ignoring the HO2S signal when calculating the air/fuel ratio. The PCM supplies the HO2S with a reference (or bias) voltage of about 450 mv. The HO2S generates a voltage within a range of 0-1000 mv that fluctuates above and below the bias voltage once in closed loop. A high HO2S voltage indicates a rich fuel mixture. A low HO2S voltage indicates a lean mixture. Heating elements in the HO2S shorten the time required for the sensor to reach normal temperature, and an accurate voltage signal. **Possible Causes:** • Air leaks in the exhaust system, intake manifold, vacuum lines • EVAP Purge system malfunction or charcoal canister problems • HO2S signal circuit is open between the sensor and the PCM • HO2S signal circuit is shorted to sensor or chassis ground • HO2S is damaged, contaminated or air reference hole clogged • PCM has failed

DTC	Trouble Code Title, Conditions & Possible Causes
DTC: P0131 **2T CCM, MIL: Yes** **Years:** 2005, 2006, 2007 **Models:** G6, GTO, LaCrosse, Malibu, Montana, Montana SV6, Relay, Rendezvous, SV6, Sky, Solstice, SRX, Terraza, Uplander **Engines:** 2.0L, 2.2L, 2.4L, 3.4L, 3.5L, 3.6L, 3.8L, 3.9L, 4.6L, 6.0L **Transmissions:** All	**HO2S-11 (Bank 1 Sensor 1) Circuit Low Input** DTC P0101, P0102, P0103, P0107, P0108, P0112, P0113, P0116, P0117, P0118, P0121, P0122, P0123, P0125, P0128, P0201, P0202, P0203, P0204, P0205, P0206, P0410, P0440, P0442, P0443, P0446, P0449 and P1441 not set, A/F ratio at 13.0-16.5:1, TP angle from 3-40%, Air Pump "off", and the PCM detected the HO2S signal was less than 175 mv in closed loop, or with the P/E mode active, the HO2S signal was under 600 mv for 15 seconds. The HO2S is used for fuel control and post-catalyst monitoring. This sensor compares the oxygen content of the surrounding air with the oxygen content of the exhaust stream. At startup, the PCM operates in open loop mode, ignoring the HO2S signal when calculating the air/fuel ratio. The HO2S voltage range is from 0-1000 mv as it fluctuates above and below 450 mv. **Possible Causes:** • Air leaks in the exhaust system, intake manifold, vacuum lines • Engine misfire condition present (look for P0300 series codes) • Fuel system too lean (possible low fuel pressure, water in fuel) • HO2S signal circuit is shorted to the sensor or chassis ground • HO2S is damaged (i.e., cracked) or air reference hole clogged • PCM has failed
DTC: P0131 **2T CCM, MIL: Yes** **Years:** 2005, 2006, 2007 **Models:** Sierra, Silverado **Engines:** 4.3L, 4.8L, 5.3L 6.0L, 6.2L, 8.1L **Transmissions:** All	**HO2S-11 (Bank 1 Sensor 1) Circuit Low Input** DTC P0101-P0103, P0106-P0108, P0112, P0113, P0116-P0118, P0121-P0123, P0200, P0300, P0401, P0404, P0405, P0440, P0442, P0446, P0452, P0453, P1120, P1125, P1220, P1221, P1258, P1404, P1441, P1514, P1515, P1516, P1517 and P1518 not set, engine started, engine running in closed loop, fuel level over 10%, system voltage over 10v, TP angle from 8-50%, or on models with TAC, the APP sensor indicated angle from 3-70%, MAP sensor more than 25 kPa, Intrusive and Scan Tool tests both off, then with the Lean Test enabled, the PCM detected the HO2S signal was less than 200 mv for 50 seconds or during the P/E Mode test, the PCM detected the HO2S signal was less than 360 mv for 10 seconds. **Possible Causes:** • Air leaks in the exhaust system, intake manifold, vacuum lines • Engine misfire condition present (look for P0300 series codes) • Fuel system too lean (possible low fuel pressure, water in fuel) • HO2S signal circuit is shorted to the sensor or chassis ground • HO2S is damaged (i.e., cracked) or air reference hole clogged • PCM has failed
DTC: P0132 **2T CCM, MIL: Yes** **Years:** 2005, 2006, 2007 **Models:** G6, GTO, LaCrosse, Malibu, Montana, Montana SV6, Relay, Rendezvous, SV6, Sky, Solstice, SRX, Terraza, Uplander **Engines:** 2.0L, 2.2L, 2.4L, 3.4L, 3.5L, 3.6L, 3.8L, 3.9L, 4.6L, 6.0L **Transmissions:** All	**HO2S-11 (Bank 1 Sensor 1) Circuit High Input** DTC P0101, P0102, P0103, P0107, P0108, P0112, P0113, P0116, P0117, P0118, P0121, P0122, P0123, P0125, P0128, P0201, P0202, P0203, P0204, P0205, P0206, P0410, P0440, P0442, P0443, P0446, P0449 and P1441 not set, A/F ratio at 12.0-16.5:1, TP angle from 3-35%, Air Pump "off", and the PCM detected the HO2S signal was more than 975 mv for 45 seconds, or the HO2S signal was more than 200 mv while in Decel Fuel Cutoff mode. **Possible Causes:** • Fuel system is too rich (fuel pressure too high, fuel pressure regulator leaking, or one or more fuel injectors sticking/leaking) • HO2S element is silicon, water or fuel contaminated • HO2S signal circuit is shorted to system power (B+) • HO2S signal tracking (water intrusion) in the connector causing a short between the HO2S signal and heater power circuits • PCM has failed
DTC: P0132 **2T CCM, MIL: Yes** **Years:** 2005, 2006, 2007 **Models:** Sierra, Silverado **Engines:** 4.3L, 4.8L, 5.3L 6.0L, 6.2L, 8.1L **Transmissions:** All	**HO2S-11 (Bank 1 Sensor 1) Circuit High Input** DTC P0101-P0103, P0106-P0108, P0112, P0113, P0116-P0118, P0121-P0123, P0200, P0300, P0401, P0404, P0405, P0440, P0442, P0446, P0452, P0453, P1120, P1125, P1220, P1221, P1258, P1404, P1441, P1514-P1517 and P1518 not set, engine started, fuel level over 10%, Intrusive and Scan Tool Tests inactive, then with the Rich Test enabled, A/F ratio from 14.5-14.7:1, TP angle from 3.5-70% for 5 seconds, or for vehicles with TAC, with the TP indicated angle from 3-70%, the PCM detected the HO2S signal was more than 775 mv for 165 seconds or with Decel Fuel Cutoff active and the time since the test started over 1 second, the PCM detected the HO2S signal was more than 540 mv for 5 seconds. **Possible Causes:** • Fuel system is too rich (fuel pressure too high, fuel pressure regulator leaking, or one or more fuel injectors sticking/leaking) • HO2S element is silicon, water or fuel contaminated • HO2S signal tracking (water intrusion) in the connector causing a short between the HO2S signal and heater power circuits • PCM has failed

DTC	Trouble Code Title, Conditions & Possible Causes
DTC: P0133 **2T O2S, MIL: Yes** **Years:** 2005, 2006, 2007 **Models:** G6, GTO, LaCrosse, Malibu, Montana, Montana SV6, Relay, Rendezvous, SV6, Sky, Solstice, SRX, Terraza, Uplander **Engines:** 2.0L, 2.2L, 2.4L, 3.4L, 3.5L, 3.6L, 3.8L, 3.9L, 4.6L, 6.0L **Transmissions:** All	**HO2S-11 (Bank 1 Sensor 1) Slow Response** DTC P0101, P0102, P0103, P0107, P0108, P0112, P0113, P0116, P0117, P0118, P0121, P0122, P0123, P0125, P0128, P0201, P0202, P0203, P0204, P0205, P0206, P0410, P0440, P0442, P0443, P0446, P0449 and P1441 not set, engine started, engine speed from 1000-3000 RPM in closed loop, A/F ratio from 14.5-14.8, system voltage over 10.0v, ECT sensor more than 122°F, MAF sensor from 10-30 g/sec, gear selector not in Reverse or P/N, Air Pump "off", and the PCM detected the HO2S lean to rich average response time was more than 94 milliseconds, or the average rich to lean response time was more than 105 ms. **Possible Causes:** • Exhaust leak present in the exhaust manifold or exhaust pipes • Fuel system is too rich (fuel pressure too high, fuel pressure regulator leaking, or one or more fuel injectors sticking/leaking) • HO2S element is silicon, water or fuel contaminated or it failed • TP sensor element broken (can cause false acceleration event) • PCM has failed
DTC: P0133 **2T O2S, MIL: Yes** **Years:** 2005, 2006, 2007 **Models:** Sierra, Silverado **Engines:** 4.3L, 4.8L, 5.3L 6.0L, 6.2L, 8.1L **Transmissions:** All	**HO2S-11 (Bank 1 Sensor 1) Slow Response** DTC P0101-P0103, P0106-P0108, P0112-P0113, P0116-P0118, P0121-P0123, P0131-135, P0151-P0155, P0200, P0300, P0401, P0404-P0405, P0440-P0446, P0452-P0453, P1120, P1125, P1220-P1221, P1258, P1404, P1441, P1514 and P1518 not set, engine started, engine speed from 1200-3000 RPM for 2 minutes in closed loop, ECT sensor more than 149°F, Purge command over 1%, MAF sensor from 23-50 g/sec, TP angle over 5% or for models with TAC, TP angle more than 5% higher than the idle value, fuel level over 10%, Scan Tool and Intrusive tests All off, conditions met for 100 seconds, and the PCM detected the HO2S rich-to-lean or the lean-to-rich response time was more than a calibrated value. **Possible Causes:** • Exhaust leak present in the exhaust manifold or exhaust pipes • Fuel system is too rich (fuel pressure too high, fuel pressure regulator leaking, or one or more fuel injectors sticking/leaking) • HO2S element is silicon, water or fuel contaminated or it failed • TP sensor element broken (can cause false acceleration event) • PCM has failed
DTC: P0134 **2T O2S, MIL: Yes** **Years:** 2005, 2006, 2007 **Models:** G6, GTO, LaCrosse, Malibu, Montana, Montana SV6, Relay, Rendezvous, SV6, Sky, Solstice, SRX, Terraza, Uplander **Engines:** 2.0L, 2.2L, 2.4L, 3.4L, 3.5L, 3.6L, 3.8L, 3.9L, 4.6L, 6.0L **Transmissions:** All	**HO2S-11 (Bank 1 Sensor 1) Insufficient Activity** DTC P0101, P0102, P0103, P0106, P0107, P0108, P0112, P0113, P0116, P0117, P0118, P0121, P0122, P0123, P0125, P0128, P0131, P0132, P0135, P0151, P0152, P0201-P0208, P0300, P0410, P0410, P0418, P0419, P0440, P0442, P0443, P0446, P0449, P1133, P1415, P1416, or P1441 not set, engine started, engine runtime over 200 seconds, system voltage over 10.0v, ECT sensor more than 122°F, and the PCM detected the HO2S signal was fixed between 408-512 mv for over 29 seconds. **Possible Causes:** • HO2S heater is damaged or has failed • HO2S signal or ground circuit has a high resistance condition • HO2S signal circuit is open or shorted to system power (B+) • HO2S has failed (i.e., it is silicon, water or fuel contaminated) • PCM has failed
DTC: P0134 **2T O2S, MIL: Yes** **Years:** 2005, 2006, 2007 **Models:** Sierra, Silverado **Engines:** 4.3L, 4.8L, 5.3L 6.0L, 6.2L, 8.1L **Transmissions:** All	**HO2S-11 (Bank 1 Sensor 1) Insufficient Activity** DTC P0101-P0103, P0106-P0108, P0112, P0113, P0116-P0118, P0121-P0123, P0200, P0300, P0401, P0404-P0405, P0440, P0442, P0446, P0452, P0453, P1120, P1125, P1220, P1221, P1258, P1404, P1441, P1514, P1515, P1516, P1517 and P1518 not set, engine started, system voltage over 10.0v, Scan Tool and Intrusive tests "off", engine runtime over 409 seconds, and the PCM detected the HO2S signal remained 350-550 mv for 60 seconds. **Possible Causes:** • HO2S heater is damaged or has failed • HO2S signal or ground circuit has a high resistance condition • HO2S signal circuit is open or shorted to system power (B+) • HO2S has failed (i.e., it is silicon, water or fuel contaminated) • PCM has failed
DTC: P0135 **2T O2S HTR, MIL: Yes** **Years:** 2005, 2006, 2007 **Models:** G6, GTO, LaCrosse, Malibu, Montana, Montana SV6, Relay, Rendezvous, SV6, Sky, Solstice, SRX, Terraza, Uplander **Engines:** 2.0L, 2.2L, 2.4L, 3.4L, 3.5L, 3.6L, 3.8L, 3.9L, 4.6L, 6.0L **Transmissions:** All	**HO2S-11 (Bank 1 Sensor 1) Heater Circuit Malfunction** DTC P0101, P0102, P0103, P0107, P0108, P0112, P0113, P0116, P0117, P0118, P0121, P0122, P0123, P0125, P0128, P0201-P0206, P0410, P0440, P0442, P0443, P0446, P0449 and P1441 not set, engine runtime over 4 minutes, engine speed from 650-2500 RPM, ECT sensor more than 158°F, system voltage from 9-18.0v, MAF sensor from 4-26 g/sec, and the PCM detected the HO2S-11 heater current was less than 0.25 amps or more than 0.90 amps. **Possible Causes:** • HO2S heater ground circuit is open or it has high resistance • HO2S heater power circuit is open (test O2S fuse in fuse block) • HO2S heater element is damaged or it has failed • PCM has failed

DTC	Trouble Code Title, Conditions & Possible Causes
DTC: P0135 **2T O2S HTR, MIL: Yes** **Years:** 2005, 2006, 2007 **Models:** Sierra, Silverado **Engines:** 4.3L, 4.8L, 5.3L 6.0L, 6.2L, 8.1L **Transmissions:** All	**HO2S-11 (Bank 1 Sensor 1) Heater Circuit Malfunction** DTC P0101-P0103, P0106-P0108, P0112, P0113, P0116-P0118, P0121-P0123, P0131, P0132, P0134, P0137, P0138, P0140, P0151, P0152, P0154, P0157, P0158, P0160, P0200, P0300, P0401, P0404, P0405, P0440, P0442, P0446, P0452, P0453, P1120, P1125, P1220, P1221, P1258, P1404, P1441, P1514, P1515, P1516, P1517 and P1518 not set, engine started, ECT and IAT sensors less than 122°F and within 14.5°F at startup, HO2S signal from 425-475 mv right after startup, Intrusive and Scan Tool tests off, MAF sensor less than 25 g/sec, and the PCM detected the HO2S signal remained within 150 mv of startup HO2S signal for a predetermined amount of time based on the ECT and airflow inputs. **Possible Causes:** • HO2S heater ground circuit is open or has high resistance • HO2S heater power circuit is open (test O2A fuse in fuse block) • HO2S heater element is damaged or has failed • PCM has failed
DTC: P0137 **2T CCM, MIL: Yes** **Years:** 2005, 2006, 2007 **Models:** G6, GTO, LaCrosse, Malibu, Montana, Montana SV6, Relay, Rendezvous, Sky, Solstice, SRX, Terraza, Uplander, Vibe **Engines:** 1.8L, 2.0L, 2.2L, 2.4L, 3.4L, 3.5L, 3.6L, 3.9L, 4.6L, 6.0L **Transmissions:** All	**HO2S-12 (Bank 1 Sensor 2) Circuit Low Input** DTC P0101, P0102, P0103, P0107, P0108, P0112, P0113, P0116, P0117, P0118, P0121, P0122, P0123, P0125, P0128, P0201, P0202, P0203, P0204, P0205, P0206, P0410, P0440, P0442, P0443, P0446, P0449 and P1441 not set, A/F ratio at 13.0-16.5:1, TP angle from 3-40%, Air Pump "off", and the PCM detected the HO2S signal was less than 10 mv in closed loop, or with the P/E mode active, the HO2S signal was under 600 mv for 15 seconds. The HO2S is used for fuel control and post-catalyst monitoring. This sensor compares the oxygen content of the surrounding air with the oxygen content of the exhaust stream. At initial startup, the PCM operates in open loop mode, ignoring the HO2S signal when calculating the air/fuel ratio. The PCM supplies the HO2S with a reference (or bias) voltage of about 450 mv. The HO2S generates a voltage within a range of 0-1000 mv that fluctuates above and below the bias voltage once in closed loop. A high HO2S voltage indicates a rich fuel mixture. A low HO2S voltage indicates a lean mixture. Heating elements in the HO2S shorten the time required for the sensor to reach normal temperature, and an accurate voltage signal. **Possible Causes:** • Air leaks in the exhaust system, intake manifold, vacuum lines • Engine misfire condition present (look for P0300 series codes) • Fuel system too lean (possible low fuel pressure, water in fuel) • HO2S signal circuit is shorted to the sensor or chassis ground • HO2S is damaged (i.e., cracked) or air reference hole clogged • PCM has failed
DTC: P0137 **2T CCM, MIL: Yes** **Years:** 2005, 2006, 2007 **Models:** Sierra, Silverado **Engines:** 4.3L, 4.8L, 5.3L 6.0L, 6.2L, 8.1L **Transmissions:** All	**HO2S-12 (Bank 1 Sensor 2) Circuit Low Input** DTC P0101, P0102, P0103, P0106, P0107, P0108, P0112, P0113, P0116, P0117, P0118, P0120, P0121, P0122, P0123, P0169, P0178, P0179, P0200, P0220, P0300, P0442, P0446, P0452, P0453, P0455, P0496, P1125, P1258, P1514, P1515, P1516, P1518, P2108 and P2135 not set, engine started, engine running in closed loop, system voltage from 10-18v, Fuel Alcohol content less than 90%, fuel level over 10%, TP angle from 3-70% over the idle value, then during the Lean Test, the PCM detected the HO2S signal was less than 80 mv for 200 seconds or with engine runtime over 30 seconds during the Power Enrichment test, the PCM detected the HO2S signal was less than 490 mv for 10 seconds. **Possible Causes:** • Air leaks in the exhaust system, intake manifold, vacuum lines • Engine misfire condition present (look for P0300 series codes) • Fuel system too lean (possible low fuel pressure, water in fuel) • HO2S signal circuit is shorted to the sensor or chassis ground • HO2S is damaged (i.e., cracked) or air reference hole clogged • PCM has failed
DTC: P0138 **2T CCM, MIL: Yes** **Years:** 2005, 2006, 2007 **Models:** G6, GTO, LaCrosse, Malibu, Montana, Montana SV6, Relay, Rendezvous, Sky, Solstice, SRX, Terraza, Uplander, Vibe **Engines:** 1.8L, 2.0L, 2.2L, 2.4L, 3.4L, 3.5L, 3.6L, 3.9L, 4.6L, 6.0L **Transmissions:** All	**HO2S-12 (Bank 1 Sensor 2) Circuit High Input** DTC P0101-P0103, P0107, P0108, P0112, P0113, P0116-P0118, P0121-P0125, P0128, P0201-P0206, P0410, P0440, P0442, P0443, P0446, P0449 and P1441 not set, A/F ratio at 12.0-16.5:1, TP angle from 3-35%, Air Pump "off", and the PCM detected the HO2S signal was over 975 mv for 45 seconds or it was more than 200 mv during Decel Fuel Cutoff mode. **Possible Causes:** • Fuel system is too rich (fuel pressure too high, fuel pressure regulator leaking, or one or more fuel injectors sticking/leaking) • HO2S element is silicon, water or fuel contaminated • HO2S signal circuit is shorted to system power (B+) • HO2S signal tracking (water intrusion) in the connector causing a short between the HO2S signal and heater power circuits • PCM has failed

DTC	Trouble Code Title, Conditions & Possible Causes
DTC: P0138 **2T CCM, MIL: Yes** **Years:** 2005, 2006, 2007 **Models:** Sierra, Silverado **Engines:** 4.3L, 4.8L, 5.3L 6.0L, 6.2L, 8.1L **Transmissions:** All	**HO2S-12 (Bank 1 Sensor 2) Circuit High Input** DTC P0101-P0103, P0106-P0108, P0112, P0113, P0116-P0118, P0121-P0123, P0200, P0300, P0401, P0404, P0405, P0440, P0442, P0446, P0452, P0453, P1120, P1125, P1220, P1221, P1258, P1404, P1441, P1514-P1517 and P1518 not set, engine started, fuel level over 10%, Intrusive and Scan Tool Tests "off", Rich Test enabled, A/F ratio from 14.5-14.7:1, TP angle from 3.5-70% for 5 seconds, or for vehicles with TAC, with the TP indicated angle from 3-70%, the PCM detected the HO2S signal was more than 930 mv for 200 seconds or while in DFCO mode, the PCM detected the HO2S signal was above 480 mv for 5 seconds. **Possible Causes:** • Fuel system is too rich (fuel pressure too high, fuel pressure regulator leaking, or one or more fuel injectors sticking/leaking) • HO2S element is silicon, water or fuel contaminated • HO2S signal circuit is shorted to system power (B+) • HO2S signal tracking (water intrusion) in the connector causing a short between the HO2S signal and heater power circuits • PCM has failed
DTC: P0140 **2T O2S, MIL: Yes** **Years:** 2005, 2006, 2007 **Models:** G6, GTO, LaCrosse, Malibu, Montana, Montana SV6, Relay, Rendezvous, SV6, Sky, Solstice, SRX, Terraza, Uplander **Engines:** 2.0L, 2.2L, 2.4L, 3.4L, 3.5L, 3.6L, 3.8L, 3.9L, 4.6L, 6.0L **Transmissions:** All	**HO2S-12 (Bank 1 Sensor 2) Insufficient Activity** DTC P0101-P0103, P0106-P0108, P0112, P0113, P0116-P0118, P0121-P0123, P0125, P0128, P0131, P0132, P0135, P0151, P0152, P0201-P0208, P0300, P0410, P0410, P0418, P0419, P0440, P0442, P0443, P0446, P0449, P1133, P1415, P1416, or P1441 not set, engine runtime over 200 seconds, system voltage over 10.0v, ECT sensor over 122°F, and the PCM detected the HO2S signal was fixed from 412-499 mv for more than 29 seconds. **Possible Causes:** • Exhaust leak present in the exhaust manifold or exhaust pipes • HO2S signal or ground circuit has a high resistance condition • HO2S element is silicon, water or fuel contaminated • PCM has failed
DTC: P0140 **2T O2S, MIL: Yes** **Years:** 2005, 2006, 2007 **Models:** Sierra, Silverado **Engines:** 4.3L, 4.8L, 5.3L 6.0L, 6.2L, 8.1L **Transmissions:** All	**HO2S-12 (Bank 1 Sensor 2) Insufficient Activity** DTC P0101-P0103, P0106-P0108, P0112, P0113, P0116-P0118, P0121-P0123, P0200, P0300, P0401, P0404, P0405, P0440, P0442, P0446, P0452, P0453, P1120, P1125, P1220, P1221, P1258, P1404, P1441, P1514-P1517 and P1518 not set, engine runtime over 409 seconds, system voltage over 10.0v, Intrusive and Scan Tool tests "off", TP angle over 5%, and the PCM detected the HO2S signal was fixed from 410-490 mv for 150 seconds. **Possible Causes:** • Exhaust leak present in the exhaust manifold or exhaust pipes • HO2S signal or ground circuit has a high resistance condition • HO2S element is silicon, water or fuel contaminated • PCM has failed
DTC: P0141 **2T O2S HTR, MIL: Yes** **Years:** 2005, 2006, 2007 **Models:** G6, GTO, LaCrosse, Malibu, Montana, Montana SV6, Relay, Rendezvous, SV6, Sky, Solstice, SRX, Terraza, Uplander **Engines:** 2.0L, 2.2L, 2.4L, 3.4L, 3.5L, 3.6L, 3.8L, 3.9L, 4.6L, 6.0L **Transmissions:** All	**HO2S-12 (Bank 1 Sensor 2) Heater Circuit Malfunction** DTC P0101, P0102, P0103, P0107, P0108, P0112, P0113, P0116, P0117, P0118, P0121, P0122, P0123, P0125, P0128, P0201-P0206, P0410, P0440, P0442, P0443, P0446, P0449, P1441 not set, ECT sensor and IAT sensor more than 95°F at engine startup, engine runtime over 200 seconds, system voltage from 9-18.0v, and the PCM detected the HO2S signal was fixed within 74 mv of the bias voltage (450 mv) for 2 minutes (depends on ECT at startup). **Possible Causes:** • HO2S assembly connector is damaged, open or shorted • HO2S heater ground circuit is open or it has high resistance • HO2S heater power circuit is open (test O2S fuse in fuse block) • HO2S heater element is damaged or has failed • PCM has failed
DTC: P0141 **2T O2S HTR, MIL: Yes** **Years:** 2005, 2006, 2007 **Models:** Sierra, Silverado **Engines:** 4.3L, 4.8L, 5.3L 6.0L, 6.2L, 8.1L **Transmissions:** All	**HO2S-12 (Bank 1 Sensor 2) Heater Circuit Malfunction** DTC P0101-P0103, P0106-P0108, P0112, P0113, P0116-P0118, P0121-P0123, P0131, P0132, P0134, P0137, P0138, P0140, P0200, P0300, P0401, P0404, P0405, P0440, P0442, P0446, P0452, P0453, P1120, P1125, P1220, P1221, P1258, P1404, P1441, P1514, P1515, P1516, P1517 and P1518 not set, ECT and IAT sensors less than 122°F and with 14.5°F at startup, engine started, HO2S signal from 425-475 mv right after startup, Intrusive and Scan Tool tests "off", MAF sensor less than 25 g/sec, and the PCM detected the HO2S signal was fixed within 150 mv of startup HO2S signal for too long (depends on ECT/MAF at startup). **Possible Causes:** • HO2S heater ground circuit is open or has high resistance • HO2S heater power circuit is open (test O2S fuse in fuse block) • HO2S heater element is damaged or has failed • PCM has failed • TSB 00-06-04-006 contains a repair procedure for this code

DTC	Trouble Code Title, Conditions & Possible Causes
DTC: P0148 **2T CCM, MIL: Yes** **Years:** 2005, 2006, 2007 **Models:** Sierra, Silverado **Engines:** 6.0L CNG **Transmissions:** All	**A/F Enable Circuit Malfunction** Key on or engine running, system voltage from 6-18v, and the PCM detected the Actual and Commanded state of the AF Fuel Enable circuit did not match for over two seconds during the test. The PCM opens the AF enable circuit when operating on CNG. When the AF enable circuit is open, the fuel injector control module (FICM) operates the CNG injectors based upon PCM fuel injector control pulse width signals. The PCM grounds the AF enable circuit when gasoline operation is desired. The switchover from one fuel to the other is always performed in an orderly, sequential manner. Since some injectors are in the middle of injecting the previous fuel, the FICM will wait until that cylinders fuel delivery is complete and then will switch over in sequential firing order to complete the operation. **Possible Causes:** • AF enable circuit is open, shorted to ground • AF enable circuit is shorted to system power (B+) • FICM connector is damaged, open or shorted • FICM assembly had failed, or the PCM has failed
DTC: P0151 **2T CCM, MIL: Yes** **Years:** 2005, 2006, 2007 **Models:** G6, SRX **Engines:** 2.4L, 3.5L, 3.6L, 3.9L, 3.9L **Transmissions:** All	**HO2S-21 (Bank 2 Sensor 1) Circuit Low Input** DTCs P0101, P0102, P0103, P0107, P0108, P0112, P0113, P0116, P0117, P0118, P0120, P0125, P0128, P0201, P0202, P0203, P0204, P0205, P0206, P0220, P0442, P0443, P0446, P0449, P0452, P0453, P0454, P0455, P0464, P0496, P2135, P2A03 are not set. DTCs P0401, P0430, and P2A03 are not commanding fuel. The system voltage is between 9-18 volts. The scan tool special functions are not active. The Air Fuel Ratio parameter is between 12:1-16.5:1. The TP sensor parameter is between 4-40 percent. The PCM detects that the HO2S 1 signal voltage is less than 78 mV for more than 51 seconds, or PCM detects that the HO2S 1 signal voltage is less than 598 mV during PE mode for more than 15 seconds. **Possible Causes:** • Air leaks in the exhaust system, intake manifold, vacuum lines • Engine misfire condition present (look for P0300 series codes) • Fuel system too lean (possible low fuel pressure, water in fuel) • HO2S signal circuit is shorted to the sensor or chassis ground • HO2S is damaged (i.e., cracked) or air reference hole clogged • PCM has failed
DTC: P0151 **2T CCM, MIL: Yes** **Years:** 2005, 2006, 2007 **Models:** Sierra, Silverado **Engines:** 4.3L, 4.8L, 5.3L 6.0L, 6.2L, 8.1L **Transmissions:** All	**HO2S-21 (Bank 2 Sensor 1) Circuit Low Input** DTC P0101-P0103, P0106-P0108, P0112, P0113, P0116-P0118, P0121-P0123, P0200, P0300, P0401, P0404, P0405, P0440, P0442, P0446, P0452, P0453, P1120, P1125, P1220, P1221, P1258, P1404, P1441, P1514, P1515, P1516, P1517 and P1518 not set, engine started, engine running in closed loop, fuel level over 10%, system voltage over 10v, TP angle from 8-50% or on models with TAC, the APP sensor indicated angle from 3-70%, MAP sensor more than 25 kPa, Intrusive and Scan Tool Tests "off", then with the Lean Test enabled, the PCM detected the HO2S signal was less than 20 mv for 50 seconds or during the P/E Mode test, the PCM detected the HO2S signal was less than 360 mv for 10 seconds. **Possible Causes:** • Air leaks in the exhaust system, intake manifold, vacuum lines • Engine misfire condition present (look for P0300 series codes) • Fuel system too lean (possible low fuel pressure, water in fuel) • HO2S signal circuit is shorted to the sensor or chassis ground • HO2S is damaged (i.e., cracked) or air reference hole clogged • PCM has failed
DTC: P0152 **2T CCM, MIL: Yes** **Years:** 2005, 2006, 2007 **Models:** G6, SRX **Engines:** 2.4L, 3.5L, 3.6L, 3.9L, 3.9L **Transmissions:** All	**HO2S-21 (Bank 2 Sensor 1) Circuit High Input** DTCs P0101, P0102, P0103, P0107, P0108, P0112, P0113, P0116, P0117, P0118, P0120, P0125, P0128, P0201, P0202, P0203, P0204, P0205, P0206, P0220, P0442, P0443, P0446, P0449, P0451, P0452, P0453, P0454, P0455, P0464, P0496, P2153 are not set. DTC P0401, P0420, and P2A04 are not commanding fuel. The system voltage is between 9-18 volts. The scan tool special functions are not active. The Air Fuel Ratio parameter is between 12:1-16.5:1. The TP sensor parameter is between 4-40 percent. The PCM detects that the HO2S 1 signal voltage is more than 889 mV for more than 75 seconds. **Possible Causes:** • Fuel system is too rich (fuel pressure too high, fuel pressure regulator leaking, or one or more fuel injectors sticking/leaking) • HO2S element is silicon, water or fuel contaminated • HO2S signal tracking in the connector causing a short to power • PCM has failed

DTC	Trouble Code Title, Conditions & Possible Causes
DTC: P0152 **2T CCM, MIL: Yes** **Years:** 2005, 2006, 2007 **Models:** Sierra, Silverado **Engines:** 4.3L, 4.8L, 5.3L 6.0L, 6.2L, 8.1L **Transmissions:** All	**HO2S-21 (Bank 2 Sensor 1) Circuit High Input** DTC P0101-P0103, P0106-P0108, P0112, P0113, P0116-P0118, P0121-P0123, P0200, P0300, P0401, P0404, P0405, P0440, P0442, P0446, P0452, P0453, P1120, P1125, P1220, P1221, P1258, P1404, P1441, P1514-P1517 and P1518 not set, engine started, fuel level over 10%, Intrusive Tests All off, then with the Rich Test enabled, A/F ratio from 14.5-14.7:1, TP angle from 3.5-70% for 5 seconds (TP indicated angle at 3-70% on vehicles with TAC), the PCM detected the HO2S signal was over 775 mv for 165 seconds or it was more than 540 mv with DFCO enabled for over 5 seconds. **Possible Causes:** • Fuel system is too rich (fuel pressure too high, fuel pressure regulator leaking, or one or more fuel injectors sticking/leaking) • HO2S element is silicon, water or fuel contaminated • HO2S signal tracking in the connector causing a short to power • PCM has failed
DTC: P0153 **2T CCM, MIL: Yes** **Years:** 2005, 2006, 2007 **Models:** G6, SRX **Engines:** 2.4L, 3.5L, 3.6L, 3.9L, 3.9L **Transmissions:** All	**HO2S-21 (Bank 2 Sensor 1) Slow Response** DTCs P0036, P0054, P0101, P0102, P0103, P0107, P0108, P0112, P0113, P0116, P0117, P0118, P0120, P0125, P0128, P0151, P0152, P0154, P0155, P0201, P0202, P0203, P0204, P0205, P0206, P0220, P0300, P0442, P0443, P0446, P0449, P0451, P0452, P0453, P0454, P0455, P0464, P0496, P2153 are not set. DTCs P0401, P0430 and P2A03 are not commanding fuel. The system voltage is between 9-18 volts. The scan tool special functions are not active. The HO2S 1 heater parameter is ON. The Loop Status parameter is closed. The MAF sensor parameter is between 15-30 g/s. The TP Indicated Angle Parameter is more than 2 percent. The evaporative emission (EVAP) system is purging. The PCM detects that the HO2S 1 rich-to-lean and lean-to-rich transition time takes longer than a calibrated value. **Possible Causes:** • Exhaust leak present in the exhaust manifold or exhaust pipes • Fuel system rich (high fuel pressure, fuel pressure regulator leaking, or leaking injectors)HO2S element is silicon, water or fuel contaminated or it failed • TP sensor element broken (can cause false acceleration event) • PCM has failed
DTC: P0153 **2T O2S, MIL: Yes** **Years:** 2005, 2006, 2007 **Models:** Sierra, Silverado **Engines:** 4.3L, 4.8L, 5.3L 6.0L, 6.2L, 8.1L **Transmissions:** All	**HO2S-21 (Bank 2 Sensor 1) Slow Response** DTC P0101-P0103, P0106-P0108, P0112-P0113, P0116-P0118, P0121-P0123, P0131-135, P0151-P0155, P0200, P0300, P0401, P0404-P0405, P0440-P0446, P0452-P0453, P1120, P1125, P1220-P1221, P1258, P1404, P1441, P1514 and P1518 not set, engine started, engine speed from 1200-3000 RPM for 2 minutes in closed loop, ECT sensor more than 149°F, Purge command over 1%, MAF sensor from 23-50 g/sec, TP angle over 5% or for models with TAC, TP angle more than 5% higher than the idle value, fuel level over 10%, Scan Tool and Intrusive tests "off", conditions met for 100 seconds, and the PCM detected the HO2S rich-to-lean or the lean-to-rich response time was more than a calibrated value. **Possible Causes:** • Exhaust leak present in the exhaust manifold or exhaust pipes • Fuel system rich (high fuel pressure, fuel pressure regulator leaking, or leaking injectors)HO2S element is silicon, water or fuel contaminated or it failed • TP sensor element broken (can cause false acceleration event) • PCM has failed
DTC: P0154 **2T CCM, MIL: Yes** **Years:** 2005, 2006, 2007 **Models:** G6, SRX **Engines:** 2.4L, 3.5L, 3.6L, 3.9L, 3.9L **Transmissions:** All	**HO2S-21 (Bank 2 Sensor 1) Insufficient Activity** DTCs P0101, P0102, P0103, P0107, P0108, P0112, P0113, P0116, P0117, P0118, P0120, P0125, P0128, P0201, P0202, P0203, P0204, P0205, P0206, P0220, P0442, P0443, P0446, P0449, P0451, P0452, P0453, P0454, P0455, P0464, P0496, P2135 are not set. DTCs P0401, P0420, and P2A04 are not commanding fuel. The system voltage is between 9-18 volts. The scan tool special functions are not active. The HO2S 1 Heater parameter is ON. The PCM detects that the HO2S 1 signal voltage is between 382-525 mV for more than 30 seconds. **Possible Causes:** • Exhaust leak present in the exhaust manifold or exhaust pipes • HO2S signal or ground circuit has a high resistance condition • HO2S element is silicon, water or fuel contaminated
DTC: P0155 **2T CCM, MIL: Yes** **Years:** 2005, 2006, 2007 **Models:** G6, SRX **Engines:** 2.4L, 3.5L, 3.6L, 3.9L, 3.9L **Transmissions:** All	**HO2S-21 (Bank 2 Sensor 1) Heater Performance** DTCs P0050, P0059, P0101, P0102, P0103, P0107, P0108, P0112, P0113, P0116, P0117, P0118, P0120, P0125, P0128, P0201, P0202, P0203, P0204, P0205, P0206, P0220, P0442, P0443, P0446, P0449, P0451, P0452, P0453, P0454, P0455, P0464, P0496, P2135 are not set. DTCs P0401, P0420, and P2A04 are not commanding fuel. The system voltage is between 9-18 volts. The scan tool special functions are not active. The Engine Run Time parameter is more than 100 seconds. ECT Sensor parameter is at least 65°C (149°F). MAF sensor parameter is between 4-30 g/s. Engine Speed parameter is between 600-3,000 RPM. HO2S heater current is less than 0.31 amp or more than 1.43 amps for at least 17 out of 20 samples. Five tests during each trip with a 30 second delay between each test. **Possible Causes:** • Exhaust leak present in the exhaust manifold or exhaust pipes • HO2S signal or ground circuit has a high resistance condition • HO2S element is silicon, water or fuel contaminated

DTC	Trouble Code Title, Conditions & Possible Causes
DTC: P0155 **2T O2S HTR, MIL: Yes** **Years:** 2005, 2006, 2007 **Models:** Sierra, Silverado **Engines:** 4.3L, 4.8L, 5.3L 6.0L, 6.2L, 8.1L **Transmissions:** All	**HO2S-21 (Bank 2 Sensor 1) Heater Circuit Malfunction** DTC P0101-P0103, P0106-P0108, P0112, P0113, P0116-P0118, P0121-P0123, P0131, P0132, P0134, P0137, P0138, P0140, P0151, P0152, P0154, P0157, P0158, P0160, P0200, P0300, P0401, P0404, P0405, P0440, P0442, P0446, P0452, P0453, P1120, P1125, P1220, P1221, P1258, P1404, P1441, P1514, P1515, P1516, P1517 and P1518 not set, ECT and IAT sensors less than 122°F and with 14.5°F at startup, engine started, engine running in closed loop right after startup, Intrusive and Scan Tool tests "off", MAF sensor less than 25 g/sec, and the PCM detected the HO2S signal remained within 150 mv of startup HO2S signal for a predetermined amount of time based on ECT and airflow signals. **Possible Causes:** • HO2S heater ground circuit is open or has high resistance • HO2S heater power circuit is open (test O2S fuse in fuse block) • HO2S heater element is damaged or has failed • PCM has failed
DTC: P0155 **2T O2S HTR, MIL: Yes** **Years:** 2005, 2006, 2007 **Models:** Sierra, Silverado **Engines:** 4.3L, 4.8L, 5.3L 6.0L, 6.2L, 8.1L **Transmissions:** All	**HO2S-21 (Bank 2 Sensor 1) Heater Circuit Malfunction** DTC P0101-P0103, P0106-P0108, P0112, P0113, P0116-P0118, P0120, P0121-P0123, P0169, P0178, P0179, P0200, P0220, P0300, P0442, P0446, P0452, P0453, P0455, P0496, P1125, P1258, P1514, P1515, P1516, P1518, P2108 and P2135 not set, engine speed from 500-3000 RPM for 120 seconds, system voltage at 10-18v, ECT sensor over 122°F, MAF sensor at 3-40 g/sec, Fuel Alcohol content below 90%, and the PCM detected the HO2S heater current was below 0.25 amps or over 3.125 amps (more than 1.375 amps on 4.8L). **Possible Causes:** • HO2S heater low control circuit is open or shorted to ground • HO2S heater circuit is open or it is shorted to ground • HO2S heater power circuit is open (test O2A fuse in fuse block) • HO2S heater element is damaged or has failed • PCM has failed
DTC: P0157 **2T CCM, MIL: Yes** **Years:** 2005, 2006, 2007 **Models:** G6, SRX **Engines:** 2.4L, 3.5L, 3.6L, 3.9L, 3.9L **Transmissions:** All	**HO2S-22 (Bank 2 Sensor 2) Circuit Low Input** DTCs P0101, P0102, P0103, P0107, P0108, P0112, P0113, P0116, P0117, P0118, P0120, P0125, P0128, P0201, P0202, P0203, P0204, P0205, P0206, P0220, P0442, P0443, P0446, P0449, P0452, P0453, P0454, P0455, P0464, P0496, P2135, P2A03 are not set. DTCs P0401, P0430, and P2A03 are not commanding fuel. The system voltage is between 9-18 volts. The scan tool special functions are not active. The Air Fuel Ratio parameter is between 12:1-16.5:1. The TP sensor parameter is between 4-40 percent. The PCM detects that the HO2S 1 signal voltage is less than 78 mV for more than 51 seconds, or PCM detects that the HO2S 1 signal voltage is less than 598 mV during PE mode for more than 15 seconds. **Possible Causes:** • Air leaks in the exhaust system, intake manifold, vacuum lines • Engine misfire condition present (look for P0300 series codes) • Fuel system too lean (possible low fuel pressure, water in fuel) • HO2S signal circuit is shorted to the sensor or chassis ground • HO2S is damaged (i.e., cracked) or air reference hole clogged • PCM has failed
DTC: P0157 **2T CCM, MIL: Yes** **Years:** 2005, 2006, 2007 **Models:** Sierra, Silverado **Engines:** 4.3L, 4.8L, 5.3L 6.0L, 6.2L, 8.1L **Transmissions:** All	**HO2S-22 (Bank 2 Sensor 2) Circuit Low Input** DTC P0101-P0103, P0106-P0108, P0112, P0113, P0116-P0118, P0120, P0121-P0123, P0169, P0178, P0179, P0200, P0220, P0300, P0442, P0446, P0452-P0496, P1125, P1258, P1514, P1515, P1516, P1518, P2108 and P2135 not set, engine started, engine running in closed loop, system voltage from 10-18v, Fuel Alcohol content less than 90%, fuel level over 10%, TP angle from 3-70% over the idle value, Lean Test enabled, the PCM detected the HO2S signal was below 80 mv for 200 seconds or with engine runtime over 30 seconds, and during the P/E test, the PCM detected the HO2S signal was below 490 mv for 10 seconds. **Possible Causes:** • Air leaks in the exhaust system, intake manifold, vacuum lines • Engine misfire condition present (look for P0300 series codes) • Fuel system too lean (possible low fuel pressure, water in fuel) • HO2S signal circuit is shorted to the sensor or chassis ground • HO2S is damaged (i.e., cracked) or air reference hole clogged • PCM has failed

DTC	Trouble Code Title, Conditions & Possible Causes
DTC: P0158 **2T CCM, MIL: Yes** **Years:** 2005, 2006, 2007 **Models:** G6, SRX **Engines:** 2.4L, 3.5L, 3.6L, 3.9L, 3.9L **Transmissions:** All	**HO2S-22 (Bank 2 Sensor 2) Circuit High Input** DTCs P0101, P0102, P0103, P0107, P0108, P0112, P0113, P0116, P0117, P0118, P0120, P0125, P0128, P0201, P0202, P0203, P0204, P0205, P0206, P0220, P0442, P0443, P0446, P0449, P0451, P0452, P0453, P0454, P0455, P0464, P0496, P2153 are not set. DTC P0401, P0420, and P2A04 are not commanding fuel. The system voltage is between 9-18 volts. The scan tool special functions are not active. The Air Fuel Ratio parameter is between 12:1-16.5:1. The TP sensor parameter is between 4-40 percent. The PCM detects that the HO2S 1 signal voltage is more than 889 mV for more than 75 seconds. **Possible Causes:** • Fuel system is too rich (fuel pressure too high, fuel pressure regulator leaking, or one or more fuel injectors sticking/leaking) • HO2S element is silicon, water or fuel contaminated • HO2S signal tracking in the connector causing a short to power • PCM has failed
DTC: P0158 **2T CCM, MIL: Yes** **Years:** 2005, 2006, 2007 **Models:** Sierra, Silverado **Engines:** 4.3L, 4.8L, 5.3L 6.0L, 6.2L, 8.1L **Transmissions:** All	**HO2S-22 (Bank 2 Sensor 2) Circuit High Input** DTC P0101, P0102, P0103, P0106, P0107, P0108, P0112, P0113, P0116, P0117, P0118, P0120, P0121, P0122, P0123, P0169, P0178, P0179, P0200, P0220, P0300, P0442, P0446, P0452, P0453, P0455, P0496, P1125, P1258, P1514, P1515, P1516, P1518, P2108 and P2135 not set, engine started, engine running in closed loop, system voltage from 10-18v, Fuel Alcohol content less than 90%, fuel level over 10%, TP angle from 3-70% more than the idle value, then during the Rich Test, the PCM detected the HO2S signal was more than 950 mv for 200 seconds or with engine runtime over 30 seconds, and during the Decel Fuel Cutoff test, the PCM detected the HO2S signal was less than 250 mv for 5 seconds. **Possible Causes:** • Fuel system rich (high fuel pressure, fuel pressure regulator leaking, or injector sticking) • HO2S element is silicon, water or fuel contaminated • HO2S signal tracking (water intrusion) in the connector causing a short between the HO2S signal and heater power circuits • PCM has failed
DTC: P0158 **2T CCM, MIL: Yes** **Years:** 2005, 2006, 2007 **Models:** G6, SRX **Engines:** 2.4L, 3.5L, 3.6L, 3.9L, 3.9L **Transmissions:** All	**HO2S-22 (Bank 2 Sensor 2) Insufficient Activity** DTCs P0101, P0102, P0103, P0107, P0108, P0112, P0113, P0116, P0117, P0118, P0120, P0125, P0128, P0201, P0202, P0203, P0204, P0205, P0206, P0220, P0442, P0443, P0446, P0449, P0451, P0452, P0453, P0454, P0455, P0464, P0496, P2135 are not set. DTCs P0401, P0420, and P2A04 are not commanding fuel. The system voltage is between 9-18 volts. The scan tool special functions are not active. The HO2S 1 Heater parameter is ON. The PCM detects that the HO2S 1 signal voltage is between 382-525 mV for more than 30 seconds. **Possible Causes:** • Exhaust leak present in the exhaust manifold or exhaust pipes • HO2S signal or ground circuit has a high resistance condition • HO2S element is silicon, water or fuel contaminated
DTC: P0160 **2T O2S, MIL: Yes** **Years:** 2005, 2006, 2007 **Models:** Sierra, Silverado **Engines:** 4.3L, 4.8L, 5.3L 6.0L, 6.2L, 8.1L **Transmissions:** All	**HO2S-22 (Bank 2 Sensor 2) Insufficient Activity** DTC P0101, P0102, P0103, P0106, P0107, P0108, P0112, P0113, P0116, P0117, P0118, P0120, P0121, P0122, P0123, P0169, P0178, P0179, P0200, P0220, P0300, P0442, P0446, P0452, P0453, P0455, P0496, P1125, P1258, P1514, P1515, P1516, P1518, P2108 and P2135 not set, engine runtime over 300 seconds, system voltage from 10-18v, Fuel Alcohol content less than 90%, then after the TP indicated angle changed more than 5% within one seconds six times on models with a TAC system, the PCM detected the HO2S signal remained between 410-490 mv for 150 seconds. **Possible Causes:** • HO2S heater is damaged or it has failed • HO2S signal or ground circuit has a high resistance condition • HO2S has failed (i.e., it is silicon, water or fuel contaminated) • PCM has failed
DTC: P0161 **2T CCM, MIL: Yes** **Years:** 2005, 2006, 2007 **Models:** G6, SRX **Engines:** 2.4L, 3.5L, 3.6L, 3.9L, 3.9L **Transmissions:** All	**HO2S-22 (Bank 2 Sensor 2) Heater Performance** DTCs P0050, P0059, P0101, P0102, P0103, P0107, P0108, P0112, P0113, P0116, P0117, P0118, P0120, P0125, P0128, P0201, P0202, P0203, P0204, P0205, P0206, P0220, P0442, P0443, P0446, P0449, P0451, P0452, P0453, P0454, P0455, P0464, P0496, P2135 are not set. DTCs P0401, P0420, and P2A04 are not commanding fuel. The system voltage is between 9-18 volts. The scan tool special functions are not active. The Engine Run Time parameter is more than 100 seconds. ECT Sensor parameter is at least 65°C (149°F). MAF sensor parameter is between 4-30 g/s. Engine Speed parameter is between 600-3,000 RPM. HO2S heater current is less than 0.31 amp or more than 1.43 amps for at least 17 out of 20 samples. Five tests during each trip with a 30 second delay between each test. **Possible Causes:** • Exhaust leak present in the exhaust manifold or exhaust pipes • HO2S signal or ground circuit has a high resistance condition • HO2S element is silicon, water or fuel contaminated

DTC	Trouble Code Title, Conditions & Possible Causes
DTC: P0161 **2T O2S HTR, MIL: Yes** **Years:** 2005, 2006, 2007 **Models:** Sierra, Silverado **Engines:** 4.3L, 4.8L, 5.3L 6.0L, 6.2L, 8.1L **Transmissions:** All	**HO2S-22 (Bank 2 Sensor 2) Heater Circuit Malfunction** DTC P0101, P0102, P0103, P0106, P0107, P0108, P0112, P0113, P0116, P0117, P0118, P0120, P0121, P0122, P0123, P0169, P0178, P0179, P0200, P0220, P0300, P0442, P0446, P0452, P0453, P0455, P0496, P1125, P1258, P1514, P1515, P1516, P1518, P2108 and P2135 not set, engine runtime 2 minutes, engine speed from 500-3000 RPM, system voltage from 10-18v, ECT sensor more than 122°F, MAF sensor from 3-40 g/sec, Fuel Alcohol content less than 90%, and the PCM detected the HO2S heater current was less than 0.25 amps, or over 3.125 amps (over 1.375 amps on 4.8L). **Possible Causes:** • HO2S heater low control circuit is open or shorted to ground • HO2S heater circuit is open or it is shorted to ground • HO2S heater power circuit is open (test O2A fuse in fuse block) • HO2S heater element is damaged or has failed • PCM has failed
DTC: P0168 **1T CCM, MIL: No** **Years:** 2005, 2006, 2007 **Models:** Sierra, Silverado **Engines:** 6.6L Diesel **Transmissions:** All	**Fuel Temperature Sensor Signal Range/Performance** Key on or engine running; and the PCM detected the Fuel Temperature sensor was under 0.10v (Scan Tool reads over 252°F). **Possible Causes:** • Inspect fuel cooler in front of fuel tank for debris restricting the airflow or damage to the cooling fins, and fuel lines for damage. • Fuel temperature sensor connector is damaged or shorted • Fuel temperature sensor signal circuit is shorted to ground • Fuel temperature sensor is damaged or it has failed • ECM has failed
DTC: P0171 **2T FUEL, MIL: Yes** **Years:** 2005, 2006, 2007 **Models:** G6, GTO, LaCrosse, Malibu, Montana, Montana SV6, Relay, Rendezvous, Sky, Solstice, SRX, Terraza, Uplander, Vibe **Engines:** 1.8L, 2.0L, 2.2L, 2.4L, 3.4L, 3.5L, 3.6L, 3.9L, 4.6L 6.0L **Transmissions:** All	**Fuel Trim System Lean (Bank 1)** DTC P0101, P0103, P0103, P0107, P0108, P0121, P0122, P0123, P0130-P0141, P0201-P0206, P0300, P0401-P0405, P0410, P0440-P0446, P0506, P0507, P1404 and P1441 not set, engine speed from 550-4000 RPM, ECT sensor from 68-230°F, IAT sensor from 64-158°F, MAF sensor at 2.8-150 gm/s, BARO sensor over 70 kPa, MAP sensor at 15-105 kPa, VSS under 82 MPH, fuel level over 10%, and the PCM detected the Short Term fuel trim was more than 20% for 6 seconds. **Possible Causes:** • Air leaks in intake manifold, exhaust pipes or exhaust manifold • Fuel control sensor is out of calibration (ECT, IAT or MAF) • Fuel component fault (fuel filter, fuel injector, low fuel pressure) • HO2S element is contaminated, deteriorated or has failed
DTC: P0171 **2T FUEL, MIL: Yes** **Years:** 2005, 2006, 2007 **Models:** Sierra, Silverado **Engines:** 4.3L, 4.8L, 5.3L 6.0L, 6.2L, 8.1L **Transmissions:** All	**Fuel Trim System Lean (Bank 1)** DTC P0101, P0102, P0103, P0108, P0135, P0137, P0141, P0200, P0300, P0410, P0420, P0430, P0440, P0442, P0443, P0446, P0449, P0506, P0507 and P1441 not set, engine started, vehicle driven at less than 85 MPH at 400-3000 RPM, BARO sensor more than 74 kPa (10.7 psi), ECT sensor from 167-239°F, IAT sensor from 4-194°F, MAF sensor from 5-90 gm/s, MAP sensor from 26-90 kPa (3.7-13 psi), TP angle less than 90%, fuel level over 10%, and the PCM detected the Long Term fuel trim value was more than +23% for 6 seconds (i.e., a lean A/F mixture existed). **Possible Causes:** • Air leaks in intake manifold, exhaust pipes or exhaust manifold • Fuel control sensor is out of calibration (ECT, IAT or MAF) • Low fuel pressure (fuel filter clogged, pressure regulator failure) • One or more injectors restricted or pressure regulator has failed • HO2S element is contaminated, deteriorated or has failed • Vacuum hose is disconnected, broken, leaking or loose
DTC: P0171 **2T FUEL, MIL: Yes** **Years:** 2005, 2006, 2007 **Models:** Sierra, Silverado **Engines:** 6.0L CNG **Transmissions:** All	**Fuel Trim System Lean (Bank 1)** DTC P0101, P0102, P0103, P0106, P0107, P0108, P0112, P0113, P0116-P0118, P0121-P0123, P0125, P0200, P0300, P0327, P0332, P0335, P0336, P0351-P0358, P0401, P0402, P0403, P0443, P0446, P0449, P0496, P0502, P0503, P1020, or P1258 not set, engine started, ECT sensor from 167-239°F, IAT sensor from 4-194°F, engine speed 400-3000 RPM, BARO sensor over 74 kPa, MAF sensor from 5-90 gm/s, TP angle under 90%, VSS less than 85 MPH, and the PCM detected the Long Term fuel trim value was over 28% for 6 seconds (indicating a lean A/F mixture was present). **Possible Causes:** • Air leaks in intake manifold, exhaust pipes or exhaust manifold • Fuel control sensor is out of calibration (ECT, IAT or MAF) • Low fuel pressure (fuel filter clogged, pressure regulator failure) • One or more injectors restricted or pressure regulator has failed • HO2S element is contaminated, deteriorated or has failed • Vacuum hose is disconnected, broken, leaking or loose

DTC	Trouble Code Title, Conditions & Possible Causes
DTC: P0172 **2T FUEL, MIL: Yes** **Years:** 2005, 2006, 2007 **Models:** G6, GTO, LaCrosse, Malibu, Montana, Montana SV6, Relay, Rendezvous, Sky, Solstice, SRX, Terraza, Uplander, Vibe **Engines:** 1.8L, 2.0L, 2.2L, 2.4L, 3.4L, 3.5L, 3.6L, 3.9L, 4.6L, 6.0L **Transmissions:** All	**Fuel Trim System Rich (Bank 1)** DTC P0101-P0103, P0107, P0108, P0121- P0123, P0130-P0135, P0137, P0138, P0140, P0141, P0201-P0206, P0300, P0401-P0405, P0410, P0440-P0446, P0506, P0507, P1404 or P1441 not set, engine started, vehicle driven at less than 82 MPH at 550-4000 RPM, BARO sensor more than 70 kPa, ECT sensor from 68-230°F, IAT sensor from 64-158°F, MAF sensor from 2.8-150 gm/s, MAP sensor from 15-105 kPa, fuel level over 10%, and the PCM detected the Long Term fuel trim value was below −13% for 40 seconds. During open loop, the PCM determines fuel delivery based on sensor signals, without the oxygen sensor input. During closed loop, the PCM adds oxygen sensor inputs to calculate Short and Long term fuel trim fuel delivery adjustments. If the oxygen sensors indicate a lean condition, the fuel trim values will be above 0 percent. If the oxygen sensors indicate a rich condition, the fuel trim values will be below 0 percent. Short Term fuel trim values change rapidly in response to HO2S signals. Long Term fuel trim makes its adjustments to maintain an A/F ratio of 14.7:1. **Possible Causes:** • Base engine "mechanical" fault affecting one or more cylinders • Excess fuel vapors in crankcase (the oil needs to be changed) • EVAP system component has failed or canister fuel saturated • Fuel control sensor is out of calibration (i.e., ECT, IAT or MAF) • Fuel delivery system supplying too much fuel during cruise or idle periods (e.g., faulty fuel pump, or faulty pressure regulator) • Fuel injector(s) is leaking or stuck partially open (one or more) • HO2S is contaminated, deteriorated or it has failed
DTC: P0172 **2T FUEL, MIL: Yes** **Years:** 2005, 2006, 2007 **Models:** Sierra, Silverado **Engines:** 4.3L, 4.8L, 5.3L 6.0L, 6.2L, 8.1L **Transmissions:** All	**Fuel Trim System Rich (Bank 1)** DTC P0101-P0103, P0108, P0135, P0137, P0141, P0200, P0300, P0410, P0420, P0440, P0442, P0443, P0446, P0449, P0506, P0507 and P1441 not set, engine started, vehicle driven at less than 85 MPH at 400-3000 RPM, BARO sensor more than 74 kPa (10.7 psi), ECT sensor from 167-239°F, IAT sensor from 4-194°F, MAF sensor from 5-90 gm/s, MAP sensor from 26-90 kPa, TP angle less than 90%, fuel level over 10%, and the PCM detected the Long Term fuel trim was less than −13% for 40 seconds. **Possible Causes:** • Base engine "mechanical" fault affecting one or more cylinders • EVAP system component has failed or canister fuel saturated • Fuel control sensor is out of calibration (i.e., ECT, IAT or MAF) • Fuel delivery system supplying too much fuel during cruise or idle periods (e.g., faulty fuel pump, or faulty pressure regulator) • Fuel injector(s) is leaking or stuck partially open (one or more) • HO2S is contaminated, deteriorated or it has failed • TSB 81-65-37 contains a repair procedure for this code
DTC: P0172 **2T FUEL, MIL: Yes** **Years:** 2005, 2006, 2007 **Models:** Sierra, Silverado **Engines:** 6.0L CNG **Transmissions:** All	**Fuel Trim System Rich (Bank 1)** DTC P0101, P0102, P0103, P0106, P0107, P0108, P0112, P0113, P0116-P0118, P0121-P0123, P0125, P0200, P0300, P0327, P0332, P0335, P0336, P0351-P0358, P0401, P0402, P0403, P0443, P0446, P0449, P0496, P0502, P0503, P1020, or P1258 not set, engine started, ECT sensor from 167-239°F, IAT sensor from 4-194°F, engine speed 400-3000 RPM, BARO sensor over 74 kPa, MAF sensor from 5-90 gm/s, TP angle under 90%, VSS under 85 MPH, and the PCM detected the Long Term fuel trim was less than −15% for 40 seconds (indicating a lean A/F mixture was present). **Possible Causes:** • Base engine "mechanical" fault affecting one or more cylinders • Excess fuel vapors in crankcase (the oil needs to be changed) • EVAP system component has failed or canister fuel saturated • Fuel control sensor is out of calibration (i.e., ECT, IAT or MAF) • Fuel delivery system supplying too much fuel during cruise or idle periods (e.g., faulty fuel pump, or faulty pressure regulator) • Fuel injector(s) is leaking or stuck partially open (one or more) • HO2S is contaminated, deteriorated or it has failed
DTC: P0174 **2T FUEL, MIL: Yes** **Years:** 2005, 2006, 2007 **Models:** G6, GTO, LaCrosse, Malibu, Montana, Montana SV6, Relay, Rendezvous, SV6, Sky, Solstice, SRX, Terraza, Uplander **Engines:** 2.0L, 2.2L, 2.4L, 3.4L, 3.5L, 3.6L, 3.9L, 4.6L, 6.0L **Transmissions:** All	**Fuel Trim System Lean (Bank 2)** DTC P0101, P0103, P0103, P0107, P0108, P0121, P0122, P0123, P0130-P0141, P0201-P0206, P0300, P0401-P0405, P0410, P0440-P0446, P0506, P0507, P1404 and P1441 not set, engine speed from 550-4000 RPM, ECT sensor from 68-230°F, IAT sensor from 64-158°F, MAF sensor at 2.8-150 gm/s, BARO sensor over 70 kPa, MAP sensor at 15-105 kPa, VSS under 82 MPH, fuel level over 10%, and the PCM detected the Short Term fuel trim was more than 20% for 6 seconds. **Possible Causes:** • Air leaks in intake manifold, exhaust pipes or exhaust manifold • Fuel control sensor is out of calibration (ECT, IAT or MAF) • Fuel component fault (fuel filter, fuel injector, low fuel pressure) • HO2S element is contaminated, deteriorated or has failed

DTC	Trouble Code Title, Conditions & Possible Causes
DTC: P0174 **2T FUEL, MIL: Yes** **Years:** 2005, 2006, 2007 **Models:** Sierra, Silverado **Engines:** 4.3L, 4.8L, 5.3L 6.0L, 6.2L, 8.1L **Transmissions:** All	**Fuel Trim System Lean (Bank 2)** DTC P0101, P0102, P0103, P0108, P0135, P0137, P0141, P0200, P0300, P0410, P0420, P0430, P0440, P0442, P0443, P0446, P0449, P0506, P0507 and P1441 not set, vehicle driven at less than 85 MPH at 400-3000 RPM, BARO sensor over 74 kPa, ECT sensor from 167-239°F, IAT sensor from 4-194°F, MAF sensor at 5-90 gm/s, MAP sensor from 26-90 kPa (3.7-13 psi), TP angle below 90%, fuel level over 10%, and the PCM detected the Long Term fuel trim was over +23% for 6 seconds (i.e., a lean A/F mixture existed). **Possible Causes:** • Air leaks in intake manifold, exhaust pipes or exhaust manifold • Fuel control sensor is out of calibration (ECT, IAT or MAF) • Low fuel pressure (fuel filter clogged, pressure regulator failure) • One or more injectors restricted or pressure regulator has failed • HO2S element is contaminated, deteriorated or has failed • Vacuum hose is disconnected, broken, leaking or loose
DTC: P0174 **2T FUEL, MIL: Yes** **Years:** 2005, 2006, 2007 **Models:** Sierra, Silverado **Engines:** 6.0L CNG **Transmissions:** All	**Fuel Trim System Lean (Bank 2)** DTC P0101-P0103, P0106-P0108, P0112, P0113, P0116-P0118, P0121-P0123, P0125, P0200, P0300, P0327, P0332, P0335, P0336, P0351-P0358, P0401, P0402, P0403, P0443, P0446, P0449, P0496, P0502, P0503, P1020, or P1258 not set, engine started, ECT sensor from 167-239°F, IAT sensor from 4-194°F, engine speed 400-3000 RPM, BARO sensor over 74 kPa, MAF sensor from 5-90 gm/s, TP angle under 90%, VSS less than 85 MPH, and the PCM detected the LT fuel trim value was over 28% for 6 seconds (e.g., a lean A/F mixture). **Possible Causes:** • Air leaks in intake manifold, exhaust pipes or exhaust manifold • Fuel control sensor is out of calibration (ECT, IAT or MAF) • Low fuel pressure (fuel filter clogged, pressure regulator failure) • One or more injectors restricted or pressure regulator has failed • HO2S element is contaminated, deteriorated or has failed • Vacuum hose is disconnected, broken, leaking or loose
DTC: P0175 **2T FUEL, MIL: Yes** **Years:** 2005, 2006, 2007 **Models:** G6, GTO, LaCrosse, Malibu, Montana, Montana SV6, Relay, Rendezvous, SV6, Sky, Solstice, SRX, Terraza, Uplander **Engines:** 2.0L, 2.2L, 2.4L, 3.4L, 3.5L, 3.6L, 3.9L, 4.6L, 6.0L **Transmissions:** All	**Fuel Trim System Rich (Bank 2)** DTC P0101-P0103, P0107, P0108, P0121-P0123, P0130-P0135, P0137, P0138, P0140, P0141, P0201-P0206, P0300, P0401-P0405, P0410, P0440-P0446, P0506, P0507, P1404 or P1441 not set, engine started, vehicle driven at less than 82 MPH at 550-4000 RPM, BARO sensor more than 70 kPa, ECT sensor from 68-230°F, IAT sensor from 64-158°F, MAF sensor from 2.8-150 gm/s, MAP sensor from 15-105 kPa, fuel level over 10%, and the PCM detected the Long Term fuel trim value was below −13% for 40 seconds. During open loop, the PCM determines fuel delivery based on sensor signals, without the oxygen sensor input. During closed loop, the PCM adds oxygen sensor inputs to calculate Short and Long term fuel trim fuel delivery adjustments. If the oxygen sensors indicate a lean condition, the fuel trim values will be above 0 percent. If the oxygen sensors indicate a rich condition, the fuel trim values will be below 0 percent. Short Term fuel trim values change rapidly in response to HO2S signals. Long Term fuel trim makes its adjustments to maintain an A/F ratio of 14.7:1. **Possible Causes:** • Base engine "mechanical" fault affecting one or more cylinders • Excess fuel vapors in crankcase (the oil needs to be changed) • EVAP system component has failed or canister fuel saturated • Fuel control sensor is out of calibration (i.e., ECT, IAT or MAF) • Fuel delivery system supplying too much fuel during cruise or idle periods (e.g., faulty fuel pump, or faulty pressure regulator) • Fuel injector(s) is leaking or stuck partially open (one or more) • HO2S is contaminated, deteriorated or it has failed
DTC: P0175 **2T FUEL, MIL: Yes** **Years:** 2005, 2006, 2007 **Models:** Sierra, Silverado **Engines:** 4.3L, 4.8L, 5.3L 6.0L, 6.2L, 8.1L **Transmissions:** All	**Fuel Trim System Rich (Bank 2)** DTC P0101, P0102, P0103, P0108, P0135, P0137, P0141, P0200, P0300, P0410, P0420, P0430, P0440, P0442, P0443, P0446, P0449, P0506, P0507 and P1441 not set, engine started, vehicle speed less than 85 MPH at 400-3000 RPM, BARO sensor over 74 kPa, ECT sensor from 167-239°F, IAT sensor from 4-194°F, MAF sensor from 5-90 gm/s, MAP sensor from 26-90 kPa (3.7-13 psi), TP angle under 90%, fuel level over 10%, and the PCM detected the LT fuel trim was less than −13% for 40 seconds (i.e., a rich A/F mixture existed). **Possible Causes:** • Base engine "mechanical" fault affecting one or more cylinders • Excess fuel vapors in crankcase (the oil needs to be changed) • EVAP system component has failed or canister fuel saturated • Fuel control sensor is out of calibration (i.e., ECT, IAT or MAF) • Fuel delivery system supplying too much fuel at cruise or idle periods (faulty regulator) • Fuel injector(s) is leaking or stuck partially open (one or more) • HO2S is contaminated, deteriorated or it has failed • TSB 76-65-04 contains a repair procedure for this code

DTC	Trouble Code Title, Conditions & Possible Causes
DTC: P0175 **2T FUEL, MIL: Yes** **Years:** 2005, 2006, 2007 **Models:** Sierra, Silverado **Engines:** 6.0L CNG **Transmissions:** All	**Fuel Trim System Rich (Bank 2)** DTC P0101-P0103, P0106-P0108, P0112, P0113, P0116-P0118, P0121-P0123, P0125, P0200, P0300, P0327, P0332, P0335, P0336, P0351-P0358, P0401-P0403, P0443, P0446, P0449, P0496, P0502, P0503, P1020 and P1258 not set, engine speed 400-3000 RPM, ECT sensor from 167-239°F, IAT sensor from 4-194°F, BARO sensor over 74 kPa, MAF sensor from 5-90 gm/s, TP angle under 90%, VSS under 85 MPH, and the PCM detected the LT fuel trim was less than −15% for 40 seconds (indicating a lean A/F mixture was present). **Possible Causes:** • Base engine "mechanical" fault affecting one or more cylinders • Excess fuel vapors in crankcase (the oil needs to be changed) • EVAP system component has failed or canister fuel saturated • Fuel delivery system supplying too much fuel at cruise or idle periods (faulty regulator) • Fuel injector(s) is leaking or stuck partially open (one or more) • HO2S is contaminated, deteriorated or it has failed
DTC: P0181 **1T CCM, MIL: Yes** **Years:** 2005, 2006, 2007 **Models:** Sierra, Silverado **Engines:** 6.6L Diesel **Transmissions:** All	**Fuel Tank Temperature Sensor Signal Range/Performance** Key off for 10 hours, DTC P0112, P0113, P0182, P0183, P0500 and P1683 not set, Fuel Tank Temperature (FTT) and ECT sensor within 18°F, IAT sensor over 59°F at startup, vehicle driven to over 15 MPH, and the PCM detected the FTT signal dropped less than 10°F after a period of 400 seconds. The PCM supplies the sensor with a 5v signal and a low reference circuit. If the fuel temperature sensor is cold, its resistance is high. The FTT signal voltage remains near the signal voltage cold and decreases as the sensor warms. The PCM monitors the FTT signal circuit to calculate the temperature of fuel entering the engine **Possible Causes:** • FTT sensor signal circuit has a high resistance fault • FTT sensor is damaged, skewed or it has failed • PCM has failed
DTC: P0182 **1T CCM, MIL: Yes** **Years:** 2005, 2006, 2007 **Models:** Sierra, Silverado **Engines:** 6.6L Diesel **Transmissions:** All	**Fuel Tank Temperature Sensor Circuit Low Input** Key on or engine running; and the PCM detected the Fuel Tank Temperature (FTT) sensor indicated more than 248°F for 2 seconds. **Possible Causes:** • FTT sensor signal circuit is shorted to chassis or sensor ground • FTT sensor is damaged, skewed or it has failed • PCM has failed
DTC: P0182 **1T CCM, MIL: Yes** **Years:** 2005, 2006, 2007 **Models:** Sierra, Silverado **Engines:** 6.0L CNG **Transmissions:** All	**Fuel Tank Temperature Sensor Circuit Low Input** DTC P1207 not set, key on or engine running, IAT sensor more than −31°F, and the PCM detected the Fuel Tank Temperature (FTT) sensor was under 0.1v (Scan Tool reads over 248°F) for 5 seconds. **Possible Causes:** • FTT sensor signal circuit is shorted to chassis or sensor ground • FTT sensor is damaged, skewed or it has failed • PCM has failed
DTC: P0183 **1T CCM, MIL: Yes** **Years:** 2005, 2006, 2007 **Models:** Sierra, Silverado **Engines:** 6.0L CNG **Transmissions:** All	**Fuel Tank Temperature Sensor Circuit High Input** DTC P0112, P0113 and P1207 not set, engine started, IAT sensor over 14°F, and the PCM detected the Fuel Tank Temperature (FTT) sensor was more than 4.95v (Scan Tool reads −22°F) for 5 seconds. **Possible Causes:** • FTT sensor signal circuit or ground circuit is open • FTT sensor signal circuit is shorted to VREF • FTT sensor is damaged, skewed or it has failed • PCM has failed
DTC: P0187 **2T CCM, MIL: Yes** **Years:** 2005, 2006, 2007 **Models:** Sierra, Silverado **Engines:** 6.0L CNG **Transmissions:** All	**Fuel Rail Temperature Sensor Circuit Low Input** Key on or engine running; and the PCM detected the Fuel Rail Temperature (FRT) sensor was less than 0.10v for 5 seconds. The FRT sensor is a variable resistor that measures the temperature of the fuel in the CNG fuel rail. The fuel injector control module (FICM) supplies 5v to the FRT signal circuit and supplies a ground to the low reference circuit. The FICM monitors the FRT sensor signal and communicates data to the PCM by a dedicated PWM circuit. This code sets when the FRT signal is below normal operating range. **Possible Causes:** • FRT sensor signal circuit shorted to chassis or sensor ground • FRT sensor is damaged, skewed or it has failed • PCM has failed

DTC	Trouble Code Title, Conditions & Possible Causes
DTC: P0188 **2T CCM, MIL: Yes** **Years:** 2005, 2006, 2007 **Models:** Sierra, Silverado **Engines:** 6.0L CNG **Transmissions:** All	**Fuel Rail Temperature Sensor Circuit High Input** DTC P0112, P0113 and P1207 not set key on or engine running, IAT sensor more than 14°F, and the PCM detected the Fuel Rail Temperature (FRT) sensor was more than 4.95v for 2 seconds. **Note: The FRT sensor should read approximately 2.20v at 86°F.** **Possible Causes:** • FRT sensor signal circuit or ground circuit is open • FRT sensor signal circuit is shorted to VREF • FRT sensor is damaged, skewed or it has failed • PCM has failed
DTC: P0191 **2T CCM, MIL: Yes** **Years:** 2005, 2006, 2007 **Models:** Sierra, Silverado **Engines:** 6.0L CNG **Transmissions:** All	**Fuel Rail Pressure Sensor Circuit Low Input** DTC P0005, P0192, P0193, P0336, P1207, P1432, P1433 and P2665 not set, then after engine startup with the engine speed over 100 RPM, ECT sensor more than 68°F, MAF sensor less than 200 g/sec, and the PCM detected the FRP sensor was less than 206 kPa (30 psi) or more than 620 kPa (90 psi) for 3 seconds. **Possible Causes:** • FRP Sensor 5v VREF circuit has a high resistance condition • FRP sensor signal circuit has a high resistance condition • FRP sensor is damaged or it has failed • PCM has failed
DTC: P0192 **1T CCM, MIL: No** **Years:** 2005, 2006, 2007 **Models:** Sierra, Silverado **Engines:** 6.6L Diesel **Transmissions:** All	**Fuel Rail Pressure Sensor Circuit Low Input** DTC P0005, P0192, P0193, P0336, P1207, P1432, P1433 and P2665 not set, key on or engine running; and the PCM detected the Fuel Rail Pressure sensor was less than 1.2 MPa. **Possible Causes:** • FRP sensor 5-volt power circuit is open or shorted to ground • FRP Sensor signal circuit is shorted to ground • FRP Sensor is damaged or has failed • PCM has failed
DTC: P0192 **1T CCM, MIL: No** **Years:** 2005, 2006, 2007 **Models:** Sierra, Silverado **Engines:** 6.0L CNG **Transmissions:** All	**Fuel Rail Pressure Sensor Circuit Low Input** DTC P0191 not set, engine started, engine speed over 100 RPM, the PCM detected the FRP sensor was less than 0.10v for 2.5 seconds. The fuel injector control module (FICM) supplies 5v on the FRP sensor reference voltage circuit. The FICM also supplies a ground circuit and a signal circuit to the FRP sensor. When the fuel rail pressure is normal, the FRP signal rises to near 2.5v. As the fuel rail pressure increases, the FRP signal voltage increases. The FICM monitors the FRP sensor and communicates the data to the PCM by a discrete PWM circuit. **Possible Causes:** • FRP sensor 5-volt power circuit is open or shorted to ground • FRP Sensor signal circuit is shorted to ground • FRP Sensor is damaged or has failed • PCM has failed
DTC: P0193 **1T CCM, MIL: Yes** **Years:** 2005, 2006, 2007 **Models:** Sierra, Silverado **Engines:** 6.6L Diesel **Transmissions:** All	**Fuel Rail Pressure Sensor Circuit High Input** DTC P1635 and P1639 not set, key on or engine running system not in Power-Down mode, and the PCM detected the Fuel Rail Pressure (FRP) sensor was more than 75 MPa during the CCM test. **Possible Causes:** • FRP sensor signal circuit shorted to VREF or system power • FRP sensor is damaged or has failed • PCM has failed
DTC: P0193 **2T CCM, MIL: Yes** **Years:** 2005, 2006, 2007 **Models:** Sierra, Silverado **Engines:** 6.0L CNG **Transmissions:** All	**Fuel Rail Pressure Sensor Circuit High Input** DTC P0336 not set, and after the engine started, engine speed over 100 RPM, the PCM detected the Fuel Rail Pressure (FRP) sensor was more than 4.95v for 10 seconds (the fault is continuous). **Possible Causes:** • FRP sensor signal circuit is open between sensor and the PCM • FRP Sensor ground circuit is open between sensor and PCM • FRP sensor signal circuit is shorted to VREF or system power • FRP Sensor is damaged or has failed • PCM has failed

DTC	Trouble Code Title, Conditions & Possible Causes
DTC: P0200 **2T CCM, MIL: Yes** **Years:** 2005, 2006, 2007 **Models:** Sierra, Silverado **Engines:** 4.3L, 4.8L, 5.3L 6.0L, 6.0L CNG, 6.2L, 8.1L **Transmissions:** All	**Fuel Injector Circuit Malfunction** Engine started; engine speed over 400 RPM, system voltage 6-18v, and the PCM detected an unexpected voltage on one or more of the Fuel Injector driver circuits for 5 seconds. Drive the vehicle at off-idle speeds and monitor the misfire current counters. Observe if more than one cylinder is misfiring. This may not be apparent until after a repair is completed. If an injector fuse is open on one cylinder bank, the Scan Tool may only display 2 or 3 cylinders as misfiring. **Possible Causes:** • Fuel injector control circuit is open between injector and PCM • Fuel injector control circuit is grounded between injector and PCM • Fuel injector power circuit is open (test INJ A, B in fuse block) • Fuel injector is damaged or has failed • PCM is damaged
DTC: P0201 **2T CCM, MIL: Yes** **Years:** 2005, 2006, 2007 **Models:** G6, GTO, LaCrosse, Malibu, Montana, Montana SV6, Relay, Rendezvous, SV6, Sky, Solstice, SRX, Terraza, Uplander **Engines:** 2.2L, 2.4L, 3.4L, 3.5L, 3.6L, 3.8L, 3.9L, 3.9L **Transmissions:** All	**Fuel Injector 1 Control Circuit Malfunction** Engine started; system voltage over 10.0v and the PCM detected an unexpected voltage on the Fuel Injector 1 driver circuit for 30 seconds. **Note: Drive the vehicle at cruise speed. Record the misfire current counters to detect if more than one cylinder is misfiring.** **Possible Causes:** • Injector 1 control circuit is open between injector and PCM • Injector 1 control circuit is grounded between injector and PCM • Injector 1 power circuit is open (test INJ fuse in fuse block) • Injector 1 is damaged or it has failed • PCM is damaged
DTC: P0202 **2T CCM, MIL: Yes** **Years:** 2005, 2006, 2007 **Models:** G6, GTO, LaCrosse, Malibu, Relay, Rendezvous, Sky, Solstice, SRX **Engines:** 2.0L, 2.2L, 2.4L, 3.4L, 3.5L, 3.6L, 3.8L, 3.9L, 4.6L, 6.0L **Transmissions:** All	**Fuel Injector 2 Control Circuit Malfunction** Engine started; system voltage over 10.0v and the PCM detected an unexpected voltage on the Fuel Injector 2 driver circuit for 30 seconds. **Note: Drive the vehicle at cruise speed. Record the misfire current counters to detect if more than one cylinder is misfiring.** **Possible Causes:** • Injector 2 control circuit is open between injector and PCM • Injector 2 control circuit is grounded between injector and PCM • Injector 2 power circuit is open (test INJ fuse in fuse block) • Injector 2 is damaged or it has failed • PCM is damaged
DTC: P0203 **2T CCM, MIL: Yes** **Years:** 2005, 2006, 2007 **Models:** G6, GTO, LaCrosse, Malibu, Montana, Montana SV6, Relay, Rendezvous, SV6, Sky, Solstice, SRX, Terraza, Uplander **Engines:** 2.0L, 2.2L, 2.4L, 3.4L, 3.5L, 3.6L, 3.8L, 3.9L, 4.6L, 6.0L **Transmissions:** All	**Fuel Injector 3 Control Circuit Malfunction** Engine started; system voltage over 10.0v and the PCM detected an unexpected voltage on the Fuel Injector 3 driver circuit for 30 seconds. **Note: Drive the vehicle at cruise speed. Record the misfire current counters to detect if more than one cylinder is misfiring.** **Possible Causes:** • Injector 3 control circuit is open between injector and PCM • Injector 3 control circuit is grounded between injector and PCM • Injector 3 power circuit is open (test INJ fuse in fuse block) • Injector 3 is damaged or it has failed • PCM is damaged
DTC: P0204 **2T CCM, MIL: Yes** **Years:** 2005, 2006, 2007 **Models:** G6, GTO, LaCrosse, Malibu, Montana, Montana SV6, Relay, Rendezvous, Sky, Solstice, SRX **Engines:** 2.0L, 2.2L, 2.4L, 3.4L, 3.5L, 3.6L, 3.8L, 3.9L, 4.6L, 6.0L **Transmissions:** All	**Fuel Injector 4 Control Circuit Malfunction** Engine started; system voltage over 10.0v and the PCM detected an unexpected voltage on the Fuel Injector 4 driver circuit for 30 seconds. **Note: Drive the vehicle at cruise speed. Record the misfire current counters to detect if more than one cylinder is misfiring** **Possible Causes:** • Injector 4 control circuit is open between injector and PCM • Injector 4 control circuit is grounded between injector and PCM • Injector 4 power circuit is open (test INJ fuse in fuse block) • Injector 4 is damaged or it has failed • PCM is damaged

DTC	Trouble Code Title, Conditions & Possible Causes
DTC: P0205 **2T CCM, MIL: Yes** **Years:** 2005, 2006, 2007 **Models:** G6, GTO, LaCrosse, Malibu, Montana, Montana SV6, Relay, Rendezvous, Sky, Solstice, SRX **Engines:** 2.0L, 2.2L, 2.4L, 3.4L, 3.5L, 3.6L, 3.8L, 3.9L, 4.6L, 6.0L **Transmissions:** All	**Fuel Injector 5 Control Circuit Malfunction** Engine started; system voltage over 10.0v and the PCM detected an unexpected voltage on the Fuel Injector 5 driver circuit for 30 seconds. **Note: Drive the vehicle at cruise speed. Record the misfire current counters to detect if more than one cylinder is misfiring** **Possible Causes:** • Injector 5 control circuit is open between injector and PCM • Injector 5 control circuit is grounded between injector and PCM • Injector 5 power circuit is open (test INJ fuse in fuse block) • Injector 5 is damaged or it has failed • PCM is damaged
DTC: P0206 **2T CCM, MIL: Yes** **Years:** 2005, 2006, 2007 **Models:** G6, GTO, LaCrosse, Malibu, Montana, Montana SV6, Relay, Rendezvous, Sky, Solstice, SRX **Engines:** 2.0L, 2.2L, 2.4L, 3.4L, 3.5L, 3.6L, 3.8L, 3.9L, 4.6L, 6.0L **Transmissions:** All	**Fuel Injector 6 Control Circuit Malfunction** Engine started; system voltage over 10.0v and the PCM detected an unexpected voltage on the Fuel Injector 6 driver circuit for 30 seconds. **Note: Drive the vehicle at cruise speed. Record the misfire current counters to detect if more than one cylinder is misfiring** **Possible Causes:** • Injector 6 control circuit is open between injector and PCM • Injector 6 control circuit is grounded between injector and PCM • Injector 6 power circuit is open (test INJ fuse in fuse block) • Injector 6 is damaged or it has failed • PCM is damaged
DTC: P0201 **1T CCM, MIL: Yes** **Years:** 2005, 2006, 2007 **Models:** Sierra, Silverado **Engines:** 6.0L CNG **Transmissions:** All	**Fuel Injector 1 Control Circuit Malfunction** U1800 and U2104 not set; engine started; system voltage from 6-18v, and the PCM detected and incorrect current level on the Fuel Injector 1 control circuit. The fuel injection control module (FICM) supplies power to each fuel injector via the ignition voltage circuit. The FICM energizes each injector by grounding the control circuit between the FICM and the injector. The FICM monitors the status of the ignition voltage and fuel injector command circuits. **Possible Causes:** • Fuel injector 1 control circuit is open, shorted to ground or shorted to power • Fuel injector 1 is damaged or it has failed, or the connector is damaged • FICM (module) has failed
DTC: P0202 **1T CCM, MIL: Yes** **Years:** 2005, 2006, 2007 **Models:** Sierra, Silverado **Engines:** 6.0L CNG **Transmissions:** All	**Fuel Injector 2 Control Circuit Malfunction** U1800 and U2104 not set; engine started; system voltage from 6-18v, and the PCM detected and incorrect current level on the Fuel Injector 2 control circuit. The fuel injection control module (FICM) supplies power to each fuel injector via the ignition voltage circuit. The FICM energizes each injector by grounding the control circuit between the FICM and the injector. The FICM monitors the status of the ignition voltage and fuel injector command circuits. **Possible Causes:** • Fuel injector 2 control circuit is open, shorted to ground or shorted to power • Fuel injector 2 is damaged or it has failed, or the connector is damaged • FICM (module) has failed
DTC: P0203 **1T CCM, MIL: Yes** **Years:** 2005, 2006, 2007 **Models:** Sierra, Silverado **Engines:** 6.0L CNG **Transmissions:** All	**Fuel Injector 3 Control Circuit Malfunction** U1800 and U2104 not set; engine started; system voltage from 6-18v, and the PCM detected and incorrect current level on the Fuel Injector 3 control circuit. The fuel injection control module (FICM) supplies power to each fuel injector via the ignition voltage circuit. The FICM energizes each injector by grounding the control circuit between the FICM and the injector. The FICM monitors the status of the ignition voltage and fuel injector command circuits. **Possible Causes:** • Fuel injector 3 control circuit is open, shorted to ground or shorted to power • Fuel injector 3 is damaged or it has failed, or the connector is damaged • FICM (module) has failed
DTC: P0204 **1T CCM, MIL: Yes** **Years:** 2005, 2006, 2007 **Models:** Sierra, Silverado **Engines:** 6.0L CNG **Transmissions:** All	**Fuel Injector 4 Control Circuit Malfunction** U1800 and U2104 not set; engine started; system voltage from 6-18v, and the PCM detected and incorrect current level on the Fuel Injector 4 control circuit. The fuel injection control module (FICM) supplies power to each fuel injector via the ignition voltage circuit. The FICM energizes each injector by grounding the control circuit between the FICM and the injector. **Possible Causes:** • Fuel injector 4 control circuit is open, shorted to ground or shorted to power • Fuel injector 4 is damaged or it has failed, or the connector is damaged • FICM (module) has failed

DTC	Trouble Code Title, Conditions & Possible Causes
DTC: P0205 **1T CCM, MIL: Yes** **Years:** 2005, 2006, 2007 **Models:** Sierra, Silverado **Engines:** 6.0L CNG **Transmissions:** All	**Fuel Injector 5 Control Circuit Malfunction** U1800 and U2104 not set; engine started; system voltage from 6-18v, and the PCM detected and incorrect current level on the Fuel Injector 5 control circuit. The fuel injection control module (FICM) supplies power to each fuel injector via the ignition voltage circuit. The FICM energizes each injector by grounding the control circuit between the FICM and the injector. **Possible Causes:** • Fuel injector 5 control circuit is open, shorted to ground or shorted to power • Fuel injector 5 is damaged or it has failed, or the connector is damaged • FICM (module) has failed
DTC: P0206 **1T CCM, MIL: Yes** **Years:** 2005, 2006, 2007 **Models:** Sierra, Silverado **Engines:** 6.0L CNG **Transmissions:** All	**Fuel Injector 6 Control Circuit Malfunction** U1800 and U2104 not set; engine started; system voltage from 6-18v, and the PCM detected and incorrect current level on the Fuel Injector 6 control circuit. The fuel injection control module (FICM) supplies power to each fuel injector via the ignition voltage circuit. The FICM energizes each injector by grounding the control circuit between the FICM and the injector. **Possible Causes:** • Fuel injector 6 control circuit is open, shorted to ground or shorted to power • Fuel injector 6 is damaged or it has failed, or the connector is damaged • FICM (module) has failed
DTC: P0207 **1T CCM, MIL: Yes** **Years:** 2005, 2006, 2007 **Models:** Sierra, Silverado **Engines:** 6.0L CNG **Transmissions:** All	**Fuel Injector 7 Control Circuit Malfunction** U1800 and U2104 not set; engine started; system voltage from 6-18v, and the PCM detected and incorrect current level on the Fuel Injector 7 control circuit. The fuel injection control module (FICM) supplies power to each fuel injector via the ignition voltage circuit. The FICM energizes each injector by grounding the control circuit between the FICM and the injector. The FICM monitors the status of the ignition voltage and fuel injector command circuits. **Possible Causes:** • Fuel injector 7 control circuit is open, shorted to ground or shorted to power • Fuel injector 7 is damaged or it has failed, or the connector is damaged • FICM (module) has failed
DTC: P0208 **1T CCM, MIL: Yes** **Years:** 2005, 2006, 2007 **Models:** Sierra, Silverado **Engines:** 6.0L CNG **Transmissions:** All	**Fuel Injector 8 Control Circuit Malfunction** U1800 and U2104 not set; engine started; system voltage from 6-18v, and the PCM detected and incorrect current level on the Fuel Injector 8 control circuit. The fuel injection control module (FICM) supplies power to each fuel injector via the ignition voltage circuit. The FICM energizes each injector by grounding the control circuit between the FICM and the injector. The FICM monitors the status of the ignition voltage and fuel injector command circuits. **Possible Causes:** • Fuel injector 8 connector is damaged, loose or shorted • Fuel injector 8 control circuit is open, shorted to ground or shorted to power • Fuel injector 8 is damaged or it has failed • FICM (module) has failed
DTC: P0218 **1T CCM, MIL: No** **Years:** 2005, 2006, 2007 **Models:** Malibu, Rendezvous **Engines:** 3.4L **Transmissions:** A/T	**Transmission Fluid Over-Temperature (4T40-E, 4T45-E)** DTC P0711, P0712 and P0713 not set, engine running, and the PCM detected the TFT sensor was more than 266°F for 10 minutes. **Possible Causes:** • ATF is low, contaminated, burnt or dirty • Engine cooling system has an airflow restriction • Transmission cooling system has an airflow restriction • Transmission cooler lines are bent, damaged or restricted • Transmission internal failure (i.e., low line pressure, TCC fault)
DTC: P0218 **1T CCM, MIL: No** **Years:** 2005, 2006, 2007 **Models:** Sierra, Silverado **Engines:** 4.3L, 4.8L, 5.0L, 5.3L, 5.3L, 5.7L, 6.0L, 6.0L CNG, 6.6L Diesel, 7.4L, 8.1L **Transmissions:** A/T	**Transmission Fluid Over-Temperature (4L60-E, 4L80-E)** DTC P0711, P0712 and P0713 not set, key on for 5 seconds or engine running; and the PCM detected the Transmission Fluid Temperature (TFT sensor indicated more than 266°F for 10 minutes. **Possible Causes:** • ATF is low, contaminated, burnt or dirty • Customer driving habits (i.e., excessive trailer towing) • Engine cooling system has an airflow restriction • Transmission cooling system has an airflow restriction • Transmission cooler lines are bent, damaged or restricted • Transmission internal failure (i.e., low line pressure, TCC fault)

DTC	Trouble Code Title, Conditions & Possible Causes
DTC: P0220 **1T CCM, MIL: No** **Years:** 2005, 2006, 2007 **Models:** All **Engines:** All **Transmissions:** All	**Throttle Position Sensor 2 Circuit Malfunction** DTP P1518 and P2108 not set, engine cranking or running; system voltage over 5.23v, and the PCM detected the TP Sensor 2 signal was less than 0.28v or more than 4.60v for one second. The PCM provides the TP sensor with a 5v, low reference and signal circuit. The signal is low at closed throttle and higher as the throttle opens. **Possible Causes:** • TP Sensor 2 signal circuit is open or shorted to ground • TP Sensor 2 VREF (5v) circuit is open, or TP Sensor 2 ground circuit is open • TP Sensor 2 is damaged or has failed • PCM is damaged • TSB 03-04-06-034 contains a repair procedure for this code
DTC: P0230 **2T CCM, MIL: Yes** **Years:** 2005, 2006, 2007 **Models:** Sierra, Silverado **Engines:** 4.3L, 4.8L, 5.0L, 5.3L, 5.3L, 5.7L, 6.0L, 6.0L CNG, 6.6L Diesel, 7.4L, 8.1L **Transmissions:** All	**Fuel Pump Relay Control Circuit Malfunction** Engine started; engine speed more than 400 RPM, system voltage from 6-18v, and the PCM detected the Actual state and the Commanded state of the Fuel Pump control circuit did not match for 2.5 seconds. **Possible Causes:** • Fuel pump relay control circuit is open or shorted to ground • Fuel pump relay power circuit is open (PCM Fuse B fuse block) • Fuel pump relay is damaged or it has failed • PCM is damaged
DTC: P0230 **1T CCM, MIL: No** **Years:** 2005, 2006, 2007 **Models:** G6, GTO, LaCrosse, Malibu, Montana, Montana SV6, Relay, Rendezvous, Sky, Solstice, SRX **Engines:** 2.0L, 2.2L, 2.4L, 3.4L, 3.5L, 3.6L, 3.8L, 3.9L, 4.6L, 6.0L **Transmissions:** All	**Fuel Pump Control Circuit Malfunction** Key on or engine running; system voltage from 9-18.0v, and the PCM detected an unexpected voltage condition on the Fuel Pump relay driver circuit for less than 1 second. **Possible Causes:** • Fuel pump relay power circuit is open (test B+ from at fuse box) • Fuel pump control circuit is open or shorted to ground • Fuel pump control circuit is shorted to system power • PCM has failed
DTC: P0230 **2T CCM, MIL: Yes** **Years:** 2005, 2006, 2007 **Models:** Sierra, Silverado **Engines:** 4.3L, 4.8L, 5.0L, 5.3L, 5.3L, 5.7L, 6.0L, 6.0L CNG, 6.6L Diesel, 7.4L, 8.1L **Transmissions:** All	**Fuel Pump Control Circuit Malfunction** Engine started; system voltage from 6-18v, and the PCM detected that the Commanded state and the Actual state of the Fuel Pump control circuit did not match for 2-5 continuous seconds. **Possible Causes:** • Fuel pump relay power circuit is open (test B+ from fuse box) • Fuel pump control circuit is open or shorted to ground • Fuel pump control circuit is shorted to system power • PCM has failed
DTC: P0234 **2T CCM, MIL: Yes** **Years:** 2005, 2006, 2007 **Models:** Sierra, Silverado **Engines:** 6.6L Diesel **Transmissions:** All	**Turbocharger Boost Circuit Range/Performance** DTC P0238 not set, engine speed over 500 RPM, less than 2700 RPM on RPO NF2, NF4, fuel quality less than 70 mm³, total fuel quality burned less than 2000 mm³, and the PCM detected the measured Boost Pressure sensor was above the expected range by 35 kPa or more for 12 seconds. This sensor responds to pressure changes in the intake manifold created by the turbocharger along with changes in the accelerator pedal position (APP) and engine speed. The ECM uses this data to assist in diagnosis of the BARO sensor, and to provide engine overboost protection. The Boost sensor has a 5-volt reference circuit, a low reference circuit, and a Boost sensor signal circuit that connect to the ECM. **Possible Causes:** • Boost sensor signal, VREF or ground circuit connection faults • Boost sensor is damaged or has failed • Pressure hose from the charged air tube to the Wastegate actuator is disconnected or ruptured • Wastegate or Turbocharger is damaged or has failed
DTC: P0236 **2T CCM, MIL: Yes** **Years:** 2005, 2006, 2007 **Models:** Sierra, Silverado **Engines:** 6.6L Diesel **Transmissions:** All	**Turbocharger Boost Circuit High Input** DTC P0237, P2227, P2228 and P2229 not set, engine speed over 500 RPM (500-2700 RPM on RPO NF2, NF4), ECT sensor from 140-158°F, total fuel quality burned under 2000 mm³, and the PCM detected the measure Boost Pressure sensor was below the expected range by more than 35 kPa for 12 seconds. **Possible Causes:** • Air cleaner or intake tube is severely restricted • Boost sensor vacuum hose is disconnected, loose or clogged • Boost sensor is damaged or has failed • Charge air pipes or intake manifold leaking • EGR throttle valve is stuck closed • Turbocharger is damaged or has failed

DTC	Trouble Code Title, Conditions & Possible Causes
DTC: P0237 **2T CCM, MIL: Yes** **Years:** 2005, 2006, 2007 **Models:** Sierra, Silverado **Engines:** 6.6L Diesel **Transmissions:** All	**Boost Sensor Circuit Low Input** DTC P1635 not set, key on or engine running and the PCM detected the Boost sensor signal was less than 38 kPa for 2 seconds. The Boost sensor responds to pressure changes in the intake manifold. This pressure is created by the turbocharger and changes to the accelerator pedal position (APP) and engine speed. The ECM uses this information to provide engine Overboost protection. The boost sensor has a 5-volt reference circuit, a low reference circuit, and a signal circuit. The ECM supplies 5 volts to the boost sensor on a 5-volt reference circuit, and provides a ground on a low reference circuit. The boost sensor provides a voltage signal to the ECM on a signal circuit relative to the pressure changes. The ECM monitors the boost sensor signal for voltage outside of the normal range. The ECM sets this code if it detects a boost sensor signal that is too low. **Possible Causes:** • Boost sensor signal circuit shorted to sensor or chassis ground • Boost sensor VREF circuit open between the sensor and PCM • Boost sensor is damaged or has failed • PCM has failed
DTC: P0238 **2T CCM, MIL: Yes** **Years:** 2005, 2006, 2007 **Models:** Sierra, Silverado **Engines:** 6.6L Diesel **Transmissions:** All	**Boost Sensor Circuit High Input** DTC P1635 not set, key on or engine running and the PCM detected the Boost sensor signal was more than 4.80v (Scan Tool reads more than 254 kPa) for 2 seconds. The Boost sensor responds to pressure changes in the intake manifold. This pressure is created by the turbocharger and changes to the accelerator pedal position (APP) and engine speed. The ECM uses this data to provide engine Overboost protection. The boost sensor has a 5-volt reference circuit, a low reference circuit, and a signal circuit. The ECM supplies 5 volts to the boost sensor on a 5-volt reference circuit, and provides a ground on a low reference circuit. The boost sensor provides a voltage signal to the ECM on a signal circuit relative to the pressure changes. The ECM monitors the boost sensor signal for voltage outside of the normal range. The ECM sets this code if it detects a boost sensor signal that is too low. **Possible Causes:** • Boost sensor signal circuit is open or it is shorted to VREF • Boost sensor ground circuit open between sensor and the PCM • Boost sensor is damaged or has failed • PCM has failed
DTC: P0300 **2T MISFIRE, MIL: Yes** **Years:** 2005, 2006, 2007 **Models:** All **Engines:** All **Transmissions:** All	**Multiple Cylinder Misfire Detected** DTC P0101-P0103, P0116-P0118, P0125, P0128, P0335, P0336, P0341, P0343, P0502, P0503, P1114, P1115, P1120, P1220, P1221 or P1336 not set, engine speed from 450-5000 RPM, system voltage over 10.0v, ECT sensor from 19-266°F, fuel level over 10%, TP angle steady (1%), ABS, AIR, Traction Control and DFCO All "off", transmission not shifting, A/C status steady, ABS signals less than the rough road thresholds, and the PCM detected a crankshaft speed variation characteristic of a misfire in more than one cylinder. **Note: If the misfire is severe, the MIL will flash on/off on the 1st trip!** **Possible Causes:** • Base engine mechanical fault that affects one or more cylinders • Fuel delivery component fault that affects more than 1 cylinder • EVAP system problem or the EVAP canister is fuel saturated • EGR valve is stuck open or PCV system has a vacuum leak • Ignition system fault (a coil) that affects more than one cylinder • TSB 03-06-04-030 contains a repair procedure for this code • TSB 03-06-04-041 contains a repair procedure for this code
DTC: P0301 **2T MISFIRE, MIL: Yes** **Years:** 2005, 2006, 2007 **Models:** Sierra, Silverado **Engines:** 4.3L, 4.8L, 5.3L 6.0L, 6.2L, 8.1L **Transmissions:** All	**Cylinder 1 Misfire Detected** DTC P0101-P0103, P0116-P0118, P0125, P0128, P0335, P0336, P0341, P0343, P0502, P0503, P1114, P1115, P1120, P1220, P1221 or P1336 not set, engine speed from 450-5001 RPM, system voltage over 10.0v, ECT sensor from 19-266°F, fuel level over 10%, TP angle steady (1%), ABS, AIR, Traction Control and DFCO All "off", transmission not shifting, A/C status steady, ABS signals less than the rough road thresholds, and the PCM detected a crankshaft speed variation in one cylinder characteristic of a misfire condition. **Note: If the misfire is severe, the MIL will flash on/off on the 1st trip!** **Possible Causes:** • Air leak in the intake manifold, or in the EGR or PCV system • Base engine mechanical fault that affects only one cylinder • Fuel delivery component fault that affects only one cylinder (i.e., a contaminated, dirty or sticking fuel injector) • Ignition system problem (coil or plug) that affects one cylinder • TSB 00-06-04-024 contains a repair procedure for this code

DTC	Trouble Code Title, Conditions & Possible Causes
DTC: P0302 **2T MISFIRE, MIL: Yes** **Years:** 2005, 2006, 2007 **Models:** Sierra, Silverado **Engines:** 4.3L, 4.8L, 5.3L 6.0L, 6.2L, 8.1L **Transmissions:** All	**Cylinder 2 Misfire Detected** DTC P0101-P0103, P0116-P0118, P0125, P0128, P0335, P0336, P0341, P0343, P0502, P0503, P1114, P1115, P1120, P1220, P1221 or P1336 not set, engine speed from 450-5001 RPM, system voltage over 10.0v, ECT sensor from 19-266°F, fuel level over 10%, TP angle steady (1%), ABS, AIR, Traction Control and DFCO All "off", transmission not shifting, A/C status steady, ABS signals less than the rough road thresholds, and the PCM detected a crankshaft speed variation in one cylinder characteristic of a misfire condition. **Note: If the misfire is severe, the MIL will flash on/off on the 1st trip!** **Possible Causes:** • Air leak in the intake manifold, or in the EGR or PCV system • Base engine mechanical fault that affects only one cylinder • Fuel delivery component fault that affects only one cylinder (i.e., a contaminated, dirty or sticking fuel injector) • Ignition system problem (coil or plug) that affects one cylinder • TSB 00-06-04-024 contains a repair procedure for this code
DTC: P0303 **2T MISFIRE, MIL: Yes** **Years:** 2005, 2006, 2007 **Models:** Sierra, Silverado **Engines:** 4.3L, 4.8L, 5.3L 6.0L, 6.2L, 8.1L **Transmissions:** All	**Cylinder 3 Misfire Detected** DTC P0101-P0103, P0116-P0118, P0125, P0128, P0335, P0336, P0341, P0343, P0502, P0503, P1114, P1115, P1120, P1220, P1221 or P1336 not set, engine speed from 450-5001 RPM, system voltage over 10.0v, ECT sensor from 19-266°F, fuel level over 10%, TP angle steady (1%), ABS, AIR, Traction Control and DFCO All "off", transmission not shifting, A/C status steady, ABS signals less than the rough road thresholds, and the PCM detected a crankshaft speed variation in one cylinder characteristic of a misfire condition. **Note: If the misfire is severe, the MIL will flash on/off on the 1st trip!** **Possible Causes:** • Air leak in the intake manifold, or in the EGR or PCV system • Base engine mechanical fault that affects only one cylinder • Fuel delivery component fault that affects only one cylinder (i.e., a contaminated, dirty or sticking fuel injector) • Ignition system problem (coil or plug) that affects one cylinder • TSB 00-06-04-024 contains a repair procedure for this code
DTC: P0304 **2T MISFIRE, MIL: Yes** **Years:** 2005, 2006, 2007 **Models:** Sierra, Silverado **Engines:** 4.3L, 4.8L, 5.3L 6.0L, 6.2L, 8.1L **Transmissions:** All	**Cylinder 4 Misfire Detected** DTC P0101-P0103, P0116-P0118, P0125, P0128, P0335, P0336, P0341, P0343, P0502, P0503, P1114, P1115, P1120, P1220, P1221 or P1336 not set, engine speed from 450-5001 RPM, system voltage over 10.0v, ECT sensor from 19-266°F, fuel level over 10%, TP angle steady (1%), ABS, AIR, Traction Control and DFCO All "off", transmission not shifting, A/C status steady, ABS signals less than the rough road thresholds, and the PCM detected a crankshaft speed variation in one cylinder characteristic of a misfire condition. **Note: If the misfire is severe, the MIL will flash on/off on the 1st trip!** **Possible Causes:** • Air leak in the intake manifold, or in the EGR or PCV system • Base engine mechanical fault that affects only one cylinder • Fuel delivery component fault that affects only one cylinder (i.e., a contaminated, dirty or sticking fuel injector) • Ignition system problem (coil or plug) that affects one cylinder • TSB 00-06-04-024 contains a repair procedure for this code
DTC: P0305 **2T MISFIRE, MIL: Yes** **Years:** 2005, 2006, 2007 **Models:** Sierra, Silverado **Engines:** 4.3L, 4.8L, 5.3L 6.0L, 6.2L, 8.1L **Transmissions:** All	**Cylinder 5 Misfire Detected** DTC P0101-P0103, P0116-P0118, P0125, P0128, P0335, P0336, P0341, P0343, P0502, P0503, P1114, P1115, P1120, P1220, P1221 or P1336 not set, engine speed from 450-5001 RPM, system voltage over 10.0v, ECT sensor from 19-266°F, fuel level over 10%, TP angle steady (1%), ABS, AIR, Traction Control and DFCO All "off", transmission not shifting, A/C status steady, ABS signals less than the rough road thresholds, and the PCM detected a crankshaft speed variation in one cylinder characteristic of a misfire condition. **Note: If the misfire is severe, the MIL will flash on/off on the 1st trip!** **Possible Causes:** • Air leak in the intake manifold, or in the EGR or PCV system • Base engine mechanical fault that affects only one cylinder • Fuel delivery component fault that affects only one cylinder (i.e., a contaminated, dirty or sticking fuel injector) • Ignition system problem (coil or plug) that affects one cylinder • TSB 00-06-04-024 contains a repair procedure for this code

DTC	Trouble Code Title, Conditions & Possible Causes
DTC: P0306 **2T MISFIRE, MIL: Yes** **Years:** 2005, 2006, 2007 **Models:** Sierra, Silverado **Engines:** 4.3L, 4.8L, 5.3L 6.0L, 6.2L, 8.1L **Transmissions:** All	**Cylinder 6 Misfire Detected** DTC P0101-P0103, P0116-P0118, P0125, P0128, P0335, P0336, P0341, P0343, P0502, P0503, P1114, P1115, P1120, P1220, P1221 or P1336 not set, engine speed from 450-5001 RPM, system voltage over 10.0v, ECT sensor from 19-266°F, fuel level over 10%, TP angle steady (1%), ABS, AIR, Traction Control and DFCO All "off", transmission not shifting, A/C status steady, ABS signals less than the rough road thresholds, and the PCM detected a crankshaft speed variation in one cylinder characteristic of a misfire condition. **Note: If the misfire is severe, the MIL will flash on/off on the 1st trip!** **Possible Causes:** • Air leak in the intake manifold, or in the EGR or PCV system • Base engine mechanical fault that affects only one cylinder • Fuel delivery component fault that affects only one cylinder (i.e., a contaminated, dirty or sticking fuel injector) • Ignition system problem (coil or plug) that affects one cylinder • TSB 00-06-04-024 contains a repair procedure for this code
DTC: P0307 **2T MISFIRE, MIL: Yes** **Years:** 2005, 2006, 2007 **Models:** Sierra, Silverado **Engines:** 4.3L, 4.8L, 5.0L, 5.3L, 5.3L, 5.7L, 6.0L, 6.0L CNG, 6.6L Diesel, 7.4L, 8.1L **Transmissions:** All	**Cylinder 7 Misfire Detected** DTC P0101-P0103, P0116-P0118, P0125, P0128, P0335, P0336, P0341, P0343, P0502, P0503, P1114, P1115, P1120, P1220, P1221 or P1336 not set, engine speed from 450-5001 RPM, system voltage over 10.0v, ECT sensor from 19-266°F, fuel level over 10%, TP angle steady (1%), ABS, AIR, Traction Control and DFCO All "off", transmission not shifting, A/C status steady, ABS signals less than the rough road thresholds, and the PCM detected a crankshaft speed variation in one cylinder characteristic of a misfire condition. **Note: If the misfire is severe, the MIL will flash on/off on the 1st trip!** **Possible Causes:** • Air leak in the intake manifold, or in the EGR or PCV system • Base engine mechanical fault that affects only one cylinder • Fuel delivery component fault that affects only one cylinder (i.e., a contaminated, dirty or sticking fuel injector) • Ignition system problem (coil or plug) that affects one cylinder • TSB 00-06-04-024 contains a repair procedure for this code
DTC: P0308 **2T MISFIRE, MIL: Yes** **Years:** 2005, 2006, 2007 **Models:** Sierra, Silverado **Engines:** 4.3L, 4.8L, 5.0L, 5.3L, 5.3L, 5.7L, 6.0L, 6.0L CNG, 6.6L Diesel, 7.4L, 8.1L **Transmissions:** All	**Cylinder 8 Misfire Detected** DTC P0101-P0103, P0116-P0118, P0125, P0128, P0335, P0336, P0341, P0343, P0502, P0503, P1114, P1115, P1120, P1220, P1221 or P1336 not set, engine speed from 450-5001 RPM, system voltage over 10.0v, ECT sensor from 19-266°F, fuel level over 10%, TP angle steady (1%), ABS, AIR, Traction Control and DFCO All "off", transmission not shifting, A/C status steady, ABS signals less than the rough road thresholds, and the PCM detected a crankshaft speed variation in one cylinder characteristic of a misfire condition. **Note: If the misfire is severe, the MIL will flash on/off on the 1st trip!** **Possible Causes:** • Air leak in the intake manifold, or in the EGR or PCV system • Base engine mechanical fault that affects only one cylinder • Fuel delivery component fault that affects only one cylinder (i.e., a contaminated, dirty or sticking fuel injector) • Ignition system problem (coil or plug) that affects one cylinder • TSB 00-06-04-024 contains a repair procedure for this code
DTC: P0300 **2T MISFIRE, MIL: Yes** **Years:** 2005, 2006, 2007 **Models:** G6, GTO, LaCrosse, Malibu, Montana, Montana SV6, Relay, Rendezvous, Sky, Solstice, SRX, Terraza, Uplander, Vibe **Engines:** 1.8L, 2.0L, 2.2L, 2.4L, 3.4L, 3.5L, 3.6L, 3.9L, 4.6L, 6.0L **Transmissions:** All	**Multiple Cylinder Misfire Detected** DTC P0101-P0103, P0107, P0108, P0116-P0118, P0121, P0122, P0123, P0125, P0336, P0341, P0502, P0503, P1106, P1107, P1114, P1115, P1121, P1122, P1336, P1351, P1352, P1361, P1362 and P1374 not set, engine speed from 525-5900 RPM, ECT sensor from 21-255°F, system voltage over 10.0v, TP angle steady, and the PCM detected a crankshaft speed variation characteristic of a misfire condition in two or more cylinders. **Note: If the misfire is severe, the MIL will flash on/off on the 1st trip!** **Possible Causes:** • Base engine mechanical or fuel metering fault that affects one or more cylinders • EVAP system problem or the EVAP canister is fuel saturated • EGR valve is stuck open or the PCV system has a vacuum leak • IC control circuit is shorted to ground (an intermittent fault) • Ignition system fault (a coil) that affects more than one cylinder • MAF sensor contamination (it can cause a very lean condition) • TSB 99-06-04-005B contains a repair procedure for this code • TSB 03-06-04-030 contains a repair procedure for this code

DTC	Trouble Code Title, Conditions & Possible Causes
DTC: P0301 **2T MISFIRE, MIL: Yes** **Years:** 2005, 2006, 2007 **Models:** G6, GTO, LaCrosse, Malibu, Montana, Montana SV6, Relay, Rendezvous, Sky, Solstice, SRX, Terraza, Uplander, Vibe **Engines:** 1.8L, 2.0L, 2.2L, 2.4L, 3.4L, 3.5L, 3.6L, 3.9L, 4.6L, 6.0L **Transmissions:** All	**Cylinder 1 Misfire Detected** DTC P0101-P0103, P0107, P0108, P0116-P0118, P0121-P0123, P0125, P0336, P0341, P0502, P0503, P1106, P1107, P1114, P1115, P1121, P1122, P1336, P1351, P1352, P1361, P1362 and P1374 not set, engine speed from 525-5900 RPM, ECT sensor from 21-255°F, system voltage over 10.0v, TP angle steady, and the PCM detected a crankshaft speed variation characteristic of a misfire in Cylinder 1. **Note: If the misfire is severe, the MIL will flash on/off on the 1st trip!** **Possible Causes:** • Air leak in the intake manifold, or in the EGR or PCV system • Base engine mechanical fault that affects only Cylinder 1 • Fuel component fault that affects only Cylinder 1 (i.e., a dirty or sticking fuel injector) • Ignition system problem (coil, plug) that affects only Cylinder 1
DTC: P0302 **2T MISFIRE, MIL: Yes** **Years:** 2005, 2006, 2007 **Models:** G6, GTO, LaCrosse, Malibu, Montana, Montana SV6, Relay, Rendezvous, Sky, Solstice, SRX, Terraza, Uplander, Vibe **Engines:** 1.8L, 2.0L, 2.2L, 2.4L, 3.4L, 3.5L, 3.6L, 3.9L, 4.6L, 6.0L **Transmissions:** All	**Cylinder 2 Misfire Detected** DTC P0101-P0103, P0107, P0108, P0116-P0118, P0121-P0123, P0125, P0336, P0341, P0502, P0503, P1106, P1107, P1114, P1115, P1121, P1122, P1336, P1351, P1352, P1361, P1362 and P1374 not set, engine speed from 525-5900 RPM, ECT sensor from 21-255°F, system voltage over 10.0v, TP angle steady, and the PCM detected a crankshaft speed variation characteristic of a misfire in Cylinder 2. **Note: If the misfire is severe, the MIL will flash on/off on the 1st trip!** **Possible Causes:** • Air leak in the intake manifold, or in the EGR or PCV system • Base engine mechanical fault that affects only Cylinder 2 • Fuel component fault that affects only Cylinder 2 (i.e., a dirty or sticking fuel injector) • Ignition system problem (coil, plug) that affects only Cylinder 2
DTC: P0303 **2T MISFIRE, MIL: Yes** **Years:** 2005, 2006, 2007 **Models:** G6, GTO, LaCrosse, Malibu, Montana, Montana SV6, Relay, Rendezvous, Sky, Solstice, SRX, Terraza, Uplander, Vibe **Engines:** 1.8L, 2.0L, 2.2L, 2.4L, 3.4L, 3.5L, 3.6L, 3.9L, 4.6L, 6.0L **Transmissions:** All	**Cylinder 3 Misfire Detected** DTC P0101-P0103, P0107, P0108, P0116-P0118, P0121-P0123, P0125, P0336, P0341, P0502, P0503, P1106, P1107, P1114, P1115, P1121, P1122, P1336, P1351, P1352, P1361, P1362 and P1374 not set, engine speed from 525-5900 RPM, ECT sensor from 21-255°F, system voltage over 10.0v, TP angle steady, and the PCM detected a crankshaft speed variation characteristic of a misfire in Cylinder 3. **Note: If the misfire is severe, the MIL will flash on/off on the 1st trip!** **Possible Causes:** • Air leak in the intake manifold, or in the EGR or PCV system • Base engine mechanical fault that affects only Cylinder 3 • Fuel component fault that affects only Cylinder 3 (i.e., a dirty or sticking fuel injector) • Ignition system problem (coil, plug) that affects only Cylinder 3
DTC: P0304 **2T MISFIRE, MIL: Yes** **Years:** 2005, 2006, 2007 **Models:** G6, GTO, LaCrosse, Malibu, Montana, Montana SV6, Relay, Rendezvous, Sky, Solstice, SRX, Terraza, Uplander, Vibe **Engines:** 1.8L, 2.0L, 2.2L, 2.4L, 3.4L, 3.5L, 3.6L, 3.9L, 4.6L, 6.0L **Transmissions:** All	**Cylinder 4 Misfire Detected** DTC P0101-P0103, P0107, P0108, P0116-P0118, P0121-P0123, P0125, P0336, P0341, P0502, P0503, P1106, P1107, P1114, P1115, P1121, P1122, P1336, P1351, P1352, P1361, P1362 and P1374 not set, engine speed from 525-5900 RPM, ECT sensor from 21-255°F, system voltage over 10.0v, TP angle steady, and the PCM detected a crankshaft speed variation characteristic of a misfire in Cylinder 4. **Note: If the misfire is severe, the MIL will flash on/off on the 1st trip!** **Possible Causes:** • Air leak in the intake manifold, or in the EGR or PCV system • Base engine mechanical fault that affects only Cylinder 4 • Fuel component fault that affects only Cylinder 4 (i.e., a dirty or sticking fuel injector) • Ignition system problem (coil, plug) that affects only Cylinder 4
DTC: P0305 **2T MISFIRE, MIL: Yes** **Years:** 2005, 2006, 2007 **Models:** G6, GTO, LaCrosse, Malibu, Relay, Rendezvous, Sky, Solstice, SRX **Engines:** 3.4L, 3.5L, 3.6L, 3.9L, 4.6L, 6.0L **Transmissions:** All	**Cylinder 5 Misfire Detected** DTC P0101-P0103, P0107, P0108, P0116-P0118, P0121-P0123, P0125, P0336, P0341, P0502, P0503, P1106, P1107, P1114, P1115, P1121, P1122, P1336, P1351, P1352, P1361, P1362 and P1374 not set, engine speed from 525-5900 RPM, ECT sensor from 21-255°F, system voltage over 10.0v, TP angle steady, and the PCM detected a crankshaft speed variation characteristic of a misfire in Cylinder 5. **Note: If the misfire is severe, the MIL will flash on/off on the 1st trip!** **Possible Causes:** • Air leak in the intake manifold, or in the EGR or PCV system • Base engine mechanical fault that affects only Cylinder 5 • Fuel component fault that affects only Cylinder 5 (i.e., a dirty or sticking fuel injector) • Ignition system problem (coil, plug) that affects only Cylinder 5

DTC	Trouble Code Title, Conditions & Possible Causes
DTC: P0306 **2T MISFIRE, MIL: Yes** **Years:** 2005, 2006, 2007 **Models:** G6, GTO, LaCrosse, Malibu, Relay, Rendezvous, Sky, Solstice, SRX **Engines:** 3.4L, 3.5L, 3.6L, 3.9L, 4.6L, 6.0L **Transmissions:** All	**Cylinder 6 Misfire Detected** DTC P0101-P0103, P0107, P0108, P0116-P0118, P0121-P0123, P0125, P0336, P0341, P0502, P0503, P1106, P1107, P1114, P1115, P1121, P1122, P1336, P1351, P1352, P1361, P1362 and P1374 not set, engine speed from 525-5900 RPM, ECT sensor from 21-255°F, system voltage over 10.0v, TP angle steady, and the PCM detected a crankshaft speed variation characteristic of a misfire in Cylinder 6. **Note: If the misfire is severe, the MIL will flash on/off on the 1st trip!** **Possible Causes:** • Air leak in the intake manifold, or in the EGR or PCV system • Base engine mechanical fault that affects only Cylinder 6 • Fuel component fault that affects only Cylinder 6 (i.e., a dirty or sticking fuel injector) • Ignition system problem (coil, plug) that affects only Cylinder 6
DTC: P0315 **1T CCM, MIL: Yes** **Years:** 2005, 2006, 2007 **Models:** Sierra, Silverado **Engines:** 4.3L, 4.8L, 5.3L, 6.0L, 6.0L CNG, 8.1L **Transmissions:** All	**Crankshaft Position Sensor Variation Not Learned** DTC P0335, P0336, P0341, P0342 and P0343 not set, engine started, ECT sensor more than 149°F, and the PCM determined the CKP sensor variation values were not stored in memory. The CKP System variation "learning" feature is used to calculate reference period errors caused by slight tolerance variations in the crankshaft and the CKP sensor. The calculated error Allows the PCM to accurately compensate for reference period variations. The PCM stores CKP variation values after a learn procedure is done. **Possible Causes:** • CKP sensor signal circuit has an interference condition (EMI) • Crankshaft main bearings worn or reluctor wheel is damaged • Crankshaft run-out is excessive or the crankshaft is damaged • ECT sensor not within the conditions for running the code test • Ignition switch is on, but the battery has insufficient voltage • PCM power disconnected with key on (erases learned values) • Debris that passes between the CKP sensor and reluctor wheel
DTC: P0325 **2T CCM, MIL: Yes** **Years:** 2005, 2006, 2007 **Models:** Sierra, Silverado, **Engines:** 4.3L, 4.8L, 5.3L 6.0L, 6.2L, 8.1L **Transmissions:** All	**Knock Sensor Circuit Malfunction** DTC P0327 not set, engine started, engine runtime from 10 seconds to 2 minutes, system voltage over 10.0v and the PCM detected an unexpected voltage condition for a period of 5-25 seconds on the diagnostic circuit used during diagnosis of the Knock sensor. **Possible Causes:** • Knock sensor signal circuit is open, shorted to ground or power • Knock sensor ground circuit is open (i.e., not mounted properly) • Knock sensor is damaged or has failed • On modules with an integrated sensor, clear the codes and retest for codes. If the same code resets, the PCM has failed.
DTC: P0325 **2T CCM, MIL: Yes** **Years:** 2005, 2006, 2007 **Models:** Sierra, Silverado **Engines:** 4.8L, 5.3L 6.0L, 6.0L CNG, 8.1L **Transmissions:** All	**Knock Sensor Circuit Malfunction** Engine started; engine runtime more than 10 seconds, system voltage over 10.0v and the PCM detected an unexpected voltage condition for 12 seconds on the Knock sensor circuit. **Possible Causes:** • Knock sensor signal circuit is open, shorted to ground or power • Knock sensor ground circuit is open (i.e., not mounted properly) • Knock sensor is damaged or has failed • On modules with an integrated sensor, clear the codes and retest for codes. If the same code resets, the PCM has failed.
DTC: P0325 **2T CCM, MIL: Yes** **Years:** 2005, 2006, 2007 **Models:** G6, GTO, LaCrosse, Malibu, Montana, Montana SV6, Relay, Rendezvous, Sky, Solstice, SRX, Terraza, Uplander, Vibe **Engines:** 1.8L, 2.0L, 2.2L, 2.4L, 3.4L, 3.5L, 3.6L, 3.9L, 4.6L, 6.0L **Transmissions:** All	**Knock Sensor Circuit Malfunction** DTC P0101, P0102, P0103, P0116, P0117, P0118, P0121, P0122, P0123, P0125, P0336, P0341, P0502, P0503, P1114, P1115, P1121, P1122 and P1336 are not set, engine speed from 1000-5000 RPM for 30 seconds, TP sensor over 15%, engine load over 45%, ECT sensor over 140°F, spark retard less than 15 degrees, and the PCM detected an unexpected voltage condition on the Knock Sensor circuit used by the PCM to test the sensor. **Possible Causes:** • Knock sensor signal circuit is open, shorted to ground or power • Knock sensor ground circuit is open (i.e., not mounted properly) • Knock sensor is damaged or has failed • On modules with an integrated sensor, clear the codes and retest for codes. If the same code resets, the PCM has failed.
DTC: P0327 **2T CCM, MIL: Yes** **Years:** 2005, 2006, 2007 **Models:** Sierra, Silverado **Engines:** 4.3L, 4.8L, 5.3L 6.0L, 6.2L, 8.1L **Transmissions:** All	**Knock Sensor Circuit Low Input (Bank 1)** DTC P0117, P0118, P0121, P0122, P0123, P0125, P1114, P1115, P1121, P1122 and P1258 not set, engine speed from 475-975 for 10 seconds, ECT sensor over 140°F, system voltage over 10.0v, minimum noise level learned, then with the engine speed from 1500-3000 RPM for 10 seconds, the MAP sensor less than 49 kPa, TP angle over 0%, and the PCM detected the Knock sensor was within an assigned average range for 9 seconds. **Possible Causes:** • Knock sensor signal circuit is open, shorted to ground or power • Knock sensor ground circuit is open (check for proper torque) • Knock sensor is damaged or has failed • PCM has failed

DTC	Trouble Code Title, Conditions & Possible Causes
DTC: P0327 **2T CCM, MIL: Yes** **Years:** 2005, 2006, 2007 **Models:** Sierra, Silverado **Engines:** 4.8L, 5.3L 6.0L CNG, 6.0L, 8.1L **Transmissions:** All	**Knock Sensor Circuit Low Input (Bank 1)** DTC P0117, P0118 and P0125 not set, engine runtime 10 seconds, minimum noise level learned with the engine speed from 475-975 RPM, then with the engine speed from 1500-3000, ECT sensor more than 140°F, MAP sensor under 49 kPa, TP angle over 0%, system voltage over 10.0v, the PCM detected the Knock Sensor signal was within a calculated voltage range or no signal existed for 9 seconds. **Possible Causes:** • Knock sensor signal circuit is open, shorted to ground or power • Knock sensor ground circuit is open (check for proper torque) • Knock sensor is damaged or it has failed • PCM has failed
DTC: P0327 **2T CCM, MIL: Yes** **Years:** 2005, 2006, 2007 **Models:** G6, GTO, LaCrosse, Malibu, Montana, Montana SV6, Relay, Rendezvous, Sky, Solstice, SRX, Terraza, Uplander, Vibe **Engines:** 1.8L, 2.0L, 2.2L, 2.4L, 3.4L, 3.5L, 3.6L, 3.9L, 4.6L, 6.0L **Transmissions:** All	**Knock Sensor Circuit Malfunction** DTC P0101, P0102, P0103, P0116, P0117, P0118, P0121, P0122, P0123, P0125, P0336, P0341, P0502, P0503, P1114, P1115, P1121, P1122 and P1336 not set, engine started, engine speed 1000-5000 RPM for over 30 seconds, ECT sensor over 140°F, engine load over 45%, TP angle over 1.5%, maximum spark retard less than 15 degrees, and the PCM detected the Knock Sensor signal was within the average voltage range for over 10 seconds. **Possible Causes:** • Knock sensor signal circuit is open, shorted to ground or power • Knock sensor ground circuit is open (check for proper torque) • Knock sensor is damaged or has failed • PCM has failed
DTC: P0332 **2T CCM, MIL: Yes** **Years:** 2005, 2006, 2007 **Models:** Sierra, Silverado **Engines:** 4.8L, 5.3L 6.0L, 6.0L CNG, 8.1L **Transmissions:** All	**Knock Sensor Circuit Low Input (Bank 2)** DTC P0117, P0118 and P0125 not set, engine runtime 10 seconds, minimum noise level learned with the engine speed from 475-975 RPM, then with the engine speed from 1500-3000, ECT sensor more than 140°F, MAP sensor under 49 kPa, TP angle over 0%, system voltage over 10.0v, the PCM detected the Knock Sensor signal was within a calculated voltage range or no signal existed for 9 seconds. **Possible Causes:** • Knock sensor signal circuit is open, shorted to ground or power • Knock sensor ground circuit is open (check for proper torque) • Knock sensor is damaged or it has failed • PCM has failed
DTC: P0335 **2T CCM, MIL: Yes** **Years:** 2005, 2006, 2007 **Models:** Sierra, Silverado **Engines:** 4.3L, 4.8L, 5.3L 6.0L, 6.2L, 8.1L **Transmissions:** All	**CKP Sensor Circuit Malfunction** DTC P0101, P0102, P0103, P0341, P0342 and P0343 not set; engine cranking, CMP signal varying, MAF sensor more than 3 g/sec, and the PCM did not detect any signals from the CKP sensor for less than 8 seconds during the CCM test period. **Possible Causes:** • CKP sensor signal circuit is open or shorted to ground • CKP sensor ground (low reference) circuit is open • CKP sensor power circuit is open between sensor and the PCM • Crankshaft reluctor wheel is damaged or improper installation • PCM has failed
DTC: P0335 **1T CCM, MIL: No** **Years:** 2005, 2006, 2007 **Models:** Sierra, Silverado **Engines:** 6.6L Diesel **Transmissions:** All	**CKP Sensor Signal Range/Performance** Engine cranking or engine running, CMP sensor signals detected, and the PCM did not detect any CKP sensor (Hall Effect 57-1) signals for less than 8 seconds in the CCM test. **Possible Causes:** • CKP sensor signal circuit is open or shorted to ground • CKP sensor VREF circuit is open between the sensor and PCM • CKP sensor ground circuit is open • CKP sensor is damaged or it failed (check crankshaft sprocket) • PCM has failed
DTC: P0335 **2T CCM, MIL: Yes** **Years:** 2005, 2006, 2007 **Models:** G6, GTO, LaCrosse, Malibu, Montana, Montana SV6, Relay, Rendezvous, Sky, Solstice, SRX, Terraza, Uplander, Vibe **Engines:** 1.8L, 2.0L, 2.2L, 2.4L, 3.4L, 3.5L, 3.6L, 3.9L, 4.6L, 6.0L **Transmissions:** All	**Crankshaft Position Sensor Circuit Malfunction** The camshaft position (CMP) sensor signal is incrementing. The mass air flow (MAF) is more than 2 g/s. The engine is cranking or running. The PCM has detected no CKP sensor pulses for more than 2 seconds **Possible Causes:** • CKP sensor signal (+) circuit or (−) circuit is open or shorted to ground • CKP sensor is damaged or has failed • PCM has failed

DTC	Trouble Code Title, Conditions & Possible Causes
DTC: P0336 **2T CCM, MIL: Yes** **Years:** 2005, 2006, 2007 **Models:** G6, GTO, LaCrosse, Malibu, Relay, Rendezvous, Sky, Solstice, SRX **Engines:** 2.0L, 2.2L, 2.4L, 3.4L, 3.5L, 3.6L, 3.8L, 3.9L, 4.6L, 6.0L **Transmissions:** All	**Crankshaft Reference 24X Circuit Malfunction** Engine started; 3X signals detected for 3 seconds, and the PCM detected an invalid ratio of 24X to 3X CKP REF pulses. The circuit uses 2 different types of crankshaft position (CKP) sensors. The CKP Sensor 'A' connects directly to the PCM through the 12v VREF, Medium Resolution engine speed signal and the low reference circuits. The CKP Sensor 'B' connects directly to the ignition control (IC) module via the CKP 'B' signal and low reference circuits. **Possible Causes:** • CKP sensor signal circuit is open or shorted to ground • CKP sensor ground (Low Reference) circuit is open • CKP sensor is damaged or it failed (check crankshaft reluctor) • PCM has failed
DTC: P0336 **2T CCM, MIL: Yes** **Years:** 2005, 2006, 2007 **Models:** Sierra, Silverado **Engines:** 4.3L, 4.8L, 5.3L 6.0L, 6.0L CNG, 6.6L Diesel, 8.1L **Transmissions:** All	**Crankshaft Reference Sensor Signal Range/Performance** Engine cranking or engine running, CMP sensor signals detected, and the PCM detected the CKP sensor signal was out-of-range for a period of less than 2 seconds during the CCM continuous test. **Possible Causes:** • CKP sensor connector is damaged, loose or shorted • CKP sensor signal circuit is open or shorted (intermittent fault) • CKP sensor contacting the reluctor wheel or it has failed • CKP sensor is damaged or it has failed • PCM has failed
DTC: P0340 **1T CCM, MIL: Yes** **Years:** 2005, 2006, 2007 **Models:** G6, GTO, LaCrosse, Malibu, Montana, Montana SV6, Relay, Rendezvous, Sky, Solstice, SRX, Terraza, Uplander, Vibe **Engines:** 1.8L, 2.0L, 2.2L, 2.4L, 3.4L, 3.5L, 3.6L, 3.9L, 4.6L, 6.0L **Transmissions:** All	**CMP Sensor Circuit Malfunction** Engine cranking (engine speed more than 50 RPM), and the PCM did not detect any CMP sensor pulses at least once for two (2) seconds. The hall effect camshaft position (CMP) sensor produces three (3) On-Off pulses for each revolution of the camshaft. The CMP output is pulsewidth encoded. The ECM uses the crankshaft position (CKP) and CMP pulses to determine engine speed and position. **Note: The engine will not start without this signal.** **Possible Causes:** • CMP sensor signal circuit is open, shorted to ground or VREF • CMP sensor VREF circuit is open between sensor and PCM • CMP sensor low reference circuit is open from sensor to PCM • CMP sensor is damaged or it failed • PCM has failed
DTC: P0340 **1T CCM, MIL: Yes** **Years:** 2005, 2006, 2007 **Models:** Sierra, Silverado **Engines:** 6.6L Diesel **Transmissions:** All	**CMP Sensor Circuit Malfunction** Engine cranking (engine speed more than 50 RPM), and the PCM did not detect any CMP sensor pulses at least once for two (2) seconds. The hall effect camshaft position (CMP) sensor produces three (3) On-Off pulses for each revolution of the camshaft. The CMP output is pulsewidth encoded. The ECM uses the crankshaft position (CKP) and CMP pulses to determine engine speed and position. **Note: The engine will not start without this signal.** **Possible Causes:** • CMP sensor signal circuit is open, shorted to ground or VREF • CMP sensor VREF circuit is open between sensor and PCM • CMP sensor low reference circuit is open from sensor to PCM • CMP sensor is damaged or it failed • PCM has failed
DTC: P0341 **2T CCM, MIL: Yes** **Years:** 2005, 2006, 2007 **Models:** G6, GTO, LaCrosse, Malibu, Montana, Montana SV6, Relay, Rendezvous, Sky, Solstice, SRX, Terraza, Uplander, Vibe **Engines:** 1.8L, 2.0L, 2.2L, 2.4L, 3.4L, 3.5L, 3.6L, 3.9L, 4.6L, 6.0L **Transmissions:** All	**CMP Sensor Signal Range/Performance** Engine started; with 3X signals received, and the PCM did not detect a CMP sensor pulse for each engine revolution. **Possible Causes:** • CMP sensor signal circuit is open, shorted to ground or shorted to VREF between the sensor and the PCM (intermittent fault) • CMP sensor signal wire is routed to close to the Generator, spark plug wires or any other possible cause of EMI/RFI • CMP sensor is cracked, damaged or has failed • PCM has failed • TSB 02-06-04-008 contains a repair procedure for this code

DTC	Trouble Code Title, Conditions & Possible Causes
DTC: P0341 **2T CCM, MIL: Yes** **Years:** 2005, 2006, 2007 **Models:** Sierra, Silverado **Engines:** 4.3L, 4.8L, 5.3L 6.0L, 6.0L CNG, 8.1L **Transmissions:** All	**CMP Sensor Signal Range/Performance** Engine speed less than 4000 RPM, and the PCM detected the CKP sensor pulses and CMP sensor pulses did not match during each engine revolution. The CMP sensor works with the 1X reluctor wheel on the camshaft. The PCM provides a 12v VREF to the CMP sensor as well as low reference and signal circuits. As the camshaft rotates, the reluctor wheel interrupts a magnetic field produced by a magnet in the sensor to produce the CMP signal. **Possible Causes:** • CMP sensor signal circuit is open, shorted to ground or VREF • CMP sensor is cracked or damaged (check the reluctor wheel) • CMP sensor wiring routed to close to Generator or plug wires • Reluctor wheel is damaged or the sensor is touching the wheel • PCM has failed
DTC: P0341 **2T CCM, MIL: Yes** **Years:** 2005, 2006, 2007 **Models:** Sierra, Silverado **Engines:** 6.6L Diesel **Transmissions:** All	**CMP Sensor Signal Range/Performance** Engine cranking (engine speed more than 50 RPM), and the ECM detected the CMP sensor pulses were out-of-range for two seconds. The hall effect camshaft position (CMP) sensor produces three (3) On-Off pulses for each revolution of the camshaft. The CMP output is pulsewidth encoded. The ECM uses the crankshaft position (CKP) and CMP pulses to determine the engine speed and position. **Note: The engine will not start without this signal.** **Possible Causes:** • CMP sensor signal circuit is open, shorted to ground or VREF • CMP sensor VREF circuit is open between sensor and PCM • CMP sensor low reference circuit is open from sensor to PCM • CMP sensor is damaged or it failed • PCM has failed
DTC: P0342 **2T CCM, MIL: Yes** **Years:** 2005, 2006, 2007 **Models:** Sierra, Silverado, **Engines:** 4.3L, 4.8L, 5.3L 6.0L, 6.0L CNG, 8.1L **Transmissions:** All	**CMP Sensor Circuit Low Input** Engine started; at less than 4000 RPM, and the PCM detected the CMP sensor signal was in a low state (when the signal should have been in a high state) for 1.5 seconds in the test. **Possible Causes:** • Camshaft reluctor wheel is damaged or foreign material present • CMP sensor signal circuit is open, shorted to ground or VREF • CMP sensor is contacting the reluctor wheel or is damaged • PCM has failed
DTC: P0343 **2T CCM, MIL: Yes** **Years:** 2005, 2006, 2007 **Models:** Sierra, Silverado **Engines:** 4.8L, 5.3L 6.0L, 6.0L CNG, 8.1L **Transmissions:** All	**CMP Sensor Circuit High Input** Engine started; engine speed less than 4000 RPM and the PCM detected the CMP sensor signal was stuck high (when the signal should have been in a low state) for 1.5 seconds in the CCM test. **Possible Causes:** • CMP sensor connector is damaged, loose or shorted • CMP sensor low reference circuit is open or shorted to VREF • Camshaft reluctor wheel is damaged or foreign material present • CMP sensor is contacting the reluctor wheel or is damaged • PCM has failed
DTC: P0351 **2T CCM, MIL: Yes** **Years:** 2005, 2006, 2007 **Models:** G6, GTO, LaCrosse, Malibu, Montana, Montana SV6, Relay, Rendezvous, Sky, Solstice, SRX, Terraza, Uplander, Vibe **Engines:** 1.8L, 2.0L, 2.2L, 2.4L, 3.4L, 3.5L, 3.6L, 3.9L, 4.6L, 6.0L **Transmissions:** All	**Ignition Coil 1 Control Circuit Malfunction** Engine started; and the PCM detected an unexpected voltage condition on the Coil Near Plug Ignition Control (IC) 1 circuit for less than one second during the CCM test period. **Possible Causes:** • IC circuit is open, shorted to ground or shorted to power (B+) • IC ground (Low REF) circuit or Module ground circuit is open • IC power circuit is open (check the INJ fuse in U/H fuse block) • Ignition Coil 1 is damaged or it has failed • PCM has failed
DTC: P0351 **2T CCM, MIL: Yes** **Years:** 2005, 2006, 2007 **Models:** Sierra, Silverado **Engines:** 4.3L, 4.8L, 5.3L 6.0L, 6.0L CNG, 8.1L **Transmissions:** All	**Ignition Coil 1 Control Circuit Malfunction** Engine started; and the PCM detected an unexpected voltage condition on the Coil Near Plug Ignition Control (IC) 1 circuit for less than one second during the CCM test period. **Possible Causes:** • IC circuit is open, shorted to ground or shorted to power (B+) • IC ground (Low REF) circuit or Module ground circuit is open • IC power circuit is open (check the INJ fuse in U/H fuse block) • Ignition Coil 1 is damaged or it has failed • PCM has failed

DTC	Trouble Code Title, Conditions & Possible Causes
DTC: P0352 **2T CCM, MIL: Yes** **Years:** 2005, 2006, 2007 **Models:** G6, GTO, LaCrosse, Malibu, Montana, Montana SV6, Relay, Rendezvous, Sky, Solstice, SRX, Terraza, Uplander, Vibe **Engines:** 1.8L, 2.0L, 2.2L, 2.4L, 3.4L, 3.5L, 3.6L, 3.9L, 4.6L, 6.0L **Transmissions:** All	**Ignition Coil 2 Control Circuit Malfunction** Engine started; and the PCM detected an unexpected voltage condition on the Coil Near Plug Ignition Control (IC) 1 circuit for less than one second during the CCM test period. **Possible Causes:** • IC circuit is open, shorted to ground or shorted to power (B+) • IC ground (Low REF) circuit or Module ground circuit is open • IC power circuit is open (check the INJ fuse in U/H fuse block) • Ignition Coil 1 is damaged or it has failed • PCM has failed
DTC: P0352 **2T CCM, MIL: Yes** **Years:** 2005, 2006, 2007 **Models:** Sierra, Silverado **Engines:** 4.3L, 4.8L, 5.3L 6.0L, 6.0L CNG, 8.1L **Transmissions:** All	**Ignition Coil 2 Control Circuit Malfunction** Engine started; and the PCM detected an unexpected voltage condition on the Coil Near Plug Ignition Control (IC) 2 circuit for less than one second during the CCM test period. **Possible Causes:** • IC circuit is open, shorted to ground or shorted to power (B+) • IC ground (Low REF) circuit or Module ground circuit is open • IC power circuit is open (check the INJ fuse in U/H fuse block) • Ignition Coil 2 is damaged or it has failed • PCM has failed
DTC: P0353 **2T CCM, MIL: Yes** **Years:** 2005, 2006, 2007 **Models:** G6, GTO, LaCrosse, Malibu, Montana, Montana SV6, Relay, Rendezvous, Sky, Solstice, SRX, Terraza, Uplander, Vibe **Engines:** 1.8L, 2.0L, 2.2L, 2.4L, 3.4L, 3.5L, 3.6L, 3.9L, 4.6L, 6.0L **Transmissions:** All	**Ignition Coil 3 Control Circuit Malfunction** Engine started; and the PCM detected an unexpected voltage condition on the Coil Near Plug Ignition Control (IC) 1 circuit for less than one second during the CCM test period. **Possible Causes:** • IC circuit is open, shorted to ground or shorted to power (B+) • IC ground (Low REF) circuit or Module ground circuit is open • IC power circuit is open (check the INJ fuse in U/H fuse block) • Ignition Coil 1 is damaged or it has failed • PCM has failed
DTC: P0353 **2T CCM, MIL: Yes** **Years:** 2005, 2006, 2007 **Models:** Sierra, Silverado **Engines:** 4.3L, 4.8L, 5.3L 6.0L, 6.0L CNG, 8.1L **Transmissions:** All	**Ignition Coil 3 Control Circuit Malfunction** Engine started; and the PCM detected an unexpected voltage condition on the Coil Near Plug Ignition Control (IC) 3 circuit for less than one second during the CCM test period. **Possible Causes:** • IC circuit is open, shorted to ground or shorted to power (B+) • IC ground (Low REF) circuit or Module ground circuit is open • IC power circuit is open (check the INJ fuse in U/H fuse block) • Ignition Coil 3 is damaged or it has failed • PCM has failed
DTC: P0354 **2T CCM, MIL: Yes** **Years:** 2005, 2006, 2007 **Models:** G6, GTO, LaCrosse, Malibu, Montana, Montana SV6, Relay, Rendezvous, Sky, Solstice, SRX, Terraza, Uplander, Vibe **Engines:** 1.8L, 2.0L, 2.2L, 2.4L, 3.4L, 3.5L, 3.6L, 3.9L, 4.6L, 6.0L **Transmissions:** All	**Ignition Coil 4 Control Circuit Malfunction** Engine started; and the PCM detected an unexpected voltage condition on the Coil Near Plug Ignition Control (IC) 1 circuit for less than one second during the CCM test period. **Possible Causes:** • IC circuit is open, shorted to ground or shorted to power (B+) • IC ground (Low REF) circuit or Module ground circuit is open • IC power circuit is open (check the INJ fuse in U/H fuse block) • Ignition Coil 1 is damaged or it has failed • PCM has failed
DTC: P0354 **2T CCM, MIL: Yes** **Years:** 2005, 2006, 2007 **Models:** Sierra, Silverado **Engines:** 4.3L, 4.8L, 5.3L 6.0L, 6.0L CNG, 8.1L **Transmissions:** All	**Ignition Coil 4 Control Circuit Malfunction** Engine started; and the PCM detected an unexpected voltage condition on the Coil Near Plug Ignition Control (IC) 4 circuit for less than one second during the CCM test period. **Possible Causes:** • IC circuit is open, shorted to ground or shorted to power (B+) • IC ground (Low REF) circuit or Module ground circuit is open • IC power circuit is open (check the INJ fuse in U/H fuse block) • Ignition Coil 4 is damaged or it has failed • PCM has failed

DTC	Trouble Code Title, Conditions & Possible Causes
DTC: P0355 **2T CCM, MIL: Yes** **Years:** 2005, 2006, 2007 **Models:** G6, GTO, LaCrosse, Malibu, Relay, Rendezvous, Sky, Solstice, SRX **Engines:** 3.4L, 3.5L, 3.6L, 3.9L, 3.9L **Transmissions:** All	**Ignition Coil 5 Control Circuit Malfunction** Engine started; and the PCM detected an unexpected voltage condition on the Coil Near Plug Ignition Control (IC) 1 circuit for less than one second during the CCM test period. **Possible Causes:** • IC circuit is open, shorted to ground or shorted to power (B+) • IC ground (Low REF) circuit or Module ground circuit is open • IC power circuit is open (check the INJ fuse in U/H fuse block) • Ignition Coil 1 is damaged or it has failed • PCM has failed
DTC: P0355 **2T CCM, MIL: Yes** **Years:** 2005, 2006, 2007 **Models:** Sierra, Silverado **Engines:** 4.3L, 4.8L, 5.3L 6.0L, 6.0L CNG, 8.1L **Transmissions:** All	**Ignition Coil 5 Control Circuit Malfunction** Engine started; and the PCM detected an unexpected voltage condition on the Coil Near Plug Ignition Control (IC) 5 circuit for less than one second during the CCM test period. **Possible Causes:** • IC circuit is open, shorted to ground or shorted to power (B+) • IC ground (Low REF) circuit or Module ground circuit is open • IC power circuit is open (check the INJ fuse in U/H fuse block) • Ignition Coil 5 is damaged or it has failed • PCM has failed
DTC: P0356 **2T CCM, MIL: Yes** **Years:** 2005, 2006, 2007 **Models:** G6, GTO, LaCrosse, Malibu, Relay, Rendezvous, Sky, Solstice, SRX **Engines:** 3.4L, 3.5L, 3.6L, 3.9L, 3.9L **Transmissions:** All	**Ignition Coil 6 Control Circuit Malfunction** Engine started; and the PCM detected an unexpected voltage condition on the Coil Near Plug Ignition Control (IC) 1 circuit for less than one second during the CCM test period. **Possible Causes:** • IC circuit is open, shorted to ground or shorted to power (B+) • IC ground (Low REF) circuit or Module ground circuit is open • IC power circuit is open (check the INJ fuse in U/H fuse block) • Ignition Coil 1 is damaged or it has failed • PCM has failed
DTC: P0356 **2T CCM, MIL: Yes** **Years:** 2005, 2006, 2007 **Models:** Sierra, Silverado **Engines:** 4.3L, 4.8L, 5.3L 6.0L, 6.0L CNG, 8.1L **Transmissions:** All	**Ignition Coil 6 Control Circuit Malfunction** Engine started; and the PCM detected an unexpected voltage condition on the Coil Near Plug Ignition Control (IC) 6 circuit for less than one second during the CCM test period. **Possible Causes:** • IC circuit is open, shorted to ground or shorted to power (B+) • IC ground (Low REF) circuit or Module ground circuit is open • IC power circuit is open (check the INJ fuse in U/H fuse block) • Ignition Coil 6 is damaged or it has failed • PCM has failed
DTC: P0357 **2T CCM, MIL: Yes** **Years:** 2005, 2006, 2007 **Models:** Sierra, Silverado **Engines:** 4.3L, 4.8L, 5.3L 6.0L, 6.0L CNG, 8.1L **Transmissions:** All	**Ignition Coil 7 Control Circuit Malfunction** Engine started; and the PCM detected an unexpected voltage condition on the Coil Near Plug Ignition Control (IC) 7 circuit for less than one second during the CCM test period. **Possible Causes:** • IC circuit is open, shorted to ground or shorted to power (B+) • IC ground (Low REF) circuit or Module ground circuit is open • IC power circuit is open (check the INJ fuse in U/H fuse block) • Ignition Coil 7 is damaged or it has failed • PCM has failed
DTC: P0358 **2T CCM, MIL: Yes** **Years:** 2005, 2006, 2007 **Models:** Sierra, Silverado **Engines:** 4.8L, 5.3L 6.0L, 6.0L CNG, 8.1L	**Ignition Coil 8 Control Circuit Malfunction** Engine started; and the PCM detected an unexpected voltage condition on the Coil Near Plug Ignition Control (IC) 8 circuit for less than one second during the CCM test period. **Possible Causes:** • IC circuit is open, shorted to ground or shorted to power (B+) • IC ground (Low REF) circuit or Module ground circuit is open • IC power circuit is open (check the INJ fuse in U/H fuse block) • Ignition Coil 8 is damaged or it has failed • PCM has failed

DTC	Trouble Code Title, Conditions & Possible Causes
DTC: P0365 **1T CCM, MIL: Yes** **Years:** 2005, 2006, 2007 **Models:** G6 **Engines:** 2.4L, 3.6L, 3.9L **Transmissions:** All	**Exhaust Camshaft Position (CMP) Sensor Circuit** The engine is running. The ECM does not receive 4 camshaft pulses within 3 seconds. **Possible Causes:** • Low reference circuit has an open/high resistance • 5-volt reference circuit has an open/high resistance or short to ground • 5-volt reference circuit has a short to voltage • Affected signal circuit has an open/high resistance or short to ground or short to voltage • CMP sensor is damaged or it failed • ECM has failed
DTC: P0366 **1T CCM, MIL: Yes** **Years:** 2005, 2006, 2007 **Models:** G6 **Engines:** 2.4L, 3.6L, 3.9L **Transmissions:** All	**Exhaust Camshaft Position (CMP) Sensor Performance** The engine is cranking. The medium resolution is less than or equal to 10 counts. The ECM detects the incorrect number of CMP sensor pulses in 2 revolutions of the crankshaft, which is usually within 1 second. **Possible Causes:** • Low reference circuit has an open/high resistance • 5-volt reference circuit has an open/high resistance or short to ground • 5-volt reference circuit has a short to voltage • Affected signal circuit has an open/high resistance or short to ground or short to voltage • CMP sensor is damaged or it failed • ECM has failed
DTC: P0370 **1T CCM, MIL: Yes** **Years:** 2005, 2006, 2007 **Models:** Sierra, Silverado **Engines:** 6.6L Diesel **Transmissions:** All	**Engine Speed Signal Circuit Malfunction** Engine cranking or running; and the FICM did not receive a crank signal, or it detected an invalid crank signal from the ECM. The CKP sensor signal is replicated and sent to the FICM as an engine speed signal. If the Engine speed signal is lost, the engine will not start. The ECM replicates the signal received from the CKP sensor. This signal is sent to the FICM through the engine speed signal circuit. The FICM uses this replicated signal to generate injection current and control the recharge of the fuel injection high voltage circuits. The FICM has full control of the fuel injectors during cranking. The only input the FICM uses at this time is the engine speed signal from the ECM. The FICM monitors the signal along with the injection request signals from the ECM after the engine is running. **Possible Causes:** • Engine speed signal circuit is open, shorted to ground or VREF • FICM has failed • PCM has failed
DTC: P0374 **1T CCM, MIL: Yes** **Years:** 2005, 2006, 2007 **Models:** Sierra, Silverado **Engines:** 6.6L Diesel **Transmissions:** All	**Engine Speed Signal Circuit Malfunction** Engine cranking or running; and the FICM did not receive a crank signal, or it detected an invalid crank signal from the ECM. The CKP sensor signal is replicated and sent to the FICM as an engine speed signal. If the Engine speed signal is lost, the engine will not start. **Possible Causes:** • Engine speed signal circuit is open, shorted to ground or VREF • FICM has failed • PCM has failed
DTC: P0380 **1T CCM, MIL: No** **Years:** 2005, 2006, 2007 **Models:** Sierra, Silverado **Engines:** 6.6L Diesel **Transmissions:** All	**Glow Plug Range/Performance** Engine cranking, Glow Plugs "on", and the PCM detected the glow plug voltage was less than 4.0v, or with the Glow plugs "off", the PCM detected the Glow plug voltage was over 4.0v or not between 5v and 6.2v (California models). The Scan Tool Glow can help to test the relay. **Possible Causes:** • Glow plug relay control circuit is open, shorted to power, or the ground circuit is open • Glow plug relay is stuck in "on" position causing constant power • Glow plug relay is damaged or has failed • ECM has failed
DTC: P0390 **1T CCM, MIL: Yes** **Years:** 2007 **Models:** G6 **Engines:** 3.6L, 3.9L **Transmissions:** All	**Exhaust Camshaft Position (CMP) Sensor Circuit Bank 2** The ECM detects engine movement by sensing the airflow through the mass air flow (MAF) sensor is more than 3 g/s, or by sensing crankshaft position (CKP) sensor pulses. The ECM detects that the starter is commanded ON and the engine has been cranking for more than 4 seconds without a CMP sensor pulse, or, ECM detects that the engine has started, but did not received a CMP sensor pulse during the first engine revolution, or, ECM detects that the engine is running, but does not receive a CMP sensor pulse for 800 of 1,000 engine cycles. **Possible Causes:** • Low reference circuit has an open/high resistance • 5-volt reference circuit has an open/high resistance or short to ground • 5-volt reference circuit has a short to voltage • Affected signal circuit has an open/high resistance or short to ground or short to voltage • CMP sensor is damaged or it failed • ECM has failed

DTC	Trouble Code Title, Conditions & Possible Causes
DTC: P0391 **1T CCM, MIL: Yes** **Years:** 2007 **Models:** G6 **Engines:** 3.6L, 3.9L **Transmissions:** All	**Exhaust Camshaft Position (CMP) Sensor Performance Bank 2** The ECM detects engine movement by sensing the airflow through the mass air flow (MAF) sensor is more than 3 g/s, or by sensing crankshaft position (CKP) sensor pulses. The ECM detects that the starter is commanded ON and the engine has been cranking for more than 4 seconds without a CMP sensor pulse, or, ECM detects that the engine has started, but did not received a CMP sensor pulse during the first engine revolution, or, ECM detects that the engine is running, but does not receive a CMP sensor pulse for 800 of 1,000 engine cycles. **Possible Causes:** • Low reference circuit has an open/high resistance • 5-volt reference circuit has an open/high resistance or short to ground • 5-volt reference circuit has a short to voltage • Affected signal circuit has an open/high resistance or short to ground or short to voltage • CMP sensor is damaged or it failed • ECM has failed
DTC: P0401 **1T EGR, MIL: Yes** **Years:** 2005, 2006, 2007 **Models:** G6, GTO, LaCrosse, Malibu, Relay, Rendezvous, Sky, Solstice, SRX **Engines:** 2.0L, 2.2L, 2.4L, 3.4L, 3.5L, 3.6L, 3.8L, 3.9L, 4.6L, 6.0L **Transmissions:** All	**Insufficient EGR Flow Detected** DTC P0101, P0102, P0103, P0107, P0108, P0112, P0113, P0116, P0117, P0118, P0121, P0122, P0123, P0125, P0201, P0202, P0203, P0204, P0205, P0206, P0300, P0336, P0403, P0404, P0405, P0502, P0503, P0506, P0507, P1106, P1107, P1111, P1112, P1114, P1115, P1121, P1122, P1374 and P1404 not set, engine runtime up to 3 minutes, engine speed of 1050-1300 RPM, VSS over 35 MPH, system voltage from 11-18v, BARO sensor over 74 kPa, ECT sensor more than 167°F, IAT sensor from 32-212°F, IAC counts stable (5 counts), A/C Clutch and current gear stable, gear selector not in Park or Neutral, Decel Fuel Cutoff and Power Enrichment not active, MAP sensor from 15-70 kPa, then during a deceleration period from over 30 MPH with the TP angle less than 1%, the PCM detected the MAP changes during testing indicated insufficient EGR flow. Note that during the test that the Desired EGR and EGR Position PID will change from 0 to a positive number (+ 0). **Possible Causes:** • Base engine problem (e.g., a severely restricted exhaust), or any other problem that causes the engine to run poorly • EGR passages or intake passages clogged or restricted • EGR pipe is clogged, dirty or otherwise restricted • EGR vacuum hoses damaged, loose or routed incorrectly • EGR solenoid valve is clogged (carbon), damaged or has failed • MAP sensor is dirty, damaged or it is "skewed"
DTC: P0401 **2T EGR, MIL: Yes** **Years:** 2005, 2006, 2007 **Models:** Sierra, Silverado **Engines:** 8.1L **Transmissions:** All	**Insufficient EGR Flow Detected** DTC P0106-P0108, P0112-P0118, P0121-P0123, P0300, P0404, P0405, P0502-P0507, P1111-P1112, P1120-P1125, P1220, P1221, P1404, P1514-P1518, P1635 and P1639 not set, engine started, vehicle driven to 25-70 MPH at 725-2000 RPM, BARO sensor over 70 kPa, ECT sensor from 140-244°F, IAT sensor from 37-167°F, altitude compensated MAP from 10-60 kPa (2-7 psi) with any change less than 0.8 kPa, IAC position and A/C Clutch both steady, followed by a deceleration period with the TP angle under 1.2% and Deceleration Fuel Cutoff off, and the PCM detected the change in the MAP sensor was less than a calculated value during the EGR flow test for 2 seconds. The PCM Allows one EGR flow test in each key cycle. To verify a repair, the PCM Allows up to 12 EGR flow test counts during the first key cycle after codes are cleared (from 9-12 EGR flow tests are needed) **Possible Causes:** • Base engine problem (e.g., a severely restricted exhaust) • EGR vacuum hoses damaged, loose or routed incorrectly • EGR passages or intake passages clogged or restricted • EGR solenoid valve is clogged (carbon), damaged or has failed
DTC: P0401 **2T EGR, MIL: Yes** **Years:** 2005, 2006, 2007 **Models:** Sierra, Silverado **Engines:** 6.6L Diesel **Transmissions:** All	**Insufficient EGR Flow Detected** DTC P0101, P0102, P0103, P0106, P0107, P0108, P0112, P0113, P0116, P0117, P0118, P0405, P0406, P0489, P0490, P0500, P0651, P2142, P2144, and P2145 not set, engine runtime over 5 seconds, ECM not operating in Reduced Engine Power mode, system voltage from 11-18v, BARO sensor over 72 kPa, engine speed from 610-820 RPM (50 RPM) for 3 seconds, ECT sensor from 140-212°F, IAT sensor more than 32°F, Calculated Fuel Rate from 3-20 mm³, Power Take Off not enabled, APP indicated angle less than 1%, vehicle speed less than 0.25 MPH, conditions met for 3 seconds, and the ECM detected a calibrated difference between the Expected MAF sensor rate and Actual MAF sensor rate during EGR system operation, or the ECM did not detect any difference between the Expected EGR Vacuum sensor signal and the Actual EGR Vacuum sensor signal for over 4 seconds. **Possible Causes:** • EGR ports are clogged or restricted • EGR throttle valve vacuum control solenoid is leaking/restricted • EGR throttle valve is binding or sticking, or it is damaged • EGR throttle valve vacuum diaphragm is damaged or has failed • Vacuum hose from vacuum pump to EGR throttle valve diaphragm leaking or restricted • Exhaust system is restricted, or exhaust system was modified

DTC	Trouble Code Title, Conditions & Possible Causes
DTC: P0403 **2T CCM, MIL: Yes** **Years:** 2005, 2006, 2007 **Models:** G6, GTO, LaCrosse, Malibu, Relay, Rendezvous, Sky, Solstice, SRX **Engines:** 2.0L, 2.2L, 2.4L, 3.4L, 3.5L, 3.6L, 3.8L, 3.9L, 4.6L, 6.0L **Transmissions:** All	**EGR Solenoid Control Circuit Malfunction** Engine started; system voltage from 9-18.0v, and the PCM detected an unexpected voltage condition on the EGR Solenoid high or low control circuit for 20 seconds in the CCM test. **Possible Causes:** • EGR solenoid control circuit is open, shorted to ground or B+ • EGR solenoid high control (VREF) circuit is open • EGR solenoid is damaged or has failed • PCM has failed • TSB 02-06-04-053 contains a repair procedure for this code
DTC: P0404 **1T CCM, MIL: Yes** **Years:** 2005, 2006, 2007 **Models:** G6, GTO, LaCrosse, Malibu, Relay, Rendezvous, Sky, Solstice, SRX **Engines:** 2.0L, 2.2L, 2.4L, 3.4L, 3.5L, 3.6L, 3.8L, 3.9L, 4.6L, 6.0L **Transmissions:** All	**EGR Open Position Signal Range/Performance** Engine started; system voltage over 11.0v, EGR solenoid enabled, EGR flow test not active, and the PCM detected the difference between the Actual EGR position and the Desired EGR position was more than 15% for over 20 seconds. The PCM will disable the EGR command if the startup ECT sensor value is less than 41°F, and will not enable the EGR solenoid until the ECT is more than 167°F. **Possible Causes:** • EGR sensor signal circuit is open, shorted to ground or power • EGR sensor ground or VREF circuit is open • EGR valve seat contains debris or carbon (inspect and clean) • EGR valve pintle contains debris or carbon (inspect and clean) • EGR valve is contaminated, clogged, damaged or has failed • PCM has failed
DTC: P0404 **2T CCM, MIL: Yes** **Years:** 2005, 2006, 2007 **Models:** Sierra, Silverado **Engines:** 4.3L, 4.8L, 5.3L, 6.0L, 8.1L **Transmissions:** All	**EGR Open Position Signal Range/Performance** Engine started; commanded EGR position over 0%, EGR flow test inactive, Desired EGR position did not change more than 20%, then after the vehicle was driven, the PCM detected the difference between the Actual EGR position and the Desired EGR position was more than 10% for over 13 seconds during the test. **Possible Causes:** • EGR sensor signal circuit is open, shorted to ground or power • EGR sensor ground or VREF circuit is open • EGR valve seat or pintle contains debris or carbon (inspect and clean) • EGR valve is contaminated, clogged, damaged or has failed • PCM has failed
DTC: P0404 **2T CCM, MIL: Yes** **Years:** 2005, 2006, 2007 **Models:** Sierra, Silverado **Engines:** 6.6L Diesel **Transmissions:** All	**Exhaust Gas Recirculation System Malfunction** DTC P0101, P0102, P0103, P0106, P0107, P0108, P0112, P0113, P0116, P0117, P0118, P0405, P0406, P0489, P0490, P0500, P0651, P2142, P2144, and P2145 not set, engine runtime over 5 seconds, PCM not operating in Reduced Engine Power mode, system voltage from 11-18v, BARO sensor over 72 kPa, engine speed from 610-820 RPM (50 RPM) for 3 seconds, ECT sensor from 140-212°F, IAT sensor more than 32°F, Calculated Fuel Rate from 3-20 mm³, PTO "off", APP indicated angle less than 1%, vehicle speed less than 0.25 MPH, conditions met for 3 seconds, and the PCM detected a lower than expected EGR Vacuum sensor signal along with a higher than expected MAF sensor rate for 8 seconds. **Possible Causes:** • Air intake pipe is clogged or damaged • EGR system vacuum lines are clogged or leaking • EGR throttle valve throttle solenoid is damaged or it had failed • EGR valve vacuum sensor is damaged or it has failed • EGR valve vent solenoid is damaged or it has failed
DTC: P0405 **1T CCM, MIL: Yes** **Years:** 2005, 2006, 2007 **Models:** G6, GTO, LaCrosse, Malibu, Relay, Rendezvous, Sky, Solstice, SRX **Engines:** 2.0L, 2.2L, 2.4L, 3.4L, 3.5L, 3.6L, 3.8L, 3.9L, 4.6L, 6.0L **Transmissions:** All	**EGR Sensor Circuit Low Input** Engine started; system voltage over 10.0v and the PCM detected the EGR Pintle Position sensor was less than 0.11v for 2 seconds. The PCM is connected to the sensor with a 5v VREF, low reference and EGR valve position signal circuit to determine the EGR valve position. This code is set if the EGR sensor voltage is pulled too low. **Possible Causes:** • EGR position sensor signal circuit is open or shorted to ground • EGR position sensor VREF circuit is open or shorted to ground • EGR position sensor is damaged or has failed • PCM has failed

DTC	Trouble Code Title, Conditions & Possible Causes
DTC: P0405 **2T CCM, MIL: Yes** **Years:** 2005, 2006, 2007 **Models:** Sierra, Silverado **Engines:** 4.3L, 4.8L, 5.3L 6.0L, 6.2L, 8.1L **Transmissions:** All	**EGR Position Sensor Circuit Low Input** Engine started; system voltage over 10.0v, EGR Position sensor VREF stable from 4-5v, and the PCM detected the EGR Position signal was less than 0.14v for a period of 5 seconds. **Possible Causes:** • EGR position sensor signal circuit is open • EGR position sensor signal circuit is shorted to ground • EGR position sensor VREF circuit is open or shorted to ground • EGR position sensor is damaged or has failed • PCM has failed • TSB 01-06-04-043 contains a repair procedure for this code
DTC: P0405 **2T CCM, MIL: Yes** **Years:** 2005, 2006, 2007 **Models:** Sierra, Silverado **Engines:** 4.3L, 4.8L, 5.3L, 6.0L, 8.1L **Transmissions:** All	**EGR Position Sensor Circuit Low Input** Engine started; system voltage over 10.0v, EGR Position sensor VREF stable from 4-5v, and the PCM detected the EGR Position signal was less than 0.14v for a period of 5 seconds. **Possible Causes:** • EGR position sensor signal circuit is open • EGR position sensor signal circuit is shorted to ground • EGR position sensor VREF circuit is open or shorted to ground • EGR position sensor is damaged or has failed • PCM has failed
DTC: P0405 **2T CCM, MIL: Yes** **Years:** 2005, 2006, 2007 **Models:** Sierra, Silverado **Engines:** 6.6L Diesel **Transmissions:** All	**EGR Vacuum Sensor Circuit Low Input** DTC P0101, P0489 and P0651 not set, engine started, system voltage from 11-18v, and the PCM detected the EGR Vacuum sensor was less than 19 kPa for 5 seconds. The EGR Vacuum sensor is used to monitor the amount of vacuum is available to the EGR valve. A low reference, 5v VREF and a Vacuum sensor signal circuit connect this sensor to the PCM. **Possible Causes:** • EGR vacuum sensor connector is damaged or shorted • EGR vacuum sensor VREF circuit is open or shorted to ground • EGR vacuum sensor signal circuit is shorted to ground • EGR vacuum sensor is damaged or it has failed • ECM has failed
DTC: P0406 **2T CCM, MIL: Yes** **Years:** 2005, 2006, 2007 **Models:** Sierra, Silverado **Engines:** 6.6L Diesel **Transmissions:** All	**EGR Vacuum Sensor Circuit High Input** DTC P0651 not set, engine started, system voltage from 11-18v, and the ECM detected the EGR Vacuum sensor was more than 158 kPa for 5 seconds during the test. The EGR Vacuum sensor is used to monitor the amount of vacuum available to the EGR valve. A low reference, 5v VREF and a sensor signal circuit connect to the ECM. **Possible Causes:** • EGR vacuum sensor connector is damaged or open • EGR vacuum sensor ground circuit is open • EGR vacuum sensor signal circuit is open • EGR vacuum sensor signal circuit is shorted to VREF • EGR vacuum sensor is damaged or it has failed • ECM has failed
DTC: P0418 **2T CCM, MIL: Yes** **Years:** 2005, 2006, 2007 **Models:** Sierra, Silverado **Engines:** 4.3L, 4.8L, 6.0L, 6.2L, 8.1L **Transmissions:** All	**Secondary Air System Pump Relay Control Circuit Malfunction (Bank 1)** Engine started; system voltage over 10.0v and the PCM detected the Actual and Commanded state of the AIR Pump Relay driver did not match for 5 seconds in the test. **Possible Causes:** • AIR relay control circuit is open, shorted to ground or power • AIR relay control circuit is shorted to system power (B+) • AIR relay power circuit is open (test power from IGN fuse) • AIR relay is damaged or has failed • PCM has failed

DTC	Trouble Code Title, Conditions & Possible Causes
DTC: P0420 **2T CAT, MIL: Yes** **Years:** 2005, 2006, 2007 **Models:** Sierra, Silverado **Engines:** 4.3L, 4.8L, 6.0L, 6.2L, 8.1L **Transmissions:** All	**Catalyst System Low Efficiency (Bank 1)** DTC P0101-P0103, P0106-P0108, P0112, P0113, P0117, P0118, P0125, P0131, P0132-P0138, P0140, P0141, P0151-P0158, P0160, P0161, P0171-P0175, P0200, P0300, P0325, P0327, P0335, P0336, P0341, P0343, P0351-P0358, P0443-P0449, P0502, P0503, P0506, P0507, P1120, P1125, P1133, P1134, P1153, P1154, P1220, P1221, P1275, P1276, P1280-P1286, P1441, P1514, P1518 not set, engine started, engine runtime over 6 minutes, engine speed over 1000 RPM for 32-40 since last idle period, BARO sensor over 72 kPa, ECT sensor more than 167°F, IAT sensor over 16°F, MAF sensor from 15-50 g/sec, Catalyst Temperature over 840°F, engine running at idle speed for under 2 minutes with the Actual idle speed within 100-125 RPM of the Desired idle speed, then vehicle driven to 22-85 MPH in closed loop, TP angle over 2% on 7.4L, Long Term fuel trim stable, any change in engine load less than 10%, and the PCM detected the Bank 1 Catalyst was degraded. **Possible Causes:** • Air leaks at the exhaust manifold or in the exhaust pipes • Base engine problems (i.e., high engine oil or coolant usage) • Catalytic converter is damaged, contaminated or has failed • Continuous engine misfire conditions, or weak or low coil output • Front HO2S or rear HO2S is contaminated with fuel or moisture • Rear HO2S is loose in the mounting hole (check it for a leak) • Front HO2S older (aged) than the rear HO2S (HO2S-12 is lazy) • TSB 81-65-37 contains a repair procedure for this code
DTC: P0420 **2T CAT, MIL: Yes** **Years:** 2005, 2006, 2007 **Models:** G6, GTO, LaCrosse, Malibu, Montana, Montana SV6, Relay, Rendezvous, Sky, Solstice, SRX, Terraza, Uplander, Vibe **Engines:** 1.8L, 2.0L, 2.2L, 2.4L, 3.4L, 3.5L, 3.6L, 3.9L, 4.6L, 6.0L **Transmissions:** All	**Catalyst System Low Efficiency (Bank 1)** DTC P0030, P0101-P0103, P0107, P0108, P0112, P0113, P0116-P0118, P0121-P0123, P0128, P0130-P0138, P0140, P0141, P0171, P0172, P0201-P0206, P0300, P0336, P0341, P0404-P0405, P0410, P0440, P0442, P0443, P0502-P0503, P0506-P0507, P1133, P1134, P1351, P1352, P1361, P1362 and P1441 not set, engine runtime over 10 minutes, system voltage over 10.0v, BARO sensor over 75 kPa, ECT sensor at 169-255°F, IAT sensor at −4°F to 212°F, MAF sensor at 12-32 g/sec, Catalyst Temperature at 788-1202°F for 3-4 minutes, engine speed at 1000-3000 RPM, engine load below 63%, VSS at 30-75 MPH, and the PCM detected the Catalyst was degraded. **Possible Causes:** • Air leaks at the exhaust manifold or in the exhaust pipes • Base engine problems (i.e., high engine oil or coolant usage) • Catalytic converter is damaged, contaminated or has failed • Continuous engine misfire conditions, or weak or low coil output • Front HO2S or rear HO2S is contaminated with fuel or moisture • Rear HO2S is loose in the mounting hole (check it for a leak) • Front HO2S older (aged) than the rear HO2S (HO2S-12 is lazy)
DTC: P0420 **2T CAT, MIL: Yes** **Years:** 2005, 2006, 2007 **Models:** Sierra, Silverado **Engines:** 4.3L, 4.8L, 5.3L, 6.0L, 6.2L, 8.1L **Transmissions:** All	**Catalyst System Low Efficiency (Bank 1)** DTC P0101-P0103, P0106-P0108, P0112, P0113, P0117, P0118, P0120, P0121-123, P0125, P0128, P0131-P0138, P0140, P0141, P0171-P0172, P0177-P0179, P0200, P0220, P0300, P0325, P0327, P0332, P0335, P0336, P0341-P0343, P0351-P0358, P0442-P0446, P0452-P0453, P0455, P0496, P0502-P0503, P1125, P1133, P1153, P1258, P1514- P1518, P2108 or P2135 not set, engine started, ECT sensor from 158-248°F, BARO sensor over 74 kPa, IAT sensor at 5-185°F, vehicle driven in closed loop at cruise speed for 40-45 seconds, and the PCM detected that the Oxygen storage capability of the Catalyst was degraded. **Possible Causes:** • Air leaks at the exhaust manifold or in the exhaust pipes • Base engine problems (i.e., high engine oil or coolant usage) • Catalytic converter is damaged, contaminated or has failed • Continuous engine misfire conditions, or weak or low coil output • Front HO2S or rear HO2S is contaminated with fuel or moisture • Rear HO2S is loose in the mounting hole (check it for a leak) • TSB 81-65-37 contains a repair procedure for this code
DTC: P0430 **2T CAT, MIL: Yes** **Years:** 2005, 2006, 2007 **Models:** Sierra, Silverado **Engines:** 4.3L, 4.8L, 5.3L, 6.0L, 6.2L, 8.1L **Transmissions:** All	**Catalyst System Low Efficiency (Bank 2)** DTC P0101-P0103, P0106-P0108, P0112, P0113, P0117, P0118, P0120, P0121-123, P0125, P0128, P0151-P0155, P0157, P0158, P0160-P0161, P0174, P0175, P0177, P0178, P0179, P0200, P0220, P0300, P0325, P0327, P0332, P0335, 336, P0341-P0343, P0351-P0358, P0442, P0443, P0446, P0452, P0453, P0455, P0496, P0502, P0503, P1125, P1133, P1153, P1258, P1514, P1516, P1518 and P2108, P2135 not set, vehicle driven at 25-75 MPH for 40-45 seconds in closed loop, BARO sensor over 74 kPa, ECT sensor at 158-248°F, IAT sensor at 5-185°F, and the PCM detected the Catalyst had degraded to below a calibrated threshold. **Possible Causes:** • Air leaks at the exhaust manifold or in the exhaust pipes • Base engine problems (i.e., high engine oil or coolant usage) • Catalytic converter is damaged, contaminated or has failed • Continuous engine misfire conditions, or weak or low coil output • Front HO2S or rear HO2S is contaminated with fuel or moisture • Rear HO2S is loose in the mounting hole (check it for a leak) • TSB 81-65-37 contains a repair procedure for this code

DTC	Trouble Code Title, Conditions & Possible Causes
DTC: P0440 **2T EVAP, MIL: Yes** **Years:** 2005, 2006, 2007 **Models:** Sierra, Silverado **Engines:** 4.3L, 4.8L, 5.3L, 6.0L, 6.2L, 8.1L **Transmissions:** All	**EVAP System No Flow During Purge** DTC P0107, P0108, P0112, P0113, P0115, P0116-P0118, P0121, P0122, P0123, P0125, P0443, P0449, P0452, P0453, P1106, P1107, P1112, P1114, P1115, P1121 and P1122 not set, engine started, ECT and IAT sensors from 39-86°F and within 16°F at startup, vehicle driven at a steady speed less than 72 MPH, system voltage over 10.0v, BARO sensor more than 75 kPa, fuel level from 15-85%, and the PCM detected the EVAP system was unable to achieve and maintain vacuum during the EVAP flow and leak test. **Possible Causes:** • Charcoal canister is loaded with fuel or moisture • Fuel filler cap is loose, cross-threaded, damaged or wrong part • Fuel tank, fuel filler neck or fuel sending unit 'O' ring is leaking • Fuel tank pressure sensor is damaged, disconnected or it failed • Fuel tank vapor line(s) is clogged, damaged or disconnected • Purge valve vapor line is clogged, damaged, or disconnected • Purge or vent solenoid power circuit is open (check the fuse) • PCM has failed
DTC: P0442 **2T EVAP, MIL: Yes** **Years:** 2005, 2006, 2007 **Models:** G6, GTO, LaCrosse, Malibu, Relay, Rendezvous, Sky, Solstice, SRX **Engines:** 2.0L, 2.2L, 2.4L, 3.4L, 3.5L, 3.6L, 3.8L, 3.9L, 4.6L, 6.0L **Transmissions:** All	**EVAP System Small Leak (0.040") Detected** DTC P0107, P0108, P0112, P0113, P0116-P0118, P0121, P0122, P0123, P0125, P0440, P0443, P0449, P0452, P0453, P1106, P1107, P1112, P1114, P1115, P1121 and P1122 not set, engine started, ECT and IAT sensors from 39-86°F and within 16°F, system voltage over 10.0v, BARO sensor more than 75 kPa, vehicle driven to a steady speed of less than 75 MPH, fuel level from 15-80%, and the PCM detected the EVAP system achieved proper vacuum, but a vacuum decay condition was detected during the EVAP leak test. **Possible Causes:** • Charcoal canister is loaded with fuel or moisture • Fuel filler cap is loose, cross-threaded, damaged or wrong part • Fuel tank, fuel filler neck or fuel sending unit 'O' ring is leaking • Fuel tank pressure sensor is damaged, disconnected or it failed • Fuel tank vapor line(s) is clogged, damaged or disconnected • Purge valve vapor line is clogged, damaged, or disconnected • Purge solenoid or Vent solenoid has a small leaking (sticking) • PCM has failed
DTC: P0442 **2T EVAP, MIL: Yes** **Years:** 2005, 2006, 2007 **Models:** Sierra, Silverado **Engines:** 4.3L, 4.8L, 5.3L, 6.0L, 6.2L, 8.1L **Transmissions:** All	**EVAP System Small Leak (0.040") Detected** DTC P0107, P0108, P0112, P0113, P0116, P0117, P0118, P0125, P0440, P0443, P0455, P0449, P0452, P0453, P1111, P1112, P1114, P1115, P1120, P1220 and P1221 not set, ECT and IAT sensors from 39-86°F and within 16°F at startup, engine started, vehicle driven at less than 75 MPH, system voltage over 10.0v, BARO sensor over 75 kPa, fuel level from 15-85%, DTC P0125 not active, and the PCM detected the EVAP system was able to achieve proper vacuum, but that a vacuum decay condition was detected. **Possible Causes:** • Charcoal canister is loaded with fuel or moisture • Fuel filler cap is loose, cross-threaded, damaged or wrong part • Fuel tank, fuel filler neck or fuel sending unit 'O' ring is leaking • Fuel tank pressure sensor is damaged, disconnected or it failed • Fuel tank vapor line(s) is clogged, damaged or disconnected • Purge valve vapor line is clogged, damaged, or disconnected • Purge solenoid or Vent solenoid has a small leaking (sticking) • PCM has failed
DTC: P0442 **2T EVAP, MIL: Yes** **Years:** 2005, 2006, 2007 **Models:** Sierra, Silverado **Engines:** 4.3L, 4.8L, 5.3L, 6.0L, 6.2L, 8.1L **Transmissions:** All	**EVAP System Small Leak (0.040") Detected** DTC P0100, P0101-P0103, P0106-P0108, P0112, P0113, P0116, P0117, P0118, P0125, P0335, P0336, P0443, P0446, P0449, P0452, P0453, P0455, P0496, P0500, P0502, P1106, P1107 and P1683 not set, engine runtime over 600 seconds, ECT and IAT sensors from 39-86°F and within 15°F at startup, vehicle driven over 3 miles this trip, BARO sensor over 74 kPa, fuel level from 15-85%, P0455 ran and passed, and the PCM detected a pressure change in the EVAP system that was less than a calibrated value. **Possible Causes:** • Charcoal canister is loaded with fuel or moisture • Fuel filler cap is loose, cross-threaded, damaged or wrong part • Fuel tank, fuel filler neck or fuel sending unit 'O' ring is leaking • Fuel tank pressure sensor is damaged, disconnected or it failed • Fuel tank or purge valve vapor lines clogged or disconnected • Purge solenoid or Vent solenoid has a small leaking (sticking) • PCM has failed

DTC	Trouble Code Title, Conditions & Possible Causes
DTC: P0443 **2T CCM, MIL: Yes** **Years:** 2005, 2006, 2007 **Models:** G6, GTO, LaCrosse, Malibu, Relay, Rendezvous, Sky, Solstice, SRX **Engines:** 2.0L, 2.2L, 2.4L, 3.4L, 3.5L, 3.6L, 3.8L, 3.9L, 4.6L, 6.0L **Transmissions:** All	**EVAP Purge Solenoid Control Circuit Malfunction** Engine started; system voltage over 10.0v and the PCM detected an unexpected voltage condition on the Purge Solenoid control circuit for over 30 seconds during the CCM test. **Possible Causes:** • Purge solenoid control circuit is open or shorted to ground • Purge solenoid control circuit is shorted to system power (B+) • Purge solenoid power circuit is open (check the IGN1 UH fuse) • Purge solenoid is damaged or has failed • PCM has failed
DTC: P0443 **2T CCM, MIL: Yes** **Years:** 2005, 2006, 2007 **Models:** Sierra, Silverado **Engines:** 4.3L, 4.8L, 5.3L, 6.0L, 6.2L, 8.1L **Transmissions:** All	**EVAP Purge Solenoid Control Circuit Malfunction** Engine started; system voltage from 6-18v, and the PCM detected the Actual and Commanded state of the EVAP Purge solenoid driver control circuit did not match for over 5 seconds during the CCM test. **Possible Causes:** • Purge solenoid control circuit is open or shorted to ground • Purge solenoid control circuit is shorted to system power (B+) • Purge solenoid power circuit is open (test the ENG1 fuse) • Purge solenoid is damaged or has failed • PCM has failed
DTC: P0443 **2T CCM, MIL: Yes** **Years:** 2005, 2006, 2007 **Models:** Sierra, Silverado **Engines:** 4.3L, 4.8L, 5.3L, 6.0L, 6.2L, 8.1L **Transmissions:** All	**EVAP Purge Solenoid Control Circuit Malfunction** Engine started; system voltage at 6-18v, and the PCM detected the Actual and Commanded state of the EVAP Purge solenoid driver control circuit did not match for over 5 seconds during the CCM test period. **Possible Causes:** • Purge solenoid control circuit is open or shorted to ground • Purge solenoid control circuit is shorted to system power (B+) • Purge solenoid power circuit is open (test the ENG1 fuse) • Purge solenoid is damaged or has failed • PCM has failed
DTC: P0446 **2T EVAP, MIL: Yes** **Years:** 2005, 2006, 2007 **Models:** G6, GTO, LaCrosse, Malibu, Relay, Rendezvous, Sky, Solstice, SRX **Engines:** 2.0L, 2.2L, 2.4L, 3.4L, 3.5L, 3.6L, 3.8L, 3.9L, 4.6L, 6.0L **Transmissions:** All	**EVAP Vent System Performance** DTC P0107, P0108, P0112, P0113, P0116-P0118, P0121-P0123, P0125, P0440, P0442, P0443, P0449, P0452, P0453, P1106, P1107, P1112, P1114, P1115, P1121 and P1122 not set, engine started, system voltage over 10.0v, fuel level from 15-85%, BARO sensor over 75 kPa, ECT and IAT sensors from 39-86°F and within 16°F at startup, VSS under 75 MPH, and the PCM detected the fuel tank pressure was less than −10 H2O for 30 seconds. **Possible Causes:** • EVAP vent fresh air hose is clogged, kinked or restricted • EVAP Vent solenoid is contaminated, damaged or has failed • FTP sensor is out-of-calibration, damaged or "skewed" • PCM has failed
DTC: P0446 **2T EVAP, MIL: Yes** **Years:** 2005, 2006, 2007 **Models:** Sierra, Silverado **Engines:** 4.3L, 4.8L, 5.3L, 6.0L, 6.2L, 8.1L **Transmissions:** All	**EVAP Vent System Performance** DTC P0106, P0107, P0108, P0112, P0113, P0116-P0118, P0125, P0440-P0453, P1111-P1115, P1120, P1220 and P1221 not set, engine started, ECT and IAT sensors from 39-86°F and within 16°F at startup, BARO over 75 kPa, fuel level from 15-85%, vehicle driven to a speed of less than 75 MPH, and the PCM detected the fuel tank pressure sensor indicated less than −10 inches H2O for 20 seconds. **Possible Causes:** • EVAP vent fresh air hose is clogged, kinked or restricted • EVAP Vent solenoid is contaminated, damaged or has failed • EVAP Canister plugged or severely restricted • Fuel Cap or EVAP Service Port leaking • Fuel vapor lines or purge lines damaged or leaking • FTP sensor is out-of-calibration, damaged or "skewed" • PCM has failed • TSB 02-06-04-037 contains a repair procedure for this code

DTC	Trouble Code Title, Conditions & Possible Causes
DTC: P0446 **2T EVAP, MIL: Yes** **Years:** 2005, 2006, 2007 **Models:** Sierra, Silverado **Engines:** 4.3L, 4.8L, 5.3L, 6.0L, 6.2L, 8.1L **Transmissions:** All	**EVAP Vent System Performance** DTC P0106, P0107, P0108, P0112, P0113, P0116, P0117, P0118, P0120, P0121, P0122, P0123, P0125, P0131, P0132, P0133, P0134, P0135, P0137, P0138, P0140, P0141, P0147, P0151, P0152, P0153, P0154, P0155, P0157, P0158, P0160, P0161, P0167, P0220, P0442, P0443, P0449, P0452, P0453, P0455, P0502, P0503, P1111, P1112, P1114, P1115, P1120 are not set, engine started, ECT and IAT sensors from 39-86°F and within 16°F at startup, BARO sensor over 75 kPa, system voltage from 10-18v, fuel level from 15-85%, and the PCM detected the fuel tank pressure sensor was less than −10 inches H2O for 30 seconds. **Possible Causes:** • EVAP vent fresh air hose is clogged, kinked or restricted • EVAP Vent solenoid is contaminated, damaged or has failed • EVAP Canister plugged or severely restricted • Fuel Cap or EVAP Service Port leaking • Fuel vapor lines or purge lines damaged or leaking • FTP sensor is out-of-calibration, damaged or "skewed" • PCM has failed • TSB 02-06-04-037 contains a repair procedure for this code
DTC: P0449 **2T CCM, MIL: Yes** **Years:** 2005, 2006, 2007 **Models:** G6, GTO, LaCrosse, Malibu, Relay, Rendezvous, Sky, Solstice, SRX **Engines:** 2.0L, 2.2L, 2.4L, 3.4L, 3.5L, 3.6L, 3.8L, 3.9L, 4.6L, 6.0L **Transmissions:** All	**EVAP Vent Solenoid Control Circuit Malfunction** Engine started; system voltage from 6-18.0v, and the PCM detected the Actual and the Commanded state of the EVAP Vent Solenoid driver control circuit did not match for over 5 seconds during the CCM test period. **Possible Causes:** • Vent solenoid control circuit is open, shorted to ground or B+ • Vent solenoid power circuit is open (test the ENG CTRL fuse) • Vent solenoid is damaged or has failed • PCM has failed
DTC: P0449 **2T CCM, MIL: Yes** **Years:** 2005, 2006, 2007 **Models:** Sierra, Silverado **Engines:** 4.3L, 6.2L **Transmissions:** All	**EVAP Vent Solenoid Control Circuit Malfunction** Engine started; system voltage from 6-18v, and the PCM detected the Actual and Commanded state of the Vent Solenoid driver control circuit did not match for over 5 seconds. **Possible Causes:** • Vent solenoid control circuit is open or shorted to ground • Vent solenoid control circuit is shorted to system power (B+) • Vent solenoid power circuit is open (test the ENG1 fuse) • Vent solenoid is damaged or has failed • PCM has failed
DTC: P0449 **2T CCM, MIL: Yes** **Years:** 2005, 2006, 2007 **Models:** Sierra, Silverado **Engines:** 4.3L, 4.8L, 5.3L, 6.0L, 6.2L, 8.1L **Transmissions:** All	**EVAP Vent Solenoid Control Circuit Malfunction** Engine started; system voltage from 6-18v, and the PCM detected the Actual and Commanded state of the Vent Solenoid driver control circuit did not match for over 5 seconds during the CCM test period. **Possible Causes:** • Vent solenoid control circuit is open or shorted to ground • Vent solenoid control circuit is shorted to system power (B+) • Vent solenoid power circuit is open (test the ENG1 fuse) • Vent solenoid is damaged or has failed • PCM has failed
DTC: P0452 **2T CCM, MIL: Yes** **Years:** 2005, 2006, 2007 **Models:** All **Engines:** All **Transmissions:** All	**Fuel Tank Pressure Sensor Circuit Low Input** Key on or engine running; and the PCM detected the Fuel Tank Pressure (FTP) sensor circuit was less than 0.10v for 5 seconds during the CCM test period. **Possible Causes:** • FTP sensor connector is damaged or shorted • FTP sensor signal circuit is open or shorted to ground • FTP sensor VREF circuit is open or shorted to ground • FTP sensor is damaged or has failed • PCM has failed
DTC: P0453 **2T CCM, MIL: Yes** **Years:** 2005, 2006, 2007 **Models:** All **Engines:** All **Transmissions:** All	**Fuel Tank Pressure Sensor Circuit High Input** Key on or engine running; and the PCM detected the Fuel Tank Pressure (FTP) sensor circuit was more than 4.90v for 5 seconds during the CCM test period. **Possible Causes:** • FTP sensor connector is damaged, loose or open • FTP sensor signal circuit is shorted to VREF (5v) • FTP sensor ground circuit is open between sensor and PCM • FTP sensor is damaged or has failed • PCM has failed

DTC	Trouble Code Title, Conditions & Possible Causes
DTC: P0455 **2T EVAP, MIL: Yes** **Years:** 2005, 2006, 2007 **Models:** All **Engines:** All **Transmissions:** All	**EVAP System Large Leak (0.080") Detected** DTC P0106-P0108, P0112, P0113, P0116-P0118, P0120-P0123, P0125, P0131-P0138, P0140, P0141, P0147, P0151-P0158, P0160, P0161, P0167, P0220, P0442-P0443, P0449, P0452-P0453, P0455, P0502, P0503, P1111, P1112, P1114, P1115, P1120 not set, engine started, ECT and IAT sensors from 39-167°F and within 16°F at startup, system voltage from 10-18v, BARO sensor more than 75 kPa, Fuel Level from 15-85%, and the PCM detected it was unable to achieve or maintain vacuum during the EVAP system. The PCM monitors the FTP sensor signal to determine the EVAP system vacuum level. Once conditions are correct, the PCM commands the Purge valve open and the EVAP vent valve closed to Allow engine vacuum to enter the system. After a calibrated time or vacuum level, the PCM commands the Purge valve closed to seal the system, and monitors the FTP sensor to determine the EVAP system vacuum level. If the system is unable to achieve the correct vacuum level, or the vacuum level decreases too rapidly, the PCM will set this code. **Possible Causes:** • Fuel filler cap is very loose, missing or the wrong part • Fuel tank, fuel filler neck or fuel sending unit 'O' ring is leaking • Fuel tank pressure sensor is damaged, disconnected or it failed • Fuel tank vapor line(s) is clogged, damaged or disconnected • Purge valve vapor line is clogged, damaged, or disconnected • Purge solenoid is not opening (it may be damaged or sticking) • Vent solenoid is not closing (it may be damaged or sticking) • PCM has failed
DTC: P0462 **1T CCM, MIL: No** **Years:** 2005, 2006, 2007 **Models:** Rendezvous **Engines:** 3.4L **Transmissions:** All	**Fuel Level Sensor Circuit Low Input** Engine started; system voltage over 10.0v and the PCM detected the Fuel Level sensor signal was less than 0.4v (less than 3%) for 10 seconds during the CCM continuous test. **Possible Causes:** • Fuel level sensor signal circuit is shorted to ground between the fuel level sensor and the PCM connector • Fuel level sender is damaged, binding or not aligned properly • PCM has failed
DTC: P0463 **1T CCM, MIL: No** **Years:** 2005, 2006, 2007 **Models:** Sierra, Silverado **Engines:** 4.3L, 4.8L, 5.3L, 6.0L, 6.2L, 8.1L **Transmissions:** All	**Fuel Level Sensor High Input** Engine started; system voltage over 10.0v and the PCM detected the Fuel Level sensor signal indicated more than 2.9-3.0v for 10-20 seconds under these conditions during the CCM test. **Possible Causes:** • Fuel level sensor signal circuit is shorted to system power • Fuel level sensor ground circuit is open • Fuel level sender is damaged, binding or not aligned properly • PCM has failed
DTC: P0463 **1T CCM, MIL: No** **Years:** 2005, 2006, 2007 **Models:** Rendezvous **Engines:** 3.4L **Transmissions:** All	**Fuel Level Sensor Circuit High Input** Engine started; system voltage over 10.0v and the PCM detected the Fuel Level sensor signal was more than 3.0v (more than 98%) for 10 seconds during the CCM continuous test. **Possible Causes:** • Fuel level sensor signal circuit is shorted to system power • Fuel level sensor ground circuit is open • Fuel level sender is damaged, binding or not aligned properly • PCM has failed
DTC: P0480 **2T CCM, MIL: Yes** **Years:** 2005, 2006, 2007 **Models:** Rendezvous **Engines:** 3.4L **Transmissions:** All	**Cooling Fan Relay 1 Control Circuit Malfunction** Key on or engine running; system voltage from 9-18v, and the PCM detected the Actual state and Commanded state of the Fan Relay 1 control circuit (Low Speed Fan) did not match for 30 seconds. **Possible Causes:** • Fan control relay control circuit is open or shorted to ground • Fan control relay control circuit is shorted to system power • Fan control relay power circuit is open (check Cool Fan 1 fuse) • Fan control relay is damaged or has failed • PCM has failed
DTC: P0480 **2T CCM, MIL: Yes** **Years:** 2005, 2006, 2007 **Models:** Malibu **Engines:** 2.2L, 2.4L **Transmissions:** All	**Cooling Fan Relay 1 Control Circuit Malfunction** Engine started, system voltage over 10.0v and the PCM detected the Commanded state and Actual state of the Fan Relay 1 control circuit (Low Speed Fan) did not match for 6 seconds. **Possible Causes:** • Fan control relay control circuit is open or shorted to ground • Fan control relay control circuit is shorted to system power • Fan control relay power circuit is open (check Cool Fan 1 fuse) • Fan control relay is damaged or has failed • PCM has failed

DTC	Trouble Code Title, Conditions & Possible Causes
DTC: P0480 **2T CCM, MIL: Yes** **Years:** 2005, 2006, 2007 **Models:** Rendezvous **Engines:** 3.4L **Transmissions:** All	**Cooling Fan Relay 2 Control Circuit Malfunction** Engine started, system voltage from 9-18v, and the PCM detected the Commanded state and Actual state of the Fan Relay 2 control circuit (High Speed Fan) did not match for 30 seconds. **Possible Causes:** • Fan control relay control circuit is open or shorted to ground • Fan control relay control circuit is shorted to system power • Fan control relay power circuit is open or shorted to ground • Fan control relay is damaged or has failed • PCM has failed
DTC: P0489 **2T CCM, MIL: Yes** **Years:** 2005, 2006, 2007 **Models:** Sierra, Silverado **Engines:** 6.6L Diesel **Transmissions:** All	**EGR Valve Vacuum Solenoid Circuit Low Input** Engine started; engine runtime over 0.5 seconds, system voltage from 11-18v, EGR solenoid command less than 71%, and the ECM detected an unexpected low voltage condition on the EGR Valve Solenoid control circuit for 2 seconds. The EGR valve is vacuum operated. A belt-driven vacuum pump is used to supply vacuum for the EGR Valve Control system. The EGR valve vacuum control solenoid and the EGR valve vacuum vent solenoid work together to control the position of the EGR valve. The PCM controls the EGR valve vacuum control solenoid with a PWM control signal. **Possible Causes:** • EGR valve solenoid connector is damaged or shorted • EGR valve solenoid control circuit is open or shorted to ground • EGR valve solenoid is damaged or it has failed • ECM has failed
DTC: P0490 **2T CCM, MIL: Yes** **Years:** 2005, 2006, 2007 **Models:** Sierra, Silverado **Engines:** 6.6L Diesel **Transmissions:** All	**EGR Valve Vacuum Solenoid Circuit High Input** Engine started; engine runtime over 0.5 seconds, system voltage from 11-18v, EGR solenoid command signal more than 10%, and the ECM detected an unexpected high voltage condition on the EGR Valve Solenoid control circuit for 2 seconds. The EGR valve is vacuum operated. A belt-driven vacuum pump is used to supply vacuum for the EGR Valve Control system. The EGR valve vacuum control solenoid and the EGR valve vacuum vent solenoid work together to control the position of the EGR valve. The PCM controls the EGR valve vacuum control solenoid with a PWM control signal. **Possible Causes:** • EGR valve solenoid connector is damaged or open • EGR valve solenoid control circuit is open or shorted to power • EGR valve solenoid is damaged or it has failed • ECM has failed
DTC: P0496 **2T EVAP, MIL: Yes** **Years:** 2005, 2006, 2007 **Models:** Sierra, Silverado **Engines:** 4.3L, 4.8L, 5.3L, 6.0L, 6.2L, 8.1L **Transmissions:** All	**EVAP Canister Purge System High Purge Flow** DTC P0106-P0108, P0112, P0113, P0116-P0118, P0120-P0123, P0125, P0131-P0138, P0140, P0141, P0147, P0151-P0158, P0160, P0161, P0167, P0220, P0442-P0443, P0449, P0452-P0453, P0455, P0502, P0503, P1111, P1112, P1114, P1115, P1120 not set, engine started, ECT and IAT sensors from 39-86°F and within 16°F at startup, system voltage from 10-18v, BARO sensor more than 75 kPa, fuel level at 15-85%, and the PCM detected a continuous open purge flow condition in the system (FTP less than −11 H2O). This diagnostic test is designed to test for undesired intake manifold vacuum flow to the EVAP system. During this test, the PCM seals the EVAP system by commanding the EVAP Purge valve closed and the EVAP canister vent valve closed. The PCM monitors the FTP sensor signal in order to determine if a vacuum is being drawn on the EVAP system. If vacuum in the EVAP system is more than a predetermined value within a certain time, this code is set. **Possible Causes:** • EVAP charcoal canister is damaged or restricted • EVAP purge pipe is damaged or restricted • FTP sensor is damaged or it has failed • Purge solenoid is damaged (it may be sticking) • Purge solenoid valve has failed
DTC: P0500 **2T CCM, MIL: Yes** **Years:** 2005, 2006, 2007 **Models:** Sierra, Silverado **Engines:** 4.3L, 4.8L, 5.3L, 6.0L, 6.2L, 8.1L **Transmissions:** M/T	**Vehicle Speed Sensor Circuit Malfunction** DTC P0106, P0107, P0108, P0335, P0336, P1120, P1125, P1128, P1220, P1221, P1514, P1515, P1516, P1517 and P1518 not set, engine started, vehicle driven at a speed over 1000 RPM, ECT sensor more than 95°F, MAP sensor from 40-100 kPa (Turbo Boost Pressure from 40-100 kPa on Diesel) TP angle from 5-95%, and the PCM did not detect any VSS signals for from 50-100 seconds. **Possible Causes:** • Output shaft rotor is chipped or damaged • Output shaft rotor is not aligned properly with the VSS unit • VSS tip contains debris or metal shavings (an intermittent fault) • VSS positive (+) signal circuit is open or shorted to ground • VSS negative (−) signal circuit is open or shorted to ground • VSS is damaged or has failed

DTC	Trouble Code Title, Conditions & Possible Causes
DTC: P0502 **2T CCM, MIL: Yes** **Years:** 2005, 2006, 2007 **Models:** Rendezvous **Engines:** 3.4L **Transmissions:** All	**VSS Circuit Low Input (4T65-E)** DTC P0107, P0108, P0121, P0122, P0123, P0716, P0717 and P1810 not set, engine started, ISS signal more than 1500 RPM, TP angle over 12%, MAP sensor from 0-150 kPa, engine torque from 40-300 ft-lbs, gearshift not in P/N, and the PCM detected the OSS sensor was less than 150 RPM for 2.5 seconds during the CCM test. **Possible Causes:** • Output shaft rotor is chipped or damaged • OSS tip contains debris or metal shavings (an intermittent fault) • OSS positive (+) signal circuit is open or shorted to ground • OSS negative (−) signal circuit is open or shorted to ground • OSS is damaged or has failed
DTC: P0502 **2T CCM, MIL: Yes** **Years:** 2005, 2006, 2007 **Models:** Sierra, Silverado **Engines:** 4.3L, 4.8L, 5.3L, 6.0L, 6.2L, 8.1L **Transmissions:** A/T	**VSS Circuit Low Input (4L60-E, 4L80-E)** DTC P0107, P0108, P0122, P0123 and P1810 not set, engine started, vehicle driven with the engine speed from 3000-4800 RPM, engine vacuum from 0-150 kPa, TP angle over 20%, engine torque from 40-400 lb ft., gear selector not in P/N, and the PCM detected the Output Shaft Speed sensor was less than 150 RPM for 3 seconds. **Possible Causes:** • Output shaft rotor is chipped or damaged • OSS tip contains debris or metal shavings (an intermittent fault) • OSS positive (+) signal circuit is open or shorted to ground • OSS negative (−) signal circuit is open or shorted to ground • OSS is damaged or has failed (an intermittent fault)
DTC: P0502 **2T CCM, MIL: Yes** **Years:** 2005, 2006, 2007 **Models:** Sierra, Silverado **Engines:** 6.6L Diesel **Transmissions:** A/T	**Vehicle Speed Sensor Low Input (4L60-E)** DTC P0107, P0108, P0122, P0123 and P1810 not set, engine speed over 3000 RPM, TP angle over 12%, not in P/N, engine vacuum from 0-15 kPa, engine torque from 40-400 lb ft., and the PCM detected the OSS signal was under 150 RPM for three seconds. **Possible Causes:** • Output shaft rotor is chipped or damaged • Output shaft rotor is not aligned properly with the VSS unit • VSS tip contains debris or metal shavings (an intermittent fault) • VSS (+) or (−) signal circuit is open or shorted to ground • VSS buffer is damaged, or one of the buffer circuits has failed • VSS is damaged or has failed
DTC: P0503 **2T CCM, MIL: Yes** **Years:** 2005, 2006, 2007 **Models:** Rendezvous **Engines:** 3.4L **Transmissions:** All	**VSS Circuit Malfunction (4T65-E)** Engine speed started, engine running, Fuel Cutoff inactive, not in Park or Neutral, time since last gear range change more than 6 seconds, Transmission Output Shaft speed rise more than 250 RPM in 2 seconds, and the PCM detected a drop in the Output Shaft Speed sensor signal of over 1500 RPM within 3 seconds. **Possible Causes:** • Output shaft rotor is chipped or damaged (intermittent fault) • OSS tip contains debris or metal shavings (intermittent fault) • OSS (+) signal circuit is open or shorted to ground (intermittent) • OSS (−) signal circuit is open or shorted to ground (intermittent) • OSS is damaged or has failed (an intermittent fault)
DTC: P0503 **2T CCM, MIL: Yes** **Years:** 2005, 2006, 2007 **Models:** Sierra, Silverado **Engines:** 4.3L, 4.8L, 5.3L, 6.0L, 6.2L, 8.1L **Transmissions:** A/T	**VSS Circuit Malfunction (4L60-E, 4L80-E)** DTC P1810 not set, engine running, 6 seconds have passed since the gear change or change in 4WD Switch status, Transmission output shaft speed did not increase over 600 RPM for 2 seconds, and the PCM detected the Output Shaft Speed decreased over 300 RPM for three seconds. **Possible Causes:** • Output shaft rotor is chipped or damaged (intermittent fault) • OSS tip contains debris or metal shavings (an intermittent fault) • OSS (+) signal circuit is open or shorted to ground (intermittent) • OSS (−) signal circuit is open or shorted to ground (intermittent) • OSS is damaged or has failed (an intermittent fault)
DTC: P0503 **2T CCM, MIL: Yes** **Years:** 2005, 2006, 2007 **Models:** Sierra, Silverado **Engines:** 6.6L Diesel **Transmissions:** A/T	**VSS Circuit Malfunction (4L60-E)** DTC P1810 not set, engine started, 6 seconds elapsed since last gear change or change in 4WD Switch status, output shaft speed no more than 600 RPM for 2 seconds, and the PCM detected the Output Shaft Speed decreased over 300 RPM for three seconds. **Possible Causes:** • Output shaft rotor is chipped or damaged (intermittent fault) • OSS tip contains debris or metal shavings (an intermittent fault) • OSS (+) signal circuit is open or shorted to ground (intermittent) • OSS (−) signal circuit is open or shorted to ground (intermittent) • OSS is damaged or has failed (an intermittent fault)

DTC	Trouble Code Title, Conditions & Possible Causes
DTC: P0506 **2T CCM, MIL: Yes** **Years:** 2005, 2006, 2007 **Models:** G6, GTO, LaCrosse, Malibu, Montana, Montana SV6, Relay, Rendezvous, Sky, Solstice, SRX, Terraza, Uplander, Vibe **Engines:** 1.8L, 2.0L, 2.2L, 2.4L, 3.4L, 3.5L, 3.6L, 3.9L, 4.6L, 6.0L **Transmissions:** All	**Idle Speed Too Low** DTC P0101-P0103, P0107-P0108, P0112-P0113, P0116-P0118, P0121-P0123, P0171-P0172, P0201-P0206, P0300, P0401-P0405 P0443, P1121, P1404 and P1441 not set, engine runtime over 2 minutes, ECT sensor over 158°F, IAT sensor over 4°F, BARO sensor over 70 kPa, system voltage over 10.0v, TPS angle under 1.5%, VSS less than 3 MPH, and the PCM detected the Actual speed was 100 RPM less than the Desired speed for 8 seconds. **Possible Causes:** • Air inlet duct is collapsed, loose or air filter element is clogged • Base engine problem (i.e., compression or misfire condition) • Idle air inlet passage or throttle bore is dirty or full of deposits • IAC valve is damaged or has failed • MAF sensor is dirty, out-of-calibration or it is "skewed" • Throttle plate, throttle shaft or linkage is damaged or sticking • PCM has failed
DTC: P0506 **2T CCM, MIL: Yes** **Years:** 2005, 2006, 2007 **Models:** Sierra, Silverado **Engines:** 4.3L, 4.8L, 5.3L, 6.0L, 6.2L, 8.1L **Transmissions:** All	**Idle Speed Too Low** DTC P0101-P0103, P0106-P0108, P0112, P0113, P0116-P0118, P0121-P0123, P0125, P0128, P0171-P0175, P0200, P0300, P0440, P0442, P0443, P0446, P0449, P1111-P1115, P1121, P1122, P1380, P1381 and P1441 not set, engine runtime over 60 seconds, ECT sensor from 140-241°F, IAT sensor over 14°F, TP angle under 0.7%, BARO sensor over 65 kPa, VSS less than 1 MPH, system voltage over 10.0v, and the PCM detected the Actual speed was 100 RPM below the Desired speed with a MAF sensor change of under 3 g/sec. **Possible Causes:** • Air inlet duct is collapsed, loose or air filter element is clogged • Base engine problem (i.e., compression or misfire condition) • IAC solenoid control circuit has a high resistance condition • IAC valve is damaged or has failed • Idle air inlet passage or throttle bore is dirty or full of deposits • MAF sensor is dirty, out-of-calibration or it is "skewed" • Throttle plate, throttle shaft or linkage is damaged or sticking • PCM has failed
DTC: P0507 **2T CCM, MIL: Yes** **Years:** 2005, 2006, 2007 **Models:** G6, GTO, LaCrosse, Malibu, Relay, Rendezvous, Sky, Solstice, SRX **Engines:** 2.0L, 2.2L, 2.4L, 3.4L, 3.5L, 3.6L, 3.8L, 3.9L, 4.6L, 6.0L **Transmissions:** All	**Idle Speed Too High** DTC P0102, P0103, P0107, P0108, P0121-P0123, P0300, P0301-P0306, P0401-P0405, P0440, P0442, P0446, P0502, P0503, P1404 and P1441 not set, engine started, engine runtime over 2 minutes, system voltage over 10.0v, vehicle speed less than 3 MPH, ECT sensor more than 158°F, IAT sensor more than 5°F, TP angle less than 1%, BARO sensor more than 65 kPa, and the PCM detected that Actual idle speed was more than 75 RPM higher than Desired idle speed for 15 seconds. The IAC valve, mounted on the throttle body, is used to control the engine idle speed. The IAC valve pintle moves in and out of an idle air passage bore to control airflow past the throttle plate. The IAC valve consists of a movable pintle, driven by a gear attached to an electric motor called a stepper motor. The stepper motor is capable of highly accurate rotation (called steps). The stepper motor has two separate windings called coils. Each coil is supplied current by two circuits from the PCM. Each time the coil changes polarity, the stepper motor moves one step. The PCM uses a predetermined number of counts to calculate IAC pintle position. **Possible Causes:** • Engine vacuum leaks, PCM valve is leaking or the wrong valve • Idle air inlet passage or throttle bore is dirty or full of deposits • IAC valve is damaged or has failed • MAF sensor is dirty, "skewed" or installed improperly • Throttle plate, throttle shaft or linkage is damaged or sticking • PCM has failed
DTC: P0507 **2T CCM, MIL: Yes** **Years:** 2005, 2006, 2007 **Models:** Sierra, Silverado **Engines:** 4.3L, 4.8L, 5.3L, 6.0L, 6.2L, 8.1L **Transmissions:** A/T	**Idle Speed Too High** DTC P0101-P0103, P0106-P0108, P0112, P0113, P0116-P0118, P0121-P0123, P0125, P0128, P0171-P0172, P0174-P0175, P0200, P0300, P0440, P0442, P0443, P0446, P0449, P1111, P1112, P1114, P1115, P1121, P1122, P1380, P1381 and P1441 not set, engine started, engine runtime over 60 seconds, ECT sensor from 140-241°F, IAT sensor more than 14°F, TP angle less than 0.7%, BARO sensor more than 65 kPa, VSS sensor less than 1 MPH, system voltage over 10.0v, and the PCM detected the Actual idle speed was more than 200 RPM higher than the Desired idle speed for 6 seconds during the CCM test. **Possible Causes:** • Engine vacuum leaks, PCM valve is leaking or the wrong valve • IAC valve is damaged or has failed • Idle air inlet passage or throttle bore is dirty or full of deposits • MAF sensor is dirty, "skewed" or installed improperly • Throttle plate, throttle shaft or linkage is damaged or sticking • TP sensor is out-of-range or "skewed" high • PCM has failed

DTC	Trouble Code Title, Conditions & Possible Causes
DTC: P0522 **1T CCM, MIL: No** **Years:** 2005, 2006, 2007 **Models:** Sierra, Silverado **Engines:** 4.3L, 4.8L, 5.3L, 6.0L, 6.2L, 8.1L **Transmissions:** All	**Engine Oil Pressure Sensor Circuit Low Input** DTC P1635 not set, engine started, and the PCM detected the Engine Oil Pressure (EOP) signal was less than 0.48v for 9 seconds. The sensor range is 0.5v (0 psi) to 4.5v (128 psi). **Possible Causes:** • Engine oil level it too low • EOP sensor signal circuit is open or shorted to ground • EOP sensor VREF circuit is open • EOP sensor is damaged or has failed • Instrument Cluster or PCM has failed
DTC: P0523 **1T CCM, MIL: No** **Years:** 2005, 2006, 2007 **Models:** Sierra, Silverado **Engines:** 4.3L, 4.8L, 5.3L, 6.0L, 6.2L, 8.1L **Transmissions:** All	**Engine Oil Pressure Sensor Circuit High Input** DTC P1635 not set, engine started, and the PCM detected the Engine Oil Pressure (EOP) signal was more than 4.60v for 9 seconds. The sensor range is 0.5v (0 psi) to 4.5v (128 psi). **Possible Causes:** • EOP sensor signal circuit is shorted to VREF or system power • EOP sensor ground circuit is open • EOP sensor is damaged or has failed • Instrument Cluster or PCM has failed
DTC: P0530 **1T CCM, MIL: No** **Years:** 2005, 2006, 2007 **Models:** G6, GTO, LaCrosse, Malibu, Relay, Rendezvous, Sky, Solstice, SRX **Engines:** 2.0L, 2.2L, 2.4L, 3.4L, 3.5L, 3.6L, 3.9L, 4.6L, 6.0L **Transmissions:** All	**A/C Refrigerant Pressure Sensor Circuit Malfunction** Engine started, engine running with A/C requested "on", and the PCM detected the A/C Pressure sensor was less than 0.10v (9 psi) or it was more than 4.94v (488 kPa) for 20 seconds during the test. **Possible Causes:** • ACP sensor signal circuit is open or shorted to ground • ACP sensor signal circuit is shorted to VREF or system power • ACP sensor ground circuit is open • ACP sensor is damaged or has failed • PCM has failed • TSB 61-65-61 contains a repair procedure for this code
DTC: P0540 **1T CCM, MIL: No** **Years:** 2005, 2006, 2007 **Models:** Sierra, Silverado **Engines:** 6.6L Diesel **Transmissions:** All	**Intake Air Heater Circuit Malfunction** Key on, engine off for over 3 seconds, ECT sensor less than 121°F, system voltage from 10-18v, or engine running with the IAT sensor signal less than 73°, and the ECM detected the Heater line voltage was more than 8.1v with the Heater relay off, or the Heater line signal was from 3.8-8.1v with the key off, or the Heater line voltage was at least 0.5v below system voltage with the ignition on, or the Heater line signal was below 3.8v with the relay on, or the reference line voltage was low with the relay off. The ECM uses an Intake Air Heater (IAH) to warm incoming air for proper cylinder combustion. **Possible Causes:** • IAT relay connector is damaged, loose or shorted • IAT heater connector is damaged, loose or shorted • IAT assembly is damaged, or it has failed • IAH relay control circuit is open, shorted to ground or power • ECM has failed
DTC: P0540 **1T CCM, MIL: No** **Years:** 2005, 2006, 2007 **Models:** Sierra, Silverado **Engines:** 6.6L Diesel **Transmissions:** All	**Intake Air Heater Diagnostic Circuit Malfunction** Key on, engine off for over 3 seconds, ECT sensor less than 121°F, system voltage from 10-18v, or engine running with the IAT sensor signal less than 73°, and the ECM detected the Heater line voltage was between 3.8-8.1v with the IAH relay "off", or the Heater line voltage was less than 0.5v below the battery voltage value with the IAH relay "on". The ECM uses an intake air heater (IAH) to warm the incoming air for proper cylinder combustion. The ECM grounds the control coil of the IAH relay to energize the heater during cold operation. The ECM sends a bias voltage on Diagnostic Circuits 1 and 2. The ECM sets this code if the voltage does not go low with the relay off, or if the voltage did not go high with the relay "on". **Possible Causes:** • IAT relay connector is damaged, loose or shorted • IAT heater connector is damaged, loose or shorted • IAT assembly is damaged, or it has failed • IAH relay control circuit is open, shorted to ground or power • Intake heater diagnostic circuit 1 or circuit 2 is open or shorted • ECM has failed

DTC	Trouble Code Title, Conditions & Possible Causes
DTC: P0560 **1T CCM, MIL: No** **Years:** 2005, 2006, 2007 **Models:** All **Engines:** All **Transmissions:** M/T	**System Voltage Malfunction** Engine started, engine speed from 1400-1550 RPM, and the PCM detected the system voltage was less than 10.5v at a maximum TFT sensor signal of 305°F, or that it was less than 6.7v at a minimum TFT sensor signal of −40°F, or that it was more than 19v at any time. **Possible Causes:** • Check for high resistance at the battery connections or at the Underhood Fuse Block power circuit connection to the PCM • Check the drive belt for excessive wear and the proper tension • Check the condition of the battery and the Generator output • Vehicle may have been used to jump-start another vehicle
DTC: P0562 **1T CCM, MIL: No** **Years:** 2005, 2006, 2007 **Models:** Sierra, Silverado **Engines:** 5.7L, 6.0L, 6.0L **Transmissions:** All	**System Voltage Too Low** Engine started, vehicle driven to a speed of over 5 MPH at an engine speed over 1000 RPM, and the PCM detected the system voltage was less than 8.0v for 5 seconds during the test. **Possible Causes:** • Check for high resistance at battery connections or the MINI fuse power circuit • Check the drive belt for excessive wear and the proper tension • Check the condition of the battery and the Generator output • Vehicle may have been used to jump-start another vehicle
DTC: P0563 **1T CCM, MIL: No** **Years:** 2005, 2006, 2007 **Models:** Sierra, Silverado **Engines:** 4.3L, 4.8L, 5.3L, 6.0L, 6.2L, 8.1L **Transmissions:** All	**System Voltage Too High** Engine started, vehicle driven to a speed of over 5 MPH at an engine speed over 1000 RPM, and the PCM detected the system voltage was more than 18.0v for 5 seconds during the CCM test. **Possible Causes:** • Check the condition of the battery (it may be worn out) • Test the operation of the Generator (it may have failed) • Vehicle may have been used to jump-start another vehicle
DTC: P0567 **1T CCM, MIL: No** **Years:** 2005, 2006, 2007 **Models:** Sierra, Silverado **Engines:** 4.3L, 4.8L, 5.3L, 6.0L, 6.2L, 8.1L **Transmissions:** All	**Cruise Control Resume Switch Circuit Malfunction** Engine started; and the PCM detected high voltage on the Cruise Resume Switch circuit with the switch off, or with the switch on; it detected the Resume Switch was "on" for 25 seconds. **Possible Causes:** • C/C resume switch is shorted to VREF or system power • C/C resume switch is stuck in the "on" position or has failed • PCM has failed
DTC: P0568 **1T CCM, MIL: No** **Years:** 2005, 2006, 2007 **Models:** Sierra, Silverado **Engines:** 4.3L, 4.8L, 5.3L, 6.0L, 6.2L, 8.1L **Transmissions:** All	**Cruise Control Set Switch Circuit Malfunction** Engine started; and the PCM detected high voltage on the Set Switch circuit with the Cruise Switch "off", or with Cruise Switch "on", the Set Switch indicated "on" for over 25 seconds. **Possible Causes:** • Set/Coast switch circuit is shorted to VREF or system power • Set/Coast switch is stuck in "on" position or it has failed • PCM has failed
DTC: P0571 **1T CCM, MIL: No** **Years:** 2005, 2006, 2007 **Models:** Sierra, Silverado **Engines:** 4.3L, 4.8L, 5.3L, 6.0L, 6.2L, 8.1L **Transmissions:** All	**Cruise/Brake Switch Circuit Malfunction** Engine started, and the PCM detected the TCC and Stop/Lamp/Cruise Brake Switch signals were different for 10 consecutive minutes, or the TCC and Cruise Brake Switch signals did not cycle open and closed for 6 brake events on one trip. **Possible Causes:** • Cruise brake switch signal circuit is shorted to ground • Cruise brake switch B+ circuit is open (test STOP/BRAKE fuse) • Cruise brake switch is damaged (closed) or has failed
DTC: P0601 **1T PCM, MIL: Yes** **Years:** 2005, 2006, 2007 **Models:** All **Engines:** All **Transmissions:** All	**Control Module ROM Malfunction** Key in crank or the run position, and the PCM detected more than 3 incorrect checksums during its initial self-test. The PCM uses an EEPROM to store software and calibration data. The PCM uses a checksum to verify the integrity of the information. At the time of programming, the PCM calculates a checksum and stores the value in the EEPROM. The PCM retrieves this data, performs a checksum test to compare the key "on" value to the value stored in EEPROM. If these two values do not match at key "on", it sets DTC P0601. **Possible Causes:** • The PCM must be replaced to correct this problem. A new PCM must be programmed with the correct software/calibration. • TSB 67-65-23 contains a repair procedure for this code

DTC	Trouble Code Title, Conditions & Possible Causes
DTC: P0602 **1T PCM, MIL:** Yes **Years:** 2005, 2006, 2007 **Models:** All **Engines:** All **Transmissions:** All	**Control Module Not Programmed** Key on, and the PCM detected it did not have the correct program to operate or that the EEPROM had been programmed incorrectly. **Possible Causes:** • Reprogram the PCM with the correct software and calibration. If this step does not correct the problem, the PCM must be replaced and programmed with the correct software/calibration.

DTC: P0603
1T PCM, MIL: Yes
Years: 2005, 2006, 2007
Models: All
Engines: All
Transmissions: All
	Control Module Long Term Memory Reset
	DTC P0604 not set, and then with the key on, the PCM detected the calculated checksum that did not match the previous checksum.
	Possible Causes:
	    • An interruption to the PCM main power and/or ground circuits
	    • Check the PCM power and ground circuits and make repairs as necessary. Clear the codes and recheck. If it resets, the PCM must be replaced and programmed with the correct software.

DTC: P0604 **1T PCM, MIL:** Yes **Years:** 2005, 2006, 2007 **Models:** All **Engines:** All **Transmissions:** All	**Control Module Random Access Memory Failure** Key on for 5 seconds, and the PCM detected the internal data test of its RAM failed. The PCM copies the program information stored in the RAM. This Allows the PCM to work with, and make any updates to this data. The PCM checks for problems in All areas of the RAM. **Possible Causes:** • The PCM must be replaced to correct this problem. A new PCM must be programmed with the correct software/calibration.
DTC: P0605 **1T PCM, MIL:** Yes **Years:** 2005, 2006, 2007 **Models:** All **Engines:** All **Transmissions:** All	**Control Module Programming Read Only Memory** Key on, and the PCM detected the data checksum did not match the expected value, or that it was unable to read its flash memory data. **Possible Causes:** • The PCM must be replaced to correct this problem. A new PCM must be programmed with the correct software/calibration.
DTC: P0606 **1T PCM, MIL:** Yes **Years:** 2005, 2006, 2007 **Models:** All **Engines:** All **Transmissions:** All	**Control Module Internal Performance** DTC P0601 and P0604 not set, key on, and the PCM determined that an internal performance problem existed within its controller. **Possible Causes:** • The PCM must be replaced to correct this problem. A new PCM must be programmed with the correct software/calibration.
DTC: P0607 **1T PCM, MIL:** Yes **Years:** 2005, 2006, 2007 **Models:** All **Engines:** All **Transmissions:** All	**Control Module Performance** Key on or engine running; then after the initial PCM power up sequence, the PCM detected an internal performance problem. **Possible Causes:** • The PCM must be replaced to correct this problem. A new PCM must be programmed with the correct software/calibration.

DTC: P0608
1T PCM, MIL: Yes
Years: 2005, 2006, 2007
Models: Sierra, Silverado
Engines: 4.3L, 4.8L, 5.3L, 6.0L, 6.2L, 8.1L
Transmissions: All
	Vehicle Speed Output Circuit Malfunction
	Engine started, engine speed over 600 RPM, and the PCM detected the Actual and Commanded state of the VSS output circuit did not match for 5 seconds. The PCM creates the VSS output signal by causing the circuit to pulse to ground, and monitoring the operation.
	Possible Causes:
	    • VSS output signal circuit is open, shorted to ground or to power
	    • VSS output signal problem related to the Instrument Cluster or the Electronic Suspension Control Module (internal problem)
	    • PCM has failed

DTC: P0611 **2T CCM, MIL:** Yes **Years:** 2005, 2006, 2007 **Models:** Sierra, Silverado **Engines:** 6.6L Diesel **Transmissions:** All	**Fuel Injection Control Module Performance** Key on, U1800 and U2104 not set, and the FICM detected an internal fault. The fuel injection control module (FICM) performs internal circuit checks on the FICM microprocessor, the status of the monitoring module, and status of the FICM A/D conversion module. If the FICM senses a problem in the FICM circuits, the FICM will send an error message to the ECM, and it will set DTC P0611 **Possible Causes:** • FICM is damaged

DTC	Trouble Code Title, Conditions & Possible Causes
DTC: P0611 **1T CCM, MIL: Yes** **Years:** 2005, 2006, 2007 **Models:** Sierra, Silverado **Engines:** 6.0L CNG **Transmissions:** All	**Control Module Performance** The Fuel Injector Control Module (FICM) monitors the CNG FTP sensor, FTT sensor, and the FRT sensor signals. The FTP, FTT, and FRT sensor values, and diagnostic data, is communicated to the PCM by two pulsewidth modulated (PWM) circuits. This code sets if the PCM detects an incorrect PWM signal from the FICM. **Possible Causes:** • FICM is damaged
DTC: P0612 **1T CCM, MIL: Yes** **Years:** 2005, 2006, 2007 **Models:** Sierra, Silverado **Engines:** 6.6L Diesel **Transmissions:** All	**Ignition Relay Control Circuit Malfunction** Key on, and the ECM detected the feedback voltage did not match the output state. The ECM monitors the condition of the ignition relay control circuit. If the ECM senses excessive voltage on the feedback circuit, it will set DTC P0612. **Possible Causes:** • Ignition relay circuit is shorted to system power • Ignition relay is damaged or it has failed • ECM has failed
DTC: P0615 **1T CCM, MIL: No** **Years:** 2005, 2006, 2007 **Models:** Sierra, Silverado **Engines:** 4.3L, 4.8L, 5.3L, 6.0L, 6.2L, 8.1L **Transmissions:** All	**Starter Relay Control Circuit Malfunction** Engine cranking, system voltage over 10.0v, and the PCM detected an unexpected voltage condition on the Starter Relay control circuit for two seconds during the CCM test. **Note: This code can set if a condition exists that prevents cranking.** **Possible Causes:** • Starter relay control circuit is open or shorted to ground • Starter relay control circuit is shorted to system power (B+) • Starter relay is damaged or has failed • PCM has failed
DTC: P0620 **1T CCM, MIL: No** **Years:** 2005, 2006, 2007 **Models:** Rendezvous **Engines:** 3.4L **Transmissions:** All	**Generator Signal Range/Performance** Engine started, the Voltage Telltale lamp is on, or less than 1000 RPM for the low duty cycle test, or more than 1000 RPM for high duty cycle test, and the PCM detected the 'L' terminal voltage was low with the Generator commanded "on", or the 'F' terminal PWM was less than 5% with the engine speed below 2500 RPM for 30 seconds. **Note: Refer to the Freeze Frame Records for additional information.** **Possible Causes:** • Generator 'L' terminal circuit is open, shorted to ground or B+ • Generator 'F' terminal circuit is open, shorted to ground or B+ • PCM has failed
DTC: P0641 **2T CCM, MIL: Yes** **Years:** 2005, 2006, 2007 **Models:** Sierra, Silverado **Engines:** 4.3L, 4.8L, 5.3L, 6.0L, 6.2L, 8.1L **Transmissions:** All	**5-Volt Reference 1 Circuit Malfunction** Key on or engine running; and the PCM detected the 5v Reference circuit was out of tolerance for 10 seconds. The 5v VREF 1 circuit from the PCM is used to provide power to the Engine Oil Pressure (EOP), Manifold Air Pressure (MAP) sensor and the Throttle Position (TP) sensor on these vehicle applications. **Possible Causes:** • 5v VREF circuit is shorted to chassis or sensor ground • 5v VREF circuit to MAP or TP sensor circuit is shorted to (B+) • PCM has failed
DTC: P0641 **2T CCM, MIL: Yes** **Years:** 2005, 2006, 2007 **Models:** Sierra, Silverado **Engines:** 6.6L Diesel **Transmissions:** All	**5-Volt Reference 1 Circuit Malfunction** Key on or engine running; and the PCM detected the 5v Reference circuit was out of tolerance for 10 seconds. The 5v VREF 1 circuit is used to provide power to the Accelerator Pedal Position (APP1) sensor, Accelerator Pedal Position 2 (APP3) sensor, Engine Oil Pressure (EOP) and Fuel Rail Pressure (FPR) sensor. **Possible Causes:** • 5v VREF circuit to APP1 or APP3 is shorted to ground or shorted to system power • FRP or EOP sensor is shorted to ground or shorted to system power • PCM has failed
DTC: P0641 **2T CCM, MIL: Yes** **Years:** 2005, 2006, 2007 **Models:** Sierra, Silverado **Engines:** 4.3L, 4.8L, 5.3L, 6.0L, 6.2L, 8.1L **Transmissions:** All	**5-Volt Reference 1 Circuit Malfunction** Key on or engine running; and the PCM detected the 5v Reference circuit was out of tolerance for 10 seconds. The 5v VREF 1 circuit is used to provide power to the Engine Oil Pressure (EOP) sensor and Manifold Air Pressure (MAP) sensor on these applications. **Possible Causes:** • 5v VREF circuit to EOP sensor or MAP sensor is shorted to ground or it is shorted to system power • PCM has failed

DTC	Trouble Code Title, Conditions & Possible Causes

DTC: P0650
1T CCM, MIL: No
Years: 2005, 2006, 2007
Models: Rendezvous
Engines: 3.4L
Transmissions: All
	Malfunction Indicator Lamp Circuit Malfunction
	Engine started, system voltage over 10.0v, and the PCM detected an unexpected voltage condition on the ODM 'D' Output 1 circuit that controls the Malfunction Indicator Lamp (MIL) for over 30 seconds.
	Possible Causes:
	  • MIL control circuit is open or shorted to ground
	  • MIL control circuit is shorted to system power
	  • MIL control power circuit is open in the Instrument Cluster
	  • MIL (the lamp) is damaged or has failed
	  • PCM has failed

DTC: P0650
1T CCM, MIL: No
Years: 2005, 2006, 2007
Models: Sierra, Silverado
Engines: 4.3L, 4.8L, 5.3L, 6.0L, 6.2L, 8.1L
Transmissions: All
	Malfunction Indicator Lamp Circuit Malfunction
	Engine started, system voltage over 10.0v, and the PCM detected the Actual state and Commanded state of the Malfunction Indicator Lamp (MIL) circuit did not match for 30 seconds during the test.
	Possible Causes:
	  • MIL control circuit is open or shorted to ground
	  • MIL control circuit is shorted to system power
	  • MIL control power circuit is open in the Instrument Cluster
	  • MIL (the lamp) is damaged or has failed
	  • Instrument Cluster or the PCM has failed

DTC: P0650
1T CCM, MIL: No
Years: 2005, 2006, 2007
Models: Sierra, Silverado,G,
Engines: 4.8L, 5.3L 6.0L, 8.1L
Transmissions: All
	Malfunction Indicator Lamp Circuit Malfunction
	Engine started, system voltage over 10.0v, and the PCM detected the Actual and Commanded state of the Malfunction Indicator Lamp (MIL) driver did not match.
	Possible Causes:
	  • MIL control circuit is open or shorted to ground
	  • MIL control circuit is shorted to system power
	  • MIL control power circuit is open in the Instrument Cluster
	  • MIL (the lamp) is damaged or has failed
	  • Instrument Cluster or the PCM has failed

DTC: P0650
1T CCM, MIL: No
Years: 2005, 2006, 2007
Models: Sierra, Silverado
Engines: 6.6L Diesel
Transmissions: All
	Malfunction Indicator Lamp Circuit Malfunction
	Engine started, system voltage from 10-18v, and the PCM detected an unexpected voltage on the MIL control circuit for 30 seconds.
	Possible Causes:
	  • MIL control circuit is open or shorted to ground
	  • MIL control circuit is shorted to system power
	  • MIL control power circuit is open in the Instrument Cluster
	  • MIL (the lamp) is damaged or has failed
	  • Instrument Cluster or the PCM has failed

DTC: P0651
1T CCM, MIL: No
Years: 2005, 2006, 2007
Models: Sierra, Silverado
Engines: 4.3L, 4.8L, 5.3L, 6.0L, 6.2L, 8.1L
Transmissions: All
	5-Volt Reference 2 Circuit Malfunction
	Key on or engine running; and the PCM detected the 5v Reference circuit was out of tolerance for 10 seconds. The 5v VREF 2 circuit is used to provide power to the Fuel Tank Pressure (FTP) sensor on this vehicle application.
	Possible Causes:
	  • 5v VREF circuit is shorted to chassis or sensor ground
	  • 5v VREF circuit to MAP or TP sensor circuit is shorted to (B+)
	  • PCM has failed

DTC: P0651
1T CCM, MIL: No
Years: 2005, 2006, 2007
Models: Sierra, Silverado
Engines: 6.6L Diesel
Transmissions: All
	5-Volt Reference 2 Circuit Malfunction
	Engine started; and the PCM detected the 5v Reference circuit was out of tolerance for 10 seconds. The 5v VREF 1 circuit is used to provide power to the Accelerator Pedal Position (APP2) sensor, BARO Sensor, Boost Pressure sensor, and the EGR Vacuum sensor.
	Possible Causes:
	  • 5v VREF circuit to APP2 or APP2, FRP or EOP sensor is shorted to ground or shorted to VREF
	  • ECM has failed

DTC: P0651
1T CCM, MIL: No
Years: 2005, 2006, 2007
Models: Sierra, Silverado
Engines: 4.3L, 4.8L, 5.3L, 6.0L, 6.2L, 8.1L
Transmissions: All
	5-Volt Reference 2 Circuit Malfunction
	Key on or engine running; and the PCM detected the 5v Reference circuit was out of tolerance for 10 seconds. The 5v VREF 2 circuit is used to provide power to the Air Conditioning Pressure (ACP) sensor and the Fuel Tank Pressure (FTP) sensor.
	Possible Causes:
	  • 5v VREF circuit to ACP sensor or FTP sensor is shorted to ground or it is shorted to system power
	  • ECM has failed

DTC	Trouble Code Title, Conditions & Possible Causes
DTC: P0654 **1T CCM, MIL: No** **Years:** 2005, 2006, 2007 **Models:** Sierra, Silverado **Engines:** 4.3L, 4.8L, 5.3L, 6.0L, 6.2L, 8.1L **Transmissions:** All	**Engine Speed Output Control Circuit Malfunction** Engine started, engine speed over 600 RPM, and the PCM detected the Commanded and Actual state of the Engine Speed Output circuit did not match for 10 seconds in the test. **Possible Causes:** • Engine speed circuit is open or shorted to ground • Engine speed is shorted to system power • Instrument Cluster has failed • PCM has failed
DTC: P0656 **1T CCM, MIL: No** **Years:** 2005, 2006, 2007 **Models:** Malibu, Rendezvous **Engines:** 3.4L **Transmissions:** All	**Fuel Gauge Output Control Circuit Malfunction** Engine started, engine speed over 600 RPM, and the PCM detected the Actual and Commanded state of the Fuel Gauge Output Control circuit did not match for 10 seconds. **Possible Causes:** • Fuel gauge circuit is open or shorted to ground • Fuel gauge control circuit is shorted to system power • Instrument Cluster has failed • PCM has failed
DTC: P0700 **1T CCM, MIL: Yes** **Years:** 2005, 2006, 2007 **Models:** Sierra, Silverado **Engines:** 4.8L, 5.3L, 5.3L, 6.0L, 6.6L Diesel, 8.1L **Transmissions:** A/T	**Malfunction Indicator Lamp Circuit Malfunction (TCM)** Key on or engine running; and the PCM received a signal from the TCM requesting that the Malfunction Indicator Lamp be illuminated. **Possible Causes:** • MIL control circuit is shorted to ground • Check the TCM for any trouble codes in memory that are responsible for the request to turn on the MIL • TCM has failed
DTC: P0706 **1T CCM, MIL: No** **Years:** 2005, 2006, 2007 **Models:** Sierra, Silverado **Engines:** 4.3L, 4.8L, 5.3L, 6.0L, 6.2L, 8.1L **Transmissions:** All	**A/T TR Switch Circuit Malfunction (4L60-E, 4L65-E)** DTC P0121, P0122, P0123, P1120, P1220 or P1221 not set, engine started; system voltage from 6-18v, and the PCM detected a Drive or a Reverse position signal at startup; or with the TP angle over 5%, VSS over 20 MPH, it detected a Park or Neutral signal for 20 seconds. The TR switch is part of the Park Neutral position and Back Up lamp switch assembly mounted on the transmission manual shaft. The TR switch is a multi-signal switch. The PCM supplies ignition voltage to the TR switch on 4 signal circuits (A, B, C, and P). Each gear selector lever position grounds one or more switch circuits. The PCM compares the voltage combinations on the signal circuits to determine the gear range selected by the driver. Switch input to the PCM is represented as HI and Low. HI indicates an ignition voltage signal. Low indicates a zero voltage signal. The four switch parameters are A, B, C and Parity. **Possible Causes:** • TR switch circuit(s) is shorted to the VREF circuit • TR switch circuit(s) is shorted to another switch circuit • TR switch is damaged or out of adjustment • PCM has failed
DTC: P0711 **1T CCM, MIL: No** **Years:** 2005, 2006, 2007 **Models:** Malibu, Rendezvous **Engines:** 3.4L **Transmissions:** A/T	**TFT Sensor Signal Range/Performance (4T65-E)** DTC P0502, P0503 and P1870 not set, engine runtime over 5 minutes, system voltage over 10.0v, ECT sensor more than 158F and changed by 90F since startup, TFT sensor from 0.2-4.92v at startup, startup TFT sensor from −40 to 69F, VSS more than 5 MPH for 409 seconds cumulative, TCC slip speed over 80 RPM for 4-9 seconds cumulative, and the PCM detected the TFT sensor did not change more than 2°F after 409 seconds cumulative since startup; or the TFT sensor changed more than 36°F in 200 ms (fault detected 14 times within a 7 second period). **Possible Causes:** • ATF fluid level too low or the fluid is contaminated or burnt • TFT sensor is contaminated, damaged or "skewed" • PCM has failed
DTC: P0711 **1T CCM, MIL: No** **Years:** 2005, 2006, 2007 **Models:** Sierra, Silverado **Engines:** 4.3L, 4.8L, 5.3L, 6.0L, 6.2L, 8.1L **Transmissions:** A/T	**TFT Sensor Range/Performance (4L60-E, 4L80-E)** DTC P0502, P0503, P0894 or P1870 not set, engine started, engine runtime over 409 seconds, system voltage over 10.0v, ECT sensor more than 158°F and a change of 90°F since startup, TFT sensor from −40 to 70°F at startup, then TFT sensor from −36 to 304°F, vehicle driven to over 5 MPH for 409 seconds cumulative, TCC slip speed over 120 RPM cumulative in the current key cycle, and the PCM detected the TFT sensor did not change more than 2.7°F for 409 seconds after startup; or the TFT sensor changed more than 36°F within 200 milliseconds (fault occurred 14 times in 7 seconds). **Possible Causes:** • ATF fluid level too low or the fluid is contaminated or burnt • TFT sensor is contaminated, damaged or "skewed" • PCM has failed

DTC	Trouble Code Title, Conditions & Possible Causes
DTC: P0712 **1T CCM, MIL:** No **Years:** 2005, 2006, 2007 **Models:** Malibu, Rendezvous **Engines:** 3.4L **Transmissions:** A/T	**TFT Sensor Circuit Low Input** DTC P0560 not set, engine started, engine running and the PCM detected the TFT sensor was more than 298°F for 10 seconds. **Possible Causes:** • TFT sensor signal circuit is shorted to sensor or chassis ground • TFT sensor is damaged or has failed (it may be shorted) • PCM has failed
DTC: P0712 **1T CCM, MIL:** No **Years:** 2005, 2006, 2007 **Models:** Sierra, Silverado **Engines:** All **Transmissions:** A/T	**TFT Sensor Circuit Low Input (4L60-E, 4L80-E)** Engine started, system voltage over 10.0v, and the PCM detected the TFT sensor was less than 0.25v for 10 seconds. **Note: A Scan Tool does not indicate the default TFT sensor reading.** **Possible Causes:** • TFT sensor signal circuit is shorted to sensor or chassis ground • TFT sensor is damaged or has failed (it may be shorted) • PCM has failed
DTC: P0713 **1T CCM, MIL:** No **Years:** 2005, 2006, 2007 **Models:** Malibu, Rendezvous **Engines:** 3.4L **Transmissions:** A/T	**TFT Sensor Circuit High Input (4T65-E)** DTC P0117, P0118 and P0560 not set, engine started, and the PCM detected the TFT sensor was less than −33°F (a voltage of 4.92v or higher) for 10 seconds during the CCM test. **Possible Causes:** • TFT sensor signal circuit is open between the sensor and PCM • TFT sensor signal circuit is shorted to VREF or system power • TFT sensor is damaged or has failed (it may be open) • PCM has failed • TSB 02-07-30-15 contains a repair procedure for this code
DTC: P0713 **1T CCM, MIL:** No **Years:** 2005, 2006, 2007 **Models:** Sierra, Silverado **Engines:** All **Transmissions:** A/T	**TFT Sensor Circuit High Input (4L60-E. 4L80-E)** Engine started; system voltage more than 10.0v, and the PCM detected the TFT sensor was more than 4.92v for 6-8 minutes. **Note: A Scan Tool does not indicate the default TFT sensor reading.** **Possible Causes:** • TFT sensor signal circuit is open between the sensor and PCM • TFT sensor signal circuit is shorted to VREF or system power • TFT sensor is damaged or has failed (it may be open) • PCM has failed
DTC: P0716 **2T CCM, MIL:** Yes **Years:** 2005, 2006, 2007 **Models:** Malibu, Rendezvous **Engines:** 3.4L **Transmissions:** A/T	**A/T Input Speed Sensor Circuit Malfunction (4T65-E)** DTC P0121, P0122, P0123, P0502, P0503, P0717, P0751, P0752, P0753, P0756, P0757 and P0758 not set, DTC P0717 test passed this key cycle, engine started, engine speed over 500 RPM for 5 seconds, Fuel Cutoff inactive, TP angle more than 14%, VSS over 5 MPH, and the PCM detected the Input Shaft Sensor speed changed by more than 1300 RPM within 800 ms during the CCM test. **Possible Causes:** • ISS positive (+) circuit is open, shorted to ground or to power • ISS negative (−) circuit is open, shorted to ground or to power • ISS is damaged or has failed • PCM has failed • TSB 02-07-30-022A contains a repair procedure for this code
DTC: P0716 **2T CCM, MIL:** Yes **Years:** 2005, 2006, 2007 **Models:** Sierra, Silverado **Engines:** All **Transmissions:** A/T	**A/T Input Shaft Speed Sensor Circuit Malfunction (4L80-E)** DTC P0121-P0123, P0502, P0503, P0717, P0751 and P0753 not set, engine running for 7 seconds while not in P/N, TP sensor over 10%, and the PCM detected the Input Shaft Speed sensor signal varied by more than 1300 RPM for a period of time over 5 seconds. **Possible Causes:** • ISS positive (+) circuit is open, shorted to ground or to power • ISS negative (−) circuit is open, shorted to ground or to power • ISS terminals are corroded or damaged (check for moisture) • ISS signal wires routed too close to the Ignition system cables • PCM has failed
DTC: P0717 **2T CCM, MIL:** Yes **Years:** 2005, 2006, 2007 **Models:** Sierra, Silverado **Engines:** All **Transmissions:** A/T	**A/T Input Shaft Speed Sensor Low Input (4L80-E)** DTC P0502 and P1810 not set, engine started, system voltage over 10.0v, Transmission not in Park or Neutral, vehicle driven to a speed of over 20 MPH, Fuel Cutoff mode inactive, and the PCM detected the Input Shaft Speed sensor was less than 100 RPM for 5 seconds. **Possible Causes:** • ISS positive (+) circuit is open, shorted to ground or to power • ISS negative (−) circuit is open, shorted to ground or to power • ISS is damaged or has failed • PCM has failed • TSB 00-07-30-015 contains a repair procedure for this code

DTC	Trouble Code Title, Conditions & Possible Causes
DTC: P0717 **2T CCM, MIL:** Yes **Years:** 2005, 2006, 2007 **Models:** Malibu, Rendezvous **Engines:** 3.4L **Transmissions:** A/T	**A/T Input Speed Sensor Circuit Low Input (4T65-E)** DTC P0502, P0503 and P1810 not set, engine started, TFP manual valve position switch not indicating Park or Neutral, system voltage over 10.0v, vehicle driven to a speed of over 5 MPH, Fuel Cutoff inactive, and the PCM detected the Input Shaft Speed sensor signal was less than 50 RPM for over 5 seconds during the CCM test. **Possible Causes:** • ISS positive (+) circuit is open, shorted to ground or to power • ISS negative (−) circuit is open, shorted to ground or to power • ISS is damaged or has failed • PCM has failed • TSB 02-07-30-022A contains a repair procedure for this code
DTC: P0719 **1T CCM, MIL:** No **Years:** 2005, 2006, 2007 **Models:** Malibu, Rendezvous **Engines:** 3.4L **Transmissions:** A/T	**TCC Brake Switch Circuit Low Input (4T60-E, 4T65-E)** DTC P0502 and P0503 not set, engine started, vehicle speed less than 5 MPH, then vehicle speed was from 5-20 MPH for 3 seconds, then after the speed more than 20 MPH for 6 seconds, the PCM detected the Brake Switch status was open for 5 minutes under these conditions. The TCC brake switch indicates brake pedal status to the PCM (i.e., when the brake pedal is applied or released). The N.C. switch supplies battery voltage signal to the PCM. Applying the brake pedal opens the TCC brake switch, interrupting voltage to the PCM. When the PCM detects 0 volts at the TCC brake switch circuit, the PCM turns OFF the TCC PWM solenoid valve. **Possible Causes:** • TCC brake switch circuit is open or shorted to ground • TCC brake switch power circuit is open (check ABS PCM fuse) • TCC brake switch is out of adjustment or damaged • PCM has failed
DTC: P0719 **1T CCM, MIL:** No **Years:** 2005, 2006, 2007 **Models:** Sierra, Silverado **Engines:** All **Transmissions:** A/T	**TCC Brake Switch Circuit Low Input (4L60-E, 4L80-E)** DTC P0502 and P0503 not set, engine started, vehicle speed less than 5 MPH, then the vehicle speed from 5-20 MPH for 4 seconds, followed by a period with the vehicle speed over 20 MPH for 6-8 seconds, and the PCM detected the Brake Switch circuit indicated zero (0) volts for 15 minutes without changing for 2 seconds. Note that this series of events must occur (8) times for this code to set. **Possible Causes:** • TCC brake switch circuit is open or shorted to ground • TCC brake switch power circuit is open (check the CRUISE, FAN ALT or other related fuse in underhood junction block) • TCC brake switch is out of adjustment or damaged • PCM has failed
DTC: P0722 **2T CCM, MIL:** Yes **Years:** 2005, 2006, 2007 **Models:** Sierra, Silverado **Engines:** 6.6L Diesel **Transmissions:** A/T	**Output Shaft Speed Sensor Circuit Low Input (4L80-E)** DTC P0106-P0108 and DTC P1810 not set, vehicle driven with the APP angle over 10% while not in P/N at an engine speed less than 3800 RPM for 7 seconds, ISS signal over 1500 RPM, and the PCM detected the OSS signal indicated less than 300 RPM for 3 seconds. **Possible Causes:** • OSS positive (+) circuit is open or shorted to ground • OSS negative (−) circuit is open or shorted to ground • OSS terminals are corroded or damaged (check for moisture) • PCM has failed
DTC: P0723 **2T CCM, MIL:** Yes **Years:** 2005, 2006, 2007 **Models:** Sierra, Silverado **Engines:** 6.6L Diesel **Transmissions:** A/T	**Output Shaft Speed Sensor Circuit High Input (4L80-E)** DTC P1810 and DTC P1810 not set, engine running with no TFP Value Position switch change for 7 seconds, vehicle not in 4WD Low position, and the PCM detected the OSS signal decreased more than 1000 RPM while driven in Drive position for over 3.5 seconds. **Possible Causes:** • OSS positive (+) circuit is open or shorted to system power • OSS negative (−) circuit is open or shorted to system power • OSS terminals are corroded or damaged (check for moisture) • PCM has failed
DTC: P0724 **1T CCM, MIL:** No **Years:** 2005, 2006, 2007 **Models:** Malibu, Rendezvous **Engines:** 3.4L **Transmissions:** A/T	**TCC Brake Switch Circuit High Input (4T65-E)** DTC P0502 and P0503 not set, vehicle speed more than 20 MPH for 6 seconds, then the speed decreased to 5 MPH for 2-6 seconds, followed by a period with the vehicle speed less than 5 MPH, and the PCM detected the Brake switch circuit was 12-14v at least 7 times. **Possible Causes:** • Check for ABS trouble codes (they can cause this code to set) • TCC brake switch circuit is shorted to system power • TCC brake switch is out of adjustment or damaged • PCM has failed

DTC	Trouble Code Title, Conditions & Possible Causes
DTC: P0724 **1T CCM, MIL: No** **Years:** 2005, 2006, 2007 **Models:** Sierra, Silverado **Engines:** All **Transmissions:** A/T	**TCC Brake Switch High Input (4L60-E, 4L80-E)** DTC P0502, P0503 and P0724 not set, engine started, then VSS signal more than 20 MPH for 6 seconds, then the VSS decreased to 5 MPH for 2-6 seconds, followed by a period with the vehicle speed less than 5 MPH, and the PCM detected the Brake switch circuit indicated from 12-14v at least 7 times (i.e., no change in the signal). **Possible Causes:** • Check for ABS trouble codes (they can cause this code to set) • TCC brake switch circuit is shorted to system power • TCC brake switch is out of adjustment or damaged • PCM has failed
DTC: P0730 **1T CCM, MIL: No** **Years:** 2005, 2006, 2007 **Models:** Malibu, Rendezvous **Engines:** 3.4L **Transmissions:** A/T	**Incorrect Gear Ratio (4T65-E)** DTC P0121, P0122, P0123, P0502, P0503, P0716, P0717 and P1810 not set, engine started, vehicle driven to over 7 MPH, Fuel Cutoff inactive, Transmission not in Park or Neutral, time since last gear select lever change over 6 seconds, TP angle over 14%, TFT sensor more than 68°F, engine torque from 50-300 ft lbs, and the PCM detected one of these conditions occurred for 7 seconds: - The gear ratio was more than 2.97:1 or it was 1.62:1 to 2.33:1 - The gear ratio was 1.05:1 to 1.52:1 or it was 0.75:1 to 0.95:1 **Possible Causes:** • ATF level is too low, or the fluid is burnt or contaminated • ISS or OSS signal circuit has an intermittent fault condition • Inspect for debris in the transmission pan or internal damaged • Possible vehicle overloading, exceeding the trailer towing limit, or towing in overdrive events occurred (discuss with customer) • TSB 02-07-30-022A contains a repair procedure for this code
DTC: P0730 **1T CCM, MIL: No** **Years:** 2005, 2006, 2007 **Models:** Sierra, Silverado **Engines:** All **Transmissions:** A/T	**Incorrect Gear Ratio (4L80-E)** DTC P0106-P0108, P0121-P0123, P0502, P0503, P0716, P0717, P1810 and P1875 not set, engine started, vehicle driven to a speed over 4 MPH, TP angle over 15%, TFT sensor signal over 68°F, delivered torque more than 400 ft lbs, and the PCM detected one or more of the following gear ratio conditions existed for four seconds: - The gear ratio was more than 2.50: 1 or less than 2.43:1 - The gear ratio was more than 1.50:1 or less than 1.44:1 - The gear ratio was more than 1.03:1 or less than 0.25:1 - The gear ratio was more than 2.12:1 or less than 2.04:1 **Possible Causes:** • ATF level is too low, or the fluid is burnt or contaminated • ISS or OSS signal circuit has an intermittent fault condition • Inspect for debris in the transmission pan or internal damaged • Possible vehicle overloading, exceeding the trailer towing limit, or towing in overdrive events occurred (discuss with customer)
DTC: P0740 **2T CCM, MIL: Yes** **Years:** 2005, 2006, 2007 **Models:** Sierra, Silverado **Engines:** 4.3L, 4.8L, 5.3L, 6.0L, 6.2L, 8.1L **Transmissions:** A/T	**TCC Solenoid Circuit Malfunction (4L60-E, 4L65-E)** Engine started, system voltage over 10.0v, Fuel Cutoff inactive, and the PCM detected the TCC feedback voltage was high with the TCC Solenoid commanded "on", or it was "low" with the TCC Solenoid commanded "off" for 5 seconds. **Possible Causes:** • TCC solenoid control circuit is open, shorted to ground or to B+ • TCC solenoid power circuit is open (test the TRANS fuse) • TCC solenoid is damaged or has failed • PCM has failed • TSB 01-07-30-002C contains a repair procedure for this code
DTC: P0741 **1T CCM, MIL: No** **Years:** 2005, 2006, 2007 **Models:** Malibu, Rendezvous **Engines:** 3.4L **Transmissions:** A/T	**TCC System Stuck Off - Mechanical (4T65-E)** DTC P0121-P0123, P0502, P0503, P0716, P0717, P0742, P1820, P1860 and P1887 not set, engine started, Fuel Cutoff inactive, Transmission gear range was D2, D3 or D4, time since last gear select lever change more than 6 seconds, TFT sensor from 68-266°F, TP angle from 4-35%, TCC PWM solenoid commanded "on" for over 500 ms, TCC commanded to maximum apply pressure, and the PCM detected the TCC slip speed was more than 180 RPM twice during a 7 second period during this key cycle. **Possible Causes:** • ATF level is too low, or the fluid is burnt or contaminated • Inspect transmission lines to radiator for bends or restrictions • Oil pressure screen is clogged or debris in the oil pan • TCC control valve is stuck "off" due to sediment or binding • TCC regulator valve is stuck "off" due to sediment or binding • TCC solenoid valve O-ring or turbine shaft seals leaking or cut • TSB 00-07-30-007A contains a repair procedure for this code

DTC	Trouble Code Title, Conditions & Possible Causes
DTC: P0741 **2T CCM, MIL: Yes** **Years:** 2005, 2006, 2007 **Models:** Sierra, Silverado **Engines:** All **Transmissions:** A/T	**TCC System Stuck Off - Mechanical (4L80-E)** DTC P0121, P0122, P0123, P0502, P0503, P0716, P0717, P0742, P1820, P1822, P1823, P1825 and P1860 not set, engine started, Fuel Cutoff inactive, time since last gear lever change more than 6 seconds, IMS indicates D2, D3 or D4, Transmission gear ratio indicates 2nd, 3rd or 4th gear, TFT sensor from 68°F-302°F, TP angle from 10-99%, engine torque from 32-159 ft lbs, TCC solenoid commanded "on", and the PCM detected the TCC slip speed was more than 125-130 RPM for a given torque for 20 seconds. **Possible Causes:** • ATF level is too low, or the fluid is burnt or contaminated • Inspect transmission lines to radiator for bends or restrictions • Oil pressure screen is clogged or debris in the oil pan • TCC control valve is stuck "off" due to sediment or binding • TCC regulator valve is stuck "off" due to sediment or binding • TCC feed valve is stuck "off" due to sediment or binding • TCC solenoid valve O-ring or turbine shaft seals leaking or cut
DTC: P0741 **2T CCM, MIL: Yes** **Years:** 2005, 2006, 2007 **Models:** Malibu, Rendezvous **Engines:** 2.2L, 3.4L, 3.5L, 3.6L, 3.9L, 3.9L **Transmissions:** A/T	**TCC System Mechanically Stuck Off (4T40, 4T45-E)** DTC P0121-P0123, P0502, P0503, P0742, P1810 and P1887 not set, engine started, TFT sensor from 70-266°F, time since last gear select lever change 6 seconds, TFP manual valve position switch indicating D2, D3 or D4, TP angle from 8-75%, commanded gear is 2nd, 3rd or 4th, TCC is "on" for 3 seconds, and the PCM detected the TCC slip speed was over 250 RPM for 8 seconds twice in 1 trip. **Possible Causes:** • ATF level is too low, or the fluid is burnt or contaminated • Inspect transmission lines to radiator for bends or restrictions • Oil pressure screen is clogged or debris in the oil pan • TCC control valve is stuck "off" due to sediment or binding • TCC regulator valve is stuck "off" due to sediment or binding • TCC feed valve is stuck "off" due to sediment or binding • TCC solenoid valve O-ring or turbine shaft seals leaking or cut • TSB 02-07-30-021 contains a repair procedure for this code
DTC: P0742 **2T CCM, MIL: Yes** **Years:** 2005, 2006, 2007 **Models:** Malibu, Rendezvous **Engines:** 2.2L, 3.4L, 3.5L, 3.6L, 3.9L, 3.9L **Transmissions:** A/T	**Torque Converter Clutch Circuit Stuck On (4T65-E)** DTC P0121, P0122, P0123, P1860 and P1887 not set, engine started, Fuel Cutoff inactive, engine torque from 70-200 ft lbs, TP position from 5-45%, TFT sensor from 68-266°F, time since last gear range change more than 6 seconds, speed ratio less than 7.0, TCC commanded "off", slip speed from −20 to 25 for 8 seconds, and the PCM detected the TCC release switch was closed 6 times for 4 seconds each time during the current key cycle. **Possible Causes:** • TCC PWM solenoid valve for the fluid exhaust is restricted • TCC regulated apply valve is stuck in the TCC apply position • TCC control valve is stuck in the TCC apply position • TCC feed limit valve is stuck (i.e., the TCC feed limit pressure, and the TCC release pressure to be low or nonexistent) • Pressure regulator valve is stuck • TCC fluid circuits leaking or abnormally low/high line pressure • TCC release switch circuit is shorted to ground • TSB 00-07-30-007A contains a repair procedure for this code
DTC: P0742 **2T CCM, MIL: Yes** **Years:** 2005, 2006, 2007 **Models:** Sierra, Silverado **Engines:** All **Transmissions:** A/T	**TCC System Stuck Off - Mechanical (4L60-E)** DTC P0122, P0123, P0502, P0503, P0740, P1810 and P1860 not set, engine speed from 1000-3000 RPM, TP angle from 17-45%, ECT sensor from 68-266°F, Fuel Cutoff off, engine vacuum from 0-105 kPa, engine torque from 50-400 ft lbs, commanded gear not in 1st, speed ratio from 0.64-1.35, gear range is D4, no gear range change for 5 seconds, TCC commanded "off", vehicle speed from 15-50 MPH, and the PCM detected the TCC slip speed was −20 to +20 RPM for over 5 seconds (the fault must occur twice for this code set). **Possible Causes:** • Exhaust orifice in the TCC solenoid valve is clogged • Converter clutch apply valve stuck in the "on" (apply) position • Valve body gasket is damaged or misaligned • Release pass is clogged or restricted • Transmission cooler line is bent or restricted

DTC	Trouble Code Title, Conditions & Possible Causes
DTC: P0748 **1T CCM, MIL: No** **Years:** 2005, 2006, 2007 **Models:** Malibu, Rendezvous **Engines:** 2.2L, 3.4L, 3.5L, 3.6L, 3.9L, 3.9L **Transmissions:** A/T	**Pressure Control Solenoid Circuit Malfunction (4T65-E)** Engine started; system voltage over 11v with the TFT sensor less than −40°F or over 13.0v with the TFT sensor more than 304°F, Pressure Control solenoid commanded "on", and the PCM detected the solenoid duty cycle was outside of its normal operating range of 0.5-95% for 200 milliseconds. The PC solenoid valve controls transmission line pressure based on current flow through its windings. The PCM determines desired line pressure based on throttle position and other inputs. The PCM then varies the duty cycle on the high side of the PC solenoid valve to control current flow to the solenoid. Current is controlled from about 0.02 amps for maximum line pressure to 1.1 amps for minimum line pressure. The PCM monitors the actual current to the solenoid. **Possible Causes:** • PC solenoid high side circuit is open, shorted to ground or B+ • PC solenoid low side circuit is open, shorted to ground or to B+ • PC solenoid high or low side driver is damaged or has failed • TSB 00-07-30-002B contains a repair procedure for this code
DTC: P0748 **1T CCM, MIL: No** **Years:** 2005, 2006, 2007 **Models:** Sierra, Silverado **Engines:** All **Transmissions:** A/T	**Pressure Control Solenoid Circuit Malfunction (4L60-E, 4L65-E)** Engine started, system voltage over 10.0v, and the PCM detected the Pressure Control solenoid duty cycle reached its high limit of around 95%, or it reached its low limit of around 0%. **Possible Causes:** • PC solenoid high side circuit is open, shorted to ground or B+ • PC solenoid low side circuit is open, shorted to ground or to B+ • PC solenoid high or low side driver is damaged or has failed
DTC: P0751 **2T CCM, MIL: Yes** **Years:** 2005, 2006, 2007 **Models:** Malibu, Rendezvous **Engines:** 2.2L, 3.4L, 3.5L, 3.6L, 3.9L, 3.9L **Transmissions:** A/T	**A/T 1-2 Shift Solenoid - No 1st or 4th Gear (4T65-E)** DTC P0121-P0123, P0502, P0503, P0716, P0717, P1820, P1822, P1823, P1825, P1842, P1843, P1845 and P1847, Engine started, Transmission not in Park, Neutral or Reverse, TFT sensor from 68-266°F, TP angle over 10%, VSS over 5 MPH, engine torque from 20-200 lb ft., ISS signal from 150-8000 RPM, OSS signal more than 300 RPM, last gear range change over 1 second, then after the PCM commanded 1st gear and the gear ratio indicates 2nd gear (1.52:1-1.62:1) for 1 second, or the PCM commanded 4th gear and the gear ratio indicated 3rd gear (0.95:1-1.05:1) for 1 second. **Possible Causes:** • ATF is burnt or contaminated • Transmission has an internal malfunction. • Shift solenoid valve seals are damaged • Transmission has failed
DTC: P0751 **1T CCM, MIL: Yes** **Years:** 2005, 2006, 2007 **Models:** Sierra, Silverado **Engines:** All **Transmissions:** A/T	**A/T 1-2 Shift Solenoid - No 1st or 4th Gear (4L60-E/4L80-E)** DTC P0122, P0123, P0502, P0503, P0740, P0742, P0753, P0758, P0785, P1810 and P1860 not set, engine started, vehicle driven to over 5 MPH, Fuel Cutoff not active, TP angle from 10-35% (7%), gear range or TFP manual valve position switch D4 with no change for 6 seconds, TFT sensor from 68-266°F, engine torque 80-400 lb ft., and the PCM detected the commanded gear equaled 1st Gear and the ratio equaled 2nd Gear; or commanded gear equaled 4th Gear with TCC locked and the ratio equaled 3rd Gear for 4 seconds. **Possible Causes:** • ATF is burnt or contaminated, or the level is incorrect • Transmission has an internal damage to the torque converter • Shift solenoid valve seals are damaged or leaking • Transmission has failed
DTC: P0751 **2T CCM, MIL: Yes** **Years:** 2005, 2006, 2007 **Models:** Sierra, Silverado **Engines:** All **Transmissions:** A/T	**A/T 1-2 Shift Solenoid - No 1st Or 4th Gear (4L60-E, 4L65-E, 4L80-E)** DTC P0122, P0123, P0502, P0503, P0740, P0742, P0753, P0758, P0785, P1810 and P1860 not set, vehicle driven to over 5 MPH, Fuel Cutoff off, TP angle over 10%, TFT sensor at 68-266°F, gear range is D4, engine torque from 50-400 lb ft., output speed over 150 RPM, Transfer Case ratio in 4WD Low from 0.9-1.2, or in 4WD High at 2.6-2.85; running in 1st gear for 2 seconds, and the PCM detected the gear ratio was 1.2-1.825 for 500 ms; or while running in 4th Gear for 1 second, the estimated gear ratio was 0.95-1.15 for 6 seconds. **Possible Causes:** • ATF is burnt or contaminated, or the level is incorrect • Transmission has an internal damage to the torque converter • Shift solenoid valve seals are damaged or leaking • Transmission has failed

DTC	Trouble Code Title, Conditions & Possible Causes

DTC: P0751
1T CCM, MIL: Yes
Years: 2005, 2006, 2007
Models: Sierra, Silverado
Engines: All
Transmissions: A/T
	A/T 1-2 Shift Solenoid - No 1st or 4th Gear (4L80-E)
	DTC P0122, P0123, P0502, P0503, P0740, P0742, P0753, P0758, P0785, P1810 and P1860 not set, engine speed below 3750 RPM, VSS over 3 MPH, APP angle or TP angle over 10%, TFT sensor at 68-266°F, engine torque at 80-475 lb ft., and the PCM detected the commanded gear equaled 1st Gear with a speed ratio equal to 2nd Gear for 2 seconds; or commanded gear equaled 4th Gear (TCC "on") with a ratio equal to 3rd Gear for 3 seconds.
	Possible Causes:
	  • ATF is burnt or contaminated, or the level is incorrect
	  • Transmission has an internal damage to the torque converter
	  • Shift solenoid valve seals are damaged or leaking
	  • Transmission has internal damage (it may need to be replaced)

DTC: P0752
2T CCM, MIL: Yes
Years: 2005, 2006, 2007
Models: Malibu, Rendezvous
Engines: 2.2L, 3.4L, 3.5L, 3.6L, 3.9L, 3.9L
Transmissions: A/T
	A/T 1-2 Shift Solenoid- No 2nd Or 3rd Gear (4T65-E)
	DTC P0121-P0123, P0502, P0503, P0716, P0717, P1820, P1822, P1823, P1825, P1842, P1843, P1845 and P1847, engine running, Transmission not in P/N or Reverse, TFT sensor from 68-266°F, TP angle over 10%, VSS over 5 MPH, engine torque from 20-200 lb ft., ISS signal from 150-8000 RPM, OSS signal over 300 RPM, 2nd Gear commanded "on" with last gear change over 1 second, and the PCM detected 1st gear (gear ratio 2.87:1-2.97:1) for 1 second, or with 3rd Gear commanded "on", the PCM detected 4th Gear (0.65:1-0.75:1).
	Possible Causes:
	  • ATF is burnt or contaminated
	  • Transmission has plugged or restricted fluid circuits
	  • Shift solenoid valve seals are leaking or damaged
	  • Transmission has failed

DTC: P0752
1T CCM, MIL: Yes
Years: 2005, 2006, 2007
Models: Sierra, Silverado
Engines: All
Transmissions: A/T
	A/T 1-2 Shift Solenoid - No 2nd Or 3rd Gear (4L80-E)
	DTC P0101-P0103, P0106-P0108, P0121-P0123, P0502, P0503, P0716, P0717, P0742, P0753, P0758, P0785, P1810, P1860 and P1870 not set, engine runtime over 5 seconds, vehicle driven to over 7 MPH, Fuel Cutoff inactive, TP angle over 10%, gear range or TFP manual valve position switch is D4 with no change for 6 seconds, TFT sensor from 68-266°F, engine torque from 80-400 lb ft., then with 2nd Gear commanded "on", the PCM detected the gear ratio equaled 1st Gear for 2.25 seconds (fault detected 5 times on 1 trip).
	Possible Causes:
	  • ATF is burnt or contaminated, or the level is incorrect
	  • Transmission has an internal damage to the torque converter
	  • Shift solenoid valve seals are damaged or leaking
	  • Transmission has failed

DTC: P0752
1T CCM, MIL: Yes
Years: 2005, 2006, 2007
Models: Sierra, Silverado
Engines: All
Transmissions: A/T
	A/T 1-2 Shift Solenoid - No 2nd Or 3rd Gear (4L80-E)
	DTC P0122, P0123, P0502, P0503, P0740, P0742, P0753, P0758, P0785, P1810 and P1860 not set, engine started, vehicle driven to over 3 MPH at an engine speed less than 3750 RPM, APP or TP angle more than 10%, TFT sensor from 68-266°F, engine torque from 80-475 lb ft., then with 2nd Gear commanded "on", the PCM detected the estimated gear ratio was 1 Gear for 2.25 seconds (fault must occur 5 times in one key cycle to set the code).
	Possible Causes:
	  • ATF is burnt or contaminated, or the level is incorrect
	  • Transmission has an internal damage to the torque converter
	  • Shift solenoid valve seals are damaged or leaking
	  • Transmission has failed

DTC: P0752
2T CCM, MIL: Yes
Years: 2005, 2006, 2007
Models: Sierra, Silverado
Engines: All
Transmissions: A/T
	A/T 1-2 Shift Solenoid - No 2nd Or 3rd Gear (4L60-E, 4L80-E)
	DTC P0122, P0123, P0502, P0503, P0740, P0742, P0753, P0758, P0785, P1810 and P1860 not set, vehicle driven to over 5 MPH, Fuel Cutoff inactive, TP angle more than 10%, gear range is D4, TFT sensor from 68-266°F, engine torque from 50-400 lb ft., transmission output speed more than 150 RPM, Transfer Case low ratio in 4WD Low at 0.9-1.2 or in 4WD High at 2.6-2.85; engine torque from 25-650 lb ft., then with 2nd Gear commanded "on" for 1 second, the PCM detected the estimated gear ratio was 3.0-3.3 for 2 seconds; or with 3rd Gear commanded "on" for 1 second, the gear ratio was 0.65-0.95 for 3 seconds.
	Possible Causes:
	  • ATF is burnt or contaminated, or the level is incorrect
	  • Transmission has an internal damage to the torque converter
	  • Shift solenoid valve seals are damaged or leaking
	  • Transmission has failed

DTC: P0753
2T CCM, MIL: Yes
Years: 2005, 2006, 2007
Models: Sierra, Silverado
Engines: All
Transmissions: A/T
	A/T 1-2 Shift Solenoid Circuit Malfunction (4L80-E)
	Engine started, Fuel Cutoff inactive, system voltage over 10.0v, and the PCM detected an unexpected voltage condition on the 1-2 Shift Solenoid control circuit during the CCM test.
	Possible Causes:
	  • 1-2 shift solenoid control circuit is open or shorted to ground
	  • 1-2 shift solenoid control circuit is shorted to system power
	  • 1-2 shift solenoid is damaged or has failed
	  • PCM has failed

DTC	Trouble Code Title, Conditions & Possible Causes
DTC: P0753 **2T CCM, MIL: Yes** **Years:** 2005, 2006, 2007 **Models:** Malibu, Rendezvous **Engines:** 2.2L, 3.4L, 3.5L, 3.6L, 3.9L, 3.9L **Transmissions:** A/T	**A/T 1-⅔ Shift Solenoid Circuit Malfunction (4T65-E)** Engine started, Fuel Cutoff inactive, system voltage over 10.0v, and the PCM detected an unexpected voltage condition on the 1- ⅔ Shift Solenoid control circuit during the CCM test. **Possible Causes:** • 1-⅔ shift solenoid control circuit is open or shorted to ground • 1-⅔ shift solenoid control circuit is shorted to system power • 1-⅔ shift solenoid is damaged or has failed • PCM has failed • TSB 02-07-30-022A contains a repair procedure for this code
DTC: P0753 **2T CCM, MIL: Yes** **Years:** 2005, 2006, 2007 **Models:** Sierra, Silverado **Engines:** 4.3L, 4.8L, 5.3L, 6.0L, 6.2L, 8.1L **Transmissions:** A/T	**A/T 1-2 Shift Solenoid Circuit Malfunction (4L60-E, 4L80-E)** Engine started, Fuel Cutoff inactive, system voltage over 10.0v, and the PCM detected an unexpected voltage condition on the 1-2 Shift Solenoid control circuit during the CCM test. **Possible Causes:** • 1-2 shift solenoid control circuit is open or shorted to ground • 1-2 shift solenoid control circuit is shorted to system power • 1-2 shift solenoid is damaged or has failed • PCM has failed • TSB 57-65-08A contains a repair procedure for this code
DTC: P0753 **2T CCM, MIL: Yes** **Years:** 2005, 2006, 2007 **Models:** Sierra, Silverado **Engines:** 4.3L, 4.8L, 5.3L, 6.0L, 6.2L, 8.1L **Transmissions:** A/T	**A/T 1-2 Shift Solenoid Circuit Malfunction (4L60-E, 4L80-E)** Engine started, Fuel Cutoff inactive, system voltage over 10.0v, and the PCM detected an unexpected voltage condition on the 1-2 Shift Solenoid control circuit during the CCM continuous test. **Possible Causes:** • 1-2 shift solenoid control circuit is open or shorted to ground • 1-2 shift solenoid control circuit is shorted to system power • 1-2 shift solenoid is damaged or has failed • PCM has failed • TSB 01-07-30-002C contains a repair procedure for this code
DTC: P0756 **1T CCM, MIL: Yes** **Years:** 2005, 2006, 2007 **Models:** Sierra, Silverado **Engines:** 4.3L, 4.8L, 5.3L, 6.0L, 6.2L, 8.1L **Transmissions:** A/T	**2-3 Shift Solenoid - No 2nd Or 3rd Gear (4L80-E)** DTC P0122, P0123, P0502, P0503, P0740, P0742, P0753, P0758, P0785, P1810 and P1860 not set, engine started, Fuel Cutoff inactive, vehicle speed over 5 MPH, TP angle from 10-35% (7%), gear range is D4, TFT sensor from 68-266°F, engine torque from 80-650 lb ft., then with 1st Gear commanded "on", the PCM detected the gear ratio indicated 4th Gear for 2.5 seconds; or with 2nd Gear commanded "on", the PCM detected the gear ratio indicated 3rd Gear for 2.7 seconds during the CCM test. **Possible Causes:** • ATF is burnt or contaminated • Transmission has plugged or restricted fluid circuits • Shift solenoid valve seals are leaking or damaged • Transmission has failed
DTC: P0756 **2T CCM, MIL: Yes** **Years:** 2005, 2006, 2007 **Models:** Sierra, Silverado **Engines:** 4.3L, 4.8L, 5.3L, 6.0L, 6.2L, 8.1L **Transmissions:** A/T	**2-3 Shift Solenoid - No 2nd Or 3rd Gear (4L60-E, 4L65-E)** DTC P0122, P0123, P0502, P0503, P0740, P0742, P0753, P0758, P0785, P1810 and P1860 not set, engine started, system voltage over 10.0v, vehicle speed over 5 MPH, TP angle over 10%, gear range is D4, TFT sensor from 68-266°F, engine torque from 50-400 lb ft., transmission output shaft speed more than 150 RPM, Fuel Cutoff inactive, then with 1st Gear commanded "on", the PCM detected the gear ratio indicated 4th Gear for 2.5 seconds; or with 2nd Gear commanded "on" for 1 second, the PCM detected the estimate gear ratio was 0.9-1.2 for 2 seconds during the CCM test **Possible Causes:** • ATF is burnt or contaminated • Transmission has plugged or restricted fluid circuits • Shift solenoid valve seals are leaking or damaged • Transmission has failed • TSB 01-07-30-036A contains a repair procedure for this code
DTC: P0756 **2T CCM, MIL: Yes** **Years:** 2005, 2006, 2007 **Models:** Sierra, Silverado **Engines:** 6.6L Diesel **Transmissions:** A/T	**2-3 Shift Solenoid - No 2nd or 3rd Gear (4L80-E)** DTC P0712, P0713, P0716, P0717, P0722, P0723, P0753, P0758, and P1810 not set, engine started, engine speed from 475-3750 RPM, system voltage over 10.0v, vehicle speed over 3 MPH, APP angle more than 10%, TFT sensor from 68-266°F, engine torque from 80-475 lb ft., then with 1st Gear commanded "on", the PCM detected he gear ratio equaled 4th Gear for 2.75 seconds; or with 2nd Gear commanded "on", the PCM detected the gear ratio equaled 3rd Gear for 2.75 at least twice; or with 3rd Gear commanded "on", the PCM detected the gear ratio equaled 2nd Gear for 3.25 seconds at least 7 times during the test. **Possible Causes:** • ATF is burnt or contaminated • Transmission has plugged or restricted fluid circuits • Shift solenoid valve seals are leaking or damaged • Transmission has failed

DTC	Trouble Code Title, Conditions & Possible Causes
DTC: P0756 **2T CCM, MIL: Yes** **Years:** 2005, 2006, 2007 **Models:** Malibu, Rendezvous **Engines:** 2.2L, 3.4L, 3.5L, 3.6L, 3.9L, 3.9L **Transmissions:** A/T	**2-3 Shift Solenoid - No 3rd Or 4th Gear (4T65-E)** DTC P0121-P0123, P0502, P0503, P0716, P0717, P0730, P0753, P0758, P1810, P1814 and P1860 not set, engine started, vehicle speed over 5 MPH, Fuel Cutoff inactive, gearshift not in Park, Neutral or Reverse, time since last gear range change 1 second, TP angle over 10%, TFT sensor at 68-264°F, engine torque from 20-200 lb ft., ISS sensor at 150-8000 RPM, OSS more than 300 RPM, then with 3rd Gear commanded "on", the PCM detected the gear ratio equaled 2nd gear (1.52:1 to 1.62:1) for 1 second; or with 4th Gear commanded "on", the PCM detected the gear ratio equaled 1st gear (2.87:1 to 2.97:1) for 1 second. **Possible Causes:** • ATF is burnt or contaminated • Transmission has plugged or restricted fluid circuits • Shift solenoid valve seals are leaking or damaged • Transmission has failed • TSB 02-07-30-13 contains a repair procedure for this code
DTC: P0757 **1T CCM, MIL: No** **Years:** 2005, 2006, 2007 **Models:** Sierra, Silverado **Engines:** 4.3L, 4.8L, 5.3L, 6.0L, 6.2L, 8.1L **Transmissions:** A/T	**2-3 Shift Solenoid - No 3rd Or 4th Gear (4T60-E, 4T65-E)** DTC P0121-P0123, P0502, P0503, P0716, P0717, P0730, P0753, P0758, P1810, P1814 and P1860 not set, VSS over 5 MPH, Fuel Cutoff "off", Transmission not in Park, Neutral or Reverse, time since last gear range change over 1 second, TP angle over 10%, TFT sensor from 68-264°F, engine torque from 20-200 lb ft., ISS sensor from 150-8000 RPM, OSS sensor more than 300 RPM, then with 3rd Gear commanded "on" for 1 second, the PCM detected the estimated gear ratio 1.6-1.8 and the engine torque was from 50-500 lb ft; or with 4th Gear commanded "on" for two seconds, the PCM detected the estimated gear ratio equaled 1.8-3.3 and the engine torque was from 50-400 lb ft for 2 seconds during the CCM test. **Possible Causes:** • ATF is burnt or contaminated • Transmission has plugged or restricted fluid circuits • Shift solenoid valve seals are leaking or damaged, or the Transmission has failed • TSB 01-07-30-038 contains a repair procedure for this code
DTC: P0758 **1T CCM, MIL: Yes** **Years:** 2005, 2006, 2007 **Models:** Sierra, Silverado **Engines:** 4.3L, 4.8L, 5.3L, 6.0L, 6.2L, 8.1L **Transmissions:** A/T	**A/T 2-3 Shift Solenoid Circuit Malfunction (4L60-E, 4L80-E)** Engine started, engine speed over 450 RPM for 5 seconds, system voltage over 10.0v, and the PCM detected an unexpected voltage condition on the 2-3 Shift Solenoid control circuit for 5 seconds. **Possible Causes:** • 2-3 shift solenoid control circuit is open or shorted to ground • 2-3 shift solenoid control circuit is shorted to system power • 2-3 shift solenoid power circuit is open (test the TRANS fuse) • 2-3 shift solenoid is damaged or has failed • PCM has failed • TSB 01-07-30-002C contains a repair procedure for this code
DTC: P0758 **1T CCM, MIL: Yes** **Years:** 2005, 2006, 2007 **Models:** Sierra, Silverado **Engines:** 4.3L, 4.8L, 5.3L, 6.0L, 6.2L, 8.1L **Transmissions:** A/T	**A/T 2-3 Shift Solenoid Circuit Malfunction (4L80-E)** Engine speed over 450 RPM for 7 seconds, system voltage over 10.0v, and the PCM detected an unexpected voltage on the 2-3 Shift Solenoid control circuit for 4-5 seconds. **Possible Causes:** • 2-3 shift solenoid control circuit is open, shorted to ground or shorted to system power • 2-3 shift solenoid power circuit is open (test the TRANS fuse) • 2-3 shift solenoid has failed, or the PCM has failed
DTC: P0758 **1T CCM, MIL: Yes** **Years:** 2005, 2006, 2007 **Models:** Sierra, Silverado **Engines:** 6.6L Diesel **Transmissions:** A/T	**A/T 2-3 Shift Solenoid Circuit Malfunction (4L80-E)** Engine speed over 450 RPM for 7 seconds, system voltage over 10.0v, and the PCM detected an unexpected voltage on the 2-3 Shift Solenoid control circuit for 4-5 seconds. **Possible Causes:** • 2-3 shift solenoid control circuit is open, shorted to ground or shorted to system power • 2-3 shift solenoid power circuit is open (test the TRANS fuse) • 2-3 shift solenoid is damaged or has failed • PCM has failed
DTC: P0785 **1T CCM, MIL: Yes** **Years:** 2005, 2006, 2007 **Models:** Sierra, Silverado **Engines:** 4.3L, 4.8L, 5.3L, 6.0L, 6.2L, 8.1L **Transmissions:** A/T	**A/T 3-2 Shift Solenoid Circuit Malfunction (4L80-E)** Engine started, engine speed over 450 RPM for 7 seconds, system voltage over 10.0v, and the PCM detected an unexpected voltage condition on the 3-2 Shift Solenoid control circuit for 4-5 seconds. **Possible Causes:** • 3-2 shift solenoid control circuit is open or shorted to ground • 3-2 shift solenoid control circuit is shorted to system power • 3-2 shift solenoid power circuit is open (test the TRANS fuse) • 3-2 shift solenoid is damaged or has failed • PCM has failed

DTC	Trouble Code Title, Conditions & Possible Causes
DTC: P0785 **1T CCM, MIL: Yes** **Years:** 2005, 2006, 2007 **Models:** Sierra, Silverado **Engines:** 6.6L Diesel **Transmissions:** A/T	**A/T 3-2 Shift Solenoid Circuit Malfunction (4L80-E)** Engine speed over 450 RPM for 7 seconds, system voltage over 10.0v, and the PCM detected an unexpected voltage on the 3-2 Shift Solenoid control circuit for 4-5 seconds. **Possible Causes:** • 3-2 shift solenoid control circuit is open or shorted to ground • 3-2 shift solenoid control circuit is shorted to system power • 3-2 shift solenoid power circuit is open (check the TRANS fuse) • 3-2 shift solenoid is damaged or has failed • PCM has failed
DTC: P0785 **1T CCM, MIL: Yes** **Years:** 2005, 2006, 2007 **Models:** Sierra, Silverado **Engines:** 4.3L, 4.8L, 5.3L, 6.0L, 6.2L, 8.1L **Transmissions:** A/T	**A/T 3-2 Shift Solenoid Circuit Malfunction (4L60-E)** Engine started, engine speed over 450 RPM for 5 seconds, system voltage over 10.0v, and the PCM detected an unexpected voltage condition on the 3-2 Shift Solenoid control circuit for 4-5 seconds. **Possible Causes:** • 3-2 shift solenoid control circuit is open, shorted to ground or shorted to system power • 3-2 shift solenoid power circuit is open (check the TRANS fuse) • 3-2 shift solenoid is damaged or has failed • PCM has failed • TSB 01-07-30-002C contains a repair procedure for this code
DTC: P0802 **1T CCM, MIL: No** **Years:** 2005, 2006, 2007 **Models:** Sierra, Silverado **Engines:** 6.6L Diesel **Transmissions:** All	**Malfunction Indicator Lamp Circuit Malfunction** Engine started and the PCM detected an incorrect voltage on the TCM MIL request circuit. **Possible Causes:** • TCM MIL Request circuit is open, shorted to ground or to B+ • ECM has failed • TCM has failed
DTC: P0850 **1T CCM, MIL: No** **Years:** 2005, 2006, 2007 **Models:** Sierra, Silverado **Engines:** All **Transmissions:** A/T	**A/T TCC PWM Solenoid Malfunction (4L60-E, 4L65-E)** DTC P0502, P0503, P0740, P0742, P0753, P0758, P1120, P1220, P1810 and P1860 not set, engine speed from 1,500-3,000 RPM for 6 seconds, VSS from 30-82 MPH, TP angle at 20-99%, speed ratio from 0.64-1.35, TFT sensor from 68-302°F, engine vacuum from 0-105 kPa, engine torque from 50-400 lb ft., not in 1st gear, gear range is D4, Shift Solenoid diagnostic counters = 0, TCC command at 40% duty cycle, TCC slip speed from 130-800 RPM for 7 seconds, then during Condition 1: With the TCC slip speed at 130-800 RPM for 7 seconds, and the PCM commanded maximum line pressure and prevented the freeze shift adapts from being updated, or during Condition 2: or with the TCC slip speed at 130-800 RPM for 7 seconds, the PCM commanded the TCC off for 1.5 seconds, or during Condition 3: with the TCC slip speed at 130-800 RPM for 7 seconds, and the current fail counter incremented. **Possible Causes:** • ATF is burnt or contaminated • Transmission has an internal malfunction, or the TCC PWM solenoid seal is damaged • TCC PWM solenoid has failed, or the Transmission has failed

OBD II Trouble Code List (P1xxx Codes)

DTC	Trouble Code Title, Conditions & Possible Causes
DTC: P1011 **1T CCM, MIL: Yes** **Years:** 2005, 2006, 2007 **Models:** Sky, Solstice, SRX **Engines:** 2.0L, 3.6L, 3.9L **Transmissions:** All	**Intake Camshaft Position (CMP) Actuator Park Position Circuit** DTCs P0010, P0013, P0341, P0342, P0343, P0366, P0367, P0368, P2088, P2089, P2090, and P2091 are not set. The engine is operating for more than 1 second. The ECM completed the CMP actuator solenoid output driver test. The ECM detects that a CMP actuator is not in the parked position on an engine start-up. **Possible Causes:** • Incorrect oil level or pressure • Other engine mechanical problems • Improper starting/stopping techniques
DTC: P1012 **1T CCM, MIL: Yes** **Years:** 2005, 2006, 2007 **Models:** Sky, Solstice, SRX **Engines:** 2.0L, 3.6L, 3.9L **Transmissions:** All	**Exhaust Camshaft Position (CMP) Actuator Park Position Circuit** DTCs P0010, P0013, P0341, P0342, P0343, P0366, P0367, P0368, P2088, P2089, P2090, and P2091 are not set. The engine is operating for more than 1 second. The ECM completed the CMP actuator solenoid output driver test. The ECM detects that a CMP actuator is not in the parked position on an engine start-up. **Possible Causes:** • Incorrect oil level or pressure • Other engine mechanical problems • Improper starting/stopping techniques

DTC	Trouble Code Title, Conditions & Possible Causes
DTC: P1013 **1T CCM, MIL: Yes** **Years:** 2005, 2006, 2007 **Models:** SRX **Engines:** 3.6L, 3.9L **Transmissions:** All	**Intake Camshaft Position (CMP) Actuator Park Position Circuit Bank 2** DTCs P0010, P0013, P0341, P0342, P0343, P0366, P0367, P0368, P2088, P2089, P2090, and P2091 are not set. The engine is operating for more than 1 second. The ECM completed the CMP actuator solenoid output driver test. The ECM detects that a CMP actuator is not in the parked position on an engine start-up. **Possible Causes:** • Incorrect oil level or pressure • Other engine mechanical problems • Improper starting/stopping techniques
DTC: P1014 **1T CCM, MIL: Yes** **Years:** 2005, 2006, 2007 **Models:** SRX **Engines:** 3.6L, 3.9L **Transmissions:** All	**Exhaust Camshaft Position (CMP) Actuator Park Position Circuit Bank 2** DTCs P0010, P0013, P0341, P0342, P0343, P0366, P0367, P0368, P2088, P2089, P2090, and P2091 are not set. The engine is operating for more than 1 second. The ECM completed the CMP actuator solenoid output driver test. The ECM detects that a CMP actuator is not in the parked position on an engine start-up. **Possible Causes:** • Incorrect oil level or pressure • Other engine mechanical problems • Improper starting/stopping techniques
DTC: P1020 **1T CCM, MIL: Yes** **Years:** 2005, 2006, 2007 **Models:** Sierra, Silverado **Engines:** 6.0L CNG **Transmissions:** All	**Camshaft Phasing System Malfunction** DTC P0148, P0611 and P1209 not set; engine operating on CNG, PCM not in Fuel Shutoff or Decel Fuel Shutoff modes, system voltage from 6-18v, and the FICM (module) detected an invalid fuel injector PWM signal. The PCM controls the fuel delivery and determines the fuel system operation on Bi-Fuel (KL6) vehicles. The FICM receives the 8 fuel injector PWM signals from the PCM, and generates duplicate PWM signals to operate the CNG injectors. **Possible Causes:** • AF fuel mode relay circuit (odd bank, even bank) is open • AF enable circuit is open or shorted to ground • FICM is damaged or it has failed
DTC: P1021 **1T CCM, MIL: Yes** **Years:** 2005, 2006, 2007 **Models:** Sierra, Silverado **Engines:** 6.0L CNG **Transmissions:** All	**CNG Fuel Injector 1 Circuit Malfunction** Engine started, system voltage from 6-18v, and the FICM detected an incorrect voltage condition on the circuit that controls the CNG Fuel Injector 1 operation during the CCM test. **Possible Causes:** • CNG fuel injector 1 control circuit is open or shorted to ground • CNG fuel injector 1 is damaged or it has failed • FICM has failed
DTC: P1022 **1T CCM, MIL: Yes** **Years:** 2005, 2006, 2007 **Models:** Sierra, Silverado **Engines:** 6.0L CNG **Transmissions:** All	**CNG Fuel Injector 2 Circuit Malfunction** Engine started, system voltage from 6-18v, and the FICM detected an incorrect voltage condition on the circuit that controls the CNG Fuel Injector 2 operation during the CCM test. **Possible Causes:** • CNG fuel injector 2 control circuit is open or shorted to ground • CNG fuel injector 2 is damaged or it has failed • FICM has failed
DTC: P1023 **1T CCM, MIL: Yes** **Years:** 2005, 2006, 2007 **Models:** Sierra, Silverado **Engines:** 6.0L CNG **Transmissions:** All	**CNG Fuel Injector 3 Circuit Malfunction** Engine started, system voltage from 6-18v, and the FICM detected an incorrect voltage condition on the circuit that controls the CNG Fuel Injector 3 operation during the CCM test. **Possible Causes:** • CNG fuel injector 3 control circuit is open or shorted to ground • CNG fuel injector 3 is damaged or it has failed • FICM has failed
DTC: P1024 **1T CCM, MIL: Yes** **Years:** 2005, 2006, 2007 **Models:** Sierra, Silverado **Engines:** 6.0L CNG **Transmissions:** All	**CNG Fuel Injector 4 Circuit Malfunction** Engine started, system voltage from 6-18v, and the FICM detected an incorrect voltage condition on the circuit that controls the CNG Fuel Injector 4 operation during the CCM test. **Possible Causes:** • CNG fuel injector 4 control circuit is open or shorted to ground • CNG fuel injector 4 is damaged or it has failed • FICM has failed
DTC: P1025 **1T CCM, MIL: Yes** **Years:** 2005, 2006, 2007 **Models:** Sierra, Silverado **Engines:** 6.0L CNG **Transmissions:** All	**CNG Fuel Injector 5 Circuit Malfunction** Engine started, system voltage from 6-18v, and the FICM detected an incorrect voltage condition on the circuit that controls the CNG Fuel Injector 5 operation during the CCM test. **Possible Causes:** • CNG fuel injector 5 control circuit is open or shorted to ground • CNG fuel injector 5 is damaged or it has failed • FICM has failed

DTC	Trouble Code Title, Conditions & Possible Causes
DTC: P1026 **1T CCM, MIL: Yes** **Years:** 2005, 2006, 2007 **Models:** Sierra, Silverado **Engines:** 6.0L CNG **Transmissions:** All	**CNG Fuel Injector 6 Circuit Malfunction** Engine started, system voltage from 6-18v, and the FICM detected an incorrect voltage condition on the circuit that controls the CNG Fuel Injector 6 operation during the CCM test. **Possible Causes:** • CNG fuel injector 6 control circuit is open or shorted to ground • CNG fuel injector 6 is damaged or it has failed • FICM has failed
DTC: P1027 **1T CCM, MIL: Yes** **Years:** 2005, 2006, 2007 **Models:** Sierra, Silverado **Engines:** 6.0L CNG **Transmissions:** All	**CNG Fuel Injector 7 Circuit Malfunction** Engine started, system voltage from 6-18v, and the FICM detected an incorrect voltage condition on the circuit that controls the CNG Fuel Injector 7 operation during the CCM test. **Possible Causes:** • CNG fuel injector 7 control circuit is open or shorted to ground • CNG fuel injector 7 is damaged or it has failed • FICM has failed
DTC: P1028 **1T CCM, MIL: Yes** **Years:** 2005, 2006, 2007 **Models:** Sierra, Silverado **Engines:** 6.0L CNG **Transmissions:** All	**CNG Fuel Injector 8 Circuit Malfunction** Engine started, system voltage from 6-18v, and the FICM detected an incorrect voltage condition on the circuit that controls the CNG Fuel Injector 8 operation during the CCM test. **Possible Causes:** • CNG fuel injector 8 control circuit is open or shorted to ground • CNG fuel injector 8 is damaged or it has failed • FICM has failed
DTC: P1093 **1T CCM, MIL: Yes** **Years:** 2005, 2006, 2007 **Models:** Sierra, Silverado **Engines:** 6.6L Diesel **Transmissions:** All	**Fuel Rail Pressure Range/Performance** DTC P0192, P0193 and P0641 not set; key on or engine running, and the ECM detected the difference between the Commanded fuel pressure and Actual fuel pressure was more than 20 MPa, or the FRP regulator fuel flow was more than 15,000 mm³ at 800 RPM, or that it was more than 38,000 mm³ at 2,000 RPM. The ECM uses the fuel rail pressure (FRP) sensor to detect the fuel pressure to the fuel injectors. This value is compared to the calculated target fuel pressure as determined by the ECM. The ECM adjusts the FRP by modulating the duty cycle of the control driver of the fuel pressure regulator. Injector pulse duration is determined by detecting the measured rail pressure and the target injection fuel to each cylinder. **Possible Causes:** • CNG fuel injector 8 connector is damaged, open or shorted • CNG fuel injector 8 control circuit is open or shorted to ground • CNG fuel injector 8 is damaged or it has failed • FICM has failed
DTC: P1094 **1T CCM, MIL: Yes** **Years:** 2005, 2006, 2007 **Models:** Sierra, Silverado **Engines:** 6.6L Diesel **Transmissions:** All	**Fuel Rail Pressure Solenoid Circuit Malfunction** DTC P0192, P0193 and P0641 not set; engine started, and the ECM detected the difference between the FRP sensor and commanded fuel injector fuel flow was more than 30 MPa. The ECM uses the fuel rail pressure sensor to detect the fuel injector fuel pressure. This value is compared to a calculated target fuel pressure in the ECM. The ECM adjusts the FRP by modulating the duty cycle of the fuel pressure regulator control driver. The pulse duration is determined by detecting the measured rail pressure and target injection fuel to each cylinder. **Possible Causes:** • Check the engine oil for fuel contamination • Fuel pressure regulator solenoid circuit is shorted to ground • If you have to prime the fuel system, inspect for a restricted fuel supply line or a fuel supply line air leak • ECM has failed
DTC: P1101 **1T CCM, MIL: Yes** **Years:** 2006, 2007 **Models:** G6 **Engines:** 2.4L, 3.6L, 3.9L, 3.9L **Transmissions:** All	**Intake Air Flow System Performance** DTCs P0102, P0103, P0107, P0108, P0112, P0113, P0116, P0117, P0118, P0125, P0128, P0335, P0336 are not set. The engine speed is between 400-6,400 RPM. The IAT Sensor parameter is between −7 and +125°C (+19 and 257°F). The ECT Sensor parameter is between 70-125°C (158-257°F). The ECM detects that the actual measured airflow from the MAF, MAP, and TP sensors is not within range of the calculated airflow that is derived from the system of models for more than 0.5 second. **Possible Causes:** • Ignition 1 voltage circuit has high resistance • MAF sensor signal circuit has high resistance or short • Failed MAF sensor • ECM has failed

DTC	Trouble Code Title, Conditions & Possible Causes
DTC: P1106 **1T CCM, MIL: No** **Years:** 2005, 2006, 2007 **Models:** Sierra, Silverado **Engines:** 4.3L, 4.8L, 5.3L, 6.0L, 6.2L, 8.1L **Transmissions:** All	**MAP Sensor Circuit Intermittent High Input** DTC P0121, P0122 and P0123 not set, engine started, system voltage over 10.0v, TP angle less than 0.4% with engine speed below 1200 RPM, or TP angle less than 20% with engine speed over 1200 RPM, and the PCM/VCM detected an unexpected "high" voltage (over 4.40v) on the MAP sensor signal circuit for over 1 second. **Possible Causes:** • MAP sensor signal circuit is shorted to VREF (intermittent fault) • MAP sensor ground circuit is open (intermittent fault) • MAP sensor is damaged or has failed • PCM has failed
DTC: P1106 **1T CCM, MIL: No** **Years:** 2005, 2006, 2007 **Models:** Malibu, Rendezvous **Engines:** 2.2L, 2.4L, 3.4L, 3.5L, 3.6L, 3.8L, 3.9L, 3.9L **Transmissions:** All	**MAP Sensor Circuit Intermittent High Input** DTC P0121, P0122 and P0123 not set, engine started, engine runtime from 1-2 minutes (depends on the ECT sensor at startup), system voltage over 10.0v, TP angle under 2% with engine speed less than 3000 RPM, or TP angle under 30% with engine speed more than 3000 RPM, and the PCM detected an intermittent high voltage (over 4.20v) condition on the MAP sensor circuit. The MAP sensor responds to pressure changes in the intake manifold that occur based on the engine load. The PCM is connected to the MAP sensor by a 5v VREF, low reference ground and MAP sensor signal circuit. **Possible Causes:** • MAP sensor signal circuit is shorted to VREF (intermittent fault) • MAP sensor ground circuit is open (intermittent fault) • MAP sensor is damaged or has failed (intermittent fault) • PCM has failed
DTC: P1107 **1T CCM, MIL: No** **Years:** 2005, 2006, 2007 **Models:** Malibu, Rendezvous **Engines:** 2.2L, 2.4L, 3.4L, 3.5L, 3.6L, 3.8L, 3.9L, 3.9L **Transmissions:** All	**MAP Sensor Circuit Intermittent Low Input** DTC P0121, P0122 and P0123 not set, engine started, system voltage over 10.0v, engine runtime from 1-2 minutes (depends on ECT sensor at startup), TP angle above 0% with engine speed less than 1000 RPM, or TP angle above 10% with engine speed more than 1000 RPM, and the PCM detected an intermittent low voltage condition (under 0.1v) on the MAP sensor signal circuit. The MAP sensor responds to pressure changes in the intake manifold that occur based on the engine load. The PCM is connected to the MAP sensor by a 5v VREF, low reference ground and MAP signal circuit. **Possible Causes:** • MAP sensor signal circuit shorted to ground (intermittent fault) • MAP sensor VREF circuit is open (intermittent fault) • MAP sensor is damaged or has failed (intermittent fault) • PCM has failed
DTC: P1107 **1T CCM, MIL: No** **Years:** 2005, 2006, 2007 **Models:** Sierra, Silverado **Engines:** 4.3L, 4.8L, 5.3L, 6.0L, 6.2L, 8.1L **Transmissions:** All	**MAP Sensor Circuit Intermittent Low Input** DTC P0121, P0122 and P0123 not set, engine started, system voltage over 10.0v, TP angle at 0% with engine speed below 800 RPM or TP angle less than 12.5% with engine speed over 800 RPM, and the PCM/VCM detected an unexpected "Low" voltage (under 0.40v) on the MAP sensor signal circuit for over 1 second. **Possible Causes:** • MAP sensor signal circuit shorted to ground (intermittent fault) • MAP sensor VREF circuit is open (intermittent fault) • MAP sensor is damaged or has failed (intermittent fault) • PCM has failed
DTC: P1111 **1T CCM, MIL: No** **Years:** 2005, 2006, 2007 **Models:** Malibu, Rendezvous **Engines:** 2.2L, 2.4L, 3.4L, 3.5L, 3.6L, 3.8L, 3.9L, 3.9L **Transmissions:** All	**IAT Sensor Circuit Intermittent High Input** DTC P0101, P0102, P0103, P0116, P0117, P0118, P0502 and P0503 not set, engine started, engine runtime over 3 minutes, MAF sensor less than 12 g/sec, VSS less than 35 MPH, ECT sensor more than 140°F, and the PCM detected an intermittent high voltage condition (Scan Tool reads −35°F) on the IAT sensor signal circuit for 3-5 seconds. The IAT sensor is a variable resistor that includes an IAT signal circuit and a low reference circuit to measure the temperature of the air entering the engine. The PCM connects to the IAT sensor with a 5v signal and a low reference ground circuit. When the IAT sensor is cold, its resistance is high. As air temperature increases, its resistance decreases. With high sensor resistance, the IAT sensor signal voltage is high. With lower sensor resistance, the IAT sensor signal voltage should be lower. **Possible Causes:** • IAT sensor signal circuit is open (intermittent fault) • IAT sensor ground circuit is open (intermittent fault) • IAT sensor is damaged (an intermittent "open" condition) • PCM has failed

DTC	Trouble Code Title, Conditions & Possible Causes
DTC: P1111 **1T CCM, MIL: No** **Years:** 2005, 2006, 2007 **Models:** Sierra, Silverado **Engines:** 4.3L, 4.8L, 5.3L, 6.0L, 6.2L, 8.1L **Transmissions:** All	**IAT Sensor Circuit Intermittent High Input** DTC P0101, P0102, P0103, P0116, P0117, P0118, P0125, P0128, P0502, P0503, P1114 and P1115 not set, engine started, engine runtime over 120 seconds, ECT sensor more than 140°F, VSS less than 7 MPH, MAF input less than 15 g/sec, and the PCM detected an intermittent high voltage condition (over 4.90v) on the IAT sensor signal circuit for 1 second during the CCM test. **Possible Causes:** • IAT sensor signal circuit is open (intermittent fault) • IAT sensor ground circuit is open (intermittent fault) • IAT sensor is damaged (an intermittent "open" condition) • PCM has failed
DTC: P1112 **1T CCM, MIL: No** **Years:** 2005, 2006, 2007 **Models:** Malibu, Rendezvous **Engines:** 2.2L, 2.4L, 3.4L, 3.5L, 3.6L, 3.8L, 3.9L, 3.9L **Transmissions:** All	**IAT Sensor Circuit Intermittent Low Input** DTC P0101, P0102, P0103, P0116, P0117, P0118, P0502 and P0503 not set, engine runtime over 10 seconds, MAF sensor less than 12 g/sec, VSS less than 25 MPH, ECT sensor more than 140°F, and the PCM detected an intermittent low voltage condition (Scan Tool reads 253°F) on the IAT sensor signal circuit for 20 seconds. **Possible Causes:** • IAT sensor signal circuit is shorted to ground (intermittent fault) • IAT sensor is damaged (an intermittent "shorted" condition) • PCM has failed
DTC: P1112 **1T CCM, MIL: No** **Years:** 2005, 2006, 2007 **Models:** Sierra, Silverado **Engines:** 4.3L, 4.8L, 5.3L, 6.0L, 6.2L, 8.1L **Transmissions:** All	**IAT Sensor Circuit Intermittent Low Input** DTC P0101, P0102, P0103, P0116, P0117, P0118, P0125, P0128, P0502, P0503, P1114 and P1115 not set, engine started, engine runtime over 120 seconds, ECT sensor more than 140°F, VSS less than 7 MPH, MAF input less than 15 g/sec, and the PCM detected an intermittent low voltage condition (Scan Tool reads 282°F) on the IAT sensor signal circuit for 6 seconds during the CCM test. **Possible Causes:** • IAT sensor signal circuit is shorted to ground (intermittent fault) • IAT sensor is damaged (an intermittent "shorted" condition) • PCM has failed
DTC: P1114 **1T CCM, MIL: No** **Years:** 2005, 2006, 2007 **Models:** Malibu, Rendezvous **Engines:** 2.2L, 2.4L, 3.4L, 3.5L, 3.6L, 3.8L, 3.9L, 3.9L **Transmissions:** All	**ECT Sensor Circuit Intermittent Low Input** Engine started, engine runtime over 5 seconds, and the PCM detected an intermittent low voltage condition (Scan Tool reads over 282°F) on the ECT sensor signal circuit for 5 seconds. The ECT sensor is a variable resistor that includes an ECT signal and a low reference circuit to measure the temperature of the engine coolant. **Possible Causes:** • ECT sensor signal circuit shorted to ground (intermittent fault) • ECT sensor has failed (possible intermittent shorted condition) • PCM has failed
DTC: P1114 **1T CCM, MIL: No** **Years:** 2005, 2006, 2007 **Models:** Sierra, Silverado **Engines:** 4.3L, 4.8L, 5.3L, 6.0L, 6.2L, 8.1L **Transmissions:** All	**ECT Sensor Circuit Intermittent Low Input** Engine started, engine runtime over 10 seconds, system voltage over 10.0v, and the PCM detected an intermittent low voltage condition (Scan Tool reads over 282°F) on the ECT sensor signal circuit for 1 second out of a 20 second period during the CCM test. **Possible Causes:** • ECT sensor signal circuit shorted to ground (intermittent fault) • ECT sensor has failed (possible intermittent shorted condition) • PCM has failed
DTC: P1133 **2T O2S, MIL: Yes** **Years:** 2005, 2006, 2007 **Models:** Malibu, Rendezvous **Engines:** 2.2L, 2.4L, 3.4L, 3.5L, 3.6L, 3.8L, 3.9L, 3.9L **Transmissions:** All	**HO2S-11 (Bank 1 Sensor 1) Insufficient Switching** DTC P0101-P0103, P0107, P0108, P0112-P0118, P0121-P0123, P0125, P0128, P0201-P0206, P0410, P0440-P0449 and P1441 not set, engine speed from 1000-3000 RPM for 3 minutes in closed loop, system voltage over 10.0v, ECT sensor over 167°F, MAF sensor from 10-30 g/sec, gear selector not in Park or Neutral, and the PCM detected the HO2S signal voltage switched from rich-lean or lean-rich less than 20 times within a 100 ms period. **Possible Causes:** • Air leaks present in the exhaust manifold or the exhaust pipes • Fuel pressure is too high (i.e., causing a rich air fuel mixture) • HO2S may be contaminated (due to improper fuel or silicone) • HO2S signal high or low reference circuit has high resistance • HO2S heater element has failed, or the heater circuit is open • PCM has failed

DTC	Trouble Code Title, Conditions & Possible Causes
DTC: P1133 **2T O2S, MIL: Yes** **Years:** 2005, 2006, 2007 **Models:** Sierra, Silverado **Engines:** 4.3L, 4.8L, 5.3L, 6.0L, 6.2L, 8.1L **Transmissions:** All	**HO2S-11 (Bank 1 Sensor 1) Insufficient Switching** DTC P0101-P0103, P0106-P0108, P0112-P0118, P0121-P0123, P0131-P0135, P0151-P0155, P0200, P0300, P0401-P0405, P0440-P0446, P0452, P0453, P1120, P1125, P1220, P1221, P1258, P1404, P1441and P01514, and P1518 not set, engine started, engine speed from 1200-3000 RPM for over 3 minutes in closed loop, system voltage over 10.0v, ECT sensor more than 149°F, fuel level over 10%, Purge command over 1%, MAF sensor from 23-50 g/sec, TP angle 5% over the idle value on models with TAC, Intrusive and Scan Tool tests inactive for 100 seconds, and the PCM detected the number of rich-to-lean or lean-to-rich HO2S signal transitions in a 100 second sample period were below a calibrated value. **Possible Causes:** • Air leaks present in the exhaust manifold or the exhaust pipes • Fuel pressure is too high (i.e., causing a rich air fuel mixture) • HO2S may be contaminated (due to improper fuel or silicone) • HO2S signal high or low reference circuit has high resistance • HO2S heater element has failed, or the heater circuit is open • PCM has failed
DTC: P1134 **2T O2S, MIL: Yes** **Years:** 2005, 2006, 2007 **Models:** Malibu, Rendezvous **Engines:** 2.2L, 2.4L, 3.4L, 3.5L, 3.6L, 3.9L, 3.9L **Transmissions:** All	**HO2S-11 (Bank 1 Sensor 1) Transition Time Ratio** DTC P0101-P0103, P0107, P0108, P0112-P0118, P0121-P0123, P0125, P0128, P0201-P0206, P0410, P0440-P0449 and P1441 not set, engine speed from 1000-3000 RPM for 3 minutes in closed loop, system voltage over 10.0v, ECT sensor over 167°F, MAF sensor from 10-30 g/sec, gear selector not in Park or Neutral, and the PCM detected the transition time ratio was less than 0.4 or more than 4.5 during a 100 second monitoring period. **Possible Causes:** • Air leaks present in the exhaust manifold or the exhaust pipes • Fuel pressure is too high (i.e., causing a rich air fuel mixture) • HO2S may be contaminated (due to improper fuel or silicone) • HO2S signal high or low reference circuit has high resistance • HO2S heater element has failed, or the heater circuit is open • PCM has failed
DTC: P1134 **2T O2S, MIL: Yes** **Years:** 2005, 2006, 2007 **Models:** Sierra, Silverado **Engines:** 4.3L, 4.8L, 5.3L, 6.0L, 6.2L, 8.1L **Transmissions:** All	**HO2S-11 (Bank 1 Sensor 1) Transition Time Ratio** DTC P0101-P0103, P0106-P0108, P0112-P0118, P0121-P0123, P0131-P0135, P0151-P0155, P0200, P0300, P0401-P0405, P0440-P0446, P0452, P0453, P1120, P1125, P1220, P1221, P1258, P1404, P1441and P01514, and P1518 not set, engine speed from 1200-3000 RPM for over 3 minutes in closed loop, system voltage over 10.0v, ECT sensor over 149°F, fuel level over 10%, Purge command over 1%, MAF sensor from 23-50 g/sec, TP angle at 5% over idle value on models with TAC, Intrusive and Scan Tool tests "off" for 100 seconds, and the PCM detected the HO2S time ratio value was not within the calibrated range. **Possible Causes:** • Air leaks present in the exhaust manifold or the exhaust pipes • HO2S may be contaminated (due to improper fuel or silicone) • HO2S signal low reference circuit has high resistance • HO2S heater element has failed, or the heater circuit is open • PCM has failed
DTC: P1153 **2T O2S, MIL: Yes** **Years:** 2005, 2006, 2007 **Models:** Sierra, Silverado **Engines:** 4.3L, 4.8L, 5.3L, 6.0L, 6.2L, 8.1L **Transmissions:** All	**HO2S-21 (Bank 2 Sensor 1) Insufficient Switching** DTC P0101-P0103, P0106-P0108, P0112-P0118, P0121-P0123, P0131-P0135, P0151-P0155, P0200, P0300, P0401-P0405, P0440-P0446, P0452, P0453, P1120, P1125, P1220, P1221, P1258, P1404, P1441and P01514, and P1518 not set, engine speed from 1200-3000 RPM for over 3 minutes in closed loop, system voltage over 10.0v, ECT sensor over 149°F, fuel level over 10%, Purge command over 1%, MAF sensor from 23-50 g/sec, TP indicated angle at 5% over the idle value (TAC models), Intrusive and Scan Tool tests "off" for 100 seconds, and the PCM detected the number of rich-to-lean or lean-to-rich HO2S signal transitions during a 100 second sample period were less than a calibrated value. **Possible Causes:** • Air leaks present in the exhaust manifold or the exhaust pipes • Fuel pressure is too high (i.e., causing a rich air fuel mixture) • HO2S may be contaminated (due to improper fuel or silicone) • HO2S signal high or low reference circuit has high resistance • HO2S heater element has failed, or the heater circuit is open • MAP sensor or TP sensor is out-of-calibration or "skewed" • PCM has failed

DTC	Trouble Code Title, Conditions & Possible Causes
DTC: P1154 **2T O2S, MIL: Yes** **Years:** 2005, 2006, 2007 **Models:** Sierra, Silverado **Engines:** 4.3L, 4.8L, 5.3L, 6.0L, 6.2L, 8.1L **Transmissions:** All	**HO2S-21 (Bank 2 Sensor 1) Transition Time Ratio** DTC P0101-P0103, P0106-P0108, P0112-P0118, P0121-P0123, P0131-P0135, P0151-P0155, P0200, P0300, P0401-P0405, P0440-P0446, P0452, P0453, P1120, P1125, P1220, P1221, P1258, P1404, P1441and P01514, and P1518 not set, engine speed from 1200-3000 RPM for over 3 minutes in closed loop, system voltage over 10.0v, ECT sensor over 149°F, fuel level over 10%, Purge command over 1%, MAF sensor from 23-50 g/sec, TP angle at 5% over idle value on models with TAC, Intrusive and Scan Tool tests "off" for 100 seconds, and the PCM detected the HO2S time ratio value was not within the calibrated range. **Possible Causes:** • Air leaks present in the exhaust manifold or the exhaust pipes • HO2S may be contaminated (due to improper fuel or silicone) • HO2S signal low reference circuit has high resistance • HO2S heater element has failed, or the heater circuit is open • PCM has failed
DTC: P1172 **1T CCM, MIL: No** **Years:** 2005, 2006, 2007 **Models:** Sierra, Silverado **Engines:** 4.3L, 4.8L, 5.3L, 6.0L, 6.2L, 8.1L **Transmissions:** All	**Secondary Fuel Pump Insufficient/No Fuel Flow** DTC P0461, P0462, P0463, P1431, P1432 and P1433 not set, engine started, vehicle not moving, primary fuel level less than 25 L (6.6 gallons), secondary fuel level between 3-10 L (0.7-2.6 gallons), conditions met for 20 seconds before secondary pump commanded "on" for 2 minutes, and the PCM detected the change in the primary and secondary fuel level sensors was less than 4 liters (1.06 gallon). The secondary fuel pump, located in the rear fuel tank, is powered by a secondary fuel pump relay. Fuel is transferred from the rear fuel tank to the front fuel tank to ensure All of the usable fuel volume is available to the primary fuel pump. Secondary fuel pump relay supply voltage is received from the primary fuel pump relay when the primary fuel pump is "on". If the PCM commands the secondary fuel pump "on", and it does not detect a predetermined change in both the front and rear fuel level sensors, it will set this trouble code. **Possible Causes:** • Fuel tank level is too low (must be within 25-75% to test relay) • Secondary F/P relay power circuit is open (test the ENG1 fuse) • Secondary F/P relay control circuit is open, shorted to ground or shorted to power • Secondary F/P relay is damaged or has failed • PCM has failed
DTC: P1172 **1T CCM, MIL: No** **Years:** 2005, 2006, 2007 **Models:** Sierra, Silverado **Engines:** 6.6L Diesel **Transmissions:** All	**Secondary Fuel Pump Insufficient/No Fuel Flow** DTC P0461, P0462, P0463, P0500, P2066, P2067 and P2068 not set, engine started, VSS at zero MPH, Primary fuel level less than 25 liters (6.6 gallons), Secondary fuel level between 3-10 liters (0.8-2.6 gallons), conditions met for 20 seconds before the fuel transfer pump was commanded on, then with the fuel transfer pump commanded on for 120 seconds, and the ECM detected a primary fuel level increase and a secondary fuel level decrease of less than 4 liters (1.06 gallons) each. **Possible Causes:** • Fuel transfer relay control circuit is open or shorted to ground • Fuel pump relay ground circuit is open • Fuel pump relay power circuit is open (check the ECB B fuse) • Fuel pump relay or the Fuel transfer pump is damaged or has failed • ECM has failed
DTC: P1174 **1T CCM, MIL: No** **Years:** 2005, 2006, 2007 **Models:** Sky **Engines:** 2.4L **Transmissions:** All	**Fuel Trim Cylinder Balance** DTCs P0030, P0053, P0068, P0101, P0102, P0103, P0106, P0107, P0108, P0116, P0117, P0118, P0120, P0121, P0122, P0123, P0128, P0131, P0132, P0133, P0134, P0135, P0220, P0222, P0223, P0201-P0204, P0300, P0442, P0443, P0446, P0449, P0451, P0452, P0453, P0454, P0455, P0496, P060D, P060E, P1133, P1516, P2101, P2119, P2120, P2122, P2125, P2127, P2128, P2135, P2138, P2176, P2A00, P2A01 are not set. The device control, intrusive diagnostics, engine overspeed protection and traction control are not active. The fuel control is in air-fuel Closed Loop. The engine speed is greater than 1,000 RPM, but less than 4,000 RPM. Multiple samples of the pre-catalyst HO2S accumulated voltage are consistently higher than the desired value. The Fuel Trim Cylinder Balance diagnostic is very sensitive to HO2S design. A non-OE sensor or an incorrect part number may set a false DTC. Monitoring the misfire current counters, or misfire graph, may help to isolate the cylinder that is causing the condition. **Possible Causes:** • Air induction system has been modified, or is damaged, leaking, or restricted • Crankcase ventilation system improper operation • Vacuum hose splits, kinks, and improper connections • Vacuum leaks at the intake manifold, the throttle body, or injector O-rings • Restricted, damaged, leaking, or modified exhaust system from the catalytic converter forward • Incorrect fuel injectors operation • Fuel contamination • Excessive fuel in the crankcase due to leaking injectors • Improper ignition system operation • Engine for any mechanical conditions which could alter the flow into the combustion chamber

DTC	Trouble Code Title, Conditions & Possible Causes
DTC: P1189 **1T CCM, MIL: Yes** **Years:** 2005, 2006, 2007 **Models:** Malibu, Rendezvous **Engines:** 2.2L, 2.4L, 3.4L, 3.5L, 3.6L, 3.9L, 3.9L **Transmissions:** All	**Engine Oil Pressure Switch Circuit Malfunction** DTC P0117, P0118, P1111 and P1114 codes set, engine started, ECT sensor less than 50°F at last key off, and the PCM detected an open EOP switch circuit for 10 seconds. Check the Failure Records. **Possible Causes:** • EOP switch circuit is open between the sensor and the PCM • Engine oil pressure switch is damaged (possible open circuit) • PCM has failed
DTC: P1204 **1T CCM, MIL: Yes** **Years:** 2005, 2006, 2007 **Models:** Sierra, Silverado **Engines:** 6.0L CNG **Transmissions:** All	**Engine Will Not Start In CNG Mode** DTC P0005, P0148, P0191, P0192, P0193, P0611, P1020, P1021-P1028, P1209, P2146 and P2665 not set, Engine started, system voltage from 6-18v, CNG operation is not inhibited, and the FICM detected the cranking time to start in CNG mode was 8 seconds. The PCM controls fuel delivery, and on KL6 vehicles, determines which fuel system the engine is operating on. The PCM controls the low-pressure lock-off (LPL) solenoid, and the high-pressure lock-off (HPL) solenoid. The PCM commands the HPL solenoid open for 1 second at key on, to prime the CNG system. The PCM commands the HPL and LPL open with the engine cranking or running on CNG. **Possible Causes:** • Diagnose the other related codes, then recheck for this code • FRP sensor parameter is out of range
DTC: P1207 **1T CCM, MIL: Yes** **Years:** 2005, 2006, 2007 **Models:** Sierra, Silverado **Engines:** 6.0L CNG **Transmissions:** All	**FICM PWM Signal To PCM Circuit Malfunction** Key on or engine running; and the PCM did not detect a Fuel Rail Pressure sensor PWM output signal for 2-5 seconds. The Fuel Injector Control Module (FICM) monitors the CNG FTP sensor, the FTT sensor, and fuel rail temperature sensor. The FTP, FTT, and FRT sensor signal and FICM diagnostic status is communicated to the PCM by two PWM circuits. **Possible Causes:** • FICM sensor PWM signal circuit is open or shorted to ground • FICM is damaged or it has failed • PCM has failed
DTC: P1208 **1T CCM, MIL: Yes** **Years:** 2005, 2006, 2007 **Models:** Sierra, Silverado **Engines:** 2.2L, 6.0L CNG **Transmissions:** All	**FICM Diagnostic Status Signal Circuit Malfunction** Engine cranking or engine running, system voltage from 6-18v, and the PCM did not receive the FICM diagnostic status signal for at least two seconds. The fuel injector control module (FICM) monitors the CNG fuel tank pressure (FTP) sensor, the fuel tank temperature (FTT) sensor, and the fuel rail temperature (FRT) sensor. The FTP, FTT, and FRT sensor values, and FICM diagnostic status, is communicated to the PCM by two PWM circuits. **Possible Causes:** • FICM diagnostic status circuit is open or shorted to ground • FICM is damaged or it has failed • PCM has failed
DTC: P1220 **1T CCM, MIL: Yes** **Years:** 2005, 2006, 2007 **Models:** Sierra, Silverado **Engines:** 4.3L, 4.8L, 5.3L, 6.0L, 6.2L, 8.1L **Transmissions:** All	**TP Sensor 2 Circuit Malfunction** DTC P1517 and P1518 not set, key in crank or run position, system voltage over 5.23v, and the PCM detected the TP2 signal was less than 0.13v or more than 4.87v for 1 second during the CCM test. **Possible Causes:** • TP2 sensor signal circuit is open, shorted to ground or to power • TP2 sensor VREF circuit is open, shorted to ground or shorted to system power (B+) • TP2 sensor ground circuit has a high resistance condition • TP2 sensor is damaged or has failed
DTC: P1221 **1T CCM, MIL: Yes** **Years:** 2005, 2006, 2007 **Models:** Sierra, Silverado **Engines:** 4.3L, 4.8L, 5.3L, 6.0L, 6.2L, 8.1L **Transmissions:** All	**TP Sensor 2 Signal Correlation** DTC P1517 and P1518 not set, key in crank or run position TP Sensor 1 (TP1) and TP Sensor 2 (TP2) more than 15% for 140 ms, and the PCM detected the TP2 signal disagreed with the TP1 signal by more than 7.5% for 1 second. The TP sensor has two separate signal, ground, and 5 volt reference circuits that are used to connect the TP sensor to the TAC module. These sensors have opposite functionality. The TP1 voltage increases from below 1.0v at 0% throttle to above 3.5v at 100% throttle opening. The TP2 voltage decreases from around 3.8v at 0 percent throttle to below 1.0v at 100% throttle opening. The TP1 signal circuit is pulled up to 5.0v and the TP2 signal circuit is pulled to ground in the TAC module. **Possible Causes:** • TP2 sensor connector is contaminated, dirty or contains water • TP2 sensor signal, ground or VREF circuit has high resistance • TP2 sensor VREF circuit has a high resistance condition • TP2 sensor ground circuit has a high resistance condition • TP2 sensor is damaged or has failed • TAC controller or the throttle body is damaged or has failed • TSB 02-06-04-005 contains a repair procedure for this code

DTC	Trouble Code Title, Conditions & Possible Causes
DTC: P1223 **1T CCM, MIL: No** **Years:** 2005, 2006, 2007 **Models:** Sierra, Silverado **Engines:** 6.6L Diesel **Transmissions:** All	**Fuel Injector 1 Control Circuit Low Input** Key on or engine running system voltage from 6-18v, and the PCM detected the Command and Actual state of the Injector 1 control circuit did not match for over 2 seconds in the test. **Possible Causes:** • FICM (module) connector is damaged, open or shorted • FICM (module) is damaged or it has failed • Fuel injector 1 control circuit is open, shorted to ground or to B+ • Fuel injector 1 is damaged or it has failed • PCM has failed
DTC: P1226 **1T CCM, MIL: No** **Years:** 2005, 2006, 2007 **Models:** Sierra, Silverado **Engines:** 6.6L Diesel **Transmissions:** All	**Fuel Injector 2 Control Circuit Low Input** Key on or engine running system voltage from 6-18v, and the PCM detected the Command and Actual state of the Injector 2 control circuit did not match for over 2 seconds in the test. **Possible Causes:** • FICM (module) connector is damaged, open or shorted • FICM (module) is damaged or it has failed • Fuel injector 2 control circuit is open, shorted to ground or to B+ • Fuel injector 2 is damaged or it has failed • PCM has failed
DTC: P1226 **1T CCM, MIL: No** **Years:** 2005, 2006, 2007 **Models:** Sierra, Silverado **Engines:** 6.6L Diesel **Transmissions:** All	**Fuel Injector 3 Control Circuit Low Input** Key on or engine running system voltage from 6-18v, and the PCM detected the Command and Actual state of the Injector 3 control circuit did not match for over 2 seconds in the test. **Possible Causes:** • FICM (module) connector is damaged, open or shorted • FICM (module) is damaged or it has failed • Fuel injector 3 control circuit is open, shorted to ground or to B+ • Fuel injector 3 is damaged or it has failed • PCM has failed
DTC: P1232 **1T CCM, MIL: No** **Years:** 2005, 2006, 2007 **Models:** Sierra, Silverado **Engines:** 6.6L Diesel **Transmissions:** All	**Fuel Injector 4 Control Circuit Low Input** Key on or engine running system voltage from 6-18v, and the PCM detected the Command and Actual state of the Injector 4 control circuit did not match for over 2 seconds in the test. **Possible Causes:** • FICM (module) connector is damaged, open or shorted • FICM (module) is damaged or it has failed • Fuel injector 4 control circuit is open, shorted to ground or to B+ • Fuel injector 4 is damaged or it has failed • PCM has failed
DTC: P1235 **1T CCM, MIL: No** **Years:** 2005, 2006, 2007 **Models:** Sierra, Silverado **Engines:** 6.6L Diesel **Transmissions:** All	**Fuel Injector 5 Control Circuit Low Input** Key on or engine running system voltage from 6-18v, and the PCM detected the Command and Actual state of the Injector 5 control circuit did not match for over 2 seconds in the test. **Possible Causes:** • FICM (module) connector is damaged, open or shorted • FICM (module) is damaged or it has failed • Fuel injector 5 control circuit is open, shorted to ground or to B+ • Fuel injector 5 is damaged or it has failed • PCM has failed
DTC: P1238 **1T CCM, MIL: No** **Years:** 2005, 2006, 2007 **Models:** Sierra, Silverado **Engines:** 6.6L Diesel **Transmissions:** All	**Fuel Injector 6 Control Circuit Low Input** Key on or engine running system voltage from 6-18v, and the PCM detected the Command and Actual state of the Injector 6 control circuit did not match for over 2 seconds in the test. **Possible Causes:** • FICM (module) connector is damaged, open or shorted • FICM (module) is damaged or it has failed • Fuel injector 6 control circuit is open, shorted to ground or to B+ • Fuel injector 6 is damaged or it has failed • PCM has failed

DTC	Trouble Code Title, Conditions & Possible Causes
DTC: P1241 **1T CCM, MIL: No** **Years:** 2005, 2006, 2007 **Models:** Sierra, Silverado **Engines:** 6.6L Diesel **Transmissions:** All	**Fuel Injector 7 Control Circuit Low Input** Key on or engine running system voltage from 6-18v, and the PCM detected the Command and Actual state of the Injector 7 control circuit did not match for over 2 seconds in the test. **Possible Causes:** • FICM (module) connector is damaged, open or shorted • FICM (module) is damaged or it has failed • Fuel injector 7 control circuit is open, shorted to ground or to B+ • Fuel injector 7 is damaged or it has failed • PCM has failed
DTC: P1244 **1T CCM, MIL: No** **Years:** 2005, 2006, 2007 **Models:** Sierra, Silverado **Engines:** 6.6L Diesel **Transmissions:** All	**Fuel Injector 8 Control Circuit Low Input** Key on or engine running system voltage from 6-18v, and the PCM detected the Command and Actual state of the Injector 8 control circuit did not match for over 2 seconds in the test. **Possible Causes:** • FICM (module) connector is damaged, open or shorted • FICM (module) is damaged or it has failed • Fuel injector 8 control circuit is open, shorted to ground or to B+ • Fuel injector 8 is damaged or it has failed • PCM has failed
DTC: P1261 **1T CCM, MIL: Yes** **Years:** 2005, 2006, 2007 **Models:** Sierra, Silverado **Engines:** 6.6L Diesel **Transmissions:** All	**Fuel Pump Relay Circuit Malfunction (Injectors 1, 4, 6 or 7)** Key on or engine running; and the PCM detected an unexpected voltage condition on one or more fuel injector circuits. The AF ECM (Alternative Fuels) monitors the status of each driver. If a circuit fault is detected on a fuel injector circuit for engine cylinders 1, 4, 6 or 7, DTC P0201, P0204, P0206, P0207 will set, along with P1261. **Possible Causes:** • One or more injector control circuits open or shorted to ground • One or more injector power circuits open or injector is damaged • Injector relay power or ground circuit is open, or relay has failed • FICM (module) has failed • ECM (module) has failed
DTC: P1262 **1T CCM, MIL: Yes** **Years:** 2005, 2006, 2007 **Models:** Sierra, Silverado **Engines:** 6.6L Diesel **Transmissions:** All	**Fuel Pump Relay Circuit Malfunction (Injectors 2, 3, 5 or 8)** Key on or engine running; and the PCM detected an unexpected voltage condition on one or more fuel injector circuits. The AF ECM (Alternative Fuels) monitors the status of each driver. If a circuit fault is detected on a fuel injector circuit for engine cylinders 2, 3, 5 or 8, then DTC P0201, P0204, P0206, P0207 will set, along with P1262. **Possible Causes:** • One or more injector control circuits open or shorted to ground • One or more injector power circuits open or injector is damaged • Injector relay power or ground circuit is open, or relay has failed • FICM (module) has failed • ECM (module) has failed
DTC: P1270 **1T CCM, MIL: No** **Years:** 2005, 2006, 2007 **Models:** Sierra, Silverado **Engines:** 6.6L Diesel **Transmissions:** All	**Fuel Pump Relay Circuit Malfunction (Injectors 2, 3, 5 or 8)** Engine cranking or running, system voltage from 7-16v, and the ECM detected that it could not process the Accelerator Pedal Position (APP) sensor analog data into digital data. **Possible Causes:** • ECM is damaged or it has failed. Clear the codes and then retest for this same trouble code. If it resets, the ECM must be replaced and reprogrammed to repair this code.
DTC: P1275 **1T CCM, MIL: No** **Years:** 2005, 2006, 2007 **Models:** Sierra, Silverado **Engines:** 4.3L, 4.8L, 5.3L, 6.0L, 6.2L, 8.1L **Transmissions:** All	**Accelerator Pedal Position Sensor 1 Circuit Malfunction** DTC P0601, P0602, P0606, P1517 and P1518 not set, key in crank or run position, system voltage over 5.23v, and the PCM detected the APP1 sensor signal voltage ranged between 0.25v and 4.22v for less than 1 second during the test. **Possible Causes:** • APP1 sensor connector is contaminated, oily or contains water • APP1 sensor signal, ground or VREF circuit high resistance • APP1 sensor VREF circuit is open, shorted to ground or to B+ • APP1 sensor signal or ground circuit has high resistance • APP1 sensor is damaged or has failed • TAC module is damaged or has failed

DTC	Trouble Code Title, Conditions & Possible Causes
DTC: P1276 **1T CCM, MIL: No** **Years:** 2005, 2006, 2007 **Models:** Sierra, Silverado **Engines:** 4.3L, 4.8L, 5.3L, 6.0L, 6.2L, 8.1L **Transmissions:** All	**Accelerator Pedal Position Sensor 1 Range/Performance** DTC P0606, P1517 and P1518 not set, key in crank or run position, system voltage over 5.23v, and the PCM detected the APP Sensor 1 and the APP Sensor 2 signals disagreed by more than 10%, or the APP Sensor 1 and APP Sensor 3 signals disagreed by over 13%. **Note: Refer to the information in the Failure Records as needed.** **Possible Causes:** • APP1 sensor connector is contaminated, oily or contains water • APP1 sensor signal circuit is open or shorted to ground • APP1 sensor signal circuit is shorted to VREF or system power • APP1 sensor ground circuit is open or has high resistance • APP1 sensor VREF circuit is open or shorted to ground • APP1 sensor is damaged or has failed
DTC: P1280 **1T CCM, MIL: No** **Years:** 2005, 2006, 2007 **Models:** Sierra, Silverado **Engines:** 4.3L, 4.8L, 5.3L, 6.0L, 6.2L, 8.1L **Transmissions:** All	**Accelerator Pedal Position Sensor 2 Circuit Malfunction** DTC P0601, P0602, P0606, P1517 and P1518 not set, key in crank or run position, system voltage over 5.23v, and the PCM detected the TP2 signal was less than 0.83v, or it was more than 4.81v for 1 second during the test. **Possible Causes:** • APP2 sensor connector is contaminated, oily or contains water • APP2 sensor signal, ground or VREF circuit high resistance • APP2 sensor VREF circuit is open, shorted to ground or to B+ • APP2 sensor signal or ground circuit has high resistance • APP2 sensor is damaged or has failed • TAC module is damaged or has failed
DTC: P1281 **1T CCM, MIL: No** **Years:** 2005, 2006, 2007 **Models:** Sierra, Silverado **Engines:** 4.3L, 4.8L, 5.3L, 6.0L, 6.2L, 8.1L **Transmissions:** All	**Accelerator Pedal Position Sensor 2 Range/Performance** DTC P1517 and P1518 not set, key in crank or run position, system voltage over 5.23v, and the PCM detected the APP sensor 2 signal disagreed with APP Sensor 1 by over 10.5% or the APP Sensor 2 disagreed with the APP Sensor 3 by over 13% for under 1 second. The APP sensor is mounted on the accelerator pedal assembly. The assembly contains three APP sensors in a single housing. Three separate signal, low-reference and 5-volt reference circuits connect the APP sensor unit to the throttle actuator control (TAC) module. Each of the three APP sensors has a unique functionality **Possible Causes:** • TP2 sensor connector is contaminated, oily or contains water • TP2 sensor signal, ground or VREF circuit has high resistance • TP2 sensor VREF circuit is open, shorted to ground or to B+ • TP2 sensor signal or ground circuit has high resistance • TP2 sensor is damaged or has failed • TAC module is damaged or has failed
DTC: P1285 **1T CCM, MIL: No** **Years:** 2005, 2006, 2007 **Models:** Sierra, Silverado **Engines:** 4.3L, 4.8L, 5.3L, 6.0L, 6.2L, 8.1L **Transmissions:** All	**Accelerator Pedal Position Sensor 3 Circuit Malfunction** DTC P0606, P1517, or P1518 not set, key in crank or run mode, system voltage over 5.23v, and the PCM detected the APP sensor 3 signal was less than 1.63v, or more than 4.28v for under 1 second. **Possible Causes:** • APP3 sensor connector is contaminated, oily or contains water • APP3 sensor signal, ground or VREF circuit high resistance • APP3 sensor VREF circuit is open, shorted to ground or to B+ • APP3 sensor signal or ground circuit has high resistance • APP3 sensor or the TAC module is damaged or has failed
DTC: P1286 **1T CCM, MIL: No** **Years:** 2005, 2006, 2007 **Models:** Sierra, Silverado **Engines:** 4.3L, 4.8L, 5.3L, 6.0L, 6.2L, 8.1L **Transmissions:** All	**Accelerator Pedal Position Sensor 3 Range/Performance** DTC P0606, P1517 and P1518 not set, key in run or crank mode, system voltage over 5.23v, and the PCM detected the APP Sensor 3 disagreed with the APP sensor 1 by over 13%, or the APP Sensor 3 signal disagreed with APP Sensor 2 by over 13% for 1 second. The APP sensor is mounted on the accelerator pedal assembly. The assembly contains three APP sensors in a single housing. Three separate signal, low-reference and 5-volt reference circuits connect the APP sensor unit to the throttle actuator control (TAC) module. **Possible Causes:** • APP3 sensor connector is contaminated, oily or moisture • APP3 sensor signal, ground or VREF circuit high resistance • APP3 sensor signal or ground circuit has high resistance • APP3 sensor or the TAC module is damaged or has failed

DTC	Trouble Code Title, Conditions & Possible Causes
DTC: P1336 **2T CCM, MIL: Yes** **Years:** 2005, 2006, 2007 **Models:** All **Engines:** All **Transmissions:** All	**CKP Sensor System Variation Not Learned** DTC P0336, P0341and P1374 not set, engine started, ECT sensor more than 158°F, and the PCM did not detect any CKP variation values. The Crankshaft Position system variation-learning feature is used to calculate reference period errors caused by slight tolerance variations in the crankshaft, and the CKP sensor(s). The calculated error Allows the PCM to accurately compensate for reference period variations to enhance the Misfire Detection capability of the system. **Possible Causes:** • Set the parking brake and block the drive wheels for safety. • Verify the hood is closed. • Read the trouble codes. If a code is set, refer to that code. • Start the engine. Allow engine temperature to reach at least 158°F (70°C). Then key off. • Select Crankshaft Position Variation Learn procedure on Scan Tool, start the vehicle. • Apply the brake pedal firmly and verify the selector is in Park. • Increase accelerator pedal position until fuel cutoff is reached at the test RPM (e.g., 5150). Quickly release the accelerator pedal after fuel cutoff is reached. The CKP system variation compensating values are learned when the engine speed (RPM) decreases back to idle speed and the procedure terminates. • Read the trouble codes and recheck for DTC P1336. • If DTC P1336 runs and passes, the CKP system variation "learn" procedure is complete. If not, look for other codes. If no codes are set, repeat the test procedure.
DTC: P1351 **1T CCM, MIL: Yes** **Years:** 2005, 2006, 2007 **Models:** Malibu, Rendezvous **Engines:** 2.2L, 2.4L, 3.4L, 3.5L, 3.6L, 3.9L, 3.9L **Transmissions:** All	**Ignition Coil Timing Circuit High Input** Engine started, engine speed over 600 RPM, and the PCM detected an unexpected open (high voltage) condition on the ICM Coil Timing control circuit for 300 3X reference periods during 100 crankshaft revolutions. The ignition control module (ICM) has independent power and ground circuits that connect to the PCM. They are the IC timing signal, IC timing control signal, low-resolution engine speed signal and the low reference (ground) signal. The ICM sends 3X signals to the PCM. The ICM controls the timing advance when the engine is cranking. The PCM controls the timing advance once it receives a second 3X signal. Then it applies 5v to the IC timing signal circuit so the timing advance can switch to PCM control. **Possible Causes:** • IC signal circuit is open, shorted to ground or shorted to power • IC module has failed
DTC: P1352 **2T CCM, MIL: Yes** **Years:** 2005, 2006, 2007 **Models:** Malibu, Rendezvous **Engines:** 2.2L, 2.4L, 3.4L, 3.5L, 3.6L, 3.9L, 3.9L **Transmissions:** All	**Ignition Signal Circuit High Input** Engine started; and the PCM detected an unexpected high voltage condition on the ICM signal circuit for at least 300 3X reference periods (100 crankshaft revolutions). The ICM has independent power and ground circuits that connect to the PCM. They are the IC timing signal, IC timing control signal, low-resolution engine speed signal and low reference (ground) signal. The ICM sends 3X signals to the PCM. The IC module controls the timing advance during engine cranking. Control of the spark timing advance changes to PCM control after the PCM receives the second 3X signal. The PCM applies 50volts to the IC timing signal circuit in order to switch the timing advance to PCM control of spark timing. **Possible Causes:** • IC signal circuit is open • IC module has failed • PCM has failed
DTC: P1361 **2T CCM, MIL: Yes** **Years:** 2005, 2006, 2007 **Models:** Malibu, Rendezvous **Engines:** 2.2L, 2.4L, 3.4L, 3.5L, 3.6L, 3.9L, 3.9L **Transmissions:** All	**ICM Ignition Control Circuit Low Input** DTC P1351 not set, engine speed over 600 RPM, and the PCM did not detect any IC pulses with IC mode advance enabled for 300 3X reference periods (100 crankshaft revolutions). **Possible Causes:** • IC timing signal circuit or control circuit is shorted to ground or shorted to power • IC module has failed, or the PCM has failed
DTC: P1362 **2T CCM, MIL: Yes** **Years:** 2005, 2006, 2007 **Models:** All **Engines:** All **Transmissions:** All	**ICM Control Circuit High Input** Engine started; and the PCM detected an intermittent high voltage condition on the IC timing signal circuit for 300 3X reference periods (100 crankshaft revolutions). The ICM has independent power and ground circuits that connect it to the PCM. Both the CMP sensor and CKP sensor signals are input directly to the ICM. The ICM sends 3X signals to the PCM, and controls the timing advance during engine cranking. The timing advance changes to PCM control after the PCM receives the second 3X signal. At this point, the PCM applies a 5v signal to the to the ignition control (IC) timing signal circuit. **Possible Causes:** • IC timing signal is shorted to system power • IC timing control circuit and IC timing signal circuits are shorted • IC module is damaged or it has failed • PCM has failed

DTC	Trouble Code Title, Conditions & Possible Causes
DTC: P1374 **2T CCM, MIL: Yes** **Years:** 2005, 2006, 2007 **Models:** Malibu, Rendezvous **Engines:** 2.2L, 2.4L, 3.4L, 3.5L, 3.6L, 3.9L, 3.9L **Transmissions:** All	**CKP Sensor High To Low Resolution Frequency Correlation** Engine started, engine running with 24X signals received, and the PCM detected the ratio of 24X REF pulses to 3X pulses did not equal 8, or the ratio of 24X pulses to CMP pulses equaled 48 for 10 seconds. The ICM (module) produces a 3X reference signal. The ICM calculates the 3X reference signal by dividing the CKP sensor 7X pulses by two (2) with the engine running with CKP synchronizing pulses received. The PCM uses the 3X reference signal to calculate the engine speed. It uses the CKP sensor signal at engine speeds above 1,600 RPM. The PCM also uses these pulses to initiate injector pulses. The PCM compares the 3X reference pulses to the 24X CKP pulses and the CMP sensor pulses. The engine can start and run using only the 24X CKP and CMP sensor signals. The PCM sets P1374 if it detects an invalid number of pulses occurred on the low-resolution engine speed circuit. **Possible Causes:** • IC 3X signal wire is routed to close to the Generator, spark plug wires or any other possible cause of EMI/RFI interference • IC 3X signal circuit is open, shorted to ground or shorted to B+ • IC module is damaged or has failed • PCM has failed
DTC: P1380 **1T CCM, MIL: No** **Years:** 2005, 2006, 2007 **Models:** Sierra, Silverado **Engines:** 4.3L, 4.8L, 5.3L, 6.0L, 6.2L, 8.1L **Transmissions:** All	**Misfire Detected, Rough Road Data Not Available** DTC P0101, P0102, P0103, P0335, P0336, P0341, P0342, P0343, P0500, P0502, P0503, P1120, P1220 and P1221 not set, engine started, vehicle driven to a speed over 10 MPH at an engine load over 60%, engine speed less than 3200 RPM, Misfire code (P0300) set with MIL requested "on", and the PCM/VCM detected a malfunction occurred that prevented it from receiving rough road detection data from the EBCM. The PCM detects engine misfire events by monitoring variations in the crankshaft rotation speed. Wheel speed changes caused by rough road conditions can cause changes in crankshaft speed. The ABS monitors the wheel speed sensors to determine if the vehicle is operating on a rough road. **Possible Causes:** • Use the Freeze Frame/Failure Records data to help find the cause on an intermittent fault. If the code cannot be duplicated, the data in the Freeze Frame/Failure Records can determine how many miles since the code set. The Fail Counter and Pass Counter can also help determine how many ignition cycles the diagnostic reported a pass or a fail. Operate the vehicle within the Freeze Frame conditions (i.e., load, engine and vehicle speed, temperature etc.). This will isolate when the code set. • Service the ABS before diagnosing a misfire because an actual engine misfire may or may not exist. An actual engine misfire may have occurred during an ABS malfunction. • Determine if the vehicle was driven on a rough road, and the ABS could not detect this due to a malfunction. The PCM may interpret variations in crankshaft speed caused by the rough road as a misfire without an actual engine misfire present. • Refer to Diagnostic System Check for Antilock Brake System • Refer to Diagnostic System Check for the Engine Controls
DTC: P1380 **1T CCM, MIL: No** **Years:** 2005, 2006, 2007 **Models:** Sierra, Silverado **Engines:** 4.3L, 4.8L, 5.3L, 6.0L, 6.2L, 8.1L **Transmissions:** All	**Misfire Detected, Rough Road Data Not Available** DTC P0101, P0102, P0103, P0120, P0335, P0336 and P0742 not set, engine started, vehicle driven to over 10 MPH at an engine load over 60%, engine speed less than 3200 RPM, Misfire code (P0300) set with MIL requested "on", and the PCM detected a malfunction occurred that prevented it from receiving rough road detection data from the EBCM. The PCM detects engine misfire events by monitoring variations in the crankshaft rotation speed. Wheel speed changes caused by rough road conditions can cause changes in crankshaft speed. The ABS (system) monitors the wheel speed sensors to determine when the vehicle is operating on a rough road. **Possible Causes:** • Use the Freeze Frame/Failure Records data to help find the cause on an intermittent fault. If the code cannot be duplicated, the data in the Freeze Frame/Failure Records can determine how many miles since the code set. The Fail Counter and Pass Counter can also help determine how many ignition cycles the diagnostic reported a pass or a fail. Operate the vehicle within the Freeze Frame conditions (i.e., load, engine and vehicle speed, temperature etc.). This will isolate when the code set. • Service the ABS before diagnosing a misfire because an actual engine misfire may or may not exist. Also, an actual engine misfire may have occurred during an ABS malfunction. • Determine if the vehicle was driven on a rough road, and the ABS could not detect this due to a malfunction. The PCM may interpret variations in crankshaft speed caused by the rough road as a misfire without an actual engine misfire present. • Refer to Diagnostic System Check for Antilock Brake System • Refer to Diagnostic System Check for the Engine Controls

DTC	Trouble Code Title, Conditions & Possible Causes
DTC: P1381 **2T CCM, MIL: Yes** **Years:** 2005, 2006, 2007 **Models:** Sierra, Silverado **Engines:** 4.3L, 4.8L, 5.3L, 6.0L, 6.2L, 8.1L **Transmissions:** All	**Misfire Detected - No Communication With The EBCM** Engine speed less than 3200 RPM (5800 RPM on some models) with the engine load less than 60%, VSS more than 10 MPH, engine misfire detected (P0300 set), and the PCM/VCM detected a serial data problem that prevented it from receiving rough road detection data, condition met for 20 seconds. The PCM detects engine misfire by detecting variations in crankshaft deceleration between firing strokes. For accurate detection of engine misfire, the PCM must distinguish between crankshaft deceleration caused by actual misfire and deceleration caused by rough road conditions. The ABS can detect if the vehicle is on a rough road based on wheel acceleration or deceleration data supplied by the wheel speed sensors. If the ABS detects rough road above a certain threshold, it sends a message to the PCM via serial data. The PCM can take the rough road into account when calculating misfire. **Possible Causes:** • Service the ABS before diagnosing a misfire because an actual engine misfire may not exist. Also, an actual engine misfire may have occurred during a period of ABS fault. • Determine if the vehicle was driven on a rough road, and the ABS could not detect this due to a malfunction. The PCM may interpret variations in crankshaft speed caused by the rough road as a misfire without an actual engine misfire present. • Refer to Diagnostic System Check for Antilock Brake System • Refer to Diagnostic System Check for the Engine Controls
DTC: P1381 **1T CCM, MIL: No** **Years:** 2005, 2006, 2007 **Models:** Sierra, Silverado **Engines:** 4.3L, 4.8L, 5.3L, 6.0L, 6.2L, 8.1L **Transmissions:** All	**Misfire Detected - No Communication With The EBCM** Engine started, engine speed less than 3200 RPM with the engine load less than 60%, VSS more than 10 MPH, engine misfire detected (P0300 set), and the PCM/VCM detected a serial data problem that prevented it from receiving rough road detection data, condition met for 20 seconds. The PCM detects engine misfire by detecting variations in crankshaft deceleration between firing strokes. For accurate detection of engine misfire, the PCM must distinguish between crankshaft deceleration caused by actual misfire and deceleration caused by rough road conditions. The ABS (system) can detect if the vehicle is on a rough road based on wheel acceleration or deceleration data supplied by the wheel speed sensors. If the ABS detects rough road above a certain threshold, it sends a message to the PCM via serial data. The PCM can then take the rough road into account when calculating misfire. Even if the ABS is malfunctioning and cannot detect rough roads, Misfire diagnostics will continue to run. However, if a misfire trouble code is set, DTC P1381 is also set to indicate that rough road data was not available during misfire calculation due to a serial data fault. **Possible Causes:** • Service the ABS before diagnosing a misfire because an actual engine misfire may not exist. Also, an actual engine misfire may have occurred during a period of ABS fault. • Determine if the vehicle was driven on a rough road, and the ABS could not detect this due to a malfunction. The PCM may interpret variations in crankshaft speed caused by the rough road as a misfire without an actual engine misfire present. • Refer to Diagnostic System Check for Antilock Brake System • Refer to Diagnostic System Check for the Engine Controls
DTC: P400 **1T CCM, MIL: No** **Years:** 2005, 2006, 2007 **Models:** Sky **Engines:** 2.4L **Transmissions:** All	**Cold Start Emission Reduction Control System** DTCs P0101, P0102, P0103, P0106, P0107, P0108, P0112, P0113, P0116, P0117, P0118, P0120, P0121, P0122, P0123, P0220, P0222, P0223, P0201, P0202, P0203, P0204, P0300, P0335, P0336, P0351, P0352, P0353, P0506, P0507, P0601, P0602, P0603, P0604, P0606, P0607, P062F, P0641, P0651, P1516, P1682, P2101, P2119, P2120, P2122, P2123, P2125, P2127, P2128, P2135, P2138, P2176, P2610 are not set. The engine is running, and a cold start has been detected. The throttle position sensor is less than 2 percent. The airflow per cylinder is greater than 80 mg. This DTC runs within 15 seconds within the first 2 minutes of start-up. This diagnostic runs once per trip when a cold start has been determined. **Possible Causes:** • Air intake system modified or restricted • Incorrect crankcase ventilation system operation • Water intrusion • Vacuum leak and other unmetered air downstream of the MAF sensor • Intake manifold leak • engine mechanical for items that could alter the air flow into the combustion chamber
DTC: P1404 **2T EGR, MIL: Yes** **Years:** 2005, 2006, 2007 **Models:** Malibu, Rendezvous **Engines:** 2.2L, 2.4L, 3.4L, 3.5L, 3.6L, 3.9L, 3.9L **Transmissions:** All	**EGR Valve Closed Position Signal Range/Performance** Engine started; system voltage from 11-18v, then after the EGR valve was commanded open at more than a 40% duty cycle for 500 ms, and then commanded to 0% (closed) for over 20 seconds, the PCM detected the EGR Position Sensor signal was 0.2 volt more than the EGR Learned Minimum Position value after the Desired EGR Position was commanded to 0% for 20 seconds, or the EGR Position Sensor signal was more than 40% and steady for 0.5 seconds after a test failure and before the next test will be run. The PCM must detect this condition 4 times to set this trouble code. The PCM monitors the EGR valve position sensor. The 5v VREF, low reference and EGR valve position signal circuits are used by the PCM to determine the EGR valve position. With the ignition switch on, the PCM records the EGR Learned Minimum Position and compares this value to the EGR Position Sensor parameter. **Possible Causes:** • EGR sensor signal circuit is open, shorted to ground or VREF • EGR sensor ground circuit is open or it has high resistance • EGR sensor is damaged or it has failed (sensor/solenoid unit) • EGR valve pintle or valve seat contains carbon deposits • PCM has failed

DTC	Trouble Code Title, Conditions & Possible Causes
DTC: P1404 **2T EGR, MIL: Yes** **Years:** 2005, 2006, 2007 **Models:** Sierra, Silverado **Engines:** 4.3L, 4.8L, 5.3L, 6.0L, 6.2L, 8.1L **Transmissions:** All	**EGR Valve Closed Position Performance** Engine started; system voltage from 11-18v, EGR valve enabled at least (6) times, and the PCM detected the EGR position sensor was 0.29v more than the EGR learned minimum position when the desired EGR position was commanded to 0% for over 2 seconds, or the EGR position sensor command is over 30% and steady for 2 seconds after a test failure and before the next test. **Possible Causes:** • EGR sensor signal circuit is shorted to VREF (5v) • EGR sensor ground circuit is open or has high resistance • EGR sensor is damaged or has failed (sensor/solenoid unit) • EGR valve pintle or valve seat contains carbon deposits • PCM has failed • TSB 01-06-04-043 contains a repair procedure for this code
DTC: P1404 **2T EGR, MIL: Yes** **Years:** 2005, 2006, 2007 **Models:** Sierra, Silverado **Engines:** 6.6L Diesel **Transmissions:** All	**EGR Valve Vacuum Sensor Range/Performance** DTC P0101, P0102, P0103, P0106, P0107, P0108, P0112, P0113, P0116, P0117, P0118, P0405, P0406, P0489, P0490, P0500, P0651, P2142, P2144, P2144 and P2145 not set, engine runtime over 5 seconds, engine speed from 610-820 RPM (50 RPM) for 3 seconds, EGR valve vacuum control solenoid commanded to over 70%, ECM not in Reduced Engine Power mode, BARO sensor more than 72 kPa, ECT sensor is from 140-212°F. Calculated Fuel Rate value between 3-20 mm^3, Power Takeoff (PTO) is disabled, IAT sensor more than 32°F, APP Indicated Angle sensor less than 1%, system voltage from 11-18v, VSS less than 0.25 MPH, and the ECM detected a higher than desired EGR vacuum sensor signal along with a lower than expected MAF sensor value for over 3 seconds. **Possible Causes:** • Check for leaking or restricted vacuum line connections • EGR vacuum sensor is damaged or it has failed • EGR vacuum vent solenoid is stuck open • EGR valve is damaged or it has failed • EGR valve vacuum control solenoid is stuck open • EGR vent solenoid is damaged or it has failed • Exhaust system may be restricted causing high back pressure
DTC: P1415 **2T AIR, MIL: Yes** **Years:** 2005, 2006, 2007 **Models:** Sierra, Silverado **Engines:** 4.3L, 4.8L, 5.3L, 6.0L, 6.2L, 8.1L **Transmissions:** All	**Secondary Air Injection System (Bank 1) Malfunction** DTC P0137, 0138 P0140-P0147, P0151-P0158, P0160, P0161, P0171, P0172, P0174, P0175, P0300, P0500, P1106, P1107, P1111-P1115, P1121, P1122, P1133, P1134, P1153, P1154, P1351 and P1361 not set, engine started, vehicle driven to an engine speed over 900 RPM at an engine load less than 33.25%, airflow less than 22 g/sec, A/F ratio at 13.125:1, ECT sensor from 158-230°F, system voltage over 10.0v, and the PCM detected the Bank 1 HO2S signal was less than 222 mv for 1 second with the AIR pump on while in closed loop. A secondary air injection (AIR) pump is used to reduce the tailpipe emissions during startup. The PCM supplies a ground to the AIR pump relay control circuit, and this action energizes the AIR pump. The PCM monitors the front HO2S signal in order to diagnose the AIR system. During the AIR test, the PCM activates the AIR pump during closed loop operation. Once the AIR pump is "on", the PCM monitors the HO2S signal and the Short Term fuel trim values of both banks of the engine. If the AIR system is operating properly, the HO2S signal should go low, and the Short Term fuel trim value should go high. If the PCM detects the HO2S signals for both banks did not respond as expected during the tests, it will set DTC P0410. If only one sensor responds, the PCM sets either a DTC P1415 or P1416 to indicate the bank where the AIR system failed. **Possible Causes:** • Air hoses disconnected, loose, kinked or failed (a burnt hose) • AIR pump is damaged or has failed (inspect air pump for water) • AIR system check valves and/or pipes are damaged or leaking • PCM has failed
DTC: P1416 **2T AIR, MIL: Yes** **Years:** 2005, 2006, 2007 **Models:** Sierra, Silverado **Engines:** 4.3L, 4.8L, 5.3L, 6.0L, 6.2L, 8.1L **Transmissions:** All	**Secondary Air Injection System (Bank 2) Malfunction** DTC P0137, 0138 P0140-P0147, P0151-P0158, P0160, P0161, P0171, P0172, P0174, P0175, P0300, P0500, P1106, P1107, P1111-P1115, P1121, P1122, P1133, P1134, P1153, P1154, P1351 and P1361 not set, engine started, vehicle driven to an engine speed over 900 RPM at an engine load less than 33.25%, airflow less than 22 g/sec, A/F ratio at 13.125:1, ECT sensor from 158-230°F, system voltage over 10.0v, and the PCM detected the Bank 2 HO2S signal was less than 222 mv for 1 second with the AIR pump on while in closed loop. The PCM supplies a ground to the AIR pump relay control circuit, and this action energizes the AIR pump. The PCM monitors the front HO2S signal in order to diagnose the AIR system. During the AIR test, the PCM activates the AIR pump during closed loop operation. Once the AIR pump is "on", the PCM monitors the HO2S signal and the Short Term fuel trim values of both banks of the engine. If the AIR system is operating properly, the HO2S signal should go low, and the Short Term fuel trim value should go high. If the PCM detects the HO2S signals for both banks did not respond as expected during the tests, it will set DTC P0410. If only one sensor responds, the PCM sets either a DTC P1415 or P1416 to indicate the bank where the AIR system failed. **Possible Causes:** • Air hoses disconnected, loose, kinked or failed (a burnt hose) • AIR pump is damaged or has failed (inspect air pump for water) • AIR system check valves and/or pipes are damaged or leaking • PCM has failed

DTC	Trouble Code Title, Conditions & Possible Causes
DTC: P1432 **1T CCM, MIL: No** **Years:** 2005, 2006, 2007 **Models:** Sierra, Silverado **Engines:** 6.0L CNG **Transmissions:** All	**Fuel Pressure Sensor Circuit Low Input** DTC P1207 not set, engine started, engine operating on alternative fuel, and the AF ECU detected the Fuel Pressure Sensor (FPS) signal was less than 0.10v for more than 1 second during the test. **Possible Causes:** • Fuel tank pressure sensor is sticking or it is damaged • Fuel tank pressure sensor signal circuit is shorted to ground • Fuel tank pressure sensor is damaged or it has failed • PCM has failed
DTC: P1432 **2T CCM, MIL: Yes** **Years:** 2005, 2006, 2007 **Models:** Sierra, Silverado **Engines:** 6.0L CNG **Transmissions:** All	**Fuel Pressure Sensor Circuit Low Input** DTC P0182 and P0183 not set; engine started, Fuel Tank temperature below 149°F, and the PCM detected the Fuel Tank Pressure (FTP) sensor was less than 0.45v for over 1 second. **Possible Causes:** • Fuel tank pressure sensor is sticking or it is damaged • Fuel tank pressure sensor signal circuit is shorted to ground • Fuel tank pressure sensor is damaged or it has failed • PCM has failed
DTC: P1433 **1T CCM, MIL: No** **Years:** 2005, 2006, 2007 **Models:** Sierra, Silverado **Engines:** 6.0L CNG **Transmissions:** All	**Fuel Pressure Sensor Circuit High Input** DTC P0182 and P0183 not set, Fuel Tank temperature below 149°F, engine started, and the PCM detected the Fuel Tank Pressure (FTP) sensor was over 4.95v for more than 1 second. **Possible Causes:** • Fuel pressure sensor is sticking or it is damaged • Fuel pressure sensor signal circuit is open or shorted to VREF • Fuel pressure sensor is damaged or it has failed • PCM has failed
DTC: P1433 **2T CCM, MIL: Yes** **Years:** 2005, 2006, 2007 **Models:** Sierra, Silverado **Engines:** 6.0L CNG **Transmissions:** All	**Fuel Pressure Sensor Circuit Low Input** DTC P0182 and P0183 not set, Fuel Tank temperature below 149°F, engine started, and the PCM detected the Fuel Tank Pressure (FTP) sensor was less than 0.45v for over 1 second. **Possible Causes:** • Fuel tank pressure sensor is sticking or it is damaged • Fuel tank pressure sensor signal circuit is shorted to ground • Fuel tank pressure sensor is damaged or it has failed • PCM has failed
DTC: P1441 **2T EVAP, MIL: Yes** **Years:** 2005, 2006, 2007 **Models:** Sierra, Silverado **Engines:** 4.3L, 4.8L, 5.3L, 6.0L, 6.2L, 8.1L **Transmissions:** All	**EVAP System Flow During Non-Purge** DTC P0107, P0108, P0112, P0113, P0116, P0117, P0118, P0125, P0440, P0442, P0443, P0446, P0449, P0452, P0453, P1111, P1112, P1114, P1115, P1120, P1220 and P1221 not set, engine started, vehicle driven to a speed of less than 75 MPH, ECT and IAT sensors from 39-86°F and within 16°F at startup, system voltage over 10.0v, BARO sensor more than 75 kPa, fuel level from 15-85%, and the PCM detected a vacuum condition present during a non-purge operating condition. The PCM seals the EVAP system by commanding the EVAP Purge valve "off" and commands the EVAP Canister Vent valve "on" (closed). The PCM monitors the FTP sensor to determine if a vacuum is being drawn on the EVAP system. If the vacuum in the EVAP system is more than a predetermined value within a calculated time, DTC P1441 will set. **Possible Causes:** • An improperly installed or damaged EVAP canister purge valve • A temporary blockage in the EVAP canister purge valve, purge pipe, or EVAP canister could cause an intermittent condition • FTP sensor is out-of-calibration, damaged or "skewed" • Purge solenoid valve is damaged or has failed • PCM has failed
DTC: P1441 **2T EVAP, MIL: Yes** **Years:** 2005, 2006, 2007 **Models:** Malibu, Rendezvous **Engines:** 2.2L, 2.4L, 3.4L, 3.5L, 3.6L, 3.9L, 3.9L **Transmissions:** All	**EVAP System Flow During Non-Purge** DTC P0107, P0108, P0110, P0112-P0118, P0121-P0123, P0125, P0440, P0442-P0449, P0452, P0453, P1106, P1107, P1111, P1112, P1114, P1115, P1121 and P1122 not set, engine started, ECT and IAT signals from 38-86°F and with 16°F at startup, vehicle driven to a speed of less than 75 MPH, BARO sensor more than 75 kPa, system voltage over 10.0v, fuel level from 15-85%, and the PCM detected vacuum in the EVAP system during a not purge condition. The PCM tests for undesired intake manifold vacuum flow to the EVAP system. The PCM seals the EVAP system by commanding the EVAP Purge valve "off" and the EVAP Canister Vent valve "on". The PCM monitors the fuel tank pressure (FTP) sensor to determine if a vacuum is being drawn on the EVAP system. If vacuum in the EVAP system is more than a preset value within a predetermined time, DTC P1441 is set. **Possible Causes:** • An improperly installed or damaged EVAP canister purge valve • A temporary blockage in the EVAP canister purge valve, purge pipe, or EVAP canister • FTP sensor is out-of-calibration, damaged or "skewed" • Purge solenoid valve is damaged or has failed • PCM has failed

DTC	Trouble Code Title, Conditions & Possible Causes
DTC: P1514 **1T CCM, MIL: Yes** **Years:** 2005, 2006, 2007 **Models:** Sierra, Silverado **Engines:** 4.3L, 4.8L, 5.3L, 6.0L, 6.2L, 8.1L **Transmissions:** All	**Throttle Body Performance** DTC P0601, P0602, P0606, P1515, P1516, P1517 and P1518 not set, P1120, P1220 and P1221 not active at the time this code set, or P1120 and P1220 not set at the same time, engine speed over 500 RPM, and the PCM detected the difference between Actual (MAF) airflow and Speed Density Calculated airflow was more than expected for 1 second. The Reduced Engine Power message displays on the Driver Information Center if this code sets. **Possible Causes:** • Inspect the throttle blade for damage and/or proper installation • Inspect the TAC module connectors for signs of water intrusion. When water intrusion occurs, multiple codes can set with no circuit or component faults apparent during diagnostic testing. • Physically and visually inspect the throttle body assembly, and throttle position sensor for damage and/or a loose mounting. Move the throttle blade from closed to wide open position without applying too much force. The throttle blade should move smoothly through the full range and should return to a slightly open position on its own. • If the TAC module detects a fault in the system, it may set more than one related code because of the many redundant tests that run continuously on this system. Locating and repairing one individual condition may fix more than one code.
DTC: P1515 **1T CCM, MIL: Yes** **Years:** 2005, 2006, 2007 **Models:** Sierra, Silverado **Engines:** 4.3L, 4.8L, 5.3L, 6.0L, 6.2L, 8.1L **Transmissions:** All	**Control Module Throttle Actuator Position Performance** DTC P0601, P0602, P0606, P1515, P1516, P1517 and P1518 not set, P1120, P1220 and P1221 not active at the time this code set, or P1120 and P1220 not set at the same time, key in crank or run mode, ETC or TAC system not in Battery Saver Mode, and the PCM detected the Actual and Commanded throttle positions were out-of-range for under 1 second. **Possible Causes:** • Throttle actuator motor CKT 1 is open, shorted to ground or B+ • Throttle actuator motor CKT 2 is open, shorted to ground or B+ • Throttle actuator motor is damaged or has failed • Throttle actuator motor control module has failed • TSB 00-06-04-035 contains a repair procedure for this code
DTC: P1516 **1T CCM, MIL: Yes** **Years:** 2005, 2006, 2007 **Models:** Sierra, Silverado **Engines:** 4.3L, 4.8L, 5.3L, 6.0L, 6.2L, 8.1L **Transmissions:** All	**TAC Module Throttle Actuator Position Performance** DTC P1518 not set, key in crank or run mode, ETC or TAC system not in Battery Saver Mode, then the ETC/TAC module detected the predicted and actual throttle positions were not within a calibrated range of each other or the PCM and ETC/TAC could not determine the throttle position or that both TP sensors signals were invalid. **Possible Causes:** • TAC motor CKT 1 or CKT 2 is open, shorted to ground or B+ • Throttle actuator motor CKT 1 is shorted to CKT 2 • Throttle actuator motor control module has failed • TSB 03-04-06-032 contains a repair procedure for this code
DTC: P1516 **1T CCM, MIL: Yes** **Years:** 2005, 2006, 2007 **Models:** Sky **Engines:** 2.4L **Transmissions:** All	**TAC Module Throttle Actuator Position Performance** DTC P0068 is not set. Engine running. The system is not in the Battery Save mode The indicated throttle position does not match the predicted throttle position for more than 0.5 second. **Possible Causes:** • Throttle blade not at rest, binding open or closed • Motor control circuit for a short to voltage or short to ground • Motor control 1 circuit has open or high resistance • Throttle actuator motor control module has failed • Throttle body has failed • ECM has failed
DTC: P1517 **1T CCM, MIL: Yes** **Years:** 2005, 2006, 2007 **Models:** Sierra, Silverado **Engines:** 4.3L, 4.8L, 5.3L, 6.0L, 6.2L, 8.1L **Transmissions:** All	**Throttle Actuator Control Module Performance** DTC P1518 not set, key in the crank or run mode, system voltage over 5.23v, and the ETC or TAC module detected that an internal data test failed (did not pass) for a time period of less than 1 second. **Possible Causes:** • Test the charging system output (low voltage can set this code) • Inspect the TAC module connectors for signs of water intrusion. If water intrusion occurs, multiple codes may set without any circuit or component conditions found during diagnostic testing. • When the TAC module detects a fault condition, several TAC related codes set because there are redundant tests running. • TAC module has failed
DTC: P1518 **1T CCM, MIL: Yes** **Years:** 2005, 2006, 2007 **Models:** Sierra, Silverado **Engines:** 4.3L, 4.8L, 5.3L, 6.0L, 6.2L, 8.1L **Transmissions:** All	**Throttle Actuator Control Module Serial Data Malfunction** Key in the crank or run mode, system voltage over 5.23v, and the ETC or TAC module detected invalid or missing serial data present for a specified amount of time, condition met for less than 1 second. **Possible Causes:** • DTC P1518 sets if the battery voltage is low. If the customer's concern is slow cranking or no crank due to low battery voltage, ignore the DTC P1518. Clear codes and retest. • DTC P1518 also sets when there is a short to B+ on the TAC module ground circuit. Inspect the Brake, Cruise fuses first. • TSB 03-04-06-032 contains a repair procedure for this code

DTC	Trouble Code Title, Conditions & Possible Causes

DTC: P1546
1T CCM, MIL: Yes
Years: 2005, 2006, 2007
Models: All
Engines: All
Transmissions: All
	A/C Clutch Relay Control Circuit
	Key on or engine running; and the PCM detected an improper voltage level on the output circuit that controls the A/C compressor clutch relay, condition met for at least 30 seconds.
	Possible Causes:
	    • A/C clutch status line is open or shorted to ground
	    • A/C clutch relay is damaged or has failed (contains not closing)
	    • A/C clutch relay power circuit is open (test the AC CLU fuse)
	    • PCM has failed

DTC: P1550
1T CCM, MIL: No
Years: 2005, 2006, 2007
Models: Sierra, Silverado
Engines: 6.6L Diesel
Transmissions: All
	Fuel Injector Control Module Power Circuit Malfunction
	U1800 and U2104 not set, key on, and the PCM detected a low supply voltage present at the Fuel Injector Control Module (FICM). The FICM activates the fuel injector. The ECM commands the FICM to turn "on" the injectors through each fuel injector control circuit.
	Possible Causes:
	    • FICM ground circuit has a high resistance condition
	    • FICM power circuit has a high resistance condition
	    • FICM (module) is damaged or it has failed

DTC: P1551
1T CCM, MIL: Yes
Years: 2005, 2006, 2007
Models: SRX
Engines: 3.6L, 3.9L
Transmissions: All
	Throttle Valve Rest Position Not Reached During Learn
	The engine speed is less than 40 RPM. The engine coolant temperature (ECT) is between 5-100°C (41-212°F). The intake air temperature (IAT) is between 5-143°C (41-290°F). The ignition 1 voltage is more than 10 volts. The accelerator pedal position (APP) is less than 15 percent. DTC P1551 runs when the throttle actuator control motor is deactivated. The ECM detects the TP sensor angle is less than 10 percent or more than 40 percent when the throttle actuator control motor is deactivated.
	Possible Causes:
	    • Incorrect throttle body and system operation
	    • throttle valve may have been held open
	    • Ice in throttle body
	    • Throttle valve is not free to move open or closed WITHOUT spring pressure
	    • Throttle body has failed

DTC: P1554
1T CCM, MIL: Yes
Years: 2005, 2006, 2007
Models: Malibu, Rendezvous
Engines: 2.2L, 2.4L, 3.4L, 3.5L, 3.6L, 3.9L, 3.9L
Transmissions: All
	Cruise Engaged Circuit High Input
	Engine started; Cruise Control commanded "off" (the Cruise Inhibit circuit is grounded), and the PCM detected the Cruise Status signal indicated that Cruise Control was enabled for one second under these operating conditions.
	Possible Causes:
	    • Cruise control inhibit circuit is open or shorted to ground
	    • SMCC II cruise control module is damaged or has failed
	    • PCM has failed

DTC: P1621
1T CCM, MIL: No
Years: 2005, 2006, 2007
Models: G6, GTO, LaCrosse, Malibu, Montana, Montana SV6, Relay, Rendezvous, Sky, Solstice, SRX, Terraza, Uplander, Vibe
Engines: 1.8L, 2.0L, 2.2L, 2.4L, 3.4L, 3.5L, 3.6L, 3.9L, 4.6L, 6.0L
Transmissions: All
	Control Module Long Term Memory Performance
	Engine cranking or running; and the PCM/VCM determined that it was unable to read data correctly from the EEPROM memory.
	Possible Causes:
	    • Serial data circuit is open between VCM and VTD (Passlock) control module, or serial data circuit is shorted to ground or B+
	    • Perform the Theft Deterrent System Check
	    • Perform the Powertrain Onboard Diagnostic System Check

DTC: P1621
1T CCM, MIL: No
Years: 2005, 2006, 2007
Models: Sierra, Silverado
Engines: 4.3L, 4.8L, 5.3L, 6.0L, 6.2L, 8.1L
Transmissions: All
	Control Module Long Term Memory Performance
	Key on, and the PCM detected a problem with its internal microprocessor integrity during the initial power-up phase.
	Possible Causes:
	    • Perform the Diagnostic System Check for Engine Controls
	    • The PCM needs to be replaced and then reprogrammed

DTC: P1621
1T CCM, MIL: No
Years: 2005, 2006, 2007
Models: Sierra, Silverado
Engines: 6.6L Diesel
Transmissions: All
	Control Module Long Term Memory Performance
	Key on, and the PCM determined that it was unable to read data correctly from the EEPROM memory in the initial power-up phase.
	Possible Causes:
	    • Perform the Powertrain Onboard Diagnostic System Check
	    • The PCM needs to be replaced

DTC	Trouble Code Title, Conditions & Possible Causes
DTC: P1626 **1T PCM, MIL: No** **Years:** 2005, 2006, 2007 **Models:** All **Engines:** All **Transmissions:** All	**Theft Deterrent System Fuel Enable Circuit Malfunction** DTC P01631 not set, engine cranking (during an attempt to start the engine and the Antitheft System Allowed fuel deliver to occur, and the PCM detected a loss of the "state of health" serial data message from the Theft Deterrent System. The VTD system is part of the BCM. The PCM monitors the "state of health" message from the VTD module to ensure that PCM to BCM communications are present. If the PCM detects a loss of the "state of health" message with the engine running, DTC P1626 will be set. DTC P1626 can cause a non-start condition or normal engine operation (depending on when the loss of VTD System communication was detected). The engine will continue to start and run if the fault that set DTC P1626 occurred "after" the PCM received a valid theft deterrent password from the BCM and already Allowed fuel during the ignition cycle. The engine will start and immediately stall if the fault that set DTC P1626 occurred "before" the PCM received a valid theft deterrent password. With this condition present, the PCM will inhibit fuel delivery and disable the starter until a valid theft deterrent password is detected. **Possible Causes:** • Perform the Onboard Diagnostic System Check • If the PCM needs replacing, it must be reprogrammed • TSB 02-08-56-002 contains a repair procedure for this code
DTC: P1626 **1T PCM, MIL: No** **Years:** 2005, 2006, 2007 **Models:** G6, GTO, LaCrosse, Malibu, Relay, Rendezvous **Engines:** 2.2L, 2.4L, 3.4L, 3.5L, 3.6L, 3.8L, 3.9L, 3.9L **Transmissions:** All	**Theft Deterrent System Fuel Enable Signal Lost** DTC P1631 not set, Engine cranking or running; VTD system has Allowed fuel delivery, and the PCM lost the health status message from the Vehicle Theft Deterrent (VTD) system. The VTD module produces the theft deterrent "fuel enable" signal with the ignition "on" and after the proper key resistor pellet is detected. The PCM monitors the fuel enable signal during cranking. If the proper signal is present on the serial data circuit, the PCM enables fuel delivery to Allow the engine to start. If the PCM detects the fuel enable signal is not present or incorrect with the engine running, DTC P1626 is set. The engine will continue to start and run as long as DTC P1626 is set. If the problem affects inputs to the VTD signal, the starter motor may be disabled. **Possible Causes:** • The most likely cause of this code is lost communications • If the engine starts and stalls, refer to VTD system diagnosis • Perform the Powertrain Onboard Diagnostic System Check
DTC: P1626 **1T PCM, MIL: No** **Years:** 2005, 2006, 2007 **Models:** Sierra, Silverado **Engines:** All **Transmissions:** All	**Analog To Digital (A/D) Performance** Key on, and the PCM detected the ECM internal Analog to Digital converter failed. The PCM monitors internal circuits for problems. If it detects a problem in the one or more circuits, DTC P1627 will set. **Possible Causes:** • Perform the Diagnostic System Check for Engine Controls • The PCM needs to be replaced
DTC: P1630 **1T CCM, MIL: No** **Years:** 2005, 2006, 2007 **Models:** Sierra, Silverado **Engines:** 6.6L Diesel **Transmissions:** All	**Theft Deterrent System - Learn Mode Enable** Key on or engine running; and the PCM determined the Theft Leaning Flag was enabled. The PCM checks for the Enable Password Learning Flag indicating it has entered learn password mode. This function during assembly when the PCM needs to learn the password from the Passlock module if either module is replaced. **Possible Causes:** • This DTC (PCM in learn mode) is used at the assembly plant, dealership or by other service personnel to indicate learn mode is enabled (i.e., the PCM is ready to lean a new password). • Perform Diagnostic System Check for Theft Deterrent System • Perform the Powertrain Onboard Diagnostic System Check • TSB 77-65-31 contains a repair procedure for this code
DTC: P1630 **1T CCM, MIL: Yes** **Years:** 2005, 2006, 2007 **Models:** G6, GTO, LaCrosse, Malibu, Relay, Rendezvous **Engines:** 2.2L, 2.4L, 3.4L, 3.5L, 3.6L, 3.8L, 3.9L, 3.9L **Transmissions:** All	**Theft Deterrent Learn Mode Active** Key on, PCM ready to learn new Pass Lock II password after it finished the 10-minute learn pending timer with the key left on for 10 minutes, and the PCM received an incorrect password from BCM or the Vehicle Theft Detection (VDC) module. If the Theft Deterrent system is replaced, the password must be relearned using approved diagnostic equipment. If the PCM is replaced, the replacement PCM should learn the password within a few seconds after the ignition is turned "on". DTC P1630 indicates the PCM is ready to learn the VTD password. The engine will start and run with DTC P1630 set. **Possible Causes:** • Refer to Programming the Theft Deterrent System • Perform the Powertrain Onboard Diagnostic System Check

DTC	Trouble Code Title, Conditions & Possible Causes
DTC: P1631 **1T CCM, MIL: No** **Years:** 2005, 2006, 2007 **Models:** Sierra, Silverado **Engines:** 4.3L, 4.8L, 5.3L, 6.0L, 6.2L, 8.1L **Transmissions:** All	**Theft Deterrent - Start Enable Signal Not Correct** DTC P1626 not active, engine cranking with the PCM not in "password learn mode", VTD (Pass Lock) system enabled, and the PCM did not receive a valid password before the fuel disable decision point was reached. When the Passlock portion of the VTD system has sensed the proper operation of the ignition switch and lock, or determined that the switch and lock have not been tampered with, the VTD (Passlock) module transmits a password to the PCM. Fuel delivery is enabled if this password matches the password stored in the PCM memory. If a component in the Theft Deterrent system has been replaced, the two modules need to relearn the password of the new components. If the relearn procedure has not been performed, DTC P1631 will set. If a VTD failure occurs during an ignition cycle on which the PCM has enabled fuel, then the PCM will enter Fail Safe mode (VTD System Failure with Fuel Enabled). The PCM remains in Fail Enable Mode for the current and future ignition cycles, until the fault is corrected, a valid password is received, or until the battery is disconnected. If the codes are cleared, the vehicle will lose its Fail Enable status and will not start until the fault is corrected or the ten minute timer expires. At this point, the PCM receives the correct fuel delivery password. **Possible Causes:** • Refer to Diagnostic System Check for Theft Deterrent Module • Perform the Powertrain Onboard Diagnostic System Check • TSB 77-65-31 contains a repair procedure for this code
DTC: P1631 **1T CCM, MIL: No** **Years:** 2005, 2006, 2007 **Models:** Sierra, Silverado **Engines:** 6.6L Diesel **Transmissions:** All	**Theft Deterrent System - Learn Mode Enable** Engine cranking, Vehicle Antitheft System enabled, and the PCM detected the Fuel Disable Flag was set because an incorrect "Fuel Continue Password has been received. The PCM checks for mismatched passwords between the VTD control module and the PCM. When the VTD control module or PCM is replaced the theft "learn" procedure must be followed so a new password is learned. **Possible Causes:** • Refer to Diagnostic System Check for Theft Deterrent Module • Perform the Powertrain Onboard Diagnostic System Check
DTC: P1631 **1T CCM, MIL: No** **Years:** 2005, 2006, 2007 **Models:** G6, GTO, LaCrosse, Malibu, Relay, Rendezvous **Engines:** 2.2L, 2.4L, 3.4L, 3.5L, 3.6L, 3.8L, 3.9L, 3.9L **Transmissions:** All	**Theft Deterrent Fuel Enable Signal Not Correct** Engine cranking and the PCM received a "Fuel Disabled" or "Undecided: password that does not match from the BCM. When the ignition switch is first turned ON, the BCM sends a password to the PCM through the serial data circuit. If the BCM password does not match the current password stored in the PCM, the PCM will disable the engine. The engine will start and stall, or it will not start. The Theft System telltale will flash on the IPC and the engine will be disabled until a matching password is received. The password is checked every 4 seconds. The engine is disabled for at least 10 minutes, and during that period, the Theft System telltale will flash on the IPC for approximately 4 seconds then will illuminate solid for 10 minutes or until a correct password is received. After the vehicle has passed theft detection, the PCM will continue a normal engine operation. If the PCM loses the BCM communication within the same ignition cycle, the vehicle will continue to run. This mode is called the fail enable mode **Possible Causes:** • Refer to Diagnostic System Check for Body Control Systems • Perform the Powertrain Onboard Diagnostic System Check
DTC: P1632 **1T CCM, MIL: No** **Years:** 2005, 2006, 2007 **Models:** G6, GTO, LaCrosse, Malibu, Relay, Rendezvous **Engines:** 2.2L, 2.4L, 3.4L, 3.5L, 3.6L, 3.9L, 3.9L **Transmissions:** All	**Theft Deterrent Fuel Disable Signal Received** Engine cranking, and the PCM received a Fuel Disabled password from the Body Control Module (BCM), or an "undecided" password was sent from the PCM to the BCM. The VTD system (the Passlock II System) is designed to prevent vehicle theft by disabling the engine unless a mechanical key is used to correctly engage the Passlock lock cylinder. This system utilizes a lock cylinder, ignition switch, the BCM and the PCM. When starting the, the PCM looks for a password from the BCM through the Class 2 serial data circuit. If the password is not recognized or not present, the PCM will disable the engine. If an incorrect or no Password is received, this indicates that the engine will start and stall and the Theft System telltale will flash on the IPC for 4 seconds. If an incorrect or disable password is received (more than three invalid passwords received) the engine will be disabled for at least 10 minutes and the Theft System telltale will turn to "solid" on the IPC for 3 seconds, and then flash on the IPC for 10 minutes. After the vehicle passes theft detection, the PCM will continue normal engine operation. If the PCM loses the BCM communication within the same ignition cycle, the vehicle will continue to run on the following ignition cycles. This mode is called the fail enable mode. **Possible Causes:** • Perform the Powertrain Onboard Diagnostic System Check • Password Learn Procedure - Attempt to start the vehicle (leave the ignition "on"). The Theft System telltale will flash for 4 seconds and then remain "on" for 10 minutes. Theft System Learn Mode will display Disabled on the Scan Tool • Turn the ignition "off" after the Theft System telltale goes "out". • Repeat steps 1 and 2 two more times. After the Theft System telltale turns "off" on the 3rd key cycle, and Theft System Learn Mode will display Enabled on the Scan Tool, attempt to start the engine. Once the engine starts the password is learned.
DTC: P1635 **2T CCM, MIL: Yes** **Years:** 2005, 2006, 2007 **Models:** G6, GTO, LaCrosse, Malibu, Relay, Rendezvous **Engines:** 2.2L, 2.4L, 3.4L, 3.5L, 3.6L, 3.9L, 3.9L **Transmissions:** All	**5-Volt Reference 'A' Circuit Malfunction** Key on or engine running; and the PCM detected the 5v REF A circuit was less than 3.5v or more than 5.5v for 10 seconds. The PCM uses the 5v Reference 1 circuit as a sensor feed to the TP sensor, MAP sensor, EGR valve pintle position and FTP sensor. **Possible Causes:** • 5v VREF circuit is shorted to sensor ground or chassis ground • 5v VREF circuit, MAP or FTP sensor circuit is shorted to (B+) • 5v VREF circuit shorted to EGR sensor High signal circuit • EGR solenoid valve (and sensor) is damaged or has failed • PCM has failed

DTC	Trouble Code Title, Conditions & Possible Causes
DTC: P1635 **2T CCM, MIL: Yes** **Years:** 2005, 2006, 2007 **Models:** Sierra, Silverado **Engines:** 4.3L, 4.8L, 5.3L, 6.0L, 6.2L, 8.1L **Transmissions:** All	**5-Volt Reference 1 Circuit Malfunction** Key on or engine running; and the PCM detected the 5v Reference 1 circuit was out of tolerance for 2 seconds. This circuit provides power to the EGR Pintle and MAP sensor. **Possible Causes:** • 5v VREF circuit is shorted to sensor ground or chassis ground • 5v VREF circuit, MAP or EOP sensor circuit is shorted to (B+) • 5v VREF circuit shorted to EGR sensor High signal circuit • EGR solenoid valve (and sensor) is damaged or has failed • PCM has failed
DTC: P1635 **2T CCM, MIL: Yes** **Years:** 2005, 2006, 2007 **Models:** Sierra, Silverado **Engines:** 6.6L Diesel **Transmissions:** All	**5-Volt Reference Circuit Low Input** Key on, and the PCM detected the 5v Reference circuit indicated less than 4.0v during the CCM (continuous monitor) test. The PCM provides a 5v supply for provide power to various engine sensors. The PCM monitors the voltage present at terminals BRD13, shared by the Boost and Crankshaft Position (CKP) sensors, and BRD14 that connects to the optical/fuel temperature sensor (Cam/HI. RES). **Possible Causes:** • 5v VREF circuit is shorted to sensor ground or chassis ground • 5v VREF circuit, Boost or CKP sensor circuit is shorted to (B+) • 5v VREF circuit shorted to the Boost sensor signal circuit • EGR solenoid valve (and sensor) is damaged or has failed • PCM has failed
DTC: P1635 **2T CCM, MIL: Yes** **Years:** 2005, 2006, 2007 **Models:** Sierra, Silverado **Engines:** 4.3L, 4.8L, 5.3L, 6.0L, 6.2L, 8.1L **Transmissions:** All	**5-Volt Reference 1 Circuit Malfunction** Key on, and the PCM detected the 5v VREF 1 circuit was out of tolerance for 2 seconds. The EGR Pintle, Fuel Level, Fuel Tank Pressure, MAP and TP sensors All connect to this circuit. **Possible Causes:** • 5v VREF circuit is shorted to sensor ground or chassis ground • 5v VREF circuit, MAP or EGR sensor circuit is shorted to (B+) • 5v VREF circuit shorted to EGR sensor High signal circuit • EGR solenoid valve (and sensor) is damaged or has failed • PCM has failed
DTC: P1637 **1T CCM, MIL: No** **Years:** 2005, 2006, 2007 **Models:** Sierra, Silverado **Engines:** 4.3L, 4.8L, 5.3L, 6.0L, 6.2L, 8.1L **Transmissions:** All	**Generator 'L' Terminal Circuit Malfunction** Engine started; and the PCM detected an incorrect voltage on the Generator 'L' terminal during the CCM test. The PCM supplies the ignition voltage to the generator lamp feed. This voltage is pulled low by the generator once the circuit is supplied voltage. Once the generator begins to turn, the PCM detects ignition voltage. If there are no Charging system faults, the lamp terminal circuit will be low (0 volts) with the ignition switch "on" and then change to the system voltage after engine startup. If the Charging system detects this circuit is shorted to ground) the IPC will display a fault message. **Possible Causes:** • A Scan Tool should display Inactive for the 'L' Terminal and 10-40% for the 'F' Terminal with the ignition "on". With the engine running, the display should indicate the 'L' Terminal is Active and the 'F' Terminal is higher than 5% on the tool display. • Generator 'L' terminal circuit shorted to ground or to power (B+) • Generator 'F' terminal circuit is open or shorted to ground • Generator is damaged or has failed or the PCM has failed
DTC: P1638 **1T CCM, MIL: No** **Years:** 2005, 2006, 2007 **Models:** Sierra, Silverado **Engines:** 4.3L, 4.8L, 5.3L, 6.0L, 6.2L, 8.1L **Transmissions:** All	**Generator 'F' Terminal Circuit Malfunction** No CKP, CMP or Generator codes set, key on and the PCM detected the PWM signal was from 10-40% for over 6 seconds; or with the engine speed under 3000 RPM, the PCM detected the PWM signal was less than 5% for 6 seconds. The PCM uses the generator field duty cycle signal circuit to monitor the duty cycle of the generator. The generator field duty cycle signal circuit connects to the high side of the field winding in the generator. A pulse width modulated (PWM) high side driver in the voltage regulator turns the field winding on/off. When the key is in run position and the engine is off, the PCM should detect a duty cycle near 0%. However, when the engine is running, the duty cycle should be from 5-100%. The PCM monitors the PWM signal using a key on test and a run test. During the tests, if the PCM detects an out of range PWM signal, DTC P1638 will set. When the DTC sets, the PCM will send a class 2 serial data message to the IPC to illuminate the charge indicator. **Possible Causes:** • Generator connector is damaged or has high resistance • Generator field duty cycle signal circuit is open or shorted • Generator is damaged or has failed • PCM has failed

DTC	Trouble Code Title, Conditions & Possible Causes
DTC: P1639 **2T CCM, MIL: Yes** **Years:** 2005, 2006, 2007 **Models:** G6, GTO, LaCrosse, Malibu, Relay, Rendezvous **Engines:** 2.2L, 2.4L, 3.4L, 3.5L, 3.6L, 3.9L, 3.9L **Transmissions:** All	**5-Volt Reference 'B' Circuit Malfunction** Key on or engine running; and the PCM detected the 5v Reference B circuit that connects to the A/C Refrigerant pressure sensor was less than 3.5v or more than 5.5v for 30 seconds. The PCM provides a 5v VREF circuit to the Air Conditioning (A/C) pressure sensor and the Fuel Tank Pressure (FTP) sensor. These 5-volt reference circuits are independent of each other outside the PCM, but are connected together inside the PCM. Therefore, a circuit condition on one sensor 5v VREF circuit may affect the other sensor 5v reference circuit. The PCM monitors the voltage on the 5v VREF circuit. If the PCM detects that the voltage is out of tolerance, it sets DTC P1639. **Possible Causes:** • A/C refrigerant pressure sensor VREF circuit is open, shorted to ground or shorted to system power • A/C refrigerant pressure sensor is damaged or PCM has failed • TSB 61-65-61 contains a repair procedure for this code
DTC: P1639 **2T CCM, MIL: Yes** **Years:** 2005, 2006, 2007 **Models:** Sierra, Silverado **Engines:** 4.3L, 4.8L, 5.3L, 6.0L, 6.2L, 8.1L **Transmissions:** All	**5-Volt Reference 2 Circuit Malfunction** Key on or engine running; and the PCM detected the 5v Reference No. 2 circuit was out of tolerance for 2 seconds. This circuit connects to the Fuel Tank Pressure (FTP) sensor. **Possible Causes:** • 5v VREF circuit is shorted to sensor ground or chassis ground • 5v VREF circuit or FTP sensor circuit is shorted to (B+) • 5v VREF circuit shorted to the FTP sensor signal circuit • FTP sensor is damaged or has failed • PCM has failed
DTC: P1639 **1T CCM, MIL: Yes** **Years:** 2005, 2006, 2007 **Models:** Sierra, Silverado **Engines:** 4.3L, 4.8L, 5.3L, 6.0L, 6.2L, 8.1L **Transmissions:** All	**5-Volt Reference 2 Circuit Malfunction** Key on or engine running; and the PCM detected the 5v Reference No. 2 circuit was out of tolerance for 2 seconds during the CCM test. This circuit is connected to the Fuel Tank Pressure (FTP) and TP sensor. **Possible Causes:** • 5v VREF circuit is shorted to sensor ground or chassis ground • 5v VREF circuit, FTP or TP sensor circuit is shorted to (B+) • 5v VREF circuit shorted to FTP or TP sensor signal circuit • FTP sensor or TP sensor is damaged or PCM has failed
DTC: P1640 **2T CCM, MIL: Yes** **Years:** 2005, 2006, 2007 **Models:** G6, GTO, LaCrosse, Malibu, Relay, Rendezvous **Engines:** 2.2L, 2.4L, 3.4L, 3.5L, 3.6L, 3.8L, 3.9L, 3.9L **Transmissions:** All	**Output Driver 1 Input Voltage High Input** Key on or engine running; and the PCM detected an unexpected high voltage condition (over 33 volts) on the Output Driver 1 circuit. The ODM (modules) are, located inside the PCM, provides grounds for output circuits that control various devices. Each output has an internal feedback circuit that connects to the PCM. The ODM 1 monitors the voltage and current condition on circuits that could cause damage to the PCM. The PCM monitors voltage through the ignition 1 input. It sets this code if it detects a fault on the ODM 1 circuit. **Possible Causes:** • EVAP Vent control circuit open, shorted to ground or to B+ • Fan relay 1 control circuit is open, shorted to ground or to B+ • Fan relay 2 or 3 control circuit is open, shorted to ground or B+ • PCM has failed
DTC: P1650 **1T CCM, MIL: Yes** **Years:** 2005, 2006, 2007 **Models:** G6, GTO, LaCrosse, Malibu, Relay, Rendezvous **Engines:** 2.2L, 2.4L, 3.4L, 3.5L, 3.6L, 3.8L, 3.9L, 3.9L **Transmissions:** All	**Output Driver 2 Input Voltage High Input** Key on or engine running; and the PCM detected an unexpected high voltage condition (over 33 volts) on the Output Driver 2 circuit. The ODM (modules) are, located inside the PCM, provides grounds for output circuits that control various devices. Each output has an internal feedback circuit that connects to the PCM. The ODM 2 monitors the voltage and current condition on circuits that could cause damage to the PCM. The PCM monitors the voltage through the ignition 1 circuit for an incorrect current value to the ODM 2. **Possible Causes:** • EGR solenoid control circuit open, shorted to ground or to B+ • TCC solenoid control circuit is open, shorted to ground or to B+ • EGR or TCC solenoid is damaged or has failed • PCM has failed
DTC: P1658 **1T CCM, MIL: Yes** **Years:** 2005, 2006, 2007 **Models:** Sierra, Silverado **Engines:** 6.6L Diesel **Transmissions:** All	**Fuel Injection Control Module Internal Malfunction** U1800, U2104 and U2106 not set; key on or engine running, and the FICM detected current through one of the Fuel Injector Control Module (FICM) internal drivers with that particular driver turned "off". **Possible Causes:** • FICM has failed. There is no external failure that can cause DTC P1658 to set. This code is due to an internal circuit failure (i.e., this code indicates a FICM replacement).

DTC	Trouble Code Title, Conditions & Possible Causes
DTC: P1660 **1T CCM, MIL: Yes** **Years:** 2005, 2006, 2007 **Models:** G6, GTO, LaCrosse, Malibu, Relay, Rendezvous **Engines:** 2.2L, 2.4L, 3.4L, 3.5L, 3.6L, 3.8L, 3.9L, 3.9L **Transmissions:** All	**Output Driver 3 Input Voltage High Input** Key on or engine running; and the PCM detected an unexpected high voltage condition (over 33 volts) on the Output Driver 3 circuit. The ODM (modules) are, located inside the PCM, provides grounds for output circuits that control various devices. Each output has an internal feedback circuit that connects to the PCM. The ODM 3 monitors the voltage and current condition on circuits that could cause damage to the PCM. The PCM monitors voltage through the ignition 1 input. Any incorrect current detected on a circuit to the ODM 3 will cause the ODM to report this trouble code. **Possible Causes:** • Cooling fan relay control circuit is open or shorted to ground • Cooling fan relay control circuit is shorted to system power • Cooling fan relay power circuit is open (check the power fuse) • Cooling fan relay is damaged or has failed • PCM has failed
DTC: P1670 **1T CCM, MIL: No** **Years:** 2005, 2006, 2007 **Models:** G6, GTO, LaCrosse, Malibu, Relay, Rendezvous **Engines:** 2.2L, 2.4L, 3.4L, 3.5L, 3.6L, 3.9L, 3.9L **Transmissions:** All	**Output Driver 4 Input Voltage High Input** Key on or engine running; and the PCM detected an unexpected high voltage condition (over 33 volts) on the Output Driver 4 circuit. The ODM (modules) are, located inside the PCM, provides grounds for output circuits that control various devices. Each output has an internal feedback circuit that connects to the PCM. The ODM 4 monitors the voltage and current condition on circuits that could cause damage to the PCM. The PCM monitors voltage through the ignition 1 input. Any incorrect current detected on a circuit to the ODM 4 will cause the ODM to report this trouble code. **Possible Causes:** • A/C relay control, Fan 1 or Fan 2 control circuit is open, shorted to ground or to power • MIL (lamp) control circuit is open, shorted to ground or to B+ • A/C Relay, Fan 1, Fan 2 and MIL power circuit(s) are open • Check for a possible battery over-charge condition • PCM has failed
DTC: P1680 **1T PCM, MIL: Yes** **Years:** 2005, 2006, 2007 **Models:** All **Engines:** All **Transmissions:** All	**Powertrain Control Module Internal Malfunction** Key on, and the PCM detected an internal malfunction had occurred. **Possible Causes:** • Clear the codes and then recheck for this trouble code. If the same code resets, the PCM is damaged and must be replaced (and the new PCM must be programmed) to repair this code.
DTC: P1681 **1T PCM, MIL: Yes** **Years:** 2005, 2006, 2007 **Models:** Sierra, Silverado **Engines:** 4.3L, 4.8L, 5.3L, 6.0L, 6.2L, 8.1L **Transmissions:** All	**Powertrain Control Module Internal Malfunction** Key on, and the PCM detected an internal malfunction had occurred. **Possible Causes:** • Clear the codes and then recheck for this trouble code. If the same code resets, the PCM is damaged and must be replaced (and the new PCM must be programmed) to repair this code.
DTC: P1683 **1T PCM, MIL: Yes** **Years:** 2005, 2006, 2007 **Models:** All **Engines:** All **Transmissions:** All	**Powertrain Control Module Internal Malfunction** Key on, and the PCM detected an internal malfunction had occurred. **Possible Causes:** • Clear the codes and then recheck for this trouble code. If the same code resets, the PCM is damaged and must be replaced (and the new PCM must be programmed) to repair this code.
DTC: P1810 **2T CCM, MIL: Yes** **Years:** 2005, 2006, 2007 **Models:** Sierra, Silverado **Engines:** 4.3L, 4.8L, 5.3L, 6.0L, 6.2L, 6.6L Diesel, 8.1L **Transmissions:** A/T	**TFP Valve Position Switch Assembly (4L60-E, 4L65-E, 4L80-E)** DTC P0502 and P0503 not set, system voltage over 10.0v, engine running for 5 seconds, Fuel Cutoff inactive, engine torque from 40-400 ft-lbs, engine vacuum from 0-105 kPa, then during Condition 1 the PCM detected an illegal TFP manual valve position switch state for 60 seconds; or during Condition 2 with the engine speed less than 80 RPM for 0.1 second, then the engine speed from 80-550 RPM for 100 ms, then the engine speed was greater than 550 RPM; then the vehicle speed was less than 2 MPH, and the PCM detected the gear range was D2, D4 or Reverse during startup for 5 seconds; or during Condition 3 with the TP angle from 10-50%, fourth gear commanded "on", TCC engaged, speed ratio from 0.6-0.75, and the PCM detected the gear range indicated Park or Neutral with the vehicle is operating in D4 for 10 seconds. The TFP manual valve position switch assembly cannot distinguish between P/N because the monitored valve body pressures are identical in both cases. **Possible Causes:** • TFP valve position switch signal circuit is open, grounded or shorted to another signal • TFP valve position switch is damaged or has failed • This code can set during fluid refilling. After refilling the fluid, cycle the key "off", then idle the engine for 20 seconds. Turn the key "off" and Allow the PCM to power down. • This code can set due to low pump pressure or due to a stuck pressure regulator. • This code can set due to a rolled forward clutch piston seal. It may Allow the PCM to see a 2.08:1 ratio (reverse) when the manual valve position is actually indicated in D4. • PCM has failed

DTC	Trouble Code Title, Conditions & Possible Causes
DTC: P1815 **1T CCM, MIL: No** **Years:** 2005, 2006, 2007 **Models:** G6, GTO, LaCrosse, Malibu, Relay, Rendezvous **Engines:** 2.2L, 2.4L, 3.4L, 3.5L, 3.6L, 3.9L, 3.9L **Transmissions:** All	**A/T Range Sensor Circuit Malfunction (4T40-E/4T45-E)** DTC P0502, P0503, P0716, P0717 and P1810 not set, engine started, engine speed in transition from 0 RPM to over 600 RPM, vehicle speed less than 5 MPH, and the PCM detected that gear shift position D2, D4 or Reverse was indicated for 250 ms after startup. **Possible Causes:** • TFP manual valve position switch circuits are open or shorted • TFP manual valve position switch is damaged or it has failed • Transmission gear selector linkage is out of adjustment • PCM has failed
DTC: P1819 **1T CCM, MIL: No** **Years:** 2005, 2006, 2007 **Models:** G6, GTO, LaCrosse, Malibu, Relay, Rendezvous **Engines:** 2.2L, 2.4L, 3.4L, 3.5L, 3.6L, 3.8L, 3.9L, 3.9L **Transmissions:** All	**Internal Mode Switch - No Start (4T65-E)** Engine cranking, system voltage over 10.0v, and the PCM detected an invalid combination from the IMS switch, or a set of signals that indicated a transitional state between gear positions for 500 ms. **Possible Causes:** • Inspect the transmission linkage from the range selector to the manual shift shaft for proper adjustment • TFP valve position switch signal circuit is open or grounded • TFP valve position switch circuit shorted to another signal • TFP valve position switch is damaged or has failed • PCM has failed
DTC: P1820 **1T CCM, MIL: No** **Years:** 2005, 2006, 2007 **Models:** G6, GTO, LaCrosse, Malibu, Relay, Rendezvous **Engines:** 2.2L, 2.4L, 3.4L, 3.5L, 3.6L, 3.9L, 3.9L **Transmissions:** All	**Internal Mode Switch Circuit 'A' Low (4T65-E)** DTC P0107 and P0108 not set, engine speed over 500 RPM for 5 seconds, system voltage over 10.0v, Fuel Shutoff not active, and the PCM detected the IMS 'A' signal was in a continuously low state, and the IMS indicated Park for 2 seconds, then the IMS indicated transitional position D4-D3 with the engine torque from 70-300 lb ft., with no engine torque defaults detected for 6 seconds. **Possible Causes:** • IMS Signal 'A' circuit is shorted to ground • The lever assembly-manual shaft detent with internal mode switch may be damaged or have failed • Transmission has internal problems (it may need an overhaul) • PCM has failed
DTC: P1822 **1T CCM, MIL: No** **Years:** 2005, 2006, 2007 **Models:** G6, GTO, LaCrosse, Malibu, Relay, Rendezvous **Engines:** 2.2L, 2.4L, 3.4L, 3.5L, 3.6L, 3.9L, 3.9L **Transmissions:** All	**Internal Mode Switch 'B' Circuit Low Input (4T65-E)** DTC P0107 and P0108 not set, system voltage from 9-18v, engine speed at least 500 RPM for 5 seconds, Fuel Shutoff inactive, and the PCM detected that the Internal Mode Switch 'B' signal was in a continuously high state for the current key cycle, and that the IMS indicated Park for 2 seconds, then the IMS indicated transitional position D2-D1 and the engine torque was 70-300 ft-lbs with no engine torque defaults for 6 seconds. **Possible Causes:** • IMS Signal 'B' circuit is open or has a high resistance condition • Transmission has internal problems / may need an overhaul
DTC: P1823 **1T CCM, MIL: No** **Years:** 2005, 2006, 2007 **Models:** G6, GTO, LaCrosse, Malibu, Relay, Rendezvous **Engines:** 2.2L, 2.4L, 3.4L, 3.5L, 3.6L, 3.9L, 3.9L **Transmissions:** A/T	**Internal Mode Switch 'P' Circuit Low Input (4T65-E)** DTC P0107 and P0108 not set, engine started, engine speed over 500 RPM for 5 seconds, system voltage over 10.0v, Fuel Shutoff inactive, and the PCM detected the Internal Mode Switch 'P' signal was in a continuously low state for the current key cycle, and that the IMS indicated Park for 2 seconds, then the IMS indicated transitional position 'N' to D4 and the engine torque was 70-300 lb ft, with no engine torque defaults for 6 seconds during the CCM test. **Possible Causes:** • IMS Signal 'P' circuit is shorted to sensor or chassis ground • Transmission has internal problems / may need an overhaul
DTC: P1825 **1T CCM, MIL: No** **Years:** 2005, 2006, 2007 **Models:** G6, GTO, LaCrosse, Malibu, Relay, Rendezvous **Engines:** 2.2L, 2.4L, 3.4L, 3.5L, 3.6L, 3.9L, 3.9L **Transmissions:** A/T	**Internal Mode Switch - Invalid Range (4T65-E)** DTC P0107 and P0108 not set, engine started, engine speed over 500 RPM for 5 seconds, system voltage over 10.0v, Fuel Shutoff inactive, and the PCM detected an invalid combination of Internal Mode Switch signals for 500 ms during the CCM test. **Possible Causes:** • IMS Signal 'A', 'B', 'C' and 'P' possible short to ground condition • IMS Signal 'A', 'B', 'C' and 'P' possible open or high resistance • Transmission has internal problems / may need an overhaul • PCM has failed
DTC: P1826 **1T CCM, MIL: No** **Years:** 2005, 2006, 2007 **Models:** G6, GTO, LaCrosse, Malibu, Relay, Rendezvous **Engines:** 2.2L, 2.4L, 3.4L, 3.5L, 3.6L, 3.9L, 3.9L **Transmissions:** A/T	**Internal Mode Switch - Invalid Range (4T65-E)** DTC P0502 and P0503 not set, DTC P1826 has passed this key cycle, system voltage from 9-18v, engine speed at least 500 RPM for 5 seconds, Fuel Shutoff inactive, engine torque more than 20 ft-lbs, and the PCM detected that the Internal Mode Switch 'C' signal was in a high state while the gear ratio indicated 1st, 2nd or 3rd gear, condition met for 0.5 seconds. **Possible Causes:** • IMS Signal 'C' circuit is open or has a high resistance condition • Transmission has internal problems / may need an overhaul

DTC	Trouble Code Title, Conditions & Possible Causes
DTC: P1860 **1T CCM, MIL: Yes** **Years:** 2005, 2006, 2007 **Models:** G6, GTO, LaCrosse, Malibu, Relay, Rendezvous **Engines:** 2.2L, 2.4L, 3.4L, 3.5L, 3.6L, 3.9L, 3.9L **Transmissions:** A/T	**TCC PWM Solenoid Circuit Malfunction (4T60-E)** DTC P0560 not set, engine started, engine runtime over 5 seconds, Fuel Shutoff inactive, and the PCM detected an unexpected "low" voltage with a 10% command or an unexpected "high" voltage with a 95% command. The Torque Converter Clutch (TCC) PWM solenoid controls fluid acting on the converter clutch valve. The clutch valve controls the application and release of the torque converter clutch. **Possible Causes:** • TCC solenoid control circuit is open or shorted to ground • TCC solenoid control circuit is shorted to system power (B+) • TCC solenoid power circuit is open (test ENG or TRANS fuse) • TCC solenoid is damaged or has failed • PCM has failed
DTC: P1860 **1T CCM, MIL: Yes** **Years:** 2005, 2006, 2007 **Models:** G6, GTO, LaCrosse, Malibu, Relay, Rendezvous **Engines:** 2.2L, 2.4L, 3.4L, 3.5L, 3.6L, 3.9L, 3.9L **Transmissions:** A/T	**TCC PWM Solenoid Circuit Malfunction (4T65-E)** Engine started, engine runtime over 5 seconds, Fuel Shutoff inactive, and the PCM detected an unexpected "low" voltage with a 10% command or unexpected "high" voltage with a 95% command. The Torque Converter Clutch (TCC) PWM solenoid controls fluid acting on the converter clutch valve. The clutch valve controls the application and release of the torque converter clutch. Ignition voltage is provided to the torque converter clutch (TCC) solenoid valve. The PCM controls the solenoid with a negative duty cycle in order to control application and release of the TCC. When the solenoid is commanded "off", the PCM senses high voltage. When it is commanded "on", the PCM senses low voltage **Possible Causes:** • TCC solenoid control circuit is open, shorted to ground or shorted to system power (B+) • TCC solenoid power circuit is open (check the TRANS fuse) • TCC solenoid is damaged or has failed • PCM has failed • TSB 02-07-30-022A contains a repair procedure for this code
DTC: P1860 **1T CCM, MIL: Yes** **Years:** 2005, 2006, 2007 **Models:** Sierra, Silverado **Engines:** 4.3L **Transmissions:** A/T	**TCM PWM Solenoid Circuit Malfunction (4L60-E)** Engine started, engine runtime over 5 seconds, system voltage over 10.0v, Fuel Cutoff inactive, 1st gear commanded "on", and the PCM detected a high voltage with the TCC solenoid commanded to 90%, or a low voltage with the TCC commanded to 0%. The TCC PWM solenoid controls fluid acting on the converter clutch valve that controls the application and release of the torque converter clutch. The solenoid attaches to the control valve body in the transmission. **Possible Causes:** • TCC solenoid control circuit is open or shorted to ground • TCC solenoid control circuit is shorted to system power (B+) • TCC solenoid power circuit is open (test TRANS or IGN fuse) • TCC solenoid is damaged or has failed • PCM has failed
DTC: P1860 **1T CCM, MIL: Yes** **Years:** 2005, 2006, 2007 **Models:** Sierra, Silverado **Engines:** 4.3L, 4.8L, 5.3L, 6.0L, 6.2L, 8.1L **Transmissions:** A/T	**TCM PWM Solenoid Circuit Malfunction (4L60-E, 4L65-E, 4L80-E)** Engine started, engine runtime over 5 seconds, system voltage over 10.0v, Fuel Cutoff inactive, 1st gear commanded "on", and the PCM detected a high voltage with the TCC solenoid commanded to 90%, or a low voltage with the TCC commanded to 0%. The TCC PWM solenoid controls fluid acting on the converter clutch valve that controls the application and release of the torque converter clutch. The solenoid attaches to the control valve body in the transmission. **Possible Causes:** • TCC solenoid control circuit is open or shorted to ground • TCC solenoid control circuit is shorted to system power (B+) • TCC solenoid power circuit is open (test TRANS or IGN fuse) • TCC solenoid is damaged or has failed • PCM has failed
DTC: P1860 **2T CCM, MIL: Yes** **Years:** 2005, 2006, 2007 **Models:** G6, GTO, LaCrosse, Malibu, Relay, Rendezvous **Engines:** 2.2L, 2.4L, 3.4L, 3.5L, 3.6L, 3.9L, 3.9L **Transmissions:** A/T	**TCC PWM Solenoid Electrical (4T40/4T45-E)** Engine runtime over 5 seconds, system voltage over 10.0v, Fuel Cutoff inactive, 1st gear commanded "on", and the PCM detected a high voltage with the TCC solenoid commanded to 90%, or a low voltage with the TCC commanded to 0%. The TCC PWM solenoid controls fluid acting on the converter clutch valve that controls the application and release of the torque converter clutch. The solenoid attaches to the control valve body in the transmission. **Possible Causes:** • TCC solenoid control circuit is open, shorted to ground or shorted to system power (B+) • TCC solenoid power circuit is open (check the TRANS fuse) • TCC solenoid is damaged or has failed • PCM has failed • TSB 02-07-30-022A contains a repair procedure for this code

DTC	Trouble Code Title, Conditions & Possible Causes
DTC: P1870 **1T CCM, MIL: Yes** **Years:** 2005, 2006, 2007 **Models:** G6, GTO, LaCrosse, Malibu, Relay, Rendezvous **Engines:** 2.2L, 2.4L, 3.4L, 3.5L, 3.6L, 3.9L, 3.9L **Transmissions:** A/T	**Transaxle Component Slipping (4T60-E)** DTC P0502, P0503, P0740, P0753, P0758, P0785 and P1860 not set, engine started, vehicle driven to a speed of 30-82 MPH at an engine speed of 1000-3000 RPM, Fuel Shutoff inactive, TP angle from 8-35%, Transaxle not in First gear, Transaxle gear range is D4, TFT sensor 68°F-266°F, engine torque from 50-200 lb ft, engine vacuum 0-105 kPa, TCC commanded "on" with maximum apply for 5 seconds, and the PCM detected the TCC slip speed was from 200-1500 RPM for over 5 seconds. The fault must be detected three times with the TCC commanded "off" each time in between cycles. **Possible Causes:** • Check the ATF level and condition (look for burnt fluid) • Transmission may have internal damage (a mechanical fault)
DTC: P1870 **1T CCM, MIL: Yes** **Years:** 2005, 2006, 2007 **Models:** Sierra, Silverado **Engines:** All **Transmissions:** A/T	**Transmission Component Slipping (4L60-E, 4L65-E, 4L80-E)** DTC P0122, P0123, P0502, P0503, P0711-P0713, P0740, P0753, P0758, P1810 and P1860 not set, vehicle driven at a speed of 30-70 MPH at an engine speed of 1500-3000 RPM, Fuel Cutoff inactive, TP angle from 9-35%, engine vacuum 0-150 kPa, speed ratio is 0.69-0.88, Transmission not 1st gear, gear range is D4, TFT sensor from 68°F-266°F, shift solenoid diagnostic counter at zero, then with the TCC solenoid commanded "on" at a 95% duty cycle for 5 seconds, the PCM detected the TCC slip speed was 130-180 RPM for 7 seconds. The fault must be detected three times with the TCC commanded "off" each time between cycles. **Possible Causes:** • 1-2 shift solenoid valve has sediment, damage or leaking seals • 2-3 shift solenoid valve has sediment, damage or leaking seals • 3-2 shift solenoid valve has sediment, damage or leaking seals • Valve body regulator apply valve stuck or regulator is scored • Torque converter front stator shaft bushing is worn, the stator roller clutch is not holding or it has external damage/leaks • Converter clutch valve is stuck or it is installed backwards • Converter clutch valve retaining ring is not positioned properly • Converter clutch outer valve spring is cocked • Pump to case gasket is not positioned properly • Orifice cup plugs are restricted or damaged • Over-tightened, or unevenly tightened pump body to cover bolts • TSB 02-07-30-001 contains a repair procedure for this code
DTC: P1875 **2T CCM, MIL: Yes** **Years:** 2005, 2006, 2007 **Models:** Sierra, Silverado **Engines:** All **Transmissions:** A/T	**4WD Low Switch Circuit Fault (4L60-E, 4L65-E, 4L80-E)** DTC P0122, P0123, P0502, P0503, P0740, P0742, P0751, P0752, P0756, P0758, P1810, P1860 and P1870 not set, engine started, vehicle driven to a speed over 7 MPH for 5 seconds, gear range is D4, Fuel Cutoff not active, TP angle from 17-50%, engine torque from 50-400 lb ft, engine vacuum from 0-105 kPa, shift solenoid performance counters at zero, TFT sensor from 68-266°F, then during Condition 1 with the 4WD Low switch in 4WD low, transfer case not in 4WD low, TCC slip speed from −3000 to −50 RPM, the PCM detected the speed ratio was 0.8-1.2; or during Condition 2 with the 4WD Low switch not in 4WD low, transfer case in 4WD low, TCC commanded "on", TCC slip speed was 100 to 3000 RPM, the PCM detected the speed ratio was 2.5-2.9 for 10 seconds. **Possible Causes:** • 4WD low switch signal circuit is open, shorted to ground or B+ • 4WD low switch is damaged or has failed • PCM has failed
DTC: P1887 **2T CCM, MIL: Yes** **Years:** 2005, 2006, 2007 **Models:** G6, GTO, LaCrosse, Malibu, Relay, Rendezvous **Engines:** 2.2L, 2.4L, 3.4L, 3.5L, 3.6L, 3.9L, 3.9L **Transmissions:** A/T	**TCC Release Switch Circuit Malfunction (4T65-E)** DTC P0716, P0717, P0741, P0742 and P1810 not set, engine started, Fuel Cutoff inactive, engine driven to a speed of 30-70 MPH, engine torque from 30-300 lb ft, Transmission gear is D4 with the TCC commanded "on", TCC pressure from 15-120 psi, TCC slip speed from −20 to +60 RPM, and the PCM detected the pressure switch was open for 6 seconds. The fault must occur twice in 1 trip to set this code. The TCC release switch is normally closed (N.C.) switch that signals the PCM that the TCC is released. This is accomplished by torque converter release fluid pressure acting on the switch contacts that open the circuit. When the circuit voltage is high, the PCM detects the TCC is no longer engaged. If the PCM determines the TCC release switch is open (indicating the TCC is not applied) and the TCC slip speed indicates the TCC is applied, then DTC P1887 sets **Possible Causes:** • TCC release switch signal circuit is open • Turbine shaft O-ring seal leaks, oil seal rings missing/damaged. • TCC control valve damaged or No. 1 check ball is damaged • Spacer plate release exhaust blocked or case cover or spacer plate gaskets damaged • TSB 02-07-30-022A contains a repair procedure for this code

OBD II Trouble Code List (P2xxx Codes)

DTC	Trouble Code Title, Conditions & Possible Causes
DTC: P2008 **1T CCM, MIL: No** **Years:** 2005, 2006, 2007 **Models:** SRX **Engines:** 3.6L, 3.9L **Transmissions:** All	**Intake Manifold Runner Control (IMRC) Solenoid Control Circuit** The ignition is ON or the engine is operating. The IMRC solenoid has been commanded ON and OFF at least once during the ignition cycle. The ECM detects that the commanded state of the driver and the actual state of the control circuit do not match for more than a cumulative of 50 seconds. **Possible Causes:** • Ignition voltage circuit of the IMRC solenoid has a short to ground or an open/high resistance • short to ground on the control circuit • short to voltage or an open/high resistance on the control circuit • open/high resistance in the ground circuit of the IMRC solenoid • Failed IMRC solenoid • Failed ECM
DTC: P2009 **1T CCM, MIL: No** **Years:** 2005, 2006, 2007 **Models:** SRX **Engines:** 3.6L, 3.9L **Transmissions:** All	**Intake Manifold Runner Control (IMRC) Solenoid Control Circuit Low Voltage** The ignition is ON or the engine is operating. The IMRC solenoid has been commanded ON and OFF at least once during the ignition cycle. The ECM detects that the commanded state of the driver and the actual state of the control circuit do not match for more than a cumulative of 50 seconds. **Possible Causes:** • Ignition voltage circuit of the IMRC solenoid has a short to ground or an open/high resistance • short to ground on the control circuit • short to voltage or an open/high resistance on the control circuit • open/high resistance in the ground circuit of the IMRC solenoid • Failed IMRC solenoid • Failed ECM
DTC: P2010 **1T CCM, MIL: No** **Years:** 2005, 2006, 2007 **Models:** SRX **Engines:** 3.6L, 3.9L **Transmissions:** All	**Intake Manifold Runner Control (IMRC) Solenoid Control Circuit High Voltage** The ignition is ON or the engine is operating. The IMRC solenoid has been commanded ON and OFF at least once during the ignition cycle. The ECM detects that the commanded state of the driver and the actual state of the control circuit do not match for more than a cumulative of 50 seconds. **Possible Causes:** • Ignition voltage circuit of the IMRC solenoid has a short to ground or an open/high resistance • short to ground on the control circuit • short to voltage or an open/high resistance on the control circuit • open/high resistance in the ground circuit of the IMRC solenoid • Failed IMRC solenoid • Failed ECM
DTC: P2066 **1T CCM, MIL: No** **Years:** 2005, 2006, 2007 **Models:** Sierra, Silverado **Engines:** 6.0L **Transmissions:** All	**Secondary Fuel Sensor Signal Range/Performance** Engine started; and the PCM did not detect a change in the Secondary fuel level of at least 0.79 gallon after the vehicle traveled a distance of 200 miles. Low fuel indicator will be "on". **Possible Causes:** • Perform the I/P Cluster Diagnostic System Check • Check the fuel tank for signs of foreign material (i.e., ice) • Fuel level sender is malfunctioning (check the fuel strainer to determine if it is interfering with the sender float arm - sticking) • Fuel level sensor is damaged or it has failed
DTC: P2067 **1T CCM, MIL: No** **Years:** 2005, 2006, 2007 **Models:** Sierra, Silverado **Engines:** 6.0L **Transmissions:** All	**Secondary Fuel Level Sensor Circuit Low Input** Key on or engine running; and the PCM detected that the Secondary fuel level sensor indicated less than 3.5% for 20 seconds. **Possible Causes:** • Perform the I/P Cluster Diagnostic System Check • Fuel level sensor connector is damaged or shorted • Fuel level sensor signal circuit is shorted to ground • Fuel level sensor is damaged or it has failed
DTC: P2068 **1T CCM, MIL: No** **Years:** 2005, 2006, 2007 **Models:** Sierra, Silverado **Engines:** 6.0L **Transmissions:** All	**Secondary Fuel Level Sensor Circuit High Input** Key on or engine running; and the PCM detected that the Secondary fuel level sensor indicated more than 98% for 20 seconds. **Possible Causes:** • Perform the I/P Cluster Diagnostic System Check • Fuel level sensor connector is damaged, open or shorted • Fuel level sensor signal circuit is open or shorted to power • Fuel level sensor is damaged or it has failed

DTC	Trouble Code Title, Conditions & Possible Causes
DTC: P2101 **1T CCM, MIL: Yes** **Years:** 2005, 2006, 2007 **Models:** LaCrosse, Sky **Engines:** 2.4L, 3.8L **Transmissions:** All	**TAC Module Throttle Actuator Position Performance** The ignition is in the crank or run position. The system is not in Battery Saver mode. The ignition voltage is more than 5.23 volts. The communication between the TAC module and the PCM must be valid. The TAC module detects that the commanded and actual throttle positions are not within a calibrated range of each other., or, TAC module or the PCM cannot determine throttle position. **Possible Causes:** • Mechanical conditions causing binding (may be temperature related) • ETC ignition 1 voltage circuit high resistance • Throttle body has failed
DTC: P2107 **1T CCM, MIL: Yes** **Years:** 2005, 2006, 2007 **Models:** LaCrosse, Sky **Engines:** 2.4L, 3.8L **Transmissions:** All	**Throttle Actuator Control (TAC) Module Internal Circuit** DTCs P0606, P2108, and U0107 are not set. The ignition is in the crank or run position. If the TAC module detects low voltage, a fault with the EEPROM or vehicle ID recorded in the TAC module does not match the vehicle ID recorded in the PCM. If the DTC is determined to be intermittent, reviewing the Failure Records can be useful in determining when the DTC was last set. **Possible Causes:** • Throttle body failed
DTC: P2108 **1T CCM, MIL: Yes** **Years:** 2005, 2006, 2007 **Models:** LaCrosse, Sky **Engines:** 2.4L, 3.8L **Transmissions:** All	**Throttle Actuator Control (TAC) Module Performance** The ignition is in the crank or run position. The ignition voltage is more than 5.23 volts. The communication between the TAC module and the powertrain control module (PCM) must be valid. The TAC module determines that an internal data test did not pass. **Possible Causes:** • Throttle body is damaged or it has failed
DTC: P2108 **1T CCM, MIL: Yes** **Years:** 2005, 2006, 2007 **Models:** Sierra, Silverado **Engines:** 4.3L, 4.8L, 5.3L, 6.0L, 6.2L, 8.1L **Transmissions:** All	**Throttle Actuator Control Module Internal Data Test Failed** DTCP1518 not set, engine cranking or running, system voltage over 6.0v, and the TAC determined that its internal data test did not pass, condition met for 1 second. The TAC module contains data that is essential for proper TAC system operation. The TAC module continuously tests the integrity of this data. When the TAC module is unable to write or read data to and from random access memory, or the TAC module was unable to correctly read data from the flash memory or internal TAC processor fault is detected, it sets P2108. **Possible Causes:** • TAC module is damaged or it has failed
DTC: P2119 **1T CCM, MIL: Yes** **Years:** 2005, 2006, 2007 **Models:** LaCrosse, Sky **Engines:** 2.4L, 3.8L **Transmissions:** All	**TAC Module Throttle Actuator Position Performance** DTC P0068 is not set. Engine running. The system is not in the Battery Save mode The ECM determines that the throttle blade did not return to the rest position within 720 milliseconds **Possible Causes:** • Throttle blade not at rest, binding open or closed • Motor control circuit for a short to voltage or short to ground • Motor control 1 circuit has open or high resistance • Throttle actuator motor control module has failed • Throttle body has failed • ECM has failed
DTC: P2120 **1T CCM, MIL: Yes** **Years:** 2005, 2006, 2007 **Models:** LaCrosse, Sky **Engines:** 2.4L, 3.8L **Transmissions:** All	**Accelerator Pedal Position Sensor 1 Signal Performance** DTC P2107 is not set. The ignition is ON. The ignition voltage is more than 5.23 volts. The APP sensor 1 voltage is less than 0.235 volt or more than 4.487 volts, or, APP sensor 2 5-volt reference voltage is less than 4.54 volts or more than 5.21 volts. **Possible Causes:** • APP sensor connector is damaged, open or shorted • APP1 sensor signal circuit is open or shorted to ground • APP1 sensor signal circuit is shorted to APP sensor 2 circuit • APP1 sensor signal circuit is open or shorted to VREF (5v) • APP sensor is damaged or it has failed • TAC module is damaged or it has failed

DTC	Trouble Code Title, Conditions & Possible Causes
DTC: P2120 **1T CCM, MIL: Yes** **Years:** 2005, 2006, 2007 **Models:** All **Engines:** All **Transmissions:** All	**Accelerator Pedal Position Sensor 1 Signal Performance** DTC P0601, P0602, P0606, P1518 and P2108 not set; engine cranking or running, system voltage more than 5.23v, and the PCM detected the APP Sensor 1 signal circuit voltage was less than 0.24v or more than 4.49v, or that the APP VREF (5v) circuit was less than 4.54v or more than 5.21v. The PCM provides the APP sensor with a 5v reference circuit and a low reference circuit. The APP sensor provides the control module a signal voltage proportional to pedal movement. The APP sensor 1 signal voltage is low at rest and increases as the pedal is depressed. When the control module detects that the APP sensor 1 signal or APP sensor 5-volt reference voltage is outside the predetermined range, it sets DTC P2120. **Possible Causes:** • APP sensor connector is damaged, open or shorted • APP1 sensor signal circuit is open or shorted to ground • APP1 sensor signal circuit is shorted to APP sensor 2 circuit • APP1 sensor signal circuit is open or shorted to VREF (5v) • APP sensor is damaged or it has failed • TAC module is damaged or it has failed
DTC: P2121 **1T CCM, MIL: Yes** **Years:** 2005, 2006, 2007 **Models:** All **Engines:** All **Transmissions:** All	**Accelerator Pedal Position Sensor 1-2 Correlation Malfunction** DTC P0606, P1518 and P2108 not set, engine cranking or running, system voltage over 5.23v, and the PCM detected the APP Sensor 1 signal disagreed with the APP Sensor 2 signal by over 10.5% for 1 second. The PCM provides the APP sensor with a 5v reference circuit and a low reference circuit. The APP sensor provides the PCM a signal proportional to pedal movement. The APP sensor 1 signal voltage is low at rest and increases as the pedal is depressed. When the control module detects that the APP sensor 1 signal or APP sensor 5-volt reference voltage is outside the predetermined range, it sets DTC P2120. **Possible Causes:** • APP sensor connector is damaged, open or shorted • APP1 sensor low reference circuit is open or high resistance • APP1 sensor VREF circuit is open or shorted to ground • APP sensor is damaged or it has failed • TAC module is damaged or it has failed
DTC: P2121 **1T CCM, MIL: No** **Years:** 2005, 2006, 2007 **Models:** Sierra, Silverado **Engines:** 6.6L Diesel **Transmissions:** All	**Accelerator Pedal Position Sensor 1 Low Input** DTC P0641 and P0651 not set, engine cranking or running, and the ECM detected the APP Sensor 1 was less than 0.25v. The accelerator pedal position (APP) sensor is made up of 3 individual sensors in a single housing. Three separate signal, low reference, and 5-volt reference circuits are used in order to interface the APP sensor with the ECM. Each sensor has a unique functionality to determine the pedal position. The ECM uses the APP sensor to determine the desired amount of acceleration or deceleration. **Possible Causes:** • APP sensor connector is damaged or shorted • APP sensor 1 signal circuit is open or shorted to ground • APP sensor is damaged or it has failed • ECM has failed
DTC: P2123 **1T CCM, MIL: Yes** **Years:** 2005, 2006, 2007 **Models:** All **Engines:** All **Transmissions:** All	**Accelerator Pedal Position Sensor 1 High Input** DTC P0641 and P0651 not set; engine cranking or running and the ECM detected the APP Sensor 1was more than 4.75v. The accelerator pedal position (APP) sensor is made up of 3 individual sensors in a single housing. Three separate signal, low reference, and 5-volt reference circuits are used in order to interface the APP sensor with the ECM. Each sensor has a unique functionality to determine the pedal position. The ECM uses the APP sensor to determine the desired amount of acceleration or deceleration. **Possible Causes:** • APP sensor 1 signal circuit is shorted to VREF • APP sensor low reference circuit is open or shorted to VREF • APP sensor is damaged or it has failed • ECM has failed
DTC: P2125 **1T CCM, MIL: Yes** **Years:** 2005, 2006, 2007 **Models:** G6, GTO, LaCrosse, Malibu, Montana, Montana SV6, Relay, Rendezvous, Sky, Solstice, SRX, Terraza, Uplander, Vibe **Engines:** 1.8L, 2.0L, 2.2L, 2.4L, 3.4L, 3.5L, 3.6L, 3.9L, 4.6L, 6.0L **Transmissions:** All	**Accelerator Pedal Position Sensor 2 Circuit Malfunction** DTC P2107 is not set. The ignition is ON. The ignition voltage is more than 5.23 volts. The APP sensor 2 voltage is less than 0.235 volt or more than 4.487 volts, or, APP sensor 2 5-volt reference voltage is less than 4.54 volts or more than 5.21 volts. **Possible Causes:** • APP2 sensor voltage out of range (0.24-2.0 volts) • APP2 sensor signal circuit is shorted • APP2 sensor signal circuit is open or shorted to VREF (5v) • APP sensor is damaged, or the TAC module is damaged or it has failed

DTC	Trouble Code Title, Conditions & Possible Causes
DTC: P2125 **1T CCM, MIL: Yes** **Years:** 2005, 2006, 2007 **Models:** Sierra, Silverado **Engines:** 4.3L, 4.8L, 5.3L, 6.0L, 6.2L, 8.1L **Transmissions:** All	**Accelerator Pedal Position Sensor 2 Circuit Malfunction** DTC P0601, P0602, P0606, P1518 and P2108 not set, engine cranking or running, system voltage over 5.23v, and the PCM detected the APP Sensor 1 signal was less than 0.24v or more than 4.49v, or the APP VREF (5v) circuit was less than 4.54v or more than 5.21v. The APP sensor provides the ECM with a signal voltage proportional to pedal movement. The APP sensor 1 is low at rest and increases as the pedal is depressed. **Possible Causes:** • APP2 sensor signal circuit is open or shorted to ground • APP2 sensor signal circuit is shorted to APP sensor 2 circuit • APP2 sensor signal circuit is open or shorted to VREF (5v) • APP sensor is damaged, or the TAC module is damaged or it has failed
DTC: P2127 **1T CCM, MIL: Yes** **Years:** 2005, 2006, 2007 **Models:** All **Engines:** All **Transmissions:** All	**Accelerator Pedal Position Sensor 2 Low Input** DTC P0641 and P0651 not set; engine cranking or running, and the ECM detected the APP Sensor 2 was less than 0.25v. The accelerator pedal position (APP) sensor is made up of 3 individual sensors in a single housing. Three separate signal, low reference, and 5-volt reference circuits are used in order to interface the APP sensor with the ECM. Each sensor has a unique functionality to determine the pedal position. The ECM uses the APP sensor to determine the amount of desired acceleration or deceleration. **Possible Causes:** • APP sensor connector is damaged or shorted • APP sensor 2 signal circuit is open or shorted to ground • APP sensor is damaged or it has failed • ECM has failed
DTC: P2128 **1T CCM, MIL: Yes** **Years:** 2005, 2006, 2007 **Models:** All **Engines:** All **Transmissions:** All	**Accelerator Pedal Position Sensor 2 High Input** DTC P0641 and P0651 not se, engine cranking or running, and the ECM detected the APP Sensor 2 was more than 4.75v. The accelerator pedal position (APP) sensor is made up of 3 individual sensors in a single housing. Three separate signal, low reference, and 5-volt reference circuits are used to interface the APP sensor with the ECM. Each sensor has a unique functionality to determine the pedal position so that the ECM can determine the amount of acceleration or deceleration desired by the driver of the vehicle. **Possible Causes:** • APP sensor connector is damaged or shorted • APP sensor 2 signal circuit is open or shorted to ground • APP sensor is damaged or it has failed • ECM has failed
DTC: P2132 **1T CCM, MIL: Yes** **Years:** 2005, 2006, 2007 **Models:** Sierra, Silverado **Engines:** 6.6L Diesel **Transmissions:** All	**Accelerator Pedal Position Sensor 3 Low Input** DTC P0641 and P0651 not set; engine cranking or running; and the ECM detected the APP Sensor 3 was less than 1.49v. The accelerator pedal position (APP) sensor is made up of 3 individual sensors in a single housing. Three separate signal, low reference, and 5-volt reference circuits are used in order to interface the APP sensor with the ECM. Each sensor has a unique functionality to determine the pedal position. The ECM uses the APP sensor to determine the amount of desired acceleration or deceleration. **Possible Causes:** • APP sensor connector is damaged or shorted • APP sensor 3 signal circuit is open or shorted to ground • APP sensor is damaged or it has failed • ECM has failed
DTC: P2133 **1T CCM, MIL: Yes** **Years:** 2005, 2006, 2007 **Models:** Sierra, Silverado **Engines:** 6.6L Diesel **Transmissions:** All	**Accelerator Pedal Position Sensor 3 High Input** DTC P0641 and P0651 not se, engine cranking or running, and the ECM detected the APP Sensor 3 was more than 4.75v. The accelerator pedal position (APP) sensor is made up of 3 individual sensors in a single housing. Three separate signal, low reference, and 5-volt reference circuits are used to interface the APP sensor with the ECM. Each sensor has a unique functionality to determine the pedal position so that the ECM can determine the amount of acceleration or deceleration desired by the driver of the vehicle. **Possible Causes:** • APP sensor connector is damaged or shorted • APP sensor 3 signal circuit is open or shorted to ground • APP sensor is damaged or it has failed • ECM has failed

DTC	Trouble Code Title, Conditions & Possible Causes

DTC: P2135
1T CCM, MIL: Yes
Years: 2005, 2006, 2007
Models: G6, GTO, LaCrosse, Malibu, Montana, Montana SV6, Relay, Rendezvous, Sky, Solstice, SRX, Terraza, Uplander, Vibe
Engines: 1.8L, 2.0L, 2.2L, 2.4L, 3.4L, 3.5L, 3.6L, 3.9L, 4.6L, 6.0L
Transmissions: All
	Throttle Position Sensor 1-2 Correlation Error
	DTCs P0606, P2108, and U0107 are not set. The ignition switch is in the CRANK or RUN position. The ignition voltage is more than 5.23 volts. The communication between the TAC module and the PCM must be valid. The throttle position indicated by TP sensor 1 disagrees with the throttle position indicated by TP sensor 2 by more than 6 percent. Or, PCM learned minimum throttle position of TP sensor 1 disagrees with the learned minimum throttle position of TP sensor 2, or, PCM detects that the TP sensor 1 signal circuit is shorted to the TP sensor 2 signal circuit
	Possible Causes:
	  • TP1 sensor signal circuit shorted to TP sensor signal 2 circuit
	  • TP1 sensor signal circuit is shorted to the low reference circuit
	  • TP2 sensor signal circuit is shorted to the low reference circuit
	  • Throttle body assembly is damaged or it has failed

DTC: P2135
1T CCM, MIL: Yes
Years: 2005, 2006, 2007
Models: Sierra, Silverado
Engines: 4.3L, 4.8L, 5.3L, 6.0L, 6.2L, 8.1L
Transmissions: All
	Throttle Position Sensor 1-2 Correlation Error
	DTC P1518 and P2108 not set, key in crank or run mode, system voltage more than 5.23v, and the PCM detected the TP Sensor 2 signal disagreed with the TP Sensor 1 signal by more than 7.5% for one second. The TP sensors are used to determine the throttle plate angle for various engine management systems. The TP sensor signals are both low at closed throttle and increase as the throttle opens. When the PCM detects that TP sensor 1 and TP sensor 2 signals disagree or signal voltages are too far apart, this code is set.
	Possible Causes:
	  • TP1 sensor signal circuit shorted to TP sensor signal 2 circuit
	  • TP1 sensor signal circuit is shorted to the low reference circuit
	  • TP2 sensor signal circuit is shorted to the low reference circuit
	  • Throttle body assembly is damaged or it has failed

DTC: P2138
1T CCM, MIL: No
Years: 2005, 2006, 2007
Models: G6, GTO, LaCrosse, Malibu, Montana, Montana SV6, Relay, Rendezvous, Sky, Solstice, SRX, Terraza, Uplander, Vibe
Engines: 1.8L, 2.0L, 2.2L, 2.4L, 3.4L, 3.5L, 3.6L, 3.9L, 4.6L, 6.0L
Transmissions: All
	Accelerator Pedal Position Sensor 1-2 Correlation Error
	DTCs P2107 and P2108 are not set. The ignition is in the CRANK or RUN position. The ignition voltage is more than 5.23 volts. The communication between the throttle actuator control (TAC) module and the powertrain control module (PCM) must be valid. The PCM detects that the difference between APP sensor 1 and APP sensor 2 is more than the predicted value.
	Possible Causes:
	  • APP sensor 1 circuit short to the signal circuit of the APP sensor 2
	  • Intermittent or poor connection at the APP pedal assembly or throttle body assembly
	  • APP sensor failed
	  • ECM has failed

DTC: P2138
1T CCM, MIL: No
Years: 2005, 2006, 2007
Models: Sierra, Silverado
Engines: 6.6L Diesel
Transmissions: All
	Accelerator Pedal Position Sensor 1-2 Correlation Error
	DTC P0641, P0651, P2122, P2123, P2132 and P2133 not set, engine cranking or running, system voltage from 7-16v, and the ECM detected the APP Sensor 1 and APP Sensor 2 was more than 10% out-of-range with each other. The APP sensor is made up of 3 sensors in one housing that connect a signal, low reference, and 5v VREF circuit to the ECM. Each sensor has a unique functionality to detect the pedal position so that the ECM can determine the amount of acceleration or deceleration desired by the driver of the vehicle.
	Possible Causes:
	  • APP sensor 3 signal circuit is open or shorted to ground
	  • APP sensor is damaged or it has failed
	  • ECM has failed

DTC: P2139
1T CCM, MIL: No
Years: 2005, 2006, 2007
Models: Sierra, Silverado
Engines: 6.6L Diesel
Transmissions: All
	Accelerator Pedal Position Sensor 2-3 Correlation
	DTC P0641, P0651, P2122, P2123, P2132 and P2133 not set, engine cranking or running, system voltage from 7-16v, and the ECM detected the APP Sensor 2 and APP Sensor 3 were more than 10% out-of-range with each other. The APP sensor is made up of 3 sensors in one housing that connect a signal, low reference, and 5v VREF circuit to the ECM. Each sensor has a unique functionality to detect the pedal position so that the ECM can determine the amount of acceleration or deceleration desired by the driver of the vehicle.
	Possible Causes:
	  • APP2 or APP3 signal circuit has a high resistance condition
	  • APP2 VREF circuit has a high resistance condition
	  • APP sensor is damaged or it has failed
	  • ECM has failed

DTC: P2140
1T CCM, MIL: No
Years: 2005, 2006, 2007
Models: Sierra, Silverado
Engines: 6.6L Diesel
Transmissions: All
	Accelerator Pedal Position Sensor 1-3 Correlation
	DTC P0641, P0651, P2122, P2123, P2132 and P2133 not set, engine cranking or running, system voltage from 7-16v, and the PCM detected the APP Sensor 1 and APP Sensor 3 were over 10% out-of-range. The APP sensor includes 3 sensors in a single housing. Each sensor has a unique functionality to detect the pedal position so that the ECM can determine the amount of acceleration or deceleration desired by the driver of the vehicle.
	Possible Causes:
	  • If DTC P2138 is also set, refer to that code repair information
	  • If DTC P2139 is also set, refer to that code repair information

DTC	Trouble Code Title, Conditions & Possible Causes
DTC: P2141 **2T CCM, MIL: Yes** **Years:** 2005, 2006, 2007 **Models:** Sierra, Silverado **Engines:** 6.6L Diesel **Transmissions:** All	**EGR Throttle Valve Vacuum Control Solenoid Low Input** Key on for 500 ms, EGR Valve Throttle Vacuum Control solenoid commanded "off", system voltage from 11-18v, and the PCM detected a low voltage on the control circuit with the EGR throttle valve vacuum control solenoid commanded "off". Diesel engines do not create sufficient engine vacuum to Allow EGR gases into the combustion process. Once the ECM commands the EGR valve open, the EGR throttle valve is closed. **Possible Causes:** • EGR vacuum solenoid circuit is open or has high resistance • EGR vacuum solenoid power circuit is open (test Fuel HT fuse) • EGR valve throttle solenoid is damaged or it has failed • ECM has failed
DTC: P2142 **2T CCM, MIL: Yes** **Years:** 2005, 2006, 2007 **Models:** Sierra, Silverado **Engines:** 6.6L Diesel **Transmissions:** All	**EGR Throttle Valve Vacuum Control Solenoid High Input** Key on for 500 ms, EGR Valve Throttle Vacuum Control solenoid commanded "on", system voltage from 11-18v, and the PCM detected a high voltage on the control circuit with the EGR throttle valve vacuum control solenoid "on". Diesel engines do not create sufficient engine vacuum to Allow EGR gases into the combustion process. Once the PCM commands the EGR valve open, the EGR throttle valve is commanded closed. The EGR throttle valve creates a restriction in the incoming fresh air to create engine vacuum. With the EGR throttle valve closed, engine vacuum develops and Allows the exhaust gases to enter the engine. **Possible Causes:** • EGR vacuum solenoid control circuit is shorted to power (B+) • EGR vacuum solenoid power circuit is open (test Fuel HT fuse) • EGR valve throttle solenoid is damaged or it has failed • PCM has failed
DTC: P2144 **2T CCM, MIL: Yes** **Years:** 2005, 2006, 2007 **Models:** Sierra, Silverado **Engines:** 6.6L Diesel **Transmissions:** All	**EGR Vacuum Vent Solenoid Low Input** Key on for 500 ms, EGR Vacuum Vent solenoid commanded "off", system voltage from 11-18v, and the PCM detected a low voltage on the control circuit with the EGR vacuum vent solenoid commanded "off". Diesel engines do not create sufficient engine vacuum to Allow EGR gases into the combustion process. Once the PCM commands the EGR valve open, the EGR throttle valve is commanded closed. The EGR throttle valve creates a restriction in the incoming fresh air to create engine vacuum. With the EGR throttle valve closed, engine vacuum develops and Allows exhaust gases to enter the engine. **Possible Causes:** • EGR vacuum vent solenoid circuit open or has high resistance • EGR vacuum solenoid power circuit is open (test Fuel HT fuse) • EGR valve throttle solenoid is damaged or it has failed • ECM has failed
DTC: P2145 **2T CCM, MIL: Yes** **Years:** 2005, 2006, 2007 **Models:** Sierra, Silverado **Engines:** 6.6L Diesel **Transmissions:** All	**EGR Vacuum Vent Solenoid Low Input** Key on for 500 ms, EGR Vacuum Vent solenoid commanded "off", system voltage from 11-18v, and the ECM detected a low voltage condition on the control circuit of the EGR vacuum vent solenoid with the ECM with the EGR vacuum vent solenoid commanded "off". **Possible Causes:** • EGR vacuum vent solenoid connector is damaged or shorted • EGR vacuum vent solenoid circuit is shorted to system power • EGR vacuum vent solenoid is damaged or it has failed • ECM has failed
DTC: P2145 **2T CCM, MIL: Yes** **Years:** 2005, 2006, 2007 **Models:** Sierra, Silverado **Engines:** 6.6L Diesel **Transmissions:** All	**EGR Vacuum Vent Solenoid High Input** Key on for 500 ms, EGR Vacuum Vent solenoid commanded "on", system voltage from 11-18v, and the ECM detected a high voltage condition on the control circuit of the EGR vacuum vent solenoid with the ECM with the EGR vacuum vent solenoid commanded "on". **Possible Causes:** • EGR vacuum solenoid circuit has a high resistance condition • EGR vacuum solenoid power circuit is open (test Fuel HT fuse) • EGR valve throttle solenoid is damaged or it has failed • ECM has failed
DTC: P2146 **2T CCM, MIL: Yes** **Years:** 2005, 2006, 2007 **Models:** Sierra, Silverado **Engines:** 6.6L Diesel **Transmissions:** All	**Fuel Pump Relay Circuit Malfunction (Injectors 1, 4, 6 or 7)** DTC U1800 and U2104 not set; key on or engine running, and the PCM detected the Actual state of the Fuel Injector control circuit did not match the Commanded state for 5 seconds. The fuel injection control module (FICM) supplies high voltage to each fuel injector on the ignition voltage circuits. The FICM energizes each fuel injector by grounding the command circuit between the FICM and the fuel injector. The FICM monitors the status of the ignition voltage circuits and the fuel injector command circuits. When a fuel injector circuit fault condition is detected by the FICM, All of the fuel injectors on the affected ignition voltage circuit will be disabled. If a circuit condition is detected on a fuel injector circuit for cylinders 1, 4, 6, or 7, DTC P0201, P0204, P0206, P0207 will set, along with DTC P2146. **Possible Causes:** • Refer to repair information for P0201, P0204, P0206 or P0207 • FICM (module) has failed (when P2146 is set All by itself)

DTC	Trouble Code Title, Conditions & Possible Causes
DTC: P2149 **1T CCM, MIL: Yes** **Years:** 2005, 2006, 2007 **Models:** Sierra, Silverado **Engines:** 6.6L Diesel **Transmissions:** All	**Fuel Pump Relay Circuit Malfunction (Injectors 2, 3, 5 or 8)** U1800 and U2104 not set; engine started, and the PCM detected an unexpected voltage condition on a Fuel Injector control circuit for 5 seconds. The fuel injection control module (FICM) supplies high voltage to each fuel injector on the ignition voltage circuits. The FICM energizes each fuel injector by grounding the command circuit between the FICM and the fuel injector. The FICM monitors the status of the ignition voltage circuits and the fuel injector command circuits. When a fuel injector circuit fault condition is detected by the FICM, All of the fuel injectors on the affected ignition voltage circuit will be disabled. If a circuit condition is detected on a fuel injector circuit for cylinders 2, 3, 5, or 8, DTC P0202, P0203, P0205, P0208 will set, along with this trouble code (DTC P2149). **Possible Causes:** • Refer to repair information for P0202, P0203, P0205 or P0208 • FICM (module) has failed (when P2149 is set All by itself)
DTC: P2176 **1T CCM, MIL: Yes** **Years:** 2005, 2006, 2007 **Models:** Sky **Engines:** 2.4L **Transmissions:** All	**TAC Module Throttle Actuator Position Performance** DTC P0068 is not set. Engine running. The system is not in the Battery Save mode The difference between the predicted and the actual throttle position is more than a calibrated amount for more than 1.5 seconds. **Possible Causes:** • Throttle blade not at rest, binding open or closed • Motor control circuit for a short to voltage or short to ground • Motor control 1 circuit has open or high resistance • Throttle actuator motor control module has failed • Throttle body has failed • ECM has failed
DTC: P2227 **1T CCM, MIL: No** **Years:** 2005, 2006, 2007 **Models:** Sierra, Silverado **Engines:** 6.6L Diesel **Transmissions:** All	**BARO Sensor Signal Range/Performance** DTC P0101, P0102, P0103, P0116, P0117, P0118, P0236, P0237, P0238, P0335, P0336, P0500, P2228 and P2229 not set, engine speed at 500-900 RPM for 20 seconds, Accelerator pedal angle under 20%, ECT sensor over 176°F, VSS under 25 MPH, MAF sensor under 50 g/sec, Power Takeoff off, conditions met for 5 seconds, and the ECM detected the difference between the BARO and Boost Pressure sensor was 10-20 kPa for 2 seconds. **Possible Causes:** • BARO sensor signal circuit is shorted to VREF • BARO sensor is damaged or it has failed • ECM has failed
DTC: P2228 **2T CCM, MIL: Yes** **Years:** 2005, 2006, 2007 **Models:** Sierra, Silverado **Engines:** 6.6L Diesel **Transmissions:** All	**BARO Sensor Circuit Low Input** DTC P0461not set, key on, and the ECM detected the BARO sensor was less than 44 kPa for two seconds during the CCM test period. **Possible Causes:** • BARO sensor signal circuit is open or shorted to ground • BARO sensor is damaged or it has failed • ECM has failed
DTC: P2228 **2T CCM, MIL: Yes** **Years:** 2005, 2006, 2007 **Models:** Sierra, Silverado **Engines:** 6.6L Diesel **Transmissions:** All	**BARO Sensor Circuit High Input** DTC P0461not set, key on, and the ECM detected the BARO sensor was more than 110 kPa for two seconds during the CCM test period. **Possible Causes:** • BARO sensor signal circuit is shorted to VREF • BARO sensor is damaged or it has failed • ECM has failed
DTC: P2279 **2T CCM, MIL: Yes** **Years:** 2005, 2006, 2007 **Models:** Sierra, Silverado **Engines:** 6.6L Diesel **Transmissions:** All	**Air Intake Leak Detected** DTC P0101, P0102, P0103, P0112, P0113, P0116, P0117, P0118, P0405, P0406, P0489, P0490, P0500, P0651, P2141, P2142, P2144, P2145, P2227, P2228 and P2229 not set, engine runtime over 60 seconds, engine speed from 600-700 RPM, BARO sensor more than 72 kPa (10 psi), system voltage from 9-16v, vehicle speed less than 1 MPH, ECT sensor from 32-176°F, and the PCM detected an engine intake leak that was over the calibrated value stored in the PCM. The MAF sensor measures the amount of air that enters the engine at any given time. The PCM uses the MAF sensor to monitor the EGR flow rate. The PCM can detect an intake leak using the MAF sensor and EGR Control Pressure sensor signals. **Possible Causes:** • Air Intake Duct is leaking somewhere after the MAF sensor • Check for an air leak in Air Induction system after the MAF sensor, in the engine intake gaskets, or the EGR tower gasket

DTC	Trouble Code Title, Conditions & Possible Causes
DTC: P2430 **2T CCM, MIL: Yes** **Years:** 2005, 2006, 2007 **Models:** LaCrosse, Sky **Engines:** 2.4L, 3.8L **Transmissions:** All	**Secondary Air Injection (AIR) System Pressure Sensor Stuck in Range** DTCs P0412, P0418, P0606, P0641, P0651, P2432, P2433 are not set. The AIR pump is commanded ON. The start-up engine coolant temperature (ECT) is between 5-50°C (41-122°F). The start-up intake air temperature (IAT) is between 5-60°C (41-140°F). The measured AIR pressure change does not meet expected pressure changes during AIR pump phase 1 or phase 2 operation. DTC P2430 sets within 8 seconds when the above condition is met. **Possible Causes:** • Low reference circuit open/high resistance • 5-volt reference circuit short to ground or an open/high resistance • 5-volt reference circuit short to voltage • Signal circuit short to voltage • Signal circuit short to ground or an open/high resistance • AIR pump inlet or outlet hoses/pipes are restricted • AIR pump has failed • AIR solenoid valve has failed • Exhaust system is restricted
DTC: P2431 **2T CCM, MIL: Yes** **Years:** 2005, 2006, 2007 **Models:** LaCrosse, Sky **Engines:** 2.4L, 3.8L **Transmissions:** All	**Secondary Air Injection (AIR) System Pressure Sensor Performance** DTCs P0107, P0108, P0412, P0418, P0606, P0641, P0651, P2432, P2433 are not set. The ignition is ON. The PCM determines that the difference between the AIR pressure sensor and the barometric pressure (BARO) sensor signals is greater than 10 kPa when the AIR pump is commanded OFF, or, PCM determines that the difference between the AIR pressure sensor and the BARO sensor signals is greater than 50 kPa when the AIR pump is commanded ON. **Possible Causes:** • Low reference circuit open/high resistance • 5-volt reference circuit short to ground or an open/high resistance • 5-volt reference circuit short to voltage • Signal circuit short to voltage • Signal circuit short to ground or an open/high resistance • AIR pump inlet or outlet hoses/pipes are restricted • AIR pump has failed • AIR solenoid valve has failed • Exhaust system is restricted
DTC: P2432 **2T CCM, MIL: Yes** **Years:** 2005, 2006, 2007 **Models:** LaCrosse, Sky **Engines:** 2.4L, 3.8L **Transmissions:** All	**Secondary Air Injection (AIR) System Pressure Sensor Circuit Low Voltage** DTCs P0606, P0641, P0651 are not set. The ignition is ON or the engine is running. The pressure sensor signal is less than 0.2 volt for at least 12.5 seconds. **Possible Causes:** • Low reference circuit open/high resistance • 5-volt reference circuit short to ground or an open/high resistance • 5-volt reference circuit short to voltage • Signal circuit short to voltage • Signal circuit short to ground or an open/high resistance • AIR pump inlet or outlet hoses/pipes are restricted • AIR pump has failed • AIR solenoid valve has failed • Exhaust system is restricted
DTC: P2433 **2T CCM, MIL: Yes** **Years:** 2005, 2006, 2007 **Models:** LaCrosse, Sky **Engines:** 2.4L, 3.8L **Transmissions:** All	**Secondary Air Injection (AIR) System Pressure Sensor Circuit High Voltage** DTCs P0606, P0641, P0651 are not set. The ignition is ON or the engine is running. The pressure sensor signal is equal to or more than 4.75 volts for at least 12.5 seconds. **Possible Causes:** • Low reference circuit open/high resistance • 5-volt reference circuit short to ground or an open/high resistance • 5-volt reference circuit short to voltage • Signal circuit short to voltage • Signal circuit short to ground or an open/high resistance • AIR pump inlet or outlet hoses/pipes are restricted • AIR pump has failed • AIR solenoid valve has failed • Exhaust system is restricted

DTC	Trouble Code Title, Conditions & Possible Causes
DTC: P2440 **2T CCM, MIL: Yes** **Years:** 2005, 2006, 2007 **Models:** LaCrosse, Sky **Engines:** 2.4L, 3.8L **Transmissions:** All	**Secondary Air Injection (AIR) System Valve Stuck Open** DTCs P0101, P0102, P0103, P0107, P0108, P0112, P0113, P0116, P0117, P0118, P0201-P0206, P0300, P0350, P0411, P0412, P0418, P0420, P0606, P0641, P0651, P1350, P2430, P2431, P2432, P2433 are not set. The system voltage is 9-18 volts. The BARO parameter is more than 60 kPa. The MAF sensor parameter is between 3-24 g/s. The AIR system is commanded ON. The start-up engine coolant temperature (ECT) is between 5-50°C (41-122°F). The start-up intake air temperature (IAT) is between 5-60°C (41-140°F). The AIR system does not meet expected pressure conditions. **Possible Causes:** • Solenoid voltage supply circuit short to voltage • AIR pump inlet or outlet hoses/pipes are restricted • AIR pump has failed • AIR solenoid valve has failed • Exhaust system is restricted
DTC: P2444 **2T CCM, MIL: Yes** **Years:** 2005, 2006, 2007 **Models:** LaCrosse, Sky **Engines:** 2.4L, 3.8L **Transmissions:** All	**Secondary Air Injection (AIR) System Pump Stuck ON** DTCs P0101, P0102, P0103, P0107, P0108, P0112, P0113, P0116, P0117, P0118, P0201-P0206, P0300, P0350, P0411, P0412, P0418, P0420, P0606, P0641, P0651, P1350, P2430, P2431, P2432, P2433 are not set. The system voltage is 9-18 volts. The BARO parameter is more than 60 kPa. The MAF sensor parameter is between 3-24 g/s. The AIR system is commanded ON. The start-up engine coolant temperature (ECT) is between 5-50°C (41-122°F). The start-up intake air temperature (IAT) is between 5-60°C (41-140°F). The AIR system pressure is more than expected. **Possible Causes:** • Switch stuck open or closed • AIR pump inlet or outlet hoses/pipes are restricted • AIR pump has failed • AIR solenoid valve has failed • Exhaust system is restricted
DTC: P2665 **2T CCM, MIL: Yes** **Years:** 2005, 2006, 2007 **Models:** Sierra, Silverado **Engines:** 6.0L **Transmissions:** All	**AF Low Pressure Lock-Off Solenoid Circuit Malfunction** Engine started, engine running, system voltage from 6-18v, and the PCM detected the Actual and Commanded state of the LPL solenoid control circuit did not match for two seconds. Ignition voltage is supplied to the Low Pressure Lock-Off (LPL) solenoid through the AF Lock-Off relay. The PCM controls the LPL solenoid by grounding the control circuit via an internal switch called a driver. The primary function of the driver is to supply ground for a controlled component. The PCM monitors the status of the driver. If it detects an incorrect voltage for the commanded state of the driver, it sets DTC P2665. **Possible Causes:** • LPL solenoid control circuit is open or shorted to ground • LPL solenoid relay power circuit is open (test the AFS fuse) • LPL solenoid relay is damaged or it has failed • AF control module has failed

OBD II Trouble Code List (Uxxxx Codes)

DTC	Trouble Code Title, Conditions & Possible Causes
DTC: U0107 **1T PCM, MIL: Yes** **Years:** 2005, 2006, 2007 **Models:** LaCrosse, Sky **Engines:** 2.4L, 3.8L **Transmissions:** All	**Throttle Actuator Control (TAC) Module Serial Data Circuit** Invalid or missing serial data messages are detected for a predetermined period of time, or, the throttle limit is exceeded while operating in the Reduced Engine Power mode. The control module illuminates the malfunction indicator lamp (MIL). The control module commands the TAC system to operate in the Reduced Engine Power mode. A message center or an indicator displays Reduced Engine Power. Under certain conditions the control module commands the engine OFF. DTC U0107 sets if the battery voltage is low or the PCM is replaced or reflashed. If the customer's concern is slow cranking, or if the engine is not cranking because the battery voltage is low, ignore DTC U0107. Clear any DTCs from memory that may have set from the low battery voltage condition. **Possible Causes:** • Intermittent and for a poor connection at the throttle body • Intermittent and for a poor connection at the PCM • TAC module ground circuits have excess resistance • Short to battery voltage in the ignition 1 voltage circuit • Short to voltage on the TAC module serial data circuit • Open or high resistance in the TAC module ground circuit • ETC ignition 1 voltage circuit high resistance • Open or short to ground in the ignition 1 voltage circuit • Open or for a short to ground in the serial data circuit • Throttle body has failed • PCM has failed

DTC	Trouble Code Title, Conditions & Possible Causes
DTC: U1000 **1T PCM, MIL: Yes** **Years:** 2005, 2006, 2007 **Models:** All **Engines:** All **Transmissions:** All	**Class 2 Communication Malfunction** Modules connected to the Class 2 circuit monitor for serial data communications during normal vehicle operation. Operating information and commands are exchanged among the modules. When a module receives a message for a critical operating parameter, the module records the identification number of the module that sent the message. These Node Alive messages are used for State of Health monitoring. A critical operating parameter is one which, when not received, requires that the module use a default value for that parameter. When a module does not associate an identification number with at least one critical parameter within 5 seconds of starting data communication, DTC U1000 or U1255 is set. When more than one critical parameter does not have an identification number associated with it, the code will only set once. **Possible Causes:** • Class 2 circuit is open, shorted to ground or shorted to power • PCM ignition power circuit(s) has a high resistance condition • PCM main ground circuit(s) has a high resistance condition • SDM (module) could be shorted pulling the voltage low
DTC: U1016 **1T PCM, MIL: Yes** **Years:** 2005, 2006, 2007 **Models:** All **Engines:** All **Transmissions:** All	**No Communication With Powertrain Control Module** Key on, and a message from a learned ID number was not detected for the five seconds. Modules on the Class 2 circuit monitor for data communications during vehicle operation. When a module receives a message for critical data, the module records the identification number of the module sending the message for State of Health monitoring (Node Alive messages). Once a module learns an ID number, it checks for that module's Node Alive message. **Note: Look for this code in All modules. The one without the code is the module that has a problem, and it may have failed.** **Possible Causes:** • PCM Class 2 circuit is open, shorted to ground or to B+ • PCM ignition power circuit(s) has a high resistance condition • PCM main ground circuit(s) has a high resistance condition • PCM (module) may have failed and is pulling the circuit low
DTC: U1026 **1T PCM, MIL: Yes** **Years:** 2005, 2006, 2007 **Models:** Sierra, Silverado **Engines:** 4.3L, 4.8L, 5.3L, 6.0L, 6.2L, 8.1L **Transmissions:** All	**Loss of ATC Class 2 Communication** Key on or engine running; and a module detected that it could not communicate with the ATC controller for 1 second. Modules connected to the Class 2 circuit monitor for data communications during normal vehicle operation. Operating information and commands are exchanged among the modules. When a module receives a message for a critical operating parameter, the module records the identification number of the module that sent the message for State of Health monitoring (Node Alive messages). Once a module learns an identification number, it will monitor for that module's Node Alive message. Each module on the Class 2 circuit that is powered and performing functions that require detection of a communications malfunction is required to send a Node Alive message every two seconds. When no message is detected from a learned identification number for five seconds, a DTC U1xxx (XXX is equal to the 3-digit identification number) is set. **Possible Causes:** • Check for a loose connection at the ATC module • Test the main power and ground circuits to the ATC module • Check the Class 2 serial data circuit to the ATC module • ATC module may have failed
DTC: U1026 **2T PCM, MIL: Yes** **Years:** 2005, 2006, 2007 **Models:** All **Engines:** All **Transmissions:** All Others	**No Communication With Transfer Case Shift Control Module** Key on, and a message from a learned ID number was not detected for the five seconds. Modules on the Class 2 circuit monitor for data communications during vehicle operation. When a module receives a message for critical data, the module records the identification number of the module sending the message for State of Health monitoring (Node Alive messages). Once a module learns an ID number, it checks for that module's Node Alive message. **Note: Look for this code in All modules. The one without the code is the module that has a problem, and it may have failed.** **Possible Causes:** • TCSCM Class 2 circuit is open, shorted to ground or to B+ • TCSCM ignition power circuit(s) has a high resistance condition • TCSCM main ground circuit(s) has a high resistance condition • TCSCM (module) may have failed and is pulling the circuit low
DTC: U1041 **2T PCM, MIL: Yes** **Years:** 2005, 2006, 2007 **Models:** All **Engines:** All **Transmissions:** All Others	**No Communication With Electronic Brake Control Module** Key on, and a message from a learned ID number was not detected for the five seconds. Modules on the Class 2 circuit monitor for data communications during vehicle operation. When a module receives a message for critical data, the module records the identification number of the module sending the message for State of Health monitoring (Node Alive messages). Once a module learns an ID number, it checks for that module's Node Alive message. **Note: Look for this code in All modules. The one without the code is the module that has a problem, and it may have failed.** **Possible Causes:** • EBCM Class 2 circuit is open, shorted to ground or to B+ • EBCM ignition power circuit(s) has a high resistance condition • EBCM main ground circuit(s) has a high resistance condition • EBCM (module) may have failed and is pulling the circuit low

DTC	Trouble Code Title, Conditions & Possible Causes
DTC: U1048 **2T PCM, MIL: Yes** **Years:** 2005, 2006, 2007 **Models:** All **Engines:** All **Transmissions:** All	**No Communication With Rear Wheel Steering Control Module** Key on, and a message from a learned ID number was not detected for the five seconds. Modules on the Class 2 circuit monitor for data communications during vehicle operation. When a module receives a message for critical data, the module records the identification number of the module sending the message for State of Health monitoring (Node Alive messages). Once a module learns an ID number, it checks for that module's Node Alive message. **Note: Look for this code in All modules. The one without the code is the module that has a problem, and it may have failed.** **Possible Causes:** • RWSCM Class 2 circuit is open, shorted to ground or to B+ • RWSCM ignition power circuit has a high resistance condition • RESCM main ground circuit(s) has a high resistance condition • RESCM (module) may have failed and is pulling the circuit low
DTC: U1064 **2T PCM, MIL: Yes** **Years:** 2005, 2006, 2007 **Models:** All **Engines:** All **Transmissions:** All	**No Communication With Body Control Module** Key on, and a message from a learned ID number was not detected for the five seconds. Modules on the Class 2 circuit monitor for data communications during vehicle operation. When a module receives a message for critical data, the module records the identification number of the module sending the message for State of Health monitoring (Node Alive messages). Look for this code in All modules. The one without this code may have failed **Possible Causes:** • BCM Class 2 circuit is open, shorted to ground or to B+ • BCM ignition power circuit has a high resistance condition • BCM main ground circuit(s) has a high resistance condition • BCM (module) may have failed and is pulling the circuit low
DTC: U1088 **2T PCM, MIL: Yes** **Years:** 2005, 2006, 2007 **Models:** All **Engines:** All **Transmissions:** All	**No Communication With SDM (Restraint Module)** Key on, and a message from a learned ID number was not detected for the five seconds. Modules on the Class 2 circuit monitor for data communications during vehicle operation. When a module receives a message for critical data, the module records the identification number of the module sending the message for State of Health monitoring (Node Alive messages). Look for this code in All modules. The one without this code may have failed. **Possible Causes:** • SDM Class 2 circuit is open, shorted to ground or to B+ • SDM ignition power circuit has a high resistance condition • SDM main ground circuit(s) has a high resistance condition • SDM (module) may have failed and is pulling the circuit low
DTC: U1092 **2T PCM, MIL: Yes** **Years:** 2005, 2006, 2007 **Models:** Sierra, Silverado **Engines:** 4.3L, 4.8L, 5.3L, 6.0L, 6.2L, 8.1L **Transmissions:** All	**Loss of VTD (Pass Lock) Communication** Key on or engine running; and a module detected that it could not communicate with the VTD controller for 1 second. Modules connected to the Class 2 circuit monitor for data communications during normal vehicle operation. Operating information and commands are exchanged among the modules. When a module receives a message for a critical operating parameter, the module records the identification number of the module that sent the message for State of Health monitoring (Node Alive messages). Once a module learns an identification number, it will monitor for that module's Node Alive message. Each module on the Class 2 circuit that is powered and performing functions that require detection of a communications malfunction is required to send a Node Alive message every two seconds. When no message is detected from a learned identification number for five seconds, a DTC U1xxx (the X's identify the 3-digit identification number) is set. **Possible Causes:** • Check for a loose connection at the VTD module • Test the main power and ground circuits to the VTD module • Check the Class 2 serial data circuit to the VTD module • VTD module may have failed
DTC: U1096 **2T PCM, MIL: Yes** **Years:** 2005, 2006, 2007 **Models:** All **Engines:** All **Transmissions:** All	**No Communication With Instrument Panel Cluster** Key on, and a message from a learned ID number was not detected for the five seconds. Modules on the Class 2 circuit monitor for data communications during vehicle operation. When a module receives a message for critical data, the module records the identification number of the module sending the message for State of Health monitoring (Node Alive messages). Once a module learns an ID number, it checks for that module's Node Alive message. **Note: Look for this code in All modules. The one without the code is the module that has a problem, and it may have failed.** **Possible Causes:** • IPC Class 2 circuit is open, shorted to ground or to B+ • IPC ignition power circuit has a high resistance condition • IPC main ground circuit(s) has a high resistance condition • IPC (module) may have failed and is pulling the circuit low

DTC	Trouble Code Title, Conditions & Possible Causes
DTC: U1097 **2T PCM, MIL: Yes** **Years:** 2005, 2006, 2007 **Models:** All **Engines:** All **Transmissions:** All	**No Communication With Driver Information Center** Key on, and a message from a learned ID number was not detected for the five seconds. Modules on the Class 2 circuit monitor for data communications during vehicle operation. When a module receives a message for critical data, the module records the identification number of the module sending the message for State of Health monitoring (Node Alive messages). Once a module learns an ID number, it checks for that module's Node Alive message. **Note: Look for this code in All modules. The one without the code is the module that has a problem, and it may have failed.** **Possible Causes:** • DIC Class 2 circuit is open, shorted to ground or to B+ • DIC ignition power circuit has a high resistance condition • DIC main ground circuit(s) has a high resistance condition • DIC (module) may have failed and is pulling the circuit low
DTC: U1151 **2T PCM, MIL: Yes** **Years:** 2005, 2006, 2007 **Models:** All **Engines:** All **Transmissions:** All	**No Communication With Vehicle Interface Unit** Key on, and a message from a learned ID number was not detected for the five seconds. Modules on the Class 2 circuit monitor for data communications during vehicle operation. When a module receives a message for critical data, the module records the identification number of the module sending the message for State of Health monitoring (Node Alive messages). Once a module learns an ID number, it checks for that module's Node Alive message. The module without this code is the module with a problem (it has failed). **Possible Causes:** • VIU Class 2 circuit is open, shorted to ground or to B+ • VIU ignition power circuit has a high resistance condition • VIU main ground circuit(s) has a high resistance condition • VIU (module) may have failed and is pulling the circuit low
DTC: U1152 **2T PCM, MIL: Yes** **Years:** 2005, 2006, 2007 **Models:** All **Engines:** All **Transmissions:** All	**No Communication With HVAC Control Module** Key on, and a message from a learned ID number was not detected for the five seconds. Modules on the Class 2 circuit monitor for data communications during vehicle operation. When a module receives a message for critical data, the module records the identification number of the module sending the message for State of Health monitoring (Node Alive messages). Once a module learns an ID number, it checks for that module's Node Alive message. The module without this code is the module with a problem (it has failed). **Possible Causes:** • HVAC Class 2 circuit is open, shorted to ground or to B+ • HVAC ignition power circuit has a high resistance condition • HVAC main ground circuit(s) has a high resistance condition • HVAC (module) may have failed and is pulling the circuit low
DTC: U1193 **2T PCM, MIL: Yes** **Years:** 2005, 2006, 2007 **Models:** Sierra, Silverado **Engines:** 4.3L, 4.8L, 5.3L, 6.0L, 6.2L, 8.1L **Transmissions:** All	**Loss of Vehicle Immobilizer Module Communications** Key on or engine running; and a module detected that it could not communicate with the VIM controller for 1 second. Modules connected to the Class 2 circuit monitor for data communications during normal vehicle operation. Operating information and commands are exchanged among the modules. When a module receives a message for a critical operating parameter, the module records the identification number of the module that sent the message for State of Health monitoring (Node Alive messages). Once a module learns an identification number, it will monitor for that module's Node Alive message. Each module on the Class 2 circuit that is powered and performing functions that require detection of a communications malfunction is required to send a Node Alive message every two seconds. When no message is detected from a learned identification number for five seconds, a DTC U1xxx (XXX is equal to the 3-digit identification number) is set. **Possible Causes:** • Test the main power and ground circuits to the VIM module for a loose connection • Check the Class 2 serial data circuit to the VIM module • VTD module may have failed
DTC: U1255 **2T PCM, MIL: Yes** **Years:** 2005, 2006, 2007 **Models:** All **Engines:** All **Transmissions:** All	**Class 2 Communications Malfunction** Modules connected to the Class 2 circuit monitor for serial data communications during normal vehicle operation. Operating data and commands are exchanged among modules. When a module receives a message for a critical operating parameter, the module records the identification number of the module that sent the message. These Node Alive messages are used for State of Health monitoring. A critical operating parameter is one which, when not received, requires the module use a default value for that parameter. If a module does not associate an ID number with at least one critical parameter in 5 seconds after starting communication, U1000 or U1255 is set. If two or more are missing, the code sets at once. **Possible Causes:** • Class 2 circuit is open, shorted to ground or shorted to power • PCM ignition power circuit(s) has a high resistance condition • PCM main ground circuit(s) has a high resistance condition

DTC	Trouble Code Title, Conditions & Possible Causes
DTC: U1300 **1T PCM, MIL: Yes** **Years:** 2005, 2006, 2007 **Models:** All **Engines:** All **Transmissions:** All	**Class 2 Circuit Short to Ground** Key on or engine running; system voltage supplied to the module is in the normal operating voltage range, vehicle power mode requires serial data communication to occur, and the PCM did no detect any valid messages on the Class 2 circuit, or the voltage condition detected on the Class 2 circuit was low for 3 seconds. Modules connected to the Class 2 circuit check for data communications during normal vehicle operation. Operating information and commands are exchanged among the modules. Each module transmits Node Alive messages on the Class 2 data circuit once every 2 seconds. When the module detects a low voltage condition on the Class 2 serial data circuit for approximately 3 seconds, it sets U1300 or U1305 if it cannot identify the problem. **Note: This code is set by loss of communication. Look in All of the modules for this trouble code - the one without it has a problem** **Possible Causes:** • Class 2 serial data line was in a low state for 3 seconds due to a short to sensor ground or chassis ground • One or more modules on the Class 2 line has a short to ground
DTC: U1301 **1T PCM, MIL: Yes** **Years:** 2005, 2006, 2007 **Models:** All **Engines:** All **Transmissions:** All	**Class 2 Circuit Short to Battery** Key on or engine running; system voltage supplied to the module is in the normal operating voltage range, vehicle power mode requires serial data communication to occur, and the PCM did no detect any valid messages on the Class 2 circuit, or the voltage condition detected on the Class 2 circuit was low for 3 seconds. Modules connected to the Class 2 circuit check for data communications during normal vehicle operation. Operating information and commands are exchanged among the modules. In addition, each module transmits Node Alive messages on the Class 2 data circuit once every 2 seconds. If the module detects a high voltage condition on the Class 2 serial data circuit for 3 seconds, it sets U1300. **Note: This code is set by loss of communication. Look in All of the modules for this trouble code - the one without it has a problem.** **Possible Causes:** • Class 2 serial data line was in a high state for 3 seconds due to a short to VREF or system power • One or more modules on Class 2 line has an short to power
DTC: U1305 **1T PCM, MIL: Yes** **Years:** 2005, 2006, 2007 **Models:** All **Engines:** All **Transmissions:** All	**Class 2 Data Link High or Low** Key on or engine running; system voltage supplied to the module is in the normal operating voltage range, vehicle power mode requires serial data communication to occur, and the PCM did no detect any valid messages on the Class 2 circuit, or the voltage condition detected on the Class 2 circuit was low for 3 seconds. Modules connected to the Class 2 circuit check for data communications during normal vehicle operation. Operating information and commands are exchanged among the modules. In addition, each module transmits Node Alive messages on the Class 2 data circuit about once every 2 seconds. When the module detects a high voltage condition on the Class 2 serial data circuit for approximately 3 seconds, it sets U1300 or U1305 if it cannot identify the problem. **Possible Causes:** • Class 2 serial data line has either a high or low voltage condition on the circuit, and the module cannot identify the fault • One or more modules on Class 2 line has an short to power • One or more modules on the Class 2 line has a short to ground

OBD II Trouble Code List (U1xxx U2xxx)

DTC	Trouble Code Title, Conditions & Possible Causes
DTC: U1800 **2T PCM, MIL: Yes** **Years:** 2005, 2006, 2007 **Models:** Sierra, Silverado **Engines:** 6.6L Diesel **Transmissions:** All	**CAN Bus Messages Missing From FICD** Key on, and the ECM did not receive any CAN messages from the FICD for 45 milliseconds. The ECM, FICD and the TCM communicate control and diagnostic data via a SAE J1939 CAN bus circuit. The ECM monitors CAN operational status by expecting a constant flow of messages from the FICM and the TCM. If the ECM fails to receive an expected message from one of these modules, U1800, U2104, or U2106 will set depending on the lost data. **Possible Causes:** • Modules that communicate on the SAE J1939 CAN system are wired parallel to each other until the respective circuits are spliced together at the ECM. An open in the CAN circuit of one module will not affect other modules. A short to ground or short to power affects All modules no matter where the failure occurs. • FICD power and/or ground circuit are open or shorted • FICD (module) has failed • ECM or TCM has failed

DTC	Trouble Code Title, Conditions & Possible Causes
DTC: U2104 **2T PCM, MIL: Yes** **Years:** 2005, 2006, 2007 **Models:** Sierra, Silverado **Engines:** 6.6L Diesel **Transmissions:** All	**CAN Bus Messages Missing From FICD, TCM** Key on, and the ECM did not receive any CAN messages from the FICD and TCM for 45 ms. The ECM, FICD and the TCM send control and diagnostic information via a SAE J1939 CAN bus circuit. The ECM monitors CAN operational status by expecting a constant flow of messages from the FICM and the TCM. If the ECM fails to receive an expected message from one of these modules, U1800, U2104, or U2106 will set; depending on the lost data. **Possible Causes:** • Modules that communicate on the SAE J1939 CAN system are wired parallel to each other until the respective circuits are spliced together at the ECM. An open in the CAN circuit of one module will not affect other modules. A short to ground or short to power affects All modules no matter where the failure occurs. • FICD power and/or ground circuit are open or shorted • FICD (module) has failed • ECM or TCM has failed

OBD II Trouble Code List (U2xxx Codes)

DTC	Trouble Code Title, Conditions & Possible Causes
DTC: U2106 **2T PCM, MIL: Yes** **Years:** 2005, 2006, 2007 **Models:** Sierra, Silverado **Engines:** 6.6L Diesel **Transmissions:** All	**CAN Bus Messages Missing From TCM** Key on, and the ECM did not receive any CAN messages from the TCM for 45 ms. The ECM, FICD and the TCM send control and diagnostic information via a SAE J1939 CAN bus circuit. The ECM monitors CAN operational status by expecting a constant flow of messages from the FICM and the TCM. If the ECM fails to receive an expected message from one of these modules, DTC U1800, U2104, or U2106 will set; depending on what data is lost. **Possible Causes:** • Modules that communicate on the SAE J1939 CAN system are wired parallel to each other until the respective circuits are spliced together at the ECM. An open in the CAN circuit of one module will not affect other modules. A short to ground or short to power affects All modules no matter where the failure occurs. • FICD power and/or ground circuit are open or shorted • FICD (module) has failed • ECM or TCM has failed

OBD II Trouble Code List (B1xxx B2xxx Codes)

DTC	Trouble Code Title, Conditions & Possible Causes
DTC: B2722 **1T CCM, MIL: No** **Years:** 2005, 2006, 2007 **Models:** Sierra, Silverado **Engines:** 6.6L Diesel **Transmissions:** All	**Powertrain Control Module Internal Malfunction** Key on or engine running; system voltage from 9-16v, Tow/Haul switch has been activated, and the ECM detected the Tow/Haul switch signal circuit was low for around 3 minutes. Tow/Haul mode enables the operator to achieve enhanced shift performance when towing or hauling a load. When tow/haul is selected, the tow/haul switch input signal to the BCM is momentarily toggled to zero volts. The BCM sends a serial data message to the PCM and instrument panel controller (IPC). The PCM extends the length of time between an upshift, increases transmission line pressure and the IPC illuminates the tow/haul indicator lamp. Cycling the tow/haul switch a second time disables the Tow/Haul mode and returns the transmission to a normal shift pattern. **Possible Causes:** • Tow/Haul switch is shorted to ground • Tow/Haul switch is damaged or it has failed • PCM has failed

Commonly Used Abbreviations

2

2WD	Two Wheel Drive

4

4WD	Four Wheel Drive

A

A/C	Air Conditioning
ABDC	After Bottom Dead Center
ABS	Anti-lock Brakes
AC	Alternating Current
ACL	Air cleaner
ACT	Air Charge Temperature
AIR	Secondary Air Injection
ALCL	Assembly Line Communications Link
ALDL	Assembly Line Diagnostic Link
AT	Automatic Transaxle/Transmission
ATDC	After Top Dead Center
ATF	Automatic Transmission Fluid
ATS	Air Temperature Sensor
AWD	All Wheel Drive

B

BAP	Barometric Absolute Pressure
BARO	Barometric Pressure
BBDC	Before Bottom Dead Center
BCM	Body Control Module
BDC	Bottom Dead Center
BPT	Backpressure Transducer
BTDC	Before Top Dead Center
BVSV	Bimetallic Vacuum Switching Valve

C

CAC	Charge Air Cooler
CARB	California Air Resources Board
CAT	Catalytic Converter
CCC	Computer Command Control
CCCC	Computer Controlled Catalytic Converter
CCCI	Computer Controlled Coil Ignition
CCD	Computer Controlled Dwell
CDI	Capacitor Discharge Ignition
CEC	Computerized Engine Control
CFI	Continuous Fuel Injection
CIS	Continuous Injection System
CIS-E	Continuous Injection System - Electronic
CKP	Crankshaft Position
CL	Closed Loop
CMP	Camshaft Position
CPP	Clutch Pedal Position
CTOX	Continuous Trap Oxidizer System
CTP	Closed Throttle Position
CVC	Constant Vacuum Control
CYL	Cylinder

D

DBC	Dual Bed Catalyst
DC	Direct Current
DFI	Direct Fuel Injection
DIS	Distributorless Ignition System
DLC	Data Link Connector
DMM	Digital Multimeter
DOHC	Double Overhead Camshaft
DRB	Diagnostic Readout Box
DTC	Diagnostic Trouble Code
DTM	Diagnostic Test Mode
DVOM	Digital Volt/Ohmmeter

E

EBCM	Electronic Brake Control Module
ECM	Engine Control Module
ECT	Engine Coolant Temperature
ECU	Engine Control Unit or Electronic Control Unit
EDIS	Electronic Distributorless Ignition System
EEC	Electronic Engine Control
EEPROM	Electrically Erasable Programmable Read Only Memory
EFE	Early Fuel Evaporation
EGR	Exhaust Gas Recirculation
EGRT	Exhaust Gas Recirculation Temperature
EGRVC	EGR Valve Control
EPROM	Erasable Programmable Read Only Memory
EVAP	Evaporative Emissions
EVP	EGR Valve Position

F

FBC	Feedback Carburetor
FEEPROM	Flash Electrically Erasable Programmable Read Only Memory
FF	Flexible Fuel
FI	Fuel Injection
FT	Fuel Trim
FWD	Front Wheel Drive

G

GND	Ground

H

HAC	High Altitude Compensation
HEGO	Heated Exhaust Gas Oxygen sensor
HEI	High Energy Ignition
HO2 Sensor	Heated Oxygen Sensor

I

IAC	Idle Air Control
IAT	Intake Air Temperature
ICM	Ignition Control Module
IFI	Indirect Fuel Injection
IFS	Inertia Fuel Shutoff
ISC	Idle Speed Control
IVSV	Idle Vacuum Switching Valve

Commonly Used Abbreviations

K

KOEO	Key On, Engine Off
KOER	Key ON, Engine Running
KS	Knock Sensor

M

MAF	Mass Air Flow
MAP	Manifold Absolute Pressure
MAT	Manifold Air Temperature
MC	Mixture Control
MDP	Manifold Differential Pressure
MFI	Multiport Fuel Injection
MIL	Malfunction Indicator Lamp or Maintenance
MST	Manifold Surface Temperature
MVZ	Manifold Vacuum Zone

N

NVRAM	Nonvolatile Random Access Memory

O

O2 Sensor	Oxygen Sensor
OBD	On-Board Diagnostic
OC	Oxidation Catalyst
OHC	Overhead Camshaft
OL	Open Loop

P

P/S	Power Steering
PAIR	Pulsed Secondary Air Injection
PCM	Powertrain Control Module
PCS	Purge Control Solenoid
PCV	Positive Crankcase Ventilation
PIP	Profile Ignition Pick-up
PNP	Park/Neutral Position
PROM	Programmable Read Only Memory
PSP	Power Steering Pressure
PTO	Power Take-Off
PTOX	Periodic Trap Oxidizer System

R

RABS	Rear Anti-lock Brake System
RAM	Random Access Memory
ROM	Read Only Memory
RPM	Revolutions Per Minute
RWAL	Rear Wheel Anti-lock Brakes
RWD	Rear Wheel Drive

S

SBC	Single Bed Converter
SBEC	Single Board Engine Controller
SC	Supercharger
SCB	Supercharger Bypass
SFI	Sequential Multiport Fuel Injection
SIR	Supplemental Inflatible Restraint
SOHC	Single Overhead Camshaft
SPL	Smoke Puff Limiter
SPOUT	Spark Output
SRI	Service Reminder Indicator
SRS	Supplemental Restraint System
SRT	System Readiness Test
SSI	Solid State Ignition
ST	Scan Tool
STO	Self-Test Output

T

TAC	Thermostatic Air Clearner
TBI	Throttle Body Fuel Injection
TC	Turbocharger
TCC	Torque Converter Clutch
TCM	Transmission Control Module
TDC	Top Dead Center
TFI	Thick Film Ignition
TP	Throttle Position
TR Sensor	Transaxle/Transmission Range Sensor
TVV	Thermal Vacuum Valve
TWC	Three-way Catalytic Converter

V

VAF	Volume Air Flow, or Vane Air Flow
VAPS	Variable Assist Power Steering
VRV	Vacuum Regulator Valve
VSS	Vehicle Speed Sensor
VSV	Vacuum Switching Valve

W

WOT	Wide Open Throttle
WU-TWC	Warm Up Three-way Catalytic Converter

ENGLISH TO METRIC CONVERSION: TORQUE

To convert foot-pounds (ft. lbs.) to Newton-meters (Nm), multiply the number of ft. lbs. by 1.36
To convert Newton-meters (Nm) to foot-pounds (ft. lbs.), multiply the number of Nm by 0.7376

ft. lbs.	Nm	ft. lbs.	Nm	ft. lbs.	Nm	ft. lbs.	Nm
0.1	0.1	34	46.2	76	103.4	118	160.5
0.2	0.3	35	47.6	77	104.7	119	161.8
0.3	0.4	36	49.0	78	106.1	120	163.2
0.4	0.5	37	50.3	79	107.4	121	164.6
0.5	0.7	38	51.7	80	108.8	122	165.9
0.6	0.8	39	53.0	81	110.2	123	167.3
0.7	1.0	40	54.4	82	111.5	124	168.6
0.8	1.1	41	55.8	83	112.9	125	170.0
0.9	1.2	42	57.1	84	114.2	126	171.4
1	1.4	43	58.5	85	115.6	127	172.7
2	2.7	44	59.8	86	117.0	128	174.1
3	4.1	45	61.2	87	118.3	129	175.4
4	5.4	46	62.6	88	119.7	130	176.8
5	6.8	47	63.9	89	121.0	131	178.2
6	8.2	48	65.3	90	122.4	132	179.5
7	9.5	49	66.6	91	123.8	133	180.9
8	10.9	50	68.0	92	125.1	134	182.2
9	12.2	51	69.4	93	126.5	135	183.6
10	13.6	52	70.7	94	127.8	136	185.0
11	15.0	53	72.1	95	129.2	137	186.3
12	16.3	54	73.4	96	130.6	138	187.7
13	17.7	55	74.8	97	131.9	139	189.0
14	19.0	56	76.2	98	133.3	140	190.4
15	20.4	57	77.5	99	134.6	141	191.8
16	21.8	58	78.9	100	136.0	142	193.1
17	23.1	59	80.2	101	137.4	143	194.5
18	24.5	60	81.6	102	138.7	144	195.8
19	25.8	61	83.0	103	140.1	145	197.2
20	27.2	62	84.3	104	141.4	146	198.6
21	28.6	63	85.7	105	142.8	147	199.9
22	29.9	64	87.0	106	144.2	148	201.3
23	31.3	65	88.4	107	145.5	149	202.6
24	32.6	66	89.8	108	146.9	150	204.0
25	34.0	67	91.1	109	148.2	151	205.4
26	35.4	68	92.5	110	149.6	152	206.7
27	36.7	69	93.8	111	151.0	153	208.1
28	38.1	70	95.2	112	152.3	154	209.4
29	39.4	71	96.6	113	153.7	155	210.8
30	40.8	72	97.9	114	155.0	156	212.2
31	42.2	73	99.3	115	156.4	157	213.5
32	43.5	74	100.6	116	157.8	158	214.9
33	44.9	75	102.0	117	159.1	159	216.2

METRIC TO ENGLISH CONVERSION: TORQUE

To convert foot-pounds (ft. lbs.) to Newton-meters (Nm), multiply the number of ft. lbs. by 1.36
To convert Newton-meters (Nm) to foot-pounds (ft. lbs.), multiply the number of Nm by 0.7376

Nm	ft. lbs.	Nm	ft. lbs.	Nm	ft. lbs.	Nm	ft. lbs.	Nm	ft. lbs.
0.1	0.1	34	25.0	76	55.9	118	86.8	160	117.6
0.2	0.1	35	25.7	77	56.6	119	87.5	161	118.4
0.3	0.2	36	26.5	78	57.4	120	88.2	162	119.1
0.4	0.3	37	27.2	79	58.1	121	89.0	163	119.9
0.5	0.4	38	27.9	80	58.8	122	89.7	164	120.6
0.6	0.4	39	28.7	81	59.6	123	90.4	165	121.3
0.7	0.5	40	29.4	82	60.3	124	91.2	166	122.1
0.8	0.6	41	30.1	83	61.0	125	91.9	167	122.8
0.9	0.7	42	30.9	84	61.8	126	92.6	168	123.5
1	0.7	43	31.6	85	62.5	127	93.4	169	124.3
2	1.5	44	32.4	86	63.2	128	94.1	170	125.0
3	2.2	45	33.1	87	64.0	129	94.9	171	125.7
4	2.9	46	33.8	88	64.7	130	95.6	172	126.5
5	3.7	47	34.6	89	65.4	131	96.3	173	127.2
6	4.4	48	35.3	90	66.2	132	97.1	174	127.9
7	5.1	49	36.0	91	66.9	133	97.8	175	128.7
8	5.9	50	36.8	92	67.6	134	98.5	176	129.4
9	6.6	51	37.5	93	68.4	135	99.3	177	130.1
10	7.4	52	38.2	94	69.1	136	100.0	178	130.9
11	8.1	53	39.0	95	69.9	137	100.7	179	131.6
12	8.8	54	39.7	96	70.6	138	101.5	180	132.4
13	9.6	55	40.4	97	71.3	139	102.2	181	133.1
14	10.3	56	41.2	98	72.1	140	102.9	182	133.8
15	11.0	57	41.9	99	72.8	141	103.7	183	134.6
16	11.8	58	42.6	100	73.5	142	104.4	184	135.3
17	12.5	59	43.4	101	74.3	143	105.1	185	136.0
18	13.2	60	44.1	102	75.0	144	105.9	186	136.8
19	14.0	61	44.9	103	75.7	145	106.6	187	137.5
20	14.7	62	45.6	104	76.5	146	107.4	188	138.2
21	15.4	63	46.3	105	77.2	147	108.1	189	139.0
22	16.2	64	47.1	106	77.9	148	108.8	190	139.7
23	16.9	65	47.8	107	78.7	149	109.6	191	140.4
24	17.6	66	48.5	108	79.4	150	110.3	192	141.2
25	18.4	67	49.3	109	80.1	151	111.0	193	141.9
26	19.1	68	50.0	110	80.9	152	111.8	194	142.6
27	19.9	69	50.7	111	81.6	153	112.5	195	143.4
28	20.6	70	51.5	112	82.4	154	113.2	196	144.1
29	21.3	71	52.2	113	83.1	155	114.0	197	144.9
30	22.1	72	52.9	114	83.8	156	114.7	198	145.6
31	22.8	73	53.7	115	84.6	157	115.4	199	146.3
32	23.5	74	54.4	116	85.3	158	116.2	200	147.1
33	24.3	75	55.1	117	86.0	159	116.9	201	147.8

ENGLISH/METRIC CONVERSION: TEMPERATURE

To convert Fahrenheit (F°) to Celsius (C°), take F° temperature and subtract 32, multiply the result by 5 and divide the result by 9
To convert Celsius (C°) to Fahrenheit (F°), take C° temperature and multiply it by 9, divide the result by 5 and add 32

F°	C°	F°	C°	C°	F°	C°	F°
-40	-40.0	150	65.6	-38	-36.4	46	114.8
-35	-37.2	155	68.3	-36	-32.8	48	118.4
-30	-34.4	160	71.1	-34	-29.2	50	122
-25	-31.7	165	73.9	-32	-25.6	52	125.6
-20	-28.9	170	76.7	-30	-22	54	129.2
-15	-26.1	175	79.4	-28	-18.4	56	132.8
-10	-23.3	180	82.2	-26	-14.8	58	136.4
-5	-20.6	185	85.0	-24	-11.2	60	140
0	-17.8	190	87.8	-22	-7.6	62	143.6
1	-17.2	195	90.6	-20	-4	64	147.2
2	-16.7	200	93.3	-18	-0.4	66	150.8
3	-16.1	205	96.1	-16	3.2	68	154.4
4	-15.6	210	98.9	-14	6.8	70	158
5	-15.0	212	100.0	-12	10.4	72	161.6
10	-12.2	215	101.7	-10	14	74	165.2
15	-9.4	220	104.4	-8	17.6	76	168.8
20	-6.7	225	107.2	-6	21.2	78	172.4
25	-3.9	230	110.0	-4	24.8	80	176
30	-1.1	235	112.8	-2	28.4	82	179.6
35	1.7	240	115.6	0	32	84	183.2
40	4.4	245	118.3	2	35.6	86	186.8
45	7.2	250	121.1	4	39.2	88	190.4
50	10.0	255	123.9	6	42.8	90	194
55	12.8	260	126.7	8	46.4	92	197.6
60	15.6	265	129.4	10	50	94	201.2
65	18.3	270	132.2	12	53.6	96	204.8
70	21.1	275	135.0	14	57.2	98	208.4
75	23.9	280	137.8	16	60.8	100	212
80	26.7	285	140.6	18	64.4	102	215.6
85	29.4	290	143.3	20	68	104	219.2
90	32.2	295	146.1	22	71.6	106	222.8
95	35.0	300	148.9	24	75.2	108	226.4
100	37.8	305	151.7	26	78.8	110	230
105	40.6	310	154.4	28	82.4	112	233.6
110	43.3	315	157.2	30	86	114	237.2
115	46.1	320	160.0	32	89.6	116	240.8
120	48.9	325	162.8	34	93.2	118	244.4
125	51.7	330	165.6	36	96.8	120	248
130	54.4	335	168.3	38	100.4	122	251.6
135	57.2	340	171.1	40	104	124	255.2
140	60.0	345	173.9	42	107.6	126	258.8
145	62.8	350	176.7	44	111.2	128	262.4

LENGTH CONVERSION

To convert inches (in.) to millimeters (mm), multiply the number of inches by 25.4

To convert millimeters (mm) to inches (in.), multiply the number of millimeters by 0.04

Inches	Millimeters	Inches	Millimeters	Inches	Millimeters	Inches	Millimeters
0.0001	0.00254	0.005	0.1270	0.09	2.286	4	101.6
0.0002	0.00508	0.006	0.1524	0.1	2.54	5	127.0
0.0003	0.00762	0.007	0.1778	0.2	5.08	6	152.4
0.0004	0.01016	0.008	0.2032	0.3	7.62	7	177.8
0.0005	0.01270	0.009	0.2286	0.4	10.16	8	203.2
0.0006	0.01524	0.01	0.254	0.5	12.70	9	228.6
0.0007	0.01778	0.02	0.508	0.6	15.24	10	254.0
0.0008	0.02032	0.03	0.762	0.7	17.78	11	279.4
0.0009	0.02286	0.04	1.016	0.8	20.32	12	304.8
0.001	0.0254	0.05	1.270	0.9	22.86	13	330.2
0.002	0.0508	0.06	1.524	1	25.4	14	355.6
0.003	0.0762	0.07	1.778	2	50.8	15	381.0
0.004	0.1016	0.08	2.032	3	76.2	16	406.4

ENGLISH/METRIC CONVERSION: LENGTH

To convert inches (in.) to millimeters (mm), multiply the number of inches by 25.4
To convert millimeters (mm) to inches (in.), multiply the number of millimeters by 0.04

Inches Fraction	Inches Decimal	Millimeters Decimal	Inches Fraction	Inches Decimal	Millimeters Decimal	Inches Fraction	Inches Decimal	Millimeters Decimal
1/64	0.016	0.397	11/32	0.344	8.731	11/16	0.688	17.463
1/32	0.031	0.794	23/64	0.359	9.128	45/64	0.703	17.859
3/64	0.047	1.191	3/8	0.375	9.525	23/32	0.719	18.256
1/16	0.063	1.588	25/64	0.391	9.922	47/64	0.734	18.653
5/64	0.078	1.984	13/32	0.406	10.319	3/4	0.750	19.050
3/32	0.094	2.381	27/64	0.422	10.716	49/64	0.766	19.447
7/64	0.109	2.778	7/16	0.438	11.113	25/32	0.781	19.844
1/8	0.125	3.175	29/64	0.453	11.509	51/64	0.797	20.241
9/64	0.141	3.572	15/32	0.469	11.906	13/16	0.813	20.638
5/32	0.156	3.969	31/64	0.484	12.303	53/64	0.828	21.034
11/64	0.172	4.366	1/2	0.500	12.700	27/32	0.844	21.431
3/16	0.188	4.763	33/64	0.516	13.097	55/64	0.859	21.828
13/64	0.203	5.159	17/32	0.531	13.494	7/8	0.875	22.225
7/32	0.219	5.556	35/64	0.547	13.891	57/64	0.891	22.622
15/64	0.234	5.953	9/16	0.563	14.288	29/32	0.906	23.019
1/4	0.250	6.350	37/64	0.578	14.684	59/64	0.922	23.416
17/64	0.266	6.747	19/32	0.594	15.081	15/16	0.938	23.813
9/32	0.281	7.144	39/64	0.609	15.478	61/64	0.953	24.209
19/64	0.297	7.541	5/8	0.625	15.875	31/32	0.969	24.606
5/16	0.313	7.938	41/64	0.641	16.272	63/64	0.984	25.003
21/64	0.328	8.334	21/32	0.656	16.669	1/1	1.000	25.400
			43/64	0.672	17.066			